CROCKF

CLERIC

2012–2013

CROCKFORD'S
CLERICAL DIRECTORY
102ND EDITION

2012–2013

A directory of the clergy
of the Church of England
the Church in Wales
the Scottish Episcopal Church
the Church of Ireland

SINCE 1858

CHURCH HOUSE
PUBLISHING

Crockford's Clerical Directory published December 2011 for The Archbishops' Council by:

Church House Publishing
Church House
Great Smith Street
London SW1P 3AZ

102nd edition (2012-2013) © The Archbishops' Council 2011.

Please send any corrections to the Compiler, Crockford (address as above), Tel (020) 7898 1012 Fax (020) 7898 1769 E-mail crockford@churchofengland.org

ISBN 978 0 7151 1053 9 (hardback)
     978 0 7151 1054 6 (paperback)

Jacket and cover design by Aubrey Design

Typeset by   Printed by
RefineCatch Ltd,   William Clowes Ltd,
Bungay, Suffolk   Beccles, Suffolk

CONTENTS

MARLBOROUGH COLLEGE

A coeducational, full boarding environment for 13-18 year olds.

CLERGY BURSARIES
AVAILABLE

www.marlboroughcollege.org

INDEX TO ADVERTISEMENTS

*Advertisements can be found
on the following pages*

"A wonderful place for a wonderful retirement"

The College of St Barnabas, set in beautiful Surrey countryside, is a residential community of retired Anglican clergy. Married couples are very welcome, as are those who have been widowed. Admission is open to licensed Church Workers and Readers; there are facilities for visitors and guests. Occasional quiet days and private retreats can also be accommodated.

Residents are encouraged to lead active, independent lives. There is a Nursing Wing, to which direct admission is also possible, providing residential and full nursing care for those who need it. This enables most residents to remain members of the College for the rest of their lives. It is sometimes possible to offer respite care here.

Sheltered 'Cloister flats' all have separate sitting rooms, bedrooms and *en suite* facilities. There are two Chapels; Mass and Evensong are celebrated daily. We have three Libraries and a well equipped Common Room. Meals are served in the Refectory or may be taken privately when necessary.

For further details or to arrange a preliminary visit please see our website or contact the Warden, Fr Howard Such, at:

The College of St Barnabas
Blackberry Lane, Lingfield, Surrey RH7 6NJ

Tel: 01342 870260   Fax: 01342 871672
Email: warden@collegeofstbarnabas.com
Website: www.st-barnabas.org.uk

or visit us at the national CRE at Sandown Park

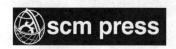

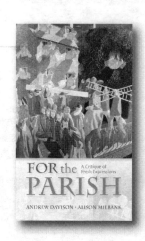

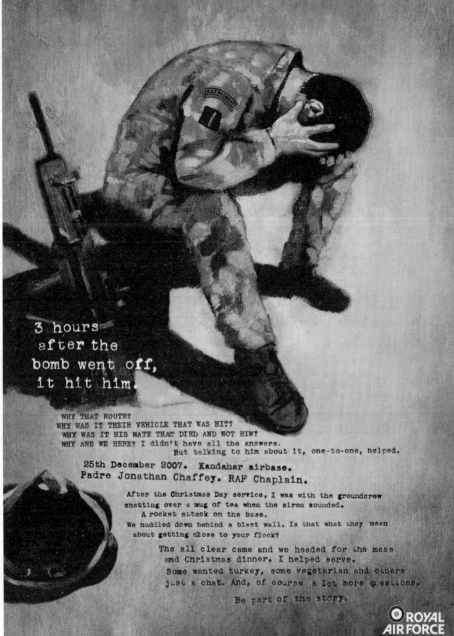

3 hours
after the
bomb went off,
it hit him.

WHY THAT ROUTE?
WHY WAS IT THEIR VEHICLE THAT WAS HIT?
WHY WAS IT HIS MATE THAT DIED AND NOT HIM?
WHY ARE WE HERE? I didn't have all the answers.
But talking to him about it, one-to-one, helped.

25th December 2007. Kandahar airbase.
Padre Jonathan Chaffey. RAF Chaplain.

After the Christmas Day service, I was with the groundcrew
chatting over a mug of tea when the siren sounded.
A rocket attack on the base.
We huddled down behind a blast wall. Is that what they mean
about getting close to your flock?

The all clear came and we headed for the mess
and Christmas dinner. I helped serve.
Some wanted turkey, some vegetarian and others
just a chat. And, of course a lot more questions.

Be part of the story.

ROYAL
AIR FORCE

Search online for RAF Chaplains

The Royal Air Force values every individual's unique contribution, irrespective
of race, ethnic origin, religion, gender, sexual orientation or social background.

The Kingdom of God belongs to such as these...

The Children's Society

God's unconditional love, as seen in the life and ministry of Jesus, inspires us to work with all children and young people. We show God's love through our work with children at risk on the streets, disabled children, young refugees, young carers and those within the youth justice system.

You can join us through:

Worship – by holding a Christingle service

Joining our Campaign – to make young runaways safe. Sign up at **www.makerunawayssafe.org.uk**

Prayer – in church or in your personal prayer time

For more information on free resources and how to get your church involved visit **www.childrenssociety.org.uk** or call our Supporter Care team on **0845 300 1128**

Charity Registration No. 221124
Photograph modelled for The Children's Society | © Laurence Dutton

A better childhood. For every child.   www.childrenssociety.org.uk

Christian Aid has produced a series of studies, written by experienced and well-informed contributors, to inspire and challenge your Church members, or home or Bible study group.

Each study considers topics of the Millennium Development Goals (MDGs) from the perspective of the Christian faith, providing a commentary, a reflection, discussion starters, a prayer and suggestions for action.

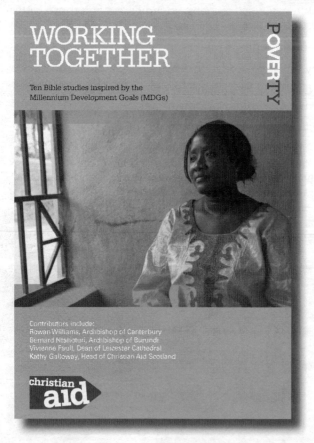

WORKING TOGETHER

POVERTY

Ten Bible studies inspired by the Millennium Development Goals (MDGs)

Contributors include:
Rowan Williams, Archbishop of Canterbury
Bernard Ntahoturi, Archbishop of Burundi
Vivienne Faull, Dean of Leicester Cathedral
Kathy Galloway, Head of Christian Aid Scotland

christian aid

For your free copy, please email **churches@christian-aid.org** giving your address and the number of copies you require. Alternatively, you can download a copy from:**christianaid.org.uk/resources/churches/ resources/working-together.aspx**

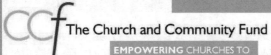

The Church and Community Fund

EMPOWERING CHURCHES TO
TRANSFORM COMMUNITIES

✠ THE CHURCH
OF ENGLAND

ARCHBISHOPS'
COUNCIL

Web: www.ccfund.org.uk ⌐ Email: ccf@churchofengland.org ⌐ Twitter: @ccf_cofe

In 2012 The CCF will support community projects that:

• Significantly expand the Church's engagement with neighbourhood renewal;

• Seek innovative ways of developing established community projects so that they either a) grow existing or b) evolve into new communities of Christian Faith, and;

• Replicate models of successful community engagement across the wider church.

We warmly welcome donations and legacies in support of our work. We support the local Church in responding to greatest needs and opportunities throughout the country bringing about lasting change in many communities across England.

The Church and Community Fund (formerly known as the Central Church Fund) is a charitable trust fund under the trusteeship of The Archbishops' Council. The Archbishops' Council is a registered charity (1074857).

INTRODUCTION

This, the one hundred and second edition of *Crockford's Clerical Directory*, provides details as at 5 August 2011 of almost 27,000 clergy and deaconesses in the Church of England (including the Diocese in Europe), the Church in Wales, the Scottish Episcopal Church, and the Church of Ireland. It also includes in the main biographical section those Michaelmas ordinands of whom we were notified in advance.

First published in 1858, the publication of *Crockford* now spans one and a half centuries. The Oxford University Press purchased the copyright for *Crockford* in 1921, publishing thirty-six editions before transferring ownership to the Church Commissioners and the Central Board of Finance, on economic grounds, sixty years later. This is the third edition under the sole ownership of the Archbishops' Council.

The publishing, design, advertising, selling and distribution of the directory are carried out by Church House Publishing in partnership with the *Crockford* Department, who are responsible for the actual compilation of the text. The information that generates the biographical entries is stored on a database, which is updated daily. Much of this information is obtained from the direct link with the Church Commissioners' central clergy pay-roll. Any alterations to this pay-roll (for example, changes of address or appointment) are automatically reflected on the *Crockford* database. However, nearly 8,500 (almost one-third) of the clergy are not on the central pay-roll. These are principally non-stipendiary ministers, those engaged in some form of ministry outside the parochial system (such as hospital, university, prison or service chaplains) and those serving in Wales, Scotland and Ireland. In maintaining the records of these clergy, we continue to rely greatly on the assistance of bishops' secretaries and diocesan offices, and information contained in diocesan directories, year books and the Church Press. We are also grateful for the help provided by the central authorities of the Church in Wales, the Scottish Episcopal Church, the Church of Ireland, the Ministry of Defence, the Hospital Chaplaincies Council, and our various overseas contacts.

A tremendous amount of help has come from the clergy themselves. We are enormously grateful to all those who have provided us with information, and have helped to minimize omissions and errors. For reasons of time, space and consistency, we are unable to include all the information clergy request us to publish, and we apologise that it has not been possible to respond to each letter individually. We are also grateful to Richard Christmas, Angela Florence and Catherine Martini, who have been responsible for most of the work in compiling the directory.

We are always glad to be informed of amendments to entries, and we particularly appreciate any information about clergy whose addresses are not currently known to us (see list on p. 1281). Information relating to omissions or amendments should be sent to the *Crockford* Department; requests for archival information from earlier editions should be addressed in writing to Lambeth Palace Library; and requests for other information which cannot be found on the Church of England's web site (at www.cofe.anglican.org) should be addressed to the Communications Office.

Crockford Department	*The Librarian*	*The Communications Office*
Church House	*Lambeth Palace Library*	*Church House*
Great Smith Street	*Lambeth Palace*	*Great Smith Street*
London SW1P 3AZ	*London SE1 7JU*	*London SW1P 3AZ*
Tel (020) 7898 1012	Tel (020) 7898 1400	Tel (020) 7898 1463
	Fax (020) 7928 7932	
E-mail crockford@churchofengland.org	E-mail lpl.staff@churchofengland.org	E-mail feedback@churchofengland.org

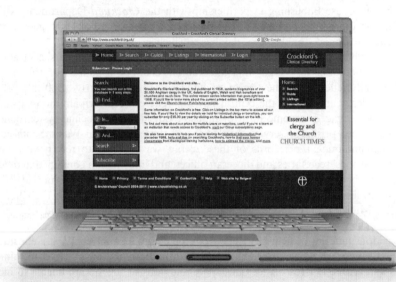

JOHN CROCKFORD

John Crockford was the eldest child of a Somerset schoolmaster and his wife, John and Hannah Crockford; and by 1841 he was working as an attorney's clerk in Taunton, Somerset. John Crockford Sr was described in 1869 as Gentleman, of Rowbarton near Taunton. By his early twenties he was in business as a printer and publisher at 29 Essex Street, Strand; and it was from that address that *Crockford* was first published in 1858. On 6 December of the same year, John Crockford moved to new business premises at 346 Strand and 19 Wellington Street North.

His private address at that time was 16 Oakley Square, Hampstead Road; though by 1865 he had moved to 10 Park Road, Haverstock Hill.

Crockford's business association of more than two decades with Edward William Cox (1809–1879) had begun in 1843, when the *Law Times* first appeared. Both men are claimed as publisher – Crockford by Boase in *Modern English Biography*; Cox by the *Athenaeum* and by *Notes and Queries*. There is similar lack of agreement over other publications, such as the ill-fated *Critic*. "[Crockford] tried to establish a literary paper, the *Critic*. To this he brought all his great ability, but after fifteen years he gave it up in despair" (*Notes and Queries*): whereas the *Dictionary of National Biography* has it that Cox became "proprietor of . . . two other papers called respectively 'The Critic' and 'The Royal Exchange'."

The truth appears to be that the two men, who shared the same business address in Essex Street, were joint founders of a number of projects. Cox – the elder, more established and richer man – was often the financier and named publisher, with Crockford as the manager of the undertaking. Each had his own specialities: Cox, called to the bar in 1843, and successively Recorder of Helston & Falmouth (1857–1868) and of Portsmouth (1868–1879), was no doubt the leader in the establishment of the *Law Times*, to which, in *DNB*'s words, he "thenceforth devoted . . . the larger portion of his time and attention." But the legend which has arisen that Cox, restrained by professional ethics from using his own name, chose, almost at random, the name of one of his clerks to bear the title of his new clerical directory in 1858 – thus, in the words of the first postwar editor (probably Newman) bestowing "a more than tomb-stone meed of remembrance" – cannot be substantiated. As the jubilee account of the *Field* notes, Crockford was an equal partner in the success of the joint enterprises: "It was John Crockford who purchased the paper for Mr Cox. He obtained it from Mr Benjamin Webster for a trifling sum . . . In a short time the net profits amounted to 20,000*l.* a year. The management was placed under Crockford's control. He was a splendid man of business" (*Notes and Queries*).

The first *Clerical Directory* (1858), "A Biographical and Statistical Book of Reference for facts relating to the clergy and the Church", seems to have been assembled in a very haphazard fashion, with names added "as fast as they could be obtained", out of alphabetical order and with an unreliable index. By 1860 the *Directory* had become a very much more useful work of reference; and by 1917, with the absorption of its only serious rival, the *Clergy List*, reigned supreme.

No more than glimpses survive of Crockford's personality, and those mostly from the account of him given by John C. Francis, in the *Field* jubilee article already referred to. "I had occasion to call upon him a short time before his death, when we joined in a hearty laugh over his former furious attacks upon the *Athenaeum*. 'Dilke's Drag' he used to call it, and would accuse it of 'vulgar insolence and coxcombry' and 'the coarsest vulgarity'. As we parted he said, 'You have the *Athenaeum* to be proud of, and we have the *Field*.'"

John Crockford died suddenly at his home on 13 January 1865, at the age of 41. He left a widow, Annie (née Ellam) whom he married on 24 December 1847 at St Pancras Old Church. A daughter, Florence Annie, was born in St Pancras in 1852. (Florence married Arthur Brownlow in 1875 and had a son called Frederick.) His very brief will, proved 6 February 1865 at the Principal Probate Registry, left everything to his widow. His personal effects were valued at less than £1,000, but the family must have lived in some style, since one of the witnesses to the will was the resident coachman. Crockford's widow moved to 4 Upper Eton Place, Tavistock Hill, and died there on 26 July 1868.

BRENDA HOUGH

A request from the *Dictionary of National Biography* for a notice of the life of John Crockford led to the preparation of this article, a shorter version of which appeared in *The Dictionary of National Biography: Missing Persons*, 1993. For the information from the 1841 Census, and the record of Crockford's daughter Florence, we are indebted to Mr Ken Rhoades, of Kent.

A USER'S GUIDE TO *CROCKFORD*

Who is included in Crockford?
Crockford includes details of over 26,000 clergy and deaconesses of the Church of England, the Church in Wales, the Scottish Episcopal Church and the Church of Ireland. Clergy currently serving overseas qualify for inclusion if they have trained or have been licensed in this country (see **Overseas clergy**). Clergy who have died since the last edition are listed on p. 1284. Generally, clergy who have resigned their offices (but not their orders) are included unless they are known to have been received into another Church. A small number of clergy are excluded at their own request.

Readers and lay workers are not included: please consult diocesan directories. The *Who's Who* section of *The Church of England Year Book* (published annually by Church House Publishing and covering most aspects of the life and institutions of the Church of England) lists members of General Synod and principal members of staff of the Church's central organizations.

Addresses and telephone numbers
Where more than one telephone number is given, the first will normally relate to the address shown.

Addressing the clergy
See p. *31*.

Appointment details in the *Biographies* section
These reflect the legal pastoral situation prevailing at 5 August 2011, the date of the compilation of this edition of *Crockford*. Conventional districts, proprietary chapels and local ecumenical projects are also recorded. Benefice names are only recorded once in a biographical entry when they apply to successive appointments.

Crockford does not record group ministries, informal local arrangements, areas of special responsibility, emeritus appointments (except as reflected in the style of address), licence or permission to officiate when held in conjunction with another appointment from the same diocese, commissary appointments, examining chaplaincies, or secular appointments (except for educational or charitable posts).

Appointments held before ordination are not included (apart from service as a deaconess) unless they straddle the date of ordination.

Archbishops overseas
The presiding (arch-)bishop or metropolitan of each of the provinces of the Anglican Communion is listed in the main *Biographies* section, cross-referenced as appropriate, together with the Moderator of each of the united churches.

Archdeaconries
See *Archdeaconries, deaneries and rural deans* on p. 1008.

Archdeacons
Look up the place name in *Biographies*: this is cross-referenced to a personal name.

Bishops (diocesan, area, suffragan, and provincial episcopal visitors)
Look up the place name in *Biographies*: this is cross-referenced to a personal name. See also p. 958, which lists the diocesan, area, suffragan and assistant bishops by diocese, as well as provincial episcopal visitors.

Bishops (assistant)
See *Bishops in England, Wales, Scotland and Ireland* on p. 958.

Bishops in the House of Lords
See p. 961.

Bishops overseas
See *Bishops of Anglican dioceses overseas* on p. 1251, and *Bishops of united churches* on p. 1273. Further information about the Anglican Communion can be found in *The Church of England Year Book.*

Bishops and archbishops, former
A list of former archbishops and bishops (diocesan and suffragan) will be found on p. 962.

Boundaries, provincial and diocesan
Maps of England and Wales, Scotland and Ireland, showing provincial and diocesan boundaries and cathedral cities, will be found on p. 1290.

Cathedral clergy
See *Cathedrals* on p. 1001 for full-time cathedral clergy. The list does not include honorary appointments.

Chapel Royal
See *Royal Peculiars* on p. 1003.

Christian names
The name by which a person prefers to be known, if not the first Christian name, is underlined (for example, SMITH, David John prefers to be called John). Names 'in religion' or names not part of a person's legal name are shown in parentheses.

Church: how to find the names of clergy responsible for a particular church
Look up the place name in the appropriate *Benefices and churches* section, see p. 1016: if the entry is in bold type, the names of all clergy are listed and can be cross-referenced in the *Biographies* section; if the place name is not in bold type, the name of the benefice is given where the names of all clergy will be found.

Church: how to find the names of clergy responsible for a particular church when there is a vacancy
If the benefice is vacant, the telephone number of the clergy house is usually given in the appropriate *Benefices and churches* section to enable contact to be made with a new incumbent or priest-in-charge. The deanery reference (e.g. *Guildf 2*) following the benefice name cross-refers to *Archdeaconries, deaneries and rural deans* on p. 1008 by means of which the name of the rural dean responsible for the vacant benefice can be found.

College chaplains
See p. 1245 for chaplains at universities, colleges of further education, colleges of higher education, sixth-form colleges, and schools.

Corrections
Please send notice of any corrections to:
Crockford Compiler, Church House, Great Smith Street, London SW1P 3AZ
Tel (020) 7898 1012 Fax (020) 7898 1769 E-mail crockford@churchofengland.org

Crockford
The full title is *Crockford's Clerical Directory. Crockford* (not *Crockford's*) is an accepted abbreviation. See also the biography of John Crockford on p. *23.*

Deaconesses
See separate section on p. 957.

Deacons
See *Biographies* section.

Deaneries
See rural or area deans below.

Deans
Look up the place name in *Biographies*: this is cross-referenced to a personal name. See also *Cathedrals* on p. 1001, and *Royal Peculiars* on p 1003.

Diocesan offices
Details of the diocesan offices in England, Wales, Scotland and Ireland can be found on p. 1004.

E-mail addresses
These are provided where known. See after the telephone and/or fax number.

Europe, chaplains in
See *Chaplains of the Diocese of Gibraltar in Europe* on p. 1228.

Fax numbers
The exchange number is only given if different from that of the preceding telephone number.

Hospital chaplains
Whole-time and part-time hospital chaplains are listed under their NHS trusts on p 1235. Cross-references have been inserted for individual hospitals.

Lay workers
Lay workers are not included in *Crockford*: please consult diocesan directories.

London churches
See *English benefices and churches* on p. 1016. City and Guild churches are listed under LONDON CITY CHURCHES and LONDON GUILD CHURCHES. In other cases, see under church name (e.g. LANGHAM PLACE (All Souls), WESTMINSTER (St Matthew)).

Married or single?
Crockford does not provide information on marital status. However, we have included the form of address Miss, Mrs or Ms where requested. Where there has been a change of surname, a cross-reference may be found from the previous name.

Non-stipendiary clergy
Non-stipendiary clergy are listed in the main *Biographies* section.

Ordination courses
See *Theological colleges and courses* on p. 1249.

Overseas clergy
Clergy who are on the *Crockford* database and who are currently serving overseas qualify for inclusion. Service overseas has in the past been recorded simply by country, though higher office (e.g. as bishop or archdeacon) has also been noted. Other eligible appointments are now being added on request.
   Overseas addresses and telephone numbers are given as required by a user in the UK, and include the international access and country codes, as well as the area code. If dialling from within the country concerned, the user will need to omit the international access and country codes, and dial zero immediately before the area code.

Patronage
The patron of each benefice is listed under the benefice name in *English benefices and churches* on p. 1016.

Prison chaplains
See p. 1233.

Proprietary chapels
See *English benefices and churches* on p. 1016.

Provincial episcopal visitors
Look up the place name in *Biographies*: this is cross-referenced to a personal name. See also p. 958, which lists the diocesan, area, suffragan and assistant bishops and provincial episcopal visitors.

Provosts
Look up the place name in *Biographies*: this is cross-referenced to a personal name. See also *Cathedrals* on p. 1001.

Queen's Chaplains
See *Royal Peculiars* on p. 1003.

Readers
Readers are not included in *Crockford*: please consult diocesan directories.

Religious orders
For members of religious orders where the Christian name alone is commonly used (e.g. Brother Aidan) a cross-reference is provided to the surname. Names 'in religion' not forming part of a person's legal name will be shown in parentheses. Details of religious communities are provided in *The Church of England Year Book*.

Retired clergy
The description 'rtd' does not imply that ministry has ceased, only that clergy so described are now in receipt of a pension. All eligible appointments are now recorded.

Rural or area deans
See *Archdeaconries, deaneries and rural deans* on p. 1008. To find who is the rural dean of a particular church, look up the place or benefice name in the appropriate *Benefices* section: the deanery reference (e.g. *Guildf 2*) following the benefice name cross-refers to *Archdeaconries, deaneries and rural deans* on p. 1008 where the name of the rural dean responsible can be found.

School chaplains
See p. 1247 for chaplains in schools.

Service chaplains
See p. 1231.

Sixth-form colleges
See p. 1246.

Theological colleges and courses
See p. 1249.

University chaplains
See p. 1245.

HOW TO ADDRESS THE CLERGY

In offering the advice below, we do not intend to imply that other practices are necessarily to be discouraged (for example, the use of Father as in 'Father Smith'). A good deal depends on circumstances, and, where a personal preference is known, it is usually good practice to follow it.

The following notes show acceptable current usage

(a) on an envelope or formal listing
(b) in starting a social letter or in speech, and
(c) when referring to a member of the clergy

Category (a) is not open to much variation, owing to the formality of the context, but categories (b) and (c) will often vary according to circumstances. It is always acceptable to use the appropriate Christian name in place of initials (for example, the Revd Alice Smith). In the absence of any style or title conferred by a post, all deacons and priests are styled 'The Reverend', and all who have been consecrated bishop are styled 'The Right Reverend'.

For abbreviations, see paragraph 13 below.

1 Deacons and Priests

(a) The Reverend A B Smith
(b) Mr/Mrs/Miss/Ms Smith (unless it is known that some other style is preferred – the title Vicar or Rector is acceptable only if the person so addressed really is the incumbent of the parish where you live or worship)
(c) The Reverend A B Smith at the first mention, and Mr/Mrs/Miss/Ms Smith thereafter

Notes 1 The form 'Reverend Smith' or 'The Reverend Smith' should *never* be used this side of the Atlantic. If the Christian name or initials are not known, the correct forms are
(a) The Reverend—Smith, *or* The Reverend Mr/Mrs/Miss/Ms Smith
(b) Mr/Mrs/Miss/Ms Smith
(c) The Reverend Mr/Mrs/Miss/Ms Smith at the first mention, and Mr/Mrs/Miss/Ms Smith thereafter

2 There is no universally accepted way of addressing an envelope to a married couple of whom both are in holy orders. We recommend the style 'The Reverend A B and the Reverend C D Smith'.

2 Prebendaries

(a) The Reverend Prebendary A B Smith
(b) Prebendary Smith
(c) Prebendary Smith

3 Canons (both Residentiary and Honorary)

(a) The Reverend Canon A B Smith
(b) Canon Smith
(c) Canon Smith

4 Archdeacons

(a) The Venerable the Archdeacon of X
(b) Archdeacon, *or more formally* Mr/Madam Archdeacon
(c) The Archdeacon of X at the first mention, and the Archdeacon thereafter

Notes 1 In the case of an archdeacon (or dean/provost, bishop, or archbishop) in office, the style above is to be preferred. The personal name should be used only for the purpose of identification.

2 For an archdeacon emeritus, the correct forms are
(a) The Venerable A B Smith
(b) Archdeacon
(c) Archdeacon Smith

5 Deans and Provosts
(a) The Very Reverend the Dean/Provost of X
(b) Dean/Provost, *or more formally* Mr/Madam Dean/Provost
(c) The Dean/Provost of X at the first mention, and the Dean thereafter (see also note 1 to paragraph 4 above)

6 Bishops, Diocesan and Suffragan
(a) The Right Reverend the Bishop of X, *or* The Right Reverend the Lord Bishop of X
(b) Bishop, *or more formally* My Lord
(c) The Bishop of X at the first mention, and the Bishop thereafter (see also note 1 to paragraph 4 above)

Notes 1 The use of 'Lord' before 'Bishop' is diminishing. It is a matter of individual preference whether it should be used.
2 The Bishop of London is a Privy Councillor, and has the style 'The Right Reverend and Right Honourable the Lord Bishop of London'.
3 The Bishop of Meath and Kildare is styled 'The Most Reverend'.

7 Assistant and Retired Bishops
(a) The Right Reverend A B Smith
(b) Bishop
(c) Bishop Smith

8 Archbishops
(a) The Most Reverend the Lord Archbishop of X
(b) Archbishop, *or more formally* Your Grace
(c) The Archbishop of X at the first mention, and the Archbishop thereafter (see also note 1 to paragraph 4 above)

Notes 1 The Archbishops of Canterbury and York, being Privy Councillors, also have 'Right Honourable' included in their style (for example, The Most Reverend and Right Honourable the Lord Archbishop of Canterbury).
2 The presiding bishop of the Scottish Episcopal Church is the Primus, and the correct forms are
  (a) The Most Reverend the Primus
  (b) Primus
  (c) Primus
3 A retired archbishop properly reverts to the status of bishop, but may be given as a courtesy the style of an archbishop.

9 Chaplains to the Armed Services
(a) The Reverend A B Smith RN (*or* CF *or* RAF)
(b) Padre, *or* Padre Smith
(c) The Padre, *or* Padre Smith

10 Titled Clerics
Where a member of the clergy also holds a temporal title, this is always preceded in writing by the ecclesiastical one.

Barons (other than retired archbishops)
(a) The Reverend the Lord Smith of Y
(b) Lord Smith
(c) The Reverend the Lord Smith at the first mention, and Lord Smith thereafter

Baronets
(a) The Reverend Sir Alan Smith Bt
(b) Sir Alan Smith or Sir Alan
(c) The Reverend Sir Alan Smith at the first mention, and Sir Alan Smith thereafter

Knights
An ordained priest may be appointed to an order of knighthood, but will not normally receive the accolade or title. The appropriate designation will follow the name or

ecclesiastical title (for example, The Right Reverend the Bishop of X, KCVO). If he was knighted *before* he was ordained, he will retain his title.

11 Ordained Members of Religious Orders

(a) The Reverend Alan/Alice Smith XYZ; The Reverend Brother Alan/Sister Alice XYZ
(b) Father, Father Smith, *or* Father Alan; Brother Alan/Sister Alice
(c) The Reverend Alan/Alice Smith; Father Alan Smith; Father Smith; Brother Alan/Sister Alice

Notes 1 A name 'in religion', shown in parentheses in the biographical entry, should be used in preference to the baptismal name or initials. Sometimes the surname is not used. In this Directory, however, the entry will be found under the surname, whether it is normally used or not, and, if appropriate, a cross-reference is given under the Christian name.
2 Some orders use 'Brother' and 'Sister' for lay and ordained members without distinction, along with Christian names.
3 It is customary to specify the religious order by giving the appropriate letters after the name.

12 Academics

When a member of the clergy holds more than one title, the ecclesiastical one is normally used.

Professor	(a)	The Reverend Canon A B Smith
also Canon	(b)	Canon Smith, *or* Professor Smith, according to context
	(c)	Canon Smith, *or* Professor Smith, according to context
Canon	(a)	The Reverend Canon A B Smith (degree)
also Doctor	(b)	Canon Smith, *or* Dr Smith, according to context
	(c)	Canon Smith, *or* Dr Smith, according to context

13 Abbreviations

The following abbreviations are in common use

Reverend:	Revd *or* Rev
Father:	Fr
Right Reverend:	Rt Revd *or* Rt Rev
Prebendary:	Preb
Venerable:	Ven

Reverend, Right Reverend, Very Reverend, Most Reverend and Venerable, whether abbreviated or not, should always be preceded by the definite article.

TACKLING POVERTY TOGETHER
CHURCH URBAN FUND

TOGETHER
WE CAN TACKLE
POVERTY IN ENGLAND

JOIN US AND SHOW YOU STAND WITH
CHRISTIANS WORKING TO TRANSFORM
THE LIVES OF THE POOREST AND MOST
MARGINALISED IN ENGLAND:
WWW.CUF.ORG.UK/TOGETHER

ABBREVIATIONS USED IN CROCKFORD'S CLERICAL DIRECTORY

A

AAAI .... Associate, Institute of Administrative Accountants
AB .... Bachelor of Arts (USA)
ABEng............. Associate Member of the Association of Building Engineers
ABIA............... Associate, Bankers' Institute of Australasia
ABIPP .... Associate, British Institute of Professional Photography
ABIST .... Associate, British Institute of Surgical Technology
ABM .... Advisory Board of Ministry (now Ministry Division)
ABPsS............. Associate, British Psychological Society (now see AFBPsS)
ABSM .... Associate, Birmingham and Midland Institute School of Music
ACA .... Associate, Institute of Chartered Accountants
ACC .... Anglican Consultative Council
ACCA .... Associate, Chartered Association of Certified Accountants (formerly AACCA)
ACCM............. Advisory Council for the Church's Ministry (now Ministry Division)
ACCS .... Associate, Corporation of Secretaries
ACCTS............. Association for Christian Conferences, Teaching, and Service
ACE.................. Associateship of the College of Education
.... Member, Association of Conference Executives
ACF.................. Army Cadet Force
ACIArb .... Associate, Chartered Institute of Arbitrators
ACIB .... Associate, Chartered Institute of Bankers (formerly AIB)
ACIBS .... Associate, Chartered Institute of Bankers in Scotland
ACII .... Associate, Chartered Insurance Institute
ACIOB .... Associate, Chartered Institute of Building
ACIPA............... Associate, Chartered Institute of Patent Agents
ACIPD .... Associate, Chartered Institute of Personnel and Development
ACIS.................. Associate, Institute of Chartered Secretaries and Administrators
ACIT .... Associate, Chartered Institute of Transport
ACMA .... Associate, Chartered Institute of Management Accountants (formerly ACWA)
ACMI................. Associate, Chartered Management Institute (formerly AIMgt)
ACORA .... Archbishops' Commission on Rural Areas
ACP.................. Associate, College of Preceptors
ACS .... Additional Curates Society
ACSM .... Associate, Camborne School of Mines
ACT.................. Australian Capital Territory
.... Australian College of Theology
ACUPA .... Archbishops' Commission on Urban Priority Areas
AD.................... Area Dean
AEdRD .... Associateship in Educational Research and Development
AFAIM .... Associate Fellow, Australian Institute of Management

AFBPsS............ Associate Fellow, British Psychological Society (formerly ABPsS)
AFC .... Air Force Cross
AFIMA............ Associate Fellow, Institute of Mathematics and its Applications
AFOM .... Associate, Faculty of Occupational Medicine
AGSM.............. Associate, Guildhall School of Music and Drama
AHSM or AHA Associate, Institute of Health Service Management (formerly Administrators)
AIA .... Associate, Institute of Actuaries
AIAS .... Associate, Incorporated Association of Architects and Surveyors
AIAT .... Associate, Institute of Animal Technicians
AIDS................. Acquired Immunity Deficiency Syndrome
AIFST .... Associate, Institute of Food Science and Technology
AIGCM............. Associate, Incorporated Guild of Church Musicians
AIIM .... Associate, Institute of Investment Management
AIL................... Associate, Institute of Linguists
AIMLS.............. Associate, Institute of Medical Laboratory Sciences
AIMSW............. Associate, Institute of Medical Social Work
AIMgt............... Associate, Institute of Management (now see ACMI)
AIPM .... Associate, Institute of Personnel Management (now see ACIPD)
AITI .... Associate, Institute of Taxation in Ireland
AKC .... Associate, King's College London
ALA .... Associate, Library Association
ALAM .... Associate, London Academy of Music
ALBC................ Associate, London Bible College
ALCD .... Associate, London College of Divinity
ALCM............... Associate, London College of Music
ALSM .... Associate, Lancashire School of Music
AM.................... Albert Medal
.... Master of Arts (USA)
AMA .... Associate, Museums Association
AMASI .... Associate Member of the Architects and Surveyors Institute
AMCST............. Associate, Manchester College of Science and Technology
AMCT............... Associate, Manchester College of Technology
AMIBF .... Associate Member, Institute of British Foundrymen
AMIC................ Associate Member, Institute of Counselling
AMICME .... Associate Member, Institute of Cast Metal Engineers
AMIDHE.......... Associate Member, Institute of Domestic Heating Engineers
AMIEHO.......... Associate Member, Institution of Environmental Health Officers
AMIM .... Associate Member, Institute of Metals
AMIMMM ...... Associate Member, Institute of Materials, Minerals and Mining
AMITD............ Associate Member, Institute of Training and Development (now see ACIPD)

AMIW.............. Associate Member, Institute of Welfare (formerly AMIWO)
AMInstT .... Associate Member, Institute of Transport
AMInstTA .... Associate Member, Institute of Transport Administration
AMRSH........... Associate Member, Royal Society of Health
AMSIA .... Associate Member, Society of Investment Analysts
AMusLCM ...... Associate in Music, London College of Music
AMusTCL......... Associate in Music, Trinity College of Music London
ANC.................. African National Congress
AO.................... Officer, Order of Australia
APhS .... Associate, Philosophical Society of England
ARAM .... Associate, Royal Academy of Music
ARCA .... Associate, Royal College of Art
ARCIC .... Anglican Roman Catholic International Commission
ARCM.............. Associate, Royal College of Music
ARCO .... Associate, Royal College of Organists
ARCO(CHM) ... Associate, Royal College of Organists with Diploma in Choir Training
ARCS .... Associate, Royal College of Science
ARCST............. Associate, Royal College of Science and Technology (Glasgow)
ARCT............... Associate, Royal Conservatory of Music Toronto
ARCUK .... Architects' Registration Council of the United Kingdom
ARHistS........... Associate, Royal Historical Society
ARIAM............ Associate, Royal Irish Academy of Music
ARMCM .... Associate, Royal Manchester College of Music
ARPS .... Associate, Royal Photographic Society
ARSCM .... Associate, Royal School of Church Music
ARSM .... Associate, Royal School of Mines
AS.................... Associate in Science (USA)
ASCA................ Associate, Society of Company and Commercial Accountants
ASSP .... Society of All Saints Sisters of the Poor
ASVA .... Associate, Incorporated Society of Valuers and Auctioneers
ATC.................. Air Training Corps
ATCL .... Associate, Trinity College of Music London
ATD .... Art Teacher's Diploma
ATI .... Associate, Textile Institute
ATII .... Associate Member, Institute of Taxation
ATL.................. Association of Teachers and Lecturers
ATV.................. Associated Television
ATh(SA)........... Associate in Theology (South Africa)
AVCM .... Associate, Victoria College of Music
Ab..................... (Diocese of) Aberdeen and Orkney
Aber.................. Aberdeen
Abp................... Archbishop
Abth .... Aberystwyth
Ad..................... Advanced
AdDipEd........... Advanced Diploma in Education
Admin............... Administration
.... Administrative
.... Administrator

Adn.................. Archdeacon
Adnry .... Archdeaconry
Adv.................. Adviser
.... Advisory
Agric................ Agricultural
.... Agriculture
Aid.................. Aidan
.... Aidan's
alt.................... alternate
Andr .... Andrew
.... Andrew's
.... Andrews
Angl................ Anglican
.... Anglicans
Ant .... Anthony
.... Anthony's
Appt .... Appointment
Arg .... (Diocese of) Argyll and The
                     Isles
Arm................. (Diocese of) Armagh
Assn................ Association
Assoc .... Associate
Asst................ Assistant
Aug................. Augustine
.... Augustine's
Aus .... Australian
Aux .... Auxiliaries
.... Auxiliary

B

b...................... Born
B & W .... (Diocese of) Bath and Wells
B or Bapt.......... Baptist
.... Baptist's
BA .... Bachelor of Arts
BA(Econ) .... Bachelor of Arts in
                     Economics
BA(Ed)............ Bachelor of Arts in
                     Education
BA(QTS)........... Bachelor of Arts (Qualified
                     Teacher Status)
BA(ThM).......... Bachelor of Arts in Theology
                     in Ministry
BA(Theol) .... Bachelor of Arts in Theology
BAI................ Bachelor of Engineering
                     (also see BE and BEng)
BAO .... Bachelor of Obstetrics
BASc .... Bachelor of Applied Science
BATM .... Bachelor of Arts in Theology
                     and Ministry
BAdmin........... Bachelor of Administration
BAgr .... Bachelor of Agriculture
BAgrSc........... Bachelor of Agricultural
                     Science
BAppSc .... Bachelor of Applied Science
BAppSc(Agric).. Bachelor of Applied Science
                     (Agriculture)
BAppSc(OT) ..... Bachelor of Applied Science
                     (Occupational Therapy)
BArch .... Bachelor of Architecture
BBA............... Bachelor of Business
                     Administration
BBC................ British Broadcasting
                     Corporation
BBS .... Bachelor of Business Studies
BC .... British Columbia (Canada)
BCA .... Bachelor of Commerce and
                     Administration
BCC............... British Council of Churches
                     (now CTBI)
BCE................ Bachelor of Civil
                     Engineering
BCL .... Bachelor of Civil Law
BCMS .... Bible Churchmen's
                     Missionary Society (now
                     Crosslinks)
BCh or BChir .... Bachelor of Surgery (also see
                     BS and ChB)
BChD .... Bachelor of Dental Surgery
BCom or .... Bachelor of Commerce
BComm...........
BCombStuds ..... Bachelor of Combined
                     Studies
BCommWelf...... Bachelor of Community
                     Welfare
BD.................. Bachelor of Divinity
BDA .... Bachelor of Dramatic Art
BDQ .... Bachelor of Divinity
                     Qualifying Examination
BDS................ Bachelor of Dental Surgery
BDSc .... Bachelor of Dental Science
BDiv .... Bachelor of Divinity

BE.................. Bachelor of Engineering
                     (also see BAI and BEng)
BEM .... British Empire Medal
BEc................. Bachelor of Economics
                     (Australia)
BEcon.............. Bachelor of Economics
                     (USA)
BEd .... Bachelor of Education
BEdSt .... Bachelor of Educational
                     Studies
BEng............... Bachelor of Engineering
                     (also see BAI and BE)
BFA .... Bachelor of Fine Arts
BFBS .... British and Foreign Bible
                     Society
BHSc .... Bachelor of Health Sciences
BIE .... Bachelor of Industrial
                     Engineering (USA)
BL.................. Bachelor of Law
BLib .... Bachelor of Librarianship
BLitt .... Bachelor of Letters
BM .... Bachelor of Medicine (also
                     see MB)
BM, BCh .... Conjoint degree of Bachelor
                     of Medicine, Bachelor of
                     Surgery
BMMF .... Bible and Medical
                     Missionary Fellowship (now
                     Interserve)
BMU .... Board for Mission and
                     Unity
BMedSci........... Bachelor of Medical Science
BMet .... Bachelor of Metallurgy
BMin .... Bachelor of Ministry
BMus.............. Bachelor of Music (also see
                     MusB and MusBac)
BMusEd .... Bachelor of Music
                     Education
BN .... Bachelor of Nursing
BNC .... Brasenose College
BPR&TM........... Bachelor of Parks,
                     Recreation and Tourism
                     Management
BPaed .... Bachelor of Paediatrics
BPh or BPhil ..... Bachelor of Philosophy
BPharm .... Bachelor of Pharmacy
BPhil(Ed).......... Bachelor of Philosophy
                     (Education)
BPl................. Bachelor of Planning
BProfStud......... Bachelor of Professional
                     Studies
BRE................ Bachelor of Religious
                     Education (USA)
BRF................ Bible Reading Fellowship
BS .... Bachelor of Science (also see
                     BSc)
.... Bachelor of Surgery (also see
                     BCh, BChir and ChB)
BSB .... Brotherhood of St Barnabas
BSE .... Bachelor of Science in
                     Engineering (also see
                     BScEng)
BSEd .... Bachelor of Science in
                     Education (USA)
BSP................. Brotherhood of St Paul
BSS .... Bachelor of Social Studies
BSSc .... Bachelor of Social Science
                     (also see BSocSc)
BST .... Bachelor of Sacred Theology
BSW .... Bachelor of Social Work
BSc .... Bachelor of Science (also see
                     BS)
BSc(Econ) .... Bachelor of Science in
                     Economics
BSc(Soc).......... Bachelor of Science
                     (Sociology)
BScAgr .... Bachelor of Science in
                     Agriculture
BScEcon........... Bachelor of Science in
                     Economics
BScEng............ Bachelor of Science in
                     Engineering (also see BSE)
BScFor............ Bachelor of Science in
                     Forestry
BScTech........... Bachelor of Technical
                     Science
BSocAdmin .... Bachelor of Social
                     Administration
BSocSc............. Bachelor of Social Science
                     (also see BSSc)
BT.................. Bachelor of Teaching
BTS .... Bachelor of Theological
                     Studies
BTech .... Bachelor of Technology
BTh or BTheol .. Bachelor of Theology (also
                     see STB)

BVM&S........... Bachelor of Veterinary
                     Medicine and Surgery
BVSc................ Bachelor of Veterinary
                     Science
BVetMed .... Bachelor of Veterinary
                     Medicine (also see VetMB)
Ball .... Balliol
Ban .... (Diocese of) Bangor
Barn................ Barnabas
.... Barnabas's
Bart.................. Bartholomew
.... Bartholomew's
Bd .... Board
Bedf .... Bedford
Belf .... Belfast
Bibl .... Biblical
Birm .... (Diocese of) Birmingham
Blackb .... (Diocese of) Blackburn
Bp .... Bishop
Br.................... British
Bradf .... (Diocese of) Bradford
Bre .... (Diocese of) Brechin
Brig................. Brigadier
Bris .... (Diocese of) Bristol
Bt.................... Baronet
BèsL .... Bachelier ès lettres

C

C...................... Curate
c...................... Consecrated
C & O .... (Diocese of) Cashel and
                     Ossory (united dioceses of
                     Cashel, Waterford,
                     Lismore, Ossory, Ferns and
                     Leighlin)
C of E............. Church of England
C of S............. Church of Scotland
C&G................ City and Guilds
C, C & R .... (Diocese of) Cork, Cloyne
                     and Ross
C-in-c.............. Curate-in-charge
c/o .... Care of
CA .... Church Army
.... Member, Institute of
                     Chartered Accountants of
                     Scotland
CA(Z)............. Member, Institute of
                     Chartered Accountants of
                     Zimbabwe
CACTM .... Central Advisory Council for
                     the Ministry (now Ministry
                     Division)
CANDL .... Church and Neighbourhood
                     Development in London
CARA .... Care and Resources for
                     people affected by
                     AIDS/HIV
CARE .... Christian Action Research
                     and Education
CASA.............. Anglican Church of the
                     Southern Cone of America
CB .... Companion, Order of the
                     Bath
CBDTI .... Carlisle and Blackburn
                     Diocesan Training
                     Institute
CBE................ Commander, Order of the
                     British Empire
CBIM .... Companion, British Institute
                     of Management
CBiol .... Chartered Biologist
CCBI .... Council of Churches for
                     Britain and Ireland (now see
                     CTBI)
CCC .... Corpus Christi College
.... Council for the Care of
                     Churches
CCCS .... Commonwealth and
                     Continental Church Society
CCWA .... Churches Community Work
                     Alliance
CChem .... Chartered Chemist
CD.................. Canadian Forces Decoration
.... Conventional District (also
                     see ED)
CDir .... Chartered Director
CECD .... Church of England Council
                     for the Deaf
CECS................ Church of England
                     Children's Society (now
                     known as the Children's
                     Society)

CEMS .... Church of England Men's Society
CETD............... Certificate in the Education of the Deaf
CEng .... Chartered Engineer
CEnv................. Chartered Environmentalist
CF .... Chaplain to the Forces
CGA .... Community of the Glorious Ascension
CGeol .... Chartered Geologist
CH .... Companion of Honour
CIO................... Church Information Office
CIPFA .... Chartered Institute of Public Finance and Accountancy
CITC .... Church of Ireland Theological College
CITP................ Chartered Information Technology Professional
CJGS .... Community of the Companions of Jesus the Good Shepherd
CMD .... Cambridge Mission to Delhi (now see USPG)
CME.................. Continuing Ministerial Education
CMG .... Companion, Order of St Michael and St George
CMJ .... Church's Ministry among Jewish People
CMP.................. Company of Mission Priests
CMS .... Church Mission Society (formerly Church Missionary Society)
CMath .... Chartered Mathematician
CNZM .... Companion, New Zealand Order of Merit
COPEC .... Conference on Politics, Economics and Community
CORAT............. Christian Organizations Research and Advisory Trust
CORE .... City Outreach through Renewal Evangelism
CP..................... Community Priest
CPA .... Chartered Patent Agent (formerly FCIPA)
CPAS................ Church Pastoral Aid Society
CPEng.............. Chartered Professional Engineer (of Institution of Engineers of Australia)
CPFA................ Member Chartered Institute of Public Finance and Accountancy (formerly IPFA)
CPM.................. Colonial Police Medal
CPhys .... Chartered Physicist of the Institute of Physics
CPsychol .... Chartered Member, British Psychological Society
CQSW .... Certificate of Qualification in Social Work
CR .... Community of the Resurrection (Mirfield)
CSA .... Community of St Andrew
CSC .... Community of the Sisters of the Church
CSD................... Community of St Denys
CSF .... Community of St Francis
CSG................... Company of the Servants of God
CSMV .... Community of St Mary the Virgin
CSP................... Community of St Peter
CSS................... Certificate in Social Service
CSSM .... Children's Special Service Mission
CSWG .... Community of the Servants of the Will of God
CSci .... Chartered Scientist
CSocSc .... Certificate in Social Science
CStat................. Chartered Statistician
CTABRSM .... Certificate of Teaching, Associated Board of the Royal Schools of Music
CTBI .... Churches Together in Britain and Ireland (formerly CCBI)
CUF .... Church Urban Fund
CVO .... Commander, Royal Victorian Order
CWME.............. Commission on World Mission and Evangelism
CY .... Church and Youth
CYCW............... Certificate in Youth and Community Work
CYFA............... Church Youth Fellowships Association

Cam.................. Cambridge
Can................... Canon
Cand................. Candidate
.... Candidate's
.... Candidates'
Cant.................. (Diocese of) Canterbury
Capt.................. Captain
carage, 42 Court Brockworth
Carl................... (Diocese of) Carlisle
Cath.................. Catharine/Catherine
.... Catharine's/Catherine's
Cathl................. Cathedral
Cdre.................. Commodore
Cen .... Centre
.... Center
.... Central
Cert................... Certificat(e)
CertEd.............. Certificate of Education
CertFE .... Certificate of Further Education
CertHE............. Certificate in Higher Education
Ch..................... Christ
.... Christ's
.... Church
Ch Ch .... Christ Church
ChB .... Bachelor of Surgery (also see BCh, BChir and BS)
Chan .... Chancellor
Chapl................ Chaplain
.... Chaplaincies
.... Chaplaincy
.... Chaplains
Chas .... Charles
.... Charles's
Chelmsf .... (Diocese of) Chelmsford
Chelt................. Cheltenham
Ches.................. (Diocese of) Chester
Chich .... (Diocese of) Chichester
Chmn................ Chairman
.... Chairwoman
Chpl.................. Chapel
Chr .... Christian
.... Christians
Chris................. Christopher
.... Christopher's
Chrys................ Chrysostom
.... Chrysostom's
Chu................... Churchill
Cl-in-c.............. Cleric-in-charge
Clem .... Clement
.... Clement's
Cllr .... Councillor/Counsellor
Clogh................ (Diocese of) Clogher
Co..................... Company
.... County
.... Counties
Co-ord .... Co-ordinator
.... Co-ordinating
Col.................... Colonel
Coll................... College
Colleg .... Collegiate
Comdr .... Commander
Comdr OM (Italy).................. Commander, Order of Merit of the Italian Republic
Commn .... Commission
Commr............. Commissioner
Comp................ Comprehensive
Conf .... Confederation
.... Conference
Conn................. (Diocese of) Connor
Corp .... Corporation
Coun................. Council
Cov .... (Diocese of) Coventry
Cttee .... Committee
Cust .... Custodian
.... Custody
Cuth .... Cuthbert
.... Cuthbert's
Cypr .... Cyprian
.... Cyprian's

D

d .... Ordained Deacon
D & D .... (Diocese of) Down and Dromore
D & G .... (Diocese of) Dublin and Glendalough
D & R............... (Diocese of) Derry and Raphoe
D&C................. Dean and Chapter

DACE............... Diploma in Adult and Continuing Education
DAES .... Diploma in Advanced Educational Studies
DAPC............... Diploma in Advanced Psychological Counselling
DASAE .... Diploma of Advanced Study in Adult Education
DASE .... Diploma in the Advanced Study of Education
DASHE .... Diploma in Advanced Studies in Higher Education
DASS .... Diploma in Applied Social Studies
DASSc .... Diploma in Applied Social Science
DArch............... Doctor of Architecture
DB .... Bachelor of Divinity (USA)
DBE .... Dame Commander, Order of the British Empire
DBF .... Diocesan Board of Finance
DBP .... Diocesan Board of Patronage
DC..................... District of Columbia (USA)
DCC .... Diploma in Crisis Counselling of the Institute of Counselling
DCE .... Diploma of a College of Education
DCL .... Doctor of Civil Law
DCYW .... Diploma in Community and Youth Work
DCnL .... Doctor of Canon Law
DD .... Doctor of Divinity
DDS .... Doctor of Dental Surgery
DEHC .... Diploma in the Education of Handicapped Children
DEd.................. Doctor of Education (also see EdD)
DEng................ Doctor of Engineering
DFC .... Distinguished Flying Cross
DFM .... Distinguished Flying Medal (Canada)
DHA .... District Health Authority
DHL.................. Doctor of Humane Letters
DHSc................ Doctor of Health Science
DHumLit .... Doctor of Humane Letters
DL..................... Deputy Lieutenant
DLC .... Diploma of Loughborough College
DLSc .... Doctor of Legal Science
DLitt .... Doctor of Letters (also see LittD)
DLitt et Phil ..... Doctor of Letters and Philosophy
DMin................ Doctor of Ministry
DMinTh........... Doctor of Ministry and Theology
DOE .... Department of the Environment
DPhil................ Doctor of Philosophy (also see PhD)
DProf................ Doctor in Professional Studies
DRCOG .... Diploma of the Royal College of Obstetricians and Gynaecologists
DSC .... Distinguished Service Cross
DSM.................. Distinguished Service Medal
DSO .... Companion, Distinguished Service Order
DST .... Doctor of Sacred Theology (also see STD)
DSc................... Doctor of Science (also see ScD)
DSc(Eng).......... Doctor of Science in Engineering
DSocSc .... Doctor of Social Science
DTI................... Department of Trade and Industry
DTech............... Doctor of Technology
DTh.................. Doctor of Theology (also see ThD)
DThM............... Doctor of Theology and Ministry
DUP................. Docteur de l'Université de Paris
DUniv .... Doctor of the University
Darw .... Darwin
Dav .... David
.... David's
Dep.................... Deputy
Dept.................. Department
Det.................... Detention
Dio .... Diocese
Dioc.................. Diocesan

Dip .... Diploma
DipAE............. Diploma in Adult Education
DipAdEd........... Diploma in Advanced
                    Education
DipCOT .... Diploma of the College of
                    Occupational Therapists
DipEd............... Diploma in Education
DipHE.............. Diploma in Higher
                    Education
DipOT .... Diploma in Occupational
                    Therapy
DipSW.............. Diploma in Social Work
Dir .... Director
Distr .... District
Div .... Divinity
Div Test .... Divinity Testimonium
Dn .... Deacon
Dn-in-c .... Deacon-in-charge
Dom .... Domestic
Down................ Downing
Dr .... Doctor
Dr rer nat......... Doctor of Natural Science
DrTheol............. Doctor of Theology
                    (Germany)
Dr Théol........... Doctor of Theology (France)
Dss.................... Deaconess
dss.................... Admitted Deaconess
Dub .... Dublin
Dur .... (Diocese of) Durham
DèS................... Docteur ès sciences
DèsL................. Docteur ès lettres

E

E .... East
.... Eastern
EAMTC .... East Anglian Ministerial
                    Training Course
EC .... Emergency Commission
ED .... Ecclesiastical District (also
                    see CD)
.... Efficiency Decoration
EMMTC.......... East Midlands Ministry
                    Training Course
EN(G).............. Enrolled Nurse (General)
EN(M).............. Enrolled Nurse (Mental)
ERD .... Emergency Reserve
                    Decoration
ERMC.............. Eastern Region Ministry
                    Course
ESC .... Ecole Superieure de
                    Commerce
ESMI................ Elderly, Sick and Mentally
                    Infirm
Ecum .... Ecumenical
.... Ecumenics
.... Ecumenism
Ed .... Editor
.... Editorial
EdD.................. Doctor of Education (also
                    see DEd)
EdM .... Master of Education (USA)
                    (also see MEd)
Edin.................. (Diocese of) Edinburgh
Edm .... Edmund
.... Edmund's
Educn .... Education
.... Educational
Edw .... Edward
.... Edward's
Eliz .... Elizabeth
.... Elizabeth's
Em .... Emanuel
.... Emmanuel
Emb................... Embassy
EngD................. Doctor of Engineering
EngTech .... Engineering Technician
Episc................. Episcopal
.... Episcopalian
Eur.................... (Diocese in) Europe
                    (formerly Diocese of
                    Gibraltar in Europe)
.... Europe
.... European
EurIng .... European Engineer
Ev .... Evangelist
.... Evangelist's
.... Evangelists
Evang .... Evangelical
.... Evangelism
Ex .... (Diocese of) Exeter
Exam .... Examining
.... Examiner
Exec.................. Executive
Exor.................. Executor
Ext .... Extension

F

F&HE .... Further and Higher
                    Education
FAA.................. Fellow, Institution of
                    Administrative Accountants
FACOG .... Fellow, American College of
                    Obstetricians and
                    Gynaecologists
FADO .... Fellow, Association of
                    Dispensing Opticians
FAEB .... Fellow, Academy of
                    Environmental Biology
                    (India)
FAIM .... Fellow, Australian Institute
                    of Management
FAIWCW .... Fellow, Australian Institute
                    of Welfare and Community
                    Workers
FASI .... Fellow, Architects' and
                    Surveyors' Institute
FBA.................. Fellow, British Academy
FBCO .... Fellow, British College of
                    Ophthalmic Opticians
                    (Optometrists)
FBCS................ Fellow, British Computer
                    Society
FBCartS .... Fellow, British Cartographic
                    Society
FBDO .... Fellow, Association of
                    British Dispensing
                    Opticians
FBEng .... Fellow, Association of
                    Building Engineers
FBIM .... Fellow, British Institute of
                    Management (formerly
                    MBIM)
FBIS .... Fellow, British Interplanetary
                    Society
FBIST .... Fellow, British Institute of
                    Surgical Technologists
FBOA .... Fellow, British Optical
                    Association
FBPICS .... Fellow, British Production
                    and Inventory Control
                    Society
FBPsS............. Fellow, British Psychological
                    Society
FBS .... Fellow, Burgon Society
FCA................. Fellow, Institute of
                    Chartered Accountants
FCCA............... Fellow, Chartered
                    Association of Certified
                    Accountants (formerly
                    FACCA)
FCFI .... Fellow, Clothing and
                    Footwear Institute
FCIArb .... Fellow, Chartered Institute
                    of Arbitrators
FCIB .... Fellow, Chartered Institute
                    of Bankers
.... Fellow, Corporation of
                    Insurance Brokers
FCIE .... Fellow, Association of
                    Charity Independent
                    Examiners
FCIH................ Fellow, Chartered Institute
                    of Housing
FCII .... Fellow, Chartered Insurance
                    Institute
FCILA .... Fellow, Chartered Institute
                    of Loss Adjusters
FCIM .... Fellow, Chartered Institute
                    of Marketing (formerly
                    FInstM)
FCIOB .... Fellow, Chartered Institute
                    of Building
FCIPD .... Fellow, Chartered Institute
                    of Personnel and
                    Development
FCIS................. Fellow, Institute of
                    Chartered Secretaries and
                    Administrators
FCIT .... Fellow, Chartered Institute
                    of Transport
FCMA.............. Fellow, Chartered Institute
                    of Management
                    Accountants
FCMI .... Fellow, Chartered
                    Management Institute
                    (formerly FIMgt)
FCO .... Foreign and Commonwealth
                    Office
FCOptom.......... Fellow, College of
                    Optometrists
FCP .... Fellow, College of Preceptors

FCT.................. Fellow, Association of
                    Corporate Treasurers
FCollP.............. Ordinary Fellow, College of
                    Preceptors
FDS.................. Fellow in Dental Surgery
FDSRCPSGlas.. Fellow in Dental Surgery,
                    Royal College of Physicians
                    and Surgeons of Glasgow
FDSRCS .... Fellow in Dental Surgery,
                    Royal College of Surgeons of
                    England
FE..................... Further Education
FEI .... Fellow, Energy Institute
FEPA................ Fellow, Evangelical
                    Preachers' Association
FFA .... Fellow, Institute of Financial
                    Accountants
FFAEM .... Fellow, Faculty of Accident
                    and Emergency Medicine
FFARCS .... Fellow, Faculty of
                    Anaesthetists, Royal College
                    of Surgeons of England
FFChM .... Fellow, Faculty of Church
                    Music
FFDRCSI .... Fellow, Faculty of Dentistry,
                    Royal College of Surgeons in
                    Ireland
FFHom .... Fellow, the Faculty of
                    Homoeopathy
FFOM .... Fellow, Faculty of
                    Occupational Medicine
FFPH .... Fellow, Faculty of Public
                    Health (formerly FFPHM)
FFPHM .... Fellow, Faculty of Public
                    Health Medicine (now see
                    FFPH)
FFPM .... Fellow, Faculty of
                    Pharmaceutical Medicine
FGA .... Fellow, Gemmological
                    Association
FGCM .... Fellow, Guild of Church
                    Musicians
FGMS .... Fellow, Guild of Musicians
                    and Singers
FGS .... Fellow, Geological Society of
                    London
FHA .... Fellow, Institute of Hospital
                    Administrators (now see
                    FHSM)
FHCIMA .... Fellow, Hotel Catering and
                    Institutional Management
                    Association
FHEA .... Fellow, Higher Education
                    Academy
FHSM .... Fellow, Institute of Health
                    Services Management
FIA.................. Fellow, Institute of Actuaries
FIBMS .... Fellow, Institute of
                    Biomedical Sciences
FIBiol .... Fellow, Institute of Biology
FICE .... Fellow, Institution of Civil
                    Engineers
FICM .... Fellow, Institution of
                    Commercial Managers
FICS................. Fellow, International College
                    of Surgeons
FIChemE .... Fellow, Institution of
                    Chemical Engineers
FIDiagE .... Fellow, Institute of
                    Diagnostic Engineers
FIED .... Fellow, Institution of
                    Engineering Designers
FIEE .... Fellow, Institution of
                    Electrical Engineers
                    (formerly FIERE)
FIEEE .... Fellow, Institute of Electrical
                    and Electronics Engineers
                    (NY)
FIERE.............. Fellow, Institution of
                    Electronic and Radio
                    Engineers (now see FIEE)
FIFireE............. Fellow, Institution of Fire
                    Engineers
FIHT .... Fellow of the Institution of
                    Highways and
                    Transportation
FIHospE .... Fellow, Institute of Hospital
                    Engineering
FIIM .... Fellow, Institution of
                    Industrial Managers
                    (formerly FIPlantE)
FIL .... Fellow, Institute of
                    Linguists
FIMA............... Fellow, Institute of
                    Mathematics and its
                    Applications

FIMI .... Fellow, Institute of the Motor Industry
FIMLS .... Fellow, Institute of Medical Laboratory Sciences
FIMM .... Fellow, Institution of Mining and Metallurgy (now see FIMMM)
FIMMM .... Fellow, Institute of Materials, Minerals and Mining
FIMS................ Fellow, Institute of Management Specialists
FIMarEST .... Fellow, Institute of Marine Engineering, Science and Technology
FIMechE......... Fellow, Institution of Mechanical Engineers
FINucE .... Fellow, Institution of Nuclear Engineers (now see FNucI)
FIOSH .... Fellow, Institute of Occupational Safety and Health
FIPD .... Fellow, Institute of Personnel Development
FIPEM .... Fellow, Institute of Physics and Engineering in Medicine
FIQA................ Fellow, Institute of Quality Assurance
FISM................ Fellow, Institute of Supervisory Management
FIST .... Fellow, Institute of Science and Technology
FIStructE .... Fellow, Institution of Structural Engineers
FInstAM .... Fellow, Institute of Administrative Management
FInstD.............. Fellow, Institute of Directors
FInstE .... Fellow, Institute of Energy
FInstLEx.......... Fellow, Institute of Legal Executives
FInstLM........... Fellow, Institute of Leadership and Management
FInstMC .... Fellow, Institute of Measurement and Control
FInstP.............. Fellow, Institute of Physics
FInstSMM .... Fellow, Institute of Sales and Marketing Management
FInstTT .... Fellow, Institute of Travel and Tourism
FKC................. Fellow, King's College London
FLA................. Fellow, Library Association
FLAME .... Family Life and Marriage Education
FLCM .... Fellow, London College of Music
FLIA .... Fellow, Life Insurance Association
FLS .... Fellow, Linnean Society
FMA .... Fellow, Museums Association
FNI.................. Fellow, Nautical Institute
FNMSM .... Fellow, North and Midlands School of Music
FNucI.............. Fellow, Nuclear Institute (formerly FINucE)
FPS.................. Fellow, Pharmaceutical Society of Great Britain
FPhS................ Fellow, Philosophical Society of England
FRACI .... Fellow, Royal Australian Chemical Institute
FRAI .... Fellow, Royal Anthropological Institute
FRAM .... Fellow, Royal Academy of Music
FRAS .... Fellow, Royal Asiatic Society
.... Fellow, Royal Astronomical Society
FRAeS .... Fellow, Royal Aeronautical Society
FRCA.............. Fellow, Royal College of Anaesthetists
FRCGP .... Fellow, Royal College of General Practitioners
FRCM .... Fellow, Royal College of Music
FRCO.............. Fellow, Royal College of Organists
FRCOG............ Fellow, Royal College of Obstetricians and Gynaecologists
FRCOphth .... Fellow, Royal College of Ophthalmologists

FRCP .... Fellow, Royal College of Physicians
FRCP(C) .... Fellow, Royal College of Physicians of Canada
FRCPCH........... Fellow, Royal College of Paediatrics and Child Health
FRCPEd........... Fellow, Royal College of Physicians Edinburgh
FRCPGlas........ Fellow, Royal College of Physicians and Surgeons, Glasgow (also see FRCSGlas)
FRCPath .... Fellow, Royal College of Pathologists
FRCPsych .... Fellow, Royal College of Psychiatrists
FRCR .... Fellow, Royal College of Radiologists
FRCS............... Fellow, Royal College of Physicians and Surgeons of England
FRCSE or .... Fellow, Royal College of
FRCSEd .... Surgeons of Edinburgh
FRCSGlas .... Fellow, Royal College of Physicians and Surgeons, Glasgow (also see FRCPGlas)
FRCSI .... Fellow, Royal College of Surgeons in Ireland
FRCVS............. Fellow, Royal College of Veterinary Surgeons
FREng.............. Fellow, Royal Academy of Engineering
FRGS .... Fellow, Royal Geographical Society
FRHS .... Fellow, Royal Horticultural Society
FRHistS .... Fellow, Royal Historical Society
FRIAS.............. Fellow, Royal Incorporation of Architects of Scotland
FRIBA .... Fellow, Royal Institute of British Architects
FRICS.............. Fellow, Royal Institution of Chartered Surveyors (formerly FLAS and FSI)
FRIN................ Fellow, Royal Institute of Navigation
FRINA............. Fellow, Royal Institution of Naval Architects
FRIPH .... Fellow, Royal Institute of Public Health
FRMetS .... Fellow, Royal Meteorological Society
FRPharmS .... Fellow, Royal Pharmaceutical Society
FRS.................. Fellow, Royal Society
FRSA .... Fellow, Royal Society of Arts
FRSAI.............. Fellow, Royal Society of Antiquaries of Ireland
FRSC .... Fellow, Royal Society of Canada
.... Fellow, Royal Society of Chemistry (formerly FRIC)
FRSCM .... Hon Fellow, Royal School of Church Music
FRSE................ Fellow, Royal Society of Edinburgh
FRSH .... Fellow, Royal Society for Public Health
FRSL............... Fellow, Royal Society of Literature
FRSM .... Fellow, Royal Society of Medicine
FRSocMed........ Fellow, Royal Society of Medicine
FRTPI .... Fellow, Royal Town Planning Institute
FSA .... Fellow, Society of Antiquaries
FSAScot .... Fellow, Royal Society of Antiquaries of Scotland
FSCA .... Fellow, Royal Society of Company and Commercial Accountants
FSJ .... Fellowship of St John the Evangelist
FSR .... Fellowship Diploma of the Society of Radiographers
FSS.................. Fellow, Royal Statistical Society
FTC................. Flying Training Command
FTCL .... Fellow, Trinity College of Music London
FTII................. Fellow, Institute of Taxation

FVCM .... Fellow, Victoria College of Music
FWeldI .... Fellow, Institute of Welding
Fell.................. Fellow
Fitzw .... Fitzwilliam
Foundn .... Foundation
Fran................. Francis
.... Francis's

G

G&C................ Gonville and Caius
GB.................... Great Britain
GBSM .... Graduate of the Birmingham School of Music
GCMG............. Knight Grand Cross, Order of St Michael and St George
GCVO .... Knight Grand Cross, Royal Victorian Order
GFS................. Girls' Friendly Society
GGSM .... Graduate Diploma of the Guildhall School of Music and Drama
GIBiol .... Graduate of the Institute of Biology
GIFireE........... Graduate of the Institute of Fire Engineers
GIMechE .... Graduate of the Institution of Mechanical Engineers
GIPE .... Graduate of the Institution of Production Engineers
GInstP .... Graduate of the Institute of Physics
GLCM .... Graduate Diploma of the London College of Music
GM.................. George Medal
GMus .... Graduate Diploma in Music
GMusRNCM ... Graduate in Music of the Royal Northern College of Music
GNSM .... Graduate of the Northern School of Music
GRIC .... Graduate Membership, Royal Institute of Chemistry
GRNCM.......... Graduate of the Royal Northern College of Music
GRSC.............. Graduate of the Royal School of Chemistry
GRSM............. Graduate of the Royal Schools of Music
GSM .... (Member of) Guildhall School of Music and Drama
GTCL.............. Graduate Diploma of Trinity College of Music, London
Gabr .... Gabriel
.... Gabriel's
Gd .... Good
Gen.................. General
Geo.................. George
.... George's
Gib .... Gibraltar
Glam .... Glamorgan
Glas .... (Diocese of) Glasgow and Galloway
.... Glasgow
Glos................. Gloucestershire
Glouc............... (Diocese of) Gloucester
Gloucester GL3 4ET
Gov.................. Governor
Gp .... Group
Gr .... Grammar
GradCIPD .... Graduate of the Chartered Institute of Personnel and Development
GradIPM.......... Graduate of the Institute of Personnel Management
Greg................. Gregory
.... Gregory's
Gt .... Great
Gtr................... Greater
Guildf.............. (Diocese of) Guildford

H

H...................... Holy
H&FE .... Higher and Further Education
HA................... Health Authority
HCIMA............ Hotel and Catering International Management Association

HDipEd............ Higher Diploma in Education
HE.................. Higher Education
HIV .... Human Immunodeficiency Virus
HM.................. Her (or His) Majesty
HMI .... Her (or His) Majesty's Inspector (or Inspectorate)
HMS.............. Her (or His) Majesty's Ship
HQ.................. Headquarters
HTV .... Harlech Television
HVCert............ Health Visitor's Certificate
Hatf................ Hatfield
Hd .... Head
Heref................ (Diocese of) Hereford
Hertf................ Hertford
Hist................. Historic
.... Historical
.... History
Ho .... House
Hon .... Honorary
.... Honourable
HonDLaws....... Honorary Doctor of Laws
HonFChS......... Honorary Fellow, Society of Chiropodists
HonRCM .... Honorary Member, Royal College of Music
Hosp................ Hospital

I

I .... Incumbent
IAAP.............. International Association for Analytical Psychology
IBA.................. Independent Broadcasting Authority
ICF.................. Industry Churches Forum (formerly Industrial Christian Fellowship)
ICM................. Irish Church Missions
ICS .... Intercontinental Church Society
IDC .... Inter-Diocesan Certificate
IDWAL .... Inter-Diocesan West Africa Link
IEAB .... Igreja Episcopal Anglicana do Brasil
IEng................ Incorporated Engineer (formerly TEng(CEI))
IFES................ International Fellowship of Evangelical Students
ILEA .... Inner London Education Authority
IME .... Initial Ministerial Education
IMMM............. Institute of Materials, Minerals and Mining
INSEAD .... Institut Européen d'Administration des Affaires
IPFA................ Member, Chartered Institute of Public Finance and Accountancy
ISO .... Imperial Service Order
IT..................... Information Technology
ITV .... Independent Television
IVF .... Inter-Varsity Fellowship of Evangelical Unions (now see UCCF)
IVS .... International Voluntary Service
Imp.................. Imperial
Inc .... Incorporated
Ind .... Industrial
.... Industry
Info.................. Information
Insp................. Inspector
Inst .... Institut
.... Institute
.... Institution
Intercon........... Intercontinental
Internat............ International
Interpr .... Interpretation
Is...................... Island
.... Islands
.... Isle
.... Isles

J

JCD .... Doctor of Canon Law
JCL.................. Licentiate in Canon Law
JD.................... Doctor of Jurisprudence

JEM................. Jerusalem and the East Mission (now see JMECA)
JMECA .... Jerusalem and Middle East Church Association (formerly JEM)
JP..................... Justice of the Peace
Jas................... James
.... James's
Jes................... Jesus
Jo .... John
.... John's
Jos................... Joseph
.... Joseph's
Jt...................... Joint
Jun .... Junior

K

K...................... King
.... King's
K, E & A .... (Diocese of) Kilmore, Elphin and Ardagh
KA................... Knight of St Andrew, Order of Barbados
KBE .... Knight Commander, Order of the British Empire
KCB................. Knight Commander, Order of the Bath
KCMG .... Knight Commander, Order of St Michael and St George
KCVO.............. Knight Commander, Royal Victorian Order
KPM .... King's Police Medal
Kath .... Katharine/Katherine
.... Katharine's/Katherine's
Kt .... Knight

L

L & K .... (Diocese of) Limerick and Killaloe (united dioceses of Limerick, Ardfert, Aghadoe, Killaloe, Kilfenora, Clonfert, Kilmacduagh and Emly)
LASI................ Licentiate, Ambulance Service Institute
LBIPP.............. Licentiate, British Institute of Professional Photography
LCC................. London County Council
LCL.................. Licentiate in Canon Law
LCP.................. Licentiate, College of Preceptors
LCST .... Licentiate, College of Speech Therapists
LCTP................ Lancashire and Cumbria Theological Partnership
LDS.................. Licentiate in Dental Surgery
LDiv................. Licentiate in Divinity
LEA.................. Local Education Authority
LEP .... Local Ecumenical Partnership
LGCM .... Lesbian and Gay Christian Movement
LGSM .... Licentiate, Guildhall School of Music and Drama
LICeram........... Licentiate, Institute of Ceramics
LIMA............... Licentiate, Institute of Mathematics and its Applications
LLA.................. Lady Literate in Arts
LLAM............... Licentiate, London Academy of Music and Dramatic Art
LLB.................. Bachelor of Laws
LLCM .... Licentiate, London College of Music
LLCM(TD)....... Licentiate, London College of Music (Teachers' Diploma)
LLD .... Doctor of Laws
LLM................. Master of Laws
LMH .... Lady Margaret Hall
LMPA .... Licentiate Master, Photographers' Association
LNSM .... Local Non-stipendary Minister (or Ministry)
LOROS............. Leicestershire Organization for the Relief of Suffering
LRAM .... Licentiate, Royal Academy of Music

LRCP .... Licentiate, Royal College of Physicians
LRCPI.............. Licentiate, Royal College of Physicians of Ireland
LRCSEng......... Licentiate of the Royal College of Surgeons in England
LRCSI .... Licentiate, Royal College of Surgeons in Ireland
LRPS .... Licentiate, Royal Photographic Society
LRSC .... Licentiate, Royal Society of Chemistry
LRSM .... Licentiate Diploma of the Royal Schools of Music
LSE .... London School of Economics and Political Science
LSHTM............ London School of Hygiene and Tropical Medicine
LSIAD .... Licentiate, Society of Industrial Artists and Designers
LSocEth .... Licence en Sociologie-Ethnologie
LTCL................ Licentiate, Trinity College of Music London
LTh................... Licentiate in Theology (also see LST)
LVCM .... Licentiate, Victoria College of Music
LVO .... Lieutenant, Royal Victorian Order
LWCMD .... Licentiate, Welsh College of Music and Drama
Lamp................ Lampeter
Lanc................. Lancaster
Laur................. Laurence
.... Laurence's
Lawr .... Lawrence
.... Lawrence's
Ld .... Lord
Ldr................... Leader
Lect.................. Lecturer
Leic.................. (Diocese of) Leicester
Leon .... Leonard
.... Leonard's
Lib.................... Librarian
.... Library
Lic .... Licence
.... Licensed
.... Licentiate
LicTh................ Licence in Theology
Lich.................. (Diocese of) Lichfield
Linc.................. (Diocese of) Lincoln
Lit .... Literature
LittD .... Doctor of Letters (also see DLitt)
Liturg............... Liturgical
Liv .... (Diocese of) Liverpool
Llan .... (Diocese of) Llandaff
Lon .... (Diocese of) London
Loughb............. Loughborough
Lt...................... Lieutenant
.... Little
Ltd................... Limited
LèsL................. Licencié ès lettres

M

M & K .... (Diocese of) Meath and Kildare
MA.................... Master of Arts
MA(Ed)............ Master of Arts in Education
MA(MM).......... Master of Arts in Mission and Ministry
MA(TS)............ Master of Arts in Theological Studies
MA(Theol)....... Master of Arts in Theology
MAAIS .... Member, Association of Archaeological Illustrators and Surveyors
MAAT.............. Member, Association of Accounting Technicians
MACC.............. Member, Australian College of Chaplains
MACE.............. Member, Australian College of Educators
MACT.............. Member, Association of Corporate Treasurers
MAE................. Member, Academy of Experts
MAJA............... Member, Association of Jungian Analysts

MAMIT .... Member, Associate of Meat Inspectors Trust
MAPM .... Member, Association for Project Management
MAPsS .... Member, Australian Psychological Society
MASI .... Member, Architects and Surveyors Institute
MAT .... Master of Arts and Teaching (USA)
MATA .... Member, Animal Technicians' Association
MATCA .... Member, Air Traffic Control Association
MATM .... Master of Arts in Theology and Ministry
MAgrSc .... Master of Agricultural Science
MArAd .... Master of Archive Administration
MArch .... Master of Architecture
MB .... Bachelor of Medicine (also see BM)
MB,BS or .... Conjoint degree of Bachelor
MB,ChB .... of Medicine, Bachelor of Surgery
MBA .... Master of Business Administration
MBACP .... Member, British Association for Counselling and Psychotherapy
MBAOT .... Member, British Association of Occupational Therapists (formerly MAOT)
MBAP .... Member, British Association of Psychotherapists
MBASW .... Member, British Association of Social Workers
MBATOD .... Member, British Association of Teachers of the Deaf
MBC................. Metropolitan (or Municipal) Borough Council
MBCS .... Member, British Computer Society
MBChA........... Member, British Chiropody Association
MBE................. Member, Order of the British Empire
MBES.............. Member, Biological Engineering Society
MBEng............ Member, Association of Building Engineers
MBIM .... Member, British Institute of Management (later MIMgt)
MBKSTS .... Member, British Kinematograph, Sound and Television Society
MBM................ Master of Business Management
MBPsS .... Member, British Psychological Society
MC .... Military Cross
MCA .... Member, Institute of Chartered Accountants
MCB................. Master in Clinical Biochemistry
MCCDRCS....... Member in Clinical Community Dentistry, Royal College of Surgeons
MCD .... Master of Civic Design
MCE................. Master of Civil Engineering
MCIArb .... Member, Chartered Institute of Arbitrators
MCIBS .... Member, Chartered Institute of Bankers in Scotland
MCIBSE .... Member, Chartered Institute of Building Service Engineers
MCIEH .... Member, Chartered Institute of Enviromental Health (formerly MIEH)
MCIH............... Member, Chartered Institute of Housing (formerly MIH)
MCIJ .... Member, Chartered Institute of Journalists
MCIM............... Member, Chartered Institute of Marketing (formerly MInstM)
MCIMA .... Member, Chartered Institute of Management Accountants
MCIOB .... Member, Chartered Institute of Building
MCIPD .... Member, Chartered Institute of Personnel and Development

MCIPS .... Member, Chartered Institute of Purchasing and Supply
MCIT .... Member, Chartered Institute of Transport
MCIWEM........ Member, Chartered Institution of Water and Enviromental Management
MCL................. Master of Canon Law
MCLIP............. Member, Chartered Institute of Library and Information Professionals
MCMI.............. Member, Chartered Management Institute (formerly MBIM and MIMgt)
MCS .... Master of Christian Spirituality
.... Master of Christian Studies
MCSD.............. Member, Chartered Society of Designers
MCSP.............. Member, Chartered Society of Physiotherapy
MCST .... Member, College of Speech Therapists
MCT................. Member, Association of Corporate Treasurers
MChOrth .... Master of Orthopaedic Surgery
MChS .... Member, Society of Chiropodists
MChem .... Master of Chemistry
MChemA .... Master in Chemical Analysis
MCollP............ Member, College of Preceptors
MCom.............. Master of Commerce
MCommH........ Master of Community Health
MD .... Doctor of Medicine
MDA .... Master of Defence Administration
MDefStud .... Master of Defence Studies
MDiv................ Master of Divinity
ME .... Master of Engineering (also see MEng)
MEHS .... Member, Ecclesiastical History Society
MEd .... Master of Education
MEng............... Master of Engineering
MFA................. Master of Fine Art
MFHom .... Member, Faculty of Homeopathy
MFOM............. Member, Faculty of Occupational Medicine
MGDSRCS....... Membership in General Dental Surgery, Royal College of Surgeons of England
MHCIMA........ Member, Hotel Catering and Institutional Management Association
MHSM............. Member, Institute of Health Services Management
MHSc .... Master of Health Science
MHort (RHS) ... Master of Horticulture, Royal Horticultural Society
MHums .... Master of Humanities
MIA .... Malawi Institute of Architects
MIAAP .... Member, International Association for Analytical Psychology
MIAAS .... Member, Incorporated Association of Architects and Surveyors
MIAM .... Member, Institute of Administrative Management
MIAP .... Member, Institution of Analysts and Programmers
MIAT .... Member, Institute of Asphalt Technology
MIBC .... Member, Institute of Business Counsellors
MIBCO .... Member, Institution of Building Control Officers
MIBF .... Member, Institute of British Foundrymen
MIBiol............. Member, Institute of Biology
MICA............... Member, International Cartographic Association
MICAS............. Member, Institute of Chartered Accountants of Scotland
MICE .... Member, Institution of Civil Engineers (formerly AMICE)
MICFM .... Member, Institute of Charity Fundraising Managers

MICFor............ Member, Institute of Chartered Foresters
MICM .... Member, Institute of Credit Management
MICS................ Member, Institute of Chartered Shipbrokers
MIChemE .... Member, Institution of Chemical Engineers
MICorrST .... Member, Institution of Corrosion Science and Technology
MIE .... Member, Institute of Engineers and Technicians
MIEAust .... Member, Institute of Engineers and Technicians Australia
MIED .... Member, Institute of Engineering Designers
MIEE .... Member, Institution of Electrical Engineers (formerly AMIEE & MIERE)
MIEEE............. Member, Institute of Electrical and Electronics Engineers (NY)
MIEEM............ Member, Institute of Ecology and Environmental Management
MIET .... Member, Institution of Engineering and Technology
MIElecIE .... Corporate Member, Institution of Electrical and Electronics Incorporated Engineers
MIEx .... Member, Institute of Export
MIGasE .... Member, Institution of Gas Engineers
MIHEEM .... Member, Institute of Healthcare Engineering and Estate Management
MIHT............... Member, Institution of Highways and Transportation
MIIExE .... Member, Institute of Incorporated Executive Engineers
MIIM .... Member, Institution of Industrial Managers
MIInfSc............ Member, Institute of Information Scientists
MIL .... Member, Institute of Linguists
MILT................ Member, Institute of Logistics and Transport
MIM................. Member, Institute of Metals (formerly Institution of Metallurgists)
MIMA.............. Member, Institute of Management Accountants
.... Member, Institute of Mathematics and its Applications
MIMC.............. Member, Institute of Management Consultants
MIMI .... Member, Institute of the Motor Industry
MIMarEST .... Member, Institute of Marine Engineering, Science and Technology
MIMechE......... Member, Institution of Mechanical Engineers (formerly AMIMechE)
MIMunE.......... Member, Institution of Municipal Engineers
MINucE .... Member, Institute of Nuclear Engineers
MIOSH .... Member, Institution of Occupational Safety and Health
MIOT .... Member, Institute of Operating Theatre Technicians
MIPI................. Member, Institute of Private Investigators
MIPR .... Member, Institute of Public Relations
MIProdE .... Member, Institution of Production Engineers
MIQA............... Member, Institute of Quality Assurance
MIRSE............. Member, Institution of Railway Signal Engineers
MISE................ Member, Institute of Sales Engineers
MISM............... Member, Institute of Supervisory Management

MISW.............. Member, Institute of Social Welfare
MIStructE........ Member, Institute of Structural Engineers
MITMA........... Member, Institute of Trade Mark Agents
MITPA............. Member, International Tax Planning Association
MIW................. Member, Institute of Welfare (formerly MIWO)
MInstC(Glas).... Member, Institute of Counselling (Glasgow)
MInstD............. Member, Institute of Directors
MInstE............. Member, Institute of Energy
MInstGA......... Member, Institute of Group Analysis
MInstP............. Member, Institute of Physics
MInstPI............ Member, Institute of Patentees and Inventors
MInstPS........... Corporate Member, Institute of Purchasing and Supply
MInstPkg......... Member, Institute of Packaging
MInstTA.......... Member, Institute of Transport Administration
ML .... Master of Leadership
MLI.................. Member, Landscape Institute
MLL.................. Master of Laws
MLS .... Master of Library Studies
MLib .... Master of Librarianship
MLitt................ Master of Letters
MM .... Military Medal
MMCET .... Martyrs' Memorial and Church of England Trust
MMS................ Member, Institute of Management Services
MMath............. Master of Mathematics
MMedSc........... Master of Medical Science
MMet .... Master of Metallurgy
MMin .... Master of Ministry
MMinTheol...... Master in Ministry and Theology
MMus.............. Master of Music (also see MusM)
MN.................. Master of Nursing
MNI .... Member, Nautical Institute
MOD................ Ministry of Defence
MPA .... Master of Public Administration
MPH .... Master of Public Health
MPS .... Master of Professional Studies
MPhil .... Master of Philosophy
MPhys .... Master of Physics
MPsychSc.......... Master of Psychological Science
MRAC .... Member, Royal Agricultural College
MRAeS .... Member, Royal Aeronautical Society
MRCGP .... Member, Royal College of General Practitioners
MRCO.............. Member, Royal College of Organists
MRCOG .... Member, Royal College of Obstetricians and Gynaecologists
MRCP .... Member, Royal College of Physicians
MRCPath .... Member, Royal College of Pathologists
MRCPsych .... Member, Royal College of Psychiatrists
MRCS .... Member, Royal College of Surgeons
MRCSE............. Member, Royal College of Surgeons of Edinburgh
MRCVS............ Member, Royal College of Veterinary Surgeons
MRIA .... Member, Royal Irish Academy
MRICS.............. Member, Royal Institution of Chartered Surveyors
MRIN .... Member, Royal Institute of Navigation
MRINA .... Member, Royal Institution of Naval Architects
MRIPHH......... Member, Royal Institute of Public Health and Hygiene
MRPharmS........ Member, Royal Pharmaceutical Society (formerly MPS)
MRSC .... Member, Royal Society of Chemistry (formerly MRIC)

MRSH.............. Member, Royal Society for the Promotion of Health
MRSL .... Member, Order of the Republic of Sierra Leone
MRST .... Member, Royal Society of Teachers
MRTPI............. Member, Royal Town Planning Institute
MRTvS............. Member, Royal Television Society
MRelSc............. Master of Religious Science
MRes................ Master of Research
MS.................... Master of Science (USA)
.... Master of Surgery
MSAICE .... Member, South African Institution of Civil Engineers
MSE .... Master of Science in Engineering (USA)
.... Minister (or Ministers) in Secular Employment
MSERT .... Member, Society of Electronic and Radio Technicians
MSHAA........... Member, Society of Hearing Aid Audiologists
MSI .... Member, Securities Institute
MSIAD .... Member, Society of Industrial Artists and Designers
MSOSc .... Member, Society of Ordained Scientists
MSOTS .... Member, Society for Old Testament Study
MSR.................. Member, Society of Radiographers
MSSCh.............. Member, School of Surgical Chiropody
MSSTh.............. Member, Society for the Study of Theology
MSSc .... Master of Social Science (also see MSocSc)
MSTSD .... Member, Society of Teachers of Speech and Drama
MSW................. Master of Social Work
MSacMus.......... Master of Sacred Music
MSc.................. Master of Science
MSc(Econ)........ Master of Science in Economics
MScRel............. Maitrise es Sciences Religieuses
MSci .... Master of Natural Sciences
MSoc .... Maitrise en Sociologie
MSocSc .... Master of Social Sciences (also see MSSc)
MSocWork .... Master of Social Work (USA)
MSt.................. Master of Studies
MTD .... Master of Transport Design
MTS .... Master of Theological Studies
MTech .... Master of Technology
MTh or MTheol Master of Theology (also see STM and ThM)
MThSt.............. Master of Theological Studies
MU.................... Mothers' Union
MVO .... Member, Royal Victorian Order
Magd .... Magdalen/Magdalene Magdalen's/Magdalene's
Man.................. (Diocese of) Manchester
Man Dir .... Managing Director
Mansf............... Mansfield
Marg................. Margaret Margaret's
Matt................. Matthew Matthew's
Mert................. Merton
MesL................. Lettres Modernes
Metrop .... Metropolitan
Mgt.................. Management
Mich .... Michael
.... Michael's
.... Michael and All Angels
Midl.................. Midlands
Mil.................... Military
Min................... Minister
.... Ministers
.... Ministries
.... Ministry
.... Minor
Minl.................. Ministerial
Miss.................. Mission
.... Missions
.... Missionary
Missr.................. Missioner

Mon.................. (Diocese of) Monmouth
Mor .... (Diocese of) Moray, Ross and Caithness
Mt..................... Mount
MusB or MusBac Bachelor of Music (also see BMus)
MusD or MusDoc Doctor of Music
MusM................ Master of Music (also see MMus)

N

N....................... North
.... Northern
NACRO .... National Association for the Care and Rehabilitation of Offenders
NASA................ National Aeronautics and Space Administration (USA)
NCEC .... National Christian Education Council
NE.................... North East
NEITE .... North East Institute for Theological Education
NEOC .... North East Oecumenical Course (formerly North East Ordination Course)
NHS .... National Health Service
NIDA .... National Institute of Dramatic Art
NJ...................... New Jersey
NOC.................. Northern Ordination Course
NS .... Nova Scotia (Canada)
NSM.................. Non-stipendiary Minister (or Ministry)
NSPCC.............. National Society for the Prevention of Cruelty to Children
NSW.................. New South Wales (Australia)
NT..................... New Testament
NTMTC............. North Thames Ministerial Training Course
NUI................... National University of Ireland
NUU.................. New University of Ulster
NW.................... North West/Northwestern
NWT .... North West Territories (Canada)
NY..................... New York (USA)
NZ..................... New Zealand
Nat .... National
Nath .... Nathanael/Nathaniel Nathanael's/Nathaniel's
Newc................. (Diocese of) Newcastle
Nic.................... Nicholas/Nicolas Nicholas's/Nicolas's
Nor.................... (Diocese of) Norwich
Northn.............. Northampton
Nottm............... Nottingham
Nuff.................. Nuffield

O

OAM .... Medal of the Order of Australia
OBE.................. Officer, Order of the British Empire
OBI................... Order of British India
OCF .... Officiating Chaplain to the Forces
OCM .... Officiating Chaplain to the Military
OGS .... Oratory of the Good Shepherd
OH..................... Ohio
OHP.................. Order of the Holy Paraclete
OLM .... Ordained Local Minister (or Ministry)
OM..................... Order of Merit
OM(Ger).......... Order of Merit of Germany
OMF .... Overseas Missionary Fellowship
ONZ.................. Order of New Zealand
OSB................... Order of St Benedict
OSP .... Order of St Paul
OT..................... Old Testament
Offg.................. Officiating
Offic.................. Officiate
Ord .... Ordained
.... Ordinands
.... Ordination

Org	Organization
....	Organizer
....	Organizing
Ox	(Diocese of) Oxford

P

P	Patron(s)
....	Priest
p	Ordained Priest
P in O	Priest in Ordinary
P-in-c	Priest-in-charge
PBS	Pengeran Bintang Sarawak (Companion of the Order of the Star, Sarawak)
PC...................	Perpetual Curate
....	Privy Counsellor
PCC	Parochial Church Council
PEV	Provincial Episcopal Visitor
PGCE	Postgraduate Certificate in Education
PGDE...............	Postgraduate Diploma in Education
PGTC	Postgraduate Teaching Certificate
PM	Priest Missioner
PO	Post Office
PQCSW	Post-Qualifying Certificate in Social Work
PV	Priest Vicar
Par	Parish
....	Parishes
Paroch	Parochial
Past..................	Pastoral
Patr..................	Patrick
....	Patrick's
....	Patronage
Pemb................	Pembroke
Penn.................	Pennsylvania (USA)
Perm.................	Permission
Pet...................	(Diocese of) Peterborough
....	Peter
....	Peter's
Peterho	Peterhouse
PhB..................	Bachelor of Philosophy
PhC..................	Pharmaceutical Chemist
PhD	Doctor of Philosophy (also see DPhil)
PhD(Educ)	Doctor of Philosophy in Education
PhL..................	Licentiate of Philosophy
Phil	Philip
....	Philip's
plc	public limited company
Poly..................	Polytechnic
Portsm	(Diocese of) Portsmouth
Preb	Prebendary
Prec..................	Precentor
Prep	Preparatory
Pres..................	President
Prin	Principal
Pris	Prison
....	Prisons
Prof..................	Professor
....	Professorial
Progr.................	Program
....	Programme
....	Programmes
Prop..................	Proprietary
Prov	Province
....	Provincial
PsychD	Professional Doctor of Counselling Psychology
Pt	Point

Q

QC...................	Queen's Counsel
QGM................	Queen's Gallantry Medal
QHC.................	Honorary Chaplain to The Queen
QN...................	Queen's Nurse
QPM.................	Queen's Police Medal
QSM.................	Queen's Service Medal
QSO.................	Queen's Service Order of New Zealand
QTS	Qualified Teacher Status
QUB	The Queen's University of Belfast
QVRM	Queen's Volunteer Reserve Medal
Qld...................	Queensland

Qu....................	Queen
....	Queen's
....	Queens'

R

R......................	Rector
....	Royal
R and D............	Research and Development
R of O	Reserve of Officers
R&SChTrust	Rochester and Southwark Church Trust
RAAF	Royal Australian Air Force
RAChD	Royal Army Chaplains' Department
RAD or RADD	Royal Association in Aid of Deaf People (formerly Deaf and Dumb)
RADA..............	Royal Academy of Dramatic Art
RADICLE	Residential and Drop-in Centre London Enterprises
RAEC	Royal Army Educational Corps
RAF	Royal Air Force
RAFVR.............	Royal Air Force Volunteer Reserve
RAM	(Member) Royal Academy of Music
RAN.................	Royal Australian Navy
RANSR.............	Royal Australian Naval Strategic Reserve
RAuxAF	Royal Auxiliary Air Force
RC	Roman Catholic
RCA	Royal College of Art
RCAF	Royal Canadian Air Force
RCM	Royal College of Music
RCN	Royal Canadian Navy
....	Royal College of Nursing
RCNT...............	Registered Clinical Nurse Teacher
RCPS	Royal College of Physicians and Surgeons
RCS	Royal College of Surgeons of England
RCSE...............	Royal College of Surgeons of Edinburgh
RD...................	Royal Navy Reserve Decoration
....	Rural Dean
RE	Religious Education
RFN	Registered Fever Nurse
RGN.................	Registered General Nurse
RHV.................	Registered Health Visitor
RIA	Royal Irish Academy
RIBA................	(Member) Royal Institute of British Architects (formerly ARIBA)
RLSMD	Royal London School of Medicine and Dentistry
RM...................	Registered Midwife
RMA or RMC..	Royal Military Academy (formerly College), Sandhurst
RMCM	Royal Manchester College of Music
RMCS	Royal Military College of Science, Shrivenham
RMHN.............	Registered Mental Health Nurse
RMN................	Registered Mental Nurse
RN...................	Registered Nurse (Canada)
....	Royal Navy
RN(MH)	Registered Nurse (for the mentally handicapped)
RNIB................	Royal National Institute for the Blind
RNLI................	Royal National Lifeboat Institution
RNMH.............	Registered Nurse for the Mentally Handicapped
RNR.................	Royal Naval Reserve
RNT.................	Registered Nurse Tutor
RNVR...............	Royal Naval Volunteer Reserve
RNZN..............	Royal New Zealand Navy
RS....................	Religious Studies
RSAMD............	Royal Scottish Academy of Music and Drama
RSCM	(Member) Royal School of Church Music
RSCN...............	Registered Sick Children's Nurse
RTCert	Certified Reality Therapist

RTE.................	Radio Telefis Eireann
RVC	Royal Veterinary College
RVO	Royal Victorian Order
Reg	Registered
Rehab	Rehabilitation
Relig	Religion(s)
....	Religious
Relns................	Relations
Rem	Remand
Rep	Representative
Res...................	Residence
....	Resident
....	Residential
....	Residentiary
Resp.................	Responsibility
Resurr	Resurrection
Revd	Reverend
Rich	Richard
....	Richard's
Ripon	Ripon and Leeds
Rob..................	Robinson
Roch	(Diocese of) Rochester
Rt	Right
Rtd or rtd	Retired

S

S......................	South
....	Southern
S & B	(Diocese of) Swansea and Brecon
S & M	(Diocese of) Sodor and Man
S'wark..............	(Diocese of) Southwark
S'well...............	(Diocese of) Southwell and Nottingham
....	Southwell
SA....................	Salvation Army
SAMS...............	South American Mission Society
SAOMC	St Albans and Oxford Ministry Course
SAP	(Member) Society of Analytical Psychologists
SCM	State Certified Midwife
....	Student Christian Movement
SE	South East
SEITE	South East Institute for Theological Education
SEN	State Enrolled Nurse
SHARE.............	Shelter Housing and Renewal Experiment
SM...................	Master of Science (USA)
SMF	Society for the Maintenance of the Faith
SNTS	Society for New Testament Studies
SNWTP............	Southern North West Training Partnership
SOAS...............	School of Oriental and African Studies
SOMA	Sharing of Ministries Abroad
SOSc................	Society of Ordained Scientists
SPCK	Society for Promoting Christian Knowledge
SPG	Society for the Propagation of the Gospel (now see USPG)
SRCh	State Registered Chiropodist
SRD	State Registered Dietician
SRN	State Registered Nurse
SROT...............	State Registered Occupational Therapist
SRP	State Registered Physiotherapist
SS	Saints
....	Saints'
....	Sidney Sussex
SSB..................	Society of the Sisters of Bethany
SSC..................	Solicitor before the Supreme Court (Scotland)
SSEES	School of Slavonic and East European Studies
SSF	Society of St Francis
SSJ...................	Society of St John of Jerusalem
SSJE.................	Society of St John the Evangelist
SSM..................	Self-supporting Minister (or Ministry)
....	Society of the Sacred Mission

STB	Bachelor of Theology (also see BTh)	TD	Team Deacon
STD	Doctor of Sacred Theology (also see DST)	,	Territorial Efficiency Decoration
STETS	Southern Theological Education and Training Scheme	TDip	Teacher's Diploma
		TEAR	The Evangelical Alliance Relief
STL	Reader (or Professor) of Sacred Theology	TEM	Territorial Efficiency Medal
STM	Master of Theology (also see MTh or MTheol and ThM)	TEng	Senior Technician Engineer
		TISEC	Theological Institute of the Scottish Episcopal Church
STV	Scottish Television	TM	Team Minister (or Ministry)
STh	Scholar in Theology (also see ThSchol)	TP	Team Priest
		TR	Team Rector
	Student in Theology	TS	Training Ship
SW	South West	TSB	Trustee Savings Bank
SWJ	Servants with Jesus	TV	Team Vicar
SWMTC	South West Ministry Training Course		Television
		TVS	Television South
Sacr	Sacrist	Tas	Tasmania
	Sacristan	Tech	Technical
Sarum	(Diocese of) Salisbury		Technological
Sav	Saviour		Technology
	Saviour's	temp	temporarily
ScD	Doctor of Science (also see DSc)	Th	Theologian
			Theological
Sch	School		Theology
Sec	Secretary	ThA	Associate of Theology
Selw	Selwyn	ThB	Bachelor of Theology (USA)
Sem	Seminary	ThD	Doctorate in Theology (also see DTh)
Sen	Senior		
Sheff	(Diocese of) Sheffield	ThL	Theological Licentiate
Shep	Shepherd	ThM	Master of Theology (also see MTh or MTheol and STM)
So	Souls		
	Souls'	ThSchol	Scholar in Theology (also see STh)
Soc	Social		
	Society	Thos	Thomas
Southn	Southampton		Thomas's
Sqn Ldr	Squadron Leader	Tim	Timothy
St	Saint		Timothy's
St Alb	(Diocese of) St Albans	Tr	Trainer
	St Alban		Training
	St Alban's	Treas	Treasurer
St And	(Diocese of) St Andrews, Dunkeld and Dunblane		Treasurer's
		Trin	Trinity
St As	(Diocese of) St Asaph		
St D	(Diocese of) St Davids		
St E	(Diocese of) St Edmundsbury and Ipswich		
Ste	Sainte	**U**	
Steph	Stephen	UAE	United Arab Emirates
	Stephen's	UCCF	Universities and Colleges Christian Fellowship of Evangelical Unions (formerly IVF)
Sub	Substitute		
Succ	Succentor		
Suff	Suffragan	UCD	University College, Dublin
Supt	Superintendent	UEA	University of East Anglia
Syn	Synod	UED	University Education Diploma
		UK	United Kingdom
		UKRC	United Kingdom Register of Counsellors
T		UMCA	Universities' Mission to Central Africa (now see USPG)
T, K & A	(Diocese of) Tuam, Killala and Achonry		
TA	Territorial Army	UMIST	University of Manchester Institute of Science and Technology
TAVR	Territorial and Army Volunteer Reserve		
TC	Technician Certificate	UNISA	University of South Africa
TCD	Trinity College, Dublin	UPA	Urban Priority Area (or Areas)
TCert	Teacher's Certificate		

URC	United Reformed Church
US or USA	United States (of America)
USCL	United Society for Christian Literature
USPG	United Society for the Propagation of the Gospel (formerly SPG, UMCA, and CMD)
UWE	University of the West of England
UWIST	University of Wales Institute of Science and Technology
Univ	University

V

V	Vicar
	Virgin
	Virgin's
VRD	Royal Naval Volunteer Reserve Officers' Decoration
VRSM	Volunteer Reserves Service Medal
Ven	Venerable
VetMB	Bachelor of Veterinary Medicine (also see BVetMed)
Vic	Victoria (Australia)
Vin	Vincent
	Vincent's
Voc	Vocational
	Vocations

W

W	West
	Western
w	with
W/Cdr	Wing Commander
WCC	World Council of Churches
WEC	Worldwide Evangelism Crusade
WEMTC	West of England Ministerial Training Course
WMMTC	West Midlands Ministerial Training Course
WRAF	Women's Royal Air Force
Wadh	Wadham
Wakef	(Diocese of) Wakefield
Westf	Westfield
Westmr	Westminster
Wilts	Wiltshire
Win	(Diocese of) Winchester
Wm	William
Wolfs	Wolfson
Wolv	Wolverhampton
Worc	(Diocese of) Worcester

Y

YMCA	Young Men's Christian Association
YOI	Young Offender Institution
YWAM	Youth with a Mission

English Clergy Association
www.clergyassoc.co.uk

Patron:
The Rt. Rev'd and Rt. Hon. The Lord Bishop of London;
President:
Professor Sir Anthony Milnes Coates, Bt., B.Sc., M.D., F.R.C.P.

Vice-Presidents:
Sir William Dugdale, The Wor. Chancellor Dr. James Behrens,
The Rt. Hon. The Lord Cormack,
The Very Rev'd Dr. Derek Hole, The Rt. Rev'd Dr. Michael Nazir-Ali,
The Lord Bishop of Portsmouth,
The Most Hon. The Marquess of Salisbury, The Venerable Tom Walker,
The Rt. Hon. The Lady Willoughby de Eresby.

The Association seeks to be a Church of England mutual resource for clergy, patrons and churchwardens requiring information or insight. Members include male and female clergy, private patrons and other lay people concerned to maintain an authentic Church of England.

Annual Address in London: 14th May 2012
previous speakers include
the Bishops of London and Rochester, the Marquess of Salisbury,
Chancellor Dr. James Behrens, Dr. Brian Hanson,
Professor Norman Doe, Sir Patrick Cormack and
The Rt. Hon. Dominic Grieve MP, the Attorney General

**Donations to the Benefit Fund provide
Clergy Holidays, Gifts, Legacies.
Church Collections are much appreciated
Registered Charity No. 258559**

**Benoporto-eca@yahoo.co.uk for Membership enquiries.
The Old School House, Norton Hawkfield, Bristol BS39 4HB**
Chairman: The Rev'd John Masding, M.A., LL.M.

The 2011 Annual Address by the Attorney General entitled The Rule of Law
is fully reported in the Members' journal **Parson & Parish.**

A

AAGAARD, Angus Robert. b 64. Moray Ho Coll of Educn CQSW86. Ripon Coll Cuddesdon BTh93. **d** 93 **p** 94. C Taunton St Andr *B & W* 93-97; TV Southampton (City Cen) *Win* 97-01; TR N Lambeth *S'wark* from 01. *St Anselm's Vicarage, 286 Kennington Road, London SE11 5DU* Tel (020) 7735 3415 Fax 7735 3403 Mobile 07810-646644
E-mail angus.aagaard@googlemail.com

ABAYOMI-COLE, Bimbisara Alfred (Bimbi). b 58. CCC Ox BA80 MA85. Trin Coll Bris BA94. **d** 94 **p** 95. C Deptford St Pet *S'wark* 94-98; V Crofton St Paul *Roch* from 98. *St Paul's Vicarage, 2 Oakwood Road, Orpington BR6 8JH* Tel and fax (01689) 852939 *or* 850697
E-mail bimbiabayomi_cole@hotmail.com

ABBEY, Canon Anthony James. b 36. Selw Coll Cam BA59 MA63 ARCO61. Ely Th Coll 59. **d** 61 **p** 62. C Wanstead St Mary *Chelmsf* 61-63; C Laindon w Basildon 63-67; R Sandon 67-76; V Epping St Jo 76-92; Hon Can Chelmsf Cathl 85-01; P-in-c Doddinghurst and Mountnessing 92-01; rtd 01; Perm to Offic *Worc* from 01. *Canons Piece, 2 The Squires, Blackminster, Evesham WR11 7XN* Tel (01386) 834119
E-mail anthony@canonspiece.fsnet.co.uk

ABBOTT, Barry Joseph. b 59. Sunderland Univ BA98 MCIEH. NEOC 89. **d** 92 **p** 93. NSM Bishopwearmouth Ch Ch *Dur* 92-98; NSM Silksworth 98-00; P-in-c Lumley 00-04; AD Chester-le-Street 02-04; P-in-c Whickham 04-08; R from 08. *The Rectory, Church Chare, Whickham, Newcastle upon Tyne NE16 4SH* Tel 0191-488 7397 Mobile 07801-074909

ABBOTT, Christopher Ralph. b 38. Univ of Wales (Lamp) BA59. Wells Th Coll 59. **d** 61 **p** 62. C Camberwell St Giles *S'wark* 61-67; C Portsea St Mary *Portsm* 67-70; V Portsea St Cuth 70-87; P-in-c Gt Milton *Ox* 87-88; P-in-c Lt Milton 87-88; R Gt w Lt Milton and Gt Haseley 88-93; R Chailey *Chich* 93-00; Chapl Chailey Heritage Hosp Lewes 95-00; rtd 00; Perm to Offic *Chich* from 01; Hon C Purbrook *Portsm* from 03. *6 Winchfield Crescent, Havant PO9 3SP* Tel (023) 9247 7376
E-mail christopherabbott@jonty.fsnet.co.uk

ABBOTT, David John. b 52. CertEd. St Jo Coll Nottm. **d** 87 **p** 88. C Biddulph *Lich* 87-90; C Tunbridge Wells St Jas *Roch* 90-92; TV Tunbridge Wells St Jas w St Phil 92-98; V Sunnyside w Bourne End *St Alb* from 98; RD Berkhamsted 04-09. *The Vicarage, Ivy House Lane, Berkhamsted HP4 2PP* Tel (01442) 865100
E-mail ssvicarage@yahoo.co.uk

ABBOTT, David Robert. b 49. Edin Univ BD72. Qu Coll Birm 72. **d** 74 **p** 75. C Kirkby *Liv* 74-78; C Ditton St Mich 78-80; R Ashton-in-Makerfield H Trin from 80. *The Rectory, North Ashton, Wigan WN4 0QF* Tel (01942) 727241

ABBOTT, Miss Geraldine Mary. b 33. SRN55 SCM58 Open Univ BA77 Lon Univ MTh85. Oak Hill Th Coll BA82. dss 86 **d** 87 **p** 94. Tutor Oak Hill Th Coll 86-96; St Alb St Paul *St Alb* 86-94; Hon Par Dn 87-94; Hon C from 94. *2 Wheatleys, St Albans AL4 9UE* Tel (01727) 860869

ABBOTT, (née ROBERTS), Ms Judith. b 55. Collingwood Coll Dur BA76 Goldsmiths' Coll Lon PGCE77. SWMTC 00. **d** 03 **p** 04. C Burrington, Chawleigh, Cheldon, Chulmleigh etc *Ex* 03-06; C Axminster, Chardstock, All Saints etc from 06. *Mill House, Chardstock, Axminster EX13 7BY* Tel (01460) 220005
E-mail judith754@btinternet.com

ABBOTT, Mrs Kathleen Frances. b 60. STETS 96. **d** 99 **p** 00. NSM St Helens and Sea View *Portsm* 99-02; P-in-c Wootton from 02. *The Rectory, 32 Church Road, Wootton Bridge, Ryde PO33 4PX* Tel and fax (01983) 882213
E-mail kath.abbott@btinternet.com

ABBOTT, Canon Nigel Douglas Blayney. b 37. Open Univ BA87. Bps' Coll Cheshunt 58. **d** 61 **p** 62. C Northampton St Mich *Pet* 61-64; C Wanstead St Mary *Chelmsf* 64-66; Chapl St Jo Sch Tiffield 66-69; V Earls Barton *Pet* 69-73; V Cov H Trin 73-80; Provost St Jo Cathl Oban 80-86; R Oban St Jo 80-86; TR Hemel Hempstead *St Alb* 86-96; RD Hemel Hempstead 94-96; R Much Hadham 96-02; Hon Can St Alb 96-02; rtd 02; Perm to Offic *Ely* from 03. *1 Cambridge Road, Ely CB7 4HJ* Tel (01353) 662256
E-mail nigel.abbott@waitrose.com

ABBOTT, Peter John. b 48. CQSW86. St Mich Coll Llan 94. **d** 96 **p** 97. C Neath w Llantwit 96-98; C Merthyr Tydfil Ch Ch 98-00; P-in-c Llangeinor w Nantymoel and Wyndham 00-02; V Cwm Ogwr 02-03; TV Ebbw Vale *Mon* from 03. *The Vicarage, 187 Badminton Grove, Ebbw Vale NP23 5UN* Tel (01495) 304546

ABBOTT, Richard. b 43. **d** 07 **p** 08. OLM Bisley and W End *Guildf* from 07. *241 Arethusa Way, Bisley, Woking GU24 9BU* Tel (01483) 481165 Mobile 07810-800114
E-mail richard_abbott@hotmail.co.uk

ABBOTT, Stephen Anthony. b 43. K Coll Cam BA65 MA69 Edin Univ BD68 Harvard Univ ThM69. Edin Th Coll 66. **d** 69 **p** 70. C Deal St Leon *Cant* 69-72; Chapl K Coll Cam 72-75; C Cambridge St Matt *Ely* 75-76; Asst Chapl Bris Univ and Hon C Clifton St Paul 77-80; Perm to Offic *Bris* 81-04; P-in-c Mangotsfield 04-10; rtd 10; Perm to Offic *Bris* from 10 and *Glouc* from 11. *24 Melrose Close, Yate, Bristol BS37 7AY* Tel (01454) 315073 E-mail abbott.steve@btinternet.com

ABBOTT, Stephen John. b 62. Qu Mary Coll Lon LLB83. Linc Th Coll BTh92. **d** 92 **p** 93. C E Dereham and Scarning *Nor* 92-95; TV Penistone and Thurlstone *Wakef* 95-97; R Brandon and Santon Downham w Elveden *St E* 97-00; P-in-c Gt Barton 00-04; Perm to Offic 04-08; R Bansfield from 08. *The Vicarage, Church Road, Wickhambrook, Newmarket CB8 8XH* Tel and fax (01440) 820288 Mobile 07742-396523
E-mail sj.abbott@lineone.net

ABBOTT, Mrs Valerie Ann. b 45. Keele Univ BA68. Trin Coll Bris MLitt00. **d** 00 **p** 01. NSM Knowle St Martin *Bris* 00-01; NSM Brislington St Chris and St Cuth 01-04; NSM Mangotsfield 04-10; rtd 10; Perm to Offic *Bris* from 10 and *Glouc* from 11. *24 Melrose Close, Yate, Bristol BS37 7AY* Tel (01454) 315073 Mobile 07979-997968
E-mail val.abbott@btinternet.com

ABDY, John Channing. b 38. Nottm Univ BA63. Cuddesdon Coll 63. **d** 65 **p** 66. C Leagrave *St Alb* 65-69; C N Mymms 69-72; V Kings Walden 72-79; V S Woodham Ferrers *Chelmsf* 79-85; V Walthamstow St Pet 85-91; V Burrington and Churchill *B & W* 91-06; rtd 06. *Sunnyside Cottage, Whitford Road, Musbury, Axminster EX13 7AP* Tel (01297) 552847
E-mail jcabdy@icdonline.co.uk

ABECASSIS, Joanna Margaret. b 54. Girton Coll Cam BA75 MA79 PhD81. WEMTC 99. **d** 02 **p** 03. C Tavistock and Gulworthy *Ex* 02-07; TV Totnes w Bridgetown, Berry Pomeroy etc 07-10; P-in-c Bradford-on-Avon H Trin *Sarum* from 10. *Holy Trinity Vicarage, 18A Woolley Street, Bradford-on-Avon BA15 1AF* Tel (01225) 864444
E-mail joanna@abecassis.freeserve.co.uk

ABEL, David John. b 31. S'wark Ord Course 71. **d** 74 **p** 75. NSM Crowhurst *S'wark* 74-85; NSM Lingfield and Crowhurst 85-92; Perm to Offic *S'wark* 92-98; *Chich* 98-07; *St E* from 03. *13 Church Street, Boxford, Sudbury CO10 5DU* Tel (01787) 211765

ABELL, Canon Brian. b 37. Nottm Univ BA61 DipEd Leeds Univ MA95. Cuddesdon Coll 61. **d** 63 **p** 64. C Lightcliffe *Wakef* 63-66; C-in-c Mixenden CD 66-68; Lect Linc Coll of Tech 68-69; Chapl Trent Coll Nottm 70-74; V Thorner *Ripon* 74-82; V Far Headingley St Chad 82-86; Deputation Appeals Org CECS 86-89; V Masham and Healey *Ripon* 89-00; Hon Can Ripon 97-00; rtd 00; Perm to Offic *Ripon* from 00. *Manor Garth, 1 Manor Road, Harrogate HG2 0HP* Tel and fax (01423) 526112
E-mail b.abell@btinternet.com

ABELL, George Derek. b 31. Selw Coll Cam BA54 MA68. Qu Coll Birm 54. **d** 56 **p** 57. C Stoke upon Trent *Lich* 56-60; C Wolverhampton 60-64; R Bridgnorth St Mary *Heref* 64-70; P-in-c Oldbury 64-70; R Atherton N Australia 70-73; R Withington w Westhide and Weston Beggard *Heref* 73-81; R Withington w Westhide 81-83; P-in-c Sutton St Nicholas w Sutton St Michael 76-81; R 81-83; Preb Heref Cathl 82-83; V Basing *Win* 83-88; rtd 88; Perm to Offic *Heref* 88-04. *25 Eastfield Court, Church Street, Faringdon SN7 8SL* Tel (01367) 240731

ABELL, Peter John. b 45. Chich Th Coll 67. **d** 70 **p** 71. C Churchdown St Jo *Glouc* 70-74; Chapl RAF 74-98; R Kilkhampton w Morwenstow *Truro* 98-09; rtd 09; Perm to Offic *York* from 11. *66 Minster Avenue, Beverley HU17 0ND* Tel (01482) 862816 E-mail 66minster@66minster.karoo.co.uk

ABERDEEN AND ORKNEY, Bishop of. See GILLIES, The Rt Revd Robert Arthur

ABERDEEN AND ORKNEY, Dean of. See NIMMO, The Very Revd Alexander Emsley

ABERDEEN, Provost of. See KILGOUR, The Very Revd Richard Eifl

✠**ABERNETHY, The Rt Revd Alan Francis.** b 57. QUB BA78 BD89. CITC. **d** 81 **p** 82 **c** 07. C Dundonald *D & D* 81-84; C

Lecale Gp 84-86; I Helen's Bay 86-90; I Ballyholme 90-07; Preb Down Cathl 00-07; Cen Dir of Ords 04-07; Bp Conn from 07. *1 Marlborough Gate, Marlborough Park, Malone, Belfast BT9 6GB* Tel (028) 9066 1942 E-mail bishop@connor.anglican.org

ABINGTON, David John Barringer. b 48. EAMTC 91. **d** 94 **p** 95. C Newport w Longford and Chetwynd *Lich* 94-96; C Newport w Longford, Chetwynd and Forton 96-98; R Adderley, Ash, Calverhall, Ightfield etc 98-02; R Brading w Yaverland *Portsm* 02-11; rtd 11; Perm to Offic *Portsm* from 11. *26 Lincoln Way, Bembridge PO35 5QJ* Tel (01983) 874690 Mobile 07855-086978 E-mail david.abington@btinternet.com

ABLETT, Edwin John. b 37. Clifton Th Coll 64. **d** 67 **p** 68. C Sneinton St Chris w St Phil *S'well* 67-70; R High and Gd Easter w Margaret Roding *Chelmsf* 70-73; SAMS Chile 73-75; C Gt Baddow *Chelmsf* 75-78; V Newchapel *Lich* 78-82; V S Westoe *Dur* 82-86; V Tibshelf *Derby* 86-00; rtd 00; Perm to Offic *St D* 00-09 and *Win* from 10. *Copihue, 18 Sherley Green, Bursledon, Southampton SO31 8FL* Tel (023) 8040 6413 E-mail john.copihue@btinternet.com

ABLETT, Mrs Jennifer Vera. b 46. **d** 00 **p** 01. OLM Henley, Claydon and Barham *St E* from 00. *10 Phillipps Road, Barham, Ipswich IP6 0AZ* Tel (01473) 830205

ABRAHAM, Brian. b 42. **d** 00 **p** 01. OLM Burscough Bridge *Liv* from 00. *4 Mere Court, Burscough, Ormskirk L40 0TQ* Tel (01704) 892547

ABRAHAM, Canon David Alexander. b 37. AKC61. **d** 62 **p** 63. C Oswestry St Oswald *Lich* 62-63; C Gt Wyrley 63-65; C Sprowston *Nor* 65-67; V Ormesby w Scratby 67-81; R Oxborough w Foulden and Caldecote 81-87; R Cockley Cley w Gooderstone 81-87; V Didlington 81-87; R Gt and Lt Cressingham w Threxton 81-87; R Hilborough w Bodney 81-87; P-in-c Nor St Giles 87-96; Chapl Asst Norfolk and Nor Hosp 87-91; V Thorpe St Matt *Nor* 96-00; Hon Can Nor Cathl 95-00; rtd 00; Perm to Offic *Nor* from 00. *170 Desmond Drive, Old Catton, Norwich NR6 7JW* Tel (01603) 402797

ABRAHAM, Estelle Pamela. b 46. C F Mott Coll of Educn TCert69. **d** 04 **p** 05. OLM Bolton Breightmet St Jas *Man* 04-06; OLM Leverhulme 06-07; NSM Witchford w Wentworth, Haddenham and Wilburton *Ely* 08-11; Canada from 11. *Address temp unknown* E-mail abrapig@hotmail.co.uk

ABRAHAM, Canon John Callis Harford. b 31. Univ of W Aus BA52. Westcott Ho Cam 53. **d** 55 **p** 56. C Wigan St Anne *Liv* 55-57; C Northam Perth Australia 57-60; R Wongan Hills 60-62; Vice-Warden Wollaston Th Coll and R Graylands 63-67; P-in-c City Beach 66-67; Lic to Offic *Birm* 67-68; R Applecross Perth Australia 68-76; Can Perth 71-84; R Leeming 76-79; Chapl Home Miss 79-81; R Wembley 81-89; R Albany 90-94; Can Bunbury 92-94; rtd 94. *10 Royston Park, Pioneer Road, Albany WA 6330, Australia* Tel (0061) (8) 9841 1809

ABRAHAM, Richard James. b 42. Liv Univ BA63. Ridley Hall Cam 64. **d** 66 **p** 67. C Warrington St Ann *Liv* 66-70; C Golborne 70-73; V Bickershaw 73-78; V Ewerby w Evedon *Linc* 78-82; R Kirkby Laythorpe w Asgarby 78-82; R Kirkby Laythorpe 82-03; rtd 03. *23 Londesborough Way, Metheringham, Lincoln LN4 3HW*

ABRAHAMS, Peter William. b 42. Southn Univ BA77. Sarum Th Coll 77. **d** 78 **p** 79. C Bitterne Park *Win* 78-82; C Old Brumby *Linc* 82-84; V Mitcham Ascension *S'wark* 84-91; TV Riverside *Ox* 91-06; rtd 06; Perm to Offic *Ox* from 06. *17 Snowberry Close, Wokingham RG41 4AQ* Tel 0118-989 3072 E-mail frapeter@aol.com

ABRAM, Paul Robert Carrington. b 36. MVO07. Keble Coll Ox BA62 MA65. Chich Th Coll 60. **d** 62 **p** 63. C Redcar *York* 62-65; CF 65-89; V Salcombe *Ex* 89-96; Miss to Seafarers from 89; rtd 96; Chapl to The Queen 96-06; Chapl St Pet-ad-Vincula at HM Tower of Lon 96-06; Dep P in O 96-06. *Paddock End, Kimpton, Andover SP11 8PG* Tel (01264) 772349

ABRAM, Steven James. b 50. Lon Univ BD76. Oak Hill Th Coll 71. **d** 76 **p** 77. C Biddulph *Lich* 76-79; C Heatherlands St Jo *Sarum* 79-83; Libya 83-84; C Stratford-on-Avon w Bishopton *Cov* 84; V Alderholt *Sarum* 84-90; V Daubhill *Man* 90-00; TV Mid Trent *Lich* from 07. *St Peter's House, 2 Vicarage Way, Hixon, Stafford ST18 0FT* Tel (01889) 270418 E-mail sj@abram.org.uk

ABREY, Mrs Barbara May. b 52. Trin Coll Bris 09. **d** 11. OLM Wroughton *Bris* from 11. *17 Edgar Row Close, Wroughton, Swindon SN4 9LR* Tel (01793) 633024 E-mail barbaraabrey@hotmail.com

ABREY, Mark Evans John. b 66. Ripon Coll Cuddesdon BTh93. **d** 93 **p** 94. C W Derby St Mary *Liv* 93-97; P-in-c Anfield St Marg 97-01; Chapl R Liverpool Children's NHS Trust 95-99; V Chase *Ox* 01-05; P-in-c Chadlington and Spelsbury, Ascott under Wychwood 01-05; R Chase from 05; P-in-c Ascott under Wychwood 01-07. *The Vicarage, Church Road, Chadlington, Chipping Norton OX7 3LY* Tel (01608) 676572 E-mail mark@abreys.com

ABREY, Philip James. b 51. NOC 82. **d** 85 **p** 86. NSM Hindley SS *Liv* 85-90; C Caversham St Pet and Mapledurham etc *Ox*

90-00; Min Caversham Park LEP 90-00; Co Ecum Officer (Berks) 96-00; Perm to Offic *Cov* 01-07; Chapl HM Pris The Mount from 02. *HM Prison, The Mount, Molyneux Avenue, Bovingdon, Hemel Hempstead HP3 0NZ* Tel (01442) 834363 E-mail philip.abrey@hmps.gsi.gov.uk

ABSALOM, Alexander James David Edward. b 69. St Jo Coll Dur BA91. Cranmer Hall Dur 92. **d** 94 **p** 95. C Cranham Park *Chelmsf* 94-98; Perm to Offic *Sheff* 98-05; Miss P Philadelphia St Thos 05-07; USA from 07. *5907 Pecan Grove Court, Edmond OK 73034, USA* Tel (001) (405) 749 8044 E-mail alex@theabsaloms.net

ABUJA, Bishop of. See AKINOLA, The Most Revd Peter Jasper

ABULEMOI, Joseph Oriho. See CHOUFAR, Joseph Oriho Abulemoi

ACARNLEY, Rita Kay. b 57. Girton Coll Cam BA79 MA83 Newc Univ MA94 St Jo Coll Dur BA98. Cranmer Hall Dur 96. **d** 99 **p** 00. NSM Humshaugh w Simonburn and Wark *Newc* 99-00; Tutor TISEC and Prov Local Collaborative Min Officer Scotland 00-03; R Stonehaven and Catterline *Bre* 03-07; P-in-c Muchalls 03-07. *13 Midtown, Poolewe, Achnasheen IV22 2LW* Tel (01445) 781315 E-mail ritaacarnley@dunelm.org.uk

ACCRA, Bishop of. See AKROFI, The Most Revd Justice Ofei

ACHESON, Denise Mary. BTh. **d** 05 **p** 06. C Ballyholme *D & D* 05-08; I Dunmurry *Conn* from 08. *The Rectory, 27 Church Avenue, Dunmurry, Belfast BT17 9RS* Tel (028) 9061 0984 E-mail denise.acheson@gmail.com

ACHESON, James Malcolm. b 48. BNC Ox BA70 MA73. Sarum & Wells Th Coll 83. **d** 85 **p** 86. C Highgate St Mich *Lon* 85-88; TV Tisbury *Sarum* 88-94; R Storrington *Chich* from 94. *The Rectory, Rectory Road, Storrington, Pulborough RH20 4EF* Tel (01903) 742888

ACHONRY, Dean of. *Vacant*

ACHURCH, Peter William Hammond. b 37. Ridley Coll Melbourne 82. **d** 82 **p** 84. C Port Lincoln Australia 82-84; P-in-c Elliston w Lock and Wuddina 86; R 87-89; Par P Leigh Creek 89-93; TV Madeley *Heref* 00-05; rtd 05. *34 Birchall Road, Goolwa Beach SA 5214, Australia* Tel (0061) (08) 8555 3279

ACKERLEY, Glyn James. b 57. Kent Univ MA04. Cranmer Hall Dur 84. **d** 87 **p** 88. C Tonbridge SS Pet and Paul *Roch* 87-90; R Willingham *Ely* 90-94; R Rampton 90-94; V Chatham St Phil and St Jas *Roch* 94-09; P-in-c Shorne from 09; Dioc Dir of Ords from 09. *The Vicarage, Butcher's Hill, Shorne, Gravesend DA12 3EB* Tel (01474) 822239 Mobile 07595-171748 E-mail g.ackerley@btconnect.com

ACKERMAN, David Michael. b 71. Westmr Coll Ox BTh95 Brighton Univ PGCE98 Cardiff Univ LLM11. Pontificium Institutum Internationale Angelicum Rome STB01 MA02. **d** 01 **p** 02. In RC Ch 01-04; C Fairford and Kempsford w Whelford *Glouc* 05-08; P-in-c Sherborne, Windrush, the Barringtons etc from 08; Dioc Ecum Officer from 08. *The Vicarage, Windrush, Burford OX18 4TS* Tel (01451) 844276 Mobile 07916-348719 E-mail dmackerman@hotmail.com

ACKFORD, Christopher Mark. b 60. Univ Coll Lon BDS83 K Coll Lon MSc89. Ripon Coll Cuddesdon 02. **d** 04 **p** 05. C Bracknell *Ox* 04-07; TV Aylesbury w Bierton and Hulcott from 07. *The Vicarage, St James Way, Bierton, Aylesbury HP22 5ED* Tel (01296) 424466 Mobile 07780-554032 E-mail mark@ackford.wanadoo.co.uk

ACKLAM, Leslie Charles. b 46. Birm Univ BEd71. Ripon Coll Cuddesdon 78. **d** 80 **p** 81. C Chingford St Anne *Chelmsf* 80-83; C Spalding *Linc* 83-85; V Spalding St Paul 85-93; P-in-c Linc St Faith and St Martin w St Pet 94-06; Chapl Linc Univ from 06. *14 Nettleham Close, Lincoln LN2 1SJ* Tel (01522) 879513 *or* 886079 E-mail leslie.acklam@ntlworld.com *or* lacklam@lincoln.ac.uk

ACKLAND, Canon John Robert Warwick. b 47. **d** 82 **p** 83. NSM Shooters Hill Ch Ch *S'wark* 82-88; NSM Mottingham St Andr w St Alban 82-94; NSM Woolwich St Thos 94-96; NSM Bellingham St Dunstan 96-03; Hon Chapl *S'wark* Cathl 98-03; P-in-c Perry Hill St Geo w Ch Ch and St Paul 03-04; V from 04; Hon Can *S'wark* Cathl from 05. *The Vicarage, Vancouver Road, London SE23 2AF* Tel (020) 8699 7676 *or* 8699 7202 Mobile 07831-516662 E-mail johnackland1@aol.com

ACKROYD, David Andrew. b 66. Coll of Ripon & York St Jo BA90 St Jo Coll Dur BA97. Cranmer Hall Dur 94. **d** 97 **p** 98. C Lilleshall and Sheriffhales *Lich* 97-01; Asst Chapl R Wolv Hosps NHS Trust 01-02; C Ogley Hay *Lich* 02-03; Perm to Offic 10-11; TR Cheswardine, Childs Ercall, Hales, Hinstock etc from 11. *The Vicarage, Childs Ercall, Market Drayton TF9 2DA* Tel (01952) 840229 E-mail andy.sandra@btinternet.com

ACKROYD, Dennis. b 36. Cranmer Hall Dur 67. **d** 70 **p** 71. C Newcastle w Butterton *Lich* 70-73; C Horsell *Guildf* 73-77; P-in-c Moreton and Woodsford w Tincleton *Sarum* 77-82; R 82-86; RD Dorchester 79-85; R Ewhurst *Guildf* 86-94; V Cleckheaton St Luke and Whitechapel *Wakef* 94-02; rtd 02; Perm to Offic *Sarum* from 03. *17 Charles Street, Weymouth DT4 7JG* Tel (01305) 778122

ACKROYD, Eric. b 29. Leeds Univ BA51 Liv Univ MA71 Leic Univ MA(Ed)86. St Jo Coll Dur 53. **d** 55 **p** 56. C Newland St Jo

York 55-58; Succ Birm Cathl 58-60; Chapl K Sch Bruton 61-66; Lect Kirkby Fields Coll of Educn Liv 67-72; Sen Lect Nene Coll of HE Northn 72-85; rtd 85. *14 Phippsville Court, St Matthew's Parade, Northampton NN2 7JW* Tel (01604) 713328

ACKROYD, John Michael Calvert. b 32. Lon Univ BSc53. Ripon Hall Ox 71. **d** 73 **p** 74. C Keighley *Bradf* 73-76; TV 76-81; V Keighley All SS 81; V Whalley *Blackb* 81-97; Chapl Calderstones Hosp Clitheroe 81-93; Chapl Calderstones NHS Trust 93-97; rtd 97; Perm to Offic *Blackb* from 97. *1 Calder Vale, Whalley, Clitheroe BB7 9SR* Tel (01254) 823943

ACKROYD, Peter Michael. b 60. Jes Coll Cam BA82 MA86 Fontainebleau MBA87 Edin Univ PhD02. Wycliffe Hall Ox BA93 MA00. **d** 94 **p** 95. C Denton Holme *Carl* 94-97; Sec Proclamation Trust 97-00; V Wootton *St Alb* from 02. *The Vicarage, Church Road, Wootton, Bedford MK43 9HF* Tel (01234) 768391 E-mail ackroyds@lineone.net

ACKROYD, Ruth. b 49. **d** 04 **p** 05. NSM Hoole *Ches* from 04. *Strathroine, Ashby Place, Hoole, Chester CH2 3AG* Tel (01244) 344529 E-mail r.ackroyd@chester.ac.uk

ACLAND, Mrs Sophia Caroline Annabel. b 61. Somerville Coll Ox BA11 MA11. Ripon Coll Cuddesdon 08. **d** 11. NSM Cam w Stinchcombe *Glouc* from 11. *The Mount House, Alderley, Wotton-under-Edge GL12 7QT* Tel (01453) 842233 E-mail nacland@nacland.fsnet.co.uk

ACONLEY, Carole Ann. b 51. Hull Univ BTh01. NEOC 99. **d** 02 **p** 03. NSM Langtoft w Foxholes, Butterwick, Cottam etc *York* from 02. *Hawthorn Farm, Langtoft, Driffield YO25 3BT* Tel (01377) 267219 E-mail caroleaconley@gmail.com

ACREMAN, John. b 53. Oak Hill Th Coll 86. **d** 88 **p** 89. C Iver *Ox* 88-92; R Hook Norton w Gt Rollright, Swerford etc from 92. *The Rectory, Hook Norton, Banbury OX15 5QQ* Tel (01608) 737223 E-mail acreman@xalt.co.uk

ACWORTH, The Ven Richard Foote. b 36. SS Coll Cam BA62 MA65. Cuddesdon Coll 61. **d** 63 **p** 64. C Fulham St Etheldreda *Lon* 63-64; C Langley All SS and Martyrs *Man* 64-66; C Bridgwater St Mary w Chilton Trinity *B & W* 66-69; V Yatton 69-81; V Yatton Moor 81; P-in-c Taunton St Jo 81-84; P-in-c Taunton St Mary 81-85; V 85-93; Preb Wells Cathl 87-93; Adn Wells, Can Res and Preb Wells Cathl 93-03; rtd 03; Perm to Offic *B & W* from 04. *Corvedale Cottage, Ganes Terrace, Croscombe, Wells BA5 3QJ* Tel (01749) 342242

ACWORTH, Richard John Philip. b 30. Ch Ch Ox BA52 MA56 Paris Univ DèsL70. **d** 63 **p** 63. In RC Ch 63-67; C Walthamstow St Mary w St Steph *Chelmsf* 68-70; P-in-c Lt Sampford 70-76; P-in-c Gt Sampford 70-76; Lect Bath Coll of HE 76-77; Lect Th Derby Lonsdale Coll 77-83; Derbyshire Coll of HE 83-88; P-in-c Newton Tracey, Alverdiscott, Huntshaw etc *Ex* 88-96; TR Newton Tracey, Horwood, Alverdiscott etc 96-98; RD Torrington 94-97; rtd 98; Perm to Offic *Portsm* from 98. *91 Oaklands Road, Havant PO9 2RL* Tel (023) 9245 0567

ADAIR, Raymond. b 33. Ripon Hall Ox 70. **d** 72 **p** 73. C Knottingley *Wakef* 72-75; C Sandal St Helen 75-77; V Sandal St Cath 77-87; V Brownhill 87-97; rtd 97; Perm to Offic *Wakef* from 99. *15 Chestnut Fold, Upper Lane, Netherton, Wakefield WF4 4NG* Tel (01924) 274640

ADAIR, Canon William Matthew. b 52. Open Univ BA. CITC 77. **d** 77 **p** 78. C Portadown St Mark *Arm* 77-78; Asst Chapl Miss to Seamen 78-80; C Lisburn Ch Ch Cathl 80-84; I Kildress w Altedesert *Arm* 84-92; I Portadown St Columba from 92; Dioc Sec Min of Healing 95-99; Can Arm Cathl from 08. *8 Ardmore Close, Portadown, Craigavon BT62 4DX* Tel (028) 3833 2746

ADAM, Canon David. b 36. Kelham Th Coll 54. **d** 59 **p** 60. C Auckland St Helen *Dur* 59-63; C Owton Manor CD 63-67; V Danby *York* 67-90; Can and Preb York Minster 89-90; V Holy Is *Newc* 90-03; rtd 03; Perm to Offic *Newc* from 03. *The Old Granary, Warren Mill, Belford NE70 7EE* Tel (01668) 214770

ADAM, Lawrence. b 38. NOC 82. **d** 82 **p** 83. C Thornton-le-Fylde *Blackb* 82-86; Dioc Video Production Co-ord 85-97; P-in-c Scorton 86-91; C W Burnley All SS 91-97; P-in-c Ashton St Jas *Man* 97-99; TV Ashton 00-03; rtd 03; Perm to Offic *Ches* from 03. *23 Dryden Avenue, Cheadle SK8 2AW*

ADAM, Lindsay Anne. *See* YATES, Lindsay Anne

ADAM, Canon Peter James Hedderwick. b 46. Lon Univ BD73 MTh76 Dur Univ PhD81. Ridley Coll Melbourne ThL69. **d** 70 **p** 71. Australia 70-72, 73-74 and from 82; C Ivanhoe St Jas 70-72; C Rosanna 72; Hon C Holborn St Geo w H Trin and St Bart *Lon* 72-73; C Essendon St Thos and Tutor Ridley Coll 73-74; Tutor St Jo Coll Dur 75-82; Hon C Dur St Cuth 75-82; P-in-c Carlton St Jude 82-88; V 88-01; Adn Melbourne 88-91; Chapl Melbourne Univ 95-01; Can Melbourne from 96; Prin Ridley Coll from 01. *160 The Avenue, Parkville Vic 3053, Australia* (0061) (3) 9207 4800 Fax 9387 5099 E-mail principal@ridley.unimelb.edu.au

ADAM, William Jonathan. b 69. Man Univ BA91 Univ of Wales (Cardiff) LLM03 PhD09. Westcott Ho Cam 92 Bossey Ecum Inst Geneva. **d** 94 **p** 95. C Beaconsfield *Ox* 94-97; C Witney 97-98; TV 98-02; P-in-c Girton *Ely* 02-07; R 07-10; Dioc Ecum

Officer 02-10; V Winchmore Hill St Paul *Lon* from 10. *St Paul's Vicarage, Church Hill, London N21 1JA* Tel (020) 8886 3545 E-mail wja@luxmundi.co.uk

ADAMS, Mrs Alison Mary. b 51. Girton Coll Cam MA73 Birm Univ BMus76 CertEd77 Sheff Univ MPhil93. EMMTC 94. **d** 97 **p** 98. NSM Burbage w Aston Flamville *Leic* 97-05; Dir Bloxham Project 00-05; Chapl HM YOI Glen Parva from 06. *HM Young Offender Institution, Glen Parva, Tiger's Road, Wigston LE18 4TN* Tel 0116-228 4100

ADAMS, Amanda Elaine. QUB BSc BTh. **d** 06 **p** 07. C Ballymena w Ballyclug *Conn* 06-09; I Ballyrashane w Kildollagh from 09. *The Rectory, 9 Sandelwood Avenue, Coleraine BT52 1JW* Tel (028) 7034 3061

ADAMS, Anthony John. b 42. St Jo Coll Nottm 83. **d** 85 **p** 86. C Wellesbourne *Cov* 85-89; R Weddington and Caldecote 89-01; P-in-c Butlers Marston and the Pillertons w Ettington 01-07; P-in-c Alderminster and Halford 01-07; P-in-c Tredington and Darlingscott w Newbold on Stour 04-07; R Stourdene Gp 07-09; rtd 09. *47 Palmer Road, Whitnash, Leamington Spa CV31 2HP* Tel (01926) 426023

ADAMS, Anthony Paul. b 41. SAOMC 95. **d** 98 **p** 99. NSM Banbury St Hugh *Ox* 98-01; P-in-c Wootton w Glympton and Kiddington 01-04; P-in-c Broughton and Duddon *Carl* 04-10; rtd 10; Perm to Offic *Ox* from 11. *10 Quarry Road, Witney OX28 1JS* Tel (01993) 775859 E-mail adamsfamily2@btinternet.com

ADAMS, Brian Hugh. b 32. Pemb Coll Ox BA54 MA57. Sarum & Wells Th Coll 77. **d** 79 **p** 80. Hon C Crediton *Ex* 79-81; Chapl St Brandon's Sch Clevedon 81-85; C Street w Walton *B & W* 86-88; RD Glastonbury 86-92 and 93-97; V Baltonsborough w Butleigh and W Bradley 88-97; rtd 97; Perm to Offic *B & W* from 97. *Manor Cottage, Weir Lane, Yeovilton, Yeovil BA22 8EU* Tel (01935) 840462 E-mail adamsbj@btinternet.com

ADAMS, Canon Brian Peter. b 47. FInstD FRSA Avery Hill Coll CertEd70. S'wark Ord Course 90. **d** 93 **p** 94. NSM Tonbridge SS Pet and Paul *Roch* 93-99; P-in-c Chatham St Mary w St Jo from 99; Hon Can Roch Cathl from 09. *The Rectory, 65 Maidstone Road, Chatham ME4 6DP* Tel (01634) 351065 *or* 351069 Mobile 07778-777824 Fax 351069 E-mail brian.adams@diocese-rochester.org

ADAMS, Bridget Ruth. b 52. Sussex Univ BSc74 DPhil78. SAOMC 03. **d** 06 **p** 07. NSM Bushey *St Alb* from 06. *Beech Tree House, The Pathway, Radlett WD7 8JB* Tel (01923) 853967 Mobile 07906-075419 E-mail bridgetbth@aol.com

ADAMS, Mrs Celia. b 39. R Holloway Coll Lon BSc60 Cam Univ CertEd61. Sarum & Wells Th Coll 86. **d** 88 **p** 94. NSM Canley *Cov* 88-91; NSM Cov N Deanery 91-92; C Coventry Caludon 92-97; Asst to Dioc Dir of Educn 92-93; Asst Chapl Geo Eliot Hosp NHS Trust Nuneaton 97-01; rtd 01; Perm to Offic *Ban* and *Cov* from 01. *Cefn-y-Mor, 102 Plas Edwards, Tywyn LL36 0AS* Tel (01654) 711604

ADAMS, The Ven Charles Alexander. b 29. MBE73 CBE82 JP. AKC59. **d** 60 **p** 61. C Bishopwearmouth St Mich w St Hilda *Dur* 60-63; C Ox SS Phil and Jas 63-66; C Tunbridge Wells St Barn *Roch* 66-68; Miss to Seafarers St Vincent from 68; Can Kingstown Cathl from 73; Adn St Vincent & The Grenadines 76-98; rtd 98. *St Mary's Rectory, Bequia, Northern Grenadines, St Vincent and the Grenadines* Tel (001784) 458 3234 Fax 457 3532 E-mail caadams@caribsurf.com

ADAMS, Christopher John. b 40. **d** 98 **p** 99. C Luton St Fran *St Alb* 98-05; rtd 06; Perm to Offic *St Alb* from 06. *91 Byron Road, Luton LU4 0HX* Tel (01582) 529373 E-mail chrisandsallyadams@ntlworld.com

ADAMS, David. *See* ADAMS, John David Andrew

ADAMS, David James. b 58. Trin Coll Bris 95. **d** 97 **p** 98. C Wirksworth *Derby* 97-00; P-in-c Seale and Lullington 00-02; R Seale and Lullington w Coton in the Elms 02-05; CF from 05. *c/o MOD Chaplains (Army)* Tel (01264) 381140 Fax 381824

ADAMS, Canon David John Anthony. b 46. QUB BSc70. Bris Sch of Min 81. **d** 84 **p** 85. NSM Sea Mills *Bris* 84-97; C Henbury 97-00; V Longwell Green from 00; AD Kingswood and S Glos 06-11; Hon Can Bris Cathl from 10. *The Vicarage, 85 Bath Road, Longwell Green, Bristol BS30 9DF* Tel 0117-932 3714 Mobile 07803-330727 E-mail djaadams@virginmedia.com

ADAMS, Donald John. b 46. St Jo Coll Nottm 86. **d** 88 **p** 89. C Byfleet *Guildf* 88-93; P-in-c E Molesey St Mary 93-03; Perm to Offic *S'wark* 96-03; rtd 03. *4 Boxbush Close, South Cerney, Cirencester GL7 5XS* Tel (01285) 852009 E-mail cada.adams@virgin.net

ADAMS, Douglas George. b 39. St Luke's Coll Ex CertEd69 MEd87 ALBC65. SWMTC 86. **d** 89 **p** 90. NSM Bude Haven and Marhamchurch *Truro* 89-93; P-in-c St Mewan 93-94; P-in-c Mevagissey and St Ewe 00-04; Chapl Mt Edgcumbe Hospice 93-96; rtd 04; Perm to Offic *Truro* from 09. *9 Arundel Terrace, Bude EX23 8LS* Tel (01288) 353842 E-mail douglasadams@tiscali.co.uk

ADAMS, Gillian. *See* WILTON, Mrs Gillian Linda

ADAMS, Godfrey Bernard. b 47. d 93 p 94. OLM Saddleworth *Man* 93-09; Perm to Offic 09-10. *Address temp unknown* E-mail godfreyadams@compuserve.com

ADAMS, Hubert Theodore. b 28. FCA. d 98 p 99. OLM Blurton *Lich* 98-11; OLM Blurton and Dresden from 11. *12 Wakefield Road, Stoke-on-Trent ST4 5PT* Tel (01782) 415364 E-mail theoadams@live.co.uk

ADAMS, Ian Robert. b 57. R Holloway Coll Lon BA79. Ridley Hall Cam 95. d 97 p 98. C Thame *Ox* 97-04; Ldr mayBe 04-09; Missional Community Developer CMS from 09. *Old Walls, Fore Street, Aveton Gifford, Kingsbridge TQ7 4LL* Tel (01548) 550388 Mobile 07889-906983 E-mail ian@thestillpoint.org.uk

ADAMS, Canon James Michael. b 49. Man Univ LLB71 Lon Univ PGCE79. St Jo Coll Nottm 80. d 82 p 83. C Luton St Mary *St Alb* 82-85; TV Cove St Jo *Guildf* 85-92; V Chislehurst Ch Ch *Roch* from 92; Hon Can Roch Cathl from 09. *Christ Church Vicarage, 62 Lubbock Road, Chislehurst BR7 5JX* Tel (020) 8467 3185 *or* tel and fax 8325 3557 E-mail mmichaelccc@aol.com

ADAMS, Mrs Jayne Maxine. b 57. Westhill Coll Birm CertEd78. WMMTC 94. d 97 p 98. NSM Cotteridge *Birm* 97-99; NSM Nechells 99-05; NSM Bournville from 05. *40 Middle Park Drive, Northfield, Birmingham B31 2FL* Tel 0121-476 0206 E-mail jane@adamsj21.freeserve.co.uk

ADAMS, John. b 38. Lon Univ DipEd66 Open Univ BA79. Linc Th Coll 68. d 70 p 71. C Skipton H Trin *Bradf* 70-72; C Bassingham *Linc* 72-73; Chapl St Piers Hosp Sch Lingfield 73-74; Hon C Keighley *Bradf* 76-79; P-in-c Bredenbury and Wacton w Grendon Bishop *Heref* 79-84; P-in-c Edwyn Ralph and Collington w Thornbury 79-84; P-in-c Pencombe w Marston Stannett and Lt Cowarne 79-84; V Macclesfield St Jo *Ches* 84-87; R Wimblington *Ely* 87-90; V Manea 87-90; R Hallaton w Horninghold, Allexton, Tugby etc *Leic* 90-96; P-in-c Moulton *Linc* 96-97; V 97-03; rtd 03; Perm to Offic *Linc* from 03. *17 Linden Drive, Burgh le Marsh, Skegness PE24 5BP* Tel (01754) 810366

ADAMS, Canon John Christopher Ronald. b 29. St Paul's Coll Grahamstown. d 55 p 56. C Bulawayo St Marg S Rhodesia 55-61; R Shabani 61-66; C Northolt Park St Barn *Lon* 67-68; C W Brompton St Mary 68-69; C Umtali Zimbabwe 69-71; R Melfort and P-in-c Cranborne 71-75; Lic to Offic 75-98; rtd 98; Perm to Offic S'wark from 01. *The College of St Barnabas, Blackberry Lane, Lingfield RH7 6NJ* Tel (01342) 872838

ADAMS, John David Andrew. b 37. TCD BA60 MA64 BD69 Div Test61 Reading Univ MEd74. d 62 p 63. C Belfast St Steph *Conn* 62-65; Asst Master Lacunza Academy Spain 65-67; Asst Master Tower Ramparts Sch Ipswich 67-70; Asst Master Robert Haining Sch Surrey 70-74; Hd Master St Paul's Secondary Sch Addlestone 74-82; Hd Master Weydon Secondary Sch Farnham 82-98; NSM Bourne *Guildf* 80-99; NSM The Bourne and Tilford 99-07; Chapl to The Queen 94-07; Consultant to Secondary Schs 98-07; Perm to Offic *Guildf* from 08. *Brookside Farm, Oast House Crescent, Farnham GU9 0NP* Tel (01252) 726888 E-mail j.david adams@ntworld.com

ADAMS, John Mark Arthur. b 67. Reading Univ BSc89. St Jo Coll Nottm MA98 MPhil07. d 99 p 00. C Skegby S'well 99-02; C Bletchley *Ox* 02-07; P-in-c Mansfield St Jo S'well 07-10; P-in-c Ladybrook 09-10; V Mansfield St Jo w St Mary from 10; AD Mansfield from 10. *The Vicarage, St John Street, Mansfield NG18 1QH* Tel (01623) 660822 *or* 625999

ADAMS, John Peter. b 42. Lon Univ BD69. Oak Hill Th Coll 65. d 70 p 71. C Whitnash *Cov* 70-73; Hon Asst Chapl Basle *Eur* 73-74; Chapl Davos 74-75; Chapl Düsseldorf 75-76; C St Baddow *Chelmsf* 77-80; Miss Eur Chr Miss 80-91; Perm to Offic *Chelmsf* 80-91; Hon Asst Chapl Vienna *Eur* 90-91; Asst Chapl Zürich 91-95; P-in-c Harmondsworth *Lon* 95-99; TV Shebbear, Buckland Filleigh, Sheepwash etc *Ex* 99-02; Perm to Offic *Ex* from 02. *The Leas, Kingscott, Torrington EX38 7JW* Tel (01805) 622161 E-mail john@adams1100.freeserve.co.uk

ADAMS, John Richard. b 38. St D Coll Lamp BA62 Lich Th Coll 62. d 64 p 65. C Falmouth K Chas *Truro* 64-68; C Bath Twerton-on-Avon *B & W* 68-72; C Milton *Win* 72-79; P-in-c Weymouth St Edm *Sarum* 79; V 90-95; Chapl Westhaven Hosp Weymouth 79-94; P-in-c The Winterbournes and Compton Valence 95-03; rtd 03. *1 Manor Barn, Bothenhampton, Bridport DT6 4BJ* Tel (01308) 422808

ADAMS, Jonathan Henry. b 48. St Andr Univ MA73. Cranmer Hall Dur 73. d 76 p 77. C Upperby St Jo *Carl* 76-78; C Sunderland St Chad *Dur* 78-82; Soc Resp Officer 83-91; TV Willington *Newc* 91-96; Local Min Development Officer 91-96; P-in-c Byker St Silas 96-01; Perm to Offic from 01. *5A Tunstall Vale, Sunderland SR2 7HP* Tel 0191-525 1881 E-mail jonathan@openroad.fsnet.co.uk

ADAMS, Margaret Anne. *See* FREEMAN, Mrs Margaret Anne

ADAMS, Mark. *See* ADAMS, John Mark Arthur

ADAMS, Martin Philip. b 57. Open Univ BA99. Sarum & Wells Th Coll 88. d 90 p 91. C Sandringham w W Newton *Nor* 90-93; P-in-c Docking w The Birchams and Stanhoe w Barwick 93-95; V Docking, the Birchams, Stanhoe and Sedgeford 95-97; V Orrell *Liv* 97-03; R Aughton St Mich 03-08; Dir Dioc OLM

Scheme from 03; Dir Studies SNWTP 08-11; Dean of Studies from 11. *The Vicarage, Intake Lane, Bickerstaffe, Ormskirk L39 0HW* Tel (01695) 727607 Mobile 07939-396934 E-mail martin.adams@snwtp.co.uk

ADAMS, Michael. *See* ADAMS, Canon James Michael

ADAMS, Canon Michael John. b 48. St Jo Coll Dur BA77. Ripon Coll Cuddesdon 77. d 79 p 80. C Falmouth K Chas *Truro* 79-81; C St Buryan, St Levan and Sennen 81-83; P-in-c Lanlivery w Luxulyan 83-84; V 84-88; V St Agnes 88-99; V Newquay from 99; RD Powder 90-96; Hon Can Truro Cathl from 03; Perm to Offic *Ex* from 94. *20 St Michael's Road, Newquay TR7 1RA* Tel and fax (01637) 872096 E-mail vicar@st-michaels-newquay.org.uk

ADAMS, Nicholas Stephen. b 68. K Coll Lon BA04. Westcott Ho Cam 06. d 09 p 10. C E Bris Partnership (Fishponds etc) 09-11; C Bris St Steph w St Jas and St Jo w St Mich etc from 11. *15 Bexley Road, Bristol BS16 3SS* Tel 0117-965 9792 Mobile 07952-005137 E-mail nickadams100@hotmail.com

ADAMS, Nigel David. b 40. Sarum & Wells Th Coll 86. d 88 p 89. C Tile Hill *Cov* 88-91; C Coventry Caludon 91-92; TV 92-97; Asst Chapl HM YOI Onley 92-95; Sub Chapl HM Pris Birm 95-01; P-in-c Nuneaton St Mary *Cov* 97-01; rtd 01; Perm to Offic *Ban and Cov* from 01; AD Ystumaner *Ban* 05-09. *Cefn-y-Mor, 102 Plas Edwards, Tywyn LL36 0AS* Tel (01654) 711604

ADAMS, Olugboyega Adeoye. b 55. Illinois Univ BSc81 Univ of Kansas MSc82 Lon Univ PhD93 Nottm Univ MA08. EMMTC 99. d 02 p 03. C Glenfield *Leic* 02-05; V Peckham St Mary Magd S'wark from 05. *St Mary's Vicarage, 22 St Mary's Road, London SE15 2DW* Tel (020) 7639 4596 E-mail oadams.smm@gmail.com

ADAMS, Peter. Bris Univ CertEd52 Lon Univ AdDipEd72. Oak Hill Th Coll 91. d 91 p 92. NSM Towcester w Easton Neston *Pet* 91-95; Perm to Offic *Ex* from 94. *Longmeads, Bovey Tracey, Newton Abbot TQ13 9LZ* Tel (01626) 832518

ADAMS, Canon Peter. b 37. K Coll Lon AKC65 Trin Coll Cam MA70. St Boniface Warminster 65. d 66 p 67. C Clapham H Trin *S'wark* 66-70; Chapl Trin Coll Cam 70-75; Warden Trin Coll Cen Camberwell 75-83; V Camberwell St Geo *S'wark* 75-83; RD Camberwell 80-83; P-in-c W Dulwich All SS and Em 83-85; V 85-92; V Addington 92-02; Hon Can S'wark Cathl 99-02; rtd 03; Perm to Offic S'wark from 04. *26 Mansfield Road, South Croydon CR2 6HN* Tel (020) 8680 3191 E-mail canon.adams@talk21.com

ADAMS, Peter Anthony. b 48. K Coll Lon BD70 AKC70 MTh72. d 72 p 74. Lic to Offic *Eur* 72-73; C Ashford *Cant* 73-79; P-in-c Ramsgate H Trin 79-86; P-in-c Ramsgate St Geo 84-86; R Ramsgate H Trin and St Geo from 86. *Holy Trinity Rectory, Winterstoke Way, Ramsgate CT11 8AG* Tel and fax (01843) 593593

ADAMS, Peter Harrison. b 41. Tyndale Hall Bris 63. d 68 p 69. C Kendal St Thos *Carl* 68-71; C W Bromwich Gd Shep w St Jo *Lich* 71-75; R Aldham *Chelmsf* 76-81; R Marks Tey 76-81; P-in-c Marks Tey w Aldham and Lt Tey 81-85; Dioc Missr 85-06; rtd 06; Through Faith Miss Ev from 06; Hon C Colchester St Jo *Chelmsf* from 85. *4 St Jude Gardens, Colchester CO4 0QJ* Tel (01206) 854041 E-mail peter@through-faith-missions.org

ADAMS, Canon Raymond William. b 58. Reading Univ BA79. Oak Hill Th Coll BA85. d 85 p 86. C Blackpool St Thos *Blackb* 85-88; C Padiham 88-90; TV Rodbourne Cheney *Bris* 90-02; RD Cricklade 97-99; V Haydon Wick from 02; Hon Can Bris Cathl from 09. *The Vicarage, 54 Furlong Close, Swindon SN25 1QP* Tel (01793) 634258 E-mail r.adams4@ntlworld.com

ADAMS, Richard. *See* ADAMS, John Richard

ADAMS, Richard John. b 48. Leeds Univ BA70. SAOMC 94. d 97 p 98. C N Hinksey and Wytham *Ox* 97-01; V Fence-in-Pendle and Higham *Blackb* 01-11; rtd 11. *Tros y Mor, LLangoed, Beaumaris LL58 8SB* Tel (01248) 490770 E-mail richard@gwyneth.net

ADAMS, Roger Charles. b 36. Em Coll Cam BA60 MA64. Tyndale Hall Bris 60. d 62 p 63. C Longfleet *Sarum* 62-65; C Uphill *B & W* 66-71; R Ramsden Crays w Ramsden Bellhouse *Chelmsf* 71-78; SW Area Sec BFBS 78-84; P-in-c Plymouth St Aug *Ex* 84-85; TV Plymouth Em w Efford 85-90; V Paignton Ch Ch 90-01; rtd 01; Perm to Offic *Ex* from 01. *171 Elburton Road, Plymouth PL9 8HY* Tel (01752) 407287

ADAMS, Ms Ruth Helen. b 73. St Jo Coll Dur BA94 TCD BTh97. CITC 94. d 97 p 98. C Drumragh w Mountfield *D & R* 97-99; Chapl Trin Coll Cam 00-06; P-in-c Bar Hill *Ely* from 06. *108 Stonefield, Bar Hill, Cambridge CB23 8TE* Tel (01954) 789369 *or* 206120 E-mail ruth.h.adams@btinternet.com

ADAMS, Stephen Paul. b 56. Ex Univ BSc78. Sarum & Wells Th Coll 85. d 87 p 88. C Swansea St Nic *S & B* 87-88; C Llwynderw 88-91; R Badby w Newham and Charwelton w Fawsley etc *Pet* 91-97; R Abington 97-06; RD Northn 01-06; Dean Min Development St Mich Coll Llan from 06. *St Michael and All Angels' College, 54 Cardiff Road, Llandaff, Cardiff CF5 2YJ* Tel (029) 2056 3379 Fax 2083 8008

ADAMS (née DABIN), Susan. b 51. NTMTC 96. d 00 p 01. NSM Hullbridge *Chelmsf* 00-03 and 07-10; NSM Rawreth w

Rettendon 07-10; NSM Ashingdon w S Fambridge 03-07; NSM Rettendon and Hullbridge from 10. *49 Crouch Avenue, Hullbridge, Hockley SS5 6BS* Tel (01702) 231825 E-mail susan@secretarybird.fslife.co.uk

ADAMS, Theo. *See* ADAMS, Hubert Theodore

ADAMS, William Thomas. b 47. Ches Coll of HE CertEd69 Open Univ BA74 Leic Univ MA91. EAMTC 97. **d** 00 **p** 01. NSM Helmdon w Stuchbury and Radstone etc *Pet* 00-03; NSM Astwell Gp 03-05; R from 05. *Brookdale, Mill Road, Whitfield, Brackley NN13 5TQ* Tel (01280) 850683 E-mail rector@astwellbenefice.co.uk

ADAMSON, Anthony Scott. b 49. Newc Univ BA70. Cranmer Hall Dur 75. **d** 78 **p** 79. C High Elswick St Paul *Newc* 78-86; C Benwell 86-92; V Tweedmouth 92-05; P-in-c Scremerston and Spittal 02-05; AD Norham 00-05; I Stranorlar w Meenglas and Kilteevogue *D & R* from 06. *The Rectory, Stranorlar, Co Donegal, Republic of Ireland* Tel (00353) (74) 913 1081 E-mail tkadamson@eircom.net

ADAMSON, Arthur John. b 38. Keble Coll Ox BA61 MA65. Tyndale Hall Bris 61. **d** 63 **p** 64. C Redhill H Trin *S'wark* 63-66; Chapl Trent Park Coll of Educn 66-69; C Enfield Ch Ch Trent Park *Lon* 66-70; Ind Chapl and V Battersea St Geo w St Andr *S'wark* 70-74; R Reedham *Nor* 74-80; Min Beighton and Moulton 75-80; P-in-c Cantley w Limpenhoe and Southwood 77-80; R Oulton St Mich 80-90; Chapl Lothingland Hosp 80-90; R Laceby *Linc* 90-98; R Laceby and Ravendale Gp 98-03; rtd 03; Perm to Offic *Pet* from 03. *24 Mill Lane, Cottesmore, Oakham LE15 7DL* Tel (01572) 812816 E-mail ajaca@compuserve.com *or* ajohnadamson@aol.com

ADAMSON, Paul. b 35. Leeds Univ BA58. Coll of Resurr Mirfield. **d** 60 **p** 61. C Southwick St Columba *Dur* 60-63; Br Guiana 63-66; Guyana 66-75; C Benwell St Jas *Newc* 75-77; V Cowgate 77-83; V Prudhoe 83-93; TV N Tyne and Redesdale 93-98; TR 98-00; RD Bellingham 98-00; rtd 00; Perm to Offic *Newc* from 01. *11 Carham Close, Corbridge NE45 5NA* Tel (01434) 633274

ADAN, Howard Keith. b 62. **d** 01 **p** 02. C Amsterdam w Den Helder and Heiloo *Eur* 01-04; Asst Chapl 04-07; Angl Chapl Amsterdam Airport Schiphol 04-07; Chapl for Min Development Ostend and Bruges 08; Old Catholic Ch The Netherlands 08-09; Asst Chapl The Hague *Eur* 09-11; R Cedar St Phil Canada from 11. *St Philip's Cedar, 1797 Cedar Road, Nanaimo BC V9X 1L6, Canada*

ADDENBROOKE, Keith Paul. b 67. Warwick Univ BSc90 MA05 Lanc Univ MA03. Qu Coll Birm BA07. **d** 07 **p** 08. C Upton (Overchurch) *Ches* 07-10; V Tranmere St Paul w St Luke from 10. *St Paul's Vicarage, 306 Old Chester Road, Birkenhead CH42 3XD* Tel 0151-645 3547

ADDENBROOKE, Peter Homfray. b 38. Trin Coll Cam BA59 MA68 Ex Univ PGCE60. Lich Th Coll. **d** 63 **p** 64. C Bakewell *Derby* 63-67; C Horsham *Chich* 67-73; P-in-c Colgate 73-98; Adv for Past Care and Counselling 73-93; rtd 98; Perm to Offic *Chich* from 99. *Oaks, Forest Road, Colgate, Horsham RH12 4SZ* Tel (01293) 851362

ADDINGTON, David John. b 47. FInstLEx72 FCIArb96. St Jo Coll Nottm 98. **d** 01 **p** 03. Asst P Warwick St Mary Bermuda 03-08; Chapl Miss to Seafarers from 05; Hon C March St Jo *Ely* from 08. *79 New Park, March PE15 8RT* Tel and fax (01354) 650139 Mobile 07775-796543 E-mail fradders@btinternet.com

ADDISON, David John Frederick. b 37. K Coll Dur BA60 DipEd62 Birm Univ MA79 Bris Univ MLitt93. Wells Th Coll 64. **d** 66 **p** 71. C Rastrick St Matt *Wakef* 66-67; Perm to Offic *Bradf* 67-71; Hon C Manningham St Luke 71-73; Perm to Offic *Glouc* 77-79; Hon C Bisley w Oakridge 79-81; V Newland and Redbrook w Clearwell 81-02; Chapl R Forest of Dean Coll 89-02; Perm to Offic *Glouc* 02-08 and *Mon* 04-08; TV Langtree *Ox* from 08. *The Vicarage, Crabtree Corner, Ipsden, Wallingford OX10 6BN* Tel (01491) 682832 Mobile 07815-806313

ADDISON, Ms Joyce Heather. b 56. Goldsmiths' Coll Lon BA81 PGCE91. Regent Coll Vancouver MDiv09. **d** 11. C Maidstone St Martin *Cant* from 11. *85 Loose Road, Maidstone ME15 7DA* Tel 07854-481259 (mobile) E-mail joyceaddisonuk@gmail.com

ADDISON, Philip Ives. b 29. K Coll Dur 49. Ely Th Coll 59. **d** 61 **p** 62. C Waltham Cross *St Alb* 61-64; C Bedford St Paul 64-66; Chapl Bedford N Wing Hosp 64-66; Chapl RN 66-70; V Foleshill St Laur *Cov* 70-74; C-in-c Halsham *York* 74-78; V Owthorne and Rimswell w Withernsea 74-99; Chapl Withernsea Hosp 74-99; rtd 99; Perm to Offic *York* from 99. *10 Park Avenue, Beverley HU17 7AT* Tel (01482) 872714

ADEKANYE, The Ven Joseph (Kehinde). b 47. Oak Hill Th Coll BA84 Liv Inst of Educn MA98. Immanuel Coll Ibadan. **d** 72 **p** 73. Nigeria 72-80, 84-97 and from 00; Lect Abp Vining Coll of Th Akure from 94; Perm to Offic *Liv* 97-00. *Archbishop Vining College, PO Box 3, Akure, Nigeria* Tel (00234) (34) 233031

ADEKUNLE, Elizabeth. b 07. **d** 07 **p** 08. C Homerton St Luke *Lon* 07-11; Chapl St Jo Coll Cam from 11. *St John's College, Cambridge CB2 1TP* Tel (01223) 338600 E-mail lizadeola@yahoo.co.uk *or* chapel@joh.cam.ac.uk

ADELOYE, The Ven Emmanuel Olufemi. b 60. Ilorin Univ Nigeria BA85 Ibadan Univ Nigeria MA95. Immanuel Coll Ibadan 89. **d** 91 **p** 92. Chapl to Bp Egba Nigeria 91-92; C Egba Cathl 92-95; V Kemta All SS 95-99; Personal Asst to Bp Ibadan S 99-00; Adn Odo-Ona and V Odo-Ona St Paul 00-06; Perm to Offic *S'wark* 07; C Lewisham St Mary 07-08; C Lagos Pentecost Nigeria 09-10; P-in-c 10; V Iju St Jo from 10; Adn Iju-Ishaga from 10. *PO Box 3616, Agege, Lagos, Nigeria* E-mail kehindevenadeloye@yahoo.com

ADEMOLA, Canon Ade. b 62. Goldsmiths' Coll Lon BA91 N Lon Univ MA94. NTMTC 95. **d** 98 **p** 99. NSM Lt Ilford St Barn *Chelmsf* 98-02; V Leyton Em from 02; Can Ibadan from 03. *Emmanuel Vicarage, 149 Hitcham Road, London E17 8HL* Tel (020) 8539 2200 Mobile 07941-029084 E-mail orison@ademola.eu

ADENEKAN, Latiff Aremu. b 38. **d** 04 **p** 05. OLM Tulse Hill H Trin and St Matthias *S'wark* 04-08; Perm to Offic 08-09. *Address temp unknown* E-mail latiff95@hotmail.com

ADESANYA, The Ven Stephen Adedotun. b 57. Ogun State Univ MEd97 Ado-Ekiti State Univ PhD03. Evang Th Faculty Osijek Croatia BTh91. **d** 91 **p** 92. Nigeria 91-07; Adn Iwade and V Italupe Em 03-07; Perm to Offic *S'wark* 07-09; P-in-c Romaldkirk w Laithkirk *Ripon* from 09; P-in-c Startforth and Bowes and Rokeby w Brignall from 09. *35 Low Startforth Road, Startforth, Barnard Castle DL12 9AU* Tel (01833) 631697 Mobile 07950-713797 E-mail dtndsny@yahoo.com

ADETAYO, Mrs Abigail Olufunke. b 47. SRN74 SCM75 Greenwich Univ PGCE07. SEITE 06. **d** 09 **p** 10. NSM Peckham St Mary Magd *S'wark* from 09. *158 Torridon Road, London SE6 1RD* Tel and fax (020) 8695 1713 Mobile 07746-035727 E-mail jadetayo@aol.com

ADEY, John Douglas. b 33. Man Univ BSc54. Coll of Resurr Mirfield 56. **d** 58 **p** 59. C Forton *Portsm* 58-64; C Northolt St Mary *Lon* 64-67; V Snibston *Leic* 67-72; V Outwood *Wakef* 72-78; V Clifton 78; V Upton Priory *Ches* 79-81; V Hyde St Thos 81-82; V Newton in Mottram 82-89; R Roos and Garton w Tunstall, Grimston and Hilston *York* 89-92; C Woodchurch *Ches* 92-95; C Coppenhall 95-98; rtd 98; Perm to Offic *Portsm* 98-09. *90A Winter Road, Southsea PO4 9BX* Tel (023) 9273 4116

ADEY HUISH, Helen Louise. b 59. Bris Univ BA81 Qu Coll Cam PhD87. SAOMC 01. **d** 04 **p** 05. NSM Banbury *Ox* 04-07; Chapl Ox Radcliffe Hosps NHS Trust from 07. *Timberhurst, The Green, Shenington, Banbury OX15 6NE* Tel (01295) 670285 *or* (01865) 229104 E-mail adey.huish@onetel.com *or* louise.adeyhuish@orh.nhs.uk

ADFIELD, Richard Ernest. b 31. Oak Hill Th Coll 62. **d** 64 **p** 65. C Bedworth *Cov* 64-67; V Whitehall Park St Andr Hornsey Lane *Lon* 67-77; V Kensington St Helen w H Trin 77-86; V Turnham Green Ch Ch 86-92; rtd 92; Perm to Offic *Chich* from 92; Chapl Brighton and Sussex Univ Hosps NHS Trust 02-03; Chapl Whittington Coll Felbridge from 03. *363 Hangleton Road, Hove BN3 7LQ* Tel (01273) 732538

✠**ADIE, The Rt Revd Michael Edgar.** b 29. CBE94. St Jo Coll Ox BA52 MA56 Surrey Univ DUniv95. Westcott Ho Cam 52. **d** 54 **p** 55 **c** 83. C Pallion *Dur* 54-57; Abp's Dom Chapl *Cant* 57-60; V Sheff St Mark Broomhall 60-69; RD Hallam 66-69; R Louth w Welton-le-Wold *Linc* 69-75; P-in-c N w S Elkington 69-75; TR Louth 75-76; V Morton w Hacconby 76-83; Adn Linc 77-83; Can and Preb Linc Cathl 77-83; Bp Guildf 83-94; rtd 95; Perm to Offic *Portsm* from 95; Hon Asst Bp Portsm from 95; Hon Asst Bp Chich from 96. *Greenslade, Froxfield, Petersfield GU32 1EB* Tel (01730) 827266

ADLAM, David John. b 47. **d** 06 **p** 07. OLM Dickleburgh and The Pulhams *Nor* from 06. *Weggs Farm, Common Road, Dickleburgh, Diss IP21 4PJ* Tel (01379) 741200 Fax 741800 Mobile 07860-417158 E-mail john@adlams.net

ADLAM, Keith Richard. b 44. STETS 00. **d** 03 **p** 04. NSM Binstead and Havenstreet St Pet *Portsm* 03-07; NSM Northwood 07-11; NSM Gurnard 07-11; NSM Cowes St Faith 07-11; P-in-c Wroxall from 11. *55 Clarence Road, Wroxall, Ventnor PO28 3BY* Tel (01983) 854325 Mobile 07552-793366 E-mail revkeith@kjr-group.co.uk

ADLEY, Ernest George. b 38. Leeds Univ BA61. Wells Th Coll 62. **d** 64 **p** 65. C Bideford *Ex* 64-67; C Yeovil St Mich *B & W* 67-70; V Taunton Lyngford 70-79; R Skegness and Winthorpe *Linc* 79-91; R Wantage Downs *Ox* 91-03; rtd 03; Perm to Offic *Ox* from 04. *13 Pixton Close, Didcot OX11 0BX* Tel (01235) 210395

ADLINGTON, David John. b 51. AKC73. K Coll Lon 70 St Aug Coll Cant 73. **d** 74 **p** 75. C Clapham St Paul *S'wark* 74-77; C Bethnal Green St Matt *Lon* 77-82; P-in-c Stepney St Pet w St Benet 80-84; PV and Succ S'wark Cathl 84-87; PV and Succ Llan Cathl 88-91; Dioc Dir of Educn 91-00; V St Hilary 91-94; TV Cowbridge 94-95; C Whitchurch 95-00; P-in-c Folkestone St Mary and St Eanswythe *Cant* 00-02; V 02-09; P-in-c Elham w Denton and Wootton from 09; Hon Min Can Cant Cathl from 01. *The Vicarage, Vicarage Lane, Elham, Canterbury CT4 6TT* Tel (01303) 840219

ADMAN, Fayaz. b 63. Pakistan Adventist Sem Sheikhupura BA94. St Thos Th Coll Karachi 97. **d** 98 **p** 99. Dn St Jo Cathl Peshawar Pakistan 98-99; P 00-03; Presbyter Peshawar City All SS 99-00; Bp's Chapl 01-03; V Charsada, Shabqadar and Ghalana 00-04; C S Rochdale *Man* 04-07; P-in-c Bolton St Paul w Em 07-11; P-in-c Daubhill 07-11; TV W Bolton from 11. *Emmanuel Vicarage, Edward Street, Bolton BL3 5LQ* Tel (01204) 393282 E-mail revfadman bpchp dop@hotmail.com

ADOYO, Miss Eugeniah Ombwayo. b 54. Lon Bible Coll 84 Westmr Coll Ox BA86 MPhil90. **dss** 82 **d** 91 **p** 91. Kenya 82-94; Internat Sec Crosslinks 94-97; Hon C Hatcham St Jas *S'wark* 94-97; C S'wark Ch Ch and Chapl S Lon Ind Miss 97-02; TV Plaistow and N Canning Town *Chelmsf* 02-09; TV Harwich Peninsula from 10. *The Vicarage, Church Hill, Ramsey, Harwich CO12 5EU* Tel (01255) 880291 Mobile 07765-278787 E-mail eugeniah@fsmail.net

ADSETTS, Ms Marilyn Ann. b 47. St Jo Coll York CertEd69 Leeds Univ BEd70 Spurgeon's Coll Lon MTh00. EAMTC 98. **d** 00 **p** 01. C Rushmere *St E* 00-03; V Rhymney *Mon* 03-07; rtd 07. *Grace House, 15 Weston Park, Weston under Penyard, Ross-on-Wye HR9 7FR* E-mail mbygrace@aol.com

ADU-BOACHIE, Francis. b 60. Oak Hill Th Coll. **d** 95 **p** 96. C Stonebridge St Mich *Lon* 95-01; V Wembley St Jo from 01. *The Vicarage, 3 Crawford Avenue, Wembley HA0 2HX* Tel (020) 8902 0273 E-mail francis@adu-boachie.freeserve.co.uk

ADYERI, James Joloba. b 58. Redcliffe Coll 96 Chelt & Glouc Coll of HE BA99. United Th Coll Bangalore 91. **d** 84 **p** 85. Uganda 85-88, 89-91, 92-96 and from 99; India 88-89 and 91-92; Perm to Offic *Glouc* 96-99. *PO Box 84, Mityana, Uganda* Tel (00256) (46) 23 36

AFFLECK, John. b 20. Liv Univ LLB48. K Coll Lon 68 St Aug Coll Cant 71. **d** 71 **p** 72. C Hutton *Chelmsf* 71-74; P-in-c Hawkchurch, Fishpond, Bettiscombe, Marshwood etc *Sarum* 74-80; R Marshwood Vale 80-86; rtd 86; Perm to Offic *Sarum* from 86. *23 St Nicholas Hospital, St Nicholas Road, Salisbury SP1 2SW* Tel (01722) 334659

AFFLECK, Stuart John. b 47. AKC69. St Aug Coll Cant. **d** 70 **p** 71. C Prittlewell St Mary *Chelmsf* 70-75; Asst Chapl Charterhouse Sch Godalming 75-78; Chapl 78-80; Warden Pilsdon Community 80-94; Perm to Offic *S'wark* from 03; rtd 07. *3 Chislehurst Road, Richmond TW10 6PW*

AGAR, George. b 40. Edin Univ BSc63 Ox Univ PGCE64. NOC 92. **d** 94 **p** 95. Hd Biddulph High Sch Stoke-on-Trent 94-96; NSM Sandbach *Ches* 94-99; NSM Hartford from 99. *128 Middlewich Road, Sandbach CW11 1FH* Tel (01270) 760191 E-mail georgea@stjohnshartford.org

AGASSIZ, David John Lawrence. b 42. St Pet Hall Ox BA64 MA67 Imp Coll Lon PhD94. Ripon Hall Ox 64. **d** 66 **p** 67. C Southampton St Mary w H Trin *Win* 66-71; V Enfield St Jas *Lon* 71-80; P-in-c Grays Thurrock *Chelmsf* 80-83; P-in-c Grays All SS 81-84; P-in-c Lt Thurrock St Mary 81-84; P-in-c W Thurrock 81-83; P-in-c Grays SS Pet and Paul, S Stifford and W Thurrock 83-84; TR Grays Thurrock 84-90; Hon Can Chelmsf Cathl 90-93; Dioc Development Rep 90-93; Kenya 98-00; Perm to Offic *S'wark* 02-07 and *B & W* from 08. *The Garden House, Stafford Place, Weston-super-Mare BS23 2QZ* Tel (01934) 620486 Mobile 07813-566957 E-mail agassiz@btinternet.com

AGBELUSI, Dele Omotayo. b 51. Ahmadu Bello Univ Zaria MSc81 Oak Hill Th Coll BA99. Immanuel Coll Ibadan. **d** 86 **p** 87. Nigeria 86-96; C Edmonton All SS w St Mich *Lon* 97-99; V Hornsey Ch Ch from 99. *Christ Church Vicarage, 32 Crescent Road, London N8 8AX* Tel (020) 8340 1656 *or* 8340 1566 E-mail agbelusi@aol.com

AGER, Mrs Christabel Ruth. b 51. Bedf Coll Lon BA73 Gipsy Hill Coll of Educn PGCE74 MCLIP98. STETS BA10. **d** 10 **p** 11. NSM Beercrocombe w Curry Mallet, Hatch Beauchamp etc *B & W* from 10. *14 Morgans Rise, Bishops Hull, Taunton TA1 5HW* Tel (01823) 335424 E-mail ager@talk21.com

AGER, David George. b 52. Lon Univ BA73 Solicitor 77. SWMTC 01. **d** 04 **p** 05. NSM Deane Vale *B & W* 04-09; NSM Taunton St Jas from 09; Bp's Officer for Ord NSM (Taunton Adnry) from 09. *14 Morgans Rise, Bishops Hull, Taunton TA1 5HW* Tel (01823) 335424 Mobile 07887-893918 E-mail ager@talk21.com

AGGETT, Miss Vivienne Cecilia. b 33. Sarum & Wells Th Coll 86. **d** 88 **p** 94. C Binley *Cov* 88-91; C Hednesford *Lich* 91-96; rtd 96; Perm to Offic *Cov* from 98 and *Lich* from 04; Asst Chapl Gtr Athens *Eur* 01-08. *Batsi, 845 03 Andros, Greece* Tel (0030) (2282) 041102 Mobile 6936-295647 E-mail aggett@otenet.gr

AGGREY, Solomon Samuel. b 49. BSc76. Immanuel Coll Ibadan MA84. **d** 80 **p** 82. Nigeria 80-88; Miss Partner CMS from 88; C Gorton Em and Gorton St Jas *Man* 93-95. *68 Booth Street, Denton, Manchester M34 3HY*

AGNEW, Kenneth David. b 33. Jes Coll Cam BA58 MA62. Clifton Th Coll 58. **d** 60 **p** 61. C Luton St Silas *Birm* 60-63; C Skellingthorpe *Linc* 63-68; C Birchwood 68-72; R Willand *Ex* 72-00; RD Cullompton 89-95; rtd 00; Perm to Offic *B & W* from 01. *Eastgate, 14 Limington Road, Ilchester, Yeovil BA22 8LX* Tel (01935) 842010

AGNEW, Kevin Raymond Christopher. b 59. Chich Th Coll. **d** 94 **p** 95. C Eastbourne St Mary *Chich* 94-98; V Roughey from 98. *Roffey Vicarage, 52 Shepherds Way, Horsham RH12 4LX* Tel (01403) 265333

AGNEW, Stephen Mark. b 54. Univ of Wales (Ban) BSc76 Southn Univ BTh81. Sarum & Wells Th Coll 76. **d** 79 **p** 80. C Wilmslow *Ches* 79-84; V Crewe St Jo 84-90; Chapl Bromsgrove Sch 90-99; V Claines St Jo *Worc* from 99. *The Vicarage, Claines Lane, Worcester WR3 7RN* Tel (01905) 754772 Mobile 07762-250749 E-mail revsmagnew@yahoo.com

AHON, Ahon Bol Nyuar. b 62. Birm Chr Coll MA06. Tyndale Th Sem Amsterdam. **d** 01 **p** 03. C St Mark's Cathl Luwero Uganda 01-03; Chapl Kiwoko Hosp 01-03; Hon Chapl Birm Cathl 03-05; P-in-c Ostend *Eur* 06-07; Sudan 08-09. *Flat 3, 45 Avenue Road, London N15 5JG* Tel 07956-165426 (mobile) E-mail de nyuar@yahoo.com

AHRENS, Irene Karla Elisabeth. b 40. Berlin Univ Bonn Univ PhD69 Lon Bible Coll BA92 K Coll Lon MTh93. SEITE 93. **d** 95 **p** 96. NSM Kew St Phil and All SS w St Luke *S'wark* 95-99; Asst Chapl Berlin *Eur* from 00. *Wildpfad 26, 14193 Berlin, Germany* Tel (0049) (30) 8972 8552 E-mail irene.ahrens@epost.de

AIDLEY, Jessica-Jil Stapleton. b 42. Westf Coll Lon BSc67 UEA PhD73 PGCE84. **d** 99 **p** 00. OLM High Oak, Hingham and Scoulton w Wood Rising *Nor* 99-04; Perm to Offic *Mon* 04-05; NSM Rockfield and Dingestow Gp 05-09; Perm to Offic *Chich* 09; NSM Brighton St Nic from 09. *21 Crown Street, Brighton BN1 3EH* Tel (01273) 723298 E-mail j.aidley@btopenworld.com

AIKEN, Canon Nicholas John. b 58. Sheff Univ BA. Wycliffe Hall Ox 80. **d** 82 **p** 83. C Ashtead *Guildf* 82-86; Dioc Youth Officer 86-93; R Wisley w Pyrford from 93; RD Woking 03-08; Hon Can Guildf Cathl from 10. *The Rectory, Aviary Road, Woking GU22 8TH* Tel (01932) 352914 E-mail rector@wisleywithpyrford.org

AIKEN, The Very Revd Simon Mark. b 62. St Andr Univ MTheol85. Ripon Coll Cuddesdon 86. **d** 88 **p** 89. C Burnley St Matt w H Trin *Blackb* 88-91; C Heyhouses on Sea 91-94; V Musbury 94-99; V Longridge 99-06; Sub Dean Bloemfontein 06-10; Chapl Free State Univ 06-10; Adn Maluti 07-09; Dean Kimberley from 10; Adn Karoo from 11. *The Deanery, 4 Park Road, Belgravia, Kimberley 8301 South Africa* Tel (0027) (53) 833 3437 E-mail kkdiocese.dean@telkomsa.net

AINGE, Canon David Stanley. b 47. Ian Ramsey Coll Brasted 68 Oak Hill Th Coll 70. **d** 73 **p** 74. C Bitterne *Win* 73-77; C Castle Church *Lich* 77-79; P-in-c Becontree St Alb *Chelmsf* 79-89; P-in-c Becontree St Jo 85-89; TR Becontree S 89-91; RD Barking and Dagenham 86-91; V Leyton St Mary w St Edw 91-96; P-in-c Leyton St Luke 91-96; V Leyton St Mary w St Edw and St Luke 96-03; RD Waltham Forest 94-00; R Gt Dunmow and Barnston from 03; Hon Can Chelmsf Cathl from 97. *The Vicarage, The Charters, Church End, Dunmow CM6 2SJ* Tel (01371) 872504 E-mail vicar@stmarysgreatdunmow.org.uk *or* davidainge@aol.com

AINSCOUGH, Malcolm Ralph. b 52. Liv Univ BEd76. St Mich Coll Llan 85. **d** 87 **p** 88. C Fleur-de-Lis *Mon* 87-90; C Chepstow 90-91; TV Cwmbran 91-95; V Newport St Steph and H Trin 95-03; R Hasland *Derby* from 03; V Temple Normanton from 03. *The Rectory, 49 Churchside, Hasland, Chesterfield S41 0JX* Tel (01246) 232486 E-mail ainscoughm@fsmail.net

AINSLEY, Canon Anthony Dixon. b 29. Oriel Coll Ox BA52 MA57 UNISA BA74. St Steph Ho Ox 53. **d** 55 **p** 56. C Burnley St Cath *Blackb* 55-60; S Africa 60-80; P-in-c Nqamakwe 62-65; P-in-c Idutywa 73-80; Adn All SS 73-80; Can St Jo Cathl Umtata 73-80; Hon Can from 81; Chapl Bordeaux w Riberac, Cahors, Duras etc *Eur* 81; V Blackpool St Steph *Blackb* 81-94; rtd 94; Perm to Offic *Bradf* 94-99. *PO Box 26239, Hout Bay, 7872 South Africa*

AINSLEY, Peter Dixon. b 32. OBE87. St Steph Ho Ox 58. **d** 60 **p** 61. C Bury St Thos *Man* 60-62; Chapl RN 62-87; Chapl HM Pris Liv 87-88; Chapl HM Pris Garth 88-95; rtd 95; Perm to Offic *Blackb* and *Liv* from 95. *21 Ridge Close, Southport PR9 8JU*

AINSWORTH, Mrs Janina Helen Margaret. b 50. Ripon Coll Cuddesdon. **d** 05 **p** 06. NSM E Farnworth and Kearsley *Man* 05-07; Chief Educn Officer Abps' Coun from 07. *Church House, Great Smith Street, London SW1P 3AZ* Tel (020) 7898 1500 Fax 7898 1520 E-mail janina.ainsworth@churchofengland.org

AINSWORTH, Mark John. b 64. Lon Univ MTh92. Wycliffe Hall Ox 86. **d** 89 **p** 90. C Chipping Barnet w Arkley *St Alb* 89-93; USA from 93. *270 Bent Road, Wyncote PA 19095-1503, USA* Tel (001) (215) 517 8568 E-mail mjaec@earthlink.net

AINSWORTH, Michael Ronald. b 50. K Coll Lon LLB71 LLM72 Trin Hall Cam BA74 MA79. Westcott Ho Cam 72. **d** 75 **p** 76. C Scotforth *Blackb* 75-78; Chapl St Martin's Coll of Educn 78-82; Chapl NOC 82-89; R Withington St Chris *Man* 89-94; TR Worsley 94-07; AD Eccles 00-05; Hon Can Man Cathl 04-07; R St Geo-in-the-East w St Paul *Lon* from 07. *St George's Rectory, 16 Cannon Street Road, London E1 0BH* Tel (020) 7680 9634 E-mail michael@ainsworth.uk.com

AINSWORTH, Paul Henry. b 46. JP. Man Poly BA81. NOC 85. **d** 88 **p** 89. NSM Salterhebble All SS *Wakef* 88-92; C Golcar 92-96; TV Moor Allerton *Ripon* 96-09; TV Moor Allerton and Shadwell 09-11; rtd 11. *Address temp unknown* E-mail batandball1@btopenworld.com

AINSWORTH, Peter. b 34. Lon Univ BD57. Coll of Resurr Mirfield 69. **d** 70 **p** 71. C Leeds St Wilfrid *Ripon* 70-74; TV Tong *Bradf* 74-77; V Fairweather Green 77-94; rtd 94; Perm to Offic *Wakef* 94-02 and *York* from 03. *34 Dulverton Hall, Esplanade, Scarborough YO11 2AR* Tel (01723) 340134

AINSWORTH-SMITH, Canon Ian Martin. b 41. MBE06. Selw Coll Cam BA64 MA68. Westcott Ho Cam 64. **d** 66 **p** 67. C Mill Hill Jo Keble Ch Lon 66-69; USA 69-71; C Purley St Mark *S'wark* 71-73; Chapl St Geo Hosp Lon 73-94; Chapl St Geo Healthcare NHS Trust Lon 94-06; Hon Can S'wark Cathl 95-06; rtd 06; Perm to Offic *B & W* from 06; Dioc Adv Hosp Chapl from 07. *Knutsford Cottage, North Street, Milverton, Taunton TA4 1LG* Tel (01823) 400365 E-mail jeanianas@btinternet.com

AIPO RONGO, Bishop of. See AYONG, The Most Revd James Simon

AIRD, Robert Malcolm. b 31. Lon Univ BSc54. Westcott Ho Cam 75. **d** 77 **p** 78. C Burnham *B & W* 77-79; P-in-c Taunton Lyngford 79-84; V 84-87; R Dulverton and Brushford 87-94; rtd 96. *Arran Cottage, East Street, Chulmleigh EX18 7DD* Tel (01769) 581042

AIRD, Wendy Elizabeth. b 41. SEITE. **d** 00 **p** 01. NSM Streatham Immanuel and St Andr *S'wark* 00-05; NSM Chevington and Shilbottle *Newc* 05-08; P-in-c Chevington 08-11; rtd 11. *12 Middle Park, Alston CA9 3AR* Tel 07711-301813 (mobile) E-mail chevvic@btinternet.com

AIREY, Robert William. b 54. **d** 99 **p** 00. OLM Holcombe *Man* 99-08; OLM Holcombe and Hawkshaw from 09. *4 Pine Street, Haslingden, Rossendale BB4 5ND* Tel (01706) 224743

AIREY, Simon Christopher. b 60. Trin Coll Bris BA87. **d** 87 **p** 88. C Wilton *B & W* 87-90; Chapl Scargill Ho 90-93; TV Kingswood *Bris* 93-96; Asst P Nether Springs Northumbria Community 96-98 and 02-03; C Bath Abbey w St Jas *B & W* 98-02; C Nailsea Ch Ch w Tickenham 03-09; Chapl Grey Coll Dur 09-11; P-in-c Criftins w Dudleston and Welsh Frankton *Lich* from 11. *The Vicarage, Criftins, Ellesmere SY12 9LN*

AISBITT, Joanne. See LISTER, Mrs Joanne

AISBITT, Michael. b 60. St Pet Coll Ox BA81 MA84. Westcott Ho Cam 81. **d** 84 **p** 85. C Norton St Mary *Dur* 84-87; C Kirkleatham *York* 87-90; V S Bank 90-96; R Whitby 96-97; TR Whitby w Aislaby and Ruswarp 97-00; R Attleborough w Besthorpe *Nor* 00-09; RD Thetford and Rockland 03-09. *16 The Acres, Stokesley, Middlesbrough TS9 5QA* E-mail m_aisbitt@hotmail.com

AISBITT, Osmond John. b 35. St Chad's Coll Dur BA57. **d** 61 **p** 62. C Ashington *Newc* 61-64; C Blyth St Mary 64-68; V Cleckheaton St Jo *Wakef* 68-75; V Horbury 75-78; V Horbury w Horbury Bridge 78-97; rtd 97; Perm to Offic *Carl* 97-00 and from 02; P-in-c Nerja and Almuñécar *Eur* 00-02. *8 Stonecross Gardens, Ulverston LA12 7HA* Tel (01229) 585622

AITCHISON, Charles Baillie. b 45. Newc Coll Dur BEd85 Bede Coll Dur TCert67 Newc Univ DAES74 ACP69. LNSM course 85. **d** 93 **p** 98. NSM Peebles *Edin* from 93; NSM Innerleithen from 93. *45 Whitehaugh Park, Peebles EH45 9DB* Tel (01721) 729750 *or* tel and fax 724008

AITKEN, Christopher William Mark. b 53. Dur Univ BA75. Westcott Ho Cam 76. **d** 79 **p** 80. C Finchley St Mary *Lon* 79-82; C Radlett *St Alb* 82-85; V Sprowston *Nor* 85-90; R Beeston St Andr 85-90; R Sprowston w Beeston 90-93; Chapl Sherborne Sch 93-04; Hd Master St Lawr Coll Ramsgate from 04. *Headmaster's House, St Lawrence College, College Road, Ramsgate CT11 7AE* Tel (01843) 572900 E-mail cwmaitken@talk21.com *or* hm@slcuk.com

AITKEN, Leslie St John Robert. b 41. Open Univ BA75. Cranmer Hall Dur 62. **d** 65 **p** 66. C Worc St Barn w Ch Ch 65-69; C Halesowen 69-73; P-in-c Whitby 77-80; R Blackley St Pet *Man* 80-99; Chapl Booth Hall Hosp Man 80-89; R Sutton, Huttoft and Anderby *Linc* 99-06; rtd 06. *17 Old School Mews, Spilsby PE23 5QU*

AITKEN, Valerie Anne. b 46. STETS 01. **d** 04 **p** 05. NSM Perivale *Lon* from 04. *22 Woodfield Road, London W5 1SH* Tel (020) 8997 6819 Mobile 07944-873168 E-mail valerie.aitken2@btinternet.com

AITKEN, William Stuart. b 35. FCFI MSIAD CertEd. Cant Sch of Min 79. **d** 82 **p** 83. NSM Roch 82-86; C Orpington All SS 86-88; R Burham and Wouldham 88-96; Dioc Communications Officer 88-96; rtd 96; Perm to Offic *Roch* from 96. *18 Commissioners Road, Rochester ME2 4EB* Tel (01634) 715892

AITON, Janice Haran. MA79 Jordanhill Coll Glas PGCE83. TISEC 98. **d** 01 **p** 02. C St Andrews St Andr *St And* 01-04; C Dunboyne and Rathmolyon *M & K* from 04. *1 The Close, Plunkett Hall, Dunboyne, Co Meath, Republic of Ireland* Tel and fax (00353) (1) 825 3288

AITON, Canon Robert Neilson. b 36. Univ of Wales BA59 DipEd60. Chich Th Coll 74. **d** 76 **p** 77. C E Grinstead St Swithun *Chich* 76-83; R Lavant 83-90; Chapl St Barn Hospice Worthing 90-95; V Durrington *Chich* 90-01; Can and Preb Chich Cathl from 99; rtd 01; Lic to Offic *Chich* from 01. *Fieldings, Joys Croft, Chichester PO19 4NJ* Tel (01243) 781728 E-mail maiton@talk21.com

AJAEFOBI, Joseph Obichukwu. b 63. Anambra State Univ of Tech Nigeria BEng88 Loughb Univ PhD04. Trin Coll Umuahia 90. **d** 92 **p** 93. Chapl Nkpor H Innocents Nigeria 92-00; Perm to Offic *Leic* from 01; Asst Chapl Loughb Univ from 05. *15 Stirling Avenue, Loughborough LE11 4LJ* Tel 07796-672212 (mobile) E-mail joeajaefobi@yahoo.co.uk

✠**AJETUNMOBI, The Rt Revd Jacob Ademola.** b 48. Middx Univ BA93. Igbaja Sem Nigeria BTh73 Lon Bible Coll BA80. **d** 83 **p** 83 **c** 99. Bp's Chapl and V Ilesa St Marg Nigeria 83-88; Chapl to Nigerian Students in UK (CMS) 88-99; Miss Partner CMS 88-99; Bp Ibadan S from 99. *59 Milton Avenue, London NW10 8PL, or c/o Bishopscourt, PO Box 166, Ibadan, Nigeria* Tel and fax (020) 8969 2379 *or* (00234) (22) 316464 E-mail jacajet@aol.com

AJIBADE, Ms Ijeoma. b 65. Univ of Nigeria LLB87 S Bank Univ MA96 Heythrop Coll Lon MA09. SEITE BA10. **d** 10 **p** 11. NSM Kensington St Mary Abbots w Ch Ch and St Phil *Lon* from 10. *25 Duffield Drive, London N15 4UH* Tel 07876-783360 (mobile) E-mail revdije@gmail.com

AJOKU, Canon Nelson Iheanacho. b 46. Trin Coll Umuahia 03. **d** 99 **p** 00. Perm to Offic Dio Egbu Nigeria 99-07; Perm to Offic *Lon* from 08; Can Egbu from 06. *187 Kneller Court, Academy Gardens, Northolt UB5 5PL* Tel (020) 8842 3840 Mobile 07946-654713 E-mail rev.nelsonajoku@yahoo.co.uk

AJUKA, Sampson. b 72. Qu Coll Birm BA08. **d** 08 **p** 09. C Venice w Trieste *Eur* from 08. *Chaplain's House, Dorsoduro 253, 30123 Venezia, Italy* Tel (0039) (049) 897 7503 Mobile 339-405 2466 E-mail sampress@yahoo.com

✠**AKINOLA, The Most Revd Peter Jasper.** b 44. Virginia Th Sem MTS81 Hon DD93. **d** 78 **p** 79 **c** 89. V Abuja St Jas Nigeria 78-79; V Suleja St Jas 81-84; Prov Missr 84-89; Bp Abuja from 89; Abp Prov III from 97; Primate All Nigeria from 00. *PO Box 212, ADCP, Abuja, Nigeria* Tel (00234) (9) 523 6928 *or* 523 0989 Fax 523 0986 Mobile 90-805853 E-mail abuja@anglican.skannet.com.ng

AKKER, Derek Alexander. b 46. Bradf Univ MA83. NOC 85. **d** 88 **p** 89. C Mossley *Man* 88-90; C Bury St Pet 90-92; V Lever Bridge 92-97; TV Wolstanton *Lich* 97-99; V Hattersley *Ches* 99-09; rtd 09; Perm to Offic *Man* from 09. *54 Purbeck Drive, Bury BL8 1JQ* Tel 0161-797 0105 E-mail d.akker@btclick.com

AKRILL, Dean. b 71. York Univ BA97. Ripon Coll Cuddesdon BTh00. **d** 00 **p** 01. C Swinton *Sheff* 00-01; C Wath-upon-Dearne 01-04; V Mosbrough 04-08; C Sprowston w Beeston *Nor* from 08. *The Newlands, 15 Blue Boar Lane, Norwich NR7 8RX* E-mail dean@sprowston.org.uk

✠**AKROFI, The Most Revd Justice Ofei.** b 42. Cen Connecticut State Univ USA BSc72 MEd73 Hon DHL00. Yale Div Sch MDiv76. **d** 76 **p** 76 **c** 96. Chapl Adisadel Coll Accra Ghana 76-78; Chapl Ridge Ch 78-81; Dean Accra 82-96; Bp Accra from 96; Abp W Africa from 03. *Bishopscourt, PO Box GP 8, Accra, Ghana* Tel (00233) (21) 662292 *or* 663595 Fax 668822 E-mail bishopakrofi@yahoo.com

ALAN MICHAEL, Brother. See PATERSON, Alan

ALASAUKKO-OJA, Tuomas. See MÄKIPÄÄ, Tuomas

ALBAN JONES, Timothy Morris. b 64. MBE03. Warwick Univ BA85. Ripon Coll Cuddesdon 85. **d** 88 **p** 89. C Tupsley *Heref* 88-93; TV Ross 93-00; P-in-c Soham *Ely* 00-01; P-in-c Wicken 00-01; V Soham and Wicken from 01; RD Fordham and Quy from 10. *The Vicarage, Cross Green, Soham, Ely CB7 5DU* Tel (01353) 720423 E-mail vicar@soham.org.uk

ALBERS, Johannes Reynoud (Joop). b 47. Hogeschool Holland BTh92 Amsterdam Univ MTh. EAMTC 99. **d** 00 **p** 01. C Voorschoten *Eur* 00-02; C Amsterdam w Den Helder and Heiloo 02-04; Asst Chapl from 04; Angl Chapl Amsterdam Airport Schiphol from 07. *Dorpsweg 134, 1697 KH Schellinkhout, The Netherlands* Tel (0031) (22) 950 1611 *or* (61) 009 8239 E-mail joopalbers@quicknet.nl

ALBON, Lionel Frederick Shapland. b 31. CEng MIMechE60. St Alb Minl Tr Scheme 80. **d** 83 **p** 84. NSM Bromham w Oakley *St Alb* 83-89; NSM Bromham w Oakley and Stagsden 88-89; Ind Chapl 89-96; rtd 96; Lic to Offic *St Alb* 96-09; Perm to Offic from 09. *38 Glebe Rise, Sharnbrook, Bedford MK44 1JB* Tel (01234) 781560 E-mail lionel@albon.fsnet.co.uk

ALBY, Harold Oriel. b 45. Witwatersrand Univ BA68 MA77. Sarum Th Coll 68. **d** 71 **p** 72. C Germiston St Boniface S Africa 71-74; C Johannesburg Cathl 74-75; R Ermelo w Pet Retief 57-78; R Potchefstroom 78-82; R Boksburg 82-89; P-in-c Forton *Portsm* 89-96; V Milton 96-10; rtd 11. *7 Plover Road, Heatherlands, George, 6529 South Africa* E-mail orielalby@hotmail.com

ALCOCK (née TOYNBEE), Mrs Claire Louise. b 65. Reading Univ BA86 Goldsmiths' Coll Lon PGTC87. Ox Min Course 07.

d 10 **p** 11. NSM Langtree *Ox* from 10. *St Mary's House, High Street, Whitchurch on Thames, Reading RG8 7DF* Tel 0118-984 3435 Mobile 07519-861040 E-mail claire alcock@hotmail.com

ALCOCK, Edwin James. b 31. AKC57. **d** 58 **p** 59. C Old St Pancras w Bedford New Town St Matt *Lon* 58-62; C Hillingdon St Andr 62-81; V N Acton St Gabr 81-01; rtd 01; Perm to Offic *Lon* from 01. *17 Westfields Road, London W3 0AX* Tel (020) 8896 2748

ALCOCK, Mrs Linda Mary. b 45. St Gabr Coll Lon TCert67. SAOMC 96. **d** 99 **p** 00. JLM Shires' Gabr *Ox* from 99. *Copperfields, Swan Lane, Great Bourton, Banbury OX17 1QR* Tel (01295) 750744

ALCOCK, Terry. **d** 08 **p** 09. NSM Narraghmore and Timolin w Castledermot etc *D & G* from 08; Asst Chapl Adelaide and Meath Hosp Dublin from 10. *Lacken, Blessington, Co Wicklow, Republic of Ireland* Tel (00353) (45) 865896 Mobile 87-054 8544

ALDCROFT, Malcolm Charles. b 44. Leeds Univ MA94. NOC 79. **d** 82 **p** 83. NSM Alverthorpe *Wakef* 82-85; NSM Horbury Junction 85-93; Sub Chapl HM Pris and YOI New Hall 94-97; Sub Chapl HM Pris Wakef 96-97; R Cupar and Ladybank *St And* 97-05; Chapl Stratheden Hosp Fife 97-05; Dioc Miss Officer and Min Development Co-ord *Mor* 05-07; Hon C Arpafeelie 05-07; Warden of Readers 06-07; Hon C St Andrews All SS *St And* from 08; TV Edin St Mich and All SS 08-11. *14 Cherry Lane, Cupar KY15 5DA* Tel (01334) 650264 E-mail m33aldcroft@tiscali.co.uk

ALDEN, Andrew Michael. b 65. Bris Univ BA88 Ex Univ PGCE89 Lon Univ MA98. Wycliffe Hall Ox 01. **d** 03 **p** 04. C Weston-super-Mare St Paul *B & W* 03-07; V from 07. *Somerset House, 20 Addiscombe Road, Weston-super-Mare BS23 4LT* Tel (01934) 621120 E-mail revandrewalden@btinternet.com

ALDEN, Mrs Pamela Ann (Pat). b 42. St Gabr Coll Lon TCert67. **d** 02 **p** 03. OLM Camberwell St Giles w St Matt *S'wark* 02-07; NSM Camberwell St Phil and St Mark from 07. *189 Upland Road, London SE22 0DG* Tel (020) 8693 5207 Fax 8693 6408 Mobile 07710-283710 E-mail pat@alphaplus.co.uk

ALDER, Mrs Anne-Louise. b 63. STETS 99. **d** 02 **p** 03. C Cowes H Trin and St Mary *Portsm* 02-05; C Cowes St Faith 05-06; C Newport St Thos 06-07; P-in-c Shipdham w E and W Bradenham *Nor* from 07; P-in-c Barnham Broom and Upper Yare from 10. *The Rectory, Church Close, Shipdham, Thetford IP25 7LX* Tel (01362) 820234 *or* 821593 E-mail louise.alder@lineone.net

ALDERMAN, Canon John David. b 49. Man Univ BA71 Selw Coll Cam BA79 MA80 Lon Inst of Educn PGCE72. Ridley Hall Cam 77. **d** 80 **p** 81. C Hartley Wintney, Elvetham, Winchfield etc 80-83; V Bursledon 83-92; R Dibden 92-05; Hon Can Win Cathl 01-05; AD Lyndhurst 04-05; Patr Sec CPAS from 05. *CPAS, Athena Drive, Tachbrook Park, Warwick CV34 6NG* Tel (01926) 458457 E-mail jalderman@cpas.org.uk

ALDERSLEY, Ian. b 42. FIBMS68. Wycliffe Hall Ox 89. **d** 91 **p** 92. C Allestree *Derby* 91-94; R Brailsford w Shirley and Osmaston w Edlaston 94-06; P-in-c Yeaveley 05-06; P-in-c Ruishton w Thornfalcon *B & W* 06-10; P-in-c Creech St Michael 08-10; rtd 10. *Tite Cottage, Main Street, Winster, Matlock DE4 2DH* Tel (01629) 650413 E-mail aldersley_ian@yahoo.co.uk

ALDERSON, Gary. ERMC. **d** 08 **p** 09. NSM Wellingborough St Mark *Pet* from 08. *75 Chatsworth Drive, Wellingborough NN8 5FD* Tel (01933) 440277 E-mail gary.alderson@btinternet.com

ALDERSON, Mrs Maureen. b 40. WMMTC 90. **d** 93 **p** 94. NSM Yardley St Cypr Hay Mill *Birm* 93-96; P-in-c 96-00; V 00-02; P-in-c Gainford and Winston *Dur* 02-07. *5 St Michaels Court, Northallerton DL7 8YX* Tel (01609) 779265

ALDERSON, Major Robin Edward Richard. b 44. **d** 04 **p** 05. OLM Alde River *St E* 04-07; NSM Brandeston w Kettleburgh and Easton from 07. *The Cloisters, Sandy Lane, Snape, Saxmundham IP17 1SD* Tel and fax (01728) 688255 Mobile 07790-242002

ALDERSON, Roger James Ambrose. b 47. Lon Univ BD70 AKC71 Man Univ 76 Liv Inst of Educn PGCE93. St Aug Coll Cant. **d** 71 **p** 72. C Lawton Moor *Man* 71-75; C Barton w Peel Green 75-76; R Heaton Norris St Thos 76-85; V Bedford Leigh 85-92; V Cleadon Park *Dur* 99-07; rtd 07. *73 West Drive, Sunderland SR6 7SL* Tel 0191-536 1236 Mobile 07710-722817

ALDERTON-FORD, Canon Jonathan Laurence. b 57. St Jo Coll Nottm BTh85. **d** 85 **p** 86. C Gaywood, Bawsey and Mintlyn *Nor* 85-87; C Herne Bay Ch Ch *Cant* 87-90; Min Bury St Edmunds St Mary *St E* 90-91; Min Moreton Hall Estate CD 91-94; V Bury St Edmunds Ch Ch from 94; Hon Can St E Cathl from 08. *18 Heldhaw Road, Bury St Edmunds IP32 7ER* Tel (01284) 769956 *or* tel and fax 725391 E-mail ccmh@iname.com *or* revdjonathanford@minister.com

ALDIS, John Arnold. b 43. Univ of Wales (Cardiff) BA65 Lon Univ BD67. Clifton Th Coll 65. **d** 69 **p** 70. C Tonbridge SS Pet and Paul *Roch* 69-72; C St Marylebone All So w SS Pet and Jo *Lon* 72-77; Overseas Service Adv CMS 77-80; C Welling *Roch* 77-80; V Leic H Trin w St Jo 80-89; Hon Can Leic Cathl 88-89; V

W Kowloon St Andr Hong Kong 89-99; Sen Chapl Protestant Ch Oman 00-01; V Watford *St Alb* 02-08; rtd 08. *146 Arrowsmith Drive, Stonehouse GL10 2QR* E-mail john.aldis@btinternet.com

ALDIS, Miss Rosemary Helen. b 40. Southn Univ BSc62 Ox Univ Inst of Educn DipEd63 Keele Univ MSc67. All Nations Chr Coll MA99. **d** 05 **p** 05. NSM Gabalfa *Llan* from 05; Hon Tutor St Mich Coll Llan from 09. *94 Glendower Court, Velindre Road, Cardiff CF14 2TZ* Tel (029) 2062 6337 E-mail aldisrosemary@omf.net

ALDOUS, Alexander Charles Victor. b 56. Southn Univ BA81 K Alfred's Coll Win PGCE83. S Dios Minl Tr Scheme 91. **d** 94 **p** 95. Chapl Oundle Sch 94-97; Chapl Benenden Sch 98-01; Chapl Oakham Sch from 02. *75 Station Road, Oakham LE15 6QT* Tel (01572) 723941 *or* 758591 E-mail aa@oakham.rutland.sch.uk

ALDOUS, John Herbert. b 37. CQSW83. Bp Otter Coll 94. **d** 96 **p** 00. NSM Gosport Ch Ch *Portsm* 96-00; NSM Rowner 00-02; R Sabie St Pet S Africa 02-05; rtd 05; Perm to Offic Dio Natal from 05. *PO Box 522, Munster, 4278 South Africa* Tel (0027) (39) 312 0415

ALDRIDGE, Mrs Anne Louise. b 59. Nottm Univ BEd80. EAMTC 96. **d** 99 **p** 00. NSM Milton *Ely* 99-04; Deputy Chapl Team Ldr Cam Univ Hosps NHS Foundn Trust from 04. *Addenbrooke's Hospital, Hills Road, Cambridge CB2 0QQ* Tel (01223) 217769 Fax 216520 E-mail r.aldridge@ntlworld.com

ALDRIDGE, Christopher John. b 35. Trin Hall Cam BA57 MA61. Ripon Hall Ox 59. **d** 60 **p** 61. C Coalville *Leic* 60-64; P-in-c Clifton St Fran *S'well* 64-72; V Gospel Lane St Mich *Birm* 72-90; V Selly Oak St Mary 90-00; rtd 00; Perm to Offic *Birm* from 00. *4 Paradise Lane, Birmingham B28 0DS* Tel 0121-777 0446

ALDRIDGE, Canon Harold John. b 42. Oak Hill Th Coll 65. **d** 69 **p** 70. C Rawtenstall St Mary *Man* 69-72; CMJ 72-76; C Woodford Wells *Chelmsf* 76-79; TV Washfield, Stoodleigh, Withleigh etc *Ex* 79-86; V Burton *Ches* 86-90; P-in-c Shotwick 90; V Burton and Shotwick 91-07; Dioc Clergy Widows and Retirement Officer 91-07; RD Wirral S 96-06; Hon Can Ches Cathl 98-07; Chapl Clatterbridge Hosp Wirral 86-91; Chapl Wirral Hosp NHS Trust 91-97; Chapl Wirral and W Cheshire Community NHS Trust 97-03; Chapl Cheshire and Wirral Partnerships NHS Trust 03-07; rtd 07. *Tedda Junction, 9 Moorhouse Close, Chester CH2 2HU* Tel (01244) 371628

ALDRIDGE, Mark Richard. b 58. Oak Hill Th Coll BA89. **d** 89 **p** 90. C Combe Down w Monkton Combe and S Stoke *B & W* 89-90; C Woodside Park St Barn *Lon* 90-94; P-in-c Cricklewood St Gabr and St Mich 94-99; V 99-04; Min Oak Tree Angl Fellowship 04-09. *100 Creffield Road, London W3 9PX* Tel (020) 8993 2060 E-mail marka@oaktree.org.uk

ALESSI, John. b 55. **d** 10 **p** 11. C Longton Hall *Lich* from 10. *The Vicarage, 131 Longton Hall Road, Blurton, Stoke-on-Trent ST3 2EL* Tel (01782) 598366 Mobile 07766-952836 E-mail johnalessi2000@hotmail.com

ALEXANDER, Ann Maria. b 58. Surrey Univ BA01. Cuddesdon Coll 07. **d** 09 **p** 10. C Chiswick St Nic w St Mary *Lon* from 09. *64A Grove Park Road, London W4 3SB* Tel (020) 8707 1979 Mobile 07961-853343 E-mail anejmi@virginmedia.com

ALEXANDER, David Graham. b 61. Ridley Hall Cam 87. **d** 89 **p** 90. C New Barnet St Jas *St Alb* 89-93; C Northwood H Trin *Lon* 93-95; V Stopsley *St Alb* from 95. *The Vicarage, 702 Hitchin Road, Luton LU2 7UJ* Tel (01582) 729194 Fax 450375 E-mail stopsley@aol.com

ALEXANDER, Douglas Keith. b 45. Ripon Coll Cuddesdon 87. **d** 89 **p** 90. C Thorpe St Matt *Nor* 89-92; P-in-c Lakenham St Alb 92-97; Chapl Nor City Coll of F&HE 92-97; TV Barnham Broom 97-00; TV Barnham Broom and Upper Yare 00-04; TR 04-10; RD Dereham in Mitford 08-10; rtd 10; Perm to Offic *Nor* from 11. *9 Thynnes Lane, Mattishall, Dereham NR20 3PN* Tel (01362) 858377 Mobile 07876-572724 E-mail doug.alexander@btinternet.com

ALEXANDER, Prof Freda. b 44. Girton Coll Cam BA62 Edin Univ PhD67 Lon Univ MSc81. TISEC 06. **d** 08. NSM Edin St Jo from 08. *79 Great King Street, Edinburgh EH3 6RN* Tel 0131-557 4474 E-mail freda.alexander1@btinternet.com

ALEXANDER, James Crighton. b 43. Qu Coll Cam BA65 MA69. Cuddesdon Coll 68. **d** 68 **p** 69. C Much Wenlock w Bourton *Heref* 68-72; V Oakington *Ely* from 72; P-in-c Dry Drayton 85-95. *The Vicarage, 99 Water Lane, Oakington, Cambridge CB24 3AL* Tel (01223) 232396 E-mail free2live@btinternet.com

ALEXANDER, Canon James Douglas. b 27. Linc Th Coll 57. **d** 58 **p** 59. C Frodingham *Linc* 58-61; V Alvingham w N and S Cockerington 61-65; V Keddington 61-65; R Gunhouse w Burringham 65-70; R Peterhead *Ab* 70-76; R Aberdeen St Mary 76-95; Miss to Seafarers 78-06; Can St Andr Cathl from 97; Chapl HM Pris Aber 82-06; P-in-c Cove Bay *Ab* 85-90; rtd 95; Dioc Supernumerary *Ab* from 95. *21 Whitehall Road, Aberdeen AB25 2PP* Tel (01224) 643202

ALEXANDER, Jane Louise. *See* MacLAREN, Mrs Jane Louise

ALEXANDER, Mrs Jean Ann. b 44. Southn Univ BTh00 SRN65 SCM67. Ripon Coll Cuddesdon 06. **d** 07 **p** 08. NSM Lytchett Minster *Sarum* 07-10; NSM The Lytchetts and Upton from 10. *1 Palmers Orchard, Lytchett Matravers, Poole BH16 6HG* Tel (01202) 631033 E-mail jean.alexander1@virgin.net

ALEXANDER, Julius Erik Louis. b 66. Wycliffe Hall Ox 89. **d** 92 **p** 93. C Hoole *Ches* 92-94; C Offerton 94-98; TV Upper Holloway *Lon* 98-03; Asst Chapl Southn Univ Hosps NHS Trust 03-06; Chapl Oakhaven Hospice Trust from 06. *Oakhaven Hospice Trust, Lower Pennington Lane, Lymington SO41 8ZZ* Tel (01590) 677773 Fax 677582 E-mail jalexander@blueyonder.co.uk

ALEXANDER, Canon Loveday Constance Anne. b 47. Somerville Coll Ox BA69 MA78 DPhil78. NOC 98. **d** 99 **p** 00. NSM Alderley Edge *Ches* from 99; Can Th Ches Cathl from 03; Perm to Offic *Sheff* from 00. *5 Nevill Road, Bramhall, Stockport SK7 3ET* Tel 0161-439 7946 E-mail loveday.alexander@btinternet.com

ALEXANDER, Canon Michael George. b 47. Open Univ BA90 DipEd91. Sarum & Wells Th Coll 74. **d** 77 **p** 78. C Wednesfield *Lich* 77-80; C Tettenhall Wood 80-83; Distr Min 83-85; Dioc Adv in Adult and Youth Educn *Derby* 85-89; V Hazlewood 85-89; V Turnditch 85-89; Par Educn Adv (Laity Development) 89-96; Dioc Laity Development Adv 96-00; Dioc Dir Studies Bp's Centres of Learning 96-00; P-in-c Ticknall, Smisby and Stanton-by-Bridge 00-01; P-in-c Barrow-on-Trent w Twyford and Swarkestone 00-01; V Ticknall, Smisby and Stanton by Bridge etc 01-07; RD Melbourne 02-07; P-in-c Loscoe from 07; C *Morley* w *Smalley* and *Horsley Woodhouse* from 07; RD Heanor 09-11; Hon Can Derby Cathl from 09. *The Vicarage, 80 Main Road, Smalley, Ilkeston DE7 6EF* Tel (01332) 880380 E-mail mike.alexander@ticvic.fsnet.co.uk

ALEXANDER, Nicholas Edward. b 68. Leic Poly BSc90. Oak Hill Th Coll BA06. **d** 06 **p** 07. C Linc Minster Gp from 06. *23 Montaigne Crescent, Lincoln LN2 4QN* Tel (01522) 529811 E-mail nickalexander110@hotmail.com

ALEXANDER, Peter John. b 36. CQSW73. Oak Hill Th Coll 92. **d** 95 **p** 96. NSM Aspenden, Buntingford and Westmill *St Alb* 95-02; rtd 02; Perm to Offic *Nor* from 02. *Dellgate, 4 The Dell, Bodham, Holt NR25 6NG* Tel (01263) 588126 E-mail peter.brenda@tiscali.co.uk

ALEXANDER, Mrs Rachel Clare. b 57. EAMTC 96. **d** 99 **p** 00. NSM Mattishall w Mattishall Burgh, Welborne etc *Nor* 99-02; Perm to Offic 02-03 and 11; NSM Rugby St Matt *Cov* 03-04; NSM Thorpe Acre w Dishley *Leic* from 11. *2 Mount Grace Road, Loughborough LE11 4FR* E-mail rachel.alexander@virgin.net

ALEXANDER, Robert. b 37. Lon Univ LLB60 St Cath Coll Ox BA62. St Steph Ho Ox 60. **d** 63 **p** 64. C Kensington St Mary Abbots w St Geo *Lon* 63-68; C Notting Hill 71-74; TV 74-79; Australia from 79; rtd 02. *302/27 Neutral Street, North Sydney NSW 2060, Australia* Tel and fax (0061) (2) 9954 0543 E-mail robalexand@bigpond.com

ALEXANDER, Sarah Louise. b 72. Wycliffe Hall Ox 02. **d** 04 **p** 05. C Enfield Ch Ch Trent Park *Lon* 04-08; C Newbury *Ox* from 08. *14 Strawberry Hill, Newbury RG14 1XJ* Tel (01635) 41922 Mobile 07889-146141 E-mail sarah-alex1@yahoo.co.uk *or* assocvicar@st-nicolas-newbury.org

ALEXANDER, Wilfred Robert Donald. b 35. TCD BA58 MA80. **d** 63 **p** 63. C Raheny w Coolock *D & G* 63-67; Min Can St Patr Cathl Dublin 65-67; Hon C Herne Hill St Paul *S'wark* 68-70; Asst Master Gosforth Gr Sch 71-76; Hon C Long Benton St Mary *Newc* 74-76; Chapl St Mary and St Anne's Sch Abbots Bromley 76-80; V Cauldon *Lich* 80-83; V Waterfall 80-83; P-in-c Calton 80-83; P-in-c Grindon 80-83; V Blackb St Luke w St Phil 83-89; V Rainhill *Liv* 89-92; R Croft w Southworth 92-99; C Croft w Southworth and Newchurch 99-01; rtd 01. *16 Hawkshaw Close, Birchwood, Warrington WA3 7NF* Tel (01925) 851472

ALEXANDER-WATTS, Tristan Nathaniel. b 66. SEITE 99. **d** 03 **p** 04. NSM Eltham H Trin *S'wark* 03-10; Asst Chapl Qu Eliz Hosp NHS Trust 07-11; Asst Chapl S Lon Healthcare NHS Trust from 11. *St Kentigern House, 31 Fairfield Grove, London SE7 8UA* Tel (020) 8853 2257 *or* 8709 9240 Mobile 07970-016009 E-mail tristalex@aol.com

ALFORD, John. b 35. Nottm Univ BSc58 DipEd76. Qu Coll Birm 74. **d** 77 **p** 78. NSM Edgmond *Lich* 77-87; C Cheadle 87-88; C Cheadle w Freehay 88-89; P-in-c Wootton Wawen *Cov* 89-95; P-in-c Grafham *Ely* 95-00; P-in-c Ellington 95-00; P-in-c Easton 95-00; P-in-c Spaldwick w Barham and Woolley 95-00; V 00-01; rtd 01; Perm to Offic *Ely* from 01. *4 Armstrong Close, Perry, Huntingdon PE28 0DF* Tel (01480) 812075 E-mail johnalford@talktalk.net

ALFORD, Mrs Rosalie Grace. b 40. Bedf Coll Lon BA61 Lon Univ PGCE62. STETS 95. **d** 98 **p** 99. NSM Wadhurst *Chich* from 98; NSM Stonegate from 98. *Content, 1 Ingoldsby Cottages, Faircrouch Lane, Wadhurst TN5 6PP* Tel (01892) 782974 E-mail rosaliealford@btinternet.com

ALIDINA (née LINGARD), Jennifer Mary. b 59. Ox Min Course 05. **d** 07 **p** 08. C Chipping Norton *Ox* 07-10. *Candleford, 4 Langston Villas, Station Road, Kingham, Chipping Norton OX7 6UW* Tel (01608) 659076 E-mail jennyalidina@freeuk.com

ALKER, Adrian. b 49. Wadh Coll Ox BA70 Lanc Univ MA71. Ripon Coll Cuddesdon 77. **d** 79 **p** 80. C W Derby St Mary *Liv* 79-83; Dioc Youth Officer *Carl* 83-88; V Sheff St Mark Broomhill 88-08; Dioc Dir of In-Service Tr 90-08; Hon Can Sheff Cathl 05-08; Dir Miss Resourcing *Ripon* from 08. *Ripon and Leeds Diocesan Office, St Mary's Street, Leeds LS9 7DP* Tel 0113-200 0559

ALKIRE, Sabina Marie. b 69. Illinois Univ BA89 Magd Coll Ox MPhil94 MSc95 DPhil99. **d** 00 **p** 02. NSM Washington St Alb and Washington St Phil USA 00-03; NSM Boston St Steph 03-07; Chapl Assoc Magd Coll Ox from 06; NSM Cowley St Jo Ox from 08. *3 Mansfield Road, Oxford OX1 3TB* Tel (01865) 271529 Fax 281801 Mobile 07792-505847 E-mail sabina.alkire@qeh.ox.ac.uk

ALLABY, Miss Mary Dorothea. b 60. Bedf Coll Lon BA82 W Sussex Inst of HE PGCE83. Trin Coll Bris 88. **d** 92 **p** 94. Par Dn Ipsley *Worc* 92-94; C 94-96; TV Bloxwich *Lich* 96-02; V Trent Vale 02-03. *Address withheld by request* E-mail mary@allaby.freeserve.co.uk

ALLABY, Simon Arnold Kenworthy. b 65. St Chad's Coll Dur BA88. Trin Coll Bris 88. **d** 90 **p** 91. C Preston on Tees *Dur* 90-93; C Chester le Street 93-99; R Ardingly *Chich* 99-05. *Briar Leigh, Rocky Lane, Haywards Heath RH16 4RN* Tel 07837-637113 (mobile) E-mail simon@sixnineteen.co.uk

ALLAIN CHAPMAN, Ms Justine Penelope Heathcote. b 67. K Coll Lon BA88 AKC88 PGCE89 Nottm Univ MDiv93. Linc Th Coll 91. **d** 93 **p** 94. C Forest Hill *S'wark* 93-96; TV Clapham Team 96-01; V Clapham St Paul 02-04; Dir Miss & Past Studies SEITE from 04; Vice Prin from 07. *SEITE Ground Floor Offices, Sun Pier House, Medway Street, Chatham ME4 4HF* Tel (01634) 846683 E-mail j.allain-chapman@seite.co.uk

ALLAN, Andrew John. b 47. Westcott Ho Cam 76. **d** 79 **p** 80. C Whitstable All SS w St Pet *Cant* 79-84; C Whitstable 84-86; P-in-c Littlebourne 86-87; P-in-c Ickham w Wickhambreaux and Stodmarsh 86-87; R Littlebourne and Ickham w Wickhambreaux etc 87-10; rtd 10. *The Moorings, Old Road, Liskeard PL14 6DL* Tel (01579) 349074

ALLAN, Canon Archibald Blackie. b 35. Edin Th Coll 57. **d** 60 **p** 61. C Aberdeen St Jo 60-63; R 82-00; Chapl St Paul's Cathl Dundee 63-68; P-in-c Aberdeen St Clem 68-76; Vice-Provost St Andr Cathl 76-82; Can 88-00; Hon Can from 01; rtd 00. *32 Craigiebuckler Terrace, Aberdeen AB15 8SX* Tel (01224) 316636

ALLAN, Donald James. b 35. Sarum & Wells Th Coll 63. **d** 65 **p** 66. C Royton St Paul *Man* 65-71; V Middleton Junction 71-78; P-in-c Finmere w Mixbury *Ox* 78-83; R Finmere w Mixbury, Cottisford, Hardwick etc 83; Chapl Westcliff Hosp 83-87; V Westcliff St Andr *Chelmsf* 83-87; R Goldhanger w Lt Totham 87-01; rtd 01; P-in-c St Goran w Caerhays *Truro* 01-06. *23 Stirrup Close, Wimborne BH21 2UQ* Tel (01202) 880645 E-mail donald.allan2@btinternet.com

ALLAN, Jeanette Winifred. b 40. ALA63. St And Dioc Tr Course 79. dss 81 **d** 86 **p** 94. NSM Hillfoot's TM *St And* 81-86; NSM Bridge of Allan *St And* 86-88; NSM Dunblane 88-98; R Glenrothes 98-06; rtd 06; Lic to Offic *St And* from 07. *Pernettya, Sinclairs Street, Dunblane FK15 0AH* Tel (01786) 821151 E-mail pernettya@googlemail.com

ALLAN, John. See ALLAN, Andrew John

ALLAN, Preb John William. b 58. St Olaf Coll Minnesota BA80 Birm Univ 86. Trin Lutheran Sem Ohio MDiv84 Qu Coll Birm 90. **d** 91 **p** 92. In Lutheran Ch (USA) 84-86; C Newport w Longford and Chetwynd *Lich* 91-94; P-in-c Longdon 94-01; Local Min Adv (Wolverhampton) 94-01; V Alrewas from 01; V Wychnor from 01; Hon Can from 04; Preb Lich Cathl from 11. *The Vicarage, Church Road, Alrewas, Burton-on-Trent DE13 7BT* Tel (01283) 790486 E-mail john.allan@lichfield.anglican.org

ALLAN, Peter Burnaby. b 52. Clare Coll Cam BA74 MA78 St Jo Coll Dur BA82. Cranmer Hall Dur 80. **d** 83 **p** 84. C Chaddesden St Mary *Derby* 83-86; C Brampton St Thos 86-89; TV Halesworth w Linstead, Chediston, Holton etc *St E* 89-94; TR Trunch *Nor* 94-03; R Ansley and Arley *Cov* from 03; RD Nuneaton from 06. *The Vicarage, 60 Birmingham Road, Ansley, Nuneaton CV10 9PS* Tel (024) 7639 9070 E-mail peter@allan49.fsworld.co.uk

ALLAN, Peter George. b 50. Wadh Coll Ox BA72 MA76. Coll of Resurr Mirfield 72. **d** 75 **p** 76. C Stevenage St Geo *St Alb* 75-78; Chapl Wadh Coll and C Ox St Mary V w St Cross and St Pet 78-82; CR from 85; Prin Coll of Resurr Mirfield from 11. *House of the Resurrection, Stocks Bank Road, Mirfield WF14 0BN* Tel (01924) 494318

ALLARD, John Ambrose. b 30. Bps' Coll Cheshunt 63. **d** 65 **p** 66. C Leigh-on-Sea St Marg *Chelmsf* 65-69; P-in-c Rawreth w Rettendon 69-70; R 70-72; V Barkingside St Fran 73-84; V E Ham St Geo 84-86; V St Osyth 86-95; rtd 95; Perm to Offic *Nor*

and *St E* 97-02; Hon C Muchalls and Stonehaven *Bre* 03-07. *23 St Nicholas Drive, Banchory AB31 5YG* Tel (01330) 822761
ALLARD, Roderick George. b 44. Lon Univ BA77 Sheff Poly MSc88 Loughb Coll of Educn CertEd96. NOC 97. **d** 99 **p** 00. NSM Charlesworth and Dinting Vale *Derby* from 99. *16 Springmeadow, Charlesworth, Glossop SK13 5HP* Tel (01457) 866278 Mobile 07798-843283
ALLARDICE, Alexander Edwin. b 49. SRN. Chich Th Coll 73. **d** 76 **p** 77. C Rugeley *Lich* 76-79; C Felixstowe St Jo *St E* 79-81; TV Ipswich St Fran 81-87; C Lostwithiel *Truro* 87-90; C Boconnoc w Bradoc 87-90; C St Veep 87-90; C St Winnow 87-90; R Lostwithiel, St Winnow w St Nectan's Chpl etc 90-97; R Mevagissey and St Ewe 97-99; rtd 99; Perm to Offic *Truro* from 99. *4 Pensylva, St Austell PL25 4RW* Tel and fax (01726) 77695 E-mail alex.allardice@classicfm.net
ALLBERRY, Samuel. b 75. Wycliffe Hall Ox BTh03. **d** 05 **p** 06. NSM Ox St Ebbe w H Trin and St Pet 05-08; C Maidenhead St Andr and St Mary from 08. *St Mary's Close, 14 High Street, Maidenhead SL6 1YY* Tel (01628) 638866 E-mail sam_allberry@yahoo.co.uk
ALLBERRY, William Alan John. b 49. Ch Coll Cam BA70 MA71. Ripon Coll Cuddesdon 84. **d** 86 **p** 87. C Brixton St Matt *S'wark* 86-90; V Wandsworth St Paul 90-98; R Esher *Guildf* from 98; RD Emly 01-06. *The Rectory, 4 Esher Place Avenue, Esher KT10 8PY* Tel and fax (01372) 462611 E-mail rector@esher.org
ALLBUTT, Mavis Miriam. **d** 98 **p** 99. OLM Meir *Lich* 98-08; P-in-c from 08. *The Vicarage, 715 Uttoxeter Road, Stoke-on-Trent ST3 5PY* Tel (01782) 313347 E-mail mavis.allbutt@btinternet.com
ALLCHIN, Miss Maureen Ann. b 50. Edge Hill Coll of HE CertEd71 Sussex Univ MA93. S Dios Minl Tr Scheme 88. **d** 91 **p** 94. Hd Past Faculty Steyning Gr Sch 79-92; NSM Southwick St Mich *Chich* 91-92; C Storrington 93-95; TV Bridport *Sarum* 95-05; Lic to Offic 05-06; P-in-c Canalside Benefice 06-08; Lic to Offic 08-09 and from 10; P-in-c Trowbridge H Trin 09-10; rtd 10. *4 Northfields, Bulkington, Devizes SN10 1SE* Tel (01380) 828931 E-mail maureen@mallchin.co.uk
ALLCOCK, Jeremy Robert. b 63. Trin Coll Bris BA92. **d** 92 **p** 93. C Walthamstow St Luke *Chelmsf* 92-96; V E Ham St Paul 96-05; V Paddington St Steph w St Luke *Lon* from 05; AD Westmr Paddington from 11. *St Stephen's Vicarage, 25 Talbot Road, London W2 5JF* Tel (020) 7792 2283 E-mail jeme6@aol.com
ALLCOCK, Peter Michael. b 37. Oak Hill Th Coll 65. **d** 68 **p** 69. C Upper Tulse Hill St Matthias *S'wark* 68-71; C Dunkeswell and Dunkeswell Abbey *Ex* 71-72; P-in-c Luppitt and Monkton 72-75; V Okehampton w Inwardleigh 75-80; TV Solihull *Birm* 80-85; V Highbury New Park St Aug *Lon* 85-99; V E and W Horndon w Lt Warley and Childerditch *Chelmsf* 99-02; rtd 02; Perm to Offic *Birm* and *Cov* 03-05; NSM Shepshed and Oaks in Charnwood *Leic* 05-07. *10 Arden Close, Balsall Common, Coventry CV7 7NY* Tel (01676) 532346 E-mail pma946078@aol.com
ALLDRED, Barbara. b 45. SNWTP. **d** 10 **p** 11. OLM Newchurch w Croft *Liv* from 10. *20 Glebelands, Culcheth, Warrington WA3 4DX* Tel (01925) 763603
ALLDRIT, Nicolas Sebastian Fitz-Ansculf. b 41. St Edm Hall Ox BA63 MA69 DPhil69. Cuddesdon Coll 72. **d** 72 **p** 73. C Limpsfield and Titsey *S'wark* 72-81; Tutor Linc Th Coll 81-96; Sub-Warden 88-96; R Witham Gp *Linc* 97-07; rtd 07; Perm to Offic *Pet* from 07. *104 Orchard Hill, Little Billing, Northampton NN3 9AG* Tel (01604) 407115
ALLEN, Andrew Michael. b 84. Ripon Coll Cuddesdon BA09. **d** 10 **p** 11. C Aston Clinton w Buckland and Drayton Beauchamp *Ox* from 10. *The Lodge, Upper Icknield Way, Aston Clinton, Aylesbury HP22 5LH* Tel (01442) 822120 E-mail andrew.curate@gmail.com
ALLEN, Andrew Stephen. b 55. Nottm Univ BPharm77 MPS. St Steph Ho Ox 78. **d** 81 **p** 82. C Gt Ilford St Mary *Chelmsf* 81-83; C Luton All SS w St Pet *St Alb* 83-86; TV Chambersbury 86-91; TV Brixham w Churston Ferrers and Kingswear *Ex* 91-01; TR 01-06; P-in-c Upton cum Chalvey *Ox* 06-08; TR from 08. *St Mary's Rectory, 34 Upton Park, Slough SL1 2DE* Tel and fax (01753) 529988 E-mail andrewallen@fastmail.com
ALLEN, Beverley Carole. See PINNELL, Ms Beverley Carole
ALLEN, Brian. See ALLEN, Frank Brian
ALLEN, Brian. b 58. Oak Hill NSM Course 90. **d** 93 **p** 94. NSM W Norwood St Luke *S'wark* 93-02; NSM Gipsy Hill Ch Ch 02-08. *76 Bradley Road, London SE19 3NS* Tel (020) 8771 4282 *or* 8686 8282
ALLEN, Brian Stanley. b 24. Roch Th Coll 65. **d** 67 **p** 68. C Roch 67-74; P-in-c Drypool St Jo *York* 74-80; TV Drypool 80; V Marlpool *Derby* 80-87; rtd 87; Perm to Offic *York* from 90. *22 Sycamore Terrace, York YO30 7DN* Tel (01904) 653418
ALLEN, Mrs Caroline Anne. b 59. ERMC 08. **d** 11. C Kesgrave *St E* from 11. *18 Fletchers Lane, Kesgrave, Ipswich IP5 2XY* Tel (01473) 623219 Mobile 07970-737639 E-mail carolineallen121@gmail.com
ALLEN, Miss Charlotte. b 79. St Jo Coll Dur BA00 Anglia Poly Univ MA03. Westcott Ho Cam 00. **d** 03 **p** 04. C Southwick

Chich 03-07; V Portchester *Portsm* from 07. *The Vicarage, 164 Castle Street, Portchester, Fareham PO16 9QH* Tel (023) 9238 1414 E-mail charlie.allen@btconnect.com
ALLEN, Christopher Dennis. b 50. Fitzw Coll Cam BA73 MA77. Cuddesdon Coll 74. **d** 76 **p** 77. C Kettering St Andr *Pet* 76-79; C Pet H Spirit Bretton 79-82; R Bardney *Linc* 82-87; V Knighton St Mary Magd *Leic* 87-11; V Cosby and Whetstone from 11. *The Vicarage, Church Lane, Whetstone, Leicester LE8 6BA* Tel 0116-286 6329 E-mail rev.c.allen@googlemail.com
ALLEN, Christopher Leslie. b 56. Leeds Univ BA78. St Jo Coll Nottm 79. **d** 80 **p** 81. C Birm St Martin 80-85; Tr and Ed Pathfinders 85-89; Hd 89-92; Midl Youth Dept Co-ord CPAS 85-89; Hon C Selly Park St Steph and St Wulstan *Birm* 86-92; V Hamstead St Bernard 92-95; NSM Kidderminster St Mary and All SS w Trimpley etc *Worc* 03-11; NSM Ribbesford w Bewdley and Dowles from 11; NSM Wribbenhall from 11. *The Brambles, Dowles Road, Bewdley DY12 2RD* Tel 07956-303037 (mobile) E-mail chris.allen@ukonline.co.uk
ALLEN, David. b 38. Llan Dioc Tr Scheme. **d** 76 **p** 77. C Fairwater *Llan* 76-84; Chapl Bp of Llan High Sch 84-97; Lic to Offic *Llan* from 84. *1 Kenley Close, Llandaff, Cardiff CF5 2PA* Tel (029) 2056 0252
ALLEN, David Edward. b 70. Van Mildert Coll Dur BSc91. Ripon Coll Cuddesdon BA94. **d** 95 **p** 96. C Grantham *Linc* 95-99; C W Hampstead St Jas *Lon* 99-01; C Kilburn St Mary w All So and W Hampstead St Jas 01-02; V Finsbury St Clem w St Barn and St Matt from 02; Chapl Moorfields Eye Hosp NHS Trust from 04. *St Clement's Vicarage, King Square, London EC1V 8DA* Tel (020) 7251 0706 E-mail davideallen@blueyonder.co.uk
ALLEN, Derek. b 57. MCIOB89. **d** 99 **p** 00. OLM Bacup Ch Ch *Man* 99-04; OLM Bacup and Stacksteads from 04. *180 New Line, Bacup OL13 9RU* Tel (01706) 875960 E-mail allen.newline@cwcom.net
ALLEN, Canon Francis Arthur Patrick. b 26. Em Coll Saskatoon Div Test 52. **d** 51 **p** 52. Miss Nipawin Canada 51-52; Miss Meadow Lake 52-54; Miss Medstead 54-57; C Bishopwearmouth St Nic *Dur* 57-59; Chapl Miss to Seamen Kobe Japan 59-63; Hon Can Kobe from 63; V Kingston upon Hull St Matt *York* 63-67; P-in-c Oberon Australia 67; R 68-73; P-in-c Cobar 73-75; Chapl Torres Strait 76-78; R Waikerie 78-82; R Willunga 82-89; R Bamaga 89-91; rtd 91. *Unit 23, Cessnock Gardens, 38 Hickey Street, Cessnock NSW 2325, Australia* Tel (0061) (2) 4995 3068
ALLEN, Frank Brian. b 47. K Coll Lon BD AKC71. **d** 71 **p** 72. C Leam Lane *Dur* 71-74; C Tynemouth Ch Ch *Newc* 74-78; Chapl Preston Hosp N Shields 74-78; Chapl Newc Poly 78-84; V Newc St Hilda 84-88; Chapl Nottm Mental Illness and Psychiatric Unit 88-89; Chapl for Mental Health Newc Mental Health Unit 89-94; Chapl Newc City Health NHS Trust 94-96; Chapl Team Leader 96-06; Chapl Team Leader Northumberland, Tyne and Wear NHS Foundn Trust from 06; Visiting Fell Newc Univ from 96. *Trust Chaplaincy Centre, St Nicholas Hospital, Gosforth, Newcastle upon Tyne NE3 3XT* Tel 0191-273 6666 ext 28465 Fax 232 2840 E-mail brian_allen63@hotmail.com *or* brian.allen@ntw.nhs.uk
ALLEN, Canon Geoffrey Gordon. b 39. Sarum Th Coll 64. **d** 66 **p** 67. C Langley Marish *Ox* 66-70; Miss to Seamen 70-82; Chapl Rotterdam w Schiedam *Eur* 78-82; Asst Chapl The Hague 84-93; Chapl Voorschoten 84-93; Can Brussels Cathl 89-04; Adn NW Eur 93-04; Chapl E Netherlands 93-04; P-in-c Haarlem 95-02; rtd 04. *Hans Brandts Buyslaan 22, 6952 BK Dieren, The Netherlands* Tel (0031) (313) 412533 E-mail g.g.allen@zonnet.nl
ALLEN, Giles David. b 70. RCM BMus91 Leeds Univ MA05. Coll of Resurr Mirfield 92. **d** 95 **p** 96. C Palmers Green St Jo *Lon* 95-99; V Lund *Blackb* from 99. *Lund Vicarage, Church Lane, Clifton, Preston PR4 0ZE* Tel (01772) 683617 E-mail giles.lund@tiscali.co.uk
ALLEN, Gordon Richard. b 29. St Jo Coll Dur BA54 MA58. **d** 55 **p** 56. C N Meols *Liv* 55-58; Uganda 58-63; V Lathom *Liv* 64-68; USA from 68; rtd 94. *237 Emerys Bridge Road, South Berwick ME 03908-1935, USA*
ALLEN, Hugh Edward. b 47. Bp Otter Coll Chich CertEd. Sarum & Wells Th Coll 79. **d** 81 **p** 82. C Frome St Jo *B & W* 81-85; R Old Cleeve, Leighland and Treborough 85-97; RD Exmoor 92-97; P-in-c The Stanleys *Glouc* 97-99; Perm to Offic *B & W* 99-05; P-in-c Charlton Musgrove, Cucklington and Stoke Trister 05-10; RD Bruton and Cary 06-10; rtd 10. *Woodpeckers, Langley Marsh, Wiveliscombe, Taunton TA4 2UL* E-mail hallenkwood@yahoo.co.uk
ALLEN, Mrs Jacqueline Lesley. b 54. EMMTC 99. **d** 02 **p** 03. NSM Huthwaite *S'well* 02-05; P-in-c Shireoaks from 05; Asst Chapl Notts Healthcare NHS Trust from 07. *1 Potter's Nook, Shireoaks, Worksop S81 8NF* Tel (01909) 479350 E-mail jackie@serv77.netscapeonline.com
ALLEN, Jamie. See ALLEN, The Very Revd Timothy James
ALLEN, Mrs Jane Rosemary. b 39. Cartrefle Coll of Educn BA83 PGCE84. St As & Ban Minl Tr Course 99. **d** 00 **p** 01. C

Llandudno *Ban* 00-05; TV 05-09; rtd 09. *29 Manor Park, Gloddaeth Avenue, Llandudno LL30 2SE* E-mail revml@hotmail.com

ALLEN, Johan. b 49. Lanc Univ CertEd75 Roehampton Inst BEd88. S'wark Ord Course 05. **d** 08 **p** 09. NSM W Streatham St Jas S'wark from 08. *54 Leigham Vale, London SW16 2JQ* Tel (020) 7564 8588 Mobile 07743-156786 E-mail johanallen@btinternet.com

ALLEN, John Catling. b 25. Leeds Univ BA50. Coll of Resurr Mirfield 50. **d** 52 **p** 53. C Knowle H Nativity *Bris* 52-54; C De Beauvoir Town St Pet *Lon* 54-57; C Beckenham St Barn *Roch* 57-60; V Orpington St Andr 60-66; V Linc St Jo 66-84; C Tynemouth Ch w H Trin *Newc* 85-87; C N Shields 87-89; rtd 89; Hon C Gt and Lt Torrington and Frithelstock *Ex* 89-05. *7 St Barnabas, Newland, Malvern WR13 5AX* Tel (01684) 899390

ALLEN, John Clement. b 32. K Coll Lon 54. **d** 58 **p** 59. C Middlesbrough St Martin *York* 58-60; C Northallerton w Kirby Sigston 60-64; V Larkfield *Roch* 64-70; R Ash 70-79; R Ridley 70-79; RD Cobham 76-79; R Chislehurst St Nic 79-97; rtd 97; Perm to Offic *Sarum* from 97. *The Peppergarth, 9 Lane Fox Terrace, Penny Street, Sturminster Newton DT10 1DE* Tel (01258) 473754

ALLEN, The Very Revd John Edward. b 32. Univ Coll Ox BA56 MA63 Fitzw Coll Cam BA68. Westcott Ho Cam 66. **d** 68 **p** 69. C Deal St Leon *Cant* 68-71; P-in-c Clifton St Paul *Bris* 71-78; Chapl Bris Univ 71-78; P-in-c Chippenham St Andr w Tytherton Lucas 78-82; Provost Wakef 82-97; rtd 97; Perm to Offic *York* from 98. *The Glebe Barn, Main Street, Sawdon, Scarborough YO13 9DY* Tel (01723) 859854 E-mail jeallen70@btinternet.com

ALLEN, Mrs Kathleen. b 46. Westmr Coll Ox MTh02. NOC 88. **d** 91 **p** 94. NSM Colne H Trin *Blackb* 91-94; NSM Colne Ch Ch 94-98; NSM Colne and Villages 98-06; rtd 06. *80 Stoddens Road, Burnham-on-Sea TA8 2DB* Tel (01278) 793627 E-mail krabos@tiscali.co.uk

ALLEN, Malcolm. b 60. Open Th Coll BA00. Trin Coll Bris 94. **d** 96 **p** 97. C Skirbeck H Trin *Linc* 96-00; TV Cheltenham St Mark *Glouc* 00-09; TR Bishop's Cleeve and Woolstone w Gotherington etc from 09. *The Rectory, 4 Church Approach, Bishops Cleeve, Cheltenham GL52 8NG* Tel (01242) 677851 E-mail malcallen147@btinternet.com

ALLEN, Matthew Frederick James. b 82. Univ of Wales (Cardiff) BSc03 St Jo Coll Dur BA09. Cranmer Hall Dur 07. **d** 10 **p** 11. C Kendal St Thos *Carl* from 10; C Crook from 10; C Crosthwaite Keswick from 10; C Cartmel Fell from 10; C Winster from 10; C Witherslack from 10. *20 Gandy Street, Kendal LA9 7AE* Tel 07739-465073 (mobile) E-mail m.f.j.allen@durham.ac.uk

ALLEN, Michael Stephen. b 37. Nottm Univ BA60. Cranmer Hall Dur 60. **d** 62 **p** 63. C Sandal St Helen *Wakef* 62-66; Hon C Tile Cross *Birm* 66-70; V 72-84; Hon C Bletchley *Ox* 70-72; Vice-Prin Aston Tr Scheme 84-91; Hon C Boldmere *Birm* 85-91; P-in-c Easton w Colton and Marlingford *Nor* 91-93; Local Min Officer 91-93; Dioc Adv in Adult Educn *S'well* 93-02; rtd 02; Perm to Offic *S'well* from 02. *8 Grenville Rise, Arnold, Nottingham NG5 8EW* Tel 0115-967 9515 E-mail msa@amd.fsnet.co.uk

ALLEN, Patricia. *See* LEWER ALLEN, Mrs Patricia

ALLEN, Peter Henry. b 34. Nottm Univ BA66. Kelham Th Coll 58. **d** 66 **p** 67. C Salisbury St Martin *Sarum* 66-70; C Melksham 70-73; C Paignton Ch Ch *Ex* 73-76; P-in-c W Holloway St Dav *Lon* 76-77; V Barnsbury St Dav w St Clem 77-84; P-in-c Brentford St Faith 84-87; TV Brentford 87-91; TV Catford (Southend) and Downham *S'wark* 91-01; rtd 01; Perm to Offic *Roch* from 01. *17 Mayfield Road, Belvedere DA17 6DX* Tel (01322) 412903 Mobile 07939-580266 E-mail peterbeth@ntlworld.com

ALLEN, Peter John. b 34. Leic Coll of Educn CertEd74 Leic Univ BEd75 MA79. EAMTC 89. **d** 92 **p** 93. NSM Ketton w Tinwell *Pet* 92-94; NSM Easton on the Hill, Collyweston w Duddington etc 94-96; Chapl St Pet Viña del Mar Chile 96-99; NSM Culworth w Sulgrave and Thorpe Mandeville etc *Pet* 00-04; rtd 04; Perm to Offic *Pet* from 04. *24 Holm Close, Weedon, Northampton NN7 4TJ* Tel (01327) 349292 E-mail peterjallen@tinyworld.co.uk

ALLEN, Canon Peter John Douglas. b 35. Jes Coll Cam BA61 MA64 PGCE67. Westcott Ho Cam 60. **d** 62 **p** 63. C Wyken *Cov* 62-65; C Boston Ch of Advent USA 65-66; Chapl Jes Coll Cam 66-72; Chapl K Sch Cant 72-87; Hon Min Can Cant Cathl 73-87; Second Master and Sen Chapl Sedbergh Sch Cumbria 87-93; P-in-c Edin St Ninian 93-06; Prec and Can St Mary's Cathl 94-06; Tutor Edin Th Coll 94-01; rtd 06; Chapl Edin Academy from 99; Chapl Fettes Coll Edin 02-07. *12A Grosvenor Crescent, Edinburgh EH12 5EL* Tel 0131-337 0027

ALLEN, Peter Richard. b 62. Qu Coll Birm BA04. **d** 04 **p** 05. C Hackenthorpe *Sheff* 04-07; TV Gleadless 07-08; Chapl for Sport from 07. *69 Hollybank Crescent, Sheffield S12 2BP* Tel 07772-926278 (mobile) E-mail prallen3@yahoo.co.uk

ALLEN, Philip Gerald. b 48. Trin Coll Bris 71. **d** 73 **p** 74. C Portsea St Luke *Portsm* 73-75; C-in-c 75-79; C Southsea St Jude 75-79; P-in-c Gatten St Paul 79-85; V from 85. *St Paul's Vicarage, St Paul's Crescent, Shanklin PO37 7AW* Tel (01983) 862027

ALLEN, Richard. BA PGCE. SWMTC. **d** 06 **p** 07. NSM Ottery St Mary, Alfington, W Hill, Tipton etc *Ex* from 06. *23 Salisbury Road, Exmouth EX8 1SL* Tel 07973-463783 (mobile) E-mail rja@millfieldprep.com

ALLEN, Richard James. b 46. Wells Th Coll 69. **d** 71 **p** 72. C Upholland *Liv* 71-75; TV 76-79; TV Padgate 79-85; V Weston-super-Mare St Andr Bournville *B & W* 85-93; V Williton 93-10; P-in-c St Decumans 08-10; Chapl Somerset Primary Care Trust 93-10; rtd 10. *26 Causeway Terrace, Watchet TA23 0HP* E-mail vicar@dickallen.freeserve.co.uk

ALLEN, Richard John. b 55. City Univ BSc76 FCOptom80. ERMC 04. **d** 07 **p** 08. NSM Lexden *Chelmsf* from 07. *22 Fitzwilliam Road, Colchester CO3 3RZ* Tel (01206) 578051 Mobile 07713-625014 E-mail richard.allen@zen.co.uk

ALLEN, Richard John Slaney. b 54. **d** 00 **p** 01. NSM Tooting All SS *S'wark* 00-04; NSM Streatham Ch Ch w St Marg 05-08; Asst Chapl SW Lon and St George's Mental Health NHS Trust from 03. *32 Burnell Avenue, Richmond TW10 7YE* Tel (020) 8549 8868

ALLEN, Richard Lee. b 41. Liv Inst of Educn TCert67. NOC 80. **d** 83 **p** 84. NSM Colne Ch Ch *Blackb* 83-90; P-in-c Trawden 91-98; NSM Colne and Villages 98-06; Chapl Burnley Health Care NHS Trust 99-03; Chapl E Lancs Hosps NHS Trust 03-06; rtd 06. *80 Stoddens Road, Burnham-on-Sea TA8 2DB* Tel (01278) 793627

ALLEN, Roger Charles Brews. b 44. Loughb Univ BTech66 Solicitor 77. **d** 92 **p** 93. OLM S Elmham and Ilketshall *St E* 92-95; OLM Bungay H Trin w St Mary from 95. *33A Earsham Street, Bungay NR35 1AF* Tel (01986) 896927 E-mail rallen@zetnet.co.uk

ALLEN, Roy Vernon. b 43. Open Univ BA81 Birm Univ MA84. Sarum Th Coll 67. **d** 70 **p** 71. C Hall Green Ascension *Birm* 70-74; V Temple Balsall 74-78; P-in-c Smethwick St Steph 78-81; V Smethwick St Mich 78-81; V Smethwick SS Steph and Mich 81-86; V Marston Green from 86. *The Vicarage, Elmdon Road, Birmingham B37 7BT* Tel 0121-779 2492 E-mail roy_v_allen@hotmail.com

ALLEN, Canon Steven. b 49. Nottm Univ BA73. St Jo Coll Nottm 73. **d** 75 **p** 76. C Gt Horton *Bradf* 75-80; V 89-02; V Upper Armley *Ripon* 80-89; RD Bowling and Horton *Bradf* 98-02; Hon Can Bradf Cathl from 00; Dioc Tr Officer from 02. *48 Toller Grove, Bradford BD9 5NP* Tel (01274) 482059 E-mail steve.allen@bradford.anglican.org

ALLEN, Stuart Philip. b 73. St Cath Coll Ox BA95. Oak Hill Th Coll BA02. **d** 02 **p** 03. C Burford w Fulbrook, Taynton, Asthall etc *Ox* 02-06; Lect Proclamation Trust 06-10; Lect Proclamation Trust and Hon C Tooting Graveney St Nic *S'wark* 06-10; R S Warks Seven Gp *Cov* from 10. *The Vicarage, Broad Street, Long Compton, Shipston-on-Stour CV36 5JH* Tel (01608) 684207 E-mail rectorsw7@gmail.com

ALLEN, Mrs Susan Rosemary. b 47. Warwick Univ BSc68 Trevelyan Coll Dur PGCE69. Sarum Th Coll 93. **d** 96 **p** 97. C Goldsworth Park *Guildf* 96-01; TV Hemel Hempstead *St Alb* 01-09; TR from 09. *33 Craigavon Road, Hemel Hempstead HP2 6BA* Tel (01442) 270585 E-mail revsue33@googlemail.com

ALLEN, Mrs Suzanna Claire. b 75. St Jo Coll Nottm 09. **d** 11. C Wareham *Sarum* from 11. *8 Wellstead Road, Wareham BH20 4EY* Tel 07773-186193 (mobile) E-mail csgl.allen@virginmedia.com

ALLEN, Thomas Davidson. b 49. QUB BA. CITC 81. **d** 84 **p** 85. C Magheralin w Dollingstown *D & D* 84-86; I Kilwarlin Upper w Kilwarlin Lower 86-91; I Maghera w Killelagh *D & R* 91-03; I Donaghcloney w Waringstown *D & D* 03-09; rtd 09; P-in-c Gweedore, Carrickfin and Templecrone *D & R* from 10. *1 Parker Gardens, Castledawson, Magherafelt BT45 8AS* Tel (028) 7946 9045 Mobile 07858-045272 E-mail tallen@talk21.com

ALLEN, Thomas Henry. b 42. NOC 87. **d** 90 **p** 91. C Upholland *Liv* 90-93; TV Walton-on-the-Hill 93-07; rtd 07. *13 Crosgrove Road, Liverpool L4 8TE* Tel 0151-476 9705

ALLEN, The Very Revd Timothy James. b 71. Warwick Univ BA93. Ripon Coll Cuddesdon BTh99. **d** 99 **p** 00. C Nuneaton St Mary *Cov* 99-02; V Seend, Bulkington and Poulshot *Sarum* 02-03; Hon C Winslow w Gt Horwood and Addington *Ox* 03-05; V Gt Cornard *St E* 05-09; V New Plymouth St Mary New Zealand 09-10; Dean Taranaki from 10. *37 Vivian Street, New Plymouth 4310, New Zealand* Tel (0064) (6) 758 3111 E-mail dean@taranakicathedral.org.nz

ALLEN, Zachary Edward. b 52. Warwick Univ BA74. Ripon Coll Cuddesdon 78. **d** 81 **p** 82. C Bognor *Chich* 81-84; C Rusper and Roughey 84-86; TV Carl H Trin and St Barn 86-90; Chapl Strathclyde Ho Hosp Carl 86-90; V Findon w Clapham and Patching *Chich* 90-01; V Rustington from 01. *The Vicarage, Claigmar Road, Rustington, Littlehampton BN16 2NL* Tel (01903) 784749

ALLERTON, Patrick. b 78. NTMTC. d 10 p 11. C Onslow Square and S Kensington St Aug *Lon* from 10. *38 Albert Mansions, Albert Bridge Road, London SW11 4QB* E-mail patallerton@hotmail.com

ALLEYNE, Sir John Olpherts Campbell, Bt. b 28. Jes Coll Cam BA50 MA55. d 55 p 56. C Southampton St Mary w H Trin *Win* 55-58; Chapl Cov Cathl 58-62; Chapl Clare Hall Cam 62-66; Chapl Bris Cathl 66-68; Area Sec (SW England) Toc H 68-71; V Speke All SS *Liv* 71-73; TR Speke St Aid 73-76; R Win St Matt 76-93; rtd 93; Perm to Offic *Guildf* from 93. *2 Ash Grove, Guildford GU2 8UT* Tel (01483) 573824

ALLFORD, Judith Mary. b 55. Sheff Univ BA Lon Univ BD. Trin Coll Bris 77. dss 86 d 87 p 94. Par Dn Deptford St Jo w H Trin *S'wark* 87-91; Asst Chapl Dulwich Hosp 91-93; Asst Chapl K Coll Hosp Lon 91-95; Asst Chapl King's Healthcare NHS Trust 93-95; Chapl N Surrey Primary Care Trust from 95. *St Peter's Hospital, Guildford Road, Chertsey KT16 0PZ* Tel (01932) 872000 ext 3324 E-mail judith.allford@asph.nhs.uk

ALLIES, Lorna Gillian. b 46. UEA BSc93 Sheff Univ EdD01. d 05 p 06. OLM Thurton *Nor* 05-07; NSM Bunwell, Carleton Rode, Tibenham, Gt Moulton etc 07-09; P-in-c Rackheath and Salhouse from 09; Dioc Rural Adv 06-09. *The Rectory, 56 Green Lane West, Rackheath, Norwich NR13 6PG* Tel (01603) 720097 or 263801 Mobile 07706-482284 E-mail l.allies@btinternet.com

ALLIN, Philip Ronald. b 43. Reading Univ MA96 Birm Univ CQSW. Lich Th Coll 71. d 71 p 72. C Sutton in Ashfield St Mary *S'well* 71-74; Chapl to Sutton Cen 74-76; Lic to Offic 74-76; P-in-c Grove 76-77; R Ordsall 76-80; V Mansfield St Mark 81-83; TR Hermitage and Hampstead Norreys, Cold Ash etc *Ox* 83-96; OCF 83-96; Chapl Nine o'clock Service *Sheff* 96-03; rtd 03; Bp's Adv in Past Care and Counselling *Sheff* 03-08; Warden of Spiritual Direction *Dur* from 08. *Hareholme House, New Brancepeth, Durham DH7 7HH* Tel 0191-373 9743

ALLINGTON, Andrew William. b 57. ACA81 Sheff Univ BA78. Cranmer Hall Dur BA95. d 95 p 96. C Clifton *York* 95-99; P-in-c Stainforth *Sheff* 99-02; V from 02. *The Vicarage, Field Road, Stainforth, Doncaster DN7 5AQ* Tel (01302) 841295 E-mail allingtonandrew@hotmail.com

ALLINSON, Capt Paul Timothy. b 63. CA Tr Coll 82 Edin Th Coll 89. d 91 p 92. C Peterlee *Dur* 91-94; C Shadforth and Sherburn w Pittington 94-97; P-in-c Byers Green 97-04; P-in-c Seaton Carew from 04; P-in-c Greatham from 09; Dioc Children's Adv from 94. *6 Front Street, Greatham, Hartlepool TS25 2ER* Tel (01429) 872626 Mobile 07888-726535 E-mail revdpaul@lineone.net

ALLISON, Elliott Desmond. b 36. UNISA BA64 K Coll Lon MTh74. S Africa Federal Th Coll. d 69 p 70. *Flat 1, 20 Southview Gardens, Worthing BN11 5JA*

ALLISON, Canon James Timothy. b 61. Man Univ BSc83. Oak Hill Th Coll BA89. d 89 p 90. C Walkden Moor *Man* 89-93; Chapl Huddersfield Univ 93-98; V Erringden from 98; RD Calder Valley from 06; Hon Can Wakef Cathl from 10. *The Vicarage, Brier Hey Lane, Mytholmroyd, Hebden Bridge HX7 5PJ* Tel (01422) 883130 E-mail erringden@aol.com

ALLISON, Keith. b 34. Dur Univ BA59. Ely Th Coll BA59 p 62. C Sculcoates *York* 61-64; C Stainton-in-Cleveland 64-65; C Leeds St Pet *Ripon* 65-70; V Micklefield *York* 70-74; V Appleton-le-Street w Amotherby 74-78; P-in-c Barton le Street 77-78; P-in-c Salton 77-80; R Amotherby w Appleton and Barton-le-Street 78-82; Chapl Lister Hosp Stevenage 82-90; P-in-c St Ippolyts *St Alb* 82-85; V 85-90; Chapl Hitchin Hosp 86-90; Chapl Shotley Bridge Gen Hosp 90-94; Chapl NW Dur HA 90-94; Sen Chapl N Dur Acute Hosps NHS Trust 94-98; Sen Chapl N Dur Healthcare NHS Trust 98-00; rtd 00. *2 Middlewood Road, Lanchester, Durham DH7 0HL* Tel (01207) 529046

ALLISON, Michael John. b 33. Leeds Univ BSc97 ATI58. Wilson Carlile Coll 05. d 05 p 06. NSM Windhill *Bradf* from 05. *33 Busy Lane, Shipley BD18 1DX* Tel (01274) 587194 E-mail m.john.allison@talktalk.net

ALLISON, Susan Ann. b 61. EMMTC 06. d 06 p 07. C Gt and Lt Coates w Bradley *Linc* 06-09; P-in-c Fotherby from 09; P-in-c Somercotes and Grainthorpe w Conisholme from 09; RD Louthesk from 11. *The Rectory, Peppin Lane, Fotherby, Louth LN11 0UG* Tel (01507) 602312 Mobile 07920-133329 E-mail susan.333allison@btinternet.com

✠**ALLISTER, The Rt Revd Donald Spargo.** b 52. Peterho Cam BA74 MA77. Trin Coll Bris 74. d 76 p 77 c 10. C Hyde St Geo *Ches* 76-79; C Sevenoaks St Nic *Roch* 79-83; V Birkenhead Ch Ch *Ches* 83-89; R Cheadle 89-02; RD Cheadle 99-02; Adn Ches 02-10; Bp Pet from 10. *Bishops Lodging, The Palace, Minster Precincts, Peterborough PE1 1YA* Tel (01733) 562492 Fax 890077 E-mail bishop@peterborough-diocese.org.uk

ALLISTER, John Charles. b 77. Ch Coll Cam MA00 MSci00 St Anne's Coll Ox PGCE01. Wycliffe Hall Ox BA08. d 09 p 10. C Hurdsfield *Ches* from 09. *138 Brocklehurst Avenue, Macclesfield SK10 2RQ* Tel (01625) 503324 or 424587 Mobile 07092-119317 E-mail john.allister@cantab.net

ALLMAN, Mrs Susan. b 56. Bris Univ BA77. WEMTC 93. d 96 p 97. NSM Henleaze *Bris* 96-99; C Southmead 99-02; V Two Mile Hill St Mich 02-08; Partnership P E Bris 08-10; P-in-c Titchfield *Portsm* from 10. *The Vicarage, 24 Frog Lane, Titchfield, Fareham PO14 4DU* Tel 07775-977298 (mobile) E-mail susanrev@hotmail.co.uk

ALLMARK, Leslie. b 48. Open Univ BA90. d 01 p 02. OLM Halliwell St Luke *Man* 01-08; rtd 08; Perm to Offic *Man* from 08. *75 Crosby Road, Bolton BL1 4EJ* Tel (01204) 845795 E-mail leslie@lallmark.freeserve.co.uk

ALLON-SMITH, Roderick David. b 51. Leic Univ BA PhD Cam Univ MA. Ridley Hall Cam 79. d 82 p 83. C Kinson *Sarum* 82-86; V Westwood *Cov* 86-96; RD Cov S 92-96; P-in-c Radford Semele 96-04; Dioc Dir Par Development and Evang 01-03; Dioc Missr *Dur* 04-10; AD Dur 08-10; R Lancercost, Walton, Gilsland and Nether Denton *Carl* from 10. *The Vicarage, Lanercost, Brampton CA8 2HQ* Tel (01697) 72478 E-mail rodallonsmith@bigfoot.com

ALLPORT, David Jack. b 55. Ox Univ BA MEd. Qu Coll Birm 78. d 80 p 81. C Abingdon w Shippon *Ox* 80-83; C-in-c Woodgate Valley CD *Birm* 83-91; Perm to Offic from 91. *122 Cherry Tree Avenue, Walsall WS5 4JL* Tel (01922) 640059

ALLRED, Frank. b 23. Tyndale Hall Bris 62. d 64 p 65. C Halliwell St Pet *Man* 64-67; V Ravenhead *Liv* 67-75; R Chadwell *Chelmsf* 75-82; TV Heworth H Trin *York* 82-86; rtd 87; Perm to Offic *York* from 87. *12 Viking Road, Bridlington YO16 6TW* Tel (01262) 677321

ALLSO, Michael Neal. b 48. FRICS72 MCIArb73 MAE00. SWMTC 95. d 98 p 99. NSM Ex St Thos and Em 98-01; NSM Colyton, Southleigh, Offwell, Widworthy etc 01-03; NSM Colyton, Musbury, Southleigh and Branscombe 03-04; C Widecombe-in-the-Moor, Leusdon, Princetown etc 04-07; C Ashburton, Bickington, Buckland in the Moor etc 07-08; NSM Dunster, Carhampton, Withycombe w Rodhuish etc *B & W* from 08. *Church House, Main Road, Carhampton, Minehead TA24 6LX* Tel (01643) 822206 E-mail revm.allso@btinternet.com

ALLSOP, Anthony James. b 37. AKC62. d 63 p 64. C Leytonstone St Marg w St Columba *Chelmsf* 63-68; V Gt Ilford St Alb 68-80; V Gainsborough St Jo *Linc* 80-85; V Hockerill *St Alb* 85-02; Chapl Herts and Essex Hosp Bp's Stortford 85-95; Chapl Essex and Herts Community NHS Trust 95-01; Chapl N Essex Mental Health Partnership NHS Trust 01-02; rtd 02; Perm to Offic *Ches* from 03. *63 Longdown Road, Congleton CW12 4QH* Tel (01260) 280628

ALLSOP, Mrs Beryl Anne. b 45. EMMTC 94. d 97 p 98. NSM Clipstone *S'well* 97-00; NSM Blidworth w Rainworth 00-10; rtd 10; Perm to Offic *S'well* from 11. *The Old Post Office, Bottom Row, Pleasley Vale, Mansfield NG19 8RS* Tel (01623) 811095 E-mail beryl@faithfulfish.co.uk

ALLSOP, David. b 50. d 10 p 11. NSM Musbury *Blackb* from 10; NSM Haslingden w Grane and Stonefold from 10; NSM Laneside from 10. *7 Elizabeth Drive, Haslingden, Rossendale BB4 4JB* Tel (01706) 224663 Mobile 07986-004401 E-mail davidallsop@hotmail.com

ALLSOP, David George. b 48. Wycliffe Hall Ox. d 99 p 00. C Chenies and Lt Chalfont, Latimer and Flaunden *Ox* 99-02; P-in-c 02-08; R from 08. *The Rectory, Chenies, Rickmansworth WD3 6ER* Tel (01923) 284433 Mobile 07818-441431 E-mail cheniesrectory@aol.com

ALLSOP, Patrick Leslie Fewtrell. b 52. Fitzw Coll Cam BA74 MA78. Ripon Coll Cuddesdon BA78 MA83. d 79 p 80. C Barrow St Matt *Carl* 79-82; Chapl Eton Coll 82-88; Chapl K Sch Roch 89-02; Hon PV Roch Cathl 89-97; Chapl St Paul's Sch Barnes from 02. *St Paul's School, Lonsdale Road, London SW13 9JT* Tel (020) 8746 5434

ALLSOP, Peter William. b 33. Kelham Th Coll 58. d 58 p 59. C Woodford St Barn *Chelmsf* 58-61; C Upholland *Liv* 61-65; V Wigan St Geo 65-71; P-in-c Marham *Ely* 71-72; TV Fincham 72-76; V Trawden *Blackb* 76-90; C Marton 90-92; C S Shore H Trin 92-98; rtd 98; Perm to Offic *Blackb* from 98. *31 Lomond Avenue, Blackpool FY3 9QL* Tel (01253) 696624 E-mail peter.w.allsop@talktalk.net

ALLSOPP, The Ven Christine. b 47. Aston Univ BSc68. S Dios Minl Tr Scheme 86. d 89 p 94. C Caversham St Pet and Mapledurham etc *Ox* 89-94; C Bracknell 94; TV 94-98; P-in-c Bourne Valley *Sarum* 98-00; TR 00-05; RD Alderbury 99-05; Can and Preb Sarum Cathl 02-05; Adn Northn *Pet* from 05; Can Pet Cathl from 05. *11 The Drive, Northampton NN1 4RZ* Tel (01604) 714015 Fax 792016 E-mail archdeacon.northampton@peterborough-diocese.org.uk

ALLSOPP, Mark Dennis. b 66. Cuddesdon Coll 93. d 96 p 97. C Hedworth *Dur* 96-98; C Gt Aycliffe 98-00; TV Gt Aycliffe and Chilton 00-04; P-in-c Kirklevington and High and Low Worsall *York* 04-08; Chapl HM YOI Kirklevington Grange 04-08; Chapl RN from 08. *Royal Naval Chaplaincy Service, Mail Point 1-2, Leach Building, Whale Island, Portsmouth PO2 8BY* Tel (023) 9262 5055 Fax 9262 5134

ALLSOPP, Mrs Patricia Ann. b 48. St Mary's Coll Chelt CertEd69. Qu Coll Birm. d 00 p 01. C Upton-on-Severn, Ripple, Earls Croome etc *Worc* 00-04; P-in-c Finstall 04-05; V 05-08; RD Bromsgrove 06-08; rtd 08. *35 Cosby Road, Littlethorpe, Leicester LE19 2HG* E-mail rev.tricia@ukonline.co.uk

ALLSOPP, Stephen Robert. b 50. BSc71 MSc72 PhD75. Mon Dioc Tr Scheme 81. d 84 p 85. NSM Trevethin *Mon* 84-88; Asst Chapl K Sch Roch 88-07; Chapl K Prep Sch 99-07; rtd 07; Hon PV Roch Cathl from 89. *117 Prince's Street, Rochester ME1 2EA* Tel (01634) 409878 E-mail stephen.allsopp@diocese-rochester.org

ALLSWORTH, Peter Thomas. b 44. St Mich Coll Llan 93. d 93 p 94. C Prestatyn *St As* 93-96; V Esclusham 96-06; C Rhyl w St Ann 06-10; P-in-c Bodelwyddan 10; P-in-c Rhuddlan and Bodelwyddan from 10. *10 Tirionfa, Rhuddlan, Rhyl LL18 6LT* Tel (01745) 590683

ALLTON, Canon Paul Irving. b 38. Man Univ BA60. d 63 p 64. C Kibworth Beauchamp *Leic* 63-66; C Reading St Mary V *Ox* 66-70; R Caston and V Griston *Nor* 70-75; P-in-c Sturston w Thompson and Tottington 70-75; V Hunstanton St Mary w Lt Ringstead 75-80; V Holme-next-the-Sea 75-80; V Hunstanton St Mary w Ringstead Parva, Holme etc 80-85; RD Heacham and Rising 81-85; Hon Can Nor Cathl 85-93; TR Lowestoft and Kirkley 85-93; TR Keynsham *B & W* 93-96; TR Gaywood *Nor* 96-01; rtd 01; Perm to Offic *Nor* from 01. *Rustic Lodge, 79 Hall Lane, West Winch, King's Lynn PE33 0PJ* Tel (01553) 840355

ALLUM, Jeremy Warner. b 32. Wycliffe Hall Ox 60. d 62 p 63. C Hornchurch St Andr *Chelmsf* 62-67; P-in-c W Derby St Luke *Liv* 67 69; V 69 75; P in o Boulton *Derby* 75 90; P-in-c *Melbourne* 86-90; V Hathersage 90-98; rtd 98; Perm to Offic *Derby* from 98. *32 Sandown Avenue, Mickleover, Derby DE3 0QQ* Tel (01332) 231253

ALLWOOD, Linda Angela Fredrika. b 76. Newc Univ BA00. Cranmer Hall Dur 01. d 03 p 04. C Northampton St Giles *Pet* 03-06; Perm to Offic *St E* from 06. *29 Warren Hill Road, Woodbridge IP12 4DU* Tel (01394) 384575 Mobile 07939-001160 E-mail linda allwood@hotmail.com

ALLWOOD, Martin Eardley. b 71. Natal Univ BSc92. Ripon Coll Cuddesdon 08. d 10 p 11. C Hundred River *St E* from 10. *The Rectory, 27 School Road, Ringsfield, Beccles NR34 8NZ* Tel 07891-478269 (mobile) E-mail meallwood110@googlemail.com

ALLWRIGHT, Mrs Janet Margaret. b 40. Oak Hill Th Coll 87. d 90 p 94. NSM Galleywood Common *Chelmsf* 90-93; NSM Downham w S Hanningfield 93-99; Chapl HM Pris Bullwood Hall 98-03; TV Canvey Is *Chelmsf* 03-06; rtd 06; Perm to Offic *Chelmsf* from 06. *26 Chaplin Close, Chelmsford CM2 8QW* Tel (01245) 265499 E-mail revdjanet@supanet.com

ALMOND, Kenneth Alfred. b 36. EMMTC 76 Linc Th Coll 78. d 79 p 80. C Boston *Linc* 79-82; V Surfleet 82-87; RD Elloe W 86-96; V Spalding St Jo w Deeping St Nicholas 87-98; rtd 98; Perm to Offic *Linc* from 99. *1 Buckingham Close, Fishtoft, Boston PE21 9QB* Tel and fax (01205) 352805 E-mail ken.hilary@btopenworld.com

ALP, Mrs Elaine Alison. b 54. Oak Hill Th Coll 87. d 00. Dn-in-c Blackb St Mich w St Jo and H Trin 00-02; Par Dn Fleetwood St Nic 02-06; Perm to Offic 06-07; Hon C Ribbleton from 07. *25 Rose Lane, Preston PR1 6HH* Tel (01772) 798483 E-mail deaconalison@hotmail.com

ALSBURY, Colin. b 56. Ch Ch Ox BA77 MA81. Ripon Coll Cuddesdon 77. d 80 p 81. C Oxton *Ches* 80-84; V Crewe All SS and St Paul 84-92; Ind Chapl 92-95; V Kettering St Andr *Pet* 95-02; V Frome St Jo *B & W* from 02; V Woodlands from 02; RD Frome from 10. *St John's Vicarage, Vicarage Close, Frome BA11 1QL* Tel (01373) 472853 E-mail colin.alsbury@zetnet.co.uk

ALSOP, Barbara. b 48. d 11. NSM Epsom St Martin *Guildf* from 11. *15 Meadow Way, Bookham, Leatherhead KT23 3NY*

ALTHAM, Donald. b 40. Liv Univ BA62. NOC 87. d 90 p 91. NSM Ramsbottom St Jo and St Paul *Man* 90-96; NSM Holcombe 99-04; NSM Walmersley, Bury from 04; NSM Bircle from 04; Chapl Asst Burnley Health Care NHS Trust 93-03; Chapl Asst E Lancs Hosps NHS Trust from 03. *387 Whalley Road, Ramsbottom, Bury BL0 0ER* Tel (01706) 822025

✠ALVAREZ-VELAZQUEZ, The Rt Revd David Andres. b 41. Inter American Univ Puerto Rico BA62 Caribbean Cen of Advanced Studies MS82. NY Th Sem MDiv65. d 65 p 65 c 87. Puerto Rico from 65; C St Mich 65; Chapl Episc Cathl Sch 65-67; R St Mark 67-70; R St Jo Cathl 70-79; R Trujillo Alto St Hilda 79-87; Bp Puerto Rico from 87. *PO Box 902, Saint Just Station, Saint Just, 00978, Puerto Rico* Tel (001) (787) 761 9800 Mobile 376 4125 Fax 761 0320 E-mail iep@spiderlinkpr.net

ALVEY, Martyn Clifford. b 53. EMMTC 96. d 99 p 00. NSM Burton Joyce w Bulcote and Stoke Bardolph *S'well* 99-02; C Worksop St Jo 02-06; P-in-c Worksop Ch Ch from 06; AD Worksop 04-06. *34 Boscombe Road, Worksop S81 7SB* Tel (01909) 473998 E-mail martynalvey@btinternet.com

AMAT-TORREGROSA, Gabriel José. b 42. R Superior Coll of Music Madrid MA63. Bapt Th Sem Ruschlikon Zürich 64. d 71 p 72. Spain 71-98; Asst Chapl Zürich *Eur* 98-07; P-in-c Marseille w Aix-en-Provence from 08. *84 boulevard Baille, 13006 Marseille, France* E-mail gjamat@hotmail.com

AMBANI, Stephen Frederick. b 45. Univ of Wales (Lamp) BA90. St Jo Coll Nottm 86 CA Tr Coll Nairobi 70. d 83 p 83. Kenya 83-93; C Glan Ely *Llan* 93-95; C Whitchurch 95-97; V Nantymoel w Wyndham 97-99; V Tonyrefail w Gilfach Goch and Llandyfodwg 99-03; V Tonyrefail w Gilfach Goch 04; rtd 05. *68 St Winfred's Road, Bridgend CF31 4PN* Tel (01656) 653589

AMBROSE, James Field. b 51. Newc Univ BA73. Cranmer Hall Dur. d 80 p 81. C Barrow St Geo w St Luke *Carl* 80-83; C Workington St Jo 83-85; R Montford w Shrawardine and Fitz *Lich* 85-88; Ch Radio Officer BBC Radio Shropshire 85-88; Chapl RAF 88-92; Voc and Min Adv CPAS 92-99; TV Syston *Leic* 99-06; C Leic Martyrs 06-07; V Heald Green St Cath *Ches* from 07; Chapl St Ann's Hospice Manchester from 07. *The Vicarage, 217 Outwood Road, Heald Green, Cheadle SK8 3JS* Tel 0161-437 4614 or 437 3685 E-mail jfambrose@btinternet.com

AMBROSE, John George. b 30. Lon Univ BD Ox Univ PGCE. d 74 p 75. C Rayleigh *Chelmsf* 74-79; V Hadleigh St Barn 79-95; rtd 95; Perm to Offic *Chelmsf* from 95. *9 Fairview Gardens, Leigh-on-Sea SS9 3PD* Tel (01702) 474632

AMBROSE, Thomas. b 47. Sheff Univ BSc69 PhD73 Em Coll Cam BA77 MA84. Westcott Ho Cam 75. d 78 p 79. C Morpeth *Newc* 78-81; C N Gosforth 81-84; R March St Jo *Ely* 84-93; RD March 89-93; P-in-c Witchford w Wentworth 93-99; Dioc Dir of Communications 93-99; Chapl K Sch Ely 94-96; V Trumpington *Ely* 99-08. *229 Arbury Road, Cambridge CB4 2JU* Tel 07711-263083 (mobile) E-mail tom.ambrose@ely.anglican.org

AMELIA, Alison. b 67. Hull Univ BA03 St Jo Coll Dur BA05. Cranmer Hall Dur 03. d 05 p 06. C Nunthorpe *York* 05-06; C Hessle 06-09; Chapl United Lincs Hosps NHS Trust from 09. *36 Peterborough Way, Sleaford NG34 8TW* Tel (01529) 414373 E-mail aamelia333@yahoo.com

AMES, Jeremy Peter. b 49. K Coll Lon BD71 AKC71. d 72 p 73. C Kennington St Jo *S'wark* 72-75; Chapl RN 75-04; Chapl RN Engineering Coll 86-89; USA 91-93; Dir of Ords RN 00-04; QHC 02-04; Master St Nic Hosp Salisbury 04-11; Perm to Offic *Sarum* from 11. *Springfield, Stratford Road, Stratford sub Castle, Salisbury SP1 3LQ*

AMES, Reginald John. b 27. Bps' Coll Cheshunt 51. d 54 p 55. C Edmonton St Alphege *Lon* 54-58; C Mill Hill Jo Keble Ch 58-60; P-in-c Northwood Hills St Edm 61-64; V 64-92; rtd 92; Hon C Moffat *Glas* 92-01; Lic to Offic from 92. *Oakbank, Lochwood, Beattock, Moffat DG10 9PS* Tel (01683) 300381

AMES-LEWIS, Richard. b 45. Em Coll Cam BA66 MA70. Westcott Ho Cam 76. d 78 p 79. C Bromley St Mark *Roch* 78-81; C Edenbridge 81-84; V 84-91; P-in-c Crockham Hill H Trin 84-91; P-in-c Barnes St Mary *S'wark* 91-97; TR Barnes 97-00; RD Richmond and Barnes 94-00; TR E Dereham and Scarning *Nor* 00-06; P-in-c Swanton Morley w Beetley w E Bilney and Hoe 02-06; TR Dereham and Distr 06-09; RD Dereham in Mitford 03-08; Hon Can Nor Cathl 06-09; rtd 09; Perm to Offic *Ely* from 09. *21 Victoria Street, Cambridge CB1 1JP* Tel (01223) 300615 E-mail ameslewis@btinternet.com

AMEY, Graham George. b 44. Lon Univ BD70. Tyndale Hall Bris 67. d 71 p 72. C Hornsey Rise St Mary *Lon* 71-74; C St Helens St Helen *Liv* 74-79; V Liv All So Springwood 79-91; V Whiston 91-02; V Aigburth from 02. *St Anne's Vicarage, 389 Aigburth Road, Liverpool L17 6BH* Tel 0151-727 1101

AMEY, John Mark. b 59. Ripon Coll Cuddesdon 98. d 00 p 01. C Winchmore Hill St Paul *Lon* 00-04; V Sutton *Ely* 04-11; R Witcham w Mepal 04-11; V St Ives from 11; Chapl ATC from 03. *The Vicarage, Westwood Road, St Ives PE27 6DH* Tel (01480) 384334 Mobile 07905-122990 E-mail fr.mark@virgin.net

AMEY, Phillip Mark. b 73. STETS 03. d 06 p 07. C Southsea H Spirit *Portsm* 06-09; P-in-c Purbrook from 09. *The Vicarage, 9 Marrels Wood Gardens, Purbrook, Waterlooville PO7 5RS* E-mail phillip.amey@ntlworld.com

AMIS, Ronald. b 37. Linc Th Coll 74. d 76 p 77. C Grantham w Manthorpe *Linc* 76-78; C Grantham 78-79; P-in-c Holbeach Hurn 79-81; V Long Bennington w Foston 81-91; V Corby Glen 91-93; RD Grantham 90-92; rtd 93; Perm to Offic *Pet* 93-03 and from 09; *Ches* 06-08. *9 Cotton End, Bretton, Peterborough PE3 9TF* Tel (01733) 261152 Mobile 07739-307865

AMOR, Peter David Card. b 28. AKC53. d 54 p 55. C St Margaret's-on-Thames *Lon* 54; C Leighton Buzzard *St Alb* 54-58; C Toxteth Park St Agnes *Liv* 58-62; C-in-c Aldershot Ascension CD *Guildf* 62-65; V Bingley H Trin *Bradf* 65-72; V The Collingbournes *Sarum* 72-75; R The Collingbournes and Everleigh 75-77; V Thorpe *Guildf* 77-85; P-in-c Monks Risborough *Ox* 85-89; R 89-94; rtd 94; Perm to Offic *Ox* from 97. *6 Saunders Meadow, Collingbourne Ducis, Marlborough SN8 3FA* Tel (01264) 850519

AMOS, Alan John. b 44. OBE79. K Coll Lon BD66 MTh67 AKC67. St Steph Ho Ox 68. d 69 p 70. C Hoxton H Trin w St Mary *Lon* 69-72; Lebanon 73-82; Lect Liturg Studies Westcott Ho Cam 82-85; Vice-Prin 85-89; Prin Cant Sch of Min

89-94; Co-Prin SEITE 94-96; Chapl Medway NHS Foundn Trust 96-09; Hon PV Roch Cathl 95-04; Hon Can 04-09; P-in-c Newington w Hartlip and Stockbury *Cant* from 09; P-in-c Upchurch w Lower Halstow from 09; P-in-c Iwade from 09. *Penny Cross, Keycol Hill, Newington, Sittingbourne ME9 8NE* Tel (01795) 842913 E-mail alanmedway@btinternet.com

AMOS, Brother. *See* YONGE, James Mohun

AMOS, Colin James. b 62. Univ of Wales (Lamp) BA83 CQSW85. Ridley Hall Cam 93. **d** 93 **p** 94. C Aberdare *Llan* 93-96; V Port Talbot St Theodore from 96; AD Margam from 08. *St Theodore's Vicarage, Talbot Road, Port Talbot SA13 1LB* Tel (01639) 883935 Fax 760104 E-mail fr.amos@ntlworld.com

AMYES, Emma Charlotte. b 65. Redcliffe Coll BA01. Ridley Hall Cam. **d** 04 **p** 05. C Hucclecote *Glouc* 04-10; TV Worle *B & W* from 10. *15 Woodpecker Drive, Weston-super-Mare BS22 8SR* Tel (01934) 517442 Mobile 07866-808635 E-mail emma.amyes@virgin.net

AMYES, Geoffrey Edmund. b 74. Bris Univ BSc96 Cam Univ BTh04. Ridley Hall Cam 01. **d** 04 **p** 05. C Hucclecote *Glouc* 04-09; Perm to Offic 09-10. *15 Woodpecker Drive, Weston-super-Mare BS22 8SR* Tel (01934) 517442 Mobile 07792-519910 E-mail g.amyes@btinternet.com

AMYS, Richard James Rutherford. b 58. Trin Coll Bris BA90. **d** 90 **p** 91. C Whitnash *Cov* 90-93; P-in-c Gravesend H Family w Ifield *Roch* 93-95; R 95-99; R Eastington, Frocester, Haresfield etc *Glouc* from 99. *The Rectory, Mill End Lane, Eastington, Stonehouse GL10 3SG* Tel and fax (01453) 822437 Mobile 07796-956050 E-mail richardjramys@aol.com

ANAN, Gabriel Jaja. b 48. Regents Th Coll BA92 Univ of E Lon MA96 PhD08 Middx Univ BA03 MCIT92. NTMTC 00. **d** 03 **p** 04. NSM Victoria Docks St Luke *Chelmsf* 03-07; NSM Forest Gate St Sav w W Ham St Matt 07-09; NSM N Woolwich w Silvertown 09-10; NSM E Ham St Geo from 10. *67 Bedale Road, Romford RM3 9TU* Tel (01708) 349564 Mobile 07734-707887 E-mail gabriel58@hotmail.com

ANAND, Jessie Nesam Nallammal. b 54. Madurai Univ BSc75 BEd76 Annamalai Univ MA84. Tamilnadu Th Sem BD91 New Coll Edin MTh94 EMMTC 02. **d** 03 **p** 04. NSM Birstall and Wanlip *Leic* 03-05; NSM Emmaus Par Team 05-07; Perm to Offic *S'wark* from 07. *All Saints' Vicarage, 100 Prince of Wales Drive, London SW11 4BD* Tel (020) 7622 3809 Mobile 07811-189358 E-mail jessieanand@yahoo.co.uk

ANAND, The Very Revd Sekar Anand Asir. b 53. Madurai Univ BSc75 Serampore Univ BD79 New Coll Edin MTh93 Annamalai Univ MA99. **d** 80 **p** 81. C Nayaith St Jo India 80-82; R Tuticorin St Paul 82-84; Sec Tirunelveli Children's Miss 84-91; C Edin St Pet 91-92; Hon C Burmantofts St Steph and St Agnes *Ripon* 92-93; C Edin St Mark 93-95; Provost Palayamcottai Cathl India 95-00; C Leic Resurr 00-07; C Battersea Fields *S'wark* from 07. *All Saints' Vicarage, 100 Prince of Wales Drive, London SW11 4BD* Tel (020) 7622 3809 E-mail anandjessie@yahoo.co.uk

ANCRUM, John. b 28. Clifton Th Coll 55. **d** 58 **p** 59. C Branksome St Clem *Sarum* 58-61; C Sparkhill St Jo *Birm* 61-63; V Tibshelf *Derby* 63-70; Canada 70-74; P-in-c Salwarpe *Worc* 74-75; P-in-c Tibberton w Bredicot and Warndon 75-76; P-in-c Hadzor w Oddingley 76-78; Lic to Offic *Chelmsf* 78-81; Chapl HM Pris Stafford 81-82; Chapl HM Pris Dartmoor 82-89; Lic to Offic *Ex* 88-89; rtd 89; Perm to Offic *Ex* from 89. *14 Merrivale View Road, Dousland, Yelverton PL20 6NS*

ANDAYI, Elphas Ombuna. b 57. St Phil Th Coll Maseno 78. **d** 79 **p** 81. Kenya 79-98 and from 99; Provost Butere 92-97; C Sparkhill w Greet and Sparkbrook *Birm* 98-99. *PO Box 199, Bukura, Kenya* Tel (00254) (333) 20038 Fax 20412

ANDERS, Mrs Erika Gertrud. b 45. ACT 88 St Jo Coll Nottm 99. **d** 92 **p** 02. C Proserpine St Paul Australia 92; C Hamburg *Eur* 99-07; Asst Chapl from 07. *Niendorfer Kirchenweg 5C, 22459 Hamburg, Germany* Tel (0049) (40) 582850 Fax 582841 Mobile 162-700 0404 E-mail erika.anders@fco.gov.uk

ANDERS, Jonathan Cyril. b 36. Wycliffe Hall Ox 69. **d** 71 **p** 72. C Prescot *Liv* 71-74; C-in-c 74-76; R Wavertree St Mary 76-81; V Aigburth 81-01; rtd 01; Perm to Offic *Liv* from 03. *3 Silverleigh, Liverpool L17 5BL* Tel 0151-728 9997

ANDERS, Roger John. b 38. Man Univ LLB61. NOC 91. **d** 94 **p** 95. NSM New Mills *Derby* 94-97; NSM Buxton w Burbage and King Sterndale 97-98; NSM Adderley, Ash, Calverhall, Ightfield etc *Lich* 98-03; R 03-10; rtd 10. *11 Mount Crescent, Whitchurch SY13 1GW* Tel (01948) 664088 E-mail anders@u.genie.co.uk

ANDERSEN, Paul John. b 49. Univ of Alabama BA. Protestant Th Sem Virginia MDiv77. **d** 77 **p** 83. USA 77-82; Belize 82-84; Chapl Zagreb *Eur* 84-85; Chapl Belgrade 85-86; USA 86-89; India 89-91; Sierra Leone 92-93; Chapl Valletta *Eur* 94-96; Chapl Skopje 96-98; NSM Worcester St Luke USA 98-00; NSM S Barre Ch Ch 00-02; R Milford Trin Ch 02-06. *Christ Church Parish (Episcopal), PO Box 15, Christchurch VA 23031, USA* Tel (001) (804) 758 2006 E-mail paulandersen@earthlink.net

ANDERSON, Albert Geoffrey (Geoff). b 42. Ex Univ BA65 MA67. Qu Coll Birm. **d** 75 **p** 76. C Helsby and Ince *Ches* 75-77;

C Helsby and Dunham-on-the-Hill 77-78; TV Gleadless *Sheff* 78-85; V Thorpe Hesley 85-92; R Ribbesford w Bewdley and Dowles *Worc* 92-03; rtd 03. *2 Waterworks Road, Worcester WR1 3EX* Tel (01905) 612634 E-mail ga@priest.com

ANDERSON, Alice Calder. b 50. Moray Ho Coll of Educn DipEd76. Local Minl Tr Course 90. **d** 93 **p** 95. NSM Edin St Barn from 93. *20 Pentland Road, Bonnyrigg EH19 2LG* Tel 0131-654 0506

ANDERSON, Mrs Ann. b 57. Cranmer Hall Dur 01. **d** 03 **p** 04. C Chester le Street *Dur* 03-07; P-in-c Hetton-Lyons w Eppleton 07; R from 07. *The Rectory, Houghton Road, Hetton-le-Hole, Houghton le Spring DH5 9PH* Tel 0191-517 3102

ANDERSON, Preb Brian Arthur. b 42. Sarum Th Coll 75. **d** 78 **p** 79. C Plymouth St Jas Ham *Ex* 78-80; Org Sec CECS *B & W, Ex* and *Truro* 80-89; TV Saltash *Truro* 89-94; RD E Wivelshire 91-94; P-in-c St Breoke and Egloshayle 94-96; R 96-02; RD Trigg Minor and Bodmin 95-02; P-in-c Torpoint 02-09; P-in-c Antony w Sheviock 02-09; Preb St Endellion 99-09; rtd 09. *44 Essa Road, Saltash PL12 4EE* Tel (01752) 511271 Mobile 07710-231219

ANDERSON, Brian Glaister. b 35. K Coll Lon 57. **d** 79 **p** 79. Chapl St Fran Sch Hooke 79; C Croydon St Jo *Cant* 80-83; Dep Chapl HM Youth Cust Cen Glen Parva 83-84; Chapl HM YOI Hewell Grange 84-89; Chapl HM Rem Cen Brockhill 84-89; Chapl HM Pris Parkhurst 89-96; rtd 96. *28 Chase Farm Close, Waltham Chase, Southampton SO32 2UD* Tel (01489) 896880 Mobile 07900-272006 E-mail brianders@btinternet.com

ANDERSON, Mrs Christine. b 42. **d** 09. OLM Skegness Gp *Linc* from 09. *14 Revesby Drive, Skegness PE25 2HT* Tel (01754) 767678

ANDERSON, David. b 19. Selw Coll Cam BA41 MA45. Wycliffe Hall Ox 47. **d** 49 **p** 50. C Bishopwearmouth St Gabr *Dur* 49-52; Tutor St Aid Birkenhead 52-56; Chapl Heswall Nautical Sch 52-53; Warden Melville Hall Ibadan Nigeria 56-58; Prin Immanuel Coll Ibadan 58-62; Can Ibadan 59-62; Prin Wycliffe Hall Ox 62-69; Sen Lect Wall Hall Coll Aldenham 70-74; Prin Lect 74-84; rtd 84; Perm to Offic *Dur* 84-02. *16 Manor Park, Borrowash, Derby DE72 3LP* Tel (01332) 664426

ANDERSON, David Graham. b 33. MICE MIStructE. St Mich Coll Llan 85. **d** 88 **p** 89. C Llanishen and Lisvane *Llan* 88-90; C Fazeley *Lich* 90-94; Perm to Offic *Heref* 96-01 and *Llan* 01-08. *7 Rowan Close, Penarth CF64 5BU* Tel (029) 2071 1013

ANDERSON, David Lee. b 75. Westmr Coll Ox BTh96. Ripon Coll Cuddesdon MTh98. **d** 98 **p** 99. C Balderton *S'well* 98-02; V Harworth 02-07; P-in-c Longridge *Blackb* from 07. *The Vicarage, Church Street, Longridge, Preston PR3 3WA* Tel (01772) 783281 E-mail vicaroflongridge@aol.com

ANDERSON, David Richard. b 58. Lanc Univ BA79. EAMTC 96. **d** 99 **p** 00. C N Walsham w Antingham *Nor* 99-02; R Stalham, E Ruston, Brunstead, Sutton and Ingham 02-06; P-in-c Smallburgh w Dilham w Honing and Crostwight 05-06; TV Wrexham *St As* 06-11; Chapl St Jos High Sch Wrexham 06-11; V Romford St Edw *Chelmsf* from 11. *St Edward's Vicarage, 15 Oaklands Avenue, Romford RM1 4DB* Tel (01708) 727002 Mobile 07956-267265 E-mail fr.anderson@ymail.com

ANDERSON, Digby Carter. b 44. Reading Univ BA Brunel Univ MPhil73 PhD77. **d** 85 **p** 86. NSM Luton St Sav *St Alb* from 85. *17 Hardwick Place, Woburn Sands, Milton Keynes MK17 8QQ* Tel (01908) 584526

ANDERSON, Donald Whimbey. b 31. Trin Coll Toronto BA54 MA58 LTh57 STB57 ThD71. **d** 56 **p** 57. Canada 57-59, 75-88 and from 96; Japan 59-74; Philippines 74-75; Dir Ecum Affairs ACC 88-96; rtd 96. *Conference on the Religious Life, PO Box 99, Little Britain ON K0M 2C0, Canada* Tel and fax (001) (705) 786 3330 E-mail dwa@nexicom.net

ANDERSON, Geoff. *See* ANDERSON, Albert Geoffrey

ANDERSON, Mrs Gillian Ann. b 52. NTMTC 05. **d** 08 **p** 09. NSM Lambourne w Abridge and Stapleford Abbotts *Chelmsf* 08-09; NSM Loughton St Jo 09-11; P-in-c High Laver w Magdalen Laver and Lt Laver etc from 11. *The Lavers Rectory, Magdalen Laver, Ongar CM5 0ES* Tel (01279) 426774 Mobile 07954-429153 E-mail gillanderson@ntlworld.com

ANDERSON, Gordon Stuart. b 49. St Jo Coll Nottm. **d** 82 **p** 83. C Hattersley *Ches* 82-86; C Dagenham *Chelmsf* 86-91; TV Mildenhall *St E* 91-01; V Southminster *Chelmsf* from 01; P-in-c Steeple from 08; RD Maldon and Dengie 06-11. *The Vicarage, Burnham Road, Southminster CM0 7ES* Tel (01621) 772300 Mobile 07759-550990 E-mail gandr42@btinternet.com

ANDERSON, Graeme Edgar. b 59. Poly of Wales BSc82. St Jo Coll Nottm MTh02. **d** 02 **p** 03. C Brislington St Luke 02-05; C Galleywood Common *Chelmsf* 05-09; P-in-c Radcliffe-on-Trent and Shelford *S'well* from 09. *The Vicarage, 2 Vicarage Lane, Radcliffe-on-Trent, Nottingham NG12 2FB* Tel 0115-923 9643 Mobile 07840-926736 E-mail graemeandjudy@gmail.com

ANDERSON, Hugh Richard Oswald. b 35. Roch Th Coll 68. **d** 70 **p** 71. C Minehead *B & W* 70-76; C Darley w S Darley *Derby* 76-80; R Hasland 80-94; V Temple Normanton 80-94; rtd 94; Perm to Offic *Derby* from 94. *32 Barry Road, Brimington, Chesterfield S43 1PU* Tel (01246) 551020

ANDERSON, James. b 36. Magd Coll Ox BA59 MA64 Leeds Univ MA00. **d** 02 **p** 03. NSM Holme and Seaton Ross Gp *York* 02-08; P-in-c The Beacon from 08. *61 Moor Lane, Carnaby, Bridlington YO16 4UT*

ANDERSON, James Frederick Wale. b 34. G&C Coll Cam BA58 MA62. Cuddesdon Coll 60. **d** 62 **p** 63. C Leagrave *St Alb* 62-65; C Eastleigh *Win* 65-70; R Sherfield-on-Loddon 70-86; P-in-c Stratfield Saye w Hartley Wespall 75-86; R Sherfield-on-Loddon and Stratfield Saye etc 86-87; R Newton Valence, Selborne and E Tisted w Colemore 87-99; rtd 99; Chapl Surrey Hants Borders NHS Trust 01-04; Hon C Farnham *Guildf* 01-04; Perm to Offic from 07. *1 Potter's Gate, Farnham GU9 7EJ* Tel (01252) 710728

ANDERSON, Canon James Raffan. b 33. FRSA90 Edin Univ MA54. Edin Th Coll 56. **d** 58 **p** 59. Chapl St Andr Cathl 58-59; Prec St Andr Cathl 59-62; CF (TA) 59-67; Chapl Aber Univ 60-62; Chapl Glas Univ 62-69; Chapl Lucton Sch 69-71; Chapl Barnard Castle Sch 71-74; Asst Dir of Educn *Blackb* 74-78; P-in-c Whitechapel 74-78; Bp's Officer for Miss *Cov* 78-87; Hon Can Cov Cathl 83-87; Miss Sec Gen Syn Bd for Miss and Unity 87-92; rtd 92; Perm to Offic *Blackb* from 98. *Eccles Moss Farm, Bleasdale Road, Whitechapel, Preston PR3 2ER* Tel and fax (01995) 641280 E-mail jamesanders@onetel.com

ANDERSON (née FLAHERTY), Mrs Jane Venitia. b 68. Oak Hill Th Coll BA92. **d** 93 **p** 94. C Timperley *Ches* 93-97; C Cheshunt *St Alb* 97-99; P-in-c N Springfield *Chelmsf* from 99. *The Vicarage, St Augustine's Way, Braddsley Drive, Springfield, Chelmsford CM1 6GX* Tel (01245) 466160 E-mail revjaney@aol.com

ANDERSON, Jeffrey. b 56. Cranmer Hall Dur. **d** 07 **p** 08. C Chester le Street *Dur* from 07. *The Rectory, Houghton Road, Hetton-le-Hole, Houghton le Spring DH5 9PH* Tel 0191-517 3102

ANDERSON, Jeremy. See ANDERSON, Brian Glaister

ANDERSON, Jeremy Dudgeon. b 41. Edin Univ BSc63. Trin Coll Bris 75. **d** 77 **p** 78. C Bitterne *Win* 77-81; TV Wexcombe *Sarum* 81-91; Evang Enabler (Reading Deanery) *Ox* 91-96; V Epsom Common Ch Ch *Guildf* 96-00; C Kinson *Sarum* 00-06; rtd 06. *The Croft, Church Road, Crowborough TN6 1ED* Tel (01892) 655825

ANDERSON, Mrs Joanna Elisabeth. b 53. St Andr Univ MTheol75. EMMTC 85. **d** 88 **p** 95. Par Dn Crosby *Linc* 88-92; Warden Iona Community *Arg* 92-95; R S Trin Broads *Nor* 95-02; Dir Body, Mind, Spirit Project 02-05; R Stiffkey and Bale *Nor* 05-09; C Hexham *Newc* from 09. *29 Robson Drive, Beaumont Park, Hexham NE46 2HZ* Tel (01434) 604935 E-mail revanderson@btinternet.com

ANDERSON, John Robert. b 75. QUB BD96 TCD MPhil98. CITC 96. **d** 98 **p** 99. C Magherafelt *Arm* 98-02; C Ballymena w Ballyclug *Conn* 02-05; I Billy w Derrykeighan from 05; Bp's Dom Chapl from 08. *The New Rectory, 231 Castlecat Road, Dervock, Ballymoney BT53 8BP* Tel (028) 2074 1241 E-mail john.eleanor@btinternet.com

ANDERSON, Julie. b 60. St Jo Coll Nottm 09. **d** 11. C Liv Ch Ch Norris Green from 11. *9 Kingsland Crescent, Liverpool L11 7AN* Tel 07540-613068 (mobile) E-mail julie_anderson51@yahoo.co.uk

ANDERSON, Canon Keith Bernard. b 36. Qu Coll Cam BA60 MA64. Tyndale Hall Bris 60. **d** 62 **p** 63. C Bootle St Leon *Liv* 62-65; Lect Can Warner Mem Coll Buye Burundi 66-73; Lect Mweya United Th Sem 74; Dir Studies Dio Nakuru Kenya 74-77; Dir RE Dio Mt Kenya E 78-83; Hon Can Mt Kenya E from 82; P-in-c Newnham and Doddington w Wychling *Cant* 83-88; Chapl Cannes w Grasse *Eur* 88-94; Dir and Chapl Mulberry Ho High Ongar 94-95; TV Horley *S'wark* 96-01; rtd 01; Perm to Offic *S'wark* 01-05 and Chich from 01. *93 Rusper Road, Horsham RH12 4BJ* Tel (01403) 262185 E-mail kb.anderson@virgin.net

ANDERSON, Canon Keith Edward. b 42. Fitzw Coll Cam BA77 MA83 MRCS83. Ridley Hall Cam 74. **d** 77 **p** 78. C Goodmayes All SS *Chelmsf* 77-80; Chapl Coll of SS Mark and Jo Plymouth *Ex* 80-87; RD Plymouth Moorside 83-86; V Northampton H Sepulchre w St Andr and St Lawr *Pet* 87-98; RD Northn 92-98; Adv for Min Willesden *Lon* 98-03; Can Res Win Cathl and Adv for Ord Min Development *Win* 03-08; rtd 08. *49 Chaundler Road, Winchester SO23 7HW* Tel (01962) 853429 E-mail keith.anderson20@btinternet.com

ANDERSON, Kenneth. b 38. G&C Coll Cam BA62 MA66. Westcott Ho Cam 63. **d** 65 **p** 66. C Nor St Steph 65-68; Chapl Norfolk and Nor Hosp 65-68; C Wareham w Arne *Sarum* 68-71; Chapl Sherborne Sch 71-83; Zimbabwe 83-94; Chapl Trevelyan and Van Mildert Coll *Dur* 95-04; Dioc Voc Adv 95-04; rtd 04. *39 Hallgarth Street, Durham DH1 3AT* Tel 0191-383 0628 or 374 3770

ANDERSON, Martin Edward. b 73. Humberside Univ BA95 St Jo Coll Dur BA02. Cranmer Hall Dur 99. **d** 02 **p** 03. C St Aycliffe and Chilton *Dur* 02-05; TV Sunderland 05-07; Chapl Sunderland Minster from 07. *21 Thornhill Terrace, Sunderland SR2 7JL* Tel 0191-567 2231 E-mail martin.anderson@durham.anglican.org

ANDERSON, Michael. b 38. **d** 06 **p** 07. NSM Dungeon Hill and The Caundles w Folke and Holwell *Sarum* 06-07; NSM Vale of White Hart 07-09; Lic to RD Sherborne 09-10; NSM Gifle Valley from 10. *Tiley House, Middlemarsh, Sherborne DT9 5QL* Tel (01300) 345375 Mobile 07966-664319 E-mail michael@tileyhouse.freeserve.co.uk

ANDERSON, Canon Michael Garland. b 42. Clifton Th Coll 62. **d** 66 **p** 67. C Fareham St Jo *Portsm* 66-69; C Worting *Win* 69-74; V Hordle 74-07; RD Lyndhurst 82-00; Hon Can Win Cathl 92-07; rtd 07. *20 Forestlake Avenue, Ringwood BH24 1QU* Tel (01425) 471490 E-mail canon.m.g.anderson@ukgateway.net

ANDERSON, Canon Michael John Austen. b 35. AKC60. **d** 66 **p** 67. C Southall Ch Redeemer *Lon* 66-69; C Hampstead Garden Suburb 69-73; V S Mimms St Giles 73-80; V The Brents and Davington w Oare and Luddenham *Cant* 80-86; V Margate All SS 86-00; Hon Can Cant Cathl 97-00; rtd 00; Perm to Offic *Cant* from 01. *Camwa Ash, Bull Lane, Boughton-under-Blean, Faversham ME13 9AH* Tel (01227) 752352 Mobile 07885-211863

ANDERSON, Canon Nicholas Patrick. b 53. Lanc Univ BA87. Allen Hall 79. **d** 81 **p** 82. In RC Ch 81-89; C Gt Crosby St Faith *Liv* 89-92; C Walton-on-the-Hill 92-95; V Pemberton St Fran Kitt Green 95-04; V Rainhill from 04; Hon Can Liv Cathl from 10. *St Ann's Vicarage, View Road, Prescot L35 0LE* Tel 0151-426 4666

ANDERSON, Mrs Pearl Ann. b 46. St Andr Univ MA68 MCIPD74. Cant Sch of Min 90. **d** 93 **p** 00. Par Dn Epping St Jo *Chelmsf* 93-95; Adv to Coun for Soc Resp *Roch* and *Cant* 95-02; Asst Chief Exec Ch in Soc *Roch* and *Cant* 02-06; Hon C Biddenden and Smarden 00-06; rtd 06; Perm to Offic *Roch* from 95 and *Cant* from 06. *1 Gibbs Hill, Headcorn, Ashford TN27 9UD* Tel (01622) 890043 Mobile 07811-209448 E-mail pearlanderson@btinternet.com

ANDERSON, Peter John. b 44. Nottm Univ BA65 BA73 Ex Univ CertEd66. St Jo Coll Nottm. **d** 74 **p** 75. C Otley *Brad* 74-77; TV Marfleet *York* 77-84; V Greasbrough *Sheff* 84-95; I Clonmel Union *C, C & R* 95-02; I Rathcooney Union 95-02; Chapl Cannes *Eur* 02-09; rtd 09. *100 route de la Colle, 06140 Tourrettes-sur-Loup, France* Tel (0033) 9 50 41 68 40 E-mail pjhmander@yahoo.com

ANDERSON, Peter Scott. b 49. Nottm Univ BTh72 CertEd. Kelham Th Coll 68. **d** 74 **p** 75. C Sheff St Cecilia Parson Cross 74-77; C Leytonstone St Marg w St Columba *Chelmsf* 77-81; P-in-c Forest Gate St Edm 81-89; V 89-90; P-in-c Plaistow 90-94; V Willesden Green St Andr and St Fran *Lon* 94-08; V Lewisham St Mary *S'wark* from 08. *Lewisham Vicarage, 48 Lewisham Park, London SE13 6QZ* Tel (020) 8690 2682 or 8690 1585 E-mail peter@scottanderson.freeserve.co.uk

ANDERSON, Philip Gregory. b 80. Keble Coll Ox BA01. Ripon Coll Cuddesdon BA04. **d** 05 **p** 06. C Prescot *Liv* 05-09; Chapl Liv Hope Univ from 09. *Liverpool Hope University, Hope Park, Liverpool L16 9JD* Tel 07773-582920 (mobile) E-mail philipanderson@merseymail.com

ANDERSON, Canon Roderick Stephen. b 43. Cant Univ (NZ) BSc63 PhD67 New Coll Ox BA72. Wycliffe Hall Ox 70. **d** 73 **p** 74. C Bradf Cathl 73-75; C Allerton 76-78; V Cottingley 78-94; V Heaton St Barn 94-09; C 09-11; RD Airedale 88-95; Chapl Bradf Univ and Bradf Coll 04-11; Hon Can Bradf Cathl 94-11; rtd 11. *40 Low Wood, Wilsden, Bradford BD15 0JS*

ANDERSON, Canon Rosemary Ann. b 36. Ex Univ BSc59. NOC 83. **dss** 86 **d** 87 **p** 94. Oldham St Paul *Man* 86-87; Hon Par Dn 87-89; Bp's Adv for Women's Min 88-99; Par Dn Roughtown 93-94; P-in-c 94-99; Hon Can Man Cathl 96-99; rtd 99; Perm to Offic *Man* from 99. *11E Rhodes Hill, Lees, Oldham OL4 5EA* Tel 0161-620 1549

ANDERSON, Scott. See ANDERSON, Peter Scott

ANDERSON, Stephen George. b 54. Liv Univ BA75 ACIB. NOC 05. **d** 08 **p** 09. NSM Gt Shelford *Ely* from 08. *3 Dukes Meadow, Stapleford, Cambridge CB22 5BH* Tel (01223) 843859 Mobile 07889-003588 E-mail fr.stephen.anderson@googlemail.com

ANDERSON, Timothy George. b 59. Ealing Coll of HE BA82. Wycliffe Hall Ox 83. **d** 86 **p** 87. C Harold Wood *Chelmsf* 86-90; V Whitfield *Derby* 90-95; P-in-c Wolverhampton St Luke *Lich* 95-98; V 98-01; I Dundonald *D & D* from 01. *St Elizabeth's Rectory, 26 Ballyregan Road, Dundonald, Belfast BT16 1HY* Tel (028) 9048 3153 or 9048 2644 E-mail t.j.anderson@btinternet.com

ANDERSON, Timothy James Lane. b 59. Pemb Coll Ox BA80 MA90. St Jo Coll Nottm 89. **d** 93 **p** 94. C Reigate St Mary *S'wark* 93-95; Perm to Offic *S'well* from 00. *3 Dale Lane, Beeston, Nottingham NG9 4EA* Tel 0115-922 4773

ANDERSON, William. CITC. **d** 09 **p** 10. NSM Killala *Arm* 09-10; C Tullaniskin w Clonoe from 10. *37 Tirmacrannon Road, Loughgall, Armagh BT61 8LW* Tel (028) 3889 1405 Mobile 07901-852565 E-mail william@apple37.plus.com

ANDERSON-MacKENZIE, Janet Melanie. b 70. Edin Univ BSc93 PhD97 Trin Coll Bris MA07. WEMTC 01. **d** 04 **p** 05. C Woolavington w Cossington and Bawdrip *B & W* 04-05; C Wellington and Distr 05-08; P-in-c Box w Hazlebury and

Ditteridge *Bris* from 08. *The Vicarage, Church Lane, Box, Corsham SN13 8NR* Tel and fax (01225) 744458 E-mail janet@anderson-mackenzie.co.uk

ANDERTON, David Edward. b 60. Leeds Poly BSc92. St Jo Coll Nottm 02. **d** 04 **p** 05. C Daybrook *S'well* 04-06; C Hucknall Torkard 06-09; TV Newark w Coddington from 09. *3 Swinderby Close, Newark NG24 2SY* Tel (01636) 610485 Mobile 07751-269412 E-mail d.anderton1@btinternet.com

ANDERTON, David Ernest. b 36. CEng68 MIMechE68. **d** 00 **p** 01. OLM Eccleston Ch Ch *Liv* 00-06; rtd 06. *16 Croxteth Drive, Rainford, St Helens WA11 8JZ* Tel (01744) 637600 Mobile 07751-038014

ANDERTON, Mrs Elaine Irene. b 73. Sussex Univ BA96. WMMTC 06. **d** 09 **p** 10. C Smestow Vale *Lich* from 09. *39 Wrottesley Road, Tettenhall, Wolverhampton WV6 8SG* Tel (01902) 741663 *or* 758894

ANDERTON, Frederic Michael. b 31. Pemb Coll Cam MA57 IAAP. Westcott Ho Cam 64. **d** 66 **p** 67. C St John's Wood *Lon* 66-69; C All Hallows by the Tower etc 70-77; C St Giles Cripplegate w St Bart Moor Lane etc 77-82; C Zürich *Eur* 82-86; Perm to Offic *Lon* 94-00; rtd 96. *61 Brassey Road, Winchester SO22 6SB* Tel (01962) 856326 Fax 852851 E-mail robin.anderton@lineone.net

ANDERTON, Peter. b 45. Sarum & Wells Th Coll 80. **d** 82 **p** 83. C Adel *Ripon* 82-86; P-in-c Dacre w Hartwith 86-90; P-in-c Thornthwaite w Thruscross and Darley 88-90; V Dacre w Hartwith and Darley w Thornthwaite 90-91; V Owton Manor *Dur* 91-02; V Torrisholme *Blackb* 02-03; P-in-c Hunslet St Mary *Ripon* 03, V Hunslet w Cross Green 03-07; rtd 07. *133 Westbrooke Avenue, Hartlepool TS25 5HZ* E-mail fr.peter@ntlworld.com

ANDREW, Brian. b 31. Oak Hill Th Coll 75. **d** 77 **p** 78. C Broadwater St Mary *Chich* 77-81; R Nettlebed w Bix and Highmore *Ox* 81-87; V Shenstone *Lich* 87-96; rtd 96; Perm to Offic *Ex* 97-00 *and* Derby 01-11. *1 Redcotts, St Botolphs Road, Worthing BN11 4JW*

ANDREW, David Neil. b 62. Down Coll Cam BA83 MA87 PhD88. Ridley Hall Cam 93. **d** 93 **p** 94. C Heatherlands St Jo *Sarum* 93-98; P-in-c White Waltham w Shottesbrooke *Ox* from 98; P-in-c Waltham St Lawrence 07-11. *The Vicarage, Waltham Road, White Waltham, Maidenhead SL6 3JD* Tel (01628) 822000

ANDREW, David Shore. b 39. Liv Univ BA61 CertEd62. OLM course 97. **d** 99 **p** 00. NSM Birkenshaw w Hunsworth *Wakef* from 99. *448 Oxford Road, Gomersal, Cleckheaton BD19 4LD* Tel (01274) 873339

ANDREW, Donald. b 35. Tyndale Hall Bris 63. **d** 66 **p** 67. C Croydon Ch Ch Broad Green *Cant* 66-69; C Ravenhead *Liv* 69-72; Scripture Union 72-77; V Rushen *S & M* 77-82; TR Heworth H Trin *York* 82-00; rtd 00; Perm to Offic *York* from 05. *60 Viking Road, Bridlington YO16 6TW* Tel (01262) 601273

ANDREW, Frank. b 17. St D Coll Lamp BA49 Ely Th Coll 50. **d** 51 **p** 52. C Howden *York* 51-55; V Mosbrough *Sheff* 55-59; C-in-c Greenhill CD 59-65; V Greenhill 65-69; R March St Jo *Ely* 69-77; R March St Mary 71-77; RD March 73-77; R Catworth Magna 77-83; R Covington 77-83; R Tilbrook 77-83; rtd 83; Perm to Offic *Chich* from 83. *The College of St Barnabas, Blackberry Lane, Lingfield RH7 6NJ*

ANDREW, Jeremy Charles Edward. b 68. St Jo Coll Dur BA01. Cranmer Hall Dur 98. **d** 01. C Newquay *Truro* 01-04; P-in-c Perranzabuloe 04-10; P-in-c Crantock 05-06; C Crantock w Cubert 06-07; P-in-c 07-10; V Perranzabuloe and Crantock w Cubert from 10. *The Vicarage, Cocks, Perranporth TR6 0AT* Tel (01872) 573375

ANDREW, John. b 60. St Mich Coll Llan 98. **d** 00 **p** 01. C Oystermouth *S & B* 00-06; V Upper Wye 06-07; P-in-c Swansea St Nic 07-08; rtd 09. *13 Park Street, Mumbles, Swansea SA3 4DA* Tel (01792) 360408

ANDREW, Canon John Gerald Barton. b 31. OBE. Keble Coll Ox BA55 MA58 Cuttington Univ Coll Liberia Hon DD76 Kentucky Sem Hon DD76 Nashotah Ho Wisconsin Hon DD77 Gen Th Sem NY Hon DD96. Cuddesdon Coll 54. **d** 56 **p** 57. C Redcar *York* 56-59; C Rumson St Geo USA 59-60; Abp's Dom Chapl *York* 60-61; Abp's Dom Chapl *Cant* 61-65; Abp's Sen Chapl 65-69; Six Preacher Cant Cathl 67-72; V Preston St Jo *Blackb* 69-72; RD Preston 70-72; R New York St Thos USA 72-96; rtd 96; Perm to Offic *B & W* 97-99. *414 East 52nd Street, New York NY 10022-6458, USA* Tel (001) (212) 355 0064

ANDREW, Jonathan William. b 50. Univ Coll Ox MA78 FCA80. Ripon Coll Cuddesdon 02. **d** 04 **p** 05. NSM Hersham *Guildf* from 04. *Orchard, 6 Westacres, Esher KT10 9JE* Tel (01372) 479776 Mobile 07968-765188 E-mail curate.stpeters@btinternet.com

ANDREW, Michael Paul. b 51. Leic Univ CertEd73. Chich Th Coll 80. **d** 83 **p** 84. C Par *Truro* 83-86; Hon Chapl Miss to Seamen 86; P-in-c Salford Ordsall St Clem *Man* 86-91; P-in-c Hammersmith St Jo *Lon* 91-04; Perm to Offic *Ex* from 06. *8 East Park Avenue, Plymouth PL4 6PF* Tel 07515-472547 (mobile) E-mail paul@dunvykryn.go-plus.net

ANDREW, Paul Roland. b 70. Oak Hill Th Coll BA06. **d** 06 **p** 07. C Plymouth Em, St Paul Efford and St Aug *Ex* 06-09; Chapl RN from 09. *Royal Naval Chaplaincy Service, Mail Point 1-2, Leach Building, Whale Island, Portsmouth PO2 8BY* Tel (023) 9262 5055 Fax 9262 5134 E-mail paulosandrews@blueyonder.co.uk

ANDREW, Philip John. b 62. Nottm Univ BSc84. St Jo Coll Nottm MTh02. **d** 02 **p** 03. C Reading Greyfriars *Ox* 02-06; V Reigate St Mary *S'wark* from 06. *St Mary's Vicarage, 76 Church Street, Reigate RH2 0SP* Tel (01737) 242973 E-mail phil.andrew@stmaryreigate.org

ANDREW, Sydney William. b 55. Cranmer Hall Dur 82. **d** 85 **p** 86. C Horncastle w Low Toynton *Linc* 85-88; V Worlaby 88-93; V Bonby 88-93; V Elsham 88-93; rtd 93; Lic to Offic *Linc* 93-95; Hon C Brocklesby Park 95-04; Hon C Croxton 96-04; Hon C Caistor Gp from 04. *10 Bentley Lane, Grasby, Barnetby DN38 6AW* Tel (01652) 628586 E-mail bridget.revdoc@clara.co.uk

ANDREW, Canon William Hugh. b 32. Selw Coll Cam BA56 MA60. Ridley Hall Cam 56. **d** 58 **p** 59. C Woking St Mary *Guildf* 58-61; C Farnborough 61-64; V Gatten St Paul *Portsm* 64-71; R Weymouth St Mary *Sarum* 71-76; V Heatherlands St Jo 76-82; Can and Preb Sarum Cathl 81-86; R Alderbury and W Grimstead 82-86; Perm to Offic *Bris* 86-88; Communications Dir Bible Soc 86-94; Communications Consultant 94-97; Hon C The Lydiards *Bris* 88-94; C W Swindon and the Lydiards 94-96; Hon C 96-98; rtd 96; Perm to Offic *Win* from 98. *31 Charnock Close, Hordle, Lymington SO41 0GU* Tel (01425) 627220

ANDREWES, Nicholas John. b 64. Southn Univ BA87 La Sainte Union Coll PGCE88. Cranmer Hall Dur BTh93. **d** 96 **p** 97. C Dovecot *Liv* 96-00; TV Pendleton *Man* 00-03; P-in-c Lower Crumpsall w Cheetham St Mark 03-10; P-in-c Oldham St Paul from 10. *St Paul's Vicarage, 55 Belgrave Road, Oldham OL8 1LU* Tel 0161-624 1068 E-mail nick.andrewes@phonecoop.coop

ANDREWES UTHWATT, Henry. b 25. Jes Coll Cam BA49 MA51. Wells Th Coll 49. **d** 51 **p** 52. C Fareham H Trin *Portsm* 51-55; C Haslemere *Guildf* 55-59; C Wimbledon *S'wark* 59-61; V W Wimbledon Ch 61-73; V Yeovil St Jo w Preston Plucknett *B & W* 73-76; TR Yeovil 76-82; V Burrington and Churchill 82-90; RD Locking 87-90; rtd 90; Perm to Offic *B & W* from 90; Chapl Partis Coll Bath 91-08; Chapl Bath and West Community NHS Trust from 91. *1 Glencairn Court, Bath BA2 4HB* Tel (01225) 482220

ANDREWS, Anthony Brian. b 33. Lon Univ BA54 AKC58. Coll of Resurr Mirfield 56. **d** 58 **p** 59. C Haggerston St Columba *Lon* 58-60; C N Hammersmith St Kath 60-63; V Goldthorpe *Sheff* 63-74; V Notting Hill St Mich and Ch Ch *Lon* from 74. *St Michael's Vicarage, 35 St Lawrence Terrace, London W10 5SR* Tel (020) 8969 0776 Fax 8969 0805 E-mail a.b.a@btinternet.com *or* archangel@supanet.com

ANDREWS, Anthony Frederick. b 25. K Coll Lon 54. **d** 55 **p** 56. C Kentish Town St Jo *Lon* 55-58; C Belmont 58-60; R Evershot, Frome St Quinton, Melbury Bubb etc *Sarum* 60-66; CF 66-69; C Bridgwater St Mary w Chilton Trinity *B & W* 69-70; R Cossington 70-73; C Highworth w Sevenhampton and Inglesham etc *Bris* 75-84; P-in-c Bishopstone w Hinton Parva 84-88; rtd 88. *Burford House, Highworth, Swindon SN6 7AD* Tel (01793) 762796

ANDREWS, Anthony John. b 35. S'wark Ord Course 75. **d** 80 **p** 81. NSM Cheam *S'wark* 80-83; C Epsom St Martin *Guildf* 83-86; V Barton *Portsm* 86-89; Chapl Northwick Park and St Mark's NHS Trust Harrow 90-98; C Regent's Park St Mark *Lon* 98-00; rtd 00; Perm to Offic *Lon* from 00. *112 Albury Drive, Pinner HA5 3RG*

ANDREWS, Benjamin. b 75. St Steph Ho Ox 97. **d** 00 **p** 01. C Whitchurch *Llan* 00-03; C Newton Nottage 03-05; C Caerphilly St Mary and St Steph w St Dyfrig etc from 05. *St Paul's Vicarage, Llanmaes Street, Cardiff CF11 7LR* Tel (029) 2022 8707 E-mail frbenandrews@aol.com

ANDREWS, Canon Brian Keith. b 39. Keble Coll Ox BA62 MA69. Coll of Resurr Mirfield 62. **d** 64 **p** 65. C Is of Dogs Ch Ch and St Jo w St Luke *Lon* 64-68; C Hemel Hempstead *St Alb* 68-71; TV 71-79; V Abbots Langley 79-05; RD Watford 88-94; Hon Can St Alb 94-05; rtd 05; Perm to Offic *Glouc* from 06. *High Pleck, Littleworth, Amberley, Stroud GL5 5AG* Tel (01453) 873068

ANDREWS, Canon Christopher Paul. b 47. Fitzw Coll Cam BA70 MA73. Westcott Ho Cam 69. **d** 72 **p** 73. C Croydon St Jo *Cant* 72-75; C Gosforth All SS *Newc* 75-79; TV Newc Epiphany 80-87; RD Newc Cen 82-87; V Alnwick and Chapl Alnwick Infirmary 87-96; R Grantham *Linc* from 96; P-in-c Grantham, Manthorpe from 11; RD Grantham from 09; Can and Preb Linc Cathl from 04; Chapl United Lincs Hosps NHS Trust 99-01; Chapl to The Queen from 09. *The Rectory, 4 Church Street, Grantham NG31 6RR* Tel (01476) 563710 *or* 572932 E-mail chris@stwulframs.com *or* chris-p-andrews@hotmail.com

ANDREWS, Clive Frederick. b 43. St Jo Coll Nottm 81. **d** 83 **p** 84. C Leic St Jas 83-86; Ind Chapl 86-90; Hon TV Melton Gt Framland 89-90; TV Clifton *S'well* 90-92; P-in-c Gamston w

Eaton and W Drayton 92-94; R 94-08; P-in-c Elkesley w Bothamsall 92-08; Chapl Bramcote Sch Notts 92-08; rtd 08. *15 Oakwood Grove, Edwinstowe, Mansfield NG21 9JT* E-mail cliveand@waitrose.com

ANDREWS, Edward **Robert**. b 33. Brasted Th Coll 60 St Mich Coll Llan 62. **d** 64 **p** 65. C Kingswinford St Mary *Lich* 64-69; Chapl RAF 69-88; R St Just-in-Roseland w Philleigh *Truro* 88-99; rtd 99; Perm to Offic *Ex* from 00. *2 Ingleside, Gunsdown Villas, Station Road, South Molton EX36 3EA* Tel (01769) 572386

ANDREWS, **Frances**. b 24. EMMTC 73. **dss** 78 **d** 87 **p** 94. Porchester *S'well* 78-86; Asst Chapl Nottm City Hosp 86-88; Hon C Gedling *S'well* 88-92; NSM Epperstone 92-95; NSM Gonalston 92-95; NSM Oxton 92-95; rtd 95; Perm to Offic *S'well* 95-05. *Address temp unknown*

ANDREWS, **Mrs Jean**. Leic Univ BSc70. NTMTC. **d** 10 **p** 11. NSM Downham w S Hanningfield *Chelmsf* from 10. *3 Sewards End, Wickford SS12 9PB*

ANDREWS, **Preb John Colin**. b 47. Open Univ BA93. Sarum & Wells Th Coll 78. **d** 80 **p** 81. C Burnham *B & W* 80-84; V Williton 84-92; P-in-c Ashwick w Oakhill and Binegar 92-02; Dioc Communications Officer from 92; TV Yatton Moor from 02; Preb Wells Cathl from 04. *Cherry Tree House, Ham Lane, Kingston Seymour, Clevedon BS21 6XE* Tel (01934) 830208 E-mail john.andrews@bathwells.anglican.org

ANDREWS, **Preb John Douglas**. b 19. Keble Coll Ox BA39 MA44. Chich Th Coll 40. **d** 42 **p** 43. C S Bermondsey St Aug *S'wark* 42-44; C Lambeth St Jo w All SS 44-46; C Towcester w Easton Neston *Pet* 46 50; C Shrewsbury H Cross *Lich* 50 52; V Ettingshall 52-59; V Walsall St Andr 59-68; V Penkhull 68-80; P-in-c Ellenhall w Ranton 80-86; P-in-c Chebsey 80-86; Preb Lich Cathl 81-86; rtd 86; Perm to Offic *Heref* and *Lich* 86-01; *York* from 01. *28 Dulverton Hall, Esplanade, Scarborough YO11 2AR* Tel (01723) 340128

ANDREWS, **John Elfric**. b 35. Ex Coll Ox BA59 MA63. Wycliffe Hall Ox 59. **d** 61 **p** 62. C Pittville All SS *Glouc* 61-66; Cand Sec Lon City Miss 66-92; Lic to Offic *S'wark* 66-92; R Kingham w Churchill, Daylesford and Sarsden *Ox* 92-99; rtd 99; Perm to Offic *St E* from 01. *4 St George's Road, Felixstowe IP11 9PL* Tel (01394) 283557 E-mail john.andrew@care4free.net

ANDREWS, **John Francis**. b 34. Jes Coll Cam BA58 MA62. S'wark Ord Course 78. **d** 81 **p** 82. NSM Upper Norwood All SS *S'wark* 81-87; NSM Dulwich St Barn 89-92; NSM S Dulwich St Steph 92-95; Perm to Offic *S'wark* 95-01 and *Sarum* from 01. *1 Kennington Square, Wareham BH20 4JR* Tel (01929) 555311

ANDREWS, **John George William**. b 42. Qu Coll Birm 65. **d** 68 **p** 69. C Smethwick St Matt w St Chad *Birm* 68-71; CF 71-97; P-in-c Lyme Regis *Sarum* 97-98; TV Golden Cap Team 98-03; rtd 03. *North Gate House, Stapledon Lane, Ashburton, Newton Abbot TQ13 7AE*

ANDREWS, **John Robert**. b 42. Nottm Coll of Educn CertEd63 FRSA92 FCMI92. **d** 04 **p** 05. OLM Farewell *Lich* 04-10; rtd 10. *1 Chaseley Gardens, Burntwood WS7 9DJ* Tel (01543) 674354 Mobile 07711-246656 E-mail johnrobert.andrews@btinternet.com

ANDREWS, **Judith Marie**. b 47. Avery Hill Coll CertEd68. **d** 00 **p** 01. OLM Wilford Peninsula *St E* 00-08; TV from 08. *Hillside, Tower Hill, Hollesley, Woodbridge IP12 3QX* Tel (01394) 411642 E-mail judith.andrews@btopenworld.com

ANDREWS, **Keith**. b 47. St Mich Coll Llan 79. **d** 81 **p** 82. C Penarth w Lavernock *Llan* 81-85; V Nantymoel w Wyndham 85-91; RD Bridgend 89-93; R Coychurch w Llangan and St Mary Hill 91-98; V Caerau St Cynfelin from 98. *The Vicarage, Cymmer Road, Caerau, Maesteg CF34 0YR* Tel (01656) 736500

ANDREWS, **Morey Alisdair Christopher**. b 66. Leic Poly BSc91 MRICS91. St Jo Coll Nottm MA99. **d** 99 **p** 00. C Yate New Town *Bris* 99-02; C Downend 02-06; V Eynsham and Cassington *Ox* from 06. *The Vicarage, 45 Acre End Street, Eynsham, Witney OX29 4PF* Tel (01865) 881323 *or* 881450 E-mail moreyandrews@onetel.com

ANDREWS, **Paul Douglas**. b 54. Univ of Wales (Abth) BLib76 PhD90. SAOMC. **d** 00 **p** 01. NSM Kempston and Biddenham *St Alb* 00-03; C Leighton Buzzard w Eggington, Hockliffe etc 03-05; TV Billington, Egginton, Hockliffe etc 06-08; P-in-c St Neots *Ely* from 08. *The Vicarage, Church Street, St Neots PE19 2BU* Tel (01480) 472297 E-mail p.d.andrews@btinternet.com

ANDREWS, **Ms Penny**. b 73. Humberside Univ BA94 Liv Univ MA05. St Jo Coll Nottm 06. **d** 08. C Much Woolton *Liv* from 08. *25 Linkside Road, Liverpool L25 9NX* Tel 0151-428 9458 Mobile 07522-472272 E-mail revpenny@gmail.com

ANDREWS, **Peter Douglas**. b 52. SEN72 SRN78. St Steph Ho Ox 86. **d** 88 **p** 89. C Perry Barr *Birm* 88-92; TV Swindon New Town *Bris* 92-98; V Streatham St Pet *S'wark* from 98. *St Peter's Vicarage, 113 Leigham Court Road, London SW16 2NS* Tel (020) 8769 2922 E-mail frpeterandrews@aol.com

ANDREWS, **Raymond Cyril**. b 50. SEITE 00. **d** 03 **p** 04. C E Dulwich St Jo *S'wark* 03-07; P-in-c S'wark St Geo w St Alphege

and St Jude from 07. *St George's Rectory, Manciple Street, London SE1 4LW* Tel (020) 7407 2796 Mobile 07930-695571 E-mail revrayandrews@aol.com

ANDREWS, **Richard John**. b 57. Bris Univ BA78 CertEd79. Ripon Coll Cuddesdon 82. **d** 84 **p** 85. C Kidderminster St Mary and All SS, Trimpley etc *Worc* 84-87; Chapl Derbyshire Coll of HE 87-89; Hon C Derby Cathl 87-89; V Chellaston 89-93; V Spondon 93-05; TR Dunstable *St Alb* from 05; RD Dunstable from 09. *The Rectory, 8 Furness Avenue, Dunstable LU6 3BN* Tel (01582) 703271 E-mail rector@dunstableparish.org.uk

ANDREWS, **Robert**. *See* ANDREWS, Edward Robert

ANDREYEV, **Michael**. b 62. Hatf Coll Dur BA85. Wycliffe Hall Ox BA93 MA03. **d** 96 **p** 97. C Surbiton Hill Ch Ch *S'wark* 96-01; NSM Stapenhill w Cauldwell *Derby* 02-03; P-in-c 03-06; V from 06. *3 Stapenhill Road, Burton-on-Trent DE15 9AF* Tel (01283) 530320 E-mail staff@st.peters.fsnet.co.uk

ANETTS, **Roy**. b 55. Qu Coll Birm 06. **d** 09 **p** 10. NSM Acocks Green *Birm* from 09. *99 Vibart Road, Birmingham B26 2AB* Tel 0121-786 1674 Mobile 07967-542237 E-mail snowyanetts@hotmail.com

ANGEL, **Andrew Richard**. b 67. St Pet Coll Ox BA89 Lon Inst of Educn PGCE90 Surrey Univ MA94 Cant Ch Ch Univ MA06. St Jo Coll Nottm PhD04. **d** 02 **p** 03. C Dartford Ch Ch *Roch* 02-05; Tutor SEITE 05-10; Tutor St Jo Coll Nottm from 10. *St John's College, Chilwell Lane, Bramcote, Nottingham NG9 3DS* Tel 0115-925 1114 E-mail a.angel@stjohns-nottm.ac.uk

ANGEL, **Gervais Thomas David**. b 36. Ch Ch Ox BA59 MA62 Bris Univ MEd78 Lon Univ PGCE72, Wycliffe Hall Ox 57. **d** 61 **p** 62. C Aberystwyth St Mich *St D* 61-65; Tutor Clifton Th Coll 65-71; Dean of Studies Trin Coll Bris 71-81; Dir of Studies 81-90; Area Sec (W and SW) SAMS 90-02; NSM Stoke Gifford *Bris* 92-02; rtd 02; Perm to Offic *Bris* from 02. *8 Oak Close, Little Stoke, Bristol BS34 6RD* Tel (01454) 618081 Mobile 07967-441426 Fax 0117-904 8588 E-mail gervais.angel@blueyonder.co.uk

ANGEL, **Robin Alan**. b 41. St Mich Coll Llan. **d** 89 **p** 90. C Whitchurch *Llan* 89-94; V Abergpergwm and Blaengwrach 94-01; V Caerau w Ely 01-03; V Porth w Trealaw 03-06; rtd 06. *54 Mardy Crescent, Caerphilly CF83 1PU*

ANGELL, **Miss Elizabeth Patricia**. b 54. Univ of Wales (Ban) BA72. Trin Coll Bris BA08. **d** 08 **p** 09. C Fosse *Leic* from 08. *St Hilda's Vicarage, 25 Ling Dale, East Goscote, Leicester LE7 3XW* Tel 0116-260 0470 E-mail elizabethangell49@btinternet.com

ANGELL, **Geoffrey**. b 63. St Jo Coll Nottm. **d** 01 **p** 02. C Daventry, Ashby St Ledgers, Braunston etc *Pet* 01-04; C Oakham, Hambleton, Egleton, Braunston and Brooke 04-07; P-in-c Barrowden and Wakerley w S Luffenham etc from 07. *The Rectory, 11 Church Lane, Barrowden, Oakham LE15 8ED* Tel (01572) 747192 E-mail rector@artangells.com

ANGELO, **Brother**. *See* DEACON, Donald

ANGIER, **Patrick John Mark**. b 61. Leic Univ BSc83. Trin Coll Bris. **d** 03 **p** 04. C Stratford-upon-Avon, Luddington etc *Cov* 03-06; V Prestbury *Ches* from 06. *Meadowside, New Road, Prestbury, Macclesfield SK10 4HP* Tel (01625) 820246 Mobile 07971-923668 E-mail patrick.angier@btinternet.com

ANGLE, **John Edwin George**. b 42. Lon Bible Coll BD65 Liv Univ AdDipEd73 Univ of Wales MEd75. WEMTC 92. **d** 94 **p** 95. NSM Clevedon St Andr and Ch Ch *B & W* 94-97; NSM Worle 97-98; P-in-c Camelot Par 98-01; R 01-06; Warden of Readers Wells Adnry 02-05; rtd 06; Perm to Offic *B & W* from 06. *14 Farthing Combe, Axbridge BS26 2DR* Tel (01934) 733695 E-mail johnangle@btinternet.com

ANGOVE, **Ms Helen Teresa**. b 71. Bath Univ BEng93. Ripon Coll Cuddesdon BTh97. **d** 97 **p** 98. C Bridgwater St Mary, Chilton Trinity and Durleigh *B & W* 97-01; P-in-c Elstree *St Alb* 01-03; USA from 03. *150 N San Marino Avenue, Pasadena CA 91107, USA* Tel (001) (626) 793 7386 E-mail htangove@yahoo.com

ANGUS, **Canon Edward**. b 39. Man Univ BA60. Qu Coll Birm. **d** 62 **p** 63. C Chorley St Geo *Blackb* 62-65; C S Shore H Trin 65-68; R Bretherton 68-76; V Altham w Clayton le Moors 76-90; V Preesall 90-04; RD Garstang 96-01; Hon Can Blackb Cathl 98-04; rtd 04; Perm to Offic *Blackb* from 04. *14 Lazenby Avenue, Fleetwood FY7 8QH* Tel (01253) 686817

ANI, **Joel Osita**. b 72. Qu Coll Birm BA08. **d** 08 **p** 10. C Telford Park *S'wark* 08-09; C Clapham Park All SS from 09. *6 Blenheim Gardens, London SW2 5DB* Tel (020) 8674 1889 Mobile 07903-234444 E-mail joel ani123@yahoo.com

ANITA, **Sister**. *See* COOK, Sister Anita Isabel

ANKER, **Malcolm**. b 39. Univ of Wales BA61. Bps' Coll Cheshunt 61. **d** 63 **p** 64. C Marfleet *York* 63-66; C Cottingham 66-69; V Skirlaugh w Long Riston 69-74; V Elloughton and Brough w Brantingham 74-84; V Tadcaster 84-86; V Tadcaster w Newton Kyme 86-91; V Oatlands *Guildf* 91-05; rtd 05; Perm to Offic *Guildf* from 05. *10 Pegasus Close, Haslemere GU27 3SZ* Tel (01428) 651630

ANKER-PETERSEN, Robert Brian. b 52. Aber Univ MTh88. Wycliffe Hall Ox BA79 MA88. **d** 93 **p** 94. C Perth St Ninian *St And* 93-96; Bp's Researcher on Ch's Min of Healing from 93; Dir Bield Retreat and Healing Cen from 93; Dioc Dir of Healing from 97. *Blackruthven House, Tibbermore, Perth PH1 1PY* Tel (01738) 583238 Fax 583828 E-mail robin@bieldatblackruthven.org.uk

ANKERS, Canon Charles William (Bill). b 42. FIMI. NEOC 89. **d** 93 **p** 95. NSM York St Luke 93-95; C Kexby w Wilberfoss 95-98; Asst Chapl HM Pris Full Sutton 95-98; V Norton juxta Malton *York* 98-11; Can and Preb York Minster from 10; rtd 11; Perm to Offic *York* from 11. *10 Beechwood Road, Norton, Malton YO17 9EJ* Tel (01653) 693930

ANKETELL, Jeyarajan. b 41. Lon Univ BSc62 PhD67 MInstP. Coll of Resurr Mirfield 69. **d** 73 **p** 74. Asst Chapl Newc Univ 73-75; Asst Chapl Lon Univ 75-77; Teacher 78-05; Lic to Offic *S'wark* 81-83; Chasetown High Sch 85-05; NSM Lich St Mary w St Mich 86-96; NSM Lich St Mich w St Mary and Wall from 96. *7 Wissage Lane, Lichfield WS13 6DQ* Tel (01543) 268897 E-mail jeyan.anketell@ntlworld.com

ANN-MARIE, Sister. See STUART, Sister Ann-Marie Lindsay

ANNANCY, Felix. b 62. **d** 87 **p** 88. C Fenton *Lich* 87-88; Ghana 88-98 and from 00; C Stalybridge St Paul *Ches* 98-00. *PO Box 329, Aksombo, Eastern Region, Ghana*

✠**ANNAS, The Rt Revd Geoffrey Peter.** b 53. Sarum & Wells Th Coll. **d** 83 **p** 84 **c** 10. C S'wark H Trin w St Matt 83-87; TV Walworth 87-94; Warden Pemb Coll Miss Walworth 87-94; V Southampton Thornhill St Chris *Win* 94-10; Hon Can Win Cathl 07-10; Area Bp Stafford *Lich* from 10. *Ash Garth, Broughton Crescent, Barlaston, Stoke-on-Trent ST12 9DD* Tel (01782) 373308 Fax 373705 E-mail bishop.stafford@lichfield.anglican.org

ANNE, Sister. See PROUDLEY, Sister Anne

ANNIS, Herman North. b 28. Lich Th Coll 62. **d** 64 **p** 65. C Kilburn St Aug *Lon* 64-67; C Toxteth Park St Agnes *Liv* 67-70; V 70-82; V Hempton and Pudding Norton 82-84; P-in-c Sculthorpe w Dunton and Doughton 82-84; V Northampton H Trin *Pet* 84-95; rtd 95; Hon C Brighton St Bart *Chich* 95-99. *13 rue des Ormeaux, 53500 Montenay, France* Tel (0033) 2 43 13 09 54

ANNIS, Jennifer Mary. b 49. Middx Univ BA95. Oak Hill Th Coll 92. **d** 95 **p** 97. NSM Digswell and Panshanger *St Alb* 95-97; NSM Codicote 97-98 and 99-00; Tanzania 98-99; Chapl ATC from 99; NSM Fishguard w Llanychar and Pontfaen w Morfil etc *St D* from 10. *Glanafon, Trecwn, Haverfordwest SA62 5XT* Tel (01348) 840689

ANNIS, Rodney James. b 43. Ex Univ BA75 MA79 PhD86. Ripon Coll Cuddesdon 75. **d** 76 **p** 77. C Brixham *Ex* 76-77; Asst Chapl Ex Univ 77-80; Chapl Ex Sch 77-80; C Boston *Linc* 80-84; Chapl Trin Hall Cam 84-87; Chapl St Edw K and Martyr Cam *Ely* 84-87; V Bush Hill Park St Steph *Lon* from 87. *St Stephen's Vicarage, 43A Village Road, Enfield EN1 2ET*

ANNON, Jacqueline. b 62. **d** 01 **p** 02. OLM Tooting All SS *S'wark* 01-04. *31 Hamilton Road, London SE27 9RZ* Tel (020) 8670 7441

ANNS, Pauline Mary. See HIGHAM, Canon Pauline Mary

ANSAH, Canon Kwesi Gyebi Ababio (George). b 54. Oak Hill Th Coll BTh97. Simon of Cyrene Th Inst 90. **d** 93 **p** 94. C Peckham St Mary Magd *S'wark* 93-96; V W Dulwich Em from 96; Hon Can Kumasi from 04. *Emmanuel Vicarage, 94 Clive Road, London SE21 8BU* Tel (020) 8670 2793 Mobile 07771-783693 E-mail gkansa@aol.com

ANSCOMBE, John Thomas. b 51. Ex Univ BA72. Cranmer Hall Dur. **d** 74 **p** 75. C Upper Armley *Ripon* 74-77; C Leeds St Geo 78-81; Exec Producer Scripture Union 81-96; Hon C Beckenham Ch Ch *Roch* from 82. *22 Hawthornedene Road, Bromley BR2 7DY* Tel and fax (020) 8462 4831 Mobile 07736-070160 E-mail john.anscombe@diocese-rochester.org

ANSELL, Antony Michael. b 40. St Jo Coll Nottm 78. **d** 80 **p** 81. C Harrow Weald St Mich *Lon* 80-84; Hon C Ches Square St Mich w St Phil 86-88; Hon C Mayfair Ch Ch 88-02; Perm to Offic *Win* from 02. *Fullerton Mill, Fullerton, Andover SP11 7LA* Tel (01264) 861076 Mobile 07855-943615 E-mail a.ansell@andover.co.uk

ANSELL, John Christopher. b 49. Sarum & Wells Th Coll 79. **d** 81 **p** 82. C Dartford St Alb *Roch* 81-84; C Leybourne and Larkfield 84-88; TV Mortlake w E Sheen *S'wark* 88-98; V Mitcham SS Pet and Paul from 98. *The Vicarage, 11 Vicarage Gardens, Mitcham CR4 3BL* Tel (020) 8646 0666 *or* 8648 1566 Mobile 07974-432562 Fax (020) 8646 0778 E-mail jsansell@hotmail.com *or* mitchamparishchurch@uk2.net

ANSELL, Mrs Mandy. b 47. **d** 04 **p** 05. OLM Rockland St Mary w Hellington, Bramerton etc *Nor* from 04. *44 The Street, Rockland St Mary, Norwich NR14 7AH* Tel (01508) 538654 E-mail mandy.ansell44@gmail.com

ANSELL, Philip Harding. b 67. LMH Ox BA89 Rob Coll Cam BA92. Ridley Hall Cam. **d** 93 **p** 94. C Rainham w Wennington *Chelmsf* 93-97; C Rodbourne Cheney *Bris* 97-01; V Moseley

St Agnes *Birm* from 01. *St Agnes' Vicarage, 5 Colmore Crescent, Birmingham B13 9SJ* Tel and fax 0121-449 0368

ANSELM, Brother. See SMYTH, Robert Andrew Laine

ANSLOW, Mrs Patricia Margaret. b 49. Yorks Min Course 08. **d** 11. NSM Bramham *York* from 11. *4 Pine Tree Avenue, Boston Spa, Wetherby LS23 6HA* Tel (01937) 844789 Mobile 07903-262880 E-mail t.anslow@hotmail.co.uk

ANSON (née DRAX), Mrs Elizabeth Margaret. b 57. St Jo Coll Nottm 91. **d** 94 **p** 95. C Kimberworth *Sheff* 94-95; C Doncaster St Mary 95-97; rtd 97; Perm to Offic *Sheff* from 10. *62 School Green Lane, Sheffield S10 4GR* Tel 0114-229 5478

ANSON, Harry. b 35. FInstFF79. St Jo Coll Nottm 83. **d** 88 **p** 03. NSM Ayr *Glas* 88-93; Hon Chapl Miss to Seamen 91-93; rtd 94. *Fairview, Balbinny, Aberlemno, Forfar DD8 3PF* Tel and fax (01307) 830446 Mobile 07790-470660 E-mail h2avro@hotmail.com

ANSTEY, Nigel John. b 55. Cranmer Hall Dur 84. **d** 87 **p** 88. C Plumstead St Jo w St Jas and St Paul *S'wark* 87-91; TV Ipswich St Fran *St E* 91-97; TV Walthamstow *Chelmsf* from 97. *St Luke's Vicarage, 17A Greenleaf Road, London E17 6QQ* Tel (020) 8520 2885 E-mail nigel.anstey@btinternet.com

ANSTICE, John Neville. b 39. Lon Univ BSc63. Cuddesdon Coll 69. **d** 71 **p** 72. C Stonebridge St Mich *Lon* 71-74; Chapl Woodbridge Sch 74-76; TV Droitwich *Worc* 76-80; P-in-c Salwarpe 76-79; Perm to Offic *Chich* from 80; rtd 99. *10 Selham Close, Crawley RH11 0EH* Tel (01293) 535654

ANTELL, Roger Howard. b 47. Lon Univ BD71 Warwick Univ MSc79 Ox Univ MTh99. Ripon Coll Cuddesdon 97. **d** 99 **p** 00. C Ashchurch *Glouc* 99-03; R Stoke Prior, Wychbold and Upton Warren *Worc* from 03. *The Rectory, Fish House Lane, Stoke Prior, Bromsgrove B60 4JT* Tel (01527) 832501 E-mail roger.antell@btinternet.com

ANTHAPURUSHA. b 53. Bangalore Univ BA77 Jnana Deepa Vidyapeeth Poona BPh80 Delhi Univ MA83 MPhil84 Serampore Th Coll BD87. Bp's Coll Calcutta 85. **d** 87 **p** 88. India 87-99; Bethany Chr Trust Edin 01-02; C Bistre *St As* 02-09; C Wrexham from 09. *The Rectory, 7 Westminster Drive, Wrexham LL12 7AT* Tel (01978) 449166 E-mail apurusha@bronyreglwys.fsnet.co.uk

ANTHONY, Ian Charles. b 47. NW Ord Course 76. **d** 79 **p** 80. NSM Lt Lever *Man* from 79. *36 Meadow Close, Little Lever, Bolton BL3 1LG* Tel (01204) 791437

ANTHONY, Peter Benedict. b 79. Magd Coll Ox BA02 MA05. St Steph Ho Ox 03 Ven English Coll Rome 05. **d** 06 **p** 07. C Hendon St Mary and Ch Ch *Lon* 06-09; Jun Dean St Steph Ho Ox from 09; Jun Chapl Mert Coll Ox from 10. *St Stephen's House, 16 Marston Street, Oxford OX4 1JX* Tel (01865) 247874 Mobile 07949-005550 E-mail peterbanthony@hotmail.com

ANTHONY, Miss Sheila Margaret. b 52. Wycliffe Hall Ox BTh04. **d** 04 **p** 05. C Bideford, Northam, Westward Ho!, Appledore etc *Ex* 04-08; P-in-c Bluntisham cum Earith w Colne and Woodhurst *Ely* 08-10; P-in-c Holywell w Needingworth 08-10; V Bluntisham cum Earith w Colne and Holywell etc from 10. *The Rectory, Rectory Road, Bluntisham, Huntingdon PE28 3LN* Tel (01487) 740456 E-mail sheila@saintintraining.co.uk

ANTHONY MARY, Father. See HIRST, Anthony Melville

ANTOINE, Emma Louise. b 72. Newc Univ BA96. Westcott Ho Cam 02. **d** 05 **p** 06. C High Wycombe *Ox* 05-06; C Wokingham All SS 06-09. *The Rectory, 6 Edge Lane, Manchester M21 9JF* Tel 0161-881 3063 E-mail revemma@hotmail.co.uk

AOKO, Mrs Olushola Ibiwunmi. b 55. SEITE 03. **d** 06 **p** 07. C Bermondsey St Mary w St Olave, St Jo etc *S'wark* 06-10; TV St Laur in Thanet *Cant* from 10. *St Christopher's House, Kimberley Road, Ramsgate CT12 6HH* Tel (01843) 594160 Mobile 07896-337578 E-mail shol1012@yahoo.co.uk

AOTEAROA, Bishop of. See TUREI, The Most Revd William Brown

ap GWILYM, Gwynn. b 50. Univ of Wales (Ban) BA71 MA76. Wycliffe Hall Ox BA84 MA89 MPhil00. **d** 84 **p** 85. C Ynyscynhaearn w Penmorfa and Porthmadog *Ban* 84-86; R Penegoes and Darowen w Llanbrynn-Mair 86-97; R Mallwyd w Cemais, Llanymawddwy, Darowen etc 97-02; P-in-c Penyfai *Llan* 02-05; P-in-c Cardiff Dewi Sant 05-07; Language Officer Ch in Wales from 07. *The Rectory, Llandough Hill, Llandough, Penarth CF64 2NA* Tel (029) 2071 0890

ap IORWERTH, Geraint. b 50. Univ of Wales (Cardiff) MPhil90 Open Univ BA78. Burgess Hall Lamp 69 Westmr Past Foundn 73 St Mich Coll Llan 73. **d** 74 **p** 75. C Holyhead w Rhoscolyn *Ban* 74-78; R Pennal w Corris and Esgairgeiliog from 78; Co-Founder and Ldr Order of Sancta Sophia from 87. *The Rectory, Pennal, Machynlleth SY20 9JS* Tel and fax (01654) 791216 E-mail apennal@ouvip.com

APOKIS, Constantinos Fotios. b 61. Monash Univ BA82. Ridley Coll Melbourne BTh87 ACT MTh96. **d** 88 **p** 88. C Greythorn Australia 88-90; C Port Melbourne 90-91; P-in-c 91-93; Res Asst World Vision 93-95; Chapl and Manager Incolink Support Services Unit 96-99; Clergy Tr Officer *S'well* from 10. *Dunham*

House, 8 Westgate, Southwell NG25 0JL Tel (01636) 817208 Mobile 07827-291725 E-mail kon@southwell.anglican.org

APPELBE, Canon Frederick Charles. b 52. CITC 87. d 87 p 88. C Waterford w Killea, Drumcannon and Dunhill *C & O* 87-90; C Taney *D & G* 90-92; I Rathmichael from 92; Can Ch Ch Cathl Dublin from 02. *Rathmichael Rectory, Shankill, Co Dublin, Republic of Ireland* Tel (00353) (1) 282 2803 Fax 258 6080 Mobile 87-248 2410 E-mail rathmichael@dublin.anglican.org

APPLEBY, Anthony Robert Nightingale. b 40. K Coll Lon AKC62. St Boniface Warminster 62. d 63 p 64. C Cov St Mark 63-67; CF 67-95; R Dulverton and Brushford *B & W* 95-02; rtd 02. *9 Ashleigh Park, Bampton, Tiverton EX16 9LF* Tel (01398) 331122

APPLEBY, David. b 60. St Jo Coll Dur BA04. Cranmer Hall Dur 02. d 04 p 05. C W Acklam *York* 04-08; R Aylestone St Andr w St Jas *Leic* from 08. *9 Springfield Road, Leicester LE2 3BB* Tel 0116-270 8295

APPLEBY, Janet Elizabeth. b 58. Bris Univ BSc80 MSc81 Newc Poly BA90. Cranmer Hall Dur 01. d 03 p 04. C Newc H Cross 03-06; TV Willington from 06. *The Vicarage, Berwick Drive, Wallsend NE28 9ED* Tel 0191-262 7518 E-mail janet.appleby@dunelm.org.uk

APPLEBY, Miss Janet Mohr. b 32. Lon Univ TCert53 BA79 Sussex Univ MA(Ed)74. Chich Th Coll 90. d 91 p 95. NSM Rottingdean *Chich* 91-95; NSM Stantonbury and Willen *Ox* 95-02; Perm to Offic 02-07. *Address temp unknown*

APPLEBY, Ms Jennie. b 58. Southlands Coll Lon CertEd81. Cranmer Hall Dur 01. d 03 p 04. C Marton-in-Cleveland *York* 03-03, C Coatham and Dormanstown 03-08, R Emmaus Par Team *Leic* from 08. *The Rectory, 9 Springfield Road, Leicester LE2 3BB* Tel 0116-270 6097

APPLEBY, Mrs Melanie Jayne. b 65. RGN86. Ripon Coll Cuddesdon 01. d 03 p 04. C Reddish *Man* 03-06; TV Wythenshawe from 06. *William Temple Vicarage, Robinswood Road, Manchester M22 0BU* Tel 0161-437 3194 Mobile 07876-191572 E-mail melanieappleby@hotmail.com

APPLEFORD, Kenneth Henry. b 30. Portsm Dioc Tr Course 91. d 92. NSM Portsea St Mary *Portsm* 92-00; rtd 00. *124 Stride Avenue, Portsmouth PO3 6HN* Tel (023) 9281 4685

APPLEFORD, Canon Patrick Robert Norman. b 25. Trin Coll Cam BA49 MA54. Chich Th Coll 50. d 52 p 53. C Poplar All SS w St Frideswide *Lon* 52-58; Chapl Bps' Coll Cheshunt 58-61; Educn Sec USPG 61-66; Dean Lusaka 66-72; P-in-c Sutton St Nicholas w Sutton St Michael *Heref* 73-75; Dir of Educn *Chelmsf* 75-90; Can Chelmsf Cathl 78-90; rtd 90; Perm to Offic *Chelmsf* from 90. *35 Sowerberry Close, Chelmsford CM1 4YB* Tel (01245) 443508

APPLEGATE, The Ven John. b 56. Bris Univ BSc78. Trin Coll Bris PhD85. d 84 p 85. C Collyhurst *Man* 84-87; Asst Chapl Monsall Hosp 84-87; C Broughton St Jas w St Clem and St Matthias 87-94; R Broughton St Jo 94-96; TR Broughton 96-02; AD Salford 97-02; Research Fell and Lect Man Univ from 00; Bp's Adv Hosp Chapl 02-08; Adn Bolton 02-08; Dir SNWTP from 08. *University of Chester, Crab Lane, Warrington WA2 0DB* Tel (01925) 534373 E-mail snwtpprincipal@chester.ac.uk

APPLETON, Mrs Bonita. b 55. Man Univ MA08. St Jo Coll Nottm 91. d 93 p 94. C Camberley St Paul *Guildf* 93-96; Chapl Elmhurst Ballet Sch 95-96; TV Cove St Jo *Guildf* 96-03; Chapl Farnborough Sixth Form Coll 97-00; Dioc Par Resources Officer *Guildf* 03-10; NSM Knaphill w Brookwood 05-10; TR S Gillingham *Roch* from 10. *The Rectory, 4 Drewery Drive, Wigmore, Gillingham ME8 0NX* Tel (01634) 231071 E-mail bonnie@babusinessconsultancy.co.uk

APPLETON, John Bearby. b 42. Linc Th Coll 74. d 76 p 77. C Selby Abbey *York* 76-79; C Epsom St Barn *Guildf* 79-82; V Line All SS 82-94; rtd 02. *33 South End, Osmotherley, Northallerton DL6 3BN*

APPLIN, David Edward. b 39. Oak Hill Th Coll 63. d 65 p 66. C Ox St Clem 65-69; C Felixstowe SS Pet and Paul *St E* 69-71; Lic to Offic 69-71; Travelling Sec Ruanda Miss 71-74; Home Sec 74-77; Gen Sec 77-81; Dir Overseas Personnel Dept TEAR Fund 82-87; Overseas Dir 87-92; Hon C Kempshott *Win* 91-92; R Awbridge w Sherfield English 92-97; Exec Dir Samaritan's Purse Internat from 95. *Flat 4, 25 Christchurch Road, St Cross, Winchester SO23 9SU* Tel (01962) 865678

APPS, Bryan Gerald. b 37. Univ of Wales (Lamp) BA59 St Cath Coll Ox BA61 MA65. Wycliffe Hall Ox 59. d 61 p 62. C Southampton St Alb *Win* 61-65; C Andover w Foxcott 65-69; P-in-c Freemantle 69-72; R 73-78; V Pokesdown All SS 78-03; rtd 03; Hon C Bournemouth Town Cen *Win* from 03. *14 Bartlett Drive, Bournemouth BH7 7JT* Tel (01202) 418360 E-mail bryanapps@talk21.com

APPS, David Ronald. b 34. Univ of Wales (Lamp) BA57. Sarum Th Coll 57. d 59 p 60. C Southbourne St Chris *Win* 59-62; C Weeke 62-67; V Alton All SS 67-80; V Charlestown *Truro* 80-97; Miss to Seamen 80-97; rtd 99. *12 Walnut Close, Exminster, Exeter EX6 8SZ* Tel (01392) 823672

APPS-HUGGINS, Mrs Lorraine Georgina. b 63. d 10 p 11. OLM Deal St Geo *Cant* from 10. *Dayspring House, 1 Gilham Grove, Deal CT14 9AX* Tel (01304) 379010 E-mail appshuggins@btinternet.com

APTHORP, The Ven Arthur Norman. b 24. Pemb Coll Cam BA47 MA50. Chich Th Coll 48. d 50 p 51. C Henfield *Chich* 50-52; C Hove All SS 52-56; R Narembeen Australia 57-60; R Boulder 60-66; R Northam 66-72; R Kalgoorlie and Boulder 72-78; Hon Can Perth 73-77 and 79-89; R Dianella 78-82; R Merredin 82-89; Adn of the Country (Perth) 82-87; Adn of the Goldfields 87-89; rtd 89. *67 Brookton Highway, Brookton WA 6306, Australia* Tel (0061) (8) 9642 1046

AQUILON-ELMQVIST, Mrs Gunilla. p 91. Sweden 91-05; C Wexford w Ardcolm and Killurin *C & O* 05-10; I Norra Asum Sweden from 10. *Kustvägen 54, 294 74 Sölvesborg, Sweden* E-mail gunilla.aquilon-elmqvist@svenskakyrkan.se

ARANZULLA, John Paul. b 71. G&C Coll Cam BA94 Oak Hill Th Coll BA01. K Coll Lon 01. d 04 p 05. C Muswell Hill St Jas w St Matt *Lon* 04-08; Crosslinks Italy from 08. *via Guibotti 14, 40134 Bologna, Italy*

ARBER, Gerald Kenneth Walter. b 37. Open Univ BA87. Oak Hill NSM Course 81. d 84 p 85. NSM Romford St Edw *Chelmsf* 84-95; NSM Cranham from 95. *5 Hill Grove, Romford RM1 4JP* Tel (01708) 750070

ARBUTHNOT, Paul Ian. b 81. TCD BA03 MA06 MLitt07. CITC BTh10. d 10 p 11. C Glenageary *D & G* from 10. *10 St Catherine's Road, Glenageary, Co Dublin, Republic of Ireland* Tel (00353) (1) 280 5478 Mobile 87-661 3383 E-mail paul.arbuthnot@gmail.com

ARCH, Ian Michael. b 75. Univ Coll Dur MSc97 Peterho Cam BA02. Westcott Ho Cam 00. d 03 p 04. C Bromborough *Ches* 03-05; Chapl Ches Univ from 05; Dean of Chpl from 10. *85 Parkgate Road, Chester CH1 4AQ* Tel (01244) 372003 or 375444 Fax 398820 E-mail ian.arch@dunelm.org.uk

ARCHER, Alan Robert. b 38. AKC56. Lich Th Coll 65. d 68 p 69. C Lower Mitton *Worc* 68-71; C Foley Park 71-74; V Warndon 74-79; P-in-c Clifton upon Teme 79-81; P-in-c Lower Sapey 79-81; P-in-c The Shelsleys 79-81; V Malvern Wells and Wyche 81-83; TV Braunstone *Leic* 83-91; P-in-c Bemerton *Sarum* 91-03; Dioc Link Officer for ACUPA 92-94; rtd 03. *15 Summerfield Road, Stourport-on-Severn DY13 9BE* Tel (01299) 822983

ARCHER, David John. b 69. Reading Univ BSc91 PhD95 Cam Univ BTh05. Ridley Hall Cam 02. d 05 p 06. C Abingdon *Ox* 05-09; R Purley from 09. *The Rectory, 1 Westridge Avenue, Purley on Thames, Reading RG8 8DE* Tel 0118-326 0839 E-mail david.archer@stmaryspurley.org.uk

ARCHER, Canon Graham John. b 58. Lanc Univ BSc79. St Jo Coll Nottm 82. d 85 p 86. C Ipswich St Matt *St E* 85-89; C Walton 89-95; P-in-c 95-99; Chapl Local Health Partnerships NHS Trust 96-99; P-in-c Portswood Ch Ch *Win* 99-05; V from 05; P-in-c Portswood St Denys 00-02; Hon Can Win Cathl from 11. *The Vicarage, 36 Brookvale Road, Southampton SO17 1QR* Tel (023) 8055 4277 E-mail vicar@highfield.org.uk

ARCHER, John Thomas. b 62. GIMechE68 CQSW83. EMMTC 79. d 80 p 81. NSM Derby St Thos 80-86; V Edlington *Sheff* 87-98; rtd 98; Perm to Offic *Lich* 04-10. *Little Croft, 20 Adderley, Cheadle, Stoke-on-Trent ST10 2NJ* Tel (01538) 751541

ARCHER, Keith Malcolm. b 40. Man Univ BA61 MA80 Magd Coll Cam BA67 MA72. Ridley Hall Cam 66. d 68 p 69. C Newland St Jo *York* 68-72; Hon C Kersal Moor *Man* 72-79; Ind Chapl 72-93; V Weaste 93-09; TV Pendleton 08-09; TV Salford All SS 09-10; rtd 10; Perm to Offic *Man* from 11. *Flat 2, 86-88 Wellington Road, Eccles, Manchester M30 9GW* Tel 07943-366502 (mobile) E-mail keitharcher@hotmail.co.uk

ARCHER, Michael James. b 67. St Jo Coll Dur BA90 St Edm Coll Cam PhD95. Ridley Hall Cam 92. d 94 p 95. C Littleover *Derby* 94-97; C Edgware *Lon* 97-98; TV 98-01; P-in-c Bletchley *Ox* 01-08; R from 08. *101 Whalley Drive, Bletchley, Milton Keynes MK3 6HX* Tel (01908) 630305

ARCHER, Michael John. b 37. Trin Coll Bris 76. d 78 p 79. C Kinson *Sarum* 78-81; C Harpenden St Nic *St Alb* 81-88; P-in-c Rashcliffe and Lockwood *Wakef* 88-00; rtd 00; Perm to Offic *Truro* from 02. *Seaview Cottage, Porthallow, Helston TR12 6PW* Tel (01326) 280502

ARCHER, Neill John. b 61. UEA BA82. NTMTC 96. d 99 p 00. C Ripley *Derby* 99-02; C Forster Tuncurry Australia 02-03; Perm to Offic *Lon* 03-04; P-in-c Malmesbury w Westport and Brokenborough *Bris* from 04; C Gt Somerford, Lt Somerford, Seagry, Corston etc from 04; AD N Wilts from 09. *The Vicarage, Holloway, Malmesbury SN16 9BA* Tel (01666) 823126 Mobile 07946-540720 E-mail neilljarcher@tiscali.co.uk

ARCHER, Sarah Elizabeth. See HARTLEY, Sarah Elizabeth

ARCHIBALD, Peter Ben. b 83. Robert Gordon Univ Aber BSc04. St Steph Ho Ox BTh08. d 08 p 09. C Middlesbrough All SS *York* from 08; Lead Chapl Middlesbrough Coll from 09. *14 Chipchase Road, Middlesbrough TS5 6EY* Tel (01642) 827196 Mobile 07793-535628 E-mail benarchibald@hotmail.com

ARCUS, Jeffrey. b 40. NW Ord Course 72. d 75 p 76. C Halliwell St Thos *Man* 75-78; C Walmsley 78-81; P-in-c Bury Ch King

81-82; TV Bury Ch King w H Trin 82-93; V Ramsbottom St Jo and St Paul '93-05; C Edenfield and Stubbins 04-05; TV Ramsbottom and Edenfield 05-08; rtd 08; Perm to Offic *Man* from 08. *The Gatehouse, Egerton House Hotel, Blackburn Road, Egerton, Bolton BL7 9PL* Tel (01204) 303149

ARDAGH-WALTER, Christopher Richard. b 35. Univ of Wales (Lamp) BA58. Chich Th Coll 58. **d** 60 **p** 61. C Heavitree *Ex* 60-64; C Redcar *York* 64-67; C King's Worthy *Win* 67-69; C-in-c Four Marks CD 70-73; V Four Marks 73-76; P-in-c Eling, Testwood and Marchwood 76-78; TR Totton 76-84; R The Sherbornes w Pamber 84-88; V Froyle and Holybourne 88-95; C Verwood *Sarum* 95-97; rtd 97; Perm to Offic *Win* from 98 and *Ox* from 01. *2 Bunkers Hill, Newbury RG14 6TF* Tel (01635) 41128 E-mail ctaw@a-walter.freeserve.co.uk

✠**ARDEN, The Rt Revd Donald Seymour.** b 16. CBE81. Leeds Univ BA37. Coll of Resurr Mirfield 37. **d** 39 **p** 40 **c** 61. C Hatcham St Cath *S'wark* 39-40; C Potten End w Nettleden *St Alb* 41-43; Asst P Pretoria African Miss S Africa 44-51; Dir Usuthu Miss Swaziland 51-61; Can Zululand 59-61; Bp Nyasaland 61-64; Bp Malawi 64-71; Bp S Malawi 71-81; Abp Cen Africa 71-80; P-in-c Uxbridge St Marg *Lon* 81-86; Asst Bp Willesden 81-94; Hon Asst Bp Lon 94-11; rtd 86; Hon C N Harrow St Alb *Lon* 86-11. *28 Mill Lane, Romsey SO51 8EU* Tel (01794) 524171 E-mail ardendj@yahoo.co.uk

ARDERN, Geoffrey. b 47. Cliff Coll MA04. SNWTP 09. **d** 11. NSM Maghull and Melling *Liv* from 11. *22 Waltho Avenue, Liverpool L31 6BE* Tel 0151-527 1383 E-mail ardernhouse@aol.com

ARDILL, Robert William Brian. b 40. QUB BSc63 PhD67 SOSc. Ox NSM Course 80 St Jo Coll Nottm 84. **d** 83 **p** 85. NSM Sunninghill *Ox* 83-84; Hon Chapl R Holloway Coll *Lon* 83-84; C Lenton *S'well* 85-87; Perm to Offic *Leic* 92-95; C Harpenden St Nic *St Alb* 95-00; R N Tawton, Bondleigh, Sampford Courtenay etc *Ex* 00-10; rtd 10. *8 Hanover Gardens, Cullompton EX15 1XA* Tel (01884) 798386 E-mail brian.ardill@googlemail.com

ARDING, Richard. b 52. ACIB84. Oak Hill Th Coll 90. **d** 92 **p** 93. C Bromley Common St Aug *Roch* 92-96; V Wilmington from 96; RD Dartford from 07. *The Vicarage, 1 Curate's Walk, Dartford DA2 7BJ* Tel (01322) 220561 Mobile 07773-104767 E-mail richard.arding@diocese-rochester.org

ARDIS, Canon Edward George. b 54. Dur Univ BA76. CITC 76. **d** 78 **p** 79. C Dublin Drumcondra w N Strand and St Barn *D & G* 78-81; C Dublin St Bart w Leeson Park 81-84; I Ardamine w Kiltennel, Glascarrig etc *C & O* 84-89; Can Tuam Cathl 89-03; Dean Killala 89-03; I Killala w Dunfeeny, Crossmolina etc 89-94; I Killala w Dunfeeny, Crossmolina, Kilmoremoy etc 94-03; Dir of Ords 95-03; I Dublin Irishtown w Donnybrook *D & G* from 03; Can Ch Ch Cathl Dublin from 08. *St Mary's Rectory, 4 Ailesbury Grove, Donnybrook, Dublin 4, Republic of Ireland* Tel (00353) (1) 269 2090 Mobile 87-419 6071 E-mail donnybrook@dublin.anglican.org

ARDIS, John Kevin. d 06 **p** 07. C Dublin Ch Ch Cathl Gp 06-08; Dean's V Cork St Fin Barre's Union *C, C & R* 08-11; Chapl Univ Coll Cork from 11. *13 The Grove, Orchard Road, Cork, Republic of Ireland* Tel (00353) (21) 434 8645 *or* 490 2444 Mobile 87-680 7289 E-mail j.ardis@ucc.ie

ARDLEY, Annett Susan. See ROSE, Annette Susan

ARDOUIN, Timothy David Peter. Univ of Wales (Lamp) BA94 Univ of Wales (Cardiff) MTh08. St Mich Coll Llan. **d** 08 **p** 09. C Gorseinon *S & B* 08-11; P-in-c Llanrhidian w Llanyrnewydd from 11. *The Vicarage, Llanrhidian, Swansea SA3 1EH* Tel (01792) 391353 Mobile 07871-420089 E-mail fr.tim.ardouin@sky.com

ARENS, Canon Johannes. b 69. Heythrop Coll *Lon* MTh97. **d** 96 **p** 97. Old Catholic Ch Germany 96-04; TV Harrogate St Wilfrid *Ripon* 04-06; V Manston 06-11; Can Res Leic Cathl from 11. *15 Rookery Close, Leicester LE5 4DQ* Tel 0116-246 1230 E-mail johannes.arens@gmx.net

ARGENTINA, Bishop of. See VENABLES, The Most Revd Gregory James

ARGLES, Mrs Christine. b 57. Bris Univ BA00. Trin Coll Bris 00. **d** 02 **p** 03. C Nailsea Ch Ch w Tickenham *B & W* 02-05; Chapl Weston Area Health Trust 05-07; Chapl Cardiff and Vale NHS Trust from 07. *Cardiff and Vale NHS Trust, Cardigan House, Heath Park, Cardiff CF14 4XW* Tel (029) 2074 7747 Mobile 07763-476127 E-mail chrisargles@aol.com

ARGUILE, Canon Roger Henry William. b 43. Dur Univ LLB64 Keble Coll Ox BA70 MA75. St Steph Ho Ox 69 Ripon Hall Ox 70. **d** 71 **p** 72. C Walsall *Lich* 71-76; TV Blakenall Heath 76-83; TV Stafford 83-95; P-in-c St Neots *Ely* 95-97; V 97-07; Hon Can Ely Cathl 01-07; RD St Neots 02-07; rtd 07. *10 Marsh Lane, Wells-next-the-Sea NR23 1EG* Tel (01328) 711788 E-mail arguile@btinternet.com

ARGYLE, Douglas Causer. b 17. St Jo Coll Cam BA39 MA43. Ridley Hall Cam 39. **d** 41 **p** 42. C Somercotes *Derby* 41-44; CF (EC) 44-47; Chapl Repton Sch *Derby* 47-59; Chapl Gresham's Sch Holt 59-74; P-in-c Eastleach w Southrop *Glouc* 74-82; rtd 82;

Perm to Offic *Glouc* from 82. *East Lynn, London Road, Fairford GL7 4AR* Tel (01285) 713235

ARGYLE, Edward Charles. b 55. Edith Cowan Univ (Aus) BSocSc99. St Barn Coll Adelaide 77. **d** 80 **p** 80. C Whitford Australia 80-82; C Gt Yarmouth *Nor* 83-85; I Kilcooley w Littleon, Crohane and Fertagh *C & O* 85-94; Can Ossory and Leighlin Cathls 90-94; Min Cranbrook w Mt Barker Australia 95-05; R Albany 02-05; P-in-c Jerramungup 05-07; P-in-c Williams from 07. *14 Adam Street, PO Box 113, Williams WA 6391, Australia* Tel (0061) (8) 9885 1174 Mobile 428-514119 E-mail edwarda@westnet.com.au

ARGYLL AND THE ISLES, Bishop of. See PEARSON, The Rt Revd Kevin

ARGYLL AND THE ISLES, Dean of. See MacCALLUM, The Very Revd Norman Donald

ARKELL, Kevin Paul. b 53. Preston Poly BTh86 Leeds Univ MA95. Sarum & Wells Th Coll 84. **d** 86 **p** 87. C S Petherton w the Seavingtons *B & W* 86-88; P-in-c Gt Harwood St Bart *Blackb* 88-90; V 90-95; TR Darwen St Pet w Hoddlesden 95-03; Acting RD Darwen 97-98; AD Blackb and Darwen 98-03; P-in-c Pokesdown All SS *Win* 03-11; P-in-c Bournemouth St Clem 08-11; V Newport St Thos *Portsm* from 11; V Newport St Jo from 11. *The Vicarage, 72A Medina Avenue, Newport PO30 1HF* Tel (01983) 539580 Mobile 07971-800083 E-mail kevin@thearkells.co.uk

ARMAGH, Archbishop of. See HARPER, The Most Revd Alan Edwin Thomas

ARMAGH, Archdeacon of. See HOEY, The Ven Raymond George

ARMAGH, Dean of. *Vacant*

ARMAN, Canon Brian Robert. b 54. St Jo Coll Dur BA77. Cranmer Hall Dur 74. **d** 78 **p** 79. C Lawrence Weston *Bris* 78-82; C Bishopston 82-88; R Filton from 88; P-in-c Horfield St Greg 03-05; Hon Can Bris Cathl from 01. *The Rectory, Station Road, Bristol BS34 7BE* Tel 0117-979 1128

ARMES, The Very Revd John Andrew. b 55. SS Coll Cam BA77 MA81 Man Univ PhD96. Sarum & Wells Th Coll 77. **d** 79 **p** 80. C Walney Is *Carl* 79-82; Chapl to Agric 82-86; TV Greystoke, Matterdale and Mungrisdale 82-86; TV Watermillock 82-86; TV Man Whitworth 86-88; TR 88-94; Chapl Man Univ 86-94; P-in-c Goodshaw and Crawshawbooth 94-98; AD Rossendale 94-98; R Edin St Jo from 98; Dean Edin from 10. *1 Ainslie Place, Edinburgh EH3 6AR* Tel 0131-225 5004 *or* 229 7565 Fax 229 2561 E-mail johnarmes@btconnect.com

ARMITAGE, Richard Norris. b 51. Birm Univ PhD10 AKC. St Aug Coll Cant 73. **d** 74 **p** 75. C Chapelthorpe *Wakef* 74-77; C W Bromwich All SS *Lich* 77-82; P-in-c Ketley 82-83; V Oakengates 82-83; V Ketley and Oakengates 83-89; V Evesham *Worc* 89-96; V Evesham w Norton and Lenchwick 96-05; RD Evesham 00-05; Chapl Wilts Constabulary *Bris* from 05. *The Rectory, Churchway, Blunsdon, Swindon SN26 7DG* Tel (01793) 729592 E-mail richard.armitage@wiltshire.pnn.police.uk

ARMITAGE, Susan. b 46. Th Ext Educn Coll 91. **d** 92 **p** 95. Pretoria Corpus Christi S Africa 92-97; C Fawley *Win* 97-00; C Chandler's Ford 00-04; TV Wylye and Till Valley *Sarum* 04-11; rtd 11. *36 St Margaret's Mead, Marlborough SN8 4BA* Tel (01672) 513678 E-mail suearmitage@savernake.com

ARMITSTEAD, Margaretha Catharina Maria. b 65. Free Univ of Amsterdam MA89. SAOMC 00. **d** 03 **p** 04. C Littlemore *Ox* 03-06; P-in-c from 06. *The Vicarage, St Nicholas Road, Oxford OX4 4PP* Tel (01865) 748003 E-mail margreetarmitstead@btinternet.com

ARMITT, Andy John. b 68. Moorlands Bible Coll 88 Trin Coll Bris BA00. **d** 00 **p** 01. C Millhouses H Trin *Sheff* 00-03; R Bisley and W End *Guildf* from 03. *The Rectory, Clews Lane, Bisley, Woking GU24 9DY* Tel and fax (01483) 473377 Mobile 07811-909782 E-mail parishofbisleyandwestend@hotmail.com

ARMSON, Canon John Moss. b 39. Selw Coll Cam BA61 MA64 St Andr Univ PhD65. Coll of Resurr Mirfield 64. **d** 66 **p** 67. C Notting Hill St Jo *Lon* 66-69; Chapl and Fell Down Coll Cam 69-73; Chapl Westcott Ho Cam 73-76; Vice-Prin 76-82; Prin Edin Th Coll 82-89; Can St Mary's Cathl 82-89; Can Res Roch Cathl 89-01; rtd 01; Member Hengrave Ecum Community 01-03; Perm to Offic *Heref* from 03. *Mill Bank, Rowlestone, Hereford HR2 0DS* Tel (01981) 241046 E-mail j.armson@virgin.net

ARMSTEAD, Geoffrey Malcolm. b 32. K Coll Lon BD56 AKC56 Nottm Univ AdDipEd73 Heythrop Coll Lon MA05. St Boniface Warminster 56. **d** 57 **p** 57. C Weymouth H Trin *Sarum* 57-60; C Mortlake w E Sheen *S'wark* 60-63; Chapl Em Sch Wandsworth 63-74; Dep Hd Master Harriet Costello Sch 74-91; Acting Hd Master 91-92; Perm to Offic *Win* 74-92 and from 01; V Win St Bart 92-01; rtd 01. *Polecat Cottage, Polecat Corner, Tunworth, Basingstoke RG25 2LA* Tel (01256) 471650 E-mail geoffrey@armstead.freeserve.co.uk

ARMSTEAD, Paul Richard. b 63. Ox Poly BA85 ACA89 FCA99. St Steph Ho Ox BTh11. **d** 08 **p** 09. C Northampton St Matt *Pet* from 08. *89 Park Avenue North, Northampton NN3 2HX* Tel (01604) 710062 E-mail curate@stmatthews-northampton.org.uk

ARMSTRONG, Adrian Christopher. b 48. LSE BSc70 K Coll Lon PhD80. EAMTC 84. **d** 87 **p** 88. NSM Linton *Ely* 87-95; P-in-c N and S Muskham *S'well* 95-00; P-in-c Averham w Kelham 95-00; Perm to Offic *B & W* 01-02; Hon C Wiveliscombe w Chipstable, Huish Champflower etc 02-06; Hon C Lydeard St Lawrence w Brompton Ralph etc 06-09; rtd 10. *Cridlands Barn, Brompton Ralph, Taunton TA4 2RU* Tel (01984) 632191 E-mail drmudpie@aol.com

ARMSTRONG, Alexander Milford. b 57. **d** 95 **p** 95. NSM Livingston LEP *Edin* 95-97; C Cleator Moor w Cleator *Carl* 97-98; C Frizington and Arlecdon 97-98; C Crosslacon 98-99; V Westfield St Mary 99-10; P-in-c Aldingham, Dendron, Rampside and Urswick from 10. *The Vicarage, Church Road, Great Urswick, Ulverston LA12 0TA* Tel (01229) 581383 E-mail amvarmstrong@hotmail.com

ARMSTRONG, The Very Revd Christopher John. b 47. Nottm Univ BTh75. Kelham Th Coll 72. **d** 75 **p** 76. C Maidstone All SS w St Phil and H Trin *Cant* 76-79; Chapl St Hild and St Bede Coll *Dur* 79-84; Abp's Dom Chapl and Dir of Ords *York* 85-91; V Scarborough St Martin 91-01; Dean Blackb from 01. *The Deanery, Preston New Road, Blackburn BB2 6PS* Tel (01254) 52502 *or* 51491 Fax 689666 E-mail dean@blackburn.anglican.org

ARMSTRONG, Christopher John Richard. b 35. Fribourg Univ LTh60 Ch Coll Cam BA64 MA68 PhD79. Edin Th Coll 74. **d** 59 **p** 59. In RC Ch 59-71; Lect Aber Univ 68-74; C Ledbury *Heref* 74-76; P-in-c Bredenbury and Wacton w Grendon Bishop 76-79; P-in-c Edwyn Ralph and Collington w Thornbury 76-79; P-in-c Pencombe w Marston Stannett and Lt Cowarne 76-79; R Cherry Burton *York* 79-80; Tutor Westcott Ho Cam 80-85; V Bottisham *Ely* 85-89; P-in-c Lode and Longmeadow 85-89; P-in-c Cropthorne w Charlton *Worc* 89-93; Dioc Local Min Sec 89-93; R Aberdaron w Rhiw and Llanfaelrhys etc *Ban* 93-99; rtd 99; Perm to Offic *Heref* and *Ban* 99-06; *Bradf* from 06. *52 Bradford Road, Burley in Wharfedale, Ilkley LS29 7PU* Tel (01943) 864761

ARMSTRONG, Eileen. **d** 95 **p** 96. NSM *M & K* from 95. *Hennigan, Nobber, Co Meath, Republic of Ireland* Tel (00353) (46) 905 2314

ARMSTRONG, John Edwin. b 51. Leic Univ CertEd73 BEd74. Ridley Hall Cam 91. **d** 93 **p** 94. C Gt Wilbraham *Ely* 93-96; P-in-c Bassingbourn 96-02; V 02-04; P-in-c Whaddon 96-02; V 02-04; P-in-c Southam *Cov* from 04; P-in-c Ufton from 04; RD Southam from 08. *The Rectory, Park Lane, Southam, Leamington Spa CV47 0JA* Tel (01926) 812413 E-mail revarmstrong@yahoo.com

ARMSTRONG, John Gordon. b 64. Man Poly BSc86 MSc91 Man Univ MA03. Wycliffe Hall Ox 95. **d** 97 **p** 98. C Pennington *Man* 97-01; P-in-c Holcombe and Hawkshaw Lane 01-07; TV Deane from 07. *St Andrew's Vicarage, Crescent Avenue, Over Hulton, Bolton BL5 1EN* Tel (01204) 651851 E-mail armstrongfamily@ntlworld.com

ARMSTRONG, Mrs Margaret Betty. b 48. SRN70 RSCN71. Westcott Ho Cam 89. **d** 92 **p** 94. NSM Linton *Ely* 92-95; NSM Shudy Camps 92-95; NSM Castle Camps 92-95; NSM Bartlow 92-95; NSM N and S Muskham and Averham w Kelham *S'well* 95-00; P-in-c Lydeard St Lawrence w Brompton Ralph etc *B & W* 01-09; rtd 10. *Cridlands Barn, Brompton Ralph, Taunton TA4 2RU* Tel (01984) 623191 E-mail wheelievicar@aol.com

ARMSTRONG, Maurice Alexander. b 62. Ulster Poly BA84. CITC 84. **d** 87 **p** 88. C Portadown St Mark *Arm* 87-90; I Sixmilecross w Termonmaguirke 90-95; I Richhill 95-01; I Tempo and Clabby *Clogh* from 01. *The Rectory, Clabby, Fivemiletown BT75 0RD* Tel (028) 8952 1697

ARMSTRONG, Nicholas Paul. b 68. Bris Univ BSc79. Trin Coll Bris 91. **d** 93 **p** 94. C Filey *York* 93-97; P-in-c Alveley and Quatt *Heref* 97-98; R from 98. *The Rectory, Alveley, Bridgnorth WV15 6ND* Tel and fax (01746) 780326 E-mail nicka@inbox.com

ARMSTRONG, Robert Charles (**Robin**). b 24. TCD BA46 HDipEd52 MA57. CITC 47. **d** 47 **p** 48. C Belfast St Luke *Conn* 48-50; Warden Gr Sch Dub 50-59; Succ St Patr Cathl Dublin 50-59; I Dublin Finglas *D & G* 59-67; I Dun Laoghaire 67-94; Dir of Ords (Dub) 74-84; USPG Area Sec 77-94; Can Ch Ch Cathl Dublin 84-88; Treas 88-94; rtd 94. *Brabazon House, 2 Gilford Road, Sandymount, Dublin 4, Republic of Ireland*

ARMSTRONG, Rosemary. See WYNN, Rosemary

ARMSTRONG, Samuel David. b 48. SD MTh. **d** 86 **p** 87. C Cambridge H Trin w St Andr Gt *Ely* 86-89; V Cambridge St Martin 89-00; I Carrigaline Union *C, C & R* 00-11; rtd 11. *11 Castlerocklands, Carrickfergus BT38 8FY*

ARMSTRONG, Samuel George. b 39. Ox Univ Inst of Educn TCert65 Open Univ BA72 Reading Univ MSc89. S Dios Minl Tr Scheme 90. **d** 93 **p** 94. NSM N Tadley St Mary *Win* 93-08; Perm to Offic from 08. *The Cedars, Blakes Lane, Tadley, Basingstoke RG26 3PU* Tel 0118-981 6593 E-mail sammie@armstrongsg.freeserve.co.uk

ARMSTRONG, Mrs Susan Elizabeth. b 45. **d** 05 **p** 06. OLM Tilstock, Edstaston and Whixall *Lich* 05-09; OLM Edstaston,

Fauls, Prees, Tilstock and Whixall from 09. *Tarragon Cottage, Shrewsbury Street, Prees, Whitchurch SY13 2DH* Tel (01948) 840039 E-mail s.armstrong01@btinternet.com

ARMSTRONG, Mrs Valri. b 50. Man Univ BA73. **d** 04 **p** 05. OLM Stoke by Nayland w Leavenheath and Polstead *St E* from 04. *Orchid House, 38 Bramble Way, Leavenheath, Colchester CO6 4UN* Tel (01206) 262814 E-mail mrsvarmstrong@hotmail.co.uk

ARMSTRONG, William. b 29. Sarum Th Coll 52. **d** 54 **p** 55. C Hebburn St Cuth *Dur* 54-55; C Ferryhill 55-57; C Gateshead H Trin 57-60; V Cassop cum Quarrington 60-66; Australia 66-81; Asst Dir of Educn *Liv* 81-90; V Aintree St Pet 81-88; TV Speke St Aid 88-90; rtd 90. *3 Downing Court, Grenville Street, London WC1N 1LX* Tel (020) 7713 7847

ARMSTRONG-MacDONNELL, Mrs Vivienne Christine. b 42. Open Univ BA89 Ex Univ MEd01 Lambeth MA05. Ripon Coll Cuddesdon 88. **d** 90 **p** 94. C Crediton and Shobrooke *Ex* 90-93; Dioc Adv in Adult Tr 93-00; rtd 00; Perm to Offic *Ex* 00-07; Bp's Adv for Spirituality 07-09. *Strand House, Woodbury, Exeter EX5 1LZ* Tel and fax (01395) 232790 E-mail spiritualityadviser@exeter.anglican.org

ARNALL-CULLIFORD, Jane Margaret. See CULLIFORD, Jane Margaret

ARNESEN, Christopher **Paul**. b 48. Lon Univ BA70. Sarum & Wells Th Coll 78. **d** 80 **p** 81. C Dalton-in-Furness *Carl* 80-83; C Ranmoor *Sheff* 83-86; R Distington *Carl* 86-93; TV Sheff Manor 93-97; Mental Health Chapl Sheff Care Trust 98-04; Perm to Offic *Sheff* from 04; Bp's Adv in Past Care and Counselling from 08. *39 Greystones Crescent, Sheffield S11 7JN* Tel 0114-266 8836 E-mail paul.arnesen@arnies.org.uk

ARNESEN, Raymond Halfdan (**Brother Ælred**). b 25. Qu Coll Cam BA49 MA54. Linc Th Coll 50. **d** 52 **p** 53. C Newc St Fran 52-55; SSF 55-66; Cistercian Monk from 66; Ewell Monastery 66-04; rtd 95. *2 Brentmead Close, London W7 3EW*

ARNOLD, Adrian Paul. b 69. St Steph Ho Ox. **d** 01 **p** 02. C Staincliffe and Carlinghow *Wakef* 01-04; V New Cantley *Sheff* 04-08; C Hesketh w Becconsall *Blackb* from 09. *All Saints' Rectory, 1 Silverdale, Hesketh Bank, Preston PR4 6RZ* Tel (01772) 811485 Mobile 07951-873597 E-mail frarnold@orange.net

ARNOLD, Brother. See NODDER, Thomas Arthur

ARNOLD, David Alun. b 78. St Andr Univ MTheol00. Coll of Resurr Mirfield 01. **d** 03 **p** 04. C Ribbleton *Blackb* 03-05; C Hawes Side and Marton Moss 05-07; Bp's Dom Chapl from 07; Asst Dir of Ords from 06. *79 Ribchester Road, Clayton le Dale, Blackburn BB1 9HT* Tel (01254) 248612 *or* 248234 Fax 246668 Mobile 07786-168261 E-mail chaplain@bishopofblackburn.org.uk

ARNOLD, Derek John. b 59. Wycliffe Hall Ox 01. **d** 03 **p** 04. C St Jo in Bedwardine *Worc* 03-06; TV Kidderminster St Jo and H Innocents 06-09; TR from 09. *The Vicarage, 33 Lea Bank Avenue, Kidderminster DY11 6PA* Tel (01562) 60250 Mobile 07789-631346 E-mail rector.kwtm@virginmedia.com

ARNOLD, Elisabeth Anne Truyens. b 44. TCert66. **d** 91 **p** 94. OLM Ipswich St Thos *St E* 91-00; Chapl Dioc Min Course 00-01; OLM Tutor 01-06; rtd 06; Perm to Offic *St E* from 06. *66 Bromeswell Road, Ipswich IP4 3AT* Tel (01473) 257406

ARNOLD, Ernest Stephen. b 27. **d** 64 **p** 65. C Aberavon *Llan* 64-68; V Ferndale 68-74; Cyprus 81-85; rtd 94; Perm to Offic *Portsm* from 94. *Barn Cottage, Apse Manor Road, Shanklin PO37 7PN* Tel (01983) 866324

ARNOLD, Frances Mary. b 64. R Holloway Coll Lon BA86 Dur Univ PGCE90 Anglia Ruskin Univ MA07. Westcott Ho Cam 01. **d** 04 **p** 05. C Biggleswade *St Alb* 04-07; Exec Officer Abps' Coun from 07; Perm to Offic *Lon* from 08. *Central Secretariat, Church House, Great Smith Street, London SW1P 3AZ* Tel (020) 7898 1372 E-mail frances.arnold@churchofengland.org

ARNOLD, Graham Thomas. b 62. Aston Tr Scheme 87 Ripon Coll Cuddesdon 89. **d** 92 **p** 93. C Margate St Jo *Cant* 92-95; TV Whitstable 95-00; Perm to Offic *S'wark* 07-09; NSM N Dulwich St Faith from 09. *62B Crawthew Grove, London SE22 9AB* Tel (020) 8693 2323 Mobile 07793-555017 E-mail graham62@btinternet.com

ARNOLD, Jane Elizabeth. b 50. **d** 11. NSM Kingswinford St Mary *Worc* from 11. *59 Buckingham Grove, Kingswinford DY6 9BT*

ARNOLD, Jennifer Anne. b 54. Univ Coll Lon BSc75 MB, BS78 FRCR85. Qu Coll Birm 00. **d** 02 **p** 03. C Aston SS Pet and Paul *Birm* 02-08; C Aston St Jas and Nechells 05-08; C Aston and Nechells from 08. *St Matthew's Vicarage, Duddeston Manor Road, Birmingham B7 4QD* Tel 0121-359 6965 Mobile 07754-449266 E-mail arnolds68@btopenworld.com

ARNOLD, The Very Revd John Robert. b 33. OBE02. SS Coll Cam BA57 MA61 Lambeth DD99. Westcott Ho Cam 58. **d** 60 **p** 61. C Millhouses H Trin *Sheff* 60-63; Chapl and Lect Southn Univ 63-72; Gen Sec Gen Syn Bd for Miss and Unity 72-78; Hon Can Win Cathl 74-78; Dean Roch 78-94; Dean Dur 89-02; rtd 03; Perm to Offic *Cant* from 02. *26 Hawks Lane, Canterbury CT1 2NU* Tel (01227) 764703

ARNOLD, Jonathan Allen. b 69. St Pet Coll Ox BA92 MA99 K Coll Lon PhD04 LTCL89 LRAM94. Ripon Coll Cuddesdon 03. **d** 05 **p** 06. NSM Chalgrove w Berrick Salome *Ox* 05-08; Chapl Worc Coll Ox from 08. *Worcester College, Oxford OX1 2HB, or Garsington Rectory, 17 Southend, Garsington, Oxford OX44 9DH* Tel (01865) 278371 Mobile 07939-093085 E-mail jonathan.arnold@worc.ox.ac.uk

✠**ARNOLD, The Rt Revd Keith Appleby.** b 26. Trin Coll Cam BA50 MA55. Westcott Ho Cam 50. **d** 52 **p** 53 c 80. C Haltwhistle *Newc* 52-55; C Edin St Jo 55-61; R 61-69; CF (TA) 58-62; V Kirkby Lonsdale w Mansergh *Carl* 69-73; RD Berkhamsted *St Alb* 73-80; TR Hemel Hempstead 73-80; Suff Bp Warw *Cov* 80-90; Hon Can Cov Cathl 80-90; rtd 90; Hon Asst Bp Ox from 97. *9 Dinglederry, Olney MK46 5ES* Tel (01234) 713044

ARNOLD, Michael John. b 44. Rhodes Univ BA68 St Edm Hall Ox BA72 MA77. St Jo Coll Nottm 93. **d** 98 **p** 98. Asst Chapl St Jo Coll Johannesburg S Africa 98-99; Chapl from 01; Chapl Clayesmore Sch Blandford 98-01. *St John's College, St David's Road, Houghton Estate, Johannesburg, 2198 South Africa* Tel (0027) (11) 648 9932 *or* 648 1350 Mobile (0) 72 3134315 Fax 487 2227 E-mail arnoldmj@hotmail.com

ARNOLD, Monica. d 11. NSM Bloxwich *Lich* from 11. *21 Tudor Close, Burntwood WS7 0BW* Tel (01543) 305199 E-mail monica.arnold@ntlworld.com

ARNOLD, Mrs Norma. b 48. SNWTP 09. **d** 11. NSM Grassendale *Liv* from 11. *28 Ambergate Road, Liverpool L19 9AU* Tel 0151-427 2320 E-mail norma.arnold@tesco.net

ARNOLD, Norman. *See* ARNOLD, Victor Norman

ARNOLD, Philip Robert. b 75. Qld Univ of Tech BN96. St Jo Coll Nottm 07. **d** 09 **p** 10. C Pudsey St Lawr and St Paul *Bradf* from 09; C Farsley from 09. *18 West Park, Pudsey LS28 7SN* Tel 07877-495111 (mobile) E-mail philarnold1@googlemail.com

ARNOLD, Richard Nicholas. b 54. AKC76. S'wark Ord Course 76. **d** 77 **p** 78. C Nunhead St Antony *S'wark* 77-80; C Walworth 80-82; P-in-c Streatham Hill St Marg 82-84; V 84-89; P-in-c Oseney Crescent St Luke *Lon* 89-93; P-in-c Kentish Town St Jo 89-93; P-in-c Kentish Town St Benet and All SS 89-93; V Kentish Town from 93; AD S Camden 00-05. *Kentish Town Vicarage, 43 Lady Margaret Road, London NW5 2NH* Tel (020) 7485 4231 Mobile 07802-730974 E-mail r.arnold@lineone.net

ARNOLD, Canon Roy. b 36. St D Coll Lamp BA62. **d** 63 **p** 64. C Brislington St Luke 63-66; C Ches St Mary 67-70; V Brinnington w Portwood 71-75; V Sale St Paul 75-82; R Dodleston 82-84; V Sheff St Oswald 84-90; Dioc Communications Officer 84-97; Chapl w the Deaf 90-97; Hon Can Sheff Cathl 95-97; rtd 97; Perm to Offic *Ches* from 97. *49 Crossfield Road, Bollington, Macclesfield SK10 5EA* Tel (01625) 575472

ARNOLD, Ms Sonja Marie. b 63. Wycliffe Hall Ox BTh98. **d** 98 **p** 99. Assoc V Hammersmith St Simon *Lon* 98-06; Dean of Women's Min Kensington Area 02-06; Network Miss P *Bris* from 07; Tutor Trin Coll Bris from 09. *6 Knole Court, Knole Lane, Bristol BS10 6TZ* Tel 0117-950 9352 Mobile 07809-636419 E-mail sonjaarnold@yahoo.com

ARNOLD, Victor Norman. b 45. Oak Hill Th Coll 91. **d** 94 **p** 95. NSM Chigwell and Chigwell Row *Chelmsf* 94-98; C W Ham 98-04; C Hornchurch St Andr 04-10; rtd 10; Perm to Offic *Chelmsf* from 10. *Spring Cottage, 6 Spring Grove, Loughton IG10 4QA* Tel (020) 8508 6572

ARNOTT, Preb David. b 44. Em Coll Cam BA66. Qu Coll Birm 68. **d** 69 **p** 70. C Charlton St Luke w St Paul *S'wark* 69-73; C S Beddington St Mich 73-78; Chapl Liv Poly 78-82; V Bridgwater St Fran *B & W* 86-02; Preb Wells Cathl 00-02; V Yealmpton and Brixton *Ex* 02-09; P-in-c from 09; RD Ivybridge from 03; rtd 09. *The Vicarage, Bowden Hill, Yealmpton, Plymouth PL8 2JX* Tel and fax (01752) 880979 E-mail revdavid.arnott@virgin.net

ARORA, Arun. b 71. Birm Univ LLB93 St Jo Coll Dur BA06 Solicitor 96. Cranmer Hall Dur 04. **d** 07 **p** 08. C Harrogate St Mark *Ripon* 07-10; Abp's Dir of Communications *York* 06-09; Pioneer Min Wolv City Cen *Lich* from 10. *65 Riches Street, Wolverhampton WV6 0EA* Tel 07984-334564 (mobile) E-mail arunarora1@yahoo.co.uk

ARRAND, The Ven Geoffrey William. b 44. K Coll Lon BD66 AKC66. **d** 67 **p** 68. C Washington *Dur* 67-70; C S Ormsby w Ketsby, Calceby and Driby *Linc* 70-73; TV Gt Grimsby St Mary and St Jas 73-79; TR Halesworth w Linstead and Chediston *St E* 79-80; TR Halesworth w Linstead, Chediston, Holton etc 80-85; R Hadleigh w Layham and Shelley 85-94; Dean Bocking 85-94; RD Hadleigh 86-94; Adn Suffolk 94-09; Hon Can St E Cathl 91-09; rtd 09; Perm to Offic *St E* from 09. *8 Elm Close, Saxilby, Lincoln LN1 2QH*

ARSCOTT, Barry James. b 36. AKC59. **d** 60 **p** 61. C Walthamstow St Andr *Chelmsf* 60-65; P-in-c Leyton St Luke 65-67; V 67-77; P-in-c Lt Ilford St Barn 77-86; V 86-01; rtd 01. *232 Fencepiece Road, Ilford IG6 2ST* Tel (020) 8502 6853

ARTHUR, Graeme Michael. b 52. Univ of NSW BCom78 Heythrop Coll Lon MA09. Linc Th Coll 93. **d** 93 **p** 94. C Witney *Ox* 93-97; R Westcote Barton w Steeple Barton, Duns Tew etc from 97. *The Rectory, 29 Enstone Road, Westcote Barton, Chipping Norton OX7 7AA* Tel (01869) 340510 E-mail graeme@arfa.clara.net

ARTHUR, Canon Ian Willoughby. b 40. Lon Univ BA63 BA66 PGCE64 Lambeth STh94 Kent Univ MA98. Ripon Coll Cuddesdon 78. **d** 80 **p** 81. C Kempston Transfiguration *St Alb* 80-83; R Potton w Sutton and Cockayne Hatley 83-96; P-in-c Sharnbrook and Knotting w Souldrop 96-98; R 98-04; RD Sharnbrook 97-04; Hon Can St Alb 99-04; rtd 04; Perm to Offic *St Alb* from 04 and *Ox* from 05. *35 London Road, Chipping Norton OX7 5AX* Tel (01608) 646839 E-mail iwarthur@supanet.com

ARTHUR, Kenneth Paul. b 64. Univ of Wales (Cardiff) BScEcon86 Roehampton Inst PGCE87 Cardiff Univ LLM08. St Steph Ho Ox BTh05. **d** 00 **p** 01. C Bodmin w Lanhydrock and Lanivet *Truro* 00-02; P-in-c Treverbyn and Boscoppa 02-06; P-in-c St Dennis from 06; RD St Austell 05-10; Warden of Readers 05-10; Deputy Warden of Readers from 10; Dir Minl Tr 06-10; Dir Minl Formation and Development from 10. *The Rectory, 16 Trelavour Road, St Dennis, St Austell PL26 8AH* Tel (01726) 822317

ARTHY, Canon Nicola Mary. b 64. St Jo Coll Ox BA85 MA93. SEITE. **d** 00 **p** 01. C Guildf H Trin w St Mary 00-01; C Farncombe 01-04; P-in-c Toddington, Stanton, Didbrook w Hailes etc *Glouc* 04-05; TV Winchcombe 05-09; AD Tewkesbury and Winchcombe 07-09; P-in-c Glouc St Mary de Lode and St Mary de Crypt etc 09-10; P-in-c Hempsted 09-10; R Glouc City and Hempsted from 10; Can Res Glouc Cathl from 09. *The Rectory, Rectory Lane, Hempsted, Gloucester GL2 5LW* Tel (01452) 523808 Mobile 07944-721835 E-mail nikkiarthy@btinternet.com

ARTLEY, Clive Mansell. b 30. St Jo Coll Dur BA56 Leeds Univ MA(Theol)01. Cranmer Hall Dur. **d** 58 **p** 59. C Eston *York* 58-61; R Burythorpe w E Acklam and Leavening 61-64; CF 64-73; Teacher 73-93; Perm to Offic *York* from 73; rtd 93. *56 High Street, Castleton, Whitby YO21 2DA* Tel (01287) 660470

ARTLEY, Miss Pamela Jean. b 47. Worc Coll of Educn CertEd68 Hull Univ MEd91 ALCM73. NEOC 99. **d** 02 **p** 03. NSM Bridlington Priory *York* 02-05; P-in-c Nafferton w Wansford from 05. *The Vicarage, 3 Middle Street, Nafferton, Driffield YO25 4JS* Tel (01377) 254372 E-mail pjartley@tiscali.co.uk

ARTUS, Stephen James. b 60. Man Poly BA82 W Midl Coll of Educn PGCE84. St Jo Coll Nottm MA95. **d** 95 **p** 96. C Altrincham St Geo *Ches* 95-99; P-in-c Norton 99-05; V 05-07; C Wybunbury and Audlem w Doddington from 10. *The Vicarage, Main Road, Wybunbury, Nantwich CW5 7LS* Tel (01270) 841178

ARUNDEL, Canon Michael. b 36. Qu Coll Ox BA60 MA64. Linc Th Coll 60. **d** 62 **p** 63. C Hollinwood *Man* 62-65; C Leesfield 65-69; R Newton Heath All SS 69-80; RD N Man 75-80; P-in-c Eccles St Mary 80-81; TR Eccles 81-91; R Man St Ann 91-01; Hon Can Man Cathl 82-01; rtd 01; Perm to Offic *Man* from 01. *20 Kiln Brow, Bromley Cross, Bolton BL7 9NR* Tel (01204) 591156

ARVIDSSON, Carl Fredrik. b 66. Regents Th Coll 88 Chich Th Coll 92. **d** 92 **p** 93. C Southsea H Spirit *Portsm* 92-94; C Botley, Curdridge and Durley 94-96; P-in-c Ringwould w Kingsdown *Cant* 9*.* R 97-01; Hon Min Can Cant Cathl from 01; Sen Chapl K Sch Cant from 01. *1 The Mint Yard, The Precincts, Canterbury CT1 2EZ* Tel (01227) 595631 *or* 595613 E-mail cfa@kings-school.co.uk

ASBRIDGE, Preb John Hawell. b 26. Dur Univ BA47. Bps' Coll Cheshunt 47. **d** 49 **p** 50. C Barrow St Geo *Carl* 49-52; C Fort William *Arg* 52-54; C Lon Docks St Pet w Wapping St Jo 54-55; C Kilburn St Aug 55-59; V Northolt Park St Barn 59-66; V Shepherd's Bush St Steph w St Thos 66-96; Preb St Paul's Cathl 89-96; rtd 96; Perm to Offic *B & W* from 05. *Crystal Glen, The Old Mineral Line, Roadwater, Watchet TA23 0RL* Tel (01984) 640211

ASBRIDGE, Nigel Henry. b 58. Bris Univ BA80. Chich Th Coll 87. **d** 89 **p** 90. C Tottenham St Paul *Lon* 89; C W Hampstead St Jas 89-94; P-in-c Hornsey H Innocents 94-04; P-in-c Stroud Green H Trin 02-04; Nat Chapl-Missr Children's Soc 04-09; NSM Edmonton St Alphege and Ponders End St Matt *Lon* 06-10; P-in-c Edmonton St Mary w St Jo from 10. *St John's Vicarage, Dysons Road, London N18 2DS* Tel (020) 8807 2767 Mobile 07905-499323 E-mail nigelasbridge@hotmail.com

ASH, Arthur Edwin. b 44. St Jo Coll Nottm 85. **d** 87 **p** 88. C Attleborough *Cov* 87-91; V Garretts Green *Birm* 91-02; rtd 02; Perm to Offic *Birm* from 02. *1 Margetts Close, Kenilworth CV8 1EN* Tel (01926) 853547 E-mail aash@tinyworld.co.uk

ASH, Brian John. b 32. ALCD62. **d** 62 **p** 63. C Plymouth St Andr *Ex* 62-66; Area Sec CMS *Cant* and *Roch* 66-73; V Bromley Common St Aug *Roch* 73-97; rtd 97; Perm to Offic *Chelmsf* 97-00. *The Vines, 95 Green Lane, Leigh-on-Sea SS9 5QU* Tel (01702) 523644 E-mail brian.ash@zen.co.uk

ASH, Christopher Brian Garton. b 53. Trin Hall Cam MA76. Wycliffe Hall Ox BA92. **d** 93 **p** 94. C Cambridge H Sepulchre *Ely*

93-97; P-in-c Lt Shelford 97-02; R 02-04; Dir Cornhill Tr Course from 04. *The Cornhill Training Course, 140-148 Borough High Street, London SE1 1LB* Tel (020) 7407 0562 E-mail cbga@proctrust.org.uk

ASH, David Nicholas. b 61. Southlands Coll Lon BA82. Wycliffe Hall Ox BTh03. **d** 03 **p** 04. C Walsall *Lich* 03-06; P-in-c Petton w Cockshutt, Welshampton and Lyneal etc from 06; Local Par Development Adv Shrewsbury Area from 10. *The Rectory, Cockshutt, Ellesmere SY12 0JQ* Tel (01939) 270211

ASH, Canon Nicholas John. b 59. Bath Univ BSc81 Nottm Univ BTh88. Linc Th Coll 85. **d** 88 **p** 89. C Hersham *Guildf* 88-93; P-in-c Flookburgh *Carl* 93-97; Dioc Officer for Stewardship 94-97; TV Cartmel Peninsula 97-98; Dir of Ords 97-03; P-in-c Dalston 98-00; P-in-c Wreay 98-00; P-in-c Raughton Head w Gatesgill 98-00; V Dalston w Cumdivock, Raughton Head and Wreay 01-03; Can Res Portsm Cathl 03-09; TR Cartmel Peninsula *Carl* from 09. *The Rectory, Hampsfell Road, Grange-over-Sands LA11 6BE* Tel (01539) 532757 E-mail nickash405@hotmail.com *or* cptmrector@googlemail.com

ASH, Nicholas Martin. b 62. Ch Ch Coll Cant BEd86. SEITE 06. **d** 09 **p** 10. NSM Faversham *Cant* from 09; NSM Preston next Faversham, Goodnestone and Graveney from 09. *15 St Catherine's Drive, Faversham ME13 8LQ* Tel (01795) 536038 Mobile 07896-006282 E-mail n.ash@virgin.net

ASHBRIDGE, Clare Patricia Esther. See KAKURU, Mrs Clare Patricia Esther

ASHBRIDGE, Miss Kathleen Mary. b 30. Alnwick Tr Coll CertEd51. **d** 03 **p** 04. NSM Caldbeck, Castle Sowerby and Sebergham *Carl* from 03. *Sharpe House, Caldbeck, Wigton CA7 8EX* Tel (01697) 478205

ASHBURNER, David Barrington. b 26. Ch Coll Cam BA51 MA55. Wycliffe Hall Ox 51. **d** 53 **p** 54. C Coalville *Leic* 53-56; C Leic H Apostles 56-58; V Bucklebury w Marlston *Ox* 58-70; V Belton *Leic* 70-75; P-in-c Osgathorpe 73-75; R Belton and Osgathorpe 75-79; V Frisby-on-the-Wreake w Kirby Bellars 79-82; V Uffington w Woolstone and Baulking *Ox* 82-91; P-in-c Shellingford 83-91; RD Vale of White Horse 87-91; rtd 91; Perm to Offic *Glouc* and *Ox* from 91. *7 Stonefern Court, Stow Road, Moreton-in-Marsh GL56 0DW* Tel (01608) 650347

✠**ASHBY, The Rt Revd Godfrey William Ernest Candler.** b 30. Lon Univ AKC54 BD54 PhD69. **d** 55 **p** 56 **c** 80. C St Helier *S'wark* 55-57; P-in-c St Mark's Miss Cape Town S Africa 58-60; Sub-Warden St Paul's Th Coll Grahamstown 60-66; R Alice 66-68; Sen Lect Rhodes Univ 68-75; Can Grahamstown Cathl 69-75; Dean and Adn Grahamstown 75-80; Bp St John's 80-85; Prof Div Witwatersrand Univ 85-88; Asst Bp Johannesburg 85-88; Asst Bp Leic 88-95; P-in-c Newtown Linford 92-95; Hon Can Leic Cathl 93-95; rtd 95; Asst Bp George S Africa 95-08; Hon Asst Bp Portsm from 08. *12 Jay Close, Waterlooville PO8 9DJ* Tel (023) 9235 9914 Mobile 07968-396195 E-mail godfreyashby@gmail.com

ASHBY, Mrs Judith Anne Stuart. b 53. Man Univ BSc74 MSc76 Ox Brookes Univ PGCE99. STETS 96. **d** 99 **p** 00. NSM Swindon Ch Ch *Bris* 99-05; P-in-c Cricklade w Latton from 05; C Ashton Keynes, Leigh and Minety from 07. *Cricklade Vicarage, 14 Bath Road, Cricklade, Swindon SN6 6EY* Tel (01793) 750300 E-mail judith.ashby@tiscali.co.uk

ASHBY, Kevin Patrick. b 53. Jes Coll Ox BA76 MA80. Wycliffe Hall Ox 76. **d** 78 **p** 79. C Market Harborough *Leic* 78-82; C Horwich H Trin *Man* 82-84; C Horwich 84; TV 84-90; R Billing *Pet* 90-01; RD Northn 98-01; R Buckingham *Ox* 01-09; AD Buckingham 04-09; TR Melton Mowbray *Leic* from 09. *57 Burton Road, Melton Mowbray LE13 1DL* Tel (01664) 410393 E-mail kevinp.ashby@virgin.net

ASHBY, Mrs Linda. b 48. Dartford Coll of Educn CertEd70. **d** 03 **p** 04. OLM N w S Wootton *Nor* from 03. *4 Melford Close, South Wootton, King's Lynn PE30 3XH* Tel (01553) 672893 E-mail linda_ashby@tiscali.co.uk

ASHBY, Peter George. b 49. Univ of Wales (Cardiff) BSc(Econ)70. Linc Th Coll 70. **d** 73 **p** 74. C Bengeo *St Alb* 73-75; Chapl Hatf Poly 76-79; C Apsley End 80; TV Chambersbury 80-82; Adn N Harare Zimbabwe 82-87; V Eskdale, Irton, Muncaster and Waberthwaite *Carl* 87-93; TR Sedgley All SS *Worc* 93-99; TV Tettenhall Regis *Lich* 99-04; V W Bromwich St Jas w St Paul 04-06; R Bradeley, Church Eaton, Derrington and Haughton 06-11; rtd 11. *24 Bryant Gardens, Clevedon BS21 5HE* E-mail peterg.ashby@gmail.com

ASHBY, Philip Charles. b 52. Birm Univ BSc73 Lon Univ MSc74 PhD93. WEMTC 05. **d** 08 **p** 09. NSM Stratton St Margaret w S Marston etc *Bris* 08-11; NSM Garsdon, Lea and Cleverton and Charlton from 11. *Cricklade Vicarage, 14 Bath Road, Cricklade, Swindon SN6 6EY* Tel (01793) 759008 E-mail phil.ashby@tiscali.co.uk

ASHCROFT, Canon Ann Christine. b 46. Cov Coll of Educn TCert68. NOC 82. **d** 87 **p** 94. Chapl Trin C of E High Sch Man 86-91; Burnage St Nic *Man* 86-91; Hon Par Dn 87-95; Dio Adv Man Coun for Educn 91-95; TV Wareham and Chapl Purbeck Sch *Sarum* 95-02; TR By Brook *Bris* 02-10; P-in-c Colerne w N

Wraxall 06-10; Hon Can Bris Cathl 08-10; rtd 10. *3 Highfield Close, Bakewell DE45 1GP* Tel (01249) 782603 E-mail annashcroft@bybrook.org.uk

ASHCROFT, The Ven Mark David. b 54. Worc Coll Ox BA77 MA82 Fitzw Coll Cam BA81. Ridley Hall Cam 79. **d** 82 **p** 83. C Burnage St Marg *Man* 82-85; Tutor St Paul's Sch of Div Kapsabet Kenya 86-89; Prin St Paul's Th Coll Kapsabet 90-96; R Harpurhey 96-09; R Harpurhey St Steph 96-09; AD N Man 00-06; Adn Man from 09; Hon Can Man Cathl from 04. *14 Moorgate Avenue, Manchester M20 1HE* Tel and fax 0161-448 1976 E-mail archdeaconmanchester@manchester.anglican.org

ASHDOWN, Andrew William Harvey. b 64. K Coll Lon BD88 AKC88. Sarum & Wells Th Coll 88. **d** 90 **p** 91. C Cranleigh *Guildf* 90-94; V Ryhill *Wakef* 94-98; P-in-c Denmead *Portsm* 98-99; V 99-05; S Asia Regional Officer USPG 05-06; Hon C Tadley S and Silchester *Win* 05-06; P-in-c Knight's Enham and Smannell w Enham Alamein 06-09; TR from 09. *The Rectory, 1 Ryon Close, Andover SP10 4DG* Tel (01264) 357032 E-mail andrew@evib.net

ASHDOWN, Anthony Hughes. b 37. AKC63. **d** 64 **p** 65. C Tettenhall Regis *Lich* 64-67; P-in-c Bassaleg *Mon* 67-70; P-in-c Gatooma Rhodesia 70-77; P-in-c Longton St Jas *Lich* 77-78; P-in-c Longton St Jo 77-78; R Longton 78-80; TR Cove St Jo *Guildf* 80-87; Chapl Lisbon *Eur* 87-90; V Wanstead H Trin Hermon Hill *Chelmsf* 90-00; rtd 02; Perm to Offic *Chich* from 00. *88 Shipppam Street, Chichester PO19 8EW* Tel (01243) 532405

ASHDOWN, Barry Frederick. b 42. St Pet Coll Ox BA65 MA69. Ridley Hall Cam 66. **d** 68 **p** 69. C Shipley St Pet *Bradf* 68-71; C Rushden w Newton Bromswold *Pet* 71-74; R Haworth *Bradf* 74-82; V Ore Ch Ch *Chich* 82-87; C Southwick St Mich 91-93. *Address temp unknown*

ASHDOWN, Ms Lucyann. b 64. LSE BSc95 RGN86 RM88. NTMTC BA08. **d** 08 **p** 09. C Stoke Newington St Mary *Lon* 08-11; C Brownswood Park 08-11; P-in-c Blaenau Irfon *S & B* from 11; P-in-c Irfon Valley from 11. *The Rectory, Maes Glas, Llangammarch Wells LD4 4EE* E-mail lucyann.ashdown@gmail.com

ASHDOWN, Philip David. b 57. Imp Coll Lon BSc79 NW Univ Chicago MS80 Cranfield Inst of Tech PhD85 ARCS79. Ripon Coll Cuddesdon 91. **d** 93 **p** 94. C Houghton le Spring *Dur* 93-96; C Stockton and Chapl Stockton Campus Dur Univ 96-02; V Stockton St Pet *Dur* from 02; P-in-c Elton from 09. *St Peter's Vicarage, 11 Lorne Court, Stockton-on-Tees TS18 3UB* Tel (01642) 670981 E-mail philip.ashdown@durham.anglican.org

ASHE, The Ven Francis John. b 53. Sheff Univ BMet74. Ridley Hall Cam 77. **d** 79 **p** 80. C Ashtead *Guildf* 79-82; S Africa 82-87; R Wisley w Pyrford *Guildf* 87-93; V Godalming 93-01; TR 01-09; RD Godalming 96-02; Hon Can Guildf Cathl 03-09; Adn Lynn *Nor* from 09. *Holly Tree House, Whitwell Road, Sparham, Norwich NR9 5PN* Tel (01362) 688032 E-mail archdeacon.lynn@norwich.anglican.org

ASHENDEN, Canon Gavin Roy Pelham. b 54. Bris Univ LLB76 Oak Hill Th Coll BA80 Heythrop Coll Lon MTh89 Sussex Univ DPhil98. **d** 80 **p** 81. C Bermondsey St Jas w Ch Ch *S'wark* 80-83; TV Sanderstead All SS 83-89; Chapl and Lect Sussex Univ from 89; Can and Preb Chich Cathl from 03; Chapl to The Queen from 08. *The Meeting House, Sussex University, Southern Ring Road, Falmer, Brighton BN1 9RH* Tel (01273) 678217 Fax 678918 Mobile 07879-493491 E-mail g.ashenden@sussex.ac.uk *or* gavin@ashenden.org

ASHFORD-OKAI, Fred. b 57. NUI BA90 Lanc Univ MA92 TCD HDipEd93. St Pet Sem Ghana 79 NTMTC 06. **d** 84 **p** 85. NSM E Ham w Upton Park *Chelmsf* 07-09. *4 Darwell Close, London E6 6BT* Tel 07940-984883 (mobile) E-mail fashfordokai@googlemail.com

ASHFORD, Archdeacon of. See DOWN, The Ven Philip Roy

ASHFORTH, David Edward. b 37. Lon Univ BSc ARCS59. Qu Coll Birm. **d** 61 **p** 62. C Scarborough St Columba *York* 61-65; C Northallerton w Kirby Sigston 65-67; V Keyingham 67-73; Chapl Imp Coll Lon 73-89; V Balderstone *Blackb* 89-01; Dir Post-Ord Tr 89-01; rtd 01; Perm to Offic *Ripon* from 02. *Sunnyholme Cottage, Preston under Scar, Leyburn DL8 4AH* Tel (01969) 622438 E-mail d.ashforth@btinternet.com

ASHLEY, Brian. b 36. S'wark Ord Course 75. **d** 77 **p** 78. NSM Horsell *Guildf* 77-07; Perm to Offic from 07. *5 Birtley House, 38 Claremont Avenue, Woking GU22 7QB* Tel (01483) 761232 E-mail brianthebusiness@onetel.com

ASHLEY, Brian Christenson. b 33. Roch Th Coll 68. **d** 70 **p** 71. C New Sleaford *Linc* 70-72; Min Basegreen CD 72-74; TV Gleadless *Sheff* 74-77; R Dinnington 77-85; RD Laughton 82-85; V Mosbrough 85-88; P-in-c Curbar and Stoney Middleton *Derby* 88-91; rtd 91; Perm to Offic *Pet* from 95. *15 Eliot Close, Saxon Fields, Kettering NN16 9XR* Tel (01536) 524457

ASHLEY, Clive Ashley. b 54. Croydon Coll of Art and Design LSIAD75 Lon Hosp SRN80 E Ham Coll of Tech TCert82. Aston Tr Scheme 81 Cranmer Hall Dur 84. **d** 86 **p** 87. C Withington St Paul *Man* 86-89; Asst Chapl Freeman Hosp

Newc 89-92; Chapl St Rich and Graylingwell Hosps Chich 92-98; Chapl Bognor Regis War Memorial Hosp 95-98; Chapl and Bereavement Cllr R W Sussex Trust 98-01; R New Fishbourne *Chich* 01-10; P-in-c Appledram 01-10; P-in-c Sandon *Chelmsf* from 10; P-in-c Lt Baddow from 10. *25 The Lintons, Sandon, Chelmsford CM2 7UA* Tel (01245) 243863 Mobile 07747-155119 E-mail cliveashley@btinternet.com
ASHLEY, Ms Rosemary Clare. b 60. Dur Univ BA82 Birkbeck Coll Lon MSc01 Brunel Univ MPhil05. Wycliffe Hall Ox 02. **d** 05 **p** 06. C Leyton St Cath and St Paul *Chelmsf* 05-09; NSM from 09. *114 Hainault Road, London E11 1EL* Tel (020) 8923 4782 Mobile 07984-618534 E-mail rosyashley@hotmail.com
ASHLEY, Miss Victoria Lesley. St Mich Coll Llan. **d** 08 **p** 09. C Tredegar *Mon* from 08. *St James's Vicarage, Poplar Road, Tredegar NP22 4LH* Tel (01495) 722510 E-mail victoria.ashley151@btinternet.com
ASHLEY-ROBERTS, James. b 53. Lon Univ BD77. Oak Hill Th Coll 75 Wycliffe Hall Ox 79. **d** 80 **p** 81. C Gt Warley Ch Ch *Chelmsf* 80-83; C E Ham St Paul 83-85; TV Holyhead w Rhoscolyn w Llanfair-yn-Neubwll *Ban* 85-88; R 88-91; V Penrhyndeudraeth w Llanfrothen w Beddgelert 91-97; R Ffestiniog w Blaenau Ffestiniog 97-01. *5 Jones Street, Blaenau Ffestiniog LL41 3YF* Tel 07881-770437 (mobile)
ASHLING, Raymond Charles. b 32. Dur Univ BA58. Linc Th Coll 58. **d** 60 **p** 61. C Halifax St Aug *Wakef* 60-63; C Farlington *Portsm* 63-65; Rhodesia 65-71; Chapl Rishworth Sch Ripponden 71-75; Lesotho 75-85; V Somercotes *Linc* 85-88; Ethiopia 88-89; R Gt w Lt Snoring w Kettlestone and Pensthorpe *Nor* 89-94; rtd 94. *6 Wells Court, Morden College, 19 St Germans Place, London SE3 0PW*
ASHMAN, Paul Andrew. b 70. Wycliffe Hall Ox 05. **d** 07 **p** 08. C Portswood Ch Ch *Win* 07-11; New Zealand from 11. *27 Searle Street, Auckland 1072, New Zealand* E-mail ashmanpaul@gmail.com
ASHMAN, Peter Michael. b 61. Ex Univ LLB83 LLM84 Called to the Bar (Inner Temple) 85. SWMTC 07. **d** 10. C Ex St Jas from 10. *17 Culverland Close, Exeter EX4 6HR* Tel (01392) 410114 E-mail peter@ashman61.info
ASHMAN, Peter Nicholas. b 52. CSS81 SEN73. Sarum & Wells Th Coll 87. **d** 89 **p** 90. C Stafford *Lich* 89-93; R Dymchurch w Burmarsh and Newchurch *Cant* 93-99; R Lyminge w Paddlesworth, Stanford w Postling etc from 99. *The Rectory, Rectory Lane, Lyminge, Folkestone CT18 8EG* Tel (01303) 862432 *or* tel and fax 862345 E-mail p.ashman@btinternet.com
ASHMAN, Mrs Vanessa Mary. b 53. Cant Ch Ch Univ BA07. **d** 03 **p** 04. NSM Lyminge w Paddlesworth, Stanford w Postling etc *Cant* from 03. *The Rectory, Rectory Lane, Lyminge, Folkestone CT18 8EG* Tel (01303) 862432 *or* tel and fax 862345 E-mail vanessa.ashman@btinternet.com
ASHTON, Anthony Joseph. b 37. Oak Hill Th Coll 62. **d** 65 **p** 66. C Crookes St Thos *Sheff* 65-68; C Heeley 68-73; V Bowling St Steph *Bradf* 73-78; R Chesterfield H Trin *Derby* 78-92; rtd 93; Perm to Offic *Derby* 93-00. *19 High Park, Stafford ST16 1BL* Tel (01785) 223943
✠**ASHTON, The Rt Revd Cyril Guy.** b 42. Lanc Univ MA86. Oak Hill Th Coll 64. **d** 67 **p** 68 **c** 00. C Blackpool St Thos *Blackb* 67-70; Voc Sec CPAS 70-74; V Lancaster St Thos *Blackb* 74-91; Lanc Almshouses 76-90; Dioc Dir of Tr *Blackb* 91-00; Hon Can Blackb Cathl 91-00; Suff Bp Doncaster *Sheff* 00-11; rtd 11. *Charis, 17C Quernmore Road, Lancaster LA1 3EB* Tel 07968-371596 (mobile) E-mail bpcg.ashton@virgin.net
ASHTON, David. b 52. Sarum Th Coll 93. **d** 96 **p** 97. NSM St Leonards Ch Ch and St Mary *Chich* 96-98; NSM Upper St Leonards St Jo 98-99; C Uckfield 99-02; V Langney from 02. *St Richard's Rectory, 7 Priory Road, Eastbourne BN23 7AX* Tel (01323) 761158 E-mail frdavidashton@aol.com
ASHTON, David William. b 51. Reading Univ BA74 Lanc Univ PGCE75. Wycliffe Hall Ox 79. **d** 82 **p** 83. C Shipley St Pet *Bradf* 82-85; C Tadley St Pet *Win* 85-88; V Sinfin *Derby* 88-91; Chapl Sophia Antipolis *Eur* 91-94; P-in-c Swanwick and Pentrich *Derby* 95-00; V 00-02; RD Alfreton 95-02; Chapl Derby Hosps NHS Foundn Trust from 02. *Chaplaincy Services, Derby City General Hospital, Uttoxeter Road, Derby DE22 3NE* Tel (01332) 340131 E-mail david.ashton@derbyhospitals.nhs.uk
ASHTON, Grant. *See* ASHTON, William Grant
ASHTON, James Paul. b 75. UWE BA97. Wycliffe Hall Ox BTh06. **d** 06 **p** 07. C Horley *S'wark* 06-09; C S Merstham 09-10; TV Merstham, S Merstham and Gatton from 10. *The Vicarage, Battlebridge Lane, Merstham, Redhill RH1 3LH* Tel (01737) 642722
ASHTON, Janet Heather Hephzibah. b 52. Westcott Ho Cam. **d** 07 **p** 08. C Wenlock *Heref* 07-11; TV Kidderminster St Mary and All SS w Trimpley etc *Worc* from 11. *50 Nursery Grove, Kidderminster DY11 5BG* Tel (01562) 741381 Mobile 07737-916499 E-mail jan@janashton.co.uk
✠**ASHTON, The Rt Revd Jeremy Claude.** b 30. Trin Coll Cam BA53 MA57. Westcott Ho Cam 53. **d** 56 **c** 76. C Bury St Mary *Man* 55-60; CF (TA) 57-60; CF (TA - R of O) 60-70; Papua New Guinea 60-86; Asst Bp Papua 76-77; Bp Aipo Rongo

77-86; rtd 86; Australia from 86. *38 Urquhart Street, Castlemaine Vic 3540, Australia* Tel and fax (0061) (3) 5472 1074
ASHTON, Miss Joan Elizabeth. b 54. Sheff Hallam Univ BA10 Eaton Hall Coll of Educn CertEd76. Cranmer Hall Dur 91. **d** 93 **p** 94. Par Dn Darnall-cum-Attercliffe *Sheff* 93-94; C Hillsborough and Wadsley Bridge 94-96; P-in-c Stainforth 96-98; P-in-c Arksey 98-03; Asst Chapl Doncaster R Infirmary and Montagu Hosp NHS Trust 98-01; Asst Chapl Doncaster and Bassetlaw Hosps NHS Trust 01-04; Co-ord Chapl Services Rotherham Gen Hosps NHS Trust from 04. *Rotherham District General Hospital, Moorgate Road, Rotherham S60 2UD* Tel (01709) 820000 E-mail joan.ashton@rothgen.nhs.uk
ASHTON, Kenneth. b 61. Ridley Hall Cam. **d** 08 **p** 09. C Walthamstow *Chelmsf* from 08; P-in-c Hainault from 11. *The Vicarage, 143 Arrowsmith Road, Chigwell IG7 4NZ* Tel (020) 8500 3366 Mobile 07932-071715 E-mail ashtonken@gmail.com
ASHTON, Lesley June. b 49. York Univ BA89. NEOC 00. **d** 04 **p** 05. C Roundhay St Edm *Ripon* 04-08; P-in-c Hawksworth Wood 08-11; TV Abbeylands from 11; Asst Dir of Ords from 10. *St Mary's Vicarage, 50 Cragside Walk, Leeds LS5 3QE* Tel 0113-258 2923 Mobile 07813-354772 E-mail lesley.ashton1@ntlworld.com
ASHTON, Mrs Margaret Lucie. b 40. St Jo Coll Nottm 79. dss 83 **d** 87 **p** 94. Billericay and Lt Burstead *Chelmsf* 83-99; NSM 87-99; rtd 99; Hon C Fordingbridge and Breamore and Hale etc *Win* 01-05; Perm to Offic from 05. *3 Stephen Martin Gardens, Fordingbridge SP6 1RF* Tel (01425) 656205 E-mail peterdashton@onetel.com
ASHTON, Mrs Mary Isabel. b 57. Robert Gordon Inst of Tech Aber BSc78 Open Univ PGCE96. St Steph Ho Ox 07. **d** 09 **p** 10. C Whitewater *Win* from 09. *The Rectory, Vicarage Lane, Hound Green, Basingstoke RG27 8LF*
ASHTON, Neville Anthony. b 45. Sarum & Wells Th Coll 78. **d** 80 **p** 81. C Hattersley *Ches* 80-82; C Lancaster Ch Ch w St Jo and St Anne *Blackb* 82-84; R Church Kirk from 84. *Church Kirk Rectory, 434 Blackburn Road, Accrington BB5 0DE* Tel (01254) 236946
ASHTON, Canon Peter Donald. b 34. Lon Univ BD62. ALCD61. **d** 62 **p** 63. C Walthamstow St Mary *Chelmsf* 62-68; V Girlington *Bradf* 68-73; Dir Past Studies St Jo Coll Nottm 73-80; TR Billericay and Lt Burstead *Chelmsf* 80-99; Chapl Mayflower Hosp Billericay 80-99; Chapl St Andr Hosp Billericay 80-93; Chapl Thameside Community Healthcare NHS Trust 93-99; RD Basildon *Chelmsf* 89-99; Hon Can Chelmsf Cathl 92-99; rtd 99; Hon C Fordingbridge and Breamore and Hale etc *Win* from 01. *3 Stephen Martin Gardens, Fordingbridge SP6 1RF* Tel (01425) 656205 E-mail peterdashton@onetel.com
ASHTON, Preb Samuel Rupert. b 42. Sarum & Wells Th Coll. **d** 83 **p** 84. C Ledbury w Eastnor *Heref* 83-86; R St Weonards w Orcop, Garway, Tretire etc 86-98; RD Ross and Archenfield 91-95 and 96-98; P-in-c Cradley w Mathon and Storridge 98-99; R 99-07; Preb Heref Cathl 97-07; rtd 07; Perm to Offic *Heref* from 08. *The Old Greyhound, Longtown, Hereford HR2 0LD* Tel (01873) 860492
ASHTON (née JONES), Mrs Susan Catherine. b 48. Qu Coll Birm 09. **d** 11. NSM Knowle *Birm* from 11. *1467 Warwick Road, Knowle, Solihull B93 9LU* Tel (01564) 776895 E-mail sueashton2003@yahoo.co.uk
ASHTON, William Grant. b 57. St Chad's Coll Dur BA79. Oak Hill Th Coll BA85. **d** 85 **p** 86. C Lancaster St Thos *Blackb* 85-89; CF from 89; Chapl R Memorial Chpl Sandhurst 06-07. *clo MOD Chaplains (Army)* Tel (01264) 381141 Fax 381824
ASHURST, Mrs Judith Anne. b 57. St Aid Coll Dur BA80 St Jo Coll Dur BA08 ACIB83. Cranmer Hall Dur 06. **d** 08 **p** 09. C Belmont and Pittington Dur from 08. *Woodlea, Percy Lane, Durham DH1 4HE* Tel 0191-386 0794
ASHWELL, Anthony John. b 42. St Andr Univ BSc65. Sarum & Wells Th Coll 86. **d** 88 **p** 89. C Plymstock *Ex* 88-91; C Axminster, Chardstock, Combe Pyne and Rousdon 91-92; TV 92-95; C Crediton and Shobrooke 95-97; TV Bride Valley *Sarum* 97-07; P-in-c Symondsbury 05-07; RD Lyme Bay 03-06; rtd 07; Perm to Offic *Sarum* from 07. *Ven Cottage, Five Acres, Charmouth, Bridport DT6 6BE* Tel (01297) 560847 E-mail anthonyashwell@aol.com
ASHWIN, Canon Vincent George. b 42. Worc Coll Ox BA65. Coll of Resurr Mirfield 65. **d** 67 **p** 68. C Shildon *Dur* 67-70; C Newc St Fran 70-72; R Mhlosheni Swaziland 72-75; R Manzini 75-79; V Shildon *Dur* 79-85; V Fenham St Jas and St Basil *Newc* 85-97; RD Newc W 89-97; V Haydon Bridge and Beltingham w Henshaw 97-04; RD Hexham 97-02; Hon Can Newc Cathl 00-04; rtd 04; Perm to Offic *S'well* from 04. *83 Westgate, Southwell NG25 0LS* Tel (01636) 813975 E-mail vincentashwin@tiscali.co.uk
ASHWIN-SIEJKOWSKI, Piotr Jan. b 64. Warsaw Univ PhD97. Coll of Resurr Mirfield 98. **d** 91 **p** 92. Poland 92-98; C Tile Hill *Cov* 99-01; Chapl and Lect Univ Coll Chich 01-04; TV Richmond St Mary w St Matthias and St Jo *S'wark* from 04.

19 Old Deer Park Gardens, Richmond TW9 2TM Tel (020) 8940 8359 E-mail piotrashwin@btinternet.com

ASHWORTH, Canon David. b 40. Nottm Univ BPharm62. Linc Th Coll 63. **d** 65 **p** 66. C Halliwell St Thos *Man* 65-69; C Heywood St Jas 69-72; C-in-c Heywood St Marg CD 72-78; V Hale *Ches* 78-87; V Hale and Ashley 87-96; V Prestbury 96-05; RD Bowdon 87-95; RD Macclesfield 98-03; Hon Can Ches Cathl 94-05; rtd 05; Perm to Offic *Ches* from 05. *12 Lime Close, Sandbach CW11 1BZ* Tel (01270) 529187 E-mail david@ashworth39.freeserve.co.uk

ASHWORTH, Graham Ernest. b 52. LCTP 07. **d** 10 **p** 11. NSM Leyland St Ambrose *Blackb* from 10. *39 Lowther Drive, Leyland PR26 6QB* Tel (01772) 495422 Mobile 07541-988288 E-mail mrgraham.ashworth@blueyonder.co.uk

ASHWORTH, James Nigel. b 55. York Univ BA77. Cranmer Hall Dur 93. **d** 93 **p** 94. C Rothwell *Ripon* 93-96; Chapl Campsfield Ho Oxon 96-99; Hon C Akeman *Ox* 96-99; V Kemsing w Woodlands *Roch* 99-08; R Man St Ann from 08. *98 Rigby Street, Salford M7 4BQ* Tel 0161-792 1123 E-mail nigelashworth@btinternet.com

ASHWORTH, John Russell. b 33. Lich Th Coll 57. **d** 60 **p** 61. C Castleford All SS *Wakef* 60-62; C Luton St Sav *St Alb* 63-67; V Clipstone *S'well* 67-70; V Bolton-upon-Dearne *Sheff* 70-82; V Thornhill Lees *Wakef* 82-98; rtd 98; Perm to Offic *Wakef* from 99. *Walsingham, 2 Vicarage Road, Savile Town, Dewsbury WF12 9PD* Tel (01924) 461269

ASHWORTH, Keith Benjamin. b 33. NW Ord Course 76. **d** 79 **p** 80. C Pennington *Man* 79-83; P-in-c Bolton St Bede 83-88; V 00-95, V Hillock 95-01; rtd 01; Perm to Offic *Man* 01-06 and *Blackb* from 06. *3 Sandpiper Place, Thornton-Cleveleys FY5 3FE* Tel (01253) 855793

ASHWORTH, Martin. b 41. AKC63. **d** 64 **p** 65. C Wythenshawe Wm Temple Ch CD *Man* 64-71; R Haughton St Anne 71-83; V Prestwich St Marg 83-06; rtd 06; Perm to Offic *Man* 06-08. *Chiserley Stile Barn, 1 Chiserley Stile, Hebden Bridge HX7 8SB* Tel (01422) 843562

ASHWORTH, Nigel. See ASHWORTH, James Nigel

ASHWORTH, Timothy. b 52. Worc Coll of Educn CertEd74. Oak Hill Th Coll BA81. **d** 82 **p** 83. C Tonbridge St Steph *Roch* 82-85; C-in-c Whittle-le-Woods *Blackb* 85-90; Chapl Scargill Ho 90-96; V Ingleton w Chapel le Dale *Bradf* 96-03; TV Yate New Town *Bris* 03-08; NSM Lostock St Thos and St Jo *Man* from 09; NSM Bolton St Bede from 09. *St Bede's Vicarage, 92 Normanby Street, Bolton BL3 3QR* Tel (01204) 654016 E-mail timashworth52@tiscali.co.uk

ASHWORTH, Mrs Vivien. b 52. Worc Coll of Educn CertEd73. Trin Coll Bris 79 Oak Hill Th Coll BA82. **dss** 82 **d** 87 **p** 94. Tonbridge St Steph *Roch* 82-85; Whittle-le-Woods *Blackb* 85-90; Hon Par Dn 87-90; Chapl Scargill Ho 90-96; Hon C Ingleton w Chapel le Dale *Bradf* 96-03; Dioc Youth Adv 96-01; Hon C Yate New Town *Bris* 03-07; TV 07-08; Sub Chapl HM Pris Ashfield 04-09; P-in-c Lostock St Thos and St Jo *Man* from 09; P-in-c Bolton St Bede from 09. *St Bede's Vicarage, 92 Normanby Street, Bolton BL3 3QR* Tel (01204) 654016 E-mail viv.ashworth01@tiscali.co.uk

ASINUGO, Mrs Christiana Chidinma. NTMTC. **d** 09 **p** 10. C Becontree St Mary *Chelmsf* from 09. *187 Barley Lane, Romford RM6 4XU* Tel (020) 8597 9246 E-mail christyasinugo@yahoo.co.uk

ASIR, Jebamani Sekar Anand. See ANAND, The Very Revd Sekar Anand Asir

ASKEW, Miss Alison Jane. b 57. Dur Univ BA78 PGCE79. S Dios Minl Tr Scheme 93. **d** 95 **p** 96. NSM Kingsclere *Win* 95-96; Asst Chapl N Hants Hosps NHS Trust 95-99; Chapl 99-04; Sen Chapl Basingstoke and N Hants NHS Foundation Trust 04-10; P-in-c Kirby-on-the-Moor, Cundall w Norton-le-Clay etc *Ripon* from 10. *The Vicarage, 13a The Croft, Kirby Hill, Boroughbridge, York YO51 9YA* Tel (01423) 326585

ASKEW, Ms Catherine Clasen. b 75. Princeton Th Sem MDiv01. Cranmer Hall Dur 08. **d** 10 **p** 11. NSM Amble *Newc* from 10. *Northumbria Community, Hetton Hall, Chatton, Alnwick NE66 5SD* Tel (01289) 388235 E-mail catherineaskew@gmail.com

ASKEW, Peter Timothy. b 68. Ridley Hall Cam 00. **d** 02 **p** 03. C Bilton *Ripon* 02-06; C Harrogate St Mark and Chapl St Aid Sch Harrogate 06-09; Perm to Offic *Newc* 10-11; NSM Felton from 11. *Croft Cottage, Acton Home Farm, Felton, Morpeth NE65 9NU* Tel 07754-046429 (mobile) E-mail pete.askew2@ntlworld.com

ASKEW, Canon Reginald James Albert. b 28. CCC Cam BA51 MA55. Linc Th Coll 55. **d** 57 **p** 58. C Highgate St Mich *Lon* 57-61; Lect and Vice-Prin Wells Th Coll 61-69; PV Wells Cathl 61-69; V Paddington Ch Ch *Lon* 69-73; Member Corrymeela Community from 71; Prin Sarum & Wells Th Coll 73-87; Chmn S Dios Minl Tr Scheme 73-87; Can and Preb Sarum Cathl 75-87; Dean K Coll Lon 88-93; rtd 93; Perm to Offic *B & W* from 93 and *Lon* 93-96. *Carters Cottage, North Wootton, Shepton Mallet BA4 4AF* Tel (01749) 890728

ASKEW, Preb Richard George. b 35. BNC Ox BA59 MA63. Ridley Hall Cam 62. **d** 64 **p** 65. C Chesham St Mary *Ox* 64-66; C Mossley Hill St Matt and St Jas *Liv* 66-67; Chapl Ox Pastorate 67-72; Asst Chapl BNC Ox 67-71; R Ashtead *Guildf* 72-83; RD Leatherhead 80-83; Can Res and Treas Sarum Cathl 83-90; Dioc Adv on Miss and Min *B & W* 83-90; R Bath Abbey w St Jas 90-00; Preb Wells Cathl 92-00; Perm to Offic *Sarum* 00-01; TV Cley Hill Warminster 01-04; rtd 04. *Shepherd's Lea, 46 The Pastures, Westwood, Bradford-on-Avon BA15 2BH* Tel (01985) 844587 E-mail askew.easter@btinternet.com

ASKEY, Gary Simon. b 64. K Coll Lon LLB99 Univ Coll Lon LLM00 Univ of S Qld MEd04. St Steph Ho Ox 88. **d** 91 **p** 92. SSM 87-99; Prior SSM Priory Kennington 96-98; C Middlesbrough All SS *York* 91-94; Sub-Chapl HM Pris Holme Ho 92-94; C Whitby Miss and Seafarer's Trust 94-96; Lic to Offic *S'wark* 96-03; Hon C Angell Town St Jo 98-03; Perm to Offic 05-07; Hon C Walworth St Jo from 07. *St John's Cottage, 16 Larcom Street, London SE17 1NQ* Tel (020) 7450 1530 E-mail simon@askey.gs

ASKEY, John Stuart. b 39. Chich Th Coll 63. **d** 66 **p** 67. C Feltham *Lon* 66-69; C Epsom Common Ch Ch *Guildf* 69-72; C Chesterton Gd Shep *Ely* 72-74; R Stretham w Thetford 74-93; Dioc Spirituality Officer 75-98; Dioc Youth Officer 80-99; P-in-c Brinkley, Burrough Green and Carlton 93-97; P-in-c Westley Waterless 93-97; P-in-c Dullingham 93-97; P-in-c Stetchworth 93-97; R Raddesby Gp 97-99; Chapl Gothenburg w Halmstad, Jönköping etc *Eur* 99-04; rtd 04. *165 Lewes Road, Brighton BN2 3LD*

ASKEY, Matthew. b 74. Loughb Coll BA96 Bretton Hall Coll MA99 Leeds Univ BA09 Huddersfield Univ PGCE06. Coll of Resurr Mirfield 07. **d** 09 **p** 10. C Elland *Wakef* from 09. *50 Victoria Road, Elland HX5 0QA* Tel (01422) 370306 Mobile 07814-502034 E-mail maskey@mirfield.org.uk

ASKEY, Mrs Susan Mary. b 44. Leeds Univ MA00. NOC 99. **d** 99 **p** 00. C Golcar *Wakef* 99-02; P-in-c Drighlington from 02. *The Vicarage, Back Lane, Drighlington, Bradford BD11 1LS* Tel 0113-285 2402 E-mail smaskey@aol.com

ASKEY, Thomas Cyril. b 29. Sheff Univ BSc50 Man Univ MA(Theol)81 ACIPA58 MITMA76. NW Ord Course 70. **d** 73 **p** 74. NSM Gawsworth *Ches* 73-76; Perm to Offic 76-80; rtd 81; Perm to Offic *Derby* 99-05. *Park Cottage, Nether End, Baslow, Bakewell DE45 1SR* Tel (01246) 583780

ASKWITH, Mrs Helen Mary. b 57. Thames Valley Univ BSc00. ERMC 04. **d** 07 **p** 08. NSM Wembley St Jo *Lon* 07-10; NSM Northolt Park St Barn from 10. *21 Roxeth Green Avenue, Harrow HA2 8AE* Tel (020) 8422 3295 Mobile 07711-643220 E-mail hdaskwith@aol.com

ASMELASH, Berhane Tesfamariam. b 56. Addis Ababa Univ MD89 Lon Bible Coll MPhil04. SEITE BA08. **d** 08 **p** 09. C Upper Holloway *Lon* from 08. *6 Zoffany Street, London N19 3ER* Tel (020) 8424 8270 Mobile 07838-167198 E-mail berhanea@fastmail.fm

ASPINALL, Philip Norman. b 51. Cam Univ MA ATI. WMMTC 86. **d** 89 **p** 90. NSM Cov E 89-98. *139 Wiltshire Court, Nod Rise, Mount Nod, Coventry CV5 7JP* Tel (024) 7646 7509

✠**ASPINALL, The Most Revd Phillip John.** b 59. Univ of Tasmania BSc80 Trin Coll Melbourne BD88 Monash Univ PhD89 Deakin Univ MBA98. Melbourne Coll of Div. **d** 88 **p** 89 c 98. C S Launceston Australia 88-89; Asst P Brighton 89-91; P-in-c Bridgewater w Gagebrook 91-94; Dir Anglicare Tas 94-98; Adn for Ch and Soc 97-98; Asst Bp Adelaide 98-02; Abp Brisbane from 02; Primate of Australia from 05. *Bishopsbourne, GPO Box 421, Brisbane Qld 4001, Australia* Tel (0061) (7) 3835 2222 Fax 3832 5030 E-mail archbishops@anglicanbrisbane.org.au

ASQUITH, Barbara Rosemary. b 37. **d** 03 **p** 04. OLM S Ossett *Wakef* 03-06; OLM Batley All SS and Purlwell from 06. *115 Teall Street, Ossett WF5 0HS* Tel (01924) 271302 Mobile 07754-859247

ASQUITH (née SHIPLEY), June Patricia. b 54. Liv Hope BA00 PGCE01. SNWTP 08. **d** 10 **p** 11. NSM Walton Breck *Liv* from 10. *50 Bidston Road, Liverpool L4 7XJ* Tel 0151-263 0316 Mobile 07999-879922 E-mail jasquith@xalt.co.uk

ASQUITH, Michael John. b 60. St D Coll Lamp BA82 MPhil91 Ch Ch Coll Cant PGCE83. Cant Sch of Min 91. **d** 94 **p** 95. C S Ashford Ch Ch *Cant* 94-98; P-in-c Weldon w Deene *Pet* 98-00; P-in-c Corby Epiphany w St Jo 98-06; Dep Dioc Dir of Educn *Leic* 06-10; R Lowestoft St Marg *Nor* from 11. *St Margaret's Rectory, 147 Hollingsworth Road, Lowestoft NR32 4BW* Tel (01502) 573046 Mobile 07503-377360 E-mail mikeasq@aol.com

ASQUITH, Rosemary. See ASQUITH, Barbara Rosemary

ASSON, Geoffrey Ormrod. b 34. Univ of Wales (Ban) BA54 St Cath Coll Ox BA56 MA61. St Steph Ho Ox 54. **d** 57 **p** 58. C Aberdare *Llan* 57-59; C Roath 59-61; R Hagworthingham w Asgarby and Lusby *Linc* 61-65; P-in-c Mavis Enderby w Raithby 62-65; V Friskney 65-69; R S Ormsby w Ketsby, Calceby and Driby 69-74; R Harrington w Brinkhill 69-74; R Oxcombe 69-74; R Ruckland w Farforth and Maidenwell 69-74; R

Somersby w Bag Enderby 69-74; R Tetford and Salmonby 69-74; P-in-c Belchford 71-74; P-in-c W Ashby 71-74; V Riverhead w Dunton Green *Roch* 75-80; R Kington w Huntington *Heref* 80-82; RD Kington and Weobley 80-86; P-in-c Almeley 81-82; P-in-c Knill 81-82; P-in-c Old Radnor 81-82; R Kington w Huntington, Old Radnor, Kinnerton etc 82-86; V Mathry w St Edren's and Grandston etc *St D* 86-97; Bp's Rural Adv and Tourist Officer 91-95; rtd 96. *Sincerity, St Dogmaels, Cardigan SA43 3JZ* Tel (01239) 615591
ASTBURY, Susan. b 61. St Hugh's Coll Ox BA82 MA85 DPhil85. SWMTC 05. d 08. C Teignmouth, Ideford w Luton, Ashcombe etc *Ex* from 08. *3 The Strand, Shaldon, Teignmouth TQ14 0DL* Tel (01626) 873807 E-mail sue.ast@btinternet.com
ASTILL, Cyril John. b 33. Oak Hill Th Coll 62. d 65 p 66. C Carl St Jo 65-68; C St Helens St Helen *Liv* 68-71; V Blackb Sav 71-85; P-in-c Blackb Ch Ch w St Matt 81-83; TR N Ferriby *York* 85-97; V 97-99; rtd 99; P-in-c Burton Agnes w Harpham and Lowthorpe etc *York* 99-03. *18 Golden Vale, Churchdown, Gloucester GL3 2LU* Tel (01452) 859771
ASTIN, Howard Keith. b 51. Warwick Univ LLB. Trin Coll Bris 83. d 83 p 84. C Kirkheaton *Wakef* 83-88; V Bowling St Jo *Bradf* from 88. *St John's Vicarage, 96 Lister Avenue, Bradford BD4 7QS* Tel (01274) 727355 E-mail howard.astin@bradford.anglican.org
ASTIN, Mrs Moira Anne Elizabeth. b 65. Clare Coll Cam BA86 MA90. Wycliffe Hall Ox BA96. d 95 p 96. C Newbury *Ox* 95-99; C Thatcham 99-01; TV 01-05; TV Woodley 05-09; V Southlake 09-11; Angl Ecum Officer (Berks) 03-11; Dioc Ecum Officer 10-11; P-in-c Frodingham *Linc* from 11. *The Vicarage, Vicarage Gardens, Scunthorpe DN15 7AZ* Tel (01724) 334873 E-mail moira.astin@btinternet.com
ASTIN, Timothy Robin. b 58. St Edm Hall Ox BA79 Darw Coll Cam PhD82 FGS. Ox Min Course 90. d 93 p 94. NSM Reading St Jo *Ox* 93-95; NSM Newbury 95-99; NSM Beedon and Peasemore w W Ilsley and Farnborough 99-05; NSM Woodley 05-09; NSM Woodley 09-11; NSM Frodingham *Linc* from 11. *The Vicarage, Vicarage Gardens, Scunthorpe DN15 7AZ* Tel (01724) 334873 E-mail t.r.astin@reading.ac.uk
ASTLEY, Prof Jeffrey. b 47. Down Coll Cam BA68 MA72 Dur Univ PhD79. Qu Coll Birm 68. d 70 p 71. C Cannock *Lich* 70-73; Lect and Chapl St Hild Coll Dur 73-75; Sen Lect and Chapl SS Hild and Bede Coll Dur 75-77; Prin Lect & Hd Relig Studies Bp Grosseteste Coll 77-81; Lic to Offic *Linc* 78-81; Dir N England Inst for Chr Educn from 81. *Carter House, Pelaw Leazes Lane, Durham DH1 1TB* Tel 0191-384 1034 *or* 374 7807 Fax 384 7529 E-mail jeff.astley@durham.ac.uk
ASTON, Glyn. b 29. Univ of Wales (Abth) BA54 TCert55. Sarum & Wells Th Coll 84. d 79 p 80. Hon C Maindee Newport *Mon* 79-85; C 85-86; V Llangwm Uchaf and Llangwm Isaf w Gwernesney etc 86-99; rtd 99; Lic to Offic *Mon* from 99. *Flat 4, 47 Caerau Road, Newport NP20 4HH*
ASTON, John Bernard. b 34. Leeds Univ BA55 PGCE56. Qu Coll Birm 72. d 75 p 76. NSM Shenstone *Lich* 75-05; NSM Stonnall 00-05; Chapl HM YOI Swinfen Hall 90-99; Perm to Offic *Lich* from 05. *4 Footherley Road, Shenstone, Lichfield WS14 0NJ* Tel (01543) 480388
ASTON, John Leslie. b 47. Open Univ BSc99 Win Univ MA07. Oak Hill Th Coll BA80. d 80 p 81. C Trentham *Lich* 80-83; C Meir Heath 83-85; V Upper Tean 85-91; CF 91-02; C Andover w Foxcott *Win* 02-05; P-in-c Felixstowe SS Pet and Paul *St E* 05-11; V from 11. *The Vicarage, 14 Picketts Road, Felixstowe IP11 7JT* Tel (01394) 284049 E-mail john.aston@oldfelixstoweparish.org
ASTON, Mrs Kim Elizabeth. b 57. Colchester Inst of Educn BA78 LRAM78. SEITE 00. d 03. C Croydon St Jo *S'wark* 03-10; V Welling from 10. *St Mary's Vicarage, Sandringham Drive, Welling DA16 3QU* Tel (020) 8856 3247 E-mail astonkim@hotmail.com
ASTON, Michael James. b 48. Loughb Univ BSc70 MBCS85. NTMTC 98. d 01 p 02. NSM Writtle w Highwood *Chelmsf* 01-07; P-in-c W Hanningfield 07-11; rtd 11; Perm to Offic *Chelmsf* from 11. *15 Weller Grove, Chelmsford CM1 4YJ* Tel (01245) 442547 Mobile 07940-417418 E-mail mikaston@globalnet.co.uk
ASTON, Roger. b 52. Ox Poly BEd83. SAOMC 96. d 99 p 00. OLM Eynsham and Cassington *Ox* from 99. *9 Bell Close, Cassington, Witney OX29 4EP* Tel (01865) 880757 E-mail rogera52@aol.com
ASTON SMITH, Anthony. b 29. Trin Coll Cam BA52 MA56 PhD55 CEng MIM FIDiagE MICorrST AMIMechE. Ox NSM Course 86. d 93 p 94. NSM Ox St Giles and SS Phil and Jas w St Marg 93-99; rtd 99; Perm to Offic *Ox* from 99. *32 Chalfont Road, Oxford OX2 6TH* Tel (01865) 557090 E-mail a.j.astonsmith@btinternet.com
ASTON, Archdeacon of. *See* RUSSELL, The Ven Brian Kenneth
ASTON, Suffragan Bishop of. *See* WATSON, The Rt Revd Andrew John
ATACK, John Philip. b 49. Lanc Univ MA91. Linc Th Coll 86. d 88 p 89. C Cleveleys *Blackb* 88-92; V Appley Bridge 92-96; P-in-c Mostyn w Ffynnongroyw *St As* 99-03; P-in-c Colwyn

03-08; R Colwyn and Llanelian from 08; AD Rhos from 09; Chapl Conwy and Denbighshire NHS Trust 05-10; Hon Chapl Miss to Seafarers 01-03. *The Vicarage, 28 Bodelwyddan Avenue, Old Colwyn, Colwyn Bay LL29 9NP* Tel (01492) 518394 E-mail phil.atack@btopenworld.com
ATALLAH, David Alexander. b 74. Ox Univ MPhys97 Ex Univ MSc99 PhD03. Wycliffe Hall Ox 09. d 11. C Okehampton w Inwardleigh, Bratton Clovelly etc *Ex* from 11. *19 Fern Meadow, Okehampton EX20 1PB* Tel (01837) 54263 E-mail dave@atallahfamily.co.uk
ATFIELD, Gladys. Univ Coll Lon BSc53. Gilmore Course. dss 79 d 87 p 94. Bexley St Mary *Roch* 79-01; Hon C 87-01; rtd 01; Perm to Offic *Roch* from 01. *6 Clarendon Mews, High Street, Bexley DA5 1JS* Tel (01322) 551741
ATFIELD, Graham Roy. b 60. Kent Univ BA82. SEITE 08. d 11. NSM Rye *Chich* from 11. *104 Elphinstone Road, Hastings TN34 2BS* Tel (01424) 717382 Mobile 07810-554268 E-mail grahamatfield@hotmail.co.uk
ATFIELD, Tom David. b 80. Qu Coll Birm 08. d 11. C Bromsgrove St Jo *Worc* from 11. *403 Stourbridge Road, Catshill, Bromsgrove B61 9LG*
ATHERFOLD, Mrs Evelyne Sara. b 43. Leeds Inst of Educn CertEd64. NOC 82. dss 85 d 92 p 94. Kirk Sandall and Edenthorpe *Sheff* 85-87; NSM Fishlake w Sykehouse and Kirk Bramwith etc 87-00; P-in-c 00-03; R from 03; P-in-c from 11; Chapl HM YOI Hatfield 96-03. *Runswick House, Hay Green, Fishlake, Doncaster DN7 5JY* Tel (01302) 841396 Mobile 07980-282270 E-mail eve.atherfold@virgin.net
ATHERLEY, Keith Philip. b 56. St Steph Ho Ox 77. d 80 p 81. C Armley w New Wortley *Ripon* 80-82; C Harrogate St Wilfrid and St Luke 82-85; V Forcett and Stanwick w Aldbrough 85-89; CF 89-03; Perm to Offic *St Alb* 05-08 and *York* from 11. *14 Station Road, Loftus, Saltburn-by-the-Sea TS13 4PX* Tel 07946-758951 (mobile) E-mail kpatherley@aol.com
ATHERSTONE, Andrew Castell. b 74. Ch Coll Cam BA95 MA98 Wycliffe Hall Ox MSt99 DPhil01 FRHistS08. d 01 p 02. C Abingdon *Ox* 01-05; NSM Eynsham and Cassington from 05; Research Fell Latimer Trust from 05; Tutor Wycliffe Hall Ox from 07. *44 Shakespeare Road, Eynsham, Witney OX29 4PY* Tel (01865) 731239 E-mail andrew.atherstone@wycliffe.ox.ac.uk
ATHERSTONE, Canon Castell Hugh. b 45. Natal Univ BA67. St Chad's Coll Dur MA79. d 70 p 70. C Pietermaritzburg St Alphege S Africa 70-72; C Berea St Thos 72-74; C Kloor 74-77; R Hillcrest 77-80; R Newcastle 80-83; Dioc Stewardship Adv *Ely* 83-87; P-in-c Doddington w Benwick 83-87; R Frant w Eridge *Chich* 87-95; P-in-c Mark Cross 94-95; RD Rotherfield 90-94; V Seaford w Sutton 95-10; RD Lewes and Seaford 97-07; Can and Preb Chich Cathl 02-10; rtd 10; Perm to Offic *Ox* from 10. *9 The Tennis, Cassington, Witney OX29 4EL* Tel (01865) 880475 E-mail hugh@atherstone.net
ATHERTON, Graham Bryson. b 47. FTCL68 GRSM69 ARMCM69 Man Univ CertEd70. Edin Th Coll 77. d 79 p 80. C Orford St Marg *Liv* 79-82; V Warrington St Barn 82-88; V Leeds Halton St Wilfrid *Ripon* 88-95; RD Whitkirk 92-95; TR Guiseley w Esholt *Bradf* from 95. *The Rectory, The Green, Guiseley, Leeds LS20 9BB* Tel (01943) 874321 E-mail graham.atherton@bradford.anglican.org
ATHERTON, Henry Anthony. b 44. Univ of Wales BSc67 DipEd68 Fitzw Coll Cam BA72 MA75 Heythrop Coll Lon MTh00 FGS68. Westcott Ho Cam 70. d 72 p 73. C Leamington Priors All SS *Cov* 72-75; C Orpington All SS *Roch* 75-78; V Gravesend St Mary 78-87; Chapl St Jas Hosp Gravesend 82-87; V Bromley St Andr *Roch* 87-10; rtd 10. *20 Laleham Road, London SE6 2HT* Tel (020) 8695 0212 E-mail anthony6atherton@btinternet.com
ATHERTON, Canon John Robert. b 39. Lon Univ BA60 Man Univ MA74 PhD79. Coll of Resurr Mirfield 60. d 62 p 63. C Aberdeen St Marg 62-64; C Bury St Mark *Man* 64-67; P-in-c Glas St Marg 67-68; R Hulme St Geo *Man* 68-74; Ind Chapl 68-74; Asst Dir Wm Temple Foundn 74-79; Dir from 79; Lic to Offic 74-84; Can Res Man Cathl 84-04; rtd 04; Perm to Offic *Man* from 04. *102 Fairview Drive, Adlington, Chorley PR6 9SB* Tel (01257) 474882 Mobile 07989-969567
ATHERTON, Lionel Thomas. b 45. Univ of Wales (Ban) BA74 St Luke's Coll Ex. St Steph Ho Ox 74. d 76 p 77. C Chenies and Lt Chalfont *Ox* 76-79; C Fleet *Guildf* 79-84; V S Farnborough 84-89; TR Alston Team *Newc* 89-96; V Chorley St Pet *Blackb* 96-10; Bp's Adv on New Relig Movements 02-10; rtd 10. *36 Windsor Park Road, Buxton SK17 7NP* Tel (01257) 263423 E-mail lionelatherton@hotmail.com
ATHERTON, Paul Christopher. b 56. Chich Th Coll. d 82 p 83. C Orford St Marg *Liv* 82-86; CR 86-88; Chapl Univ of Wales (Cardiff) *Llan* 88-89; TV Walton St Mary *Liv* 89-92; C Westmr St Matt *Lon* 92-96; C Somers Town 96-97; V Bush Hill Park St Mark from 97; Chapl N Middx Hosp NHS Trust from 97. *The Vicarage, St Mark's Road, Enfield EN1 1BE* Tel (020) 8363 2780 E-mail paul.atherton@blueyonder.co.uk
ATHERTON, Philip Gordon. b 54. NTMTC BA07. d 07 p 08. NSM Hornsey H Innocents *Lon* from 07; NSM Stroud Green H

Trin from 07; NSM Harringay St Paul from 10. *4 Pensilver Close, Barnet EN4 9BE* Tel (020) 8441 5524 Mobile 07901-355235 E-mail philipatherton@tiscali.co.uk

ATKIN, Arthur Courtney Qu'appelle. b 19. Dur Univ BA44. Lich Th Coll 59. **d** 59 **p** 60. Chapl Bromsgrove Jun Sch 59-64; C Kidderminster St Geo *Worc* 59-60; C Bromsgrove All SS 60-64; Chapl RN 64-69; Chapl R Hosp Sch Holbrook 69-72; P-in-c Brixham *Ex* 72-74; Chapl Colston's Sch Bris 74-79; P-in-c Pitcombe w Shepton Montague and Bratton St Maur *B & W* 79-85; rtd 86; Perm to Offic *B & W* 86-93; Perm to Offic *Heref* from 93. *6 Leadon Bank, Orchard Lane, Ledbury HR8 1BY*

ATKINS, Andrew John. b 72. St Jo Coll Nottm 09. **d** 11. C Ex St Dav from 11. *5 Hove Villas, Haven Road, Exeter EX2 8BP* Tel (01392) 202024 Mobile 07599-058129 E-mail andya4jc@gmail.com

ATKINS, Austen Shaun. b 55. St Pet Coll Ox MA82 Selw Coll Cam MA85. Ridley Hall Cam 79. **d** 82 **p** 83. C S Mimms Ch Ch *Lon* 82-86; C Fulham St Matt 86-91; P-in-c Fulham St Dionis 91-03; V 03-04; C Ox St Andr 05-09; Chapl Bedford Sch from 09. *The Chaplaincy, Bedford School, De Parys Avenue, Bedford MK40 2TU* Tel (01234) 362239 E-mail chaplain@bedfordschool.org.uk

ATKINS, Canon David John. b 43. Kelham Th Coll 64. **d** 68 **p** 69. C Lewisham St Mary *S'wark* 68-72; Min Motspur Park 72-77; P-in-c Mitcham Ascension 77-82; V 82-83; P-in-c Downham w S Hanningfield *Chelmsf* 83-88; R 88-01; P-in-c W Hanningfield 90-93; RD Chelmsf S 93-01; V Maldon All SS w St Pet 01-09; Hon Can Chelmsf Cathl 00-09; rtd 09; Perm to Offic *Chelmsf* from 09. *19 The Green, Hadleigh, Ipswich IP7 6AE* Tel (01473) 822535 E-mail atkins.d@btinternet.com

ATKINS, Dean John. b 70. Univ of Wales (Cardiff) BD93. St Steph Ho Ox 93. **d** 95 **p** 96. C Merthyr Dyfan *Llan* 95-99; V Aberaman and Abercwmboi w Cwmaman 99-01; Dioc Youth Officer from 01; P-in-c Roath St Sav from 08. *St Anne's, 1 North Church Street, Cardiff CF10 5HB* Tel (029) 2049 9867

ATKINS, Mrs Diana. b 31. K Coll Lon BD54 DipEd55. Qu Coll Birm 81. **dss** 83 **d** 87. De Beauvoir Town St Pet *Lon* 83-85; Gleadless *Sheff* 85-93; Par Dn 87-93; rtd 93; Perm to Offic *Sheff* from 93. *27 Stannington Glen, Sheffield S6 6NA* Tel 0114-234 0543

ATKINS, Forrest William (Bill). b 59. Ch Coll Cam MA85 Lon Univ BD84. Ridley Hall Cam 83. **d** 86 **p** 87. C Normanton *Derby* 86-90; C Stratford St Jo and Ch Ch w Forest Gate St Jas *Chelmsf* 90-97; Asst Chapl Dubai and Sharjah w N Emirates 97-03; 1 Mohill w Farnaught, Aughavas, Oughteragh etc *K, E & A* from 03. *St Mary's Rectory, Mohill, Co Leitrim, Republic of Ireland* Tel (00353) (71) 963 2959 E-mail fwatkins@eircom.net

ATKINS, Francis John. b 47. CEng MIStructE. S Dios Minl Tr Scheme. **d** 89 **p** 90. NSM Studley *Sarum* 89-92; Lic to RD Bradford from 92. *Church Cottage, 344 Frome Road, Trowbridge BA14 0EF* Tel (01225) 761757

ATKINS, Jane Elizabeth. b 51. EMMTC 98. **d** 01 **p** 02. NSM Fenn Lanes Gp *Leic* 01-05; Sub Chapl HM Pris Leic 03-05; P-in-c Ashill w Saham Toney *Nor* 05-07; V Ashill, Carbrooke, Ovington and Saham Toney from 07. *The Rectory, Swaffham Road, Ashill, Thetford IP25 7BT* Tel (01760) 441191

ATKINS, Joy Katherine. b 75. Lon Sch of Th BTh97 Dur Univ PGCE98. St Jo Coll Nottm MTh09. **d** 09 **p** 10. C Uxbridge *Lon* from 09. *St Andrew's Vicarage, 32A Greenway, Uxbridge UB8 2PJ* Tel (01895) 200252 Mobile 07799-835696 E-mail joy.atkins@uxbridgeparish.org

ATKINS, Nicholas Steven. b 60. Oak Hill Th Coll BA88. **d** 88 **p** 89. C Shepton Mallet w Doulting *B & W* 88-91; C Combe Down w Monkton Combe and S Stoke 91-93; TV N Wingfield, Clay Cross and Pilsley *Derby* 93-98; V Essington *Lich* 98-05; P-in-c Ipswich St Matt *St E* 05-06; R Triangle, St Matt and All SS from 06. *St Matthew's Rectory, 3 Portman Road, Ipswich IP1 2ES* Tel (01473) 251630

ATKINS, Canon Paul Henry. b 38. St Mich Coll Llan 62. **d** 65 **p** 66. C Sheringham *Nor* 65-68; V Southtown 68-84; RD Flegg (Gt Yarmouth) 78-84; P Aylmerton w Runton 84-99; P-in-c Beeston Regis 98-99; P-in-c Gresham 98-99; R Aylmerton, Runton, Beeston Regis and Gresham 99-03; RD Repps 86-95; Hon Can Nor Cathl 88-03; rtd 03; Perm to Offic *Nor* from 03. *34 Regis Avenue, Beeston Regis, Sheringham NR26 8SW* Tel (01263) 820147 E-mail amdd24@dial.pipex.com

ATKINS, Peter. b 29. Edin Univ MA52. Edin Th Coll 52. **d** 54 **p** 55. C Edin Old St Paul 54-59; P-in-c Edin St Dav 59-64; Chapl Fulbourn Hosp Cam 64-66; R Galashiels *Edin* 66-69; Perm to Offic 69-72; Divisional Dir Soc Services Brighton 72-83; Asst Dir Soc Services E Sussex from 83. *Address temp unknown*

ATKINS, Robert Brian. b 49. Open Univ BA94 CIPFA78. SAOMC 94. **d** 97 **p** 98. NSM Bicester w Bucknell, Caversfield and Launton *Ox* from 97. *8 Tubb Close, Bicester OX26 2BN* Tel (01869) 600504 Mobile 07905-814401

ATKINS, Roger Francis. b 30. AKC54. **d** 55 **p** 56. C Bromley All Hallows *Lon* 55-58; C Eastleigh *Win* 58-62; Missr The Murray Australia 62-65; R Mossman 65-69; Adn Carpentaria 69-71; V

Wolverley *Worc* 71-76; V S Hackney St Mich w Haggerston St Paul *Lon* 76-85; TV Gleadless *Sheff* 85-93; rtd 93; Perm to Offic *Sheff* from 93. *27 Stannington Glen, Sheffield S6 6NA* Tel 0114-234 0543

ATKINS, Shaun. See ATKINS, Austen Shaun

ATKINS, Timothy David. b 45. Ridley Hall Cam 71. **d** 74 **p** 75. C Stoughton *Guildf* 74-79; C Chilwell *S'well* 79-84; R Eastwood 84-91; V Finchley Ch Ch *Lon* 91-10; Chapl Barnet Healthcare NHS Trust 92-01; Chapl Enfield Primary Care Trust 01-10; rtd 10. *106 Ashurst Road, London N12 9AB* Tel (020) 8445 7185 E-mail ta.atkins@hotmail.co.uk

ATKINS, Timothy James. b 38. Worc Coll Ox BA62. Cuddesdon Coll 62. **d** 64 **p** 65. C Stafford St Mary *Lich* 64-67; C Loughborough St Pet *Leic* 67-69; C Usworth *Dur* 69-71; Lic to Offic *Newc* 71-76; P-in-c Slaley 76-87; P-in-c Shotley 87-05; Dioc Child Protection Adv 98-06. *5 Railway Terrace, Witton le Wear, Bishop Auckland DL14 0AL* Tel (01388) 488626

ATKINS, Timothy Samuel. b 22. DSC44. Em Coll Cam BA46 MA52. Ridley Hall Cam 47. **d** 49 **p** 50. C Melton Mowbray w Burton Lazars, Freeby etc *Leic* 49-51; C Preston St Jo *Blackb* 51-54; V Baxenden 54-58; R Mildenhall *St E* 58-63; V Bunbury *Ches* 63-87; RD Malpas 85-87; rtd 87; Perm to Offic *Ches* 87-01. *7 Fosbrooke House, 8 Clifton Drive, Lytham St Annes FY8 5RQ* Tel (01253) 667052

ATKINS, William. See ATKINS, Forrest William

ATKINSON, Adam. b 67. Birm Univ BA89. Wycliffe Hall Ox 05. **d** 07 **p** 08. C Shadwell St Paul w Ratcliffe St Jas *Lon* 07-11; C Bethnal Green St Pet w St Thos from 11. *St Peter's Vicarage, St Peter's Close, London E2 7AE* Tel (020) 7229 0550 Mobile 07780-992112 E-mail adam@spbg.info

ATKINSON, Ms Audrey. b 54. Univ of Wales (Lamp) BA97 Trin Coll Carmarthen PGCE98. Coll of Resurr Mirfield 06. **d** 08 **p** 09. C Beadnell and N Sunderland *Newc* 08-11; Dep Warden Launde Abbey *Leic* from 11. *South Cottage, Launde Abbey, Launde Road, Launde, Leicester LE7 9XB* Tel (01572) 717009 Mobile 07833-198968 E-mail audreyatkinson@hotmail.co.uk

ATKINSON, Brian Colin. b 54. Sarum & Wells Th Coll 85. **d** 87 **p** 88. C Up Hatherley *Glouc* 87-90; R Upper Stour *Sarum* 90-95; TR Trowbridge H Trin 95-04; P-in-c Fairford and Kempsford w Whelford *Glouc* 04-08; TR Fairford Deanery from 09; AD Fairford from 04. *The Vicarage, The Croft, Fairford GL7 4BB* Tel and fax (01285) 712467 E-mail katki01225@aol.com

ATKINSON, Christopher John. b 57. Man Univ BA80. Qu Coll Birm 82. **d** 85 **p** 86. C Stalybridge *Man* 85-88; P-in-c Westhall w Brampton and Stoven *St E* 88-89; P-in-c Sotterley, Willingham, Shadingfield, Ellough etc 88-90; P-in-c Hundred River Gp of Par 90-92; R Hundred River 92-97; P-in-c Eye w Braiseworth and Yaxley 97-00; P-in-c Occold 97-00; P-in-c Bedingfield 97-00; R Eye 00-03; RD Hartismere 97-03; V Bourne *Linc* from 03. *Vicarage, Church Walk, Bourne PE10 9UQ* Tel (01778) 422412 E-mail chris atk@yahoo.com

ATKINSON, Canon Christopher Lionel Varley. b 39. K Coll Lon 63. Chich Th Coll 65. **d** 67 **p** 68. C Sowerby Bridge w Norland *Wakef* 67-70; P-in-c Flushing *Truro* 70-73; Dioc Adv in RE 70-73; Perm to Offic *Worc* 74-78; TR Halesowen 78-88; RD Dudley 79-87; Hon Can Worc Cathl 83-88; V Cartmel *Carl* 88-97; TV Cartmel Peninsula 97-98; RD Windermere 94-98; Hon Can Carl Cathl 94-98; TR Bensham *Dur* 98-03; AD Gateshead 99-03; rtd 03; Bp's Adv Spiritual Development *Dur* 03-08; Hon Can Dur Cathl from 01. *4 Attwood Place, Tow Law, Bishop Auckland DL13 4ER* Tel (01388) 731749

ATKINSON, Clive James. b 68. QUB BSc90. CITC 90. **d** 93 **p** 94. C Belfast H Trin and Ardoyne *Conn* 93-97; I Belfast Upper Falls 97-02; Chapl Vevey w Château d'Oex *Eur* from 02. *The Parsonage, chemin de Champsavaux 1, 1807 Blonay, Vaud, Switzerland* Tel (0041) (21) 943 2239 E-mail info@allsaints.ch

ATKINSON, Prof David. b 44. Hull Univ BSc66 Newc Univ PhD69 CBiol FIBiol FRSA MIEEM. TISEC 03. **d** 05 **p** 06. C Aberdeen St Andr 05-07; P Bieldside 07-09; P Auchindoir from 09; P Inverurie from 09; P Kemnay from 09. *33 Norman Gray Park, Blackburn, Aberdeen AB21 0ZR* Tel (01224) 791163 E-mail atkinson390@btinternet.com

ATKINSON, David. b 64. St Cuth Soc Dur BA02. Cranmer Hall Dur 02. **d** 04 **p** 05. C Dunston *Dur* 04-07; C Pelton and W Pelton 07-10; P-in-c Dunston 10-11; V from 11. *St Nicholas' Vicarage, Willow Avenue, Dunston, Gateshead NE11 9UN* Tel 0191-460 9327 E-mail revd.atkinson@btinternet.com

ATKINSON, Canon David James. b 41. K Coll Lon BD63 AKC63 Selw Coll Cam BA65 MA72. Linc Th Coll 65. **d** 66 **p** 67. C Linc St Giles 66-70; Asst Chapl Newc Univ 70-73; P-in-c Adbaston *Lich* 73-80; Adult Educn Officer 73-75; Dioc Dir of Educn 75-82; Preb Lich Cathl 79-82; Chapl Hull Univ 82-87; Dioc Dir of Educn *Linc* 87-94; P-in-c Bishop Norton, Wadingham and Snitterby 94-01; Perm to Offic from 01; Can and Preb Linc Cathl 89-06; rtd 06. *4 The Orchards, Middle Rasen, Market Rasen LN8 3TL* Tel (01673) 849979

✠**ATKINSON, The Rt Revd David John.** b 43. K Coll Lon BSc65 AKC65 PhD69 Bris Univ MLitt73 Ox Univ MA85 MSOSc. Trin Coll Bris and Tyndale Hall Bris 69. **d** 72 **p** 73 **c** 01. C

Halliwell St Pet *Man* 72-74; C Harborne Heath *Birm* 74-77; Lib Latimer Ho Ox 77-80; Chapl CCC Ox 80-93; Fell 84-93; Visiting Lect Wycliffe Hall Ox 84-93; Can Res and Chan S'wark Cathl 93-96; Adn Lewisham 96-01; Suff Bp Thetford *Nor* 01-09; rtd 09; Asst Bp S'wark from 09. *6 Bynes Road, South Croydon CR2 0PR* Tel (020) 8406 0895 E-mail davidatkinson43@virginmedia.com

ATKINSON, Derek Arthur. b 31. K Coll Lon BD59 AKC59. **d** 60 **p** 61. C Ashford *Cant* 60-64; C Deal St Leon 64-68; R E w W Ogwell *Ex* 68-81; Asst Dir of RE 68-78; Dep Dir and Children's Adv 78-88; R Ogwell and Denbury 81-84; R Kenton w Mamhead and Powderham 84-88; rtd 88; Perm to Offic *Ex* 88-98. *High Trees, Fulford Road, Fulford, Stoke-on-Trent ST11 9QT* Tel (01782) 397156 E-mail derek-atkinson@lineone.net

ATKINSON, Mrs Heather Dawn. b 69. Leeds Univ BA02. NOC 03. **d** 05 **p** 06. C Morley *Wakef* 05-08; P-in-c Moldgreen and Rawthorpe from 08. *The Vicarage, 35 Church Street, Huddersfield HD5 9DL* Tel (01484) 424432 Mobile 07766-575371 E-mail heatherwood19@yahoo.co.uk

ATKINSON, Ian. b 33. BNC Ox BA58 MA63. Coll of Resurr Mirfield 56. **d** 58 **p** 59. C Welling S'wark 58-62; C Camberwell St Giles 62-63; V Wandsworth Common St Mary 63-67; C Pretoria Cathl S Africa 67-68; C Oxted *S'wark* 68-69; Asst Chapl Ch Hosp Horsham 70-85; NSM Dalmahoy *Edin* 85-91; Asst Master Clifton Hall Sch 85-91; NSM Dunkeld *St And* from 92; rtd 98. *2 Pinel Lodge, Druids Park, Murthly, Perth PH1 4ES* Tel (01738) 710561

ATKINSON, Canon Prof James. b 14. St Jo Coll Dur BA36 MA39 MLitt50 Univ of Munster DTh55 Hull Univ Hon DD97. **d** 37 **p** 38. C Newc H Cross 37-41; Succ Sheff Cathl 41-42; Prec 42-44; V Shiregreen St Jas and St Chris 44-51; Fell Sheff Univ from 51; Can Th Leic Cathl 54-70; Lect Th Hull Univ 56-64; Reader 64-67; Prof Bibl Studies Sheff Univ 67-79; Lic to Offic *Sheff* 68-06; Perm to Offic from 07; Can Th Sheff Cathl 70-93; rtd 79; Latimer Ho Ox 81-84. *Leach House, Leadmill Bridge, Hathersage, Hope Valley S32 1BA* Tel (01433) 650570

ATKINSON, Canon John Dudley. b 38. ACA60 FCA71. Qu Coll Birm 63. **d** 66 **p** 67. C Bishop's Stortford St Mich *St Alb* 66-70; C Norton 70-73; V Markyate Street 73-80; R Baldock w Bygrave 80-94; RD Stevenage 83-89; TR Bride Valley *Sarum* 94-03; RD Lyme Bay 98-03; Can and Preb Sarum Cathl 02-03; rtd 03; Perm to Offic *Heref* from 04. *48 Prince Rupert Road, Ledbury HR8 2FA* Tel (01531) 632014 E-mail canonjda@btinternet.com

ATKINSON, Ms Judith Angela. b 70. Leeds Univ BA92 Fitzw Coll Cam BA95 MA02. Ridley Hall Cam 93. **d** 96 **p** 97. C Chester le Street *Dur* 96-00; Community Employment Development Worker 00-01; NSM Dunston 01-02; Ch Partnership Co-ord N Tyneside 00-02; Lic to Offic *Birm* 03-06; Regional Manager KeyRing Living Support Networks 03-05; Dir (Research and Projects) 05-07; Perm to Offic Canberra & Goulburn Australia from 07. *United Theological College, 16 Masons Drive, North Parramatta, NSW 2151, Australia* E-mail juditha_stephenh@hotmail.com

ATKINSON, Mrs Kate Bigwood. b 56. Cranmer Hall Dur 94. **d** 96 **p** 97. C Woking St Jo *Guildf* 96-00; NSM Haslemere and Grayswood 00-03; Assoc P Incline Village USA from 03. *818 Barbara Street, Incline Village NV 89451-8514, USA*

ATKINSON, Canon Lewis Malcolm. b 34. St Jo Coll Dur. **d** 82 **p** 83. C Chapeltown *Sheff* 82-85; V Sheff St Paul 85-93; Ind Chapl 85-99; RD Ecclesfield 90-93; V Oughtibridge 93-99; RD Tankersley 96-99; Hon Can Sheff Cathl 98-99; rtd 99; Perm to Offic *Sheff* from 99. *14 Rowan Close, Chapeltown, Sheffield S35 1QE*

ATKINSON, Margaret Ann. d 07 **p** 08. OLM Fawdon *Newc* from 07. *48 Brotherlee Road, Newcastle upon Tyne NE3 2SL*

ATKINSON, Marianne Rose. b 39. Girton Coll Cam BA61 CertEd62 MA64. Linc Th Coll 86. **d** 88 **p** 94. C S w N Hayling *Portsm* 88-91; C Rainham *Roch* 91-92; Asst Chapl Salford R Hosps NHS Trust 92-97; Hon C Prestwich St Marg *Man* 94-97; Chapl R United Hosp Bath NHS Trust 97-00; rtd 00; Perm to Offic *B & W* 00-03 and *St E* from 03. *68 Barons Road, Bury St Edmunds IP33 2LW* Tel (01284) 752075 E-mail torrensatkinson@aol.com

ATKINSON, Megan Annice. b 37. SRN58. STETS 95. **d** 98 **p** 01. NSM Bridgemary *Portsm* 98-02; NSM Locks Heath 02-04; rtd 04; Perm to Offic *Portsm* from 05. *23 Home Rule Road, Locks Heath, Southampton SO31 6LH* Tel (01489) 575331 E-mail meganatkinson1@msn.com

ATKINSON, Michael Hubert. b 33. Qu Coll Ox BA57 MA60. Ripon Hall Ox 56. **d** 58 **p** 59. C Attercliffe w Carbrook *Sheff* 58-60; Ind Chapl 60-66; C Sharrow St Andr 60-66; Ind Chapl *Pet* 66-71; Sen Ind Chapl *Cant* 71-79; Research Officer Gen Syn Bd for Soc Resp 79-87; Representation Sec USPG 88-92; TV High Wycombe *Ox* 92-97; Chapl Bucks Coll of HE 94-97; rtd 97. *7 Birch Court, Old Bridge Rise, Ilkley LS29 9HH* Tel (01943) 609891

ATKINSON, Nigel Terence. b 60. Sheff Univ BA82 St Jo Coll Dur MA96. Westmr Th Sem (USA) MDiv87 Cranmer Hall Dur

ATKINSON, Canon Patricia Anne. b 47. EAMTC 86. **d** 89 **p** 01. NSM Nor St Steph 89-94; Lic to Offic from 94; Chapl Norfolk Primary Care Trust from 00; Chapl Norfolk and Nor Univ Hosp NHS Trust 01-11; NSM Brundall w Braydeston and Postwick *Nor* 01-02; Hon Can Nor Cathl from 06. *32 Berryfields, Brundall, Norwich NR13 5QE* Tel (01603) 714720 E-mail revpat@live.co.uk

ATKINSON, Paul William. b 64. St Steph Ho Ox 07. **d** 09 **p** 10. C Castleford *Wakef* from 09; C Smawthorpe from 11. *St Paul's Vicarage, Churchfield Lane, Castleford WF10 4BP* Tel (01977) 512404 E-mail aldextra@sky.com

ATKINSON, Peter Duncan. b 41. Univ Coll Dur BA62. Linc Th Coll 63. **d** 65 **p** 66. C Beckenham St Geo *Roch* 65-69; C Caversham *Ox* 69-75; P-in-c Millfield St Mark *Dur* 76-86; V Dedworth *Ox* 86-93; TV Aylesbury w Bierton and Hulcott 93-05; rtd 05. *24 Grimbald Road, Knaresborough HG5 8HD* Tel (01423) 866593

ATKINSON, The Very Revd Peter Gordon. b 52. St Jo Coll Ox BA74 MA78 FRSA06. Westcott Ho Cam 77. **d** 79 **p** 80. C Clapham Old Town *S'wark* 79-83; P-in-c Tatsfield 83-90; R Bath H Trin *B & W* 90-91; Prin Chich Th Coll 91-94; Can and Preb Chich Cathl 91-97; R Lavant 94-97; Can Res and Chan Chich Cathl 97-07; Dean Worc from 07. *The Deanery, 10 College Green, Worcester WR1 2LH* Tel (01905) 732939 *or* 732909 Fax 732906 E-mail peteratkinson@worcestercathedral.org.uk

ATKINSON, Philip Charles. b 50. Hull Univ BA71 PhD76 Chorley Coll of Educn CertEd77. NOC 81. **d** 84 **p** 85. NSM Bolton SS Simon and Jude *Man* 84-87; Chapl R Wolv Sch 87-05; rtd 05. *22 Kirton Grove, Tettenhall, Wolverhampton WV6 8RX*

ATKINSON, Philip John. b 69. Birkbeck Coll Lon PhD04. Ridley Hall Cam 08. **d** 10 **p** 11. C Ox St Aldate from 10. *St Aldate's Parish Office, 40 Pembroke Street, Oxford OX1 1BP* Tel (01865) 254800 E-mail pja.online@gmail.com

ATKINSON, Philip Stephen. b 58. K Coll Lon BD80 AKC80 Dur Univ MA97. Ridley Hall Cam 81. **d** 83 **p** 84. C Barrow St Matt *Carl* 83-86; C Kirkby Lonsdale 86-89; R Redmarshall *Dur* 89-95; V Bishopton w Gt Stainton 89-95; C Kirkby Lonsdale *Carl* 95-97; Chapl Casterton Sch Lancs 95-09; NSM Kirkby Lonsdale *Carl* 97-09; Chapl Taunton Sch 09-11; R Odd Rode *Ches* from 11. *Odd Rode Rectory, Church Lane, Scholar Green, Stoke-on-Trent ST7 3QN* Tel (01270) 882195

ATKINSON, The Ven Richard William Bryant. b 58. OBE02. Magd Coll Cam MA. Ripon Coll Cuddesdon. **d** 84 **p** 85. C Abingdon w Shippon *Ox* 84-87; TV Sheff Manor 87-91; TR 91-96; Hon Tutor Ripon Coll Cuddesdon 87-92; V Rotherham *Sheff* 96-02; Hon Can Sheff Cathl 98-02; Adn Leic from 02. *46 Southernhay Road, Leicester LE2 3TJ* Tel and fax 0116-270 4441 *or* tel 248 7419 E-mail richard.atkinson@leccofe.org

ATKINSON, Miss Ruth Irene. b 58. Worc Coll of Educn BEd80 Cant Ch Ch Univ MA08. Qu Coll Birm 06. **d** 09 **p** 10. C Old Swinford Stourbridge *Worc* from 09. *58 Arlington Court, Stourbridge DY8 1NN* Tel (01384) 373286 Mobile 07913-849532 E-mail home@riatkinson.plus.com

ATKINSON, Canon Samuel Charles Donald. b 30. TCD BA54. **d** 55 **p** 56. C Belfast St Simon *Conn* 55-62; I Ballynaclough *L & K* 62-68; I Cloughjordan w Modreeny 68-87; Dioc Youth Adv (Killaloe) 75-83; Dioc Info Officer 76-88; Can Killaloe Cathl 76-82; Chan *K & A* 82-96; I Cloughjordan w Borrisokane etc 87-96; rtd 96. *Dromore Lodge, Rockcorry, Co Monaghan, Republic of Ireland* Tel (00353) (42) 42356

ATKINSON, Simon James. b 71. St Chad's Coll Dur BA93 Ustinov Coll Dur PGCE04 PGDE08. St Steph Ho Ox 93. **d** 95 **p** 96. C Norton St Mary *Dur* 95-96; C Hartlepool H Trin 96-99; TV Jarrow 99-01; V Chich St Wilfrid 01-03; Perm to Offic *Dur* 03-09 and *Lon* 09-10; NSM Old St Pancras *Lon* from 10; Headteacher Hampstead Paroch C of E Primary Sch from 10; CMP from 98. *Hampstead Parochial Primary School, Holly Bush Vale, London NW3 6TX* Tel (020) 7435 4135 E-mail head@hampsteadprim.camden.sch.uk

ATKINSON, Terence Harry. b 52. Coll of Resurr Mirfield 88. **d** 90 **p** 91. C Bottesford w Ashby *Linc* 90-93; TV Cleethorpes 93-98; C-in-c Cleethorpes St Fran CD 98-01; V Chapel St Leonards w Hogsthorpe 01-03; Perm to Offic *Gt Grimsby St Andr w St Luke and All SS* from 03. *St Andrew's Vicarage, 2A Albion Street, Grimsby DN32 7DY* Tel (01472) 348200

ATKINSON, Wendy Sybil. b 53. Man Univ BA95. NOC 95. **d** 97 **p** 98. NSM Brinnington w Portwood *Ches* 97-99; C 99-01; NSM Werneth from 01. *8 Freshfield Close, Marple Bridge, Stockport SK6 5ES* Tel 0161-427 5612

ATKINSON-JONES, Mrs Susan Florence. b 64. Univ of Wales (Cardiff) BD93. St Mich Coll Llan 96. **d** 98 **p** 99. C Bargoed and

Deri w Brithdir *Llan* 98-05; TV Sanderstead *S'wark* from 05. *35 Audley Drive, Warlingham CR6 9AH* Tel (020) 8657 5505 E-mail susan@sanderstead-parish.org.uk

ATLING, Canon Edwood Brian. b 46. ACIB FCMI. Westcott Ho Cam 00. **d** 02 **p** 03. NSM Godmanchester *Ely* 02-04; P-in-c Abbots Ripton w Wood Walton from 04; P-in-c Kings Ripton from 04; P-in-c Houghton w Wyton from 04; RD Huntingdon from 06; Hon Can Ely Cathl from 10. *Blue Cedars, 70 Common Lane, Hemingford Abbots, Huntingdon PE28 9AW* Tel (01480) 493975 Fax 496240 Mobile 07775-544679 E-mail atling@btopenworld.com

ATTA-BAFFOE, Victor Reginald. b 59. Trin Coll Toronto BTh88 Episc Div Sch Cambridge (USA) MA92 Yale Univ STM93. St Nic Th Coll Ghana LTh87. **d** 88 **p** 89. Ghana 88-90 and 93-98; USA 90-93; Lect St Nic Th Coll 88-90 and 93-98; NSM Finsbury Park St Thos *Lon* from 99. *20 Great Peter Street, London SW1P 2BU* Tel (020) 7222 3704 Fax 7233 0255

ATTAWAY, Mrs Elizabeth Ann. b 36. Herts Coll CertEd56. Cant Sch of Min 93 Bp Otter Coll 57. **d** 96 **p** 97. NSM Maidstone St Paul *Cant* 96-02; NSM Boxley w Detling from 02. *1 Staplers Court, Penenden Heath, Maidstone ME14 2XB* Tel (01622) 762656 E-mail glattaway@btinternet.com

ATTFIELD, David George. b 31. Magd Coll Ox BA54 MA58 BD61 K Coll Lon MPhil72 Dur Univ MA81. Westcott Ho Cam 57. **d** 58 **p** 59. C Edgbaston St Aug *Birm* 58-61; C Ward End 61-62; Lect Div St Kath Coll Tottenham 62-64; All SS Coll Tottenham 64-68; Sen Lect St Bede Coll Dur 68-75; St Hild and St Bede Coll 75-80; TV Drypool *York* 80-86; R Newton Heath All SS *Man* 86-96; rtd 97; Perm to Offic *Dur* from 97. *19 Laburnum Avenue, Durham DH1 4HA* Tel 0191-383 0509

ATTLEY, Ronald. b 46. Open Univ BA87. Brasted Th Coll 66 Chich Th Coll 68. **d** 70 **p** 71. C Heworth St Mary *Dur* 70-73; C Hulme Ascension *Man* 73-75; R Corozal and Orange Walk Belize 76-79; V Leadgate *Dur* 79-84; Chapl HM Rem Cen Ashford 84-87; Chapl HM Pris Ashwell and Stocken 87-89; Chapl HM Pris Frankland 89-92; Chapl HM YOI Deerbolt 92-96; V Bath St Barn w Englishcombe *B & W* 96-00; Belize 00; V Brinnington w Portwood *Ches* 01-06; P Narrogin Australia 06-11; rtd 11. *103 Clayton Road, Narrogin WA 6312, Australia* Tel (0061) (8) 0881 1041 E-mail frrona@hotmail.com

ATTWATER, Mrs Sallyanne. b 48. Westmr Coll Ox MTh98. S Dios Minl Tr Scheme 86. **d** 94 **p** 95. Chapl Asst Eastbourne Distr Gen Hosp 94-95; Asst Chapl Princess Alice Hosp and All SS Hosp 94-95; C E Grinstead St Swithun *Chich* 95-98; P-in-c Bishop's Cannings, All Cannings etc *Sarum* 98-10; RD Devizes 07-10; rtd 10. *51 St Kitts Drive, Eastbourne BN23 5TL* Tel (01323) 472266 E-mail sally.attwater@gmail.com

ATTWATER, Canon Stephen Philip. b 47. ALCM67. Linc Th Coll 85. **d** 87 **p** 88. C Warrington St Elphin *Liv* 87-90; P-in-c Eccleston St Thos 90-94; V 94-99; V Padgate from 99; AD Warrington from 05; Hon Can Liv Cathl from 05. *The Rectory, Station Road South, Padgate, Warrington WA2 0PD* Tel (01925) 821555 E-mail stephen@attwater1.freeserve.co.uk

ATTWOOD, Andrew Michael. b 66. Derby Coll of Educn BEd91. Trin Coll Bris BA02. **d** 02 **p** 03. C Leamington Priors St Mary *Cov* 02-10; V Kenilworth St Jo from 10. *St John's Vicarage, Clarke's Avenue, Kenilworth CV8 1HX* Tel (01936) 853203 E-mail a.attwood@talk21.com

ATTWOOD, Anthony Norman. b 47. Univ of Wales (Abth) BSc(Econ)69 Hull Univ MA82. Qu Coll Birm 69. **d** 72 **p** 73. C Greenhill *Sheff* 72-75; V Elsecar 76-81; Ind Missr 81-95; TV Maltby 81-86; Ind Chapl 86-95; RD Adwick 89-95; Teesside Ind Miss *Dur* 95-99; P-in-c Swindon St Aug *Bris* 99-03; Soc Resp Adv 99-03; P-in-c Dudley St Barn *Worc* 03-09; P-in-c Dudley St Thos and St Luke 04-09; TR Dudley 09-11; rtd 11. *St Francis's Vicarage, 50 Laurel Road, Dudley DY1 3EZ* Tel 07967-604435 (mobile)

ATTWOOD, Preb Carl Norman Harry. b 53. Bris Univ BA74. Cuddesdon Coll BA76 MA80. **d** 77 **p** 78. C Tupsley *Heref* 77-82; R Colwall w Upper Colwall and Coddington 82-08; Bp's Voc Officer 83-89; RD Ledbury 90-96; Chapl St Jas Sch Malvern 86-08; Preb Heref Cathl 97-08; rtd 08; Perm to Offic *Worc* from 82 *and Heref* from 08. *The Lodge, Old Colwall, Malvern WR13 6HF* Tel (01604) 540788 E-mail carl@attwoods.org

ATTWOOD, David John Edwin. b 51. Dur Univ BA76 Em Coll Cam BA73 MA77. Cranmer Hall Dur 74. **d** 77 **p** 78. C Rodbourne Cheney *Bris* 77-79; C Lydiard Millicent w Lydiard Tregoz 79-85; Dir and Lect Trin Coll Bris 85-97; V Prenton *Ches* 97-02; R Sundridge w Ide Hill and Toys Hill *Roch* from 02. *The Rectory, Chevening Road, Sundridge, Sevenoaks TN14 6AB* Tel (01959) 563749 E-mail david.attwood@diocese-rochester.org

ATTWOOD, Mrs Jennifer. **d** 08 **p** 09. NSM Lingfield and Crowhurst *S'wark* from 08. *28 Headland Way, Lingfield RH7 6BP* Tel (01342) 833100 E-mail jennyattwood@aol.com

ATTWOOD, Leslie Thomas. b 42. UWE MA94 Cranfield Univ MBA MCIPD76. St Steph Ho Ox. **d** 83 **p** 84. C Ascot Heath *Ox* 83-86; Dioc Tr Officer *Truro* 86-88; C Walsall St Hilary *Ches* 98-00; C Devizes St Pet *Sarum* 00-02; TV Godrevy *Truro* 02-07; TR 07-09; rtd 09. *Chyrempter, Perranuthnoe, Penzance*

TR20 9NQ Tel (01736) 710449 E-mail attwood99@lineone.net

ATTWOOD, Peter John. b 44. ACIB68. SEITE 00. **d** 03 **p** 04. NSM Langton Green *Roch* 03-06; C S Molton w Nymet St George, High Bray etc *Ex* from 06; RD S Molton from 09. *The Vicarage, East Street, North Molton, South Molton EX36 3HX* Tel (01598) 740325 E-mail rev@podlea.co.uk

ATTY, Norman Hughes. b 40. Dur Univ BA62. Cranmer Hall Dur 62. **d** 65 **p** 66. C Blackb St Gabr 65-67; Asst Master Billinge Sch Blackb 67-71; City of Leic Boys' Sch 71-73; P-in-c Elmley Lovett w Hampton Lovett *Worc* 73-78; P-in-c Elmbridge w Rushock 74-78; R Elmley Lovett w Hampton Lovett and Elmbridge etc 78-85; Hon Can Worc Cathl 81-85; rtd 05; Perm to Offic *Blackb* from 05. *The Dog Inn, King Street, Whalley, Clitheroe BB7 9SP* Tel (01254) 823009

ATWELL, The Rt Revd Robert Ronald. b 54. St Jo Coll Dur BA75 Dur Univ MLitt79. Westcott Ho Cam 76. **d** 78 **p** 79 **c** 08. C Mill Hill Jo Keble *Ch Lon* 78-81; Chapl Trin Coll Cam 81-87; OSB 87-98; Lic to Offic *Ox* 87-97; Perm to Offic *Ely* 97-98; V Primrose Hill St Mary w Avenue Road St Paul *Lon* 98-08; Suff Bp Stockport *Ches* from 08. *Bishop's Lodge, Back Lane, Dunham Town, Altrincham WA14 4SG* Tel 0161-928 5611 Fax 929 0692 E-mail bpstockport@chester.anglican.org

AUBREY-JONES, Adrian Frederick. b 51. ERMC 04. **d** 07 **p** 08. NSM Dersingham w Anmer and Shernborne *Nor* 07-10; TV Dereham and Distr from 10. *The Vicarage, Woodgate Lane, Swanton Morley, Dereham NR20 4NS* Tel (01362) 638378 Mobile 07775-514567 E-mail a3351adrian@aol.com

AUCHMUTY, John Robert. b 67. ACCA. CITC 89. **d** 92 **p** 93. C Dundela St Mark *D & D* 92-96; I Eglish w Killylea *Arm* 96-01; I Killaney w Carryduff *D & D* 01-07; I Knock from 07. *St Columba's Rectory, 29 King's Road, Knock, Belfast BT5 6JG* Tel (028) 9047 1514 E-mail johnauchmuty@btinternet.com

AUCKLAND, Bishop of. *See* PATERSON, The Rt Revd John Campbell

AUCKLAND, Archdeacon of. *See* BARKER, The Ven Nicholas John Willoughby

AUDEN, Lawson Philip. b 45. DL06. Qu Coll Birm 73. **d** 78 **p** 81. C Spalding *Linc* 78-81; TV Wordsley *Lich* 81-82; TV Kidderminster St Mary and All SS, Trimpley etc *Worc* 82-87; Ind Chapl 82-87; Perm to Offic *Cov* and *Worc* 87-97; *Birm*, *Lich* and *Glouc* 94-97; Chapl Worcs Community Healthcare NHS Trust 91-97; P-in-c Pebworth w Dorsington and Honeybourne *Glouc* 97-99; Perm to Offic *Cov* 98-01; *B & W* 00-04; *Glouc* from 01; Chapl Miss to Seafarers 99-10; Millennium Officer *Glouc* 99-01; rtd 10. *351 Nore Road, Portishead, Bristol BS20 8EX* Tel (01275) 390305 E-mail philipauden@ukf.net

AUDIBERT, Mrs Janice Elizabeth. b 56. **d** 99 **p** 00. OLM Oakdale *Sarum* 99-02; C N Poole Ecum Team 02-06; TV from 06. *24 Blackbird Close, Poole BH17 7YA* Tel and fax (01202) 389751 E-mail janice.audibert@christ-church-creekmoor.org.uk

AULD, The Very Revd Jeremy Rodger. b 66. Edin Univ LLB87 Solicitor 89 Barrister 97. TISEC BD04. **d** 04 **p** 05. C Edin St Pet 04-06; Hon Chapl Edin Univ 04-06; R Dollar *St And* 06-10; Provost St Paul's Cathl Dundee from 10. *4 Richmond Terrace, Dundee DD2 1BQ* Tel (01382) 646296 Mobile 07976-707253 E-mail jeremy.auld@btinternet.com

AULD, Mrs Sheila Edith. b 38. Newc Poly BA87 Univ of Northumbria at Newc MA99. NEOC 91. **d** 94 **p** 95. Project Worker Cedarwood Trust 88-02; NSM Newc St Gabr 94-02; rtd 02; NSM Newc St Gabr from 02. *5 Gibson Fields, Hexham NE46 1AS* Tel (01434) 602297

AUSSANT, Mrs Jill Amaryllis. MA LLB. Ripon Coll Cuddesdon. **d** 07 **p** 08. NSM Crawley and Littleton and Sparsholt w Lainston *Win* 07-08; NSM Downs Benefice from 08. *121 Hocombe Road, Chandler's Ford, Eastleigh SO53 5QD* Tel (023) 8026 9799

AUSTEN, Glyn Benedict. b 54. UEA BA77 MPhil80. Ripon Coll Cuddesdon BA81 MA85. **d** 82 **p** 83. C Newport w Longford and Chetwynd *Lich* 82-85; C Hawley H Trin *Guildf* 85-87; R Barnack w Ufford and Bainton *Pet* 87-03; Asst Master Stamford High Sch from 03. *31 Hill View Road, South Witham, Grantham NG33 5QW* Tel (01572) 767944 *or* (01780) 484200 Fax (01780) 484201 E-mail g.b.austen@ukf.net

AUSTEN, Canon John. b 46. St Cath Coll Cam BA69 MA72. Qu Coll Birm. **d** 71 **p** 72. C Birmingham St Geo *Birm* 71-74; C Aston St Jas *Birm* 74-82; Chapl Aston Univ 82-88; C Handsworth St Andr 88-11; Hon Can Birm Cathl 06-11; rtd 11; Perm to Offic *Birm* from 11. *151 Church Lane, Handsworth, Birmingham B20 2RU* Tel 0121-554 8882 E-mail john@jausten.freeserve.co.uk

AUSTEN, Simon Neil. b 67. Warwick Univ BSc88. Wycliffe Hall Ox BA93 MA97. **d** 94 **p** 95. C Gt Chesham *Ox* 94-98; Chapl Stowe Sch 98-02; V Houghton *Carl* from 02. *12 Brunstock Close, Carlisle CA3 0HL* Tel (01228) 810076 *or* 515972 E-mail simon@hkchurch.org.uk

AUSTERBERRY, Preb David Naylor. b 35. Birm Univ BA58. Wells Th Coll 58. **d** 60 **p** 61. C Leek St Edw *Lich* 60-63; Iran 64-70; Chapl CMS Foxbury 70-73; V Walsall Pleck and Bescot *Lich* 73-82; R Brierley Hill 82-88; R Kinnerley w Melverley and Knockin w Maesbrook 88-99; RD Oswestry 92-95; Preb Lich Cathl 96-00; rtd 00; Perm to Offic *Heref* and *Lich* from 00. *Chad Cottage, Dovaston, Kinnerley, Oswestry SY10 8DT* Tel (01691) 682039

AUSTERBERRY, John Maurice. b 62. Birm Univ BA83. Sarum & Wells Th Coll 84. **d** 86 **p** 87. C Clayton *Lich* 86-89; Asst Chapl Withington Hosp Man 89-95; Chapl Tameside and Glossop NHS Trust 95-99; Chapl N Staffs Hosp NHS Trust from 99. *City General Hospital, Newcastle Road, Stoke-on-Trent ST4 6QG* Tel (01782) 715444 *or* 552252 Fax 552017 E-mail john.austerberry@uhns.nhs.uk

AUSTIN, Canon Alfred George. b 36. Ridley Coll Melbourne ThL61. **d** 61 **p** 62. C Bendigo All SS Australia 63-64; R W End 64-70; R Eaglehawk and Bp's Dom Chapl 70-77; C Dartford St Alb *Roch* 77-79; R Tatura Australia 79-84; R W Bendigo 84-90; R Kyneton 90-93; Can Bendigo Cathl 83-97; I Essendon Ch Ch 97-00; rtd 01. *Brocklyn, 3 Alpina Place, Kangaroo Flat Vic 3555, Australia* Tel (0061) (3) 5447 0174

AUSTIN, Mrs Catherine Brenda. b 57. **d** 00 **p** 01. OLM Henley, Claydon and Barham *St E* from 00. *Fait Accompli, 7 Freeman Avenue, Henley, Ipswich IP6 0RZ* Tel (01473) 830100

AUSTIN, David Samuel John. b 63. St Jo Coll Dur BATM11. Cranmer Hall Dur 09. **d** 11. C Silsden *Bradf* from 11. *12 Westerley Crescent, Silsden, Keighley BD20 0BW* Tel 07740-922468 (mobile) E-mail dsj.austin@hotmail.com

AUSTIN, The Ven George Bernard. b 31. St D Coll Lamp BA53 Chich Th Coll 53. **d** 55 **p** 56. C Chorley St Pet *Blackb* 55-57; C Notting Hill St Clem *Lon* 57-60; Asst Chapl Lon Univ 60-61; C Dunstable *St Alb* 61-64; V Eaton Bray 64-70; V Bushey Heath 70-88; Hon Can St Alb 78-88; Adn York 88-99; Can and Preb York Minster 98-99; rtd 99; Perm to Offic *York* from 99 and *St Alb* from 10. *1 Priory Court, 169 Sparrows Herne, Bushey WD23 1EF* Tel (020) 8420 4116 E-mail george.austin@virgin.net

AUSTIN, Miss Jane. b 43. SRN64 SCM66. dss 81 **d** 87 **p** 94. Tonbridge SS Pet and Paul *Roch* 81-98; C 87-98; Hon Can Roch Cathl 96-98; P-in-c Meltham *Wakef* 98-01; V 01-07; P-in-c Helme 00-01; RD Almondbury 01-06; rtd 07; Perm to Offic *Wakef* from 08. *177 Bourne View Road, Netherton, Huddersfield HD4 7JS* Tel (01484) 664212 E-mail j.austin.meltham@care4free.net

AUSTIN, Leslie Ernest. b 46. Trin Coll Bris 72. **d** 74 **p** 75. C Paddock Wood *Roch* 74-79; C Upper Armley *Ripon* 79-81; V Horton *Bradf* 81-85; V Long Preston w Tosside 85-97; TR Shirwell, Loxhore, Kentisbury, Arlington, etc *Ex* from 97. *The Parsonage, 1 The Glebe, Bratton Fleming, Barnstaple EX31 4RE* Tel (01598) 710807 E-mail les@austin85.freeserve.co.uk

AUSTIN, Margaret Rose. b 41. Qu Coll Birm 01. **d** 03 **p** 04. NSM Farewell *Lich* 03-09; NSM Gentleshaw 03-09; NSM Hammerwich 03-09; rtd 09. *137 Highfields Road, Chasetown, Burntwood WS7 4QT* Tel (01543) 686883

AUSTIN, Canon Michael Ridgwell. b 33. Lon Univ BD57 PhD69 Birm Univ MA66 FRHistS. Lon Coll of Div ALCD56. **d** 57 **p** 58. C Ward End *Birm* 57-60; PC Derby St Andr 60-66; Lect Th Derbyshire Coll of HE 66-73; Prin Lect 73-85; Chapl Derby Cathl 66-81; Can Res Derby Cathl 81-85; Bp's Adv on Tr *S'well* 85-88; Dir Post-Ord Tr 86-94; Can Res S'well Minster 88-96; Dioc Dir of Tr 88-94; Abps' Adv for Bps' Min 94-98; rtd 98; Perm to Offic *S'well* from 04. *7 Dudley Doy Road, Southwell NG25 0NJ* Tel (01636) 812604

AUSTIN, Mrs Rosemary Elizabeth. b 68. K Alfred's Coll Win BEd91. SWMTC 08. **d** 11. C Fremington, Instow and Westleigh *Ex* from 11. *19 Lane End Close, Instow, Bideford EX39 4LG* Tel (01271) 861405 Mobile 07810-036236 E-mail rosieaustin@live.co.uk

AUSTIN, Mrs Susan Frances. b 47. Open Univ BA81. Cant Sch of Min 87. **d** 92 **p** 94. Chapl Ch Ch High Sch Ashford 90-94; C Gt Chart *Cant* 92-94; C Ashford 92-94; C Estover *Ex* 94-96; V Stevenage All SS Pin Green *St Alb* 96-98; P-in-c Bredgar w Bicknor and Frinsted w Wormshill etc *Cant* 00-04; rtd 04; Perm to Offic *Cant* from 04. *9 Pheasant Lane, Maidstone ME15 9QR* Tel (01622) 745276 E-mail susanandralphaustin@hotmail.com

AUSTRALIA, Primate of. See ASPINALL, The Most Revd Phillip John

AVANN, Canon Penelope Joyce. b 46. dss 83 **d** 87 **p** 98. Southborough St Pet w Ch Ch and St Matt *Roch* 83-89; Par Dn 87-89; Warden Past Assts 89-10; Par Dn Beckenham St Jo 89-94; C 94-02; C Green Street Green and Pratts Bottom from 02; Hon

Can Roch Cathl from 94. *9 Ringwood Avenue, Orpington BR6 7SY* Tel and fax (01689) 861742 Mobile 07710-418839 E-mail penny.avann@rochester.anglican.org

AVENT, Raymond John. b 28. St D Coll Lamp BA55 Coll of Resurr Mirfield 55. **d** 57 **p** 58. C Bury H Trin *Man* 57-60; C Holborn St Alb w Saffron Hill St Pet *Lon* 60-66; C Munster Square St Mary Magd 66-67; V Tottenham St Paul 67-77; RD E Haringey 73-77; V Kilburn St Aug w St Jo 77-87; AD Westmr Paddington 79-84; R St Vedast w St Mich-le-Querne etc 87-94; rtd 94; Perm to Offic *Lon* 94-00; *Glouc* from 00. *Maryvale House, Catbrook, Chipping Campden GL55 6DE* Tel (01386) 841323 E-mail avent@campadene.fsnet.co.uk

AVERY, Andrew James. b 58. Dudley Coll of Educn CertEd79 Open Univ BA81. St Jo Coll Nottm 06. **d** 08 **p** 09. C Brundall w Braydeston and Postwick *Nor* 08-11; TV Gt Yarmouth from 11. *18 Royal Avenue, Great Yarmouth NR30 4EB* Tel 07976-523554 (mobile) E-mail crandajavery@hotmail.co.uk

AVERY, Mrs Lydia Dorothy Ann. b 57. Sheff Univ MA03 Bath Spa Univ Coll PGCE97. STETS BA08. **d** 08 **p** 09. C Pilton w Croscombe, N Wootton and Dinder *B & W* from 08. *Hill House, Fayre Way, Croscombe, Wells BA5 3RA* Tel (01749) 343427 E-mail lydiaavery@aol.com

AVERY, Richard Julian. b 52. Keble Coll Ox BA73. St Jo Coll Nottm 74. **d** 77 **p** 78. C Macclesfield St Mich *Ches* 77-80; Asst P Prince Albert St Dav Canada 82-83; C Becontree St Mary *Chelmsf* 84-87; R Hudson Bay Canada 87-90; R Duncan 90-97; TV Cheltenham St Mark *Glouc* 97-03; Perm to Offic 03-06; P-in-c Berkeley w Wick, Breadstone, Newport, Stone etc 06-11; V from 11. *The Vicarage, Church Lane, Berkeley GL13 9BN* Tel (01453) 810294 E-mail averyfamily@yahoo.com

AVERY, Robert Edward. b 69. Magd Coll Cam BA90. Ripon Coll Cuddesdon 90. **d** 93 **p** 94. C Cen Telford *Lich* 93-96; C Cambridge Gt St Mary w St Mich *Ely* 96-99; V Tamerton Foliot Ex 99-03; V Tunbridge Wells K Chas *Roch* from 03. *The Vicarage, 5D Frant Road, Tunbridge Wells TN2 5SB* Tel (01892) 525455 E-mail robert.avery@diocese-rochester.org

AVERY, Canon Russel Harrold. b 46. JP74. Moore Th Coll Sydney 66. **d** 77 **p** 77. C Curtin Australia 77; C S Queanbeyan 77-78; C Prenton *Ches* 78-79; Chapl Tunis St Geo Tunisia 79-82; Chapl Maisons-Laffitte *Eur* 82-88; R Lane Cove Australia 88-98; Chapl Nord Pas de Calais *Eur* 98-00; Chapl Lille 00-02; Ind Chapl Australia 02-06; Chapl RAAF 04-09; Sen State Chapl NSW Police from 09; Hon Can Goulburn Cathl from 09. *1A Alliedale Close, Hornsby NSW 2077, Australia* Tel (0061) (2) 9487 5580 E-mail rhavery@cia.com.au

AVES, Peter Colin. b 57. Qu Mary Coll Lon BSc79 CertEd80 Lon Univ BD89. Wycliffe Hall Ox 85. **d** 88 **p** 89. C Thames Ditton *Guildf* 88-90; C Chertsey 90-93; R Stockbridge and Longstock and Leckford *Win* 93-00; Chapl to the Deaf *Sarum* 00-03; TV Beaminster Area 03-07. *Address temp unknown* E-mail peteraves@excite.co.uk

AVESON, Ian Henry. b 55. Jes Coll Ox BA77 MA81 Univ Coll Dur PGCE78 Birkbeck Coll Lon MSc85. St Mich Coll Llan BD97. **d** 97 **p** 98. C Penarth All SS *Llan* 97-99; TV Aberystwyth *St D* 99-07; V Llandingat w Myddfai from 07. *The Vicarage, 42 Broad Street, Llandovery SA20 0AY* Tel (01550) 720524

AVEYARD, Ian. b 46. Liv Univ BSc68 Sheff Univ MEd00. ALCD72 St Jo Coll Nottm 71. **d** 71 **p** 72. C Bradley *Wakef* 71-74; C Knowle *Birm* 74-79; P-in-c Cofton Hackett 79; P-in-c Barnt Green 79; V Cofton Hackett w Barnt Green 80-94; Dioc Dir of Reader Tr 85-94; Warden of Readers 91-94; Course Leader St Jo Coll Nottm 96-99; P-in-c Thanington and Dioc Dir of Ords *Cant* 99-09; rtd 09. *19 The Damsells, Tetbury GL8 8JA* Tel (01666) 502278 E-mail ian.aveyard1@btinternet.com

AVIS, Canon Paul David Loup. b 47. Lon Univ BD70 PhD76. Westcott Ho Cam 73. **d** 75 **p** 76. C S Molton, Nymet St George, High Bray etc *Ex* 75-80; V Stoke Canon, Poltimore w Huxham and Rewe etc 80-98; Preb Ex Cathl 93-08; Sub Dean Ex Cathl 97-08; Can Th Ex Cathl from 08; Gen Sec Coun for Chr Unity from 98; Chapl to The Queen from 08. *Church House, Great Smith Street, London SW1P 3AZ, or Lea Hill, Membury, Axminster EX13 7AQ* Tel (020) 7898 1470 Fax 7898 1483 E-mail paul.avis@churchofengland.org

AWRE, Canon Richard William Esgar. b 56. Univ of Wales BA78. Wycliffe Hall Ox 78. **d** 81 **p** 82. C Blackpool St Jo *Blackb* 81-84; Asst Dir of Ords and Voc Adv 84-89; C Altham w Clayton le Moors 84-89; V Longridge 89-99; V Kenilworth St Nic *Cov* from 99; RD Kenilworth 01-09; Hon Can Cov Cathl from 11. *The Vicarage, 7 Elmbank Road, Kenilworth CV8 1AL* Tel (01926) 854367 *or* 857509 E-mail stnicholasken@aol.com

AXFORD, Mrs Christine Ruth. b 53. Glam Coll of Educn BEd75. STETS BTh00. **d** 00 **p** 02. NSM Yeovil w Kingston Pitney *B & W* 00-01; NSM N Hartismere *St E* 02-08; NSM Wotton-under-Edge w Ozleworth, N Nibley etc *Glouc* from 08. *The Vicarage, Culverhay, Wotton-under-Edge GL12 7LS* Tel (01453) 842175 E-mail chris.axford@metronet.co.uk

AXFORD, Robert Henry. b 50. Univ of Wales BEng72 CEng85. Sarum & Wells Th Coll 89. **d** 91 **p** 92. C Castle Cary w Ansford *B & W* 91-95; P-in-c Queen Camel w W Camel, Corton Denham etc 95-01; R 01-02; R N Hartismere *St E* 02-08; RD Hartismere 04-08; P-in-c Wotton-under-Edge w Ozleworth, N Nibley etc *Glouc* 08-11; V from 11; AD Wotton from 09. *The Vicarage, Culverhay, Wotton-under-Edge GL12 7LS* Tel (01453) 842175 E-mail rob@robaxford.plus.com

AXON, Andrew John. b 76. Univ of Wales (Lamp) BTh97 Univ of Wales (Ban) MTh09. Trin Coll Bris 99. **d** 01 **p** 02. C Sevenhampton w Charlton Abbots, Hawling etc *Glouc* 01-05; V Ruddington *S'well* 05-10; P-in-c Hucclecote *Glouc* from 10. *102A Hucclecote Road, Gloucester GL3 3RX* Tel (01452) 612509 E-mail ajaxon@mail.com

AXTELL, Ronald Arthur John. b 33. Lon Univ BSc54 St Cath Soc Ox BA58 MA62. Wycliffe Hall Ox 56. **d** 58 **p** 59. C Walton Breck *Liv* 58-61; Iran 63-78; Chapl Tehran 63-67; Chapl Kerman 67-68; Chapl Shiraz 69-78; Chr Witness to Israel Miss in Man 78-82; Perm to Offic *Man* 79-82; TV Man Resurr 82; TV Man Gd Shep 82-88; R Levenshulme St Pet 88-98; rtd 98; Perm to Offic *Man* from 98. *15 Berwick Avenue, Stockport SK4 3AA* Tel 0161-432 5943 E-mail axtell@ntlworld.com

AXTELL, Stephen Geoffrey. b 57. Open Univ BSc96. St Jo Coll Nottm 00. **d** 02 **p** 03. C Coseley Ch Ch *Worc* 02-06; Chapl Rotterdam *Eur* from 06; Chapl Rotterdam w Schiedam Miss to Seafarers from 06. *Jan Steenstraat 69, 3117 TC Schiedam, The Netherlands* Tel (0031) (10) 426 0933 *or* tel and fax 476 4043 E-mail missiontoseafarers@kabelfoon.nl *or* stmarys@hetnet.nl

AYERS, Canon John. b 40. FCollP Bris Univ BEd75 Newton Park Coll Bath MEd89 FRSA94. **d** 77 **p** 78. NSM Corsham *Bris* 77-79; NSM Gtr Corsham 79-88; NSM Ditteridge 88-92; NSM Box w Hazlebury and Ditteridge 93-10; Hon Can Bris Cathl 94-10; rtd 10. *Toad Hall, Middlehill, Box, Corsham SN13 8QP* Tel (01225) 742123 E-mail johnayers@middlehill.netlineuk.net

AYERS, Martin John. b 79. Trin Hall Cam MA03 Solicitor 04. Oak Hill Th Coll 08. **d** 11. C Preston All SS *Blackb* from 11. *226 Tag Lane, Ingol, Preston PR2 3TX* Tel 07976-170916 (mobile) E-mail martin.ayers@talk21.com

AYERS, Paul Nicholas. b 61. St Pet Coll Ox BA82 MA86. Trin Coll Bris 83. **d** 85 **p** 86. C Clayton *Bradf* 85-88; C Keighley St Andr 88-91; V Wrose 91-97; V Pudsey St Lawr and St Paul from 97. *The Vicarage, Vicarage Drive, Pudsey LS28 7RL* Tel 0113-256 4197 *or* 257 7843 E-mail paul.ayers@bradford.anglican.org

AYERS-HARRIS, Mrs Rebecca Theresa. b 70. Nottm Univ BA91 Birm Univ PGCE92. WEMTC 01. **d** 04 **p** 05. NSM Leominster *Heref* 04-08; Chapl Sherborne Sch for Girls from 08. *Sherborne School for Girls, Bradford Road, Sherborne DT9 3QN* Tel (01935) 812245

AYERST, Gabrielle Mary. b 52. St Luke's Coll Ex BEd74. SEITE 97. **d** 00 **p** 01. NSM Surbiton St Andr and St Mark *S'wark* 00-08. *6 Bell Tower Park, Berwick-upon-Tweed TD15 1ND* Tel (01289) 302680 E-mail gadrillea@paff.nsf.org.uk

AYKROYD, Harold Allan. b 22. DFC. Man Univ BA48. Qu Coll Birm 73. **d** 76 **p** 76. NSM Moseley St Agnes *Birm* 76-82; NSM Bournville 82-96; Perm to Offic from 96. *108 Middleton Hall Road, Birmingham B30 1DG* Tel 0121-451 1365 *or* 569 4687

AYLETT, Graham Peter. b 59. Qu Coll Cam BA81 MA84 PhD85 St Jo Coll Dur BA88. Cranmer Hall Dur 86 All Nations Chr Coll 96. **d** 90 **p** 91. C Wilton *B & W* 90-94; C Runcorn All SS *Ches* 94-96; C Thetford *Nor* 97-98; Mongolia from 98. *clo JCS, PO Box 49/532, Ulaanbaatar 210349, Mongolia*

AYLETT, Mrs Nicola Jane. b 63. St Anne's Coll Ox BA84 St Jo Coll Dur BA88. Cranmer Hall Dur 87 All Nations Chr Coll 96. **d** 90 **p** 94. C Wilton *B & W* 90-94; NSM Runcorn All SS *Ches* 94-96; Perm to Offic *Nor* 97-98; Mongolia from 98. *clo JCS, PO Box 49/532, Ulaanbaatar 210349, Mongolia*

AYLING, Mrs Ann Margaret. b 39. Edge Hill Coll of HE TCert59. STETS 07. **d** 10 **p** 11. NSM Bridport *Sarum* from 10. *4 Manor Farm Court, Walditch, Bridport DT6 4LQ* Tel (01308) 424896 E-mail annay@storr.eclipse.co.uk

AYLING, Miss Dallas Jane. b 53. Trin Coll Bris BA94. **d** 98 **p** 99. C Ellesmere Port *Ches* 98-02; TV Birkenhead Priory 02-06; TR 06-07; R from 07. *10 Cavendish Road, Birkenhead CH41 8AX* Tel 0151-653 6092 E-mail revdallasayling@yahoo.co.uk

AYLING, Canon John Michael. b 37. St Cath Coll Cam BA60 MA64. Linc Th Coll 60. **d** 62 **p** 63. C Stoke upon Trent *Lich* 62-66; C Codsall 66-67; Australia 67-71; Solomon Is 71-72; Lic to Offic *St Alb* 72-91; TR Boscastle w Davidstow *Truro* 91-98; R 98-02; RD Stratton 98-02; Hon Can Truro Cathl 01-02; rtd 02; Perm to Offic *Heref* from 03. *Woodstock House, Church Street, Leominster HR6 8ED* Tel (01568) 611523 E-mail john.ayling@virgin.net

AYLING, Mrs Susan Pamela. b 48. OBE03. SEITE 95. **d** 98 **p** 99. NSM Oxshott *Guildf* 98-02; NSM Cuddington 02-10; NSM Long Ditton from 10. *114 Edenfield Gardens, Worcester Park KT4 7DY* Tel (020) 8337 6347 *or* 7438 6589 E-mail sue.ayling@btinternet.com

AYLWARD, James Gareth. b 45. St Cath Coll Cam BA68 MA72. St As Minl Tr Course 94. **d** 97 **p** 98. NSM Wrexham *St As* 97-00; V Broughton 00-05; V Broughton and Berse Drelincourt from

05. *The Vicarage, Bryn-y-Gaer Road, Pentre Broughton, Wrexham LL11 6AT* Tel (01978) 756210

AYOK-LOEWENBERG, Joseph. b 60. DipEd91. Trin Coll Bris 85. **d** 88 **p** 89. C Swanage and Studland *Sarum* 88-90; Cam Univ Miss Bermondsey 90; Crowther Hall CMS Tr Coll Selly Oak 90-91; C Barnes St Mary *S'wark* 91-92; C Earlsfield St Jo 92; CMS Uganda 92-95; P-in-c Symondsbury and Chideock *Sarum* 96-98; TV Golden Cap Team 98-01; CMS Egypt 02-06; Hon C Barnes *S'wark* 06-09; TV Kidderminster St Geo *Worc* from 09. *38 Comberton Avenue, Kidderminster DY10 3EG* Tel (01562) 637645 E-mail ayokloewenberg@dataxprs.com.eg

✠AYONG, The Most Revd James Simon. b 44. Newton Th Coll Martin Luther Sem BTh. **d** 82 **p** 84 **c** 96. Papua New Guinea from 82; Asst P Popondetta Resurr 85-86; Lect Newton Th Coll 87-88; Prin 89-93; Par P Gerehu 94-95; Bp Aipo Rongo from 95; Abp Papua New Guinea from 96. *PO Box 893, Mount Hagen, Western Highlands Province, Papua New Guinea* Tel (00675) 542 1131 *or* 542 3727 Fax 542 1181 E-mail acpnghgn@global.net.pg

AYRE, Richard. b 40. Liv Inst of Educn CertEd61 Newc Univ BPhil(Ed)88. **d** 04 **p** 05. OLM Chapel House *Newc* from 04. *57 Grosvenor Court, Newcastle upon Tyne NE5 1RY* Tel 0191-267 2096

AYRES, Anthony Lawrence. b 47. Trin Coll Bris 69. **d** 73 **p** 74. C Plumstead All SS *S'wark* 73-77; Hon C 77-00; Member of Counselling Team CA from 83. *37 Donaldson Road, London SE18 4JZ* Tel (020) 8856 1542

AYRES, Dean Matthew. b 68. Bris Univ BSc89. Ridley Hall Cam 00. **d** 02 **p** 03. C Epsom Common Ch Ch *Guildf* 02-06; Chapl W Lon Univ from 06. *The Chaplaincy, University of West London, St Mary's Road, London W5 5RF* Tel (020) 8231 2365 E-mail ayresnograces@yahoo.co.uk

AZER, Ms Helen. b 77. Ch Ch Ox BA00 MA03. Wycliffe Hall Ox BTh04. **d** 04 **p** 05. C Ox St Aldate 04-07; C Cumnor from 07. *St Michael's Church Office, 1 Abingdon Road, Cumnor, Oxford OX2 9QN* Tel (01865) 861541 E-mail gryphius2000@hotmail.com

B

BABB, Ann Elizabeth. b 38. Battersea Coll of Educn TDip59. Qu Coll Newfoundland 96 St Steph Ho Ox 05. **d** 06. C Antwerp St Boniface *Eur* from 06. *Leo van Hullebuschstraat 37, 2900 Schoten, Belgium* Tel (0032) (3) 685 3420 E-mail ann.babb@skynet.be

BABB, Canon Geoffrey. b 42. Man Univ BSc64 MA74 Linacre Coll Ox BA67. Ripon Hall Ox 65. **d** 68 **p** 69. C Heywood St Luke *Man* 68-71; C-in-c Loundsley Green Ascension CD *Derby* 71-76; TV Old Brampton and Loundsley Green 76-77; TV Stafford and Dioc Soc Resp Officer *Lich* 77-88; Preb Lich Cathl 87-88; P-in-c Salford Sacred Trin *Man* 88-99; Dir CME 88-99; TR Wythenshawe 99-06; TV 06-07; Hon Can Man Cathl 97-06; rtd 07; Perm to Offic *Man* 07-08; *Newc* 07-10; *Derby* from 10. *The Rectory, 84 Church Street North, Old Whittington, Chesterfield S41 9QP* Tel (01246) 450651 E-mail gandjbabb@btinternet.com

BABB, Mrs Julia Bebbington. b 69. Man Univ BA98 St Jo Coll Dur MA00. Cranmer Hall Dur. **d** 00 **p** 01. C Langley and Parkfield *Man* 00-04; V Cowgate *Newc* 04-10; P-in-c Whittington *Derby* from 10. *The Rectory, 84 Church Street North, Old Whittington, Chesterfield S41 9QP* Tel (01246) 450651 E-mail gandjbabb@btinternet.com

BABBAGE, Canon Stuart Barton. b 16. AM95. St Jo Coll Auckland 35 Univ of NZ BA35 MA36 K Coll Lon PhD42. Tyndale Hall Bris 37 ACT ThD50. **d** 39 **p** 40. C Havering-atte-Bower *Chelmsf* 39-41; Tutor and Lect Oak Hill Th Coll 39-41; Chapl-in-Chief RAF 42-46; Australia 46-63; Dean Sydney 47-53; Dean Melbourne 53-62; Prin Ridley Coll Melbourne 53-63; USA 63-73; V Atlanta and Austell 63-65; Visiting Prof Columbia Th Sem 63-67; Pres Conwell Th Sch Philadelphia 67-69; Vice-Pres and Dean Gordon-Conwell Th Sem 69-73; Australia from 73; Master New Coll Univ of NSW 73-82; Registrar ACT 77-92; rtd 83; Hon Can Sydney from 83. *46 St Thomas Street, Waverley NSW 2024, Australia* Tel (0061) (2) 9665 1882

BABINGTON, Canon Gervase Hamilton. b 30. Keble Coll Ox BA57 MA57. Wells Th Coll 55. **d** 57 **p** 58. C Sheff St Geo and St Steph 57-60; P-in-c Manor Park CD 60-65; R Waddington *Linc* 65-81; RD Graffoe 74-81; Can and Preb Linc Cathl 77-95; V Gainsborough All SS 81-90; RD Corringham 82-87; R Walesby 90-95; rtd 95; Perm to Offic *Linc* 95-98. *15 Highfields, Nettleham, Lincoln LN2 2ST* Tel (01522) 595702

BABINGTON, Peter Gervase. b 69. Aston Univ BSc91 Birm Univ MPhil03. Cuddesdon Coll BTh98. **d** 98 **p** 99. C Salter Street and Shirley *Birm* 98-02; V Bournville from 02; AD Moseley from 07. *The Vicarage, 61 Linden Road, Birmingham B30 1JT* Tel 0121-472 1209 *or* 472 7215
E-mail vicar@bournvilleparishchurch.org.uk
BACH, Mrs Frances Mary. b 48. Open Univ BA AIL. CITC BTh. **d** 94 **p** 95. NSM Ballynure and Ballyeaston *Conn* 94-96; C Larne and Inver 96-99; C Glynn w Raloo 96-99; I Armoy w Loughguile and Drumtullagh from 99. *The Rectory, 181 Glenshesk Road, Armoy, Ballymoney BT53 8RJ* Tel (028) 2075 1226 *or* 2082 3348
E-mail frances.bach@btinternet.com
BACH, John Edward Goulden. b 40. JP. Dur Univ BA66. Cranmer Hall Dur 66. **d** 69 **p** 70. C Bradf Cathl 69-72; Chapl and Lect NUU 73-84; Chapl and Lect Ulster Univ from 84. *The Anglican Chaplaincy, 70 Hopefield Avenue, Portrush BT56 8HE* Tel (028) 2075 1226, 2032 4549 *or* 2082 3348
E-mail revjegbach@hotmail.com *or* jeg.bach@ulst.ac.uk
BACHELL, Kenneth George. b 22. Lon Univ BD49. K Coll Lon 55. **d** 56 **p** 57. C Bitterne Park *Win* 56-60; C-in-c Andover St Mich CD 60-64; V Andover St Mich 64-68; V Southampton St Alb 68-76; Warden Dioc Conf Ho Crawshawbooth *Man* 76-79; P-in-c Crawshawbooth 76-79; V Holdenhurst *Win* 79-83; V Froyle and Holybourne 83-87; rtd 87; Perm to Offic *Blackb* 88-98. *18 Cherrylea, Auchterarder PH3 1QG* Tel (01764) 663824
BACHU, Jagjit. b 66. Man Univ BSc88 Leeds Univ MBA98 MA07. NOC 04. **d** 07 **p** 08. NSM Wales *Sheff* 07-09. *10 Catherine's Hill, Coddenham, Ipswich IP6 9QG* Tel (01449) 761980 E-mail helen.bachu@tesco.net
BACK, Esther Elaine. *See* McCAFFERTY, Mrs Esther Elaine
BACKHOUSE, Alan Eric. b 37. Keble Coll Ox BA61 MA67. Tyndale Hall Bris 61. **d** 64 **p** 65. C Burnage St Marg *Man* 64-67; C Cheadle Hulme St Andr *Ches* 67-70; V Buglawton 70-80; V New Ferry 80-87; V Tarvin 87-93; V Knypersley *Lich* 93-99; Patr Sec Ch Soc Trust 99-00; C Watford *St Alb* 99-02; rtd 02. *Perelandra, Church Pitch, Llandyssil, Montgomery SY16 6LQ* Tel (01686) 669963
BACKHOUSE, Colin. b 41. Birm Coll of Art & Design BA67 MCSD82. Oak Hill Th Coll 85. **d** 87 **p** 88. C Branksome St Clem *Sarum* 87-91; P-in-c Bluntisham cum Earith w Colne and Woodhurst *Ely* 91-92; R 92-07; rtd 07. *13 Hillside View, Midsomer Norton, Bath BA3 2TB* Tel 07811-960048 (mobile)
E-mail colin.backhouse@googlemail.com
BACKHOUSE, John. b 30. Univ Coll Southn BA50. Wycliffe Hall Ox 51. **d** 53 **p** 54. C Eccleston St Luke *Liv* 53-55; C Maghull 55-58; V Lathom 58-64; Area Sec CMS *Linc* and *Ely* 64-71; *Leic* 72-78; *Cov* 75-78; V Thorpe Acre w Dishley *Leic* 78-83; R Ab Kettleby Gp 83-89; P-in-c Bitteswell 89-94; RD Guthlaxton II 90-94; rtd 94; Perm to Offic *Leic* from 94. *29 Peashill Close, Sileby, Loughborough LE12 7PT* Tel (01509) 812016
BACKHOUSE, Jonathan Roland. b 60. Jes Coll Cam BA82 MA85. Trin Coll Bris 01. **d** 03 **p** 04. C Nailsea H Trin *B & W* 03-07; Chapl RN from 07. *Royal Naval Chaplaincy Service, Mail Point 1-2, Leach Building, Whale Island, Portsmouth PO2 8BY* Tel (023) 9262 5055 Fax 9262 5134
E-mail jcbackhouse@bigfoot.com
BACKHOUSE, Robert. b 35. ALCD70. **d** 70 **p** 71. C Harold Wood *Chelmsf* 70-74; Publicity Sec CPAS 74-78; rtd 00; Perm to Offic *Sarum* 01-05. *10 Eccleston Square, London SW1V 1NP*
BACON, David Gary. b 62. Leic Univ BA83 Southn Univ BTh88. Sarum & Wells Th Coll 85. **d** 88 **p** 89. C Bromley St Mark *Roch* 88-92; C Lynton, Brendon, Countisbury, Lynmouth etc *Ex* 92; TV 92-95; P-in-c Lapford, Nymet Rowland and Coldridge 95-99; P-in-c Dartford St Alb *Roch* 99-05; P-in-c Bramshaw and Landford w Plaitford *Sarum* 05-06; TV Forest and Avon from 06. *The Rectory, Bramshaw, Lyndhurst SO43 7JF* Tel (01794) 390256 E-mail david.bacon@tesco.net
BACON, Derek Robert Alexander. b 44. Birkbeck Coll Lon BA92 MSc94 Ulster Univ PhD04. TCD Div Sch 69. **d** 71 **p** 72. C Templemore *D & R* 71-73; V Choral Derry Cathl 72-73; C Heeley *Sheff* 74-76; V Sheff St Pet Abbeydale 76-82; Chapl Gt Ormond Street Hosp for Children NHS Trust 82-95; Visiting Fell Ulster Univ 95-97; Perm to Offic *Conn* from 04. *14A Heathmount, Portstewart BT55 7AP* Tel (028) 7083 4987
E-mail dra.bacon@btinternet.com
BACON, Eric Arthur. b 23. Qu Coll Birm 68. **d** 69 **p** 70. C Linc St Pet-at-Gowts and St Andr 69-71; C Asterby Gp 71-74; V Anwick 74-78; V S Kyme 74-78; P-in-c Kirkby Laythorpe w Asgarby 76-78; P-in-c Ewerby w Evedon 76-78; P-in-c Burton Pedwardine 76-78; V Messingham 78-89; rtd 89; Perm to Offic *Linc* 89-01. *2 Curtois Close, Branston, Lincoln LN4 1LJ* Tel (01522) 794265
BACON, Janet Ann. b 57. Man Univ LLB78. NTMTC 95. **d** 98 **p** 99. NSM Stifford *Chelmsf* 98-01; P-in-c Sandbach Heath w Wheelock *Ches* 01-03; V from 03. *Heath Vicarage, School Lane, Sandbach CW11 2LS* Tel (01270) 768826
E-mail j.bacon@virgin.net
BACON, John Martindale. b 22. St Aid Birkenhead 54. **d** 57 **p** 58. C Bury St Paul *Man* 57-59; C-in-c Clifton Green St Thos CD

59-71; V Astley Bridge 71-87; rtd 87; Perm to Offic *Man* from 87-00 and *Blackb* from 87. *21 Lichen Close, Charnock Richard, Chorley PR7 5TT* Tel (01257) 792535
E-mail johnandcon.bacon@tiscali.co.uk
BADDELEY, The Ven Martin James. b 36. Keble Coll Ox BA60 MA64. Linc Th Coll 60. **d** 62 **p** 63. C Stretford St Matt *Man* 62-64; Lect Linc Th Coll 65-66; Tutor 66-69; Chapl 68-69; Chapl Fitzw Coll and New Hall Cam 69-74; Can Res Roch Cathl 74-80; Hon Can 80-96; Prin S'wark Ord Course 80-94; Co-Prin SEITE 94-96; Adn Reigate *S'wark* 96-00; rtd 00; Perm to Offic *Heref* from 00 and *Worc* from 01. *34 The Quadrangle, Newland, Malvern WR13 5AX* Tel (01684) 568690
BADEN, Peter Michael. b 35. CCC Cam BA59 MA62. Cuddesdon Coll 58. **d** 60 **p** 61. C Hunslet St Mary and Stourton *Ripon* 60-63; Lic to Offic *Wakef* 63-64; C E Grinstead St Swithun *Chich* 65-68; V Brighton St Martin 68-74; TR Brighton Resurr 74-76; R Westbourne and V Stansted 76-84; V Copthorne 84-91; V Clifton and R Dean *Carl* 91-00; P-in-c Mosser 99-00; rtd 00; Perm to Offic *Pet* from 00; *Carl* from 01. *62 Springfield Avenue, Thrapston, Kettering NN14 4TN* Tel (01832) 733186
E-mail p.baden36@btinternet.com
BADGER, Mark. b 65. Qu Coll Birm BTh96. **d** 96 **p** 97. C Barbourne *Worc* 96-01; P-in-c Worc St Geo w St Mary Magd 01-05; Chapl R Gr Sch Worc 02-05; Chapl Thames Valley Police Force *Ox* 05-07; Man Dir Motov8 from 04. *Motov8, Unit 2, Mill Works, Gregory's Mill Street, Worcester WR3 8BA* Tel and fax (01905) 619068 E-mail motov8@supanet.com
BADHAM, Prof Paul Brian Leslie. b 42. Jes Coll Ox BA65 MA69 Jes Coll Cam BA68 MA72 Birm Univ PhD73. Westcott Ho Cam 66. **d** 68 **p** 69. C Edgbaston St Bart *Birm* 68-69; C Rubery 69-73; Lic to Offic *St D* from 73; Lect Th Univ of Wales (Lamp) 73-83; Sen Lect 83-88; Reader 88-91; Prof Th 91-07; rtd 07; Dir Alister Hardy Relig Experience Research Cen from 02. *4 Coed y Bryn, Aberaeron SA46 0DW* Tel (01545) 571244 Mobile 07968-626902 E-mail pblbadham@hotmail.com
BAGE, Damon John. b 71. Teesside Univ BA95. St Steph Ho Ox 01. **d** 03 **p** 04. C Stockton St Jo *Dur* 03-07; P-in-c Norton St Mich from 07; Chapl John Snow Coll Dur from 06. *St Michael's Vicarage, 13 Imperial Avenue, Norton, Stockton-on-Tees TS20 2EW* Tel (01642) 553984 *or* 0191-334 0034
E-mail damon_j_bage@hotmail.com
BAGG, Marcus Christopher. b 75. Bath Univ BSc96. Trin Coll Bris BA07. **d** 07 **p** 08. C Stanmore *Win* 07-11; P-in-c Gatcombe *Portsm* from 11; P-in-c Carisbrooke St Nic from 11; P-in-c Carisbrooke St Mary from 11. *The Vicarage, 56 Castle Road, Carisbrooke, Newport PO30 1DP* Tel (01983) 522095
E-mail rev.marcus.bagg@yahoo.co.uk
BAGGALEY, Mrs Patricia Anne. b 45. Open Univ BSc96 RGN68. ERMC 05. **d** 07 **p** 08. NSM Trunch *Nor* from 07. *Anglesea, Rosebery Road, West Runton, Cromer NR27 9QW* Tel (01263) 837490 E-mail baggaley157@btinternet.com
BAGGS, Steven. b 70. **d** 09 **p** 10. NSM White Horse *Sarum* from 09. *37 Timor Road, Westbury BA13 2GA* Tel (01373) 826509
E-mail stevenbaggs@hotmail.com
BAGLEY, Roy Victor. b 33. **d** 03 **p** 04. OLM Chasetown *Lich* 03-11; rtd 11. *65 Oakdene Road, Burntwood WS7 4SA* Tel (01543) 686000 E-mail rv.bagley@btinternet.com
BAGNALL, Katherine Janet. b 67. Sunderland Univ BEd92. NEOC 02. **d** 05 **p** 06. NSM Monkwearmouth *Dur* 05-06; C Darlington St Mark w St Paul 06-10; P-in-c Sunderland St Mary and St Pet from 10. *The Clergy House, Springwell Road, Sunderland SR3 4DY* Tel 0191-528 3754
E-mail katherine.bagnall@ntlworld.com
BAGOTT, Paul Andrew. b 61. Leeds Univ BA85. Westcott Ho Cam 86. **d** 88 **p** 89. C Chingford SS Pet and Paul *Chelmsf* 88-91; C Pimlico St Sav *Lon* 91-95; P-in-c Clerkenwell H Redeemer and St Mark 95-01; V Clerkenwell H Redeemer from 02; V Clerkenwell St Mark from 02; PV Westmr Abbey from 08. *Holy Redeemer Clergy House, 24 Exmouth Market, London EC1R 4QE* Tel and fax (020) 7837 1861
E-mail holyredeemermerstmark@tiscali.co.uk
BAGSHAW, Paul Stanley. b 55. Selw Coll Cam BA78 MA81 CQSW80. NOC 85. **d** 88 **p** 89. Ind Missr *Sheff* 86-90; C Handsworth Woodhouse 88-90; NSM 91-93; C Newark *S'well* 93-96; P-in-c Ordsall 96-08. *12 Rosewood Crescent, Newcastle upon Tyne NE6 4PQ* Tel 0191-262 7158
E-mail paulbagshaw@gmail.com
BAGSHAWE, John Allen. b 45. St Jo Coll Dur BA70. Cranmer Hall Dur 67. **d** 71 **p** 72. C Bridlington Priory *York* 71-75; C N Ferriby 75-79; V Kingston upon Hull St Matt w St Barn 79-10; AD W Hull 00-10; rtd 10. *334 Southcoates Lane, Hull HU9 3TR* Tel (01482) 702220
BAGULEY, David Mark. b 61. Man Univ BSc83 MSc86 Open Univ MBA94 Wolfs Coll Cam PhD05. ERMC 09. **d** 11. Visiting Prof Anglia Ruskin Univ from 10; NSM Milton *Ely* from 11; NSM Waterbeach from 11; NSM Landbeach from 11. *272 Cherry Hinton Road, Cambridge CB1 7AJ* E-mail dmb29@cam.ac.uk

BAGULEY, Paul. b 36. NTMTC 94. **d** 98 **p** 99. NSM N Harrow St Alb *Lon* from 98. *86 Central Avenue, Pinner HA5 5BP* Tel (020) 8866 3454 E-mail paulbaguley@waitrose.com

BAILES, Kenneth. b 35. Dur Univ BA69 DPhil. **d** 71 **p** 72. C Redcar *York* 71-73; TV Redcar w Kirkleatham 73-74; P-in-c Appleton Roebuck w Acaster Selby 74-80; P-in-c Sutton on the Forest 80-82; R Stamford Bridge Gp 82-90; V Healaugh w Wighill, Bilbrough and Askham Richard 90-95; rtd 95; Perm to Offic *York* 98-11. *Lawnwith House, Stuton Grove, Tadcaster LS24 9BD* Tel (01937) 831245 Mobile 07764-614139 E-mail kb13@btinternet.com

BAILES, Mrs Rachel Jocelyn. b 60. Huddersfield Sch of Music BA81 Kingston Poly PGCE83 Leeds Univ MEd96 BA07. NOC 04. **d** 07 **p** 08. C Thornes and Lupset *Wakef* 07-11; Chapl Mid Yorks Hosps NHS Trust from 11. *Trust HQ and Education Centre, Pinderfields Hospital, Aberford Road, Wakefield WF1 4DG* Tel 08448-118110 E-mail rjbailes@btinternet.com

BAILEY, Adrian Richard. b 57. St Jo Coll Dur 89. **d** 91 **p** 92. C Oswestry St Oswald *Lich* 91-94; C Shobnall 94-99; C Burton 94-99; Town Cen Chapl 94-99; P-in-c Shobnall 99-01; P-in-c Hengoed w Gobowen 01-08; C Weston Rhyn and Selattyn 05-07; P-in-c Selattyn 07-08; P-in-c Selattyn and Hengoed w Gobowen from 08; Chapl Robert Jones/Agnes Hunt Orthopaedic NHS Trust from 01; RD Oswestry *Lich* from 09. *The Vicarage, Old Chirk Road, Gobowen, Oswestry SY11 3LL* Tel and fax (01691) 661226 E-mail arb2@totalise.co.uk

BAILEY, Alan George. b 40. Open Univ BA93. Ripon Hall Ox 62. **d** 64 **p** 65. C Formby H Trin *Liv* 64-67; C Longhulord 67-70; P-in-c Edgehill St Dunstan 70-74; V 74-81; RD Toxteth 78-81; Perm to Offic 81-83; Asst Chapl Liv Cathl 83-85; C Liv Our Lady and St Nic w St Anne 85-89; V Waddington *Bradf* 89-03; rtd 03. *66 Woone Lane, Clitheroe BB7 1BJ* Tel (01200) 425699

BAILEY, Andrew Henley. b 57. AKC78. Sarum & Wells Th Coll 79. **d** 80 **p** 81. C Romsey *Win* 80-83; V Bournemouth St Alb 83-93; R Milton from 93. *The Rectory, Church Lane, New Milton BH25 6QN* Tel and fax (01425) 615150 E-mail andrew@miltonrectory.freeserve.co.uk

BAILEY, Andrew John. b 37. Trin Coll Cam BA61 MA. Ridley Hall Cam 60. **d** 63 **p** 64. C Drypool *York* 63-66; C Melton Mowbray w Thorpe Arnold *Leic* 66-69; C-in-c Skelmersdale Ecum Cen *Liv* 69-79; V Langley Mill *Derby* 79-90; V Gt Faringdon w Lt Coxwell *Ox* 90-02; AD Vale of White Horse 97-01; rtd 02; Perm to Offic *Ches* from 02. *58 Manor Road, Sandbach CW11 2ND* Tel (01270) 764076 E-mail baileyaj@talk21.com

BAILEY, Canon Angela. b 61. Kent Univ BA82. Qu Coll Birm 83. **dss** 85 **d** 87 **p** 94. Reculver and Herne Bay St Bart *Cant* 85-88; Par Dn 87-88; Asst Chapl Hull Univ 88-92; Sen Chapl 94-98; Perm to Offic 92-94; P-in-c Rowley w Skidby 98-09; R from 10; V Walkington from 10; P-in-c Bishop Burton from 10; RD Beverley from 07; Chapl E Riding Community Health Trust 98-04; Can and Preb York Minster from 03; Dioc Ecum Officer 07-09. *The Rectory, 31 Old Village Road, Little Weighton, Cottingham HU20 3US* Tel (01482) 843317 E-mail angela@petermichael.karoo.co.uk

BAILEY, Bertram Arthur. b 20. Tyndale Hall Bris 65. **d** 67 **p** 68. C Bath St Luke *B & W* 67-72; C Bickenhill w Elmdon *Birm* 72-73; R N Tawton *Ex* 73-79; R N Tawton and Bondleigh 79-87; rtd 87; Perm to Offic *B & W* from 87; Clergy Retirement and Widows' Officer 89-06. *4 Uphill Road South, Weston-super-Mare BS23 4SD* Tel (01934) 633552

BAILEY, Mrs Bethan. b 54. Univ of Wales CertEd93 BTh07 MCSP75. St Jo Coll Nottm 04. **d** 06 **p** 07. C Dolgellau w Llanfachreth and Brithdir etc *Ban* 06-10; Dioc Children's Officer from 10; C Ardudwy Deanery 10; P-in-c Penrhyndeudraeth and Llanfrothen w Maentwrog etc from 11. *Corsygedol Farm, Dyffryn Ardudwy LL44 2RJ* Tel (01341) 247499 E-mail bethbaileydol@tiscali.co.uk

BAILEY, Brendan John. b 61. Strathclyde Univ BSc83 K Coll Lon MA99. Ripon Coll Cuddesdon BTh93. **d** 94 **p** 95. C Purley *Ox* 94-99; R Nettlebed w Bix, Highmoor, Pishill etc from 99; P-in-c Nuffield from 06. *The Rectory, High Street, Nettlebed, Henley-on-Thames RG9 5DD* Tel (01491) 641575 E-mail baileybj@ndo.co.uk

BAILEY, Canon Brian Constable. b 36. K Coll Lon AKC62. **d** 63 **p** 64. C Mill Hill Jo Keble Ch *Lon* 63-66; C Gt Stanmore 66-69; C Gt Marlow *Ox* 69-72; R Burghfield 72-81; R Wokingham All SS 81-96; Hon Can Ch Ch 94-96; TV Pinhoe and Broadclyst *Ex* 96-00; rtd 00; V of Close Sarum Cathl 00-01. *2 Rose Cottages, Maudlin Road, Totnes TQ9 5TG* Tel (01803) 865992 E-mail brianbailey579@btinternet.com

BAILEY, Mrs Carolyn. b 64. Ox Min Course 07. **d** 10 **p** 11. NSM Gt Missenden w Ballinger and Lt Hampden *Ox* from 10. *Mill House, 81 Aylesbury Road, Wendover, Aylesbury HP22 6JJ* Tel (01296) 624814 Mobile 07841-583303 E-mail carolyn.bailey1@virgin.net

BAILEY, The Ven David Charles. b 52. Linc Coll Ox BA75 MA78 MSc77. St Jo Coll Nottm BA79. **d** 80 **p** 81. C Worksop St Jo *S'well* 80-83; C Edgware *Lon* 83-87; V S Cave and Ellerker w

Broomfleet *York* 87-97; RD Howden 91-97; V Beverley Minster 97-08; P-in-c Routh 97-08; Can and Preb York Minster 98-08; Adn Bolton *Man* from 08. *14 Springside Road, Bury BL9 5JE* Tel 0161-761 6117 Fax 763 7973 E-mail archdeaconbolton@manchester.anglican.org

BAILEY, David Ross. b 58. UNISA BTh82. St Bede's Coll Umtata 80. **d** 82 **p** 82. S Africa 82-08; C Somerset West S Africa 82-85; C Elgin 85-87; R Atlantis 87-95; R Salt River 95-08; P-in-c Honicknowle *Ex* from 08; C Ernesettle from 08; C Whitleigh from 08. *St Francis's Presbytery, 53 Little Dock Lane, Plymouth PL5 2LP* Tel and fax (01752) 773874 Mobile 07864-059302 E-mail fr.david@blueyonder.co.uk

BAILEY, Derek Gilbert. b 42. Div Hostel Dub 65. **d** 68 **p** 69. C Cork St Luke w St Ann *C, C & R* 68-72; CF 72-06; Rtd Officer Chapl RAChD from 06; Perm to Offic *York* from 98; *Sheff* 97-01 and from 03. *c/o MOD Chaplains (Army)* Tel (01980) 615804 Fax 615800

BAILEY, Derek William. b 39. Man Univ BA96. Cranmer Hall Dur 64. **d** 67 **p** 68. C Sutton *Liv* 67-69; C Chapel-en-le-Frith *Derby* 69-73; V Hadfield 73-90; R Collyhurst *Man* 90-95; V Chaddesden St Mary *Derby* 95-02; rtd 02; Perm to Offic *York* from 03. *187 Bishopthorpe Road, York YO23 1PD* Tel (01904) 628080

BAILEY, Canon Edward Ian. b 35. CCC Cam BA59 MA63 Bris Univ MA69 PhD77. United Th Coll Bangalore 59 Westcott Ho Cam 61. **d** 63 **p** 64. C Newc St Jo 63-65; Asst Chapl Marlborough Coll 65-68; Perm to Offic *Bris* 69-70; R Winterbourne 70-06; P-in-c Winterbourne Down 75-81; RD Stapleton 77-83; Chapl Frenchay Hosp Bris 79-84; Hon Can Bris Cathl 84-06; Warden of Readers 95-03; rtd 06; Visiting Prof Middx Univ from 97; Perm to Offic *Ox* from 07. *The Old School, Church Lane, Yarnton, Kidlington OX5 1PY* Tel (01865) 841772 E-mail eibailey@csircs.freeserve.co.uk

BAILEY, Edward Peter. b 35. Nottm Univ MA93. Qu Coll Birm. **d** 62 **p** 63. C Ordsall *S'well* 62-66; C Clifton w Glapton 66-71; V Lady Bay 71-83; Relig Affairs Adv to Radio Trent 83-85; C Gedling 86-89; C Bilborough St Jo 89-00; rtd 00; Perm to Offic *York* from 00. *Cragside Cottage, 18 Egton Road, Aislaby, Whitby YO21 1SU*

BAILEY, Elizabeth. b 47. **d** 03 **p** 04. OLM Bishop's Cannings, All Cannings etc *Sarum* 03-09; rtd 09. *Lynden, The Street, Bishop's Cannings, Devizes SN10 2LD* Tel (01380) 860400 E-mail liz@iftco.com

BAILEY, Mrs Elizabeth Carmen. b 45. EAMTC 89. **d** 93 **p** 94. NSM Roughton and Felbrigg, Metton, Sustead etc *Nor* 93-95 and 99-02; P-in-c 02-06; NSM Cromer and Gresham 95-99; C Buxton w Oxnead, Lammas and Brampton 06-07; C Bure Valley 07-10; rtd 10. *5 Warren Road, Southrepps, Norwich NR11 8UN* Tel (01263) 833785 E-mail elizabeth.bailey2@btconnect.com

BAILEY, Eric Arthur. b 14. AKC37. **d** 37 **p** 38. C S'wark St Geo 37-39; C Waltham Cross *St Alb* 39-41; C Diss *Nor* 41-42; Chapl CF (EC) 42-43; C Kingsbury *Birm* 44-45; V Dordon 45-52; R Londesborough *York* 52-60; P-in-c Nunburnholme 53-54; R 54-60; P-in-c Burnby 53-54; R 54-60; V Gt w Lt Ouseburn *Ripon* 60-65; V Stonegate *Chich* 65-79; rtd 79; Perm to Offic *St E* 81-88. *Hill End, Sapiston, Bury St Edmunds IP31 1RR* Tel (01359) 269638

BAILEY, Ms Helen Margaret. b 69. Hull Univ BA92 PGCE99 SS Coll Cam BA09. Westcott Ho Cam 07. **d** 10 **p** 11. C High Harrogate Ch Ch *Ripon* from 10. *2A St Clements Road, Harrogate HG2 8LU* E-mail helen.bailey5@googlemail.com

BAILEY, Ian Arthur. b 53. York Univ BA74 DPhil78. WEMTC. **d** 01 **p** 02. NSM Clifton H Trin, St Andr and St Pet *Bris* 01-02; NSM Henleaze from 02. *5 Queens Gate, Stoke Bishop, Bristol BS9 1TZ* Tel 0117-968 6251 E-mail iandfbailey@blueyonder.co.uk

BAILEY, Canon Ivan John. b 33. Keble Coll Ox BA57 MA65. St Steph Ho Ox 57. **d** 59 **p** 60. C Ipswich All Hallows *St E* 59-62; Clerical Sec CEMS 62-66; V Cringleford *Nor* 66-81; RD Humbleyard 73-81; R Colney 80-81; Relig Adv Anglia TV 81-91; P-in-c Kirby Bedon w Bixley and Whitlingham *Nor* 81-92; Hon Can Nor Cathl 84-98; Chapl St Andr Hosp Norwich 92-94; Chapl Mental Health Unit Nor HA 92-94; Chapl Norfolk Mental Health Care NHS Trust 94-98; rtd 98; Perm to Offic *Nor* from 98. *21 Cranleigh Rise, Norwich NR4 6PQ* Tel (01603) 453565 E-mail ivan@bailey1966.freeserve.co.uk

BAILEY, Ms Jane Rome. b 50. Univ of Wales (Ban) BA99 BTh03. Ban Ord Course 00. **d** 03 **p** 04. C Llifon and Talybolion Deanery *Ban* 03-06; P-in-c Trefdraeth w Aberffraw, Llangadwaladr etc 06-10; TV Holyhead from 10. *St Seiriol's House, 25 Gors Avenue, Holyhead LL65 1PB* Tel (01407) 764780 E-mail jane.r.bailey@btinternet.com

BAILEY, Joyce Mary Josephine. See OUTEN, Mrs Joyce Mary Josephine

BAILEY, Judith Elizabeth Anne. See MILLER, Judith Elizabeth Anne

BAILEY, Justin Mark. b 55. Birm Univ BA77 Southn Univ MTh97 Wolv Poly PGCE78. Ripon Coll Cuddesdon 90. **d** 92 **p** 93. C Oakdale *Sarum* 92-96; P-in-c Milton Abbas, Hilton w

Cheselbourne etc 96-05; P-in-c Piddletrenthide w Plush, Alton Pancras etc 02-05; V Piddle Valley, Hilton, Cheselbourne etc 05-06; P-in-c Bruton and Distr *B & W* from 06. *The Rectory, Plox, Bruton BA10 0EF* Tel (01749) 812616 E-mail frjustin@btinternet.com

BAILEY, Mark David. b 62. Ripon Coll Cuddesdon 87. **d** 90 **p** 91. C Leigh Park *Portsm* 90-93; C Fleet *Guildf* 93-95; TV Basingstoke *Win* 95-00; P-in-c Twyford and Owslebury and Morestead 00-08; R Lower Dever from 08. *The Rectory, 6 Green Close, South Wonston, Winchester SO21 3EE* Tel (01962) 880650 E-mail revd.bailey@ukgateway.net

BAILEY, Canon Mark Robert. b 60. St Paul's Coll Chelt BA81. Trin Coll Bris BA89. **d** 89 **p** 90. C Heigham H Trin *Nor* 89-94; Chapl UEA 92-93; TV Cheltenham St Mary, St Matt, St Paul and H Trin *Glouc* 94-07; TR Cheltenham H Trin and St Paul from 07; Hon Can Glouc Cathl from 04. *100 Hewlett Road, Cheltenham GL52 6AR* Tel (01242) 582398 *or* 262306 E-mail mark.bailey@trinityuk.org

BAILEY, Martin Tristram. b 57. Oak Hill Th Coll 89. **d** 91 **p** 92. C Brundall w Braydeston and Postwick *Nor* 91-95; TV Plymouth St Andr and Stonehouse *Ex* 95-06; Chapl St Dunstan's Abbey Sch Plymouth 02-05; V Riseley w Bletsoe *St Alb* from 06. *The Vicarage, 16 Church Lane, Riseley, Bedford MK44 1ER* Tel (01234) 708234 E-mail martin@7baileys.freeserve.co.uk

BAILEY, Michael Joseph. b 78. Open Univ BSc01 City Univ MSc05 RN96. St Steph Ho Ox 08. **d** 10 **p** 11. C Holbrooks *Cov* from 10. *9 John Shelton Drive, Coventry CV6 4PE* Tel (02476) 637722 E-mail mjdtb4v@aol.com

BAILEY, Nicholas Andrew. b 55. Open Univ BA84 Nottm Univ CertEd80. Ripon Coll Cuddesdon 88. **d** 90 **p** 91. C Guisborough *York* 90-92; Chapl Repton Prep Sch from 92. *Repton Preparatory School, Foremarke Hall, Milton, Derby DE65 6EJ* Tel (01283) 703269

BAILEY, Miss Patricia Laura. b 49. Wall Hall Coll Aldenham CertEd72. NTMTC 95. **d** 98 **p** 99. NSM Hackney Marsh *Lon* 98-01; NSM S Hackney St Jo w Ch 01-04; NSM Cosby and Whetstone *Leic* from 04. *16 The Plantation, Countesthorpe, Leicester LE8 5ST* Tel 0116-277 4362

BAILEY, Peter. *See* BAILEY, Edward Peter

BAILEY, Canon Peter Robin. b 43. St Jo Coll Dur BA64. Trin Coll Bris 72. **d** 74 **p** 75. C Corby St Columba *Pet* 74-77; C Bishopsworth *Bris* 77-82; V Sea Mills 82-97; RD Westbury and Severnside 91-97; P-in-c Bishopston 97-98; P-in-c Bris St Andr w St Bart 97-98; TR Bishopston and St Andrews 98-09; Hon Can Bris Cathl 97-09; rtd 09. *4 The Croft, Backwell, Bristol BS48 3LY* Tel (01275) 790611 E-mail peterandheather@blueyonder.co.uk

BAILEY, Richard William. b 38. Man Univ BSc59. Ripon Hall Ox 63. **d** 65 **p** 66. C Tonge *Man* 65-68; C Stretford St Matt 68-71; R Abbey Hey 71-80; V E Crompton 80-86; V Chadderton St Matt 86-98; R Stand 98-04; rtd 04; Perm to Offic *Bradf* from 07. *Address withheld by request* E-mail jean_richard@btinternet.com

BAILEY, Richard William. b 47. Oak Hill Th Coll BA84. **d** 84 **p** 85. C Huyton St Geo *Liv* 84-87; V Wombridge *Lich* 87-97; P-in-c Shenstone and Stonnall 97-06; Chapl HM Pris Dovegate from 06. *HM Prison Dovegate, Uttoxeter ST14 8XR* Tel (01283) 829525 E-mail ricthevic@madasafish.com

BAILEY, Robert Henry. b 45. FCA69. NOC 99. **d** 02 **p** 03. NSM Dewsbury *Wakef* 02-05; Sub Chapl HM Pris Leeds 02-05; NSM Kinsley w Wragby *Wakef* from 05; P-in-c from 06. *The Vicarage, George Street, South Hiendley, Barnsley S72 9BX* Tel (01226) 715315 E-mail robertbailey.minster@btinternet.com

BAILEY, Canon Robert William. b 49. Open Univ BA91. Bernard Gilpin Soc Dur 68 Lich Th Coll 69. **d** 72 **p** 73. C Stoke *Cov* 72-75; Chapl RAF 75-99; RD Calne *Sarum* 97-98; TV Cartmel Peninsula *Carl* 99-11; Hon Can Carl Cathl 05-11; rtd 11. *Longmead, The Cartway, Wedhampton, Devizes SN10 3QD*

BAILEY, Simon. b 56. Man Univ MusB Nottm Univ BCombStuds. Linc Th Coll. **d** 83 **p** 84. C Armley w New Wortley *Ripon* 83-86; C Harrogate St Wilfrid and St Luke 86-90; R Harby, Long Clawson and Hose *Leic* 90-94; V Woodhall *Bradf* 94-03; RD Calverley 98-01; R N Adelaide Ch Ch Australia 03-07; R Glen Osmond from 07. *2 Pridmore Road, Glen Osmond SA 5064, Australia* Tel (0061) (8) 8379 1494 *or* 8379 4114 Fax 8338 3442 E-mail rector@stsavoursgo.net

BAILEY, Stella. b 76. Westhill Coll Birm BTheol98. Ripon Coll Cuddesdon 07. **d** 09 **p** 10. C Walsgrave on Sowe *Cov* from 09. *33 Brookshaw Way, Coventry CV2 2NJ* E-mail chacethedog@sky.com

BAILEY, Stephen. b 39. Leic Univ BA61. Clifton Th Coll 61. **d** 62 **p** 63. C Wellington w Eyton *Lich* 62-66; C Rainham *Chelmsf* 66-69; V Ercall Magna *Lich* 69-75; V Rowton 69-75; RD Wrockwardine 72-75; V W Bromwich Gd Shep w St Jo 75-83; P-in-c W Bromwich St Phil 80-81; V 81-83; R Chadwell *Chelmsf* 83-96; RD Thurrock 92-96; V Galleywood Common 96-04; rtd 04; Perm to Offic *Chelmsf* from 04. *64 Bridport Way, Braintree CM7 9FJ* Tel (01376) 550859

BAILEY, Stephen Andrew. b 75. St Jo Coll Nottm 05. **d** 07 **p** 08. C Walton-on-Thames *Guildf* 07-11; TV Oadby *Leic* from 11.

St Paul's House, Hamble Road, Oadby, Leicester LE2 4NX E-mail steveandangiebailey@tiscali.co.uk

BAILEY, Stephen John. b 57. Sarum & Wells Th Coll 88. **d** 90 **p** 91. C Redhill H Trin *S'wark* 90-95; Chapl E Surrey Coll 91-93; P-in-c Betchworth *S'wark* 95-00; V 00-06; P-in-c Buckland 95-00; R 00-06; R Hamilton H Trin Bermuda from 06. *PO Box CR 186, Hamilton Parish CR BX, Bermuda* Tel (001441) 293 1710 E-mail holytrinitychurch@logic.bm

BAILEY, Mrs Susan Mary. b 40. F L Calder Coll Liv CertEd61. EAMTC 89. **d** 92 **p** 94. NSM Chelmsf Cathl 92-93; NSM Needham Market w Badley *St E* 93-95; NSM Belper *Derby* 96-00; NSM Allestree St Nic and Quarndon 00-05; Chapl Morley Retreat and Conf Ho Derby 00-05; rtd 05. *28 Burleigh Way, Wickwar, Wotton-under-Edge GL12 8LR* Tel (01454) 294112 E-mail susan.m.bailey@gmail.com

BAILEY, Yvonne Mary. *See* HOBSON, Mrs Yvonne Mary

BAILIE, Alison Margaret. b 62. Leeds Univ LLB83. Trin Coll Bris BA98. **d** 98 **p** 99. C Halliwell St Pet *Man* 98-05; P-in-c Droylsden St Mary 05-09; R from 09. *St Mary's Rectory, Dunkirk Street, Droylsden, Manchester M43 7FB* Tel 0161-370 1569 E-mail alison@bailie.free-online.co.uk

BAILLIE, Canon Frederick Alexander. b 21. FRGS Open Univ BA75 QUB MA86 PhD87. CITC 53. **d** 55 **p** 56. C Belfast St Paul *Conn* 55-59; C Dunmurry 59-61; RAChD 57-84; I Eglantine *Conn* 61-69; I Belfast Whiterock 69-74; Hd of S Ch Miss Ballymacarrett 74-79; I Magheraculmoney *Clogh* 79-87; Dioc Communications Officer 80-86; Hon CF from 84; Can Clogh Cathl 85-87; rtd 87. *2 Raasay Court, Portree IV51 9TG* Tel (01478) 611376 E-mail fabaillie@btinternet.com

BAILLIE, Terence John. b 46. New Coll Ox BA69 MA78 Man Univ MSc72. St Jo Coll Nottm 74. **d** 77 **p** 78. C Chadwell *Chelmsf* 77-80; C Bickenhill w Elmdon *Birm* 80-84; V Bedminster St Mich *Bris* 84-96; V Clevedon St Andr and Ch Ch *B & W* from 96. *The Vicarage, 10 Coleridge Road, Clevedon BS21 7TB* Tel (01275) 872982 E-mail terry.baillie@tesco.net

BAILY, Linda Rosemary. **d** 06 **p** 07. NSM Llanaber w Caerdeon *Ban* from 06. *Llwyn Gloddaeth, Abermaw, Barmouth LL42 1DX* Tel (01341) 280524

BAILY, Canon Robert Spencer Canning. b 21. G&C Coll Cam BA42 MA46. Westcott Ho Cam 42. **d** 44 **p** 45. C Sherborne w Castleton and Lillington *Sarum* 44-46; C Heacham *Nor* 46-47; C Bedford All SS *St Alb* 48-50; C-in-c Hayes St Edm CD *Lon* 50-56; R Blofield w Hemblington *Nor* 56-69; P-in-c Perlethorpe *S'well* 69-87; Dir of Educn 69-87; Hon Can S'well Minster 80-87; rtd 87; Perm to Offic *Linc* 87-02; *S'well* 87-00. *17 Ravendale Close, Grantham NG31 8BS* Tel (01476) 568614

BAIN, Alan. b 48. Thames Poly BSc72. St Jo Coll Nottm. **d** 77 **p** 78. C Wakef St Andr and St Mary 77-81; V Bath Odd Down *B & W* 81-82; P-in-c Combe Hay 81-82; V Bath Odd Down w Combe Hay from 82. *The Vicarage, 39 Frome Road, Bath BA2 2QF* Tel (01225) 832838 *or* tel and fax 835228 E-mail alanbain@stphilipstjames.org

BAIN, Andrew John. b 55. Newc Poly BA77 Edin Univ MTh89. Edin Th Coll 86. **d** 88 **p** 89. Chapl St Mary's Cathl 88-91; C Edin St Mary 88-91; R Edin St Jas 91-98; P-in-c Edin St Marg 93-98; R Haddington 98-06; P-in-c Edin St Ninian 06-10; Dioc Dir of Ords 95-98 and 06-07. *Emmaus House, 14 Gilmore Place, Edinburgh EH3 9NQ* E-mail andrewbain99@hotmail.com

BAIN, David Roualeyn Findlater (Roly). b 54. Bris Univ BA75. Ripon Coll Cuddesdon 76. **d** 78 **p** 79. C Perry Hill St Geo *S'wark* 78-81; Chapl Asst Guy's Hosp Lon 81-84; Succ S'wark Cathl 81-84; V Streatham St Paul 84-90; Perm to Offic *Bris* 90-08; Hon C Almondsbury and Olveston from 08. *The Vicarage, The Street, Olveston, Bristol BS35 4DA* Tel and fax (01454) 616593

BAIN, The Ven John Stuart. b 55. Van Mildert Coll Dur BA77. Westcott Ho Cam 78. **d** 80 **p** 81. C Washington *Dur* 80-84; C Dunston 84-86; V Shiney Row 86-92; V Herrington 86-92; P-in-c Whitworth w Spennymoor 92-97; P-in-c Merrington 94-97; AD Auckland 96-02; V Spennymoor, Whitworth and Merrington 97-02; Hon Can Dur Cathl 98-02; Adn Sunderland from 02; P-in-c Hedworth from 02; P-in-c E Boldon from 09; P-in-c Boldon from 10. *St Nicholas' Vicarage, Hedworth Lane, Boldon Colliery NE35 9JA* Tel 0191-536 2300 Fax 519 3369 E-mail archdeacon.of.sunderland@durham.anglican.org

BAIN, Lawrence John Weir. b 60. NTMTC BA05. **d** 05 **p** 06. C Stoughton *Guildf* 05-09; P-in-c Camberley Heatherside from 09. *30 Yockley Close, Camberley GU15 1QH* Tel (01276) 691127 Fax 678015 E-mail revlarrybain@aol.com

BAIN-DOODU, Canon Joseph Justice. b 56. Cape Coast Univ Ghana MEd09. St Nic Th Coll Ghana LTh86. **d** 86 **p** 86. Ghana 86-97 and 99-08; Hon C Sheldon *Birm* 97-98; Perm to Offic *Portsm* from 09. *The Rectory, 3A Wadham Road, Portsmouth PO2 9ED* Tel (023) 9234 2661 Mobile 07532-104795 E-mail josephbaindoodu@gmail.com

BAINBRIDGE, Mrs Christine Susan. b 48. St Aid Coll Dur BA70 K Coll Lon MA99. SEITE 93. **d** 96 **p** 97. C S'wark H Trin w St Matt 96-99; Asst to Bp Woolwich (Greenwich Area) 99-03; C Lee Gd Shep w St Pet 99-03; P-in-c Deptford St Jo w H Trin 03-06; TR Deptford St Jo w H Trin and Ascension from 06.

St John's Vicarage, St John's Vale, London SE8 4EA Tel (020) 8692 2857 Fax 8318 1915 Mobile 07939-662980 E-mail bainbridge.c@tiscali.co.uk

BAINBRIDGE, David George. b 42. Wadh Coll Ox BA63 MA67 Lon Inst of Educn PGCE67. Ridley Hall Cam 84. **d** 86 **p** 87. C Downend *Bris* 86-90; TV Yate New Town 90-01; Warden Lee Abbey Internat Students' Club Kensington 01-07; rtd 07; Perm to Offic *Glouc* from 08. *2 Kingsmead, Lechlade GL7 3BW* Tel (01367) 250347 E-mail bainbridge1973@yahoo.co.uk

BAINBRIDGE, John Richard. b 35. Pemb Coll Cam BA59 MA63. Clifton Th Coll 65. **d** 67 **p** 68. C Ex St Leon w H Trin 67-70; P-in-c Penge St Paul *Roch* 70-73; Chapl Uppingham Sch 73-87; V Stevenage St Nic and Graveley *St Alb* 87-98; rtd 98; Perm to Offic *Pet* from 99. *Willowdown Cottage, 8 Laxton, Corby NN17 3AT* Tel (01780) 450308

BAINBRIDGE, Mrs Phyllis Marion. Aber Univ BSc81. St Jo Coll Nottm 10. **d** 11. NSM Littleover *Derby* from 11. *33 Broadway, Duffield, Belper DE56 4BU* Tel (01332) 840128 Mobile 07899-984254 E-mail phyllis@bainbridges.net

BAINBRIDGE, Richard Dennis. b 49. Ch Coll Cam BA71 MA75 Edge Hill Coll of HE PGCE72. S'wark Ord Course 91. **d** 94 **p** 95. C Bermondsey St Jas w Ch Ch *S'wark* 94-99; V Lee Gd Shep w St Pet from 99; AD E Lewisham from 06. *The Vicarage, 47 Handen Road, London SE12 8NR* Tel (020) 8318 2363 Fax 8318 1915 E-mail revrdb@yahoo.com

BAINES, Alan William. b 50. S Bank Poly BSc72. Trin Coll Bris 92. **d** 94 **p** 95. C Chenies and Lt Chalfont, Latimer and Flaunden *Ox* 94-98; V Eye *Pet* 98-05; Post Ord Tr Co-ord 00-05; TV Duston from 05. *The Rectory, 3 Main Road, Duston, Northampton NN5 6JB* Tel (01604) 752591 E-mail a.baines93@ntlworld.com

BAINES, Derek Alfred. b 53. MCSP75. CBDTI 99. **d** 02 **p** 03. NSM Lostock Hall *Blackb* 02-09; NSM Lostock Hall and Farington Moss 09-11; P-in-c Hoole from 11. *16 Middlefield, Leyland PR26 7AE* Tel and fax (01772) 641521 Mobile 07774-200885 E-mail baines5253@btinternet.com

BAINES, Edward. *See* BAINES, Noel Edward

BAINES, John Charles. b 68. Ripon Coll Cuddesdon 00. **d** 02 **p** 03. C Morton and Stonebroom w Shirland *Derby* 02-06; P-in-c New Mills from 06; RD Glossop from 10. *St George's Vicarage, Church Lane, New Mills, High Peak SK22 4NP* Tel (01663) 743225 E-mail vicar@newmillschurch.co.uk

BAINES, Keith. b 46. **d** 99 **p** 00. OLM Atherton and Hindsford *Man* 99-02; OLM Atherton and Hindsford w Howe Bridge 02-05; TV from 05. *6 Marton Drive, Atherton, Manchester M46 9WA* Tel (01942) 897668 E-mail baines1@supanet.com

✠**BAINES, The Rt Revd Nicholas.** b 57. Bradf Univ BA80. Trin Coll Bris BA87. **d** 87 **p** 88 **c** 03. C Kendal St Thos *Carl* 87-91; C Leic H Trin w St Jo 91-92; V Rothley 92-00; RD Goscote 96-00; Adn Lambeth *S'wark* 00-03; Area Bp Croydon 03-11; Bp Bradf from 11. *Bishopscroft, Ashwell Road, Heaton, Bradford BD9 4AU* Tel (01274) 545414 Fax 544831 E-mail bishop@bradford.anglican.org

BAINES, Noel Edward (Ted). b 29. St Jo Coll Dur BSc52 MA62. **d** 54 **p** 55. C Rainham *Chelmsf* 54-58; C Surbiton Hill Ch Ch *S'wark* 58-61; V Southborough St Matt *Roch* 61-67; V Beckenham St Jo 67-74; Hd RE Taunton Manor High Sch Caterham 74-83; Keston Coll 85-91; Hon C Bromley Ch Ch *Roch* 91-98; Hon C New Beckenham St Paul from 98; rtd 94. *10 Bromley Avenue, Bromley BR1 4BQ* Tel and fax (020) 8460 8256 E-mail ted.baines@diocese-rochester.org

BAINES, Mrs Sharon June. b 52. Sheff Hallam Univ MSc05 MCSP74. LCTP 06. **d** 09 **p** 10. NSM Penwortham St Leon *Blackb* from 09. *16 Middlefield, Leyland PR26 7AE* Tel and fax (01772) 641521 E-mail baines5253@btinternet.com

BAIRD, Agnes Murry (Nancy). Man Univ CertEd70. EAMTC 93. **d** 96 **p** 97. NSM Bramford *St E* 96-98; NSM Haughley w Wetherden and Stowupland 98-09; rtd 09; Perm to Offic *St E* from 09. *32 Maple Road, Stowupland, Stowmarket IP14 4DG* Tel (01449) 674734 E-mail nancy@ctlconnect.co.uk

BAIRD, Paul Drummond. b 48. St Chad's Coll Newc CertEd71 Open Univ BA85. Ripon Coll Cuddesdon 88. **d** 90 **p** 91. C Chandler's Ford *Win* 90-93; V Hythe 93-03; P-in-c Compton and Otterbourne 03-06; rtd 08. *5 Kensington Close, Eastleigh SO50 6NS* Tel (023) 8064 7536 Mobile 07802-431012 E-mail paulbaird@aol.com

BAIRD, Robert Douglas. b 21. ERD56. Cam Univ MA64. Ripon Coll Cuddesdon. **d** 85 **p** 86. NSM Charlbury w Shorthampton *Ox* 85-87; Asst Chapl HM Pris Grendon and Spring Hill 85; Lic to Offic *Ox* 87-91; Perm to Offic 91-07. *Glebe House, Ibstone, High Wycombe HP14 3XZ* Tel (01491) 638642 E-mail robert@baird1921.freeserve.co.uk

BAIRD, Mrs Sally. b 53. St As Minl Tr Course 04. **d** 06. NSM Bistre *St As* from 06. *100 Park Avenue, Bryn-y-Baal, Mold CH7 6TP* Tel (01352) 758831 E-mail sally.baird@btinternet.com

BAIRD, Canon William Stanley. b 33. TCD BA54 Div Test. **d** 56 **p** 57. C Carlow *C & O* 56-59; I Dunganstown *D & G* 59-64; C Knock *D & D* 64-69; P-in-c Kilwarlin Upper w Kilwarlin Lower

69-71; I 71-72; Warden Ch Min of Healing (Ireland) 72-79; I Dublin Drumcondra w N Strand *D & G* 79-91; Dir of Ords (Dub) 84-99; Can Ch Ch Cathl Dublin 88-99; I Swords w Donabate and Kilsallaghan 91-99; rtd 99. *5 Weavers Way, Wheaton Hall, Dublin Road, Drogheda, Co Louth, Republic of Ireland* Tel (00353) (41) 984 6645 E-mail stanleybaird1@eircom.net

BAISLEY, George. b 45. Sarum & Wells Th Coll 78. **d** 80 **p** 81. C Glouc St Geo w Whaddon 80-83; R Welford w Weston and Clifford Chambers 83-87; Chapl Myton Hamlet Hospice 87-91; Chapl Warw Univ 87-91; R Berkswell 91-03; RD Kenilworth 96-01; Chapl Bromley Coll 03-04; P-in-c Doddington, Newnham and Wychling *Cant* 04-07; P-in-c Lynsted w Kingsdown 04-07; P-in-c Norton 04-07; rtd 07; Perm to Offic *Chelmsf* 07-08; P-in-c N Ockendon from 08. *52 Birch Crescent, South Ockendon RM15 6TZ* Tel (01708) 850525 Mobile 07974-151056 E-mail george@baisley45.co.uk

BAKER, Alan. b 42. Liv Univ BA64. Carl Dioc Tr Inst 93. **d** 96 **p** 97. NSM Flookburgh *Carl* 96-97; NSM Cartmel Peninsula 97-07; Perm to Offic *Blackb* from 98 and *Carl* from 11. *1 Church View, Priest Lane, Cartmel, Grange-over-Sands LA11 6PU* Tel (01539) 536551

BAKER, Albert George. b 30. Qu Coll Birm. **d** 61 **p** 62. C Merton St Mary *S'wark* 61-64; C Limpsfield and Titsey 64-65; C Chapel-en-le-Frith *Derby* 65-68; R Odd Rode *Ches* 68-76; V Holme Cultram St Mary *Carl* 76-78; R Blofield w Hemblington *Nor* 78-94; rtd 94. *240 Raedwald Drive, Bury St Edmunds IP32 7DN* Tel (01284) 701802

BAKER, Alexander David Laing. **d** 11. C Edin Ch Ch from 11. *4 Arden Street, Edinburgh EH9 1BP* Tel 0131-229 0054 E-mail dradlbaker@gmail.com

BAKER, Alicia Mary. b 63. Trin Coll Bris BA03. **d** 03 **p** 04. C E Ham St Paul *Chelmsf* 03-07; P-in-c Abercarn and Cwmcarn *Mon* from 07. *The Vicarage, Twyn Road, Abercarn, Newport NP11 5GU* Tel (01495) 243919 E-mail aliciabakeruk@btinternet.com

BAKER, Angela Mary. b 42. **d** 91. Par Dn Battersea St Sav and St Geo w St Andr *S'wark* 91-94; C 94-96; C Battersea Fields 96-02; rtd 02; Perm to Offic *Roch* from 03. *Finches, Ide Hill, Sevenoaks TN14 6JW* Tel (01732) 750470

BAKER, Mrs Ann Christine. b 49. Edin Univ BEd71. CBDTI 98. **d** 01 **p** 02. NSM St Bees *Carl* 01-04; P-in-c Eskdale, Irton, Muncaster and Waberthwaite 04-09; V from 09. *Eskdale Vicarage, Boot, Holmrook CA19 1TF* Tel (019467) 23242 E-mail j.baker@can-online.org.uk

BAKER, Anne-Marie Clare. *See* BIRD, Mrs Anne-Marie Clare

BAKER, Anthony Peter. b 38. Hertf Coll Ox BA59 MA63. Clifton Th Coll 60. **d** 63 **p** 64. C Ox St Ebbe w St Pet 63-66; C Welling *Roch* 66-70; V Redland *Bris* 70-79; Lect Tyndale Hall Bris 70-71; Lect Trin Coll Bris 71-77; V Beckenham Ch Ch *Roch* 79-94; Chapl Beckenham Hosp 79-94; V Hove Bp Hannington Memorial Ch *Chich* 94-03; rtd 03; Perm to Offic *Chich* from 04. *12 Paradise Close, Eastbourne BN20 8BT* Tel (01323) 438783

BAKER, Miss Barbara Ann. b 36. Linc Th Coll 85. **d** 87 **p** 94. Par Dn Hornchurch St Andr *Chelmsf* 87-94; C 94-97; rtd 97; Perm to Offic *Chelmsf* from 97. *120 Devonshire Road, Hornchurch RM12 4LN* Tel (01708) 447759

BAKER, Canon Bernard George Coleman. b 36. Lon Univ BD61. Oak Hill Th Coll 61. **d** 63 **p** 64. C Broadwater St Mary *Chich* 63-66; Tanzania 66-84 and 96-01; BCMS Miss P and Chapl Morogoro Em Ch 66-79; V Moshi St Marg 79-84; Hon Can Morogoro from 77; Hon Can Mt Kilimanjaro from 82; C-in-c Ryde St Jas Prop Chpl *Portsm* 84-96; Crosslinks 96-01; Asst P Ruaha Cathl and Teacher Amani Chr Tr Cen 96-01; rtd 01; Perm to Offic *Ex* from 02. *104 Merafield Road, Plympton, Plymouth PL7 1SJ* Tel (01752) 339879

BAKER (formerly BARTON), Mrs Caroline Janet. b 61. Ex Univ BA83. Westcott Ho Cam 93. **d** 96 **p** 97. C Ivybridge w Harford *Ex* 96-02; P-in-c Torquay St Luke and Dioc Adv in Adult Tr 02-05; rtd 05. *11 Arundel Close, Exeter EX2 8UG* Tel (01392) 426781

BAKER, Charles Edward. b 47. **d** 87 **p** 88. NSM Dublin Clontarf *D & G* 87-90; NSM Delgany 90-94; NSM Dublin Sandford w Milltown 94-97; NSM Dublin St Patr Cathl Gp from 97. *12 Aranleigh Vale, Rathfarnham, Dublin 14, Republic of Ireland* Tel (00353) (1) 494 6251

BAKER, Prof Christopher James. b 54. St Cath Coll Cam BA75 MA78 PhD78 CEng83 FICE96 FIHT95. EMMTC 85. **d** 88 **p** 89. NSM Matlock Bath *Derby* 88-95; NSM Matlock Bath and Cromford 95; NSM Beeston *S'well* 95-98; Perm to Offic *Lich* 98-00; NSM Lich St Mich w St Mary and Wall 00-10; NSM Lich Ch Ch from 10. *28 Grosvenor Close, Lichfield WS14 9SR* Tel (01543) 256320 or 262211 E-mail cjsmbaker@btinternet.com

BAKER, Christopher Peter. b 64. St Cuth Soc Dur BA95 Greenwich Univ PGCE96. SEITE 99. **d** 02 **p** 03. C Kennington St Mark *S'wark* 02-06; Chapl Greenwich Univ from 07. *St Mark's Vicarage, 10 Church Road, Biggin Hill, Westerham TN16 3LB* Tel (01959) 540482

BAKER, Christopher Richard. b 61. Man Univ BA83 PhD02 Southn Univ BTh90 Heythrop Coll Lon MTh92. Sarum & Wells Th Coll 86. **d** 89 **p** 93. C Dulwich St Barn *S'wark* 89-92; Tutor Sarum & Wells Th Coll 92-94; Dir Chr Tr Milton Keynes *Ox* 94-98; Dir Tr OLM 98-99; Development Officer Wm Temple Foundn 01-04; Research Dir from 04. *Luther King House, Brighton Grove, Rusholme, Manchester M14 5JP* Tel 0161-249 2502 Mobile 07779-000021 E-mail temple@wtf.org.uk

BAKER, David. b 63. SWMTC 99. **d** 02. NSM Parkham, Alwington, Buckland Brewer etc *Ex* from 02. *4 Ashley Terrace, Bideford EX39 3AL* Tel (01237) 473453 E-mail bakerbuzz@hotmail.com

BAKER, David Ayshford. b 66. St Aid Coll Dur BA88. Wycliffe Hall Ox BTh97. **d** 97 **p** 98. C Chadwell Heath *Chelmsf* 97-01; C Surbiton Hill Ch Ch *S'wark* 01-09; R E Dean w Friston and Jevington *Chich* from 09. *The Rectory, Gilberts Drive, East Dean, Eastbourne BN20 0DL* Tel (01323) 423266

BAKER, David Clive. b 47. Sarum & Wells Th Coll 76. **d** 78 **p** 79. C Shirley *Birm* 78-82; R Wainfleet All SS w St Thos *Linc* 82-83; P-in-c Wainfleet St Mary 82-83; P-in-c Croft 82-83; R The Wainfleets and Croft 83-86; V Stirchley *Birm* 86-96; Perm to Offic 97-98; V Handsworth St Mich 98-02; Chapl Aston Univ 99-02; C Codsall *Lich* 02-05; P-in-c Coven 04-05; V Bilbrook and Coven from 05. *The New Vicarage, Church Lane, Coven, Wolverhampton WV9 5DE* Tel (01902) 790230 Mobile 07958-468819

BAKER, David Frederick. b 32. Clifton Th Coll 67. **d** 69 **p** 70. C Bilton *Ripon* 69-71; C Heworth w Peasholme St Cuth *York* 71-75; V Sand Hutton w Gate and Upper Helmsley 75-77; P-in-c Bossall w Buttercrambe 75-77; V Sand Hutton 77-80; R Preston in Holderness 80; P-in-c Sproatley 80; R Preston and Sproatley in Holderness 80-89; C Topcliffe w Dalton and Dishforth 89; V Baldersby w Dalton, Dishforth etc 89-96; rtd 96; Perm to Offic *York* and *Ripon* 96-08. *6 Mains Court, Westhill AB32 6QZ* Tel (01224) 743070

BAKER, David John. b 27. LRAM50 GRSM51. Ely Th Coll 53. **d** 55 **p** 56. C Swanley St Mary *Roch* 55-58; C Guildf St Nic 58-63; Prec St Alb Abbey 63-67; P-in-c Colney St Pet 67-68; V 68-73; V Tattenham Corner and Burgh Heath *Guildf* 73-84; R Fetcham 84-96; rtd 96; Perm to Offic *Guildf* from 96. *1 Terra Cotta Court, Quennels Hill, Wrecclesham, Farnham GU10 4SL* Tel (01252) 734202

BAKER, David Jordan. b 35. Univ of Wales (Lamp) BA59. Ely Th Coll 59. **d** 61 **p** 62. C Spalding *Linc* 61-66; C Gainsborough All SS 66-69; V Wrawby 69-78; V Melton Ross w Newby 70-78; V Linc St Pet-at-Gowts and St Andr 78-94; rtd 98; Perm to Offic *Linc* from 01. *Fartherwell, The Paddock, Canwick, Lincoln LN4 2RX* Tel (01522) 526903

BAKER, Dilly. *See* BAKER, Ms Hilary Mary

BAKER, Mrs Elizabeth May Janet Margaret. b 51. Bretton Hall Coll CertEd73. Ox Min Course 04. **d** 07 **p** 08. NSM Watling Valley *Ox* 07-10; NSM Stantonbury and Willen from 10. *The Well, Newport Road, Willen, Milton Keynes MK15 9AA* Tel (01908) 662092 E-mail beth@willenbakers.co.uk

BAKER, Frank Thomas. b 36. Selw Coll Cam BA61. Coll of Resurr Mirfield. **d** 63 **p** 64. C Mackworth St Fran *Derby* 63-66; C Leeds St Pet *Ripon* 66-73; P-in-c Stanley *Dur* 73-74; R Crook 73-74; Chapl Bucharest *Eur* 74-75; C Tewkesbury w Walton Cardiff *Glouc* 75-81; Min Can Windsor 81-86; rtd 86. *15 Hartford Court, 33 Filey Road, Scarborough YO11 2TP* Tel (01723) 352466

BAKER, Frederick Peter. b 24. Bps' Coll Cheshunt 58. **d** 60 **p** 61. C Peckham St Jude *S'wark* 60-63; C Mitcham St Mark 63-66; C Northampton St Pet w Upton 66-69; P-in-c Northampton St Lawr 69-71; V Northampton St Edm 71-78; V Spratton 78-83; R Walgrave w Hannington and Wold 83-89; rtd 89; Perm to Offic *Win* 89-98 and *Ely* 00-08. *73 Five Arches, Orton Wistow, Peterborough PE2 6FQ* Tel (01733) 371349

BAKER, Gillian Devonald. b 40. S Dios Minl Tr Scheme 88. **d** 91 **p** 94. NSM Redhorn *Sarum* 91-07; TV 02-07; Chapl HM Pris Erlestoke 94-01. *11 The Street, Chirton, Devizes SN10 3QS* Tel (01380) 848170 Fax 840152 E-mail davidb@atlanticbridge.co.uk

BAKER, The Very Revd Graham Brinkworth. b 26. AKC54. **d** 55 **p** 56. C Wandsworth St Anne *S'wark* 55-58; Canada from 58. *1280 Tracksell Avenue, Victoria BC V8P 2C9, Canada*

BAKER, Mrs Heather Elizabeth. b 48. WEMTC 94. **d** 97 **p** 98. NSM Ewyas Harold w Dulas, Kenderchurch etc *Heref* 97-98; C Burghill and Stretton Sugwas 00-01; P-in-c Glasbury and Llowes w Clyro and Betws *S & B* 02-08. *Park Lodge, Pontrilas, Hereford HR2 0HE*

BAKER, Ms Hilary Mary (Dilly). b 61. Man Univ BA83 CQSW86. Sarum & Wells Th Coll 86. **d** 89 **p** 94. Par Dn E Dulwich St Jo *S'wark* 89-92; Tutor Sarum & Wells Th Coll 92-94; TV Stantonbury and Willen *Ox* 94-01; Warden Scargill Ho 01-08; P-in-c Kirkby-in-Malhamdale w Coniston Cold *Bradf* 08-09; P-in-c Kirkby-in-Malhamdale from 09. *The Vicarage, Kirkby Malham, Skipton BD23 4BS* Tel (01729) 830144 E-mail dillybaker@gmail.com

BAKER, Hugh Crispin. b 58. Open Univ BA92. Linc Th Coll 95. **d** 95 **p** 96. C Birstall and Wanlip *Leic* 95-99; V Middlestown *Wakef* 99-09; P-in-c Mirfield from 09; Dioc Rural Officer from 04. *The Vicarage, 3 Vicarage Meadow, Mirfield WF14 9JL* Tel (01924) 505790 E-mail hughcbaker@googlemail.com

BAKER, Hugh John. b 46. Birm Univ BSocSc68. Cuddesdon Coll 69. **d** 71 **p** 72. C Binley *Cov* 71-74; C Pemberton St Mark Newtown *Liv* 74-78; TV Sutton 78-90; V Hints *Lich* 90-05; V Fazeley from 90; V Canwell from 05; R Drayton Bassett from 05; Chapl S Staffs Healthcare NHS Trust from 00. *St Paul's Vicarage, 9 West Drive, Bonehill, Tamworth B78 3HR* Tel (01827) 287701 *or* 289414 E-mail elizabethatthevicarage@supanet.com

BAKER, Iain. b 70. St D Coll Lamp BA91. Oak Hill Th Coll BA99. **d** 99 **p** 00. C Gt Clacton *Chelmsf* 99-03; V Kidsgrove *Lich* from 03. *St Thomas's Vicarage, The Avenue, Kidsgrove, Stoke-on-Trent ST7 1AG* Tel (01782) 772895 *or* 771727 E-mail ib.ib@virgin.net

BAKER, Ivon Robert. b 28. St Aug Coll Cant 59. **d** 60 **p** 61. C Sutton in Ashfield St Mary *S'well* 60-62; V Gringley-on-the-Hill 62-94; Chapl HM YOI Gringley 82-91; RD Bawtry *S'well* 85-90; rtd 94; Perm to Offic *York* 94-11. *2 Willowgate, Pickering YO18 7BE* Tel (01751) 472281

BAKER, Canon James Henry. b 39. MBE02. Kelham Th Coll 62. **d** 67 **p** 68. C Sheff Arbourthorne 67-70; C Pemberton St Jo *Liv* 70-71; Chapl and Prec St Mary's Cathl 71-74; R Lochgelly *St And* 74-84; P-in-c Rosyth and Inverkeithing 76-84; Can St Ninian's Cathl Perth 83-84; TR Whitehaven *Carl* 84-04; RD Calder 96-01; Hon Can Carl Cathl from 96; rtd 04. *Eskdale Vicarage, Boot, Holmrook CA19 1TF* Tel (019467) 23242 E-mail j.baker@can-online.org.uk

BAKER, James Roger. b 71. Bucks Chilterns Univ Coll BA99 RMN99. St Steph Ho Ox 05 Ripon Coll Cuddesdon 06. **d** 07 **p** 08. C Didcot St Pet *Ox* 07-10; V Yeovil St Mich *B & W* from 10. *133 Sherborne Road, Yeovil BA21 4HF* Tel (01935) 475752 E-mail jamesbaker 364@fsmail.net

BAKER, Jean Margaret. b 47. Sheff Univ BSc69 DipEd70 Lon Univ BD78. All Nations Chr Coll 75 Gilmore Course 81. **dss** 82 **d** 87 **p** 97. Liv Our Lady and St Nic w St Anne 82-87; Chapl Huyton Coll 87; Chapl St Mary and St Anne's Sch Abbots Bromley 87-91; Chapl Howell's Sch Denbigh 91-98; C Denbigh *St As* 97-08; rtd 08. *Lle Braf, 28 Abrams Lane, Denbigh LL16 3SS* Tel (01745) 812262 E-mail margaret@smallrev.demon.co.uk

BAKER, Jenifer Marlene. b 44. Bris Univ BSc65 Univ of Wales (Swansea) PhD71 York St Jo Coll BA05. **d** 05 **p** 06. OLM Ruyton XI Towns w Gt and Lt Ness *Lich* from 05. *Clock Cottage, Church Street, Ruyton XI Towns, Shrewsbury SY4 1LA* Tel (01939) 260910

BAKER, John Albert. b 29. St Edm Hall Ox BA52 MA56 Lon Univ BSc68 S Bank Poly MSc76. Cuddesdon Coll 52. **d** 54 **p** 55. C Battersea St Luke *S'wark* 54-58; C Richmond St Mary 58-62; V Battersea Park All SS 62-83; Tutor Roehampton Inst 83-91; rtd 94; Hon C Battersea St Luke *S'wark* 84-02. *44 Wroughton Road, London SW11 6BG* Tel (020) 7585 2492

BAKER, John Alfred. b 41. **d** 02 **p** 03. OLM Herne *Cant* 02-05; OLM St Nicholas at Wade w Sarre and Chislet w Hoath from 05; OLM Minster w Monkton from 05. *Oakfield, 219 Canterbury Road, Herne Bay CT6 7HB* Tel (01227) 362519 Mobile 07960-107169 E-mail john-baker@kent35.fslife.co.uk

✠**BAKER, The Rt Revd John Austin.** b 28. Oriel Coll Ox BA52 MA55 BLitt55 MLitt. Lambeth DD91 Cuddesdon Coll 52. **d** 54 **p** 55 **c** 82. C Cuddesdon *Ox* 54-57; Tutor Cuddesdon Coll 54-57; C Hatch End St Anselm *Lon* 57-59; Lect K Coll Lon 57-59; Chapl CCC Ox 59-73; Lect Th Ox Univ 59-73; Can Westmr Abbey 73-82; Sub Dean Westmr 78-82; R Westmr St Marg 78-82; Chapl to Speaker of Ho of Commons 78-82; Bp Sarum 82-93; Can and Preb Sarum Cathl 82-93; rtd 93; Hon Asst Bp Win from 94. *4 Mede Villas, Kingsgate Road, Winchester SO23 9QQ* Tel (01962) 861388 Fax 843089

BAKER, John Carl. b 55. Chich Th Coll 77. **d** 80 **p** 81. C Wigan St Andr *Liv* 80-83; V Hollinfare 83-85; TV Seacroft *Ripon* 85-89; TV Bottesford w Ashby *Linc* 89-94; V Liv St Paul Stoneycroft 94-02; V Altcar and Hightown 02-09; rtd 09. *49 Moor Lane, Southport PR8 3NY* Tel (01704) 570639 E-mail revjcb@btopenworld.com

BAKER, John Reginald. b 62. Hatf Coll Dur BSc83. Wycliffe Hall Ox 86. **d** 89 **p** 90. C Amersham *Ox* 89-92; C Greenford H Cross *Lon* 92-97. *11A Lakeside Road, London W14 0DX* Tel (020) 8574 3762

✠**BAKER, The Rt Revd Jonathan Mark Richard.** b 66. St Jo Coll Ox BA88 MPhil90. St Steph Ho Ox BA92. **d** 93 **p** 94 **c** 11. C Ascot Heath *Ox* 93-96; C Reading St Mark 96; P-in-c 96-99; V 99-02; P-in-c Reading H Trin 96-99; V 99-02; Prin Pusey Ho from 03; Hon C Ox St Thos from 08; Suff Bp Ebbsfleet (PEV) *Cant* from 11. *Pusey House, Oxford OX1 3LZ* Tel (01865) 278415 Fax 278416 E-mail jonathan.baker@stx.ox.ac.uk

BAKER, Canon Jonathan William. b 61. SS Coll Cam MA85. Wycliffe Hall Ox BA91. **d** 92 **p** 93. C Sanderstead All SS *S'wark*

BALDOCK

92-96; P-in-c Scalby w Ravenscar and Staintondale *York* 96-97; V Scalby 97-04; P-in-c Hackness w Harwood Dale 96-97; V 97-04; P-in-c Scarborough St Luke 03-04; Can Res Pet Cathl from 04. *The Chapter Office, Minster Precincts, Peterborough PE1 1XS* Tel (01733) 897335 *or* 355310 Fax 355316 E-mail jonathan.baker@peterborough-cathedral.org.uk
BAKER, Mrs Julie Ann Louise. b 77. Univ of Wales (Lamp) BA98. St Mich Coll Llan BTh06. **d** 06 **p** 07. C Barry All SS *Llan* 06-09; PV Llan Cathl from 09. *2 White House, The Cathedral Green, Cardiff CF5 2EB* Tel (029) 2055 2313 E-mail julie@treeherder.co.uk
BAKER, Lambert William. b 38. EMMTC 92. **d** 96 **p** 97. NSM Welford w Sibbertoft and Marston Trussell *Pet* 96-99; P-in-c 98-01; P-in-c N w S Kilworth and Misterton *Leic* 01-03; P-in-c Swinford w Catthorpe, Shawell and Stanford 01-03; TR Gilmorton, Peatling Parva, Kimcote etc 03-11; RD Guthlaxton 05-11; Hon Can Leic Cathl 06-11; rtd 11; Perm to Offic *Pet* from 11. *Homestead, 9 The Green, Lilbourne, Rugby CV23 0SR* Tel (01788) 860409 E-mail kw.baker@btinternet.com
BAKER, Marc Crispin. b 75. Westmr Coll Ox BTh96. Oak Hill Th Coll 00. **d** 02 **p** 03. C Upton (Overchurch) *Ches* 02-06; TV Cheltenham St Mary, St Matt, St Paul and H Trin *Glouc* 06-07; C Cheltenham St Mary w St Matt from 07. *38 College Road, Cheltenham GL53 7HX* Tel (01242) 525994 E-mail marc.baker@virgin.net
BAKER, Margaret. b 55. **d** 08 **p** 09. C Herringthorpe *Sheff* 08-10; C Rivers Team from 10. *40 Flat Lane, Whiston, Rotherham S60 4EF* Tel (01709) 363959 E-mail margaret.baker@sheffield.anglican.org
BAKER, Canon Michael Robert Henry. b 39. Keele Univ MA88. Lich Th Coll 63. **d** 66 **p** 67. C Wellingborough All SS *Pet* 66-68; C Pet All SS 68-73; V Earls Barton 73-87; RD Wellingborough 76-87; P-in-c Gt Doddington 77-82; TR Kingsthorpe w Northampton St Dav 87-95; V Towcester w Easton Neston 95-04; RD Towcester 98-03; Can Pet Cathl 85-04; rtd 04; Perm to Offic *Pet* from 04. *Magdalene Cottage, 56 Queen Street, Geddington, Kettering NN14 1AZ* Tel (01536) 741091 E-mail mnmbaker@googlemail.com
BAKER, Michael William. b 38. Roch Th Coll 68. **d** 70 **p** 71. C Woodmansterne *S'wark* 70-75; TV Danbury *Chelmsf* 75-78; P-in-c Barrington *Ely* 78-90; V 90-97; P-in-c Shepreth 78-90; V 90-97; rtd 97; Perm to Offic *Nor* from 98. *The White House, Church Street, Elsing, Dereham NR20 3EB* Tel (01362) 637370 E-mail hmb@waitrose.com
BAKER, Miles Anthony. b 71. Brunel Univ BA92. Ridley Hall Cam 99. **d** 02 **p** 03. C Paignton Ch Ch and Preston St Paul *Ex* 02-05; P-in-c Upton 05-08; Dioc Miss Enabler *Pet* from 08. *The Rectory, 32 West Street, Ecton, Northampton NN6 0QF* Tel (01604) 407899 E-mail miles.baker@peterborough-diocese.org.uk
BAKER, Canon Neville Duff. b 35. St Aid Birkenhead 60. **d** 63 **p** 64. C Stranton *Dur* 63-66; C Houghton le Spring 66-68; V Tudhoe Grange 68-07; P-in-c Merrington 91-94; RD Auckland 83-94; Hon Can Dur Cathl 90-07; rtd 07. *2 The Bents, Sunderland SR6 7NX*
BAKER, Noel Edward Lloyd. b 37. Sarum & Wells Th Coll 73. **d** 75 **p** 76. C Charlton Kings St Mary *Glouc* 75-79; V Clearwell 79-81; R Eastington and Frocester 81-97; RD Stonehouse 90-94; P-in-c Eastington and Frocester 97-98; P-in-c Standish w Haresfield and Moreton Valence etc 97-98; rtd 98; Perm to Offic *Glouc* from 00. *46 Dozule Close, Leonard Stanley, Stonehouse GL10 3NL* Tel (01453) 823569 E-mail noelbaker@greenbee.net
BAKER, Mrs Pamela. Ox Min Course. **d** 08. NSM Blackbird Leys *Ox* from 08. *27 Exeter Road, Kidlington OX5 2DY*
BAKER, Paul Anthony. b 64. St Chad's Coll Dur BA85. St Steph Ho Ox BA88 MA98. **d** 89 **p** 90. C Hartlepool St Aid *Dur* 89-93; TV Jarrow 93-98; V Sunderland Pennywell St Thos 98-04; V Darlington St Mark w St Paul from 04. *St Mark's Vicarage, 394 North Road, Darlington DL1 3BH* Tel (01325) 382400
BAKER, Peter Colin. b 43. Sarum & Wells Th Coll. **d** 82 **p** 83. C Bridgemary *Portsm* 82-86; V Ash Vale *Guildf* 86-99; P-in-c Earlham St Anne *Nor* 99-08; P-in-c Earlham St Mary 99-08; rtd 08. *15 Linden Close, Laverstock, Salisbury SP1 1PN* Tel 07710-844243 (mobile) E-mail peter.baker854@ntlworld.com
BAKER, Peter Graham. b 55. MA PhD. St Steph Ho Ox. **d** 82 **p** 83. C Ches H Trin 82-86; C Holborn St Alb w Saffron Hill St Pet *Lon* 86-91; V Golders Green 91-01; AD W Barnet 95-00; V Regent's Park St Mark from 01; rtd 11. *Address temp unknown* E-mail petergbaker@freeuk.com
BAKER, Robert James. b 80. Oriel Coll Ox BA04 MA08. Wycliffe Hall Ox BA07. **d** 08 **p** 09. C Chesham Bois *Ox* from 08. *19 Milton Lawns, Amersham HP6 6BJ* Tel 07855-774384 (mobile) E-mail robert.baker robertj@hotmail.com
BAKER, Canon Robert John Kenneth. b 50. Southn Univ BSc71 MICE79. Oak Hill Th Coll 88. **d** 90 **p** 91. C Cromer *Nor* 90-94; R Pakefield from 94; Hon Can Nor Cathl from 07. *The Rectory, The Causeway, Pakefield, Lowestoft NR33 0JZ* Tel (01502) 574040

BAKER, Canon Robert Mark. b 50. Bris Univ BA73. St Jo Coll Nottm 74. **d** 76 **p** 77. C Portswood Ch Ch *Win* 76-80; R Witton w Brundall and Braydeston *Nor* 80-89; P-in-c Buckenham w Hassingham and Strumpshaw 80-86; R Brundall w Braydeston and Postwick 89-05; RD Blofield 89-94; TV Thetford from 05; Hon Can Nor Cathl from 93. *The Rectory, 6 Redcastle Road, Thetford IP24 3NF* Tel (01842) 762291 E-mail bob-baker@homecall.co.uk
BAKER, Ronald Kenneth. b 43. Open Univ BA80. St Jo Coll Nottm LTh87. **d** 87 **p** 88. C Paddock Wood *Roch* 87-90; V Ramsgate St Mark *Cant* 90-95; P-in-c Ewhurst and Bodiam *Chich* 95-98; V 98-03; rtd 03; Perm to Offic *Chich* from 03. *49 Coneyburrow Gardens, St Leonards-on-Sea TN38 9RZ* Tel (01424) 851870 E-mail revronbaker@talktalk.net
BAKER, Roy David. b 36. St Aid Birkenhead 59. **d** 62 **p** 63. C Garston *Liv* 62-64; C N Meols 64-68; V Newton-le-Willows 68-73; V Crossens 73-82; V Blundellsands St Nic 82-01; rtd 01; Perm to Offic *Liv* from 03. *18 Ennerdale Road, Formby, Liverpool L37 2EA* Tel (01704) 830622
BAKER, Sarah Jane. b 59. Lon Univ MB, BS82 Sheff Univ MPhil00 Coll of Ripon & York St Jo MA02. NOC 99. **d** 02 **p** 03. NSM Kinsley w Wragby *Wakef* 02-04; NSM Sandal St Cath 04-07; Perm to Offic from 07. *Address temp unknown* Tel 07885-376182 (mobile) E-mail sarah.baker17@btinternet.com
BAKER, Canon Simon Nicholas Hartland. b 57. K Coll Lon BD78. Qu Coll Birm 79. **d** 82 **p** 83. C Tupsley *Heref* 81-85; V Shinfield *Ox* 85-98; Prin Berks Chr Tr Scheme 93-98; Lay Min Adv and Warden of Readers *Win* 98-02; Dir of Min Development 02-07; Dir of Min and Past Planning from 07; Hon Can Win Cathl from 08. *The Rectory, Trinity Hill, Medstead, Alton GU34 5LT* Tel (01420) 568191
BAKER, Stuart. b 44. MATA63 AIAT65. Ripon Coll Cuddesdon 92. **d** 93 **p** 94. C Whitchurch *Bris* 93-97; R Brightling, Dallington, Mountfield etc *Chich* 97-10; rtd 10. *8 Ayscue Close, Eastbourne BN23 6HE* Tel (01323) 720168
BAKER, Canon William John. b 45. FCII80. Cranmer Hall Dur 87. **d** 89 **p** 90. C Sale St Anne *Ches* 89-93; V Crewe St Andr w St Jo from 93; P-in-c Crewe Ch Ch from 07; RD Nantwich from 06; Hon Can Ches Cathl from 08. *St John's Vicarage, 14 Dane Bank Avenue, Crewe CW2 8AA* Tel (01270) 569000 Fax 650209 E-mail bill@revbaker.fsnet.co.uk
BAKERE, The Very Revd Ronald Duncan. b 35. TCD BA58 MA61 BD62 Ch Ch Ox MA66 FRSA68 FBIM79. Div Test 59. **d** 59 **p** 60. C Knockbreda *D & D* 59-61; C Dublin Zion Ch *D & G* 61-63; Min Can St Patr Cathl Dublin 62-64; CF (TA) 65-67; Lect Th Ex Univ Inst Educn 67-72; Prin Kuka Teachers' Coll Nigeria 73-77; Cen Org Red Cross Ex 78-81; Perm to Offic *Ex* 82-85; P-in-c Chew Magna w Dundry *B & W* 86-87; Hd RS Sir John Cass Foundn Lon 88-93; Dean Port Moresby Papua New Guinea 93-96; Visiting Prof H Spirit RC Sem 94-96; Hospitaller and Sen Chapl St Barts Hosp Lon 96-97; rtd 97; Perm to Offic *Lon* 96-04. *12 Dumbarton Road, London SW2 5LU* Tel 07958-061962 (mobile)
BAKKER, Gregory Kendall. b 66. California State Univ BA89. Trin Episc Sch for Min Penn MDiv92 Trin Coll Bris 99. **d** 92 **p** 93. C Tariffville USA 92-96; Lect St Phil Coll Kongwa Tanzania 96-99; C Wroughton *Bris* 00-02; TV Stratton St Margaret w S Marston etc 02-08; V Sholing *Win* from 08. *The Vicarage, 41 Station Road, Southampton SO19 8FN* Tel (023) 8044 8337 E-mail gbakker@tiscali.co.uk *or* sholingvicarage@googlemail.com
BAKKER (née CAMPBELL), Mrs Jane Judith. b 68. Trin Coll Bris BA01. **d** 01 **p** 02. NSM Lyddington and Wanborough and Bishopstone etc *Bris* 01-03; NSM Stratton St Margaret w S Marston etc 03-08; NSM Sholing *Win* from 08. *The Vicarage, 41 Station Road, Southampton SO19 8FN* Tel (023) 8044 8337 E-mail jjbakker@tiscali.co.uk
BALCH, John Robin. b 37. Lon Univ BSc61 Bris Univ CertEd62. ALCD68. **d** 68 **p** 69. C Bath Walcot *B & W* 68-71; C Fulwood *Sheff* 71-76; V Erith St Paul *Roch* 76-93; RD Erith 90-93; P-in-c Fairlight *Chich* 93-94; R Fairlight, Guestling and Pett 94-01; rtd 01; Perm to Offic *Derby* from 01. *29 Whitecotes Park, Chesterfield S40 3RT* Tel (01246) 297099
BALCHIN, Michael John. b 38. Selw Coll Cam BA60 MA64. Wells Th Coll 60. **d** 62 **p** 63. C Bournemouth H Epiphany *Win* 62-65; C Bris St Mary Redcliffe w Temple etc 65-69; R Norton sub Hamdon *B & W* 69-70; P-in-c Chiselborough w W Chinnock 69-70; R Norton sub Hamdon w Chiselborough 70-77; P-in-c Chipstable w Huish Champflower and Clatworthy 77-82; R 82-88; Perm to Offic *Ban* from 88; rtd 03. *The Barn, Middle Penygelly, Kerry, Newtown SY16 4LX* Tel (01686) 670710
BALDOCK, Charles William Martin. b 52. Nottm Univ BPharm73 York St Jo Coll MA07. St Jo Coll Nottm LTh. **d** 85 **p** 86. C Nailsea Ch Ch *B & W* 85-89; V Brampton Bierlow *Sheff* 89-00; RD Wath 95-00; Hon Can Sheff Cathl 98-00; V Dringhouses *York* from 00; RD City of York from 04; Chapl St Leon Hospice York from 02. *The Vicarage, Tadcaster Road,*

Dringhouses, York YO24 1QG Tel (01904) 706120 *or* tel and fax 709111 E-mail ms@msbaldock.plus.com *or* parishoffice@care4free.net
BALDOCK, Canon Norman. b 29. K Coll Lon BD52 AKC52. **d** 53 **p** 54. C Cant St Pet w H Cross 53-54; C Thornton Heath St Jude 54-58; V Ash w W Marsh 58-67; V Sheerness H Trin w St Paul 67-75; V Margate St Jo 75-94; RD Thanet 80-86; Hon Can Cant Cathl 82-94; Chapl Margate Gen Hosp 82-94; rtd 94; Perm to Offic *Cant* from 94. *9 Beach Avenue, Birchington CT7 9VS* Tel (01843) 841173
BALDOCK, Reginald David. b 48. Oak Hill Th Coll 72. **d** 75 **p** 76. C Plymouth St Jude *Ex* 75-79; C Ardsley *Sheff* 79-85; V Rawthorpe *Wakef* 85-96; C Salterhebble All SS 96-98; P-in-c Bournemouth St Jo w St Mich *Win* from 98. *The Vicarage, 13 Durley Chine Road South, Bournemouth BH2 5JT* Tel (01202) 761962 E-mail r.baldock1@ntlworld.com
BALDRY, John Netherway. b 19. Lon Univ BA53. **d** 79 **p** 80. NSM Brighton St Paul *Chich* from 79. *81 Windsor Court, Tongdean Lane, Brighton BN1 5JS* Tel (01273) 501268
BALDWICK, Frank Eric. b 24. Ripon Hall Ox 54. **d** 55 **p** 56. C Newark Ch Ch and Hawton *S'well* 55-58; C W Bridgford 58-60; V Oldham St Barn *Man* 60-65; R Gt Lever 65-78; V Hindsford 78-81; TV Clifton *S'well* 81-89; rtd 89; Perm to Offic *S'well* 89-10. *35 Lady Bay Road, West Bridgford, Nottingham NG2 5BJ* Tel 0115-982 1273
BALDWIN, Colin Steven. b 61. Brighton Poly BA85. St Jo Coll Nottm MTh01. **d** 01 **p** 02. C Billericay and Lt Burstead *Chelmsf* 01-05; P-in-c Prittlewell St Steph from 05. *26 Eastbourne Grove, Westcliff-on-Sea SS0 0QF* Tel (01702) 352448 Mobile 07714-048450 E-mail csbald@aol.com
BALDWIN, David Frederick Beresford. b 57. Ripon Coll Cuddesdon 93. **d** 95 **p** 96. C Uttoxeter w Bramshall *Lich* 95-97; C Uttoxeter Area 97-98; V Tilstock, Edstaston and Whixall 98-08; P-in-c Prees 03-08; P-in-c Fauls 03-08; Rural Chapl (Salop Adnry) 00-08; RD Wem and Whitchurch 06-08; P-in-c The Lulworths, Winfrith Newburgh and Chaldon *Sarum* 08-10; C Wool and E Stoke 09-10; TR Beaminster Area from 10. *The Rectory, 3 Clay Lane, Beaminster DT8 3BU* Tel (01308) 862150 E-mail revddavidbaldwin@yahoo.co.uk
BALDWIN, Derek Wilfred Walter. b 23. Lon Univ LTh74. ALCD56. **d** 52 **p** 53. C Sharrow St Andr *Sheff* 52-54; C Woodlands 54-56; V Shepley *Wakef* 56-59; V Earl's Heaton 59-66; Org Sec CECS *B & W, Ex* and *Truro* 66-72; R Morchard Bishop *Ex* 72-73; Org Sec CECS *St Alb* and *Ox* 73-77; C Portishead *B & W* 77-79; R Wymondham w Edmondthorpe *Leic* 79-80; P-in-c St Mewan *Truro* 80-81; V Crowan w Godolphin 81-83; C Cockington *Ex* 83-87; rtd 87; Perm to Offic *Ex* 90-09. *7 Case Gardens, Seaton EX12 2AP*
BALDWIN, Mrs Frances Mary. b 49. SRN71. SEITE 99. **d** 02 **p** 03. NSM Caterham *S'wark* 02-10. *3 Hillhurst Gardens, Caterham CR3 5HX* Tel (020) 8660 7534 E-mail francesb3@btinternet.com
BALDWIN, John Charles. b 39. Bris Univ BSc61 Sussex Univ DPhil65 FBCS CEng. St Steph Ho Ox 82. **d** 83 **p** 84. C Llandaff w Capel Llanilltern 83-90; V Ewenny w St Brides Major 90-92; Lic to Offic from 92; Hon Chapl Llan Cathl from 96; rtd 04. *60 Llantrisant Road, Llandaff, Cardiff CF5 2PX* Tel (029) 2055 4457 Fax 2038 7835 E-mail dovemaster@gmail.com
BALDWIN, Jonathan Michael. b 58. Chich Th Coll 92. **d** 94 **p** 95. C Crawley *Chich* 94-96; C New Shoreham 96-02; C Old Shoreham 96-02; Chapl Gatwick Airport from 02; C Crawley from 02. *18 Aldingbourne Close, Ifield, Crawley RH11 0QJ* Tel (01293) 406001 E-mail jonathan@theairport.wanadoo.co.uk
BALDWIN, Miss Julia Clare. b 81. St Chad's Coll Dur BA02 Darw Coll Cam PGCE05. Ripon Coll Cuddesdon BA09. **d** 10 **p** 11. C Bridge *Cant* from 10. *21 High Street, Bridge, Canterbury CT4 5JZ* Tel (01227) 830265 E-mail curate@bridgechurch.co.uk
BALDWIN, Peter Alan. b 48. Bede Coll Dur BA70. Qu Coll Birm 72. **d** 73 **p** 74. C Hartlepool St Oswald *Dur* 73-75; C Darlington H Trin 75-78; OGS from 77; C-in-c Bishop Auckland Woodhouse Close CD *Dur* 78-82; V Ferryhill 82-88; V Pendleton St Thos *Man* 88-89; P-in-c Charlestown 88-89; TR Pendleton St Thos w Charlestown 89-90; TR Newton Aycliffe *Dur* 90-96; TR Gt Aycliffe 96-97; V The Trimdons 97-99; AD Sedgefield 96-99; P-in-c Bramley *Ripon* 99-00; TR 00-02; Hon C Harrogate St Wilfrid 02-03; Hon C Methley w Mickletown 03-04; Dom Chapl to Bp Horsham *Chich* 04-06; P-in-c Buncton and Wiston 05-06; P-in-c Brightlingsea *Chelmsf* from 06; rtd 11; Hon C Halifax *Wakef* from 11. *12 Warren Lodge Gardens, Halifax HX3 0RB* E-mail peterabaldwin5@btinternet.com
BALDWIN, Shaun. b 64. Man Univ BA04. Ushaw Coll Dur 82. **d** 89 **p** 90. In RC Ch 89-00; NSM Hawes Side and Marton Moss *Blackb* from 11. *4 Mythop Village, Mythop Road, Blackpool FY4 4XA* Tel (01253) 836181 Mobile 07720-722263 E-mail shaunbaldwin64@hotmail.com
BALDWIN, Mrs Vivien Lindsay. b 50. SAOMC 97. **d** 98 **p** 99. NSM Westbury w Turweston, Shalstone and Biddlesden *Ox* 98-00; C W Buckingham 00-02; P-in-c Stoneleigh w Ashow *Cov*

02-07; Rural Life Officer 02-06; Chapl W Midl Police *Birm* 07-09; Perm to Offic *Pet* from 07. *20 Castle Road, Woodford Halse, Daventry NN11 3RS* Tel (01327) 264722 Mobile 07720-811477 E-mail vivthevic@earthling.net
BALDWIN, William. b 48. RMN73 FRSH83. NW Ord Course 75. **d** 78 **p** 79. C Royton St Anne *Man* 78-82; V Halliwell St Thos 82-87; TR Atherton 87-99; TR Atherton and Hindsford 99-02; TV Atherton and Hindsford w Howe Bridge 02-08; AD Leigh 01-08; TV Turton Moorland Min from 08. *Walmsley Vicarage, Blackburn Road, Egerton, Bolton BL7 9RZ* Tel and fax (01204) 304283 E-mail frbill@fsmail.net
BALE, Edward William Carre. b 22. AKC55. **d** 55 **p** 56. C Mansfield SS Pet and Paul *S'well* 55-59; C Corby St Jo *Pet* 59-61; R Corby SS Pet and Andr 61-69; V Wollaston and Strixton 69-87; rtd 88; Perm to Offic *Pet* 89-94 and *Ox* from 88. *27 The Crescent, Haversham, Milton Keynes MK19 7AN* Tel (01234) 391443 E-mail tedcarrebale@lineone.net
BALE, Kenneth John. b 34. Univ of Wales (Lamp) BA58. Qu Coll Birm. **d** 60 **p** 61. C Mitcham St Olave *S'wark* 60-63; C Warlingham w Chelsham and Farleigh 63-67; V Battersea Rise St Mark 67-85; Perm to Offic 85-88; Hon C Balham St Mary and St Jo 88-90; V S Wimbledon All SS 90-01; Dioc Adv Min of Healing 91-01; rtd 01; Perm to Offic *Sheff* from 01. *23 Selhurst Crescent, Bessacarr, Doncaster DN4 6EF* Tel 07710-212263 (mobile) Fax (01302) 371850
BALE, Susannah. b 67. Univ of Wales (Cardiff) BA90 BTh06. St Mich Coll Llan 03. **d** 06 **p** 07. C Betws w Ammanford *St D* 06-08; C Bro Teifi Sarn Helen 08-10; P-in-c Llanybydder and Llanwenog w Llanllwni from 10. *The Vicarage, Llanllwni, Pencader SA39 9DR* Tel (01559) 395413 E-mail suzybale@hotmail.com
BALFOUR, Andrew Crispin Roxburgh. b 49. Coll of Resurr Mirfield 93. **d** 95 **p** 96. C S Lafford *Linc* 95-99; P-in-c St Neot and Warleggan *Truro* 99-00; P-in-c Cardynham 99-00; R St Neot and Warleggan w Cardynham from 00; P-in-c Altarnon w Bolventor, Laneast and St Clether from 10. *The Vicarage, St Neot, Liskeard PL14 6NG* Tel (01579) 320472
BALFOUR, Hugh Rowlatt. b 54. SS Coll Cam BA76. Ridley Hall Cam 78. **d** 81 **p** 82. C Bedford Ch Ch *St Alb* 81-86; P-in-c Camberwell Ch Ch *S'wark* 86-90; V from 90. *Christ Church Vicarage, 79 Asylum Road, London SE15 2RJ* Tel (020) 7639 5662 E-mail hrbalfours@btinternet.com
BALFOUR, Mark Andrew. b 66. Yourk Univ BA88 R Holloway Coll Lon PhD98. Trin Coll Bris BA01. **d** 02 **p** 03. C Churchdown *Glouc* 02-06; V Furze Platt *Ox* from 06. *The Vicarage, 259 Courthouse Road, Maidenhead SL6 6HF* Tel (01628) 621961 E-mail thebalfours@btinternet.com
BALFOUR, Mrs Penelope Mary. b 47. St Andr Univ MA69 St Jo Coll York DipEd72. Coates Hall Edin 89 St Jo Coll Nottm 84. **d** 88 **p** 95. C Dundee St Marg *Bre* 88-94; Dioc AIDS Officer 90-94; NSM Invergowrie 94-96; C 00-07; Chapl Abertay Univ 94-97; C Dundee St Marg 96-00. *10 Strathaird Place, Dundee DD2 4TN* Tel (01382) 643114 E-mail pennybalfour@btinternet.com
BALKWELL, Judith Alison. b 59. **d** 10 **p** 11. NSM Musbury *Blackb* from 10. *15 Hyacinth Close, Haslingden, Rossendale BB4 6JU* Tel (01706) 223652 E-mail judithbalkwell@nhs.net
BALKWILL, Canon Michael Robert. b 67. Univ of Wales (Lamp) BD89 Univ of Wales (Cardiff) MTh92. St Mich Coll Llan 89 Bp Tucker Coll Mukono 91. **d** 91 **p** 92. C Llanrhos *St As* 91-97; Bp's Visitor from 94; R Llanfyllin and Bwlchycibau 97-11; AD Llanfyllin 05-11; Bp's Chapl and Press Officer from 11; Can Cursal and Can Res St As Cathl from 11. *The Vicarage, 1 Llys Trewithan, St Asaph LL17 0DJ* Tel (01745) 583503 E-mail michaelbalkwill@churchinwales.org.uk
BALKWILL, Roger Bruce. b 41. St Mich Coll Llan 61. **d** 64 **p** 65. C Llantrisant 64-68; C Caerphilly 68-73; Youth Chapl Dio Matabeleland Rhodesia 73-76; P-in-c Ilam w Blore Ray and Okeover *Lich* 76-81; P-in-c Alstonfield 81-82; V 82-08; P-in-c Beckbury 89-90; P-in-c Badger 89-90; P-in-c Ryton 89-90; P-in-c Kemberton, Sutton Maddock and Stockton 89-90; RD Shifnal 89-98; P-in-c Donington 00-08; P-in-c Boningale 97-08; V Albrighton, Boningale and Donington 08-10; RD Edgmond and Shifnal 08-10; rtd 10; Perm to Offic *Lich* from 10. *3 Ainsdale Drive, Priorslee, Telford TF2 9QJ* Tel (01952) 274713
BALL, Alan. b 26. Qu Coll Birm 72. **d** 75 **p** 75. NSM Hamstead St Paul *Birm* 75-93; rtd 93; Perm to Offic *Portsm* from 93. *25 Tebourba Drive, Alverstoke, Gosport PO12 2NT* Tel (023) 9260 1694
BALL, Andrew Thomas. b 54. K Coll Lon BD75 AKC75. Sarum & Wells Th Coll 76. **d** 77 **p** 78. C Ribbleton *Blackb* 77-80; C Sedgley All SS *Lich* 80-84; V Pheasey 84-90; Chapl Gd Hope Distr Gen Hosp Sutton Coldfield 90-94; Chapl Gd Hope Hosp NHS Trust Sutton Coldfield from 94. *Chaplain's Office, Good Hope Hospital, Rectory Road, Sutton Coldfield B75 7RR* Tel 0121-378 2211 ext 2676 *or* 243 1948
BALL, Anthony Charles. b 46. Lon Univ BD71. Chich Th Coll 72. **d** 73 **p** 74. C Heref St Martin 73-76; C Ealing St Pet Mt Park *Lon*

76-82; V Ruislip Manor St Paul 82-11; rtd 11. *44 Ashdown, Eaton Road, Hove BN3 3AQ*
BALL, Canon Anthony James. b 68. St Chad's Coll Dur BA89 Heythrop Coll Lon MA10. NTMTC 97. **d** 00 **p** 01. NSM Madrid *Eur* 00-03; Chapl Damascus 03-05; Abp's Asst Sec for Internat, Ecum and Angl Affairs *Cant* 05-08; Abp's Sec for Internat and Inter-Relig Relns 08-09; Abp's Chapl from 09; Hon Can All SS Cathl Cairo from 07; Hon Can Madrid Cathl from 07; Lic Preacher *Lon* from 07; Perm to Offic *S'wark* 09-10; Public Preacher from 10. *Lambeth Palace, London SE1 7JU* Tel (020) 7898 1220 Fax 7401 9886
E-mail anthony.ball@lambethpalace.org.uk
BALL, Anthony Michael. b 46. Kelham Th Coll 66. **d** 70 **p** 71. C Kingswinford St Mary *Lich* 70-74; C W Bromwich All SS 74-76; P-in-c Priorslee 76-80; V 80-82; Asst Chapl HM Pris Liv 82-83; Chapl 88-95; Chapl HM Pris Lewes 83-88; Featherstone 95-00; The Verne 00-06; rtd 06. *La Providence, 21 Portland Road, Weymouth DT4 9ES* Tel (01305) 787027
E-mail tonyball2008@hotmail.co.uk
BALL, Mrs Carol Maureen. b 58. NTMTC BA08. **d** 08 **p** 09. C Danbury *Chelmsf* from 08. *40 Millfields, Danbury, Chelmsford CM3 4LE* Tel (01245) 227260 Mobile 07860-894139
E-mail revcarolball@googlemail.com
BALL, Christopher Jonathan. b 61. Ripon Coll Cuddesdon. **d** 07 **p** 08. C Bedford St Andr *St Alb* 07-11; P-in-c Ashwell w Hinxworth and Newnham from 11. *The Rectory, Hodwell, Ashwell, Baldock SG7 5QQ* Tel (01462) 742277
E-mail c.j.ball@mac.com
BALL, Christopher Rowland. b 40. Wycliffe Hall Ox. **d** 82 **p** 83. C Heysham *Blackb* 82-86; TV Swanborough *Sarum* 86-90; R Llanyblodwel and Trefonen *Lich* 90-99; rtd 99; Perm to Offic *Lich* 00-03. *27 Wallace Lane, Forton, Preston PR3 0BA* Tel (01524) 791619
BALL, Geoffrey Ernest. b 49. Ox Min Course 00. **d** 03. NSM Winslow w Gt Horwood and Addington *Ox* from 03. *4 Fledgelings Walk, Winslow, Buckingham MK18 3QU*
E-mail geoffball@btinternet.com
BALL, Ian Raymond. b 45. CertEd Univ of Wales MPhil. Glouc Th Course 81. **d** 85 **p** 87. NSM Churchstoke w Hyssington and Sarn *Heref* from 85; Lic to Bp Ludlow from 87; Lic to Offic *St As* from 93. *Bachaethlon Cottage, Sarn, Newtown SY16 4HH* Tel (01686) 670505 Mobile 07966-022404
E-mail ian@pathways-development.com
BALL, Mrs Jane. b 68. Charlotte Mason Coll of Educn BEd91. St Steph Ho Ox 01. **d** 03 **p** 04. C Bedale and Leeming *Ripon* 03-05; Hon C Devizes St Jo w St Mary *Sarum* 05-07; Chapl Godolphin Sch from 07. *The Godolphin School, Milford Hill, Salisbury SP1 2RA* Tel (01722) 430614 Mobile 07771-804324
E-mail jandjball@btinternet.com
BALL, John Kenneth. b 42. Lon Univ BSc64 AKC64. Linc Th Coll 69. **d** 71 **p** 72. C Garston *Liv* 71-74; C Eastham *Ches* 74-75; C Barnston 75-77; V Over St Jo 77-82; V Helsby and Dunham-on-the-Hill 82-94; RD Frodsham 88-94; P-in-c Alvanley 92-94; V Hoylake 94-98; rtd 98; P-in-c Downholme and Marske *Ripon* 00-05; C Richmond w Hudswell and Downholme and Marske 05-07; Perm to Offic *Blackb* from 06. *2 King Street, Longridge, Preston PR3 3RQ* Tel (01772) 783172
✠**BALL, The Rt Revd John Martin.** b 34. Univ of Wales BA55. Tyndale Hall Bris. **d** 59 **p** 60 **c** 95. C Blackb St Jude 59-63; Kenya 63-79; Dep Gen Sec BCMS 79-81; Gen Sec 81-93; Gen Sec Crosslinks 93-95; Hon C Sidcup Ch Ch *Roch* 81-95; Hon Can Karamoja from 88; Asst Bp Tanzania 95-00; rtd 00; Hon Asst Bp *Chelmsf* from 00. *5 Hill View Road, Chelmsford CM1 7RS* Tel (01245) 268296 E-mail ball john@onetel.com
BALL, John Roy. b 47. Fitzw Coll Cam MA71. Wycliffe Hall Ox 83. **d** 85 **p** 86. C Stockport St Mary *Ches* 85-88; C Fazeley *Lich* 88-94; Res Min Drayton Bassett 89-94; Chapl Grenoble *Eur* 94-00; P-in-c Lithuania 00-05; Asst Chapl Amsterdam w Den Helder and Heiloo from 05. *De Kuilenaar 60, 1851 RZ Heiloo, The Netherlands* Tel (0031) (72) 532 5720
E-mail jroyball@christchurch.nl
BALL, Jonathan. b 63. BNC Ox BA85 MA01 Leeds Univ BA87 Cardiff Univ MTh06. Coll of Resurr Mirfield 85. **d** 88 **p** 89. C Blakenall Heath *Lich* 88-92; TV Rugeley 92-96; CF 96-08; Bp's Chapl *Sarum* from 08. *68A The Close, Salisbury SP1 2EN* Tel (01722) 334031 Mobile 07500-872081
E-mail bishops.chaplain@salisbury.anglican.org
BALL, Mrs Judith Anne. b 48. Nottm Univ BA70 Liv Univ PGCE71. NOC 98. **d** 01 **p** 02. C Upholland *Liv* from 01. *8 Beacon View Drive, Upholland, Skelmersdale WN8 0HL* Tel (01695) 622181
BALL, Kevin Harry. b 55. Linc Th Coll 92. **d** 94 **p** 95. C New Mills *Derby* 94-96; C Walthamstow St Sav *Chelmsf* 96-98; V Stocksbridge *Sheff* 98-00; C Barnsley St Mary *Wakef* 00-01; Chapl Barnsley Coll 00-01; P-in-c Sneinton St Cypr *S'well* 01-05; Chapl Notts Fire and Rescue Service 04-05; Sen Chapl Man Airport from 05. *The Chaplaincy, Manchester Airport, Manchester M90 1QX* Tel 0161-489 2838

BALL, Mrs Marion Elaine. b 68. Hertf Coll Ox BA90 St Jo Coll Dur BA99. Cranmer Hall Dur 97. **d** 02 **p** 03. C Kingston upon Hull H Trin *York* from 02. *12 Church Lane, Hook, Goole DN14 5PN* Tel (01405) 767721
E-mail revdmball@holyapostles-hull.co.uk
BALL, Mark Francis. b 72. St Jo Coll Dur BA94. St Steph Ho Ox BA00. **d** 01 **p** 02. C Poulton-le-Fylde *Blackb* 01-04; TV Loughton St Jo *Chelmsf* 04-08; P-in-c Cant St Pet w St Alphege and St Marg etc from 08; P-in-c Cant St Dunstan w H Cross from 10; Asst Dir of Ords from 09; Jt AD Cant from 11. *83 St Peter's Lane, Canterbury CT1 2BO* Tel (01227) 472557
E-mail mark@canterburycityparish.org.uk
BALL, Martin Francis. b 62. Wycliffe Hall Ox 06. **d** 08 **p** 09. C Woking Ch Ch *Guildf* from 08. *59 Brushfield Way, Knaphill, Woking GU21 2TQ* Tel (01483) 800128 Mobile 07816-398459
E-mail martball@gmail.com
✠**BALL, The Rt Revd Michael Thomas.** b 32. Qu Coll Cam BA55 MA59. **d** 71 **p** 71 **c** 80. CGA from 60; Prior Stroud Priory 64-76; C Whiteshill *Glouc* 71-76; Lic to Offic 76; P-in-c Stanmer w Falmer *Chich* 76-80; Chapl Sussex Univ 76-80; Suff Bp Jarrow *Dur* 80-90; Asst Bp Truro 90-97; rtd 97; Perm to Offic *B & W* 01-10. *The Coach House, The Manor, Aller, Langport TA10 0RA* Tel (01458) 250495
E-mail aller.ball@tiscali.co.uk
BALL, Nicholas Edward. b 54. Man Univ BA75 Ox Univ MA85. Ripon Coll Cuddesdon 79. **d** 80 **p** 81. C Yardley Wood *Birm* 80-83; C Moseley St Mary 83-86; Chapl Cen 13 83-85; V Bartley Green 86-95; P-in-c Hall Green St Pet 95-97; Perm to Offic 00 03; Chapl Birm Children's Hosp NHS Trust and Birm Heartlands and Solihull NHS Trust 99; rtd 09. *5 Princethorpe Close, Shirley, Solihull B90 2LP* Tel 0121-243 1336
E-mail nicholasball@hotmail.com
BALL, Norman. b 41. Liv Univ BA63 Ch Coll Liv CertEd72. Cuddesdon Coll 65. **d** 68 **p** 69. C Broseley w Benthall *Heref* 68-72; Hd RS Christleton High Sch 72-75; V Plemstall w Guilden Sutton *Ches* 75-79; Hd RS Neston Co High Sch 79-94; NSM Dodleston 86-91; NSM Buckley *St As* 91-94; TV Hawarden 94-00; rtd 00; Perm to Offic *St As* from 00. *White Cottage, Lower Mountain Road, Penyffordd, Chester CH4 0EX* Tel (01244) 661132
BALL, Peter Edwin. b 44. Lon Univ BD65 DipEd. Wycliffe Hall Ox 75. **d** 77 **p** 78. C Prescot *Liv* 77-80; R Lawford *Chelmsf* 80-99; RD Harwich 91-96; P-in-c Broomfield 99-04; V 04-10; rtd 10; Perm to Offic *Chelmsf* from 10. *14 Merriam Close, Brantham, Manningtree CO11 1RY*
E-mail brian@theworboys.freeserve.co.uk
✠**BALL, The Rt Revd Peter John.** b 32. Qu Coll Cam BA54 MA58. Wells Th Coll 54. **d** 56 **p** 57 **c** 77. C Rottingdean *Chich* 56-58; Novice SSM 58-60; CGA from 60; Prior CGA 60-77; Lic to Offic *Birm* 65-66; P-in-c Hoar Cross *Lich* 66-69; Lic to Offic *B & W* 69-77; Suff Bp Lewes *Chich* 77-84; Area Bp Lewes 84-92; Can and Preb Chich Cathl 79-92; Bp Glouc 92-93; rtd 93; Perm to Offic *B & W* 01-10. *The Coach House, The Manor, Aller, Langport TA10 0RA* Tel (01458) 250495
BALL, Peter Terence. b 49. **d** 07 **p** 08. OLM Hanborough and Freeland *Ox* from 07. *137 Wroslyn Road, Freeland, Witney OX29 8HP* Tel (01993) 882859 E-mail ptb49@yahoo.co.uk
BALL, Canon Peter William. b 30. Worc Coll Ox BA53 MA57. Cuddesdon Coll 53. **d** 55 **p** 56. C Poplar All SS w St Frideswide *Lon* 55-61; V Preston Ascension 61-68; R Shepperton 68-84; RD Staines 72-74; RD Spelthorne 74-83; Preb St Paul's Cathl 76-84; Can Res and Chan 84-90; Perm to Offic *Sarum* from 90; rtd 95. *Whittonedge, Whittonditch Road, Ramsbury, Marlborough SN8 2PX* Tel (01672) 520259
BALL, Philip John. b 52. Bris Univ BEd75 Ox Univ MTh98. Ripon Coll Cuddesdon 79. **d** 82 **p** 83. C Norton St Mich *Dur* 82-84; C Greenford H Cross *Lon* 84-88; V Hayes St Edm 88-97; AD Hillingdon 94-97; TR Bicester w Bucknell, Caversfield and Launton *Ox* 97-07; AD Bicester and Islip 00-05; R Abington *Pet* from 07. *The Rectory, 5 Abington Park Crescent, Northampton NN3 3AD* Tel (01604) 631041
E-mail philipjball@btinternet.com
BALL, Philip John. b 63. Coll of Ripon & York St Jo BA91. Cranmer Hall Dur 97. **d** 99 **p** 00. C Linthorpe *York* 99-02; C Kingston upon Hull H Trin 02-07; N Humberside Ind Chapl 08-11; V Airmyn, Hook and Rawcliffe *Sheff* from 11. *The Vicarage, 12 Church Lane, Hook, Goole DN14 5PN* Tel (01405) 767721 E-mail meandpj@meandpj.karoo.co.uk
BALL, Phillip Eric. b 53. Open Univ BA91. Qu Coll Birm 07. **d** 09 **p** 10. NSM Walsall St Matt *Lich* 09-11; NSM Walsall St Martin from 11. *Dinglebank, 13 Bodmin Rise, Walsall WS5 3HY* Tel 07775-518879 (mobile) E-mail phillipball53@hotmail.com
BALL, Mrs Rita Enid. b 49. Sheff Univ LLB69. SAOMC 94. **d** 97 **p** 98. NSM Newbury *Ox* 97-03; R Wantage Downs 03-09; TR Hermitage from 09; AD Newbury from 10. *The Rectory, High Street, Hermitage, Thatcham RG18 9ST* Tel (01635) 202967
E-mail rita@ritaball.wanadoo.co.uk
BALL, Roy. *See* BALL, John Roy

BALL, Stephen Andrew. b 54. Wycliffe Hall Ox. **d** 05 **p** 06. C Hilperton w Whaddon and Staverton etc *Sarum* 05-07; C Canalside Benefice 07-08; P-in-c from 08. *22 Warren Road, Staverton, Trowbridge BA14 8UZ* Tel (01225) 774903 E-mail sb54rev@gmail.com

BALL, Timothy William. b 60. Trin Coll Bris 96. **d** 96 **p** 97. C Harlow St Mary and St Hugh w St Jo the Bapt *Chelmsf* 96-99; V Springfield H Trin from 99; Ind Chapl 00-11; TR Loughrigg *Carl* from 11. *The Vicarage, Millans Park, Ambleside LA22 9AD* Tel (015394) 33205 E-mail timmyball@tesco.net

BALL, Vernon. b 34. Ox Min Course 87. **d** 90 **p** 91. NSM Banbury *Ox* 90-99. *20 Springfield Avenue, Banbury OX16 9HT* Tel (01295) 265740

BALLANTINE, Peter Sinclair. b 46. Nottm Univ MTh85. K Coll Lon BA68 AKC68 St Jo Coll Nottm 70 Lon Coll of Div ALCD71 BD73 LTh74. **d** 73 **p** 74. C Rainham *Chelmsf* 73-77; C Wennington 73-77; TV Barton Mills *St E* 77-80; TV Barton Mills, Beck Row w Kenny Hill etc 80-82; Chapl Liv Poly 83-86; Tr Officer Rugby Deanery *Cov* 86-97; P-in-c Churchover w Willey 86-97; P-in-c Clifton upon Dunsmore and Newton 86-97; Dir Buckingham Adnry Chr Tr Progr *Ox* 97-02; TV Stantonbury and Willen from 02. *The Rectory, The Green, Great Linford, Milton Keynes MK14 5BD* Tel (01908) 605892 Mobile 07984-902641 E-mail pballarev@aol.com

BALLANTINE, Roderic Keith. b 44. Chich Th Coll 66. **d** 69 **p** 70. C Nunhead St Antony *S'wark* 69-72; C S Hackney St Jo w Ch Ch *Lon* 72-75; P-in-c Kensal Town St Thos w St Andr and St Phil 75-79; V Stoke Newington St Andr 79-05; rtd 05; Perm to Offic *Lon* from 06. *67 Savernake Road, London NW3 2LA* Tel (020) 7267 2744

BALLANTYNE, Jane Elizabeth. See KENCHINGTON, Canon Jane Elizabeth Ballantyne

BALLARD, The Ven Andrew Edgar. b 44. Dur Univ BA66. Westcott Ho Cam 66. **d** 68 **p** 69. C St Marylebone St Mary *Lon* 68-72; C Portsea St Mary *Portsm* 72-76; V Haslingden w Haslingden Grane *Blackb* 76-82; V Walkden Moor *Man* 82-93; TR Walkden Moor w Lt Hulton 93-98; AD Farnworth 90-98; Chapl Salford Coll 82-92; P-in-c Rochdale *Man* 98-99; TR 00; Adn Rochdale 00-05; Adn Man 05-09; Hon Can Man Cathl 98-09; rtd 09. *30 Swift Drive, Scawby Brook, Brigg DN20 9FL* Tel (01652) 659560 E-mail ae.ballard@btinternet.com

BALLARD, Ann. d 09 **p** 10. NSM Norton in the Moors *Lich* from 09. *94 Chatterley Drive, Kidsgrove, Stoke-on-Trent ST7 4LL* Tel (01782) 785586

BALLARD, Miss Anne Christina. b 54. LRAM76 HonRCM93 ARAM94. Wycliffe Hall Ox 82. dss85 **d** 87 **p** 94. Hove Bp Hannington Memorial Ch *Chich* 85-87; Chapl St Mich Sch Burton Park 87-89; Chapl RCM and Imp Coll *Lon* 89-93; Prec Ch Ch *Ox* 93-98; P-in-c Ivinghoe w Pitstone and Slapton 98-03; P-in-c Llanbadarn Fawr, Llandegley and Llanfihangel etc *S & B* 03-08; V Alstonfield, Butterton, Ilam etc *Lich* from 08. *The Vicarage, Alstonefield, Ashbourne DE6 2FX* Tel (01335) 310216 Mobile 07773-734201 E-mail annieballard@supanet.com

BALLARD, Charles Martin. b 29. Jes Coll Cam BA52 MA56. **d** 58 **p** 59. C Doncaster St Geo *Sheff* 58-61; V Balne 61-62; rtd 94; Perm to Offic *Ely* 95-00. *35 Abbey Road, Cambridge CB5 8HH*

BALLARD, Duncan Charles John. b 65. Sheff Univ BSc87. St Mich Coll Llan 00. **d** 02 **p** 03. C Worc St Barn w Ch Ch 02-06; TV Worc SE 06-11; P-in-c Hampton in Arden *Birm* from 11; P-in-c Bickenhill from 11; Chapl Birm Airport from 11. *The Vicarage, 1 High Street, Hampton-in-Arden, Solihull B92 0AE* Tel (01675) 442339

BALLARD, Canon Michael Arthur. b 44. Lon Univ BA66. Westcott Ho Cam 68. **d** 70 **p** 71. C Harrow Weald All SS *Lon* 70-73; C Aylesbury *Ox* 73-78; V Eastwood *Chelmsf* 78-90; RD Hadleigh 83-90; R Southchurch H Trin from 90; RD Southend 94-00; Hon Can Chelmsf Cathl from 89. *The Rectory, 8 Pilgrims Close, Southend-on-Sea SS2 4XF* Tel (01702) 466423 E-mail michael@ballard4701.fsnet.co.uk

BALLARD, Nigel Humphrey. b 48. Linc Th Coll 92. **d** 94 **p** 95. C Old Brumby *Linc* 94; C Bottesford w Ashby 94-97; P-in-c Helpringham w Hale 97-01; rtd 02. *Tamarisk Cottage, 5 Homelands Avenue, East Preston, Littlehampton BN16 1PS*

BALLARD, Peter James. b 55. SS Hild & Bede Coll Dur BEd78. Sarum & Wells Th Coll 85. **d** 87 **p** 88. C Grantham *Linc* 87-90 and 91; R Port Pirie Australia 90; V Lancaster Ch Ch *Blackb* 91-98; RD Lancaster 94-98; Can Res Blackb Cathl 98-06; Adn Lancaster 06-10; Dioc Dir of Educn 98-10. *Address temp unknown* Tel 07970-923141 (mobile) E-mail peter.j.ballard@btinternet.com

BALLARD, Steven Peter. b 52. Man Univ BA73 MA74 Philipps Univ Marburg DrTheol98. St Steph Ho Ox 76. **d** 78 **p** 79. C Lancaster St Mary *Blackb* 78-81; C Blackpool St Mich 81-84; V Brierfield 84-94; Perm to Offic *Carl* 95-07. *1 St Catherines Court, Drovers Lane, Penrith CA11 9JA* Tel (01768) 890976

BALLENTINE, Ian Clarke. b 46. Aston Univ BSc71 CEng. BTh. **d** 91 **p** 92. C Lurgan St Jo *D & D* 91-95; I Mallusk *Conn* 95-07;

Nat Dir (Ireland) SOMA UK from 07. *12 Gordonville, Coleraine BT52 1EF* Tel (028) 7035 8328 E-mail ian ballentine@bigfoot.com

BALLENTYNE, Mrs Fiona Virginia Grace. b 61. ALAM80 R Holloway Coll Lon BA83 Dur Univ PGCE90. EAMTC 95. **d** 97 **p** 98. NSM Halesworth w Linstead, Chediston, Holton etc *St E* 97-98; C Sole Bay 98-00; Chapl St Felix Sch Southwold 99-00; Chapl HM YOI Castington 00-05; Chapl Northumbria Healthcare NHS Trust 00-05; Chapl HM Pris Sudbury from 05; Chapl HM Pris Foston Hall from 11. *Chaplain's Office, HM Prison, Sudbury, Ashbourne DE6 5HW* Tel (01283) 584088 E-mail jvfb27@aol.com

BALLINGER, Miss Charlotte Emily. b 85. Pemb Coll Ox BA07 Em Coll Cam MPhil09. Westcott Ho Cam 07. **d** 10 **p** 11. C Chipping Barnet *St Alb* from 10. *13 Cedar Lawn Avenue, Barnet EN5 2LW* Tel (020) 8449 4797 Mobile 07890-038722 E-mail ceballinger@gmail.com

BALLINGER, Francis James. b 43. AKC70. **d** 71 **p** 85. C Weston-super-Mare St Sav *B & W* 71-72; Dir Bd Soc Resp *Leic* 85-88; Hon C Bringhurst w Gt Easton 85-88; TV Melksham *Sarum* 88-93; P-in-c Coughton and Spernall, Morton Bagot and Oldberrow *Cov* 93-98; Dioc Rural Adv 93-98; R Kingstone w Clehonger, Eaton Bishop etc *Heref* 98-03; rtd 04. *4 Broxburn Road, Warminster BA12 8EX* Tel (01985) 300316 E-mail f.ballinger@midnet.com

BALLISTON THICKE, James. See THICKE, James Balliston

BALMER, Walter Owen. b 30. NOC 83. **d** 86 **p** 87. NSM Gateacre *Liv* 86-91; NSM Hale 91-00; Perm to Offic from 00. *38 Grangemeadow Road, Liverpool L25 4SU* Tel 0151-421 1189

BALOGUN, Olusegun Joseph. b 69. Ogun State Univ BSc91 Lagos Univ MSc96. Immanuel Coll Ibadan 96. **d** 98 **p** 99. Nigeria 98-02; C Mansfield St Jo *S'well* 04-06; V Beckton St Mark *Chelmsf* from 06. *10 Yarrow Crescent, London E6 5UH* Tel (020) 7473 6059 Mobile 07960-050923 E-mail vicar@stmarkscofebeckton.org.uk

BAMBER, Jeremy John. b 56. St Jo Coll Cam MA82. STETS 06. **d** 09 **p** 10. NSM Southover *Chich* from 09. *29 Montacute Road, Lewes BN7 1EN* Tel (01273) 474923 E-mail jjbj@bambers.net

BAMBER, Patrick Herbert. b 71. Dundee Univ MA93. Wycliffe Hall Ox BTh02. **d** 02 **p** 03. C St Austell *Truro* 02-09; I Calry *K, E & A* from 09. *Calry Rectory, The Mall, Sligo, Co Sligo, Republic of Ireland* Tel (00353) (71) 914 6513 E-mail patrick.bamber@talktalk.net

BAMBER, Canon Sheila Jane. b 54. Univ of Wales (Lamp) BA75 Sheff Univ MA77 Open Univ MBA94. Ripon Coll Cuddesdon 96. **d** 98 **p** 99. C Dur St Cuth 98-01; C Sacriston and Kimblesworth 01-02; TV Dur N 02-09; Hon C Lanchester 09-10; Dioc Dir of Educn 04-10; Adv for Women's Min 09-10; Hon Can Dur Cathl 06-10; Can Res Newc Cathl from 10. *2A Holly Avenue, Jesmond, Newcastle upon Tyne NE2 2PY* Tel 0191-281 4329 *or* 232 1939 Mobile 07989-542565 E-mail sheilabamber@stnicnewcastle.co.uk

BAMBERG, Robert William. b 43. Chu Coll Cam BA65 PGCE68. SWMTC 98. **d** 01 **p** 02. NSM Kingsteignton *Ex* 01-08; Perm to Offic 08-10. *Address temp unknown*

BAMFORD, Geoffrey Belk. b 35. Lon Univ BA57 Leic Coll of Educn PGCE58. **d** 99 **p** 00. OLM Upper Holme Valley *Wakef* from 99. *11 Flushoase, Holmbridge, Holmfirth HD9 2QY* Tel (01484) 682532 E-mail jmgbbamford@tiscali.co.uk

BAMFORD, Mrs Marion. b 35. K Coll Lon BA56 AKC56. NOC 81. dss 84 **d** 90 **p** 94. Baildon *Bradf* 84-85; S Kirkby *Wakef* 85-90; Dn-in-c Brotherton 90-94; P-in-c 94-96; Chapl Pontefract Gen Infirmary 89-96; rtd 96; Perm to Offic *Bradf* and *Wakef* from 96. *170 Warren Lane, Eldwick, Bingley BD16 3BY* Tel (01274) 564925

BAMFORTH, Canon Marvin John. b 48. NOC 78. **d** 81 **p** 82. C Barnoldswick w Bracewell *Bradf* 81-84; V Cullingworth 84-88; V Mornington New Zealand 88-89; V Thornton in Lonsdale w Burton in Lonsdale *Bradf* 89-98; P-in-c Bentham St Jo 93-98; Dioc Chapl MU 91-94; Chapl Paphos Cyprus 98-05; rtd 06; Chapl Miss to Seafarers Limassol Cyprus from 06; Hon Can Kinkizi from 08. *PO Box 59358, Pissouri, 4610 Limassol, Cyprus* Tel (00357) (25) 222649 E-mail marvinandsue@cytanet.com.cy

BAMFORTH, Stuart Michael. b 35. Hertf Coll Ox BA58 MA61. Sarum Th Coll 60. **d** 62 **p** 63. C Adel *Ripon* 62-67; V Hampton and Pudding Norton 67-71; V Toftrees w Shereford 67-71; P-in-c Pensthorpe 67-71; P-in-c Colkirk 69-70; Lic to Offic *Derby* 72-77 and *Ripon* from 77; rtd 95; Perm to Offic *York* from 01. *52 Beverley Road, Market Weighton, York YO43 3JP* Tel (01430) 874105

BAMPING, Mrs Susan Janet. b 49. LCTP 08. **d** 11. NSM Cross Fell Gp *Carl* from 11. *Croft House Barn, Kirkland, Skirwith, Penrith CA10 1RL* Tel (01768) 879085 E-mail alan.sue.bamping@btinternet.com

BANBURY, David Paul. b 62. Coll of Ripon & York St Jo BA84. Ridley Hall Cam 85. **d** 88 **p** 89. C Blackb St Jas 88-90; C Preston St Cuth 90-95; P-in-c Bradf St Clem 95-00; V 00; CPAS Evang 01-08; Dir Miss and Faith Stratford-upon-Avon, Luddington etc

Cov from 08. *3 Coopers Close, Stratford-upon-Avon CV37 0RS* Tel (01789) 415410 E-mail banbury.family@btinternet.com

BANCROFT, Mrs Patricia Ann. b 64. STETS. **d** 10 **p** 11. C Kingsclere and Ashford Hill w Headley *Win* from 10. *The Vicarage, Ashford Hill, Thatcham RG19 8AZ* Tel (01635) 269180 E-mail sbancroft49@aol.com

BANDAWE, Mrs Christine. b 57. NOC 01. **d** 04 **p** 05. C Middleton St Mary *Ripon* 04-08; TV Seacroft from 08. *30 Fearnville Road, Leeds LS8 3EA*

BANDS, Canon Leonard Michael. b 40. Rhodes Univ BA64. St Paul's Coll Grahamstown. **d** 69 **p** 70. C Uitenhage S Africa 69-72; R Alexandria 72-75; Chapl Rhodes Univ 75-80; Chapl Dioc Sch for Girls Grahamstown 80-86; Chapl Dioc Coll Cape Town 87-94; Dean Bloemfontein 94-02; C Lockerbie *Glas* from 03; C Moffat from 03. *The Rectory, Ashgrove Terrace, Lockerbie DG11 2BQ* Tel and fax (01576) 202484 Mobile 07766-341094 E-mail michael.bands@btinternet.com

BANFIELD, Andrew Henry. b 48. AKC71. St Aug Coll Cant 72. **d** 73 **p** 74. C Crayford *Roch* 73-76; Youth Chapl *Glouc* 77-89; Soc Services Development Officer Glos Co Coun from 89. *18 East Approach Drive, Cheltenham GL52 3JE*

BANFIELD, The Ven David John. b 33. ALCD56. **d** 57 **p** 58. C Middleton *Man* 57-62; Chapl Scargill Ho 62-65; Asst Warden 65-67; V Addiscombe St Mary *Cant* 67-80; V Luton St Mary *St Alb* 80-90; Hon Can St Alb 89-90; RD Luton 89-90; Adn Bris 90-98; Hon Can Bris Cathl 90-98; rtd 98; Perm to Offic *Bris* from 98. *47 Avon Way, Stoke Bishop, Bristol BS9 1SL* Tel 0117-968 4227

BANGAY, Edward Newman. b 37. CQSW75. New Coll Lon BD60. **d** 98 **p** 98. NSM Yeovil w Kingston Pitney *B & W* 98-02; Chapl E Somerset NHS Trust 98-02; Perm to Offic *B & W* from 02. *Castle Cottage, Main Street, Mudford, Yeovil BA21 5TE* Tel (01935) 850452 E-mail edward@bangay.com

BANGAY (formerly REAST), Mrs Eileen Joan. b 40. Open Univ BA93. EMMTC 81. **dss** 84 **d** 87 **p** 94. Linc St Mary-le-Wigford w St Benedict etc 80-90; C 87-90; C Stamford All SS w St Jo 90-93; NSM Walesby 93-95; P-in-c Sutton Bridge 95-00; V 00; RD Elloe E 99-00; rtd 01; Perm to Offic *Linc* from 01. *35 Welland Mews, Stamford PE9 2LW* Tel (01780) 765115

BANGOR, Archdeacon of. *Vacant*

BANGOR, Bishop of. *See* JOHN, The Rt Revd Andrew Thomas Griffith

BANGOR, Dean of. *See* JONES, The Very Revd Susan Helen

BANHAM, Richard Mark. b 69. Sheff City Poly BSc92. Trin Coll Bris 04. **d** 06 **p** 07. C Wroughton *Bris* 06-10; P-in-c Wheathampstead *St Alb* from 10. *The Rectory, Old Rectory Gardens, Wheathampstead, St Albans AL4 8AD* Tel (01582) 833144 E-mail richard@banham.org

BANISTER, Desmond Peter. b 52. K Coll Lon BA75 AKC75. SAOMC 02. **d** 05 **p** 06. Hd Master Quainton Hall Sch Harrow 98-09; NSM Hatch End St Anselm *Lon* 05-08; NSM Hillingdon All SS 09; V from 09; Perm to Offic *Ox* from 05. *All Saints' Vicarage, Ryefield Avenue, Uxbridge UB10 9BT* Tel (01895) 239457 E-mail ppash@uk2.net

BANISTER, Jane Catherine. b 67. Man Univ BA90 Em Coll Cam BA96. Westcott Ho Cam 94. **d** 97 **p** 98. C Addington *S'wark* 97-00; C Wisley w Pyrford *Guildf* 00-02; Perm to Offic *St Alb* 03-08; NSM Tring from 08. *The Rectory, 2 The Limes, Station Road, Tring HP23 5NW* Tel (01442) 822170

BANISTER, Canon Martin John. b 39. Worc Coll Ox BA62 MA68. Chich Th Coll 62. **d** 64 **p** 65. C Wellingborough All Hallows *Pet* 64-67; C Heene *Chich* 67-70; V Denford w Ringstead *Pet* 70-78; P-in-c Wilshamstead *St Alb* 78-80; P-in-c Houghton Conquest 78-80; V Wilshamstead and Houghton Conquest 80-89; RD Elstow 86-89; V Waltham Cross 89-04; RD Cheshunt 00-04; Hon Can St Alb 03-04; rtd 04; Perm to Offic *St Alb* from 04. *35 Cottonmill Lane, St Albans AL1 2BT* Tel (01727) 847082

BANKS, Aleck George. b 18. Lon Univ BD42 AKC42. **d** 42 **p** 43. C Colchester St Jas, All SS, St Nic and St Runwald *Chelmsf* 42-45; C Leigh St Clem 45-51; V Bradfield 51-56; PC Becontree St Geo 56-61; V S Benfleet 61-83; rtd 83; Perm to Offic *Chelmsf* from 83 and *St E* from 85. *5 Gosford Close, Clare, Sudbury CO10 8PT* Tel (01787) 277088

BANKS, Allen James. b 48. CBDTI 98. **d** 01 **p** 02. OLM Kells *Carl* from 01. *36 Basket Road, Whitehaven CA28 9AH* Tel (01946) 61470

BANKS, Brian William Eric. b 35. Lon Univ BD69 Open Univ BA94. Wycliffe Hall Ox 63. **d** 65 **p** 66. C Swindon Ch Ch *Bris* 65-68; C Halesowen *Worc* 68-71; R Wychbold and Upton Warren 71-77; V Bengeworth 77-87; RD Evesham 81-87; V Freshwater *Portsm* 87-00; R Yarmouth 95-00; rtd 00; Perm to Offic *Sarum* 01-09. *12 St Davids Close, Leyland PR25 4XX* Tel (01772) 435707

BANKS, Mrs Dawn. b 56. CBDTI 01. **d** 04 **p** 05. OLM Preesall *Blackb* 04-05; OLM Waterside Par 05-07; NSM from 07. *Squires Gate Farm, Head Dyke Lane, Pilling, Preston PR3 6SD* Tel (01253) 790250

BANKS, Geoffrey Alan. b 43. St Andr Univ MA66. NOC 84. **d** 87 **p** 88. NSM Shelley and Shepley *Wakef* 87-89; C Halifax 89-91; V Holmfield 91-98; TV Upper Holme Valley 98-09; rtd 09; Perm to Offic *Wakef* from 09. *3 Brookside Fold, Oxenhope, Keighley BD22 9HQ* Tel (01535) 244876 E-mail geoff@banksvicarage.fsnet.co.uk

BANKS, Helen. b 52. Yorks Min Course. **d** 09 **p** 10. NSM Garforth *Ripon* from 09. *Westfield Cottage, Carr Lane, Thorner, Leeds LS14 3HD* Tel 0113-289 2668 E-mail helen.banks@yahoo.co.uk

BANKS, John Alan. b 32. Hertf Coll Ox BA54 MA58. Westcott Ho Cam 56. **d** 58 **p** 59. C Warsop *S'well* 58-61; C Ox St Aldate w H Trin 61-64; V Ollerton *S'well* 64-75; V Boughton 64-75; R Wollaton 75-83; RD Beeston 77-81; Lic to Offic 83-85; C Bramcote 85-86; C Arnold 86-95; rtd 95; Perm to Offic *S'well* from 95. *247 Oxclose Lane, Nottingham NG5 6FB* Tel 0115-926 6814

BANKS, Michael Lawrence. b 40. Open Univ BA72 Brunel Univ MA82. Westcott Ho Cam 84. **d** 86 **p** 87. C Cheshunt *St Alb* 86-89; Chapl HM Pris Blundeston 89-90; V Leagrave *St Alb* 90-94; V Hatfield Hyde 95-01; rtd 01; Perm to Offic *Nor* 01-03 and 05-11; P-in-c Barningham w Matlaske w Baconsthorpe etc 03-05; Chapl Beeston Sch from 11. *Quarndon, Post Office Lane, Saxthorpe, Norwich NR11 7BL* Tel (01263) 587319 E-mail mbanks@tiscali.co.uk

BANKS, Canon Michael Thomas Harvey. b 35. Ushaw Coll Dur 58 Open Univ BA75. **d** 63 **p** 64. In RC Ch 63-69; C Winlaton *Dur* 69-71; P-in-c Bishopwearmouth Gd Shep 71-75; TV Melton Mowbray w Thorpe Arnold *Leic* 75-80; TR Loughborough Em 80-88; Dir of Ords 83-97; Hon Can Leic Cathl 83-87; Can Res and Chan 87-03; Assoc P Christianity S 93-95; Hon C Leic H Spirit 01-03; rtd 03; Perm to Offic *Glouc* from 04. *Harvard House, 7 Harvard Close, Moreton-in-Marsh GL56 0JT* Tel (01608) 650706

✠**BANKS, The Rt Revd Norman.** b 54. Oriel Coll Ox BA76 MA80. St Steph Ho Ox 79. **d** 82 **p** 83 **c** 11. C Newc Ch Ch w St Ann 82-87; P-in-c 87-90; V Tynemouth Cullercoats St Paul 90-00; V Walsingham, Houghton and Barsham *Nor* 00-11; P-in-c from 11; RD Burnham and Walsingham 08-11; Chapl to The Queen 09-11; Suff Bp Richborough (PEV) *Cant* from 11. *The Vicarage, Church Street, Walsingham NR22 6BL* Tel (01328) 821316 E-mail bishop@richborough.org.uk

BANKS, Philip Charles. b 61. NE Lon Poly BSc85 Nottm Univ BTh93 MRICS87. Linc Th Coll 90. **d** 93 **p** 94. C Chelmsf Ascension 93-94; C Brentwood St Thos 94-98; P-in-c Elmstead 98-03; V Coggeshall w Markshall from 03; Bp's Press Officer 97-05; Bp's Dom Chapl 01-04; RD Dedham and Tey from 08. *The Vicarage, 4 Church Green, Coggeshall, Colchester CO6 1UD* Tel (01376) 561234 Mobile 07798-681886 E-mail fr-philip@st-peter-ad-vincula.org.uk

BANKS, Stephen John. b 65. Newc Univ BSc87. St Jo Coll Nottm MA96. **d** 97 **p** 98. C Sheldon *Birm* 97-00; P-in-c Austrey and Warton 00-07; P-in-c Newton Regis w Seckington and Shuttington 06-07; R N Warks from 07; AD Polesworth 02-07. *The Vicarage, 132 Main Road, Austrey, Atherstone CV9 3EB* Tel (01827) 839022 E-mail sbanks4@sky.com

BANKS, Susan Angela. *See* GRIFFITHS, Mrs Susan Angela

BANKS, Mrs Susan June. b 60. NOC 03. **d** 06 **p** 07. C Medlock Head *Man* 06-09; TV Heywood 09-10; P-in-c Heywood St Marg and Heap Bridge from 10. *St Margaret's Vicarage, 27 Heys Lane, Heywood OL10 3RD* Tel (01706) 368053 E-mail sbanks@sky.com

BANNARD-SMITH, Dennis Ronald. b 22. Birm Univ BSc42. St Alb Minl Tr Scheme 80. **d** 83 **p** 84. NSM Pavenham *St Alb* 83-88; NSM Odell and Pavenham 88-92; Perm to Offic from 92. *Goodly Heritage, 10 The Bury, Pavenham, Bedford MK43 7PX* Tel (01234) 822992

BANNER, John William. b 36. Open Univ BA78. Tyndale Hall Bris 61. **d** 64 **p** 65. C Bootle St Leon *Liv* 64-66; C Wigan St Jas 66-69; C Stapleton *Bris* 69-70; Gen Sec Scripture Union Australia 70-72; V Liv Ch Ch Norris Green 72-82; V Tunbridge Wells H Trin w Ch Ch *Roch* 82-05; rtd 05. *Kingsmead, Burwash Common, Etchingham TN19 7NA* Tel (01435) 882977 E-mail john@secondremake.plus.com

BANNER, Michael Charles. b 61. Ball Coll Ox BA83 MA86 DPhil87. **d** 86 **p** 87. Fell St Pet Coll Ox 85-88; Dean Peterho Cam 88-94; Prof Moral and Soc Th K Coll Lon 94-04; NSM Balsham, Weston Colville, W Wickham etc *Ely* 01-04; Prof Edin Univ 04-06; Dean Trin Coll Cam from 06. *Trinity College, Cambridge CB2 1TQ* Tel (01223) 338563 Fax 338564

BANNISTER, Preb Anthony Peter. b 40. Ex Univ BA62. Clifton Th Coll 63. **d** 65 **p** 66. C Uphill *B & W* 65-69; C Hove Bp Hannington Memorial Ch *Chich* 69-74; V Wembdon *B & W* 74-91; Youth Chapl 80-83; RD Bridgwater 80-89; V Taunton St Jas 91-05; Preb Wells Cathl 97-05; rtd 05; Perm to Offic *B & W* from 05. *12 Mitre Court, Taunton TA1 3ER* Tel (01823) 259110 E-mail apbannister@ukonline.co.uk

BANNISTER, Clifford John. b 53. Hatf Coll Dur BA76. Ripon Coll Cuddesdon 84. **d** 86 **p** 87. C Weymouth H Trin *Sarum* 86-89; TV Basingstoke *Win* 89-94; V Hedge End St Jo 94-09; AD

Eastleigh 07-09; P-in-c Win St Bart 09-10; R Win St Bart and St Lawr w St Swithun from 10. *St Lawrence Rectory, Colebrook Street, Winchester SO23 9LH* Tel (01962) 852032 E-mail cliffbannister@tiscali.co.uk

BANNISTER, John Leslie. b 55. Lanc Univ MA99. CBDTI 95. **d** 98 **p** 99. C Flimby and Netherton *Carl* 98-00; C Whitehaven 00-02; TV 02-04; TR from 04. *The Rectory, Autumn Garth, Harras Road, Harras Moor, Whitehaven CA28 6SG* Tel (01946) 693474 Mobile 07788-562488 E-mail johnlbannister@tiscali.co.uk

BANNISTER, Lesley. b 30. **d** 99 **p** 00. OLM Gt Cornard *St E* 99-07; Perm to Offic from 07. *58 Broom Street, Great Cornard, Sudbury CO10 0JT* Tel (01787) 372889

BANNISTER, Peter. *See* BANNISTER, Preb Anthony Peter

BANNISTER, Peter Edward. b 38. Leeds Univ BSc60, Linc Th Coll 72. **d** 74 **p** 75. C Norbury St Steph *Cant* 74-77; C Allington and Maidstone St Pet 77-80; R Temple Ewell w Lydden 80-86; TV Bracknell *Ox* 86-93; P-in-c Swallowfield 93-03; rtd 03; Perm to Offic *Bradf* from 04. *15 Ryeland Street, Cross Hills, Keighley BD20 8SR* Tel (01535) 636036 E-mail peterandlesleyb@btinternet.com

BANNISTER-PARKER, Mrs Charlotte. b 63. Trevelyan Coll Dur BA84 Dur Univ MA92 Middx Univ BA05. Westmr Past Foundn 00. **d** 05 **p** 06. NSM Ox St Mary V w St Cross and St Pet from 05. *8 Belbroughton Road, Oxford OX2 6UZ* Tel (01865) 512252 E-mail charlotte@thegbps.co.uk

BANNON, Lyndon Russell. b 73. Ches Coll of HE BA95 Univ Coll Ches PGCE96 Leeds Univ MA06. NOC 04. **d** 06 **p** 07. NSM Leasowe *Ches* 06-10; NSM Willaston from 10. *7 Nelson's Croft, Wirral CH63 3DU* Tel 0151-334 9931 E-mail revlrbannon@talktalk.net

BANTING, Canon David Percy. b 51. Magd Coll Cam MA74. Wycliffe Hall Ox MA79. **d** 80 **p** 81. C Ox St Ebbe w H Trin and St Pet 80-83; Min St Jos Merry Hill CD *Lich* 83-90; V Chadderton Ch Ch *Man* 90-98; V Harold Wood *Chelmsf* from 98; Hon Can Chelmsf Cathl from 09. *The Vicarage, 15 Athelstan Road, Harold Wood, Romford RM3 0QB* Tel (01708) 376400 *or* 342080 E-mail david.banting@stpetersharoldwood.org

BANTING, The Ven Kenneth Mervyn Lancelot Hadfield. b 37. Pemb Coll Cam BA61 MA65. Cuddesdon Coll 64. **d** 65 **p** 66. Asst Chapl Win Coll 65-70; C Leigh Park *Portsm* 70-72; TV Hemel Hempstead *St Alb* 73-79; V Goldington 79-88; P-in-c Renhold 80-82; RD Bedford 84-87; V Portsea St Cuth *Portsm* 88-96; RD Portsm 94-96; Adn Is of Wight 96-03; Hon Can Portsm Cathl 95-96; rtd 03; Perm to Offic *Portsm* from 03 and *Chich* from 04; RD Westbourne *Chich* 09-11. *Furzend, 38A Bosham Hoe, Bosham PO18 8ET* Tel (01243) 572340 E-mail merlinbanting@f2s.com

BANYARD, Douglas Edward. b 21. S'wark Ord Course 69. **d** 71 **p** 72. NSM Selsdon St Jo w St Fran *Cant* 71-77; Perm to Offic *Chich* 77-08 and *Portsm* from 77. *22 Lower Wardown, Petersfield GU31 4NY* Tel (01730) 261004

BANYARD, Michael George. b 47. Ch Ch Coll Cant CertEd69 Birm Univ BPhil79 Open Univ MA92. Westcott Ho Cam 01. **d** 03 **p** 04. NSM Chippenham *Ely* 03-08; NSM Fordham St Pet 07-08; NSM Isleham 07-08; NSM Kennett 07-08; NSM Snailwell 07-08; TR Three Rivers Gp from 08; Dioc Spirituality Officer from 10. *The Vicarage, High Street, Chippenham, Ely CB7 5PP* Tel (01638) 721616 E-mail banyardmg1@yahoo.co.uk

BANYARD, Peter Vernon. b 35. Sarum Th Coll 57. **d** 59 **p** 60. C Southampton Maybush St Pet *Win* 59-63; C Tilbury Docks *Chelmsf* 63-65; Miss to Seamen 63-65; Namibia 65-68; V Chesterfield St Aug *Derby* 68-74; TV Grantham w Manthorpe *Linc* 74-78; TV Grantham 78-79; Chapl Warminster Sch 79-85; V Hykeham *Linc* 85-88; rtd 88; Perm to Offic *Linc* from 88. *56 Western Avenue, Lincoln LN6 7SY* Tel and fax (01522) 829026 E-mail ppbanyard@hotmail.com

BANYARD (or BRUNSKILL), Canon Sheila Kathryn. b 53. Univ of Wales (Ban) BA75 K Coll Lon MA83 Ox Univ MTh99. Cranmer Hall Dur 78. **dss** 82 **d** 92 **p** 94. Sunbury Lon 82-85; Asst Chapl Ch Hosp Horsham 85-90; Chapl Malvern Girls' Coll 90-95; TV Droitwich Spa *Worc* 95-00; TR 00-10; RD Droitwich 99-02; RD Droitwich from 10; Hon Can Worc Cathl from 03. *The Rectory, 205 Worcester Road, Droitwich WR9 8AS* Tel and fax (01905) 773134 *or* tel 794952 E-mail sk.banyard@virgin.net *or* droitwich.parish@virgin.net

✠**BARAHONA, The Most Revd Martin de Jesus.** c 92. Bp El Salvador from 92; Primate Cen America from 02. *47 Avenida Sur, 723 Col Flor Blanca, Apt Postal (01), 274 San Salvador, El Salvador* Tel (00503) 223 2252 *or* 224 6136 Fax 223 7952 E-mail anglican@saltel.net

BARBARA JUNE, Sister. *See* KIRBY, Barbara Anne June

BARBER, Ann. *See* BARBER, Mrs Margaret Ann

BARBER, Ms Annabel Ruth. b 58. Leeds Univ BSc80. NEOC 01. **d** 04 **p** 05. C Scawby, Redbourne and Hibaldstow *Linc* 04-07; Chapl N Lincs and Goole Hosps NHS Trust from 07. *Chaplains' Office, Diana Princess of Wales Hospital, Scartho Road, Grimsby DN33 2BA* Tel (01472) 874111

BARBER, Canon Christopher Albert. b 33. Ch Coll Cam BA53 MA57. Coll of Resurr Mirfield 56. **d** 58 **p** 59. C Cov St Pet 58-61; C Stokenchurch and Cadmore End *Ox* 61-64; V Royton St Paul *Man* 64-70; V Stapleford *Ely* 70-80; RD Shelford 76-80; V Cherry Hinton St Andr 80-88; Hon Can Ely Cathl 88-98; R Cottenham 88-92; RD N Stowe 90-92; V Terrington St John 92-98; V Tilney All Saints 92-98; rtd 98; Perm to Offic *Ely* from 98; Asst Rtd Clergy and Clergy Widow(er)s' Officer 00-07; Retired Clergy Officer from 07; PV Ely Cathl from 03. *20 King Edgar Close, Ely CB6 1DP* Tel (01353) 612338 E-mail chrisbarber2@ntlworld.com

BARBER, Craig John Francis. b 71. STETS 98. **d** 02 **p** 03. NSM Brighton St Bart *Chich* 02-03; C Brighton St Geo w St Anne and St Mark 03-06; TV Worth 06-08; C Worth, Pound Hill and Maidenbower 08-10; Chapl Lon Metrop Univ from 10. *St Luke's House, Roscoe Street, London EC1Y 8PT* Tel (020) 7250 0891

BARBER, Garth Antony. b 48. Southn Univ BSc69 Lon Univ MSc79 FRAS MSOSc. St Jo Coll Nottm. **d** 76 **p** 77. C Hounslow H Trin *Lon* 76-79; Chapl City of Lon Poly 79-86; P-in-c Twickenham All Hallows 86-97; Chapl Richmond Coll 87-97; Chapl UEA *Nor* 97-02; P-in-c Kingswood *S'wark* 02-11; V from 11; AD Reigate from 06. *The Vicarage, Woodland Way, Kingswood, Tadworth KT20 6NW* Tel (01737) 832164 E-mail garth.barber@virgin.net

BARBER, Canon Hilary John. b 65. Aston Tr Scheme 92 Sarum Th Coll 94. **d** 96 **p** 97. C Moston St Jo *Man* 96-00; R Chorlton-cum-Hardy St Clem 00-07; P-in-c Chorlton-cum-Hardy St Werburgh 05-07; Dioc Music Adv 03-07; V Halifax *Wakef* from 07; Hon Can Wakef Cathl from 11. *The Vicarage, Kensington Road, Halifax HX3 0HN* Tel (01422) 365477 E-mail h.barber@halifaxminster.org.uk

BARBER, John Eric Michael. b 30. Wycliffe Hall Ox 63. **d** 65 **p** 66. C Lupset *Wakef* 65-68; C Halifax St Jo Bapt 68-70; V Dewsbury St Matt and St Jo 70-80; V Perry Common *Birm* 80-95; rtd 95; Perm to Offic *Sarum* from 95. *21A Westhill Road, Weymouth DT4 9NB* Tel (01305) 786553

BARBER, Mrs Margaret Ann. b 31. GTCL52. Dalton Ho Bris 55 Sarum & Wells Th Coll 82. **dss** 83 **d** 87 **p** 94. Wimborne Minster and Holt *Sarum* 83-90; Par Dn 87-90; rtd 90; Hon Par Dn Hampreston *Sarum* 90-94; Hon C 94-02; Perm to Offic from 02. *1 Highbarn Place, 2 St Mary's Road, Ferndown BH22 9HB* Tel (01202) 873626

BARBER, Miss Marion. b 50. Birkbeck Coll Lon BSc97 K Coll Lon MSc03. **d** 07 **p** 08. NSM Lee St Mildred *S'wark* from 07. *12B Beechfield Road, London SE6 4NE* Tel (020) 8690 6035

BARBER, Martin John. b 35. Univ Coll Lon BA61. Linc Th Coll 61. **d** 63 **p** 64. C Stepney St Dunstan and All SS *Lon* 63-67; Chapl K Sch Bruton 67-93; rtd 93; Perm to Offic *B & W* from 93. *1 Plox Green, Bruton BA10 0EY* Tel (01749) 812290

BARBER, Michael. *See* BARBER, John Eric Michael

BARBER, Michael. b 40. Open Univ BA83. Oak Hill Th Coll 69. **d** 71 **p** 72. C Rothley *Leic* 71-74; C Leic Martyrs 74-76; V Queniborough 76-82; V Monkwearmouth All SS *Dur* 82-92; V Mirehouse *Carl* 92-05; rtd 05. *Allonby, 34 Victoria Park, Kirkcudbright DG6 4EN* Tel (01557) 339305

BARBER, Neil Andrew Austin. b 63. Ealing Coll of Educn BA85. NTMTC 94. **d** 98 **p** 98. St Mary's Chr Workers' Trust from 95; NSM Eastrop *Win* 98-01; V Normanton *Derby* from 01. *St Giles's Vicarage, 16 Browning Street, Derby DE23 8DN* Tel (01332) 767483 E-mail neil.barber@stgiles-derby.org.uk

✠**BARBER, The Rt Revd Paul Everard.** b 35. St Jo Coll Cam BA58 MA66. Wells Th Coll 58. **d** 60 **p** 61 **c** 89. C Westborough *Guildf* 60-66; V York Town St Mich 66-73; V Bourne 73-80; RD Farnham 74-79; Hon Can Guildf Cathl 80-89; Adn Surrey 80-89; Suff Bp Brixworth *Pet* 89-01; Can Pet Cathl 89-01; rtd 01; Hon Asst Bp B & W from 01. *Hillside, 41 Somerton Road, Street BA16 0DR* Tel (01458) 442916

BARBER, Philip Kenneth. b 43. St Jo Coll Dur BA65 Sheff Univ DipEd66. NW Ord Course 74. **d** 76 **p** 77. NSM Burscough Bridge *Liv* 76-84; Asst Master Ormskirk Gr Sch 76-84; P-in-c Brigham *Carl* 84-85; V 85-89; P-in-c Mosser 84-85; V 85-89; P-in-c Borrowdale 89-94; Chapl Keswick Sch 89-94; P-in-c Beetham and Educn Adv *Carl* 94-99; P-in-c Brampton and Farlam and Castle Carrock w Cumrew 99-02; P-in-c Irthington, Crosby-on-Eden and Scaleby 99-02; P-in-c Hayton w Cumwhitton 99-02; TR Eden, Gelt and Irthing 02-04; rtd 04; Perm to Offic *Carl* from 04 and *Blackb* from 05. *18 Holbeck Avenue, Morecambe LA4 6NP* Tel (01524) 401695 E-mail philipbarber326@btinternet.com

BARBER, Ralph Warwick. b 72. Lon Guildhall Univ BA94. Ripon Coll Cuddesdon 03. **d** 05 **p** 06. C Newquay *Truro* 05-08; Chapl RN from 08. *Royal Naval Chaplaincy Service, Mail Point 1-2, Leach Building, Whale Island, Portsmouth PO2 8BY* Tel (023) 9262 5055 Fax 9262 5134 E-mail ralphwbarber@aol.com

BARBER, Royston Henry. b 38. Univ of Wales (Abth) BD86. United Th Coll Abth 83. **d** 86 **p** 87. NSM Tywyn w Aberdyfi *Ban* 86-92; NSM Cannington, Otterhampton, Combwich and Stockland *B & W* 93-98; Perm to Offic *B & W* from 98 and *Ex*

from 00. *Brambledown, Silver Street, Culmstock, Cullompton EX15 3JE* Tel (01884) 841041
BARBER, Sheila. b 50. NOC 96. **d** 99 **p** 00. C Dinnington *Sheff* 99-02; V Woodhouse St Jas 02-09; rtd 09. *5 Gannow Close, Killamarsh, Sheffield S21 2BB* Tel 0114-247 6537
E-mail sheilab@uwclub.net
BARBER, Thelma Naomi. b 53. Portsm Univ CertEd98. STETS 03. **d** 06 **p** 07. NSM Purbrook *Portsm* 06-07; C Carew *St D* 07-08; TV from 08. *The Vicarage, Lamphey, Pembroke SA71 5NR* Tel (01646) 672020
E-mail thelma.barber@ntlworld.com
BARBOUR, Mrs Jennifer Louise. b 32. JP67. Barrister-at-Law 55 St Hugh's Coll Ox BA54 MA57. Gilmore Course 80. dss 81 **d** 87 **p** 94. Bray and Braywood *Ox* 81-84; Hermitage and Hampstead Norreys, Cold Ash etc 84-87; Chapl Leeds Poly *Ripon* 87-92; Chapl Leeds Metrop Univ 92-95; rtd 95; NSM Shipton Moyne w Westonbirt and Lasborough *Glouc* 95-99; Perm to Offic *Bris* from 95; *Glouc* from 99; *Cov* and *Worc* from 00. *Cheriton, Aston Road, Chipping Campden GL55 6HR* Tel (01386) 840279
BARBOUR, Walter Iain. b 28. FICE65 Pemb Coll Cam BA48 MA53. Ox NSM Course 78. **d** 81 **p** 82. NSM Bray and Braywood *Ox* 81-84; NSM Thatcham 84-87; TV Moor Allerton *Ripon* 87-95; rtd 95; NSM Shipton Moyne w Westonbirt and Lasborough *Glouc* 95-98; Perm to Offic *Bris* from 95; *Glouc* 98-01; *Cov* and *Worc* from 00. *Cheriton, Aston Road, Chipping Campden GL55 6HR* Tel (01386) 840279
BARBY, Canon Sheana Braidwood. b 38. Bedf Coll Lon BA59. EMMTC 81. dss 84 **d** 87 **p** 94. Derby St Paul 84-87; NSM Derby Cathl 87 03; Dioc Dir of Orde 90 97; Par Educn Adv 93-01; rtd 03; Hon Can Derby Cathl from 96; RD Derby N 00-05; Perm to Offic from 05. *2 Margaret Street, Derby DE1 3FE* Tel (01332) 383301 E-mail sheana@talktalk.net
BARCLAY, Mrs Christine Ann. b 54. TISEC. **d** 07 **p** 08. C St Andrews All SS *St And* 07-10; NSM from 08; R Tayport from 10. *12 Millfield, Cupar KY15 5UU* Tel (01334) 656154
E-mail christine.barclay1@btopenworld.com
BARCLAY, Ian Newton. b 33. Clifton Th Coll 58. **d** 61 **p** 62. C Cullompton *Ex* 61-63; C Ashill w Broadway *B & W* 63-66; V Chatham St Phil and St Jas *Roch* 66-69; C St Helen Bishopsgate w St Martin Outwich *Lon* 70-73; V Prestonville St Luke *Chich* 73-81; Lic to Offic 82-93; rtd 93; P-in-c Cannes *Eur* 98-02. *35 Marine Avenue, Hove BN3 4LH*
E-mail ibarclay692@btinternet.com
BARCLAY, Mrs Susan Molly. Wycliffe Hall Ox. **d** 87 **p** 99. Hon Par Dn March St Wendreda *Ely* 87-96; Tutor Past Studies Ridley Hall Cam 96-05; Perm to Offic *Ely* from 05. *42 Greystoke Road, Cambridge CB1 8DS* Tel (01223) 246877
E-mail sigb2@medschl.cam.ac.uk
BARCROFT, The Very Revd Ian David. b 60. UMIST BSc83 Edin Univ BD88 Glas Univ MTh01. Edin Th Coll 85. **d** 88 **p** 89. Prec St Ninian's Cathl Perth 88-92; Min Perth St Ninian 88-92; P-in-c Aberdeen St Clem 92-97; R Hamilton *Glas* from 97; Dean Glas from 10. *The Rectory, 4C Auchingramont Road, Hamilton ML3 6JT* Tel and fax (01698) 429895
E-mail ian.barcroft@btinternet.com
BARDELL, Alan George. City Univ BSc. **d** 92 **p** 93. OLM Addlestone *Guildf* 92-06; rtd 06; Perm to Offic *Guildf* from 07. *14 Dickens Drive, Addlestone KT15 1AW* Tel (01932) 847574
E-mail alanbardell@aol.com
BARDELL, Terence Richard. b 51. EMMTC 04. **d** 01 **p** 02. OLM Coningsby w Tattershall *Linc* 01-05; C Gt Grimsby St Mary and St Jas 05-06; TV 06-09; P-in-c Chapel St Leonards w Hogsthorpe from 09. *The Vicarage, Church Lane, Chapel St Leonards, Skegness PE24 5UJ* Tel (01754) 871176
BARDSLEY, Warren Nigel Antony. b 52. AKC74. St Aug Coll Cant 74. **d** 75 **p** 76. C Leeds St Aid *Ripon* 75-78; C Cov St Jo 78-80; P-in-c Stoke Golding w Dadlington *Leic* 80-89; TV Swinton and Pendlebury *Man* 90-94. *Orchard House, 22 Upper Olland Street, Bungay NR35 1BH* Tel (01986) 895760
BARDWELL, Mrs Elaine Barbara. b 60. K Coll Lon BA81 AKC81. St Steph Ho Ox BA85 MA90. dss 86 **d** 87 **p** 95. Heref H Trin 86-89; C 87-89; Dir Past Studies St Steph Ho Ox 89-96; V New Marston *Ox* from 96; AD Cowley 02-07. *The Vicarage, 8 Jack Straws Lane, Headington, Oxford OX3 0DL* Tel (01865) 434340 E-mail elaine.bardwell@virgin.net
BARDWELL, John Edward. b 53. Jes Coll Cam BA75 MA79 Ox Univ BA85 MA90. St Steph Ho Ox 83. **d** 86 **p** 87. C Heref H Trin 86-89; Perm to Offic Ox 90-96. *The Vicarage, 8 Jack Straws Lane, Headington, Oxford OX3 0DL* Tel (01865) 434340
BAREHAM, Miss Sylvia Alice. b 36. Hockerill Coll Cam CertEd59 Open Univ BA83 Ox Univ DipEd84. Ox Min Course 86. **d** 89 **p** 94. NSM N Leigh *Ox* 89-93; NSM Bampton w Clanfield 93-95; NSM Kedington *St E* 95-97; NSM Hundon w Barnardiston 95-97; NSM Haverhill w Withersfield, Wrattings etc 95-97; NSM Stourhead 97-05; NSM Lark Valley 05-07; rtd 07; Perm to Offic *Chelmsf* from 05 and *St E* from 07. *Davaar, Old Hall Lane, Fornham St Martin, Bury St Edmunds IP31 1SS* Tel (01284) 724899

BARFOOT, John Henry. b 38. **d** 08 **p** 09. NSM Tintagel *Truro* from 08. *Brambly Hedge, Castle Heights, Atlantic Road, Tintagel PL34 0DE* Tel (01840) 779047
BARFORD, Patricia Ann. b 47. Univ of Wales (Cardiff) BSc68 PhD73. WMMTC 95. **d** 98 **p** 99. NSM Stoke Prior, Wychbold and Upton Warren *Worc* 98-05; C Redditch H Trin 05-08; TV 08-09; rtd 09; Perm to Offic *Worc* from 09. *Greenfields, Church Road, Dodford, Bromsgrove B61 9BY* Tel (01527) 871614
E-mail thebarfords@hotmail.com
BARGE, Mrs Ann Marina. b 42. S'wark Ord Course 89. **d** 96 **p** 97. C Ludlow, Ludford, Ashford Carbonell etc *Heref* from 96. *8 Old Street, Ludlow SY8 1NP* Tel (01584) 877307
BARGE, David Robert. b 45. S Dios Minl Tr Scheme 92. **d** 95 **p** 96. NSM Westfield *B & W* 95-00; C Frome St Jo and St Mary 00; V Frome St Mary 01-10; RD Frome 08-10; rtd 10. *26 Charolais Drive, Bridgwater TA6 6EX* Tel (01278) 431655
E-mail dbarge@btinternet.com
BARGE, Marian Elizabeth. **d** 00. OLM Mynyddislwyn *Mon* from 00. *8 Pinewood Court, Pontllanfraith, Blackwood NP12 2PA* Tel (01495) 227208
BARGH, George Edward Norman. b 25. St Jo Coll Cam BA48 MA53 Leeds Univ LLB51. Carl Dioc Tr Course 80. **d** 83 **p** 84. NSM Ulverston St Mary w H Trin *Carl* 83-86; P-in-c Egton w Newland 86-87; P-in-c Blawith w Lowick 86-87; P-in-c Egton-cum-Newland and Lowick 87-89; rtd 90; Perm to Offic *Carl* from 90. *8 Highfield Road, Grange-over-Sands LA11 7JA* Tel (015395) 35755
BARHAM, Ian Harold. b 40. Clifton Th Coll 64. **d** 66 **p** 67. C Broadwater St Mary *Chich* 66-69 and 72-76; Burundi 71-72; R Beyton and Hessett *St E* 76-79; Perm to Offic 79-81; Hon C Bury St Edmunds St Mary 81-84; Chapl St Aubyn's Sch Tiverton 84-96; Chapl Lee Abbey 96-99; rtd 00; Perm to Offic *Ex* from 00. *53 Sylvan Road, Exeter EX4 6EY* Tel (01392) 251643
BARHAM, Mrs Jennifer Mary. b 43. RN65. Oak Hill Th Coll 92. **d** 95 **p** 96. NSM Leigh-on-Sea St Aid *Chelmsf* 95-02; NSM Gt Burstead 02-07; Chapl Basildon and Thurrock Gen Hosps NHS Trust 01-03; Perm to Offic *Chelmsf* 07-08; NSM Canvey Is from 08. *47 Walker Drive, Leigh-on-Sea SS9 3QT* Tel (01702) 558766
E-mail jen-john@barham47.freeserve.co.uk
✠**BARHAM, The Rt Revd Kenneth Lawrence.** b 36. OBE01. Clifton Th Coll BD63. **d** 63 **p** 64 **c** 93. C Worthing St Geo *Chich* 63-65; C Sevenoaks St Nic *Roch* 65-67; C Cheltenham St Mark *Glouc* 67-70; V Maidstone St Luke *Cant* 70-79; S Area Sec Rwanda Miss 79-84; P-in-c Ashburnham w Penhurst *Chich* 84-01; Asst Bp Cyangugu (Rwanda) 93-96; Bp 96-01; rtd 01; Hon Asst Bp Chich from 05. *Rosewood, Canadia Road, Battle TN33 0LR* Tel and fax (01424) 773073
E-mail bishopken@btinternet.com
BARHAM, Peter. b 62. Selw Coll Cam MA83. Linc Th Coll BTh94. **d** 94 **p** 95. C Fornham All SS and Fornham St Martin w Timworth *St E* 94-97; P-in-c Cockfield w Bradfield St Clare, Felsham etc 97-01; Min Can St E Cathl 98-03; Chapl 01-03; Can Res St E Cathl 03-08; V Ponteland *Newc* from 08. *The Vicarage, Thornhill Road, Ponteland, Newcastle upon Tyne NE20 9PZ* Tel (01661) 822140 E-mail revpeterbarham@aol.com
BARKER, Arthur John Willoughby. b 10. Lon Coll of Div 46. **d** 48 **p** 49. C Addiscombe St Mary *Cant* 48-53; V Westgate St Jas 53-58; Warden Scargill Ho 58-61; V Dent w Cowgill *Bradf* 61-76; rtd 76; Perm to Offic 76-99. *Manormead, Tilford Road, Hindhead GU26 6RA* Tel (01428) 602500
BARKER, Brian Wallwork. b 26. G&C Coll Cam BA50 MA55. Wells Th Coll 51. **d** 52 **p** 53. C Bradford cum Beswick *Man* 52-55; Singapore 55-61; Malaya 62-63; Malaysia 63-64; V Ashton St Jas *Man* 65-71; R Burnage St Nic 71-85; R Heaton Reddish 85-91; rtd 91; Perm to Offic *Man* and *Ches* from 91. *Room 4, Abbeyfield House, Dovedale Close, High Lane, Stockport SK6 8DU* Tel (01663) 766950 *or* 764498
BARKER, Cameron Timothy. b 62. Rhodes Univ BA83 Nottm Univ MA(TS)96. St Jo Coll Nottm 94. **d** 96 **p** 97. C W Streatham St Jas *S'wark* 96-00; V Herne Hill from 00. *The Vicarage, 1 Finsen Road, London SE5 9AX* Tel (020) 7771 0381
E-mail vicar@hernehillparish.org.uk
BARKER, Prof Charles Philip Geoffrey. b 50. Lon Univ MB, BS75 MS91 FRCS79 FICS92. S Dios Minl Tr Scheme 95. **d** 98 **p** 99. NSM Alverstoke *Portsm* 98-02; NSM The Lickey *Birm* 02-06; NSM Empangeni H Cross S Africa from 06. *PO Box 11032, Empangeni, 3880 South Africa* Tel and fax (0027) (35) 772 1211 E-mail barker@kznmail.co.za
✠**BARKER, The Rt Revd Clifford Conder.** b 26. TD71. Oriel Coll Ox BA50 MA55. St Chad's Coll Dur. **d** 52 **p** 53 **c** 76. C Falsgrave *York* 52-55; C Redcar 55-57; V Sculcoates 57-63; CF (TA) 58-74; P-in-c Sculcoates St Silas *York* 59-61; V Rudby in Cleveland w Middleton 63-70; RD Stokesley 65-70; V York St Olave w St Giles 70-76; RD City of York 71-75; Can and Preb York Minster 73-76; Suff Bp Whitby 76-83; Suff Bp Selby 83-91; rtd 91; Hon Asst Bp York from 95. *29 Dulverton Hall, The Esplanade, Scarborough YO11 2AR* Tel (01723) 340129
BARKER, David Robert. b 45. Cam Univ BA67 MA70. Virginia Th Sem BD72. **d** 72 **p** 73. C Roehampton H Trin *S'wark* 72-75; Chapl Goldsmiths' Coll Lon 75-79; Min Tr Officer *Cov*

79-85; Selection Sec and Sec for Continuing Minl Educn ACCM 85-90; V Sutton Valence w E Sutton and Chart Sutton *Cant* 90-08; rtd 09. *1 Colletts Close, Corfe Castle, Wareham BH20 5HG* Tel (01929) 481477 E-mail david_pennybarker@hotmail.com

BARKER, Edward. See BARKER, William Edward

BARKER, Gillian Ann. b 52. Portsm Univ MA02. Portsm Dioc Tr Course 91. d 92 p 98. NSM Alverstoke *Portsm* 92-95; NSM Bridgemary 95-96; Asst Chapl Portsm Hosps NHS Trust 96-98; Chapl 98-01; Chapl Ox Radcliffe Hosps NHS Trust 01-06; R Aynho and Croughton w Evenley etc *Pet* from 06. *The Rectory, Croughton Road, Aynho, Banbury OX17 3BD* Tel (01869) 810903 E-mail barkergill@hotmail.com

BARKER, Gordon Frank. b 43. Heriot-Watt Univ MSc75 Sheff Univ MA98. S & M Dioc Tr Inst 91. d 94 p 95. NSM Malew *S & M* 94-00; V Grain w Stoke *Roch* 00-04; Through Faith Miss Ev 00-04; P-in-c Andreas and Jurby S & M 04-08; P-in-c Lezayre 04-05; rtd 08; Perm to Offic *S & M* from 10. *The Harp Inn, Cross Four Ways, Ballasalla, Isle of Man IM9 3DH* Tel (01624) 824116

BARKER, Howard. See BARKER, Canon John Howard

BARKER, Canon John Howard. b 36. Southn Univ BA58. Ripon Coll Cuddesdon 80. d 82 p 83. C W Leigh *Portsm* 82-84; V Cosham 84-88; Bp's Dom Chapl 88-96; Hon Can Portsm Cathl 93-02; V St Helens and Sea View 96-02; rtd 02; Perm to Offic *Portsm* from 02. *Coniston Lodge, 3 Coniston Drive, Ryde PO33 3AE* Tel (01983) 618674 Mobile 07802-281797 E-mail jhbarker@netcomuk.co.uk

BARKER, John Stuart. b 30. Keele Univ BA55. Wells Th Coll 55. d 57 p 58. C Oswestry St Oswald *Lich* 57-60; C Portishead *B & W* 60-63; V Englishcombe *B & W* 60-63; R Priston 63-69; V Chew Magna w Dundry 70-85; rtd 94. *9 West Street, Axbridge BS26 2AA* Tel (01934) 732740

BARKER, Jonathan. b 55. Hull Univ BA79. Westcott Ho Cam 79. d 83 p 84. C Sketty *S & B* 83-86; Chapl Sport and Leisure 83-86; C Swansea St Mary w H Trin 85-86; Bermuda 86-90; TV Liv Our Lady and St Nic w St Anne 90-93; P-in-c S Shore St Pet *Blackb* 93-98; Chapl Blackpool Victoria Hosp NHS Trust 93-98; V Chislehurst St Jo *Wakef* 98-08; Chapl St Pancras Internat and K Cross Stations *Lon* from 08. *3 Carleton Villas, Leighton Grove, London NW5 2QU* Tel (020) 7485 2472 E-mail jonathanbarker2004@tesco.net

BARKER, Ms Joyce. b 46. Nottm Univ BPharm68. Yorks Min Course 09. d 11. NSM Barnby Dun *Sheff* from 11. *52A Harpenden Drive, Dunscroft, Doncaster DN7 4HN* Tel (01302) 844970 (mobile) E-mail joycebarkertwin@aol.com

BARKER, Julian Roland Palgrave. b 37. Magd Coll Cam BA61 MA65. Westcott Ho Cam 61. d 63 p 64. C Stafford St Mary *Lich* 63-66; Chapl Clare Hall Cam 66-69; Chapl Clare Coll Cam 66-70; Tutor St Aug Coll Cant 70-71; TV Raveningham *Nor* 71-78; TR 78-82; V Foremark *Derby* 82-02; V Repton 82-02; P-in-c Newton Solney 01-02; V Foremark and Repton w Newton Solney 02-03; RD Repton 91-95; rtd 03; Perm to Offic *St E* from 06. *Old Bank House, 12 Market Hill, Framlingham, Woodbridge IP13 9AN* Tel (01728) 621057

BARKER, Mark. b 62. ACIB90. St Jo Coll Nottm BTh95. d 95 p 96. C Barking St Marg w St Patr *Chelmsf* 95-98; C Cranham Park 98-04; V Tonbridge St Steph *Roch* from 04. *St Stephen's Vicarage, 6 Brook Street, Tonbridge TN9 2PJ* Tel (01732) 353079 E-mail mark.barker@diocese-rochester.org

BARKER, Miriam Sarah Anne. b 62. d 11. C Southborough St Pet w Ch Ch and St Matt etc *Roch* from 11. *St Stephen's Vicarage, 6 Brook Street, Tonbridge TN9 2PJ* Tel (01732) 353079

BARKER, Neil Anthony. b 52. St Andr Univ BSc73. Ridley Hall Cam 74. d 77 p 78. C Leic H Apostles 77-81; C Camberley St Paul *Guildf* 81-86; R Bradfield *Ox* 86-88; R Bradfield and Stanford Dingley 88-92; R Woodmansterne *S'wark* 92-05; AD Reigate 05; Chapl MU 96-02; TR Modbury, Bigbury, Ringmore w Kingston etc *Ex* from 05; RD Woodleigh from 07. *The Vicarage, Church Lane, Modbury, Ivybridge PL21 0QN* Tel (01548) 830260 E-mail revneil@i.am

BARKER, The Ven Nicholas John Willoughby. b 49. Oriel Coll Ox BA73 BA75 MA77. Trin Coll Bris 75. d 77 p 78. C Watford *St Alb* 77-80; TV Didsbury St Jas and Em *Man* 80-86; TR Kidderminster St Geo *Worc* 86-07; RD Kidderminster 01-07; Hon Can Worc Cathl 03-07; Adn Auckland and Can Dur Cathl from 07; P-in-c Darlington H Trin from 07. *Holy Trinity Vicarage, 45 Milbank Road, Darlington DL3 9NL* Tel (01325) 480444 E-mail archdeacon.of.auckland@durham.anglican.org

BARKER, Philip. See BARKER, Prof Charles Philip Geoffrey

BARKER, Canon Roy Thomas. b 33. K Coll Lon BD57 AKC57. d 58 p 59. C Headingley *Ripon* 58-62; C Hawksworth Wood 62-66; Chapl Cape Town Univ S Africa 66-72; Sub-Dean St Geo Cathl Cape Town 73-80; Can 74-80; Dean and Adn Grahamstown 80-92; Hon Can from 92; V Southmead *Bris* 92-98; rtd 98; Perm to Offic *Bris* from 98. *7 Cleeve Avenue, Downend, Bristol BS16 6BT* Tel 0117-956 9057 E-mail rtbarker@talktalk.net

BARKER, The Ven Timothy Reed. b 56. Qu Coll Cam BA79 MA82. Westcott Ho Cam 78. d 80 p 81. C Nantwich *Ches* 80-83; V Norton 83-88; V Runcorn All SS 88-94; Urban Officer 88-90;

Dioc Communications Officer 91-98; Bp's Chapl 94-98; Hon P Asst Ches Cathl 94-98; V Spalding *Linc* 98-09; P-in-c Spalding St Paul 07-09; RD Elloe W 00-09; RD Elloe E 08-09; Adn Linc from 09; Can and Preb Linc Cathl from 03. *Archdeacon's House, 1A Northfield Road, Quarrington, Sleaford NG34 8RT* Tel (01529) 304348 Mobile 07590-950041 E-mail tim@tjkc.co.uk *or* archdeacon.lincoln@lincoln.anglican.org

BARKER, William Edward. b 28. Kelham Th Coll 49. d 54 p 55. C Warsop *S'well* 54-55; C Bawtry w Austerfield 55-57; V Frizington *Carl* 57-64; V Barrow St Jas 64-70; V Applethwaite 70-93; P-in-c Troutbeck 78-93; rtd 93; Perm to Offic *Carl* from 93. *114 Burneside Road, Kendal LA9 4RZ* Tel (01539) 734787

BARKING, Area Bishop of. See HAWKINS, The Rt Revd David John Leader

BARKS, Jeffrey Stephen. b 45. Cranmer Hall Dur 66. d 71 p 72. C Wootton *St Alb* 71-74; C Boscombe St Jo *Win* 74-76; C Ringwood 76-80; P-in-c Spaxton w Charlynch *B & W* 80; P-in-c Enmore w Goathurst 80; P-in-c Spaxton w Goathurst, Enmore and Charlynch 80-81; R 81-92; RD Bridgwater 89-94; V Wembdon 92-07; rtd 07. *77 Alfoxton Road, Bridgwater TA6 7NW* Tel (01278) 423647 E-mail stephenbarks@dsl.pipex.com

BARLEY, Ann Christine. b 47. d 93 p 94. OLM Walton *St E* 93-00; OLM Walton and Trimley 00-08; rtd 08; Perm to Offic *St E* from 08. *Carmel, 13 New Road, Trimley St Mary, Felixstowe IP11 0TQ* Tel (01394) 283752 E-mail ann.carmel@lineone.net

BARLEY, Canon Christopher James. b 56. St Steph Ho Ox BA90 MA93. d 93 p 94. C Upton cum Chalvey *Ox* 93-96; TV High Wycombe 96-01; V Swinton *Sheff* from 01; Dioc Chapl MU from 08; Hon Can Sheff Cathl from 10. *The Vicarage, 50 Golden Smithies Lane, Swinton, Mexborough S64 8DL* Tel (01709) 582259 E-mail chris.barley@sheffield.anglican.org

BARLEY, Gordon Malcolm. b 59. Aston Tr Scheme 94 Oak Hill Th Coll 96. d 98 p 99. C Walthamstow St Jo *Chelmsf* 98-02; TV Barking St Marg w St Patr from 02. *St Patrick's Vicarage, 79 Sparsholt Road, Barking IG11 7YG* Tel (020) 8594 1960 E-mail revgbarley@eggconnect.net

BARLEY, Ivan William. b 48. Loughb Univ MA01 CEng74 MIET74. d 93 p 94. OLM Walton *St E* 93-00; OLM Walton and Trimley from 00; Dioc NSM/OLM Officer 02-10. *Carmel, 13 New Road, Trimley St Mary, Felixstowe IP11 0TQ* Tel (01394) 283752 E-mail iwbarley@gmail.com

BARLEY, Preb Lynda Mary. b 53. York Univ BA74 PGCE75 Lon Univ MSc76 FSS77. S'wark Ord Course 93. d 96 p 97. NSM Lower Nutfield *S'wark* 96-97; NSM Littleham w Exmouth 97-98; NSM Tedburn St Mary, Whitestone, Oldridge etc 98-00; Hd Research and Statistics Abps' Coun from 00; NSM Cullompton, Willand, Uffculme, Kentisbeare etc *Ex* from 03; Preb Ex Cathl from 09. *Church House, Great Smith Street, London SW1P 3AZ* Tel (020) 7898 1540 Fax 7898 1532 E-mail lynda.barley@churchofengland.org

BARLEY, Victor Laurence. b 41. St Jo Coll Cam MA66 Ch Ch Ox DPhil72 FRCSEd75 FRCR76. d 02 p 03. NSM Flax Bourton and Barrow Gurney *B & W* 02-06; NSM Clevedon St Jo 06-09; NSM Chew Stoke w Nempnett Thrubwell from 09. *1 Home Orchard, Chew Stoke, Bristol BS40 8UZ* Tel (01275) 332914 E-mail victor.barley@tiscali.co.uk

BARLING, Michael Keith. b 38. Oak Hill Th Coll 63. d 66 p 67. C Portman Square St Paul *Lon* 66-70; C Enfield Ch Ch Trent Park 70-74; V Sidcup St Andr *Roch* 74-78; Dir Fountain Trust 78-81; Chapl Bethany Fellowship and Roffey Place 81-88; Hon C Kennington St Mark *S'wark* 88-89; rtd 03. *10 Copper Beeches, Taunton TA1 5HS* Tel (01823) 272092 E-mail michael@kingdomfaithsw.com

BARLOW, Alan David. b 36. Worc Coll Ox BA59 MA65. Wycliffe Hall Ox 59. d 61 p 62. C Wealdstone H Trin *Lon* 61-67; V Neasden cum Kingsbury St Cath 67-73; Chapl Cranleigh Sch Surrey 73-81; Chapl Cheltenham Ladies' Coll 82-01; rtd 01; Perm to Offic *Glouc* from 02. *22 Moorend Road, Leckhampton, Cheltenham GL53 0EU* Tel and fax (01242) 584668 E-mail revdavid@globalnet.co.uk

BARLOW, Clive Christopher. b 42. Linc Th Coll 67. d 70 p 71. C Surbiton St Mark *S'wark* 70-74; C Spring Park *Cant* 74-77; V Ash w Westmarsh 77-92; R Chartham 92-08; RD E Bridge 86-92; RD W Bridge 95-01; rtd 08; Perm to Offic *Cant* from 08. *5 Barton Road, Canterbury CT1 1YG* Tel (01227) 784779 E-mail c.barlow@btinternet.com

BARLOW, Darren. b 65. Ridley Hall Cam 96. d 98 p 99. C Rayleigh *Chelmsf* 98-01; TV Billericay and Lt Burstead 01-06; TR Grays Thurrock from 06; RD Thurrock from 11. *The Rectory, 10 High View Avenue, Grays RM17 6RU* Tel (01375) 377379 E-mail revbarlow@talktalk.net

BARLOW, David. See BARLOW, Alan David

BARLOW, David. b 50. Leeds Univ BA71 MA99. Wycliffe Hall Ox 71. d 73 p 74. C Horninglow *Lich* 73-75; C Wednesfield St Thos 75-77; C Bloxwich 77-78; Chapl RN 78-08; Prin Armed Forces Chapl Cen Amport Ho 05-08; P-in-c Baughurst, Ramsdell, Wolverton w Ewhurst etc *Win* from 08; QHC from 04. *The Rectory, Crabs Hill, Wolverton, Tadley RG26 5RU* Tel (01635) 297543 E-mail barlow857@btinternet.com

BARLOW, Canon Edward Burnley. b 29. St Aid Birkenhead 56. d 58 p 59. C Lenton Abbey S'well 58-61; C Ipswich All SS St E 61-63; R Fishtoft Linc 63-76; V Linc St Giles 76-96; Can and Preb Linc Cathl 92-05; rtd 96; Perm to Offic Linc 96-99. 8 Pynder Close, Washingborough, Lincoln LN4 1EX Tel (01522) 793762

BARLOW, James Derek. b 64. Ex Univ BA87. Ripon Coll Cuddesdon 09. d 11. C Burnham Ox from 11. 12 Hatchgate Gardens, Burnham, Slough SL1 8DD

BARLOW, Paul Andrew. b 59. Imp Coll Lon BSc80 UMIST PhD84 Bolton Inst of HE PGCE85. Aston Tr Scheme 89 Chich Th Coll 91. d 93 p 94. C Hale Guildf 93-97; C Christchurch Win 97-01; P-in-c Alton All SS 01-09; C Alton from 10. All Saints' Vicarage, Queen's Road, Alton GU34 1HU Tel (01420) 83458 E-mail paul@paulbarlow.plus.com

BARLOW, Paul Benson. b 31. Fitzw Coll Cam BA73 MA77 FRSA74. d 64 p 65. C Bath Abbey w St Jas B & W 64-74; Dep Hd Master Leys High Sch Redditch 74-81; Hd Master Jo Kyrle High Sch Ross-on-Wye 82-96; Perm to Offic Heref 82-85; Lic to Offic 85-92; NSM Walford and St John w Bishopswood, Goodrich etc 92-97; Perm to Offic 97-08. The Coach House, Hentland, Ross-on-Wye HR9 6LP

BARLOW, Robert Mark. b 53. St Jo Coll Nottm 84. d 86 p 87. C Colwich w Gt Haywood Lich 86-91; R Crick and Yelvertoft w Clay Coton and Lilbourne Pet 91-04; Bp's Rural Officer 98-04; Chapl to Agric and Rural Life Worc 04-10; C Worcs W 05-10; P-in-c Teme Valley S from 10. The Rectory, Broadheath, Tenbury Wells WR15 8QW Tel (01886) 853286 Mobile 07947-600627 E-mail temevalleyvicar@gmail.com

BARLOW, Canon Timothy David. b 46. Univ Coll Ox BA67 MA71 Lon Univ BD71. Oak Hill Th Coll 71. d 71 p 72. C Marple All SS Ches 71-74; C Northwood Em Lon 74-78; Chapl Vevey w Château d'Oex and Villars Eur 78-84; Switzerland 84-89; V Romiley Ches from 89; Hon Can Ches Cathl 08-11; rtd 11. Bryn Araul, Winllan Road, Llansanffraid SY22 6TS E-mail timdbarlow@gmail.com

BARLOW, William George. b 40. Liv Univ BSc62 Univ of Wales BD65. St Mich Coll Llan 76. d 76 p 77. C Roath Llan 76-79; TV Cyncoed Mon 79-83; R Radyr Llan 83-05; RD Llan 95-04; rtd 05. 15 Cae Tymawr, Whitchurch, Cardiff CF14 2HB

BARNARD, Canon Anthony Nevin. b 36. St Jo Coll Cam BA60 MA64. Wells Th Coll 61. d 63 p 64. C Cheshunt St Alb 63-65; Tutor Wells Th Coll 65-66; Chapl 66-69; Vice-Prin 69-71; Dep Prin Sarum & Wells Th Coll 71-77; Dir S Dios Minl Tr Scheme 74-77; Can Res and Chan Lich Cathl 77-06; Warden of Readers 77-91; Dir of Tr 86-91; rtd 06; Perm to Offic Lich from 06. 1 The Stables, The Knoll, Barton under Needwood, Burton-on-Trent DE13 8AB

BARNARD, Catherine Elizabeth. b 54. York Univ BA76 Dur Univ BA79. Cranmer Hall Dur 77. dss 80 d 87 p 94. Mexborough Sheff 80-83; Sheff Manor 83-90; Hon Par Dn 87-90; Hon Par Dn Bolsterstone 90-94; C 94-08; P-in-c Stocksbridge from 08. The Vicarage, Stone Moor Road, Bolsterstone, Sheffield S36 3ZN Tel and fax 0114-288 2149

BARNARD, Jonathan Dixon. b 46. St Cath Coll Cam BA68. Cuddesdon Coll 69. d 71 p 72. C Silksworth Dur 71-74; C Hatfield Hyde St Alb 74-78; TV Hitchin 78-86; TR Penrith w Newton Reigny and Plumpton Wall Carl 86-91; rtd 91. 4 Hallin Croft, Penrith CA11 8AA Tel (01768) 63000

BARNARD, Kevin James. b 52. Keble Coll Ox BA77 MA79. Cranmer Hall Dur 77. d 79 p 80. C Swinton Sheff 79-83; TV Sheff Manor 83-90; V Bolsterstone from 90; Bp's Adv on Issues Relating to Ageing from 94. The Vicarage, Stone Moor Road, Bolsterstone, Sheffield S36 3ZN Tel and fax 0114-288 2149

BARNARD, Leslie William. b 24. St Cath Coll Ox BA50 MA55 Southn Univ PhD70. Cuddesdon Coll 51. d 51 p 52. C Portswood Ch Ch Win 51-55; V Shaw and Whitley Sarum 55-61; R Chilcomb w Win All SS and Chesil 61-68; Sen Lect Leeds Univ 69-83; Dioc Dir of Tr Ripon 70-76; Chapl Harrogate Gen Hosp 83-89; rtd 89; Perm to Offic Ripon from 89. 24 High St Agnesgate, Ripon HG4 1QR Tel (01765) 604420

BARNDEN, Saskia Gail. b 50. Waterloo Univ (Canada) BA70 Victoria Univ (BC) MA71 Indiana Univ PhD88 Westmr Coll Ox CertEd75. SAOMC 97. d 00 p 01. Asst Chapl Wycombe Abbey Sch 00-01; Chapl Haberdashers' Monmouth Sch for Girls from 01. 47 Elvetham Road, Birmingham B15 2LY Tel 0121-440 5677 or (01600) 711100 Mobile 07813-616574 E-mail headsec@hmsg.org

BARNES, Alan Duff. b 42. St Steph Ho Ox 75. d 77 p 78. C Wanstead H Trin Hermon Hill Chelmsf 77-80; C Clacton St Jas 80-82; R Cranham 82-89; V Calcot Ox 89-07; rtd 07; Perm to Offic Ox from 07. 18 Hartleys, Silchester, Reading RG7 2QE

BARNES, Canon Brian. b 42. Sussex Univ MA82. Cant Sch of Min 79. d 82 p 83. NSM Maidstone All SS and St Phil w Tovil Cant 82-89; C 89-92; FE Adv Gen Syn Bd of Educn 86-92; R Staplehurst Cant 92-02; V Hythe 02-08; RD W Charing 95-99; AD Cranbrook 99-01; Hon Can Cant Cathl 01-08; rtd 08. 9 Egerton Road, Lincoln LN2 4PJ Tel (01522) 569508 E-mail brian.barnes@virgin.net

BARNES, Brian. b 49. St Mich Coll Llan 93. d 93 p 94. C Betws w Ammanford St D 93-96; V Llanwnda, Goodwick w Manorowen and Llanstinan from 96. The Vicarage, Dyffryn, Goodwick SA64 0AN Tel (01348) 873758

BARNES, Christopher. d 06 p 07. NSM Bowling St Jo Bradf from 06. 257 Bowling Hall Road, Bradford BD4 7TJ Tel (01274) 306230 E-mail chrisbarnes257@hotmail.co.uk

BARNES, Christopher Charles. b 51. Victoria Univ Wellington BA79 TDip79. Trin Coll Bris. d 00 p 01. C Langport Area B & W 00-03; P-in-c Burton and Rosemarket St D 03-07; Chapl Miss to Seafarers Milford Haven 03-07; Port Chapl Kobe Japan 07-09; Port Chapl Auckland New Zealand from 09. PO Box 465, Shortland Street, Auckland 1140, New Zealand Tel (0064) (9) 373 4352 Fax 373 4010 E-mail portchaplain1@gmail.com

BARNES, Colin. b 33. St Jo Coll York CertEd58. St Aid Birkenhead 61. d 64 p 65. C Eccles St Mary Man 64-66; C Barrow St Geo w St Luke Carl 66-68; V Goodshaw Man 68-80; P-in-c Wythenshawe St Martin 80-83; New Zealand 83-98; rtd 98; Perm to Offic Man 98-10 and Blackb 08-10. 7 Louis Street, Trentham, Upper Hutt 5018, New Zealand

BARNES, David John. b 37. Kent Univ MA96. Chich Th Coll 65. d 68 p 69. C Crayford Roch 68-71; Chapl RAF 71-75; Chapl Sutton Valence Sch Kent 75-87; C Minster-in-Sheppey Cant 87-93; V Ash w Westmarsh 93-01; RD E Bridge 98-01; rtd 01; Perm to Offic Cant 02-10 and Roch from 02. 15 Meadow Lane, Edenbridge TN8 6HT Tel and fax (01732) 300561 E-mail davidjbarnes@blueyonder.co.uk

BARNES, David Keith. b 53. Linc Th Coll. d 89 p 90. C E Crompton Man 89-93; V Belfield 93-99; V Honley Wakef from 99. The Vicarage, St Mary's Road, Honley, Holmfirth HD9 6AZ Tel (01484) 661178 E-mail d.barnes645@btinternet.com

BARNES, Derek Ian. b 44. Leeds Univ BA66. Westcott Ho Cam 66. d 68 p 69. C Far Headingley St Chad Ripon 68-71; Chapl Qu Eliz Coll Lon 72-77; Warden Lee Abbey Internat Students' Club Kensington 77-81; Hon C Willesden Green St Gabr Lon 81-83; P-in-c Southall H Trin 84-98; P-in-c Southall St Geo 89-92; Perm to Offic 99-02; Chapl W Lon Mental Health NHS Trust 02-11; rtd 11. 19 Wimborne Avenue, Hayes UB4 0HG Tel (020) 8354 8974 E-mail derekibarnes@gmail.com

BARNES, Duncan Christopher. b 64. Warwick Univ BA90. Trin Coll Bris BA93. d 93 p 94. C Hornchurch St Andr Chelmsf 93-98; V Bicker Linc 98-00; V Donington 98-00; TV Woughton Ox 00-08. 61 Green Lane, Wolverton, Milton Keynes MK12 5HW Tel (01908) 226886 E-mail dbgreenleys@gmail.com

BARNES, Mrs Enid Mabel. b 38. Homerton Coll Cam Dip Teaching58. WMMTC 87. d 90 p 94. Par Dn Walsall St Paul Lich 90-94; C 94-96; TV Chell Heath 96-02; rtd 02; Perm to Offic Lich 02-04. 10 Hind Avenue, Breaston, Derby DE72 3DG Tel (01332) 873665 E-mail enidbarnes@hotmail.com

BARNES, Harvey Thomas. b 61. SWMTC 02. d 05 p 06. C Plympton St Mary Ex 05-08; P-in-c Whitchurch 08-09. 9 Dawlish Walk, Plymouth PL6 8PZ

BARNES, Miss Heather Dawn. b 75. Liv Hope BA96 PGCE97. Ridley Hall Cam 03. d 05 p 06. C Luton Lewsey St Hugh St Alb 05-09; P-in-c Hartshill and Galley Common Cov from 09. The New Vicarage, Church Road, Hartshill, Nuneaton CV10 0LY Tel (024) 7639 2266

BARNES, Mrs Helen Clark. b 61. Worc Coll of Educn BA82. Ox Min Course 07. d 10 p 11. NSM Haddenham w Cuddington, Kingsey etc Ox from 10. 30 Dovecote, Haddenham, Aylesbury HP17 8BP Tel (01844) 292595 E-mail helen.barnes19@btinternet.com

BARNES, Jennifer. b 45. Leeds Univ MA96. NOC 94. d 96 p 97. C Thorne Sheff 96-99; C Clifton St Jas 99-01; Chapl HM Pris Featherstone 01-04; Chapl HM YOI Swinfen Hall 04-05; P-in-c Barnsley St Edw Wakef 05-07; Chapl HM Pris and YOI New Hall 07-08; rtd 08; Perm to Offic Wakef 07-09; NSM Lundwood 09-11. Carlton House, 71 Woodhead Road, Honley, Holmfirth HD9 6PP Tel (01484) 660876 E-mail jbjcb@tiscali.co.uk

BARNES, Jeremy Paul Blissard. b 70. Southn Univ BSc92. Wycliffe Hall Ox BTh99. d 99 p 00. C Brompton H Trin w Onslow Square St Paul Lon 99-05; C Shadwell St Paul w Ratcliffe St Jas 05-09; V E Twickenham St Steph from 09. 17 Claremont Road, Twickenham TW1 2QX

BARNES, Canon John Barwick. b 32. AKC58. d 59 p 60. C Brentwood St Thos Chelmsf 59-65; R Arkesden w Wicken Bonhunt 65-71; V Gt Ilford St Mary 71-99; Hon Can Chelmsf Cathl 95-99; rtd 99; Perm to Offic Chelmsf from 99. 352 Henley Road, Ilford IG1 1TJ Tel (020) 8478 1954

BARNES, John Christopher. b 43. MA ATI. Linc Th Coll 78. d 80 p 81. C Guiseley Bradf 80-83; TV Guiseley w Esholt 83-86; V Rawdon 86-92; R Armthorpe Sheff 92-98; TR Maltby 98-01; RD Doncaster 96-98; Hon Can Sheff Cathl 00-01; TR Blakenall Heath Lich 01-05; P-in-c Gomersal Wakef 05-09; P-in-c Cleckheaton St Jo 08-09; rtd 09; P-in-c Lundwood Wakef 09-11. Carlton House, 71 Woodhead Road, Honley, Holmfirth HD9 6PP Tel (01484) 660876 E-mail jbjcb@tiscali.co.uk

BARNES, John Seymour. b 30. Qu Coll Birm 58. d 61 p 62. C Bromsgrove St Jo Worc 61-64; C Kingsthorpe Pet 64-66; C

Styvechale *Cov* 66-69; P-in-c Avon Dassett w Farnborough 69-75; P-in-c Cov St Alb 75-84; R Weddington and Caldecote 84-89; P-in-c Wilnecote *Lich* 89-90; V Bentley 90-96; rtd 96; Perm to Offic *Lich* 96-04. *10 Hind Avenue, Breaston, Derby DE72 3DG* Tel (01332) 873665

BARNES, Jules Ann. b 60. St Mary's Coll Dur BA83 Dur Univ MSc84 RGN95. Ripon Coll Cuddesdon 08. d 10 p 11. C Wilton w Netherhampton and Fugglestone *Sarum* from 10. *Dairy Cottage, Netherhampton, Salisbury SP2 8PJ* Tel (01722) 743395 E-mail barnesjules@hotmail.com

BARNES, Canon Katrina Crawford. b 52. K Coll Lon BA98 AKC98. Oak Hill Th Coll 90. d 93 p 94. NSM Bromley H Trin *Roch* 93-98; C Meopham w Nurstead 98-00; Assoc Staff Tutor SEITE 99-03; R Longfield *Roch* 01-06; V Bromley Common St Aug from 06; Bp's Adv for Ord Women's Min from 05; Hon Can Roch Cathl from 05. *St Augustine's Vicarage, Southborough Lane, Bromley BR2 8AT* Tel (020) 8467 1351 E-mail katrina.barnes@diocese-rochester.org

BARNES, Lee. b 74. Trin Coll Bris BA03 MA09. d 09 p 10. C Malmesbury w Westport and Brokenborough *Bris* from 09; C Gt Somerford, Lt Somerford, Seagry, Corston etc from 09. *1 Park Close, Malmesbury SN16 0EB* Tel (01666) 823371 Mobile 07959-467359 E-mail mrleebarnes@gmail.com

BARNES, Mrs Mary Jane. b 48. St Jo Coll Nottm 97. d 99 p 00. C Harefield *Lon* 99-02; TV New Windsor *Ox* 02-10; C from 10; P-in-c Old Windsor from 10. *The Vicarage, Church Road, Old Windsor, Windsor SL4 2PQ* Tel (01753) 865778 Mobile 07930-337407 E-mail mary@harefield9.fsnet.co.uk

BARNES, Matthew John. b 68. Leeds Univ MA99. St Jo Coll Nottm BA93. d 96 p 97. C Stanley *Wakef* 96-99; TV N Wingfield, Clay Cross and Pilsley *Derby* 99-08; R Brampton St Thos from 08. *The Rectory, 674 Chatsworth Road, Chesterfield S40 3NU* Tel (01246) 567634 Mobile 07977-976348

BARNES, Neal Duncan. b 63. Leeds Univ BSc84 Cranfield Inst of Tech PhD92. Oak Hill Th Coll 93. d 95 p 96. C Biggleswade *St Alb* 95-99; V Anlaby St Pet *York* 99-10; P-in-c Kingston upon Hull H Trin from 10; Hon Chapl Ambulance Service Hull from 99. *Holy Trinity Vicarage, 66 Pearson Park, Hull HU5 2TQ* E-mail neal@anvic.karoo.co.uk

BARNES, Canon Neil. b 42. Kelham Th Coll 61 Bps' Coll Cheshunt 65. d 68 p 69. C Poulton-le-Fylde *Blackb* 68-72; C Ribbleton 72-75; V Knuzden 75-81; Chapl Prestwich Hosp Man 81-88; Chapl Salford Mental Health Services NHS Trust 88-04; Manager Chapl Services 94-04; Hon Can Man Cathl 96-04; rtd 04; Perm to Offic *Blackb* and *Man* from 04. *Leads Cottage, Bacup Road, Cliviger, Burnley BB11 3QZ.* Tel (01282) 451533 E-mail neilbarnes@bigfoot.com

BARNES, Paul. See BYLLAM-BARNES, Preb Paul William Marshall

BARNES, Paul Nicholas. b 58. Qu Coll Birm 89. d 91 p 92. C Weymouth H Trin *Sarum* 91-95; P-in-c Studley 95-07; P-in-c Mere w W Knoyle and Maiden Bradley from 07. *The Vicarage, Angel Lane, Mere, Warminster BA12 6DH* Tel (01747) 863313

BARNES, Peter Frank. b 52. St Jo Coll Nottm LTh81. d 81 p 82. C Colne St Bart *Blackb* 81-83; C Melton Mowbray w Thorpe Arnold *Leic* 83-86; P-in-c Barlestone 86-89; V Broughton and Duddon *Carl* 89-98; V Shrewsbury St Geo w Greenfields *Lich* 98-08; P-in-c Bicton, Montford w Shrawardine and Fitz 98-00; P-in-c Myddle from 08; P-in-c Broughton from 08; P-in-c Loppington w Newtown from 08. *The Rectory, Myddle, Shrewsbury SY4 3RX* Tel (01939) 291801 E-mail peter.barnes@lineone.net

BARNES, Philip John. b 52. Cant Ch Ch Univ BA08. SEITE 01. d 04 p 05. NSM Gravesend St Mary *Roch* 04-06; C Gravesend St Aid 06-09; TV S Gillingham from 09. *58 Parkwood Green, Gillingham ME8 9PP* Tel (01634) 306806 Mobile 07764-151833 E-mail philip.barnes@diocese-rochester.org

BARNES, Philip Richard. b 73. Westmr Coll Ox BTh94 Heythrop Coll Lon MA99. St Steph Ho Ox 98. d 00 p 01. C Ruislip St Martin *Lon* 00-03; Shrine P Shrine of Our Lady of Walsingham 03-08; V Northwood Hills St Edm *Lon* from 08. *St Edmund's Vicarage, 2 Pinner Road, Northwood HA6 1QS* Tel (020) 8866 9230 E-mail frphilipbarnes@btinternet.com

BARNES, Robin James. b 52. d 05 p 06. NSM Debenham and Helmingham *St E* from 05. *119 Gardeners Road, Debenham, Stowmarket IP14 6RZ* Tel (01728) 861498 E-mail robin@rbarnes.fsnet.co.uk

BARNES, Roland Peter. b 59. Ban Ord Course 01. d 03 p 04. NSM Bro Ddyfi Uchaf *Ban* from 03; P-in-c from 05. *Y Rheithordy, Mallwyd, Machynlleth SY20 9HJ* Tel (01650) 531650

BARNES, Stephen. b 46. Hull Univ BA69. Clifton Th Coll 69. d 72 p 73. C Girlington *Bradf* 72-74; TV Glyncorrwg w Afan Vale and Cymmer Afan *Llan* 74-79; R 79-86; V Aberavon 86-01; V Dulais Valley from 01. *The Vicarage, 86 Church Road, Seven Sisters, Neath SA10 9DT* Tel and fax (01639) 700286 E-mail stephen.cwmdulais@btinternet.com

BARNES, Stephen John. b 59. Univ of Wales (Cardiff) BSc80. Chich Th Coll 83. d 86 p 87. C Neath w Llantwit 86-89; C Coity

w Nolton 89-95; V Troedyrhiw w Merthyr Vale from 95. *The Vicarage, Nixonville, Merthyr Vale, Merthyr Tydfil CF48 4RF* Tel (01443) 690249

BARNES, Stephen William. b 53. Man Univ BSc. St Jo Coll Nottm. d 83 p 84. C Chadwell Heath *Chelmsf* 83-87; C Becontree St Alb 88-89; Deanery Youth Chapl 88-91; C Becontree S 89-91; TV Worth *Chich* 91-98; Chapl Willen Hospice Milton Keynes from 99. *90 Bradwell Road, Bradville, Milton Keynes MK13 7AD* E-mail chaplain@willen-hospice.org.uk

BARNES, Mrs Sylvia Frances. b 43. Shoreditch Coll Lon CertEd75. S Tr Scheme 92. d 96 p 97. Hon C Cusop w Blakemere, Bredwardine w Brobury etc *Heref* from 96. *Pwll Cwm, Arthur's Stone Lane, Dorstone, Hereford HR3 6AY* Tel (01981) 500252

BARNES, Thomas. See BARNES, Canon William Thomas

BARNES, Timothy. b 56. Birm Univ BSc78. Westcott Ho Cam 96 Lon Bible Coll 82. d 98 p 99. C Shrub End *Chelmsf* 98-02; V Leigh-on-Sea St Aid 02-11; P-in-c Bocking St Pet from 11. *The House, The Street, Bradwell, Braintree CM77 8EL* Tel (01376) 563800 E-mail timbarnes1@btinternet.com

BARNES, William Joseph Athanasius. b 57. St Andr Univ MTheol84 Newc Univ MA02 RGN89. Westcott Ho Cam 91. d 92 p 93. C S Bank *York* 92-95; C Northallerton w Kirby Sigston 95-97; V Dormanstown 97-01; P-in-c Netherton St Andr *Worc* 01-06; P-in-c Darby End 03-06. *20 Cropton Close, Redcar TS10 4HU* Tel (01642) 471772 E-mail bja.barnes@btopenworld.com

BARNES, Canon William Thomas. b 39. Dur Univ BA60. Wycliffe Hall Ox 60. d 62 p 63. C Scotforth *Blackb* 62-66; C Cleveleys 66-67; V Colne Ch 67-74; V Bamber Bridge St Sav 74-04; Hon Can Blackb Cathl 00-04; rtd 04; Perm to Offic *Blackb* from 04. *12 Little Close, Farington Moss, Leyland PR26 6QU* Tel (01772) 457646 E-mail tom.beryl.barnes@hotmail.co.uk

BARNES-CLAY, Peter John Granger. b 43. Cam Univ CertEd69 MCollP. Chich Th Coll 72. d 75 p 82. C Earlham St Anne *Nor* 75-76; Asst Master Hewett Sch Nor 76-83; Chapl Nor Cathl from 80; Hon C Eaton 81-83; C 83-87; R Winterton w E and W Somerton and Horsey 87-92; R Weybourne Gp 92-03; RD Holt 95-02; rtd 03; Perm to Offic *Nor* 03-05; C Smallburgh w Dilham w Honing and Crostwight 05-06; P-in-c 06-08; Perm to Offic from 08. *Hunters End, 1 Danby Close, Eaton Rise, Norwich NR4 6RH* Tel (01603) 501199 E-mail becketsthree1@aol.com

BARNETT, Alec James Leon. b 44. Em Coll Cam BA66 MA70 PGCE71. Cuddesdon Coll 66. d 69 p 70. C Preston St Jo *Blackb* 69-72; Asst Master Hutton Grammar Sch 70-72; Asst Chapl Uppingham Sch 72-80; Hd of RE 72-80; Dir of Farmington/Ampleforth Project 79-83; C Witney *Ox* 80-84; P-in-c Lt Compton w Chastleton, Cornwell etc 84-88; Prin Ox Chr Tr Scheme 84-88; P-in-c St Michael Penkevil *Truro* 88-95; P-in-c Lamorran and Merther 88-95; Dioc Tr Officer 88-95; Chapl Strasbourg *Eur* 95-01; Abp Cant's Rep at Eur Inst from 95; Perm to Offic *Truro* from 95; rtd 01. *7 rue des Magnolias, La Croix, 17800 St Léger, France* Tel (0033) 5 46 94 99 25 Fax 5 46 94 95 01 E-mail james.barnett@wanadoo.fr

BARNETT, Ann. See BARNETT, Miss Patricia Ann

BARNETT, David John. b 33. Magd Coll Ox BA56 MA61. St Steph Ho Ox BA58. d 59 p 60. C Styvechale *Cov* 59-62; Chapl Rhodes Univ S Africa 62-68; P-in-c Grahamstown St Bart 62-68; Lic to Offic Cape Town 68-69; Chapl and Lect Univ of Rhodesia 70-76; V Colindale St Matthias *Lon* 77-90; R Finchley St Mary 90-98; rtd 98; Perm to Offic *Ex* 98-08. *2 Curlew Way, Exeter EX4 4SW* Tel (01392) 431486

BARNETT, Dudley Graham. b 36. Ch Ch Ox BA62 MA65. St Steph Ho Ox 62. d 64 p 65. C Abbey Hey *Man* 64-68; V Swinton H Rood 68-90; R Old Trafford St Hilda 90-01; R Firswood and Gorse Hill 01-02; rtd 02; Perm to Offic *Man* from 02. *6A Gilda Crescent Road, Eccles, Manchester M30 9AG* Tel 0161-707 9767

BARNETT, James. See BARNETT, Alec James Leon

BARNETT, James Andrew McWilliam. b 76. Leeds Univ BA99. Trin Coll Bris BA01. d 02 p 03. C Bolton St Paul w Em *Man* 02-05; TV Leeds St Geo *Ripon* 05-10; Pioneer Min to New Communities from 10. *14 Parkside Green, Leeds LS6 4NY* Tel 0113-243 8498 Mobile 07747-892192

BARNETT, John. See BARNETT, David John

BARNETT, John Raymond. b 51. Lon Univ LLB74 BD86 Birm Univ MA98. Westcott Ho Cam 74. d 77 p 78. C Northfield *Birm* 77-81; V Hamstead St Bernard 81-91; R The Quinton 91-03; AD Edgbaston 98-03; P-in-c Oldbury 03-07; P-in-c Langley St Jo 03-07; P-in-c Langley St Mich 03-07; P-in-c Londonderry 04-07; V Oldbury, Langley and Londonderry 07-09; Hon Can Birm Cathl 01-09; P-in-c Darlaston All SS *Lich* from 09; Inter-Faith Officer Wolverhampton Area from 09. *All Saints' Vicarage, 255 Walsall Road, Wednesbury WS10 9SQ* Tel 0121-552 6898 Mobile 07969-114132 E-mail barnett4@jajolohe.freeserve.co.uk

BARNETT, John Richard. b 28. Open Univ BA99. Portsm Dioc Tr Course 86. d 88 p 98. NSM Droxford and Meonstoke w

Corhampton cum Exton *Portsm* 88-91; NSM W Meon and Warnford 91-01; rtd 01. *5 The Croft, 10 St Annes Road, Eastbourne BN21 2DL* Tel (01323) 731711

BARNETT (*née* JACKSON), **Mrs Lisa Helen.** b 79. Reading Univ BA(Ed)01 Cam Univ BA06. Ridley Hall Cam 04. **d** 07 **p** 08. C Patcham *Chich* 07-11; P-in-c Scaynes Hill from 11. *The Vicarage, Vicarage Lane, Scaynes Hill, Haywards Heath RH17 7PB* Tel (01444) 831827 Mobile 07989-761575 E-mail revlisa@btinternet.com

BARNETT, Michael. *See* BARNETT, Preb Raymond Michael

BARNETT, Miss Patricia Ann. b 38. Whitelands Coll Lon CertEd. St Jo Coll Dur 75. **dss** 78 **d** 87 **p** 94. Gateacre *Liv* 78-82; Litherland St Paul Hatton Hill 82-88; Par Dn 87-88; Par Dn Platt Bridge 88-94; C 94-95; V Skelmersdale Ch at Cen 95-98; rtd 98; Perm to Offic *Liv* from 00. *93 Alder Hey Road, St Helens WA10 4DW* Tel (01744) 607609

BARNETT, Peter Geoffrey. b 46. AKC71. St Aug Coll Cant 71. **d** 72 **p** 73. C Wolverhampton *Lich* 72-77; P-in-c Caldmore 77-83; TR Bris St Agnes and St Simon w St Werburgh 83-87; P-in-c Bris St Paul w St Barn 83-87; TR Bris St Paul's 87-94; Warden Pilsdon Community 94-04; Ewell Monastery from 04. *Ewell Monastery, Water Lane, West Malling, Maidstone ME19 6HH* Tel (01732) 843089 Fax 870279 E-mail community@ewell-monastery.co.uk

BARNETT, Preb Raymond Michael. b 31. Man Univ BA54. Wells Th Coll 54. **d** 56 **p** 57. C Fallowfield *Man* 56-59; Madagascar 59-60; V Blackrod *Man* 60-67; V Woolavington *B & W* 67-76; RD Bridgwater 72-76; V St Decumans 76-96; RD Quantock 78-86 and 93-95; Preb Wells Cathl 89-96; rtd 96; Perm to Offic *B & W* 96-08. *22 Fosbrooke House, Clifton Drive, Lytham St Annes FY8 5RQ*

BARNETT-COWAN, Bruce Edgar. b 52. BA MDiv. **d** 78 **p** 78. R Schefferville Canada 78-83; Co-President Henry Budd Coll for Min 83-91; P-in-c Runnymede St Paul 92-02; Interim P Toronto St Clem w St Matt 03-07; Interim P Coldwater-Medonte 08-09; NSM Ealing All SS *Lon* from 10; NSM W Acton St Martin from 10. *St Martin's Cottage, Hale Gardens, London W3 9SQ* Tel (020) 8896 9009 E-mail bruce_barnett_cowan@hotmail.com

BARNFATHER, Thomas Fenwick. b 52. Cant Ch Ch Univ BSc09. Linc Th Coll 86. **d** 88 **p** 89. C Sedgefield *Dur* 88-91; TV E Darlington 91-92; CF 92-96; V Heybridge w Langford *Chelmsf* 96-98; Chapl HM YOI Dover 98-00; Chapl HM Pris Swaleside 00-01; P-in-c Aylesham w Adisham *Cant* 01-04; Asst Dir of Ords 02-05; Perm to Offic 04-09; P-in-c Westgate St Sav from 09. *Vicarage, Thanet Road, Westgate on Sea CT8 8PB* Tel (01843) 832717 E-mail tom_barnfather@btinternet.com

BARNSHAW, Anthony James. b 72. Man Univ BA97. St Jo Coll Nottm 03. **d** 05 **p** 06. C Kersal Moor *Man* 05-08; TV Ramsbottom and Edenfield from 08. *The Vicarage, 16 Maple Grove, Ramsbottom, Bury BL0 0AN* Tel (01706) 821036 E-mail a.barnshaw@btopenworld.com

BARNSLEY, Mrs Angela Vera. b 47. St Hild Coll Dur BA70. St Alb Minl Tr Scheme 90. **d** 93. NSM Codicote *St Alb* 93-94. *Address temp unknown*

BARNSLEY, David Edward. b 75. Ox Brookes Univ BSc97. Oak Hill Th Coll BA03. **d** 03 **p** 04. C Kilnhurst *Sheff* 03-06; C Duffield and Lt Eaton *Derby* from 06. *107 Duffield Road, Little Eaton, Derby DE21 5DT* Tel (01332) 843177 E-mail davidb@rnsley.freeserve.co.uk

BARNSLEY, Canon Melvyn. b 46. Dur Univ BA67 Lon Univ CertEd. St Chad's Coll Dur 64. **d** 71 **p** 72. C Cov St Thos 71-74; C Cov St Jo 71-75; V New Bilton 75-82; R Stevenage St Andr and St Geo *St Alb* from 82; RD Stevenage 89-99; Hon Can St Alb from 00. *The Rectory, Cuttys Lane, Stevenage SG1 1UP* Tel (01438) 351631

BARNSTAPLE, Archdeacon of. *See* GUNN-JOHNSON, The Ven David Allan

BARON, Thomas Michael. b 63. St Steph Ho Ox 85. **d** 88 **p** 89. C Hartlepool St Paul *Dur* 88-92; Chapl Asst Hartlepool Gen Hosp 89-92; Asst Chapl Whittington Hosp Lon 92-95; Chapl Enfield Community Care NHS Trust 95-01; Chapl Chase Farm Hosps NHS Trust 95-99; Chapl Barnet and Chase Farm Hosps NHS Trust from 99; Chapl Barnet, Enfield and Haringey Mental Health Trust from 01; Chapl Enfield Primary Care Trust from 01. *The Chaplaincy, Chase Farm Hospital, The Ridgeway, Enfield EN2 8JL* Tel (020) 8375 1078 *or* 8882 1195 E-mail frtom.baron@btinternet.com

BARON, Mrs Vanessa Lillian. b 57. City Univ BSc79 Fitzw Coll Cam BA84 MA85 Birkbeck Coll Lon MA06 SRN79. Ridley Hall Cam 83. **dss** 86 **d** 87 **p** 94. Roxbourne St Andr *Lon* 86-89; Par Dn 87-89; NSM Roxeth 92-95; Lic Preacher from 95; Asst Chapl Harrow Sch 95-04; Chapl St Paul's Girls' Sch Hammersmith from 04. *2 Kennet House, Harrow Park, Harrow HA1 3JE* Tel (020) 8872 8182 *or* 7603 2288 E-mail vbaron@spgs.org

BARR, Alan. b 59. TCD BTh07. **d** 07 **p** 08. C Bray *D & G* 07-09; I Sixmilecross w Termonmaguirke *Arm* from 09. *St Michael's Rectory, 104 Cooley Road, Sixmilecross, Omagh BT79 9DH* Tel (028) 8075 7097 Mobile 87-948 4408 E-mail alnbarr@gmail.com *or* sixmilecross@armagh.anglican.org

BARR, John. *See* BARR, Michael John Alexander

BARR (*née* HAYTER), **Mary Elizabeth.** b 58. Jes Coll Ox BA80 CertEd81 MA84 Qu Coll Ox DPhil85. Ridley Hall Cam 84. **dss** 86 **d** 87 **p** 94. Chapl Cam Univ Pastorate 86-91; Cambridge H Trin w St Andr Gt *Ely* 86-87; Par Dn 87-91; Perm to Offic 91-92; Perm to Offic *Ex* 92-94; NSM Torquay St Luke 94-97; NSM Gt Malvern St Mary *Worc* from 97; Chapl Worcs Community Healthcare NHS Trust 99-01; Chapl Worcs Community and Mental Health Trust from 01. *Priory Vicarage, Clarence Road, Malvern WR14 3EN* Tel and fax (01684) 563707 *or* 561020 E-mail jmbarr@ukonline.co.uk *or* office@greatmalvernpriory.org.uk

BARR, Michael John Alexander. b 60. Qu Coll Ox BA82 MA86 Pemb Coll Cam BA86 MA90. Ridley Hall Cam 84. **d** 87 **p** 88. C Earley St Pet *Ox* 87-89; C Cambridge Gt St Mary w St Mich *Ely* 89-92; Chapl Girton Coll Cam 90-92; P-in-c Torquay St Luke *Ex* 92-97; Dioc Communications Officer 92-97; P-in-c Gt Malvern St Mary *Worc* 97-99; V from 99; RD Malvern 01-07. *Priory Vicarage, Clarence Road, Malvern WR14 3EN* Tel and fax (01684) 563707 *or* 561020 E-mail jmbarr@ukonline.co.uk *or* office@greatmalvernpriory.org.uk

BARR, Norma Margaret. b 41. Trin Coll Bris BA99. **d** 00 **p** 01. C Aberdour *St And* 01-03; P-in-c Pontiac Grace Ch USA 03-05. *3300 W Kinnickinnic Rover Parkway, Apartment #2, Milwaukee WI 53215, USA* E-mail normabarr@gmail.com

BARR-HAMILTON, Nicholas James. b 74. Oak Hill Th Coll. **d** 08 **p** 09. C Linthorpe *York* from 08. *26 Emerson Avenue, Middlesbrough TS5 7QH* Tel (01642) 813386 E-mail nickbarr-hamilton@o2.co.uk

BARRACLOUGH, Mrs Barbara Amanda Juliet. b 61. Stirling Univ BA83 Ches Coll of HE MA00. NOC 97. **d** 00 **p** 01. C Lupset *Wakef* 00-04; V W Ardsley from 04. *Woodkirk Vicarage, 1168 Dewsbury Road, Dewsbury WF12 7JL* Tel (01924) 472375 Fax 475758 Mobile 07890-614579 E-mail amanda.barraclough1@btinternet.com

BARRACLOUGH, Dennis. b 35. St Jo Coll York CertEd58 Lambeth STh68 LCP62 FCP74. Ripon Hall Ox 66. **d** 68 **p** 69. C Woodhouse *Wakef* 68-71; V Gildersome 71-83; V Kirkburton 83-00; RD Kirkburton 92-98; rtd 00; Perm to Offic *Wakef* from 00. *8 Clough Park, Fenay Bridge, Huddersfield HD8 0JH* Tel (01484) 325515

BARRACLOUGH, Canon Owen Conrad. b 32. Pemb Coll Cam BA55 MA59. Westcott Ho Cam 56. **d** 57 **p** 58. C Chippenham St Andr w Tytherton Lucas *Bris* 57-62; V Harringay St Paul *Lon* 62-70; Bp's Chapl for Community Relns *Cov* 70-77; P-in-c Baginton 72-77; V Swindon Ch Ch *Bris* 77-97; Chapl Princess Marg Hosp Swindon 77-89; Hon Can Bris Cathl 87-97; rtd 98; Perm to Offic *Bris* from 98 and *Glouc* 98-01; Jt P-in-c Staverton w Boddington and Tredington etc *Glouc* 01-04; Hon C Twigworth, Down Hatherley, Norton, The Leigh etc 04-06; Hon C Leckhampton SS Phil and Jas w Cheltenham St Jas 06-09; Hon C S Cheltenham 10-11. *Robin Hollow, 10A Church Road, St Marks, Cheltenham GL51 7AN* Tel (01242) 230855 E-mail obarraclough@btinternet.com

BARRAND, George William (Bill). b 33. Lon Coll of Div 59. **d** 62 **p** 63. C Bucknall and Bagnall *Lich* 62-65; C Parr *Liv* 65-69; Australia from 70; rtd 98. *2/20 Riversdale Road, Yarra Junction Vic 3797, Australia* Tel (0061) (3) 5967 2592

BARRAS, June. **d** 10 **p** 11. OLM Warkworth and Acklington *Newc* from 10. *8 St Omer Road, Acklington, Morpeth NE65 9DA* Tel (01670) 760650

BARRATT, Mrs Elizabeth June. b 32. ACP65. Trin Coll Bris 75. **dss** 78 **d** 87 **p** 94. W Kilburn St Luke w St Simon and St Jude *Lon* 78-87; Par Dn 87-94; C 94-98; rtd 98; Hon C Kensal Rise St Mark and St Martin *Lon* 99-11; Hon C Kensal Rise St Martin from 11. *68A Bathhurst Gardens, London NW10 5HY* Tel (020) 8968 5951 Mobile 07763-474602 E-mail ejbarratt@hotmail.co.uk

BARRATT, Philip Norman. b 62. Aston Tr Scheme 87 St Steph Ho Ox 89 Coll of Resurr Mirfield 90. **d** 92 **p** 93. C Heywood St Luke w All So *Man* 92-96; V Thornham St Jas from 96. *St James's Vicarage, 129 Shaw Road, Rochdale OL16 4SQ* Tel (01706) 645256 Mobile 07775-646733 E-mail pn.barratt@zen.co.uk

BARRELL, Adrian Edward. b 36. Keble Coll Ox BA59. Ely Th Coll 59. **d** 62 **p** 63. C Plymouth St Jas Ham *Ex* 62-66; C Bideford 66-70; V Walkhampton 70-80; rtd 01. *Cartref, Dousland, Yelverton PL20 6PA* Tel (01822) 852612

BARRETT, Alan. b 48. Southn Univ BA69. Wycliffe Hall Ox 74. **d** 77 **p** 78. C Conisbrough *Sheff* 77-80; C Lower Homerton St Paul *Lon* 80-81; C-in-c Hounslow Gd Shep Beavers Lane CD 81-87; R Langdon Hills *Chelmsf* 87-97; P-in-c Tamworth *Lich* 97-03; V from 03; RD Tamworth 99-04. *The Vicarage, Hospital Street, Tamworth B79 7EE* Tel and fax (01827) 62446 *or* tel 68339 E-mail alan.barrett@breathemail.net

BARRETT, Alastair David. b 75. Fitzw Coll Cam BA97 MA01 Birm Univ BD00. Qu Coll Birm MA01. **d** 01 **p** 02. C Sutton Coldfield St Chad *Birm* 01-04; C Oldbury, Langley and Londonderry 04-10; P-in-c Hodge Hill from 10. *8 Dreghorn Road, Hodge Hill, Birmingham B36 8LJ* Tel 0121-747 6982 E-mail hodgehillvicar@hotmail.co.uk

BARRETT, Mrs Alexandra Mary. b 75. Clare Coll Cam BA96 MA99. Westcott Ho Cam 00. **d** 03 **p** 04. C Godmanchester *Ely* 03-07; R Buckden w the Offords from 07. *The Vicarage, Church Street, Buckden, St Neots PE19 5TL* Tel (01480) 810371 Mobile 07896-175631 E-mail ally.barrett@ely.anglican.org

BARRETT, Arthur. *See* BARRETT, Kenneth Arthur Lambart

BARRETT, Mrs Brigid. b 44. RN90. STETS MA11. **d** 11. NSM Parkstone St Pet and St Osmund w Branksea *Sarum* from 11. *1 Wyatts Lane, Wareham BH20 4NH* Tel (01929) 553460 E-mail brigidbrrtt@gmail.com

BARRETT, Christopher Paul. b 49. AKC71 St Aug Coll Cant 71. **d** 72 **p** 73. C Tupsley *Heref* 72-75; C Ex St Thos 75-79; R Atherington and High Bickington 79-83; V Burrington 79-83; Asst Dir of Educn 79-87; P-in-c Sticklepath 83-85; P-in-c Barnstaple 83-85; TV 85-90; V Whipton 90-99; TV Ex St Thos and Em 99-05; Chapl Burton Hosps NHS Trust from 05. *Queen's Hospital, Belvedere Road, Burton-on-Trent DE13 0RB* Tel (01283) 566333 *or* (01332) 516345 E-mail paul.barrett@burtonh-tr.wmids.nhs.uk

BARRETT, Clive. b 55. Ox Univ BA76 MA80 CertEd77 Leeds Univ PhD98. St Steph Ho Ox 80. **d** 83 **p** 84. C Wakef Cathl 83-87; Asst Chapl Leeds Univ 87-97; Dioc Development Rep 89-92; P-in-c Middleton St Cross 98-07; Co Ecum Development Officer W Yorks from 07; Hon C Headingley from 08. *West Yorkshire Ecumenical Council, Hinsley Hall, 62 Headingley Lane, Leeds LS6 2BX* Tel 0113-261 8053 Mobile 07966-540699 E-mail clivebarrett@wyec.co.uk

BARRETT, Canon Derek Leonard. b 25. St Fran Coll Brisbane ThL57. **d** 57 **p** 58. Australia 53-63; C Ramsgate St Geo *Cant* 64-65; C Putney St Mary *S'wark* 65-67; V Kidderminster St Jo *Worc* 67-77; V Stourbridge St Thos 77-90; RD Stourbridge 83-89; Hon Can Worc Cathl 87-90; rtd 90; Perm to Offic *Glouc* and *Worc* 90-02. *Lotty Leven, Crystal Waters, M/S 16, Maleny Qld 4552, Australia* Tel (0061) (7) 5494 4710

BARRETT, Mrs Diane Joan. b 46. **d** 10. OLM Bolton St Bede *Man* from 10; OLM Lostock St Thos and St Jo from 10. *6 Whitland Avenue, Bolton BL1 5FB* Tel (01204) 847870 E-mail dianejoanbarrett@sky.com

BARRETT, Gary John. b 46. Sarum & Wells Th Coll 87. **d** 90 **p** 91. NSM Guernsey St Peter Port *Win* 90-97; Chapl Eliz Coll Guernsey 93-97; P-in-c Westham *Chich* 97-98; V from 98. *The Vicarage, 6 Rattle Road, Westham, Pevensey BN24 5DE* Tel (01323) 762294

BARRETT, John Joseph James. b 38. Lon Univ BD65. Sarum & Wells Th Coll. **d** 78 **p** 78. C Danbury *Chelmsf* 78-80; Ind Chapl 80-89; C Dovercourt 80-83; TV Dovercourt and Parkeston 83-89; V Rubery *Birm* 89-04; rtd 04; Perm to Offic *Sheff* from 04. *4 Arran Hill, Thrybergh, Rotherham S65 4BH* Tel (01709) 850288 E-mail rev.barrett@btinternet.com

BARRETT, Jonathan Murray. b 68. Oak Hill Th Coll BA98. **d** 98 **p** 99. C Pennycross *Ex* 98-02; TV Plymouth Em, St Paul Efford and St Aug 02-08; V Thurnby w Stoughton *Leic* from 08. *The Vicarage, Thurnby, Leicester LE7 9PN* Tel 0116-241 2263

BARRETT, Canon Kenneth. b 42. Univ of Wales (Lamp) BA64. St Steph Ho Ox 65. **d** 67 **p** 68. C Poulton-le-Fylde *Blackb* 67-69; C S Shore H Trin 69-72; V Brierfield 72-83; V Chorley St Geo 83-07; Hon Can Blackb Cathl 03-07; rtd 07; Perm to Offic *Blackb* from 07. *24 Astley Road, Chorley PR7 1RR* Tel (01257) 233421

BARRETT, Kenneth Arthur Lambart. b 60. CITC BTh94. **d** 97 **p** 98. C Seagoe *D & D* 97-00; I Dublin Booterstown *D & G* 00-04; I Dublin Mt Merrion 00-04; I Boyle and Elphin w Aghanagh, Kilbryan etc *K, E & A* 04-08; I Taunagh w Kilmactranny, Ballysumaghan etc 04-08; I Rossorry *Clogh* from 08; Dir of Ords from 11. *Rossorry Rectory, Rossorry, Enniskillen BT74 7JZ* Tel (028) 6632 0239

BARRETT, Canon Kenneth Sydney. b 26. Roch Th Coll 60. **d** 62 **p** 63. C Wollaton *S'well* 62-65; C Hucknall Torkard 65-67; R Collie Australia 67-73; R Mandurah 73-92; Can Bunbury 76-92; rtd 92. *PO Box 818, 2 Loxton Street, Mandurah WA 6210, Australia* Tel and fax (0061) (8) 9581 2519 E-mail joykenb@westnet.com.au

BARRETT, Mrs Marion Lily. b 54. Ex Univ BA01 SRN75. SWMTC 91. **d** 94 **p** 95. C St Mawgan w St Ervan and St Eval *Truro* 94-97; C St Breoke and Egloshayle 97-98; Asst Chapl R Cornwall Hosps Trust 98-99; Chapl 00-05; R St Mewan w Mevagissey and St Ewe *Truro* from 05; RD St Austell from 10. *The Rectory, St Mewan Lane, St Mewan, St Austell PL26 7DP* Tel (01726) 72679 E-mail marionstmewan@btinternet.com

BARRETT, Paul. *See* BARRETT, Christopher Paul

BARRETT, Mrs Rachel Jeanne Alexandra. b 56. Ex Univ BA78 PGCE79. SWMTC 92. **d** 95 **p** 96. NSM Ex St Mark 95-96; NSM Ex St Mark, St Sidwell and St Matt 96-00; Chapl St Margaret's Sch Ex 00-05; Chapl Derby High Sch from 05. *Derby High*

School, Hillsway, Littleover, Derby DE23 3DT Tel (01332) 514267 Fax 516085

BARRETT, Robert David. b 48. **d** 11. OLM Alford w Rigsby *Linc* from 11. *14 East Street, Alford LN13 9EQ* Tel (01507) 462135 E-mail frbob@btinternet.com

BARRETT, Ronald Reginald. b 30. Roch Th Coll 61. **d** 64 **p** 65. C Spring Park *Cant* 64-66; C Thornton Heath St Jude 66-68; V Greengates *Bradf* 68-73; V Shelf 73-79; V Embsay w Eastby 79-87; V Farndon and Coddington *Ches* 87-92; rtd 92; Perm to Offic *Bradf* 92-10 and *Man* from 10. *27 Rivington Road, Springhead, Oldham OL4 4RJ* Tel (0161) 620 8124

BARRETT, Stephen David Norman. b 54. Aber Univ BSc75 Edin Univ BD78. Edin Th Coll 75. **d** 78 **p** 79. C Ardrossan *Glas* 78-80; R Peterhead *Ab* 80-81; Chapl HM Pris Peterhead 80-81; R Renfrew *Glas* 81-87; R Bishopbriggs 87-94; Chapl HM Pris Glas (Barlinnie) 87-94; Chapl Stobhill Gen Hosp 87-94; P-in-c Port Glas 94-99; R 99-08; rtd 08; Perm to Offic *Glas* from 09. *9 Birnock Avenue, Renfrew PA4 0YW* Tel 0141-886 6796

BARRETT, Mrs Susan Lesley. b 56. E Sussex Coll of HE CertEd77 BEd78. WMMTC 03. **d** 06. NSM Bowbrook N *Worc* 06-07; NSM Droitwich Spa 07-10; NSM Ombersley w Doverdale from 10; NSM Hartlebury from 10; NSM Elmley Lovett w Hampton Lovett and Elmbridge etc from 10. *55-57 High Street, Feckenham, Redditch B96 6HU* Tel and fax (01527) 893866 Mobile 07717-412441 E-mail sue@artmetal.co.uk

BARRIBAL, Richard James Pitt. b 45. Trin Coll Bris. **d** 80 **p** 81. C Northampton St Giles *Pet* 80-82; V Long Buckby w Watford 82-86; Perm to Offic *Pet* 86-00 and *Leic* 00-08; P-in-c Welham, Glooston and Cranoe and Stonton Wyville *Leic* 08-10. *45 Knights End Road, Great Bowden, Market Harborough LE16 7EY* Tel (01858) 431495 E-mail r.barribal@ntlworld.com

BARRIE, John Arthur. b 38. K Coll Lon 58 Bps' Coll Cheshunt 59. **d** 63 **p** 64. C Southgate St Mich *Lon* 63-66; CF 66-88; Sen CF 88-93; Chapl Guards Chpl Lon 88-92; QHC 91-93; P-in-c Heref H Trin 93-96; P-in-c Breinton 95-96; V St Marylebone St Mark Hamilton Terrace *Lon* 96-10; Ecum Adv Two Cities Area 99-10; rtd 10; Perm to Offic *Lon* from 10. *27 Strafford Road, Twickenham TW1 3AD* Tel (020) 8892 6847 E-mail john.barrie1@btopenworld.com

BARRIE, Mrs Rosemary Joan. b 62. Bris Univ BA83 PGCE84. Qu Coll Birm 87 Perkins Sch of Th (USA) 89. **d** 07 **p** 08. NSM W Kilburn St Luke and Kilburn St Mary w All So and W Hampstead St Jas *Lon* 07-08; NSM St Marylebone St Mark Hamilton Terrace 08-10; C Twickenham St Mary from 10; Chapl St Mary's Sch Twickenham from 10. *27 Strafford Road, Twickenham TW1 3AD* Tel (020) 8892 6847 E-mail rosybarrie1@btinternet.com

BARRINGTON, Dominic Matthew Jesse. b 62. Hatf Coll Dur BA84 MSc85 LTCL. Ripon Coll Cuddesdon BA94 MA98 Ch Div Sch of Pacific MTS95. **d** 95 **p** 96. C Mortlake w E Sheen *S'wark* 95-98; Chapl St Chad's Coll Dur 98-03; P-in-c Kettering SS Pet and Paul 03-10; R from 10. *The Rectory, Church Walk, Kettering NN16 0DJ* Tel and fax (01536) 513385 Mobile 07720-704953 E-mail dominic@peterandpaul.org.uk

✠**BARRINGTON-WARD, The Rt Revd Simon.** b 30. KCMG01. Magd Coll Cam BA53 MA57. Wycliffe Coll Toronto Hon DD Westcott Ho Cam 54. **d** 56 **p** 57 **c** 85. Chapl Magd Coll Cam 56-60; Nigeria 60-63; Fell and Dean of Chpl Magd Coll Cam 63-69; Prin Crowther Hall CMS Tr Coll Selly Oak 69-74; Gen Sec CMS 75-85; Hon Can Derby Cathl 75-85; Chapl to The Queen 84-85; Bp Cov 85-97; rtd 97; Hon Fell Magd Coll Cam 87; Hon Asst Chapl from 98; Hon Asst Bp Ely from 97. *4 Searle Street, Cambridge CB4 3DB* Tel (01223) 740460 E-mail sb292@cam.ac.uk

BARRODALE, Canon George Bryan. b 44. St Mich Coll Llan 67. **d** 69 **p** 70. C Maindee Newport *Mon* 69-72; TV Merthyr Tydfil and Cyfarthfa *Llan* 72-76; R Cotgrave and P-in-c Owthorpe *S'well* 76-00; RD Bingham 94-00; CF (TA) 76-86; V Beeston *S'well* 00-06; Hon Can S'well Minster 97-06; rtd 06; Perm to Offic *Linc* and *S'well* from 06. *2 Daphne Close, Branston, Lincoln LN4 1PQ* Tel (01522) 826381 E-mail canonbryan.barrodale@btinternet.com

BARRON, Arthur Henry. b 45. Solicitor 72. SEITE 99. **d** 02 **p** 03. NSM Addiscombe St Mary Magd w St Martin *S'wark* 02-06; Perm to Offic 06-07; NSM Woodmansterne from 07; Chapl Asst St Mary's NHS Trust Paddington 05-09; Chapl Guy's and St Thos' NHS Foundn Trust from 09. *23 Little Woodcote Lane, Purley CR8 3PZ* Tel (020) 8660 1921 Mobile 07710-275977 E-mail art.barron@hotmail.com *or* art.barron@gstt.nhs.uk

BARRON, John William. b 66. Imp Coll Lon BSc88. Cranmer Hall Dur 06. **d** 08 **p** 09. C Whickham *Dur* from 08. *7A Coalway Drive, Whickham, Newcastle upon Tyne NE16 4BT* Tel 0191-488 6661 E-mail john.barron@ntlworld.com

BARRON, Kurt Karl. b 60. Chich Th Coll BTh92. **d** 92 **p** 93. C Bulwell St Mary *S'well* 92-97; TV Southend *Chelmsf* 97-01; P-in-c Mansfield St Lawr *S'well* 01-08. *Address temp unknown* E-mail kurt.barron@btopenworld.com

BARRON, Leslie Gill. b 44. ACII69. Lich Th Coll 67. **d** 70 **p** 71. C Bishopwearmouth Ch Ch *Dur* 70-72; C Bishopwearmouth

St Mary V w St Pet CD 72-75; C Harton 75-77; V Lumley 77-88; P-in-c Hendon and Sunderland 88-90; R Hendon 90-94; P-in-c Ushaw Moor 94-95; V Bearpark and Ushaw Moor 95-04; rtd 08. *34 Brecongill Close, Hartlepool TS24 8PH* Tel (01429) 291197 E-mail l.barron@ntlworld.com

BARRON, Richard Davidson. b 51. Lon Univ BSc74. Trin Coll Bris 75. d 78 p 79. C Bradley *Wakef* 78-81; C Heworth H Trin *York* 81-82; TV 82-89; Chapl York Distr Hosp 82-86; R Greenhithe St Mary *Roch* from 89. *The Rectory, 131 Mounts Road, Greenhithe DA9 9ND* Tel (01322) 382031 E-mail richard.barron@diocese-rochester.org

BARRON, Sonia Patricia. b 55. NTMTC. d 11. C Chilwell *S'well* from 11. *29 Farm Road, Beeston, Nottingham NG9 5BZ* Tel 07800-583824 (mobile) E-mail sbarron55@gmail.com

BARRON, Canon Victor Robert. b 45. St Luke's Coll Ex CertEd70. Trin Coll Bris 76. d 78 p 79. C Rainham *Chelmsf* 78-81; V Easton H Trin w St Gabr and St Lawr and St Jude *Bris* 81-89; TR Kinson *Sarum* 89-90; RD Poole 94-00; Can and Preb Sarum Cathl 98-00; rtd 00; Perm to Offic *Sarum* 00-05; Hon C Witchampton, Stanbridge and Long Crichel etc 05-07. *159 Middlehill Road, Wimborne BH21 2HJ* Tel (01202) 885434 E-mail vicbarron@onetel.com

BARROW, Miss Gillian Stephanie. b 77. Regent's Park Coll Ox BA98. Westcott Ho Cam 08. d 10 p 11. C Gainsborough w Morton *Linc* from 10. *The Vicarage, Morton Front, Gainsborough DN21 3AD*

BARROW (née DONSON), Mrs Margaret Christine. b 44. Homerton Coll Cam CertEd65. Westcott Ho Cam 08. d 09 p 10. NSM Girton *Ely* from 09. *2 Cockerton Road, Girton, Cambridge CB3 0QW* Tel (01223) 575089 E-mail mcbarrow@mac.com

BARROW, Paul Beynon. b 48. Liv Univ LLB69 Man Univ MA01. St Steph Ho Ox 02. d 04 p 05. NSM Ches H Trin 04-05; P-in-c Hargrave 05-11; V from 11. *The Vicarage, Church Lane, Hargrave, Chester CH3 7RN* Tel (01829) 781378 Mobile 07792-154388 E-mail paul.barrow6@btopenworld.com

BARRY, Colin Lionel. b 49. Open Univ BSc94. Bp Attwell Tr Inst 85. d 96 p 97. NSM Arbory *S & M* from 96. *80 Ballanorris Crescent, Ballabeg, Castletown, Isle of Man IM9 4ER* Tel (01624) 823080

BARRY, Ms Jacqueline Françoise. Univ of Bordeaux II LSocEth86 MSoc87 York Univ PGCE91. Ridley Hall Cam. d 99 p 00. C Sydenham H Trin *S'wark* 99-03; C Paddington Em Harrow Road *Lon* from 03; C W Kilburn St Luke w St Simon and St Jude from 03. *Emmanuel Vicarage, 44C Fermoy Road, London W9 3NH* Tel (020) 8969 0438 E-mail jackie.barry@lineone.net

BARRY, Canon Jonathan Peter Oulton. b 47. TCD BA70 MA73 Hull Univ BA73 QUB PhD84. Ripon Hall Ox 73. d 74 p 75. C Dundela St Mark *D & D* 74-79; I Ballyphilip w Ardquin 79-85; Dioc Info Officer 80-90; I Comber from 85; Preb St Audoen St Patr Cathl Dublin from 01. *The Rectory, 12 Windmill Hill, Comber, Newtownards BT23 5WH* Tel (028) 9187 2283 E-mail comber@down.anglican.org

BARRY, Keith Gordon. b 67. TCD BA92. CITC 92. d 94 p 95. C Templemore *D & R* 94-97; V Choral Derry Cathl 94-95; Dean's V 95-97; P-in-c 97; CF 97-07; Sen CF from 07. *c/o MOD Chaplains (Army)* Tel (01980) 615804 Fax 615800

BARRY, Nicholas Brian Paul. b 61. Leic Univ BA83. St Steph Ho Ox 84. d 87 p 88. C St John's Wood *Lon* 87-90; Chapl RAF from 90. *Chaplaincy Services, HQ Personnel and Training Command, RAF High Wycombe HP14 4UE* Tel (01494) 496800 Fax 496343 E-mail nicholas.barry247@mod.uk

BARSLEY, Canon Margaret Ann. b 39. Totley Hall Coll CertEd60. EMMTC 79. dss 83 d 87 p 94. Kirton in Holland *Linc* 83-89; NSM 87-89; NSM Skirbeck Quarter 89-96; P-in-c Swineshead 96-99; V 99-04; RD Holland W 97-04; Can and Preb Linc Cathl from 00; rtd 04. *44 Sentance Crescent, Kirton, Boston PE20 1XF* Tel (01205) 723824 E-mail margaret@churchlane8539.freeserve.co.uk

BARTER, Christopher Stuart. b 49. Chich Th Coll. d 84 p 85. C Margate St Jo *Cant* 84-88; V Whitwood and Chapl Castleford, Normanton and Distr Hosp 88-95; P-in-c Ravensthorpe and AIDS Cllr W Yorks HA 95-98; TV Gt Yarmouth *Nor* 98-02; R Somersham w Pidley and Oldhurst *Ely* 02-10; V Somersham w Pidley and Oldhurst and Woodhurst from 10; P-in-c Holywell w Needingworth 07-08; RD St Ives 06-10. *The Rectory, Rectory Lane, Somersham, Huntingdon PE28 3EL* Tel (01487) 840676 E-mail christopher.barter@btopenworld.com

BARTER, The Very Revd Donald. b 34. St Fran Coll Brisbane ThL69 ACT ThSchol74. d 69 p 70. C Townsville Australia 69-72; R Mareeba 72-76; R Ingham 76-81; Adn of the W and R Mt Isa 81-86; Dean Townsville 86-90; Chapl Miss to Seamen 86-90; Chapl HM Police Service 88-90; Appeals Dir SPCK 90-93; Lic to Offic *Leic* 90-93; Australia from 93; Asst to Dean St Jas Cathl 94-00. *49 Macrossan Street, South Townsville Qld 4810, Australia* Tel and fax (0061) (7) 4772 7036 Mobile 414-989593 E-mail dba18613@bigpond.net.au

BARTER, Geoffrey Roger. b 41. Bris Univ BSc63. Clifton Th Coll 65. d 67 p 68. C Normanton *Derby* 67-70; C Rainham *Chelmsf*

70-75; V Plumstead St Jo w St Jas and St Paul *S'wark* 75-82; V Frogmore *St Alb* 82-01; rtd 01; Perm to Offic *Chich* from 02. *45 West Front Road, Pagham, Bognor Regis PO21 4SZ* Tel (01243) 262522

BARTER, Leonard Reginald Treseder. b 38. d 95 p 96. OLM St Stythians w Perranarworthal and Gwennap *Truro* from 95. *Vellandrucia Foundry, Stithians, Truro TR3 7BU* Tel (01209) 860341

BARTER, Michael Christopher Charles. b 74. Coll of Resurr Mirfield 07. d 09 p 10. C Hangleton *Chich* from 09. *139 Godwin Road, Hove BN3 7FS* E-mail mikeccbarter@hotmail.co.uk

BARTER, Susan Kathleen. b 53. Open Univ MBA97 Anglia Ruskin Univ MA09. Ridley Hall Cam 01. d 03 p 04. C Happisburgh, Walcott, Hempstead w Eccles etc *Nor* 03-06; C Bacton w Edingthorpe w Witton and Ridlington 04-06; C Ward End w Bordesley Green *Birm* from 06. *St Paul's Vicarage, 405 Belchers Lane, Birmingham B9 5SY* Tel 0121-772 0418 Mobile 07778-063644 E-mail susan@sbarter777.co.uk

BARTHOLOMEW, Craig Gerald. b 61. UNISA BTh82 Potchefstroom Univ MA92 Bris Univ PhD97. Wycliffe Hall Ox BA84 MA88. d 86 p 87. S Africa 86-92; C Pinetown Ch Ch 87-89; Lect Geo Whitefield Coll Cape Town 89-92; Research Fell Glos Univ 97-04; Perm to Offic *Glouc* 98-04; Canada from 04. *Redeemer University College, 777 Garner Road, Ancaster ON L9K 1J4, Canada* Tel (001) (905) 648 2139 ext 4270 E-mail cbartho@redeemer.ca

BARTHOLOMEW, David Grant. b 50. Univ of Wales (Lamp) BA77. Chich Th Coll 91. d 93 p 94. C Petersfield *Portsm* 93-96; R Fitton w Helpston and Maxey *Pet* 96-98; R Burghclere w Newtown and Ecchinswell w Sydmonton *Win* from 98. *The Rectory, Well Street, Burghclere, Newbury RG20 9HS* Tel (01635) 278470 E-mail davidrectory@aol.com

BARTLAM, Alan Thomas. b 51. Bris Univ BEd74. Linc Th Coll 88. d 90 p 91. C Longdon-upon-Tern, Rodington, Uppington etc *Lich* 90-92; C Tilstock and Whixall 92-95; V Tilstock, Edstaston and Whixall 95-98; R Bewcastle, Stapleton and Kirklinton etc *Carl* 98-06; V Shnestly *Lich* 06-11; rtd 11. *45-47 Main Street, New Deer, Turriff AB53 6TA*

BARTLE, Canon David Colin. b 29. Em Coll Cam BA53 MA57. Ridley Hall Cam 53. d 55 p 56. C Birm St Martin 55-57; C Boscombe St Jo *Win* 57-60; V Lowestoft St Jo *Nor* 60-70; P-in-c Thetford St Cuth w H Trin 70-72; P-in-c Thetford St Mary 70-72; P-in-c Thetford St Pet w St Nic 70-72; TR Thetford 72-75; P-in-c Kilverstone 70-75; P-in-c Croxton 70-75; Teacher Bournemouth Sch 75-83; R Brantham w Stutton *St E* 83-90; RD Samford 86-90; P-in-c Roxwell *Chelmsf* 90-93; Dioc Dir of Ords 90-93; Dioc Lay Min Adv 90-93; Hon Can Chelmsf Cathl 91-93; rtd 93; Perm to Offic *Win* 93-98; Chapl R Bournemouth and Christchurch Hosps NHS Trust 98-00. *26 Gracey Court, Woodland Road, Broadclyst, Exeter EX5 3GA* E-mail dbartle8@aol.com

BARTLE, Canon Reginald Stephen. b 24. K Coll Lon AKC51 BD52. d 52 p 53. C Penge Ch Ch w H Trin *Roch* 52-55; SAMS 55-79; Chile 55-70; Adn Chile 64-70; Hon Can Chile from 64; NW Area Sec SAMS 70-73; Home Sec 73-79; C Tunbridge Wells St Jas *Roch* 80-83; rtd 83; Perm to Offic *St D* 84-94; *Chelmsf* 94-00; *S'wark* 00-01; *Cant* 01-03. *24 Bromley College, London Road, Bromley BR1 1PE* Tel (020) 8460 7128

BARTLE-JENKINS, Canon Leonard Christmas. b 13. Univ of Wales (Lamp) BA35. Lich Th Coll 35. d 38 p 39. C Fleur-de-Lis *Mon* 38-41; C Trevethin 41-47; V Llangattock-vibon-Avel 47-55; V Bassaleg 55-74; Can St Woolos Cathl 64-82; RD Bassaleg 67-82; R Michaelston-y-Fedw and Rudry 74-82; rtd 82; Lic to Offic *Mon* from 82; Perm to Offic *Llan* from 82. *c/o Mrs C Judd, 13 Grove Road, Bridgend CF31 3GF*

BARTLE-JENKINS, Paul. b 43. Bris & Glouc Tr Course. d 84 p 86. NSM Bris St Agnes and St Simon w St Werburgh 84-87; NSM Bris St Paul's 87-09; P-in-c 07-09. *188A Henleaze Road, Westbury-on-Trym, Bristol BS9 4NE* Tel 0117-962 0286 E-mail fatherpaul00@hotmail.com

BARTLEM, Gregory John. b 68. Ox Brookes Univ BA05. Qu Coll Birm 07. d 09 p 10. NSM Cheylesmore *Cov* 09-11; C Cov Cathl from 11. *17 Courtleet Road, Coventry CV3 5GS* Tel (024) 7650 5524 Mobile 07967-662184 E-mail greg.bartlem@covcofe.org

BARTLES-SMITH, The Ven Douglas Leslie. b 37. St Edm Hall Ox BA61 MA65. Wells Th Coll 61. d 63 p 64. C Westmr St Steph w St Jo *Lon* 63-68; P-in-c Camberwell St Mich w All So w Em *S'wark* 68-72; P-in-c Battersea St Luke 75-85; RD Battersea 81-85; Adn S'wark 85-04; rtd 04; Chapl to The Queen 96-07; Perm to Offic *Lich* from 04. *18 Vane Road, Shrewsbury SY3 7HB* Tel (01743) 363282

BARTLETT, Alan Bennett. b 58. G&C Coll Cam BA81 MA85 Birm Univ PhD87 St Jo Coll Dur BA90. Cranmer Hall Dur 88. d 91 p 92. C Newc H Cross 91-94; C Newburn 94-96; Tutor Cranmer Hall Dur 96-08; V Dur St Giles from 08; P-in-c Shadforth and Sherburn from 08. *St Giles's Vicarage, Gilesgate, Durham DH1 1QQ* Tel 0191-384 2452 E-mail vicarsgss@live.co.uk

BARTLETT, Anthony Martin. b 43. Cranmer Hall Dur 74. **d** 77 **p** 78. C Heworth St Mary *Dur* 77-80; V Cleadon 80-84; CF (TA) 81-90; Prec Dur Cathl 85-87; V Harton 87-95; P-in-c Hendon 95-96; R 96-97; V Greenlands *Blackb* from 01. *St Anne's House, Salmesbury Avenue, Blackpool FY2 0PR* Tel (01253) 353900 E-mail bcressell@aol.com

BARTLETT, David John. b 36. Pemb Coll Ox BA61. Linc Th Coll 63. **d** 65 **p** 66. C Wollaton *S'well* 65-70; V Woodthorpe 70-83; V Farnsfield 83-01; P-in-c Kirklington w Hockerton 83-01; RD S'well 83-93; Chapl Rodney Sch Kirklington 83-01; rtd 01; Perm to Offic *S'well* from 01. *6 De Havilland Way, Farndon Road, Newark NG24 4RF* Tel (01636) 651582

BARTLETT, David William. b 59. Trin Coll Bris 89. **d** 91 **p** 92. C Frinton *Chelmsf* 91-95; TV Eston w Normanby *York* 95-96; Assoc P Worksop St Jo *S'well* 96-01; TV Trunch *Nor* from 01. *The Rectory, Clipped Hedge Lane, Southrepps, Norwich NR11 8NS* Tel (01263) 833404

BARTLETT, George Frederick. b 34. Clifton Th Coll 61. **d** 64 **p** 65. C Branksome St Clem *Sarum* 64-71; V Gt Baddow *Chelmsf* 71-72; Perm to Offic *Win* 81-87; rtd 99. *8 Glencarron Way, Southampton SO16 7EF* Tel (023) 8032 5162 E-mail george.bartlett@cwcom.net

BARTLETT, Prof John Raymond. b 37. BNC Ox BA59 MA62 BLitt62 TCD MA70 LittD94. Linc Th Coll 61. **d** 63 **p** 64. C W Bridgford *S'well* 63-66; Lect Div TCD 66-86; Assoc Prof Bibl Studies 86-92; Fell 75-92; Prof Past Th 90-01; Prin CITC 89-01; Treas Ch Ch Cathl Dublin 86-88; Prec 88-01; rtd 01. *102 Sorrento Road, Dalkey, Co Dublin, Republic of Ireland* Tel (00353) (1) 284 7786 E-mail jrbartlett@eircom.net

BARTLETT, Kenneth Vincent John. b 36. OBE93. Oriel Coll Ox BA61 BTh63. Ripon Hall Ox 61. **d** 63 **p** 64. C Paddington St Jas *Lon* 63-67; Lic to Offic from 67; rtd 01. *25 Tudor Road, Kingston-upon-Thames KT2 6AS* Tel (020) 8541 0378 E-mail shaa4949@aol.com

BARTLETT, Canon Maurice Edward. b 33. G&C Coll Cam BA59 MA63. Wells Th Coll 59. **d** 60 **p** 61. C Batley All SS *Wakef* 60-64; Bp's Dom Chapl 64-66; Dir of Ords 64-66; Asst Chapl HM Pris Wakef 64-66; V Allerton *Liv* 66-81; V Lancaster St Mary *Blackb* 81-97; Chapl HM Pris Lanc 81-97; Hon Can Blackb Cathl 87-97; rtd 97. *Waverley House, West Common, Bowness-on-Solway, Carlisle CA7 5AG*

BARTLETT, Michael Fredrick. b 52. Ex Univ BA74 Liv Univ BPhil75. Ven English Coll Rome 78 Ripon Coll Cuddesdon BA79 MA. **d** 79 **p** 80. C Kirkby *Liv* 79-82; C Wordsley *Lich* 82-83; TV 83-88; Chapl Wordsley Hosp 82-88; TV Redditch, The Ridge *Worc* 88-05; TR Redditch Ch the K from 05. *St Peter's House, Littlewoods, Redditch B97 5LB* Tel (01527) 545709

BARTLETT, Preb Michael George. b 35. S Dios Minl Tr Scheme 84. **d** 87 **p** 88. NSM Wimborne Minster and Holt *Sarum* 87-90; C Charlestown *Truro* 90-91; R St Endellion w Port Isaac and St Kew 91-06; Preb St Endellion 91-06; rtd 06; Perm to Offic *Truro* from 07; PV Truro Cathl from 10. *Chapel House, St Austell Road, Probus, Truro TR2 4LF* Tel (01726) 884310

☩**BARTLETT, The Rt Revd Peter.** b 54. **d** 96 **p** 97 **c** 08. SAMS Bolivia 96-05; TV Parr *Liv* 05-08; Bp Paraguay from 08. *Iglesia Anglicana Paraguay, Casilla de Correo 1124, Asunción, Paraguay* Tel (00595) (21) 200934 *or* 214795 E-mail iapar@sce.cnc.una.py

BARTLETT, Canon Richard Charles. b 68. St Kath Coll Liv BA90 Surrey Univ MA01. Westcott Ho Cam 91. **d** 94 **p** 95. C Wareham *Sarum* 94-98; Assoc V Ealing All SS *Lon* 98-02; Chapl Twyford C of E High Sch Acton 98-02; USPG Brazil 02-05; Hon Can Brasilia Cathl from 05; V Northwood H Trin *Lon* from 05; AD Harrow from 07. *Holy Trinity Vicarage, Gateway Close, Northwood HA6 2RP* Tel (01923) 825732 E-mail richard.bartlett@london.anglican.org

BARTON, Allan Benjamin. b 77. Univ Coll Lon BA98 York Univ MA99 PhD04. Ripon Coll Cuddesdon 05. **d** 08 **p** 09. C Louth *Linc* 08-09; C Saxilby Gp from 09; P-in-c Aylmerton, Runton, Beeston Regis and Gresham *Nor* from 11. *The Rectory, Cromer Road, West Runton, Cromer NR27 9QT* E-mail vitrearum@googlemail.com

BARTON, Andrew Edward. b 53. St Jo Coll Ox MA77 DPhil80 Idaho Univ MTh06 MRSC. Ridley Hall Cam 87. **d** 90 **p** 91. C Ringwood *Win* 90-94; R Baughurst, Ramsdell, Wolverton w Ewhurst etc 95-07; Lect K Alfred's Coll Win 95-98; R Auchterarder *St And* from 07; R Muthill from 07. *St Kessog's Rectory, High Street, Auchterarder PH3 1AD* Tel (01764) 662525 Mobile 07778-771651 E-mail james.kessog@gmail.com

BARTON, Anne. *See* BARTON, Margaret Anne

BARTON, Canon Arthur Michael. b 33. CCC Cam BA57 MA61. Wycliffe Hall Ox 57. **d** 59 **p** 60. Min Can Bradf Cathl 59-61; C Maltby *Sheff* 61-63; V Silsden *Bradf* 63-70; V Moor Allerton *Ripon* 70-81; TR 81-82; V Wetherby 82-98; Chapl HM YOI Wetherby 82-89; RD Harrogate *Ripon* 88-95; Hon Can Ripon Cathl 89-98; rtd 98; Perm to Offic *Ripon* from 98. *22 Ash Road, Harrogate HG2 8EG* Tel (01423) 870799 E-mail teambarton@aol.com

BARTON, The Ven Charles John Greenwood. b 36. ALCD63. **d** 63 **p** 64. C Cant St Mary Bredin 63-66; V Whitfield w W

Langdon 66-75; V S Kensington St Luke *Lon* 75-83; AD Chelsea 80-83; Chief Broadcasting Officer for C of E 83-90; Adn Aston *Birm* 90-03; Can Res Birm Cathl 90-02; P-in-c Bickenhill 02-03; rtd 03; Perm to Offic *Cant* from 03; Abp's Communications Adv York 05-06; Acting Prin Adv to Abp York 07; Abp's Chapl and Researcher 08. *10 Stuart Court, Puckle Lane, Canterbury CT1 3LA* Tel (01227) 379688 Mobile 07743-118544 E-mail johnbarton@waitrose.com

BARTON, Dale. b 49. Selw Coll Cam BA71 MA76. Linc Th Coll 71. **d** 73 **p** 74. C Gosforth All SS *Newc* 73-77; Lesotho 77-81; Dep Warden CA Hostel Cam 82-83; C Shepton Mallet w Doulting *B & W* 83-88; TV Preston St Steph *Blackb* 88-96; V 96-99; Bp's Adv on Inter-Faith Relns 99-07; P-in-c Bradf St Clem from 07; P-in-c Bradf St Aug Undercliffe from 07. *The Vicarage, 294A Barkerend Road, Bradford BD3 9DF* Tel (01274) 665109 E-mail st.barton@ukonline.co.uk

BARTON, David Gerald Story. b 38. Selw Coll Cam BA62 MA66. Cuddesdon Coll 63. **d** 65 **p** 66. C Cowley St Jas *Ox* 65-67; C Hambleden 67-70; Hon C Hammersmith St Jo *Lon* 72-77; Hon C Paddington St Jas 77-81; Hd Master Soho Par Sch 81-88; Hon C Westmr St Jas 81-92; RE Project Officer Lon Dioc Bd for Schs 88-92; Dioc Schs Adv *Ox* 93-99; rtd 00; Hon C Iffley *Ox* 93-06; Perm to Offic from 06. *254 Iffley Road, Oxford OX4 1SE* Tel (01865) 240059 E-mail daviebarton@aol.com

BARTON, Edward. b 23. **d** 75 **p** 76. C Budock *Truro* 75-79; P-in-c St Stithians w Perranarworthal 79-80; V St Stythians w Perranarworthal and Gwennap 80-82; rtd 88; Perm to Offic *Truro* from 98. *Riversmeet, 5 Riviera Estate, Malpas, Truro TR1 1SR* Tel (01872) 271686

BARTON, Canon Geoffrey. b 27. Oriel Coll Ox BA48 MA52. Chich Th Coll 49. **d** 51 **p** 52. C Arnold *S'well* 51-53; C E Retford 53-54; V Mirfield Eastthorpe St Paul *Wakef* 54-60; V Boroughbridge w Roecliffe *Ripon* 60-73; V Aldborough w Boroughbridge and Roecliffe 73; P-in-c Farnham w Scotton and Staveley and Copgrove 73-74; R 74-77; Chapl Roundway Hosp Devizes 77-92; Can and Preb Sarum Cathl 86-92; rtd 92; Perm to Offic *Sarum* from 01. *4B Willow House, Downlands Road, Devizes SN10 5EA* Tel (01380) 725311

BARTON (née CRABB), Helen Maria. b 56. Lon Bible Coll BA83 St Jo Coll Dur MA04 St Mary's Coll Strawberry Hill PGCE98. Cranmer Hall Dur 01. **d** 03 **p** 04. C Wisley w Pyrford *Guildf* 03-04; C Lanchester *Dur* 04-06; C Hexham *Newc* 06-08; V Ulgham from 08; V Widdrington from 08. *The Vicarage, Grangemoor Road, Widdrington, Morpeth NE61 5PU* Tel (01670) 790389 E-mail hmbarton@fsmail.net

BARTON, Mrs Jean Valerie. b 42. Wycliffe Hall Ox BTh01. **d** 02 **p** 03. NSM Harwell w Chilton *Ox* 02-07; Perm to Offic *Man* 07-10; NSM Saddleworth 10-11; rtd 11. *16 Sykes Close, Greenfield, Oldham OL3 7PT* Tel (01457) 878995 E-mail jeanbarton@onetel.com

BARTON, John. *See* BARTON, The Ven Charles John Greenwood

BARTON, Canon John. b 25. MBE91. Keble Coll Ox BA48 MA50. Ely Th Coll 48. **d** 50 **p** 51. C Worksop St Anne *S'well* 50-53; C Harrogate St Wilfrid *Ripon* 53-56; V Beeston Hill H Spirit 56-60; Chapl Stanley Royd and Pinderfields Hosps Wakef 60-72; RD Wakef 68-72; Chapl Jo Radcliffe Hosp and Radcliffe Infirmary 72-90; Chapl Chu Hosp Ox 72-89; Hon Can Ch Ch *Ox* 77-94; RD Cowley 89-94; rtd 90; Perm to Offic *Ox* 94-01 and *Roch* from 01. *150A Longlands Road, Sidcup DA15 7LF* Tel (020) 8300 7073

BARTON, Prof John. b 48. Keble Coll Ox BA69 MA73 Mert Coll Ox DPhil74 St Cross Coll Ox DLitt88. **d** 73 **p** 73. Jun Research Fell Mert Coll Ox 73-74; Lect St Cross Coll Ox 74-89; Fell 74-91; Chapl 79-91; Lect Th Ox Univ 74-89; Reader 89-91; Oriel and Laing Prof of Interpr of H Scrip from 91; Fell Oriel Coll Ox from 91; Can Th Win Cathl 91-03. *11 Withington Court, Abingdon OX14 3QA* Tel (01235) 525925 E-mail johnbarton@oriel.ox.ac.uk

BARTON, Canon John Christopher Peter. b 28. Trin Hall Cam BA51 MA56. Ridley Hall Cam 51. **d** 53 **p** 54. C Erith St Paul *Roch* 53-56; C Cockfosters Ch Ch CD *Lon* 56-64; V Welling *Roch* 64-75; P-in-c Malmesbury w Westport *Bris* 75-84; P-in-c Charlton w Brokenborough and Hankerton 80-84; V Malmesbury w Westport and Brokenborough 84-94; Hon Can Kigezi from 92; rtd 94; Perm to Offic *B & W* 94-07. *Orchard House, Orchard Road, Crewkerne TA18 7AF* Tel (01460) 72536

BARTON, John Michael. b 40. TCD BA62 Div Test. **d** 63 **p** 64. C Coleraine *Conn* 63-68; C Portadown St Mark *Arm* 68-71; I Carnteel and Crilly 71-83; I Derryloran 83-97; Bp's C Acton and Drumbanagher 97-09; Can Arm Cathl 94-09; Treas 98-01; Chan 01-09; rtd 09. *23 Strand Cottages, Sheskburn Avenue, Ballycastle BT54 6HR* Tel (028) 2076 9673

BARTON, Mrs Margaret Ann Edith. b 48. Newc Univ BA71. EMMTC 95. **d** 98 **p** 99. NSM Castle Bytham w Creeton *Linc* 98-04; P-in-c Corby Glen from 04. *Blanchland House, Swinstead Road, Corby Glen, Grantham NG33 4NU* Tel (01476) 550765

BARTON, Margaret Anne. b 54. St Anne's Coll Ox BA76 MA80 DPhil81 Selw Coll Cam BA89 MA94. Ridley Hall Cam 87. **d** 90

p 94. Par Dn Burley Ville *Win* 90-94; Chapl K Alfred Coll 94-98; Dioc Development and Research Officer for Liturg Matters 99-01; NSM Baughurst, Ramsdell, Wolverton w Ewhurst etc 99-01; Asst Chapl Gen Synod 96-00; rtd 01. *St Kessog's Rectory, High Street, Auchterarder PH3 1AD* Tel (01764) 662525
E-mail rev.anne.barton@ntlworld.com
BARTON, Michael. See BARTON, Canon Arthur Michael
BARTON, Patrick Michael. Huddersfield Univ BA. BTh. **d** 05 **p** 06. C Arm St Mark 05-08; I Ballintoy w Rathlin and Dunseverick *Conn* from 08. *The Rectory, 2 Ballinlea Road, Ballintoy, Ballycastle BT54 6NQ* Tel (028) 2076 8155
E-mail patribart@aol.com
BARTON, Peter. See BARTON, Canon John Christopher Peter
BARTON, Canon Samuel David. b 45. **d** 84 **p** 85. C Ballywillan *Conn* 84-86; I Aghadowey w Kilrea *D & R* 86-92; Bp's C Fahan Lower and Upper from 92; Dioc Educn Co-ord from 94; Dioc Communications Officer from 98; Can Raphoe Cathl from 98. *The Rectory, Cahir O'Doherty Avenue, Buncrana, Co Donegal, Republic of Ireland* Tel (00353) (74) 936 1154 Fax 936 3726
E-mail fahan@raphoe.anglican.org
BARTON (*née* McVEIGH), **Mrs Sandra.** b 58. Reading Univ BA80. Cranmer Hall Dur 95. **d** 95 **p** 96. C Stranton *Dur* 95-98; P-in-c Blackhall, Castle Eden and Monkhesleden 98-99; R 99-02; Perm to Offic *St E* 08-11; NSM Mildenhall from 11. *The Old Village Stores, 6 The Street, Freckenham, Bury St Edmunds IP28 8HZ* Tel (01638) 720048
E-mail revsandiebarton@gmail.com
BARTON, Stephen Christian. b 52. Macquarie Univ (NSW) BA75 DipEd75 Lanc Univ MA78 K Coll Lon PhD92. Cranmer Hall Dur 91. **d** 93 **p** 94. NSM Neville's Cross St Jo CD *Dur* 93-00; NSM Dur St Marg and Neville's Cross St Jo 00-06; Perm to Offic *Newc* from 06. *The Vicarage, Grangemoor Road, Widdrington, Morpeth NE61 5PU* Tel (01670) 790389
E-mail s.c.barton@durham.ac.uk
BARTON, Stephen William. b 50. St Jo Coll Cam BA73 Leeds Univ MPhil81. Coll of Resurr Mirfield 75. **d** 77 **p** 78. C Horton *Bradf* 77-80; USPG 80-92; Presbyter Dhaka St Thos Bangladesh 81-88; St Andr Th Coll Dhaka 88-92; TV Southampton (City Cen) *Win* 92-98; Chapl Manager Birm Women's Healthcare NHS Trust 99-06; rtd 06. *290 City Road, Birmingham B16 0NE* Tel 0121-429 2176 E-mail notrabnehpets@yahoo.co.uk
BARTON, Timothy Charles. b 47. Sarum & Wells Th Coll 73. **d** 76 **p** 77. C Upholland *Liv* 76-80; V Dalton from 80. *88 Lyndhurst Avenue, Skelmersdale WN8 6UH* Tel (01695) 733148
BARTON, Trevor James. b 50. St Alb Minl Tr Scheme 79. **d** 87 **p** 88. NSM Hemel Hempstead *St Alb* from 87. *46 Crossfell Road, Hemel Hempstead HP3 8RQ* Tel and fax (01442) 251537
E-mail trevorbarton@hotmail.com
BARWELL, Brian Bernard Beale. b 30. Preston Poly CertEd79. AKC59 St Boniface Warminster 59. **d** 60 **p** 61. C Heywood St Jas *Man* 60-63; V Smallbridge *Blackb* 63-69; V Farington *Blackb* 69-72; C-in-c Blackb St Luke w St Phil 72-75; C Standish 75-76; Lic to Offic 76-92; rtd 92; Perm to Offic *Blackb* from 92. *70 Claytongate, Coppull, Chorley PR7 4PS* Tel (01257) 794251
BARZEY, Ms Michele Alison Lesley. b 63. Trin Coll Bris BA94. **d** 94. C Gravelly Hill *Birm* 94-96; Perm to Offic from 00. *6 Topcliffe House, Yatesbury Avenue, Birmingham B35 6DU* Tel 0121-730 3094
BASAVARAJ, Mrs Patricia Margaret. b 37. SRN61 SCM62. **d** 00. OLM Verwood *Sarum* 00-07; Perm to Offic 07-08. *Hope Cottage, Church Hill, Verwood BH31 6HT* Tel (01202) 822920
BASFORD HOLBROOK, Colin Eric. b 42. St Steph Ho Ox 73. **d** 75 **p** 76. C Dovecot *Liv* 75-78; V Hollinfare 79-83; CMS 83-88; Cyprus 83-91; Chapl Athens w Kifissia, Patras, Thessaloniki etc *Eur* 91-93; Chapl Athens w Patras, Thessaloniki and Voula 93-94; rtd 02. *7 St Catherine's Close, Uttoxeter ST14 8EF*
BASH, Anthony. b 52. Bris Univ LLB73 LLM76 Glas Univ BD88 Clare Hall Cam PhD96. Westcott Ho Cam 94. **d** 96 **p** 97. C Kingston upon Hull H Trin *York* 96-99; V N Ferriby 99-04; Chapl to Legal Profession 97-04; Hon Fell Hull Univ 97-04; Chapl and Fell Univ Coll Dur 05-06; TR Dur N 06-08; Chapl and Tutor Hatf Coll Dur from 08; Hon Research Fell Univ Coll Dur from 08. *Hatfield College, North Bailey, Durham DH1 3RQ* Tel 0191-334 2636 E-mail anthony.bash@durham.ac.uk
BASHFORD, Richard Frederick. b 36. Clifton Th Coll. **d** 68 **p** 69. C Bedworth *Cov* 68-71; C Lower Homerton St Paul *Lon* 71-75; V Bordesley Green *Birm* 75-81; R Birm Bp Latimer w All SS 81-06; rtd 06. *244 Adams Hill, Birmingham B32 3PD* Tel 0121-421 1807 E-mail domusmariae@blueyonder.co.uk
BASHFORD, Robert Thomas. b 49. Ch Coll Cam BA70 CertEd72 MA74 Lon Univ BD84 MPhil89. Oak Hill Th Coll 86. **d** 88 **p** 89. C Frinton *Chelmsf* 88-91; C Galleywood Common 91-96; V Clapham *St Alb* 96-02; P-in-c Westgate St Jas *Cant* 02-06; V from 06. *St James's Vicarage, Orchard Gardens, Margate CT9 5JT* Tel (01843) 832380
BASHFORTH, Alan George. b 64. Ex Univ MA. Ripon Coll Cuddesdon BTh96. **d** 96 **p** 97. C Calstock *Truro* 96-98; C St Ives 98-01; V St Agnes and Mount Hawke w Mithian from 01; RD

Powder from 04. *The Vicarage, 6 Penwinnick Parc, St Agnes TR5 0UQ* Tel (01872) 553391
BASINGSTOKE, Suffragan Bishop of. See HANCOCK, The Rt Revd Peter
BASKERVILLE, John. b 45. Open Univ BA78. Sarum & Wells Th Coll 92. **d** 93 **p** 94. C Wanstead St Mary w Ch Ch *Chelmsf* 93-96; C Chingford SS Pet and Paul 96-98; V Felkirk w Brierley *Wakef* 98-04; rtd 04. *131 Howard Road, Upminster RM14 2UQ* Tel (01708) 641242 Mobile 07710-209469
BASKERVILLE, Philip Duncan. b 58. St Chad's Coll Dur BSc79 Oriel Coll Ox PGCE80. Trin Coll Bris BA87. **d** 88 **p** 89. C Roby *Liv* 88-93; Tutor St Paul's Th Coll Kapsabet Kenya 93-98; C Barnston *Ches* 98-05; Chapl St Andr Sch Turi Kenya 05-08; P-in-c Guernsey St Sampson *Win* from 08. *The Rectory, Grandes Maisons Road, St Sampsons, Guernsey GY2 4JS* Tel (01481) 244710 Mobile 07839-213096
E-mail philbaskerville@cwgsy.net
BASON, Brian Vaudrey. b 27. Leeds Univ BA49 Lon Univ BD69 AMusTCL97. Coll of Resurr Mirfield 49. **d** 51 **p** 52. C Haggerston St Aug w St Steph *Lon* 51-55; C Bow w Bromley St Leon 55-56; V Audenshaw St Hilda *Man* 56-89; Audenshaw High Sch 89-92; rtd 92; Perm to Offic *Ches* from 89; *Man* 89-95 and from 99. *78 Windsor Road, Denton, Manchester M34 2HE* Tel 0161-320 4408
BASON, Mrs Carol. b 44. De Montfort Univ BSc96. **d** 09 **p** 10. OLM S Lawres Gp *Linc* from 09. *Walnut Tree Cottage, 15 Church Lane, Reepham, Lincoln LN3 4DQ* Tel (01522) 753282 Mobile 07749-211397 E-mail cbason@tiscali.co.uk
BASS, Colin Graham. b 41. Liv Univ BSc62 Fitzw Ho Cam BA61 MA68. Ox NSM Course 84. **d** 87 **p** 88. Dir of Studies Leighton Park Sch Reading 87-97; NSM Earley St Pet *Ox* 87-92; NSM Reading Deanery from 92. *9 Bramley Close, Reading RG6 7PL* Tel 0118-966 3732 E-mail colin.bass@lineone.net
BASS, George Michael. b 39. Ely Th Coll 62. **d** 65 **p** 66. C Romaldkirk *Ripon* 65-68; C Kenton Ascension *Newc* 68-71; CF 71-94; Chapl Northumbria Healthcare NHS Trust 95-02; rtd 02; Perm to Offic *Newc* from 02. *35 Kelso Drive, North Shields NE29 9NS* Tel 0191-258 2514
BASS, Mrs Marguerite Rowena. b 61. MA BD ARCM. St Jo Coll Nottm. **d** 05 **p** 06. C Wellingborough All SS *Pet* 05-08; Perm to Offic 08-11; Chapl HM Pris Rye Hill 08; Chapl St Andr Hosp Northn 08-10; Chapl Cambs and Pet NHS Foundn Trust from 10. *29 Northfield Avenue, Ringstead, Kettering NN14 4DX* Tel (01933) 460213 E-mail bassrowena@btopenworld.com
BASS, Mrs Rosemary Jane. b 38. Linc Th Coll 76. **dss** 79 **d** 87 **p** 94. Bedford *St Alb St Alb* 79-84; Leavesden 84-94; Par Dn 87-94; C 94-95; V Luton St Andr 95-01; rtd 01; Perm to Offic *St Alb* from 01. *3 Highfield Road, Oakley, Bedford MK43 7TA* Tel (01234) 822126 E-mail roanj@btinternet.com
BASSETT, John Edmund. b 33. St Aid Birkenhead 63. **d** 66 **p** 67. C Guiseley *Bradf* 66-67; C Stechford *Birm* 67-71; C Ross *Heref* 71-72; P-in-c Brampton Abbotts 73-75; P-in-c Weston under Penyard 73-75; P-in-c Hope Mansell 73-75; TR Halesworth w Linstead and Chediston *St E* 75-78; R Laceby *Linc* 78-83; V Sale St Paul *Ches* 83-88; P-in-c Southport All SS *Liv* 88-94; P-in-c Southport All So 88-94; V Southport All SS So 94-98; P-in-c Aspull 98-99; V Aspull and New Springs 99-02; rtd 02; Hon C Lower Wharfedale *Ripon* 02-09. *1 St Martin's Field, Otley LS21 2FN* Tel (01943) 461389
BASSETT, Mrs Rosemary Louise. b 42. STETS. **d** 00 **p** 01. NSM The Winterbournes and Compton Valence *Sarum* 00-08; P-in-c 03-08; NSM Dorchester from 08. *12 Lime Close, Dorchester DT1 2HQ* E-mail trl@bassett-online.com
BASTABLE, Richard Michael. b 83. Ex Univ BA04 St Edm Coll Cam MPhil08. Westcott Ho Cam 06. **d** 08 **p** 09. C Ruislip St Martin *Lon* 08-10; C St Andr Holborn from 10. *The Lodge, St Andrew's Vicarage, 5 St Andrew Street, London EC4A 3AB* Tel (020) 7353 8189 Mobile 07816-074597
E-mail rbastable@gmail.com
BASTEN, Richard Henry. b 40. Codrington Coll Barbados 60. **d** 63 **p** 64. Br Honduras 63-67; Barbados 68-72; C Hartlepool H Trin *Dur* 72-73; Chapl Bedstone Coll 73-88; C Clun w Chapel Lawn *Heref* 73-77; P-in-c Clungunford 77-78; R Clungunford w Clunbury and Clunton, Bedstone etc 78-88; R Rowde and Poulshot *Sarum* 88-95; rtd 95; Perm to Offic *Glouc* from 95. *41 Bewley Way, Churchdown, Gloucester GL3 2DU* Tel (01452) 859738
BASTIDE, Derek. b 44. Dur Univ BA65 Reading Univ DipEd66 Sussex Univ MA77. Chich Th Coll 76. **d** 77 **p** 78. Hon C Lewes All SS, St Anne, St Mich and St Thos *Chich* 77-84; Prin Lect Brighton Poly 80-92; Prin Lect Brighton Univ from 92; P-in-c Hamsey *Chich* from 84. *The Rectory, Offham, Lewes BN7 3PX* Tel (01273) 474356 E-mail dandj@bastide8.wanadoo.co.uk
BASTON, The Ven Caroline. b 56. Birm Univ BSc78 CertEd79. Ripon Coll Cuddesdon 87. **d** 89 **p** 94. Par Dn Southampton Thornhill St Chris *Win* 89-94; C 94-95; R Win All SS w Chilcomb and Chesil 95-06; Dioc Communications Officer 95-98; Dioc Dir of Ords 99-06; Hon Can Win Cathl 00-06; Adn

Is of Wight *Portsm* from 06. *5 The Boltons, Wootton Bridge, Ryde PO33 4PB* Tel (01983) 884432
E-mail adiow@portsmouth.anglican.org
BATCHELOR, Alan Harold. b 30. Bris Univ BA54 Hull Univ MA63. Linc Th Coll 54. **d** 56 **p** 57. C Kingston upon Hull St Alb *York* 56-60; C Attercliffe w Carbrook *Sheff* 60-62; India 63-87; Ind Chapl *Ripon* 87-95; C Kirkstall 92-95; rtd 95; Perm to Offic *Ripon* from 01. *16 Moor Grange Rise, Leeds LS16 5BP* Tel 0113-226 9671
BATCHELOR, Andrew George. b 59. St Jo Coll Nottm 07. **d** 09 **p** 10. C Ulverston St Mary w H Trin *Carl* from 09. *21 Victoria Park, Ulverston LA12 7TT* Tel 07934-483439 (mobile)
E-mail andy.batchelor@yahoo.co.uk
BATCHELOR, John Millar. CITC 76. **d** 78 **p** 79. C Belfast All SS *Conn* 78-80; I Eglish w Killylea *Arm* 80-96; I Ballyhalbert w Ardkeen *D & D* 96-01; rtd 01. *Rhone Brae, 102 Eglish Road, Dungannon BT70 1LB* Tel (028) 8775 0177
E-mail jm_batchelor@lineone.net
BATCHELOR, Martin John. b 67. Plymouth Poly BSc91. St Jo Coll Nottm MA95. **d** 95 **p** 96. C Brecon St Mary and Battle w Llanddew *S & B* 95-97; Min Can Brecon Cathl 95-97; C Sketty 97-00; TV Hawarden *St As* 00-05; V Bistre from 05; AD Hawarden from 10. *Bistre Vicarage, Mold Road, Buckley CH7 2NH* Tel (01244) 550947
E-mail martin_batchelor@bigfoot.com
BATCHELOR, Veronica. b 48. Mon Dioc Tr Scheme 91. **d** 94 **p** 95. NSM Fleur-de-Lis *Mon* 94-96; NSM Bedwellty 96-97; C Pontypool 97-99; C Tenby *St D* 99-02; R Begelly w Ludchurch and Crunwere 02-05; C Risca *Mon* from 05. *18 Commercial Street, Risca, Newport NP11 6AY* Tel (01633) 614084
BATE, Preb Lawrence Mark. b 40. Univ Coll Ox BA63. Coll of Resurr Mirfield 65. **d** 67 **p** 68. C Benwell St Jas *Newc* 67-69; C Monkseaton St Pet 69-72; TV Withycombe Raleigh *Ex* 72-84; RD Aylesbeare 81-84; R Alphington 84-00; RD Christianity 95-99; TV Heavitree w Ex St Paul 00-02; TV Heavitree and St Mary Steps 02-05; Preb Ex Cathl 02-10; rtd 05. *Chapple Court, Kenn, Exeter EX6 7UR* Tel (01392) 833485
E-mail morleybate@freeuk.com
BATE, Michael Keith. b 42. Lich Th Coll 67. **d** 69 **p** 70. C W Bromwich St Jas *Lich* 69-73; C Thornhill *Wakef* 73-76; V Wrenthorpe 76-82; V Upper Gornal *Lich* 82-93; V Upper Gornal *Worc* 93-05; TV Gornal and Sedgley 05-08; Chapl Burton Hosp Dudley 82-94; Chapl Dudley Gp of Hosps NHS Trust 94-00; rtd 08; Perm to Offic *Lich* from 09. *44 Wentworth Road, Wolverhampton WV10 8EF*
E-mail michael.bate@tesco.net
BATE, Stephen Donald. b 58. Sheff Univ BSc79 Cov Univ PhD92 CEng97 MIET97. **d** 05 **p** 06. OLM Whitnash *Cov* from 05. *73 Golf Lane, Whitnash, Leamington Spa CV31 2QB* Tel (01926) 334134 Mobile 07773-583356 E-mail sbate@aol.com
BATEMAN, James Edward. b 44. Sheff Univ Coll Lon BSc65. Trin Coll Bris 71. **d** 74 **p** 75. C Woodlands *Sheff* 74-77; C Rushden w Newton Bromswold *Pet* 77-84; R Vange *Chelmsf* 84-94; V Southminster 94-01; P-in-c Nazeing and Roydon 01-03; Warden Stacklands Retreat Ho W Kingsdown 03-05; C Rainham *Roch* 05-09; rtd 09; Perm to Offic *Pet* from 11. *11 Ryeburn Way, Wellingborough NN8 3AH* Tel (01933) 440106
BATEMAN, Kenneth William. b 34. ACII58. NOC 85. **d** 88 **p** 89. Hon C Pilling *Blackb* 88-91; Chapl Lanc Moor Hosp 88-92; Chapl Lanc Priority Services NHS Trust 92-95; C Kirkby Lonsdale *Carl* 91-95; NSM 95-98; rtd 95; Perm to Offic *Carl* from 98. *Greenside, Barbon, Carnforth LA6 2LT* Tel (015242) 76318
BATEMAN, Martyn Henry. b 31. Jes Coll Cam BA54 MA58. Clifton Th Coll 54. **d** 56 **p** 57. C Heatherlands St Jo *Sarum* 56-59; C New Malden and Coombe *S'wark* 59-60; Iran 60-62; V Charsfield and R Monewden and Hoo *St E* 62-69; V Wickham Market 69-82; Hon Can St E Cathl 80-85; V Felixstowe SS Pet and Paul 82-85; TR Lydford, Brent Tor, Bridestowe and Sourton *Ex* 85-92; RD Tavistock 90-92; rtd 92; Lic to Offic *Mor* from 01. *Ardochy, Whitebridge, Inverness IV2 6UR* Tel (01456) 486273
BATEMAN, Nest Wynne. Univ of Wales (Cardiff) BA71 CQSW73. Westcott Ho Cam 08. **d** 09 **p** 10. NSM Lich Cathl from 09. *21 Christchurch Lane, Lichfield WS13 8BA* Tel (01543) 257681 Mobile 07729-256364 E-mail nestbateman@aol.com

BATEMAN, Patrick John. b 64. St Jo Coll Nottm 99. **d** 01 **p** 02. C Wallington *S'wark* 01-05; P-in-c Chipstead 05-11; R from 11. *The Rectory, Starrock Lane, Chipstead, Coulsdon CR5 3QD* Tel (01737) 552157 Mobile 07764-171400
E-mail patrick@batemannet.co.uk
BATES, Derek Alvin. b 27. St Mich Coll Llan 57. **d** 59 **p** 60. C Bishop's Cleeve *Glouc* 59-63; V Shebbear *Ex* 67-71; R Buckland Filleigh 67-71; R Coates *Ely* 72-80; R Clovelly *Ex* 80-92; V Woolfardisworthy and Buck Mills 80-92; rtd 92; Perm to Offic *Ex* 92-06 and *Portsm* 09-11. *Lonicera, Erw Haf, Llanwrtyd Wells LD5 4RT* Tel (01591) 610169
BATES, Elaine Austwick. b 57. Newc Univ BSc79 MSc80 Lanc Univ PGCE00. LCTP 06. **d** 10 **p** 11. NSM Barrow St Paul *Carl* from 10. *17 Harrel Lane, Barrow-in-Furness LA13 9LN* Tel (01229) 822149 E-mail ebates12@hotmail.co.uk
✠**BATES, The Rt Revd Gordon.** b 34. Kelham Th Coll 54. **d** 58 **p** 59 **c** 83. C New Eltham All SS *S'wark* 58-62; Asst Youth Chapl *Glouc* 62-64; Youth Chapl *Liv* 65-69; Chapl Liv Cathl 65-69; V Huyton St Mich 69-73; Can Res and Prec Liv Cathl 73-83; Dir of Ords 73-83; Suff Bp Whitby *York* 83-99; rtd 99; Hon Asst Bp *Carl* and *Blackb* 99-09; NSM Kirkby Lonsdale *Carl* 03-09. *19 Fernwood Close, Brompton, Northallerton DL6 2UX* Tel (01609) 761586
BATES, James. b 46. Linc Th Coll 73. **d** 75 **p** 76. C Ewell *Guildf* 75-77; C Farncombe 77-80; V Pet St Mary Boongate 80-92; V Kingston All SS w St Jo *S'wark* 92-05; P-in-c Win St Cross w St Faith 05-07; Master St Cross Hosp 05-07; V Offerton *Ches* from 07. *St Alban's Vicarage, 1A Salcombe Road, Stockport SK2 5AG* Tel 0161-480 3773 E-mail vicarofferton@aol.com
BATES, James Paul. QUB BSc PGCE Cranfield Univ MSc MPhil. **d** 06. NSM Bangor Abbey *D & D* 06-07. *16 Craigowen Road, Holywood BT18 0DL* Tel (028) 9042 2077
E-mail paul_tssf@hotmail.com
BATES, Mrs Nichola Jane. b 63. Trin Coll Bris 09. **d** 11. C Freiston, Butterwick w Bennington, and Leverton *Linc* from 11; C Old Leake w Wrangle from 11; C Friskney from 11. *The Vicarage, 1 Giles Close, Old Leake, Boston PE22 9NN* Tel (01205) 872089 Mobile 07760-484793
BATES, Miss Phyllis Edith. b 29. S'wark Ord Course 80. dss 83 **d** 87 **p** 94. Registrar S'wark Ord Course 83-89; Fulham St Dionis *Lon* 83-94; Hon Par Dn 87-94; rtd 89; NSM Hammersmith St Paul *Lon* 94-99; Perm to Offic *S'wark* 89 and *Lon* from 99. *26 St Dionis Road, London SW6 4TT* Tel (020) 7731 6935
BATES, Robert John. b 50. FRICS81. EAMTC 99. **d** 02 **p** 03. NSM Pet St Mary Boongate 02-05; C Ketton, Collyweston, Easton-on-the-Hill etc 05-09; Chapl Algarve *Eur* from 09. *Apartado 2135, Casa Sao Vincente, Boliqueime, Algarve 8100-170, Portugal* Tel (00351) (289) 366720
E-mail rev.bobbates@virgin.net or stvincentsbq@sapo.pt
BATES, Mrs Rosemary Eileen Hamilton. b 45. Ripon Coll Cuddesdon 87. **d** 89 **p** 94. Par Dn Brackley St Pet w St Jas 89-94; C 94-95; P-in-c N Hinksey and Wytham *Ox* 95-04; rtd 04; Perm to Offic *Ely* 04-08. *45 Spring Lane, Bottisham, Cambridge CB25 9BL* Tel (01223) 813902 E-mail revrosie@rosiebates.com
BATES, Stuart Geoffrey. b 61. Univ of Wales (Lamp) BA82. St Steph Ho Ox 83. **d** 85 **p** 86. C Bromley St Mark *Roch* 85-88; C Westmr St Matt *Lon* 88-89; C Gt Ilford St Mary *Chelmsf* 89-95; V Crofton Park St Hilda w St Cypr *S'wark* from 95. *St Hilda's Vicarage, 35 Buckthorne Road, London SE4 2DG* Tel (020) 8699 1277
BATES, William Frederic. b 49. St Jo Coll Dur BSc72 BA74 MA97. Cranmer Hall Dur. **d** 75 **p** 76. C Knutsford St Jo and Toft *Ches* 75-78; C Ripley *Derby* 78-80; R Nether and Over Seale 81-93; V Lullington 81-93; V Allestree St Nic from 93; Bp's Adv on New Relig Movements from 99; P-in-c Quarndon from 00; RD Duffield 09-10. *The Vicarage, 4 Lawn Avenue, Allestree, Derby DE22 2PE* Tel (01332) 550224
E-mail williambates@btconnect.com
BATES, William Hugh. b 36. Keble Coll Ox BA56 MA59. Westcott Ho Cam 59. **d** 60 **p** 61. C Horsforth *Ripon* 60-63; Tutor St Chad's Coll Dur 63-70; V Bishop Wilton *York* 70-76; RD Pocklington 74-76; V Pickering 76-82; Prin NEOC 79-94; P-in-c Crayke w Brandsby and Yearsley *York* 82-94; P-in-c Stillington and Marton w Moxby 82-94; rtd 94; Perm to Offic *York* from 94. *2 The Bungalows, Main Street, Bugthorpe, York YO41 1QG* Tel (01759) 368402
BATESON, Canon Geoffrey Frederick. b 27. K Coll Lon BD51 AKC51. **d** 52 **p** 53. C Tynemouth Cullercoats St Paul *Newc* 52-56; C Gosforth All SS 56-60; V Monkseaton St Pet 60-68; V Newc St Geo 68-77; RD Newc 75-77; R Morpeth 77-89; Chapl St Geo and Cottage Hosp Morpeth 77-89; Hon Can Newc Cathl 80-89; rtd 89; Perm to Offic *York* from 91. *1 Netherby Close, Sleights, Whitby YO22 5HD* Tel (01947) 810997
BATESON, Canon James Howard. b 36. Qu Mary Coll Lon BSc57 MSOSc88. EMMTC 85. **d** 87 **p** 88. NSM W Bridgford *S'well* 87-88; NSM Wilford Hill 88-95; Dioc Officer for NSMs 94-04; P-in-c Kilvington and Staunton w Flawborough 96-04; Hon Can S'well Minster 99-04; rtd 04; Perm to Offic *S'well* from

04. *45 Stamford Road, West Bridgford, Nottingham NG2 6GD*
Tel and fax 0115-923 1820 E-mail h bateson@primeuk.net
BATESON, Keith Nigel. b 43. d 00 p 01. OLM Wonersh w
Blackheath *Guildf* from 00. *Advent Cottage, Blackheath Lane,*
Wonersh, Guildford GU5 0PN Tel (01483) 892753
E-mail keith@batesonfamily.net
BATESON, Tracey Jane. b 74. St Mark & St Jo Coll Lon BEd96
MPhil04. Trin Coll Bris BA03. d 04 p 05. C Holdenhurst and
Iford *Win* 04-07; CF from 07. *c/o MOD Chaplains (Army)* Tel
(01264) 381140 Fax 381824
BATEY, Caroline. d 08. OLM Warrington H Trin *Liv* from 08.
22 Fairclough Avenue, Warrington WA1 2JS
E-mail cabethbatey@hotmail.com
BATEY, Canon Herbert Taylor. b 22. Qu Coll Ox BA46 MA48.
Linc Th Coll 48. d 48 p 49. C Dalton-in-Furness *Carl* 48-50; C
Egremont 50-52; V Cleator Moor w Cleator 52-59; Chapl St
Bees Sch Cumbria 59-64; Chapl Culham Coll Abingdon 64-68;
Prin Lect 68-75; P-in-c Culham *Ox* 68-75; Vice-Prin Coll of
Ripon and York St Jo 75-92; Hon Can Ripon Cathl 85-92; rtd
87; Perm to Offic *Ripon* from 92. *Clova House Care Home, 2*
Clotherholme Road, Ripon HG4 2DA Tel (01765) 603678
BATH, David James William. b 43. Oak Hill NSM Course 87.
d 89 p 90. NSM Henley *Ox* 89-90; Gen Manager Humberside
Gd News Trust 90-96; NSM Anlaby St Pet *York* 96-04; P-in-c
Anlaby Common St Mark 04-10; rtd 10. *24 Lawnswood, Hessle*
HU13 0PT E-mail davidjwbath@hotmail.com
BATH AND WELLS, Bishop of. *See* PRICE, The Rt Revd Peter
Bryan
BATH, Archdeacon of. *See* PIGGOTT, The Ven Andrew John
BATHURST, Bishop of. *See* HURFORD, The Rt Revd Richard
Warwick
BATLEY-GLADDEN, Dane Christopher. b 68. St Steph Ho Ox
96. d 99 p 00. C Hendon St Alphage *Lon* 99-01; C-in-c Grahame
Park St Aug CD from 01. *St Augustine's House, Great Field,*
London NW9 5SY Tel (020) 8205 1979 Fax 8205 6127
E-mail frdane@dcbg.org.uk
BATSON, David Frederick Edward. b 38. K Coll Lon AKC61
BD69 FSAScot97. St Boniface Warminster. d 62 p 63. C
Southport H Trin *Liv* 62-64; Asst Chapl Hurstpierpoint Coll
64-65; C Cleator Moor w Cleator *Carl* 65-66; Asst Master K Geo
V Sch Southport 66-67; NSM Leigh w Bransford *Worc* 68-79;
Hon Asst Chapl Convent of H Name Malvern Link 68-72; Prin
Soc Work Tr Dept Dumfries and Galloway Coun 84-94; Lect
and Tutor Langside Coll Glas 95-97; Lect Soc Studies Dumfries
and Galloway Coll 96-04; Visiting Lect Paisley Univ 02-07.
Kindar House, New Abbey, Dumfries DG2 8DB Tel (01387)
850514 Fax 850556
BATSON, Lee Paul. b 77. R Holloway Coll Lon BA99 MA00
Selw Coll Cam BA03. Westcott Ho Cam 01. d 04 p 05. C Saffron
Walden w Wendens Ambo, Littlebury etc *Chelmsf* 04-08; P-in-c
Boreham from 08; Co Ecum Officer from 08. *The Vicarage,*
Church Road, Boreham, Chelmsford CM3 3EG Tel (01245)
451087 E-mail lbatson@chelmsford.anglican.org
BATSON, Paul Leonard. b 47. Southn Univ BTh79. Sarum &
Wells Th Coll 73. d 75 p 76. C Chesham St Mary *Ox* 75-79; Dioc
Youth Adv *Newc* 79-85; V Earley St Pet *Ox* 85-93; Perm to Offic
Sarum 01-08. *Maple Cottage, 78 Murhill, Limpley Stoke, Bath*
BA2 7FB Tel (01225) 722721
E-mail paul.and.linds@btinternet.com
BATSON, William Francis Robert. b 43. St Jo Coll Dur BA72.
Cranmer Hall Dur. d 73 p 74. C Eastwood *S'well* 73-77; R Long
Marton w Dufton and w Milburn *Carl* 77-79; V Flimby 79-85;
TR Raveningham *Nor* 85-91; R Kinver and Enville *Lich* 91-00; V
Ledsham w Fairburn *York* 00-08; rtd 08. *8 Langdale Avenue,*
Carlisle CA2 5QG Tel (01228) 537798
E-mail bob@ledvic.fsnet.co.uk
BATSTONE, Bruce. b 70. Bris Univ BA92. St Steph Ho Ox 98.
d 00 p 01. C Leigh-on-Sea St Marg *Chelmsf* 00-03; C Old
St Pancras *Lon* 03-07; TV from 07; Chapl Camden and Islington
Community Health NHS Trust from 03. *23 Albert Street,*
London NW1 7LU Tel (020) 7387 4193
E-mail bruce.batstone@ic24.net
BATT, Canon Joseph William. b 39. Keele Univ BA62. Ripon
Hall Ox 63. d 64 p 65. C Bushbury *Lich* 64-68; C Walsall 68-71;
Tr Officer and Youth Chapl Dio Ibadan Nigeria 71-75; Hon Can
Oke-Osun from 94; Area Sec CMS *Guildf* and Chich 75-84; V
Ottershaw *Guildf* 84-04; rtd 04; Perm to Offic *Bradf* from 07.
8 Parkwood Road, Shipley BD18 4SS Tel (01274) 589775
BATT, Canon Kenneth Victor. b 41. Wycliffe Hall Ox 68. d 71 p 72.
C Yateley *Win* 71-76; R The Candover Valley 76-82; R
Durrington *Sarum* 82-89; V Kempshott *Win* 89-00; P-in-c
Bournemouth H Epiphany 00-05; V 05-08; rtd 08; Hon Can Win
Cathl from 07; Hon C Tadley S and Silchester from 08.
St Mary's House, 10 Romans Field, Silchester, Reading
RG7 2QH Tel 0118-970 2353
BATTE, Mrs Kathleen. b 47. Homerton Coll Cam TCert68.
NEOC 91. d 94 p 95. NSM Newc St Gabr *Newc* 94; NSM Wilford
Hill *S'well* 96-99; P-in-c Cinderhill 99-05; Bp's Adv for Self-
Supporting Min 05-07; Chapl Crowhurst Chr Healing Cen 07-10

and from 10. *The Old Rectory, Forewood Lane, Crowhurst, Battle*
TN33 9AD Tel (01424) 830762 E-mail kath.batte@talk21.com
BATTEN, Stuart William. b 73. Univ of Wales (Abth) BD94
MTh96. Trin Coll Bris 96. d 98 p 99. C Northolt St Jos *Lon*
98-01; TV Hucknall Torkard *S'well* 01-06; P-in-c Wickham
Bishops w Lt Braxted *Chelmsf* from 06; Asst Dir of Ords from
06. *The Rectory, 1 Church Road, Wickham Bishops, Witham*
CM8 3LA Tel (01621) 891360
E-mail stuart.batten@btinternet.com
BATTERSBY, David George Sellers. b 32. AKC57. St Boniface
Warminster 57 Lambeth STh80. d 58 p 59. C Glas St Marg
58-60; C Burnley St Pet *Blackb* 60-62; V Warton St Paul 62-71;
Chapl K Wm's Coll Is of Man 71-91; C Ashchurch *Glouc* 91-97;
rtd 97; Perm to Offic *Glouc* and *Worc* from 97, *Ox* from 03. *Shill*
Brook Cottage, Buckland Road, Bampton OX18 2AA Tel (01993)
851414 E-mail dgsb@fan.com
BATTERSBY, Simon Charles. b 64. Wycliffe Hall Ox BTh01. d 01
p 02. C Askern *Sheff* 01-03; Chapl Bethany Sch Goudhurst
03-07; Chapl Culford Sch Bury St Edmunds from 08. *Culford*
School, Bury St Edmunds IP28 6TX Tel (01284) 728615 Mobile
07900-242757 E-mail chaplain@culford.co.uk
BATTERSHELL, Mrs Anne Marie. b 33. Ox Poly BEd83.
SAOMC 95. d 98 p 99. NSM Goring w S Stoke *Ox* 98-01; NSM
Brafferton w Pilmoor, Myton-on-Swale etc *York* 01-03; rtd 03;
Perm to Offic *Wakef* from 04 and *Man* from 07. *26 Winterbutlee*
Grove, Todmorden OL14 7QU Tel (01706) 839848
E-mail revanne@battershell.fsnet.co.uk
BATTERSHELL, Rachel Damaris. b 65. SNWTP. d 11. C
Coldhurst and Oldham St Steph *Man* from 11. *The Vicarage, 46*
Godson Street, Oldham OL1 2DB Tel 0161-622 1423
E-mail rev.rachel@hotmail.co.uk
BATTEY, Alexander Robert Fenwick. b 77. St Andr Univ MA99.
Ripon Coll Cuddesdon BA05. d 05 p 06. C Whitby w Aislaby
and Ruswarp *York* 05-08; CF from 08. *c/o MOD Chaplains*
(Army) Tel (01264) 381140 Fax 381824
E-mail alexander.battey370@mod.uk *or* arfbattey@aol.com
BATTIN (*née* WEBB), Mrs Frances Mary. b 52. WEMTC 92.
d 95 p 96. NSM Inkberrow w Cookhill and Kington w
Dormston *Worc* 95-98; Asst Chapl HM Pris Brockhill 98-03;
Perm to Offic *Worc* 03-07; NSM Church Lench w Rous Lench
and Abbots Morton etc from 07. *2 The Rowans, Harvington,*
Evesham WR11 8SX
BATTISON, David John. b 62. ACIB93. St Jo Coll Nottm 07. d 09
p 10. C Matlock Bath and Cromford *Derby* from 09. *Blossom*
House, 67 Morledge, Matlock DE4 3SB Tel (01629) 580850
Mobile 07971-506088 E-mail davidbattison12@ntlworld.com
BATTISON, Mark Richard. b 62. EMMTC 01. d 04 p 05. NSM
Leic St Jas 04-07; NSM Oadby 07-09; NSM Guilsborough and
Hollowell and Cold Ashby etc *Pet* 09-11; R from 11. *The*
Vicarage, 15 Church Street, Guilsborough, Northampton
NN6 8QA Tel 07717-200777 (mobile)
E-mail markbattison@btinternet.com
BATTLE, Dean of. *See* EDMONDSON, The Very Revd John
James William
BATTMAN, John Brian. b 37. ALCD61. d 61 p 62. C Fulham
Ch Ch *Lon* 61-64; SAMS Argentina 64-69; Paraguay 69-76; Adn
Paraguay 70-76; Ext Sec SAMS 77-80; V Romford Gd Shep
Chelmsf 80-92; V Werrington *Pet* 92-02; rtd 02; Perm to Offic
St E from 02. *57 Glencoe Road, Ipswich IP4 3PP* Tel (01473)
717902 E-mail john.battman@ntlworld.com
BATTY, John Ivan. b 35. Clifton Th Coll 59. d 62 p 63. C Clayton
Bradf 62-67; V Toxteth Park St Clem *Liv* 67-73; R Darfield *Sheff*
73-90; Chapl Düsseldorf *Eur* 90-95; V The Marshland *Sheff*
95-00; rtd 00; Perm to Offic *Sheff* and *Linc* from 00.
4 St Lawrence Way, Tallington, Stamford PE9 4RH Tel and fax
(01780) 740151
BATTY, Mark Alan. b 56. BSc. Ripon Coll Cuddesdon. d 82 p 83.
C Bottesford w Ashby *Linc* 82-86; V Scunthorpe All SS 86-95;
P-in-c N Wolds Gp 95-97; V from 97. *The Vicarage, St Barnabas*
Road, Barnetby DN38 6JE Tel (01652) 688182
BATTY, Canon Stephen Roy. b 58. Chich Th Coll 88. d 90 p 91. C
Wimborne Minster and Holt *Sarum* 90-94; P-in-c Yetminster w
Ryme Intrinseca and High Stoy 94-02; V Branksome St Aldhelm
from 02; Perm to Offic *Win* from 02; Can and Preb Sarum Cathl
from 10. *The Vicarage, St Aldhelm's Road, Poole BH13 6BT* Tel
(01202) 764420
BATTYE, John Noel. b 42. TCD BA64 MA73. CITC 66. d 66
p 67. C Drumglass *Arm* 66-69; C Ballynafeigh St Jude *D & D*
70-73; Chapl Pemb Coll Cam 73-78; Bp's C Knocknagoney
D & D 78-80; I Cregagh 80-08; Preb Castleknock St Patr Cathl
Dublin 94-08; rtd 08. *The Vicarage, 2 Whitechurch Road,*
Ballywalter, Newtownards BT22 2JY
BATTYE, Ms Lisa Katherine. b 55. Man Univ BN78
MA(Theol)96 Liv Univ MTh00 RM79. NOC 96. d 99 p 00. C
Clifton *Man* 99-02; R Kersal Moor from 02. *St Paul's Rectory,*
1 Moorside Road, Salford M7 3PJ Tel 0161-792 5362
E-mail lisa@battye.fsbusiness.co.uk
BATY, Edward. b 30. Open Univ BA77 UEA PhD88 MRICS59.
St Aid Birkenhead 60. d 62 p 63. C Acomb St Steph *York* 62-64;

Succ Chelmsf Cathl 64-67; V Becontree St Cedd 67-71; R Hope Bowdler w Eaton-under-Heywood *Heref* 71-79; R Rushbury 71-79; P-in-c Cardington 71-79; R Fincham *Ely* 79-82; OCF 79-94; R Long Stanton w St Mich *Ely* 82-94; P-in-c Lolworth 85-88; CF(V) 86-95; rtd 95; Perm to Offic *Guildf* from 95. *25 Martindale Avenue, Camberley GU15 1BB* Tel (01276) 20315
BAUDAINS, Mrs Geraldine Louise. b 58. Ex Univ BTh07. SWMTC 02. **d** 05 **p** 06. NSM Jersey All SS *Win* from 05; NSM Jersey St Simon from 05. *Le Chataignier, La Rue du Flicquet, St Martin, Jersey JE3 6BP* Tel (01534) 855556
E-mail baudains@jerseymail.co.uk
✠**BAUERSCHMIDT, The Rt Revd John Crawford.** b 59. Kenyon Coll Ohio BA81. Gen Th Sem (NY) MDiv84. **d** 84 **p** 85 **c** 07. C Worcester All SS USA 84-87; Lib Pusey Ho 87-91; R Albemarle Ch Ch USA 92-97; R Covington Ch Ch 97-07; Bp Tennessee from 07. *50 Vantage Way, Suite 107, Nashville TN 37228-1524, USA* Tel (001) (615) 251 3322 Fax 251 8010
E-mail info@episcopaldiocese-tn.org
BAUGHAN, Emma Louise Langley. See LANGLEY, Ms Emma Louise
BAUGHEN, Andrew Jonathan. b 64. Lon Guildhall Univ BA87. Wycliffe Hall Ox BTh94. **d** 94 **p** 95. C Battersea Rise St Mark *S'wark* 94-97; P-in-c Clerkenwell St Jas and St Jo w St Pet *Lon* 97-00; V from 00. *St James's Church, Clerkenwell Close, London EC1R 0EA* Tel (020) 7251 1190 E-mail vicar@jc-church.org
✠**BAUGHEN, The Rt Revd Michael Alfred.** b 30. Lon Univ BD55. Oak Hill Th Coll 51. **d** 56 **p** 57 **c** 82. C Hyson Green *S'well* 56-59; C Reigate St Mary *S'wark* 59-61; Ord Cand Sec CPAS 61-64; R Rusholme H Trin *Man* 64-70; TV St Marylebone All So w SS Pet and Jo *Lon* 70-75; R 75-82; AD Westmr St Marylebone 78-82; Preb St Paul's Cathl 79-82; Bp Ches 82-96; rtd 96; Hon Asst Bp Lon 96-06; Asst Bp Guildf from 06; Perm to Offic *S'wark* 97-02. *42 Rookwood Court, Guildford GU2 4EL* Tel (01483) 457061 E-mail michaelmyrtle@tiscali.co.uk
BAULCOMB, Canon Geoffrey Gordon. b 46. K Coll Lon BD86. AKC68. **d** 69 **p** 70. C Crofton Park St Hilda w St Cypr *S'wark* 69-74; TV Padgate *Liv* 74-79; R Whitton and Thurleston w Akenham *St E* 79-03; Hon Can St E Cathl 03; rtd 03; Perm to Offic *St E* from 03 and *Chich* from 04. *Greenlands, 39 Filching Road, Eastbourne BN20 8SE* Tel (01323) 641746 Mobile 07880-731232 E-mail geoffreybaulcomb@hotmail.com
BAUN, Jane. b 60. **d** 10 **p** 11. NSM Abingdon *Ox* from 10. *68 Vicarage Road, Oxford OX1 4RE* Tel (01865) 244559
E-mail jane.baun@theology.ox.ac.uk
BAVERSTOCK, David John. b 76. K Coll Lon BA00 MA01. Westcott Ho Cam 07. **d** 09 **p** 11. C Mill End and Heronsgate w W Hyde *St Alb* 09-10; C Cheshunt from 10. *114 Trinity Lane, Waltham Cross EN8 7EN* Tel 07921-887513 (mobile)
E-mail david.baverstock@kcl.ac.uk
✠**BAVIN, The Rt Revd Timothy John.** b 35. Worc Coll Ox BA59 MA61. Cuddesdon Coll 59. **d** 61 **p** 62 **c** 74. S Africa 61-69 and 73-85; C Uckfield *Chich* 69-71; V Brighton Gd Shep Preston 71-73; Dean and Adn Johannesburg 73-74; Bp Johannesburg 74-85; Bp Portsm 85-95; OGS from 87; Community of Our Lady and St John from 96; Perm to Offic *Win* from 96; rtd 98. *Alton Abbey, Abbey Road, Beech, Alton GU34 4AP* Tel (01420) 562145 *or* 563575 Fax 561691
BAVINGTON, John Eduard. b 68. Loughb Univ BEng91. Trin Coll Bris BA99. **d** 99 **p** 00. C W Ealing St Jo w St Jas *Lon* 99-02; V Bradf St Clem 02-06; Chapl Giggleswick Sch from 06. *Tems House, Tems Bank, Giggleswick, Settle BD24 0BP* Tel (01729) 893000 Mobile 07704-854978
E-mail jebavington@giggleswick.org.uk
BAWDEN, Sheila Irene. b 55. **d** 11. NSM Bodmin w Lanhydrock and Lanivet Truro from 11. *Chimes, 8 Church Lane, Lostwithiel PL22 0EQ* Tel 07879-551046
E-mail sheila.stevens55@btinternet.com
BAWTREE, Andrew James. b 66. Univ of Wales BD91 Ch Ch Coll Cant PGCE92. St Jo Coll Nottm MA95. **d** 96 **p** 97. C Hoddesdon *St Alb* 96-99; R S Boston Trin Ch USA 00-07; P-in-c River Cant from 07. *The Vicarage, 23 Lewisham Road, Dover CT17 0QG* Tel (01304) 822037
E-mail rockabillyrev@hotmail.com
BAWTREE, Canon Robert John. b 39. Oak Hill Th Coll 62. **d** 67 **p** 68. C Foord St Jo *Cant* 67-70; C Boscombe St Jo *Win* 70-73; C Kinson *Sarum* 73-75; TV Bramerton w Surlingham *Nor* 76-82; R Arborfield w Barkham *Ox* 82-91; V Hildenborough *Roch* 91-04; RD Tonbridge 95-01; Hon Can Roch Cathl 02-04; rtd 04; Hon C Camelot Par *B & W* 04-08. *47 Mount Pleasant Road, Weald, Sevenoaks TN14 6QB* Tel (01732) 464427
E-mail robert.bawtree@virgin.net
BAXANDALL, Canon Peter. b 45. Tyndale Hall Bris 67. **d** 70 **p** 72. C Kidsgrove *Lich* 70-71; C St Helens St Mark *Liv* 71-75; C Ardsley *Sheff* 76-77; Rep Leprosy Miss E Anglia 77-86; P-in-c March St Wendreda *Ely* 86-87; R from 87; P-in-c March St Jo from 09; RD March 93-09; Hon Can Ely Cathl from 07. *St Wendreda's Rectory, 21 Wimblington Road, March PE15 9QW* Tel (01354) 653377
E-mail peter.baxandall@sky.com

BAXENDALE, John Richard. b 48. Cranmer Hall Dur 89. **d** 91 **p** 92. C Carl St Jo 91-94; C Dalston 94-95; P-in-c Monton *Man* 95-96; TV Eccles 96-04; V Clifton from 04. *St Anne's Vicarage, 237 Manchester Road, Manchester M27 6PP* Tel 0161-794 1939
BAXENDALE, Paul Gordon. b 70. Leeds Univ BA91. Ridley Hall Cam 93. **d** 96 **p** 97. C Kendal St Thos *Carl* 96-01; P-in-c Burton and Holme from 01. *St James's Vicarage, Glebe Close, Burton, Carnforth LA6 1PL* Tel (01524) 781391
BAXENDALE, Rodney Douglas. b 45. Ex Univ BA66 Cardiff Univ MTh10 Leeds Univ PGCE68. Linc Th Coll 78. **d** 80 **p** 81. C Maidstone All SS and St Phil w Tovil *Cant* 80-83; Chapl RN 83-03; Chapl Plymouth Hosps NHS Trust 06-08; Sen Chapl from 08. *Derriford Hospital, Derriford Road, Plymouth PL6 8DH* Tel 08451-558155 *or* (01752) 792313
E-mail rodney.baxendale@nhs.net
BAXTER, Anthony. b 54. SEITE 99. **d** 02 **p** 08. NSM Romford Ascension Collier Row *Chelmsf* 02-07; NSM Hutton from 07. *44 Prower Close, Billericay CM11 2BU* Tel (01277) 655514 Mobile 07909-984675 E-mail tonybaxter54@aol.com
BAXTER, Carlton Edwin. **d** 07 **p** 08. NSM Lurgan Ch the Redeemer *D & D* 07-10; NSM Maghaberry from 10. *33 Charnwood Grange, Portadown, Craigavon BT63 5TU*
BAXTER, David. See BAXTER, Canon Richard David
BAXTER, David Norman. b 39. Open Univ BA87. Kelham Th Coll 59. **d** 64 **p** 65. C Tonge Moor *Man* 64-68; Chapl RN 68-84; P-in-c Becontree St Pet *Chelmsf* 84-85; TV Becontree W 85-86; TR 86-94; Spain from 94; rtd 99. *Cl Vidal i Barraquer, 10, Escalera B, 1-2, 08870 Sitges (Barcelona), Spain* Tel (0034) 938 946 151 Fax 938 943 800 E-mail dnbaxter@teleline.es
BAXTER, Dennis Alexander. b 56. Sheff Univ BA96. St Mich Coll Llan 03. **d** 05 **p** 06. C Tenby *St D* 05-09; P-in-c Llanedi w Tycroes and Saron from 09. *The Vicarage, 37 Hendre Road, Tycroes, Ammanford SA18 3LA* Tel (01269) 592315 Mobile 07963-447702 E-mail aarowkosky2@aol.com
BAXTER (née AVIS), Elizabeth Mary. b 49. Leeds Metrop Univ BA93 CYCW77. NOC 81. **dss** 84 **d** 87 **p** 94. Leeds St Marg and All Hallows *Ripon* 84-93; Par Dn 87-93; Chapl Abbey Grange High Sch 85-93; Par Dn Topcliffe *York* 93-94; C 94-96; C Thirsk 96-07; Jt Dir H Rood Ho Cen for Health and Past Care 93-07; Exec Dir from 07; Perm to Offic *Ripon* from 93; *Dur* and *Newc* from 94; *Bradf* 97-04; *Sheff* from 95; *York* from 08. *5 Glendale Road, Wooler NE71 6DN* Tel (01668) 283125 *or* (01845) 522580 E-mail elizabeth.baxter@tiscali.co.uk
BAXTER, Harold Leslie. b 11. Roch Th Coll 62. **d** 64 **p** 65. C Corsham *Bris* 64-67; C Bath Lyncombe *B & W* 67-70; V Shapwick w Ashcott 70-88; P-in-c Burtle 75-88; V Shapwick w Ashcott and Burtle 88-95; rtd 96; Perm to Offic *Truro* from 97. *Tredole, Prussia Cove Lane, Rosudgeon, Penzance TR20 9AX* Tel (01736) 762133
BAXTER, Jane Elizabeth. b 51. EAMTC 98. **d** 01 **p** 02. C Clare w Poslingford, Cavendish etc *St E* 01-04; P-in-c Lyddington w Stoke Dry and Seaton etc *Pet* 04-10; C Bulwick, Blatherwycke w Harringworth and Laxton 04-10; V Lyddington, Bisbrooke, Caldecott, Glaston etc from 10. *The Rectory, 4 Windmill Way, Lyddington, Oakham LE15 9LY* Tel (01572) 822717 E-mail revjanebaxter@gmail.com
BAXTER, John Richard. b 44. ACII66. STETS 96. **d** 99 **p** 00. NSM Banstead *Guildf* 99-03; TV Surrey Weald 03-11; rtd 11. *High Lea, 54 The Street, Capel, Dorking RH5 5LE* Tel (01306) 711260 Mobile 07974-609233
E-mail johnbaxter@eastewell.freeserve.co.uk
BAXTER, Leslie. See BAXTER, Harold Leslie
BAXTER, Canon Richard David. b 33. Kelham Th Coll 53. **d** 57 **p** 58. C Carl St Barn 57-59; C Barrow St Matt 59-64; V Drighlington *Wakef* 64-73; V Penistone 73-80; V Carl St Aid and Ch Ch 80-86; Can Res Wakef Cathl 86-97; Prec from 86; Vice-Provost 92-97; rtd 97; Perm to Offic *Carl* from 97; Hon V Choral Carl Cathl from 04. *20 Summerfields, Dalston, Carlisle CA5 7NW* Tel and fax (01228) 710496
E-mail canondavidbaxter@btinternet.com
BAXTER, Stanley Robert. b 31. Leeds Univ MA90 FRSA96 MICM93 MInstD97 FRSH99 FRSM02 FCIM07. Chich Th Coll 79. **d** 80 **p** 81. In Lutheran Ch 71-79; C Far Headingley St Chad *Ripon* 80-82; P-in-c Leeds St Marg 82-87; P-in-c Leeds All Hallows w Wrangthorn 85-87; P-in-c Leeds St Marg and All Hallows 87-93; P-in-c Topcliffe *York* 93-95; NSM 95-96; NSM Thirsk 96-07; Dir Leeds Cen for Urban Th Studies 88-93; Assoc Chapl Leeds Univ 91-93; Jt Dir H Rood Ho Cen for Health and Past Care 93-07; Dir Miss from 07; Perm to Offic *Ripon* from 93; Perm to Offic *Dur* and *Newc* from 94; *Bradf* and *Sheff* from 95; Chapl N Yorks and York Primary Care Trust 03-07; Chief Exec Hexthorpe Manor Community from 07. *5 Glendale Road, Wooler NE71 6DN* Tel (01668) 283125 *or* (01845) 522580
E-mail stanleybaxter@holyroodhouse.org.uk
BAXTER, Stuart. b 43. Liv Univ BA65 Nottm Univ PGCE66. Cuddesdon Coll 66. **d** 70 **p** 71. C Kirkby *Liv* 70-73; C Ainsdale 73-76; CMS 76-77 and 83-84; Sierra Leone 77-83; V Nelson in Lt Marsden *Blackb* 84-92; V Lostock Hall 92-99; P-in-c Hatton

Derby 99-04; Asst Chapl HM Pris Sudbury 99-03; Asst Chapl HM Pris Foston Hall 03-06; rtd 06; Perm to Offic *Derby* from 06. *11 Pingle Crescent, Belper DE56 1DY* Tel (01773) 827309
BAXTER, Terence Hugh. b 48. Leeds Poly BSc74. NOC 89. **d** 92 **p** 93. NSM Guiseley w Esholt *Bradf* 92-04; NSM Weston w Denton 04-08; NSM Leathley w Farnley, Fewston and Blubberhouses 04-08; NSM Washburn and Mid-Wharfe from 08. *The Rectory, Stainburn Lane, Leathley, Otley LS21 2LF* Tel 0113-284 3744 Mobile 07985-391298
E-mail terry.baxter@bradford.anglican.org
BAYCOCK, Philip Louis. b 33. Wells Th Coll 64. **d** 66 **p** 67. C Kettering SS Pet and Paul 66-68; C St Peter-in-Thanet *Cant* 68-72; V Bobbing w Iwade 72-73; Perm to Offic 73-76; V Thanington w Milton 77-84; R Chagford w Gidleigh and Throwleigh *Ex* 84-01; rtd 01; Perm to Offic *Ex* from 01. *7 Grove Meadow, Sticklepath, Okehampton EX20 2NE* Tel (01837) 840617 E-mail louisb@care4free.net
BAYES, Frederick Alan. b 60. Imp Coll Lon BSc81. St Jo Coll Dur BA92 Cranmer Hall Dur 93. **d** 93 **p** 94. C Talbot Village *Sarum* 93-97; Chapl St Hild and St Bede Coll *Dur* 97-03; Bp's Adv in Interfaith Matters 02-03; V Penllergaer *S & B* from 03. *The Vicarage, 16 Swansea Road, Penllergaer, Swansea SA4 9AQ* Tel (01792) 892603
✠**BAYES, The Rt Revd Paul.** b 53. Birm Univ BA75. Qu Coll Birm 76. **d** 79 **p** 80 **c** 10. C Tynemouth Cullercoats St Paul *Newc* 79-82; Chapl Qu Eliz Coll Lon 82-87; Chapl Chelsea Coll 85-87; TV High Wycombe *Ox* 87-90; TR 90-94; TR Totton *Win* 95-04; AD Lyndhurst 00-04; Nat Miss and Evang Adv Abps' Coun 04 10; Hon Can Worc Cathl 07-10; Suff Bp Hertford *St Alb* from 10. *Bishopswood, 3 Stobarts Close, Knebworth SG3 6ND* Tel (01438) 817260 E-mail bishophertford@stalbans.anglican.org
BAYFORD, Terence Michael. b 48. Westmr Coll Ox MTh96. Wilson Carlile Coll 70 NOC 97. **d** 99 **p** 00. Dep Chapl HM Pris Wakef 99-01; NSM Alverthorpe *Wakef* 99-01; Chapl HM Pris Moorland 01-05; Chapl HM Pris Wealstun from 05. *The Chaplain's Office, HM Prison Wealstun, Thorp Arch, Wetherby LS23 7AZ* Tel (01937) 444400
BAYLDON, Roger. b 38. MBE74 TD99. **d** 04 **p** 05. OLM Parkstone St Pet and St Osmund w Branksea *Sarum* 04-08. *37 Blake Dene Road, Poole BH14 8HF* Tel and fax (01202) 730683 Mobile 07831-272773
E-mail r.bayldon@btinternet.com *or* roger@bayldon.com
BAYLEY, Anne Christine. b 34. OBE86. Girton Coll Cam BA55 MB, ChB58 FRCS66 FRCSEd86. St Steph Ho Ox 90. **d** 91 **p** 94. NSM Wembley Park St Aug *Lon* 91-97; Perm to Offic *York* 97-05 and *Heref* 05-08. *52 Frome Court, Bartestree, Hereford HR1 4DX* Tel (01432) 850220
BAYLEY, David Francis. b 47. **d** 99 **p** 00. OLM Wriggle Valley *Sarum* 99-04; NSM Weaverthorpe w Helperthorpe, Luttons Ambo etc *York* 04-08; P-in-c 06-08; rtd 09; Perm to Offic *York* from 09. *62 Newbiggin, Malton YO17 7JF* Tel 07817-023108 (mobile) E-mail bayley7jf@btinternet.com
BAYLEY, Michael John. b 36. CCC Cam BA60 MA64 Sheff Univ PhD73. Linc Th Coll 60. **d** 62 **p** 63. C Leeds Gipton Epiphany *Ripon* 62-66; NSM Sheff St Mark Broomhill 67-93; C Sheff St Mary w Highfield Trin 93-95; C Sheff St Mary Bramall Lane 95-00; rtd 00. *27 Meadowbank Avenue, Sheffield S7 1PB* Tel 0114-258 5248
BAYLEY, Oliver James Drummond. b 49. Mansf Coll Ox MA PGCE. St Jo Coll Nottm 81. **d** 83 **p** 84. C Bath Weston St Jo w Kelston *B & W* 83-88; P-in-c Bathampton 88-93; P-in-c Claverton 92-93; R Bathampton w Claverton 93-96; Chapl Dauntsey's Sch Devizes 96-02; rtd 02; Perm to Offic *Win* from 01. *19 Treeside Road, Southampton SO15 5FY* Tel (023) 8078 6498 E-mail ojdb80@hotmail.com
BAYLEY, Canon Raymond. b 46. Keble Coll Ox BA68 MA72 Ex Univ PhD86. St Chad's Coll Dur 68. **d** 69 **p** 70. C Mold *St As* 69-74; Lay Tr Officer 71-74; C Llandaff w Capel Llanilltern 74; PV Llan Cathl and Lay Tr Officer 74-77; V Cwmbach 77-80; Dir Past Studies St Mich Coll Llan 80-84; Lect Univ of Wales (Cardiff) *Llan* 80-84; V Ynysddu *Mon* 84-86; V Griffithstown 86-92; Tutor Dioc Minl Tr Course 84-92; V Rhosymedre *St As* 92-96; Warden and R Ruthin w Llanrhydd 96-09; Tutor Dioc Minl Tr Course 92-06; Dir CME 94-01; Warden of Readers 02-09; Hon Can St As Cathl 04-09; rtd 09. *11 Maes Glanrafon, Brook Street, Mold CH7 1RJ* Tel (01352) 752345
E-mail raymond.bayley@virgin.net
BAYLIS (née LOFTS), Mrs Sally Anne. b 55. Kent Univ BA78 K Coll Lon MA80 Nottm Univ PGCE93. St Jo Coll Nottm 01. **d** 03 **p** 04. C Gedling *S'well* 03-07; P-in-c Daybrook from 07. *St Paul's Vicarage, 241 Oxclose Lane, Nottingham NG5 6FB* Tel 0115-926 2686 E-mail k.baylis@ntlworld.com
BAYLISS, Geoffrey Brian Tudor. b 60. R Holloway Coll Lon BSc83 Univ of Wales (Swansea) PGCE85 Univ of Wales (Ban) MA11. EAMTC 96. **d** 99 **p** 00. NSM Panfield and Rayne *Chelmsf* 99-04; TV Halstead Area 04-10; RD Hinckford 08-10; P-in-c Tolleshunt D'Arcy and Tolleshunt Major 10-11; P-in-c Tollesbury w Salcot Virley 10-11; V N Blackwater from 11; RD

Witham from 11. *The Vicarage, 37 Church Street, Tolleshunt D'Arcy, Maldon CM9 8TS* Tel (01621) 869895
E-mail g.bayliss41@btinternet.com
BAYLISS, Grant David. b 75. Ex Univ BA96 Wolfs Coll Ox DPhil05 Ox Univ MA05. Ripon Coll Cuddesdon BA99. **d** 03 **p** 04. C Prestbury and All SS *Glouc* 03-07; Chapl St Jo Coll Cam 07-11; Lect Ripon Coll Cuddesdon from 11. *Ripon College, Cuddesdon, Oxford OX44 9EX* Tel (01895) 874404
E-mail grant.bayliss@ripon-cuddesdon.ac.uk
BAYLOR, Nigel Peter. b 58. NUI BA80 TCD MPhil88. **d** 84 **p** 86. C Carrickfergus *Conn* 84-87; C Dundela St Mark *D & D* 87-89; I Galloon w Drummully *Clogh* 89-94; Adult Educn Adv 91-94; I Carnmoney *Conn* 94-03; I Jordanstown from 03. *The Rectory, 120A Circular Road, Jordanstown, Newtownabbey BT37 0RH* Tel (028) 9086 2119 E-mail revbaylor munster@hotmail.co.uk
BAYLY, Mrs Janet. b 48. **d** 08. OLM Schorne *Ox* from 08. *Crandon Farm, North Marston, Buckingham MK18 3PQ* Tel (01296) 670245 E-mail crancon@dial.pipex.com
BAYLY, Samuel Niall Maurice. b 36. TCD BA64 MA. CITC Div Test65. **d** 65 **p** 66. C Belfast St Matt *Conn* 65-68; Miss to Seamen 68-69; C Belfast St Pet *Conn* 69-74; I Belfast Ch Ch 74-02. *81 Dunluce Avenue, Belfast BT9 7AW* Tel (028) 9066 8732
BAYMAN, Ann Bernette. b 45. **d** 04 **p** 05. OLM Yoxmere *St E* 04-10; rtd 10; Perm to Offic *St E* from 10. *Dove Cottage, 4 South Road, Beccles NR34 9NN* Tel (01502) 471709 Mobile 07884-072944 E-mail annie@dovecottage.orangehome.co.uk
BAYMAN, Brynn. b 66. **d** 11. OLM Finchampstead *Ox* from 11. *Bevirs, Mordaunt Drive, Wellington College, Crowthorne RG45 7QQ*
BAYNE, Canon David William. b 52. St Andr Univ MA75. Edin Th Coll 88. **d** 90 **p** 91. C Dumfries *Glas* 90-92; P-in-c 92-93; R 93-99; Chapl Dumfries and Galloway Primary Care NHS Trust 92-99; Chapl Crichton R Hosp Dumfries 92-99; Chapl HM Pris Dumfries 96-99; P-in-c Castle Douglas *Glas* from 99; Can St Mary's Cathl from 99. *The Rectory, 68 St Andrew Street, Castle Douglas DG7 1EN* Tel and fax (01556) 503818
E-mail dwbayne@aol.com
BAYNE, Mrs Felicity Meriel. b 47. WEMTC 91. **d** 94 **p** 95. NSM Cheltenham Ch Ch *Glouc* 94-98; NSM Leckhampton St Pet 98-09; Chapl Glenfall Ho from 09. *Glenfall House, Mill Lane, Charlton Kings, Cheltenham GL54 4EP* Tel (01242) 583654 Fax 251314 E-mail felicity.bayne@btinternet.com
BAYNE-JARDINE, Anthea Mary. *See* GRIGGS, Mrs Anthea Mary
BAYNES, Mrs Clare. b 57. Reading Univ BA79. SAOMC 01. **d** 04 **p** 05. NSM Chambersbury *St Alb* 04-08; NSM St Alb St Steph from 08. *4 Pilgrim Close, Park Street, St Albans AL2 2JD* Tel (01727) 875524 E-mail clare@simonbaynes.fsnet.co.uk
BAYNES, Canon Matthew Thomas Crispin. b 62. UEA BA83 Qu Coll Cam BA86 MA91. Westcott Ho Cam 85. **d** 87 **p** 88. C Southgate Ch Ch *Lon* 87-90; C Gt Berkhamsted *St Alb* 90-95; V Coseley Ch Ch *Worc* 95-99; R Bredon w Bredon's Norton from 99; P-in-c Overbury w Teddington, Alstone etc from 09; RD Pershore from 05; Hon Can Worc Cathl from 10. *The Rectory, Bredon, Tewkesbury GL20 7LT* Tel (01684) 772237
E-mail matthew@tcbaynes.fsnet.co.uk
BAYNES, Simon Hamilton. b 33. New Coll Ox BA57 MA62. Wycliffe Hall Ox 57. **d** 59 **p** 60. C Rodbourne Cheney *Bris* 59-62; Japan 63-80; C Keynsham *B & W* 80-84; P-in-c Winkfield *Ox* 84-85; V Winkfield and Cranbourne 85-99; rtd 99; Lic to Offic *Ox* 99-02; Hon C Thame from 02. *23 Moorend Lane, Thame OX9 3BQ* Tel (01844) 213673 E-mail baynes@psa-online.com
BAYNES, Timothy Francis de Brissac. b 29. Ely Th Coll 59. **d** 61 **p** 62. C Hockerill *St Alb* 61-65; C Mansfield Woodhouse *S'well* 65-67; Ind Chapl *Man* 67-94; P-in-c Miles Platting St Jo 67-72; rtd 94; Perm to Offic *Man* 94-97. *46 Kirkbie Green, Kendal LA9 7AJ* Tel (01539) 740605
BAYNES, William Hendrie. b 39. Adelaide Univ BA60. S'wark Ord Course 77. **d** 79 **p** 80. C Notting Hill All SS w St Columb *Lon* 79-85; Perm to Offic 86-87 and 99-00; Hon C Paddington St Sav 88-98; Asst Chapl St Mary's NHS Trust Paddington 94-99; Hon C Paddington St Jas *Lon* 00-10; Perm to Offic from 10. *39E Westbourne Gardens, London W2 5NR* Tel (020) 7727 9530 E-mail will.baynes@london.anglican.org
BAYNHAM, Matthew Fred. b 57. BNC Ox BA78 Birm Univ MPhil00. Wycliffe Hall Ox 81. **d** 83 **p** 84. C Halesowen *Birm* 83-87; TV Bath Twerton-on-Avon *B & W* 87-93; V Reddal Hill St Luke *Worc* 93-00; RD Dudley 98-00; Chapl Bp Grosseteste Coll Linc 00-05; Assoc Chapl Liv Univ 05-07; Sen Res Tutor 05-07; P-in-c Llanllwchaearn and Llanina *St D* from 11. *Fronnant, Nanternis, New Quay SA45 9RW* Tel (01545) 560500 E-mail matthewbaynham@hotmail.com
BAYS, Mrs Helen Margaret. b 48. Kent Univ BA69 RGN71 RHV73. STETS 97. **d** 00 **p** 01. NSM Calne and Blackland *Sarum* 00-02; NSM Dawlish *Ex* from 02. *14 Stockton Hill, Dawlish EX7 9LP* Tel (01626) 862860
E-mail hbays@talktalk.net

BAZELY, Stephen William. b 80. Ox Brookes Univ BSc06. Oak Hill Th Coll BA11. **d** 11. C Deane *Man* from 11. *1 Somerset Road, Bolton BL1 4NE* Tel 07980-367731 (mobile) E-mail sbazely@hotmail.com

BAZELY, William Francis. b 53. Sheff Univ BEng75. St Jo Coll Nottm 78. **d** 81 **p** 82. C Huyton St Geo *Liv* 81-84; TV Netherthorpe *Sheff* 84-92; Chapl Lambeth Healthcare NHS Trust 92-98; Chapl Guy's and St Thos' Hosps NHS Trust Lon 98-01; C Rotherham *Sheff* 01-03; Chapl Rotherham Gen Hosps NHS Trust 01-03; Chapl Rotherham Priority Health Services NHS Trust 01-03; Sen Chapl Norfolk & Waveney Mental Health NHS Foundn Trust from 03. *34 Woodcock Road, Norwich NR3 3TX* Tel (01603) 421345 Mobile 07786-734519 E-mail bill_bazely@hotmail.com

✠**BAZLEY, The Rt Revd Colin Frederick.** b 35. St Pet Coll Ox BA57 MA61. Tyndale Hall Bris 57. **d** 59 **p** 60 **c** 69. C Bootle St Leon *Liv* 59-62; SAMS Miss Chile 62-00; Adn Cautin and Malleco 67-69; Asst Bp Cautin and Malleco 69-75; Asst Bp Santiago 75-77; Bp Chile 77-00; Primate CASA 77-83; Primate Iglesia Anglicana del Cono Sur 89-95; rtd 00; Hon Asst Bp Ches from 00; Warden of Readers 00-05; RD Wallasey 09-11. *121 Brackenwood Road, Higher Bebington, Wirral CH63 2LU* Tel 0151-608 1193 Mobile 07866-391333 E-mail colin@colbarb.fsnet.co.uk

BAZLINTON, Stephen Cecil. b 46. Lon Univ BDS RCS LDS. Ridley Hall Cam 78. **d** 85 **p** 86. NSM Stebbing w Lindsell *Chelmsf* 85-04; NSM Stebbing and Lindsell w Gt and Lt Saling 04-08; Perm to Offic from 08. *St Helens, High Street, Stebbing, Dunmow CM6 3SE* Tel (01371) 856495 E-mail revbaz@care4free.co.uk

BEACH, Jonathan Mark. b 67. Essex Univ BSc89. Trin Coll Bris BA94. **d** 94 **p** 95. C Oulton Broad *Nor* 94-97; Chapl RAF from 97. *Chaplaincy Services, Valiant Block, HQ Air Command, RAF High Wycombe HP14 4UE* Tel (01494) 496800 Fax 496343

BEACH, Mark Howard Francis. b 62. Kent Univ BA83 Nottm Univ MA95 K Coll Lon DMin11. St Steph Ho Ox 85. **d** 87 **p** 88. C Beeston *S'well* 87-90; C Hucknall Torkard 90-93; R Gedling 93-01; R Netherfield 96-01; Bp's Chapl *Wakef* 01-03; TR Rugby *Cov* from 03. *The Rectory, Church Street, Rugby CV21 3PH* Tel (01788) 542936 or 565609 Mobile 07930-577248 E-mail mark.beach@o2.co.uk or rector@rugbyteam.org.uk

BEACH, Stephen John. b 58. Man Univ BA81 BD88 Didsbury Coll of Educn PGCE82. NOC 92. **d** 93 **p** 94. C Harwood *Man* 93-97; TV Westhoughton and Wingates 97-01; P-in-c Devonport St Budeaux *Ex* 01-02; V from 02. *St Budeaux Vicarage, Agaton Road, Plymouth PL5 2EW* Tel (01752) 361019 or 351087 E-mail steph.beach@xalt.co.uk

BEACHAM, Peter Martyn. b 44. Ex Coll Ox BA65 MA70 Lon Univ MPhil67 FSA92 MRTPI69. Sarum Th Coll 70. **d** 73 **p** 74. NSM Ex St Martin, St Steph, St Laur etc 73-74; NSM Cen Ex 74-90; Perm to Offic from 99. *Bellever, Barrack Road, Exeter EX2 6AB* Tel (01392) 435074

BEACON, Canon Ralph Anthony. b 44. St Mich Coll Llan 70. **d** 71 **p** 72. C Neath w Llantwit 71-74; TV Holyhead w Rhoscolyn *Ban* 74-78; R Llanenddwyn w Llanddwywe, Llanbedr w Llandanwg 78-99; V Harlech and Llanfair-juxta-Harlech etc 99-11; RD Ardudwy 89-02; AD from 02; Hon Can Ban Cathl 91-97; Can Cursal 97-03; Can and Preb Ban Cathl 03-11; rtd 11. *The Rectory, Môn Dirion, Ffordd Uchaf, Harlech LL46 2SS* Tel (01766) 781336 Mobile 07713-421858

BEACON, Mrs Stephanie Kathleen Nora. b 49. Univ of Wales (Ban) BA70 PGCE71. NW Ord Course 94. **d** 96 **p** 97. NSM Llanenddwyn w Llanddwywe, Llanbedr w Llandanwg *Ban* 96-98; C Ardudwy 99-09; P-in-c Llanenddwyn w Llanddwywe, Llanbedr w Llandanwg 99-01; R from 01. *The Rectory, Môn Dirion, Ffordd Uchaf, Harlech LL46 2SS* Tel (01766) 781336 Mobile 07713-421858

BEADLE, David Alexander. b 37. St And Dioc Tr Course. **d** 88 **p** 89. NSM St Andrews St Andr *St And* from 88. *48 Clayton Caravan Park, St Andrews KY16 9YB* Tel (01334) 870001 E-mail dabeadle@lineone.net

BEADLE, Canon Janet Mary. b 52. Philippa Fawcett Coll CertEd74. EAMTC 91. **d** 94 **p** 95. C Kingston upon Hull H Trin *York* 94-98; V Ness Gp *Linc* from 98; Bp's Adv in Women's Min 00-08; Can and Preb Linc Cathl from 03. *The Vicarage, 10 Church Street, Thurlby, Bourne PE10 0EH* Tel (01778) 422475 E-mail janet.beadle@talk21.com

BEADLE, Liam Paul. b 84. St Pet Coll Ox BA07 MA11 St Jo Coll Dur MA10. Cranmer Hall Dur 07. **d** 09 **p** 10. C Enfield St Andr *Lon* from 09. *159 Parsonage Lane, Enfield EN1 3UJ* E-mail liam.beadle@gmail.com

BEADLE, Mrs Lorna. b 40. NEOC 92. **d** 95 **p** 96. NSM Ashington *Newc* from 95; Chapl MU from 02. *9 Arundel Square, Ashington NE63 8AW* Tel (01670) 816467

BEAHAN, Alan. b 64. Birm Univ BA87 York Univ PGCE89 St Jo Coll Dur BA07. Cranmer Hall Dur 05. **d** 07 **p** 08. C Warrington St Elphin *Liv* 07-10; P-in-c Hindley All SS from 10. *The Vicarage, 192 Atherton Road, Hindley, Wigan WN2 3XA* Tel (01942) 255175 E-mail alanbeahan@yahoo.co.uk

✠**BEAK, The Rt Revd Robert Michael Cawthorn.** b 25. OBE90. Lon Bible Coll. **d** 53 **p** 54 **c** 84. C Tunbridge Wells St Jo *Roch* 53-55; BCMS 55-56 and 84-89; Kenya 56-69 and 84-89; R Heanton Punchardon *Ex* 70-84; Offg Chapl RAF 70-80; RD Barnstaple *Ex* 77-81; R Heanton Punchardon w Marwood 79-84; Preb Ex Cathl 82-84; Asst Bp Mt Kenya E 84-89; rtd 90; Hon Asst Bp Derby from 91. *Ashcroft Cottage, Butts Road, Ashover, Chesterfield S45 0AX* Tel (01246) 590048

BEAK, Stephen Robert. b 64. City Univ BSc86. Wycliffe Hall Ox BTh94. **d** 94 **p** 95. C Lache cum Saltney *Ches* 94-97; C Howell Hill *Guildf* 97-01; NSM Woking St Mary 01-05; V from 05. *St Mary's Vicarage, Bethany House, West Hill Road, Woking GU22 7UJ* Tel (01483) 761269 E-mail stephen.beak@ntlworld.com

BEAKE, the Ven Stuart Alexander. b 49. Em Coll Cam BA72 MA76. Cuddesdon Coll 72. **d** 74 **p** 75. C Hitchin St Mary *St Alb* 74-76; C Hitchin 77-79; TV Hemel Hempstead 79-85; Bp's Dom Chapl *S'well* 85-87; V Shottery St Andr *Cov* 87-00; RD Fosse 93-99; Dioc Dir of Ords 96-00; Hon Can Cov Cathl 98-00; Can Res and Sub-Dean Cov Cathl 00-05; Adn Surrey *Guildf* from 05; Hon Can Guildf Cathl 05-10; Can Res from 10; Warden CSP from 08. *Archdeacon's House, Lime Grove, West Clandon, Guildford GU4 7UT* Tel (01483) 211924 or 790352 E-mail stuart.beake@cofeguildford.org.uk or sabeake@msn.com

BEAKEN, Robert William Frederick. b 62. SS Paul & Mary Coll Cheltenham BA83 Lambeth STh90 MA01 K Coll Lon PhD09 FSAScot01. Ripon Coll Cuddesdon 85 Ven English Coll & Pontifical Gregorian Univ Rome 87. **d** 88 **p** 89. C Forton *Portsm* 88-92; C Shepshed *Leic* 92-94; V Colchester St Barn *Chelmsf* 94-02; P-in-c Gt and Lt Bardfield from 02. *The Vicarage, Braintree Road, Great Bardfield, Braintree CM7 4RN* Tel (01371) 810267 E-mail robert@webform.com

BEAL, David Michael. b 61. St Jo Coll Nottm BTh89. **d** 89 **p** 90. C Marton *Blackb* 89-92; C Darwen St Pet w Hoddlesden 92-93; TV 93-97; R Itchingfield w Slinfold *Chich* 97-09; R W Chiltington from 09. *The Rectory, East Street, West Chiltington, Pulborough RH20 2JY* E-mail beals@tesco.net

BEALES, Christopher Leader Day. b 51. St Jo Coll Dur BA72. Cranmer Hall Dur 72. **d** 76 **p** 77. C Upper Armley and Ind Chapl *Ripon* 76-79; Ind Chapl *Dur* 79-84; Sen Chapl 82-84; Sec Ind Cttee of Gen Syn Bd for Soc Resp 85-91; Sec Inner Cities Relig Coun (DOE) 92-94; Dir Churches' Regional Commn in the NE *Newc* and *Dur* 94-98; Consultant Dir 98; Chief Exec Employment Focus 99-07; C Thamesmead *S'wark* 99-01; Perm to Offic from 01; Chief Exec Afghan Action from 05; P-in-c Woburn Sands *St Alb* from 08. *St Michael's Vicarage, 30 Church Road, Woburn Sands, Milton Keynes MK17 8TR* Tel (01908) 582581 E-mail chrisbeales@afghanaction.com

BEALES, John David. b 55. SS Hild & Bede Coll Dur BA77 Univ of W Aus DipEd79. St Jo Coll Nottm 81. **d** 83 **p** 84. Australia 83-89 and 95-00; C Scarborough 83-86; Dioc Youth Chapl Perth 86-89; Dir Educn and Tr Philo Trust 89-90; NSM Nottingham St Nic *S'well* 89-95; Dir Evang Melbourne 95-00; Perm to Offic *Chelmsf* 99-01. *52 Wellesley Road, Colchester CO3 3HF* Tel (01206) 530934 E-mail davidbeales@ntlworld.com

BEALING, Andrew John. b 42. Sarum Th Coll 67. **d** 69 **p** 70. C Auckland St Andr and St Anne *Dur* 69-73; P-in-c Eastgate and Rookhope 73-76; V Frosterley 76-85; V Rekendyke 85-09; Chapl S Tyneside Distr Hosp 90-93; Chapl S Tyneside Healthcare Trust 93-09; Chapl Miss to Seafarers 02-09; rtd 09. *31 Cedar Drive, Jarrow NE32 4BF* Tel 0191-519 2588

BEALING, Mrs Patricia Ramsey. b 39. Lightfoot Ho Dur IDC63. **dss** 63 **d** 87 **p** 94. Rekendyke *Dur* 85-06; Par Dn 87-94; C 94-06; Chapl S Tyneside Distr Hosp 88-93; Chapl S Tyneside Healthcare Trust from 93. *31 Cedar Drive, Jarrow NE32 4BF* Tel 0191-519 2588

BEAMENT, Canon Owen John. b 41. MBE01. Bps' Coll Cheshunt 61. **d** 64 **p** 65. C Deptford St Paul *S'wark* 64-68; C Peckham St Jo 69-73; C Vauxhall St Pet 73-74; V Hatcham Park All SS from 74; Hon Can S'wark Cathl from 97. *All Saints' Vicarage, 22 Erlanger Road, London SE14 5TG* Tel (020) 7639 3497 E-mail owenbeament@aol.com

BEAMER, Neville David. b 40. Univ of Wales (Lamp) BA62 Jes Coll Ox BA65 MA70. Wycliffe Hall Ox 64. **d** 65 **p** 66. C Hornchurch St Andr *Chelmsf* 65-68; C Warwick St Mary *Cov* 68-72; V Holton-le-Clay *Linc* 72-75; P-in-c Stoneleigh w Ashow *Cov* 75-79; P-in-c Baginton 77-79; V Fletchamstead 79-86; Warden Whatcombe Ho Blandford Forum 86-90; R Jersey St Lawr and V Jersey Millbrook St Matt *Win* 90-95; V Yateley 95-03; P-in-c Eversley 00-03; R Yateley and Eversley 03-05; rtd 05; Perm to Offic *Cov* from 05. *8 Aintree Road, Stratford-upon-Avon CV37 9FL* Tel (01789) 263435 E-mail nevillebeamer@aol.com

BEAN, Douglas Jeyes Lendrum. b 25. Worc Coll Ox BA50 MA53. Ely Th Coll 50. **d** 51 **p** 52. C Croydon Woodside *Cant* 51-54; Min Can Windsor 54-59; V Reading St Laur *Ox* 59-68; Chapl HM Borstal Reading 61-68; RD Reading 65-68; Min Can St Paul's Cathl 68-72; Hon Min Can from 72; V St Pancras w

St Jas and Ch Ch 72-93; PV Westmr Abbey 75-80; rtd 93; Perm to Offic *Lon* from 99. *3 Bishop Street, London N1 8PH* Tel (020) 7226 8340

BEAN, James Corey. b 35. Centenary Coll New Jersey BA58 Long Is Univ MS74. Seabury-Western Th Sem LTh61. **d** 61 **p** 62. USA 61-79 and from 90; Chapl Wiesbaden *Eur* 79-90. *PO Box 490, Pomeroy WA 99347-0490, USA* Tel (001) (509) 843 1871

BEAN, Canon John Victor. b 25. Down Coll Cam BA47 MA51. Sarum Th Coll 48. **d** 50 **p** 51. C Milton *Portsm* 50-55; C Fareham SS Pet and Paul 55-59; V St Helens 59-66; V Cowes St Mary 66-91; RD W Wight 68-72; Hon Can Portsm Cathl 70-91; P-in-c Cowes St Faith 77-80; C-in-c Gurnard All SS CD 78-91; Chapl to The Queen 80-95; rtd 91; Perm to Offic *Portsm* from 91. *23 Queens Road, Ryde PO33 3BG* Tel (01983) 562856

BEANE, Andrew Mark. b 72. St Jo Coll Nottm BA02. **d** 02 **p** 03. C Thorpe St Matt *Nor* 02-05; P-in-c Horsham St Faith, Spixworth and Crostwick 05-06; R from 06. *The Rectory, Buxton Road, Spixworth, Norwich NR10 3PR* Tel (01603) 898258 E-mail andrewbeane@onetel.com

BEANEY, Canon John. b 47. Trin Coll Bris 77. **d** 79 **p** 80. C Bromley Ch Ch *Roch* 79-84; V Broadheath *Ches* 84-08; Chapl Altrincham Gen Hosp 91-94; Chapl Trafford Healthcare NHS Trust 94-98; P-in-c Norton *Ches* from 08; Ecum Officer (Gtr Man) from 02; Hon Can Ches Cathl from 10. *The Vicarage, Windmill Hill, Runcorn WA7 6QE* Tel (01928) 715225

BEARCROFT, Bramwell Arthur. b 52. Homerton Coll Cam BEd82. EAMTC 87. **d** 90 **p** 91. Chapl and Hd RS Kimbolton Sch Cambs 88-94; NSM Tilbrook *Ely* 90-94; NSM Covington 90-94, NSM Catworth Magna 90-94, NSM Keyston and Bythorn 90-94; NSM Cary Deanery *B & W* 94-02; Hd Master Hazlegrove Sch 94-02; Asst Chapl Aquitaine *Eur* from 10. *Clé de Tève, Devillac, 47210 Lot et Garonne, France* Tel (0033) 5 53 71 46 24 E-mail jenniferbearcroft@hotmail.com

BEARD, Christopher Robert. b 47. Chich Th Coll 81. **d** 83 **p** 84. C Chich St Paul and St Pet 83-86; TV Ifield 86-91; V Haywards Heath St Rich 91-99; P-in-c Donnington from 99; Chapl St Wilfrid's Hospice Eastbourne from 99. *The Vicarage, 34 Graydon Avenue, Donnington, Chichester PO19 8RF* Tel (01243) 776395 Mobile 07845-482779

BEARD, Laurence Philip. b 45. Lon Univ BA68. Trin Coll Bris 88. **d** 90 **p** 91. C Trentham *Lich* 90-94; V Wolverhampton St Matt 94-01; P-in-c Hartshill *Cov* 01-08; rtd 08. *14 Beechcroft Avenue, Croxley Green, Rickmansworth WD3 3EQ* Tel (01923) 222312 E-mail lpbeard@talk21.com

BEARD, Robert John Hansley. b 61. St Andr Univ BD85. Ripon Coll Cuddesdon 86 Ch Div Sch of the Pacific (USA) 87. **d** 88 **p** 89. C Sheff Manor 88-91; C Rotherham 91-94; V Sheff St Pet Abbeydale 94-02; Assoc Chapl Sheff Hallam Univ 95-98; Bp's Adv on Interfaith Issues 96-02; Intercultural Regeneration Development Worker Simunye from 02. *18 Arnside Road, Sheffield S8 0UX* Tel 0114-255 6335 E-mail arjay61@hotmail.com

BEARDALL, Raymond. b 32. St Jo Coll Nottm 70. **d** 72 **p** 73. C Ilkley All SS *Bradf* 72-74; C Seasalter *Cant* 74-79; V Farndon *S'well* 79-84; R Thorpe 79-84; V Farndon 84-97; rtd 97; Perm to Offic *S'well* from 03. *4 Winster Avenue, Ravenshead, Nottingham NG15 9DD* Tel (01623) 408205 E-mail ray@beardallhome.fsnet.co.uk

BEARDMORE, John Keith. b 42. FCP85 Bris Univ BEd74 K Coll Lon MA90. **d** 77 **p** 78. NSM Maindee Newport *Mon* from 77. *16 Hove Avenue, Newport NP19 7QP* Tel (01633) 263272

BEARDSHAW, David. b 37. JP. Wells Th Coll 65. **d** 67 **p** 68. C Wood End *Cov* 67-69; C Stoke 70-73; V Whitley 73-77; Dioc Educn Officer 77-87; P-in-c Offchurch and Warden Offa Retreat Ho 87-93; rtd 93. *188 Ashington Grove, Coventry CV3 4DB*

BEARDSLEY, Christina. b 51. Sussex Univ BA73 St Jo Coll Cam PhD99 Leeds Univ MA07. Westcott Ho Cam 76. **d** 78 **p** 79. C Portsea N End St Mark *Portsm* 78-85; V Catherington and Clanfield 85-00; Chapl Worthing and Southlands Hosps NHS Trust 00-01; Asst Chapl Chelsea and Westmr Hosp NHS Found Trust 01-04; Chapl 04-08; Hd Multi-Faith Chapl from 08; Visiting Lect St Mary's Univ Coll Twickenham from 10. *Chaplains' Office, Chelsea and Westminster Hospital, 369 Fulham Road, London SW10 9NH* Tel (020) 8746 8083 E-mail christina.beardsley@chelwest.nhs.uk

BEARDSLEY, Nigel Andrew. b 61. Sheff Hallam Univ BSc88 Nottm Univ MA00. EMMTC 97. **d** 00 **p** 01. C Bath Bathwick *B & W* 00-05; Chapl RN from 05. *Royal Naval Chaplaincy Service, Mail Point 1-2, Leach Building, Whale Island, Portsmouth PO2 8BY* Tel (023) 9262 5055 Fax 9262 5134

BEARE, William. b 33. TCD BA58. **d** 59 **p** 60. C Waterford St Patr *C & O* 59-62; C Cork H Trin w Shandon St Mary *C, C & R* 62-64; I Rathcormac 64-68; I Marmullane w Monkstown 68-76; Dioc C 76-82; I Stradbally w Ballintubbert, Coraclone etc *C & O* 82-99; Can Ossory and Leighlin Cathls 88-90; Chan 90-92; Prec 92-99; Dean Lismore and I Lismore w Cappoquin, Kilwatermoy, Dungarvan etc 99-08; Preb Stagonil St Patr Cathl Dublin 95-08; rtd 09. *24 Lapp's Court, Hartland's*

Avenue, Glasheen, Cork, Republic of Ireland Tel (00353) (21) 497 5980 Mobile 87-233 1508

BEARN, Hugh William. b 62. Man Univ BA84 MA98. Cranmer Hall Dur 86. **d** 89 **p** 90. C Heaton Ch Ch *Man* 89-92; Chapl RAF 92-96; V Tottington *Man* from 96; CF (TA) 96-02; Chapl Bury Hospice 99-03; CF (ACF) from 06; Chapl to The Queen from 06. *St Ann's Vicarage, Chapel Street, Tottington, Bury BL8 4AP* Tel (01204) 883713 E-mail hughbearn@aol.com

BEARPARK, Canon John Michael. b 36. Ex Coll Ox BA59 MA63. Linc Th Coll 59. **d** 61 **p** 62. C Bingley H Trin *Bradf* 61-64; C Baildon 64-67; V Fairweather Green 67-77; Chapl Airedale Gen Hosp 77-94; V Steeton 77-94; Hon Can Bradf Cathl 89-01; V Bentham St Marg 94-01; P-in-c Bentham St Jo 99-01; RD Ewecross 94-00; rtd 01; Perm to Offic *Bradf* from 01. *31 Northfields Crescent, Settle BD24 9JP* Tel (01729) 822712

BEASLEY, Noel Michael Roy. b 68. Imp Coll Lon BSc91 Oriel Coll Ox DPhil96 St Jo Coll Dur BA98. Cranmer Hall Dur. **d** 99 **p** 00. C Newport w Longford, Chetwynd and Forton *Lich* 99-03; Chapl Westcott Ho Cam 03-07; Tutor 07-10; Dioc Dir of Miss *Ox* from 10. *39 The Motte, Abingdon OX14 3NZ* Tel (01235) 539265 E-mail nmrb2@cam.ac.uk

BEASLEY, Canon Walter Sydney. b 33. Nottm Univ BA57. Linc Th Coll 57. **d** 59 **p** 60. C Harworth *S'well* 59-64; V Forest Town 64-70; R Bulwell St Mary 70-97; Hon Can S'well Minster 85-97; rtd 97; Perm to Offic *S'well* from 04. *3 Clayton's Drive, Nottingham NG7 2PF* Tel 0115-970 2717 Mobile 07889-350442

BEATER, David MacPherson. b 41. Chich Th Coll 66. **d** 69 **p** 70. C Withington St Crispin *Man* 69-72; C Lightbowne 72-74; V Prestwich St Hilda 74-81; V Northfleet *Roch* 81-85; C Bickley 86-90; TV Stanley *Dur* 90-97; CMP from 91; SSF 97-01; C Seaton Hirst *Newc* 01-05; rtd 05; Perm to Offic *Cant* 07-10. *7 Ferndown, 146 Minnis Road, Birchington CT7 9QE* Tel (01843) 842166

BEATON, Mark Timothy. b 61. Univ of Wales (Ban) BA83. Trin Coll Bris 03. **d** 05 **p** 06. C Swindon St Jo and St Andr *Bris* 05-08; P-in-c New Radnor and Llanfihangel Nantmelan etc *S & B* from 08. *The Rectory, School Lane, New Radnor, Presteigne LD8 2SS* Tel (01544) 350342 E-mail mark.beaton@tesco.net

BEATTIE, David George. b 42. MIMechE76. CITC 01. **d** 04 **p** 05. NSM Belfast H Trin and St Silas *Conn* 04-09; NSM Whitehouse 09-10; Chapl Belfast Health and Soc Care Trust from 10; NSM Ematris w Rockcorry, Aghabog and Aughnamullan *Clogh* from 11. *6 Blackthorn Way, Newtownabbey BT37 0GW* Tel (028) 9086 3406 Mobile 07812-718080 E-mail beattie5@talktalk.net

BEATTIE, Ian David. b 36. Univ of NZ BA58. St Jo Coll Auckland LTh60. **d** 60 **p** 61. C Epsom St Andr New Zealand 60-64; C Shirley St Jo *Cant* 64-65; V S Wimbledon St Andr S'wark 65-71; C Napier St Aug New Zealand 71-73; V Onehunga 73-96; rtd 96. *1/148A Tasman Street, Nelson 7010, New Zealand* Tel (0064) (3) 546 7507

BEATTIE, Margaret. *See* BREWSTER, Margaret

BEATTIE, Canon Noel Christopher. b 41. TCD BTh65 Cranfield Inst of Tech MSc86. **d** 68 **p** 69. C Belfast H Trin *Conn* 68-70; C Belfast St Bart 70-73; C Doncaster St Mary *Sheff* 73-77; TV Northampton Em *Pet* 77-88; Ind Chapl 85-88; Ind Chapl *Linc* 88-92; Ind Chapl *Roch* 92-04; Hon Can Roch Cathl 00-04; rtd 04; Perm to Offic *Heref* from 05. *6 Oaks Road, Church Stretton SY6 7AX* Tel (01694) 725530 E-mail noelbt@globalnet.co.uk

BEAUCHAMP, Anthony Hazlerigg Proctor. b 40. Trin Coll Cam BA62 MA66 MICE68. St Jo Coll Nottm 73. **d** 75 **p** 76. C New Humberstone *Leic* 75-77; C-in-c Polegate *Chich* 77-80; Chapl Bethany Sch Goudhurst 80-86; Chapl Luckley-Oakfield Sch Wokingham 86-88; Chapl Clayesmore Sch Blandford 89-93; R Kirby-le-Soken w St Holland *Chelmsf* 93-00; Asst P Wetheral w Warwick *Carl* 00-01; rtd 01; Perm to Offic *Carl* 00-01 and *Chich* from 01. *2 Stelvio Cottages, 17 Beachy Head Road, Eastbourne BN20 7QP* Tel (01323) 732743

BEAUCHAMP, Gerald Charles. b 55. Hull Univ BA78 K Coll Lon MA96. Coll of Resurr Mirfield 78. **d** 80 **p** 81. C Hatcham St Cath *S'wark* 80-83; S Africa 83-86; C Ealing St Steph Castle Hill *Lon* 86-88; P-in-c Brondesbury St Anne w Kilburn H Trin 88-89; V 89-93; Chapl Kilburn Coll 88-93; C Chelsea St Luke and Ch Ch *Lon* 93-96; V W Brompton St Mary w St Pet 96-04; AD Chelsea 02-04; SSJE 04-07; C St Marylebone All SS *Lon* 07-10; P-in-c St Marylebone St Cypr from 10; P-in-c St Marylebone Annunciation Bryanston Street from 10. *16 Clarence Gate Gardens, Glentworth Street, London NW1 6AY* Tel (020) 7258 0031 or 7258 0724 E-mail gerald.beauch@btconnect.com

BEAUCHAMP, John Nicholas. b 57. Wycliffe Hall Ox 92. **d** 94 **p** 95. C Ipswich St Jo *St E* 94-97; TV Beccles St Mich 97-05; P-in-c Beccles St Mich and St Luke 05-08; R from 08. *44 Ringsfield Road, Beccles NR34 9PF* Tel (01502) 712317

BEAUCHAMP, Julian Thomas Proctor. b 68. Ex Univ BA91. Oak Hill Th Coll BA05. **d** 05 **p** 06. C Cheadle *Ches* 05-08; R Waverton w Aldford and Bruera from 08. *The Rectory, Village Road, Waverton, Chester CH3 7QN* Tel (01244) 336668 Mobile 07974-397022

BEAUMONT, Canon Brian Maxwell. b 34. Nottm Univ BA56. Wells Th Coll 58. **d** 59 **p** 60. C Clifton *S'well* 59-62; C E Stoke w Syerston 62; C Edgbaston St Geo *Birm* 62-65; V Smethwick St Alb 65-70; V Blackb H Trin 70-77; Asst Dir RE 70-73; Dir RE 73-92; Hon Can Blackb Cathl 73-77 and 92-99; Can Res 77-92; V Goosnargh w Whittingham 92-99; Bp's Adv for Rural Areas 92-99; rtd 99; Perm to Offic *Blackb* from 00. *14 Green Drive, Barton, Preston PR3 5AT* Tel (01772) 861131

BEAUMONT, Mrs Catherine Grace La Touche. b 60. SS Coll Cam MA83 Darw Coll Cam PGCE83 Solicitor 87. **d** 09 **p** 10. OLM Clopton w Otley, Swilland and Ashbocking *St E* from 09. *Otley Hall, Hall Lane, Otley, Ipswich IP6 9PA* Tel (01473) 890264 Mobile 07801-342336 E-mail catherine.beaumont@otleyhall.co.uk

BEAUMONT, Mrs Jane. b 56. Ches Coll of HE BTh. NOC 01. **d** 04 **p** 05. NSM Chadkirk *Ches* 04-08; NSM Ashton-upon-Mersey St Mary Magd from 08. *23 Rydal Avenue, Sale M33 6WN* E-mail janebeaumont@romileylifecentre.co.uk

BEAUMONT, Canon John Philip. b 32. Leeds Univ BA55. Coll of Resurr Mirfield 55. **d** 57 **p** 58. C Leeds St Marg *Ripon* 57-60; C Wellingborough All Hallows *Pet* 60-64; V Wellingborough St Andr 64-70; Chapl HM Borstal Wellingborough 64-70; V Finedon *Pet* 70-96; Can Pet Cathl 80-96; RD Higham 83-87; rtd 96; Perm to Offic *Pet* from 96. *9 Warren Bridge, Oundle, Peterborough PE8 4DQ* Tel (01832) 273863 E-mail john@beaumont.plus.com

BEAUMONT, Stephen Martin. b 51. K Coll Lon BD73 AKC74. St Aug Coll Cant 73. **d** 74 **p** 75. C Benwell St Jas *Newc* 74-77; Asst Chapl Marlborough Coll 77-81; R Ideford, Luton and Ashcombe *Ex* 81-84; Bp's Dom Chapl 81-84; Chapl Taunton Sch 85-91; Chapl Haileybury Coll 92-00; Second Chapl and Hd Div Tonbridge Sch 00-04; Sen Chapl 04-11; P-in-c Chiddingstone w Chiddingstone Causeway *Roch* from 11. *The Rectory, Chiddingstone, Edenbridge TN8 7AH* Tel (01892) 870478

BEAUMONT, Canon Terence Mayes. b 41. Lon Univ BA63. Linc Th Coll 68. **d** 71 **p** 72. C Hitchin St Mary *St Alb* 71-74; C Harpenden St Nic 75-79; V Stevenage St Pet Broadwater 79-87; V St Alb St Mich 87-06; Hon Can St Alb 05-06; rtd 06. *65 Weatherby, Dunstable LU6 1TP* Tel (01582) 661333 E-mail y.beaumont123@btinternet.com

BEAUMONT, Mrs Veronica Jean. b 38. Ox Min Course 90. **d** 93 **p** 94. NSM High Wycombe *Ox* 93-03; NSM W Wycombe w Bledlow Ridge, Bradenham and Radnage from 03; Fundraising Manager (Oxon) Children's Soc from 95. *Edgehill, Upper Stanley Road, High Wycombe HP12 4DB* Tel (01494) 523697 E-mail veronica.beaumont@virgin.net

BEAVAN, Canon Edward Hugh. b 43. Ex Coll Ox BA70 MA74 Solicitor 66. Cuddesdon Coll 69. **d** 71 **p** 72. C Ashford St Hilda *Lon* 71-74; C Newington St Mary *S'wark* 74-76; R Sandon *Chelmsf* 76-86; V Thorpe Bay 86-98; P-in-c Bradwell on Sea 98-05; P-in-c St Lawrence 98-05; V Burnham 05-09; Ind Chapl 98-05; RD Maldon and Dengie 00-05; Hon Can Chelmsf Cathl 02-09; rtd 09; Perm to Offic *Chelmsf* from 09. *19 Wordsworth Road, Colchester CO3 4HR* Tel (01206) 564577 E-mail hugh@beavan.go-plus.net

BEAVER, William Carpenter. b 45. Colorado Coll BA Wolfs Coll Ox DPhil76. Ox NSM Course 79. **d** 82 **p** 83. NSM Kennington St Jo w St Jas *S'wark* 82-95; NSM Avonmouth St Andr *Bris* 96-97; NSM Bris St Mary Redcliffe w Temple etc 95-08; NSM St Andr Holborn *Lon* 01-04; Dir Communications for C of E 97-02; Dir Communications for Br Red Cross 02-04; Speech Writer to the Ld Mayor of Lon from 04; OCM from 09. *The Mansion House, Mansion House Street, London EC4N 8BH* Tel (020) 7626 2500 E-mail william.beaver@cityoflondon.gov.uk

BEAVIS, Adrian Neill. b 74. Worc Coll Ox BA97. Wycliffe Hall Ox MTh00. **d** 00 **p** 01. C E Twickenham St Steph *Lon* 00-08; V S Kensington St Luke from 08. *12 Wharfedale Street, London SW10 9AL* Tel (020) 7370 0338 E-mail adrian@stlukeschurch.co.uk

BEAVIS, Sandra Kathleen. b 51. Univ Coll Chich BA01. **d** 98 **p** 07. C Southbourne w W Thorney *Chich* 98-05; C Bedhampton *Portsm* 05-09; Perm to Offic 09-10; P-in-c Soberton w Newtown from 10; OCM from 02. *The Vicarage, Webbs Green, Soberton, Southampton SO32 3PY* Tel (01489) 877400 E-mail sandrabeavis@btinternet.com

BEAZLEY, Prof John Milner. b 32. Man Univ MB, ChB57 MRCOG62 FRCOG73 FACOG89 MD64. St Deiniol's Hawarden 83. **d** 86 **p** 87. NSM W Kirby St Bridget *Ches* 86-89; NSM Newton 89-92; NSM Hayton w Cumwhitton *Carl* 92-98; rtd 99; Perm to Offic *Carl* 99-07. *High Rigg, Faugh, Heads Nook, Carlisle CA8 9EA* Tel (01228) 70353

BEAZLEY, Miss Margaret Sheila Elizabeth Mary. b 32. Nor City Coll CertEd59. St Alb Minl Tr Scheme 86. **d** 89 **p** 94. NSM Ware St Mary *St Alb* from 89; Perm to Offic *St E* from 08. *38 Fanshawe Crescent, Ware SG12 0AS* Tel (01920) 462349

BEAZLEY-LONG, Clive. b 77. Greenwich Univ BSc99. Trin Coll Bris 08. **d** 10 **p** 11. C Chertsey, Lyne and Longcross *Guildf* from

10. *The Manse, 25 Abbey Road, Chertsey KT16 8AL* Tel (01932) 565535 E-mail gospelguy77@hotmail.com

BEBB, Erica Charlotte. STETS. **d** 09 **p** 10. NSM Sea Mills *Bris* from 09. *21 Bramble Drive, Bristol BS9 1RE*

BEBBINGTON, Julia. See BABB, Mrs Julia Bebbington

BECHTOLD, Bryant Coffin. b 51. Georgia Inst of Tech BCE73 MCE75 Univ of Utah PhD78 Univ of the S (USA) MDiv86. **d** 86 **p** 87. C Atlanta St Luke USA 86-87; C Deltona 87-89; V Price and E Carbon 90-97; V Fort Worth Ch the K 97-00; R 00-06; Perm to Offic *St Alb* 06-07; P-in-c The Wainfleet Gp *Linc* from 07. *The Rectory, Vicarage Lane, Wainfleet St Mary, Skegness PE24 4JJ* Tel (01754) 880401 E-mail frbryant@btinternet.com

BECK, Alan. b 28. AKC50. **d** 53 **p** 54. C N Harrow St Alb *Lon* 53-56; C Northolt St Mary 56-59; C Loughborough All SS *Leic* 59-61; V Crookham *Guildf* 61-69; V Puriton *B & W* 69-78; P-in-c Pawlett 74-78; V Puriton and Pawlett 78-79; P-in-c Staplegrove 79-84; R 84-88; rtd 88; Perm to Offic *B & W* 88-97 and 04-07. *Redwing, Creech Heathfield, Taunton TA3 5EG* Tel (01823) 443030

BECK, Amanda Ruth. b 68. Liv Univ BA91 Birm Univ BD93. Qu Coll Birm 91. **d** 94 **p** 95. C W Derby Gd Shep *Liv* 94-99; Asst Chapl Voorschoten *Eur* 99-02; P-in-c Kingston Vale St Jo *S'wark* from 03. *St John's Vicarage, Robin Hood Lane, London SW15 3PY* Tel (020) 8546 4079 E-mail mandy.beck@alty.org

BECK, Mrs Gillian Margaret. b 50. Sheff Univ CertEd71 Nottm Univ BTh78. Linc Th Coll 74. dss 78 **d** 87. Gt Grimsby St Mary and St Jas *Linc* 78-83; St Paul's Cathl 84-87; Hon Par Dn St Botolph Aldgate w H Trin Minories 87-88; Par Dn Monkwearmouth St Andr *Dur* 88-94; C 94-97; NSM Eppleton and Hetton le Hole 97-04; NSM E Rainton from 04; NSM W Rainton from 04. *The Rectory, South Street, West Rainton, Houghton le Spring DH4 6PA* Tel 0191-584 7595

BECK, John Edward. b 28. ARCM52 FRCO59 St Jo Coll Ox BA56 MA59. Wells Th Coll 56. **d** 58 **p** 59. C Dursley *Glouc* 58-61; C Glouc St Paul 61-63; S Rhodesia 63-65; Rhodesia 65-70; C Cheltenham Ch Ch *Glouc* 70-77; C Cirencester 77-93; rtd 93; Perm to Offic *Glouc* from 93. *25 Bowling Green Road, Cirencester GL7 2HD* Tel (01285) 653778

BECK, Ms Karen Maureen. b 53. R Holloway Coll Lon BA74. St Alb Minl Tr Scheme 88. **d** 92 **p** 94. Par Dn Royston *St Alb* 92-94; C 94-96; TV Chipping Barnet w Arkley 96-02; P-in-c Heddon-on-the-Wall *Newc* 02-07; Chapl Northumbria Police 02-07; P-in-c Didcot All SS *Ox* from 07. *The Rectory, 140 Lydalls Road, Didcot OX11 7EA* Tel (01235) 813244 E-mail karenandgod@yahoo.co.uk

BECK, Michael Leonard. b 50. K Coll Lon BD77 AKC77. Linc Th Coll 77. **d** 78 **p** 79. C Gt Grimsby St Mary and St Jas *Linc* 78-83; Min Can and Succ St Paul's Cathl 83-88; V Monkwearmouth St Andr *Dur* 88-96; TR Monkwearmouth 96-97; R Eppleton and Hetton le Hole 97-04; AD Houghton 97-04; P-in-c Lyons 00-04; P-in-c W Rainton from 04; P-in-c E Rainton from 04; Dir Reader Min 04-09; Tutor Lindisfarne Regional Tr Partnership from 09. *The Rectory, South Street, West Rainton, Houghton le Spring DH4 6PA* Tel 0191-584 7595

BECK, The Very Revd Peter John. b 48. Mert Coll Ox BA69 MA73. Sarum Th Coll 69. **d** 72 **p** 73. C Banbury *Ox* 72-75; TV 75-78; Dioc Youth and Community Officer 75-78; P-in-c Lon St Mary-le-Wigford w St Benedict etc 78-81; City Cen Chapl 78-81; New Zealand from 81; TV Glenfield 81-85; V Mt Albert St Luke 86-93; Adn Waitemata 87-93; V Auckland St Matt 93-00; Adn Auckland 98-00; Hon Asst P Wellington Cathl 00-02; Dir Vaughan Park Retreat Cen 02; Dean Christchurch from 02; V Gen from 03. *25 Springfield Road, St Albans, Christchurch, New Zealand* Tel (0064) (3) 377 6095 *or* 366 0046 Mobile 21-654445 E-mail peterbeck@xtra.co.nz

BECK, Roger William. b 48. Chich Th Coll 79. **d** 81 **p** 82. C St Marychurch *Ex* 81-85; TV Torre 85-88; V Torquay St Jo and Ellacombe 88-94; C Plympton St Mary from 94. *27 Pinewood Close, Plympton, Plymouth PL7 2DW* Tel (01752) 336393

BECK, Mrs Sandra Veronica. b 52. St Jo Coll Nottm 97. **d** 00 **p** 01. NSM Digswell and Panshanger *St Alb* 00-04; NSM Codicote 04-08; Perm to Offic 08-09; Chapl E and N Herts NHS Trust from 09. *The Chaplaincy, Lister Hospital, Coreys Mill Lane, Stevenage SG1 4AB* Tel (01438) 314333 E-mail csbeck@btinternet.com

BECKERLEG, Barzillai. b 20. Selw Coll Cam BA43 MA46. Westcott Ho Cam 42. **d** 44 **p** 45. C Golders Green St Alb *Lon* 44-48; Chapl St Jo Coll Dur 48-52; Lic to Offic *Dur* 49-52; V Battersea St Mary *S'wark* 52-58; V Wentworth *Sheff* 58-59; Hd Master Newc Cathl Choir Sch 59-62; Prec Newc Cathl 59-62; R Duncton *Chich* 62-64; R Burton w Coates 62-64; V Kippington *Roch* 64-75; R E Bergholt *St E* 75-79; Chapl St Mary's Sch Wantage 79-85; rtd 85; Perm to Offic *Truro* from 85; *Roch* 86-93; *Chich* from 93; *S'wark* and *Roch* from 00. *17 Ramsay Hall, 9-13 Byron Road, Worthing BN11 3HN*

BECKETT, George. b 26. Scawsby Coll of Educn CertEd76 Sheff Univ BEd77 Hull Univ MEd84. **d** 91 **p** 92. NSM Hatfield *Sheff*

from 91. *10 Norman Drive, Hatfield, Doncaster DN7 6AQ* Tel (01302) 841091

BECKETT, Glynis. d 10 **p** 11. OLM Radley and Sunningwell *Ox* from 10. *18 Sadlers Court, Abingdon OX14 2PA* Tel (01235) 529505 E-mail glynis.beckett@lmh.ox.ac.uk

BECKETT, Graham. b 49. St As Minl Tr Course 95. **d** 99 **p** 00. NSM Hawarden *St As* 99-01; C 01-07; V Gorsedd w Brynford, Ysgeifiog and Whitford from 07. *The Vicarage, Gorsedd, Holywell CH8 8QZ* Tel (01352) 711675

BECKETT, John Adrian. b 61. Bris Univ BVSc85. Trin Coll Bris. **d** 00 **p** 01. C Harrogate St Mark *Ripon* 00-04; P-in-c Sevenhampton w Charlton Abbots, Hawling etc *Glouc* from 04. *The Rectory, Station Road, Andoversford, Cheltenham GL54 4LA* Tel (01242) 820230

BECKETT, Michael Shaun. b 55. ACA79. Oak Hill Th Coll BA88. **d** 88 **p** 89. C Cambridge St Barn *Ely* 88-93; P-in-c Cambridge St Paul 93-94; V from 94. *St Paul's Vicarage, 15 St Paul's Road, Cambridge CB1 2EZ* Tel (01223) 354186 *or* 315832 Fax 471792 E-mail church@centrestpauls.org.uk

BECKETT, Mrs Patricia Anne. b 44. **d** 00 **p** 01. NSM Cheddleton *Lich* 00-06; NSM Upper Tean from 06. *The Vicarage, Vicarage Road, Tean, Stoke-on-Trent ST10 4LE* Tel (01538) 722227

BECKETT, Canon Stanley. b 20. Linc Th Coll. **d** 64 **p** 65. C Barnston *Ches* 64-71; V Daresbury 71-87; P-in-c Aston by Sutton 86-87; Hon C 87-90; Hon Can Ches Cathl 82-87; rtd 87; Hon C Grappenhall *Ches* 90-98; Perm to Offic *Linc* from 98. *107 Barclay Court, Trafalgar Road, Cirencester GL7 2EN*

BECKHAM, John Francis. b 25. Bps' Coll Cheshunt 65. **d** 67 **p** 68. C Leytonstone St Jo *Chelmsf* 67 70; C Colchester St Mary V 70-73; R Lawford 73-80; V Gt w Lt Chesterford 80-90; rtd 90; Perm to Offic *St E* from 91. *North Barn, Reckford Road, Westleton, Saxmundham IP17 3BE* Tel (01728) 648969

BECKINSALE, Mrs Pamela Rachel. b 46. Man Univ BSc69. Cant Sch of Min 88. **d** 91 **p** 94. NSM Sittingbourne St Mich *Cant* 91-96; Hon Chapl N Kent Health Care NHS Trust 96-98; Chapl Thames Gateway NHS Trust from 98. *8 Glovers Crescent, Bell Road, Sittingbourne ME10 4DU* Tel (01795) 471632 *or* 418300

BECKLEY, Peter William (Pedr). b 52. Lon Univ BSc73 CertEd. Trin Coll Bris 76. **d** 79 **p** 80. C Plymouth St Jude *Ex* 79-83; C Ecclesall *Sheff* 83-88; V Greystones from 88; P-in-c Endcliffe from 11. *The Vicarage, 1 Cliffe Farm Drive, Sheffield S11 7JW* Tel 0114-266 7686 E-mail pedr@talktalk.net

BECKLEY, Simon Richard. b 38. Lon Univ BA61. Oak Hill Th Coll 58. **d** 63 **p** 64. C Watford St Luke *St Alb* 63-67; C New Ferry *Ches* 67-70; C Chadderton Ch Ch *Man* 70-73; V Friarmere 73-80; V Tranmere St Cath *Ches* 80-03; Chapl Wirral Community Healthcare NHS Trust 80-97; Chapl Wirral and W Cheshire Community NHS Trust 97-03; rtd 03; Perm to Offic *Ches* from 04. *162 Heathbank Avenue, Wirral CH61 4YG* Tel 0151-648 7767

BECKWITH, Ian Stanley. b 36. Nottm Univ BA58 Selw Coll Cam CertEd59 Westmr Coll Ox MTh96. Linc Th Coll 78. **d** 79 **p** 80. NSM Linc Cathl 79-85; Sen Lect Bp Grosseteste Coll Linc 80-86; NSM Wallingford w Crowmarsh Gifford etc *Ox* 91-97; OLM Tr Officer (Berks) 96-02; C Coxwell w Buscot, Coleshill etc 97-02; rtd 02; Perm to Offic *Heref* and *Lich* from 02. *2 Affcot Mill, Affcot, Church Stretton SY6 6RL* Tel (01694) 781667

BECKWITH, Canon John Douglas. b 33. AKC57. **d** 58 **p** 65. C Streatham St Leon *S'wark* 58-59; Lic to Offic *Ripon* 59-60; Tutor Ijebu-Igbo Gr Sch and Molusi Coll Nigeria 60-62; C Bedale *Ripon* 62-63; C Mottingham St Andr w St Alban *S'wark* 64-69; Chapl Gothenburg w Halmstad and Jönköping *Eur* 69-70; Chapl to Suff Bp Edmonton 70-77; Dir of Ords *Lon* 70-77; V Brookfield St Anne, Highgate Rise 77-88; Can Gib Cathl 84-88; Hon Can Gib Cathl 88-05; P-in-c Bladon w Woodstock *Ox* 88-93; P-in-c Wootton and Kiddington w Asterleigh 88; C Kidlington w Hampton Poyle 93-94; rtd 98; Perm to Offic *Lon* from 94 and *Eur* from 98. *4 St James's Close, Bishop Street, London N1 8PH* Tel and fax (020) 7226 6672 Mobile 07710-277124 E-mail malbis@dircon.co.uk

BECKWITH, John James. b 53. UMIST BSc74 Newc Univ PGCE88. **d** 02 **p** 03. OLM Bothal and Pegswood w Longhirst *Newc* 02-04; C Morpeth 04-07; V Belford and Lucker from 07. *The Vicarage, North Bank, Belford NE70 7LY* Tel (01668) 213545 E-mail johnange@ne61yg.wanadoo.co.uk

BECKWITH, Roger Thomas. b 29. St Edm Hall Ox BA52 MA56 BD85 Lambeth DD92. Ripon Hall Ox 51 Tyndale Hall Bris 52 Cuddesdon Coll 54. **d** 54 **p** 55. C Harold Wood *Chelmsf* 54-57; C Bedminster St Luke w St Silas *Bris* 57-59; Tutor Tyndale Hall Bris 59-63; Lib Latimer Ho Ox 63-73 and from 94; Warden 73-94; Lect Wycliffe Hall Ox 71-94; Hon C Wytham *Ox* 88-90; Hon C N Hinksey and Wytham 90-96; rtd 94; Hon C Ox St Mich w St Martin and All SS 97-03; Perm to Offic from 03. *310 Woodstock Road, Oxford OX2 7NR* Tel (01865) 557340

BEDDINGTON, Peter Jon. b 36. ACP68 DipEd81. NW Ord Course 71. **d** 74 **p** 75. C Bury St Pet *Man* 74-77; Hon C Bury Ch

King 77-82; Hon C Elton All SS 82-09; Hon C Kirklees Valley from 09. *9 Hebburn Drive, Bury BL8 1ED* Tel 0161-764 3292

BEDEAU (née MILLS), Mrs Melina. b 40. Local Minl Tr Course. **d** 00 **p** 04. NSM W Bromwich St Phil *Lich* 00-03; NSM W Bromwich Gd Shep w St Jo from 03. *4 Jervoise Street, West Bromwich B70 9LY* Tel 0121-553 6833

BEDELL, Anthony Charles John. b 59. Worc Coll Ox BA81 Univ Coll Chich PGCE05 ACA84 QTS05. Linc Th Coll BTh90. **d** 90 **p** 91. C Newbold w Dunston *Derby* 90-94; C Bedford Leigh *Man* 94-98; V Blackb St Luke w St Phil 98-03; Min Partnership Development Officer *Pet* 03; L'Arche Bognor Community 03-04; Perm to Offic *Chich* 03-04; Lic to Offic from 04; Teacher Bognor Regis Community Coll from 05. *22 Armada Way, Littlehampton BN17 6QY* Tel (01903) 717719 E-mail abedell@wsgfl.org.uk

BEDFORD, Christopher John. b 40. CEng68 MIStructE68. **d** 05 **p** 06. OLM Chobham w Valley End *Guildf* from 05. *23 Swallow Rise, Knaphill, Woking GU21 2LG* Tel (01483) 480127 E-mail ahbedford@hotmail.com

BEDFORD, Mrs Linda. b 43. **d** 07. NSM Hanley Castle, Hanley Swan and Welland *Worc* from 06. *Linton, Roberts End, Hanley Swan, Worcester WR8 0DL* Tel (01684) 311324

BEDFORD, Michael Anthony. b 38. Reading Univ BSc59 Heythrop Coll Lon MA00. **d** 01 **p** 02. NSM Ruislip St Martin *Lon* from 01. *7 Chandos Road, Eastcote, Pinner HA5 1PR* Tel (020) 8866 4332 E-mail mabedford7cr@waitrose.com

BEDFORD, Richard Derek Warner. b 27. Clare Coll Cam BA52. ALCD54. **d** 54 **p** 55. C Wallington *S'wark* 54-57; C Sanderstead All SS 57; C Weybridge *Guildf* 57-59; C Addlestone 59-62; C-in-c New Haw CD 62-66; V Epsom Common Ch Ch 66-81; R Walton-on-the-Hill 81-87; Asst Chapl Burrswood Chr Cen 87-92; rtd 92; Perm to Offic *Chich* and *Roch* from 92. *2 Lealands Close, Groombridge, Tunbridge Wells TN3 9ND* Tel (01892) 864550

BEDFORD, Archdeacon of. See HUGHES, The Ven Paul Vernon
BEDFORD, Suffragan Bishop of. See INWOOD, The Rt Revd Richard Neil

BEE, Mrs Judith Mary. b 52. STETS 03. **d** 06 **p** 07. NSM Hambledon *Portsm* 06-10; NSM Buriton from 10. *St Mary's House, 41 North Lane, Buriton, Petersfield GU31 4RS* Tel (01730) 269390 E-mail judith.bee@clara.co.uk

BEEBEE, Meyrick Richard Legge. b 43. SAOMC 99. **d** 02 **p** 03. NSM Gerrards Cross and Fulmer *Ox* from 02. *Oak House, 86 Fulmer Road, Gerrards Cross SL9 7EG* Tel (01753) 882524 E-mail mbeebee@aol.com

BEEBY, Lawrence Clifford. b 28. S'wark Ord Course 70. **d** 73 **p** 74. C Notting Hill St Jo *Lon* 73-74; C Sunbury 74-76; C-in-c Hounslow Gd Shep Beavers Lane CD 76-80; Chapl Botleys Park Hosp Chertsey 80-96; rtd 96; Perm to Offic *Guildf* 96-99 and *Lon* from 96. *24 Bingley Road, Sunbury-on-Thames TW16 7RB* Tel (01932) 788922

BEEBY, Matthew. b 57. Oak Hill Th Coll. **d** 11. NSM Mayfair Ch Ch *Lon* from 11. *Address temp unknown*

BEECH, Miss Ailsa. b 44. N Co Coll Newc TDip65. Trin Coll Bris 78. **dss** 80 **d** 87 **p** 94. Pudsey St Lawr and St Paul *Bradf* 80-88; Par Dn 87-88; C Attleborough *Cov* 88-89; Par Dn Cumnor *Ox* 89-92; Asst Chapl Walsgrave Hosp Cov 92-94; Asst Chapl Walsgrave Hosps NHS Trust 94-96; Chapl 96-00; Chapl Univ Hosps Cov and Warks NHS Trust 00-04; rtd 04; Perm to Offic *York* from 04. *Oxenby, Whitby Road, Pickering YO18 7HL* Tel (01751) 472689 E-mail ailsab@btopenworld.com

BEECH, Mrs Charmian Patricia. b 45. RGN66 RHV70 TCert74. St As Minl Tr Course 99. **d** 02 **p** 03. C Connah's Quay *St As* 02-04; P-in-c Hodnet w Weston under Redcastle *Lich* from 04; Dioc Child Protection Officer from 04; RD Hodnet from 11. *The Rectory, Abbots Way, Hodnet, Market Drayton TF9 3NQ* Tel (01630) 685491 E-mail charmian.beech@virgin.net

BEECH, Derek Charles. b 49. EMMTC 99. **d** 02 **p** 03. NSM Horsley and Denby *Derby* 02-11; NSM Ambergate and Heage from 11. *39 Brook Street, Heage, Belper DE56 2AG* Tel (01773) 850168 Mobile 07967-582661

BEECH, Frank Thomas. b 36. Tyndale Hall Bris 64. **d** 66 **p** 67. C Penn Fields *Lich* 66-70; C Attenborough w Chilwell *S'well* 70-74; P-in-c 74-75; P-in-c Attenborough 75-76; V 76-84; V Worksop St Anne 84-03; Chapl Welbeck Coll 84-03; rtd 04; Perm to Offic *S'well* from 04. *43 Bescar Lane, Ollerton, Newark NG22 9BS* Tel 07743-592012 (mobile) E-mail frank.beech@lineone.net

BEECH, John. b 41. St Jo Coll Nottm. **d** 83 **p** 83. C York St Pet 83-84; P-in-c Bubwith w Ellerton and Aughton 84-85; P-in-c Thorganby w Skipwith and N Duffield 84-85; V Bubwith w Skipwith 85-87; V Acomb H Redeemer 87-00; P-in-c Westleigh St Pet *Man* 00-01; rtd 01; Perm to Offic *York* from 04. *6 Water Ark Cottages, Goathland, Whitby YO22 5JZ* E-mail jobe65@talktalk.net

BEECH, John Thomas. b 38. St Aid Birkenhead 64. **d** 67 **p** 68. C Burton St Paul *Lich* 67-70; Chapl RN 70-85; V Ellingham and Harbridge and Ibsley *Win* 85-94; Chapl Whiteley Village *Guildf* 94-03; rtd 03. *10 Friars Walk, Barton-on-Sea, New Milton BH25 7DA*

BEECH, Mrs Linda. d 06 **p** 07. NSM Lapley w Wheaton Aston *Lich* 06-09; NSM Blymhill w Weston-under-Lizard 06-09; NSM Watershed from 09. *The New Rectory, School Lane, Blymhill, Shifnal TF11 8LH* Tel (01952) 850149
E-mail beeches7@tiscali.co.uk

BEECH, Peter John. b 34. Bps' Coll Cheshunt 58. **d** 61 **p** 62. C Fulham All SS *Lon* 61-64; S Africa 64-67; V S Hackney St Mich *Lon* 68-71; P-in-c Haggerston St Paul 68-71; V S Hackney St Mich w Haggerston St Paul 71-75; V Wanstead H Trin Hermon Hill *Chelmsf* 75-89; P-in-c St Mary-at-Latton 89-90; V 90-99; rtd 99; Perm to Offic *Ely* from 99. *9 Fitzgerald Close, Ely CB7 4QB* Tel (01353) 666269

BEECH-GRÜNEBERG, Keith Nigel. b 72. CCC Ox BA93 MA96 St Jo Coll Dur BA97 PhD02. Cranmer Hall Dur 95. **d** 01 **p** 02. C Pangbourne w Tidmarsh and Sulham *Ox* 01-04; Dir Studies Dioc Bd Stewardship from 04. *47 Stockey End, Abingdon OX14 2NF* Tel (01235) 528661
E-mail keith.gruneberg@oxford.anglican.org

BEECHAM, Clarence Ralph. b 35. S'wark Ord Course. **d** 83 **p** 84. NSM Leigh-on-Sea St Jas *Chelmsf* 83-86. *27 Scarborough Drive, Leigh-on-Sea SS9 3ED* Tel (01702) 574923

BEECROFT, Benjamin Harold. b 77. Trin Coll Bris BA98. **d** 00 **p** 01. C Stapleford *S'well* 00-04; C Warfield *Ox* 04-07; V Addlestone *Guildf* from 07. *The Vicarage, 140 Church Road, Addlestone KT15 1SJ* Tel (01932) 842879
E-mail ben.beecroft@btinternet.com

BEECROFT, Mrs Christine Mary. b 62. RGN85. Trin Coll Bris BA97 MA99. **d** 98 **p** 99. C Roxeth *Lon* 98-00; Perm to Offic *S'well* 00-02; C Stapleford 02-04; NSM Warfield *Ox* 04-07; C Addlestone *Guildf* from 09. *The Vicarage, 140 Church Road, Addlestone KT15 1SJ* Tel (01932) 842879
E-mail christine.beecroft@btinternet.com

BEEDELL, Trevor Francis. b 31. ALCD65. **d** 65 **p** 66. C Walton *St E* 65-68; R Hartshorne *Derby* 68-79; RD Repton 74-79; V Doveridge 79-86; Chapl HM Det Cen Foston Hall 79-80; Dioc Dir of Chr Stewardship *Derby* 79-97; rtd 97; Perm to Offic *Derby* from 97. *185 High Lane West, West Hallam, Ilkeston DE7 6HP* Tel 0115-932 5589

BEEDON, David Kirk. b 59. Birm Univ BA89 MPhil93. Qu Coll Birm 86. **d** 89 **p** 90. C Cannock *Lich* 89-92; V Wednesbury St Bart 92-99; R Lich St Mich w St Mary and Wall from 99; P-in-c Lich Ch C 07-09. *St Michael's Rectory, St Michael Road, Lichfield WS13 6SN* Tel and fax (01543) 262420 or 262211
E-mail dkbeedon@aol.com

BEER, Anthony. b 72. St Mich Coll Llan. **d** 09 **p** 10. NSM Caerau w Ely *Llan* 09-11; C Llantwit Major from 11. *The New Rectory, Trepit Road, Wick, Cowlbridge CF71 7QL* Tel (01656) 895068
E-mail amber0049@yahoo.com

BEER, Mrs Janet Margaret. b 43. Goldsmiths' Coll Lon CertEd64. Oak Hill Th Coll 83. **dss** 86 **d** 87 **p** 94. London Colney St Pet *St Alb* 86-97; Hon C 87-97; Chapl St Alb High Sch for Girls 87-89; Chapl Middx Univ 94-97; NSM Northaw and Cuffley *St Alb* 97-09; rtd 09; Perm to Offic *Portsm* from 09. *L'Auberge, 15 Seymour Road, Lee-on-the-Solent PO13 9EG* Tel (023) 9255 0264 E-mail j.m.beer@btinternet.com

BEER, The Ven John Stuart. b 44. Pemb Coll Ox BA65 MA70 Fitzw Coll Cam MA78. Westcott Ho Cam 69. **d** 71 **p** 72. C Knaresborough St Jo *Ripon* 71-74; Chapl Fitzw Coll and New Hall Cam 74-80; Fell Fitzw Coll 77-80; Bye-Fell from 01; P-in-c Toft w Caldecote and Childerley *Ely* 80-83; R 83-87; P-in-c Hardwick 80-83; R 83-87; V Grantchester 87-97; Dir of Ords, Post-Ord Tr and Student Readers from 88; Hon Can Ely Cathl from 89; Adn Huntingdon 97-04; Acting Adn Wisbech 02-04; Adn Cam from 04. *St Botolph's Rectory, 1A Summerfield, Cambridge CB3 9HE* Tel (01223) 350424 Fax 360929
E-mail archdeacon.cambridge@ely.anglican.org

BEER, Michael Trevor. b 44. Chich Th Coll. **d** 69 **p** 70. C Leagrave *St Alb* 69-73; C St Geo Cathl Kingstown St Vincent 73-74; C Thorley w Bishop's Stortford H Trin *St Alb* 74-80; V London Colney St Pet 80-97; V Northaw and Cuffley 97-09; rtd 09; Perm to Offic *Portsm* from 09. *L'Auberge, 15 Seymour Road, Lee-on-the-Solent PO13 9EG* Tel (023) 9255 0264
E-mail j.m.beer@btinternet.com

BEER, Nigel David. b 62. Portsm Poly BSc84. St Jo Coll Nottm MA93. **d** 93 **p** 94. C Rastrick St Matt *Wakef* 93-96; C Bilton *Ripon* 96-98; TV Moor Allerton 98-09; TV Moor Allerton and Shadwell from 09; Asst Dir of Ords from 05. *73 The Avenue, Leeds LS17 7NP* Tel 0113-267 8487
E-mail ndbeer@btinternet.com

BEER, William Barclay. b 43. ACT ThA68 St Steph Ho Ox. **d** 71 **p** 72. C St Marychurch *Ex* 71-76; V Pattishall w Cold Higham *Pet* 76-82; V Northampton St Benedict 82-85; V Chislehurst Annunciation *Roch* from 85. *The Vicarage, 2 Foxhome Close, Chislehurst BR7 5XT* Tel and fax (020) 8467 3606
E-mail williambbeer@tiscali.co.uk

BEESLEY, John Stanley. b 70. St Martin's Coll Lanc BSc92 QTS92. WEMTC 06. **d** 09 **p** 10. C Ludlow Heref from 09. *St Giles's Vicarage, Sheet Road, Ludlow SY8 1LR* Tel (01584) 874383 E-mail john.beesley@lineone.net

BEESLEY, Michael Frederick. b 37. K Coll Cam BA59. Westcott Ho Cam 60. **d** 61 **p** 64. C Eastleigh *Win* 61-69; rtd 02. *24 Charmouth Grove, Poole BH14 0LP* Tel (01202) 773471

BEESLEY, Ramon John. b 27. Magd Coll Ox BA51 MA55. Wycliffe Hall Ox 51. **d** 53 **p** 56. C Gerrards Cross *Ox* 53-54; Asst Chapl Embley Park Sch Romsey 54-58; Perm to Offic *Win* 54-58; Asst Master Farnham Sch 58-62; Perm to Offic *Guildf* 58-62; Perm to Offic *Win* from 63; Hd Science Gore Sch New Milton 63-69; Dep Hd Applemore Sch Dibden Purlieu 69-74; Hd Master Bellemoor Sch Southn 74-84; rtd 84. *Wayfarers, Burley, Ringwood BH24 4HW* Tel (01425) 402284

BEESON, Christopher George. b 48. Man Univ BSc70. Qu Coll Birm 72. **d** 75 **p** 76. C Flixton St Mich *Man* 75-78; C Newton Heath All SS 78-80; R Gorton St Jas 80-90; Dioc Communications Officer *Blackb* 91-92; C Ribbleton 92-93; rtd 93; Perm to Offic *Blackb* from 93. *24 Arnold Close, Ribbleton, Preston PR2 6DX* Tel (01772) 702675
E-mail cbeeson@cix.co.uk

BEESON, The Very Revd Trevor Randall. b 26. OBE97. K Coll Lon MA76 FKC87 Southn Univ Hon DLitt99. **d** 51 **p** 52. C Leadgate *Dur* 51-54; C Norton St Mary 54-56; C-in-c Stockton St Chad CD 56-60; V Stockton St Chad 60-65; C St Martin-in-the-Fields *Lon* 65-71; V Ware St Mary *St Alb* 71-76; Can Westmr Abbey 76-87; Treas 78-82; R Westmr St Marg 82-87; Chapl to Speaker of Ho of Commons 82-87; Dean *Win* 87-96; rtd 96; Perm to Offic *Win* from 96. *69 Greatbridge Road, Romsey SO51 8FE* Tel (01794) 514627

BEESTON, Andrew Bernard. b 41. RMN64 RGN67. NEOC 99. **d** 01 **p** 02. NSM Cullercoats St Geo *Newc* 01-06; NSM Long Benton 06-09; NSM Earsdon and Backworth from 09. *21 Deepdale Road, Cullercoats, North Shields NE30 3AN* Tel 0191-259 0431 E-mail abeeston@ukf.net

BEET, Duncan Clive. b 65. LLB. Ridley Hall Cam 98. **d** 01 **p** 02. C Northampton Em *Pet* 01-04; P-in-c Mears Ashby and Hardwick and Sywell etc from 04. *The Vicarage, 46 Wellingborough Road, Mears Ashby, Northampton NN6 0DZ* Tel (01604) 812907
E-mail avsy17@dsl.pipex.com

BEETHAM, Anthony. b 32. Lon Univ BSc53. Ox NSM Course. **d** 75 **p** 76. Dir Chr Enquiry Agency 88-97; NSM Ox St Clem 75-02; rtd 02; Perm to Offic *Ox* from 03. *44 Rose Hill, Oxford OX4 4HS* Tel (01865) 770923

BEETON, David Ambrose Moore. b 39. Chich Th Coll 62. **d** 65 **p** 66. C Forest Gate St Edm *Chelmsf* 65-71; V Rush Green 71-81; V Coggeshall w Markshall 81-02; rtd 02; Perm to Offic *Nor* from 03. *Le Strange Cottages, 2 Hunstanton Road, Heacham, King's Lynn PE31 7HH* Tel (01485) 572150

BEETY, Arthur Edward. b 38. Sheff Univ BA60. Cant Sch of Min 92. **d** 95 **p** 96. NSM Cobham w Luddesdowne and Dode *Roch* from 95. *The Old Forge, 4 The Street, Cobham, Gravesend DA12 3BN* Tel (01474) 816684
E-mail arthur.beety@diocese-rochester.org

BEEVER, Miss Alison Rosemary. b 59. Man Univ BA80. Linc Th Coll 83. **d** 90 **p** 94. Par Dn Watford Ch Ch *St Alb* 90-94; C 94-96; V Tilehurst St Cath *Ox* 96-01; P-in-c Cen Ex and Dioc Dir of Ords *Ex* 01-04; rtd 04. *7 Langridge Road, Paignton TQ3 3PT* Tel (01803) 553645

BEEVERS, Preb Colin Lionel. b 40. K Coll Lon BSc62 PhD66 CEng70 MIET70 MBIM73. Sarum & Wells Th Coll 87. **d** 89 **p** 90. C Ledbury w Eastnor *Heref* 89-93; C Lt Marcle 89-93; Asst Dir of Tr 92-96; P-in-c Kimbolton w Hamnish and Middleton-on-the-Hill 93-96; P-in-c Bockleton w Leysters 93-96; P-in-c Ledbury w Eastnor 96-98; P-in-c Much Marcle 96-98; TR Ledbury 98-05; RD Ledbury 96-02; Preb Heref Cathl 02-05; Chapl Herefordshire Primary Care Trust 96-05; rtd 05; Perm to Offic *Worc* from 06. *55 Lion Court, Worcester WR1 1UT* Tel (01905) 24132 E-mail annandcolin.beevers@virgin.net

BEGBIE, Jeremy Sutherland. b 57. Edin Univ BA77 Aber Univ BD80 PhD87 LRAM80 ARCM77 MSSTh. Ridley Hall Cam 80. **d** 82 **p** 83. C Egham *Guildf* 82-85; Chapl Ridley Hall Cam 85-87; Dir Studies 87-92; Vice-Prin 93-00; Assoc Prin 00-09; Hon Reader St Andr Univ 00-09; Research Prof Th Duke Div Sch USA from 09. *Duke University Divinity School, Box 90968, Durham NC 27708, USA* Tel (001) (919) 660 3591
E-mail jeremy.begbie@duke.edu

BEGGS, Norman Lindell. b 32. N Lon Poly CQSW77. S Dios Minl Tr Scheme 86. **d** 89 **p** 90. NSM Milborne St Andrew w Dewlish *Sarum* 89-92; C 92-95; C Piddletrenthide w Plush, Alton Pancras etc 92-95; C Puddletown and Tolpuddle 92-95; rtd 95; Perm to Offic *Sarum* from 95. *Wallingford House, Dewlish, Dorchester DT2 7LX* Tel (01258) 837320

BEGLEY, Mrs Helen. b 59. Kingston Poly BA81. NOC 87. **d** 89 **p** 94. Par Dn Leeds H Trin *Ripon* 89-90; Chapl to the Deaf 89-96; Par Dn Leeds City 91-94; C 94-96; Chapl to the Deaf (Wilts) *Sarum* 96-06; NSM Upper Wylye Valley 03-11; NSM Melksham from 11. *The Vicarage, Green Lane, Codford, Warminster BA12 0NY* Tel (01985) 850019
E-mail helenbegley@tiscali.co.uk

BEGLEY, Peter Ernest Charles. NTMTC. **d** 10 **p** 11. NSM New Thundersley *Chelmsf* from 10. *58 Marguerite Drive, Leigh-on-Sea SS9 1NW*

BEHENNA, Preb Gillian Eve. b 57. CertEd78. St Alb Minl Tr Scheme 82. **dss** 85 **d** 87 **p** 94. Chapl to the Deaf *Sarum* 85-90; Chapl w Deaf People *Ex* 90-04; Preb Ex Cathl 02-04; Chapl w Deaf Community *Bris* from 05. *1 Saxon Way, Bradley Stoke, Bristol BS32 9AR* Tel (01454) 202483 Mobile 07715-707135 E-mail gillbehenna@me.com

BEHREND, Michael Christopher. b 60. St Jo Coll Cam BA82 MA86 PGCE83. Oak Hill Th Coll 93. **d** 97 **p** 98. C Hensingham *Carl* 97-02; TV Horwich and Rivington *Man* from 02; C Blackrod from 11. *St Catherine's House, Richmond Street, Horwich, Bolton BL6 5QT* Tel (01204) 697162

BELCHER, Mrs Catherine Jane Allington. b 53. Charlotte Mason Coll of Educn CertEd75. EAMTC 02. **d** 05 **p** 06. NSM Norwich St Mary Magd w St Jas 05-11; Perm to Offic from 11. *70 Mill Hill Road, Norwich NR2 3DS* Tel 07708-650897 (mobile) E-mail revkatebelcher@yahoo.co.uk

BELCHER, David John. b 44. Ch Ch Ox BA65 MA69. Cuddesdon Coll 68. **d** 70 **p** 71. C Gateshead St Mary *Dur* 70-73; C Stockton St Pet 73-76; Lic to Offic *Lich* 76-81; P-in-c W Bromwich Ch Ch 81-85; P-in-c W Bromwich Gd Shep w St Jo 85-89; V 89-95; RD W Bromwich 90-94; R Bratton, Edington and Imber, Erlestoke etc *Sarum* 95-03; rtd 03; Hon C Smestow Vale *Lich* 03-07; Perm to Offic from 09. *81 The Lindens, Newbridge Crescent, Wolverhampton WV6 0LS* Tel (01902) 750903

BELCHER, Canon Derek George. b 50. Univ of Wales (Cardiff) MEd86 LLM04 Lon Univ PGCE82 MRSH73 MBIM82 FRSH00. Chich Th Coll 74. **d** 77 **p** 78. C Newton Nottage *Llan* 77-81; PV Llan Cathl 81-87; V Margam 87-01; RD Margam 99-01; TR Cowbridge from 01; Can Llan Cathl from 97; AD Vale of Glam 08-11. *The Rectory, 85 Broadway, Llanblethian, Cowbridge CF71 7EY* Tel (01446) 771625 Mobile 07796-170671 E-mail derek@cowbridge.plus.com *or* rector@cowbridgeparish.com

BELFAST, Archdeacon of. See DODDS, The Ven Norman Barry

BELFAST, Dean of. See MANN, The Very Revd John Owen

BELHAM, John Edward. b 42. K Coll Lon BSc65 AKC65 PhD70. Oak Hill Th Coll 69. **d** 72 **p** 73. C Cheadle Hulme St Andr *Ches* 72-75; C Cheadle 75-83; R Gressenhall w Longham w Wendling etc *Nor* 83-08; P-in-c Mileham 07-08; rtd 08; Perm to Offic *Nor* from 08. *6 Brentwood, Norwich NR4 6PW* E-mail johnbelham@lords-prayer.co.uk

BELHAM, Michael. b 23. Lon Univ BScEng50. **d** 67 **p** 68. C Northwood Hills St Edm *Lon* 67-69; C Hendon St Mary 69-73; V Tottenham H Trin 73-78; V Hillingdon St Jo 78-85; P-in-c Broughton *Ox* 85; R Broughton w N Newington and Shutford 85-90; Chapl Horton Gen Hosp 85-90; rtd 90; Perm to Offic *Ox* and *Pet* 90-01; *B & W* from 01; Sec DBP *Ox* 95-01. *14 Holly Court, Frome BA11 2SQ* Tel (01373) 462941 E-mail michael-belham@supanet.com

BELING, David Gibson. b 30. Fitzw Ho Cam BA54 MA58. **d** 56 **p** 57. C Radipole *Sarum* 56-59; C Broadwater St Mary *Chich* 59-61; R W Knighton w Broadmayne *Sarum* 61-73; V Paignton St Paul Preston *Ex* 73-91; rtd 91; Perm to Offic *Ex* 91-09. *51 Manor Road, Paignton TQ3 2HZ*

BELITHER, John Roland. b 36. Oak Hill Th Coll 83. **d** 86 **p** 87. NSM Bushey Heath *St Alb* 86-91; V Marsh Farm 91-06; rtd 06; Perm to Offic *St Alb* from 06. *43 Mallard Road, Abbots Langley WD5 0GE* Tel (01923) 494399

BELL, Adrian Christopher. b 48. AKC70. St Aug Coll Cant 70. **d** 71 **p** 72. C Sheff St Aid w St Luke 71-74; C Willesborough w Hinxhill *Cant* 74-78; P-in-c Wormshill 78; P-in-c Hollingbourne w Hucking 78-82; P-in-c Leeds w Broomfield 79-82; V Hollingbourne and Hucking w Leeds and Broomfield 82-84; V Herne Bay Ch Ch 84-91; R Washingborough w Heighington and Canwick *Linc* 91-01; R Fakenham w Alethorpe *Nor* from 01. *The Rectory, Gladstone Road, Fakenham NR21 9BZ* Tel and fax (01328) 862268 E-mail adrian.bell4@btopenworld.com

BELL, Canon Alan John. b 47. Liv Univ BA68. Ridley Hall Cam 69. **d** 72 **p** 73. C Speke St Aid *Liv* 72-77; P-in-c Halewood 77-81; R Wavertree St Mary 81-88; Chapl Mabel Fletcher Tech Coll and Olive Mt Hosp 81-88; R Fakenham w Alethorpe *Nor* 88-00; RD Burnham and Walsingham 92-00; TR Stockport SW *Ches* 00-07; V Stockport St Geo from 07; RD Stockport from 05; Hon Can Ches Cathl from 08. *St George's Vicarage, 7 Corbar Road, Stockport SK2 6EP* Tel and fax 0161-456 0918 *or* tel 480 2453 E-mail vicaralanbell@aol.com

BELL, Alan McRae. b 49. Moray Ho Teacher Tr Coll Edin CertEd80 E Lon Univ BA90. S'wark Ord Course 86. **d** 92 **p** 95. NSM Bow H Trin and All Hallows *Lon* 91-93; NSM R Foundn of St Kath in Ratcliffe 93-95; USA 95-97; Chapl Univ of California 95-96; P-in-c Bolinas St Aidan 96-97. *177 Well Street, London E9 6QU* Tel (020) 8985 1978

BELL, Andrew Thomas. b 58. Ripon Coll Cuddesdon 93. **d** 95 **p** 96. C Leighton Buzzard w Eggington, Hockliffe etc *St Alb* 95-98; TV Schorne *Ox* 98-10. *Address temp unknown*

BELL, Anne Elizabeth. b 38. RGN60. SAOMC 98. **d** 08 **p** 08. NSM Shrivenham and Ashbury *Ox* from 08. *Whitcot, Shotover Corner, Uffington, Faringdon SN7 7RH* Tel (01367) 820091 E-mail anne@shotover.fsnet.co.uk

BELL, Anthony Lawson. b 47. AKC72. St Aug Coll Cant 71. **d** 72 **p** 73. C Peterlee *Dur* 72-77; C-in-c Stockton St Jas CD 82-89; P-in-c Byers Green 89-96; Ind Chapl Teesside 89-96; P-in-c Ault Hucknall *Derby* 96-99; V Ault Hucknall and Scarcliffe from 99. *The Vicarage, 59 The Hill, Glapwell, Chesterfield S44 5LX* Tel (01246) 850371 Fax 857530 E-mail glapwell@btconnect.com

BELL, Antony Fancourt. b 28. Magd Coll Ox BA51 MA58. Wells Th Coll 54. **d** 56 **p** 57. C Clapham H Trin *S'wark* 56-59; C Gillingham *Sarum* 59-61; R Stanway *Chelmsf* 61-94; RD Dedham and Tey 81-91; rtd 94. *7 Postern Close, Portchester, Fareham PO16 9NB* Tel (023) 9237 8272

BELL, Arthur James. b 33. Ch Coll Cam BA57 MA60. Coll of Resurr Mirfield 57. **d** 59 **p** 60. C New Cleethorpes *Linc* 59-63; C Upperby St Jo *Carl* 63-66; P-in-c Wabasca Canada 67-72 and 77-83; Perm to Offic *Ely* 73-75; Lic to Offic *Carl* 75-76; Warden Retreat of the Visitation Rhandirmwyn 83-99; Perm to Offic *Dur* from 00. *Burnside, 22 Rose Terrace, Stanhope, Bishop Auckland DL13 2PE* Tel (01388) 526514

BELL, Barnaby. See BELL, Simon Barnaby

BELL, Bede. See BELL, Canon William Wealands

BELL, Brian Thomas Benedict. b 64. Newc Poly BA87 Newc Univ PGCE88 Univ of Northumbria at Newc MA93 Leeds Univ BA97. Coll of Resurr Mirfield. **d** 97 **p** 98. C Tynemouth Cullercoats St Paul *Newc* 97-01; V Horton 01-08; V Horbury w Horbury Bridge *Wakef* from 08. *2 Elm Grove, Horbury, Wakefield WF4 5EP* Tel (01924) 273671 E-mail frbrian@ourladyandbenedict.fsnet.co.uk

BELL, Catherine Ann. See MOSS, Mrs Catherine Ann

BELL, Charles William. b 43. TCD Div Test 66 BA66 MA69. CITC 64. **d** 67 **p** 68. C Newtownards *D & D* 67-70; C Larne and Inver *Conn* 70-74; C Ballymena w Ballyclug 74-80; Bp's C Belfast Ardoyne 80-88; Bp's C Belfast Ardoyne w H Redeemer 88-89; I Eglantine 89-11; Dioc Info Officer (S Conn) 89-11; Preb Conn Cathl 04-11; rtd 11. *2 Beechwood Crescent, Moira, Craigavon BT67 0LA* Tel (028) 9261 9834

BELL, Colin Douglas. b 65. QUB BTh94 TCD MPhil96. CITC 94. **d** 96 **p** 97. C Dundonald *D & D* 96-98; C Knock 98-00; I Lack *Clogh* 00-02; I Rathcoole *Conn* 02-05; CF 05-07 and from 08; I Aghadrumsee w Clogh and Drumsnatt 07-08. *c/o MOD Chaplains (Army)* Tel (01264) 381140 Fax 381824

BELL, Cyril John. b 22. Lon Univ BA48. Wycliffe Hall Ox 52. **d** 53 **p** 54. C Monkwearmouth St Pet *Dur* 53-56; Asst Master Bede Gr Sch Sunderland 53-56; Lect and Chapl Union Chr Coll Alwaye S India 56-60; Lic to Offic *Ches* 62-87; Hon C Westlands St Andr *Lich* 66-71; Hd RE Marple Comp Sch 71-87; rtd 87; Perm to Offic *Lich* 87-96. *49 Delamere Road, Nantwich CW5 7DF* Tel (01270) 628910

BELL, David Bain. b 57. Bp Otter Coll BEd82. Ox Min Course 04. **d** 07 **p** 08. NSM Stantonbury and Willen *Ox* 07-10; TV Watling Valley from 10. *6 Edgecote, Great Holm, Milton Keynes MK8 9ER* Tel (01908) 564434 E-mail fivebells2007@hotmail.co.uk

BELL, David James. b 62. QUB BSc84 BTh. **d** 91 **p** 92. C Ballyholme *D & D* 91-94; C Coleraine *Conn* 94-00; I Ardtrea w Desertcreat *Arm* from 00. *Tullyhogue Rectory, 50 Lower Grange Road, Cookstown BT80 8SL* Tel and fax (028) 8676 1163 E-mail bell.david@talk21.com

BELL, Canon David Owain. b 49. Dur Univ BA69 Fitzw Coll Cam BA72 MA80. Westcott Ho Cam 70. **d** 72 **p** 73. C Houghton le Spring *Dur* 72-76; C Norton St Mary 76-78; P-in-c Worc St Clem 78-84; R 84-85; R Old Swinford Stourbridge 85-97; RD Stourbridge 90-96; Hon Can Worc Cathl from 96; TR Kidderminster St Mary and All SS w Trimpley etc from 97. *The Vicarage, 22 Roden Avenue, Kidderminster DY10 2RF* Tel (01562) 823265 E-mail dowainbell@yahoo.co.uk

BELL, Canon Donald Jon. b 50. Sarum & Wells Th Coll 73. **d** 76 **p** 77. C Jarrow *Dur* 76-80; C Darlington St Cuth w St Hilda 80-83; V Wingate Grange 83-89; V Sherburn w Pittington 89-95; R Shadforth 94-95; P-in-c Dur St Cuth 95-97; V 97-02; R Witton Gilbert 97-02; TR Dur N 02-05; AD Dur 93-05; Chapl Dur and Darlington Fire and Rescue Brigade 95-05; Bp's Sen Chapl and Exec Officer from 05; Hon Can Dur Cathl from 01. *Auckland Castle, Market Place, Bishop Auckland DL14 7NR* Tel (01388) 602576 Fax 605264 Mobile 07973-829491 E-mail chaplain@bishopdunelm.co.uk

BELL, Dorothy Jane. b 53. Teesside Univ BSc93. Cranmer Hall Dur 01. **d** 03 **p** 04. C Washington *Dur* 03-07; P-in-c Stockton St Jo from 07; P-in-c Stockton St Jas from 07. *St John the Baptist Vicarage, 190 Durham Road, Stockton-on-Tees TS19 0PS* Tel (01642) 674119

BELL, Evelyn Ruth. b 52. Univ of Wales (Cardiff) BSc(Econ). SAOMC 97. **d** 00 **p** 01. C Waltham Cross *St Alb* 00-03; Chapl HM Pris Edmunds Hill 03-11; Chapl HM Pris Highpoint from 11. *HM Prison Edmunds Hill, Stradishall, Newmarket CB8 9YN* Tel (01440) 743595 E-mail eve.bell@hmps.gsi.gov.uk

BELL, Canon Francis William Albert. b 28. TCD BA52 MA57 BD57. d 53 p 54. C Belfast St Mich *Conn* 53-55; C Belfast All SS 55-61; C Ballynafeigh St Jude *D & D* 61-63; P-in-c Ballyhalbert 63-71; P-in-c Ardkeen 67-71; I Ballyhalbert w Ardkeen 71-95; Miss to Seamen 71-95; Can Belf Cathl 89-95; rtd 95. *Stationbanks, 18 Kilmore Road, Crossgar, Downpatrick BT30 9HJ* Tel (028) 4483 1665

BELL, Mrs Glynis Mary. b 44. Leeds Univ BA66. SAOMC 99. d 02 p 03. OLM Newport Pagnell w Lathbury and Moulsoe *Ox* from 02. *6 Kipling Drive, Newport Pagnell MK16 8EB* Tel (01908) 612971

BELL, Godfrey Bryan. b 44. Oak Hill Th Coll 72. d 75 p 76. C Penn Fields *Lich* 75-79; R Dolton *Ex* 79-89; R Iddesleigh w Dowland 79-89; R Monkokehampton 79-89; R Tollard Royal w Farnham, Gussage St Michael etc *Sarum* 89-96; TV Washfield, Stoodleigh, Withleigh etc *Ex* 96-06; TR 06-09; rtd 09. *Bethany, 3 Alstone Road, Tiverton EX16 4JL* Tel (01884) 252874 E-mail gomar@stoodleigh.freeserve.co.uk

BELL, Graham Dennis Robert. b 42. K Coll Lon BSc63 AKC63 Nottm Univ MTh73 ALCM76 Lambeth STh01. Tyndale Hall Bris 65. d 68 p 69. C Stapleford *S'well* 68-71; C Barton Seagrave *Pet* 71-73; C Barton Seagrave w Warkton 73-76; Perm to Offic *Nor* 76-82; V Wickham Market *St E* 82-86; V Wickham Market w Pettistree and Easton 86-98; R Thrapston *Pet* 98-07; rtd 07; Perm to Offic *Pet* from 11. *22 Cottesmore Avenue, Barton Seagrave, Kettering NN15 6QX* Tel (01536) 725924 E-mail grahambellgood@talktalk.net

BELL, Canon Jack Gorman. b 23. Lon Univ BSc48. Oak Hill Th Coll 51. d 53 p 54. C Blackpool Ch Ch *Blackb* 53-55; C Chadderton Ch Ch *Man* 55-59; R Man St Jerome w Ardwick St Silas 59-69; V Mosley Common 69-89; Hon Can Man Cathl 87-89; rtd 89; Perm to Offic *Carl* 89-11. *39 The Moorings, Stafford Street, Stone ST15 8QZ* Tel (01785) 286126

✠**BELL, The Rt Revd James Harold.** b 50. St Jo Coll Dur BA72 St Pet Hall Ox BA74 MA78. Wycliffe Hall Ox 72. d 75 p 76 c 04. Hon C Ox St Mich w St Martin and All SS 75-76; Chapl and Lect BNC Ox 76-82; R Northolt St Mary *Lon* 82-93; AD Ealing 91-93; Adv for Min Willesden 93-97; Dioc Dir of Min and Tr *Ripon* 97-99; Dioc Dir of Miss 99-04; Can Res Ripon Cathl 97-99; Hon Can from 99; Suff Bp Knaresborough from 04. *Thistledown, Main Street, Exelby, Bedale DL8 2HD* Tel and fax (01677) 423525 E-mail bishop.knaresb@btinternet.com

BELL, James Samuel. b 40. MBE71. RMA 59 St Chad's Coll Dur BA69. Coll of Resurr Mirfield 71. d 72 p 73. C Lambeth St Phil *S'wark* 72-74; C N Lambeth 74; P-in-c Invergordon St Ninian *Mor* 74-77; P-in-c Dornoch 74-77; P-in-c Brora 74-77; V Pet H Spirit Bretton 77-83; P-in-c Marholm 82-83; Sen Chapl Tonbridge Sch 83-00; rtd 00. *Clocktower House, Edderton, Tain IV19 1LJ* Tel (01862) 821305

BELL, Jane. See BELL, Dorothy Jane

BELL, Canon Jeffrey William. b 37. Buckingham Univ MA94. Sarum Th Coll 60. d 63 p 64. C Northampton St Matt *Pet* 63-66; C Portishead *B & W* 66-68; C Digswell *St Alb* 68-72; V Pet St Jude 72-79; V Buckingham *Ox* 79-93; RD Buckingham 84-88 and 89-90; V Portsea N End St Mark *Portsm* 93-03; Hon Can Portsm Cathl 00-03; rtd 03; Hon C The Bourne and Tilford *Guildf* from 03. *All Saints' Vicarage, Tilford, Farnham GU10 2DA* Tel (01252) 792333

BELL, Jennifer Kathryn. See McWHIRTER, Jennifer Kathryn

BELL, John. See BELL, Cyril John

BELL, John. See BELL, Canon Donald Jon

BELL, John Christopher. b 33. TCD BA56 MA66. TCD Div Sch Div Test. d 56 p 57. C Newtownards *D & D* 56-59; C Willowfield 59-62; I Carrowdore 62-70; I Drumbo 70-98; Chapl Young Offender Cen Belf 79-98; Can Down Cathl 87-98; Treas 91-98; rtd 98. *Ashwell House, 6 Ballywillin Road, Crossgar, Downpatrick BT30 9LE* Tel (028) 4483 1907

BELL, John Edward. b 34. Cranmer Hall Dur. d 67 p 68. C Harraby *Carl* 67-70; C Dalton-in-Furness 70-72; V Pennington 72-75; V Carl St Herbert w St Steph 75-84; V Wreay 84-85; rtd 99; Perm to Offic *Carl* from 01. *189 Brampton Road, Carlisle CA3 9AX* Tel (01228) 522746

BELL, John Holmes. b 50. Sheff City Coll of Educn CertEd71. Oak Hill Th Coll BA80. d 80 p 81. C Leic St Phil 80-83; C Portswood Ch Ch 83-86; TV S Molton w Nymet St George, High Bray etc *Ex* 86-01; V Stoke Fleming, Blackawton and Strete from 01. *The Rectory, Rectory Lane, Stoke Fleming, Dartmouth TQ6 0QB* Tel (01803) 771050 E-mail john@ding-dong.fsnet.co.uk

BELL, Karl Edwin. b 33. Minnesota Univ BA56. Seabury-Western Th Sem MDiv61. d 61 p 62. USA 61-71 and 76-92; Venezuela 71-76; Chapl Wiesbaden *Eur* from 92. *St Augustine of Canterbury, Frankfurterstrasse 3, 65189 Wiesbaden, Germany* Tel (0049) (611) 306674 Fax 372270 E-mail bell@wiesbaden.netsurf.de

BELL, Kenneth Murray. b 30. Sarum & Wells Th Coll 75. d 74 p 76. Perm to Offic *Guildf* 74-76; C Hartley Wintney and Elvetham 76-77; C Hartley Wintney, Elvetham, Winchfield etc 77-80; V Fair Oak 80-95; rtd 96; Perm to Offic *Win* from 96.

12 Hill Meadow, Overton, Basingstoke RG25 3JD Tel (01256) 770890 E-mail keny12@talk21.com

BELL, Kevin David. b 58. Newc Univ MA93 Univ of Wales (Lamp) MA06 FInstLM11 FRSA11. Aston Tr Scheme 78 Sarum & Wells Th Coll 80. d 83 p 84. C Weoley Castle *Birm* 83-87; C Acocks Green 87-89; CF 89-07; Asst Chapl Gen from 07; Dir of Ords 07-11. *c/o MOD Chaplains (Army)* Tel (01980) 615804 Fax 615800

BELL, Canon Nicholas Philip Johnson. b 46. St Jo Coll Dur BSc69. St Jo Coll Nottm 70. d 73 p 74. C Chadderton Ch Ch *Man* 73-77; C Frogmore *St Alb* 77-81; V Bricket Wood 81-91; RD Aldenham 87-91; V Luton St Mary from 91; Hon Can St Alb from 01. *The Vicarage, 48 Crawley Green Road, Luton LU2 0QX* Tel and fax (01582) 728925 E-mail nickbell@stmarysluton.org

BELL, Owain. See BELL, Canon David Owain

BELL, Paul Joseph. b 35. Dur Univ BA56 DipEd57. Trin Coll Bris 77. d 77 p 78. Burundi 77-81; C Highbury Ch Ch w St Jo and St Sav *Lon* 82-85; V Middleton w E Winch *Nor* 85-95; P-in-c Barningham w Matlaske w Baconsthorpe etc 95-99; R 99-02; rtd 02; Perm to Offic *Portsm* from 02. *21 Hurst Point View, Totland Bay PO39 0AQ* Tel (01983) 756180

BELL, Prof Richard Herbert. b 54. Univ Coll Lon BSc75 PhD79 Tubingen Univ DrTheol91. Wycliffe Hall Ox BA82 MA87. d 83 p 84. C Edgware *Lon* 83-86; W Germany 86-90; Lect Th Nottm Univ 90-97; Sen Lect 97-05; Reader 05-08; Prof from 08. *Department of Theology and Religious Studies, University Park, Nottingham NG7 2RD* Tel 0115-951 5858 Fax 951 5887 E-mail richard.bell@nottingham.ac.uk

BELL, Robert Clarke. b 30. Roch Th Coll 63. d 65 p 66. C Leeds All SS *Ripon* 65-67; C Claxby w Normanby-le-Wold *Linc* 67-69; R Newark St Leon *S'well* 69-71; V Gosberton Clough *Linc* 71-74; P-in-c Quadring 73-74; Chapl to the Deaf 74-85; V Harmston and Coleby 85-94; RD Graffoe 92-94; rtd 94; Perm to Offic *Blackb* 94-05 and *Carl* 94-98. *10 Upper Close, Sturton by Stow, Lincoln LN1 2DZ* Tel (01427) 787962

BELL, Robert Mason. b 35. Lon Coll of Div 66. d 68 p 69. C Burgess Hill St Andr *Chich* 68-78; R Lewes St Jo sub Castro 78-00; rtd 00. *10 Rufus Close, Lewes BN7 1BG* Tel (01273) 470561

BELL, Ross Kinninmonth. b 64. Bradf and Ilkley Coll BA87. Aston Tr Scheme 89 Westcott Ho Cam 91. d 94 p 95. C W Bromwich All SS *Lich* 94-98; TV Cen Wolverhampton 98-02; Chapl Bilston Street Police Station 04-06; Perm to Offic *Edin* from 06. *Flat 4, 5 Colonsay Close, Edinburgh EH5 1BT* Tel 0131-552 3060 Mobile 07976-157022 E-mail ro.bell@btinternet.com

BELL, Mrs Shena Margaret. b 49. EAMTC. d 00 p 01. C Earls Barton *Pet* 00-04; P-in-c Raunds 04-07; P-in-c Ringstead and Stanwick w Hargrave 04-07; R Raunds, Hargrave, Ringstead and Stanwick from 07. *The Vicarage, High Street, Raunds, Wellingborough NN9 6HS* Tel (01933) 461509 E-mail shena.bell@virgin.net

BELL, Simon Barnaby. b 48. Bris Univ CertEd70. Sarum & Wells Th Coll 87. d 89 p 90. C Ewyas Harold w Dulas *Heref* 89-90; C Ewyas Harold w Dulas, Kenderchurch etc 90-93; P-in-c Clungunford w Clunbury and Clunton, Bedstone etc 93-01; R from 01. *The Rectory, Clungunford, Craven Arms SY7 0PN* Tel (01588) 660342

BELL, Canon Stuart Rodney. b 46. Ex Univ BA67. Tyndale Hall Bris 69. d 71 p 72. C Henfynyw w Aberaeron and Llanddewi Aberarth *St D* 71-74; V 81-88; V Llangeler 74-80; TR Aberystwyth from 88; Chapl Univ of Wales (Abth) from 94; Ev St Teilo Trust from 95; Can St D Cathl from 01. *The Rectory, Laura Place, Aberystwyth SY23 2AU* Tel and fax (01970) 617184 *or* tel 625080

BELL (née STEWART), Mrs Susan Catherine. b 57. St Martin's Coll Lanc BEd80. LCTP 08. d 10 p 11. C Longridge *Blackb* from 10. *8 Clayton Court, Longridge, Preston PR3 3UD* Tel (01772) 780803 Mobile 07738-305129 E-mail bellsue9@gmail.com

BELL, Terrance James. b 63. Toronto Univ BA92. Trin Coll Toronto MDiv97. d 97 p 98. C Wedmore w Theale and Blackford *B & W* 97-01; C Hampstead St Jo *Lon* 01-06; Chapl Eden Hall Marie Curie Hospice 01-06; P-in-c King's Walden and Offley w Lilley *St Alb* from 06. *Millstone Corner, Salusbury Lane, Offley, Hitchin SG5 3EG* Tel (01462) 768123 E-mail kwol@btinternet.com

BELL, Timothy John Keeton. b 59. Trin Coll Bris BA02. d 02 p 03. C Saltford w Corston and Newton St Loe *B & W* 02-06; Chapl Bath Spa Univ 04-06; P-in-c Wick w Doynton and Dyrham *Bris* from 06. *The Vicarage, 57 High Street, Wick, Bristol BS30 5QQ* Tel 0117-937 3581 E-mail tim.vicar@gmail.com

BELL, Canon William Wealands. b 63. York Univ BA86 Dur Univ PGCE87 Leeds Univ BA99. Coll of Resurr Mirfield 97. d 99 p 00. C Jarrow *Dur* 99-02; Novice CR 02-04; Chapl Aldenham Sch Herts 04-07; Can Res Lich Cathl from 07. *23 The Close, Lichfield WS13 7LD* E-mail wealands.bell@lichfield-cathedral.org

BELL-RICHARDS, Douglas Maurice. b 23. St Steph Ho Ox 59. **d** 61 **p** 62. C Chipping Campden *Glouc* 61-62; C Thornbury 62-67; V Dymock w Donnington 67-75; V Fairford 75-91; rtd 91. *21 Capel Court, The Burgage, Prestbury, Cheltenham GL52 3EL* Tel (01242) 578030

BELLAMY, David Quentin. b 62. Univ of Wales (Cardiff) BMus84 Univ of Wales (Ban) MA93. Ripon Coll Cuddesdon 87 Ch Div Sch of the Pacific (USA). **d** 90 **p** 91. C Rhyl w St Ann *St As* 90-94; V Llay 94-04; V Prestatyn from 04; AD St As from 10. *The Vicarage, 109 High Street, Prestatyn LL19 9AR* Tel (01745) 853780 E-mail vicar@parishofprestatyn.org.uk

BELLAMY, Mrs Dorothy Kathleen. b 33. Gilmore Course 74. **dss** 82 **d** 87 **p** 94. Feltham *Lon* 82-84; Twickenham St Mary 84; Hampton St Mary 84-85; Hampton Wick 85-88; Par Dn 87-88; Par Dn Teddington St Mark and Hampton Wick 88-90; Par Dn Westbury *Sarum* 90-94; C 94-96; rtd 97; NSM Freshwater and Yarmouth *Portsm* 97-09. *9 Strathwell Crescent, Whitwell, Ventnor PO38 2QZ* Tel (01983) 731545

BELLAMY, Mrs Janet Mary. b 45. Westf Coll Lon BA66 Birm Univ BLitt98 MEd93 Cam Univ PGCE67. **d** 09 **p** 10. NSM Hope Bowdler w Eaton-under-Heywood *Heref* from 09. *Orchard House, Diddlebury, Craven Arms SY7 9DH* Tel (01584) 841511 E-mail janetmbellamy@googlemail.com

BELLAMY, John Stephen. b 55. Jes Coll Ox BA77 MA81 Liv Univ PhD06. St Jo Coll Nottm. **d** 84 **p** 85. C Allerton *Liv* 84-87; C Southport Ch Ch 87-89; Bp's Dom Chapl 89-91; V Birkdale St Jas 91-08; V Dur St Nic from 08. *11 Beechways, Durham DH1 4LG* Tel 0191-384 6066 E-mail jsbellamy@onetel.com

BELLAMY, Canon Mervyn Roger Hunter. b 47. Sussex Univ CertEd Heythrop Coll Lon MA04. St Mich Coll Llan 81. **d** 81 **p** 82. C Frecheville and Hackenthorpe *Sheff* 81-85; V Shiregreen St Hilda 85-94; RD Ecclesfield 93-94; R Rawmarsh w Parkgate 94-01; P-in-c King's Sutton and Newbottle and Charlton *Pet* 01-09; V from 09; RD Brackley from 05; Can Pet Cathl from 09. *The Vicarage, Church Avenue, King's Sutton, Banbury OX17 3RJ* Tel (01295) 811364 E-mail rogerbellamy@hotmail.co.uk

BELLAMY, Mrs Norma Edna. b 44. Birm Univ CertEd75 Open Univ BA83. **d** 10 **p** 11. OLM Shareshill *Lich* from 10. *10 Meadowlark Close, Hednesford, Cannock WS12 1UE* Tel (01543) 876809 Mobile 07866-431211 E-mail robert.jbellamy@virgin.net

BELLAMY, Peter Charles William. b 38. Birm Univ MA70 PhD79 AKC61. **d** 62 **p** 63. C Allestree *Derby* 62-65; Chapl All SS Hosp Birm 65-73; Chapl St Pet Coll of Educn Saltley 73-78; Chapl and Lect Qu Eliz Hosp Birm 78-90; Lect Past Psychology Birm Univ 79-92; Manager HIV Services Birm Cen HA 90-92; Commr for Public Health Cen and S Birm HA 92-96; Research Fell Birm Univ 97-02; Local Min Development Adv *Heref* 01-06; Dioc Co-ord for Min of Deliverance from 06. *Orchard House, Diddlebury, Craven Arms SY7 9DH* Tel (01584) 841511 E-mail peterbellamy@googlemail.com

BELLAMY, Quentin. *See* BELLAMY, David Quentin

BELLAMY, Richard William. b 62. SEITE 07. **d** 10 **p** 11. NSM Cheriton St Martin *Cant* from 10. *5 Papworth Close, Folkestone CT19 5LZ* Tel (01303) 271059 Mobile 07952-958247 E-mail r.w.bellamy@btinternet.com

BELLAMY, Robert John. b 40. Ripon Hall Ox 64. **d** 66 **p** 67. C Fishponds St Jo *Bris* 66-70; C Oldland 70-74; P-in-c Coalpit Heath 74-76; TV Cannock *Lich* 90-96; Perm to Offic 96-98 and 03-04; Hon C Longdon 98-03; Hon C Shareshill 04-11; Perm to Offic from 11. *10 Meadowlark Close, Hednesford, Cannock WS12 1UE* Tel (01543) 876809 E-mail robert.jbellamy@virgin.net

BELLAMY, Roger. *See* BELLAMY, Canon Mervyn Roger Hunter

BELLAMY, Stephen. *See* BELLAMY, John Stephen

BELLAMY-KNIGHTS, Peter George. b 41. Leic Univ BSc63 Man Univ MSc67 PhD70 Lon Univ BD03 CMath91 FIMA91 CEng94 FRAeS98. Man OLM Scheme 03. **d** 04 **p** 05. NSM Man Cathl from 04. *113 Old Hall Lane, Manchester M14 6HL* Tel 0161-224 2702

BELLENES, Peter Charles. b 49. Thurrock Coll Essex CQSW72. Linc Th Coll 79. **d** 81 **p** 90. C Penistone *Wakef* 81-82; Hon C Liskeard, St Keyne, St Pinnock, Morval etc *Truro* 89-91; Hon C Menheniot 91-99; P-in-c Marldon *Ex* 99-03; TV Totnes w Bridgetown, Berry Pomeroy etc 03-09; rtd 09. *Little Grove, Harrow Barrow, Callington PL17 8JN* Tel (01822) 833508 E-mail pbellenes@aol.com

BELLENGER, Peter John Russell. b 74. New Coll Ox BA96 MA02 St Jo Coll Dur BA03 St Andr Univ MPhil09. Cranmer Hall Dur 01. **d** 04 **p** 05. C Tollington *Lon* 04-07; P-in-c from 10. *1 Moray Road, London N4 3LD* Tel (020) 7561 5462 E-mail pete.bellenger@tollingtonparish.org.uk

BELLINGER, Canon Denys Gordon. b 29. Sheff Univ BA49. Westcott Ho Cam 51. **d** 53 **p** 54. C Ribbleton *Blackb* 53-56; C Lancaster St Mary 56-58; V Colne H Trin 58-68; V Scotforth 68-93; RD Lancaster 82-89; Hon Can Blackb Cathl 86-93; rtd 93; Perm to Offic *Blackb* from 93. *40 Yewlands Drive, Garstang, Preston PR3 1JP* Tel (01995) 601539

BELLINGER, Richard George. b 47. Univ of Wales (Abth) BSc(Econ)69. S Dios Minl Tr Scheme 91. **d** 94 **p** 95. NSM Guernsey St Steph *Win* 94-96; NSM Guernsey St Martin from 96. *La Maison des Vinaires, Rue des Vinaires, St Peter's, Guernsey GY7 9EZ* Tel (01481) 63203 Fax 66989

BELLIS, Huw. b 72. Univ of Wales (Lamp) BA94. Westcott Ho Cam 96. **d** 98 **p** 99. C Merrow *Guildf* 98-02; TV Tring *St Alb* 02-08; TR from 08. *The Rectory, 2 The Limes, Station Road, Tring HP23 5NW* Tel (01442) 822170 E-mail huwbellis@btinternet.com

BELOE, Mrs Jane. b 46. STETS. **d** 04 **p** 05. NSM Shedfield *Portsm* 04-06; NSM Bishop's Waltham from 06; NSM Upham from 06. *Roughay Cottage, Popes Lane, Upham, Southampton SO32 1JB* Tel (01489) 860452 E-mail janebeloe@btinternet.com

BELOE, Robert Francis. b 39. Sarum Th Coll. **d** 65 **p** 71. C Nor Heartsease St Fran 65-66; C Edmonton St Mary w St Jo *Lon* 68-70; C St Marylebone Ch Ch w St Paul 70-74; P-in-c Wicken *Ely* 74-76; V 76-00; rtd 00; Perm to Offic *Ely* 00-08 and *Carl* from 08. *20 Lakehead Court, Keswick CA12 5EU* Tel (017687) 74796

BELSHAW, Patricia Anne. b 47. **d** 05 **p** 06. OLM Leyland St Jas *Blackb* 05-07; NSM 07-10; NSM Darwen St Pet from 10. *9 The Laund, Leyland, Preston PR26 7XX* Tel (01772) 453624 E-mail patriciabelshaw@yahoo.co.uk

BEMENT, Peter James. b 43. Univ of Wales (Cardiff) BA64 PhD69. Wycliffe Hall Ox 92. **d** 94 **p** 95. C Hubberston *St D* 94-97; V Llandeilo Fawr and Taliaris 97-08; rtd 08. *21 Chandler's Yard, Burry Port SA16 0FE* Tel (01554) 833905

BENCE, Helen Mary. b 44. Leic Univ BA65 PGCE66. EMMTC 93. **d** 97 **p** 98. NSM Humberstone *Leic* 97-02; NSM Thurnby Lodge 01-02; TV Oadby 03-08; NSM Thurnby w Stoughton from 08. *The Grange, 126 Shanklin Drive, Leicester LE2 3QB* Tel 0116-270 7820 E-mail helenbence@leicester.freeserve.co.uk

BENCE, Norman Murray. b 34. Ripon Hall Ox 63. **d** 63 **p** 64. C Eling *Win* 63-66; Australia 66 and 75; NSM Holdenhurst and Iford *Win* from 81. *72 Corhampton Road, Bournemouth BH6 5PB* Tel (01202) 421992 Fax 420154

BENDALL, Robin Andrew. b 64. Qu Mary Coll Lon BA86. SEITE 08. **d** 11. NSM Sandwich *Cant* from 11. *24 Delfside, Sandwich CT13 9RL* Tel (01304) 617458 E-mail robinbendall@hotmail.com

BENDELL, David James. b 38. ACIB74. S'wark Ord Course 84. **d** 87 **p** 88. NSM Surbiton Hill Ch Ch *S'wark* 87-03; Perm to Offic from 10. *3 Pine Walk, Surbiton KT5 8NJ* Tel (020) 8399 7143 E-mail bendell@talktalk.net

BENDING, Richard Clement. b 47. Southn Univ BSc68. Ridley Hall Cam 87. **d** 89 **p** 90. Par Dn St Neots *Ely* 89-92; V Buckden 92-99; P-in-c Hail Weston 97-99; P-in-c Terrington St John 99-02; P-in-c Tilney All Saints 99-02; P-in-c Wiggenhall St Germans and Islington 99-02; P-in-c Wiggenhall St Mary Magd 99-02; V E Marshland 02-05; rtd 05; Perm to Offic *Nor* from 05. *Dawn Cottage, Newgate Green, Cley, Holt NR25 7TT* Tel (01263) 741603 E-mail rcbending@hotmail.com

BENDREY (née BRIGNALL), Elizabeth Jane. b 69. St Mary's Coll Twickenham BA(QTS)91 Heythrop Coll Lon MA02 Cam Univ BTh06. Westcott Ho Cam 04. **d** 06 **p** 07. C Witham *Chelmsf* 06-09; P-in-c Black Notley from 09. *The Rectory, 265C London Road, Black Notley, Braintree CM77 8QQ* Tel (01376) 567971 Mobile 07940-516741 E-mail revbethbendrey@hotmail.co.uk

BENDREY, Iain Robert. b 73. Bp Grosseteste Coll BA96 Birm Univ MEd03. ERMC 06. **d** 08 **p** 09. NSM Wickham Bishops w Lt Braxted *Chelmsf* from 08. *The Rectory, 265C London Road, Black Notley, Braintree CM77 8QQ* Tel (01376) 567971 Mobile 07960-810687 E-mail curate@churchinwickhambishops.org.uk

BENEDICT, Brother. *See* WINSPER, Arthur William

BENFIELD, Paul John. b 56. Newc Univ LLB77 Southn Univ BTh89 Barrister-at-Law (Lincoln's Inn) 78. Chich Th Coll 86. **d** 89 **p** 90. C Shiremoor *Newc* 89-92; C Hexham 92-93; TV Lewes All SS, St Anne, St Mich and St Thos *Chich* 93-97; R Pulborough 97-00; V Fleetwood St Nic *Blackb* from 00. *St Nicholas' Vicarage, Highbury Avenue, Fleetwood FY7 7DJ* Tel and fax (01253) 874402 E-mail benfield@btinternet.com

BENFORD, Steven Charles. b 61. Leic Univ MB, ChB86. NEOC 97. **d** 00 **p** 01. NSM Northallerton w Kirby Sigston *York* 00-04; P-in-c York St Luke from 04. *St Luke's Vicarage, 79 Burton Stone Lane, York YO30 6BZ* Tel (01904) 641058 E-mail benford@doctors.org.uk

BENGE, Charles David. b 40. Cranmer Hall Dur 63. **d** 68 **p** 69. C Millfield St Mark *Dur* 68-72; C Hensingham *Carl* 72-75; TV Maghull *Liv* 75-82; V Bootle St Leon 82-97; NSM Ormskirk 97-01; rtd 01; Perm to Offic *Liv* from 03. *26 Drummersdale Lane, Scarisbrick, Ormskirk L40 9RB* Tel (01704) 880956

BENHAM, Ms Sandra Rhys. b 59. Westcott Ho Cam 04. **d** 06 **p** 07. C Gainsborough and Morton *Linc* 06-09; P-in-c Quarrington w Old Sleaford from 09; P-in-c Silk Willoughby from 09; P-in-c Cranwell 09-11. *The Rectory, 5 Spire View, Sleaford NG34 7RN* Tel (01529) 306776 E-mail sandrabenham@btinternet.com

BENIAMS, Alec Charles. b 28. AKC52. **d** 53 **p** 54. C Gosforth All SS *Newc* 53-56; C Cullercoats St Geo 56-58; C Eltham St Jo *S'wark* 58-59; C-in-c Lynemouth St Aid CD *Newc* 59-61; CF (TA) 60-67; V Lynemouth *Newc* 61-63; V Whittingham 63-67; V Willington 67-71; CF (TA - R of O) from 67; V Haydon Bridge *Newc* 71-85; R Yardley Hastings, Denton and Grendon etc *Pet* 85-90; rtd 90; Perm to Offic *Newc* from 90. *12 Dickson Drive, Highford Park, Hexham NE46 2RB* Tel (01434) 600226

BENISON, Canon Brian. b 41. K Coll Lon 61. Bps' Coll Cheshunt 63. **d** 66 **p** 67. C Tynemouth Ch Ch *Newc* 66-70; C Gosforth All SS 70-72; TV Cullercoats St Geo 73-81; V Denton 81-93; V Blyth St Mary 93-04; RD Bedlington 98-03; Chapl Cheviot and Wansbeck NHS Trust 93-98; Chapl Northumbria Healthcare NHS Trust 98-04; Hon Can Newc Cathl from 01; rtd 04. *64 Monks Wood, North Shields NE30 2UA* Tel 0191-257 1631 E-mail brian.benison@btinternet.com

BENJAMIN, Adrian Victor. b 42. Wadh Coll Ox BA66 MA68. Cuddesdon Coll 66. **d** 68 **p** 69. C Gosforth All SS *Newc* 68-71; C Stepney St Dunstan and All SS *Lon* 71-75; V Friern Barnet All SS from 75; Relig Ed ITV Oracle from 83. *All Saints' Vicarage, 14 Oakleigh Park South, London N20 9JU* Tel (020) 8445 4654 *or* 8445 8388 Mobile 07889-83298 Fax 8445 6831 E-mail allsaints@mcmail.com

✠**BENN, The Rt Revd Wallace Parke.** b 47. UCD BA69. Trin Coll Bris 69. **d** 72 **p** 73 **c** 97. C New Ferry *Ches* 72-76; C Cheadle 76-82; V Audley *Lich* 82-87; V Harold Wood *Chelmsf* 87-97; Chapl Harold Wood Hosp Chelmsf 87-96; Area Bp Lewes *Chich* from 97; Can and Preb Chich Cathl from 97. *Bishop's Lodge, 16A Prideaux Road, Eastbourne BN21 2NB* Tel (01323) 648462 Fax 641514 E-mail bishop.lewes@diochi.org.uk

BENNELL, Canon Richard. b 25. Leeds Univ BA45 DipEd45. Coll of Resurr Mirfield 46. **d** 48 **p** 49. C Bedminster *Bris* 48-51; C Brislington St Anne 51-56; V Fishponds St Jo 56-68; V Knowle St Martin 68-73; TR Knowle 73-80; RD Brislington 73-79; Hon Can Bris Cathl 76-91; Chapl St Monica Home Westbury-on-Trym 80-91; rtd 91; Perm to Offic *Bris* from 91. *1B Cooper Road, Bristol BS9 3QZ* Tel 0117-962 2364

BENNET, Hadley Jane. b 66. **d** 09 **p** 10. NSM Grayshott *Guildf* from 09. *Landfall, Three Gates Lane, Haslemere GU27 2ET* Tel (01428) 658166 E-mail hadleybennet@yahoo.co.uk

BENNET, Mark David. b 62. SS Coll Cam BA84 MA92 Anglia Poly Univ MA04 ACA89. Westcott Ho Cam 98. **d** 01 **p** 02. C Chapel Allerton *Ripon* 01-05; TV Gt Parndon *Chelmsf* 05-07; P-in-c 07-09; TR from 09; TR Thatcham *Ox* from 11. *The Rectory, 17 Church Gate, Thatcham RG19 3PN* E-mail markbennet@btinternet.com

BENNETT, Alan Robert. b 31. Roch Th Coll 62. **d** 64 **p** 65. C Asterby w Goulceby *Linc* 64-67; C St Alb St Pet *St Alb* 67-70; R Banham *Nor* 70-72; CF 72-77; P-in-c Colchester St Mary Magd *Chelmsf* 77; TV Colchester St Leon, St Mary Magd and St Steph 77-81; R Colne Engaine 81-88; P-in-c Stoke Ferry w Wretton *Ely* 88-89; V 89-96; V Whittington 88-96; rtd 96; Hon C Wimbotsham w Stow Bardolph and Stow Bridge etc *Ely* 96-00; Perm to Offic from 00. *34 West Way, Wimbotsham, King's Lynn PE34 3PZ* Tel (01366) 385958

BENNETT, Canon Alan William. b 42. Sarum Th Coll 65. **d** 68 **p** 69. C Fareham H Trin *Portsm* 68-71; C Brighton St Matthias *Chich* 71-73; C Stanmer w Falmer and Moulsecoomb 73-75; C Moulsecoomb 76; V Lower Sandown St Jo *Portsm* 76-80; V Soberton w Newtown 80-87; R Aston Clinton w Buckland and Drayton Beauchamp *Ox* 87-07; RD Wendover 94-04; Hon Can Ch Ch 03-07; rtd 07; Hon Asst Chapl Costa Almeria and Costa Calida *Eur* from 10. *2 Chapman Close, Aylesbury HP21 8FY* E-mail canonbennett@hotmail.co.uk

BENNETT, Alexander Steven Frederick. b 69. Hull Univ BA91. Westcott Ho Cam 93. **d** 95 **p** 96. C Whitton and Thurleston w Akenham *St E* 95-99; OGS from 99; C Oswestry *Lich* 99-01; V Oswestry H Trin 01-04; CF from 04. *clo MOD Chaplains (Army)* Tel (01264) 381140 Fax 381824 E-mail armypadre@hotmail.com

BENNETT, Mrs Alison. b 63. Open Univ BSc03 DipSW99. STETS 05. **d** 08 **p** 09. C Bramshott and Liphook *Portsm* from 08. *2 Meadow End, Liphook GU30 7UA* Tel (01428) 725390

BENNETT, Ms Anne Yvonn. b 62. Open Univ MSc95 Imp Coll Lon MBA00. Cranmer Hall Dur 06. **d** 08 **p** 09. C Harton *Dur* from 08; C Cleadon Park from 09. *218 Sunderland Road, South Shields NE34 6AT* Tel 0191-456 2875 E-mail timeshift@btinternet.com

BENNETT, Anton Wayne. b 69. SW Poly Plymouth BSc90. Westcott Ho Cam 00. **d** 02 **p** 03. C Pendleton *Man* 02-05; R Abberton, The Flyfords, Naunton Beauchamp etc *Worc* 05-07; rtd 07. *18 Victoria Street, Settle BD24 9HD* Tel (01729) 822349 E-mail father.anton@virgin.net

BENNETT, Arnold Ernest. b 29. K Coll Lon BD59 AKC53. **d** 54 **p** 55. C S w N Hayling *Portsm* 54-59; C Stevenage *St Alb* 59-64; R N w S Wootton *Nor* 64-74; V Hykeham *Linc* 74-85; V Heckfield w Mattingley and Rotherwick *Win* 85-99; rtd 99; Perm to Offic *Win* from 99. *24 Cricket Green, Hartley Wintney, Basingstoke RG27 8PP* Tel (01252) 843147

BENNETT, Arthur Harling. b 22. Ripon Hall Ox 70. **d** 71 **p** 72. C Standish *Blackb* 71-74; TV Darwen St Pet w Hoddlesden 75-79; V Whitechapel 79-89; V Whitechapel w Admarsh-in-Bleasdale 89-90; rtd 90; Perm to Offic *Blackb* from 90. *1 Eden Gardens, Longridge, Preston PR3 3WF* Tel (01772) 784924

BENNETT, Avril Elizabeth Jean. b 63. BEd. **d** 00 **p** 01. NSM Dublin Crumlin w Chapelizod *D & G* 00-03; NSM Tallaght from 03. *17 Ardeevin Court, Lucan, Co Dublin, Republic of Ireland* Tel (00353) (1) 628 2353

BENNETT, Bernard Michael. b 27. Leeds Univ CertEd52. St Aid Birkenhead 55. **d** 58 **p** 59. C Hemsworth *Wakef* 58-60; C Chapelthorpe 60-62; V Birkenhead St Bede w All SS *Ches* 62-71; V Latchford St Jas 71-75; Chapl HM Pris Appleton Thorn 75-82; V Appleton Thorn and Antrobus *Ches* 75-86; Chapl HM Rem Cen Risley 81-84; rtd 86; Perm to Offic *Ches* from 86-01 and *Blackb* 91-03. *8 Hanover Close, Prenton CH43 1XR* Tel 0151-652 8968

BENNETT, Charles William. b 38. LTh. St Jo Coll Auckland 60. **d** 63 **p** 64. C Tauranga New Zealand 63-68; V Clive 68-71; C St Jo Cathl Napier 71-74; V Waipaoa 74-79; C N Walsham w Antingham *Nor* 80-81; V Waipaoa New Zealand 81-82; V Te Puke 82-87; V Dannevirke and P-in-c Woodville 87-91; V Westshore 91-93; Min Enabler 94-03; V Waipawa from 05. *59 McGrath Street, Napier South, Napier 4110, New Zealand* Tel (0064) (6) 835 9924 Fax 835 9920 E-mail bwbennett@inspire.net.nz

BENNETT, Mrs Christina Mary. b 45. **d** 07 **p** 08. NSM Henfield w Shermanbury and Woodmancote *Chich* from 07. *17 Gresham Place, Henfield BN5 9QJ* Tel (01273) 492222 E-mail christina@cmb45.wanadoo.co.uk

BENNETT, Christopher Ian. b 75. TCD BA98 BTh00. CITC 97. **d** 00 **p** 01. C Larne and Inver *Conn* 00-03; C Holywood *D & D* 03-09; Bp's C Belfast Titanic Quarter from 09. *29 Loughview Terrace, Greenisland, Carrickfergus BT38 8RE* Tel (028) 9085 2895 Mobile 07980-885991 E-mail cands2000@hotmail.com

BENNETT, Clifford Orford. b 32. St Mich Coll Llan 73. **d** 75 **p** 76. C Holywell *St As* 75-79; V Pontblyddyn 79-99; rtd 99. *4 Bryn Teg, Brynford, Holywell CH8 8AP* Tel (01352) 719028

BENNETT, David Edward. b 35. Fitzw Ho Cam BA56 MA60 Lon Univ PGCE. Wells Th Coll 58. **d** 60 **p** 61. C Lightcliffe *Wakef* 60-62; NE Area Sec Chr Educn Movement 62-68; Gen Insp RE Nottm Co Coun 68-00; Hon C Holme Pierrepont w Adbolton *S'well* 71-85; NSM Radcliffe-on-Trent and Shelford etc 85-00; rtd 00; Perm to Offic *S'well* from 04. *The Old Farmhouse, 65 Main Street, Gunthorpe, Nottingham NG14 7EY* Tel 0115-966 3451

BENNETT, Donovan Harry. b 27. Qu Mary Coll Lon BScEng52 FGS61 AMICE61 CEng61 FICE72. Moray Ord Course 88. **d** 92 **p** 93. Hon C Dingwall *Mor* 92-93; Hon C Strathpeffer 92-93; Hon C Inverness St Mich 93-95; Assoc Chapl Raigmore Hosp NHS Trust Inverness 94-96; P-in-c Grantown-on-Spey *Mor* 96-99; Can St Andr Cathl Inverness 98-00; Perm to Offic from 99. *8 Brewster Drive, Forres IV36 2JW* Tel (01309) 671478 E-mail donovan.bennett@btinternet.com

BENNETT, Edwin James. b 23. St Barn Coll Adelaide ThL47 STh52. **d** 47 **p** 48. Australia 47-74; V Oldham St Barn *Man* 74-78; V Alderney *Win* 78-84; R Hatherden w Tangley, Weyhill and Penton Mewsey 84-89; rtd 89; Perm to Offic *Win* from 89. *Kalgoorlie, 33 Hatherden Road, Charlton, Andover SP10 4AP* Tel (01264) 356358

BENNETT, Elizabeth Mary. **d** 10 **p** 11. NSM Broughton Gifford, Gt Chalfield and Holt *Sarum* from 10. *388 Gaston, Holt, Trowbridge BA14 6QA* Tel (01225) 783119

BENNETT, Garry Raymond. b 46. K Coll Lon 66 St Aug Coll Cant 69. **d** 70 **p** 71. C Mitcham St Mark *S'wark* 70-73; C Mortlake w E Sheen 73-75; TV 76-78; V Herne Hill St Paul 78-88; P-in-c Ruskin Park St Sav and St Matt 82-88; V Herne Hill 89; Sen Dioc Stewardship Adv *Chelmsf* 89-94; TR Southend 94-98; Dir and Chapl Herne Hill Sch *S'wark* 98-04; Perm to Offic *St D* from 00. *Hendre House, Llandeloy, Haverfordwest SA62 6LW* Tel (01348) 831160 E-mail phyll.bennett@btinternet.com

BENNETT, Geoffrey Kenneth. b 56. Ex Univ MA01. Oak Hill Th Coll. **d** 89 **p** 90. C Ipswich St Matt *St E* 89-92; R St Ruan w St Grade and Landewednack *Truro* 92-98; V Budock from 98; P-in-c Mawnan from 03. *The Vicarage, Merry Mit Meadow, Budock Water, Falmouth TR11 5DW* Tel (01326) 376422 E-mail g.k.bennett@amserve.net

BENNETT, Canon George Edward. b 51. Univ of Wales (Abth) BA72. St Steph Ho Ox 73. **d** 76 **p** 77. C Clifton All SS w Tyndalls Park *Bris* 76-78; C Clifton All SS w St Jo 78-82; Chapl Newbury and Sandleford Hosps 82-93; TV Newbury *Ox* 82-93; V Llwynderw *S & B* 93-06; V Newton St Pet from 06; AD Clyne from 98; Hon Can Brecon Cathl 00-02; Can Res Brecon Cathl from 02. *The Vicarage, Marytwill Lane, Mumbles, Swansea SA3 4RB* Tel (01792) 368348

BENNETT, Graham Eric Thomas. b 53. Sarum & Wells Th Coll 88. **d** 90 **p** 91. C Baswich *Lich* 90-94; C Codsall 94-00; P-in-c Willenhall St Steph 00-05; V from 05; AD Wolverhampton

05-11. *St Stephen's Vicarage, 27 Wolverhampton Street, Willenhall WV13 2PS* Tel (01902) 605239 E-mail grahambennett.69@btinternet.com

BENNETT, Handel Henry Cecil. b 33. MCIM. Cant Sch of Min 79. **d** 82 **p** 83. NSM St Margarets-at-Cliffe w Westcliffe etc *Cant* 82-85; Dir Holy Land Chr Tours 85-94; Holy Land Consultant F T Tours 95-96; Sen Travel Consultant Raymond Cook Chr Tours from 96; Perm to Offic *St Alb* 85-99 and *Ex* from 99. *Camps Bay, 2 Victoria Road, Sidmouth EX10 8TZ* Tel and fax (01395) 514211 Mobile 07774-981569

BENNETT, Helen Anne. See EDWARDS, Helen Anne

BENNETT, Canon Ian Frederick. b 30. Ch Coll Cam BA54 MA62. Westcott Ho Cam 61. **d** 63 **p** 64. C Hemel Hempstead *St Alb* 63-68; Asst Chapl Man Univ 69-73; Sen Chapl 73-79; C Chorlton upon Medlock 69-73; P-in-c 73-79; TR Man Whitworth 79; Dioc Tr Officer *Birm* 79-88; Hon Can Birm Cathl 86-88; Can Res Newc Cathl 88-98; Dioc Dir of Min and Tr 90-98; Dir Post-Ord Tr 97-98; rtd 98; Perm to Offic *Newc* from 98. *21 Otterburn Avenue, Gosforth, Newcastle upon Tyne NE3 4RR* Tel 0191-285 1967

BENNETT, John David. b 58. Ox Univ BA79 MA83. Westcott Ho Cam 81. **d** 83 **p** 84. C Taunton St Andr *B & W* 83-86; Chapl Trowbridge Coll *Sarum* 86-90; Asst P Studley 86-90; V Yeovil H Trin *B & W* 90-95; R Yeovil H Trin w Barwick 95-02; R Sprowston w Beeston *Nor* 02-10; RD Nor N 05-10; V Spalding *Linc* from 10; P-in-c Spalding St Paul from 10. *The Parsonage, 1 Halmer Gate, Spalding PE11 2DR* Tel (01775) 719668 E-mail jdbennett@gmail.com

BENNETT, John Dudley. b 44. Open Univ BA87 Lanc Univ MA92 Huddersfield Univ PGCE04. Coll of Resurr Mirfield 08. **d** 09 **p** 09. NSM Bolton Abbey *Bradf* from 09. *Honeysuckle Cottage, The Green, Linton, Skipton BD23 5HJ* Tel (01756) 753763 E-mail brj.linton@virgin.net

BENNETT, John Seccombe. b 59. Wye Coll Lon BSc81 Leic Poly CertEd84. Trin Coll Bris. **d** 00 **p** 01. C Llanrhian w Llanhywel and Carnhedryn etc *St D* 00-01; C Dewisland 01-02; TV from 02; Min Can St D Cathl from 00. *The Vicarage, Llanrhian, Haverfordwest SA62 5BG* Tel (01348) 831354

BENNETT, Joyce Mary. b 23. OBE79. Westf Coll Lon BA44 DipEd45 Hong Kong Univ Hon DSocSc84. **d** 62 **p** 71. C Kowloon St Thos 62-66; C Hong Kong Crown of Thorns 67-68; C Kwun Tong St Barn 68-83; Lect Union Th Sem Hong Kong 63-66; Prin St Cath Girls Sch Kwun Tong 68-83; NSM St Martin-in-the-Fields *Lon* 84-87; Perm to Offic *Ox* 87-07. *The Cornerstone, 72 The Crescent, High Wycombe HP13 6JP* Tel (01494) 539016

BENNETT, Marian Joyce. b 53. BEd. EMMTC. **d** 06 **p** 07. NSM Castle Donington and Lockington cum Hemington *Leic* 06-10; NSM Mountsorrel Ch Ch and St Pet from 10. *174 Leicester Road, Loughborough LE11 2AH* Tel (01509) 263601 E-mail marian@bennett54.freeserve.co.uk

BENNETT, Mark Ian. b 61. K Coll Cam BA83 MA86. Trin Coll Bris BA94. **d** 94 **p** 95. C Selly Park St Steph and St Wulstan *Birm* 94-97; C Harrow Trin St Mich *Lon* 97-99; Hon C Redland *Bris* 99-00; TV Drypool *York* 00-06; V Gee Cross Ches from 06. *16 Higham Lane, Hyde SK14 5LX* Tel 0161-368 2337 E-mail mark@holytrinitychurch-gx.org.uk

BENNETT, Mark Stephen. b 66. Cant Univ (NZ) MusB89. SEITE 07. **d** 10 **p** 11. NSM Staplehurst *Cant* from 10; Chapl Dulwich Prep Sch Cranbrook from 10; Hon Min Can Cant Cathl from 11. *Lodge Tutor's Flat, Coursehorn Lane, Cranbrook TN17 3NR* Tel (01580) 710144 Mobile 07709-376668 E-mail sbennett@dcpskent.org

BENNETT, Michael John. b 43. AKC66. St Boniface Warminster 66. **d** 67 **p** 68. C Chester le Street *Dur* 67-71; C Portland All SS w St Pet *Sarum* 71-74; V Portland St Jo 74-85; Chapl Portland Hosp Weymouth 74-85; R Alveley and Quatt *Heref* 85-92; Dep Chapl HM YOI Glen Parva 93-95; TV Wrexham *St As* 95-99; V Llansantffraid-ym-Mechain and Llanfechain 99-05; C Rhyl w St Ann 05-09; rtd 09; Hon C Redmarley D'Abitot, Bromesberrow, Pauntley etc *Glouc* from 09. *The Vicarage, St Mary's Close, Dymock GL18 2AX* Tel (01531) 892967 E-mail smbennett@talktalk.net

BENNETT, Nigel John. b 47. Oak Hill Th Coll 66. **d** 71 **p** 72. C Tonbridge St Steph *Roch* 71-75; C Heatherlands St Jo *Sarum* 75-79; P-in-c Kingham w Churchill, Daylesford and Sarsden *Ox* 79; R 80-85; Chapl Blue Coat Sch Reading 85-08; rtd 08; Perm to Offic *Ox* 08-09; Hon C Southsea St Jude *Portsm* from 09. *Address temp unknown* E-mail revnjb@nigel58.wanadoo.co.uk

BENNETT, Osmond Shirley. b 36. Oriel Coll Ox BA67. Ripon Hall Ox 64. **d** 68 **p** 69. C Stocking Farm *Leic* 68-71; C Thurcaston 71-72; V Leic St Marg 72-82; V Leic St Marg and All SS 83-89; R Houghton-on-the-Hill, Keyham and Hungarton 89-00; rtd 00. *48 Wide Lane, Hathern, Loughborough LE12 5LN* Tel (01509) 553644

BENNETT, Paul. b 55. Southn Univ BTh94. St Steph Ho Ox 95. **d** 97 **p** 98. C Willingdon *Chich* 97-00; C Hangleton 00-04; R Letchworth *St Alb* from 04. *St Michael's Rectory, 39 South View,*

Letchworth Garden City SG6 3JJ Tel (01462) 684822 Fax 643592 E-mail revpaulbennett@ntlworld.com

BENNETT, Paul Jonathan. b 61. Ex Univ BA85. Ripon Coll Cuddesdon 85. **d** 87 **p** 88. C Henleaze *Bris* 87-91; P-in-c Swindon All SS 91-94; V Swindon All SS w St Barn 94-96; V Patrick, Foxdale and German St Jo *S & M* 96-00. *Address temp unknown*

BENNETT, Paul William. b 61. Linc Th Coll 95. **d** 95 **p** 96. C Thornton-le-Fylde *Blackb* 95-00; V Wesham 00-03; P-in-c Treales 00-03; V Wesham and Treales 03-08; Chapl Dunkirk Miss to Seafarers *Eur* from 08. *Princess Alice House, 130 rue de l'Ecole Maternelle, 59140 Dunkerque, France* Tel (0033) 3 28 59 04 36 Fax 3 28 66 09 13 E-mail mowbreck@aol.com

BENNETT, Miss Rachel Elizabeth. b 56. W Sussex Inst of HE CertEd79. **d** 04. NSM Littlehampton and Wick *Chich* 04-05; C Durrington 05-07; Chapl Worthing and Southlands Hosps NHS Trust from 08. *Worthing Hospital, Lyndhurst Road, Worthing BN11 2DH* Tel (01903) 205111 Mobile 07810-350098 E-mail rachel.bennett3@tesco.net

BENNETT, Robert Geoffrey. b 43. FCA. **d** 05 **p** 06. OLM Woking St Jo *Guildf* from 05. *10 Barricane, Woking GU21 7RB* Tel (01483) 722832 E-mail robgbennett@tiscali.co.uk

BENNETT, Roger Sherwood. b 35. Nottm Univ BA56. Wells Th Coll 58. **d** 59 **p** 60. C Mansfield Woodhouse *S'well* 59-60; C Spalding *Linc* 60-63; V Gedney 63-69; Chapl RNR 65-68; Chapl RN 69-90; V Amport, Grateley, Monxton and Quarley *Win* 90-95; rtd 96; Perm to Offic *Win* from 96. *Le Reduit, School Lane, Nether Wallop, Stockbridge SO20 8EH* Tel (01264) 782336

BENNETT, Roy Donald. b 40. Nottm Univ MA97. St Jo Coll Nottm 78. **d** 80 **p** 81. C Fletchamstead *Cov* 80-83; C Bedworth 83-87; P-in-c Studley 87-93; Chapl Univ Hosp Nottm 93-96; Chapl Qu Medical Cen Nottm 94-96; Chapl Bassetlaw Hosp and Community Services NHS Trust 96-01; Chapl Doncaster and Bassetlaw Hosps NHS Trust 01-02; rtd 02; Perm to Offic *Sarum* 03-08. *21 High Street, Puddletown, Dorchester DT2 8RT* Tel (01305) 848144

BENNETT, Shirley. See BENNETT, Osmond Shirley

BENNETT (née FORD), Ms Simone Louise. b 70. Warwick Univ BA92. Westcott Ho Cam 00. **d** 02 **p** 03. C Stockingford *Cov* 02-03; C Didsbury Ch Ch and Withington St Chris *Man* 03-05; Hon C Abberton, The Flyfords, Naunton Beauchamp etc *Worc* 06-09. *18 Victoria Street, Settle BD24 9HD* Tel (01729) 822349 Mobile 07946-548366 E-mail simone.bennett@virgin.net

BENNETT, Stephen. See BENNETT, Mark Stephen

BENNETT, Ms Toni Elizabeth. b 56. Worc Coll of Educn BA81 Sheff Poly 87. St Jo Coll Nottm MA94. **d** 96 **p** 97. C Heanor *Derby* 96-00; TV Bedworth *Cov* 00-08; R Montgomery and Forden and Llandyssil *St As* from 08; AD Pool from 10. *The Rectory, Lions Bank, Montgomery SY15 6PT* Tel (01686) 668243 E-mail toni.rev@btinternet.com

BENNETT, William Leslie. b 52. TCD Div Sch. **d** 90 **p** 91. C Carrickfergus *Conn* 90-93; I Lisnaskea *Clogh* 93-00; I Newcastle w Newtownmountkennedy and Calary *D & G* from 00. *The Rectory, Church Lane, Newcastle, Greystones, Co Wicklow, Republic of Ireland* Tel (00353) (1) 281 9300 Mobile 87-948 0317 E-mail bennettwilliam1@gmail.com

BENNETT-REES, Catherine Mary. See MEAKIN, Catherine Mary

BENNETT-SHAW, Miss Anne Elizabeth. b 38. **d** 02 **p** 03. OLM Upper Wylye Valley *Sarum* from 02. *5 Hospital of St John, Heytesbury, Warminster BA12 0HW* Tel (01985) 840339 E-mail revannebennettshaw@btinternet.com

✠BENNETTS, The Rt Revd Colin James. b 40. Jes Coll Cam BA63 MA67. Ridley Hall Cam 63. **d** 65 **p** 66 **c** 94. C Tonbridge St Steph *Roch* 65-69; Chapl Ox Pastorate 69-79; C Ox St Aldate w H Trin 69-73; Asst Chapl Jes Coll Ox 73-75; Chapl 75-78; P-in-c Ox St Jonathan *Ny* V 80-90; RD Ox 84-89; Can Res Ches Cathl and Dioc Dir of Ords 90-94; Area Bp Buckm *Ox* 94-98; Bp Cov 98-08; rtd 08; Asst Bp Guildf from 09. *23 Brox Road, Ottershaw, Chertsey KT16 0HG* Tel (01932) 875324 E-mail colinbennetts682@btinternet.com

BENNETTS, John Barrington. b 32. **d** 92 **p** 93. NSM Falmouth K Chas *Truro* 92-04; rtd 04; Perm to Offic *Truro* from 04. *39 Budock Terrace, Falmouth TR11 3NE* Tel (01326) 314961 or 312111 E-mail kcmvestry@onetel.com

BENNETTS, Ms Rachel Mary. b 69. Homerton Coll Cam BEd91. Trin Coll Bris BA01. **d** 02 **p** 03. C Wroughton *Bris* 02-06; TV N Farnborough *Guildf* from 06; Chapl Farnborough Sixth Form Coll from 07. *The Vicarage, 45 Sand Hill, Farnborough GU14 8ER* Tel (01252) 543789 Mobile 07749-045449 E-mail racheagle@yahoo.co.uk

BENNIE, Stanley James Gordon. b 43. Edin Univ MA65. Coll of Resurr Mirfield 66. **d** 68 **p** 69. C Ashington *Newc* 68-70; Prec St Andr Cathl Inverness 70-74; Itinerant Priest 74-81; R Portsoy *Ab* 81-84; R Buckie 81-84; R Stornoway *Arg* 84-10; R Eorropaidh 84-95; Miss to Seafarers from 84; rtd 10. *St Lennan, 13A Scotland Street, Stornoway HS1 2JN* Tel 07768-660612 (mobile) E-mail gm4ptq@btinternet.com

BENNISON, Philip Owen. b 42. Dur Univ BA64. Coll of Resurr Mirfield 64. **d** 66 **p** 67. C Guisborough *York* 66-67; C S Bank

67-71; C Thornaby on Tees St Paul 71-72; TV Thornaby on Tees 72-74; R Skelton in Cleveland 74-78; R Upleatham 75-78; Chapl Freeman Hosp Newc 78-84; V Ashington *Newc* 84-93; Chapl N Tees Health NHS Trust Stockton-on-Tees 93-02; P-in-c Newton Flowery Field *Ches* 02-10; P-in-c Hyde St Thos 02-10; rtd 10; Perm to Offic *York* from 10. *62 Glaisdale Road, Yarm TS15 9RP* E-mail philip bennison@hotmail.com

BENNISON, Timothy Paul. b 63. Aber Univ BD94. Edin Th Coll 95. **d** 97 **p** 98. C St Andr Cathl 97-00; Asst Chapl Aberdeen Univ 97-00; P-in-c Aberdeen St Jas 00-03; Dioc Miss 21 Co-ord 00-03; P-in-c Glencarse *Bre* 05-08; R Dunfermline *St And* from 08. *The Rectory, 17 Ardeer Place, Dunfermline KY11 4YX* Tel (01383) 723901 Mobile 07707-353526

BENOY, Stephen Michael. b 66. Clare Coll Cam BA87 MA90. Trin Coll Bris BA93. **d** 96 **p** 97. C New Malden and Coombe *S'wark* 96-02; Kingston Borough Youth Project 00-02; V Kettering Ch the King *Pet* 02-11; Dir of Ords and Voc from 11. *Bouverie Court, 6 The Lakes, Bedford Road, Northampton NN4 7YD* E-mail steve.benoy@virgin.net

BENSON, Christopher Hugh. b 53. Bath Academy of Art BA75 Keble Coll Ox BA78 MA87. Chich Th Coll 78. **d** 80 **p** 81. C Heavitree w Ex St Paul 80-83; P-in-c Broadclyst 83-85; TV Pinhoe and Broadclyst 85-90; V Kingsteignton and Teigngrace 90-08; Chapl Plymouth Univ 92-95; RD Newton Abbot and Ipplepen 01-07; C Baslow w Curbar and Stoney Middleton *Derby* 08-11; C Ashford w Sheldon and Longstone 08-11; V Longstone, Curbar and Stony Middleton from 11. *The Vicarage, Church Lane, Great Longstone, Bakewell DE45 1TB* Tel (01629) 640257 E-mail chrishbenson@hotmail.com

BENSON, David. *See* BENSON, John David

BENSON, Gareth Neil. b 47. Jordan Hill Coll Glas TCert80. St And NSM Tr Scheme 77. **d** 81 **p** 82. NSM Glenrothes *St And* 81-88; NSM Kirkcaldy from 88; NSM Kinghorn from 88; P-in-c from 04. *The Rectory, 1 Longbraes Gardens, Kirkcaldy KY2 5YJ* Tel (01592) 204208 *or* 568518 E-mail fathergareth@btinternet.com

BENSON, The Ven George Patrick. b 49. Ch Ch Ox BA70 Lon Univ BD77 Open Univ MPhil94. All Nations Chr Coll 78 St Jo Coll Nottm 89. **d** 91 **p** 92. C Upton (Overchurch) *Ches* 91-95; V Barnston 95-11; RD Wirral N 98-08; Hon Can Ches Cathl 09-11; Adn Heref from 11. *3 Hatterall Close, Hereford HR1 1GA* Tel (01432) 265659 E-mail paddy@kabare.freeserve.co.uk

BENSON, Mrs Hilary Christine. b 51. Man Univ BA72 Hughes Hall Cam PGCE73. Trin Coll Bris 81. **dss** 84 **d** 87 **p** 94. Starbeck *Ripon* 84-86; Birm St Martin w Bordesley St Andr 86-91; NSM 87-91; NSM Brandwood 91-97; Chapl Birm Univ 92-97; Chapl St Edw Sch Ox 97-00; Chapl Qu Anne's Sch Caversham from 00. *Queen Anne's School, Henley Road, Caversham, Reading RG4 6DX* Tel 0118-947 1582 *or* 954 5026 E-mail saintben@ntlworld.com

BENSON, John David. b 36. St Aid Birkenhead 58. **d** 61 **p** 62. C Kingston upon Hull St Martin *York* 61-65; C Marfleet 65-68; V Ingleby Greenhow 68-72; P-in-c Kildale 68-72; Asst Youth Chapl 68-72; Dioc Youth Chapl *Sheff* 72-78; V Thorne 78-91; V Totley 91-98; rtd 98; Perm to Offic *Sheff* from 98. *14 Ash Hill Crescent, Hatfield, Doncaster DN7 6HY* Tel (01302) 846359

BENSON, John Patrick. b 51. Univ of Wales (Ban) BSc72. Trin Coll Bris 83. **d** 85 **p** 86. C Stoke Damerel *Ex* 85-88; P-in-c Petrockstowe, Petersmarland, Merton and Huish 88; TV Shebbear, Buckland Filleigh, Sheepwash etc 89-94; RD Torrington 93-94; P-in-c Newport, Bishops Tawton and Tawstock 94-97; TV Barnstaple 97-07; R Knockholt w Halstead *Roch* from 07. *The Rectory, Church Road, Halstead, Sevenoaks TN14 7HQ* Tel (01959) 532133 E-mail john.benson3@btinternet.com

BENSON, Canon John Patrick. b 52. Ch Coll Cam BA73 MA76 PhD76. Trin Coll Bris 78. **d** 81 **p** 82. C Walmley *Birm* 81-84; C Chadkirk *Ches* 84-86; V St Geo Singapore 87-95; Dir of Tr 95-01; V Chpl of Resurr 01-07; Hon Can Singapore 96-07; Dean Cambodia 93-05; Dean Laos 98-00; rtd 07; Perm to Offic *Ches* from 09. *Cherry Trees, Queens Park Road, Chester CH4 7AD* Tel (01244) 671170 E-mail johnpbenson@gmail.com

BENSON, Nicholas Henry. b 53. Man Univ BSc75 Leeds Univ MSc77. Trin Coll Bris 81. **d** 84 **p** 85. C Starbeck *Ripon* 84-86; C Birm St Martin w Bordesley St Andr 86-91; Chapl to the Markets 86-91; V Brandwood 91-97; Perm to Offic *Ox* 99-01; NSM Reading St Jo from 01. *Hillside, 2 Henley Road, Caversham, Reading RG4 6DS* Tel 0118-954 5026 E-mail saintben@ntlworld.com

BENSON, Paddy. *See* BENSON, The Ven George Patrick

BENSON, Philip Steven. b 59. Ulster Univ BSc81 LLCM80. S Dios Minl Tr Scheme 88. **d** 92 **p** 93. Producer Relig Broadcasting Dept BBC 91-94; NSM W Ealing St Jo w St Jas *Lon* 92-94; Relig Progr Producer BBC Man from 94. *4 Cranford Avenue, Knutsford WA16 0EB* Tel (01565) 652513 Fax 641695

BENSON, Mrs Rachel Candia. b 43. JP76. TCD MA66 Lon Univ PGCE67. S'wark Ord Course 84. **d** 87 **p** 94. NSM Putney St Marg *S'wark* 87-97; NSM Sand Hutton and Whitwell w Crambe, Flaxton and Foston *York* 97-07; Perm to Offic from 07.

Grange Farm, Westow, York YO60 7NJ Tel (01653) 658296 Fax 658456 E-mail rachelbenson4@btopenworld.com

BENSON, Richard John. b 55. Birm Coll of Educn CertEd78. Ripon Coll Cuddesdon 92. **d** 94 **p** 95. C Alford w Rigsby *Linc* 94-97; R Partney Gp from 97. *The Rectory, Partney, Spilsby PE23 4PG* Tel (01790) 753570

BENSON, Steven. *See* BENSON, Philip Steven

BENSON, Thomas Henry Frank. b 66. SWMTC 06. **d** 09 **p** 10. C Bideford, Northam, Westward Ho!, Appledore etc *Ex* from 09. *The Vicarage, Mines Road, Bideford EX39 4BZ* Tel (01237) 423918

BENT, David Michael. b 55. Leeds Univ BSc77. Trin Coll Bris BA94. **d** 96 **p** 97. C Gorleston St Andr *Nor* 96-00; TR Brinsworth w Catcliffe and Treeton *Sheff* 00-03; TR Rivers Team from 03. *The Vicarage, 61 Whitehill Lane, Brinsworth, Rotherham S60 5JR* Tel (01709) 363850 E-mail david.bent@btinternet.com

BENT, Mrs Helen Margaret. b 56. Sheff Univ BMus77 Trent Poly PGCE78 Suffolk Poly BA00. EAMTC 97. **d** 98 **p** 99. C Gorleston St Mary *Nor* 98-00; C Brightside w Wincobank *Sheff* 00-04; Bp's Adv in Music and Worship from 05. *The Vicarage, 61 Whitehill Lane, Brinsworth, Rotherham S60 5JR* Tel (01709) 363850 E-mail helen@thebents.co.uk

BENT, The Very Revd Michael Charles. b 31. Kelham Th Coll 51. **d** 55 **p** 56. C Wellingborough St Mary *Pet* 55-60; New Zealand 60-85, 89-94 and from 96; Papua New Guinea 94-96; Adn Taranaki 76-85; Dean H Trin Cathl Suva Fiji 85-89; Can St Pet Cathl Hamilton 90-94. *34 Brooklands Road, New Plymouth 4601, New Zealand* Tel (0064) (6) 753 5507 E-mail miro@clear.net.nz

BENTALL, Canon Jill Margaret. b 44. MCSP66. S Dios Minl Tr Scheme 91. **d** 94 **p** 95. NSM Knights Enham *Win* 94-02; C Andover w Foxcott 02-09; P-in-c Pastrow from 09; RD Andover 06-10; Hon Can Win Cathl from 11. *The Rectory, Chalkcroft Lane, Penton Mewsey, Andover SP11 0RD* Tel (01264) 773554 E-mail jill.bentall@btinternet.com

BENTHAM, Canon John William. b 58. Loughb Univ BSc80 Nottm Univ LTh85. St Jo Coll Nottm 82. **d** 85 **p** 86. C Burmantofts St Steph and St Agnes *Ripon* 85-88; C Horsforth 88-90; P-in-c Nottingham St Sav *S'well* 90-92; V 92-98; Chapl Nottm Univ from 98; AD Nottingham W 06-08; AD W Bingham from 08; Hon Can S'well Minster from 10. *51 Chaworth Road, West Bridgford, Nottingham NG2 7AE* Tel 0115-846 1054 *or* 846 6037 E-mail john.bentham@nottingham.ac.uk

BENTHAM, Philip John (Ben). b 55. Hull Univ BA83 PGCE85. Trin Coll Bris MA96. **d** 96 **p** 97. C Wrockwardine Deanery *Lich* 96-00; P-in-c Chipinge and Chimanimani Zimbabwe 00-03; Chapl Viña del Mar St Pet Chile 03-07; Chapl Bethany Sch Goudhurst from 08. *1 Providence Cottages, Curtisden Green, Goudhurst, Cranbrook TN17 1LD* Tel (01580) 212994 E-mail benbentham@yahoo.com.uk

✠**BENTLEY, The Rt Revd David Edward.** b 35. Leeds Univ BA56. Westcott Ho Cam 58. **d** 60 **p** 61 **c** 86. C Bris St Ambrose Whitehall 60-62; C Guildf H Trin w St Mary 62-66; R Headley All SS 66-73; R Esher 73-86; RD Emly 77-82; Hon Can Guildf Cathl 80-86; Chmn Dioc Coun Soc Resp 80-86; Suff Bp Lynn *Nor* 86-93; Chmn Cand Cttee ACCM 87-91; ABM 91-93; Bp Glouc 93-03; rtd 04; Hon Asst Bp Lich from 04; Perm to Offic *Cov* from 04. *19 Gable Croft, Lichfield WS14 9RY* Tel (01543) 419376

BENTLEY, Frank Richard. b 41. K Coll Lon BD67 AKC67. **d** 68 **p** 69. C Feltham *Lon* 68-72; P-in-c Bethnal Green St Bart 72-77; R Bow w Bromley St Leon 77-88; P-in-c Mile End Old Town H Trin 77-88; P-in-c Bromley All Hallows 77-88; AD Tower Hamlets 83-88; TR E Ham w Upton Park *Chelmsf* 88-97; P-in-c Petersham *S'wark* 97-07; Chapl HM Pris Latchmere Ho 97-07; rtd 07; Perm to Offic *St E* from 08. *104 Cannon Street, Bury St Edmunds IP33 1JU* Tel (01284) 766063 E-mail richardbentley.41@virgin.net

BENTLEY, The Ven Frank William Henry. b 34. AKC57. **d** 58 **p** 59. C Shepton Mallet *B & W* 58-62; R Kingsdon w Podymore-Milton 62-66; P-in-c Yeovilton 62-66; P-in-c Babcary 64-66; V Wiveliscombe 66-76; RD Tone 73-76; V St Jo in Bedwardine *Worc* 76-84; P-in-c Worc St Mich 82-84; RD Martley and Worc W 80-84; Hon Worc Cathl 81-84; Adn Worc and Can Res Worc Cathl 84-04; Hon Can Worc Cathl from 04; Chapl to The Queen 94-04. *Willow Cottage, Station Road, Fladbury, Pershore WR10 2QW* Tel (01386) 861847 E-mail f.bentley@virgin.net

BENTLEY, Graham John. b 29. S'wark Ord Course 77. **d** 80 **p** 81. NSM Merton St Mary *S'wark* 80-83; C Balham St Mary 83-84; C Wimbledon 85-86; V Raynes Park St Sav 86-95; rtd 95; Perm to Offic *Guildf* from 95. *61 Clarence Road, Fleet, Aldershot GU51 3RY* Tel (01252) 613574

BENTLEY, Canon Ian Robert. b 55. Sheff Univ BA76 Sheff City Poly PGCE78. Cranmer Hall Dur 93. **d** 95 **p** 96. C Mattishall w Mattishall Burgh, Welborne etc *Nor* 95-98; R Ditchingham, Hedenham, Broome, Earsham etc 98-06; V Oulton Broad from 06; RD Lothingland from 10; Hon Can Nor Cathl from 10.

St Mark's Vicarage, 212 Bridge Road, Lowestoft NR33 9JX Tel (01502) 572563 E-mail ian@revbentley.freeserve.co.uk

BENTLEY, Ian Ronald. b 51. BA79. Oak Hill Th Coll 76. **d** 79 **p** 80. C Inartwood Em *Lon* 79-85; C St Marylebone All So w SS Pet and Jo 85-88; C Langham Place All So 88-91; V Eynsham and Cassington *Ox* 91-05; V Chineham *Win* from 05. *The Vicarage, 1 Hartswood, Chineham, Basingstoke RG24 8SJ* Tel (01256) 474285

BENTLEY, Lesley. b 55. Univ of Wales (Lamp) BA76 RMN80. St Jo Coll Nottm MTh82. **dss** 82 **d** 87 **p** 94. Mickleover St Jo *Derby* 82-84; Thornton *Liv* 84-89; Par Dn 87-89; Dir Diaconal Mins 89-92; Par Dn Farnworth 92-94; C 94-95; V Westbrook St Phil 95-01; Hon Can Liv Cathl 99-01; V Bilton *Ripon* 01-03; TR 03-09; Initial Minl Educn Officer 03-09; Dir Min Development *Lich* 09-10; Dir Min from 10. *The Vicarage, Salt Lane, Salt, Stafford ST18 0BW* Tel (01889) 508066 E-mail lesley.bentley@btinternet.com

BENTLEY, Canon Paul. b 48. Sarum & Wells Th Coll. **d** 93 **p** 94. C Ex St Dav 93-96; P-in-c Marlpool *Derby* 96-01; V 01-02; Chapl Derbyshire Community Health Services 96-00; Chapl Amber Valley Primary Care Trust 00-02; Chapl Mansfield Distr Primary Care Trust from 02; Hon Can S'well Minster from 11. *The Pilgrim Centre, Mansfield Community Hospital, Stockwell Gate, Mansfield NG18 5QJ* Tel (01623) 785011 E-mail paul.bentley@mansfield-pct.nhs.uk *or* revpaulb@aol.com

BENTLEY, Richard. See BENTLEY, Frank Richard

BENTON, John Anthony. b 27. Ex Coll Ox BA48 MA52. Sarum Th Coll 49. **d** 50 **p** 51. C N Keyham *Ex* 50-52; C Tavistock and Gulworthy 52-55; C Heavitree 55-56; R Lower Gravenhurst *St Alb* 56-61; V Silsoe 56-61; V Upper Gravenhurst 56-61; C Port Elizabeth St Cuth S Africa 61-63; R Port Elizabeth St Sav 64-68; R Moretonhampstead *Ex* 68-74; RD Moreton 73-74; R Holsworthy w Cookbury and Hollacombe 74-80; TR Withycombe Raleigh 80-92; RD Aylesbeare 84-89; rtd 92; Perm to Offic *Ex* from 92. *38 Wreford's Close, Exeter EX4 5AY* Tel (01392) 211428

BENTON, Canon Michael John. b 38. Lon Univ BSc60 FRSA93 MSOSc. Sarum & Wells Th Coll 72. **d** 74 **p** 74. Sen Lect K Alfred Coll *Win* 74-76; NSM Weeke 74-76; C Bursledon 76-78; R Over Wallop w Nether Wallop 78-83; Dir of Educn 79-96; R Win St Lawr and St Maurice w St Swithun 83-90; Hon Can Win Cathl 89-03; P-in-c Kingsclere 96-03; Chapl to The Queen 98-08; rtd 03; Perm to Offic *Win* from 03. *South Lodge, Auchterarder House, Auchterarder PH3 1ER* Tel (01764) 662991

BENTON-EVANS, Martin James William. b 69. K Coll Lon BA90 Anglia Poly Univ PGCE97. Ripon Coll Cuddesdon BTh03. **d** 03 **p** 04. C Ivybridge w Harford *Ex* 03-06; P-in-c St Teath *Truro* 06; P-in-c Lanteglos by Camelford w Advent from 06; Chapl Sir Jas Smith's Community Sch Camelford from 10. *The Rectory, Trefrew Road, Camelford PL32 9TP* Tel (01840) 214877 Mobile 07915-650434 E-mail jim@benton-evans1.demon.co.uk

BENWELL, John Desmond. Jes Coll Cam BA54 MA58. St Jo Coll Nottm. **d** 89 **p** 89. Somalia 89-90; Chapl Fontainebleau *Eur* 91-93; Hon C Portswood Ch Ch *Win* 93-99; rtd 99; Perm to Offic *Win* from 04. *14 Furzedown Road, Southampton SO17 1PN* Tel (023) 8055 7622

BENWELL, Michael Patrick. b 55. Jes Coll Cam BA77 Glas Univ PhD80. Sarum & Wells Th Coll BTh92. **d** 92 **p** 93. C Eastleigh *Win* 92-95; Chapl Leeds Metrop Univ 95-99; TV Seacroft 99-06; TR from 06; AD Whitkirk from 09. *St Luke's Vicarage, Stanks Lane North, Leeds LS14 5AS* Tel 0113-273 1302 E-mail benwell@ndirect.co.uk

BENZIES, Neil Graham. Bede Coll Dur. Cranmer Hall Dur 93. **d** 95 **p** 96. NSM Stockton St Pet *Dur* 95-08. *62 Fairwell Road, Stockton-on-Tees TS19 7HX* Tel (01642) 582322

BERDINNER, Clifford. b 24. SS Mark & Jo Univ Coll Plymouth BA88 Ex Univ MPhil95. **d** 64 **p** 65. C Leic St Pet 64-67; R Heather 67-72; NSM Totnes and Berry Pomeroy *Ex* 86-91; NSM Totnes, Bridgetown and Berry Pomeroy etc 91-94; rtd 89; Perm to Offic *Ex* from 89. *Little Croft, 30 Droridge, Dartington, Totnes TQ9 6JQ* Tel (01803) 732518

BERESFORD, Charles Edward. b 45. St Jo Coll Nottm. **d** 86 **p** 87. C Bushbury *Lich* 86-90; TV Glascote and Stonydelph 90-98; TR N Wingfield, Clay Cross and Pilsley *Derby* 98-11; rtd 11. *8 Spring Close, Belper DE56 2TY* Tel (01773) 826519

BERESFORD, David Charles. b 56. Leeds Univ BA09 ACIB93. Coll of Resurr Mirfield 07. **d** 09 **p** 10. C Lancing w Coombes *Chich* 09-11; C Bury w Houghton and Coldwaltham and Hardham from 11. *The Vicarage, Church Lane, Coldwaltham, Pulborough RH20 1LW* Tel (01798) 872844 E-mail davidberesford@gmail.com

BERESFORD, Canon Eric Brian. b 57. Liv Univ BSc78 Univ of K Coll Halifax NS Hon DD. Wycliffe Hall Ox BA82 MA86. **d** 82 **p** 83. C Upton (Overchurch) *Ches* 82-85; Canada from 85; Asst Prof Ethics McGill Univ Montreal 88-96; Consultant Ethics and Interfaith Relns Gen Syn 96-04; President Atlantic Sch of Th Halifax NS from 05; Consultant Ethics ACC 99-05;

Hon Can Montreal from 99. *Atlantic School of Theology, 660 Francklyn Street, Halifax NS B3H 3B5, Canada* Tel (001) (902) 423 6801 E-mail eberesford@astheology.ns.ca

BERESFORD, Mrs Florence. b 33. Cranmer Hall Dur 75. **dss** 87 **d** 87 **p** 94. Eighton Banks *Dur* 78-86; Lobley Hill 86-87; Par Dn 87-90; Par Dn Chester le Street 90-91; rtd 91. *Gilead, 39 Picktree Lodge, Chester-le-Street DH3 4DH* Tel 0191-388 7425

BERESFORD, Patrick Larner. b 53. Lon Bible Coll BA77. **d** 10 **p** 11. NSM Weston super Mare St Jo *B & W* from 10. *23 Old Church Road, Uphill, Weston-super-Mare BS23 4UP* Tel (01934) 620964 Mobile 07590-230797 E-mail paddyjfj04@btinternet.com

BERESFORD, Peter Marcus de la Poer. b 49. Cranmer Hall Dur 74. **d** 77 **p** 78. C Walney Is *Carl* 77-80; C Netherton 80-83; TV Wednesfield *Lich* 83-88; TV Rugby *Cov* 88-97; Chapl Rugby Hosps 88-97; R Barby w Kilsby *Pet* from 97. *The Rectory, Rectory Lane, Barby, Rugby CV23 8TZ* Tel (01788) 890252 E-mail petermberesford@hotmail.co.uk

BERESFORD JONES, Gareth Martin. b 70. Ex Univ BA93 Fitzw Coll Cam BTh01. Westcott Ho Cam 98. **d** 01 **p** 02. C Sidcup St Jo *Roch* 01-05; Chapl Ealing Hosp NHS Trust 05-06; Perm to Offic *Ely* 08-11; NSM Beetham *Carl* from 11. *6 Leighton Beck Road, Slack Head, Milnthorpe LA7 7AX* Tel (015395) 62912 Mobile 07810-272076 E-mail gmbj27@mac.com

BERESFORD-PEIRSE, Mark de la Poer. b 45. Qu Coll Birm 73. **d** 76 **p** 77. C Garforth *Ripon* 76-79; C Beeston 79-83; V Barton and Manfield w Cleasby 83-90; V Pannal w Beckwithshaw 90-01; Dioc Chapl MU 91-98; R W Tanfield and Well w Snape and N Stainley 01-09; rtd 09. *15 Eastfield Avenue, Richmond DL10 4NH* Tel (01748) 826649

BERG, John Russell. b 36. MBE78. Sarum Th Coll 57. **d** 60 **p** 61. C Ipswich St Aug *St E* 60-64; C Whitton and Thurleston w Akenham 64-65; Miss to Seafarers 65-04; Hong Kong 65-68; Japan 68-04; rtd 01; Perm to Offic *St E* from 04. *23 Old Maltings Court, Old Maltings Approach, Melton, Woodbridge IP12 1AE* Tel (01394) 383748 E-mail jrberg@tiscali.co.uk

BERGQUIST, Anders Karim. b 58. Peterho Cam BA79 MA83 PhD90. St Steph Ho Ox BA85 MA90. **d** 86 **p** 87. C Abbots Langley *St Alb* 86-89; Hon C Cambridge St Mary Less *Ely* 89-97; Tutor Westcott Ho Cam 89-95; Vice-Prin 95-97; Can Res St Alb 97-02; Minl Development Officer 97-02; V St John's Wood *Lon* from 02. *St John's House, St John's Wood High Street, London NW8 7NE* Tel (020) 7722 4378 or 7586 3864 E-mail vicar.stjohnswood@london.anglican.org

BERKSHIRE, Archdeacon of. See RUSSELL, The Ven Norman Atkinson

BERMUDA, Archdeacon of. See DOUGHTY, The Ven Andrew William

BERMUDA, Bishop of. See WHITE, The Rt Revd Patrick George Hilliard

BERNARD, Miss Moina Suzanne. b 56. Cranmer Hall Dur 07. **d** 09 **p** 10. NSM Tong *Bradf* from 09. *36 Wenborough Lane, Bradford BD4 0PD* Tel 07967-709444 (mobile) E-mail moinab@googlemail.com

BERNARDI, Frederick John. b 33. JP75. Chich Th Coll 55. **d** 58 **p** 59. C Blackb St Luke 58-60; C Ribbleton 60-63; V Brinsley w Underwood *S'well* 63-66; V St Leon Barbados 67-71; V Sparkbrook St Agatha *Birm* 71-77; P-in-c Sparkbrook Ch Ch 73-75; V Haywards Heath St Wilfrid *Chich* 77-80; TR 80-87; Chapl Madrid *Eur* 87-90; NSM Tooting All SS *S'wark* 90-91; V Hanger Hill Ascension and W Twyford St Mary *Lon* 91-95; rtd 95; Perm to Offic *Chich* from 95. *42 Woodlands Way, Southwater, Horsham RH13 9HZ* Tel (01403) 733335 E-mail stella@knights-templar.org.uk *or* john@bernardi.co.uk

BERNERS-WILSON (or SILLETT), Preb Angela Veronica Isabel. b 54. St Andr Univ MTheol76. Cranmer Hall Dur 77. **dss** 79 **d** 87 **p** 94. Southgate Ch Ch *Lon* 79-82; St Marylebone Ch Ch 82-84; Ind Chapl 82-84; Chapl Thames Poly *S'wark* 84-91; Chapl Bris Univ 91-95; C Bris St Mich and St Paul 94-95; P-in-c Colerne w N Wraxall 95-01; R 01-04; Chapl Bath Univ from 04; Preb Wells Cathl from 09. *Chaplain's House, The Avenue, Claverton Down, Bath BA2 7AX* Tel (01225) 386193 E-mail a.berners-wilson@bath.ac.uk *or* colrec.freeserve.co.uk

BERNHARD, Peter James. b 55. Magd Coll Ox BA76 MA80. SAOMC 03. **d** 06 **p** 07. NSM Homerton St Luke *Lon* 06-08; Hon Chapl Homerton Univ Hosp NHS Trust Lon 07-08; Perm to Offic *Ox* 08-10 and *Lon* from 09. *16 Doves Yard, London N1 0HQ* Tel 07970-855354 (mobile) E-mail souldernspring@aol.com

BERRETT, Michael Vincent. b 56. St Chad's Coll Dur BA78. Ox Min Course 06. **d** 09. NSM Wantage *Ox* from 09. *Old Stock Cottage, Farnborough, Wantage OX12 8NT* Tel (01488) 639635 E-mail mvberrett@googlemail.com

BERRIDGE, Grahame Richard. b 38. S'wark Ord Course 71. **d** 72 **p** 73. NSM S Beddington St Mich *S'wark* 72-75; NSM Merton St Jas 75-81; Perm to Offic from 81. *11 Cedar Walk, Kingswood, Tadworth KT20 6HW* Tel (01737) 358882

BERRIMAN, Brinley John. b 50. Univ Coll Lon BSc71. SWMTC 95. **d** 98 **p** 99. NSM St Ives and Halsetown *Truro* 98-00; P-in-c Lanteglos by Camelford w Advent 00-05; P-in-c St Buryan, St Levan and Sennen from 05. *The Rectory, Rectory Road, St Buryan, Penzance TR19 6BB* Tel (01736) 810216 E-mail brin@dreckly.net

BERRIMAN, Gavin Anthony. b 60. S'wark Ord Course 87. **d** 90 **p** 91. C Greenwich St Alfege w St Pet and St Paul *S'wark* 90-94; V Lee St Aug from 94. *St Augustine's Vicarage, 336 Baring Road, London SE12 0DU* Tel (020) 8857 4941

BERRY, Canon Adrian Charles. b 50. Mert Coll Ox BA71 MA78. Cuddesdon Coll 72. **d** 75 **p** 76. C Prestbury *Glouc* 75-79; C Cirencester 79-83; V Cam w Stinchcombe 83-88; Dioc Ecum Officer 83-95; P-in-c Twyning 88-95; R Leckhampton St Pet 95-02; Dioc Min Development Officer *Llan* from 02; P-in-c Wenvoe and St Lythans 02-09; R Barry All SS from 09; Can Llan Cathl from 02. *The Rectory, 3 Park Road, Barry CF62 6NU* Tel (01446) 701206 E-mail barryallsaints@btinternet.com

BERRY, Alan Peter. b 36. NW Ord Course 74. **d** 77 **p** 78. NSM Headingley *Ripon* 77-78; NSM Chapel Allerton 78-91; Perm to Offic from 91. *17 High Street, Spofforth, Harrogate HG3 1BQ* Tel (01937) 590503 E-mail apeterberry@btinternet.com

BERRY, Anthony Nigel. b 53. Lon Bible Coll BA80. Sarum & Wells Th Coll 84. **d** 87 **p** 88. NSM Howell Hill *Guildf* 87-90; C 90; C Farnham 90-93; R Abinger cum Coldharbour from 93; Dioc Tr Officer for Past Assts from 94. *The Rectory, Abinger Lane, Abinger Common, Dorking RH5 6HZ* Tel (01306) 730746 E-mail revanberry@aol.com

BERRY, David Llewellyn Edward. b 39. St Jo Coll Cam BA61 MA65. Wells Th Coll 64. **d** 66 **p** 67. C Poplar All SS w St Frideswide *Lon* 66-69; C Ellesmere Port *Ches* 69-73; V Brafferton w Pilmoor and Myton-on-Swale *York* 73-79; P-in-c Thormanby 78-79; R Skelton w Upleatham 79-87; V Barrow St Aid *Carl* 87-97; Chapl Rotterdam *Eur* 97-99; rtd 99; Perm to Offic *Carl* from 04. *2 The Croft, Warcop, Appleby-in-Westmorland CA16 6PH* Tel (01768) 342175

BERRY, David Nicholas. b 73. York Univ BA00 St Jo Coll Dur BA10. Cranmer Hall Dur 08. **d** 10 **p** 11. C Mansfield St Jo w St Mary *S'well* from 10. *St Mary's Vicarage, Bancroft Lane, Mansfield NG18 5LZ* Tel 07733-127698 (mobile) E-mail revddavidberry@gmail.com

BERRY, Mrs Eleanor Shields. b 48. Derby Univ BEd95. EMMTC 01. **d** 04 **p** 05. NSM Morley w Smalley and Horsley Woodhouse *Derby* 04-09; NSM Spondon from 09. *5 Gilbert Close, Spondon, Derby DE21 7GP* Tel (01332) 675265 E-mail es.berry@ukonline.co.uk

BERRY, Prof Frank John. b 47. Lon Univ BSc72 PhD75 DSc88 FRSC84. Qu Coll Birm 96. **d** 99 **p** 00. Prof Inorganic Chemistry Open Univ from 91; Hon Prof Chemistry Birm Univ from 07; NSM Rednal 99-04; NSM Birm St Martin w Bordesley St Andr 04-07; NSM Moseley St Mary and St Anne from 07. *44 Middle Park Road, Selly Oak, Birmingham B29 4BJ* Tel 0121-475 2718 E-mail frank@berry44.fsworld.co.uk

BERRY, Miss Heather Evelyn. b 45. Lon Univ BA67 Ex Univ PGCE68. **d** 00 **p** 01. OLM Gaywood *Nor* from 00. *12 Kent Road, King's Lynn PE30 4AF* Tel (01553) 764098 E-mail heberry@talktalk.net

BERRY, Canon Ian Thomas Henry. b 73. QUB BSc94. CITC BTh98. **d** 98 **p** 99. C Bangor Abbey *D & D* 98-02; I Monaghan w Tydavnet and Kilmore *Clogh* from 02; Preb Clogh Cathl from 11. *The Rectory, Clones Road, Monaghan, Republic of Ireland* Tel (00353) (47) 81136 E-mail monaghan@clogher.anglican.org

BERRY, John. b 41. Dur Univ BA62. Oak Hill Th Coll 63. **d** 65 **p** 66. C Burnage St Marg *Man* 65-68; C Middleton 68-70; Travelling Sec IVF 70-73; V Derby St Pet 73-76; P-in-c Derby Ch Ch and H Trin 73-76; V Derby St Pet and Ch Ch w H Trin 76-81; Bp's Officer for Evang *Carl* 81-86; P-in-c Bampton and Mardale 81-86; TR N Wingfield, Pilsley and Tupton *Derby* 86-89; Evang Sec Evang Alliance 89-92; V Guernsey H Trin *Win* 92-98; TR Broadwater *Chich* 98-07; rtd 07. *27 Blythe Close, Newport Pagnell MK16 9DN* Tel (01908) 217631 E-mail reverendjohn@sky.com

BERRY, Paul Edward. b 56. NOC 91. **d** 94 **p** 95. C Halliwell St Luke *Man* 94-98; TV Horwich and Rivington 98-08; TV Edgware *Lon* from 08. *1 Beulah Close, Edgware HA8 8SP* Tel (020) 8958 9730

BERRY, The Very Revd Peter Austin. b 35. Keble Coll Ox BA59 BTh61 MA63 Birm Univ Hon DD97. St Steph Ho Ox 59. **d** 62 **p** 63. C Cov St Mark 62-66; Dioc Community Relns Officer 64-70; C Cov Cathl 66-73; Can Res Cov Cathl 73-86; Vice-Provost Cov Cathl 77-86; Bp's Adv for Community Relns 77-86; Provost Birm 86-99; rtd 99; Perm to Offic *Cov* from 99 and *Birm* from 00. *Reed Lodge, D5 Kenilworth Court, Hagley Road, Birmingham B16 9NU* Tel 0121-454 0021

BERRY, Mrs Philippa Raines. b 51. Man Univ BA72 Univ of Wales (Cardiff) CertEd73. St Jo Coll Nottm 82. **d** 95 **p** 96. NSM Leic H Apostles 95-04; P-in-c from 04. *The Vicarage, 281 Fosse Road South, Leicester LE3 1AE* Tel 0116-282 4336 E-mail pipberry@hotmail.com

BERRY, Sister Susan Patricia (Sister Sue). b 49. Bris Univ BA70 Hughes Hall Cam PGCE72. Qu Coll Birm 77. **dss** 86 **d** 87 **p** 94. Chapl Barn Fellowship Whatcombe Ho 86-89; Chapl Lee Abbey 89-91; NSM Thatcham *Ox* 93-95; CSF from 95; Perm to Offic *B & W* 96-97 and 98-10; Chapl Guy's and St Thos' Hosps NHS Trust Lon 97-98; Perm to Offic *S'wark* 97-98 and from 10. *St Alphege Clergy House, Pocock Street, London SE1 0BJ* Tel (020) 7928 8910 E-mail suecsf@franciscans.org.uk

BERRY, Timothy Hugh. b 50. Reading Univ BA72. Oak Hill NSM Course 81. **d** 84 **p** 85. NSM Swanley St Paul *Roch* 84-88; C Gorleston St Andr *Nor* 88-93; V Grain w Stoke *Roch* 93-95; rtd 95; Perm to Offic *Roch* from 01. *26 Cyclamen Road, Swanley BR8 8HJ* Tel (01322) 613385

BERRY-DAVIES, Charles William Keith. b 48. MIOT71. Linc Th Coll. **d** 83 **p** 84. C Hythe *Cant* 83-86; Chapl RAF 86-09. *Address temp unknown*

BERRYMAN, William Arthur David. b 47. Lon Univ BD69 St Pet Coll Ox CertEd71. Sarum & Wells Th Coll 75. **d** 76 **p** 77. Asst Master Preston Sch Yeovil 76-80; Hon C Yeovil St Mich *B & W* 76-80; C Ex St Dav and Chapl Ex Coll 80-83; Chapl RN 83-89; V Highertown and Baldhu *Truro* 89-95; TR Cov E 95-97; TR The Abbey and P-in-c Leic St Paul 97-01; R Banchory and P-in-c Kincardine O'Neil *Ab* 01-05; P-in-c Beeston *Ripon* from 05. *Beeston Vicarage, 16 Town Street, Beeston, Leeds LS11 8PN* Tel 0113-272 3337 E-mail davidberryman@hotmail.com

BERSON, Alan Charles. b 31. Univ of Michigan BA52 MA53 Lon Univ PhD62. St Steph Ho Ox 63. **d** 65 **p** 66. C Leeds St Pet *Ripon* 65-68; C St Giles-in-the-Fields *Lon* 68; Lic to Offic 69-80; Perm to Offic 80-88. *32 Bath Hill Court, Bath Road, Bournemouth BH1 2HP* Tel (01202) 319122

BERSWEDEN, Judith Anne. b 63. St Jo Coll Dur BA84. Ripon Coll Cuddesdon BA91. **d** 92 **p** 94. Par Dn Mirfield *Wakef* 92-94; NSM Robert Town 94-97; NSM Roberttown w Hartshead 97-00; NSM Alderbury Deanery from 00; Chapl Bp Wordsworth Sch Salisbury from 01. *The Rectory, Winterslow, Salisbury SP5 1RE* Tel (01980) 862231 E-mail judith.bersweden@dsl.pipex.com

BERSWEDEN, Nils Herry Stephen. b 57. Newc Univ BSc78. Ripon Coll Cuddesdon 88. **d** 90 **p** 91. C Mirfield *Wakef* 90-93; P-in-c Purlwell 93-94; P-in-c Robert Town 94-97; V Roberttown w Hartshead 97-00; P-in-c Winterslow *Sarum* 00-01; TV Clarendon 01-08; TR from 08. *The Rectory, Winterslow, Salisbury SP5 1RE* Tel (01980) 862231 E-mail nils.bersweden@breathemail.net

BERTRAM, Canon Richard Henry. b 27. TCD BA50 MA64. CITC 50. **d** 53 **p** 54. C Sligo Cathl 53-56; C Dublin Booterstown *D & G* 56-58; I Stranorlar w Meenglas and Kilteevogue *D & R* 58-65; I Dublin St Cath w St Jas *D & G* 65-73; I Dublin Irishtown 73-74; I Dublin Irishtown w Donnybrook 74-02; Can Ch Ch Cathl Dublin 86-02; Treas 95-02; rtd 02. *Glencoe, The Harbour, North Beach, Greystones, Co Wicklow, Republic of Ireland* Tel (00353) (1) 287 5320

BESSANT, Brian Keith. b 32. Roch Th Coll 65. **d** 67 **p** 68. C Chatham St Wm *Roch* 67-70; C Cove St Jo *Guildf* 71-74; V Frimley Green 74-97; rtd 97; Perm to Offic *Guildf* from 97. *14 Tay Close, Farnborough GU14 9NB* Tel (01252) 376530

BESSANT, Christopher Dixon. b 69. Ridley Hall Cam 07. **d** 09 **p** 10. C Gt Bookham *Guildf* from 09. *19 The Lorne, Bookham, Leatherhead KT23 4JY* Tel (01372) 453729 Mobile 07800-719405 E-mail c.bessant@hotmail.com

BESSANT, Canon Idwal Brian. b 39. Cardiff Coll of Art ATD62. St Mich Coll Llan 65. **d** 68 **p** 69. C Llantwit Major and St Donat's 68-73; R Llangammarch w Garth, Llanlleonfel etc *S & B* 73-77; V Crickhowell 77-78; CMS Miss 78-83; Cyprus 80-83; V Crickhowell w Cwmdu and Tretower *S & B* 83-91; RD Crickhowell 86-91; V Llanwrtyd w Llanddulas in Tir Abad etc 91-04; Can Res Brecon Cathl 98-04; RD Builth 02-04; rtd 04. *10 Bronant, Bronllys Road, Talgarth, Brecon LD3 0HF* Tel (01874) 712380

BESSANT, Canon Simon David. b 56. Sheff Univ BMus77 MA00. St Jo Coll Nottm. **d** 81 **p** 82. C Litherland St Jo and St Jas *Liv* 81-84; C Holloway Em w Hornsey Road St Barn *Lon* 84-86; C Holloway St Mark w Em 86-91; V Blackb Redeemer 91-98; Acting RD Blackb 97-98; Dir Miss and Evang 98-07; Dir CME 02-07; Hon Can Blackb Cathl 06-07; V Ecclesall *Sheff* from 07. *Ecclesall Vicarage, Ringinglow Road, Sheffield S11 7PQ* Tel 0114-236 0084 E-mail simon.bessant@sheffield.anglican.org

BESSENT, Preb Stephen Lyn. b 53. Bris Univ BA75. Wycliffe Hall Ox 75. **d** 77 **p** 78. C Patchway *Bris* 77-80; TV Swindon St Jo and St Andr 80-83; TV Eston w Normanby *York* 83-90; V Cogges *Ox* 90-94; P-in-c S Leigh 90-94; V Cogges and S Leigh 94-01; P-in-c Alphington, Shillingford St George and Ide *Ex* from 01; Preb Ex Cathl from 09. *The Rectory, 6 Lovelace Gardens, Exeter EX2 8XQ* Tel (01392) 437662 E-mail rectory6ssmgi@btinternet.com

BEST, Miss Karen Belinda. b 62. Qu Coll Birm 92. **d** 94 **p** 95. C Southall Green St Jo *Lon* 94-97; C Northolt Park St Barn 97-00; V Gillingham St Barn *Roch* 00-08; P-in-c Roxwell *Chelmsf* from 08; Lay Discipleship Adv (Bradwell Area) from 08. *The Vicarage,*

Vicarage Road, Roxwell, Chelmsford CM1 4NB Tel (01245) 248157 E-mail revkbest@aol.com

BEST, Canon Raymond. b 42. Sarum & Wells Th Coll 71. **d** 74 **p** 75. C Whorlton *Newc* 74-78; C Seaton Hirst 78-83; C Benwell St Jas 83-85; TV Benwell 85-89; V Walker 89-00; P-in-c Byker St Martin 96-99; V Haltwhistle and Greenhead 00-10; Hon Can Newc Cathl 97-10; AD Hexham 02-06; rtd 10. *The Annexe, 3 Admiral Close, Swarland, Morpeth NE65 9GZ* Tel (01670) 783434 E-mail canonbest@aol.com

BEST, Mrs Ruth Helen. b 54. **d** 05 **p** 06. NSM Ipswich St Matt *St E* 05-06; NSM Triangle, St Matt and All SS from 06. *2 Newson Street, Ipswich IP1 3NY* Tel (01473) 424121

BESTELINK, Canon William Meindert Croft. b 48. Hull Univ BA70 FRSA78. Cuddesdon Coll 71. **d** 73 **p** 74. C Holt *Nor* 73-74; C E Dereham w Hoe 74-76; C Thorpe St Andr 76-80; R Colby w Banningham and Tuttington 80-90; R Felmingham 80-90; R Suffield 80-90; P-in-c Roydon St Remigius 90-04; P-in-c Scole, Brockdish, Billingford, Thorpe Abbots etc 02-04; P-in-c Gillingham w Geldeston, Stockton, Ellingham etc 04-09; RD Redenhall 00-03; Dioc Rural Officer 99-09; Hon Can Nor Cathl 02-09; rtd 09; Perm to Offic *Nor* from 09. *3 Linkside, 26 Park Road, Cromer NR27 0EA* Tel (01263) 511278 Mobile 07909-690073 E-mail wmcbestelink@hotmail.com

BESTLEY, Peter Mark. b 60. Qu Coll Cam MA Univ of Wales (Cardiff) MPhil92. St Mich Coll Llan 89. **d** 92 **p** 93. C Hampton All SS *Lon* 92-95; Chapl W Middx Univ Hosp NHS Trust 95-99; Hon C Bracknell *Ox* 04-06; C Easthampstead from 06. *4 Qualitas, Bracknell RG12 7QG* Tel (01344) 426741 E-mail peter.bestley@lineone.net

BESWETHERICK, Andrew Michael. b 55. Ex Univ BEd80. S'wark Ord Course 87. **d** 90 **p** 91. Dep Hd Maze Hill Sch Greenwich 88-98; NSM Blackheath St Jo *S'wark* from 90; Hd Sixth Form Rosemary Sch Islington from 98. *112 Charlton Road, London SE7 7EY* Tel (020) 8853 0853 E-mail aj@4bes.eclipse.co.uk

BESWICK, Canon Gary Lancelot. b 38. ALCD63. **d** 63 **p** 64. C Walthamstow St Mary *Chelmsf* 63-67; C Laisterdyke *Bradf* 67-70; V Idle 70-78; Area Sec (NW England) SAMS 78-92; Area Sec (N Thames) 92-97; Hon Can N Argentina from 87; R Gt Smeaton w Appleton Wiske and Birkby etc *Ripon* 97-03; rtd 03. *17 Gustory Road, Crantock, Newquay TR8 5RG* Tel (01637) 831361

BESWICK, Jane. *See* VOST, Mrs Jane

BESWICK, Joseph Hubert. b 25. Birm Univ MB, ChB48. **d** 59 **p** 60. Lic to Offic *S'well* 59-00. *38 Hallams Lane, Beeston, Nottingham NG9 5FH* Tel 0115-925 6719

BETHELL, Catherine Anita. *See* MACKRELL, Ms Catherine Anita

BETSON, Christopher James. b 81. Writtle Agric Coll BSc03. Cranmer Hall Dur 06 St Jo Coll Dur BA09. **d** 09 **p** 10. C Anston *Sheff* from 09. *The Vicarage, 27 Skipton Road, Swallownest, Sheffield S26 4NQ* Tel 0114-287 2903 E-mail chrisbetson@hotmail.com

BETSON (née BIDDINGTON), Mrs Laura Claire. b 84. Trin Coll Cam BA05 St Jo Coll Dur MA08. Cranmer Hall Dur 06. **d** 08 **p** 09. C Aston cum Aughton w Swallownest and Ulley *Sheff* from 08. *The Vicarage, 27 Skipton Road, Swallownest, Sheffield S26 4NQ* Tel 0114-287 2903 Mobile 07984-960749 E-mail laura.biddington@yahoo.co.uk

BETSON, Mark John. b 77. Univ Coll Lon BSc99 Birkbeck Coll Lon PhD Cam Univ BA06. Westcott Ho Cam 04. **d** 07 **p** 08. C Southwick *Chich* 07-10; P-in-c Lower Beeding from 10. *The Vicarage, Handcross Road, Plummers Plain, Horsham RH13 6NU* Tel (01403) 891367 Mobile 07801-273074 E-mail m.betson@clara.co.uk

BETSON, Stephen. b 53. Sarum & Wells Th Coll 89. **d** 91 **p** 92. C Sittingbourne St Mich *Cant* 91-95; V Fairweather Green *Bradf* 95-01; R Hockwold w Wilton *Ely* 01-06; R Weeting 01-06; P-in-c Stanground from 06. *38 Riverside Mead, Peterborough PE2 8JN* Tel (01733) 315461 E-mail betson1@tesco.net

BETTELEY, John Richard. b 46. Sarum & Wells Th Coll 81. **d** 83 **p** 84. C Auchterarder *St And* 83-85; C Dunblane 83-85; Chapl RAF 85-89; R Callander *St And* 89-94; P-in-c Aberfoyle 89-94; P-in-c Doune 89-94; R Ballachulish *Arg* 94-04; R Glencoe 94-04; R Onich 94-04; Dioc Youth Officer 94-01; Syn Clerk 99-04; Can St Jo Cathl Oban 99-04; Can Cumbrae 99-04; R Aboyne 04-06; R Ballater 04-06; R Braemar 04-06. *3 School Street, Fearn, Tain IV20 1SX* Tel 07713-914602 (mobile) E-mail johnrbetteley@aol.com

BETTERIDGE, Kelly Anne. b 69. Roehampton Inst BA92. Qu Coll Birm 08. **d** 10 **p** 11. C Nuneaton St Nic *Cov* from 10. *17 Trinity Walk, Nuneaton CV11 4PH* Tel (024) 7634 4304 Mobile 07709-400213 E-mail kells612@yahoo.co.uk

BETTERIDGE, Simon Frank. b 66. St Jo Coll Nottm. **d** 00 **p** 01. C Studley *Cov* 00-02; C Leamington Priors St Paul 02-04; Chapl Univ Hosps Cov and Warks NHS Trust from 04. *17 Trinity Walk, Nuneaton CV11 4PH* Tel (024) 7634 4304 Mobile 07743-870601 E-mail simon.betty@yahoo.com *or* simon.betteridge@uhcw.nhs.uk

BETTINSON, Philip Keith. b 79. Univ of Wales (Abth) BEng01. St Mich Coll Llan BTh11. **d** 11. C Cilcain, Gwernaffield, Llanferres etc *St As* from 11. *9 Pen y Coed, Nannerch, Mold CH7 5RS* Tel (01352) 741791 E-mail rev@jara23.co.uk

BETTIS, Canon Margaret Jean. b 42. Gilmore Ho 72. **dss** 77 **d** 87 **p** 94. Kenya 77-79; Tutor Crowther Hall CMS Tr Coll Selly Oak 79-82; Hodge Hill *Birm* 82-87; Par Dn 87; Par Dn Flitwick *St Alb* 87-93; P-in-c Westoning w Tingrith 93-94; V 94-04; Hon Can St Alb 97-04; rtd 04; Perm to Offic *St Alb* 04-05 and *Glouc* 05-06; Hon C Cirencester *Glouc* from 06. *19 Bathurst Road, Cirencester GL7 1SA* Tel (01285) 658695

BETTRIDGE, Canon Graham Winston. b 39. Kelham Th Coll 60. **d** 65 **p** 66. C Burley in Wharfedale *Bradf* 65-67; C Baildon 67-70; V Harden and Wilsden 70-81; TR Kirkby Lonsdale *Carl* 81-06; Hon Can Carl Cathl 89-06; rtd 06; Chapl Cumbria Constabulary *Carl* from 96; Perm to Offic *Bradf* from 07. *Moorgate Cottage, Maypole Green, Long Preston, Skipton BD23 4PJ* Tel (01729) 841113 E-mail canongraham@mintegrity.co.uk

BETTS, Alan John. b 55. Portsm Poly BSc77 St Martin's Coll Lanc PGCE81. St Jo Coll Nottm 93. **d** 93 **p** 94. C Cannock *Lich* 93-01; P-in-c Endon w Stanley 01-04; V Bagnall w Endon from 04. *St Luke's Vicarage, Leek Road, Endon, Stoke-on-Trent ST9 9BH* Tel (01782) 502166

BETTS, Canon Anthony Clive. b 40. Wells Th Coll 63. **d** 65 **p** 66. C Leeds All Hallows w St Simon *Ripon* 65-67; C Wetherby 67-70; C Adel 70-73; V Leeds All SS 73-79; V Leeds Richmond Hill 79-84; R Knaresborough 84-03; TR 03-05; RD Harrogate 95-98; Hon Can Ripon Cathl 04-05; rtd 05; Perm to Offic *Ripon* from 06. *1 Bilsdale Close, Romanby, Northallerton DL7 8FT* Tel (01609) 760378 E-mail tonybetts@bettst.freeserve.co.uk

BETTS, Canon Anthony Percy. b 26. Lon Univ BD52. ALCD52. **d** 52 **p** 53. C Guildf St Sav 52-56; C Hanworth St Geo *Lon* 56-59; V Derby St Aug 59-74; RD Derby 71-74; V Bracebridge *Linc* 74-83; R Fenny Bentley, Kniveton, Thorpe and Tissington *Derby* 83-91; RD Ashbourne 86-91; Hon Can Derby Cathl 87-91; rtd 91; Perm to Offic *Derby* from 91. *Otterbourne House, Windley, Belper DE56 2LP* Tel (01773) 550677

BETTS, David John. b 38. Lon Univ BSc61. Oak Hill Th Coll 63. **d** 65 **p** 66. C Slough *Ox* 65-70; C Welling *Roch* 70-75; V Swanley St Paul 75-93; R Nottingham St Nic *S'well* 93-98; TV Canford Magna *Sarum* 98-04; rtd 04. *290 Rempstone Road, Wimborne BH21 1SZ* Tel (01202) 840537

BETTS, Edmund John. b 51. St Chad's Coll Dur BA72 Lanc Univ MA81. Qu Coll Birm 73. **d** 76 **p** 77. C Leagrave *St Alb* 76-79; Asst Chapl R Albert Hosp Lanc 79-81; Chapl Lea Castle Hosp and Kidderminster Gen Hosp 81-86; Prov Officer Educn for Min Ch in Wales 86-88; Exec Sec for Min Ch in Wales 88-90; TR Haverhill w Withersfield, the Wrattings etc *St E* 90-97; V Haverhill w Withersfield 97-06; RD Clare 91-06; Hon Can St E Cathl 02-06; CUF Link Officer 02-06; V Altrincham St Geo *Ches* from 06; P-in-c Altrincham St Jo from 07. *St George's Vicarage, Townfield Road, Altrincham WA14 4DS* Tel 0161-928 1279 E-mail edmund.betts1@btinternet.com

BETTS, George William John. b 23. Ex Univ BA51. Westcott Ho Cam 51. **d** 53 **p** 54. C Wallsend St Luke *Newc* 53-54; C Benwell St Jas 54-56; C Plumstead St Jas w St Jo *S'wark* 56; C Peckham St Andr w All SS 56; C Eltham St Jo 57-60; C Findon *Chich* 60-67; Rhodesia 67-68; C Sherborne w Castleton and Lillington *Sarum* 68-69; C Brookfield St Anne, Highgate Rise *Lon* 69; rtd 88. *72 Westmount Road, London SE9 1JE* Tel (020) 8850 2116

BETTS, Ivan Ringland. b 38. TCD BA61 MA67. **d** 62 **p** 63. C Ballyholme *D & D* 62-65; C Dundela St Mark 65-69; Miss to Seamen 69-73; Sudan 69-71; Trinidad and Tobago 71-73; C Drumglass *Arm* 73-81; I Augher w Newtownsaville and Eskrahoole *Clogh* 81-86; Bp's C Ballymacarrett St Martin *D & D* 86-02; rtd 02. *56 Norwood Drive, Belfast BT4 2EB* Tel (028) 9065 0723 E-mail ivanbetts@btinternet.com

BETTS, Mrs Patricia Joyce. b 43. St Kath Coll Lon CertEd64 FRSA96. S Dios Minl Tr Scheme 90. **d** 96 **p** 97. NSM Bath Widcombe *B & W* 96-00; P-in-c 00-05; Perm to Offic from 05. *Hunters Lodge, North Road, Bath BA2 6HP* Tel (01225) 464918 E-mail candpbetts@talktalk.net

BETTS, Paul Robert. b 31. Lon Univ BSc51. Oak Hill Th Coll 53. **d** 56 **p** 57. C Plymouth St Jude *Ex* 56-59; C Cheltenham St Mark *Glouc* 59-63; V Finchley St Paul Long Lane 63-76; Warden St Columba Cen Cam 76-79; R Datchworth w Tewin *St Alb* 79-96; rtd 96; Perm to Offic *Ex* from 96. *2 Penny Close, Exminster, Exeter EX6 8SU* Tel (01392) 824403

BETTS, Richard Alan. b 56. ACA83 UEA BA77. Sarum & Wells Th Coll 93. **d** 93 **p** 94. C Mile Cross *Nor* 93-97; TV Dorchester *Sarum* from 97. *St George's Vicarage, 59 Fordington High Street, Dorchester DT1 1LB* Tel (01305) 262394 E-mail richard@betts39.fsnet.co.uk

BETTS, Canon Steven James. b 64. York Univ BSc86. Ripon Coll Cuddesdon 87. **d** 90 **p** 91. C Bearsted w Thurnham *Cant* 90-94; Bp's Chapl *Nor* 94-97; V Old Catton 97-05; RD Nor N 01-05; Bp's Officer for Ord and Initial Tr from 05; Hon Can Nor Cathl

from 08. *Emmaus House, 65 The Close, Norwich NR1 4DH* Tel (01603) 628103 E-mail stevenbetts@norwich.anglican.org
BEVAN, Alan John. b 29. Bris Univ BA54. Oak Hill Th Coll 54. **d** 56 **p** 59. C Penn Fields *Lich* 56-57; C Corsham *Bris* 58-61; C Wath-upon-Dearne w Adwick-upon-Dearne *Sheff* 61-68; C Darfield 68-71; C Drypool St Columba w St Andr and St Pet *York* 71-79; Chapl HM Pris Wandsworth 79-83; Chapl HM Pris Kirkham 83-86; rtd 86; Perm to Offic *Ex* 86-09. *c/o the Revd J Ancrum, 14 Merrivale Road, Dousland, Yelverton PL20 6NS*
BEVAN, Mrs Angela Ruth. b 56. Qu Coll Birm. **d** 07 **p** 08. NSM Shenley Green *Birm* from 07. *204 Shenley Fields Road, Birmingham B29 5BL* Tel 0121-477 9924
BEVAN, Christopher Jeremy. Lon Inst BA89 Lon Guildhall Univ MA97 Cardiff Univ BA11. **d** 11. C Llanelli *S & B* from 11. *Llanelly Rectory, Abergavenny Road, Gilwern, Abergavenny NP7 0AD* Tel (01873) 830280
BEVAN, David Graham. b 34. Univ of Wales (Lamp) BA54 LTh56. Gen Th Sem (NY) MDiv57. **d** 57 **p** 58. C Llanelli *St D* 57-60; CF 60-76; rtd 99. *148 Bromley Heath Road, Bristol BS16 6JJ* Tel 0117-956 0946
BEVAN, Gareth Edward. **d** 10 **p** 11. NSM Wembley Park *Lon* from 10. *57 Oakington Avenue, Wembley HA9 8HX* Tel (020) 8908 3719 Mobile 07876-133314 E-mail gbevan76@googlemail.com
BEVAN, Hubert Basil Henry. b 24. Univ of Wales (Lamp) BA52 LTh54 MTh75 PhD78. **d** 54 **p** 55. C Knighton and Heyope *S & B* 54-60; C Toxteth Park St Marg *Liv* 60-61; V Walsall St Mary and All SS Palfrey *Lich* 61-64; R Sunderland *Dur* 64-66; V Hendon St Paul 64-66; V Gilfach Goch w Llandyfodwg 66-73; R Cregina *S & B* 73-78; V Bettws Disserth w Llansantffraed in Elwell 73-78; V Glascwm and Rhulen 76-78; R Llanferres, Nercwys and Eryrys *St As* 78-80; Tutor St Deiniol's Lib Hawarden 79-89; V Treuddyn and Nercwys and Eryrys *St As* 80-85; R Llanfynydd 85-89; rtd 89. *Bryn Heulog, Bryniau Duon, Old Llandegfan, Menai Bridge LL59 5PP*
BEVAN, Janet Mary. See MOORE, Ms Janet Mary
BEVAN, Judith Anne. See EGAR, Miss Judith Anne
BEVAN, Paul John. b 49. Bris Sch of Min 84. **d** 87. NSM Bishopsworth *Bris* 87-96. *10 Brookdale Road, Headley Park, Bristol BS13 7PZ* Tel 0117-964 6330
BEVAN, Peter John. b 54. K Coll Lon BA76 AKC76 MA86. St Steph Ho Ox BA79. **d** 80 **p** 81. C Brighouse *Wakef* 80-83; C Chapelthorpe 83-86; V Scholes 86-95; V Potters Bar *St Alb* from 95. *The Vicarage, 15 The Walk, Potters Bar EN6 1QN* Tel (01707) 644539 *or* 645080
BEVAN, Philip Frank. b 41. Brasted Th Coll 63 Chich Th Coll 65. **d** 67 **p** 68. C Walton St Mary *Liv* 67-71; P-in-c Long Is SS Pet and Paul Bahamas 71-73; R Nassau St Matt 73-78; Perm to Offic *S'wark* from 00. *5 Dunstable Road, Richmond TW9 1UH* Tel (020) 8940 3622 Mobile 07970-961539 E-mail fr.philip@btinternet.com
BEVAN, Mrs Rebecca Anne. b 64. Reading Univ BA86. Ox Min Course 04. **d** 07 **p** 08. NSM Thatcham *Ox* 07-10; R Aldermaston and Woolhampton from 10. *The Rectory, Wasing Lane, Aldermaston, Reading RG7 4LX* Tel 0118-971 2281 E-mail beckywinterbevan@aol.com
BEVAN, Canon Richard Justin William. b 22. LTh42 St Chad's Coll Dur BA45 DTh72 PhD80. St Aug Coll Cant 39. **d** 45 **p** 46. C Stoke upon Trent *Lich* 45-49; Chapl Aberlour Orphanage 49-51; Lic to Offic *Mor* 49-51; Lic to Offic *Blackb* 51-52; C Church Kirk 52-56; C Whalley 56-61; R Dur St Mary le Bow w St Mary the Less 61-64; Chapl Dur Univ 61-74; V Dur St Oswald 64-74; P-in-c Dur St Mary le Bow w St Mary the Less 64-67; R 67-74; R Grasmere *Carl* 74-82; Can Res, Lib and Treas Carl Cathl 82-89; Vice-Dean Carl 86-89; Chapl to The Queen 86-93; rtd 89; Perm to Offic *Carl* from 89. *Beck Cottage, West End, Burgh-by-Sands, Carlisle CA7 6BT* Tel (01228) 576781
BEVAN, Rodney. b 57. Leeds Univ BA80 Keele Univ PGCE81 Open Univ MA99. St Jo Coll Dur 97. **d** 99 **p** 00. C Ogley Hay *Lich* 99-03; TV Rossendale Middle Valley *Man* 03-04; TR from 04. *St Anne's Vicarage, Ashworth Road, Rossendale BB4 9JE* Tel (01706) 221889 E-mail revrodbev@hotmail.com
BEVER, Canon Michael Charles Stephen. b 44. Selw Coll Cam BA66 MA70. Cuddesdon Coll 67. **d** 69 **p** 70. C Steeton *Bradf* 69-72; C Northampton St Mary *Pet* 72-74; Niger 75-79; P-in-c Elmstead *Chelmsf* 80-83; V 83-85; V Bocking St Pet 85-96; P-in-c Odiham *Win* 96-07; rtd 07; Hon Can Awka from 93; Perm to Offic *Win* from 07 and *Portsm* from 08. *68A Drift Road, Waterlooville PO8 0NX* Tel and fax (023) 9259 6895 E-mail mcsb@ozala.plus.com
BEVERIDGE, Mrs Freda Joy. b 38. Qu Mary Coll Lon BA59 Lon Inst of Educn PGCE60. Ripon Coll Cuddesdon 83. **dss** 85 **d** 87 **p** 94. Ox St Giles and SS Phil and Jas w St Marg 85-88; Par Dn 87-88; Par Dn Woughton 88-94; C 94-95; TR 95-97; C Woodham *Guildf* 97-00; rtd 00; Perm to Offic *Sarum* from 01. *Moonraker Cottage, 27 New Road, Chiseldon, Swindon SN4 0LY* Tel (01793) 741064
BEVERIDGE, Simon Alexander Ronald. b 61. Nottm Univ BA84. Chich Th Coll 84. **d** 87 **p** 88. C Braunton *Ex* 87-90; TV N Creedy 90-93; Chapl RN from 93. *Royal Naval Chaplaincy Service, Mail Point 1-2, Leach Building, Whale Island, Portsmouth PO2 8BY* Tel (023) 9262 5055 Fax 9262 5134
BEVERLEY, David John. b 46. Univ of Wales (Lamp) BA68. Linc Th Coll 71. **d** 73 **p** 74. C Cov E 73-76; C Immingham *Linc* 76-84; V Bracebridge Heath 84-86; Ind Chapl 86-97; P-in-c Scunthorpe Resurr 97-01; V 01-02; R Trentside E 02-11; rtd 11. *73 Peveril Avenue, Scunthorpe DN17 1BG* Tel (01724) 279914 E-mail davejbev@aol.com
BEVERLEY, Sister. See DAVIES, Sister Beverley
BEVERLEY, Suffragan Bishop of (Provincial Episcopal Visitor). See JARRETT, The Rt Revd Martyn William
BEVERLY, Mrs Sue Jane. b 53. Cardiff Univ BTh08. St Mich Coll Llan 05. **d** 07 **p** 08. NSM Coity, Nolton and Brackla *Llan* from 07; Asst Dir of Min 10; AD Bridgend from 11. *Y Llety, Heol yr Ysgol, Coity, Bridgend CF35 6BL* Tel (01656) 652540 E-mail sue.beverly@zen.co.uk
BEVINGTON, Canon Colin Reginald. b 36. ALCD63. **d** 63 **p** 64. C Devonport St Budeaux *Ex* 63-65; C Attenborough w Chilwell *S'well* 65-68; R Benhall w Sternfield *St E* 68-74; P-in-c Snape w Friston 73-74; V Selly Hill St Steph *Birm* 74-81; P-in-c Selly Oak St Wulstan 80-81; V Selly Park St Steph and St Wulstan 81-88; Dioc Adv on Miss *St E* 88-95; Dioc and Co Ecum Officer 88-99; Hon Can St E Cathl 93-00; Bp's Dom Chapl and Personal Asst 95-99; R Holbrook, Freston, Woolverstone and Wherstead 99-00; RD Samford 99-00; rtd 01; Perm to Offic *St E* 01-05 and *Blackb* from 07. *4 Highgrove Road, Lancaster LA1 5FS* Tel (01524) 64851 E-mail bevington@capel19.freeserve.co.uk
BEVINGTON, David John. b 51. Ch Coll Cam BA72 MA76. Trin Coll Bris 73. **d** 76 **p** 77. C Tulse Hill H Trin *S'wark* 76-79; C Galleywood Common *Chelmsf* 79-82; TV Hanley H Ev *Lich* 82-90; TV Hemel Hempstead *St Alb* 90-99; V Calbourne w Newtown *Portsm* from 99; V Shalfleet from 99. *The Vicarage, 4 Manor Green, Shalfleet, Newport PO30 4QT* Tel (01983) 531238 E-mail dbevington@lineone.net
BEVIS, Anthony Richard. b 34. Chich Th Coll 87. **d** 87 **p** 89. NSM Hamble le Rice *Win* 87-94; NSM Woolston from 94; Chapl Southn Community Services NHS Trust 90-01; Chapl Southn City Primary Care Trust from 01. *Lynwood, High Street, Hamble, Southampton SO31 4HA* Tel (023) 8045 3102 *or* 8047 2258
BEWES, Anthony Charles Neill. b 71. Birm Univ BA93. Wycliffe Hall Ox 96. **d** 99 **p** 00. C Sevenoaks St Nic *Roch* 99-05; Team Ldr Titus Trust from 05. *45 Lonsdale Road, Oxford OX2 7ES* Tel (01865) 553625 E-mail anthony@bewes.com
BEWES, Helen Catherine. See SCAMMAN, Mrs Helen Catherine
BEWES, Preb Richard Thomas. b 34. OBE05. Em Coll Cam BA58 MA61. Ridley Hall Cam 57. **d** 59 **p** 60. C Beckenham Ch *Ch Roch* 59-65; V Harold Wood *Chelmsf* 65-74; V Northwood Em *Lon* 74-83; R St Marylebone All So w SS Pet and Jo 83-88; P-in-c Portman Square St Paul 87-88; R Langham Place All So 88-04; Preb St Paul's Cathl 88-04; rtd 04; Perm to Offic *Lon* from 05. *50 Curzon Road, London W5 1NF* Tel (020) 8998 1723
BEWLEY, Robin John. b 63. St Jo Coll Ox BA86 MA95 Fitzw Coll Cam BA99 PhD05. Ridley Hall Cam. **d** 00 **p** 01. NSM Histon and Impington *Ely* 00-04; C Harborne Heath *Birm* 04-11; V Kettering Ch the King *Pet* from 11. *The Vicarage, Deeble Road, Kettering NN15 7AA* Tel (01536) 512828 Mobile 07733-346631 E-mail rob@thebewleys.co.uk
BEXON, Mrs Valerie Joan. b 60. Chelt & Glouc Coll of HE BA96. Wycliffe Hall Ox 07. **d** 09 **p** 10. C Wotton-under-Edge w Ozleworth, N Nibley etc *Glouc* from 09. *9 Coombe Road, Wotton-under-Edge GL12 7LU* Tel (01453) 521417 Mobile 07882-882796 E-mail valeriebexon@onetel.com
BEYNON, Malcolm. b 36. Univ of Wales (Lamp) BA56 Univ of Wales (Cardiff) PGCE71. St Mich Coll Llan 56. **d** 59 **p** 60. C Aberavon *Llan* 59-62; C Whitchurch 63-68; V Llanwynno 68-73; Chapl Old Hall Sch Wellington Shropshire 74-75; Chapl Nevill Holt Sch Market Harborough 75-82; Chapl Denstone Coll Prep Sch Uttoxeter 82-93; V Dale and St Brides w Marloes *St D* 93-01; rtd 01. *22 Ostrey Bank, St Clears, Carmarthen SA33 4AH* Tel (01994) 231872
BEYNON, Nigel David. b 68. Collingwood Coll Dur BSc90 Fitzw Coll Cam BA94. Ridley Hall Cam 92. **d** 95 **p** 96. C Fulham St Matt *Lon* 95-98; Assoc V St Helen Bishopsgate w St Andr Undershaft etc 98-07; Student Team Ldr 01-07. *78 Aubert Park, London N5 1TS*
BEYNON, Vincent Wyn. b 54. CertEd76 Lambeth STh97 Anglia Poly Univ MA04. St Mich Coll Llan 78. **d** 81 **p** 82. C Llantrisant 81-83; C Caerphilly 84-85; R Gelligaer 85-88; TV Cwmbran *Bris* 88-97; R Potton w Sutton and Cockayne Hatley *St Alb* 97-08; RD Biggleswade 01-06. *6 Minnis Green, Stelling Minnis, Canterbury CT4 6AA* Tel (01227) 709762 Mobile 07595-313035 E-mail wynbeynon@gmail.com
BHUTTA, Mrs Patricia Frances Mary. b 52. Kent Univ BA74. Ox Min Course 08. **d** 10 **p** 11. NSM Cumnor *Ox* from 10. *67 Eynsham Road, Botley, Oxford OX2 9BU* Tel (01865) 865739 Fax 865052 Mobile 07968-089566 E-mail pat@patbhutta.co.uk

BIANCHI, Mrs Margaret Ruth. b 56. St Mary's Coll Dur BA77. Cranmer Hall Dur 78. **dss** 80 **d** 91 **p** 94. Chester le Street *Dur* 80-83; W Pelton 83-91; NSM 91-95; Perm to Offic from 95. *8 Lindisfarne, Washington NE38 7JR* Tel 0191-417 0852
BIANCHI, Robert Frederick. b 56. St Jo Coll Dur BA77. Cranmer Hall Dur 78. **d** 80 **p** 81. C Chester le Street *Dur* 80-83; C W Pelton 83-86; P-in-c 86-95; Perm to Offic from 95. *8 Lindisfarne, Washington NE38 7JR* Tel 0191-417 0852
BIBBY, Paul Benington. b 27. Magd Coll Cam BA51 MA56. Westcott Ho Cam 55. **d** 57 **p** 58. C Flixton St Mich *Man* 57-60; C Woolwich St Mary w H Trin *S'wark* 60-62; V Hurst *Man* 62-69; Hd of Cam Ho Camberwell 69-76; R Shepton Mallet *B & W* 76-81; P-in-c Doulting w E and W Cranmore and Downhead 78-81; R Shepton Mallet w Doulting 81-82; Sen Chapl Eton Coll 82-87; R Hambleden Valley *Ox* 87-93; rtd 93; Perm to Offic *Nor* from 94. *Vine Cottage, Cross Lane, Stanhoe, King's Lynn PE31 8PS* Tel (01485) 518291
BICK, David Jim. b 33. ALCD59 LTh74. **d** 59 **p** 60. C Glouc St Cath 59-61; C Coleford w Staunton 61-63; R Blaisdon w Flaxley 63-72; V Coaley 72-83; P-in-c Arlingham 80-83; P-in-c Frampton on Severn 80-83; Hon C Saul w Fretherne and Framilode 83-84; Perm to Offic from 84; rtd 98. *St Joseph's, Prinknash Park, Cranham, Gloucester GL4 8EU* Tel (01452) 812973
BICK (née GRIFFITHS), Mrs Sarah. b 75. Ex Univ BA96 Homerton Coll Cam PGCE99. Qu Coll Birm 07. **d** 09 **p** 10. C Coleford, Staunton, Newland, Redbrook etc *Glouc* from 09. *20 North Road, Broadwell, Coleford GL16 7DR* Tel (01594) 835476 Mobile 07773-651893 E-mail sarahbick@enterprise.net
BICKERSTETH, David Craufurd. b 50. Wycliffe Hall Ox 71. **d** 75 **p** 76. C Beverley Minster *York* 75-79; C Farnborough *Guildf* 79-81; P-in-c Dearham *Carl* 81-85; V 85-86; R Gosforth w Nether Wasdale and Wasdale Head 86-93; P-in-c Harraby 93-97; V Maryport 98-04; TR Maryport, Netherton and Flimby 04-06; Dioc Chapl MU 94-97; R Draycott-le-Moors w Forsbrook *Lich* from 06; P-in-c Upper Tean from 08. *3 Willowcroft Rise, Blythe Bridge, Stoke-on-Trent ST11 9ST* Tel (01782) 397985 E-mail david.bickersteth@btinternet.com
BICKERSTETH, Edward Piers. b 56. MRICS80. Wycliffe Hall Ox 89. **d** 91 **p** 92. NSM Bebington *Ches* 91-92; C 92-94; Proclamation Trust 94-98; P-in-c Arborfield w Barkham *Ox* 98-02; R from 02. *The Rectory, Church Lane, Arborfield, Reading RG2 9HZ* Tel 0118-976 0285
✠**BICKERSTETH, The Rt Revd John Monier.** b 21. KCVO89. Ch Ch Ox BA49 MA53 Open Univ BA97. Wells Th Coll 48. **d** 50 **p** 51 **c** 70. C Moorfields *Bris* 50-54; C-in-c Hurst Green CD *S'wark* 54-62; V Chatham St Steph *Roch* 62-70; Hon Can Roch Cathl 68-70; Suff Bp Warrington *Liv* 70-75; Bp B & W 75-87; ChStJ and Sub-Prelate from 77; Clerk of the Closet 79-89; rtd 87. *Beckfords, Newtown, Tisbury, Salisbury SP3 6NY* Tel (01747) 870479
BICKERSTETH, Simon Craufurd. b 77. St Jo Coll Dur BA98. Wycliffe Hall Ox 99. **d** 01 **p** 02. C Windermere *Carl* 01-05; TV Walsall St Matt *Lich* 05-11; V Walsall St Martin from 11. *St Martin's House, 17 Daffodil Road, Walsall WS5 3DQ* Tel (01922) 611909 Mobile 07752-853148 E-mail simon.bickersteth@tiscali.co.uk
BICKLEY, Mrs Alice Elizabeth Ann. b 60. Qu Coll Birm 06. **d** 09 **p** 10. C Leagrave *St Alb* from 09. *39 Butely Road, Luton LU4 9EW* Tel (01582) 572054 Mobile 07977-601437 E-mail lizbickley@btinternet.com
BICKLEY, Mrs Pamela. b 59. Birm Univ BPhil99. WEMTC 06. **d** 09 **p** 10. NSM Minsterley *Heref* from 09. *High Ridge, Gorsty Bank, Snailbeach, Shrewsbury SY5 0LX* Tel (01743) 792824 E-mail shepherdstock@aol.com
BICKNELL, Carl Royston. Wycliffe Hall Ox. **d** 10 **p** 10. NSM Stapenhill w Cauldwell *Derby* from 10. *Bungalow 2, Drakelow House, Walton Road, Burton-on-Trent DE15 9UA* Tel (01283) 534288 E-mail carl@stpetersstapenhill.org.uk
BICKNELL, Jonathan Richard. b 62. Wycliffe Hall Ox. **d** 00 **p** 01. C Chesham Bois *Ox* 00-02. *210 High Street, Berkhamsted HP4 1AG* Tel (01442) 872447
BICKNELL (née RIDING), Mrs Pauline Alison. b 61. SEN82. Oak Hill Th Coll BA90. **d** 90 **p** 96. Par Dn Moor Allerton *Ripon* 90-93; Par Dn Leeds St Aid 93-94; C 94-96; C Rothwell 96-99; TV Drypool *York* 99-05; P-in-c Slyne w Hest *Blackb* 05-06; R Slyne w Hest and Halton w Aughton from 06. *The Vicarage, Summerfield Drive, Slyne, Lancaster LA2 6AQ* Tel (01524) 822128 E-mail pauline@thebicknells.org
BIDDELL, Canon Christopher David. b 27. Ch Coll Cam BA48 MA52. Ridley Hall Cam 51. **d** 51 **p** 52. C Hornchurch St Andr *Chelmsf* 51-54; Succ S'wark Cathl 54-56; P-in-c Wroxall *Portsm* 56-61; R Bishop's Waltham 62-75; RD Bishop's Waltham 69-74; V Stockport St Geo *Ches* 75-86; Hon Can Ches Cathl 81-86; Can Res 86-93; RD Stockport 85-86; Vice-Dean Ches 91-93; rtd 93; P-in-c Duncton *Chich* 95-98; P-in-c Tillington 95-98; P-in-c Up Waltham 95-98; Perm to Offic from 98. *3 Park Terrace, Tillington, Petworth GU28 9AE* Tel (01798) 342008
BIDDINGTON, Laura Claire. *See* BETSON, Mrs Laura Claire

BIDDINGTON, Terence Eric. b 56. Hull Univ BA77 Trin & All SS Coll Leeds PGCE78 Leeds Univ PhD86 Nottm Univ BTh88 Man Univ MA(Theol)96 MCollP83. Linc Th Coll 85. **d** 88 **p** 89. C Harpenden St Jo *St Alb* 88-90; Chapl Keele Univ 90-93; Freelance Th Educator and Asst Lect Keele Univ 94-99; Assoc Min Betley and Keele 90-93; Asst Dir Cornerstone St Aug *Man* 95-96; Mental Health Advocate Stockport 96-98; Dir and Sen Advocate Stockport MIND from 99; Perm to Offic *Man* 99-01; P-in-c Heaton Norris Ch w All SS 01-02; C Heatons 02-03; Asst Chapl Man Mental Health Partnership 01-03; Chapl Man Univ from 03; Chapl Man Metrop Univ from 03. *St Peter's House, Oxford Road, Manchester M13 9GH* Tel 0161-275 2894 E-mail terry.biddington@manchester.ac.uk
BIDDINGTON, Mrs Wendy Elizabeth. b 51. Cov Univ BSc93 SRN73 SCM74. Qu Coll Birm 07. **d** 09 **p** 10. OLM Wellesbourne *Cov* from 09. *72 Mountford Close, Wellesbourne, Warwick CV35 9QQ* Tel (01789) 840953 E-mail nlb@biddington.spacomputers.com
BIDDLE, Canon Nicholas Lawrence. b 71. K Coll Lon BA94 Leeds Univ MA98. Coll of Resurr Mirfield 96. **d** 98 **p** 99. C Bedford St Andr *St Alb* 98-01; Bp's Dom Chapl and Research Asst *Chich* 01-04; P-in-c Brighton Gd Shep Preston 04-05; TV Putney St Mary *S'wark* 07-10; PV Westmr Abbey 08-10; Can Res Portsm Cathl from 10. *32 Woodville Drive, Portsmouth PO1 2TG* Tel (023) 9234 8139 Mobile 07825-322326 E-mail nicklb@hotmail.co.uk
BIDDLE, Miss Rosemary. b 44. CertEd67. St Jo Coll Dur 76. **dss** 79 **d** 87 **p** 94. Sheldon *Birm* 79-83; Burntwood *Lich* 83-87; Par Dn 87 89; Par Dn Gt Wyrley 89 94; C 94 99; rtd 99; Perm to Offic *Lich* from 00. *8 Brook Lane, Great Wyrley, Walsall WS6 6BQ* Tel (01922) 419032
BIDDLECOMBE, Francis William. b 30. St Mich Coll Llan 57. **d** 59 **p** 60. C Llangynwyd w Maesteg 59-62; C Roath 62-65; V Llanddewi Rhondda w Bryn Eirw 65-71; V Berse and Southsea *St As* 71-79; P-in-c Teme Valley S *Worc* 79-85; rtd 92; Perm to Offic *Heref* and *Worc* from 92. *Four Winds, New Road, Highley, Bridgnorth WV16 6NN* Tel (01746) 861746 E-mail francis@sagainternet.co.uk
BIDE, Mary Elizabeth. b 53. St Anne's Coll Ox BA74 MA78. S Dios Minl Tr Scheme 91. **d** 94 **p** 95. C Gt Bookham *Guildf* 94-98; Year Tutor Dioc Min Course 96-03; P-in-c Frimley Green 98-01; V Frimley Green and Mytchett 02-03; Prec Ch Ch *Ox* 03-07; TR Wimbledon *S'wark* from 07. *The Rectory, 14 Arthur Road, London SW19 7DZ* Tel (020) 8946 2830 or 8946 2605 Fax 8946 6293 E-mail rector.wimbledon@stmaryswimbledon.org
BIDEN, Neville Douglas. b 31. S'wark Ord Course 76. **d** 79 **p** 80. C Ash *Guildf* 79-82; NSM Surbiton St Andr and St Mark *S'wark* 87-91; Chapl Asst Long Grove Hosp Epsom 90-91; C Coulsdon St Jo *S'wark* 91-96; rtd 96; Perm to Offic *Heref* 95-97; *Guildf* from 97; *Win* from 01. *5 Taylor Drive, Bramley, Tadley RG26 5XB* Tel (01256) 880459 E-mail rev.nev@virgin.net
BIDGOOD, Julian Paul. b 71. Sussex Univ BA92. Oak Hill Th Coll BA03. **d** 03 **p** 04. C Ox St Ebbe w H Trin and St Pet 03-08; C Arborfield w Barkham from 08. *22 Church Hams, Finchampstead, Wokingham RG40 4XF* Tel 07779-296511 (mobile) E-mail julianbidgood@hotmail.com
BIELBY, Canon Elaine Elizabeth. b 57. Surrey Univ MSc83. Ripon Coll Cuddesdon 96. **d** 98 **p** 99. C Marton-in-Cleveland *York* 98-01; P-in-c Welton w Melton from 01; Tr Officer E Riding from 01; Dean of Women's Min from 08; Can and Preb York Minster from 10. *St Helen's Vicarage, Cowgate, Welton, Brough HU15 1ND* Tel (01482) 666677 E-mail ebielby@ebielby.karoo.co.uk
BIENFAIT, Alexander. b 61. Hatf Poly BSc86. Sarum & Wells Th Coll BTh94. **d** 94 **p** 95. C Battersea St Luke *S'wark* 94-96; C Clapham Team 96-99; TV Whitstable *Cant* 99-07; P-in-c Biddenden and Smarden from 07. *The Rectory, High Street, Biddenden, Ashford TN27 8AH* Tel (01580) 291454 E-mail alex.bienfait@virgin.net
BIERBAUM, Ms Ruth Anne. b 67. RN89. Trin Coll Bris BA98. **d** 99 **p** 00. C Filey *York* 99-02; C Coxheath, E Farleigh, Hunton, Linton etc *Roch* 02-08; Lead Mental Health Chapl Kent & Medway NHS and Soc Care Partnership Trust from 08. *52 Stag Road, Chatham ME5 8LG* Tel (01634) 670715 or 838944 Mobile 017954-227184 E-mail ruth@bierbaumfreeserve.co.uk or ruth.bierbaum@kmpt.nhs.uk
BIGG, Andrew John. b 82. Jes Coll Ox MPhys05 Leeds Univ BA10 Sheff Univ MA11. Coll of Resurr Mirfield. **d** 11. C Cottingham *York* from 11. *10 Kingtree Avenue, Cottingham HU16 4DS* Tel 07854-706551 (mobile) E-mail bigg.andrew@gmail.com
BIGG, Howard Clive. b 40. Fitzw Coll Cam BA68 MA72. Ridley Hall Cam 73. **d** 74 **p** 75. C Worksop St Jo *S'well* 74-76; Min Can St Alb 76-77; Perm to Offic *Ches* 78-82; *Ely* 82-99 and 01-05; Vice-Prin Romsey Ho Cam 86-89; NSM Cambridge St Benedict *Ely* 99-01; rtd 05; Perm to Offic *Ely* from 08. *55 Hemingford Road, Cambridge CB1 3BY* Tel (01223) 514155 E-mail hcb29@cam.ac.uk

BIGGAR, Prof Nigel John. b 55. Worc Coll Ox BA76 MA88 Chicago Univ AM80 PhD86 Regent Coll Vancouver MCS81. d 90 p 91. Lib Latimer Ho Ox 85-91; Asst Lect Chr Ethics Wycliffe Hall Ox 87-94; Chapl Oriel Coll Ox 90-99; Prof Th Leeds Univ 99-04; Prof Th TCD 04-07; Can Ch Ch Cathl Dublin 05-07; Regius Prof Moral and Past Th Ox Univ from 07; Can Res Ch Ch Ox from 07. *Christ Church, Oxford OX1 1DP* Tel (01865) 276219 E-mail nigel.biggar@chch.ox.ac.uk

BIGGIN, Ronald. b 20. NW Ord Course 70. d 73 p 74. C Thelwall *Ches* 73-79; V 79-87; rtd 87; NSM Lt Leigh and Lower Whitley *Ches* 90-93; Perm to Offic from 93. *12 Wilmslow Crescent, Thelwall, Warrington WA4 2JE* Tel (01925) 261531

BIGGS, David James. b 55. St Jo Coll Auckland LTh82. d 81 p 82. New Zealand 81-86; C Stevenage St Andr and St Geo *St Alb* 86-89; TV Moulsecoomb *Chich* 89-99; C Brighton St Pet w Chpl Royal 99-02; P-in-c 02-09; P-in-c Brighton Chpl Royal from 09; Chapl St Mary's Hall Brighton from 03. *4 Parochial Mews, Princes Street, Brighton BN2 1WF* Tel (01273) 774492 E-mail david@crbtn.freeserve.co.uk

BIGGS, George Ramsay. b 45. Liv Univ BA67 Qu Coll Cam BA73. Westcott Ho Cam 72. d 74 p 75. C Lee St Aug *S'wark* 74-78; TV Eling, Testwood and Marchwood *Win* 78; TV Totton 78-93; V E and Wellow 93-98; V E w W Wellow and Sherfield English 98-11; Hosp Chapl Adv (Bournemouth Adnry) 02-11; rtd 11. *10 Bowerhill Road, Salisbury SP1 3DN* Tel (01722) 329215

BIGGS, Laurence John. b 60. Leeds Univ BSc81. Trin Coll Bris 92. d 94 p 95. C St Alb St Paul *St Alb* 94-99; V Codicote from 99. *The Vicarage, 4 Bury Lane, Codicote, Hitchin SG4 8XT* Tel (01438) 820266 Fax 822007 E-mail lbiggs@enterprise.net

BIGGS, Stewart Richard. b 58. SEITE. d 01 p 02. C Tunbridge Wells St Jas w St Phil *Roch* 01-04; C Tunbridge Wells St Jas 04-05; V St Mary Cray and St Paul's Cray 05-06. *46 Watson Avenue, Chatham ME5 9SN* Tel 07967-979559 (mobile) E-mail revstewb@xalt.co.uk

BIGMORE, Graeme Paul. b 57. Univ of Wales (Cardiff) BTh95. St Mich Coll Llan 89. d 92 p 93. C Cardiff St Jo *Llan* 92-96; Cardiff City Cen Chapl 94-96; C Rhondda 96-98; V Tylorstown w Ynyshir 98-05; V Ynyshir from 05. *The Vicarage, Graig Road, Porth CF39 0NS* Tel (01443) 684148

BIGNELL, Alan Guy. b 39. Lon Univ BA64. Ox NSM Course 78. d 81 p 82. NSM Upton cum Chalvey *Ox* 81-90; NSM Burnham and Slough Deanery 90-10; Perm to Offic from 10. *Little Gidding, 2 Turners Road, Slough SL3 7AN* Tel (01753) 523005 E-mail abignell@waitrose.com

BIGNELL, David Charles. b 41. EMMTC 76. d 79 p 80. C Porchester *S'well* 79-82; V Awsworth w Cossall 82-86; V Edwalton 86-06; Bp's Ecum Officer 84-06; rtd 06; C Nottingham All SS, St Mary and St Pet *S'well* 08-09. *6 Allendale Avenue, Beeston, Nottingham NG9 6AN* Tel 0115-925 0060

BIGWOOD, Kate Elizabeth. *See* ATKINSON, Mrs Kate Bigwood

BILES, David George. b 35. AKC58 Open Univ BA75 Lambeth STh91 Leeds Univ MA96. d 59 p 60. C Cockerton *Dur* 59-62; C Winlaton 62-67; P-in-c Dipton 67-74; R Wolviston 74-89; P-in-c Thirkleby w Kilburn and Bagby *York* 89-90; V 90-00; RD Thirsk 90-91; RD Mowbray 91-00; rtd 00; Perm to Offic *York* from 00 and *Sheff* from 11. *10 King Rudding Close, Riccall, York YO19 6RY* Tel and fax (01757) 248829

BILES, Mrs Kathleen Anne. b 52. Bradf Univ BA74. St Jo Coll Nottm 98. d 04 p 06. C Ch Ch Cathl Stanley Falkland Is from 04. *PO Box 166, 14 Kent Road, Stanley FIQQ 1ZZ, Falkland Islands* Tel and fax (00500) 21897 E-mail kbiles@horizon.co.fk

BILES, Canon Timothy Mark Frowde. b 35. St Mich Coll Llan 60. d 64 p 66. C Middleton St Cross *Ripon* 64-66; Chapl St Fran Sch Hooke 66-72; P-in-c Toller Porcorum w Hooke *Sarum* 72-79; P-in-c Melplash w Mapperton 74-79; P-in-c Beaminster 77-79; TR Beaminster Area 79-00; Can and Preb Sarum Cathl 83-00; RD Beaminster 84-89; rtd 00; Perm to Offic *Sarum* from 01. *36 Hound Street, Sherborne DT9 3AA* Tel (01935) 816247

BILL, Alan. b 29. K Coll Lon BD66 AKC66. d 67 p 68. C St Burstead *Chelmsf* 67-70; TV Thornaby on Tees *York* 71-76; R E Gilling 76-81; V Ormesby 81-91; rtd 91; Perm to Offic *Newc* from 91. *13 Wilmington Close, Tudor Grange, Newcastle upon Tyne NE3 2SF* Tel 0191-242 4467

BILL, Canon Thomas Andrew Graham. b 47. Dur Univ BA76. Cranmer Hall Dur. d 77 p 78. C Penwortham St Mary *Blackb* 77-80; C Torrisholme 80-82; P-in-c Accrington St Pet 82-89; P-in-c Haslingden St Jo Stonefold 82-89; V Skerton St Chad 89-03; R Burnley St Pet 03-11; P-in-c Burnley St Steph 08-11; R Burnley St Pet and St Steph from 11; Hon Can Blackb Cathl from 03. *St Peter's Rectory, 1 Ridge Court, Burnley BB10 3LN* Tel and fax (01282) 413599 E-mail tom@tombill.entadsl.com

BILLAM, John. b 38. St Aid Birkenhead 63. d 66 p 67. C Wellington Ch Ch *Lich* 66-70; P-in-c Colwyn *S & B* 03-08. *Melin y Cwm, Beulah, Llanwrtyd Wells LD5 4TT* Tel (01591) 620493

BILLETT, Canon Anthony Charles. b 56. Bris Univ BEd. Wycliffe Hall Ox 83. d 85 p 86. C Waltham Abbey *Chelmsf* 85-88; C Nor St Pet Mancroft w St Jo Maddermarket 88-91; V Stalham and E

Ruston w Brunstead 91-00; R Stalham, E Ruston, Brunstead, Sutton and Ingham 00-01; R Diss from 01; RD Redenhall from 06; Hon Can Nor Cathl from 10. *The Rectory, 26 Mount Street, Diss IP22 3QG* Tel (01379) 642072 E-mail tbillett@diss26.freeserve.co.uk

BILLETT (née RANDALL), Mrs Elizabeth Nicola. b 55. RGN75 SCM81. EAMTC 94. d 97 p 98. C Loddon, Sisland w Hales and Heckingham *Nor* 97-98; C Loddon, Sisland, Chedgrave, Hardley and Langley 98-01; TV Hempnall from 02. *The Flat, George's House, The Street, Woodton, Bungay NR35 1LZ* Tel (01508) 482366

BILLIN, David Robert. b 55. S Bank Poly BSc77 CEng82 MIET82 MIRSE86 EurIng89. d 06 p 07. NSM Carshalton *S'wark* from 06. *33 Beeches Avenue, Carshalton SM5 3LJ* Tel (020) 8647 5046 Mobile 07946-609387 E-mail davidbillin1955@btinternet.com

BILLIN, Mrs Susan Lynn. b 59. S Bank Univ BSc99 Greenwich Univ CertEd96 RGN82. SEITE 02. d 05 p 06. NSM S Beddington and Roundshaw *S'wark* from 05. *33 Beeches Avenue, Carshalton SM5 3LJ* Tel (020) 8647 5046 E-mail lynn billin@lineone.net

BILLINGHURST, Richard George. b 48. St Jo Coll Cam BA70 MA74 FIA76. Ridley Hall Cam 76. d 79 p 80. C Caverswall *Lich* 79-81; C Cullompton *Ex* 81-84; R Redgrave cum Botesdale w Rickinghall St E 84-92; R Skellingthorpe w Doddington *Linc* from 92; RD Graffoe 94-02. *The Rectory, 50 Lincoln Road, Skellingthorpe, Lincoln LN6 5UY* Tel (01522) 682520 Fax 693330 Mobile 07971-590378 E-mail acorns@clara.co.uk

BILLINGS, Canon Alan Roy. b 42. Em Coll Cam BA65 MA69 Bris Univ PGCE66 Leic Univ MEd75 NY Th Sem DMin87. Linc Th Coll 66. d 68 p 69. C Knighton St Mary Magd *Leic* 68-72; P-in-c Sheff Gillcar St Silas 72-76; V Beighton 76-77; Hd RE Broadway Sch Barnsley 77-81; Perm to Offic 77-81; V Walkley 81-86; Dir Ox Inst for Ch and Soc 86-92; Perm to Offic *Ox* 86-92; Vice-Prin Ripon Coll Cuddesdon 88-92; Prin WMMTC 92-94; V Kendal St Geo *Carl* 94-07; C Grayrigg 06-07; Warden of Readers 96-03; Dir Cen for Ethics and Relig Lanc Univ 00-07; Hon Can Carl Cathl 05-07; rtd 07. *43 Northfield Court, Sheffield S10 1QR* Tel 0114-267 6549 E-mail alanbillingsuk@yahoo.co.uk

BILLINGS, Derek Donald. b 30. Fitzw Ho Cam BA54 MA59. Tyndale Hall Bris 55. d 56 p 57. C Attenborough w Bramcote and Chilwell *S'well* 56-58; R Ashley w Silverley *Ely* 59-66; V Bottisham 66-80; R Houghton w Wyton 80-97; rtd 97; Perm to Offic *Ely* from 97. *The Limes, 59 Cambridge Street, Godmanchester, Huntingdon PE29 2AY* Tel (01480) 414244

BILLINGS, Roger Key. b 41. ACIB. Oak Hill Th Coll BA80. d 80 p 81. C Tunbridge Wells St Jas *Roch* 80-84; V Chatham St Paul w All SS 84-95; V Carterton *Ox* 95-03; TR Brize Norton and Carterton 03-07; AD Witney 03-07; rtd 07; Perm to Offic *Nor* from 07. *Maudville, Norwich Road, Cromer NR27 9JU* Tel (01263) 519055 E-mail rogerb2006@tiscali.com

BILLINGS, Mrs Valerie Ann. b 52. Nottm Trent Univ CertEd02. EMMTC 07. d 09 p 10. NSM Ockbrook *Derby* from 09. *14 Conway Avenue, Borrowash, Derby DE72 3GT* Tel (01332) 726285 E-mail val-billings@excite.com

BILLINGSLEY, Raymond Philip. b 48. FCMA80 Open Univ BA98 DASS98. Qu Coll Birm 87. d 89 p 90. C Yardley St Edburgha *Birm* 89-92; V Ward End 92-96; V Brymbo *St As* 96-04; V Northop from 04. *The Vicarage, Sychdyn Road, Northop, Mold CH7 6AW* Tel (01352) 840235 Mobile 08315-39896 E-mail northopvicarage@hotmail.co.uk

BILLINGTON, Charles Alfred. b 30. St Jo Coll Dur BA55. Coll of Resurr Mirfield 53. d 55 p 56. C Carl H Trin 55-59; CR 59-64; R Man St Aid 64-66; V Gt Crosby St Faith *Liv* 66-72; R Harrold and Carlton w Chellington *St Alb* 72-80; R Tintinhull w Chilthorne Domer, Yeovil Marsh etc *B & W* 80-81; Chapl Leybourne Grange Hosp W Malling 81-85; V Walsden *Wakef* 85-88; R Llanfair Talhaearn and Llansannan etc *St As* 88-97; rtd 97. *5 Sunningdale, Abergele LL22 7UB* Tel (01745) 824563

BILLINGTON, George. b 45. St Jo Coll Nottm 92. d 94 p 95. C Accrington St Jo w Huncoat *Blackb* 94-98; C Whittle-le-Woods 98-00; V Stalmine w Pilling 00-10; rtd 10. *Brookvale, Sterridge Valley, Berrynarnor, Ilfracombe EX34 9TB* E-mail g.billington@btconnect.com

BILLOWES, David. b 20. Chich Th Coll. d 76 p 77. NSM Cowes St Mary *Portsm* 76-91; Chapl St Mary's Hosp Newport 82-91; rtd 91; Perm to Offic *Portsm* 91-06. *3 Greenfields, Gosfield, Halstead CO9 1TR* Tel (01787) 472823

BILLSON, Kevin Michael. b 58. Lon Univ BD81 QTS01. Qu Coll Birm 10. d 11. C Brereton and Rugeley *Lich* from 11. *4 St George Drive, Hednesford, Cannock WS12 0FB* Tel (01543) 426028 Mobile 07941-341911 E-mail kevin.billson@eraith.net

BILNEY, Kenneth Henry. b 25. FBCS. St Deiniol's Hawarden 75. d 75 p 76. Hon C Knighton St Mary Magd *Leic* 75-78; C Leic St Jas 78-80; R Leire w Ashby Parva and Dunton Bassett 80-90; rtd 90; Perm to Offic *Leic* from 90. *20 Ferndale Road, Leicester LE2 6GN* Tel 0116-257 0436

BILSTON, Barbara Bradley. b 35. Man Univ BA58 Essex Univ MA75. EAMTC 96. **d** 97 **p** 98. NSM Bacton w Wyverstone and Cotton *St E* 97-00; NSM Bacton w Wyverstone, Cotton and Old Newton etc 00-04; Asst to RD Stowmarket 04-05; RD from 05. *Boy's Hall, Ward Green, Old Newton, Stowmarket IP14 4EY* Tel and fax (01449) 781253 Mobile 07889-516674
E-mail b.b.bilston@open.ac.uk

BILTON, Canon Paul Michael. b 52. AKC74. St Aug Coll Cant 74. **d** 75 **p** 76. C Skipton Ch Ch *Bradf* 75-79; Ind Chapl *Worc* 79-81; V Greetland and W Vale *Wakef* 81-88; R Mablethorpe w Trusthorpe *Linc* 88-91; V Bradf St Wilfrid Lidget Green 91-04; P-in-c Bradf St Columba w St Andr 00-04; V Bradf St Wilfrid w St Columba from 04; RD Bowling and Horton from 02; Hon Can Bradf Cathl from 04. *St Wilfrid's Vicarage, St Wilfrid's Road, Bradford BD7 2LU* Tel (01274) 572504
E-mail paul.bilton@bradford.anglican.org

BIMSON, Sara Margaret. b 56. St Jo Coll Nottm BA. **d** 03 **p** 04. C Maidstone St Martin *Cant* 03-08; rtd 08; Voc Officer *Cant* 08-10; Perm to Offic from 08. *39 Ivy Lane, Canterbury CT1 1TU* Tel (01227) 760655 E-mail sara-mary@hotmail.co.uk *or* sbimson@diocant.org

BINDING, Ms Frances Mary. b 59. York Univ BA81 Newc Poly PGCE82. WEMTC 98. **d** 02 **p** 03. C Bromyard *Heref* 02-07; TV Worc SE from 07. *33 Aconbury Close, Worcester WR5 1JD* Tel (01905) 763378 E-mail franbinding@lineone.net

BINDOFF, Ms Anna. b 70. Leeds Univ BA94. Ripon Coll Cuddesdon BA97. **d** 98 **p** 99. Asst Chapl New Coll Ox 98-01; Hon C Blackbird Leys *Ox* 98-01; C 01-04. *23 Brook Street, Watlington OX49 5JH* Tel (01491) 613327

BING, Canon Alan Charles. b 56. St Edm Hall Ox BA78 MA91 Ex Univ MA96. Oak Hill Th Coll 89. **d** 91 **p** 92. C Fremington *Ex* 91-94; C-in-c Roundswell CD 94-97; TV Barnstaple 97-99; Chapl N Devon Coll Barnstaple 96-99; P-in-c Ulverston St Mary w H Trin *Carl* 99-04; R from 04; RD Furness from 10; Hon Can Carl Cathl from 09. *The Rectory, 15 Ford Park Crescent, Ulverston LA12 7JR* Tel and fax (01229) 584331

BINGHAM, Mrs Marie Joyce Phyllis. b 27. Glouc Sch of Min 80. **dss** 84 **d** 87 **p** 94. Glouc St Mary de Crypt w St Jo and Ch Ch 84-85; Glouc St Mary de Lode and St Nic 85-87; Hon C 87-95; Hon C Glouc St Mary de Crypt w St Jo and Ch Ch 94-95; Hon C Glouc St Mary de Crypt w St Jo, Ch Ch etc 95-98; Perm to Offic from 98. *Clematis Cottage, 1 Queenwood Grove, Prestbury, Cheltenham GL52 3NG* Tel (01452) 242252

BINGHAM, Norman James Frederick. b 26. Lon Univ BSc51. Tyndale Hall Bris 61. **d** 63 **p** 64. C Chell *Lich* 63-67; C Macclesfield St Mich *Ches* 67-71; P-in-c Macclesfield St Pet 71-73; V Leyton St Mary w St Edw *Chelmsf* 73-81; RD Waltham Forest 81-86; P-in-c Leyton St Luke 82-91; rtd 91; Perm to Offic *St Alb* from 91. *97 Monks Walk, Buntingford SG9 9DP* Tel (01763) 272275

BINKS, Andrew John. b 49. Open Univ BA Leeds Univ MA06. NOC 03. **d** 06 **p** 07. NSM Haslingden w Grane and Stonefold *Blackb* 06-09; NSM Accrington St Jo w Huncoat from 09. *18 Sandown Road, Haslingden, Rossendale BB4 6PL* Tel (01706) 229285 E-mail jmbinks@tiscali.co.uk

BINKS, Canon Edmund Vardy. b 36. K Coll Lon BD61 AKC61 Liv Univ Hon LLD98 FRSA89. **d** 62 **p** 63. C Selby Abbey *York* 62-65; Asst Chapl Univ Coll of Ripon and York St Jo 65-83; Hd St Kath Coll Liv 83-87; Prin Ches Coll of HE 87-98; Hon Can Ches Cathl 95-98; Perm to Offic *Chich* from 98; rtd 01. *2 Lodge Close, Lewes BN7 1AR* Tel (01273) 487136

BINKS, Robert Peter. b 73. Trin Coll Bris 08. **d** 10 **p** 11. C Basildon St Andr w H Cross *Chelmsf* from 10. *57 Halstow Way, Pitsea, Basildon SS13 2NY* Tel (01268) 559722
E-mail rob.binks@me.com

BINLEY, Miss Teresa Mary. b 37. Dalton Ho Bris 61. **d** 87 **p** 94. Par Dn Ashton-upon-Mersey St Mary Magd *Ches* 87-92; Bp's Officer for Women in Min 87-92; C Chaddesden St Mary *Derby* 92-98; rtd 98; Perm to Offic *Derby* from 98. *27 Hindscarth Crescent, Mickleover, Derby DE3 9NN* Tel (01332) 511146

BINNEY, Mark James Gurney. b 58. K Coll Lon BD80. Qu Coll Birm 84. **d** 86 **p** 87. C Hornchurch St Andr *Chelmsf* 86-89; C Hutton 89-91; V Pheasey *Lich* 91-96; TV Wombourne w Trysull and Bobbington 96-99; V Wilnecote 99-08; P-in-c Hampton w Sedgeberrow and Hinton-on-the-Green *Worc* from 08. *St Andrew's Vicarage, 54 Pershore Road, Evesham WR11 2PQ* Tel (01386) 446381
E-mail reverend-mark-binney@hotmail.co.uk

BINNS, Miss Catherine Dorothy. b 70. Univ of Cen England in Birm BSc04 Leeds Univ BA07 RN99. NOC 04. **d** 07 **p** 08. NSM Stand *Man* from 07. *23 Scott Street, Radcliffe, Manchester M26 1EX* Tel (01204) 707922
E-mail cath@chazfrog.fsnet.co.uk

BINNS, David John. b 39. Moore Th Coll Sydney ThL64. **d** 64 **p** 65. Australia 64-67 and from 70; C Norbiton *S'wark* 67-69; R Adelaide St Luke 80-98; Assoc Min 98-00; rtd 00. *Unit 4/2 Spence Avenue, Myrtle Bank SA 5064, Australia* Tel (0061) (8) 8338 5779 Mobile 0417-860560 E-mail djb29@ozemail.com.au

BINNS, Miss Elizabeth Ann. b 55. MBE06. Man Metrop Univ BA87 RGN77. **d** 05 **p** 06. OLM Bury St Jo w St Mark *Man* 05-10; OLM Walmersley Road, Bury from 10. *36 Raymond Avenue, Bury BL9 6NN* Tel 0161-764 5071 Mobile 07976-818157 E-mail elizabethbinns@aol.com

BINNS, Mrs Janet Victoria. b 57. ACIB96. Ox Min Course 04. **d** 07 **p** 08. C Slough *Ox* 07-10; C Eton w Eton Wick, Boveney and Dorney from 10. *209 Stoke Road, Slough SL2 5AX* Tel (01753) 528672 E-mail janet.binns@talktalk.net

BINNS, Canon John Richard Elliott. b 51. St Jo Coll Cam MA76 K Coll Lon PhD89. Coll of Resurr Mirfield 74. **d** 76 **p** 77. C Clapham Old Town *S'wark* 76-80; TV Mortlake w E Sheen 80-87; V Upper Tooting H Trin 87-94; V Cambridge Gt St Mary w St Mich *Ely* from 94; RD Cambridge N 07-11; Hon Can Ely Cathl from 07. *Great St Mary's Vicarage, 39 Madingley Road, Cambridge CB3 0EL* Tel (01223) 355285 *or* 741716 Fax 462914 E-mail jb344@cam.ac.uk

BINNS, Peter Rodney. b 44. St Andr Univ MA66. Ox NSM Course 72. **d** 75 **p** 76. NSM Amersham on the Hill *Ox* 75-90; NSM Wingrave w Rowsham, Aston Abbotts and Cublington 90-97; NSM Hawridge w Cholesbury and St Leonard 90-97; NSM Amersham on the Hill from 97. *16 Turnfurlong Row, Turnfurlong Lane, Aylesbury HP21 7FF* Tel (01296) 330836 Fax 337965

BINNY, John Wallace. b 46. Univ of Wales (Lamp) BA70. St Mich Coll Llan 69. **d** 71 **p** 72. C Llantrisant 71-77; V Troedyrhiw w Merthyr Vale 77-82; R Eglwysbrewis w St Athan, Flemingston, Gileston 82-95; R Eglwysbrewis w St Athan w Gileston 95-03; V Pentyrch w Capel Llanillterne from 03. *The Vicarage, Church Road, Pentyrch, Cardiff CF15 9QF* Tel (029) 2089 0318

BINSLEY, Michael. **d** 09 **p** 10. OLM Yoxall *Lich* from 09. *83 Lightwood Road, Yoxall, Burton-on-Trent DE13 8QE* Tel (01543) 472761

BIRBECK, Anthony Leng. b 33. MBE90. Linc Coll Ox BA59 MA61. Linc Th Coll 58. **d** 60 **p** 61. C Redcar *York* 60-74; Chapl Teesside Ind Miss 62-74; Can Res and Treas Wells Cathl 74-78; NSM Wells St Thos w Horrington 89-98; rtd 98; Perm to Offic *B & W* from 98; RD Shepton Mallet 07-11. *Beeches, Cannard's Grave Road, Shepton Mallet BA4 4LX* Tel (01749) 330382 Mobile 07802-725024 E-mail tonybirbeck@hotmail.co.uk

BIRBECK, John Trevor. b 49. ACIB77. St Jo Coll Nottm 86. **d** 88 **p** 89. C Eccleshill *Bradf* 88-92; V Hurst Green and Mitton 92-93; R Rawmarsh w Parkgate *Sheff* from 03; C Kimberworth from 10; C Greasbrough from 10; C Kimberworth Park from 10. *The Rectory, 2 High Street, Rawmarsh, Rotherham S62 6NE* Tel (01709) 527160 E-mail john.birbeck@ntlworld.com

BIRCH, Barry. b 46. Sheff Univ CertEd69 Lon Univ BA74 MIL84 MCollP85. **d** 06 **p** 07. NSM Cantley *Sheff* 06-08; NSM Eastchurch w Leysdown and Harty *Cant* from 08. *The Rectory, Warden Road, Eastchurch, Sheerness ME12 4EJ* Tel (01795) 880205 Mobile 07711-514671 E-mail barrybirch@hotmail.com

BIRCH, Derek. b 31. Univ of Wales (Lamp) BA58. Coll of Resurr Mirfield 58. **d** 60 **p** 61. C S Elmsall *Wakef* 60-62; C Penistone w Midhope 62-66; V Silkstone 66-89; Chapl Stainborough 76-89; P-in-c Hoyland Swaine 85-89; V Hoylandswaine and Silkstone w Stainborough 89-97; rtd 98; Perm to Offic *Wakef* from 98. *46 Pengeston Road, Penistone, Sheffield S36 6GW* Tel (01226) 761523

BIRCH, Mrs Elizabeth Ann Marie. b 65. Ball Coll Ox BA88 MA05. NTMTC BA06. **d** 06 **p** 07. NSM Pinner *Lon* 06-09; R Wantage Downs *Ox* from 09. *The Rectory, Church Street, East Hendred, Wantage OX12 8LA* Tel (01235) 833235

BIRCH, Graham James. b 62. NOC BTh94. **d** 97 **p** 98. C Southport St Phil and St Paul *Liv* 97-01; P-in-c Wigan St Cath 01-07; V Ainsdale from 07. *The Vicarage, 708 Liverpool Road, Southport PR8 3QE* Tel (01704) 577760
E-mail madrebgra@aol.com

BIRCH, Henry Arthur. b 24. St Jo Coll Dur BA48. Tyndale Hall Bris 48. **d** 49 **p** 50. C Edin St Thos 49-51; C Surbiton Hill Ch Ch *S'wark* 51-54; R Uphill *B & W* 54-69; C-in-c Sylvania Heights Australia 69-77; R 77-81; R Mowbray S Africa 81-84; P-in-c Rose Bay Australia 84-85; R Hurstville 85-90; rtd 90. *12/184 Salisbury Road, Camperdown NSW 2050, Australia*

BIRCH, Mark Russell. b 70. Bris Univ BVSc93 Em Coll Cam BA99. Westcott Ho Cam 97. **d** 00 **p** 01. C Cirencester *Glouc* 00-03; Chapl and Fell Ex Coll Ox 03-06; Chapl Helen and Douglas Ho Ox 06-10; Chapl Treloar Coll Alton from 10. *Treloar College, Holybourne, Alton GU34 4GL* Tel (01420) 547400 Fax 542708

BIRCH, Richard Arthur. b 51. Brighton Poly BSc73 Chelsea Coll Lon MSc76. SEITE 98. **d** 01 **p** 02. NSM Foord St Jo *Cant* 01-04; NSM Hawkinge w Acrise and Swingfield 04-07; NSM Hythe 07-08; NSM Doddington, Newnham and Wychling from 08. *The Vicarage, The Street, Doddington, Sittingbourne ME9 0BH* Tel (01795) 886265 E-mail richarda.birch@btinternet.com

BIRCH, Shirley Anne. b 34. EMMTC 88. **d** 91 **p** 94. Hon Par Dn Melton Gt Framland *Leic* 91-93; NSM Melton Mowbray 93-01; NSM Minster-in-Sheppey *Cant* 02-09; rtd 09. *St Peter's House, 2*

St Peter's Close, Minster on Sea, Sheerness ME12 3DD Tel (01795) 662399 E-mail shirley@stpeters02.freeserve.co.uk

BIRCH, Thomas Reginald. b 33. AKC57. St Boniface Warminster 67. **d** 68. C Basildon St Andr CD *Chelmsf* 68-69; Ind Chapl 69-88; rtd 88. *29 Muspole Street, Norwich NR3 1DJ* Tel (01603) 631446

BIRCHALL, John Dearman. b 70. St Andr Univ MA93. Wycliffe Hall Ox BTh99. **d** 99 **p** 00. C Purley Ch Ch *S'wark* 99-02; C Fisherton Anger *Sarum* 02-08; V Surbiton Hill Ch Ch *S'wark* from 08. *Christ Church Vicarage, 7 Christ Church Road, Surbiton KT5 8JJ* Tel (020) 8399 3733 *or* 8390 7215 E-mail john.birchall@ccsurbiton.org

BIRCHALL, Robert Gary. b 59. Sheff Univ BA81. St Jo Coll Nottm 85. **d** 88 **p** 89. C Manston *Ripon* 88-91; C Leic Martyrs 91-94; C New Humberstone 94-95; V Burnopfield *Dur* from 95; AD Lanchester from 06. *The Vicarage, Front Street, Burnopfield, Newcastle upon Tyne NE16 6HQ* Tel (01207) 270261 E-mail gary.birchall@dsl.pipex.com

BIRCHARD, Canon Thaddeus Jude. b 45. Louisiana State Univ BA66. Kelham Th Coll 66. **d** 70 **p** 71. C Devonport St Mark Ford *Ex* 70-73; C Southend St Jo w St Mark, All SS w St Fran etc *Chelmsf* 73-76; TV Poplar *Lon* 76-80; V Paddington St Jo w St Mich 80-01; Hon Can Louisiana from 90; rtd 01; Perm to Offic *Lon* from 02. *142 Dibdin House, Maida Vale, London W9 1QG* Tel (020) 7328 2380 E-mail thaddeus@birchard.co.uk

BIRD, Mrs Ann Maud. b 39. **d** 00 **p** 01. OLM W Bromwich All SS *Lich* from 00. *16 Caldwell Street, West Bromwich B71 2DN* Tel 0121-588 4335

BIRD (née BAKER), Mrs Anne-Marie Clare. b 56. Wye Coll Lon BSc78 Glas Univ MSc80. St Jo Coll Nottm 88. **d** 90 **p** 94. Par Dn Levenshulme St Pet *Man* 90-94; C 94-95; P-in-c Crumpsall 95-03; TV Keynsham *B & W* 03-05; rtd 05; Perm to Offic *B & W* from 05. *26 Culvers Road, Keynsham, Bristol BS31 2DW* Tel 0117-904 8585 E-mail pjbird@blueyonder.co.uk

BIRD, Anthony Peter. b 31. St Jo Coll Ox BA54 BTh55 MA57 Birm Univ MB, ChB70. Cuddesdon Coll 55. **d** 57 **p** 58. C Stafford St Mary *Lich* 57-60; Chapl Cuddesdon Coll 60-61; Vice-Prin 61-64; C Selly Oak St Wulstan *Birm* 64-68; Lic to Offic 68-79; Prin Qu Coll Birm 74-79; Perm to Offic *Birm* from 85. *93 Bournbrook Road, Birmingham B29 7BX*

BIRD, Brian Edward. b 37. Rhodes Univ BA. **d** 75. S Africa 75-99 and from 08; Bp's C Mt Merrion *D & D* 99-05; rtd 05. *17 Hillcrest, League Street, Telfin Heights, Knysna, 6570 South Africa* E-mail brian_bird23@hotmail.com

BIRD, The Very Revd David John. b 46. St D Coll Lamp BA70 Duquesne Univ PhD87. Gen Th Sem (USA) STM74. **d** 70 **p** 71. C Kidderminster St Geo *Worc* 70-72; USA from 72; Chapl Trin Sch New York 72-78; V Rochdale Ch Ch 78-79; R New Kensington St Andr 79-89; R Washington Grace Ch 89-03; Dean Trin Cathl San Jose from 03. *Trinity Cathedral, 81 North 2nd Street, San Jose, CA 95113-1205, USA* Tel (001) (408) 293 7953 Fax 293 4993 E-mail david3933@aol.com

BIRD, Canon David Ronald. b 55. York Univ BA76. St Jo Coll Nottm 83. **d** 86 **p** 87. C Kinson *Sarum* 86-90; R Thrapston *Pet* 90-97; P-in-c Islip 94-95; RD Higham 94-97; V Northampton St Giles from 97; Can Pet Cathl from 01. *St Giles's Vicarage, 2 Spring Gardens, Northampton NN1 1LX* Tel (01604) 634060 Fax 628623 E-mail drbird@talktalk.net

BIRD, Douglas Norman. b 38. **d** 92 **p** 93. OLM New Bury *Man* 92-06; Perm to Offic *Blackb* and *Man* from 06. *4 Oak Avenue, Horwich, Bolton BL6 6JE* Tel (01204) 695916

BIRD, Canon Frederick Hinton. b 38. St Edm Hall Ox BA62 MA66 Univ of Wales MEd81 PhD86. St D Coll Lamp BD65. **d** 65 **p** 66. C Mynyddislwyn *Mon* 65-67; Min Can St Woolos Cathl 67-70; Chapl Anglo-American Coll Farringdon 70-71; Perm to Offic *Ox* 70-78; Cant 72-78 and *Mon* 76-82; V Rushen *S & M* 82-03; Can St German's Cathl 93-03; rtd 03; Perm to Offic *S & M* from 04. *Conrhenny, 56 Selborne Drive, Douglas, Isle of Man IM2 3NL* Tel (01624) 621624

BIRD, Geoffrey. b 44. Dioc OLM tr scheme 97. **d** 99 **p** 00. Asst Chapl HM YOI and Remand Cen Brinsford 99; Sen Chapl 99-04; Chapl HM Pris Shepton Mallet 04-09; rtd 09. *2 Hosey Road, Sturminster Newton DT10 1QP* Tel (01258) 472904

BIRD, Henry John Joseph. b 37. ARCO58 Qu Coll Cam BA59 MA63. Linc Th Coll 62. **d** 64 **p** 65. C Harbledown *Cant* 64-68; C Skipton H Trin *Bradf* 68-70; V Oakworth 70-81; Chapl Abingdon Sch 81-82; P-in-c Doncaster St Geo *Sheff* 82-85; V 85-02; rtd 02. *332 Thorne Road, Doncaster DN2 5AL* Tel (01302) 365589

BIRD, Hinton. *See* BIRD, Canon Frederick Hinton

BIRD, Hugh Claud Handley. b 24. FRCGP SS Coll Cam MA MB BCh. Ridley Hall Cam. **d** 86 **p** 86. NSM Coxheath w E Farleigh, Hunton and Linton *Roch* 86-95; Perm to Offic *Cant* from 95. *The Slate Barn, Seamark Road, Brooksend, Birchington CT7 0JL* Tel (01843) 846619

BIRD, Ian Nicholas. b 62. Qu Eliz Coll Lon BSc83 Newc Univ PhD87 Heythrop Coll Lon MA10. SAOMC 03. **d** 06 **p** 07. C Chandler's Ford *Win* 06-10; V from 10. *The Vicarage, 30 Hursley Road, Chandler's Ford, Eastleigh SO53 2FT* Tel (023) 8025 4739 Mobile 07733-213535 E-mail ianbird@parishofchandlersford.org.uk

BIRD, Jeffrey David. b 54. Nottm Univ BCombStuds85. Linc Th Coll 82. **d** 85 **p** 86. C Frome St Jo *B & W* 85-88; Asst Chapl HM Pris Pentonville 88-89; Chapl HM Pris Dartmoor 89-95; Chapl HM Pris Albany 95-03; Chapl HM Pris Linc 03-07; Chapl HM Pris Stafford from 07. *HM Prison, 54 Gaol Road, Stafford ST16 3AW* Tel (01785) 773000 Fax 773001

BIRD, Jeremy Paul. b 56. Ex Univ BSc77 Hull Univ MA88. Sarum Th Coll 78. **d** 80 **p** 81. C Tavistock and Gulworthy *Ex* 80-83; Chapl Teesside Poly *York* 83-88; R Chipstable w Huish Champflower and Clatworthy *B & W* 88-93; Rural Affairs Officer 88-93; V Uffculme *Ex* 93-01; P-in-c Dawlish 01-09; P-in-c Exwick from 09. *The Vicarage, Exwick Hill, Exeter EX4 2AQ* Tel (01392) 255500 E-mail jerry@credamus.freeserve.co.uk

BIRD, John. *See* BIRD, Henry John Joseph

BIRD, John Anthony. b 45. EMMTC 00. **d** 03 **p** 04. NSM Thringstone St Andr *Leic* 03-09; NSM Whitwick and Swannington 07-09; NSM Whitwick, Thringstone and Swannington 09-11; NSM Shepshed and Oaks in Charnwood from 11. *8 Buckingham Drive, Loughborough LE11 4TE* Tel (01509) 234962 E-mail curate.thringstone@tiscali.co.uk

BIRD, Mrs Margaret Kathleen. b 48. SAOMC 04. **d** 06 **p** 07. NSM Cox Green *Ox* 06-10; NSM New Windsor from 10. *73 Alma Road, Windsor SL4 3HD* Tel (01753) 315397 Mobile 07881-712611 E-mail margaret.bird@talktalk.net

BIRD, Nicholas William Randle. b 70. Univ of Cen England in Birm BSc99 RGN92. NEOC 02. **d** 05 **p** 06. C Thirsk *York* 05-09; P-in-c Dunnington from 09; P-in-c Stockton-on-the-Forest w Holtby and Warthill from 09. *The Rectory, 30 Church Street, Dunnington, York YO19 5PW* Tel (01904) 489349 E-mail frnick.bird@btinternet.com

BIRD, Norman David. b 32. CQSW73. Coll of Resurr Mirfield 87. **d** 89 **p** 90. NSM Willesden Green St Andr and St Fran *Lon* 89-92; NSM Preston Ascension 93-98; rtd 98; Perm to Offic *Lon* from 99. *5 Oldfield Road, London NW10 9UD* Tel (020) 8451 4160

BIRD, Canon Peter Andrew. b 40. Wadh Coll Ox BA62 MA68. Ridley Hall Cam 63. **d** 65 **p** 66. C Keynsham w Queen Charlton *B & W* 65-68; C Strood St Nic *Roch* 68-72; TV Strood 72-79; V S Gillingham 79-89; V Westerham 89-02; Hon Can Roch Cathl 01-02; Perm to Offic *Roch* 02-05 and *Derby* from 05. *Iona, Prospect Terrace, Stanedge Road, Bakewell DE45 1DG* Tel (01629) 813508

BIRD, Canon Roger Alfred. b 49. AKC72. St Aug Coll Cant 72. **d** 73 **p** 74. C Prestatyn *St As* 73-78; R Llandysilio and Penrhos and Llandrinio etc 78-92; Dioc RE Adv from 84; Dioc Dir of Educn from 89; R Guilsfield 92-97; R Guilsfield w Pool Quay 97-02; V Guilsfield w Buttington from 02; Hon Can St As Cathl from 93; RD Pool 96-01 and 07-10. *The New Vicarage, Guilsfield, Welshpool SY21 9NF* Tel and fax (01938) 554245 E-mail rogerb_790@fsmail.net

BIRDSEYE, Miss Jacqueline Ann. b 55. Sussex Univ BEd78 Southn Univ BTh88 K Coll Lon MTh93. Sarum & Wells Th Coll 85. **d** 88 **p** 94. C Egham Hythe *Guildf* 88-91; C Fleet 91-92; C Shottermill 92-95; C Leavesden *St Alb* 95-98; R Knaphill w Hinxworth and Newnham 98-05; R Moreton and Woodsford w Tincleton *Sarum* from 05. *The Rectory, 17 Warmwell Road, Crossways, Dorchester DT2 8BS* Tel (01305) 854046

BIRDWOOD, William Halhed. b 51. St Jo Coll Dur BA73. Sarum & Wells Th Coll 76. **d** 78 **p** 79. C Royston *St Alb* 78-82; C Thorley w Bishop's Stortford H Trin 82-89; Chapl HM Pris Ex 89-96; Chapl HM Pris Dartmoor from 96; Lic to Offic *Ex* from 89. *HM Prison Dartmoor, Princetown, Yelverton PL20 6RR* Tel (01822) 890261 Fax 890679

BIRKENHEAD, Suffragan Bishop of. *See* SINCLAIR, The Rt Revd Gordon Keith

BIRKETT, Christine Joy. b 53. Univ of Wales (Cardiff) BTheol99 PGCE02. Trin Coll Bris 07. **d** 08 **p** 09. NSM Berkeley w Wick, Breadstone, Newport, Stone etc *Glouc* 08-10; NSM Cainscross w Selsley from 10. *The House, Middle Street, Uplands, Stroud GL5 1TH* Tel 07962-304018 (mobile) E-mail cjoyb1953@yahoo.co.uk

BIRKETT, Mrs Joyce. b 38. WMMTC 84. **d** 87 **p** 94. Par Dn Hill *Birm* 87-91; Asst Chapl Highcroft Hosp Birm 87-91; Par Dn Rowley Regis *Birm* 91-94; C 94-96; V Londonderry 96-01; rtd 01; Perm to Offic *Birm* from 01. *83 Callowbrook Lane, Rubery, Rednal, Birmingham B45 9HP* Tel 0121-457 9759

BIRKETT, Mrs Julie Anne. b 56. SWMTC. **d** 10 **p** 11. NSM Hutton and Locking *B & W* from 10. *19 Stanhope Road, Weston-super-Mare BS23 4LP* Tel (01934) 625587 E-mail rebelrevd@gmail.com

BIRKETT, Neil Warren. b 45. Lanc Univ BEd74 Southn Univ MA84. Kelham Th Coll 65. **d** 77 **p** 77. NSM Win St Matt from 77. *Corrymeela, 132 Teg Down Meads, Winchester SO22 5NS* Tel (01962) 864919

BIRKIN, Mrs Elspeth Joyce (Joy). b 36. CertEd58. WMMTC 95. **d** 96 **p** 97. NSM Hanley Castle, Hanley Swan and Welland *Worc*

96-01; NSM Berrow w Pendock, Eldersfield, Hollybush etc 01-04; Perm to Offic from 04. *9 Hastings Road, Malvern WR14 2SS* Tel (01684) 569493

BIRKINSHAW, Ian George. b 58. Pemb Coll Ox BA81 Leeds Univ MA97 Sheff Univ PGCE82. NOC 93. **d** 96 **p** 97. NSM Chapeltown *Sheff* 96-97; C Normanton *Wakef* 98-01; C York St Mich-le-Belfrey 01-08; TR Huntington 08-10; R from 10. *The Rectory, Chestnut Court, Huntington, York YO32 9RD* Tel (01904) 766550 *or* 768160

BIRMINGHAM, Archdeacon of. *See* OSBORNE, The Ven Hayward John

BIRMINGHAM, Bishop of. *See* URQUHART, The Rt Revd David Andrew

BIRMINGHAM, Dean of. *See* OGLE, The Very Revd Catherine

BIRNIE, Ms Ruth Burdett. b 41. Glas Univ MA64 Jordanhill Coll Glas PGCE65 Leeds Univ MA73. NEOC 02. **d** 04 **p** 05. NSM Gosforth All SS *Newc* from 04. *27 Delaval Terrace, Newcastle upon Tyne NE3 4RT* Tel 0191-284 1393 E-mail ruth@birnie27.fsnet.co.uk

BIRT, David Edward. b 26. St Steph Ho Ox 86. **d** 86 **p** 87. NSM Ealing Ch the Sav *Lon* 86-99; Perm to Offic from 99. *10 Manor Court Road, London W7 3EL* Tel (020) 8579 4871

BIRT, Patrick. b 34. Glouc Th Course 71. **d** 75 **p** 75. NSM Bisley *Glouc* 75-76; NSM Whiteshill 76-81; C Stroud H Trin 81; R Ruardean 81-86; V Newbridge-on-Wye and Llanfihangel Brynpabuan *S & B* 86-88; TV Gillingham *Sarum* 88-99; rtd 99; Perm to Offic *Sarum* from 01. *Hornbeam Cottage, Green Lane, Stour Row, Shaftesbury SP7 0QD* Tel (01747) 839716

BIRT, Richard Arthur. b 43. Ch Ch Ox BA66 MA69 Cuddesdon Coll 67. **d** 69 **p** 70. C Sutton St Mich *York* 69-71; C Wollaton S'well 71-75; R Kirkby in Ashfield 75-80; P-in-c Duxford *Ely* 80-87; R 87-88; P-in-c Hinxton 80-87; V 87-88; P-in-c Ickleton 80-87; V 87-88; V Weobley w Sarnesfield and Norton Canon *Heref* 88-00; P-in-c Letton w Staunton, Byford, Mansel Gamage etc 88-00; rtd 00; Perm to Offic *Heref* from 00. *7 Great Western Court, Canonmoor Street, Hereford HR4 9YA* Tel (01432) 360804

BIRTWISTLE, Canon James. b 33. FCA66. Ely Th Coll 57. **d** 59 **p** 60. C Southport St Luke *Liv* 59-63; V Cleator Moor w Cleator *Carl* 63-70; R Letchworth *St Alb* 70-73; P-in-c Wareside 73-80; Dep Dir of Educn 77-80; Dioc Dir of Educn 80-98; Hon Can St Alb 85-98; P-in-c Hertingfordbury 88-98; rtd 98; Perm to Offic *Ex* from 99. *9 Stoneborough Lane, Budleigh Salterton EX9 6HL* Tel (01395) 442517

BIRTWISTLE, Lesley Sutherland. b 44. LLB. EMMTC 00. **d** 00 **p** 01. NSM Appleby Gp *Leic* 00-07; NSM Measham 07-08; NSM Packington w Normanton-le-Heath 07-08; NSM Donisthorpe and Moira w Stretton-en-le-Field 07-08; NSM Woodfield from 08. *14 Nethercroft Drive, Packington, Ashby-de-la-Zouch LE65 1WT* Tel (01530) 413309 E-mail lesley@bwistle.f9.co.uk

BISASO-SEKITOLEKO, Capt Samuel. b 66. Cheltenham & Glouc Coll of HE BA99. St Paul's Coll Limuru. **d** 99 **p** 02. NSM Matson *Glouc* 99; NSM Ponders End St Matt *Lon* 01-02; NSM Brownswood Park 02-06; Chapl Miss to Seafarers from 06. *24 Victoria Road, Keelby, Grimsby DN41 8EH* Tel 07944-800605 (mobile) E-mail sambisaso@aol.com

BISCOE, Clive. b 45. St Deiniol's Hawarden 85. **d** 86 **p** 87. C Llansamlet *S & B* 86-90; V Landore 90-91. *6 Hazelwood Row, Cwmavon, Port Talbot SA12 9DP*

BISCOE, Ian Rowland. b 68. Ox Min Course 06. **d** 07 **p** 08. C Cherwell Valley *Ox* from 07. *9 Soden Road, Upper Heyford, Bicester OX25 5LR* Tel (01869) 232439 Mobile 07971-529234 E-mail ian.biscoe@googlemail.com

BISH, Donald. b 26. Ripon Hall Ox. **d** 75 **p** 75. C S Gillingham *Roch* 75-79; R Wateringbury w Teston and W Farleigh 79-92; rtd 92; Perm to Offic *Cant* 92-09; *Roch* 92-98 and 00-04. *5 Eynesford Road, Allington, Maidstone ME16 0TD* Tel (01622) 661847

BISHOP, Mrs Alice Margaret Marion. b 67. Newnham Coll Cam BA89 MA93 Lon Univ MTh92. St Steph Ho Ox 92. **d** 94. C Stepney St Dunstan and All SS *Lon* 94-99. *The Vicarage, Church Lane, Old Basing, Basingstoke RG24 7DJ* Tel (01256) 473762

BISHOP, Andrew Scott. b 70. Leeds Univ BA93 Heythrop Coll Lon MTh02. St Steph Ho Ox BTh93. **d** 96 **p** 97. C Westmr St Steph w St Jo *Lon* 96-99; C Kensington St Mary Abbots w St Geo 99-03; V Old Basing and Lychpit *Win* from 03; AD Basingstoke 08-11. *The Vicarage, Church Lane, Old Basing, Basingstoke RG24 7DJ* Tel (01256) 473762 E-mail as.bishop@tiscali.co.uk

BISHOP, Canon Anthony John. b 43. G&C Coll Cam BA66 MA69 Lon Univ MTh69. ALCD67. **d** 69 **p** 70. C Eccleston St Luke *Liv* 69-73; C Gt Baddow *Chelmsf* 73-77; CMS Nigeria 77-84; Lect Lon Bible Coll 84-85; TV Chigwell *Chelmsf* 85-93; P-in-c Walthamstow St Jo 93-98; V 98-09; Hon Can Kano from 00. *7 High Meadows, Chigwell IG7 5JY* Tel (020) 8501 4998 E-mail tony.bishop@talktalk.net

BISHOP, The Ven Anthony Peter. b 46. CB01. Nottm Univ MPhil84 ALCD71 FRSA87. St Jo Coll Nottm 71. **d** 71 **p** 72. C Beckenham St Geo *Roch* 71-75; Chapl RAF 75-91; Command Chapl RAF 91-98; Chapl-in-Chief RAF 98-01; Can and Preb Linc Cathl 98-01; Hon C Tewkesbury w Walton Cardiff and Twyning *Glouc* 01-03; C 03-06; rtd 06. *La Croix Blanche, 50810 St Germain d'Elle, France*

BISHOP, Canon Christopher. b 48. St Aug Coll Cant 71. **d** 72 **p** 73. C Gt Ilford St Mary *Chelmsf* 72-75; C Upminster 75-78; Adn's Youth Chapl 77-80; Dioc Youth Officer 80-86; Chapl Stansted Airport from 86; P-in-c Manuden w Berden 86-03; P-in-c Manuden w Berden and Quendon w Rickling from 03; RD Newport and Stansted from 89; Hon Can Chelmsf Cathl from 99. *The Vicarage, 24 Mallows Green Road, Manuden, Bishops Stortford CM23 1DG* Tel (01279) 812228 E-mail chrismitre@hotmail.com

BISHOP, Craig. *See* BISHOP, Stephen Craig

BISHOP, David. b 65. St Jo Coll Nottm 01. **d** 03 **p** 04. C Boulton *Derby* 03-07; V Ogley Hay *Lich* from 07. *St James's Vicarage, 37 New Road, Brownhills, Walsall WS8 6AT* Tel (01543) 372187 *or* 373251

BISHOP, David Henry Ryder. b 27. MRAC50. Tyndale Hall Bris 54. **d** 57 **p** 58. C Sevenoaks St Nic *Roch* 57-59; C Branksome St Clem *Sarum* 59-63; Chapl Jinja Uganda 64-67; Dep Sec CCCS 68; R Ox St Clem 69-91; Zimbabwe 91-93; rtd 93; Perm to Offic *Ox* from 99. *40 Old High Street, Headington, Oxford OX3 9HN* Tel (01865) 760099 E-mail david@bishox.go-plus.net

BISHOP, Donald. b 22. Lon Univ BSc48. Qu Coll Birm 56. **d** 57 **p** 58. C Trowbridge H Trin *Sarum* 57-60; CF (TA) 58-68; V Bodicote *Ox* 60-87, P-in-c Broughton 71-83, rtd 87, Perm to Offic *Cov* 87-01 and *Wakef* from 01. *17 Westminster Road, Halifax HX3 8DH* Tel (01422) 200844

BISHOP, Mrs Evelyn Joy. b 43. **d** 01 **p** 02. NSM Penkridge *Lich* 01-04; NSM Baswich from 04. *21 Farmdown Road, Stafford ST17 0AP* Tel (01785) 603074

BISHOP, Huw Daniel. b 49. Univ of Wales (Lamp) BA71. Bp Burgess Hall Lamp 71. **d** 73 **p** 74. C Carmarthen St Pet *St D* 73-77; Prov Youth Chapl Wales 77-79; V Llanybydder and Llanwnog w Llanwnnen 79-80; Youth and Community Officer 80-81; Hd RS Carre's Gr Sch Sleaford 81-85; Hd RS K Sch Pet 85-91; Assoc Hd Teacher St Pet Colleg Sch Wolv 91-98; Hd Teacher St Teilo's High Sch Cardiff 98-01; Prin St Pet Colleg Sch Wolv from 01; CF (TA) from 85; Asst Dioc Dir of Educn *Lich* from 10. *St Peter's Collegiate School, Compton Road West, Wolverhampton WV3 9DU* Tel (01902) 558600

BISHOP, The Ven Ian Gregory. b 62. Portsm Poly BSc84 MRICS87. Oak Hill Th Coll BA91. **d** 91 **p** 92. C Purley Ch Ch S'wark 91-95; P-in-c Saxlingham Nethergate and Shotesham *Nor* 95-97; TR Newton Flotman, Swainsthorpe, Tasburgh, etc 98-01; V Middlewich w Byley *Ches* 01-11; RD Middlewich 05-10; Adn Macclesfield from 11. *57A Sandbach Road, Congleton CW12 4LH* Tel 07715-102519 (mobile) E-mail ian.bishop@chester.anglican.org

BISHOP, Jeffrey Paul. b 67. Texas A&M Univ BA88 MD93 Dallas Univ MTh00. **d** 99 **p** 00. C Dallas Incarnation USA 99-05; Perm to Offic *Ex* 05-06; PV Ex Cathl 06-07; USA from 07. *1106 Lawrence Avenue, Nashville TN 37204, USA* Tel (001) (615) 942 7074

BISHOP, Jeremy Simon. b 54. Nottm Univ BSc75 Yonsei Univ S Korea 84. All Nations Chr Coll 82 Wycliffe Hall Ox 89. **d** 91 **p** 92. C Macclesfield Team *Ches* 91-98; R Carlton Colville w Mutford and Rushmere *Nor* 98-99; V Carlton Colville and Mutford from 99. *The Rectory, Rectory Road, Carlton Colville, Lowestoft NR33 8BB* Tel (01502) 565217 E-mail jbishop771@aol.com

BISHOP, John Charles Simeon. b 46. Chich Th Coll 77. **d** 79 **p** 79. SSF 66-86; P-in-c Edin St Dav 82-86; Chapl to the Deaf *Birm* 86-99; C Portsea N End St Mark *Portsm* 99-01; Chapl to the Deaf *Linc* 01-11; rtd 11. *7 Rowley Drive, Ushaw Moor, Durham DH7 7QR* Tel 0191-373 0205 E-mail jcsbishop@btinternet.com

BISHOP, John David. b 36. Liv Univ BEng MIMechE. EMMTC. **d** 85 **p** 86. NSM Ockbrook *Derby* 85-07; Perm to Offic from 07. *143 Victoria Avenue, Borrowash, Derby DE7 3HF* Tel (01332) 663828

BISHOP, Kathleen Rachel. b 51. Open Univ BA88 Saffron Walden Coll CertEd76. ERMC 05. **d** 08 **p** 09. NSM Raddesley Gp *Ely* from 08. *4 The Woodlands, Linton, Cambridge CB21 4UF* Tel (01223) 892288 E-mail michael.bishop@virgin.net

BISHOP, Keith William. b 64. SEITE 00. **d** 03 **p** 04. NSM Balham St Mary and St Jo *S'wark* 03-07; NSM Clapham Common St Barn from 07. *43 Magdalen Road, London SW18 3ND* Tel (020) 8870 7267 E-mail keithwilliambishop@hotmail.com

BISHOP, Mark Andrew. b 58. Down Coll Cam BA80 MA83 Barrister 81. EAMTC 99. **d** 02 **p** 03. Dep Chan *Roch* from 01; NSM Cambridge St Mary Less *Ely* from 02. *10 Wordsworth Grove, Cambridge CB3 9HH* Tel (01223) 362281 E-mail mark.bishop@btinternet.com

BISHOP, Mark Christopher. b 81. Sheff Hallam Univ BA03. **d** 08 **p** 09. C Oak Tree Angl Fellowship *Lon* 08-11; Lic to Offic from 11. *32 Hereford Road, London W3 9JW* Tel 07779-585105 (mobile) E-mail revmarkbishop@gmail.com

BISHOP, Philip Michael. b 47. Lon Univ BD69 AKC69. St Aug Coll Cant 70. **d** 71 **p** 72. C Mansfield Woodhouse *S'well* 71-76; C Liscard St Mary w St Columba *Ches* 76-78; V Thornton-le-Moors w Ince and Elton 78-90; V Sutton w Carlton and Normanton upon Trent etc *S'well* 90-96; P-in-c Ch Broughton w Barton Blount, Boylestone etc *Derby* 96-98; P-in-c Longford, Long Lane, Dalbury and Radbourne 96-98; R Boylestone, Church Broughton, Dalbury, etc from 98. *The Vicarage, Chapel Lane, Church Broughton, Derby DE65 5BB* Tel (01283) 585296 E-mail rev@michael.bishop.name

BISHOP, Phillip Leslie. b 44. K Coll Lon BD66 AKC66. **d** 67 **p** 68. C Albrighton *Lich* 67-70; C St Geo-in-the-East St Mary *Lon* 70-71; C Middlesbrough Ascension *York* 71-73; P-in-c Withernwick 73-77; Ind Chapl 73-82; V Gt Ayton w Easby and Newton-in-Cleveland 82-89; RD Stokesley 85-89; R Guisborough 89-08; Chapl S Tees Community and Mental NHS Trust 90-99; Chapl Tees and NE Yorks NHS Trust 99-08; Chapl Langbaurgh Primary Care Trust 02-08; rtd 08; Perm to Offic *York* from 08. *2 Sunny Side Grove, Stockton-on-Tees TS18 5DH* Tel (01642) 582281

BISHOP, Roger John. b 49. SEITE 06. **d** 09 **p** 10. NSM Lamberhurst and Matfield *Roch* from 09. *Brambletye, Maidstone Road, Five Oak Green, Tonbridge TN12 6QR* Tel (01892) 833232 E-mail rogerjbishop@hotmail.com

BISHOP, Simeon. *See* BISHOP, John Charles Simeon

BISHOP, Stephen Craig. b 68. Wye Coll Lon BSc90 Man Univ MA92 Ex Univ MPhil97 Glos Univ PGCE98. Wycliffe Hall Ox 03. **d** 05 **p** 06. C Thornbury and Oldbury-on-Severn w Shepperdine *Glouc* 05-09; TV Fairford Deanery from 09. *The Vicarage, Coln St Aldwyns, Cirencester GL7 5AG* Tel (01285) 750013 E-mail scraigbishop@hotmail.com

BISHOP, Stephen John. b 62. Hull Univ BA84 PGCE86. Ripon Coll Cuddesdon 90 Ch Div Sch of the Pacific (USA) 90. **d** 92 **p** 93. C Syston *Leic* 92-95; C Market Harborough 95-97; TV Market Harborough and The Transfiguration etc 97-00; R Six Saints circa Holt from 00; Rural Officer (Leic Adnry) from 01. *The Rectory, Rectory Lane, Medbourne, Market Harborough LE16 8DZ* Tel (01858) 565933 E-mail stephenjbishop@btopenworld.com

BISHOP, Stephen Patrick. b 60. Dioc OLM tr scheme 99. **d** 02 **p** 03. OLM Purley Ch Ch *S'wark* from 02. *Elmwood, 117 Mitchley Avenue, South Croydon CR2 9HP* Tel (020) 8651 2840 *or* 7337 3135 E-mail elmwood@tinyonline.co.uk

BISHOP, Miss Waveney Joyce. b 38. Westf Coll Lon BSc60. Cranmer Hall Dur. **dss** 82 **d** 87 **p** 94. Leyton St Mary w St Edw *Chelmsf* 82-84; Bishopsworth *Bris* 84-96; Hon Par Dn 87-94; Hon C 94-96; rtd 96; Perm to Offic *Bris* 96-99 and *B &W* from 98. *14 Saxby Close, Clevedon BS21 7YF* Tel (01275) 343533

BISIG (*née* BOULNOIS)**, Linda Dianne.** b 59. Trin Coll Bris 92. **d** 96 **p** 97. C Brampton Bierlow *Sheff* 96-99; Asst Chapl Berne w Neuchâtel *Eur* from 00. *Jubiläumsplatz 2, CH-3066 Bern, Switzerland* Tel (0041) (31) 352 8567 Fax 351 0548

BISSET, Michael Davidson. b 55. NTMTC 96. **d** 99 **p** 00. C Ickenham *Lon* 99-03; P-in-c Penn *Ox* 03-04; P-in-c Tyler's Green 03-04; V Penn and Tylers Green from 04. *The Vicarage, Church Road, Penn, High Wycombe HP10 8NU* Tel (01895) 676092 E-mail mike.bisset@talk21.com

BISSEX, Mrs Janet Christine Margaret. b 50. Westhill Coll Lon CertEd72. Trin Coll Bris 76. **dss** 86 **d** 87 **p** 94. Toxteth Park St Bede *Liv* 86-93; Par Dn 87-93; Dn-in-c Kirkdale St Mary and St Athanasius 93-94; P-in-c 94-03; C Litherland St Andr 03; TV Bootle from 04. *The Vicarage, 4 St Andrews Road, Bootle L20 5EX* Tel 0151-922 7916 Fax 944 1121 E-mail revjanetb@yahoo.co.uk

BISSON, Joyce Elaine. b 52. Liv Univ BTh98 Nottm Coll of Educn TCert73. NOC 06. **d** 08 **p** 09. NSM Gt Meols *Ches* from 08. *14 Howbeck Drive, Prenton CH43 6UY* Tel 0151-652 7888 E-mail elainebisson@yahoo.co.uk

BLACK, Canon Alexander Stevenson. b 28. Glas Univ MA53. Edin Th Coll 53. **d** 55 **p** 56. C Dumfries *Glas* 55-58; Chapl Glas Univ 58-61; C Glas St Mary 58-61; P-in-c E Kilbride 61-69; C Edin St Columba 69-79; TV Edin St Jo 79-83; R Haddington 83-93; R Dunbar 83-93; Can St Mary's Cathl from 88; rtd 93. *3 Bass Rock View, Canty Bay, North Berwick EH39 5PJ* Tel (01620) 894771 E-mail maags@tiscali.co.uk

BLACK, Dominic Paul. b 70. S Bank Univ BSc95 St Jo Coll Dur BA98 MA11. Cranmer Hall Dur 95. **d** 98 **p** 99. C N Hull St Mich *York* 98-04; V N Ormesby from 04; RD Middlesbrough from 11. *The Vicarage, James Street, North Ormesby, Middlesbrough TS3 6LD* Tel (01642) 271814 E-mail dominic.black@trinitycentre.org

BLACK, Douglas John. b 58. Middx Poly BA80. Ridley Hall Cam 89. **d** 91 **p** 92. C Wrexham *St As* 91-01; Chapl NE Wales Inst of

HE 93-01; V Thelwall *Ches* from 02. *All Saints' Vicarage, Bell Lane, Thelwall, Warrington WA4 2SX* Tel (01925) 261166 E-mail revdouglasblack@aol.com

BLACK, Canon Ian Christopher. b 62. Kent Univ BA85 Nottm Univ MDiv93. Linc Th Coll 91. **d** 93 **p** 94. C Maidstone All SS and St Phil w Tovil *Cant* 93-96; P-in-c The Brents and Davington w Oare and Luddenham 96-02; Hon Min Can Cant Cathl 97-02; Asst Dir Post-Ord Tr 98-02; V Whitkirk *Ripon* from 02; Capitular Can Ripon Cathl from 08. *Whitkirk Vicarage, 386 Selby Road, Leeds LS15 0AA* Tel 0113-264 5790 E-mail vicar.whitkirk@btinternet.com

BLACK, Ian Forbes. b 29. St Aid Birkenhead 55. **d** 58 **p** 59. C Bramhall *Ches* 58-61; C Witton 61-63; P-in-c Prestonpans *Edin* 63-68; R Edin Ch Ch-St Jas 68-71; Asst Chapl HM Pris Liv 71-72; Chapl HM Pris Haverigg 72-73; R Bootle w Corney *Carl* 73-75; P-in-c Whicham w Whitbeck 73-75; R Bootle, Corney, Whicham and Whitbeck 75-86; P-in-c Orton St Giles 86-89; R 89-94; P-in-c Aikton 86-89; R 89-94; rtd 94; Perm to Offic *Carl* from 98. *Solwayside, Port Carlisle, Wigton CA7 5BU* Tel (01697) 351964

BLACK, Miss Imogen Nadine Laura. b 79. Trin Coll Ox BA02 MA05 MSt03. St Steph Ho Ox 08. **d** 11. C Belper Ch Ch w Turnditch *Derby* from 11. *26 Leighton Way, Belper DE56 1SX* E-mail imogen.black@trinity-oxford.com

BLACK (*formerly* NAPIER), **Jennifer Beryl.** b 39. S Dios Minl Tr Scheme 89. **d** 93 **p** 96. NSM Itchen Valley *Win* 93-01; Perm to Offic 02-05; C Cupar *St And* from 05. *Edenwood, Cupar KY15 5NX* Tel (01334) 653159

BLACK, Canon Neville. b 36. MBE97. Oak Hill Th Coll 61. **d** 64 **p** 65. C Everton St Ambrose w St Tim *Liv* 64-69; P-in-c Everton St Geo 69-71; V 71-81; P-in-c Everton St Benedict 70-72; P-in-c Everton St Chad w Ch 70-72; Nat Project Officer Evang Urban Tr Project 74-81; TR St Luke in the City 81-04; Chapl Liv Women's Hosp 82-92; Chapl Liv Women's Hosp NHS Trust 92-04; Tutor NOC 82-89; Dir Gp for Urban Min and Leadership *Liv* 84-95; Hon Can Liv Cathl 87-04; P-in-c Edgehill St Dunstan 98-02; rtd 05. *445 Aigburth Road, Liverpool L19 3PA* Tel 0151-427 9803 Fax 494 0736 Pager 07699-727640 E-mail neville.black@btinternet.com

BLACK, Canon Robert John Edward Francis Butler. b 41. TCD BA65 HDipEd70 MA85. CITC 66. **d** 66 **p** 67. C Jordanstown *Conn* 66-68; C Dublin St Steph and St Ann *D & G* 68-73; C Stillorgan w Blackrock 73-85; Hd Master Dundalk Gr Sch *Arm* 85-96; Lic to Offic from 85; Hd Master Kilkenny Coll *C & O* from 96; Can Ossory Cathl from 96. *Kilkenny College, Kilkenny, Co Kilkenny, Republic of Ireland* Tel (00353) (56) 772 2213 *or* 776 1544 Fax 777 0918 E-mail robertblack05@eircom.net

BLACK, Samuel James. b 38. CITC. **d** 68 **p** 69. C Cloughfern *Conn* 68-72; C Lisburn St Paul 72-78; I Rasharkin w Finvoy 78-82; I Belfast Upper Malone (Epiphany) 82-95; I Ballymore *Arm* 95-05; rtd 05. *Toberhewny Hall, 22 Toberhewny Lane, Lurgan, Craigavon BT66 8JZ* Tel (028) 3834 3267

BLACK, William Henry. St Deiniol's Hawarden. **d** 88 **p** 89. NSM Malahide w Balgriffin *D & G* 88-89; NSM Dublin St Ann and St Steph 89-94; C 94-00; Hon Asst Chapl Miss to Seamen 89-00; I Dublin Drumcondra w N Strand *D & G* 00-07; rtd 07. *27 Greendale Avenue, Dublin 5, Republic of Ireland* Tel (00353) (1) 832 3141 Mobile 86-150 3747 E-mail willieblack@eircom.net

BLACKALL, Mrs Margaret Ivy. b 38. St Kath Coll Lon CertEd58. EAMTC 82. **dss** 86 **d** 87 **p** 94. NSM Wickham Market w Pettistree and Easton *St E* 86-88; Par Dn Leiston 88-92; Par Dn Gt and Lt Glemham, Blaxhall etc 92-94; P-in-c 94-96; R 96-02; P-in-c Snterwell w Benhall and Snape 98-02; rtd 03; Perm to Offic *St E* from 03. *6 Orchard Place, Wickham Market, Woodbridge IP13 0RU* Tel (01728) 747326 Mobile 07850-632900 E-mail mgtblack@globalnet.co.uk

BLACKALL, Robin Jeremy McRae. b 35. Ridley Hall Cam 67. **d** 69 **p** 70. C Stowmarket *St E* 69-72; R Stanstead w Shimplingthorne and Alpheton 72-77; R Bradwell on Sea *Chelmsf* 77-79; R St Lawrence 77-79; Warden Bede Ho Staplehurst 79-81; Chapl HM Det Cen Blantyre Ho 81-82; R Edith Weston w N Luffenham and Lyndon w Manton *Pet* 86-95; P-in-c Upwell St Pet *Ely* 95-99; P-in-c Outwell 95-99; Dioc Rural Miss Officer 95-01; P-in-c Barton Bendish w Beachamwell and Shingham 99-01; P-in-c Boughton 99-01; P-in-c Wereham 99-01; rtd 01; Perm to Offic *Ely* from 01 and *Nor* from 02. *The Pightle House, Eastmoor Road, Eastmoor, Oxborough, King's Lynn PE33 9PZ* Tel (01366) 328663 Fax 328163 E-mail rjmb@globalnet.co.uk

BLACKALL, Susan Elizabeth. b 52. Qu Univ Kingston Ontario BA74 MA75 CCC Ox DPhil82. SEITE 00. **d** 03 **p** 04. NSM Eltham St Barn *S'wark* from 03. *8 Park Place House, Park Vista, London SE10 9ND* Tel (020) 8853 3302 *or* 7656 5000 E-mail s.blackall@research-int.com

BLACKBURN, David James. b 45. Hull Univ BA67. Trin Coll Bris 85. **d** 87 **p** 88. C Bromsgrove St Jo *Worc* 87-90; V Cradley

90-01; R Kinver and Enville *Lich* from 01. *The Vicarage, Vicarage Drive, Kinver, Stourbridge DY7 6HJ* Tel (01384) 872556
BLACKBURN, Frederick John Barrie. b 28. TD73. Lich Th Coll 52. **d** 55 **p** 56. C Hebburn St Cuth *Dur* 55-58; C Bishopwearmouth St Mary V w St Pet CD 58-61; V Hunwick 61-64; CF (TA) 61-87; V Eighton Banks *Dur* 64-75; R Stella 75-87; TV Bellingham/Otterburn Gp *Newc* 87-89; rtd 89. *26 Kepier Chare, Ryton NE40 4UW* Tel and fax 0191-413 7365 Mobile 07745-028780
BLACKBURN, Helen Claire. b 55. Leeds Univ BA76 MA99 PGCE78 ARCM75. NOC 96. **d** 99 **p** 00. C Sheff Cathl 99-01; Asst Chapl Cen Sheff Univ Hosps NHS Trust 01-04; Chapl Sheff Teaching Hosps NHS Trust 04-06; C Ranmoor *Sheff* 06-07; P-in-c Abbeydale St Jo 07-09; Lead Chapl Willowbrook Hospice from 10. *Bishop's House, 34 Central Avenue, Eccleston Park, Prescot L34 2QP* Tel 0151-426 1897
E-mail helen_blackburn@hotmail.co.uk
BLACKBURN, The Ven John. b 47. CB04. Open Univ BA88. St Mich Coll Llan 66. **d** 71 **p** 72. C Risca *Mon* 71-76; CF (TA) 73-76; CF 76-99; Dep Chapl Gen 99-00; Chapl Gen 00-04; Adn for the Army 99-04; QHC from 96; Hon Can Ripon Cathl 01-04; V Risca *Mon* from 04. *The Vicarage, 1 Gelli Crescent, Risca, Newport NP11 6QG* Tel (01633) 612307
E-mail northmanor@btinternet.com
BLACKBURN, Sister Judith Elizabeth. b 58. SEITE 99. **d** 02 **p** 03. NSM Old Ford St Paul and St Mark *Lon* 02-05; P-in-c Bethnal Green St Pet w St Thos 05-11; NSM Bethnal Green St Matt w St Jas the Gt from 11. *St Saviour's Priory, 18 Queensbridge Road, London E2 8NX* Tel (020) 7739 9976 Mobile 07855-510393 E-mail judithblackburn@aol.com
BLACKBURN, Keith Christopher. b 39. K Coll Lon BD63 AKC63. St Boniface Warminster 63. **d** 64 **p** 65. C Surbiton St Andr *S'wark* 64-66; C Battersea St Mary 67-70; Teacher Sir Walter St John Sch Battersea 67-70; Hon C Eltham H Trin 70-76; Hd of Ho Crown Woods Sch Eltham 70-76; Dep Hd Master Altwood C of E Sch 76-82; Chapl and Hd Master St Geo Sch Gravesend 83-93; Hon C Fawkham and Hartley *Roch* 83-93; V Seal SS Pet and Paul 93-05; rtd 05; Perm to Offic *Heref* from 05. *The Tythe Barn, St Weonards, Hereford HR2 8NT* Tel (01981) 580389 E-mail revkcb@aol.com
BLACKBURN, Peter James Whittaker. b 47. Sydney Univ BA69. Coll of Resurr Mirfield. **d** 72 **p** 73. C Felixstowe St Jo *St E* 72-76; C Bournemouth St Pet w St Swithun, H Trin etc *Win* 76-79; R Burythorpe, Acklam and Leavening w Westow *York* 79-85; Chapl Naples Ch Ch *Eur* 85-91; Chapl Algarve 91-97; Perm to Offic *Lon* 07-09; Hon C Hampstead Ch Ch from 09. *8 Hampstead Square, London NW3 1AB* Tel (020) 7435 5818 E-mail peter.blackburn@virgilio.it
✠**BLACKBURN, The Rt Revd Richard Finn.** b 52. St Jo Coll Dur BA74 Hull Univ MA97. Westcott Ho Cam 81. **d** 83 **p** 84 **c** 09. C Stepney St Dunstan and All SS *Lon* 83-87; P-in-c Isleworth St Jo 87-92; V Mosbrough *Sheff* 92-99; RD Attercliffe 96-99; Hon Can Sheff Cathl 98-99; Adn Sheff and Rotherham 99-09; Can Res Sheff Cathl 99-05; Suff Bp Warrington *Liv* from 09. *Bishop's House, 34 Central Avenue, Eccleston Park, Prescot L34 2QP* Tel 0151-705 2140 Fax 709 2885
E-mail bishopofwarrington@liverpool.anglican.org
BLACKBURN, Archdeacon of. See HAWLEY, The Ven John Andrew
BLACKBURN, Bishop of. See READE, The Rt Revd Nicholas Stewart
BLACKBURN, Dean of. See ARMSTRONG, The Very Revd Christopher John
BLACKDEN, Mrs Diane Janice. b 40. **d** 06. NSM Buxted and Hadlow Down *Chich* from 06. *Oak Hill, Five Ashes, Mayfield TN20 6HL* Tel (01435) 872082
BLACKER, Herbert John. b 36. Bris Univ BSc59. Cranmer Hall Dur. **d** 61 **p** 62. C Wednesbury St Bart *Lich* 61-63; C Chasetown 63-65; C Chigwell *Chelmsf* 65-69; TV Barnham Broom w Kimberley, Bixton etc *Nor* 69-76; R Burgh Parva w Briston 76-92; P-in-c Melton Constable w Swanton Novers 86-92; R Briston w Burgh Parva and Melton Constable 92-01; rtd 01; Perm to Offic *Nor* from 01 and *St E* from 04. *8 Lloyds Avenue, Kessingland, Lowestoft NR33 7TP*
BLACKETT, James Gilbert. b 27. Tyndale Hall Bris 52. **d** 55 **p** 56. C Heworth H Trin *York* 55-57; C Newburn *Newc* 57-58; C Newc St Barn and St Jude 58-61; V Broomfleet *York* 61-67; V Ledsham 67-74; V Burton All SS *Lich* 74-82; V Burton All SS w Ch Ch 82-92; rtd 92; Perm to Offic *Ox* and *Pet* from 92. *103 Milford Avenue, Stony Stratford, Milton Keynes MK11 1EZ* Tel (01908) 265149
BLACKETT, Robert Peter. b 63. Dur Univ BSc85 Open Univ BSc07. Ripon Coll Cuddesdon BTh95. **d** 95 **p** 96. C Wigton *Carl* 95-00; R Bowness-on-Solway, Kirkbride and Newton Arlosh from 00. *The Rectory, Church Road, Kirkbride, Carlisle CA7 5HY* Tel (01697) 351256
BLACKFORD, Barry Douglas. b 52. Southn Inst BSc96 MCMI00 MBCS04. STETS 05. **d** 08 **p** 09. C N Poole Ecum

Team *Sarum* from 08. *6 Wingfield Avenue, Oakdale, Poole BH15 3DQ* Tel 07866-430428 (mobile)
E-mail bdblackford@hotmail.com
BLACKIE, Richard Footner (Brother Edmund). b 37. St Cath Coll Cam BA59 MA63 Worc Coll Ox BA59 BSc61. Ely Th Coll 60. **d** 62 **p** 63. C Saffron Walden *Chelmsf* 62-65; SSF from 66. *Society of St Francis, 42 Balaam Street, London E13 8AQ* Tel (020) 7476 5189
BLACKLEDGE, David John. b 51. Oak Hill Th Coll 89. **d** 92 **p** 93. NSM Woodford Wells *Chelmsf* from 92. *Hornbeam, 143 Monkhams Lane, Woodford Green IG8 0NW* Tel (020) 8262 7690
E-mail davidjblackledge@aol.com
BLACKLEDGE, Philip Vincent Patrick. b 74. Edin Univ BMus92 BD02. TISEC 99. **d** 02 **p** 03. C Edin St Mary 02-06; Chapl St Mary's Cathl 03-06; P-in-c Linlithgow from 06; P-in-c Bathgate from 06. *The Rectory, 85 Acredales, Linlithgow EH49 6JA* Tel (01506) 848726
E-mail philipblackledge@aol.com
BLACKLEY, Miles. b 69. Wycliffe Hall Ox. **d** 05 **p** 06. C Ches Square St Mich w St Phil *Lon* 05-08; C St Olave Hart Street w All Hallows Staining etc 08-10; C St Kath Cree 08-10; Perm to Offic *S'wark* from 11. *22 Assembly Apartments, 24 York Grove, London SE15 2NZ* E-mail milesblackley@hotmail.com
BLACKMAN, Brian David Eric. b 38. Ox NSM Course 82. **d** 85 **p** 86. NSM Reading St Luke *Ox* 85-86; NSM Reading St Luke w St Bart 86-08; Perm to Offic from 08. *13 Avebury Square, Reading RG1 5JH* Tel 0118-926 0345
BLACKMAN (née PRATT), Christine Fiona. b 60. Reading Univ BSc81. Ox Min Course 88. **d** 91 **p** 94. NSM Reading St Luke w St Bart *Ox* 91-94; NSM Earley St Pet 94-95; NSM Reading St Luke w St Bart from 95. *13 Avebury Square, Reading RG1 5JH* Tel 0118-926 0345
BLACKMAN, Clive John. b 51. Hull Univ BSc73 MSc74. Qu Coll Birm 75. **d** 78 **p** 79. C Folkestone St Sav *Cant* 78-81; Chapl Birm Univ 81-86; V Thorpe St Matt *Nor* 86-94; R Cringleford w Colney and Bawburgh 94-98; Asst Dir Lay and Reader Tr 98-03; Dir Reader Tr 03-11; Chapl Nor City Coll of F&HE from 03. *13 Norvic Drive, Norwich NR4 7NN* Tel (01603) 505776 *or* 773538 E-mail cblackman@ccn.ac.uk
BLACKMAN, Michael Orville. b 46. Univ of W Ontario BMin80. Codrington Coll Barbados 67. **d** 71 **p** 71. C St Jo Cathl Antigua 71-73; R H Innocents w St Sav Barbados 73-78; Hon C Westminster St Jas Canada 78-80; P-in-c St Patr Barbados 80-86; TV E Ham w Upton Park *Chelmsf* 86-91; R St Pet Barbados 91-97; V Dalton *Sheff* 97-03; P-in-c Raynes Park St Sav *S'wark* 03-10; P-in-c S Wimbledon All SS 03-10; V Raynes Park St Sav and S Wimbledon All SS from 10. *St Saviour's Vicarage, Church Walk, London SW20 9DG* Tel (020) 8542 2787
E-mail michael.blackman1@btopenworld.com
BLACKMAN, Peter Richard. b 28. Sarum Th Coll 52. **d** 55 **p** 56. C Aylestone *Leic* 55-60; V Ratby cum Groby 60-84; TR 84-93; rtd 93; Perm to Offic *Chich* from 93. *25 Turnbull Road, Chichester PO19 7LY* Tel (01243) 787299
BLACKMORE, Frank Ellis. b 43. Univ of Wales (Lamp) BA66. Wells Th Coll 65. **d** 67 **p** 68. C S'wark St Geo 67-70; Hon C Camberwell St Giles 70-79; NSM Paddington St Sav from 79. *35 Leith Mansions, Grantully Road, London W9 1LH* Tel (020) 7289 3020 E-mail ellisblackmore@btinternet.com
BLACKMORE, Robert Ivor. b 37. Univ of Wales (Lamp) 59 Open Univ BA78 Univ of Wales MTh94. **d** 62 **p** 63. C Llangynwyd w Maesteg 62-65; C Dowlais 65-67; C Neath w Llantwit 67-71; V Fochriw w Deri 71-73; V Troedrhiwgarth 73-80; V Seven Sisters 80-00; rtd 02. *28 Hen Parc Lane, Upper Killay, Swansea SA2 7EY*
BLACKMORE, Vernon John. b 50. Southn Univ BSc Man Univ MSc K Coll Lon MTh. Oak Hill Th Coll. **d** 82 **p** 83. C Ecclesall *Sheff* 82-87; Bp's Adv on Youth 85-87; Ed Lion Publishing 87-90; Dir Publications, Tr and Sales CPAS 90-99. *6 Guy Street, Warwick CV34 4LN* Tel (01926) 498351
BLACKSHAW, Brian Martin. b 43. Lanc Univ MA74 Ch Ox BA95 MA96. Ox NSM Course 87. **d** 90 **p** 91. NSM Amersham *Ox* 90-93; C Hatch End St Anselm *Lon* 93-95; V Cheshunt *St Alb* 96-07; rtd 07. *Holly Bush, Flaunden Lane, Flaunden, Hemel Hempstead HP3 0PQ* Tel (01442) 832254
E-mail brianblackshaw@f2s.com
BLACKSHAW, Trevor Roland. b 36. GIMechE59. Lon Coll of Div 67. **d** 69 **p** 70. C New Catton St Luke *Nor* 69-73; C Luton Lewsey St Hugh *St Alb* 73-78; V Llandinam w Trefeglwys w Penstrowed *Ban* 78-85; Dioc Dir of Adult Educn 83-85; Consultant Dir Wholeness Through Ch Min 86-92; Midl Regional Co-ord Crosslinks 92-97; Dir and Warden Divine Healing Miss Crowhurst 97-02; rtd 02; Perm to Offic *Lich* 04-06 and from 07; P-in-c Weston Rhyn and Selattyn 06-07. *Mayland, 2 Balmoral Crescent, Oswestry SY11 2XG* Tel (01691) 659645
E-mail trevor@blackshawt.freeserve.co.uk
BLACKSTONE, James Christopher. b 75. Peterho Cam BA97. Westcott Ho Cam 06. **d** 10 **p** 11. C Eltham H Trin *S'wark* from 10. *59A Southend Crescent, London SE9 2SD* Tel (020) 3342 1302 E-mail jim.blackstone47@gmail.com

BLACKTOP, Graham Leonard. b 33. St Alb Minl Tr Scheme 82. **d** 85 **p** 86. NSM Rickmansworth *St Alb* 85-92; Perm to Offic *Sarum* from 92. *Dairy House, Wolfeton, Dorchester DT2 9QN* Tel and fax (01305) 262184

BLACKWALL, David d'Arcy Russell. b 35. Southn Univ BSc60. Wycliffe Hall Ox 63. **d** 65 **p** 66. C Southampton Thornhill St Chris *Win* 65-68; V Long Sutton 69-72; Chapl Ld Wandsworth Coll Hants 69-74; Hon C Odiham w S Warnborough *Win* 72-75; Chapl St Lawr Coll Ramsgate 75-95; Hd Jun Sch 95-97; rtd 97; Perm to Offic *Sarum* from 98. *Cookwell, Back Lane, Okeford Fitzpaine, Blandford Forum DT11 0RD* Tel (01258) 860157

BLACKWELL, Geoffrey Albert. b 27. Lon Coll of Div 62. **d** 65 **p** 66. C Clifton *York* 65-69; Chapl RN 69-73; Warden St Mich Home of Healing Cleadon 73-75; V S Hetton *Dur* 75-82; CSWG 83-94; P-in-c Burpham *Chich* 95-96; rtd 96; Perm to Offic *Chich* 96-05. *1 Highfield Gardens, Rustington, Littlehampton BN16 2PZ* Tel (01903) 782219

BLACKWELL, Nicholas Alfred John. b 54. Warwick Univ MA97. St Jo Coll Nottm BTh85. **d** 85 **p** 86. C Birkenhead Priory *Ches* 85-88; C Stratford-on-Avon w Bishopton *Cov* 88-91; TV Cov E 91-98. *74 Brays Lane, Coventry CV2 4DW* Tel (024) 7626 1161

BLACKWELL-SMYTH, Charles Peter Bernard. b 42. TCD BA64 MA71 MB73. Gen Th Sem (NY) MDiv65. **d** 65 **p** 66. C Bangor Abbey *D & D* 65-67; C Dublin Ch Ch Leeson Park *D & G* 67-69; P-in-c Carbury *M & K* 73-75; Hon C St Stephen in Brannel *Truro* 87-94; Perm to Offic from 94. *Parcgwyn, Rectory Road, St Stephen, St Austell PL26 7RL* Tel (01726) 822465

BLACOE, Brian Thomas. b 36. Open Univ BA. Oak Hill Th Coll 63. **d** 66 **p** 67. C Dundonald *D & D* 66-69; C Drumcree *Arm* 69-74; I Annahavna w Desertcreat 74-78; I Annalong *D & D* 78-95; I Knocknamuckley 95-08; Can Dromore Cathl 93-08; Prec 02-08; rtd 08. *91 Richmond Drive, Tandragee, Craigavon BT62 2GW* Tel (028) 3884 2029 Mobile 07745-564056 E-mail eablacoe@tiscali.co.uk

BLADE, Brian Alan. b 24. ACCS55 ASCA66. Roch Th Coll 67. **d** 69 **p** 70. C Barnehurst *Roch* 69-71; C Crayford 71-76; V Buttershaw St Aid *Bradf* 76-80; R Etton w Helpston *Pet* 80-86; V Hardingstone and Horton and Piddington 86-90; rtd 90; Perm to Offic *Cant* and *Roch* from 90. *25 Dan Drive, Faversham ME13 7SW* Tel (01795) 531842 E-mail revbrianblade@tesco.net

BLADE, Mrs Susan Joan. b 58. SEITE 97. **d** 00 **p** 01. NSM Wateringbury and Teston *Roch* 00-02; Asst Chapl Maidstone and Tunbridge Wells NHS Trust 00-02; Sen Chapl 02-06; Chapl Cant Ch Ch Univ 07-10; P-in-c Sampford Peverell, Uplowman, Holcombe Rogus etc *Ex* 10-11; TR from 11. *The Rectory, Blackdown View, Sampford Peverell, Tiverton EX16 7BP* Tel (01884) 829461 E-mail sue.blade@gmail.com

BLAGDEN, Ms Susan. b 64. Ox Min Course 89 Ripon Coll Cuddesdon 97. **d** 99 **p** 00. C Grantham *Linc* 99-03; Asst Chapl Stoke Mandeville Hosp NHS Trust 03-10; R Bangor Monachorum, Worthenbury and Marchwiel *St As* from 10. *The Rectory, 8 Ludlow Road, Bangor-on-Dee, Wrexham LL13 0JG* Tel (01978) 780608 E-mail blagdensm@aol.com

BLAGG, Colin. b 31. Leeds Univ BA57. Coll of Resurr Mirfield 57. **d** 59 **p** 60. C Edin Old St Paul 59-63; R Gourock *Glas* 63-68; Chapl to the Deaf RADD Lon 68-74; Hon C Stoke Newington St Olave *Lon* 73-74; Chapl to the Deaf *Chich* 74-80; V Shoreham Beach 80-96; rtd 97; Perm to Offic *Chich* from 97. *2 Greenfields, Bognor Regis PO22 7SS* Tel (01243) 582742

BLAIN, Anne Sharon. b 46. RGN89. Dioc OLM tr scheme 98. **d** 01 **p** 02. OLM Tadworth *S'wark* from 01. *Watts Cottage, Watts Lane, Tadworth KT20 5RW* Tel (01737) 355347 Fax 351546 Mobile 07811-267238 E-mail breusis@aol.com

BLAIR, Mrs Catherine Jill. b 62. Nottm Univ BA84 BArch87 RIBA88. St Jo Coll Nottm MA02. **d** 02 **p** 03. C Goldsworth Park *Guildf* 02-06; C Woking St Paul from 06; RD Woking from 10. *St Paul's Vicarage, Pembroke Road, Woking GU22 7ED* Tel (01483) 850489 E-mail cathy@stpaulswoking.org.uk

BLAIR, Henry. See BLAIR, William Henry

BLAIR, Canon John Wallace. b 48. Lon Univ BSc70. Qu Coll Birm 79. **d** 81 **p** 82. C Chorlton-cum-Hardy St Werburgh *Man* 81-83; CF 83-97; I Faughanvale *D & R* from 97; Can Derry Cathl from 09. *21 Main Street, Eglinton, Londonderry BT47 3AB* Tel (028) 7181 0217

BLAIR, Jonathan Lewis. b 62. Nottm Univ BA84 ACA88. St Jo Coll Nottm. **d** 02 **p** 03. C Goldsworth Park *Guildf* 02-06; P-in-c Woking St Paul from 06. *St Paul's Vicarage, Pembroke Road, Woking GU22 7ED* Tel (01483) 850489 *or* 888611 E-mail jonny.blair@tiscali.co.uk

BLAIR, Patrick Allen. b 31. Trin Coll Cam BA54 MA58. Ridley Hall Cam 54. **d** 56 **p** 57. C Harwell *Ox* 56-59; Chapl Oundle Sch 59-64; Tutor St Geo Coll and Chapl to Abp in Jerusalem 64-66; Provost Khartoum Sudan 67-71; R Chester le Street *Dur* 71-77; TR Barking St Marg w St Patr *Chelmsf* 77-87; Chapl Barking Hosp 77-87; Chapl Tunis 87-91; Provost Nicosia Cyprus 91-96; rtd 96. *Grace Cottage, Pilley Green, Boldre, Lymington SO41 5QG* Tel (01596) 677015

BLAIR, Philip Hugh. b 39. St Edm Hall Ox BA62 MA67 Ex Univ DipEd75 PhD84. Ridley Hall Cam 62. **d** 64 **p** 65. C Camborne *Truro* 64-68; C Kenwyn 68-70; Sudan 70-73; P-in-c Probus *Truro* 73-74; P-in-c St Enoder 74-75; Perm to Offic Cyprus and the Gulf 90-94; rtd 04. *St Martin's, 121 Newland, Sherborne DT9 3DU* Tel and fax (01935) 816022 E-mail philip@philipblair.net

BLAIR, William Henry. b 66. QUB BAgr89 TCD BTh04. CITC 01. **d** 04 **p** 05. C Monaghan w Tydavnet and Kilmore *Clogh* 04-06; C Magheraculmoney 06-11; I from 11. *The Rectory, 47 Main Street, Kesh, Enniskillen BT93 1TF* Tel (028) 6863 1820 E-mail henryblair@utvinternet.co.uk

BLAIR-CHAPPELL, Mrs Elcineide. b 47. Sao Paulo Univ Brazil 74 Birm Poly PGCE88. WMMTC 00. **d** 03 **p** 04. NSM Erdington *Birm* from 03; NSM Birm St Martin w Bordesley St Andr from 08; Hon Chapl Birm Children's Hosp NHS Trust from 07. *18 Kempson Avenue, Sutton Coldfield B72 1HJ* Tel 0121-682 5340

BLAKE, Colin David. b 52. Rolle Coll CertEd Ex Univ BEd Lon Univ BD. Trin Coll Bris 81. **d** 84 **p** 85. C Hucclecote *Glouc* 84-88; C Patchway and Min Bradley Stoke N CD *Bris* 88-00; TV Worle *B & W* 00-09; Miss P Bradf Adnry from 09; Adv in Fresh Expressions Min from 09. *6 Glenhurst Road, Shipley BD18 4DZ* Tel (01274) 592180 E-mail colinblake1@aol.com

BLAKE, Ian Martyn. b 57. BA79. Oak Hill Th Coll 76. **d** 80 **p** 81. C Widford *Chelmsf* 80-84; C Barton Seagrave w Warkton *Pet* 84-90; V Sneinton St Chris w St Phil *S'well* 90-01; C Howell Hill w Burgh Heath *Guildf* 01-06; Perm to Offic *Guildf* from 06 and *S'wark* from 08. *87 Ambleside Gardens, Sutton SM2 5HN* Tel (020) 8643 2817 Mobile 07904-340783 E-mail iannablake@yahoo.co.uk

BLAKE, Ms Katharine Naomi. b 67. Southn Univ BA89. Westcott Ho Cam 09. **d** 11. C Pinner *Lon* from 11. *37 Eastcote Road, Pinner HA5 1EL*

BLAKE, Mrs Margaret. b 48. Open Univ BA87. S'wark Ord Course 92. **d** 95 **p** 96. C Farnham *Guildf* 95-01; P-in-c Farncombe 01-05; R 05-09; rtd 09. *Haul y Bryn, Llanfihangel Nant Bran, Brecon LD3 9NA* Tel (01874) 636390 E-mail revmargaretblake@aol.com

BLAKE, Preb Patrick John. b 30. Univ of Wales BA51 DipEd52 St Edm Hall Ox BA54 MA58. St Mich Coll Llan 54. **d** 55 **p** 56. C Buckley *St As* 55-59; C Oystermouth *S & B* 59-63; V Cleeve *B & W* 63-71; R Bruton w Lamyatt, Wyke and Redlynch 71-83; Dioc Ecum Officer 79-84; Preb Wells Cathl 79-03; TR Yeovil 83-88; P-in-c Backwell 88-89; R 89-92; R Backwell w Chelvey and Brockley 92-95; RD Portishead 92-95; rtd 95; Perm to Offic *B & W* from 95; Clergy Retirement and Widows' Officer 96-06. *The Firs, 47 Lower Street, Merriott TA16 5NN* Tel (01460) 78932

BLAKE, Peta Ruth. b 44. Lambeth STh89 Episc Div Sch Cam Mass MA89 DMin90. Trin Coll Bris 82. **dss** 83 **d** 87. New Swindon St Barn Gorse Hill *Bris* 83-88; Par Dn 87-88; Perm to Offic 88-93. *303 Beckett Condo, 220 Beckett Street, Arcadia, Pretoria, 0083 South Africa*

BLAKE, Philip Charles. b 29. Mitchell Coll of Adv Educn (NSW) BA80 Macquarie Univ (NSW) MA86 FAIWCW88 MACC88. Oak Hill Th Coll 54. **d** 57 **p** 58. C Slough *Ox* 57-60; C Uphill *B & W* 60-62; V Branston *Lich* 62-69; C-in-c Marsfield Australia 69-72; R Denistone E w Marsfield 72-75; Chal Long Bay Pris 75-80; Chapl W Metrop Pris 81-83; Sen Chapl Dept Corrective Services 81-85; Chapl Parramatta Hosp 86-91; Chapl Tas Univ 91-94; rtd 94. *74/217 Vimiera Road, Eastwood NSW 2122, Australia* Tel (0061) (2) 9868 4340

BLAKE, Stephen. b 59. Ch Coll Cam MA85 Wadh Coll Ox BM, BCh84 MRCGP88. Ox Min Course 07. **d** 10 **p** 11. NSM Burford w Fulbrook, Taynton, Asthall etc *Ox* from 10. *Morecroft, Hastings Hill, Churchill, Chipping Norton OX7 6NA* Tel (01608) 658545 E-mail stephenblake@burfordchurch.org

BLAKE, Steven Robert (Max). b 53. Furzedown Coll of Educn CertEd74 Brentwood Coll of Educn BEd91. NTMTC 98. **d** 01 **p** 02. NSM Orsett and Bulphan and Horndon on the Hill *Chelmsf* from 01. *Oakfield, Victoria Road, Horndon-on-the-Hill, Stanford-le-Hope SS17 8ND* Tel (01375) 360522 E-mail max@hobnob.org.uk

BLAKELEY, Julian Graham. b 60. Oak Hill Th Coll BA88. **d** 88 **p** 89. C Bedworth *Cov* 88-91; C Harlow St Mary and St Hugh w St Jo the Bapt *Chelmsf* 91-95; R Darfield *Sheff* 95-03; TR Eston w Normanby *York* from 03. *429 Normanby Road, Middlesbrough TS6 0ED* Tel (01642) 206264 E-mail julianblakeley@hotmail.co.uk

BLAKELY, Denise Irene. See CADDOO, Mrs Denise Irene

BLAKEMAN, Mrs Janet Mary. b 36. Man Univ BA57 CertEd58. Carl Dioc Tr Course 87. **d** 90 **p** 97. NSM Wetheral w Warwick *Carl* 90-97; NSM Thornthwaite cum Braithwaite, Newlands etc 97-01; Perm to Offic 01-07. *1 The Coach House, Romaldkirk, Barnard Castle DL12 9ED*

BLAKEMAN, Walter John. b 37. Qu Coll Birm 74. **d** 76 **p** 77. C Gnosall *Lich* 76-83; C Cheadle 83-86; Res Min Hednesford 86-90; Min Roundshaw LEP *S'wark* 90-94; TV E Scarsdale

Derby 94-98; rtd 98. *10 Maes Madog, Pontfadog, Llangollen LL20 7BN* Tel (01691) 718173

BLAKESLEY, John. b 50. Keble Coll Ox BA72 MA76. St Steph Ho Ox 72. **d** 74 **p** 75. C Egremont *Carl* 74-77; C Doncaster Ch Ch *Sheff* 77-79; V Auckland St Helen *Dur* 79-94; Chapl Tindale Crescent Hosp Dur 90-94; Lect Th Dur Univ from 91; Tutor St Chad's Coll Dur 95-00; C Ch the King *Newc* 00-03; V Cambois and Sleekburn from 03. *St John's Vicarage, North View, Bedlington NE22 7ED* Tel (01670) 822309

BLAKEWAY-PHILLIPS, Richard John. b 19. St Chad's Coll Dur BA43. **d** 43 **p** 44. C Ledbury *Heref* 43-45; C Cirencester *Glouc* 45-50; C Lydney w Aylburton 50-52; R Dumbleton w Wormington 52-58; V Crawley Down All SS *Chich* 58-69; V Arrington *Ely* 69-77; R Orwell and Wimpole 69-77; P-in-c Hildersham and Gt w Lt Abington 77-86; rtd 86; Perm to Offic *Heref* 86-04 and *Ox* from 07. *Glanthus Cottage, 61 Long Row, Latchford Lane, Great Haseley, Oxford OX44 7LE* Tel (01844) 278035

BLAKEY, Canon Cedric Lambert. b 54. Fitzw Coll Cam BA76 MA80. St Jo Coll Nottm 77. **d** 79 **p** 80. C Cotmanhay *Derby* 79-83; C-in-c Blagreaves St Andr CD 83-89; P-in-c Sinfin Moor 84-89; V Heanor 89-97; RD Heanor 94-97; Bp's Dom Chapl 97-05; NSM Derby Cathl 05-11; Hon Can 02-11; Vice Provost St Mary's Cathl from 11. *St Mary's Cathedral, 300 Great Western Road, Glasgow G4 9JB* Tel 0141-339 6691 Fax 334 5669 E-mail cedric.blakey@googlemail.com *or* viceprovost@thecathedral.org

BLAKEY, William George. b 51. Southn Univ BSc72 PGCE73. Oak Hill Th Coll BA82. **d** 82 **p** 83. C Cheltenham St Mark *Glouc* 82-85; P-in-c Parkham, Alwington, Buckland Brewer etc *Ex* 85-86; R 86-94; TR 94-01; P-in-c Lundy Is 92-01; RD Hartland 89-96; TR Wareham *Sarum* 01-07; TR Brize Norton and Carterton *Ox* from 07; AD Witney from 08. *St John's Vicarage, 6 Burford Road, Carterton OX18 3AA* Tel (01993) 846996 E-mail rector@theblakeys.co.uk

BLAMEY, Mark Kendall. b 62. Bris Poly BSc84 MRICS86. Ripon Coll Cuddesdon 99. **d** 01 **p** 02. C Cowley St Jo *Ox* 01-04; P-in-c Goring w S Stoke 04-07; V Goring and Streatley w S Stoke from 07. *The Vicarage, Manor Road, Goring, Reading RG8 9DR* Tel (01491) 872196 E-mail mark@blamey.fslife.co.uk

BLAMIRE, Jean. See PROSSER, Jean

BLAMIRE, Philip Gray. b 50. St Pet Coll Birm CertEd71 Wall Hall Coll Aldenham BEd76 UEA MA91. EAMTC 00. **d** 03 **p** 04. C Swaffham *Nor* 03-07; P-in-c Weybourne Gp 07-10; R from 10. *The Rectory, The Street, Weybourne, Holt NR25 7SY* Tel (01263) 588268 E-mail philgb@lineone.net

BLAMIRE-BROWN, Charles Richard. b 21. St Cath Soc Ox BA49 MA53. Cuddesdon Coll 49. **d** 51 **p** 52. C Bedale *Ripon* 51-53; C Welwyn *St Alb* 53-58; P-in-c Tewin 58-67; R 67-75; RD Hatfield 71-75; V Chipperfield St Paul 75-86; rtd 86. *7 Willoughby Avenue, Kenilworth CV8 1DG* Tel (01926) 850808

BLANCH, Michael Dennis. b 46. TD and Bar 88. Birm Univ BSocSc69 PGCE70 PhD75. NOC 07. **d** 09 **p** 10. NSM Askrigg w Stallingbusk *Ripon* from 09; NSM Hawes and Hardraw from 09. *Strands, Simonstone, Hawes DL8 3LY* Tel (01969) 667573 Mobile 07792-240684 E-mail mike@blanch.org

BLANCH, Paul Frederick. b 56. St Cuth Soc Dur BA97. Chich Th Coll 83. **d** 86 **p** 87. C Chaddesden St Phil *Derby* 86-88; C Auckland St Andr and St Anne *Dur* 88-91; P-in-c Hunwick 91-94; Chapl HM Pris Edin 98-02; P-in-c Edin St Salvador 98-00; R 00-02; P-in-c Wester Hailes St Luke 00-02; P-in-c Melton *St E* 02-03; P-in-c Ufford w Bredfield and Hasketon 02-03; R Melton and Ufford 03-05; V Meir Heath and Normacot *Lich* 05-09; R Schenectady St Geo USA from 09. *St George's Rectory, 23 Front Street, Schenectady NY 12305-1301, USA* Tel (001) (518) 374 3163 E-mail frpaul@meltuff.freeserve.co.uk

BLANCHARD, Christopher John. b 46. Univ of Wales (Lamp) BA70. St Mich Coll Llan 86. **d** 79 **p** 80. NSM Chepstow *Mon* 79-81; NSM Itton and St Arvans w Penterry and Kilgwrrwg etc 81-86; TV Ebbw Vale 87-89; R Llangenni and Llanbedr Ystrad Yw w Patricio *S & B* 89-98; V Chepstow *Mon* from 98. *The Vicarage, 25 Mount Way, Chepstow NP16 5NF* Tel (01291) 620980

BLANCHARD, Frank Hugh. b 30. St Jo Coll Dur BA54 MA62. **d** 55 **p** 56. C Bottesford *Linc* 55-58; CMS 58-65; C Kirby Grindalythe *York* 65-67; V 67-71; C N Grimston w Wharram Percy and Wharram-le-Street 65-67; V 67-71; P-in-c Thorpe Bassett 67-71; P-in-c Settrington 67-68; V Scarborough St Jas 71-79; P-in-c Scarborough H Trin 78-79; V Scarborough St Jas and H Trin 79-86; R Stockton-on-the-Forest w Holtby and Warthill 87-94; rtd 94; P-in-c Rothesay *Arg* 94-96; Perm to Offic *York* from 00. *23 Front Street, Sowerby, Thirsk YO7 1JG* Tel (01845) 574446

BLANCHARD, Mrs Jean Ann. b 43. St Alb Minl Tr Scheme 79. **dss** 83 **d** 87 **p** 94. Horsham and Heronsgate w W Hyde *St Alb* 85-92; Hon Par Dn 87-92; Par Dn Luton All SS w St Pet 92-94; C 94-95; P-in-c Skirbeck Quarter *Linc* 96-97; V 97-01; P-in-c Digby

Gp 01-08; rtd 08. *92 High Street, Billingborough, Sleaford NG34 0QD* Tel (01529) 240536 E-mail jean.blanchard@btinternet.com

BLANCHARD, Canon Lawrence Gordon. b 36. Edin Univ MA60. Linc Th Coll 63. **d** 65 **p** 66. C Woodhouse *Wakef* 65-67; C Cannock *Lich* 67-70; Chapl Waterford Sch Mbabane Swaziland 70-72; R Mbabane All SS 72-75; Lic to Offic 75-76; TV Raveningham *Nor* 76-80; V Ancaster *Linc* 80-87; Dir LNSM 80-87; Can and Preb Linc Cathl 85-88; Dir of Tr CA 88-93; V Roxton w Gt Barford *St Alb* 93-98; rtd 98; Perm to Offic *St E* 99-09 and *Ely* from 09. *7A Barton Road, Ely CB7 4HZ* Tel (01353) 654133 E-mail sonialaurie3@hotmail.com

BLANCHARDE, Hilary Mary. STETS. **d** 09 **p** 10. NSM Horfield H Trin *Bris* from 09. *149 Abbey Road, Bristol BS9 3QH*

BLAND, Mrs Elizabeth Anne. b 63. Collingwood Coll Dur BA85. SAOMC 01. **d** 04 **p** 05. C N Shields *Newc* 04-08; V Ashington from 08. *Holy Sepulchre Vicarage, Wansbeck Road, Ashington NE63 8HZ* Tel (01670) 813358 E-mail seat@seatbland.freeserve.co.uk

BLAND, Jean Elizabeth. b 42. K Coll Lon BA63. Glouc Sch of Min 87. **d** 90 **p** 94. Par Dn Cen Telford *Lich* 90-94; Asst Chapl HM Pris Shrewsbury 92-94; Chapl HM Pris Doncaster 94-98; C Goole *Sheff* 99; P-in-c Purleigh, Cold Norton and Stow Maries *Chelmsf* 99-08; rtd 08. *33 Seagers, Great Totham, Maldon CM9 8PB* Tel (01621) 829646 E-mail ebland@prowselyan.plus.com

BLANDFORD-BAKER, Neil James. b 64. Dundee Univ BSc86. St Jo Coll Nottm BTh92. **d** 93 **p** 94. C The Quinton *Birm* 93-96; V E Acton St Dunstan w St Thos *Lon* 96-06; Dir of Ords Willesden Area 02-06; V Histon *Ely* from 06; P-in-c Impington from 06; RD N Stowe from 07. *The Vicarage, 9A Church Street, Histon, Cambridge CB24 9EP* Tel (01223) 233456 *or* 232255 E-mail jamesbb@btinternet.com

BLANEY, Laurence. b 41. Open Univ BA85 Essex Univ MA88 PhD95. Oak Hill Th Coll 66. **d** 69 **p** 70. C Leyton St Mary w St Edw *Chelmsf* 69-73; P-in-c Wimbish w Thunderley 73-77; P-in-c Mayland 77-82; P-in-c Steeple 77-82; R Pitsea 82-95; R Pitsea w Nevendon 95-96; P-in-c Mayland 96-06; P-in-c Steeple 96-06; rtd 06; Perm to Offic *Chelmsf* from 06. *14 Piercys, Basildon SS13 3HN* Tel (01268) 552254

BLANKENSHIP, Charles Everett. b 42. Santa Clara Univ BA64. Cuddesdon Coll 71. **d** 74 **p** 75. C Catford (Southend) and Downham *S'wark* 74-78; P-in-c Battersea St Phil w St Bart 78-83; V 83-85; TV Wimbledon 85-91; P-in-c Welling 91-92; V 92-99; P-in-c S Norwood St Alb 99-06; RD Croydon N 02-06; rtd 06; Perm to Offic *S'wark* from 06. *10 Bromley College, London Road, Bromley BR1 1PE* Tel (020) 8464 2443 E-mail charles.blankenship@btinternet.com

BLANKLEY, Roger Henry. b 32. MRICS60. Clifton Th Coll 62. **d** 66 **p** 67. C Peckham St Mary Magd *S'wark* 66-69; SAMS 70-74; Brazil 74-80; R Gillingham w Geldeston, Stockton, Ellingham etc *Nor* 80-91; P-in-c Charmouth and Catherston Leweston *Sarum* 91-97; rtd 97; Perm to Offic *Cov* 98-00 and 02-06; Glouc from 97, *Ox* from 00; Asst Area Sec SAMS 98-00. *12 Hubbard Close, Buckingham MK18 1YS* Tel (01280) 814710 E-mail mblankley@rblankley.freeserve.co.uk

BLATCHLEY, Ms Elizabeth. b 62. Wycliffe Hall Ox 01. **d** 03 **p** 04. C Northolt St Jos *Lon* 03-06; C Telford Park *S'wark* 06-11; V Homerton St Luke *Lon* from 11. *St Luke's Vicarage, 23 Cassland Road, London E9 7AL* Tel (020) 8985 2263 E-mail betsyblatchley@btinternet.com

BLATCHLY, Owen Ronald Maxwell. b 30. Bps' Coll Cheshunt 62. **d** 64 **p** 65. C Boxmoor St Jo *St Alb* 64-67; C Boreham Wood All SS 67-69; C Frimley *Guildf* 69-77; V Manaccan w St Anthony-in-Meneage *Truro* 77-82; R Binfield *Ox* 82-97; rtd 97; Perm to Offic *Truro* from 97. *1 Rose Cottages, East Road, Stithians, Truro TR3 7BD* Tel (01209) 860845

BLATHERWICK, Mrs Jane Lesley. b 63. St Jo Coll Nottm. **d** 05 **p** 06. C Arnold *S'well* 05-09; P-in-c Carlton-in-Lindrick and Langold w Oldcotes from 09. *The Rectory, 21 Grange Close, Carlton-in-Lindrick, Worksop S81 9DX* Tel (01909) 730398 E-mail janeblatherwick@aol.com

BLAY, Ian. b 65. Man Univ BA88. Westcott Ho Cam 89. **d** 91 **p** 92. C Withington St Paul *Man* 91-94; C Elton All SS 94-96; R Droylsden St Andr 96-05; Dioc Ecum Officer 98-05; R Mobberley Ches from 05. *The Rectory, Church Lane, Mobberley, Knutsford WA16 7RA* Tel (01565) 873218 Mobile 07879-004033 E-mail ianblay@btinternet.com

BLAY, Kenneth Neil. b 72. Leeds Univ BA07. Coll of Resurr Mirfield 05. **d** 07 **p** 08. C E Crompton *Man* 07-08; C Dearnley 08-10. *Address temp unknown* E-mail nkblay@btinternet.com

BLEAKLEY, Melvyn Thomas. b 43. K Coll Lon BD66 AKC66 Reading Univ TCert78. **d** 67 **p** 68. C Cross Heath *Lich* 67-70; TV High Wycombe *Ox* 70-77; Perm to Offic 77-00; NSM Chalfont St Giles from 00. *294 Hughenden Road, High Wycombe HP13 5PE* Tel (01494) 529315 E-mail melvyn_bleakley@hotmail.com

BLEAZARD, John George. b 57. Univ of Wales (Abth) BA79 Qu Coll Birm MA06. Ripon Coll Cuddesdon 06. **d** 08 **p** 09. C Gt

Cornard *St E* from 08. *58 Canhams Road, Great Cornard, Sudbury CO10 0ER* Tel (01787) 377397 E-mail johnbleazard@hotmail.com

BLEE, Peter Michael. b 64. St Jo Coll Cam BA86. St Steph Ho Ox BTh94. **d** 94 **p** 95. C Guildf St Nic 94-97; C Whipton *Ex* 97-03; P-in-c Berwick w Selmeston and Alciston *Chich* 03-07; R 07-10; R Arlington, Berwick, Selmeston w Alciston etc from 10. *The Parsonage, Berwick, Polegate BN26 6SR* Tel (01323) 870512 E-mail peterblee@btinternet.com

BLEWETT, Martin Arthur. b 60. Keele Univ BA82 Glos Univ MA04. Trin Coll Bris 07. **d** 09 **p** 10. C Seaford w Sutton *Chich* from 09. *2 Benenden Close, Seaford BN25 3PG* Tel (01323) 891831 Mobile 07854-273489 E-mail prospero888@clara.co.uk

BLEWETT, Roy. b 32. K Coll Lon BSc54 MPhil74. Edin Th Coll 81. **d** 82 **p** 83. C Newc St Fran 82-85; P-in-c Branxton and Cornhill w Carham 85-91; rtd 92; Perm to Offic *Truro* 92-08. *37 Summerland Park, Upper Killay, Swansea SA2 7HU*

BLEWETT, Timothy John. b 67. Surrey Univ BA88 Cam Univ BA92 MA92 Coll of Ripon & York St Jo MA96. Westcott Ho Cam 89. **d** 92 **p** 93. C Knaresborough *Ripon* 92-95; V Hanmer, Bronington, Bettisfield, Tallarn Green *St As* 95-98; Can Res and Can Cursal St As Cathl 98-03; Asst Dioc Dir of Ords 98-00; Dioc Dir of Ords 00-03; Dioc Officer for Min and Adv for CME 98-03; CF 03-04; P-in-c Loddington *Leic* from 04; Warden Launde Abbey from 04. *The Warden's House, Launde Abbey, Launde Road, Launde, Leicester LE7 9XB* Tel (01572) 717254 E-mail tim.blewett@virgin.net

BLICK, John Harold Leslie. b 36. Univ of Wales (Lamp) BA61. Bps' Coll Cheshunt 61. **d** 63 **p** 64. C Radlett *St Alb* 63-66; Min St Cem Miss Labrador Canada 66-71; Min Marsh Farm CD *St Alb* 71-76; R Shaw cum Donnington *Ox* 76-89; rtd 96; Perm to Offic *Mon* from 99. *Springwood, Cleddon, Trelleck NP25 4PN* Tel (01600) 860094 Fax 869045 E-mail revdjblick@aol.com

BLIGH, Philip Hamilton. b 36. Lon Univ BSc57 PhD61 MEd79 St Cath Coll Ox BA63 MInstP75. S'wark Ord Course 86. **d** 88 **p** 89. C Abington *Pet* 88-90; V Bozeat w Easton Maudit 90-99; R Hackett Australia 99-01; rtd 01; Perm to Offic *Nor* from 02. *Harmony House, 40 Cromwell Road, Cromer NR27 0BE* Tel (01263) 511385 E-mail philaud@blighp.freeserve.co.uk

BLIGHT, Francis Charles. b 71. Newc Univ BA94. Oak Hill Th Coll BA08. **d** 08 **p** 09. C Virginia Water *Guildf* from 08. *6 Beechmont Avenue, Virginia Water GU25 4EY* E-mail francis@cc-vw.org

BLISS, Allan Ernest Newport. b 29. K Coll Lon AKC50. St Boniface Warminster 54. **d** 54 **p** 57. C Wooburn *Ox* 54-56; C Whitley Ch 56-58; C Hatcham Park All SS *S'wark* 63-68; C Sundon w Streatley *St Alb* 68-78; C Caldecote All SS 74-78; V 78-91; V Old Warden 81-91; Perm to Offic 91-05; rtd 94. *6 Jubilee Gardens, Biggleswade SG18 0JW* Tel (01767) 313797

BLISS, Canon David Charles. b 52. Aston Univ BSc75 Cranfield Inst of Tech MSc82. St Jo Coll Nottm 87. **d** 89 **p** 90. C Burntwood *Lich* 89-93; Chapl St Matt Hosp Burntwood 89-93; TV Aston cum Aughton w Swallownest, Todwick etc *Sheff* 93-02; R Todwick 02-08; AD Laughton 03-08; Chapl among Deaf People 97-08; V Rotherham from 08; AD Rotherham from 08; Hon Can Sheff Cathl from 06. *51 Hallam Road, Rotherham S60 3ED* Tel (01709) 364341 E-mail david.bliss@sheffield.anglican.org

BLISS, John Derek Clegg. b 40. Sarum Th Coll. **d** 68 **p** 69. C Wymondham *Nor* 68-73; V Easton 73-80; R Colton 73-80; R Madera H Trin USA 80-89; Human Outreach Agency Hayward 92-96; rtd 01; C Coconut Grove St Steph from 01. *4 Edgewater Hillside, Westport CT 06880-6101, USA* Tel (001) (203) 222 1879 E-mail jb106600@aol.com

BLISS, Mrs Lyn Elizabeth. b 54. SS Mark & Jo Univ Coll Plymouth CertEd76. Ox Min Course 06. **d** 09 **p** 10. NSM Bradfield and Stanford Dingley *Ox* from 09; NSM Bucklebury w Marlston from 09. *Holly Hedges, 2 Broad Lane, Upper Bucklebury, Reading RG7 6QJ* Tel (01635) 862281 Mobile 07824-741225 E-mail lyn.bliss@virgin.net

BLISSARD-BARNES, Christopher John. b 36. ARCO55 Linc Coll Ox BA61 MA64. Ridley Hall Cam 61. **d** 63 **p** 64. C Woking St Paul *Guildf* 63-67; C Orpington Ch Ch *Roch* 67-71; P-in-c Heref St Jas 71-78; Chapl Heref Gen Hosp 71-78; R Hampreston *Sarum* 78-88; TR 88-89; RD Wimborne 80-85; P-in-c Hambledon *Guildf* 89-94; R Newdigate 94-01; Warden of Readers 93-99; rtd 01; Perm to Offic *Win* from 02. *148 Olivers Battery Road South, Winchester SO22 4LF* Tel and fax (01962) 862082 E-mail chrisandfreda@virginmedia.com

BLOCK, Robert Allen. b 62. Univ of Wales (Lamp) BA84. Coll of Resurr Mirfield 86. **d** 88 **p** 89. C Hampton *Worc* 88-91; C Notting Hill St Mich and Ch Ch *Lon* 91-96; P-in-c Hammersmith St Luke 96-02; C-in-c Hammersmith SS Mich and Geo White City Estate CD 96-02. *Address temp unknown*

BLOCKLEY, Christopher John Hamilton. b 72. UWE LLB96 Rob Coll Cam BTh04 Barrister-at-Law (Gray's Inn) 98. Ridley Hall Cam 01. **d** 04 **p** 05. C Kingswood *Bris* 04-07; Chapl Bps'

Coll Glouc from 07. *29 Wellesley Street, Gloucester GL1 4QP* Tel (01452) 539956 *or* 524879 ext 137 Mobile 07795-266674 E-mail chris.blockley@hotmail.com

BLODWELL, Ms Christine Maria. b 46. Open Univ BA Jo Dalton Coll Man CertEd71. NOC 04. **d** 05 **p** 06. NSM Marple All SS *Ches* from 05. *12 Ventura Court, Ollersett Avenue, New Mills, High Peak SK22 4LL* Tel (01663) 746523 Mobile 07931-714130 E-mail cmblodwell@aol.com

BLOFELD, Thomas Guest. *See* GUEST-BLOFELD, Thomas

BLOGG, Kevin Derek. b 55. Ch Ch Coll Cant BSc82 PGCE87. Franciscan Ho of Studies. **d** 84 **p** 85. NSM Eythorne and Elvington w Waldershare etc *Cant* 89-92; Orchard Sch Cant 89-90; Harbour Sch Dover 92-93; NSM Colkirk w Oxwick w Pattesley, Whissonsett etc *Nor* 95-02; NSM Gressenhall w Longham w Wendling etc from 02; Sidestrand Hall Sch Nor from 94. *The Rectory Barn, Rectory Road, Gressenhall, Dereham NR19 2QG* Tel (01362) 861084 E-mail bloggbarn@aol.com

BLOOD, David John. b 36. G&C Coll Cam BA60 MA64. Westcott Ho Cam 60. **d** 62 **p** 63. C Rushmere *St E* 62-66; C Harringay St Paul *Lon* 66-70; Lic to Offic 71-81; rtd 01. *42 Churston Gardens, London N11 2NL*

BLOOD, Canon Michael William. b 44. AKC67. **d** 69 **p** 70. C Moseley St Agnes *Birm* 69-75; V Cotteridge 75-09; Relig Progr Producer BBC Radio W Midl 76-06; Hon Can Birm Cathl 97-09; rtd 09; Perm to Offic *Birm* from 09. *19 Nursery Drive, Birmingham B30 1DR* Tel 0121-458 2815 E-mail michaelblood@blueyonder.co.uk

BLOOD, Stephen John. b 28. Keble Coll Ox BA53 MA58. Coll of Resurr Mirfield 53. **d** 55 **p** 56. C Greenford H Cross *Lon* 55-58; C Forest Gate St Edm *Chelmsf* 58-61; C-in-c Ashford St Hilda CD *Lon* 61-73; V Ashford St Hilda 73-00; rtd 00; Perm to Offic *St Alb* from 00. *69 Hampstead Road, Kings Langley WD4 8BS* Tel (01923) 268453

BLOOMER, Ms Sherry Lesley. b 50. TD91. Liv Jo Moores Univ BA91 Wolv Poly CertEd83 RN73 RM74 RHV78. Westcott Ho Cam 95. **d** 97 **p** 98. C Llangollen w Trevor and Llantysilio *St As* 97-00; R Cilcain and Nannerch and Rhydymwyn 00-04; V Worc St Clem and Lower Broadheath from 04; Chapl Worc Univ from 04. *St Clement's Rectory, 124 Laugherne Road, Worcester WR2 5LT* Tel (01905) 339455 E-mail sherry@sbloomer.freeserve.co.uk

BLOOMFIELD, Mrs Brenda Elizabeth. b 41. Gipsy Hill Coll of Educn TCert63. **d** 07 **p** 08. NSM Upper Weardale *Dur* from 07. *1 Broadwood View, Frosterley, Bishop Auckland DL13 2RT* Tel (01388) 527980

BLOOMFIELD, Mrs Christine Louise. b 52. ERMC 05. **d** 08 **p** 09. C Strasbourg *Eur* from 08. *28 rue Principale, 67270 Kienheim, France* Tel (0033) 3 88 62 61 05 Fax 6 67 45 20 56 E-mail bloomfieldhilaire@wanadoo.fr

BLOOMFIELD, John Michael. b 35. Univ of Wales (Lamp) BA57. Sarum Th Coll 59. **d** 61 **p** 62. C Fordington *Sarum* 61-64; C Branksome St Aldhelm 64-66; Youth Chapl *Win* 66-69; R Win w St Mich and Chesil 71-79; P-in-c Corsley *Sarum* 79-81; P-in-c Studland 83-86; Chapl HM Pris Dorchester 87-89; C Dorchester *Sarum* 87-89; Chapl HM Pris The Verne 89-00; rtd 00; Perm to Offic *Sarum* from 01. *Green Acres, Valley Road, Corfe Castle, Wareham BH20 5HU* Tel (01929) 480924 Fax 481699 E-mail swanbeck@aol.com

BLOOMFIELD, John Stephen. b 56. Chich Th Coll 83. **d** 86 **p** 87. C Chich St Paul and St Pet 86-89; TV Littlehampton and Wick 89-98; V Hunstanton St Edm w Ringstead *Nor* from 98. *St Edmund's Vicarage, 53 Northgate, Hunstanton PE36 6DS* Tel (01485) 532531 E-mail bloomfield545@btinternet.com

BLOOR, Ms Amanda Elaine. b 62. Leic Univ BA83 Open Univ PGCE96 York Univ MA02. Ripon Coll Cuddesdon 02. **d** 04 **p** 05. C Hambleden Valley *Ox* 04-07; Bp's Dom Chapl from 07. *Diocesan Church House, North Hinksey, Oxford OX2 0NB* Tel (01865) 208221 E-mail amanda.bloor@oxford.anglican.org

BLOOR, Terence Bernard. b 62. Liv Univ BTh02. NOC 99. **d** 02 **p** 03. C Hadley *Lich* 02-06; P-in-c Basford from 06; RD Newcastle from 11; Chapl N Staffs Hosp NHS Trust from 06. *211 Basford Park Road, Newcastle ST5 0PG* Tel (01782) 619045 Mobile 07890-980749 E-mail terry.bloor@btinternet.com

BLORE, Canon John Francis. b 49. Jes Coll Ox BA72 MA76. Wycliffe Hall Ox 73. **d** 75 **p** 76. C Waltham Abbey *Chelmsf* 75-78; C E Ham St Geo 78-81; R Colchester St Mich Myland 81-00; Chapl Oxley Parker Sch Colchester 81-00; P-in-c Halstead St Andr w H Trin and Greenstead Green *Chelmsf* 00-04; TR Halstead Area from 04; RD Hinckford 03-08; Hon Can Chelmsf Cathl from 09. *The Vicarage, Parsonage Street, Halstead CO9 2LD* Tel (01787) 472171 E-mail john@johnfblore.freeserve.co.uk

BLOUNT, Robin George. b 38. Lon Coll of Div 61 Wycliffe Hall Ox 67. **d** 68 **p** 69. C Bletchley *Ox* 68-71; C Washington *Dur* 71-74; TV Chelmsley Wood *Birm* 74-76; Ind Chapl *Worc* 76-89; Asst P Dudley St Jo 76-88; Asst P Dudley St Thos and St Luke 88-89; Ind Chapl (Eurotunnel Development) *Cant* 89-03; rtd 03;

Perm to Offic *Cant* from 03. *6 Lyn Court, Shorncliffe Road, Folkestone CT20 2PE* Tel (01303) 250028 E-mail robin.blount@virgin.net

BLOWS, Canon Derek Reeve. b 26. Linc Coll Ox BA50 MA52 SAP75. Cuddesdon Coll 50. **d** 52 **p** 53. C Cov St Mark 52-56; Lic to Offic *Sarum* 56-58; Chapl Warlingham Park Hosp Croydon 58-65; V Purley St Mark *S'wark* 65-70; Dir Past Care and Counselling 70-80; Hon Can S'wark Cathl 72-80; Dir Westmr Past Foundn 80-91; rtd 91; Perm to Offic *Roch* 91-09. *30 St James Street, Shaftesbury SP7 8HE* Tel (01747) 853088

BLOXAM-ROSE, Canon Simon Franklyn. b 61. Southn Univ BTh MA92 PhD99 HonFLCM88. Chich Th Coll 85. **d** 88 **p** 89. C Bassaleg *Mon* 88-89; Chapl Aldenham Sch Herts 89-94; Sen Chapl Millfield Sch Somerset 94-06; CF from 06; Can St Jo Pro-Cathl Katakwa from 95. *c/o MOD Chaplains (Army)* Tel (01264) 381140 Fax 381824

BLOXHAM, Oliver. b 27. Ely Th Coll 60. **d** 62 **p** 63. C Newc H Cross 62-65; C Ponteland 65-69; V Dudley 69-79; P-in-c Balkwell 79-81; V 81-92; rtd 92; Perm to Offic *Newc* from 92. *25 Dawson Place, Morpeth NE61 1AQ* Tel (01670) 514841

BLUNDELL, Catherine. b 62. SAOMC 96. **d** 99 **p** 00. C Furze Platt *Ox* 99-03; TV Bracknell 03-09; V Winkfield and Cranbourne from 09. *The Vicarage, Winkfield Street, Winkfield, Windsor SL4 4SW* Tel (01344) 884271 E-mail catherine.blundell@btinternet.com

BLUNDELL, Peter Grahame. b 61. Ealing Coll of Educn BA83. Oak Hill NSM Course 91. **d** 94 **p** 95. NSM Kensington St Barn *Lon* 94-97; Zimbabwe 97-99; Assoc Min Romford Gd Shep *Chelmsf* 99-04; 1 Oak Ridges Canada from 04. *19 Waldron Crescent, Richmond Hill ON L4E 4A3, Canada*

BLUNDEN, Jacqueline Ann. See MILLER, Mrs Jacqueline Ann

BLUNDEN, Jeremy Augustine. b 61. BSc CEng88 MIStructE88. SEITE 99. **d** 99 **p** 00. NSM Sydenham St Bart *S'wark* 99-01; C 01-03; V Clapham H Spirit from 03. *15 Elms Road, London SW4 9ER* Tel (020) 7622 8703 E-mail jeremy.blunden@btopenworld.com

BLUNSUM, Charles Michael. b 28. ACIB51 MBIM86. **d** 74 **p** 75. C Stoke Bishop *Bris* 74-79; Chapl Brunel Manor Chr Cen Torquay 79-94; rtd 94; Perm to Offic *Ex* from 94. *16A Hollywater Close, Torquay TQ1 3TN* Tel (01803) 214371

BLUNT, Jeremy William. b 49. Birm Univ MEd85 GRNCM73. **d** 07 **p** 08. OLM Streetly *Lich* from 07. *63 Lindrosa Road, Sutton Coldfield B74 3LB* Tel 0121-353 9712 Mobile 07849-689180 E-mail jeremy.blunt@virgin.net

BLYDE, Ian Hay. b 52. Liv Univ BSc74 Edin Univ BD80. Edin Th Coll 77. **d** 80 **p** 81. C Ainsdale *Liv* 80-83; Chapl Birkenhead Sch Merseyside 83-90; V Over St Chad *Ches* 90-93; Chapl Ex Sch and St Marg Sch 93-98; NSM Littleham w Exmouth 03-06; TV Brixham w Churston Ferrers and Kingswear from 06. *The Vicarage, 13 Warborough Road, Churston Ferrers, Brixham TQ5 0JY* Tel (01803) 844663

BLYTH, Andrew Kenneth Eric. b 63. Roehampton Inst BA86 Middx Univ PGCE87. Ridley Hall Cam 98. **d** 00 **p** 01. C Luton St Mary *St Alb* 00-04; P-in-c Walton H Trin *Ox* 04-09; V Walton H Trin from 09; AD Aylesbury from 10. *The Rectory, 42 Redwood Drive, Aylesbury HP21 7TN* Tel (01296) 394906 Mobile 07905-181002 E-mail hta_vicar@yahoo.co.uk

BLYTH, Bryan Edward Perceval. b 22. Linc Coll Ox BA49 MA52. Wells Th Coll 48. **d** 50 **p** 51. C Timperley *Ches* 50-52; C Talbot Village *Sarum* 52-55; C-in-c Weymouth St Edm 55; P-in-c 56-63; Asst Dir of Educn *Chelmsf* 64-67; Hon C Mountnessing 67-68; Hon C Ingatestone w Buttsbury 67-68; Teacher Ingatestone Sec Modern Sch 67-68; Teacher Westwood Co Jun Sch 68-72; Dep Hd 72-87; Hon C Thundersley 80-84; rtd 87; Perm to Offic *Sarum* and *Win* from 98. *Greenways, 19 Chiltern Drive, New Milton BH25 7JY* Tel (01425) 611140

BLYTH, Mrs Geraldine Anne. b 50. Llan Dioc Tr Scheme 90. **d** 94 **p** 97. C Llantrisant 94-01; P-in-c Llanharry 01-06; Chapl Pontypridd and Rhondda NHS Trust 01-06; V Llangynwyd w Maesteg from 06. *Yr Hen Ficerdy, Llangynwyd, Maesteg CF34 9SB* Tel (01656) 733194

BLYTH, Graham. See BLYTH, Canon Michael Graham

BLYTH, Ian John. b 40. Rhodes Univ BA66 Natal Univ BEd81 MEd96. **d** 82 **p** 83. S Africa 82-01; Dioc Educn Officer Natal 83-85; R Pietermaritzburg St Luke 85-87; Lic to Offic 88-01; NSM W Woodhay w Enborne, Hampstead Marshall etc *Ox* 02-09; NSM Kintbury w Avington 05-09; rtd 09; Hon C Burstwick w Thorngumbald *York* from 09. *The Rectory, Ottringham Road, Keyingham, Hull HU12 9RX* Tel (01964) 622907 Mobile 07900-857096 E-mail ianblyth0801@btinternet.com

BLYTH, John Reddie. b 25. Wadh Coll Ox BA48 MA50. Ridley Hall Cam 48. **d** 50 **p** 51. C Enfield Ch Ch *Lon* 50-52; C Enfield Ch Ch Trent Park *Lon* 52-55; V Plymouth St Jude *Ex* 55-63; E Midl Area Sec CPAS 63-70; V Parkstone St Luke *Sarum* 70-90; Chapl Uplands Sch Parkstone 70-73; rtd 90; Perm to Offic *Chich* from 90. *5 Powell Road, Newick, Lewes BN8 4LS* Tel (01825) 722011

BLYTH, Kenneth Henry. b 35. Oak Hill Th Coll 58. **d** 61 **p** 62. C St Alb St Paul *St Alb* 61-65; P-in-c Aspenden and Layston w Buntingford 65-66; R 66-72; R Washfield, Stoodleigh, Withleigh etc *Ex* 72-82; P-in-c Cruwys Morchard 72-74; RD Tiverton 76-82; V Eastbourne H Trin *Chich* 82-00; rtd 00; Perm to Offic *Ex* from 00. *Hamslade House, Bampton, Tiverton EX16 9JA*

BLYTH, Canon Michael Graham. b 53. Jes Coll Ox BA75 MA78 Dur Univ PhD79. Qu Coll Birm 82. **d** 84 **p** 85. C Nantwich *Ches* 84-86; C Coppenhall 86-88; TV Southend *Chelmsf* 88-95; P-in-c Danbury 95-11; R from 11; RD Chelmsf S 01-07; Hon Can Chelmsf Cathl from 07. *St John's Rectory, 55 Main Road, Danbury, Chelmsford CM3 4NG* Tel (01245) 223140 E-mail michaelg@canongate.org.uk

BOAG, David. b 46. Edin Th Coll 69. **d** 72 **p** 73. C Edin Old St Paul 72-75; P-in-c Edin St Andr and St Aid 75-88; Lic to Offic from 88. *7 Starch Mill, Ford Road, Haddington EH41 4AR* Tel (01620) 826839

BOAG, Michael John. b 61. Leeds Univ BA00. Coll of Resurr Mirfield 98. **d** 00 **p** 01. C Howden *York* 00-03; Min Can and Succ Windsor from 03; Chapl St Geo Sch Windsor 03-06; Dean's V from 06. *3 The Cloisters, Windsor Castle, Windsor SL4 1NJ* Tel (01753) 848737 E-mail succentor@stgeorges-windsor.org

BOAK, Canon Donald Kenneth. b 30. MBAOT53. S'wark Ord Course 82. **d** 85 **p** 86. C Tulse Hill H Trin and St Matthias *S'wark* 85-88; C Surbiton St Matt 88-91; Intercon Ch Soc, SAMS and Miss to Seamen 91-95; Peru 91-95; Dean Lima 93-95; rtd 95; Hon Can Peru from 95; Hon C Bournemouth St Andr *Win* 96-99; Perm to Offic *Sarum* 98-01 and from 99. *3 Hymans Way, Totton, Southampton SO40 3DL* Tel (023) 8086 8265

BOAKES, Canon Norman. b 50. Univ of Wales (Swansea) BA71 Univ of Wales (Lamp) LTh73 Ox Univ MTh96. Bp Burgess Hall Lamp 71. **d** 73 **p** 74. C Swansea St Mary w H Trin *S & B* 73-78; Chapl Univ of Wales (Swansea) 76-78; Chapl K Alfred Coll *Win* 78-82; V Colbury 82-91; Chapl Ashurst Hosp 82-91; Chapl Mental Handicap Services Unit 82-91; V Southampton Maybush St Pet *Win* 91-06; P-in-c Southampton St Jude 04-06; V Maybush and Southampton St Jude 06-07; Bp's Adv for Hosp Chapl 87-00; AD Southampton 02-07; Continuing Minl Development Officer from 08; Hon Can Win Cathl from 11. *33 Shepherds Down, Alresford SO24 9PP* Tel (01962) 734599 E-mail norman.boakes@winchester.anglican.org

BOARDMAN, Frederick Henry. b 25. Liv Univ BSc46 St Cath Soc Ox BA49 MA54 Birm Univ MEd71 PhD77 Lon Univ PGCE68. Wycliffe Hall Ox 47. **d** 50 **p** 51. C Bootle Ch Ch *Liv* 50-52; C-in-c Netherton CD 52-57; V Stechford *Birm* 57-63; Lic to Offic *Birm* 63-69 and *Liv* 71-89; Hon C Sutton *Liv* 76-89; Hon C Burtonwood 89-02; rtd 92; Perm to Offic *Liv* from 92. *Woodside, Burtonwood Road, Great Sankey, Warrington WA5 3AN* Tel (01925) 635079

BOARDMAN, The Ven Jonathan. b 63. Magd Coll Cam BA89 Magd Coll Ox MA90. Westcott Ho Cam 87. **d** 90 **p** 91. C W Derby St Mary *Liv* 90-93; Prec St Alb Abbey 93-96; TR Catford (Southend) and Downham *S'wark* 96-99; RD E Lewisham 99; Chapl Rome *Eur* from 99; Sen Tutor Angl Cen Rome from 00; Can Gib Cathl from 07; Adn Italy and Malta from 09. *All Saints, via del Babuino 153, 00187 Rome, Italy* Tel (0039) (06) 3600 2171 *or* tel and fax 3600 1881 E-mail j.boardman@allsaintsrome.org *or* office@allsaintsrome.org

BOARDMAN, Preb Philippa Jane. b 63. Jes Coll Cam BA85 MA89. Ridley Hall Cam 87. **d** 90 **p** 94. Par Dn Walthamstow St Mary w St Steph *Chelmsf* 90-93; C Hackney Wick St Mary of Eton w St Aug *Lon* 93-96; P-in-c Old Ford St Paul and St Mark 96-03; V from 03; Dean of Women's Min Stepney Area 94-02; Preb St Paul's Cathl from 02. *The Vicarage, St Stephen's Road, London E3 5JL* Tel (020) 8980 9020

BOCKING (Essex), Dean of. See NEED, The Very Revd Philip Alan

BOCKING (Suffolk), Dean of. See THROWER, The Very Revd Martin Charles

BODDAM-WHETHAM, Tudor Alexander. b 76. St Aid Coll Dur BA97. Wycliffe Hall Ox 06. **d** 08 **p** 09. C Houghton *Carl* from 08. *167 Kingstown Road, Carlisle CA3 0AX* Tel 07910-754394 (mobile)

BODDINGTON, Canon Alan Charles Peter. b 37. Oak Hill Th Coll 63. **d** 66 **p** 67. C Bedworth *Cov* 66-69; P-in-c Bp's Officer for Min 69-75; Bp's Chapl for Miss 69-73; P-in-c Wroxall and Honiley 72-75; V Westwood 75-85; Asst Chapl Warw Univ 78-85; TR N Farnborough *Guildf* 85-02; RD Aldershot 88-93; Hon Can Guildf Cathl 92-02; rtd 02; Perm to Offic *Cov* from 02. *Tremar, Hathaway Lane, Stratford-upon-Avon CV37 9BJ* Tel (01789) 263643 Mobile 07866-909092

BODDY, Alan Richard. b 47. Ripon Coll Cuddesdon. **d** 84 **p** 85. C Eastcote St Lawr *Lon* 84-87; C Kensington St Mary Abbots w St Geo 87-90; Chapl HM Pris Brixton 90-91; Chapl HM Pris Send and Downview 91-92; Chapl HM Pris High Down 92-98; Chapl HM Pris Wormwood Scrubs 98-02; rtd 02; Perm to Offic *Lon* and *S'wark* from 02; PV Westmr Abbey from 02. *105 Valiant House, Vicarage Crescent, London SW11 3LX* E-mail alanboddy@dsl.pipex.com

BODDY, David. b 57. Linc Th Coll 92. **d** 92 **p** 93. C Peterlee *Dur* 92-95; C Penshaw 95-97; P-in-c Shiney Row 95-98; P-in-c Herrington 95-98; TV S Shields All SS 98-04; V Haswell, Shotton and Thornley from 04. *The Vicarage, Shotton Colliery, Durham DH6 2JW* Tel 0191-526 1156 Mobile 07971-304622 E-mail davidboddy@lineone.net

BODLE, Richard Talbot. b 70. Southn Univ LLB91. Wycliffe Hall Ox BTh98. **d** 98 **p** 99. C S Mimms Ch Ch *Lon* 98-02; TV Edgware 02-08; V Churt and Hindhead *Guildf* from 08. *St Alban's Vicarage, Wood Road, Hindhead GU26 6PX* Tel (01428) 605305 E-mail richard@bodle.plus.com

BODMIN, Archdeacon of. *See* ELKINGTON, The Ven Audrey Anne

BODY, Andrew. b 46. Pemb Coll Cam BA68 MA71. Ridley Hall Cam 68. **d** 70 **p** 71. C New Bury *Man* 70-73; TV Droylsden St Mary 73-78; V Low Harrogate St Mary *Ripon* 78-92; TR Redhorn *Sarum* 92-97; V Chobham w Valley End *Guildf* from 97; RD Surrey Heath from 06. *Chobham Vicarage, Bagshot Road, Chobham, Woking GU24 8BY* Tel (01276) 858197 E-mail ab@tasoma.orangehome.co.uk

BODY, Mrs Shuna Jane. b 67. SEITE 98. **d** 01 **p** 02. NSM Appledore w Brookland, Fairfield, Brenzett etc *Cant* from 01. *Hope Farm, Snargate, Romney Marsh TN29 9UQ* Tel (01797) 343977 Mobile 07977-981990 E-mail shunabody@hotmail.com

BODYCOMBE, Stephen John. b 58. Lanchester Poly Cov BA. St Mich Coll Llan. **d** 83 **p** 84. C Cardiff St Jo *Llan* 83-86; V Dinas and Penygraig w Williamstown 86-00; V Dyffryn from 00. *The Vicarage, Dyffryn, Neath SA10 7AZ* Tel (01792) 814237

BOFFEY, Ian. b 40. Glas Univ MA63. Glas NSM Course 75. **d** 75 **p** 78. NSM Dalry *Glas* 75-78; P-in-c 78-97; N Ayrshire TM from 97. *2 Kinloch Avenue, Stewarton, Kilmarnock KA3 3HF* Tel (01560) 482586 E-mail ian.boffey2@btinternet.com

BOGA, Bishop of. *See* NJOJO, The Rt Revd Patrice Byankya

BOGGUST, Mrs Patricia Anne. b 42. Portsm Dioc Tr Course. **d** 90 **p** 98. NSM Hook w Warsash *Portsm* 90-94; NSM Locks Heath 94-09; Chapl Southn Univ Hosps NHS Trust from 01. *21 Beverley Close, Park Gate, Southampton SO31 6QU* Tel (01489) 573586

BOGLE, Ms Elizabeth. b 47. York Univ BA68 Leeds Univ PGCE69. S'wark Ord Course 93. **d** 96 **p** 97. NSM E Greenwich *S'wark* 96-00; NSM Hatcham St Jas 00; NSM Newington St Paul from 06. *96 Grierson Road, London SE23 1NX* Tel (020) 8699 9996 E-mail elizabethbogle@hotmail.com

BOGLE, James Main Lindam Linton. b 33. Peterho Cam BA56 MA60. Wells Th Coll 59. **d** 61 **p** 62. C Bermondsey St Anne *S'wark* 61-65; Chapl York Univ 65-72; V Brayton 72-76; V Forest Hill St Aug *S'wark* 76-83; C Hatcham St Cath 83-85; Hon C 91-03; C Herne Hill St Paul 86-87; rtd 87; Perm to Offic *S'wark* from 04. *96 Grierson Road, London SE23 1NX* Tel (020) 8699 9996 E-mail jamesmllbogle@hotmail.com

BOGLE, Paul David. b 57. CITC BTh10. **d** 10. C Dunboyne and Rathmolyon *M & K* from 10. *Curragha, Ashbourne, Co Meath, Republic of Ireland* Tel (00353) (1) 835 1037 E-mail pdbogle@gmail.com

BOHAN, Kimberley. b 72. St Andr Univ MA93 Smith Coll (USA) MAT94 St Andr Univ BD99 Edin Univ MTh03. **d** 03 **p** 04. C Glas St Ninian 03-06; R Dunoon *Arg* 06-09; P-in-c Rothesay 06-09; P-in-c Tighnabruaich 06-09; R Dunblane *St And* from 09. *The Rectory, Smith Loan, Dunblane FK15 0HQ* E-mail kbohan@btinternet.com

BOIT, Mervyn Hays. b 38. Univ of Wales (Lamp) BA59. St Mich Coll Llan 59. **d** 61 **p** 62. C Roath St German *Llan* 61-63; C Skewen 63-69; V Pontycymer and Blaengarw 69-03; rtd 03; P-in-c Biarritz *Eur* 06-07. *St Andrew's House, Troed-y-Bryn, Caerphilly CF83 2PX* Tel (029) 850140

BOLAND, Christopher Paul. b 75. Hertf Coll Ox MPhys97. Ridley Hall Cam BTh01. **d** 01 **p** 02. C Skirbeck H Trin *Linc* 01-05; P-in-c Grantham, Harrowby w Londonthorpe from 05. *The Vicarage, Edinburgh Road, Grantham NG31 9QZ* Tel (01476) 564781 Mobile 07791-702537 E-mail cpboland@btinternet.com

BOLAND, Geoffrey. b 56. Open Univ BA03. Oak Hill Th Coll 87. **d** 89 **p** 90. C Ormskirk *Liv* 89-94; C Woodside Park St Barn *Lon* 94-99; TV Canford Magna *Sarum* from 99. *11 Plantagenet Crescent, Bournemouth BH11 9PL* Tel (01220) 573872

BOLD, Peter Edward. b 64. Sheff Univ BEng86 PhD90. Cranmer Hall Dur BA94. **d** 95 **p** 96. C Grenoside *Sheff* 95-97; C Rotherham and Dioc Communications Officer 97-01; P-in-c Brampton Bierlow 01-05; V from 05. *Brampton Vicarage, Christchurch Road, Wath-upon-Dearne, Rotherham S63 6NW* Tel (01709) 873210 E-mail pebold@talk21.com

BOLDING, Alan Frederick. b 40. NTMTC. **d** 07 **p** 07. NSM Woodford Bridge *Chelmsf* from 07. *21 Portman Drive, Woodford Green IG8 8QN* Tel (020) 8550 2070 Mobile 07932-797983 E-mail apbolding@onetel.com

BOLE, Malcolm Dennis. b 30. Oak Hill Th Coll 65. **d** 67 **p** 68. C Bridlington Priory *York* 67-70; Lect Stanley Smith Th Coll Gahini Rwanda 71; Prin 71-72; Lect École de Théologie Butare

72-73; P-in-c Combe Hay *B & W* 74-81; V Bath Odd Down 74-81; P-in-c Taunton St Jas 81-84; V 84-90; R Bicknoller w Crowcombe and Sampford Brett 90-98; rtd 98; Perm to Offic *B & W* from 01. *7 Putsham Mead, Kilve, Bridgwater TA5 1DZ* Tel (01278) 741297

BOLLARD, Canon Richard George. b 39. Fitzw Ho Cam BA61 MA65 K Coll Lon BD63 AKC63. **d** 64 **p** 65. C Southampton Maybush St Pet *Win* 64-68; Chapl Aston Univ 68-74; TR Chelmsley Wood 74-82; V Coleshill and Maxstoke 82-04; RD Coleshill 82-92; Hon Can Birm Cathl 85-04; Dioc Ecum Officer 97-02; rtd 04; Perm to Offic *Heref* from 05. *Moreton Cottage, 12 Prince Edward Road, Hereford HR4 0LG* Tel (01432) 267414

BOLLEY, Michael Francis. b 55. St Cath Coll Ox BA76 MSc77 MA92. Ripon Coll Cuddesdon 90. **d** 92 **p** 93. C Pinner *Lon* 92-95; C Eastcote St Lawr 95-99; P-in-c Southall H Trin 99-06; V from 06. *Holy Trinity Vicarage, Park View Road, Southall UB1 3HJ* Tel (020) 8574 3839 E-mail michael@bolley.freeserve.co.uk

BOLSTER, Chris David. b 77. St Mary's Coll Twickenham BA99. STETS MA11. **d** 11. C Stanwix *Carl* from 11. *54 Eden Street, Stanwix, Carlisle CA3 9LH* Tel 07970-943244 (mobile) E-mail cdbolster2000@tiscali.co.uk

BOLSTER, David Richard. b 50. BA. St Jo Coll Nottm. **d** 84 **p** 85. C Luton Lewsey St Hugh *St Alb* 84-87; V Woodside w E Hyde 87-01; V Edmonton St Aldhelm *Lon* 01-10. *Address temp unknown*

BOLT, George Henry. b 34. MInstP75 CPhys75 Lon Univ BSc60 Bath Univ MSc75. S Dios Minl Tr Scheme 85. **d** 88 **p** 89. NSM Oldbury *Sarum* 88-89; Chapl Chippenham Tech Coll 89-90; C Kington St Michael *Bris* 90-92; P-in-c Aldenham *St Alb* 92-98; rtd 98; Perm to Offic *Ban* from 98. *Ty Capel Ffrwd, Llanfachreth, Dolgellau LL40 2NR* Tel (01341) 422006

BOLT, Mrs Mary Veronica. b 36. S Dios Minl Tr Scheme 90. **d** 93 **p** 94. NSM Aldenham *St Alb* 93-98; Sub-Chapl HM Pris The Mount 93-98; rtd 98; Perm to Offic *Ban* 98-99; P-in-c Maentwrog w Trawsfynydd 99-03. *Ty Capel Ffrwd, Llanfachreth, Dolgellau LL40 2NR* Tel (01341) 422006 E-mail mary.bolt@care4free.net

BOLTON, Canon Christopher Leonard. b 60. St Mich Coll Llan. **d** 83 **p** 84. C Lampeter *St D* 83-86; P-in-c Llanarth and Capel Cynon w Talgarreg etc 86-87; V from 87; AD Glyn Aeron from 02; Hon Can St D Cathl from 09. *The Vicarage, Llanarth SA47 0NJ* Tel (01545) 580745

BOLTON, Canon Jane Elizabeth. b 53. Leic Univ BA75. Ripon Coll Cuddesdon 95. **d** 97 **p** 98. C Sheff St Mark Broomhill 97-02; P-in-c Dinnington 02-04; P-in-c Laughton w Throapham 03-04; P-in-c Dinnington w Laughton and Throapham 04-05; R 05-11; AD Laughton 08-11; P-in-c Ravenfield, Hooton Roberts and Braithwell from 11; SSM Officer from 11; Hon Can Sheff Cathl from 10. *The Rectory, Micklebring Lane, Braithwell, Rotherham S66 7AS* Tel (01709) 812665 E-mail mail@janebolton.co.uk *or* jane.bolton@sheffield.anglican.org

BOLTON, John. b 43. SS Paul & Mary Coll Cheltenham DipEd64. Trin Coll Bris 83. **d** 85 **p** 86. C Minehead *B & W* 85-89; R Winford w Felton Common Hill 89-98; C-in-c Locking Castle CD 98-06; rtd 06; Perm to Offic *B & W* from 06. *The Poppies, 13 Cornlands, Sampford Peverell, Tiverton EX16 7UA* Tel (01884) 821445 E-mail john20011ccp@aol.com

BOLTON, Kelvin. b 53. Wilson Carlile Coll 88 Trin Coll Bris BA98. **d** 98 **p** 99. C Walton Breck Ch Ch *Liv* 98-01; V Goose Green 01-08; P-in-c Walton Breck from 08. *Christ Church Vicarage, 157 Hartnup Street, Liverpool L5 1UW* Tel 0151-263 2518 E-mail kelvb@uwclub.net

BOLTON, Paul Edward. b 53. St Jo Coll Ox BA94 MA98 Peterho Cam BA97. Ridley Hall Cam 95. **d** 98 **p** 99. C Lowestoft Ch Ch *Nor* 98-01; Titus Trust from 01. *33 Wharton Road, Headington, Oxford OX3 8AL* Tel (01865) 756334 E-mail paul_bolton@lineone.net

BOLTON, Peter Richard Shawcross. b 58. Warwick Univ BA79. Sarum & Wells Th Coll 80. **d** 83 **p** 84. C Beckenham St Jas *Roch* 83-86; C Bedford Leigh *Man* 86-88; V Royton St Paul 88-94; AD Tandle 93-94; P-in-c Lower Broughton Ascension 95-01; P-in-c Salford Ordsall St Clem 99-01; P-in-c Ardwick St Benedict 99-01; V Leavesden *St Alb* 01-07; V Weston super Mare All SS and St Sav *B & W* 07-10; rtd 10; CMP 99-10. *Address withheld by request* E-mail prsb58@gmail.com

BOLTON, Richard David Edward. b 52. MA. St Steph Ho Ox 79. **d** 81 **p** 82. C Rawmarsh w Parkgate *Sheff* 81-84; Chapl Wellingborough Sch 85-92; Chapl Merchant Taylors' Sch Northwood from 91; Perm to Offic *Lon* from 91; P in O from 96. *1 Askew Road, Sandy Lodge, Northwood HA6 2JE* Tel (01923) 821136 *or* 820644

BOLTON, Archdeacon of. *See* BAILEY, The Ven David Charles

BOLTON, Suffragan Bishop of. *See* EDMONDSON, The Rt Revd Christopher Paul

BOMFORD, Canon Rodney William George. b 43. BNC Ox BA64 MA68. Coll of Resurr Mirfield 67 Union Th Sem (NY) STM69. **d** 69 **p** 70. C Deptford St Paul *S'wark* 69-77; V Camberwell St Giles w St Matt 77-01; RD Camberwell 87-97;

Hon Can S'wark Cathl 93-01; rtd 01. *The Manor House, Modbury, Ivybridge PL21 0RA* Tel (01548) 831277

BOMYER, Julian Richard Nicholas Jeffrey. b 55. AKC78 Sarum & Wells Th Coll 78. **d** 79 **p** 80. C Rugby *Cov* 79-84; TV 85-88; P-in-c Clifton upon Dunsmore w Brownsover 84-85; Prec Ch Ch *Ox* 88-93; V Hampton *Worc* 93-01; P-in-c Sedgeberrow w Hinton-on-the-Green 00-01; R Hampton w Sedgeberrow w Hinton-on-the-Green 01-06; rtd 06. *52 Elmside, Evesham WR11 3DZ* Tel (01386) 421559 E-mail julian@bomyer.co.uk

BOND, Alan Richard. b 49. Lon Univ BSc71 Imp Coll Lon ARCS71 MCMI75 MIMA75 CMath98 CSci05. S Dios Minl Tr Scheme 80. **d** 83 **p** 84. NSM Westbourne *Chich* 83-86. *Address temp unknown* E-mail alan.r.bond@btopenworld.com

✠**BOND, The Rt Revd Charles Derek.** b 27. AKC51. **d** 52 **p** 53 **c** 76. C Friern Barnet St Jas *Lon* 52-56; Lic to Offic *Birm* 56-58; Midl Sch Sec SCM 56-58; V Harringay St Paul *Lon* 58-62; V Harrow Weald All SS 62-72; P-in-c Pebmarsh *Chelmsf* 72-73; Adn Colchester 72-76; Suff Bp Bradwell 76-84; Area Bp Bradwell 84-92; rtd 92; Hon Asst Bp Glouc and Worc 92-06; Perm to Offic *Chelmsf* from 06; Hon Asst Bp Chelmsf from 07. *52 Horn Book, Saffron Walden CB11 3JW* Tel (01799) 521308 E-mail derekbond@greenbee.net

BOND, Daniel Michael. b 75. Bp Grosseteste Coll BA(QTS)97 Cam Univ BTh02. Ridley Hall Cam 99. **d** 02 **p** 03. C Ranworth w Panxworth, Woodbastwick etc *Nor* 02-05; R Acle w Fishley, N Burlingham, Beighton w Moulton 05-07; Chapl Aldenham Sch Herts from 07. *1 The Orchard, Aldenham School, Aldenham Road, Elstree, Borehamwood WD6 3AJ* Tel (01923) 858122 E-mail dmb40@cam.ac.uk

BOND, David. b 36. Oak Hill Th Coll 72. **d** 74 **p** 75. C Leyton St Mary w St Edw *Chelmsf* 74-78; C Slough *Ox* 78-80; V Selby St Jas *York* 80-93; P-in-c Wistow 80-82; V 82-93; RD Selby 89-93; P-in-c Northiam *Chich* 93-94; R 94-99; rtd 99; Perm to Offic *Chich* from 00. *32 Reginald Road, Bexhill-on-Sea TN39 3PH* Tel (01424) 731845

BOND, David Matthew. b 38. Leic Univ BA59 Leeds Univ PGCE67 Nottm Univ MA85. Sarum Th Coll 59. **d** 61 **p** 62. C Leic St Anne 61-64; E England Sec SCM 64-66; Hon C Nor St Pet Mancroft 64-67; Lect and Hd of Section Pet Regional Coll 67-96; Lect Pet Coll of Adult Educn from 96; Hon C Stamford All SS w St Pet *Linc* 74-81; Hon C Stamford All SS w St Jo from 81; Perm to Offic *Pet* 85-07. *2 The Courtyard, Cotterstock, Peterborough PE8 5HD* Tel (01832) 226255

BOND, David Warner. b 32. MA BSc(Econ). Cant Sch of Min 79. **d** 82 **p** 83. NSM Otham w Langley *Cant* 82-10; Perm to Offic from 11. *6 Denton Close, Maidstone ME15 8ER* Tel (01622) 202239 Fax 205149 E-mail dwbond@blueyonder.co.uk *or* dwbond@bigfoot.com

BOND, Derek. See BOND, The Rt Revd Charles Derek

BOND, Mrs Gita Devi. b 57. N Lon Poly BSc80 Chelsea Coll Lon PGCE81. Ridley Hall Cam 06. **d** 08 **p** 09. C The Ramseys and Upwood *Ely* from 08. *23 Signal Road, Ramsey, Huntingdon PE26 1NG* Tel (01487) 821105 Mobile 07977-555895 E-mail gita.bond@hotmail.com

BOND, Gordon. b 44. Chich Th Coll 68. **d** 71 **p** 72. C Wisbech St Aug *Ely* 71-74; C Wembley Park St Aug *Lon* 74-77; C York Town St Mich *Guildf* 77-80; TV Haywards Heath St Wilfrid *Chich* 80-82; V Lower Beeding 82-86; V E Grinstead St Mary 86-06; RD E Grinstead 98-04; rtd 06. *6 St Andrew's Close, Reigate RH2 7JF*

BOND, Mrs Jill Margaret. b 45. Newton Park Coll Bath TCert67. WEMTC 04. **d** 06 **p** 07. OLM Redmarley D'Abitot, Bromesberrow, Pauntley etc *Glouc* from 06. *Southfield, Hawcross, Redmarley, Gloucester GL19 3JQ* Tel (01452) 840202 E-mail revjmbond@googlemail.com

BOND, Canon John Albert. b 35. LRAM55 GGSM56 St Cath Soc Ox BA61 MA65 MPhil77 Seabury-Western Th Sem BD62. Wycliffe Hall Ox 58. **d** 62 **p** 63. C Chelmsf Cathl 62-63; Succ 63-64; Prec 64-66; Lect St Osyth Coll Clacton-on-Sea 66-69; Lect Ch Ch Coll Cant 69-73; Sen Lect 73-85; Prin Lect and Hd RS Cant Ch Ch Univ Coll 85-00; Hon Min Can Cant Cathl 70-85; Hon Can 85-00; rtd 00; Perm to Offic *Cant* from 03. *1 St Lawrence Forstal, Canterbury CT1 3PA* Tel (01227) 765575

BOND, The Very Revd John Frederick Augustus. b 45. Open Univ BA75. CITC 64. **d** 67 **p** 69. C Lisburn St Paul *Conn* 67-70; C Finaghy 70-77; I Ballynure and Ballyeaston 77-99; I Skerry w Rathcavan and Newtowncrommelin from 99; Can Conn Cathl 96-98; Prec 98-01; Dean Conn from 01. *The Rectory, 49 Rectory Gardens, Broughshane, Ballymena BT42 4LF* Tel and fax (028) 2586 1215 Mobile 07711-285728 E-mail jfa.bond@btinternet.com *or* dean@connor.anglican.org

BOND, Kim Mary. See BURGESS, Mrs Kim Mary

BOND, Lawrence. b 53. ACIB77. Sarum & Wells Th Coll 92. **d** 92 **p** 93. C Saffron Walden w Wendens Ambo and Littlebury *Chelmsf* 92-95; TV 96-00; P-in-c Takeley w Lt Canfield 00-04; R 04-09; RD Dunmow and Stansted 02-09; P-in-c Sible Hedingham w Castle Hedingham from 09; RD Hinckford from 10. *The Vicarage, Queen Street, Castle Hedingham, Halstead CO9 3EZ* Tel (01787) 460274 E-mail revlbond@hotmail.com

BOND, Linda. b 52. Nottm Univ BEd80 Lon Inst of Educn MA89. EAMTC 96. **d** 99 **p** 00. C Brackley St Pet w St Jas 99-03; C Skegness Gp *Linc* 03-09; P-in-c Bromham w Oakley and Stagsden *St Alb* from 09. *The Vicarage, 47 Stagsden Road, Bromham, Bedford MK43 8PY* Tel (01234) 823268 E-mail revdlinda@talktalk.net

BOND, Mrs Marian Nancy Hamlyn. b 49. Univ of Wales (Cardiff) BSc(Econ)71 Westmr Coll Ox PGCE72 Ex Univ MEd77. SEITE BA06. **d** 06 **p** 07. NSM Marden *Cant* 06-09; NSM Len Valley 09-11; NSM Bredgar w Bicknor and Frinsted w Wormshill etc from 11; NSM Tunstall w Rodmersham from 11; Asst Dir of Ords from 09. *The Vicarage, Parsonage Lane, Bredgar, Sittingbourne ME9 8HA* Tel 07966-442181 (mobile) E-mail mnhbond@googlemail.com

BOND, Mark Francis Wilson. b 53. Sarum & Wells Th Coll 89. **d** 91 **p** 92. C Taunton Lyngford *B & W* 91-95; V Highbridge 95-02; R Jersey St Brelade *Win* from 02. *The Rectory, La Marquanderie Hill, St Brelade, Jersey JE3 8EP* Tel (01534) 742302 Fax 490878 E-mail rector@stbreladeschurch.com

BOND, Norman. b 23. Wycliffe Hall Ox. **d** 70 **p** 71. C Warrington St Ann *Liv* 70-73; P-in-c 73-77; P-in-c Warrington St Pet 73-77; V Wigan St Cath 77-88; rtd 88; Perm to Offic *Carl* 88-01; *Liv* 88-98; *S & M* 00-09. *Longs Croft, Gate Lane, Freshwater PO40 9QD* Tel (01983) 760799

BOND, Paul Maxwell. b 36. TD73. Open Th Coll BA00 ACIB56. Oak Hill Th Coll 76. **d** 79 **p** 80. NSM Wisley w Pyrford *Guildf* 79-91; Org Children's Soc SW Lon 88-91; C Egham *Guildf* 91-93; C Horsell 93-94; V Rockfield and St Maughen's w Llangattock etc *Mon* 94-99; rtd 99; Hon C Islip w Charlton on Otmoor, Oddington, Noke etc *Ox* 99-01; Hon C Ray Valley 01-04; Nat Liaison Officer Ch Tourism Assn 99-04; Perm to Offic *Guildf* from 08. *Fosters, Pyrford Heath, Pyrford, Woking GU22 8SS* Tel (01932) 351137 E-mail paul_bond@bigfoot.com

BOND, Mrs Susan Fraser. b 55. SS Hild & Bede Coll Dur BEd78 Leeds Univ MA00. NOC 96. **d** 99 **p** 00. C Tickhill w Stainton *Sheff* 99-02; R Warmsworth 02-10; AD W Doncaster 06-07; V Ampleforth w Oswaldkirk, Gilling E etc *York* from 10. *The Vicarage, West End, Ampleforth, York YO62 4DU* Tel (01439) 788876 E-mail sue@bond007.fslife.co.uk

BONE, David Hugh. b 39. Worc Coll Ox BA63 MA67. **d** 06 **p** 07. OLM Almondsbury and Olveston *Bris* from 06. *3 Hardy Lane, Tockington, Bristol BS32 4LJ* Tel (01454) 614601 Mobile 07958-414729 E-mail david.bone10@btinternet.com

BONE, Mrs Evelyn Mary. b 48. WEMTC 05. **d** 08 **p** 09. NSM Draycot *Bris* from 08. *Somerford House, 2 Fairleigh Rise, Kington Langley, Chippenham SN15 5QF* Tel (01249) 750519 E-mail langley@gebone.maill.co.uk

BONE, Janet. **d** 05 **p** 06. NSM Trellech and Penallt *Mon* 05-09; NSM Monmouth w Overmonnow etc from 09. *Ty Ffynnon, The Narth, Monmouth NP25 4QJ* Tel (01600) 860466

✠**BONE, The Rt Revd John Frank Ewan.** b 30. St Pet Coll Ox BA54 MA59 Whitelands Coll Lon PGCE71. Ely Th Coll 54. **d** 56 **p** 57 **c** 89. C Pimlico St Gabr *Lon* 56-60; C Henley *Ox* 60-63; V Datchet 63-76; RD Burnham 74-77; R Upton cum Chalvey 76-78; Adn Buckingham 77-89; Area Bp Reading 89-96; rtd 97; Hon Asst Bp Ox from 97. *4 Grove Road, Henley-on-Thames RG9 1DH* Tel (01491) 413482 E-mail jbone@talktalk.net

BONE, Simon Adrian. b 78. Ripon Coll Cuddesdon BA09. **d** 09 **p** 10. C Newquay *Truro* from 09. *127 Penmere Drive, Newquay TR7 1NS* Tel (01637) 879419 Mobile 07971-270615 E-mail fathersimon@btinternet.com

BONHAM, Mrs Valerie. b 47. ALA94. SAOMC 94. **d** 97 **p** 98. NSM Newbury *Ox* 97-98; C Cookham 98-02; P-in-c Coleford w Holcombe *B & W* from 02. *The Vicarage, Church Street, Coleford, Radstock BA3 5NG* Tel (01373) 813382

BONHAM-CARTER, Gerard Edmund David. b 31. Lon Univ BSc53. S'wark Ord Course 84. **d** 87 **p** 88. NSM Wandsworth St Paul *S'wark* 87-04; Chapl R Hosp for Neuro-Disability 92-04; Perm to Offic *St E* from 87 and *S'wark* from 04. *2 Fleur Gates, Princes Way, London SW19 6QQ* Tel and fax (020) 8788 1230 *or* 8780 5075 E-mail gerard.bonham-carter@ukgateway.net

BONIFACE, Lionel Ernest George. b 36. Lon Coll of Div ALCD63 BD64. **d** 64 **p** 65. C Attenborough w Chilwell *S'well* 64-69; C Farndon 69-71; C Thorpe 69-71; P-in-c Mansfield St Aug 71-77; V Oughtibridge *Sheff* 77-92; Ind Chapl 79-81; P-in-c Treeton 92-93; TV Brinsworth w Catcliffe and Treeton 93-98; rtd 98; Perm to Offic *Sheff* from 99. *30 Everard Avenue, Bradway, Sheffield S17 4LZ* Tel 0114-235 0415

BONIWELL, Timothy Richard. b 51. AKC73. St Aug Coll Cant 74. **d** 75 **p** 76. C Walthamstow St Mich *Chelmsf* 75-78; C Wigmore Abbey *Heref* 78-83; C Studley and Chapl Trowbridge Coll *Sarum* 83-86; V Bath St Barn w Englishcombe *B & W* 86-95; R Tintinhull w Chilthorne Domer, Yeovil Marsh etc 95-02; V Enfield St Geo *Lon* 02-05; Chapl Convent of St Mary at the Cross Edgware 05-10; Chapl Barnet and Chase Farm Hosps NHS Trust from 10. *Chase Farm Hospital, The Ridgeway, Enfield EN2 8JL* Tel 08451-114000 E-mail boniwell@btinternet.com

BONNER, David Robert. b 28. ASCA66 FCIS72 FCIB74. S'wark Ord Course 74. **d** 77 **p** 78. NSM Hampton All SS *Lon* 77-84; P-in-c Twickenham All SS 84-91; rtd 91; Perm to Offic *Lon* 91-05. *17 St James's Road, Hampton Hill, Hampton TW12 1DH* Tel (020) 8979 1565

BONNER, James Maxwell Campbell. b 28. Sydney Univ BSc48 DipEd49. Oak Hill Th Coll BD59. **d** 60 **p** 61. C Walthamstow St Mary *Chelmsf* 60-63; C Morden S'wark 63-65; Australia from 65; rtd 98. *120615 Albert Road, Strathfield NSW 2135, Australia* Tel (0061) (2) 9763 7535

BONNET, Tom. b 51. Univ of Wales (Cardiff) BTh90. St Mich Coll Llan 90. **d** 90 **p** 91. C Criccieth w Treflys *Ban* 90-91; C Denio w Abererch 91-93; R Llanfachraeth 93-94; R Valley w Llanfachraeth 94-98; R Valley w Llechylched and Caergeiliog 98-07; AD Llifon and Talybolion 04-07; V Caerhun and Llangelynnin and Llanbedr-y-Cennin from 07. *Caerhun Vicarage, Tyn-y-Groes, Conwy LL32 8UG* Tel (01492) 650250 Mobile 07713-548941 E-mail rev@tbonnet.freeserve.co.uk

BONNEY, Canon Mark Philip John. b 57. St Cath Coll Cam BA78 MA82. St Steph Ho Ox BA84 MA89. **d** 85 **p** 86. C Stockton St Pet *Dur* 85-88; Chapl St Alb Abbey 88-90; Prec 90-92; V Eaton Bray w Edlesborough 92-96; R Gt Berkhamsted 96-04; RD Berkhamsted 02-04; Can Res and Treas Sarum Cathl from 04. *Loders, 23 The Close, Salisbury SP1 2EH* Tel (01722) 322172 E-mail treasurer@salcath.co.uk

BONNEY, Prof Richard John. b 47. Ox Univ DPhil73. **d** 96 **p** 97. NSM Knighton St Mary Magd *Leic* from 96. *7 Carisbrooke Park, Leicester LE2 3PQ* Tel 0116-212 5677 E-mail hon@leicester.anglican.org

BONNEY, Stuart Campbell. b 51. Edin Univ BD83. Edin Th Coll 81. **d** 83 **p** 84. C Edin St Luke 83-86; C Edin St Martin 83-86; P-in-c Auchterarder *St And* 86-90; P-in-c Muthill 86-90; Dep Chapl HM Pris Leeds 90-91; Chapl HM Pris Moorland 91-96; P-in-c Bathgate *Edin* 96-01; P-in-c Linlithgow 96-01. *Circlebay Cottage, 159 Main Street, Pathhead EH37 5SQ* Tel (01875) 320336

BONNEYWELL, Miss Christine Mary. b 57. Univ of Wales (Lamp) BA78 LTh80. Sarum & Wells Th Coll 80. **d** 81 **p** 94. C Swansea St Pet *S & B* 81-84; C Llangyfelach 84-86; Chapl Univ of Wales (Lamp) *St D* 86-90; Educn Officer Wells Cathl 90-95; C Yeovil H Trin w Barwick 95-97; Chapl Yeovil Distr Hosp 95-97; Chapl Pilgrim Health NHS Trust Boston 97-01; Chapl United Lincs Hosps NHS Trust from 01. *The Chaplaincy, Pilgrim Hospital, Sibsey Road, Boston PE21 9QT, or 4 Hospital Lane, Boston PE21 9BY* Tel (01205) 364801 ext 2243 *or* 355151 Fax 354395

BONSALL, Charles Henry Brash. b 42. Ex Univ BA66. Ridley Hall Cam 66. **d** 68 **p** 69. C Cheltenham St Mary *Glouc* 68-72; Sudan 72-77 and 79-83; Perm to Offic *Nor* 78; Development and Miss Sec Intercon Ch Soc 83-93; rtd 93; Perm to Offic *Birm* from 91. *3 Pakenham Road, Birmingham B15 2NE* Tel 0121-440 6143

BONSEY, Hugh Richmond Lowry. b 49. Sarum & Wells Th Coll 74. **d** 76 **p** 77. C Bris St Mary Redcliffe w Temple etc 76-80; TV Sutton *Liv* 80-88; P-in-c Sutton Keynell *Bris* 88-89; P-in-c Biddestone w Slaughterford 88-89; P-in-c Castle Combe 88-89; P-in-c W Kington 88-89; P-in-c Nettleton w Littleton Drew 88-89; C Westbury-on-Trym H Trin 89-90; V Peasedown St John w Wellow *B & W* 90-04; TV Wylye and Till Valley *Sarum* from 04. *The Rectory, West Street, Great Wishford, Salisbury SP2 0PQ* Tel (01722) 790363 E-mail hbonsey@wylye.net

BONTING, Prof Sjoerd Lieuwe. b 24. Amsterdam Univ BSc44 MSc50 PhD52 Lon Univ BD58 SOSc. Washington Dioc Course 63. **d** 63 **p** 64. C Bethesda St Luke *USA* 63-65; Prof Biochemistry Nijmegen Univ 65-85; Chapl Nijmegen, Eindhoven, Arnhem and Twenthe *Eur* 80-85; Asst Sunnyvale St Thos *USA* 85-90; Asst Palo Alto St Mark 90-93; Perm to Offic *Eur* from 93. *Specreyse 12, 7471 TH Goor, The Netherlands* Tel (0031) (547) 260947 E-mail s.l.bonting@wxs.nl

BOOKER, Ms Alison Susan Wray. b 74. Worc Coll of Educn BA95 York St Jo Coll MA04. Westcott Ho Cam 06. **d** 08 **p** 09. C Countesthorpe w Foston *Leic* from 08. *7 Borrowcup Close, Countesthorpe, Leicester LE8 5XJ* Tel 0116-277 6066 E-mail abooker@leicester.anglican.org

BOOKER, Gerald Dennis. b 30. St Pet Coll Ox BA52 MA56. Ridley Hall Cam 53 Oak Hill Th Coll 80. **d** 81 **p** 82. Hon C Hertford All SS *St Alb* 81-83; R Bramfield w Stapleford and Waterford 83-96; Chapl Herts Univ 90-96; rtd 96; Perm to Offic *St Alb* from 96. *The Garden House, Churchfields, Hertford SG13 8AE*

BOOKER, Mrs Margaret Katharine. b 20. MCSP42. Westcott Ho Cam 82. **dss** 83 **d** 87 **p** 94. Stansted Mountfitchet *Chelmsf* 83-95; Par Dn 87-90; NSM 90-95; rtd 90; Perm to Offic *Ely* from 95. *49 Home Farm Road, Houghton, Huntingdon PE28 2BN* Tel (01480) 469167

BOOKER, Michael Charles. b 36. LLCM57 ARCO58. Lon Coll of Div LTh63. **d** 63 **p** 64. C Royston *St Alb* 63-66; C Mildenhall *St E* 66-68; Min Can St E Cathl 68-83; Prec 70-83; Chapl Framlingham Coll 84-99; rtd 99; Perm to Offic *St E* from 99.

BOOKER, Michael Paul Montague. b 57. Jes Coll Ox BA79 Bris Univ PGCE80. Trin Coll Bris BA87. **d** 87 **p** 88. C Cant St Mary Bredin 87-91; V Leamington Priors St Mary *Cov* 91-96; Dir Miss and Past Studies Ridley Hall Cam 96-05; P-in-c Comberton *Ely* 05-10; P-in-c Toft w Caldecote and Childerley 05-10; TR Lordsbridge from 10. *The Vicarage, 92 Swaynes Lane, Comberton, Cambridge CB3 7EF* Tel (01223) 260095 E-mail mpmb2@yahoo.co.uk

BOOKLESS, Andrew Pitcairn. b 63. Sheff Univ BA85. St Jo Coll Nottm 90. **d** 92 **p** 93. C Llantrisant 92-95; C Llangynwyd w Maesteg 95-97; V Bargoed and Deri w Brithdir from 97. *The Vicarage, Vicarage Lane, Bargoed CF81 8TR* Tel (01443) 831069 E-mail ahbookless@googlemail.com

BOOKLESS, David John Charles. b 62. Jes Coll Cam MA83 PGCE. Trin Coll Bris MA91. **d** 91 **p** 92. C Southall Green St Jo *Lon* 91-99; P-in-c Southall St Geo 99-01; Nat Dir A Rocha UK (Christians in Conservation) from 01; Hon C Southall Green St Jo from 03. *13 Avenue Road, Southall UB1 3BL* Tel (020) 8571 0981 E-mail dave.bookless@arocha.org *or* uk@arocha.org

BOOKLESS, Mrs Rosemary. b 26. Westf Coll Lon BA47 DipEd49 Serampore Univ BD72. St Mich Ho Ox 56. **dss** 80 **d** 91 **p** 94. Willoughby-on-the-Wolds w Wysall and Widmerpool *S'well* 80-85; rtd 85; Perm to Offic *Leic* 85-89; Loughborough Em 89-91; NSM 91-95; NSM Loughborough Em and St Mary in Charnwood 95-97; Perm to Offic 97-03. *7 Oakland Gardens, Bargoed CF81 8QF* Tel (01443) 832546 E-mail rosemary@rbookless.freeserve.co.uk

BOON, Miss Hilary Joy. b 44. Bath Coll of HE TCert65 Birm Univ BPhil83. Yorks Min Course 08. **d** 10 **p** 11. NSM Hutton Cranswick w Skerne, Watton and Beswick *York* from 10. *Homefield, 1 Laburnum Avenue, Cranswick, Driffield YO25 9QH* Tel (01377) 202084 Mobile 07970-370913 E-mail hilaryboon@hilaryboon.karoo.co.uk

BOON, Marion. *See* SIMMONS, Mrs Marion

BOON, Nigel Francis. b 39. St Jo Coll Nottm. **d** 83 **p** 84. C St Helens St Helen *Liv* 83-86; V Kirkdale St Lawr 86-92; V Huyton Quarry 92-99; rtd 01. *13/81 Lake Road, Devenport, North Shore, Auckland 0624, New Zealand* E-mail nigelfboon@hotmail.com

BOON, William John. b 54. Glouc Sch of Min 84. **d** 88 **p** 89. NSM Matson *Glouc* 88-91; C Gt Witcombe 91-95; C Brockworth 91-96; P-in-c Sharpness w Purton and Brookend 96-99; P-in-c Slimbridge 97-99; R Sharpness, Purton, Brookend and Slimbridge from 00; AD Dursley 02-07. *The Vicarage, Sanigar Lane, Newtown, Berkeley GL13 9NF* Tel (01453) 811360 E-mail bill.boon@lineone.net

BOORMAN, Hugh Ronald. b 58. Ox Min Course 07. **d** 08 **p** 08. C Didcot All SS *Ox* from 08. *Barnabas House, 12 Trent Road, Didcot OX11 7RB* Tel (01235) 819036 Mobile 07980-046162 E-mail huh.boorman1@btinternet.com

BOOT, Felicity Olivia. b 43. TCert64. STETS 94. **d** 97 **p** 98. NSM Lyndhurst and Emery Down and Minstead *Win* 97-04; Chapl Southn Univ Hosps NHS Trust 04-09; rtd 09; Perm to Offic *Win* from 09. *The Firs, Pikes Hill, Lyndhurst SO43 7AY* Tel (023) 8028 2616 E-mail felicityboot@hotmail.com

BOOTES, Michael Charles Edward. b 35. ACP70. Sarum Th Coll 58. **d** 61 **p** 62. C Winchmore Hill St Paul *Lon* 61-64; Switzerland 64-67; C St Marylebone All SS *Lon* 67-68; OGS from 68; Chapl Kingsley St Mich Sch W Sussex 69-75; V Brandon *Dur* 75-78; Chapl Shoreham Gr Sch 78-79; C Clayton w Keymer *Chich* 80-84; TV Ovingdean w Rottingdean and Woodingdean 84-85; R Ovingdean 85-88; V Lundwood *Wakef* 88-92; C Pontefract St Giles 92-95; P-in-c Kellington w Whitley 95-00; rtd 00; Hon C Castleford *Wakef* 00-05; Hon C Methley w Mickletown *Ripon* 05-09; Perm to Offic *Wakef* from 09. *39 Minden Close, Pontefract WF8 4EH* Tel (01977) 793717 Mobile 07515-387938 E-mail mb@ogs.net

BOOTH, Charles. *See* BOOTH, Ewart Charles

BOOTH, Charles Robert. b 48. Leeds Univ CertEd75. NOC 79. **d** 82 **p** 83. C Eccleshill *Bradf* 82-84; C Jersey St Brelade *Win* 84-88; C Newman Australia 88-90; V Blurton *Lich* 90-93; Chapl Frederick Irwin Angl Communion Sch Mandurah Australia 94-98; R Spearwood 99-03; rtd 03. *PO Box 1474, Toodyay WA 6566, Australia* E-mail boothimages@hotmail.com

BOOTH, David. b 44. Coll of Resurr Mirfield 72. **d** 74 **p** 75. C Osmondthorpe St Phil *Ripon* 74-77; C Armley w New Wortley 77-79; V Leeds St Wilfrid 79-95; V Royton St Paul *Man* 95-09; rtd 09. *13 Lyon Street, Shaw, Oldham OL2 7RU* Tel (01706) 661172

BOOTH, Derek. b 36. LTCL ALCM AKC61. **d** 62 **p** 63. C Woodchurch *Ches* 62-65; C Penrith St Andr *Carl* 65-67; C Tranmere St Paul *Ches* 67-70; C Wilmslow 70-72; V Micklehurst 73-97; C Staveley and Barrow Hill *Derby* 97-01; rtd 01; Perm to Offic *Derby* from 01. *9 Ilam Close, Inkersall, Chesterfield S43 3EW* Tel (01246) 475421

BOOTH, Eric James. b 43. Open Univ BA84. NOC 86. **d** 89 **p** 90. NSM Nelson St Phil *Blackb* 89-93; NSM Fence and Newchurch-in-Pendle 93-97; NSM Padiham w Hapton and Padiham Green 97-03; rtd 03; Perm to Offic *Blackb* from 04. *5 Round Hill Place, Cliviger, Burnley BB10 4UA* Tel (01282) 450708

BOOTH, Ewart Charles. b 67. LTCL85 K Coll Lon LLB88. Sarum & Wells Th Coll BTh93. **d** 93 **p** 95. NSM Tadley St Pet *Win* 93-95; C Highcliffe w Hinton Admiral 95-00; R W Parley *Sarum* from 00. *The Rectory, 250 New Road, West Parley, Ferndown BH22 8EW* Tel (01202) 873561

BOOTH, Graham Richard. b 55. Birm Univ BSocSc75. St Jo Coll Nottm 89. **d** 91 **p** 92. C Woodthorpe *S'well* 91-96; P-in-c Trowell 96-02; P-in-c Awsworth w Cossall 00-02; R Trowell, Awsworth and Cossall 02-05; Community of Aid and Hilda from 05. *The Lifeboat House, Holy Island, Berwick-upon-Tweed TD15 2SQ* Tel and fax (01289) 389110 E-mail g.r.booth@ntlworld.com

BOOTH, Ian George. b 64. Chich Th Coll 85 Linc Th Coll 87. **d** 88 **p** 89. C Pet St Mary Boongate 88-90; C Hawley H Trin *Guildf* 90-94; V Willesden St Mary *Lon* 94-03; P-in-c Gosport H Trin *Portsm* 03-05; V 05-06; V Gosport Ch Ch 05-06; RD Gosport 03-06; V Leigh-on-Sea St Marg *Chelmsf* from 09. *St Margaret's Vicarage, 1465 London Road, Leigh-on-Sea SS9 2SB* Tel (01702) 471773 E-mail frianbooth@hotmail.com

BOOTH, Jon Alfred. b 42. Nottm Univ BA64 Lon Univ MPhil72. Coll of Resurr Mirfield 78. **d** 80 **p** 81. C Elland *Wakef* 80-84; C Royston and Carlton 84-09; rtd 09; Perm to Offic *Wakef* from 09 and *York* from 10. *Millbank Cottage, Thorpe Bassett, Malton YO17 8LU* Tel (01944) 758518

BOOTH, Kenneth Neville. b 41. Otago Univ BA62 MA63 BD66 MTh69 St Andr Univ PhD74. St Jo Coll Auckland 63. **d** 65 **p** 66. C St Paul's Cathl Dunedin New Zealand 65-69; Perm to Offic *St And* 70-71; Lect St Andr Univ 70-71; Lect St Jo Coll Auckland 72-80; Asst P Tamaki St Thos 73-80; Warden Selwyn Coll Dunedin 81-85; Lect 85-97; V Roslyn 85-97; Adn Dunedin 86-95; V Gen 92-97; Dir Th Ho 97-06. *30 Church Lane, Merivale, Christchurch 8014, New Zealand* Tel (0064) (3) 355 9145 Fax 355 6140

BOOTH, Martin Allison. b 54. K Coll Lon MA06. SEITE. **d** 09 **p** 10. C Wimbledon *S'wark* from 09. *9 Thornton Road, London SW19 4NE* Tel (020) 8946 4494

BOOTH, Michael Kevin. b 47. Louvain Univ Belgium BA. St Jo Coll Nottm 88 Oscott Coll (RC) 65. **d** 71 **p** 72. In RC Ch 71-87; C N Reddish *Man* 88-89; R Heaton Norris Ch w All SS 89-99; rtd 99; Perm to Offic *Man* 00-08 and *Derby* from 06. *3 Potter Road, Hadfield, Hyde SK13 2RA* Tel (01457) 853963

BOOTH, Paul Harris. b 49. St Jo Coll Nottm. **d** 79 **p** 80. C Thorpe Edge *Bradf* 79-82; P-in-c Frizinghall 82-83; TV Shipley St Paul and Frizinghall 83-97; rtd 97; Perm to Offic *Bradf* from 97. *11 Derwent Avenue, Wilsden, Bradford BD15 0LY* Tel (01535) 958939 E-mail paul.booth@bradford.anglican.org

BOOTH, Terrence Richard. b 44. Edith Cowan Univ (Aus) BA98. St Jo Coll Morpeth. **d** 69 **p** 70. Australia 69-79 and from 81; C Corowa 69-71; Asst Broken Hill 72-74; P-in-c Urana/Jerilderie 74-79; C Chesterfield St Mary and All SS *Derby* 79-81; Chapl Chesterfield R Hosp 79-81; R Coolamon/Ganmain 82; RD Murrumbidgee 83-84; Chapl Bunbury Cathl Gr Sch 85-93; Chapl Edith Cowan Univ 86-92; R Casino 94-98; V Ithaca-Ashgrove 98-01; AD from 01. *286 Waterworks Road, PO Box 31, Ashgrove Qld 4060, Australia* Tel (0061) (7) 3366 2320 Fax 3366 9793 E-mail stpaulsash@iprimus.com.au

BOOTHBY, Frank. b 29. St D Coll Lamp 56. **d** 58 **p** 59. C Maghull *Liv* 58-61; C N Meols 61-64; Miss to Seamen 64; rtd 94. *7 Belsfield Drive, Hesketh Bank, Preston PR4 6YB*

BOOTHBY, Mrs Julia. b 64. St Andr Univ MTheol87. SAOMC 02. **d** 04 **p** 05. C Welwyn *St Alb* 04-08; TV Ouzel Valley 08-11; TV Bp's Hatfield, Lemsford and N Mymms from 11. *The Vicarage, North Mymms Park, North Mymms, Hatfield AL9 7TN* Tel (01727) 822887 Mobile 07952-514228 E-mail juliabby@sky.com

BOOTHMAN, Ms Olive. b 31. TCD BA. **d** 94 **p** 95. NSM Clondalkin w Rathcoole *D & G* from 94. *Miley Hall, Blessington, Co Wicklow, Republic of Ireland* Tel (00353) (45) 865119

BOOTS, Claude Donald Roy. b 26. Roch Th Coll 67. **d** 69 **p** 70. C Midsomer Norton *B & W* 69-73; V Westfield 73-80; R Ilton w Hambridge, Earnshill, Isle Brewers etc 80-91; rtd 91; Perm to Offic *B & W* from 91. *41 Furlong Close, Midsomer Norton, Bath BA3 2PR* Tel (01761) 419263 E-mail pairofboots@uwclub.net

BOOYS, Canon Susan Elizabeth. b 56. Bris Univ BA78 LMH Ox PGCE79. SAOMC 92. **d** 95 **p** 96. C Kidlington w Hampton Poyle *Ox* 95-99; TV Dorchester 99-05; TR from 05; TV Warborough 99-05; TR from 05; AD Aston and Cuddesdon from 07; Hon Can Ch Ch from 08. *The Rectory, Manor Farm Road, Dorchester-on-Thames, Wallingford OX10 7HZ* Tel and fax (01865) 340007 E-mail sue@booys.fsnet.co.uk

BOREHAM, Harold Leslie. b 37. S'wark Ord Course. **d** 72 **p** 73. C Whitton and Thurleston w Akenham *St E* 72-77; R Saxmundham 77-85; V Felixstowe SS Pet and Paul 85-96; Chapl Felixstowe Hosp 85-96; Chapl Bartlet Hosp Felixstowe 95-96; P-in-c Ramsgate St Mark *Cant* 96-01; V 01-03; Chapl E Kent NHS and Soc Care Partnership Trust 98-03; rtd 03; Perm to

Offic *St E* from 03. *313 St John's Road, Colchester CO4 0JR* Tel (01206) 853769 E-mail harry@borehamclan.fsnet.co.uk

BORLEY, Mark Letchford. b 61. Lon Univ BSc83 PhD87. St Jo Coll Nottm MTh03. **d** 04 **p** 05. C W Swindon and the Lydiards *Bris* 04-05; C Swindon St Aug and Swindon All SS w St Barn 05-07; C Cricklade w Latton 07-09; P-in-c Allington and Maidstone St Pet *Cant* from 09. *The Rectory, 35 Poplar Grove, Allington, Maidstone ME16 0DE* Tel (01622) 758704 Mobile 07811-124237

BORROWDALE, Geoffrey Nigel. b 61. Southn Univ BSc83 W Sussex Inst of HE PGCE94. Chich Th Coll 87. **d** 90 **p** 99. C Tilehurst St Mich *Ox* 90-91; Perm to Offic *Chich* 93-97; NSM Sunninghill *Ox* 98-99; C Bracknell 99-01; P-in-c Theale and Englefield 01-11; C The Churn from 11. *The Rectory, Church Lane, South Moreton, Didcot OX11 9AF* Tel (01235) 812042

BORTHWICK, Alexander Heywood. b 36. Open Univ BA80 Surrey Univ MSc89 MBPsS90. Lich Th Coll 57. **d** 60 **p** 61. C Glas Ch Ch 60-62; C Landore *S & B* 62-64; C Swansea St Thos and Kilvey 64-65; Br Guiana 65-66; Guyana 66-70; C Oystermouth *S & B* 70-71; USPG 71-83; Area Sec *Man* and *Liv* 71-76; Area Sec *Blackb* and *S & M* 73-76; Sch and Children's Work Sec 76-83; Chapl Tooting Bec Hosp Lon 83-91; Chapl Charing Cross Hosp Lon 92-94; Chapl Hammersmith Hosps NHS Trust 94-00; TR Catford (Southend) and Downham *S'wark* 00-04; rtd 04. *Le Roc de Brolange, 5 Brolange, 17150 Soubran, France* Tel (0033) 5 46 48 46 23

BORTHWICK, Ms Anne Christine. b 50. Lanc Univ BA96 Leeds Univ MA10 Huddersfield Univ PGCE99. Yorks Min Course 07. **d** 10 **p** 11. NSM Dunnington *York* from 10. *1 Bonington Court, York YO26 4QN* Tel (01904) 790344 E-mail anne.christine@virgin.net

BOSHER, Philip Ross. b 61. Sarum & Wells Th Coll 84. **d** 87 **p** 88. C Warminster St Denys *Sarum* 87-90; P-in-c Farley w Pitton and W Dean w E Grimstead 90-91; TV Alderbury Team 91-96; CF from 96. *c/o MOD Chaplains (Army)* Tel (01264) 381140 Fax 381824

BOSS, Mrs Ann. b 42. Cen Lancs Univ BA93. CBDTI 99. **d** 02 **p** 03. NSM Scorton and Barnacre and Calder Vale *Blackb* 02-05; P-in-c Hanmer Springs New Zealand 05-10; Perm to Offic *Blackb* from 10. *School House Barn, Inglewhite Road, Inglewhite, Preston PR3 2LD* Tel (01995) 643146 E-mail ann.boss227@btinternet.com

BOSSCHAERT, Anthony John. b 34. St Fran Coll Brisbane 65 ACT ThL69. **d** 68 **p** 69. C Maryborough Australia 68-72; C Roath *Llan* 72-73; C Leckhampton SS Phil and Jas w Cheltenham St Jas *Glouc* 73-76; R Skipton Australia 76-80; C Westmr St Steph w St Jo *Lon* 80-82; TV Wood Green St Mich w Bounds Green St Gabr etc 82-89; In URC 89-03; rtd 03. *55 Willow Way, Potters Bar EN6 2PR* E-mail anton4.bosschaert@gmail.com

BOSSWARD, Eric Paul. b 63. CQSW90. Trin Coll Bris BA99. **d** 99 **p** 00. C Ecclesall *Sheff* 99-01; C Netherthorpe St Steph 01-04; Co-ord Chapl HM YOI Castington from 04. *HM Young Offender Institution, Castington, Morpeth NE65 9XG* Tel (01670) 762100 E-mail eric.bossward@talktalk.net

BOSTOCK, Peter Anthony. b 64. Nottm Univ BA85 Fitzw Coll Cam BA89. Westcott Ho Cam 87. **d** 90 **p** 91. C Brighton St Matthias *Chich* 90-94; C Leytonstone St Marg w St Columba *Chelmsf* 94-98; P-in-c Bishopwearmouth Gd Shep *Dur* 98-02; V Monk Bretton *Wakef* 02-03; P-in-c Ryhill from 03; P-in-c Sharlston from 03; CMP from 99. *The Vicarage, 20 School Lane, Ryhill, Wakefield WF4 2DW* Tel (01226) 722363 Mobile 07752-886039 E-mail pbostock@tiscali.co.uk

BOSTON, Jonathan Bertram. b 40. Ely Th Coll 61. **d** 64 **p** 65. C Eaton *Nor* 64-70; Sen Chapl ACF Norfolk 66-05; Chapl Norfolk Constabulary from 94; V Horsham St Faith w Newton St Faith 70-90; V Horsford 71-90; V Horsford and Horsham w Newton St Faith 90-97; P-in-c Litcham w Kempston, E and W Lexham, Mileham etc 97-06; rtd 06; Perm to Offic *Nor* from 06. *Bevan House, Front Street, Litcham, King's Lynn PE32 2QG* Tel (01328) 701200

BOSWELL, Canon Colin John Luke. b 47. Sarum & Wells Th Coll 72. **d** 74 **p** 75. C Upper Tooting H Trin *S'wark* 74-78; C Sydenham St Phil 78-79; C St Helier 80-83; P-in-c Caterham 83-95; P-in-c Chaldon 85-95; RD Caterham 85-95; V Croydon St Jo from 95; RD Croydon Cen 00-06; Hon Can S'wark Cathl from 99. *Croydon Vicarage, 20A Haling Park Road, South Croydon CR2 6NE* Tel (020) 8688 1387 or 8688 8104 Fax 8688 5877 Mobile 07931-850905 E-mail croydon.parishchurch@lineone.net

BOTHAM, Arthur. b 53. St Jo Coll Nottm. **d** 00 **p** 01. C Hartley Wintney, Elvetham, Winchfield etc 00-04; TV Basingstoke from 04; AD Basingstoke from 11. *The Vicarage, 25 Tewkesbury Close, Popley, Basingstoke RG24 9DU* Tel (01256) 324734 E-mail arthur.botham@btinternet.com

BOTT, Graham Paul. b 49. Staffs Univ MBA95. NOC 00. **d** 03 **p** 04. NSM Rickerscote *Lich* from 03. *24 Wayfield Drive, Stafford ST16 1TR* Tel (01785) 255658 E-mail graham.pbott@btopenworld.com

BOTT, Theodore Reginald. b 27. MBE03. Birm Univ BSc52 PhD68 DSc84 CEng58 FIChemE68. WMMTC 85. **d** 86 **p** 87. NSM Harborne St Faith and St Laur *Birm* 86-97; Perm to Offic from 97. *17 Springavon Croft, Birmingham B17 9BJ* Tel 0121-427 4209

BOTTERILL, David Darrell. b 45. Open Univ BA. Sarum & Wells Th Coll. **d** 83 **p** 84. C Blandford Forum and Langton Long etc *Sarum* 83-86; TV Shaston 86-00; Chapl HM YOI Guys Marsh 89-91; P-in-c Portland St Jo *Sarum* 00-09; Asst Chapl Dorset Community NHS Trust 01-09; rtd 09; Hon Chapl Miss to Seafarers from 02. *41 Hawthorn Avenue, Gillingham SP8 4ST* Tel (01747) 821601 E-mail david.botterill45@btinternet.com

BOTTING, Canon Michael Hugh. b 25. K Coll Lon BSc51 AKC K Coll Lon PGCE52. Ridley Hall Cam 54. **d** 56 **p** 57. C Onslow Square St Paul *Lon* 56-61; V Fulham St Matt 61-72; RD Hammersmith 67; V Leeds St Geo *Ripon* 72-84; RD Headingley 81-84; Hon Can Ripon Cathl 82-84; R Aldford and Bruera *Ches* 84-90; rtd 90; Jt Dir Lay Tr *Ches* 90-95; Perm to Offic 95-07. *12 Hazelhurst, 24 Eldorado Road, Cheltenham GL50 2PT* Tel (01242) 541125 E-mail michael.botting@btinternet.com

BOTTING, Paul Lloyd. b 43. Brasted Th Coll 67 St Mich Coll Llan 69. **d** 71 **p** 72. C Hucknall Torkard *S'well* 71-74; C Cen Torquay *Ex* 74-76; P-in-c Sutton in Ashfield St Mich *S'well* 76; V 77-88; Chapl King's Mill Hosp Sutton-in-Ashfield 85-88; Perm to Offic *Leic* 95-97; NSM Vale of Belvoir Gp 95-97; C High Framland Par 97-01; C Waltham on the Wolds, Stonesby, Saxby etc 97-01; C Wymondham w Edmondthorpe, Buckminster etc 97-01; P-in-c High Framland Par 01-10; rtd 10; Perm to Offic *Leic* from 10 and *S'well* from 11. *9 Orchard Close, Radcliffe-on-Trent, Nottingham NG12 2BN* Tel 0115-933 2591 Mobile 07770-853762 E-mail plb@pixie-cat.fslife.co.uk

BOTTLEY, Mrs Kate. b 75. Trin & All SS Coll Leeds BA(QTS)97 Open Univ MTh08. St Jo Coll Nottm LTh08. **d** 08 **p** 09. C Skegby w Teversal *S'well* from 08. *64 Fackley Way, Stanton Hill, Sutton-in-Ashfield NG17 3HT* Tel (01623) 516160 Mobile 07910-242404 E-mail kate@skegbyparish.org.uk

BOTTOMLEY, Gordon. b 31. Oak Hill Th Coll 51. **d** 55 **p** 56. C Kinson *Sarum* 55-58; Lic to Offic *Man* 58-63; N Area Sec BCMS 58-63; V Hemswell w Harpswell *Linc* 63-72; V Glentworth 63-72; Chapl RAF 63-71; R Bucknall and Bagnall *Lich* 72-80; TR 80-82; P-in-c Worthing H Trin *Chich* 82-88; V Camelsdale 88-96; rtd 96; Perm to Offic *Portsm* from 98. *6 Jay Close, Fareham PO14 3TA*

BOTWRIGHT, Canon Adrian Paul. b 55. St Jo Coll Ox MA PGCE. Westcott Ho Cam 80. **d** 82 **p** 83. C Chapel Allerton *Ripon* 82-85; Chapl Chapel Allerton Hosp 82-85; C Bourne *Guildf* 85-88; V Weston 88-94; R Skipton H Trin *Bradf* from 94; P-in-c Embsay w Eastby from 05; Hon Can Bradf Cathl from 02. *The Rectory, Rectory Lane, Skipton BD23 1ER* Tel (01756) 793622 E-mail adrian.botwright@bradford.anglican.org

BOUCHER, Brian Albert. b 39. Univ of Wales (Lamp) BA61. Chich Th Coll 61. **d** 63 **p** 64. C Hoxton H Trin w St Mary *Lon* 63-67; Chapl RN 67-68; Asst Chapl Harrow Sch 68-73; Chapl 73-86; P-in-c Clerkenwell H Redeemer w St Phil *Lon* 86-91; P-in-c Myddleton Square St Mark 86-91; Chapl Hurstpierpoint Coll 92-96; rtd 96; Perm to Offic *Chich* from 01. *20 Summervale Road, Tunbridge Wells TN4 8JB* Tel (01892) 530342

BOUCHER, Geoffrey John. b 61. Warwick Univ BA82 K Coll Lon 94. Ridley Hall Cam 94. **d** 96 **p** 97. C Tavistock and Gulworthy *Ex* 96-01; P-in-c W Monkton *B & W* 01-11; R W Monkton w Kingston St Mary, Broomfield etc from 11; RD Taunton from 10. *The Rectory, West Monkton, Taunton TA2 8QT* Tel (01823) 412226 E-mail geoffboucher@btinternet.com

BOUGHEY, Richard Keith. b 26. Man Univ MEd71. Qu Coll Birm 77. **d** 80 **p** 82. NSM Upper Tean *Lich* 80-81; NSM Stoke-upon-Trent 80-81; NSM Uttoxeter w Bramshall 82-88; rtd 88; Perm to Offic *Lich* from 88. *Kontokali, The Old Lane, Deadman's Green, Checkley, Stoke-on-Trent ST10 4NQ* Tel (01538) 722013

BOUGHTON, Mrs Elisabeth Mary Victoria. b 66. St Anne's Coll Ox BA87 MA93. Ridley Hall Cam 89. **d** 91 **p** 94. C Guildf Ch Ch 91-95; Chapl St Cath Sch Bramley 92-97; NSM Fetcham *Guildf* from 97; Chapl Guildf YMCA from 04; Tutor CME *Guildf* from 08. *The Rectory, 10A The Ridgeway, Fetcham, Leatherhead KT22 9AZ* Tel (01372) 375000

BOUGHTON, Canon Michael John. b 37. Kelham Th Coll 57. **d** 62 **p** 63. C Grantham St Wulfram *Linc* 62-66; C Kingsthorpe *Pet* 66-68; C Linc St Nic w St Jo Newport 68-72; V Scunthorpe All SS 72-79; V Crowle 79-89; TR Bottesford w Ashby 89-02; Can and Preb Linc Cathl from 00; rtd 02; Perm to Offic *Linc* from 02. *45 Albion Crescent, Lincoln LN1 1EB* Tel (01552) 569653 E-mail mboughton@aol.com

BOUGHTON, Paul Henry. b 55. Imp Coll Lon BScEng77 ARSM77 ACA80. Ridley Hall Cam 89. **d** 91 **p** 92. C Guildf Ch Ch 91-96; R Fetcham from 96. *The Rectory, 10A The Ridgeway, Fetcham, Leatherhead KT22 9AZ* Tel (01372) 375000 E-mail boughtonfamily@yahoo.com

BOUGHTON, Miss Ruth Frances. b 52. Ox Brookes Univ BA10. Birm Bible Inst 71. **d** 07 **p** 08. OLM Chenies and Lt Chalfont,

Latimer and Flaunden *Ox* 07-10; NSM from 10. *17 Bell Lane, Amersham HP7 9PF* Tel (01494) 764221

BOULCOTT, Thomas William. b 16. Bps' Coll Cheshunt 47. **d** 49 **p** 50. C Hitchin St Mary *St Alb* 49-51; C Kempston All SS 51-54; Chapl Bedf Gen Hosp 52-54; V Newfoundpool *Leic* 54-61; V N Evington 61-73; Chapl Leic Gen Hosp 62-73; V Loppington w Newtown *Lich* 73-85; RD Wem and Whitchurch 83-85; rtd 85; Perm to Offic *Lich* from 85. *Silver Birch, Tilley Road, Wem, Shrewsbury SY4 5HA* Tel (01939) 233602

BOULD, Preb Arthur Roger. b 32. Selw Coll Cam BA54 MA58 Wadh Coll Ox BA55 DipEd57 MA58. St Steph Ho Ox 54. **d** 57 **p** 58. C Wednesfield St Thos *Lich* 57-64; V Wellington Ch Ch 64-71; R Cheadle 71-88; P-in-c Freehay 84-88; R Cheadle w Freehay 88-91; Chapl Cheadle Hosp 71-91; Chapl HM Pris Moorcourt 72-82; RD Cheadle 72-91; Preb Lich Cathl 83-99; Asst to Bp Wolv 91-97; Bp Lich's Past Aux 97-99; C Stafford 97-99; rtd 99; Perm to Offic *Lich* 00-10. *The College of St Barnabas, Blackberry Lane, Lingfield RH7 6NJ*

BOULLIER, Kenneth John. b 51. Trin Coll Bris 82. **d** 84 **p** 85. C Heref St Pet w St Owen and St Jas 84-87; V Nutley *Chich* 88-93; R Maresfield 88-93; New Zealand 93-97; R Nailsea H Trin *B & W* 97-08; P-in-c St Just-in-Roseland and St Mawes *Truro* from 08. *16 Waterloo Close, St Mawes, Truro TR2 5BD* Tel (01326) 270248 E-mail revkjb@hotmail.co.uk

BOULNOIS, Linda Dianne. *See* BISIG, Linda Dianne

BOULT, David Ronald. b 51. Bris Univ BSc73. St Mich Coll Llan 04. **d** 07 **p** 08. NSM Llantwit Major 07-10; NSM Cowbridge from 11. *52 The Verlands, Cowbridge CF71 7BY* Tel and fax (01446) 772166 Mobile 07767-818257 E-mail daveboult@aol.com

BOULT, Geoffrey Michael. b 56. Southn Univ BTh88 Bris Univ MA90 Birm Univ MSc96. Sarum & Wells Th Coll 77. **d** 80 **p** 81. C Newark w Hawton, Cotham and Shelton *S'well* 80-83; TV Melksham *Sarum* 83-90; P-in-c Charminster and Stinsford 90-95; Perm to Offic *Birm* 95-96 and *Sarum* 95-98; Hon C Bradford Peverell, Stratton, Frampton etc from 09. *The Rectory, 4 Meadow Bottom, Stratton, Dorchester DT2 9WH* Tel (01305) 257972 E-mail geoff@boultco.freeserve.co.uk

BOULTBEE, John Michael Godolphin. b 22. Oak Hill Th Coll 66. **d** 68 **p** 69. C Hawkwell *Chelmsf* 68-71; C St Keverne *Truro* 71-73; V Constantine 74-79; P-in-c St Merryn 79-81; V 81-87; rtd 87; Perm to Offic *Ex* from 87. *July Cottage, 8 Williams Close, Dawlish EX7 9SP* Tel (01626) 865761

BOULTER, Adam Charles. b 71. Bath Coll of HE BA93 Kingston Univ MA04 Fitzw Coll Cam BA07 MA11. Westcott Ho Cam 05. **d** 08 **p** 09. C Battersea St Mary *S'wark* from 08. *35 Kerrison Road, London SW11 2QG* Tel and fax (020) 7228 9648 E-mail adamboulter@me.com or office@stmarysbattersea.org.uk

BOULTER, Michael Geoffrey. b 32. Lon Univ BD56. Tyndale Hall Bris 53. **d** 57 **p** 58. C Tranmere St Cath *Ches* 57-60; R Cheetham Hill *Man* 60-65; R Tollard Royal w Farnham *Sarum* 65-66; Chapl Alderney Hosp Poole 66-96; V Branksome St Clem *Sarum* 66-96; rtd 96. *7 Temple Trees, 13 Portarlington Road, Bournemouth BH4 8BU* Tel (01202) 768718

BOULTER, Robert George. b 49. Man Univ MA90. St Aug Coll Cant 72. **d** 75 **p** 76. C Langley All SS and Martyrs *Man* 75-80; V Lower Kersal 80-84; Oman 84-86; Slough Community Chapl *Ox* 86-87; R Whalley Range St Marg *Man* 87-99; P-in-c Whalley Range St Marg from 99; Chapl Trin and All SS Coll Leeds from 07. *St Margaret's Rectory, Rufford Road, Manchester M16 8AE* Tel 0161-226 1289

BOULTON, Christopher David. b 50. Keble Coll Ox BA71 MA80. Cuddesdon Coll 71. **d** 74 **p** 75. C St Mary-at-Latton *Chelmsf* 74-77; C Shrub End 77-80; P-in-c St Bentley 80-83; V 83-89; V Cherry Hinton St Andr *Ely* 89-04; P-in-c Teversham 90-04; P-in-c Much Hadham *St Alb* 04-05; TR Albury, Braughing, Furneux Pelham, Lt Hadham etc from 06; RD Bishop's Stortford from 07. *The Rectory, High Street, Much Hadham SG10 6DA* Tel (01279) 842609 E-mail rectory@muchhadham.com

BOULTON, Ms Louise Jane. b 72. Goldsmiths' Coll Lon BA93 Heythrop Coll Lon MA98. SEITE 02. **d** 05 **p** 06. NSM Wandsworth St Anne *S'wark* 05-08; NSM Wandsworth St Anne w St Faith 08-10. *17 Somers Road, London SW2 2AE* Tel (020) 7096 1646

BOULTON, Wallace Dawson. b 31. MCIJ86. Lon Coll of Div 65. **d** 67 **p** 68. C Bramcote *S'well* 67-71; Dioc Public Relns Officer 69-71; Hon C St Bride Fleet Street w Bridewell etc *Lon* 71-86; Guild Chapl from 86; Publicity Sec CMS 71-79; Media Sec 79-86; Ed C of E Newspaper 86-88; Lic to Offic *Chich* 84-94; Perm to Offic 94-96; rtd 96; Hon C St Leonards St Leon *Chich* 96-01 and 04-09; P-in-c 01-03; Hon C St Leonards St Ethelburga and St Leon from 09. *44 Winterbourne Close, Hastings TN34 1XQ* Tel (01424) 713743 E-mail revw.boulton@talktalk.net

BOULTON-LEA, Peter John. b 46. St Jo Coll Dur BA68. Westcott Ho Cam 69. **d** 71 **p** 72. C Farlington *Portsm* 72-75; C Darlington St Jo *Dur* 75-77; R E and W Horndon w Lt Warley

Chelmsf 77-82; V Hersham *Guildf* 82-91; R Kirk Sandall and Edenthorpe *Sheff* 91-96; RD Doncaster 95-96; V Campsall 96-97; R Burghwallis and Campsall 97-98; V Tattenham Corner and Burgh Heath *Guildf* 98-03; V Thorne *Sheff* 03-08; rtd 08; Perm to Offic *Ox* from 08. *25 Larkfields, Headington, Oxford OX3 8PF* Tel (01865) 744302

BOULTON-REYNOLDS, Mrs Jean. b 49. Sarum Th Coll 93. **d** 96 **p** 97. C Harnham *Sarum* 96-99; C Salisbury St Mark 99-01; TV Westborough *Guildf* 01-05; TV Barnes S'wark from 05. *The Vicarage, 162 Castelnau, London SW13 9ET* Tel (020) 8741 7330 E-mail revjbr@sarum26.freeserve.co.uk

BOUNDY, David. b 34. Kelham Th Coll 55. **d** 59 **p** 60. C Stirchley *Birm* 59-64; Chapl E Birm Hosp 64-74; V Bordesley St Oswald 64-70; V S Yardley St Mich 70-74; R Bideford *Ex* 74-82; RD Hartland 80-82; R Northfield *Birm* 82-88; P-in-c Penzance St Mary w St Paul *Truro* 88-90; V 90-94; rtd 94; Chapl Convent of St Mary at the Cross Edgware 94-99; Perm to Offic *Ex* 00-05. *34 Milford Hill, Salisbury SP1 2QX* Tel (01722) 410341 E-mail retreat5@btopenworld.com

BOUNDY, Canon Gerald Neville. b 36. BA. Linc Th Coll. **d** 65 **p** 66. C Bris St Mary Redcliffe w Temple etc 65-70; P-in-c Southmead 70-72; V 72-81; V Cotham St Sav w St Mary 81-99; Hon Can Bris Cathl 96-99; rtd 99; Perm to Offic *Bris* from 99. *10 Morley Road, Southville, Bristol BS3 1DT* Tel 0117-966 3337

BOURDEAUX, Canon Michael Alan. b 34. St Edm Hall Ox BA57 MA61 Lambeth DD96. Wycliffe Hall Ox BA59. **d** 60 **p** 61. C Enfield St Andr *Lon* 60-64; P-in-c Charlton St Luke w St Paul S'wark 64-65; Lic to Offic *Roch* 65-91 and *Ox* 91-04; Visiting Prof St Bernard's Sem Rochester NY 69; Gen Dir Keston Inst 69-99; Hon Can Roch Cathl 90-99; rtd 99; Perm to Offic *Ox* from 04. *101 Church Way, Iffley, Oxford OX4 4EG* Tel (01865) 777276 E-mail mbourdeaux@freenet.co.uk

✠**BOURKE, The Rt Revd Michael Gay.** b 41. CCC Cam BA63 MA67. Cuddesdon Coll 65. **d** 67 **p** 68 **c** 93. C Grimsby St Jas *Linc* 67-71; C Digswell St Alb 71-73; C-in-c Panshanger CD 73-78; Course Dir St Alb Minl Tr Scheme 75-87; V Southill 78-86; Adn Bedford 86-93; Area Bp Wolverhampton *Lich* 93-06; rtd 07; Perm to Offic *Heref* from 07. *The Maltings, Little Stretton, Church Stretton SY6 6AP* Tel (01694) 722910

BOURKE, Peter Charles. b 80. Union Th Coll Belf BTh02. Oak Hill Th Coll 07. **d** 09 **p** 10. C Moreton *Ches* from 09. *9 Kinnerton Close, Wirral CH46 6HT* Tel 0151-605 1241 Mobile 07816-974454 E-mail peter.bourke@hotmail.com

BOURKE, Canon Ronald Samuel James. b 50. MA HDipEd. **d** 79 **p** 80. C Portadown St Mark *Arm* 79-83; I Carnteel and Crilly 83-90; I Mountmellick w Coolbanagher, Rosenallis etc *M & K* 90-97; I Kingscourt w Syddan 97-09; Chan Kildare Cathl 00-09; Can Meath 00-09; I Boyle and Elphin w Aghanagh, Kilbryan etc *K, E & A* from 09; Preb Tipper St Patr Cathl Dublin from 00. *The Rectory, Riverstown, Co Sligo, Republic of Ireland*

BOURKE, Canon Stanley Gordon. b 48. CITC 78. **d** 78 **p** 79. C Dundonald *D & D* 78-80; C Lurgan Ch the Redeemer 81-82; I Dungiven w Bovevagh *D & R* 82-89; I Lurgan St Jo *D & D* 89-03; I Inishmacsaint *Clogh* from 03; Preb Clogh Cathl from 06; Chan from 11. *The Rectory, Main Street, Derrygonnelly, Enniskillen BT93 6HW* Tel (028) 6864 1638 E-mail sgbourke@hotmail.co.uk

BOURNE, Anne Clare. b 63. Univ of Wales (Cardiff) BEd85. SEITE 08. **d** 11. NSM Sevenoaks St Luke *Roch* from 11. *Charein, 27 St James's Road, Sevenoaks TN13 3NQ* Tel (01732) 456788 Mobile 07512-734234 E-mail rev.annebourne@talktalk.net

BOURNE, Mrs Carole Sylvia. b 47. York Univ BA68 LSE MSc79 PhD85. SEITE 99. **d** 02 **p** 03. C Epsom St Martin *Guildf* 02-05; NSM E Molesey from 05; RD Emly from 10. *The Vicarage, St Mary's Road, East Molesey KT8 0ST* Tel (020) 8979 0677 *or* 8783 1441 Mobile 07957-295842 E-mail cbmole@msn.com

BOURNE, Colin Douglas. b 56. Culham Coll of Educn CertEd77. Oak Hill Th Coll BA04. **d** 04 **p** 05. C Wellington All SS w Eyton *Lich* 04-08; P-in-c Toton *S'well* from 08. *95 Stapleford Lane, Beeston, Nottingham NG9 6FZ* Tel 0115-973 1138 Mobile 07821-967879 E-mail colin@bournesenf.supanet.com

BOURNE, David James. b 54. Reading Univ BA76. Trin Coll Bris 77. **d** 79 **p** 80. C W Bromwich Gd Shep w St Jo *Lich* 79-84; V Riseley w Bletsoe *St Alb* 84-05; V Hailsham *Chich* from 05. *St Mary's Vicarage, Vicarage Road, Hailsham BN27 1BL* Tel (01323) 842381 E-mail davidjbourne@googlemail.com

BOURNE, Canon Dennis John. b 32. Ridley Hall Cam 58. **d** 60 **p** 61. C Gorleston St Andr *Nor* 60-64; Min Gorleston St Mary CD 64-79; V Costessey 79-86; R Hingham w Wood Rising w Scoulton 86-97; RD Hingham and Mitford 90-95; Hon Can Nor Cathl 93-97; rtd 97; Perm to Offic *Nor* 97-06. *Amron, Star Lane, Long Stratton, Norwich NR15 2XH* Tel (01508) 530301 E-mail johnbourne@onetel.com

BOURNE, Mrs Diana Mary. b 46. St Jo Coll York BEd68. S Dios Minl Tr Scheme 92. **d** 95 **p** 96. C Pinner *Lon* 95-00; V Lamberhurst and Matfield *Roch* 00-06; rtd 07; Perm to Offic

Cant from 07. *The Pump House, Angley Road, Cranbrook TN17 2PN* Tel (01580) 712005 E-mail revdbourne@hotmail.com

BOURNE, Henry. b 34. Spurgeon's Coll 55. **d** 64 **p** 65. C Handsworth St Mary *Birm* 64-67; Chapl RAF 67-85; Asst Chapl-in-Chief RAF 85-87; P-in-c Bourn *Ely* 87-88; P-in-c Kingston 87-88; R 88-89; V Caxton 88-89; R Bourn and Kingston w Caxton and Longstowe 89-91; rtd 91; Perm to Offic *Truro* 95-00 and from 01; Hon C Sampford Peverell, Uplowman, Holcombe Rogus etc *Ex* 00-01. *13 The Bowjey Hill, Newlyn, Penzance TR18 5LW* Tel (01736) 330742

BOURNE, Ian Grant. b 32. Univ of NZ BA55 Otago Univ BD75. **d** 56 **p** 57. New Zealand 56-65 and from 67; Adn Wellington 78-86 and 90-95; C Epsom St Martin *Guildf* 65-67. *26 Annan Grove, Papakowhai, Porirua 5024, New Zealand* Tel (0064) (4) 233 0466 E-mail ian.marg@bourne.co.nz

BOURNE, John. *See* BOURNE, Canon Dennis John

BOURNE, John Mark. b 49. Cant Sch of Min 88. **d** 91 **p** 92. C Allington and Maidstone St Pet *Cant* 91-94; V Marden 94-03; Chapl HM Pris Blantyre Ho 94-02; rtd 03. *9 Eylesden Court, Bearsted, Maidstone ME14 4BF* Tel (01622) 734420 E-mail revjohnbourne@classicfm.net

BOURNE, Nigel Irvine. b 60. St Jo Coll Ox BA82 MA86 Open Univ MBA09. Trin Coll Bris BA92. **d** 92 **p** 93. C Bedhampton *Portsm* 92-94; C Newport St Jo 94-98; V Chalk *Roch* from 98. *The Vicarage, 2A Vicarage Lane, Gravesend DA12 4TF* Tel (01474) 567906 Fax 745147 E-mail nigel.bourne@diocese-rochester.org

BOURNE, Philip John. b 61. Sussex Univ BEd83 Aber Univ MLitt86 Ex Univ MEd96 FRSA97. Cranmer Hall Dur 85. **d** 87 **p** 88. C Gildersome *Wakef* 87-89; Chapl Ex Univ 89-93; Assoc Chapl The Hague and Voorschoten *Eur* 94 and 95; Chapl Voorschoten 96-06; Can Brussels Cathl 04-06; Dir of Ords *Chich* from 07. *6 Patcham Grange, Brighton BN1 8UR* Tel (01273) 564057 E-mail philipbourne@btinternet.com

BOURNEMOUTH, Archdeacon of. *See* ROUCH, The Ven Peter Bradford

BOURNER, Paul. b 48. CA Tr Coll. **d** 90 **p** 91. CA from 79; C Ipswich St Mary at Stoke w St Pet *St E* 90-93; R Ufford w Bredfield and Hasketon 93-01; V Ipswich St Thos from 01. *St Thomas's Vicarage, 102 Cromer Road, Ipswich IP1 5EP* Tel (01473) 741215 E-mail paul.bourner@ntlworld.com

BOUSFIELD, Andrew Michael. b 70. Middx Univ BA92. Oak Hill Th Coll BA00. **d** 00 **p** 01. C Beckenham Ch Ch *Roch* 00-03; C Surbiton Hill Ch Ch *S'wark* 03-07; C Patcham *Chich* from 07. *32 Fairway Rise, Brighton BN1 5GL* Tel (01273) 503926 Mobile 07866-434117 E-mail andybousfield@yahoo.co.uk

BOUSKILL, David Walter. b 72. Westcott Ho Cam 95. **d** 98 **p** 99. C Henley w Remenham *Ox* 98-02; TV Bicester w Bucknell, Caversfield and Launton 02-08; TV Horsham *Chich* from 08. *Holy Trinity House, Blunts Way, Horsham RH12 2BL* Tel (01403) 265401 E-mail fr.david@bouskill.co.uk

BOUTAN, Marc Robert. b 53. Univ of Iowa BA74. Fuller Th Sem California MD87 Virginia Th Sem 90. **d** 91 **p** 92. USA 91-96 and from 99; Asst Chapl Brussels *Eur* 96-99. *St James Episcopal Church, 1872 Camp Road, Charleston, SC 29412, USA*

BOUTLE, David Francis. b 44. Leeds Univ BSc67. Cuddesdon Coll 69. **d** 72 **p** 73. C Boston *Linc* 72-77; C Waltham 77-80; P-in-c Morton 80-81; V 81-94; Chapl W Lindsey NHS Trust 80-94; Local Mental Health Chapl 88-94; P-in-c Heckington *Gp Linc* 94-10; rtd 10. *3 Hengist Close, Quarrington, Sleaford NG34 8WU* Tel (01529) 415384 E-mail boutle.heck@btinternet.com

BOVEY, Denis Philip. b 29. Ely Th Coll 50. **d** 53 **p** 54. C Southwick St Columba *Dur* 53-57; Perm to Offic *Ox* 57-59; Lic to Offic *Chich* 62-64; C W Hartlepool St Aid *Dur* 64-66; R Aberdeen St Jas 66-74; R Old Deer 74-89; R Longside 74-89; R Strichen 74-89; Can St Andr Cathl 75-88; Syn Clerk 78-83; Dean Ab 83-88; R Alford 89-94; R Auchindoir 89-94; R Inverurie 89-94; P-in-c Dufftown 89-94; P-in-c Kemnay 89-94; rtd 94. *15 Loskin Drive, Glasgow G22 7QW* Tel 0141-574 3603

BOVILL, Francis William. b 34. St Aid Birkenhead 55. **d** 58 **p** 59. C Bispham *Blackb* 58-61; C Crosthwaite Keswick *Carl* 61-64; V Radcliffe St Andr *Man* 64-68; P-in-c Woodside St Steph *Glouc* 68; V 69-73; V Scotby *Carl* 73-96; P-in-c Cotehill and Cumwhinton 94-96; rtd 96; Perm to Offic *Carl* from 96. *Crosthwaite, West Road, Wigton CA7 9RG* Tel (016973) 43410

BOWCOTT, Jonathan Michael William. b 67. Trin Coll Bris. **d** 01 **p** 02. C Cricklewood St Gabr and St Mich *Lon* 01-04. *Top Flat, 13 Florence Park, Bristol BS6 7LS* E-mail jonathan@jonathanbowcott.com

BOWDEN, Andrew. *See* BOWDEN, Canon Robert Andrew

BOWDEN, Andrew David. b 59. Newc Univ BA80 BArch83. Cranmer Hall Dur 95. **d** 97 **p** 98. C Monkseaton St Pet *Newc* 97-01; V Whorlton 01-09; Perm to Offic *York* 10-11; P-in-c Weaverthorpe w Helperthorpe, Luttons Ambo etc from 11; C Old Malton from 11; C New Malton from 11. *Chapel House, Back Lane, West Lutton, Malton YO17 8TF* E-mail andy@lovelyland.plus.com

BOWDEN, Andrew John. b 77. Nottm Trent Univ BSc99. Wycliffe Hall Ox 09. **d** 11. C Laleham *Lon* from 11. *169 Elizabeth Avenue, Staines TW18 1JN* Tel (01784) 880271 E-mail andrew.bowden@allsaintslaleham.org.uk

BOWDEN, John-Henry David. b 47. Magd Coll Cam BA69 MA73 MIL78. S Dios Minl Tr Scheme 81. **d** 84 **p** 85. NSM Redlynch and Morgan's Vale *Sarum* 84-88; NSM Cuckfield *Chich* 88-92; NSM St Mary le Bow w St Pancras Soper Lane etc *Lon* 92-98; NSM Chailey *Chich* 98-04; P-in-c Venice w Trieste *Eur* 04-09; rtd 09. *Dene House, South Chailey, Lewes BN8 4AB* Tel (01273) 401076

BOWDEN, Lynne. b 53. Bris Univ BA77 PGCE78. **d** 06 **p** 07. OLM Oatlands *Guildf* from 06. *Ulverstone House, Broom Way, Weybridge KT13 9TG* Tel (01932) 842216 Fax 842238 Mobile 07931-599045 E-mail a.curate@btinternet.com *or* lynne@bowden.freeserve.co.uk

BOWDEN, Mrs Mary Eiluned. **d** 07 **p** 08. NSM Gipsy Hill Ch Ch *S'wark* 07-09; C W Dulwich All SS from 09; P-in-c Haslemere and Grayswood *Guildf* from 11. *Church Hill Gate, Tanners Lane, Haslemere GU27 1BL* Tel 07921-315894 (mobile) E-mail mebowden@btinternet.com

BOWDEN, Philip William. b 76. Ripon Coll Cuddesdon 08. **d** 10 **p** 11. C Portsea St Mary *Portsm* from 10. *166 Shearer Road, Portsmouth PO1 5LS* Tel (023) 9235 0245

BOWDEN, Canon Robert Andrew. b 38. Worc Coll Ox BA62 MA67 BDQ68. Cuddesdon Coll 63. **d** 65 **p** 66. C Wolverhampton St Geo *Lich* 65-69; C Duston *Pet* 69-72; R Byfield 72-79; Chapl R Agric Coll Cirencester 79-93; R Coates, Rodmarton and Sapperton etc *Glouc* 79-04; Bp's Adv on Rural Soc 81-93; Local Min Officer 93-04; rtd 04; Hon C Kemble, Poole Keynes, Somerford Keynes etc *Glouc* 04-08; Chapl to The Queen 92-08; Hon Can Glouc Cathl 90-08; Perm to Offic from 08. *Washbrook Cottage, Caudle Green, Cheltenham GL53 9PW* Tel (01285) 821067 E-mail bowdencoates@care4free.net

BOWDEN-PICKSTOCK, Mrs Susan Mary. b 63. Bp Otter Coll BA85 RGN88. Ridley Hall Cam 09. **d** 11. C Bluntisham cum Earith w Colne and Holywell etc *Ely* from 11. *73 Greenfields, Earith, Huntingdon PE28 3QH* Tel 07912-293905 (mobile) E-mail revroses@gmail.com

BOWEN, Canon Colin Wynford. b 48. St D Coll Lamp. **d** 71 **p** 72. C Hubberston *St D* 71-75; R Cosheston w Nash and Upton 75-77; V Carew and Cosheston w Nash and Upton 77-85; V Pembroke St Mary w St Mich 85-01; V Haverfordwest St Martin w Lambston 01-09; P-in-c Camrose 04-09; Can St D Cathl 01-09; R Llangenni and Llanbedr Ystrad Yw w Patricio *S & B* from 09. *The Rectory, Llangenny, Crickhowell NP8 1HD* Tel (01873) 812593 Mobile 07770-572464

BOWEN, Daniel Joseph George. b 51. St Mich Coll Llan 96. **d** 98 **p** 99. C Gorseinon *S & B* 98-00; C Cen Swansea 00-01; TV 01-02; V Birchfield *Birm* 02-07; rtd 07. *Dryslwyn, 41 Station Road, Ystradgynlais, Swansea SA9 1NX* Tel (01639) 843020 E-mail daniel@bowen4515.freeserve.co.uk

BOWEN, David Gregory. b 47. Lanchester Poly Cov BSc69. Cuddesdon Coll 70. **d** 74 **p** 75. C Rugby St Andr *Cov* 74-77; C Charlton St Luke w H Trin *S'wark* 78-80; TV Stantonbury *Ox* 80-82; Perm to Offic *B & W* 89-07 and *Ab* from 08. *Erraid Station House, Stronsay, Orkney KW17 2AS* Tel (01857) 616435 E-mail dbowenuk@btinternet.com

BOWEN, David John. b 46. Glouc Th Course 83. **d** 86 **p** 88. NSM Ross w Brampton Abbotts, Bridstow and Peterstow *Heref* 86-88; C Kingstone w Clehonger, Eaton Bishop etc 88-93; P-in-c Lugwardine w Bartestree and Weston Beggard 93-94; V Lugwardine w Bartestree, Weston Beggard etc 94-10; P-in-c Withington w Westhide 04-10; RD Heref Rural 99-05; rtd 10. *2 Tavern Meadow, Hope-under-Dinmore, Leominster HR6 0NP* E-mail david@bowen.demon.co.uk

BOWEN, Ms Delyth. b 54. St D Coll Lamp BA90. St Mich Coll Llan. **d** 91 **p** 97. C Llandybie *St D* 91-95; Din-in-c Llanllwni 95-97; V Llanybydder and Llanwenog w Llanllwni 97-02; V Betws w Ammanford from 02. *The Rectory, 78 High Street, Ammanford SA18 2NB* Tel (01269) 592084 E-mail delyth.amman@btopenworld.com

BOWEN, Gareth James. b 60. Lon Guildhall Univ BA99 ARPS00. NTMTC 99. **d** 02 **p** 04. C Leyton St Cath and St Paul *Chelmsf* 02-05; C Upminster 05-07; V Barnehurst *Roch* from 07. *St Martin's Vicarage, 93 Pelham Road, Bexleyheath DA7 4LY* Tel (01322) 523344 Mobile 07775-674504 E-mail gareth@bowen.to

BOWEN, Canon Jennifer Ethel. b 46. Liv Univ BSc68 CertEd69. NOC 80. **dss** 83 **d** 87 **p** 94. Blundellsands St Nic *Liv* 83-86; W Derby St Mary 86-94; Par Dn 87-94; C 94-08; AD W Derby 01-08; Hon Can Liv Cathl 03-08; rtd 08. *6 Springhill Court, Liverpool L15 9EJ* Tel 0151-291 0845 E-mail jenny@happyserver.w.uk

BOWEN, John. b 39. **d** 68 **p** 69. C Aberavon *Llan* 68-73; Australia from 73. *3 Sculptor Street, Giralang ACT 2617, Australia* Tel (0061) (2) 6241 5317 *or* 6234 2252 Fax 6234 2263 E-mail john.bowen@radford.com.au

BOWEN, John Roger. b 34. St Jo Coll Ox BA59 MA62. Tyndale Hall Bris 59. **d** 61 **p** 62. C Cambridge St Paul *Ely* 61-65; Tanzania 65-76; Kenya 76-80; Dir Past Studies St Jo Coll Nottm 80-85; Tutor 85-95; Gen Sec Crosslinks 96-00; rtd 99; Perm to Offic *Ely* from 01; Asst Retired Clergy Officer from 09. *26 Lingholme Close, Cambridge CB4 3HW* Tel (01223) 352592 E-mail bowenrw@onetel.com

BOWEN, Mark Franklin. b 61. Coll of H Cross (USA) BA79 Univ of S Florida MA89. **d** 93. Asst Chapl Univ of S Florida USA 93-96; C Tampa St Andr 96-97; Perm to Offic *S'wark* 07-09; Co-ord Inclusive Ch *Eur* from 09; Teacher Internat Sch of Basel from 09. *309 Guterstrasse, Basel 4053, Switzerland* Tel (0041) (61) 331 0961 E-mail markfbowen@hotmail.com

BOWEN, Canon Roger William. b 47. Magd Coll Cam BA69 MA73 Heythrop Coll Lon MA01 ALCD72. St Jo Coll Nottm 69. **d** 72 **p** 73. C Rusholme H Trin *Man* 72-75; Rwanda Miss (CMS) Burundi 75-84; Tutor and Lect All Nations Chr Coll Ware 85-91; Hon C Ware Ch Ch *St Alb* 86-91; Gen Sec Mid-Africa Min (CMS) 91-97; V Lt Amwell *St Alb* 97-04; RD Hertford and Ware 99-04; CMS Burundi 04-07; rtd 07. *The Outlook, Porteynon, Swansea SA3 1NL* Tel (01792) 391591

BOWEN, Canon Stephen Allan. b 51. Leic Univ BA72. Glouc Sch of Min 88. **d** 91 **p** 92. NSM Bream *Glouc* 91-92; NSM Tidenham w Beachley and Lancaut 91-94; C Glouc St Jas and All SS 94-97; P-in-c Woodchester and Brimscombe 97-00; R from 00; AD Stonehouse 07-08; AD Stroud from 08; Hon Can Glouc Cathl from 09. *The Vicarage, Walls Quarry, Brimscombe, Stroud GL5 2PA* Tel (01453) 882204 E-mail bowen_stcphcn@hotmail.com

BOWEN, Stephen Guy. b 47. Qu Coll Cam BA68 MA72 Bris Univ MA72. Clifton Th Coll 69. **d** 71 **p** 72. C Chelsea St Jo *Lon* 71-73; C Guildf St Sav 73-76; C Guildf St Sav w Stoke-next-Guildford 76-77; C Wallington *S'wark* 77-79; V Felbridge from 79. *The Vicarage, 8 The Glebe, Felbridge, East Grinstead RH19 2QT* Tel (01342) 321524 Fax 07006-022399 E-mail vicar@stjohnsfelbridge.co.uk

BOWER, Brian Mark. b 60. QUB BA. **d** 85 **p** 86. C Orangefield w Moneyreagh *D & D* 85-87; I Inver w Mountcharles, Killaghtee and Killybegs *D & R* 87-93; Miss to Seafarers from 87; I Augher w Newtownsaville and Eskrahoole *Clogh* 93-03. *48 Campsie Road, Omagh BT79 0AG* Tel 07816-449399 (mobile)

BOWER, Jonathan James. b 72. Bp Grosseteste Coll BA96. Ripon Coll Cuddesdon 97. **d** 00 **p** 01. C Spalding *Linc* 00-02; C Sanderstead St Mary *S'wark* 02-03; P-in-c 03-05; TV Sanderstead 05-06; V E Crompton *Man* 06-09; R Broughty Ferry *Bre* 09-11; Chapl St Mich Hospice Harrogate from 11. *Crimple House, Hornbeam Park Avenue, Harrogate HG2 8QL* Tel (01423) 879687 Fax 872654 E-mail jonathanbower@clergy.net

BOWERING, John Anthony (Tony). b 34. SS Coll Cam BA57 MA. Wycliffe Hall Ox 57. **d** 59 **p** 60. C Hornchurch St Andr *Chelmsf* 59-62; Succ Chelmsf Cathl 62; Prec 63; V Brampton Bierlow *Sheff* 64-70; V Norton Woodseats St Paul 70-80; V Tickhill w Stainton 80-97; RD W Doncaster 87-92; rtd 97; Perm to Offic *S'well* and *Sheff* from 97. *Linthwaite Cottage, Main Street, Kirklington, Newark NG22 8ND* Tel (01636) 816995 E-mail john.bowering@which.net

BOWERING, The Ven Michael Ernest. b 35. Kelham Th Coll 55. **d** 59 **p** 60. C Middlesbrough St Oswald *York* 59-62; C Huntington 62-64; V Brayton 64-72; RD Selby 71-72; V Saltburn-by-the-Sea 72-81; Can Res York Minster 81-87; Sec for Miss and Evang 81-87; Adn Lindisfarne *Newc* 87-00; rtd 00; Perm to Offic *York* from 00. *Robin's Nest, Crabmill Lane, Easingwold, York YO61 3DD* Tel (01347) 823682 E-mail mbwrng@aol.com

BOWERMAN, Andrew Mark. b 67. Southn Univ BSc88 Brunel Univ MSW91. Wycliffe Hall Ox 00. **d** 02 **p** 03. C Bradf St Aug Undercliffe 02-05; Miss P Bradf Adnry 05-09; P-in-c Wareham *Sarum* from 09. *The Rectory, 19 Pound Lane, Wareham BH20 4LQ* Tel (01929) 552684 Mobile 07720-398659 E-mail andy.bowerman@virgin.net

BOWERS, Dale Arthur. b 69. St Steph Ho Ox BTh04. **d** 04 **p** 07. C St Paul's St Helena 04-10; V from 10. *China Lane, Jamestown STHL 122, St Helena* Tel (00290) 2960 E-mail dale.penny@cwimail.sh

BOWERS, David. b 56. Man Univ BA79. Wycliffe Hall Ox 82. **d** 84 **p** 85. C Lawton Moor *Man* 84-87; C Walmsley 87-93; V Milnrow 93-98; P-in-c Deerhurst and Apperley w Forthampton etc *Glouc* 98-04; V 04-08; Assoc Dir of Ords 98-07; V S Cerney w Cerney Wick, Siddington and Preston from 08. *The Vicarage, Silver Street, South Cerney, Cirencester GL7 5TP* Tel (01285) 860221 E-mail dbowers@btinternet.com

BOWERS, Canon Francis Malcolm. b 44. Chan Sch Truro 79. **d** 82 **p** 83. NSM Penzance St Mary w St Paul *Truro* 82-83; C 86-88; NSM Madron 83-86; TV Redruth w Lanner and Treleigh 88-91; V St Blazey from 91; P-in-c Luxulyan w Luxulyan 01-08; P-in-c Luxulyan from 08; P-in-c Tywardreath w Tregaminion from 02; RD St Austell 96-05; Hon Can Truro Cathl from 01.

Church House, 2 Nursery Close, Tywardreath, Par PL24 2QW Tel and fax (01726) 817665 Mobile 07974-818631 E-mail fathermalcolmorrightee@tiscali.co.uk

BOWERS, Canon John Edward. b 23. TD68. AKC50. **d** 51 **p** 52. C Leic St Pet 51-55; Sacr S'wark Cathl 55-57; CF (TA) 56-67; V Loughborough St Pet *Leic* 57-63; V Ashby-de-la-Zouch St Helen w Coleorton 63-88; CF (R of O) 67-78; RD Akeley W *Leic* 76-88; Hon Can Leic Cathl 78-88; rtd 88; Perm to Offic *Derby* and *Leic* 88-94; *Ely* 94-00. *19 Curtis Drive, Heighington, Lincoln LN4 1GF* Tel (01522) 791330

BOWERS, Canon John Edward William. b 32. St Aid Birkenhead 60. **d** 63 **p** 64. C Bromborough *Ches* 63-68; Ind Chapl 68-74; P-in-c Crewe St Pet 69-71; V Crewe St Mich 71-74; TR Ellesmere Port 74-79; V Hattersley 79-91; Hon Can Ches Cathl 80-02; RD Mottram 88-91; V Bunbury and Tilstone Fearnall 91-98; P-in-c Leasowe 98-02; rtd 02; Perm to Offic *Ches* from 02. *2 Shalford Grove, Wirral CH48 9XY* Tel 0151-625 4831

BOWERS, Canon Julian Michael. b 48. Middx Univ BA97 Goldsmiths' Coll Lon MA00. Edin Th Coll 69. **d** 72 **p** 73. C Chippenham St Andr w Tytherton Lucas *Bris* 72-74; C Henbury 74-77; Chapl Kandy H Trin Sri Lanka 77-82; P-in-c Evercreech w Chesterblade and Milton Clevedon *B & W* 82-83; V 83-89; V Enfield St Jas *Lon* 89-94; Chapl St Andr Hosp Northn from 04; Can Pet Cathl from 10. *The Chaplaincy, St Andrew's Hospital, Billing Road, Northampton NN1 5DG* Tel (01604) 616000 E-mail jbowers@standrew.co.uk

BOWERS, Michael Charles. b 52. Sarum & Wells Th Coll 89. **d** 91 **p** 92. C St Peter-in-Thanet *Cant* 91-95; V Reculver and Herne Bay St Bart 95-02; P-in-c Fen Ditton *Ely* from 02; P-in-c Horningsea from 02; P-in-c Teversham from 04. *The Rectory, 29 High Street, Fen Ditton, Cambridge CB5 8ST* Tel (01223) 295927 E-mail michael@mcbvic.demon.co.uk

BOWERS, Preb Peter. b 47. Linc Th Coll 72. **d** 76 **p** 77. C Mackworth St Fran *Derby* 76-78; C Maidstone St Martin *Cant* 78-83; V Elmton *Derby* 83-89; R Swimbridge w W Buckland and Landkey *Ex* 89-10; RD Shirwell 01-10; Preb Ex Cathl 07-10; rtd 10. *30 Kingsgate, Bridlington YO15 3PU* E-mail pebo@live.co.uk

BOWERS, Peter William Albert. b 36. K Coll Lon BD61 AKC61. **d** 62 **p** 63. C Chorley St Pet *Blackb* 62-64; C New Sleaford *Linc* 64-67; C Folkestone H Trin w Ch Ch *Cant* 67-72; V Deal St Geo 72-80; Dir Galilee Community 80-85; R River 86-02; RD Dover 93-00; rtd 02; Perm to Offic *Cant* from 02. *7 River Street, River, Dover CT16 0RB* Tel (01304) 822808 E-mail pbowers4@aol.com

BOWERS, Mrs Rosemary Christine. b 49. Ripon Coll Cuddesdon 99. **d** 01 **p** 02. C Rossendale Middle Valley *Man* 01-04; P-in-c Micklehurst *Ches* 04-09; P-in-c Kinnerley w Melverley and Knockin w Maesbrook *Lich* from 09. *The Rectory, Vicarage Lane, Kinnerley, Oswestry SY10 8DE* Tel (01691) 682351 E-mail revrosie@btinternet.com

BOWES, Mrs Beryl Sylvia. b 48. Hull Univ BTh89 Leeds Univ MA06 SRN70 RSCN71. NEOC 89. **d** 91 **p** 94. NSM Kirk Ella *York* 91-99; Chapl R Hull Hosps NHS Trust 93-99; P-in-c Kexby w Wilberfoss *York* 99-04; R The Street Par from 04. *The Rectory, Church Street, Amotherby, Malton YO17 6TN* Tel (01653) 690663 E-mail rector@thestreetparishes.org

BOWES, Canon John Anthony Hugh. b 39. Ch Ch Ox BA62 MA65. Westcott Ho Cam 63. **d** 65 **p** 66. C Langley All SS and Martyrs *Man* 65-68; Asst Chapl Bris Univ 68-73; TV Cramlington *Newc* 73-76; P-in-c Oldland *Bris* 76-80; TR 80-84; V Westbury-on-Trym St Alb 84-05; Hon Can Bris Cathl 02-05; rtd 05. *4 Royal Albert Road, Bristol BS6 7NY* Tel 0117-973 5844

BOWES, Peter Hugh. b 48. Hull Univ LLB69 Dur Univ MA05 Solicitor 72. Cranmer Hall Dur 02. **d** 03 **p** 04. NSM Pocklington and Owsthorpe and Kilnwick Percy etc *York* 03-04; NSM The Street Par 04-07; NSM New Malton 06-07; P-in-c from 07; C Old Malton from 10; C Weaverthorpe w Helperthorpe, Luttons Ambo etc from 11; Assoc Dir of Ords 05-10; RD S Ryedale from 11. *The Rectory, Church Street, Amotherby, Malton YO17 6TN* Tel (01653) 690663 Mobile 07775-757723 E-mail vicar@stmichaelsmalton.org.uk

BOWES-SMITH, Edward Michael Crispin. b 67. K Coll Lon LLB89 AKC89 Solicitor 90 Selw Coll Cam BA96. Ridley Hall Cam 94. **d** 97 **p** 98. C Combe Down w Monkton Combe and S Stoke *B & W* 97-00; C Enfield Ch Ch Trent Park *Lon* 00-03; P-in-c Linc Minster Gp from 03. *St Peter's Vicarage, Lee Road, Lincoln LN2 4BH* Tel (01522) 568529 E-mail bowessmith@waitrose.com

BOWETT, Canon Richard Julnes. b 45. EAMTC 86. **d** 89 **p** 90. C Hunstanton St Mary w Ringstead Parva, Holme etc *Nor* 89-93; C King's Lynn St Marg w St Nic 93-95; V Watton w Carbrooke and Ovington 95-02; RD Breckland 99-02; P-in-c Ashill w Saham Toney 00-01; Dioc Sec 02-09; rtd 09; Hon Can Nor Cathl from 05. *Willow House, 6 Barnby Road, RAF Coltishall, Norwich NR10 5JN* Tel (01603) 736916

BOWIE, Michael Nicholas Roderick. b 59. Sydney Univ BA78 CCC Ox DPhil90. St Steph Ho Ox MA90. **d** 91 **p** 92. C Swanley St Mary *Roch* 91-93; C Penarth w Lavernock *Llan* 93-96;

Australia 96-00; R Norton *Sheff* 00-05; TR Gt Berkhamsted, Gt and Lt Gaddesden etc *St Alb* from 05; RD Berkhamsted from 09. *The Rectory, Rectory Lane, Berkhamsted HP4 2DH* Tel (01442) 864194 E-mail mnrbowie@hotmail.com

BOWIE, Sara. b 53. Open Univ BA83 Surrey Univ BA02. STETS 99. **d** 02 **p** 03. NSM Camberley St Mich Yorktown *Guildf* 02-07; C Coity, Nolton and Brackla *Llan* 07-10; P-in-c Essington *Lich* from 10; P-in-c Shareshill from 10. *The Vicarage, 11 Brookhouse Lane, Featherstone, Wolverhampton WV10 7AW* Tel (01902) 727579

BOWKER, Prof John Westerdale. b 35. Worc Coll Ox BA58. Ripon Hall Ox. **d** 61 **p** 62. C Endcliffe *Sheff* 61-62; Fell Lect and Dir of Studies CCC Cam 62-74; Lect Div Cam Univ 70-74; Prof RS Lanc Univ 74-86; Hon Prov Can Cant Cathl 85-03; Dean of Chpl Trin Coll Cam 86-91; rtd 91; Lic to Offic *Cant* 91-94; Perm to Offic *Ely* 94-00. *14 Bowers Croft, Cambridge CB1 8RP*

BOWKETT, Graham Philip. b 67. Open Univ BSc99. NEOC 06. **d** 09 **p** 10. C Thirsk *York* from 09. *3 Herriot Way, Thirsk YO7 1FL* Tel (01845) 523812 E-mail bowkett520@hotmail.co.uk

✠**BOWLBY, The Rt Revd Ronald Oliver.** b 26. Trin Coll Ox BA50 MA54. Westcott Ho Cam 50. **d** 52 **p** 53 **c** 73. C Pallion *Dur* 52-56; C Billingham St Cuth 56-57; C-in-c Billingham St Aid CD 57-60; V Billingham St Aid 60-66; V Croydon St Jo *Cant* 66-73; Hon Can Cant Cathl 70-73; Bp Newc 73-80; Bp S'wark 80-91; rtd 91; Hon Asst Bp Lich 91-10. *4 Uppington Avenue, Shrewsbury SY3 7JL* Tel (01743) 244192 E-mail rbowlby@phonecoop.coop

BOWLER, Christopher William. See JAGE-BOWLER, Canon Christopher William

BOWLER, David Edward. b 53. Northumbria Univ BA04 RMN80. NEOC 05. **d** 08 **p** 09. NSM Cramlington *Newc* 08-10; Chapl Northgate and Prudhoe NHS Trust from 10; Chapl Northumberland, Tyne and Wear NHS Foundn Trust from 10. *1 Hickstead Grove, Cramlington NE23 2FF* Tel (01670) 716271 E-mail djbowler@sky.com

BOWLER, David Henderson. b 54. Kent Univ BA75. St Jo Coll Nottm 75. **d** 78 **p** 79. C Bramcote *S'well* 78-82; TV Kirby Muxloe *Leic* 82-88; V Quorndon from 88. *27 Mansfield Avenue, Quorn, Loughborough LE12 8BD* E-mail dhb300154@aol.com

BOWLER, Preb Kenneth Neville. b 37. K Coll Lon 57. **d** 61 **p** 62. C Buxton *Derby* 61-67; R Sandiacre 67-75; V E Bedfont *Lon* 75-87; AD Hounslow 82-87; V Fulham All SS 87-02; Preb St Paul's Cathl 85-02; rtd 02; Perm to Offic *St Alb* from 03. *The Coach House, 22 Brincliffe Crescent, Sheffield S11 9AW* Tel 0114-250 0043

BOWLER, Neil. b 70. Nottm Trent Univ LLB92 Leeds Univ BA05 Solicitor 93. Coll of Resurr Mirfield 03. **d** 05 **p** 06. C Doncaster St Jude *Sheff* 05-08; R Whiston from 09. *The Rectory, Rectory Drive, Whiston, Rotherham S60 4JG* Tel (01709) 364430

BOWLES, Arthur William. b 36. **d** 96 **p** 97. OLM Gt Yarmouth *Nor* 96-06; Perm to Offic from 06. *4 Onslow Avenue, Great Yarmouth NR30 4DT* Tel (01493) 842360 E-mail revawb@talktalk.net

BOWLES, Preb Michael Hubert Venn. b 36. Selw Coll Cam BA59 MA63. Ridley Hall Cam 59. **d** 61 **p** 62. C Woodside Park St Barn *Lon* 61-64; C Swanage *Sarum* 64-67; Lect St Mich Coll Llan 67-72; Chapl 67-70; Lib 70-72; Lect Th Univ of Wales (Cardiff) 67-72; R St Stanmore *Lon* 72-01; Preb St Paul's Cathl 85-01; rtd 01; Perm to Offic *St Alb* from 02. *15 The Limes, St Albans AL1 4AT* Tel (01727) 832555

BOWLES, Peter John. b 39. Lon Univ BA60. Linc Th Coll 71. **d** 73 **p** 74. C Clay Cross *Derby* 73-76; C Boulton 76-79; R Brailsford w Shirley 79-85; P-in-c Osmaston w Edlaston 81-85; R Brailsford w Shirley and Osmaston w Edlaston 85-89; TR Old Brampton and Loundsley Green 89-98; V Hope, Castleton and Bradwell 98-04; rtd 04; Perm to Offic *Nor* from 04. *3 Blackhorse Yard, Wells-next-the-Sea NR23 1BN* Tel (01328) 711119

BOWLEY, Canon John Richard Lyon. b 46. MRTPI76 Dur Univ BA68 QUB MSc72. CITC. **d** 79 **p** 80. C Knock *D & D* 79-81; Bp's C Knocknagoney 81-90; I Ballywalter w Inishargie from 90; Can Down Cathl from 03. *The Vicarage, 2 Whitechurch Road, Ballywalter, Newtownards BT22 2JY* Tel (028) 9175 8416

BOWMAN, Miss Alison Valentine. b 57. St Andr Univ MA79. St Steph Ho Ox 86. **d** 89 **p** 94. Par Dn Peacehaven *Chich* 89-94; C 94-95; Chapl to Bp Lewes 93-95; TV Rye 95-03; P-in-c Preston St Jo w Brighton St Aug and St Sav 03-09; V from 09. *33 Preston Drove, Brighton BN1 6LA* Tel (01273) 555033

BOWMAN, Clifford William. b 57. St Jo Coll Dur BA78 Nottm Univ MA96. Ridley Hall Cam 80. **d** 82 **p** 83. C Sawley *Derby* 82-85; C Hucknall Torkard *S'well* 85-89; R Warsop 89-00; Dioc Chapl amongst Deaf People 00-06; TV Uxbridge *Lon* from 06. *St Andrew's Vicarage, Nursery Waye, Uxbridge UB8 2BJ* Tel (01895) 239055 E-mail c.bowman@dunelm.org.uk

BOWMAN, Canon Ivelaw Alexander. b 46. **d** 97 **p** 98. OLM Stockwell Green St Andr *S'wark* 97-03; OLM Stockwell St Andr and St Mich from 03; Chapl S Lon and Maudsley NHS Foundn Trust 03-07; Hon Can S'wark Cathl from 05. *16 Horsford Road, London SW2 5BN* Tel (020) 7733 2309

BOWMAN, Prof John. b 16. Glas Univ MA38 BD41 Ch Ch Ox DPhil45. **d** 50 **p** 54. Hon C Leeds St Geo *Ripon* 51-53; Hon C Kirkstall 53-54; Perm to Offic *York* 54-59; Australia from 59; rtd 73. *15 Haines Street, North Melbourne Vic 3051, Australia* Tel and fax (0061) (3) 9329 0794 E-mail mbowman@vicnet.net.au

BOWMAN-EADIE, Preb Russell Ian. b 45. K Coll Lon BD71 AKC71 ACP68 FCP. St Aug Coll Cant 71. **d** 72 **p** 73. C Hammersmith St Pet *Lon* 72-74; V Leic St Nic 74-81; Chapl Leic Univ 74-81; Adult Educn Adv *Dur* 81-84; Dir of Tr *B & W* 84-09; Preb Wells Cathl 90-09; Can Res and Treas Wells Cathl 02-09; rtd 10. *8 Shaftesbury Place, Rustington, Littlehampton BN16 2GA* Tel (01903) 774580 E-mail russell.bowmaneadie@googlemail.com

BOWN, Mrs Marcia Helen. EMMTC. **d** 10 **p** 11. NSM N Wingfield, Clay Cross and Pilsley *Derby* from 10. *43 Rupert Street, Lower Pilsley, Chesterfield S45 8DB* Tel (01773) 872550 E-mail marciabown@hotmail.co.uk

BOWNASS (née FRYER), Alison Jane. b 56. Univ Coll of Swansea BSc78 Birm Poly PGCE90. Qu Coll Birm 05. **d** 07 **p** 08. C The Quinton *Birm* 07-10; Perm to Offic 10-11; C Hill from 11. *41 Silvermead Road, Sutton Coldfield B73 5SR* Tel 0121-321 1600 Mobile 07958-911378 E-mail alison@bownass.co.uk

BOWNESS, William Gary. b 48. Warwick Univ BSc69 Chicago State Univ DMin98. Ripon Coll Cuddesdon 80. **d** 82 **p** 83. C Lancaster St Mary *Blackb* 82-86; V Lostock Hall 86-91; V Whittington w Arkholme and Gressingham 91-02; RD Tunstall 93-99; Dir Post-Ord Tr 00-02; R Alderley w Birtles *Ches* 02-07; P-in-c Henbury from 07. *St Thomas's Vicarage, Church Lane, Henbury, Macclesfield SK11 9NN* Tel (01625) 424113 E-mail gary@bowness1792.freeserve.co.uk

BOWRING, Stephen John. b 55. R Holloway Coll Lon BMus77 St Mary's Coll Twickenham PGCE78. EMMTC 89. **d** 92 **p** 93. C Thurmaston *Leic* 92-95; V Shepshed 95-02; R River *Cant* 02-06; P-in-c Charlton-in-Dover 05-06; AD Dover 03-06; Hon Min Can Cant Cathl 04-06; V Chesterton St Geo *Ely* 06-11; R Kym Valley from 11. *The Vicarage, 3 St Andrew's Court, Kimbolton, Huntingdon PE28 0DF* Tel (01480) 860792 E-mail stephenbowring@btinternet.com

BOWRON, Hugh Mark. b 52. Cant Univ (NZ) BA74 MA76. Coll of Resurr Mirfield 76. **d** 79 **p** 80. C Northampton St Mary *Pet* 79-82; V Ellesmere New Zealand 82-86; V Addington St Mary 86-95; V Wellington St Pet 95-05; V Avonside H Trin from 05. *2/142 Avonside Drive, Christchurch, New Zealand* Tel (0064) (3) 389 3024 E-mail office@holytrinityavonside.co.nz

BOWSER, Alan. b 35. Univ of Wales (Lamp) BA60. **d** 63 **p** 64. C Gateshead St Chad Bensham *Dur* 63-67; C Owton Manor CD 67-72; V Horden 72-02; rtd 02. *Kengarth House, Coast Road, Blackhall Colliery, Hartlepool TS27 4HF* Tel 0191-586 1753

BOWSHER, Andrew Peter. b 59. Reading Univ BA81. St Jo Coll Nottm 83. **d** 86 **p** 87. C Grenoside *Sheff* 86-89; C Darfield 89-91; P-in-c Haley Hill *Wakef* 91-96; V Bradf St Aug Undercliffe 96-99; Chapl Bradf Univ and Bradf Coll 99-04; Perm to Offic *Dur* from 04; Tutor St Jo Coll Nottm 07-11; Chapl Northumbria Univ from 11. *282 Wingrove Road North, Fenham, Newcastle upon Tyne NE4 9EE* Tel 0191-227 3284 Mobile 07876-401339 E-mail andii.bowsher@northumbria.ac.uk

BOWSKILL, Mrs Amanda. b 49. STETS 96. **d** 99 **p** 00. NSM Winklebury 99-03; NSM Tadley S and Silchester 03-04; NSM Kempshott from 05. *10 Portway Place, Basingstoke RG23 8DT* Tel (01256) 327301 E-mail mandy.bowskill@cwcom.net

BOWSKILL, Robert Preston. b 48. S Dios Minl Tr Scheme 88. **d** 91 **p** 92. NSM Eastrop *Win* 91-94; NSM Winklebury 94-05; NSM Kempshott from 05. *10 Portway Place, Basingstoke RG23 8DT* Tel (01256) 327301 E-mail bob.bowskill@cwcom.net

BOWTELL, Paul William. b 47. Lon Univ BSc68. St Jo Coll Nottm 80. **d** 82 **p** 83. C Gorleston St Andr *Nor* 82-85; TV Forest Gate St Sav w W Ham St Matt *Chelmsf* 85-91; R Spitalfields Ch Ch w All SS *Lon* 91-02; Co-ord Transform Newham 02-06; Chapl to Bp Barking *Chelmsf* from 06; C Leyton St Cath and St Paul from 07. *Barking Lodge, 35A Verulam Avenue, London E17 8ES* Tel (020) 8509 7377 E-mail pbowtell@chelmsford.anglican.org

BOWYER, Arthur Gustavus Frederick. b 36. **d** 00 **p** 01. NSM Kingswood *S'wark* from 00. *41 Tattenham Grove, Epsom KT18 5QT* Tel (01737) 357913 Mobile 07939-533506 E-mail abowyer@onetel.com

BOWYER, Geoffrey Charles. b 54. ACA79 ATII82 Lanc Univ BA76. St Jo Coll Nottm 85. **d** 87 **p** 88. C Walton *St E* 87-89; C Macclesfield Team *Ches* 89-91; V Cinderford St Steph w Littledean *Glouc* 91-95; V Brockenhurst *Win* 95-98; Hon C Trull w Angersleigh *B & W* from 00. *36 Bakers Close, Bishops Hull, Taunton TA1 5HD* Tel (01823) 335289 E-mail us4bowyers@aol.com

BOWYER, Gerry. b 60. Cliff Th Coll MA10. **d** 10 **p** 10. C Aberdeen St Ninian 10; Bp's Ev for Fresh Expressions and Ch Planting from 11. *2 Buckie Road, Bridge of Don, Aberdeen AB22 8DG* Tel (01224) 706916 Mobile 07956-098566 E-mail gerry.bowyer@live.com

BOX, Reginald Gilbert (Brother Reginald). b 20. Lon Univ BD41 AKC41 Em Coll Cam BA52 MA57 Lambeth STh91. Westcott Ho Cam 41. **d** 43 **p** 44. C Chingford SS Pet and Paul *Chelmsf* 43-47; Chapl Bps' Coll Cheshunt 47-50; SSF from 51; Lic to Offic *Ely* 51-55 and *Sarum* 55-61; C Cambridge St Benedict *Ely* 61-67; Chapl Coll of SS Mark and Jo Chelsea 67-69; New Zealand, Australia and Melanesia 69-84; Perm to Offic *Sarum* from 84 and *Ely* 85-97; Chapl Chich Th Coll 90-93; Perm to Offic *Cant* from 05. *The Friary, 6A Stour Street, Canterbury CT1 2NR* Tel (01227) 479364

BOXALL, David John. b 41. Dur Univ BA63. Sarum Th Coll 65. **d** 66 **p** 67. C Ipswich St Aug *St E* 66-69; C Bourne *Linc* 69-71; C Woodside Park St Barn *Lon* 71-72; C Thundersley *Chelmsf* 72-76; P-in-c Farcet *Ely* 76-77; TV Stanground and Farcet 77-85; V Guyhirn w Ring's End 85-90; V Southea w Murrow and Parson Drove 85-90; P-in-c Fletton 90-94; Perm to Offic 94-00 and 05-08; rtd 99. *11 Plover Drive, March PE15 9HY* Tel (01354) 659905

BOXALL, Keith Michael. b 37. Trin Coll Bris. **d** 82 **p** 83. C Staines St Pet *Lon* 82-83; C Staines St Mary and St Pet 83-85; C Lydiard Millicent w Lydiard Tregoz *Bris* 85-86; TV The Lydiards 86-93; V Mangotsfield 93-03; rtd 03; Perm to Offic *Bris* from 03. *25 Parc Plas, Blackwood NP12 1SJ* Tel (01495) 222572 Mobile 07745-016038 E-mail keith.boxall1@btinternet.com

BOXALL, Canon Martin Alleyne. b 37. Wells Th Coll 65. **d** 67 **p** 68. C Crowthorne *Ox* 67-70; C Tilehurst St Mich 70-76; V Tilehurst St Cath 76-78; V Padstow *Truro* 78-00; Miss to Seafarers from 78; RD Pydar *Truro* 93; Hon Can Truro Cathl from 93; rtd 01; Dioc Officer for Unity *Truro* from 01. *Goonhilland Farmhouse, Burnthouse, St Gluvias, Penryn TR10 9AS* Tel (01872) 863241 E-mail martinboxall@aol.com

BOXALL, Simon Roger. b 55. St Jo Coll Cam BA76 MA80. Ridley Hall Cam 77. **d** 79 **p** 80. C Eaton *Nor* 79-82; SAMS Brazil 82-04; P-in-c Belo Horizonte St Pet 84-88; P-in-c Santiago St Tim and Horizontina H Spirit 88-91; C Bagé Crucifixion 93-94; R Jaguarao Ch Ch 94-98; English Chapl Rio de Janeiro 99-04; TV Thamesmead *S'wark* from 05. *62-64 Battery Road, London SE28 0JT* Tel (020) 8836 9069

BOXLEY, Christopher. b 45. K Coll Lon BD68 AKC68 Southn Univ CertEd73 Reading Univ MA84. **d** 69 **p** 70. C Bitterne Park *Win* 69-73; Hd RS Midhurst Gr Sch from 73; Dir Midhurst and Petworth RS Cen from 78; Perm to Offic *Chich* 73-78; P-in-c Heyshott from 78. *The Rectory, Heyshott, Midhurst GU29 0DH* Tel (01730) 814405 E-mail boxley@talktalk.net

BOYCE, Christopher Allan. b 44. ARIBA69. S Dios Minl Tr Scheme 84. **d** 87 **p** 88. NSM Eastbourne All SS *Chich* 87-93; C Upton (Overchurch) *Ches* 93-96; V New Brighton St Jas w Em 96-02; P-in-c New Brighton All SS 98-02; TV Bicester w Bucknell, Caversfield and Launton *Ox* from 02. *4 Orpine Close, Bicester OX26 3ZJ* Tel (01869) 244918 Mobile 07989-269175 E-mail revcab@lineone.net

BOYCE, John Frederick. b 33. ALCD57. **d** 57 **p** 58. C Earlsfield St Andr *S'wark* 57-60; C Westerham *Roch* 60-63; C Farnborough 63-66; V Sutton at Hone 66-73; P-in-c Chiddingstone 73-74; R Chiddingstone w Chiddingstone Causeway 74-84; V Brenchley 84-98; rtd 98; Perm to Offic *Chich* from 99. *3 Orchard Rise, Groombridge, Tunbridge Wells TN3 9RU* Tel (01892) 864633

BOYCE, Joy. b 46. **d** 05 **p** 06. NSM Streatham Ch Ch w St Marg *S'wark* 05-09; NSM Southfields St Barn from 09. *60 Westover Road, London SW18 2RH* Tel (020) 8874 1905 Mobile 07867-830273 E-mail joy.boyce@fujitsu.com

BOYCE, Canon Kenneth Albert. b 51. St Edm Hall Ox BA72 MA76 Selw Coll Cam BA75 MA79. Westcott Ho Cam 73. **d** 75 **p** 76. C Evington *Leic* 75-78; P-in-c Gt Bowden w Welham 78-81; Dioc Stewardship Adv 78-81; Chapl Leic Poly 81-86; TV Leic H Spirit 82-86; P-in-c Astwood Bank and Chapl to the Deaf *Worc* 86-93; R Fladbury, Wyre Piddle and Moor 93-98; P-in-c Cropthorne w Charlton 94-98; R Fladbury w Wyre Piddle and Moor etc 98-00; RD Pershore 97-00; TR Worc SE from 00; RD Worc E from 05; Hon Can Worc Cathl from 07. *The Rectory, 6 St Catherine's Hill, Worcester WR5 2EA* Tel (01905) 355119 E-mail ken@kenboyce.fsnet.co.uk

BOYCE, Ms Susan. b 59. Ch Ch Coll Cant MA00 Birm Univ BPhil06. Ripon Coll Cuddesdon 05. **d** 06 **p** 07. NSM Rushall *Lich* 06-11; Perm to Offic from 11. *c/o the Lord Bishop of Lichfield, 22 The Close, Lichfield WS13 7LG* Tel 07941-927245 (mobile) E-mail sueboyceca@hotmail.com

BOYCE, William Alexander. **d** 03 **p** 04. C Willowfield *D & D* 03-04; C Bangor Abbey 04-07; I Mallusk *Conn* from 07. *The Rectory, 6 Carwood Drive, Newtownabbey BT36 5LP* Tel (028) 9087 9029 E-mail weebill@hotmail.com

BOYCE-TILLMAN, Prof June Barbara. b 43. MBE. St Hugh's Coll Ox BA65 Lon Inst of Educn PGCE66 PhD87 LRAM74. Dioc OLM tr scheme. **d** 06 **p** 07. NSM Streatham St Paul *S'wark* 06-10; Perm to Offic from 10. *108 Nimrod Road, London SW16 6TQ* Tel 07850-208721 (mobile) Fax (020) 8677 8752 E-mail junebt@globalnet.co.uk

BOYD, Alan McLean. b 50. St Jo Coll Nottm BTh79. **d** 79 **p** 80. C Bishop's Waltham *Portsm* 79-83; Chapl Reading Univ 83-88; Chapl E Birm Hosp 88-94; Chapl Birm Heartlands and Solihull NHS Trust from 94. *Solihull Hospital, Lode Lane, Solihull B91 2JL* Tel 0121-424 4099

BOYD, Canon Alexander Jamieson. b 46. St Chad's Coll Dur BSc68 Nottm Univ PGCE69 MIBiol FSAScot. Coll of Resurr Mirfield 69. **d** 79 **p** 80. NSM Musselburgh *Edin* 79-83; CF 83-00; P-in-c Loddington *Leic* 00-03; Warden Launde Abbey 00-03; P-in-c Mareham-le-Fen and Revesby *Linc* 03-06; P-in-c Mareham on the Hill 03-06; R Fen and Hill Gp from 06; RD Horncastle from 06; Can and Preb Linc Cathl from 09. *The Rectory, Fieldside, Mareham-le-Fen, Boston PE22 7QU* Tel (01507) 568215 E-mail alec@ajboyd.wanadoo.co.uk

BOYD, Allan Gray. b 41. St Jo Coll Nottm 84. **d** 87 **p** 88. Hon Chapl Miss to Seafarers from 87; NSM Glas St Gabr 87-93; NSM Greenock 93-96; NSM Paisley St Barn 96-00; NSM Paisley H Trin 96-00; NSM Alexandria 00-01; NSM Clydebank 02-08. *47 Holms Crescent, Erskine PA8 6DJ* Tel 0141-812 2754

BOYD, Canon David Anthony. b 42. Sarum & Wells Th Coll 72. **d** 75 **p** 76. C Ches H Trin 75-79; R 85-93; V Congleton St Jas 79-85; V Farndon and Coddington 93-07; RD Malpas 97-04; Hon Can Ches Cathl 02-07; rtd 07. *68 St James Avenue, Upton, Chester CH2 1NL* Tel (01244) 348800

BOYD, James. *See* BOYD, William James

BOYD, Michael Victor. b 53. St Chad's Coll Dur BA57 DipAdEd69 MEd77 PhD81. Coll of Resurr Mirfield 57. **d** 59 **p** 60. C Warsop *S'well* 59-61; Chapl St Geo Coll Quilmes Argent 62-63; Chapl Wolsingham Sch 63-67; Lect St Hild Coll Dur 67-75; Lect SS Hild and Bede Dur 75-79; Lect Dur Univ 79-84; rtd 98. *4 Aykley Green, Durham DH1 4LN* Tel 0191-384 9473

BOYD, Robert Henry. b 36. **d** 66 **p** 67. C Drumcree *Arm* 66-69; I Annaghmore 69-83; Bp's C Lissan 83-90; I 90-06; rtd 06. *Lillybank, 19 Killymaddy Knox, Dungannon BT70 1NL* Tel (028) 8772 2351

BOYD, Samuel Robert Thomas. b 62. **d** 90 **p** 91. NSM Derryloran *Arm* 90-95; C 95-97; I Woodschapel w Gracefield 97-05; I Killyman from 05. *St Andrew's Rectory, 85 Dungorman Road, Dungannon BT71 6SE* Tel and fax (028) 8772 2500 E-mail killyman@armagh.anglican.org

BOYD, Stephen William. b 71. Aston Tr Scheme 95 Ripon Coll Cuddesdon BTh00. **d** 00 **p** 01. C Walton-on-the-Hill *Liv* 00-04; V Westbrook St Jas 04-09; P-in-c Orford St Marg from 09. *St Margaret's Vicarage, 2 St Margaret's Avenue, Warrington WA2 8DT* Tel (01925) 631937

BOYD, Stuart Adrian. b 51. Open Univ BA99 UWE MA02. STETS 02. **d** 05 **p** 07. NSM Brent Knoll, E Brent and Lympsham *B & W* 05-06; NSM Knowle H Nativity *Bris* 06-09. *29 Stafford Road, Weston-super-Mare BS23 3BN* Tel (01934) 627897

BOYD, William James. **d** 07 **p** 08. C Magheralin w Dollingstown *D & D* 07-11; I Dromore *Clogh* from 11. *The Rectory, 19 Galbally Road, Dromore, Omagh BT78 3EE* Tel (028) 8289 8246 E-mail jamesthegrey@hotmail.com

BOYD, Canon William John Peter. b 28. Lon Univ BA48 BD53 PhD77 Birm Univ MA60. **d** 57 **p** 58. C Aston SS Pet and Paul *Birm* 57-60; V W Smethwick 60-63; V St Breward *Truro* 63-68; Adult Educn Chapl 64-85; Dioc Ecum Officer 65-83; R St Ewe 68-73; Preb St Endellion 73-85; V St Kew 73-77; R Falmouth K Chas 77-85; RD Carnmarth S 84-85; Dir of Tr 85-93; Prin SWMTC 85-93; Can Res and Chan Truro Cathl 85-93; rtd 93; Perm to Offic Truro from 93. *7 Chapel Crescent, Zelah, Truro TR4 9HN*

BOYD-WILLIAMS, Anthony Robert. b 46. St Mich Coll Llan 86. **d** 88 **p** 89. C Tonyrefail w Gilfach Goch *Llan* 88-91; V Treharris w Bedlinog 91-96; V Ocker Hill *Lich* 96-05; RD Wednesbury 03-05; rtd 06; Perm to Offic *Cov* from 05. *36 Kendall Avenue, Stratford-upon-Avon CV37 6SQ*

BOYDEN, Peter Frederick. b 41. Lon Univ BSc62 AKC62 Em Coll Cam BA64 MA68 MLitt69. Ridley Hall Cam 63. **d** 66 **p** 67. C Chesterton St Andr *Ely* 66-68; C Wimbledon *S'wark* 68-72; Chapl K Sch Cant 72-89; Asst Chapl Radley Coll 89-02; rtd 02; Perm to Offic *Derby* from 02. *30 Chesterfield Road, Shirland, Alfreton DE55 6BN* Tel (01773) 830552 E-mail pandjboyden@aol.com

BOYES, Canon David Arthur Stiles. b 30. Lon Coll of Div 62. **d** 63 **p** 64. C Islington St Mary *Lon* 63-71; V Canonbury St Steph 71-75; V St Paul's Cray St Barn *Roch* 75-85; P-in-c Earl Soham w Cretingham and Ashfield *St E* 85-96; Dioc Development Officer 86-92; RD Loes 91-95; Hon Can St E Cathl 95-96; rtd 96; Perm to Offic *St E* from 96. *13 Magdalen Drive, Woodbridge IP12 4EF* Tel (01394) 383389

BOYES, Matthew John. b 70. Roehampton Inst BA91. Wycliffe Hall Ox 89. **d** 99 **p** 00. C Bury St Edmunds Ch Ch *St E* 99-02; P-in-c Penn Street *Ox* 02-06; V Turnham Green Ch Ch *Lon* 06-11; Chapl HM YOI Feltham from 11. *HM Young Offender Institution, Bedfont Road, Feltham TW13 4ND* Tel (020) 8844 5000 Fax 8844 5001 E-mail matt_boyz@dsl.pipex.com

BOYES, Michael Charles. b 27. Lon Univ BA53 BD58. Wells Th Coll 53. **d** 55 **p** 56. C Heavitree *Ex* 55-61; C Exwick 61-68; V Broadclyst 68-83; RD Aylesbeare 77-81; TV Sampford Peverell, Uplowman, Holcombe Rogus etc 83-85; TR 85-92; rtd 92; Perm to Offic *Ex* from 92. *Old Brewery Cottage, 1 East Street, Uffculme, Cullompton EX15 3AL* Tel (01884) 840492

BOYLAND, Alice Teresa. b 41. **d** 99 **p** 05. NSM Llangybi and Coedypaen w Llanbadoc *Mon* 99-04; NSM Chard and Distr *B & W* 05-06; NSM Chaffcombe, Cricket Malherbie etc 06-11; rtd 11. *62 Link Hay Orchard, South Chard, Chard TA20 2QS* Tel (01460) 221010 E-mail daveterri@waitrose.com

BOYLAND, David Henry. b 58. TCD BA79 BAI79. TCD Div Sch BTh91. **d** 91 **p** 92. C Seapatrick *D & D* 91-94; I Celbridge w Straffan and Newcastle-Lyons *D & G* 94-98; I Kilmakee *Conn* from 98. *Kilmakee Rectory, 60 Killeaton Park, Dunmurry, Belfast BT17 9HE* Tel (028) 9061 0505 *or* 9061 1024

BOYLAND, Henry Hubert. b 23. CITC. **d** 84 **p** 85. NSM Dunboyne Union *M & K* 84-87; Bp's C Carrickmacross w Magheracloone *Clogh* 87-90; I 90-93; rtd 93. *2 Spring View, Wheaton Hall, Dublin Road, Drogheda, Co Louth, Republic of Ireland* Tel (00353) (41) 984 4724

BOYLAND, Peter James. b 68. TCD BA92 MA07. St Steph Ho Ox 07. **d** 09 **p** 10. C Towcester w Caldecote and Easton Neston etc *Pet* from 09. *35 Hazel Crescent, Towcester NN12 6UQ* Tel (01327) 323018 Mobile 07798-501847 E-mail frbovland@gmail.com

BOYLE, Andrew McKenzie. b 45. Down Coll Cam BA67 MA71 CEng72 MICE72. WMMTC 82. **d** 85 **p** 86. NSM Woodthorpe *S'well* 85-87; Perm to Offic *Roch* 88-90; 91-96; Hon C Sevenoaks St Luke CD 90-91; NSM Sundridge w Ide Hill and Toys Hill from 96. *Greenridge, 35 Garth Road, Sevenoaks TN13 1RU* Tel (01732) 456546 Fax 450060 E-mail andrew.boyle@diocese-rochester.org

BOYLE, Charles Robert. b 69. Edin Univ MA92. Ridley Hall Cam 08. **d** 10 **p** 11. C Kea *Truro* from 10. *169 Treffry Road, Truro TR1 1UF* Tel (01872) 274362 Mobile 07979-857200 E-mail keacurate@gmail.com

✠**BOYLE, The Rt Revd Christopher John.** b 51. AKC75. St Aug Coll Cant 75. **d** 76 **p** 77 **c** 01. C Wylde Green *Birm* 76-80; Bp's Dom Chapl 80-83; R Castle Bromwich SS Mary and Marg 83-01; AD Coleshill 92-99; P-in-c Shard End 96-97; Hon Can Birm Cathl 96-01; Bp N Malawi 01-09; Asst Bp Leic from 09. *5 The Pastures, Anstey, Leicester LE7 7QR* E-mail bishopboyle@googlemail.com

BOYLE, Mrs Lynn. b 58. Leeds Univ BEd79 BA07. NOC 04. **d** 07 **p** 08. NSM Stockport St Sav *Ches* 07-11; V Werneth from 11. *St Paul's Vicarage, Compstall Brow, Compstall, Stockport SK6 5HU* Tel 0161-427 1259 Mobile 07971-390019 E-mail lynnboyle1@aol.com

BOYLE, Paul. **d** 01 **p** 02. C Cen Cardiff *Llan* 01-03; C Barry All SS 03-05; P-in-c Pontypridd St Matt and Cilfynydd w Llanwynno 05-08; P-in-c Burton and Rosemarket *St D* 08-11; P-in-c Camrose from 11; Asst Dioc Officer for Soc Resp from 11. *The Vicarage, Camrose, Haverfordwest SA62 6JE* Tel (01437) 710558

BOYLE, Robert Leslie. b 52. EMMTC 97. **d** 00 **p** 01. NSM Derby St Anne and St Jo 00-08; C Paignton St Jo *Ex* from 08. *73 Dartmouth Road, Paignton TQ4 5AF* Tel (01803) 698412 E-mail robert.boyle7@btinternet.com

BOYLES, Peter John. b 59. Univ of Wales (Lamp) BA84. Sarum & Wells Th Coll 86. **d** 88 **p** 89. C Ches St Mary 88-91; C Neston 91-95; R Lavendon w Cold Brayfield, Clifton Reynes etc *Ox* 95-99; V Dent w Cowgill *Bradf* from 99. *The Vicarage, Flintergill, Dent, Sedbergh LA10 5QR* Tel (015396) 25226

BOYLING, Canon Denis Hudson. b 16. Keble Coll Ox BA38 MA42. Cuddesdon Coll 39. **d** 40 **p** 41. C Sheff St Cuth 40-46; Chapl K Coll Hosp Lon 46-49; Chapl United Sheff Hosps 49-57; V Endcliffe *Sheff* 57-68; Hon Can Sheff Cathl 58-68; V Almondbury *Wakef* 68-75; RD Almondbury 68-75; Hon Can Wakef Cathl 72-75; Can Res Wakef Cathl 75-82; rtd 82; Perm to Offic *Heref* from 82. *5 St Mary's Close, Tenbury Wells WR15 8ES* Tel (01584) 811633

BOYLING, The Very Revd Mark Christopher. b 52. Keble Coll Ox BA74 MA78. Cuddesdon Coll 74. **d** 77 **p** 78. C Kirkby *Liv* 77-79; P-in-c 79-80; TV 80-85; Bp's Dom Chapl 85-89; V Formby St Pet 89-94; Can Res and Prec Liv Cathl 94-04; Dean Carl from 04. *The Deanery, The Abbey, Carlisle CA3 8TZ* Tel (01228) 523335 Fax 548151 E-mail dean@carlislecathedral.org.uk

BOYNS, Martin Laurence Harley. b 26. St Jo Coll Cam BA49 MA51. Ridley Hall Cam 50. **d** 52 **p** 53. C Woodmansterne *S'wark* 52-55; C Folkestone H Trin w Ch Ch Cant 55-58; V Duffield *Derby* 58-71; V Rawdon *Bradf* 71-76; Chapl Woodlands Hosp Rawdon 71-76; R Melton *St E* 76-85; R Gerrans w St Anthony in Roseland *Truro* 85-92; Miss to Seamen 85-92; rtd 92; Perm to Offic *Truro* from 92. *Bojunda, Boscaswell Village, Pendeen, Penzance TR19 7EP* Tel (01736) 788390

BOYNS, Timothy Martin Harley. b 58. Warwick Univ BA80 Nottm Univ BCombStuds84. Linc Th Coll 81. **d** 84 **p** 85. C Oxhey St Matt *St Alb* 84-87; TV Solihull *Birm* 87-94; V Lillington *Cov* 94-06; RD Warwick and Leamington 99-06; V Hessle *York* from 06; AD W Hull from 10; RD Hull from 11. *All Saints' Vicarage, 4 Chestnut Avenue, Hessle HU13 0RH* Tel (01482) 648555 E-mail timboyns@timboyns.karoo.co.uk

BOYSE, Felix Vivian Allan. b 17. LVO78. CCC Cam BA39 MA42. Cuddesdon Coll 39. **d** 40 **p** 41. C New Mills *Derby* 40-43; P-in-c 43-45; Vice-Prin Cuddesdon Coll 46-51; V Kingswood *S'wark* 51-58; V St Mary Abchurch *Lon* 58-61; Prin St Geo Coll Jerusalem 61-64; Chapl Chpl Royal Hampton Court Palace 65-82; Preacher Lincoln's Inn 82-93; rtd 93; Perm to Offic *Chich* from 83. *Rose Cottage, Rookwood Road, West Wittering, Chichester PO20 8LT* Tel (01243) 514320

BRABIN-SMITH, Ms Lorna Daphne. b 54. Leeds Univ BSc75. Westcott Ho Cam 03. **d** 05 **p** 06. C Emmaus Par Team *Leic* 05-08; TV Fosse from 08. *The Parsonage, 20 Hoby Road, Thrussington, Leicester LE7 4TH* Tel (01664) 424962

BRABY (*née* QUINTON), **Rosemary Ruth.** b 53. Univ Coll Lon BA75 Lon Inst of Educn PGCE79. **d** 06 **p** 07. OLM Old Catton *Nor* 06-09; Perm to Offic 09-10; NSM Trowse from 10. *49 Woodland Drive, Norwich NR6 7AZ* Tel (01603) 427165 Fax 479556 E-mail rosemary.braby@ntlworld.com

BRACE, Alistair Andrew. b 53. Newc Univ MB, BS76. WMMTC 90. **d** 94. NSM Broseley w Benthall, Jackfield, Linley etc *Heref* 94-98. *58 Spout Lane, Benthall, Broseley TF12 1QY* Tel (01952) 884031

BRACE, Stuart. b 49. Open Univ BSc01. Bp Burgess Hall Lamp. **d** 74 **p** 75. C Llanelli Ch Ch *St D* 74-76; C Tenby w Gumfreston 76-77; V Ystradmeurig and Strata Florida 77-79; CF 79-86; CF(V) 86-93; Chapl HM Youth Cust Cen Everthorpe 86-88; Chapl HM Pris Stafford 88-93; Chapl HM Pris Long Lartin 93-95; Ecum Tr Officer HM Pris Service Chapl Pris 95-99; Chapl HM Pris Glouc 99-03; Chapl HM Pris Leyhill 03-11; rtd 11; Perm to Offic *Worc* from 95. *Address temp unknown* E-mail brace3@chap0.freeserve.co.uk

BRACEGIRDLE, Canon Christopher Andrew. b 56. Dur Univ BEd79 St Edm Ho Cam BA84 MA89 Cov Univ PhD05. Ridley Hall Cam 82. **d** 85 **p** 86. C Livesey *Blackb* 85-88; TV E Farnworth and Kearsley *Man* 88-92; V Astley and Chapl Wigan and Leigh Health Services NHS Trust 92-98; P-in-c Walkden Moor w Lt Hulton *Man* 98-99; TR Walkden and Lt Hulton 99-03; V Heaton Ch Ch 03-10; Tutor Dioc OLM and Reader Course 97-06; AD Bolton 05-10; Bp's Sen Chapl from 10; Warden of Readers from 08; Hon Can Man Cathl from 07. *Bishopscourt, Bury New Road, Salford M7 4LE* Tel 0161-792 2096 E-mail chaplain@bishopscourt.manchester.anglican.org

BRACEGIRDLE, Canon Cynthia Wendy Mary. b 52. LMH Ox BA73 MA77 Liv Univ DipAE82. NOC. **d** 87 **p** 94. Chapl Asst Man R Infirmary 85-88; Dir Dioc OLM Scheme *Man* 89-02; Hon Can Man Cathl 98-02; rtd 03; Perm to Offic *Carl* from 03. *The Vicarage, St George's Road, Millom LA18 4JA* Tel (01229) 772889 E-mail ignatius@globalnet.co.uk

BRACEGIRDLE, Robert Kevin Stewart. b 47. Univ Coll Ox BA69 MA73. St Steph Ho Ox 70. **d** 73 **p** 74. C Dorchester *Sarum* 73-75; C Woodchurch *Ches* 75-78; V Bidston 78-82; P-in-c Salford St Ignatius *Man* 82-86; R Salford St Ignatius and Stowell Memorial 86-02; P-in-c Salford Ordsall St Clem 99-02; P-in-c Millom *Carl* 02-06; V from 06. *The Vicarage, St George's Road, Millom LA18 4JA* Tel (01229) 772889 E-mail robert.bracegirdle@btinternet.com

BRACEWELL, Canon David John. b 44. Leeds Univ BA66 Man Univ MA82. Tyndale Hall Bris 67. **d** 69 **p** 70. C Tonbridge St Steph *Roch* 69-72; C Shipley St Pet *Bradf* 72-75; V Halliwell St Paul *Man* 75-84; R Guildf St Sav 84-10; Hon Can Guildf Cathl 05-10; rtd 10. *9 Nutcroft Grove, Fetcham, Leatherhead KT22 9LA* Tel (01372) 383036 E-mail djbracewell@gmail.com

BRACEWELL, Howard Waring. b 35. FRGS73. Tyndale Hall Bris. **d** 63 **p** 63. Canada 63-72; Travel Missr World Radio Miss Fellowship 72-77; P-in-c Ashill *Nor* 72-74; Hon C Bris St Phil and St Jacob w Em 77-84; Perm to Offic *St Alb* 84-86; R Odell 86-88; V Pavenham 86-88; Lic to Offic *Man* 88-93; Assoc Min St Andrew's Street Bapt Ch Cambridge 94-99; Assoc Min Halliwell St Luke 99-01; rtd 01; Perm to Offic *Man* 01-08. *10 Fairfields, Egerton, Bolton BL7 9EE* Tel (01204) 304028 E-mail howard@igloovut.fsnet.co.uk

BRACEWELL, Mrs Norma Lesley. b 47. SEITE 08. **d** 10 **p** 11. OLM Cant All SS from 10. *3 Metcalfe Mews, Canterbury CT1 1JD* Tel (01227) 452033 E-mail norma@bracewell.org

BRACEY, David Harold. b 36. AKC63. **d** 64 **p** 65. C Westleigh St Pet *Man* 64-67; C Dunstable *St Alb* 67-70; V Benchill *Man* 70-76; V Elton St Steph 76-87; V Howe Bridge 87-00; rtd 00; Perm to Offic *Ban* from 06. *Rhiw Awel, Sarn, Pwllheli LL53 8EY* Tel (01758) 730381

BRACEY, Dexter Lee. b 70. Lanc Univ BA92. St Steph Ho Ox 07. **d** 09 **p** 10. C St Marychurch *Ex* from 09. *28 Barewell Road, Torquay TQ1 4PA* Tel (01803) 326203 E-mail dexter_bracey@yahoo.co.uk

BRACHER, Paul Martin. b 59. Solicitor 84 Ex Univ LLB80. Trin Coll Bris BA90. **d** 90 **p** 91. C Sparkhill St Jo *Birm* 90; C Sparkhill w Greet and Sparkbrook 90-93; Chapl Birm Women's Hosp 92-93; P-in-c Lea Hall *Birm* 93-98; V from 98. *St Richard's Vicarage, Hallmoor Road, Birmingham B33 9QY* Tel 0121-783 2319 E-mail richard1552@aol.com

BRACKENBURY, The Ven Michael Palmer. b 30. Linc Th Coll 64. **d** 66 **p** 67. C S Ormsby w Ketsby, Calceby and Driby *Linc* 66-69; V Scothern w Sudbrooke 69-77; RD Lawres 73-78; Bp's Personal Asst 77-88; Dioc Dir of Ords 77-87; Can and Preb Linc Cathl 79-95; Dioc Lay Min Adv 86-87; Adn Linc 88-95; rtd 95. *18 Lea View, Ryhall, Stamford PE9 4HZ* Tel (01780) 752415

✠BRACKLEY, The Rt Revd Ian James. b 47. Keble Coll Ox BA69 MA73. Cuddesdon Coll 69. **d** 71 **p** 72 **c** 96. C Bris Lockleaze St Mary Magd w St Fran 71-74; Asst Chapl Bryanston Sch 74-77; Chapl 77-80; V E Preston w Kingston *Chich* 80-88; RD Arundel and Bognor 82-87; TR Haywards Heath St Wilfrid 88-96; RD Cuckfield 89-95; Suff Bp Dorking *Guildf* from 96; Hon Can Guildf Cathl from 96. *13 Pilgrim's Way, Guildford GU4 8AD* Tel (01483) 570829 Fax 567268 E-mail bishop.ian@cofeguildford.org.uk

BRACKLEY, Mark Ozanne. b 53. Boro Road Teacher Tr Coll CertEd75. S'wark Ord Course 90. **d** 93 **p** 94. C Hampstead St Steph w All Hallows *Lon* 93-97; V W Green Ch Ch w St Pet 97-04; Chapl Univ Coll Lon Hosps NHS Foundn Trust 04-08; Chapl Bolton Hospice from 08. *Bolton Hospice, Queens Park Street, Bolton BL1 4QT* Tel (01204) 663066 Fax 663060

BRACKNALL, Richard David Guy. b 43. Ian Ramsey Coll Brasted 71 Ripon Hall Ox 73. **d** 75 **p** 76. C Pocklington w Yapham-cum-Meltonby, Owsthorpe etc *York* 75-78; TV Thornaby on Tees 78-84; V New Marske 84-90; P-in-c Wilton 84-90; Ind Chapl 90-95; Perm to Offic from 05. *34 Margrove Park, Boosbeck, Saltburn-by-the-Sea TS12 3BX* Tel (01287) 653417

BRADBERRY, John Stephen. b 47. Hull Univ BSc70 Leeds Univ CertEd71 MEd86 Bradf Univ PhD91. NW Ord Course 76. **d** 79 **p** 80. NSM Warley *Wakef* from 79; Chapl H Trin Sch Holmfield 91-06; Chapl Rishworth Sch Ripponden from 06; Bp's Officer for NSMs *Wakef* 95-04; RD Halifax from 07. *129 Paddock Lane, Halifax HX2 0NT* Tel (01422) 358282 E-mail sbradberry@tiscali.co.uk

BRADBROOK, Mrs Averyl. b 46. Girton Coll Cam BA67 MA88 Man Univ PGCE69 MA(Theol)96. NOC 90. **d** 93 **p** 94. C Heaton Ch Ch *Man* 93-96; P-in-c Elton St Steph 96-02; Bp's Adv for Women's Min 01-02; V Moseley St Mary *Birm* 02-05; P-in-c Moseley St Anne 04-05; TR Eden, Gelt and Irthing *Carl* 05-10; rtd 10. *2 Ellerbank, Cowan Head, Burneside, Kendal LA8 9HX* Tel 07808-290817 (mobile) E-mail abradbrook@btinternet.com

BRADBROOK, Peter David. b 33. Kelham Th Coll 54. **d** 60 **p** 61. C Ches St Oswald St Thos 60-63; C Fulham St Etheldreda *Lon* 64-65; V Congleton St Jas *Ches* 65-79; V Wheelock 79-92; V Crewe All SS and St Paul 92-98; rtd 98; Perm to Offic *Ches* from 00. *20 Magdalen Court, College Fields, Dane Bank Avenue, Crewe CW2 8FF* Tel (01270) 669420

BRADBURY, George Graham. b 35. AKC58. **d** 59 **p** 60. C Portsea St Mary *Portsm* 59-62; C Melksham *Sarum* 62-64; R Winfrith Newburgh w Chaldon Herring 64-68; CF 68-71; rtd 99. *Wayside, Brook Street, Shipton Gorge, Bridport DT6 4NA* Tel (01308) 897714

BRADBURY, Julian Nicholas Anstey. b 49. BNC Ox BA71 MA75 Birm Univ MA84 Cardiff Univ PhD07. Cuddesdon Coll 71. **d** 73 **p** 74. C S'wark H Trin 73-75; In RC Ch in USA 76-79; V Tottenham H Trin *Lon* 79-85; Dir Past Th Sarum & Wells Th Coll 85-90; P-in-c Yatton Keynell *Bris* 90-97; P-in-c Biddestone w Slaughterford 90-97; P-in-c Castle Combe 90-97; P-in-c W Kington 90-97; P-in-c Nettleton 90-97; R Horfield H Trin 97-02; Fell K Fund 02-07; Sen Fell from 07; Perm to Offic *Ox* 02-09; Hon C Ox St Giles and SS Phil and Jas w St Marg from 09. *12 St Bernards Road, Oxford OX2 6EH* Tel (01865) 316825 E-mail n.bradbury@kingsfund.org.uk

BRADBURY, Justin Robert Grant. b 66. St Andr Univ MA92. Wycliffe Hall Ox 06. **d** 08 **p** 09. C Southbroom *Sarum* from 08. *73 Chivers Road, Devizes SN10 3FP* Tel (01380) 720149 E-mail justinrgbradbury@hotmail.co.uk

BRADBURY, Nicholas. See BRADBURY, Julian Nicholas Anstey

BRADBURY, Paul. b 72. St Cath Coll Cam BA93 N Lon Univ MA99. Trin Coll Bris BA04. **d** 04 **p** 05. C Bitterne Park *Win* 04-08; C Pioneer Min Poole Old Town *Sarum* from 08. *67 Green Road, Poole BH1 1QH*

BRADBURY, Robert Douglas. b 50. Ripon Coll Cuddesdon 75. **d** 76 **p** 77. C Harlescott *Lich* 76-81; V Ruyton 81-88; P-in-c Gt w Lt Ness 84-88; V Ruyton XI Towns w Gt and Lt Ness 88-99. *Fairview, Hindford Road, Froncysyllte, Llangollen LL20 7PU* Tel (01691) 777898

BRADDICK-SOUTHGATE, Charles Anthony Michael. b 70. K Coll Lon BD92. Chich Th Coll 92. **d** 94 **p** 95. C Catford St Laur *S'wark* 94-97; V Nunhead St Antony w St Silas 97-09. *Address temp unknown*

BRADDOCK, Canon Andrew Jonathan. b 71. SS Coll Cam BA92 MA96. Ridley Hall Cam 95. **d** 98 **p** 99. C Ranworth w Panxworth, Woodbastwick etc *Nor* 98-01; R Cringleford and Colney 01-08; RD Humbleyard 04-08; Dioc Missr *Glouc* from 08; Hon Can Glouc Cathl from 11. *Church House, College Green, Gloucester GL1 2LY* Tel (01452) 610346
E-mail abraddock@glosdioc.org.uk

BRADDY, Andrew (Richard). b 67. SEITE. **d** 10 **p** 11. C Whitstable *Cant* from 10. *19 Queen's Road, Whitstable CT5 2JE* Tel (01227) 272156 E-mail arichard.braddy@googlemail.com

BRADFORD, Alan. b 57. Southn Univ BSc79 Warwick Univ PGCE80. St Jo Coll Nottm MTh04. **d** 04 **p** 05. C Countesthorpe w Foston *Leic* 04-08; C Warfield *Ox* from 08. *2 Dorset Vale, Warfield, Bracknell RG42 3JL* Tel (01344) 425000 Mobile 07902-925826 E-mail abradford@hotmail.co.uk

BRADFORD, John. b 34. Lon Univ BA60 Birm Univ MEd81 FRSA FRGS. Oak Hill Th Coll 55. **d** 60 **p** 61. C Walcot *B & W* 60-64; Ass Master Wendover C of E Primary Sch 64-65; Hd RE Dr Challoner's High Sch Lt Chalfont 65-69; Perm to Offic *Ox* 66-70; Lect St Pet Coll of Educn Saltley 70-77; Perm to Offic *Birm* 70-71 and from 05; Lic to Offic 71-03; Perm to Offic *Cov* from 77; Nat Chapl-Missr Children's Soc 77-99; Gen Perm to Offic Ch in Wales from 89; rtd 99. *27 Marsh Lane, Solihull B91 2PG* Tel 0121-704 9895 *or* (020) 7837 4299
E-mail revjohnbradford@aol.com

BRADFORD, Peter. b 38. Sarum Th Coll 69. **d** 70 **p** 71. C Holdenhurst *Win* 70-73; C Stanmore 73-77; P-in-c Eling, Testwood and Marchwood 77-78; R Marchwood 78-86; C Christchurch 86-90; C Andover w Foxcott 90-92; V E and W Worldham, Hartley Mauditt w Kingsley etc 92-04; rtd 04. *Old Forge House, 22 Church Street, Helston TR13 8TQ* Tel (01326) 560576

BRADFORD, Phillip James. b 81. York Univ BA02 MA04 PhD08. Westcott Ho Cam 07. **d** 10 **p** 11. C Worc SE from 10. *99 Sebright Avenue, Worcester WR5 2HJ* Tel (01905) 350098
E-mail phillipbradford@yahoo.com

BRADFORD, Steven John. b 59. Open Univ MBA01. St Jo Coll Nottm 06. **d** 08 **p** 09. C Bearsted w Thurnham *Cant* from 08. *66 Peverel Drive, Bearsted, Maidstone ME14 4PS* Tel 07909-560070 (mobile) E-mail stevejbradford@btinternet.com

BRADFORD, Archdeacon of. *See* LEE, The Ven David John

BRADFORD, Bishop of. *See* BAINES, The Rt Revd Nicholas

BRADFORD, Dean of. *See* ISON, The Very Revd David John

BRADING, Jeremy Clive. b 74. Birm Univ BA95 MPhil98. Westcott Ho Cam 00. **d** 02 **p** 03. C Man Clayton St Cross w St Paul 02-05; TV Pendleton 05-07; P-in-c Daisy Hill from 07; C Westhoughton and Wingates from 11. *The Vicarage, 30 Lower Leigh Road, Westhoughton, Bolton BL5 2EH* Tel (01942) 857251 Mobile 07786-567140
E-mail jeremybrading@stjamesdaisyhill.co.uk

BRADISH, Paul Edward. b 61. Reading Univ LLB83. Ripon Coll Cuddesdon MA07. **d** 07 **p** 08. C Wokingham St Sebastian *Ox* 07-08; C Upper Kennet *Sarum* 08-10; R Shiplake w Dunsden and Harpsden *Ox* from 10. *The Rectory, Church Lane, Shiplake, Henley-on-Thames RG9 4BS* Tel 0118-940 1549 Mobile 07766-813661 E-mail revpaulbradish@gmail.com

BRADLEY, Andrew Robert. b 65. Clare Coll Cam BA88. St Jo Coll Nottm MA94. **d** 94 **p** 95. C Burnage St Marg *Man* 94-98; TV Didsbury St Jas and Em 98-04; Nat Co-ord Acorn Chr Foundn from 04. *Acorn Christian Foundation, Whitehill Chase, Bordon GU35 0AP* Tel (01420) 478121 Fax 478122

BRADLEY, Anthony David. b 56. Wye Coll Lon BSc76. St Jo Coll Nottm 86. **d** 88 **p** 89. C Southchurch Ch Ch *Chelmsf* 88-91; C Cov H Trin 91-97; P-in-c Budbrooke 97-06; Dioc Lay Tr Adv 93-06; Development Dir Forward Vision 06-07; rtd 07; Perm to Offic *Carl* from 06. *12 St George's Road, Millom LA18 5BA* Tel (01229) 770535 E-mail tony.bradley@dial.pipex.com

BRADLEY, Anthony Edward. b 39. Perth Bible Coll 93. **d** 89 **p** 96. Dn-in-c Ravensthorpe Australia 95-96; P-in-c 96-99; C Wotton St Mary *Glouc* 00-04; rtd 04. *PO Box 1083, Bridgetown WA 6255, Australia* Tel (0061) (8) 9761 2917
E-mail tonychris@westnet.com.au

BRADLEY, Brian Hugh Granville. b 32. Univ Coll Ox 51. Lon Coll of Div 59. **d** 62 **p** 63. C E Twickenham St Steph *Lon* 62-65; C Herne Bay Ch Ch *Cant* 65-69; Miss to Seamen Teesside 69-71; Ceylon 71-72; Sri Lanka 72-74; Chapl Amsterdam w Haarlem and Den Helder *Eur* 75-79; Chapl Lyon w Grenoble and Aix-les-Bains 79-85; TV Bucknall and Bagnall *Lich* 87-93; Assoc Chapl Dubai and Sharjah w N Emirates 93-97; rtd 97; Perm to Offic *Win* 97-03. *1 Maer Bay Court, Douglas Avenue, Exmouth EX8 2BX* Tel (01395) 263969

BRADLEY, Clifford David. b 36. Lon Univ BA60. St Aid Birkenhead 60. **d** 62 **p** 63. C Stoneycroft All SS *Liv* 62-65; C Chipping Sodbury and Old Sodbury *Glouc* 65-68; Br Honduras 68-70; C Leckhampton SS Phil and Jas *Glouc* 70-71; V Badgeworth w Shurdington 71-79; Dioc Missr *S & M* 79-84; V Santan 79-84; V Braddan 79-84; Bp's Dom Chapl 81-84; V Stroud and Uplands w Slad *Glouc* 84-89; C Shepshed *Leic* 90-92; R Leire w Ashby Parva and Dunton Bassett 92-99; rtd 99; P-in-c

Renhold *St Alb* 99-06; Perm to Offic from 06. *47 Paddock Close, Clapham, Bedford MK41 6BD* Tel (01234) 305981

BRADLEY, Colin John. b 46. Edin Univ MA69. Sarum & Wells Th Coll 72. **d** 75 **p** 76. C Easthampstead *Ox* 75-79; V Shawbury *Lich* 79-90; R Moreton Corbet 80-90; P-in-c Stanton on Hine Heath 81-90; Can Res Portsm Cathl and Dir of Ords *Portsm* 90-98; C Chich 98-00; C Chich St Paul and Westhampnett 00-01; P-in-c Cocking, Bepton and W Lavington from 01. *The Rectory, Mill Lane, Cocking, Midhurst GU29 0HJ* Tel (01730) 817340 E-mail zen101842@zen.co.uk

BRADLEY (née DRAPER), Mrs Elizabeth Ann. b 38. Nottm Univ BTh75. Linc Th Coll 71. **dss** 84 **d** 87 **p** 94. Ind Chapl *Linc* 84-91; Bracebridge 84-91; Hon C 87-91; GFS Ind Chapl *Lon* 91-96; Hon Chapl GFS 96-98; Riverside Chapl *S'wark* 96; C Leighton Buzzard w Eggington, Hockliffe etc *St Alb* 98-01; Perm to Offic 01-02; Chapl Luton and Dunstable Hosp NHS Trust from 02. *26 Dew Pond Road, Flitwick, Bedford MK45 1RT* Tel (01525) 712369
E-mail elizabeth.bradley@ldh-tr.anglox.nhs.uk

BRADLEY, Gary Scott. b 53. Lon Univ LLB75. Ripon Coll Cuddesdon 75. **d** 78 **p** 79. C St John's Wood *Lon* 78-83; V Paddington St Sav from 83; P-in-c Paddington St Mary from 95; P-in-c Paddington St Mary Magd 98-03. *6 Park Place Villas, London W2 1SP* Tel (020) 7723 1968 Fax 7724 5332 Mobile 07957-140371 E-mail bottlerot@aol.com

BRADLEY, Joy Elizabeth. *See* COUSANS, Mrs Joy Elizabeth

BRADLEY, Mrs Julie Caroline. b 59. Ex Univ BSc80. WEMTC 00. **d** 03 **p** 04. NSM Stoke Gifford *Bris* from 03. *113 North Road, Stoke Gifford, Bristol BS34 8PE* Tel 0117-979 3418
E-mail cjcbradley@deltats.co.uk

BRADLEY, Canon Michael Frederick John. b 44. Qu Coll Birm 76. **d** 77 **p** 78. C Sheff St Cuth 77-78; C Alford w Rigsby *Linc* 78-83; V Bracebridge 83-90; V Flitwick *St Alb* from 90; RD Ampthill and Shefford from 08; Hon Can St Alb from 10. *The Vicarage, 26 Dew Pond Road, Flitwick, Bedford MK45 1RT* Tel (01525) 712369 E-mail mfjbradley@btopenworld.com

BRADLEY, Michael Louis. Dartington Coll of Arts BA77 K Coll Lon MMus84. ERMC. **d** 11. NSM Loughton St Jo *Chelmsf* from 11. *Chigwell School, High Road, Chigwell IG7 6QF*

BRADLEY, The Ven Peter David Douglas. b 49. Nottm Univ BTh79. Ian Ramsey Coll Brasted 74 Linc Th Coll 75. **d** 79 **p** 80. C Upholland *Liv* 79-83; TR 94-01; V Dovecot 83-94; Dir CME 89-02; Hon Can Liv Cathl from 00; Adn Warrington from 01; TR Upholland 01-11. *30 Sandbrook Road, Orrell, Wigan WN5 8UD* Tel (01695) 624131
E-mail archdeacon@peterbradley.fsnet.co.uk

BRADLEY, The Very Revd Peter Edward. b 64. Trin Hall Cam BA86 MA90 FRSA02. Ripon Coll Cuddesdon 86. **d** 88 **p** 89. C Northampton St Mich w St Edm *Pet* 88-91; Chapl G&C Coll Cam 91-95; TV Abingdon *Ox* 95-98; TV High Wycombe 98-03; TR 03; Dean Sheff from 03. *Sheffield Cathedral, Church Street, Sheffield S1 1HA* Tel 0114-263 6063 Fax 263 6075
E-mail dean@sheffield-cathedral.org.uk

BRADLEY, Philip John Paul. b 64. Birm Univ BSc85. Trin Coll Bris 09. **d** 11. C Oldland *Bris* from 11. *30 Church Road, Hanham, Bristol BS15 3AE* Tel 0117-329 1404 Mobile 07947-030808
E-mail fivebradleys@yahoo.co.uk

BRADLEY, Ronald Percival. b 25. ACP51 FRSA52 TCert49. Ex & Truro NSM Scheme 80. **d** 83 **p** 84. C Honiton, Gittisham, Combe Raleigh, Monkton etc *Ex* 83-86; P-in-c Halberton 86-87; rtd 90. *Abbeyfield House, Trehill Road, Ivybridge PL21 0AZ* Tel (01752) 691567

BRADLEY, Susan Frances. b 59. Wolv Univ BSc92 Liv Univ MSc96 RGN81 RSCN81. Trin Coll Bris BA10. **d** 10 **p** 11. C Glenfield *Leic* from 10. *8 Lynmouth Close, Glenfield, Leicester LE3 8RW* Tel 0116-287 8224 Mobile 07855-095060
E-mail suebradley@onetel.com

BRADLEY, Mrs Susan Kathleen. b 47. Hull Coll of Educn TCert68 Open Univ BA84 MA96. **d** 05 **p** 06. OLM S Lawres Gp *Linc* from 05. *17 Holly Close, Cherry Willingham, Lincoln LN3 4BH* Tel (01522) 750292 E-mail rev.s.bradley@gmail.com

BRADLEY (née NAYLOR), Ms Vivien Frances Damaris. b 55. New Hall Cam BA78 MA82 RGN86. Ripon Coll Cuddesdon. **d** 93 **p** 94. C Northampton St Jas *Pet* 93-95; Chapl Asst Southn Univ Hosps NHS Trust 95-98; Chapl 98-00; Chapl Addenbrooke's NHS Trust 00-03; Perm to Offic *Nor* from 03. *7 Station Road, Kimberley, Wymondham NR18 9HB* Tel (01603) 757807

BRADNUM, Canon Ella Margaret. b 41. CertEd64 St Hugh's Coll Ox MA65. **dss** 69 **d** 87 **p** 94. Illingworth *Wakef* 69-72; Batley All SS 72-73; Lay Tr Officer 77-82; Min Tr Officer 82-88; Sec Dioc Bd of Min 88-06; Warden of Readers 88-02; Co-ord Lay Tr 88-02; Hon Can Wakef Cathl 94-06; Prin Wakef Min Scheme 97-06; rtd 06. *4 Southlands Drive, Huddersfield HD2 2LT* Tel (01484) 420721

BRADNUM, Richard James. b 39. Pemb Coll Ox BA62 MA67. Ridley Hall Cam 62. **d** 64 **p** 65. C Birm St Martin 64-68; C Sutton St Jas *York* 68-69; Perm to Offic *Wakef* 71-72; C Batley All SS 72-74; V Gawthorpe and Chickenley Heath 74-86; V

Mixenden 86-97; rtd 97; Perm to Offic *Wakef* 97-99; Hon Retirement Officer from 99. *4 Southlands Drive, Huddersfield HD2 2LT* Tel (01484) 420721

BRADSHAW, Charles Anthony. b 44. Qu Coll Birm MA76. **d** 75 **p** 76. C Whickham *Dur* 75-78; C Bilton *Cov* 78-81; TV Coventry Caludon 81-89; V Birstall and Wanlip *Leic* 89-99; TR Vale of Belvoir 00-04; TV Caterham *S'wark* from 04. *The Rectory, Station Road, Woldingham, Caterham CR3 7DD* Tel (01883) 652192 E-mail cab@paxchristi.wanadoo.co.uk

BRADSHAW, Denis Matthew. b 52. Chich Th Coll 77. **d** 80 **p** 81. C Ruislip St Martin *Lon* 80-84; C Northolt Park St Barn 84-86; V Northolt St Jos 86-01; P-in-c Hayes St Nic CD 94-00; V Kennington St Jo w St Jas *S'wark* 01-09; V Burgess Hill St Edw Chich from 09. *St Edward's Vicarage, 7 Bramble Gardens, Burgess Hill RH15 8UQ* Tel (01444) 241300 E-mail denis.bradshaw1@btinternet.com

BRADSHAW, Graham. b 58. Edin Univ BD86. Edin Th Coll 83. **d** 86 **p** 87. C Thornton-le-Fylde *Blackb* 86-89; C Kirkby Lonsdale *Carl* 89-91; V Langford *St Alb* 91-97; Papua New Guinea 97-99; R Aspley Guise w Husborne Crawley and Ridgmont *St Alb* from 00. *The Rectory, Church Street, Aspley Guise, Milton Keynes MK17 8HN* Tel (01908) 583169 E-mail gbradshaw@tinyworld.co.uk

BRADSHAW, Miss Jennie McNeille. b 47. UEA BA69. Cranmer Hall Dur 85. **d** 90 **p** 94. Par Dn Herne *Cant* 90-94; C 94-95; P-in-c Claybrooke cum Wibtoft and Frolesworth *Leic* 95-96; R 96-06; P-in-c Burham and Wouldham *Roch* from 06. *The Rectory, 266 Rochester Road, Burham, Rochester ME1 3RJ* Tel (01634) 666862

BRADSHAW (née DAY), Mrs Jennifer Ann. b 67. Aber Univ BSc89. Wycliffe Hall Ox BTh95. **d** 95 **p** 96. C Whitburn *Dur* 95-98; C Monkwearmouth 98-99; TV 99-01; Hon C Silksworth from 02. *St Matthew's Vicarage, Silksworth Road, Sunderland SR3 2AA* Tel 0191-521 1167

BRADSHAW, Canon Malcolm McNeille. b 45. Kelham Th Coll 65. **d** 70 **p** 71. C New Addington *Cant* 70-76; Chapl Milan w Cadenabbia, Varese and Lugano *Eur* 77-82; V Boxley w Detling *Cant* 82-99; Sen Chapl Gtr Athens *Eur* from 99; Hon Can Malta Cathl from 01. *c/o the British Embassy, Plutarchou 1, 106-75 Athens, Greece* Tel and fax (0030) (210) 721 4906 E-mail anglican@otenet.gr

BRADSHAW, Canon Prof Paul Frederick. b 45. Clare Coll Cam BA66 MA70 K Coll Lon PhD71 Ox Univ DD94 FRHistS91. Westcott Ho Cam 67. **d** 69 **p** 70. C W Wickham St Jo *Cant* 69-71; C Cant St Martin and St Paul 71-73; Tutor Chich Th Coll 73-78; V Flamstead *St Alb* 78-82; Dir of Minl Tr Scheme 78-82; Vice-Prin Ripon Coll Cuddesdon 83-85; USA 85-95; Prof Th Notre Dame Univ from 85; Hon Can N Indiana from 90; PV Westmr Abbey from 95; Perm to Offic *Guildf* from 95; Dioc Liturg Officer *Eur* from 07; rtd 10. *Little Ledbury, Oatlands Avenue, Weybridge KT13 9TW* Tel (01932) 844102 E-mail bradshaw.1@nd.edu

BRADSHAW, Philip Hugh. b 39. Qu Coll Ox BA64 MA67. S'wark Ord Course 88. **d** 91 **p** 92. NSM Bletchingley *S'wark* 91-98; Ldr Community of Celebration 91-98; NSM Redhill St Jo 98-10; Perm to Offic from 10. *35 Cavendish Road, Redhill RH1 4AL* Tel (01737) 778760

BRADSHAW, Richard Gordon Edward. b 66. Southn Univ LLB90. Wycliffe Hall Ox BTh94. **d** 97 **p** 98. C Bishopwearmouth St Gabr *Dur* 97-00; C Silksworth 00-01; P-in-c 01-03; V from 03; AD Wearmouth from 08. *St Matthew's Vicarage, Silksworth Road, Sunderland SR3 2AA* Tel 0191-521 1167

BRADSHAW, Roy John. b 49. Sarum & Wells Th Coll 85. **d** 87 **p** 88. C Gainsborough All SS *Linc* 87-90; V New Waltham 90-94; R Killamarsh *Derby* 94-06; C Barlborough and Renishaw 05-06; rtd 06; Perm to Offic *Derby* from 07. *22 St Peter's Close, Duckmanton, Chesterfield S44 5JJ* Tel (01246) 822280

BRADSHAW, Timothy. b 50. Keble Coll Ox BA72 MA78 PhD. St Jo Coll Nottm BA75. **d** 76 **p** 77. C Clapton Park All So *Lon* 76-79; Lect Trin Coll Bris 80-91; Hon C Sea Mills *Bris* 83-91; Tutor Regent's Park Coll Ox from 91; NSM Ox St Aldate w St Matt 91-94; NSM Ox St Matt 95-07. *54 St Giles, Oxford OX1 3LU* Tel (01865) 288147 E-mail timothy.bradshaw@regents.ox.ac.uk

BRADSHAW, Veronica. See CAROLAN, Mrs Veronica

BRADWELL, Area Bishop of. See WRAW, The Rt Revd John Michael

BRADY, Frederick Herbert James. b 33. Sydney Univ BSc55 DipEd56 Lon Univ BD65. Moore Th Coll Sydney ThL59. **d** 60 **p** 60. Australia 60-63 and from 69; Lic to Offic *Lon* 63-69; rtd 00. *18 Capel Street, West Melbourne Vic 3003, Australia* Tel (0061) (3) 9328 8487 *or* 9650 3791 Fax 9650 4718 E-mail brady@ioville.net.au

BRADY, Ian. b 59. Ridley Hall Cam. **d** 01 **p** 02. C Cromer *Nor* 01-04; V Belmont *Lon* 04-09; P-in-c Douglas St Thos *S & M* from 09. *St Thomas's Vicarage, Marathon Avenue, Douglas, Isle of Man IM2 4JA* Tel (01624) 611503 E-mail i.bradybunch@btopenworld.com

BRADY, Mrs Lynda. b 60. SRN83. SA Internat Tr Coll 87 Oak Hill Th Coll 07. **d** 07 **p** 08. NSM Belmont *Lon* 07-09; NSM Douglas St Thos *S & M* from 09; Chapl Hospice Is of Man from 09. *St Thomas's Vicarage, Marathon Avenue, Douglas, Isle of Man IM2 4JA* Tel (01624) 611503 Mobile 07974-995561 E-mail revbrady@btopenworld.com

BRADY, Canon Madalaine Margaret. b 45. Univ of Wales (Ban) BD88 CertEd91 MA92. **d** 89 **p** 97. Asst Chapl Univ of Wales (Ban) 89-96; Dioc Communications Officer from 94; Dioc Lay Min Officer from 95; C Arllechwedd 96-97; P-in-c Llanfaelog 97-02; R Llanfaelog and Llangwyfan from 02; AD Llifon and Talybolion from 07; Can Cursal Ban Cathl 03-09; Can and Treas from 09. *The Rectory, Station Road, Rhosneigr LL64 5JX* Tel (01248) 354999 Fax 353882 *or* tel and fax (01407) 810412 E-mail dmbrady@btinternet.com

BRAE, David. b 80. Trin Coll Bris BA09. **d** 10 **p** 11. C Bishop's Cleeve and Woolstone w Gotherington etc *Glouc* from 10. *2A Orchard Road, Bishops Cleeve, Cheltenham GL52 8LX* Tel 07793-714882 (mobile) E-mail wonderfulworld@me.com

BRAE, Mrs Yvonne Rosetta. b 45. WEMTC 05. **d** 08 **p** 09. NSM Cheltenham St Luke and St Jo *Glouc* from 08; NSM Cheltenham St Mich from 08. *86 Arle Road, Cheltenham GL51 8LB* Tel (01242) 519780 Mobile 07940-452211 E-mail jmyr@blueyonder.co.uk

BRAGG, Marie-Elsa Beatrice Roche. b 65. Ripon Coll Cuddesdon. **d** 07 **p** 09. NSM St Marylebone St Paul *Lon* 07-09; NSM Kilburn St Mary w All So and W Hampstead St Jas from 09. *12 Woodside, London NW11 6HH* E-mail meboxford@hotmail.com

BRAGG, Mrs Rosemary Eileen. b 41. MRPharmS64. St Steph Ho Ox 99. **d** 00 **p** 01. NSM Boyne Hill *Ox* 00-06; NSM Golden Cap Team *Sarum* 06-11; rtd 11. *Dove Inn Cottage, 48 Silver Street, Lyme Regis DT7 3HR* Tel (01297) 442403 E-mail rosie@brag.eu

BRAID, Simon. b 54. SS Coll Cam MA76 FCA79. SEITE 06. **d** 09 **p** 10. NSM Hildenborough *Roch* from 09. *Petresfield, Fordcombe Road, Penshurst, Tonbridge TN11 8DL* Tel (01892) 870480 Fax 871453 Mobile 07802-809849 E-mail simonbraid@aol.com

BRAILSFORD, Matthew Charles. b 64. Newc Univ BSc86 St Jo Coll Dur BA95. Cranmer Hall Dur 92. **d** 95 **p** 96. C Hull St Jo Newland *York* 95-06; P-in-c N Ferriby from 06. *The Vicarage, 20 Aston Hall Drive, North Ferriby HU14 3EB* Tel (01482) 631306 E-mail matthew.brailsford@ukgateway.net

BRAIN, Mrs Marina. b 52. **d** 01 **p** 02. OLM Wokingham St Sebastian *Ox* 01-05; Chapl HM Pris Reading, Grendon and Spring Hill 05-06; Chapl HM Pris High Down 06-10; Chapl HM Pris Coldingley from 10. *H M Prison Coldingley, Shaftesbury Road, Bisley, Woking GU24 9EX* Tel (01483) 344300

BRAIN, Michael Charles. b 39. Culham Coll Ox TCert61 ACP65. Lich Th Coll 68. **d** 70 **p** 71. C Stone St Mich *Lich* 70-73; C Harlescott 73-76; C Longton St Jas 76-77; P-in-c Dudley St Edm *Worc* 77-79; V 79-04; Chapl Dudley Coll of Tech 77-04; rtd 04; Perm to Offic *Worc* from 04. *33 Dibdale Road, Dudley DY1 2RX* Tel (01384) 232774

BRAITHWAITE, Albert Alfred. b 24. Clifton Th Coll. **d** 59 **p** 60. C Bestwood St Matt *S'well* 59-62; Chapl RN 62-81; QHC from 77; C Southsea St Jude *Portsm* 82-90; rtd 90; Perm to Offic *Portsm* from 90. *16 Charminster, 46 Craneswater Park, Southsea PO4 0NU*

BRAITHWAITE, Canon Michael Royce. b 34. Linc Th Coll 71. **d** 73 **p** 74. C Barrow St Geo w St Luke *Carl* 73-77; V Kells 77-88; RD Calder 84-88; V Lorton and Loweswater w Buttermere 88-99; Ldr Rural Life and Agric Team 93-96; Member Rural Life and Agric Team 96-99; RD Derwent 94-98; Hon Can Carl Cathl 94-99; rtd 99; Perm to Offic *Carl* from 00. *High Green Farm, Bothel, Carlisle CA7 2JA* Tel (01697) 32349

BRAITHWAITE, Canon Roy. b 34. Dur Univ BA56. Ridley Hall Cam 58. **d** 60 **p** 61. C Blackb St Gabr 60-63; C Burnley St Pet 63-66; V Accrington St Andr 66-74; V Blackb St Jas 74-95; RD Blackb 86-91; Hon Can Blackb Cathl 93-98; V Garstang St Helen Churchtown 95-98; Dioc Ecum Officer 95-98; rtd 98; Perm to Offic *Blackb* from 98. *9 Barker Lane, Mellor, Blackburn BB2 7ED* Tel (01254) 240724

BRALEY, Robert James. See RILEY-BRALEY, Robert James

BRAMHALL, Eric. b 39. St Cath Coll Cam BA61 MA65. Tyndale Hall Bris 61. **d** 63 **p** 64. C Eccleston St Luke *Liv* 63-66; C Bolton Em *Man* 66-69; Perm to Offic *Ches* 70-74; V Aughton Ch Ch *Liv* 75-92; Chapl Ormskirk Children's Hosp 75-92; V Childwall All SS *Liv* 92-04; rtd 04. *Henfaes, Prior Street, Ruthin LL15 1LT* Tel (01824) 702757

BRAMHALL, John. **d** 08. NSM Greenham *Ox* from 08. *56 Greyberry Copse Road, Thatcham RG19 8XB* Tel (01635) 42348 E-mail johnbramuk@yahoo.co.uk

BRAMLEY, Thomas Anthony. b 44. BSc PhD. TISEC. **d** 96 **p** 97. NSM Penicuik *Edin* from 96; NSM W Linton from 96. *44 Bavelaw Crescent, Penicuik EH26 9AT*

BRAMMER, David John. b 62. **d** 99 **p** 00. C Acton St Mary *Lon* 99-02; C Ealing All SS and Chapl Twyford C of E High Sch Acton 02-09; R Acton St Mary *Lon* from 09. *The Rectory, 14 Cumberland Park, London W3 6SX* Tel (020) 8992 8876 E-mail rev.d.brammer@btinternet.com

BRAMPTON, Canon Fiona Elizabeth Gordon. b 56. St Jo Coll Dur BA78 BA83. Cranmer Hall Dur 81. **dss** 84 **d** 87 **p** 94. Bris St Andr Hartcliffe 84-90; Par Dn 87-90; C Orton Waterville *Ely* 90-96; C-in-c Orton Goldhay CD 90-96; TV The Ortons, Alwalton and Chesterton 96-00; V Haddenham from 00; V Wilburton from 00; P-in-c Witchford w Wentworth from 08; RD Ely 03-09; Hon Can Ely Cathl from 05. *The Vicarage, Church Lane, Haddenham, Ely CB6 3TB* Tel (01353) 740309 E-mail fiona.brampton@ely.anglican.org

BRANCHE, Brian Maurice. b 32. Chich Th Coll 73. **d** 75 **p** 76. C Brighton Resurr *Chich* 75-78; C Upper Norwood St Jo *Cant* 78-81; P-in-c Croydon St Martin 81-84; V Croydon St Martin *S'wark* 85-88; V St Helier 88-93; V New Eltham All SS 93-97; V Barkingside H Trin *Chelmsf* 97-02; rtd 02; Perm to Offic *Man* from 03. *113 Tong Road, Little Lever, Bolton BL3 1PU* E-mail bbranche@aol.com

BRAND, Peter John. b 32. Lon Univ BSc54. Edin Dioc NSM Course 75. **d** 83 **p** 84. NSM Edin St Jo from 83. *24 Drum Brae Park, Edinburgh EH12 8TF* Tel 0131-339 4406

BRAND, Richard Harold Guthrie. b 65. Dur Univ BA87. Ripon Coll Cuddesdon 87. **d** 89 **p** 90. C N Lynn w St Marg and St Nic *Nor* 89-92; C King's Lynn St Marg w St Nic 92-93; C Croydon St Jo *S'wark* 93-96; TV Fendalton New Zealand 96-98; P-in-c Hambledon *Portsm* 98-06; Dir of Ords 98-06; P-in-c Market Harborough and The Transfiguration etc *Leic* 06-08; TR from 08. *The Rectory, Rectory Lane, Market Harborough LE16 8AS* Tel (01858) 462926 E-mail richard.brand@virgin.net

BRAND, Stuart William. b 30. Leeds Univ BSc53. Coll of Resurr Mirfield 53. **d** 55 **p** 56. C Stepney St Dunstan and All SS *Lon* 55-59; C Acton Green St Pet 59-60; C-in-c Godshill CD *Portsm* 60-63; Malawi 63-67; V Widley w Wymering *Portsm* 67-72; Chapl Fieldhead Hosp Wakef 72-80; Chapl Pinderfields & Stanley Royd Hosps Wakef 72-80; Chapl Brook Gen Hosp Lon 80-95; Chapl Greenwich Distr Hosp Lon 80-95; rtd 95; Perm to Offic *Ox* from 96. *17 Hayfield Road, Oxford OX2 6TX* Tel (01865) 316456

BRANDES, Simon Frank. b 62. Univ of Wales (Ban) BA83. Edin Th Coll 83. **d** 85 **p** 86. C Barton w Peel Green *Man* 85-88; C Longsight St Jo w St Cypr 88-90; R 90-94; Asst Dioc Youth Officer 88-94; V Lt Lever 94-02; P-in-c Lydgate w Friezland 02-03; TR Saddleworth 03-07; V Chiswick St Nic w St Mary *Lon* from 07. *Chiswick Vicarage, Chiswick Mall, London W4 2PJ* Tel (020) 8995 4717 Mobile 07775-526285

BRANDIE, Canon Beaumont Lauder. b 40. MBE07. K Coll Lon AKC64 BD66. **d** 65 **p** 66. C Whitton St Aug *Lon* 65-71; C Portsea St Mary *Portsm* 71-77; TR Brighton Resurr *Chich* 77-09; V Brighton St Martin w St Wilfrid and St Alban 09-11; RD Brighton 97; Can and Preb Chich Cathl 87-11; rtd 11. *48 A'Becket Gardens, Worthing BN13 2BN* Tel (01903) 264471 Mobile 07789-044476 E-mail beaumont.brandie@btinternet.com

BRANDON, Mrs Helen Beatrice. b 55. Heythrop Coll Lon MA02. SAOMC 03. **d** 06 **p** 07. NSM Burton Latimer *Pet* 06-07; NSM Earls Barton 07-09; Abps' Adv for Healing Min from 07; Perm to Offic *Lon* from 07 and *Pet* from 09. *Clopton Manor, Clopton, Kettering NN14 3DZ* Tel (01832) 720346 Fax 720446 E-mail beatrice@healingministry.org.uk

BRANDON, Milesius. b 69. Heythrop Coll Lon BA92 MA07 City Univ MSc04 RMN97 PGCE98. St Steph Ho Ox MTh09. **d** 09 **p** 10. C Clerkenwell H Redeemer *Lon* from 09. *Most Holy Redeemer Church, 24 Exmouth Market, London EC1R 4QE* Tel (020) 7837 1861 E-mail mbrandon51@hotmail.com

BRANDRETH, Mrs Jacqueline. b 59. **d** 07 **p** 08. OLM Pendlebury St Jo *Man* from 07. *36 Asten Fold, Salford M6 7JH*

BRANSCOMBE, Michael Peter. b 65. Cranmer Hall Dur BA95. **d** 95 **p** 96. C Ogley Hay *Lich* 95-01; Dioc Voc Officer 99-01; Asst R Palm Harbor USA 01-04; Assoc R Clearwater Ascension from 04. *1010 Charles Street, Clearwater FL 33755-1008, USA* Tel (001) (727) 447 3469 E-mail mikeb@churchofascension.org

BRANSON, Robert David. b 46. Linc Th Coll 74. **d** 77 **p** 78. C Kempston Transfiguration *St Alb* 77-80; C Goldington 80-82; V Marsh Farm 82-91; V Aylsham *Nor* from 91; RD Ingworth 00-10; Chapl Norfolk Primary Care Trust 99-11; rtd 11. *28 Alford Grove, Sprowston, Norwich NR7 8XB* E-mail rdlbransons@btinternet.com

BRANT, Anthony William. b 31. TD67. Linc Th Coll 73. **d** 75 **p** 76. C Cove St Jo *Guildf* 75-79; P-in-c Puttenham and Wanborough 79-83; V Lightwater 83-93; rtd 93; Perm to Offic *Chich* from 93. *2 Southcourt Avenue, Bexhill-on-Sea TN39 3AR* Tel (01424) 217526

BRANT, Jonathan David. b 70. K Coll Lon MA02 Trin Coll Ox MPhil06 DPhil09. St Mellitus Coll 09. **d** 11. NSM Ox St Clem from 11; Chapl Ox Pastorate from 11. *33 Jack Straw's Lane, Headington, Oxford OX3 0DL* Tel 07854-771041 (mobile) E-mail jonathan.brant@oxfordpastorate.org

BRANT, Ms Karlyn Lee. b 72. Birm Univ BA99 MA01. Ripon Coll Cuddesdon 01. **d** 03 **p** 04. C Gaywood *Nor* 03-07; R Dunster, Carhampton, Withycombe w Rodhuish etc *B & W* from 07. *The Rectory, St George's Street, Dunster, Minehead TA24 6RS* Tel (01643) 821812 E-mail revd.lee@btinternet.com

BRASIER, Ralph Henry (Jim). b 30. Cant Sch of Min 82. **d** 85 **p** 86. C S Ashford Ch Ch *Cant* 85-89; V Pembury *Roch* 95-97; rtd 95; Perm to Offic *Portsm* and *Win* from 95. *72 Jenkyns Close, Botley, Southampton SO30 2UU* Tel (01489) 788332

BRASSELL, Canon Kenneth William. b 23. Kelham Th Coll 46. **d** 50 **p** 51. C Woodbridge St Mary *St E* 50-53; C-in-c Bury St Edmunds All SS CD 53-57; V Ipswich St Thos 57-63; V Beckenham St Jas *Roch* 63-88; P-in-c Beckenham St Aug 66-77; P-in-c Beckenham St Mich w St Aug 77-78; Hon Can Roch Cathl 82-88; rtd 88; Perm to Offic *Glouc* from 88. *20 College Green, Gloucester GL1 2LR* Tel (01452) 309080

BRASSIL, Seán Adrian. b 56. Westf Coll Lon BSc79. STETS 97. **d** 00 **p** 01. NSM Westborough *Guildf* 00-04; NSM Woking St Jo 04-05; C Addlestone 05-10; P-in-c Whitchurch *Ex* from 10. *The Vicarage, 204 Whitchurch Road, Tavistock PL19 9DQ* Tel (01822) 615650 Mobile 07984-299333 E-mail sean.brassil@btinternet.com

BRATLEY, David Frederick. b 42. Linc Th Coll 80. **d** 82 **p** 83. C Holbeach *Linc* 82-85; R Fleet w Gedney 85-07; RD Elloe E 01-05; rtd 07. *1 Setts Green, Bourne PE10 0FZ* Tel (01778) 392567

BRATTON, Mark Quinn. b 62. Lon Univ BA84 K Coll Lon MA98 Barrister-at-Law (Middle Temple) 87. Wycliffe Hall Ox BA94. **d** 94 **p** 95. C W Ealing St Jo w St Jas *Lon* 94-98; Chapl Warw Univ 95-09; AD Cov S 02-09; P-in-c Berkswell from 09. *The Rectory, Meriden Road, Berkswell, Coventry CV7 7BE* Tel (01676) 533766 *or* 533605 Mobile 07540-604225 E-mail markbratton@berkswellchurch.org.uk

BRAUN, Thomas Anthony. b 53. St Jo Coll Ox BA76 MA76 Univ Coll Lon PhD80. S'wark Ord Course 89. **d** 92 **p** 93. NSM Surbiton St Andr and St Mark *S'wark* 92-05. *8 Kings Drive, Surbiton KT5 8NG* Tel (020) 8399 6898

BRAVINER, William Edward. b 66. Leic Poly BSc88 St Jo Coll Dur BA94 ACA91. Cranmer Hall Dur 92. **d** 95 **p** 96. C Royton St Anne *Man* 95-99; R Lansallos and V Talland *Truro* 99-03; P-in-c Duloe, Herodsfoot, Morval and St Pinnock 01-03; TR Jarrow *Dur* from 03; P-in-c S Shields St Simon from 09; AD Jarrow from 05. *St Peter's House, York Avenue, Jarrow NE32 5LP* Tel 0191-489 3279 E-mail bill.braviner@durham.anglican.org

BRAVINGTON, Timothy Frederick Desmond. b 34. Trin Coll Cam BA56 MA70. Cuddesdon Coll 56. **d** 58 **p** 59. C Caledon S Africa 58-61; Asst Chapl St Andr Coll Grahamstown 61-64; R Namaqualand 64-71; R Bellville Transfiguration 71-76; R Durban N St Martin-in-the-Fields 76-83; R Stellenbosch St Mary 84-88; R Elgin St Mich 88-98; Perm to Offic Cape Town 99-06; *Eur* 06-09; *Ox* from 08. *63 Cutteslowe House, Park Close, Oxford OX2 8NP* Tel (01865) 511416 E-mail timbrav@gmail.com

BRAY, Christopher Laurence. b 53. Leeds Univ BSc74 Qu Univ Kingston Ontario MSc76. St Jo Coll Nottm 78. **d** 81 **p** 82. C Aughton Ch Ch *Liv* 81-84; Hon C Scarborough St Mary w Ch Ch and H Apostles *York* 84-88; Chapl Scarborough Coll 84-88; V St Helens St Matt Thatto Heath *Liv* 88-98; V Southport All SS and All So 98-02; rtd 02; Perm to Offic *Liv* from 03. *9 Arbour Street, Southport PR8 6SB* Tel (01704) 530486 E-mail chrislbray@aol.com

BRAY, Gerald Lewis. b 48. McGill Univ Montreal BA69 Sorbonne Univ Paris LittD73. Ridley Hall Cam 76. **d** 78 **p** 79. C Canning Town St Cedd *Chelmsf* 78-80; Tutor Oak Hill Th Coll 80-92; Ed *Churchman* from 83; Angl Prof Div Beeson Div Sch Samford Univ Alabama from 93. *16 Manor Court, Cambridge CB3 9BE* Tel (01223) 311804 *or* (001) (205) 726 2585 Fax (01223) 566608 *or* (001) (205) 726 2234 E-mail glbray@samford.edu

BRAY, Jason Stephen. b 69. SS Hild & Bede Coll Dur BA90 MA91 Fitzw Coll Cam PhD96 MSOTS97. Westcott Ho Cam 95. **d** 97 **p** 98. C Abergavenny St Mary w Llanwenarth Citra *Mon* 97-99; Min Can St Woolos Cathl 99-02; V Blaenavon w Capel Newydd from 02; P-in-c Abersychan and Garndiffaith 09-11. *The Vicarage, Llanover Road, Blaenavon, Pontypool NP4 9HR* Tel (01495) 790292 E-mail jasonbray@aol.com

BRAY, Jeremy Grainger. b 40. Man Univ BA62. Wells Th Coll 62. **d** 64 **p** 65. C Bris St Andr w St Bart 64-67; C Bris H Cross Inns Court 67-71; C-in-c Stockwood CD 71-73; V Bris Ch the Servant Stockwood 73-83; RD Brislington 79-83; P-in-c Chippenham St Pet 83-88; V 88-93; V Fishponds St Jo 93-04; rtd 04. *46 Charter Road, Chippenham SN15 2RA* Tel (01249) 655661 E-mail jg.bray@btinternet.com

BRAY, Joyce. b 32. CA Tr Coll. **dss** 80 **d** 87 **p** 94. Bloxwich *Lich* 80-84; Derringham Bank *York* 84-03; Par Dn 87-94; Hon C 94-03; rtd 94; Perm to Offic *York* from 03. *413 Willerby Road, Hull HU5 5JD* Tel (01482) 502193

BRAY, Kenneth John. b 31. St Mich Coll Llan 65. **d** 67 **p** 72. C Killay *S & B* 67-68; C S Harrow St Paul *Lon* 71-73; C Hillingdon St Jo 73-76; C Chipping Sodbury and Old Sodbury *Glouc* 76-79; C Worle *B & W* 79-80; Lic to Offic *Ches* 80-83; TV Wrexham *St As* 83-85; V Llay 85-94; rtd 94. *c/o M Bray Esq, 18 Springfield Road, Poole BH14 0LQ* Tel (01202) 741206

BRAY, Richard Antony. b 77. CCC Ox MA05. Oak Hill Th Coll BA09. **d** 09 **p** 10. C St Botolph without Aldersgate *Lon* from 09. *82 Saunders Ness Road, London E14 3EA* Tel 07798-940554 (mobile) E-mail brayra2001@yahoo.co.uk

BRAYBROOKE, Marcus Christopher Rossi. b 38. Magd Coll Cam BA62 MA65 Lon Univ MPhil68 Lambeth DD04. Wells Th Coll 63. **d** 64 **p** 65. C Highgate St Mich *Lon* 64-67; C Frindsbury w Upnor *Roch* 67-72; TV Frindsbury w Upnor 72-73; P-in-c Swainswick w Langridge and Woolley *B & W* 73-76; R 76-79; Dir of Tr 79-84; Hon C Bath Ch Ch Prop Chpl 84-91; Exec Dir Coun of Chrs and Jews 84-87; rtd 88; Perm to Offic *Bris* 88-93; Preb Wells Cathl 90-93; Chapl Bath St Mary Magd Holloway 92-93; Hon C Dorchester *Ox* 93-05. *17 Courtiers Green, Clifton Hampden, Abingdon OX14 3EN* Tel (01865) 407566 E-mail marcusbray@aol.com

BRAZELL, Denis Illtyd Anthony. b 42. Trin Coll Cam BA64 MA68. Wycliffe Hall Ox 78. **d** 80 **p** 81. C Cheltenham Ch Ch *Glouc* 80-84; V Reading St Agnes w St Paul *Ox* 84-96; Perm to Offic *Guildf* 96-97; Warden and Chapl Acorn Chr Healing Trust 97-99; rtd 99; Co-Dir Word for Life Trust from 99; Perm to Offic *Glouc* 02-09; Lead Chapl St Andr Healthcare from 09. *32 Oakham Road, Harborne, Birmingham B17 9DG* Tel 0121-427 2934 *or* 432 2100 E-mail denisbrazell@mac.com

BRAZIER, Eric James Arthur. b 37. Qu Coll Birm 84. **d** 86 **p** 87. C Lighthorne *Cov* 86-89; P-in-c 89-92; P-in-c Chesterton 89-92; P-in-c Newbold Pacey w Moreton Morrell 89-92; R Astbury and Smallwood *Ches* 92-99; rtd 99; Perm to Offic *Ches* from 99; *Lich* 00-11 and *Heref* from 00. *Wolf's Head Cottage, Chirbury, Montgomery SY15 6BP* Tel (01938) 561450

BRAZIER, Canon Raymond Venner. b 40. Wells Th Coll 68. **d** 71 **p** 72. C Horfield St Greg *Bris* 71-75; P-in-c Bris St Matt and St Nath 75-79; V 79-05; RD Horfield 85-91; P-in-c Bishopston 93-97; Hon Can Bris Cathl 94-05; rtd 05; Perm to Offic *Bris* from 05; Chapl to The Queen from 98. *51 Chalks Road, Bristol BS5 9EP* Tel 0117-952 3209 E-mail rayvb@tiscali.co.uk

BRAZIER-GIBBS, Samantha Elizabeth. b 78. Ridley Hall Cam 03. **d** 06 **p** 08. C Grays Thurrock *Chelmsf* 06-09; Hon C Harlow St Mary and St Hugh w St Jo the Bapt from 10; Hon C Church Langley from 10. *The Vicarage, Broomfields, Hatfield Heath, Bishop's Stortford CM22 7EH* Tel (01279) 730288 Mobile 07876-301307 E-mail revsbg@mac.com

BREADEN, Robert William. b 37. Edin Th Coll 58. **d** 61 **p** 62. C Broughty Ferry *Bre* 61-65; R 72-07; R Carnoustie 65-72; Can St Paul's Cathl Dundee 77-07; Dean Bre 84-07; rtd 07; P-in-c Portree *Arg* from 07. *The Rectory, Somerled Square, Portree IV51 9EH* Tel (01478) 613135 E-mail ateallach@aol.com

BREADMORE, Martin Christopher. b 67. Lon Univ LLB89. Wycliffe Hall Ox BTh93. **d** 93 **p** 94. C Herne Bay Ch Ch *Cant* 93-97; C Camberley St Paul *Guildf* 97-01; Chapl Elmhurst Ballet Sch 97-98; C Wallington *S'wark* 01-10; Dir Lic Min Kensington Area *Lon* from 10. *207 London Road, Twickenham TW1 1EJ* Tel (020) 8891 0324 E-mail martin.breadmore@london.anglican.org

BREADON, John Desmond. b 73. St Andr Univ BD96 Birm Univ PhD02. Westcott Ho Cam 99. **d** 01 **p** 02. C W Bromwich All SS *Lich* 01-05; Chapl St Geo Post 16 Cen *Birm* 05-08; Nat Adv for FE/Chapl Abps' Coun from 08. *Church House, Great Smith Street, London SW1P 3AZ* Tel (020) 7898 1513 E-mail john.breadon@churchofengland.org

BREAR, Alvin Douglas. b 43. **d** 87 **p** 96. NSM Leic H Spirit 87-88; NSM Leic Ch Sav 88-96; NSM Leic Presentation 96-10; Perm to Offic *Blackb* from 10; Finland from 98. *Sahurintie 44, SF28800 Pori, Finland* Tel (00358) (2) 648 2060 E-mail douglas.brear@tse.fi

BREARLEY, Canon Janet Mary. b 48. Cranmer Hall Dur 88. **d** 90 **p** 94. C Prudhoe *Newc* 90-91; C Fenham St Jas and St Basil 91-95; Chapl MU 93-95; V Warkworth and Acklington *Newc* from 95; AD Alnwick 05-11; Hon Can Newc Cathl from 04. *The Vicarage, 11 Dial Place, Warkworth, Morpeth NE65 0UR* Tel and fax (01665) 711217 E-mail jmbrearley@stlawrence-church.org.uk

BREBNER, Martin James. b 47. OBE02. Imp Coll Lon BSc68 ARCS68. St Alb Minl Tr Scheme 87. **d** 90 **p** 91. Hon C Letchworth St Paul w Willian *St Alb* 90-94; Hon C St Ippolyts 95-01; Perm to Offic *St Alb* 01-02 and *Linc* from 02. *Willowcroft, Greatford, Stamford PE9 4QA* Tel (01778) 561145 Fax 561157 E-mail martinbrebner@yahoo.com

BRECH, Miss Suzy Zelda. b 73. Man Univ BSc95 Roehampton Inst PGCE97. SEITE 06. **d** 09 **p** 10. NSM Battersea St Mich

S'wark from 09. *St Michael's Church, Cobham Close, London SW11 6SP*

BRECHIN, Bishop of. See PEYTON, The Rt Revd Nigel

BRECHIN, Dean of. See MUMFORD, The Very Revd David Christopher

BRECKLES, Robert Wynford. b 48. St Edm Hall Ox BA72 MA74 CertEd. Cranmer Hall Dur. **d** 79 **p** 80. C Bulwell St Mary *S'well* 79-84; V Lady Bay 84-05; V Lady Bay w Holme Pierrepont and Adbolton from 06. *The Vicarage, 121 Holme Road, Nottingham NG2 5AG* Tel 0115-981 3565

BRECKNELL, David Jackson. b 32. Keble Coll Ox BA53 MA57. St Steph Ho Ox 56. **d** 58 **p** 59. C Streatham St Pet *S'wark* 58-62; C Sneinton St Steph w St Alb *S'well* 62-64; C Solihull *Birm* 64-68; V Streatham St Paul *S'wark* 68-75; R Rumboldswyke *Chich* 75-81; P-in-c Portfield 79-81; R Whyke w Rumboldswhyke and Portfield 81-95; rtd 95; Perm to Offic *Chich* from 95; P-in-c Boxgrove 98-99. *8 Priory Close, Boxgrove, Chichester PO18 0EA* Tel (01243) 784841 E-mail david.brecknell@tesco.net

BRECKWOLDT, Peter Hans. b 57. Man Poly BA79. Oak Hill Th Coll BA88. **d** 88 **p** 89. C Knutsford St Jo and Toft *Ches* 88-92; V Moulton *Pet* from 92. *The Vicarage, 30 Cross Street, Moulton, Northampton NN3 1RZ* Tel (01604) 491060 E-mail peterbreckwoldt@aol.com

BRECON, Archdeacon of. See THOMAS, The Ven Alfred James Randolph

BRECON, Dean of. See MARSHALL, The Very Revd Geoffrey Osborne

BREED, Mrs Verena. b 69. **d** 02 **p** 02. NSM Prestbury *Ches* 02-04; V Bosley and N Rode w Wincle and Wildboarclough from 04. *The Vicarage, Wincle, Macclesfield SK11 0QH* Tel (01260) 227234 E-mail verenabreed@onetel.com

BREEDS, Christopher Roger. b 51. Lon Univ CertEd73 LGSM83. Chich Th Coll 84. **d** 87 **p** 88. C E Grinstead St Swithun *Chich* 87-90; TV Aldrington 90-92; P-in-c Hove St Andr Old Ch 92-93; TV Hove 93-99; V Wivelsfield from 99; RD Cuckfield from 06. *New Vicarage, Church Lane, Wivelsfield, Haywards Heath RH17 7RD* Tel (01444) 471783 E-mail christopher.breeds@virgin.net

BREENE, Timothy Patrick Brownell. b 59. Kent Univ BA81 CCC Cam BA89 MA90. Ridley Hall Cam 87. **d** 90 **p** 93. C Hadleigh w Layham and Shelley *St E* 90-95; C Martlesham w Brightwell 95-03; rtd 03. *85 Cliff Road, Felixstowe IP11 9SQ* Tel (01394) 283718

BREFFITT, Geoffrey Michael. b 46. CChem MRIC72 Trent Poly CertEd77. Qu Coll Birm 87. **d** 89 **p** 90. C Prenton *Ches* 89-92; V Frankby w Greasby 92-01; Dioc Ecum Officer 00-01; V German St Jo *S & M* 01-08; V Foxdale 01-08; V Patrick 01-08; RD Castletown and Peel 04-08; P-in-c Weston *Ches* from 08. *The Vicarage, 13 Cemetery Road, Weston, Crewe CW2 5LQ* Tel (01270) 582585

BRENDON-COOK, John Lyndon. b 37. FRICS. SWMTC. **d** 81 **p** 82. NSM Bodmin *Truro* 81-82; NSM St Breoke and Egloshayle 82-90; NSM Helland 90-94; P-in-c 94-98; NSM Cardynham 90-94; rtd 98; Perm to Offic *Truro* from 98. *Treworder Byre, 119 Egloshayle Road, Wadebridge PL27 6AG* Tel (01208) 812468

BRENNAN, John Lester. b 20. MRCP51 FRCPath77 Barrister-at-Law (Middle Temple) 71 Lon Univ MB, BS44 MD52 LLM86. St Aug Coll Cant 54. **d** 55 **p** 56. India 55-65; Hon C Woodside Park St Barn *Lon* 65-69; Lic to Offic *Lich* 69-88; P-in-c Chrishall *Chelmsf* 88-89; Hon C 89-91; Hon C Heydon, Gt and Lt Chishill, Chrishall etc 91-93; Perm to Offic *St Alb* from 93. *16 Butterfield Road, Wheathampstead AL4 8PU* Tel (01582) 832230

BRENNAN, Samuel James. b 16. St Aid Birkenhead. **d** 57 **p** 58. C Magheralin *D & D* 57-60; C Down H Trin 60-63; Min Can Down Cathl 60-63; I Scarva 63-69; I Aghalee 69-84; rtd 84. *Mitchell Court, 50 West Street, Newtownards BT23 4EN* Tel (028) 9181 9139

BRENNAND (née PUNSHON), Ms Carol Mary. b 59. Liv Inst of Educn BEd83. Ridley Hall Cam 92. **d** 94 **p** 95. C Bushey *St Alb* 94-97; C Watford Ch Ch 97-00; P-in-c Ash Vale *Guildf* 00-06; V 06-07; P-in-c Claybrooke cum Wibtoft and Frolesworth *Leic* 07-08; P-in-c Leire w Ashby Parva and Dunton Bassett 07-08; C Upper Soar 08-09; R from 09. *The Vicarage, Main Road, Claybrooke Parva, Lutterworth LE17 5AE* Tel (01455) 208878 E-mail carolbrennand@btinternet.com

BRENNAND, Ian Peter. b 55. STETS 01. **d** 04 **p** 05. C Frimley *Guildf* 04-07; Chapl Univ Hosps Leic NHS Trust from 08. *The Vicarage, Main Road, Claybrooke Parva, Lutterworth LE17 5AE* Tel (01455) 202262 E-mail ianbrennand@btinternet.com

BRENNEN, Canon Colin. b 15. Lon Univ BA47 BD56 Dur Univ PhD88. Linc Th Coll 46. **d** 48 **p** 49. C Seaton Hirst *Newc* 48-50; C Bishopwearmouth Ch Ch *Dur* 50-52; V Grangetown 52-58; V Whitworth w Spennymoor 58-78; RD Auckland 74-82; Hon Can Dur Cathl 78-93; V Hamsterley 78-82; rtd 82. *10 Maes lal, Llanarmon-yn-ial, Mold CH7 4PZ*

BRENT, Philip. b 68. K Coll Lon BD89. Cuddesdon Coll 94. **d** 96 **p** 97. C Sawbridgeworth *St Alb* 96-99; C Skegness and

Winthorpe *Linc* 99-03; Chapl United Lincs Hosps NHS Trust 00-03; R Market Deeping *Linc* from 03. *The Rectory, 13 Church Street, Market Deeping, Peterborough PE6 8DA* Tel (01778) 342237 E-mail philip@candace.fsnet.co.uk

BRENTNALL, David John. b 53. UEA BA75 MPhil82. Ridley Hall Cam 84. **d** 86 **p** 87. C Eaton *Nor* 86-90; V Stevenage St Pet Broadwater *St Alb* 90-96; V St Alb St Pet 96-09. *Address temp unknown*

BRERETON, Catherine Louise. See WILLIAMS, Mrs Catherine Louise

BRETEL, Keith Michael. b 51. St Mich Coll Llan 79. **d** 81 **p** 82. C Thundersley *Chelmsf* 81-84; CF 84-06; Chapl Guards Chpl Lon 03-05; P-in-c St Raphaël *Eur* from 11. *St John the Evangelist, avenue Paul Doumer, 83700 St Raphaël, France* Tel (0033) (4) 94 95 45 78

BRETHERTON, Canon Anthony Atkinson. b 51. Cant Univ (NZ) BA74 Waikato Univ (NZ) MMS97. St Jo Th Coll (NZ) LTh74 STh76. **d** 75 **p** 76. Asst C Ashburton New Zealand 75-78; Asst P St Geo-in-the-East w St Paul *Lon* 79-80; V Te Kauwhata New Zealand 80-85; V Cam 85-91; Can St Pet Cathl Waikato 88-90; Offg Min Waikato 91-01; Lic to Offic *L & K* 02-07; Perm to Offic *B & W* from 07. *18 Vicars Close, Wells BA5 2UJ* Tel 07738-993809 (mobile) E-mail tonybretherton@hotmail.com

BRETHERTON, Donald John. b 18. Lon Univ BD57. Handsworth Coll Birm 38 Headingley Coll Leeds 38 St Aug Coll Cant 59. **d** 60 **p** 61. In Methodist Ch 42-59; C Cant St Martin w St Paul 60-62; V Thornton Heath St Jude 62-70; V Herne 70-82; RD Reculver 74-80; rtd 82; Perm to Offic *Cant* from 84. *Martin's, The Green. Chartham, Canterbury CT4 7JW* Tel (01227) 730255

BRETT, Dennis Roy Anthony. b 46. Sarum & Wells Th Coll 86. **d** 88 **p** 89. C Bradford-on-Avon H Trin *Sarum* 88-92; P-in-c Bishopstrow and Boreham 92-01; R from 01; Chapl Warminster Hosp from 92. *50 Gypsy Lane, Warminster BA12 9LR* Tel (01985) 213000

BRETT, Canon Paul Gadsby. b 41. St Edm Hall Ox BA62 MA66. Wycliffe Hall Ox 64. **d** 65 **p** 66. C Bury St Pet *Man* 65-68; Asst Ind Chapl 68-72; Ind Chapl *Worc* 72-76; Sec Ind Cttee of Gen Syn Bd for Soc Resp 76-84; Dir Soc Resp *Chelmsf* 85-94; Can Res Chelmsf Cathl 85-94; R Shenfield 94-08; rtd 08. *Ore Cottage, Mill Road, Friston, Saxmundham IP17 1PH* Tel (01728) 687767 E-mail paul.brett@btinternet.com

BRETT, Canon Peter Graham Cecil. b 35. Em Coll Cam BA59 MA63. Cuddesdon Coll 59. **d** 61 **p** 62. C Tewkesbury w Walton Cardiff *Glouc* 61-64; C Bournemouth St Pet *Win* 64-66; Chapl Dur Univ 66-72; R Houghton le Spring 72-83; RD Houghton 80-83; Can Res Cant Cathl 83-01; rtd 01; Perm to Offic *Cant* from 01. *3 Appledore Road, Tenterden TN30 7AY* Tel (01580) 761794 E-mail pandgbrett@btinternet.com

BRETT YOUNG (née ROBIN), Ms Helen Mary Kathleen. b 67. St Martin's Coll Lanc BEd96. Cranmer Hall Dur BA98. **d** 98 **p** 99. C Gd Shep TM *Carl* 98-02; TV from 02. *The Rectory, Patterdale, Penrith CA11 0NL* Tel (01768) 482209 E-mail hmbrettyoung@hotmail.com

BREUILLY, Mrs Elizabeth Linda. b 48. York Univ BA70. WMMTC 02. **d** 05 **p** 06. NSM Bournville *Birm* 05-10; NSM Water Eaton *Ox* from 10. *18 Bradwell Road, Loughton, Milton Keynes MK5 8AJ* Tel (01908) 606983 E-mail lizbreuilly@btinternet.com

BREW, William Kevin Maddock. b 49. **d** 78 **p** 79. C Raheny w Coolock *D & G* 78-80; Bp's C Dublin Finglas 80-83; I Mountmellick w Coolbanagher, Rosenallis etc *M & K* 83-89; I Ahoghill w Portglenone *Conn* 89-05; I Howth *D & G* from 05. *The Rectory, 94 Howth Road, Howth, Co Dublin, Republic of Ireland* Tel (00353) (1) 832 3019 *or* tel and fax 832 6346 E-mail howth@dublin.anglican.org

BREW, William Philip. b 43. Derby Coll of Educn CertEd64 FCollP84. NOC 84. **d** 87 **p** 88. In Independent Methodist Ch 70-83; Hd Master Birtenshaw Sch 78-90; NSM Holcombe *Man* 87-90; TV Horwich 91-93; TV Horwich and Rivington 93-97; V Lostock St Thos and St Jo 97-08; P-in-c Bolton St Bede 04-08; AD Deane 98-05; rtd 08; Perm to Offic *Wakef* from 08. *22 Deganwy Drive, Kirkheaton, Huddersfield HD5 0NG* Tel (01484) 301295 E-mail wp.brew@ntlworld.com

BREWER, Barry James. b 44. Oak Hill Th Coll 72. **d** 75 **p** 76. C Hove Bp Hannington Memorial Ch *Chich* 75-78; C Church Stretton *Heref* 78-81; TV Bishopsnympton, Rose Ash, Mariansleigh etc *Ex* 81-87; R Swynnerton and Tittensor *Lich* 87-07; RD Stone 01-07; rtd 07. *Les Nouhouds, 16500 Saint-Maurice-des-Lions, France* E-mail barry.brewer@orange.fr

BREWER, Christina Anne. b 51. SEITE. **d** 11. C Crofton St Paul *Roch* from 11. *55 Place Farm Avenue, Orpington BR6 8DG* E-mail ca.brewer@tesco.net

BREWER, Mrs Susan Comport. b 55. LMH Ox MA76. SEITE 99. **d** 02 **p** 03. C Dartford St Edmn *Roch* 02-07; V Milton next Gravesend Ch Ch from 07. *The Vicarage, 48 Old Road East, Gravesend DA12 1NR* Tel (01474) 352643 Mobile 07930-492323 E-mail suec@brewer86.plus.com

BREWERTON, Andrew Robert. b 70. Oak Hill Th Coll BA05. **d** 05 **p** 06. C Gt Clacton *Chelmsf* 05-09; V Kilnhurst *Sheff* from

09. *The Vicarage, Highthorn Road, Kilnhurst, Mexborough S64 5TX* Tel (01709) 589674 E-mail andy@brewerton.org

BREWIN, David Frederick. b 39. Leic Poly BSc PhD. Lich Th Coll 63. **d** 66 **p** 67. C Shrewsbury H Cross *Lich* 66-69; C Birstall *Leic* 69-73; V Eyres Monsell 73-79; V E Goscote 79-82; V E Goscote w Ratcliffe and Rearsby 82-90; R Thurcaston 90-91; R Thurcaston w Cropston 92-05; rtd 05; Perm to Offic *Leic* from 05 and *Pet* from 06. *28 Welland Way, Oakham LE15 6SL* Tel (01572) 720073

BREWIN, Donald Stewart. b 41. Ch Coll Cam BA62 MA66. Ridley Hall Cam 68. **d** 71 **p** 72. C Ecclesall *Sheff* 71-75; V Anston 75-81; V Walton H Trin *Ox* 81-89; TR 89-94; RD Aylesbury 90-94; Nat Dir SOMA UK 94-07; Perm to Offic *St Alb* from 94; rtd 07. *Wickham Cottage, Gaddesden Turn, Great Billington, Leighton Buzzard LU7 9BW* Tel (01525) 373644 Mobile 07816-362797 E-mail donbrewin@compuserve.com

BREWIN, Karan Rosemary. b 42. CA Tr Coll 77 Glas NSM Course 80. **dss** 84 **d** 85. Clarkston *Glas* 84-89; Hon C 86-89 and 91-97; OHP 89 and 98-02; Perm to Offic *York* 01-02; Swaziland from 02. *St Hilda's House, PO Box 1272, Manzini, Swaziland* Tel (0026) (85) 053323 E-mail jdean@africaonline.co.sz

BREWIN, Wilfred Michael. b 45. Nottm Univ BA69. Cuddesdon Coll 69. **d** 70 **p** 71. C Walker *Newc* 70-73; C Alnwick St Paul 73-74; C Alnwick w Edlingham and Bolton Chpl 74-77; Fell Sheff Univ 77-79; C Greenhill *Sheff* 79; P-in-c Eggleston *Dur* 79-81; V Norton St Mich 81-87; V Headington *Ox* 87-10; rtd 10. *Rose Cottage, New Road, Chatton, Alnwick NE66 5PU* Tel (01668) 215319 E-mail michael.brewin@hotmail.com

BREWIS, Robert David. b 81. Lanc Univ BSc03. Oak Hill Th Coll MTh11. **d** 11. C Washfield, Stoodleigh, Withleigh etc *Ex* from 11. *3 Court Gardens, Stoodleigh, Tiverton EX16 9PL* Tel (01398) 351552 E-mail rbrewis02@hotmail.com

BREWSTER, Christine Elaine. b 45. Newc Univ BA67 CertEd68 Lon Univ DipEd82 MA84 Univ of Wales (Ban) PhD07 ALCM76 LTCL78. SAOMC 95. **d** 98 **p** 99. NSM Aylesbury w Bierton and Hulcott *Ox* 98-00; NSM Dacre w Hartwith and Darley w Thornthwaite *Ripon* 00-01; C Wetherby 01-04; Perm to Offic 04-08; P-in-c Llanwnnog and Caersws w Carno *Ban* from 08. *The Vicarage, Llanwnog, Caersws SY17 5JG* Tel (01686) 688318 E-mail cbholly@supanet.com

BREWSTER, David Pearson. b 30. Clare Coll Cam BA54 MA58 Lon Univ BA65 Oriel Coll Ox MA66 DPhil76. Ridley Hall Cam. **d** 58 **p** 59. C Southampton St Mary w H Trin *Win* 58-61; C N Audley Street St Mark *Lon* 61-62 and 63-65; Tunisia 62-63; Home Sec JEM 65-66; C Ox St Mary V w St Cross and St Pet 66-68; Lect Lady Spencer-Churchill Coll Ox 68-71; New Zealand 71-78; V Brockenhurst *Win* 78-95; rtd 95; Perm to Offic *Win* from 95. *4 Saxonford Road, Christchurch BH23 4ES* Tel (01425) 277860

BREWSTER, David Thomas. b 68. GLCM90 ALCM89. Cranmer Hall Dur BA99. **d** 99 **p** 00. C Bidston *Ches* 99-03; TV Stockport SW 03-07; V Edgeley and Cheadle Heath from 07. *St Mark's Vicarage, 66 Berlin Road, Stockport SK3 9QF* Tel 0161-480 5896

BREWSTER, Jonathan David. b 67. Bucks Coll of Educn BA89 Bris Univ BA94 K Coll Lon MA01. Trin Coll Bris 91. **d** 94 **p** 95. C Gt Horton *Bradf* 94-98; Chapl Univ of Westmr *Lon* 98-03; V Highbury Ch w St Jo and St Sav from 03. *Christ Church Vicarage, 155 Highbury Grove, London N5 1SA* Tel (020) 7226 4544 Mobile 07977-127244 E-mail vicar@dsl.pipex.com

BREWSTER (née BEATTIE), Margaret. b 43. S'wark Ord Course 90. **d** 93 **p** 94. NSM S'wark H Trin w St Matt 93-97; NSM Newington St Paul 97-04; NSM Dunstable *St Alb* 04-07. *39 Glen Drive, Boston PE21 7QB* Tel (01205) 351298 E-mail brew95906@aol.com

BREWSTER, Mrs Susan Jacqueline. b 48. SEITE 94. **d** 97 **p** 98. NSM Goodmayes St Paul *Chelmsf* 97-01; TV Loughton St Jo 01-09; P-in-c Cranham from 09. *51 Courtenay Gardens, Upminster RM14 1DH* Tel (01708) 250854 E-mail sue@brewster6441.fsnet.co.uk

BRIAN, Brother. See HARLEY, Brother Brian Mortimer

BRIAN, Stephen Frederick. b 44. Sussex Univ BEd77 Open Univ MA90 Lanc Univ MPhil97 Surrey Univ PhD03. Qu Coll Birm 82. **d** 85 **p** 86. C Scotforth *Blackb* 85-88; V Freckleton 88-97; V Bagshot *Guildf* 97-06; Chapl Heathfield St Mary's Sch Wantage 06-07; P-in-c Mid Loes *St E* 07-08; R from 08. *The Rectory, Church Lane, Earl Soham, Woodbridge IP13 7SD* Tel (01728) 685308 E-mail sfb4510@aol.com

BRICE, Christopher John. b 48. St Edm Ho Cam MA80. Wycliffe Hall Ox 82. **d** 82 **p** 83. C N Hinksey *Ox* 82-86; Chapl Nuff Coll Ox 84-86; V S Hackney St Mich w Haggerston St Paul *Lon* 86-93; Dir Dioc Bd for Soc Resp 93-01; Adv for Soc Justice 01-08; Hon C De Beauvoir Town St Pet 93-08; P-in-c Kentish Town St Martin w St Andr from 08. *9 Beresford Road, London N5 2HS* Tel (020) 7226 3834 *or* 7932 1121 E-mail chris.brice@london.anglican.org

BRICE, Derek William Fred. b 39. Poly Cen Lon MA87 MCIM89 FCMI82. **d** 02 **p** 03. OLM Cheam *S'wark* from 02.

Mallow, Parkside, Cheam, Sutton SM3 8BS Tel (020) 8642 0241 *or* 8693 4324 E-mail derek.brice@ukgateway.net
BRICE, Jonathan Andrew William. b 61. **d** 92 **p** 93. C Buckhurst Hill *Chelmsf* 92-96; C Victoria Docks Ascension 96; P-in-c 96-98; V 98-06; Chapl Felsted Sch from 06. *Felsted School, Felsted, Dunmow CM6 3LL* Tel (01371) 822600 Fax 822607
BRICE, Neil Alan. b 59. Man Univ BA81 Hughes Hall Cam CertEd87. Westcott Ho Cam 82. **d** 84 **p** 85. C Longton *Lich* 84-86; Hd of Relig Studies Coleridge Community Coll Cam 87-89; NSM Cherry Hinton St Andr *Ely* 88-89; C Fulbourn 89-92; C Gt Wilbraham 89-92; C Lt Wilbraham 89-92; V Arrington 92-00; R Orwell 92-00; R Wimpole 92-00; R Croydon w Clopton 92-00; P-in-c Barrington 98-00; R Orwell Gp 00-09. *St Magnus' Rectory, Greenfield Place, Lerwick, Shetland ZE1 0AQ* E-mail neil@neilbrice.co.uk
BRICE, Paul Earl Philip. b 54. Bath Univ BSc77. Wycliffe Hall Ox 83. **d** 86 **p** 87. C Gt Baddow *Chelmsf* 86-89; Chapl Imp Coll Lon and St Mary's Hosp Med Sch 89-95; Chapl RCA 90-95; Sec HE/Chapl C of E Bd of Educn 95-02; Hon C S Kensington St Jude *Lon* 95-02; R Hartfield w Coleman's Hatch *Chich* from 02. *The Rectory, Church Street, Hartfield TN7 4AG* Tel (01892) 770850
BRIDGE, John Jeremy. b 74. Ripon Coll Cuddesdon 07. **d** 09 **p** 10. C Four Oaks *Birm* from 09. *2 Knightsbridge Close, Sutton Coldfield B74 4UQ* Tel 0121-352 0441 E-mail john.100bridge@btinternet.com
BRIDGE, Martin. b 45. Lon Univ BA66 Linacre Coll Ox BA71 MA73. St Steph Ho Ox 69. **d** 72 **p** 73. C St Peter-in-Thanet *Cant* 72-77; New Zealand from 77. *PO Box 87-145, Meadowbank, Auckland, New Zealand* Tel and fax (0064) (9) 521 5013 *or* 521 0636 E-mail martin.bridge@xtra.co.nz
BRIDGE, Mrs Sheila Margaret. b 62. St Jo Coll Nottm. **d** 11. C Rugby W *Cov* from 11. *89 Sidney Road, Rugby CV22 5LD* Tel (01788) 336763
BRIDGEN, Andrew Grahame. b 57. Aston Univ BSc81 Surrey Univ BA03 FCCA95. STETS 00. **d** 03 **p** 04. NSM Portchester *Portsm* 03-04; C Portsea St Luke 05-07; Perm to Offic from 08. *9 Campbell Road, Southsea PO5 1RH* Tel (023) 9234 8617 E-mail andrew.bridgen@ntlworld.com
BRIDGEN, John William. b 40. K Coll Cam BA62 MA66. Ripon Hall Ox 66. **d** 70 **p** 72. C Headstone St Geo *Lon* 70-71; C Hanwell St Mary 71-75; C Tolladine *Worc* 75; TV Worc St Barn w Ch Ch 76; R Barrow *St E* 76-83; V Denham St Mary 76-83; Perm to Offic *Ely* 84-88 and from 91; rtd 88; Perm to Offic *Glas* 89-91. *57 St Philip's Road, Cambridge CB1 3DA* Tel (01223) 571748
BRIDGEN, Mark Stephen. b 63. K Coll Lon BD85. Cranmer Hall Dur 86. **d** 88 **p** 89. C Kidderminster St Jo and H Innocents *Worc* 88-92; C Nor St Pet Mancroft w St Jo Maddermarket 92-94; V Longbridge *Birm* 94-00; V Wednesbury St Bart *Lich* 00-07; P-in-c Gnosall and Moreton 08-10; R Adbaston, High Offley, Knightley, Norbury etc from 10. *The Vicarage, Glebe Lane, Gnosall, Stafford ST20 0ER* Tel (01785) 822213 E-mail mark.bridgen@btinternet.com
BRIDGER, Francis William. b 51. Pemb Coll Ox BA73 MA78 Bris Univ PhD81. Trin Coll Bris 74. **d** 78 **p** 79. C Islington St Jude Mildmay Park *Lon* 78-82; Lect St Jo Coll Nottm 82-90; V Woodthorpe *S'well* 90-99; Prin Trin Coll Bris 99-05; Prof Fuller Th Sem USA 05-08; Perm to Offic *Nor* from 11. *10 The Avenue, Snettisham, King's Lynn PE31 7QT* Tel 07507-885476 (mobile) E-mail fbridger@yahoo.ie
BRIDGER, Canon Gordon Frederick. b 32. Selw Coll Cam BA53 MA58. Ridley Hall Cam 54. **d** 56 **p** 57. C Islington St Mary *Lon* 56-60; C Cambridge St Sepulchre *Ely* 60-62; V Fulham St Mary N End *Lon* 62-69; C Edin St Thos 69-76; R Heigham H Trin *Nor* 76-87; RD Nor S 79-86; Hon Can Nor Cathl 84-87; Prin Oak Hill Th Coll 87-96; rtd 96; Perm to Offic *Nor* from 96. *The Elms, 4 Common Lane, Sheringham NR26 8PL* Tel (01263) 823522 E-mail gebridger@lineone.net
BRIDGER, Mrs Helen Ruth. b 68. Bradf Univ BA91. Trin Coll Bris BA06. **d** 05 **p** 06. C Altadena USA 05-06; C Arcadia Transfiguration 06-08; C Nuthall and Kimberley *S'well* 08-10; Chapl Qu Eliz Hosp King's Lynn NHS Trust from 10. *The Chaplain's Office, Queen Elizabeth Hospital, Gayton Road, King's Lynn PE30 4ET* Tel (01553) 613613 E-mail helenbridger@yahoo.com
✠**BRIDGES, The Rt Revd Dewi Morris.** b 33. Univ of Wales (Lamp) BA54 CCC Cam BA56 MA60. Westcott Ho Cam 57. **d** 57 **p** 58 **c** 88. C Rhymney *Mon* 57-60; C Chepstow 60-63; V Tredegar St Jas 63-65; Lect Kidderminster Coll 65-69; Lic to Offic *Worc* 65-69; V Kempsey 69-79; RD Upton 74-79; RD Narberth *St D* 80-82; R Tenby 79-88; Adn St D 82-88; Bp S & B 88-98; rtd 98. *11 Wimbledon Court, St Florence Parade, Tenby SA70 7DZ* Tel (01834) 844087
BRIDGES, Mrs Gillian Mary. b 43. EAMTC 85. **d** 88 **p** 94. NSM Hellesdon *Nor* 88-96; NSM Lakenham St Jo 96-97; Assoc V Lakenham St Alb 97-99; Assoc V Sprowston w Beeston 99-08;

rtd 08; Perm to Offic *Nor* from 08. *2 Vera Road, Norwich NR6 5HU* Tel (01603) 789634 E-mail sgbridges63v@talktalk.net
BRIDGES, John Malham. b 57. TD. Goldsmiths' Coll Lon BSc80. Ridley Hall Cam 03. **d** 05 **p** 06. C Cranleigh *Guildf* 05-08; Chapl RN from 08. *Royal Naval Chaplaincy Service, Mail Point 1-2, Leach Building, Whale Island, Portsmouth PO2 8BY* Tel (023) 9262 5055 Fax 9262 5134 E-mail jmbridges@cantab.net
BRIDGES, The Ven Peter Sydney Godfrey. b 25. ARIBA51. Linc Th Coll 56. **d** 58 **p** 59. C Hemel Hempstead *St Alb* 58-64; Warden Angl Chapl Birm Univ 64-68; Perm to Offic *Birm* 65-72; Lect Aston Univ 68-72; Adn Southend *Chelmsf* 72-77; P-in-c Southend St Jo w St Mark, All SS w St Fran etc 72-73; Dir Dioc Research and Development Unit 73-77; Adn Cov 77-83; Can Th Cov Cathl 77-90; Adn Warwick 83-90; rtd 90; Dioc Adv for Chr Spirituality 90-93; Perm to Offic *Win* from 01. *St Clare, 25 Rivermead Close, Romsey SO51 8HQ* Tel (01794) 512889
BRIDGES (née BANKS), Mrs Vivienne Philippa. b 46. Somerville Coll Ox BA69. SAOMC 02. **d** 05 **p** 06. NSM Wolvercote *Ox* 05-10; NSM Wolvercote and Wytham from 10. *6 Haslemere Gardens, Oxford OX2 8EL* Tel (01865) 558705
BRIDGEWATER, Guy Stevenson. b 60. Ch Ch Ox BA83. Trin Coll Bris BA87. **d** 87 **p** 88. C Radipole and Melcombe Regis *Sarum* 87-90; Chapl Lee Abbey 90-93; V Cranbrook *Cant* 93-98; Dioc Officer for Par Resources (Miss and Lay Tr) *Glouc* 98-07; Dioc Can Res Glouc Cathl 02-07; TR Horsham *Chich* from 07; RD Horsham from 09. *The Vicarage, Causeway, Horsham RH12 1HE* Tel (01403) 272919 *or* 253762
BRIDGEWOOD, Bruce William. b 41. K Coll Lon BA02 Heythrop Coll Lon MA06. St Paul's Coll Grahamstown LTh67. **d** 67 **p** 68. C Plumstead S Africa 67-69; C Somerset W 70-71; Hon C Stanmer w Falmer *Chich* 81-86; Hon C Westmr St Matt *Lon* 90-93; Hon C Alexandra Park 93-04; P-in-c Friern Barnet St Pet le Poer from 04. *81 Warwick Road, London N11 2SP* Tel (020) 8211 9709 E-mail brucebridgewood@talktalk.net
BRIDGMAN, Canon Gerald Bernard. b 22. St Cath Coll Cam BA50 MA55. Bible Churchmen's Coll Bris 46 Wycliffe Hall Ox 50. **d** 51 **p** 52. C Broadwater St Mary *Chich* 51-54; C Ox St Aldate 54-56; C-in-c Southgate CD *Chich* 56-59; V Southgate 59-67; V Kingston upon Hull H Trin *York* 67-87; Chapl Hull R Infirmary 67-87; AD Cen and N Hull 81-86; Can and Preb York Minster 83-87; rtd 87; Perm to Offic *Chich* from 87. *129 The Welkin, Lindfield, Haywards Heath RH16 2PL* Tel (01444) 484563
BRIDGMAN, James William. b 85. Man Univ BA06. Trin Coll Bris BA09 MA10. **d** 10 **p** 11. C Heswall *Ches* from 10. *The Croft, 4 Croftsway, Wirral CH60 9JP* Tel 0151-342 6579 Mobile 07531-768081 E-mail jim bridgman@hotmail.com
BRIDGMAN, Mrs Jennifer Claire. b 84. Man Univ BA06. Trin Coll Bris BA08 MPhil10. **d** 10 **p** 11. C Heswall *Ches* from 10; Young Voc Adv from 11. *The Croft, 4 Croftsway, Wirral CH60 9JP* Tel 0151-342 6579 Mobile 07709-471494 E-mail jenb@heswallparish.co.uk
BRIDGWATER, Philip Dudley. b 31. St Alb Minl Tr Scheme 88. **d** 91 **p** 92. NSM Buxton w Burbage and King Sterndale *Derby* 91-94 and 98-01; NSM Fairfield 94-98; Perm to Offic from 01. *Millstone, 9 College Road, Buxton SK17 9DZ* Tel (01298) 72876
BRIDLE, Geoffrey Peter. b 52. CITC 87. **d** 87 **p** 88. C Lurgan Ch the Redeemer *D & D* 87-91; I Carnteel and Crilly *Arm* 91-99; I Cleenish w Mullaghdun *Clogh* from 99. *Cleenish Rectory, Bellanaleck, Enniskillen BT92 2BA* Tel (028) 6634 8259 Fax 6634 8620 E-mail geoffreypbridle@email.com
BRIDSON, Canon Raymond Stephen. b 58. Southn Univ BTh82. Chich Th Coll. **d** 82 **p** 83. C St Luke in the City *Liv* 82-86; TV Ditton St Mich 86-98; V Anfield St Columba from 98; AD Walton from 02; Hon Can Liv Cathl from 03. *St Columba's Vicarage, Pinehurst Avenue, Liverpool L4 2TZ* Tel 0151-474 7231 E-mail frray@blueyonder.co.uk
BRIDSTRUP, Juergen Walter. b 44. St Alb Minl Tr Scheme 84. **d** 87 **p** 88. C Leagrave *St Alb* 87-90; V Goff's Oak St Jas 90-08; TV Cheshunt 08-09; rtd 09. *4 The Vineyard, Lower Broad Street, Ludlow SY8 1PH* Tel (01584) 876992 E-mail juergen.bridstrup@btinternet.com
BRIEN, John Richard. b 57. Kingston Poly BSc80. EAMTC 98. **d** 01 **p** 02. NSM Mistley w Manningtree and Bradfield *Chelmsf* from 01. *1 East View, Crown Street, Dedham, Colchester CO7 6AN* Tel (01206) 322706 E-mail brienfamily@tiscali.co.uk
BRIERLEY, Charles Ian. b 46. MIMI69. S Dios Minl Tr Scheme 90. **d** 93 **p** 94. NSM Wellington and Distr *B & W* 93-11; rtd 11. *Shady Oak, 19 Immenstadt Drive, Wellington TA21 9PT* Tel (01823) 666101 E-mail brierley@aol.com
BRIERLEY, John Michael. b 32. Lon Univ BD71. Lich Th Coll 57. **d** 60 **p** 61. C Lower Mitton *Worc* 60-62; C-in-c Dines Green St Mich CD 62-68; V Worc St Mich 69-71; R Eastham w Rochford 71-79; P-in-c Knighton-on-Teme 76-79; P-in-c Reddal Hill St Luke 79-81; V 81-92; rtd 92; Perm to Offic *Worc* from 92. *10 Woodhouse Way, Cradley Heath, Warley B64 5EL* Tel (01384) 633527

BRIERLEY, Michael William. b 73. CCC Cam BA94 MA98 Birm Univ PhD07. Ripon Coll Cuddesdon BA98. d 98 p 99. C Marnhull *Sarum* 98-01; C Okeford 98-01; Bp's Dom Chapl *Ox* 01-07; P-in-c Tavistock and Gulworthy *Ex* from 07. *The Vicarage, 5A Plymouth Road, Tavistock PL19 8AU* Tel (01822) 617432 E-mail mwbrierley@aol.com

BRIERLEY, Philip. b 49. Salford Univ BSc74. d 92 p 93. OLM Stalybridge *Man* from 92. *Burnside, 30 Cranworth Street, Stalybridge SK15 2NW* Tel 0161-303 0809 E-mail irenephilipbrierley@yahoo.com

BRIERLEY, William David. b 64. Kent Univ BA87 New Coll Ox DPhil93. Ripon Coll Cuddesdon. d 93 p 94. C Amersham *Ox* 93-97; TV Wheatley 97-05. *37 Chessbury Road, Chesham HP5 1JT* E-mail william.brierley@tesco.net

BRIGGS, Christopher Ronald. b 58. K Coll Lon BD79 AKC79 PGCE80. Sarum & Wells Th Coll 87. d 89 p 90. C Horsell *Guildf* 89-93; Hong Kong 93-97; V Norton *St Alb* 97-00; Sen Chapl Haileybury Coll from 00. *Lawrence Cottage, 2 Hailey Lane, Hertford Heath, Hertford SG13 7NX* Tel and fax (01992) 462922 *or* tel 706314 E-mail chrisbriggs@freenet.co.uk

BRIGGS, Enid. b 50. CBDTI 03. d 06 p 07. NSM Walton-le-Dale St Leon w Samlesbury St Leon *Blackb* from 06. *85 Plantation Street, Accrington BB5 6RT* Tel (01254) 383568 E-mail enid briggs@hotmail.com

BRIGGS, George William. b 76. Wadh Coll Ox BA98 Fitzw Coll Cam BA02. Ridley Hall Cam 00. d 03 p 04. C Old Trafford St Bride *Man* 03-06; P-in-c Clapham Park All SS S'wark from 06. *All Saints' Vicarage, 250 Lyham Road, London SW2 5NP* Tel (020) 8678 6020 E-mail george.briggs@bigfoot.com

BRIGGS, Gordon John. b 39. CIPFA. SAOMC 95. d 98 p 99. OLM Farnham Royal w Hedgerley *Ox* 98-11; Perm to Offic from 11. *52 Freemans Close, Stoke Poges, Slough SL2 4ER* Tel (01753) 662536

BRIGGS, Canon John. b 39. Edin Univ MA61. Ridley Hall Cam 61. d 63 p 64. C Jesmond Clayton Memorial *Newc* 63-66; Schs Sec Scripture Union 66-79; Tutor St Jo Coll Dur 67-74; Lic to Offic *Dur* 67-74 and *Edin* 74-79; V Chadkirk *Ches* 79-88; RD Chadkirk 85-88; TR Macclesfield Team 88-04; Hon Can Ches Cathl 96-04; Chapl W Park Hosp Macclesfield 90-99; rtd 04; Perm to Offic *Ches* from 04. *16 Lostock Hall Road, Poynton, Stockport SK12 1DP* Tel (01625) 267228 E-mail john.briggs20@ntlworld.com

BRIGGS, Michael Weston. b 40. Edin Th Coll 61. d 64 p 65. C Sneinton St Steph w St Alb S'well 64-67; C Beeston 67-70; P-in-c Kirkby Woodhouse 70-74; V Harworth 74-81; R Harby w Thorney and N and S Clifton 81-94; R N Wheatley, W Burton, Bole, Saundby, Sturton etc 94-05; P-in-c Clarborough w Hayton 03-05; CF (ACF) 74-97; rtd 05; Perm to Offic S'well from 06. *3 Monkwood Close, Collingham, Newark NG23 7SY* Tel (01636) 893344 E-mail m_w_briggs@lineone.net

BRIGGS, The Very Revd Roger Edward. b 36. ALCD61. d 61 p 61. Canada 61-71; C Upper Armley *Ripon* 71-72; Canada 72-99; Dean Arctic 96-99; rtd 99. *Apartment 1207, 415 Greenview Avenue, Ottawa ON K2B 8G5, Canada*

BRIGHAM, John Keith. b 48. Man Univ CertEd70 FSAScot. St Steph Ho Ox 71. d 74 p 75. C Ches H Trin 74-77; C Ealing Ch the Sav *Lon* 77-85; P-in-c Fulwell St Mich and St Geo 85-88; P-in-c Upper Teddington SS Pet and Paul 85-88; V Southport St Luke *Liv* 88-94; Dioc Chapl to the Deaf 88-94; V Lund *Blackb* 94-98. *17 South Meade, Timperley, Altrincham WA15 6QL* Tel 0161-973 6684 E-mail keebee@aol.com

BRIGHOUSE, George Alexander (Alex). b 46. NOC 87. d 90 p 91. NSM Ingrow w Hainworth *Bradf* 90-91; NSM Keighley All SS 92; NSM Bradf St Wilfrid Lidget Green 92-94; NSM Bradf St Wilfrid w St Columba from 04. *38 Thirsk Grange, Clayton, Bradford BD14 6HS* Tel 07960-114534 (mobile)

BRIGHT, George Frank. b 50. Peterho Cam BA71 MA75 LSE MSc83 SAP99. Coll of Resurr Mirfield 71. d 74 p 75. C Notting Hill *Lon* 74-77; Perm to Offic 77-84; P-in-c Kentish Town St Benet and All SS 84-89; P-in-c Kensington St Jo 89-93; V 93-06. *The Vicarage, 176 Holland Road, London W14 8AH* Tel (020) 7602 4655 E-mail gfb@dircon.co.uk

BRIGHT, Reginald. b 26. Tyndale Hall Bris 57. d 60 p 61. C Toxteth Park St Philemon w St Silas *Liv* 60-63; P-in-c Everton St Polycarp 63-65; R Orton St Giles *Carl* 65-72; V Holme 72-79; P-in-c W Newton 79-81; V Bromfield w Waverton 79-81; R Bowness 81-93; rtd 93; Perm to Offic *Carl* from 93. *Spinney House, Cannonfield, Roadhead, Carlisle CA6 6NB* Tel (01697) 748645

BRIGHTMAN, Peter Arthur. b 30. ALCD61 LTh74. d 64 p 65. C Westgate St Jas *Cant* 64-67; C Lydd 67-70; C Lt Coates *Linc* 70; C Heaton Ch Ch *Man* 71-72; V Bolton SS Simon and Jude 72-77; R Bath St Sav *B & W* 77-85; R Farmborough, Marksbury and Stanton Prior 85-90; C Coney Hill *Glouc* 90-93; C Hardwicke, Quedgeley and Elmore w Longney 93-95; rtd 95; Perm to Offic *B & W* from 95. *2 Westmead Cottages, Dean Hill Lane, Weston, Bath BA1 4DT* Tel (01225) 315076

BRIGHTON, Margaret Elizabeth. b 53. Qu Coll Birm BA07. WMMTC 04. d 07 p 08. C Boldmere *Birm* 07-10; V The Lickey

from 10. *The Vicarage, 30 Lickey Square, Lickey, Birmingham B45 8HB* Tel 0121-445 6781 E-mail margaret.brighton@ntlworld.com

BRIGHTON, Terrence William. b 43. SWMTC 85. d 88 p 89. C Dawlish *Ex* 88-92; P-in-c Newton Poppleford w Harpford 92-94; V Newton Poppleford, Harpford and Colaton Raleigh 94-98; RD Ottery 96-98; P-in-c W Lavington and the Cheverells *Sarum* 98-02; Rural Officer (Ramsbury Area) 98-02; P-in-c Charleton w Buckland Tout Saints etc *Ex* 02-05; R 05-08; RD Woodleigh 03-07; rtd 08. *30 Millway, Chudleigh, Newton Abbot TQ13 0JN* Tel 07974-294044 (mobile) E-mail twb@madasafish.com

BRIGHTWELL, Johanna Clare. See CLARE, Ms Johanna Howard

BRIGNALL, Elizabeth Jane. See BENDREY, Elizabeth Jane

BRIGNALL, Simon Francis Lyon. b 54. St Jo Coll Dur BA78. Wycliffe Hall Ox 80. d 83 p 84. C Colne St Bart *Blackb* 83-86; SAMS Peru 86-96; P-in-c Tetsworth, Adwell w S Weston, Lewknor etc *Ox* 96-98; TV Thame 98-09; P-in-c Wriggle Valley *Sarum* from 09. *The Rectory, Church Street, Yetminster, Sherborne DT9 6LG* Tel (01935) 872237 Mobile 07718-627674

BRIGNELL, Roger. b 39. CertEd65 ACP88 MCollP89. St Aid Birkenhead 60 St As Minl Tr Course 95. d 98 p 99. NSM Montgomery and Forden and Llandyssil *St As* from 98. *Cedar Lea, Caerhowel, Montgomery SY15 6HE* Tel and fax (01686) 668539

BRIMACOMBE, Keith John. b 59. Open Univ BA92 Westmr Coll Ox MTh00. SWMTC 99. d 01 p 03. NSM Ottery St Mary, Alfington, W Hill, Tipton etc *Ex* from 01. *Banklea, Exeter Road, Newton Poppleford, Sidmouth EX10 0BJ* Tel (01395) 568404 E-mail brims@kjbrims.fsnet.co.uk

BRIMICOMBE, Mark. b 44. Nottm Univ BA66 CertEd. SWMTC 83. d 85 p 86. NSM Plympton St Mary *Ex* from 85. *4 David Close, Stoggy Lane, Plympton, Plymouth PL7 3BQ* Tel (01752) 338454 E-mail mark@thebrambles.eclipse.co.uk

BRIMSON, Mrs Dawn Diana. b 44. Ex Univ BTh08. SWMTC 02. d 05 p 06. NSM Quantoxhead *B & W* 05-07; NSM Quantock Coast from 07. *Ridges, Holford, Bridgwater TA5 1DU* Tel (01278) 741413 E-mail dawnbrimson@googlemail.com

BRINDLE, Peter John. b 47. MIStructE72 FLS05. NOC 78. d 81 p 82. NSM Bingley All SS *Bradf* 81-84; NSM Bingley H Trin 84-86; V Keighley All SS 86-91; V Kirkstall *Ripon* 91-96; V Beeston 96-02; TR 02-04; TR Leic Presentation 04-09; P-in-c Leic St Chad 04-07; P-in-c N Evington 07-09; rtd 09. *5 Showfield Close, Sherburn in Elmet, Leeds LS25 6LW* Tel (01977) 680026 Mobile 07860-157363 E-mail brindle16@hotmail.co.uk

BRINDLEY, Angela Mary. See SPEEDY, Mrs Angela Mary

BRINDLEY, The Very Revd David Charles. b 53. K Coll Lon BD75 AKC75 MTh76 MPhil81. St Aug Coll Cant 75. d 76 p 77. C Epping St Jo *Chelmsf* 76-79; Lect Coll of SS Paul and Mary Cheltenham 79-82; Dioc Dir of Tr *Leic* 82-86; V Quorndon 82-86; Prin Glouc Sch for Min 87-92; Prin WEMTC 92-94; Dir of Minl Tr 87-94; Dioc Officer for NSM 88-94; Hon Can Glouc Cathl 92-94; TR Warwick *Cov* 94-02; Dean Portsm from 02. *The Deanery, 13 Pembroke Road, Portsmouth PO1 2NS* Tel (023) 9282 4400 *or* 9234 7605 Fax 9229 5480 E-mail david.brindley@portsmouthcathedral.org.uk

BRINDLEY, Canon Stuart Geoffrey Noel. b 30. St Jo Coll Dur BA53. d 55 p 56. C Newc St Anne 55-58; C Tynemouth Cullercoats St Paul 58-60; C Killingworth 60-63; V Newsham 63-69; W Germany 69-76; Asst Master Wyvern Sch Weston-super-Mare 76-80; V Stocksbridge *Sheff* 80-88; RD Tankersley 85-88; V Rotherham 88-96; Hon Can Sheff Cathl 95-96; rtd 96; Perm to Offic *Newc* from 96. *Hambury, Backcrofts, Rothbury, Morpeth NE65 7XY* Tel (01669) 621472

BRINKWORTH, Canon Christopher Michael Gibbs. b 41. Lanc Univ BA70. Kelham Th Coll 62. d 67 p 68. C Lancaster St Mary *Blackb* 67-70; C Milton *Portsm* 70-74; V Ault Hucknall *Derby* 74-84; V Derby St Anne and St Jo 84-06; Hon Can Derby Cathl 00-06; rtd 06; Perm to Offic *Derby* from 06. *3 Westfield Drive, Derby DE22 3SG* Tel (01332) 208478 E-mail michaelbrinkworth@btinternet.com

BRION, Martin Philip. b 33. Ex Univ BA55. Ridley Hall Cam 57. d 59 p 60. C Balderstone *Man* 59-62; C Morden S'wark 62-66; V Low Elswick *Newc* 66-73; P-in-c Giggleswick *Bradf* 73-77; V 77-80; V Camerton H Trin W Seaton *Carl* 80-86; V Dearham 86-95; rtd 95; Perm to Offic *Carl* from 95. *7 Falcon Place, Moresby Parks, Whitehaven CA28 8YF* Tel (01946) 691912

BRISBANE, Archbishop of. See ASPINALL, The Most Revd Phillip John

BRISCOE, Allen. b 42. Liv Univ BSc64 CertEd65. Coll of Resurr Mirfield 90. d 92 p 93. C Shiremoor *Newc* 92-95; V Barnsley St Pet and St Jo *Wakef* 95-10; Asst Dioc Ecum Officer 01-03; Bp's Adv for Ecum Affairs 03-06; RD Barnsley 04-09; rtd 10; Hon C Goldthorpe w Hickleton *Sheff* from 11. *37 Holly Grove, Goldthorpe, Rotherham S63 9LA* Tel (01709) 896739 E-mail abriscoe@talk21.com

BRISCOE, Canon Frances Amelia. b 35. Univ of Wales CertEd55 Man Univ BA71 MA74. Gilmore Course 74. dss 77 d 87 p 94. Gt Crosby St Luke *Liv* 77-81; Dioc Lay Min Adv 81-87; Chapl

Liv Cathl 81-89; Dir Diaconal Mins 87-89; Lect St Deiniol's Minl Tr Scheme 88-00; Hon Can Liv Cathl 88-00; AD Sefton 89-00; Dir of Reader Studies 89-00; Dn-in-c Hightown 92-94; P-in-c 94-00; rtd 00; Perm to Offic *Liv* from 01. *5 Derwent Avenue, Formby, Liverpool L37 2JT* Tel (01704) 830075

BRISCOE, Mark. b 71. Coll of Ripon & York St Jo BA(QTS)95. Ripon Coll Cuddesdon 05. **d** 07 **p** 08. C Saxilby Gp *Linc* 07-10; P-in-c Corringham and Blyton Gp from 10; P-in-c Glentworth Gp from 10. *The Vicarage, Church Lane, Blyton, Gainsborough DN21 3JZ*

BRISON, The Ven William Stanly. b 29. Alfred Univ NY BSc51 Connecticut Univ MDiv57 STM71. Berkeley Div Sch. **d** 57 **p** 57. USA 57-72; V Davyhulme Ch Ch *Man* 72-81; R Newton Heath All SS 81-85; AD N Man 81-85; Hon Can Man Cathl 82-85; Adn Bolton 85-92; TV E Farnworth and Kearsley 85-89; C Bolton St Thos 89-92; CMS 92-94; Nigeria 92-94; P-in-c Pendleton St Thos w Charlestown *Man* 94-95; TR Pendleton 95-98; rtd 98; Perm to Offic *Man* from 99. *2 Scott Avenue, Bury BL9 9RS* Tel 0161-764 3998

BRISTOL, Archdeacon of. See McCLURE, The Ven Timothy Elston

BRISTOL, Bishop of. See HILL, The Rt Revd Michael Arthur

BRISTOL, Dean of. See HOYLE, The Very Revd David Michael

BRISTOW, Keith Raymond Martin. b 56. Ex Univ BA78. Chich Th Coll 87. **d** 89 **p** 90. C Kirkby *Liv* 89-93; C Portsea St Mary *Portsm* 93-03; R Ash *Guildf* from 03. *The Rectory, Ash Church Road, Ash, Aldershot GU12 6LU* Tel (01252) 321517 E-mail frkeithbristow@ntlworld.com

BRISTOW, Peter Edmund. b 49. Pontificium Institutum Internationale Angelicum Rome JCL77 St Jos Coll Upholland 67. **d** 72 **p** 73. In RC Ch 72-87; C Poplar *Lon* 89-92; Lay Tr Officer 89-90; TV Droitwich Spa *Worc* 92-94; TR 94-00; V Boston Spa *York* 00-11; P-in-c Bramham 09-11; P-in-c Thorp Arch w Walton 00-11; V Bramham from 11; RD New Ainsty from 06. *The Vicarage, 86 High Street, Boston Spa, Wetherby LS23 6EA* Tel (01937) 842454 E-mail peterbristow1@ntlworld.com

BRISTOW, Roger. b 60. Aston Tr Scheme 81 Ridley Hall Cam 83. **d** 86 **p** 87. C Leyton St Mary w St Edw *Chelmsf* 86-90; TV Kings Norton *Birm* 90-98; V Bromley H Trin *Roch* from 98. *Holy Trinity Vicarage, Church Lane, Bromley BR2 8LB* Tel and fax (020) 8462 1280 Mobile 07778-397224 E-mail roger.bristow@diocese-rochester.org

BRITT, Eric Stanley. b 47. St Jo Coll Nottm BTh75. **d** 74 **p** 75. C Chorleywood Ch Ch *St Alb* 74-78; C Frimley *Guildf* 78-80; P-in-c Alresford *Chelmsf* 80-88; R Takeley w Lt Canfield 88-93; Asst Chapl R Free Hosp Lon 93-96; Chapl Mid-Essex Hosp Services NHS Trust 96-00; Chapl Algarve *Eur* 01-06; rtd 06. *5 De Lisle Close, Papworth Everard, Cambridge CB23 3UT* E-mail e.britt@btinternet.com

BRITT, Sister Mary Stephen. b 44. Stockwell Coll of Educn TCert65 Open Univ BA76. SAOMC 02. **d** 05 **p** 06. CSJB from 05; NSM Hanborough and Freeland *Ox* from 05. *The Priory, 2 Spring Hill Road, Begbroke, Kidlington OX5 1RX* Tel (01865) 855324 E-mail marycsjb@csjb.org.uk

BRITT, William Thomas. b 60. Westmr Coll Fulton (USA) BA82. St Mellitus Coll BA11. **d** 11. C Kempston Transfiguration *St Alb* from 11. *16 Rosedale Way, Kempston, Bedford MK42 8JE* Tel (01234) 308682 E-mail revd.bill.britt@gmail.com

BRITTAIN, John. b 23. St Aug Coll Cant 59. **d** 60 **p** 61. C Heref St Martin 60-62; V Highley 62-88; rtd 88. *26 Stuart Court, High Street, Kibworth, Leicester LE8 0LR*

BRITTEN, Mrs Diana. d 07 **p** 08. OLM Cley Hill Villages *Sarum* from 07. *69 Lane End, Corsley, Warminster BA12 7PG* Tel (01373) 832515 E-mail dianabritten@ukonline.co.uk

BRITTLE, Miss Janice Lilian. b 50. Man Poly BA74 Open Univ BA84 Sheff Univ MMedSc00 RGN76. **d** 04 **p** 05. OLM Rugeley *Lich* 04-06; OLM Brereton and Rugeley from 06. *3 Norwood House, Peakes Road, Rugeley WS15 2ND* Tel (01889) 586138 E-mail janice.brittle@btinternet.com

BRITTON, Christine Mary. See BEECROFT, Mrs Christine Mary

BRITTON, David Robert. b 80. Leeds Univ BA03 Fitzw Coll Cam BA09. Ridley Hall Cam 07. **d** 10 **p** 11. C W Streatham St Jas S'wark from 10. *63 Chillerton Road, London SW17 9BE* Tel 07841-237908 (mobile) E-mail rev.britton@gmail.com

BRITTON, John Timothy Hugh. b 50. Dundee Univ BSc73. Trin Coll Bris 73. **d** 76 **p** 77. C Cromer *Nor* 76-79; P-in-c Freethorpe w Wickhampton 79-82; P-in-c Beighton and Moulton 79-82; P-in-c Halvergate w Tunstall 79-82; CMS 82-89; Uganda 83-89; R Allesley *Cov* 89-02; P-in-c Long Itchington and Marton from 02; P-in-c Wappenbury w Weston under Wetherley from 02; P-in-c Hunningham from 02; P-in-c Offchurch from 02. *The Vicarage, Leamington Road, Long Itchington, Southam CV47 9PL* Tel (01926) 812518 E-mail timbritton@myrealbox.com

BRITTON, Neil Bryan. b 35. Em Coll Cam BA59 MA63. Clifton Th Coll 61. **d** 63 **p** 64. C Eastbourne All SS *Chich* 63-67; C Ashtead *Guildf* 67-70; Chapl Scargill Ho 70-74; Chapl Aiglon Coll and Asst Chapl Villars *Eur* 74-78; In Reformed Ch of Switzerland 78-98; rtd 00; USA 01-05. *Rose Cottage, 7 Newbury Way, Kingsclere, Newbury RG20 5SP* Tel (01635) 297687 Mobile 07903-120368 E-mail britton.neil@googlemail.com

BRITTON, Canon Paul Anthony. b 29. SS Coll Cam BA52 MA57. Linc Th Coll 52. **d** 54 **p** 55. C Upper Norwood St Jo *Cant* 54-57; C Wantage *Ox* 57-61; V Stanmore *Win* 61-70; V Bitterne Park 70-80; Can Res Win Cathl 80-94; Lib 81-85; Treas 85-94; rtd 94; Perm to Offic *Sarum* from 94. *Pemberton, High Street, Hindon, Salisbury SP3 6DR* Tel (01747) 820406

BRITTON, Robert. b 37. Oak Hill Th Coll 78. **d** 79 **p** 80. C St Helens St Helen *Liv* 79-83; V Lowton St Mary 83-02; AD Winwick 89-01; rtd 02; Perm to Offic *Liv* and *Man* from 03. *15 Balmoral Avenue, Lowton, Warrington WA3 2ER* Tel (01942) 711135

BRITTON, Ronald George Adrian Michael (Robert). b 24. Univ of State of NY BSc78 Lambeth STh82. St D Coll Lamp 63. **d** 82 **p** 82. Arabia 82-85; Chapl Alassio *Eur* 85-90 and 92-93; Chapl San Remo 86; Hon C Southbourne St Kath *Win* 90-92; rtd 96; Perm to Offic *Bris* from 97. *2 Cherry Tree Road, Bristol BS16 4EY* Tel 0117-965 5734 E-mail robert@britton320.fsnet.co.uk

BRITTON, Timothy. See BRITTON, John Timothy Hugh

BRIXTON, Miss Corinne Jayne. b 63. Ex Univ BSc84. Wycliffe Hall Ox BTh95. **d** 95. C Leytonstone St Jo *Chelmsf* 95-00; C Buckhurst Hill from 00. *63 High Road, Buckhurst Hill IG9 5SR* Tel (020) 8504 6652 E-mail cbrixton@aol.com

BRIXWORTH, Suffragan Bishop of. See HOLBROOK, The Rt Revd John Edward

BROAD, Mrs Christine Jane. b 63. Leeds Univ BSc86 BA06. NOC 03. **d** 06 **p** 07. C Newchapel *Lich* 06-09; TV Hanley H Ev from 09. *19 Widecombe Road, Birches Head, Stoke-on-Trent ST1 6SL* Tel (01782) 852280 E-mail christine@broad1959.freeserve.co.uk

BROAD, David Nicholas Andrew. b 59. Man Univ BA. Edin Th Coll. **d** 87 **p** 88. C Fulham All SS *Lon* 87-90; TV Clare w Poslingford, Cavendish etc *St E* 90-93; TV Totton *Win* 93-99; R Abbotts Ann and Upper and Goodworth Clatford from 99. *The Rectory, Upper Clatford, Andover SP11 7QP* Tel and fax (01264) 352906 E-mail dna.broad@virgin.net

BROAD, Canon Hugh Duncan. b 37. Lich Th Coll 64. **d** 67 **p** 68. C Heref H Trin 67-72; Asst Master Bp's Sch Heref 72-73; C Fareham SS Pet and Paul *Portsm* 74-76; V Heref All SS 76-90; R Matson *Glouc* 90-97; V Glouc St Geo w Whaddon 97-03; Hon Can Glouc Cathl 02-03; rtd 03; P-in-c Costa Almeria and Costa Calida *Eur* from 03. *6A Calla la Mata, Apartado 617, 04638 Mojácar Playa (Almeria), Spain* Tel (0034) 950 478 432 Mobile 617 779 327 E-mail fr.hugh@hotmail.co.uk

BROAD, Hugh Robert. b 49. St Mich Coll Llan 67. **d** 72 **p** 73. C Tenby w Gumfreston *St D* 72-75; C Caerau w Ely *Llan* 75-79; V Llanharan w Peterston-super-Montem 79-89; RD Bridgend 88-89; Ex-Paroch Officer 90; V Whatborough Gp *Leic* 90-08; rtd 08. *12 Cooke Close, Thorpe Astley, Braunstone, Leicester LE3 3RG* E-mail hugh.broad@hotmail.com

BROAD, Canon William Ernest Lionel. b 40. Ridley Hall Cam 64. **d** 66 **p** 67. C Ecclesfield *Sheff* 66-69; Chapl HM Pris Wormwood Scrubs 69; Chapl HM Pris Albany 70-74; Chapl HM Rem Cen Risley 74-76; V Ditton St Mich *Liv* 76-81; TR 82-83; P-in-c Mayland and Steeple *Chelmsf* 83-91; V Blackhall *Dur* 91-97; TR Gt Aycliffe 97-03; P-in-c Chilton 03; TV Gt Aycliffe and Chilton 03-04; Hon Can Dur Cathl 02-04; rtd 04. *Moorcote, Thornley, Tow Law, Bishop Auckland DL13 4NU* Tel (01388) 731350 E-mail bill@deagol.fsnet.co.uk

BROADBENT, Mrs Doreen. b 36. **d** 94 **p** 95. OLM Stalybridge *Man* 94-02; Perm to Offic from 02. *37 Ladysmith Road, Ashton-under-Lyne OL6 9DJ* Tel 0161-330 9085

BROADBENT, Hugh Patrick Colin. b 53. Selw Coll Cam BA75 MA. **d** 78 **p** 79. C Chatham St Steph *Roch* 78-82; C Shortlands 82-84; C Edenbridge 84-87; C Crockham Hill H Trin 84-87; V Bromley H Trin 87-97; V Bromley St Jo 97-09; Chapl St Olave's Gr Sch Orpington 95-09; R Snodland All SS w Ch Ch *Roch* from 09. *The Vicarage, 11 St Katherine's Lane, Snodland ME6 5EH* Tel (01634) 240232 E-mail hugh.broadbent@diocese-rochester.org

BROADBENT, Neil Seton. b 53. Qu Coll Birm. **d** 81 **p** 82. C Knaresborough *Ripon* 81-84; C Leeds Gipton Epiphany 84-87; Lic to Offic 87-89; Chapl Minstead Community *Derby* 89; Perm to Offic from 89; Dir Sozein from 93. *The Old Vicarage, Church Lane, Horsley Woodhouse, Ilkeston DE7 6BB* Tel (01332) 780598 E-mail neil.broadbent@sozein.org.uk

BROADBENT, Paul John. b 41. Oak Hill Th Coll 83. **d** 85 **p** 86. C Duston *Pet* 85-88; TV Ross w Brampton Abbotts, Bridstow and Peterstow *Heref* 88-91; R Pattishall w Cold Higham and Gayton w Tiffield *Pet* 91-10; rtd 10; P-in-c Fairwarp *Chich* from 10. *The Vicarage, Fairwarp, Uckfield TN22 3BL* Tel (01825) 712277 Mobile 07786-865015 E-mail pjbroadbent@aol.com

✠**BROADBENT, The Rt Revd Peter Alan.** b 52. Jes Coll Cam BA74 MA78. St Jo Coll Nottm 74. **d** 77 **p** 78 **c** 01. C Dur St Nic 77-80; C Holloway Em w Hornsey Road St Barn *Lon* 80-83; Chapl N Lon Poly 83-89; Hon C Islington St Mary 83-89; V

Harrow Trin St Mich 89-94; AD Harrow 94; Adn Northolt 95-01; P-in-c Southall H Trin 98-99; Area Bp Willesden from 01. *173 Willesden Lane, London NW6 7YN* Tel (020) 8451 0189 Fax 8451 4606 Mobile 07957-144674 E-mail bishop.willesden@btinternet.com

BROADBENT, Ralph Andrew. b 55. K Coll Lon BD76 AKC76 Birm Univ PhD04. Chich Th Coll 77. **d** 78 **p** 79. C Prestwich St Mary *Man* 78-82; R Man Miles Platting 82-84; CF 84-87; TV Wordsley *Lich* 88-93; Chapl Wordsley and Ridge Hill Hosps 88-93; V Wollescote *Worc* from 93. *St Andrew's Vicarage, Oakfield Road, Wollescote, Stourbridge DY9 9DG* Tel (01384) 422695

BROADBENT, Thomas William. b 45. Chu Coll Cam BA66 MA70 PhD70. Ridley Hall Cam 75. **d** 78 **p** 79. C Allington and Maidstone St Pet *Cant* 78-82; Chapl Mid Kent Coll of H&FE 80-82; C Kings Heath *Birm* 82-84; Hon C Pendleton St Thos *Man* 84-89; TV Pendleton St Thos w Charlestown 89-92; Chapl Salford Univ 84-92; P-in-c Claydon and Barham *St E* 92-08; P-in-c Henley 99-08; P-in-c Gt Blakenham 02-08; Chapl Suffolk Coll 92-00; P-in-c Witham Gp *Linc* from 08. *The Rectory, 15 Hillview Road, South Witham, Grantham NG33 5QW* Tel (01572) 767240

BROADBERRY, Canon Richard St Lawrence. b 31. TCD BA53 BD59 MLitt66. **d** 54 **p** 55. C Dublin St Thos *D & G* 54-56; C Dublin Grangegorman 56-62; Min Can St Patr Cathl Dublin 58-62; Hon Clerical V Ch Ch Cathl Dublin 62-66; C Dublin Clontarf 62-64; C Thornton Heath St Jude *Cant* 64-66; V Norwood All SS 66-82; V Upper Norwood All SS w St Marg 82-84; RD Croydon N 81-84; Hon Can Cant Cathl 82-84; V Merton St Mary *S'wark* 85-92; RD Croydon N 85; Hon Can S'wark Cathl 85-01; V Riddlesdown 92-01; rtd 01; Perm to Offic *S'wark* from 01. *73 Court Avenue, Coulsdon CR5 1HG* Tel (01737) 551109 E-mail r-m.broadberry@tiscali.co.uk

BROADHEAD, Mrs Lynn. b 59. Yorks Min Course 08. **d** 11. NSM Thorpe Hesley *Sheff* from 11. *20 Chambers Grove, Chapeltown, Sheffield S35 2TD* Tel 0114-245 1164 E-mail lynn.broadhead@sky.com

BROADHURST, Jonathan Robin. b 58. Univ Coll Ox BA81 MA86. Wycliffe Hall Ox 85. **d** 88 **p** 89. C Hull St Jo Newland *York* 88-91; P-in-c Burton Fleming w Fordon, Grindale etc 91-92; V 92-98; C Kingston upon Hull H Trin 98-01; P-in-c Rastrick St Jo *Wakef* 01-06; rtd 06. *1 Moravian Terrace, Halifax HX3 8AL* Tel (01422) 209549 Mobile 07790-899195 E-mail jonathan@broadhurst-jr.freeserve.co.uk

BROADLEY, Michael John. b 66. Roehampton Inst BA87. Trin Coll Bris 93. **d** 96 **p** 97. C Egham *Guildf* 96-01; TV Horsham *Chich* 01-10; TR Loughborough Em and St Mary in Charnwood *Leic* from 10. *Emmanuel Rectory, 47 Forest Road, Loughborough LE11 3NW* Tel (01509) 263264 E-mail broadley@bigfoot.com

BROCK, Michael John. b 52. Birm Univ BSc74. St Jo Coll Nottm BA77. **d** 78 **p** 79. C Stapleford *S'well* 78-82; C Bestwood St Matt 82-86; TV Bestwood 86-90; R Epperstone and Gonalston and V Oxton 90-05; P-in-c Woodborough 02-05; RD S'well 93-96; Dioc Adv in Rural Affairs 97-02; R Dersingham w Anmer and Shernborne *Nor* from 05; RD Heacham and Rising 07-11. *The Vicarage, Sherborne Road, Dersingham, King's Lynn PE31 6JA* Tel (01485) 540214 E-mail mjb65@btinternet.com

BROCKBANK, Arthur Ross. b 51. NOC 87. **d** 90 **p** 91. C Haughton St Mary *Man* 90-93; V Bircle from 93; P-in-c Walmersley 04; Chapl Bury Healthcare NHS Trust 93-02; Chapl Co-ord 02-03. *The Vicarage, 33 Castle Hill Road, Bury BL9 7RW* Tel 0161-764 3853

BROCKBANK, Donald Philip. b 56. Univ of Wales (Ban) BD78. Sarum & Wells Th Coll 79. **d** 81 **p** 82. C Prenton *Ches* 81-85; TV Birkenhead Priory 85-91; V Altrincham St Jo 91-96; Urban Officer 91-96; Dioc Ecum Officer *Lich* 96-98; C Lich St Mich w St Mary and Wall 96-98; V Acton and Worleston, Church Minshull etc *Ches* 98-06; rtd 07; Dioc Adv in Spirituality *Ches* from 07. *1 Plover Avenue, Winsford CW7 1LA* Tel (01606) 593651 E-mail donald@brockbankrev.freeserve.co.uk

BROCKBANK, John Keith. b 44. Dur Univ BA65. Wells Th Coll 66. **d** 68 **p** 69. C Preston St Matt *Blackb* 68-71; C Lancaster St Mary 71-73; V Habergham All SS 73-83; P-in-c Gannow 81-83; V W Burnley All SS 83-86; Dioc Stewardship Adv 86-92; P-in-c Shireshead 86-92; V Kirkham 92-09; rtd 09; Perm to Offic *Blackb* from 09. *44 Esthwaite Gardens, Lancaster LA1 3RG* Tel (01524) 847520 E-mail revjkb@talktalk.net

BROCKBANK, John Stanley. b 41. CBDTI 97. **d** 00 **p** 01. OLM Arnside *Carl* 00-11; rtd 11. *Hough Close, 5 Ash Meadow Road, Arnside, Carnforth LA5 0AE* Tel (01524) 761634

BROCKHOUSE, Canon Grant Lindley. b 47. Adelaide Univ BA71 Ex Univ MA81. St Barn Coll Adelaide 70. **d** 73 **p** 74. C Edwardstown w Ascot Park Australia 73-74; Tutor St Barn Coll Belair 74-78; C Ex St Jas 78-80; Asst Chapl Ex Univ 80-83; V Marldon 83-98; Dep PV Ex Cathl 81-98; RD Torbay 95-98; V Higham Ferrers w Chelveston *Pet* from 98; RD Higham from 03; Can Pet Cathl from 07. *The Vicarage, Wood Street, Higham Ferrers, Rushden NN10 8DL* Tel (01933) 312433 E-mail grantbrockhouse@care4free.net

BROCKIE, Canon William James Thomson. b 36. Pemb Coll Ox BA58 MA62. Linc Th Coll 58. **d** 60 **p** 61. C Lin St Jo Bapt CD *Linc* 60-63; V Gt Staughton *Ely* 63-68; Chapl HM Borstal Gaynes Hall 63-68; TV Edin St Jo 68-76; Chapl Edin Univ 71-76; USA 76; R Edin St Martin 76-01; P-in-c Edin St Luke 79-90; Hon Can St Mary's Cathl from 98; rtd 00; Hon C Edin St Hilda and Edin St Fillan 02-03. *31 Holly Bank Terrace, Edinburgh EH11 1SP* Tel 0131-337 6482 E-mail billjennybrockie@hotmail.com

BROCKLEBANK, John. b 32. NOC 83. **d** 86 **p** 87. NSM Warrington St Barn *Liv* 86-93; NSM Orford St Marg 93-97; Perm to Offic from 97. *53 St Mary's Road, Penketh, Warrington WA5 2DT* Tel (01925) 722063

BROCKLEHURST, John Richard. b 51. Univ Coll Ox BA72 Lon Univ CertEd74. Oak Hill Th Coll BA81. **d** 81 **p** 82. C Harwood *Man* 81-85; V Hopwood 85-97; P-in-c Friarmere 97-03; TV Saddleworth 03-08; P-in-c Waddington *Bradf* from 08; Hon C Hurst Green and Mitton from 08; Hon C Bolton by Bowland w Grindleton from 08. *The Vicarage, Slaidburn Road, Waddington, Clitheroe BB7 3JQ* Tel and fax (01200) 422481 E-mail waddowvicar@talktalk.net

BROCKLEHURST, Simon. b 63. Cranmer Hall Dur 86. **d** 89 **p** 90. C Clifton *S'well* 89-93; TV 93-96; P-in-c Mabe *Truro* 96-99; Miss to Seamen 96-99; V Ham St Andr *S'wark* from 99; Inland Hon Chapl Miss to Seafarers from 00. *St Andrew's Vicarage, Church Road, Ham, Richmond TW10 5HG* Tel and fax (020) 8940 9017 E-mail revsimonb@btinternet.com

BRODDLE, Christopher Stephen Thomas. b 57. **d** 87 **p** 88. C Lisburn St Paul *Conn* 87-90; CF 90-07; Sen CF from 07. *c/o MOD Chaplains (Army)* Tel (01980) 615804 Fax 615800

BRODIE, Miss Ann. b 55. Ex Univ BA76 PGCE77. St Jo Coll Nottm 03. **d** 05 **p** 06. C Putney St Marg *S'wark* 05-09; P-in-c from 09. *St Margaret's Vicarage, 46 Luttrell Avenue, London SW15 6PE* Tel (020) 8788 5522 E-mail vicar@stmargaretsputney.org.uk

BRODIE, Frederick. b 40. Leic Teacher Tr Coll TCert61. St Jo Coll Nottm 90. **d** 92 **p** 93. C Lutterworth w Cotesbach *Leic* 92-95; P-in-c Mountsorrel Ch Ch and St Pet 95-97; V 97-03; rtd 03; Perm to Offic *Leic* from 03. *11 Cooper Lane, Ratby, Leicester LE6 0QG* Tel 0116-238 7959

BRODRIBB, Carolyn Ann. b 48. Plymouth Univ MA CQSW. **d** 04 **p** 05. NSM Plymstock and Hooe *Ex* 04-06; C Dolton 06-07; P-in-c from 07; C Iddesleigh w Dowland 06-07; P-in-c from 07; C Monkokehampton 06-07; P-in-c from 07. *The Rectory, Cleave Hill, Dolton, Winkleigh EX19 8QT* Tel (01805) 804264 E-mail carolynbrodribb@aol.com

BRODY, Paul. b 40. NOC 85. **d** 88 **p** 89. C Leigh St Mary *Man* 88-90; C Peel 90-91; TR 91-97; TV Worsley 97-07; rtd 07; Perm to Offic *Man* from 07. *29 Parkfield Avenue, Tyldesley, Manchester M29 7BE* Tel (01942) 700102 E-mail brendabrody@blueyonder.co.uk

BROGGIO, Bernice Muriel Croager. b 35. Bedf Coll Lon BA57 K Coll Lon BD66. dss 84 **d** 87 **p** 94. Bris St Paul w St Barn 84-87; Hon Par Dn Bris St Paul's 87-88; C Charlton St Luke w H Trin *S'wark* 88-95; V Upper Tooting H Trin 95-03; Hon Can S'wark Cathl 95-03; RD Tooting 96-02; TV Bensham *Dur* 03-05; Hon C 06-07; rtd 06; Hon C Birtley *Dur* from 07. *86 Woodburn, Gateshead NE10 8LY* Tel 0191-495 0959 Mobile 07900-327316 E-mail bernicebroggio@hotmail.com

BROMAGE, Kenneth Charles. b 51. EAMTC. **d** 90 **p** 91. NSM Woolpit w Drinkstone *St E* 90-92; Chapl RN from 92. *Royal Naval Chaplaincy Service, Mail Point 1-2, Leach Building, Whale Island, Portsmouth PO2 8BY* Tel (023) 9262 5055 Fax 9262 5134

BROMFIELD, Michael. b 32. Kelham Th Coll 54 Lich Th Coll 59. **d** 62 **p** 63. C Sedgley All SS *Lich* 62-64; C Tunstall Ch Ch 64-67; P-in-c Grindon 67-70; R 70-80; P-in-c Butterton 67-70; V 70-80; R Hope Bowdler w Eaton-under-Heywood *Heref* 80-97; R Rushbury 80-97; V Cardington 80-97; rtd 98; Perm to Offic *Lich* from 98. *11 Walklate Avenue, Newcastle ST5 0PR* Tel (01782) 630716 E-mail bromfield@stoke54.freeserve.co.uk

BROMFIELD, Nicholas Robert. b 60. St Jo Coll Cam MA82. WEMTC 98. **d** 02 **p** 03. C Tidenham w Beachley and Lancaut *Glouc* 02-07; C St Briavels w Hewelsfield 05-07; R Drybrook, Lydbrook and Ruardean from 07. *The Rectory, Oakland Road, Harrow Hill, Drybrook GL17 9JX* Tel (01594) 542232 E-mail bromfields@email.msn.com

BROMFIELD, Richard Allan. b 47. Sussex Univ MA96 LVCM85. Chich Th Coll 86. **d** 88 **p** 89. C Durrington *Chich* 88-95; V Woodingdean from 95; Chapl Nuffield Hosp Brighton from 96. *Woodingdean Vicarage, 2 Downsway, Brighton BN2 6BD* Tel (01273) 681582 E-mail r.a.bromfield@btinternet.com

BROMILEY, Paul Nigel. b 49. Univ of Wales (Cardiff) BSc71. Oak Hill Th Coll 88. **d** 90 **p** 91. C Gee Cross *Ches* 90-94; P-in-c Millbrook 94-03; Master Wyggeston's Hosp *Leic* from 03. *Master's House, Wyggeston's Hospital, Hinckley Road, Leicester LE3 0UX* Tel 0116-254 8682 or 255 9174 E-mail wyggeston.hospital@connectfree.co.uk

BROMILEY, Philip Arthur. b 73. Westmr Coll Ox BTh94 St Jo Coll Dur MA98. Cranmer Hall Dur 95. **d** 98 **p** 99. C Marton *Blackb* 98-01; Assoc P Calne and Blackland *Sarum* 01-06; P-in-c Oldbury 06-08; R from 08. *The Rectory, The Street, Cherhill, Calne SN11 8XR* Tel (01249) 820062
E-mail philbromiley@cybermail.uk.com
BROMILEY, Mrs Janet Catherine Gay. b 45. Surrey Univ BSc68 Bradf Univ MSc72 Brunel Tech Coll Bris FE TCert86. S Dios Minl Tr Scheme 91. **d** 94 **p** 96. C Westbury-on-Trym H Trin *Bris* 94-96; C Wroughton 96-00; Dean of Women's Min 98-00; R Dursley *Glouc* from 00; AD Dursley 07-09. *The Rectory, Broadwell, Dursley GL11 4JE* Tel (01453) 542053
E-mail revjanet@dursleyparishchurch.freeserve.co.uk
BROMILEY, Richard. b 60. Birm Chr Coll MA02. **d** 08 **p** 09. NSM Binley *Cov* from 08. *22 Chaceley Close, Coventry CV2 2SF* Tel (024) 7660 4152 Mobile 07803-888257
E-mail richard@yehright.com
BROMILEY AND BEXLEY, Archdeacon of. *See* WRIGHT, The Ven Paul
BRONNERT, Preb David Llewellyn Edward. b 36. Ch Coll Cam BA57 MA61 PhD61 Lon Univ BD62. Tyndale Hall Bris 60. **d** 63 **p** 64. C Cheadle Hulme St Andr *Ches* 63-67; C Islington St Mary *Lon* 67-69; Chapl N Lon Poly 69-75; V Southall Green St Jo 75-01; Preb St Paul's Cathl 89-01; P-in-c Southall St Geo 92-99; AD Ealing W 84-90; rtd 01; Perm to Offic *Ox* from 04. *101 Walton Way, Aylesbury HP21 7JP* Tel (01296) 484048
E-mail david.bronnert@talk21.com
BRONNERT, John. b 33. Man Univ MA(Theol)84 Univ of Wales (Lamp) PhD98 ACA57 FCA68. Tyndale Hall Bris 65. **d** 68 **p** 69. C Hoole *Ches* 68-71; P-in-c Parr *Liv* 71-73; TV 73-85; V Runcorn St Jo Weston *Ches* 85-98; rtd 98; Perm to Offic *Liv* 85-04; *Man* from 98. *Tyndale, 15 Craig Avenue, Flixton, Urmston, Manchester M41 5RS* Tel 0161-748 7061
E-mail revddrjohn.bronnert@tiscali.co.uk
BROOK, David Thomas. b 46. **d** 11. OLM Lt Aston *Lich* from 11. *35 Kensington Drive, Sutton Coldfield B74 4UD* Tel 0121-353 6106 E-mail d brook@sky.com
BROOK, John Brendan Paul. b 79. CCC Ox MEng01. Oak Hill Th Coll BA06. **d** 06 **p** 07. C Hailsham *Chich* 06-10; Min The Haven CD from 10. *1 Columbus Drive, Eastbourne BN23 6RR* Tel (01323) 325989 E-mail jbrook@gmail.com
BROOK, Jonathan Roger Wilson. b 67. St Jo Coll Nottm 05. **d** 07 **p** 08. C Ripley *Derby* 07-10; TV N Wingfield, Clay Cross and Pilsley from 10. *The Vicarage, Stretton Road, Clay Cross, Chesterfield S45 9AQ* Tel 07939-472799 (mobile)
E-mail jonathan-susie.brook@tiscali.co.uk
BROOK, Neville. *See* BROOK, William Neville
BROOK, Peter Geoffrey (Brother Simon). b 47. NOC 91. **d** 94 **p** 95. CGA from 71; NSM Heywood and Middleton Deanery 94-96; Perm to Offic *Ex* from 96. *The Priory, Lamacraft Farm, Start Point, Chivelstone, Kingsbridge TQ7 2NG* Tel (01548) 511474
BROOK, Priestly. b 42. CBDTI 04. **d** 07 **p** 08. NSM Colne and Villages *Blackb* from 07. *The Coach House, Foulds Road, Trawden, Colne BB8 8NT* Tel (01282) 869876
E-mail philbybrook1@btinternet.com
BROOK, Stephen Edward. b 44. Univ of Wales (Abth) BSc65 DipEd66. Wycliffe Hall Ox 71 All Nations Chr Coll 85. **d** 74 **p** 75. C Haworth H Trin *York* 74-77; C Linthorpe 77-80; TV Deane *Man* 80-85; Crosslinks 86-96; Portugal 88-96; P-in-c Bacup St Sav *Man* 96-03; P-in-c Tunstead 99-03; V Blackpool St Mark *Blackb* from 03; P-in-c Blackpool St Mich from 10. *St Mark's Vicarage, 163 Kingscote Drive, Blackpool FY3 8EH* Tel (01253) 392895 E-mail stephen.brook2@virgin.net
BROOK, William *Neville*. b 31. S'wark Ord Course 66. **d** 69 **p** 70. C Maidstone St Martin *Cant* 69-75; V Hartlip w Stockbury 75-80; R Willesborough w Hinxhill 80-87; R Willesborough 87-89; V Gt Staughton and Hail Weston *Ely* 89-96; rtd 96; Perm to Offic *Chich* from 96. *27 Middleton Drive, Eastbourne BN23 6HD* Tel (01323) 731243
BROOKE, Miss Bridget Cecilia. b 31. Coll of Resurr Mirfield 88. **d** 89 **p** 94. Hon Par Dn Ranmoor *Sheff* 89-94; Hon C 94-04; Bp's Adv for NSMs 94-01; Perm to Offic from 04. *166 Tom Lane, Sheffield S10 3PG* Tel 0114-230 2147
BROOKE, David Fewsdale. b 43. St Paul's Coll Grahamstown 80. **d** 90 **p** 90. Asst Chapl Dioc Coll Cape Town S Africa 90-92; NSM Crawford St Jo 93-97; NSM Sea Point St Jas 98-99; Perm to Offic *Newc* 00; C Norham and Duddo 01-04; C Cornhill w Carham 01-04; C Branxton 01-04; R Dunkeld *St And* from 04; R Strathtay from 04. *Spoutside, Snaigow, Dunkeld PH8 0RD* Tel (01738) 710726 E-mail stmarys.birnam@btinternet.com
BROOKE, David Martin. b 58. Selw Coll Cam BA80 MA83 Lon Inst of Educn PGCE81. SAOMC 96. **d** 99 **p** 00. C Luton Lewsey St Hugh *St Alb* 99-00; NSM Sunnyside w Bourne End 00-02; C 02-04; V Bishopton w Gt Stainton *Dur* from 04; R Redmarshall from 04; R Grindon, Stillington and Wolviston from 04; P-in-c Billingham St Mary from 10; AD Stockton from 07. *The*

Rectory, Church Lane, Redmarshall, Stockton-on-Tees TS21 1ES Tel (01740) 630810 Mobile 07967-326085
E-mail revdbrooke@stocktonsix.org.uk *or* david@revd.co.uk
BROOKE, Katherine Margaret. b 58. GRSM79 LRAM80 ARCM80. SAOMC 01. **d** 04 **p** 05. C Auckland St Andr and St Anne *Dur* 04-07; C Stranton 07-11; Chapl HM Pris Holme Ho from 11. *HM Prison Holme House, Holme House Road, Stockton-on-Tees TS18 2QU* Tel (01642) 744115 Mobile 07973-539729 E-mail katherine.brooke@hmps.gsi.gov.uk
BROOKE, Canon Robert. b 44. Qu Coll Birm 70. **d** 73 **p** 74. C Man Resurr 73-76; C Bournville *Birm* 76-77; Chapl Qu Eliz Coll *Lon* 77-82; C Bramley *Ripon* 82-85; TV 85-86; V Hunslet Moor St Pet and St Cuth 86-93; Chapl People w Learning Disabilities from 86; TV Seacroft 93-03; TV Beeston 03-10; Chapl Leeds Mental Health Teaching NHS Trust 94-03; Hon Can Ripon Cathl 01-10; rtd 10. *103 Crossgates Road, Leeds LS15 7PA* E-mail bob.brooke@another.com
BROOKE, Canon Rosemary Jane. b 53. Cam Univ BEd75 Open Univ BA83. NOC 86. **d** 89 **p** 94. NSM Poynton *Ches* 89-05; Bp's Adv for Women in Min 96-05; P-in-c Werneth 05-10; Can Res Ches Cathl from 10. *3 Bridge Place, Chester CH1 1SA* Tel (01244) 351432 E-mail scrolls2@btinternet.com
BROOKE, Timothy Cyril. b 38. Jes Coll Cam BA60 MA70 Middx Poly CQSW76. Ripon Coll Cuddesdon 84. **d** 86 **p** 87. C Hillmorton *Cov* 86-90; V Earlsdon 90-98; V Cov St Fran N Radford 98-05; Perm to Offic *Cov* from 05. *80 Broadway, Coventry CV5 6NU* Tel (024) 7667 9126
E-mail brookenet@zetnet.co.uk
BROOKE, Vernon. b 41. St Aid Birkenhead 62. **d** 65 **p** 66. C Crofton Park St Hilda w St Cypr *S'wark* 65-68; C Eccleshill *Bradf* 68-70; Ind Chapl *Linc* 70-84; Ind Chapl *Derby* 84-97; Ind Chapl *Chich* 97-06; rtd 06; Perm to Offic *Pet* from 06. *5 Blakesley Close, Northampton NN2 8PA* Tel (01604) 845585
E-mail vernonbrooke@yahoo.co.uk
BROOKE, Canon William Edward. b 13. Birm Univ BA34 MA35. Westcott Ho Cam 35. **d** 37 **p** 38. C Wylde Green *Birm* 37-40; C Sparkbrook St Agatha 40-44; P-in-c Birm St Jude 44-50; V 50-60; R Castle Bromwich SS Mary and Marg 60-78; Hon Can Birm Cathl 61-78; rtd 78; Perm to Offic *Heref* from 78. *clo V T Jordan Esq, New House Farm, Much Marcle, Ledbury HR8 2PH*
BROOKER, Mrs Anna Lesley. b 56. York Univ BA78 MA79 Homerton Coll Cam PGCE80. Ridley Hall Cam 01. **d** 03 **p** 04. C Brentford *Lon* 03-06; P-in-c Isleworth All SS from 06. *Butterfield House, 61 Church Street, Isleworth TW7 6BE* Tel (020) 8560 6379 E-mail albrooker@email.com
BROOKER, Ruth Muriel. b 53. Wycliffe Hall Ox 96. **d** 98 **p** 99. C Beverley Minster *York* 98-02; R Haddlesey w Hambleton and Birkin 02-03; Perm to Offic *S'well* 03-04 and *Lich* from 05. *13 West Park Court, Connaught Road, Wolverhampton WV1 4SQ* Tel (01902) 711782 *or* (01384) 233511
E-mail ruth@christianvocations.org
BROOKER, Mrs Wendy Ann. b 41. St Alb Minl Tr Scheme 82. **dss** 85 **d** 87 **p** 94. Pinner *Lon* 85-87; Par Dn Greenhill St Jo 87-88; Ind Chapl 89-94; C Hayes St Edm 95-99; Chapl R Nat Orthopaedic Hosp NHS Trust from 99. *16 Rosecroft Walk, Pinner HA5 1LL* Tel (020) 8866 0795
E-mail wd.brooker@ukf.net
BROOKES, Arthur George. b 21. ACIB52. Worc Ord Coll 64. **d** 66 **p** 67. C Lower Mitton *Worc* 66-67; C Fladbury w Throckmorton, Wyre Piddle and Moor 67-70; C Abberton w Bishampton 67-70; R 70-73; V Cradley 73-78; P-in-c Castle Morton 78-79; P-in-c Holly Bush w Birtsmorton 78-79; P-in-c Castlemorton, Hollybush and Birtsmorton 79-80; P-in-c Norton w Whittington 80-81; TV Worc St Martin w St Pet, St Mark etc 81-86; rtd 86; Perm to Offic *Worc* from 86. *13 Capel Court, The Burgage, Prestbury, Cheltenham GL52 3EL* Tel (01242) 580523
BROOKES, Colin Stuart. b 70. Lon Bible Coll BA93. Ridley Hall Cam 00. **d** 02 **p** 03. C Cambridge St Barn *Ely* 02-06; C Woodside Park St Barn *Lon* from 06. *12 Courthouse Road, London N12 7PJ* Tel (020) 8446 1002 Mobile 07973-840340
E-mail colinbrookes@stbarnabas.co.uk
BROOKES, David Charles. b 45. St Mich Coll Llan 84. **d** 86 **p** 87. C Llanishen and Lisvane 86-88; TV Brighouse St Martin *Wakef* 89-92; TV Brighouse and Clifton 92-94; V Hollingbourne w Hucking w Leeds and Broomfield *Cant* 94-03; rtd 03. *19 Orchards Rise, Richards Castle, Ludlow SY8 4EZ* Tel (01584) 831276 E-mail david@dcbrookes.freeserve.co.uk
BROOKES, Edwin William. b 39. St Mark & St Jo Coll Lon TCert63 Birm Univ BPhil(Ed)85 Open Univ BA73 BA93. OLM course 95. **d** 98 **p** 99. OLM Cen Wolverhampton *Lich* from 98. *23 Chetwynd Road, Blakenhall, Wolverhampton WV2 4NZ* Tel (01902) 654979 Fax 562616
E-mail ed.brookes@blueyonder.co.uk
BROOKES, Geoffrey John Denis. b 24. CMS Tr Coll Crowther Hall 78 Ridley Hall Cam 84. **d** 85 **p** 86. Bahrain 85-88; Project Officer Ch Action w the Unemployed 88-91; Hon C Hastings All So *Chich* 88-91; Asst Chapl Milan w Genoa and Varese *Eur* 91-94; Canada 94-97; Perm to Offic *Chich* 97-99 and 01-02;

Guildf from 03. *50 Chapel Court, Church Street, Dorking RH4 1BT* Tel (01306) 884287

BROOKES, Keith Roy. b 37. JP74. Leeds Univ DipEd72 MHCIMA MRSH. St Aid Birkenhead 64. **d** 80 **p** 81. Hon C Stockport St Thos *Ches* 80-86; Hon C Stockport St Thos w St Pet 86-91; C 91-98; Hon C from 99. *42 Derby Road, Stockport SK4 4NE* Tel 0161-442 0301

BROOKES, Laurence. b 33. **d** 02 **p** 03. OLM Flockton cum Denby Grange *Wakef* 02-06; OLM Emley 02-06; Perm to Offic from 06. *Treetops, 6 Chessington Drive, Flockton, Wakefield WF4 4TJ* Tel (01924) 848238
E-mail lauriemarybrookes@supanet.com

BROOKES, Robin Keenan. b 47. Trin Coll Bris 72. **d** 75 **p** 76. C Livesey *Blackb* 75-78; C Burnley St Pet 78-80; P-in-c Bawdeswell w Foxley *Nor* 80-83; I Donagh w Tyholland and Errigal Truagh *Clogh* 83-91; Dioc Communications Officer 90-91; I Dublin Drumcondra w N Strand *D & G* 91-99; Chapl Ayia Napa Cyprus 99-06; Chapl Famagusta 06-10; Perm to Offic *Nor* from 11. *69 Beresford Road, Lowestoft NR32 2NQ* Tel (01502) 446301 E-mail rkbc1947@gmail.com

BROOKES, Steven David. b 60. Lanc Univ BA81. Ripon Coll Cuddesdon 82. **d** 85 **p** 86. C Stanley *Liv* 85-88; C W Derby St Mary 88-90; Chapl RN 90-94; R Weybridge *Guildf* 94-03; P-in-c Liv Our Lady and St Nic w St Anne 03-07; R Liv Our Lady and St Nic from 07. *The Rector's Lodging, 233 South Ferry Quay, Liverpool L3 4EE* Tel 0151-709 2551 Mobile 07903-505639 E-mail rector@livpc.co.uk

BROOKFIELD, Alun John. b 50. Lon Univ BMus72 Spurgeon's Coll Lon BA82. **d** 00 **p** 01. NSM Stratton St Margaret w S Marston etc *Bris* 00-02; P-in-c Cwmtawe Uchaf *S & B* from 03. *The Vicarage, Heol Tawe, Abercrave, Swansea SA9 1TJ* Tel (01639) 730640 E-mail a.brookfield@virgin.net

BROOKFIELD, Patricia Anne. See HARDACRE, Mrs Patricia Anne

BROOKS, Alan Leslie. b 43. Nor City Coll TCert65. Dioc OLM tr scheme 98. **d** 01 **p** 02. OLM Waterloo Ch Ch and St Jo *Liv* from 01. *6 Kingsway, Waterloo, Liverpool L22 4RQ* Tel 0151-920 8770 E-mail alanbrooks@blueyonder.co.uk

BROOKS, Mrs Alison Margaret. b 46. EMMTC. **d** 03 **p** 04. Asst Chapl Qu Medical Cen Nottm Univ Hosp NHS Trust from 03. *12 Russell Avenue, Nottingham NG8 2BL*

BROOKS, Catherine Elizabeth. b 57. LCTP. **d** 08 **p** 09. C Blackb St Jas from 08. *4 Hawkshaw Bank Road, Blackburn BB1 8JS* Tel (01254) 681175

BROOKS, Mrs Christine Anne. b 62. STETS. **d** 09 **p** 10. C N Poole Ecum Team *Sarum* from 09. *87 Verity Crescent, Poole BH17 8TT* E-mail christine.brooks@ntlworld.com

BROOKS, Mrs Christine Ellen. b 43. Sheff Univ BA65 Lon Univ BD81 Lambeth STh81. EAMTC 86. **d** 88 **p** 94. NSM Palgrave w Wortham and Burgate *St E* 88-89; Par Dn Thorndon w Rishangles, Stoke Ash, Thwaite etc 89-94; P-in-c Aldringham w Thorpe, Knodishall w Buxlow etc 94-04; R Whinlands from 04; Asst P Sternfield w Benhall and Snape 98-03; P-in-c Alde River 03-06. *The Rectory, Aldeburgh Road, Friston, Saxmundham IP17 1NP* Tel (01728) 688972 Mobile 07752-652833 E-mail christine@brook7463.freeserve.co.uk

BROOKS, David Edward. b 73. **d** 09 **p** 10. OLM Middleton and Thornham *Man* from 09. *The Vicarage, Boardman Lane, Middleton, Manchester M24 4TU* Tel 07904-520906 (mobile) E-mail dave@thelaunch.org.uk

BROOKS, Dorothy Anne. See MOORE BROOKS, Dorothy Anne

BROOKS, Canon Francis Leslie. b 35. Kelham Th Coll 55. **d** 59 **p** 60. C Woodlands *Sheff* 59-61; Ind Missr S Yorkshire Coalfields 61-66; V Moorends 66-72; Chapl HM Borstal Hatfield 67-72; Chapl HM Pris Acklington 72-75; Chapl HM Borstal Wellingborough 75-79; Chapl HM Pris Wakef 79-83; Area Sec USPG *Wakef* and *Bradf* 83-88; V Carleton and E Hardwick *Wakef* 88-96; Can Mara (Tanzania) from 88; rtd 96; Perm to Offic *Wakef* 03-04; Hon C Chevington *Newc* from 04. *20 Robsons Way, Amble, Morpeth NE65 0GA* Tel (01665) 712765

BROOKS, Ian George. b 47. Selw Coll Cam BA68 MA72. Chich Th Coll 68. **d** 70 **p** 71. C Stoke Newington St Mary *Lon* 70-74; C Hoxton St Anne w St Sav and St Andr 74-75; C Hoxton St Anne w St Columba 75-80; P-in-c Croxteth St Paul CD *Liv* 80-81; V Croxteth from 81. *St Paul's Vicarage, Delabole Road, Liverpool L11 6LG* Tel and fax 0151-548 9009
E-mail frigb@blueyonder.co.uk

BROOKS, Jeremy Paul. b 67. Leic Univ LLB88 Clare Coll Cam BA96 MA01 K Coll Lon MA00. Ridley Hall Cam 94. **d** 97 **p** 98. C Highgate St Mich *Lon* 97-01; P-in-c Hoddesdon *St Alb* 01-07; V 07-10; TR Beaconsfield *Ox* from 10. *The Rectory, Wycombe End, Beaconsfield HP9 1NB* Tel (01494) 673949 E-mail jpbrooks@ntlworld.com

BROOKS, Jonathan Thorburn. b 53. Solicitor 76 G&C Coll Cam BA75. Trin Coll Bris 84. **d** 86 **p** 87. C Dagenham *Chelmsf* 86-88; Perm to Offic *Glouc* 03; NSM Thornbury and Oldbury-on-

Severn w Shepperdine 03-05. *12 Hyde Avenue, Thornbury, Bristol BS35 1JA* Tel (01454) 411853

BROOKS, Malcolm David. b 45. **d** 71 **p** 72. C Pontllotyn w Fochriw *Llan* 71-72; C Caerphilly 72-78; V Ferndale w Maerdy 78-81; C Port Talbot St Theodore 82-84; V Ystrad Mynach 84-85; V Ystrad Mynach w Llanbradach 85-06. *33 Heol y Gors, Whitchurch, Cardiff CF14 1HF*

BROOKS, Patrick John. b 27. Man Univ BA49 DipEd. Oak Hill Th Coll 78. **d** 77 **p** 79. Burundi 77-80; Perm to Offic *Ex* 80-85; P-in-c Phillack w Gwithian and Gwinear *Truro* 83-88; R 88-93; rtd 93; Perm to Offic *Chich* from 93. *Abbots, Claigmar Road, Rustington, Littlehampton BN16 2NL*

BROOKS, Paul John. b 59. Loughb Univ BSc81. St Jo Coll Nottm 87. **d** 90 **p** 91. C Long Eaton St Jo *Derby* 90-94; Min Jersey St Paul Prop Chpl *Win* from 94. *5 Claremont Avenue, St Saviour, Jersey JE2 7SF* Tel (01534) 880393
E-mail pjbvic@aol.com

BROOKS, Peter. b 55. St Mich Coll Llan 97. **d** 99 **p** 00. C Morriston *S & B* 99-01; P-in-c Rhayader and Nantmel 01-02; P-in-c Cwmdauddwr w St Harmon and Llanwrthwl 02-05; P-in-c Llanwrthwl w St Harmon, Rhayader, Nantmel etc 05-08; P-in-c Gwastedyn from 08. *The Vicarage, Dark Lane, Rhayader LD6 5DA* Tel (01597) 810223
E-mail peter.brooks256@btinternet.com

BROOKS, Philip David. b 52. MA Cam Univ MTh. St Jo Coll Nottm 80. **d** 83 **p** 84. C Ipsley *Worc* 83-87; V Fulford w Hilderstone *Lich* 87-95; Chapl Stallington Hosp 87-95; P-in-c Crich *Derby* 95-01; V Crich and S Wingfield from 01; Dioc Adv Past Care and Counselling from 03; RD Alfreton from 09. *The Vicarage, 19 Coasthill, Crich, Matlock DE4 5DS* Tel (01773) 852449 E-mail philipdbro@aol.com

BROOKS, Mrs Susan Margaret. b 50. Philippa Fawcett Coll CertEd71 Open Univ BA95. SEITE 00. **d** 03 **p** 11. NSM Chatham St Paul w All SS *Roch* 03-05; NSM Snodland All SS w Ch Ch from 11. *189 Malling Road, Snodland ME6 5EE* (01634) 241350 E-mail suebrooks@talk21.com

BROOKS, Mrs Susan Vera. b 51. NOC 87. **d** 90 **p** 94. Par Dn Carleton and E Hardwick *Wakef* 90-93; TV Almondbury w Farnley Tyas 93-98; Chapl Huddersfield NHS Trust 98-01; Chapl Calderdale and Huddersfield NHS Trust 01-03; Lead Chapl from 03. *Royal Infirmary, Acre Street, Huddersfield HD3 3EA* Tel (01484) 342092 *or* 323839
E-mail susan.brooks@cht.nhs.uk

BROOKS, Mrs Vivien June. b 47. Univ of Wales (Ban) BA68 Southn Univ MA70. Ridley Hall Cam 87. **d** 89 **p** 90. C Exning St Martin w Landwade *St E* 89-92; Par Dn Hermitage and Hampstead Norreys, Cold Ash etc *Ox* 92-94; C 94-95; P-in-c Cox Green 95-03; Co Ecum Officer (Berks) 00-03; P-in-c Earls Colne w White Colne and Colne Engaine *Chelmsf* 03-04; TV Halstead Area from 04. *St Andrew's Rectory, 5 Shut Lane, Earls Colne, Colchester CO6 2RE* Tel (01787) 220347
E-mail vbrooks@minnieb.com

BROOKS, Vivienne Christine. See ARMSTRONG-MacDONNELL, Mrs Vivienne Christine

BROOKSBANK, Alan Watson. b 43. Univ of Wales (Lamp) BA64 Edin Univ MEd76. Edin Th Coll 64. **d** 66 **p** 67. C Cleator Moor w Cleator *Carl* 66-70; V Dalston 70-80; P-in-c Greystoke, Matterdale and Mungrisdale 80-81; R 81-83; R Watermillock 81-83; R Hagley *Worc* 83-95; Bp's Officer for NSM 88-95; V Claines St Jo 95-98; rtd 98. *169 Northfields Lane, Brixham TQ5 8RD*

BROOKSHAW, Miss Janice Chitty. b 48. MCIPD90. Ripon Coll Cuddesdon 96. **d** 98 **p** 99. C Beaconsfield *Ox* 98-02; P-in-c The Stodden Churches *St Alb* 02-03; R from 03. *Stodden Rectory, High Street, Upper Dean, Huntingdon PE28 0ND* Tel and fax (01234) 708531 E-mail jan@revbrookshaw.freeserve.co.uk

BROOM, Canon Andrew Clifford. b 65. Keele Univ BSocSc86. Trin Coll Bris BA92. **d** 92 **p** 93. C Wellington All SS w Eyton *Lich* 92-96; C Brampton St Thos *Derby* 96-00; V Walton St Jo 00-09; Dir of Miss and Min from 09; Hon Can Derby Cathl from 11. *15 Old Pheasant Court, Chesterfield S40 3GY*
E-mail andy@atdc.wanadoo.co.uk

BROOM, Jacqueline Anne. b 52. R Holloway Coll Lon BSc73. Trin Coll Bris 79. dss 82 **d** 95 **p** 95. Easton H Trin w St Gabr and St Lawr and St Jude *Bris* 82-86; OMF Internat 87-01; Hong Kong 87-95; Macao China 96-01; rtd 01; Perm to Offic *B & W* from 02. *30 Wesley Drive, Weston-super-Mare BS22 7TH* Tel (01934) 521180

BROOME, David Curtis. b 36. Leeds Univ BA63. Coll of Resurr Mirfield. **d** 65 **p** 66. C Winshill *Derby* 65-69; C Leigh-on-Sea St Marg *Chelmsf* 69-74; V Leek St Marg *Ripon* 74-81; V Stoke H Cross w Dunston *Nor* 81-93; P-in-c Arminghall 92-93; P-in-c Caistor w Markshall 92-93; R Stoke H Cross w Dunston, Arminghall etc 93-00; rtd 00; Perm to Offic *Nor* from 00. *13 Greenacres Drive, Poringland, Norwich NR14 7JG* Tel (01508) 493201

BROOME, Mildred Dorothy. b 43. **d** 00 **p** 01. NSM Malden St Jo *S'wark* from 00. *124 The Manor Drive, Worcester Park KT4 7LW* Tel (020) 8337 1572

BROOMFIELD, David John. b 37. Reading Univ BA59. Oak Hill Th Coll 64. **d** 66 **p** 67. C Gresley *Derby* 66-71; C Rainham *Chelmsf* 71-77; R High Ongar w Norton Mandeville 77-88; RD Ongar 83-88; P-in-c Stanford Rivers 84-86; P-in-c Loughton St Mary and St Mich 88-95; P-in-c Loughton St Mary 95-97; V 97-03; rtd 03; Perm to Offic *Glouc* from 03. *15 Oriel Grove, Moreton-in-Marsh GL56 0ED* Tel (01608) 651023 E-mail david@dabroomfield.freeserve.co.uk

BROOMFIELD, Iain Jonathan. b 57. Univ Coll Ox MA87. Wycliffe Hall Ox 80. **d** 83 **p** 84. C Beckenham Ch Ch *Roch* 83-87; Sen Schs Worker Titus Trust 87-00; V Bromley Ch Ch *Roch* from 00. *Christ Church Vicarage, 18 Highland Road, Bromley BR1 4AD* Tel (020) 8313 9882 *or* 8464 1898 Fax 8464 5846 E-mail iain.broomfield@christchurchbromley.org

BROOMHEAD, Mark Roger. b 71. Nottm Univ BSc00. St Jo Coll Nottm 06. **d** 08 **p** 09. C N Wingfield, Clay Cross and Pilsley *Derby* 08-10; C Brampton St Thos from 10. *35 Whitecotes Park, Chesterfield S40 3RT* Tel (01246) 555988

BROSNAN, Mark. b 61. St Martin's Coll Lanc BA83 RMN88 Otley Agric Coll. EAMTC 92. **d** 95 **p** 96. C Rushmere *St E* 95-98; Perm to Offic *Chelmsf* 01-05; Hon C W w E Mersea 05-08; Hon C Peldon w Gt and Lt Wigborough 05-08; P-in-c Hadleigh St Barn from 08. *The Vicarage, 169 Church Road, Hadleigh, Benfleet SS7 2EJ* Tel (01702) 554658 E-mail gohiking@hotmail.co.uk

BROSTER, Godfrey David. b 52. Ealing Tech Coll BA75. Ripon Coll Cuddesdon 78. **d** 81 **p** 82. C Crayford *Roch* 81-82; C Brighton Resurr *Chich* 82-86; C-in-c The Hydneye CD 86-91; R Plumpton w E Chiltington 91-93; R Plumpton w F. Chiltington cum Novington from 93. *The Rectory, Station Road, Plumpton Green, Lewes BN7 3BU* Tel (01273) 890570

BROTHERSTON, Miss Isabel Mary. b 42. Cranmer Hall Dur 81. **dss** 83 **d** 87 **p** 94. Coleshill *Birm* 83-87; Par Dn Duddeston w Nechells 87-92; Par Dn Harlescott *Lich* 92-94; C 94-04; R Llanddulas and Llysfaen *St As* 04-08; rtd 08. *3 Marlow Terrace, Mold CH7 1HH* Tel (01352) 756011 E-mail mbrother@live.co.uk

BROTHERTON, The Ven John Michael. b 35. St Jo Coll Cam BA59 MA63. Cuddesdon Coll 59. **d** 61 **p** 62. C Chiswick St Nic w St Mary *Lon* 61-65; Chapl Trin Coll Port of Spain Trinidad 65-69; R Diego Martin 69-75; V Cowley St Jo and Chapl St Hilda's Coll Ox 76-81; RD Cowley 78-81; V Portsea St Mary *Portsm* 81-91; Hon Can Kobe Japan from 86; Adn Chich 91-02; rtd 02; Perm to Offic *Chich* and *Lon* from 03. *Flat 2, 23 Gledhow Gardens, London SW5 0AZ* Tel (020) 7373 5147 E-mail jmbrotherton@amserve.com

BROTHERTON, Michael. b 56. MBE93. Univ of Wales (Abth) BD80. Wycliffe Hall Ox 80. **d** 81 **p** 82. Hon Chapl Miss to Seamen 81-84; C Pembroke Dock *St D* 81-84; Chapl RN from 84. *Royal Naval Chaplaincy Service, Mail Point 1-2, Leach Building, Whale Island, Portsmouth PO2 8BY* Tel (023) 9262 5055 Fax 9262 5134

BROTHERWOOD, Nicholas Peter. b 50. Oak Hill Th Coll BA83. **d** 83 **p** 84. C Nottingham St Nic *S'well* 83-86; Canada from 86; Dir Quebec Lodge 86-89; Angl Chapl McGill Univ 89-91; Assoc R Westmount St Steph from 91. *3498 Harvard Avenue, Montreal QC H4A 2W3, Canada* Tel (001) (514) 489 4158 Fax 932 0550 E-mail st.stephens@qc.aira.com

BROTHWELL, Paul David. b 37. Lich Th Coll 62. **d** 65 **p** 66. C Honley *Wakef* 65-68; Min Can Wakef Cathl 68-71; V Whittington St Giles *Lich* 71-83; P-in-c Weeford 78-83; V Whittington w Weeford 83-92; Chapl Kidderminster Gen Hosp 92-94; Chapl Kidderminster Health Care NHS Trust 94-01; Chapl Worcs Community and Mental Health Trust 01-02; Hon Can Antananarivo 02; rtd 02; Perm to Offic *Worc* from 02. *8 Hillside Close, Stourport-on-Severn DY13 0JW* Tel (01299) 823495 *or* (01562) 823424 ext 3306

BROTHWELL, Ruth. b 10. NSM Merrow *Guildf* from 10. *Foxgrove, Burnt Common Lane, Ripley, Woking GU23 6HD* Tel (01483) 223571 E-mail ruthbrothwell@yahoo.com

BROTHWOOD, Ian Sidney. b 56. K Coll Lon BD84. Linc Th Coll 87. **d** 89 **p** 90. C Selsdon St Jo w St Fran *S'wark* 89-93; P-in-c S Norwood St Alb 93-97; V 97-99; V Reigate St Mark 99-04; P-in-c Selsdon St Jo w St Fran 04-06; R from 06. *St John's Rectory, Upper Selsdon Road, South Croydon CR2 8DD* Tel (020) 8657 2343 E-mail iansb@aol.com

BROTHWOOD, John. b 31. Peterho Cam MA55 MB, BChir55. S'wark Ord Course 89. **d** 91 **p** 92. NSM Dulwich St Barn *S'wark* 91-04. *98 Woodwarde Road, London SE22 8UT* Tel (020) 8693 8273

BROUGH, Gerald William. b 32. Trin Coll Cam BA55 MA59. Ridley Hall Cam 55. **d** 57 **p** 58. C Westgate St Jas *Cant* 57-60; C New Addington 60-62; V Mancetter *Cov* 62-73; P-in-c Bourton w Frankton and Stretton on Dunsmore etc 73-74; R 74-93; rtd 93; Perm to Offic *Cov* from 93. *17 Brookhurst Court, Beverley Road, Leamington Spa CV32 6PB* Tel (01926) 430759 E-mail gwbris@aol.com

BROUGH (née CROWLE), Mrs Sarah Ann. b 65. Ripon Coll Cuddesdon BTh99. **d** 99 **p** 00. C Godalming *Guildf* 99-03; Chapl

Godalming Coll 01-03; R Chiddingfold *Guildf* from 03. *The Rectory, Coxcombe Lane, Chiddingfold, Godalming GU8 4QA* Tel (01428) 682008 Mobile 07747-031524 E-mail sarahbrough@btinternet.com

BROUGHALL, Rodney John. b 32. **d** 96 **p** 97. OLM Watton w Carbrooke and Ovington *Nor* 96-02; rtd 02; Perm to Offic *Nor* from 02. *15 Garden Close, Watton, Thetford IP25 6DP* Tel (01953) 881989 E-mail rodbroughall@hotmail.com

BROUGHTON, James Roger. b 48. Leeds Univ BA71 Nottm Univ CertEd72 Liv Univ MEd00. Wycliffe Hall Ox 87. **d** 89 **p** 90. C Stoneycroft All SS *Liv* 89-92; P-in-c Carr Mill 92-94; V 94-96; Chapl Duke of York's R Mil Sch Dover 96-08; rtd 08; Perm to Offic *Cant* from 08. *Woodstock, St Vincent Road, St Margarets-at-Cliffe, Dover CT15 6ET* Tel (01304) 853840

BROUGHTON, Lynne Mary. b 46. Melbourne Univ BA67 PhD79. EAMTC 99. **d** 00 **p** 01. NSM Wood Ditton w Saxon Street *Ely* 00-07; NSM Kirtling 00-07; NSM Cheveley 00-07; NSM Ashley w Silverley 00-07; Perm to Offic from 07. *85 Richmond Road, Cambridge CB4 3PS* Tel (01223) 322014 E-mail lmb27@hermes.cam.ac.uk

BROUGHTON, Canon Stuart Roger. b 36. Wilson Carlile Coll 59 St Mich Coll Llan 61. **d** 64 **p** 65. C Bromley Ch Ch *Roch* 64-67; SAMS 67-79 and 86-95; Miss Paraguayan Chaco Paraguay 67-70; R Salvador Gd Shep Brazil 70-79; V Stoke sub Hamdon *B & W* 79-83; Hon CF 82-86; V Blackb Ch Ch w St Matt 83-86; R Alcacer do Sal Portugal 86-91; Chapl Rio de Janeiro Brazil 91-95; rtd 96; Chapl Aigla Napa Cyprus 96; Chapl Ch Ch Cathl Falkland Is 97-98; P-in-c Corfu *Eur* 98-01; Hon C Jersey St Paul Prop Chpl *Win* 01-03; Chapl to Abp Congo from 03; Hon Can Bukavu from 04. *c/o P Broughton Esq, Point Cottage, 29 Fir Tree Lane, Littleton, Chester CH3 7DN* E-mail stuartrbroughton@hotmail.com

BROUN, Canon Claud Michael. b 30. BNC Ox BA55. Edin Th Coll 56. **d** 58 **p** 59. Chapl St Mary's Cathl 58-62; Can St Mary's Cathl 84-95; Hon Can from 95; P-in-c Cambuslang 62-70; R 70-75; R Hamilton 75-88; R Gatehouse of Fleet 88-95; R Kirkcudbright 88-95; rtd 95. *Martin Lodge, Ardross Place, Alness IV17 0PX* Tel (01349) 882442

BROWELL (née SHILLINGTON), Mrs Maureen Lesley. b 57. MIH89. NEOC 02. **d** 05 **p** 06. Soc Resp Officer *Ripon* 99-08; NSM Hoylandswaine and Silkstone w Stainborough *Wakef* 05-08; TV Almondbury w Farnley Tyas from 08; Dioc Co-ord for Soc Resp from 08. *The Vicarage, 150 Fleminghouse Lane, Huddersfield HD5 8UD* Tel (01484) 545085 Mobile 07930-194421 E-mail maureenbrowell@talktalk.net

BROWN, Mrs Ailsa Elizabeth. b 64. Hull Univ BA94 Nottm Univ MA10. EMMTC 07. **d** 10 **p** 11. NSM Barton upon Humber *Linc* from 10. *21 Ferriby Road, Barton-upon-Humber DN18 5LE* Tel (01652) 634855 E-mail brown5le@btinternet.com

BROWN, Canon Alan. b 37. Tyndale Hall Bris 59. **d** 63 **p** 64. C Braintree *Chelmsf* 63-66; C Tooting Graveney St Nic *S'wark* 66-68; C Chesham St Mary *Ox* 68-70; V Hornsey Rise St Mary *Lon* 70-75; V Sidcup Ch Ch *Roch* 75-88; V Newport St Jo *Portsm* 88-01; P-in-c Newport St Thos 96-99; V 99-01; RD W Wight 91-96; Hon Can Portsm Cathl 95-01; rtd 01. *65 Sherbourne Avenue, Ryde PO33 3PW* Tel (01983) 566956

BROWN, Alan George. b 51. Bradf Univ BSc84 Leeds Univ CertEd81 MBA92 SRN72 RMN75 RNT81. NOC 92. **d** 95 **p** 96. NSM Ilkley St Marg *Bradf* from 95; Hd of Division Applied Health Studies Leeds Univ from 98; Bp's Adv for Hosp Chapl from 03. *Waverley, Wheatley Road, Ilkley LS29 8TS* Tel and fax (01943) 601115 E-mail alan.brown@bradford.anglican.org

BROWN, Alan Michael Ernest. b 52. St Chad's Coll Dur BA74. St Jo Coll Nottm 81. **d** 83 **p** 84. C Bridlington Priory *York* 83-86; V Morton St Luke *Bradf* 86-02; Perm to Offic from 02; Mental Health Worker Bradf City Primary Care Trust 02-07. *6 South View Terrace, Bingley BD16 3EJ* Tel (01274) 511970

BROWN, Albert Harry Alfred Victor. b 12. **d** 81 **p** 83. OLM Kennington Park St Agnes *S'wark* 81-92; Perm to Offic 92-00 and 05-07. *23/20 The Royal Hospital, London SW3 4SI* Tel (020) 7274 5982

BROWN, Alec George. b 53. Univ of Zimbabwe DipSW80 Univ of Wales (Cardiff) MSc(Econ)87. St Deiniol's Hawarden 88 NOC 90. **d** 92 **p** 93. C Stockton Heath *Ches* 95-96; C Thelwall 96-97; V 97-01; V Gt Budworth from 01; RD Gt Budworth from 10. *The Vicarage, High Street, Great Budworth, Northwich CW9 6HF* Tel (01606) 891324 E-mail alec.brown@tiscali.co.uk

BROWN, Mrs Alison Louise. b 60. RGN83. STETS 05. **d** 08 **p** 09. C Horsell *Guildf* from 08. *6 Waldens Park Road, Woking GU21 4RN* Tel (01483) 764094 E-mail alison@slbalb.co.uk

BROWN, Allan James. b 47. K Coll Lon BD69 AKC69 MTh70. St Aug Coll Cant 69. **d** 73 **p** 74. Chapl St Geo Sch Jerusalem 73-74; Chapl St Marg Sch Nazareth 74-75; C Clifton *S'well* 75-77; CF 77-99; Asst Chapl Gen 99-00; V Ilkeston St Mary *Derby* 00-10; P-in-c Ilkeston St Jo 05-10; rtd 10; Perm to Offic *S'well* from 10. *63 Highfield Road, Nottingham NG2 6DR* E-mail brown@lorisallan.freeserve.co.uk

BROWN, Canon Andrew. b 55. St Pet Hall Ox BA80 MA82. Ridley Hall Cam 79. d 80 p 81. C Burnley St Pet *Blackb* 80-82; C Elton All SS *Man* 82-86; P-in-c Ashton St Pet 86-93; V 94-96; V Halliwell St Luke 96-03; Can Th Derby Cathl from 03; Dioc CME Adv from 03. *149 Church Road, Quarndon, Derby DE22 5JA* Tel (01332) 553424 E-mail andie.brown@tiscali.co.uk

BROWN, Andrew. b 65. d 95 p 96. OLM Heywood *Man* 95-05. *24 Honiton Close, Heywood OL10 2PF* Tel (01706) 623091

BROWN, Andrew. b 71. d 11. C Walton Breck *Liv* from 11. *83 Crosswood Crescent, Liverpool L36 2QF*

BROWN, Andrew (Bod). b 66. Man Univ BSc87. Oak Hill Th Coll BA02. d 03 p 04. C Hyde St Geo *Ches* 03-06; V Weaverham from 06. *The Vicarage, Church Street, Weaverham, Northwich CW8 3NJ* Tel (01606) 852110

BROWN, Andrew James. b 60. Univ of Wales (Ban) BA81. Ripon Coll Cuddesdon 07. d 09 p 10. C Castle Bromwich SS Mary and Marg *Birm* from 09. *16 Oldington Grove, Solihull B91 3NF* Tel 05602-710769 Mobile 07974-947126 E-mail father.brown@btinternet.com

BROWN, Anne Elizabeth. b 61. SWMTC 06. d 09 p 10. C Probus, Ladock and Grampound w Creed and St Erme *Truro* from 09. *The Rectory, Ladock, Truro TR2 4PL* Tel (01726) 883593 E-mail ladockrectory@btinternet.com

BROWN, Anthony Frank Palmer. b 31. Fitzw Ho Cam BA56 Fitzw Coll Cam MA84. Cuddesdon Coll 56. d 58 p 59. C Aldershot St Mich *Guildf* 58-61; C Chiswick St Nic w St Mary *Lon* 61-66; Asst Chapl Lon Univ 65-70; Lic to Offic 70-72; C-in-c Hammersmith SS Mich and Geo White City Estate CD 72-74; P-in-c Upper Sunbury St Sav 74-80; V 80-01; rtd 01; Perm to Offic *Chich* from 02. *6 Church Lane, Ditchling, Hassocks BN6 8TB* Tel (01273) 843847

BROWN, Preb Anthony Paul. b 55. Reading Univ BSc75 MRICS87. Qu Coll Birm 77. d 80 p 81. C Pelsall *Lich* 80-83; C Leighton Buzzard w Eggington, Hockliffe etc *St Alb* 83-87; TV Langley Marish *Ox* 87-93; V Pet St Mary Boongate 93-98; TR Wombourne w Trysull and Bobbington *Lich* 98-02; TR Smestow Vale from 02; Preb Lich Cathl from 09. *The Vicarage, School Road, Wombourne, Wolverhampton WV5 9ED* Tel (01902) 892234 *or* 897700 E-mail revpbrown@aol.com

BROWN, Antony William Keith. b 26. RN Coll Dartmouth 43. Trin Coll Bris 86. d 87 p 88. NSM Lawrence Weston *Bris* 87-89; Chapl Casablanca *Eur* 89-93; Asst Chapl Paris St Mich 94-00; rtd 00; Perm to Offic *Bris* from 01. *13 Marklands, 37 Julian Road, Bristol BS9 1NP* Tel and fax 0117-377 6543 E-mail ansh.brown@blueyonder.co.uk

BROWN, Arthur Basil Etheredge. b 17. Reading Univ BA39. Wycliffe Hall Ox 46. d 47 p 48. C Camborne *Truro* 47-50; Org Sec (Midl) CPAS 50-53; PC Scarborough H Trin *York* 53-58; V Heworth H Trin 58-66; R Camborne *Truro* 66-82; rtd 82; Perm to Offic *Truro* from 82. *14 Tregenna Fields, Camborne TR14 7QS* Tel (01209) 716196

BROWN, Arthur William Stawell. b 26. St Jo Coll Ox BA50 MA51. Cuddesdon Coll 63. d 65 p 66. C Edin St Jo 65-66; C Petersfield w Sheet *Portsm* 67-75; V Portsea St Alb 75-79; R Smithfield St Bart Gt *Lon* 79-91; R St Sepulchre w Ch Ch Greyfriars etc 81-91; Chapl Madeira *Eur* 90-93; rtd 91; Perm to Offic *Ex* 93-09. *Clare Park, Crondall, Farnham GU10 5DT* Tel (01252) 851200

BROWN, Barry Ronald. b 48. Ridley Coll Melbourne ThL72. d 73 p 74. Australia 73-77 and 82-95; C Richmond St Mary *S'wark* 78-79; C Richmond St Mary w St Matthias and St Jo 79; C Edin Old St Paul 79-80; Chapl Belgrade w Zagreb *Eur* 81-82; Canada from 95. *52 Queen Street, Belleville ON K8N 1T7, Canada* Tel (001) (613) 968 9873 E-mail bbrownhome@hotmail.com

BROWN, Canon Bernard Herbert Vincent. b 26. Mert Coll Ox BA50 MA52. Westcott Ho Cam 50. d 52 p 53. C Rugby St Andr *Cov* 52-56; C Stoke Bishop *Bris* 56-59; Youth Chapl 56-62; Ind Chapl *Roch* 62-73; Bp's Dom Chapl 66-73; R Crawley *Chich* 73-79; TR 79-83; Ind Chapl *Bris* 83-92; Bp's Soc and Ind Adv 84-92; Hon Can Bris Cathl 85-92; RD Bris City 85-91; rtd 92; Perm to Offic *Sarum* from 92. *33B London Road, Dorchester DT1 1NF* Tel (01305) 260806

BROWN, Bernard Maurice Newall. b 26. Oak Hill Th Coll 47. d 51 p 52. C Penn Fields *Lich* 51-53; S Area Sec BCMS 53-55; Kenya 55-62; R Hartshorne *Derby* 62-68; V Stapenhill w Cauldwell 68-72; C Weston-super-Mare Ch Ch B & W 72-74; R Spaxton w Charlynch 74-80; rtd 80. *12 Ewart Road, Weston-super-Mare BS22 8NU* Tel (01934) 412170

BROWN, Bill Charles Balfour. b 44. Linc Th Coll 87. d 89 p 90. C Moulsham St Luke *Chelmsf* 89-91; C Prittlewell 91-94; V Worksop St Paul *S'wark* from 95. *St Paul's Vicarage, Cavendish Road, Worksop S80 2QY* Tel (01909) 473289 E-mail fatherbill@btopenworld.com

BROWN, Bod. *See* BROWN, Andrew

BROWN (*née* BRYCE), Mrs Brenda Dorothy. b 48. d 11. NSM Trowell, Awsworth and Cossall *S'well* from 11. *41 Park Hill, Awsworth, Nottingham NG16 2RD* Tel 0115-932 9328

BROWN, Brian Ernest. b 36. ALA64. Oak Hill NSM Course 82. d 85 p 86. NSM Wallington *S'wark* 85-91; C 91-00; rtd 00; Perm to Offic *Nor* from 00. *6 Burnside, Necton, Swaffham PE37 8ER* Tel (01760) 721292

BROWN, Mrs Caroline Jane. b 59. Sussex Univ BA80. Westcott Ho Cam 05. d 09 p 10. C Prittlewell *Chelmsf* 09-10; C Hadleigh St Jas from 10. *201 Ambleside Drive, Southend-on-Sea SS1 2UE* Tel (01702) 464152 Mobile 07511-632903 E-mail cjbrown42@hotmail.co.uk

BROWN, Charles Henry. b 48. Tulane Univ (USA) BA70 Ch Coll Cam BA75 MA81. Westcott Ho Cam. d 00 p 01. C Boston *Linc* 00-03; Lect 03-05; Lic Preacher 05-06; P-in-c Crowland from 06. *The Abbey Rectory, East Street, Crowland, Peterborough PE6 0EN* Tel (01733) 211763

BROWN, Charles Hubert. b 21. S'wark Ord Course 82. d 84 p 85. NSM Shortlands *Roch* 84-86; P-in-c Seal St Lawr 86-90; P-in-c Underriver 86-90; rtd 90; Perm to Offic *Roch* 90-02. *c/o A Brown Esq, 47 Goodhart Way, West Wickham BR4 0ER* Tel (01732) 882893

BROWN, Mrs Christine Ann. b 42. Keele Univ CertEd72. LCTP 10. d 11. NSM Dent w Cowgill *Bradf* from 11. *Dale View, Laning, Dent, Sedbergh LA10 5QJ* Tel (015396) 25418 E-mail christinea.brown@tiscali.co.uk

BROWN, Mrs Christine Lilian. b 54. Ex Univ BA75 Newc Univ MA93. NEOC 01. d 04 p 05. NSM Ponteland *Newc* from 04; Chapl St Oswald's Hospice Newc from 08. *4 Woodlands, Ponteland, Newcastle upon Tyne NE20 9EU* Tel (01661) 824196

BROWN, Christopher. b 38. AKC62 CQSW68. St Boniface Warminster 62. d 63 p 64. C Crofton Park St Hilda w St Cypr *S'wark* 63-64; C S Beddington St Mich 64-67; C Herne Hill St Paul 67-68; Lic to Offic *S'wark* 68-72; Lich 72-74; *Birm* 74-76; *Worc* 76-79; Perm to Offic *Chelmsf* from 86; Dir and Chief Exec NSPCC 89-95. *7 Baronia Croft, Colchester CO4 9EE* Tel (01206) 852904 E-mail chribrow@yahoo.co.uk

BROWN, Christopher. b 43. Linc Th Coll 79. d 81 p 82. C Stafford St Jo *Lich* 81-85; V Alton w Bradley-le-Moors and Oakamoor w Cotton 85-94; Chapl Asst Nottm City Hosp NHS Trust 94-05; Sen Chapl 05-06; rtd 06. *3 Kingsbury Drive, Nottingham NG8 3EP* Tel 0115-929 4821 E-mail revbrowncj@aol.com

BROWN, Christopher Charles. b 58. Univ of Wales (Cardiff) LLB79 Solicitor 82. Westcott Ho Cam 87. d 90 p 91. C Taunton St Mary *B & W* 90-94; R Timsbury and Priston 94-00; P-in-c Urmston *Man* 00-10; AD Stretford 05-10; TR Radcliffe from 10. *St Thomas's Vicarage, Vicarage Street, Radcliffe, Manchester M26 2TR* Tel 0161-723 2123 E-mail christopher56.brown@mypostoffice.co.uk

BROWN, Christopher David. b 49. Birm Univ BEd72. St Mich Coll Llan 92. d 94 p 95. C Swansea St Thos and Kilvey *S & B* 94-96; C Swansea St Jas 96-98; St Helena 99-01; Chapl and Hd RS Epsom Coll 01-03; Chapl Ellesmere Coll 03-05. *Flat 1, 13 Worcester Road, Malvern WR14 4QY* E-mail kristophdavid@hotmail.com

BROWN, Christopher Edgar Newall. b 31. Oak Hill Th Coll 51. d 55 p 56. C Surbiton Hill Ch Ch *S'wark* 55-57; C Gipsy Hill Ch Ch 57-61; V Plumstead All SS 61-70; V Sissinghurst *Cant* 70-73; P-in-c Frittenden 72-73; V Sissinghurst w Frittenden 73-76; Perm to Offic *S & M* 84-91 and from 96; Bp's Dom Chapl 91-95; rtd 96. *21 College Green, Castletown, Isle of Man IM9 1BE* Tel (01624) 822364

BROWN, Canon Christopher Francis. b 44. Sarum Th Coll 68. d 71 p 72. C High Wycombe *Ox* 71-74; C Sherborne w Castleton and Lillington *Sarum* 74-77; P-in-c Wylye, Fisherton Delamere and the Langfords 77-79; R Yarnbury 79-82; R Portland All SS w St Pet 82-88; RD Weymouth 85-88; R Trowbridge St Jas 88-07; R Trowbridge St Jas and Keevil 07-09; Chapl Trowbridge and Distr Hosp 88-95; RD Bradford 94-01; Can and Preb Sarum Cathl 98-09; rtd 09; Perm to Offic *B & W* and *Sarum* from 09. *4 Alum Close, Trowbridge BA14 7HD* Tel (01225) 354811

BROWN, Christopher Howard. b 49. d 03 p 04. OLM Uttoxeter Area *Lich* from 03. *21 Carter Street, Uttoxeter ST14 8EY* Tel (01889) 567492 E-mail revchrishbrown@aol.co.uk

BROWN, Christopher James. b 50. Open Univ BA92. Trin Coll Bris 91. d 93 p 94. C Skelmersdale St Paul *Liv* 93-97; Chapl Asst Salford R Hosps NHS Trust 97-03; Chapl Trafford Healthcare NHS Trust from 03. *Trafford Healthcare NHS Trust, Moorside Road, Davyhulme, Manchester M41 5SL* Tel 0161-748 4022 *or* 746 2624

BROWN, Clive Lindsey. b 33. Southn Univ BA55. Oak Hill Th Coll 57. d 59 p 60. C Becontree St Mary *Chelmsf* 59-62; P-in-c Balgowlah w Manly Vale Australia 62-69; P-in-c Balgowlah Heights 66-69; R 69-72; R Roseville E 72-98; rtd 98. *14/11 Addison Road, Manly NSW 2095, Australia*

BROWN, Prof Colin. b 32. Liv Univ BA53 Lon Univ BD58 Nottm Univ MA61 DD94 Bris Univ PhD70. Tyndale Hall Bris 55. d 58 p 59. C Chilwell *S'well* 58-61; Lect Tyndale Hall Bris 61-78; Vice Prin 67-70; Dean Studies 70-71; Prof Systematic Th Fuller Th Sem California USA from 78; Assoc R Altadena St Mark from 80; Assoc Dean Adv Th Studies 88-97; rtd 00.

1024 Beverly Way, Altadena CA 91001-2516, USA Tel (001) (626) 798 7180 E-mail colbrn@fuller.edu

BROWN, David Andrew. b 72. York Univ BA93. Wycliffe Hall Ox BTh04. **d** 04 **p** 05. C Rugby St Matt *Cov* 04-08; P-in-c Budbrooke from 08. *23 Robins Grove, Warwick CV34 6RF* Tel (01926) 497298

BROWN, David Charles Girdlestone. b 42. Solicitor 67. S'wark Ord Course 87. **d** 90 **p** 91. NSM Milford *Guildf* 90-92; NSM Haslemere 92-00; NSM Haslemere and Grayswood 00-01; Perm to Offic *Chich* 02-04; Lic to Offic 04-08; P-in-c Barlavington, Burton w Coates, Sutton and Bignor from 08. *The Rectory, The Street, Sutton, Pulborough RH20 1PS* Tel (01798) 869220 E-mail david.brown@bignor.net

BROWN, David Frederick. b 38. Illinois Univ BA60. Seabury-Western Th Sem MDiv67. **d** 67 **p** 67. C Evanston St Mark USA 67-68; C Camarillo St Columba 68-69; P-in-c 69-70; C San Francisco H Innocents and C Grace Cathl 70-75; Hon C Battersea Ch Ch and St Steph *S'wark* 78-83; Sen Chapl R Marsden NHS Trust 83-00; rtd 00; Perm to Offic *Lon* from 02. *12 Caversham House, 21-25 Caversham Street, London SW3 4AE* Tel (020) 7352 3457

BROWN, Canon David Lloyd. b 44. TCD BTh90. **d** 86 **p** 87. C Cregagh *D & D* 86-91; Bp's C Knocknagoney from 91; Can Down Cathl from 07. *The Aslan Centre, 13A Knocknagoney Road, Belfast BT4 2NR* Tel and fax (028) 9076 3343 E-mail davidlloydbrown@googlemail.com

BROWN, David Mark. b 67. Bp Grosseteste Coll BSc93. Oak Hill Th Coll 05. **d** 07. C Sidmouth, Woolbrook, Salcombe Regis, Sidbury etc *Ex* 07-11; P-in-c Stevenage St Nic and Graveley *St Alb* from 11. *St Nicholas' House, 2A North Road, Stevenage SG1 4AT* Tel (01438) 354355 Mobile 07814-911937 E-mail revdmb@aol.com

BROWN, David Victor Arthur. b 44. Em Coll Cam BA66 MA70 CertEd. Linc Th Coll 72. **d** 74 **p** 75. C Bourne *Linc* 74-77; Chapl St Steph Coll Broadstairs 77-79; Chapl Asst N Gen Hosp Sheff 81-84; C Sheff St Cuth 81-84; Chapl Ridge Lea Hosp Lanc 84-92; Chapl Lanc Moor Hosp 84-92; Chapl Lanc R Infirmary 87-92; Chapl Lanc Priority Services NHS Trust and Lanc Acute Hosps NHS Trust 92-98; Chapl Morecambe Bay Hosps NHS Trust and Morecambe Bay Primary Care Trust 98-09; Hon C Scorton and Barnacre and Calder Vale *Blackb* 06-09; P-in-c from 09. *The Vicarage, Snow Hill Lane, Scorton, Preston PR3 1AY* Tel (01524) 791229 E-mail dlgbrown@aol.com

BROWN, Prof David William. b 48. Edin Univ MA70 Oriel Coll Ox BA72 Clare Coll Cam PhD76 FBA02. Westcott Ho Cam 75. **d** 76 **p** 77. Chapl, Fell and Tutor Oriel Coll Ox 76-90; Van Mildert Prof Div Dur Univ 90-07; Can Res Dur Cathl 90-07; Wardlaw Prof St Andr Univ from 07. *St Mary's College, University of St Andrews, St Andrews KY16 9JU* E-mail dwb21@st-andrews.ac.uk

BROWN (née BOWERS), Lady (Denise Frances). b 50. City Univ BSc72. SAOMC 99. **d** 02 **p** 03. NSM Beedon and Peasemore w W Ilsley and Farnborough *Ox* 02-10; NSM Brightwalton w Catmore, Leckhampstead etc 05-10; NSM E Downland from 10. *Bridleway Cottage, Stanmore, Beedon, Newbury RG20 8SR* Tel and fax (01635) 281825 Mobile 07901-914975

BROWN, Dennis Cockburn. b 27. Hatf Coll Dur BSc48 K Coll Dur PhD54. WMMTC 79. **d** 82 **p** 83. C Bilton *Cov* 82-84; V Wolford w Burmington 84-96; R Cherington w Stourton 84-96; R Barcheston 84-96; rtd 96; Perm to Offic *Cov* from 96; Dioc Rtd Clergy and Widows Officer from 98. *13 Cleveland Court, 41 Kenilworth Road, Leamington Spa CV32 6JA* Tel (01926) 423771

BROWN, Derek. *See* BROWN, John Derek

BROWN, Derek. b 42. Lindisfarne Regional Tr Partnership 10. **d** 10 **p** 11. NSM Gateshead St Helen *Dur* from 10. *29 Heathfield Road, Gateshead NE9 5HH* Tel 0191-487 5922 Mobile 07985-512766 E-mail derekderekb@aol.com

BROWN, Derek Henry Pridgeon. b 46. Cam Coll of Art and Tech BA67 Leeds Univ PGCE73. St Steph Ho Ox 90. **d** 92 **p** 93. C Finchley St Mary *Lon* 92-95; C W Hampstead St Jas 95-99; V Eyres Monsell *Leic* 99-08; TV Leic Presentation 08-09; Min Leic St Barn CD from 09. *11 Dixon Drive, Leicester LE2 1RA* Tel 0116-270 9750 E-mail dbrown@leicester.anglican.org

BROWN, Canon Donald Fryer. b 31. St Jo Coll Dur BA56. Cranmer Hall Dur 60. **d** 61 **p** 62. Min Can Bradf Cathl 61-64; C Bingley All SS 64-66; V Low Moor H Trin 66-97; Hon Can Bradf Cathl 85-97; RD Bowling and Horton 87-95; rtd 97; Perm to Offic *Bradf* from 98. *3 Northfield Gardens, Wibsey, Bradford BD6 1LQ* Tel (01274) 671869 E-mail don-iris@supanet.com

BROWN, Mrs Doreen Marion. b 39. Cam Univ CertEd67. NOC 85. **d** 88 **p** 94. Par Dn Axminster, Chardstock, Combe Pyne and Rousdon *Ex* 88-92; Ind Chapl *Linc* 92-98; TV Brumby 98-05; rtd 05. *7 Thorngarth Lane, Barrow-upon-Humber DN19 7AW* Tel (01469) 532102 E-mail doreen.bn@lineone.net

BROWN, Douglas Adrian Spencer. b 29. Univ of W Aus BA50 MA71 K Coll Lon MTh90. St Mich Th Coll Crafers 50. **d** 53 **p** 54. SSM 54-00; Chapl St Mich Th Coll Crafers Australia

54-60; Chapl Kelham Th Coll 60-66; Chapl Univ of W Aus 66-71; P-in-c Canberra St Alb 71-75; Warden St Mich Th Coll Crafers 75-82; P-in-c Adelaide St Jo 78-82; Academic Dean Adelaide Coll of Div 79-81; President 88; Visiting Scholar Union Th Sem NY 82; Perm to Offic *Lon* 88-90; Chapl Bucharest w Sofia *Eur* 90-91; Dir Angl Cen Rome 91-95; Chapl Palermo w Taormina *Eur* 95-96; Lect Newton Th Coll Papua New Guinea 97; Perm to Offic *Dur* 97-00 and *S'wark* 99-00; Dir Nor Cathl Inst and Hon PV Nor Cathl 00-02. *75/6 Manning Terrace, South Perth WA 6151, Australia* Tel (0061) (8) 9368 0014 E-mail brown.douglas75@gmail.com

BROWN, Mrs Elizabeth Alexandra Mary Gordon. b 67. Westcott Ho Cam 06. **d** 08 **p** 09. C Merrow *Guildf* 08-11. *Address temp unknown* Tel 07768-075803 (mobile)

BROWN, Ms Elizabeth Ann. b 43. **d** 00 **p** 01. OLM W Bromwich All SS *Lich* 01-08; OLM Wednesbury St Paul Wood Green 08-10; rtd 10. *367 Beaconview Road, West Bromwich B71 3PS* Tel 0121-588 7530 E-mail e.a.brown@talktalk.net

BROWN, Miss Elizabeth Charlotte (Beth). b 54. Bris Univ BSc76 PGCE77. Trin Coll Bris 93. **d** 95 **p** 96. C Taunton Lyngford *B & W* 95-99; TV Bath Twerton-on-Avon 99-06; C N Swindon St Andr *Bris* 06-11; C Swindon Dorcan from 11. *6 Vespasian Close, Swindon SN3 4BX* Tel (01793) 826444 E-mail beth@revbethbrown.org.uk

BROWN, Mrs Elizabeth Mary Godwin. b 48. St Matthias Coll Bris CertEd69. WEMTC 07. **d** 10. NSM Leominster *Heref* from 10. *Fairleigh House, Hereford Terrace, Leominster HR6 8JP* Tel (01568) 613636 Mobile 07971-917141 E-mail elizabethmgbrown@hotmail.com

BROWN, Eric. b 28. Leeds Univ BA98. NW Ord Course 73. **d** 76 **p** 77. NSM S Kirkby *Wakef* 76-83; NSM Knottingley 83-94; NSM Kellington w Whitley 89-94; Sub Chapl HM Pris Lindholme 90-94; Perm to Offic from 94. *Wynberg, Barnsley Road, South Kirkby, Pontefract WF9 3BG* Tel (01977) 643683

BROWN, Canon Ernest George. b 23. Em Coll Cam BA51 MA56. Oak Hill Th Coll 52. **d** 53 **p** 54. C Darfield *Sheff* 53-56; V Ardsley 56-66; V Thurnby w Stoughton *Leic* 66-79; RD Gartree II 78-90; Hon Can Leic Cathl 82-90; rtd 90; Perm to Offic *Leic* 90-04. *16 Holbeck Drive, Broughton Astley, Leicester LE9 6UR* Tel (01455) 285458

BROWN, Ernest Harry. b 32. St Mich Coll Llan. **d** 59 **p** 60. C Swansea St Pet *S & B* 59-62; C Gowerton w Waunarlwydd 62-68; CF (TA) 62-68; Chapl to the Deaf *S & B* 68-78; rtd 98. *Montreaux, 30 Lon Cedwyn, Sketty, Swansea SA2 0TH* Tel (01792) 207628

BROWN, Geoffrey Alan. b 34. **d** 99 **p** 00. OLM Bury St Edmunds St Mary *St E* 99-07; rtd 07; Perm to Offic *St E* from 07. *Rodenkirchen, 12 Sharp Road, Bury St Edmunds IP33 2NB* Tel (01284) 769725

BROWN, Geoffrey Gilbert. b 38. Dur Univ BA62 DipEd63 Fitzw Coll Cam BA69 MA73 FBIS. Westcott Ho Cam 67. **d** 70 **p** 71. C Gosforth All SS *Newc* 70-73; Chapl Dauntsey's Sch Devizes 73-76; Chapl St Paul's Colleg Sch Hamilton NZ 76-78; V Barrow St Aid *Carl* 79-86; Chapl Ch Coll Canterbury NZ 86-90; C Digswell and Panshanger *St Alb* 91-93; Chapl E Herts Hospice Care 94-97; rtd 07. *32 Uplands, Welwyn Garden City AL8 7EW* Tel (01707) 327565

BROWN, Canon Geoffrey Harold. b 30. Trin Hall Cam BA54 MA58. Cuddesdon Coll 54. **d** 56 **p** 57. C Plaistow St Andr *Chelmsf* 56-60; C Birm St Pet 60-63; R Birm St Geo 63-73; TR Gt Grimsby St Mary and St Jas *Linc* 73-85; Can and Preb Linc Cathl 79-85; V St Martin-in-the-Fields *Lon* 85-95; rtd 95; Perm to Offic *Worc* from 95. *Greenacres, Little Shurdington, Cheltenham GL51 4TX* Tel (01452) 864972

BROWN, Graham Stanley. *See* REAPER-BROWN, Graham Stanley

BROWN, Mrs Harriet Nina. b 37. Open Univ BA77 Lon Univ CertEd57. Gilmore Course 80 Oak Hill Th Coll 83. **dss** 83 **d** 87 **p** 94. Greenstead *Chelmsf* 83-90; Par Dn 87-90; Asst Chapl R Hosp Sch Holbrook 90-93; Perm to Offic *Chelmsf* from 93 and *St E* 93-96; P-in-c Gt and Lt Blakenham w Baylham and Nettlestead *St E* 96-01; rtd 01. *22 Gainsborough Road, Colchester CO3 4QN* Tel (01206) 523072

BROWN, Ian Barry. b 53. St Cuth Soc Dur BA80 PGCE81. Sarum & Wells Th Coll 84. **d** 86 **p** 87. C Winchmore Hill St Paul *Lon* 86-89; Hon Chapl Chase Farm Hosp Enfield 86-88; Hon Chapl Harley Street Area Hosps 88-90; Hon Chapl RAM 89; C St Marylebone w H Trin 89-94; rtd 94; Hon Chapl Regent's Coll *Lon* 96-05. *Flat 4, 9 Welbeck Street, London W19 9YB*

BROWN, Ian David. b 53. UEA BA76. Wycliffe Hall Ox BA80. **d** 81 **p** 82. C Southsea St Jude *Portsm* 81-84; Chapl Coll of SS Paul and Mary Cheltenham 84-89; V Lt Heath *St Alb* 89-05; V Frindsbury w Upnor and Chattenden *Roch* from 05. *Frindsbury Vicarage, 4 Parsonage Lane, Rochester ME2 4UR* Tel (01634) 717580

BROWN, Canon Jack Robin. b 44. Linc Th Coll 67. **d** 69 **p** 70. C Hanning Town St Cedd *Chelmsf* 69-72; C Dunstable *St Alb* 72-78; V Luton St Andr 78-85; V Kempston Transfiguration 85-00; RD Bedford 92-98; Hon Can St Alb 97-09; Dioc Officer for Local Min 00-09; rtd 10; P-in-c Mill End and Heronsgate w W Hyde *St Alb* 10-11; Perm to Offic from 11; Dir of Ords from 11. *9 Westmead, Princes Risborough HP27 9HP*   Tel (01844) 347178   E-mail randvbrown@btinternet.com

BROWN, Mrs Jacqueline Kay. b 43. Saffron Walden Coll CertEd65. **d** 08   **p** 09. OLM Newton Longville, Mursley, Swanbourne etc *Ox* from 08. *5 Berry Way, Newton Longville, Milton Keynes MK17 0AS*   Tel (01908) 270159

BROWN, James Douglas. b 52. S'wark Ord Course 93. **d** 96 **p** 97. NSM Shooters Hill Ch Ch *S'wark* 96-01; P-in-c E Malling *Roch* 02-07; P-in-c Wateringbury and Teston 02-07; V E Malling, Wateringbury and Teston from 07; RD Malling from 07. *The Vicarage, 2 The Grange, East Malling, West Malling ME19 6AH*   Tel and fax (01732) 843282   Mobile 07957-906297   E-mail james.brown@diocese-rochester.org

BROWN, Canon James Philip. b 30. Ex Coll Ox BA54 MA55. Westcott Ho Cam 54. **d** 56 **p** 57. C Hemel Hempstead *St Alb* 56-63; V Hellesdon *Nor* 63-71; P-in-c Kirkley w Lowestoft St Jo 71-79; TV Lowestoft St Marg 76-78; TV Lowestoft and Kirkley 79-81; P-in-c Northleach w Hampnett and Farmington *Glouc* 81-95; RD Northleach 83-92; P-in-c Cold Aston w Notgrove and Turkdean 86-95; Hon Can Glouc Cathl 91-95; rtd 95; Perm to Offic *Ex* from 95. *The Priest's House, 1 St Scholastica's Abbey, Teignmouth TQ14 8FF*   Tel (01626) 773623

BROWN, Jane Madeline. See SHARP, Mrs Jane Madeline

BROWN, Mrs Jean. b 49. WEMTC 05. **d** 08 **p** 09. NSM Lechlade *Glouc* 08; NSM Fairford Deanery from 09. *The Colt, Whelford, Fairford GL7 4EA*   Tel (01285) 712503   Mobile 07957-657935   E mail jeanbrown50@email.com

BROWN, Jennifer. b 44. Guy's Hosp Medical Sch MSc91 Southn Univ BDS67 Open Univ BA81. Ripon Coll Cuddesdon 08. **d** 09 **p** 10. NSM Downs Benefice *Win* from 09. *18A Main Road, Littleton, Winchester SO22 6PS*   Tel (01962) 888593   Mobile 07870-772905   E-mail jenniferandjosie@hotmail.com

BROWN, Mrs Jennifer Elizabeth. b 70. Geo Mason Univ Virginia BSc91. SAOMC 02. **d** 05 **p** 06. C Ox St Clem 05-08; Chapl Jes Coll Ox 09. *49 Laburnum Road, Oxford OX2 9EN*   Tel (01865) 279757   E-mail chaplain@jesus.ox.ac.uk *or* chaplain@jenbrown.org.uk

BROWN, Jenny. b 78. St Martin's Coll Lanc BA99. Oak Hill Th Coll BA03. **d** 03 **p** 04. C Hyde St Geo *Ches* 03-06; C Weaverham from 06. *The Vicarage, Church Street, Weaverham, Northwich CW8 3NJ*   Tel (01606) 852110   E-mail revjennybrown@yahoo.co.uk

BROWN, Mrs Joan Leslie. b 31. SS Hild & Bede Coll Dur CertEd53. Oak Hill Th Coll BA85. dss 85 **d** 87 **p** 94. Fulwood *Sheff* 85-88; Par Dn 87-88; TD Netherthorpe 88-93; NSM Ellesmere St Pet 93-99; rtd 99; Perm to Offic *Sheff* from 00. *15 Dover Gardens, Sheffield S3 7LB*   Tel 0114-273 1364

BROWN, John. b 64. Kent Univ BA86. Westcott Ho Cam 87. **d** 90 **p** 91. C Lt Ilford St Mich *Chelmsf* 90-94; C E Ham w Upton Park 94; TV 94-01; P-in-c Gt Ilford St Luke from 01. *St Luke's Vicarage, Baxter Road, Ilford IG1 2HN*   Tel (020) 8478 1248 *or* 8553 7606   E-mail livingfaith@stluke-ilford.org.uk

BROWN, Canon John Bruce. b 42. Nottm Univ BA64 MA68. Cuddesdon Coll 64. **d** 66 **p** 67. C Warwick St Nic *Cov* 66-71; C Bp's Hatfield *St Alb* 71-78; V Watford St Mich 78-08; RD Watford 94-99; Hon Can St Alb 02-08; rtd 08; Perm to Offic *Ox* from 09. *Broomfield Cottage, Poffley End, Hailey, Witney OX29 9US*   Tel (01993) 703029   E-mail patandjohnb@yahoo.co.uk

BROWN, John Derek. b 41. Linc Th Coll 71. **d** 73 **p** 74. C Rotherham *Sheff* 73-76; P-in-c V W Pinchbeck *Linc* 76-78; V Surfleet 76-82; R Boultham 83-94; RD Christianity 85-92; P-in-c Epworth and Wroot 94-97; R Epworth Gp 97-05; RD Is of Axholme 96-05; Can and Preb Linc Cathl 88-05; rtd 05. *3 Walnut Cottages, Yorkshireside, Eastoft DN17 4PG*   Tel (01724) 798659   E-mail jbrown@wanadoo.fr

BROWN, John Dixon. b 28. Pemb Coll Cam BA52. Oak Hill Th Coll 52. **d** 54 **p** 55. C Worthing St Geo *Chich* 54-57; C S w N Bersted 57-63; V W Hampnett 63-91; rtd 91; Perm to Offic *Chich* from 91. *3 Manor Way, Elmer, Bognor Regis PO22 6LA*   Tel (01243) 583449

BROWN, Canon John Duncan. b 43. St Pet Coll Ox BA64 BA66 MA68 Lon Univ BSc. Wycliffe Hall Ox 65. **d** 67 **p** 68. C Kingston upon Hull H Trin *York* 67-69; C St Leonards St Leon *Chich* 69-72; Hon C Norbiton *S'wark* 72-75; C Kirkcaldy *St And* 75-78; Prec and Chapl Chelmsf Cathl 78-86; P-in-c Kelvedon Hatch 86-92; P-in-c Navestock 86-92; P-in-c Fryerning w Margaretting 92-99; Bp's ACORA Officer 92-99; Hon Can Chelmsf Cathl 93-03; rtd 99. *556 Galleywood Road, Chelmsford CM2 8BX*   Tel (01245) 358185

✠**BROWN, The Rt Revd John Edward.** b 30. Lon Univ BD68. Kelham Th Coll 50. **d** 55 **p** 56 **c** 87. Chapl St Geo Colleg Ch Jerusalem 55-57; C Reading St Mary V *Ox* 57-60; Sudan 60-64; V Stewkley *Ox* 64-69; V Maidenhead St Luke 69-73; V Bracknell 73-77; RD Sonning 73-77; Adn Berks 78-87; Warden Ascot Priory 80-87; Bp Cyprus and the Gulf 87-95; rtd 95; Hon Asst

Bp *Linc* from 95; RD Grimsby and Cleethorpes 03-04. *130 Oxford Street, Cleethorpes DN35 0BP*   Tel (01472) 698840   E-mail bishopjohnsaints@tiscali.co.uk

BROWN, Canon John Roger. b 37. AKC60. **d** 61 **p** 62. C New Eltham All SS *S'wark* 61-64; C Bexhill St Pet *Chich* 64-68; V Eastbourne St Elisabeth 68-75; V E Grinstead St Swithun 75-97; Chapl Qu Victoria Hosp NHS Trust East Grinstead 75-97; Perm to Offic *Chich* 97-99; RD E Grinstead 82-93; Can and Preb Chich Cathl 89-98; TV Worth 00-04; rtd 05. *120 Malthouse Road, Crawley RH10 6BH*   Tel (01293) 520454   E-mail jroger.brown@tesco.net

BROWN, Jonathan. b 60. Univ Coll Dur BA83 MA85 Ex Univ CertEd86. Ripon Coll Cuddesdon 86 Ch Div Sch of the Pacific (USA) 88. **d** 89 **p** 90. C Esher *Guildf* 89-97; TV Crawley *Chich* 97-04; Chapl St Cath Hospice 97-04; V Earlsfield St Andr *S'wark* from 04. *22 St Andrew's Court, Waynflete Street, London SW18 3QF*   Tel (020) 8946 4214

BROWN, Prof Judith Margaret. b 44. Girton Coll Cam MA69 PhD68 Natal Univ Hon DSocSc01. Ripon Coll Cuddesdon 09. **d** 09 **p** 10. NSM Osney *Ox* from 09; Asst Chapl Ball Coll Ox from 09. *97 Victoria Road, Oxford OX2 7QG*   Tel (01865) 514486

BROWN, Mrs Kathleen Margaret. b 40. MBE07. QUB BD BTh. **d** 88 **p** 90. C Carrickfergus *Conn* 88-92; I Belfast St Paul w St Barn 92-07; Can Belf Cathl 00-07; rtd 07. *3 The Avenue, Carrickfergus BT38 8LT*   Tel (028) 9336 6787   E-mail kbrown117@btinternet.co.uk

BROWN, Keith Michael. b 42. **d** 07 **p** 08. OLM Earlham *Nor* from 07. *115 Colman Road, Norwich NR4 7HF*   Tel (01603) 464707   E mail keith.brown93@ntlworld.com

BROWN, Kenneth Arthur Charles. b 27. ACP65. **d** 84 **p** 85. OLM Ingoldsby *Linc* 84-97. *11 Ingoldsby Road, Lenton, Grantham NG33 4HB*   Tel (01476) 85763

BROWN, Kenneth Roger. b 48. St Chad's Coll Dur BA69. Liturg Inst Trier 72. **d** 73 **p** 74. C Patchway *Bris* 73-77; C Fishponds St Jo 77-79; Chapl RAF 79-95; Chapl HM Pris Pentonville 95-96; Chapl HM Pris Wellingborough 96-98; Perm to Offic *B & W* 99-00; P-in-c Crook Peak 00-11; R from 11. *The Rectory, Sparrow Hill Way, Weare, Axbridge BS26 2LE*   Tel (01934) 733140   E-mail rev_ken_brown@hotmail.com

BROWN, Miss Louise Margaret. b 53. MBE05. Trin Coll Bris 80. **dss** 83 **d** 87 **p** 94. Woodley St Jo the Ev *Ox* 84-87; Par Dn Woodley 87-92; Asst Chapl Reading Hosps 92-94; C Shinfield 93-94; P-in-c Dedworth from 94; P-in-c Clewer St Andr from 04. *3 Convent Court, Hatch Lane, Windsor SL4 3QR*

BROWN, Malcolm Arthur. b 54. Oriel Coll Ox BA76 MA82 Man Univ PhD00. Westcott Ho Cam 77. **d** 79 **p** 80. C Riverhead w Dunton Green *Roch* 79-83; TV Southampton (City Cen) *Win* 83-91; Assoc Dir Wm Temple Foundn 91-93; Exec Sec 93-00; Hon C Heaton Moor *Man* 95-00; Prin EAMTC *Ely* 00-05; Prin ERMC 05-07; Dir Miss and Public Affairs Abps' Coun from 07. *Church House, Great Smith Street, London SW1P 3AZ*   Tel (020) 7898 1000   E-mail malcolm.brown@churchofengland.org

BROWN, Mandy Kathleen. b 57. SEITE. **d** 10 **p** 11. C Bp's Hatfield, Lemsford and N Mymms *St Alb* from 10. *St Michael's Vicarage, 31 Homestead Road, Hatfield AL10 0QJ*   Tel 07772-121277 (mobile)   E-mail brownm05@hotmail.com

BROWN, Marcus Clement. b 51. SEITE 08. **d** 10 **p** 11. NSM Iford w Kingston and Rodmell *Chich* from 10. *Abergavenny House, Mill Lane, Rodmell, Lewes BN7 3HS*   Tel (01273) 473939   Mobile 07815-157756   E-mail marcusandjennyrodmell@gmail.com

BROWN (née PATTERSON), Mrs Marjorie Jean. b 54. Wooster Coll USA BA76 K Coll Lon MA04. S Dios Minl Tr Scheme 92. **d** 95 **p** 96. C Poplar *Lon* 95-99; P-in-c Stamford Hill St Thos 99-02; V 02-09; P-in-c Upper Clapton St Matt 06-08; Dean of Women's Min Stepney Area 02-07; V Primrose Hill St Mary w Avenue Road St Paul from 09. *St Mary's Vicarage, 44 King Henry's Road, London NW3 3RP*   Tel (020) 7722 3062   E-mail revmarjorie@gmail.com

BROWN, Mark Edward. b 61. Southn Univ BSc83 Cam Univ PGCE84 Brunel Univ MTh98. Trin Coll Bris BA88. **d** 88 **p** 89. C Egham *Guildf* 88-92; C Northwood Em *Lon* 92-96; Assoc V 96-02; Bp's Officer for Evang 96-02; Can Missr *S'well* 02-07; Hon Can S'well Minster 02-07; P-in-c Tonbridge SS Pet and Paul *Roch* 07-10; V from 10; RD Tonbridge from 10. *The Vicarage, Church Street, Tonbridge TN9 1HD*   Tel (01732) 770962   E-mail mark@tonbridgeparishchurch.org.uk

BROWN, Martin Warwick. b 65. BSc MA. ERMC. **d** 07 **p** 08. NSM St Alb St Mary Marshalswick *St Alb* 07-09; NSM Leavesden from 09. *Waterdell, Chequers Lane, Watford WD25 0GR*   Tel (01923) 682763 *or* 672782

BROWN, Michael Brian. b 56. Trin Coll Bris BA97 Coll of Resurr Mirfield 98. **d** 99 **p** 00. C Trowbridge St Jas *Sarum* 99-02; C Bruton and Distr *B & W* 02-09; C Bickleigh and Shaugh Prior *Ex* from 09; Chapl Plymouth Hosps NHS Trust from 09. *2 Blackeven Close, Roborough, Plymouth PL6 7AX*   Tel (01752) 782926   E-mail fr.michaelbrown@btopenworld.com

BROWN, Murray. See BROWN, Phillip Murray

BROWN, Nicholas Francis Palgrave. b 23. Fitzw Ho Cam BA51 MA54. d 53 p 54. C Warwick St Nic *Cov* 53-55; C Birm St Paul 55-60; V Temple Balsall 60-66; Gen Sec Ind Chr Fellowship 66-76; V St Kath Cree *Lon* 66-71; Chapl and Dir of Studies Holland Ho Cropthorne 76-80; P-in-c Cropthorne w Charlton *Worc* 76-88; Adult Educn Officer 80-85; rtd 88; Perm to Offic *Worc* from 88. *Bredon View, Rear of 40 Bridge Street, Pershore WR10 1AT* Tel (01386) 556816

BROWN, Nicholas James Watson. b 76. R Holloway Coll Lon BMus98 Lon Inst of Educn PGCE99. Ripon Coll Cuddesdon 08. d 09 p 10. C Warminster St Denys and Upton Scudamore *Sarum* from 09. *22 Minster View, Warminster BA12 8TD* Tel (01985) 211049 Mobile 07901-852198 E-mail njwbrown@btinternet.com

BROWN, Nina. *See* BROWN, Mrs Harriet Nina

BROWN, Canon Norman Charles Harry. b 27. Univ of Wales BSc46. St Mich Coll Llan 48. d 50 p 51. C Canton St Jo *Llan* 50-57; C Llanishen and Lisvane 58-63; V Miskin 63-97; RD Aberdare 82-97; Can Llan Cathl 86-97; rtd 97. *33 Bron y Deri, Mountain Ash CF45 4LL* Tel (01443) 476631

BROWN, Canon Norman John. b 34. Thames Poly MA90. Ripon Hall Ox 72. d 74 p 75. C High Wycombe *Ox* 74-78; V Tilehurst St Cath 78-82; V Boyne Hill 82-04; Chapl Windsor and Maidenhead Coll 87-89; Hon Can Ch Ch *Ox* 03-04; rtd 04; Perm to Offic *Ox* from 04. *Chantry House, Radley Road, Abingdon OX14 3SL* Tel (01235) 553454 E-mail revbrown@waitrose.com

BROWN, Patricia Valerie. b 37. CertEd58. STETS BTh95. d 98 p 99. NSM Tadley St Pet *Win* 98-02; NSM Tadley S and Silchester 02-07; rtd 07. *58 Bowmonts Road, Tadley, Basingstoke RG26 3SB* Tel 0118-981 6109

BROWN, Paul. *See* BROWN, Preb Anthony Paul

BROWN, Paul David Christopher. b 50. Lon Univ LLB71. EMMTC 81. d 84 p 85. NSM Wollaton *S'well* from 84. *32 Benington Drive, Wollaton, Nottingham NG8 2TF* Tel 0115-928 4493

BROWN, Canon Penelope Jane. b 57. St Steph Ho Ox 94. d 96 p 97. C Croydon St Jo *S'wark* 96-99; V Croydon St Matt 99-05; AD Croydon Cen 07-09; P-in-c Limpsfield and Titsey 09-10; TR Limpsfield and Tatsfield from 10; Hon Can S'wark Cathl from 08. *The Rectory, High Street, Limpsfield, Oxted RH8 0DG* Tel (01883) 722351 E-mail canpennyb@btinternet.com

BROWN, Peter. b 38. Leeds Univ BSc62 PhD65. Nashotah Ho 85. d 87 p 88. R Minneapolis St Andr USA 87-89; C Sprowston w Beeston *Nor* 89-92; P-in-c W Winch w Setchey and N Runcton 92-98; P-in-c Middleton w E Winch 96-98; P-in-c Nor St Andr and Nor St Geo Colegate 98-99; Chapl Norfolk and Nor Health Care NHS Trust 98-99; rtd 00; Perm to Offic *Leic* from 00. *41 Main Street, Cosby, Leicester LE9 1UW* Tel 0116-286 6184 E-mail peterbrown@tesco.net

BROWN, Canon Peter. b 47. RMN69. Kelham Th Coll 69. d 74 p 75. CMP from 75; C Hendon *Dur* 74-80; C Byker St Ant *Newc* 80-90; C Brandon and Ushaw Moor *Dur* 90-05; V from 05; Hon Can Dur Cathl from 01. *The Clergy House, Sawmill Lane, Brandon, Durham DH7 8NS* Tel 0191-378 0845

BROWN, Peter. b 53. St Chad's Coll Dur BA75. Sarum & Wells Th Coll 75. d 77 p 78. C Tunstall Ch Ch *Lich* 77-79; C Tunstall 79-80; C Willenhall H Trin 80-83; V Weston Rhyn 83-88; Australia 88-90; R Hubberston *St D* 90-01; V Chilvers Coton w Astley *Cov* 01-10; rtd 10. *43C Albany Street, Loughborough LE11 5NB* Tel (01509) 214815

BROWN, Peter Russell. b 43. Oak Hill Th Coll. d 71 p 72. C Gt Faringdon w Lt Coxwell *Ox* 71-73; C Reading Greyfriars 73-74; V Forty Hill Jes Ch *Lon* 74-81; V Laleham 81-09; rtd 09; Perm to Offic *Cant* from 10. *42A Tothill Street, Minster, Ramsgate CT12 4AJ* Tel (01843) 822294 E-mail revprb43@yahoo.com

BROWN, Peter Thomas. b 43. Leic Univ BSc64. WEMTC 00. d 03 p 04. OLM Prestbury and All SS *Glouc* 03-08; NSM N Cheltenham from 08. *32 Gallops Lane, Prestbury, Cheltenham GL52 5SD* Tel (01242) 529774 E-mail pete.brown@northchelt.org.uk

BROWN, Philip. *See* BROWN, Canon James Philip

BROWN, Philip Anthony. b 54. Oak Hill Th Coll BA91. d 91 p 92. C Rock Ferry *Ches* 91-95; V Hattersley 95-98; V Harold Hill St Geo *Chelmsf* 98-09; P-in-c Chartham *Cant* from 09; Asst Dir of Ords from 09. *The Rectory, The Green, Chartham, Canterbury CT4 7JW* Tel (01227) 738256 E-mail filbrown@btinternet.com

BROWN, Canon Philip Roy. b 41. St Steph Ho Ox 78. d 80 p 81. C Highters Heath *Birm* 80-83; P-in-c Washwood Heath 83-87; V Tysoe w Oxhill and Whatcote *Cov* 87-93; R Harbury and Ladbroke 93-07; RD Southam 95-97 and 99-02; Hon Can Cov Cathl 00-07; rtd 07; Perm to Offic *Cov* 07-11; Hon C Aston Cantlow and Wilmcote w Billesley from 11. *3 Margetts Close, Kenilworth CV8 1EN* Tel (01926) 850638 E-mail canon.roybrown@lineone.net

BROWN, Phillip John. b 75. Univ of Wales (Lamp) BTh10. WEMTC 05. d 08 p 09. C Heref S Wye from 08. *1 Holme Lacy Road, Hereford HR2 6DD* Tel (01432) 353275 E-mail pbrown777@aol.com

BROWN, Phillip Murray. b 59. Keele Univ BSc80. Trin Coll Bris. d 87 p 88. C Greasbrough *Sheff* 87-91; Ind Chapl 87-93; V Thorne 91-99; V Norton Lees St Paul from 99. *St Paul's Vicarage, 6 Angerford Avenue, Sheffield S8 9BG* Tel 0114-255 1945 E-mail murray.stpauls@btinternet.com

BROWN, Raymond John. b 49. Ox Univ BEd71. Wycliffe Hall Ox 72. d 75 p 76. C Barking St Marg w St Patr *Chelmsf* 75-78; C Walton H Trin *Ox* 78-82; V Enfield St Mich *Lon* 82-91; Chapl St Mich Hosp Enfield 82-91; R Springfield All SS *Chelmsf* from 91. *The Rectory, 4 Old School Field, Chelmsford CM1 7HU* Tel (01245) 356720 E-mail raymondjohnbrown@talktalk.net

BROWN, Richard George. b 38. Dur Univ BSc63. Wells Th Coll 63. d 65 p 66. C Norton St Mary *Dur* 65-69; C N Gosforth *Newc* 69-71; Chapl Wells Cathl Sch 71-81; P-in-c Dulverton and Brushford *B & W* 81-83; R 83-86; Chapl Millfield Jun Sch Somerset 86-89; Chapl Brighton Coll 89-92; Chapl Benenden Sch 92-94; Perm to Offic *Chich* 94-97; P-in-c Poynings w Edburton, Newtimber and Pyecombe 97-04; rtd 04. *4 Standean Farm Cottages, Standean Farm, Brighton BN1 8ZA* Tel (01273) 501469 E-mail richardgb@ukgateway.net

BROWN, Robert. b 47. Man Univ BSc72 Open Univ BA86 Dur Univ MA87. NEOC 95. d 98 p 99. C Yarm *York* 98-01; V Ormesby from 01. *The Vicarage, 54 Church Lane, Ormesby, Middlesbrough TS7 9AU* Tel (01642) 314445

BROWN, Robert Peter Cameron. b 63. K Coll Lon BSc84 Imp Coll Lon MSc87 Lon Bible Coll BA97. Cranmer Hall Dur 01. d 03 p 04. C Upper Weardale *Dur* 03-08. *Stapleton House, Roweltown, Carlisle CA6 6LD*

BROWN, Robin. *See* BROWN, Canon Jack Robin

BROWN, Robin. b 38. Leeds Univ BA60 MPhil69. Qu Coll Birm 89. d 91 p 92. C Far Headingley St Chad *Ripon* 91-94; V Hawksworth Wood 94-00; rtd 00; Perm to Offic *Ripon* from 00. *Dale Edge, 2A Harbour View, Bedale DL8 2DQ* Tel and fax (01677) 425483 Mobile 07960-277495 E-mail robin.stel1@btinternet.com

BROWN, Roger. *See* BROWN, Canon John Roger

BROWN, Capt Roger George. b 37. CQSW. CA Tr Coll SEITE 92. d 95 p 96. C Maidstone St Martin *Cant* 95-97; C Oakham, Hambleton, Egleton, Braunston and Brooke *Pet* 97-04; Chapl Leics and Rutland Healthcare NHS Trust 97-04; rtd 04; Asst Chapl Kettering Gen Hosp NHS Trust from 04. *5 Valley Walk, Kettering NN16 0LY* Tel (01536) 524954

BROWN, Canon Roger Lee. b 42. Univ of Wales (Lamp) BA63 Univ Coll Lon MA73. Wycliffe Hall Ox 66. d 68 p 69. C Dinas w Penygraig *Llan* 68-70; C Bargoed and Deri w Brithdir 70-72; TV Glyncorrwg w Afan Vale and Cymmer Afan 72-74; R 74-79; V Tongwynlais 79-93; R Welshpool w Castle Caereinion *St As* 93-07; AD Pool 01-07; Can Cursal St As Cathl 02-07; rtd 07. *14 Berriew Road, Welshpool SY21 7SS* Tel (01938) 552161

✠**BROWN, The Rt Revd Ronald.** b 26. St Jo Coll Dur BA50. d 52 p 53 c 74. A C Chorley St Laur *Blackb* 52-56; V Whittle-le-Woods 56-61; V Halliwell St Thos *Man* 61-69; R Ashton St Mich 69-74; RD Ashton-under-Lyne 69-74; Suff Bp Birkenhead *Ches* 74-92; rtd 92; Perm to Offic *Ches* 92-00. *16 Andrew Crescent, Chester CH4 7BQ* Tel (01244) 629955

BROWN, Canon Rosalind. b 53. Lon Univ BA74. Yale Div Sch MDiv97. d 97 p 97. V Canonsburg St Thos USA 97-99; Vice-Prin OLM Scheme *Sarum* 99-05; Tutor STETS 99-05; Can Res Dur Cathl from 05. *6A The College, Durham DH1 3EQ* Tel 0191-384 2415 Fax 386 4267 E-mail rosalind.brown@durhamcathedral.co.uk

BROWN, Mrs Rosémia. b 53. Ripon Coll Cuddesdon 97. d 99 p 00. C Shoreditch St Leon and Hoxton St Jo *Lon* 99-00; C Shoreditch St Leon w St Mich 00-02; TV Hackney 02-03; V Clapton St Jas from 03. *134 Rushmore Road, London E5 0EY* Tel (020) 8985 1750

BROWN, Roy. *See* BROWN, Canon Philip Roy

BROWN, Sandra Ann. b 51. d 04 p 05. OLM Linc St Geo Swallowbeck from 04. *10 Station Road, North Hykeham, Lincoln LN6 9AQ* Tel (01522) 877065 E-mail sandra.brown77@ntlworld.com

BROWN, Mrs Sarah Romilly Denner. b 65. Nottm Univ BA86. ERMC 05. d 08 p 09. NSM Welford w Sibbertoft and Marston Trussell *Pet* 08-11; TV Daventry, Ashby St Ledgers, Braunston etc from 11. *The Rectory, 71 High Street, Braunston, Daventry NN11 7HS* Tel (01788) 823052 Mobile 07803-902864 E-mail sarah@talkingdirect.co.uk

BROWN, Canon Simon Nicolas Danton. b 37. Clare Coll Cam BA61 MA65. S'wark Ord Course 61 Linc Th Coll 63. d 64 p 65. C Lambeth St Mary the Less *S'wark* 64-66; Chapl and Warden LMH Settlement 66-72; P-in-c Southampton St Mary w H Trin *Win* 72-73; TV Southampton (City Cen) 73-79; R Gt Brickhill w Bow Brickhill and Lt Brickhill *Ox* 79-84; TR Burnham w Dropmore, Hitcham and Taplow 84-04; RD Burnham and Slough 87-02; Hon Can Ch Ch 94-04; Dioc Consultant for Deanery Development 97-04; Sen Exec Asst to Bp Buckingham 02-04; rtd 04; Perm to Offic *St E* from 04. *Seagulls, Pin Mill Road, Chelmondiston, Ipswich IP9 1JN* Tel (01473) 780051 E-mail simon.brown1@orange.net

BROWN, Sonya Helen Joan. b 77. Liv Jo Moores Univ BA00. St Mich Coll Llan 07. **d** 10 **p** 11. C Leic St Phil from 10. *St Chad's Vicarage, 145 Coleman Road, Leicester LE5 4LH* Tel 07947-509423 (mobile) E-mail son.the.rev@me.com

BROWN, Stephen Charles. b 60. Leeds Univ BA83 BA89 Reading Univ PGCE89. Coll of Resurr Mirfield 87. **d** 90 **p** 91. C Whitkirk *Ripon* 90-93; Asst Youth Chapl 92-95; C Chapel Allerton 93-95; R Stanningley St Thos 95-01; Chapl MU 98-01; V Laneside *Blackb* from 01; Hon Chapl ATC 03-07. *St Peter's Vicarage, Helmshore Road, Haslingden, Rossendale BB4 4BG* Tel (01706) 213838 E-mail highlow@talktalk.net

BROWN, Stephen James. b 44. Bradf Univ BSc69. Westcott Ho Cam 71. **d** 72 **p** 73. C Seaton Hirst *Newc* 72-75; C Marton-in-Cleveland *York* 75-77; Dioc Youth Adv *Dur* 77-82; V Thorner *Ripon* 82-92; Dioc Officer for Local Min 90-01; P-in-c Ripley w Burnt Yates 92-09; Chapl Yorkshire TV 89-09; rtd 09; Perm to Offic *York* from 10. *88 Prince Rupert Drive, Tockwith, York YO26 7QS* Tel (01423) 359142 Mobile 07521-705350 E-mail stephen.brown83@hotmail.co.uk

BROWN, Susan Gertrude. b 48. Univ of Wales (Swansea) BA71 Roehampton Inst PGCE72. St Mich Coll Llan 98. **d** 02 **p** 03. NSM Gelligaer *Llan* 02-04; NSM Eglwysilan 04-07; Lic to Offic 07-08; NSM Caerphilly from 08; Dioc Adv for NSM from 10. *2 Caerleon Court, Caerphilly CF83 2UF* Tel (029) 2140 3773 E-mail suebrown27 uk@yahoo.com

BROWN, Terence George Albert. b 49. SS Mark & Jo Univ Coll Plymouth BEd75. ERMC 04. **d** 06 **p** 09. NSM Langdon Hills *Chelmsf* 06-09; NSM Gt Wakering w Foulness from 09; NSM Barling w Lt Wakering from 09. *201 Ambleside Drive, Southend-on-Sea SS1 2UE* Tel (01702) 464152 Mobile 07944-444675 E-mail tgabrown@hotmail.com

✠**BROWN, The Rt Revd Thomas John.** b 43. San Francisco Th Sem DMin84. St Jo Coll Auckland. **d** 72 **p** 73 **c** 91. C Christchurch St Alb New Zealand 72-74; C Leic St Jas 74-76; V Upper Clutha New Zealand 76-79; V Roslyn 79-85; V Lower Hutt St Jas 85-91; Adn Belmont 87-91; Asst Bp Wellington 91-97; Bp Wellington from 97. *20 Eccleston Hill, Wellington 6011, New Zealand* Tel (0064) (4) 472 3183 *or* 472 1057 Fax 499 1360 E-mail bishoptom@paradise.net.nz

BROWN, Mrs Verity Joy. b 68. Qu Mary Coll Lon BA89. Ripon Coll Cuddesdon BTh93. **d** 93 **p** 94. C Barnard Castle w Whorlton *Dur* 93-95; C Bensham 95-97; Perm to Offic from 97. *75 Eamont Gardens, Hartlepool TS26 9JE* Tel (01429) 423186 E-mail verity.brown@virgin.net

BROWN, Victor Charles. b 31. S'wark Ord Course 67. **d** 71 **p** 72. C Pinhoe *Ex* 71-73; C Egg Buckland 73-74; C Oakdale St Geo *Sarum* 74-77; R Old Trafford St Hilda *Man* 77-83; R Chigwell Row *Chelmsf* 83-92; R Fenny Bentley, Kniveton, Thorpe and Tissington *Derby* 92-96; rtd 96; Perm to Offic *Sarum* 96-08. *5 Gracey Court, Woodland Road, Broadclyst, Exeter EX5 3GA* Tel (01392) 462799

BROWN, Wallace. b 44. Oak Hill Th Coll 77. **d** 79 **p** 80. C Oadby *Leic* 79-85; V Quinton Road W St Boniface *Birm* 85-03; Hon Can Birm Cathl 01-03; TR Ipsley *Worc* 03-09; rtd 09. *2 Coppice Close, Withington, Hereford HR1 3PP* E-mail wallace@rncb.ac.uk

BROWN, Miss Wendy Anne. b 71. Homerton Coll Cam BEd89. Trin Coll Bris 09. **d** 11. C Summerfield *Birm* from 11; C Edgbaston St Germain from 11. *410 Gillott Road, Birmingham B16 9LP* Tel 07825-288779 (mobile) E-mail wendyannebrown@googlemail.com

BROWNBRIDGE, Bernard Alan. b 19. NW Ord Course 74. **d** 77 **p** 78. NSM Huntington *York* 77-80; V Sand Hutton 80-86; rtd 87; Hon C Birdsall w Langton *York* 87-92; Perm to Offic 92-11. *2 Duncombe Close, Malton YO17 7YY* Tel (01653) 697626

BROWNE, Arnold Samuel. b 52. St Jo Coll Cam BA77 MA77 SS Coll Cam PhD87 Surrey Univ MSc89 MBPsS92. Westcott Ho Cam 76. **d** 78 **p** 79. C Esher *Guildf* 78-81; C Worplesdon 81-86; Chapl R Holloway and Bedf New Coll 86-92; Fell and Dean of Chpl Trin Coll Cam 92-06; Perm to Offic *Nor* from 06. *18 Riverside Road, Norwich NR1 1SN* Tel (01603) 629362 E-mail arnoldbrowne@btinternet.com

BROWNE, Aubrey Robert Caulfeild. b 31. Moore Th Coll Sydney 54. **d** 55 **p** 56. Australia 55-71; Producer of Relig Radio Progr USPG 72-84; Hon C S Kensington St Steph *Lon* 78-88; Hd of Area Sec Dept USPG 84-87; P-in-c Nunhead St Antony *S'wark* 88-90; V Nunhead St Antony w St Silas 90-96; rtd 97; Australia from 97. *15 Caroma Avenue, Kyeemagh NSW 2216, Australia* Tel (0061) (2) 9567 5371

BROWNE, Miss Christine Mary. b 53. Nottm Univ BEd75. EMMTC 87. **d** 90 **p** 94. C Bulwell St Mary *S'well* 90-95; TV Hucknall Torkard 95-00; Dep Chapl HM Pris Nor 00-01; Chapl HM YOI Swinfen Hall 01-03; Perm to Offic *Derby* 03-05; P-in-c Dudley St Aug Holly Hall *Worc* 05-09; TV Dudley from 09; Chapl Merry Hill Shopping Cen from 05. *St Augustine's Vicarage, 1 Hallchurch Road, Dudley DY2 0TG* Tel (01384) 261026

BROWNE, Herman Beseah. b 65. Cuttington Univ Coll BTh86 K Coll Lon BD90 AKC90 Heythrop Coll Lon PhD94. **d** 87 **p** 97. C N Lambeth *S'wark* 90-91; Tutor Simon of Cyrene Th Inst 90-96;

Abp's Asst Sec for Ecum and Angl Affairs *Cant* 96-01; Abp's Officer for Angl Communion 01-05; Perm to Offic *S'wark* 96-04; Hon Prov Can Cant Cathl 01-04; Liberia from 05. *Trinity Cathedral, PO Box 10-0277, 1000 Monrovia 10, Liberia* Tel (00231) 224760 Fax 227519

BROWNE, Ian Cameron. b 51. St Cath Coll Ox BA74 MA78 Fitzw Coll Cam BA76 MA80. Ridley Hall Cam 74. **d** 77 **p** 78. C Cheltenham Ch Ch *Glouc* 77-80; Hon C Shrewsbury St Chad *Lich* 80-83; Asst Chapl Shrewsbury Sch 80-83; Chapl Bedford Sch 83-96; Sen Chapl Oundle Sch from 97. *The School, Oundle, Peterborough PE8 4EN* Tel (01832) 273372 *or* 273541 E-mail icb@oundleschool.org.uk

BROWNE, Mrs Karen. b 64. Ox Min Course 06. **d** 09 **p** 10. NSM Newport Pagnell w Lathbury and Moulsoe *Ox* from 09. *94 Lakes Lane, Newport Pagnell MK16 8HR* Tel (01908) 217703 E-mail karen browne@btopenworld.com

BROWNE, Leonard Joseph. b 58. St Cath Coll Cam BA81 MA84. Trin Coll Bris 87. **d** 89 **p** 90. C Reading Greyfriars *Ox* 89-92; V Cambridge St Barn *Ely* 92-00; Sen Chapl and Hd Div Dean Close Sch Cheltenham 00-03; Hd Master Dean Close Prep Sch from 03. *Dean Close Preparatory School, Lansdown Road, Cheltenham GL51 6QS* Tel (01242) 512217 E-mail hmdcps@deanclose.org.uk *or* lj-browne@supanet.com

BROWNE, Peter Clifford. b 59. Bris Univ BA80 SRN82. Ripon Coll Cuddesdon 88. **d** 90 **p** 91. C Southgate Ch Ch *Lon* 90-92; NSM Kemp Town St Mary *Chich* 93-95; Chapl United Bris Healthcare NHS Trust 96-98; NSM Southmead *Bris* 98-02; Chapl HM Pris Preston 02-10; Chapl HM Pris Shepton Mallet from 10. *HM Prison Shepton Mallet, Cornhill, Shepton Mallet BA4 5LU* Tel (01749) 823300

BROWNE, Robert. *See* BROWNE, Aubrey Robert Caulfeild

BROWNHILL, Mrs Diane. b 56. Dioc OLM tr scheme 03. **d** 06 **p** 07. C Man Apostles w Miles Platting 06-09; TV Heatons from 09. *St Thomas' Rectory, 6 Heaton Moor Road, Stockport SK4 4NS* Tel 0161-432 1912 Mobile 07505-781530 E-mail gldbrownhill@aol.com

BROWNING, Derek. *See* BROWNING, Robert Derek

BROWNING, Edward Barrington Lee (Barry). b 42. St Pet Coll Saltley TCert65. Ripon Coll Cuddesdon 90. **d** 92 **p** 93. C Falmouth K Chas *Truro* 92-96; R Roche and Withiel 96-01; P-in-c Manaccan w St Anthony-in-Meneage and St Martin 01-06; P-in-c Cury and Gunwalloe w Mawgan 01-06; rtd 06; Perm to Offic *Truro* 06-10; P-in-c St Goran w Caerhays from 10. *The Vicarage, Gorran, St Austell PL26 6HN* Tel (01726) 842040 E-mail barry.browningbtinternet.com

✠**BROWNING, The Rt Revd George Victor.** b 42. Chas Sturt Univ NSW DLitt07. St Jo Coll Morpeth ThL66. **d** 66 **p** 67 **c** 85. C Inverell Australia 66-68; C Armidale 68-69; V Warialda 69-73; Vice Prin St Jo Coll Morpeth 73-76; R Singleton and Adn Upper Hunter 76-84; R Woy Woy and Adn Cen Coast 84-85; Asst Bp Brisbane 85-93; Prin St Fran Th Coll 88-91; Bp Canberra and Goulburn 93-08; Dir Aus Cen Christianity and Culture 96-08; P-in-c Wriggle Valley *Sarum* 08-09; rtd 09. *24 Henry Place, Long Beach NSW 2536, Australia* Tel (0061) (2) 4472 7470 E-mail gandmbrowning@bigpond.com

BROWNING, Canon Jacqueline Ann. b 44. Sarum Th Coll 93. **d** 96 **p** 97. NSM New Alresford w Ovington and Itchen Stoke *Win* 96-02; Past Asst Win Cathl from 02; Min Can 06-09; Hon Can from 09. *1 Paddock Way, Alresford SO24 9PN* Tel (01962) 734372 *or* 857237 E-mail jackie.browning@winchester-cathedral.org.uk

BROWNING, Canon John William. b 36. Keele Univ BA61. Ripon Hall Ox 61. **d** 63 **p** 64. C Baswich *Lich* 63-66; Chapl Monyhull Hosp Birm 67-72; Chapl Wharncliffe Hosp Sheff 72-78; Chapl Middlewood Hosp Sheff 72-94; Hon Can Sheff Cathl 84-97; Chapl Sheff Mental Health Unit 85-94; Chapl Community Health Sheff NHS Trust 94-97; Chapl Sheff (South) Mental Health Centres 94-97; rtd 97; Perm to Offic *Sheff* from 97. *1 Anvil Close, Sheffield S6 5JN* Tel 0114-234 3740 E-mail johnpatbrowning@hotmail.com

BROWNING, Julian. b 51. St Jo Coll Cam BA72 MA76. Ripon Coll Cuddesdon 77. **d** 80 **p** 81. C Notting Hill *Lon* 80-81; C W Brompton St Mary w St Pet 81-84; Perm to Offic 84-91; NSM Paddington St Sav 99-06; NSM St Marylebone St Cypr from 06. *82 Ashworth Mansions, Grantully Road, London W9 1LN* Tel (020) 7286 6034

BROWNING, Kevin John. b 56. Ridley Hall Cam 96. **d** 98 **p** 99. C Northampton Em *Pet* 98-01; P-in-c Hardwick *Ely* 01-09; C Cranham Park *Chelmsf* from 10. *226 Moor Lane, Upminster RM14 1HN* E-mail kevin browning@hotmail.co.uk

BROWNING, Miss Rachel. b 69. Oak Hill Th Coll BA08. **d** 09. NSM Hastings Em and St Mary in the Castle *Chich* from 09. *11A Emmanuel Road, Hastings TN34 3LB* Tel (01424) 430980 Mobile 07939-126955 E-mail rach.browning@gmail.com *or* rach@emmanuelhastings.org.uk

BROWNING, Robert Derek. b 42. Guildf Dioc Min Course 98. **d** 01 **p** 02. OLM Lightwater *Guildf* from 01. *16 Guildford Road, Lightwater GU18 5SN* Tel (01276) 474345 E-mail derekandcarol.b@tiscali.co.uk

BROWNING, Canon Wilfrid Robert Francis. b 18. Ch Ch Ox BA40 MA44 BD49. Cuddesdon Coll 40. d 41 p 42. C Towcester w Easton Neston *Pet* 41-44; C Woburn Square Ch Ch *Lon* 44-46; Chapl St Deiniol's Lib Hawarden 46-48; Chapl Heswall Nautical Sch 46-48; C-in-c Hove St Rich CD *Chich* 48-51; Lect Cuddesdon Coll 51-59; R Gt Haseley *Ox* 51-59; Ed *Bulletin Anglican* 55-60; Warden Whalley Abbey 59-63; Can Res Blackb Cathl 59-65; Dir Post-Ord Tr 62-65; Lect Cuddesdon Coll 65-70; Can Res Ch Ch *Ox* 65-87; Hon Can 87-89; Dir Post-Ord Tr 65-85; Dir of Ords 65-85; Dir Ox NSM Course 72-89; rtd 87; Hon C N Hinksey and Wytham *Ox* 89-09; Tutor Westmr Coll Ox 93-99. *The College of St Barnabas, Blackberry Lane, Lingfield RH7 6NJ* Tel (01342) 872853

BROWNLESS, Brian Paish. b 25. TD72. Keble Coll Ox BA50 MA50. Wells Th Coll 50. d 52 p 53. C Man St Aid 52-54; C Chorlton-cum-Hardy St Clem 54-56; C Swinton St Pet 56-58; V Elton St Steph 58-66; CF (TA) 60-66; Area Sec USPG *Lich* 66-77; Lic to Offic *Lich* 66-77; CF (TA - R of O) 66-72; R Yoxall *Lich* 77-82; V S Ramsey St Paul *S & M* 82-87; rtd 87; Perm to Offic *Heref* from 87. *10 Caple Avenue, Kings Caple, Hereford HR1 4UL* Tel (01432) 840246

BROWNLESS, Philip Paul Stanley. b 19. Selw Coll Cam BA41 MA45. Ridley Hall Cam 46. d 47 p 48. C Prittlewell St Mary *Chelmsf* 47-50; Min Prittlewell St Luke CD 50-54; Chapl and Hd Master Lambrook Sch Bracknell 54-71; V Heckfield cum Mattingley *Win* 71-74; V Heckfield w Mattingley and Rotherwick 74-84; RD Odiham 83-84; rtd 85; Perm to Offic *Chich* from 85. *The Hornpipe, Oak Meadow, Birdham, Chichester PO20 7BH* Tel (01243) 512177

BROWNLIE, Miss Caroline Heddon. b 47. CQSW75. Qu Coll Birm IDC81. d 87 p 94. Asst Chapl Fairfield Hosp Hitchin 87-91; NSM Ashwell w Hinxworth and Newnham *St Alb* 92-98; Chapl HM Rem Cen Low Newton 90-01; Perm to Offic *St Alb* 04-05; P-in-c Gilling and Kirkby Ravensworth *Ripon* 05-07; rtd 07; Perm to Offic *Ely* from 07. *9 Mount Pleasant, Cambridge CB3 0BL* Tel (01223) 350663
E-mail carolineatno9@talktalk.net

BROWNRIDGE, David Leonard Robert. b 76. Univ of Wales (Lamp) BA97. Trin Coll Bris 98. d 00 p 01. C Henfynyw w Aberaeron and Llanddewi Aberarth *St D* 00-04; V Laugharne w Llansadwrnen and Llandawke from 04. *The Vicarage, King Street, Laugharne, Carmarthen SA33 4QE* Tel (01994) 427218
E-mail davidbecky@brownridge97.freeserve.co.uk

BROWNSELL, Preb John Kenneth. b 48. Hertf Coll Ox BA69 BA72 MA89. Cuddesdon Coll 70. d 73 p 74. C Notting Hill All SS w St Columb *Lon* 73-74; C Notting Hill 74-76; TV 76-82; V Notting Hill All SS w St Columb from 82; AD Kensington 84-92; Preb St Paul's Cathl from 92; Dir of Ords from 95. *The Vicarage, Powis Gardens, London W11 1JG* Tel (020) 7727 5919
E-mail johbrwnsll@aol.com

BROXHAM, Ms Ann. b 47. York St Jo Coll BA03. Westcott Ho Cam 10. d 10. NSM Littleport *Ely* from 10. *22 Dexter Lane, Littleport, Ely CB6 1GE* Tel (01353) 862483
E-mail annbroxham@yahoo.co.uk

BROXTON, Alan. b 40. UMIST BSc72 CEng MICE79 MIStructE77. d 96 p 97. OLM Rhodes *Man* 96-09; Perm to Offic from 09. *241 Heywood Old Road, Middleton, Manchester M24 4QR* Tel and fax 0161-643 6319

BRUCE, Miss Amanda Jane. b 67. Liv Univ BSc87 Southn Univ PGCE89 Chelt & Glouc Coll of HE AdDipEd01. Wycliffe Hall Ox 06. d 08. C Haydock St Mark *Liv* from 08. *303 Park Street, Haydock, St Helens WA11 0BG* Tel (01744) 634026 Mobile 07921-461381 E-mail mandylou@bluebottle.com

BRUCE, David Ian. b 47. St Mich Coll Llan 70. d 73 p 74. C Bordesley St Benedict *Birm* 73-74; C Llanishen and Lisvane 74-81; V Canley *Cov* 81-90; V Longford 90-97; rtd 97; Perm to Offic *Cov* from 97. *122 Hugh Road, Coventry CV3 1AF* Tel (024) 7644 5789

BRUCE, Francis Bernard. b 30. Trin Coll Ox BA52 MA56. Westcott Ho Cam 52. d 54 p 55. C Bury St Mary *Man* 54-59; C Sherborne w Castleton and Lillington *Sarum* 59-61; R Croston *Blackb* 61-86; V Bibury w Winson and Barnsley *Glouc* 86-95; rtd 95; Perm to Offic *Glouc* from 95. *6 Gloucester Street, Cirencester GL7 2DG* Tel (01285) 641954

BRUCE, James Hamilton. b 57. Dur Univ BSc78 Newc Univ MSc79 St Andr Univ PhD99. Trin Coll Bris 81. d 84 p 85. C Walmley *Birm* 84-86; Perm to Offic *Carl* 87-95; W Cumbria Sch Worker N Schs Chr Union 87-93; Nat Development Officer Wales Scripture Union 93-94; Chapl Turi St Andr Kenya 95-96; NSM St Andrews St Andr *St And* 96-99; R Penicuik and W Linton *Edin* 99-03; Perm to Offic *Win* 03-06; V Lyndhurst and Emery Down and Minstead from 06. *The Vicarage, 5 Forest Gardens, Lyndhurst SO43 7AF* Tel (023) 8028 2154
E-mail bruces@talktalk.net

BRUCE, John. b 26. d 50 p 51. Canada 50-62; V Broughton Moor *Carl* 63-66; V Carl St Herbert w St Steph 66-74; P-in-c Kendal St Geo 74-76; V 76-83; V Coundon *Dur* 83-86; rtd 86; Perm to Offic *Carl* 86-93. *9 Penton Close, Carlisle CA3 0PX*

BRUCE, John Cyril. b 41. EMMTC 95. d 98 p 99. NSM Spalding *Linc* 98-05; P-in-c Grantham, Manthorpe 05-08; rtd 09. *5 Welwyn Close, Grantham, Grantham NG31 7JU* Tel (01476) 561546 Mobile 07947-156933 E-mail john@john-bruce.co.uk

BRUCE, Ms Kathrine Sarah. b 68. Leeds Univ BA89 St Jo Coll Dur BA01 Trin & All SS Coll Leeds PGCE91. Cranmer Hall Dur 98. d 01 p 02. C Ripon H Trin 01-04; Chapl Trevelyan Coll Dur 04-08; Chapl Van Mildert Coll 04-08; NSM Dur St Oswald 04-08; Chapl St Jo Coll Dur from 08. *St John's College, 3 South Bailey, Durham DH1 3RJ* Tel 0191-334 3500

BRUCE, Leslie Barton. b 23. Liv Univ MB, ChB48. d 71 p 72. NSM Wavertree H Trin *Liv* 71-05. *3 Childwall Park Avenue, Liverpool L16 0JE* Tel 0151-722 7664

BRUCE, Rosemary. d 09 p 10. NSM Drayton St Pet (Berks) *Ox* from 09. *4 Greenacres, Drayton, Abingdon OX14 4JU*
E-mail rosie-bruce@hotmail.co.uk

BRUCE, Mrs Susan Elizabeth. b 52. d 08 p 09. OLM Haughton le Skerne *Dur* from 08. *14 Haughton Green, Darlington DL1 2DF* Tel (01325) 281567 Mobile 07810-720490
E-mail s.bruce178@ntlworld.com

BRUECK, Ms Jutta. b 61. LSE MSc89 Heythrop Coll Lon MA92 Fitzw Coll Cam BA96 MA00. Westcott Ho Cam 94. d 97 p 98. C Is of Dogs Ch Ch and St Jo w St Luke *Lon* 97-01; Chapl Guildhall Sch of Music and Drama 01-06; Chapl Fitzw Coll Cam 06-08; P-in-c Cambridge St Jas *Ely* from 08. *St James's Vicarage, 110 Wulfstan Way, Cambridge CB1 8QJ* Tel (01223) 246419 E-mail jb200@cam.ac.uk

BRUNN, Steven. b 67. Ridley Hall Cam. d 05 p 06. C Chertsey, Lyne and Longcross *Guildf* 05-09; V Oatlands from 10. *The Vicarage, 5 Beechwood Avenue, Weybridge KT13 9TE*
E-mail steve.brunn@ntlworld.com

BRUNNING, Canon David George. b 32. St D Coll Lamp BA53. St Mich Coll Llan 53. d 55 p 56. C Llantwit Major and St Donat's 55-59; C Usk and Monkswood w Glascoed Chpl and Gwehelog 59-62; V Abercarn 62-71; V Pontnewydd 71-89; RD Pontypool 89-97; R Panteg 90-98; Can St Woolos Cathl from 94; rtd 98; Lic to Offic *Mon* from 98. *6 Spitzkop, Llantwit Major CF61 1RD* Tel (01446) 792124

BRUNNING, Neil. b 29. NW Ord Course 73. d 76 p 77. C Cheadle Hulme All SS *Ches* 76-79; V 79-88; V Glentworth *Linc* 88-93; P-in-c Hemswell w Harpswell 88-93; V Glentworth Gp 93-94; rtd 94; Perm to Offic *Linc* from 94. *11 Cavendish Drive, Lea, Gainsborough DN21 5HU* Tel and fax (01427) 617938
E-mail neilbrun@aol.com

BRUNO, Canon Allan David. b 34. AKC59. St Boniface Warminster 59. d 60 p 61. C Darlington H Trin *Dur* 60-64; C Kimberley Cathl and Chapl Bp's Hostel S Africa 64-65; Asst Chapl Peterhouse Dioc Boys' Sch Rhodesia 65-70; Overseas Chapl Scottish Episc Ch 70-75; C Edin Old St Paul 75-76; Dir of Miss Prov of S Africa 76-80; Namibia 80-86; Dean Windhoek 81-86; R Falkirk *Edin* 86-95; Hon Can Kinkizi from 95; Bp's Dom Chapl *Bradf* 96-99; Bp's Past Asst 99-01; rtd 01; Perm to Offic *Bradf* from 01 and *Blackb* from 02. *Pond House, 5 Twine Walk, Burton in Lonsdale, Carnforth LA6 3LR* Tel (015242) 61616 E-mail david@bruno81.freeserve.co.uk

BRUNSKILL, Mrs Sheila Kathryn. See BANYARD, Canon Sheila Kathryn

BRUNSWICK, Canon Robert John. b 38. TD86. St Aid Birkenhead 60. d 63 p 64. C Neston *Ches* 63-66; CF (TA - R of O) 65-96; C Warrington St Paul *Liv* 66-68; V Liv St Paul Stoneycroft 68-78; V Southport St Luke 78-87; R Croston *Blackb* 87-01; R Croston and Bretherton 01-05; Chapl Bp Rawstorne Sch Preston 88-05; Hon Can Koforidua from 94; rtd 05. *50 St Clements Avenue, Farington, Leyland PR25 4QU* Tel (01772) 426094

BRUNT, Prof Peter William. b 36. CVO01 OBE94. Liv Univ MB59 MD67 Lon Univ FRCP74 FRCPEd. Ab Dioc Tr Course. d 96 p 97. NSM Bieldside *Ab* 96-07. *Flat 4, 1 Hillpark Rise, Edinburgh EH4 7BB*

BRUNT, Canon Philippa Ann. b 53. Leeds Univ BA74 Leeds and Carnegie Coll PGCE75. WEMTC 95. d 98 p 99. C Cinderford St Steph w Littledean *Glouc* 98-01; V Parkend and Viney Hill from 01; AD Forest S from 09; Hon Can Glouc Cathl from 10. *The Vicarage, Lower Road, Yorkley, Lydney GL15 4TN* Tel (01594) 562828 E-mail pabrunt@btinternet.com

BRUNYEE, Miss Hilary. b 46. Linc Th Coll 76. dss 81 d 87 p 94. Longsight St Jo w St Cypr *Man* 81-87; Par Dn Peel 87-94; TV 94-99; TV Walkden and Lt Hulton 99-00; rtd 00; Perm to Offic *Man* from 00. *38 Holly Avenue, Worsley, Manchester M28 3DW* Tel 0161-790 7761

BRUSH, Canon Sally. b 47. Lon Univ BD75 Univ of Wales MPhil96. Trin Coll Bris 73. dss 76 d 80 p 97. Flint *St As* 76-83; C 80-83; C Cefn 83-87; C St As and Tremeirchion 83-87; Chapl St As Cathl 83-87; Dn-in-c Cerrigydrudion w Llanfihangel Glyn Myfyr etc 87-97; V 97-07; RD Edeirnion 98-04; Hon Can St As Cathl 01-07; rtd 07. *Persondy, 1 Tyddyn Terrace, Cerrigydrudion, Corwen LL21 9TN* Tel (01490) 420048

BRYAN, Angela. b 82. York Univ BA03 York St Jo Coll PGCE04. St Jo Coll Nottm 07. **d** 10 **p** 11. C Tipton St Matt *Lich* from 10. *54 Oxford Way, Tipton DY4 8AL* Tel 0121-439 9679 E-mail tiptoncurate@googlemail.com

BRYAN, Cecil William. b 43. TCD BA66 MA73. CITC 66. **d** 68 **p** 69. C Dublin Zion Ch *D & G* 68-72; Chapl RAF 72-75; Dioc Info Officer *D & G* 75-90; I Castleknock w Mulhuddart, Clonsilla etc 75-89; Chapl K Hosp Dub 89-99; I Tullow *D & G* 99-07; Can Ch Ch Cathl Dublin 03-07; rtd 07. *2 Grange Heights, Green Road, Newbridge, Co Kildare, Republic of Ireland* Tel (00353) (45) 435572 Mobile 87-221 2004 E-mail c.bryan@iol.ie

BRYAN, Christopher Paul. b 75. Univ Coll Ox BA96 St Jo Coll Dur BA99. Cranmer Hall Dur 97. **d** 00 **p** 01. C Old Swinford Stourbridge *Worc* 00-04; P-in-c Lechlade *Glouc* 04-08; TV Fairford Deanery 09-10; P-in-c Sherston Magna, Easton Grey, Luckington etc *Bris* from 10; P-in-c Hullavington, Norton and Stanton St Quintin from 10. *The Rectory, 1 Rectory Close, Stanton St Quintin, Chippenham SN14 6DT* Tel (01666) 837522 Mobile 07906-175331 E-mail christopher.bryan123@btinternet.com

BRYAN, David John. b 56. Liv Univ BSc77 Hull Univ BTh85 Qu Coll Ox DPhil89. Ox Min Course 89. **d** 90 **p** 91. C Abingdon *Ox* 90-93; Tutor Qu Coll Birm 93-01; Dean of Studies 95-01; R Haughton le Skerne *Dur* 01-11; Dir Studies Lindisfarne Reg Tr Partnership from 11. *2 Kingfisher Close, Esh Winning, Durham DH7 9AN*

BRYAN, Helen Ann. b 68. NTMTC BA07. **d** 07 **p** 08. NSM Laindon w Dunton *Chelmsf* from 07. *21 Ozonia Way, Wickford SS12 0PQ* Tel (01268) 562372 Mobile 07747-397973 E-mail hbryan@talktalk.net

BRYAN, Judith Claire. *See* STEPHENSON, Judith Claire

BRYAN, Michael John Christopher. b 35. Wadh Coll Ox BA58 BTh59 MA63 Ex Univ PhD83. Ripon Hall Ox 59. **d** 60 **p** 61. C Reigate St Mark *S'wark* 60-64; Tutor Sarum & Wells Th Coll 64-69; Vice-Prin 69-71; USA 71-74; Sen Officer Educn and Community Dept *Lon* 74-79; Chapl Ex Univ 79-83; USA from 83; rtd 95; Perm to Offic *Ex* from 95. *148 Proctors Hall Road, Sewanee TN 37375-0860, USA* Tel (001) (931) 598 0860

BRYAN, Canon Philip Richard. b 40. Dur Univ BA61. Wycliffe Hall Ox 72. **d** 74 **p** 75. C Macclesfield St Mich *Ches* 74-77; V St Bees *Carl* 77-06; Chapl St Bees Sch Cumbria 77-06; RD Calder *Carl* 88-96; Hon Can Carl Cathl 91-00; rtd 06. *18 Old Forde, Whitehead, Carrickfergus BT38 9XY* Tel (028) 9337 8438

BRYAN, Canon Sherry Lee. b 49. WMMTC 88. **d** 91 **p** 94. Par Dn St Columb Minor and St Colan *Truro* 91-94; C 94-96; P-in-c St Teath 96-05; P-in-c Blisland w St Breward from 05; P-in-c Helland from 05; Chapl Cornwall Healthcare NHS Trust 99-02; RD Trigg Minor and Bodmin from 02; Hon Can Truro Cathl from 03. *The Rectory, Green Briar, Coombe Lane, St Breward, Bodmin PL30 4LT* Tel (01208) 851829

BRYAN, Timothy Andrew. b 56. St Edm Hall Ox MA80. S'wark Ord Course 93. **d** 96 **p** 97. NSM Morden *S'wark* 96-99; NSM Carshalton Beeches 99-05; NSM Sutton 05-08; Resettlement Chapl HM Pris Wandsworth 07-08; Co-ord Chapl from 08. *HM Prison Wandsworth, PO Box 757, Heathfield Road, London SW18 3HS* Tel (020) 8588 4000 E-mail timbryan7@aol.com

BRYAN, William Terence. b 38. Dudley Coll of Educn CertEd68. Chich Th Coll 73. **d** 75 **p** 76. C Shrewsbury St Giles *Lich* 75-79; V Churchstoke w Hyssington and Sarn *Heref* 79-03; rtd 04; Hon C Betws Cedewain and Tregynon and Llanwyddelan *St As* from 07. *29 Llys Melyn, Tregynon, Newtown SY16 3EE* Tel (01686) 650899

BRYANT, Andrew Watts. b 57. St Jo Coll Dur BA78 Birm Univ MA81. Qu Coll Birm 80. **d** 83 **p** 84. C Pelsall *Lich* 83-87; NSM 91-94; Perm to Offic 87-92; NSM Streetly 94-96; NSM Beckbury, Badger, Kemberton, Ryton, Stockton etc 96-99; R Worplesdon *Guildf* 99-09; Chapl Merrist Wood Coll of Agric and Horticulture 01-09; TR Portishead *B & W* from 09. *The Rectory, 2 Brambling Lane, Portishead, Bristol BS20 7NN* Tel and fax (01275) 848934 E-mail andybryant3@virgin.net

BRYANT, Canon Christopher. b 32. K Coll Lon AKC60. **d** 61 **p** 62. C Fareham H Trin *Portsm* 61-65; C Yatton Keynell *Bris* 65-71; C Biddestone w Slaughterford 65-71; C Castle Combe 65-71; V Chirton, Marden and Patney *Sarum* 71-76; V Chirton, Marden, Patney, Charlton and Wilsford 76-78; P-in-c Devizes St Jo w St Mary 78-87; R 79-97; RD Devizes 83-93; Can and Preb Sarum Cathl 87-04; rtd 97; Master St Nic Hosp Salisbury 97-04. *34 Mill Road, Salisbury SP2 7RZ* Tel (01722) 502336

BRYANT, David Henderson. b 37. K Coll Lon BD60 AKC60. **d** 61 **p** 62. C Trowbridge H Trin *Sarum* 61-63; C Ewell *Guildf* 63-67; V Leiston *St E* 67-73; Chapl RN 73; C Northam *Ex* 74-75; P-in-c Clavering w Langley *Chelmsf* 76-77; Teacher Mountview High Sch Harrow 77-85; P-in-c Boosbeck w Moorsholm *York* 85-89; V 89-90; V Sowerby 90-95; P-in-c Sessay 90-95; V Lastingham w Appleton-le-Moors, Rosedale etc 95-99; rtd 99. *35 West End, Kirkbymoorside, York YO62 6AD* Tel (01751) 430269

BRYANT, Canon Edward Francis Paterson. b 43. S'wark Ord Course 73. **d** 78 **p** 79. NSM Hadlow *Roch* 78-84; C Dartford St Alb 84-87; R Hollington St Leon *Chich* 87-93; V Bexhill

St Aug 93-99; TR Bexhill St Pet from 99; P-in-c Sedlescombe w Whatlington 02-05; RD Battle and Bexhill 98-04 and from 10; Can and Preb Chich Cathl from 00. *The Rectory, Old Town, Bexhill-on-Sea TN40 2HE* Tel (01424) 211115 Fax 07970-991268 Mobile 07824-859044 E-mail bexhillrector@gmail.com

BRYANT, Graham Trevor. b 41. Keble Coll Ox BA63 MA67. Chich Th Coll 64. **d** 66 **p** 67. C Leeds St Wilfrid *Ripon* 66-69; C Haywards Heath St Wilfrid *Chich* 69-74; V Crawley Down All SS 74-79; V Bexhill St Aug 79-85; V Charlton Kings St Mary *Glouc* 85-02; rtd 02; Perm to Offic *Glouc* from 03. *6 The Close, Cheltenham GL53 0PQ* Tel (01242) 520313

✠**BRYANT, The Rt Revd Mark Watts.** b 49. St Jo Coll Dur BA72. Cuddesdon Coll 72. **d** 75 **p** 76 c 07. C Addlestone *Guildf* 75-79; C Studley *Sarum* 79-83; V 83-88; Chapl Trowbridge Coll 79-83; Voc Development Adv and Dioc Dir of Ords *Cov* 88-96; Hon Can Cov Cathl 93-01; TR Coventry Caludon 96-01; AD Cov E 99-01; Adn Cov 01-07; Can Res Cov Cathl 06-07; Suff Bp Jarrow *Dur* from 07. *Bishop's House, Ivy Lane, Gateshead NE9 6QD* Tel 0191-491 0917 Fax 491 5116 E-mail bishop.of.jarrow@durham.anglican.org

BRYANT, Patricia Ann. b 36. Qu Mary Coll Lon BA58. St Mich Coll Llan 94. **d** 91 **p** 92. NSM Llanbadoc *Mon* 91-93; NSM Llangybi and Coedypaen w Llanbadoc 93-94; C 94-98; Asst Chapl Gwent Tertiary Coll 94-98; V Merthyr Cynog and Dyffryn Honddu etc *S & B* 98-02; rtd 03. *5 Trebarried Court, Llandefalle, Brecon LD3 0NB* Tel (01874) 754087 E-mail bryants@surfaid.org

BRYANT, Peter James. b 35. Jes Coll Cam BA58 MA64 UWIST 59 FInstM. St Deiniol's Hawarden 86 St Mich Coll Llan 96. **d** 97 **p** 98. NSM Raglan-Usk *Mon* 97-98; NSM Merthyr Cynog and Dyffryn Honddu etc *S & B* 98-02. *5 Trebarried Court, Llandefalle, Brecon LD3 0NB* Tel (01874) 754087 E-mail bryants@surfaid.org

BRYANT, Canon Richard Kirk. b 47. Ch Coll Cam BA68 MA72. Cuddesdon Coll 70. **d** 72 **p** 73. C Newc St Gabr 72-75; C Morpeth 75-78; C Benwell St Jas 78-82; V Earsdon and Backworth 82-93; V Wylam 93-97; Prin Local Min Scheme 97-11; Prin Reader Tr 97-11; Hon Can Newc Cathl 97-11; rtd 11. *10 Highworth Drive, Newcastle upon Tyne NE7 7FB* Tel 0191-240 1510 E-mail rk.bryant@virginmedia.com

BRYANT, Richard Maurice. b 46. MAAIS80. WMMTC 90. **d** 93 **p** 94. NSM The Stanleys *Glouc* 93-98; NSM Glouc St Geo w Whaddon 98-04; NSM Twigworth, Down Hatherley, Norton, The Leigh etc 04-08; NSM Bisley, Chalford, France Lynch, and Oakridge from 08. *6 Church Street, Kings Stanley, Stonehouse GL10 3HW* Tel (01453) 823172

BRYANT, Miss Sarah Elizabeth. b 82. Grey Coll Dur BA05 Wolfs Coll Cam MPhil07. Westcott Ho Cam 06. **d** 08 **p** 09. C Branksome St Aldhelm *Sarum* 08-11; Chapl St Jo Sch Leatherhead from 11. *St John's School, Epsom Road, Leatherhead KT22 8SP* Tel (01372) 373000 E-mail sarah.bryant82@googlemail.com

BRYARS, Peter John. b 54. BA MEd PhD. St Jo Coll Nottm. **d** 84 **p** 85. C Hull St Martin w Transfiguration *York* 84-87; TV Drypool 87-90; TV Glendale Gp *Newc* 90-94; P-in-c Heddon-on-the-Wall 94-01; Adult Educn Adv 94-01; V Delaval from 01; AD Bedlington from 03; Chapl MU from 02; Bp's Adv for Healing Min *Newc* from 06. *The Vicarage, The Avenue, Seaton Sluice, Whitley Bay NE26 4QW* Tel 0191-237 1982 E-mail pjbryars@btinternet.com

BRYCE, Michael Adrian Gilpin. b 47. TCD BA71 MA95. CITC 74. **d** 77 **p** 78. C Clondalkin w Tallaght *D & G* 77-79; C Ch Ch Cathl and Chapl Univ Coll Dub 79-82; I Ardamine w Kiltennel, Glascarrig etc *C & O* 82-84; CF 84-00; I Lisbellaw *Clogh* 00-05; R Bolam w Whalton and Hartburn w Meldon *Newc* from 05; V Nether Witton from 05. *The Rectory, Whalton, Morpeth NE61 3UX* Tel (01670) 775360

BRYCE, Paul Russell. b 79. SS Mark & Jo Univ Coll Plymouth BA00. Wycliffe Hall Ox MTh. **d** 06 **p** 07. C Paignton Ch Ch and Preston St Paul *Ex* 06-10; P-in-c Charles w Plymouth St Matthias from 10. *The Vicarage, 6 St Lawrence Road, Plymouth PL4 6HN* Tel (01752) 225516

BRYDON, Michael Andrew. b 73. St Chad's Coll Dur BA95 MA96 PhD00. St Steph Ho Ox BA01. **d** 02 **p** 03. C Bexhill St Pet *Chich* 02-06; C Brighton St Paul 06-08; C Brighton St Mich 06-08; Dioc Adv for Educn and Tr of Adults 06-08; R Catsfield and Crowhurst from 08. *The Rectory, Church Lane, Catsfield, Battle TN33 9DR* Tel (01424) 892988

BRYER, Anthony Colin. b 51. Qu Eliz Coll Lon BSc72. Trin Coll Bris 72. **d** 75 **p** 76. C Preston St Cuth *Blackb* 75-78; C Becontree St Mary *Chelmsf* 78-81; TV Loughton St Mary and St Mich 81-88; C Clifton St Paul *Bris* 88-91; P-in-c 91-94; R Bris St Mich and St Paul 94-96; In C of S and Lic to Offic *Edin* 96-04; P-in-c Towcester w Caldecote and Easton Neston Pet 04-07; C Greens Norton w Bradden and Lichborough 06-07; V Towcester w Caldecote and Easton Neston etc 07-11; Ind Chapl *Edin* from 11. *21A Balfour Street, North Berwick EH39 4JY* Tel (01620) 893175 Mobile 07814-832004 E-mail tsbryer@waitrose.com

BRYER, Paul Donald. b 58. Sussex Univ BEd80 Nottm Univ MA96. St Jo Coll Nottm. **d** 90 **p** 91. C Tonbridge St Steph *Roch* 90-94; TV Camberley St Paul *Guildf* 94-99; V Camberley St Mary 99-01; V Dorking St Paul from 01; RD Dorking from 09. *St Paul's Vicarage, 7 South Terrace, Dorking RH4 2AB* Tel (01306) 881998 E-mail paul@stpaulsdorking.org.uk
BRYN-THOMAS, John. b 37. Lich Th Coll 63. **d** 66 **p** 67. C Stoke upon Trent *Lich* 66-71; R Wotton *Guildf* 71-79; P-in-c Holmbury St Mary 78-79; R Wotton and Holmbury St Mary 79-86; C Easthampstead *Ox* 86-88; TV Chambersbury *St Alb* 88-01; rtd 01; Perm to Offic *Guildf* from 02. *Hillmount, 9 Llanway Road, Godalming GU7 3EB* Tel (01483) 527990 E-mail jbrynthomas@tiscali.co.uk
BRYSON, James Ferguson. b 55. NE Lon Poly BSc79 RIBA93. SEITE 04. **d** 07 **p** 08. C Old Ford St Paul and St Mark *Lon* 07-10; P-in-c Eltham St Jo *S'wark* from 11. *The Vicarage, Sowerby Close, London SE9 6HB* E-mail fergusonbryson@btinternet.com
BUCHAN, Geoffrey Herbert. b 38. CEng MIMechE. NOC 91. **d** 94 **p** 95. NSM Barnton *Ches* 94-96; NSM Goostrey 96-99; C Stretton and Appleton Thorn from 99. *12 Hough Lane, Anderton, Northwich CW9 6AB* Tel (01606) 74512 E-mail gbuchan@tiscali.co.uk
BUCHAN, Ms Janet Elizabeth Forbes. b 56. Ex Univ BA79 K Coll Lon MSc90 Surrey Univ PGCE93. SEITE 08. **d** 11. C W Hackney St Barn *Lon* from 11. *9 Stanford Mews, London E8 1JA* Tel (020) 7254 0619 Mobile 07749-104870 E-mail janetbuchan@gmail.com
BUCHAN, Matthew Alexander John. b 69. St Andr Univ MA92. Wycliffe Hall Ox BTh95. **d** 98 **p** 99. C Horninglow *Lich* 98-01; TV Moulsecoomb *Chich* 01-04; Bp's Chapl *Glouc* 04-06; P-in-c Leybourne *Roch* from 06. *The Rectory, 73 Rectory Lane North, Leybourne, West Malling ME19 5HD* Tel (01732) 842187 E-mail frbuchan@frbuchan.force9.co.uk
BUCHANAN, Andrew Derek. b 64. Stirling Univ BA90. Wycliffe Hall Ox 98. **d** 01 **p** 02. C Plas Newton *Ches* 01-03; C Ches Ch Ch 03-06; C Plas Newton w Ches Ch Ch 07-11; Asst Chapl Ches Univ 03-11; V Ruddington *S'well* from 11. *The Vicarage, Wilford Road, Ruddington, Nottingham NG11 6EL* Tel 0115-921 4522 E-mail rev buchanan@hotmail.com
✠**BUCHANAN, The Rt Revd Colin Ogilvie.** b 34. Linc Coll Ox BA MA Lambeth DD93. Tyndale Hall Bris 59. **d** 61 **p** 62 **c** 85. C Cheadle *Ches* 61-64; Tutor St Jo Coll Nottm 64-85; Lib 64-69; Registrar 69-74; Dir of Studies 74-75; Vice-Prin 75-78; Prin 79-85; Hon Can S'well Minster 81-85; Suff Bp Aston *Birm* 85-89; Asst Bp Roch 89-96; Asst Bp S'wark 90-91; V Gillingham St Mark *Roch* 91-96; Area Bp Woolwich *S'wark* 96-04; rtd 04; Hon Asst Bp Bradf from 04; Hon Asst Bp Ripon and Leeds from 05. *21 The Drive, Alwoodley, Leeds LS17 7QB* Tel 0113-267 7721 E-mail colinbuchanan101@btinternet.com
BUCHANAN, Eoin George. b 59. Qu Coll Birm 98. **d** 00 **p** 01. C Dovercourt and Parkeston w Harwich *Chelmsf* 00-04; C Ramsey w Lt Oakley 02-04; TR N Hinckford from 04. *The Rectory, Gages Road, Belchamp St Paul, Sudbury CO10 7BT* Tel (01787) 277850 Mobile 07766-605489 E-mail belchamp@googlemail.com *or* rectory@vodafoneemail.co.uk
BUCHANAN, James Kenyon. b 79. Qu Coll Cam BA02 MA06. Oak Hill Th Coll MTh10. **d** 10 **p** 11. C Clerkenwell St Mark *Lon* from 10. *100 Copenhagen Street, London N1 0RX* Tel (020) 7837 6993 Mobile 07912-227719 E-mail jameskbuchanan@googlemail.com
BUCHANAN, John Fraser Walter. b 32. Em Coll Cam BA55. **d** 93 **p** 94. OLM Wainford *St E* 93-07; rtd 07; Perm to Offic *St E* from 07. *The Hermitage, Bridge Street, Beccles NR34 9BA* Tel (01502) 712154
BUCHANAN, Stephanie Joan. b 65. Linc Coll Ox BA88 MA02 Selw Coll Cam BA01 Goldsmiths' Coll Lon PGCE93. Ridley Hall Cam 99. **d** 02 **p** 03. C Mirfield *Wakef* 02-06; TV Em TM from 06. *The Vicarage, 42 Beaumont Park Road, Huddersfield HD4 5JS* Tel (01484) 431163 E-mail stephanie.buchanan@btinternet.com
BUCK, Ashley. See BUCK, William Ashley
BUCK, David Andrew. b 64. GMusRNCM88. Ripon Coll Cuddesdon 97. **d** 99 **p** 00. C Poulton-le-Sands w Morecambe St Laur *Blackb* 99-03; V Hednesford *Lich* 03-10. *The Vicarage, Wakefield Road, Lightcliffe, Halifax HX3 8TH* Tel (01422) 202424
BUCK, Mrs Jacqueline Rosemary. b 66. ERMC 06. **d** 09 **p** 10. NSM Cople, Moggerhanger and Willington *St Alb* from 09. *54 Henderson Way, Kempston, Bedford MK42 8NP* Tel (01234) 407020 E-mail jackiebuck@hotmail.co.uk
BUCK (née JONES), Kathryn Mary. b 59. Birm Univ BA81 MEd91 Sheff Univ PGCE92. Ripon Coll Cuddesdon. **d** 99 **p** 00. C Uttoxeter Area *Lich* 99-00; C Scotforth *Blackb* 00-03; TV Cannock *Lich* 03-10; C Hednesford 05-10; V Lightcliffe and Hove Edge *Wakef* from 11. *The Vicarage, Wakefield Road, Lightcliffe, Halifax HX3 8TH* Tel (01422) 202424

BUCK, Canon Nicholas John. b 57. Leic Univ BScEng79. Ridley Hall Cam 81. **d** 84 **p** 85. C Oakwood St Thos *Lon* 84-87; C Darnall and Attercliffe *Sheff* 87-90; V Kimberworth 90-96; Chapl Scargill Ho 96-01; P-in-c Bassingham Gp *Linc* 01-06; R from 06; RD Graffoe from 09; Can and Preb Linc Cathl from 10. *The Rectory, 11 Torgate Lane, Bassingham, Lincoln LN5 9HF* Tel (01522) 788383 E-mail nick buck@tiscali.co.uk
BUCK, Canon Richard Peter Holdron. b 37. AKC64. Lambeth Hon MA93. **d** 65 **p** 66. C Mill Hill Jo Keble Ch *Lon* 65-68; C St Marylebone All SS 68-74; Can Res and Treas Truro Cathl 74-76; V Primrose Hill St Mary w Avenue Road St Paul *Lon* 76-84; Bp's Ecum Adv *S'wark* 84-91; P-in-c Dulwich Common St Pet 84-86; Hon Can S'wark Cathl 90-98; C Rotherhithe St Kath w St Barn 91-92; C Bermondsey St Kath w St Bart 92-94; C Greenwich St Alfege w St Pet and St Paul 94-98; rtd 98. *50 Viceroy Lodge, 143 Kingsway, Hove BN3 4RB* Tel (01273) 710155
BUCK, William Ashley. b 61. Man Univ BA82 Ox Univ BA86 MA91. Ripon Coll Cuddesdon 84. **d** 87 **p** 88. C Addington *S'wark* 87-91; C Pimlico St Pet w Westmr Ch Ch *Lon* 91-94; TV Wenlock *Heref* 94-03; RD Condover 00-03; R Cleobury Mortimer w Hopton Wafers etc from 03. *The Rectory, The Hurst, Cleobury Mortimer, Kidderminster DY14 8EG* Tel (01299) 270264
BUCKINGHAM, The Ven Hugh Fletcher. b 32. Hertf Coll Ox BA57 MA60. Westcott Ho Cam 55. **d** 57 **p** 58. C Halliwell St Thos *Man* 57-60; C Sheff Gillcar St Silas 60-65; V Hindolveston *Nor* 65-70; V Guestwick 65-70; R Fakenham w Alethorpe 70-88; Chmn Dioc Bd Soc Resp 81-88; RD Burnham and Walsingham 81-87; Hon Can Nor Cathl 85-88; Adn E Riding *York* 88-98; Can and Preb York Minster 88-01; rtd 98; Perm to Offic *York* from 01. *2 Rectory Corner, Brandsby, York YO61 4RJ* Tel (01347) 888202
BUCKINGHAM, Paul John. b 63. Bris Univ BVSc87. WMMTC 94. **d** 98. NSM Kington w Huntington, Old Radnor, Kinnerton etc *Heref* from 98. *The Cottage, Prospect Lane, Kington HR5 3BE* Tel (01544) 231357
BUCKINGHAM, Richard Arthur John. b 49. Univ of Wales (Cardiff) BA71 PGCE72. Chich Th Coll 73. **d** 76 **p** 77. C Llantwit Major 76-80; C Leigh-on-Sea St Marg *Chelmsf* 80-84; C Westmr St Matt *Lon* 84-87; R Stock Harvard *Chelmsf* 87-02; Perm to Offic *Lon* from 02. *3 Priory Close, London N3 1BB* Tel (020) 8371 0178 E-mail rbuckingham@waitrose.com
BUCKINGHAM, Terence John. b 52. Aston Univ BSc73 MSc75 PhD78 FCOptom74. Coll of Resurr Mirfield 01. **d** 03 **p** 04. NSM Harrogate St Wilfrid *Ripon* 03-09; P-in-c Nidd 09-10; NSM Leeds St Wilfrid from 10. *29 Dalesway, Guiseley, Leeds LS20 8JN* Tel (01943) 876066 Mobile 07815-994017 E-mail terry.j.buckingham@btopenworld.com
BUCKINGHAM, Archdeacon of. See GORHAM, The Ven Karen Marisa
BUCKINGHAM, Area Bishop of. See WILSON, The Rt Revd Alan Thomas Lawrence
BUCKLE, Graham Charles. b 59. ERMC 08. **d** 11. NSM Silverstone and Abthorpe w Slapton etc *Pet* from 11. *5 Orchard Close, Milton Malsor, Northampton NN7 3AY* Tel (01604) 858152 Mobile 07901-660593 E-mail gdjlg@tiscali.co.uk
BUCKLE, Graham Martin. b 62. Southn Univ BTh89 Sheff Univ MMinTheol04. Sarum & Wells Th Coll 85. **d** 89 **p** 90. C Paddington St Jas *Lon* 89-94; P-in-c Paddington St Pet 94-00; R St Marylebone St Paul from 00; Dir of Ords Two Cities Area from 99. *St Paul's House, 9 Rossmore Road, London NW1 6NJ* Tel and fax (020) 7262 9443 Pager 07654-327687 E-mail buckle@freeuk.com
BUCKLER, Andrew Jonathan Heslington. b 68. Trin Coll Ox BA89 MA96. Wycliffe Hall Ox BTh93. **d** 96 **p** 97. C Ox St Aldate 96-00; Crosslinks France from 00. *12 rue de Gassicourt, 78200 Mantes la Jolie, France* Tel (0033) 1 30 33 07 95 E-mail bucklers@clara.net
BUCKLER, George Anthony (Tony). b 35. Open Univ BA74. Lich Th Coll 58. **d** 61 **p** 62. C Old Swinford *Worc* 61-65; C Droitwich St Nic w St Pet 65-67; C Droitwich St Andr w St Mary 65-67; Chapl Claybury Hosp Woodford Bridge 67-78; Chapl St Geo and Co Hosps Linc 78-87; Chapl Lawn Hosp Linc 78-81; Chapl Wexham Park Hosp Slough 87-90; Chapl Mapperley Hosp Nottm 90-94; Chapl Nottm Mental Illness and Psychiatric Unit 90-96; Chapl Wells Rd Cen Nottm 94-96; Chapl Qu Medical Cen Nottm 94-96; Chapl Highbury Hosp Nottm 94-96; rtd 96. *73 Westfield Drive, Lincoln LN2 4RE*
BUCKLER, Canon Guy Ernest Warr. b 46. ACA69 FCA79. Linc Th Coll 71. **d** 74 **p** 75. C Dunstable *St Alb* 74-77; C Houghton Regis 77-86; TV Willington *Newc* 86-88; TR 88-95; Chapl N Tyneside Coll of FE 88-95; R Bedford St Pet w St Cuth *St Alb* 95-05; R Bushey from 05; RD Aldenham 08-11; Hon Can St Alb 10-11; rtd 11. *Address temp unknown* E-mail guybuckl@hotmail.com
BUCKLER, Kenneth Arthur. b 50. S Bank Univ MSc94. NTMTC 95. **d** 98 **p** 99. C Welwyn w Ayot St Peter *St Alb* 98-01; P-in-c Kimpton w Ayot St Lawrence 01-05; Asst Chapl E Herts NHS

Trust 99-00; Asst Chapl E and N Herts NHS Trust 00-04; Chapl Team Ldr 04-05; V Hounslow W Gd Shep *Lon* from 05. *Good Shepherd House, 360 Beavers Lane, Hounslow TW4 6HJ* Tel (020) 8570 4035 Mobile 07909-970545 E-mail vicargoodshepherd@yahoo.co.uk

BUCKLER, The Very Revd Philip John Warr. b 49. St Pet Coll Ox BA70 MA74. Cuddesdon Coll 70. **d** 72 **p** 73. C Bushey Heath *St Alb* 72-75; Chapl Trin Coll Cam 75-81; Min Can and Sacr St Paul's Cathl 81-87; V Hampstead St Jo 87-99; AD N Camden 93-98; Can Res St Paul's Cathl 99-07; Treas 00-07; Dean Linc from 07. *The Deanery, 11 Minster Yard, Lincoln LN2 1PJ* Tel (01522) 561611 E-mail dean@lincolncathedral.com

BUCKLES, Ms Jayne Elizabeth. b 53. **d** 07 **p** 08. NSM Penrhyndeudraeth and Llanfrothen w Maentwrog etc *Ban* 07-10; R St Edm Way *St E* from 10. *The Rectory, Harrow Green, Lawshall, Bury St Edmunds IP29 4PB* Tel (01284) 830513 E-mail jaynebuckles@btinternet.com

BUCKLEY, Alexander Christopher Nolan. b 67. Univ of Wales (Abth) BD89 Man Univ MA06. St Mich Coll Llan. **d** 91 **p** 94. C Llandudno *Ban* 91-92; C Ynyscynhaearn w Penmorfa and Porthmadog 92-93 and 94-96; Jesuit Volunteer Community Manchester 93-94; C Caerau w Ely *Llan* 96-01; V Trowbridge Mawr *Mon* 01-03; Chapl ATC 96-03; Perm to Offic *Mon* 03-09 and *Man* 04-09; R Llanllyfni *Ban* from 09; CMP from 02. *V Rheithordy, 2 Mor Awel, Penygroes, Caernarfon LL54 6RA* Tel (01286) 881124 E-mail rheithor@llanllyfni.plus.com

BUCKLEY, Anthony Graham. b 63. Keble Coll Ox BA84 MA90 PGCE85. Wycliffe Hall Ox 96. **d** 98 **p** 99. C Foord St Jo *Cant* 98-00; V 00-08; AD Elham 05-08; Hon Can Cant Cathl 08; Chapl Alleyn's Sch Dulwich from 08; Hon C Dulwich St Barn *S'wark* from 08; Dir of IME Woolwich Area from 09. *53 Gilkes Crescent, London SE21 7PB* E-mail antmon64@hotmail.com

BUCKLEY, Christopher Ivor. b 48. Chich Th Coll 84. **d** 86 **p** 87. C Felpham w Middleton *Chich* 86-89; C Jersey St Brelade *Win* 89-93; V Jersey St Mark 93-06; Chapl Jersey Airport 00-06; V Knighton, Norton, Whitton, Pilleth and Cascob *S & B* 06-10; rtd 11; Perm to Offic *Win* from 10. *1 Les Petites Champs, La Rue du Flicquet, St Martin, Jersey JE3 6BP* Tel (01534) 738265 Mobile 07797-714595 E-mail christopher.buckley@jerseymail.co.uk

BUCKLEY, David Rex. b 47. Ripon Coll Cuddesdon 75. **d** 77 **p** 78. C Witton *Ches* 77-81; V Backford 81-85; Youth Chapl from 81; V Barnton 85-93; P-in-c Bickerton w Bickley 93-97; P-in-c Harthill and Burwardsley 93-97; V Bickerton, Bickley, Harthill and Burwardsley 97-01; P-in-c Sandbach 01-03; V 03-07; rtd 08; Chapl Cheshire Constabulary from 08. *308 Swanlow Lane, Winsford CW7 4BN* Tel (01606) 559437 E-mail rex@chazandrex.freeserve.co.uk

BUCKLEY, Ms Debra. b 59. Birm Poly BA81. Qu Coll Birm 08. **d** 10 **p** 11. C Balsall Heath and Edgbaston SS Mary and Ambrose *Birm* from 10. *23 Westridge Road, Birmingham B13 0DU* Tel 0121-702 2063 E-mail dbuckley@afairworld.co.uk

BUCKLEY, Ernest Fairbank. b 25. Jes Coll Cam BA49 MA50 Jes Coll Ox BLitt53. Westcott Ho Cam 55. **d** 55 **p** 56. C Rochdale *Man* 55-58; V Hey 58-64; V Baguley 64-79; V Clun w Chapel Lawn, Bettws-y-Crwyn and Newcastle *Heref* 79-87; RD Clun Forest 82-87; rtd 88. *The Old Barn, Brassington, Matlock DE4 4HL* Tel (01629) 540821 E-mail buckley@w3z.co.uk

BUCKLEY, Heather Eileen. b 52. **d** 11. NSM Prenton *Ches* from 11. *57 Field Road, Wallasey CH45 5BG*

BUCKLEY, John. b 42. **d** 95 **p** 96. C Macclesfield Team *Ches* 95-01; P-in-c Pott Shrigley from 01; Chapl E Cheshire NHS Trust from 01. *The Vicarage, Spuley Lane, Pott Shrigley, Macclesfield SK10 5RS* Tel (01625) 573316

BUCKLEY, Michael. b 49. St Jo Coll Dur Cranmer Hall Dur 77. **d** 79 **p** 80. C Birkdale St Jo *Liv* 79-82; TV Maghull 82-88; V Earlestown 88-98; V Gt Sankey from 98. *The Parsonage, Parsonage Way, Great Sankey, Warrington WA5 1RP* Tel (01925) 723235

BUCKLEY, Rex. See BUCKLEY, David Rex

BUCKLEY, Richard Francis. b 44. Ripon Hall Ox 69. **d** 72 **p** 73. C Portsea St Cuth *Portsm* 72-75; C Portsea All SS w St Jo Rudmore 75-79; Chapl RN 79-00; Perm to Offic *B & W* from 00. *Ste Croix, Coryate Close, Higher Odcombe, Yeovil BA22 8UJ* Tel and fax (01935) 864039 Mobile 07810-123065 E-mail rfbuckley@onetel.com

BUCKLEY, Richard John. b 43. Hull Univ BSc(Econ)64 PhD87 Strathclyde Univ MSc69. Sarum Th Coll 64. **d** 66 **p** 67. C Huddersfield St Jo *Wakef* 66-68; C Sutton St Jas *York* 69-71; TV Sutton St Jas and Wawne 71-75; V Handsworth Woodhouse *Sheff* 75-85; R Adwick-le-Street 85-91; V Wentworth and Area Co-ord (S Yorks) Chr Aid 91-97; Area Co-ord (S and E Yorkshire) Chr Aid 97-07; rtd 07; Perm to Offic *York* 97-07 and *Sheff* from 97. *2 Kirkstead Abbey Mews, Thorpe Hesley, Rotherham S61 2UZ* Tel 0114-246 5064

BUCKLEY, Richard Simon Fildes. b 63. WMMTC 97. **d** 00 **p** 01. NSM Moseley St Mary *Birm* 00-04; NSM Soho St Anne w

St Thos and St Pet *Lon* from 05. *12 College Green Court, 55 Barrington Road, London SW9 7JG* Tel (020) 7095 1810 Mobile 07976-290351 E-mail puppet.buckley@virgin.net

BUCKLEY, Canon Robert William. b 50. Grey Coll Dur BSc70 PhD73 DipEd73 CPhys75 MInstE91 FCollP92 FInstP97. NOC 85. **d** 87 **p** 88. NSM N Greenford All Hallows *Lon* 87-91; P-in-c 91-94; NSM W Acton St Martin 94-95; NSM Ealing All SS 94-95; C 95-97; P-in-c Preston Ascension 97-99; TR Wembley Park 99-03; AD Brent 00-03; TR Atherton and Hindsford w Howe Bridge *Man* from 03; AD Leigh from 08; Hon Can Man Cathl from 10. *St Michael's Vicarage, Leigh Road, Atherton, Manchester M46 0PH* Tel (01942) 883359

BUCKLEY, Stephen Richard. b 45. Cranmer Hall Dur 82. **d** 84 **p** 85. C Iffley *Ox* 84-88; TV Halesowen *Worc* 88-00; TR Sedgley All SS 00-05; TR Gornal and Sedgley from 05; P-in-c Sedgley St Mary from 10. *All Saints' Vicarage, Vicar Street, Sedgley, Dudley DY3 3SD* Tel (01902) 882255 E-mail stephen@presbyter.freeserve.co.uk

BUCKLEY, Timothy Denys. b 57. BA. St Jo Coll Nottm. **d** 83 **p** 84. C S Westoe *Dur* 83-85; C Paddington Em Harrow Road *Lon* 85-88; C Binley *Cov* 88-98; Min Binley Woods LEP 88-98; V Belton Gp *Linc* from 98; P-in-c Crowle Gp from 09. *The Old Rectory, 118 High Street, Belton, Doncaster DN9 1NS* Tel (01427) 872207 E-mail timothybuckley@breathe.com

BUCKLEY, Timothy John. b 67. Jes Coll Cam BA90 MA94 ACA94. Wycliffe Hall Ox BTh99. **d** 99 **p** 00. C Langham Hills *Chelms* 99-02; P-in-c Devonport St Mich and St Barn *Ex* from 02. *St Barnabas' Vicarage, 10 De la Hay Avenue, Plymouth PL3 4HU* Tel (01752) 666544 E-mail rev tim@virgin net

BUCKLEY, Timothy Simon. b 72. St Mellitus Coll. **d** 11. C Combe Down w Monkton Combe and S Stoke *B & W* from 11; C Bath Widcombe from 11. *162 Bradford Road, Combe Down, Bath BA2 5BZ* Tel (01225) 840397 E-mail tim.buckley@htcd.org

BUCKMAN, Rossly David. b 36. TCD BA64 MA67 St Pet Coll Ox BA65 MA98. Moore Th Coll Sydney. **d** 59 **p** 60. C Eastwood Australia 59-60; C Port Kembla 60-61; C Dublin Harold's Cross *D & G* 61-64; C Ox St Mich 64-65; Lect Clifton Th Coll 65-69; CF 69-76; Tutor Canberra Coll of Min Australia 77-80; P-in-c Mid Marsh Gp *Linc* 81-82; R 82-89; P-in-c Blakehurst Australia 89-91; R 91-00; Chapl Düsseldorf *Eur* 00-05; rtd 05. *1/40 Bundoran Parade, Mont Albert North Vic 3129, Australia* Tel (0061) (3) 9890 4340 Fax 9899 9849 E-mail buckmen@bigpond.com

BUCKNALL, Ms Alison Mary. b 55. Leeds Univ BA76 Trin Coll Bris MA94. Qu Coll Birm 94. **d** 96 **p** 97. C The Quinton *Birm* 96-00; C Sutton Coldfield H Trin 00-01; Asst Chapl N Bris NHS Trust from 01. *North Bristol NHS Trust, Beckspool Road, Frenchay, Bristol BS16 1LE* Tel 0117-970 1070

BUCKNALL, Allan. b 35. St Matthias Coll Bris CertEd73. ALCD62. **d** 62 **p** 63. C Harlow New Town w Lt Parndon *Chelmsf* 62-69; Chapl W Somerset Miss to Deaf 69-71; Perm to Offic *Bris* 71-77; P-in-c Wisborough Green *Chich* 77-79; R Tillington 78-86; R Duncton 82-86; R Up Waltham 82-86; C Henfield w Shermanbury and Woodmancote 86-89; Asst Chapl Princess Marg Hosp Swindon 89-96; rtd 00; Perm to Offic *Bris* from 00. *5 The Willows, Highworth, Swindon SN6 7PG* Tel (01793) 762721

BUCKNALL, Miss Ann Gordon. b 32. K Coll Lon BSc53 Hughes Hall Cam DipEd54. Qu Coll Birm 80. **dss** 81 **d** 87 **p** 94. Birm St Aid Small Heath 81-85; Balsall Heath St Paul 85-92; Par Dn 87-92; C Handsworth St Jas 92-95; rtd 95; Perm to Offic *Lich* from 95. *20 St Margaret's Road, Lichfield WS13 7RA* Tel (01543) 257382

BUDD, Canon John Christopher. b 51. QUB BA73. CITC. **d** 82 **p** 83. C Ballymena *Conn* 82-85; C Jordanstown w Monkstown 85-88; I Craigs w Dunaghy and Killagan 88-97; Dioc Info Officer 89-97; Bp's Dom Chapl from 94; I Derriaghy w Colin from 97; Can Conn Cathl from 11. *Derriaghy Rectory, 20 Derriaghy Road, Magheralave, Lisburn BT28 3SH* Tel (028) 9061 0859

BUDD, Philip John. b 40. St Jo Coll Dur BA68 MLitt71 Bris Univ PhD78. Cranmer Hall Dur. **d** 66 **p** 67. C Attenborough w Chilwell *S'well* 66-69; Lect Clifton Th Coll 69-71; Lect Trin Coll Bris 72-80; Tutor Ripon Coll Cuddesdon 80-88; Asst Chapl and Tutor Westmr Coll Ox 80-00; Lect 88-00; Asst Chapl and Tutor Ox Brookes Univ 00-03; Lect 00-03; Hon C N Hinksey and Wytham 03-06; Perm to Offic from 06. *4 Clover Close, Oxford OX2 9JH* Tel (01865) 863682 E-mail budds@talk21.com

BUDDEN, Alexander Mark. b 60. UEA BA84. SEITE 01. **d** 04 **p** 05. NSM Mitcham St Barn *S'wark* 04-08; Perm to Offic from 09. *29 Dane Road, London SW19 2NB* Tel (020) 8542 0622 Mobile 07738-290534 E-mail markbudden@sky.com

BUDDEN, Clive John. b 39. Lon Univ DipEd Liv Univ BA. Chich Th Coll. **d** 84 **p** 86. C Gaywood, Bawsey and Mintlyn *Nor* 84-87; TV Brixham w Churston Ferrers and Kingswear *Ex* 87-90; R Exton and Winsford and Cutcombe w Luxborough *B & W* 90-99; Perm to Offic *Truro* 00-02; P-in-c Veryan w Ruan

Lanihorne 02-07; rtd 07. *Carennac House, Polbreen Lane, St Agnes TR5 0UL* Tel (01872) 554313

BUDGELL, Mrs Anne Margaret. b 44. RGN66. STETS 07. **d** 10 **p** 11. NSM Vale of White Hart *Sarum* from 10. *7 Fox's Close, Holwell, Sherborne DT9 5LH* Tel (01963) 23428 E-mail budgells@hotmail.co.uk

BUDGELL, Peter Charles. b 50. Lon Univ BD74. **d** 83 **p** 84. C Goodmayes All SS *Chelmsf* 83-86; C Chipping Barnet w Arkley *St Alb* 86-88; V Luton St Anne 88-06; V Luton St Anne w St Chris from 06. *The Vicarage, 7 Blaydon Road, Luton LU2 0RP* Tel and fax (01582) 720052 E-mail pcbudgell@aol.com

BUDGET, Preb Anthony Thomas. b 26. TD60. Oriel Coll Ox BA50 MA57. Wells Th Coll 57. **d** 59 **p** 60. C Hendford *B & W* 59-63; PC Lopen 63-68; R Seavington St Mich w St Mary 63-68; V Somerton 68-80; RD Ilchester 72-81; P-in-c Compton Dundon 76-80; R Somerton w Compton Dundon 80-81; R Somerton w Compton Dundon, the Charltons etc 81-84; Preb Wells Cathl 83-90; P-in-c Bruton w Lamyatt, Wyke and Redlynch 84-85; P-in-c Batcombe w Upton Noble 84-85; P-in-c S w N Brewham 84-85; TR Bruton and Distr 85-90; rtd 90; Perm to Offic *Ex* 90-09 and *B & W* from 94. *Cornerways, White Ball, Wellington TA21 0LS* Tel (01823) 672321

BUFFREY, Canon Samuel John Thomas. b 28. Keble Coll Ox BA52 MA57. Cuddesdon Coll 52. **d** 54 **p** 55. C Lower Tuffley St Geo CD *Glouc* 54-56; C Branksome St Aldhelm *Sarum* 56-61; R Gussage St Michael and Gussage All Saints 61-69; V Amesbury 69-80; RD Avon 77-80; P-in-c Broadstone 80-82; V 82-93; Can and Preb Sarum Cathl 87-93; rtd 93; Perm to Offic *Sarum* from 93. *34 Woolslope Road, West Moors, Ferndown BH22 0PD* Tel (01202) 875522

BUFTON (née FORSHAW), Mrs Janet Elisabeth. b 41. Redland Coll of Educn CertEd61. **d** 99 **p** 00. OLM Debenham w Aspall and Kenton *St E* 99-04; OLM Helmingham w Framsden and Pettaugh w Winston 99-04; OLM Debenham and Helmingham 04-07; rtd 07; Perm to Offic *St E* from 09. *Harkaway Cottage, 9 Fenn Street, Winston, Stowmarket IP14 6LD* Tel (01728) 860535

BUGDEN, Ernest William. b 16. Lich Th Coll 56. **d** 58 **p** 59. C Esher *Guildf* 58-68; Hon C 68-81; rtd 81; Perm to Offic *Ely* 91-03. *Room 25, Cambridge Manor Care Home, 33 Milton Road, Cambridge CB4 1UZ* Tel (01223) 363904

BUGG, Canon Peter Richard. b 33. Univ of BC BA62. Wells Th Coll 63. **d** 64 **p** 64. C Whitley Ch *Ox* 64-67; C Ludlow *Heref* 67-69; Lic to Offic Zambia 69-72; P-in-c Brill w Boarstall *Ox* 72-78; P-in-c Chilton w Dorton 77-78; V Brill, Boarstall, Chilton and Dorton 78-97; Hon Can Ch Ch 92-97; rtd 97; Lic to Offic Kimberley and Kuruman S Africa 95-98; Perm to Offic *Ox* 04-09. *6 Woodward Parks, Fladbury, Pershore WR10 2RB* Tel (01386) 860531 E-mail pjbugg@btinternet.com

BUGLER, Canon Derek Leslie. b 25. Gen Th Sem NY 62. **d** 64 **p** 64. USA 64-90 and from 04; rtd 90; Lic to Offic *Win* 90-04. *51 Raymond Road, Brunswick ME 04011, USA* E-mail dbugler@gwi.net

BUIK, Canon Allan David. b 39. St Andr Univ BSc61. Coll of Resurr Mirfield 66. **d** 68 **p** 69. Perm to Offic *Win* 68-69; CMP from 69; C Eastleigh *Win* 69-72; C Brighton St Bart *Chich* 72-74; C Lavender Hill Ascension *S'wark* 74-78; V Kingstanding St Mark *Birm* 78-86; Guyana 86-91; V Tunstall *Lich* 91-07; rtd 07; P-in-c Hempton and Pudding Norton from 07; Chantry P Shrine of Our Lady of Walsingham from 06; Hon Can Georgetown Guyana from 10. *20 Cleaves Drive, Walsingham NR22 6EQ* Tel (01328) 820030 Mobile 07703-479715 E-mail allanbuik@googlemail.com

BUIKE, Desmond Mainwaring. b 32. Ex Coll Ox BA55 MA69 Leeds Univ CertEd72. **d** 57 **p** 58. C Man St Aid 57-60; C Ox SS Phil and Jas 60-63; V Queensbury *Bradf* 63-71; Perm to Offic *Bradf* 71-85 and *York* from 93; V Glaisdale *York* 85-93; rtd 93. *Wayside, 3 White Bridge Road, Whitby YO21 3JQ* Tel (01947) 821440

BULCOCK, Andrew Marcus. b 62. **d** 03 **p** 04. OLM Elton St Steph *Man* 03-06; Perm to Offic 06-08; OLM Turton Moorland Min from 08. *5 Fieldhead Avenue, Bury BL8 2LX* Tel 0161-761 6347

BULL, Andrew David. b 70. Hull Univ BSc91 Sheff Univ PGCE92. Regents Th Coll BA99. **d** 07 **p** 08. C Macclesfield Team *Ches* 07-10; P-in-c Bredbury St Mark from 10. *St Mark's Vicarage, 61 George Lane, Bredbury, Stockport SK6 1AT* Tel 0161-406 6552 E-mail ukbulls@aol.com

BULL, Mrs Christine. b 45. Bedf Coll Lon BA67. NOC 91. **d** 94 **p** 95. NSM High Lane *Ches* 94-98; NSM Stockport SW 98-99; Perm to Offic *Derby* 98-04; *Ches* 99-04; *Man* from 00; C Hale and Ashley 04-07; NSM Wormhill, Peak Forest w Peak Dale and Dove Holes *Derby* 07-08; P Pastor Ches Cathl from 08. *Flat 4, 15 Abbey Street, Chester CH1 2JF* Tel (01663) 740847 E-mail revchristinebull@yahoo.co.uk

BULL (née ADAMS), Mrs Christine Frances. b 53. Cam Inst of Educn CertEd74. NEOC 97. **d** 00 **p** 01. NSM St Oswald in Lee w Bingfield *Newc* from 00; P-in-c from 07. *East Side Lodge, Bingfield, Newcastle upon Tyne NE19 2LE* Tel (01434) 672303 E-mail pc.bull@ukonline.co.uk

BULL, Christopher Bertram. b 45. Lon Bible Coll BA87. Wycliffe Hall Ox 88. **d** 90 **p** 91. C Leominster *Heref* 90-95; P-in-c Westbury 95-02; R 02-10; P-in-c Yockleton 95-02; R 02-10; P-in-c Gt Wollaston 95-02; V 02-10; P-in-c Worthen 07-10; rtd 10. *12 Aldersley Way, Ruyton XI Towns, Shrewsbury SY4 1NE* Tel (01939) 260059 E-mail cbbull@fsmail.net

BULL, Christopher David. b 59. Univ of Wales MA08. St Jo Coll Nottm 89. **d** 91 **p** 92. C Bowbrook S *Worc* 91-95; P-in-c Flackwell Heath *Ox* 95-00; V from 00; RD Wycombe 97-05. *The Vicarage, 9 Chapel Road, Flackwell Heath, High Wycombe HP10 9AA* Tel (01628) 522795 or 533004 E-mail vicar@ccfh.org.uk

BULL, David. b 72. Worc Coll Ox BA94. Wycliffe Hall Ox BA07. **d** 08 **p** 09. C Reigate St Mary *S'wark* from 08. *3 St Clair Close, Reigate RH2 0QB* Tel (01737) 221100

BULL, George. See BULL, William George

BULL, John. See BULL, Michael John

BULL, Malcolm George. b 35. Portsm Dioc Tr Course 87. **d** 87 **p** 98. NSM Farlington *Portsm* 87-90; NSM Widley w Wymering 92-93; NSM S Hayling 93-97; NSM Hayling Is St Andr 97-00; Bp's Adv for Cults and New Relig Movements 99-00; rtd 00; Perm to Offic *Portsm* 00-01 and from 04; P-in-c Greatworth and Marston St Lawrence etc *Pet* 01-04. *20 Charleston Close, Hayling Island PO11 0JY* Tel (023) 9246 2025 E-mail bullmg@bushinternet.com

BULL, Martin Wells. b 37. Worc Coll Ox BA61 MA68. Ripon Hall Ox 61. **d** 63 **p** 64. C Blackley St Andr *Man* 63-67; C Horton *Bradf* 67-68; V Ingrow w Hainworth 68-78; RD S Craven 74-77; V Bingley All SS 78-80; TR 80-92; P-in-c Gargrave 92-02; rtd 02; Perm to Offic *Ripon* from 03. *Mallard Cottage, Grewelthorpe, Ripon HG4 3BT* Tel (01765) 650473 Mobile 07870-138386

BULL, Michael John. b 35. Roch Th Coll 65. **d** 67 **p** 68. C N Wingfield *Derby* 67-69; C Skegness *Linc* 69-72; R Ingoldmells w Addlethorpe 72-79; Area Sec USPG *S'wark* 79-85; Area Org RNLI (Lon) 86-88; C Croydon St Jo *S'wark* 89-93; P-in-c Mitcham Ch Ch 93-97; V Colliers Wood Ch Ch 97-00; rtd 00; Perm to Offic *Nor* 00-04; Hon C Guiltcross 04-08; P-in-c from 08. *The Rectory, Back Street, Garboldisham, Diss IP22 2SD* Tel (01953) 688347 E-mail mjbull@waitrose.com

BULL, Canon Robert David. b 51. Westmr Coll Ox MTh03. Ripon Coll Cuddesdon 74. **d** 77 **p** 78. C Worsley *Man* 77-80; C Peel 80-81; TV 81-86; P-in-c Wisbech St Aug *Ely* 86-88; V 88-02; RD Wisbech 92-02; R Lich St Chad 02-11; P-in-c Longdon 08-10; Can Res Bris Cathl from 11. *41 Salisbury Road, Bristol BS6 7AR* Tel 0117-926 4879 E-mail canon.pastor@bristol-cathedral.co.uk

BULL, Mrs Ruth Lois Clare. b 54. Univ of Wales (Lamp) BA76 W Midl Coll of Educn PGCE77. Qu Coll Birm 08. **d** 11. NSM Burntwood *Lich* from 11. *36 Broadlands Rise, Lichfield WS14 9SF* Tel (01543) 319296 E-mail dkbrlcb@hotmail.com

BULL, Stephen Andrew. b 58. St Jo Coll Nottm 91. **d** 93 **p** 94. C Wroughton *Bris* 93-96; P-in-c Eyemouth *Edin* 96-98; Lic to Offic from 98. *12 Craigs Court, Torphichen, Bathgate EH48 4NU* Tel (01506) 650070 E-mail stvbull@btinternet.com

BULL, Miss Susan Helen. b 58. Qu Mary Coll Lon BSc79 ACIS84. STETS BTh98. **d** 98 **p** 99. NSM Epsom St Barn *Guildf* 98-04; Chapl Surrey and Borders Partnership NHS Trust from 04. *41 Stamford Green Road, Epsom KT18 7SR* Tel (01372) 742703 E-mail rev@suebull.freeserve.co.uk

BULL, Timothy Martin. b 65. Worc Coll Ox BA87 MA93 Dur Univ PhD94 Fitzw Coll Cam BA98 MA07 FRSA96 CEng96 MBCS96. Ridley Hall Cam 96. **d** 99 **p** 00. C Bath Walcot *B & W* 99-03; P-in-c Langham w Boxted *Chelmsf* from 03; Colchester Area CME Adv from 03. *The Rectory, Wick Road, Langham, Colchester CO4 5PG* Tel (01206) 230666 E-mail revdrtim@gmail.com

BULL, William George. b 28. Sarum Th Coll 65. **d** 66 **p** 67. C Salisbury St Mich *Sarum* 66-69; V Swallowcliffe w Ansty 69-75; Dioc Youth Officer 69-71; P-in-c Laverstock 75-81; V 81-93; rtd 94; Perm to Offic *Sarum* from 94. *Bungalow 1, Boreham Field, Warminster BA12 9EB* Tel (01985) 847830

BULLAMORE, John Richard. b 41. Linc Coll Ox BA69 MA69. Wycliffe Hall Ox 74. **d** 95 **p** 95. NSM Eorropaidh *Arg* 95-98; NSM Bath St Sav w Swainswick and Woolley *B & W* 98-08; NSM Knaresborough *Ripon* from 08. *39 Birkdale Close, Knaresborough HG5 0LS* Tel (01423) 864484 E-mail john.bullamore@homecall.co.uk

BULLIMORE, Canon Christine Elizabeth. b 46. Nottm Univ BA67. St Jo Coll Nottm 96. **d** 96 **p** 97. Bp's Adv Past Care and Counselling *Wakef* 92-99 and from 01; NSM S Ossett 96-99; P-in-c Emley and Flockton cum Denby Grange 99-11; RD Kirkburton 05-11; Hon Can Wakef Cathl 08-11; rtd 11. *5 Snowgate Head, New Mill, Holmfirth, Huddersfield HD9 7DH* Tel (01484) 686812 Mobile 07921-588276 E-mail chrisbullimore@talktalk.net

BULLIMORE, Matthew James. b 77. Em Coll Cam BA99 MA03 PhD07 Man Univ MPhil02. Harvard Div Sch 99 Westcott Ho Cam 01. **d** 05 **p** 06. C Robertstown w Hartshead *Wakef* 05-07; Bp's Dom Chapl 07-11; V Royston from 11. *The Clergy House,*

Church Street, Royston, Barnsley S71 4QZ Tel (01226) 722410
E-mail mjb56@cantab.net
BULLIVANT, Ronald. b 32. CertEd. St Mich Coll Llan. d 59 p 60.
C Roath St German *Llan* 59-61; P-in-c Bradf H Trin 61-66; V
Horbury *Wakef* 66-69; Lic to Offic *Ripon* 70-78; Perm to Offic
Nor 78-81; Lic to Offic 81-98; Perm to Offic *Man* 99-11. *6 rue des
Chênes, Grande Romelière, 79600 Saint-Loup-Lamaire, France*
Tel (0033) 5 49 64 30 71
BULLOCH, William Gillespie. b 68. St Steph Ho Ox. d 01 p 02. C
Bognor *Chich* 01-05; V Leigh-on-Sea St Jas *Chelmsf* from 05.
St James's Vicarage, 103 Blenheim Chase, Leigh-on-Sea SS9 3BY
Tel (01702) 471786 E-mail frbill.bulloch@gmail.com
BULLOCK, Andrew Belfrage. b 50. Univ of Wales (Ban) BSc73
MEd81 Westmr Coll Ox PGCE79. Wycliffe Hall Ox 94. d 97
p 98. C Sandhurst *Ox* 97-02; P-in-c Alfrick, Lulsley, Suckley,
Leigh and Bransford *Worc* 02-08; TV Worcs W from 09. *The
Rectory, Leigh, Worcester WR6 5LE* Tel (01886) 832355
Mobile 07958-654331 E-mail abullock@waitrose.com
BULLOCK, Andrew Timothy. b 56. Southn Univ BTh91. Sarum
& Wells Th Coll 89. d 91 p 92. C Erdington St Barn *Birm* 91-94;
TV Solihull 94-03; P-in-c Acocks Green 03-08; V from 08. *The
Vicarage, 34 Dudley Park Road, Acocks Green, Birmingham
B27 6QR* Tel and fax (0121-706 9764
E-mail andrewbullock2@blueyonder.co.uk
BULLOCK, Ian. b 74. Cranmer Hall Dur. d 08 p 09. C Pontefract
St Giles *Wakef* 08-11; P-in-c Heckmondwike from 11; P-in-c
Liversedge w Hightown from 11. *The Vicarage, 25 Church Street,
Heckmondwike WF16 0AX* Tel (01924) 401275
E-mail ianb@mailshack.com
BULLOCK, Jude Ross. b 58. Heythrop Coll Lon BD89. Allen
Hall 84. d 89 p 90. In RC Ch 89-97; C Lt Ilford St Mich *Chelmsf*
01-05; V Chingford St Anne from 05. *St Anne's Vicarage, 200A
Larkshall Road, London E4 6NP* Tel (020) 8529 4740 Mobile
07976-395732 E-mail juderbullock1@yahoo.co.uk
BULLOCK, Kenneth Poyser. b 27. Down Coll Cam BA50 MA55.
Ridley Hall Cam 50. d 52 p 53. C Aston SS Pet and Paul *Birm*
52-56; R Openshaw *Man* 56-63; V Ainsworth 63-91; rtd 91.
26 Plas Penrhyn, Penrhyn Bay, Llandudno LL30 3EU Tel
(01492) 543343
BULLOCK, Canon Michael. b 49. Hatf Coll Dur BA71. Coll of
Resurr Mirfield 72. d 75 p 76. C Pet St Jo 75-79; Zambia 79-86; V
Longthorpe *Pet* 86-91; Chapl Naples *Eur* 91-99; OGS from 93;
P-in-c Liguria *Eur* 99-00; Chapl Gtr Lisbon from 00; Can Malta
Cathl from 98. *rua João de Deus 5, Alcoitão, 2645-128
Alcabideche, Portugal* Tel and fax (00351) (21) 469 2303
E-mail padre@lisbonanglicans.org
BULLOCK, Philip Mark. b 59. Qu Coll Birm 05. d 08 p 09. C Cov
E 08-10; TV from 10. *The Vicarage, Mercer Avenue, Coventry
CV2 4PQ* Tel 07831-147822 (mobile)
E-mail philip.bullock00@btinternet.com
BULLOCK, Miss Rosemary Joy. b 59. Portsm Poly BA81 Southn
Univ BTh94. Sarum & Wells Th Coll 89. d 91 p 94. Par Dn
Warblington w Emsworth *Portsm* 91-94; C 94-95; C Gt Parndon
Chelmsf 95-98; TV Beaminster Area *Sarum* 98-03; P-in-c
Ridgeway 03-04. *82 Green Lane, Shanklin PO37 7HD* Tel
(01983) 863345
BULLOCK (*née* WHEALE), **Canon Sarah Ruth.** b 64. Surrey
Univ BA86 St Jo Coll Dur BA93. Cranmer Hall Dur 90. d 93
p 94. C Kersal Moor *Man* 93-98; P-in-c Whalley Range St Edm
98-04; P-in-c Moss Side St Jas w St Clem 99-04; R Whalley
Range St Edm and Moss Side etc from 04; Dioc Voc Adv 98-05;
Chapl MU 00-06; Bp's Adv for Women's Min *Man* from 09;
Borough Dean Man from 10; Hon Can Man Cathl from 07.
St Edmund's Rectory, 1 Range Road, Manchester M16 8FS Tel
0161-226 1291 E-mail revsbullock@aol.com
BULLOCK, Stephanie Clair. b 46. St Mary's Hosp Medical Sch
Lon MB, BS70. Ripon Coll Cuddesdon 90. d 92 p 94. Par Dn
Cuddesdon *Ox* 92-94; Tutor Ripon Coll Cuddesdon 92-94; Asst
Chapl Ox Radcliffe Hosp NHS Trust 94-97; Chapl Ox Radcliffe
Hosps NHS Trust 97-03; Hon C Headington St Mary *Ox* 03-09;
rtd 09; Perm to Offic *Ox* from 09. *Church Farm, Church Lane,
Old Marston, Oxford OX3 0PT* Tel (01865) 722926
E-mail stephaniebullock9@gmail.com
BULLOCK, Victor James Allen. b 67. Southn Univ BTh90
St Mary's Coll Twickenham PGCE91. St Steph Ho Ox 92. d 94
p 95. C Cowley St Jas *Ox* 94-95; C Reading St Giles 95-99; V
Fenny Stratford from 99. *The Vicarage, Manor Road, Milton
Keynes MK2 2HW* Tel (01908) 372825
BULLWORTHY, Rita Irene. b 48. Glos Univ BA09. SWMTC 09.
d 11. NSM N Tawton, Bondleigh, Sampford Courtenay etc *Ex*
from 11. *Rivendell House, Sampford Courtenay, Okehampton
EX20 2TF* Tel (01837) 89168
E-mail ritabullworthy@yahoo.co.uk
BULMAN, Madeline Judith. *See* STRONG, Ms Madeline Judith
BULMAN, Michael Thomas Andrew. b 34. Jes Coll Cam BA59
MA61. Ridley Hall Cam 58. d 60 p 61. C Blackpool St Mark
Blackb 60-63; C Branksome St Clem *Sarum* 63-67; V York
St Barn 67-84; CMJ Israel 84-93; R Jerusalem Ch Ch 85-87; Can
Jerusalem 87-93; R Maresfield and V Nutley *Chich* 94-00; rtd 00;

Perm to Offic *Portsm* from 06. *Oate Villa, Western Road,
Ivybridge PL21 9AT* Tel (01752) 691941
E-mail michael.bulman@sky.com
BUNCE (*née* HOW), **Gillian Carol.** b 53. K Coll Lon MB, BS77
MRCGP82 MFHom96. STETS 04. d 07 p 08. NSM Worle
B & W from 07. *85 Clevedon Road, Tickenham, Clevedon
BS21 6RD* Tel (01275) 810610
E-mail gill.how@blueyonder.co.uk
BUNCE, Michael John. b 49. Westcott Ho Cam. d 80 p 81. C
Grantham *Linc* 80-83; TV 83-85; R Tarfside *Bre* 85-92; R
Brechin 85-92; R Auchmithie 91-92; Provost St Paul's Cathl
Dundee 92-97; Chapl Menorca *Eur* from 00. *Apartado de
Correos 102, 07720 Es Castell, Menorca, Spain* Tel (0034) 971
352 378 Fax 971 150 173
BUNCE, Raymond Frederick. b 28. Ely Th Coll 54. d 57 p 58. C
Hillingdon St Andr *Lon* 57-62; C Greenford H Cross 62-67; V
Ealing All SS 67-89; Chapl Ascot Priory 89-90; rtd 90; Perm to
Offic *Portsm* from 91 and *Chich* from 99. *45 Guillards Oak,
Midhurst GU29 9JZ* Tel (01730) 816282
BUNCH, Canon Andrew William Havard. b 53. Selw Coll Cam
BA74 MA78 PhD79. Ox NSM Course 84. d 87 p 88. NSM
Wantage *Ox* 87-91; C New Windsor 91-93; TV 93-97; V Ox
St Giles and SS Phil and Jas w St Marg from 97; Hon Can Ch Ch
from 09. *The Vicarage, Church Walk, Oxford OX2 6LY* Tel
(01865) 510460 E-mail vicar@churchwalk.eclipse.co.uk
BUNDAY, Mrs Janet Lesley. b 56. Nottm Univ BA78 Univ of
Wales (Lamp) MA08 Lon Inst of Educn PGCE79. Ridley Hall
Cam 08. d 10 p 11. NSM Potton w Sutton and Cockayne Hatley
St Alb from 10. *The Barnyard, Silver Street, Litlington, Royston
SG8 0QE* Tel (01763) 853213 E-mail jan@bunday.co.uk
BUNDAY, Canon Paul. b 30. Wadh Coll Ox BA54 MA58.
ALCD56. d 56 p 57. C Woking St Jo *Guildf* 56-60; Chapl Reed's
Sch Cobham 60-66; R Landford w Plaitford *Sarum* 66-77; RD
Alderbury 73-77; TR Radipole and Melcombe Regis 77-86; RD
Weymouth 82-85; Can and Preb Sarum Cathl 83-95; TV
Whitton 86-91; TR 91-95; Chapl Duchess of Somerset Hosp
Froxfield 86-94; rtd 95; Perm to Offic *Sarum* from 95.
4 Springfield Park, Tisbury, Salisbury SP3 6QN Tel (01747)
871530
BUNDAY, Richard William. b 76. Lanc Univ BA98 MA04.
Cranmer Hall Dur 98. d 00 p 01. C Redcar *York* 00-01; C
Marton *Blackb* 01-04; P-in-c Ashton-on-Ribble St Mich w
Preston St Mark 04-06; TR W Preston 06-10; P-in-c Kirkham
10-11; V from 11. *The Vicarage, Church Street, Kirkham, Preston
PR4 2SE* E-mail bundays@blueyonder.co.uk
BUNDOCK, Canon Anthony Francis. b 49. Qu Coll Birm 81. d 83
p 84. C Stansted Mountfitchet *Chelmsf* 83-86; TV
Borehamwood *St Alb* 86-94; TR Seacroft *Ripon* 94-05; AD
Whitkirk 00-05; TR Leeds City from 05; Hon Can Ripon Cathl
from 05. *Leeds Rectory, 1 Vicarage View, Leeds LS5 3HF* Tel
0113-278 6237 E-mail tony.pat.bundock@virgin.net
BUNDOCK, Edward Leigh. b 52. Keble Coll Ox BA73 Open
Univ PhD94 MAAT. St Steph Ho Ox 74. d 76 p 77. C Malvern
Link w Cowleigh *Worc* 76-80; C-in-c Portslade Gd Shep CD
Chich 80-88; V Wisborough Green 88-94; Perm to Offic *Guildf*
96-97; P-in-c E and W Rudham, Houghton-next-Harpley etc
Nor 97-99; R E w W Rudham, Helhoughton etc from 99. *The
Rectory, South Raynham Road, West Raynham, Fakenham
NR21 7HH* Tel (01328) 838385
BUNDOCK, Canon John Nicholas Edward. b 45. Wells Th Coll
66. d 70 p 71. C Chingford SS Pet and Paul *Chelmsf* 70-74; P-in-c
Gt Grimsby St Matt Fairfield CD *Linc* 74-81; V Hindhead
Guildf 81-99; RD Farnham 91-96; V Bramley and Grafham from
99; RD Cranleigh from 04; Chapl Gosden Ho Sch from 99; Hon
Can Guildf Cathl from 09. *The Vicarage, Birtley Rise, Bramley,
Guildford GU5 0HZ* Tel (01483) 892109
E-mail jnebundock@tiscali.co.uk
BUNDOCK, Nicholas John. b 73. Sheff Univ BSc94 PhD98 Fitzw
Coll Cam BA01. Ridley Hall Cam 99. d 02 p 03. C Mortomley
St Sav High Green *Sheff* 02-05; TV Didsbury St Jas and Em
Man 05-10; TR from 10. *St James's Rectory, 9 Didsbury Park,
Manchester M20 5LH* Tel 0161-434 6518 or 446 4150
E-mail nickbundock@stjamesandemmanuel.org
BUNDOCK, Ronald Michael. b 44. Leeds Univ BSc65. Ox NSM
Course 87. d 90 p 91. NSM Buckingham *Ox* 90-98; NSM Stowe
from 98; P-in-c from 03; AD Buckingham from 11. *1 Holton
Road, Buckingham MK18 1PQ* Tel (01280) 813887
E-mail ron@bundock.com
BUNKER (*née* HARDING), **Mrs Elizabeth.** Chelsea Coll Lon
BSc67 MSc69. SAOMC 04. d 06 p 07. NSM Baldock w Bygrave
and Weston *St Alb* 06-10; NSM St Paul's Walden from 10.
Arana, 6 Hitchin Road, Letchworth Garden City SG6 3LL Tel
(01462) 686808 Fax 679276 Mobile 07850-413724
E-mail elizabethbunker@hotmail.com
BUNKER, Janet Constance. b 59. Qu Mary Coll Lon BSc81 (R
Holloway & Bedf New Coll Lon PhD85 Open Univ MA(Ed).
Westcott Ho Cam 05. d 07 p 08. C Cambridge Ascension *Ely*
07-10; TV from 10. *Ascension Rectory, 95 Richmond Road,*

Cambridge CB4 3PS Tel (01223) 229976 Mobile 07811-357564
E-mail janet ascension@yahoo.com
BUNKER, John Herbert George. b 31. AKC56. **d** 57 **p** 58. C Newc
St Jo 57-60; C Cullercoats St Geo 61-65; V Byker St Mich 65-74;
V Ashington 74-84; V Halifax St Aug *Wakef* 84-93; rtd 93; Perm
to Offic *Wakef* 93-98. *1 Hebble Dean, Hebble Lane, Halifax
HX3 5JL* Tel (01422) 251484
E-mail thebunkers@blueyonder.co.uk
BUNKER, The Very Revd Michael. b 37. Oak Hill Th Coll 59.
d 63 **p** 64. C Alperton *Lon* 63-66; C St Helens St Helen *Liv* 66-70;
V Muswell Hill St Matt *Lon* 70-79; V Muswell Hill St Jas 78-79;
V Muswell Hill St Jas w St Matt 79-92; AD W Haringey 85-90;
Preb St Paul's Cathl 90-92; Dean Pet 92-06; rtd 06; Perm to Offic
Pet from 10. *21 Black Pot Lane, Oundle, Peterborough PE8 4AT*
Tel (01832) 273032 E-mail mandmbbythesea@btinternet.com
BUNN, Mrs Rosemary Joan. b 60. EAMTC 94. **d** 97 **p** 98. NSM
Sprowston w Beeston *Nor* 97-01; R Stoke H Cross w Dunston,
Arminghall etc 01-11; R Belton and Burgh Castle from 11. *The
Rectory, Beccles Road, Belton, Great Yarmouth NR31 9JQ* Tel
(01493) 780210
BUNNELL, Adrian. b 49. Univ of Wales (Abth) BSc72. St Mich
Coll Llan 74. **d** 75 **p** 76. C Wrexham *St As* 75-78; C Rhyl w
St Ann 78-79; CF 79-95; R Aberfoyle and Callander *St And*
95-03; R Newport-on-Tay 03-06; rtd 06. *Gauger Hall Cottage,
Forneth, Blairgowrie PH10 6SP* Tel (01350) 724317
E-mail adrian.bunnell@tesco.net
BUNTING, Edward Garth. b 70. TCD BTh99. CITC 96. **d** 99
p 00. C Clooney w Strathfoyle *D & R* 99-02; I Leckpatrick w
Dunnalong 02-06; I Belfast Upper Malone (Epiphany) *Conn*
06-10; I Finaghy 06-10; PV Ch Ch Cathl Dublin from 10.
67 Brookfield Green, Kimmage, Dublin 12, Republic of Ireland
Tel (00353) (1) 677 9099 Fax 679 8991
E-mail garth.bunting@cccdub.ie
BUNTING, Canon Ian David. b 33. Ex Coll Ox BA58 MA61.
Tyndale Hall Bris 57 Princeton Th Sem ThM60. **d** 60 **p** 61. C
Bootle St Leon *Liv* 60-63; V Waterloo St Jo 64-71; Dir Past
Studies St Jo Coll Dur 71-78; R Chester le Street *Dur* 78-87; RD
Chester-le-Street 79-84; Kingham Hill Fellow 87-89; Dioc Dir of
Ords *S'well* 90-99; C Lenton 90-97; Hon Can S'well Minster
93-99; Bp's Research Officer 97-00; rtd 00; Perm to Offic *S'well*
from 00. *8 Crafts Way, Southwell NG25 0BL* Tel (01636) 813688
E-mail ibunting@waitrose.com
BUNTING, Jeremy John. b 34. St Cath Coll Cam BA56 MA60
Worc Coll Ox BA58 MA60. St Steph Ho Ox 57. **d** 59 **p** 60. C
Bickley *Roch* 59-62; C Cambridge St Mary Less *Ely* 62-66; Fell
and Tutor Gen Th Sem New York USA 66-68; R Stock Harvard
Chelmsf 68-87; RD Wickford 73-79; V Hampstead Garden
Suburb *Lon* 87-94; rtd 99. *Fairview, 82 New Road, Haslingfield,
Cambridge CB23 1LP* Tel (01223) 871602
BUNTING (née BYRNE), Mrs Lynda. b 47. STETS 06. **d** 08 **p** 09.
NSM Chandler's Ford *Win* from 08. *18 Queen's Road,
Chandler's Ford, Eastleigh SO53 5AH* Tel (023) 8026 9418
E-mail lyndabunting@aol.com
BUNYAN, David Richard. b 48. Edin Th Coll 93. **d** 96 **p** 97. NSM
Musselburgh *Edin* 96-98; NSM Prestonpans 96-98; C Edin
St Dav 98-00; R Grangemouth from 00; P-in-c Bo'ness from 00.
The Rectory, 33 Carronflats Road, Grangemouth FK3 9DG Tel
and fax (01324) 482438 E-mail drbdoe@blueyonder.co.uk
BUNYAN, Richard Charles. b 43. Oak Hill Th Coll 63 Ridley Hall
Cam 69. **d** 71 **p** 72. C Luton Ch Ch *Roch* 71-74; C Bexleyheath
Ch Ch 74-76; C Bexley St Jo 76-79; TV Northampton Em *Pet*
79-81; V Erith St Jo *Roch* 81-86; V S Woodham Ferrers *Chelmsf*
86-89; Chapl Scargill Ho 89-90; Sub Chapl HM Pris Swaleside
91-94; Dep Chapl HM Pris Belmarsh 94-96; Chapl HM Pris
Littlehey 96-08; rtd 08; Perm to Offic *Ely* from 08; Dioc
Spirituality Officer 07-10. *6 Swan End, Buckden, St Neots
PE19 5SW* Tel (01480) 812950
E-mail rbunyan@btinternet.com
BUR, Patricia Margaret. See CAPRIELLO, Patricia Margaret
BURBERRY, Miss Frances Sheila. b 60. ACII83. TISEC 03. **d** 06
p 07. C Edin St Pet 06-11; R Edin St Ninian from 11; Hon Chapl
Edin Univ from 06. *131 Craiglea Drive, Edinburgh EH10 5PP*
Tel 07803-602394 (mobile) E-mail frances.burberry@ed.ac.uk
BURBIDGE, Barry Desmond. b 52. STETS 94. **d** 97 **p** 98. NSM
Fleet *Guildf* 97-03; NSM Crondall and Ewshot from 03; Chapl
Frimley Park Hosp NHS Foundn Trust from 07. *34 Ashbury
Drive, Hawley, Camberley GU17 9HH* Tel (01276) 32776
E-mail b.burbidge@ntlworld.com
or barry.burbidge@fph-tr.nhs.uk
BURBIDGE, Richard John. b 77. Lon Guildhall Univ BSc00.
Oak Hill Th Coll BTh11. **d** 11. C Lowestoft Ch Ch *Nor* from 11.
10 Station Road, Lowestoft NR32 4QF Tel 07973-801254
(mobile) E-mail richburbidge@googlemail.com
BURBRIDGE, The Very Revd John Paul. b 32. K Coll Cam BA54
MA58 New Coll Ox BA54 MA58 FSA89. Wells Th Coll 58. **d** 59
p 60. C Eastbourne St Mary *Chich* 59-62; V Choral York
Minster 62-66; Can Res and Prec 66-76; Adn Richmond *Ripon*
76-83; Can Res Ripon Cathl 76-83; Dean Nor 83-95; rtd 95;

Perm to Offic *Ripon* 95-06. *The Clachan Bothy, Newtonairds,
Dumfries DG2 0JL*
BURBRIDGE, Richard James. b 47. Univ of Wales (Ban) BSc68.
Oak Hill Th Coll 68. **d** 72 **p** 73. C Rodbourne Cheney *Bris* 72-75;
C Downend 75-78; P-in-c Bris H Cross Inns Court 78-83; P-in-c
Fishponds All SS 83-86; V 86-97; RD Stapleton 89-95; C
Bishopston 97-98; C Bris St Andr w St Bart 97-98; TV
Bishopston and St Andrews from 98. *10 Scandrett Close, Bristol
BS10 7SS* Tel 0117-950 4945
E-mail burbridge466@btinternet.com
BURBURY, Janet. b 56. Sunderland Univ CertEd02. Cranmer
Hall Dur 05. **d** 07 **p** 08. C Hart w Elwick Hall *Dur* 07-11; P-in-c
from 11. *West Holling Carr, Trimdon, Trimdon Station, Durham
TS29 6NN* Tel (01429) 880334 Mobile 07958-131271
E-mail janetb 231@hotmail.co.uk
BURCH, Charles Edward. b 57. Trin Coll Cam MA80 Lon
Business Sch MBA87. ERMC 05. **d** 07 **p** 08. NSM Harpenden
St Jo *St Alb* from 07; Dioc Voc Officer from 11. *12 Poynings
Close, Harpenden AL5 1JD* Tel (01582) 712776 *or* 461481
E-mail charlesburch57@hotmail.com
or dvo@stalbans.anglican.org
BURCH, Christopher. See BURCH, Canon John Christopher
BURCH, Canon John Christopher. b 50. Trin Coll Cam BA71
MA76 Leeds Univ MPhil95. St Jo Coll Nottm 73. **d** 76 **p** 77. C
Sheff St Jo 76-79; C Holbeck *Ripon* 79-82; V Burmantofts
St Steph and St Agnes 82-95; Can Res and Prec Cov Cathl 95-02;
Chapl to Clergy of UPA 99-02; C-in-c Braunstone Park CD *Leic*
02-08; V Braunstone Park from 08; RD Christianity S 04-08; AD
City of Leic 08-09. *St Peter's Vicarage, Main Street, Leicester
LE3 3AL* Tel 0116-289 3377 E-mail chris@burches.co.uk
BURCH, Canon Peter John. b 36. ACA60 FCA71. Ripon Hall Ox
62. **d** 64 **p** 65. C Brixton St Matt *S'wark* 64-67; Chapl Freetown
St Aug Sierra Leone 68-72; P-in-c Chich St Pet 72-76; V
Broadwater Down 76-85; V Steyning 85-94; R Ashurst 85-94;
Hon Can Bauchi from 93; V Broadway *Worc* 94-96; V Broadway
w Wickhamford 96-02; rtd 02; Perm to Offic *Glouc* from 03 and
Worc from 04. *6 Jordan's Close, Willersey, Broadway WR12 7QD*
Tel (01386) 853837 E-mail pj pjburch@hotmail.com
BURCH, Stephen Roy. b 59. St Jo Coll Nottm 82. **d** 85 **p** 86. C
Ipswich St Aug *St E* 85-89; Youth Chapl *Cov* 89-94; P-in-c
Kinwarton w Gt Alne and Haselor 89-99; R 99-04; P-in-c
Coughton 02-04; RD Alcester 99-04; V Fletchamstead from 04;
AD Cov S from 10; AD Kenilworth from 10. *St James's
Vicarage, 395 Tile Hill Lane, Coventry CV4 9DP* Tel (024) 7646
6262 E-mail stephen.burch@btinternet.com
BURCHELL, Mrs Elizabeth Susan. b 53. Sheff Univ BSc74.
SAOMC 04. **d** 07 **p** 08. NSM Banbury St Leon *Ox* 07-10; P-in-c
from 10. *St Leonard's Vicarage, 46 Middleton Road, Banbury
OX16 4RG* Tel (01295) 271008 Mobile 07709-754914
E-mail revsueb@btinternet.com
BURCHILL, Jane. b 31. Dalhousie Univ Canada BSc54 Aber
Univ PhD81. Moray Ho Edin CertEd56 St Jo Coll Nottm 85.
d 88 **p** 94. NSM Inverurie *Ab* from 88; NSM Auchindoir from
88; NSM Alford from 88; NSM Kemnay from 88. *5 Hopetoun
Avenue, Bucksburn, Aberdeen AB21 9QU* Tel (01224) 712931
BURDEN, Miss Anne Margaret. b 47. Ex Univ BSc69 CQSW72.
Linc Th Coll 89. **d** 91 **p** 94. Par Dn Mill Hill Jo Keble Ch *Lon*
91-94; C 94; TV Basingstoke *Win* 94-02; Dioc Adv for Women's
Min 00-02; TV Brixham w Churston Ferrers and Kingswear *Ex*
02-10; rtd 10. *Ainsdale, Dornafield Road, Ipplepen, Newton Abbot
TQ12 5SJ* Tel (01803) 813520 E-mail anne-burden@virgin.com
BURDEN, Derek Ronald. b 37. Sarum Th Coll 59. **d** 62 **p** 63. C
Cuddington *Guildf* 62-64; C Leamington Priors All SS *Cov*
64-66; C Stamford All SS w St Pet *Linc* 66-74; C-in-c Stamford
Ch Ch CD 71-74; P-in-c Ashbury w Compton Beauchamp *Ox*
74-77; V 77-81; V Ashbury, Compton Beauchamp and Longcot
w Fernham 81-84; V Wokingham St Sebastian 84-97; P-in-c
Wooburn 97-02; rtd 02; Perm to Offic *Sarum* 03-05. *5 Cranford
Park Drive, Yateley GU46 6JR* Tel (01276) 512343
BURDEN, Joanna Mary. See INGRAM, Mrs Joanna Mary
BURDEN, Michael Henry. b 36. Selw Coll Cam BA59 MA62
Hull Univ MEd79. Ridley Hall Cam 59. **d** 61 **p** 62. C Ashton-
upon-Mersey St Mary Magd *Ches* 62-65; Chapl St Pet Sch York
65-70; Asst Master Beverley Gr Sch 70-74; R Walkington *York*
74-77; Chapl Asst Berwick R Infirmary 82-94; P-in-c Berwick H
Trin *Newc* 82-87; V 87-89; P-in-c Berwick St Mary 82-87; V
Berwick H Trin and St Mary 89-94; P-in-c Skirwith, Ousby and
Melmerby w Kirkland *Carl* 94-98; Sec Guild of St Raphael
94-98; rtd 99; Perm to Offic *Newc* 99-09. *The College of
St Barnabas, Blackberry Lane, Lingfield RH7 6NJ* Tel (01342)
872849
BURDEN, Paul. b 62. Rob Coll Cam BA84 MA88
AMIMechE87. Wycliffe Hall Ox BA91. **d** 92 **p** 93. C Clevedon
St Andr and Ch Ch *B & W* 92-96; R Bathampton w Claverton
from 96; Warden of Readers Bath Adnry from 06. *The Vicarage,
Bathampton Lane, Bath BA2 6SW* Tel (01225) 463570
E-mail p.burden@tiscali.co.uk
BURDETT, John Fergusson. b 25. Pemb Coll Cam BA47 MA79.
d 79 **p** 80. C Edin St Jo 79-87 and 90-95; Cyprus 87-90; rtd 95.

80/1 Barnton Park View, Edinburgh EH4 6HJ Tel 0131-339 7226 Fax 317 1179 E-mail revjb@blueyonder.co.uk

BURDETT, Canon Stephen Martin. b 49. AKC72. St Aug Coll Cant 73. **d** 74 **p** 75. C Walworth St Pet *S'wark* 74-75; C Walworth 75-77; C Benhilton 77-80; P-in-c Earlsfield St Jo 80-83; V 83-89; V N Dulwich St Faith 89-99; Ldr Post Ord Tr Woolwich Area 96-99; TR Southend *Chelmsf* from 99; Hon Can Chelmsf Cathl from 09; RD Southend from 10. *144 Alexandra Road, Southend-on-Sea SS1 1HB* Tel (01702) 342687 E-mail stephenburdett@btinternet.com

BURDON, Anthony James. b 46. Ex Univ LLB67 Lon Univ BD73. Oak Hill Th Coll 71. **d** 73 **p** 74. C Ox St Ebbe w St Pet 73-76; C Church Stretton *Heref* 76-78; Voc Sec CPAS and Hon C Bromley Ch Ch *Roch* 78-81; V Filkins w Broadwell, Broughton, Kelmscot etc *Ox* 81-84; R Broughton Poggs w Filkins, Broadwell etc 84-85; V Reading St Jo 85-96; C California and Adv for Spirituality (Berks) 96-98; Warden and P-in-c Cumbrae (or Millport) *Arg* 98-04; V Burstwick w Thorngumbald *York* from 04; P-in-c Roos and Garton w Tunstall, Grimston and Hilston from 08; RD S Holderness 06-09; rtd 11. *22 Wheatlands Close, Pocklington, York YO42 2UT* E-mail tony@tonyburdon.karoo.co.uk

BURDON, Canon Christopher John. b 48. Jes Coll Cam BA70 MA74 Glas Univ PhD95. Coll of Resurr Mirfield 71. **d** 74 **p** 75. C Chelmsf All SS 74-78; TV High Wycombe *Ox* 78-84; P-in-c Olney w Emberton 84-90; R 90-92; Lic to Offic *Glas* 92-94; Lay Tr Officer *Chelmsf* 94-99; Prin NOC 00-07; Can Th and CME Adv *St E* from 07. *3 Crown Street, Bury St Edmunds IP33 1QX* Tel and fax (01284) 706813 E-mail chris@stedmundsbury.anglican.org

BURDON, Mrs Pamela Muriel. b 46. Ex Univ BA68 Reading Univ DipEd69. Wycliffe Hall Ox 88. **d** 90 **p** 94. Par Dn Reading St Jo *Ox* 90-94; C 94-96; P-in-c California 96-98; NSM Cumbrae (or Millport) *Arg* 98-04; NSM Burstwick w Thorngumbald *York* 04-11; C Preston and Sproatley in Holderness 05-06; P-in-c from 06; C Roos and Garton w Tunstall, Grimston and Hilston from 08; rtd 11. *22 Wheatlands Close, Pocklington, York YO42 2UT* E-mail pam@tonyburdon.karoo.co.uk

BURFITT, Edward Ronald. b 42. MIMA64. Cranmer Hall Dur 91. **d** 93 **p** 94. C Monkseaton St Mary *Newc* 93-97; rtd 97. *Cragston Court, Cragston Close, Blakelaw, Newcastle upon Tyne NE5 3SR* Tel 0191-286 4443 Mobile 07870-762522 E-mail revburf@aol.com

BURFORD, Anthony Francis. b 55. Oak Hill Th Coll BA98. **d** 98 **p** 99. C Cov H Trin 98-02; P-in-c Rye Park St Cuth *St Alb* 02-07; V 07-11; V S Hornchurch St Jo and St Matt *Chelmsf* from 11. *St John's Vicarage, South End Road, Rainham RM13 7XT* Tel (01708) 555260 Mobile 07500-007479 E-mail revdtonyburford@googlemail.com

BURGE, Edward Charles Richard. b 70. Liv Univ BA92. Ridley Hall Cam 93. **d** 96 **p** 97. C Cayton w Eastfield *York* 96-99; P-in-c Lythe w Ugthorpe 99-03; Children's Officer (Cleveland Adnry) 99-03; Hon Chapl Miss to Seafarers 02-03; Dioc Youth and Children's Work Co-ord *Wakef* 04-10; P-in-c Roberttown w Hartshead from 10; P-in-c Scholes from 10. *The Vicarage, Scholes Lane, Scholes, Cleckheaton BD19 6PA* Tel (01924) 873024 E-mail richard.burge@wakefield.anglican.org

BURGE-THOMAS, Mrs Ruth. b 66. **d** 04 **p** 05. NSM Clapham H Spirit *S'wark* from 04; Chapl St Mark's C of E Academy Mitcham from 10. *86 Englewood Road, London SW12 9NY* Tel (020) 8675 6594 E-mail ruththomas@claphamhome.freeserve.co.uk

BURGER, David Joseph Cave. b 31. Selw Coll Cam BA58 MA62 Leic Univ 68. Coll of Resurr Mirfield 58. **d** 60 **p** 61. C Chiswick St Paul Grove Park *Lon* 60-63; C Charlton St Luke w H Trin *S'wark* 63-65; Warden St Luke Tr Ho Charlton 63-65; Chapl Moor Park Coll Farnham 66; Teacher Ysgol y Gader Dolgellau 68-85; Resettlement Officer Ches Aid to the Homeless 88-93; rtd 92; Perm to Offic *Ban* from 96. *Pwllygele Mawr, Llanfachreth, Dolgellau LL40 2DP* Tel (01341) 450350

BURGESS, Alan James. b 51. Ridley Hall Cam 87. **d** 89 **p** 90. C Glenfield *Leic* 89-92; V Donisthorpe and Moira w Stretton-en-le-Field 92-06; RD Akeley W 00-06; C Ravenstone and Swannington 06-09; P-in-c Thringstone St Andr 06-09; P-in-c Whitwick St Jo the Bapt 07-09; R Whitwick, Thringstone and Swannington from 09. *4 Badger's Croft, Thringstone, Coalville LE67 8JB* Tel (01530) 223481 E-mail sunergos@bigfoot.com

BURGESS, Mrs Anne. b 52. STETS 04. **d** 07 **p** 08. NSM Isleworth St Fran *Lon* from 07. *24 Penwerris Avenue, Isleworth TW7 4QX* Tel (020) 8570 4238 E-mail anne@ivanburgess.co.uk

BURGESS, Charles Anthony Robert. STETS. **d** 11. NSM Bath Weston All SS w N Stoke and Langridge *B & W* from 11. *The Vicarage, 27 Church Street, Bathford, Bath BA1 7RS* E-mail cj.burgess@lineone.net

BURGESS, Clive Brian. b 63. Trin Coll Bris BA00. **d** 00 **p** 01. C Oxton *Ches* 00-03; V Brewood *Lich* 03-08; V Bishopswood 03-08; R Bentham *Bradf* 08-11; Rural Miss Adv 08-11; V Onchan *S & M* from 11. *St Peter's Vicarage, Church Road, Onchan, Isle of Man IM3 1BF* Tel (01624) 675797 E-mail revdcliveburgess@btinternet.com

BURGESS, David James. b 58. Southn Univ BSc80. St Jo Coll Nottm. **d** 89 **p** 90. C S Mimms Ch Ch *Lon* 89-93; C Hanwell St Mary w St Chris 93-97; P-in-c Hawridge w Cholesbury and St Leonard *Ox* 97-08; R from 08; P-in-c The Lee 97-08; V from 08. *The Vicarage, The Lee, Great Missenden HP16 9LZ* Tel (01494) 837315 E-mail d.burgess@clara.net

BURGESS, Preb David John. b 39. Trin Hall Cam BA62 MA66 Univ Coll Ox MA66 FRSA91. Cuddesdon Coll 62. **d** 65 **p** 66. C Maidstone All SS w St Phil *Cant* 65; Asst Chapl Univ Coll Ox 66-70; Chapl 70-78; Can and Treas Windsor 78-87; V St Lawr Jewry *Lon* 87-08; Preb St Paul's Cathl 02-08; Chapl to The Queen 87-09; rtd 08. *62 Orbel Street, London SW11 3NZ* Tel (020) 7585 1572

BURGESS, Mrs Denise. b 49. **d** 00 **p** 01. OLM Glascote and Stonydelph *Lich* 00-06; NSM 06-07; NSM Elford from 07. *23 Croft Close, Elford, Tamworth B79 9BU* Tel 07818-890184 (mobile) E-mail burgess.denise@virgin.net

BURGESS, Canon Edwin Michael. b 47. Ch Coll Cam BA69 MA73. Coll of Resurr Mirfield 70. **d** 72 **p** 73. C Beamish *Dur* 72-77; C Par *Truro* 77-80; P-in-c Duloe w Herodsfoot 80-83; R 83-86; Jt Dir SWMTC 80-86; Subwarden St Deiniol's Lib Hawarden 86-91; R Oughtrington *Ches* 91-05; P-in-c Warburton 93-05; R Oughtrington and Warburton from 05; CME Officer 99-03; Asst Chapl (Warrington) Ches Univ from 03; Dioc Chapl MU from 02; Hon Can Ches Cathl from 10. *The Rectory, Stage Lane, Lymm WA13 9JB* Tel (01925) 752388 E-mail m.e.burgess@tesco.net

BURGESS, Canon Henry Percival. b 21. Leeds Univ BA48. Coll of Resurr Mirfield 48. **d** 50 **p** 51. C Northfield *Birm* 50-54; V Shaw Hill 54-62; V Wylde Green 62-89; Hon Can Birm Cathl 75-90; RD Sutton Coldfield 76-88; rtd 90; Perm to Offic *Birm* from 90. *39 Chestnut Drive, Birmingham B36 9BH* Tel 0121-747 9926

BURGESS, Hugh Nigel. b 55. Edin Univ BSc76 Aber Univ MA79. St As Minl Tr Course. **d** 06 **p** 07. NSM Halkyn w Caerfallwch w Rhesycae *St As* from 06; P-in-c from 07. *The Chimneys, 7 Leete Park, Rhydymwyn, Mold CH7 5JJ* Tel (01352) 741646 E-mail hugh@halkynparish.wanadoo.co.uk

BURGESS, Jane Ellen. b 63. STETS BA10. **d** 07 **p** 08. C Frome H Trin *B & W* 07-10; P-in-c Bathford from 10. *The Vicarage, 27 Church Street, Bathford, Bath BA1 7RS* Tel (01225) 858325 E-mail jane@stswithunsbathford.co.uk

BURGESS, Mrs Jean Ann. b 62. Nottm Univ MA03. EMMTC 00. **d** 03 **p** 04. C Gresley *Derby* 03-09; C Derby St Alkmund and St Werburgh from 09. *The Vicarage, 25 Highfield Road, Derby DE22 1GX* Tel (01332) 332681

BURGESS, John David. b 51. Ex Univ BSc73 Sussex Coll of Tech PGCE94. Trin Coll Bris 07. **d** 08 **p** 09. NSM Westfield *Chich* 08-09; NSM Fairlight, Guestling and Pett from 09. *Bethel, Eight Acre Lane, Three Oaks, Hastings TN35 4NL* Tel 07963-406854 (mobile) E-mail jbtescom@hotmail.com

BURGESS, The Ven John Edward. b 30. Lon Univ BD57. ALCD56. **d** 57 **p** 58. C Bermondsey St Mary w St Olave and St Jo *S'wark* 57-60; C Southampton St Mary w H Trin *Win* 60-62; V Dunston w Coppenhall *Lich* 62-67; Chapl Stafford Coll of Tech 63-67; V Keynsham w Queen Charlton *B & W* 67-75; R Burnett 67-75; RD Keynsham 72-75; Adn Bath and Preb Wells Cathl 75-95; rtd 96; Perm to Offic *B & W* and *Sarum* from 96. *12 Berryfield Road, Bradford-on-Avon BA15 1SX* Tel (01225) 868905

BURGESS, John Henry William. b 35. Wells Th Coll 65. **d** 67 **p** 68. C Teddington St Alb *Lon* 67-72; C Northolt St Jos 72-74; Perm to Offic *B & W* 93-99 and 00-06; rtd 95; C Bruton and Distr *B & W* 99-00; Perm to Offic *Nor* from 04. *9 Fairview Drive, Colkirk, Fakenham NR21 7NT* Tel (01328) 863410 E-mail burgess@walsingham9.wanadoo.co.uk

BURGESS, John Michael. b 36. ALCD61. **d** 61 **p** 62. C Eccleston St Luke *Liv* 61-64; C Avondale St Mary Magd Rhodesia 64-68; R Marlborough 68-74; V Nottingham St Andr *S'well* 74-79; Bp's Adv on Community Relns 77-79; V Earlestown *Liv* 79-87; RD Warrington 82-87; TR Halewood 87-94; V Southport St Phil and St Paul 94-01; AD N Meols 95-00; rtd 01; Perm to Offic *Liv* from 03. *3 Glencoyne Drive, Southport PR9 9TS* Tel (01704) 506843

BURGESS, John Mulholland. b 32. Cranmer Hall Dur 58. **d** 61 **p** 62. C Frimley *Guildf* 61-67; C Cheltenham St Luke and St Jo *Glouc* 67-69; P-in-c Withington w Compton Abdale 69-74; R Woolstone w Gotherington and Oxenton 74-75; Chapl Rotterdam w Schiedam etc *Eur* 75-78; Chapl Sliema 78-80; C Nottingham All SS *S'well* 80; C Rolleston w Morton 80-83; C Rolleston w Fiskerton, Morton and Upton 83-84; V Mansfield St Aug 84-99; Asst RD Mansfield 88-92; RD 92-98; rtd 99; Perm to Offic *S'well* from 03. *278 Westfield Lane, Mansfield NG19 6NQ* Tel (01623) 421163

BURGESS, Kate Lamorna. b 64. Man Poly BA86 Leeds Univ MA97. NEOC 99. **d** 02 **p** 03. OHP 92-03; C Hessle *York* 02-06;

TV Howden 06-10; P-in-c Stretford St Matt *Man* from 10. *St Matthew's Rectory, 39 Sandy Lane, Stretford, Manchester M32 9DB* Tel 0161-865 2535 E-mail kburgess1@tiscali.co.uk

BURGESS (*née* BOND), Mrs Kim Mary. b 58. SRN79. Trin Coll Bris BA87. **d** 87 **p** 94. Par Dn Cullompton *Ex* 87-91; Asst Chapl N Staffs R Infirmary Stoke-on-Trent 91-95; NSM Audley *Lich* 95-00. *38 Birch Avenue, Alsager, Stoke-on-Trent ST7 2QY*

BURGESS, Miss Laura Jane. b 74. Imp Coll Lon BSc95 ARSM95. Ripon Coll Cuddesdon BTh00. **d** 00 **p** 01. C St Alb Abbey 00-01; C Boxmoor St Jo 01-04; Min Can and Sacr St Paul's Cathl 04-09; V St Botolph Aldgate w H Trin Minories from 09; PV Westmr Abbey from 10. *St Botolph's Church, Aldgate High Street, London EC3N 1AB* Tel (020) 7283 2154 E-mail rector@stbotolphs.org.uk

BURGESS, Michael. *See* BURGESS, Canon Edwin Michael

BURGESS, Michael Anglin. b 34. St Deiniol's Hawarden 81. **d** 83 **p** 84. C Habergham Eaves St Matt *Blackb* 83-85; C Burnley St Matt w H Trin 85-86; V Preston St Matt 86-93; V Nelson St Bede 93-99; rtd 99; Perm to Offic *Blackb* from 99. *39 Reedley Road, Reedley, Burnley BB10 2LU* Tel (01282) 449727 E-mail revmab1@ntlworld.com

BURGESS, Canon Michael James. b 42. Coll of Resurr Mirfield 74. **d** 76 **p** 77. C Leigh-on-Sea St Marg *Chelmsf* 76-79; C St Peter-in-Thanet *Cant* 79-82; Chapl Royal St Geo Coll Toronto Canada 82-89; R Toronto Epiphany and St Mark 89-04; R Toronto Transfiguration from 04; Can Toronto from 01. *318W-118 Montgomery Avenue, Toronto ON M4R 1E3, Canada* Tel (001) (416) 482 2462 *or* 489 7798 Fax 489 3272 E-mail michaelburgess@sympatico.ca

BURGESS, Neil. b 53. Univ of Wales (Lamp) BA75 Nottm Univ MTh87 PhD93. St Mich Coll Llan 75. **d** 77 **p** 78. C Cheadle *Lich* 77-79; C Longton 79-82; TV Hanley H Ev 82-86; C Uttoxeter w Bramshall 86-87; Lect Linc Th Coll 87-95; Hon C Linc Minster Gp 88-95; Dioc Dir of Clergy Tr *S'well* 95-00; C Newark 97-00; Perm to Offic *Linc* 00-06; Hon C Linc St Pet-at-Gowts and St Andr from 06; Hon C Linc St Botolph from 06; Hon C Linc St Mary-le-Wigford w St Benedict etc from 06; Hon C Linc St Faith and St Martin w St Pet from 06; Hon C Linc St Swithin from 06. *23 Drury Lane, Lincoln LN1 3BN* Tel (01522) 539408 E-mail ann.burgess@btinternet.com

BURGESS, Sister Patricia Jean. b 16. Edin Univ BSc38. New Coll Edin 65. **dss** 69 **d** 86. NSM Roslin (Rosslyn Chpl) *Edin* 69-73; Community of the Transfiguration Midlothian from 72. *Hermitage of the Transfiguration, 70E Clerk Street, Loanhead EH20 9RG*

BURGESS, Paul Christopher James. b 41. Qu Coll Cam BA63 MA67. Lon Coll of Div 66. **d** 68 **p** 69. C Islington St Mary *Lon* 68-72; C Church Stretton *Heref* 73-74; Lect Gujranwala Th Sem Pakistan 74-83; Warden Carberry Tower (Ch of Scotland) 84-86; Progr Co-ord 86-88; TV Livingston LEP *Edin* 88-92; Prof and Lib Gujranwala Th Sem from 94. *Gujranwala Theological Seminary, Civil Lines, Gujranwala, Pakistan* Tel (0092) (53) 254770 E-mail burgess@brain.net.pk

BURGESS, Peter Alan. b 40. St Edm Ho Cam BA86 MA89 MPhil86 St Jo Coll York MA99. Cranmer Hall Dur 02. **d** 03 **p** 04. NSM Wheldrake w Thorganby *York* 03-08; NSM Derwent Ings from 08. *2 Derwent Drive, Wheldrake, York YO19 6AL* Tel (01904) 448309 E-mail burgesspr@btinternet.com

BURGESS, Roy. b 32. S Dios Minl Tr Scheme 80. **d** 83 **p** 84. NSM Bentworth and Shalden and Lasham *Win* 83-89; R Ingoldsby *Linc* 89-97; RD Beltisloe 93-97; rtd 97; Perm to Offic *Nor* from 98. *4 Melton Gate, Wymondham NR18 0PQ* Tel (01953) 606449

BURGESS, Roy Graham. b 47. Birm Univ CertCYW72. Ox Min Course 91. **d** 94 **p** 95. C Easthampstead *Ox* 94-99; C Wokingham St Paul 99-04; P-in-c Owlsmoor 04-09; V from 09. *The Vicarage, 107 Owlsmoor Road, Owlsmoor, Sandhurst GU47 0SS* Tel (01344) 780110 *or* 771286 E-mail revroy@compriest.freeserve.co.uk

BURGHALL, Kenneth Miles. b 34. Selw Coll Cam BA57 MA61. Qu Coll Birm 57. **d** 59 **p** 60. C Macclesfield St Mich *Ches* 59-63; CF 63-66; P-in-c Birkenhead Priory *Ches* 67-71; V Macclesfield St Paul 71-87; V Lower Peover 87-04; P-in-c Over Peover 92-04; rtd 04; Perm to Offic *Ches* from 04. *45 Ullswater Road, Congleton CW12 4JE* Tel (01260) 289277

BURGON, Canon George Irvine. b 41. Open Univ BA92. Edin Th Coll 62. **d** 65 **p** 66. C Dundee St Mary Magd *Bre* 65-68; C Wellingborough All Hallows *Pet* 68-71; P-in-c Norton 71-73; TV Daventry w Norton 73-75; V Northampton St Mary 75-98; R Rothwell w Orton, Rushton w Glendon and Pipewell 98-08; Can Pet Cathl 95-08; rtd 08; Perm to Offic *Pet* from 09. *47 Woodlands Avenue, Barton Seagrave, Kettering NN15 6QS* Tel (01536) 722193 E-mail georgeburgon@yahoo.co.uk

BURGON, Mrs Lynne. b 58. RGN80 RM83. SWMTC 03. **d** 06 **p** 07. NSM Fremington *Ex* 06-07; C Okehampton w Inwardleigh, Bratton Clovelly etc 07-11; V Bampton, Morebath, Clayhanger, Petton etc from 11. *The Vicarage, Station Road, Bampton, Tiverton EX16 9NG* Tel (01398) 332443 E-mail l.burgon@btinternet.com

BURKE, Charles Michael. b 28. Keble Coll Ox BA51 MA54 Ox Univ DipEd52. Glouc Th Course. **d** 84 **p** 85. C Colwall w Upper Colwall and Coddington *Heref* 84-88; V Canon Pyon w Kings Pyon and Birley 88-98; P-in-c Wellington 96-98; rtd 98; Perm to Offic *Heref* from 98. *Pyons, 7 Stretton Close, Fayre Oakes, Hereford HR4 0QN* Tel (01432) 270068

BURKE, Canon Christopher Mark. b 65. Cov Poly LLB87 Heythrop Coll Lon MA06. Ripon Coll Cuddesdon 89. **d** 92 **p** 93. C Northorpe *York* 92-96; V S Bank 96-02; R Stepney St Dunstan and All SS *Lon* 02-10; Can Res Sheff Cathl from 10. *49 Broomgrove Road, Sheffield S10 2NA* Tel 0114-263 6066 E-mail christopher.burke@sheffield-cathedral.org.uk

BURKE, Colin Douglas. b 41. Bp Otter Coll CertEd64. **d** 92 **p** 93. OLM Fressingfield, Mendham etc *St E* 92-99; P-in-c Oare w Culbone *B & W* from 99. *The Rectory, Oare, Lynton EX35 6NX* Tel (01598) 741270

BURKE, Elisabeth Ann. b 44. St Matthias Coll Bris CertEd66. **d** 05 **p** 06. OLM E Horsley and Ockham w Hatchford and Downside *Guildf* from 05. *39 Copse Road, Cobham KT11 2TW* Tel (01932) 863886

BURKE, Eric John. b 44. Llan Dioc Tr Scheme 81. **d** 85 **p** 86. NSM Cardiff St Jo *Llan* 85-95; Chapl Asst Univ Hosp of Wales and Llandough NHS Trust 95-00; Chapl Asst Cardiff and Vale NHS Trust from 00. *Chaplaincy Department, University Hospital of Wales, Heath Park, Cardiff CF4 4XW* Tel (029) 2074 3230 *or* 2079 8147

BURKE, Jonathan. b 53. Lon Univ BEd. Westcott Ho Cam 79. **d** 82 **p** 83. C Weymouth H Trin *Sarum* 82-85; R Bere Regis and Affpuddle w Turnerspuddle 85-92; NSM Talbot Village 04-08; TR White Horse from 08. *The Vicarage, Bitham Lane, Westbury BA13 3BU* Tel (01373) 822209 E-mail jonathan.burke@whitehorseteam.org

BURKE, Kelvin Stephen. b 56. Man Univ BA77 FCA81. Cranmer Hall Dur. **d** 99 **p** 00. C Stanley *Wakef* 99-02; P-in-c Wakef St Andr and St Mary 02-06; Asst Chapl Leeds Teaching Hosps NHS Trust 06-10; Perm to Offic *Portsm* from 11. *7 Steephill Court Road, Ventnor PO38 1UH* Tel (01983) 854261 Mobile 07793-979907

BURKE, Michael Robert. b 61. Leeds Univ BA83. Trin Coll Bris BA89. **d** 89 **p** 90. C Anston *Sheff* 89-92; V Crosspool 92-00; V Hucclecote *Glouc* 00-09. *Address temp unknown*

BURKE, Patrick. CITC. **d** 09 **p** 10. C Douglas Union w Frankfield *C, C & R* from 09. *64 Willowbank, Church Road, Blackrock, Cork, Republic of Ireland* Tel (00353) (21) 435 8226 E-mail pathos@eircom.net

BURKE, Wayne Jackson. b 51. San Francisco State Univ BA76 MA78 Univ of Wales (Cardiff) PhD91. St Steph Ho Ox 01. **d** 02 **p** 03. Hon C Gtr Athens *Eur* from 02. *1 Iridos, Amarousion, 151-22 Athens, Greece* Tel and fax (0030) (210) 614 8198 E-mail paterw@hol.gr

BURKE, Canon William Spencer Dwerryhouse. b 46. Ripon Coll Cuddesdon 90. **d** 92 **p** 93. C Watford St Mich *St Alb* 92-95; R Castor w Sutton and Upton w Marholm *Pet* from 95; Can Pet Cathl from 07; Perm to Offic *Ely* from 11. *The Rectory, 5 Church Hill, Castor, Peterborough PE5 7AU* Tel (01733) 380244 E-mail wburke@btinternet.com

BURKETT, Canon Christopher Paul. b 52. Warwick Univ BA75 Westmr Coll Ox MTh93 Liv Univ PhD10. Qu Coll Birm 75. **d** 78 **p** 79. C Streetly *Lich* 78-81; C Harlescott 81-83; TV Leek and Meerbrook 83-89; Chapl Leek Moorlands Hosp 83-89; Area Sec USPG *Ches* 89-92; V Whitegate w Lt Budworth *Ches* 92-00; Asst CME Officer 93-00; Can Res Ches Cathl 00-10; Bp's Chapl 00-10; Dioc Dir of Min from 10; C Ches H Trin from 10; Hon Can Ches Cathl from 11. *36 Abbots Park, Chester CH1 4AN* Tel (01244) 399941 E-mail christopher.burkett@chester.anglican.org

BURKILL, Mark Edward. b 56. MA PhD. Trin Coll Bris. **d** 84 **p** 85. C Cheadle *Ches* 84-88; C Harold Wood *Chelmsf* 88-91; V Leyton Ch Ch from 91. *The Vicarage, 52 Elm Road, London E11 4DW* Tel (020) 8539 4980 E-mail m.burkill@ntlworld.com

BURKITT, Paul Adrian. b 49. RMN75 SRN77. St Steph Ho Ox 84. **d** 86 **p** 87. C Whitby *York* 86-90; V Egton w Grosmont 90-93; V Newington w Dairycoates 93-96; P-in-c Kingston upon Hull St Mary 96-07; P-in-c Sculcoates 04-07; rtd 07; Perm to Offic *York* from 07. *The Loft, Flat 6, 12 The Esplanade, Whitby YO21 3HH*

BURKITT, Richard Francis. b 49. Leeds Univ BA71 CertEd72. Sarum & Wells Th Coll 82. **d** 90 **p** 90. R Fraserburgh w New Pitsligo *Ab* 90-95; R Fortrose *Mor* 95-08; R Cromarty 95-08; R Arpafeelie 95-08; C Inverness St Mich 08-09. *Mews Flat, Farmsteading, Wester Templands, Fortrose IV10 8RA* Tel 07717-457247 (mobile) E-mail burkitt@supanet.com

BURKITT-GRAY, Mrs Joan Katherine. b 47. Portsm Poly BSc68 Southn Univ MPhil74. SEITE 00. **d** 04 **p** 05. NSM Lee St Marg *S'wark* from 04; Hon Asst Chapl St Chris Hospice Lon 08-09. *7 Foxes Dale, London SE3 9BD* Tel (020) 8463 0365 *or* 8768 4500 E-mail mail@burkitt-gray.com

BURLAND, Clive Beresford. b 37. Sarum & Wells Th Coll 81. **d** 85 **p** 86. C Warblington w Emsworth *Portsm* 85-87; C Cowes

St Mary 87-92; V Gurnard 92-98; R Northwood 93-98; rtd 98; Perm to Offic *Portsm* from 98. *5A Orchard Close, Freshwater PO40 9BQ* Tel (01983) 753949

BURLEIGH, David John. b 42. FCII69. St Deiniol's Hawarden 84. **d** 87 **p** 88. NSM Lache cum Saltney *Ches* 87-88; NSM Eastham 89-92; C Birkenhead Priory 92-95; P-in-c Duloe w Herodsfoot *Truro* 95-99; TV Liskeard, St Keyne, St Pinnock, Morval etc 95-99; R Duloe, Herodsfoot, Morval and St Pinnock 99-01; V Bath St Barn w Englishcombe *B & W* 01-10; rtd 10. *1 Vine Gardens, Frome BA11 2LX* E-mail david.burleigh@hotmail.co.uk

BURLEIGH, Walter Coleridge. b 41. WMMTC 89. **d** 89 **p** 90. NSM N Evington *Leic* 90-96; Perm to Offic from 96. *20 Border Drive, Leicester LE4 2JH* Tel 0116-235 9230

BURLES, Robert John. b 54. Bris Univ BSc75. St Jo Coll Nottm LTh86. **d** 88 **p** 89. C Mansfield SS Pet and Paul *S'well* 88-91; C The Lydiards *Bris* 91-92; TV W Swindon and the Lydiards 92-97; TR Swindon St Jo and St Andr 97-11; AD Swindon 06-11; Hon Can Bris Cathl 04-11; P-in-c Takeley w Lt Canfield *Chelmsf* from 11. *The Rectory, Parsonage Road, Takeley, Bishop's Stortford CM22 6QX* Tel (01279) 870214 Mobile 07946-496418 E-mail rob@burles.org.uk

BURLEY, John Roland James. b 46. St Jo Coll Cam BA67 MA70. Trin Episc Sch for Min Ambridge Penn MDiv88. **d** 81 **p** 82. SAMS Chile 81-90; TV Southgate *Chich* 90-99; R Alfold and Loxwood *Guildf* 99-07; P-in-c 08-11; rtd 11. *72 Dahn Drive, Ludlow SY8 1XZ* Tel (01584) 873155 E-mail john@burleys.co.uk

BURLEY, Michael. b 58. Ridley Hall Cam 86. **d** 89 **p** 90. C Scarborough St Mary w Ch Ch and H Apostles *York* 89-92; C Drypool 93; TV 93-97; V Sutton St Mich 97-03; V Burley in Wharfedale *Bradf* from 03; Assoc Dioc Dir of Ords from 07. *The Vicarage, 21 Southfield Road, Burley in Wharfedale, Ilkley LS29 7PB* Tel (01943) 863216 E-mail michael.burley@btinternet.com

BURLEY, Richard Alexander. b 80. Warwick Univ BA01 Fitzw Coll Cam BA07. Ridley Hall Cam 05. **d** 08 **p** 09. C Bilton *Cov* from 08. *10 Monks Close, Cawston, Rugby CV22 7FP* Tel 07875-123867 (mobile) E-mail rich@burley.biz

BURLTON, Aelred Harry. b 49. Sarum & Wells Th Coll 75. **d** 78 **p** 79. C Feltham *Lon* 78-82; Chapl Heathrow Airport 83-94; P-in-c Harmondsworth 92-94; R St Buryan, St Levan and Sennen *Truro* 94-05; rtd 05. *Farway Barn, Hellangove Farm, Gulval, Penzance TR20 8XD* Tel (01736) 330426

BURMAN, Philip Harvey. b 47. Kelham Th Coll 66. **d** 70 **p** 71. C Huyton St Mich *Liv* 70-75; C Farnworth 75-77; TV Kirkby 77-83; V Hindley All SS 83-93; V Middlesbrough St Martin *York* 93-97; V Middlesbrough St Martin w St Cuth 97-99; P-in-c Eccleston St Thos *Liv* 99-08; V Liv St Chris Norris Green from 08. *St Christopher's Vicarage, Lorenzo Drive, Liverpool L11 1BQ* Tel 0151-226 1637 E-mail philip.h.burman@googlemail.com

BURMAN, Thomas George. b 41. S'wark Ord Course 86. **d** 89 **p** 90. NSM Forest Hill *S'wark* 89-03; NSM Perry Hill St Geo w Ch Ch and St Paul 03-07; Perm to Offic from 07. *131 Como Road, London SE23 2JN* Tel (020) 8699 8929

BURMAN, William Guest. b 26. St Cath Coll Cam MA55 Worc Coll Ox MA63. St Steph Ho Ox 81. **d** 83 **p** 84. C Weymouth H Trin *Sarum* 83-86; R Exton and Winsford and Cutcombe w Luxborough *B & W* 86-89; TV Langport Area 89-91; rtd 91; Perm to Offic *B & W* 91-98 and from 02; Master Bath St Mary Magd Holloway from 94. *8 Stoneleigh Court, Lansdown Road, Bath BA1 5TL* Tel (01225) 312140

BURMESTER, Stephen John. b 66. Leeds Univ BSc87. Wycliffe Hall Ox 96. **d** 98 **p** 99. C Lenton *S'well* 98-02; C Bebington *Ches* 02-08; V Handforth from 08. *The Vicarage, 36 Sagars Road, Handforth, Wilmslow SK9 3EE* Tel (01625) 250559 or 532145 E-mail steve.burmester@gmail.com

BURN, Geoffrey Livingston. b 60. Sydney Univ BSc83 Imp Coll Lon PhD87 St Jo Coll Dur BA95. Cranmer Hall Dur 93. **d** 96 **p** 97. C St Austell *Truro* 96-03; Perm to Offic *Cant* 03-06; P Forest S Deanery *Glouc* from 06; Hon C Cinderford St Jo 06-10; Hon C Cinderford w Littledean from 10; Chapl Glos Primary Care Trust from 06. *St John's Vicarage, 1 Abbots View, Buckshaft, Cinderford GL14 3EG* Tel (01594) 825446 E-mail geoffrey@burn.eclipse.co.uk

BURN, Mrs Helen Mary. b 64. Down Coll Cam BA86 Ox Univ PGCE88 Ex Univ MA02. SWMTC 00. **d** 03 **p** 04. C Eythorne and Elvington w Waldershare etc *Cant* 03-06; Tutor WEMTC *Glouc* from 06; Sen Lect Glos Univ from 06. *St John's Vicarage, 1 Abbots View, Buckshaft, Cinderford GL14 3EG* Tel (01594) 829602 E-mail helen@burn.eclipse.co.uk

BURN, Leonard Louis. b 44. K Coll Lon BD67 AKC67. **d** 68 **p** 69. C Kingswinford St Mary *Lich* 68-70; C S Ascot *Ox* 70-72; C Caversham 72-76; Chapl Selly Oak Hosp Birm 76-81; Bris City Hosp 81-82; P-in-c Bris St Mich 81-83; R Peopleton and White Ladies Aston w Churchill etc *Worc* 83-88; V Bengeworth 88-97; Chapl St Mark's Hospice Worc 88-97; Chapl Evesham Coll 90-97; rtd 97; Perm to Offic *Glouc* from 97 and *Worc* 97-98; Chapl Worcs Community and Mental Health Trust from 98.

Beckford Rise, Beckford, Tewkesbury GL20 7AN Tel and fax (01386) 881160 Mobile 07734-505663

BURN, Richard James Southerden. b 34. Pemb Coll Cam BA56. Wells Th Coll 56. **d** 58 **p** 59. C Cheshunt *St Alb* 58-62; C Leighton Buzzard 65-66; C Glastonbury St Jo *B & W* 66-68; P-in-c Prestonpans *Edin* 68-71; P-in-c Stokesay *Heref* 71-75; P-in-c Dorrington 75-81; P-in-c Stapleton 75-81; P-in-c Leebotwood w Longnor 75-81; P-in-c Smethcott w Woolstaston 81; TR Melbury *Sarum* 81-87; P-in-c Quendon w Rickling and Wicken Bonhunt *Chelmsf* 87-92; R Quendon w Rickling and Wicken Bonhunt etc 92-95; rtd 95; V Isleworth St Fran *Lon* 95-00; Hon C S Warks Seven Gp *Cov* 06-09. *The Old Rectory House, 29 Lydbury North, Craven Arms SY7 8AU* Tel (01588) 680465 E-mail richard.burn58@yahoo.co.uk

BURN, Robert Pemberton. b 34. Peterho Cam BA56 MA60 Lon Univ PhD68. CMS Tr Coll Chislehurst 60. **d** 63 **p** 81. India 63-71; Perm to Offic *Ely* 71-81; P-in-c Foxton 81-88; Perm to Offic *Ex* from 89. *Sunnyside, Barrack Road, Exeter EX2 6AB* Tel (01392) 430028

BURN-MURDOCH, Aidan Michael. b 35. Trin Coll Cam BA60 MA63. Ridley Hall Cam 59. **d** 61 **p** 62. C Bishopwearmouth St Gabr *Dur* 61-63; Tutor Ridley Hall Cam 63-67; CMS Miss 67-70; India 68-70; R Hawick *Edin* 70-77; Bp's Co-ord of Evang *S & B* 77-81; R Reynoldston w Penrice and Llangennith 77-83; R Port Eynon w Rhosili and Llanddewi and Knelston 83-89; R Uddingston and Cambuslang *Glas* 89-97; rtd 97; Missr Eyemouth *Edin* 98-00. *19 Blairston Avenue, Bothwell, Glasgow G71 8RZ* Tel (01698) 853377

BURNAGE, Arthur Gavin. b 63. Ulster Univ BA85 Cam Univ MA05. Wycliffe Hall Ox 05. **d** 07 **p** 08. C Aldridge *Lich* from 07; NSM from 11. *Betel of Britain, Windmill House, Weatheroak Hill, Alvechurch, Birmingham B48 7EA* Tel (01564) 822356 E-mail gav.burnage@googlemail.com

BURNE, Sambrooke Roger. b 47. Lon Univ MB, BS70 MRCGP74. SAOMC 03. **d** 06 **p** 07. NSM Blackbird Leys *Ox* from 06. *5 Eleanor Close, Oxford OX4 3ND* E-mail roger.burne@ntlworld.com

BURNET, Norman Andrew Gray. b 32. Aber Univ BEd77 Cam Univ MLitt92. Edin Th Coll 53. **d** 55 **p** 56. C Ayr *Glas* 55-58; S Africa 58-69; C St Jo Cathl Umtata 58-63; R Mt Frere 63-69; R Leven *St And* 69-72; Perm to Offic *Ab, Bre* and *Ely* 73-81; P-in-c Brinkley, Burrough Green and Carlton *Ely* 82-83; P-in-c Westley Waterless 82-83; Australia 83-84; R Fraserburgh w New Pitsligo *Ab* 85-89; P-in-c Bicker *Linc* 89; V Bicker and Wigtoft 89-97; rtd 97; Perm to Offic *Nor* 97-99; *Linc* 97-00. *61 Westlode Street, Spalding PE11 2AE* Tel and fax (01775) 767429

BURNETT, Canon John Capenhurst. b 19. AKC49. **d** 49 **p** 50. C Shirehampton *Bris* 49-53; C Stoke Bishop 53-56; V Wroughton 56-76; RD Cricklade 70-76; Hon Can Bris Cathl 74-85; V Bris St Andr w St Bart 76-85; rtd 85; Perm to Offic *Bris* from 85. *57 Upper Cranbrook Road, Bristol BS6 7UR* Tel 0117-924 5284

BURNETT, Mrs Patricia Kay. b 38. Newnham Coll Cam MA60. Sarum Th Coll 94. **d** 97 **p** 98. NSM Jarvis Brook *Chich* 97-08; rtd 08. *20 St Richards Road, Crowborough TN6 3AT* Tel (01892) 655668

BURNETT, Susan Mary. b 50. Lon Univ BEd73. St Jo Coll Dur 76. **dss** 78 **d** 87 **p** 94. Welling *S'wark* 78-83; E Greenwich Ch Ch w St Andr and St Mich 83-91; Par Dn 87-91; Par Dn Sydenham All SS 91-94; C 94-95; C Lower Sydenham St Mich 91-95; V 95-09; rtd 09. *9 Grove Park, Chichester PO19 3HY* Tel (01243) 532748

BURNETT-CHETWYND, Mrs Gemma Claire. b 82. Westcott Ho Cam. **d** 11. C Plaistow St Mary *Roch* from 11. *The Vicarage, 1 Lake Avenue, Bromley BR1 4EN* Tel (020) 8460 0481 E-mail gemmaburnettchetwynd@gmail.com

BURNETT-HALL, Mrs Karen. b 46. Bp Grosseteste Coll CertEd68 Lon Univ BD82. Oak Hill Th Coll 86. **d** 89 **p** 94. Par Dn Norbury *Ches* 89-92; NSM York St Paul 93-95; NSM York St Barn 95-99; P-in-c 00-09; P-in-c Wimbotsham w Stow Bardolph and Stow Bridge etc *Ely* from 11. *The Rectory, Church Road, Wimbotsham, King's Lynn PE34 3QG* Tel (01366) 384342 E-mail karen.bh@btinternet.com

BURNHAM, Frank Leslie. b 23. Edin Th Coll 52. **d** 55 **p** 56. C York St Mary Bishophill Senior 55-58; C Marfleet 58-62; V York St Mary Bishophill Senior 55-58; C Marfleet 58-62; V 62-72; TR 72-74; V Acomb St Steph 74-85; C Fulford 85-88; rtd 88; Perm to Offic *York* from 88. *Dulverton Hall, Esplanade, Scarborough YO11 2AR* Tel (01723) 340101

BURNHAM, Stephen Patrick James. b 75. Ch Ch Ox BA97. Westcott Ho Cam 00. **d** 02 **p** 03. C Vale of Belvoir *Leic* 02-05; TV Leic Resurr from 05. *445A Loughborough Road, Birstall, Leicester LE4 4BH* Tel 0116-267 7074 Mobile 07905-882805

BURNIE, Judith. See SWEETMAN, Ms Judith

BURNINGHAM, Frederick George. b 34. ALCD60. **d** 60 **p** 61. C New Beckenham St Paul *Roch* 60-63; Canada 63-68 and 89-95; C Wisley w Pyrford *Guildf* 68-69; P-in-c Sydenham H Trin *S'wark* 69-71; C Broadwater St Mary *Chich* 72-77; R Sotterley, Willingham, Shadingfield, Ellough etc *St E* 77-82; R Ipswich St Clem w H Trin 82-89; P-in-c Thorndon w Rishangles, Stoke

BURNINGHAM

Ash, Thwaite etc 95-99; rtd 99; Perm to Offic *Bradf* from 99. *8 Meadow Rise, Skipton BD23 1BT* Tel (01756) 794440 E-mail f.burningham@btopenworld.com

BURNINGHAM, Richard Anthony. b 47. Keele Univ BA70 Aber Univ CQSW77 Roehampton Inst PGCE85. All Nations Chr Coll 82 Oak Hill Th Coll 94. d 96 p 97. C Reigate St Mary *S'wark* 96-00; V Weston *Win* from 00. *The Vicarage, Weston Lane, Southampton SO19 9HG* Tel (023) 8044 8421 E-mail richardb@ukonline.co.uk

BURNISTON, Aubrey John. b 53. St Jo Coll Dur BA92 Leeds Univ MA03. Cranmer Hall Dur 79. d 83 p 84. C Owton Manor *Dur* 83-86; TV Rugby *Cov* 86-93; V Heaton St Martin *Bradf* 93-09; Bp's Adv in Liturgy 00-09; V Islington St Jas w St Pet *Lon* from 09. *St James's Vicarage, 1A Arlington Square, London N1 7DS* Tel (020) 7226 4108 E-mail vicar@stjamesislington.org

BURNLEY, Suffragan Bishop of. See GODDARD, The Rt Revd John William

BURNS, Arthur. See BURNS, Williams Arthur

BURNS, Dane. b 51. d 85 p 86. C Enniskillen *Clogh* 85-87; I Augher w Newtownsaville and Eskrahoole 87-92; Dioc Communications Officer 91-92; I Camus-juxta-Bann *D & R* 92-96. *86 Donneybrewer Road, Eglinton, Londonderry BT47 3PD*

BURNS, Canon Edward Joseph. b 38. Liv Univ BSc58 St Cath Soc Ox BA61 MA64. Wycliffe Hall Ox 58. d 61 p 62. C Leyland St Andr *Blackb* 61-64; C Burnley St Pet 64-67; V Chorley St Jas 67-75; V Fulwood Ch Ch 75-03; RD Preston 79-86; Chapl Sharoe Green Hosp Preston 81-94; Hon Can Blackb Cathl 86-03; Bp's Adv on Hosp Chapls 89-94; rtd 03; Perm to Offic *Blackb* from 03. *17 Greenacres, Fulwood, Preston PR2 7DA* Tel (01772) 864741 E-mail eddieandsheila@ejburns.freeserve.co.uk

BURNS, Canon James Denis. b 43. Lich Th Coll 69. d 72 p 73. C Gt Wyrley *Lich* 72-75; C Atherton *Man* 75-76; Asst Chapl Sheff Ind Miss 76-79; C-in-c Masborough St Paul w St Jo 76-78; C-in-c Northfield St Mich 76-78; V Rotherham St Paul, St Mich and St Jo Ferham Park 78-79; V Lancaster Ch Ch *Blackb* 79-81; V Lancaster Ch Ch w St Jo and St Anne 81-86; V Chorley St Pet 86-96; R Rufford 96-07; Warden Past Assts 96-06; C Croston and Bretherton 06-07; rtd 07; Hon C Hesketh w Becconsall *Blackb* 07-09; Hon Can Blackb Cathl 99-09; Perm to Offic *Blackb* and *Man* from 09. *7 Devon Drive, Diggle, Oldham OL3 5PP* Tel (01457) 810074

BURNS, John Macdonald. See ODA-BURNS, John Macdonald

BURNS, Mrs Lucinda Roberte. b 56. Qu Coll Birm BA11. d 11. NSM Gt Hanwood *Heref* from 11; NSM Longden and Annscroft w Pulverbatch from 11. *Church House, Church Close, Cruckton, Shrewsbury SY5 8PP* E-mail lucinda.burns@virgin.net

BURNS, Matthew. Leeds Univ BA. Coll of Resurr Mirfield. d 05 p 06. C Wrexham *St As* 05-08; V Towyn 08-10; P-in-c 10-11; TV Wrexham from 11. *55 Princess Street, Wrexham LL13 7US* Tel (01978) 264834 *or* 266145 E-mail matthew.burns@wrexhamparish.org.uk

BURNS, Michael John. b 53. AKC76. Chich Th Coll 76. d 77 p 78. C Broseley w Benthall *Heref* 77-81; C Stevenage All SS Pin Green *St Alb* 81-84; V Tattenham Corner and Burgh Heath *Guildf* 84-92; C and Chapl Younger People Milton Keynes *Ox* 92-00; P-in-c Potters Bar K Chas *St Alb* from 00; AD Barnet from 11. *The Vicarage, 8 Dugdale Hill Lane, Potters Bar EN6 2DW* Tel (01707) 661266

BURNS, Robert Joseph. b 34. Wycliffe Hall Ox 67. d 71 p 72. C Portswood Ch Ch *Win* 71-73; C Woking St Jo *Guildf* 73-77; C Glas St Mary 77; Bp's Dom Chapl 77-78; R Glas Gd Shep and Ascension 78-92; rtd 92. *The Vicarage, Church Street, Chipping Campden GL55 6JG* Tel (01386) 840671

BURNS, Stephen. b 70. Grey Coll Dur BA92 MA94 Clare Coll Cam MLitt96 Dur Univ PhD03. Ridley Hall Cam 93. d 96 p 97. C Houghton le Spring *Dur* 96-99; TV Gateshead 99-02; Dir Urban Miss Cen Cranmer Hall 99-02; Tutor Qu Coll Birm 03-06; Chapl and Lect St Jo Coll Dur 06-07; Fell Chas Sturt Univ Australia from 07. *United Theological College, 16 Masons Drive, North Parramatta, NSW 2151 Australia*

BURNS, Stuart Keith. b 66. Bp Grosseteste Coll BEd88 Lon Univ BD94 Leeds Univ MA95 PhD99. St Jo Coll Nottm. d 03 p 04. C Gt Bowden w Welham, Glooston and Cranoe etc *Leic* 03-06; Hd Sch for Min from 06. *The Rectory, 3 Stonton Road, Church Langton, Market Harborough LE16 7SZ* Tel (01858) 540202 E-mail sburns@zetnet.co.uk

BURNS, The Rt Revd Stuart Maitland. b 46. Leeds Univ BA67. Coll of Resurr Mirfield 67. d 69 p 70. C Wyther *Ripon* 69-73; Asst Chapl Leeds Univ and Leeds Poly 73-77; P-in-c Thornthwaite w Thruscross and Darley 77-84; V Leeds Gipton Epiphany 84-89; OSB from 89; Prior Burford Priory 96-01; Abbot from 01; Lic to Offic *Ox* 89-08; Perm to Offic *Worc* from 10. *Mucknell Abbey, Mucknell Farm Lane, Stoulton, Worcester WR7 4RB* Tel (01905) 345900 E-mail abbot@mucknellabbey.org.uk

BURNS, Stuart Sandeman. b 62. Natal Univ BA85 Ball Coll Ox BA89 MA94. St Paul's Coll Grahamstown. d 89 p 90. S Africa 89-99; C Stanger 90-91; Dir Scripture Union Ind Schs 92-94; R

Drakensberg 95-97; Chapl W Prov Prep Sch 98-99; I Kinneigh Union *C, C & R* 99-02; TV Bourne Valley *Sarum* 02-08; I Down H Trin w Hollymount *D & D* from 08; Min Can Down Cathl from 10. *The Rectory, 12 The Meadows, Strangford Road, Downpatrick BT30 6LN* Tel (028) 4461 2286 E-mail stuart.burns01@btinternet.com

BURNS, Williams Arthur. b 51. CITC 08. d 11. NSM Glendermott *D & R* from 11. *33 Sevenoaks, Londonderry BT47 6AL* Tel (028) 7134 4354 Mobile 07917-358317 E-mail arthurburns33@hotmail.co.uk

BURR, Mrs Ann Pamela. b 39. S Dios Minl Tr Scheme 83. dss 86 d 87 p 94. Fareham H Trin *Portsm* 86-06; Hon C 87-06; Hon Asst Chapl Knowle Hosp Fareham 86-90; Asst Chapl Qu Alexandra Hosp Portsm 90-92; Chapl Portsm Hosps NHS Trust 92-00; rtd 06; Perm to Offic *Portsm* from 06. *3 Bruce Close, Fareham PO16 7QJ* Tel (01329) 281375 E-mail ann.burr@hotmail.co.uk

BURR, Mrs Anna Victoria. b 58. Southn Univ BA80 Leeds Univ MA07. NOC 04. d 07 p 08. NSM Fulford *York* 07-11; P-in-c Haddlesey w Hambleton and Birkin from 11. *The Rectory, Millfield Road, Chapel Haddlesey, Selby YO8 8QF* Tel (01757) 270325 E-mail avburr@btinternet.com

BURR, Christopher Edward. b 68. Univ of Wales (Cardiff) BTh01. St Mich Coll Llan 98. d 01 p 02. C Llantrisant 01-04; P-in-c Pwllgwaun and Llanddewi Rhondda 04-10; V Lisvane from 10. *The Vicarage, Green Gables, 2 Llwyn y Pia Road, Lisvane, Cardiff CF14 0SY* Tel (029) 2075 3338 E-mail chris.burr1@ntlworld.com

BURR, Paul David. b 62. Birm Univ LLB83. St Jo Coll Nottm MA99. d 99 p 00. C Newark *S'well* 99-02; C Eaton *Nor* 02-05; P-in-c Swardeston w E Carleton, Intwood, Keswick etc 05-09; R from 09. *The Vicarage, The Common, Swardeston, Norwich NR14 8EB* Tel (01508) 570550 E-mail paul.burr@tiscali.co.uk

BURR, Raymond Leslie. b 43. NEOC 82 Edin Th Coll 84. d 85 p 86. C Hartlepool St Paul *Dur* 85-87; C Sherburn w Pittington 87-89; R Lyons 89-95; RD Houghton 94-96; V S Shields St Hilda w St Thos 95-08; rtd 08. *57 Pierremont Road, Darlington DL3 6DN* Tel (01325) 463666 E-mail ray@burr.org.uk

BURRELL, David Philip. b 56. Southn Univ BTh90. Sarum & Wells Th Coll 85. d 88 p 89. C Ixworth and Bardwell *St E* 88-91; P-in-c Haughley w Wetherden 91-96; P-in-c Culford, W Stow and Wordwell w Flempton etc 96-98; R Lark Valley from 98. *The Rectory, West Stow, Bury St Edmunds IP28 6ET* Tel (01284) 728556

BURRELL, Godfrey John. b 49. Reading Univ BSc70 Qu Coll Ox CertEd71. Wycliffe Hall Ox 84. d 86 p 87. C Didcot All SS *Ox* 86-89; Chapl St Alb Coll Pretoria 90-95; Chapl Pretoria Cen Pris 90-94; R Lynnwood Trin Ch 96-01; Adn Pretoria E 00-01; R Lighthorne *Cov* 01-11; V Chesterton 01-11; V Newbold Pacey w Moreton Morrell 01-11; RD Fosse 07-11; V Benson *Ox* from 11. *Benson Vicarage, Church Road, Benson, Wallingford OX10 6SF* Tel (01491) 201668 E-mail gjburrell@btinternet.com

BURRELL, Martin John. b 51. Cant Ch Ch Univ Coll MA00 ARCM71. Trin Coll Bris BA95. d 95 p 96. C Cant St Mary Bredin 95-99; V Cranbrook 99-09; Asst Dir of Ords 06-09; P-in-c Bushmead *St Alb* from 09. *Church House, 73 Hawkfields, Luton LU2 7NW* Tel (01582) 487327 Mobile 07791-536713 E-mail mburrell51@googlemail.com

BURRELL, Timothy Graham. b 43. JP83. St Steph Ho Ox 69. d 72 p 07. C Haltwhistle *Newc* 72-73; NSM Harrogate St Wilfrid *Ripon* from 06; Chapl to Suff Bp Beverley (PEV) *York* from 10. *8 St Hilda's Road, Harrogate HG2 8JY* Tel (01423) 883832 Mobile 07885-681379 E-mail tim.burrell@virgin.net

BURRETT, Miss Gaynor Elizabeth. b 59. St Jo Coll Nottm 04. d 06 p 07. C Branksome St Clem *Sarum* 06-10; P-in-c Kingston, Langton Matravers and Worth Matravers from 11. *The Rectory, St George's Close, Langton Matravers, Swanage BH19 3HZ* Tel (01929) 422559 E-mail gaynorburrett@btinternet.com

BURRIDGE, Matthew Guy. b 73. Univ Coll Lon BSc94 MB, BS97. NTMTC BA08. d 08 p 09. NSM Kentish Town St Silas and H Trin w St Barn *Lon* from 08. *Health E1 Homeless Medical Centre, 9-11 Brick Lane, London E1 6PU* Tel (020) 7247 0090 E-mail fr.matthewburridge@googlemail.com

BURRIDGE, Richard Alan. b 55. Univ Coll Ox BA77 MA81 Nottm Univ CertEd78 PhD89. St Jo Coll Nottm 82. d 85 p 86. C Bromley SS Pet and Paul *Roch* 85-87; Chapl Ex Univ 87-94; Dean K Coll Lon from 94; Lic Preacher *Lon* from 94; Perm to Offic *S'wark* from 98 and *Chelmsf* from 05. *King's College, Strand, London WC2R 2LS* Tel (020) 7848 2333 Fax 7848 2344 E-mail dean@kcl.ac.uk

BURRIDGE-BUTLER, Paul David. See BUTLER, Paul David

BURROW, Miss Alison Sarah. b 59. Homerton Coll Cam BEd82. Westcott Ho Cam 84. d 87 p 03. Par Dn Hebden Bridge *Wakef* 87-88; Par Dn Prestwood and Gt Hampden *Ox* 88-90; Par Dn Olney w Emberton 90-92; rtd 92; Hon C Bedford St Pet w St Cuth *St Alb* 02-07; P-in-c Renhold from 07. *The Vicarage, Church Road, Renhold, Bedford MK41 0LU* Tel (01234) 771317 E-mail as.burrow@ntlworld.com

BURROW, Mrs Margaret Anne. b 46. Open Univ BA82 Leeds Univ MSc85 Lon Univ TCert68. Coll of Resurr Mirfield 06. d 07

p 08. NSM Douglas St Ninian *S & M* 07-08; NSM St German's Cathl from 08. *1 Thorny Road, Douglas, Isle of Man IM2 5EF* Tel (01624) 662173 Mobile 07624-235711 E-mail margaret.burrow@mcb.net

BURROW, Ronald. b 31. Univ Coll Dur BA55. St Steph Ho Ox 83. **d** 85 **p** 86. C Dawlish *Ex* 85-87; TV Ottery St Mary, Alfington, W Hill, Tipton etc 87-91; P-in-c Pyworthy, Pancrasweek and Bridgerule 91-95; rtd 95; Perm to Offic *Ex* from 95. *3 Riverside, Dolphin Street, Colyton EX24 6LU* Tel and fax (01297) 553882

BURROW, Stephen Paul. b 62. Univ Coll Dur BA84. Trin Coll Bris 09. **d** 11. C Chilcompton w Downside and Stratton on the Fosse *B & W* from 11. *1 Mendip Fields, Stockhill Road, Chilcompton, Radstock BA3 4LT* Tel 07511-544375 (mobile) E-mail s_p_burrow@yahoo.co.uk

BURROWS, Canon Brian Albert. b 34. Atlantic Sch of Th BTh83. St Aid Birkenhead 56. **d** 59 **p** 60. C Sutton St Geo *Ches* 59-62; Canada 62-69 and from 74; V Stratton St Margaret *Bris* 70-74; Hon Can Frobisher Bay 78-80; rtd 99. *334 Mary Street, Niagara on the Lake ON L0S 1J0, Canada*

BURROWS, Christopher Mark. b 75. St Mellitus Coll 08. **d** 11. C W Hampstead Trin *Lon* from 11. *2nd Floor Flat, 51 Gascony Avenue, London NW6 4ND* Tel 07939-130151 (mobile) E-mail chris@htsc.org

BURROWS, Prof Clifford Robert. b 37. OBE05. Univ of Wales BSc62 Lon Univ PhD69 DSc(Eng)89 Aston Univ Hon DSc01 MIMechE68 FIMechE82 FIEE98 FREng98. Chich Th Coll 75. **d** 76 **p** 77. NSM Brighton St Pet *Chich* 76-78; NSM Brighton St Pet w Chpl Royal 78-80; NSM Brighton St Pet w Chpl Royal and St Jo 80-82; Perm to Offic *Glas* 82-85 and 86-89; NSM Clarkston 85-86; NSM Bath Ch Ch Prop Chpl *B & W* 90-10; rtd 10. *Stonecroft, Entry Hill Drive, Bath BA2 5NL* Tel (01225) 334743 Fax 429990 E-mail c.r.burrows@bath.ac.uk

BURROWS, Clive Robert. b 60. Bath Coll of HE BEd82 Ches Coll of HE BA04. NOC 01. **d** 04 **p** 05. C N Wingfield, Clay Cross and Pilsley *Derby* 04-09; P-in-c Hyson Green and Forest Fields *S'well* from 09. *St Stephen's Vicarage, 18 Russell Road, Nottingham NG7 6HB* Tel 0115-978 4480 E-mail clive@revburrows.plus.com

BURROWS, Canon David. b 62. Leeds Univ BA85 MA03. Linc Th Coll 86. **d** 88 **p** 89. C Kippax w Allerton Bywater *Ripon* 88-91; C Manston 91-95; Chapl Killingbeck Hosp 94; V Halifax St Anne Southowram *Wakef* 95-00; P-in-c Charlestown 95-00; V Southowram and Claremount 00-02; TV Elland 02-05; TR from 05; C Stainland w Outlane from 06; C Greetland and W Vale from 08; RD Brighouse and Elland from 08; Chapl Overgate Hospice from 02; Hon Can Wakef Cathl from 10. *All Saints' Vicarage, Charles Street, Elland HX5 0JF* Tel (01422) 373184 Mobile 07932-694555 E-mail rectorofelland@btinternet.com

BURROWS, David MacPherson. b 43. NOC. **d** 82 **p** 83. NSM Newburgh *Liv* 82-93; NSM Newburgh w Westhead from 93; Dioc Adv NSM 03-11. *34 Woodrow Drive, Newburgh, Wigan WN8 7LB* Tel (01257) 462948 E-mail davidmacburrows@msn.com

BURROWS, Diane. b 48. **d** 05 **p** 06. NSM Saltash *Truro* from 05. *20 Andrews Way, Hatt, Saltash PL12 6PE* Tel (01752) 842540 E-mail di.burrows@connells.co.uk

BURROWS, Graham Charles. b 47. Leeds Univ CertEd69 Open Univ BA81. NOC 87. **d** 90 **p** 91. C Chorlton-cum-Hardy St Clem *Man* 90-93; TV Horwich 93; TV Horwich and Rivington 93-94. *29 Heaton Road, Lostock, Bolton BL6 4EE* Tel (01204) 494826

BURROWS, Graham John. b 63. Jes Coll Cam BA84 MA88 Goldsmiths' Coll Lon PGCE94. Oak Hill Th Coll 07. **d** 09 **p** 10. C Polegate *Chich* from 09. *99 Greenleaf Gardens, Polegate BN26 6PH* Tel (01323) 489666 Mobile 07740-622962 E-mail curate@polegate.org.uk

BURROWS, Jean. b 54. CertEd75. Trin Coll Bris 89. **d** 91 **p** 94. C Allesley *Cov* 91-95; C Thorley *St Alb* 95-99; P-in-c Harrold and Carlton w Chellington 99-06; R 06-07; P-in-c Boughton under Blean w Dunkirk and Hernhill *Cant* from 07. *The Vicarage, 101 The Street, Boughton-under-Blean, Faversham ME13 9BG* Tel (01227) 751410 E-mail jeanburrows@jeanius.me.uk

BURROWS, Canon John Edward. b 36. Leeds Univ BA60 PGCE63. Coll of Resurr Mirfield. **d** 63 **p** 65. C Much Hadham *St Alb* 63-65; Hon C Haggerston St Mary w St Chad *Lon* 65-73; P-in-c Finsbury St Clem w St Barn and St Matt 73-76; Chapl Woodbridge Sch 76-83; V Ipswich St Bart *St E* 83-03; Hon Can St E Cathl 01-03; rtd 03; Perm to Offic *St E* from 03. *55 Berners Street, Ipswich IP1 3LN* Tel (01473) 216629 E-mail burrows@freenetname.co.uk

BURROWS, Joseph Atkinson. b 32. St Aid Birkenhead 58. **d** 61 **p** 62. C Hoole *Ches* 61-67; Jamaica 67-68; C Ayr *Glas* 68-74; R Prestwick 74-78; Hon Chapl RAF 74-78; Hon Chapl RN 74-78; C Cronulla Australia 78-81; R Naremburn and Cammeray 81-87; Asst Min St Ives 87-02; Sen Asst Min from 02. *1/23 Ayres Road, St Ives NSW 2075, Australia* Tel (0061) (2) 0144 3019

✠**BURROWS, The Rt Revd Michael Andrew James.** b 61. TCD BA82 MA85 MLitt86. **d** 87 **p** 88 **c** 06. C Douglas Union w Frankfield *C, C & R* 87-91; Dean of Res TCD 91-94; Min Can St Patr Cathl Dublin 91-94; I Bandon Union *C, C & R* 94-02; Can Cork and Cloyne Cathls 96-02; Dean Cork and I Cork St Fin Barre's Union 02-06; Bp C & O from 06. *Bishop's House, Troysgate, Kilkenny, Republic of Ireland* Tel (00353) (56) 778 6633 E-mail cashelossorybishop@eircom.net

BURROWS, Canon Paul Anthony. b 55. Nottm Univ BA77 Gen Th Sem NY STM88. St Steph Ho Ox 77. **d** 79 **p** 80. C Camberwell St Giles *S'wark* 79-81; C St Helier 81-83; C Fareham SS Pet and Paul *Portsm* 83-85; V Union St Luke and All SS New Jersey USA 85-90; R Temple Hills St Barn Maryland 90-95; P-in-c Des Moines St Mark Iowa 95-01; Can Des Moines Cathl 98-01; R San Francisco Advent of Ch the K from 01. *162 Hickory Street, San Francisco CA 94102, USA* E-mail rector@advent-sf.org

BURROWS, The Ven Peter. b 55. BTh. Sarum & Wells Th Coll 80. **d** 83 **p** 84. C Baildon *Bradf* 83-87; R Broughton Astley *Leic* 87-95; TR Broughton Astley and Croft w Stoney Stanton 95-00; RD Guthlaxton I 94-00; Dir of Ords 97-03; Par Development Officer 00-03; Dir Min, Tr and Par Development 03-05; Hon Can Leic Cathl 98-05; Adn Leeds *Ripon* from 05. *Archdeacon's Lodge, 3 West Park Grove, Leeds LS8 2HQ* Tel and fax 0113-269 0594 E-mail archdeacon.leeds@riponleeds.anglican.org

BURROWS, Philip Geoffrey. b 59. Birm Univ BSc80. Oak Hill Th Coll 90. **d** 92 **p** 93. C Poynton *Ches* 92-96; Min Cheadle Hulme Em CD 96-03; V Mottram in Longdendale from 03. *30A Broadbottom Road, Mottram, Hyde SK14 6JB* Tel (01457) 762268 E-mail philipburrows@man4god.co.uk

BURROWS, Samuel Reginald. b 30. AKC37. **d** 38 **p** 39. C Shildon *Dur* 58-62; C Heworth St Mary 62-67; C-in-c Leam Lane CD 67-72; C-in-c Bishopwearmouth St Mary V w St Pet CD 72-77; R Bewcastle and Stapleton *Carl* 77-82; R Harrington 82-90; P-in-c Millom 90; V 90-95; rtd 95. *40 Lindisfarne Road, Durham DH1 5YQ*

✠**BURROWS, The Rt Revd Simon Hedley.** b 28. K Coll Cam BA52 MA56. Westcott Ho Cam 52. **d** 54 **p** 55 **c** 74. C St John's Wood *Lon* 54-57; Chapl Jes Coll Cam 57-60; V Wyken *Cov* 60-67; V Fareham H Trin *Portsm* 67-71; TR 71-74; Suff Bp Buckingham *Ox* 74-87; Area Bp Buckm 87-94; rtd 94; Hon Asst Bp Win from 94. *8 Quarry Road, Winchester SO23 0JF* Tel (01962) 853332

BURROWS, Victoria Elizabeth. b 61. STETS 01. **d** 04 **p** 05. C The Bourne and Tilford *Guildf* 04-07; R Long Ditton from 07. *The Rectory, Church Meadow, Surbiton KT6 5EP* Tel (020) 8398 1583 E-mail vicki@stmaryslongditton.org.uk *or* vicki@williamburrows.com

BURSELL, Michael Hingston McLaughlin. b 70. K Coll Cam MA96 Open Univ MBA02. ERMC 05. **d** 08 **p** 09. NSM Halstead Area *Chelmsf* from 08. *Bowyer's, North Road, Great Yeldham, Halstead CO9 4QD* Tel (01787) 237486 Mobile 07971-926937 Fax 08700-517360 E-mail mike.bursell@anglicanpriest.org

BURSELL, Canon Rupert David Hingston. b 42. QC86. Ex Univ LLB63 St Edm Hall Ox BA67 MA72 DPhil72. St Steph Ho Ox 67. **d** 68 **p** 69. NSM St Marylebone w H Trin *Lon* 68-69; NSM Almondsbury *Bris* 69-71; NSM Bedminster St Fran 71-75; NSM Bedminster 75-82; NSM Bris Ch Ch w St Ewen and All SS 83-88; NSM City of Bris 83-88; Lic to Offic 88-95; Lic to Offic *B & W* 72-92; Chan *Dur* from 89; Chan *B & W* 92; Chan *St Alb* 92-02; Hon Can St Alb 96-02; NSM Cheddar *B & W* 93-11; Dep Chan *York* from 94; Hon CF 96-01; Chan *Ox* from 02; Hon Can Ch Ch from 11. *Brookside, 74 Church Road, Winscombe BS25 1BP*

BURSLEM, Christopher David Jeremy Grant. b 35. AKC85. **d** 59 **p** 60. C Bocking St Mary *Chelmsf* 59-63; C Glouc All SS 64-67; R Amberley 67-87; P-in-c Withington and Compton Abdale w Haselton 87-98; rtd 98; Perm to Offic *Derby* from 98. *44 Vestry Road, Oakwood, Derby DE21 2BL* Tel (01332) 830146

BURSON-THOMAS, Michael Edwin. b 52. Sarum & Wells Th Coll 84. **d** 86 **p** 87. C Bitterne Park *Win* 86-89; V Lockerley and E Dean w E and W Tytherley 89-95; P-in-c Fotherby *Linc* 95-99; Asst Local Min Officer 95-99; V Horncastle w Low Toynton 99-06; R Greetham w Ashby Puerorum 99-06; V High Toynton 99-06; R Horncastle Gp 06-07; RD Horncastle 01-06; P-in-c Scotton w Northorpe from 07; RD Is of Axholme from 11; RD Manlake from 11. *The Rectory, Church Lane, Scotter, Gainsborough DN21 3RZ* Tel (01724) 762951 E-mail m.bursonthomas@btinternet.com

BURSTON, Richard John. b 46. MRICS70 MRTPI73. S Dios Minl Tr Scheme 86. **d** 93 **p** 94. Hon C Stratton St Margaret w S Marston etc *Bris* from 93. *17 Crawley Avenue, Swindon SN3 4LB* Tel (01793) 822403

BURSTON, Canon Robert Benjamin Stuart. b 45. St Chad's Coll Dur BA68. **d** 70 **p** 71. C Whorlton *Newc* 70-77; V Alwinton w Holystone and Alnham 77-83; TR Glendale Gp from 83; Hon Can Newc Cathl from 95. *The Rectory, 5 Fenton Drive, Wooler NE71 6DT* Tel and fax (01668) 281551

BURT, David Alan. b 44. Southn Univ BTh98. STETS 95. **d** 98 **p** 99. C Goring-by-Sea *Chich* 98-06; P-in-c Lyminster 06-10; rtd 10. *15 Fernhurst Drive, Goring-by-Sea, Worthing BN12 5AH*

BURT, Paul Andrew. b 52. Leeds Univ BA74 K Coll Lon MA02 Univ of Wales (Ban) PhD09. Ridley Hall Cam 82. **d** 84 **p** 85. C Edin St Thos 84-88; CMS Bahrain 88-90; R Melrose *Edin* 91-00; Chapl Borders Gen Hosp NHS Trust 93-98; Ho Master Win Coll 00-04; Hd RS Pilgrims' Sch 00-04; Chapl and Hd RE K Coll Sch Cam 04-06; Sen Chapl Win Coll from 06. *Winchester College, College Street, Winchester SO23 9NA* Tel (01962) 862374 E-mail pab@wincoll.ac.uk

BURT, Roger Malcolm. b 45. MBE91. St Jo Coll Auckland. **d** 73 **p** 74. V Tinui New Zealand 73-80; P-in-c Colton *Nor* 80; P-in-c Easton 80; V Easton w Colton and Marlingford 80-88; CF 88-01; P-in-c E Coker w Sutton Bingham and Closworth *B & W* 01-10; rtd 10. *PO Box 200, Port Macquarie NSW 2444, Australia*

BURTON, Andrew John. b 63. St Kath Coll Liv BA84. Cranmer Hall Dur 86. **d** 88 **p** 89. C Harlescott *Lich* 88-91; C Ches H Trin 91-94; P-in-c Congleton St Jas 94-01; R Calton, Cauldon, Grindon, Waterfall etc *Lich* 01-08; RD Alstonfield 03-08; V Bushey Heath *St Alb* from 08. *St Peter's Vicarage, 19 High Road, Bushey Heath, Bushey WD23 1EA* Tel (020) 8950 1424 E-mail ajburton63@btinternet.com

BURTON, Antony William James. b 29. Ch Coll Cam BA52 MA56. Cuddesdon Coll 52. **d** 54 **p** 55. C Linc St Nic w St Jo Newport 54-57; C Croydon St Jo *Cant* 57-62; V Winterton *Linc* 62-82; V Roxby w Risby 70-82; RD Manlake 76-82; V Nettleham 82-94; rtd 94; Perm to Offic *Linc* 94-02. *28 Eastfield Road, Messingham, Scunthorpe DN17 3PG* Tel (01724) 763916

BURTON, Miss Barbara Louise. b 57. Leic Univ LLB81 Solicitor 84. ERMC 03. **d** 06 **p** 07. NSM March St Jo *Ely* 06-10; P-in-c Barton Bendish w Beachamwell and Shingham from 10; P-in-c Wereham from 10; P-in-c Fincham from 10; P-in-c Shouldham from 10; P-in-c Shouldham Thorpe from 10; P-in-c Boughton from 10; P-in-c Marham from 10. *The Rectory, High Street, Fincham, King's Lynn PE33 9EL* Tel (01366) 347321 E-mail barbaraburton@btinternet.com

BURTON, Christopher Paul. b 38. FCA75 Bris Univ PhD00. Clifton Th Coll 67. **d** 69 **p** 70. C Wandsworth All SS *S'wark* 69-72; C York St Paul 72-75; V Castle Vale *Birm* 75-82; R Gt Parndon *Chelmsf* 82-99; TR 99-03; rtd 03; Perm to Offic *St E* 04-07. *Damson Cottage, 69B London Road North, Poynton, Stockport SK12 1AG* Tel (01625) 875266

BURTON, Daniel John Ashworth. b 63. Regent's Park Coll Ox BA88 MA93 Heythrop Coll Lon MTh93. St Mich Coll Llan 93. **d** 94 **p** 95. C Mountain Ash *Llan* 94-97; R St Brides Minor w Bettws 97-02; R St Brides Minor w Bettws w Aberkenfig 02-03; P-in-c Cheetham *Man* from 03; AD N Man from 10. *The Vicarage, 105 Brideoak Street, Manchester M8 0AY* Tel 0161-205 1734 E-mail daniel.burton2@virgin.net

BURTON, David Alan. b 53. St Jo Coll Dur BA75. Westcott Ho Cam 81. **d** 84 **p** 85. C Bedford St Andr *St Alb* 84-87; C Leighton Buzzard w Eggington, Hockliffe etc 87-91; V Kingsbury Episcopi w E Lambrook *B & W* 91-94; V Kingsbury Episcopi w E Lambrook, Hambridge etc 94-95; R Bishops Lydeard w Bagborough and Cothelstone 95-03; rtd 04; C Dawlish *Ex* from 06; C Kenton, Mamhead, Powderham, Cofton and Starcross from 06. *The Rectory, 1 Staplake Rise, Starcross, Exeter EX6 8SJ* Tel (01626) 891777 E-mail david burton@dsl.pipex.com

BURTON, Desmond Jack. b 49. Sarum & Wells Th Coll 70. **d** 73 **p** 74. C Lakenham St Jo *Nor* 73-77; C Gt Yarmouth 77-80; R Tidworth *Sarum* 80-83; Chapl HM Pris Pentonville 83-84; Chapl HM Pris Standford Hill 84-88; Chapl HM Pris Swaleside 88-93; Chapl HM Pris Roch 93-99; Chapl HM Pris Whitemoor 99-05; Chapl HM Pris Whatton 05-09; P-in-c Balcombe *Chich* from 09. *The Rectory, Haywards Heath Road, Balcombe, Haywards Heath RH17 6PA* Tel (01444) 811249

BURTON, Graham John. b 45. Bris Univ BA69. Tyndale Hall Bris 69. **d** 71 **p** 72. C Leic St Chris 71-75; C Southall Green St Jo Lon 75-79; CMS Pakistan 80-92; P-in-c Basford w Hyson Green *S'well* 92-99; P-in-c Hyson Green and Forest Fields 99-01; Assoc P 01-07; Dir Rainbow Project 01-07; rtd 07; Perm to Offic *S'well* from 07. *6 Meadow Brown Road, Nottingham NG7 5PH*

BURTON, Hugh Anthony. b 56. Edin Univ BD79. Cranmer Hall Dur 81. **d** 83 **p** 84. C Coalville and Bardon Hill *Leic* 83-87; P-in-c Packington w Normanton-le-Heath 87-92; V 92-96; TV Kidderminster St Geo *Worc* 96-08; P-in-c from 08. *The Rectory, 30 Leswell Street, Kidderminster DY10 1RP* Tel (01562) 824490 E-mail hburton@wfcsmail.com

BURTON, Leslie Samuel Bertram. b 23. **d** 91 **p** 92. NSM St Cleer *Truro* 91-93; Perm to Offic 93-00. *29 Vivian Court, Truro TR1 2TR*

BURTON, Michael John. b 55. Leeds Univ BSc76 Leeds Poly BSc80. St Jo Coll Nottm 86. **d** 88 **p** 89. C Charles w Plymouth St Matthias *Ex* 88-92; V Paignton St Paul Preston 92-99; TV Almondbury w Farnley Tyas *Wakef* 99-02; V Roade and Ashton w Hartwell *Pet* from 02; RD Towcester 03-09; C Collingtree w Courteenhall and Milton Malsor from 09. *The Vicarage, 18 Hartwell Road, Roade, Northampton NN7 2NT* Tel (01604) 862284 E-mail michaelburton5@aol.com

BURTON, Nicholas Guy. b 69. Bris Univ BSc91 ACCA00. Ridley Hall Cam 03. **d** 05 **p** 06. C Ore St Helen and St Barn *Chich* 05-09; C Bexhill St Steph from 09. *St George's Flat, St George's Church, Cantelupe Road, Bexhill-on-Sea TN40 1PP* Tel (01424) 210260 Mobile 07851-742049 E-mail ngb.cofe@tiscali.co.uk

BURTON, Nicholas John. b 52. St Steph Ho Ox 77. **d** 80 **p** 81. C Leic St Matt and St Geo 80-82; C Leic Resurr 82-83; TV 83-88; C Narborough and Huncote 88-90; R 90-10; rtd 10. *Address withheld by request*

BURTON, Norman George. b 30. NOC. **d** 83 **p** 84. C Rothwell w Lofthouse *Ripon* 83-86; C Rothwell 86-87; V Lofthouse 87-96; rtd 96; Perm to Offic *Ripon* from 96. *28 Temple Row Close, Leeds LS15 9HR* Tel 0113-260 1129

BURTON, Mrs Sarah Elizabeth. b 59. Nottm Univ BMedSci80 Dur Univ PGCE82. NOC 05. **d** 08 **p** 09. C Eastham *Ches* from 08. *6 Elizabeth Crescent, Chester CH4 7AZ* Tel (01244) 659874 E-mail seburton@fsmail.net

BURTON, Mrs Virginia Ann. b 55. St As Minl Tr Course 00. **d** 03 **p** 04. C Llanrhos *St As* 03-08; C Colwyn Bay w Brynymaen from 08. *The Rectory, 1 Rhodfa Sant Elian, Colwyn Bay LL29 8PY* Tel (01492) 512160

BURTON, Mrs Zoe. b 66. Open Univ BSc99. EMMTC 07. **d** 10 **p** 11. NSM Ravenshead *S'well* from 10. *Mar-Ann, 348 Mansfield Road, Sutton-in-Ashfield NG17 4HS* Tel 07505-773694 (mobile) E-mail zoe.burton@ntlworld.com

BURTON EVANS, David. *See* EVANS, David Burton

BURTON-JONES, The Ven Simon David. b 62. Em Coll Cam BA84 MA88. St Jo Coll Nottm BTh92 MA93. **d** 93 **p** 94. C Darwen St Pet w Hoddlesden *Blackb* 93-96; C Biggin Hill *Roch* 96-98; P-in-c Plaistow St Mary 98-00; V 00-05; R Chislehurst St Nic 05-10; AD Bromley 01-06; Adn Roch from 10; Can Res Roch Cathl from 10. *The Archdeaconry, King's Orchard, Rochester ME1 1TG* Tel (01634) 813533 E-mail simon.burtonjones@diocese-rochester.org

BURTT, Andrew Keith. b 50. Massey Univ (NZ) BA72 MA74 DipEd76. St Jo Coll (NZ) LTh82. **d** 81 **p** 82. New Zealand 81-83; CF 84-92; Sen Chapl Brighton Coll 93-03; Chapl Portsm Gr Sch from 03. *8 Penny Street, Portsmouth PO1 2NH* Tel (023) 9268 1395

BURTWELL, Stanley Peter. b 32. Leeds Univ BA55. Coll of Resurr Mirfield 55. **d** 57 **p** 58. C Leeds St Hilda *Ripon* 57-61; S Africa 61-72; P-in-c Gt Hanwood *Heref* 72-78; R 78-83; RD Pontesbury 80-83; V Upper Norwood St Jo *Cant* 83-84; V Upper Norwood St Jo *S'wark* 85-90; RD Croydon N 85-90; TR Bourne Valley *Sarum* 90-97; rtd 97; Perm to Offic *Sarum* from 97. *Splinters, 116 High Street, Swanage BN19 2NY* Tel (01929) 421785

BURUNDI, Archbishop of. *See* NTAHOTURI, The Most Revd Bernard

BURY, Miss Dorothy Jane. b 53. Lanc Univ BA96 MA98 St Hild Coll Dur CertEd75. Ripon Coll Cuddesdon 00. **d** 02 **p** 03. C Thornton-le-Fylde *Blackb* 02-06; P-in-c Wigan St Anne *Liv* from 06; Chapl Deanery C of E High Sch Wigan from 06. *St Anne's Vicarage, 154 Beech Hill Avenue, Wigan WN6 7TA* Tel (01942) 241930 Mobile 07715-560031 E-mail tillybury@tiscali.co.uk

BURY, The Very Revd Nicholas Ayles Stillingfleet. b 43. Qu Coll Cam BA65 MA69 Ch Ch Ox MA71. Cuddesdon Coll. **d** 68 **p** 69. C Liv Our Lady and St Nic 68-71; Chapl Ch Ch *Ox* 71-75; V Stevenage St Mary Shephall *St Alb* 75-84; V St Peter-in-Thanet *Cant* 84-97; RD Thanet 93-97; Hon Can Cant Cathl 94-97; Dean Glouc 97-10; rtd 10. *122 The Homend, Ledbury HR8 1BZ* Tel (01531) 636075

BUSBY, Ian Frederick Newman. b 32. Roch Th Coll 61. **d** 64 **p** 65. C Bedale *Ripon* 64-67; C Stevenage St Geo *St Alb* 67-71; V Stevenage St Mary Shephall 71-75; V Kildwick *Bradf* 75-92; rtd 93; Perm to Offic *Bradf* from 93. *12 Currergate Mews, Skipton Road, Steeton, Keighley BD20 6PE* Tel (01535) 652099

BUSBY, John. b 38. St Cath Coll Cam MA60 CEng. **d** 93 **p** 94. OLM Worplesdon *Guildf* 93-02; OLM Pirbright 02-04; Perm to Offic from 06. *Iona, Fox Corner, Worplesdon, Guildford GU3 3PP* Tel (01483) 234562

BUSFIELD, Miss Lynn Maria. b 60. Trin Coll Bris BA99. **d** 99 **p** 00. C Scartho *Linc* 99-03; TV Marlborough *Sarum* 03-05; Chapl Mt Edgcumbe Hospice 05-08; P-in-c Fladbury, Hill and Moor, Wyre Piddle etc *Worc* from 09; P-in-c Peopleton and White Ladies Aston w Churchill etc from 11; C Fladbury, Hill and Moor, Wyre Piddle etc from 11; C Abberton, The Flyfords, Naunton Beauchamp etc from 11. *The Rectory, Peopleton, Pershore WR10 2EE* E-mail lynn.busfield@virgin.net

BUSH, Mrs Ann Kathleen. b 47. MATCA65. Ox Min Course 90. **d** 93 **p** 94. NSM Warfield *Ox* 93-96; Dep Chapl HM Pris Wormwood Scrubs 96-97; Chapl HM Pris Reading 97-99; Sen Chapl HM Pris Feltham 99-01; R Fort Smith Canada from 01. *PO Box 64, Fort Smith NT X0E 0P0, Canada* Tel (001) (867) 872 3438 E-mail abush@auroranet.nt.ca

BUSH, David. b 25. FRIBA47 Liv Univ BArch47. S'wark Ord Course 73. **d** 77 **p** 77. C Douglas St Geo and St Barn *S & M*

77-80; Chapl Ballamona Hosp and Cronk Grianagh 80-86; V Marown 80-87; R The Rissingtons *Glouc* 87-92; rtd 92; Perm to Offic *Glouc* 92-98 and *Ely* from 99. *12 Kentwell Place, Burwell, Cambridge CB25 0RT* Tel (01638) 741839 E-mail dandac.bush@care4free.net

BUSH, Esther Rachma Hartley. b 66. LMH Ox BA88 St Jo Coll Dur BA04. Cranmer Hall Dur 02. **d** 04 **p** 05. C Bethnal Green St Matt w St Jas the Gt *Lon* 04-07; C Staines 07-10; P-in-c Westfield *B & W* from 10; Chapl Norton Radstock Coll of FE from 10. *5 Wellsway, Wells Road, Bath BA3 3UW* Tel (01784) 450861 Mobile 07854-852806 E-mail rachmasaid@yahoo.co.uk

BUSH, George Raymond. b 57. St Jo Coll Cam BA81 MA84 Univ of Wales LLM95. Ripon Coll Cuddesdon BA84 MA88. **d** 85 **p** 86. C Leeds St Aid *Ripon* 85-89; Chapl St Jo Coll Cam 89-94; V Hoxton St Anne w St Columba *Lon* 94-02; R St Mary le Bow w St Pancras Soper Lane etc from 02. *The Rector's Lodgings, Cheapside, London EC2V 6AU* Tel (020) 7248 5139 Fax 7248 0509 E-mail grbush@london.anglican.org

BUSH, Mrs Glenda. b 41. NOC 92. **d** 95 **p** 96. NSM Bolton St Phil *Man* 95-99; C 99-02; C Bolton SS Simon and Jude 99-02; P-in-c 02-06; rtd 06; Perm to Offic *Man* from 06. *46 Mary Street West, Horwich, Bolton BL6 7JU* Tel (01204) 691539

BUSH, Mrs Kathryn Ann. b 60. OLM course 95. **d** 99 **p** 00. OLM Mareham-le-Fen and Revesby *Linc* 99-06; OLM Mareham on the Hill 99-06; OLM Hameringham w Scrafield and Winceby 99-06; OLM Fen and Hill Gp from 06. *Wheatsheaf Farm, Chapel Lane, New Bolingbroke, Boston PE22 7LF* Tel (01205) 480631 Mobile 07775-736344

BUSH, Kieran John Christopher. b 80. Ch Coll Cam BA01 MA05. Oak Hill Th Coll MTh11. **d** 11. C Dagenham *Chelmsf* from 11. *8 Church Lane, Dagenham RM10 9UL* Tel (020) 8595 3485 Mobile 07709-119325 E-mail kieranbush@hotmail.com

BUSH, Rachma. *see* BUSH, Esther Rachma Hartley

BUSH, The Ven Roger Charles. b 56. K Coll Lon BA78 Leeds Univ BA85. Coll of Resurr Mirfield 83. **d** 86 **p** 87. C Newbold w Dunston *Derby* 86-90; TV Leic Resurr 90-94; TR Redruth w Lanner and Treleigh *Truro* 94-04; RD Carnmarth N 96-03; Hon Can Truro Cathl 03-04; Can Res Truro Cathl from 04; Adn Cornwall from 06. *Westwood House, Tremorvah Crescent, Truro TR1 1NL* Tel (01872) 225630 E-mail roger@truro.anglican.org

BUSH, Lt Col Walter Patrick Anthony. b 39. **d** 07 **p** 08. OLM Watercombe *Sarum* from 07. *Holworth Farmhouse, Holworth, Dorchester DT2 8NH* Tel (01305) 852242 E-mail bushinarcadia@yahoo.co.uk

BUSHAU, Reginald Francis. b 49. Shimer Coll Illinois AB71. St Steph Ho Ox BA73 MA98. **d** 74 **p** 75. C Deptford St Paul *S'wark* 74-77; C Willesden St Andr and Gladstone Park St Fran *Lon* 77-82; P-in-c Brondesbury St Anne w Kilburn H Trin 83-88; V Paddington St Mary Magd 88-97; AD Westmr Paddington 92-97; P-in-c S Kensington St Steph 96-98; V from 98. *9 Eldon Road, London W8 5PU* Tel (020) 7937 5083 or 7370 3418 E-mail bushrf@aol.com

BUSHBY, Michael Reginald. b 42. LSE BSc70 Leeds Univ MA97. **d** 02 **p** 03. NSM S Cave and Ellerker w Broomfleet *York* 02-05; P-in-c Newbald from 05. *The Vicarage, 7 Dot Hill Close, North Newbald, York YO43 4TS* Tel (01430) 801088

BUSHELL, Anthony Colin. b 59. Pemb Coll Ox MA82 Barrister 83. S'wark Ord Course 93. **d** 96 **p** 97. NSM Felsted and Lt Dunmow *Chelmsf* 96-98; NSM Stanway 98-06; NSM Greenstead w Colchester St Anne from 06. *Pump Hall, Middle Green, Wakes Colne, Colchester CO6 2BJ* Tel (01787) 222487 Fax 222361 E-mail vicartone@aol.com

BUSHELL, Mrs Linda Mary. b 52. Bradf and Ilkley Coll BEd91. STETS 06. **d** 09 **p** 10. NSM Bembridge *Portsm* from 09. *2 Rowborough Cottages, Rowborough Lane, Brading, Sandown PO36 0AY* Tel (01983) 400261 E-mail linda.bushell1@btinternet.com

BUSHELL, Roy. b 32. NW Ord Course 75. **d** 79 **p** 80. NSM Croft w Southworth *Liv* 79-87; C Netherton 87-89; R Newton in Makerfield Em 89-97; rtd 97; Perm to Offic *Bradf* from 98. *34 Maple Avenue, Whitley Bay NE25 8JS* Tel 0191-251 9816

BUSHELL, Stephen Lionel. b 60. K Coll Lon BA84. Ripon Coll Cuddesdon 92. **d** 94 **p** 95. C Exhall *Cov* 94-97; Asst P Shelswell Ox 97-05; Asst Chapl Aylesbury Vale Community Healthcare NHS Trust 97-05; Chapl Oxon & Bucks Mental Health Partnership NHS Trust from 05. *6 Aris Way, Buckingham MK18 1FX* Tel (01280) 823772 E-mail tostephenbushell@hotmail.com *or* stephen.bushell@obmh.nhs.uk

BUSHYAGER, Ronald Robert. b 77. Belmont Univ Nashville BSc00. Wycliffe Hall Ox BTh04. **d** 04 **p** 05. C Gamston and Bridgford *S'well* 04-07; C Abingdon Ox 07-10; Chapl to Bp Kensington *Lon* from 10. *Dial House, Riverside, Twickenham TW1 3DT* Tel (020) 8892 7781 E-mail ronbushyager@ntlworld.com

BUSHYAGER (née TWITCHEN), Mrs Ruth Kathleen Frances. b 77. Bris Univ MSci99. Wycliffe Hall Ox BA04. **d** 05 **p** 06. C Wilford *S'well* 05-07; NSM Abingdon Ox 08; Asst Chapl St Edw

Sch Ox 08-10; Area Missr Kensington Area *Lon* from 10. *Dial House, Riverside, Twickenham TW1 3DT* Tel (020) 8892 7781 E-mail ruth.bushyager@london.anglican.org

BUSK, David Westly. b 60. Magd Coll Cam BA83 St Jo Coll Dur BA88. Cranmer Hall Dur 86. **d** 89 **p** 90. C Old Swinford Stourbridge *Worc* 89-93; USPG Japan 94-95; C Fukuoka Cathl 95-96; P-in-c Nagasaki H Trin 96-06; P-in-c Godmanchester *Ely* from 06; P-in-c Hilton from 11. *The Vicarage, 59 Post Street, Godmanchester, Huntingdon PE29 2AQ* Tel (01480) 436400 *or* tel and fax 453354 Mobile 07765-851757 E-mail dwbusk@hotmail.com

BUSK, Horace. b 36. Clifton Th Coll 56. **d** 60 **p** 61. C Burton All SS *Lich* 60-63; Paraguay 63-66; C Silverhill St Matt *Chich* 66-67; Lic to Offic *Sarum* 67-69; C W Kilburn St Luke w St Simon and St Jude *Lon* 69-74; TV Ashwellthorpe w Wreningham *Nor* 74-81; P-in-c Meysey Hampton w Marston Meysey and Castle Eaton *Glouc* 81-82; R 82-04; rtd 04; Perm to Offic *Glouc* from 04. *23 Eastcote Road, Cirencester GL7 2DB* Tel (01285) 650884

BUSS, Gerald Vere Austen. b 36. CCC Cam PhD87. St Steph Ho Ox 59. **d** 63 **p** 64. C Petersham *S'wark* 63-66; C Brompton H Trin *Lon* 66-69; Asst Chapl Hurstpierpoint Coll 70-73; Chapl 74-90; Ho Master 90-94; History teacher 94-96; rtd 96. *Souches, The Street, Albourne, Hassocks BN6 9DJ* Tel and fax (01273) 832465

BUSSELL, Ian Paul. b 62. Reading Univ BA84 Kingston Poly PGCE85. Qu Coll Birm MA98. **d** 98 **p** 99. C Twickenham St Mary *Lon* 98-01; TV Godalming *Guildf* 01-07; P-in-c Leckhampton SS Phil and Jas w Cheltenham St Jas *Glouc* 07-09; TV S Cheltenham 10-11; Dioc Dir of Ords from 11. *56 Leckhampton Road, Cheltenham GL53 0BG* Tel (01242) 256104 E-mail ianbussell@googlemail.com

BUSSELL, Ronald William. b 34. CA Tr Coll 57 St Deiniol's Hawarden 81. **d** 83 **p** 84. C Claughton cum Grange *Ches* 83-85; P-in-c Preston St Oswald *Blackb* 85-87; V Fleetwood St Nic 87-93; Dioc Chapl MU 91-95; R Tarleton 93-95; rtd 95; Perm to Offic *Blackb* from 95. *4 Willoughby Avenue, Thornton-Cleveleys FY5 2BW* Tel (01253) 820067 E-mail ron.bussell@talk21.com

BUSSEY, Diane Jean. b 57. **d** 07 **p** 08. OLM Clifton w Newton and Brownsover *Cov* from 07; Chapl Rainsbrook Secure Tr Cen from 09. *2 Teasel Close, Rugby CV23 0TJ* Tel (01788) 339278 E-mail diane.bussey1@ntlworld.com

BUSSEY, Norman. b 22. Clifton Th Coll 63. **d** 65 **p** 66. C Upton (Overchurch) *Ches* 65-69; V Bradley *Wakef* 69-88; rtd 88; Perm to Offic *Glouc* from 88. *43 Crispin Road, Winchcombe, Cheltenham GL54 5JX* Tel (01242) 602754

BUSSEY, Rachel Anne. STETS 00. **d** 03 **p** 04. NSM Durrington *Sarum* from 03; NSM Avon Valley from 08. *3 Birchwood Drive, Durrington, Salisbury SP4 8ER* Tel 07899-926034 (mobile) E-mail rachel.bussey@ntlworld.com

BUSSMANN, Mrs Mary Elizabeth. b 52. Leeds Univ MA06. Trin Coll Bris. **d** 06 **p** 07. C Otham w Langley *Cant* 06-10; R E Horsley and Ockham w Hatchford and Downside *Guildf* from 10. *The Rectory, Ockham Road South, East Horsley, Leatherhead KT24 6RL* Tel (01483) 282359 E-mail ebussmann@btinternet.com

BUSTARD, Guy Nicholas. b 51. K Coll Lon BD77 AKC77. St Steph Ho Ox 77. **d** 78 **p** 79. C Hythe *Cant* 78-81; Chapl RN 81-85; V Haddenham and Wilburton *Ely* 85-89; Chapl Qu Eliz Hosp Welwyn Garden City 89-92; Chapl E Herts NHS Trust 92-00; Chapl E and N Herts NHS Trust 00-02; Perm to Offic *St Alb* from 02. *2 Copper Beeches, Welwyn AL6 0SS* Tel (01438) 717916

BUSTIN, Canon Peter Ernest. b 32. Qu Coll Cam BA56 MA60. Tyndale Hall Bris 56. **d** 57 **p** 58. C Welling *Roch* 57-60; C Farnborough *Guildf* 60-62; V Hornsey Rise St Mary *Lon* 62-70; R Barnwell *Pet* 70-78; RD Oundle 76-84; P-in-c Luddington w Hemington and Thurning 77-78; R Barnwell w Thurning and Luddington 78-84; V Southwold *St E* 84-97; RD Halesworth 90-95; Hon Can St E Cathl 91-97; rtd 97; Perm to Offic *St E* from 97. *55 College Street, Bury St Edmunds IP33 1NH* Tel (01284) 767708 E-mail bustin@saintedmunds.vispa.com

BUSTIN, Peter Laurence. b 54. St Steph Ho Ox. **d** 83 **p** 84. C Northolt St Mary *Lon* 83-86; C Pimlico St Pet w Westmr Ch Ch 86-88; C Heston 88-91; P-in-c Twickenham All SS 91-98; V 98-11; rtd 11; P-in-c Beaulieu-sur-Mer and Cannes from 11. *St Michael, 11 chemin des Myrtes, 06310 Beaulieu-sur-Mer, France* Tel and fax (0033) (4) 93 01 45 61 E-mail peter@padova.fsnet.co.uk

BUSTIN, Timothy Mark. b 75. UWE BA98. Wycliffe Hall Ox 05. **d** 07 **p** 08. C Bletchley Ox 07-10; C Waikanae New Zealand from 10. *2 Pemi Kupa Street, Waikanae 5036, New Zealand* E-mail tim.busters@freeserve.co.uk

BUTCHER, Andrew John. b 43. Trin Coll Cam BA66 MA69. Cuddesdon Coll 66. **d** 68 **p** 69. C Sheff St Mark Broomhall 68-70; P-in-c Louth H Trin *Linc* 70-72; Chapl RAF 72-87; Lic to Offic *Ox* 85-87; TR Cove St Jo *Guildf* 87-91; V Egham Hythe 91-98; V Docking, the Birchams, Stanhoe and Sedgeford *Nor* 98-08; rtd 08; Perm to Offic *Nor* from 08. *67 The Street, Hindringham, Fakenham NR21 0PR* Tel (01328) 878526 Mobile 07887-506876 E-mail andrewj.butcher@btinternet.com

BUTCHER, Miss Ann Lesley. b 46. Lon Coll of Printing BA67 Ex Univ BTh09. SWMTC 06. **d** 09 **p** 10. NSM St Michael Penkevil *Truro* from 09; NSM Tregony w St Cuby and Cornelly from 09; NSM Tresillian and Lamorran w Merther from 09. *Burnwithian House, Burnwithian, St Day, Redruth TR16 5LG* Tel (01209) 820788 E-mail mail@annbutcher.demon.co.uk

BUTCHER, Edwin William. b 39. Portsm Dioc Tr Course 91 STETS 04. **d** 92 **p** 05. NSM Ryde All SS *Portsm* from 92. *23 Quarry Road, Ryde PO33 2TX* Tel (01983) 616889

BUTCHER (née POTTS), Mrs Heather Dawn. b 52. **d** 98 **p** 99. C Attleborough w Besthorpe *Nor* 98-01; R Bunwell, Carleton Rode, Tibenham, Gt Moulton etc 01-09; Bp's Adv for Women's Min from 11. *The Vicarage, 7A Newmarket Road, Cringleford, Norwich NR4 6UE* Tel (01603) 458467 E-mail vicarage.cringleford@btinternet.com

BUTCHER, Philip Warren. b 46. Trin Coll Cam BA68 MA70. Cuddesdon Coll 68. **d** 70 **p** 71. C Bris St Mary Redcliffe w Temple etc 70-73; Hon C W Wickham St Fran *Cant* 73-78; Chapl Abingdon Sch 78-85; Chapl Nor Sch 85-98; V Horsford and Horsham w Newton St Faith *Nor* 98-04; rtd 04; P-in-c Barningham w Matlaske w Baconsthorpe etc *Nor* 05-09; Perm to Offic from 09. *The Vicarage, 7A Newmarket Road, Cringleford, Norwich NR4 6UE* Tel (01603) 458467

BUTCHER, Richard Peter. b 50. St Chad's Coll Dur BA71. Chich Th Coll 73. **d** 74 **p** 75. C Yeovil St Mich *B & W* 74-77; Chapl Wellingborough Sch 77-83; R Gt w Lt Billing *Pet* 83-88; Chapl Bp Stopford Sch Kettering 88-90; Perm to Offic *Pet* 90-01. *55 Field Street, Kettering NN16 8EN*

BUTCHERS, Mark Andrew. b 59. Trin Coll Cam BA81 K Coll Lon MTh90 PhD06. Chich Th Coll BTh87. **d** 87 **p** 88. C Chelsea St Luke and Ch Ch *Lon* 87-90; C Mitcham SS Pet and Paul *S'wark* 90-93; R N Tawton, Bondleigh, Sampford Courtenay etc *Ex* 93-99; Chapl and Fell Keble Coll Ox 99-05; C Wolvercote w Summertown *Ox* 05-07; P-in-c Wolvercote 07-10; V Wolvercote and Wytham from 10. *The Vicarage, 1 Mere Road, Oxford OX2 8AN* Tel (01865) 515640 E-mail mark.butchers@dsl.pipex.com

BUTLAND, Cameron James. b 58. BA. Ripon Coll Cuddesdon 81. **d** 84 **p** 85. C Tettenhall Regis *Lich* 84-88; V Bodicote *Ox* 88-95; TR Witney 95-04; RD Witney 97-02; R Grasmere *Carl* from 04; V Rydal from 04; Chapl Rydal Hall from 04. *The Rectory, Grasmere, Ambleside LA22 9SW* Tel (01539) 435326 E-mail cameron@butland555.fsnet.co.uk

BUTLAND, Godfrey John. b 51. Grey Coll Dur BA72. Wycliffe Hall Ox 73. **d** 75 **p** 76. C Much Woolton *Liv* 75-78; Bp's Dom Chapl 78-81; V Everton St Geo 81-94; AD Liv N 89-94; V Allerton 94-05; P-in-c Mossley Hill St Barn 04-05; TV Mossley Hill 05-06; TR from 06; AD Liv S 00-06; Hon Can Liv Cathl 03-06. *Allerton Vicarage, Harthill Road, Liverpool L18 3HU* Tel 0151-724 1561

BUTLER, Canon Alan. b 53. Carl Dioc Tr Inst 89. **d** 89 **p** 90. NSM Flookburgh *Carl* 89-93; C Maryport 93-96; C Flimby 93-96; P-in-c 96-98; TV Saltash *Truro* 98-09; TR from 09; Hon Can Truro Cathl from 10. *The Vicarage, St Stephen by Saltash, Saltash PL12 4AB* Tel (01752) 842323

BUTLER, Canon Alan. b 57. Leic Univ BA78. Coll of Resurr Mirfield 80. **d** 83 **p** 84. C Skerton St Luke *Blackb* 83-87; C Birch w Fallowfield *Man* 87-90; V Claremont H Angels 90-95; Chapl Pendleton Coll 95-99; TV Pendleton *Man* 95-99; P-in-c High Crompton from 99; AD Oldham E from 09; Hon Can Man Cathl from 11. *St Mary's Vicarage, 18 Rushcroft Road, Shaw, Oldham OL2 7PR* Tel and fax (01706) 847455 E-mail alanbutler@freenetname.co.uk

BUTLER, Ms Angela Elizabeth. b 31. Gilmore Ho 60 Lambeth STh64. **dss** 81 **d** 87 **p** 94. Cookham *Ox* 81-86; Wheatley w Forest Hill and Stanton St John 86-97; Hon Par Dn 87-89; NSM 89-97; NSM Wheatley 97-01; Perm to Offic from 02. *10 River Gardens, Purley-on-Thames, Reading RG8 8BX* Tel 0118-942 2055

BUTLER, Angela Madeline. b 47. Oak Hill NSM Course 87. **d** 90 **p** 94. Hon Par Dn Chipperfield St Paul *St Alb* 90-93; Dn-in-c 93-94; P-in-c 94-01; Staff Oak Hill Th Coll 93-97; Springboard Missr 97-01; P-in-c Hempsted and Dioc Springboard Missr *Glouc* 01-07; rtd 07. *22 Esplanade Road, Newquay TR7 1QB* Tel (01637) 859238 E-mail angelambutler@btinternet.com

BUTLER, Catherine Elizabeth. b 46. **d** 06 **p** 07. NSM Waltham *Linc* from 06. *8 Danesfield Avenue, Waltham, Grimsby DN37 0QE* Tel (01472) 587692 E-mail elsiebutlerdane@msn.com

BUTLER, Cecil Anthony. b 37. Sarum Th Coll 65. **d** 68 **p** 69. C Gillingham *Sarum* 68-70; CF 70-74; R Whittington St Jo *Lich* 74-83; rtd 02; Perm to Offic *S & M* from 10. *The Mines House, The Mines Yard, Laxey, Isle of Man IM4 7NJ* Tel (01624) 860085 Mobile 07967-497721

BUTLER, Christine Jane. b 66. Cranmer Hall Dur. **d** 10 **p** 11. C Cheddar *B & W* from 10; C Draycott w Rodney Stoke from 10. *4 Southfield, Cheddar BS27 3HT* Tel 07910-479145 (mobile) E-mail butlerchristine19@gmail.com

BUTLER, Christopher. b 67. St Jo Coll Nottm 99. **d** 01 **p** 02. C Retford *S'well* 01-05; P-in-c Holbeck *Ripon* from 05. *St Luke's Vicarage, Malvern View, Leeds LS11 8SG* Tel 0113-271 7996 E-mail vicar@stlukesholbeck.org.uk or crbutler@bigfoot.com

BUTLER, Christopher John. b 25. Leeds Univ BA50. Chich Th Coll 50. **d** 52 **p** 53. C Kensington St Mary Abbots w St Geo *Lon* 52-57; Australia 57-59; V Blackmoor *Portsm* 60-70; V Wellingborough St Andr *Pet* 70-79; P-in-c Garsington *Ox* 79-83; R Garsington and Horspath 83-95; rtd 95; Perm to Offic *Portsm, Chich, Guildf* and *Win* from 95. *33 Oak Tree Road, Whitehill, Bordon GU35 9DF* Tel (01420) 475311

BUTLER, Colin Sydney. b 59. Bradf Univ BSc81. Wycliffe Hall Ox 81. **d** 84 **p** 85. C Farsley *Bradf* 84-87; C Bradf St Aug Undercliffe 87-89; P-in-c Darlaston All SS *Lich* 89-95; Ind Missr 89-95; TR Chell 95-99; CF from 99. *c/o MOD Chaplains (Army)* Tel (01264) 381140 Fax 381824

BUTLER, David Edwin. b 56. Jes Coll Ox BA79 BA86 ACA83. St Steph Ho Ox MA87. **d** 87 **p** 88. C Hulme Ascension *Man* 87-90; V Patricroft 90-94; Perm to Offic *Liv* 97-03; *Man* 03-08; *Blackb* from 03; Hon C Prestwich St Hilda *Man* 00-01. *16 St George's Road, Nelson BB9 0YA*

BUTLER, Derek John. b 53. Aston Univ BSc74 St Jo Coll York PGCE75. St Jo Coll Dur 79. **d** 82 **p** 83. C Bramcote *S'well* 82-86; Lon and SE Co-ord CPAS 86-88; NSM Bromley Ch Ch *Roch* 88-91; NSM Chesham Bois *Ox* 92-10; Perm to Offic from 10. *121 Woodside Road, Amersham HP6 6AL* Tel (01494) 724577

BUTLER, Donald Arthur. b 31. **d** 79 **p** 80. Hon C Apsley End *St Alb* 79-80; Hon C Chambersbury 80-04; Perm to Offic from 04. *143 Belswains Lane, Hemel Hempstead HP3 9UZ*

BUTLER, George James. b 53. AKC74 Kent Univ MA95. St Aug Coll Cant 75. **d** 76 **p** 77. C Ellesmere Port *Ches* 76-79; C Eastham 79-81; Chapl RAF 81-83; C W Kirby St Bridget *Ches* 83-84; V Newton 84-86; CF 86-91; V Folkestone St Sav *Cant* 91-99; P-in-c Wool and E Stoke *Sarum* 99-04; P-in-c Mansfield St Mark *S'well* 04-10; AD Mansfield 06-10; V Goring-by-Sea *Chich* from 10. *The Vicarage, 12 Compton Avenue, Goring-by-Sea, Worthing BN12 4UJ* Tel (01903) 242525 E-mail revgjb@btinternet.com

BUTLER, Canon George William. b 52. CITC. **d** 90 **p** 91. C Drung w Castleterra, Larah and Lavey etc *K, E & A* 90-93; I 93-95; I Castlemacadam w Ballinaclash, Aughrim etc *D & G* from 95; Can Ch Ch Cathl Dublin from 03. *The Rectory, Castlemacadam, Avoca, Co Wicklow, Republic of Ireland* Tel and fax (00353) (402) 35127 Mobile 87-679 5625 E-mail gwb2@hotmail.com

BUTLER, Mrs Helen Carole. b 66. Bath Coll of HE BEd87. Dioc OLM tr scheme 02. **d** 04 **p** 05. NSM Mirfield *Wakef* from 04. *1A Holmdene Drive, Mirfield WF14 9SZ* Tel (01924) 496189 Mobile 07764-187988 E-mail curate-stmary@cofe-mirfield.org.uk

BUTLER, Henry. b 25. Ridley Hall Cam 73. **d** 75 **p** 76. C Cambridge St Paul *Ely* 75-77; P-in-c Stilton w Denton and Caldecote 77-83; P-in-c Folksworth w Morborne 77-83; V Histon 83-90; P-in-c Impington 84-90; rtd 90; Perm to Offic *Ely* from 90. *48 Church Road, Hauxton, Cambridge CB22 5HS* Tel (01223) 874184

BUTLER, Huw. b 63. Univ of Wales (Ban) BSc84. St Mich Coll Llan BTh95. **d** 95 **p** 96. C Llantwit Fardre 95-00; R Llangynhafal w Llanbedr DC and Llanychan *St As* 00-02; R Llanbedr DC w Llangynhafal, Llanychan etc 02-10; P-in-c Llanynys 10; AD Dyffryn Clwyd 10; TR Llantwit Major from 10. *The Rectory, High Street, Llantwit Major CF61 1SS* Tel (01446) 794670 E-mail huw.butler@tesco.net

BUTLER, Ian Malcolm. b 39. Bris Univ BA67 BA69. Clifton Th Coll 67. **d** 69 **p** 70. C Clapham Common St Barn *S'wark* 69-73; C Reigate St Mary 73-78; V Sissinghurst w Frittenden *Cant* 78-93; Chapl Dulwich Prep Sch Cranbrook 90-05; rtd 92. *20 Kingsmead Road, Bognor Regis PO22 6NE* Tel 07786-935469 (mobile) E-mail ian@butler08.fsnet.co.uk

BUTLER, Jane. See BUTLER, Linda Jane

BUTLER, John. b 38. Gwent Coll Newport CertEd77. St Mich Coll Llan. **d** 68 **p** 69. C Ebbw Vale *Mon* 68-70; TV 70-75; Perm to Offic 76-77 and 79-88; P-in-c Crumlin 77-78; R Gt and Lt Casterton w Pickworth and Tickencote *Pet* 88-91; R Woolstone w Gotherington and Oxenton etc *Glouc* 91-97; Hon C Dawlish *Ex* 98-01; P-in-c Chevington w Hargrave, Chedburgh w Depden etc *St E* 01-02; R 02-03; rtd 03; C Shaldon, Stokeinteignhead, Combeinteignhead etc *Ex* 03-06. *3 Peak Coach House, Cotmaton Road, Sidmouth EX10 8SY* Tel (01395) 577248

BUTLER, John Philip. b 47. Leeds Univ BA70. Coll of Resurr Mirfield 70. **d** 72 **p** 73. C Elton All SS *Man* 72-75; C Bolton St Pet 75-78; Chapl Bolton Colls of H&FE 75-78; Asst Chapl Bris Univ 78-81; Hon C Clifton St Paul 78-81; V Llansawel w Briton Ferry 81-84; Warden Bp Mascall Cen *Heref* 84-88; Vice-Prin Glouc Sch for Min 85-88; Chapl Univ of Wales (Ban) 88-07; rtd 07. *Cefn Engan, Llangybi, Pwllheli LL53 6LZ* Tel (01766) 810046

BUTLER, Mrs Lesley Ann. b 52. Cov Univ BSc75 Nottm Univ MA05. EMMTC 08. **d** 10. NSM Loughborough Em and St Mary in Charnwood *Leic* 10-11; NSM Kegworth, Hathern,

Long Whatton, Diseworth etc from 11. *1 Cheriborough Road, Castle Donington, Derby DE74 2RY* Tel (01332) 391780 Mobile 07505-384527 E-mail revlesley.butler@gmail.com

BUTLER, Mrs Linda. b 51. Liv Univ CertEd72. Cranmer Hall Dur 01. **d** 03 **p** 04. C Middlewich w Byley *Ches* 03-06; R Ditchingham, Hedenham, Broome, Earsham etc *Nor* from 06. *The Rectory, School Road, Earsham, Bungay NR35 2TF* Tel (01986) 892147 E-mail franandlinda@googlemail.com

BUTLER, Linda Jane. b 56. SRN77. St Jo Coll Nottm 85. **d** 88 **p** 94. C Burbage w Aston Flamville *Leic* 88-91; Asst Chapl Leic R Infirmary 91-93; Asst Chapl Towers Hosp Humberstone 93-95; Chapl 95-97; Chapl Leics and Rutland Healthcare NHS Trust 97-03; Chapl amongst Deaf People *Pet* 03-10; P-in-c Kingsthorpe w Northampton St Dav from 10. *The Rectory, 16 Green End, Kingsthorpe, Northampton NN2 6RD* Tel (01604) 717133 Mobile 07773-018260 E-mail janebutler01@tiscali.co.uk

BUTLER, Mrs Louise Gail Nesta. d 04 **p** 05. OLM Blewbury, Hagbourne and Upton *Ox* 04-06; OLM S w N Moreton, Aston Tirrold and Aston Upthorpe 05-06; OLM The Churn from 06. *Penridge, Church Road, Blewbury, Didcot OX11 9PY* Tel (01235) 851011 E-mail louisegbutler@aol.com

BUTLER, Malcolm. b 40. Linc Th Coll 76. **d** 78 **p** 79. C Whickham *Dur* 78-82; V Leam Lane 82-87; R Penshaw 87-90; rtd 90. *Lincoln Lodge, Front Street, Castleside, Consett DH8 9AR* Tel (01207) 507672

BUTLER, Canon Michael. b 41. St Mich Coll Llan 62 St Deiniol's Hawarden 63. **d** 64 **p** 65. C Welshpool *St As* 64; C Welshpool w Castle Caereinion 65-73; TV Aberystwyth *St D* 73-80; Chapl Univ of Wales (Abth) 73-80; V St Issell's and Amroth 80-09; V St Issell's and Amroth w Crunwere from 09; AD Narberth 94-10; AD Pembroke from 10; Can St D Cathl from 01. *St Issell's Vicarage, Saundersfoot SA69 9BD* Tel (01834) 812375

BUTLER, Canon Michael John. b 32. Keble Coll Ox BA58 MSW. Coll of Resurr Mirfield. **d** 59 **p** 60. C Poplar All SS w St Frideswide *Lon* 59-68; Hon C St Steph Walbrook and St Swithun etc 68-73; C Godalming *Guildf* 73-76; P-in-c Brighton St Anne *Chich* 77-79; Dioc Communications Officer and Dir Soc Resp 77-83; Dir Dioc Bd of Soc Resp 83-94; Soc Resp Adv 94-00; Hon C Brighton St Pet w Chpl Royal 94-00; Can and Preb Chich Cathl 85-00; rtd 00; Perm to Offic *Nor* from 00. *Railway Cottage, 2 Buxton Road, Aylsham, Norwich NR11 6JD* Tel (01263) 734820

BUTLER, Canon Michael Weeden. b 38. Clare Coll Cam BA60 MA65. Westcott Ho Cam 63. **d** 65 **p** 66. C Bermondsey St Mary w St Olave, St Jo etc *S'wark* 65-68; Ind Chapl 68-72; Sierra Leone 73-77; Ind Chapl and R Gt Chart *Cant* 77-86; RD E Charing 81-86; V Glouc St Jas and All SS 86-04; RD Glouc City 94-99; Hon Can Glouc Cathl 96-04; rtd 04; Clergy Retirement Officer *Glouc* from 05. *121 London Road, Gloucester GL2 0RR* Tel (01452) 421563 E-mail michael121@blueyonder.co.uk

BUTLER, Ms Pamela. b 53. Nottm Univ BTh86 CertEd74. Linc Th Coll 83. **dss** 86 **d** 87 **p** 94. Rotherhithe H Trin *S'wark* 86-87; Par Dn 87-88; Par Dn Old Trafford St Jo *Man* 88-89; Par Dn Claremont H Angels 90-94; C 94-95; C Pendleton 95-97; Chapl Asst S Man Univ Hosps NHS Trust from 96. *St Mary's Vicarage, 18 Rushcroft Road, Shaw, Oldham OL2 7PR* Tel (01706) 847455, 0161-291 2298 *or* 998 7070

BUTLER, Patrick. b 61. All Nations Chr Coll 89. **d** 07 **p** 07. V Asuncion St Andr Paraguay 07-09; C Stoughton *Guildf* from 09. *12 Grange Close, Guildford GU2 9QJ* Tel (01483) 531148 Mobile 07847-121092 E-mail patrickbutler61@hotmail.com

BUTLER, Paul David. b 67. Sheff Univ BA88. Linc Th Coll 92. **d** 92 **p** 93. C Handsworth Woodhouse *Sheff* 92-96; V Bellingham St Dunstan *S'wark* 96-06; AD E Lewisham 99-06; R Deptford St Paul from 06. *St Paul's Rectory, Mary Ann Gardens, London SE8 3DP* Tel (020) 8692 7449 E-mail paulredbutler@btinternet.com

BUTLER, Paul Harnett. b 58. Perkins Sch of Th (USA) MTS95 Girton Coll Cam MPhil98. Ridley Hall Cam 05. **d** 07 **p** 08. C Histon *Ely* from 07; C Impington from 07. *The Vicarage, 60 Impington Lane, Impington, Cambridge CB24 9NJ* Tel (01223) 236887 Mobile 07903-904599 E-mail revpbutler@gmail.com

✠**BUTLER, The Rt Revd Paul Roger.** b 55. Nottm Univ BA77. Wycliffe Hall Ox BA82. **d** 83 **p** 84 **c** 04. C Wandsworth All SS *S'wark* 83-87; Inner Lon Ev Scripture Union 87-92; Dep Hd of Miss 92-94; NSM E Ham St Paul *Chelmsf* 87-94; P-in-c Walthamstow St Mary w St Steph 94-97; P-in-c Walthamstow St Luke 94-97; TR Walthamstow 97-04; AD Waltham Forest 00-04; Hon Can Byumba from 01; Suff Bp Southampton *Win* 04-09; Bp S'well and Nottm from 09. *Bishop's Manor, Bishop's Drive, Southwell NG25 0JR* Tel (01636) 812112 Fax 815401 E-mail bishop@southwell.anglican.org

BUTLER, Perry Andrew. b 48. York Univ BA70 Lon Univ PGCE75 Jes Coll Ox DPhil78 FRHistS. Linc Th Coll 78. **d** 80 **p** 81. C Chiswick St Nic w St Mary *Lon* 80-83; C S Kensington St Steph 83-87; V Bedford Park 87-95; Angl Adv Lon Weekend TV 87-99; P-in-c Bloomsbury St Geo w Woburn Square Ch Ch *Lon* 95-02; R 02-09; Dioc Dir of Ords 96-09; rtd 09. *6 Mikyle*

Court, 39 South Canterbury Road, Canterbury CT1 3LH Tel (01227) 767692 E-mail holmado@aol.com

BUTLER, Richard Charles Burr. b 34. St Pet Hall Ox BA59 MA62. Linc Th Coll 58. **d** 60 **p** 61. C St John's Wood *Lon* 60-63; V Kingstanding St Luke *Birm* 63-75; R Lee St Marg *S'wark* 75-00; rtd 00. *21 Defoe House, Barbican, London EC2Y 8DN* Tel (020) 7628 0527 E-mail eleanorandrichardbutler@btinternet.com

BUTLER, Robert Clifford. b 25. AKC54. **d** 55 **p** 56. C Gt Berkhamsted *St Alb* 55-59; C Dunstable 59-63; V Stanbridge w Tilsworth 63-73; R Maulden 73-80; R Oldbury *Sarum* 80-93; rtd 93; Perm to Offic *Sarum* from 93. *3 Mithras Close, Dorchester DT1 2RF* Tel (01305) 264817

BUTLER, Canon Robert Edwin. b 37. Ely Th Coll 60. **d** 62 **p** 63. C Lewisham St Jo Southend *S'wark* 62-65; C Eastbourne St Elisabeth *Chich* 65-69; V Langney 69-86; TR 86-96; Can and Preb Chich Cathl 94-97; rtd 96; Perm to Offic *Chich* from 97. *10 Langdale Close, Langney, Eastbourne BN23 8HS* Tel (01323) 461135

BUTLER, Sandra. *See* BARTON, Mrs Sandra

BUTLER, Canon Simon. b 64. UEA BSc86 RN Coll Dartmouth 86. St Jo Coll Nottm MA92. **d** 92 **p** 93. C Chandler's Ford *Win* 92-94; C Northolt St Jos *Lon* 94-97; V Streatham Immanuel and St Andr *S'wark* 97-04; RD Streatham 01-04; Lambeth Adnry Ecum Officer 99-02; P-in-c Sanderstead All SS 04-05; TR Sanderstead from 05; V Battersea St Mary from 11; Hon Can S'wark Cathl from 06. *St Mary's Vicarage, 32 Vicarage Crescent, London SW11 3LD* Tel (020) 7585 3986 E mail simon.butler7@gmail.com

BUTLER, Simon Richard. b 80. Oak Hill Th Coll BA03 Ripon Coll Cuddesdon MTh06. **d** 06 **p** 07. C W Bridgford *S'well* 06-10; C Ashtead *Guildf* from 10. *1 Oakfield Road, Ashtead KT21 2RE* Tel 07803-909284 (mobile) E-mail sib@christiansinmotorsport.org.uk

BUTLER, Stephen Ian. b 59. Edin Univ BA BSc80. Trin Coll Bris BA84. **d** 97 **p** 98. C Edin St Pet 97-99; R Edin St Jas 99-08. *Greenbrae, Durisdeer, Thornhill DG3 5BJ* Tel (01848) 500322 Mobile 07939-069699

BUTLER, Mrs Susan Jane. Anglia Ruskin Univ BA99. Ridley Hall Cam 08. **d** 11. NSM Cambridge St Phil *Ely* from 11. *The Vicarage, 60 Impington Lane, Impington, Cambridge CB24 9NJ* Tel (01223) 236887 Mobile 07958-406371 E-mail susybu@gmail.com

✠**BUTLER, The Rt Revd Thomas Frederick.** b 40. Leeds Univ BSc61 MSc62 PhD72. Coll of Resurr Mirfield 62. **d** 64 **p** 65 **c** 85. C Wisbech St Aug *Ely* 64-66; C Folkestone St Sav *Cant* 66-67; Lect Univ of Zambia 68-73; Chapl Kent Univ 73-80; Six Preacher Cant Cathl 79-84; Adn Northolt *Lon* 80-85; Area Bp Willesden 85-91; Bp Leic 91-98; Bp S'wark 98-10; rtd 10; Hon Asst Bp Wakef from 10. *Overtown Grange Cottage, The Balk, Walton, Wakefield WF2 6JX*

BUTLER, Valerie Joyce. *See* WHITE, Mrs Valerie Joyce

BUTLER-SMITH, Basil George (Bob). b 30. Bps' Coll Cheshunt 66. **d** 67 **p** 68. C Bray and Braywood *Ox* 67-71; R Norton *St E* 71-74; P-in-c Tostock 71-74; R Rotherfield Peppard *Ox* 76-02; P-in-c Rotherfield Greys 79-80; R 80-02; rtd 02. *40 Westleigh Drive, Sonning Common, Reading RG4 9LB* Tel 0118-972 1871

BUTLIN, David Francis Grenville. b 55. Bris Univ BA77 Ox Univ CertEd78. Sarum & Wells Th Coll 85. **d** 87 **p** 88. C Bedford St Andr *St Alb* 87-90; C Milton *Portsm* 90-92; V Hurst Green *S'wark* from 92; RD Godstone 04-08. *The Vicarage, 14 Oast Road, Oxted RH8 9DU* Tel (01883) 712674 E-mail dfgbutlin@14oastroad.freeserve.co.uk

BUTLIN, Timothy Greer. b 53. St Jo Coll Dur BA75 Ox Univ CertEd76 Spurgeon's Coll MTh05. Wycliffe Hall Ox 85. **d** 87 **p** 88. C Eynsham and Cassington *Ox* 87-91; V Loudwater from 91. *The Vicarage, Treadaway Hill, Loudwater, High Wycombe HP10 9QL* Tel (01628) 526087 Fax 529354 E-mail vicar@loudwater.org

BUTT, Adrian. b 37. **d** 71 **p** 72. C Umtata Cathl S Africa 71-76; C Ilkeston St Mary *Derby* 76-79; R N and S Wheatley w W Burton *S'well* 79-84; P-in-c Bole w Saundby 79-84; P-in-c Sturton w Littleborough 79-84; R N Wheatley, W Burton, Bole, Saundby, Sturton etc 84-85; R Kirkby in Ashfield 85-05; rtd 05. *25 Searby Road, Sutton-in-Ashfield NG17 5JQ* Tel (01623) 555650 E-mail adrian@shopfront.freeserve.co.uk

BUTT, Mrs Catherine. b 76. St Hilda's Coll Ox BA99 MA02 St Jo Coll Dur BA02. Cranmer Hall Dur 00. **d** 03 **p** 04. C Bletchley *Ox* from 03. *1 Ashburnham Close, Bletchley, Milton Keynes MK3 7TR* Tel (01908) 631050 Mobile 07971-714223 E-mail butties01@yahoo.co.uk

BUTT, The Very Revd Christopher Martin. b 52. St Pet Coll Ox BA74 Fitzw Coll Cam BA77. Ridley Hall Cam 75. **d** 79 **p** 80. C Cambridge St Barn *Ely* 79-82; Hong Kong 82-89; P-in-c Windermere *Carl* 89-98; TR S Gillingham *Roch* 98-09; Dean St Chris Cathl Bahrain from 09. *St Christopher's Cathedral, PO Box 36, Manama, Bahrain* Tel (00973) 253866 Fax 246436 E-mail revbutt@ymail.com

BUTT, Edward. b 46. CQSW80. Trin Coll Bris 86. **d** 88 **p** 89. C Erith St Paul *Roch* 88-92; C Shirley *Win* 92-99; V Stourbridge St Mich Norton *Worc* from 99. *St Michael's House, Westwood Avenue, Stourbridge DY8 3EN* Tel (01384) 376477

BUTT, Martin James. b 52. Sheff Univ LLB75. Trin Coll Bris 75. **d** 78 **p** 79. C Aldridge *Lich* 78-84; C Walsall 84-87; TV 87-94; P-in-c Farewell from 94; P-in-c Gentleshaw from 94; C Hammerwich 96-03; P-in-c from 03. *The Vicarage, Budds Road, Rugeley WS15 4NB* Tel (01543) 684329

BUTT, William Arthur. b 44. Kelham Th Coll 70 Linc Th Coll 71. **d** 71 **p** 72. C Mackworth St Fran *Derby* 71-75; C Aston cum Aughton *Sheff* 76-79; V Dalton 79-88; TR Staveley and Barrow Hill *Derby* from 88. *The Rectory, Staveley, Chesterfield S43 3XZ* Tel (01246) 472270

BUTTANSHAW, Graham Charles. b 59. TCD BA(Econ)80 BA85. St Jo Coll Nottm 88. **d** 91 **p** 92. C Toxteth St Cypr w Ch Ch *Liv* 91-94; CMS 94-99; Uganda 95-99; V Otley *Bradf* from 99. *The Vicarage, Vicarage Gardens, Otley LS21 3PD* Tel (01943) 462240
E-mail graham.buttanshaw@bradford.anglican.org

BUTTERFIELD, The Ven David John. b 52. Lon Univ BMus73. St Jo Coll Nottm. **d** 77 **p** 78. C Southport Ch Ch *Liv* 77-81; Min Aldridge St Thos CD *Lich* 81-91; V Lilleshall, Muxton and Sheriffhales 91-07; RD Edgmond 97-01; RD Shifnal 99-01; RD Edgmond and Shifnal 01-06; Adn E Riding *York* from 07; Can and Preb York Minster from 07. *Brimley Lodge, 27 Molescroft Road, Beverley HU17 7DX* Tel and fax (01482) 881659
E-mail archdeacon.of.eastriding@yorkdiocese.org

BUTTERFIELD, John Kenneth. b 52. Nottm Univ BCombStuds. Linc Th Coll 79. **d** 82 **p** 83. C Cantley *Sheff* 82-84; C Doncaster St Leon and St Jude 84-86; TV Ilfracombe, Lee, Woolacombe, Bittadon etc *Ex* 86-88; V Thurcroft *Sheff* 88-96; Chapl Chesterfield and N Derbyshire NHS Trust from 96. *Chesterfield and North Derbyshire Royal Hospital, Calow, Chesterfield S44 5BL* Tel (01246) 277271 ext 3398

BUTTERWORTH, Canon Antony James. b 51. Hull Univ BSc73. Trin Coll Bris 73. **d** 76 **p** 77. C Halliwell St Pet *Man* 76-81; V Werneth 81-90; V Tonge Fold 90-06; V Pennington from 06; Hon Can Man Cathl from 11. *Pennington Vicarage, Schofield Street, Leigh WN7 4HT* Tel (01942) 673619
E-mail tony@penningtonchurch.com

BUTTERWORTH, David Frederick. b 48. Oak Hill Th Coll BA88. **d** 88 **p** 89. R Telegraph Creek Canada 88-92; R Barrhead and Westlock 92-94; R Yellowknife 94-98; V Hanmer, Bronington, Bettisfield, Tallarn Green *St As* 98-04. *Bettisfield Hall, Bettisfield, Whitchurch SY13 2LB* Tel (01948) 710525

BUTTERWORTH, Elsie. b 27. Linc Th Coll 81. dss 83 **d** 87 **p** 94. OHP 83-85; Derringham Bank *York* 85-87; Par Dn 87-88; Par Dn Filey 88-94; C 94-97; rtd 93; Perm to Offic *York* from 97. *3 Brooklands Close, Filey YO14 9BJ* Tel (01723) 515781

BUTTERWORTH, Frederick. See BUTTERWORTH, David Frederick

BUTTERWORTH, George John. b 58. Liv Univ BA85. Chich Th Coll 92. **d** 92 **p** 93. C Mayfield *Chich* 92-93; C Hastings St Clem and All SS 93-96; TV Brighton Resurr 96-02; P-in-c Saltdean 02-09; V from 09. *St Nicholas' Vicarage, Saltdean Vale, Saltdean, Brighton BN2 8HE* Tel (01273) 302345
E-mail butt21158@aol.com

BUTTERWORTH, Canon George Michael. b 41. Man Univ BSc63 Lon Univ BD67 PhD89 Nottm Univ MPhil71. Tyndale Hall Bris. **d** 67 **p** 68. C S Normanton *Derby* 67-71; India 72-79; Lect United Th Coll Bangalore 72-77; Lect Oak Hill Th Coll 80-96; Prin SAOMC *Ox* 97-05; Prin Ox Min Course 05-06; Prin ERMC 05-06; Hon Can St Alb 02-06; Perm to Offic from 06; Hon C Walton H Trin *Ox* 06-09; Hon C Broughton 09-11. *3 Horseshoe Close, Cheddington, Leighton Buzzard LU7 0SB* Tel 07870-242250 (mobile) E-mail mikebutterworth@waitrose.com

BUTTERWORTH, Canon Gillian. b 49. Man Univ BA71 Dur Univ PGCE72. NOC 96. **d** 99. C Barnsley St Mary *Wakef* 99-03; Min Development Officer from 03; Hon Par Dn Outwood from 03; Asst Chapl Wakefield Hospice from 03; Hon Can Wakef Cathl from 10. *Outwood Vicarage, 424 Leeds Road, Wakefield WF1 2JB* Tel (01924) 823150

BUTTERWORTH, Ian Eric. b 44. Aber Univ MA67 MTh79. Edin Th Coll 67. **d** 69 **p** 70. C Langley All SS and Martyrs *Man* 69-71; Prec St Andr Cathl 71-75; V Bolton St Matt w St Barn *Man* 75-85; C-in-c Lostock CD 85-92; Laity Development Officer (Bolton Adnry) 85-92; Teacher Fairfield High Sch Droylsden 92-99; Perm to Offic *Man* 96-99; Hon C Sudden St Aidan 00-05; P-in-c Castleton Moor 00-05; V 05-10; AD Heywood and Middleton 07-10; rtd 10; Perm to Offic *Man* from 10. *7 Bruce Street, Rochdale OL11 3NH* Tel (01706) 522264
E-mail i.butterworth@tesco.net

BUTTERWORTH, James Frederick. b 49. St Chad's Coll Dur BA70 Birm Univ MA99. Cuddesdon Coll 70. **d** 72 **p** 73. C Kidderminster St Mary *Worc* 72-76; P-in-c Dudley St Barn 76-79; V 79-82; Prec and Min Can Worc Cathl 82-88; TR Bridgnorth, Tasley, Astley Abbotts, etc *Heref* 88-94; Can Res and Treas Heref Cathl 94-99; Preb 94-06; P-in-c Ewyas Harold w

Dulas, Kenderchurch etc 99-06; RD Abbeydore 02-06; V Cirencester *Glouc* 06-08; rtd 08. *Meadows View, Orcop, Hereford HR2 8SF* Tel (01981) 540887

BUTTERWORTH, James Kent. b 49. Southn Univ BTh79. Chich Th Coll 75. **d** 79 **p** 80. C Heckmondwike *Wakef* 79-83; V Wrenthorpe 83-95; V Staincross from 95. *St John's Vicarage, 48 Greenside, Staincross, Barnsley S75 6GU* Tel (01226) 382261
E-mail jim@radiouk.com

BUTTERWORTH, John Walton. b 49. St Jo Coll Dur BSc70. Cranmer Hall Dur. **d** 74 **p** 75. C Todmorden *Wakef* 74-77; Chapl Wakef Cathl 77-78; C Wakef Cathl 77-78; V Outwood from 78. *Outwood Vicarage, 424 Leeds Road, Wakefield WF1 2JB* Tel (01924) 823150 E-mail johnbutterworth@blueyonder.co.uk

BUTTERWORTH, Canon Julia Kay. b 42. Edin Univ MA64 Bris Univ CertEd66. Linc Th Coll 73. dss 77 **d** 87 **p** 94. Cov E 77-79; Cant Cathl 79-84; Dioc Adv in Women's Min 82-92; Faversham 84-92; Par Dn 87-92; TD Whitstable 92-94; TV 94-97; P-in-c Tenterden St Mich 97-07; Dioc Adv in Spirituality 97-07; Hon Can Cant Cathl 96-07; rtd 07; Perm to Offic *Cant* from 07. *14 Cobham Close, Canterbury CT1 1YL* Tel (01227) 472806
E-mail jkbutterworth@btinternet.com

BUTTERWORTH, Michael. See BUTTERWORTH, Canon George Michael

BUTTERWORTH, Mildred Jean. b 42. Leeds Univ MB, ChB65 FRCOG84. St Jo Coll Nottm. **d** 00 **p** 01. NSM Moldgreen and Rawthorpe *Wakef* 00-03; NSM Almondbury w Farnley Tyas 03-11; rtd 11. *1 Furnbrook Gardens, Kirkheaton, Huddersfield HD5 0DY* Tel (01484) 664455
E-mail mildred@mildredjb.plus.com

BUTTERWORTH, Roy. b 31. Selw Coll Cam BA55 MA59. Wells Th Coll 55. **d** 57 **p** 58. C Bathwick w Woolley *B & W* 57-61; Prec St Paul's Cathl Dundee 61-63; V Dearnley *Man* 63-81; V Tyldesley w Shakerley 81-83; V Healey 83-94; rtd 94. *102 Greenbank Road, Rochdale OL12 0EN* Tel (01706) 350808

BUTTERY, Bernard. b 36. Culham Coll Ox CertEd58 LCP75. OLM course 96. **d** 99 **p** 00. OLM Stafford *Lich* from 99. *7 Dearnsdale Close, Tillington, Stafford ST16 1SD* Tel (01785) 244771 E-mail bb.ngb@talktalk.net

BUTTERY, Graeme. b 62. York Univ BA84. St Steph Ho Ox 85. **d** 88 **p** 89. C Peterlee *Dur* 88-91; C Sunderland 91-92; TV 92-94; V Horsley Hill St Lawr 94-05; AD Jarrow 01-05; V Hartlepool St Oswald from 05. *St Oswald's Clergy House, Brougham Terrace, Hartlepool TS24 8EY* Tel (01429) 273201
E-mail buttery.stl@virgin.net

BUTTERY, Nathan James. b 72. Em Coll Cam BA94 MA97. Wycliffe Hall Ox BA98. C 00 **p** 01. C Hull St Jo Newland *York* 00-08; C Cambridge H Sepulchre *Ely* from 09. *1 Pretoria Road, Cambridge CB4 1HD* Tel (01223) 518299
E-mail nathan.buttery@stag.org

BUTTIMER, Mrs Cynthia Margaret. b 45. STETS 07. **d** 08 **p** 09. OLM Clarendon *Sarum* from 08. *Willow Cottage, Gunville Road, Winterslow, Salisbury SP5 1PP* Tel (01980) 862017
E-mail cynthiabuttimer@hotmail.com

BUTTIMORE, Canon John Charles. b 27. St Mich Coll Llan 55. **d** 57 **p** 58. C Treherbert *Llan* 57-60; C Aberdare St Fagan *Llan* 60-64; V Williamstown 64-71; Chapl Ely Hosp Cardiff 71-98; V Caerau w Ely *Llan* 71-97; RD Cardiff 83-89; Can Llan Cathl 87-97; rtd 97; Perm to Offic *Llan* from 97. *3 Nant y Pepra, Cardiff CF5 4UB* Tel (029) 2065 9333

BUTTLE, Leslie Albert. b 32. Open Univ BA89. Edin Th Coll 61. **d** 64 **p** 65. C Sowerby Bridge w Norland *Wakef* 64-66; C Plymstock *Ex* 66-69; C Ilfracombe H Trin 69-71; V Woolfardisworthy and Buck Mills 71-76; C Sticklepath 76-77; Asst Chapl HM Pris Leeds 77-80; Lic to Offic *Ripon* 77-80; Chapl HM Youth Cust Cen Hindley 80-84; Perm to Offic *Ex* 86-93; Hon C Braunton from 93; rtd 97. *63 Caen View, Braunton EX33 1FE* Tel (01271) 817022

BUTTON, David Frederick. b 27. St Chad's Coll Dur BA53. **d** 54 **p** 55. C S Shields St Mary *Dur* 54-58; C Seacroft *Ripon* 58-60; V Holland Fen *Linc* 60-64; V Surfleet 64-71; R Belton SS Pet and Paul 71-78; V Barkston w Syston 72-78; V Honington 73-78; R Gunhouse w Burringham 78-82; P-in-c Gt w Lt Hockham w Wretham w Illington *Nor* 82-84; P-in-c Shropham w Larling and Snetterton 82-84; V Hockham w Shropham Gp of Par 84-91; rtd 91; Perm to Offic *Nor* 91-96. *6 Vallibus Close, Oulton, Lowestoft NR32 3DS*

BUXTON, Alyson Christina. b 65. Chelt & Glouc Coll of HE BA00 Nottm Univ MA03 RGN86. St Jo Coll Nottm MTh01. **d** 02 **p** 03. C New Sleaford *Linc* 02-05; Dioc Lay Min Co-ord and PV Linc Cathl 05-08; P-in-c Horncastle Gp 08-10; R from 10; R Asterby Gp from 10; R Hemingby Gp from 11. *The Vicarage, 2 Millstone Close, Horncastle LN9 5SU* Tel (01507) 525974
E-mail alybux@mac.com

BUXTON, Canon Derek Major. b 31. Lon Univ BD63. Ripon Hall Ox 58. **d** 60 **p** 61. C Leic St Nic 60-64; Chapl Leic Univ 60-64; Chapl Leic Coll of Art and Tech 61-65; Min Can Leic Cathl 64-69; Prec 67; R Ibstock 69-76; R Ibstock w Heather 76-87; Chapl ATC from 78; OCF and Cen and E Regional Chapl from 87; RD Akeley S *Leic* 84-87; P-in-c Woodhouse Eaves

87-91; V Woodhouse and Woodhouse Eaves 91-98; Chapl Roecliffe Manor Cheshire Home from 87; Hon Can Leic Cathl from 88; rtd 98; Perm to Offic *Leic* from 99. *Shepherd's Hill, 74 Pitsford Drive, Loughborough LE11 4NY* Tel (01509) 216663

BUXTON, Francis Edmund. b 42. Trin Coll Cam MA68 Sheff Univ MA93. Linc Th Coll 65. **d** 67 **p** 68. C Wanstead St Mary *Chelmsf* 67-70; C Cambridge Gt St Mary w St Mich *Ely* 70-73; C Barking St Marg w St Patr *Chelmsf* 74-75; Chapl Vellore Hosp S India 75-79; Chapl Bath Univ 79-89; TR Willenhall H Trin *Lich* 89-96; Chapl Team Leader Univ Hosp Birm NHS Foundn Trust 96-07; rtd 07; Hon C St Briavels w Hewelsfield *Glouc* from 08. *3 St Anne's Way, St Briavels, Lydney GL15 6UE* Tel (01594) 531052 Mobile 07899-673096 E-mail fjbuxton@yahoo.co.uk

BUXTON, Graham. b 45. York Univ BA66 Bradf Univ MSc71. St Jo Coll Nottm 83 Melbourne Coll of Div MMin97. **d** 83 **p** 84. C Ealing Dean St Jo *Lon* 83-84; C W Ealing St Jo w St Jas 84-86; C S Harrow St Paul 86-89; P-in-c 89-91; Sen Lect Tabor Coll Australia from 91. *5 Heron Place, Flagstaff Hill SA 5159, Australia* Tel (0061) (8) 8370 6038 *or* 8373 8777 Fax 8373 1766 E-mail gbuxton@adelaide.tabor.edu.au

BUXTON, James Andrew Denis. b 64. Newc Univ BA86. Westcott Ho Cam 95. **d** 97 **p** 98. C Portsea St Mary *Portsm* 97-01; Succ S'wark Cathl 01-07; Chapl Guy's Campus K Coll Lon 01-07; Chapl CCC Cam from 07; Tutor Westcott Ho Cam from 08. *Corpus Christi College, Trumpington Street, Cambridge CB2 1RH* Tel and fax (01223) 338002 E-mail jb225@cam.ac.uk

BUXTON, Nicholas. b 66. Wolfs Coll Cam BA02 Trin Hall Cam MPhil03 PhD07. St Steph Ho Ox MTh08. **d** 08 **p** 09. C Ripon Cathl from 08. *17 High St Agnesgate, Ripon HG4 1QR* Tel (01765) 602923 E-mail buxton.nicholas@googlemail.com

BUXTON, Richard Fowler. b 40. Lon Univ BSc62 Linacre Coll Ox BA67 MA71 Ex Univ PhD73. St Steph Ho Ox 65. **d** 68 **p** 69. C Whitley Ch Ch *Ox* 68-70; C Pinhoe *Ex* 70-71; Asst Chapl Ex Univ 71-73; Tutor Sarum & Wells Th Coll 73-77; Vice-Prin 77; Perm to Offic *Ches* 77-97; Lect Liturgy Man Univ 80-94; Subwarden St Deiniol's Lib Hawarden 94-97; Perm to Offic *Ban* from 96; *St As* from 97; rtd 00. *Golygfa'r Orsaf, 6 Rhesdai Garth, Porthmadog LL49 9BE* Tel (01766) 514782

BUXTON, James Trevor George. b 57. Ex Univ BEd78. Chich Th Coll 81. **d** 83 **p** 84. C Hove All SS *Chich* 83-87; C Burgess Hill St Jo 87-91; V Brighton St Aug and St Saw 91-03; P-in-c Sidley 02-04; V from 04; Can and Preb Chich Cathl from 01. *All Saints' Vicarage, All Saints Lane, Bexhill-on-Sea TN39 5HA* Tel (01424) 221071 Mobile 07885-942901 E-mail hojoe@waitrose.com

BUYERS, Stanley. b 39. Leeds Univ CertEd71 Sunderland Poly BEd78 Newc Univ MEd90. NEOC 97. **d** 00 **p** 01. NSM E Boldon *Dur* 00-03; P-in-c Boldon 03-09; rtd 09. *37 Tarragon Way, South Shields NE34 8TB* Tel 0191-519 0370 Mobile 07979-693153 E-mail stanbuyers@btinternet.com

BYARD, Nigel Gordon. b 65. Leic Poly BEng88 CEng MIMechE. Ox Min Course 06. **d** 09 **p** 10. NSM Sunningdale *Ox* 09-11; TV Penrith w Newton Reigny and Plumpton Wall *Carl* from 11. *7 Park Close, Penrith CA11 8ND* Tel 07902-217144 (mobile) E-mail nigelbyard@btinternet.com

BYATT, John William. b 55. St Jo Coll Nottm 99. **d** 01 **p** 02. C Heanor *Derby* 01-05; C Ilkeston St Jo 05-07; P-in-c Whipton *Ex* from 07. *The Vicarage, 9 Summer Lane, Exeter EX4 8BY* Tel (01392) 462206 Mobile 07773-906919

BYE, Canon Peter John. b 39. Lon Univ BD65. Clifton Th Coll 62. **d** 67 **p** 68. C Hyson Green *S'well* 67-70; C Dur St Nic 70-73; V Lowestoft Ch Ch *Nor* 73-80; V Carl St Jo 80-04; Hon Can Carl Cathl 98-04; RD Carl 00-04; Chapl Carl Gen Hosp 80-94; Chapl Carl Hosps NHS Trust 94-98; rtd 04. *21 McIlmoyle Way, Carlisle CA2 5GY* Tel (01228) 596256 E-mail peterbye@mcilmoyleway.plus.com

BYERS, Canon Christopher Martin. b 33. Jes Coll Ox BA59 MA62. Wycliffe Hall Ox 59. **d** 60 **p** 61. C Bermondsey St Mary w St Olave, St Jo etc *S'wark* 60-66; R Mottingham St Andr w St Alban 66-86; TR Thamesmead 86-99; C 99-00; Hon Can S'wark Cathl 96-00; rtd 01; Perm to Offic *Cant* from 01. *36 Faversham Road, Whitstable CT5 4AR* Tel (01227) 272786

BYFIELD, Andrew Thornton Janes. b 77. St Pet Coll Ox MA99 Selw Coll Cam BTh09. Ridley Hall Cam 07. **d** 09 **p** 10. C Wimbledon Em Ridgway Prop Chpl *S'wark* from 09. *11 Preston Road, London SW20 0SS* Tel 07925-421085 (mobile) E-mail a.byfield@spc.oxon.org

BYFORD, The Ven Edwin Charles. b 47. Aus Nat Univ BSc70 Melbourne Univ of Div BD73 Univ of Chicago MA76 Man Univ PhD85. Trin Coll Melbourne 70. **d** 73 **p** 73. C Qeanbeyan Ch Ch Australia 73-75; Chapl Univ of Chicago USA 75-76; Hon C Chorlton-cum-Hardy St Werburgh *Man* 76-79; Australia from 79; Chapl Woden Valley Hosp 80-83; Asst P Wagga Wagga 83-84; Asst P Ainslie All SS 84-87; Chapl Aus Nat Univ 87-91; R Binda 91-95; R Broken Hill St Pet and Adn The Darling from 95. *PO Box 185, Broken Hill NSW 2880, Australia* Tel and fax (0061) (8) 8087 3221 Mobile 409-467981 E-mail e-byford-4@alumni.uchicago.edu

BYLES, Canon Raymond Vincent. b 30. Univ of Wales (Lamp) BA52. St Mich Coll Llan 52. **d** 54 **p** 55. C Llanfairisgaer *Ban* 54-57; C Llandudno 57-59; V Carno 59-64; V Trefeglwys 63; V Newmarket and Gwaenysgor *St As* 64-72; R Llysfaen 72-80; V Bodelwyddan and St George 80-85; V Bodelwyddan 85-95; Hon Can St As Cathl from 89; rtd 95. *20 Lon Dderwen, Tan-y-Goppa Parc, Abergele LL22 7DW* Tel (01745) 833604

BYLLAM-BARNES, Preb Paul William Marshall. b 38. Birm Univ BCom Lon Univ MSc. Sarum & Wells Th Coll. **d** 84 **p** 85. C Gt Bookham *Guildf* 84-87; R Cusop w Blakemere, Bredwardine w Brobury etc *Heref* 87-03; RD Abbeydore 96-00; Preb Heref Cathl 99-03; rtd 03. *90 Granger Avenue, Maldon CM9 6AN* Tel (01621) 858978

BYNON, William. b 43. St Aid Birkenhead 63. **d** 66 **p** 67. C Huyton St Mich *Liv* 66-69; C Maghull 69-72; TV 72-75; V Highfield 75-82; V Southport All SS 82-88; P-in-c Southport All So 86-88; V Newton in Makerfield St Pet 88-94; V Caerhun w Llangelynin w Llanbedr-y-Cennin *Ban* 94-96; rtd 06. *Swn-y-Don, Maes Hyfryd, Moelfre LL72 8LR* Tel (01248) 410749 E-mail william@pontwgan.freeserve.co.uk

BYRNE, Bryn. See BYRNE, Ronald Brendan Anthony

BYRNE, David Patrick. b 48. PGCE96. St Jo Coll Nottm 74. **d** 77 **p** 78. C Bordesley Green *Birm* 77-79; C Weoley Castle 79-82; TV Kings Norton 82-92; TV Hodge Hill 92-94; Perm to Offic 94-97; Chapl Asst Birm Heartlands and Solihull NHS Trust 96-98; Chapl NW Lon Hosp NHS Trust from 98; Chapl Harrow and Hillingdon Healthcare NHS Trust from 98; Hon C Greenhill St Jo *Lon* from 11. *Chaplaincy Department, Northwick Park Hospital, Watford Road, Harrow HA1 3UJ* Tel (020) 8869 2111 E-mail david.byrne@nwlh.nhs.uk

BYRNE, David Rodney. b 47. St Jo Coll Cam BA70 MA73. Cranmer Hall Dur 71. **d** 73 **p** 74. C Maidstone St Luke *Cant* 73-77; C Patcham *Chich* 77-83; TV Stantonbury *Ox* 83-87; TV Stantonbury and Willen 87-92; TV Woodley 92-02; V Patchway *Bris* 02-10; rtd 11. *4 Pound Lane, Topsham, Exeter EX3 0NA* Tel (01392) 758557

BYRNE, Canon Georgina Ann. b 72. Trin Coll Ox BA92 MA96 CCC Cam MPhil98. Westcott Ho Cam. **d** 97 **p** 98. NSM W Bromwich All SS *Lich* 97-98; C 98-01; Hon Asst Chapl CCC Cam 97-98; Chapl to Bp Kensington *Lon* 01-04; Hon C Twickenham St Mary 01-04; TV Halas *Worc* 04-09; Can Res Worc Cathl from 09; Dir of Ords from 09; Convenor for Women's Min from 05. *15B College Green, Worcester WR1 2LH* Tel (01905) 20909

BYRNE, Ian Barclay. b 53. Ripon Coll Cuddesdon 01. **d** 03 **p** 04. C Blyth Valley *St E* 03-06; P-in-c Bungay H Trin w St Mary from 06; C Wainford from 06. *The Vicarage, 3 Trinity Gardens, Bungay NR35 1HH* Tel (01986) 892553 E-mail rev.ib@btinternet.com

BYRNE, Canon John Victor. b 47. FCA. St Jo Coll Nottm LTh73. **d** 73 **p** 74. C Gillingham St Mark *Roch* 73-76; C Cranham Park *Chelmsf* 76-80; V Balderstone *Man* 80-87; V Southsea St Jude *Portsm* 87-06; P-in-c Southsea St Pet 95-03; Hon Can Portsm Cathl 97-06; RD Portsm 01-06; V Branksome Park All SS *Sarum* from 06; Chapl to The Queen from 03. *The Vicarage, 28 Western Road, Poole BH13 7BP* Tel (01202) 708202 E-mail byrne.jv@gmail.com

BYRNE, The Very Revd Matthew. b 27. Man Univ MA69 TCD HDipEd81. Tyndale Hall Bris 47. **d** 51 **p** 52. C Rawtenstall St Mary *Man* 51-54; OCF 54-57; R Moss Side St Jas *Man* 57-62; R Whalley Range St Marg 62-80; P-in-c Chapelizod *D & G* 80-83; Chapl K Hosp Dub 83-89; Dean Kildare *M & K* 89-93; I Kildare w Kilmeague and Curragh 89-93; Producer Relig Dept RTE 83-92; Chapl Defence Forces 89-92; rtd 92. *5 Fairfield Park, Greystones, Co Wicklow, Republic of Ireland* Tel and fax (00353) (1) 287 3622

BYRNE, Miriam Alexandra Frances. b 46. Westcott Ho Cam. **d** 87 **p** 94. Par Dn Beoley *Worc* 87-90; C Ayr *Glas* 90-92; Dn-in-c Dumbarton 92-94; P-in-c 94-98; Provost St Paul's Cathl Dundee 98-06; R Dundee St Paul 98-06; rtd 06. *rue de la Bonnacherie, 16700 Salles-de-Villefagnan, France* Tel (0033) 6 31 66 58 34

BYRNE, Rodney Edmund. b 18. **d** 84 **p** 84. Hon C Leckhampton SS Phil and Jas w Cheltenham St Jas *Glouc* 84-88; rtd 88; Perm to Offic *Glouc* 88-03. *39 Collum End Rise, Cheltenham GL53 0PA* Tel (01242) 526428

BYRNE, Ronald Brendan Anthony (Bryn). b 31. Reading Univ BA72. Westcott Ho Cam 86. **d** 64 **p** 65. Chapl Cov Cathl 87-91; Chapl Lanchester Poly 87-91; Lic to Offic 91-94; Chapl Limerick Univ 94-98; Chapl Villier's Sch Limerick 95-98; rtd 96; Chapl Lanzarote *Eur* 98-00; Perm to Offic *Lon* 02-07. *6 Newton Terrace, Crown Lane, Bromley BR2 9PH* Tel 07960-319294 (mobile) E-mail brynbyrne@aol.com *or* roybyrne@eircom.net

BYRNE, Roy Harold. b 71. Westmr Coll Ox BTh97 Irish Sch of Ecum MPhil00. CITC 97. **d** 99 **p** 00. C Dublin Ch Ch Cathl Gp 99-03; I Killeshin w Cloydagh and Killabban *C & O* 03-08; I Dublin Drumcondra w N Strand *D & G* from 08. *The Rectory, 74 Grace Park Road, Drumcondra, Dublin 9, Republic of Ireland* Tel (00353) (1) 837 2505 E-mail roybyrne@eircom.net

BYROM, Alan. b 51. Magd Coll Ox BA72 Leeds Univ PGCE73 Bris Univ MA85 Man Univ MPhil99. NOC 97. **d** 99 **p** 00. C Leyland St Andr *Blackb* 99-03; TV Solway Plain *Carl* 03-10;

P-in-c Blackpool Ch Ch w All SS *Blackb* from 10. *The Vicarage, 23A North Park Drive, Blackpool FY3 8LR* Tel (01253) 391235 E-mail arm@abyrom.freeserve.co.uk

BYROM, Canon Malcolm Senior. b 37. Edin Th Coll 65. **d** 67 **p** 68. C Allerton *Bradf* 67-69; C Padstow *Truro* 69-72; V Hessenford 72-77; P-in-c St Martin by Looe 72-77; V Kenwyn 77-91; R Kenwyn w St Allen 91-99; Hon Can Truro Cathl 92-00; RD Powder 88-90; Sub-Warden Community of the Epiphany Truro 85-01; Warden from 01; rtd 99; Perm to Offic *Truro* from 00. *West Haven, Dobbin Lane, Trevone, Padstow PL28 8QP* Tel (01841) 520242 E-mail malcolmbyrom@supanet.com

BYRON, Terence Sherwood. b 26. Keble Coll Ox BA50 MA54. Linc Th Coll 50. **d** 52 **p** 53. C Melton Mowbray w Burton Lazars, Freeby etc *Leic* 52-55; C Whitwick St Jo the Bapt 55-60; India 60-76; C-in-c Beaumont Leys (Extra-paroch Distr) *Leic* 76-85; V Beaumont Leys 85-86; RD Christianity N 86-92; P-in-c Leic St Phil 86-88; V 88-92; rtd 93; Perm to Offic *Leic* from 93. *84 Flax Road, Leicester LE4 6QD* Tel 0116-266 1922

BYSOUTH, Paul Graham. b 55. Oak Hill Th Coll. **d** 84 **p** 85. C Gorleston St Andr *Nor* 84-87; C Ripley *Derby* 87-91; TV N Wingfield, Clay Cross and Pilsley 91-00; V Blagreaves from 00. *St Andrew's Vicarage, 5 Greenburn Close, Littleover, Derby DE23 1FF* Tel (01332) 773877 E-mail paulbysouth4@yahoo.co.uk

BYTHEWAY, Phillip James. b 35. MIIExE89 BA93. **d** 97. OLM Church Stretton *Heref* 97-00; rtd 00; Perm to Offic *Heref* from 00. *Ivy Glen, 55 Watling Street South, Church Stretton SY6 7BQ* Tel (01694) 723901 Mobile 07778-391088 Fax 724440

BYWORTH, Canon Christopher Henry Briault. b 39. Oriel Coll Ox BA61 MA65 Bris Univ BA63. Lon Coll of Div 64. **d** 65 **p** 66. C Low Leyton *Chelmsf* 65-68; C Rusholme H Trin *Man* 68-70; Lic to Offic *Lon* 71-75; TR Thetford *Nor* 75-79; Warden Cranmer Hall Dur 79-83; TR Fazakerley Em *Liv* 83-90; P-in-c St Helens St Helen 90-94; TR 94-04; AD St Helens 90-00; Hon Can Liv Cathl 99-04; rtd 04. *11 Oakleigh, Skelmersdale WN8 9QU* Tel (01744) 886481

BYWORTH, Mrs Ruth Angela. b 49. Cranmer Hall Dur BA82. dss 83 **d** 92 **p** 94. Kirkby *Liv* 83-89; Aintree St Pet 89-97; Dn-in-c 92-94; P-in-c 94-97; P-in-c St Helens St Mark 97-98; C Sutton 98-03; TV 03-04; rtd 04. *11 Oakleigh, Skelmersdale WN8 9QU* Tel (01744) 886481

C

CABLE, Kevin John. b 74. Ripon Coll Cuddesdon BA08. **d** 08 **p** 09. C Bromley Common St Aug *Roch* 08-11. *Address temp unknown* Tel 07739-539448 (mobile)

CABLE, Patrick John. b 50. AKC72. **d** 74 **p** 75. C Herne *Cant* 74-78; CF 78-06; Rtd Officer Chapl RAChD from 06. *c/o MOD Chaplains (Army)* Tel (01980) 615804 Fax 615800

CACKETT, Janice Susan. b 39. Goldsmiths' Coll Lon BA76 Surrey Univ MSc83. SWMTC 99. **d** 99 **p** 00. NSM Clyst St Mary, Clyst St George etc *Ex* 99-03; P-in-c E Budleigh w Bicton and Otterton 03-10; rtd 10. *27 Elm Grove Road, Topsham, Exeter EX3 0EJ* Tel (01392) 877468 E-mail jcackett@ukgateway.net

CADDELL, Richard Allen. b 54. Auburn Univ Alabama BIE77. Trin Coll Bris BA88. **d** 88 **p** 89. C Uphill *B & W* 88-94; Perm to Offic 94-96; TV Beaconsfield *Ox* 96-07; P-in-c Lamp 07-09; R from 09. *The Rectory, High Street, Haversham, Milton Keynes MK19 7DT* Tel (01908) 312136 E-mail caddells@holtspur.plus.com

CADDEN, Brian Stuart. b 58. BSc BTh TCD. **d** 89 **p** 90. C Lecale Gp *D & D* 89-92; C Killowen *D & R* 92-95; I Muckamore *Conn* 95-06; I Castlewellan w Kilcoo *D & D* from 06. *5 Cedar Heights, Bryansford, Newcastle BT33 0PJ* Tel (028) 4372 3198 E-mail castlewellan@dromore.anglican.org

CADDEN, Canon Terence John. b 60. TCD BTh89. CITC 86. **d** 89 **p** 90. C Coleraine *Conn* 89-92; C Lurgan Ch the Redeemer *D & D* 92-93; Past Dir 93-01; I Gilford 01-06; I Seagoe from 06; Can Dromore Cathl from 10. *Seagoe Rectory, 8 Upper Church Lane, Portadown, Craigavon BT63 5JE* Tel (028) 3833 2538 *or* 3835 0583 Fax 3833 0773 Mobile 07894-987702 E-mail cadden@talktalk.net *or* seagoechurch@btinternet.com

CADDICK, Jeremy Lloyd. b 60. St Jo Coll Cam BA82 MA86 K Coll Lon MA93. Ripon Coll Cuddesdon BA86 MA91. **d** 87 **p** 88. C Kennington St Jo w St Jas *S'wark* 87-90; Chapl Lon Univ 90-94; Chapl R Free Medical Sch 90-94; Chapl R Veterinary Coll Lon 90-94; PV Westmr Abbey 92-94; Dean Em Coll Cam from 94. *Emmanuel College, Cambridge CB2 3AP* Tel (01223) 334264 *or* 330195 Fax 334426 E-mail jlc24@cam.ac.uk

CADDICK, Canon Lloyd Reginald. b 31. Bris Univ BA56 St Cath Coll Ox BA58 MA62 Nottm Univ MPhil73 K Coll Lon PhD78 Open Univ Hon MA79. St Steph Ho Ox 56. **d** 59 **p** 59. C N Lynn w St Marg and St Nic *Nor* 59-62; Chapl Oakham Sch 62-66; P-in-c Bulwick, Harringworth w Blatherwycke and Laxton *Pet* 66-67; R Bulwick, Blatherwycke w Harringworth and Laxton 67-77; V Oundle 77-96; Can Pet Cathl 94-96; rtd 96; Perm to Offic *Pet* from 96. *102 West Street, Kings Cliffe, Peterborough PE8 6XA* Tel (01780) 470332

CADDOO (née BLAKELY), Mrs Denise Irene. b 69. QUB BD91 PGCE92. CITC 93. **d** 95 **p** 96. C Holywood *D & D* 95-99; C Portadown St Columba *Arm* 99-00; I Carrowdore w Millisle *D & D* 00-04; C Holywood 04-06; I Gilford from 06. *The Vicarage, 18 Scarva Road, Gilford, Craigavon BT63 6BG* Tel (028) 3883 1130

CADDY, Canon Michael George Bruce Courtenay. b 45. K Coll Lon. **d** 71 **p** 72. C Walton St Mary *Liv* 71-76; C Solihull *Birm* 76-79; TV 79-81; V Shard End 81-87; TR Shirley 87-00; P-in-c Tanworth St Patr Salter Street 97-00; TR Salter Street and Shirley from 00; AD Shirley 97-02; Hon Can Birm Cathl from 99; Dioc Chapl MU from 07. *The Vicarage, 2 Bishopton Close, Shirley, Solihull B90 4AH* Tel 0121-744 3123 *or* 745 8896 E-mail stjames@shirleyparishoffice.freeserve.co.uk

CADDY, Ms Susan. b 50. Westcott Ho Cam 99. **d** 01 **p** 02. C Sutton in Ashfield St Mary *S'well* 01-05; P-in-c Shelton and Oxon *Lich* 05-10; TV Retford Area *S'well* from 10. *The Rectory, All Hallows Street, Retford DN22 7TP* Tel (01777) 703322 E-mail sue.cee@talktalk.net

CADE, Mrs Margaret Elizabeth. b 34. Dioc OLM tr scheme 99. **d** 00. OLM Portland All SS w St Andr *Sarum* 00-07. *27 Avalanche Road, Portland DT5 2DJ* Tel (01305) 821317 Fax 826453 Mobile 07974-696892

CADE, Simon Peter Vincent. b 69. Univ of Wales BA90. Westcott Ho Cam 92. **d** 94 **p** 95. C Calne and Blackland *Sarum* 94-98; Chapl St Mary's Sch Calne 94-97; TV Basingstoke *Win* 98-05; TR Redruth w Lanner and Treleigh *Truro* from 05. *Chycarn, West Trewirgie Road, Redruth TR15 2TJ* Tel (01209) 215258 E-mail simon@simoncade.org.uk

CADMAN, Robert Hugh. b 49. St Jo Coll Nottm 77. **d** 78 **p** 79. C Ecclesall *Sheff* 78-82; C Worting *Win* 82-84; C-in-c Winklebury CD 84-87; R Widford *Chelmsf* 87-94; Chapl Anglia Poly Univ 94-95; NSM Brentwood St Thos 01-03; TV Southend 03-08; V Prittlewell St Pet w Westcliff St Cedd from 08. *The Vicarage, 122 Mendip Crescent, Westcliff-on-Sea SS0 0HN* Tel (01702) 525126 E-mail robcadman@blueyonder.co.uk

CADMORE, Albert Thomas. b 47. Open Univ BA81 UEA MA94 Lon Inst of Educn CertEd68. EAMTC 85. **d** 88 **p** 89. NSM Gorleston St Andr *Nor* 88-96; NSM Winterton w E and W Somerton and Horsey 94-96; NSM Flegg Coastal Benefice from 96. *10 Upper Cliff Road, Gorleston, Great Yarmouth NR31 6AL* Tel (01493) 668762 E-mail acadmore@ntlworld.com

CADOGAN, Paul Anthony Cleveland. b 47. AKC74. **d** 75 **p** 76. C Fishponds St Jo *Bris* 75-79; C Swindon New Town 79-81; P-in-c Swindon All SS 81-82; V 82-90; R Lower Windrush *Ox* 90-94. *2 Malthouse Close, Ashbury SN6 8PB* Tel (01793) 710488

CADOGAN, Percil Lavine. b 41. WMMTC. **d** 01 **p** 02. NSM Bournville *Birm* 01-05; NSM Bordesley St Benedict from 05. *76 Highbury Road, Birmingham B14 7QW* Tel 0121-680 9595

CADWALLADER, Michael Godfrey. b 56. Bris Univ BEd79 St Jo Coll Dur BA06. Cranmer Hall Dur 05. **d** 07 **p** 08. C Kingston upon Hull St Aid Southcoates *York* 07-11; P-in-c Burton Dassett *Cov* from 11; P-in-c Avon Dassett w Farnborough and Fenny Compton from 11; P-in-c Gaydon w Chadshunt from 11. *Burton Dassett Vicarage, Bottom Street, Northend, Southam CV47 2TH* Tel (01295) 770400 E-mail cadwalladermg@waitrose.com

CAESAR, Canon Anthony Douglass. b 24. LVO87 CVO91. Magd Coll Cam BA47 MA49 MusB47 FRCO47. St Steph Ho Ox 59. **d** 61 **p** 62. C Kensington St Mary Abbots w St Geo *Lon* 61-65; Chapl RSCM Addington 65-70; Asst Sec CACTM 65-66; ACCM 65-70; Dep P in O 67-68; P-in-O 68-70; C Bournemouth St Pet *Win* 70-73; Prec and Sacr Win Cathl 74-79; Hon Can 75-76 and 79-91; Can Res 76-79; Dom Chapl to The Queen 79-91; Extra Chapl to The Queen from 91; Sub Almoner and Dep Clerk of the Closet 79-91; Sub Dean of HM Chpls Royal 79-91; rtd 91; Chapl St Cross Hosp Win 91-93; Perm to Offic *Portsm* 93-06. *26 Chapel Court, The Burgage, Prestbury, Cheltenham GL52 3EL* Tel (01242) 577541

CAFFYN, Douglas John Morris. b 36. Peterho Cam MA60 Nairobi Univ MSc69 Westmr Coll Ox DipEd61 ACIS77. S Dios Minl Tr Scheme 87. **d** 90 **p** 91. NSM Hampden Park *Chich* 90-94; Chapl among Deaf People 94-97; Jt Sec Cttee for Min among Deaf People 95-97; Perm to Offic from 97; rtd 01. *255 King's Drive, Eastbourne BN21 2UR* Tel (01323) 500977

CAHILL, Canon Nigel. b 59. St Mich Coll Llan. **d** 82 **p** 83. C Whitchurch *Llan* 82-86; V Tonypandy w Clydach Vale 86-96; RD Rhondda 93-96; V Fairwater 96-03; V Caerau w Ely 03-08; AD Llan 06-08; TR Aberavon from 08; Can Llan Cathl from 09.

The Rectory, Forge Road, Port Talbot SA13 1US Tel (01639) 883630 E-mail ncahill@talktalk.net

CAHUSAC, Henry William James. b 73. Wycliffe Hall Ox BTh06. **d** 06 **p** 07. C Tollington *Lon* 06-10; C Onslow Square and S Kensington St Aug from 10. *13 Lyminge Gardens, London SW18 3JS*

CAIN, Andrew David. b 63. Aber Univ BSc86. Ripon Coll Cuddesdon BA89. **d** 90 **p** 91. C Walworth St Jo *S'wark* 90-94; Bp's Dom Chapl *Ox* 94-98; P-in-c Kilburn St Mary w All So *Lon* 98-01; P-in-c W Hampstead St Jas 98-01; V Kilburn St Mary w All So and W Hampstead St Jas from 01; AD N Camden from 07. *St Mary's Vicarage, 134A Abbey Road, London NW6 4SN* Tel and fax (020) 7624 5434 E-mail vicaragekilburn@btopenworld.com

CAIN, Andrew Paul. b 76. St Jo Coll Nottm. **d** 08 **p** 09. C Hinckley H Trin *Leic* 08-11; C Bosworth and Sheepy Gp from 11. *6 Springfield Avenue, Market Bosworth, Nuneaton CV13 0NS* Tel (01455) 293650

CAIN, Frank Robert. b 56. Oak Hill Th Coll BA88. **d** 88 **p** 89. C Aughton Ch Ch *Liv* 88-91; P-in-c Toxteth Park St Clem 91-99; V Toxteth St Bede w St Clem 99-04; AD Toxteth and Wavertree 01-04; Hon Can Liv Cathl 03-04; Chapl N Mersey Community NHS Trust 96-04; V New Brighton St Jas w Em *Ches* from 04; RD Wallasey 07-09. *The Vicarage, 14 Albion Street, Wallasey CH45 9LF* Tel 0151-639 5844 E-mail frankandsuecain@ukgateway.net

CAIN, Michael Christopher. b 68. St Jo Coll Dur BA90 K Coll Lon MA92 Selw Coll Cam BA94. Ridley Hall Cam 92. **d** 95 **p** 96. C Wimbledon Em Ridgway Prop Chpl *S'wark* 95-99; Asst Chapl Leipzig *Eur* 99-02; C Clifton Ch Ch w Em *Bris* 02-10; Pioneer Min Clifton Em from 11. *60 Clifton Park Road, Bristol BS8 3HN* Tel 0117-973 3729 E-mail mike@emmanuelbristol.org.uk

CAIN, Michael John Patrick. b 62. Chich Th Coll 88. **d** 91 **p** 92. C Cainscross w Selsley *Glouc* 91-94; C Mackworth St Fran *Derby* 94-97; V Derby St Luke 97-02; C Paignton St Jo *Ex* 02-07; rtd 07. *124 Forest Road, Torquay TQ1 4JY* Tel (01803) 316046 E-mail cainfamily@toucansurf.co.uk

CAINES, Julia Clare. See CHARD, Mrs Julia Clare

CAINK, Richard David Somerville. b 37. Lich Th Coll 68. **d** 71 **p** 72. C Prittlewell St Mary *Chelmsf* 71-74; C Gt Yarmouth *Nor* 74-76; P-in-c Blickling w Ingworth 76-80; P-in-c Saxthorpe and Corpusty 76-80; P-in-c Oulton SS Pet and Paul 76-80; R Cheddington w Mentmore and Marsworth *Ox* 80-87; P-in-c Wooburn 87-90; V 90-96; P-in-c Lacey Green 96-98; TV Risborough 98-02; rtd 02. *1 Whitlock Drive, Great Yeldham, Halstead CO9 4EE* Tel (01787) 236091

✠**CAIRD, The Rt Revd Prof Donald Arthur Richard.** b 25. TCD BA49 MA55 BD55 HDipEd59 Hon DD88 Hon LLD93. TCD Div Sch 49. **d** 50 **p** 51 **c** 70. C Dundela St Mark *D & D* 50-53; Chapl and Asst Master Portora R Sch Enniskillen 53-57; Lect St D Coll Lamp 57-59; I Rathmichael *D & G* 60-69; Asst Master St Columba's Coll Dub 60-62; Lect TCD 62-64; Lect in Philosophy of Relig Div Hostel Dub 64-69; Dean Ossory *C & O* 69-70; Can Leighlin Cathl 69-70; I Kilkenny 69-70; Bp Limerick, Ardfert and Aghadoe *L & K* 70-76; Bp M & K 76-85; Abp Dublin *D & G* 85-96; Preb Cualaun St Patr Cathl Dublin 85-96; rtd 96; Visiting Prof Gen Th Sem New York from 97. *3 Crofton Avenue, Dun Laoghaire, Co Dublin, Republic of Ireland* Tel (00353) (1) 280 7869 Fax 230 1053

CAIRNS, Dorothy Elizabeth. b 66. Wilson Carlile Coll 87 CITC 07. **d** 09 **p** 10. CA from 90; C Portadown St Columba *Arm* from 09. *19 Derryvinney Road, Portadown, Craigavon BT62 1SX* Tel (028) 3885 1231 Mobile 07719-857187 E-mail ecairns@talk21.com

CAIRNS, Henry Alfred (Jim). Melbourne Univ BA49. ACT ThL43. **d** 42 **p** 43. Australia 42-81; Can Gippsland 59-60; Perm to Offic *Cant* 81-83; Perm to Offic *St Alb* 81-83 and from 85; Hon C Radlett 83-85. *47 Westminster Court, St Stephen's Hill, St Albans AL1 2DX* Tel (01727) 850949

CAISSIE, Mrs Elizabeth Anne. b 40. CBDTI 07. **d** 08 **p** 09. NSM Keighley St Andr *Bradf* from 08. *School House, Haworth Road, Cross Roads, Keighley BD22 9DL* Tel (01535) 645800

CAITHNESS, Mrs Joyce Marigold. b 45. **d** 06 **p** 07. OLM Bris St Matt and St Nath from 06. *383 Southmead Road, Westbury-on-Trym, Bristol BS10 5LT* Tel 0117-983 3755 E-mail jm.caithness@blueyonder.co.uk

CAKE, Nichola Carla. See CHATER, Nichola Carla

CAKE, Simon Charles Eagle. b 61. Wilson Carlile Coll 91 Cranmer Hall Dur 08. **d** 10 **p** 11. C Hebburn St Jo *Dur* from 10. *St Oswald's Vicarage, St Oswald's Road, Hebburn NE31 1HR* Tel 0191-485 6806 Mobile 07710-523856 E-mail cakekands@btinternet.com

CALCOTT-JAMES, Colin Wilfrid. b 25. Bris Univ BSc48. S'wark Ord Course 77. **d** 80 **p** 81. NSM Barnes H Trin *S'wark* 80-85; C Hykeham *Linc* 85-88; R Barrowby 88-92; rtd 92; Perm to Offic *Lon* 93-94 and *S'wark* from 95. *23 Gwendolen Avenue, London SW15 6ET* Tel (020) 8788 6591

CALDECOURT, Ms Frances Ann. b 51. RGN72. Ridley Hall Cam 05. **d** 07 **p** 08. C Harlington Ch Ch CD *Lon* 07-08; C W Hayes 08-11; V Northolt St Jos from 11. *St Joseph's Vicarage, 430 Yeading Lane, Northolt UB5 6JS* Tel (020) 8845 6161 Mobile 07885-749422 E-mail francaldecourt@btinternet.com

CALDER, David Ainsley. b 60. NE Lon Poly BSc86 St Jo Coll Dur BA95. Cranmer Hall Dur 93. **d** 96 **p** 97. C Ireland Wood *Ripon* 96-00; V Woodhouse and Wrangthorn 00-10; Chapl Leeds Metrop Univ 02-10. *Address temp unknown* Tel 07947-535044 (mobile) E-mail david.calder@lineone.net

CALDER, Canon Ian Fraser. b 47. York Univ BA68 CertEd69. Glouc Sch of Min 84. **d** 87 **p** 88. NSM Lydney w Aylburton *Glouc* 87-91; C Cirencester 91-95; V Coney Hill 95-01; RD Glouc City 99-01; R Bishop's Cleeve 01-08; AD Tewkesbury and Winchcombe 02-07; Hon Can Glouc Cathl 03-08; rtd 08. *11 Riversley Road, Elmbridge, Gloucester GL2 0QU* Tel (01452) 537845 E-mail revian@blueyonder.co.uk

CALDER, Roger Paul. b 53. Hatf Coll Dur BA75. Chich Th Coll 76. **d** 79 **p** 80. C Addlestone *Guildf* 79-82; C Grangetown *Dur* 82-84; TV Brighton Resurr *Chich* 84-87; CF 87-92; P-in-c Cocking, Bepton and W Lavington *Chich* 92-95; P-in-c Bognor 95-98; V 98-05; P-in-c Portsea St Sav *Portsm* 05-07; V from 07; P-in-c Portsea St Alb 05-07; V from 07. *St Saviour's Vicarage, Twyford Avenue, Portsmouth PO2 8PB* Tel (023) 9266 3664 E-mail fr.roger@stalban.org.uk

CALDERHEAD, Christopher Conrad. b 62. Princeton Univ AB84. Seabury-Western Th Sem MDiv98. **d** 98 **p** 99. C Chesterton Gd Shep *Ely* 98-02; USA from 02. *3075 Thirty-third Street Apt 4A, Astoria NY 11102, USA* Tel (001) (718) 278 3098 E-mail cccalderhead@yahoo.com

CALDERWOOD, Emma Louise. See WILLIAMS, Emma Louise

CALDICOTT, Anthony. b 31. St Jo Coll Dur BA53 ARCO52 FRCO62. Ripon Hall Ox 55. **d** 57 **p** 58. C Finham *Cov* 57-61; C Bedford St Andr *St Alb* 61-64; Chapl Lindisfarne Coll 64-67; C W Bromwich All SS *Lich* 67-69; Lic to Offic *Cov* 69-75; Hon C Twickenham St Mary *Lon* 75-89; Perm to Offic from 91; rtd 96. *38 Lyndhurst Avenue, Twickenham TW2 6BX* Tel (020) 8894 6859

CALDWELL, Alan. b 29. Oak Hill Th Coll 65. **d** 67 **p** 68. C Aldershot H Trin *Guildf* 67-69; C New Malden and Coombe *S'wark* 69-73; C-in-c Edgware St Andr CD *Lon* 73-78; P-in-c Pettaugh and Winston *St E* 78; R Helmingham w Framsden and Pettaugh w Winston 78-87; R Cowden w Hammerwood *Chich* 87-94; rtd 94; Perm to Offic *Ban* from 95. *Ael-y-Bryn, Druid Road, Menai Bridge LL59 5BY* Tel (01248) 713550 E-mail alancaldwell3d@btinternet.com

CALDWELL, Alan Alfred. b 48. Loughb Univ BSc70 PhD83. Linc Th Coll 70. **d** 73 **p** 74. C Bulwell St Mary *S'well* 73-80; Chapl Nottm Univ 80-87; R Baxterley w Hurley and Wood End and Merevale etc *Birm* 87-91; Perm to Offic *S'well* from 06. *33 The Spinney, Bulcote, Nottingham NG14 5GX* Tel 0115-931 4556

CALDWELL, Ian Charles Reynolds. b 43. St Mich Coll Llan 68. **d** 70 **p** 71. C Oakham w Hambleton and Egleton *Pet* 70-74; C Swindon New Town *Bris* 74-78; P-in-c Honicknowle *Ex* 78-80; V 80-88; V Norton St Mich *Dur* 88-94; rtd 03. *Address withheld by request*

CALDWELL, Mrs Jill. b 47. Lon Univ BPharm69 MRPharmS70. S Dios Minl Tr Scheme 89. **d** 92 **p** 94. NSM Yiewsley *Lon* 92-97; NSM St Marylebone w H Trin 97-02; Chapl St Marylebone Girls' Sch Lon 97-98; Chapl R Academy of Music 97-98; Chapl Lon Sch of Pharmacy 97-98; Chapl Liv Cathl 03-04; Perm to Offic *Derby* 04-05; NSM Darley Abbey 05-10; NSM Allestree St Edm and Darley Abbey from 10. *3 Brick Row, Darley Abbey, Derby DE22 1DQ* Tel (01332) 550676 E-mail jill-caldwell@talk21.com

CALDWELL, Roger Fripp. b 31. Cranmer Hall Dur. **d** 64 **p** 65. C Gosforth St Nic *Newc* 64-67; C Sugley 67-74; R Greatworth and Helmdon w Stuchbury and Radstone *Pet* 74-91; rtd 91. *Silver House, Silver Street, Ditcheat, Shepton Mallet BA4 6QY* Tel (01749) 860239

CALE, Canon Clifford Roy Fenton. b 38. St Mich Coll Llan 65. **d** 67 **p** 68. C Griffithstown *Mon* 67-72; V Cwm 72-73; V Abersychan 73-79; V Abersychan and Garndiffaith 79-82; R Goetre w Llanover and Llanfair Kilgeddin 82-85; R Goetre w Llanover 85-01; RD Raglan-Usk 90-01; Can St Woolos Cathl 98-01; rtd 01. *3 Trelawny Close, Usk NP15 1SP* Tel (01291) 672252

CALE, Nicholas. b 66. St Mich Coll Llan. **d** 92 **p** 93. C Tenby *St D* 92-95; R Begelly w Ludchurch and Crunwere 95-01; V Wiston w Walton E and Clarbeston from 01. *The Vicarage, Wiston, Haverfordwest SA62 4PL* Tel (01437) 731266 E-mail cale@tinyonline.co.uk

CALITIS, Juris. Maryland Univ BA Latvia Univ DD. Harvard Div Sch STB. **d** 98 **p** 98. Chapl Riga, Latvia *Eur* from 98; Dean Faculty of Th Univ of Latvia from 99; Assoc Prof Bibl Studies from 99; Co-ord Bible Translation (Latvian Bible Soc) from 99.

Anglikanu iela 2A, Riga, LV1050, Latvia Tel and fax (00371) 721 1390 *or* 721 1288 E-mail juris.calitis@lu.lv

CALLADINE, Joanne Elizabeth. b 71. Liv Inst of Educn BA93. Cranmer Hall Dur 95. **d** 97 **p** 98. NSM Blurton *Lich* 97-98; C Stoke-upon-Trent 98-01; Perm to Offic *Man* from 07. *St Mary's Rectory, 47 Nuthurst Road, Moston, Manchester M40 0EW* Tel 0161-681 1201 E-mail jo.calladine@lineone.net

CALLADINE, Matthew Robert Michael. b 65. St Jo Coll Dur BSc87 BA95 Reading Univ MSc89. Cranmer Hall Dur 93. **d** 96 **p** 97. C Blurton *Lich* 96-01; P-in-c Moston St Mary *Man* from 01. *St Mary's Rectory, 47 Nuthurst Road, Moston, Manchester M40 0EW* Tel 0161-681 1201 E-mail matthew.calladine@lineone.net

CALLAGHAN, Canon Harry. b 34. AKC59 Open Univ BA83. **d** 60 **p** 61. C Sheff St Cecilia Parson Cross 60-63; Br Guiana 63-66; Guyana 66-70; Barbados 70-74; Lic to Offic *Man* 74-84; Miss to Seamen 74-76; Area Sec USPG *Blackb, Man* and *S & M* 76-84; P-in-c Wythenshawe St Martin *Man* 84-85; V 85-91; V Bolton St Jo 91-98; Hon Can Massachusetts from 92; rtd 98; Perm to Offic *Man* from 98 and *Derby* from 99. *5 Manor Park View, Glossop SK13 7TL* Tel (01457) 868886 Mobile 07778-988523 E-mail harry@harrycallaghan.wanadoo.co.uk

CALLAGHAN, Martin Peter. b 57. Edin Th Coll 91. **d** 93 **p** 94. C Ayr *Glas* 93-96; C Girvan 93-96; C Maybole 93-96; P-in-c Gretna from 96; P-in-c Eastriggs from 96; P-in-c Annan from 97; P-in-c Lockerbie from 97; P-in-c Moffat from 97; Clergy Ldr Annandale Gp from 03. *South Annandale Rectory, 28 Northfield Park, Annan DG12 5EZ* Tel (01461) 202924 E-mail martinpcallaghan@btinternet.com

CALLAGHAN, Michael James. b 63. Clare Coll Cam BA85. SEITE 94. **d** 97 **p** 98. NSM Blackheath Park St Mich *S'wark* 97-08. *Address temp unknown*

CALLAGHAN, Robert Paul. b 59. K Coll Lon BD81 Kent Univ MA04. Linc Th Coll 81. **d** 83 **p** 85. C Winchmore Hill St Paul *Lon* 83-85; C Paddington St Jo w St Mich 85-91; V Dartford St Edm *Roch* 91-11; Nat Co-ordinator Inclusive Ch from 11. *2 Mount Pleasant, Buckland Lane, Staple, Canterbury CT3 1LA* Tel (01304) 813263 E-mail bobcallaghan@tiscali.co.uk

CALLAGHAN, Yvonne Susan. b 58. St Jo Coll Nottm 06. **d** 08 **p** 09. C Middleham w Coverdale and E Witton etc *Ripon* from 08. *The Rectory, The Springs, Middleham, Leyburn DL8 4RB* Tel (01969) 620206 E-mail callaghans1992@ntlworld.com

CALLAN, Canon Terence Frederick. b 26. CITC 55. **d** 57 **p** 58. C Monaghan *Clogh* 57-58; I Clogh 58-64; C Derriaghy *Conn* 64-66; P-in-c Ballymacash 67-70; I Belfast St Aid 70-79; I Agherton 79-94; Can Conn Cathl from 86; Treas from 90; rtd 94. *18 Central Avenue, Portstewart BT55 7BS* Tel (028) 7083 2704

CALLAN, Ms Wendy Mary. b 52. Ox Brookes Univ BA93. SAOMC 96. **d** 99 **p** 00. C Bicester w Bucknell, Caversfield and Launton *Ox* 99-03; V Shipton-under-Wychwood w Milton, Fifield etc 03-10; I Killala w Dunfeeny, Crossmolina, Kilmoremoy etc *T, K & A* from 10. *St Michael's Rectory, Church Road, Ballina, Co Mayo, Republic of Ireland* Tel (00353) (96) 77894

CALLAN-TRAVIS, Anthony. b 46. NOC 90. **d** 93 **p** 94. C Tong *Bradf* 93-97; C Harrogate St Wilfrid *Ripon* 97-03; TV Knaresborough 03-08; rtd 09. *3 Providence Terrace, Harrogate HG1 5EX* Tel (01423) 529266

CALLARD, Canon David Kingsley. b 37. St Pet Coll Ox BA61 MA65. Westcott Ho Cam 61. **d** 63 **p** 64. C Leamington Priors H Trin *Cov* 63-66; C Wyken 66-68; C Bp's Hatfield *St Alb* 68-73; R Bilton *Cov* 73-83; TR Swanage and Studland *Sarum* 83-93; TR Oakdale 93-02; Can and Preb Sarum Cathl 95-02; rtd 02; Perm to Offic *B & W* from 05. *Woodlands, 29 Folkestone Road, Salisbury SP2 8JP* Tel (01722) 501200

CALLEN, Mrs Nicola Geraldine. d 11. OLM Fishponds St Jo *Bris* from 11. *164 Ridgeway Road, Bristol BS16 3EG* E-mail ng.callen@gmail.com

CALLENDER, Francis Charles. b 48. TCD BA70 DipEd71 MA73. TCD Div Sch 76. **d** 79 **p** 80. C Bandon *C, C & R* 79-82; New Zealand 82-88 and from 90; USA 88-90. *31 Grampian Street, Casebrook, Christchurch 8051, New Zealand* Tel (0064) (3) 359 4568 Fax 337 8236

CALLER, Laurence Edward Harrison. b 19. Lon Univ BMus77 MA82. Lich Th Coll 39. **d** 42 **p** 43. C Ipswich St Matt *St E* 42-45; C Walsall St Pet *Lich* 45-46; C Hednesford 46-48; R Stafford St Mary 48-55; Subchanter Lich Cathl 55-57; V Shrewsbury St Alkmund 57-63; V Harlescott 63-67; rtd 84. *103 Fronks Road, Dovercourt, Harwich CO12 4EG* Tel (01255) 504501

CALLIS, Gillian Ruth. *See* TURNER-CALLIS, Mrs Gillian Ruth

CALLIS, Stephen Harby. b 49. Keele Univ MA97. SNWTP 10. **d** 11. NSM Prestbury *Ches* from 11. *2 Fieldbank Road, Macclesfield SK11 8PZ* Tel (01625) 427002 Mobile 07720-181978 E-mail paraprexis@sky.com

CALLON, Andrew McMillan. b 56. Chich Th Coll 77. **d** 80 **p** 81. C Wigan All SS *Liv* 80-85; V Abram 85-90; V Bickershaw 89-90; Chapl RN from 90. *Royal Naval Chaplaincy Service, Mail Point*

1-2, Leach Building, Whale Island, Portsmouth PO2 8BY Tel (023) 9262 5055 Fax 9262 5134

CALLWAY, Peter Stanley. b 55. SEITE 06. **d** 09 **p** 10. C Paddock Wood *Roch* from 09. *3 Ashcroft Road, Paddock Wood, Tonbridge TN12 6LG* Tel (01892) 833194 Mobile 07595-378715

CALOW, Jacqueline. b 60. SNWTP. **d** 11. C Langley *Man* from 11. *The Vicarage, 316 Windermere Road, Middleton, Manchester M24 4LA* E-mail jackie.2026309@hotmail.com

CALOW, Timothy. b 10 **p** 11. NSM Sutton w Cowling and Lothersdale *Bradf* from 10. *3 Laurel Close, Embsay, Skipton BD23 6RS* Tel (01756) 799517

CALVELEY, Mrs Susan. b 47. **d** 02 **p** 03. OLM Birkdale St Pet *Liv* 02-06; NSM 06-11; rtd 11. *1 Balfour Road, Southport PR8 6LE* E-mail revd.sue@gmail.com

CALVER, Canon Gillian Margaret. b 47. Qu Eliz Coll Lon BSc68. Cant Sch of Min 89. **d** 92 **p** 94. NSM Folkestone H Trin w Ch Ch *Cant* 92-95; P-in-c Alkham w Capel le Ferne and Hougham 95-01; V 01-02; Chapl Dover Coll 95-99; R Staplehurst *Cant* 02-11; AD Weald 06-10; Hon Can Cant Cathl 08-11; rtd 11; Chapl to The Queen from 08. *6 Grand Court, Grand Parade, Littlestone, New Romney TN28 8NT* Tel (01797) 366082 E-mail gill.calver@btinternet.com

CALVER, Nicholas James. b 58. Nottm Univ BTh83 Dur Univ MA90. Cranmer Hall Dur 86. **d** 88 **p** 89. C Forest Hill Ch Ch *S'wark* 88-91; C Forest Hill 91-92; P-in-c Mottingham St Edw 92-95; V 95-97; Voc Adv Lewisham Adnry 94-97; V Redhill St Jo from 97. *St John's Vicarage, Church Road, Redhill RH1 6QA* Tel (01737) 766562

CALVERT, Geoffrey Richard. b 58. Edin Univ BSc79 PhD84 Leeds Univ BA86. Coll of Resurr Mirfield 84. **d** 87 **p** 88. C Curdworth w Castle Vale *Birm* 87-90; C Barnsley St Mary *Wakef* 90-92; TV Halifax 92-94; V Halifax H Trin 95-99; V Luton St Aug Limbury *St Alb* 99-09; P-in-c Watford St Mich from 09. *St Michael's Vicarage, 5 Mildred Avenue, Watford WD18 7DY* Tel (01923) 232460 E-mail calvert@dsl.pipex.com

CALVERT, Canon Jean. b 34. Lightfoot Ho Dur IDC63. **dss** 78 **d** 87 **p** 94. S Bank *York* 78-84; Chapl Asst Rampton Hosp Retford 84-88; Dn-in-c Dunham w Darlton, Ragnall, Fledborough etc *S'well* 88-94; P-in-c 94-04; Hon Can S'well Minster 93-04; rtd 04; Perm to Offic *S'well* from 06. *The Rafters, Lincoln Road, Darlton, Newark NG22 0TF* Tel (01777) 228758

CALVERT, John Raymond. b 42. Lon Coll of Div 64. **d** 67 **p** 68. C Kennington St Mark *S'wark* 67-70; C Southborough St Pet *Roch* 70-72; C Barton Seagrave *Pet* 72-75; Asst Master Shaftesbury High Sch 78-79; Dioc Children's Officer *Glouc* 79-87; P-in-c S Cerney w Cerney Wick and Down Ampney 87-89; V 89-07; P-in-c Siddington w Preston 02-07; rtd 07. *46 Penn Lane, Brixham TQ5 9NR*

CALVERT, John Stephen. b 27. Lon Univ BSc53. Wycliffe Coll Toronto BTh61. **d** 61 **p** 62. Canada 61-63; C Preston St Jo *Blackb* 63-70; rtd 92; Perm to Offic *Blackb* from 92. *17 Leyster Street, Morecambe LA4 5NF* Tel (01524) 424491

CALVERT, Mrs Judith. b 50. NOC 04. **d** 07 **p** 08. NSM Woodchurch *Ches* from 07. *33 Centurion Drive, Wirral CH47 7AL* Tel 0151-632 4729 E-mail rev.judithcalvert@btinternet.com

CALVERT, Canon Peter Noel. b 41. Ch Coll Cam BA63 MA67. Cuddesdon Coll 64. **d** 66 **p** 67. C Brighouse *Wakef* 66-71; V Heptonstall 71-82; V Todmorden 82-07; P-in-c Cross Stone 83-93; RD Calder Valley 86-90; Hon Can Wakef Cathl 92-07; rtd 07; P-in-c Leven Valley *Carl* from 07; Chapl to The Queen from 98. *Leven Valley Vicarage, Haverthwaite, Ulverston LA12 8AJ* Tel (01539) 531476 E-mail pncalvert@btinternet.com

CALVERT, Philip. b 62. St Steph Ho Ox 00. **d** 02 **p** 03. C Holbrooks *Cov* 02-06; P-in-c Kingstanding St Mark *Birm* 06-10; V from 10. *St Mark's Clergy House, Bandywood Crescent, Birmingham B44 9JX* Tel 0121-360 7288 Mobile 07969-362577 E-mail frphilipcalvert@aol.com

CALVIN, Alison. CITC. **d** 09 **p** 10. C Killeshandra w Killegar and Derrylane *K, E & A* from 09. *The Rectory, Killeshandra, Co Cavan, Republic of Ireland* Tel (00353) (49) 433 4307 E-mail alisoncalvin@gmail.com *or* killeshandra@kilmore.anglican.org

CALVIN-THOMAS, David Nigel. b 43. Univ of Wales (Cardiff) BSc64 Lon Univ BD77. St Mich Coll Llan 77. **d** 78 **p** 79. C Pontypridd St Cath *Llan* 78-80; Malawi 81-84; V Rastrick St Matt *Wakef* 84-88; V Birchencliffe 88-93; Chapl Huddersfield R Infirmary 88-93; R Aberdeen St Pet 93-01; P-in-c Cove Bay 93-01; TV Glenrothes *St And* 01-07; R 07-09; R Leven and Lochgelly 07-09; rtd 09. *2 Ruthin Way, Tonteg, Pontypridd CF38 1TF* Tel (01443) 203633 E-mail davidcalvinthomas@btinternet.com

CALWAY, Geoffrey. b 45. Bris Sch of Min 84. **d** 87 **p** 88. NSM Cotham St Sav w St Mary *Bris* 87-94; NSM Horfield H Trin 94-97; P-in-c Publow w Pensford, Compton Dando and Chelwood *B & W* 97-07; P-in-c Instow and Westleigh *Ex* 08-10; C Fremington, Instow and Westleigh from 10. *10 South Road, Appledore, Bideford EX39 1QH* Tel (01237) 459729

CAM, Julian Howard. b 48. York Univ BA69 Man Univ MA99. Qu Coll Birm 73. **d** 75 **p** 76. C St Ives *Truro* 75-80; C Lelant 78-80; V Flookburgh *Carl* 80-82; V St Stephen by Saltash *Truro* 82-83; V Low Marple *Ches* 83-08; rtd 08; Perm to Offic *Derby* and *Ches* from 08. *14 High Lea Road, New Mills, High Peak SK22 3DP* Tel (01663) 744065
E-mail julian.angela.cam08@btinternet.com

CAMBER, Mrs Victoria Clare. b 69. Man Univ BA91 Leeds Univ BA10. Yorks Min Course 07. **d** 10 **p** 11. C Wales *Sheff* from 10. *1 Clarke Avenue, Dinnington, Sheffield S25 3PJ* Tel (01909) 567746 Mobile 07810-798087
E-mail vicky_camber@yahoo.co.uk

CAMBRIDGE, Benedict Howard. b 73. Westmr Coll Ox BTh95. Cranmer Hall Dur 99. **d** 01 **p** 02. C Chilwell *S'well* 01-05; Sen Chapl Staffs Univ from 05. *10 Fenton Hall Close, Stoke-on-Trent ST4 4PU* Tel (01782) 294974
E-mail b.h.cambridge@staffs.ac.uk

CAMBRIDGE, Archdeacon of. *See* BEER, The Ven John Stuart

✠**CAMERON, The Rt Revd Andrew Bruce.** b 41. Edin Th Coll 61. **d** 64 **p** 65 **c** 92. C Helensburgh *Glas* 64-67; C Edin H Cross 67-71; Prov and Dioc Youth Chapl 69-75; Chapl St Mary's Cathl 71-75; R Dalmahoy 75-82; Chapl Heriot-Watt Univ 75-82; TV Livingston LEP 82-88; R Perth St Jo *St And* 88-92; Convener Prov Miss Bd 88-92; Bp Ab 92-06; Primus 00-06; rtd 06. *2 Newbigging Grange, Coupar Angus, Blairgowrie PH13 9GA* Tel (01821) 650482 E-mail bruce2541@gmail.com

CAMERON, David Alan. b 59. Glas Univ MA81 DipEd82 PGCE82. Ripon Coll Cuddesdon 88. **d** 91 **p** 92. C Farncombe *Guildf* 91-93, C Guildf H Trin w St Mary 93-96, V Fenton *Lich* from 96. *The Vicarage, 65 Glebedale Road, Stoke-on-Trent ST4 3AQ* Tel and fax (01782) 412417

CAMERON, David Alexander. b 42. Reading Univ BA63 MRTPI. St And Dioc Tr Course 80. **d** 90 **p** 93. NSM Blairgowrie *St And* from 90; NSM Coupar Angus from 90; NSM Alyth from 90. *Firgrove, Golf Course Road, Blairgowrie PH10 6LF* Tel (01250) 873272 E-mail dacameron@talk21.com

CAMERON, Donald Eric Nelson. b 29. St Jo Coll Dur 68. **d** 70 **p** 71. C Kingston upon Hull H Trin *York* 70-73; V Eston 73-82; R Balerno *Edin* 82-87; rtd 94. *The Granary, Crauchie, East Linton EH40 3EB* Tel (01620) 860067

✠**CAMERON, The Rt Revd Douglas MacLean.** b 35. Edin Th Coll 59. **d** 62 **p** 63 **c** 93. C Falkirk *Edin* 62-65; Miss P Eiwo Papua New Guinea 66-67; Miss P Movi 67-72; R Goroka and Adn New Guinea Mainland 72-74; P-in-c Edin St Fillan 74-78; R 78-88; R Edin St Hilda 77-88; R Dalkeith 88-92; R Lasswade 88-92; Can St Mary's Cathl 90-91; Syn Clerk 90-91; Dean Edin 91-92; Bp Arg 93-03; rtd 03; Lic to Offic *Edin* from 04. *23 Craigs Way, Rumford, Falkirk FK2 0EU* Tel (01324) 714137

✠**CAMERON, The Rt Revd Gregory Kenneth.** b 59. Linc Coll Ox BA80 MA84 Down Coll Cam BA82 MA85 Univ of Wales (Cardiff) MPhil92 LLM95. St Mich Coll Llan 82. **d** 83 **p** 84 **c** 09. C Newport St Paul *Mon* 83-86; Tutor St Mich Coll Llan 86-89; C Llanmartin *Mon* 86-87; TV 87-88; Chapl Wycliffe Coll Glos 88-94; Dir Bloxham Project 94-00; Research Fell Cardiff Univ Cen for Law and Relig 98-00; Chapl to Abp Wales 00-03; Dir Ecum Relns ACC 03-04; Dep Sec 04-09; Hon Can St Woolos Cathl 03-09; Bp St As from 09. *Esgobty, St Asaph LL17 0TW* Tel (01745) 583503
E-mail bishop.stasaph@churchinwales.org.uk

CAMERON, Mrs Janice Irene. b 43. Reading Univ BA. TISEC 93. **d** 96 **p** 96. C Blairgowrie *St And* 96-98; C Coupar Angus 96-98; C Alyth 96-98; R Dunblane 99-08; Can St Ninian's Cathl Perth 05-08; rtd 08. *Firgrove, Golf Course Road, Blairgowrie PH10 6LF* Tel (01250) 873272
E-mail rector@stmarysdunblane.org

CAMERON, Preb Margaret Mary. b 48. Qu Mary Coll Lon BA69 Ex Univ MA95. SWMTC 87. **d** 90 **p** 94. NSM Budleigh Salterton *Ex* 90-95; C Whipton 95-97; R Hemyock w Culm Davy, Clayhidon and Culmstock 97-03; RD Cullompton 99-03; V Plympton St Mary from 03; Preb Ex Cathl from 05. *St Mary's Vicarage, 209 Ridgeway, Plymouth PL7 2HP* Tel (01752) 336157 *or* 348525 E-mail revd.cameron@tesco.net

CAMERON, Michael John. b 41. Linc Th Coll 91. **d** 92 **p** 93. C Dinnington *Sheff* 92-96; V Beighton 96-06; AD Attercliffe 99-02; rtd 07. *17 Western Street, Barnsley S70 2BP* Tel (01226) 249573

CAMERON, Peter Scott. b 45. Edin Univ LLB67 BD76 Cam Univ PhD79 LRAM64. **d** 97 **p** 97. C Perth St Jo *St And* 97-98; R Dunkeld 98-04; R Strathtay 98-04; rtd 04. *Hope Cottage, Strathtay, Pithlochry PH9 0PG* Tel and fax (01887) 840212

CAMERON, Ms Sheila. b 34. TCert54. Gilmore Ho 65. **d** 98 **p** 99. NSM Catford St Laur *S'wark* 98-02; Perm to Offic from 02. *52 Engleheart Road, London SE6 2HW* Tel (020) 8698 9282 *or* 8698 9706

CAMERON, Sheila Helen MacLeod. b 46. St Andr Univ MA68 Stirling Univ MLitt83 Cam Univ MA96 Anglia Ruskin Univ MA06. ERMC 04. **d** 06 **p** 07. NSM Cherry Hinton St Andr *Ely* 06-07; NSM Chesterton St Geo 07-09; P-in-c Dunbar *Edin* from

09. *St Anne's House, 1 Westgate, Dunbar EH42 1JL* Tel (01368) 865711 Mobile 07776-334250
E-mail cameron3dr@btinternet.com

CAMERON, Thomas Edward. b 46. **d** 06. NSM St Paul's Cathl from 06. *26 Grove Road, London E17 9BN* Tel (020) 8925 9332
E-mail tomecam1@aol.com

CAMERON, William Hugh Macpherson. b 59. Edin Univ LLB82 BD86. Edin Th Coll 83. **d** 86 **p** 87. C Cheadle Hulme All SS *Ches* 86-89; Asst Chapl and Hd RS Wellington Coll Berks 89-93; Chapl K Sch Bruton 93-00; Perm to Offic *Chich* from 01. *Cranesden, West Street, Mayfield TN20 6DS* Tel (01435) 872991

CAMINER, Mrs Miriam. b 54. Lanc Univ BA77. Ox Min Course 09. **d** 11. OLM Old Windsor *Ox* from 11. *9 The Grange, Old Windsor, Windsor SL4 2PS*

CAMMELL, William John. b 36. Glouc Sch of Min 89. **d** 92 **p** 93. OLM Ruardean *Glouc* 92-07; OLM Drybrook, Lydbrook and Ruardean from 07. *The Beeches, High Beech Road, The Pludds, Ruardean GL17 9UD* Tel (01594) 860603

CAMP, Brian Arthur Leslie. b 50. St Jo Coll Nottm. **d** 83 **p** 84. C Blackheath *Birm* 83-86; TV Halesowen *Worc* 86-96; P-in-c Sheldon *Birm* 96-97; R from 97. *The Rectory, 165 Church Road, Sheldon, Birmingham B26 3TT* Tel 0121-743 2033
E-mail rector@stgilessheldon.org

CAMP, Mrs Carole Ann. b 48. Qu Coll Birm. **d** 08 **p** 09. NSM Chelmsley Wood *Birm* from 08. *The Rectory, 165 Church Road, Sheldon, Birmingham B26 3TT* Tel 0121-743 2033

CAMP, Lin. b 47. Loughb Univ MA07. SNWTP 07. **d** 10 **p** 11. OLM Ormskirk *Liv* from 10. *9 Whiterails Drive, Ormskirk L39 3BE* Tel (01695) 574152
E-mail lin.camp@mypostoffice.co.uk

CAMP, Canon Michael Maurice. b 52. Southn Univ BTh83 K Coll Lon MA99 Brentwood Coll of Educn CertEd70. Sarum & Wells Th Coll 78. **d** 81 **p** 82. C Loughton St Jo *Chelmsf* 81-84; C Chingford SS Pet and Paul 84-87; V Northfleet *Roch* 87-94; V Hadlow 94-01; RD Paddock Wood 99-01; V Bromley SS Pet and Paul from 01; AD Bromley from 06; Hon Can Roch Cathl from 11. *The Vicarage, 9 St Paul's Square, Bromley BR2 0XH* Tel and fax (020) 8460 6275 Mobile 07734-424996
E-mail michael.mcamp@diocese-rochester.org

CAMPBELL, Mrs Brenda. b 47. St Jo Coll Nottm 92. **d** 94 **p** 95. C Rothley *Leic* 94-97; C Market Bosworth, Cadeby w Sutton Cheney etc 97-00; TV Bosworth and Sheepy Gp 00-07; rtd 07. *28 Ashfield Drive, Moira, Swadlincote DE12 6HQ* Tel (01530) 413534 E-mail brendajones101@tiscali.co.uk

CAMPBELL, David. b 70. St Andr Univ MTheol92 New Coll Edin MTh94. Edin Th Coll 92. **d** 94 **p** 95. C Perth St Jo *St And* 94-96; P-in-c Tayport and Newport-on-Tay 96-99; R Dunfermline 99-07; Dioc Youth Officer 96-07; Chapl Fettes Coll Edin from 07. *Fettes College, Carrington Road, Edinburgh EH4 1QX* Tel 0131-332 2281 E-mail d.campbell@fettes.com *or* frdavid.campbell@btinternet.com

CAMPBELL, Miss Elizabeth Hume. b 53. Glas Univ MA74 Hamilton Coll of Educn TCert75. St Jo Coll Nottm 01. **d** 02 **p** 03. NSM Alstonfield, Butterton, Ilam etc *Lich* 02-08; NSM Stonehaven and Catterline *Bre* 08-10; P-in-c Dundee St Luke from 10. *3 Ramsay Road, Stonehaven AB39 2HJ* Tel (01569) 764264 E-mail lizziecampbell@o2.co.uk

CAMPBELL, George St Clair. b 32. Lon Univ BSc53. Clifton Th Coll 58. **d** 60 **p** 61. C Tunbridge Wells St Pet *Roch* 60-64; C Clitheroe St Jas *Blackb* 64-70; V Tibshelf *Derby* 70-86; V W Bromwich H Trin *Lich* 86-97; Chapl Heath Lane Hosp 87-97; rtd 97; Perm to Offic *Guildf* from 98. *2 Doreen Close, Farnborough GU14 9HB* Tel (01276) 31639

CAMPBELL, Mrs Hilary Anne. b 56. UMIST BSc80. SAOMC. **d** 01 **p** 02. C Goring w S Stoke *Ox* 01-05; TV Kidlington w Hampton Poyle from 05. *St John's Vicarage, 16 The Broadway, Kidlington OX5 1EF* Tel (01865) 375611
E-mail vicar@thecampbells.demon.co.uk

CAMPBELL, Ian George. b 47. FRICS74 FBEng93. SEITE 96. **d** 99 **p** 00. NSM Chilham w Challock and Molash *Cant* 99-01; P-in-c Crundale w Godmersham from 01. *The Forge, Godmersham Park, Godmersham, Canterbury CT4 7DT* Tel (01227) 730925 *or* (01622) 761605
E-mail campbellkent@fsmail.net

CAMPBELL, James Duncan. b 55. Qu Eliz Coll Lon BSc77. St Jo Coll Dur 85 Oak Hill Th Coll MA00. **d** 87 **p** 88. C Hendon St Paul Mill Hill *Lon* 87-92; V Stevenage St Hugh and St Jo *St Alb* from 92. *St Hugh's House, 4 Mobbsbury Way, Chells, Stevenage SG2 0HL* Tel (01438) 354307
E-mail shsj@nildram.co.uk

CAMPBELL, James Larry. b 46. Indiana Univ BSc69 E Kentucky Univ MA73 Hull Univ MA91. Linc Th Coll 86. **d** 88 **p** 89. C N Hull St Mich *York* 88-92; C Hessle 92-95; V Burton Pidsea and Humbleton w Elsternwick from 95. *The New Vicarage, Back Lane, Burton Pidsea, Hull HU12 9AN* Tel (01964) 671074 E-mail campbell822@aol.com

CAMPBELL, James Malcolm. b 56. MRICS81. Wycliffe Hall Ox 89. **d** 91 **p** 92. C Scole, Brockdish, Billingford, Thorpe Abbots etc *Nor* 91-95; R Bentley and Binsted *Win* 95-08; RD Alton 02-08;

Hon Can Win Cathl 08; R The Lavingtons, Cheverells, and Easterton *Sarum* from 08. *The Vicarage, 14 Church Street, Market Lavington, Devizes SN10 4DT*
CAMPBELL, Canon James Norman Thompson. b 49. BTh MA. d 86 p 87. C Arm St Mark w Aghavilly 86-89; I Belfast H Trin and Ardoyne *Conn* 89-95; I Dundela St Mark *D & D* 95-01; I Portadown St Mark *Arm* from 01; Can Arm Cathl from 09. *The Rectory, Brownstown Road, Portadown, Craigavon BT62 3QA* Tel (028) 3833 2368 E-mail j.campbell147@btinternet.com
CAMPBELL, Jane Judith. See BAKKER, Mrs Jane Judith
CAMPBELL, Kenneth Scott. b 47. BA82. Oak Hill Th Coll. d 82 p 83. C Aughton St Mich *Liv* 82-85; V Brough w Stainmore *Carl* 85-90; R Brough w Stainmore, Musgrave and Warcop 90-92; rtd 92. *4 Quarry Close, Kirkby Stephen CA17 4SS* Tel (01768) 372390
CAMPBELL, Kenneth William. b 66. Oak Hill Th Coll. d 10. C Leyland St Andr *Blackb* from 10. *1 Bridgewater Drive, Buckshaw Village, Chorley PR7 7EU* Tel (01772) 456494 E-mail ken.campbell@standrewsleyland.org.uk
CAMPBELL, Lawrence Henry. b 41. TCD BA63 MA66. d 63 p 65. C Larne and Inver *Conn* 63-66; C Finaghy 66-67; Chapl RN 67-83; R Brancaster w Burnham Deepdale and Titchwell *Nor* 83-95; P-in-c Hunstanton St Mary w Ringstead Parva, Holme etc 94-95; R Hunstanton St Mary w Ringstead Parva etc 95-08; RD Heacham and Rising 01-07; rtd 08; Perm to Offic *Nor* from 08. *5 Park Hill, Dersingham, King's Lynn PE31 6NE* Tel (01485) 543542 E-mail lawcor@talktalk.net
CAMPBELL, Mrs Margaret Ruth. b 62. Trin Coll Bris BA02. d 02 p 03. C Yeovil w Kingston Pitney *B & W* 02-06; TV Wellington and Distr 06-11; R Backwell w Chelvey and Brockley from 11. *The Rectory, 12 Church Lane, Backwell, Bristol BS48 3JJ* Tel (01275) 462391 E-mail jmbt2001@hotmail.com
CAMPBELL, Patrick Alistair. b 36. Qu Coll Birm 64. d 67 p 68. C Paston *Pet* 67-71; C Stockton Heath *Ches* 71-73; V Egremont St Jo 73-78; V Bredbury St Mark 78-85; R Astbury and Smallwood 85-91; V Wybunbury w Doddington 91-97; rtd 97; Perm to Offic *Ches* from 97; Warden Coll of St Barn Lingfield 01-07. *8 Brookside, Crawley Down, Crawley RH10 4UU* Tel (01342) 713667
CAMPBELL, Robin William. b 41. TCD BA63 MA67. Ridley Hall Cam 63. d 65 p 66. C Netherton *Liv* 65-68; C Liv Our Lady and St Nic w St Anne 68-70; V Hooton *Ches* 70-99; rtd 99. *77 Seaview Parade, Lakes Entrance Vic 3909, Australia* Tel (0061) (3) 5155 2157
CAMPBELL, Roger Stewart. b 40. Birm Univ BSc61 PhD65 St Jo Coll Dur BA71. Cranmer Hall Dur 68. d 71 p 72. C Jesmond Clayton Memorial *Newc* 71-77; V Singapore St Jo and St Marg 78-85; C Nottingham St Nic *S'well* 86-90; V Holloway St Mark w Em *Lon* 90-92; TR Tollington 92-97; Chapl Leeds Teaching Hosps NHS Trust 97-04; rtd 04; Perm to Offic *Carl* from 05. *Redesdale Cottage, Lazonby, Penrith CA10 1AJ* Tel (01768) 870695
CAMPBELL, Stephen James. b 60. TCD BTh91. CITC 88. d 91 p 92. C Lisburn Ch Ch *Conn* 91-95; I Kilcronaghan w Draperstown and Sixtowns *D & R* 95-00; I Dunluce *Conn* 00-03; Perm to Offic *Eur* from 04; C Killowen *D & R* from 06. *94A Mountsandel Road, Coleraine BT52 1TA* E-mail sjmimc@yahoo.com
CAMPBELL, Stephen Lloyd. b 46. St Andr Univ LLB67 Solicitor 72. SEITE 95. d 98 p 99. NSM Quantoxhead *B & W* 98-07; NSM Quantock Coast from 07; RD Quantock from 06. *Hodderscombe Lodge, Holford, Bridgwater TA5 1SA* Tel and fax (01278) 741329 Mobile 07808-967046 E-mail stephencampbell0@tiscali.co.uk
CAMPBELL-SMITH, Robert Campbell. b 38. CCC Cam BA61 MA66 Ibadan Univ Nigeria 62. Linc Th Coll 61. d 63 p 64. C Norbury St Steph *Cant* 63-66; C W Wickham St Mary 66-71; Ind Chapl 65-76; V Croydon St Aug 71-81; Acting RD Croydon Cen 77-81; Spiritual Development Adv Nat Assn of Boys' Clubs 77-89; V Goudhurst *Cant* 81-87; Chapl Kent Assn of Boys' Clubs 81-97; RD W Charing *Cant* 82-89; P-in-c Kilndown 83-87; V Goudhurst w Kilndown 87-99; Hon Can Cant Cathl 94-99; Chapl Kent Youth Trust 97-99; TR Modbury, Bigbury, Ringmore w Kingston etc *Ex* 99-04; rtd 04. *Even Keel, Pillory Hill, Noss Mayo, Plymouth PL8 1ED* Tel (01752) 872559
CAMPBELL-TAYLOR, William Goodacre. b 65. Ox Univ BA87 Cam Univ BA93. Westcott Ho Cam 90. d 94 p 95. C Chingford SS Pet and Paul *Chelmsf* 94-97; Chapl Lon Guildhall Univ 97-02; Chapl Lon Metrop Univ 02-04; Hon C Hoxton St Anne w St Columba 05-09; V Stamford Hill St Thos from 09. *The Vicarage, 1 Clapton Terrace, London E5 9BW* Tel (020) 8806 1463
CAMPBELL-WILSON, Allan. b 43. Dur Univ BEd74. NEOC 79. d 82 p 83. NSM Boosbeck w Moorsholm *York* 82-85; R Easington w Skeffling, Kilnsea and Holmpton 85-87; P-in-c Middlesbrough St Jo the Ev 89-95; V 95-99; V Cayton w Eastfield from 99. *The Vicarage, 90 Main Street, Cayton, Scarborough YO11 3RP* Tel (01723) 586569 E-mail frallancayton@aol.com

CAMPEN, William Geoffrey. b 50. Liv Univ CertEd71 Southn Univ BTh81 Lon Univ MA08. Sarum & Wells Th Coll 76. d 79 p 80. C Peckham St Jo w St Andr *S'wark* 79-83; P-in-c Mottingham St Edw 83-92; R Charlwood from 92; R Sidlow Bridge from 92. *The Rectory, The Street, Charlwood, Horley RH6 0EE* Tel (01293) 862343 E-mail w.g.campen@bigfoot.com
CAMPION, Keith Donald. b 52. S Dios Minl Tr Scheme. d 84 p 87. NSM Is of Scilly *Truro* 84-96. *20 Launceston Close, St Mary's TR21 0LN* Tel (01720) 422606
CAMPION (formerly HOUSEMAN), Mrs Patricia Adele. b 39. St Mich Coll Llan. d 93 p 97. C St Issell's and Amroth *St D* 93-95; C Llanegryn w Aberdyfi w Tywyn *Ban* 95-97; rtd 97. *3 Mariners Reach, The Strand, Saundersfoot SA69 9EX* Tel (01834) 811047
CAMPION, Canon Peter Robert. b 64. Bp's Univ Canada BA87 TCD BTh90 MA93 MPhil97 Homerton Coll Cam PGCE94. d 90 p 91. C Belfast H Trin and Ardoyne *Conn* 90-93; C Taney *D & G* 94-00; Dean's V St Patr Cathl Dublin 96-00; Chapl Netherwood Sch Rothesday Canada 00-05; Chapl K Hosp Dub from 05; Treas V St Patr Cathl Dublin from 05; Prec Ch Ch Cathl Dublin from 08. *The King's Hospital, Palmerstown, Dublin 20, Republic of Ireland* Tel (00353) (1) 626 5933 Fax 623 0349
CAMPION-SPALL, Ms Kathryn May. b 79. York Univ BA02 Fitzw Coll Cam BA09. Westcott Ho Cam 07. d 10. C Merton St Mary *S'wark* from 10. *30 Kenley Road, London SW19 3JQ* Tel (020) 3490 3895 Mobile 07960-588015 E-mail curate@stmarysmerton.org.uk
CAMPLING, The Very Revd Christopher Russell. b 25. St Edm Hall Ox BA50 MA54. Cuddesdon Coll 50. d 51 p 52. C Basingstoke *Win* 51-55; Chapl K Sch and Min Can Ely Cathl 55-60; Chapl Lancing Coll 60-68; P-in-c Birlingham w Nafford *Worc* 68-75; V Pershore w Wick 68-75; V Pershore w Pinvin, Wick and Birlingham 75-76; RD Pershore 70-76; Hon Can Worc Cathl 74-84; Dioc Dir of Educn 76-84; Adn Dudley 76-84; P-in-c Dodderhill 76-84; Dean Ripon 84-95; Chmn CCC 88-94; rtd 95; Perm to Offic *Chich* from 95. *Pebble Ridge, Aglaia Road, Worthing BN11 5SW* Tel (01903) 246598
CAMPLING, Doreen Elizabeth. b 31. K Coll Lon BSc55. d 01 p 02. OLM Bridport *Sarum* 01-08. *Harbour Lights, Coneygar Park, Bridport DT6 3BA* Tel (01308) 425670
CAMPLING, Michael. b 27. Trin Coll Cam BA50 MA61. Wells Th Coll 51. d 53 p 54. C Calne *Sarum* 53-57; C Roehampton H Trin *S'wark* 57-61; V Crowthorne *Ox* 61-75; P-in-c Foleshill St Laur *Cov* 75-81; V 81-83; R Old Alresford and Bighton *Win* 83-92; rtd 92; Chapl St Marg Convent E Grinstead 92-99; Hon C Bexhill St Pet *Chich* 99-05. *9 Orchard Grove, Bloxham, Banbury OX15 4NZ* Tel (01295) 721599
CAMPLING-DENTON, Camilla Anne. b 76. St Andr Univ MA98 Jes Coll Cam MPhil04. Westcott Ho Cam 02. d 05 p 06. C Fountains Gp *Ripon* 05-07; C Caerleon w Llanhennock *Mon* 07-09; C Caerleon and Llanfrechfa 09-10; Hon C Washburn and Mid-Wharfe *Bradf* from 10. *The Rectory, Stainburn Lane, Leathley, Otley LS21 2LF* Tel 0113-284 3744 Mobile 07779-429351 E-mail milly@c-d.eclipse.co.uk
CANADA, Primate of. See HUTCHISON, The Most Revd Andrew Sandford
CANBERRA AND GOULBURN, Bishop of. See ROBINSON, The Rt Revd Stuart Peter
CANDELAND, Thomas Blyde. b 37. d 99 p 00. OLM Lyng, Sparham, Elsing, Bylaugh, Bawdeswell etc *Nor* 99-08; RD Sparham 05-08; Perm to Offic from 08. *2 Hammond Place, Lyng, Norwich NR9 5RQ* Tel (01603) 871674
CANDOW, Brian Gordon. b 58. Memorial Univ Newfoundland BComm82 BEd83. Qu Th Coll Newfoundland MDiv89. d 89 p 89. C Fogo Is Canada 89-91; R Botwood 91-95; R Summerside and St Eleanor 00-04; Hon C Skirbeck Quarter *Linc* 04-05; Assoc P Gander Canada from 05. *2 Lindberg Road, Gander NL A1V 2E7, Canada* Tel (001) (709) 256 3700 E-mail candows@bostonengland.freeserve.co.uk
CANDY, Julia Elaine. b 80. K Coll Cam BA01 QUB PhD06 Jes Coll Cam BA09. Westcott Ho Cam 07. d 10 p 11. C Dur St Giles from 10; C Shadforth and Sherburn from 10. *St Nicholas' Vicarage, Kepier Villas, Durham DH1 1JP* E-mail jec1492@hotmail.com
CANE, Canon Anthony William Nicholas Strephon. b 61. Cape Town Univ BA81 Birm Univ MPhil93 PhD03. Westcott Ho Cam 87. d 90 p 91. C Kings Heath *Birm* 90-93; Chapl Brighton Univ 93-99; P-in-c Torquay St Luke *Ex* 99-01; Dioc Adv in Adult Tr 99-01; C Ringmer and Dioc Adv for Educn and Tr of Adults *Chich* 01-07; Can Res and Chan Chich Cathl from 07. *The Residentiary, 2 Canon Lane, Chichester PO19 1PX* Tel (01243) 813594 E-mail chancellor@chichestercathedral.org.uk
CANEY, Canon Robert Swinbank. b 37. St Jo Coll Cam 57. Lich Th Coll 58. d 61 p 62. C Kingswinford H Trin *Lich* 61-64; C Castle Church 64-67; V Bradwell *Derby* 67-73; V Fairfield 73-84; RD Buxton 78-84; P-in-c Peak Forest and Wormhill 79-83; R Wirksworth w Alderwasley, Carsington etc 84-92; TR Wirksworth 92-02; Hon Can Derby Cathl 93-02; rtd 02; Perm to

Offic *Derby* from 02. *2 Erica Drive, South Normanton, Alfreton DE55 2ET* Tel (01773) 581106 E-mail randjcaney@aol.co.uk
CANHAM, Frances Elizabeth. b 55. MCIPD93. St Mich Coll Llan 05. **d** 07 **p** 08. NSM Thanington *Cant* 07-10; Asst Chapl Salisbury NHS Foundn Trust from 10. *c/o Col T W Canham, Head C41SR, British Defence Staff, BFPO 2* Tel and fax (001) (703) 242 3782 E-mail frances.canham@cox.net
CANHAM, Francis. *See* CANHAM, Robert Edwin Francis
CANHAM, John Graham. b 33. Univ of Wales (Lamp) BA55. Chich Th Coll 55. **d** 57 **p** 58. C Hawarden *St As* 57-64; Asst Chapl Ellesmere Coll 64-66; Chapl Ches Cathl Choir Sch 66-73; Chapl Choral Ches Cathl 66-73; Asst Chapl Rossall Sch Fleetwood 73-76 and 83-93; Chapl 76-83; V Minera *St As* 93-05; V Bwlchgwyn and Minera 05-08; AD Minera 01-08; rtd 08. *2 Parkers Close, Wrexham LL11 2RR* Tel (01978) 291166
CANHAM, Robert Edwin Francis. b 24. FRCO59 ARCM. **d** 74 **p** 75. NSM Newlyn St Pet *Truro* 74-75; C Phillack w Gwithian 75-79; P-in-c Phillack w Gwithian and Gwinear 79-83; V Greenham *Ox* 83-93; rtd 93; Perm to Offic *Chich* from 93. *Cross Way, 1A Torton Hill Road, Arundel BN18 9HF* Tel (01903) 883614
CANHAM, William Alexander. b 26. Clare Coll Cam BA47 MA56. Roch Th Coll 65. **d** 67 **p** 68. C Orpington St Andr *Roch* 67-70; C Guernsey St Steph *Win* 70-75; Chapl Eliz Coll Guernsey 72-75; R Tadley St Pet *Win* 75-83; V Bournemouth St Luke 83-91; R Guernsey St Marguerite de la Foret 91-96; rtd 96; Perm to Offic *Portsm* 96-09 and *Win* from 96. *56 The Causeway, Petersfield GU31 4JS* Tel (01730) 269413
CANN, Christopher James. b 64. St Andr Univ BA MA. St Steph Ho Ox. **d** 91 **p** 92. C Newport St Julian *Mon* 91-93; Chapl Smallwood Manor Sch Uttoxeter from 93; Hd Master from 97. *Smallwood Manor Preparatory School, Uttoxeter ST14 8NS* Tel (01889) 562083 E-mail headmaster@smallwoodmanor.co.uk
CANNAM, Martin Stafford John. b 68. Jes Coll Ox BA90 MA95. Wycliffe Hall Ox 93. **d** 96 **p** 97. C Childwall All SS *Liv* 96-00; V Biddulph *Lich* from 00. *The Vicarage, 7 Wrexham Close, Biddulph, Stoke-on-Trent ST8 6RZ* Tel (01782) 513247 or 513891 E-mail martin@cannam.fsnet.co.uk
CANNELL, Anthea Marjorie. b 45. UEA MA85. EAMTC 01. **d** 02 **p** 03. NSM Theydon Bois *Chelmsf* 02-10; P-in-c Roydon from 10. *118 High Street, Roydon, Harlow CM19 5EF* Tel (01279) 792543 E-mail amcannell@btinternet.com
CANNER, Canon Peter George. b 24. St Chad's Coll Dur BA49 MA55. **d** 51 **p** 52. C Stoke *Cov* 51-53; S Africa 53-63; R Piet Retief 53-56; R Eshowe 56-63; Can Eshowe 62-63; V Tynemouth Ch Ch *Newc* 63-77; V Ponteland 77-89; Hon Can Newc Cathl 80-89; rtd 89; Perm to Offic *Newc* from 89. *c/o P J Canner Esq, 15 Benlaw Grove, Felton, Morpeth NE65 9NG*
CANNING, Canon Arthur James. b 45. St Jo Coll Dur BA66 Linacre Coll Ox BA70 MA74 Lambeth STh90. Ripon Hall Ox 67. **d** 71 **p** 72. C Coleshill *Birm* 71-74; C Frome St Jo *B & W* 75-76; V Frizington and Arlecdon *Carl* 76-80; P-in-c Foleshill St Paul *Cov* 80-81; V from 81; Hon Can Cov Cathl from 00. *St Paul's Vicarage, 13 St Paul's Road, Coventry CV6 5DE* Tel (024) 7668 8283 E-mail jimcanningstpcov@aol.com
CANNING, Graham Gordon Blakeman. b 33. S'wark Ord Course 73. **d** 76 **p** 77. NSM Mill Hill Jo Keble *Ch Lon* 76-78; TV Dorchester *Ox* 78-85; V Shipton-under-Wychwood w Milton, Fifield etc 85-98; RD Chipping Norton 95-00; rtd 98; Perm to Offic *Ox* from 00. *Moredays, 36 The Slade, Oxford OX7 3SJ* Tel and fax (01608) 810421 E-mail gcanning@gcanning.u-net.com
CANNING, Peter Christopher. b 52. Birm Poly CQSW. St Jo Coll Nottm 87. **d** 89 **p** 90. C Cov St Mary 89-93; V Hartshill 93-96; rtd 96. *11 Thackeray Close, Galley Common, Nuneaton CV10 9RT* Tel (024) 7639 8828
CANNON, Elizabeth Mary. b 50. EAMTC 94. **d** 97 **p** 98. NSM New Catton Ch Ch *Nor* 97-00; P-in-c Cross Roads cum Lees *Bradf* 00-06; TV Blyth Valley St E from 06. *The Vicarage, Beccles Road, Holton, Halesworth IP19 8NG* Tel (01986) 874548
CANNON, Mark Harrison. b 60. Keble Coll Ox BA82. Cranmer Hall Dur 83. **d** 85 **p** 86. C Skipton Ch Ch *Bradf* 85-88; Dioc Youth Officer 88-92; C Baildon 88-92; P-in-c Church Coniston *Carl* 92-00; P-in-c Torver 92-00; P-in-c Brindle *Blackb* 00-10; Dioc Voc Adv 00-05; P-in-c E Lonsdale from 10. *The Rectory, Main Street, Wray, Lancaster LA2 8QF* Tel (01524) 221030 E-mail mhcannon@fsmail.net
CANNON, Ms Rebekah Lindsey. b 77. Man Metrop Univ BA99 Middx Univ MA06 PGCE06 SS Coll Cam BTh09. Westcott Ho Cam 07. **d** 10 **p** 11. C Whyke w Rumboldswhyke and Portfield *Chich* from 10. *4 Little London, Chichester PO19 1PH* Tel (01243) 790556 E-mail cannonis@cantab.net
CANNON, Tony Arthur. b 57. Oak Hill Th Coll 94. **d** 96 **p** 97. C Church Stretton *Heref* 96-00; P-in-c Kingham w Churchill, Daylesford and Sarsden *Ox* 00-01; TV Chipping Norton 01-10; V Woking St Jo *Guildf* from 11. *The Vicarage, St John's Hill Road, Woking GU21 7RQ* Tel (01483) 761253 E-mail tonycannon@tiscali.co.uk
CANSDALE, George Graham. b 38. Mert Coll Ox BA60 MA64 DipEd61. Clifton Th Coll 62. **d** 64 **p** 65. C Heatherlands St Jo

Sarum 64-67; BCMS Kenya 68-76; P-in-c Clapham *St Alb* 76-80; V 80-89; Asst Chapl Bedford Sch 89-97; Lic to Offic *St Alb* 93-01; Perm to Offic *Wakef* from 01; rtd 03. *7 Stubbins Close, Mytholmroyd, Hebden Bridge HX7 5HP* Tel (01422) 881693 E-mail graham.cansdale@virgin.net
CANSDALE, Michael Cranmer. b 70. Bradf Univ BA93 St Jo Coll Dur BA06. Cranmer Hall Dur 04. **d** 06 **p** 07. C Silsden *Bradf* 06-09; P-in-c Riddlesden from 09; P-in-c Morton St Luke from 09. *The Vicarage, St Mary's Road, Riddlesden, Keighley BD20 5PA* Tel (01535) 603419 Mobile 07545-566898 E-mail mike@stlukesmorton.org.uk
CANSDALE, Philip John. b 73. Keble Coll Ox BA95 MA99. Trin Coll Bris BA98 MA99. **d** 99 **p** 00. C Cant St Mary Bredin 99-03; C Penn Fields *Lich* 03-09; V Meole Brace from 09. *The Vicarage, Vicarage Road, Shrewsbury SY3 9EZ* Tel (01743) 231744
CANSDALE, Simon James Lee. b 68. Keble Coll Ox BA90. Wycliffe Hall Ox 93. **d** 95 **p** 96. C Bletchley *Ox* 95-98; C Cambridge H Trin *Ely* 98-01; R W Bridgford *S'well* 01-08; TR Gt Chesham *Ox* from 08. *The Rectory, Church Street, Chesham HP5 1HY* Tel and fax (01494) 783629 Mobile 07914-361911 E-mail rector@cheshamchurch.co.uk
CANT, Anthony David. b 59. Middx Univ BA04. NTMTC 01. **d** 04 **p** 05. C Walthamstow *Chelmsf* 04-07; TV 07-10; Chapl Anglia Ruskin Univ from 10. *4 Bishops Court Gardens, Chelmsford CM2 6AZ* Tel (01245) 261700 Mobile 07980-291940 E-mail revtonyc@googlemail.com
CANT, Christopher Somerset Travers. b 51. Keble Coll Ox BA72 MA76 Ex Univ PGCE77. All Nations Chr Coll 80 Wycliffe Hall Ox 93. **d** 87 **p** 90. Pakistan 87-92; Lic to Offic *Cov* 92-93; Warden St Clem Family Cen Ox 93-95; C Gt Ilford St Andr *Chelmsf* 95-98; V Hainault 98-10; rtd 10; C Clyst St Mary, Clyst St George etc *Ex* from 11; C Aylesbeare, Rockbeare, Farringdon etc from 11; C Lympstone and Woodbury w Exton from 11. *15 Stoneborough Lane, Budleigh Salterton EX9 6HL* Tel (01395) 488178 E-mail chriscant@tiscali.co.uk
CANT, David Edward. b 49. Sheff Univ LLB70. Oak Hill Th Coll 87. **d** 89 **p** 90. C Newburn *Newc* 89-92; C N Shields 92-93; TV 93-98; Chapl Tynemouth Coll 94-98; P-in-c Wylam *Newc* 98-11; Dioc Ecum Officer 08-11; rtd 11. *17 Farrier's Rise, Shilbottle, Alnwick NE66 2EN* Tel (01665) 575349
CANT, Joseph Clifford. b 72. UEA BA94 MA98 DipSW98 Cam Univ BTh08. Westcott Ho Cam 06. **d** 08 **p** 09. C Hilton w Marston-on-Dove *Derby* from 08; TV Uttoxeter Area *Lich* from 11. *The Vicarage, Moisty Lane, Marchington, Uttoxeter ST14 8JY* Tel 07847-125341 (mobile) E-mail cant740@btinternet.com
CANTACUZENE, Mrs Mary. b 52. **d** 05 **p** 06. NSM Bures w Assington and Lt Cornard *St E* from 05. *Peartree Barn, Peartree Hill, Mount Bures, Bures CO8 5BA* Tel (01787) 227616 Fax 227220 Mobile 07932-033019 E-mail mary@cantacuzene.co.uk
CANTERBURY, Archbishop of. *See* WILLIAMS, The Most Revd and Rt Hon Rowan Douglas
CANTERBURY, Archdeacon of. *See* WATSON, The Ven Sheila Anne
CANTERBURY, Dean of. *See* WILLIS, The Very Revd Robert Andrew
CANTI, Mrs Christine. b 24. St Alb Minl Tr Scheme 82. dss 85 **d** 87 **p** 94. Radlett *St Alb* 85-86; Hon C Pitminster w Corfe *B & W* 87-90; Perm to Offic from 90. *Tresawsen, Mill Lane, Corfe, Taunton TA3 7AH* Tel (01823) 421623
CANTRELL, David Grindon. b 59. Bris Univ BSc80 Nottm Univ PhD83 Pemb Coll Cam BA88. Ridley Hall Cam 86. **d** 89 **p** 90. C Low Harrogate St Mary *Ripon* 89-90; C Horsforth 90-94; Chapl Nottm Trent Univ 94-97; V Porchester 97-00; Chapl York Univ 00-04; Perm to Offic 04-11. *52 Tranby Avenue, York YO10 3NJ* Tel (01904) 427146 E-mail david.cantrell@ukgateway.net
CANTRILL, Mark James. b 67. Lanc Univ BEd89. St Jo Coll Nottm 00. **d** 02 **p** 03. C Warsop *S'well* 02-07; TV Retford Area from 07. *Clarborough Vicarage, Church Lane, Clarborough, Retford DN22 9NA* Tel (01777) 711530 Mobile 07985-160694 E-mail revmark.cantrill@btinternet.com
CANTY, Mrs Katherine Anne. b 52. York Univ BA74 Coll of Ripon & York St Jo PGCE75. NOC 05. **d** 07 **p** 08. Asst Chapl HM Pris Altcourse 03-07; Chapl from 07; NSM Gateacre *Liv* from 07. *HM Prison Altcourse, Higher Lane, Liverpool L9 7LH* Tel 0151-522 2000 ext 2395
CAPEL, Luke Thomas. *See* IRVINE-CAPEL, Luke Thomas
CAPEL-EDWARDS, Maureen. b 36. Southn Univ BSc60 Reading Univ PhD69. St Alb Minl Tr Scheme 84. **d** 87 **p** 94. NSM Ware St Mary *St Alb* 87-90; Chapl Hertf Regional Coll of FE 87-00; NSM Hertford All SS *St Alb* 90-94; NSM Aspenden and Layston w Buntingford 94-95; NSM Aspenden, Buntingford and Westmill 95-00; P-in-c Ardeley and Cottered w Broadfield and Throcking 00-05; rtd 05; Perm to Offic *Portsm* from 05. *Capeland, High Street, Soberton, Southampton SO32 3PN* Tel (01489) 878192 E-mail capeland@waitrose.com
CAPELIN-JONES, Kevin Stuart. b 73. Huddersfield Univ BMus96. Oak Hill Th Coll BA02. **d** 02 **p** 03. C Croglin and Holme Eden and Wetheral w Warwick *Carl* 02-06; Chapl RAF

from 06. *Chaplaincy Services, Valiant Block, HQ Air Command, RAF High Wycombe HP14 4UE* Tel (01494) 496800 Fax 496343 E-mail rev.kev@virgin.net

CAPERON, John Philip. b 44. Bris Univ BA66 Open Univ MPhil80 Ox Univ MSc83 Kent Univ MA99. Ox NSM Course 80. **d** 83 **p** 84. NSM Hook Norton w Gt Rollright, Swerford etc *Ox* 83-86; NSM Knaresborough *Ripon* 86-92; Dep Hd St Aid Sch Harrogate 86-92; Hd and Chapl Bennett Memorial Dioc Sch Tunbridge Wells 92-04; rtd 04; Perm to Offic *Chich* 98-03; Hon C Mayfield from 03; Dir Bloxham Project from 06. *Sarum, 5 Twyfords, Beacon Road, Crowborough TN6 1YE* Tel (01892) 667207 E-mail johncaperon@btinternet.com

CAPES, Dennis Robert. b 34. Handsworth Coll Birm 55 Linc Th Coll 65. **d** 64 **p** 65. In Methodist Ch (Sarawak) 59-63; C Lt Coates *Linc* 64-66; R Miri Malaysia 66-69; V Gosberton Clough *Linc* 69-71; V Kirton in Holland 71-80; Area Sec USPG *Cov, Heref* and *Worc* 80-87; Chapl Copenhagen w Aarhus *Eur* 87-93; TV Liv Our Lady and St Nic w St Anne 93-99; rtd 99. *35 Hardwick Avenue, Newark NG24 4AW* Tel (01636) 672874

CAPIE, Fergus Bernard. b 47. Auckland Univ BA68 MA71. Wycliffe Hall Ox BA77. **d** 77 **p** 78. C Ox St Mich w St Martin and All SS 77-80; Chapl Summer Fields Sch Ox 80-91; Hon C Wolvercote w Summertown *Ox* 87-91; Perm to Offic *St E* 91; TV E Ham w Upton Park *Chelmsf* 91-95; P-in-c Brondesbury St Anne w Kilburn H Trin *Lon* 95-01; V from 01; Chapl NW Lon Coll from 95. *125 Salusbury Road, London NW6 6RG* Tel (020) 7625 7470, 7372 6864 *or* 7604 3053 Fax 7604 3052 E-mail fergus.capie@london.anglican.org

CAPITANCHIK, Sophie Rebecca. *See* JELLEY, Mrs Sophie Rebecca

CAPLE, Stephen Malcolm. b 55. Chich Th Coll 86. **d** 88 **p** 89. C Newington St Mary *S'wark* 88-92; V Eltham St Sav 92-97; V Salfords 97-07; P-in-c S Kensington St Aug *Lon* 07-10; V Whitton St Aug from 10; Dir Evang Kensington Area from 07. *St Augustine's Vicarage, Hospital Bridge Road, Twickenham TW2 6DE* Tel (020) 8894 3764 E-mail stephencaple@blueyonder.co.uk

CAPON, Canon Anthony Charles. b 26. Trin Coll Cam BA51 MA55. Wycliffe Coll Toronto BD65 DD82 Oak Hill Th Coll 51. **d** 53 **p** 54. C Portman Square St Paul *Lon* 53-56; Canada from 56; Hon Can Montreal from 78; Prin Montreal Dioc Th Coll 78-91; rtd 91. *5 Loradean Crescent, Kingston ON K7K 6X9, Canada* Tel (001) (613) 545 9781 E-mail acapon@cgocable.net

CAPON, Gerwyn Huw. b 65. Liv Jo Moores Univ BSc92 St Steph Ho Ox 01. **d** 03 **p** 04. C W Derby St Mary *Liv* 03-07; Chapl to Abp Wales and Dir of Ords *Llan* 07-09; P-in-c Bolton-le-Sands *Blackb* from 09. *The Vicarage, 117 Main Road, Bolton le Sands, Carnforth LA5 8DX* Tel (01524) 823106

CAPPER, Alan. *See* CAPPER, William Alan

CAPPER, Mrs Elizabeth Margaret. b 31. St Chris Coll Blackheath 52. **dss** 79 **d** 87 **p** 94. The Dorothy Kerin Trust Burrswood 79; Whitstable *Cant* 80-96; Hon Par Dn 87-94; Hon C 94-96; rtd 91. *Brocastle Manor Care Home, Brocastle Estate, Ewenny, Bridgend CF35 5AU* Tel (01656) 679120

CAPPER, Mrs Katherine Frances. b 64. Warwick Univ BA(QTS)86. SEITE 07. **d** 10. NSM Horley *S'wark* from 10. *12 Beaufort Close, Reigate RH2 9DG* Tel (01737) 217191 E-mail kate@thecappers.co.uk

CAPPER, Lorraine. **d** 10. C Drumragh w Mountfield *D & R* from 10. *12 Crevenagh Way, Omagh BT79 0JE* Tel (028) 8224 1527 E-mail lorraine.capper@googlemail.com

CAPPER, Canon Richard. b 49. Leeds Univ BSc70 Fitzw Coll Cam BA72 MA79. Westcott Ho Cam 70. **d** 73 **p** 74. C Wavertree H Trin *Liv* 73-76; P-in-c Ince St Mary 76-79; V 79-83; V Gt Crosby St Faith 83-97; AD Bootle 89-97; Can Res Wakef Cathl 97-05; Can Res Nor Cathl from 05; P-in-c Nor St Mary in the Marsh from 05. *52 The Close, Norwich NR1 4EG* Tel (01603) 665210

CAPPER, Robert Melville. b 52. Chu Coll Cam BA74 MA80. Wycliffe Hall Ox 74. **d** 77 **p** 78. C Maindee Newport *Mon* 77-81; TV Aberystwyth *St D* 81-87; Chapl Univ of Wales (Abth) 81-87; V Malpas *Mon* 87-00; V Gabalfa *Llan* from 00; P-in-c Tremorfa St Phil CD from 05. *St Mark's Vicarage, 208 North Road, Gabalfa, Cardiff CF14 3BL* Tel (029) 2061 3286

CAPPER, William Alan. QUB BTh. **d** 88 **p** 89. C Dundonald *D & D* 88-91; C Lisburn Ch Ch *Conn* 91-94; I Tamlaght O'Crilly Upper w Lower *D & R* 94-96; I Lack *Clogh* 03-09; I Lisnaskea from 09. *3 Castlebalfour Road, Lisnaskea, Enniskillen BT92 0LT* Tel (028) 6772 2413 *or* 6772 3977 E-mail lisnaskea24@clogher.anglican.org

CAPPLEMAN, Graham Robert (Sam). b 56. Chelsea Coll Lon BSc79 Sheff Univ PhD83. SAOMC 94. **d** 97 **p** 98. NSM Bedf St Mark *St Alb* from 97. *107 Dover Crescent, Bedford MK41 8QR* Tel (01234) 266952 Fax 402624 Mobile 07836-784051 E-mail samc@tesco.net *or* nsm@thisischurch.com

CAPPLEMAN, Mrs Jennifer Margaret. b 53. Liv Univ CertEd74. SAOMC 94. **d** 00 **p** 01. NSM Bedford St Pet w St Cuth *St Alb* 00-03; C Goldington 03-07; TV Ouzel Valley

from 07. *The Vicarage, 2 Reach Lane, Heath and Reach, Leighton Buzzard LU7 0AL* Tel (01525) 237633 Mobile 07714-701008 E-mail jennie.cappleman@btinternet.com

CAPRIELLO (*née* BUR), **Patricia Margaret.** b 59. SEITE. **d** 99 **p** 01. C Clapham Team *S'wark* 99-01; C Nunhead St Antony w St Silas 01-03; P-in-c N Woolwich w Silvertown *Chelmsf* from 03; Ind Chapl from 04. *St John's Vicarage, Manwood Street, London E16 2JY* Tel (020) 7476 2388 E-mail stjohnse16@hotmail.co.uk

CAPRON, Canon David Cooper. b 45. Open Univ BA80. Sarum & Wells Th Coll 71. **d** 75 **p** 76. C Cov St Mary 75-79; V Shottery St Andr 79-86; TV Stratford-on-Avon w Bishopton 79-86; V Shottery St Andr 86; V Newton Aycliffe *Dur* 86-89; TR 89-90; P-in-c Alcester and Arrow w Oversley and Weethley *Cov* 90-95; R from 95; P-in-c Kinwarton w Gt Alne and Haselor from 06; P-in-c Coughton from 06; Hon Can Cov Cathl from 07; Chapl Warks Fire and Rescue Service 93-09. *St Nicholas' Rectory, Old Rectory Garden, Alcester B49 5DB* Tel (01789) 764261 Mobile 07780-707521 E-mail canon@caprons.co.uk

CAPRON, Ronald Beresford. b 35. Clifton Th Coll. **d** 62 **p** 63. Canada 62-65; C Evington *Leic* 65-67; R Gaddesby w S Croxton 67-71; R Beeby 67-71; Chapl RAF 71-83; rtd 95. *107 Coverside Road, Great Glen, Leicester LE8 9EB* Tel 0116-259 2809

CAPSTICK, Mrs Jean Rose. **d** 09 **p** 10. NSM Sodbury Vale *Glouc* 09-11; rtd 11. *Lerryn, Wotton Road, Rangeworthy, Bristol BS37 7LZ* Tel (01454) 228236 E-mail jean.capstick@homecall.co.uk

CAPSTICK, John Nowell. b 30. AKC54. **d** 55 **p** 56. C Skipton Ch Ch *Bradf* 55-57; C Buxton *Derby* 57-61; V Codnor and Loscoe 61-63; C-in-c Rawthorpe CD *Wakef* 63-64; V Rawthorpe 64-70; V Netherthong 70-89; TV Upper Holme Valley 89-95; rtd 95; Perm to Offic *Wakef* from 96. *8 Town End Avenue, Holmfirth HD9 1QW* Tel (01484) 688708

CAPSTICK, William Richard Dacre. b 32. Pemb Coll Ox. Chich Th Coll 61. **d** 64 **p** 65. C Hunslet St Mary and Stourton St Andr *Ripon* 64-67; C Knaresborough H Trin 67-71; V Stratfield Mortimer *Ox* 71-76; P-in-c St Marylebone Ch Ch w St Paul *Lon* 76-78; TV St Marylebone Ch Ch 78-79; TR Newbury *Ox* 79-89; TV Brighton St Pet and St Nic w Chpl Royal *Chich* 89-97; rtd 97. *28 Bloomsbury Street, Brighton BN2 1HQ* Tel (01273) 681171

CARBERRY, Derek William. b 65. Leeds Univ BA03 SEN88. Coll of Resurr Mirfield 01. **d** 03 **p** 04. C Tynemouth Cullercoats St Paul *Newc* 03-08; P-in-c Horton from 08. *St Benedict's Vicarage, Brierley Road, Blyth NE24 5AU* Tel (01670) 544455 E-mail d.wc@btopenworld.com

CARBERRY, Leon Carter. b 54. Penn State Univ BSc76. St Steph Ho Ox 81. **d** 84 **p** 85. C Peterlee *Dur* 84-87; C Newton Aycliffe 87-89; V Choral York Minster 89-94; Chapl St Pet Sch York 94-95; V Fylingdales and Hawsker cum Stainsacre *York* 95-01; Chapl Burrswood Chr Cen *Roch* 01-03; V Beckenham St Jas from 03. *The Vicarage, 15 St James' Avenue, Beckenham BR3 4HF* Tel and fax (020) 8650 0420 E-mail leoncarberry@googlemail.com

CARBY, Stuart Graeme. b 51. CBiol77 MIBiol77 LRSC78 Man Univ BSc73 Leeds Univ PGCE74 Open Univ MA96. St Jo Coll Nottm 92. **d** 92 **p** 93. C Magor w Redwick and Undy *Mon* 92-96; TV Cyncoed from 96. *100 Hillrise, Llanederyn, Cardiff CF23 6UL* Tel (029) 2073 3915

CARD, Terence Leslie. b 37. K Coll Lon BD68 AKC68 Heythrop Coll Lon MTh84. **d** 69 **p** 70. C Thundersley *Chelmsf* 69-72; Lic to Offic *Bradf* 72-75; V Chingford St Anne *Chelmsf* 75-81; RD Waltham Forest 78-81; R Springfield All SS 81-83; C Becontree St Jo 85-87; rtd 87; Perm to Offic *Ely* 96-00. *11 Harvey Goodwin Gardens, Cambridge CB4 3EZ* Tel (01223) 367715

CARD-REYNOLDS, Charles Leonard. b 67. Lon Univ BD92 Hughes Hall Cam BA94 MA98. St Steph Ho Ox 96. **d** 98 **p** 99. C Reading H Trin *Ox* 98-06; C Reading St Mark 98-06; V Stamford Hill St Bart *Lon* from 06. *St Bartholomew's Vicarage, 31 Craven Park Road, London N15 6AA* Tel (020) 8800 1554

CARDALE, Charles Anthony. b 21. St D Coll Lamp BA47 Lich Th Coll 55. **d** 56 **p** 57. C Honicknowle CD *Ex* 56-58; C Bideford 58-60; R Wembworthy w Eggesford 60-69; V Brushford 63-69; V Staverton w Landscove 69-87; R Broadhempston, Woodland, Staverton etc 88-89; Perm to Offic 89-06; rtd 90. *1 Barnetts Well, Draycott, Cheddar BS27 3TF*

CARDALE, Edward Charles. b 50. CCC Ox BA72 MA73. Cuddesdon Coll 72 Union Th Sem (NY) STM74. **d** 74 **p** 75. C E Dulwich St Jo *S'wark* 74-77; Asst P Bainbridge Is USA 77-81; V Ponders End St Matt *Lon* 80-84; V Lytchett Minster *Sarum* 84-98; Dir Past Studies Coll of the Resurr Mirfield 98-02; P-in-c Lemsford *St Alb* 02-05; TV Bp's Hatfield, Lemsford and N Mymms from 05; Tutor SAOMC 02-05; Dir Past Studies ERMC from 05. *7 High Oaks Road, Welwyn Garden City AL8 7BJ* Tel (01707) 322521 E-mail edward.cardale@btopenworld.com

CARDELL-OLIVER, John Anthony. b 43. Em Coll Cam BA67 MA72 Univ of W Aus BEd75 MEd85. Westcott Ho Cam 86. **d** 86 **p** 88. C Subiaco w Leederville Australia 86-88; Perm to Offic *Ely* 88-89; C Stansted Mountfitchet *Chelmsf* 89-92; R Langham w Boxted 92-02; rtd 02. *40 Halesworth Road, Jolimont, Perth WA 6014, Australia* Tel and fax (0061) (8) 9383 7381 E-mail jcardelloliver@optusnet.com.au

CARDEN, Edwin William. b 54. Cranmer Hall Dur 85. d 87 p 88. C Thundersley *Chelmsf* 87-91; CUF 91-93; NSM Poplar *Lon* 91-93; Chapl Pathfinder Mental Health Services NHS Trust 93-99; Chapl SW Lon and St George's Mental Health NHS Trust 99-00; Selection Sec Min Division 00-05; NSM Maldon St Mary w Mundon *Chelmsf* 00-02; Dioc Dep Chief Exec 03-08; Perm to Offic from 08; Chief Exec WHCM from 08. *21 Plume Avenue, Maldon CM9 6LB* Tel (01621) 854908 E-mail mudmonkeys4@btinternet.com

CARDIGAN, Archdeacon of. See STRANGE, The Ven William Anthony

CARDINAL, Ian Ralph. b 57. Qu Coll Birm 81. d 84 p 85. C Whitkirk *Ripon* 84-87; C Knaresborough 87-89; R Ancaster Wilsford Gp *Linc* 89-94; P-in-c Wigginton *Lich* 94-07; Warden of Readers 96-03; P-in-c Stone St Mich and St Wulfad w Aston St Sav 07-08; R from 08. *11 Farrier Close, Stone ST15 8XP* Tel (01785) 812747 Mobile 07778-055993 E-mail ian.cardinal@ukonline.co.uk

CARDWELL, Edward Anthony Colin. b 42. Trin Coll Cam BA63 MA68. St Jo Coll Nottm 73. d 75 p 76. C Stapenhill w Cauldwell *Derby* 75-78; C Bramcote *S'well* 78-81; V S'well H Trin 81-92; R Eastwood 92-07; rtd 07. *49 Bramcote Road, Beeston, Nottingham NG9 1DW* Tel 0115-925 5866

CARDWELL, Joseph Robin. b 47. Qu Coll Cam BA68 MA77. Trin Coll Bris 73. d 76 p 77. C Bromley Ch Ch *Roch* 76-79; C Shirley *Win* 79-82; V Somborne w Ashley 82-90; V Derry Hill *Sarum* 90-94; V Derry Hill w Bremhill and Foxham 94-00; Community Affairs Chapl 90-94; V Lyddington and Wanborough and Bishopstone etc *Bris* from 00. *The Vicarage, 19 Church Road, Wanborough, Swindon SN4 0BZ* Tel (01793) 790242 E-mail robin@cardwell99.fsnet.co.uk

CARE, Canon Charles Richard. b 21. Univ of Wales (Lamp) BA42. St Mich Coll Llan 42. d 44 p 45. C Grangetown *Llan* 44-57; R St Brides Minor 57-88; RD Bridgend 75-88; Can Llan Cathl 83-88; Prec 87-88; rtd 88; Perm to Offic *Llan* from 88. *31 Laburnum Drive, Porthcawl CF36 5UA* Tel (01656) 785446

CAREW, Bryan Andrew. b 38. ACIB63. St D Coll Lamp. d 67 p 68. C Pembroke Dock *St D* 67-70; CF 70-74; P-in-c Gt and Lt Henny w Middleton *Chelmsf* 74-76; P-in-c Wickham St Paul w Twinstead 75-76; R Gt and Lt Henny w Middleton, Wickham St Paul etc 76-99; P-in-c Alphamstone w Lamarsh 99; Perm to Offic *Chelmsf* from 03. *The Hinckford Margin, 4 Raydon Way, Great Cornard, Sudbury CO10 0LE*

CAREW, Richard Clayton. b 72. York Univ BA94 PGCE96 St Jo Coll Dur BA04. Cranmer Hall Dur 02. d 05 p 06. C Beverley Minster *York* 05-10; Abp's Dom Chapl from 10. *Bishopthorpe Palace, Bishopthorpe, York YO23 2GE* Tel (01904) 707021 Fax 709204 E-mail richard.carew@archbishopofyork.org

CAREY, Alan Lawrence. b 29. K Coll Lon AKC53. d 54 p 55. C Radford *Cov* 54-57; C Burnham *Ox* 57-65; C-in-c Cippenham CD 65-77; rtd 94. *12 Ormsby Street, Reading RG1 7YR* Tel 0118-961 2309

CAREY, Charles John. b 29. K Coll Lon BD53 AKC53. St Aug Coll Cant 71. d 72 p 73. C Spring Park *Cant* 72-74; C Ifield *Chich* 74-78; C Burgess Hill St Jo 78-80; Chapl Rush Green Hosp Romford 80-94; Chapl Oldchurch Hosp Romford 80-94; rtd 94. *Address withheld by request*

CAREY, Christopher Lawrence John. b 38. St Andr Univ BSc61 Lon Univ BD64. Clifton Th Coll 61. d 64 p 65. C Battersea Park St Sav *S'wark* 64-67; CMS Kenya 68-79; Overseas Regional Sec for E and Cen Africa CMS 79-98; NSM Chislehurst Ch Ch *Roch* 79-98; R Stickney Gp *Linc* 99-04; RD Bolingbroke 02-03; rtd 04; Perm to Offic *Mon* from 04. *83 Wentwood View, Caldicot NP26 4QH* Tel (01291) 425010 E-mail crcandkili@tiscali.co.uk

CAREY, Donald Leslie. b 50. ACII78. CBDTI 01. d 04 p 05. OLM Ashton-on-Ribble St Mich w Preston St Mark *Blackb* 04-06; OLM W Preston 06-07; NSM 07-08; P-in-c Fairhaven from 08. *Fairhaven Vicarage, 83 Clifton Drive, Lytham St Annes FY8 1BZ* Tel (01253) 734562 E-mail fr.donaldcarey@tiscali.co.uk

CAREY, Mark Jonathan. b 65. St Jo Coll Nottm BTh94. d 94 p 95. C S Ossett *Wakef* 94-97; C Chapeltown *Sheff* 97-99; V Grenoside 99-07; P-in-c Low Harrogate St Mary *Ripon* from 07. *St Mary's Vicarage, 22 Harlow Moor, Harrogate HG2 0DS* Tel (01423) 701848 E-mail mpjcarey@aol.com *or* mark@stmarysharrogate.org

CAREY, Canon Ronald Clive Adrian. b 21. K Coll Lon BA46 MA48. Chich Th Coll 47. d 48 p 49. C Harborne St Pet *Birm* 48-50; Bp's Dom Chapl *Chich* 50-52; C Keighley *Bradf* 52-55; V Illingworth *Wakef* 55-59; Asst in Relig Broadcasting BBC 59-68; Perm to Offic *S'wark* 59-68; V Claygate *Guildf* 68-78; RD Emly 72-77; Hon Can Guildf Cathl 78-86; R Guildf H Trin w St Mary 78-86; RD Guildf 84-86; rtd 86; Perm to Offic *Roch* 86-04 and *Linc* from 04. *23 Moores Court, Jermyn Street, Sleaford NG34 7UL* Tel (01529) 303698

CAREY, Mrs Wendy Marion. b 45. Bris Univ BA66 Lon Inst of Educn CertEd67. WMMTC 90. d 93 p 94. NSM Milton Keynes *Ox* 93-96; Sub Chapl HM Pris Woodhill 93-96; Chapl HM Pris Bullingdon 96-00; Ecum Tr Officer HM Pris Service Chapl 00-06; rtd 06; Perm to Offic *Ox* from 00. *46 Parklands, Great Linford, Milton Keynes MK14 5DZ* Tel (01908) 605997

✠**CAREY OF CLIFTON, The Rt Revd and Rt Hon Lord (George Leonard).** b 35. PC91. Lon Univ BD62 MTh65 PhD71 Dur Univ Hon DD93 Open Univ Hon DD95 FRSA91 FKC93. ALCD61. d 62 p 63 c 87. C Islington St Mary *Lon* 62-66; Lect Oak Hill Th Coll 66-70; Lect St Jo Coll Nottm 70-75; V Dur St Nic 75-82; Chapl HM Rem Cen Low Newton 77-81; Prin Trin Coll Bris 82-87; Hon Can Bris Cathl 84-87; Bp B & W 87-91; Abp Cant 91-02; rtd 02. *Rosemount, Garden Close Lane, Newbury RG14 6PR* E-mail carey.george01@googlemail.com

CARGILL, Christine Elizabeth. b 68. Chas Sturt Univ NSW BA(Ed)91 New England Univ NSW MLitt99 Sydney Univ MA03. NTMTC 07. d 10 p 11. C Kilburn St Mary w All So and W Hampstead St Jas *Lon* from 10. *1 St James's House, 2 Sherriff Road, London NW6 2AP* Tel (020) 7372 6441 Mobile 07906-067569 E-mail motherchristinenw6@gmail.co.uk

CARGILL THOMPSON, Edmund Alwyn James. b 72. St Jo Coll Ox BA94. Cranmer Hall Dur 98. d 00 p 01. C St Jo on Bethnal Green *Lon* 00-03; V Barkingside H Trin *Chelmsf* from 03. *Barkingside Vicarage, 36 Mossford Green, Ilford IG6 2BJ* Tel (020) 8550 2669 E-mail father.edmund@ntlworld.com

CARHART, John Richards. b 29. Bris Univ BA50 Salford Univ MSc77 Liv Univ MTh99 FRSA. St Deiniol's Hawarden 63. d 65 p 66. C Ches St Oswald w Lt St Jo 65-72; Lect Ches Coll of HE 63-72; Prin Lect from 72; Dean Academic Studies 88-94; C Ches 72; Lic to Offic 73-85; Hon C Ches St Mary 85-00; rtd 00; Perm to Offic Ches from 00. *29 Abbot's Grange, Chester CH2 1AJ* Tel (01244) 380923 E-mail jcarhart@nepc.co.uk

CARLESS, Canon Frank. b 22. Lon Univ BD56. St Aid Birkenhead 53. d 56 p 57. C Normanton *Wakef* 56-59; V Rashcliffe 59-64; V Warley 64-87; RD Halifax 82-86; Hon Can Wakef Cathl 86-87; rtd 87; Perm to Offic *Wakef* from 87. *8 Joseph Crossley Almshouses, Arden Road, Halifax HX1 3AA* Tel (01422) 348379

CARLILL, Adam Jonathan. b 66. Keble Coll Ox BA88. Linc Th Coll 88. d 90 p 91. C Romford St Edw *Chelmsf* 90-94; C Uckfield *Chich* 94-98; V Tilehurst St Geo *Ox* from 98; P-in-c Tilehurst St Mary from 02. *St George's Vicarage, 98 Grovelands Road, Reading RG3 2PD* Tel 0118-958 8354

CARLILL, Richard Edward. b 38. Westcott Ho Cam 77. d 79 p 80. C Prittlewell *Chelmsf* 79-83; TV Saffron Walden w Wendens Ambo and Littlebury 83-89; V Langtoft w Foxholes, Butterwick, Cottam etc *York* 89-94; V Gt and Lt Driffield 94-03; RD Harthill 99-02; rtd 03; Perm to Offic *Newc* from 03. *31 Riverdene, Tweedmouth, Berwick-upon-Tweed TD15 2JD* Tel (01289) 303701

CARLIN, Philip Charles. b 49. St Cath Coll Cam MA71 Didsbury Coll of Educn PGCE72. d 09 p 10. OLM Hurst *Man* from 09. *1 Sunderland Avenue, Ashton-under-Lyne OL6 8PF* Tel 0161-330 5530 Mobile 07708-398699 E-mail carlin@phonecoop.coop

CARLIN, William Patrick Bruce. b 53. St Steph Ho Ox 75. d 78 p 79. C Penistone *Wakef* 78-81; C Barnsley St Mary 81-83; V Stockton St Chad *Dur* 83-93; V Hedworth 93-01; TR Kippax w Allerton Bywater *Ripon* from 01. *The Rectory, Church Lane, Kippax, Leeds LS25 7HF* Tel 0113-286 2710 Fax 286 7339 E-mail brucecarlin@cooptel.net

CARLING, Mrs Bronwen Noël. b 43. SRN65 SCM73. Linc Th Coll 89. d 91 p 94. C Blakeney w Cley, Wiveton, Glandford etc *Nor* 91-94; C Trunch 94-96; TV 96-01; rtd 01; Perm to Offic *Nor* 01-04. *Meadowbank, Rathdermot, Bansha, Co Tipperary, Republic of Ireland* Tel (00353) (62) 54891 E-mail bncarling@sagainternet.co.uk

CARLISLE, Matthew David. b 74. Man Univ BA96. Westcott Ho Cam 99. d 02 p 03. C E Crompton *Man* 02-06; TV Heywood 06-11; V Heywood St Jo and St Luke from 11. *St John's Vicarage, Manchester Road, Heywood OL10 2EQ* Tel (01706) 369324 Mobile 07870-760746 E-mail matthewcarlisle@aol.com

CARLISLE, Archdeacon of. See ROBERTS, The Ven Kevin Thomas

CARLISLE, Bishop of. See NEWCOME, The Rt Revd James William Scobie

CARLISLE, Dean of. See BOYLING, The Very Revd Mark Christopher

CARLSON, Blair Truett. b 52. Wheaton Coll Illinois BA74. Cranmer Hall Dur 00. d 02 p 03. C Hailsham *Chich* 02-05; USA from 05. *4619 Arden Avenue, Edina MN 55424, USA* Tel (001) (952) 924 9062 E-mail btcarlson@gmail.com

CARLSSON, Miss Siw Ebba Christina. b 43. d 92 p 94. Par Dn Barnes St Mary *S'wark* 92-93; C Mitcham SS Pet and Paul 93-98; Asst Chapl SW Lon and St George's Mental Health NHS Trust 99-00; Chapl Ipswich Hosp NHS Trust 00-08; rtd 08; Perm to Offic *St E* from 08. *60 Bury Hill, Melton, Woodbridge IP12 1JD* Tel (01394) 384281

CARLTON, Preb Roger John. b 51. **d** 80 **p** 81. NSM Downend *Bris* 80-83; NSM Heavitree w Ex St Paul 83-87; Chapl Ex Sch and St Marg Sch 83-87; TV Bickleigh (Plymouth) *Ex* 87-91; TR 91-93; TR Bickleigh and Shaugh Prior 94-10; RD Ivybridge 93-98; V Paignton St Jo from 10; Preb Ex Cathl from 06. *The Vicarage, Palace Place, Paignton TQ3 3AQ* Tel (01803) 551866 E-mail roger.carlton@btinternet.com

CARLYON, Miss Catherine Rachel. b 67. RN89. Ripon Coll Cuddesdon BTh06. **d** 02 **p** 03. C Launceston *Truro* 02-06; C Crediton, Shobrooke and Sandford etc *Ex* from 06; Chapl w Deaf People from 06. *12 Linhay Park, Sandford, Crediton EX17 4LL* Tel (01363) 772163 E-mail catherinecarlyon@btopenworld.com

CARMAN, Jill Youde. b 37. Cartrefle Coll of Educn CertEd69 Liv Univ DipEd86. SAOMC 97. **d** 99 **p** 00. NSM Markyate Street *St Alb* 99-02; NSM Quinton *Glouc* 02-05; NSM Quinton and Welford w Weston 05-06; NSM Bourton-on-the-Water w Clapton etc from 06. *6 De Havilland Road, Upper Rissington, Cheltenham GL54 2NZ* Tel (01451) 824389 E-mail jill.carman@virgin.net

CARMAN, Philip Gordon. b 80. York St Jo Coll BA01 St Jo Coll Dur BA07. Cranmer Hall Dur 04. **d** 07 **p** 08. C Acomb St Steph *York* 07-10; C Huntington from 10. *402 Huntington Road, York YO31 9HU* Tel (01904) 619852 E-mail philcarman3@gmail.com

CARMARTHEN, Archdeacon of. See EVANS, The Ven Alun Wyn

CARMICHAEL, Elizabeth Dorothea Harriet. b 46. MBE95. LMH Ox MA73 BM73 BCh73 Worc Coll Ox BA83 Ox Univ DPhil91. **d** 91 **p** 92. S Africa 91-96; Chapl and Tutor St Jo Coll Ox from 96. *St John's College, Oxford OX1 3JP* Tel (01865) 277300 Fax 277435 E-mail liz.carmichael@sjc.ox.ac.uk

CARMICHAEL, Peter Iain. b 28. Chich Th Coll. **d** 75 **p** 76. C Rye w Rye Harbour and Playden *Chich* 75-79; C Rye, Rye Harbour and Playden and Iden 79-80; R Earnley and E Wittering 80-94; rtd 94; Perm to Offic *Chich* from 94. *20 East Street, Selsey, Chichester PO20 0BJ* Tel (01243) 606197

CARMODY, Canon Dermot Patrick Roy. b 41. CITC 77. **d** 77 **p** 78. C Dublin Zion Ch *D & G* 77-79; I Dunganstown w Redcross 79-84; TV Dublin Ch Ch Cathl Gp 84-93; Can Ch Ch Cathl Dublin 84-92; Preb Ch Ch Cathl Dublin 92-93; I Mullingar, Portnashangan, Moyliscar, Kilbixy etc *M & K* 93-08; Dir of Ords (Meath) 97-08; Can Meath 98-08; Can Kildare Cathl 98-08; Treas 00-08; P-in-c Rathmolyon w Castlerickard, Rathcore and Agher 00-08; rtd 08. *15 Gleann Alain, Collinstown, Mullingar, Co Westmeath, Republic of Ireland* Tel and fax (00353) (44) 966 6232 Mobile 86-829 0183 E-mail patkcarmody@gmail.com

CARMYLLIE, Mrs Kathryn Ruth. b 61. Cov Poly BA84 CQSW84 Univ Coll Ches BTh04. NOC 01. **d** 04 **p** 05. C Leigh St Mary *Man* 04-07; TV Worsley from 07. *St Stephen's Vicarage, 7 Holbeck, Astley, Tyldesley, Manchester M29 7DU* Tel (01942) 883313

CARMYLLIE, Robert Jonathan. b 63. Cov Poly BSc85. St Jo Coll Dur 85. **d** 88 **p** 89. C Horwich *Man* 88-92; P-in-c Edgeside 92-99; P-in-c Astley 99-06; TR Astley, Tyldesley and Mosley Common from 06. *St Stephen's Vicarage, 7 Holbeck, Astley, Tyldesley, Manchester M29 7DU* Tel (01942) 883313

CARNALL, Mrs Nicola Jane. b 66. St Jo Coll Nottm 99. **d** 01 **p** 02. C Edwinstowe *S'well* 01-05; P-in-c Sowerby *York* from 05; P-in-c Sessay from 05. *The Vicarage, 5 The Close, Sowerby, Thirsk YO7 1JA* Tel (01845) 522814 E-mail vicar@stoswaldsowerby.org.uk *or* njcarnall@tiscali.co.uk

CARNE, Canon Brian George. b 29. FSA Liv Univ BCom50. Qu Coll Birm 53. **d** 55 **p** 56. C Swindon St Aug *Bris* 55-58; C Bris St Andr w St Bart 58-60; R Lydiard Millicent w Lydiard Tregoz 60-68; V Bris St Andr Hartcliffe 68-74; V Almondsbury 74-91; RD Westbury and Severnside 80-86; Hon Can Bris Cathl 82-91; P-in-c Littleton on Severn w Elberton 83-91; P-in-c Olveston 83-91; rtd 91; Perm to Offic *Bris* from 92; *Glouc* 92-98 and from 01. *Whitehouse Farm, English Bicknor, Coleford GL16 7PA* Tel (01594) 860200

CARNE, Norman David John. b 27. Roch Th Coll 59. **d** 62 **p** 63. C Roch St Justus 62-66; C Strood St Mary 66-68; R Westcote Barton and Steeple Barton *Ox* 68-74; P-in-c Enstone and Heythrop 74-82; R 82-92; rtd 92; Perm to Offic *Leic* 93-98. *45 Beckingthorpe Drive, Bottesford, Nottingham NG13 0DN* Tel (01949) 843890

CARNEGIE, Ms Rachel Clare. b 62. New Hall Cam BA84 Sussex Univ MA94. SEITE 01. **d** 04 **p** 05. NSM Richmond St Mary w St Matthias and St Jo *S'wark* 04-09; Abp's Sec for Internat Development *Cant* from 09. *Lambeth Palace, London SE1 7JU* Tel (020) 7898 1200 E-mail rachel.carnegie@churchofengland.org

CARNELL, Canon Geoffrey Gordon. b 18. St Jo Coll Cam BA40 MA44. Cuddesdon Coll 40. **d** 42 **p** 43. C Abington *Pet* 42-49;

Chapl and Lect St Gabr Coll Camberwell 49-53; R Isham and V Gt w Lt Harrowden *Pet* 53-71; Dir of Post-Ord Tr and Dir of Ords 62-85; Can Pet Cathl 65-85; R Boughton 71-85; Dioc Lib Ecton Ho 67-93; Chapl to The Queen 81-88; rtd 85; Perm to Offic *Pet* 86-07. *52 Walsingham Avenue, Kettering NN15 5ER* Tel (01536) 511415

CARNELLEY, The Ven Desmond. b 29. Open Univ BA77 Leeds Univ CertEd. Ripon Hall Ox 59. **d** 60 **p** 61. C Aston cum Aughton *Sheff* 60-63; C-in-c Ecclesfield St Paul CD 63-67; V Balby w Hexthorpe 67-73; P-in-c Mosbrough 73-74; V 74-85; RD Attercliffe 79-84; Adn Doncaster 85-94; Dioc Dir of Educn 91-94; rtd 94; Perm to Offic *Sheff* and *Derby* from 94. *11 Fairways, Wickersley, Rotherham S66 1AE* Tel (01709) 544927

CARNELLEY, Ms Elizabeth Amy. b 64. St Aid Coll Dur BA85 Selw Coll Cam MPhil87. Ripon Coll Cuddesdon 88. **d** 90 **p** 94. Par Dn Sharrow St Andr *Sheff* 90-93; Par Dn Is of Dogs Ch Ch and St Jo w St Luke *Lon* 93-94; C 94-95; P-in-c Woolfold *Man* 95-99; TV Man Whitworth 99-02; Chapl Man Univ and Man Metrop Univ 99-02; Policy Officer Chs' Regional Commn for Yorks and the Humber 02-06; Chief Exec from 06; Perm to Offic *Ripon* from 02. *20 New Market Street, Leeds LS1 6DG* Tel 0113-244 3413 Mobile 07734-149725 E-mail liz.carnelley@crc-online.org.uk

CARNEY, David Anthony. b 42. Salford Univ BSc77. Linc Th Coll 77. **d** 79 **p** 80. C Wythenshawe St Martin *Man* 79-81; CF 81-84; Chapl Canadian Armed Forces 84-87; R Burford H Trin Ontario 87-91; P-in-c Whaplode *Linc* 91-97; V 97-02; P-in-c Holbeach Fen 91-97; V 97-02; R Colsterworth Gp 02-05; P-in-c Kirton in Holland 05-09; rtd 09. *6 South Road, Bourne PE10 9JD* Tel (01778) 426061

CARNEY, Mrs Mary Patricia. b 42. Univ of Wales (Ban) BSc62. Wycliffe Hall Ox. **d** 90 **p** 94. Par Dn Carterton *Ox* 90-93; Par Dn Harwell w Chilton 93-94; C 94-01; P-in-c Ray Valley 01-07; rtd 07; Perm to Offic *Ox* from 07. *344B Woodstock Road, Oxford OX2 8BZ* Tel (01865) 515325 E-mail marypcarney@tiscali.co.uk

CARNEY, The Ven Richard Wayne. b 52. Lon Teachers' Coll Ontario TCert73 Toronto Univ BA79. Trin Coll Toronto MDiv84. **d** 84 **p** 85. Canada 84-95; C Scarborough St Andr 84-86; I Roche's Pt 86-91; P Asst Newmarket St Paul 91-93; Assoc P 93-95; I Clonfert Gp *L & K* 95-03; I Birr w Lorrha, Dorrha and Lockeen from 03; Adn Killaloe, Kilfenora, Clonfert etc from 02. *The Rectory, Birr, Co Offaly, Republic of Ireland* Tel (00353) (57) 912 0021 Mobile 87-786 5234 E-mail mapleire@eircom.net *or* archdeacon@killaloe.anglican.org

✠**CARNLEY, The Rt Revd Peter Frederick.** b 37. AO98. Melbourne Univ BA66 Cam Univ PhD69 Gen Th Sem NY Hon DD84 Newc Univ Aus Hon DLitt00 Univ of W Aus Hon DLitt00. St Jo Coll Morpeth. **d** 62 **p** 64 **c** 81. Lic to Offic Melbourne 63-65; C Parkes 66; Lic to Offic *Ely* 66-69; Chapl Mitchell Coll Bathurst 70-71; Research Fell St Jo Coll Cam 71-72; Warden St Jo Coll Brisbane 72-81; Can Res Brisbane 75-81; Abp Perth 81-05; Primate of Australia 00-05; rtd 05. *PO Box 221, Nannup WA 6275, Australia* Tel (0061) (8) 9756 0420

CAROLAN (née STUART-BLACK), Mrs Veronica. b 52. St Jo Coll Dur BA75. Cranmer Hall Dur. dss 82 **d** 87 **p** 08. Borehamwood *St Alb* 82-84; Watford Ch Ch 84-85; Stevenage St Mary Shephall 85-87; Par Dn Stevenage St Mary Shephall w Aston 87-88; Hon C from 08; Perm to Offic 98-08. *18 Randalls Hill, Shephall, Stevenage SG2 9YN* Tel (01438) 235597

CAROLAN-EVANS, Stewart James. b 65. Salford Univ BSc88 CEng95 MICE95. SEITE 04. **d** 06 **p** 07. NSM Dover St Mary *Cant* from 06. *Springfield, Eythorne Road, Shepherdswell, Dover CT15 7PW* Tel (01304) 832248 Fax 830641 Mobile 07940-544748 E-mail sjkgcarolan@tesco.net

CARPANI, Karl Augustus. b 65. St Jo Coll Nottm 96. **d** 98 **p** 99. C Biggin Hill *Roch* 98-01; V Green Street Green and Pratts Bottom from 01. *The Vicarage, 46 World's End Lane, Orpington BR6 6AG* Tel (01689) 852905 E-mail karl.carpani@diocese-rochester.org *or* karl@carpani.org

CARPENTER, Canon Bruce Leonard Henry. b 32. Lon Univ BA54. St Chad's Coll Dur. **d** 59 **p** 60. C Portsea N End St Mark *Portsm* 59-63; C Fareham SS Pet and Paul 63-67; V Locks Heath 67-74; TR Fareham H Trin 74-84; RD Alverstoke 71-76; Hon Can Portsm Cathl 78-84; V Richmond St Mary w St Matthias and St Jo *S'wark* 84-91; Chapl Ch Ch High Sch Ashford 91-93; P-in-c S Ashford Ch Ch *Cant* 94-97; rtd 97; Chapl Huggens Coll Northfleet 97-02; Perm to Offic *Portsm* from 02; Hon Chapl MU from 03. *Pistachio, 96 Festing Grove, Southsea PO4 9QF* Tel (023) 9229 4128

CARPENTER, David James. b 52. Trin Coll Carmarthen CertEd74. St Steph Ho Ox 74. **d** 76 **p** 77. C Newport St Julian *Mon* 76-77; C Pontypool 77-79; C Ebbw Vale 79-81; TV 81-85; V Pontnewynydd 85-88; V Bedwellty 88-00; Chapl Aberbargoed Hosp 88-99; V Staincliffe and Carlinghow *Wakef* 00-05; Chapl Yorks Ambulance Service 05-11; Perm to Offic 10-11; P-in-c

Birkby and Woodhouse from 11. *The Vicarage, 43 Ashbrow Road, Huddersfield HD2 1DX* Tel (01484) 424669 E-mail carpenterdj@aol.com

CARPENTER, Canon Derek George Edwin. b 40. K Coll Lon BD62 AKC62. **d** 63 **p** 64. C Friern Barnet All SS *Lon* 63-66; C Chingford SS Pet and Paul *Chelmsf* 66-70; V Dartford St Alb *Roch* 70-79; R Crayford 79-90; RD Erith 82-90; R Beckenham St Geo 90-02; Hon Can Roch Cathl 97-02; rtd 02; Perm to Offic *Roch* from 04. *39 Chatfield Way, East Malling, West Malling ME19 6QD* Tel (01732) 874420

CARPENTER, Donald Arthur. b 35. Roch Th Coll 65. **d** 67 **p** 68. C Thornton Heath St Jude *Cant* 67-73; V Earby *Bradf* 73-78; V Skipton Ch Ch 78-88; V Baildon 88-91; P-in-c Perivale *Lon* 91-96; rtd 96; Perm to Offic *Lon* 96-05. *Le Moulin Verneau, 49390 Parcay-les-Pins, France* Tel (0033) 2 41 51 42 22 Mobile 6 77 98 48 07 E-mail sue.carpenter@numeo.fr

CARPENTER, Giles Michael Gerard. b 67. Trin Coll Bris BA10. **d** 10 **p** 11. C Shottermill *Guildf* from 10. *33 Sunvale Avenue, Haslemere GU27 1PJ* Tel (01428) 651134 Mobile 07710-498906 E-mail giles.carpenter@blueyonder.co.uk

CARPENTER, Canon Judith Margaret. b 47. Bris Univ BA68 CertEd69. Trin Coll Bris BA95. **d** 95 **p** 96. C Warmley, Syston and Bitton *Bris* 95-99; V Withywood from 99; Hon Can Bris Cathl from 06. *Withywood Church House, 63 Turtlegate Avenue, Bristol BS13 8NN* Tel 0117-964 7763 E-mail judith.carpenter1@btinternet.com

CARPENTER, Leonard Richard. b 32. EMMTC 82. **d** 85 **p** 86. NSM Leic H Apostles 85-90; P-in-c Barlestone 90-98; rtd 98; Perm to Offic *Leic* and *Derby* from 98. *10 Main Street, Albert Village, Swadlincote DE11 8EW* Tel (01283) 229335

CARPENTER, Michael John Anselm. b 77. Leeds Univ BA02. Coll of Resurr Mirfield 99. **d** 02 **p** 03. C Cudworth and Lundwood *Wakef* 02-03; C Castleford 03-06; In RC Ch 06-09; C Hanging Heaton from 10; C Batley St Thos from 10. *The Vicarage, 16 Stockwell Drive, Batley WF17 5PA* Tel 07970-821438 (mobile) E-mail michael.carpenter1@mypostoffice.co.uk

CARPENTER, William Brodie. b 35. St Alb Minl Tr Scheme 76. **d** 79 **p** 80. NSM Hemel Hempstead *St Alb* 79-85; C Bp's Hatfield 85-88; C Caversham St Pet and Mapledurham etc *Ox* 88-89; V Caversham St Andr 89-99; rtd 99; Perm to Offic *St Alb* 00-02; P-in-c Wigginton 02-05; Perm to Offic *Ox* from 07. *33 Elm Tree Walk, Tring HP23 5EB* Tel (01442) 824585 E-mail billcarp@supanet.com

CARR, Alan Cobban. b 49. Nottm Univ BTh88. Linc Th Coll 85. **d** 88 **p** 89. C Rustington *Chich* 88-92; V Highbrook and W Hoathly 92-10; C St Giles-in-the-Fields *Lon* from 10. *16 Ashmere Grove, London SW2 5UJ* Tel (020) 7274 0407 E-mail alancarr17@hotmail.com

CARR, Mrs Amanda Helen. b 70. Univ of Wales (Cardiff) BA91 Kent Univ MA97. SEITE 01. **d** 04 **p** 05. C Meopham w Nurstead *Roch* 04-07; P-in-c Lamberhurst and Matfield from 07. *The Vicarage, Old Town Hill, Lamberhurst, Tunbridge Wells TN3 8EL* Tel (01892) 891538 Mobile 07866-675015 E-mail mandy.carr@diocese-rochester.org

CARR, Anthony Howard. b 62. Ex Univ BA. **d** 92 **p** 93. C Taverham w Ringland *Nor* 92-97; P-in-c S Darley, Elton and Winster *Derby* 97-03; R E Peckham and Nettlestead *Roch* 03. *The Rectory, Bush Road, East Peckham, Tonbridge TN12 5LL* Tel (01622) 871278

CARR, The Very Revd Arthur Wesley. b 41. KCVO06. Jes Coll Ox BA64 MA67 Jes Coll Cam BA66 MA70 Sheff Univ PhD75 Hon DLitt03 UWE Hon DLitt07. Ridley Hall Cam 65. **d** 67 **p** 68. C Luton w E Hyde *St Alb* 67-71; Tutor Ridley Hall Cam 70-71; Chapl 71-72; Hon C Ranmoor *Sheff* 72-74; Chapl Chelmsf Cathl 74-78; Can Res 78-87; Dep Dir Cathl Cen for Research and Tr 74-82; Dioc Dir of Tr 76-84; Dean Bris 87-97; Dean Westmr 97-06; rtd 06. *16 Church Road, Romsey SO51 8EY* E-mail wesleycarr.wanadoo.co.uk

CARR, David Scott. b 72. Derby Univ BA97 MCIM05. NEOC 06. **d** 09 **p** 10. NSM Horden *Dur* from 09. *Glen View, 26 Station Avenue, Brandon, Durham DH7 8QQ* Tel 07990-775054 (mobile) E-mail david@carrd.fsbusiness.co.uk

CARR, Derrick Charles. b 43. MCIPD. SAOMC 99. **d** 02 **p** 03. NSM Amersham *Ox* from 02; AD Amersham from 09. *52 Warren Wood Drive, High Wycombe HP11 1EA* Tel and fax (01494) 452389 Mobile 07768-507391 E-mail dcarr@globalnet.co.uk

CARR, Mrs Elaine Susan. b 46. LTCL82. SAOMC 99. **d** 02 **p** 03. NSM High Wycombe *Ox* 02-09; Bp's NSM Officer (Bucks) from 09. *52 Warren Wood Drive, High Wycombe HP11 1EA* Tel and fax (01494) 452389 E-mail revcarr@btinternet.com

CARR, Miss Eveline. b 45. St Jo Coll Dur 91. **d** 93 **p** 95. NSM Eighton Banks *Dur* 93-98; NSM Gateshead from 98. *10 Lanchester Avenue, Gateshead NE9 7AJ* Tel 0191-482 1157 E-mail e-carr@supnet.com

CARR, John Henry Percy. b 52. NTMTC 95. **d** 98 **p** 99. C Hackney Wick St Mary of Eton w St Aug *Lon* 98-01; R Walesby

Linc from 01. *The Rectory, Otby Lane, Walesby, Market Rasen LN8 3UT* Tel (01673) 838513 E-mail carr.ide@boltblue.com

CARR, John Robert. b 40. ACII62. Oak Hill Th Coll 63. **d** 66 **p** 67. C Tonbridge St Steph *Roch* 66-70; C Cheadle Hulme St Andr *Ches* 70-79; R Widford *Chelmsf* 79-87; TV Becontree W 87-93; V Basildon St Andr w H Cross 93-05; rtd 05; Perm to Offic *Chelmsf* from 06. *3 Windsor Way, Rayleigh SS6 8PE* Tel (01268) 741065 E-mail johnwendycarr@ukgateway.net

CARR, Miss Joy Vera. b 32. DipEd52. Dalton Ho Bris 56. **dss** 80 **d** 87 **p** 94. Scarborough St Jas and H Trin *York* 80-82; Kingston upon Hull St Matt w St Barn 82-87; Par Dn 87-89; Par Dn Elloughton and Brough w Brantingham 89-92; rtd 92; Perm to Offic *York* from 92. *15 Sea View Gardens, Scarborough YO11 3JD* Tel (01723) 376986

CARR, Leighton Westwood. b 60. Trin Coll Bris. **d** 09 **p** 10. NSM Kingswood *Bris* from 09. *19 Nutgrove Avenue, Bristol BS3 4QE* Tel 0117-983 2605

CARR, Mandy. *See* CARR, Mrs Amanda Helen

CARR, Paul Anthony. b 62. Aston Tr Scheme 93 Oak Hill Th Coll 95. **d** 97 **p** 98. C Handforth *Ches* 97-01; V Chadwell Heath *Chelmsf* 01-08; TR Billericay and Lt Burstead from 08. *The Rectory, 40 Laindon Road, Billericay CM12 9LD* Tel (01277) 658055 E-mail revpaulcarr@btinternet.com

CARR, Richard George. b 43. AKC65. St Boniface Warminster 65. **d** 66 **p** 67. C Fenham St Jas and St Basil *Newc* 66-69; C Alnwick St Mich 69-73; Ind Chapl *Llan* 73-77; Perm to Offic *Chelmsf* from 80. *Nelmes, Mill Lane, Birch, Colchester CO2 0NG* Tel (01206) 330521 E-mail richardcarr@nelmes.fsnet.co.uk

CARR, Wesley. *See* CARR, The Very Revd Arthur Wesley

CARRINGTON, David John. b 63. Trin Coll Bris. **d** 09 **p** 10. C Bovey Tracey SS Pet, Paul and Thos w Hennock *Ex* from 09. *Orchard Meadow, Coombe Cross, Bovey Tracey, Newton Abbot TQ13 9EP* Tel (01626) 830770

CARRINGTON, Mrs Elizabeth Ashby. b 46. EMMTC 86. **d** 90 **p** 94. NSM Nottingham St Ann w Em *S'well* 90-91; C Basford w Hyson Green 92-97; Lect Nottingham St Mary and St Cath 97-00; Assoc P W Bingham Deanery 00; Perm to Offic 00-01; Chapl Woodford Ho Sch New Zealand 01-11; NSM Napier Cathl 03-11; rtd 11. *98 Repton Road, West Bridgford, Nottingham NG2 7EL* Tel 0115-914 2504 E-mail carringtonpe@yahoo.co.uk

CARRINGTON, Margaret Elizabeth. **d** 09. NSM York St Luke from 09. *202 Boroughbridge Road, York YO26 6BD* Tel (01904) 798916 E-mail carringtone@btinternet.com

CARRINGTON, Philip John. b 48. MBE03. Leeds Univ MA96 Leeds Poly CEng MCML Chich Th Coll 83. **d** 85 **p** 86. C W Acklam *York* 85-88; V Middlesbrough St Agnes 88-92; Chapl S Cleveland Hosp 88-92; Trust Chapl S Tees Hosps NHS Trust 92-06; V Guernsey St Steph *Win* from 06; Hd Chapl Services States of Guernsey Bd of Health from 07. *St Stephen's Vicarage, Les Gravees, St Peter Port, Guernsey GY1 1RN* Tel (01481) 720268 E-mail thecarringtons@cwgsy.net

CARRIVICK, Derek Roy. b 45. Birm Univ BSc66. Ripon Hall Ox 71. **d** 74 **p** 75. C Enfield St Jas *Lon* 74-78; C-in-c Woodgate Valley CD *Birm* 78-83; TR Chelmsley Wood 83-92; Dioc Ecum Officer 86-96; R Baxterley w Hurley and Wood End and Merevale etc 92-99; AD Polesworth 96-99; P-in-c Helland and Blisland w St Breward *Truro* 99-04; P-in-c Devoran 04-11; Hon C from 11; Hon C Chacewater w St Day and Carharrack from 11; Hon C St Stythians w Perranarworthal and Gwennap from 11; Hon C Feock from 11; Bp's Dom Chapl 04-09; rtd 09. *The Vicarage, Devoran Lane, Devoran, Truro TR3 6PA* Tel (01872) 863116 E-mail pjc87@tutor.open.ac.uk

CARROLL, The Ven Charles William Desmond. b 19. TCD BA43 MA46. St Chad's Coll Dur. **d** 48 **p** 49. C Stanwix *Carl* 48-50; V 50-59; Hon Can Blackb Cathl 59-64; Dir RE 59-73; Can Res Blackb Cathl 64-75; Adn Blackb 73-86; V Balderstone 73-86; rtd 86; Perm to Offic *Blackb* from 86. *11 Assheton Road, Blackburn BB2 6SF* Tel (01254) 51915

CARROLL, Frederick Albert. b 16. Worc Coll Ox BA51 MA55. Ripon Hall Ox 46. **d** 51 **p** 52. C Oldbury *Birm* 51-56; V Cotteridge 56-65; C-in-c Castle Vale CD 65-68; V Castle Vale 68-74; V Coughton *Cov* 74-87; R Spernall, Morton Bagot and Oldberrow 74-87; RD Alcester 84-87; rtd 87. *8 Gracey Court, Woodland Road, Broadclyst, Exeter EX5 3GA* Tel (01392) 460788

CARROLL, James Thomas. b 41. Pittsburgh Univ MA85. St Deiniol's Hawarden 89 Oblate Fathers Sem Dub 59. **d** 63 **p** 64. C Dublin St Patr Cathl Gp 89-92; Min Can St Patr Cathl Dublin 90-96; I Raheny w Coolock *D & G* from 92; Chan V St Patr Cathl Dublin from 96. *403 Howth Road, Raheny, Dublin 5, Republic of Ireland* Tel (00353) (1) 831 3929 E-mail midnight@indigo.ie

CARROLL, John Hugh. b 31. Bris Univ BA57. Tyndale Hall Bris 54. **d** 58 **p** 59. C Slough *Ox* 58-61; V S Lambeth St Steph *S'wark* 61-72; V Norwood St Luke 72-81; P-in-c Purley Ch Ch 81-85; V 85-93; rtd 93. *75 Court Avenue, Coulsdon CR5 1HJ* Tel (01737) 553471 E-mail jonthel.carroll@virgin.net

CARROLL, Laurence William. b 44. Birm Univ CertEd66 Open Univ BA73 Leic Univ BEd74 FRHS66 ACP67 LCP68. **d** 95 **p** 96. OLM Mid Marsh Gp *Linc* from 95. *15 Grantavon House, Brayford Wharf East, Lincoln LN5 7WA* Tel (01522) 523643

CARROLL WALLIS, Ms Joy Ann. b 59. SS Mark & Jo Univ Coll Plymouth BEd82. Cranmer Hall Dur 85. **d** 88 **p** 94. Par Dn Hatcham St Jas *S'wark* 88-93; Par Dn Streatham Immanuel and St Andr 93-94; C 94-97; USA from 97. *1305 Fairmont Street NW, Washington DC 20009, USA* Tel (001) (202) 483 0119 E-mail joycwallis@aol.com

CARRUTHERS, Arthur Christopher (Kester). b 35. Lon Coll of Div ALCD60 LTh73. **d** 60 **p** 61. C Addiscombe St Mary *Cant* 60-62; Prec Bradf Cathl 62-64; CF 64-92; R W Tanfield and Well w Snape and N Stainley *Ripon* 92-00; rtd 00; Perm to Offic *Guildf* from 00. *3 Park View Court, Woking GU22 7SE* Tel (01483) 721995

CARSON, Christopher John. b 69. QUB BA91 TCD BTh94. **d** 94 **p** 95. C Bangor St Comgall *D & D* 94-97; Bp's C Kilmegan w Maghera 97-98; I from 98. *The Rectory, 50 Main Street, Dundrum, Newcastle BT33 0LY* Tel (028) 4375 1225 Mobile 07758-722617

CARSON, Claire. b 76. St Martin's Coll Lanc BA98 Birm Univ MA99. Qu Coll Birm 00. **d** 03 **p** 04. C Streetly *Lich* 03-04; C Stafford 04-05; C Lich St Mich w St Mary and Wall 05-07; Chapl R Free Hampstead NHS Trust 07-10; Chapl Imp Coll Healthcare NHS Trust 10-11; Chapl SW Lon and St George's Mental Health NHS Trust from 11. *20 Courthope Road, London NW3 2LB* Tel 07891-180023 (mobile) E-mail claire.carson3@btinternet.com

CARSON, Ernest. b 17. S'wark Ord Course 68. **d** 71 **p** 72. C Baldock w Bygrave and Clothall *St Alb* 71-75; R Hertingfordbury 75-86; rtd 86; Perm to Offic *Worc* from 86. *16 Woodward Close, Pershore WR10 1LP* Tel (01386) 553511

CARSON, Gerald James Alexander. b 24. TCD BA49 MA52. **d** 49 **p** 50. C Belfast St Phil *Conn* 49-51; C Derry Cathl 51-54; I Kilteevogue 54-57; I Dunfanaghy 57-68; Can Raphoe Cathl 67-81; I Urney w Sion Mills 68-85; Can Derry Cathl 81-85; I Clonallon w Warrenpoint *D & D* 85-90; rtd 90. *30 Killowen House, 20 Killowen Street, Coleraine BT51 3BT* Tel (028) 7035 6047

CARSON, James Irvine. b 59. TCD BA MTh. **d** 84 **p** 85. C Willowfield *D & D* 84-87; C Lecale Gp 87-89; I Devenish w Boho *Clogh* 89-95; Dioc Youth Adv 91-95; Dioc Communications Officer 93-95; I Belfast Upper Malone (Epiphany) *Conn* 95-99; I Lisburn St Paul from 99. *St Paul's Rectory, 3 Ballinderry Road, Lisburn BT28 1UD* Tel (028) 9266 3520 E-mail jamescarson203@btinternet.com

CARSON-FEATHAM, Lawrence William. b 53. AKC. **d** 78 **p** 79. SSM from 77; C Walton St Mary *Liv* 78-82; Chapl Bolton Colls of H&FE 82-87; C Bolton St Pet *Man* 82-87; TV Oldham 87-92; V Ashton St Jas 92-95; Perm to Offic *Liv* 95-97; C Leeds Belle Is St Jo and St Barn *Ripon* 97-01; TV Accrington Ch the King *Blackb* from 01. *St Mary Magdalen's Vicarage, 5 Queen's Road, Accrington BB5 6AR* Tel (01254) 233763 E-mail carsonfeatham@btinternet.com

CARTER, Arthur Edward. b 32. CITC. **d** 97 **p** 98. C Clonmel w Innislounagh, Tullaghmelan etc *C & O* from 97. *Suir Villa, Barnora, Cahir, Co Tipperary, Republic of Ireland* Tel (00353) (52) 744 1524 E-mail nacarter@eircom.net

CARTER, Barry Graham. b 54. K Coll Lon BD76 AKC76. St Steph Ho Ox 76. **d** 77 **p** 78. C Evesham *Worc* 77-81; C Amblecote 81-84; TV Ovingdean w Rottingdean and Woodingdean *Chich* 84-85; V Woodingdean 85-95; V Lancing St Mich from 95. *The Vicarage, 117 Penhill Road, Lancing BN15 8HD* Tel (01903) 753653 E-mail frbaz@saintmichaels.plus.com

CARTER, Benjamin Huw. b 77. Ex Univ BA99 St Cath Coll Cam MPhil00 Middx Univ PhD04. Cranmer Hall Dur 08. **d** 10 **p** 11. C Monkseaton St Mary *Newc* from 10. *89 Queen's Road, Monkseaton, Whitley Bay NE26 3AS* Tel 07985-412542 (mobile) E-mail benj.carter@yahoo.co.uk

CARTER, Celia. b 38. JP74. Glouc Sch of Min 86. **d** 89 **p** 94. NSM Avening w Cherington *Glouc* from 89; Asst Chapl Stroud Gen Hosp 89-93; Asst Chapl Severn NHS Trust 93-06; Asst Chapl Glos Primary Care Trust from 06. *Avening Park, West End, Avening, Tetbury GL8 8NE* Tel (01453) 836390

CARTER (née SMITH), Mrs Christine Lydia. b 43. SRN64 SCM67. Trin Coll Bris 89. **d** 91 **p** 94. Par Dn Penkridge *Lich* 91-94; C 94-96; Perm to Offic *Blackb* 96-97; NSM Blackb Sav 97-01; Chapl Asst St Helens and Knowsley Hosps NHS Trust 97-01; NSM Elmdon St Nic *Birm* 01-11. *4 Goods Station Lane, Penkridge, Stafford ST19 5AU*

CARTER, Christopher Franklin. b 37. Wadh Coll Ox BA59 MA63. Wycliffe Hall Ox 60. **d** 64 **p** 65. C Clifton St Jas *Sheff* 64-67; C Handsworth 67-70; C Clun w Chapel Lawn *Heref* 70-74; Lic to Offic 74-76; P-in-c Ironbridge 76-78; C Coalbrookdale, Iron-Bridge and Lt Wenlock 78-80; V Llansilin

w Llangadwaladr and Llangedwyn *St As* 80-05; RD Llanfyllin 88-05; rtd 05. *Ysgubor Goch, Cefn Coch, Llanrhaeadr-ym-Mochnant, Oswestry SY10 0BQ* Tel (01691) 860577

CARTER, Christopher Paul. b 43. CCC Cam BA64. SAOMC 02. **d** 05 **p** 06. NSM W Buckingham *Ox* from 05. *The Mount, Upper Street, Tingewick, Buckingham MK18 4QN* Tel and fax (01280) 848291 E-mail lorraine.carter@btinternet.com

CARTER, Colin John. b 56. Fitzw Coll Cam BA77 MB, BChir80 MA81 FRCS86 FRCOphth89. Trin Coll Bris BA93. **d** 93 **p** 94. C Ripley *Derby* 93-97; TV Horsham *Chich* 97-00. *Duke Elder Eye Unit, Blackshaw Road, London SW17 0QT* Tel (020) 8266 6111

CARTER, David John. b 37. Chich Th Coll 64. **d** 67 **p** 68. C Plaistow St Andr *Chelmsf* 67-70; C Wickford 70-73; Chapl Asst Runwell Hosp Wickford 71-73; Chapl Basingstoke Distr Hosp 73-80; R E Woodhay and Woolton Hill *Win* 80-02; rtd 02; Perm to Offic *Win* from 02. *24 Sandford Close, Kingsclere, Newbury RG20 5LZ* Tel (01635) 299455

CARTER, Dudley Herbert. b 25. Peterho Cam BA49 MA51. Ridley Hall Cam 49. **d** 51 **p** 52. C Longfleet *Sarum* 51-53; C Rainham *Chelmsf* 54-56; R Tollard Royal w Farnham *Sarum* 60-64; Chapl Colston's Sch Bris 65-67; Lic to Offic *B & W* 67-85; Perm to Offic from 85; rtd 90. *9 Beaufort House, Rectory Road, Burnham-on-Sea TA8 2BY* Tel (01278) 789096

CARTER, Duncan Robert Bruton. b 58. Univ of Wales (Cardiff) BA79 Cam Univ BA83 MA89. Ridley Hall Cam 81. **d** 84 **p** 85. C Harold Wood *Chelmsf* 84-88; C S Kensington St Luke *Lon* 88-90; V Henley H Trin *Ox* from 90; AD Henley 02-06. *Holy Trinity Vicarage, Church Street, Henley-on-Thames RG9 1SE* Tel (01491) 574822 E-mail drbcarter@hotmail.com

CARTER, Edward John. b 67. Ex Univ BA88. Ripon Coll Cuddesdon BA96 MA01. **d** 97 **p** 98. C Thorpe St Matt *Nor* 97-00; Min Can and Dean's V Windsor 00-04; P-in-c Didcot St Pet *Ox* from 04; AD Wallingford from 07. *St Peter's Vicarage, 47A Newlands Avenue, Didcot OX11 8QA* Tel (01235) 812114 E-mail priest-in-charge@stpeters-didcot.org.uk

CARTER, Frank Howard James. b 23. Chich Th Coll 58. **d** 59 **p** 60. C Bethnal Green St Matt *Lon* 59-64; V Ipstones *Lich* 64-65; V Haggerston All SS *Lon* 65-75; V Alexandra Park St Andr 75-88; rtd 88; Perm to Offic Lon 91-98. *53 Naylor Road, London N20 0HE* Tel (020) 8445 0982

CARTER, Grayson Leigh. b 53. Univ of S California BSc76 Ch Ch Ox DPhil90. Fuller Th Sem California MA84 Wycliffe Hall Ox 89. **d** 90 **p** 91. C Bungay H Trin w St Mary *St E* 90-92; Chapl BNC Ox 92-96; Hon C Ox St Mary V w St Cross and St Pet 93-96; USA from 96; Assoc Prof Methodist Coll Fayetteville 96-03; Asst R Fayetteville H Trin 96-03; Assoc Prof Fuller Th Sem from 03. *1602 Palmcroft Drive SW, Phoenix AZ 85007-1738, USA* Tel (001) (602) 252 5582 *or* 220 0400 Fax 220 0444 E-mail gcarter10@yahoo.com *or* gcarter@fuller.edu

CARTER, Hazel June. b 48. Doncaster Coll of Educn CertEd72. Carl Dioc Tr Inst 89. **d** 92 **p** 94. C Wreay *Carl* 92-94; C Dalston and Raughton Head w Gatesgill 92-98; TV Carl H Trin and St Barn 98-02; TR 02-07; rtd 07. *4 Wandales Lane, Natland, Kendal LA9 7QY* Tel (01228) 526284

CARTER, Heather Ruth. b 62. SEN82. Trin Coll Bris 85. **d** 02 **p** 04. Dn Montevideo Cathl Uruguay 02-04; NSM Dalston w Cumdivock, Raughton Head and Wreay *Carl* from 04; Chapl to the Deaf and Hard of Hearing 05-08; Chapl N Cumbria Acute Hosps NHS Trust 05-07. *The Vicarage, Townhead Road, Dalston, Carlisle CA5 7JF* Tel (01228) 710215 Fax 710288 E-mail revhev@tiscali.co.uk

CARTER, Ian Sutherland. b 51. Trin Coll Ox BA73 MA77 DPhil77 Leeds Univ BA80. Coll of Resurr Mirfield 78. **d** 81 **p** 82. C Shildon *Dur* 81-84; C Darlington H Trin 84-87; Chapl Liv Univ 87-93; V Hindley St Pet 93-98; Chapl Oldham NHS Trust 98-03; Chapl Salford R Hosps NHS Foundn Trust from 03. *Hope Hospital, Stott Lane, Salford M6 8HD* Tel 0161-206 5167 *or* 789 7373 E-mail ian.carter@srht.nhs.uk

CARTER (née O'NEILL), Mrs Irene. b 44. Worc Coll of Educn CertEd65. EMMTC 92. **d** 93. NSM N and S Leverton *S'well* 93-11; NSM Retford Area from 11. *38 St Martin's Road, North Leverton, Retford DN22 0AU*

CARTER, Mrs Jacqueline Ann. b 50. St Mich Coll Llan 01. **d** 03 **p** 04. C Ebbw Vale *Mon* 03-06; TV 06-11; V Rhosllannerchrugog *St As* from 11. *The Vicarage, Wrexham Road, Johnstown, Wrexham LL14 1PE* Tel (01978) 844535 E-mail jackiecarter16@hotmail.com

CARTER, Canon John Howard Gregory. b 55. York Univ BA76 Leeds Univ CertEd77 Nottm Univ MA96. St Jo Coll Nottm LTh87. **d** 87 **p** 88. C Nailsea H Trin *B & W* 87-91; TV Camberley St Paul *Guildf* 91-97; Chapl Elmhurst Ballet Sch 91-97; Dioc Communications Officer *Ripon* from 97; Bp's Press Officer from 00; Hon Can Ripon Cathl from 10. *7 Bish, Cam Court, Harrogate HG2 9DT* Tel (01423) 530369 Fax 08717-333778 Mobile 07798-652707 E-mail jhgcarter@aol.com

CARTER, Mrs Joy. **d** 09. OLM Didcot St Pet *Ox* from 09. *St Peter's Vicarage, 47A Newlands Avenue, Didcot OX11 8QA* Tel (01235) 812114

CARTER, Marian. b 40. Whitelands Coll Lon TCert61 Lon Univ BD67 Nottm Univ MPhil79 Man Univ MA84 Ex Univ PhD05. N Bapt Coll 81. **d** 92 **p** 94. Par Dn Kempshott *Win* 92-93; Tutor SWMTC 92-96; Tutor Coll of SS Mark and Jo Plymouth 93-00; NSM Plymstock and Hooe *Ex* 94-98; NSM Widecombe-in-the-Moor, Leusdon, Princetown etc 98-00; Chapl St Eliz Hospice Ipswich 00-05; rtd 05; Perm to Offic *St E* from 06. *Shalom, 80 Woodlands, Chelmondiston, Ipswich IP9 1DU* Tel (01473) 780259

CARTER, Canon Michael John. b 32. St Alb Minl Tr Scheme 81. **d** 84 **p** 85. NSM Radlett *St Alb* 84-88; Chapl SW Herts HA 88-94; Chapl Watford Gen Hosp 88-94; Lic to Offic *St Alb* 88-99; Chapl Mt Vernon and Watford Hosps NHS Trust 94-99; Bp's Adv for Hosp Chapl *St Alb* 95-99; Hon Can St Alb 96-99; rtd 99; Perm to Offic *St Alb* from 99; Hon Chapl Peace Hospice Watford from 99. *4 Field View Rise, Bricket Wood, St Albans AL2 3RT* Tel (01923) 279870 E-mail mail@mjcarter.com

CARTER, Michael William. b 33. Newland Park Teacher Tr Coll TCert56. Dioc OLM tr scheme 98. **d** 01 **p** 02. OLM Lingfield and Crowhurst *S'wark* 01-04; rtd 04; Perm to Offic *S'wark* from 04. *Redwood House, 76 Godstone Road, Lingfield RH7 6BT* Tel (01342) 833843

CARTER, Nicholas Adrian. b 47. Ripon Hall Ox 71. **d** 74 **p** 75. C Sowerby *Wakef* 74-79; V Hanging Heaton 79-83; CF 83-86; V Elton All SS *Man* 86-90; C Milton *Win* 90-94; P-in-c Boscombe St Andr 94-00; V 00-09; rtd 09; TV Winchcombe *Glouc* from 09. *The Vicarage, Church Road, Alderton, Tewkesbury GL20 8NR* Tel (01242) 620238 E-mail cdevildom@aol.com

CARTER, Nigel John. b 53. Bolton Inst of Educn CertEd89. Sarum & Wells Th Coll 91. **d** 93 **p** 94. C Burntwood *Lich* 93-96; V Bentley 96-04; RD Wolverhampton 00-02; V Walsall Wood from 04. *The Vicarage, 2 St John's Close, Walsall Wood, Walsall WS9 9NH* Tel (01543) 360558 or 372284 E-mail nigel.carter@02.co.uk

CARTER, Noel William. b 53. Birm Univ BSc75 Bris Univ CertEd76 Nottm Univ BSc83. Linc Th Coll. **d** 83 **p** 84. C Penrith w Newton Reigny and Plumpton Wall *Carl* 83-86; C Barrow St Matt 86-87; V Netherton 87-91; TR Penrith w Newton Reigny and Plumpton Wall 91-97; P-in-c Jersey St Brelade *Win* 97-98; R 98-01; Vice-Dean Jersey 00-01; P-in-c Brymbo and Southsea *St As* 05-07; P-in-c Brymbo, Southsea and Tanyfron from 07; AD Minera from 08. *The Bryn, Bryn Road, Moss, Wrexham LL11 6EL*

CARTER, Canon Norman. b 23. Leeds Univ BSc48. Coll of Resurr Mirfield 48. **d** 50 **p** 51. C Liv Our Lady and St Nic w St Anne 50-54; C Orford St Marg 54-56; V 56-71; PC Knotty Ash H Spirit 71-74; V Dovecot 74-83; RD W Derby 78-83; Hon Can Liv Cathl 82-88; V Formby St Pet 83-88; rtd 88; Perm to Offic *Liv* from 88. *34 Granby Close, Southport PR9 9QG* Tel (01704) 232821

CARTER, Canon Paul Brian. b 22. AKC49. **d** 50 **p** 51. C Scarborough St Columba *York* 50-53; C Pocklington w Yapham-cum-Meltonby, Owsthorpe etc 53-55; V Kingston upon Hull St Jo Newington 55-60; R Ainderby Steeple and Scruton *Ripon* 60-79; P-in-c Yafforth 76-79; R Ainderby Steeple w Yafforth and Scruton 79-87; Hon Can Ripon Cathl 86-87; rtd 87; Perm to Offic *Ripon* 87-09. *Cliffe Cottage, West Tanfield, Ripon HG4 5JR* Tel (01677) 470203

CARTER, Paul Joseph. b 67. St Chad's Coll Dur BA88. St Steph Ho Ox 89. **d** 91 **p** 92. C Ipswich All Hallows *St E* 91; C Newmarket St Mary w Exning St Agnes 91-94; V Thorpe-le-Soken *Chelmsf* 94-04; V Ipswich St Bart *St E* from 04. *St Bartholomew's Vicarage, Newton Road, Ipswich IP3 8HQ* Tel (01473) 727441 E-mail frpaul@stbarts.freeserve.co.uk

CARTER, Paul Mark. b 56. BA78 MA90 Cranfield Univ MBA95. Ridley Hall Cam 79. **d** 81 **p** 82. C Kidsgrove *Lich* 81-84; CF 84-00; Asst P Vancouver St Phil Canada 00-03. *1655 West 41st Avenue, Vancouver BC V6M 1X9, Canada* Tel (001) (604) 222 4497 E-mail paulcarter@acinw.org

CARTER, Paul Rowley. b 45. Lon Univ BD69 Lon Bible Coll ALBC69 Southn Univ PGCE70. Trin Coll Bris. **d** 91 **p** 92. C Penkridge *Lich* 91-96; V Blackb Sav 96-01; R Elmdon St Nic *Birm* 01-11; rtd 11; Perm to Offic *Birm* from 11. *4 Goods Station Lane, Penkridge, Stafford ST19 5AU* E-mail paul@tworevs.co.uk

CARTER, Richard Anthony. b 59. Univ of Wales (Abth) BA80 Melbourne Coll of Div BD94 Leeds Univ MA02 Lon Inst of Educn PGCE87. Bp Patteson Th Coll (Solomon Is) 90. **d** 91 **p** 92. Asst Bp Patteson Th Coll 91-00; Miss and Tr Co-ord Melanesian Brotherhood 00-05; Chapl 94-00 and 02-05; Perm to Offic *Lon* 00-06; C St Martin-in-the-Fields from 06. *Flat 1, 6 St Martin's Place, London WC2N 4JJ* Tel (020) 7766 1100 Fax 7839 5163 E-mail richard.carter@smitf.org

CARTER, Richard William. b 75. Newc Univ BSc96. Westcott Ho Cam 04. **d** 07 **p** 08. C Llaneddir DC w Llangynhafal, Llanychan etc *St As* 07-10; P-in-c 10; P-in-c Clocaenog and Gyffylliog from 10; P-in-c Llanfair DC, Derwen, Llanelidan and Efenechtyd from 10. *The Vicarage, Bron y Clwyd, Llanfair Dyffryn Clwyd,*

CARTER, Robert Desmond. b 35. Cranmer Hall Dur 62. **d** 65 **p** 66. C Otley *Bradf* 65-69; C Keighley 69-73; V Cowling 73-00; rtd 00; Perm to Offic *Bradf* from 00. *1 Quincy Close, Eccleshill, Bradford BD2 2EP* Tel (01274) 638385

CARTER, Robert Edward. b 44. Univ of Wales (Ban) BSc66. St Jo Coll Nottm 79. **d** 81 **p** 82. C Caverswall *Lich* 81-86; V Biddulph 86-94; V Wolverhampton St Jude 94-10; rtd 11; Perm to Offic *Lich* from 11. *17 The Spinney, Wolverhampton WV3 9HE*

CARTER, Robert Thomas. b 49. Moore Th Coll Sydney 72 Ridley Coll Melbourne ThL75. **d** 75 **p** 76. C Traralgon St Jas Australia 75-76; P-in-c Endeavour Hills St Matt 77-79; V 80-84; Assoc Min Kew St Hilary 85-91; V Blackburn N St Alfred 92-00; C Fisherton Anger *Sarum* 00-02; Australia from 02. *224 Maroondah Highway, Croydon, Melbourne Vic 3136, Australia*

CARTER, Robin. b 46. Cam Univ MSt02. Chich Th Coll 71. **d** 74 **p** 75. C Wortley de Leeds *Ripon* 74-76; C Hutton *Chelmsf* 76-78; C Wickford 78-81; TV Wickford and Runwell 81-83; Chapl HM Pris Leeds 83-85; Chapl HM Pris Reading 85-89; Chapl HM YOI Huntercombe and Finnamore 85-89; Chapl HM YOI Finnamore Wood Camp 86-89; Gov 5, Hd of Operations, HM Pris Channings Wood 89-94; Gov 4, Hd of Operations/Régime and Throughcare, HM Pris Woodhill 94-99; Gov HM Pris E Sutton Park 99-05; Sen Operational Pris Service Manager 05-08; Chapl Costa Blanca *Eur* from 08. *Ptl 3 1°G, Edif El Valle, Calle Nou de Octubre 2, 03520 Polop, Spain* Tel (0034) 695 321 866 E-mail robincarter@yahoo.com

CARTER, Ronald George. b 31. Leeds Univ BA58. Coll of Resurr Mirfield 58. **d** 60 **p** 61. C Wigan St Anne *Liv* 60-63; Prec Wakef Cathl 63-66; V Woodhall *Bradf* 66-77; Chapl Qu Marg Sch Escrick Park 77-83; Min Can, Prec and Sacr Pet Cathl 83-88; R Upper St Leonards St Jo *Chich* 88-94; rtd 94; Perm to Offic *York* from 95. *5 Greenwich Close, York YO30 5WN* Tel (01904) 610237

CARTER, Russell James Wigney. b 29. Chich Th Coll 80. **d** 82 **p** 83. C Aldwick *Chich* 82-86; R Buxted and Hadlow Down 86-90; rtd 90; Perm to Offic *Chich* from 90. *6 Lucerne Court, Aldwick, Bognor Regis PO21 4XL* Tel (01243) 862858

CARTER, Samuel. b 49. St Jo Coll Dur BA71. Cranmer Hall Dur 73. **d** 74 **p** 75. C Kingswinford St Mary *Lich* 74-77; C Shrewsbury H Cross 77-84; V Normacot 84-94. *Address withheld by request*

CARTER, Sarah Helen Buchanan. See GORTON, Sarah Helen Buchanan

CARTER, Stanley Reginald. b 24. St Jo Coll Dur BA49. **d** 50 **p** 51. C Stoughton *Guildf* 50-53; C Bucknall and Bagnall *Lich* 53-56; R Salford St Matthias w St Simon *Man* 56-62; V Highbury New Park St Aug *Lon* 62-69; V Sneinton St Chris w St Phil *S'well* 69-89; rtd 89; Perm to Offic *S'well* from 89. *31 Pateley Road, Nottingham NG3 5QF* Tel 0115-953 2122 E-mail stan.carter@dunelm.org.uk

CARTER, Canon Stephen. b 56. Univ of Wales (Lamp) BA77 Southn Univ BTh81. Sarum & Wells Th Coll 78. **d** 81 **p** 82. C Halstead St Andr w H Trin and Greenstead Green *Chelmsf* 81-84; C Loughton St Jo 84-89; V N Shoebury 89-95; R Lexden 95-09; RD Colchester 01-06; V Maldon All SS w St Pet from 09; Hon Can Chelmsf Cathl from 07. *All Saints' Vicarage, Church Walk, Maldon CM9 4PY* Tel (01621) 854179 E-mail revscarter@googlemail.com

CARTER, Stephen Howard. b 47. City Univ BSc72. St Jo Coll Nottm 83. **d** 85 **p** 86. C Hellesdon *Nor* 85-88; Chapl Asst Birm Children's Hosp 88-91; Chapl Asst Birm Maternity Hosp 88-91; TV Tettenhall Wood *Lich* 91-98; Chapl Compton Hospice 91-98; P-in-c Coalbrookdale, Iron-Bridge and Lt Wenlock *Heref* 98-00; R 00-07; Asst Dioc Co-ord for Evang 00-01; P-in-c Netherton St Andr *Worc* 07-08; V from 08; P-in-c Darby End 07-08; V from 08; RD Dudley from 10. *St Andrew's Vicarage, Highbridge Road, Netherton, Dudley DY2 0HT* Tel and fax (01384) 257097 E-mail stevecarter@fastmail.net

CARTER, Stephen Paul. b 55. Cartrefle Coll of Educn CertEd76. Trin Coll Bris BA88. **d** 98 **p** 99. Dn-in-c Montevideo H Spirit Uruguay 99-99; P-in-c 00-04; V Dalston w Cumdivock, Raughton Head and Wreay *Carl* from 04. *The Vicarage, Townhead Road, Dalston, Carlisle CA5 7JF* Tel and fax (01228) 710215 E-mail spc55@tiscali.co.uk

CARTER, Stuart Conway. b 58. Lon Bible Coll 81 St Jo Coll Nottm 90. **d** 92 **p** 93. C Birm St Luke 92-96; C The Quinton 96-10; V Castle Bromwich St Clem from 10. *The Vicarage, Lanchester Way, Castle Bromwich, Birmingham B36 9JG* Tel 0121-281 6118 E-mail stuwecarter@btinternet.com

CARTER, Terence John. b 31. K Coll Lon BD57 AKC57 Lon Univ BA68 PGCE69. **d** 58 **p** 59. C Winchmore Hill H Trin *Lon* 58-60; PV S'wark Cathl 60-63; Sacr S'wark Cathl 60-61; Succ S'wark Cathl 61-63; R Ockham w Hatchford *Guildf* 63-69; Lic to

Ruthin LL15 2SB Tel (01824) 703867 Mobile 07769-727985 E-mail reverendcarter@gmail.com

Offic *S'wark* 69-78 and *Portsm* 78-82; Perm to Offic *Portsm* from 82; rtd 91. *15 Balliol Road, Portsmouth PO2 7PP* Tel (023) 9269 9167 Mobile 07811-474020
E-mail terence.carter1@ntlworld.com

CARTER, Timothy Stephen. b 76. Somerville Coll Ox MEng99. St Jo Coll Nottm 06. **d** 08 **p** 09. C Hanley H Ev *Lich* from 08. *23 Mereside Close, Stoke-on-Trent ST1 5GH* Tel (01782) 208735 Mobile 07772-956146 E-mail tim@carterclan.me.uk

CARTER, Mrs Wendy Elise Grace. b 46. Battersea Coll of Educn TCert67. Qu Coll Birm 01. **d** 04 **p** 05. C Kingshurst *Birm* 04-07; P-in-c High Wych and Gilston w Eastwick *St Alb* 07-10; rtd 10. *45 Woodside Way, Solihull B91 1HH* Tel 07753-676973 (mobile) E-mail revwendy@sky.com

CARTLEDGE, Margery. See TOLLER, Elizabeth Margery

CARTLEDGE, Mark John. b 62. Lon Bible Coll BA85 Univ of Wales PhD00. Oak Hill Th Coll MPhil89. **d** 88 **p** 89. C Formby H Trin *Liv* 88-91; Miss Partner CMS 91-93; Nigeria 91-93; Chapl Liv Univ 93-98; Chapl and Tutor St Jo Coll Dur 98-03; Lect Univ of Wales (Lamp) 03-06; Sen Lect Th Birm Univ from 08. *Department of Theology, University of Birmingham, Edgbaston, Birmingham B15 2TT* Tel 0121-414 7512
E-mail m.j.cartledge@bham.ac.uk

CARTMELL, Canon Richard Peter Watkinson. b 43. Cranmer Hall Dur 77. **d** 79 **p** 80. C Whittle-le-Woods *Blackb* 79-85; V Lower Darwen St Jas 85-03; RD Darwen 91-96; P-in-c S Shore H Trin 03-08; Hon Can Blackb Cathl 98-08; rtd 08; Perm to Offic *Blackb* from 08. *4 Salwick Avenue, Blackpool FY2 9BT* Tel (01253) 590083

CARTMILL, Canon Ralph Arthur. b 40. St Jo Coll Dur BA62 Em Coll Cam MA64. Ridley Hall Cam 63. **d** 65 **p** 66. C Dukinfield St Jo *Ches* 65-68; C Wilmslow 68-69; Warden Walton Youth Cen Liv 69-70; Asst Master Aylesbury Gr Sch 70-74; Perm to Offic *Ox* 72-74; V Terriers 74-85; P-in-c Chinnor w Emmington and Sydenham 85-86; R Chinnor w Emmington and Sydenham etc 86-98; Hon Can Ch 97-98; rtd 98; Perm to Offic *Nor* from 00. *6 Longview Close, Snettisham, King's Lynn PE31 7RD* Tel (01485) 543357

CARTWRIGHT, Alan John. b 44. Liv Univ BEng66 Birm Univ MSc68 Warwick Univ PhD95 CEng72 MIMechE72. WMMTC 04. **d** 07 **p** 08. OLM Rugby W *Cov* from 07. *39 Buchanan Road, Rugby CV22 6AZ* Tel (01788) 574071 Mobile 07981-667534 E-mail alan@stmatthews.org.uk

CARTWRIGHT, Mrs Amanda Jane. b 58. St Jo Coll Nottm 00. **d** 02 **p** 03. C Beeston *S'well* 02-07; P-in-c Bilborough St Jo from 07; P-in-c Bilborough w Strelley from 07. *St John's Vicarage, Graylands Road, Nottingham NG8 4FD* Tel 0115-854 3628 E-mail revdmand@hotmail.com

CARTWRIGHT, Julia Ann. b 58. Nottm Univ BA80. Linc Th Coll 84. **dss** 86 **d** 87 **p** 94. Asst Chapl HM Pris Morton Hall 85-90; Linc St Jo 86-88; Hon C 87-88; Hon C Bardney 88-97; Chapl Linc Co Hosp 90-93; Chapl St Geo Hosp Linc 90-93; Chapl Linc Distr Health Services and Hosps NHS Trust 93-97; Chapl S Bucks NHS Trust 97-04; Lic to Offic *Ox* 97-04; Chapl S Warks Combined Care NHS Trust from 04. *St Michael's Hospital, St Michael's Road, Warwick CV34 5QW* Tel (01926) 496241 *or* 406789 Fax 406700

CARTWRIGHT, Michael. See CARTWRIGHT, William Michael

CARTWRIGHT, Michael John. b 42. Qu Coll Birm 67. **d** 70 **p** 71. C Astwood Bank w Crabbs Cross *Worc* 70-75; P-in-c Worc St Mich 75-77; V Stockton St Paul *Dur* 77-87; V Market Rasen *Linc* from 87; R Linwood from 87; V Legsby from 87; RD W Wold 89-01; R Wickenby Gp 95-00; V Lissington from 00. *The Vicarage, 13 Lady Frances Drive, Market Rasen LN8 3JJ* Tel (01673) 843424

CARTWRIGHT, Paul. b 71. Leeds Metrop Univ BA99 Huddersfield Univ PGCE02 Leeds Univ BA08. Coll of Resurr Mirfield 06. **d** 08 **p** 09. C Athersley *Wakef* from 08; C Carlton from 10. *Priory House, 24 Kirkland Gardens, Barnsley S71 2GD* Tel (01226) 285209 Mobile 07852-174303
E-mail fr.paul.cartwright@gmail.com

CARTWRIGHT, Samuel. b 27. Cuddesdon Coll 71. **d** 72 **p** 72. C Rochdale *Man* 72-76; V Roundthorn 76-83; V Ashton Ch Ch 83-93; rtd 93; Perm to Offic *Derby* from 93. *8 Wentworth Avenue, Walton, Chesterfield S40 3JB* Tel (01246) 232252

CARTWRIGHT, Sidney Victor. b 22. Launde Abbey 73. **d** 74 **p** 75. C Braunstone *Leic* 74-78; P-in-c Arnesby w Shearsby 78-86; R Arnesby w Shearsby and Bruntingthorpe 86-87; rtd 87; Perm to Offic *Leic* and *Pet* from 87. *32 Northleigh Grove, Market Harborough LE16 9QX* Tel (01858) 463915

CARTWRIGHT, Simon John. b 71. R Holloway Coll Lon BA93 Sheff Univ MA95. St Jo Coll Nottm MTh05. **d** 06 **p** 07. C Ward End w Bordesley Green *Birm* from 06. *The Vicarage, St Margarets Avenue, Birmingham B8 2BH* Tel 0121-327 9089 Mobile 07720-769631 E-mail simon@ccbl.org.uk

CARTWRIGHT, William Michael. b 44. Birm Univ CertEd67. Coll of Resurr Mirfield 83. **d** 83 **p** 84. Hd Master Chacombe Sch 83-85; Hon C Middleton Cheney w Chacombe *Pet* 83-85; Hd Master Chacombe Sch Banbury 83-85; C Kettering SS Pet and

Paul 85-86; Perm to Offic 86-88; Chapl Northaw Prep Sch Win 89-92; P-in-c Altarnon w Bolventor, Laneast and St Clether *Truro* 92-97; V Treverbyn 97-01; V Bempton w Flamborough, Reighton w Speeton *York* 01-03; V Ampleforth w Oswaldkirk, Gilling E etc 03-09; rtd 09; P-in-c Barningham w Matlaske w Baconsthorpe etc *Nor* from 09. *The Rectory, The Street, Matlaske, Norwich NR11 7AQ* Tel (01263) 577455
E-mail williamcartwright606@btinternet.com

CARUANA, Mrs Rosemary Anne. b 38. St Alb Minl Tr Scheme 81. **dss** 84 **d** 87 **p** 94. Hertford St Andr *St Alb* 84-87; Par Dn Hertingfordbury 87-94; C 94-98; P-in-c 98-05; rtd 05. *36 Holly Croft, Hertford SG14 2DR* Tel (01992) 306427 Mobile 07769-658756 E-mail r.caruana@ntlworld.com

CARVER, Miss Elizabeth Ann. b 36. Bp Otter Coll BA00 Chich Univ MA09 ACIB73. **d** 99. NSM Littlehampton and Wick *Chich* from 99. *13 Hearnfield Road, Littlehampton BN17 7PR* Tel (01903) 713169

CARVETH, Mrs Marlene. b 51. Ex Univ BA07. SWMTC 04. **d** 07 **p** 08. NSM Camborne *Truro* from 07. *Trelowarren, 5 Rosevale Crescent, Camborne TR14 7LU* Tel (01209) 713175 E-mail roseyvale@tiscali.co.uk

CARVOSSO, John Charles. b 45. ACA71 FCA79. Oak Hill Th Coll 75. **d** 78 **p** 79. C Chelsea St Jo w St Andr *Lon* 78-81; Chapl RAF 81-84; P-in-c Tawstock *Ex* 84-85; TV Newport, Bishops Tawton and Tawstock 85-96; TV Newton Tracey, Horwood, Alverdiscott etc 96-11; RD Torrington 97-02; rtd 11. *45 Trafalgar Drive, Torrington EX38 7AD* Tel 07507-369127 (mobile) E-mail revjcc@gmail.com

CASE, Preb Catherine Margaret. b 44. Ripon Coll Cuddesdon 86. **d** 88 **p** 94. C Blurton *Lich* 88-92; TD Hanley H Ev and Min to Hanley Care Agencies 92-94; P-in-c Wrockwardine Wood 95-98; R 98-00; V Gnosall 00-06; V Gnosall and Moreton 06-07; Preb Lich Cathl 02-07; rtd 07; Perm to Offic *Lich* 07-11; C Mow Cop from 11. *2 Fulmar Place, Stoke-on-Trent ST3 7QF* Tel (01782) 399291

CASE, Clive Anthony. b 70. St Andr Univ MTheol93 Surrey Univ BA05 St Jo Coll Dur PGCE94. STETS 02. **d** 05 **p** 06. NSM Epsom St Martin *Guildf* 05-11; Asst Chapl Epsom Coll 05-07; Chapl St Jo Sch Leatherhead 08-11; Sen Chapl Charterhouse Sch Godalming from 11. *Charterhouse School, Brook Hall, Charterhouse, Godalming GU7 2DX* Tel (01483) 291741 Mobile 07801-288943 E-mail cac@charterhouse.org.uk

CASEBOW, Ronald Philip. b 31. Roch Th Coll 59. **d** 61 **p** 62. C Southgate Ch Ch *Lon* 61-64; C Oseney Crescent St Luke w Camden Square St Paul 64-70; Warden St Paul's Ho Student Hostel 64-70; V Colchester St Steph *Chelmsf* 70-74; V Burnham 74-89; rtd 89; Perm to Offic *Nor* from 95. *The Priory, Priory Road, Palgrave, Diss IP22 1AJ* Tel (01379) 651804

CASEY, Christopher Noel. b 61. Open Univ BA95. St Jo Coll Nottm BA01. **d** 01 **p** 02. C Penrith w Newton Reigny and Plumpton Wall *Carl* 01-06; P-in-c Mirehouse from 06. *The Vicarage, Hollins Close, Whitehaven CA28 8EX* Tel (01946) 693565 E-mail kc.family@btopenworld.com

CASH, Simon Andrew. b 62. St Jo Coll Nottm 99. **d** 01 **p** 02. C Aston cum Aughton w Swallownest and Ulley *Sheff* 01-04; P-in-c Worksop St Anne *S'well* from 04; P-in-c Norton Cuckney from 05. *The Vicarage, 11 Poplar Close, Worksop S80 3BZ* Tel (01909) 472069 E-mail s.cash@freenet.co.uk

CASHEL, Dean of. See KNOWLES, The Very Revd Philip John

CASHEL, WATERFORD AND LISMORE, Archdeacon of. See MURRAY, The Ven John Grainger

CASHEL, WATERFORD, LISMORE, OSSORY, FERNS AND LEIGHLIN, Bishop of. See BURROWS, The Rt Revd Michael Andrew James

CASIOT, David John. b 39. St Pet Coll Ox BA63 MA67. Clifton Th Coll 63. **d** 65 **p** 66. C Drypool St Columba w St Andr and St Pet *York* 65-67; C Barking St Marg *Chelmsf* 67-71; R Whalley Range St Edm *Man* 71-84; V Wandsworth St Mich *S'wark* 84-00; Perm to Offic *Roch* from 00; rtd 04. *52 High Street, Otford, Sevenoaks TN14 5PQ* Tel (01959) 522588
E-mail david@oakside.idps.co.uk

CASON, Preb Ronald Arthur. b 28. Kelham Th Coll 48. **d** 53 **p** 54. C Fenton *Lich* 53-56; V Brereton 56-63; V Hugglescote w Donington *Leic* 63-67; R Blakenall Heath *Lich* 67-74; R Stoke upon Trent 74-80; Preb Lich Cathl 75-93; RD Stoke 78-88; TR Stoke-upon-Trent 80-91; Lect Tettenhall Par 91-93; rtd 93; Perm to Offic *Lich* 93-00. *Talbot House Nursing Home, 28-30 Talbot Street, Rugeley WS15 2EG* Tel (01889) 570527

CASSAM, Victor Reginald. b 33. Chich Univ BA05. Chich Th Coll 59. **d** 62 **p** 63. C Portsea St Jo Rudmore *Portsm* 62-64; C W Leigh CD 64-66; C Torquay St Martin Barton *Ex* 66-69; C Stanmer w Falmer and Moulsecoomb *Chich* 69-73; P-in-c Catsfield 73-76; R Catsfield and Crowhurst 76-81; R Selsey 81-01; RD Chich 96-01; rtd 01; Perm to Offic *Chich* and *Portsm* from 01. *195 Oving Road, Chichester PO19 7ER* Tel and fax (01243) 783998 Mobile 07976-757451
E-mail vrc@vicas.demon.co.uk

CASSELTON, John Charles. b 43. Univ of Wales (Swansea) MA95. Oak Hill Th Coll 64. **d** 68 **p** 69. C Upton *Ex* 68-73; C

Braintree *Chelmsf* 73-80; V Ipswich St Jo *St E* 80-92; RD Ipswich 86-92; Chapl St Clem Hosp Ipswich 92-98; Chapl St Eliz Hospice Ipswich 92-00; Dir Inspire Chr Counselling from 00; Perm to Offic *St E* from 00. *Rose Cottage, 41 North Hill Road, Ipswich IP4 2PN* Tel (01473) 401638
E-mail inspire.ipswich@btclick.com

CASSIDY, Brian Ross. b 31. Cape Town Univ. St Bede's Coll Umtata 88. **d** 89 **p** 91. S Africa 89-92; C Lymington *Win* 92-93; P-in-c Hyde Common 93-96; P-in-c Ellingham and Harbridge and Ibsley 95-96; V Ellingham and Harbridge and Hyde w Ibsley 96-03; rtd 03. *The Vicarage, Hyde, Fordingbridge SP6 2QJ* Tel (01425) 653216 E-mail cassidy@btinternet.com

✠CASSIDY, The Rt Revd George Henry. b 42. QUB BSc65 Lon Univ MPhil67. Oak Hill Th Coll 70. **d** 72 **p** 73 **c** 99. C Clifton Ch Ch w Em *Bris* 72-75; V Sea Mills 75-82; V Portman Square St Paul *Lon* 82-87; Adn Lon and Can Res St Paul's Cathl 87-99; P-in-c St Ethelburga Bishopgate 89-91; Bp S'well and Nottm 99-09; rtd 09; Hon Asst Bp B & W from 10. *Darch House, 17 St Andrew's Road, Stogursey, Bridgwater TA5 1TE* Tel (01278) 732625
E-mail georgecassidy123@btinternet.com

CASSIDY, Herbert. b 35. TCD BA57 MA65. CITC 58. **d** 58 **p** 59. C Belfast H Trin *Conn* 58-60; C Londonderry Ch Ch *D & R* 60-62; I Aghavilly w Derrynoose *Arm* 62-65; Hon V Choral Arm Cathl 63-85; C Portadown St Columba 65-67; I 67-85; Dean Kilmore *K, E & A* 85-89; I Kilmore w Ballintemple 85-86; I Kilmore w Ballintemple, Kildallan etc 86-89; Dir of Ords 89; Dean Arm and Keeper of Public Lib 89-06; rtd 06; Hon Sec Gen Syn from 90. *2 Kilmore Meadows, Kilmore, Armagh BT61 8PA* Tel (028) 3887 0825 Mobile 07759-323733
E-mail herbieandanncassidy@hotmail.co.uk

CASSIDY, Ian David. b 59. NOC 94. **d** 97 **p** 98. NSM Everton St Geo *Liv* 97-07; NSM Liv N Deanery 07-11; NSM Liv All SS from 11. *79 Gilroy Road, Liverpool L6 6BG* Tel 0151-263 9751 Mobile 0780-1933654

CASSIDY, Canon Joseph Patrick. b 54. Concordia Univ Montreal BA76 Detroit Univ MA80 Toronto Univ STB86 MDiv86 St Paul Univ Ottawa LTh89 DTh95 Ottawa Univ PhD95 FRSA. Regis Coll Toronto 82. **d** 85 **p** 86. Canada 85-96; NSM Laverstock *Sarum* 96-97; NSM Salisbury St Martin 96-97; Prin St Chad's Coll Dur from 97; Hon Can Dur Cathl from 01. *St Chad's College, University of Durham, 18 North Bailey, Durham DH1 3RH* Tel 0191-334 3345 *or* 384 7317 Fax 334 3371 E-mail j.p.cassidy@durham.ac.uk

CASSIDY, Patrick Nigel. b 40. TCD BA63 MA66. Sarum Th Coll 64. **d** 66 **p** 67. C Heaton St Barn *Bradf* 66-68; Asst Chapl Brussels *Eur* 68-70; Chapl SW France 70-72; V Oseney Crescent St Luke w Camden Square St Paul *Lon* 72-83; Chapl Strasbourg w Stuttgart and Heidelberg *Eur* 83-84; Perm to Offic *Chich* 86-90; Chapl Marseille w Aix-en-Provence *Eur* 90-05; Hon Chapl Miss to Seafarers 90-05; rtd 05; Perm to Offic *Eur* from 05. *73 La Canebière (Appt 83), 13001 Marseille, France* Tel (0033) 4 91 90 18 81

CASSIDY, Canon Ronald. b 43. Lon Univ BD66 Man Univ MPhil85 Liv Univ PhD00. Tyndale Hall Bris 63. **d** 68 **p** 69. C Kirkdale St Lawr *Liv* 68-70; C Bolton Em *Man* 70-74; V Roughtown 74-89; R Denton St Lawr 89-07; AD Ashton-under-Lyne 97-03; Hon Can Man Cathl 02-07; rtd 07; Perm to Offic *Man* from 07. *19 Broomfields, Denton, Manchester M34 3TH* Tel 0161-320 6955 E-mail roncass 99@talktalk.net

CASSON, David Christopher. b 41. Qu Coll Cam BA64 MA68. Ridley Hall Cam 65. **d** 67 **p** 68. C Birm St Martin 67-72; C Luton St Mary *St Alb* 72-77; P-in-c Luton St Fran 77; V 77-84; V Richmond H Trin and Ch Ch *S'wark* 84-97; R Acle w Fishley, N Burlingham, Beighton w Moulton *Nor* 97-04; rtd 04; Perm to Offic *Nor* from 04. *70 The Street, Brundall, Norwich NR13 5LH* Tel (01603) 712092

CASSON, Canon James Stuart. b 32. Liv Univ BA54 Nottm Univ MPhil70. Ridley Hall Cam. **d** 61 **p** 62. C Eccleston Ch Ch *Liv* 61-64; C Littleover *Derby* 64-67; V Dearham *Carl* 67-76; V Holme Eden 76-98; RD Brampton 91-96; Hon Can Carl Cathl 93-98; P-in-c Croglin 93-98; rtd 98; Perm to Offic *Carl* from 01. *5 High Woodbank, Brisco, Carlisle CA4 0QR* Tel (01228) 525692

CASSWELL, David Oriel. b 52. Loughb Coll of Educn DipEd74 CQSW79. Oak Hill Th Coll 85. **d** 87 **p** 88. C Acomb St Steph *York* 87-91; Dep Chapl HM Pris Leeds 91-92; Chapl HM Pris Everthorpe 92; Chapl HM Pris Wolds 92-98; V Clifton *York* from 98. *Clifton Vicarage, Clifton, York YO30 6BH* Tel (01904) 655071 Fax 654796
E-mail david.casswell@cliftonparish.org.uk

CASSWELL, Peter Joyce. b 22. Trin Coll Cam BA48 MA50. Ridley Hall Cam 48. **d** 50 **p** 51. C Addiscombe St Mildred *Cant* 50-53; C-in-c New Addington CD 53-55; V New Addington 55-64; R Buckhurst Hill *Chelmsf* 64-78; Hon Can Chelmsf Cathl 75-78; Chapl Forest Gate Hosp Lon 64-78; R Lutterworth w Cotesbach *Leic* 78-90; R Guthlaxton II 89-90; rtd 90; Perm to Offic *Leic* from 90. *1 Spring Close, Lutterworth LE17 4DD* Tel (01455) 554197 *or* 282630

CASTER, John Forristall. b 71. Texas A&M Univ BA93. St Steph Ho Ox BTh05. **d** 05 **p** 06. C Hendon St Alphage *Lon* 05-09; TV Old St Pancras from 09. *St Mary's House, Eversholt Street, London NW1 1BN* Tel (020) 7267 8631

✠CASTLE, The Rt Revd Brian Colin. b 49. Lon Univ BA72 Ox Univ BA77 MA80 Birm Univ PhD89. Cuddesdon Coll 74. **d** 77 **p** 78 **c** 02. C Limpsfield and Titsey *S'wark* 77-81; USPG Zambia 81-84; Lect Ecum Inst WCC Geneva 84-85; V N Petherton w Northmoor Green *B & W* 85-92; Dir Past Studies and Vice-Prin Cuddesdon Coll 92-01; Suff Bp Tonbridge *Roch* from 02; Hon Can Roch Cathl from 02. *Bishop's Lodge, 48 St Botolph's Road, Sevenoaks TN13 3AG* Tel (01732) 456070 Fax 741449
E-mail bishop.tonbridge@rochester.anglican.org

CASTLE, Brian Stanley. b 47. Oak Hill Th Coll 70. **d** 73 **p** 74. C Barnsbury St Andr w St Thos and St Matthias *Lon* 73-76; C Lower Homerton St Paul 76-79; P-in-c Bethnal Green St Jas Less 79-82; V 82-98; V Tile Cross *Birm* 98-08; P-in-c Garretts Green 03-08; V Garretts Green and Tile Cross from 08; AD Coleshill from 06. *The Vicarage, Haywood Road, Birmingham B33 0LH* Tel and fax 0121-779 2739 Mobile 07710-251790
E-mail revbcastle@aol.com

CASTLE, John Arthur. b 61. G&C Coll Cam BA83 St Jo Coll Dur BA95. Aston Tr Scheme 90 Cranmer Hall Dur 92. **d** 95 **p** 96. C Southborough St Pet w Ch Ch and St Matt *Roch* 95-99; Miss Partner CMS 99-04; P-in-c Sandhurst *Ox* 04-10; R from 10. *The Rectory, 155 High Street, Sandhurst GU47 8HR* Tel (01252) 872168 E-mail rector@stmichaels-sandhurst.org.uk

CASTLE, Martin Roger. b 69. Leic Univ BA92 Liv Univ MCD95 St Edm Coll Cam BTh09. Ridley Hall Cam **d** 09 **p** 10. C Leic Martyrs from 09. *62 Ashleigh Road, Leicester LE3 0FB* Tel 0116-254 1341 E-mail curate.martin@martyrs.org.uk

CASTLE, Michael David. b 38. Wells Th Coll 69. **d** 71 **p** 72. C Acocks Green *Birm* 71-75; C Weoley Castle 76-78; V 78-08; rtd 08. *12 West Pathway, Birmingham B17 9DU* Tel 0121-427 2914

CASTLE, Phillip Stanley. b 43. **d** 97 **p** 98. OLM E Farnworth and Kearsley *Man* 97-09; OLM Farnworth, Kearsley and Stoneclough from 09. *73 Bradford Street, Farnworth, Bolton BL4 9JY* Tel (01204) 571439
E-mail phillip@stjohnsfarnworth.co.uk

CASTLE, Roger James. b 39. St Jo Coll Cam BA62 MA66. Clifton Th Coll 63. **d** 65 **p** 66. C Rushden w Newton Bromswold *Pet* 65-68; C Stapenhill w Cauldwell *Derby* 68-72; V Hayfield 72-89; R Coxheath, E Farleigh, Hunton, Linton etc *Roch* 89-04; Chapl Invicta Community Care NHS Trust 91-04; rtd 04; Perm to Offic *Bris* from 04. *10 College Park Drive, Bristol BS10 7AN* Tel 0117-950 7028

CASTLETON, David Miles. b 39. Oak Hill Th Coll 69. **d** 72 **p** 73. C Canonbury St Steph *Lon* 72-76; C Guildf St Sav w Stoke-next-Guildford 76-89; rtd 04. *15 Locks Ride, Ascot SL5 8RA*

CASTLETON, Mark Peter. b 82. Bath Spa Univ BA04 Cam Univ BTh09. Ridley Hall Cam 06. **d** 09 **p** 10. C Salisbury St Mark *Sarum* from 09. *4 St Joseph's Close, Bishopdown, Salisbury SP1 3FX* E-mail castletonmark@yahoo.co.uk

CASWELL, Brian John. b 47. St Chad's Coll Dur BA70. St Steph Ho Ox 75. **d** 77 **p** 78. C Brighton Resurr *Chich* 77-83; TV Crawley 83-90; TR Littlehampton and Wick from 90; Chapl Littlehampton Hosp 90-93; Chapl Worthing Priority Care NHS Trust from 93. *St Mary's Vicarage, 18 Church Street, Littlehampton BN17 5PX* Tel (01903) 724410 *or* 726875

CASWELL, Thomas Hubert. b 55. Aston Tr Scheme 90 Coll of Resurr Mirfield 92. **d** 94 **p** 95. C Sheff St Leon Norwood 94-97; P-in-c Sheff St Cecilia Parson Cross 97-04; V Masbrough from 04. *St Paul's Vicarage, 256 Kimberworth Road, Rotherham S61 1HG* Tel (01709) 557810

CATCHPOLE, Geoffrey Alan. b 53. AKC. Westcott Ho Cam 76. **d** 77 **p** 78. C Camberwell St Luke *S'wark* 77-80; C Dulwich St Barn 80-82; TV Canvey Is *Chelmsf* 82-87; Ind Chapl 83-87; P-in-c Bradwell on Sea 87-92; P-in-c St Lawrence 87-92; V Holland-on-Sea 92-00; P-in-c Witchford w Wentworth *Ely* 00-02; Adult Educn and Tr Officer 00-02; R Colchester St Mich Myland *Chelmsf* 02-07; rtd 07; Perm to Offic *Chelmsf* from 09. *Shobita's Ship, 21 Empire Road, Harwich CO12 3QA* Tel (01255) 508525 E-mail pole@pole97.fsnet.co.uk

CATCHPOLE, Guy St George. b 30. **d** 82 **p** 83. Kenya 82-89; C Woodford Wells *Chelmsf* 89-95; rtd 95; Perm to Offic *Cant* 95-08. *67 Trevor Drive, Allington, Maidstone ME16 0QW* Tel (01622) 761378

CATCHPOLE, Richard James Swinburne. b 65. St Steph Ho Ox 92. **d** 95 **p** 96. C Eastbourne St Andr *Chich* 95-98; C Eastbourne St Mary 98-00; C E Grinstead St Swithun 00-07. *23 Nineveh Shipyard, Arundel BN18 9SU* Tel 07951-427384 (mobile) E-mail rjscatchpole@hotmail.co.uk

CATCHPOLE, Roy. b 46. Sheff Univ MMinTheol95. St Jo Coll Nottm LTh74 ALCD74. **d** 74 **p** 75. C Rainham *Chelmsf* 74-76; C Hyson Green *S'well* 76-79; V Broxtowe 79-86; V Calverton 86-94; Hilfield Friary Dorchester 95-01; rtd 01; Perm to Offic *Sarum* from 06. *60 Gainsborough, Milborne Port, Sherborne DT9 5BB* Tel (01963) 250040 E-mail rev.catch@virgin.net

CATER, Lois May. b 37. S Dios Minl Tr Scheme 81. **dss** 84 **d** 87 **p** 94. Calne and Blackland *Sarum* 84-89; Hon Par Dn 87-89; Hon Par Dn Devizes St Jo w St Mary 89-94; Hon C 94-96; Hon TV Alderbury Team 96-01; Hon TV Clarendon 01-07. *18 St Margaret's Close, Calne SN11 0UQ* Tel (01249) 819432

CATERER, James Albert Leslie Blower. b 44. New Coll Ox BA67 MA81. Sarum & Wells Th Coll 79. **d** 81 **p** 82. C Cheltenham St Luke and St Jo *Glouc* 81-85; V Standish w Haresfield and Moreton Valence etc 85-96; P-in-c Glouc St Steph 96-09; rtd 09. *Copelands, 180 Stroud Road, Gloucester GL1 5JX* Tel and fax (01452) 524694 E-mail jimscicaterer@googlemail.com

CATHCART, Adrian James. *See* MATTHEWS, Adrian James

CATHERALL, Mark Leslie. b 64. Chich Th Coll BTh93. **d** 93 **p** 94. C Lancing w Coombes *Chich* 93-95; C Selsey 95-98; Chapl RN 98-04; V S Thornaby *York* from 04. *St Peter's Rectory, White House Road, Thornaby, Stockton-on-Tees TS17 0AJ* Tel (01642) 888403 E-mail frmark.catherall@ntlworld.com

CATHERINE JOY, Sister. *See* MOON, Sister Catherine Joy

CATHIE, Sean Bewley. b 43. Dur Univ BA67 Birkbeck Coll Lon MSc04. Cuddesdon Coll 67. **d** 69 **p** 70. C Kensal Rise St Martin *Lon* 69-73; C Paddington H Trin w St Paul 73-75; P-in-c Bridstow w Peterstow *Heref* 76-79; Hon C Westmr St Jas *Lon* 85-97; Hon C St Marylebone w H Trin 99-06; Hon C St Marylebone St Cypr 99-06; rtd 06. *22 Southwood Park, Southwood Lawn Road, London N6 5SG* Tel (020) 8350 4372 *or* tel and fax 8347 7050 E-mail scathie@waitrose.com

CATLEY, John Howard. b 37. AKC60. K Coll Lon 57 St Boniface Warminster 60. **d** 61 **p** 62. C Sowerby Bridge w Norland *Wakef* 61-64; C Almondbury 64-67; V Earl's Heaton 67-75; V Brownhill 75-86; V Morley St Pet w Churwell 86-92; V St Annes St Marg *Blackb* 92-98; RD Kirkham 94-98; rtd 98; Perm to Offic *Blackb* from 98. *Flat 6, Herne Hill Lodge, 598 Lytham Road, Blackpool FY4 1RB* Tel (01253) 408129

CATLEY, Marc. b 59. Liv Univ BA82 Lon Bible Coll BA85 Man Poly PGCE90. St Jo Coll Nottm MTh06. **d** 07 **p** 08. C E Green *Cov* 07-11; V Packwood w Hockley Heath *Birm* from 11. *The Vicarage, Nuthurst Lane, Hockley Heath, Solihull B94 5RP* Tel (01564) 783121 Mobile 07952-456846 E-mail marc.catley@yahoo.co.uk

CATLING, Michael David. b 56. Goldsmiths' Coll Lon CertEd77 DipEd84 Newc Univ MLitt06. Cranmer Hall Dur 88. **d** 90 **p** 91. C Cullercoats St Geo *Newc* 90-94; TV Glendale Gp 94-01; V Whittingham and Edlingham w Bolton Chapel 01-09; R Wigmore Abbey *Heref* from 09. *The Rectory, Dark Lane, Leintwardine, Craven Arms SY7 0LJ* Tel (01547) 540235 E-mail mikecat7@btinternet.com

CATLING, Canon Robert Mason. b 19. St Jo Coll Ox BA41 MA44. St Steph Ho Ox 41. **d** 43 **p** 44. C Falmouth All SS *Truro* 43-57; Lib Pusey Ho and Asst Chapl Univ Coll Ox 57-61; C Falmouth All SS 61-64; V Beckenham St Barn *Roch* 64-72; V Devoran *Truro* 72-87; Hon Can Truro Cathl 77-87; rtd 87; Perm to Offic *Ex* and *Truro* from 87. *Ground Floor Flat, 31 Cranford Avenue, Exmouth EX8 2QA* Tel (01395) 267896

CATO (*formerly* LEGGETT), Ms Vanessa Gisela. b 51. St Osyth Coll of Educn TCert75. Westcott Ho Cam 93. **d** 93 **p** 94. C Southchurch H Trin *Chelmsf* 93-97; R Orsett and Bulphan and Horndon on the Hill 97-03; Chapl Basildon and Thurrock Gen Hosps NHS Trust 99-03; P-in-c Sandridge *St Alb* from 03; Herts Area Children's Work Adv from 03. *The Vicarage, 2 Anson Close, Sandridge, St Albans AL4 9EN* Tel (01727) 866089 E-mail vicarsleonards03@btinternet.com

CATON, Philip Cooper. b 47. Oak Hill Th Coll 79. **d** 81 **p** 82. C Much Woolton *Liv* 81-85; TV Parr 85-98; V Birkdale St Jo from 98; rtd 11. *Cooper's Cottage, 23 Alma Road, Southport PR8 4AN* Tel (01704) 565785 E-mail p.caton@sky.com

CATTELL, The Ven Jack. b 15. Univ Coll Dur BA37 MA40 Lon Univ BD53. Sarum & Wells Th Coll 38. **d** 39 **p** 40. C Royston *Wakef* 39-41; Perm to Offic *Sarum* 41-42; CF (EC) 42-46; Lic to Offic *Ripon* 46-49; Chapl R Wanstead Sch 49-53; Bermuda 53-82; Adn Bermuda 61-82; Perm to Offic *Mon* 82-89. *39A Risca Road, Newport NP9 4HX* Tel (01633) 54529

CATTERALL, David Arnold. b 53. Lon Univ BSc74 ARCS74. Cranmer Hall Dur. **d** 78 **p** 79. C Swinton St Pet *Man* 78-81; C Wythenshawe St Martin 81-83; R Heaton Norris Ch w All SS 83-88; I Fanlobbus Union *C, C & R* 88-95; Can Cork and Ross Cathls 90-95; Warden Ch's Min of Healing in Ireland 95-02; I Templemichael w Clongish, Clooncumber etc *K, E & A* from 02. *Amberley, The Belfry, Co Longford, Republic of Ireland* Tel (00353) (43) 334 6442 E-mail djcatt@eircom.net

CATTERALL, Canon Janet Margaret. b 53. Univ of Wales (Ban) BA74. Cranmer Hall Dur 77. **dss** 81 **d** 87 **p** 90. Wythenshawe St Martin *Man* 81-83; Heaton Norris Ch w All SS 83-88; Par Dn 87-88; C Bandon Union *C, C & R* 88-89; Dioc Youth Adv (Cork) 89-94; Dioc Youth Chapl 94-95; I Drung w Castleterra, Larah and Lavey etc *K, E & A* 95-02; P-in-c Mostrim w Granard, Clonbroney, Killoe etc from 02; Preb Mulhuddart St Patr Cathl Dublin from 05. *Amberley, The Belfry, Co Longford, Republic of Ireland* Tel (00353) (43) 334 6442 E-mail djcatt@eircom.net

CATTERICK, Matthew John. b 68. W Sussex Inst of HE BA90. St Steph Ho Ox BTh95. **d** 95 **p** 96. C Colchester St Jas and St Paul w All SS etc *Chelmsf* 95-98; C Leic Resurr 98-99; TV 99-04; TR Wembley Park *Lon* from 04. *The Rectory, 319 Preston Road, Harrow HA3 0QQ* Tel (020) 8904 4062 E-mail matthew.catterick@gmail.com

CATTLE, David James. b 75. ACCA00 FCCA05. Trin Coll Bris BA06 MA07. **d** 07 **p** 08. C Firswood and Gorse Hill *Man* 07-10; TV Digswell and Panshanger *St Alb* from 11. *71 Haldens, Welwyn Garden City AL7 1DH* Tel (01707) 372316 Mobile 07891-148884 E-mail david cattle@hotmail.com

CATTLE, Canon Richard John. b 40. WMMTC 88. **d** 90 **p** 91. NSM Brixworth Deanery *Pet* 90-91; NSM Welford w Sibbertoft and Marston Trussell 91-92; V 92-97; Bp's Dioc Chapl 97-00; Dioc Sec 98-00; Can Pet Cathl 98-02; rtd 01; Perm to Offic *Pet* from 02; Dean's Asst from 05. *18 Minster Precincts, Peterborough PE1 1XX* Tel (01733) 209275 *or* 355315 Fax 355316 E-mail richard.cattle@peterborough-cathedral.org.uk

CATTLEY, Richard Melville. b 49. Trin Coll Bris. **d** 73 **p** 74. C Kendal St Thos *Carl* 73-77; Nat Sec Pathfinders CPAS 77-82; Exec Sec 82-85; V Dalton-in-Furness *Carl* 85-90; V Dulwich St Barn *S'wark* 90-99; Chapl Alleyn's Foundn Dulwich 90-99; V Milton Keynes *Ox* 99-05; AD Milton Keynes 01-05; V Dorking w Ranmore *Guildf* 05-10; rtd 11. *9 St Margaret's Road, Maidenhead SL6 5DZ*

CATTON, Canon Cedric Trevor. b 36. JP. Lambeth STh94. Wells Th Coll 70. **d** 72 **p** 73. C Solihull *Birm* 72-74; R Whepstead w Brockley *St E* 74-75; R Hawstead and Nowton w Stanningfield etc 74-79; Dioc Stewardship Adv 77-83; R Cockfield 79-83; V Exning St Martin w Landwade 83-99; Chapl Newmarket Gen Hosp 85-93; Chapl Mid Anglia Community Health NHS Trust 93-99; Hon Can St E Cathl 90-02; Dioc Par Resources and Stewardship Officer 99-02; Asst Can Past St E Cathl 02; Acting Can Past 03-05; rtd 02; Dioc Clergy Retirement Officer *St E* 02-10. *60 Sextons Meadows, Bury St Edmunds IP33 2SB* Tel and fax (01284) 749429 E-mail moretee@vicar1.freeserve.co.uk

CATTON, Stanley Charles. b 44. **d** 99 **p** 00. OLM Bermondsey St Jas w Ch Ch and St Crispin *S'wark* from 99. *4 Reverdy Road, London SE1 5QE* Tel (020) 7237 7703 *or* 7274 0913 E-mail stan@pat-catton.freeserve.co.uk

CAUDWELL, Juliet Lesley. *See* STRAW, Mrs Juliet Lesley

CAUNT, Mrs Margaret. b 55. Coll of Ripon & York St Jo MA97. NOC 93. **d** 97 **p** 98. NSM Brightside w Wincobank *Sheff* 97-00; C Ecclesfield 00-02; TV Gleadless 02-07; V Anston from 07. *The Vicarage, 17 Rackford Road, North Anston, Sheffield S25 4DE* Tel (01909) 563447 *or* 519459 E-mail caunt@sky.com

CAVAGAN, Raymond. b 35. Hull Univ MA86 PhD87. **d** 63 **p** 64. C Upper Holloway St Pet *Lon* 63-66; C Hurworth *Dur* 66-68; V New Shildon 68-76; V Toxteth Park St Mich *Liv* 76-77; P-in-c Toxteth Park St Andr Aigburth Road 76-77; V Toxteth Park St Mich w St Andr 78-88; V Stamfordham w Matfen *Newc* 88-05; Hon CF from 90; rtd 05; Perm to Offic *Ches* from 05. *1 Leys Road, Timperley, Altrincham WA14 5AT* Tel 0161-969 5603

CAVAGHAN, Dennis Edgar. b 45. Ex Univ MA99. St Jo Coll Nottm BTh74. **d** 74 **p** 75. C Hartford *Ches* 74-77; C Plymouth St Andr w St Paul and St Geo *Ex* 77-80; V Cofton w Starcross 80-88; P-in-c W Exe 88-93; Perm to Offic *B & W* 94-02; Hon C Taunton St Mary from 02. *Combe House, Corfe, Taunton TA3 7BU* Tel (01823) 421013 Mobile 07810-796025 E-mail dennis.cavaghan@btinternet.com

CAVALCANTI, Joabe Gomes. b 69. Federal Univ of Pernambuco BA97 Trin Coll Bris MA00. Nordeste Th Sem BA91. **d** 98 **p** 98. Perm to Offic *Bris* 99 and *S'wark* 01-05; Chapl St Sav and St Olave's Sch Newington *S'wark* 05-08; C Bermondsey St Hugh CD 05-08; V Mitcham St Barn from 08. *St Barnabas' Vicarage, 46 Thirsk Road, Mitcham CR4 2BD* Tel (020) 8648 2571 Mobile 07940-444241 E-mail joabec@gmail.com

CAVALIER, Mrs Sandra Jane. b 48. Guildf Dioc Min Course 98. **d** 00 **p** 01. OLM Guildf Ch Ch w St Martha-on-the-Hill 00-04; NSM Westborough 04-08; NSM Wrecclesham from 08. *107 Campbell Fields, Aldershot GU11 3TZ* Tel (01252) 325567 Mobile 07990-658445 E-mail revcav@hotmail.co.uk

CAVAN, Lawrence Noel. b 38. Trin Coll Bris 72. **d** 75 **p** 76. C Lurgan Ch the Redeemer *D & D* 75-78; C Chorleywood Ch Ch *St Alb* 78-82; I Durrus *C, C & R* 82-85; I Portarlington w Cloneyhurke and Lea *M & K* 85-90; TV Eston w Normanby *York* 90-03; rtd 03; Perm to Offic *Derby* from 05 and *Sheff* from 11. *22 Wentworth Road, Dronfield Woodhouse, Dronfield S18 8ZU* Tel (01246) 418814 E-mail thecavans@hotmail.com

CAVANAGH, Anthony James. b 49. Ushaw Coll Dur 72. **d** 79 **p** 80. In RC Ch 79-95; C Goole *Sheff* 99-01; TV Cullercoats St Geo *Newc* 01-06; V Billy Mill 06-09; V Marden w Preston Grange 06-09; P-in-c Shilbottle from 09; P-in-c Gosforth St Hugh from 11. *The Vicarage, 24 Hepple Way, Newcastle upon Tyne NE3 3HS* Tel 0191-285 8792 E-mail cavanaghtony@aol.com

CAVANAGH, Capt Kenneth Joseph. b 41. CA Tr Coll 60. d 77 p 77. CA from 64; Paraguay 70-83; P-in-c Gt w Lt Snoring *Nor* 83-85; R Gt w Lt Snoring w Kettlestone and Pensthorpe 85-88; R Glencarse *Bre* 88-94; CA Co-ord (Scotland/Ireland) & Regional Voc Adv 90-95; R Dundee St Luke 95-06; rtd 06. *PD Barranquets, Calle 38 Casa 18, 03779 Els Poblets (Alicante), Spain* E-mail kscavanagh@tiscali.co.uk

CAVANAGH, Lorraine Marie. b 46. Lucy Cavendish Coll Cam BA97 MA01 PhD03. Ridley Hall Cam 00. d 01 p 02. Perm to Offic *Ely* 01-03; Chapl Fitzw Coll Cam 03; Chapl Cardiff Univ 04-09; rtd 09. *Cae Hedd, Talycoed Lane, Llantilio Crossenny, Abergavenny NP7 8TL* Tel (01600) 780244

CAVANAGH, Michael Richard. b 49. Salford Univ MSc00. NOC 89. d 92 p 93. NSM Stalybridge H Trin and Ch Ch *Ches* 92-98; P-in-c Over Tabley and High Legh 98-03; V 03-10; P-in-c Kenmare w Sneem, Waterville etc *L & K* from 10. *St Patrick's Rectory, Kenmare, Co Kerry, Republic of Ireland* Tel (00353) (64) 664 8566 Mobile 87-160 6312 E-mail michael@balmoralconsulting.co.uk

CAVANAGH, Canon Peter Bernard. b 49. Sarum & Wells Th Coll 71. d 73 p 74. C Gt Crosby St Faith *Liv* 73-76; C Stanley 76-79; V Anfield St Columba 79-97; V Lancaster St Mary w St John and St Anne *Blackb* 97-09; P-in-c Scorton and Barnacre and Calder Vale 06-09; Hon Can Blackb Cathl 00-09; rtd 09; Perm to Offic *Blackb* from 09. *6 Lunesdale Court, Derwent Road, Lancaster LA1 3ET* Tel (01524) 62786 E-mail manderley552@btinternet.com

CAVE, Anthony Sidney. b 32. EMMTC. d 84 p 85. C Immingham *Linc* 84-88; V Keelby 88-89; V Riby 88-89; V Keelby w Riby and Aylesby 89-98; rtd 99; Perm to Offic *Linc* from 00. *Polruan, The Bungalow, Cherry Lane, Barrow-upon-Humber DN19 7AX* Tel (01469) 532350

CAVE, Bill. See CAVE-BROWNE-CAVE, Bernard James William

CAVE, Brian Malcolm. b 37. St Cath Soc Ox BA60 MA64. Oak Hill Th Coll. d 63 p 64. C Streatham Park St Alb *S'wark* 63-66; C Ruskin Park St Sav and St Matt 66-68; C Tunbridge Wells St Jas *Roch* 68-71; V Bootle St Leon *Liv* 71-75; Min St Mary w St John Bootle 71-75; Area Sec Leprosy Miss 75-81; V Hurst Green *Bradf* 81-82; P-in-c Mitton 81-82; V Hurst Green and Mitton 82-91; rtd 91; Perm to Offic *B & W* from 97. *63 Westway, Nailsea, Bristol BS48 2NB* Tel (01275) 854892

CAVE, Douglas Lionel. b 26. Lon Bible Coll 50 Lon Coll of Div 64. d 66 p 67. C Upper Holloway St Jo *Lon* 66-69; C Barking St Marg *Chelmsf* 69-73; V Blackb St Barn 73-81; Ind Chapl *Lon* 81-91; rtd 91; Perm to Offic *Lon* from 93. *8 Wood Rise, Pinner HA5 2JD* Tel (01895) 677426

CAVE, Mrs Margaret. b 62. Van Mildert Coll Dur BSc84. SEITE 07. d 10 p 11. NSM Kidbrooke St Jas *S'wark* from 10. *3 Hardy Road, London SE3 7NS* Tel (020) 8858 5964 Mobile 07740-859958 E-mail margaret.cave@btinternet.com

CAVE BERGQUIST, Julie Anastasia. b 59. St Jo Coll Dur BA80 Franciscan Univ Rome STL87. St Steph Ho Ox 85. d 87 p 89. Par Dn Kennington *Cant* 87-89; Chapl Trin Coll Cam 89-94; Chapl Westcott Ho Cam 94-97; C St Alb St Steph *St Alb* 98-02; P-in-c S Kensington H Trin w All SS *Lon* 02-06; Dir of Ords Two Cities Area 02-06; Nat Voc Adv and Selection Sec Min Division 06-10; Perm to Offic *Lon* from 06; Dioc Dir of Ords *Ox* from 10. *Diocesan Church House, North Hinksey Lane, Botley, Oxford OX2 0NB* Tel (01865) 208291

CAVE-BROWNE-CAVE, Bernard James William (Bill). b 54. Trin Hall Cam BA76 MA80 Bradf Univ MA90. Westcott Ho Cam 77. d 79 p 80. C Chesterton Gd Shep *Ely* 79-83; Chapl Lanc Univ 83-95; Chapl HM Pris Service from 95. *Chaplaincy HQ, Room 410, Abell House, John Islip Street, London SW1P 4LH* Tel (020) 7217 5685 Fax 7217 5090 E-mail bill@cave browne cave.freeserve.co.uk

CAVEEN, David Francis. b 44. Univ of Wales (Cardiff) BSc66 DipEd67. STETS 95. d 98 p 99. C Swaythling *Win* 98-02; V Lord's Hill 02-09; rtd 09. *35A Bassett Row, Southampton SO16 7FT* E-mail davidcaveen@tinyworld.co.uk

✠CAVELL, The Rt Revd John Kingsmill. b 16. Qu Coll Cam BA39 MA44. Wycliffe Hall Ox 39. d 40 p 41 c 72. C Folkestone H Trin *Cant* 40; C Addington 40-44; Lic to Offic *Ox* 45-52; Area Sec (Dio Ox) CMS 44-52; Dio Perm 44-49; Tr Officer 49-52; V Cheltenham Ch Ch *Glouc* 52-62; V Plymouth St Andr *Ex* 62-72; RD Plymouth 67-72; Preb Ex Cathl 67-72; V E Stonehouse 68-72; Suff Bp Southampton *Win* 72-84; Hon Can Win Cathl 72-84; rtd 84; Perm to Offic *Win* from 84; Hon Asst Bp Sarum from 88; Can and Preb Sarum Cathl from 88. *143 The Close, Salisbury SP2 1EY* Tel (01722) 334782 Fax 413112

CAVELL-NORTHAM, Canon Cavell Herbert James. b 32. St Steph Ho Ox 53. d 56 p 57. C W Wycombe *Ox* 56-61; CF (TA) 60-63; V Lane End *Ox* 61-68; V Stony Stratford 68-97; P-in-c Calverton 69-72; R 72-97; Hon Can Ch Ch 91-97; rtd 97; Lic to Offic *Ox* 97-04; Perm to Offic from 04. *The Glebe House, Finings Road, Lane End, High Wycombe HP14 3EU* Tel (01494) 881913

CAW (née FINLAY), Alison Mary. b 40. Natal Univ BA62 Ox Univ PGCE64. Ox Min Course 90. d 93 p 94. NSM Beaconsfield

Ox 93-04; NSM Penn and Tylers Green 04-08; Perm to Offic from 08. *1 Westway, Beaconsfield HP9 1DQ* Tel (01494) 674524

CAW, Hannah Mary. See JEFFERY, Mrs Hannah Mary

CAWDELL, Mrs Sarah Helen Louise. b 65. St Hugh's Coll Ox BA88 St Hugh's Coll Ox MA91 Trin Coll Cam BA94 MA99 K Coll Lon MA99. Ridley Hall Cam 92. d 95 p 96. C Belmont *S'wark* 95-98; Perm to Offic *Heref* 98-00; Hon C Claverley w Tuckhill 00-10; CME Officer 06-09; Public Preacher from 10. *The Rectory, 16 East Castle Street, Bridgnorth WV16 4AL* Tel (01746) 761573 E-mail s.h.cawdell@btinternet.com

CAWDELL, Simon Howard. b 65. Univ Coll Dur BA86 K Coll Lon MA99. Ridley Hall Cam 91. d 94 p 95. C Cheam Common St Phil *S'wark* 94-98; V Claverley w Tuckhill *Heref* 98-10; TR Bridgnorth, Tasley, Astley Abbotts, etc from 10; V Morville w Aston Eyre from 10; RD Bridgnorth from 09. *The Rectory, 16 East Castle Street, Bridgnorth WV16 4AL* Tel (01746) 761573 E-mail s.h.cawdell@btinternet.com

CAWLEY, David Lewis. b 44. AKC71 FSA81. St Aug Coll Cant 71. d 72 p 73. C Sprowston *Nor* 72-75; Chapl HM Pris Nor 74-75; C Wymondham *Nor* 75-77; C Buckland in Dover w Buckland Valley *Cant* 77-83; V Eastville St Anne w St Mark and St Thos *Bris* 83-95; V Leic St Mary 95-09; TV Leic H Spirit 97-02; Chapl Trin Hosp Leic 96-09; rtd 09; Hon C Margate All SS *Cant* from 09. *All Saints' Vicarage, All Saints' Avenue, Margate CT9 5QL* Tel (01843) 290845 E-mail david.l.cawley@btinternet.com

CAWRSE, Christopher William. b 60. Birkbeck Coll Lon BA97 Qu Mary and Westf Coll Lon MA00. Westcott Ho Cam 82. d 84 p 85. C Stoke Newington St Mary *Lon* 84-86; Chapl St Mark's Hosp Lon 86-90; C Islington St Jas w St Pet Lon 86-90; Chapl Asst Charing Cross Hosp Lon 90-93; Perm to Offic *Lon* 93-06; P-in-c St Pancras H Cross w St Jude and St Pet from 06. *Holy Cross Vicarage, 47 Argyle Square, London WC1H 8AL* Tel (020) 7278 6263 E-mail chriscawrse@blueyonder.co.uk

CAWTE, Canon David John. b 30. St Mich Coll Llan. d 65 p 66. C Chorley St Laur *Blackb* 65-67; C Boyne Hill *Ox* 67-74; C-in-c Cox Green CD 75-78; V Cox Green 78-94; Hon Can Ch Ch 88-94; rtd 94; Perm to Offic *Win* from 94. *6 Broadfields Close, Milford on Sea, Lymington SO41 0SE* Tel (01590) 642793 E-mail david.cawte@tinyworld.co.uk

CAWTE, Martin Charles. b 51. Jes Coll Ox BA73 MA77 IPFA77. SEITE 97. d 00 p 01. NSM Sanderstead All SS *S'wark* 00-03; NSM Greenham *Ox* 03-06; NSM Hermitage from 06. *The Rectory, 8 Yew Tree Mews, High Street, Compton, Newbury RG20 6NQ* Tel 07775-706976 (mobile) E-mail martin_cawte@hotmail.com

CAWTHORNE, Jack. b 22. ATD50. Cuddesdon Coll 69. d 71 p 72. NSM Newchurch *Man* 71-86; NSM Garforth *Ripon* 87-88; Perm to Offic from 88. *15 Arran Drive, Garforth, Leeds LS25 2BU* Tel 0113-286 9527 Mobile 077451-325559

CAWTHORNE, Paul Howarth. b 66. St Hild Coll Dur BA88. Cuddesdon Coll 98. d 98 p 99. C Cen Telford *Lich* 98-01; TV Wrockwardine Deanery from 01. *The Vicarage, Eaton Constantine, Shrewsbury SY5 6RF* Tel (01952) 510333 E-mail paul@cawthorne52.fsnet.co.uk

CAYTON, John. b 32. Bps' Coll Cheshunt 54. d 57 p 58. C Hindley All SS *Liv* 57-59; C Littleham w Exmouth 59-63; V Burnley St Cath *Blackb* 63-72; V Marton 72-87; V Fleetwood St Pet 87-97; Miss to Seamen 87-97; rtd 97; Perm to Offic *Blackb* from 97. *19 Parkstone Avenue, Thornton-Cleveleys FY5 5AE* Tel (01253) 854088

CECIL, Kevin Vincent. b 54. BA PGCE. St Mich Coll Llan. d 82 p 83. C Llanilid w Pencoed 82-85; C Coity w Nolton 85-88; Area Co-ord CMS St D, Llan, Mon and S & B 88-05; P-in-c Dixton *Heref* 05-08; V Dixton, Wyesham, Bishopswood, Whitchurch etc from 08. *The Vicarage, 38 Hillcrest Road, Wyesham, Monmouth NP25 3LH* Tel (01600) 713459 E-mail vincent_cecil@yahoo.com

CECILE, Sister. See HARRISON, Sister Cécile

CERMAKOVA, Ms Helena Maria Alija. b 43. d 88 p 95. NSM Roath *Llan* 88-91; Asst Chapl Univ Hosp of Wales Cardiff 92-95; Chapl United Bris Healthcare NHS Trust 95-99; Lead Chapl Jersey Gp of Hosps 99-06; Tutor St Mich Coll Llan from 06. *62A Heol Lewis, Cardiff CF14 6QB* Tel (029) 2061 2475 E-mail helenacermakova@talktalk.net

CERRATTI, Christa Elisabeth. See PUMFREY, Canon Christa Elisabeth

CHABALA, Patches. b 78. St Jo Coll Nottm BA11. d 11. C Plas Newton w Ches Ch Ch from 11. *13 Mannings Lane South, Chester CH2 3RX* Tel 07791-250300 (mobile)

CHADD, Jeremy Denis. b 55. Jes Coll Cam BA77 MA81. Coll of Resurr Mirfield 78. d 81 p 82. C Seaton Hirst *Newc* 81-84; C N Gosforth 84-88; V Sunderland St Chad *Dur* from 88. *St Chad's Vicarage, Charter Drive, Sunderland SR3 3PG* Tel 0191-528 2397

CHADD, Canon Leslie Frank. b 19. Leeds Univ BSc41. Coll of Resurr Mirfield 41. d 43 p 44. C Portsea All SS w St Jo Rudmore *Portsm* 43-46; Chapl RNVR 46-48; C Greenford H Cross *Lon* 48-54; C Littlehampton St Mary *Chich* 54-58; V Hanworth All

SS *Lon* 58-65; V Fareham SS Pet and Paul *Portsm* 65-92; Relig Adv STV 72-81; Hon Can Portsm Cathl 81-92; rtd 92; Perm to Offic *Portsm* from 92. *Tree Tops, Hoads Hill, Wickham, Fareham PO17 5BX* Tel (01329) 834397

CHADDER, Philip Thomas James. b 66. Ex Univ BA88. Oak Hill Th Coll 01. **d** 03 **p** 04. C Gt Chesham *Ox* 03-07; Chapl HM Pris Brixton from 07. *HM Prison Brixton, Jebb Avenue, London SW2 5XF* Tel (020) 8588 6052 Mobile 07796-815285 E-mail philchadder@yahoo.co.uk

CHADWICK, Alan Michael. b 61. St Cath Coll Cam BA83 MA87. Wycliffe Hall Ox 96. **d** 98 **p** 99. C Hubberston *St D* 98-01; R 01-11; P-in-c Llanstadwell from 11; AD Roose from 10. *The Vicarage, 68 Church Road, Llanstadwell, Milford Haven SA73 1EB* Tel (01646) 600227

CHADWICK, Arnold. *See* CHADWICK, Francis Arnold Edwin

CHADWICK, Carolyn Ann. b 52. Westhill Coll Birm CertEd73 Birm Univ BMus93 ABSM78. WMMTC 04. **d** 07 **p** 08. NSM Pontesbury I and II *Heref* from 07. *The Hermitage, Asterley, Minsterley, Shrewsbury SY5 0AW* Tel and fax (01743) 792421 Mobile 07766-832547 E-mail carolyn@thechadwickfamily.net

CHADWICK, Preb Charles John Peter. b 59. Birm Univ BA81 Southn Univ BTh90. Sarum & Wells Th Coll 85. **d** 88 **p** 89. C Chalfont St Peter *Ox* 88-91; C Gt Marlow 91-93; TV Gt Marlow w Marlow Bottom, Lt Marlow and Bisham 93-95; P-in-c Stokenchurch and Ibstone 95-01; Asst Dir Chiltern Ch Tr Course 95-01; V Bridgwater St Mary and Chilton Trinity *B & W* from 01; Preb Wells Cathl from 11. *The Vicarage, 7 Durleigh Road, Bridgwater TA6 7HU* Tel (01278) 422437 *or* 424972 E-mail cjpchad9@aol.com

CHADWICK, David Emmerson. b 73. Lincs & Humberside Univ BA96. Ridley Hall Cam BTh00. **d** 00 **p** 01. C Whickham *Dur* 00-06; V Ryhope from 06. *St Paul's Vicarage, Ryhope Street North, Sunderland SR2 0HH* Tel 0191-523 7884

CHADWICK, David Guy Evelyn St Just. b 36. Bps' Coll Cheshunt 65. **d** 68 **p** 69. C Edmonton All SS *Lon* 68-71; C Edmonton St Mary w St Jo 71-72; C Greenhill St Jo 72-74; Bp's Dom Chapl *Truro* 74-79; Chapl Community of the Epiphany Truro 77-78; P-in-c Crantock *Truro* 79-83; R Clydebank *Glas* 83-87; R Renfrew 87-94; rtd 94. *Alverna, 1 Nithsdale Crescent, Bearsden, Glasgow G61 4DF*

CHADWICK, Francis Arnold Edwin. b 30. AKC54. **d** 55 **p** 56. C Chapel Allerton *Ripon* 55-58; C Hayes *Roch* 58-61; V Arreton *Portsm* 61-67; V Newchurch 61-67; V Kingshurst *Birm* 67-73; V York Town St Mich *Guildf* 73-83; P-in-c Long Sutton w Long Load *B & W* 83-87; R Stockbridge and Longstock and Leckford *Win* 87-93; rtd 93; Chapl Helsinki w Tallinn *Eur* 95-98; Perm to Offic *B & W* 98-02 and *Sarum* from 02. *Hillway, Wickfield, Devizes SN10 5DU* Tel (01380) 721489

CHADWICK, Helen Jane. *See* MARSHALL, Mrs Helen Jane

CHADWICK, Mark William Armstrong. Coll of Resurr Mirfield. **d** 05 **p** 06. C Colwyn Bay w Brynymaen *St As* 05-08; V Kerry, Llanmerewig, Dolfor and Mochdre from 08. *The Vicarage, 47 Willan's Drive, Kerry, Newtown SY16 4DB*

CHADWICK, Owen. *See* CHADWICK, Prof William Owen

CHADWICK, Peter MacKenzie. b 21. Lich Th Coll 63. **d** 65 **p** 66. C Buckhurst Hill *Chelmsf* 65-66; Jt Hd Master Forres Sch Swanage 56-81; Chapl 66-85; NSM Kingston, Langton Matravers and Worth Matravers *Sarum* 85-92; rtd 89; Perm to Offic *Sarum* from 92. *Flat 4, 18 Victoria Avenue, Swanage BH19 1AN* Tel (01929) 422258

CHADWICK, Philip Edward. b 41. AMICE63 IEng65. **d** 07 **p** 08. OLM Elland *Wakef* from 07. *26 Crestfield Avenue, Elland HX5 0LN* Tel (01422) 373298 E-mail pechadwick@hotmail.com

CHADWICK, Prof William Owen. b 16. OM83 KBE82. St Jo Coll Cam BA39 MA42 BD51 DD55 St Andr Univ Hon DD60 Ox Univ Hon DD73 Univ of Wales Hon DD93 FBA62. Cuddesdon Coll 39. **d** 40 **p** 41. C Huddersfield St Jo *Wakef* 40-42; Chapl Wellington Coll Berks 42-46; Fell Trin Hall Cam 47-56; Dean 49-56; Master Selw Coll Cam 56-83; Fell from 83; Dixie Prof Ecclesiastical Hist Cam 58-68; Regius Prof Modern Hist Cam 68-83; Pres Br Academy 81-85; Chan UEA 85-94; Perm to Offic *Ely* from 94. *67 Grantchester Street, Cambridge CB7 9HZ* Tel (01223) 314000

CHAFFEY, Jane Frances. b 59. Somerville Coll Ox BA80 MA84 St Jo Coll Dur BA86. Cranmer Hall Dur 84. **d** 88 **p** 94. Par Dn Roby *Liv* 88-90; NSM Finningley w Auckley *S'well* 95-96; Perm to Offic *Pet* 96-99 and *Linc* 98-01; Perm to Offic RAF from 98; Chapl Wycombe Abbey Sch from 08. *Wycombe Abbey School, Abbey Way, High Wycombe HP11 1PE* Tel (01494) 520381

CHAFFEY, Jonathan Paul Michael. b 62. St Chad's Coll Dur BA83. Cranmer Hall Dur 84. **d** 87 **p** 88. C Gateacre *Liv* 87-90; Chapl RAF from 90. *Chaplaincy Services, HQ Personnel and Training Command, RAF High Wycombe HP14 4UE* Tel (01494) 496800 Fax 496343

CHAFFEY, Michael Prosser. b 30. Lon Univ BA51. St Steph Ho Ox 53. **d** 55 **p** 56. C Victoria Docks Ascension *Chelmsf* 55-59; C Leytonstone H Trin and St Aug Harrow Green 59-62; V Walthamstow St Mich 62-69; R Cov St Jo 69-85; P-in-c Cov

St Thos 69-75; Hon C Bideford *Ex* 85; P-in-c Charlestown *Man* 85-88; V Sutton St Mich *York* 88-96; rtd 96; Perm to Offic *York* from 96. *7 Shirley Court, South Marine Drive, Bridlington YO15 3JJ* Tel (01262) 602758

CHALCRAFT, Christopher Warine Terrell (Kit). b 37. Oak Hill Th Coll. **d** 67 **p** 68. C Egham *Guildf* 67-70; P-in-c Slough *Ox* 70-73; TV Bramerton w Surlingham *Nor* 73-87; P-in-c Cockley Cley w Gooderstone 87-95; P-in-c Gt and Lt Cressingham w Threxton 87-95; P-in-c Didlington 87-95; P-in-c Hilborough w Bodney 87-95; P-in-c Oxborough w Foulden and Caldecote 87-95; Perm to Offic from 02. *The Malthouse, 39 London Street, Swaffham PE37 7DD* Tel (01760) 724805 E-mail k.chalcraft@btinternet.com

CHALCRAFT, Mrs Sharon Anita. b 62. Ex Univ BTh09. SWMTC 05. **d** 08 **p** 09. NSM Carbis Bay w Lelant, Towednack and Zennor *Truro* 08-09; NSM Breage w Godolphin and Germoe from 09. *Summerhill Cottage, Nancledra, Penzance TR20 8AY* Tel (01736) 350779 Mobile 07889-406326 E-mail sharon@m8trix.ltd.uk

CHALK, Francis Harold. b 25. Lich Th Coll 61. **d** 62 **p** 63. C Linc St Nic w St Jo Newport 62-64; R Kirkby Laythorpe w Asgarby 64-69; V Ewerby w Evedon 65-69; R Gt Gonerby 69-89; rtd 89; Perm to Offic *Truro* from 90. *Chalkleigh, 3 Church Street, St Just, Penzance TR19 7HA* Tel (01736) 787925

CHALKLEY, Andrew William Guy. b 64. Aston Tr Scheme 90 St Jo Coll Nottm BTh92. **d** 95 **p** 96. C Liskeard, St Keyne, St Pinnock, Morval etc *Truro* 95-99; TV Uphill *B & W* 99-07; P-in-c Beckington w Standerwick, Berkley, Rodden etc 07-10; R from 10. *8 Church Street, Beckington, Frome BA11 6TG* Tel (01373) 830314

CHALLEN, Canon Peter Bernard. b 31. Clare Coll Cam BA56 MA60 FRSA94. Westcott Ho Cam 56. **d** 58 **p** 59. C Goole *Sheff* 58-61; V Dalton 61-67; Sen Ind Chapl *S'wark* 67-96; R S'wark Ch Ch 67-96; Hon Can S'wark Cathl 74-96; rtd 96; Perm to Offic *S'wark* from 96. *21 Bousfield Road, London SE14 5TP* Tel and fax (020) 7207 0509 E-mail peterchallen@gmail.com

CHALLENDER, John Clifford. b 32. CITC 67. **d** 67 **p** 68. C Belfast St Luke *Conn* 67-70; Bp's V and Lib Kilkenny Cathl and C Kilkenny w Aghour and Odagh *C & O* 70-71; I Fenagh w Myshall and Kiltennel 71-76; I Fenagh w Myshall, Aghade and Ardoyne 76-79; I Crosspatrick Gp 79-95; Preb Ferns Cathl 85-88; Dioc Glebes Sec (Ferns) 86-91; Treas Ferns Cathl 88-91; Chan 91-95; I Killeshin w Cloydagh and Killabban 95-02; Can Ossory and Leighlin Cathls 00-02; rtd 02. *3 Adare Close, Killincarrig, Greystones, Co Wicklow, Republic of Ireland* Tel (00353) (1) 201 7268 *or* 287 6359 Mobile 86-243 3678 E-mail challen1@eircom.net

CHALLENGER, Ann. b 54. Leeds Univ BA09. NOC 06. **d** 09 **p** 10. NSM Bradf St Aug Undercliffe from 09; NSM Bradf St Clem from 09. *304 Undercliffe Street, Bradford BD3 0PH* Tel (01274) 640410 Mobile 07832-293751 E-mail ann_challenger@hotmail.co.uk

CHALLENGER, Peter Nelson. b 33. St Jo Coll Cam BA57 MA61. Ripon Hall Ox 57. **d** 59 **p** 60. C Bushbury *Lich* 59-62; V Horsley Woodhouse *Derby* 62-67; V Derby St Barn 67-75; Brazil 75-80; TV New Windsor *Ox* 80-89; V Wootton (Boars Hill) 89-98; rtd 99. *39 Moorland Road, Witney OX28 6LS* Tel (01993) 774630

CHALLICE, John Richard. b 34. ACP65. Sarum & Wells Th Coll 73. **d** 75 **p** 76. C Warminster St Denys *Sarum* 75-78; R Longfield *Roch* 78-00; rtd 00; Perm to Offic *Roch* from 00. *Magnolia, Allhallows Road, Lower Stoke, Rochester ME3 9SL* Tel (01634) 272468

CHALLIS, Douglas James. b 21. Selw Coll Cam BA48 MA55. Cuddesdon Coll 49. **d** 51 **p** 58. Kimbolton Sch 53-58; Chapl Summer Fields Sch Ox 58-60; Asst Chapl Stowe Sch 60-64; Chapl St Bees Sch Cumbria 64-67; Chapl Reed's Sch Cobham 67-80; rtd 80; Perm to Offic *Cant* 89-07; Chapl Crowhurst Chr Healing Cen 05-06; Lic to Offic *Mor* 07-10; Perm to Offic from 10. *7 Milinclarin Way, Church Hill Road, Lairg IV27 4BL* Tel (01549) 402168

CHALLIS, Ian. b 46. St Jo Coll Nottm 82. **d** 84 **p** 85. C Heatherlands St Jo *Sarum* 84-86; C Lytchett Minster 86-88; Perm to Offic 88-95 and 00-08; NSM Canford Magna 95-00. *50 Constitution Hill Road, Poole BH14 0QD* Tel (01202) 691300

CHALLIS, John William Anthony. b 68. St Steph Ho Ox 98. **d** 00 **p** 01. C Ifield *Chich* 00-04; P-in-c Buxted and Hadlow Down 04-09; R Beeding and Bramber w Botolphs from 09. *The Rectory, Sele Priory Church, Church Lane, Upper Beeding BN44 3HP* Tel (01903) 810265

CHALLIS, Terence Peter. b 40. St Aid Birkenhead 65. **d** 68 **p** 69. C Billericay St Mary *Chelmsf* 68-71; Admin Sec Dio Maseno S Kenya 72-75; Bp's Chapl 72-74; P-in-c Sparkbrook Ch Ch *Birm* 76-80; V Enfield St Jas *Lon* 80-89; V Astley Bridge *Man* 89-98; P-in-c Leigh St Mary and Leigh St Jo 99-02; rtd 02; Perm to Offic *Blackb* from 03. *48 Wilson Square, Thornton-Cleveleys FY5 1RF* Tel (01253) 864534

CHALLIS, William George. b 52. Keble Coll Ox BA73 K Coll Lon MTh75. Oak Hill Th Coll 73. **d** 75 **p** 76. C Islington

St Mary *Lon* 75-79; Lect Trin Coll Bris 79-81; C Stoke Bishop *Bris* 79-81; Lect Oak Hill Th Coll 82; Burundi 82-85; P-in-c Bishopston *Bris* 86-89; TR 89-92; Vice-Prin Wycliffe Hall Ox 93-98; V Bitterne *Win* 98-03; Dir of Ords *Guildf* from 03. *80 York Road, Woking GU22 7XR* Tel (01483) 769759 *or* 790322 E-mail ddo@cofeguildford.org.uk

CHALMERS, Canon Brian. b 42. Oriel Coll Ox BA64 MA68 DPhil70 BA71. Wycliffe Hall Ox 71. **d** 72 **p** 73. C Luton St Mary *St Alb* 72-76; Chapl Cranfield Inst of Tech 76-81; Chapl Kent Univ 81-89; Six Preacher Cant Cathl 85-96; V Charing w Charing Heath and Lt Chart 89-05; AD Ashford 98-03; Hon Can Cant Cathl 97-05; rtd 05; Perm to Offic *Cant* from 05. *The Chantry, Pilgrims Lane, Chilham, Canterbury CT4 8AB* Tel (01227) 730669 E-mail brian.chalmers@tesco.net

CHAMBERLAIN, Allen Charles William. b 29. Lon Univ CertEd52 Birkbeck Coll Lon BSc56. **d** 96 **p** 97. OLM Gunton St Pet *Nor* 96-99; rtd 99; Perm to Offic *Nor* from 99. *28 Yarmouth Road, Lowestoft NR32 4AG* Tel (01502) 573637

CHAMBERLAIN, David (**Bernard**). b 28. Fitzw Ho Cam BA51. Linc Th Coll 52. **d** 54 **p** 55. C Brighouse *Wakef* 54-57; C Sheff St Cecilia Parson Cross 57-61; CR 63-85; S Africa 68-70; Bp's Adv on Community Relns *Wakef* 71-85; Bp's Adv Community Relns & Inter-Faith Dialogue *Bris* 86-93; V Easton All Hallows 86-93; rtd 93; Perm to Offic *B & W* from 94. *43 Bath Road, Wells BA5 3HR* Tel (01749) 679369

CHAMBERLAIN, David Murray. b 22. Cuddesdon Coll 55. **d** 57 **p** 58. C Barkingside H Trin *Chelmsf* 57-60; Japan 60-71 and 76-81; V Edgbaston St Germain *Birm* 71-76; Miss to Seamen N Australia 81-88; rtd 88; Perm to Offic *Truro* from 88. *42 Tresawls Road, Truro TR1 3LE* Tel (01872) 272270

CHAMBERLAIN, Elizabeth Ann. b 58. St Jo Coll Nottm 08. **d** 10 **p** 11. C Walsall St Matt *Lich* from 10. *21 Buchanan Road, Walsall WS4 2EW* Tel (01922) 443362 E-mail lizchamberlainuk@yahoo.co.uk

CHAMBERLAIN, Eric Edward. b 34. Tyndale Hall Bris 62. **d** 65 **p** 66. C Chell *Lich* 65-73; P-in-c Preston St Mary *Blackb* 73-76; V 76-89; P-in-c Preston St Luke 81-83; R S Normanton *Derby* 89-99; rtd 99; Perm to Offic *Ox* 00-11. *10 Hailes Wood, Elsenham, Bishop's Stortford CM22 6DQ* Tel (01279) 814375

CHAMBERLAIN, Frederick George. b 19. Univ of Wales (Lamp) BA50. Chich Th Coll 50. **d** 52 **p** 53. C Weybridge *Guildf* 52-54; C Bourne 54-57; V Blindley Heath *S'wark* 57-63; V Tilshead *Sarum* 63-71; R The Orchestons 66-71; V Chitterne 69-71; R Tilshead, Orcheston and Chitterne 71-80; P-in-c Handley w Pentridge 80-82; R 82-84; rtd 84; Perm to Offic *Sarum* 84-04. *22 Gracey Court, Woodland Road, Broadclyst, Exeter EX5 3GA* Tel (01392) 462633

CHAMBERLAIN, Helen. **d** 09 **p** 10. NSM Farnham Royal w Hedgerley *Ox* from 09. *18 Frensham Walk, Farnham Common, Slough SL2 3QG* E-mail helen@daven.demon.co.uk

CHAMBERLAIN, Jane Louise. b 62. Bedf Coll Lon BSc84. WEMTC 04. **d** 07 **p** 08. NSM Blagdon w Compton Martin and Ubley *B & W* 07-11; R from 11. *Grove House, The Street, Compton Martin, Bristol BS40 6JF* Tel (01761) 220070 Mobile 07949-037548 E-mail jlchamberlain@tiscali.co.uk

CHAMBERLAIN, Malcolm Leslie. b 69. York Univ BA92. Wycliffe Hall Ox 93. **d** 96 **p** 97. C Walsall Pleck and Bescot *Lich* 96-99; C Mossley Hill St Matt and St Jas *Liv* 99-02; Asst Chapl Liv Univ 99-02; Chapl Liv Univ and Dioc 18-30s Officer 02-08; P-in-c Wavertree St Mary from 08; V from 11. *St Mary's Rectory, 1 South Drive, Wavertree, Liverpool L15 8JJ* Tel 0151-735 1615

✠CHAMBERLAIN, The Rt Revd Neville. b 39. Nottm Univ BA61 MA73 CQSW73. Ripon Hall Ox 61. **d** 63 **p** 64 **c** 97. C Balsall Heath St Paul *Birm* 63-64; C Hall Green Ascension 64-66; C-in-c Gospel Lane CD 66-69; V Gospel Lane St Mich 69-72; Lic to Offic *Linc* 73-74; Soc Resp Sec 74-82; Can and Preb Linc Cathl 79-98; R Edin St Jo 82-97; Bp Bre 97-05; rtd 05; Master Hugh Sexey's Hosp Bruton from 05. *The Master's House, Hugh Sexey's Hospital, Bruton BA10 0AS* Tel (01749) 813369

CHAMBERLAIN, Nicholas Alan. b 63. St Chad's Coll Dur BA85 PhD91 New Coll Edin BD91. Edin Th Coll 88. **d** 91 **p** 92. C Cockerton *Dur* 91-94; C Newton Aycliffe 94-95; TV 95-96; TV Gt Aycliffe 95-98; P-in-c Burnmoor 98-06; Bp's Adv for CME 98-06; V Newc St Geo and St Hilda from 06. *St George's Vicarage, St George's Close, Newcastle upon Tyne NE2 2TF* Tel 0191-281 1628

CHAMBERLAIN, Paul Martin. b 74. Southn Univ MChem97 Bris Univ PhD02. Ripon Coll Cuddesdon 08. **d** 10 **p** 11. C Thame *Ox* from 10. *8 Victoria Mead, Thame OX9 3HY* Tel (01844) 330402 E-mail revdr.paulchamberlain@googlemail.com

CHAMBERLAIN, Roger Edward. b 53. Culham Coll of Educn BEd75. Trin Coll Bris BA87. **d** 87 **p** 88. C Plymouth Em w Efford *Ex* 87-90; C Selly Park St Steph and St Wulstan *Birm* 90-94; V Yardley St Cypr Hay Mill 94-96; Perm to Offic 96-10; P-in-c Baddesley Ensor w Grendon from 10. *The Vicarage, 75*

Newlands Road, Baddesley Ensor, Atherstone CV9 2BY Tel (01827) 713245 E-mail revrog@hotmail.co.uk

CHAMBERLAIN, Roy Herbert. b 44. Oak Hill Th Coll 91 NOC 95. **d** 96 **p** 97. C Gee Cross *Ches* 96-98; Perm to Offic *Blackb* from 01. *125 Lancaster Road, Morecambe LA4 5QJ* Tel (01524) 409070

CHAMBERLAIN, Russell Charles. b 51. Univ of Wales (Cardiff) LLM00. Oak Hill Th Coll 76. **d** 78 **p** 79. C Harold Hill St Geo *Chelmsf* 78-80; C Uckfield *Chich* 80-83; R Balcombe 83-90; V Okehampton w Inwardleigh *Ex* 90-94; TR Okehampton w Inwardleigh, Bratton Clovelly etc 94-01; RD Okehampton 93-98; R Wolborough and Ogwell from 01. *The Rectory, 5 Coach Place, Newton Abbot TQ12 1ES* Tel (01626) 368889 E-mail russell@chamberlain70.fsnet.co.uk

CHAMBERLIN, David John. b 56. St Jo Coll Nottm. **d** 94 **p** 95. C Chatham St Phil and St Jas *Roch* 94-97; R Swardeston w E Carleton, Intwood, Keswick etc *Nor* 97-04; RD Humbleyard 03-04; R Milton *Ely* from 04. *The Rectory, 24 Church Lane, Milton, Cambridge CB24 6AB* Tel (01223) 861511 Mobile 07805-083300 E-mail rector@allsaintsmilton.org.uk

CHAMBERLIN, John Malcolm. b 38. Carl Dioc Tr Course 84. **d** 87 **p** 88. NSM Cockermouth w Embleton and Wythop *Carl* 87-97; Master St Mary Magd and H Jes Trust 97-05; Hon C Newc St Jo 98-05; rtd 05. *45 Wansbeck Avenue, North Shields NE30 3DU* Tel 0191-253 0022 E-mail johnchamberlin@btinternet.com

CHAMBERS, Canon Anthony Frederick John. b 40. ACII69. Sarum Th Coll 69. **d** 71 **p** 72. C Hall Green St Pet *Birm* 71-74; C Holdenhurst *Win* 74-77; P-in-c Ropley w W Tisted 77-79; R Bishop's Sutton and Ropley and W Tisted 79-83; V Pokesdown St Jas 83-99; RD Bournemouth 95-99; P-in-c Heckfield w Mattingley and Rotherwick 99-02; V 02-04; Chapl N Foreland Lodge Sch Basingstoke 99-04; Hon Can Win Cathl 03-04; rtd 05; Perm to Offic *Ex* from 05. *4 J H Taylor Drive, Northam, Bideford EX39 1TU* Tel (01237) 421306 E-mail anthony.chambers1@virgin.net

CHAMBERS, Miss Barbara Ada. b 51. **d** 98 **p** 99. OLM Gt Crosby St Luke *Liv* from 98. *12 Vale Road, Crosby, Liverpool L23 5RZ* Tel 0151-924 5851

CHAMBERS, Mrs Barbara Mary Sinnott. b 43. SRN65 RM67 HVCert75 Keele Univ TCert77. WMMTC 87. **d** 93 **p** 94. Par Dn Blurton *Lich* 93-94; C 94-96; Chapl Asst Qu Medical Cen Nottm Univ Hosp NHS Trust 96-03; Chapl 03-07; Chapl United Lincs Hosps NHS Trust from 07. *51 Mill Lane, Woodhall Spa LN10 6QZ* Tel (01526) 354872 E-mail barbara.chambers@ulh.nhs.uk

CHAMBERS, Carl Michael. b 68. Pemb Coll Cam BA90 Oak Hill Th Coll BA00. **d** 01 **p** 02. C Hove Bp Hannington Memorial Ch *Chich* 01-05; C Preston St Jo w Brighton St Aug and St Sav from 05. *24 Stanford Avenue, Brighton BN1 6EA* Tel (01273) 553207

CHAMBERS, Mrs Christine. b 55. St Mellitus Coll BA10. **d** 10 **p** 11. C E Ham St Paul *Chelmsf* from 10. *153 Burges Road, London E6 2BL* Tel (020) 8552 7660 Mobile 07941-823783 E-mail christinechambers@hotmail.co.uk

CHAMBERS, George William. b 24. TCD BA46 MA57. CITC 47. **d** 47 **p** 48. C Conwall *D & R* 47-50; Chapl Portora R Sch Enniskillen 51-56; I Tullyaughnish w Milford *D & R* 51-61; I Adare *L & K* 61-81; Dioc Registrar (Limerick etc) 62-81; Adn Limerick 69-81; Dean Limerick 81-86; I Limerick City 81-86; I Killeshin w Cloydagh and Killabban *C & O* 86-95; Can Ossory and Leighlin Cathls 90-92; Treas Ossory and Leighlin Cathls 92-95; rtd 95. *52 Rathdown Court, Greystones, Co Wicklow, Republic of Ireland* Tel (00353) (1) 287 1140

CHAMBERS, John Richard. b 50. EMMTC 01. **d** 04 **p** 05. C Farnsfield *S'well* 04-07; C Kirklington w Hockerton 04-07; C Bilsthorpe 04-07; C Eakring 04-07; C Maplebeck 04-07; C Winkburn 04-07; P-in-c E Bridgford and Kneeton 07-10; P-in-c Flintham 08-10; P-in-c Car Colston w Screveton 08-10; R Richmond w Hudswell and Downholme and Marske *Ripon* from 10. *The Rectory, Church Wynd, Richmond DL10 7AQ* Tel (01748) 821241 Mobile 07875-348245 E-mail j_echambers@btinternet.com

CHAMBERS, Mrs Lynn. b 53. Northd Coll of Educn TCert74 Greenwich Univ MA96. St Mich Coll Llan 03. **d** 05 **p** 06. Dioc Children's Officer *St D* 01-06; NSM Carmarthen St Pet 05-08; P-in-c Brechfa w Abergorlech etc from 08. *Llwyn Aderyn, Brechfa, Carmarthen SA32 7BL* Tel (01267) 202763 E-mail chambers@bromihangel.freserve.co.uk

CHAMBERS, Canon Peter Lewis. b 43. Imp Coll Lon BScEng64. St Steph Ho Ox 64. **d** 66 **p** 67. C Llandaff w Capel Llanilltern 66-70; Chapl Ch in Wales Youth Coun 70-73; Youth Chapl *Bris* 73-78; V Bedminster St Mich 78-84; Bp Bedminster 81-84; Adv Ho of Bps Marriage Educn Panel Gen Syn 84-88; Dir Dioc Coun for Soc Resp *Guildf* 88-94; Hon Can Guildf Cathl 89-94; Dir Tr *Sheff* 95-00; P-in-c Harthill and Thorpe Salvin 00-07; Dioc Min Teams Officer 00-04; Hon Can Sheff Cathl 96-07; rtd 07. *5 Henley Grove, Bristol BS9 4EQ* Tel 0117-307 9427

CHAMBERS, Robert Anthony. b 46. d 05 p 06. OLM Kirkburton *Wakef* from 05. *4 Clough Park, Fenay Bridge, Huddersfield HD8 0JH* Tel (01484) 605920 Mobile 07968-279351 E-mail robert.chambers27@ntlworld.com

CHAMBERS, Simon Paul. b 65. Liv Univ BEng87 PhD91. Ripon Coll Cuddesdon 00. d 02 p 03. C Parkstone St Pet and St Osmund w Branksea *Sarum* 02-05; P-in-c Ashwell w Hinxworth and Newnham *St Alb* 05-10; TV Shaftesbury *Sarum* from 10. *St James's Vicarage, 34 Tanyards Lane, Shaftesbury SP7 8HW* Tel (01747) 852193 E-mail simon@simonchambers.me.uk

CHAMBEYRON, Mrs Julia Lynne. Univ of Wales (Ban) BTh06. ERMC 03. d 06 p 07. C La Côte *Eur* from 06. *1199 rue Guy de Maupassant, 01220 Divonne les Bains, France* Tel (0033) 4 50 20 19 37 E-mail julia.chambeyron@orange.fr

CHAMP, Darren David. b 60. Kent Univ BA93. Linc Th Coll MA95. d 95 p 96. C Ashford *Cant* 95-97; Perm to Offic 02-03. *154 Beaver Road, Ashford TN23 7SS* Tel (01233) 663090 E-mail daz@dazchamp.co.uk

CHAMPION, Arthur. b 51. Loughb Univ BSc76 Aston Univ MSc77 CEng88 MIMechE88 FIOSH88. WEMTC 03. d 08 p 09. NSM Badgeworth, Shurdington and Witcombe w Bentham *Glouc* from 08. *21 Glynrosa Road, Charlton Kings, Cheltenham GL53 8QS* Tel (01242) 263081 Mobile 07768-658723 E-mail championarthur@gmail.com

CHAMPION, Canon John Oswald Cecil. b 27. St Chad's Coll Dur BA49. d 51 p 52. C Worc St Martin 51-53; Chapl RN 53-57; C Cant St Martin w St Paul 57-60; C-in-c Stourbridge St Mich Norton CD *Worc* 60-64; V Astwood Bank w Crabbs Cross 64-68; V Redditch St Steph 68-75; R Fladbury, Wyre Piddle and Moor 75-93; RD Pershore 79-85; Hon Can Worc Cathl 81-93; rtd 93; Perm to Offic *Worc* from 93. *Black Horse Cottage, 3 Church Row, Pershore WR10 1BL* Tel (01386) 552403

CHAMPNEYS, Michael Harold. b 46. LRAM66 GRSM67 ARCO67. Linc Th Coll 69. d 72 p 73. C Poplar *Lon* 72-73; C Bow w Bromley St Leon 73-75; P-in-c Bethnal Green St Barn 75-76; C Tewkesbury w Walton Cardiff *Glouc* 76-78; V Bedford Park *Lon* 78-83; V Shepshed *Leic* 84-87; Community Educn Tutor Bolsover 88-93; Perm to Offic *Derby* 90-92; NSM Bolsover 92-93; V Potterspury, Furtho, Yardley Gobion and Cosgrove *Pet* 93-98; RD Towcester 94-98; V Shap w Swindale and Bampton w Mardale *Carl* 98-01; R Calow and Sutton cum Duckmanton *Derby* 01-10; rtd 10. *1 New Road, Holymoorside, Chesterfield S42 7EW* Tel (01246) 566172 E-mail michaelchampneys@yahoo.co.uk

CHANCE, David Newton. b 44. Univ of Wales (Lamp) BA68. St Steph Ho Ox 68. d 70 p 71. C Selsdon St Jo w St Fran *Cant* 70-73; C Plymstock *Ex* 73-77; P-in-c Northam 77-79; TR Northam w Westward Ho! and Appledore 79-93; V Banstead *Guildf* 93-10; rtd 10. *3 Norman Road, Westgate-on-Sea CT8 8RR* Tel (01843) 836882 E-mail david.chance93@ntlworld.com

CHAND, Richard. b 62. SAOMC 02. d 05 p 06. NSM Headington St Mary *Ox* 05-09; NSM Cowley St Jas from 09. *Moores House, 15 Beauchamp Lane, Oxford OX4 3LF* Tel 07966-659270 (mobile) E-mail richardchandrw@ministry.fsbusiness.co.uk

CHAND, Wazir. b 29. Punjab Univ BA56 BT59. Ox NSM Course. d 90 p 91. NSM Cowley St Jas *Ox* 90-04; Perm to Offic from 04. *38 Garsington Road, Oxford OX4 2LG* Tel (01865) 714160 or 433015

CHANDA, Daniel Khazan. b 28. Punjab Univ BA57 MA62 Saharanpur Coll. d 70 p 70. Hon C Handsworth St Jas *Birm* 70-83; Hon C Perry Barr 83-89; C Small Heath 89-98; rtd 98; Perm to Offic *Birm* from 98. *173 Wood Lane, Handsworth, Birmingham B20 2AG* Tel 0121-551 0725

CHANDLER, Anthony. b 43. Lon Inst of Educn CertEd65. EAMTC 94. d 97 p 98. Dioc Youth Officer *Ely* 96-00; NSM March St Mary 97-00; R from 00; NSM March St Pet 97-00; R from 00. *17 St Peter's Road, March PE15 9NA* Tel and fax (01354) 652894 E-mail anthony.chandler@ely.anglican.org

CHANDLER, Barbara Janet. b 58. Newc Univ BMedSci79 MB, BS82 MD93 FRCP00. NEOC 04. d 07 p 08. NSM Ponteland *Newc* 07-11; Perm to Offic *Mor* from 11. *Oak Cottage, Mount Gerald, Dingwall IV15 9TT* E-mail chandlernorth@googlemail.com

CHANDLER, Derek Edward. b 67. Southn Univ BTh91 Nottm Univ MDiv93. Linc Th Coll 91. d 93 p 94. C Bitterne Park *Win* 93-97; C Sholing 97-00; R Emmer Green w Caversham Park *Ox* from 00. *20 St Barnabas Road, Emmer Green, Reading RG4 8RA* Tel 0118-947 8239 E-mail rev.derek.chandler@virgin.net

CHANDLER, The Ven Ian Nigel. b 65. K Coll Lon BD89 AKC89. Chich Th Coll 92. d 92 p 93. C Hove *Chich* 92-96; Bp's Dom Chapl 96-00; V Haywards Heath St Rich 00-10; RD Cuckfield 04-06; Adn Plymouth *Ex* from 10. *St Mark's House, 46A Cambridge Road, Plymouth PL2 1PU* Tel (01752) 202401 E-mail archdeacon.of.plymouth@exeter.anglican.org

CHANDLER, John. b 49. ACIB73. NTMTC 05. d 07 p 08. NSM Colchester St Mich Myland *Chelmsf* from 07. *4 Longdryve, Wavell Avenue, Colchester CO2 7HH* Tel (01206) 249154 Mobile 07951-160558 E-mail john@mylandchurch.org.uk

CHANDLER, John Charles. b 46. Solicitor. Oak Hill Th Coll 91. d 94 p 95. C Tonbridge St Steph *Roch* 94-98; V Felsted and Lt Dunmow *Chelmsf* 98-05; V Hildenborough *Roch* from 05. *The Vicarage, 194 Tonbridge Road, Hildenborough, Tonbridge TN11 9HR* Tel (01732) 833569 E-mail jm@chandler464.freeserve.co.uk

CHANDLER, The Very Revd Michael John. b 45. Lambeth STh80 K Coll Lon PhD87. Linc Th Coll 70. d 72 p 73. C Cant St Dunstan w H Cross 72-75; C Margate St Jo 75-78; V Newington w Bobbing and Iwade 78-83; P-in-c Hartlip w Stockbury 80-83; V Newington w Hartlip and Stockbury 83-88; RD Sittingbourne 84-88; R Hackington 88-95; RD Cant 94-95; Can Res Cant Cathl 95-03; Dean Ely from 03. *The Deanery, The College, Ely CB7 4DN* Tel (01353) 667735 or 660300 Fax 665668 E-mail dean@cathedral.ely.anglican.org

CHANDLER, Quentin David. b 62. Aston Tr Scheme 87 Trin Coll Bris BA92. d 92 p 93. C Goldington *St Alb* 92-96; TV Rushden w Newton Bromswold *Pet* 96-00; V Rushden St Pet 00-03; Dir Tr for Past Assts from 03; R Burton Latimer 03-11; Continuing Minl Development Officer from 11. *The Rectory, Preston Court, Burton Latimer, Kettering NN15 5LR* Tel and fax (01536) 722959 E-mail q.chandler@btopenworld.com

CHANDLER, Stephen Michael. NTMTC. d 09 p 10. NSM Victoria Docks St Luke *Chelmsf* from 09. *117 Atkinson Road, London E16 3LT*

CHANDLER, Mrs Susan May. b 54. WMMTC 06. d 09 p 10. NSM Olton *Birm* from 09. *14 Hollyberry Avenue, Solihull B91 3UA* Tel 0121-709 1512 Mobile 07970-791288 E-mail j14chand@aol.com

CHANDRA, Kevin Douglas Naresh. b 65. Lon Bible Coll BA91. Qu Coll Birm 94. d 96 p 97. C Walmley *Birm* 96-00; P-in-c Erdington St Chad 00-02; TV Erdington 02-05; Chapl St Pet Sch Ex from 06. *St Peter's C of E Aided School, Quarry Lane, Exeter EX2 5AP* Tel (01392) 204764 E-mail kc@chandra.plus.com

CHANDY, Sugu John Mathai. b 40. Kerala Univ BSc61 Serampore Univ BD66. Wycliffe Coll Toronto 67. d 66 p 68. India 66-74 and from 80; C Ormesby *York* 74-77; C Sutton St Jas and Wawne 78-80; rtd 99. *Matteethra, Muttambalam, Kottayam, Kerala 686 004, India* Tel (0091) (481) 572434 or 572590

✠**CHANG-HIM, The Rt Revd French Kitchener.** b 38. Lich Th Coll. d 62 p 63 c 79. C Goole *Sheff* 62-63; R Praslin Seychelles 63-67; C Sheff St Leon Norwood 67-68; C Mahé Cathl Mauritius 68-70; Missr Praslin 70-73; R Anse Royale St Sav and Adn Seychelles 73-79; Bp Seychelles 79-04; rtd 04. *PO Box 44, Victoria, Seychelles* Tel and fax (00248) 248151 E-mail changhim@seychelles.sc

CHANNER, Christopher Kendall. b 42. K Coll Lon BD64 AKC64. St Boniface Warminster 64. d 65 p 66. C Norbury St Steph *Cant* 65-68; C S Elmsall *Wakef* 68-70; V Dartford St Edm *Roch* 70-75; Chapl Joyce Green Hosp Dartford 73-75; V Bromley St Andr *Roch* 75-81; V Langton Green 81-94; Chapl Holmewood Ho Sch Tunbridge Wells 94-98; P-in-c Lewes All SS, St Anne, St Mich and St Thos *Chich* 98-00; R Lewes St Mich and St Thos at Cliffe w All SS 00-08; rtd 08. *Willow Cottage, 3 Oakland Drive, Robertsbridge TN32 5EX* Tel (01580) 881478

CHANT, Edwin John. b 14. Lon Univ BA62. K Coll Lon 39 Clifton Th Coll 46. d 47 p 48. C Erith St Paul *Roch* 47-49; C Darfield *Sheff* 49-51; C Conisbrough 51-53; C Cliftonville *Cant* 53-56; V Gentleshaw *Lich* 56-80; V Farewell 56-80; rtd 80; Perm to Offic *Lich* from 80. *31 Huntsmans Gate, Burntwood WS7 9LL*

CHANT, Harry. b 40. Oak Hill Th Coll. d 78 p 79. C Heatherlands St Jo *Sarum* 78-81; P-in-c Bramshaw 81-83; P-in-c Landford w Plaitford 81-83; R Bramshaw and Landford w Plaitford 83-87; V Fareham St Jo *Portsm* 87-00; rtd 00; Perm to Offic *Truro* from 00. *Paradise Cottage, 34 Nanscober Place, Helston TR13 0SP* Tel and fax (01326) 561916 E-mail handrchant@aol.com

CHANT, Kenneth William. b 37. St Deiniol's Hawarden 67. d 70 p 71. C Ynyshir *Llan* 70-74; C Bargoed and Deri w Brithdir 74; P-in-c Aberpergwm and Blaengwrach 74-77; V 77-81; V Cwmavon 81-02; rtd 02. *22 Chalice Court, Port Talbot SA12 7DA* Tel (01639) 813456

CHANT, Maurice Ronald. b 26. Chich Th Coll 51. d 54 p 55. C Mitcham St Mark *S'wark* 54-57; C Surbiton St Matt 57-60; P-in-c Cookridge CD Ripon 60-64; V Cookridge H Trin 64-67; Chapl Miss to Seamen Tilbury 67-71; Gt Yarmouth 71-77; Australia 77-84 and from 85; Seaga 84-85; rtd 91. *Unit 4, 150 Oceana Terrace, Lota Qld 4179, Australia*

CHANTER, Canon Anthony Roy. b 37. ACP60 Open Univ BA72 Lon Univ MA75. Sarum Th Coll 64. d 66 p 67. C W Tarring *Chich* 66-69; Chapl St Andr Sch Worthing 69-70; Hd Master Bp King Sch Linc 70-73; Hon PV Linc Cathl 70-73; Hd Master Grey Court Comp Sch Richmond 73-76; Hon C Kingston All SS *S'wark* 73-76; Hd Master Bp Reindorp Sch Guildf 77-84; Dir of Educn *Guildf* 84-01; Hon Can Guildf Cathl 84-01; rtd 02; Perm to Offic *Chich* from 02. *Thalassa, 62 Sea Avenue, Rustington, Littlehampton BN16 2DJ* Tel (01903) 774288 E-mail tonychanter@hotmail.com

CHANTREY, Preb David Frank. b 48. K Coll Cam BA70 PhD73 MA74. Westcott Ho Cam 83. d 86 p 87. C Wordsley *Lich* 86-89;

C Beckbury 89-90; P-in-c 90-93; C Badger 89-90; P-in-c 90-93; C Kemberton, Sutton Maddock and Stockton 89-90; P-in-c 90-93; C Ryton 89-90; P-in-c 90-93; R Beckbury, Badger, Kemberton, Ryton, Stockton etc 93-08; TR Wrockwardine Deanery from 08; RD Wrockwardine from 08; Preb Lich Cathl from 99. *The Rectory, Wrockwardine, Telford TF6 5DD* Tel (01952) 251857 Mobile 07785-524495 E-mail david@wdtm.org.uk

CHANTRY, Canon Helen Fiona. b 59. Bradf Univ BSc82 Leeds Univ CertEd83. Trin Coll Bris BA89. d 89 p 94. NSM Hyde St Geo *Ches* 89-92; Dioc Youth Officer 92-00; NSM Barrow 94-99; C Acton and Worleston, Church Minshull etc 00-04; P-in-c Audlem 04-11; V Wybunbury and Audlem w Doddington from 11; Bp's Adv for Women in Min from 05; Hon Can Ches Cathl from 10. *The Rectory, Church Lane, Nantwich CW5 5RQ* Tel (01270) 625268 *or* 811543 E-mail helenchantry@btopenworld.com

CHANTRY, Peter Thomas. b 62. Bradf Univ BSc83. Trin Coll Bris BA89. d 89 p 90. C Hyde St Geo *Ches* 89-92; Dioc Youth Officer 91-99; P-in-c Barrow 94-99; R Nantwich from 99. *The Rectory, Church Lane, Nantwich CW5 5RQ* Tel (01270) 625268 E-mail peterchantry@hotmail.com

CHANTRY, Mrs Sandra Mary. b 41. Cam Inst of Educn CertEd63. EMMTC 83. dss 86 d 87 p 94. Loughb Gd Shep *Leic* 86-87; Par Dn 87-89; Par Dn Belton and Osgathorpe 89-90; Par Dn Hathern, Long Whatton and Diseworth w Belton etc 90-94; C 94-97; P-in-c 97-01; rtd 01; Perm to Offic *Derby* from 07. *4 The Toft, Mill Lane, Belton, Loughborough LE12 9UL* Tel (01530) 222678 E-mail sandrachantry@aol.com

CHAPLIN, Ann. b 39. Em Coll Boston (USA) MA93 LRAM59 TCert75. WEMTC 95. d 98 p 99. NSM Heref S Wye 98-02; NSM St Weonards w Orcop, Garway, Tretire etc 02-05; P-in-c Belmont St Andr USA 06-09; Asst R Cambridge St Pet from 09. *St Peter's Church, PO Box 390390, Cambridge MA 02139, USA* Tel (001) (617) 547 7788

CHAPLIN, Colin. b 33. Edin Dioc NSM Course 74. d 76 p 77. NSM Penicuik *Edin* 76-91; P-in-c Peebles 89-90; NSM Bathgate 91-95; rtd 95; Asst P Edin St Mark 97-00; Asst P Innerleithen from 00; Asst P Peebles from 00. *26 Broomhill Road, Penicuik, Edinburgh EH26 9EE* Tel (01968) 672050

CHAPLIN, Douglas Archibald. b 59. Em Coll Cam BA81. St Jo Coll Nottm. d 86 p 87. C Glouc St Geo w Whaddon 86-89; C Lydney w Aylburton 89-93; R Worc St Clem 93-01; TV Droitwich Spa from 01. *The Vicarage, 29 Old Coach Road, Droitwich WR9 8BB* Tel (01905) 798929 Mobile 07905-842565 E-mail fatherdoug@actually.me.uk

CHAPLIN, Paul. b 57. Hull Univ BA80 CertEd81 K Coll Lon MA89. St Steph Ho Ox 85. d 87 p 88. C Ex St Jas 87-90; C Wokingham St Paul *Ox* 90-98; V Stratfield Mortimer 98-99; V Stratfield Mortimer and Mortimer W End etc from 99. *The Vicarage, 10 The Avenue, Mortimer, Reading RG7 3QY* Tel 0118-933 2404 *or* 933 3704

CHAPMAN, Andrew John. b 81. Leeds Univ BA03 St Jo Coll Dur BA09. Cranmer Hall Dur 06. d 09 p 10. C Hykeham *Linc* from 09. *120A Station Road, Waddington, Lincoln LN5 9QS* Tel (01522) 723094 E-mail a.j.chapman@live.co.uk

CHAPMAN, Ms Ann Beatrice. b 53. Hull Coll of Educn BEd77 Leeds Univ BA87. St Jo Coll Nottm MA95. d 95 p 96. C Burley *Ripon* 95-98; TV Sheff Manor 98-01; P-in-c Askrigg w Stallingbusk *Ripon* from 01; Dir Practical Th NEOC 04-08; P-in-c Hawes and Hardraw *Ripon* from 09. *The Vicarage, Burtersett Road, Hawes DL8 3NP* Tel (01969) 667553 E-mail ann81@btinternet.com

CHAPMAN, Barry Frank. b 48. Trin Coll Bris 83. d 82 p 83. NSM Bradford-on-Avon Ch Ch *Sarum* 82-11; Assoc Chapl Bath Univ from 83; NSM N Bradford on Avon and Villages *Sarum* from 11. *16 Church Acre, Bradford-on-Avon BA15 1RL* Tel (01225) 866861 *or* 461244 E-mail pysbfc@bath.ac.uk

CHAPMAN, Mrs Celia. b 32. Whitelands Coll Lon TCert53 Open Univ BA82. WMMTC 84. d 87 p 94. NSM Bilston *Lich* 87-93; Chapl St Pet Colleg Sch Wolv and Ind Chapl Black Country Urban Ind Miss 93-98; rtd 99; Perm to Offic *Glouc* and *Worc* from 99. *5 Tyne Drive, Evesham WR11 7FG* Tel (01386) 765878

CHAPMAN, Canon Christopher Robin. b 37. Ripon Hall Ox 72. d 73 p 74. C Kidbrooke St Jas *S'wark* 73-77; V Corton *Nor* 77-80; V Hopton 77-80; V Hopton w Corton 80-92; RD Lothingland 80-86; P-in-c Loddon w Sisland 92-93; P-in-c Loddon, Sisland w Hales and Heckingham 93-98; P-in-c Chedgrave w Hardley and Langley 97-98; V Loddon, Sisland, Chedgrave, Hardley and Langley 98-03; RD Loddon 95-98; Hon Can Nor Cathl 96-03; Chapl Langley Sch Nor 00-03; rtd 04; Perm to Offic *Chelmsf* 04-06 and *St E* from 06. *Preveli, 16 Riley Close, Ipswich IP1 5QD* Tel (01473) 462109

CHAPMAN, Colin Gilbert. b 38. St Andr Univ MA60 Lon Univ BD62 Birm Univ MPhil94. Ridley Hall Cam 62. d 64 p 65. C Edin St Jas 64-67; Asst Chapl Cairo Cathl Egypt 68-73; Tutor Crowther Hall CMS Tr Coll Selly Oak 73-75; Prin 90-97; Lebanon 75-82; Chapl Limassol St Barn 82-83; Lect Trin Coll Bris 83-90; Dir Faith to Faith Consultancy 97-99; Lect Near E

Sch of Th Lebanon 99-03; rtd 04; Perm to Offic *Ely* from 07. *West Lodge, 17 Knights Way, Milton, Cambridge CB24 6DE* Tel (01223) 862169 E-mail beirutchapman@hotmail.com

CHAPMAN, Mrs Deborah Herath. b 55. Fort Lewis Coll (USA) BA76 Lon Bible Coll MA94. NTMTC 04. d 05 p 06. C Hanwell St Mellitus w St Mark *Lon* 05-08; C Northolt St Jos from 08. *St Hugh's House, 22 Gosling Close, Greenford UB6 9UE* Tel (020) 8813 0162 E-mail bee@rechord.com

CHAPMAN, Canon Derek. b 22. Westcott Ho Cam 52. d 53 p 54. C Earlsdon *Cov* 53-56; C Rugby St Andr 56-58; V E Malling *Roch* 58-79; CF (TA) 60-67; R Hever w Mark Beech *Roch* 79-89; P-in-c Four Elms 80-89; Hon Can Roch Cathl 84-89; rtd 89; Perm to Offic *Roch* 89-98 and *Chich* from 89. *1 Moat Lane, Sedlescombe, Battle TN33 0RZ* Tel (01424) 754455

CHAPMAN, Mrs Dorothy. b 38. EMMTC. d 89 p 94. Par Dn Bingham *S'well* 89-92; Sub-Chapl HM Pris Whatton 89-92; C Lenton 92-98; rtd 98; Perm to Offic *S'well* from 04. *86 Kenrick Road, Nottingham NG3 6FB* Tel 0115-950 3088

CHAPMAN, Drummond John. b 36. Cant Sch of Min 80. d 83 p 86. C Kington w Huntington, Old Radnor, Kinnerton etc *Heref* 83-84; C Llanidloes w Llangurig *Ban* 86-90; V Llanwnnog and Caersws w Carno 90-06; rtd 06. *Wgi Fawr, Carno, Caersws SY15 5LX*

CHAPMAN, Mrs Elizabeth Ann. b 57. SEITE 05. d 09 p 10. NSM Gillingham St Mary *Roch* 09-11; Chapl Pilgrims Hospice Cant from 11; NSM Cant St Pet w St Alphege and St Marg etc from 11. *Pilgrims Hospice, 10-12 Pilgrims Way, Canterbury CT1 1XT* Tel (01227) 812610 Mobile 07961-337083 E-mail l.chapman431@btinternet.com

CHAPMAN, Preb Gorran. b 55. Dur Univ BA. Westcott Ho Cam 78. d 80 p 81. C Par *Truro* 80-82; C Kenwyn 82-84; P-in-c Penwerris 84-89; V 89-92; V Torquay St Martin Barton *Ex* from 92; Perm to Offic *Truro* from 99; Preb Ex Cathl from 07. *St Martin's Vicarage, Beechfield Avenue, Barton, Torquay TQ2 8HU* Tel (01803) 327223

CHAPMAN, Guy Godfrey. b 33. Southn Univ BSc57. Clifton Th Coll 60. d 62 p 63. C Chadderton Ch Ch *Man* 62-67; V Edgeside 67-70; P-in-c Shipton Bellinger *Win* 70-72; V 72-83; RD Andover 75-85; Hon Can Win Cathl 79-91; R Over Wallop w Nether Wallop 83-91; V Ambrosden w Merton and Piddington *Ox* 91-00; RD Bicester and Islip 95-00; rtd 00; Perm to Offic *Sarum* and *Win* from 01. *65 St Ann Place, Salisbury SP1 2SU* Tel (01722) 335339

CHAPMAN, Henry Davison. b 31. Bris Univ BA55. Tyndale Hall Bris 52. d 56 p 57. C St Helens St Mark *Liv* 56-60; R Clitheroe St Jas *Blackb* 60-67; V Tipton St Martin *Lich* 67-68; SW Area Sec CPAS 68-72; V Eccleston St Luke *Liv* 72-78; P-in-c Ringshall w Battisford, Barking w Darmsden etc *St E* 78-80; R 80-93; RD Bosmere 87-91; rtd 93; Perm to Offic *Sarum* from 93. *Daracombe, 4 The Clays, Market Lavington, Devizes SN10 4AY* Tel (01380) 813774

CHAPMAN (née CRAVEN), Canon Janet Elizabeth. b 58. St Jo Coll Dur BSc80 MA92. Cranmer Hall Dur 84. d 87 p 95. Par Dn Darlington St Cuth *Dur* 87-92; NSM Edin Gd Shep 93-95; NSM Long Marston and Rufforth w Moor Monkton and Hessay *York* 95-98; Chapl Qu Ethelburga's Coll York 97-99; Chapl Harrogate Ladies' Coll 00; P-in-c Banbury *Ox* 01-08; Can Res Birm Cathl from 08. *4 Nursery Drive, Handsworth, Birmingham B20 2SW* Tel 0121-262 1840 E-mail canonliturgist@birminghamcathedral.com

CHAPMAN, John Brown. b 54. Strathclyde Univ BSc76 Lon Bible Coll BA80. NTMTC 00. d 02 p 03. C W Ealing St Jo w St Jas *Lon* 02-05; C Northolt St Mary 05-08; Chapl for internat churches from 08. *St Hugh's House, 22 Gosling Close, Greenford UB6 9UE* Tel (020) 8813 0162 E-mail john@lchaimcommunity.com

CHAPMAN (née WHITFIELD), Mrs Joy Verity. b 46. SRN67 SCM71. Trin Coll Bris BA88. d 88 p 94. C Littleover *Derby* 88-92; Par Dn Bucknall and Bagnall *Lich* 92-94; TV Bucknall and Bagnall 94-97; Chapl LOROS Hospice 97-03; rtd 03; Perm to Offic *Leic* from 03. *15 Templar Way, Rothley, Leicester LE7 7RB* Tel 0116-230 1994 E-mail joychapman@btinternet.com

CHAPMAN, Mrs Lesley. b 61. NEOC 02. d 05 p 06. C Fenham St Jas and St Basil *Newc* 05-09; P-in-c Kenton Ascension from 09. *Kenton Vicarage, Creighton Avenue, Newcastle upon Tyne NE3 4UN* Tel 0191-285 7803 E-mail lesley.chapman414@btopenworld.com

CHAPMAN, Mrs Linda. b 46. Lon Univ BSc67 Lon Inst of Educn PGCE68. Guildf Dioc Min Course 98. d 00 p 01. NSM Ewell St Fran *Guildf* 00-04; NSM Cheswardine, Childs Ercall, Hales, Hinstock etc *Lich* from 04. *The Vicarage, High Street, Cheswardine, Market Drayton TF9 2RS* Tel (01630) 661204 E-mail rev.linda.chapman@dsl.pipex.com

CHAPMAN, Miss Lynn Marie. b 71. Coll of Ripon & York St Jo BEd93 Cant Ch Ch Univ MA98. ERMC 08. d 11. C Sheringham *Nor* from 11. *11 Scotter Rise, Sheringham NR26 8YD* Tel (01263) 824274 E-mail chapman.lynn@btinternet.com

CHAPMAN, Margaret. *See* FLINTOFT-CHAPMAN, Mrs Margaret

CHAPMAN, Mrs Margaret. b 34. Univ Coll Lon BA72 Qu Mary Coll Lon MA74. EAMTC 94. **d** 95 **p** 96. NSM Theydon Bois *Chelmsf* 95-01; P-in-c Gt Hallingbury and Lt Hallingbury 01-06; Perm to Offic from 06. *Broadacres, Cannons Lane, Hatfield Broad Oak, Bishop's Stortford CM22 7HJ* Tel (01279) 723341 E-mail revd.m.chapman@btinternet.com

CHAPMAN, Mark David. b 60. Trin Coll Ox MA83 DPhil89. Ox Min Course 93. **d** 94 **p** 95. Lect Ripon Coll Cuddesdon from 92; NSM Dorchester *Ox* 94-99; NSM Wheatley from 99. *Ripon College, Cuddesdon, Oxford OX44 9EX* Tel (01865) 874310 E-mail mchapman@ripon-cuddesdon.ac.uk

CHAPMAN, The Ven Michael Robin. b 39. Leeds Univ BA61. Coll of Resurr Mirfield 61. **d** 63 **p** 64. C Southwick St Columba *Dur* 63-68; Chapl RN 68-84; V Hale *Guildf* 84-91; RD Farnham 88-91; Adn Northn and Can Pet Cathl 91-04; rtd 04; Perm to Offic *Pet* 04-07. *Dolphin House, High Street, Caenby, Market Rasen LN8 2EE* Tel (01673) 876190 E-mail chapmanhome@btinternet.com

CHAPMAN, Nigel Leonard. b 58. York St Jo Coll MA02. Cranmer Hall Dur 04. **d** 05 **p** 06. Dioc Youth Officer *York* from 00; NSM Coxwold and Husthwaite from 05. *The Vicarage, Coxwold, York YO61 4AD* Tel (01347) 868287 Mobile 07877-793179 E-mail nigel.chapman@yorkdiocese.org

CHAPMAN, Miss Patricia Ann. b 42. dss 84 **d** 87 **p** 94. Rainworth *S'well* 84-96; Par Dn 87-94; C 94-96; P-in-c Mansfield Oak Tree Lane 96-07; rtd 07. *28 St John's View, Mansfield NG18 1QP*

CHAPMAN, Peter Harold White. b 40. AKC64. **d** 65 **p** 66. C Havant *Portsm* 65-69; C Stanmer w Falmer and Moulsecoomb *Chich* 69-73; Chapl RN 73-86; Chapl Chigwell Sch Essex 86-90; P-in-c Stapleford Tawney w Theydon Mt *Chelmsf* 87-01. *Unit F, 33/F, Block 6, Tung Chung Crescent, 2 Mei Tung Street, Lantau, Hong Kong, China* E-mail phwchapman@aol.com

CHAPMAN, Peter John. b 33. Dur Univ BA56. Cranmer Hall Dur. **d** 59 **p** 60. C Boulton *Derby* 59-62; Uganda 63-70; P-in-c Southampton St Matt *Win* 71-73; TV Southampton (City Cen) 73-78; V Bilston St Leon *Lich* 78-79; P-in-c Bilston St Mary 78-79; TR Bilston 80-98; RD Wolverhampton 89-98; rtd 99; Perm to Offic *Glouc* and *Worc* from 99. *5 Tyne Drive, Evesham WR11 6FG* Tel (01386) 765878

CHAPMAN, Peter John. b 50. ERMC 05. **d** 08 **p** 09. NSM Lt Barningham, Blickling, Edgefield etc *Nor* 08-11; NSM Trunch from 11. *Pump Cottage, The Street, Bessingham, Norwich NR11 7JR* Tel (01263) 577782 E-mail peternina@mypostoffice.co.uk

CHAPMAN, Prof Raymond. b 24. Jes Coll Ox BA45 MA59 Lon Univ MA47 BD75 PhD78. S'wark Ord Course 72. **d** 74 **p** 75. NSM St Mary le Strand w St Clem Danes *Lon* 74-82; NSM Barnes St Mary *S'wark* 82-94; Perm to Offic *Lon* 82-91 and *S'wark* from 94. *6 Kitson Road, London SW13 9HJ* Tel (020) 8748 9901

CHAPMAN, Raymond. b 41. Linc Th Coll 68. **d** 71 **p** 72. C Dronfield *Derby* 71-74; C Delaval *Newc* 75-76; TV Whorlton 76-79; V Newc St Hilda 79-83; V Blyth St Cuth 83-89; Hon C Fareham SS Pet and Paul *Portsm* 95-98; Perm to Offic 98-00 and from 05; C Purbrook 00-05. *170 White Hart Lane, Fareham PO16 9AX* Tel (023) 9232 4537 Fax 9264 4237 Mobile 07944-1245467

CHAPMAN, Canon Rex Anthony. b 38. Univ Coll Lon BA62 St Edm Hall Ox BA64 MA68. Wells Th Coll 64. **d** 65 **p** 66. C Stourbridge St Thos *Worc* 65-68; Chapl Aber Univ 68-78; Can St Andr Cathl 76-78; Bp's Adv for Educn *Carl* 78-85; Dir of Educn 85-04; Can Res Carl Cathl 78-04; rtd 04; Lic to Offic *Ab* from 06; Chapl to The Queen 97-08. *The Cottage, Myreside, Finzean, Banchory AB31 6NB* Tel (01330) 850645 E-mail rex.chapman@btinternet.com

CHAPMAN, Robert Bertram. b 68. St Jo Coll Nottm BA00. **d** 00 **p** 01. C Daybrook *S'well* 00-03; P-in-c Colwick from 03; P-in-c Netherfield from 03. *St George's Rectory, 93 Victoria Road, Netherfield, Nottingham NG4 2NN* Tel 0115-961 5566 E-mail robertsarah@talktalk.net

CHAPMAN, Rodney Andrew. b 53. AKC75. St Aug Coll Cant 75. **d** 76 **p** 77. C Hartlepool St Aid *Dur* 76-81; Lic to Offic 81-83; C Owton Manor 83-87; P-in-c Kelloe 87-92; V Sharlston *Wakef* 92-01; V Stainland w Outlane from 01; C Elland from 06. *The Vicarage, 345 Stainland Road, Stainland, Halifax HX4 9HF* Tel (01422) 311848

CHAPMAN, Roger. b 60. Leic Univ BSc82. Westcott Ho Cam 04. **d** 06 **p** 07. C Norton *St Alb* 06-09; P-in-c Eaton Bray w Edlesborough 09-10; rtd 10. *13 The Pastures, Hatfield AL10 8PB* Tel 07905-891890 (mobile) E-mail r.chapman27@ntlworld.com

CHAPMAN, Roger John. b 34. AKC58. **d** 59 **p** 60. C Guildf Ch Ch 59-61; Kenya 61-67; R S Milford *York* 68-77; RD Selby 72-77; V Beverley St Mary 77-88; RD Beverley 85-88; V Desborough *Pet* 88-95; R Brampton Ash w Dingley and Braybrooke 88-95; rtd 95; Perm to Offic *York* from 95. *14 Scrubwood Lane, Beverley HU17 7BE* Tel (01482) 881267

CHAPMAN, Sally Anne. b 55. Lanchester Poly Cov BSc76 Univ of Wales (Swansea) PGCE77. WMMTC 87. **d** 90 **p** 94. Par Dn Glascote and Stonydelph *Lich* 90-93; Par Dn Willenhall H Trin 93-94; C 94-96; TV 96-99; V Streetly 99-05; Dioc Adv for Women in Min 99-04; RD Walsall 04-05; Preb Lich Cathl 04-05; Lect Stourbridge Coll from 05. *41 Hunters Gate, Much Wenlock TF13 6BW* Tel (01952) 727569 E-mail robert@furzebank.freeserve.co.uk

CHAPMAN, Mrs Sarah Jean. b 55. Lon Univ DipCOT77. Sarum & Wells Th Coll 86. **d** 89 **p** 94. NSM Rogate w Terwick and Trotton w Chithurst *Chich* 89-94; NSM Easebourne 94-96; Perm to Offic *Portsm* 96-97; V Sheet 97-02; V Bitterne Park *Win* from 02. *Bitterne Park Vicarage, 7 Thorold Road, Southampton SO18 1HZ* Tel (023) 8055 1560 E-mail revsarah@sargil.co.uk

CHAPMAN, Simon Jon. b 75. Bris Bapt Coll 04 Trin Coll Bris 07. **d** 08 **p** 09. C Broxbourne w Wormley *St Alb* 08-11; CF(V) 09-11; Chapl RAF from 11. *Chaplaincy Services, Valiant Block, HQ Air Command, RAF High Wycombe HP14 4UE* Tel (01494) 496800 Fax 496343 E-mail curate@chapsters.org.uk

CHAPMAN *(formerly* **WOOD), Canon Sylvia Marian.** b 40. Univ of Wales (Lamp) BA09. Gilmore Ho 77. dss 80 **d** 87 **p** 94. Tolleshunt Knights w Tiptree *Chelmsf* 80-83; Leigh-on-Sea St Jas 83-86; Canvey Is 86-92; Par Dn 87-92; Miss to Seamen 87-92; Warden of Ords *Chelmsf* 89-92; C Hutton and CME Officer 92-97; Ind Chapl 97; V Moulsham St Luke 99-06; rtd 06; Hon Can Chelmsf Cathl 01-06; Perm to Offic *Nor* 00-05 and *St E* from 05. *Preveli, 16 Riley Close, Ipswich IP1 5QD* Tel (01473) 462109 E-mail canons.chapman@btinternet.com

CHAPMAN, Thomas Graham. b 33. Trin Coll Bris 73. **d** 75 **p** 76. C Branksome St Clem *Sarum* 75-81; V Quarry Bank *Lich* 81-93; V Quarry Bank *Worc* 93-99; rtd 99; Perm to Offic *Worc* from 99. *8 Somerset Drive, Wollaston, Stourbridge DY8 4RH* Tel (01384) 373921 E-mail thomas.chapman1@btinternet.com

CHAPMAN, Timothy Mark. b 69. Clare Coll Cam BA91. Oak Hill Th Coll BA02. **d** 02 **p** 03. C Lt Shelford *Ely* from 02. *6 Wakelin Avenue, Sawston, Cambridge CB22 3DS* Tel (01223) 830169 *or* 820116 Mobile 07815-686072 E-mail timandlucy@gmail.com

CHAPMAN, Tristan David. b 79. K Alfred's Coll Win BA01. Ripon Coll Cuddesdon BTh07. **d** 07 **p** 08. C Bocking St Mary *Chelmsf* 07-10; TV Chipping Barnet *St Alb* from 10. *St Mark's Vicarage, 56 Potters Road, Barnet EN5 5HY* Tel (020) 8440 7490 E-mail fr.tristan@googlemail.com

CHAPMAN, Miss Yvonne Hazel. b 35. Serampore Th Coll BRE63 Brighton Coll of Educn CertEd55. EAMTC 95. **d** 96 **p** 97. NSM Duston *Pet* 96-02; NSM Officer 99-02; rtd 02; Perm to Offic *Pet* from 02. *18 Sundew Court, Northampton NN4 9XH* Tel (01604) 762091 E-mail rev.ychapman@virgin.net

CHAPPELL, Allan. b 27. Selw Coll Cam BA51 MA56. Coll of Resurr Mirfield 51. **d** 53 **p** 54. C Knowle *Bris* 53-57; Zanzibar 57-63; C Long Eaton St Laur *Derby* 64-67; C-in-c Broxtowe CD *S'well* 67-73; P-in-c Flintham 73-82; R Car Colston w Screveton 73-82; V Mansfield St Lawr 82-92; rtd 93; Perm to Offic *S'well* from 93 and *Derby* from 00. *c/o A M Chappell Esq, 9 Rosetta Road, New Basford, Nottingham NG7 7GX*

CHAPPELL, Edward Michael. b 32. Glouc Sch of Min 84. **d** 87 **p** 88. NSM Wotton-under-Edge w Ozleworth and N Nibley *Glouc* 87-01; Perm to Offic from 01. *5 Parklands, Wotton-under-Edge GL12 7LT* Tel (01453) 844250

CHAPPELL, Frank Arnold. b 37. Dur Univ BA58. Bps' Coll Cheshunt. **d** 60 **p** 61. C Headingley *Ripon* 60-65; V Beeston Hill St Luke 65-73; R Garforth 73-91; V Dacre w Hartwith and Darley w Thornthwaite 91-02; rtd 02; Perm to Offic *York* and *Ripon* from 02. *14 Nelsons Lane, York YO24 1HD* Tel (01904) 709566

CHAPPELL, Michael. *See* CHAPPELL, Edward Michael

CHAPPELL, Michael Paul. b 35. Selw Coll Cam BA57 MA61. Cuddesdon Coll 60. **d** 62 **p** 63. C Pershore w Pinvin, Wick and Birlingham *Worc* 62-65; Malaysia 65-67; V Choral and Chapl Heref Cathl 67-71; Min Can Dur Cathl 71-76; Prec 72-76; Chapl H Trin Sch Stockton 76-87; C-in-c Stockton Green Vale H Trin CD *Dur* 82-87; V Scarborough St Luke *York* 87-01; Chapl Scarborough Gen Hosp 87-97; rtd 01; Perm to Offic *York* from 01. *26 Dulverton Hall, Esplanade, Scarborough YO11 2AR* Tel (01723) 340126

CHARD, Mrs Julia Clare. b 54. Trin Coll Bris 09. **d** 11. OLM Soundwell *Bris* from 11. *8 Glenside Close, Bristol BS16 2QY* Tel 0117-902 1774 E-mail juliachard@hotmail.com

CHARD, Reginald Jeffrey. b 40. Univ of Wales (Lamp) BA62 CQSW75. Coll of Resurr Mirfield 62. **d** 64 **p** 65. C Ystrad Mynach *Llan* 64-67; C Aberdare St Fagan 67-71; V Hirwaun 71-74; Hon C Stechford *Birm* 74-78; TV Banbury *Ox* 78-86; Ind Chapl 86-09; P-in-c Claydon w Mollington 86-96; R Ironstone 96-09; rtd 09. *5 The Glen, Yarmouth PO41 0PZ* Tel (01983) 760554 E-mail jeffreychard@btinternet.com

CHARING CROSS, Archdeacon of. *See* JACOB, The Ven William Mungo

CHARKHAM, Rupert Anthony. b 59. Ex Univ BA81. Wycliffe Hall Ox 83. **d** 89 **p** 89. C Ox St Aldate w St Matt 89-92; P-in-c

Fisherton Anger *Sarum* 92-99; R 99-03; V Cambridge H Trin *Ely* from 03. *Holy Trinity Vicarage, 1 Selwyn Gardens, Cambridge CB3 9AX* Tel (01223) 354774 *or* 355397
E-mail rupert.charkham@htcambridge.org.uk

CHARLES, Cecilia. *See* CHARLES, Mary Cecilia

CHARLES, David Gordon. b 79. Ex Coll Ox BA01 MA04 CCC Cam BA05 MA09. Westcott Ho Cam 03. **d** 06 **p** 07. C Willingdon *Chich* 06-10; P-in-c Waldron from 10; Chapl to Bp Lewes from 10. *Waldron Rectory, Sheepsetting Lane, Cross in Hand, Heathfield TN21 0UY* Tel (01435) 862816
E-mail davidgcharles@hotmail.com

CHARLES, George Edward. b 41. St Jo Coll Morpeth 63. **d** 66 **p** 67. C Bentleigh St Jo Australia 66-67; C Broadmeadows 67-70; I Montmorency 70-74; I Mooroolbark 74-81; I Bacchus Marsh 81-86; I Sorrento 86-93; I Altona 93-98; I Inverleigh, Bannockburn and Meredith 98-01; TV Hanley H Ev *Lich* 02-06; rtd 06; Perm to Offic *Lich* 06-10; RD Alstonfield 09-10. *140 Geelong Road, Portarlington Vic 3223, Australia*
E-mail gpsecharles@ntlworld.com

CHARLES, James Richard. b 67. St Edm Hall Ox BA90 CertEd91. Oak Hill Th Coll BA03. **d** 03 **p** 04. C Throop *Win* 03-07; P-in-c Bexleyheath St Pet *Roch* from 07. *St Peter's Vicarage, 50 Bristow Road, Bexleyheath DA7 4QA* Tel (020) 8303 8713 E-mail jimrcharles@mac.com

CHARLES, Canon Jonathan. b 42. St Luke's Coll Ex CertEd64. Ripon Hall Ox 72 Ripon Coll Cuddesdon 78. **d** 79 **p** 80. C Leagrave *St Alb* 79-82; Chapl Denstone Coll Uttoxeter 82-86; Chapl Malvern Girls' Coll 86-89; Chapl K Sch Worc 89-95; Min Can Worc Cathl 89-95; R Burnham Gp of Par *Nor* 95-09; RD Burnham and Walsingham 00-08; Hon Can Nor Cathl 05-09; rtd 09; Perm to Offic *Nor* from 09. *Michaelmas Cottage, 8 Back Street, South Creak, Fakenham NR21 9PG* Tel (01328) 823072
E-mail revj.charles@virgin.net

CHARLES, Kevin. b 58. EMMTC 08. **d** 11. NSM Annesley w Newstead *S'well* from 11. *6 Boughton Close, Sutton-in-Ashfield NG17 4NJ* Tel (01623) 514294
E-mail kevin.charles1@btinternet.com

CHARLES, Martin. *See* CHARLES, William Martin Darrell

CHARLES, Mary Cecilia. b 49. Univ of Wales BEd. Trin Coll Carmarthen. **d** 96 **p** 97. NSM Letterston w Llanfair Nant-y-Gof etc *St D* 96-08; NSM Maenclochog and New Moat etc 08-09; V Borth and Eglwys-fach w Llangynfelyn from 09. *8 Clos Winifred, Borth SY24 5LE* Tel (01970) 871889

CHARLES, Meedperdas Edward. b 28. Fitzw Ho Cam BA60 MA64. Bangalore Th Coll BD54. **d** 54 **p** 55. C Malacca Malaya 54-55; P-in-c Singapore St Paul and St Pet 55-58; Perm to Offic *Ely* 58-60; V Sheff St Bart Langsett Road 60-64; Chapl Univ of Singapore 64-66; V Gravelly Hill *Birm* 66-78; V Endcliffe *Sheff* 79-90; rtd 91; Perm to Offic *Sheff* from 91. *60 Ringinglow Road, Sheffield S11 7PQ* Tel 0114-266 4980

CHARLES, Robert Sidney James. b 40. Lon Univ CertEd77 Open Univ BA79 Univ of Wales LLM97. St Mich Coll Llan. **d** 65 **p** 66. C Merthyr Tydfil *Llan* 65-68; C Shotton *St As* 68-70; R Stock and Lydlinch *Sarum* 70-74; R Hubberston *St D* 74-76; Perm to Offic *Chelmsf* 81-83; V Crossens *Liv* 83-97; V Budleigh Salterton *Ex* 97-10; rtd 10; Perm to Offic *Ex* from 11. *8 Old Bystock Drive, Exmouth EX8 5RB* Tel (01395) 223419
E-mail robert.charles@homecall.co.uk

CHARLES, Robin. b 50. Sarum & Wells Th Coll. **d** 86 **p** 87. C Chesterton *Lich* 86-89; C Rugeley 89-90; TV 90-97; TV E Scarsdale *Derby* 97-01; C Chesterfield St Mary and All SS 01-04; V Worc Dines Green St Mich and Crowle E, Rushwick from 04. *3 Grove Farm, Farmbrook Close, Worcester WR2 5UG* Tel and fax (01905) 749995 Mobile 07788-724581
E-mail robin@maize45.freeserve.co.uk

CHARLES, Mrs Susan Jane. b 67. SEITE 05. **d** 08 **p** 09. NSM Eltham H Trin *S'wark* from 08. *109 Tarnwood Park, London SE9 5PE* Tel (020) 8850 0189 E-mail susanjcharles@aol.com

CHARLES, William Martin Darrell. b 40. **d** 90 **p** 91. C Market Harborough *Leic* 90-91; P-in-c Higham-on-the-Hill w Fenny Drayton and Witherley 91-99; P-in-c Breedon cum Isley Walton and Worthington 99-02; rtd 02. *37 Whatton Road, Kegworth, Derby DE74 2EZ* Tel (01509) 672040

CHARLES-EDWARDS, David Mervyn. b 38. Trin Coll Cam BA61. Linc Th Coll 62. **d** 64 **p** 89. C Putney St Mary *S'wark* 64-65; Chief Exec Officer Br Assn for Counselling 82-87; Gen Manager Lon Lighthouse AIDS Project 87-88; Consultant in leadership and team building from 88; NSM Rugby *Cov* 89-99; P-in-c Clifton upon Dunsmore and Newton 99-03; Perm to Offic from 03. *236 Hillmorton Road, Rugby CV22 5BG* Tel (01788) 569212 E-mail cwa.david@btinternet.com

CHARLESWORTH, Eric Charlesworth. b 29. Kelham Th Coll 49. **d** 54 **p** 56. C Woodbridge St Mary *St E* 54-57; Asst Chapl Oslo St Edm *Eur* 57-59; Canada 60-66; R Huntingfield w Cookley *St E* 66-70; R Slimbridge *Glouc* 70-96; rtd 96; Perm to Offic *Glouc* from 96 and *Ox* from 04. *Gardener's Cottage, Fairford Park, Fairford GL7 4JQ* Tel (01285) 712141

CHARLESWORTH, Ian Peter. b 65. Lanc Univ BA87. St Mich Coll Llan. **d** 93 **p** 94. C Caereithin *S & B* 93-95; C

Oystermouth 95-97; R Llandefalle and Llyswen w Boughrood etc from 97. *The Rectory, Church Lane, Llyswen, Brecon LD3 0UU* Tel (01874) 754255
E-mail ian.charlesworth@btinternet.com

CHARLESWORTH, Philip. b 55. Sheff City Poly BSc85 Anglia Poly MSc92. **d** 07 **p** 08. OLM Sprowston w Beeston *Nor* from 07. *63 Wroxham Road, Norwich NR7 8TN* Tel (01603) 411316 Mobile 07983-911958 E-mail pc111@tiscali.co.uk

CHARLEY, Canon Julian Whittard. b 30. New Coll Ox BA55 MA58. Ridley Hall Cam 55. **d** 57 **p** 58. C St Marylebone All So w SS Pet and Jo *Lon* 57-64; Lect Lon Coll of Div 64-70; Vice-Prin St Jo Coll Nottm 70-74; TR Everton St Pet *Liv* 74-87; Warden Shrewsbury Ho 74-87; P-in-c Gt Malvern St Mary *Worc* 87-97; Hon Can Worc Cathl 91-97; rtd 97; Perm to Offic *Heref* and *Worc* from 97. *155A Old Hollow, Malvern WR14 4NN* Tel (01684) 569801

CHARLTON, Mrs Elizabeth Anne. b 55. STETS BA08. **d** 08 **p** 09. C W Moors *Sarum* 08-11; C Budleigh Salterton *Ex* from 11; C E Budleigh w Bicton and Otterton from 11. *The New Vicarage, Vicarage Road, East Budleigh, Budleigh Salterton EX9 7EF* Tel (01395) 444276 Mobile 07541-069078
E-mail eacharlton@btinternet.com

CHARLTON, Helen. **d** 09 **p** 10. NSM Wokingham All SS *Ox* from 09. *36 Rances Lane, Wokingham RG40 2LH* Tel 0118-978 9153 E-mail helenjcharlton@btinternet.com

CHARMAN, Canon Jane Ellen Elizabeth. b 60. St Jo Coll Dur BA81 Selw Coll Cam BA84 MA88. Westcott Ho Cam 82. **d** 87 **p** 94. C Glouc St Geo w Whaddon 87-90; Chapl and Fell Clare Coll Cam 90-95; R Duxford *Ely* 95-04; V Hinxton 95-04; V Ickleton 95-04; RD Shelford 03-04; Dir of Min *Sarum* 04-07; Dir of Learning for Discipleship and Min from 07; Can and Preb Sarum Cathl from 07. *4 The Sidings, Downton, Salisbury SP5 3QZ* Tel (01722) 411944 Mobile 07867-146524
E-mail jane.charman@salisbury.anglican.org

CHARMLEY, Mark Richard. b 71. Ex Univ BA93. Qu Coll Birm MA01. **d** 01 **p** 02. C Blurton *Lich* 01-04; P-in-c Banbury St Leon *Ox* 04-10; P-in-c Guernsey St Sav *Win* from 10; P-in-c Guernsey St Marguerite de la Foret from 10. *The Rectory, Le Neuf Chemin Road, St Saviour, Guernsey GY7 9FQ* Tel (01481) 263045
E-mail charmley@totalise.co.uk

CHARMLEY, Mrs Tracy-Belinda. b 72. Ex Univ BA93 St Luke's Coll Ex PGCE95 Birm Univ MEd. Ripon Coll Cuddesdon 07. **d** 10 **p** 11. NSM Guernsey St Martin *Win* from 10. *The Rectory, La Neuf Chemin Road, St Saviour, Guernsey GY1 1SB* Tel (01481) 263045 E-mail charmley@cwgsy.net

CHARNOCK, Deryck Ian. b 47. Oak Hill Th Coll 78. **d** 80 **p** 81. C Rowner *Portsm* 80-84; TV Southgate *Chich* 84-90; V Penge St Paul *Roch* 90-98; V Whitwick St Jo the Bapt *Leic* 98-06; R Hollington St Leon *Chich* from 06. *The Rectory, Tile Barn Road, St Leonards-on-Sea TN38 9PA* Tel (01424) 852257
E-mail deryck8@aol.com

CHARNOCK, Ms Tracy. b 75. Leeds Univ BA97 BA08. Coll of Resurr Mirfield 06. **d** 08 **p** 09. C Man Victoria Park from 08; P-in-c S Shore H Trin *Blackb* from 11; P-in-c S Shore St Pet from 11. *92 Watson Road, Blackpool FY4 2DE* Tel 07778-163920 (mobile) E-mail tracy.charnock@hotmail.co.uk

CHARRETT, Geoffrey Barton. b 36. ALCM Nottm Univ BSc57. Ridley Hall Cam 63. **d** 67 **p** 68. C Clifton *York* 67-68; Lic to Offic *Blackb* 69-80; C Walthamstow St Mary w St Steph *Chelmsf* 81-82; TV 82-87; Chapl Gordon's Sch Woking 87-94; P-in-c Hambledon *Guildf* 94-97; rtd 97; Perm to Offic *Linc* from 00. *2 Station Road, Sutton-on-Sea, Mablethorpe LN12 2HN* Tel (01507) 443525

CHARRINGTON, Nicholas John. b 36. MA. Cuddesdon Coll 60. **d** 62 **p** 63. C Shrewsbury St Chad *Lich* 62-65; C Gt Grimsby St Mary and St Jas *Linc* 65-72; P-in-c Wellington Ch Ch *Lich* 72-78; R Edgmond 78-89; R Edgmond w Kynnersley and Preston Wealdmoors 89-91; C Plymstock *Ex* 91-94; Chapl St Luke's Hospice Plymouth 91-94; P-in-c Longden and Annscroft w Pulverbatch *Heref* 94-00; rtd 00; Perm to Offic *Heref* from 00 and *Lich* from 11. *Domas Cottage, Harley, Shrewsbury SY5 6LX* Tel (01952) 510721
E-mail nick@charrington.enta.net

CHARTERIS, Hugo Arundale. b 64. Witwatersrand Univ BA88. Cranmer Hall Dur 90. **d** 93 **p** 94. C Byker St Mark and Walkergate St Oswald *Newc* 93-97; P-in-c New Ferry *Ches* 97-02; V 02-05. *26 Rothbury Terrace, Newcastle upon Tyne NE6 5XH* Tel 0191-209 2508 E-mail hugo@charteris.org.uk

CHARTERS, Alan Charles. b 35. Trin Hall Cam BA60 MA63 FCollP88. Linc Th Coll 60. **d** 62 **p** 63. C Gt Grimsby St Mary and St Jas *Linc* 62-65; Chapl and Hd RE Eliz Coll Guernsey 65-70; P-in-c Guernsey St Jas the Less 65-70; Dep Hd Master Park Sen High Sch Swindon 70-73; Chapl St Jo Sch Leatherhead 73-83; Dep Hd Master 76; Visiting Lect and Tutor Lon Univ Inst of Ed 76-80; Headmaster The K Sch Glouc 83-92; V Aberedw w Llandeilo Graban and Llanbadarn etc *S & B* 92-00; Bp's Visitor to Schs 92-00; rtd 00; Perm to Offic *Eur* 00-03; P-in-c Dinard 03-06. *Crescent House, Church Street, Talgarth, Brecon LD3 0BL* Tel (01874) 711135 E-mail alan@ccharters.net.uk

✠**CHARTRES, The Rt Revd and Rt Hon Richard John Carew.** b 47. KCVO09 PC96. Trin Coll Cam BA68 MA73 BD83 Hon DLitt98 Hon DD99 FSA99 Hon FGCM97. Cuddesdon Coll 69 Linc Th Coll 72. **d** 73 **p** 74 **c** 92. C Bedford St Andr *St Alb* 73-75; Bp's Dom Chapl 75-80; Abp's Chapl *Cant* 80-84; P-in-c Westmr St Steph w St Jo *Lon* 84-85; V 86-92; Dir of Ords 85-92; Prof Div Gresham Coll 86-92; Six Preacher Cant Cathl 91-97; Area Bp Stepney *Lon* 92-95; Bp Lon from 95; Dean of HM Chpls Royal and Prelate of OBE from 95. *The Old Deanery, Dean's Court, London EC4V 5AA* Tel (020) 7248 6233 Fax 7248 9721 E-mail bishop@londin.clara.co.uk

CHASE, Mrs Elizabeth. Wycliffe Hall Ox. **d** 09 **p** 10. NSM Headbourne Worthy *Win* from 09; NSM King's Worthy from 09. *The Greetings, Grange Road, Winchester SO23 9RT*

CHATER, John Augustus. b 43. SEITE 99. **d** 04 **p** 05. NSM St Peter-in-Thanet *Cant* 04-07; Ramsgate Town Cen Missr from 07. *25 High Street, Ramsgate CT11 9UA* Tel (01843) 596175 E-mail johnchater@rya-online.net

CHATER, John Leathley. b 29. Qu Coll Cam BA54 MA58. Ridley Hall Cam 54. **d** 56 **p** 57. C Bath Abbey w St Jas *B & W* 56-60; V Bermondsey St Anne S'*wark* 60-64; Ind Chapl 60-64; V Heslington *York* 64-69; Chapl York Univ 64-69; V Lawrence Weston *Bris* 69-73; Perm to Offic 74-80; P-in-c Wraxall *B & W* 80-82; R 82-84; V Battle *Chich* 84-90; Dean Battle 84-90; RD Battle and Bexhill 86-90; R St Marylebone w H Trin *Lon* 90-96; rtd 96; Perm to Offic *Chich* 96-11. *High Ridge, London Road, Halesworth IP19 8LR* Tel (01986) 875876

CHATER (née CAKE), Nichola Carla. b 58. Liv Univ BSc79 MB, ChB85 MRCGP FRCP08. Cranmer Hall Dur 05. **d** 07 **p** 08. NSM Dur St Marg and Neville's Cross St Jo from 07. *37 Hill Meadows, High Shincliffe, Durham DH1 2PE* Tel 0191-383 1869 E-mail nicky.chater@yahoo.co.uk

CHATFIELD, Adrian Francis. b 49. Leeds Univ BA71 MA72 MPhil89 PhD97. Coll of Resurr Mirfield 71. **d** 72 **p** 73. Trinidad and Tobago 72-83; TV Barnstaple, Goodleigh and Landkey *Ex* 83-85; TR Barnstaple 85-88; Lect St Jo Coll Nottm 88-98; S Africa 99-05; Tutor Wycliffe Hall Ox 05-07; Hon C Wallingford *Ox* 05-07; Dir Simeon Cen and Co-ord Mixed Mode Tr Ridley Hall Cam from 07. *12 Barrons Way, Comberton, Cambridge CB23 7EQ* Tel (01223) 263009 *or* 746590 E-mail adrian.chatfield@btinternet.com *or* ac588@cam.ac.uk

CHATFIELD, Mrs Gillian. b 50. Leeds Univ BA71 PGCE72. St Jo Coll Nottm MA94. **d** 94 **p** 95. C Greasley S'*well* 94-98; S Africa 99-05; TV Wallingford *Ox* 05-07; Past Tutor Ridley Hall Cam from 07. *12 Barrons Way, Comberton, Cambridge CB23 7EQ* Tel (01223) 263009 Mobile 07758-591430 E-mail jill.chatfield@btinternet.com

CHATFIELD, Michael Francis. b 75. York Univ BSc96 Fitzw Coll Cam BA99 MA03. Ridley Hall Cam. **d** 00 **p** 01. C Attenborough S'*well* 00-03; P-in-c Chaguanas St Thos Trinidad and Tobago 04-09; Chapl RAF from 09. *Chaplaincy Services, Valiant Block, HQ Air Command, RAF High Wycombe HP14 4UE* Tel (01494) 496800 Fax 496343 Mobile 07540-848758 E-mail thechatalots@hotmail.com

CHATFIELD, Canon Norman. b 37. Fitzw Coll Cam BA59 MA68. Ripon Hall Ox 60. **d** 62 **p** 63. C Burgess Hill St Jo *Chich* 62-65; C Uckfield 65-69; V Lower Sandown St Jo *Portsm* 69-76; V Locks Heath 76-83; R Alverstoke 83-91; Hon Can Portsm Cathl 85-91; Can Res Glouc Cathl 91-02; rtd 02; Perm to Offic *Portsm* from 03. *Ellwood, Garfield Road, Bishop's Waltham SO32 1AT* Tel (01489) 891995 E-mail chat.field@btinternet.com

CHATFIELD, Thomas William. b 19. Chich Th Coll 44. **d** 46 **p** 47. C Hanworth All SS *Lon* 46-49; C Woolwich St Mich S'*wark* 49-51; C Eastbourne St Andr *Chich* 51-55; V Halton in Hastings St Clem 55-68; P-in-c Hastings St Mary Magd 68-71; R 71-78; P-in-c Bishopstone 78-84; rtd 84; Perm to Offic *Chich* from 84. *Lauriston Christian Nursing Home, 40 The Green, St Leonards-on-Sea TN38 0SY* Tel (01424) 441590

CHATTELL, David Malcolm. b 63. St Luke's Coll Ex BEd93. Wycliffe Hall Ox 03. **d** 05 **p** 06. C Bucklebury w Marlston *Ox* 05-11; R Farleigh, Candover and Wield *Win* from 11. *The Rectory, Alresford Road, Preston Candover, Basingstoke RG25 2EE* Tel (01256) 389474 E-mail davidchattell172@btinternet.com

CHATTERLEY, Mrs Marion Frances. b 55. Edin Th Coll 95. **d** 98 **p** 99. C Edin Gd Shep 98-00; C Edin Ch Ch 00-05; Hon C Edin St Mich and All SS from 07; Chapl Napier Coll from 00; Dioc Dir of Ords from 06. *102 Relugas Road, Edinburgh EH9 2LZ* Tel (0131) 667 6847 Mobile 07771-982163 E-mail marion.chatterley@blueyonder.co.uk

CHATTERTON, Thomas William. b 50. SEITE. **d** 99 **p** 00. OLM Blackheath All SS S'*wark* from 99. *44 Harland Road, London SE12 0JA* Tel (020) 8851 6813 *or* 7525 7912 ext 4482 E-mail trev2@amserve.com

CHATWIN, Ronald Ernest. b 34. St Aid Birkenhead 58. **d** 60 **p** 61. C Selsdon *Cant* 60-64; C Crawley *Chich* 64-68; V Coldwaltham 68-74; TV Ovingdean w Rottingdean and Woodingdean 74-83; V Saltdean 83-91; V Hellingly and Upper Dicker 91-02; rtd 02;

Perm to Offic *Chich* from 03. *Cold Waltham, 29A New Road, Hellingly, Hailsham BN27 4EW* Tel (01323) 843346

CHAUDHARY, Jaisher Masih. b 56. Qu Coll Birm. **d** 08 **p** 09. NSM Handsworth St Mich *Birm* from 08. *29 George Street, Handsworth, Birmingham B21 0EG* Tel 0121-551 6279

CHAVE, Preb Brian Philip. b 51. Open Univ BA. Trin Coll Bris. **d** 84 **p** 85. C Cullompton *Ex* 84-87; TV Bishopsnympton, Rose Ash, Mariansleigh etc 87-93; Chapl for Agric *Heref* 93-96; Communications Adv and Bp's Staff Officer 97-01; Bp's Dom Chapl 97-01; TV W Heref from 01; Preb Heref Cathl from 97; Can 97-01; RD Heref City 04-07. *The Vicarage, Vowles Close, Hereford HR4 0DF* Tel (01432) 273086 E-mail chave@hfddiocesan.freeserve.co.uk

CHAVE-COX, Guy. b 56. St Andr Univ BSc79. Wycliffe Hall Ox 83. **d** 86 **p** 87. C Wigmore Abbey *Heref* 86-88; C Bideford *Ex* 88-91; TV Barnstaple from 91. *St Paul's Vicarage, Old Sticklepath Hill, Barnstaple EX31 2BG* Tel (01271) 344400 E-mail vicar@barnstaple-st-paul.org.uk

CHAVNER, Robert. b 59. ALCM82 AGSM85 FGMS00 FRSA05. Linc Th Coll 90. **d** 92 **p** 93. C Beckenham St Geo *Roch* 92-96; V Sevenoaks St Luke 96-06; P-in-c Brighton St Nic *Chich* 06-11; V from 11. *The Vicarage, 8 Prestonville Road, Brighton BN1 3TL* Tel (01273) 709045 E-mail robert.chavner@ntlworld.com

CHEADLE, Preb Robert. b 24. MBE71 TD66. Leeds Univ BA49. Coll of Resurr Mirfield 49. **d** 51 **p** 52. C Newbury St Jo *Ox* 51-55; C Tunstall Ch Ch *Lich* 55-57; TR Hanley H Ev 57-60; V Bloxwich 60-72; V Penkridge w Stretton 72-89; Preb Lich Cathl 79-89; P-in-c Dunston w Coppenhall 79-82; V 82-89; P-in-c Acton Trussell w Bednall 80-82; V 82-89; rtd 89; Perm to Offic *Lich* 89-09. *19 Andrews Close, Tarvin, Chester CH3 8LN* Tel (01829) 741679

CHEATLE, Adèle Patricia. b 46. York Univ BA73. Trin Coll Bris 76. **d** 87 **p** 98. Par Dn Harborne Heath *Birm* 87; NSM 92-93; Perm to Offic *Heref* 96-97; NSM Burghill and Stretton Sugwas 97-99; NSM Heref St Pet w St Owen and St Jas 99-04; NSM Ches Square St Mich w St Phil *Lon* 04-07. *26 Oakham Road, Harborne, Birmingham B17 9DG* E-mail adele@cheatle.fslife.co.uk

CHEDZEY, Derek Christopher. b 67. Trin Coll Bris BA93. **d** 93 **p** 94. C Bedgrove *Ox* 93-95; C Haddenham w Cuddington, Kingsey etc 95-98; TV High Wycombe 98-01; Deanery Tr Officer and C Washfield, Stoodleigh, Withleigh etc *Ex* 01-04; P-in-c Frenchay and Winterbourne Down *Bris* 04-06; Dioc Dir Lay Min 04-08; Adv for Initial Minl Educn from 08; Warden of Readers from 04; Hon C Yate New Town from 09. *The Rectory, Rectory Road, Frampton Cotterell, Bristol BS36 2BP* Tel 0117-906 0100 Mobile 07811-878774 E-mail derek.chedzey@bristoldiocese.org

CHEEK, Jane Elizabeth. *See* VLACH, Jane Elizabeth

CHEEK, Richard Alexander. b 35. Lon Univ LDS60 RCS 60. Ox NSM Course 72. **d** 75 **p** 76. NSM Maidenhead St Luke *Ox* 75-94; Asst Chapl Heatherwood and Wexham Park Hosp NHS Trust from 94. *Windrush, 26 Sheephouse Road, Maidenhead SL6 8EX* Tel (01628) 628484 E-mail r.a.cheek@dialpipex.com

CHEESEMAN (née DUNHAM), Mrs Angela May. b 40. New Hall Cam MB, BChir66 MRCOG74 FRCSEd75 FRCOG96. **d** 05 **p** 06. OLM Eastling w Ospringe and Stalisfield w Otterden *Cant* 05-10. *New House Farm, Otterden Road, Eastling, Faversham ME13 0BN* Tel (01795) 892124 E-mail angiecheeseman45@hotmail.com

CHEESEMAN, Colin Henry. b 47. Reading Univ BA69 Kent Univ PhD00. Sarum & Wells Th Coll 82. **d** 84 **p** 85. C Cranleigh *Guildf* 84-87; C Godalming 87-89; V Cuddington 89-96; Chapl HM Pris Wealstun 96-97; P-in-c Tockwith and Bilton w Bickerton *York* 97-01; RD New Ainsty 99-01; P-in-c Roundhay St Jo *Ripon* from 01; Dioc Ecum Adv from 09. *The Vicarage, 2A Ryder Gardens, Leeds LS8 1JS* Tel 0113-266 9747 E-mail colin@stjohnsroundhay.co.uk

CHEESEMAN, Janet. *See* GOODAIR, Jan

CHEESEMAN, John Anthony. b 50. Oriel Coll Ox BA73 MA75. Trin Coll Bris. **d** 76 **p** 77. C Sevenoaks St Nic *Roch* 76-79; C Egham *Guildf* 79-82; V Leyton Ch Ch *Chelmsf* 82-90; V Westgate St Jas *Cant* 90-01; V Eastbourne H Trin *Chich* 01-10; rtd 10; Perm to Offic *Cant* from 11. *7 Meadow Road, Margate CT9 5JJ* Tel (01843) 230733 E-mail jcpreach@gmail.com

CHEESEMAN, Kenneth Raymond. b 29. Roch Th Coll 63. **d** 66 **p** 67. C Crayford *Roch* 66-69; C Beckenham St Jas 69-75; V Belvedere St Aug 75-83; V Thorley *Portsm* 83-94; R Yarmouth 83-94; rtd 94; Perm to Offic *Portsm* from 94. *10 St Catherine's View, Godshill, Ventnor PO38 3JJ* Tel (01983) 840700

CHEESEMAN, Nicholas James. b 72. Qu Mary and Westf Coll Lon BA94 Leeds Univ BA02. Coll of Resurr Mirfield 00. **d** 03 **p** 04. C Wantage *Ox* 03-07; V Reading All SS from 07. *All Saints' Vicarage, 14 Downshire Square, Reading RG1 6NH* Tel 0118-957 2000 Mobile 07732-252709

CHEESEMAN, Trevor Percival. b 38. Auckland Univ PhD64 Lon Univ BD67. K Coll Lon and St Boniface Warminster AKC67. **d** 68 **p** 69. C Warmsworth *Sheff* 68-71; New Zealand from 71. *49 Birdwood Avenue, Papatoetoe, Manukau 2025, New Zealand* Tel (0064) (9) 277 6145 E-mail tpandhmc@middleearth.net.nz

CHEESMAN, Canon Andrew Walford. b 36. St Mark's Coll Adelaide BA58. Cuddesdon Coll 59. d 61 p 62. C Man St Aid 61-63; P-in-c Keith Australia 64-68; Prec St Pet Cathl Adelaide 68-70; Chapl Flinders Univ 68-70; Asst Chapl St Pet Coll Adelaide 70-73; P-in-c Tea Tree Gully 73-76; R Mitcham Adelaide 76-01; Adn Torrens 85-93; Can Adelaide from 85. *1/4 Torrens Street, Mitcham SA 5062, Australia* Tel and fax (0061) (8) 8272 1864 E-mail mousal@bigbutton.com.au

CHEESMAN, Peter. b 43. ACA65 FCA76 MCMI. Ridley Hall Cam 66. d 69 p 70. C Herne Bay Ch Ch *Cant* 69-74; TV Lowestoft St Marg *Nor* 75-78; TV Lowestoft and Kirkley 79-81; Ind Chapl *Glouc* 81-84; P-in-c Saul w Fretherne and Framilode 84-85; V Frampton on Severn, Arlingham, Saul etc 85-08; rtd 08. *Frampton Court, The Green, Frampton on Severn, Gloucester GL2 7EX* Tel (01452) 740533 E-mail peter@the-cheesman.net

CHEETHAM (née MUMFORD), Mrs Lesley Anne. b 51. Man Univ BA73. NOC 01. d 04 p 05. C Halifax *Wakef* 04-08; V Easby w Skeeby and Brompton on Swale etc *Ripon* from 08. *The Vicarage, St Paul's Drive, Brompton on Swale, Richmond DL10 7HQ* Tel (01748) 811748 Mobile 07963-620391 E-mail lesley.cheetham3@btinternet.com

✠**CHEETHAM, The Rt Revd Richard Ian.** b 55. CCC Ox BA77 CertEd78 MA82 Lon Univ PhD99. Ripon Coll Cuddesdon 85. d 87 p 88 c 02. C Newc H Cross 87-90; V Luton St Aug Limbury *St Alb* 90-99; RD Luton 95-98; Adn St Alb 99-02; Area Bp Kingston *S'wark* from 02. *Kingston Episcopal Area Office, 620 Kingston Road, London SW20 8DN* Tel (020) 8545 2440 or 8789 3218 Fax 8545 2441 E-mail bishop.richard@southwark.anglican.org

CHEEVERS, George Alexander. b 42. CITC 70. d 73 p 74. C Carrickfergus *Conn* 73-81; C Kilroot 78-81; I Kilmakee 82-91; I Magheragall 91-04; Can Belf Cathl 01-04; rtd 04. *1 Hampton Court, Dromore BT25 1SB* Tel (028) 9269 0701 E-mail bistokids@btinternet.com

CHEGE, James Gathioro. b 57. St Paul's Coll Limuru BD94. NTMTC. d 09 p 10. NSM Grays Thurrock *Chelmsf* from 09. *35 Oakley Close, Grays RM20 4AN* Tel (01375) 381513 Mobile 07983-607574 E-mail captjchege@aol.com

CHELASHAW, Godfrey Kiprotich (Kip). b 76. Oak Hill Th Coll BA08 MA10. d 10 p 11. C Audley *Lich* from 10. *St John's Vicarage, High Street, Alsagers Bank, Stoke-on-Trent ST7 8BQ* E-mail kchelashaw@yahoo.com

CHELMSFORD, Bishop of. *See* COTTRELL, The Rt Revd Stephen Geoffrey

CHELMSFORD, Dean of. *See* JUDD, The Very Revd Peter Somerset Margesson

CHELTENHAM, Archdeacon of. *See* SPRINGETT, The Ven Robert Wilfred

CHENERY, Mrs Janice Marienne. b 46. d 07 p 08. OLM Mid Loes *St E* from 07. *White House Cottage, Dallinghoo, Woodbridge IP13 0JP* Tel (01473) 737425

CHERRY, David. b 30. Roch Th Coll 59. d 61 p 62. C Seacroft *Ripon* 61-67; R Bamford *Derby* 67-75; Chapl Málaga w Almuñecar and Nerja *Eur* 83-91; rtd 91; NSM Waltham St Lawrence *Ox* 97-01; Perm to Offic *Leic* from 01. *2 Church Lane, Rearsby, Leicester LE7 4YE* Tel (01664) 424099

CHERRY, David Warwick. b 61. Cape Town Univ BMus86 Leeds Univ BA91. Coll of Resurr Mirfield 92. d 92 p 93. C Hammersmith SS Mich and Geo White City Estate CD *Lon* 92-01; C Hammersmith St Luke 94-01; Chapl Greenwich Univ 01-03; Chapl Univ of Westmr *Lon* 03-10; Hon C St Marylebone St Cypr 06-08; V Pimlico St Mary Bourne Street from 10; V Pimlico St Barn from 10. *St Mary's Presbytery, 30 Bourne Street, London SW1W 8JJ* Tel (020) 7730 2423 Mobile 07939-553547 E-mail vicar@stmarysbournest.com

CHERRY, Malcolm Stephen. b 28. Open Univ BA81. Sarum Th Coll 51. d 54 p 55. C Mill Hill Jo Keble Ch *Lon* 54-57; C Hendon All SS Childs Hill 57-59; Min Colchester St Anne CD *Chelmsf* 59-68; V Horndon on the Hill 68-79; Ind Chapl 69-79; Voc Officer Southend Adnry 74-79; R Lochgilphead *Arg* 79-82; V Mill End and Heronsgate w W Hyde *St Alb* 82-90; TV Chipping Barnet w Arkley 90-94; rtd 94; Perm to Offic *St E* from 04. *Nether Hankleys, Barrow Road, Higham, Bury St Edmunds IP28 6NN* Tel (01284) 810269 E-mail mandpcherry@waitrose.com

CHERRY, Canon Stephen Arthur. b 58. St Chad's Coll Dur BSc79 Fitzw Coll Cam BA85 MA90 K Coll Lon PhD95. Westcott Ho Cam 83. d 86 p 87. C Baguley and Asst Chapl Wythenshawe Hosp Man 86-89; Chapl K Coll Cam 89-94; R Loughborough All SS w H Trin *Leic* 94-06; RD Akeley E 96-99; Hon Can Leic Cathl 04-06; Dir Min and Tr *Dur* from 06; Can Res Dur Cathl from 06. *St Margaret's House, 30 South Street, Durham DH1 4QP* Tel 0191-384 3623 E-mail sacherry@btinternet.com

CHERRY, William Gerald. b 32. MIMechE55. Wells Th Coll 61. d 63 p 64. C Ashford *Cant* 63-66; C Edgbaston St Bart *Birm* 66-68; V Smethwick 68-72; Lic to Offic *Heref* 72-78; TV

Glendale Gp *Newc* 78-84; rtd 84; Hon Asst Chapl Algarve *Eur* 84-97; Perm to Offic *Sarum* from 97. *Flat 10, Manormead, Tilford Road, Hindhead GU26 6RA*

CHESHER, Michael. b 52. Open Univ BA84. EAMTC. d 00 p 01. C Littleport *Ely* 00-03; V Chelmsf All SS 03-04; P-in-c Walpole St Peter w Walpole St Andrew *Ely* 04-11; P-in-c W Walton 04-11. *The Rectory, Church Road, Walpole St Peter, Wisbech PE14 7NS* Tel (01945) 780252 E-mail m.chesher559@btinternet.com

CHESNEY, David Vince. b 69. UMIST BSc99. NTMTC BA08. d 08 p 09. C Springfield H Trin *Chelmsf* from 08. *49 Patching Hall Lane, Chelmsford CM1 4BU* Tel (01245) 352206 E-mail dave.chesney@btinternet.com

✠**CHESSUN, The Rt Revd Christopher Thomas James.** b 56. Univ Coll Ox BA78 MA82 Trin Hall Cam BA82. Westcott Ho Cam. d 83 p 84 c 05. C Sandhurst *Ox* 83-87; C Portsea St Mary *Portsm* 87-89; Min Can and Chapl St Paul's Cathl 89-93; Voc Adv 90-05; R Stepney St Dunstan and All SS 93-01; AD Tower Hamlets 97-01; Adn Northolt 01-05; Area Bp Woolwich *S'wark* 05-11; Bp S'wark from 11. *Bishop's House, 38 Tooting Bec Gardens, London SW16 1QZ* Tel (020) 8769 3256 or 7939 9420 Fax 8769 4126 E-mail bishop.christopher@southwark.anglican.org

CHESTER, David Kenneth. b 50. Dur Univ BA73 Aber Univ PhD78 CGeol92 FGS88. NOC 93. d 96 p 97. NSM Hoylake *Ches* 96-04; NSM W Kirby St Bridget from 04. *Yenda, Grange Old Road, West Kirby, Wirral CH48 4ET* Tel 0151-625 8004 E-mail jg54@liv.ac.uk

CHESTER, Mark. b 55. Lanc Univ BA79. Wycliffe Hall Ox 86. d 88 p 89. C Plymouth St Andr w St Paul and St Geo *Ex* 88-94; V Burney Lane *Birm* 94-99; V Camberley St Paul *Guildf* from 99; CF (TA) from 07. *The Vicarage, Sandy Lane, Camberley GU15 2AG* Tel (01276) 21100 or 700211 E-mail mark@stpaulscamb.co.uk

CHESTER, Maureen Olga. b 47. Univ of Wales (Swansea) BA70. NEOC 94. d 97 p 98. NSM Morpeth *Newc* from 97. *10 Leland Place, Morpeth NE61 2AN* Tel (01670) 514569 E-mail mochester@classicfm.net

CHESTER, Philip Anthony Edwin. b 55. Birm Univ LLB76. Cranmer Hall Dur 77. d 80 p 81. C Shrewsbury St Chad *Lich* 80-85; C St Martin-in-the-Fields *Lon* 85-88; Chapl K Coll Lon 88-95; PV Westmr Abbey from 90; P-in-c Westmr St Matt *Lon* 95-03; V from 03; AD Westmr St Marg from 05. *St Matthew's House, 20 Great Peter Street, London SW1P 2BU* Tel (020) 7222 3704 Fax 7233 0255 E-mail office@stmw.org

CHESTER, Mrs Violet Grace. b 50. WEMTC 97. d 00 p 01. OLM Dymock w Donnington and Kempley *Glouc* 00; OLM Redmarley D'Abitot, Bromesberrow, Pauntley etc from 00. *1 Longbridge, Dymock GL18 2DA* Tel (01531) 890633 Fax 635919 E-mail vi@vichester.orangehome.co.uk

CHESTER, Archdeacon of. *See* GILBERTSON, The Ven Michael Robert

CHESTER, Bishop of. *See* FORSTER, The Rt Revd Peter Robert Ferguson

CHESTER, Dean of. *See* McPHATE, The Very Revd Gordon Ferguson

CHESTERFIELD, Archdeacon of. *See* WILSON, The Ven Christine Louise

CHESTERMAN, Canon George Anthony (Tony). b 38. Man Univ BSc62 DipAdEd Nottm Univ PhD89. Coll of Resurr Mirfield 62. d 64 p 65. C Newbold w Dunston *Derby* 64-68; C Derby St Thos 68-70; Adult Educn Officer 70-79; R Mugginton and Kedleston 70-89; Vice-Prin EMMTC 79-86; Can Res Derby Cathl and Dioc Clergy In-Service Tr Adv *Derby* 89-03; rtd 03; Chapl to The Queen 98-08. *7 Hillside, Lesbury, Alnwick NE66 3NR* Tel (01665) 833124

✠**CHESTERS, The Rt Revd Alan David.** b 37. CBE07. St Chad's Coll Dur BA59 St Cath Soc Ox BA61 MA65. St Steph Ho Ox 59. d 62 p 63 c 89. C Wandsworth St Anne *S'wark* 62-66; Hon C 66-68; Chapl Tiffin Sch Kingston 66-72; Hon C Ham St Rich *S'wark* 68-72; Dioc Dir of Educn *Dur* 72-85; R Brancepeth 72-85; Hon Can Dur Cathl 75-85; Adn Halifax *Wakef* 85-89; Bp Blackb 89-03; rtd 03; Hon Asst Bp Ches 03-10; Hon Asst Bp Eur 05-09; Hon Asst Bp St As 09-10; Hon Asst Bp S'wark from 11. *The College of St Barnabas, Blackberry Lane, Lingfield RH7 6NJ* Tel (01342) 872861 E-mail alanandjenniechesters@googlemail.com

CHESTERS, David Nigel. b 45. d 04 p 05. NSM Wallasey St Hilary *Ches* 04-06; V Ches St Pet w St Jo from 06. *48 Elizabeth Crescent, Chester CH4 7AZ* Tel (01244) 676567 E-mail rectorofchester@btinternet.com

CHESTERS, Simon. b 66. Rob Coll Cam BA87 MA91. Wycliffe Hall Ox BA94. d 95 p 96. C Bidston *Ches* 95-99; P-in-c Runcorn St Jo Weston 99-03; Dioc Min Development Officer 03-09; Hon C Lache cum Saltney 03-09; Dir Reader Tr 99-09; Regional Leadership Development Adv (NW) CPAS 10-11; Dir Studies Dioc Lifelong Learning *Liv* from 11; Lic Preacher *Man* from 10. *St James' House, 20 St James Road, Liverpool L1 7BY* Tel 0151-705 2120 E-mail simon.chesters@liverpool.anglican.org

CHESTERTON, Robert Eric. b 31. St Aid Birkenhead 63. **d** 65 **p** 66. C Kirby Muxloe *Leic* 65-67; Miss Cambridge Bay Canada 67-68; C St Annes St Thos *Blackb* 68-69; V Southminster *Chelmsf* 69-75; R Ashcroft and Savona Canada 75-78; V Wythenshawe Wm Temple Ch *Man* 78-82; TV Marfleet *York* 82-85; V Marshchapel *Linc* 85-88; R N Coates 85-88; V Grainthorpe w Conisholme 85-88; V Langtoft Gp 88-91; V Kingsbury *Birm* 91-94; rtd 94; Perm to Offic *Pet* 95-08; *Leic* 96-99 and from 03. *20 David Royce House, South Street, Oakham LE15 6HD* Tel (01572) 757262

CHESWORTH (*née* **NAYLOR**), **Mrs Alison Louise.** b 68. St Andr Univ MTheol97 Edin Univ MTh99. TISEC 98. **d** 00 **p** 01. C Ayr, Girvan and Maybole *Glas* 00-03; R Glas All SS and P-in-c Glas H Cross 03-10; TV Ipswich St Mary at Stoke w St Pet and St Fran *St E* from 10. *St Francis' House, 190 Hawthorn Drive, Ipswich IP2 0QQ* Tel (01473) 688339 E-mail alichesworth@sky.com

CHESWORTH, John Martin. b 44. Leeds Univ BSc67 PhD71 FRSC80. S Dios Minl Tr Scheme 90. **d** 92 **p** 93. Oman 92-95; Perm to Offic *Ab* 96-98 and *Ches* 98-03; C Egremont St Jo *Ches* 03-04; V Tranmere St Paul w St Luke 04-09; rtd 09; Perm to Offic *Lich* from 10. *21 Oerley Way, Oswestry SY11 1TD* Tel (01691) 653922 E-mail jchesworth44@tiscali.co.uk

CHEUNG, Anita Yen. b 40. **d** 98 **p** 99. OLM St Luke in the City *Liv* 99-06; rtd 06. *10 Pine Walks, Prenton, Birkenhead CH42 8LQ* Tel and fax 0151-609 1459

CHEVERTON, Miss Jill. b 48. Cranmer Hall Dur 93. **d** 93 **p** 94. Par Dn Bilton *Ripon* 93-94; C 94-96; V Burmantofts St Steph and St Agnes 96-03; Min Binley Woods LEP *Cov* from 03. *20 Daneswood Road, Binley Woods, Coventry CV3 2BJ* Tel (024) 7654 3003 E-mail revchev@email.com

CHEVILL, Elizabeth Jane. *See* PITKETHLY, Elizabeth Jane

✠**CHEW, The Most Revd John Hiang Chea.** b 47. Nanyang Tech Univ Singapore BA69 MA77 Lon Univ BD77 Sheff Univ PhD82. **d** 77 **p** 78 **c** 00. C St Andr Cathl Singapore 77-85; Hon Can 85-00; Lect Trin Th Coll Singapore 82-99; Dean of Studies 85-88; Prin 91-99; Bp Singapore from 00; Abp SE Asia from 06. *1 Francis Thomas Drive, #01-01 Singapore 359340, Republic of Singapore* Tel (0065) 6288 7585 Fax 6288 5574 E-mail bpoffice@anglican.org.sg

CHEW, Philip Vivian Frederick. b 62. St Martin's Coll Lanc BA96. Qu Coll Birm 96. **d** 98 **p** 99. C Chorley St Laur *Blackb* 98-02; V Burnley St Steph 02-08; P-in-c Blackb St Fran and St Aid 08-10; R Llanbedr DC, Llangynhafal, Llanychan etc *St As* from 10; AD Dyffryn Clwyd from 10. *The Rectory, Llanbedr Dyffryn Clwyd, Ruthin LL15 1UP* Tel (01824) 705755 E-mail chewphilip@aol.com

CHEW, Susan. **d** 10 **p** 11. OLM Haughton le Skerne *Dur* from 10. *59 Saltersgate Road, Darlington DL1 3DX* Tel (01325) 355520 E-mail suechew@f2s.com

CHICHESTER, Caroline Margaret. STETS. **d** 09 **p** 10. NSM Winterborne Valley and Milton Abbas *Sarum* from 09. *Kingston Farmhouse, West Street, Winterborne Kingston, Blandford Forum DT11 9AX* E-mail cmchichester@tiscali.co.uk

CHICHESTER, Archdeacon of. *See* McKITTRICK, The Ven Douglas Henry

CHICHESTER, Bishop of. *See* HIND, The Rt Revd John William

CHICHESTER, Dean of. *See* FRAYLING, The Very Revd Nicholas Arthur

CHIDLAW, Richard Paul. b 49. St Cath Coll Cam BA71 MA. Ripon Hall Ox 72. **d** 74 **p** 81. C Ribbesford w Bewdley and Dowles *Worc* 74-76; NSM Coaley *Glouc* 81-83; NSM Frampton on Severn 81-83; NSM Arlingham 81-83; NSM Saul w Fretherne and Framilode 83-84; NSM Cam w Stinchcombe 85-90; Perm to Offic 90-91; NSM Berkeley w Wick, Breadstone and Newport 91-02; NSM Berkeley w Wick, Breadstone, Newport, Stone etc from 02. *38 May Lane, Dursley GL11 4HU* Tel (01453) 547838 E-mail richardandpauline@chidlaw.freeserve.co.uk

CHIDWICK, Alan Robert. b 49. MA MIL. Oak Hill NSM Course. **d** 84 **p** 85. NSM Pimlico St Pet w Westmr Ch Ch *Lon* 84-06; rtd 06; Perm to Offic *Nor* from 06. *The Croft House, The Croft, Costessey, Norwich NR8 5DT* Tel (01603) 745654 E-mail thecrofthouse@btinternet.com

CHIGUMIRA, Godfrey. St Mich Coll Llan. **d** 08. C Hawarden *St As* from 08. *3 Ffordd Tegid, Ewloe, Deeside CH5 3UD* Tel (01244) 530571 E-mail gchigumira@hotmail.co.uk

CHIKE, Chigor. b 66. Glos Univ BA93. St Jo Coll Nottm 05. **d** 06 **p** 07. C Victoria Docks St Luke *Chelmsf* 06-10; V Forest Gate Em w Upton Cross from 10. *Emmanuel Vicarage, 2B Margery Park Road, London E7 9JY* Tel (020) 8534 8780 Mobile 07905-155494 E-mail chigor.chike@aol.com

CHILCOTT, Mark David. b 62. Ch Coll Cam BA83 MA87 PhD88. Ripon Coll Cuddesdon BA92. **d** 93 **p** 94. C Warrington St Elphin *Liv* 93-99; P-in-c Westbrook St Jas 99-01; V 01-02. *Estates Branch, Sedgley Park Centre, Sedgley Park Road, Prestwich, Manchester M25 0JT* Tel 0161-856 0505 Fax 856 0506

CHILD, Corin James. b 73. Man Univ BA95. Trin Coll Bris BA02 MA03. **d** 03 **p** 04. C Sanderstead *S'wark* 03-07; V King's Lynn St Jo the Ev *Nor* from 07; Chapl Coll of W Anglia from 07. *St John's Vicarage, Blackfriars Road, King's Lynn PE30 1NT* Tel (01553) 773034 E-mail corin@childfamily.wanadoo.co.uk

CHILD, David Francis. Univ Coll Lon MB, ChB67 FRCP88. St As Minl Tr Course 02. **d** 04 **p** 05. NSM Gresford *St As* 04-07; NSM Bangor Isycoed Deanery from 08. *Whitegate Farm, Gyfelia, Wrexham LL13 0YH* Tel (01978) 823396 E-mail d_f_child@yahoo.co.uk

CHILD, James John. b 79. St Jo Coll Ox BA00. Oak Hill Th Coll BTh10. **d** 10 **p** 11. C St Helen Bishopsgate w St Andr Undershaft etc *Lon* from 10. *26 Walcot Square, London SE11 4TZ* Tel (020) 7283 2231 E-mail jamiejchild@hotmail.com

CHILD, Margaret Mary. *See* MASLEN, Mrs Margaret Mary

CHILDS, Christopher. b 59. **d** 05 **p** 06. NSM Gt Finborough w Onehouse, Harleston, Buxhall etc *St E* 05-11; P-in-c from 11. *Rectory Bungalow, Buxhall, Stowmarket IP14 3DJ* Tel (01449) 736093 E-mail revcchilds@aol.com

CHILDS, David Robert. b 64. Univ Coll Lon BSc86 Regent's Park Coll Ox MA95. Ripon Coll Cuddesdon 99. **d** 99 **p** 00. C Bloxham w Milcombe and S Newington *Ox* 99-02; TV Witney 02-06; TR 06-08; P-in-c Hadleigh St Jas *Chelmsf* from 08. *The Rectory, 50 Rectory Road, Hadleigh, Benfleet SS7 2ND* Tel (01702) 389532 E-mail dekm@sky.com

CHILDS, Emma Jane. *See* WESTERMANN-CHILDS, Miss Emma Jane

CHILDS, Ernest Edmund. b 23. Lich Th Coll 63. **d** 65 **p** 66. C Billesley Common *Birm* 65-68; C Elland *Wakef* 68-69; Clerical Org Sec CECS *Pet, Leic* and *Ely* 69-72; V Staverton w Helidon and Catesby *Pet* 72-76; rtd 77; Perm to Offic *Nor* 77-91; Hon C W Lynn *Ely* 92-94; P-in-c 94-95; Perm to Offic *Ely* from 95; *Nor* from 96. *4 Fieldview Court, Fakenham NR21 8PB* Tel (01328) 856595

CHILDS, Michael Thomas. b 79. Hull Univ BA01. St Steph Ho Ox BTh10. **d** 10 **p** 11. C Swinton *Sheff* from 10. *14 St Mary's Crescent, Swinton, Mexborough S64 8QL* Tel (01709) 591411 E-mail michaelchilds79@gmail.com

CHILLINGTON, Barbara Ann. b 42. RGN84. WEMTC. **d** 00 **p** 01. NSM Madley w Tyberton, Peterchurch, Vowchurch etc *Heref* from 00. *Cephas House, 2 Princes Orchard, Peterchurch, Hereford HR2 0RW* Tel and fax (01981) 550979 Mobile 07891-248723 E-mail barbarathrv@aol.com

✠**CHILLINGWORTH, The Most Revd David Robert.** b 51. TCD BA73 Oriel Coll Ox BA75 MA81. Ripon Coll Cuddesdon 75. **d** 76 **p** 77 **c** 05. C Belfast H Trin *Conn* 76-79; Ch of Ireland Youth Officer 79-83; C Bangor Abbey *D & D* 83-86; I Seagoe 86-05; Dean Dromore 95-02; Adn Dromore 02-05; Bp St And from 05; Primus from 09. *Perth Diocesan Centre, 28A Balhousie Street, Perth PH1 5HJ* Tel (01738) 443173 *or* 564432 Fax 443174 Mobile 07921-168666 E-mail bishop@standrews.anglican.org

CHILLMAN, David James. b 59. Southn Univ BA82. Trin Coll Bris 93. **d** 95 **p** 96. C Yateley *Win* 95-99; V Halifax All So and St Aug *Wakef* 99-07; V Bagshot *Guildf* from 07. *The Vicarage, 43 Church Road, Bagshot GU19 5EQ* Tel (01276) 473348 E-mail vicar.bagshot@virgin.net

CHILTON, Janice. **d** 08. NSM Wallingford *Ox* from 08. *2 Fairthorne Memorial, West End, Brightwell-cum-Sotwell, Wallingford OX10 0RY* Tel (01491) 836661 E-mail jchilton894@btinternet.com

CHIN, Michael Shoon Chion. b 41. Lon Univ BD71 Melbourne Univ BA76 DipEd79. Trin Th Coll Singapore BTh64 Melbourne Coll of Div. **d** 64 **p** 65. Malaysia 64-68; Australia 69-80, 87-91 and from 97; Miss to Seamen 72-81 and 83-89; USA 81-82; Gen Sec Internat Chr Maritime Assn 91-96. *711 Bouverie Street, Charlton Vic 3053, Australia* Tel and fax (0061) (3) 9347 0005 Mobile 40-859 7966 E-mail mschin22@goldenit.net.au

CHING, Derek. b 37. St Cath Coll Cam BA58 MA Cam Inst of Educn CertEd59. Qu Coll Birm 81. **d** 83 **p** 84. C Finham *Cov* 83-87; V Butlers Marston and the Pillertons w Ettington 87-96; rtd 96; Perm to Offic *Ripon* from 96. *25 Kirkby Road, Ripon HG4 2EY* Tel (01765) 609419

CHIPLIN, Christopher Gerald. b 53. Lon Univ BSc75. St Steph Ho Ox BA77 MA81. **d** 78 **p** 79. C Chesterfield St Mary and All SS *Derby* 78-80; C Thorpe St Andr *Nor* 80-84; V Highbridge *B & W* 84-94; V Midsomer Norton w Clandown from 94. *The Vicarage, 42 Priory Close, Midsomer Norton, Radstock BA3 2HZ* Tel (01761) 412118 E-mail cchi759070@aol.com

CHIPLIN, Gareth Huw. b 50. Worc Coll Ox BA71 MA. Edin Th Coll 71. **d** 73 **p** 74. C Friern Barnet St Jas *Lon* 73-75; C Eastcote St Lawr 76-79; C Notting Hill St Mich and Ch Ch 79-84; V Hammersmith St Matt from 84. *St Matthew's Vicarage, 1 Fielding Road, London W14 0LL* Tel (020) 7603 9769

CHIPLIN, Howard Alan. b 43. Sarum & Wells Th Coll 84. **d** 86 **p** 87. C Caerleon *Mon* 86-89; V Ferndale w Maerdy *Llan* 89-91; V Ysbyty Cynfyn w Llantrisant and Eglwys Newydd *St D* 91-95; R Narberth w Mounton w Robeston Wathen and Crinow 95-02;

V Grwp Bro Ystwyth a Mynach 02-08; rtd 08; AD Arwystli *Ban* from 11. *Minffordd, 15 Hafren Terrace, Llanidloes SY18 6AT*
CHIPLIN, Malcolm Leonard. b 42. St Mich Coll Llan 86. **d** 88 **p** 89. C Newton Nottage *Llan* 88-91; V Pwllgwaun w Llanddewi Rhondda 91-03; V Mountain Ash and Miskin 03-08; rtd 08. *3 Maes y Ffynon Grove, Aberaman, Aberdare CF44 6PH* Tel (01685) 874720 E-mail malcolmchiplin@aol.com
CHIPPENDALE, Peter David. b 34. Dur Univ BA55. Linc Th Coll 57. **d** 59 **p** 60. C Claines St Jo *Worc* 59-63; V Defford w Besford 63-73; P-in-c Eckington 66-69; V 69-73; V Kidderminster St Geo 73-76; V The Lickey *Birm* 76-96; rtd 96. *1 Fairways, Pershore WR10 1HA* Tel (01386) 553478
CHIPPENDALE, Robert William. b 42. Ox Univ BA79 Dip Teaching84. St Fran Coll Brisbane 64. **d** 67 **p** 68. C Maryborough Australia 67-69; C Hollinwood 70-72; V Shaw *Man* 72-78; R Beaudesert Australia 79-84; Chapl St Hilda's Sch Southport 85-03; rtd 03. *31 Gladioli Court, PO Box 1124, Caboolture Qld 4510, Australia* Tel (0061) (7) 5495 4514
CHISHOLM, Canon Ian Keith. b 36. AKC62. **d** 63 **p** 64. C Lich St Chad 63-66; C Sedgley All SS 66-69; V Rough Hills 69-77; V Harrow Weald All SS *Lon* 77-88; V W Moors *Sarum* 88-01; Can and Preb Sarum Cathl 00-01; rtd 01; Perm to Offic *Sarum* from 02. *33 Meadoway, Shrewton, Salisbury SP3 4HE* Tel (01980) 620579
CHISHOLM, Ian Stuart. b 37. ALCD63. **d** 63 **p** 64. C Worksop St Jo *S'well* 63-66; Succ Sheff Cathl 66-68; Bp's Chapl for Soc Resp 68-72; C Ox St Andr 72-76; Tutor Wycliffe Hall Ox 72-76; V Conisbrough *Sheff* 76-94; Chapl Conisbrough Hosp 76-94; RD W Doncaster 82-87 and 93-94; V Chilwell *S'well* 94-99; Perm to Offic *Sheff* from 94; *Linc* from 00; *S'well* from 03. *72 Broadbank, Louth LN11 0EW* Tel (01605) 605970 E-mail ichisholm@waitrose.com
CHISHOLM, Canon Reginald Joseph. b 13. TCD BA40 MA51. TCD Div Sch 42. **d** 42 **p** 43. C Belfast St Donard *D & D* 42-45; C Bangor St Comgall 45-48; I Ardglass w Dunsford 48-51; I Newtownards 51-82; Min Can Belf Cathl 52-62; Treas Down Cathl 80-82; rtd 82. *20 Glendun Park, Bangor BT20 4UX* Tel (028) 9145 0100
CHISHOLM, Samuel James. b 20. Edin Th Coll 74 St Jo Coll Nottm 86. **d** 86 **p** 87. NSM Eastriggs *Glas* 87-92; NSM Gretna 90-91; rtd 92; Perm to Offic *Chich* from 95. *36 Peterhouse, Church Street, Bexhill-on-Sea TN40 2HF* Tel (01424) 219294
CHISLETT, David Norman Hilton. b 61. Kingston Poly BSc83 UEA PGCE84. Ridley Hall Cam 00. **d** 02 **p** 03. C Highley w Billingsley, Glazeley etc *Heref* 02-05; TV Eston w Normanby *York* 05-09; C Bridlington Quay Ch Ch from 09; C Bessingby from 09. *Bessingby Vicarage, West Hill, Bridlington YO16 4RU* Tel (01262) 400253 E-mail dave.chislett@btinternet.com
CHITHAM, Ernest John. b 57. LSE BSc79 Leeds Univ PGCE80 Dur Univ MA84. NEOC 88. **d** 91 **p** 92. C Swanborough *Sarum* 91-94; CMS Lebanon 95-98; TV Worthing Ch the King *Chich* 99-08; V Worthing St Matt from 08. *85 Heene Road, Worthing BN11 4PP* Tel (01903) 218026 E-mail john.chitham@ntlworld.com
CHITTENDEN, John Bertram d'Encer. b 24. ASCA. Lon Coll of Div 56. **d** 58 **p** 59. C St Mary-at-Lambeth *S'wark* 58-64; R Acrise *Cant* 64-82; R Hawkinge 64-82; R Hawkinge w Acrise and Swingfield 82-90; rtd 91; Perm to Offic *Cant* from 91. *19 Harbourland Road, Folkestone CT19 6BQ* Tel (01303) 241773
✠**CHIU, The Rt Revd Joshua Ban It.** b 18. K Coll Lon LLB41 AKC41 Barrister-at-Law (Inner Temple) 41. Westcott Ho Cam 43. **d** 45 **p** 46 **c** 66. C Bournville *Birm* 45-47; Malaya 47-50; Singapore 50-59 and 66-82; Hon Can St Andr Cathl Singapore 56-59; Australia 59-62; Service Laymen Abroad WCC Geneva 62-65; Fell St Aug Coll Cant 65-66; Bp Singapore and Malaya 66-70; Bp Singapore 70-82; Member Cen Cttee 68-75; Member ACC 75-79; rtd 82; Perm to Offic *Sarum* 82-00 and *Chelmsf* from 02. *40 Beverley Crescent, Woodford Green IG8 9DD* Tel (020) 8924 6490
CHIUMBU, Esther Tamisa. See PRIOR, Esther Tamisa
CHIVERS, Canon Christopher Mark. b 67. Magd Coll Ox BA88 MA92 Selw Coll Cam BA96 MA00. Westcott Ho Cam 94. **d** 97 **p** 98. C Friern Barnet St Jas *Lon* 97-99; Can Prec St Geo Cathl Cape Town 99-01; Min Can and Prec Westmr Abbey 01-05; Can Res and Chan Blackb Cathl 05-10; V Mill Hill Jo Keble Ch *Lon* from 10; C Mill Hill St Mich from 11. *John Keble Vicarage, 142 Deans Lane, Edgware HA8 9NT* Tel (020) 8959 1312 Mobile 07706-632508 E-mail chris.chivers@johnkeble.org.uk
CHIVERS, Ernest Alfred John. b 32. Bris & Glouc Tr Course. **d** 83 **p** 84. NSM Bedminster *Bris* 83-87; NSM Whitchurch 87-98; NSM Knowle St Martin 98-00; Sen Asst P Chard and Distr *B & W* 00-04; P-in-c 04-05; rtd 05; Perm to Offic *B & W* from 05. *40 Calcott Road, Bristol BS4 2HD* Tel 0117-977 7867
CHIVERS, Royston George. b 34. Glouc Th Course. **d** 83 **p** 84. NSM Gorsley w Cliffords Mesne *Glouc* 83-85; NSM Newent and Gorsley w Cliffords Mesne from 85. *Mayfield, Gorsley, Ross-on-Wye HR9 7SJ* Tel (01989) 720492
CHO, Paul Hang-Sik. b 61. Kent Univ MA96 PhD04. Chr Th Sem & Div Sch of Korea BTh93. **d** 00 **p** 01. C Munster Square

Ch Ch and St Mary Magd *Lon* 00-07; Chapl Angl Korean Community 00-07; Consultant for Institutional Advancement Ox Cen for Miss Studies 08-11; Prof St Andr Th Sem from 10. *25 Corunna Crescent, Oxford OX4 2RB* E-mail frpaulcho@hotmail.com
CHOI, Soon-Han. b 64. Bapt Sem Seoul BA74 Surrey Univ MA99. **d** 10. NSM St Marylebone Annunciation Bryanston Street *Lon* from 10. *Flat 8, 33 Lexham Gardens, London W8 5JR* Tel (020) 7373 5025 Mobile 07984-452169 E-mail soonpray@gmail.com
CHOLDCROFT, Graham Charles. b 49. Ripon Coll Cuddesdon 07. **d** 10 **p** 11. Minister Ox from 10; Chapl Thames Valley Police Force from 10. *100 Aylesbury Road, Thame OX9 3AY* Tel (01844) 216979 Mobile 07851-191842 E-mail graham-choldcroft@supanet.com
CHORLTON, John Samuel Woodard. b 45. Newc Univ BSc67. Wycliffe Hall Ox 89. **d** 89 **p** 91. Jerusalem 79-92; C Ox St Aldate w St Matt 92-94; C Ox St Aldate 95-04; Voc Adv from 98; AD Ox 99-04; TV W Slough 04-08; V Britwell from 08. *St George's House, Long Furlong Drive, Slough SL2 2LX* Tel (01753) 554684 Mobile 07709-873831 E-mail jsw@chorlton.org
CHOUFAR, Joseph Oriho Abulemoi. b 57. Nile Th Coll Khartoum BA95 ICI Univ Amman BA98. **d** 87 **p** 88. Sudan 87-96; All SS Cathl Khartoum 87-88 and 91-96; Torit Congregation Lologo Displaced Camp 88-90; NSM Ealing St Pet Mt Park *Lon* from 00. *11 Bromyard House, Bromyard Avenue, London W3 7BE* Tel (020) 8762 0714 E-mail abulemoi@hotmail.com
CHOW, Ting Suie Roy. b 46. Brasted Th Coll 68 Sarum & Wells Th Coll 70. **d** 72 **p** 73. C Weaste *Man* 72-74; C Swinton St Pet 74-78; R Blackley St Paul 78-85; Sec SPCK (Dio Man) from 80; R Burnage St Nic *Man* 85-95; P-in-c Man Gd Shep 95-97; P-in-c Openshaw 95-97; R Manchester Gd Shep and St Barn from 97. *All Soul's Rectory, Every Street, Ancoats, Manchester M4 7DQ* Tel 0161-273 6582
CHOW, Wai Meng. b 65. Bris Univ BSc89 ACA93. Trin Coll Bris BA97 MA02. **d** 02 **p** 03. NSM Westminster St Jas the Less *Lon* from 02. *29 Carillon Court, Oxford Road, London W5 3SX* Tel (020) 8810 1651 *or* 7630 6282 Mobile 07968-776557 E-mail waimeng.chow@sjtl.org
CHOWN, William Richard Bartlett. b 27. AKC54. **d** 55 **p** 56. C Egremont *Carl* 55-58; C Upminster *Chelmsf* 58-61; R Romford St Andr 61-78; R Newton Longville w Stoke Hammond, Whaddon etc *Ox* 78-83; P-in-c Kidmore End 83-85; V 85-90; rtd 90; NSM Harpsden *Ox* 93-94; Perm to Offic 94-03; Hon C Shiplake w Dunsden and Harpsden 03-05; Perm to Offic *Guildf* from 07. *3 Coniston Court, Weybridge KT13 9YR* Tel (01932) 821936
CHRICH, Andrew James. b 70. Girton Coll Cam BA92 MA96. Cranmer Hall Dur BA96. **d** 96 **p** 97. C Gerrards Cross and Fulmer *Ox* 96-99; Chapl Trin Coll Cam 99-04; R Linton in Craven *Bradf* 04-09; P-in-c Burnsall w Rylstone 04-09; V Trumpington *Ely* from 09. *The Vicarage, 28 Wingate Way, Trumpington, Cambridge CB2 9HD* Tel 07540-108240 (mobile) E-mail andychrich@virginmedia.com
CHRICH-SMITH, Joanne Elizabeth. b 71. Qu Coll Cam BA93 MA97. Cranmer Hall Dur BA96 Ripon Coll Cuddesdon 96. **d** 97 **p** 98. C Amersham on the Hill *Ox* 97-99; Perm to Offic *Ely* 99-04; Chapl Girton Coll Cam 00-02; Perm to Offic *Bradf* 04-09. *The Vicarage, 28 Wingate Way, Trumpington, Cambridge CB2 9HD*
CHRISMAN, John Aubrey. b 33. US Naval Academy BS58. Westcott Ho Cam 86. **d** 88 **p** 89. NSM Orwell *Ely* 88-89; NSM Wimpole 88-89; NSM Arrington 88-89; NSM Croydon w Clopton 88-89; Asst Chapl Oslo St Edm *Eur* 89-91; R Newport St Geo USA 91-01; rtd 01. *7118 Treymore Court, Sarasota FL 34243, USA* Tel (001) (941) 351 3177 E-mail fatherjack@comcast.net
CHRIST THE KING, Bishop of. See LEE, The Rt Revd Peter John
CHRISTCHURCH, Bishop of. See COLES, The Rt Revd David John
CHRISTENSEN, Mrs Carole Glenda. b 45. Qu Coll Birm 07. **d** 09 **p** 10. NSM Blackheath *Birm* from 09. *73 John Street, Rowley Regis B65 0EN* Tel 0121-561 5761 E-mail christensen_250@hotmail.com
CHRISTENSEN, Canon Norman Peter. b 37. St D Coll Lamp BA63. Ridley Hall Cam 63. **d** 65 **p** 66. C Barnston *Ches* 65-70; V Over St Jo 70-77; R Bromborough 77-92; RD Wirral S 86-92; Hon Can Ches Cathl 90-02; Chapl Arrowe Park Hosp Wirral 92-96; V Higher Bebington *Ches* 96-02; rtd 02; Perm to Offic *Ches* from 02. *13 Howbeck Close, Prenton CH43 6TH* Tel 0151-652 9869 E-mail canonpc@aol.com
CHRISTIAN, Mrs Alison Jean. b 51. S Dios Minl Tr Scheme 88. **d** 91 **p** 94. Par Dn Uxbridge *Lon* 91-94; C 94-95; Chapl Uxbridge Coll 91-95; V Sudbury St Andr *Lon* 95-02; R Gt Stanmore from 02. *St John's Rectory, Rectory Lane, Stanmore HA7 4AQ* Tel (020) 8954 0276 E-mail alison.christian1@btopenworld.com

CHRISTIAN, Anthony Clive Hammond. b 46. Kent Univ BA74 Sussex Univ MA95 DPhil99 FRSA01. K Coll Lon 74 St Aug Coll Cant 74. **d** 76 **p** 77. C Faversham *Cant* 76-79; C St Laur in Thanet 79-81; P-in-c 81-84; R Gt Mongeham w Ripple and Sutton by Dover 84-88; V Pevensey *Chich* 88-94; P-in-c 94-01; V from 01. *4 Chiswick Place, Eastbourne BN21 4NH* Tel (01323) 724505 Mobile 07711-170350

CHRISTIAN, Brother. *See* PEARSON, Christian David John

CHRISTIAN, Mark Robert. b 58. Linc Th Coll 95. **d** 95 **p** 96. C Stockport SW *Ches* 95-98; CF 98-08; Sen CF from 08. *c/o MOD Chaplains (Army)* Tel (01980) 615802 Fax 615800 E-mail mark@padre.me.uk

CHRISTIAN, Paul. b 49. Cant Sch of Min 84. **d** 87 **p** 88. C Folkestone St Sav *Cant* 87-91; R Temple Ewell w Lydden from 91. *The Rectory, Green Lane, Temple Ewell, Dover CT16 3AS* Tel (01304) 822865

CHRISTIAN, Richard. b 37. Nottm Univ DipEd74 Ox Univ MA81. AKC62. **d** 63 **p** 65. C Camberwell St Mich w All So w Em *S'wark* 63-66; C Woolwich St Mary w H Trin 66-70; Chapl and Lect Bp Lonsdale Coll Derby 70-74; P-in-c Hurley *Ox* 76-79; Chapl Lancing Coll 79-81; Chapl Harrow Sch 82-89; Chapl R W Sussex Hosp Chich 89-91; P-in-c Cowley *Lon* 91-95; Chapl Hillingdon Hosp NHS Trust 91-11. *St John's Rectory, Rectory Lane, Stanmore HA7 4AQ* Tel (020) 8954 0276

CHRISTIAN-EDWARDS, Canon Michael Thomas. b 36. Down Coll Cam BA60 MA64. Clifton Th Coll 60. **d** 62 **p** 63. C Ex St Leon w H Trin 62-67; V Trowbridge St Thos *Sarum* 67-75; R Wingfield w Rowley 67-75; P-in-c Fisherton Anger 75-81; R 81-92; Ind Chapl 85-92; RD Salisbury 85-90; Can and Preb Sarum Cathl 87-92; V Crofton *Portsm* 92-00; rtd 00; Perm to Offic *Win* from 02. *Rivendell, Westbeams Road, Sway, Lymington SO41 6AE* Tel (01590) 682353 E-mail mmce@ukpiglet.com

CHRISTIAN-IWUAGWU, Canon Amatu Onundu. b 73. Port Harcourt Univ Nigeria BEng93. **d** 00 **p** 01. NSM Stonebridge St Mich *Lon* 00-03; NSM Welwyn *St Alb* 04-05; NSM Stonebridge St Mich *Lon* 05-07; V Harmondsworth from 07; Can Ideato from 03. *St Mary's Vicarage, High Street, Harmondsworth, West Drayton UB7 0AQ* Tel (020) 8897 2385 Mobile 07961-593880 E-mail iwuagwuoa@yahoo.co.uk

CHRISTIANSON, Canon Rodney John (Bill). b 47. St Paul's Coll Grahamstown. **d** 72 **p** 73. C St Sav Cathl Pietermaritzburg S Africa 72-76; Miss to Seafarers 76-09; Min Sec 93-00; Sec Gen 00-09; Hon C Milton next Gravesend Ch Ch *Roch* 78-82; R Richard's Bay S Africa 82-91; Chapl Hull Miss to Seamen 91-93; Lic to Offic *Lon* 94-97; V St Mich Paternoster Royal 00-09; rtd 09; Perm to Offic *Lon* from 09; Hon Can Bloemfontein Cathl from 93. *45 Wimbledon Park Court, Wimbledon Park Road, London SW19 6NN* E-mail bill.christianson@mtsmail.org

CHRISTIE, Alexander Robert. b 58. Qu Coll Cam BA79 LLM80. Oak Hill Th Coll 92. **d** 94 **p** 95. C W Norwood St Luke *S'wark* 95-02; C Wandsworth All SS 98-03; V Blackheath Park St Mich from 03. *St Michael's Vicarage, 2 Pond Road, London SE3 9JL* Tel (020) 8852 5287 E-mail ar.christie@virgin.net

CHRISTIE, David James. b 58. York Univ BA80 MA83 PGCE81 Leeds Univ MPhil88. Cranmer Hall Dur 89. **d** 91 **p** 92. C Drypool *York* 91-95; V Patrick Brompton and Hunton *Ripon* 95-09; V Hornby 95-09; V Crakehall 95-09. *Address temp unknown* E-mail dc@christiepb.fsnet.co.uk

CHRISTIE, Canon Thomas Richard. b 31. CCC Cam BA53 MA57. Linc Th Coll 55. **d** 57 **p** 58. C Portsea N End St Mark *Portsm* 57-60; C Cherry Hinton St Andr *Ely* 60-62; C-in-c Cherry Hinton St Jas CD 62-66; V Wisbech St Aug 66-73; V Whitstable All SS *Cant* 73-75; V Whitstable All SS w St Pet 75-80; Can Res and Treas Pet Cathl 80-01; Perm to Offic *Ely* from 80; RD Pet 87-96; Chapl to Rtd Clergy from 00; rtd 01; P-in-c Thornhaugh and Wansford *Pet* from 01. *16 College Park, Peterborough PE1 4AW* Tel (01733) 344228 E-mail thomaschristie@talktalk.net

CHRISTODOULOU, Kostakis. b 53. Southn Univ CertEd76 BEd76. St Mellitus Coll BA10. **d** 10 **p** 11. NSM Edgware *Lon* from 10. *226 East End Road, London N2 8AX* Tel (020) 8883 9971

CHRISTOPHER, Miss Barbara. b 58. Univ of Wales (Swansea) BA80. **d** 09 **p** 10. OLM Saddleworth *Man* from 09. *2 St Mary's Crest, Greenfield, Oldham OL3 7DS* Tel (01457) 876802 E-mail barbara.christopher@tiscali.co.uk

CHRISTOPHER, Richard. b 53. NTMTC 94. **d** 97 **p** 98. C Southall Green St Jo *Lon* 97-04; C Reading St Luke w St Bart *Ox* from 04. *107 Anderson Avenue, Earley, Reading RG6 1HA* Tel 0118-987 1495 E-mail rev.r.christopher@yahoo.com

CHRISTOU, Sotirios. b 51. St Jo Coll Nottm 84. **d** 88 **p** 92. C Berechurch St Marg w St Mich *Chelmsf* 88-89; C Goodmayes All SS 89-90; NSM Harston w Hauxton *Ely* 92-94; Lic to Offic 94-95; C Burgess Hill St Andr *Chich* 95-98; Perm to Offic *Ely* from 98. *18 Bullen Close, Cambridge CB1 8YU* Tel (01223) 246349 E-mail christousotirios@hotmail.co.uk

CHUBB, John Nicholas. b 33. St Cath Soc Ox BA55 MA58. Qu Coll Birm 57. **d** 59 **p** 60. C Kirby Moorside w Gillamoor *York* 59-62; C Scarborough St Mary 62-64; V Potterspury w Furtho

and Yardley Gobion *Pet* 64-69; V Brixworth 69-74; P-in-c Holcot 73-74; V Brixworth w Holcot 74-81; V Hampton Hill *Lon* 81-88; Chapl Pet Distr Hosp 88-97; Chapl Edith Cavell Hosp 88-97; rtd 97. *12 Alness Drive, York YO24 2XZ*

CHUBB, Richard Henry. b 45. Univ of Wales (Cardiff) BMus67 Bris Univ PGCE76. Linc Th Coll 67. **d** 70 **p** 71. C Chippenham St Andr w Tytherton Lucas *Bris* 71-72; C-in-c Stockwood CD 72-73; C Bris Ch the Servant Stockwood 73-76; Perm to Offic 76-79; Min Can and Succ Bris Cathl 79-88; Chapl w Deaf People 83-02; Chapl Qu Eliz Hosp Sch Bris 87-92; rtd 02. *22B Westfield Road, Westbury-on-Trym, Bristol BS9 3HG* Tel and fax 0117-983 2842 E-mail richard.chubb@lineonet.net

CHUDLEY, Cyril Raymond. b 29. Lon Univ BA53 DipEd. Wells Th Coll 70. **d** 72 **p** 73. C Newark St Mary *S'well* 72-75; C Egg Buckland *Ex* 75-77; P-in-c Plymouth St Aug 77-80; V 80-83; V Milton Abbot, Dunterton, Lamerton etc 83-91; TV Wickford and Runwell *Chelmsf* 91-95; rtd 95; Perm to Offic *Truro* from 95. *Ten Acres, Coxpark, Gunnislake PL18 9BB* Tel (01822) 832345

CHUMU MUTUKU, Norbert. b 68. Urbanian Univ Rome BA89 St Jo Fisher Coll USA MSc00. St Mathias Mulumba Sem Kenya 89. **d** 93 **p** 94. Ngong Kenya 93-98; Rochester USA 98-02; C Milton *Portsm* 03-06; C Pitsea w Nevendon *Chelmsf* from 06. *34 St Michael's Avenue, Basildon SS13 3DE* E-mail nchumu@yahoo.com

CHURCH, Mrs Annette Marie. b 56. **d** 09 **p** 10. C Caldicot *Mon* from 09. *Belle Grove, Manor Court, Rogiet, Caldicot NP26 3TU* Tel (01291) 431392 Mobile 07789-778312 E-mail anniechurch@hotmail.com *or* revannie@hotmail.co.uk

CHURCH, Mrs Linda Ann. b 51. MCSP73. EMMTC 88. **d** 91 **p** 94. NSM Kirkby in Ashfield St Thos *S'well* 91-95; NSM Skegby and Teversal 95-98; P-in-c Annesley w Newstead 98-03; TR Hucknall Torkard 03-09; Hon Can S'well Minster 07-09; R Fowlmere, Foxton, Shepreth and Thriplow *Ely* from 09. *The Rectory, High Street, Fowlmere, Royston SG8 7SU* Tel (01763) 208195 E-mail canonlinda.church@btinternet.com

CHURCH, William John. b 41. Qu Coll Cam MA62 Solicitor. SAOMC 96. **d** 99 **p** 00. NSM Bengeo *St Alb* 99-01; NSM Gt Amwell w St Margaret's and Stanstead Abbots 01-05; NSM Hertford from 05. *115 Queen's Road, Hertford SG13 8BJ* Tel (01992) 410469 Fax 583079 E-mail bill.church@hertscc.gov.uk *or* churchwj@hotmail.com

CHURCHER, Ms Mandy. b 54. RN75 RM77 Surrey Univ PGCE87 Brunel Univ MEd92. NTMTC 96. **d** 99 **p** 00. C Wolverhampton St Matt *Lich* 99-02; Assoc Chapl Plymouth Hosps NHS Trust 02-06; Chapl S Devon Healthcare NHS Foundn Trust 06-11; NSM Malmesbury w Westport and Brokenborough *Bris* from 11; NSM Gt Somerford, Lt Somerford, Seagry, Corston etc from 11. *Address temp unknown*

CHURCHMAN, David Ernest Donald. b 21. Univ of Wales MTh01. Clifton Th Coll 45. **d** 48 **p** 49. C Preston All SS *Blackb* 48-49; C Braintree *Chelmsf* 50-52; V Harold Wood 52-59; V Southsea St Jude *Portsm* 59-74; V Enfield Ch Ch Trent Park *Lon* 74-86; RD Enfield 75-82; rtd 86; Perm to Offic *Portsm* from 87. *The Wedge, 8 Park Road, Hayling Island PO11 0HU* Tel (023) 9246 7338 E-mail don.churchman@btinternet.com

CHYNCHEN, John Howard. b 38. FRICS72. Sarum & Wells Th Coll 88. **d** 89 **p** 90. Bp's Dom Chapl *Sarum* from 89; Hon Chapl Hong Kong Cathl 90-07; Chapl from 07. *St John's Cathedral, 4-8 Garden Road, Hong Kong* Tel (00852) 2523 4157 Fax 2855 0420 E-mail chynchen@stjohnscathedral.org.hk

CIANCHI, Dalbert Peter. b 28. Lon Univ BSc57. Westcott Ho Cam 69. **d** 70 **p** 71. C Harpenden St Nic *St Alb* 70-74; TV Woughton *Ox* 74-80; P-in-c Wavendon w Walton 74-80; P-in-c Lavendon w Cold Brayfield 80-84; R Lavendon w Cold Brayfield, Clifton Reynes etc 84-94; rtd 94. *20 Fisken Crescent, Kambah ACT 2902, Australia* Tel (0061) (2) 6231 8556 E-mail pcianchi@cyberone.com.au

CIECHANOWICZ, Edward Leigh Bundock. *See* BUNDOCK, Edward Leigh

CINNAMOND, Andrew Victor. b 71. St Andr Univ MA94. Wycliffe Hall Ox BA00. **d** 01 **p** 02. C Clapham H Trin and St Pet *S'wark* 01-05; C Wandsworth All SS 05-11; TV Fairford Deanery *Glouc* from 11. *The Vicarage, Sherborne Street, Lechlade GL7 3AH* Tel (01367) 253651 E-mail andrew_cinnamond@hotmail.com

CLABON, Ronald Oliver Edwin. b 30. **d** 97. NSM Pontnewydd *Mon* 97-03. *22 Anthony Drive, Caerleon, Newport NP18 3DX* Tel (01633) 420790

CLACEY, Derek Phillip. b 48. St Jo Coll Nottm 76. **d** 79 **p** 80. C Gt Parndon *Chelmsf* 79-82; C Walton H Trin *Ox* 82-88; R Bramshaw and Landford w Plaitford *Sarum* 88-94; P-in-c Redlynch and Morgan's Vale 03-04; TV E Greenwich *S'wark* from 04. *The Vicarage, 52 Eastcombe Street, London SE10 9ES* Tel (020) 8853 5950 E-mail derekclacey@aol.com

CLACK (née JERWOOD), Mrs Eleanor Alice Jerwood. b 80. Bath Univ BSc03. St Jo Coll Nottm 05. **d** 08 **p** 09. C New Milverton *Cov* 08-11; Perm to Offic from 11. *62 Whitemoor Road, Kenilworth CV8 2BP* E-mail ellieclack@hotmail.co.uk

CLACK, Robert John Edmund. b 63. Lanc Univ BA85. Coll of Resurr Mirfield 89. **d** 92 **p** 93. C Bury St Pet *Man* 92-95; Chapl Bury Colls of FE 93-95; TV New Bury 95-97; R Ashton-upon-Mersey St Martin *Ches* from 97. *St Martin's Rectory, 367 Glebelands Road, Sale M33 5GG* Tel 0161-973 4204
E-mail rjec@fsmail.net

CLACKER, Martin Alexander. b 56. Trin Coll Bris 93. **d** 95 **p** 96. C Yate New Town *Bris* 95-98; V Southmead 98-00; C Portishead *B & W* 00-02; TV 02-03; Perm to Offic *Bris* 06-08; P-in-c Winterbourne from 08; C Frenchay and Winterbourne Down from 08; C Frampton Cotterell and Iron Acton from 08. *Orchard House, 70 High Street, Winterbourne, Bristol BS36 1JQ* Tel (01454) 771856 E-mail martinclacker@hotmail.com

CLAMMER, Thomas Edward. b 80. Sussex Univ BA01 CCC Cam BA04 MA09. Westcott Ho Cam 02. **d** 05 **p** 06. C Wotton St Mary *Glouc* 05-08; P-in-c Deerhurst and Apperley w Forthampton etc from 08; Dioc Worship Officer from 08; C Tewkesbury w Walton Cardiff and Twyning from 10. *The Vicarage, 1 The Green, Apperley, Gloucester GL19 4DQ* Tel (01452) 780880 E-mail tomclammer@gmail.com

CLANCY, Michael. b 24. Kensington Univ (USA) BA82. Glas NSM Course 76. **d** 79 **p** 80. Hon C Glas St Silas 79-96; Perm to Offic from 96. *33 Highfield Drive, Clarkston, Glasgow G76 7SW* Tel 0141-638 4469

CLAPHAM, Christopher Charles. b 69. Man Univ BA91 St Jo Coll Dur BA96. Cranmer Hall Dur 94 Union Th Sem (NY) STM98. **d** 99 **p** 00. NSM Withington St Chris *Man* 99-01; C Didsbury Ch Ch 01-03; P-in-c Swinton H Rood 03-08; Chapl Keele Univ from 08. *Berachah House, 51 Quarry Bank, Keele, Newcastle ST5 5AG* Tel (01782) 583393
E-mail charlesclapham@lineone.net

CLAPHAM, George Henry James. b 52. Trin Coll Bris. **d** 08 **p** 09. C Wellington and Distr *B & W* from 08. *15 Shuteleigh, Wellington TA21 8PG* Tel (01823) 664841
E-mail jamesclapham@talktalk.net

CLAPHAM, John. b 47. Open Univ BA76. Sarum & Wells Th Coll 77. **d** 80 **p** 81. Dep PV Ex Cathl from 80; C Lympstone 85-87; P-in-c 87-99; P-in-c Woodbury 97-99; RD Aylesbeare 96-01; R Lympstone and Woodbury w Exton 99-09; rtd 09. *375 Topsham Road, Exeter EX2 6HB* Tel (01392) 873345
E-mail johnclaphamuk@btinternet.com

CLAPHAM, Kenneth. b 47. Trin Coll Bris 76. **d** 78 **p** 79. C Pemberton St Mark Newtown *Liv* 78-81; C Darfield *Sheff* 81-83; P-in-c Over Kellet *Blackb* 83-88; V from 88. *The Vicarage, 3 Kirklands Road, Over Kellet, Carnforth LA6 1DJ* Tel and fax (01524) 734189 E-mail ukvicar@gmail.com

CLAPHAM, Stephen James. b 61. Portsm Poly BSc84 Ches Coll of HE BTh04. NOC 01. **d** 04 **p** 05. C Nantwich *Ches* 04-06; V Crewe All SS and St Paul w St Pet from 07. *All Saints' Vicarage, 79 Stewart Street, Crewe CW2 8LX* Tel (01270) 560310
E-mail steve.clapham@yahoo.co.uk

CLAPPERTON, Mrs Carolin Beryl. b 43. Westcott Ho Cam 04. **d** 05 **p** 06. NSM Faversham *Cant* 05-08; NSM The Brents and Davington w Oare and Luddenham 08-11; rtd 11. *5 Provender Walk, Belvedere Road, Faversham ME13 7NF* Tel (01795) 538334 Mobile 07946-420745
E-mail carolinclapperton226@btinternet.com

CLAPSON, Clive Henry. b 55. Leeds Univ BA76. Trin Coll Toronto MDiv79. **d** 79 **p** 80. C Belleville St Thos Canada 79-80; R Loughborough 80-83; V Alpine Ch the K USA 83-88; C Hawley H Trin *Guildf* 88-90; R Invergordon St Ninian *Mor* 90-00; Prin Moray Ord and Lay Tr Course 90-94; Can St Andr Cathl Inverness 97-00; R Aberdeen St Mary 00-05; P-in-c Dundee St Salvador *Bre* from 05. *9 Minard Crescent, Dundee DD3 6LH* Tel (01382) 221785
E-mail father.clive@blueyonder.co.uk

CLAPTON, Timothy. b 59. Westmr Coll Ox MTh92. Westcott Ho Cam 96. **d** 98 **p** 99. C Wimborne Minster *Sarum* 98-02; Ecum Chapl Milton Keynes Gen NHS Trust 02-05; Milton Keynes Miss Partnership Development Chapl *Ox* 05-10; Perm to Offic *S'wark* from 11. *78 Ruskin Park House, Champions Hill, London SE5 8TH* Tel 07958-182077 (mobile)
E-mail timclapton@talktalk.net

CLARE, Christopher. b 52. Sheff Univ BSc73 Nottm Univ PGCE74. Ox Min Course 89. **d** 92 **p** 93. NSM Chesham Bois *Ox* from 92. *5 Lime Tree Walk, Amersham HP7 9HY* Tel (01494) 766513

CLARE, Ms Johanna Howard. b 64. Bris Univ BSc86 Heythrop Coll Lon MA98. Ridley Hall Cam 97. **d** 99 **p** 00. C Coulsdon St Jo *S'wark* 99-02; TV Morden 02-09; Dioc Continuing Professional Development Officer from 09. *47 West Square, London SE1 4SP* Tel (020) 7207 2170 *or* 7939 9472
E-mail johanna.clare@southwark.anglican.org

CLARE, Sister. *See* LOCKHART, Clare Patricia Anne

CLARIDGE, Antony Arthur John. b 37. Hull Univ MA LRAM. Bris & Glouc Tr Course. **d** 84 **p** 85. NSM Keynsham *B & W* 84-97; Bp's Officer for NSMs 90-10; Min Bath Ch Ch Prop Chpl 97-10; rtd 10. *62 Cranwells Park, Bath BA1 2YE* Tel (01225) 427462 E-mail antony.claridge@btinternet.com

CLARIDGE, Michael John. b 61. MCIEH. Qu Coll Birm 89 Bossey Ecum Inst Geneva 91. **d** 92 **p** 93. C Harlescott *Lich* 92-95; P-in-c Wellington Ch Ch 95-97; V 97-03; V W Bromwich St Andr w Ch Ch from 03. *St Andrew's Vicarage, Oakwood Street, West Bromwich B70 9SN* Tel 0121-553 1871
E-mail mjclaridge@tiscali.co.uk

CLARINGBULL, Canon Denis Leslie. b 33. K Coll Lon BD57 AKC57 Univ of Cen England in Birm DUniv98 MCIPD85 FCIPD01. **d** 58 **p** 59. C Croydon St Aug *Cant* 58-62; Ind Chapl to Bp Croydon 62-71; Ind Chapl *Cov* 71-75; Chapl Cov Cathl 71-75; Succ 72-75; V Norbury St Phil *Cant* 75-80; Sen Ind Chapl *Birm* 80-98; P-in-c Birm St Paul 85-88; V 88-98; Hon Can Birm Cathl 87-98; rtd 98; Perm to Offic *Birm* and *Heref* from 98. *17 Merrivale Crescent, Ross-on-Wye HR9 5JU* Tel (01989) 567771 E-mail gms58@dial.pipex.com

CLARINGBULL (née DAVID), Canon Faith Caroline. b 55. St Aid Coll Dur BA77. Ripon Coll Cuddesdon 87. **d** 89 **p** 94. Par Dn Is of Dogs Ch Ch and St Jo w St Luke *Lon* 89-93; Asst Chapl R Lon Hosps NHS Trust 93-98; NSM Wheatley *Ox* 98-00; Asst Dioc Dir of Ords *Worc* 00-04; Dioc CME Officer 02-04; Dioc Dir of Ords *Birm* from 04; Dean of Women's Min from 04; Hon Can Birm Cathl from 05. *175 Harborne Park Road, Birmingham B17 0BH* Tel 0121-426 0445
E-mail faith@birmingham.anglican.org

CLARINGBULL, Keith. b 49. Ripon Coll Cuddesdon 98. **d** 00 **p** 01. SSF 69-89; C Droitwich Spa *Worc* 00-04; P-in-c Hampton in Arden *Birm* 04-10; P-in-c Bickenhill 04-10. *14 Asbury Road, Balsall Common, Coventry CV7 7QN* Tel (01676) 530197
E-mail claring.bull@virgin.net

CLARK, Andrew. b 76. Anglia Poly Univ BA97. Oak Hill Th Coll BA08. **d** 08 **p** 09. C Heref St Pet w St Owen and St Jas from 08. *10 St Barnabas Close, Hereford HR1 1EY* Tel (01432) 266588
E-mail lurpak@aol.com

CLARK, Andrew James. b 50. ACIB72 ACIS76. EMMTC 91. **d** 94 **p** 95. NSM Allestree *Derby* 94-97; NSM Allenton and Shelton Lock 97-03; NSM Walbrook Epiphany 03-05. *Address temp unknown*

CLARK, Antony. b 61. York Univ BA83. Wycliffe Hall Ox 84. **d** 88 **p** 89. C Ashton-upon-Mersey St Mary Magd *Ches* 88-92; Chapl Lee Abbey 92-95; Lic to Offic *Ex* 92-95; Chapl Univ of Westmr *Lon* 95-98; C Bletchley *Ox* 98-00. *Address temp unknown*

CLARK, Arthur. b 30. MIBiol FRSC Sheff Univ BSc MCB. St D Dioc Tr Course. **d** 88 **p** 89. NSM Haverfordwest St Mary and St Thos w Haroldston *St D* 88-91; C 91-92; V Llawhaden w Bletherston and Llancefn 92-96; rtd 96. *84 Portfield, Haverfordwest SA61 1BT* Tel (01437) 762694

CLARK, Bernard Charles. b 34. Open Univ BA81. S'wark Ord Course 65. **d** 68 **p** 69. C Pemberton St Jo *Liv* 68-71; C Winwick 71-73; P-in-c Warrington St Barn 74-76; V 76-78; V Hindley All SS 78-83; Perm to Offic 86-94; R Glazebury w Hollinfare 94-99; rtd 99; Perm to Offic *Man* 00-08. *31 Linkfield Drive, Worsley, Manchester M28 1JU* Tel 0161-799 7998
E-mail bckathcain31@aol.com

CLARK, Brian John. b 48. Portsm Poly CQSW89 Portsm Univ MA94. STETS 97. **d** 00 **p** 01. NSM Titchfield *Portsm* 00-01; NSM Helston and Wendron *Truro* 01-02; Perm to Offic *Portsm* 02-06. *Address temp unknown*

CLARK, Ms Caroline Robbins (Robbin). b 45. Mt Holyoke Coll USA BA67 Columbia Univ BS70 Univ of California MS74. Ch Div Sch of Pacific MDiv81 Ripon Coll Cuddesdon 79. **d** 81 **p** 82. C Upland St Mark USA 81-84; R Santa Fé St Bede 85-93; R Berkeley St Mark 93-10; Dean of Women Clergy *Glouc* from 11. *36 Larkhay Road, Hucclecote, Gloucester GL3 3NS* Tel (01452) 547469 Mobile 07986-148701 E-mail rclark@glosdioc.org.uk

CLARK, Cecil. b 44. Sarum Th Coll. **d** 98 **p** 99. OLM Canford Magna *Sarum* from 98. *Fermain Cottage, 133 Magna Road, Bearwood, Bournemouth BH11 9NE* Tel (01202) 577898 *or* 663275 E-mail firmain@ntlworld.com

CLARK, Mrs Christine Margaret. b 44. SAOMC 01. **d** 01 **p** 02. NSM Croxley Green St Oswald *St Alb* 01-06; P-in-c Odell from 06. *The Rectory, 3 Church Lane, Odell, Bedford MK43 7AA* Tel (01234) 720234 Mobile 07812-524992

CLARK, Daughter Austin. b 52. **d** 10 **p** 11. NSM Worthing St Geo *Chich* from 10. *34A Forest Road, Worthing BN14 9NB*

CLARK, Daniel Alastair. b 74. St Jo Coll Dur BA96. Wycliffe Hall Ox BA99. **d** 00 **p** 01. C Rusholme H Trin *Man* 00-06; NSM 04-06; C Clifton Ch Ch w Em *Bris* from 06. *5 Clifton Park Road, Bristol BS8 3HN* Tel 0117-973 2128
E-mail dan@christchurchclifton.org.uk

CLARK, David. b 30. Nottm Univ BSc51. St Aid Birkenhead 55. **d** 57 **p** 58. C Tyldesley w Shakerley *Man* 57-60; V Ashton St Jas 60-64; rtd 93; Perm to Offic *Eur* from 07. *30 Dulverton Hall, Esplanade, Scarborough YO11 2AR* Tel (01723) 340130
E-mail d2aclark@wanadoo.fr

CLARK, Canon David George Neville. b 25. Linc Coll Ox BA49 MA59. Wells Th Coll 49. **d** 51 **p** 52. C Sanderstead All SS *S'wark* 51-54; C Lewisham St Jo Southend 54-59; V Sutton New Town St Barn 59-72; R Charlwood 72-90; P-in-c Sidlow Bridge 76-77; R 77-90; P-in-c Buckland 85-87; P-in-c Leigh 87-90; Hon Can

S'wark Cathl 88-90; rtd 90; Perm to Offic *Cov* from 90. *12 Marlborough Road, Coventry CV2 4EP* Tel (024) 7644 2400

CLARK, David Gordon. b 29. Clare Coll Cam BA52 MA57. Ridley Hall Cam 52. **d** 54 **p** 55. C Walthamstow St Jo *Chelmsf* 54-57; V 60-69; C Gt Ilford St Andr 57-60; R Stansted *Roch* 69-82; R Stansted w Fairseat and Vigo 82-94; rtd 94; Perm to Offic *Sarum* 94-06. *4 St Marys Close, Platt, Sevenoaks TN15 8NH* Tel (01732) 883191

CLARK, David Humphrey. b 39. G&C Coll Cam BA60. Wells Th Coll 62. **d** 64 **p** 65. C Leigh St Mary *Man* 64-68; Min Can and Prec Man Cathl 68-70; Ind Chapl *Nor* 70-85; P-in-c Nor St Clem and St Geo 70-76; P-in-c Nor St Sav w St Paul 70-76; V Norwich-over-the-Water Colegate St Geo 76-79; Hon Asst P Nor St Pet Mancroft 79-85; TR Oladby *Leic* 85-98; C Leic St Jas 98-04; rtd 04; Perm to Offic *Leic* from 04. *46 St James Road, Leicester LE2 1HQ* Tel 0116-255 8988
E-mail dhclark@leicester.anglican.org

CLARK, David John. b 40. Surrey Univ MPhil75 CEng MIStructE. Ridley Hall Cam 81. **d** 83 **p** 84. C Combe Down w Monkton Combe and S Stoke *B & W* 83-89; Voc Adv Bath Adnry 89-96; R Freshford, Limpley Stoke and Hinton Charterhouse 89-05; rtd 05; Perm to Offic *B & W* from 05. *14 Barn Close, Frome BA11 4ER* Tel (01373) 461073
E-mail david@freshford313.freeserve.co.uk

CLARK, Dennis Henry Graham. b 26. St Steph Ho Ox 52. **d** 55 **p** 56. C Southall St Geo *Lon* 55-58; C Barbourne *Worc* 58-61; Chapl RAF 61-78; Asst Chapl-in-Chief RAF 78-82; Chapl St Clem Danes (RAF Ch) 79-82; V Godmanchester *Ely* 82-91; rtd 91; Perm to Offic *Ely* from 91. *8 Arran Way, St Ives PE27 3DT* Tel (01480) 301951

CLARK, Diane Catherine. See FITZGERALD CLARK, Mrs Diane Catherine

CLARK, Edward Robert. b 39. Ex Coll Ox BA61 MA65. St Steph Ho Ox 61. **d** 63 **p** 64. C Solihull *Birm* 63-67; Perm to Offic *Bris* 67-69; *Leic* 69-71; *Ox* 71-80; *St Alb* 80-84; *Cant* from 84; rtd 04. *3 Hunters Bank, Old Road, Elham, Canterbury CT4 6SS* Tel (01303) 840134 E-mail edward.clark@virgin.net

CLARK, Ellen Jane. See CLARK-KING, Ellen Jane

CLARK, Frederick Albert George. b 15. MBE68. ACP66. **d** 67 **p** 68. Hon C Stroud *Glouc* 67-84; Hon C Stroud and Uplands w Slad 84-85; Perm to Offic 85-97. *2 Terrace Cottages, Thrupp, Stroud GL5 2BN* Tel (01453) 882060

CLARK, Harold Clive. b 28. Witwatersrand Univ LTh53. St Paul's Coll Grahamstown. **d** 54 **p** 55. C Orange Grove S Africa 54-56; R Mayfair 56-60; P-in-c Morden S'wark 60-62; R Verulam S Africa 62-68; Chapl Michaelhouse 68-77; V Green Island New Zealand 77-85; V Kaitaia 85-92; Chapl Kristin Sch Albany from 92. *351 East Coast Road, Mairangi Bay, North Shore City 0630, New Zealand* Tel (0064) (9) 479 3434
E-mail hr.clark@clear.net.nz

CLARK, Ian Duncan Lindsay. b 35. K Coll Cam BA59 MA63 PhD64. Ripon Hall Ox 62. **d** 64 **p** 65. C Willington *Newc* 64-66; India 66-76; Lect Bp's Coll Calcutta 66; Vice-Prin 69-74; Chapl St Cath Coll Cam 76; Fell 77-85; Tutor 78-85; Dean of Chpl and Lect 80-85; Select Preacher Cam Univ 82; Hon Asst P Kelso *Edin* 85-06. *4 Yewtree Lane, Yetholm, Kelso TD5 8RZ* Tel (01573) 420323

CLARK, Jacqueline Mary. b 58. **d** 08 **p** 09. OLM Canalside Benefice *Sarum* from 08. *3 Stonelea, Trowbridge Road, Hilperton, Trowbridge BA14 7QQ* Tel (01225) 769940 Mobile 07948-089865 E-mail revjclark@hotmail.co.uk

CLARK, Jeremy James. b 66. Cant Univ (NZ) BA88. St Jo Coll Auckland BTh97. **d** 94 **p** 95. C Shirley St Steph New Zealand 94-97; C Upton (Overchurch) *Ches* 97-01; P-in-c Ilfracombe SS Phil and Jas w W Down *Ex* 01-08; C Alphington, Shillingford St George and Ide from 08. *c/o Crockford, Church House, Great Smith Street, London SW1P 3AZ* E-mail pipjimcalix@aol.com *or* jemkiwi@aol.com

CLARK, John David Stanley. b 36. Dur Univ BA64. Ridley Hall Cam 64. **d** 66 **p** 67. C Benchill *Man* 66-69; C Beverley Minster *York* 69-74; Perm to Offic *S'well* 74-76; Lic to Offic 76-77; Miss to Seamen 77-80; Perm to Offic *York* 80-83; V Egton w Grosmont 83-89; R Thornton Dale w Ellerburne and Wilton 89-01; R Thornton Dale w Allerston, Ebberston etc 01-05; rtd 05; Perm to Offic *York* from 05. *22 Swainsea Lane, Pickering YO18 8AP* Tel (01751) 476118 E-mail jdsclark@btinternet.com

CLARK, John Edward Goodband. b 49. Leeds Univ MA01. Chich Th Coll 70. **d** 73 **p** 74. C Thorpe St Andr *Nor* 73-76; C Earlham

St Anne 76-78; Chapl RN 78-82; P-in-c Tittleshall w Godwick, Wellingham and Weasenham *Nor* 82-85; P-in-c Helhoughton w Raynham 82-85; R S Raynham, E w W Raynham, Helhoughton, etc 85-90; R Taverham w Ringland 90-96; V Eggleston and R Middleton-in-Teesdale w Forest and Frith *Dur* 96-03; AD Barnard Castle 00-03; R Caston, Griston, Merton, Thompson etc *Nor* 03-05; Perm to Offic from 07. *98 Norwich Road, Dereham NR20 3AR* Tel (01362) 698948

CLARK, John Michael. b 35. EMMTC 87. **d** 90 **p** 91. Chapl to the Deaf *Linc* 86-00; NSM Bracebridge Heath 90-00; rtd 00; Perm to Offic *Linc* from 00. *3 Hawthorn Road, Cherry Willingham, Lincoln LN3 4JU* Tel (01522) 751759

CLARK, John Patrick Hedley. b 37. St Cath Coll Cam BA61 MA65 Worc Coll Ox BA63 MA72 BD74 Lambeth Hon DD89. St Steph Ho Ox 61. **d** 64 **p** 65. C Highters Heath *Birm* 64-67; C Eglingham *Newc* 67-72; P-in-c Newc St Anne 72-77; V Longframlington w Brinkburn 77-95; V Chevington 95-02; rtd 02; Perm to Offic *Dur* from 02. *6 The Cottage, West Row, Greatham, Hartlepool TS25 2HW* Tel (01429) 870203

CLARK, Canon John Ronald Lyons. b 47. TCD BA69 MA72. Div Hostel Dub 67. **d** 70 **p** 71. C Dundela St Mark *D & D* 70-72; CF 72-75; C Belfast St Aid *Conn* 75-76; I Stranorlar w Meenglas and Kilteevogue *D & R* 76-81; Chapl Wythenshawe Hosp Man 81-95; I Kilgariffe Union *C, C & R* 95-96; Chapl Blackb, Hyndburn and Ribble Valley NHS Trust 96-03; Chapl Co-ord E Lancs Hosps NHS Trust 03-09; Chapl E Lancs Hospice 96-05; Hon Can Blackb Cathl 06-09; rtd 09. *Inishfree, Lefka Ori View, Xerosterni, 73008 Vamos, Chania, Crete, Greece* Tel (0030) (282) 502 2914 Mobile 6970-862858
E-mail rcronnieclark@googlemail.com

CLARK, Jonathan Dunnett. b 61. Ex Univ BA83 Bris Univ MLitt90 Southn Univ MA96. Trin Coll Bris 84. **d** 88 **p** 89. C Stanwix *Carl* 88-92; Chapl Bris Univ 92-93; Dir of Studies S Dios Minl Tr Scheme 94-97; Chapl Univ of N Lon 97-02; Chapl Lon Metrop Univ 02-03; AD Islington 99-03; R Stoke Newington St Mary from 03; P-in-c Brownswood Park from 04. *St Mary's Rectory, Stoke Newington Church Street, London N16 9ES* Tel (020) 7254 6072 Fax 7923 4135 Mobile 07968-845698 E-mail rectorofstokey@btinternet.com

CLARK, Jonathan Jackson. b 57. Linc Coll Ox 79 Down Coll Cam 83. Ridley Hall Cam 81. **d** 84 **p** 85. C W Derby St Luke *Liv* 84-87; C Gt Clacton *Chelmsf* 87-93; V Hammersmith St Simon *Lon* 93-03; AD Hammersmith and Fulham 96-01; TR Leeds St Geo *Ripon* from 03. *St George's Vicarage, 208 Kirkstall Lane, Leeds LS5 2AB* Tel 0113-274 4367
E-mail jonathan.clark@stgeorgesleeds.org.uk

CLARK, The Ven Kenneth James. b 22. DSC44. St Cath Soc Ox BA48 MA52. Cuddesdon Coll 52. **d** 52 **p** 53. C Brinkworth *Bris* 52-53; C Cricklade w Latton 53-56; C-in-c Filwood Park CD 56-59; V Bris H Cross Inns Court 59-61; V Westbury-on-Trym H Trin 61-72; V Bris St Mary Redcliffe w Temple etc 72-82; P-in-c Bedminster St Mich 73-78; RD Bedminster 73-79; Hon Can Bris Cathl 74-92; Adn Swindon 82-92; rtd 92; Perm to Offic *Sarum* 92-04. *c/o Miss R C Clark, 33 Beachgrove Road, Bristol BS16 4AU*

CLARK, Kenneth William. b 69. R Holloway Coll Lon BA92 Trin Coll Cam BA99 MA04. Westcott Ho Cam 97. **d** 00 **p** 01. C Bromley St Mark *Roch* 00-04; R Stone from 04. *The Rectory, Church Road, Greenhithe DA9 9BE* Tel (01322) 382076
E-mail kenneth.clark@diocese-rochester.org

CLARK, Lance Edgar Dennis. b 52. MBE93. Linc Th Coll 74. **d** 77 **p** 78. C Arnold *S'well* 77-82; V Brinsley w Underwood 82-87; Chapl RAF 87-02; Chapl Cardiff and Vale NHS Trust 02-10; rtd 10. *Hafod, Gileston, Vale of Glamorgan CF62 4HX* Tel (01446) 751077 E-mail lanceedclark@aol.co.uk

CLARK, Lynn. See PURVIS, Lynn

CLARK, Canon Martin Hudson. b 46. K Coll Lon BD68 AKC68 MTh91 Birm Univ PGCE89. **d** 71 **p** 72. C S'wark H Trin 71-74; C Parkstone St Pet w Branksea and St Osmund *Sarum* 74-77; V E Wickham *S'wark* 77-86; V Wandsworth St Anne 86-98; RD Wandsworth 90-95; V Angell Town St Jo 98-07; RD Brixton 01-05; Hon Can S'wark Cathl 05-07; rtd 07; Perm to Offic *Cant* 07-08 and from 11; Hon C Deal St Leon w St Rich and Sholden etc 08-10. *27 Century Walk, Deal CT14 6AL* Tel (01304) 366586 E-mail eveandmartin@hotmail.com

CLARK, Michael Arthur. b 46. S Dios Minl Tr Scheme. **d** 83 **p** 84. NSM Monkton Farleigh, S Wraxall and Winsley *Sarum* 83-05; Perm to Offic *Chich* from 05. *5 Park West, Southdowns Park, Haywards Heath RH16 4SG* Tel (01444) 440831 E-mail mike clark55@hotmail.com

CLARK, Michael David. b 45. Ox Univ MA68. Trin Coll Bris. **d** 72 **p** 73. C Cheadle *Ches* 72-76; Brazil 77-86; Bolivia 86-88; C Wilton *B & W* 89-90; TV 90-99; C Tollington *Lon* 99-01; TR Edgware from 01. *The Rectory, Rectory Lane, Edgware HA8 7LG* Tel (020) 8952 1081 *or* tel and fax 8952 4066
E-mail edgware@london.anglican.org

CLARK, Michael James. b 71. Univ of Wales (Cardiff) BSc92. Trin Coll Bris BA02. **d** 02 **p** 03. C Tiverton St Geo and St Paul *Ex* 02-07; TV Newton Tracey, Horwood, Alverdiscott etc from

07. *The Rectory, High Bickington, Umberleigh EX37 9AY* Tel (01769) 560870 E-mail revmikeclark@yahoo.co.uk

CLARK, Pamela Ann. b 45. Garnett Coll Lon CertEd72 Ch Ch Coll Cant PGCE93. SEITE 03. St Jo Coll Nottm 03. **d** 04 **p** 05. NSM Orlestone w Snave and Ruckinge w Warehorne etc *Cant* 04-06; NSM Hythe 06-09; Asst Chapl St Mich Hospice 06-07; Perm to Offic *Cant* 09-10; Chapl Dover Immigration Removal Cen from 10. *Chaplaincy Office, The Citadel, Western Heights, Dover CT17 0DR* Tel (01304) 246472

CLARK, Miss Patricia Mary. b 36. Liv Univ BSc. **d** 88 **p** 94. Par Dn Leasowe *Ches* 88-92; Bp's Officer for Women in Min 89-97; Par Dn Davenham 92-94; C 94-97; rtd 97; Perm to Offic *Ches* from 97. *18 Farmstead Way, Great Sutton, Ellesmere Port CH66 2RU* Tel 0151-339 1450

CLARK, Canon Peter. b 39. Ch Coll Cam BA61 MA65. Chich Th Coll 61. **d** 63 **p** 64. C Huddersfield SS Pet and Paul *Wakef* 63-67; C Notting Hill St Jo *Lon* 67-74; Grenada 75-79; C Hove All SS *Chich* 79; P-in-c Hove St Patr 79-82; V Hove St Patr w Ch Ch and St Andr 82-83; V Battersea Ch Ch and St Steph *S'wark* 83-08; RD Battersea 86-88; Can Hon S'wark Cathl 96-08; rtd 08; Perm to Offic *S'wark* from 08. *46 Havil Street, London SE5 7RS* Tel 020-7708 8915 Mobile 07773-164134 E-mail peterclark263@btinternet.com

CLARK, Peter. b 45. Sarum & Wells Th Coll 87. **d** 89 **p** 90. C Portsea St Cuth *Portsm* 89-92; TV Rye *Chich* 92-96 and 04-08; P-in-c Chiddingly w E Hoathly 96-98; R 98-04; rtd 08. *44 Ingrams Way, Hailsham BN27 3NP* Tel (01323) 841809 E-mail clucksville@tiscali.co.uk

CLARK, Peter. b 47. DipCOT92. ERMC 04. **d** 07 **p** 08. NSM Vange *Chelmsf* from 07. *283 Church Road, Basildon SS14 2NE* Tel (01268) 527570 Mobile 07786-125795 E-mail pclark@blueyonder.co.uk

CLARK, Peter Norman. b 53. Qu Coll Cam BA79. Westcott Ho Cam 78. **d** 80 **p** 81. C Bris St Mary Redcliffe w Temple etc 80-83; C Potternewton *Ripon* 83-86; R Longsight St Luke *Man* from 86; AD Ardwick 00-03. *St Luke's Rectory, Stockport Road, Longsight, Manchester M13 9AB* Tel 0161-273 6662

CLARK, Peter Rodney. b 58. Oriel Coll Ox BA81 MCIH93. NOC 97. **d** 00 **p** 01. C Stone St Mich and St Wulfad w Aston St Sav *Lich* 00-03; TV Hanley H Ev from 03; RD Stoke N from 08. *Christ Church Vicarage, 10 Emery Street, Stoke-on-Trent ST6 2JJ* Tel (01782) 212639 E-mail revrod@tiscali.co.uk

CLARK, Mrs Prudence Anne. b 44. Man Coll of Educn CertEd78. NOC 89. **d** 92 **p** 94. NSM Royton St Anne *Man* 92-94; Hon C 94-95; NSM Haughton St Anne 95-09; Perm to Offic from 09. *1 Hereford Way, Stalybridge SK15 2TD* Tel 0161-338 5275

CLARK, Richard Martin. b 60. Ch Coll Cam MA81 Nottm Univ MA99. Trin Coll Bris BA86. **d** 86 **p** 87. C Orpington Ch Ch *Roch* 86-89; C Marple All SS *Ches* 89-92; V Nottingham St Andr *S'well* from 92; AD Nottingham Cen from 08. *St Andrew's Vicarage, Chestnut Grove, Nottingham NG3 5AD* Tel 0115-912 0098 Mobile 07970-823462 E-mail standrews.office@ntlworld.com

CLARK, Robert Henry. b 32. Oak Hill Th Coll 61. **d** 64 **p** 65. C Haydock St Mark *Liv* 64-67; C Tranmere St Cath *Ches* 67-75; V Platt Bridge *Liv* 75-84; V Litherland St Paul Hatton Hill 84-94; rtd 94; Perm to Offic *Liv* from 94. *9 Lime Vale, Ince, Wigan WN3 4PE* Tel (01942) 861751

CLARK, Rodney. See CLARK, Peter Rodney

CLARK, Ronald. See CLARK, Canon John Ronald Lyons

CLARK, Canon Sarah Elizabeth. b 65. Loughb Univ BA86 Keele Univ MBA94. St Jo Coll Nottm MA97. **d** 98 **p** 99. C Porchester *S'well* 98-02; R Carlton-in-Lindrick and Langold w Oldcotes 02-09; AD Worksop 06-09; TR Clifton from 09; Dean of Women's Min from 10; Hon Can S'well Minster from 10. *The Rectory, 569 Farnborough Road, Nottingham NG11 9DG* Tel 0115-878 0541 E-mail sarahclark@ntlworld.com

CLARK, Simon Peter John. b 68. Westcott Ho Cam 95. **d** 98 **p** 99. C Bocking St Mary *Chelmsf* 98-02; C Edmonton St Alphege *Lon* 02-07; C Ponders End St Matt 02-07; P-in-c Noel Park St Mark from 07; Chapl NE Lon Coll from 07. *St Mark's Vicarage, Ashley Crescent, London N22 6LJ* Tel (020) 8888 3442 E-mail fr.simon@btinternet.com

CLARK, Canon Stephen Kenneth. b 52. Bris Univ BEd74. Wycliffe Hall Ox 80. **d** 83 **p** 84. C Pitsea *Chelmsf* 83-86; Chapl Scargill Ho 86-89; R Elmley Castle w Bricklehampton and Combertons *Worc* 89-96; Chapl Burrswood Chr Cen *Roch* 96-01; Chapl Team Ldr 01-07; I Annagh w Drumaloor, Cloverhill and Drumlane *K, E & A* from 07; Can Kilmore Cathl from 10. *The Rectory, 2 Creen, Belturbet, Co Cavan, Republic of Ireland* Tel (00353) (49) 952 4778 Mobile 86-382 6454 E-mail skclar@googlemail.com

CLARK, Terence Paul. b 62. Leeds Univ BSc85 PGCE94 St Jo Coll Ox DPhil91. Wycliffe Hall Ox 98. **d** 00 **p** 01. C Whitfield *Derby* 00-10; TR Deane *Man* from 10. *Deane Rectory, 234 Wigan Road, Bolton BL3 5QE* Tel (01204) 61819 E-mail rector@deaneparish.co.uk

CLARK-KING (*née* CLARK), **Ellen Jane.** b 62. Newnham Coll Cam BA85 MA89 Lon Univ MA99 Lanc Univ PhD03. Ripon Coll Cuddesdon 89. **d** 92 **p** 94. C Colwall w Upper Colwall and Coddington *Heref* 92-95; Chapl SS Coll Cam 95-00; NSM N Shields *Newc* 00-05; Asst Dioc Dir of Ords 01-05; Canada from 05. *195 East Windsor Road, North Vancouver BC V7N 1J9, Canada* Tel (001) (604) 985 5919 Fax 985 7667 E-mail ejck@lineone.net

CLARK-KING (formerly KING), Jeremy Norman. b 66. K Coll Lon BD88 AKC88 Lon Univ MA99. Ripon Coll Cuddesdon 88. **d** 90 **p** 91. C Ashby-de-la-Zouch St Helen w Coleorton *Leic* 90-93; C Ledbury w Eastnor *Heref* 93-96; C Cambridge Gt St Mary w St Mich *Ely* 96-00; Chapl Girton Coll Cam 96-99; Chapl Cam Univ 96-99; V Byker St Ant *Newc* 00-05; R N Vancouver St Martin Canada from 05. *195 East Windsor Road, North Vancouver BC V7N 1J9, Canada* Tel (001) (604) 985 5919 Fax 985 7667 E-mail anglican@uniserve.com

CLARKE, Alan John. b 55. St Jo Coll Dur BA77 MA85 PGCE. Westcott Ho Cam 78. **d** 80 **p** 81. C Heworth St Mary *Dur* 80-83; C Darlington St Jo 83-87; Asst Chapl Bryanston Sch 87-91; Chapl St Pet High Sch Ex 93-99; Lic to Offic *Ex* 93-99; Chapl and Hd RS Reed's Sch Cobham from 99. *Clover, Reed's School, Sandy Lane, Cobham KT11 2BL* Tel (01932) 869006 or 869080

CLARKE, Alexandra Naomi Mary. b 75. Trin Coll Cam BA96 MA99 MPhil97 SS Hild & Bede Coll Dur PhD02 Anglia Poly Univ BA04. Westcott Ho Cam 02. **d** 05 **p** 06. C Papworth *Ely* 05-09; R Upper Itchen *Win* from 09. *The Rectory, Cheriton, Alresford SO24 0QH* Tel (01962) 771226 E-mail rector@upperitchen.plus.com

CLARKE, Miss Alison Clare. b 33. MCST54 Open Univ BA85. EAMTC 90. **d** 93 **p** 94. NSM Lt Ilford St Mich *Chelmsf* 93-98; Asst Chapl Newham Healthcare NHS Trust Lon 93-98; Perm to Offic *Lon* 94-98; NSM Woodford St Mary w St Phil and St Jas *Chelmsf* 98-03; rtd 03; Perm to Offic *Chelmsf* 03-04. *29 Glengall Road, Woodford Green IG8 0DN* Tel (020) 8504 5106

CLARKE, Andrew John. b 58. New Coll Edin BD82 Graduate Soc Dur PGCE89. Linc Th Coll 84. **d** 86 **p** 87. C High Harrogate Ch Ch *Ripon* 86-88; RE Teacher Royds Hall High Sch Huddersfield 89-91; C Thornbury *Bradf* 91-93; P-in-c Bingley H Trin 93-99; V from 99; RD Airedale 00-05. *6 Woodvale Crescent, Bingley BD16 4AL* Tel (01274) 562278 E-mail andrew.clarke@bradford.anglican.org

CLARKE, Ann. See CLARKE, Geraldine Ann

CLARKE (*née* HARWOOD), Mrs Ann Jane. b 73. SEITE. **d** 08. C Winslow w Gt Horwood and Addington *Ox* 08-11; C Lee Gd Shep w St Pet *S'wark* from 11. *56 Weigall Road, London SE12 8HF* Tel 07903-652927 (mobile) E-mail annharwood73@googlemail.com

CLARKE, Anne. b 51. **d** 04 **p** 05. OLM E Dulwich St Jo *S'wark* from 04. *62 Oakhurst Grove, London SE22 9AQ* Tel (020) 8693 1276 E-mail apsy73@dsl.pipex.com

CLARKE, Arthur. b 34. Lon Univ BD66 Nottm Univ MPhil75 DipEd. Sarum & Wells Th Coll 75. **d** 76 **p** 77. C Wollaton *S'well* 76-79; R Sutton Bonington 79-91; P-in-c Normanton on Soar 79-91; R Sutton Bonington w Normanton-on-Soar 91-93; P-in-c Arnold 93-94; V 94-02; rtd 02; Perm to Offic *S'well* from 02 and *Leic* from 03. *16 Kegworth Road, Kingston-on-Soar, Nottingham NG11 0DB* Tel (01509) 674545 E-mail aclarke@kos16.fsnet.co.uk

CLARKE, Miss Audrey May. b 35. Gilmore Ho 65. **dss** 75 **d** 87 **p** 94. Crofton Park St Hilda w St Cypr *S'wark* 75-79; Chapl Asst Middx Hosp Lon 80-84; Mottingham St Andr w St Alban *S'wark* 84-87; Par Dn 87-89; C Westborough *Guildf* 89-95; rtd 95; Hon C St Mary's Bay w St Mary-in-the-Marsh etc *Cant* 95-98; Hon C New Romney w Old Romney and Midley 95-98; Perm to Offic *Pet* 98-10. *3 Stuart Court, High Street, Kibworth, Leicester LE8 0LR* Tel 0116-279 2592 E-mail audrey@revaclarke.freeserve.co.uk

CLARKE, Barbara. b 51. Bradf Univ BA87 Leeds Univ PGCE89 MA07. NOC 04. **d** 07 **p** 08. NSM Addingham *Bradf* from 07. *8 Brighton Road, Ilkley LS29 8PS* Tel (01943) 605253 E-mail bclarke@talktalk.net

CLARKE, Bernard Ronald. b 53. FRGS. Ridley Hall Cam 74. **d** 77 **p** 78. C Leigh Park *Portsm* 77-78; C Petersfield w Sheet 78-81; Chapl RN from 81; Dir of Ords RN 93-03. *Royal Naval Chaplaincy Service, Mail Point 1-2, Leach Building, Whale Island, Portsmouth PO2 8BY* Tel (023) 9262 5055 Fax 9262 5134

CLARKE, Mrs Caroline Anne. b 49. Girton Coll Cam BA75 MA79 K Coll Lon PGCE76. SEITE 97. **d** 00 **p** 01. NSM Clapham H Trin and St Pet *S'wark* from 00; Chapl Trin Hospice Lon from 03. *42 The Chase, London SW4 0NH* Tel (020) 7622 0765 Fax 7652 4555 Mobile 07808-858674 E-mail clarkecaroline@hotmail.com

CLARKE, Charles David. b 37. Univ of Wales BA76 MA93 PhD98 Cam Univ DipEd77 MEd Lambeth MA95 LCP77. St Mich Coll Llan 88. **d** 90 **p** 91. C Whitchurch *Llan* 90-93; V Graig 93-96; P-in-c Cilfynydd 93-96; TV Cyncoed *Mon* 96-98; R Neath w Llantwit 98-01; TR Neath 01-02; rtd 02. *Lough Cutra,*

11 Davies Andrews Road, Tonna, Neath SA11 1EU Tel (01639) 638049

CLARKE, Canon Christopher George. b 43. Sarum Th Coll 67. **d** 68 **p** 69. C Sprowston *Nor* 68-72; V Hemsby 72-77; V Sutton Courtenay w Appleford *Ox* 77-84; TR Bracknell 84-97; RD Bracknell 90-96; Hon Can Ch Ch 95-08; P-in-c Sonning 97-98; V 98-08; rtd 08. *Oak Lodge, Upton Snodsbury, Worcester WR7 4NH* Tel (01905) 381146 E-mail cgandcgclarke@googlemail.com

CLARKE, Canon David James. b 55. Univ of Wales (Abth) BSc(Econ)77 Keele Univ MA78 PhD83. Trin Coll Bris. **d** 84 **p** 85. C Cardigan w Mwnt and Y Ferwig *St D* 84-87; P-in-c Llansantffraed and Llanbadarn Trefeglwys etc 87-88; V 88-91; Chapl Coll of SS Mark and Jo Plymouth 91-96; V Lindfield *Chich* from 96; Can and Preb Chich Cathl from 06. *The Vicarage, High Street, Lindfield, Haywards Heath RH16 2HR* Tel (01444) 482386

CLARKE, Dominic James. b 71. Surrey Univ BA07. STETS 04. **d** 07 **p** 08. C Petersfield *Portsm* from 07. *38 Larcombe Road, Petersfield GU32 3LS* Tel (01730) 260213

CLARKE, Douglas Charles. b 33. Bps' Coll Cheshunt 65. **d** 66 **p** 67. C Chingford SS Pet and Paul *Chelmsf* 66-72; V Romford Ascension Collier Row 72-79; V Bembridge *Portsm* 79-83; V Bournemouth St Mary *Win* 83-87; R High Wych and Gilston w Eastwick *St Alb* 87-00; rtd 00; Perm to Offic *Linc* and *St Alb* from 00. *36 Tennyson Drive, Bourne PE10 9WD* Tel (01778) 394840

CLARKE, Dudley Barrington. b 22. OBE. Em Coll Cam BA46 MA48 PhD. Ridley Hall Cam 46. **d** 48 **p** 49. C Aldershot H Trin *Guildf* 48-50; Chapl Monkton Combe Sch Bath 50-58; Australia from 59; rtd 87. *c/o D G Clarke Esq, PO Box 116, Elsternwick Vic 3185, Australia*

CLARKE, Duncan James Edward. b 54. Wycliffe Hall Ox 75. **d** 78 **p** 79. C Newport St Andr *Mon* 78-80; C Griffithstown 80-82; Trinidad and Tobago 82-84 and 95-99; NSM Fleckney and Kilby *Leic* 92-95; USPG 95-99; C Wednesfield *Lich* 99; TV 99-01; Asst Chapl HM Pris Wormwood Scrubs 01-02; Chapl HM Pris Haverigg 02-07; Chapl HM Pris Garth 07-09; P-in-c Leyland St Ambrose *Blackb* 09-11; V from 11. *St Ambrose Vicarage, 85 Moss Lane, Leyland, Preston PR25 4XA* Tel (01772) 623426 Mobile 07946-668786 E-mail namabiah@msn.com

CLARKE, Mrs Elizabeth Hazel. b 55. Ridley Hall Cam 02. **d** 04 **p** 05. C Frankby w Greasby *Ches* 04-09; P-in-c Dodleston from 09. *St Mary's Rectory, Pulford Lane, Dodleston, Chester CH4 9NN* Tel (01244) 660257

CLARKE, Eric Samuel. b 26. Nottm Univ BSc51 St Cath Coll Ox BA69 MA69. Wycliffe Hall Ox 51. **d** 54 **p** 55. C Gedling *S'well* 54-57; C Nottingham St Pet and St Jas 57-69; Perm to Offic *Derby* 63-02; rtd 02. *Hillcrest, Cottington Mead, Sidmouth EX10 8HB*

CLARKE (née GILMARTIN), Mrs Frances. b 53. Reading Univ BSc75 PGCE92. **d** 11. OLM Skellingthorpe w Doddington *Linc* from 11. *12 Shaftesbury Avenue, Lincoln LN6 0QN* Tel (01522) 685487 E-mail frances_clarke@hotmail.co.uk

CLARKE, Frank. b 21. St Jo Coll Nottm. **d** 85 **p** 87. NSM Farnsfield *S'well* 85-97; rtd 98; Perm to Offic *S'well* from 03. *Belvedere, Tippings Lane, Farnsfield, Newark NG22 8EP* Tel (01623) 882528 E-mail doreen@onetel.com

CLARKE, Frank Alfred. b 46. MCLIP67 MCMI82. **d** 08 **p** 09. OLM Weybourne Gp *Nor* from 08. *7 Alexandra Road, Sheringham NR26 8HU* Tel (01263) 825677 E-mail f.clarke46@tiscali.co.uk

CLARKE, Geoffrey. b 53. CA Tr Coll 84 Trin Coll Bris 94. **d** 97 **p** 98. C Belmont *Lon* 97-00; C Tonbridge SS Pet and Paul *Roch* 00-05; V Erith St Paul from 05. *The Vicarage, 44A Colyers Lane, Erith DA8 3NP* Tel (01322) 332809 E-mail geofftherev@ntlworld.com

CLARKE, Geraldine Ann. b 46. Hockerill Coll of Educn CertEd68 ACP81. NTMTC 93. **d** 96 **p** 97. NSM Aldersbrook *Chelmsf* 96-01; TR Becontree S 01-09; P-in-c N Bersted *Chich* from 09. *The Vicarage, 330 Chichester Road, North Bersted, Bognor Regis PO21 5AU* Tel (01243) 823800 E-mail annclarke@talktalk.net

CLARKE, Canon Harold George. b 29. St D Coll Lamp 58. **d** 61 **p** 62. C Ebbw Vale Ch Ch *Mon* 61-64; C Roath St German *Llan* 64-73; Chapl Wales Poly 73-74; V Glyntaff 73-84; V Roath St Martin 84-00; RD Cardiff 89-99; Can Res Llan Cathl 91-99; rtd 00. *12 St Margaret's Crescent, Cardiff CF23 5AU* Tel (029) 2046 2280

CLARKE, Hazel. See CLARKE, Mrs Elizabeth Hazel

CLARKE, Hilary James. b 41. JP. Univ of Wales (Lamp) BA64 Ox Univ DipEd65. St Steph Ho Ox 64. **d** 66 **p** 67. C Kibworth Beauchamp *Leic* 66-68; Chapl to the Deaf 68-71; Prin Officer Ch Miss for Deaf Walsall 71-73; Prin Officer & Sec Leic and Co Miss for the Deaf 73-89; Hon C Leic St Anne 73-98; TV Leic H Spirit 82-89; Hon Can Leic Cathl 88-96; Bp's Press Relns and Dio Communications Officer 95-96; Sec Gen Syn Coun for the Deaf 88-02; rtd 02. *The Gate House, Brough, Kirkby Stephen CA17 4DS* Tel 07730-002570 (mobile)

CLARKE, James. See CLARKE, Canon David James

CLARKE, Jason Philip. b 66. Lon Hosp BDS. Oak Hill Th Coll 99. **d** 01 **p** 02. C Fulwood *Sheff* 01-06; Dir Staff Tr UCCF from 06; Perm to Offic *Sheff* from 06. *469 Redmires Road, Sheffield S10 4LF* Tel 0114-230 9345

CLARKE, Jason Scott. b 65. Leeds Univ BA87. Coll of Resurr Mirfield 89. **d** 91 **p** 92. C Hendon St Mary *Lon* 91-95; V Enfield St Geo 95-01; V Ditchling *Chich* 01-06; CF from 06. *c/o MOD Chaplains (Army)* Tel (01264) 381140 Fax 381824

CLARKE, John Charles. b 31. St Jo Coll Nottm 91. **d** 92 **p** 93. NSM Winshill *Derby* 92-95; P-in-c Stanley 95-98; rtd 98. *5 The Tyleshades, Tadburn, Romsey SO51 5RJ* Tel (01794) 523945

CLARKE, Canon John David Maurice. b 60. **d** 89 **p** 90. C Dublin Whitechurch *D & G* 89-92; Asst Chapl St Vin Hosp Donnybrook 89-92; I Navan w Kentstown, Tara, Slane, Painestown etc *M & K* from 92; Can Meath from 00; Can Kildare Cathl from 00; Can St Patr Cathl Dublin from 09. *The Rectory, Boyne Road, Navan, Co Meath, Republic of Ireland* Tel and fax (00353) (46) 902 1172 E-mail johndmclarke@eircom.net

CLARKE, The Very Revd John Martin. b 52. Edin Univ BD76 Hertf Coll Ox BA89 MA89. Edin Th Coll 73. **d** 76 **p** 77. C Kenton Ascension *Newc* 76-79; Prec St Ninian's Cathl Perth 79-82; Info Officer to Gen Syn of Scottish Episc Ch 82-87; Greece 87-88; V Battersea St Mary *S'wark* 89-96; Prin Ripon Coll Cuddesdon 97-04; Can and Preb Linc Cathl 00-04; Dean Wells *B & W* from 04. *The Dean's Lodging, 25 The Liberty, Wells BA5 2SZ* Tel and fax (01749) 670278 E-mail dean@wellscathedral.uk.net

CLARKE, John Patrick Hatherley. b 46. Pemb Coll Ox BA68 Man Univ MBA73. St Jo Coll Nottm. **d** 83 **p** 84. C Leic H Trin w St Jo 83-87; C Selly Park St Steph and St Wulstan *Birm* 87-92; Hon C Woking St Mary *Guildf* 92-94; V Greenham *Ox* from 94. *Greenham Vicarage, New Road, Greenham, Thatcham RG19 8RZ* Tel (01635) 41075

CLARKE, Canon John Percival. b 44. TCD BA67 MA98. **d** 69 **p** 70. C Belfast St Simon *Conn* 69-72; C Monkstown *D & G* 72-76; Asst Chapl TCD 76-78; I Durrus *C, C & R* 79-82; I Carrigrohane Union 82-89; Tanzania 89-92; I Wicklow w Killiskey *D & G* from 92; Abp's Dom Chapl 95-97; Can Ch Ch Cathl Dublin from 97. *The Rectory, Wicklow, Republic of Ireland* Tel (00353) (404) 67132

CLARKE, John Philip. b 31. Trin Hall Cam BA54 MA62. Linc Th Coll. **d** 57 **p** 58. C Walworth Lady Marg w St Mary *S'wark* 57-59; C Warlingham w Chelsham and Farleigh 59-62; V Mottingham St Andr w St Alban 62-67; C Eltham Park St Luke 67-72; Chapl Leeds Gen Infirmary 72-91; C Far Headingley St Chad *Ripon* 91-96; Bp's Adv on Chr Healing 91-96; rtd 96; Perm to Offic *Ripon* from 96. *13 Bishop Garth, Pateley Bridge, Harrogate HG3 5LL* Tel (01423) 711646

CLARKE, Mrs Joy Ann. b 48. **d** 98 **p** 02. OLM Ditton St Mich w St Thos *Liv* 98-10; rtd 10. *55 Spinney Avenue, Widnes WA8 8LB* Tel 0151-424 8747

CLARKE, Judith Irene. b 46. SRN67 SCM69. EAMTC 97. **d** 00 **p** 01. NSM Shingay Gp *Ely* 00-02; P-in-c Gt Staughton 02-05; P-in-c Hail Weston and Southoe 04-05; R Gt Staughton w Hail Weston w Southoe from 05. *The Vicarage, Causeway, Great Staughton, St Neots PE19 5BF* Tel (01480) 861215 E-mail judi195@btinternet.com

CLARKE (née PULLIN), Kathleen Jean Rebecca. b 58. Qu Coll Birm BA07. **d** 07 **p** 08. C Kings Norton *Birm* 07-11; V Highters Heath from 11. *Immanuel Vicarage, 5 Pickenham Road, Birmingham B14 4TG* Tel 0121-430 7578 E-mail rebeccapullin@hotmail.com

✠**CLARKE, The Rt Revd Kenneth Herbert.** b 49. TCD BA71. **d** 72 **p** 73 **c** 01. C Magheralin *D & D* 72-75; C Dundonald 75-78; Chile 78-81; I Crinken *D & G* 82-86; I Coleraine *Conn* 86-01; Chmn SAMS (Ireland) from 94; Can Conn Cathl 96-98; Adn Dalriada 98-01; Bp K, E & A from 01. *48 Carrickfern, Cavan, Republic of Ireland* Tel (00353) (49) 437 2759 Fax 436 2829 E-mail ken@atnaf.freeserve.co.uk *or* bishop@kilmore.anglican.org

CLARKE, Mrs Lynnette Jean. b 46. Qu Coll Birm 05. **d** 08 **p** 09. OLM Allesley Park and Whoberley *Cov* from 08. *14 High Park Close, Coventry CV5 7BE* Tel (024) 7646 7097 Mobile 07890-048210 E-mail lynnette@mountnod.co.uk

CLARKE, Canon Margaret Geraldine. b 33. Dalton Ho Bris 62. dss 68 **d** 87 **p** 94. Wells St Thos w Horrington *B & W* 68-74; Easthampstead *Ox* 74-94; Par Dn 87-94; C 94; Hon Can Ch Ch 90-94; rtd 94; Hon C Bracknell *Ox* from 97. *Hermon, London Road, Bracknell RG12 2XH* Tel (01344) 427451

CLARKE, Martin Howard. b 47. AKC70. St Aug Coll Cant 70. **d** 71 **p** 72. C Saffron Walden w Wendens Ambo *Chelmsf* 71-74; C Ely 74-78; V Messing w Inworth *Chelmsf* 78-90; V Layer de la Haye 90-02; R Layer de la Haye and Layer Breton w Birch etc from 03. *The Vicarage, 45 Malting Green Road, Layer-de-la-Haye, Colchester CO2 0JJ* Tel (01206) 734243 E-mail stationmaster@thelayers.fsnet.co.uk

CLARKE, Ms Mary Margaret. b 65. K Coll Lon BD86 AKC86. Linc Th Coll 89. **d** 89 **p** 94. Par Dn Northampton St Jas *Pet* 89-93; Chapl Nene Coll of HE Northn 92-93; TD Coventry Caludon 93-94; TV 94-01; Perm to Offic *Lon* 01-08. *1 Porchester Gardens, London W2 3LA* Tel (020) 7229 6359 E-mail mary-andrew@clarkewillson.fsnet.co.uk

CLARKE, Maurice Harold. b 30. K Alfred's Coll Win CertEd56 Sussex Univ MA79 LCP69. Cuddesdon Coll 65. **d** 67 **p** 68. Hd Master Co Sec Sch Cowplain (Lower Sch) 67-72; Dep Hd Master Thamesview High Sch 72-80; Hd Master Eltham Green Comp Sch 80-83; Hon C Waterlooville *Portsm* 67-70; Hon C Fareham SS Pet and Paul 70-72; Hon C Higham and Merston *Roch* 72-83; V Hamble le Rice *Win* 83-90; rtd 91; Perm to Offic *Win* from 91 and *Chich* from 92. *10 Worcester Road, Chichester PO19 8DJ* Tel (01243) 775646

CLARKE, Michael. b 39. Ely Th Coll 60. **d** 62 **p** 63. C S Stoneham *Win* 62-64; C N Greenford All Hallows *Lon* 64-69; Hon C Milton *Portsm* 69-74; Chapl St Jas Hosp Portsm 69-91; Chapl Hurstpierpoint Coll 91-92; R Highnam, Lassington, Rudford, Tibberton etc *Glouc* 92-98; rtd 99; Perm to Offic *Glouc* 99-01 and *Portsm* from 02. *Little Barns, 77 Fishbourne Lane, Ryde PO33 4EX* Tel (01983) 883858

CLARKE, Canon Neil Malcolm. b 53. OBE05. Solicitor 79. WMMTC 89. **d** 92 **p** 93. NSM Desborough, Brampton Ash, Dingley and Braybrooke *Pet* from 92; Can Pet Cathl from 04. *53 Breakleys Road, Desborough, Kettering NN14 2PT* Tel (01536) 760667 E-mail revnclarke@aol.com

CLARKE, Nicholas John. b 57. Lon Univ BA78 Lon Inst of Educn PGCE80. Ridley Hall Cam 95. **d** 97 **p** 98. C Attleborough *Cov* 97-00; V Fillongley and Corley 00-07; Chapl Chantilly *Eur* from 07. *7A avenue du Bouteiller, 60500 Chantilly, France* Tel (0033) 3 44 58 53 22 E-mail chaplain@stpeterschantilly.info

CLARKE, Norman. b 28. Keble Coll Ox BA52 MA58. St Steph Ho Ox 52. **d** 54 **p** 55. C Ellesmere Port *Ches* 54-57; C Kettering St Mary *Pet* 57-60; Chapl and Tutor St Monica Mampong Ghana 60-62; C Friern Barnet All SS *Lon* 62-63; Lic to Offic *Leic* 63-74; C Knighton St Mary Magd 74-81; Dioc Communications Officer 81-88; P-in-c Sproughton w Burstall *St E* 81-88; P-in-c Dunsford and Doddiscombsleigh *Ex* 88-95; P-in-c Churston Ferrers w Churston Ferrers *Ex* 95-08; RD Ottery 02-03; Perm to Offic St Helena from 96. *78 Malden Road, Sidmouth EX10 9NA* Tel (01395) 515849

CLARKE, Paul Ian. b 72. W Suffolk Coll BA09. Trin Coll Bris BA11. **d** 11. C Haughley w Wetherden and Stowupland *St E* from 11. *1 Church View, Haughley, Stowmarket IP14 3NU* Tel 07590-121122 (mobile) E-mail paul@theclarkehouse.net

CLARKE, Paul Wordsworth. b 74. Trevelyan Coll Dur LLB97. Oak Hill Th Coll BA06. **d** 07. C St Helen Bishopsgate w St Andr Undershaft etc *Lon* from 07. *4 Merrick Square, London SE1 4JB* Tel (020) 7283 2231 E-mail p.clarke@st-helens.org.uk

CLARKE, Preb Peter Gerald. b 38. Cuddesdon Coll 74. **d** 76 **p** 77. NSM Marston Magna w Rimpton *B & W* 76-79; NSM Queen Camel, Marston Magna, W Camel, Rimpton etc 79-87; NSM Chilton Cantelo, Ashington, Mudford, Rimpton etc 87-88; R Tintinhull w Chilthorne Domer, Yeovil Marsh etc 88-94; TV Weston-super-Mare Cen Par 94-95; V Weston super Mare All SS and St Sav 96-06; Preb Wells Cathl 02-08; rtd 06; Perm to Offic *B & W* from 06. *6 West Camel Farm, West Camel, Yeovil BA22 7HH* Tel (01935) 850408 E-mail peter2117@lycos.com

CLARKE, Peter John. b 36. Qu Coll Ox BA60 MA64 Lon Univ BD79. Clifton Th Coll 62. **d** 62 **p** 63. C Upper Tulse Hill St Matthias *S'wark* 62-64; CMJ 64-96; Dir for S America 88-96; rtd 97. *Pedro Moran 4414, C 1419 HLH Buenos Aires, Argentina* Tel and fax (0054) (11) 4501 4629

CLARKE, Philip John. b 44. Bris Univ BA65 Univ of Wales (Abth) DipEd66. NOC 84. **d** 87 **p** 88. NSM Crewe Ch Ch and St Pet *Ches* 87-88; NSM Coppenhall 88-90; Lic to Offic 90-91; C Altrincham St Geo 91-95; C Odd Rode 95-97; P-in-c Peterchurch w Vowchurch, Turnastone and Dorstone *Heref* 97-98; V Llansantffraid Glyn Ceirog and Llanarmon etc *St As* 98-09; rtd 09; P-in-c Caerwys and Bodfari *St As* 09-11; P-in-c Lowther and Askham and Clifton and Brougham *Carl* from 11. *The Rectory, Clifton, Penrith CA10 2EA* Tel (01768) 895201 E-mail revphilipjclarke@aol.com

CLARKE, Richard Leon. b 37. Sarum Th Coll 62. **d** 65 **p** 66. C Fordington *Sarum* 65-68; C Haywards Heath St Rich *Chich* 68-72; C Goring-by-Sea 72-76; P-in-c Southwick St Pet 76-77; P-in-c Portslade St Andr 76-77; V Portslade St Pet and St Andr 77-79; R Clayton w Keymer 79-02; RD Hurst 90-98; rtd 02; Perm to Offic *Chich* 03-05; Hon C Brighton Annunciation from 05. *107 Freshfield Road, Brighton BN2 0BL* Tel (01273) 628086

✠**CLARKE, The Most Revd Richard Lionel.** b 49. TCD BA71 MA79 PhD90 K Coll Lon BD75 AKC75. **d** 75 **p** 76 **c** 96. C Holywood *D & D* 75-77; C Dublin St Bart w Leeson Park *D & G* 77-79; Dean of Residence TCD 79-84; I Bandon Union *C, C & R* 84-93; Dir of Ords 85-93; Cen Dir of Ords 82-97; Can Cork and Ross Cathls 91-93; Dean Cork 93-96; I Cork St Fin Barre's Union 93-96; Chapl Univ Coll Cork 93-96; Bp M & K from 96; Hon Can St Ninian's Cathl Perth from 04. *Bishop's House, Moyglare, Maynooth, Co Kildare, Republic of Ireland* Tel (00353) (1) 628 9354 E-mail bishop@meath.anglican.org

CLARKE, Canon Robert George. b 36. St Jo Coll Dur BA65 Natal Univ PhD83. Cranmer Hall Dur 65. **d** 67 **p** 68. C Basingstoke *Win* 67-70; R Ixopo 71-74; C Pietermaritzburg Cathl 75-80; Dir Pietermaritzburg Urban Min Project 77-83; R Grahamstown St Bart 84-87; Lect St Paul's Coll 84-87; Ecum Officer Albany Regional Coun of Chs 88-95; Hon Can Grahamstown from 05. *26 Somerset Street, Grahamstown, 6139 South Africa* Tel (0027) (046) 622 7803 E-mail bobandmaggy@imaginet.co.za

CLARKE, Robert Graham. b 28. S Dios Minl Tr Scheme 78. **d** 81 **p** 82. NSM Woolston *Win* 81-89; NSM Portswood St Denys 89-93; Chapl Torrevieja *Eur* 93-95; Perm to Offic *Win* 95-05 and *Eur* from 95. *10 River Green, Hamble, Southampton SO31 4JA* Tel (023) 8045 4230

CLARKE, Robert Michael. b 45. Oak Hill Th Coll BD71 Sarum & Wells Th Coll 78. **d** 78 **p** 79. Hon C Glastonbury St Jo w Godney *B & W* 78-81; Asst Hd Master Edington Sch 78-81; Chapl Felsted Sch 81-84; Asst Chapl and Ho Master 85-92; Hd Master Brocksford Hall 92-94; Hd Master The Park Sch Bath 94-96; Chapl Seaford Coll Petworth 96-99; Hd Master Bredon Sch 99-00; Perm to Offic *Lich* from 01. *17 Top Street, Whittington, Oswestry SY11 4DR* Tel (01691) 662548

CLARKE, Robert Sydney. b 35. OBE00. K Coll Lon AKC64 MA65. **d** 65 **p** 66. C Hendon St Mary *Lon* 65-69; C Langley Marish *Ox* 69-70; Chapl New Cross Hosp Wolv 70-74; Chapl Dorchester Hosps 74-79; Sen Chapl Westmr Hosp Lon 80-85; Sen Chapl Win Hosps 88-94; Sen Chapl Win and Eastleigh Healthcare NHS Trust 94-00; Chapl to The Queen 87-05; Sec and Dir Tr Gen Syn Hosp Chapl Coun 94-00; rtd 00; Perm to Offic *Lon* and *S'wark* 95-00; *Eur* from 00; *Win* from 05. *3 Brook Court, Middlebridge Street, Romsey SO51 8HR* Tel (01794) 524215

CLARKE, Canon Robert William. b 56. CITC. **d** 83 **p** 84. C Cloughfern *Conn* 83-85; C Drumragh w Mountfield *D & R* 85-87; I Edenderry w Clanabogan from 87; Can Derry Cathl from 05. *Edenderry Rectory, 91 Crevenagh Road, Omagh BT79 0EZ* Tel (028) 8224 5525

CLARKE, Roger David. b 58. Man Univ BA Ox Univ MA. Ripon Coll Cuddesdon 80. **d** 83 **p** 84. C Frodsham *Ches* 83-86; C Wilmslow 86-88; V High Lane 88-93; V Heald Green St Cath 93-99; R W Kirby St Bridget 99-10; V Hale Barns w Ringway from 10. *Ringway Vicarage, 35 Burnside, Hale Barns, Altrincham WA15 0SG* Tel 0161-980 8944

CLARKE, Ronald George. b 31. Oak Hill Th Coll. **d** 64 **p** 65. C Carlton-in-the-Willows *S'well* 64-68; V Bestwood St Matt 68-76; V Barnsbury St Andr w St Thos and St Matthias *Lon* 76-77; V Barnsbury St Andr 77-78; V Barnsbury St Andr w H Trin 79-80; P-in-c Battle Bridge All SS w Pentonville St Jas 79-80; V Barnsbury St Andr and H Trin w All SS 81-86; TR Bath Twerton-on-Avon *B & W* 86-94; rtd 94; P-in-c Churchstanton, Buckland St Mary and Otterford *B & W* 94-97; Perm to Offic from 97. *Myrtle Cottage, 35 High Street, Chard TA20 1QL* Tel (01460) 65495

CLARKE, Stephen Robert. b 77. Southn Univ BA99. Trin Coll Bris BA10. **d** 10 **p** 11. C Pioneer Min Glouc City from 10. *35 St Mary's Square, Gloucester GL1 2QT* Tel (01452) 451023 E-mail steveclarkey@gmail.com

CLARKE, Steven Peter. b 61. Oak Hill Th Coll 93. **d** 97 **p** 98. C Frinton *Chelmsf* 97-01; C Woodford Wells from 01. *80 Montalt Road, Woodford Green IG8 9SS* Tel (020) 8505 1431

CLARKE (formerly GARDNER), Mrs Susan Carol. b 54. SRN75. St Jo Coll Nottm 02. **d** 04 **p** 05. C Abington *Pet* 04-07; P-in-c Woodhouse *Wakef* 07-08; V Birkby and Woodhouse 08-10; P-in-c Thornhill and Whitley Lower from 10. *Thornhill Rectory, 51 Frank Lane, Dewsbury WF12 0JW* Tel (01924) 520861 Mobile 07732-189485 E-mail sue@suegardner1.wanadoo.co.uk

CLARKE (née DAVIS), Susan Elizabeth Mary. b 50. St Thos Hosp Lon MB, BS74 Univ Coll Lon MSc81 FRCP84 FRCR03. SEITE 03. **d** 06 **p** 07. NSM W Streatham St Jas *S'wark* from 06; NSM Streatham St Paul from 10. *26 Abbotsleigh Road, London SW16 1SP* Tel (020) 8769 5117 Mobile 07710-744006 E-mail sue.clarke@kcl.ac.uk

CLARKE, Timothy John. b 69. Jes Coll Cam BA91 MA95 Barrister 92. WMMTC 00. **d** 03 **p** 04. NSM Birm Cathl from 03. *15B College Green, Worcester WR1 2LH* E-mail timclarke@waitrose.com

CLARKE, Ms Valerie Diane. b 45. St Jo Coll Nottm BA00. NOC 91. **d** 95 **p** 96. C Sherburn in Elmet w Saxton *York* 95-97; C Brayton 97-99; Chapl Scargill Ho 00-03; P-in-c Barnburgh w Melton on the Hill etc *Sheff* 03-09; rtd 09; Perm to Offic *Wakef* from 09. *1 Arrunden Court, Holmfirth HD9 2AP* Tel (01484) 688609 Mobile 07974-698468 E-mail valclarke@googlemail.com

CLARKE, Mrs Yvonne Veronica. b 58. CA Tr Coll. **dss** 85 **d** 87 **p** 94. Nunhead St Silas *S'wark* 86-90; Par Dn 87-90; Par Dn Nunhead St Antony w St Silas 90-91; Par Dn Mottingham

St Andr w St Alban 91-94; C 94-98; V Spring Park All SS from 98. *All Saints' Vicarage, 1 Farm Drive, Croydon CR0 8HX* Tel (020) 8777 2775 Fax 8777 5228

CLARKSON, The Ven Alan Geoffrey. b 34. Ch Coll Cam BA57 MA61. Wycliffe Hall Ox 57. **d** 59 **p** 60. C Penn *Lich* 59-60; C Oswestry St Oswald 60-63; C Wrington *B & W* 63-65; V Chewton Mendip w Emborough 65-74; Dioc Ecum Officer 65-75; V Glastonbury St Jo w Godney 74-84; P-in-c W Pennard 80-84; P-in-c Meare 81-84; P-in-c Glastonbury St Benedict 82-84; V Glastonbury w Meare, W Pennard and Godney 84; Hon Can Win Cathl 84-99; Adn Win 84-99; V Burley Ville 84-99; rtd 99; Perm to Offic *Chelmsf, Ely* and *St E* from 99. *Cantilena, 4 Harefield Rise, Linton, Cambridge CB21 4LS* Tel (01223) 892988 E-mail agclarkson@hotmail.co.uk

CLARKSON, David James. b 42. St Andr Univ BSc66. NOC 85. **d** 88 **p** 89. NSM Slaithwaite w E Scammonden *Wakef* 88-89; C Morley St Pet w Churwell 89-91; R Cumberworth w Denby Dale 91-93; P-in-c Denby 91-93; R Cumberworth, Denby and Denby Dale 93-02; rtd 03; Lic to Offic *Glas* from 04. *Waulkmill Cottage, Westerkirk, Langholm DG13 0NJ* Tel (01387) 370279

CLARKSON, Eric George. b 22. St Jo Coll Dur BA48. **d** 50 **p** 51. C Birkdale St Jo *Liv* 50-52; C Grassendale 52-54; PC W Derby St Luke 54-66; V Blackb St Mich 66-75; V Blackb St Mich w St Jo 75; V Chapeltown *Sheff* 75-86; C Ranmoor 86-87; V Crosspool 87-92; rtd 92; Perm to Offic *York* 92-10. *2 Harewood Drive, Filey YO14 0DE* Tel and fax (01723) 513957

CLARKSON, Geoffrey. b 35. AKC61. **d** 62 **p** 63. C Shildon *Dur* 62-65; Asst Chapl HM Pris Liv 65-66; Chapl HM Borstal Feltham 66-71; Development Officer Br Assn of Settlements 71-74; Dir Community Projects Foundn 74-87; Chapl HM Rem Cen Ashford 88-90; Chapl HM Pris Coldingley 90-99; Chapl HM Pris Send 92-94; rtd 00; Hon C Hampton St Mary *Lon* 71-05; Perm to Offic from 05. *109 Cambridge Road, Teddington TW11 8DF* Tel (020) 8977 1434 E-mail gfclarkson@aol.com

CLARKSON, Canon John Thomas. b 30. AKC53. St Boniface Warminster 54. **d** 54 **p** 55. C Luton St Sav *St Alb* 54-59; Australia 59-73 and from 77; Brotherhood of St Barn 59-64; R Mundingburra 64-72; V Dallington *Pet* 73-77; R W Wyalong St Barn 77-82; R Blayney Ch Ch 82-95; Hon Can Bathurst 95-96; rtd 96. *134 Mitre Street, Bathurst NSW 2795, Australia* Tel (0061) (2) 6332 6032 E-mail clarkson@netwit.net.au

CLARKSON, Michael. See CLARKSON, Richard Michael

CLARKSON, Michael Livingston. b 48. California Univ BA70 Loyola Univ JD73. Wycliffe Hall Ox 87. **d** 89 **p** 90. C Kensington St Barn *Lon* 89-93; Min Oak Tree Angl Fellowship 93-04; Oman 04-08; R Johns Island Our Sav USA from 08. *4416 Betsy Kerrison Parkway, Johns Island SC 29455-7125, USA* Tel (001) (843) 768 2046 Mobile 298 0003 E-mail mclarkson@our-saviour.net

CLARKSON, Canon Richard. b 33. Man Univ BSc54 Ball Coll Ox DPhil57. Oak Hill Th Coll 89. **d** 91 **p** 92. NSM Sunnyside w Bourne End *St Alb* from 91; RD Berkhamsted 97-02; Hon Can St Alb from 02. *Kingsmead, Gravel Path, Berkhamsted HP4 2PH* Tel (01442) 873014 E-mail r.sclarkson@btopenworld.com

CLARKSON, Richard Michael. b 38. St Jo Coll Dur BA60 Lanc Univ PGCE68. Cranmer Hall Dur 60. **d** 62 **p** 63. C Heyhouses on Sea *Blackb* 62-66; C Lancaster St Mary 66-68; Asst Master Kirkham Gr Sch 68-90; Asst Master Hurstpierpoint Coll 90-91; Asst Master St Mary's Hall Brighton 92-98; Chapl 96-98; rtd 93; Perm to Offic *Chich* from 93. *121 College Lane, Hurstpierpoint, Hassocks BN6 9AF* Tel (01273) 834117

CLARKSON, Robert Christopher. b 32. Dur Univ BA53 DipEd54. S Dios Minl Tr Scheme 85. **d** 87 **p** 88. NSM Lower Dever Valley *Win* 87-03; Perm to Offic from 03. *27 Wrights Way, South Wonston, Winchester SO21 3HE* Tel (01962) 881692

CLARRIDGE, Mrs Ann. b 44. Bournemouth Univ BSc89 S Bank Univ MSc94. SEITE 01. **d** 04 **p** 05. NSM Shepherd's Bush St Steph w St Thos *Lon* 04-07; NSM Whitton St Aug 07-11; NSM Northwood H Trin from 11. *3 Lees Avenue, Northwood HA6 1HT* E-mail annclarridge@hotmail.co.uk

CLARRIDGE, Donald Michael. b 41. DipOT86. Oak Hill Th Coll 63. **d** 66 **p** 67. C Newc St Barn and St Jude 66-70; C Pennycross *Ex* 70-76; R Clayhanger 76-83; R Petton 76-83; R Huntsham 76-83; V Bampton 76-83. *Winkley, Broad Road, Hambrook, Chichester PO18 8RF* Tel (01243) 573821 E-mail donclarridge@tiscali.co.uk

CLASBY, Michael Francis Theodore. b 37. Univ Coll Lon BA59. Chich Th Coll 59. **d** 61 **p** 62. C Leigh-on-Sea St Marg *Chelmsf* 61-64; C Forest Gate St Edm 64-69; V Walthamstow St Mich 69-70; Chapl Community of Sisters of the Love of God 87-89; Perm to Offic *St Alb* 87-89; NSM Hemel Hempstead 90-93; Perm to Offic 93-98; rtd 02. *14 Richmond Walk, St Albans AL4 9BA* Tel (01727) 853513

CLASPER, John. b 42. AKC67. **d** 68 **p** 69. C Leeds All Hallows w St Simon *Ripon* 68-71; C Hawksworth Wood 72-74; Ind Chapl *Dur* 74-97; TV Jarrow St Paul 75-77; TV Jarrow 77-91; Dioc Urban Development Officer 90-91; TR E Darlington 91-97; V Fenham St Jas and St Basil *Newc* 97-02; RD Newc W 98-02; rtd 03; Perm to Offic *Newc* from 03. *103 Warkworth Woods,*

Newcastle upon Tyne NE3 5RB Tel 0191-217 1325 Mobile 07710-078945 E-mail john.clasper@virgin.net

CLASSON, Michael Campbell. b 32. TCD BA52 HDipEd54 MA55. CITC 87. **d** 89 **p** 91. NSM Conwal Union w Gartan *D & R* 89-90; NSM Ardara w Glencolumbkille, Inniskeel etc from 90. *Summy, Portnoo, Co Donegal, Republic of Ireland* Tel (00353) (74) 954 5242

CLATWORTHY, Jonathan Richard. b 48. Univ of Wales BA70. Sarum & Wells Th Coll 71. **d** 76 **p** 77. C Man Resurr 76-78; C Bolton St Pet 78-81; V Ashton St Pet 81-85; Chapl Sheff Univ 85-91; V Denstone w Ellastone and Stanton *Lich* 91-98; Chapl Liv Univ 98-02; rtd 02; Perm to Offic *Liv* from 04. *9 Westward View, Aigburth, Liverpool L17 7EE* Tel 0151-727 6291 E-mail jonathan@clatworthy.org

CLAUSEN, John Frederick. b 37. Sarum Th Coll 65. **d** 68 **p** 69. C Kentish Town St Jo *Lon* 68-71; C Rainham *Roch* 71-77; R Stone 77-89; Lic to Dartford RD 89-02; rtd 02. *24 Spring Vale North, Dartford DA1 2LL* Tel (01322) 279570

CLAY, Canon Colin Peter. b 32. Ch Coll Cam BA55 MA59. Em Coll Saskatoon Hon DD91 Wells Th Coll 55. **d** 57 **p** 58. C Malden St Jas *S'wark* 57-59; Canada from 59; C Sudbury Epiphany 59-60; R Sudbury St Jas 60-69; R Sudbury St Geo 60-64; R French River St Thos 64-69; Asst Prof RS Laurentian Univ 69-72; R Capreol St Alb 70-77; Chapl Saskatchewan Univ 77-00; Hon Can Saskatoon from 97; Interim I St Jo Cathl 00-01; Hon Asst from 01. *812 Colony Street, Saskatoon SK SN7 0S1, Canada* Tel (001) (306) 664 4628 E-mail clay@sask.usask.ca

CLAY, Canon Elizabeth Jane. b 50. MBE06. Ridley Hall Cam. dss 86 **d** 87 **p** 94. Birstall *Wakef* 86-87; Hon Par Dn Lupset 87-90; Par Dn 90-94; C 94-96; Chapl HM Pris and YOI New Hall 96-10; Hon Can Wakef Cathl 00-10; rtd 10. *43 Hollybank Avenue, Upper Cumberworth, Huddersfield HD8 8NY* Tel (01484) 603051 E-mail ejclay@ejclay.demon.co.uk

CLAY, Geoffrey. b 51. CertEd. Ridley Hall Cam. **d** 86 **p** 87. C Birstall *Wakef* 86-90; V Lupset 90-03; P-in-c Marsden 03-10; P-in-c Kirkburton from 10; P-in-c Cumberworth, Denby and Denby Dale from 10; Min Development Officer from 03. *43 Hollybank Avenue, Upper Cumberworth, Huddersfield HD8 8NY* Tel (01484) 603051 E-mail geoff@ejclay.demon.co.uk

CLAY, Peter Herbert. b 31. Lich Th Coll 62. **d** 64 **p** 65. C Ross Heref 64-67; C Leamington Priors All SS *Cov* 67-70; P-in-c Temple Grafton w Binton 70-73; V 73-75; P-in-c Exhall w Wixford 70-73; R 73-75; TV Cen Telford *Lich* 75-86; USPG 86-90; V Loughb Gd Shep *Leic* 90-96; rtd 96; Perm to Offic *Cov* and *Leic* from 96. *78 Eastlands Road, Rugby CV21 3RR* Tel (01788) 569138

CLAY, Timothy Francis. b 61. St Mark & St Jo Coll Lon BA85 Ealing Coll of Educn 89. Linc Th Coll 95. **d** 95 **p** 96. C Wickford and Runwell *Chelmsf* 95-98; C S Ockendon 98-01; C S Ockendon and Belhus Park 01-02; P-in-c Ashingdon w S Fambridge 02-10; P-in-c Canewdon w Paglesham 03-10; R Ashingdon w S Fambridge, Canewdon and Paglesham from 10. *The Rectory, Church Road, Rochford SS4 3HY* Tel (01702) 549318 E-mail tim@tclay.fslife.co.uk

CLAYDEN, David Edward. b 42. Oak Hill Th Coll 74. **d** 76 **p** 77. C Worksop St Jo *S'well* 76-79; V Clarborough w Hayton 79-84; C Bloxwich *Lich* 87-90; TV 90-93; TV Tollington *Lon* 93-99; P-in-c Thorndon w Rishangles, Stoke Ash, Thwaite etc *St E* 99-00; P-in-c Thornhams Magna and Parva, Gislingham and Mellis 99-00; R S Hartismere 00-06; rtd 06. *151 Southview Road, Carlton, Nottingham NG4 3QT* Tel 0115-987 2690 E-mail david.clayden@boltblue.com

CLAYDON, Preb Graham Leonard. b 43. K Coll Lon BA65. Clifton Th Coll 66. **d** 68 **p** 69. C Walthamstow St Mary w St Steph *Chelmsf* 68-71; C St Marylebone All So w SS Pet and Jo *Lon* 71-73; Hon C 73-81; Warden All So Clubhouse 71-81; V Islington St Mary 81-99; Dioc Ev (Stepney) and C Highbury Ch Ch w St Jo and St Sav 99-03; TV Hackney Marsh 03-06; Preb St Paul's Cathl 92-06; rtd 07. *Acre End, Tangmere Road, Tangmere, Chichester PO20 2HW* Tel (01243) 536789 E-mail graham@lclaydon.fsnet.co.uk

CLAYDON, John Richard. b 38. St Jo Coll Cam BA61 MA65. Trin Coll Bris 71. **d** 73 **p** 74. C Finchley Ch Ch *Lon* 73-76; Asst Chapl K Edw Sch Witley 76-77; C Macclesfield St Mich *Ches* 77-81; V Marple All SS 81-91; CMJ Israel 91-99; V Blackb Redeemer 99-02; rtd 02; Perm to Offic *Chelmsf* from 03. *54 Old Forge Road, Layer-de-la-Haye, Colchester CO2 0LH* Tel (01206) 734056 E-mail john.claydon4295.freeserve.co.uk

CLAYTON, Adam. b 78. Keble Coll Ox BA99. Westcott Ho Cam 00. **d** 02 **p** 03. C Far Headingley St Chad *Ripon* 02-06; TV Seacroft 06-08; Chapl Leeds Teaching Hosps NHS Trust from 10. *47 St James Approach, Leeds LS14 6JJ* Tel 0113-294 0414 Mobile 07834-827294 E-mail revdaclayton@aol.com

CLAYTON, Adam Jonathan Barnett. b 56. **d** 06 **p** 07. OLM Icknield Ox from 06. *5 Watlington Road, Shirburn, Watlington OX49 5DR* Tel (01491) 612210 E-mail adam@ajbc.fsnet.co.uk

CLAYTON, Canon Anthony Edwin Hay. b 36. Sarum Th Coll 61. **d** 63 **p** 64. C Tooting All SS *S'wark* 63-68; Perm to Offic *Leic*

69-74; Perm to Offic *S'well* 73-80; Hon C Lockington w Hemington *Leic* 74-80; P-in-c Eastwell 80-83; P-in-c Eaton 80-83; P-in-c Croxton Kerrial, Knipton, Harston, Branston etc 83-84; R 84-93; R High Framland Par 93-96; RD Framland 90-94; Hon Can Leic Cathl 92-96; rtd 97; Perm to Offic *Leic* 97-00. *18 Commerce Square, Nottingham NG1 1HS* Tel and fax 0115-988 1920

CLAYTON, Geoffrey Buckroyd. b 26. Newc Univ BA67. Roch Th Coll 62. **d** 64 **p** 65. C Newc St Geo 64-67; C Byker St Ant 67-68; Chapl Salonika *Eur* 68-69; C Cheddleton *Lich* 69-72; V Arbory *S & M* 72-97; RD Castletown 82-97; V Santan 88-97; rtd 97; Perm to Offic *St D* from 97. *Y Rheithordy, Llangeitho, Tregaron SY25 6TR* Tel (01974) 821388

CLAYTON, Canon John. b 11. Leeds Univ BA33 MA43. Wells Th Coll 34. **d** 35 **p** 36. C Dewsbury Moor *Wakef* 35-38; C Halifax St Jo Bapt 38-41; Lect 40-41; V Lupset 41-51; Chapl Snapethorpe Hosp 49-51; V Bolton St Jas *Bradf* 51-65; RD Calverley 56-65; V Otley 65-76; RD Otley 68-73; Hon Can Bradf Cathl 63-76; rtd 76; Perm to Offic *Bradf* and *Ripon* from 76. *10 Sandy Walk, Bramhope, Leeds LS16 9DW* Tel 0113-261 1388

CLAYTON, Melanie Yvonne. See SANTORINI, Melanie Yvonne

CLAYTON, Paul. b 47. Cranmer Hall Dur 03. **d** 04 **p** 05. NSM Elton and Preston-on-Tees and Longnewton *Dur* 04-06; NSM Bishopton w Gt Stainton from 06; NSM Redmarshall from 06; NSM Grindon, Stillington and Wolviston from 06; NSM Billingham St Mary from 09. *144 Darlington Lane, Stockton-on-Tees TS19 0NG* Tel (01642) 607233 E-mail pclayton@tinyonline.co.uk

CLAYTON, Sydney Cecil Leigh. b 39. Pemb Coll Ox BA62 MA65 Lon Univ BD65. Linc Th Coll. **d** 65 **p** 66. C Birch St Jas *Man* 65-68; Lect Bolton Par Ch 68-77; V Denshaw 77-09; rtd 09; Perm to Offic *Man* from 09. *The Vicarage, Huddersfield Road, Denshaw, Oldham OL3 5SB* Tel (01457) 874575

CLAYTON, William Alan. b 32. Liv Univ BSc54 Lon Univ BD60. **d** 63 **p** 64. C Wallasey St Hilary *Ches* 63-67; R Burton Agnes w Harpham *York* 67-69; V Batley St Thos *Wakef* 69-72; Lic to Offic *Ripon* 73-85; Hon C Grinton 75-85; R Barningham w Hutton Magna and Wycliffe 85-97; rtd 97; Perm to Offic *Newc* from 00. *Halidon View, 1 The Pastures, Tweedmouth, Berwick-upon-Tweed TD15 2NT*

CLEALL-HILL, Malcolm John. b 51. Salford Univ Man Metrop Univ. **d** 01 **p** 02. OLM Chorlton-cum-Hardy St Werburgh *Man* from 01. *62 Buckingham Road, Chorlton cum Hardy, Manchester M21 0RP* Tel 0161-881 7024 or 247 2288 E-mail m.cleall-hill@mmu.ac.uk

CLEATON, John. b 39. Open Univ BA86. S Dios Minl Tr Scheme 89. **d** 92 **p** 93. NSM Wareham *Sarum* 92-02. *1 Avon Drive, Wareham BH20 4EL* Tel (01929) 553149

CLEATON, Mrs Nancy. b 45. Lon Bible Coll BD67. WEMTC 05. **d** 07 **p** 08. NSM Church Stretton *Heref* from 07. *39 Swain's Meadow, Church Stretton SY6 6HT* Tel (01694) 723387 E-mail nancy.cleaton@tiscali.co.uk

CLEATON, Sheena Faith. b 74. Colchester Inst BA97 R Holloway Coll Lon MMus02 PhD07. Ripon Coll Cuddesdon 09. **d** 11. C Bourne *Linc* from 11. *20 Tilia Way, Bourne PE10 0QR* Tel (01778) 395626 E-mail sheena_cleaton@hotmail.com

CLEAVER, Gerald. b 20. Lon Univ BSc52. St Jo Coll Nottm 85. **d** 86 **p** 87. NSM W Bridgford *S'well* 86-96; NSM Clifton 96-02; rtd 02; Perm to Offic *S'well* from 02. *62 South Road, West Bridgford, Nottingham NG2 7AH* Tel 0115-914 3558 E-mail gerald.cleaver@ntlworld.com

CLEAVER, Gordon Philip. b 29. SWMTC. **d** 78 **p** 79. NSM St Ruan w St Grade *Truro* 78-86; Perm to Offic from 86. *Bryn-Mor, Cadgwith, Ruan Minor, Helston TR12 7JZ* Tel (01326) 290328

CLEAVER, John Martin. b 42. K Coll Lon BD64 AKC64. St Boniface Warminster 61. **d** 65 **p** 66. C Bexley St Mary *Roch* 65-69; C Ealing St Steph Castle Hill *Lon* 69-71; P-in-c Bostall Heath *Roch* 71-76; V Green Street Green 76-85; Primary Adv Lon Dioc Bd for Schs 85-92; V Teddington St Mary w St Alb 92-08; rtd 08. *5 Oaklands, Westham, Pevensey BN24 5AW* Tel (01323) 769964 E-mail jm.cleaver@amserve.net

CLEAVER, Stuart Douglas. b 46. ACIS. Oak Hill Th Coll. **d** 83 **p** 84. C Portsdown *Portsm* 83-86; C Blendworth w Chalton w Idsworth etc 86-88; P-in-c Whippingham w E Cowes 88-98; R 98-01; rtd 01. *The Crest, Soake Road, Waterlooville PO7 6HY* Tel (023) 9226 2277

CLEEVE, Admire William. b 43. Ox Univ MTh96 ACIS78 MBIM81. Sierra Leone Th Hall 78. **d** 82 **p** 83. Sierra Leone 82-86; NSM Douglas St Geo and St Barn *S & M* 87-91; TV Langley Marish *Ox* 91-97; P-in-c Tilehurst St Mary 97-02; rtd 02. *5346 Bressler Drive, Hilliard OH 43026-9401, USA* Tel (001) (614) 219 8407

CLEEVE, Martin. b 43. Bp Otter Coll TCert65 ACP67 Open Univ BA80. Oak Hill Th Coll 69. **d** 72 **p** 73. C Margate H Trin *Cant* 72-76; V Southminster *Chelmsf* 76-86; Teacher Castle View Sch Canvey Is 86-91; Hd RE Bromfords Sch Wickford 91-94; Hd RE Deanes Sch Thundersley 94-98; P-in-c Gt Mongeham w

Ripple and Sutton by Dover *Cant* 99-04; rtd 04; Perm to Offic *Cant* from 04; Chapl Kent & Medway NHS and Soc Care Partnership Trust from 08. *Euphony, Waldershare Road, Ashley, Dover CT15 5JA* E-mail martincleeve@mcleeve.freeserve.co.uk

CLEEVES, David John. b 56. Univ of Wales (Lamp) BA Fitzw Coll Cam MA85. Westcott Ho Cam. **d** 82 **p** 83. C Cuddington *Guildf* 82-85; C Dorking w Ranmore 85-87; V Ewell St Fran 87-94; P-in-c Rotherfield w Mark Cross *Chich* 94-01; V Masham and Healey *Ripon* from 01; Jt AD Ripon 04-05; AD 05-09. *The Vicarage, Rodney Terrace, Masham, Ripon HG4 4JA* Tel (01765) 689255 E-mail cleevesmasham@onetel.com

CLEGG, Anthony. See CLEGG, Canon John Anthony Holroyd

CLEGG, Canon John Anthony Holroyd. b 44. Kelham Th Coll 65. **d** 70 **p** 71. C Heyhouses on Sea *Blackb* 70-74; C Lancaster St Mary 74-76; V Lower Darwen St Jas 76-80; TV Shaston *Sarum* 80-86; Chapl HM Youth Cust Cen Guys Marsh 80-86; R Poulton-le-Sands w Morecambe St Laur *Blackb* 86-97; RD Lancaster 89-94; TR Cartmel Peninsula *Carl* 97-04; RD Windermere 01-04; P-in-c Appleby 04-08; P-in-c Ormside 04-08; TR Heart of Eden 08-09; RD Appleby 04-09; Hon Can Carl Cathl 01-09; rtd 09; Perm to Offic *Blackb* from 10. *33 Mayfield Road, Holme, Carnforth LA6 1PT* Tel (01524) 784752 E-mail anthonyclegg@talktalk.net

CLEGG, John Lovell. b 48. Qu Coll Ox BA70 MA74. Trin Coll Bris. **d** 75 **p** 76. C Barrow St Mark *Carl* 75-79; R S Levenshulme *Man* 79-98; P-in-c Blackley St Paul 98-10; rtd 10; Perm to Offic *Man* from 11. *5 Mough Lane, Chadderton, Oldham OL9 9NT* Tel 0161-684 1226

CLEGG, Patricia Ann. b 45. STETS 96. **d** 99 **p** 00. NSM Harnham *Sarum* 99-03; Perm to Offic 03-05; NSM Bemerton 05-07; NSM Arle Valley *Win* 07-11; rtd 11. *24 Arle Close, Alresford SO24 9BG* Tel (01962) 736566 E-mail pat@newsarum.fsnet.co.uk

CLEGG, Peter Douglas. b 49. Sarum & Wells Th Coll 83. **d** 85 **p** 86. C Hangleton *Chich* 85-88; C-in-c Portslade Gd Shep CD 88-94; V Portslade Gd Shep 94-09; rtd 10. *8B Hangleton Road, Hove BN3 7GE* Tel (01273) 382913 E-mail fatherpeterclegg_ssc@yahoo.co.uk

CLEGG, Roger Alan. b 46. St Jo Coll Dur BA68 Nottm Univ CertEd69. St Jo Coll Nottm 75. **d** 78 **p** 79. C Harwood *Man* 78-81; TV Sutton St Jas and Wawne *York* 81-87; V Kirk Fenton w Kirkby Wharfe and Ulleskelfe 87-09; Chapl HM Pris Askham Grange from 95; Perm to Offic *York* from 09. *HM Prison Askham Grange, Askham Richard, York YO23 3FT* Tel (01904) 772014 or (01757) 268060 Mobile 07957-474030 E-mail rogclegg@dunelm.org.uk

CLELAND, Miss Lucy Eleanor. b 74. Aston Univ BSc97 Anglia Poly Univ BTh05. Ridley Hall Cam 02. **d** 05 **p** 06. C Yaxley and Holme w Conington *Ely* 05-08; P-in-c Landbeach from 08; P-in-c Waterbeach from 08. *The Vicarage, 8 Chapel Street, Waterbeach, Cambridge CB25 9HR* Tel (01223) 440501 Mobile 07986-685792 E-mail lecleland@hotmail.com

CLELAND, Richard. b 26. Belf Coll of Tech MPS47. St Aid Birkenhead 58. **d** 60 **p** 61. C Lisburn Ch Ch *Conn* 60-63; C Ballynafeigh St Jude *D & D* 63-66; C Portman Square St Paul *Lon* 66-67; V Ilkley All SS *Bradf* 67-83; Master Wyggeston's Hosp Leic 83-97; Perm to Offic *S'well* 97-02; rtd 97. *23 Stuart Court, High Street, Kibworth, Leicester LE8 0LR* Tel 0116-279 6245

CLELAND, Trevor. b 66. QUB BTh94 TCD MPhil97. CITC 94. **d** 96 **p** 97. C Lisburn Ch Ch *Conn* 96-99; C Carrickfergus 99-03; I Belfast Upper Falls from 03. *31 Dunmurry Lane, Belfast BT17 9RP* Tel (028) 9062 2400

CLEMAS, Nigel Antony. b 53. Wycliffe Hall Ox. **d** 83 **p** 84. C Bootle St Mary w St Paul *Liv* 83-87; V Kirkdale St Mary and St Athanasius 87-91; TV Netherthorpe *Sheff* 91-93; V Netherthorpe St Steph 93-98; R Chapel Chorlton, Maer and Whitmore *Lich* from 98; RD Eccleshall from 00. *The Rectory, Snape Hall Road, Whitmore, Newcastle ST5 5HS* Tel (01782) 680258 E-mail nclemas@hotmail.com

CLEMENCE, Paul Robert Fraser. b 50. St Edm Hall Ox MA90 MRTPI82. Wycliffe Hall Ox 88. **d** 90 **p** 91. C Lancaster St Mary *Blackb* 90-94; Chapl HM Pris Lanc Castle 90-94; V Lt Thornton *Blackb* from 94; AD Poulton 00-09. *St John's Vicarage, 35 Station Road, Thornton-Cleveleys FY5 5HY* Tel and fax (01253) 825107 E-mail p.clemence@tiscali.co.uk

CLEMENT, Miss Barbara Winifred. b 20. Gilmore Ho 49. **dss** 56 **d** 87. Frimley Green *Guildf* 53-66; Hd Dss 66-74; Dioc Adv Lay Min 74-82; Frimley 74-82; Frimley Hosp 74-87; rtd 82; Perm to Offic *Guildf* 82-99 and from 01. *9 Merlin Court, The Cloisters, Frimley, Camberley GU16 5JN* Tel (01276) 22527

CLEMENT, Geoffrey Paul. b 69. **d** 94 **p** 96. Jardines del Hipódromo St Aug Uruguay 94-96; Colon St Jas Miss 95-97; Barrio Fátima Salto St Luke w H Spirit 97-01; TV Wilford Peninsula *St E* 01-07; R Holbrook, Stutton, Freston, Woolverstone etc from 07. *The Rectory, 15 Denmark Gardens, Holbrook, Ipswich IP9 2BG* Tel (01473) 327141 Mobile 07766-601011 E-mail revgclement@btinternet.com

CLEMENT, Paskal. b 63. Punjab Univ BA92 Univ of Wales MA08. Nat Catholic Inst of Th Karachi 82. **d** 88 **p** 88. Pakistan 88-01; NSM Hounslow H Trin w St Paul *Lon* 04-08; C Oadby *Leic* from 08. *62 Fairstone Hill, Oadby, Leicester LE2 5RJ* Tel 0116-271 6474 Mobile 07727-286905
E-mail paskalm@yahoo.com
CLEMENT, Peter James. b 64. UMIST BSc88 Man Univ MA98. Qu Coll Birm 89. **d** 92 **p** 93. C Grange St Andr *Ches* 92-95; C Man Apostles w Miles Platting 95-97; TV Uggeshall w Sotherton, Wangford and Henham *St E* 97-99; TV Sole Bay 99-00; Dioc Youth Officer 01-02; V Fairweather Green *Bradf* 02-07; Assoc Dioc Dir of Ords 04-07; Dioc Dir of Ords *Ripon* from 07; C Ripon Cathl from 07. *16 Orchard Close, Sharow, Ripon HG4 5BE* Tel (01765) 607017
E-mail peterc@riponleeds-diocese.org.uk
CLEMENT, Richard Percy. b 63. Bris Univ BA85. ERMC 04. **d** 06 **p** 08. C Framlingham w Saxtead *St E* 06-09; Chapl RAF from 09. *Chaplaincy Services, Valiant Block, HQ Air Command, RAF High Wycombe HP14 4UE* Tel (01494) 496800 Fax 496343
E-mail revd.richard@btinternet.com
CLEMENT, Thomas Gwyn. b 51. Lon Univ BMus73 Goldsmiths' Coll Lon PGCE74 LRAM73 LTCL74. St Steph Ho Ox. **d** 93 **p** 94. C Friern Barnet St Jas *Lon* 93-96; V Edmonton St Alphege 96-04; P-in-c Ponders End St Matt 02-04; AD Enfield 01-04; V Hendon St Mary and Ch Ch from 04; Warden of Readers Edmonton Area from 08; AD W Barnet from 09. *The Vicarage, 34 Parson Street, London NW4 1QR* Tel (020) 8203 2884
E-mail fr.gwyn@btinternet.com
CLEMENT, Canon Timothy Gordon. b 54. Trin Coll Bris 92. **d** 94 **p** 95. C Chepstow *Mon* 94-97; R Bettws Newydd w Trostrey etc from 97; Rural Min Adv from 02; AD Raglan-Usk from 05; Can St Woolos Cathl from 08. *The Rectory, Bettws Newydd, Usk NP15 1JN* Tel (01873) 880258
CLEMENTS, Alan Austin. b 39. Newc Univ MA93 ACIB66 FCIE05. Linc Th Coll 74. **d** 76 **p** 77. C Woodley St Jo the Ev *Ox* 76-79; C Wokingham All SS 79-83; V Felton *Newc* 83-95; P-in-c Wallsend St Pet 95-01; rtd 01; Perm to Offic *Newc* 01-06; *Blackb* from 07; *Man* from 09. *15 Carleton Road, Chorley PR6 8TQ* Tel and fax (01257) 271782 E-mail fr alan@btinternet.com
CLEMENTS, Andrew. b 48. K Coll Lon BD72 AKC72 Leeds Univ MA02. St Aug Coll Cant 72. **d** 73 **p** 74. C Langley All SS and Martyrs *Man* 73-76; C Westhoughton 76-81; R Thornton Dale w Ellerburne and Wilton *York* 81-89; Prec Leic Cathl 89-91; V Market Weighton *York* 91-97; R Goodmanham 91-97; V Osbaldwick w Murton from 97; RD Derwent from 11. *The Vicarage, 80 Osbaldwick Lane, York YO10 3AX* Tel (01904) 416763 E-mail andrew@ozmurt.freeserve.co.uk
CLEMENTS, Miss Christine Hilda. b 49. Ex Univ BTh04. SWMTC 99. **d** 02 **p** 03. C Halsetown *Truro* 05-06; Zambia 05-07; Perm to Offic *Nor* 07; TR Thamesmead *S'wark* from 07. *Thamesmead Rectory, 22 Manor Close, London SE28 8EY* Tel (020) 8312 0731 Mobile 07852-476805
CLEMENTS, Canon Doris Thomasina Sara. b 46. TCD BA68 MA90. CITC 92. **d** 95 **p** 96. NSM Killala w Dunfeeny, Crossmolina, Kilmoremoy etc *T, K & A* from 95; Can Achonry Cathl 05-11; Can Tuam Cathl from 11. *Doobeg House, Bunninadden, Ballymote, Co Sligo, Republic of Ireland* Tel (00353) (71) 918 5425 Fax 918 5255 Mobile 86-249 7806
E-mail dcolhoun@gofree.indigo.ie
CLEMENTS, Canon Edwin George. b 41. Chich Th Coll 77. **d** 79 **p** 80. C Didcot St Pet *Ox* 79-83; C Brixham w Churston Ferrers *Ex* 83; TV 84-86; TV Brixham w Churston Ferrers and Kingswear 86-87; P-in-c Hagbourne *Ox* V 88-90; P-in-c Blewbury 89-90; P-in-c Upton 89-90; R Blewbury, Hagbourne and Upton 90-06; P-in-c S w N Moreton, Aston Tirrold and Aston Upthorpe 05-06; R The Churn 06-07; AD Wallingford 99-07; Hon Can Ch Ch 07; rtd 07; Hon C Uffington, Shellingford, Woolstone and Baulking *Ox* 07-09; Hon C Shrivenham and Ashbury from 09. *St Mary's House, Chapel Lane, Ashbury, Swindon SN6 8LS* Tel (01793) 710811 Mobile 07703-342950 E-mail revedwin@btinternet.com
CLEMENTS, Miss Mary Holmes. b 43. Bedf Coll Lon BA64 Lon Inst of Educn PGCE69. Ox Min Course 92. **d** 94 **p** 95. NSM High Wycombe *Ox* 94-01; C N Petherton w Northmoor Green and N Newton w St Michaelchurch, Thurloxton etc *B & W* 01-03; C Alfred Jewel 03-10; rtd 10. *18 Meadway, Woolavington, Bridgwater TA7 8HA* Tel (01278) 662905
E-mail circeclements@btinternet.com
CLEMENTS, Philip Christian. b 38. K Coll Lon BD64 AKC64. **d** 65 **p** 66. C S Norwood St Mark *Cant* 65-68; Chapl R Russell Sch Croydon 68-75; Asst Chapl Denstone Coll Uttoxeter 75-76; Chapl 76-81; Chapl Lancing Coll 82-90; R Ninfield *Chich* 90-99; V Hooe 90-99; rtd 99; Perm to Offic *Cant* from 95; Chapl St Bart Hosp Sandwich from 04. *21 Swaynes Way, Eastry, Sandwich CT13 0JP* Tel (01304) 617413 or 613982
E-mail philip@clements3739.freeserve.co.uk
CLEMENTS, Philip John Charles. b 42. Nottm Univ CertEd64 Loughb Univ Hon BA09. Ridley Hall Cam. **d** 85 **p** 86. C

Aylestone St Andr w St Jas *Leic* 85-87; P-in-c Swinford w Catthorpe, Shawell and Stanford 87-91; V 91-99; Dioc Rural Officer 91-96; RD Guthlaxton II 94-99; P-in-c N w S Kilworth and Misterton 96-99; P-in-c Barrowden and Wakerley w S Luffenham *Pet* 99-02; R Barrowden and Wakerley w S Luffenham etc 03-06; RD Barnack 00-06; rtd 06; Perm to Offic *Pet* from 06 and *Leic* from 07. *Clementine Cottage, 51 Laughton Road, Lubenham, Market Harborough LE16 9TE* Tel and fax (01858) 432548 E-mail pipclements2@tiscali.co.uk
CLEMENTS, Canon Roy Adrian. b 44. St Chad's Coll Dur BA68 MA74. **d** 69 **p** 70. C Royston *Wakef* 69-73; V Clifton 73-77; V Rastrick St Matt 77-84; Dioc Communications Officer 84-98; V Horbury Junction 84-92; Bp's Chapl 92-00; V Battyeford 00-08; Hon Can Wakef Cathl 94-08; rtd 08; Perm to Offic *Wakef* from 08. *12 Castle Crescent, Sandal, Wakefield WF2 7HX* Tel (01924) 251834 E-mail royaclements@tiscali.co.uk
CLEMETT, Peter Thomas. b 33. Univ of Wales (Lamp) BA60. Sarum Th Coll 59. **d** 61 **p** 62. C Tredegar St Geo *Mon* 61-63; Chapl St Woolos Cathl 63-66; CF 66-99; Chapl R Memorial Chpl Sandhurst 84-88; rtd 88; OCM from 99. *Silver Birches, Gardeners Lane, East Wellow, Romsey SO51 6AD* Tel (023) 8081 4261
CLEMOW (*née* **WINDER**)**, Cynthia Frances.** b 48. SWMTC 02. **d** 05 **p** 06. NSM Bodmin w Lanhydrock and Lanivet *Truro* from 05. *Denton, 2 Boxwell Park, Bodmin PL31 2BB* Tel (01208) 73306
CLENCH, Brian Henry Ross. b 31. Ripon Coll Cuddesdon. **d** 82 **p** 83. C Fulham All SS *Lon* 82-85; Ind Chapl *Truro* 85-92; P-in-c St Mewan 85-92; rtd 92; Perm to Offic *Sarum* from 96. *Tamworth Barn, Hampton Lane, Whitford, Axminster EX13 7NJ*
CLEPHANE, Alexander Honeyman. b 48. **d** 97 **p** 98. OLM Flixton St Mich *Man* 97-11; NSM from 11. *306 Church Road, Urmston, Manchester M41 6JJ* Tel 0161-747 8816 Mobile 07798-613291
CLEUGH, David Robert. b 80. New Coll Ox BA07. Ripon Coll Cuddesdon BTh09. **d** 09 **p** 10. C Dorchester *Ox* from 09. *26 Windrush Road, Berinsfield, Wallingford OX10 7PF* Tel (01865) 341382 E-mail yellow3927@yahoo.co.uk
CLEUGH, Hannah Felicity. b 81. Worc Coll Ox MA08 MSt04 DPhil07. Ripon Coll Cuddesdon 07. **d** 09 **p** 10. C Dorchester *Ox* from 09. *26 Windrush Road, Berinsfield, Wallingford OX10 7PF* Tel (01865) 341382 E-mail hannah.cleugh@googlemail.com
CLEVELAND, Mrs Lorna Christina (Dickie). b 39. State Univ NY BSc60. SEITE 99. **d** 02 **p** 03. NSM Wye w Brook and Hastingleigh etc *Cant* 02-10; NSM Mersham w Hinxhill and Sellindge 08-10; Perm to Offic from 10. *2 Church Street, Wye, Ashford TN25 5BJ* Tel (01233) 813051
E-mail dickie@clevelp.freeserve.co.uk
CLEVELAND, Michael Robin. b 52. Warwick Univ BA73. St Jo Coll Nottm 86 Serampore Th Coll BD88. **d** 88 **p** 89. C Bushbury *Lich* 88-92; V Foleshill St Laur *Cov* from 92. *St Laurence's Vicarage, 142 Old Church Road, Coventry CV6 7ED* Tel (024) 7668 8271
CLEVELAND, Archdeacon of. See FERGUSON, The Ven Paul John
CLEVERLEY, Michael Frank. b 36. Man Univ BScTech57. Wells Th Coll 61. **d** 63 **p** 64. C Halifax St Aug *Wakef* 63; C Huddersfield St Jo 63-66; C Brighouse 66-69; V Gomersal 69-83; P-in-c Clayton W w High Hoyland 83-89; P-in-c Scissett St Aug 83-89; R High Hoyland, Scissett and Clayton W 89-96; rtd 96; Hon C Leathley w Farnley, Fewston and Blubberhouses *Bradf* 96-08; Hon C Washburn and Mid-Wharfe from 08. *86 Riverside Park, Otley LS21 2RW*
E-mail michael.cleverley@bradford.anglican.org
CLEVERLY, Charles St George. b 51. St Jo Coll Ox MA75 Goldsmiths' Coll Lon PGCE76. Trin Coll Bris 79. **d** 82 **p** 83. C Cranham Park *Chelmsf* 82-89; V 89-92; Crosslinks Paris 92-02; R Ox St Aldate from 02. *Holy Trinity House, 19 Turn Again Lane, Oxford OX1 1QL* Tel (01865) 244713 Fax 201543
E-mail charlie.cleverly@staldates.org.uk
CLEWS, Nicholas. b 57. SS Coll Cam BA80 MA84 Leeds Univ BA87 CIPFA85. Coll of Resurr Mirfield 85. **d** 88 **p** 89. C S Elmsall *Wakef* 88-91; V Featherstone 91-07; P-in-c Purston cum S Featherstone 04-07; P-in-c Thornbury *Bradf* from 07; P-in-c Woodhall from 07. *St James's Vicarage, Galloway Lane, Pudsey LS28 8JR* Tel (01274) 662735
E-mail nicholas.clews@bradford.anglican.org
CLIFF, Frank Graham. b 38. St Paul's Coll Chelt TCert60. Clifton Th Coll 63. **d** 66 **p** 67. C Leic St Chris 66-69; C Whitton and Thurleston w Akenham *St E* 69-71; USA from 71; Asst R Houston St Thos 71-72; Asst R Waco St Alb 72-74; Asst R Potomac St Jas 74-78; R Denton Ch Ch 78-85; V Pittsburgh St Phil 86-87; R Pittsburgh Advent Ch 87-94; R Honesdale Grace Ch 94-03. *15 Bede Circle, Honesdale PA 18431-7625, USA* Tel (001) (570) 253 4535 E-mail cliffam@ptd.net
CLIFF, Julian Arnold. b 41. Univ Coll Ches BEd86. Cranmer Hall Dur 63. **d** 66 **p** 67. C Bowdon *Ches* 66-69; C Poynton 69-73; P-in-c Crewe St Barn 73-74; V 74-79; Hon C Higher Bebington

98-00; Perm to Offic from 06. *15 Sandy Lane, Heswall, Wirral CH60 5SX* Tel 0151-342 3230 Mobile 07980-379699 E-mail julianann.cliff@talktalk.net

CLIFFE, Canon Christopher George. b 47. CITC 94. **d** 97 **p** 98. C Fiddown w Clonegam, Guilcagh and Kilmeaden *C & O* 97-00; I from 00; Bp's Dom Chapl from 97; Can Ossory Cathl from 07. *The Rectory, Piltown, Carrick-on-Suir, Co Kilkenny, Republic of Ireland* Tel (00353) (51) 643275 Mobile 87-236 8682 E-mail fiddown@lismore.anglican.org *or* cgc2@eircom.net

CLIFFORD, Bruce Douglas. Trin Coll Bris. **d** 11. NSM Glouc St Cath from 11. *10 Carne Place, Gloucester GL4 3BE* Tel (01452) 302238

CLIFFORD, Erin Chrisanne. b 77. James Madison Univ USA BS98. Gordon-Conwell Th Sem MDiv06. **d** 08 **p** 09. C Ches Square St Mich w St Phil *Lon* 08-11; C Onslow Square and S Kensington St Aug from 11. *107B Pimlico Road, London SW1W 8PH* Tel 07515-433746 (mobile) E-mail clifford_erin@yahoo.com

CLIFFORD, Paula. b 45. **d** 11. NSM Ox St Giles and SS Phil and Jas w St Marg from 11. *3 Pound Close, Kirtlington, Kidlington OX5 3JR*

CLIFFORD, Raymond Augustine. b 45. Coll of Resurr Mirfield 91. **d** 93 **p** 94. C Saltdean *Chich* 93-96. *124 Arnold Estate, Druid Street, London SE1 2DT* Tel (020) 7232 2439 E-mail raylondonbb@hotmail.com

CLIFFORD, Miss Susan Frances. b 58. Qu Univ Kingston Ontario BA87. Westcott Ho Cam 02. **d** 04 **p** 05. C Winchmore Hill St Paul *Lon* 04-08; Canada from 08. *54 Kinsman Crescent, Arnprior ON K7S 1V6, Canada* E-mail susanclif@hotmail.com

CLIFTON, Canon Robert Walter. b 39. Solicitor. Westcott Ho Cam 82. **d** 84 **p** 85. C Bury St Edmunds St Geo *St E* 84-87; P-in-c Culford, W Stow and Wordwell 87-88; R Culford, W Stow and Wordwell w Flempton etc 88-95; P-in-c Fornham All SS and Fornham St Martin w Timworth 93-95; RD Thingoe 93-95; P-in-c Orford w Sudbourne, Chillesford, Butley and Iken 95-00; P-in-c Eyke w Bromeswell, Rendlesham, Tunstall etc 98-99; TR Wilford Peninsula 00-05; RD Woodbridge 96-04; Hon Can St E Cathl 00-05; rtd 05; Perm to Offic *Nor* and *St E* from 05. *12 Stan Petersen Close, Norwich NR1 4QJ* Tel (01603) 631758 Mobile 07713-237754

CLIFTON, Canon Roger Gerald. b 45. ACA70 FCA. Sarum & Wells Th Coll 70. **d** 73 **p** 74. C Winterbourne *Bris* 73-76; P-in-c Brislington St Cuth 76-83; P-in-c Colerne w N Wraxall 83-95; RD Chippenham 88-94; Hon Can Bris Cathl 94-09; TR Gtr Corsham 95-01; TR Gtr Corsham and Lacock 01-09; rtd 09. *Flat 1, 7 Bathwick Street, Bath BA2 6NX* Tel (01225) 330211 E-mail rogerclifton@btinternet.com

CLIFTON, Sharon. b 66. **d** 07 **p** 08. C St Illogan *Truro* from 07. *Church House, 46 Bosmeor Park, Redruth TR15 3JN* Tel (01209) 218753

CLIFTON-SMITH, Gregory James. b 52. GGSM73 Lon Univ TCert74 Goldsmiths' Coll Lon BMus82. Sarum & Wells Th Coll 87. **d** 89 **p** 90. C Welling *S'wark* 89-93; V Tattenham Corner and Burgh Heath *Guildf* 93-97; Asst Chapl R Berks and Battle Hosps NHS Trust 97-99; Chapl Isle of Wight NHS Primary Care Trust from 99. *The Chaplaincy, St Mary's Hospital, Parkhurst Road, Newport PO30 5TG* Tel (01983) 534639 *or* 856781 Mobile 07790-089981 E-mail gregory.clifton-smith@iow.nhs.uk

CLINCH, Christopher James. b 60. Nottm Univ BEd82 BTh89. Linc Th Coll 86. **d** 89 **p** 90. C Newc St Geo 89-92; C Seaton Hirst 92-94; TV Ch the King 94-00; V Newc St Fran 00-09; Chapl K Sch Tynemouth from 09. *The King's School, Huntingdon Place, North Shields NE30 4RF* Tel 0191-258 5995 E-mail ccne12747@blueyonder.co.uk

CLINCH, Kenneth Wilfred. b 22. Bps' Coll Cheshunt 62. **d** 64 **p** 65. C Old Shoreham *Chich* 64-67; C Lancing St Mich 67-73; R Upper St Leonards St Jo 73-88; rtd 88; Perm to Offic *Chich* from 88. *7 The Leas, Essenden Road, St Leonards-on-Sea TN38 0PU* Tel and fax (01424) 438286 E-mail ken22@globalnet.co.uk

CLINES, Emma Christine. *See* LOUIS, Ms Emma Christine

CLINES, Jeremy Mark Sebastian. b 68. Cranmer Hall Dur. **d** 97 **p** 98. C Birm St Martin w Bordesley St Andr 97-99; Chapl York St Jo Univ 99-10; Chapl Sheff Univ from 10. *119 Ashdell Road, Sheffield S10 3DB* Tel 0114-266 9243 E-mail jeremyclines@gmail.com

CLITHEROW, Canon Andrew. b 50. St Chad's Coll Dur BA72 Ex Univ MPhil87. Sarum & Wells Th Coll 78. **d** 79 **p** 80. Hon C Bedford Ch Ch *St Alb* 79-84; Asst Chapl Bedford Sch 79-84; Chapl Caldicott Sch Farnham Royal 84-85; C Penkridge w Stretton *Lich* 85-88; Min Acton Trussell w Bednall 85-88; Chapl Rossall Sch Fleetwood 89-94; V Scotforth *Blackb* 94-00; Dioc Dir of Tr and Can Res Blackb Cathl 00-07; Hon Can from 07; P-in-c Lytham St Cuth from 07; P-in-c Lytham St Jo from 08; Chapl to The Queen from 08. *St Cuthbert's Vicarage, Church Road, Lytham, Lytham St Annes FY8 5PX* Tel (01253) 736168 E-mail clitherow814@btinternet.com

CLOAKE, David Michael. b 72. Ripon Coll Cuddesdon 07. **d** 08 **p** 09. C Aylesbury w Bierton and Hulcott *Ox* from 08; CF (ACF)

from 10. *4 Cubb Field, Aylesbury HP19 7SH* Tel (01296) 582331 Mobile 07758-289702 E-mail fatherdavid@ntlworld.com

CLOCKSIN (née HOYLE), Mrs Pamela Margaret. b 61. Nottm Univ BA82. St Jo Coll Nottm 84. **d** 87 **p** 94. Par Dn Bulwell St Jo *S'well* 87-91; Cam Pastorate Chapl 91-95; C Cambridge H Trin *Ely* 91-95; Perm to Offic 95-01. *5 Stansfield Close, Oxford OX3 8TH* Tel (01865) 426022

CLOCKSIN, Prof William Frederick. b 55. BA76 St Cross Coll Ox MA81 Trin Hall Cam MA87 PhD93. EAMTC 91. **d** 94 **p** 95. Asst Chapl Trin Hall Cam 94-01; Acting Dean 00-01. *5 Stansfield Close, Oxford OX3 8TH* Tel (01865) 426022 E-mail wfc@brookes.ac.uk

CLODE, Arthur Raymond Thomas. b 35. Roch Th Coll 67. **d** 69 **p** 70. C Blackheath *Birm* 69-72; V Londonderry 73-75; R Kirkbride *S & M* 75-79; UAE 80-83; Min Stewartly LEP 86-90; C Wootton *St Alb* 86-90; C St Alb St Paul 90-94; rtd 94; Perm to Offic *Glouc* from 01. *60 Albemarle Gate, Cheltenham GL50 4PJ* Tel (01242) 577521

CLOETE, Richard James. b 47. AKC71. St Aug Coll Cant 72. **d** 72 **p** 73. C Redhill St Matt *S'wark* 72-76; V Streatham St Paul 76-84; P-in-c W Coker w Hardington Mandeville, E Chinnock etc *B & W* 84-88; R 88; R Wincanton and Pen Selwood 88-97; Sec and Treas Dioc Hosp Chapl Fellowship 91-97; Perm to Offic *Lon* 97-98 and *Ex* 99-02; C Sampford Peverell, Uplowman, Holcombe Rogus etc *Ex* 02-11; rtd 11. *19 Mount Nebo, Taunton TA1 4HG* Tel (01823) 338428 Mobile 07855-493868 E-mail r.j.cloete@btinternet.com

CLOGHER, Archdeacon of. *See* PRINGLE, The Ven Cecil Thomas

CLOGHER, Bishop of. *See* McDOWELL, The Rt Revd Francis John

CLOGHER, Dean of. *See* HALL, The Very Revd Kenneth Robert James

CLONMACNOISE, Dean of. *See* JONES, The Very Revd Robert William

CLOSE, Brian Eric. b 49. St Chad's Coll Dur BA74 MA76. Ridley Hall Cam 74. **d** 76 **p** 77. C Far Headingley St Chad *Ripon* 76-79; C Harrogate St Wilfrid 79-80; C Harrogate St Wilfrid and St Luke 80-82; P-in-c Alconbury cum Weston *Ely* 82-83; V 83-86; P-in-c Buckworth 82-83; R 83-86; P-in-c Upton and Copmanford 82-83; Chapl Reed's Sch Cobham 86-96; Chapl Malvern Coll 96-01; Chapl Uppingham Sch 01-04; R Easington, Easington Colliery and S Hesleden *Dur* 04-09; rtd 09. *Burnside, Calgary, Ardvasar, Isle of Skye IV45 8RU*

CLOSE (née HITCHEN), Mrs Carol Ann. b 47. St Mary's Coll Ban CertEd69 St Martin's Coll Lanc DipEd91 Ches Coll of HE BTh02. NOC 99. **d** 02 **p** 03. NSM Hindley St Pet *Liv* 02-07; Perm to Offic *Man* 08-11; NSM Hindley Green *Liv* from 11. *271 Warrington Road, Abram, Wigan WN2 5RQ* Tel (01942) 861670

CLOSE, Mrs Jane. b 48. WMMTC 00. **d** 03 **p** 04. NSM Fillongley and Corley *Cov* 03-06; P-in-c Leam Valley from 06. *The Rectory, Lower Street, Willoughby, Rugby CV23 8BX* Tel (01926) 632455 Mobile 07957-233502 E-mail j-b.close@ntlworld.com

CLOSE, Canon Timothy John. b 68. QUB BA91 Leic Univ MSc95 TCD BTh00. CITC 97. **d** 00 **p** 01. C Glenageary *D & G* 00-03; Dean's V Belf Cathl 03-09; Can Belf Cathl from 07. *The Vicarage, 11 Woodfield, Newtownabbey BT37 0ZH* Tel (028) 9086 0023

CLOSS-PARRY, The Ven Selwyn. b 25. Univ of Wales (Lamp) BA50. St Mich Coll Llan 50. **d** 52 **p** 53. C Dwygyfylchi *Ban* 52-58; V Treuddyn *St As* 58-66; R Llangystennin 66-71; V Holywell 71-77; Can St As Cathl 76-82; Prec 82-84; Preb 82-90; V Colwyn 77-84; Adn St As 84-90; R Trefnant 84-90; rtd 91. *3 Llys Brompton, Brompton Avenue, Rhos-on-Sea LL28 4TB* Tel (01492) 545801

CLOTHIER, Gerald Harry. b 34. Oak Hill Th Coll 75. **d** 78 **p** 79. Hon C Highwood *Chelmsf* 78-79; Hon C Writtle w Highwood 79-83; P-in-c Westhall w Brampton and Stoven *St E* 83-86; TV Beccles St Mich 86-93; R Rougham, Beyton w Hessett and Rushbrooke 93-97; rtd 97; Perm to Offic *Nor* from 97; P-in-c Tenerife Sur *Eur* 01-02. *4 Wiggs Way, Corton, Lowestoft NR32 5JJ* Tel (01502) 733231

CLOUSTON, Eric Nicol. b 63. G&C Coll Cam BA85 MA88 PhD89. Ridley Hall Cam 03. **d** 05 **p** 06. C Chatham St Phil and St Jas *Roch* 05-08; CMS India from 09. *c/o V Duraikan Esq, 29 Aylesford Way, Stapleford, Cambridge CB22 5DP* E-mail eclouston@btinternet.com

CLOVER, Brendan David. b 58. G&C Coll Cam BA79 MA83 LTCL74. Ripon Coll Cuddesdon 79. **d** 82 **p** 83. C Friern Barnet St Jas *Lon* 82-85; C W Hampstead St Jas 85-87; Chapl Em Coll Cam 87-92; Dean 92-94; P-in-c St Pancras w St Jas and Ch Ch *Lon* 94-99; P-in-c St Pancras H Cross w St Jude and St Pet 96-99; Can Res Bris Cathl 99-06; Sen Provost Woodard Corp from 06; Perm to Offic *Lich* from 06. *The Woodard Corporation, High Street, Abbots Bromley, Rugeley WS15 3BW* Tel (01283) 840670 *or* 840120 E-mail brendanclover@woodard.co.uk

CLOW, Laurie Stephen. b 65. Man Univ BA86 MA88. Wycliffe Hall Ox 96. **d** 98 **p** 99. C Trentham *Lich* 98-01; TV Hampreston *Sarum* from 01. *19 Canford Bottom, Wimborne Minster BH21 2HA* Tel (01202) 884796 E-mail w.m.clow@uclan.ac.uk *or* isclow@ccssite.freeserve.co.uk

CLOWES, John. b 45. AKC67. **d** 68 **p** 69. C Corby St Columba *Pet* 68-71; R Itchenstoke w Ovington and Abbotstone *Win* 71-74; V Acton w Gt and Lt Waldingfield *St E* 74-80; Asst Dioc Chr Stewardship Adv 75-80; TV Southend St Jo w St Mark, All SS w St Fran etc *Chelmsf* 80-82; TV Southend 82-85; Ind Chapl 80-85; R Ashwick w Oakhill and Binegar *B & W* 85-91; P-in-c Brompton Regis w Upton and Skilgate 91-97; rtd 98. *The Tythings, Tythings Court, Minehead TA24 5NT* Tel 07808-200619 (mobile)

CLOYNE, Dean of. See MARLEY, The Very Revd Alan Gordon

CLUCAS, Anthony John. b 56. Portsm Poly BA77. WMMTC 96. **d** 99 **p** 00. NSM Erdington *Birm* 99-04; NSM Nechells 04-05; P-in-c Shard End from 05. *Apartment 1, 11 York Crescent, Birmingham B34 7NS* Tel 0121-747 3299 E-mail clucas@btinternet.com

CLUCAS, Robert David. b 55. Cranmer Hall Dur. **d** 82 **p** 83. C Gateacre *Liv* 82-86; P-in-c Bishop's Itchington *Cov* 86-93; CPAS Staff 93-98; Freelance Tr GodStuff from 99; Perm to Offic *Cov* 93-09; C Priors Hardwick, Priors Marston and Wormleighton from 09; C Napton-on-the-Hill, Lower Shuckburgh etc from 09. *1 Church Hill, Leamington Spa CV32 5AZ* Tel (01926) 887792 E-mail bob@godstuff.org.uk

CLUER, Donald Gordon. b 21. S'wark Ord Course 61. **d** 64 **p** 65. C Malden St Jas *S'wark* 64-68; C Bexhill St Pet *Chich* 68-73; V Shoreham Beach 73-77; V Heathfield St Rich 77-86; C Eastbourne St Mary 86-90; rtd 90; Perm to Offic *Ox* from 90. *St John's Home, St Mary's Road, Oxford OX4 1QE* Tel (01865) 241658

CLUES, David Charles. b 66. K Coll Lon BD87 Lon Univ PGCE95. St Steph Ho Ox 88. **d** 90 **p** 91. C Notting Hill All SS w St Columb *Lon* 90-94; NSM 94-96; NSM Notting Hill St Mich and Ch Ch 96-98; Asst Chapl HM Pris Wormwood Scrubs 97-98; C Paddington St Mary Magd *Lon* 98-03; C Paddington St Mary 98-03; C Paddington St Sav 98-03; V Willesden St Mary from 03. *St Mary's Vicarage, 18 Neasden Lane, London NW10 2TT* Tel (020) 8459 2167 E-mail transpontem@aol.com *or* stmarywillesden@aol.com

CLUETT, Preb Michael Charles. b 53. Kingston Poly BSc78. St Steph Ho Ox 84. **d** 86 **p** 87. C Pontesbury I and II *Heref* 86-90; TV Wenlock 90-99; P-in-c Canon Pyon w Kings Pyon and Birley 99-04; V Canon Pyon w King's Pyon, Birley and Wellington from 04; RD Leominster from 08; Preb Heref Cathl from 10. *The Vicarage, Brookside, Canon Pyon, Hereford HR4 8NY* Tel (01432) 830802 E-mail mccluett@aol.com

CLUNE, David Julian. b 60. Open Univ BSc03. Wilson Carlile Coll 99 St Jo Coll Nottm LTh07. **d** 07 **p** 08. C Spalding *Linc* 07-11; TV Sutton St Jas and Wawne *York* from 11. *The Rectory, Church Street, Sutton, Hull HU7 4TL* E-mail david@clune.org.uk

CLUNIE, Grace. b 60. Ulster Univ BA82 MA91. CITC BTh95. **d** 95 **p** 96. C Newtownards *D & D* 95-99; C Seagoe 99-01; I Belfast St Nic *Conn* 01-07; Dir Celtic Spirituality Arm Cathl from 07; Dom Chapl to Abp Arm from 09. *The Garden House, 23 Drumilly Road, Armagh BT61 8RG* Tel (028) 3887 0667 E-mail contact@celtic-spirituality.net

CLUTTERBUCK, Herbert Ivan. b 16. Ch Coll Cam BA38 MA42. Chich Th Coll 38. **d** 39 **p** 40. C Lamorbey H Trin *Roch* 39-41; Hon CF 41-44; Chapl and Sen Classics Master Wellingborough Sch 44-47; Chapl RN 47-62; V Lanteglos by Fowey *Truro* 62-66; Org Sec Ch Union 66-74; Chapl Qu Marg Sch Escrick Park 74-76; Chapl and Dir Relig Studies Roedean Sch Brighton 76-81; rtd 82; Master St Jo Hosp *Lich* 82-91; Perm to Offic *Truro* 99-05 and *Roch* 00-05. *The College of St Barnabas, Blackberry Lane, Lingfield RH7 6NJ* Tel (01342) 872827

CLUTTERBUCK, Miss Marion Isobel. b 56. Oak Hill Th Coll BA91. **d** 92 **p** 94. C Lindfield *Chich* 92-96; TV Alderbury Team *Sarum* 96-01; TV Clarendon 01-05. *3 Hillside Close, West Dean, Salisbury SP5 1EX* Tel (01794) 342377 E-mail marion@mclutterbuck.fsnet.co.uk

CLUTTON, Canon Barbara Carol. b 47. WMMTC 00. **d** 04 **p** 05. NSM Bourton w Frankton and Stretton on Dunsmore etc *Cov* from 04; P-in-c from 08; Rural Life Officer from 07; Hon Can Cov Cathl from 11. *Church Cottage, Main Street, Grandborough, Rugby CV23 8DQ* Tel 07808-137550 (mobile) E-mail barbaraclutton@gilberthouse.co.uk

CLYDE, John. b 39. Univ of Wales (Lamp) MA99 Greenwich Univ PhD. CITC. **d** 71 **p** 72. C Belfast St Aid *Conn* 71-74; I Belfast St Barn 74-80; I Belfast H Trin 80-89; Bp's C Acton and Drumbanagher *Arm* 89-94; I Desertlyn w Ballyeglish 94-02; rtd 02. *25 Castleoak, Castledawson, Magherafelt BT45 8RX* Tel (028) 7946 9153 E-mail jc@rclyde.freeserve.co.uk

CLYNES, William. b 33. Sarum & Wells Th Coll 78. **d** 79 **p** 80. C Winterbourne *Bris* 79-83; TV Swindon St Jo and St Andr 83-91;

rtd 91. *34 Sandown Court, 22-62 Bromley Drive, Cardiff CF5 5EZ*

COAKLEY (née FURBER), Prof Sarah Anne. b 51. New Hall Cam BA73 PhD82. Harvard Div Sch ThM75. **d** 00 **p** 01. Edw Mallinckrodt Jr Prof Div Harvard Div Sch 95-07; Visiting Prof 07-08; Hon C Waban The Gd Shep 00-08; Hon C Littlemore *Ox* 00-07; Norris-Hulse Prof Div Cam Univ from 07; Lic to Offic *Ely* from 08. Faculty of Divinity, West Road, Cambridge *CB3 9BS* Tel (01223) 763002 E-mail sc545@cam.ac.uk

COATES, Alan Thomas. b 55. St Jo Coll Nottm 87. **d** 89 **p** 90. C Heeley *Sheff* 89-90; C Bramley and Ravenfield 90-92; V Askern 92-96; Chapl RAF from 96; Perm to Offic *Ripon* from 96. *Chaplaincy Services, Valiant Block, HQ Air Command, RAF High Wycombe HP14 4UE* Tel (01494) 496800 Fax 496343

COATES, Archie. See COATES, Richard Michael

COATES, Canon Christopher Ian. b 59. Qu Coll Birm 81. **d** 84 **p** 85. C Cottingham *York* 84-87; TV Howden 87-91; V Sherburn in Elmet 91-94; V Sherburn in Elmet w Saxton 94-02; V Bishopthorpe from 02; V Acaster Malbis from 02; P-in-c Appleton Roebuck w Acaster Selby from 07; Hon Can Ho from 10. *The Vicarage, 48 Church Lane, Bishopthorpe, York YO23 2QG* Tel (01904) 707840 E-mail chriscoates@hotmail.co.uk

COATES, David Martin. b 57. Sheff Univ BSc78 Reading Univ MSc80 Birm Univ PhD83. STETS 04. **d** 07 **p** 08. NSM Salisbury St Mark *Sarum* 07-10; NSM Bourne Valley from 10. *2 St Matthew's Close, Bishopdown, Salisbury SP1 3FJ* Tel (01980) 613207 E-mail dmc50@waitrose.com

COATES, Canon Jean Margaret. b 47. Sussex Univ BSc68 Reading Univ PhD77 MIBiol CBiol. SAOMC 93. **d** 96 **p** 97. C Wallingford *Ox* 96-99; P-in-c Watercombe *Sarum* 99-02; R from 02; Rural Officer (Dorset) from 99; Can and Preb Sarum Cathl from 05. *The Rectory, Main Street, Broadmayne, Dorchester DT2 8EB* Tel (01305) 852435 E-mail jeancoates@macunlimited.net

COATES, John David Spencer. b 41. St Jo Coll Dur BA64. Cranmer Hall Dur 64. **d** 66 **p** 67. C Chipping Campden w Ebrington *Glouc* 66-68; CF 69-96; rtd 96; Perm to Offic *B & W* from 96. *4 The Poplars, Hawkcombe, Porlock, Minehead TA24 8QN* Tel (01643) 862772

COATES, Maxwell Gordon. b 49. Lon Univ CertEd70 Open Univ BA83 UEA MA86. Trin Coll Bris. **d** 77 **p** 78. C Blackheath Park St Mich *S'wark* 77-79; Chapl Greenwich Distr Hosp Lon 77-79; Asst Teacher Saintbridge Sch Glouc 79-81; Teacher Gaywood Park High Sch King's Lynn 81-85; NSM Lynn St Jo *Nor* 85-85; Dep Hd Teacher Winton Comp Sch Bournemouth 85-90; Hd Teacher St Mark's Comp Sch Bath 90-97; NSM Canford Magna *Sarum* 85-90 and 99-05; NSM Stoke Gifford *Bris* 93-96; Perm to Offic *B & W* 91-96; rtd 96. *3 Oakley Road, Wimborne BH21 1QJ* Tel (01202) 883162

COATES, Michael David. b 60. Ches Coll of HE BTh01. NOC 98. **d** 01 **p** 02. C Orrell Hey St Jo and St Jas *Liv* 01-07; P-in-c Edge Hill St Cypr w St Mary 07-10; C Liv All SS from 11. *The Vicarage, 48 John Lennon Drive, Liverpool L6 9HT* Tel 0151-260 6351 E-mail evertonmike.c@sky.com

COATES, Canon Nigel John. b 51. Reading Univ BSc MA. Trin Coll Bris. **d** 83 **p** 84. C Epsom St Martin *Guildf* 83-86; C Portswood Ch Ch *Win* 86-88; Chapl Southn Univ 89-97; Chapl Southn Inst of HE 89-95; P-in-c Freemantle 97-00; R 00-05; Can Res S'well Minster from 05. *3 Vicars Court, Southwell NG25 0HP* Tel (01636) 817296 E-mail nigelcoates@southwellminster.org

COATES, Canon Peter Frederick. b 50. K Coll Lon BD79 AKC79. St Steph Ho Ox 79. **d** 80 **p** 81. C Woodford St Barn *Chelmsf* 80-83; C E and W Keal *Linc* 83-86; R The Wainfleets and Croft 86-94; R The Wainfleet Gp 94-03; RD Calcewaithe and Candleshoe 92-03; P-in-c Spilsby Gp from 03; RD Bolingbroke from 03; Can and Preb Linc Cathl from 02. *The Vicarage, Church Street, Spilsby PE23 5DU* Tel (01790) 752526 E-mail peter.coates@onetel.net

COATES, Richard Michael (Archie). b 70. Birm Univ BA92. Wycliffe Hall Ox BA99. **d** 00 **p** 01. C Ashtead *Guildf* 00-03; C Brompton H Trin w Onslow Square St Paul *Lon* 03-09; V Brighton St Pet *Chich* from 09. *10 West Drive, Brighton BN2 0GD* Tel (01273) 695064 E-mail coates@archieandson.co.uk

COATES, Robert. b 63. Aston Tr Scheme 87 St Steph Ho Ox 89. **d** 92 **p** 93. C Heavitree w Ex St Paul 92-95; Chapl RN 95-00; V Bexhill St Aug *Chich* from 00. *St Augustine's Vicarage, St Augustine's Close, Bexhill-on-Sea TN39 3AZ* Tel and fax (01424) 210785 E-mail erl@rcoates42.freeserve.co.uk

COATES, Robert Charles. b 44. Open Univ BA76. Cant Sch of Min 83. **d** 86 **p** 87. C Deal St Leon and St Rich and Sholden *Cant* 86-89; V Linside 89-00; V Rawmarsh *Glouc* 00-06; rtd 06; Perm to Offic *B & W* from 06. *70 Barrington Place, Shepton Mallet BA4 5GH* Tel (01749) 344698 E-mail robert.coates2@virgin.net

COATES, Stuart Murray. b 49. Lon Univ BA70 Edin Univ MTh91. Wycliffe Hall Ox 72. **d** 75 **p** 76. C Rainford *Liv* 75-78; C Orrell 78-79; V 79-86; Chapl Strathcarron Hospice Denny from

86; Hon C Stirling *Edin* 86-90; NSM Doune *St And* from 89; NSM Aberfoyle 89-94. *Westwood Smithy, Chalmerston Road, Stirling FK9 4AG* Tel (01786) 860531 *or* (01324) 826222 E-mail stuart@stuartcoates.wanadoo.co.uk

COATS, Maureen Quin. b 43. **d** 10 **p** 11. NSM Eastham *Ches* from 10. *24 Stanley Lane, Wirral CH62 0AG*

COATSWORTH, Nigel George. b 39. Trin Hall Cam BA61 MA. Cuddesdon Coll 61. **d** 63 **p** 64. C Hellesdon *Nor* 63-66; Ewell Monastery 66-80; TV Folkestone H Trin and St Geo w Ch Ch *Cant* 83-85; C Milton next Sittingbourne 85-86; P-in-c Selattyn *Lich* 86-91; P-in-c Weston Rhyn 88-91; R Weston Rhyn and Selattyn 91-05; rtd 05; Perm to Offic *Lich* from 05. *Oakmere House, 69 Hill Park, Dudleston Heath, Ellesmere SY12 9LB* Tel (01691) 690261 E-mail rev.coatsworth@micro-plus-web.net

COBB, George Reginald. b 50. Oak Hill Th Coll BA81. **d** 81 **p** 82. C Ware Ch Ch *St Alb* 81-84; C Uphill *B & W* 84-89; R Alresford *Chelmsf* 89-99; Chapl Mt Vernon and Watford Hosps NHS Trust 99-00; Chapl W Herts Hosps NHS Trust from 00. *Mount Vernon Hospital, Rickmansworth Road, Northwood HA6 2RN* Tel (01923) 844447 *or* (020) 8861 2720 E-mail gcobb83618@aol.com *or* george.cobb@whht.nhs.uk

COBB, Canon John Philip Andrew. b 43. Man Univ BSc65 New Coll Ox BA67 MA71. Wycliffe Hall Ox 66. **d** 68 **p** 69. C Reading St Jo *Ox* 68-71; C Romford Gd Shep *Chelmsf* 71-73; SAMS Chile 74-08; Can from 99; Dioc Ecum Officer 00-06; rtd 08; Lic to Offic Chile from 08. *Casilla 330, Correo Paine, Paine, Region Metropolitana, Chile* Tel (0056) (2) 259 4099 E-mail jn.cobb@yahoo.co.uk

COBB, Miss Marjorie Alice. b 24. St Chris Coll Blackheath IDC52. **dss** 61 **d** 87. CSA 56-85; rtd 85; Perm to Offic *Cant* from 87; Chapl Jes Hosp Cant from 90. *2 John Boys Wing, Jesus Hospital, Sturry Road, Canterbury CT1 1BS* Tel (01227) 472615

COBB, Mark Robert. b 64. Lanc Univ BSc86 Keele Univ MA99. Ripon Coll Cuddesdon 88. **d** 91 **p** 92. C Hampstead St Jo *Lon* 91-94; Asst Chapl Derbyshire R Infirmary NHS Trust 94-96; Palliative & Health Care Chapl Derbyshire R Infirmary NHS Trust 96-98; Chapl Manager Cen Sheff Univ Hosps NHS Trust 98-02; Sen Chapl 98-04; Sen Chapl Sheff Teaching Hosps NHS Foundn Trust from 04. *Chaplaincy Services, Royal Hallamshire Hospital, Glossop Road, Sheffield S10 2JF* Tel 0114-271 2718 *or* 271 1900 E-mail mark.cobb@sth.nhs.uk

COBB, Peter Graham. b 27. St Jo Coll Cam BA48 MA52. Ridley Hall Cam 66. **d** 68 **p** 69. C Porthkerry *Llan* 68-71; P-in-c Penmark 71-72; V Penmark w Porthkerry 72-81; V Magor w Redwick and Undy *Mon* 82-95; rtd 95. *2 Talycoed Court, Talycoed, Monmouth NP25 5HR* Tel (01600) 780309

COBBOLD, Richard Nevill. b 55. Bris Univ BScEng76. Local Minl Tr Course. **d** 11. NSM N Farnborough *Guildf* from 11. *4 Penns Wood, Farnborough GU14 6RB* Tel (01252) 515547 Mobile 07776-352240 E-mail richard@cobbold.plus.com

COCHLIN, Maurice Reginald. b 19. TCert57 FVCM57 ACP60 FFChM Sussex Univ CertEd70 Lambeth STh74. Chich Th Coll 70. **d** 70 **p** 71. C Rowlands Castle *Portsm* 70-72; Chapl Paulsgrove Sch Cosham 71; C Warblington w Emsworth *Portsm* 72-75; C S w N Bersted *Chich* 76-78; Hd Littlemead Upper Sch Chich 78-79; C Saltdean *Chich* 79-83; V Kirdford 83-88; rtd 88; Perm to Offic *Chich* from 88. *56 Farnhurst Road, Barnham, Bognor Regis PO22 0JW* Tel (01243) 553584

COCHRANE, Alan George. b 28. S'wark Ord Course. **d** 82 **p** 83. NSM Clapham Old Town *S'wark* 82-85; C Spalding St Jo w Deeping St Nicholas *Linc* 85-87; R Southery and Hilgay *Ely* 87-98; V Fordham St Mary 87-91; rtd 98; Perm to Offic *Nor* from 99. *34 Pightle Way, Lyng, Norwich NR9 5RL* Tel (01603) 872795

COCHRANE, Mrs Anthea Mary. b 38. **d** 02 **p** 03. OLM Clarendon *Sarum* 02-07; Perm to Offic 07-08. *Old Timbers, Silver Street, Alderbury, Salisbury SP5 3AN* Tel (01722) 710503 E-mail anthea.cochrane@tiscali.co.uk

COCHRANE, Philip Andrew. b 74. Reading Univ BA92. Trin Coll Bris BA07. **d** 07 **p** 08. C Fareham H Trin *Portsm* 07-09; TV from 09. *12 Greenwood Close, Fareham PO16 7UF* Tel·(01329) 318665 E-mail philip@scfareham.org.uk

COCHRANE, Canon Roy Alan. b 25. AKC53. **d** 54 **p** 55. C Linc St Faith 54-56; C Skegness 56-59; R Thurlby w Norton Disney 59-65; V Swinderby 59-65; Chapl HM Borstal Morton Hall 59-65; R N Coates *Linc* 65-69; Chapl RAF 65-69; V Marshchapel *Linc* 65-69; V Grainthorpe w Conisholme 65-69; V Glanford Bridge 69-89; Chapl Glanford Hosp 69-89; RD Yarborough 76-81; Can and Preb Linc Cathl 77-97; Chapl and Warden St Anne's Bedehouses 89-93; rtd 90. *4 Trinity Hospital, Hospital Road, Retford DN22 7BD* Tel (01777) 702882

COCKAYNE, Gordon. b 34. RMN73. **d** 92 **p** 93. NSM Owlerton *Sheff* 92-94; Ind Chapl 92-94; NSM Brightside w Wincobank 94-99; Perm to Offic from 99. *6 Austin Close, Loxley, Sheffield S6 6QD* Tel 0114-220 6626

COCKAYNE, Canon Mark Gary. b 62. UEA LLB82. St Jo Coll Nottm BTh92 MA93. **d** 93 **p** 94. C Armthorpe *Sheff* 93-96; V Malin Bridge 96-05; AD Hallam 02-05; C Haydock St Mark *Liv* 05-08; V from 08; AD St Helens from 06; Hon Can Liv Cathl

from 06. *St Mark's Vicarage, 2 Stanley Bank Road, St Helens WA11 0UW* Tel (01744) 808301

COCKBILL, Douglas John. b 53. Chicago Univ BA75. Gen Th Sem (NY) MDiv78. **d** 78 **p** 79. Virgin Is 79-80; Bahamas 80-83; USA 84-90 and 05-06; P-in-c Roxbourne St Andr *Lon* 90-92; V 92-04; Chapl Larnaca St Helena Cyprus from 06. *16 Agiou Georgiou Makri, 6306 Larnaca, Cyprus* Tel (00357) (2) 465 1327 *or* (9) 965 8147 E-mail dcockbill22@yahoo.com

COCKBURN, Kathleen. b 50. NEOC 04. **d** 07 **p** 08. NSM Walker *Newc* 07-10; NSM N Shields from 10. *92 Paignton Avenue, Whitley Bay NE25 8SZ* Tel 0191-252 0710 E-mail kath.c@blueyonder.co.uk

COCKE, James Edmund. b 26. Wadh Coll Ox BA50 MA55. Wells Th Coll 50. **d** 52 **p** 53. C Christchurch *Win* 52-57; V Highfield *Ox* from 57; Chapl Wingfield-Morris Hosp Ox 57-90; Chapl Nuffield Orthopaedic Centre NHS Trust from 90. *All Saints' Vicarage, 85 Old Road, Oxford OX3 7LB* Tel (01865) 62536

COCKELL, Ms Helen Frances. b 69. Trin Hall Cam BA90 MA94. Qu Coll Birm BD94. **d** 95. C Bracknell *Ox* 95-98; Perm to Offic *Cov* from 00; Chapl S Warks Gen Hosps NHS Trust from 09. *The New Rectory, Pool Close, Rugby CV22 7RN* Tel (01788) 812613 E-mail nell.cockell@btinternet.com

COCKELL, Timothy David. b 66. Qu Coll Birm BTheol95. **d** 95 **p** 96. C Bracknell *Ox* 95-98; C Rugby *Cov* 98-99; TV 99-04; P-in-c Bilton 04-08; R from 08. *The New Rectory, Pool Close, Rugby CV22 7RN* Tel (01788) 812613 E-mail tim.cockell@btopenworld.com

COCKER (née BENTLEY), Mrs Frances Rymer (Sister Frances Anne). b 22. Man Univ BSc48 TDip49 PGCE49. **d** 95 **p** 95. Mother Superior C3D 87-00; Perm to Offic *Sarum* from 95. *7 St Nicholas Hospital, St Nicholas Road, Salisbury SP1 2SW* Tel (01722) 339761 Mobile 07702-659609

COCKERELL, David John. b 47. Univ of Wales (Cardiff) BA51 Univ of Wales (Swansea) MA74 Qu Coll Cam BA75. Westcott Ho Cam 73. **d** 76 **p** 77. C Chapel Allerton *Ripon* 76-79; C Farnley 79-81; TV Hitchin *St Alb* 81-89; TV Dorchester *Ox* 89-92; Adult Educn and Tr Officer *Ely* 92-00; R Raddesley Gp 00-06; rtd 06. *44 Humberley Close, Eynesbury, St Neots PE19 2SE* Tel (01480) 218225 E-mail david@cockerell.co.uk

COCKERTON, Canon John Clifford Penn. b 27. Liv Univ BA48 St Cath Soc Ox BA54 MA58. Wycliffe Hall Ox 51. **d** 54 **p** 55. C St Helens St Helen *Liv* 54-58; Tutor Cranmer Hall Dur 58-60; Chapl 60-63; Warden 68-70; Vice-Prin St Jo Coll Dur 63-70; Prin 70-78; R Wheldrake *York* 78-84; R Wheldrake w Thorganby 84-92; Can and Preb York Minster 87-92; rtd 92; Perm to Offic *York* from 98. *42 Lucombe Way, New Earswick, York YO32 4DS* Tel (01904) 765555

COCKETT, The Ven Elwin Wesley. b 59. Aston Tr Scheme 86 Oak Hill Th Coll BA91. **d** 91 **p** 92. C Chadwell Heath *Chelmsf* 91-94; Chapl W Ham United Football Club from 92; C Harold Hill St Paul 94-95; P-in-c 95-97; V 97-00; TR Billericay and Lt Burstead 00-07; RD Basildon 04-07; Adn W Ham from 07. *86 Aldersbrook Road, London E12 5DH* Tel (020) 8989 8557 E-mail a.westham@chelmsford.anglican.org

COCKFIELD, Mrs Myrtle Jacqueline. b 51. S Bank Univ BSc96. SEITE 03. **d** 08 **p** 09. NSM Mitcham SS Pet and Paul *S'wark* from 08. *28 Garden Avenue, Mitcham CR4 2EA* Tel (020) 8646 2333 Mobile 07722-568604 E-mail jackiecockfield@yahoo.co.uk

COCKING, Ann Louisa. b 44. **d** 03 **p** 04. OLM The Lavingtons, Cheverells, and Easterton *Sarum* from 03. *High Acre, Eastcott, Devizes SN10 4PH* Tel (01980) 812763

COCKING, Martyn Royston. b 53. Trin Coll Bris 83. **d** 85 **p** 86. C Weston-super-Mare Cen Par *B & W* 85-88; C Kingswood *Bris* 88-89; TV 89-93; V Pill w Easton in Gordano and Portbury *B & W* 93-96. *68 Friary Grange Park, Winterbourne, Bristol BS36 1NB* Tel (01454) 886771

COCKMAN, David Willie. b 32. Ex & Truro NSM Scheme 89. **d** 82 **p** 83. C Christow, Ashton, Trusham and Bridford *Ex* 82; NSM Exwick 83-84; Warden Mercer Ho 83-97; Lic to Offic from 83; rtd 97. *4 The Fairway, Pennsylvania, Exeter EX4 5DW* Tel (01392) 278590

COCKRAM, Anthony John. b 44. Leeds Univ BSc65 Birm Univ MEd83 Ex Univ BA04. SWMTC 98. **d** 01 **p** 02. NSM Seaton *Ex* 01-03; NSM Seaton and Beer 03-04; Asst Chapl R Devon and Ex NHS Foundn Trust 04-05; TV Aberavon *Llan* 05-10; rtd 10. *1 Hillymead, Seaton EX12 2LF* Tel (01297) 21887 E-mail ajcockram@hotmail.co.uk

COCKS, Canon Howard Alan Stewart. b 46. St Barn Coll Adelaide 78. **d** 80 **p** 81. C Portland Australia 80-82; C Prestbury *Glouc* 82-87; P-in-c Stratton w Baunton 87-94; P-in-c N Cerney w Bagendon 91-94; R Stratton, N Cerney, Baunton and Bagendon 95-98; V Leic St Aid 98-04; RD Christianity S 01-04; R Winchelsea and Icklesham *Chich* from 04; Can The Murray from 06. *The Rectory, St Thomas Street, Winchelsea TN36 4EB* Tel (01797) 226254

COCKS, Michael Dearden Somers. b 28. Univ of NZ MA50 St Cath Coll Ox BA53 MA57. Ripon Hall Ox. **d** 53 **p** 54. C Merivale New Zealand 53-56; V Geraldine 56-58; V Ross and S

Westland 58-60; V Hinds 60-63; V St Martins 63-70; V Barrington Street w Speydon St Nic 70-79; V Hororata 79-93; Chapl Gothenburg w Halmstad, Jönköping etc *Eur* 93-98; rtd 98. *23 Fairfield Avenue, Addington, Christchurch 8020, New Zealand* Tel and fax (0064) (3) 377 7053 E-mail michaelandgertrud@gmail.com

COCKSEDGE, Hugh Francis. b 26. Magd Coll Cam BA50 MA52. **d** 88 **p** 89. NSM Alton All SS *Win* 88-89; Lic to Offic 89-91; Chapl Ankara *Eur* 91-96; rtd 96; Perm to Offic *Win* 96-01; *Eur* from 97; *Portsm* from 01; *Guildf* from 06. *Stancomb, Stancomb Lane, Medstead, Alton GU34 5QB* Tel (01420) 563624 E-mail hughcocksedge@talktalk.net

COCKSEDGE, Simon Hugh. b 56. Univ Coll Lon BSc78 New Coll Ox 86. Birm Univ MD03 FRCGP96. NOC 05. **d** 07 **p** 08. NSM Hayfield and Chinley w Buxworth *Derby* 07-11; NSM Edale from 11. *Corrour, Hall Hill, Chapel-en-le-Frith, High Peak SK23 9RX*

COCKSHAW, Evan David. b 74. Sussex Univ BSc95. St Jo Coll Nottm MA99. **d** 00 **p** 01. C Horncastle w Low Toynton *Linc* 00-02; C Pennington *Man* 02-07; Pioneer Min W Bromwich *Lich* 07-09; C Aldridge from 09. *14 St Thomas Close, Aldridge, Walsall WS9 8SL* Tel (01922) 453342 Mobile 07958-050009

✠**COCKSWORTH, The Rt Revd Christopher John.** b 59. Man Univ BA80 PhD89 PGCE81. St Jo Coll Nottm 84. **d** 88 **p** 89 **c** 08. C Epsom Common Ch Ch *Guildf* 88-92; Chapl R Holloway and Bedf New Coll 92-97; Dir STETS 97-01; Hon Can Guildf Cathl 99-01; Prin Ridley Hall Cam 01-08; Bp Cov from 08. *The Bishop's House, 23 Davenport Road, Coventry CV5 6PW* Tel (024) 7667 2244 Fax 7671 3271 E-mail bishcov@btconnect.com

CODLING, Timothy Michael. b 62. Trin Coll Ox BA84 MA91. St Steph Ho Ox 89. **d** 91 **p** 92. C N Shoebury *Chelmsf* 91-97; V Tilbury Docks from 97; Hon Chapl Miss to Seafarers from 97. *St John's Vicarage, Dock Road, Tilbury RM18 7PP* Tel (01375) 842417 E-mail tim@frcodling.fsnet.co.uk

CODRINGTON-MARSHALL, Louise. b 64. Westcott Ho Cam 06. **d** 08 **p** 09. C Mortlake w E Sheen *S'wark* 08-11; P-in-c Deptford St Nic and St Luke from 11. *11 Evelyn Street, London SE8 5RQ* Tel (020) 8876 7162 E-mail revdlouise@blueyonder.co.uk

CODY, Paul James Luke. b 73. Westcott Ho Cam. **d** 08 **p** 09. C Cen Wolverhampton *Lich* from 08. *1B Claremont Road, Wolverhampton WV3 0EA* Tel 07834-345269 (mobile) E-mail paulcody@hotmail.co.uk

COE, Andrew Derek John. b 58. Nottm Univ BTh86. St Jo Coll Nottm 83. **d** 86 **p** 87. C Pype Hayes *Birm* 86-88; C Erdington St Barn 88-91; C Birm St Martin w Bordesley St Andr 91-96; P-in-c Hamstead St Bernard 96; V 96-02; P-in-c Newdigate *Guildf* 02-03; TR Surrey Weald from 03; RD Dorking 04-09. *The Rectory, Church Road, Newdigate, Dorking RH5 5DL* Tel (01306) 631469 E-mail revdandrewdj.coe@btinternet.com

COE, David. b 45. **d** 69 **p** 70. C Belfast St Matt *Conn* 69-72; C Belfast St Donard *D & D* 72-75; I Tullylish 75-81; I Lurgan St Jo 81-89; I Ballymacarrett St Patr 89-02; I Richhill *Arm* from 02. *The Rectory, 15 Annareagh Road, Richhill BT61 9JT* Tel (028) 3887 1232 E-mail davidcoe144@aol.com

COE, John Norris. b 31. Oak Hill Th Coll 57. **d** 59 **p** 60. C Stoughton *Guildf* 59-61; C Guernsey St Michel du Valle *Win* 61-63; C Norbiton *S'wark* 63-67; V Bath Widcombe *B & W* 67-84; R Publow w Pensford, Compton Dando and Chelwood 84-96; rtd 96; Perm to Offic *B & W* from 96. *12 Stirtingale Road, Bath BA2 2NF* Tel (01225) 789752

COE, Michael Stephen. b 63. Bath Univ BSc85. Wycliffe Hall Ox. **d** 00 **p** 01. C Moulton *Pet* 00-03; P-in-c Silverhill St Matt *Chich* 03-05; R from 05. *The Rectory, 9 St Matthew's Road, St Leonards-on-Sea TN38 0TN* Tel (01424) 430262 E-mail mikelisac@aol.com

COE, Noelle Elizabeth. b 60. Anglia Ruskin Univ BA10. **d** 08 **p** 09. NSM N Holmwood *Guildf* 08-10; NSM Westcott from 10. *The Rectory, Church Road, Newdigate, Dorking RH5 5DL* Tel (01306) 631469 E-mail noellecoe@btinternet.com

COE, Stephen David. b 49. Ch Coll Cam MA72 Oak Hill Th Coll MA99. Ox Min Course 90. **d** 93 **p** 94. NSM Abingdon *Ox* 93-97; Assoc Min Ox St Andr 97-05; V Wallington *S'wark* from 05. *Holy Trinity Vicarage, Maldon Road, Wallington SM6 8BL* Tel (020) 8401 8177 E-mail sdcoe@btinternet.com

COEKIN, Philip James. b 64. Wye Coll Lon BScAgr87. Oak Hill Th Coll BA93. **d** 96 **p** 97. C Eastbourne All SS *Chich* 96-00; V Hastings Em and St Mary in the Castle 00-11; V Eastbourne H Trin from 11. *Holy Trinity Vicarage, 2 Hartington Place, Eastbourne BN21 3BE* Tel (01323) 325421 E-mail philipcoekin@talktalk.net

COEKIN, Richard John. b 61. Solicitor 86 Jes Coll Cam BA83 MA87. Wycliffe Hall Ox 89. **d** 91 **p** 92. C Cheadle *Ches* 91-95; NSM Wimbledon Em Ridgway Prop Chpl *S'wark* from 95; Perm to Offic *Lon* from 02. *264 Worple Road, London SW20 8RG* Tel (020) 8545 2734 E-mail richard.coekin@dundonald.org

COFFEY, Hubert William (Bill). b 15. MBE46. TCD BA37 MA40. TCD Div Sch Div Test38. **d** 38 **p** 39. C Errigle Keerogue

w Ballygawley and Killeshil *Arm* 38-41; Chapl RN 41-47; I Milltown *Arm* 47-52; Chapl Miss to Seamen 52-64; Australia from 53; V Melbourne S 64-80; rtd 80; Perm to Offic *Melbourne* from 80. *23 Hawthorn Avenue, Caulfield North Vic 3161, Australia* Tel (0061) (3) 9527 7875

COFFIN, Pamela. See PENNELL, Ms Pamela

COFFIN, Stephen. b 52. Pemb Coll Ox BA74 MA79. Trin Coll Bris 74. **d** 77 **p** 78. C Illogan *Truro* 77-80; C Liskeard w St Keyne and St Pinnock 80-82; CMS Burundi 82-86; V St Germans *Truro* 86-00; Chapl Grenoble *Eur* from 00. *14 rue Gérard Philippe, 38100 Grenoble, France* Tel (0033) 4 76 25 33 79 E-mail chaplain@grenoble-church.org *or* coffin@onetelnet.fr

COGGINS, Glenn. b 60. Warwick Univ BA81. St Jo Coll Dur 93. **d** 95 **p** 96. C Cley Hill Warminster *Sarum* 95-99; R Doddington w Benwick and Wimblington *Ely* 99-06; V E Ardsley *Wakef* from 06; Bp's Adv for Ecum Affairs from 07. *The Vicarage, Church Lane, East Ardsley, Wakefield WF3 2LJ* Tel (01924) 822184 Mobile 07951-651952 E-mail glenn.coggins@ely.anglican.org

COGHLAN, Jennifer Mary. See WILTSHIRE, Mrs Jennifer Mary

COGHLAN, Canon Patrick John. b 47. Down Coll Cam BA69. St Jo Coll Nottm MA73. **d** 73 **p** 74. C Crookes St Thos *Sheff* 73-78; Brazil 78-92; V Anston *Sheff* 92-96; V Malin Bridge from 06; Hon Can Sheff Cathl from 01. *St Polycarp's Vicarage, 33 Wisewood Lane, Sheffield S6 4WA* Tel 0114-234 3450 E-mail rev.patrick@btinternet.com

COHEN, The Ven Clive Ronald Franklin. b 46. ACIB71. Sarum & Wells Th Coll 79. **d** 81 **p** 82. C Esher *Guildf* 81-85; R Winterslow *Sarum* 85-00; RD Alderbury 89-93; Can and Preb Sarum Cathl 92-00; Adn Bodmin *Truro* 00-11; Hon Can Truro Cathl 00-11; rtd 11. *86 Moor View Drive, Teignmouth TQ14 9UZ* E-mail clive@truro.anglican.org

COHEN, Canon David Mervyn Stuart. b 42. Sydney Univ BA63 MA78. **d** 67 **p** 68. Exec Sec Bible Soc Mauritius 67-69; Dep Gen Sec Bible Soc New Zealand 70-72; Regional Sec (Africa) Bible Soc 73-75; C-in-c Sylvania Australia 75-77; R Manly St Matt 78-85; Gen Dir Scripture Union (England and Wales) 86-93; Tear Fund UK 93-96; Nat Dir Chr Nationals Evang Coun Australia from 96; Hon Can Antsiranana from 06. *1 Currawong Place, East Blaxland NSW 2774, Australia* E-mail davidc@moringa-au.com

COHEN, Grant Geoffrey. b 71. Regents Th Coll BA08. Ridley Hall Cam 09. **d** 11. C Sale St Anne *Ches* from 11. *3 Windermere Avenue, Sale M33 3FP* Tel 07717-170386 (mobile) E-mail grant_cohen@hotmail.co.uk

COHEN, Canon Ian Geoffrey Holland. b 51. Nottm Univ BA74. Ripon Coll Cuddesdon 77. **d** 79 **p** 80. C Sprowston *Nor* 79-83; TV Wallingford w Crowmarsh Gifford etc *Ox* 83-88; V Chalgrove w Berrick Salome from 88; Hon Can Ch Ch from 11. *The Vicarage, 58 Brinkinfield Road, Chalgrove, Oxford OX44 7QX* Tel (01865) 890392 E-mail ianghcohen@hotmail.com

COHEN, Malcolm Arthur. b 38. Canberra Coll of Min. **d** 78 **p** 79. Australia 79-84; C Moruya, Bega and Cootamundra 79-80; R Braidwood 82-83; R Stifford *Chelmsf* 84-92; Chapl Asst Thurrock Community Hosp Grays 84-86; Hon Chapl ATC from 86; P-in-c Mayland and Steeple *Chelmsf* 92-95; C Prittlewell 95-99; C Greenstead 99-00; TV Greenstead w Colchester St Anne 00-03; rtd 03. *177 Straight Road, Colchester CO3 5DG* Tel (01206) 573231

COHEN, Michael Neil. b 45. Ripon Coll Cuddesdon 79. **d** 81 **p** 82. C Gt Bookham *Guildf* 81-84; C York Town St Mich 84-93; V Camberley St Martin Old Dean 93-95; Regional Adv (SE) CMJ 96-99; R Jerusalem Ch Ch 99-03; rtd 10. *6/32 Hagvish, 98558 Ma'aleh Adumim, Israel* Tel (00972) (2) 535 1088 E-mail michaelfrancohen@gmail.com

COKE, Canon William Robert Francis. b 46. St Edm Hall Ox BA68 MA79 Lon Univ BD78. Trin Coll Bris 75. **d** 79 **p** 80. C Blackb Sav 79-83; V Fence in Pendle 83-84; P-in-c Newchurch-in-Pendle 83-84; V Fence and Newchurch-in-Pendle 84-89; Switzerland 89-95; Chapl Ardingly Coll 95-96; V Ambleside w Brathay *Carl* 96-10; P-in-c Langdale 97-08; TR Loughrigg 10-11; RD Windermere 04-10; Hon Can Carl Cathl 08-11; rtd 11. *Anancaun Cottage, Kinlochewe, Achnasheen IV22 2PA* Tel (01445) 760364 E-mail robertricia.coke@homecall.co.uk

COKE-WOODS, Sylvia Jessie. b 47. Sheff Univ BA69. Qu Coll Birm 81 NOC 98. **d** 99 **p** 00. C Widnes St Mary *Liv* 99-03; Perm to Offic *B & W* from 04. *29 Southwoods, Yeovil BA20 2QQ* Tel (01935) 474542

COKER, Alexander Bryan. b 48. Fourah Bay Coll (Sierra Leone) LDiv73 K Coll Lon BD75 MTh76 Brunel Univ MA84 MEd89 AKC76 MCollP84. St Aug Coll Cant 75. **d** 86 **p** 87. NSM Belsize Park *Lon* 86-90; C Croydon Woodside *S'wark* 90-93; C Cheam Common St Phil 93-94; Perm to Offic *Lon* 02-04. *The Mission House, 19 Rosehill Park West, Sutton SM1 3LA* Tel (020) 8641 8690

COKER, Canon Barry Charles Ellis. b 46. K Coll Lon BD69 AKC69. **d** 70 **p** 71. C Newton Aycliffe *Dur* 70-74; Trinidad and

Tobago 74-78; R Matson *Glouc* 78-90; V Stroud and Uplands w Slad from 90; RD Bisley 94-06; P-in-c The Edge, Pitchcombe, Harescombe and Brookthorpe 00-01; Hon Can Glouc Cathl 98-11; rtd 11. *St Petroc, 30 Highfield Road, Lydney GL15 5NA*

COLAM (*née* **TAVERNER**), **Mrs Lorraine Dawn.** b 61. SRN82 RSCN86. d 07 p 08. OLM Tilehurst St Cath and Calcot *Ox* from 07. *120 Chapel Hill, Tilehurst, Reading RG31 5DH* Tel 0118-943 2001 Mobile 07790-076450 E-mail lorraine@colam.supanet.com

COLBOURN, John Martin Claris. b 30. Selw Coll Cam BA52 MA56. Ridley Hall Cam 52. d 54 p 55. C Cheadle *Ches* 54-58; V Trowbridge St Thos *Sarum* 59-65; V Fareham St Jo *Portsm* 65-87; V Crich *Derby* 87-95; RD Alfreton 88-95; rtd 95; Perm to Offic *Derby* from 95. *Stanton View Cottage, Dale Road North, Darley Dale, Matlock DE4 2HX* Tel (01629) 733284

COLBY, David Allan. b 33. Ox NSM Course 78. d 81 p 82. NSM Gt Faringdon w Lt Coxwell *Ox* 81-83; TV Ewyas Harold w Dulas, Kenderchurch etc *Heref* 83-91; V Westbury-on-Severn w Flaxley and Blaisdon *Glouc* 91-99; rtd 99; Perm to Offic *Ox* 01-10. *Solway House, Faringdon Road, Kingston Bagpuize, Abingdon OX13 5AQ* Tel (01865) 820360

COLCHESTER, Archdeacon of. *See* COOPER, The Ven Annette Joy

COLCHESTER, Area Bishop of. *See* MORGAN, The Rt Revd Christopher Heudebourck

✠**COLCLOUGH, The Rt Revd Michael John.** b 44. Leeds Univ BA69. Cuddesdon Coll 69. d 71 p 72 c 96. C Burslem St Werburgh *Lich* 71-75; C Ruislip St Mary *Lon* 75-79; P-in-c Hayes St Anselm 79-85; V 85-86; AD Hillingdon 85-92; P-in-c Uxbridge St Marg 86-88; P-in-c Uxbridge St Andr w St Jo 86-88; TR Uxbridge 88-92; Adn Northolt 92-94; P-in-c St Vedast w St Mich-le-Querne etc 94-96; Bp's Sen Chapl 94-96; Dean of Univ Chapls from 94; Dep P in O 95-96; Area Bp Kensington *Lon* 96-08; Can Res St Paul's Cathl from 08. *2 Amen Court, London EC4M 7BU* Tel (020) 7236 0199 E-mail canonpastor@stpaulscathedral.org.uk

COLDERWOOD, Alfred Victor. b 26. Bps' Coll Cheshunt 58. d 60 p 61. C Oakwood St Thos *Lon* 60-63; C Enfield St Jas 63-66; V Edmonton St Aldhelm 66-91; rtd 91; Perm to Offic *Cant* 91-09. *28 Elliot Close, South Woodham Ferrers, Chelmsford CM3 5YN* Tel (01245) 324758

COLDHAM, Miss Geraldine Elizabeth. b 35. FLA66 Trevelyan Coll Dur BA80. Cranmer Hall Dur 82. dss 83 d 87 p 94. S Normanton *Derby* 83-87; Par Dn 87; Par Dn Barking St Marg w St Patr *Chelmsf* 87-90; Par Dn Stifford 90-94; C 94-95; rtd 95; Perm to Offic *Glouc* from 01. *27 Capel Court, The Burgage, Prestbury, Cheltenham GL52 3EL* Tel (01242) 576425

COLDICOTT, Mrs Christine Mary. b 51. EMMTC 04. d 07 p 08. NSM Ascension TM *Leic* 07-11; NSM Fosse from 11. *5 Wayfarer Drive, East Goscote, Leicester LE7 3QZ* Tel 0116-260 2437 E-mail chris_grand2004@yahoo.co.uk

COLDICOTT, Richard Spencer. b 69. Leeds Univ BSc90 PhD93 PGCE94. Trin Coll Bris 06. d 08 p 09. C Aspley *S'well* 08-11; TV Horsham *Chich* from 11. *St Mark's House, North Heath Lane, Horsham RH12 4PJ* Tel (01403) 260435 Mobile 07742-014444 E-mail richardcoldicott@btinternet.com

COLDWELL, John Philip. b 62. Trin Coll Bris 04. d 06 p 07. C Inglewood Gp *Carl* 06-09; P-in-c Douglas St Ninian *S & M* from 09; Dioc Communications Officer from 10. *St Ninian's Vicarage, 58 Ballanard Road, Douglas, Isle of Man IM2 5HE* Tel (01624) 621694 E-mail media@sodorandman.im

COLDWELL, Rosemary Anne. b 52. Bretton Hall Coll CertEd75 Open Univ BA82 LTCL74 LLCM74. STETS 04. d 07 p 08. NSM Blandford Forum and Langton Long *Sarum* from 07. *12 Stileham Bank, Milborne St Andrew, Blandford Forum DT11 0LE* Tel (01258) 837600 Mobile 07929-090948 E-mail rosemarycoldwell@btinternet.com

COLE, Adrian Peter. *See* ROBBINS-COLE, Adrian Peter

COLE, Canon Alan John. b 35. Bps' Coll Cheshunt 63. d 66 p 67. C Bearwood Wood All SS *St Alb* 66-69; C St Alb St Mich 69-72; V Redbourn 72-80; R Thorley w Bishop's Stortford H Trin 80-87; Chapl St Edw K and Martyr Cam *Ely* 87-94; Chapl Arthur Rank Hospice Cam 87-94; P-in-c Gamlingay w Hatley St George and E Hatley *Ely* 94-99; Hon Can Ely Cathl 96-00; P-in-c Everton w Tetworth 98-99; R Gamlingay and Everton 99-00; rtd 01; Perm to Offic *St E* and *Ely* from 01. *73 Finchams Close, Linton, Cambridge CB21 4ND* Tel (01223) 892286 E-mail alan73@waitrose.com

COLE, Alan Michael. b 40. Melbourne Univ DipEd74 BA74. ACT. d 66 p 67. Australia 66-75 and 80-97; Chapl Bp Otter Coll Chich 76-77; Chapl Ardingly Coll 77-82; Chapl Bonn w Cologne *Eur* 82-86; Chapl Helsinki w Moscow 86-90; P-in-c Ilkeston H Trin *Derby* 97-01; V 02-10; rtd 10; Perm to Offic *Pet* from 10. *30 St Mary's Paddock, Wellingborough NN8 1HJ*

COLE, Canon Brian Robert Arthur. b 35. Nottm Univ BA57. Ridley Hall Cam 59. d 61 p 62. C Tye Green w Netteswell *Chelmsf* 61-64; C Kendal H Trin *Brad* 64-67; V Copley *Wakef* 67-73; Chapl Halifax Gen Hosp 67-73; R Gt w Lt Dunham *Nor* 73-82; R Gt w Lt Fransham 74-82; P-in-c Sporle w Gt and Lt Palgrave

81-82; R Gt and Lt Dunham w Gt and Lt Fransham and Sporle 83-03; P-in-c 03-06; rtd 06; Perm to Offic *Nor* from 06; RD Brisley and Elmham 93-08; Hon Can Nor Cathl 98-08. *Stone Cottage, The Street, Mileham, King's Lynn PE32 2RA* Tel (01328) 701466 E-mail brian@cole4235.freeserve.co.uk

COLE, Charles Vincent. b 26. Kelham Th Coll 47. d 51 p 52. C Harton *Dur* 51-54; C Gateshead St Jas 54-56; V Blackhall 56-91; rtd 91; Perm to Offic *Wakef* 91-06. *66 Scott Green Crescent, Gildersome, Morley, Leeds LS27 7DF* Tel 0113-253 0021

COLE, David Henry. *See* GIFFORD-COLE, David Henry

COLE, Guy Spenser. b 63. Univ of Wales (Ban) BA84 Jes Coll Cam BA88 MA91. Westcott Ho Cam 85. d 88 p 89. C Eastville St Anne w St Mark and St Thos *Bris* 88-92; P-in-c Penhill 92-95; V 95-01; R Easthampstead *Ox* from 01. *The Rectory, Crowthorne Road, Easthampstead, Bracknell RG12 7ER* Tel (01344) 423253 *or* 425205 E-mail guycole@guycole.freeserve.co.uk

COLE, Jennifer Ann. b 52. Open Univ MBA04. STETS 07. d 09 p 10. NSM Radstock w Writhlington *B & W* from 09; NSM Kilmersdon w Babington from 09. *51 Under Knoll, Peasedown St John, Bath BA2 8TY* Tel (01761) 437768 Mobile 07749-079276 E-mail jennifer.cole@bathwells.anglican.org

COLE, John Gordon. b 43. Magd Coll Cam BA65 MA69. Cuddesdon Coll 66. d 68 p 69. C Leeds St Pet *Ripon* 68-71; C Moor Allerton 71-75; P-in-c Pendleton *Blackb* 75-86; Dioc Communications Officer 75-86; Dioc Missr *Linc* 86-98; Ecum Development Officer 98-02; Nat Adv for Unity in Miss 03-08; rtd 08. *Pelham House, Little Lane, Wrawby, Brigg DN20 8RW* Tel (01652) 657484 E-mail johngcole@btinternet.com

COLE, John Spensley. b 39. Clare Coll Cam BA62 MA66 FCA65. Linc Th Coll 78. d 80 p 81. C Cowes St Mary *Portsm* 80-83; C Portchester 83-87; V Modbury *Ex* 87-95; R Aveton Gifford 87-95; TR Modbury, Bigbury, Ringmore w Kingston etc 95-98; P-in-c Alne and Brafferton w Pilmoor, Myton-on-Swale etc *York* 98-05; rtd 05. *11 Long Meadow, Farnsfield, Newark NG22 8DR* Tel (01623) 883595 E-mail johnlizcole@firenet.uk.net

COLE, Michael Berkeley. b 44. Cuddesdon Coll. d 72 p 73. C Shepshed *Leic* 72-76; V Leic St Chad 76-79; Hon C Painswick w Sheepscombe *Glouc* 94-97; Hon C Painswick w Sheepscombe and Cranham 97-98; Hon C Fairford and Kempsford w Whelford 98-04; TR Redhorn *Sarum* 04-09; rtd 09. *Homestead, Church End, Twyning, Tewkesbury GL20 6DA* E-mail mbcole@uwclub.net

COLE, Michael George. b 35. CD75. Wesley Th Sem Washington DMin88. Kelham Th Coll 56 Lich Th Coll 57. d 60 p 61. C Doncaster Ch Ch *Sheff* 60-63; Chapl RAF 63-68; Canada 68-82; USA from 82; rtd 98. *1202 Stonegate Way, Crozet VA 22932-3150, USA* E-mail mvgrcr6@comcast.net

COLE, Canon Michael John. b 34. St Pet Hall Ox BA56 MA60. Ridley Hall Cam 56. d 58 p 59. C Finchley Ch Ch *Lon* 58; C Leeds St Geo *Ripon* 58-61; Travelling Sec IVF 61-64; V Crookes St Thos *Sheff* 64-71; R Rusholme H Trin *Man* 71-75; V Woodford Wells *Chelmsf* 75-00; Chapl Leytonstone Ho Hosp 85-00; Hon Can Chelmsf Cathl 89-00; RD Redbridge 95-00; rtd 00; Perm to Offic *Chelmsf* 00-06. *1 Paradise Drive, Eastbourne BN20 7SX* Tel (01323) 723425

COLE, Canon Norma Joan. b 46. EAMTC 93. d 96 p 97. C Ipswich St Mary at Stoke w St Pet *St E* 96-97; C Ipswich St Mary at Stoke w St Pet and St Fran 97-99; V Gt Cornard 99-04; V Rushen *S & M* 04-10; Hon Can St German's Cathl 09-10; rtd 10. *Rushen Vicarage, Barracks Road, Port St Mary, Isle of Man IM9 5LP* Tel (01624) 832275

COLE, Canon Peter George Lamont. b 27. Pemb Coll Cam BA49 MA52. Cuddesdon Coll 50. d 52 p 53. C Aldershot St Mich *Guildf* 52-55; C St Jo Cathl Bulawayo S Rhodesia 55-59; P-in-c Riverside All SS 55-59; R 59-62; Chapl St Steph Coll Balla Balla 63-65; V Bromley St Andr *Roch* 65-72; V Folkestone St Mary and St Eanswythe *Cant* 72-87; Hon Can Cant Cathl 80-87; V E and W Worldham, Hartley Mauditt w Kingsley etc *Win* 87-92; RD Alton 89-92; rtd 92; RD Petworth *Chich* 94-95; Perm to Offic from 95. *29 Swan View, Pulborough RH20 2BF* Tel (01798) 873238

COLE, Stanley Westley Tom. b 28. d 97 p 98. NSM Chalke Valley *Sarum* 97-10; rtd 10. *Cranborne Farm, Old Blandford Road, Coombe Bissett, Salisbury SP5 4LF* Tel and fax (01722) 718240 E-mail revcolecb@talktalk.net

COLE, Timothy Alexander Robertson. b 60. Aber Univ MA83 Edin Univ BD86. Edin Th Coll 83. d 86 p 87. C Dunfermline *St And* 86-89; Vice-Provost St Andr Cathl Inverness 89-90; R Inverness St Andr 89-90; R Edin St Mich and All SS 90-95; CF from 95; Chapl R Memorial Chpl Sandhurst 07-08. *c/o MOD Chaplains (Army)* Tel (01264) 381140 Fax 381824

COLE, Mrs Vanessa Anne. b 73. K Alfred's Coll Win BA94. Trin Coll Bris BA03. d 04 p 05. C Congresbury w Puxton and Hewish St Ann *B & W* 04-09; TV Portway and Danebury *Win* from 09. *The Rectory, Over Wallop, Stockbridge SO20 8HT* Tel (01264) 782615 E-mail vanessa@cole.org.uk

COLE, William. b 45. Oak Hill Th Coll BA96. d 96 p 97. NSM St Keverne *Truro* 96-99; P-in-c St Ruan w St Grade and

Landewednack 99-10; rtd 10. *16 Copperas Close, Lowca, Whitehaven CA28 6QU* E-mail billcole124@btinternet.com

COLE-BAKER, Peter Massey. b 58. New Univ of Ulster BSc80 TCD BTh98. CITC 95. **d** 98 **p** 99. C Ballywillan *Conn* 98-01; I Templemore w Thurles and Kilfithmone *C & O* from 01. *The Rectory, Roscrea Road, Templemore, Co Tipperary, Republic of Ireland* Tel and fax (00353) (504) 31175 E-mail pcolebaker@eircom.net

COLEBROOK, Canon Christopher John. b 36. Qu Mary Coll Lon BA60 BD69. St D Coll Lamp 60. **d** 62 **p** 63. C Llandeilo Tal-y-bont *S & B* 62-66; C Llansamlet 66-71; V Nantmel w St Harmon's and Llanwrthwl 71-76; V Glantawe 76-85; V Gowerton 85-01; RD Llwchwr 93-00; Hon Can Brecon Cathl 97-01; Prec 00-01; rtd 01. *79 Vivian Road, Sketty, Swansea SA2 0UN*

COLEBROOK, Peter Acland. b 29. Coates Hall Edin 52. **d** 55 **p** 56. C Northfield *Birm* 58-62; C Bideford *Ex* 62-66; rtd 89; Perm to Offic *Sarum* from 01. *Danes Lee, Ham Lane, Marnhull, Sturminster Newton DT10 1JN* Tel (01258) 820246

COLEBROOKE, Andrew. b 50. Imp Coll Lon BSc71 MSc72 PhD75. Ridley Hall Cam 92. **d** 94 **p** 95. C Shrub End *Chelmsf* 94-98; R Mistley w Manningtree and Bradfield 98-09; RD Harwich 04-09; R Icknield Way Villages from 09. *The Rectory, 1 Hall Lane, Great Chishill, Royston SG8 8SG* Tel (01763) 838703 E-mail a.colebrooke@btinternet.com

COLEBY, Andrew Mark. b 59. Linc Coll Ox MA85 DPhil85 Dur Univ BA90 FRHistS88. Cranmer Hall Dur 88. **d** 91 **p** 92. C Heeley *Sheff* 91-93; TV Gleadless 94-97; Chapl Ox Brookes Univ 97-01; P-in-c Didcot All SS 01-06; Dioc FE Officer and Chapl Abingdon and Witney Coll 06-09; Soc Resp Adv *St Alb* from 09; Perm to Offic *Ox* from 11. *Silver Birches, Picklers Hill, Abingdon OX14 2BA* Tel (01235) 528374 E-mail acoleby@stalbans.anglican.org

COLEMAN, Aidan William. b 56. St Jo Coll Nottm 97. **d** 99 **p** 00. C Llandudno *Ban* 99-02; TV Bangor and P-in-c Llandygai and Maes y Groes 02-05; P-in-c Rhosymedre w Penycae *St As* from 05. *The Vicarage, Church Street, Rhosymedre, Wrexham LL14 3EA* Tel (01978) 810786

COLEMAN, Mrs Ann Valerie. b 51. K Coll Lon BD72 Heythrop Coll Lon MA03. St Aug Coll Cant. **dss** 80 **d** 87 **p** 94. Hampstead Garden Suburb *Lon* 80-84; Golders Green 85-87; Selection Sec and Voc Adv ACCM 87-91; Teacher Bp Ramsey Sch 92-93; Chapl 93-99; Dir of Ords Willesden Area *Lon* 96-99; Course Leader NTMTC 99-04; Hon C Eastcote St Lawr *Lon* 93-04; Dir Wydale Hall *York* 04-08; Dioc Moderator Reader Tr 05-08; Tutor St Mellitus Coll *Lon* from 08. *12 Craneswater Park, Southall UB2 5RP* Tel (020) 8574 8352 E-mail annvc@tiscali.co.uk

COLEMAN, Brian James. b 36. K Coll Cam BA58 MA61. Ripon Hall Ox 58. **d** 60 **p** 61. C Allestree *Derby* 60-65; V Allestree St Nic 65-69; Chapl and Lect St Mich Coll Salisbury 69-77; P-in-c Matlock Bank *Derby* 77-86; R Frimley *Guildf* 86-92; V Guildf All SS 92-02; rtd 02; Perm to Offic *Sarum* from 03. *6 Kingfisher Close, Salisbury SP2 8JE* Tel (01722) 410034

COLEMAN, Brian Ray. b 71. California State Univ Fullerton BPhil94. Seabury-Western Th Sem MDiv98. **d** 98 **p** 99. Assoc R Los Angeles St Jas USA 98-01; C Sheff St Leon Norwood 01-03; Chapl N Gen Hosp NHS Trust Sheff 01-03; P-in-c Sheff St Pet Abbeydale 03-08; P-in-c Sheff St Oswald 03-08; R Battle Creek St Thos USA from 08. *St Thomas's Rectory, 252 Chestnut Street, Battle Creek MI 49017-3348, USA* E-mail frbrian@btopenworld.com

COLEMAN, David. b 49. K Coll Lon BD72 AKC72. St Aug Coll Cant 72. **d** 73 **p** 74. C Is of Dogs Ch ch and St Jo w St Luke *Lon* 73-77; C Greenford H Cross 77-80; V Cricklewood St Pet 80-85; V Golders Green 85-90; V Eastcote St Lawr 90-04; P-in-c Upper Ryedale and CME Officer Cleveland Adnry *York* 04-08; V Heston *Lon* from 08. *12 Craneswater Park, Southall UB2 5RP* Tel (020) 8574 8352 E-mail frdavid.coleman@tiscali.co.uk

COLEMAN, David Kenneth. b 60. SWMTC 06. **d** 09 **p** 10. NSM Bickleigh and Shaugh Prior *Ex* from 09. *4 Torbridge Road, Horrabridge, Yelverton PL20 7SD* Tel (01822) 853311 E-mail deekaycee@hotmail.com

COLEMAN, Frank. b 58. Hull Univ BA79. St Steph Ho Ox BA83 MA87. **d** 83 **p** 84. C Brandon *Dur* 83-85; C Newton Aycliffe 85-88; V Denford w Ringstead *Pet* 88-00; P-in-c Islip 95-00; V Caldecote, Northill and Old Warden *St Alb* from 00. *The Vicarage, 2A Biggleswade Road, Upper Caldecote, Biggleswade SG18 9BL* Tel (01767) 315578 Fax 317988 Mobile 07738-357458 E-mail frankcoleman@ntlworld.com

COLEMAN, John Harold. b 58. Univ of Wales BTh03. **d** 86 **p** 87. NSM Dover St Martin *Cant* 86-92; V St Mary's Bay w St Mary-in-the-Marsh etc 92-03; P-in-c New Romney w Old Romney and Midley 95-03; rtd 03; Perm to Offic *Cant* from 03. *119 Canterbury Road, Hawkinge, Folkestone CT18 7BS* Tel (01303) 893952 E-mail john.coleman8@btinternet.com

COLEMAN, Jonathan Mark. b 59. Kent Univ BA81. Qu Coll Birm MA99. **d** 99 **p** 00. C Warrington St Elphin *Liv* 99-02; P-in-c Liv St Chris Norris Green 02-07; Area Dean W Derby and Hon Can Liv Cathl 06-07; P-in-c W Derby St Mary 07-09; P-in-c W Derby St Jas 07-09; V W Derby St Mary and St Jas from 09. *The Rectory, Meadow Lane, West Derby, Liverpool L12 5EA* Tel 0151-256 6600 E-mail markcoleman@bigfoot.com

COLEMAN, Ms Julie Victoria. b 62. Cant Ch Ch Univ PGCE08. St Jo Coll Nottm 09. **d** 11. C Aylesham w Adisham *Cant* from 11; C Nonington w Wymynswold and Goodnestone etc from 11. *61 The Street, Adisham, Canterbury CT3 3JN* Tel 07583-774857 (mobile) E-mail jvcoleman@btinternet.com

COLEMAN, Michael. b 28. Nat Coll Div LTh90. **d** 95. NSM E Kilbride *Glas* 95-99; NSM Motherwell 99-01; NSM Wishaw 99-01; rtd 01; Lic to Offic *Glas* from 01. *51 Lammermoor, Calderwood, East Kilbride, Glasgow G74 3SE* Tel (01355) 902523

COLEMAN, Neil Geoffrey. b 77. Trin Coll Bris BA11. **d** 11. C N Mundham w Hunston and Merston *Chich* from 11. *3 Willowmead Close, Runcton, Chichester PO20 1NH* Tel (01243) 785629 Mobile 07826-850273 E-mail n-coleman@hotmail.co.uk

COLEMAN, Ms Nicola Jane. b 63. Goldsmiths' Coll Lon BA86. Ripon Coll Cuddesdon 99. **d** 01 **p** 02. C Croydon St Jo *S'wark* 01-05; P-in-c S Norwood H Innocents from 05. *Holy Innocents' Vicarage, 192A Selhurst Road, London SE25 6XX* Tel (020) 8653 2063 E-mail holyinnocents@btinternet.com

COLEMAN, Patrick Francis. b 58. Reading Univ Pontifical Univ Rome STL STB PhB. Ven English Coll Rome 77. **d** 82 **p** 83. In RC Ch 82-91; NSM Abergavenny St Mary w Llanwenarth Citra *Mon* 96-99; Asst Chapl Milan w Genoa and Varese *Eur* 99-01; R Goetre w Llanover *Mon* 01-06; Dir CME 02-06; P-in-c Abertillery w Cwmtillery 06-11, V Abertillery w Cwmtillery w Llanhilleth etc from 11. *The Vicarage, Church Street, Abertillery NP13 1DA* Tel (01495) 212246

COLEMAN, Canon Peter Nicholas. b 42. St Mich Coll Llan 83. **d** 85 **p** 86. C Skewen *Llan* 85-88; R Ystradyfodwg 88-07; P-in-c Treorchy and Treherbert 04-07; RD Rhondda 96-04; Can Llan Cathl 04-07; rtd 07. *15 Pant Hendre, Pencoed, Bridgend CF35 6LN*

COLEMAN, Richard Ian. b 70. Open Univ BSc00. Wycliffe Hall Ox 05. **d** 07 **p** 08. C Peterlee *Dur* 07-11; P-in-c Barton in Fabis *S'well* from 11; P-in-c Gotham from 11; P-in-c Kingston and Ratcliffe-on-Soar from 11; P-in-c Thrumpton from 11. *The New Rectory, 39 Leake Road, Gotham, Nottingham NG11 0HW* Tel 0115-983 0608 E-mail coleman@orpheusmail.co.uk

COLEMAN, Canon Sybil Jean. b 30. St Deiniol's Hawarden 83. **d** 85 **p** 97. NSM Manselton *S & B* 85-90; C Swansea St Mark and St Jo 90-94; P-in-c 94-98; V 98-00; Hon Can Brecon Cathl 98-00; rtd 00. *Beckley, 25 Beverley Gardens, Fforestfach, Swansea SA5 5DR* Tel (01792) 584280

COLEMAN, Terence Norman. b 37. St Mich Coll Llan 83. **d** 85 **p** 86. C Machen *Mon* 85-87; C Penmaen and Crumlin 87-89; V 89-93; V Newbridge 93-02; rtd 02. *2 Fox Avenue, Newbridge, Newport NP11 4HP* Tel (01495) 243839

COLEMAN, Timothy. b 57. Southn Univ BSc79 MBACP. Ridley Hall Cam 87. **d** 89 **p** 90. C Bisley and W End *Guildf* 89-93; C Hollington St Jo *Chich* 93-97; V Aldborough Hatch *Chelmsf* 97-02; Chapl Princess Alexandra Hosp NHS Trust 02-04; Chapl Barking Havering and Redbridge Hosps NHS Trust from 04. *The Chaplain's Office, Queen's Hospital, Rom Valley Way, Romford RM7 0AG* Tel (01708) 503201 E-mail tim.coleman@bhrhospitals.nhs.uk

COLERIDGE, William Paul Hugh. b 76. Newc Univ LLB98 Solicitor 01. Wycliffe Hall Ox 07. **d** 09 **p** 10. C Ches Square St Mich w St Phil *Lon* from 09. *24 Sullivan Road, London SE11 4UH* Tel 07968-078432 (mobile) E-mail william@coleridge129.freeserve.co.uk

COLES, Alasdair Charles. b 67. St Andr Univ BSc90 Homerton Coll Cam PGCE91 Heythrop Coll Lon PhD03. Ripon Coll Cuddesdon 06. **d** 96 **p** 97. C Wymondham *Nor* 96-99; Min Can and Sacr St Paul's Cathl 99-04; P-in-c Pimlico St Mary Bourne Street 04-07; V 07-09; P-in-c Pimlico St Barn 04-07; V 07-09; Asst Vice Prin and Chapl All SS Academy Dunstable from 09; PV Westmr Abbey from 04. *All Saints Academy, Houghton Road, Dunstable LU5 5AB* Tel (01582) 619700 ext 205 Fax 619701 Mobile 07729-962723 E-mail alasdaircoles@allsaintsacademydunstable.org

COLES, Alasdair John. b 66. Pemb Coll Ox BA87 Green Coll Ox BM, BCh90 CCC Cam PhD98 MRCP94. ERMC 05. **d** 08 **p** 09. NSM Chesterton St Andr *Ely* from 08. *Department of Neurology, Box 165, Addenbrooke's Hospital, Cambridge CB2 2QQ* Tel (01223) 216751 Fax 336941 E-mail ajc1020@medschl.cam.ac.uk

COLES, Miss Alison Elizabeth. b 60. St Mary's Coll Dur BA81. Ripon Coll Cuddesdon 95. **d** 97 **p** 98. C Leckhampton SS Phil and Jas w Cheltenham St Jas *Glouc* 97-00; Asst Chapl Dudley Gp of Hosps NHS Trust 00-04; Chapl Walsall Hosps NHS Trust from 04. *Walsall Hospitals NHS Trust, Manor Hospital, Moat Road, Walsall WS2 9PS* Tel (01922) 656216

COLES, Christopher Wayne. b 58. St Mich Coll Llan 97. **d** 99 **p** 00. C Coity w Nolton *Llan* 99-02; C Canton Cardiff 02-07;

P-in-c Porth Newydd from 07. *St John's Vicarage, Cymmer, Porth CF39 9HW* Tel (01443) 682219

✠COLES, The Rt Revd David John. b 43. Auckland Univ MA67 Otago Univ BD69 MTh71 Man Univ PhD74. St Jo Coll Auckland 66. **d** 68 **p** 69 **c** 90. C Remuera New Zealand 68-70; Chapl Selwyn Coll Dunedin 70-71; Hon C Fallowfield *Man* 72-74; Chapl Hulme Hall 73-74; V Glenfield New Zealand 74-76; V Takapuna 76-80; Dean Napier 80-84; Dean Christchurch 84-90; Bp Christchurch from 90. *PO Box 4438, Christchurch 8140, New Zealand* Tel (0064) (3) 351 7711 *or* 363 0913 Fax 372 3357 E-mail bishop@chch.ang.org.nz

COLES, Preb Francis Herbert. b 35. Selw Coll Cam BA59 MA63. Coll of Resurr Mirfield 59. **d** 61 **p** 62. C Wolvercote *Ox* 61-65; C Farnham Royal 65-69; V Lynton and Brendon *Ex* 69-73; V Countisbury 70-73; TR Lynton, Brendon, Countisbury, Lynmouth etc 73-76; P-in-c Iffley *Ox* 76-88; V Ivybridge w Harford *Ex* 88-00; Preb Ex Cathl from 98; rtd 00; Perm to Offic *Ex* from 00. *8 Glenthorne Road, Exeter EX4 4QU* Tel (01392) 420238

COLES, Graham Robert. b 60. Qu Coll Birm 07. **d** 09 **p** 10. C Lillington and Old Milverton *Cov* from 09; C Leamington Spa H Trin from 09. *10 Sandown Close, Leamington Spa CV32 7SX* Tel 07786-774881 (mobile)

COLES, John Spencer Halstaff. b 50. Hertf Coll Ox BA72 MA76. Wycliffe Hall Ox 72. **d** 75 **p** 76. C Reading Greyfriars *Ox* 75-79; C Clifton Ch Ch w Em *Bris* 79-82; V Woodside Park St Barn *Lon* 82-06; C 06-11; Dir New Wine Internat Min from 11. *33 Arnos Road, London N11 1AP* Tel (020) 3441 5264

COLES, Matthew Simon Robert. b 79. UEA BA02. Ridley Hall Cam 06. **d** 09 **p** 10. C Gt Chesham *Ox* from 09. *31 Chapmans Crescent, Chesham HP5 2QT* Tel 07736-464537 (mobile) E-mail mattsr7@yahoo.com

COLES, Mrs Pamela. b 39. Nottm Univ CertEd59. NOC 04. **d** 05 **p** 06. NSM Clayton *Bradf* 05-09; Perm to Offic from 09. *4 Ferndale Avenue, Clayton, Bradford BD14 6PG* Tel (01274) 427956 E-mail geoffandpamcoles@yahoo.com

COLES, Richard Keith Robert. b 62. K Coll Lon BA94 AKC94 Leeds Univ MA05. Coll of Resurr Mirfield 03. **d** 05 **p** 06. C Boston *Linc* 05-07; C Wilton Place St Paul *Lon* 07-11; Chapl R Academy of Music 07-08; P-in-c Finedon *Pet* from 11. *St Mary's Vicarage, Church Hill, Finedon, Wellingborough NN9 5NR* Tel (01933) 681786 E-mail revdrichardcoles@yahoo.co.uk

COLES, Canon Robert Reginald. b 47. Surrey Univ BSc69. Cant Sch of Min 82. **d** 85 **p** 86. NSM Sittingbourne St Mich *Cant* 85-87; C St Laur in Thanet 87-93; P-in-c St Nicholas at Wade w Sarre and Chislet w Hoath from 93; P-in-c Minster w Monkton from 96; Hon Can Cant Cathl from 09. *The Vicarage, St Mildred's Road, Minster, Ramsgate CT12 4DE* Tel (01843) 821250

COLES, Stephen Richard. b 49. Univ Coll Ox BA70 MA74 Leeds Univ BA80. Coll of Resurr Mirfield 78. **d** 81 **p** 82. C Stoke Newington St Mary *Lon* 81-84; Chapl K Coll Cam 84-89; V Finsbury Park St Thos *Lon* from 89. *25 Romilly Road, London N4 2QY* Tel (020) 7359 5741 E-mail cardinal.jeoffry@btconnect.com

COLES, Mrs Sylvia Margaret. b 48. ERMC 04. **d** 07 **p** 08. NSM Northampton St Benedict *Pet* 07-10; NSM Duston from 10. *37 Delapre Crescent Road, Northampton NN4 8NG* Tel (01604) 767305 E-mail lizziesgranny@talktalk.net

COLEY (née JOHNSON), Mrs Emma Louise. b 76. Ex Univ BA97 PGCE98. Wycliffe Hall Ox BTh04. **d** 04 **p** 05. C Wendover and Halton *Ox* 04-09; C Kennington from 09; C Radley and Sunningwell from 09. *The Vicarage, Ross Court, The Avenue, Kennington, Oxford OX1 5AD* Tel (01865) 735135 E-mail emcoley@me.com

COLEY, Peter Leonard. b 45. Bath Univ BSc67 City Univ MSc84 CEng MIMechE. Oak Hill Th Coll 85. **d** 87 **p** 88. C Mile Cross *Nor* 87-92; R Stratton St Mary w Stratton St Michael etc 92-01; R Kirby-le-Soken w Gt Holland *Chelmsf* 01-10; rtd 10. *6 Forest Rise, Liss GU33 7AU* Tel (01730) 300659 Mobile 07706-037108 E-mail rev.petercoley@gmail.com

COLLARD, Canon Harold. b 27. Wycliffe Hall Ox 51. **d** 53 **p** 54. C Rainham *Chelmsf* 53-56; C Kingston upon Hull H Trin *York* 56-59; V Upper Armley *Ripon* 59-68; R Chesterfield H Trin *Derby* 68-77; P-in-c Matlock Bath 77-83; V 83-92; Hon Can Derby Cathl 87-92; RD Wirksworth 88-92; rtd 92; Perm to Offic *Ripon* from 92. *10 Kirkby Avenue, Ripon HG4 2DR* Tel (01765) 606306

COLLARD, Norton Harvey. b 22. Open Univ BA80. Roch Th Coll 63. **d** 65 **p** 66. C Swanley St Mary *Roch* 65-67; C Dartford H Trin 67-70; V Grantham St Anne *Linc* 70-87; rtd 87; Perm to Offic *Linc* 87-02. *1 Kenwick Drive, Grantham NG31 9DP* Tel (01476) 577345

COLLAS, Canon Victor John. b 23. Pemb Coll Ox BA44 MA48. Wycliffe Hall Ox 49. **d** 51 **p** 52. C Milton *Win* 51-58; R Guernsey St Andr 58-81; Hon Can Win Cathl 78-81; Perm to Offic from 81; rtd 88. *Paradis, La Rue du Paradis, Vale, Guernsey GY3 5BL* Tel (01481) 244450

COLLEDGE, Ms Anthea June. b 78. St Jo Coll Ox BA00 Imp Coll Lon MSc06 MPhil09 St Jo Coll Dur BA10. Cranmer Hall Dur 08. **d** 10 **p** 11. C Wortley de Leeds *Ripon* from 10. *Farnley Rectory, 16 Cross Lane, Leeds LS12 5AA* Tel 0113-263 9225 Mobile 07518-319475 E-mail a.j.colledge@googlemail.com

COLLEDGE, Christopher Richard. b 58. Chich Th Coll. **d** 82 **p** 83. C Deal St Leon *Cant* 82-83; C Deal St Leon and St Rich and Sholden 83-85; Bermuda 85-88; TV Wickford and Runwell *Chelmsf* 88-90; Chapl Runwell Hosp Wickford 88-90; Chapl RAD 90-03; rtd 04. *Address withheld by request* E-mail chriscolledge@aol.com

COLLESS, Mrs Salma. b 55. SRN77 RM80. EAMTC 89. **d** 92 **p** 94. NSM Chesterton St Andr *Ely* 92-93; Australia from 93; Hon Dn Chapman 93; C Curtin 94-96; Chapl Brindabella Gardens 96; P Worker Bernie Court 97; Asst P Woden 97-98. *12 Sollya Place, Rivett ACT 2611, Australia* Tel (0061) (2) 6288 7835 Mobile 414-755756

COLLETT, George Ernest. b 48. Cant Sch of Min 01. **d** 04 **p** 05. NSM Bromley H Trin *Roch* from 04. *Holy Trinity Cottage, 1 Church Lane, Bromley BR2 8LB* Tel (020) 8462 7561 E-mail george.collett@diocese-rochester.org

COLLETT-WHITE, Thomas Charles. b 36. Trin Coll Cam BA61 MA86. Ridley Hall Cam 60. **d** 62 **p** 63. C Gillingham St Mark *Roch* 62-66; V 79-90; C Normanton *Wakef* 66-69; V Highbury New Park St Aug *Lon* 69-76; R Huntingdon w Ormstown Canada 76-79; Chapl Medway Hosp Gillingham 79-85; P-in-c Clerkenwell St Jas and St Jo w St Pet *Lon* 90-96; rtd 01; Perm to Offic *Cant* from 06. *77 The Street, Boughton-under-Blean, Faversham ME13 9BE* Tel (01227) 750770

COLLICUTT McGRATH, Joanna Ruth. b 54. LMH Ox BA76 MA85 Lon Univ MPhil78 Ox Brookes Univ PhD98. Wycliffe Hall Ox 00 Ripon Coll Cuddesdon 05. **d** 06 **p** 07. NSM Witney *Ox* 06-10; Dioc Adv for Spiritual Care for Older People from 10. *Heythrop College, Kensington Square, London W8 5HQ* Tel (020) 7795 6600 E-mail jcollicutt@aol.com

COLLIE, Canon Bertie Harold Guy. b 28. Glas Univ MB, ChB56. Glas NSM Course 75. **d** 76 **p** 77. NSM Ayr *Glas* 76-84; NSM Maybole 76-04; NSM Girvan 84-04; NSM Pinmore 84-04; Dioc Supernumerary 91-99; Can St Mary's Cathl 96-99; Hon Can from 99. *4 Savoy Park, Ayr KA7 2XA* Tel (01292) 285889 E-mail b.collie@sky.com

COLLIER, Anthony Charles. b 45. Peterho Cam BA68 MA72 Whitelands Coll Lon PGCE76. Cuddesdon Coll 68. **d** 71 **p** 72. C N Holmwood *Guildf* 71-75; Perm to Offic S'*wark* 75-79; Chapl Colfe's Sch Lon 80-10; rtd 10; Hon C Shirley St Jo *Cant* 80-84; Hon C Shirley St Jo S'*wark* from 85. *56 Bennetts Way, Croydon CR0 8AB* Tel (020) 8777 6456 E-mail accollier@hotmail.com

COLLIER, Clive. *See* COLLIER, Paul Clive

COLLIER, Mrs Janice Margaret. b 57. MCSP79. Cam Th Federation 99. **d** 01 **p** 02. C Formby H Trin *Liv* 01-05; P-in-c Hale 05-10; TR S Widnes from 10. *The Vicarage, 2 Vicarage Close, Hale Village, Liverpool L24 4BH* Tel 0151-425 3195

COLLIER, Michael Francis. b 29. Wycliffe Hall Ox 71. **d** 73 **p** 74. C Hamstead St Paul *Birm* 73-75; P-in-c Castleton *Derby* 75-80; P-in-c Hope 78-80; V Hope and Castleton 80-97; RD Bakewell and Eyam 90-95; rtd 97; Perm to Offic *Derby* from 97. *Buffers Cottage, Station Road, Hope, Hope Valley S33 6RR* Tel (01433) 620915

COLLIER, Paul Clive. b 53. Trin Coll Bris 80. **d** 82 **p** 83. C Hazlemere *Ox* 82-90; V from 90. *The New Vicarage, 260 Amersham Road, High Wycombe HP15 7PZ* Tel (01494) 439404

COLLIER, Paul Edward. b 63. Mert Coll Ox BA85 Lon Univ PGCE87 Solicitor 93. S'wark Ord Course 91. **d** 94 **p** 95. C E Dulwich St Jo S'*wark* 94-97; C-in-c Bermondsey St Hugh CD 97-02; Chapl Goldsmiths' Coll Lon 03-09; Hon C Dulwich St Barn 09-11; C Peckham St Sav from 11. *5 Wickham Road, London SE4 1PF* Tel (020) 8692 1821 E-mail paul.collier3@virgin.net

COLLIER, Richard John Millard. b 45. FRSA92. EAMTC 78. **d** 81 **p** 82. NSM Nor St Pet Mancroft w St Jo Maddermarket 81-97; NSM Thurton from 99. *Old Manor Farm, Fox Road, Framingham Pigot, Norwich NR14 7PZ* Tel (01508) 492916 E-mail rjsjc@yahoo.com

COLLIER, Stefan John. b 74. Man Univ BSc95 St Andr Univ PhD99 Cam Univ BTh09. Ridley Hall Cam 07. **d** 09 **p** 10. C E Win from 09. *28 Longfield Road, Winchester SO23 0NT* E-mail curateastwinchester@googlemail.com

COLLIER, Stephen John. b 45. Trin Coll Ox MA68 Univ of Wales (Cardiff) DipSW74. Qu Coll Birm 92. **d** 94 **p** 95. C Thorpe St Andr *Nor* 94-98; C Nor St Pet Mancroft w St Jo Maddermarket 98-01; R Kessingland, Gisleham and Rushmere 01-05; rtd 05; Hon C N Greenford All Hallows *Lon* from 06. *9 Drew Gardens, Greenford UB6 7QF* Tel (020) 8903 9697

COLLIER, Susan Margaret. b 42. Cam Univ MB, BChir73. NOC 95. **d** 98 **p** 99. NSM Dringhouses *York* from 98. *12 St Helen's Road, York YO24 1HP* Tel (01904) 706064 Fax 708052

COLLIN, Terry. b 39. St Aid Birkenhead 65. **d** 67 **p** 68. C Bolton St Jas w St Chrys *Bradf* 67-71; C Keighley 71-74; V Greengates

74-04; rtd 04; Perm to Offic *Bradf* from 05. *275 Leeds Road, Eccleshill, Bradford BD2 3LD* Tel (01274) 200855

COLLING, Canon James Oliver (Joc). b 30. MBE95. Man Univ BA50. Cuddesdon Coll 52. **d** 54 **p** 55. C Wigan All SS *Liv* 54-59; V Padgate Ch Ch 59-71; R Padgate 71-73; RD Warrington 70-82 and 87-89; AD 89-95; R Warrington St Elphin 73-97; Hon Can Liv Cathl 76-97; Chapl to The Queen 90-00; rtd 97; Perm to Offic *Ches* 99-11. *The College of St Barnabas, Blackberry Lane, Lingfield RH7 6NJ* Tel (01342) 870260

COLLING, Terence John. b 47. Linc Th Coll 84. **d** 86 **p** 87. C Wood End *Cov* 86-90; V Willenhall 90-02; V Wolvey w Burton Hastings, Copston Magna etc from 02. *St John's Vicarage, School Lane, Wolvey, Hinckley LE10 3LH* Tel (01455) 220385 Fax 221590 E-mail tc@vicwolvey.fsnet.co.uk

COLLINGBOURNE, David Edward. b 42. St D Coll Lamp. **d** 01. Treas Dioc Coun of Educn *Mon* from 94; NSM Bishton 01-06; NSM Newport Ch Ch 06-08; NSM Bedwas w Machen w Rudry from 08. *The Rectory, Rectory Gardens, Machen, Caerphilly CF83 8SU* Tel (01633) 440321 E-mail davidcollingbourne42@tiscali.co.uk

COLLINGBOURNE, Mrs Susan Lynne. b 48. Caerleon Coll of Educn TCert75 Univ of Wales (Cardiff) BEd82 MEd94. **d** 09 **p** 10. NSM Maesglas and Duffryn *Mon* from 09; Dioc Child Protection Officer from 98. *The Rectory, Rectory Gardens, Machen, Caerphilly CF83 8SU* Tel (01633) 440321 E-mail susan.collingbourne@tinyworld.co.uk

COLLINGE, Mrs Christine Elizabeth. b 47. Doncaster Coll of Educn CertEd68. SAOMC 95. **d** 98 **p** 99. NSM W Slough *Ox* 98-04; TV Stantonbury and Willen from 04. *29 Bradwell Road, Bradville, Milton Keynes MK13 7AX* Tel (01908) 314224 E-mail chriscollinge@hotmail.com

COLLINGRIDGE, Graham Ian. b 58. Pemb Coll Ox BA80 MA84 Bedf Coll Lon MSc84 Anglia Ruskin Univ MA10. Ridley Hall Cam 07. **d** 09 **p** 10. C Bitterne Park *Win* from 09. *24 Lacon Close, Southampton SO18 1JA* Tel (023) 8058 4640 E-mail g.collingridge@btinternet.com

COLLINGS, Ms Helen Mary. b 67. Warwick Univ BA88 St Jo Coll Dur BA06 Jes Coll Ox PGCE90. Cranmer Hall Dur 04. **d** 06 **p** 07. C Ossett and Gawthorpe *Wakef* 06-09; P-in-c Sandal St Cath from 09. *10C Westfield Drive, Ossett WF5 8HJ* Tel (01924) 276640 Mobile 07708-066063 E-mail helen@trinityossett.org.uk

COLLINGS, Robert Frank. b 26. Lon Univ BD53. ALCD52. **d** 52 **p** 53. C Bayswater *Lon* 52-55; Australia from 55; rtd 87. *Unit 5, 2 Wattle Street, Bunbury WA 6230, Australia* Tel (0061) (8) 9721 4520

COLLINGTON, Cameron James. b 69. Wycliffe Hall Ox BTh01. **d** 01 **p** 02. C Ealing St Paul *Lon* 01-05; V Hammersmith St Simon from 05. *153 Blythe Road, London W14 0HL* Tel (020) 7602 1043 E-mail bagpipes.collington@xalt.co.uk

COLLINGWOOD, Christopher Paul. b 54. Birm Univ BMus76 PGCE77 Ox Univ BA82 MA87 K Coll Lon MA01 PhD07 LRSM04. Ripon Coll Cuddesdon 80. **d** 83 **p** 84. C Tupsley *Heref* 83-86; Prec St Alb Abbey 86-90; V Bedford St Paul 90-97; Can Res and Prec Guildf Cathl 97-99; Hon C Loughton St Jo *Chelmsf* 99-09; Chapl Chigwell Sch Essex 99-09; Sen Tutor 01-09; R Minchinhampton w Box and Amberley *Glouc* from 09. *The Rectory, Butt Street, Minchinhampton, Stroud GL6 9JP* Tel (01453) 882289 E-mail rector@minchchurch.org.uk

COLLINGWOOD, Deryck Laurence. b 50. St Jo Coll Cam BA72. Edin Th Coll BD85. **d** 85 **p** 85. Chapl Napier Poly *Edin* 85-88; C Edin Ch Ch 85-88; TV 88-89; Tutor Edin Th Coll 89-94; Asst P Edin St Hilda and Edin St Fillan 94-03; Chapl Napier Univ 95-03; P-in-c Dalmahoy 03-06; R from 06. *St Mary's Rectory, Dalmahoy, Kirknewton EH27 8EB* Tel 0131-333 1312 E-mail collingwoods@supanet.com

COLLINGWOOD, Graham Lewis. b 63. Open Univ BA92 Ex Univ MA98. St Steph Ho Ox 92. **d** 95 **p** 96. C Heavitree w Ex St Paul 95-97; CF 97-99; C St Marychurch *Ex* 99-00; C Cottingham *York* 00-02; Chapl RAF from 02. *Chaplaincy Services, Valiant Block, HQ Air Command, RAF High Wycombe HP14 4UE* Tel (01494) 496800 Fax 496343

COLLINGWOOD, John Jeremy Raynham. b 37. Barrister 64 CCC Cam BA60 MA68 Lon Univ BD78. Trin Coll Bris 75. **d** 78 **p** 79. C Henleaze *Bris* 78-80; P-in-c Clifton H Trin, St Andr and St Pet 80-81; V 81-91; RD Clifton 84-87; Bp's Officer for Miss and Evang 87-91; V Guildf Ch Ch 91-98; V Guildf Ch Ch w St Martha-on-the-Hill 98-02; RD Guildf 95-00; rtd 02. *The Old Manse, 55 Audley Road, Saffron Walden CB11 3HD* Tel (01799) 529055 E-mail mporokoso@aol.com

COLLINS, Adelbert Andrew. b 15. Lich Th Coll. **d** 61 **p** 62. C Sedgley All SS *Lich* 61-77; P-in-c Enville 77-81 and 86-88; R 81-86; C Kinver and Enville 88-90; rtd 90; Perm to Offic *Lich* and *Worc* from 90. *West Cottage, Bridgnorth Road, Enville, Stourbridge DY7 5JA* Tel (01384) 873733

COLLINS, Anthony James. b 63. NEOC 04. **d** 07 **p** 08. NSM Fountains Gp *Ripon* 07-08; NSM Dacre w Hartwith and Darley w Thornthwaite from 08. *Harvest Cottage, Sawley, Ripon HG4 3EQ* Tel (01765) 620393 Mobile 07971-245780

COLLINS, Barry Douglas. b 47. Kelham Th Coll 66. **d** 70 **p** 71. C Peel Green *Man* 70-73; C Salford St Phil w St Steph 73-75; R Blackley H Trin 75-79; Perm to Offic *Ripon* 80-82; *Pet* 83-93; *Cov* 85-93; *Ox* 93-97; P-in-c Bengeworth *Worc* 98-99; V from 99. *The Vicarage, 1 Broadway Road, Evesham WR11 3NB* Tel and fax (01386) 446164 E-mail barry.collins@tesco.net

COLLINS, Bruce Churton. b 47. BSc. Oak Hill Th Coll. **d** 83 **p** 84. C Notting Hill St Jo *Lon* 83-87; C Notting Hill St Jo and St Pet 87-90; V Roxeth Ch Ch and Harrow St Pet 90-93; P-in-c S Harrow St Paul 91-93; TR Roxeth 93-03; Overseer New Wine Internat Min 03-07; Hon C Roxeth 03-07; Perm to Offic *St D* from 07. *Address temp unknown* Tel 07989-402012 (mobile) E-mail bruce@collinsbruce.orangehome.co.uk

COLLINS, Ms Cheryl Anne. b 62. Rob Coll Cam BA85 MA89 MCA90. Ripon Coll Cuddesdon 91. **d** 93 **p** 94. C Sharrow St Andr *Sheff* 93-95; Chapl Sheff Univ 95-01; Hon C Endcliffe 96-01; P-in-c Barton *Ely* 01-10; P-in-c Coton 01-10; P-in-c Dry Drayton 01-10; RD Bourn 03-10; Miss P Red Lodge *St E* from 10; Perm to Offic *Ely* from 11. *28 Acorn Way, Red Lodge, Mildenhall IP28 8FY* Tel (01638) 551638 E-mail revcherylc@aol.com

COLLINS, Christopher. b 46. K Coll Lon BSc67 AKC67 Pemb Coll Ox BA70. St Steph Ho Ox 68. **d** 71 **p** 72. C Pennywell St Thos and Grindon St Oswald CD *Dur* 71-74; C Pallion 74-76; C Millfield St Mary 74-76; C Bishopwearmouth Gd Shep 74-76; C Harton Colliery 76-78; TV Winlaton 78-85; V Grangetown from 85. *15 Linthorpe Avenue, Seaham SR7 7JW* Tel 0191-581 7186

COLLINS, Canon Christopher David. b 43. Sheff Univ BA(Econ)64. Tyndale Hall Bris 65. **d** 68 **p** 69. C Rusholme H Trin *Man* 68-71; C Bushbury *Lich* 71-74; V Fairfield *Liv* 74-81; V Tunbridge Wells St Jo *Roch* 81-92; R Luton Ch Ch and Chapl Thames Gateway NHS Trust 92-05; Chapl Medway NHS Trust 92-99; RD Roch 94-00; P-in-c Cobham w Luddesdowne and Dode 05-08; Hon Can Roch Cathl 98-08; rtd 08. *2 Courtenay Gardens, Alphington, Exeter EX2 8UH* Tel (01392) 203975 E-mail canonchris@blueyonder.co.uk

COLLINS, Darren Victor. b 69. NTMTC. **d** 05 **p** 06. C Chingford SS Pet and Paul *Chelmsf* 05-07; Min Can St Alb Abbey 07-11; P-in-c Norton from 11. *Norton Vicarage, 17 Norton Way North, Letchworth Garden City SG6 1BY* Tel (01462) 685059 *or* 678133 E-mail frdarren@yahoo.com

COLLINS, Debra Michelle. b 67. **d** 11. NSM Cofton Hackett w Barnt Green *Birm* from 11. *72 Brookvale Road, Solihull B92 7HZ* Tel 0121-246 2877

COLLINS, Donard Michael. b 55. Oak Hill Th Coll BA83. **d** 83 **p** 84. C Lurgan Ch the Redeemer *D & D* 83-87; I Ardmore w Craigavon 87-98; I Killowen *D & R* from 98. *St John's Rectory, 4 Laurel Hill, Coleraine BT51 3AT* Tel (028) 7034 2629 E-mail revdonard@yahoo.com

COLLINS, The Ven Gavin Andrew. b 66. Trin Hall Cam BA89 MA93. Trin Coll Bris BA96 MA97. **d** 97 **p** 98. C Cambridge St Barn *Ely* 97-02; V Chorleywood Ch Ch *St Alb* from 02; RD Rickmansworth 06-11; Hon Can St Alb 09-11; Adn The Meon Portsm from 11. *Victoria Lodge, 36 Osborn Road, Fareham PO16 7DS* Tel (01329) 608895 E-mail gavin-collins@supanet.com *or* admeon@portsmouth.anglican.org

COLLINS, Guy James Douglas. b 74. St Andr Univ MTheol96 Peterho Cam PhD00. Westcott Ho Cam 96. **d** 00 **p** 01. C Barnes *S'wark* 00-03; R Huntington Valley USA from 03. *The Rectory, 2122 Washington Lane, Huntingdon Valley PA 19006-5824, USA*

COLLINS, Canon Ian Geoffrey. b 37. Hull Univ BA60 CertEd. Sarum Th Coll 60. **d** 62 **p** 63. C Gainsborough All SS *Linc* 62-65; Min Can Windsor 65-81; Succ Windsor 67-81; R Kirkby in Ashfield *S'well* 81-85; Can Res S'well Minster 85-02; P-in-c Edingley w Halam 91-00; rtd 02. *2 Marston Moor Road, Newark NG24 2GN* Tel (01636) 702866

COLLINS, Miss Janet May. b 55. Qu Mary Coll Lon BA78 St Jo Coll Dur BA84. Cranmer Hall Dur 82. **dss** 85 **d** 87 **p** 94. Willington *Newc* 85-88; C 87-88; Par Dn Stevenage St Hugh Chells *St Alb* 88-90; Par Dn Goldington 90-93; TD Witney *Ox* 93-94; TV 94-96; Tutor SAOMC 96-01; TV Langtree 99-01; P-in-c Weldon w Deene *Pet* 01-08; P-in-c Gt and Lt Oakley 01-08; RD Corby 02-07; P-in-c Pet H Spirit Bretton 08-10; P-in-c Corby SS Pet and Andr from 10; P-in-c Gt and Lt Oakley from 10. *The Rectory, 40 Beanfield Avenue, Corby NN18 0EH* Tel (01536) 267620 *or* 402442 E-mail rev.jan@talktalk.net

COLLINS, John Gilbert. b 32. S'wark Ord Course 67. **d** 71 **p** 72. C Coulsdon St Jo *S'wark* 71-75; Chapl St Fran Hosp Haywards Heath 75-84; Chapl Hurstwood Park Hosp Haywards Heath 75-84; R Stedham w Iping, Elsted and Treyford-cum-Didling *Chich* 84-92; rtd 92; Perm to Offic *Chich* 94-00. *12 Exeter Road, Broyle, Chichester PO19 5EF* Tel (01243) 536861

COLLINS, Preb John Theodore Cameron Bucke. b 25. Clare Coll Cam BA49 MA52. Ridley Hall Cam 49. **d** 51 **p** 52. C St Marylebone All So w SS Pet and Jo *Lon* 51-57; V Gillingham St Mark *Roch* 57-71; Chapl Medway Hosp Gillingham 70-71; V Canford Magna *Sarum* 71-80; RD Wimborne 79-80; V

Brompton H Trin w Onslow Square St Paul *Lon* 80-85; C 85-89; AD Chelsea 84-88; Preb St Paul's Cathl 85-89; rtd 89; Perm to Offic *Lon* 89-90; Perm to Offic *Win* 89-97. *27 Woodstock Close, Oxford OX2 8DB* Tel (01865) 556228

COLLINS, John William Michael. b 54. Bp Otter Coll 95. **d** 98 **p** 07. NSM S Patcham *Chich* 98-06; NSM Moulsecoomb from 06. *2 Buxted Rise, Brighton BN1 8FG* Tel (01273) 509388

COLLINS, Ms Kathryne Broncy. b 51. Portland State Univ BSc75 Lon Univ MSc76. Linc Th Coll 92. **d** 94 **p** 95. C Bishop's Castle w Mainstone *Heref* 94-98; P-in-c 98-01; V Bishop's Castle w Mainstone, Lydbury N etc 01-03; TV Wrexham *St As* 03-05; NSM from 05; Chapl NE Wales NHS Trust from 03. *Chaplain's Office, Wrexham Maelor Hospital, Croesnewydd Road, Wrexham LL13 7TD* Tel (01978) 725590 E-mail kathy.collins@virgin.net

COLLINS, Ms Linda Kathleen. b 56. Girton Coll Cam BA77 MA80 Bris Univ PGCE78. WMMTC 99. **d** 02 **p** 03. C Harborne St Pet *Birm* 02-05; C Cen Wolverhampton *Lich* 05-09; TV 09-10; C Lich St Mich w St Mary and Wall from 10; Chapl K Sch Wolv from 05; Chapl St Pet Colleg Sch Wolv from 05. *9 Sanstone Road, Walsall WS3 3SJ* Tel (01922) 711225 Mobile 07985-033476 E-mail tobycol@aol.com

COLLINS, Mrs Lindsay Rosemary Faith. b 70. K Coll Lon BD91 AKC91 PGCE92. Ripon Coll Cuddesdon MTh95. **d** 97 **p** 98. C Witney *Ox* 97-99; NSM 00-01; Chapl Cokethorpe Sch Witney 00-01; Chapl and Hd RE St Paul's Girls' Sch Hammersmith 01-04; Chapl K Coll Sch Wimbledon 04-10; Hon C Barnes *S'wark* 04-10; Chapl Sherborne Sch from 10. *Rosslyn House, 11 Acreman Street, Sherborne DT9 3NU* Tel (01935) 813846

COLLINS, Louise Ridley. b 59. Lanc Univ BA81 LGSM83. Cranmer Hall Dur 01. **d** 03 **p** 04. C Sheff St Cuth 03-07; V from 07. *St Cuthbert's Vicarage, 7 Horndean Road, Sheffield S5 6UJ* Tel 0114-261 1605

COLLINS, Martin. See COLLINS, Canon William Francis Martin

COLLINS, Canon Norman Hilary. b 33. Mert Coll Ox BA55 MA58. Wells Th Coll 58. **d** 60 **p** 61. C Ystrad Mynach *Llan* 60-62; C Gelligaer 62-67; V Maerdy 67-77; R Penarth w Lavernock 77-98; RD Penarth and Barry 87-98; Can Llan Cathl 92-98; rtd 98. *4 Llys Steffan, Llantwit Major CF61 2UF* Tel (01446) 794976

COLLINS, Paul David Arthur. b 50. Lanc Univ MSc91. K Coll Lon BD72 AKC72 St Aug Coll Cant 73. **d** 73 **p** 74. C Rotherhithe St Mary w All SS *S'wark* 73-76; C Stocking Farm *Leic* 76-78; V 78-83; R Husbands Bosworth w Mowsley and Knaptoft etc 83-87; Soc Resp Officer *Blackb* 87-94; R Worc City St Paul and Old St Martin etc 94-03; Min Can Worc Cathl 95-03; P-in-c Bishop's Castle w Mainstone, Lydbury N etc *Heref* 03-10; RD Clun Forest 05-08; rtd 10. *2 College Precincts, Worcester WR1 2LG* E-mail nb.wcycrown@hotmail.co.uk

COLLINS, Paul Michael. b 71. St Jo Coll Nottm 06. **d** 08 **p** 09. C Chenies and Lt Chalfont, Latimer and Flaunden *Ox* 08-10; Chapl RAF from 11. *Chaplaincy Services, Valiant Block, HQ Air Command, RAF High Wycombe HP14 4UE* Tel (01494) 496800 Fax 496343 Mobile 07973-838003 E-mail pmcollins2@yahoo.co.uk

COLLINS, Paul Myring. b 53. St Jo Coll Dur BA75 Ox Univ BA78 MA83 K Coll Lon PhD95. St Steph Ho Ox 76. **d** 79 **p** 80. C Meir *Lich* 79-82; C Fenton 82-83; TV Leek and Meerbrook 83-87; Tutor in Th and Liturgy Chich Th Coll 87-94; Dir of Studies 90-94; V Brighton Gd Shep Preston *Chich* 94-96; Tutor Qu Coll Birm 96-01; V Bournville *Birm* 01-02; Reader Chr Th Chich Univ 02-11; V Holy Is *Newc* from 11. *The Vicarage, Holy Island, Berwick-upon-Tweed TD15 2RX* E-mail pmcollins1@btinternet.com

COLLINS, Peter Graham. b 60. Anglia Ruskin Univ MA07. EMMTC 99 Westcott Ho Cam 05. **d** 07 **p** 08. C S Lawres Gp *Linc* 07-11; P-in-c Upper Wreake *Leic* from 11. *The Rectory, 2 Carrfields Lane, Frisby on the Wreake, Melton Mowbray LE14 2NT* Tel 07896-066302 (mobile) E-mail revdpeter@msn.com

COLLINS, Peter John. b 33. Open Univ BA. Oak Hill Th Coll 64. **d** 66 **p** 67. C Low Leyton *Chelmsf* 66-69; C Portsdown *Portsm* 69-72; V Gatten St Paul 72-79; C-in-c Ingrave St Steph CD *Chelmsf* 79-85; V Roydon 85-98; rtd 98; Perm to Offic *S'wark* from 00. *14 Glyndale Grange, Mulgrave Road, Sutton SM2 6LP* Tel (020) 8770 7683

COLLINS, Philip Howard Norton. b 50. AKC73. St Aug Coll Cant 73. **d** 74 **p** 75. C Stamford Hill St Thos *Lon* 74-78; C Upwood w Gt and Lt Raveley *Ely* 78-81; C Ramsey 78-81; R Leverington 81-92; P-in-c Wisbech St Mary 89-92; RD Wisbech 90-92; TR Whittlesey and Pondersbridge 92-95; TR Whittlesey, Pondersbridge and Coates 95-02; R New Alresford w Ovington and Itchen Stoke *Win* 02-07; R Arle Valley from 07; RD Alresford from 09. *The Rectory, 37 Jacklyns Lane, Alresford SO24 9LF* Tel (01962) 732105 E-mail philip_nortoncollins@hotmail.com

COLLINS (née SHIRRAS), Rachel Joan. b 66. Univ of Wales (Abth) BSc88. St Jo Coll Nottm 88. **d** 91 **p** 94. Par Dn Ockbrook *Derby* 91-94; C Bris St Matt and St Nath 94-97; V Beckton

St Mark *Chelmsf* 97-02; NSM Wandsworth St Steph *S'wark* 02-06; NSM Wandsworth St Mich 02-06; NSM Wandsworth St Mich w St Steph from 06. *11 Combemartin Road, London SW18 5PP* Tel (020) 8788 1851 E-mail rshirras@aol.com

COLLINS, Richard Andrew. b 65. K Coll Lon BD92 AKC92 Dur Univ MA00. St Steph Ho Ox 92. **d** 94 **p** 95. C Whickham *Dur* 94-97; C Bensham 97-98; TV 98-03; P-in-c Greatham and Chapl Greatham Hosp 03-09; Local Min Officer *Dur* 03-09; P-in-c Lumley from 09; Dir of Ords from 09. *Christ Church Vicarage, Great Lumley, Chester le Street DH3 4ER* Tel 0191-388 2228 *or* 374 6015 E-mail richard.collins@durham.anglican.org

COLLINS, Roger Richardson. b 48. Birm Univ BPhil88. WMMTC 78. **d** 81 **p** 82. NSM Cotteridge *Birm* from 81. *6 Chesterfield Court, Middleton Hall Road, Birmingham B30 1AF* Tel 0121-459 4009 E-mail roger@rrcollins.freeserve.co.uk

COLLINS, Ross Nicoll Ferguson. b 64. Edin Univ MA87 Ven English Coll Rome 91 Pontifical Univ Rome 91. Ripon Coll Cuddesdon BA91. **d** 92 **p** 93. C Goring w S Stoke *Ox* 92-96; P-in-c N Leigh 96-01; TR Barnes *S'wark* 01-10; NSM Sherborne w Castleton, Lillington and Longburton *Sarum* from 10. *Rosslyn House, 11 Acreman Street, Sherborne DT9 3NU* Tel (01935) 812077 Mobile 07738-478548 E-mail rossnfcollins@btinternet.com

COLLINS, Canon Stella Vivian. b 32. S Dios Minl Tr Scheme 74. **dss** 77 **d** 87 **p** 94. Harnham *Sarum* 77-88; Hon Par Dn 87-88; Dioc Lay Min Adv 82-97; Adv for Women's Min 82-97; Hon Par Dn Wilton w Netherhampton and Fugglestone 88-94; Hon C 94-97; RD Wylye and Wilton 89-94; Can and Preb Sarum Cathl 93-97; rtd 97; Perm to Offic *Sarum* 97-07. *1 Meadowslde, Hanging Langford, Salisbury SP3 4NW* Tel (01722) 790743

COLLINS, Canon William Francis Martin. b 43. St Cath Coll Cam BA66 MA70. Cuddesdon Coll 68. **d** 70 **p** 71. C Man Victoria Park 70-73; P-in-c Ancoats 73-78; Chapl Abraham Moss Cen 78-91; Hon C Cheetham Hill 81-84; Chs' FE Officer for Gtr Man 84-91; V Norbury *Ches* 91-08; Hon Can Ches Cathl 05-08; rtd 08. *9 Milldale Avenue, Buxton SK17 9BE* Tel (01298) 74906 Mobile 07866-505589

COLLINS, Winfield St Clair. b 41. Univ of W Indies BA83 Man Univ BA88 MEd91. Codrington Coll Barbados. **d** 76 **p** 76. Asst Chapl HM Pris Wakef 76; Barbados 76-84; C St Jo 76; P-in-c St Mark and St Cath 77-84; Asst Chapl HM Pris Wandsworth 85; Chapl HM YOI Thorn Cross 85-91; Chapl HM Pris Pentonville 91-01; Can Res Barbados 01-02; rtd 02. *92 Barclay Road, London N18 1EQ* Tel (020) 8245 4145

COLLINSON, Mrs Amanda. b 74. Luton Univ BA96. Ripon Coll Cuddesdon 07. **d** 09 **p** 10. C Catherington and Clanfield *Portsm* from 09. *23 Pipers Mead, Clanfield, Waterlooville PO8 0ST* Tel (023) 9236 7924 E-mail amanda.collinson@ntlworld.com

COLLINSON, Leslie Roland. b 47. St Jo Coll Nottm 90. **d** 92 **p** 93. C Gorleston St Andr *Nor* 92-96; TV Banbury *Ox* 96-98; V Banbury St Fran 98-00; V Darwen St Barn *Blackb* from 00. *St Barnabas' Vicarage, 68 Park Road, Darwen BB3 2LD* Tel (01254) 702732 E-mail revles@talktalk.net

COLLINSON, Mark Peter Charles. b 68. City Univ BSc90 Fitzw Coll Cam BA97 MA01. Ridley Hall Cam 95. **d** 98 **p** 99. C Ashton-upon-Mersey St Mary Magd *Ches* 98-01; Chapl Amsterdam w Den Helder and Heiloo *Eur* from 01. *Bouwmeester 2, 1188 DT Amstelveen, The Netherlands* Tel (0031) (20) 441 0355 Fax 453 7431 E-mail mark@christchurch.nl

COLLINSON, Roger Alfred. b 36. St Jo Coll Dur BA58 Cranmer Hall Dur 60. **d** 63 **p** 97. C Liv St Mich 63-64; NSM Ormside *Carl* 97-06; NSM Appleby 97-06; Perm to Offic from 06. *1 Caesar's View, Appleby-in-Westmorland CA16 6SH* Tel (01768) 352886

COLLIS, Janet Mary. b 57. Plymouth Poly BA78 PhD83 SS Mark & Jo Univ Coll Plymouth MA03. SWMTC 08. **d** 10. NSM Plympton St Mary *Ex* from 10. *Chelsea House, 4 Longbrook Street, Plymouth PL7 1NJ* Tel 07899-995683 (mobile) E-mail jan.collis@gmail.com

COLLIS, Jonathan. b 69. Selw Coll Cam BA91 MA94. Aston Tr Scheme 96 Westcott Ho Cam 97. **d** 99 **p** 00. C St Neots *Ely* 99-02; Chapl Jes Coll Cam 02-09; V Thorpe Bay *Chelmsf* from 09. *The Vicarage, 86 Tyrone Road, Southend-on-Sea SS1 3HB* Tel (01702) 587597 E-mail jonathan.collis@cantab.net

COLLIS, Michael Alan. b 35. K Coll Lon BD60 AKC60. **d** 61 **p** 62. C Worc St Martin 61-63; C Dudley St Thos 63-66; C St Peter-in-Thanet *Cant* 66-70; V Croydon H Trin 70-77; P-in-c Norbury St Steph 77-81; V 81-82; V Sutton Valence w E Sutton and Chart Sutton 82-89; R New Fishbourne *Chich* 89-00; P-in-c Appledram 89-00; rtd 00; Perm to Offic *Chich* from 00. *66 Orchard Way, Barnham, Bognor Regis PO22 0HY* Tel (01243) 552429

COLLIS, Canon Stephen Thomas. b 47. MHCIMA94. Cranmer Hall Dur 80. **d** 82 **p** 83. C Crewe All SS and St Paul *Ches* 82-84; C Wilmslow 84-86 and 95-98; Chapl RAF 86-95; P-in-c Barthomley *Ches* 98-00; S Cheshire Ind Chapl 98-00; Chapl Abu Dhabi UAE 00-02; Dean St Paul's Cathl and Chapl Nicosia

02-09; Hon Can Malta Cathl from 09; Adn Cyprus 06-09; R Montrose *Bre* from 09; R Inverbervie from 09. *5 Martins Lane, Brechin DD9 6AS*

COLLISHAW, Ashley Stuart. b 66. Wycliffe Hall Ox 03. d 05 p 06. C Worc City 05-09; Hon C Cheltenham H Trin and St Paul *Glouc* from 09. *22 Greatfield Drive, Charlton Kings, Cheltenham GL53 9BY* Tel 07932-045598 (mobile) E-mail crockfords@collishaw.net

COLLISON, Christopher John. b 48. Oak Hill Th Coll 68. d 72 p 73. C Cromer *Nor* 72-75; C Costessey 76-78; V 87-95; C Heckmondwike *Wakef* 78-79; P-in-c Shepley and Dioc Communications Officer 79-83; Chapl Flushing Miss to Seamen *Eur* 83-85; Asst Min Sec Miss to Seamen 85-87; C St Mich Paternoster *Lon* 85-87; P-in-c Swainsthorpe w Newton Flotman *Nor* 95-97; TV Newton Flotman, Swainsthorpe, Tasburgh, etc 98-02; R Henfield w Shermanbury and Woodmancote *Chich* 02-09; Dioc Evang Officer *Nor* 95-01; RD Hurst *Chich* 04-09; P-in-c Hartlepool St Hilda *Dur* from 09; RD Hartlepool from 10; Chapl Miss to Seafarers from 09. *The Rectory, Church Close, Hartlepool TS24 0PW* Tel (01429) 267030

COLLISON, Ms Elizabeth. b 38. Man Univ CertEd58. NOC 85. d 88 p 94. C Huyton St Mich *Liv* 88-94; C Rainhill 94-05; rtd 05. *25 Lowther Drive, Rainhill, Prescot L35 0NG* Tel 0151-426 3853 E-mail liz collison@yahoo.co.uk

COLLYER, David John. b 38. JP. Keble Coll Ox BA61 MA86. Westcott Ho Cam 61. d 63 p 64. C Perry Beeches *Birm* 63-65; P-in-c Deritend 66-70; Bp's Chapl for Special Youth Work 65-70; Bp's Youth Chapl and Dioc Youth Officer 70-73; R Northfield 73-78; Hon Chapl Birm Cathl 78-81; Hon C Birm St Geo 81-86; V Handsworth St Andr 86-97; Dioc Development Officer 97-01; Hon Can Birm Cathl 95-06; Perm to Offic from 01. *19 Birch Close, Bournville, Birmingham B30 1NA*

COLLYER, Leon John. b 72. SS Hild & Bede Coll Dur BSc95 Leeds Univ BA00. Coll of Resurr Mirfield 98. d 01 p 02. C Airedale w Fryston *Wakef* 01-04; P-in-c Crofton and Warmfield 04-10; C Reading St Agnes w St Paul and St Barn *Ox* from 10. *St Barnabas' Rectory, 14 Elm Road, Reading RG6 5TS* Tel 0118-327 9389 Mobile 07714-986462 E-mail leoncollyer@gmail.com

COLMAN, Geoffrey Hugh. b 29. Univ Coll Ox BA53 MA68. Wells Th Coll 67. d 68 p 69. C Wanstead St Mary *Chelmsf* 68-72; V Barking St Erkenwald 72-77; Youth Chapl 78-81; C Maidstone All SS and St Phil w Tovil *Cant* 85-88; P-in-c Norton 88-93; R 93-96; P-in-c Teynham 88-93; P-in-c Lynsted w Kingsdown 88-93; V Teynham w Lynsted and Kingsdown 93-96; rtd 96; Perm to Offic *Cant* 98-99. *c/o Mrs G H Fulcher, 98 Barnham Road, Barnham, Bognor Regis PO22 0EW*

COLMER, Andrew John. b 68. De Montfort Univ Leic BSc90. St Jo Coll Nottm MA96 LTh97. d 97 p 98. C Roby *Liv* 97-01; C Litherland St Andr 01-02; P-in-c Liv All So Springwood 02-10; Chapl Enterprise S Liv Academy from 10. *Enterprise South Liverpool Academy, Horrocks Avenue, Liverpool L19 5PF* E-mail andrew.colmer@virgin.net

COLMER, The Ven Malcolm John. b 45. Sussex Univ MSc67. St Jo Coll Nottm BA73. d 73 p 74. C Egham *Guildf* 73-76; C Chadwell *Chelmsf* 76-79; V S Malling *Chich* 79-85; V Hornsey Rise St Mary w St Steph *Lon* 85-87; TR Hornsey Rise Whitehall Park Team 87-96; AD Islington 90-94; Adn Middx 96-05; Adn Heref 05-10; Can Res Heref Cathl 05-10; rtd 10. *Pantdafydd, Maesllyn, Llandysul SA44 5LL* Tel (01239) 851731 E-mail malcom colmer@hotmail.com

COLPUS (*née* EDWARDS), Mrs Anita Carolyn. b 71. Trin Coll Bris 01. d 03 p 04. C Notting Hill St Pet *Lon* 03-06; NSM Sittingbourne St Mary and St Mich *Cant* 07-10; P-in-c Reigate St Luke w Doversgreen *S'wark* from 10. *St Luke's House, 3 Church Road, Reigate RH2 8HY* Tel (01737) 243846 E-mail anitacolpus@tesco.net

COLSON, Ian Richard. b 65. Wolv Poly BSc86 Nottm Univ BTh89 Warwick Univ MA03. Linc Th Coll 86. d 89 p 90. C Nunthorpe *York* 89-92; C Thornaby on Tees 92-93; Chapl RAF 93-00; V Sunbury *Lon* 00-02; Chapl Ardingly Coll 02-09; Sen Chapl Ch Hosp Horsham from 09. *Christ's Hospital, Horsham RH13 0YP* Tel (01403) 252547 E-mail ianrcolson@aol.com

COLSTON, Canon John Edward. b 42. Open Univ BA91 Leeds Univ MA94. Lich Th Coll 65. d 68 p 69. C Bromsgrove All SS *Worc* 68-71; C Tettenhall Wood *Lich* 71-74; V Alrewas and Wychnor 74-88; R Ainderby Steeple w Yafforth and Kirby Wiske etc *Ripon* 88-95; V High Harrogate Ch Ch 95-07; Warden of Readers 90-96; AD Harrogate 01-05; Hon Can Ripon Cathl 06-07; rtd 08. *15 Sycamore Road, Ripon HG4 2LR* Tel (01765) 600747 E-mail john.colston@yahoo.co.uk

COLTON, Mrs Christine Ann. b 56. Univ of Wales (Cardiff) BA00 MTh06. St Mich Coll Llan 01. d 06 p 07. NSM Cen Cardiff *Llan* 06-07; NSM Radyr from 07. *Canton Vicarage, 3A Romilly Road, Cardiff CF5 1FH* Tel (029) 2022 9683 E-mail chris.colton@ntlworld.com

COLTON, Martin Philip. b 67. Sheff Univ BMus89 MMus92 FRCO92 Open Univ PGCE97. St Mich Coll Llan BA03. d 03

p 04. C Whitchurch *Llan* 03-06; TV Canton Cardiff from 06. *Canton Vicarage, 3A Romilly Road, Cardiff CF5 1FH* Tel (029) 2022 9683 E-mail martin.colton@which.net

✠COLTON, The Rt Revd William Paul. b 60. NUI BCL81 TCD MPhil87 Univ of Wales (Cardiff) LLM06. d 84 p 85 c 99. C Lisburn St Paul *Conn* 84-87; Bp's Dom Chapl 85-90; V Choral Belf Cathl 87-90; Min Can Belf Cathl 89-90; PV, Registrar and Chapter Clerk Ch Ch Cathl Dub 90-95; I Castleknock and Mulhuddart w Clonsilla 90-99; Co-ord Protestant Relig Progr RTE 93-99; Hon Chapl Actors' Ch Union 94-96; Area Chapl (Ireland) Actors' Ch Union 96-97; Can Ch Ch Cathl Dublin 97-99; Bp C, C & R from 99. *St Nicholas' House, 14 Cove Street, Cork, Republic of Ireland* Tel (00353) (21) 500 5080 Fax 432 0960 E-mail bishop@ccrd.ie

COLVILLE, Gary Stanley. b 59. Sarum & Wells Th Coll 90. d 92 p 94. C Plaistow St Mary *Roch* 92-94; P-in-c Foots Cray 94-96; R 96-00; P-in-c N Cray 97-00; R Pembroke Bermuda 01-04; V Roch from 04. *The Vicarage, 138 Delce Road, Rochester ME1 2EH* Tel (01634) 845122 E-mail moiracolville@hotmail.com

COLWELL, Ms Katherine Elizabeth. b 57. Man Univ BA78 Nottm Univ MA08 Man Poly PGCE79. EMMTC 05. d 08 p 09. C Barton upon Humber *Linc* from 08. *82 West Acridge, Barton-upon-Humber DN18 5AN* Tel (01652) 632318 E-mail katherine.colwell@virgin.net

COLWILL, James Patrick (Jay). b 68. Man Poly BA91. St Jo Coll Nottm BTh93 MA94. d 94 p 95. C Reading St Agnes w St Paul *Ox* 94-97; C Easthampstead 97-03; V Orpington Ch Ch *Roch* from 03; AD Orpington from 10. *The Vicarage, 165 Charterhouse Road, Orpington BR6 9EP* Tel (01689) 870923 Mobile 07941-752513 E-mail jay.colwill@diocese-rochester.org

COMBE, The Very Revd John Charles. b 33. TCD BA53 MA56 BD57 MLitt65 PhD70. d 56 p 57. C Cork St Luke w St Ann *C, C & R* 56-58; C Ballynafeigh St Jude *D & D* 58-61; I Crinken *D & G* 61-66; Hon Clerical V Ch Ch Cathl Dublin 63-66; C Belfast St Bart *Conn* 66-70; I Belfast St Barn 70-74; I Portadown St Mark *Arm* 74-84; I Arm St Mark w Aghavilly 84-90; Can Arm Cathl 85-90; Dean Kilmore *K, E & A* 90-96; I Kilmore w Ballintemple, Kildallan etc 90-96; rtd 96. *24 Kensington Park, Maxwell Road, Bangor BT20 3RF* Tel (028) 9146 6123

COMBER, Mrs Alison. d 94 p 95. OLM New Bury *Man* 94-04; Perm to Offic from 04. *12 Seymour Grove, Farnworth, Bolton BL4 0HF* Tel (01204) 397745

COMBER, The Ven Anthony James. b 27. Leeds Univ BSc49 MSc52. St Chad's Coll Dur 53. d 56 p 57. C Manston *Ripon* 56-60; V Oulton 60-69; V Hunslet St Mary 69-77; RD Armley 72-75 and 79-81; R Farnley 77-82; Hon Can Ripon Cathl 80-92; Adn Leeds 82-92; rtd 92; Perm to Offic *Ripon* from 92 and *Bradf* 93-99. *28 Blayds Garth, Woodlesford, Leeds LS26 8WN* Tel 0113-288 0489 Mobile 07840-763818 E-mail tony.comber@btinternet.com

COMBER, Michael. b 35. Carl Dioc Tr Inst. d 72 p 72. CA 59-72; C Carl H Trin and St Barn 72-73; C Upperby St Jo 73-76; V Dearham 76-81; V Harraby 81-84; R Orton and Tebay w Ravenstonedale etc 84-90; I Clonfert Gp *L & K* 90-94; I Convoy w Monellan and Donaghmore *D & R* 94-97; I Tamlaght O'Crilly Upper w Lower 97-02; rtd 02; Perm to Offic *Carl* from 03. *87 Pinecroft, Kingstown, Carlisle CA3 0DB* Tel (01228) 401428 Mobile 07742-392124 E-mail m.comber@talk21.com

COMBES, The Ven Roger Matthew. b 47. K Coll Lon LLB69. Ridley Hall Cam 72. d 74 p 75. C Onslow Square St Paul *Lon* 74-77; C Brompton H Trin 76-77; C Cambridge H Sepulchre w All SS *Ely* 77-86; R Silverhill St Matt *Chich* 86-03; RD Hastings 98-02; Adn Horsham from 03. *3 Danehurst Crescent, Horsham RH13 5HS* Tel (01403) 262710 Fax 210778 E-mail archhorsham@diochi.org.uk

COMER, Michael John. b 30. St Mich Coll Llan 79. d 81 p 82. C Bistre *St As* 81-84; R Llanfyllin and Bwlchycibau 84-91; V Hattersley *Ches* 91-94; rtd 94. *8 Cae Camlas, Newtown SY16 2HT* Tel (01686) 624557

COMERFORD, Canon Patrick. b 52. Pontifical Univ Maynooth BD87 FRSAI87. CITC 99. d 00 p 01. NSM Dublin Whitechurch *D & G* from 00; Dir Spiritual Formation CITC 06-11; Lect from 11; Can Ch Ch Cathl Dublin from 10. *75 Glenvara Park, Knocklyon, Dublin 16, Republic of Ireland* Tel (00353) (1) 495 0934 Mobile 87-663 5116 E-mail patrickcomerford@citc.ie

COMERFORD, Mrs Suzanne Lyn. b 46. SAOMC 97. d 00 p 01. OLM Woodley Ox 00-08. *110 Lower Drayton Lane, Portsmouth PO6 2HE* Tel 07786-224247 (mobile)

COMFORT, Alan. b 64. Ridley Hall Cam 91. d 94 p 95. C Chadwell Heath *Chelmsf* 94-97; C Buckhurst Hill 97-98; TV 98-03; V Loughton St Mary 03-09; TR Gt Baddow 09-10; V Walthamstow St Jo from 10. *St John's Vicarage, 18 Brookscroft Road, London E17 4LH* Tel (020) 8531 9411 E-mail alancomfort11@tiscali.co.uk

COMLEY, Thomas Hedges. b 36. Leeds Univ BA62. Coll of Resurr Mirfield 62. d 64 p 65. C Eastgate *Dur* 64-67; C Shirley *Birm* 67-71; V Smethwick St Alb 71-76; Perm to Offic 76-82; V N Wembley St Cuth *Lon* 82-92; V Taddington, Chelmorton and

Flagg, and Monyash *Derby* 92-01; rtd 01; Perm to Offic *Derby* from 01. *19 Wentworth Avenue, Walton, Chesterfield S40 3JB* Tel (01246) 270911 E-mail tom comley@lineone.net
COMMANDER, David James. b 58. Cranfield Inst of Tech MSc84. SEITE 07. **d** 10 **p** 11. C Tunbridge Wells St Jas *Roch* from 10. *3 Andrews Close, Tunbridge Wells TN2 3PA* Tel and fax (01892) 531297 Mobile 07710-416978 E-mail david@dc-uk.co.uk
COMMIN, Robert William. b 47. Cape Town Univ BA79. St Paul's Coll Grahamstown. **d** 70 **p** 71. S Africa 70-80 and from 89; Chapl Loretto Sch Musselburgh 80-84; TV Thetford *Nor* 84-89. *42 Earl Street, Woodstock, 7925 South Africa* Tel (0027) 82-202 5303 (mobile) E-mail bcommin@netactive.co.za
COMPTON, Barry Charles Chittenden. b 33. Linc Th Coll 60. **d** 62 **p** 63. C Beddington *S'wark* 62-65; C Limpsfield and Titsey 66-68; Hon C 71-94; R Ridley *Roch* 69-70; R Ash 69-70; Perm to Offic *S'wark* from 70; rtd 94. *14 Hallsland Way, Oxted RH8 9AL* Tel (01883) 714896 Fax 722842
COMYNS, Clifford John. b 28. TCD BA50 HDipEd53 MA53 BD67. **d** 51 **p** 52. C Chapelizod *D & G* 51-55; CF 55-75; Asst Master Eastbourne Coll 75-06; Asst Chapl 85-06; rtd 06. *6 Nursery Way, Heathfield TN21 0UW* Tel (01435) 864941 E-mail helen@dormand.fsworld.co.uk
CONALTY, Julie Anne. b 63. SEITE. **d** 99 **p** 00. NSM Wickham *S'wark* 99-04; NSM Charlton 04-10; C Plumstead Common from 10. *12 Little Heath, London SE7 8HU* Tel (020) 8317 7166 E-mail julie@littleheath.demon.co.uk
CONANT, Alan Richard. b 67. Kent Univ BSc89 PhD92. St Jo Coll Nottm 09 **d** 11. C Maghull and Melling *Liv* from 11. *1B Rock View, Maghull, Liverpool L31 1JF* Tel 07804-450925 (mobile) E-mail alan.conant@tesco.net
CONANT, Frane Charles. b 44. Oak Hill Th Coll 83. **d** 85 **p** 86. C Hoole *Ches* 85-89; V Kelsall 89-01; P-in-c Seer Green and Jordans *Ox* 01-06; rtd 06; Partner Evang Luis Palau Evang Assn from 06. *1 Spring Bank, Shrewsbury Road, Church Stretton SY6 6HA* Tel (01694) 722610 E-mail fanesue@aol.com
CONAWAY, Barry Raymond. b 41. CertEd69 Nottm Univ BEd70. Sarum & Wells Th Coll 86. **d** 88 **p** 89. C Ross w Brampton Abbotts, Bridstow and Peterstow *Heref* 88-91; R Bishop's Frome w Castle Frome and Fromes Hill 91-96; P-in-c Acton Beauchamp and Evesbatch 91-96; P-in-c Charminster and Stinsford *Sarum* 96-01; rtd 01; Perm to Offic *Glouc* 01-02 and *Sarum* from 03. *9 Constable Way, West Harnham, Salisbury SP2 8LN* Tel (01722) 334870
CONDER, Paul Collingwood Nelson. b 33. St Jo Coll Cam BA56 MA60. Ridley Hall Cam 56. **d** 58 **p** 59. C Grassendale *Liv* 58-61; Tutor St Jo Coll Dur 61-67; R Sutton *Liv* 67-74; TR 74-75; V Thames Ditton *Guildf* 75-86; RD Emly 82-86; V Blundellsands St Mich *Liv* 86-99; rtd 99; Perm to Offic *York* from 00. *112 Strensall Road, Earswick, York YO32 9SJ* Tel (01904) 763071
CONDRY, Canon Edward Francis. b 53. UEA BA74 Ex Coll Ox BLitt77 DPhil80 Open Univ MBA02. Linc Th Coll 80. **d** 82 **p** 83. C Weston Favell *Pet* 82-85; V Bloxham w Milcombe and S Newington *Ox* 85-93; TR Rugby *Cov* 93-02; Can Res Cant Cathl from 02; Dir Post-Ord Tr 02-06; Treas and Dir of Educn from 06. *15 The Precincts, Canterbury CT1 2EL* Tel (01227) 865228 E-mail edwardc@canterbury-cathedral.org
CONEY, Joanna Margery. b 39. Culham Coll of Educn CertEd75 Open Univ BA83. Ox Min Course 90. **d** 93 **p** 94. C Wolvercote w Summertown *Ox* 93-97; Hon C New Marston 97-06; Hon C Wolvercote w Summertown 06-07; Hon C Wolvercote 07-10; OLM Tr Officer (Ox Adnry) 97-00; Dioc Portfolio Officer 00-04; rtd 04; Dioc Adv to Lic Lay Min *Ox* 02-09; NSM Voc Adv from 09; Min Prov (Eur) Third Order SSF from 09; Hon C Wolvercote and Wytham *Ox* from 10. *4 Rowland Close, Wolvercote, Oxford OX2 8PW* Tel and fax (01865) 556456 E-mail joanna.coney@gmail.com
CONEYS, Canon Stephen John. b 61. Sheff Univ LLB82. St Jo Coll Nottm 87. **d** 90 **p** 91. C Plymouth Em w Efford *Ex* 90-92; C Plymouth Em, Efford and Laira 93-94; TV Whitstable *Cant* 94-02; TR from 02; Hon Can Cant Cathl from 08. *The Vicarage, 11 Kimberley Grove, Seasalter, Whitstable CT5 4AY* Tel (01227) 276795 E-mail steveconeys@btinternet.com
CONGDON, John Jameson. b 30. St Edm Hall Ox BA53 MA57. Wycliffe Hall Ox 53. **d** 55 **p** 56. C Aspley *S'well* 55-58; C-in-c Woodthorpe CD 58-63; V Woodthorpe 63-61; V Spring Grove St Mary *Lon* 70-84; V Woodley St Jo the Ev *Ox* 84-89; Chapl W Middx Univ Hosp Isleworth 89-95; rtd 95; Perm to Offic *Lon* from 95 and *Ox* 06-09. *23 Pates Manor Drive, Feltham TW14 8JJ* Tel (020) 8893 1823
CONLEY, James Alan. b 29. Dur Univ BSc51. St Jo Coll Nottm. **d** 87 **p** 88. NSM Cropwell Bishop w Colston Bassett, Granby etc *S'well* 87-97; Perm to Offic *Sarum* 97-07. *30 The Waldrons, Thornford, Sherborne DT9 6PX* Tel (01935) 872672
CONLIN, Tiffany Jane Kate. b 71. K Coll Lon BA93 MA94 PhD00 AKC93. Westcott Ho Cam 03. **d** 05 **p** 06. C Wisbech St Aug and Wisbech SS Pet and Paul *Ely* 05-08; Chapl Fitzw

Coll Cam from 08. *Fitzwilliam College, Cambridge CB3 0DG* Tel (01223) 332013 E-mail tiffanyjkconlin@yahoo.com
CONLON, Shaun. b 69. Birm Univ BA90. Ripon Coll Cuddesdon 91. **d** 93 **p** 94. C Castle Bromwich SS Mary and Marg *Birm* 93-97; C Hockerill *St Alb* 97-00; V St Mary-at-Latton *Chelmsf* 00-07; V Prittlewell from 07. *Prittlewell Vicarage, 489 Victoria Avenue, Southend-on-Sea SS2 6NL* Tel (01702) 343470 E-mail shaunconlon@tiscali.co.uk
CONN, Alistair Aberdein. b 37. Down Coll Cam BA60 MA64. Linc Th Coll 60. **d** 62 **p** 63. C W Hartlepool St Paul *Dur* 62-65; Uganda 65-66; Chapl Shrewsbury Sch 66-73; R Coupar Angus *St And* 73-78; V Ravenshead *S'well* 78-93; RD Newstead 90-93; R Collingham w S Scarle and Besthorpe and Girton 93-02; RD Newark 95-02; rtd 02; Perm to Offic *S'well* from 02. *17 Beacon Heights, Newark, Newark NG24 2JS* Tel (01636) 706291
CONNELL, Clare. See CONNELL, Mrs Penelope Clare
CONNELL, Frederick Philip Richard John. b 45. St Jo Coll Nottm MA98. **d** 99 **p** 00. Deacon Jos St Piran Nigeria 99-00; V 00-01; NSM Nottingham St Pet and All SS *S'well* 01-03; Perm to Offic 03-04; NSM Nottingham St Nic 04-07; C Leic Martyrs 07-09; TV Vale of Belvoir from 09. *Colston Bassett House, Church Gate, Colston Bassett, Nottingham NG12 3FE* Tel (01949) 81424 E-mail frederick.connell@tiscali.co.uk
CONNELL, Miss Heather Josephine. b 38. Open Univ BA93 SRN60 SCM61. S'wark Ord Course. **dss** 79 **d** 87 **p** 94. Heston *Lon* 79-84; Gillingham St Barn *Roch* 84-90; Par Dn 87-90; Distr Chapl Medway NHS Trust 91-96; NSM Gillingham H Trin *Roch* 94-07; rtd 98; Perm to Offic *Chelmsf* from 08. *27 Norman Close, St Osyth, Clacton-on-Sea CO16 8PN* Tel (01255) 820537 E-mail h.connell@tesco.net
CONNELL, John Richard. b 63. K Coll Lon BD84. St Mich Coll Llan 92. **d** 94 **p** 96. C Caldicot *Mon* 94-97; C Risca 97-00; V Llantilio Pertholey w Bettws Chpl etc 00-05; P-in-c Wokingham St Paul *Ox* 05-11. *Ty Enfys, 15 Angus Close, Wokingham RG41 5GS* Tel 0118-978 0629 E-mail johntyenfys@gmail.com
CONNELL, Julie. **d** 08 **p** 09. NSM Brixton Road Ch Ch *S'wark* from 08. *8 Helix Road, London SW2 2JS* Tel (020) 8671 0481 *or* 7587 0375 Fax 7582 7421
CONNELL, Mrs Penelope Clare. b 44. EMMTC. **d** 03 **p** 04. NSM Whatton w Aslockton, Hawksworth, Scarrington etc *S'well* 03-06; NSM Nottingham St Nic 06-07; NSM Ironstone Villages *Leic* from 07. *Colston Bassett House, Church Gate, Colston Bassett, Nottingham NG12 3FE* Tel (01949) 81424 Mobile 07866-495720 E-mail clare.connell@tiscali.co.uk
CONNELL, Ms Sharon Margaret. b 65. St Jo Coll Nottm BA03. **d** 03 **p** 04. C S Hackney St Jo w Ch Ch *Lon* 03-06; C Stepney St Dunstan and All SS 06-08; Ecum Chapl Chelsea and Westmr Hosp NHS Found Trust from 08. *Chelsea and Westminster Hospital, 369 Fulham Road, London SW10 9NH* Tel (020) 8746 8083 E-mail sharon.connell@chelwest.nhs.uk
CONNER, Mrs Cathryn. b 42. Birm Univ BSc64. NEOC 91. **d** 94 **p** 95. NSM Bainton w N Dalton, Middleton-on-the-Wolds etc *York* 94-98; NSM Woldsburn 98-04; rtd 04; Perm to Offic *York* from 04. *Centre House, North Dalton, Driffield YO25 9XA* Tel (01377) 217265
CONNER, Charles Borthwick. b 20. Keble Coll Ox BA43 MA49. St Steph Ho Ox 48. **d** 50 **p** 51. C Saltburn-by-the-Sea *York* 50-52; Chapl Ely Th Coll 52-53; CF 53-70. *Angel Cottage, West Knighton, Dorchester DT2 8PE* Tel (01305) 852465
✠**CONNER, The Rt Revd David John.** b 47. KCVO10. Ex Coll Ox BA69 MA77. St Steph Ho Ox 69. **d** 71 **p** 72 **c** 94. Asst Chapl St Edw Sch Ox 71-73; Chapl 73-80; Hon C Summertown *Ox* 71-76; TV Wolvercote w Summertown 76-80; Chapl Win Coll 80-87; V Cambridge Gt St Mary w St Mich *Ely* 87-94; RD Cambridge 89-94; Suff Bp Lynn *Nor* 94-98; Dean Windsor and Dom Chapl to The Queen from 98; Bp HM Forces 01-09. *The Deanery, Windsor Castle, Windsor SL4 1NJ* Tel (01753) 865561 Fax 819002 E-mail david.conner@stgeorges-windsor.org
CONNING, Dowell Paul. b 64. Ripon Coll Cuddesdon BTh00. **d** 00 **p** 01. C Leckhampton St Pet *Glouc* 00-03; CF from 03; Hon Min Can Ripon Cathl from 05. *c/o MOD Chaplains (Army)* Tel (01264) 381140 Fax 381824 E-mail dconning@googlemail.com
CONNOLL, Miss Helen Dorothy. b 45. Oak Hill Th Coll BA86. **dss** 86 **d** 87 **p** 94. Leytonstone St Jo *Chelmsf* 86-90; Par Dn 87-90; Asst Chapl Grimsby Distr Gen Hosp 90-93; Chapl Kent and Cant Hosp 93-94; Chapl Kent and Cant Hosps NHS Trust 94-99; Chapl E Kent Hosps NHS Trust from 99; Hon C Aylesham w Adisham and Nonington w Wymynswold and Goodnestone etc *Cant* 01-09; rtd 09; Perm to Offic *Cant* from 09. *5 White House, Farm Court, Easole Street, Nonington, Dover CT15 4NJ* Tel (01304) 840271 E-mail helen.therev@virgin.net
CONNOLLY, Daniel. b 51. BEng. St Jo Coll Nottm 82. **d** 84 **p** 85. C Bedgrove *Ox* 84-87; C-in-c Crookhorn Ch Cen CD *Portsm* 87-88; V Crookhorn 88-97; R Sutton Coldfield H Trin *Birm* 97-98; V Reigate St Mary *S'wark* 98-05; RD Reigate 03-05; P-in-c Kenilworth St Jo *Cov* 05-08; Adnry Miss Enabler 08-09; P-in-c Blackpool St Jo *Blackb* from 09. *32 Forest Gate, Blackpool FY3 9AW* Tel (01253) 623190 E-mail dan@famcon.co.uk

CONNOLLY, Miss Lynne. b 53. Aston Tr Scheme 88 Linc Th Coll 92. **d** 92 **p** 94. Par Dn Hurst *Man* 92-94; C 94-96; R Burnage St Nic 96-02; V Spotland 02-10; P-in-c E Crompton from 10. *St James's Vicarage, Vicarage Street, Shaw, Oldham OL2 7TE* Tel (01706) 847454 E-mail tyc@clara.co.uk

CONNOLLY, Canon Sydney Herbert. b 40. Leeds Univ BA66. Coll of Resurr Mirfield 66. **d** 68 **p** 69. C W Derby St Mary *Liv* 68-71; C Prescot 71-74; V Burtonwood 74-80; V Walker *Newc* 80-89; TR Whorlton 89-96; V Chapel House 96-99; TR N Shields 99-06; Hon Can Newc Cathl 04-06; rtd 06. *222 Brunton Walk, Newcastle upon Tyne NE3 2TL* Tel 0191-271 1473 E-mail sydandpat@blueyonder.co.uk

CONNOP PRICE, Martin Randall. See PRICE, Martin Randall Connop

CONNOR, Geoffrey. b 46. K Coll Lon BD73 AKC73. St Aug Coll Cant. **d** 74 **p** 75. C Cockerton *Dur* 74-79; Dioc Recruitment Officer 79-87; Chapl St Chad's Coll 84-87; R Edin St Mary and Vice Provost St Mary's Cathl 87-90; Dioc Dir of Ords *Edin* and *Arg* 87-90; V Whitechapel w Admarsh-in-Bleasdale *Blackb* 90-00; Dir of Ords 90-00; TR Epping Distr *Chelmsf* from 00; RD Epping Forest 04-10. *The Rectory, Hartland Road, Epping CM16 4PD* Tel and fax (01992) 572906 E-mail geoffrey_connor@priest.com

CONNOR, Archdeacon of. See McBRIDE, The Ven Stephen Richard

CONNOR, Bishop of. See ABERNETHY, The Rt Revd Alan Francis

CONNOR, Dean of. See BOND, The Very Revd John Frederick Augustus

CONRAD, Canon Paul Derick. b 54. Worc Coll Ox BA76 MA82. St Steph Ho Ox 78. **d** 80 **p** 81. C Wanstead St Mary *Chelmsf* 80-83; C Somers Town *Lon* 83-85; P-in-c Kentish Town St Martin w St Andr 85-91; V 91-95; P-in-c Hampstead Ch Ch 95-97; V from 97; Chapl R Free Hampstead NHS Trust from 95; Can Wiawso Ghana from 09. *Christ Church Vicarage, 10 Cannon Place, London NW3 1EJ* Tel and fax (020) 7435 6784 E-mail paulconrad@btinternet.com

CONSTABLE, Douglas Brian. b 40. Lon Univ BA62 Southn Univ MPhil05. Linc Th Coll 63. **d** 65 **p** 66. C Stockwood CD *Bris* 65-70; Asst Chapl Bris Univ 70-72; Hon C Clifton St Paul 70-72; Chapl Lee Abbey 72-77; V Derby St Thos 77-85; TV Southampton (City Cen) *Win* 85-92; rtd 92; Perm to Offic *Win* 92-05. *Y Bwthyn, 9 Church Street, Llandeilo SA19 6BH* Tel (01558) 823518 E-mail douglasconstable@btinternet.com

CONSTABLE, Mrs Sharon Joanne. b 57. STETS 95. **d** 98 **p** 99. NSM Hutton *B & W* 98-01; Bp's Officer for NSMs 01-04; C E Clevedon w Clapton in Gordano etc 01-04; Chapl St Jo Cathl Hong Kong 04-10; TV Melton Mowbray *Leic* from 10; Bp's Adv for Women's Min from 10. *26 Firwood Road, Melton Mowbray LE13 1SA* Tel (01664) 481793 E-mail sharonconstable@msn.com

CONSTABLE, Mrs Sybil Margaret. b 43. **d** 00 **p** 01. NSM Montgomery and Forden and Llandyssil *St As* 00-04; P-in-c Slindon, Eartham and Madehurst *Chich* 04-09; rtd 09. *Stubbs Oak, Straight Half Mile, Maresfield, Uckfield TN22 3DN* Tel (01825) 760715

CONSTANTINE, Miss Elaine Muriel. b 50. Univ of Wales (Swansea) BSc72 CertEd73 DipEd75 Lon Univ MEd78. St Alb Minl Tr Scheme. **dss** 86 **d** 87 **p** 94. Bedford St Martin *St Alb* 86-88; Par Dn 87-88; Par Dn Leighton Buzzard w Eggington, Hockliffe etc 88-94; C 94-98; TV Dunstable 98-04; P-in-c Earlham St Eliz *Nor* 04-08; R Earlham 08-10; rtd 10; Perm to Offic *Nor* from 10. *4 Doughty's Cottages, Golden Dog Lane, Norwich NR3 1BS* Tel (01603) 219764 E-mail elaine.constantine@btinternet.com

CONSTANTINE, Leonard. b 30. AKC57. **d** 58 **p** 59. C W Hartlepool St Aid *Dur* 58-61; C Sheff St Geo and St Steph 61-62; Nyasaland 62-64; Malawi 64-69; V W Pelton *Dur* 69-73; V Shotton 73-78; V Stillington 78-80; V Grindon and Stillington 80-82; V Corbridge w Halton and Newton Hall *Newc* 82-95; Chapl Charlotte Straker Hosp 82-95; rtd 95; Perm to Offic *Wakef* 95-10. *18 Stuart Court, High Street, Kibworth, Leicester LE8 0LR* Tel 0116-279 2347

CONVERY, Canon Arthur Malcolm. b 42. Sheff Univ BSc63 DipEd64. NOC 79. **d** 82 **p** 83. NSM Parr *Liv* 82-87; V Marown *S & M* 87-04; V Onchan 04-10; Can St German's Cathl 99-10; rtd 10; P-in-c German St Jo *S & M* from 10; C Michael from 10. *50 Faaie ny Cabbal, Kirk Michael, Isle of Man IM6 2HU* Tel (01624) 878855

CONWAY, Alfred Sydney. b 22. Kelham Th Coll 40. **d** 45 **p** 46. C Fulham St Oswald w St Aug *Lon* 45-49; PC Allenton and Shelton Lock *Derby* 49-55; P-in-c Chaddesden St Phil 55-63; V Croxley Green All SS *St Alb* 63-81; V Watton St Jo *Liv* 81-89; rtd 89; Perm to Offic *Ex* from 89. *58 Millhead Road, Honiton EX14 1RA* Tel (01404) 46052

CONWAY, Canon Glyn Haydn. b 38. St Mich Coll Llan. **d** 65 **p** 66. C Wrexham *St As* 65-71; TV 71-77; V Holywell 77-83; V Upton Ascension *Ches* 83-05; rtd 05; Hon Can Accra from 03;

Perm to Offic *St As* from 07. *15 Penygraig, Aberystwyth SY23 2JA* Tel (01970) 612637 E-mail glyn.conway@btinternet.com

CONWAY, John Arthur. b 67. Leeds Univ BEng90 Edin Univ BD97. Linc Th Coll 94 TISEC 95. **d** 97 **p** 98. C Edin St Mary 97-01; R Edin St Martin from 01; Chapl Edin Sick Children's NHS Trust 98-01. *15 Ardmillan Terrace, Edinburgh EH11 2JW* Tel 0131-337 5471 E-mail jaconway@talktalk.net

CONWAY, Philip James. b 66. Lin Inst of Educn BA91. St Steph Ho Ox 92. **d** 95 **p** 96. C High Harrogate Ch Ch *Ripon* 95-99; P-in-c Menheniot *Truro* 99-08; C St Ive and Pensilva w Quethiock 02-08; P-in-c Lostwithiel, St Winnow w St Nectan's Chpl etc from 08; P-in-c Lanlivery from 08. *The Rectory, 3 Springfield Close, Lostwithiel PL22 0ER* E-mail lostwithielrectory@live.co.uk

CONWAY, Mrs Sandra Coralie. b 45. Bris Univ BA66. S'wark Ord Course 89. **d** 92 **p** 00. NSM Kenley *S'wark* 92-05; Perm to Offic *S'wark* 06-07 and *Guildf* 07-09; NSM E Horsley and Ockham w Hatchford and Downside *Guildf* from 09. *Rowan Tree Cottage, Norrels Drive, East Horsley, Leatherhead KT24 5DR* Tel (01483) 281497 E-mail sandyconwayrtc@btinternet.com

✠**CONWAY, The Rt Revd Stephen David.** b 57. Keble Coll Ox BA80 MA84 CertEd81 Selw Coll Cam BA85. Westcott Ho Cam 83. **d** 86 **p** 87 **c** 06. C Heworth St Mary *Dur* 86-89; C Bishopwearmouth St Mich w St Hilda 89-90; Dir of Ords and Hon C Dur St Marg 90-94; P-in-c Cockerton 94-96; V 96-98; Bp's Sen Chapl and Communications Officer 98-02; Adn Dur and Can Res Dur Cathl 02-06; Area Bp Ramsbury *Sarum* 06-10; Bp Ely from 10. *The Bishop's House, The College, Ely CB7 4DW* Tel (01353) 662749 Fax 669477 E-mail bishop@ely.anglican.org

CONWAY, Thomas Robertson. b 36. **d** 86 **p** 87. C Bangor Abbey *D & D* 86-95; I Dungiven w Bovevagh *D & R* 89-95; I Carrowdore w Millisle *D & D* 95-00; rtd 00. *6 Rosstulla Drive, Newtownabbey BT37 0QJ* Tel (028) 9086 0523

CONWAY-LEE, Stanley. b 17. Linc Th Coll 68. **d** 70 **p** 71. C Dedham *Chelmsf* 70-72; C Lt Ilford St Mich 72-74; V Tollesbury 74-75; V Tollesbury w Salcot Virley 75-79; V Bocking St Pet 79-85; rtd 85; Perm to Offic *Chelmsf* from 85. *10 Northumberland Close, Braintree CM7 9NL* Tel and fax (01376) 550117

COOGAN, The Ven Robert Arthur William. b 29. Univ of Tasmania BA51. St Jo Coll Dur 51. **d** 53 **p** 54. C Plaistow St Andr *Chelmsf* 53-56; R Bothwell Australia 56-62; V N Woolwich *Chelmsf* 62-73; P-in-c W Silvertown St Barn 62-73; V Hampstead St Steph *Lon* 73-77; P-in-c N St Pancras All Hallows 74-77; RD S Camden 75-81; P-in-c Old St Pancras w Bedford New Town St Matt 76-80; V Hampstead St Steph w All Hallows 77-85; P-in-c Kentish Town St Martin w St Andr 78-81; AD N Camden 78-83; Preb St Paul's Cathl 82-85; Adn Hampstead 85-94; rtd 94; Perm to Offic *Chich* 94-00 and *St E* from 03. *Salters Hall West, Stour Street, Sudbury CO10 2AX* Tel (01787) 370026

COOK, Alan. b 27. St Deiniol's Hawarden 79. **d** 80 **p** 81. Hon C Gatley *Ches* 80-83; Chapl Man R Eye Hosp 83-86; Chapl Asst Man R Infirmary 80-83 and 86-88; V Congleton St Jas *Ches* 89-93; rtd 93; Perm to Offic *Ches* from 93. *15 Buttermere Road, Gatley, Cheadle SK8 4RQ* Tel 0161-428 4350

COOK, Sister Anita Isabel. b 44. Whitelands Coll Lon CertEd66 Toronto Univ BA93. **d** 06 **p** 07. CSC from 67; Hon C E Clevedon w Clapton in Gordano etc *B & W* from 10. *St Gabriel's, 27A Dial Hill Road, Clevedon BS21 7HL* E-mail anita@sistersofthechurch.org.uk

COOK, Canon Brian Edwin. b 36. Sarum & Wells Th Coll 78. **d** 80 **p** 81. C E Wickham *S'wark* 80-83; C Petersfield w Sheet *Portsm* 83-86; R Liss 86-01; RD Petersfield 91-96 and 99; Hon Can Portsm Cathl 96-01; rtd 01; Perm to Offic *Chich* from 01. *Daubeney Cottage, Bersted Street, South Bersted, Bognor Regis PO22 9QE* Tel (01243) 828379 E-mail daubeney@tesco.net

COOK, Brian Robert. b 43. Chich Th Coll 83. **d** 85 **p** 86. C Whyke w Rumboldswhyke and Portfield *Chich* 85-87; C Worth 87-90; TV 90-94; P-in-c Chidham 94-99; V 99-04; RD Westbourne 99-04; P-in-c E Blatchington 04-08; R E Blatchington and Bishopstone 08-11; rtd 11; Hon C Wymering *Portsm* from 11; Hon C Cosham from 11. *269 Hawthorn Crescent, Cosham, Portsmouth PO6 2TL*

COOK, Celia Jane. b 66. DipCOT94. ERMC 07. **d** 10 **p** 11. C Aldeburgh w Hazlewood *St E* from 10. *1 The Birches, Aldeburgh IP15 5PW* Tel (01728) 453946 Mobile 07857-823617 E-mail thecooksonline@hotmail.co.uk

COOK, Canon Charles Peter. b 32. St Jo Coll Dur BA54. Cranmer Hall Dur. **d** 58 **p** 59. C Kingston upon Hull H Trin *York* 58-64; V High Elswick St Paul *Newc* 64-74; V Cheadle Hulme St Andr *Ches* 74-98; Hon Can Ches Cathl 91-98; rtd 98; Perm to Offic *Newc* 00-05; Carl 01-05; *Ches* from 05. *4 Moseley Grange, Cheadle Hulme, Cheadle SK8 5EZ* Tel 0161-485 1702

COOK, Christopher. See COOK, Canon James Christopher Donald

COOK, Christopher. b 44. Qu Coll Birm 68. **d** 69 **p** 70. C Gt Ilford St Mary *Chelmsf* 69-72; C Corringham 72-77; R E Donyland

77-84; R Pentlow, Foxearth, Liston and Borley 84-88; Chapl RAD Essex Area 88-89; rtd 89; Perm to Offic *Chelmsf* 89-04. *Oak Mill, Field View Drive, Little Totham, Maldon CM9 8ND* Tel (01621) 893280

COOK, Canon Christopher Arthur. Edin Th Coll 53. **d** 56 **p** 58. C Motherwell *Glas* 56-59; S Africa 59-64 and from 70; Clydesdale Miss 59-60; Matatiele St Steph 60-61; Idutywa St Barn 61-64; Area Sec USPG *Wakef* and *Sheff* 65-70; R Grahamstown St Matt Miss 70-95; Adn Grahamstown 80-95; Hon Can Grahamstown from 96; rtd 96. *PO Box 7641, East London, 5200 South Africa* Tel (0027) (431) 385357

COOK, Christopher Charles Holland. b 56. K Coll Lon BSc77 MB, BS81 MD95 MRCPsych87. SEITE 97. **d** 00 **p** 01. Prof Psychiatry Alcohol Misuse Kent Inst of Medicine and Health Science 97-03; NSM Otham w Langley *Cant* 00-03; Chapl and Prof Fell St Chad's Coll Dur 03-05; Prof Research Fell Dur Univ from 05; Tutor and Lect Cranmer Hall Dur from 08. *Department of Theology and Religion, Abbey House, Palace Green, Durham DH1 3RS* Tel 0191-334 3885 E-mail c.c.h.cook@durham.ac.uk

COOK, David. b 46. Hertf Coll Ox BA MA72. Wycliffe Hall Ox 69. **d** 73 **p** 74. C Hartlepool All SS Stranton *Dur* 74-75; Lect Qu Coll Birm 75-81; Chapl Cranbrook Sch Kent 81-11; rtd 11. *33 Oatfield Drive, Cranbrook TN17 3LA* Tel (01580) 713310 E-mail senor aardvark@hotmail.com

COOK, David Arthur. b 50. St Jo Coll Dur BA74. St Steph Ho Ox 86. **d** 88 **p** 89. C S Bank *York* 88-91; C Up Hatherley *Glouc* 91-93; P-in-c Cumbernauld *Glas* 93-04; P-in-c Helensburgh from 04. *The Rectory, 16 William Street, Helensburgh G84 8BD* Tel (01436) 672300 E-mail rector@stmichaelhelensburgh.org.uk

COOK, Canon David Charles Murray. b 41. MA. Wycliffe Hall Ox 65. **d** 67 **p** 68. C Chatham St Phil and St Jas *Roch* 67-71; S Africa 71-89; TR Newbury *Ox* 89-02; RD Newbury 98-02; Hon Can Ch Ch 02; P-in-c Chipping Campden w Ebrington *Glouc* from 02. *The Vicarage, Church Street, Chipping Campden GL55 6JG* Tel (01386) 840671

COOK, David Smith. b 47. Hull Univ BTh88 MA93. Lich Th Coll 68. **d** 71 **p** 72. C Tudhoe Grange *Dur* 71-75; C Bishopwearmouth St Mary V w St Pet CD 75-77; V Copley *Wakef* 77-80; V Birstall 80-83; V Holme upon Spalding Moor *York* 83-98; R Holme and Seaton Ross Gp 98-01; RD S Wold 96-01; V Copmanthorpe 01-07; P-in-c Askham Bryan 01-07; Chapl Askham Bryan Coll 01-04; P-in-c Eskdaleside w Ugglebarnby and Sneaton *York* 07-09; V Lower Esk from 09; RD Whitby from 08. *The Vicarage, 22 Eskdaleside, Sleights, Whitby YO22 5EP* Tel (01947) 810349 E-mail revcook@btinternet.com

COOK, Elspeth Jean. b 34. Edin Univ BSc56 PhD66. S Dios Minl Tr Scheme 85. **d** 88 **p** 94. C Yateley *Win* 88-91; Assoc Chapl Ld Mayor Treloar Hosp Alton 91-93; NSM Dunfermline *St And* 93-99; P-in-c Aberdour 96-01; rtd 01. *12 River View, Dalgety Bay, Dunfermline KY11 9YE* Tel (01383) 825222 E-mail andrewandjean.cook@tesco.net

COOK, Geoffrey John Anderson. b 64. St Steph Ho Ox. **d** 97 **p** 98. C St Leonards Ch Ch and St Mary *Chich* 97-99; Hon Asst P Brighton St Mich 00-02; Hon C Southwick St Mich 02-03; Asst Chapl Univ Coll Lon Hosps NHS Foundn Trust 03-05; Chapl W Herts Hosps NHS Trust 05-06; Chapl E Sussex Hosps NHS Trust from 06. *The Chaplain's Office, Eastbourne District General Hospital, King's Drive, Eastbourne BN21 2UD* Tel (01323) 417400

COOK, Ian. b 63. Trin Coll Bris. **d** 09 **p** 10. C Plymouth St Jude *Ex* from 09. *120 Salisbury Road, Plymouth PL4 8TB* Tel (01752) 665653

COOK, Ian Bell. b 38. NW Ord Course 70. **d** 73 **p** 74. C Oldham St Paul *Man* 73-75; Ind Chapl 76-79; P-in-c Newton Heath St Wilfrid and St Anne 76-79; V Middleton Junction 79-08; rtd 08; Perm to Offic *Man* from 09. *109 Hollin Lane, Middleton, Manchester M24 5LA* Tel 0161-654 0283 E-mail ian.cook13@btopenworld.com

COOK, Preb Ian Brian. b 38. Aston Univ MSc72 Birm Univ MA76 MBIM73. Kelham Th Coll 58. **d** 63 **p** 64. C Langley Marish *Ox* 63-66; C Stokenchurch and Cadmore End 66-68; V Lane End 68-72; P-in-c Ibstone w Fingest 68-72; Tutor W Bromwich Coll of Comm and Tech 72-74; Sen Tutor 74-80; NSM W Bromwich St Pet *Lich* 77-80; R Wednesbury St Jas and St Jo 80-03; Dir St Jas Tr Inst 81-03; RD Wednesbury 88-03; Preb Lich Cathl 94-03; rtd 03; Perm to Offic *Lich* from 03; RD Penkridge 06-11. *4 Orams Lane, Brewood, Stafford ST19 9EA* Tel (01902) 850960

COOK, Canon James Christopher Donald. b 49. Ch Ch Ox BA70 MA74. St Steph Ho Ox 79. **d** 80 **p** 81. C Witney *Ox* 80-83; CF 83-04; P-in-c Toxteth Park St Agnes and St Pancras *Liv* 04-06; V from 06; Can Wiawso Ghana from 09. *St Agnes's Vicarage, 1 Buckingham Avenue, Liverpool L17 3BA* Tel and fax 0151-733 1742 E-mail leoclericus@aol.com

COOK, James Robert. b 45. ACCA68 FCCA73. Ox Min Course 05. **d** 08 **p** 09. NSM Newbury *Ox* 08-10; NSM W Woodhay w Enborne, Hampstead Marshall etc 10-11; NSM Walbury

Beacon from 11. *St Laurence's Rectory, West Woodhay, Newbury RG20 0BL* Tel (01488) 668122 E-mail jamesrobertcook@aol.com

COOK, Jean. *See* COOK, Elspeth Jean

COOK, Mrs Joan Lindsay. b 46. SRN70. St Jo Coll Dur 86. **d** 88 **p** 94. Par Dn Hartlepool St Hilda *Dur* 88-93; Dn-in-c 93-94; P-in-c 94-96; rtd 96. *10 Peakston Close, Hartlepool TS26 0PN* Tel (01429) 231778

COOK, John. b 32. Linc Th Coll 87. **d** 89 **p** 90. C Bourne *Linc* 89-92; R Colsterworth Gp 92-02; rtd 02. *24 Portrush Drive, Grantham NG31 9GD* Tel (01476) 569063

COOK, John Edward. b 35. AKC61. **d** 62 **p** 63. C York Town St Mich *Guildf* 62-67; Singapore 67-77; P-in-c Beoley *Worc* 78-83; V 83-89; V Bromsgrove All SS 89-01; rtd 01; Perm to Offic *Cov* from 02. *61 Newport Drive, Alcester B49 5BJ* Tel (01789) 762553 Fax 400040 E-mail jcook120@btinternet.com

COOK, John Henry. b 11. Mert Coll Ox BA34 BSc35 MA39 MSc81. Clifton Th Coll 36. **d** 38 **p** 39. C Gt Faringdon w Lt Coxwell *Ox* 38-42; C Newbury St Nic 42-45; V Winkfield 45-52; V Furze Platt 52-68; R Witney 68-78; rtd 79; Hon C Witney *Ox* from 79. *7 Madley Park House, Madley Way, Witney OX28 1AT* Tel (01993) 704609

COOK, John Michael. b 48. Coll of Resurr Mirfield 72. **d** 74 **p** 75. C Weymouth H Trin *Sarum* 74-76; C Felixstowe St Jo *St E* 76-79; P-in-c Gt and Lt Whelnetham 79-84; P-in-c Cockfield 84-85; P-in-c Bradfield St George w Bradfield St Clare etc 84-85; R Cockfield w Bradfield St Clare, Felsham etc 85-87; V Workington St Jo *Carl* from 87. *St John's Vicarage, 59 Thorncroft Gardens Workington CA14 4DP* Tel (01900) 602383

COOK, John Richard Millward. b 61. St Jo Coll Dur BA. Wycliffe Hall Ox 83. **d** 85 **p** 86. C Brampton St Thos *Derby* 85-89; C Farnborough *Guildf* 89-92; C Langham Place All So *Lon* 92-98; V Chelsea St Jo w St Andr 98-08; V Wargrave w Knowl Hill *Ox* from 08. *The Vicarage, Station Road, Wargrave, Reading RG10 8EU* Tel 0118-940 2202 E-mail johnrmcook@btinternet.com

COOK (*née* OBLESBY), Mrs Judith Mary. b 43. Cranmer Hall Dur 07. **d** 08 **p** 09. NSM Middlesbrough St Martin w St Cuth *York* from 08. *8 Windsor Crescent, Nunthorpe, Middlesbrough TS7 0AN* Tel (01642) 315482 E-mail judycook.nunthorpe@googlemail.com

COOK, Kenneth Hugh. b 30. ALAM. AKC55. **d** 56 **p** 57. C Netherfield *S'well* 56-59; C Newark w Coddington 59-61; V Basford St Aid 61-67; V Gargrave *Bradf* 67-77; Dir of Ords 77-89; Can Res Bradf Cathl 77-95; rtd 95; Perm to Offic *Ripon* from 95. *25 Hollins Close, Hampsthwaite, Harrogate HG3 2EH* Tel (01423) 772521

COOK (*née* McCLEAN), Mrs Lydia Margaret Sheelagh. b 72. Ball Coll Ox BA94 MA98. Cuddesdon Coll 94. **d** 96 **p** 97. C Brackley St Pet w St Jas 96-99; Chapl Cranford Ho Sch Ox 99-02; NSM Wallingford *Ox* 99-01; NSM Wallingford Deanery 01-04; NSM Sandford-on-Thames 04-06. *Tower View Farm, Kingston, Sturminster Newton DT10 2AR* Tel (01258) 817914 E-mail simonandlydia@towerviewfarm.co.uk

COOK, Marcus John Wyeth. b 41. Chich Th Coll 67. **d** 70 **p** 71. C Friern Barnet St Jas *Lon* 70-73; Hon C St Geo-in-the-East w St Paul 73-00; Perm to Offic 73-00. *St George-in-the-East Church, Cannon Street Road, London E1 0BH* Tel (020) 7481 1345

COOK, Matthew. b 78. Oak Hill Th Coll. **d** 06 **p** 07. C Bispham *Blackb* 06-10; P-in-c Preston St Steph 10-11; V from 11. *St Stephen's Vicarage, 32 West Cliff, Preston PR1 8HU* Tel (01772) 555762 E-mail matthewcook14@btinternet.com

COOK, Mrs Myrtle Bridget Weigela. b 47. BA LLM. EMMTC. **d** 04 **p** 05. NSM Kibworth and Smeeton Westerby and Saddington *Leic* 04-08; NSM Church Langton cum Tur Langton etc from 08; P-in-c from 11. *1 Highcroft, Husbands Bosworth, Lutterworth LE17 6LF* Tel (01858) 880935 E-mail mchighcroft@aol.com

COOK, Neil John. b 70. Wolv Univ BA93. Wycliffe Hall Ox 05. **d** 06 **p** 07. C Roby *Liv* 06-07; C Huyton Quarry 07-10; P-in-c Goose Green from 10. *21 Colby Road, Wigan WN3 5NP* Tel 07733-296850 (mobile) E-mail cookrnj@googlemail.com

COOK, Nicholas Leonard. b 59. Nottm Univ BCombStuds84. Linc Th Coll 81. **d** 84 **p** 85. C Leic St Pet 84-85; C Knighton St Mich 85-86; Chapl Asst Towers Hosp Humberstone 86-89; Chapl Leics Mental Health Service Unit 89-91; Chapl Quantin Hall Sch Harrow 91-94; CF(V) 88-94; CF from 94. *clo MOD Chaplains (Army)* Tel (01264) 381140 Fax 381824

COOK, Paul Raymond. *See* McLAREN-COOK, Paul Raymond

COOK, Peter John. b 57. Ridley Hall Cam 93. **d** 95 **p** 96. C Romford Gd Shep *Chelmsf* 95-98; C Colchester St Jo 98-06; V Bangkok Ch Ch Thailand from 06. *11 Convent Road, Bangkok 10500, Thailand* Tel (0066) (2) 266 2887 E-mail vicar@christchurchbangkok.org

COOK, Peter Ralph. b 69. Portsm Univ BA92 Kent Univ BA06. SEITE 03. **d** 06 **p** 07. C Hadlow *Roch* 06-09; V Docking, the Birchams, Stanhoe and Sedgeford *Nor* from 09. *The Vicarage,*

COOK

Sedgeford Road, Docking, King's Lynn PE31 8PN Tel (01485) 517157 E-mail t2andnor@supanet.com

COOK, Mrs Rachel Elizabeth. d 11. NSM Haydon Wick *Bris* from 11. *7 Capesthorne Drive, Swindon SN25 1UP* Tel (01793) 706142 Mobile 07584-094104 E-mail rachelecook@btinternet.com

COOK, Canon Richard John Noel. b 49. Univ Coll Ox BA70 MA74 PGCE72. Wycliffe Hall Ox MA77. **d** 78 **p** 79. C Fulwood *Sheff* 78-80; C Bolton St Paul w Em *Man* 81-86; TV 86-93; V Goldsworth Park *Guildf* from 93; RD Woking 99-03; Hon Can Guildf Cathl from 10. *St Andrew's Vicarage, 8 Cardingham, Woking GU21 3LN* Tel (01483) 764523 E-mail cookingwok@tiscali.co.uk

COOK, Canon Robert Bond. b 28. Dur Univ BSc54. Ripon Hall Ox 54. **d** 56 **p** 57. C Benwell St Jas *Newc* 56-60; C Sugley 60-64; V Denton 64-75; V Haltwhistle 75-88; P-in-c Greenhead 84-88; V Haltwhistle and Greenhead 88-93; RD Hexham 88-93; Hon Can Newc Cathl 92-93; rtd 93; Perm to Offic *St E* from 94; RD Lavenham 03-05. *Ashcroft, Heath Road, Woolpit, Bury St Edmunds IP30 9RN* Tel (01359) 240670

COOK, Mrs Ruth Anna Margaret. b 52. Bedf Coll of Educn CertEd74. **d** 08 **p** 09. OLM Smestow Vale *Lich* from 08. *10 Dowells Gardens, Stourbridge DY8 5QA* Tel (01384) 835311 Mobile 07796-615982 E-mail ruthfromstourbridge@googlemail.com

COOK, Simon David James. b 74. St Cath Coll Ox BA97 St Jo Coll Dur BA08. Cranmer Hall Dur 06. **d** 08 **p** 09. C Broughton *Man* 08-11; V Kirklees Valley from 11. *All Saints' Vicarage, 10 Kirkburn View, Bury BL8 1DL* Tel 0161-797 1595 Mobile 07745-232662 E-mail simondjcook@aol.com

COOK, Stephen. b 62. JP05. Brunel Univ BSc(Econ)84. S'wark Ord Course 89. **d** 92 **p** 93. Hon C Forest Hill St Aug *S'wark* 92-98; P-in-c Eltham St Barn 98-10; V from 11; CF (TA) from 00. *St Barnabas' Vicarage, 449 Rochester Way, London SE9 6PH* Tel (020) 8856 8294 E-mail cooksca@aol.com

COOK, Stephen William. b 57. Bris Univ BA80 Lambeth STh86. Trin Coll Bris 82. **d** 85 **p** 86. C Heref St Pet w St Owen and St Jas 85-89; TV Keynsham *B & W* 89-95; V Hanham *Bris* 95-02; RD Bitton 98-99; AD Kingswood and S Glos 99-02; TR Okehampton w Inwardleigh, Bratton Clovelly etc *Ex* from 02; RD Okehampton from 05. *The Rectory, 1 Church Path, Okehampton EX20 1LW* Tel (01837) 659297

COOK, Timothy John. b 62. Cranmer Hall Dur 95. **d** 95 **p** 96. C Dorchester *Sarum* 95-99; TV Ilminster and Distr *B & W* 99-03; R Yeovil H Trin w Barwick from 03. *Holy Trinity Vicarage, 24 Turners Barn Lane, Yeovil BA20 2LM* Tel (01935) 423774 E-mail timcook@tesco.net

COOK, Trevor Vivian. b 43. Sarum Th Coll 67. **d** 69 **p** 70. C Lambeth St Phil *S'wark* 69-73; C St Buryan, St Levan and Sennen *Truro* 73-75; V The Ilketshalls *St E* 75-79; P-in-c Rumburgh w S Elmham 75-79; R Rumburgh w S Elmham w the Ilketshalls 79-84; TR Langport Area *B & W* 84-96; P-in-c Rode Major 96-02; C Hardington Vale 02-04; rtd 04; Perm to Offic *B & W* from 04. *Hedge End, 5 Queen Street, Keinton Mandeville, Somerton TA11 6EH* Tel (01458) 224448

COOKE, Alan. b 50. Nottm Univ BTh74 Lanc Univ PGCE75. Kelham Th Coll 69. **d** 75 **p** 76. C Tyldesley w Shakerley *Man* 75-78; C Langley All SS and Martyrs 80-82; TV Langley and Parkfield 82-83; P-in-c Chadderton St Mark 83-85; V from 85. *St Mark's Vicarage, Milne Street, Chadderton, Oldham OL9 0HR* Tel 0161-624 2005

COOKE, Angela Elizabeth. b 42. SRN65 SCM67. St Jo Coll Nottm 85. **d** 87 **p** 94. Par Dn Walton H Trin *Cov* 87-92; Par Dn Bexleyheath Ch Ch *Roch* 92-94; C 94-97; V St Mary Cray and St Paul's Cray 97-05; rtd 05. *7 Maytree Gardens, Bexhill-on-Sea TN40 2PE* Tel (01424) 213268 E-mail angelacooke@hotmail.com

COOKE (née LEA), Mrs Carolyn Jane. b 65. Nottm Univ BA88 PGCE90. St Jo Coll Nottm MTh02. **d** 02 **p** 03. C Hyson Green and Forest Fields *S'well* 02-06; TV Clifton 06-10; Chapl La Côte Eur from 10. *Address temp unknown* E-mail d.cooke3@ntlworld.com

COOKE, Christopher Stephen. b 54. Lon Univ BA76 MA77 Ox Univ BA81 MA88. Ripon Coll Cuddesdon 79. **d** 82 **p** 83. C Cen Telford *Lich* 82-86; R Uffington, Upton Magna and Withington 86-95; RD Wrockwardine 92-01; TR Wrockwardine Deanery 95-01; P-in-c Wem from 01; P-in-c Lee Brockhurst from 01; P-in-c Loppington w Newtown 01-02. *The Rectory, Ellesmere Road, Wem, Shrewsbury SY4 5TU* Tel (01939) 232550 E-mail christopher@csc2000.f9.co.uk

COOKE, Daniel. b 84. Hull Univ BA06. St Jo Coll Nottm 06. **d** 08 **p** 09. C W Acklam *York* 08-11; R Brimington *Derby* from 11. *The Rectory, Church Street, Brimington, Chesterfield S43 1JG* Tel (01246) 273103 E-mail danielbcooke@hotmail.com

COOKE, David John. b 31. Linc Th Coll 60. **d** 62 **p** 63. C Brighton Gd Shep Preston *Chich* 62-65; C Clayton w Keymer 65-70; R Stone w Hartwell w Bishopstone *Ox* 70-77; R Stone w Dinton

and Hartwell 77-07; rtd 07; Perm to Offic *Ox* from 08. *5 Astronomy Way, Aylesbury HP19 7WD* Tel (01296) 748215

COOKE, David Michael Randle. b 68. Newc Univ BA90. Wycliffe Hall Ox 05. **d** 07 **p** 08. C Richmond H Trin and Ch Ch *S'wark* from 07. *Holy Trinity Church, Sheen Park, Richmond TW9 1UP* Tel (020) 8404 1112 Mobile 07766-900267 E-mail davidcooke2003@hotmail.com *or* david.cooke@htrichmond.org.uk

COOKE, Francis Theodore. b 34. Tyndale Hall Bris 53 Clifton Th Coll 58. **d** 02 **p** 03. Ind Missr Bentley Motors *Ches* from 02; NSM Woodford from 02; NSM Poynton 02-03. *13 Maple Avenue, Poynton, Stockport SK12 1PR* Tel (01625) 859246

COOKE, Frederic Ronald. b 35. Selw Coll Cam BA58 MA61. Ridley Hall Cam 59. **d** 61 **p** 62. C Flixton St Mich *Man* 61-64; C-in-c Flixton St Jo CD 64-67; V Flixton St Jo 68-74; R Ashton St Mich 74-77; Jerusalem 77-80; V Walmsley *Man* 80-85; AD Walmsley 81-85; Malaysia 85-90; Prin Ho of Epiphany Th Coll Borneo 85-90; P-in-c Accrington *Blackb* 90-91; TR 91-96; P-in-c Ringley w Prestolee *Man* 96-01; rtd 01; Perm to Offic *S & M* from 09. *314 Queens Court, St Pauls Square, Ramsey, Isle of Man IM8 1LF* Tel (01624) 816747

COOKE, Geoffrey. b 38. Sarum Th Coll. **d** 64 **p** 65. C Eastover *B & W* 64-67; Chapl RAF 67-71; C Bridgwater St Jo *B & W* 71-76; R N Newton w St Michaelchurch and Thurloxton 76-78; R N Newton w St Michaelchurch, Thurloxton etc 78-83; TV Yeovil 83-88; V Yeovil H Trin 88-89; R Staple Fitzpaine, Orchard Portman, Thurlbear etc 89-96; rtd 96; Perm to Offic *B & W* from 96. *34 Bluebell Close, Taunton TA1 3XQ* Tel (01823) 324235 E-mail endymion.99@virgin.net

COOKE (married name SHEARD), Ms Gillian Freda. b 39. Lon Univ BD73 Leeds Univ MA87. Linc Th Coll 74. **dss** 78 **d** 87 **p** 94. Cricklewood St Pet CD *Lon* 78-80; Chapl Middx Poly 78-80; Chapl Leeds Poly *Ripon* 80-87; N Humberside Ind Chapl *York* 87-90; Asst Chapl HM Pris Hull 90-94; Chapl Keele Univ 94-97; Assoc Min Betley and Keele 94-97; Chapl Rampton Hosp Retford 97-99; rtd 99; Perm to Offic *York* from 00; Chapl HM Pris Wolds from 05. *The Chaplain's Office, HM Prison Wolds, Everthorpe, Brough HU15 2JZ* Tel (01430) 428000 E-mail gilalsrd@gilalsrd.karoo.co.uk

COOKE (née MORRALL), Mrs Heather Lynne. b 55. LMH Ox BA76 MA80 MIPR88. Open Th Coll 94 Dioc OLM tr scheme 96. **d** 99 **p** 00. OLM Martlesham w Brightwell *St E* from 99. *9 Swan Close, Martlesham Heath, Ipswich IP5 3SD* Tel (01473) 623770 Mobile 07703-568051 E-mail hcookema@aol.com

COOKE, James Martin. b 46. Trin Coll Ox BA67 Ox Univ DipEd68. **d** 07 **p** 08. OLM Wonersh w Blackheath *Guildf* from 07. *7 Durnsford Way, Cranleigh GU6 7LN* Tel (01483) 276049 E-mail james.cooke20@virgin.net

COOKE, John Stephen. b 35. K Coll Lon BD58 AKC58. **d** 60 **p** 60. C W Bromwich St Fran *Lich* 59-62; C Chalfont St Peter *Ox* 62-66; V Cross Heath *Lich* 66-72; R Haughton 72-86; P-in-c Ellenhall w Ranton 72-80; V Eccleshall 86-00; Sub Chapl HM Pris Drake Hall 89-95; rtd 00; Perm to Offic *Lich* from 00. *50 High Street, Eccleshall, Stafford ST21 6BZ* Tel (01785) 850570

COOKE, Canon Kenneth John. b 29. Linc Coll Ox BA53 MA57. Ely Th Coll 53. **d** 55 **p** 56. C Nuneaton St Mary *Cov* 55-58; C Cov St Thos 58-61; V Willenhall 61-66; V Meriden 66-76; V Cov St Geo 76-84; V Leamington Spa H Trin and Old Milverton 84-94; Hon Can Cov Cathl 92-94; rtd 94; Perm to Offic *Cov* from 94. *2 Chantry Crescent, Alcester B49 5BT* Tel (01789) 763460

COOKE, Michael David. b 46. New Coll Ox BA68 MA71 DPhil71. Ox NSM Course 75. **d** 78 **p** 79. NSM Newport Pagnell *Ox* 78-85; NSM Newport Pagnell w Lathbury and Moulsoe 85-88; NSM Beckenham Ch Ch *Roch* 90-96; P-in-c Seal St Lawr 96-10; P-in-c Underriver 96-10; rtd 10; Perm to Offic *Cant* from 11. *92 Dumpton Park Drive, Broadstairs CT10 1RL* Tel (01843) 863293 E-mail mcooke.92@btinternet.com

COOKE, Michael John. b 39. Ab Dioc Tr Course 78. **d** 80 **p** 81. NSM St Andr Cathl 80-81; Chapl Miss to Seamen 81-88; Miss to Seamen Tilbury 88-91; Hon C Immingham *Linc* 81-88; Ind Chapl Teesside *Dur* 91-97; V Kelloe and Coxhoe 97-06; rtd 06. *24 West Pasture, Kirkbymoorside, York YO62 6BR* E-mail mikecooke8@yahoo.co.uk

COOKE, Miss Priscilla Garland Hamel. b 24. Gilmore Ho 69. **dss** 80 **d** 87 **p** 94. Bromsgrove St Jo *Worc* 80-82; Lee Abbey 82-85; Torquay St Matthias, St Mark and H Trin *Ex* 86-87; NSM 87-92 and 94-98; Perm to Offic 92-94 and 98-08. *7 Woodrow, Asheldon Road, Torquay TQ1 2QN* Tel (01803) 297366

COOKE, Raymond. b 34. Liv Univ BSc56. Wells Th Coll 58. **d** 60 **p** 61. C Newton Heath All SS *Man* 60-64; C-in-c Failsworth H Family CD 64-75; R Failsworth H Family 75-83; P-in-c Man Gd Shep 83-88; V Westleigh St Pet 88-99; rtd 99; Perm to Offic *Man* from 99. *136 Victoria Avenue East, Manchester M9 6HF* Tel 0161-740 0664

COOKE, Richard James. b 60. Pemb Coll Ox BA82 MA88 Bris Univ PhD96. Trin Coll Bris 85. **d** 88 **p** 89. C Rugby St Matt *Cov* 88-92; V Fletchamstead 92-04; Dir Initial Tr for Readers 97-02;

CME Adv 04-07; CME Lay Development and Local Min Adv 07-08; Dir of Discipleship Development from 09; C Warmington w Shotteswell and Radway w Ratley from 07; C Kineton from 07; C Combroke w Compton Verney from 07. *Diocesan Office, 1 Hill Top, Coventry CV1 5AB* Tel (024) 7652 1200 E-mail richard.cooke@covcofe.org

COOKE, Roger. b 68. Heriot-Watt Univ BA90 BArch91 Edin Univ MTh02. TISEC 98. **d** 99 **p** 00. C Prestonpans *Edin* 99-02; R 02-09; C Musselburgh 99-02; R 02-09; I Coleraine *Conn* from 09. *St Patrick's Rectory, 28 Mountsandel Road, Coleraine BT52 1JE* Tel (028) 7034 3429 E-mail carrington20@aol.com

COOKE, Stephen. *See* COOKE, John Stephen

COOKE, Mrs Suzanne. b 65. Westmr Coll Ox BTh96. Westcott Ho Cam 08. **d** 10 **p** 11. C Watton *Nor* from 10. *44 Jubilee Road, Watton, Thetford IP25 6BS* Tel (01953) 889905 E-mail suzanne@cookehouse.co.uk

COOKSEY, Miss Diane Marie. b 75. Univ of Cen England in Birm BA(QTS)97. St Jo Coll Nottm 09. **d** 11. C Churchill-in-Halfshire w Blakedown and Broome *Worc* from 11. *14 The Croft, Blakedown, Kidderminster DY10 3JP* Tel 07974-556514 (mobile) E-mail diane cooksey@hotmail.com

COOKSON, Canon Diane Veronica. b 51. NOC 81. **dss** 84 **d** 87 **p** 94. Gt Sutton *Ches* 84-86; Neston 86-87; Par Dn 87-94; C 94-96; V Stockport St Sav from 96; Ecum Adv (Gtr Man) 00-02; Hon Can Ches Cathl from 04. *St Saviour's Vicarage, 22 St Saviour's Road, Great Moor, Stockport SK2 7QE* Tel 0161-483 2633 E-mail st.saviours@virgin.net

COOKSON, Canon Graham Leslie. b 37. Sarum Th Coll 64. **d** 67 **p** 68. C Upton Ascension *Ches* 67-69; C Timperley 69-75; V Godley cum Newton Green 75-83; R Tarporley 83-07; Hon Can Ches Cathl 04-07; rtd 07. *15 Dolphin Court, Chester CH4 8JX* Tel (01244) 671044

COOKSON, Matthew. **d** 09 **p** 10. NSM Kintbury w Avington *Ox* 09-11; NSM W Woodhay w Enborne, Hampstead Marshall etc 09-11; NSM Walbury Beacon from 11. *84 Church Street, Great Bedwyn, Marlborough SN8 3PF* Tel (01672) 871013 E-mail mjgcookson@gmail.com

COOKSON, William. b 61. **d** 98 **p** 99. C Haydock St Mark *Liv* 98-02; Min Wallington Springfield Ch *S'wark* from 02. *49 Stanley Park Road, Carshalton SM5 3HT* Tel (020) 8404 6064 E-mail willcookson@blueyonder.co.uk

COOLING, Derrick William. b 35. AKC58 Heref Coll of Educn TCert68 Lon Univ BD69 DipEd71 Univ of Wales (Cardiff) MEd81. St Boniface Warminster 58. **d** 59 **p** 60. C Haydock St Jas *Liv* 59-61; C Hove St Barn *Chich* 61-63; V Llangattock w St Maughan's etc *Mon* 63-68; R Blaina 68-70; Perm to Offic *Sarum* 70-74; Chapl Windsor Girls' Sch Hamm 74-75; Asst Master Croesyceiliog Sch Cwmbran 75-81; Chapl Epsom Coll 81-84; V Bettws *Mon* 84-95; P-in-c Purleigh, Cold Norton and Stow Maries *Chelmsf* 95-98; rtd 98; Perm to Offic *Mon* from 98 and *Glouc* from 05. *St Thomas Cottage, The Fence, St Briavels, Lydney GL15 6QG* Tel and fax (01594) 530926 E-mail clericderrick@aol.com

COOLING (*née* YOUNG), **Mrs Margaret Dorothy.** b 37. K Coll Lon BA59 AKC Lon Univ BD69 DipEd71 Univ of Wales (Cardiff) MEd81. Mon Dioc Tr Scheme 89. **d** 90 **p** 95. NSM Bettws *Mon* 95; NSM Purleigh, Cold Norton and Stow Maries *Chelmsf* 95-98; rtd 98; Perm to Offic *Mon* from 98 and *Glouc* from 01; Warden, Lect and Preacher Newland Almshouses from 04. *St Thomas Cottage, The Fence, St Briavels, Lydney GL15 6QG* Tel and fax (01594) 530926 E-mail clericderrick@aol.com

COOMBE, James Anthony. b 31. Em Coll Cam BA53 MA57 Lon Univ BD60. Tyndale Hall Bris 57. **d** 60 **p** 61. C Chadderton Ch Ch *Man* 60-63; C Worthing St Geo *Chich* 63-65; V Wandsworth St Mich *S'wark* 65-74; P-in-c Warboys *Ely* 74-76; R 76-87; RD St Ives 83-87; P-in-c Broughton and Wistow 84-87; R Buckworth and V Alconbury cum Weston 87-96; rtd 96; Perm to Offic *Cant* from 06. *12 Nursery Fields, Hythe CT21 4DL* Tel (01303) 262151

COOMBE, John Morrell (Brother Martin). b 25. Chich Th Coll 56. **d** 57 **p** 58. SSF from 49; Lic to Offic *Sarum* 57-59; C-in-c Hillfield and Hermitage 59-66; Asst Chapl Ellesmere Coll 66-69; Chapl Ranby Ho Sch Retford 69-71; V Cambridge St Benedict *Ely* 71-85; Perm to Offic Jerusalem 85-86; Prov Sec SSF 86-94; Sec for Miss SSF from 99; Lic to Offic *Linc* 86-95; Perm to Offic *Ely* 97-05; *Lon* from 06; *Chelmsf* from 09. *The Vicarage, 11 St Mary's Road, London E13 9AE* Tel (020) 8552 4019 E-mail martin@stmaryscssf.plus.com

COOMBE, Canon Michael Thomas. b 31. Lon Univ BA64. Ox NSM Course 73. **d** 75 **p** 76. Chapl St Piran's Sch Maidenhead 75-81; NSM Furze Platt *Ox* 75-81; C 86-88; Asst Chapl Oslo St Edm *Eur* 81-84; Chapl Belgrade w Zagreb 84-86; Chapl Marseille w St Raphaël, Aix-en-Provence etc 88-89; Chapl Reading Gp of Hosps 89-91; P-in-c Clewer St Andr *Ox* 91-92; C New Windsor 92-93; C Reading St Mark 93-95; C Reading H Trin 93-95; Prec Gib Cathl and Port Chapl 95-03; Can Gib Cathl 00-03; rtd 03. *28 Gipsy Lane, Exmouth EX8 3HN* Tel (01395) 272923

COOMBER, Ian Gladstone. b 47. Ch Ch Coll Cant CertEd68 Southn Univ BTh79. Sarum & Wells Th Coll 73. **d** 76 **p** 77. C Weeke *Win* 76-79; TV Saffron Walden w Wendens Ambo and Littlebury *Chelmsf* 79-82; V Weston *Win* 82-90; R Bedhampton *Portsm* 90-96; R Botley and Durley 96-05; V Curdridge 96-05; RD Bishop's Waltham 98-03; TR Cartmel Peninsula *Carl* 05-09; rtd 09. *Elder Cottage, Throop Road, Templecombe BA8 0HR* Tel (01963) 371205

COOMBER, Matthew James McKinnon. **d** 06. Perm to Offic *Sheff* from 06. *Flat 9, 36 Oakholme Road, Sheffield S10 3DF* Tel 0114-268 0707

COOMBES, Frederick Brian John. b 34. Nottm Univ BA56 Plymouth Poly MPhil73 FRGS. SWMTC 85. **d** 88 **p** 89. NSM Bodmin w Lanhydrock and Lanivet *Truro* 88-07; Perm to Offic from 07. *191 Boslowick Road, Falmouth TR11 4QF* Tel (01326) 210788

COOMBES, Gareth John. **d** 10 **p** 11. NSM Bedwas w Machen w Rudry *Mon* from 10. *6 Blaen Ifor, Energlyn, Caerphilly CF83 2NW* Tel (029) 2088 3979 E-mail revgareth@aol.com

COOMBS, Edward Neve. b 66. Bris Univ BSc88. Cranmer Hall Dur BA93. **d** 94 **p** 95. C Edin St Thos 94-96; C Dagenham *Chelmsf* 97-01; P-in-c Banbury St Paul *Ox* from 01. *St Paul's House, Bretch Hill, Banbury OX16 0LR* Tel (01295) 264003 E-mail encoombs@tesco.net

COOMBS, John Allen. b 46. Portsm Poly BSc70. Oak Hill Th Coll 86 Sarum & Wells Th Coll 87. **d** 89 **p** 90. C Leverington and Wisbech St Mary *Ely* 89-93; P-in-c Emneth 93-96; V Emneth and Marshland St James 96-99; P-in-c Papworth Everard 99-00; TV Papworth 00-02; Chapl Papworth Hosp NHS Foundn Trust 99-06; P-in-c Roche and Withiel *Truro* from 06. *The Rectory, Fore Street, Roche, St Austell PL26 8EP* Tel (01726) 890301 E-mail john@familycoombs.freeserve.co.uk

COOMBS, John Kendall. b 47. Culham Coll Ox BEd73. Sarum & Wells Th Coll 75. **d** 77 **p** 78. C Fareham H Trin *Portsm* 77-80; C Petersfield w Sheet 80-83; TV Beaminster Area *Sarum* 83-87; TR Preston w Sutton Poyntz and Osmington w Poxwell 87-97; TR Hermitage *Ox* 97-05; P-in-c Hurst 05-11; rtd 11. *29 Waxes Close, Abingdon OX14 2NG* E-mail jkcoombs@yahoo.co.uk

COOMBS, Martin. *See* COOMBS, Canon Walter James Martin

COOMBS, The Ven Peter Bertram. b 28. Bris Univ BA58 MA61. Clifton Th Coll 55. **d** 60 **p** 61. C Beckenham Ch Ch *Roch* 60-63; R Nottingham St Nic *S'well* 63-68; V New Malden and Coombe *S'wark* 68-75; RD Kingston 71-75; Adn Wandsworth 75-88; Adn Reigate 88-95; rtd 95; Perm to Offic *Portsm* from 97. *92 Locks Heath Park Road, Locks Heath, Southampton SO31 6LZ* Tel (01489) 577288

COOMBS, Richard Murray. b 63. St Chad's Coll Dur BSc85 Rob Coll Cam BA89 MA90. Ridley Hall Cam 87. **d** 90 **p** 91. C Enfield Ch Ch Trent Park *Lon* 90-94; C St Helen Bishopsgate w St Andr Undershaft etc 94-98; P-in-c St Pet Cornhill 95-98; V Burford w Fulbrook, Taynton, Asthall etc *Ox* from 98. *The Vicarage, Church Lane, Burford OX18 4SD* Tel (01993) 822275 Fax 824699 E-mail rmcoombs@btinternet.com

COOMBS, Stephen John. b 54. Open Univ BA86. Trin Coll Bris 85. **d** 87 **p** 88. C Norton Canes *Lich* 87-90; Chapl Trowbridge Coll *Sarum* 90-94; C Studley 90-94. *48 Whitstone Rise, Shepton Mallet BA4 5QB* Tel (01749) 343750

COOMBS, Canon Walter James Martin. b 33. Keble Coll Ox BA57 MA61. Cuddesdon Coll 59. **d** 61 **p** 62. C Kennington St Jo *S'wark* 61-64; Chapl Em Coll Cam 64-68; Bp's Dom Chapl *S'wark* 68-70; V E Dulwich St Jo 70-77; V Pershore w Pinvin, Wick and Birlingham *Worc* 77-92; Hon Can Worc Cathl 84-92; RD Pershore 85-91; TV Dorchester *Ox* 92-98; rtd 98; Perm to Offic *Ox* from 01. *54 Divinity Road, Oxford OX4 1LJ* Tel (01865) 243865

COONEY, Craig Stephen. Ulster Univ BSc98 TCD BTh06. **d** 06 **p** 07. C Lurgan Ch the Redeemer *D & D* from 06. *136 Lough Road, Lurgan, Craigavon BT66 6JL* Tel (028) 3834 4402 Mobile 07708-905560 E-mail cooneycraig@hotmail.com

COONEY, Canon Michael Patrick. b 55. City of Lon Poly BA77. Ripon Coll Cuddesdon 77. **d** 80 **p** 81. C Cov E 80-83; C Old Brumby *Linc* 83-85; V Linc St Jo 85-90; V Frodingham 90-05; RD Manlake 99-10; RD Is of Axholme 05-10; Ind Chapl from 05; Can and Preb Linc Cathl from 04. *16 Neap House Road, Gunness, Scunthorpe DN15 8TT* Tel (01724) 784245 E-mail mike.cooney@btinternet.com

COONEY, William Barry. b 47. K Coll Lon 69. **d** 70 **p** 71. C W Bromwich All SS *Lich* 70-73; C Wolverhampton St Pet 73-75; C Rugeley 75-78; V Sneyd Green 78-87; R Sandiacre *Derby* 87-11; rtd 11. *15 Newthorpe Common, Nottingham NG16 2BX*

COOPER, Alexander James Goodenough. b 47. Bath Univ BSc69. WEMTC 04. **d** 06 **p** 07. NSM Soundwell *Bris* from 06. *1 Deerhurst, Bristol BS15 1XH* Tel 0117-973 9441 E-mail linsand@blueyonder.co.uk

COOPER, Alfred Philip. b 50. Bris Univ BA71. All Nations Chr Coll 72. **d** 77 **p** 78. Chile from 75; SAMS from 77. *Iglesia Anglicana del Chile, Casilla 50675, Correo Central, Santiago, Chile* Tel (0056) (2) 226 8794

COOPER, Mrs Alison Beryl. b 51. Ripon Coll Cuddesdon 03. d 04 p 05. NSM Ascot Heath *Ox* 04-07; NSM Sunninghill and S Ascot 07-10; NSM Limpsfield and Tatsfield *S'wark* from 10; C-in-c Limpsfield Chart St Andr CD from 10. *St Andrew's Vicarage, Kent Hatch Road, Oxted RH8 0TB* Tel (01883) 723153 Mobile 07747-682139 E-mail allison@talktalk.net

COOPER, Andrew John. b 62. W Sussex Inst of HE BA87 Greenwich Univ PGCE03. St Steph Ho Ox 88. d 91 p 92. C Rawmarsh w Parkgate *Sheff* 91-93; C Mosbrough 93-95; P-in-c Donnington Wood *Lich* 95-96; CF from 96. *c/o MOD Chaplains (Army)* Tel (01264) 381140 Fax 381824

COOPER, Andrew John Gearing. b 48. Sir John Cass Coll Lon BSc70. Ripon Coll Cuddesdon 73. d 76 p 77. C Potternewton *Ripon* 76-79; Antigua 79-81; Anguilla 81-87; V W Bromwich St Andr w Ch Ch *Lich* 88-92. *45 Dimbles Lane, Lichfield WS13 7HW* Tel (01543) 416020 E-mail andrew.cooper@lichfield.anglican.org

COOPER, Andrew Richard James. b 81. Lon Metrop Univ BSc04. Ridley Hall Cam 07. d 10 p 11. C S Harrow St Paul *Lon* from 10. *39 Eastcote Lane, Harrow HA2 8DE* E-mail arjcooper@aim.com

COOPER, The Ven Annette Joy. b 53. Open Univ BA80 CQSW84. S'wark Ord Course 85. d 88 p 94. NSM Pembury *Roch* 88; Chapl Asst Kent and Sussex Hosp Tunbridge Wells 88-91; Chapl Asst Leybourne Grange Hosp W Malling 88-91; Chapl Bassetlaw Hosp and Community Services NHS Trust 91-96; P-in-c Edwinstowe *S'well* 96-04; Chapl Center Parcs Holiday Village 96-01; AD Worksop 99-04; Hon Can S'well Minster 02-04; Adn Colchester *Chelmsf* from 04. *63 Powers Hall End, Witham CM8 1NH* Tel (01376) 513130 Fax 500789 E-mail a.colchester@chelmsford.anglican.org

COOPER, Barrie Keith. b 56. Oak Hill Th Coll. d 85 p 86. C Partington and Carrington *Ches* 85-89; V Stockport St Mark 89-93; Chapl HM YOI Stoke Heath 93-01; Chapl HM Pris Acklington 01-08; Chapl HM Pris Dur from 08. *HM Prison, Old Elvet, Durham DH1 3HU* Tel 0191-332 3400

COOPER, Canon Bede Robert. b 42. Ex Univ BA69. Coll of Resurr Mirfield 69. d 71 p 72. C Weymouth H Trin *Sarum* 71-74; P-in-c Broad Town 74-79; V Wootton Bassett 74-86; R Wilton w Netherhampton and Fugglestone 86-07; Can and Preb Sarum Cathl 88-07; rtd 07. *205 High Street, Milborne Port, Sherborne DT9 5AG* Tel (01963) 250503

COOPER, Benedict Christopher. b 68. K Coll Cam BA90 Wolfs Coll Ox MPhil94 DPhil97 W Sydney Univ PhD10. Oak Hill Th Coll BA03. d 03 p 04. C St Helen Bishopsgate w St Andr Undershaft etc *Lon* 03-07; Australia 07-10; C Fulwood *Sheff* from 10. *522 Fulwood Road, Sheffield S10 3QD* Tel 0114-230 4444 *or* 229 5567 Mobile 07402-065857 E-mail bencooper@fulwoodchurch.co.uk

COOPER, Bert. *See* COOPER, Herbert William

COOPER, Brian Hamilton. b 35. Keble Coll Ox BA58 MA67. Ripon Hall Ox 58. d 60 p 61. C Woolwich St Mary w H Trin *S'wark* 60-64; Canada 64-66; Vice-Prin Westcott Ho Cam 66-71; R Downham Market w Bexwell *Ely* 71-82; RD Fincham 80-82; V Chesterfield St Mary and All SS *Derby* 82-91; V Herringthorpe *Sheff* 91-00; RD Rotherham 93-98; rtd 00. Perm to Offic *Sheff* from 00. *51 Anston Avenue, Worksop S81 7HU* Tel (01909) 479306 E-mail m.y.cooper1723@aol.com

✠**COOPER, The Rt Revd Carl Norman.** b 60. Univ of Wales (Lamp) BA82 Trin Coll Carmarthen MPhil99. Wycliffe Hall Ox 82. d 85 p 86 c 02. C Llanelli St D 85-87; P-in-c Llanerch Aeron w Ciliau Aeron and Dihewyd etc 87-88; R 88-93; R Dolgellau w Llanfachreth and Brithdir etc *Ban* 93-02; Warden of Readers 88-02; Adn Meirionnydd 00-02; Bp St D 02-08. *Hafod Lon, 35 Llandeilo Road, Llandybie, Ammanford SA18 3JA*

COOPER, Cecil Clive. b 26. TD75. AKC52. d 53 p 54. C Chipping Campden *Glouc* 53-55; C Cheltenham St Mary 55-60; V Stroud 60-65; CF (TA) 63-75; R Woodmansterne *S'wark* 65-91; RD Sutton 80-90; rtd 91; Perm to Offic *Cov* and *Pet* from 91. *10 Mill Close, Braunston, Daventry NN11 7HY* Tel (01788) 890596

COOPER, Canon Cecil William Marcus. b 32. TCD BA58 MA66. CITC 57. d 59 p 60. C Cork St Fin Barre and St Nic *C, C & R* 59-62; Bp's V, Lib and Registrar Kilkenny Cathl 62-64; C Knockbreda *D & D* 65-67; Asst Ed *Church of Ireland Gazette* 66-82; Ed 82-00; I Magheradroll 67-82; Dioc Registrar 81-90; I Drumbeg 82-00; Can Down Cathl 86-00; Prec 90-91; Chan 91-00; rtd 00. *35 Manor Drive, Lisburn BT28 1JH* Tel (028) 9263 4425

COOPER, Clive Anthony Charles. b 38. Lon Univ BEd74. ALCD62. d 62 p 63. C Morden *S'wark* 62-65; SAMS Argentina 65-71; Asst Master St Nic Sch Cranleigh 74-92; Hon C Cranleigh *Guildf* 78-79; Hon C Ewhurst 80-82; Hon Chapl Duke of Kent Sch 83-92; Chapl Felixstowe Coll 92-93; Perm to Offic *Ex* 94-95; Chapl Puerto Pollensa *Eur* 95-02; P-in-c Instow and Westleigh *Ex* 03-07; rtd 08; Perm to Offic *Eur* from 08 and *Ex* from 09. *1 Stanbridge Park, Bideford EX39 3RS* Tel (01237) 424617 E-mail csa.cooper@hotmail.co.uk

COOPER, Colin. b 55. Open Univ BA. St Jo Coll Nottm 83. d 86 p 87. C Cheadle Hulme St Andr *Ches* 86-89; C Tunbridge Wells St Jo *Roch* 89-93; V Whitfield *Derby* from 93. *The Vicarage, 16 Scotty Brook Crescent, Glossop SK13 8KG* Tel (01457) 864938 E-mail colin@glossop.org

COOPER, Colin Charles. b 40. Middx Univ BA94. Oak Hill Th Coll 62. d 66 p 67. C Islington St Andr w St Thos and St Matthias *Lon* 66-69; Bermuda 69-76; V Gorleston St Andr *Nor* 77-94; R Emporia Ch Ch w Purdy Grace USA from 94. *111 Battery Avenue, Emporia VA 23847-2001, USA* Tel (001) (434) 348 3863 E-mail christandgrace@cs.com

COOPER, Mrs Corynne Elizabeth. b 54. Kent Univ BA76 PGCE77 Nottm Univ MA98. EMMTC 95. d 98 p 99. NSM Kneesall w Laxton and Wellow *S'well* 98-01; C Woodombe-in-the-Moor, Leusdon, Princetown etc *Ex* 01-05; TV Ashburton, Bickington, Buckland in the Moor etc from 05. *The Vicarage, Holne, Newton Abbot TQ13 7RT* Tel (01364) 631522 E-mail corynne.cooper@virgin.net

COOPER, David Philip. b 65. York Univ BA86. Qu Coll Birm BTheol94. d 94 p 95. C Burslem *Lich* 94-98; TV Cen Wolverhampton and Dioc Inter-Faith Officer 98-05; P-in-c Arnside *Carl* from 05. *The Vicarage, 45 Church Hill, Arnside, Carnforth LA5 0DW* Tel (01524) 761319

COOPER, Derek Edward. b 30. Bps' Coll Cheshunt 61. d 62 p 63. C Bishop's Stortford St Mich *St Alb* 62-66; V Westcliff St Cedd *Chelmsf* 66-89; R Camerton w Dunkerton, Foxcote and Shoscombe *B & W* 89-95; rtd 95; Perm to Offic *Win* from 95. *6 Caerleon Drive, Andover SP10 4DE* Tel (01264) 362807

COOPER, Eric John. b 22. Cam Univ MA47. Chich Th Coll 52. d 53 p 54. C Tottenham St Paul *Lon* 53-55; C Hillingdon St Jo 55-62; C Knowle St Martin *Bris* 62-66; V Bedminster Down 66-72; rtd 87. *6 Deveron Grove, Keynsham, Bristol BS31 1UJ* Tel 0117-986 7339

COOPER, Frederick. b 30. Cranmer Hall Dur 68. d 70 p 71. C Preston All SS *Blackb* 70-72; C Preston St Jo 72-76; TV 76-78; V Higher Walton 78-91; P-in-c Preston All SS 91-95; rtd 95; Perm to Offic *Blackb* from 96. *10 Guardian Close, Fulwood, Preston PR2 8EX* Tel (01772) 713808

COOPER, Gavin Ashley. b 85. Chich Univ BA06. St Steph Ho Ox BA10. d 11. C Old St Pancras *Lon* from 11. *33B Crowndale Road, London NW1 1TN* Tel (020) 7388 4354 E-mail fr.gavin@posp.co.uk

COOPER, Gordon William. b 54. Aston Tr Scheme 93 Ripon Coll Cuddesdon 95. d 97 p 98. C Kippax w Allerton Bywater *Ripon* 97-01; V Wyther 01-08; P-in-c Garforth from 08. *The Rectory, Church Lane, Garforth, Leeds LS25 1NR* Tel 0113-286 3737 E-mail gordon@williamcooper.freeserve.co.uk

COOPER, Graham Denbigh. b 48. Nottm Univ BTh75. St Jo Coll Nottm LTh75. d 75 p 76. C Collyhurst *Man* 75-78; C Stambermill *Worc* 78-80; V The Lye and Stambermill 80-90; P-in-c Frome H Trin *B & W* 90; V 91-95; Appeals Organiser Children's Soc 95-97; Area Manager Save the Children Fund from 97. *2 Coombe View, Shepton Mallet BA4 5YF* Tel (01749) 343157

COOPER, Mrs Gwenda. d 11. NSM Colwyn and Llanelian *St As* from 11. *Bron Digain, Llangernyw, Abergele LL22 8PP* Tel (01745) 860349 E-mail brondigain@googlemail.com

COOPER, Herbert William. b 29. Chich Th Coll 77. d 79 p 80. C Leigh Park *Portsm* 79-82; C-in-c Hayling St Pet CD 82-85; V Whitwell and R St Lawrence 85-94; P-in-c Niton 89-94; rtd 94; Perm to Offic *Heref* 94-04 and *Chich* from 05. *10 Andrew Avenue, Felpham, Bognor Regis PO22 7QS* Tel (01243) 584212

COOPER, Ian. b 57. St Jo Coll Nottm 00. d 02 p 03. C Mildenhall *St E* 02-05; TV 05-06; V Blacklands Hastings Ch Ch and St Andr *Chich* 06-10; P-in-c Peacehaven and Telscombe Cliffs from 10. *The Vicarage, 41 Bramber Avenue, Peacehaven BN10 8HR* Tel (01273) 583149 E-mail ian@rpmo.co.uk

COOPER, Ian Clive. b 48. Ex Univ BA76 K Coll Lon MTh94 FCA. Linc Th Coll 76. d 78 p 79. C Sunbury *Lon* 78-81; P-in-c Astwood Bank *Worc* 81-85; P-in-c Feckenham w Bradley 82-85; TV Hemel Hempstead *St Alb* 85-95; R Bushey 95-04; TR Witney *Ox* 04-06; TV Marlborough *Sarum* from 06. *Preshute Vicarage, 7 Golding Avenue, Marlborough SN8 1TH* Tel (01672) 513408 *or* 512357 E-mail iancoopermrlboro@aol.com

COOPER, Jack. b 44. St Jo Coll Nottm 76. d 78 p 79. C Roundhay St John *Ripon* 78-80; C Ripley *Derby* 80-82; V Willington 82-88; V Findern 82-88; P-in-c Parwich w Alsop-en-le-Dale 88-94; Perm to Offic *York* from 95; rtd 04. *3 Arundel Howe Court, Stakesbury Road, Whitby YO21 1YJ* Tel (01947) 604213 E-mail estuaryjuac@googlemail.com

COOPER, James Peter. b 61. Westf Coll Lon BSc82. Sarum & Wells Th Coll 82. d 85 p 86. C Durrington *Chich* 85-88; C Clayton w Keymer 88-95; TV Chich and Chapl Chich Coll of Tech 95-01; Chapl R W Sussex NHS Trust from 01. *St Richard's Hospital, Spitalfield Lane, Chichester PO19 6SE* Tel (01243) 788122 Fax 531269 Mobile 07989-741004 E-mail james.cooper@rws-tr.nhs.uk

COOPER, Mrs Jennifer Ann Lisbeth. b 45. MCSP67. d 04 p 05. OLM Ashwellthorpe, Forncett, Fundenhall, Hapton etc *Nor*

from 04. *10 Boileau Avenue, Tacolneston, Norwich NR16 1DQ* Tel (01953) 789702

COOPER, Jennifer Elaine. b 62. Toronto Univ BA83 Ottawa Univ MA90 Keble Coll Ox DPhil05. Ripon Coll Cuddesdon 05. **d** 06 **p** 07. C Cotham St Sav w St Mary and Clifton St Paul *Bris* 06-09; Lect and Tutor Coll of Resurr Mirfield from 09; Visiting Lect Leeds Univ from 09. *College of the Resurrection, Stocks Bank Road, Mirfield WF14 0BW* Tel (01924) 481904 E-mail jcooper@mirfield.org.uk

COOPER, Jeremy John. b 45. Kelham Th Coll 65 Linc Th Coll 71. **d** 71 **p** 72. C Derby St Luke 71-76; TV Malvern Link w Cowleigh *Worc* 76-79; P-in-c Claypole *Linc* 79-80; P-in-c Westborough w Dry Doddington and Stubton 79-80; C Eye w Braiseworth and Yaxley *St E* 80-82; P-in-c Hundon w Barnardiston 82-83; R 83-97; V Hundon 97-99; Chapl St Marg Convent E Grinstead 99-03; Warden, Lect and Preacher Newland Almshouses 03-04. *The College of St Barnabas, Blackberry Lane, Lingfield RH7 6NJ* Tel (01342) 870260

COOPER, Jeremy Llewellyn John. b 51. Lanc Univ BA73 Sussex Univ PGCE74 York Univ MSc87. **d** 07 **p** 08. OLM Morpeth *Newc* 07-11; Chapl Northumbria Healthcare NHS Trust from 11. *Southdown, 13 Curlew Hill, Morpeth NE61 3SH* E-mail jeremylcooper@aol.com

COOPER, John. b 34. BEd. NOC. **d** 83 **p** 84. C Tong *Bradf* 83-87; V Bingley H Trin 87-92; V Silsden 92-99; rtd 99; Perm to Offic *Bradf* 01-08 and *Blackb* from 10. *15 Fosbrooke House, 8 Clifton Drive, Lytham St Annes FY8 5RQ* Tel (01253) 667052

COOPER, John. b 47. Sarum & Wells Th Coll 71. **d** 74 **p** 75. C Spring Grove St Mary *Lon* 74-77; C Shepherd's Bush St Steph w St Thos 77-82; V Paddington St Pet 82-89; V Darwen St Cuth w Tockholes St Steph *Blackb* 89-96; V Northampton St Mich w St Edm *Pet* 96-99; Perm to Offic *St Alb* from 99 and *Lon* from 02. *8B Hampstead Square, London NW3 1AB* Tel (020) 7209 4165 E-mail jco4328743@yahoo.co.uk

COOPER, John Edward. b 40. K Coll Lon BD63 AKC63. **d** 64 **p** 65. C Prittlewell St Mary *Chelmsf* 64-67; C Up Hatherley *Glouc* 67-69; C-in-c Dorridge CD *Birm* 69-71; V Longford and P-in-c Alkmonton w Yeaveley *Derby* 71-76; TV Canvey Is *Chelmsf* 76-82; R Spixworth w Crostwick *Nor* 82-91; R Frettenham w Stanninghall 82-91; V Gt w Lt Harrowden and Orlingbury *Pet* 91-01; rtd 01; Perm to Offic *Leic* and *Pet* from 01. *Staveley House, 30 Brooke Road, Braunston, Oakham LE15 8QR* Tel (01572) 770984

COOPER, Canon John Leslie. b 33. Lon Univ BD65 MPhil78. Chich Th Coll 59. **d** 62 **p** 63. C Kings Heath *Birm* 62-65; Asst Chapl HM Pris Wandsworth 65-66; Chapl HM Borstal Portland 66-68; Chapl HM Pris Bris 68-72; P-in-c Balsall Heath St Paul *Birm* 73-81; V 81-82; Adn Aston and Can Res Birm Cathl 82-90; Adn Coleshill 90-93; C Sutton Coldfield H Trin 93-97; Hon Can Birm Cathl 93-97; rtd 97; Perm to Offic *Derby* from 98. *4 Ireton Court, Kirk Ireton, Ashbourne, Derby DE6 3JP* Tel (01335) 370459

COOPER, John Northcott. b 44. Ox Min Course 89. **d** 92 **p** 93. NSM Burghfield *Ox* 92-99; P-in-c Wootton (Boars Hill) 99-00; V Wootton and Dry Sandford 00-10; AD Abingdon 02-07; rtd 10. *Dinosaur Footprints, 21 Townend Road, Swanage BH19 2PU* Tel (01929) 421342 E-mail dinofoot@hotmail.co.uk

COOPER, Jonathan Mark Eric. b 62. Man Univ BSc83 Edin Univ BD88. Edin Th Coll 85. **d** 88 **p** 89. C Stainton-in-Cleveland *York* 88-91; C W Bromwich All SS *Lich* 91-93; P-in-c Ingleby Barwick CD *York* 93-98; P-in-c Hinderwell w Roxby 98-03; R Kirby Misperton w Normanby, Edston and Salton 03-10; V Brompton w Deighton from 10; R Rounton w Welbury from 10. *The Vicarage, Northallerton Road, Brompton, Northallerton DL6 2QA* Tel (01609) 772436 E-mail j.m.e.c.@btinternet.com

COOPER, Joseph Trevor. b 32. Linc Th Coll 65. **d** 67 **p** 68. C Fletchamstead *Cov* 67-69; Ind Chapl 69-90; rtd 92; Perm to Offic *Cov* 92-00. *16 Trevor Close, Tile Hill, Coventry CV4 9HP* Tel (024) 7646 2341

COOPER, Judith Mary. b 52. Leeds Univ BA09. NOC 06. **d** 09 **p** 10. C Prestwich St Mary *Man* from 09. *25 Rectory Lane, Prestwich, Manchester M25 1RB* Tel 07752-676007 (mobile) E-mail cooper.j@blueyonder.co.uk

COOPER, Ms Louise Helena. b 68. Leeds Univ BA90. Qu Coll Birm. **d** 93 **p** 94. Par Dn Dovecot *Liv* 93-94; C 94-96; Dep Chapl HM YOI Glen Parva 96-01; Chapl HM Pris Styal 01-02; Chapl HM Pris Man 02-09; Chapl HM Pris Nottm 09-11; Chapl HM Pris Dartmoor from 11. *The Chaplaincy, HM Prison Dartmoor, Princetown, Yelverton PL20 6RR* Tel (01822) 322000

COOPER, Malcolm Tydeman. b 37. Pemb Coll Ox BA61 MA64. Linc Th Coll 63. **d** 63 **p** 64. C Spennithorne *Ripon* 63-66; C Caversham *Ox* 66-71; Hon C Blackbird Leys CD 71-75; Lic to Offic *Sarum* 75-78 and *B & W* 78-82; NSM Sutton and Witcham w Mepal *Ely* 82-97; P-in-c Coveney 97-06. *8 The Coppice, Merrington, Bomere Heath, Shrewsbury SY4 3QE* E-mail mtcm4@waitrose.com

COOPER, Marc Ashley Rex. b 62. Leeds Univ BA85 MA95. Linc Th Coll 92. **d** 92 **p** 93. C Bolton St Jas w St Chrys *Bradf* 92-96; P-in-c Fishtoft *Linc* 96-97; R from 97; RD Holland E 03-09. *The Rectory, Rectory Close, Fishtoft, Boston PE21 0RZ* Tel and fax (01205) 363216 E-mail revmarccooper@dsl.pipex.com

COOPER, Sister Margery. b 26. CA Tr Coll 49. **dss** 79 **d** 87 **p** 94. CA from 52; Evang Family Miss *Dur, Newc* and *York* 79-86; Perm to Offic *York* 86-91 and 00-11; NSM Fulford 91-00; rtd 00. *3 Grimston Court, Hull Road, York YO19 5LE* Tel (01904) 489343

COOPER, Canon Mark Richard. b 69. Kent Univ BA98. St Jo Coll Morpeth. **d** 95 **p** 95. C Hamilton Australia 95-96; C Rainham *Roch* 96-98; Assoc P Kincumber Australia 98-02; P-in-c Blue Gum Hills 02-06; Chapl Bp Tyrell Angl Coll 06; Can Res Goulbourn Cathl from 07; Chapl Goulbourn Mental Health Service from 07. *55 Reign Street, Goulbourn NSW 2580, Australia* Tel (0061) (2) 4821 1506 *or* 4821 2206 Fax 4822 2634 Mobile 40-982 8006 E-mail markcooper1969@hotmail.com

COOPER, Canon Michael Leonard. b 30. St Jo Coll Cam BA53 MA58. Cuddesdon Coll 53. **d** 55 **p** 56. C Croydon St Jo *Cant* 55-61; V Spring Park 61-71; V Boxley 71-82; RD Sutton 74-80; V Cranbrook 82-92; Hon Chapl to Bp Dover 93-97; Asst Chapl Kent and Cant Hosps NHS Trust 94-97; Hon Can Cant Cathl 76-97; Perm to Offic *Roch* 97-06; rtd 00. *The Rectory, Bellingham, Hexham NE48 2JS* Tel (01434) 220019

COOPER, Canon Michael Sydney. b 41. Univ of Wales (Lamp) BA63. Westcott Ho Cam 63. **d** 65 **p** 66. C Farlington *Portsm* 65-69; Pakistan 70-71; Mauritius 71-73; C-in-c Hayling St Pet CD *Portsm* 74-81; V Carisbrooke St Mary 81-92; V Carisbrooke St Nic 81-92; V Hartplain 92-98; V Portchester 98-06; RD Fareham 99-04; Hon Can Portsm Cathl 02-06; rtd 06; Perm to Offic *Portsm* from 06. *122 Paxton Road, Fareham PO14 1AE* Tel (01329) 822152

COOPER, Nicholas. b 62. Wycliffe Hall Ox. **d** 06 **p** 07. C Tenterden St Mildred w Smallhythe *Cant* 06-09; C Tenterden St Mich 07-09; P-in-c Saltwood from 09; C Aldington w Bonnington and Bilsington etc from 10. *The Rectory, Rectory Lane, Saltwood, Hythe CT21 4QA* Tel (01303) 266932

COOPER, Nigel Scott. b 53. Qu Coll Cam BA75 MA79 PGCE76 CEnv MIEEM CBiol FIBiol FLS. Ripon Coll Cuddesdon BA83 MA88. **d** 83 **p** 84. C Moulsham St Jo *Chelmsf* 83-88; R Rivenhall 88-05; Chapl Anglia Ruskin Univ from 05; Bp's Adv on Further Educn from 08. *The Chaplaincy Office, Anglia Ruskin University, East Road, Cambridge CB1 1PT* Tel 08451-962398 E-mail nigel.cooper@anglia.ac.uk

COOPER, Noel. b 49. Oak Hill Th Coll. **d** 88 **p** 89. C Plymouth St Jude *Ex* 88-92; V Clapham Park All SS *S'wark* 92-99; R Bedford St Jo and St Leon *St Alb* from 99. *St John's Rectory, 36 St John's Street, Bedford MK42 0DH* Tel (01234) 354818 E-mail stjohns@nascr.net

COOPER, Canon Peter David. b 48. Sarum & Wells Th Coll 70. **d** 73 **p** 74. C Yateley *Win* 73-78; C Christchurch 78-81; P-in-c Southampton St Mark 81-83; V 83-98; P-in-c Tadley St Pet 98-02; Hon Can Ife Nigeria from 00; R Tadley S and Silchester *Win* from 02. *The Rectory, The Green, Tadley RG26 3PB* Tel 0118-981 4860 E-mail peter.cooper@xaltmail.com

COOPER, Peter Timothy. b 65. Brunel Univ BSc95. Ridley Hall Cam 01. **d** 03 **p** 04. C Edgware *Lon* 03-07; China from 07. *4 Mount Orchard, Tenbury Wells WR15 8DW* E-mail pandmcooper@tiscali.co.uk

COOPER, Canon Richard Thomas. b 46. Leeds Univ BA69. Coll of Resurr Mirfield 69. **d** 71 **p** 72. C Rothwell *Ripon* 71-75; C Adel 75-78; C Knaresborough 78-81; P-in-c Croft 81-90; P-in-c Eryholme 81-90; P-in-c Middleton Tyas and Melsonby 81-90; RD Richmond 86-90; V Aldborough w Boroughbridge and Roecliffe 90-98; RD Ripon 93-96; R Richmond w Hudswell 98-05; R Richmond w Hudswell and Downholme and Marske 05-09; Hon Can Ripon Cathl 97-09; rtd 09; Chapl to The Queen from 03. *14 Hargill Drive, Redmire, Leyburn DL8 4DZ* Tel (01969) 623844 E-mail richard@hargill.plus.com

COOPER, Canon Robert Gerard. b 68. Univ of Wales (Abth) BD91. Linc Th Coll 93. **d** 93 **p** 94. C Whitkirk *Ripon* 93-96; C Leeds Richmond Hill 96-97; Chapl Agnes Stewart C of E High Sch Leeds 96-97; Chapl Chigwell Sch Essex 97-98; V Lightcliffe *Wakef* 98-05; V Pontefract St Giles from 05; RD Pontefract from 06; Hon Can Wakef Cathl from 08. *The Vicarage, 9 The Mount, Pontefract WF8 1NE* Tel (01977) 706803 Mobile 07931-565516 E-mail robert cooper@msn.com

COOPER, Robert James. b 52. Bris Univ BA75. Ridley Hall Cam 76. **d** 78 **p** 79. C Street w Walton *B & W* 78-82; C Batheaston w St Cath 82-86; P-in-c Sadberge *Dur* 86-03; Asst Chapl Arts and Recreation 86-05; Chapl 05-08; Lic to AD Stockton from 08. *24 Front Close, Thorpe Thewles, Stockton-on-Tees TS21 3JY* Tel (01740) 630015 E-mail robert@cooperphoto.co.uk

COOPER, Canon Roger Charles. b 48. GRSM ARMCM69 PGCE70. Coll of Resurr Mirfield 79. **d** 81 **p** 82. C Monkseaton St Mary *Newc* 81-83; C Morpeth 83-87; Min Can and Prec Man Cathl 87-90; V Blackrod from 90; AD Deane from 05; Hon Can Man Cathl from 11; C Horwich and Rivington from 11. *St Katharine's Vicarage, Blackhorse Street, Blackrod, Bolton BL6 5EN* Tel (01204) 468150

COOPER, Seth William. b 62. Westcott Ho Cam 94. **d** 96 **p** 97. C Golders Green *Lon* 96-00; TV Uxbridge 00-05; V Walmer *Cant* from 05; AD Sandwich from 10. *Elizabeth House, 32 St Mary's Road, Walmer, Deal CT14 7QA* Tel (01304) 366605 E-mail sethandjen@tinyworld.co.uk

COOPER, Shirley Ann. *See* RUSSELL, Alexandra Blaise

COOPER, Stephen. b 54. Bernard Gilpin Soc Dur 73 Chich Th Coll 74. **d** 77 **p** 78. C Horbury *Wakef* 77-78; C Horbury w Horbury Bridge 78-81; C Barnsley St Mary 81-84; TV Elland 84-91; Hon C Huddersfield St Thos 93-94; P-in-c Middlesbrough St Columba w St Paul *York* 94-08; V from 09; P-in-c Middlesbrough St Jo the Ev 05-08; V from 09; Chapl S Tees Hosps NHS Trust 94-05. *St Columba's Vicarage, 115 Cambridge Road, Middlesbrough TS5 5HF* Tel (01642) 824779 E-mail fr_s_cooper@hotmail.com

COOPER, Stephen Paul Crossley. b 58. Trin Coll Bris 91. **d** 93 **p** 94. C Blackb Redeemer 93-95; C Altham w Clayton le Moors 95-98; V Langho Billington 98-03; Chapl Rossall Sch Fleetwood 03-09; TV Fellside Team *Blackb* from 09. *The Vicarage, Goosnargh Lane, Goosnargh, Preston PR3 2BN* Tel (01722) 865274 E-mail revscooper@googlemail.com

COOPER, Mrs Susan Mary. b 45. Westcott Ho Cam 01. **d** 03 **p** 04. C Syston *Leic* 03-06; R Chipping Ongar w Shelley *Chelmsf* from 06. *The Rectory, Shakletons, Ongar CM5 9AT* Tel (01277) 362173 E-mail scoople@btinternet.com

COOPER, Susan Mira. *See* RAMSARAN, Susan Mira

COOPER, Thomas Joseph Gerard Strickland. b 46. Lanc Univ PhD85. Ven English Coll & Pontifical Gregorian Univ Rome PhB66 PhL67 STB69 STL71. **d** 70 **p** 70. In RC Ch 70-92; Chapl St Woolos Cathl 93-95; V Llandaff N 95-08; rtd 08. *Arwel, Cwmdegwel, St Dogmaels, Cardigan SA43 3JH* Tel (01239) 614156 E-mail teilo@woolos.supanet.com

COOPER, Trevor. *See* COOPER, Joseph Trevor

COOPER, Trevor Jann. b 51. Ex Univ MA95. Wycliffe Hall Ox 75. **d** 79 **p** 95. C Southsea St Pet *Portsm* 79-80; NSM Heavitree w Ex St Paul 93-96; C Standish *Blackb* 96-99; V Burnley St Cuth 99-03; P-in-c Lytham St Jo 03-06; rtd 06. *119 Emsworth Road, Portsmouth PO2 0BT* E-mail trevor.j.cooper@btinternet.com

COOPER, William Douglas. b 42. Open Univ BA83 St Andr Univ MA08 Aber Univ MA09. St Jo Coll Nottm 88 Qu Coll Birm 93. **d** 94 **p** 95. NSM Melbourne *Derby* 94-97; C Penwortham St Mary *Blackb* 97-00; P-in-c Smeeth w Monks Horton and Stowting and Brabourne *Cant* 00-04; rtd 04. *18A Market Street, St Andrews KY16 9NS* Tel (01334) 460678

COORE, Jonathan. b 71. Lon Inst of Educn PGCE97 GTCL94. Trin Coll Bris 05. **d** 07 **p** 08. C Heref St Pet w St Owen and St Jas from 07; Bp's Dom Chapl from 08. *61 Lichfield Avenue, Hereford HR1 2RL* Tel (01432) 270293 *or* 276320 E-mail jonathancoore@msn.com

COOTE, Anthony John. b 54. Qu Coll Birm 95. **d** 97 **p** 98. C Malvern H Trin and St Jas *Worc* 97-01; TV Heref S Wye 01-02; P-in-c Cradley *Worc* 02-04; rtd 04. *43 The Poplars, Stourbridge DY8 5SN* Tel (01384) 482446

COOTE, Bernard Albert Ernest. b 28. Lon Univ BD53. Chich Th Coll 54. **d** 55 **p** 56. C Addiscombe St Mary *Cant* 55-57; C Hawkhurst 57-59; C Sanderstead All SS *S'wark* 59-63; Chapl HM Borstal E Sutton Park 63-74; V Sutton Valence w E Sutton *Cant* 63-76; P-in-c Chart next Sutton Valence 71-76; Chapl and Dir R Sch for the Blind Leatherhead 76-91; rtd 91; Perm to Offic *Chich* and *Guildf* from 91. *6 Coxham Lane, Steyning BN44 3JG* Tel (01903) 813762

COPE, James Brian Andrew. b 58. Chich Th Coll 80. **d** 83 **p** 84. C Poulton-le-Fylde *Blackb* 83-86; C Fleetwood St Pet 86-87; V Fleetwood St Dav 87-94; P-in-c Somercotes *Derby* 94-99; V Watford St Jo *St Alb* 99-07; V Castle Vale w Minworth *Birm* from 07. *St Cuthbert's Vicarage, St Cuthbert's Place, Birmingham B35 7PL* Tel 0121-747 4041 E-mail fr.jamescopessc@sky.com

COPE, Judith Diane. b 50. St Hilda's Coll Ox BA72 Lon Univ MB, B75 MRCGP80. SAOMC 00. **d** 03 **p** 04. NSM Lt Berkhamsted and Bayford, Essendon etc *St Alb* from 03. *18 Hatherleigh Gardens, Potters Bar EN6 5HZ* Tel (01707) 644391 E-mail m.cope@btinternet.com

COPE, Mrs Melia Lambrianos. b 53. Cape Town Univ BSocSc73. St Jo Coll Nottm 78 WMMTC 83. **dss** 86 **d** 93 **p** 94. W Bromwich All SS *Lich* 86-93; NSM 93-94; NSM W Bromwich St Mary Magd CD 93-94; TV Cen Telford 94-02; Chapl HM Pris Shrewsbury 95-98; P-in-c Stokesay *Heref* from 02; P-in-c Halford w Sibdon Carwood from 02; P-in-c Acton Scott from 02; P-in-c Wistanstow from 06. *Stokesay Vicarage, Clun Road, Craven Arms SY7 9QW* Tel (01588) 673463 E-mail melia.cope@emailuk.biz

COPE, Miss Olive Rosemary. b 29. Gilmore Ho 63. **dss** 69 **d** 87 **p** 94. Kentish Town St Martin w St Andr *Lon* 69-72; Enfield St Andr 73-99; Par Dn 87-89; Hon Par Dn 89-94; Hon C 94-99; Perm to Offic from 99. *7 Calder Close, Enfield EN1 3TS* Tel (020) 8363 8221 E-mail oliveclose2003@yahoo.co.uk

COPE, Peter John. b 42. Mert Coll Ox BA64 MA68 Lon Univ MSc74 Man Univ PhD91. Cuddesdon Coll 64. **d** 66 **p** 67. C

Chapel Allerton *Ripon* 66-69; Ind Chapl *Lon* 69-76; Ind Chapl *Worc* 76-85; Min Can Worc Cathl 76-85; P-in-c Worc St Mark 76-81; Min W Bromwich St Mary Magd CD *Lich* 85-94; Ind Chapl 85-94; Telford Town Cen Chapl 94-07; W Midl FE Field Officer 94-97; Churches Ind Officer 97-07; rtd 07; Perm to Offic *Heref* from 96 and *Lich* 07-10. *Stokesay Vicarage, Clun Road, Craven Arms SY7 9QW* Tel and fax (01588) 673463 E-mail peterjcope@hotmail.co.uk

COPE, Ralph Bruce. Sir Geo Williams Univ Montreal BA60 McGill Univ Montreal BD62. **d** 60 **p** 61. Canada 60-99 and from 00; P-in-c Sophia Antipolis *Eur* 99-00. *407-4701 Uplands Drive, Nanaimo BC V9T 5Y2, Canada* Tel (001) (250) 758 3296 E-mail ralglo@compuserve.com

COPE, Canon Stephen Victor. b 60. St Jo Coll Ox BA81 MA87. Chich Th Coll 86. **d** 89 **p** 90. C Newmarket St Mary w Exning St Agnes *St E* 89-92; C Northampton St Matt *Pet* 92-94; V Rudston w Boynton and Kilham *York* 94-98; V Rudston w Boynton, Carnaby and Kilham 98-06; P-in-c Burton Fleming w Fordon, Grindale etc 00-06; RD Bridlington 98-03; P-in-c Owthorne and Rimswell w Withernsea 06-07; P-in-c Easington w Skeffling, Kilnsea and Holmpton 06-07; R Withernsea w Owthorne and Easington etc from 07; RD S Holderness from 09; Can and Preb York Minster from 10. *The Vicarage, 28 Park Avenue, Withernsea HU19 2JU* Tel (01964) 611462 E-mail stephenvcope@tiscali.co.uk

COPELAND, Annabel Susan Mary. b 64. Roehampton Inst BEd87. Wycliffe Hall Ox 03. **d** 05 **p** 06. C Billericay and Lt Burstead *Chelmsf* 05-08; TV Gt Baddow from 08. *124 Beehive Lane, Chelmsford CM2 9SH* Tel (01245) 269026 E-mail annabel.c@bun.com

COPELAND, Christopher Paul. b 38. AKC64. **d** 65 **p** 66. C Luton St Andr *St Alb* 65-67; C Droitwich St Nic w St Pet *Worc* 67-71; C Kings Norton *Birm* 71-72; TV 73-78; V Tyseley 78-88; P-in-c Grimley w Holt *Worc* 88-96; Dioc Stewardship Missr 88-96; P-in-c Forest of Dean Ch Ch w English Bicknor *Glouc* 95; rtd 03; Perm to Offic *Worc* from 03. *24 Players Avenue, Malvern WR14 1DU* Tel (01684) 563323

COPELAND, Derek Norman. b 38. Worc Coll Ox BA62 MA68. Westcott Ho Cam 63. **d** 64 **p** 65. C Portsea St Mary *Portsm* 64-71; P-in-c Avonmouth St Andr *Bris* 71-77; P-in-c Chippenham St Paul w Langley Burrell 78-79; Ind Chapl from 78; TR Chippenham St Paul w Hardenhuish etc 79-89; V Kington St Michael 79-89; Perm to Offic *Bris*; *B & W* and *Sarum* from 89; rtd 03. *51B Lowden, Chippenham SN15 2BG* Tel (01249) 443879

COPELAND, Ian Trevor. b 51. FCA83. **d** 99 **p** 00. OLM Werrington *Lich* 99-09; OLM Werrington and Wetley Rocks from 09. *4 Heather Close, Werrington, Stoke-on-Trent ST9 0LU* Tel (01782) 303525 E-mail it.copeland@ntlworld.com

COPELAND, Trevor. b 57. St Jo Coll Nottm 04. **d** 07 **p** 08. C Westfield St Mary *Carl* from 07. *68 Rowe Terrace, Workington CA14 3SR* Tel (01900) 873303

COPLAND, Miss Carole Jean. b 37. Man Univ BA60. Wm Temple Coll Rugby 65. **d** 87 **p** 94. NSM Northallerton w Kirby Sigston *York* 87-90; Dioc Adv in Children's Work 81-90; Par Dn Dunnington 90-94; Faith in the City Link Officer 90-96; C Dunnington 94-96; V Ledsham w Fairburn 96-99; rtd 99; Perm to Offic *York* from 99. *4 Jedwell Close, New Earswick, York YO32 4DQ* Tel (01904) 767110 E-mail carolecopland@hotmail.com

COPLETON, Roger Boyd. b 62. Edin Univ BD87. TISEC 97. **d** 97 **p** 98. NSM Haddington and Dunbar *Edin* 97-06. *30 Couston Drive, Dalgety Bay, Dunfermline KY11 9NX* Tel 07759-952618 (mobile)

COPLEY, Colin. b 30. FRSA85. Kelham Th Coll 51. **d** 55 **p** 56. C Linc St Swithin 55-58; C Bottesford 58-60; Chapl HM Borstal Hollesley Bay 60-66; Chapl HM Pris Liv 66-70; Chapl HM Pris Styal 70-73; N Regional Chapl HM Pris and Borstals 70-73; Midl Region 73-75; Chapl HM Pris Drake Hall 73-75; Asst Chapl Gen of Pris (Midl) 75-90; Chapl HM Pris Sudbury and Foston Hall 90-95; Chapl HM Pris Stafford 95-00; rtd 00; Perm to Offic *Lich* from 90; Lect Potchefstroom Univ from 98. *67 Porlock Avenue, Stafford ST17 0HT* Tel (01785) 663162 E-mail colincopley7@btinternet.com

COPLEY, Paul. b 58. NEOC 97. **d** 99 **p** 00. C Hessle *York* 99-02; TV Sutton St Jas and Wawne 02-07; P-in-c Kingston upon Hull St Nic from 07; P-in-c Newington w Dairycoates 07-10. *St Nicholas' Vicarage, 898 Hessle High Road, Hull HU4 6SA* Tel (01482) 504088 E-mail copleypaul@hotmail.com

COPPEN, Colin William. b 53. BCombStuds85. Linc Th Coll. **d** 85 **p** 86. C Tokyngton St Mich *Lon* 85-88; C Somers Town 88-90; P-in-c Edmonton St Alphege 90-92; V 92-95; P-in-c W Hampstead St Jas 95-97; P-in-c Kilburn St Mary w All So 95-97; TR Wood Green St Mich w Bounds Green St Gabr etc from 97. *St Michael's Rectory, 1A Selborne Road, London N22 7TL* Tel (020) 8888 1968 E-mail rector@woodgreenparish.com

COPPEN, George. *See* COPPEN, Brian Richards

COPPEN, Canon Martin Alan. b 48. Ex Univ BA69. St Jo Coll Nottm 83. **d** 85 **p** 86. C Bitterne *Win* 85-88; V St Mary Bourne and Woodcott 88-99; V Hurstbourne Priors, Longparish etc from 00; RD Whitchurch 98-03; Hon Can Win Cathl from 04. *The Vicarage, St Mary Bourne, Andover SP11 6AY* Tel and fax (01264) 738308 E-mail church@1and3.org.uk

COPPEN, Robert George. b 39. Cape Town Univ BA66. St Jo Coll Dur 79. d 81 p 82. C Douglas St Geo and St Barn *S & M* 81-84; TV Kidlington w Hampton Poyle *Ox* 84-05; Chapl HM YOI Campsfield Ho 84-91; rtd 05. *Taobh Mol, Kildary, Invergordon IV18 0NJ* Tel (01862) 842381 E-mail coppen@dunelm.org.uk

COPPIN, Canon Ronald Leonard. b 30. Birm Univ BA52. Ridley Hall Cam 54. d 56 p 57. C Harrow Weald All SS *Lon* 56-59; Bp's Dom Chapl *Man* 59-63; Chapl St Aid Birkenhead 63-65; Vice-Prin 65-68; Selection Sec ACCM 68-74; Sec Cttee for Th Educn 71-74; Can Res and Lib Dur Cathl 74-97; Dir of Clergy Tr 74-96; Warden NEOC 76-84; Dir Post-Ord Tr 86-97; rtd 97; Perm to Offic *Lon* from 02. *157 Defoe House, London EC2Y 8ND* Tel (020) 7588 9228 E-mail ronald.coppin@virgin.net

COPPING, Adrian Walter Alexander. b 52. Ridley Hall Cam. d 00 p 01. C Royston *St Alb* 00-04; R Bangor Monachorum, Worthenbury and Marchwiel *St As* 04-09; AD Bangor Isycoed 05-09; R Cilcain, Gwernaffield, Llanferres etc from 09; AD Mold from 11. *The New Rectory, Rectory Lane, Llanferres, Mold CH7 5SR* Tel (01352) 810936 E-mail adriancopping@hotmail.com

COPPING, John Frank Walter Victor. b 34. K Coll Lon BD58 AKC58. d 59 p 60. C Hampstead St Jo *Lon* 59-62; C Bray and Braywood *Ox* 62-65; V Langley Mill *Derby* 65-71; V Cookham Dean *Ox* 71-03; RD Maidenhead 87-94; rtd 03; Perm to Offic *Ox* from 03. *41 Golden Ball Lane, Pinkneys Green, Maidenhead SL6 6NW* Tel (01628) 674433 E-mail johnfcopping@talktalk.net

COPPING, Raymond. b 36. St Mark & St Jo Coll Lon TCert59. Wycliffe Hall Ox 72. d 74 p 75. C High Wycombe *Ox* 74-77; TV 77-87; TV Digswell and Panshanger *St Alb* 87-95; P-in-c Charlton Kings H Apostles *Glouc* 95-00; rtd 00; Hon C Thame *Ox* from 04. *20 Friars Furlong, Long Crendon, Aylesbury HP18 9DQ* Tel (01844) 208509

COPPINGER, Mrs Kristina Yvette. b 62. US Air Force Academy Colorado Spring BS86. Trin Episc Sch for Min Penn MDiv94. d 94 p 94. C Lees Summit St Paul USA 94-95; C Charleston St Mich 95-97; V Lebanon Trin Ch 97-00; Chapl US Air Force from 98; Perm to Offic *Ely* and *St E* from 10. *118A Main Street, Hockwold, Thetford IP26 4NB* Tel (01842) 827527 E-mail kcoppinger@satx.rr.com

COPPINGER, Timothy Ronald. b 65. Kansas Wesleyan Univ (USA) BS88. Trin Episc Sch for Min Penn MDiv97. d 97 p 97. R Camdenton USA 97-04; P-in-c Burkburnett 04-08; P-in-c Wichita Falls St Steph 04-07; Perm to Offic *Ely* and *St E* from 10. *118A Main Street, Hockwold, Thetford IP26 4NB* Tel (01842) 827527 E-mail kcoppinger@satx.rr.com

COPSEY, Mrs Christine. b 51. Nottm Univ CertEd73. ERMC 04. d 07 p 08. NSM Fakenham w Alethorpe *Nor* 07-08; NSM King's Lynn St Marg w St Nic 08-11; Chapl Ind Miss from 11. *5 Back Lane, Castle Acre, King's Lynn PE32 2AR* Tel (01760) 755558 E-mail chriscopsey@btinternet.com

COPSEY, Mrs Janette. d 11. NSM Ben Rhydding *Bradf* from 11. *23 Wheatley Avenue, Ilkley LS29 8PT* Tel (01943) 607113

COPSEY, Nigel John. b 52. K Coll Lon BD75 AKC75 Surrey Univ MSc88 Middx Univ DProf01. St Aug Coll Cant 72. d 76 p 77. C Barkingside St Fran *Chelmsf* 76-78; C Canning Town St Cedd 78-80; P-in-c Victoria Docks Ascension 80-87; Chapl E Surrey Mental Health Care NHS Trust from 90; Co-ord Past Care Surrey Priority Care NHS Trust from 90; Co-ord Past Care Surrey Oaklands NHS Trust 99-05; Hd Past and Spiritual Care Surrey and Borders Partnership NHS Trust from 08; Co-ord Relig Care Newham Community Health Services NHS Trust 99-01; Co-ord Relig Care Newham Primary Care Trust from 01; Team Ldr Spiritual, Relig & Cultural Care E Lon NHS Foundation Trust from 08. *Newham Centre for Mental Health, Glen Road, London E13 8SP* Tel (020) 7540 4380 Fax 7540 2970 E-mail nigel.copsey@eastlondon.nhs.uk

COPUS, Brian George. b 36. AKC59. d 60 p 61. C Croydon St Mich *Cant* 60-63; C Swindon New Town *Bris* 63-69; V Colebrooke *Ex* 69-73; P-in-c Hittisleigh 69-73; R Perivale *Lon* 73-82; V Ruislip St Mary 82-01; rtd 01; Perm to Offic *Win* from 02. *Le Bec, 84 Carbery Avenue, Bournemouth BH6 3LQ* Tel (01202) 428943

COPUS, John Cecil. b 38. TCert64 Maria Grey Coll Lon DipEd71 Open Univ BA78. Cant Sch of Min. d 83 p 84. Hon C Folkestone H Trin and St Geo w Ch Ch *Cant* 83-85; Hon C Midsomer Norton w Clandown *B & W* 85-91; Dioc Adv for Children's Work *Ex* 91-98; Hon C Aylesbeare, Rockbeare, Farringdon etc 95-98; P-in-c 98-01; rtd 01; Perm to Offic *Ex* from 01; Clergy Widow(er)s Officer from 02; C N Creedy 08-10. *The Sidings, Park Road, Lapford, Crediton EX17 6QJ* Tel (01363) 83408

COPUS, Jonathan Hugh Lambert. b 44. BNC Ox BA66 MA71 LGSM66 MInstPI94. S'wark Ord Course 68. d 71 p 72. C

Horsell *Guildf* 71-73; Producer Relig Progr BBC Radio Solent 73-87; V Maenclochog and New Moat etc *St D* 06-07; V Martletwy w Lawrenny and Minwear etc 07; Perm to Offic from 07. *Llys Myrddin, Efailwen, Clynderwen SA66 7XG* Tel (01994) 419834 Mobile 07828-510283 E-mail revjc@dentron.co.uk

CORBAN-BANKS, Edrick Hale. b 53. Victoria Univ Wellington BMus74 LTCL79 FTCL81. St Jo Coll Auckland BTh91. d 91 p 92. New Zealand 91-99; P Asst Johnsonville St Jo 92-94; Ch Planter Churton Park 93-94; V Katikati 94-99; P Missr Alicante Spain 99; R Alicante St Paul 99-00; Chapl Ibiza *Eur* 00-03; V Stoke New Zealand from 04. *523 Main Road, Stoke, Nelson 7001, New Zealand* Tel (0064) (3) 547 3478 E-mail vicar.stbarnabas@paradise.net.nz

CORBETT, George. b 18. Bible Churchmen's Coll Bris 47. d 50 p 51. C Wednesfield Heath *Lich* 50-52; R Salford St Matthias w St Simon *Man* 52-55; N Area Sec BCMS 55-58; V S Lambeth St Steph *S'wark* 58-61; Assoc Home Sec BCMS 61-63; V Hatherleigh *Ex* 63-78; P-in-c Ringmore and Kingston 78-84; R Bigbury, Ringmore and Kingston 84-86; rtd 86; Perm to Offic *Heref* from 87. *2 Quantock Close, Hereford HR4 0TD* Tel (01432) 269211

CORBETT, Canon Henry. b 53. CCC Cam BA75. Wycliffe Hall Ox. d 78 p 79. C Everton St Pet *Liv* 78-84; TV 84-87; TR 87-02; R Everton St Pet w St Chrys from 02; AD Liv N from 03; Hon Can Liv Cathl from 03. *Shrewsbury House, Langrove Street, Liverpool L5 3LT* Tel 0151-207 1948 E-mail hjcorbett@shewsy.freeserve.co.uk

CORBETT, The Very Revd Ian Deighton. b 42. St Cath Coll Cam BA64 MA67 Cam Univ PGCE65. Westcott Ho Cam 67. d 69 p 70. C New Bury *Man* 69-72; C Bolton St Pet 72-75; Chapl Bolton Colls of H&FE 72-75; R Man Victoria Park 75-80; Chapl Salford Univ 80-83; Dioc FE Officer 74-83; R Salford Sacred Trin 83-87; Dir CME and Hon Can Man Cathl 83-87; Warden Lelapa la Jesu Sem Lesotho 88-91; Can Missr Harare Zimbabwe 92-93; Can Missr Botswana 93-95; R Kuruman St Mary S Africa 95-97; Dean Tuam and I Tuam w Cong and Aasleagh *T, K & A* 97-99; R Whitesands Canada 99-01; V Utah Region USA 01-08; Hon C E Clevedon w Clapton in Gordano etc *B & W* from 09. *5 Chestnut Grove, Clevedon BS21 7LA* Tel (01275) 872723 E-mail iancorbett123@btinternet.com

CORBETT, Jocelyn Rory. d 05 p 06. Aux Min Aghalee *D & D* 05-06; Aux Min Donaghcloney w Waringstown from 06. *Badger Hill, 23 Magherabeg Road, Dromore BT25 1RS* Tel (028) 9269 2067 E-mail rory.corbett23@gmail.com

CORBETT, John David. b 32. Oriel Coll Ox BA55 MA59. St Steph Ho Ox 55. d 57 p 58. C Plymouth St Pet *Ex* 57-64; V Marldon 64-74; TV Bournemouth St Pet w St Swithun, H Trin etc *Win* 74-83; V Beckenham St Barn *Roch* 83-88; V King's Sutton and Newbottle and Charlton *Pet* 88-97; rtd 97; Perm to Offic *Portsm* and *Win* from 98. *119 St Augustine Road, Southsea PO4 9AA* Tel (023) 9275 3212 E-mail jdc.augustine@virgin.net

CORBETT, Philip Peter. b 81. St Andr Univ MTheol03 Yale Univ STM04 Keble Coll Ox MPhil06. Coll of Resurr Mirfield 06. d 08 p 09. C Worksop Priory *S'well* from 08. *6 Conrad Close, Worksop S80 2EN* Tel (01909) 530860 E-mail philippetercorbett@googlemail.com

CORBETT, Miss Phyllis. b 34. Cranmer Hall Dur 76. dss 80 d 87 p 94. Walsall Wood *Lich* 80-87; Par Dn Baswich 87-94; C 94-95; rtd 95; Perm to Offic *Lich* from 95. *9 Redhill Gorse, Crab Lane, Trinity Fields, Stafford ST16 1SW*

CORBETT, Rory. See CORBETT, Jocelyn Rory

CORBETT, Stephen Paul. b 57. BA80. St Jo Coll Nottm 83. d 85 p 86. C Tollington Park St Mark w St Anne *Lon* 85-86; C Holloway St Mark w Em 86-91; V Chitts Hill St Cuth 91-93; V Springfield *Birm* 93-04; AD Moseley 02-04; V Walmley 04-09; P-in-c Blackb St Gabr 09-11; V from 11. *St Gabriel's Vicarage, 6 Charnwood Close, Blackburn BB2 7BT* Tel (01254) 581412

CORBIN, Frederick Athelston. b 42. S Dios Minl Tr Scheme 80. d 83 p 85. NSM Basingstoke *Win* 83-84; C Hulme Ascension *Man* 84-86; Lic to Hulme Deanery 86-87; C E Crompton 87-89; V Oldham St Barn 89-00; rtd 00; Grenada 00-01; Perm to Offic *Man* 01-07. *St Alban's and St Silas's Rectory, Lower Carlton, St James, Barbados* Tel (001) (246) 422 2913

CORBYN, John. b 58. Man Univ BA79 Ven English Coll & Pontifical Gregorian Univ Rome 83. Wycliffe Hall Ox BA83 MA87. d 84 p 85. C Deane *Man* 84-87; C Lancaster St Mary *Blackb* 87-90; Sub-Chapl HM Pris Lanc 89-90; V Blackb St Gabr 90-01; V Bearsted w Thurnham *Cant* from 01. *The Vicarage, Church Lane, Bearsted, Maidstone ME14 4EF* Tel (01622) 737135 E-mail vicar@holycrosschurch.co.uk

CORBYN, John Robert. b 54. Qu Coll Birm. d 82 p 83. C Northolt St Jos *Lon* 82-86; C Sutton St Mich and Urban Miss P *York* 86-88; V Dalton *Sheff* 88-96; R Cressing *Chelmsf* 96-99; R Cressing w Stisted and Bradwell etc 99-09; V Harlow St Mary Magd from 09. *The Vicarage, 3 Oaklands Drive, Harlow CM17 9BE* Tel (01279) 453848 E-mail johncorbyn@btinternet.com

CORCORAN, Daniel Chad. b 71. Man Metrop Univ BA93. St Jo Coll Nottm 04. d 06 p 07. C Stapleford *S'well* 06-10; C

Bilborough w Strelley from 10. *St Barnabas' Vicarage, Derby Road, Beeston, Nottingham NG9 2SN* Tel 0115-808 2656 Mobile 07963-332221 E-mail danchadcorcoran@hotmail.com
CORCORAN, Jennifer Miriam. b 78. Lanc Univ BA01. St Jo Coll Nottm MA(MM)07. **d** 07 **p** 08. C Chilwell *S'well* from 07; NSM from 10; NSM Lenton Abbey from 10. *St Barnabas' Vicarage, Derby Road, Beeston, Nottingham NG9 2SN* Tel 0115-808 2656
CORCORAN, Mrs Valerie A'Court. b 46. UEA BA68 Lon Inst of Educn PGCE69. STETS 99. **d** 02 **p** 03. NSM Boyatt Wood *Win* 02-10; rtd 10. *Ashley, Finches Lane, Twyford, Winchester SO21 1QB* Tel (01962) 712951 Fax 715770 Mobile 07736-459500 E-mail v.corcoran@btinternet.com
CORDELL, Derek Harold. b 34. Chich Th Coll 57. **d** 60 **p** 61. C Whitstable All SS *Cant* 60-63; C Moulsecoomb *Chich* 63-69; Chapl Bucharest *Eur* 69-71; V Brighton St Wilfrid *Chich* 71-74; Chapl HM Borstal Roch 74-80; Asst Chapl HM Pris Man 80-81; Chapl HM Pris The Verne 81-89; Chapl HM Pris Channings Wood 89-90; Chapl Milan w Genoa and Varese *Eur* 90-91; Chapl Mojácar 91-94; Perm to Offic from 95; rtd 97. *27 Scalwell Mead, Seaton EX12 2DW* Tel (01297) 624182
CORDINER, Alan Dobson. b 61. Westmr Coll Ox BA87. **d** 92 **p** 93. C Upperby St Jo *Carl* 92-98; P-in-c Bootle, Corney, Whicham and Whitbeck 98-05; Asst Chapl HM Pris Haverigg 98-03. *32 Summer Hill, Bootle, Millom LA19 5UB* Tel (01229) 718605
CORDINGLEY, Canon Brian Lambert. b 30. St Aid Birkenhead 55. **d** 57 **p** 58. Ind Chapl *Sheff* 57-63; C Clifton St Jas 57-61; C Rotherham 61-63; Ind Chapl *Man* 63-92; R Old Trafford St Cuth 63-81; V Hamer 81-92; Hon Can Man Cathl 87-92; rtd 92; Perm to Offic *Man* from 99. *Wellsprings, 27 Fernthorpe Avenue, Uppermill, Oldham OL3 6EA* Tel (01457) 820130
CORFE, David Robert. b 35. Pemb Coll Cam BA58 MA60 Lambeth STh70. Cuddesdon Coll 58. **d** 60 **p** 61. C Wigan All SS *Liv* 60-63; SPG Miss India 63-68; V Lucknow Ch Ch w All SS and St Pet 70-75; C Northwood Em *Lon* 75; V Westwell and Eastwell w Boughton Aluph *Cant* 75-80; V Hildenborough *Roch* 80-91; Lic Preacher Stretford St Bride *Man* 91-98; Team Ldr Interserve 98-00; rtd 00; Perm to Offic *Win* from 03. *1 Hartley Court, 12 Winn Road, Southampton SO17 1EN* Tel (023) 8058 5557 E-mail drcorfe@freedomland.co.uk
CORK, Ronald Edward. b 43. Plymouth Poly CQSW72. NOC 89. **d** 92 **p** 93. Hon C Altrincham St Geo *Ches* 92-96; P-in-c Altrincham St Jo 96-01; rtd 01. *15 Emmasfield, Exmouth EX8 2LS* Tel (01395) 223489 E-mail roncork@aol.com
CORK, CLOYNE AND ROSS, Archdeacon of. See WHITE, The Ven Robin Edward Bantry
CORK, CLOYNE AND ROSS, Bishop of. See COLTON, The Rt Revd William Paul
CORK, Dean of. See DUNNE, The Very Revd Nigel Kenneth
CORKE, Andrew John. b 55. Bris Univ LLB77. **d** 98 **p** 99. NSM Canford Magna *Sarum* 98-10; TV Swanage and Studland from 10. *The Vicarage, 5 Redcliffe Road, Swanage BH19 1LZ* Tel (01929) 421836 Mobile 07711-898723 E-mail vicar@allsaints-swanage.org
CORKE, Bryan Raymond. b 49. Westmr Coll Lon 81. **d** 95 **p** 96. OLM Flixton St Jo *Man* from 95. *40 Daresbury Avenue, Manchester M41 8GL* Tel 0161-748 1827
CORKE, Colin John. b 59. St Pet Coll Ox BA81. Cranmer Hall Dur 83. **d** 85 **p** 86. C Chapel Allerton *Ripon* 85-88; C Burmantofts St Steph and St Agnes 88-91; P-in-c Tatsfield *S'wark* 91-01; Reigate Adnry Ecum Officer 92-01; V Longbridge *Birm* from 01; Dioc Ecum Officer from 02; AD Kings Norton from 06. *St John's Vicarage, 220 Longbridge Lane, Birmingham B31 4JT* Tel 0121-475 3484 E-mail ado67@btinternet.com
CORKE, Francis Bonny. See RODRIGUEZ-VEGLIO, Francis Bonny
CORKE, Louise Dorothy. b 59. Southn Univ BSc80 PGCE81. Trin Coll Bris BA94. **d** 97 **p** 98. C Ipsley *Worc* 97-01; TV Bradgate Team *Leic* from 01. *The Rectory, 58 Pymm Ley Lane, Groby, Leicester LE6 0GZ* Tel 0116-231 3090 E-mail standstill@btopenworld.com
CORKE, Roderick Geoffrey. b 58. UEA BEd79 Open Univ MA96. St Jo Coll Nottm 90. **d** 92 **p** 93. C Trimley *St E* 92-95; C Walton 95-00; TR Walton and Trimley 00-05; P-in-c Taunton St Mary *B & W* 05-08; V from 08. *St Mary's Vicarage, Church Square, Taunton TA1 1SA* Tel (01823) 272441 E-mail rodcorke@tiscali.co.uk
CORKER, Mrs Elizabeth Jane. b 42. **d** 99 **p** 00. OLM Martlesham w Brightwell *St E* 99-10; OLM Felixstowe St Jo from 10. *12 Fairfield Avenue, Felixstowe IP11 9JN* Tel (01394) 210793 E-mail e.corker@ntlworld.com
CORKER, John Anthony. b 37. TD93. ACIB75 AKC63. **d** 64 **p** 65. C Lindley *Wakef* 64-68; V Brotherton 68-72; Perm to Offic 72-82; CF (TA) 80-93; Hon C Askham Bryan *York* 82-91; TV York All SS Pavement w St Crux and St Martin etc 91-96; Chapl York Health Services NHS Trust 91-96; Chapl Dudley Gp of Hosps NHS Trust 96-99; Asst P Amblecote *Worc* 96-01; Asst P

Dudley St Barn 01-02; rtd 02; Perm to Offic *Worc* from 02. *69 Lakeside Court, Brierley Hill DY5 3RQ* Tel (01384) 897378
CORLEY, Canon Samuel Jon Clint. b 76. St Aid Coll Dur BA97 MA98 Hughes Hall Cam PGCE99. St Jo Coll Nottm MA04. **d** 04 **p** 05. C Lancaster St Thos *Blackb* 04-08; Asst Dioc Missr 08-11; P-in-c Ellel w Shireshead 08-11; Can Res Bradf Cathl from 11; Chapl Bradf Univ from 11. *3 Cathedral Close, Bradford BD1 4EG* Tel (01274) 777733 *or* 777731 Mobile 07966-524683 E-mail sam.corley@bradfordcathedral.org
CORMACK, Donald Stuart. b 45. Brock Univ Ontario TCert67 McMaster Univ Ontario BA71. Regent Coll Vancouver MTh85. **d** 92 **p** 93. C Singapore St Geo 92-93; P-in-c Phnom Penh Cambodia 93-96; Perm to Offic *Glouc* from 06. *305 Gloucester Road, Cheltenham GL51 7AR* Tel (01242) 699506 E-mail don.cormack@hotmail.co.uk
CORNE, Ronald Andrew. b 51. Sarum & Wells Th Coll 87. **d** 89 **p** 90. C Bitterne Park *Win* 89-93; R Headbourne Worthy and King's Worthy 93-01; P-in-c Broughton, Bossington, Houghton and Mottisfont 01-03; R from 03; RD Romsey from 06. *The Rectory, Rectory Lane, Broughton, Stockbridge SO20 8AB* Tel (01794) 301287 E-mail cronandrew@aol.com
CORNECK, Canon Warrington Graham. b 35. MBE05. ACA60 FCA62. Clifton Th Coll. **d** 65 **p** 66. C Islington St Jude Mildmay Park *Lon* 65-67; C Southgate *Chich* 67-73; P-in-c Deptford St Nic w Ch Ch *S'wark* 73-76; P-in-c Deptford St Luke 73-76; V Deptford St Nic and St Luke 76-05; RD Deptford 85-05; Hon Can S'wark Cathl 91-05; rtd 05. *42 Nadine Street, London SE7 7PG* Tel (020) 8465 5316 E-mail grahamcorneck@corneck.freeserve.co.uk
CORNELIUS, Donald Eric. b 31. K Coll Lon BD52 AKC. Linc Th Coll 84. **d** 84 **p** 85. NSM Crowle *Linc* 84-97; NSM Crowle Gp 97-02; NSM Flixborough w Burton upon Stather 91-02; P-in-c Gunhouse w Burringham 91-02; Perm to Offic 02-04. *4 Mulberry Drive, Crowle, Scunthorpe DN17 4JF* Tel (01724) 710279
CORNELL, Miss Jean Cranston. b 36. Man Univ CertEd59 BA64 York Univ BPhil71. Ripon Coll Cuddesdon 87 MTh00. **d** 89 **p** 94. C Matson *Glouc* 89-92; C Bishop's Cleeve 92-96; rtd 96; NSM Winchcombe, Gretton, Sudeley Manor etc *Glouc* 96-01; Perm to Offic 01-02. *11 Willow Close, Woodmancote, Cheltenham GL52 9TU* Tel (01242) 662869 E-mail naej@chris47.freeserve.co.uk
CORNELL, Michael Neil. See COHEN, Michael Neil
CORNELL, Nicholas Simon. b 78. Trin Hall Cam BA00 MA03. Oak Hill Th Coll MTh08. **d** 08 **p** 09. C Eastbourne All SS *Chich* from 08. *1F Grassington Road, Eastbourne BN20 7BP* Tel (01323) 721231 Mobile 07946-220638 E-mail nscornell@gmail.com
CORNES, Alan Stuart. b 70. Open Univ BA98. St Jo Coll Nottm MA00. **d** 01 **p** 02. C Meole Brace *Lich* 01-04; P-in-c Halliwell St Luke *Man* 04-11; P-in-c Halliwell 06-11; TR W Bolton from 11. *St Matthew's Vicarage, Stowell Street, Bolton BL1 3RQ* Tel (01204) 522810 E-mail stuart.cornes@new-wine.net
CORNES, Canon Andrew Charles Julian. b 49. CCC Ox BA70 MA74. Wycliffe Hall Ox 70 Cranmer Hall Dur 72. **d** 73 **p** 74. C York St Mich-le-Belfrey 73-76; C St Marylebone All So w SS Pet and Jo *Lon* 76-85; R Pittsburgh Ascension USA 85-88; V Crowborough *Chich* from 89; RD Rotherfield 97-03; Can and Preb Chich Cathl from 00; Chapl Eastbourne and Co Healthcare NHS Trust 89-02; Chapl Sussex Downs and Weald Primary Care Trust from 02. *All Saints' Vicarage, Chapel Green, Crowborough TN6 1ED* Tel (01892) 667384 *or* 652081
CORNESS, Andrew Stuart. b 69. Bp Otter Coll Chich BA91 Westmr Coll Ox PGCE93. Wycliffe Hall Ox BA00 MA05. **d** 01 **p** 02. C Ewood *Blackb* 01-04; Chapl RN from 04. *Royal Naval Chaplaincy Service, Mail Point 1-2, Leach Building, Whale Island, Portsmouth PO2 8BY* Tel (023) 9262 5055 Fax 9262 5134 E-mail andrewcorness@hotmail.com
CORNFIELD, Richard James. b 67. St Jo Coll Nottm BA96. **d** 96 **p** 97. C Cheltenham Ch Ch *Glouc* 96-00; C Aldridge *Lich* 00-03; R 03-11; C Edin St Paul and St Geo from 11. *76 Morningside Drive, Edinburgh EH10 5NU* Tel 07966-165043 (mobile) E-mail richard.cornfield@virgin.net
CORNISH, Anthony. b 30. Roch Th Coll 64. **d** 67 **p** 68. C Goodmayes All SS *Chelmsf* 67-71; C Buckhurst Hill 71-73; V Westcliff St Andr 73-83; R Rawreth w Rettendon 83-96; rtd 96; Perm to Offic *Chelmsf* from 99. *12 Fleetwood Avenue, Clacton-on-Sea CO15 5SE* Tel (01255) 813826
CORNISH, Dennis Henry Ronald. b 31. FCIB72 FCIS81. S'wark Ord Course 83. **d** 86 **p** 87. NSM Uxbridge *Lon* 86-89; R Lurgashall, Lodsworth and Selham *Chich* 89-96; rtd 96; Perm to Offic *Chich* from 96. *Peerley Lodge, 1 Peerley Road, East Wittering, Chichester PO20 8DW* Tel (01243) 672481
CORNISH, Gillian Lesley. b 45. ACIB77. **d** 96 **p** 97. OLM Moston St Mary *Man* 96-08; OLM Blackley St Pet 08-10; rtd 10; Perm to Offic *Man* from 10. *11 Rishworth Drive, New Moston, Manchester M40 3PS* Tel 0161-681 2839 E-mail gl.cornish@ntlworld.com

CORNISH, Graham Peter. b 42. Dur Univ BA67 FLA. NEOC 82. **d** 84 **p** 85. NSM Harrogate St Wilfrid and St Luke *Ripon* 84-96; Perm to Offic *York* from 84; NSM Bilton *Ripon* 96-09. *33 Mayfield Grove, Harrogate HG1 5HD* Tel (01423) 562747 Fax 529928 E-mail gp-jm.cornish@virgin.net

CORNISH, Ivor. b 40. Reading Univ BSc61 DipEd62. Ox Min Course 86. **d** 89 **p** 90. NSM Aston Clinton w Buckland and Drayton Beauchamp *Ox* 89-97; NSM The Lee and Hawridge w Cholesbury and St Leonard 97-10; Perm to Offic from 10. *79 Weston Road, Aston Clinton, Aylesbury HP22 5EP* Tel (01296) 630345

CORNISH, John Douglas. b 42. Lich Th Coll 67. **d** 70 **p** 71. C Lt Stanmore St Lawr *Lon* 70-73; C Harefield 73-96; Perm to Offic from 96. *46 Arnos Grove, London N14 7AR*

CORNISH, Peter Andrew. b 55. Ch Ch Ox BA77 MA80 Ex Univ CertEd78. St Jo Coll Nottm 84. **d** 87 **p** 88. C Sanderstead All SS *S'wark* 87-92; TV Cen Telford *Lich* from 92; R Sturry w Fordwich and Westbere w Hersden *Cant* from 98; Jt AD Cant from 11. *The Rectory, 2 The Hamels, Sturry, Canterbury CT2 0BL* Tel (01227) 710320 E-mail rector@sturrychurch.org.uk

CORNWALL, Archdeacon of. *See* BUSH, The Ven Roger Charles

CORNWELL, Christopher Richard. b 43. Dur Univ BA67. Cuddesdon Coll 67. **d** 69 **p** 70. C Cannock *Lich* 69-75; P-in-c Hadley 75-80; V 80-81; Bp's Dom Chapl 81-86; Subchanter Lich Cathl 81-86; V Ellesmere 86-89; V Welsh Frankton 86-89; V Ellesmere and Welsh Frankton 89-92; TV Leeds City *Ripon* 92-00; AD Allerton 94-97; V Ireland Wood 00-08; AD Headingley 01-07; Hon Min Can Ripon Cathl from 08. *The Vicarage, Knaresborough Road, Bishop Monkton, Harrogate HG3 3QQ* Tel (01765) 676367 E-mail christophercornwell08@btinternet.com

CORNWELL, Lisa Michele. b 70. Lon Bible Coll BA94 Westmr Coll Ox PGCE95 K Coll Lon MA99. Ridley Hall Cam 00. **d** 02 **p** 03. C Newport Pagnell w Lathbury and Moulsoe *Ox* 02-06; V Crowthorne from 06. *The Vicarage, 56 Duke's Ride, Crowthorne RG45 6NY* Tel (01344) 772413 E-mail revlisacornwell@aol.com

CORP, Ronald Geoffrey. b 51. Ch Ch Ox MA77. STETS. **d** 98 **p** 99. NSM Kilburn St Mary w All So and W Hampstead St Jas *Lon* 98-02; NSM Hendon St Mary and Ch Ch 02-07; NSM Holborn St Alb w Saffron Hill St Pet from 07. *The Clergy House, 18 Brooke Street, London EC1N 7RD* Tel 07956-847792 (mobile) E-mail ronald.corp@btconnect.com

CORRIE, Jennifer Sylvia. b 46. RMN68 SRN76. **d** 99 **p** 00. OLM Broughton *Man* from 99. *6 Briardene, Back Hilton Street, Salford M7 2GQ*

CORRIE, John. b 48. Imp Coll Lon BScEng69 MSc70 PhD73 Nottm Univ MTh86. Trin Coll Bris 74. **d** 77 **p** 78. C Kendal St Thos *Carl* 77-80; C Attenborough *S'well* 80-86; ICS Peru 86-91; Tutor and Lect All Nations Chr Coll Ware 91-02; Lect/Development Officer Cen for Angl Communion Studies Selly Oak 02-05; Abp's Internat Project Officer *Cant* 05-06; Tutor Trin Coll Bris from 07; Perm to Offic *Birm* from 03. *9 Longton Road, Kings Heath, Birmingham B13 9UL* Tel 0121-444 2767

CORRIE, Paul Allen. b 43. St Jo Coll Nottm 77. **d** 79 **p** 80. C Beverley Minster *York* 79-82; V Derby St Werburgh 82-84; V Derby St Alkmund and St Werburgh 84-95; Singapore 95-99; R Hawkwell *Chelmsf* 00-05; rtd 06; Perm to Offic *Bradf* from 06. *5 Airedale Ings, Cononley, Keighley BD20 8LF* E-mail plcorrie@btopenworld.com

CORRIGAN, The Ven Thomas George. b 28. TCD BTh91. CITC 56. **d** 58 **p** 59. C Cavan and Drung *K, E & A* 58-60; I Drung 60-67; I Belfast St Mich *Conn* 67-70; I Kingscourt w Syddan *M & K* 70-96; Adn Meath 81-96; Dioc Registrar (Meath) 87-90; rtd 96. *The Beeches, Turner's Hill, Kingscourt, Co Cavan, Republic of Ireland* Tel (00353) (42) 966 8348 E-mail adngcorrigan@eircom.net

CORRY, Mrs Sarah. b 57. Sussex Univ BEd78. SEITE 06. **d** 09 **p** 10. NSM Crayford *Roch* from 09. *20 Glebelands, Dartford DA1 4RZ* Tel (01322) 523907 E-mail sarahcorry@aol.com

CORSIE, Andrew Russell. b 57. Middx Univ BA97. Trin Coll Bris 91. **d** 93 **p** 94. C Northolt Park St Barn *Lon* 93-97; C Perivale 97-01; P-in-c 01-06; R from 06; AD Ealing 03-10. *Perivale Rectory, Federal Road, Perivale, Greenford UB6 7AP* Tel (020) 8997 1948 E-mail acorsie@aol.com *or* andrew.corsie@perivalechurch.org.uk

CORWIN, Nigel Trevor. b 47. EAMTC 95. **d** 97 **p** 98. NSM Bury St Edmunds Ch Ch *St E* from 97. *121 Raedwald Drive, Bury St Edmunds IP32 7DG* Tel (01284) 725284 Fax 725391 Mobile 07713-769816 E-mail nigel@corwin.fsnet.co.uk

CORY, Valerie Ann. *See* DAWSON, Mrs Valerie Ann

COSBY, Ingrid St Clair. b 34. ALCM LLCM DipEd. **dss** 71 **d** 86 **p** 96. Cumbernauld *Glas* 71-73; Asst CF 73-78; Stromness *Ab* 83-86; NSM from 86. *Quarrybrae, Hillside Road, Stromness KW16 3HR* Tel and fax (01856) 850832

COSENS, William Edward Hyde. b 38. Lich Th Coll 61. **d** 64 **p** 65. C W Drayton *Lon* 64-68; C Roehampton H Trin *S'wark* 68-70; ILEA Youth Ldr 69-70; Miss to Seamen 70-94; Rotterdam 70-72; Tilbury 72-76; Dampier Seafarers' Cen

Australia 76-81; Auckland New Zealand 81-89; Chapl Immingham Seafarers' Cen 89-94; Hon C Immingham *Linc* 89-94; Chapl Felixstowe Seafarers' Cen 94-97; Chapl Avonmouth Miss to Seamen 97-99; Sen Chapl Melbourne Miss to Seafarers Australia 99-03; Chapl State of Vic 99-03; rtd 03; Perm to Offic *Sarum* 04-05 and *Chich* from 05. *8 Barford Road, Chichester PO19 7DP* Tel (01243) 789698 Mobile 07963-093816 E-mail ted.caroline.cosens@virgin.net

COSGRAVE-HANLEY, Máirt Joseph. *See* HANLEY, Máirt Joseph

COSH, Roderick John. b 56. Lon Univ BSc78 Heythrop Coll Lon MA03. St Steph Ho Ox 78. **d** 81 **p** 82. C Swindon New Town *Bris* 81-86; Chapl Asst R Marsden Hosp Lon and Surrey 86-91; V Whitton St Aug *Lon* 91-00; P-in-c Staines St Mary and St Pet 00-05; P-in-c Staines Ch Ch 04-05; V Staines from 06; AD Spelthorne 04-10. *St Peter's Vicarage, 14 Thames Side, Staines TW18 2HA* Tel (01784) 453039 *or* 469155 E-mail rod@stainesparish.org

COSLETT, Anthony Allan. b 49. Cuddesdon Coll. **d** 84 **p** 85. C Notting Hill St Clem and St Mark *Lon* 84-85; C Brentford 85-87; C-in-c Hounslow Gd Shep Beavers Lane CD 87-90; V Hounslow W Gd Shep 90-92; CF 92-08; TR Leic Resurr from 08. *St Alban's House, Weymouth Street, Leicester LE4 6FN* Tel 0116-268 0255

COSLETT (*née* SLATER), Mrs Carol Ann. b 63. Univ of Wales (Ban) BD85 Jes Coll Cam PGCE86 Lon Inst of Educn MA92. Ripon Coll Cuddesdon 01. **d** 03 **p** 04. C Horsell *Guildf* 03-07; R Betchworth and Buckland *S'wark* from 08. *The Rectory, Old Reigate Road, Betchworth RH3 7DE* Tel (01737) 842102 Mobile 07803-671256 E-mail carolcoslett@tiscali.co.uk

COSS, Oliver James. b 82. Hull Univ BSc04 Leeds Univ BA06 MA09. Coll of Resurr Mirfield 04. **d** 07 **p** 08. C Cottingham *York* 07-11; V Small Heath *Birm* from 11. *The Clergy House, 85 Jenkins Street, Small Heath, Birmingham B10 0PQ* Tel 0121-772 0621 E-mail oliver.coss@gmail.com

COSSAR, David Vyvyan. b 34. Lon Univ BA63. Chich Th Coll 63. **d** 65 **p** 66. C Upper Clapton St Matt *Lon* 65-68; C Withycombe Raleigh *Ex* 68-72; V Honicknowle 72-78; V Brixham w Churston Ferrers 78-86; P-in-c Kingswear 85-86; TR Brixham w Churston Ferrers and Kingswear 86-90; V Lamorbey H Trin *Roch* 90-03; rtd 03; Perm to Offic *Roch* from 03. *25 Bromley College, London Road, Bromley BR1 1PE* Tel (020) 8464 6911 E-mail dvanddlcossar@tiscali.co.uk

COSSAR, Canon Heather Jillian Mackenzie. b 27. dss 83 **d** 91 **p** 94. CMS Kenya 83-90; NSM Slindon, Eartham and Madehurst *Chich* 90-99; Perm to Offic from 99; Can Nyahururu from 03. *Gwitu, 38 Spinney Walk, Barnham, Bognor Regis PO22 0HT* Tel (01243) 552718

COSSINS, John Charles. b 43. Hull Univ BSc65. Oak Hill Th Coll 65. **d** 67 **p** 68. C Kenilworth St Jo *Cov* 67-70; C Huyton St Geo *Liv* 70-73; TV Maghull 73-79; Chapl Oakwood Hosp Maidstone 79-85; Maidstone Hosp 85-88; Chapl Park Lane Hosp Maghull 88-03; Chapl Moss Side Hosp Liv 88-03; Chapl Ashworth Hosp Maghull 88-03; rtd 03; Perm to Offic *Liv* from 03. *9 Longton Drive, Liverpool L37 7ET* Tel (01704) 833136 E-mail jcossins@jcossins.demon.co.uk

COSSINS, Roger Stanton. b 40. K Coll Lon BD67 AKC67. **d** 68 **p** 69. C Bramley *Ripon* 68-71; C W End *Win* 71-76; V Bramley 76-91; P-in-c Bournemouth H Epiphany 91-94; V 94-00; rtd 00. *5 Allen Court, Trumpington, Cambridge CB2 9LU* Tel (01223) 841726

COSSTICK, Mrs Helen Mary Vaux. b 47. K Alfred's Coll Win TCert05. NTMTC 06. **d** 09 **p** 10. NSM Hanwell St Mary w St Chris *Lon* from 09. *22 Shakespeare Road, London W7 1LR* Tel (020) 8579 6367 Mobile 07727-902309 E-mail helen.cosstick@btinternet.com

COSTER, Mrs Catherine Anne. b 47. Bris Poly BEd85. WEMTC 97. **d** 00 **p** 01. NSM Yate New Town *Bris* 00-04; NSM Warmley, Syston and Bitton from 04; Hon Min Can Bris Cathl from 04. *31 Vayre Close, Chipping Sodbury, Bristol BS37 6NT* Tel (01454) 314858 Fax 0117-927 7454 E-mail catherine.coster@bristoldiocese.org

COSTER, David John. b 65. Derby Univ BSc98. NTMTC BA09. **d** 09 **p** 10. C Leigh St Clem *Chelmsf* from 09. *32 Sandown Road, Thundersley, Benfleet SS7 3SE* Tel (01268) 777501 Mobile 07747-391083 E-mail david@coster.ms

COSTERTON, Alan Stewart. b 40. Bris Univ BA67. Clifton Th Coll 67. **d** 69 **p** 70. C Peckham St Mary Magd *S'wark* 69-73; C Forest Gate St Sav w W Ham St Matt *Chelmsf* 73-76; TV 76-79; V Thornton cum Bagworth *Leic* 79-85; V Thornton, Bagworth and Stanton 85-95; TR Sileby, Cossington and Seagrave 95-04; R 04-05; rtd 05. *59 Station Road, Cropston, Leicester LE7 7HG* Tel 0116-234 1026 E-mail alan@costerton.freeserve.co.uk

COSTIGAN, Esther Rose. *See* FOSS, Esther Rose

COSTIN, Pamela Lindsay. b 49. Ridley Hall Cam 06. **d** 07 **p** 08. C Immingham, Habrough Gp and Keelby Gp *Linc* 07-09; C Scawby, Redbourne and Hibaldstow 09-10; C Bishop Norton, Wadingham and Snitterby 09-10; C Kirton in Lindsey w Manton 09-10; C Grayingham 09-10; S Wolds Community

Chapl from 10. *The Rectory, 6 Simons Close, Donington-on-Bain, Louth LN11 9TX* Tel (01507) 343345 Mobile 07756-852907 E-mail pamcostin@yahoo.co.uk

COSTIN, Richard George Charles. b 38. Liv Univ CertEd59 Anglia Poly BEd85 ACP67 FCollP82. Coll of Resurr Mirfield 04. **d** 05 **p** 06. NSM Scarborough St Martin *York* from 05. *12 Lightfoots Close, Scarborough YO12 5NR* Tel (01723) 376141 Mobile 07768-856175 E-mail rcos38@hotmail.com

COTMAN, John Sell Granville (Jan). b 44. St Jo Coll Dur BA69. Wells Th Coll 70. **d** 73 **p** 74. C Leigh St Mary *Man* 73-76; P-in-c Coldhurst 76-78; TV Oldham 78-82; TV E Ham w Upton Park *Chelmsf* 82-85; C Hove All SS *Chich* 88-93; TV Hove 93-00; TV W Slough *Ox* 01-08; V Manor Park and Whitby Road from 08. *298 Stoke Poges Lane, Slough SL1 3LL* Tel (01753) 578503

COTSON, Tony Arthur. b 53. NEOC 00. **d** 03 **p** 04. C Kingston upon Hull St Nic *York* 03-10; P-in-c Kingston upon Hull St Matt w St Barn from 10; C Newington w Dairycoates 08-10; P-in-c from 10. *11 Kipling Walk, Summergroves Way, Hull HU4 6SX* Tel (01482) 504189 Mobile 07718-567675 E-mail tony@cotson.karoo.co.uk

COTTAM, Kenneth Michael David. b 46. St Mich Coll Llan 93. **d** 93 **p** 94. Lic to Offic Llangadog and Llandeilo Deanery *St D* 93-96; V Llangadog and Gwynfe w Llanddeusant from 96. *The Vicarage, Walters Road, Llangadog SA19 9AE* Tel (01550) 777604

COTTEE, Christopher Paul. b 54. Newc Univ BSc75. Wycliffe Hall *Ox* 77. **d** 80 **p** 81. C Much Woolton *Liv* 80-84; C Prescot 84-88; NSM Parr 89-91; V Watford St Pet *St Alb* from 91. *St Peter's Vicarage, 61 Westfield Avenue, Watford WD24 7HF* Tel (01923) 226717 E-mail chris.cottee1@ntlworld.com

COTTEE, Mary Jane. b 43. Open Univ BA81 CertEd64. Oak Hill Th Coll 87. **d** 90 **p** 94. NSM Gt Baddow *Chelmsf* 90-95; P-in-c Woodham Ferrers and Bicknacre 95-11; rtd 11. *20 Elm Road, South Woodham Ferrers, Chelmsford CM3 5QE* Tel 07735-975423 (mobile) E-mail marycottee@btinternet.com

COTTELL, Avril Jane. *See* GAUNT, Mrs Avril Jane

COTTER, Graham Michael. b 50. Univ of Wales (Ban) BA72. Ridley Hall Cam 75. **d** 78 **p** 79. C Headley All SS *Guildf* 78-81; C Plymouth St Andr w St Paul and St Geo *Ex* 81-84; V Buckland Monachorum from 84; RD Tavistock 93-98. *The Vicarage, Buckland Monachorum, Yelverton PL20 7LQ* Tel (01822) 852227 E-mail cotters@onetel.com

COTTER, James England. b 42. G&C Coll Cam BA64 MA67. Linc Th Coll 65. **d** 67 **p** 68. C Stretford St Matt *Man* 67-70; Lect Linc Th Coll 70-73; Perm to Offic *Lon* 73-74; Chapl G&C Coll Cam 74-77; C Leavesden *St Alb* 77-83; Asst Prin St Alb Minl Tr Scheme 77-83; Course Dir 83-86; Perm to Offic *Ex* 88-95; Lic to Offic *Sheff* 88-01; Perm to Offic *Ban* 99-08; P-in-c Aberdaron and Llanfaelrhys from 08. *Gernant, Aberdaron, Pwllheli LL53 8BG* Tel (01758) 760296 E-mail jim@cottercairns.co.uk

COTTER, Robert Edmund. d 05 p 06. NSM Mossley *Conn* 05-09; NSM Skerry w Rathcavan and Newtowncrommelin from 09. *33 Deerfin Road, Ballymena BT42 4HP* Tel (028) 2563 1303 E-mail robertcotter76@btinternet.com

COTTERELL, Michael Clifford. b 54. Oak Hill Th Coll 81. **d** 84 **p** 85. C Lutterworth w Cotesbach *Leic* 84-87; C Belper *Derby* 87-91; V Locking *B & W* 91-98; V Slough *Ox* from 98. *St Paul's Vicarage, 196 Stoke Road, Slough SL2 5AY* Tel (01753) 521497 E-mail mchtterell@toucansurf.com

COTTERILL, John Glyn. d 10 p 11. NSM Baswich *Lich* from 10. *11 Bracken View, Brocton, Stafford ST17 0TF* Tel (01785) 664072 E-mail john-cotterill@btinternet.com

COTTERILL, Joseph Charles. b 17. AMCT38 Lon Univ BD California Coll Peking MA46. Ox Min Course 92. **d** 93 **p** 94. NSM Marcham w Garford *Ox* 93-98; Perm to Offic from 98. *8 Draycott Road, Southmoor, Abingdon OX13 5BY* Tel (01865) 820436

COTTINGHAM, Peter John Garnet. b 24. Wadh Coll Ox BA48 MA50. Ridley Hall Cam 48. **d** 50 **p** 51. C Cheadle *Ches* 50-55; R Ox St Clem 55-68; V S Mimms Ch Ch *Lon* 68-81; V Derby St Pet and Ch Ch w H Trin 81-89; rtd 89; Perm to Offic *Ban* 89-07. *2 Sherwood Avenue, Potters Bar EN6 2LD*

COTTON, Charles Anthony. b 50. Linc Coll Ox BA72 MA77 PGCE73. Ridley Hall Cam 89. **d** 91 **p** 92. C Hendon St Paul Mill Hill *Lon* 91-96; C Wandsworth All SS *S'wark* 96-97; V Clapham St Jas 97-08; Perm to Offic from 08. *9 Woodcote Avenue, Wallington SM6 0QR* Tel (020) 8669 1143 E-mail revdcharlie@btinternet.com

COTTON, John Horace Brazel. b 28. MIMechE St Jo Coll Cam BA50 MA76. St Alb Minl Tr Scheme 78. **d** 81 **p** 82. NSM Lt Berkhamsted and Bayford, Essendon etc *St Alb* 81-87; P-in-c 87-96; rtd 96; Perm to Offic *St Alb* from 96. *49 Sherrardspark Road, Welwyn Garden City AL8 7LD* Tel (01707) 321815

COTTON, John William. b 53. Oak Hill Th Coll 86. **d** 86 **p** 87. C New Clee *Linc* 86-89; Chapl St Andr Hospice Grimsby 88-89; R Middle Rasen Gp 89-95; P-in-c Broughton 95-97; R 97-10; Chapl Humberside Airport 99-00; rtd 11. *47 Ridgeway, Nettleham, Lincoln LN2 2TL* E-mail revcottonj@yahoo.co.uk

COTTON, Mrs Margaret Elizabeth. b 30. JP79. Newnham Coll Cam BA53 MA66. St Alb Minl Tr Scheme 78. **dss** 82 **d** 87 **p** 94. Lt Berkhamsted and Bayford, Essendon etc *St Alb* 82-87; Hon Par Dn 87-94; Hon C 94-96; rtd 96; Perm to Offic *St Alb* from 96. *49 Sherrardspark Road, Welwyn Garden City AL8 7LD* Tel (01707) 321815

COTTON, Miss Michelle Susan. b 77. Ripon Coll Cuddesdon 09. **d** 11. C Weston Favell *Pet* from 11. *5 Kestrel Close, Northampton NN3 3JG* Tel 07817-905423 (mobile) E-mail michelle.cotton123@btinternet.com

COTTON, Norman Joseph. b 39. Kelham Th Coll 59. **d** 64 **p** 65. C Auckland St Helen *Dur* 64-67; C Withington St Chris *Man* 67-68; C Hucknall Torkard *S'well* 69-71; TV 71-73; TV Fenny Stratford *Ox* 73-75; TV Fenny Stratford and Water Eaton 75-82; R Walton 82-90; TR Walton Milton Keynes 90-92; V Stewkley w Soulbury and Drayton Parslow 92-04; RD Mursley 94-01; rtd 04; Perm to Offic *Ox* 05-10. *5 Whites Close, Steeple Claydon, Buckingham MK18 2HN* Tel (01296) 738602 E-mail nomo uk@yahoo.co.uk

COTTON, Miss Patricia Constance. b 32. Gilmore Ho 54. **dss** 60 **d** 87 **p** 94. Forest Gate St Edm *Chelmsf* 60-64; Reading St Giles *Ox* 64-65; Basildon St Martin w H Cross and Laindon *Chelmsf* 65-79; Gt Burstead 79-87; Par Dn Maldon All SS w St Pet 87-91; rtd 92; NSM Holland-on-Sea *Chelmsf* 94-96; Perm to Offic from 96. *67 Copperfield Gardens, Brentwood CM14 4UD* Tel (01277) 224274

COTTON, Patrick Arthur William. b 46. Essex Univ BA67 Down Coll Cam MA73 Homerton Coll Cam PGCE96. Linc Th Coll 68. **d** 71 **p** 72. C Earlham St Anne *Nor* 71-73; Chapl Down Coll Cam 73-78; V Eaton Socon *St Alb* 78-84; TR Newc Epiphany 84-90; V Tunstall w Melling and Leck *Blackb* 90-95; Chapl Pet High Sch 01-05; P-in-c Debenham and Helmingham *St E* from 06. *The Vicarage, 6 Raedwald Way, Debenham, Stowmarket IP14 6SN* Tel (01728) 861073

COTTON, Peter John. b 45. BNC Ox BA66 CQSW76. Cuddesdon Coll 67. **d** 69 **p** 70. C Salford St Phil w St Steph *Man* 69-73; Asst Educn Officer *St Alb* 73-75; C Bris St Geo 75-76; C-in-c Portsea St Geo CD *Portsm* 76-80; Soc Resp Adv 78-88; Can Res Portsm Cathl 84-88; V St Laur in Thanet *Cant* 88-93; TR 93-97; Hon Min Can Cant Cathl 93-97; TR Hemel Hempstead *St Alb* 97-09; RD Hemel Hempstead 03-08; Hon Can St Alb 08-09; rtd 09. *45 Bepton Down, Petersfield GU31 4PR* Tel (01730) 233785 E-mail petercotton2@tiscali.co.uk

COTTON, Canon Richard William. b 35. Hertf Coll Ox BA58 MA62. Clifton Th Coll 58. **d** 60 **p** 61. C Harold Wood *Chelmsf* 60-64; C Higher Openshaw *Man* 64-67; Lic to Offic 67-71; Ch Youth Fellowships Assn and Pathfinders 67-71; Nat Sec Pathfinders CPAS 71-76; Lic to Offic *St Alb* 73-76; V Chislehurst Ch Ch *Roch* 76-92; V Herne Bay Ch Ch *Cant* 92-01; RD Reculver 93-01; Hon Can Cant Cathl 99-01; rtd 01; Perm to Offic *Cant* from 01. *16 Crundale Way, Cliftonville, Margate CT9 3YH* Tel (01843) 221970 E-mail rwcotton67@hotmail.com

COTTON, Canon Robert Lloyd. b 58. Mert Coll Ox MA79. Westcott Ho Cam 81. **d** 83 **p** 84. C Plaistow St Mary *Roch* 83-86; C Bisley and W End *Guildf* 87-89; P-in-c E Molesey St Paul 89-96; Dir of Reader Tr from 90; R Guildf H Trin w St Mary from 96; Hon Can Highveld S Africa from 06; Hon Can Guildf Cathl from 10. *Holy Trinity Rectory, 9 Eastgate Gardens, Guildford GU1 4AZ* Tel (01483) 575489 E-mail rector@holytrinityguildford.org.uk

COTTON-BETTERIDGE, Mrs Fiona Jane Marson. b 56. Nottm Univ MA05. EMMTC 02. **d** 05 **p** 06. NSM Burton Joyce w Bulcote and Stoke Bardolph *S'well* 05-08; P-in-c Old Leake w Wrangle *Linc* from 08; P-in-c Friskney from 08. *The Vicarage, Yawling Gate Road, Friskney, Boston PE22 8QF* Tel (01205) 820104 E-mail fionacb@aol.com

⧾**COTTRELL, The Rt Revd Stephen Geoffrey.** b 58. Poly Cen Lon BA79. St Steph Ho Ox 81. **d** 84 **p** 85 **c** 04. C Forest Hill Ch Ch *S'wark* 84-88; P-in-c Parklands St Wilfrid CD *Chich* 88-93; Asst Dir Past Studies Chich Th Coll 88-93; Dioc Missr *Wakef* 93-98; Bp's Chapl for Evang 93-98; Springboard Missr and Consultant in Evang 98-01; Can Res Pet Cathl 01-04; Area Bp Reading *Ox* 04-10; Bp Chelmsf from 10. *Bishop's Court, Main Road, Margaretting, Ingatestone CM4 0HD* Tel (01277) 352001 Fax 355374 E-mail bishopscourt@chelmsford.anglican.org

COTTRILL, Derek John. b 43. MA. Qu Coll Birm. **d** 82 **p** 83. C Southampton Maybush St Pet *Win* 82-85; V Barton Stacey and Bullington etc 85-92; R Bishopstoke 92-06; Asst Chapl Win and Eastleigh Healthcare NHS Trust 92-06; rtd 06. *7 The Old Green, Sherborne DT9 3JY* Tel (01935) 816746

COUCH, Ms Felicity Anne. b 59. CQSW85. SEITE 00. **d** 03 **p** 04. NSM Stockwell St Andr and St Mich *S'wark* 03-08; P-in-c Ulceby Gp, Croxton and Brocklesby Park *Linc* 08-11; R Orwell Gp *Ely* from 11. *The Rectory, Fishers Lane, Orwell, Royston SG8 5QX* Tel (01223) 207212 Mobile 07745-905417 E-mail fcouch@btinternet.com

COUCHMAN, Anthony Denis. b 37. Sarum Th Coll 66. **d** 69 **p** 70. C Barkingside St Fran *Chelmsf* 69-71; C Chingford SS Pet and

Paul 71-76; P-in-c Walthamstow St Barn and St Jas Gt 76-80; V 80-07; rtd 07; Perm to Offic *Nor* from 08. *Friarscot, Church Street, King's Lynn PE30 5EB* Tel (01553) 766643 E-mail anthony.couchman@yahoo.co.uk

COUCHMAN, Kathryn. b 60. Open Univ BA92 Coll of Ripon & York St Jo MA00. NOC 02. **d** 06 **p** 07. C Wetherby *Ripon* 06-08; C Spofforth w Kirk Deighton 08-10; Chapl HM YOI Wetherby 08-11; Chapl Harrogate and Distr NHS Foundn Trust from 11. *Harrogate District Hospital, Lancaster Park Road, Harrogate HG2 7SX* Tel (01423) 553045 E-mail kathycouchman@fsmail.net

COUGHTREY, Miss Sheila Frances. b 48. RSCN73 SRN73 S Bank Poly BSc79. Qu Coll Birm 79. **dss** 81 **d** 87 **p** 94. Sydenham St Bart *S'wark* 81-85; Roehampton H Trin 85-91; Par Dn 87-91; Par Dn Brixton Hill St Sav 91-94; P-in-c 94-01; Min King's Acre LEP 91-01; RD Brixton 99-01; P-in-c Pleshey *Chelmsf* from 01; Warden Dioc Retreat Ho from 01. *The Vicarage, The Street, Pleshey, Chelmsford CM3 1HA* Tel (01245) 237576 E-mail sheila@scoughtrey.fsnet.co.uk

COULDRIDGE, Janice Evelyn. *See* FOX, Mrs Janice Evelyn

COULING, Canon David Charles. b 36. Open Univ BA89. Qu Coll Birm 61. **d** 63 **p** 64. C Harborne St Faith and St Laur *Birm* 63-66; C E Grinstead St Mary *Chich* 66-70; V Copthorne 70-75; V Eastbourne St Mich 75-82; V Brighton St Matthias 82-83; C-in-c Harton St Lawr CD *Dur* 84-90; V Horsley Hill St Lawr 91-94; P-in-c Greatham 94-97; V 97-01; AD Hartlepool 95-01; Master Greatham Hosp 94-00; Hon Can Dur Cathl 99-01; rtd 01; P-in-c Brancepeth *Dur* 01-04; Chapl Dur Cathl from 04. *11 Shropshire Drive, Durham DH1 2LT* Tel 0191-375 7367

COULSON, Renée. b 45. **d** 03 **p** 04. OLM Potterne w Worton and Marston *Sarum* 03-09; P-in-c Seend, Bulkington and Poulshot from 09. *The Rectory, High Street, Seend, Melksham SN12 6NR* Tel (01380) 828615 E-mail rycoulson@talktalk.net

COULSON, Canon Stephen Hugh. b 60. St Edm Hall Ox BA82 MA88 Lon Univ CertEd83. Wycliffe Hall Ox 85. **d** 88 **p** 89. C Summerfield *Birm* 88-91; Perm to Offic 91-92; CMS Uganda 92-01; Asst V Namirembe 92-96; Can from 99; Prin Uganda Martyrs Sem Namugongo 96-01; V Mitcham St Mark *S'wark* from 01; AD Merton from 09. *St Mark's Vicarage, Locks Lane, Mitcham CR4 2JX* Tel (020) 8648 2397 E-mail steve@scoulson.freeserve.co.uk

COULSON, Thomas Stanley. b 32. TCD BA54 MA68. TCD Div Sch 55. **d** 55 **p** 56. C Maghera *D & R* 55-62; I Aghalurcher and Tattykeeran *Clogh* 62-63; I Woodschapel w Gracefield *Arm* 63-97; Preb Arm Cathl 88-97; Treas Arm Cathl 94-96; Chan Arm Cathl 96-97; rtd 97. *Lisadian, 84 Coleraine Road, Portrush BT56 8HN* Tel (028) 7082 4202 E-mail canoncoulson@btinternet.com

COULSON, Tony Erik Frank. b 32. St Edm Hall Ox BA55 MA59. Wycliffe Hall Ox 55. **d** 57 **p** 58. C Walthamstow St Mary *Chelmsf* 57-60; C Reading St Jo *Ox* 60-63; V Iver 63-86; R White Waltham w Shottesbrooke 86-97; rtd 97; Perm to Offic *Ox* from 98. *30 Ravensbourne Drive, Reading RG5 4LH* Tel 0118-969 3556

COULTER, Edmond James. b 60. QUB BSc82 BD96. **d** 87 **p** 88. C Ballymena w Ballyclug *Conn* 87-90; C Knockbreda *D & D* 90-92; I Belfast Upper Falls *Conn* 92-97; I Milltown *Arm* 97-03; Supt Dublin Irish Ch Miss *D & G* from 03. *38 Woodpark, Castleknock, Dublin 15, Republic of Ireland* Tel no (00353) (1) 821 2336 *or* 873 0829 Fax 878 4049 E-mail ejcoulter@iolfree.ie *or* eddie@icm-online.ie

COULTER, Ian Herbert Young. b 54. TCD BA77 HDipEd78. **d** 99 **p** 00. Lic to Offic Cashel, Waterford and Lismore *C & O* 99-10; NSM Castlecomer w Colliery Ch, Mothel and Bilboa from 10. *22 Rose Hill Court, Kilkenny, Co Kilkenny, Republic of Ireland* Tel and fax (00353) (56) 776 2675 Mobile (86) 8130290 E-mail ianhycoulter@gmail.com *or* iancoulter@ireland.com

COULTER, Mrs Kirsten Ruth. b 43. Univ of Wales (Abth) BSc64 Homerton Coll Cam CertEd65 Lon Univ BD89 Newc Univ MA93. **d** 01 **p** 02. OLM Tweedmouth *Newc* from 01. *90 Shielfield Terrace, Tweedmouth, Berwick-upon-Tweed TD15 2EE* Tel (01289) 308485 E-mail timothy.coulter@btinternet.com

COULTER (née REEVES), Mrs Maria Elizabeth Ann. b 72. Leeds Univ BA95 Heythrop Coll Lon MTh03. St Steph Ho Ox 96. **d** 98 **p** 99. C Newington St Mary *S'wark* 98-02; V Dulwich St Clem w St Pet from 02. *St Clement's Vicarage, 140 Friern Road, London SE22 0AY* Tel (020) 8693 1890 E-mail meareeves@hotmail.com

COULTER, Miss Marilyn Judith. b 48. City of Birm Coll BEd70 Qu Coll Birm BA05. WMMTC 02. **d** 05 **p** 06. NSM Brewood *Lich* from 05; NSM Bishopswood from 05; Chapl Mid Staffs NHS Foundn Trust from 08. *14 St Chad's Close, Brewood, Stafford ST19 9DA* Tel (01902) 851168 E-mail coulter14@aol.com

COULTER, Stephen Paul. b 53. Nottm Univ BSc76 CEng MIMechE. **d** 92 **p** 93. C Oakwood St Thos *Lon* 92-95; V Grange Park St Pet 95-99; I Kells Union *M & K* 99-01; R Pimperne, Stourpaine, Durweston and Bryanston *Sarum* from 01. *The Vicarage, Shaston Road, Stourpaine, Blandford Forum DT11 8TA* Tel (01258) 480580

COULTHARD, Miss Nina Marion. b 50. CertEd71 Bp Lonsdale Coll BEd72. Trin Coll Bris 89. **d** 91 **p** 94. Par Dn Cant St Mary Bredin 91-94; C 94-95; C Bath Abbey w St Jas *B & W* 95-99; Chapl R Nat Hosp for Rheumatic Diseases NHS Trust 95-99; C Northwood Em *Lon* 99-06; V Loughton St Mich *Chelmsf* from 06. *St Michael's House, Roding Road, Loughton IG10 3EJ* Tel (020) 8508 1489

COULTHURST, Jeffrey Evans. b 38. Man Univ BA61 Leeds Univ PGCE62. **d** 84 **p** 85. OLM Ancaster *Linc* 84-89; OLM Ancaster Wilsford Gp 89-05. *5 North Drive, Ancaster, Grantham NG32 3RB* Tel (01400) 230280 E-mail jeff@jcoulthurst.fsnet.co.uk

COULTON, David John. b 45. St Jo Coll Cam BA67 MA71 Glos Univ MA04 CertEd69. WEMTC 07. **d** 09 **p** 10. NSM Tewkesbury w Walton Cardiff and Twyning *Glouc* from 09. *4 Conigree Lane, Abbots Road, Tewkesbury GL20 5TF* Tel (01684) 293523 E-mail davidcoulton@btinternet.com

COULTON, David Stephen. b 41. Bernard Gilpin Soc Dur 63 Sarum Th Coll 64. **d** 67 **p** 68. C Guildf H Trin w St Mary 67-70; Asst Chapl St Luke's Hosp Guildf 67-70; Asst Chapl Radley Coll 70-83; Chapl Eton Coll 83-01; Chapl Eton Coll 01-04; rtd 04. *20 The Oakbournes, Bishopdown, Salisbury SP1 3FZ* Tel (01722) 333928

COULTON, The Very Revd Nicholas Guy. b 40. Lon Univ BD72 Ox Univ MA07. Cuddesdon Coll 65. **d** 67 **p** 68. C Pershore w Wick *Worc* 67-70; Bp's Dom Chapl *St Alb* 71-75; P-in-c Bedford St Paul 75-79; V 79-90; Hon Can St Alb 89-90; Provost Newc 90-01; Dean Newc 01-03; Can Res and Sub-Dean Ch Ch *Ox* 03-08; rtd 08. *123 Merewood Avenue, Headington, Oxford OX3 8EQ* Tel (01865) 763790 E-mail ngc@proscenia.co.uk

COULTON, Philip Ernest. b 31. St Cath Coll Cam BA54 MA58 TCD BD68 Open Univ BA84. Ely Th Coll 55. **d** 57 **p** 58. Asst Master Perse Sch Cam 54-55; Asst Master Bradf Gr Sch 57; C Newark w Coddington *S'well* 57-61; Min Can and Sacr Cant Cathl 61-63; Min Can Ripon Cathl 63-68; Hd of RE Ashton-under-Lyne Gr Sch 69-84; V Ulceby Gp *Linc* 85-89; P-in-c Ingatestone w Buttsbury *Chelmsf* 89-99; P-in-c Fryerning w Margaretting 89-92; rtd 99; Perm to Offic *Sarum* from 01 and *B & W* 02-06. *90 Boreham Road, Warminster BA12 9JW* Tel (01985) 219353 E-mail pecoulton@talktalk.net

COUNSELL, Edwin Charles Robert. b 63. Univ of Wales (Cardiff) BA84 MTh97. St Steph Ho Ox 85. **d** 88 **p** 89. C Cardiff St Mary and St Steph w St Dyfrig etc *Llan* 88-94; V Pendoylan w Welsh St Donats 94-06; Dioc Dir Statutory Educn from 00; Prov Adv on Educn Ch in Wales from 06. *The Vicarage, 9 Heol St Cattwg, Pendoylan, Cowbridge CF71 7UG* Tel (01446) 760195 *or* tel and fax 760210 E-mail post@llandaffschools.fs.net.co.uk

COUNSELL, Michael John Radford. b 35. Pemb Coll Cam BA59 MA63. Ripon Hall Ox 59. **d** 61 **p** 62. C Handsworth St Mary *Birm* 61-63; Singapore 64-68; Vietnam and Cambodia 68-71; Seychelles 72-76; Dean Mahé 73-76; V Harborne St Pet *Birm* 76-89; Relig Consultant Inter-Ch Travel Ltd 89-90; V Forest Hill St Aug *S'wark* 90-00; Perm to Offic *Cant* 91-00; rtd 00; Perm to Offic *Birm* and *Eur* from 05. *Flat 2, 340 Tessall Lane, Birmingham B31 5EN* Tel and fax 0121-628 2028 Mobile 07891-860473 E-mail mjrcounsell@hotmail.com

COUPAR, Thomas. b 50. BA71 ACE80. Edin Dioc NSM Course 77. **d** 80 **p** 81. NSM Dunbar *Edin* 80-86; NSM Haddington 80-86; Hd Master Pencaitland Primary Sch E Lothian 80-81; Hd Master K Meadow Sch E Lothian 81-87; Asst Dioc Supernumerary *Edin* 87-89; Primary Educn Adv Fife from 88; Dioc Supernumerary 90-96; Chapl Robin Chapel Edin from 06. *21/9 Rennie's Isle, Edinburgh EH6 6QB* Tel 0131-551 1800 E-mail tcoupar@hotmail.com

COUPER (née WOOD), Mrs Audrey Elizabeth. b 54. Edin Univ BSc75 Westmr Coll of Educn PGCE76. ERMC 05. **d** 08 **p** 09. NSM Digswell and Panshanger *St Alb* from 08. *18 Netherfield Road, Harpenden AL5 2AG* Tel (01582) 346901 E-mail audrey@tizmoi.net

COUPER, Jeanette Emily (Jean). b 40. S'wark Ord Course 85. **d** 88. Par Dn Mitcham SS Pet and Paul *S'wark* 88-93; Chapl Asst Guy's Hosp Lon 93-94; Perm to Offic *S'wark* 93-04; rtd 04. *Rose Cottage, Wentnor, Bishops Castle SY9 5EE* Tel (01588) 650590

COUPER, Jonathan George. b 51. St Jo Coll Dur BA73. Wycliffe Hall Ox 73. **d** 75 **p** 76. C Clifton *York* 75-78; C Darfield *Sheff* 78-81; V Bridlington Quay Ch Ch *York* from 81; P-in-c Bessingby from 99. *21 Kingston Road, Bridlington YO15 3NF* Tel (01262) 400259 *or* 404100 E-mail jonathan.couper@christchurchbridlington.co.uk

COUPLAND, Simon Charles. b 59. St Jo Coll Cam BA82 PGCE83 MA85 PhD87. Ridley Hall Cam 88. **d** 91 **p** 92. C Bath St Luke *B & W* 91-95; TV Broadwater *Chich* 95-04; V Kingston Hill St Paul *S'wark* from 04. *The Vicarage, 33 Queen's Road, Kingston upon Thames KT2 7SF* Tel (020) 8549 8597 *or* 8549 5444 E-mail simon.coupland@stpaulskingston.org.uk

COURT, Canon David Eric. b 58. Southn Univ BSc80 PhD83 PGCE84. Oak Hill Th Coll BA91. **d** 91 **p** 92. C Barton Seagrave w Warkton *Pet* 91-94; C Kinson *Sarum* 94-97; P-in-c Mile Cross *Nor* 97-99; V 99-03; V Cromer from 03; RD Repps from 10; Hon Can Nor Cathl from 10. *The Vicarage, 30 Cromwell Road, Cromer NR27 0BE* Tel (01263) 512000 E-mail revdavidcourt@btinternet.com

COURT, Canon Kenneth Reginald. b 36. AKC60. d 61 p 62. C Garforth *Ripon* 61-63; C Harrogate St Wilfrid 63-65; V Thornbury *Bradf* 65-73; Prec Leic Cathl 73-76; V Douglas St Matt *S & M* 76-84; V Syston *Leic* 84-93; TR 93-98; RD Goscote 90-95; Hon Can Leic Cathl 92-98; rtd 98; Perm to Offic *Leic* from 99; *Linc* 01-03; *Pet* 03-08. *12 Lord Burghley's Hospital, Station Road, Stamford PE9 2LD* Tel (01780) 754372 E-mail kenneth@kcourt.wanadoo.co.uk

COURT, Martin Jeremy. b 61. GRNCM84 Nottm Univ BTh89. Linc Th Coll 86. d 89 p 90. C Thurmaston *Leic* 89-92; C Leic St Jas 92-93; TV Leic Resurr 93-98; V Scraptoft from 98; P-in-c Leic St Chad from 08; Dioc Info Tech Co-ord from 96. *All Saints' Vicarage, 331 Scraptoft Lane, Scraptoft, Leicester LE5 2HU* Tel 0116-241 3205 Mobile 07798-876837 E-mail mcourt@leicester.anglican.org

COURT, Martin John. b 64. Ridley Hall Cam 03. d 05 p 06. C Blandford Forum and Langton Long *Sarum* 05-09; V Chadwell Heath *Chelmsf* from 09. *The Vicarage, 7 Chadwell Heath Lane, Romford RM6 4LS* Tel (020) 8590 2391 Mobile 07905-612542

COURT, Nicholas James Keble. b 56. Chich Th Coll 86. d 88 p 89. C Golders Green *Lon* 88-91; C Westbury-on-Trym H Trin *Bris* 91-94; PV Llan Cathl 94-96; V Graig 96-02; P-in-c Cilfynydd 96-01; Miss P *Mor* from 09. *Cair Paravel, Ardmuir, Ullapool IV26 2TN* Tel (01854) 612506

COURT, Richard Leonard. b 54. Univ of Wales (Ban) BTh04. EAMTC 94. d 97 p 98. NSM Framlingham w Saxtead *St E* 97-05; V Badsey w Aldington and Offenham and Bretforton *Worc* from 05; RD Evesham from 10. *The Vicarage, High Street, Badsey, Evesham WR11 7EW* Tel (01386) 834550 Mobile 07751-775917 E-mail richard.court@btinternet.com

COURTAULD, Augustine Christopher Caradoc. b 34. Trin Coll Cam BA58 MA61. Westcott Ho Cam 58. d 60 p 61. C Oldham St Mary *Man* 60-63; Chapl Trin Coll Cam 63-68; Chapl The Lon Hosp (Whitechapel) 68-78; V Wilton Place St Paul *Lon* 78-99; AD Westmr St Marg 92-97; rtd 99; Perm to Offic *St E* from 00. *Broke House, The Drift, Levington, Ipswich IP10 0LF* Tel (01473) 659773

COURTIE, John Malcolm. b 42. BNC Ox BA65 DPhil72 St Jo Coll Dur BA76. Cranmer Hall Dur 74. d 77 p 78. C Mossley Hill St Matt and St Jas *Liv* 77-80; V Litherland St Paul Hatton Hill 80-84; Wellingborough Sch 84-89; Hon C Wollaston and Strixton *Pet* 84-89; V Woodford Halse w Eydon 89-99; R Blisworth and Stoke Bruerne w Grafton Regis etc 99-02; rtd 02; Hon C NW Hants *Win* 09-10. *Brooksong, Longmeadow Road, Lympstone, Exmouth EX8 5LF* Tel (01395) 260242 E-mail thecourties@yahoo.co.uk

COURTNEY (*née* JORDAN), Mrs Avril Marilyn. b 35. Lon Univ DipEd56. SWMTC 79. dss 82 d 87 p 94. Highweek and Teigngrace *Ex* 82-88; Par Dn 87-88; Par Dn Ottery St Mary, Alfington, W Hill, Tipton etc 88-94; C 94-99; rtd 99; Perm to Offic *Ex* 00-09. *Fairholme, Exeter Road, Newton Poppleford, Sidmouth EX10 0BJ* Tel (01395) 568691

COURTNEY, Canon Brian Joseph. b 44. BD92 MA97. CITC 70. d 73 p 74. C Willowfield *D & D* 73-75; P-in-c Knocknagoney 75-78; I Aghavea *Clogh* 78-83; I Carrickfergus *Conn* 83-95; I Enniskillen *Clogh* 95-09; Prec Clogh Cathl 95-09; rtd 09. *10 Berkeley Road, Carrickfergus BT38 9DS* Tel (028) 9335 5139 E-mail briancourtney@nireland.com

COURTNEY, Miss Louise Anita Hodd. b 48. Ex Univ BTh04. SWMTC 99. d 02 p 03. C St Keverne *Truro* 02-05; P-in-c Lanteglos by Fowey from 05; P-in-c Lansallos from 05; P-in-c Talland from 10. *The Vicarage, 4 Ocean View, Polruan, Fowey PL23 1QJ* Tel (01726) 870988 E-mail louisecourtney@tiscali.co.uk

COURTNEY, Martin Horace. b 34. SAOMC 95. d 98 p 99. OLM Flackwell Heath *Ox* from 98. *1 Green Crescent, Flackwell Heath, High Wycombe HP10 9JQ* Tel (01628) 526354

COURTNEY, Michael Monlas. b 44. Coll of Resurr Mirfield 58. d 60 p 61. C Shrewsbury St Chad *Lich* 60-63; P-in-c N Keyham *Ex* 63-68; V 68-73; TV Sidmouth, Woolbrook, Salcombe Regis etc 73-84; rtd 84; Perm to Offic *Ex* from 86. *Fairholme, Exeter Road, Newton Poppleford, Sidmouth EX10 0BJ* Tel (01395) 568691

COUSANS (*née* BRADLEY), Mrs Joy Elizabeth. b 63. Sheff Univ BA85 Fitzw Coll Cam BA91 MA95. Ridley Hall Cam 89. d 92 p 94. Par Dn Wadsley *Sheff* 92-94; C 94-96; C Mosbrough 96-97; V Hillsborough and Wadsley Bridge 97-06; P-in-c High Hoyland, Scissett and Clayton W *Wakef* from 06; Asst Dioc Dir of Ords from 08. *The Rectory, Church Lane, Clayton West, Huddersfield HD8 9LY* Tel (01484) 862321 E-mail joy@daveandjoy.plus.com

COUSINS, Christopher William. b 44. Ox Univ MTh95. d 87 p 88. C Wallasey St Hilary *Ches* 87-90; R Rollesby w Burgh w Billockby w Ashby w Oby etc *Nor* 90-94; P-in-c Ormesby w

Scratby 92-94; V Ormesby St Marg w Scratby, Ormesby St Mich etc 94-98; RD Gt Yarmouth 94-98; V Altham w Clayton le Moors *Blackb* 98-03; P-in-c Rochford *Chelmsf* 03-10; P-in-c Stambridge 03-10; P-in-c Sutton w Shopland 03-10; RD Rochford 04-08; rtd 10; Perm to Offic *Chelmsf* from 10. *180 Manners Way, Southend-on-Sea SS2 6QB* Tel (01702) 351584 E-mail c4cousins@yahoo.com

COUSINS, Mrs Deborah Ann. b 52. LCST74. ERMC 06. d 09 p 10. C Earlham *Nor* from 09. *St Mary's Vicarage, Douglas Haig Road, Norwich NR5 8LD* Tel (01603) 457751 E-mail deb@madmotorbike.fsnet.co.uk

COUSINS, Graham John. b 55. Oak Hill Th Coll BA91. d 91 p 92. C Birkenhead St Jas w St Bede *Ches* 91-95; C Bebington 95-01; R Moreton from 01; RD Wallasey from 11. *The Rectory, Dawpool Drive, Moreton, Wirral CH46 0PH* Tel 0151-641 0303 E-mail rector@christchurchmoreton.org.uk

COUSINS, Peter Gareth. b 37. d 95 p 96. NSM Cwmparc *Llan* 95-02. *15 Conway Road, Cwmparc, Treorchy CF42 6UW* Tel (01443) 773669

COUSINS, Canon Philip John. b 35. K Coll Cam BA58 MA62. Cuddesdon Coll 59. d 61 p 62. C Marton *Blackb* 61-63; PV Truro Cathl 63-67; USPG Ethiopia 67-75; V Henleaze *Bris* 75-84; RD Clifton 79-84; Provost All SS Cathl Cairo 84-89; Chan Malta Cathl 89-95; Chapl Valletta w Gozo 89-95; R Llandudno *Ban* 95-04; rtd 04; Perm to Offic *York* from 04 and *Eur* from 05. *17 Chalfonts, York YO24 1EX* Tel (01904) 700316

COUSINS, Stephen Michael. b 53. SAOMC 98. d 01 p 02. OLM Caversham St Jo *Ox* 01-03; Perm to Offic 03-04; NSM Shiplake w Dunsden and Harpsden 04-11; Chapl Shiplake Coll Henley from 09. *15 Champion Road, Caversham, Reading RG4 8EL* Tel 0118-948 1679 Mobile 07753-166687 E-mail stephen.cousins@btinternet.com

COUSSENS, Mervyn Haigh Wingfield. b 47. St Jo Coll Nottm BTh74. d 74 p 75. C Clifton Ch Ch w Em *Bris* 74-77; C Morden *S'wark* 77-83; V Patchway *Bris* 83-91; R Lutterworth w Cotesbach *Leic* 91-98; P-in-c Bitteswell 95-98; R Lutterworth Cotesbach and Bitteswell from 99; RD Guthlaxton II 01-05. *The Rectory, Coventry Road, Lutterworth LE17 4SH* Tel (01455) 552669 *or* 558797 E-mail rector.stmarys.lutterworth@care4free.net

COUSSMAKER, Canon Colin Richard Chad. b 34. OBE99. Worc Coll Ox BA57 BSc58 MA63 MSc85. Chich Th Coll 59. d 60 p 61. C Newtown St Luke *Win* 60-64; C Whitley Ch Ch *Ox* 64-67; Chapl Istanbul *Eur* 67-72; Chapl Sliema 72-77; Chapl Antwerp St Boniface 77-93; Can Brussels Cathl 81-00; Chapl Moscow 93-99; rtd 99; Hon Asst Chapl Nice w Vence *Eur* 99-00; Perm to Offic from 00. *533 route des Vallettes Sud, 06140 Tourrettes-sur-Loup, France* Tel (0033) 4 93 59 28 74

COUTTS, Diana. d 07 p 08. Chapl S Lon Healthcare NHS Trust from 08. *Queen Mary's Hospital, Frognal Avenue, Sidcup DA14 6LT* Tel (020) 8302 2678 ext 4399 E-mail diana.coutts@nhs.net

COUTTS, Ian Alexander. b 56. Warwick Univ BA77 Jes Coll Ox MSc80 CQSW80. St Jo Coll Nottm 87. d 89 p 90. C Hamstead St Bernard *Birm* 89-92; C Warlingham w Chelsham and Farleigh *S'wark* 92-97; TV 97-00; Perm to Offic *S'wark* 00-03 and *Ox* from 03. *220 Headley Way, Headington, Oxford OX3 7TB* Tel (01865) 742655

COUTTS, James Allan. b 58. Fitzw Coll Cam MA. St Jo Coll Nottm MTh84. d 84 p 85. C Thorpe Acre w Dishley *Leic* 84-88; TV Kirby Muxloe 88-99; P-in-c Trowbridge St Thos and W Ashton *Sarum* 99-07; V from 07; Chapl Wilts and Swindon Healthcare NHS Trust from 99. *St Thomas's Vicarage, York Buildings, Trowbridge BA14 8SF* Tel (01225) 754826

COUTTS, Canon James Walter Cargill. b 35. Univ of Wales (Lamp) BA57 CCC Cam BA59. St Mich Coll Llan 59. d 60 p 61. C Cardiff St Mary *Llan* 60-63; C Greenford H Cross *Lon* 63-67; C Swansea St Gabr *S & B* 67-71; V Llanwrtyd w Llanddulas in Tir Abad etc 71-78; V Brecon St Dav 78-80; V Brecon St David w Llanspyddid and Llanilltyd 80-84; V Monmouth 84-02; Can St Woolos Cathl 94-02; RD Monmouth 99-01; rtd 02. *The Reynolds, Penallt, Monmouth NP25 4RX* Tel (01600) 860277

COUTTS, Mrs Mandy Rosalind. b 65. Ox Poly BSc87 Bath Univ PGCE88 St Jo Coll Dur BA06. Cranmer Hall Dur 04. d 06 p 07. C Chapel Allerton *Ripon* 06-10; TV Bramley from 10. *The Rectory, Stanningley Road, Stanningley, Pudsey LS28 6NB* Tel 0113-257 5111 E-mail mandy.coutts@virgin.net

COUTTS, Richard Ian Marcus. b 65. Bath Univ BSc87 PGCE88 St Jo Coll Dur BA06. Cranmer Hall Dur 04. d 06 p 07. C Leeds City *Ripon* 06-10; R Stanningley St Thos from 10. *The Rectory, Stanningley Road, Stanningley, Pudsey LS28 6NB* Tel 0113-257 5111 Mobile 07736-180461 E-mail richard.coutts@virgin.net

COUTTS, Canon Robin Iain Philip. b 52. Portsm Univ MA00. Sarum & Wells Th Coll 80. d 83 p 84. C Alverstoke *Portsm* 83-86; Min Leigh Park St Clare CD 86-89; V Warren Park 89-91; V Purbrook 91-04; RD Havant 00-04; P-in-c Blendworth w Chalton w Idsworth 04-06; P-in-c Hambledon from 06; Dioc Dir NSM from 04; Dioc Dir of Ords from 06; Hon Can Portsm

Cathl from 06. *The Vicarage, Church Lane, Hambledon, Waterlooville PO7 4RT* Tel (023) 9263 2717
E-mail robin.rocket@btinternet.com

COUTURE (*née* MAWBEY), **Mrs Diane.** b 55. Birm Univ MMedSc97. Cranmer Hall Dur. **d** 89 **p** 94. Par Dn Menston w Woodhead *Bradf* 89-92; C Barnoldswick w Bracewell 92-93; Chapl Asst Birm Children's Hosp 93-96; Chapl Asst Birm Maternity Hosp 93-96; Chapl Birm Women's Healthcare NHS Trust 96-98; R The Whitacres, Lea Marston, and Shustoke *Birm* from 98. *The Rectory, Dog Lane, Coleshill, Birmingham B46 2DU* Tel (01675) 481252 Mobile 07710-281648

COUVELA, Ms Stephanie Joy. b 68. Sheff City Poly BA89. Ridley Hall Cam 95. **d** 98 **p** 99. C Upper Holloway *Lon* 98-01; TV 01-04; C Busbridge and Hambledon *Guildf* 04-10; Chapl Scargill Ho from 10. *Scargill House, Kettlewell, Skipton BD23 5HU* Tel (01756) 761323

COVENTRY, Archdeacon of. *See* WATSON, The Ven Ian Leslie Stewart

COVENTRY, Bishop of. *See* COCKSWORTH, The Rt Revd Christopher John

COVENTRY, Dean of. *See* IRVINE, The Very Revd John Dudley

COVERLEY, **Mrs Cheryl Joy.** b 62. SS Hild & Bede Coll Dur BA83 PGCE84. St Jo Coll Nottm MA07. **d** 05 **p** 06. C Birkenhead St Jas w St Bede *Ches* 05-07; V Newton from 07; Asst Warden of Readers from 08. *St Michael's Vicarage, 56 Queensbury, Wirral CH48 6EP* Tel 0151-625 8517

COVINGTON, **Canon Michael William Rock.** b 38. Open Univ BA78. Sarum Th Coll 60. **d** 63 **p** 64. C Daventry *Pet* 63-66; C Woolwich St Mary w H Trin *S'wark* 66-68; C Northampton All SS w St Kath *Pet* 68-71; V Longthorpe 71-86; Hon Min Can Pet Cathl 75-86; V Warmington, Tansor, Cotterstock and Fotheringhay 86-95; Warden of Readers 87-95; RD Oundle 89-95; P-in-c Langham 97-03; RD Rutland 02-03; Can Pet Cathl 86-03; rtd 03; Perm to Offic *Leic* 05-06; C Burrough Hill Pars 07-10. *Hall Farm House, Burrough Road, Little Dalby, Melton Mowbray LE14 2UG* Tel (01664) 454015

COWAN, **David John.** b 47. Selw Coll Cam BA69 MA73. SEITE 06. **d** 09 **p** 10. NSM Dorking w Ranmore *Guildf* from 09. *Dolphin House, Harrow Road West, Dorking RH4 3BE* Tel (01306) 885341 Fax 740183 E-mail david@cowansdorking.co.uk

COWAN, **Helen Jane.** b 42. **d** 00 **p** 01. OLM Redhill H Trin *S'wark* from 00. *15 Westway Gardens, Redhill RH1 2JA* Tel (01737) 762543

COWAN, **John Conway.** b 71. Trin Coll Bris. **d** 03 **p** 04. C Redcar *York* 03-07; V Hull St Cuth from 07; Chapl Hull Univ from 10. *The Vicarage, 112 Marlborough Avenue, Hull HU5 3JX* Tel (01482) 342848 E-mail cowanjohnc@aol.com

COWAN, **Mrs Lynda Barbette.** b 55. ALAM77. Ban Ord Course 02. **d** 05 **p** 06. C Arwystli Deanery *Ban* 05-08; P-in-c Llandinam w Trefeglwys w Penstrowed *Ban* 08-10; V from 10. *The Coach House, Old Hall Road, Llanidloes SY18 6PQ* Tel (01686) 413099

COWAN, **Malcolm.** b 45. CBDTI. **d** 00 **p** 01. NSM Keswick St Jo *Carl* 00-05; TV Whitehaven 05-07; P-in-c Kirkby Ireleth from 07; C Dalton-in-Furness and Ireleth-with-Askam from 07. *The Vicarage, School Road, Kirkby-in-Furness LA17 7UQ* Tel (01229) 889256

COWAN, **Malcolm.** b 60. Ches Coll of HE BTh04. NOC 01. **d** 04 **p** 05. C W Kirby St Bridget *Ches* 04-07; V Witton 07-11; R Christleton from 11. *The Rectory, Birch Heath Lane, Christleton, Chester CH3 7AP* Tel (01244) 335663
E-mail jandmcowan@ukonline.co.uk

COWAN, **Paul Hudson.** b 69. Ripon Coll Cuddesdon BTh05. **d** 02 **p** 03. C Wokingham All SS *Ox* 02-05; C Kimberley Cathl S Africa 05-06; TV Newbury *Ox* from 06. *St George's Vicarage, 206 Andover Road, Newbury RG14 6NU* Tel (01635) 41249
E-mail vicar@st-george-newbury.org

COWARD, **Colin Charles Malcolm.** b 45. Kingston Poly DArch72. Westcott Ho Cam 75. **d** 78 **p** 79. C Camberwell St Geo *S'wark* 78-82; P-in-c Wandsworth St Faith 82-90; V 90-96; Chapl Richmond, Twickenham and Roehampton NHS Trust 96-97; Co-ord Changing Attitude 97-03; Dir from 03. *6 Norney Bridge, Mill Road, Worton, Devizes SN10 5SF* Tel (01380) 724908
E-mail colin@changingattitude.org

COWARD, **Raymond.** b 41. NW Ord Course 79. **d** 82 **p** 83. C Turton *Man* 82-84; C Heaton Ch Ch 84-86; V Rochdale St Geo w St Alb 86-92; V Daisy Hill 92-06; rtd 06; Perm to Offic *Man* from 06. *48 Eastbourne Grove, Bolton BL1 5LH*
E-mail coward@tinyworld.co.uk

COWBURN, **John Charles.** b 48. Sarum & Wells Th Coll 88. **d** 90 **p** 91. C Andover w Foxcott *Win* 90-94; C Christchurch 94-96; Chapl to the Deaf 96-09; P-in-c Church Aston 01-09; Chapl to the Deaf *Sarum* from 09. *The Vicarage, 25 White Street, West Lavington, Devizes SN10 4LW* Tel (01380) 816878

COWELL, **Anthony.** *See* COWELL, Neil Anthony

COWELL, **Christopher Douglas.** b 47. Ex Univ BA90 K Coll Lon PGCE92 Brunel Univ PGDE99. **d** 08 **p** 09. OLM Frimley Green and Mytchett *Guildf* from 08. *29 The Glade, Mytchett, Camberley GU16 6BG* Tel (01252) 513434

COWELL, **Irene Christine.** b 58. RGN80. Ridley Hall Cam 92. **d** 94 **p** 95. C Litherland St Phil *Liv* 94-98; R Sefton and Thornton from 98; Dioc Adv on HIV/AIDS and Sexual Health 97-06; Dioc Dir CME from 02; Dir Leadership and Management Tr from 05. *The Vicarage, Water Street, Liverpool L23 1TB* Tel 0151-931 4676
E-mail irene.cowell@btinternet.com

COWELL, **Neil Anthony.** b 61. **d** 98 **p** 99. OLM New Bury *Man* 98-06; OLM New Bury w Gt Lever from 06. *166 Harrowby Street, Farnworth, Bolton BL4 7DE* Tel (01204) 706957

COWELL, **Peter James.** b 58. Peterho Cam BA80 MA84. Coll of Resurr Mirfield 80. **d** 82 **p** 83. C Folkestone St Sav *Cant* 82-86; Chapl Asst St Thos Hosp Lon 86-90; Co-ord Chapl R Lon Hosp 90-94; Lead Trust Chapl Barts and The Lon NHS Trust 94-09; Hospitaller 05-09; PV Westmr Abbey 94-05; V St Bart Less *Lon* 05-09; New Zealand from 09. *Address temp unknown*

COWEN, **Canon Brian.** b 45. Nottm Univ BTh77. Linc Th Coll 73. **d** 77 **p** 78. C Hexham *Newc* 77-80; C Eastnor *Heref* 80-81; C Ledbury 80-81; TV Glendale Gp *Newc* 81-90; V Lesbury w Alnmouth 90-08; V Longhoughton w Howick 98-08; AD Alnwick 93-05; Hon Can Newc Cathl 01-08; rtd 08. *13 Fenton Grange, Wooler NE71 6AW* Tel (01668) 281991
E-mail rev.cowen@btopenworld.com

COWGILL, **Canon Michael.** b 48. Linc Th Coll 84. **d** 86 **p** 87. C Bolton St Jas w St Chrys *Bradf* 86-89; V Buttershaw St Paul 89-93; P-in-c Cullingworth and Dir Dioc Foundn Course 93-97; V Sutton 97-07; V Sutton w Cowling and Lothersdale from 07; Hon Can Bradf Cathl from 07. *The Vicarage, Main Street, Sutton-in-Craven, Keighley BD20 7JS* Tel (01535) 633372
E-mail michael.cowgill@bradford.anglican.org

COWIE, **Andrew Cameron.** b 66. Wycliffe Hall Ox. **d** 11. C Claygate *Guildf* from 11. *Cranwood, Raleigh Drive, Claygate KT10 9DE* E-mail thecowies@btinternet.com

COWIE, **Derek Edward.** b 33. S'wark Ord Course 70. **d** 73 **p** 74. C Maldon All SS w St Pet *Chelmsf* 73-76; R Bowers Gifford w N Benfleet 76-79; V Chelmsf Ascension 79-84; V Shrub End 84-95; P-in-c Gosfield 95-03; RD Hinckford 01-03; rtd 03; Perm to Offic *Nor* from 03. *Bruar Cottage, 68 Wash Lane, Kessingland, Lowestoft NR33 7QY* Tel (01502) 740989 Mobile 07788-662211
E-mail decow@lineone.net *or* derekecowie@tiscali.co.uk

COWIE, **John William Stephen.** b 64. Wycliffe Hall Ox BTh97. **d** 97 **p** 98. C Shoreditch St Leon and Hoxton St Jo *Lon* 97-00. *Address withheld by request* E-mail williamcowie@onetel.com

COWLES, **Richard Martin.** b 53. Birm Univ BSc74. Ripon Coll Cuddesdon 91. **d** 93 **p** 94. C Iffley *Ox* 93-96; TV Wheatley 96-08; V Bray and Braywood from 08. *The Vicarage, High Street, Bray, Maidenhead SL6 2AB* Tel (01628) 621527
E-mail vicar@cowles.globalnet.co.uk

COWLEY, **Anne.** *See* COWLEY, Mrs Judith Anne

COWLEY, **Charles Frederick.** *See* HOWARD-COWLEY, Joseph Charles

COWLEY, **Mrs Elizabeth Mary.** b 47. Bris Univ PQCSW84. WMMTC 89. **d** 92 **p** 94. NSM Wolston and Church Lawford *Cov* 92-97; Soc Resp Officer 97-02; P-in-c Churchover w Willey 97-02; TV Daventry, Ashby St Ledgers, Braunston etc *Pet* from 02; Adv for Healing Min (Northn Adnry) from 06. *The Vicarage, 19 Church Street, Staverton, Daventry NN11 6JJ* Tel (01327) 702466 E-mail liz.cowley@btinternet.com

COWLEY, **Herbert Kenneth.** b 20. Glouc Sch of Min 75. **d** 79 **p** 80. Hon C Lydney w Aylburton *Glouc* 79-89; rtd 89; Perm to Offic *B & W* 89-98. *108 Waverley Court, Forth Avenue, Portishead BS20 7NY* Tel (01275) 856198

COWLEY, **Ian Michael.** b 51. Natal Univ BCom72 BA75 Sheff Univ MA83. Wycliffe Hall Ox 75. **d** 78 **p** 79. C Scottsville S Africa 78-81; C Norton Woodseats St Chad *Sheff* 81-83; R Hilton S Africa 83-94; R Milton *Ely* 94-03; RD Quy 00-02; V Yaxley and Holme w Conington 03-08; Co-ord of Voc and Spirituality *Sarum* from 08. *The Vicarage, Common Road, Whiteparish, Salisbury SP5 2SU* Tel (01794) 884315
E-mail iancowley@ukonline.co.uk

COWLEY, **Mrs Jean Louie Cameron.** *See* HERRICK, Mrs Jean Louie Cameron

COWLEY, **Mrs Judith Anne.** b 59. Nottm Univ BSc80. Ox Min Course. **d** 08 **p** 09. NSM Shepherd's Bush St Steph w St Thos *Lon* from 08. *10 Barlby Road, London W10 6AR* Tel (020) 8960 9587 Mobile 07824-511029 E-mail anne.cowley@ntlworld.com

COWLEY, **Kenneth.** *See* COWLEY, Herbert Kenneth

COWLEY, **Paul William.** b 55. Middx Univ BA02. NTMTC 99. **d** 02 **p** 03. C Brompton H Trin w Onslow Square St Paul *Lon* 02-11; C Onslow Square and S Kensington St Aug from 11. *72 Archel Road, London W14 9QP* Tel (020) 7386 5140 *or* 08456-447544 Mobile 07860-146552
E-mail amanda.wilkie@htb.org.uk

COWLEY, **Peter.** b 53. NOC 06. **d** 08 **p** 09. NSM Prescot *Liv* from 08. *17 Kingsway, Prescot L35 5BG* Tel 0151-426 5441
E-mail petercowley@blueyonder.co.uk

COWLEY, **Samuel Henry.** b 44. St Jo Coll Nottm 85. **d** 87 **p** 88. C Hadleigh w Layham and Shelley *St E* 87-91; P-in-c Ipswich St Mich 91-99; P-in-c Westerfield and Tuddenham w Witnesham

99-10; rtd 10; Perm to Offic *St E* from 10. *44 Hunters End, Trimley St Mary, Felixstowe IP11 0XH* Tel (01394) 200462 E-mail sam@familycowley.co.uk

COWLING, Canon Douglas Anderson. b 19. Leeds Univ BA40. Coll of Resurr Mirfield 40. **d** 42 **p** 43. C Linc St Andr 42-45; R Candlesby w Scremby 47-53; R Carlton Scroop w Normanton 53-61; V Spalding St Paul 61-84; Can and Preb Linc Cathl 77-93; rtd 84; Perm to Offic *Linc* from 84. *24 Campbell's Close, Spalding PE11 2UH* Tel (01775) 767044

COWLING, John Francis. b 32. K Coll Cam BA56. Linc Th Coll 56. **d** 58 **p** 59. C Leigh St Mary *Man* 58-61; Sec SCM in Schs Liv and Ches 61-65; V Bolton St Matt 65-71; V Bolton St Matt w St Barn 71-75; V Southport H Trin *Liv* 75-91; R St Olave Hart Street w All Hallows Staining etc *Lon* 91-05; P-in-c St Kath Cree 02-05; Dir of Ords 92-02; rtd 05; Perm to Offic *Cant* from 05. *Sankey Farm, Shear Way, Burmarsh, Romney Marsh TN29 0JJ* Tel (01303) 872312

COWLING, Mark Alasdair. b 71. Loughb Univ BA92 Man Metrop Univ MA94. Trin Coll Bris BA10. **d** 10 **p** 11. C Halliwell St Pet *Man* from 10. *9 Capitol Close, Bolton BL1 6LU* Tel (01204) 848229 E-mail mark@stpetersparish.info

COWLING, Canon Simon Charles. b 59. G&C Coll Cam BA80 MA88 K Coll Lon PGCE82. Linc Th Coll BTh91. **d** 91 **p** 92. C Potternewton *Ripon* 91-94; C Far Headingley St Chad 94-96; V Roundhay St Edm 96-07; AD Allerton 04-07; Can Res and Prec Sheff Cathl from 07. *62 Kingfield Road, Sheffield S11 9AU* Tel 0114-275 3434 E-mail simon.cowling@sheffield-cathedral.org.uk

COWMEADOW, Derek Lowe. b 28. Wells Th Coll 68. **d** 70 **p** 71. C Ledbury *Heref* 70-72; C Llanrhos *St As* 72-74; V Bringhurst w Gt Easton *Leic* 74-77; P-in-c Coln St Aldwyn w Hatherop and Quenington *Glouc* 77-82; V Coln St Aldwyns, Hatherop, Quenington etc 82-93; rtd 93; Perm to Offic *Glouc* from 93. *2 Hampton Grove, Meysey Hampton, Cirencester GL7 5JN* Tel (01285) 851645

COWPER, Christopher Herbert. b 44. Open Univ BA76. AKC67. **d** 68 **p** 69. C Pitsmoor *Sheff* 68-71; C Ulverston St Mary w H Trin *Carl* 71-74; R Kirklinton w Hethersgill and Scaleby 74-83; V Bridekirk and Chapl Dovenby Hall Hosp Cockermouth 83-94; P-in-c Wetheral w Warwick *Carl* 94-98; R Barningham w Hutton Magna and Wycliffe *Ripon* 98-09; rtd 09. *6 Darnborough Gate, Ripon HG4 2TF* Tel (01765) 692221 E-mail chrisjchrish@gmail.com

COWPER, Peter James. *See* SELLICK, Peter James

COX, Alan John. b 34. Lon Coll of Div ALCD65 LTh. **d** 65 **p** 66. C Kirkheaton *Wakef* 65-67; C Keynsham w Queen Charlton *B & W* 67-71; R Chipstable w Huish Champflower and Clatworthy 71-76; TV Strood *Roch* 76-80; V Strood St Fran 80-83; R Keston 83-95; rtd 95; Perm to Offic *Roch* from 00. *12 Beech Court, 46 Copers Cope Road, Beckenham BR3 1LD* Tel (020) 8639 0082

COX, The Very Revd Albert Horace Montague. b 26. **d** 86 **p** 87. C Masvingo Zimbabwe 86-94; P-in-c Mucheke 91-94; Dean Gweru 95-02; V Gen Cen Zimbabwe 96-03; Hon C Winchelsea and Icklesham *Chich* 03-10; Perm to Offic *Cant* from 10. *Address temp unknown*

COX, Ms Alison Clare. b 63. MHort(RHS)89. Ripon Coll Cuddesdon 01. **d** 03 **p** 04. C Spalding *Linc* 03-07; P-in-c Dukinfield St Mark *Ches* from 07. *The Vicarage, 2 Church Square, Dukinfield SK16 4PX* Tel 0161-330 2783 E-mail alisoncox19@hotmail.com

COX, Alison Hilda. b 57. Coll of Ripon & York St Jo BEd79 Nottm Univ MA02. EMMTC 99. **d** 02 **p** 03. NSM Bakewell *Derby* 02-04; NSM Walton St Jo 04-05; TV Buxton w Burbage and King Sterndale 05-07; Lay Tr Officer *S'well* from 07. *7 Macclesfield Road, Buxton SK17 9AH* Tel (01298) 77699 E-mail alison.cox@southwell.anglican.org

COX, Canon Anthony James Stuart. b 46. BNC Ox BA68 MA74. Qu Coll Birm 69. **d** 71 **p** 72. C Smethwick St Matt w St Chad *Birm* 71-74; Chapl Liv Univ 74; Chapl Malosa Secondary Sch Malawi 75-79; Hd Master 80-87; Hon Can S Malawi from 80; Chapl Loughborough Gr Sch 87-09; rtd 09; Perm to Offic *Leic* from 87 and *S'well* from 97. *Orchard House, 169 Main Street, Willoughby on the Wolds, Loughborough LE12 6SY* Tel (01509) 880861 E-mail tonycox169@gmail.com

COX, Brian Leslie. b 49. S Dios Minl Tr Scheme 91. **d** 94 **p** 95. C Southampton Maybush St Pet *Win* 94-98; P-in-c Knights Enham 98-05; R Knight's Enham and Smannell w Enham Alamein 05-06; P-in-c Freemantle from 06. *The Rectory, 129 Paynes Road, Southampton SO15 3BW* Tel (023) 8022 1804

COX, David John. b 51. Lon Univ BD97 Man Univ MA04. Qu Coll Birm 76. **d** 79 **p** 80. C Brampton Bierlow *Sheff* 79-82; Miss Partner CMS 82-88; V N Perak W Malaysia 83-88; V Friarmere *Man* 88-96; P-in-c Denton Ch Ch 96-06; rtd 06; Perm to Offic *Carl* from 07. *5 Main Street, St Bees CA27 0DE* Tel (01946) 821601 E-mail cox.davidj@btinternet.com

COX (née FRANKLIN), Mrs Dianne Mary. b 48. UEA BA69 Univ Coll of Swansea PGCE70. NEOC 03. **d** 06 **p** 07. NSM Osbaldwick w Murton *York* 06-09; Chapl Aiglon Coll

Switzerland from 09. *Aiglon College, CH-1885 Chesières-Villars, Switzerland* Tel (0041) (24) 496 6161 E-mail diannecoxuk@yahoo.co.uk

COX, Elizabeth Anne. b 55. SEITE 01. **d** 04 **p** 05. NSM Newington w Hartlip and Stockbury *Cant* from 04. *Appleden, 20 Pear Tree Walk, Newington, Sittingbourne ME9 7NG* Tel (01795) 844241 Mobile 07789-510499 E-mail lizapple@btopenworld.com

COX, Canon Eric William. b 30. Dur Univ BA54. Wells Th Coll 54. **d** 56 **p** 57. C Sutton in Ashfield St Mary *S'well* 56-59; Asst Chapl Brussels *Eur* 59-62; V Winnington *Ches* 62-71; V Middlewich 71-76; Chapl Mid Cheshire Hosps Trust 73-95; P-in-c Biley *Ches* 73-76; V Middlewich w Byley 76-95; RD Middlewich 80-94; Hon Can Ches Cathl 84-95; rtd 95; Perm to Offic *Ches* from 95 and *Lich* from 96. *Lovel Hollow, Church Road, Baschurch, Shrewsbury SY4 2EE* Tel (01939) 261258 E-mail canoneric@lovelhollow.fsnet.co.uk

COX, Geoffrey Sidney Randel. b 33. Mert Coll Ox BA56 MA60. Tyndale Hall Bris. **d** 58 **p** 59. C St Paul's Cray St Barn CD *Roch* 58-61; C Bromley Ch Ch 61-64; V Gorsley w Cliffords Mesne *Glouc* 64-79; V Hucclecote 79-89; V Wollaston and Strixton *Pet* 89-96; rtd 96; Perm to Offic *Glouc* from 96. *32 Murvagh Close, Cheltenham GL53 7QY* Tel (01242) 251604

COX, Hugh Teversham. b 42. Keble Coll Ox BA76 MA82 Trin Evang Div Sch (USA) DMin99. Moore Th Coll Sydney. **d** 69 **p** 70. C Manuka St Paul Australia 70-71; P-in-c Kameruka 71-74; Perm to Offic *Ox* 75-76; P-in-c Canberra Ch Ch Australia 76-82; Tutor and Lect St Mark's Nat Th Cen 77-82; R Lane Cove 82-87; R Castle Hill St Paul 87-01; Tervuren *Eur* 01-06; R E Sydney Australia from 06. *PO Box 465, Kings Cross NSW 1340, Australia* Tel (0061) (2) 9360 6844 Fax 9360 1759 E-mail rector@stjohnsanglican.org.au

COX, James David Robert. b 65. Lanc Univ BA88. Qu Coll Birm BD92. **d** 93 **p** 94. C Harborne St Pet *Birm* 93-96; C Chelmsley Wood 96-97; TV 97-00; V Smethwick Resurr 00-07; V Taunton St Andr *B & W* 07-09; V Selly Oak St Mary *Birm* from 09. *St Mary's Vicarage, 923 Bristol Road, Selly Oak, Birmingham B29 6ND* Tel 0121-472 0250 E-mail jimcox11@googlemail.com

COX, Janet. b 48. CBDTI 04. **d** 05 **p** 06. NSM Long Marton w Dufton and w Milburn *Carl* 05-08; NSM Heart of Eden from 08. *Broom Cottage, Long Marton, Appleby-in-Westmorland CA16 6JP* Tel (017683) 62896 E-mail peter_janet_cox@hotmail.com

COX, John Anthony. b 45. Hull Univ BA67. Qu Coll Birm 71. **d** 73 **p** 74. C Buckingham *Ox* 73-76; C Whitley Ch Ch 76-81; V Reading St Agnes w St Paul 81-83; V Chaddesley Corbett and Stone *Worc* 83-10; rtd 10. *7 Burlington Close, Kidderminster DY10 3DQ* Tel (01562) 637966 E-mail jacm.cox@ukgateway.net

COX, John Edgar. b 26. Lon Univ BSc50 MSc69 CEng MIET56. Bps' Coll Cheshunt 67. **d** 68 **p** 69. NSM Harlow St Mary Magd *Chelmsf* 68-76; C S Petherwin w Trewen *Truro* 77-79; P-in-c 79-82; P-in-c Lawhitton 81-82; P-in-c Lezant 81-82; R Lezant w Lawhitton and S Petherwin w Trewen 82-83; V Breage w Germoe 83-91; rtd 91; Perm to Offic *Truro* from 91. *Manderley, 8 Trewartha Road, Praa Sands, Penzance TR20 9ST* Tel (01736) 762582

COX, The Ven John Stuart. b 40. Fitzw Ho Cam BA62 MA66 Linacre Coll Ox BA67. Wycliffe Hall Ox 64. **d** 68 **p** 69. C Prescot *Liv* 68-71; C Birm St Geo 71-73; R 73-78; Selection Sec ACCM 78-83; Hon C Orpington All SS *Roch* 78-83; Dioc Dir of Ords *S'wark* 83-91; Can Res and Treas S'wark Cathl 83-91; V Roehampton H Trin 91-95; Adn Sudbury *St E* 95-06; rtd 06; Perm to Offic *St E* from 06; Dioc Dir of Educn from 07. *2 Bullen Close, Bury St Edmunds IP33 3JP* Tel and fax (01284) 766796 E-mail archdeacon.john@stedmundsbury.anglican.org

COX, Jonathan James. b 63. Wollongong Univ BA85 Univ of NSW DipEd86. Ridley Hall Cam. **d** 00 **p** 01. C Tonbridge SS Pet and Paul *Roch* 00-03; R Oxley Vale Australia from 03. *95 Glengarrin Drive, Tamworth NSW 2340, Australia* Tel (0061) (2) 6761 7271

COX, Julie Margaret. b 55. SAOMC. **d** 00 **p** 01. NSM Luton St Chris Round Green *St Alb* 00-08; Perm to Offic from 08. *29 Maple Close, Pulloxhill, Bedford MK45 5EF* Tel (01525) 717002 E-mail revjuliecox@hotmail.com

COX, Martin Brian. b 64. Keele Univ BA91 CQSW91. St Jo Coll Nottm 01. **d** 03 **p** 04. C Sale St Anne *Ches* 03-05; V Sandiway 05-10; P-in-c Chorley St Laur *Blackb* 10-11; R from 11. *The Rectory, Rectory Close, Chorley PR7 1QW* Tel (01257) 263114 E-mail martin_b_cox@btopenworld.com

COX, Martin Lloyd. b 57. Wilson Carlile Coll and Sarum & Wells Th Coll. **d** 88 **p** 89. C Risca *Mon* 88-91; TV Pontypool 91-96; V Monkton *St D* 96-04; TR 04-10; V Gorseinon *S & B* from 10. *40 Princess Street, Gorseinon, Swansea SA4 4US* Tel (01792) 892849

COX, Nicholas. **d** 10. C Ayr *Glas* from 10; C Girvan from 10; C Maybole from 10. *30 Queens Terrace, Ayr KA7 1DX*

COX, Ms Patricia Jean. b 44. WEMTC. **d** 00 **p** 01. NSM Coleford, Staunton, Newland, Redbrook etc *Glouc* 00-07; NSM Lydney from 07. *67 Primrose Hill, Lydney GL15 5SW* Tel (01594) 843852 E-mail revp cox@tiscali.co.uk

COX, Canon Paul Graham. b 40. Keele Univ BA62 DipEd62. Westcott Ho Cam 77. **d** 78 **p** 79. NSM Kemsing w Woodlands *Roch* 78-80; Hd Master and Chapl St Mich Sch Otford 81-90; C Petham and Waltham w Lower Hardres etc *Cant* 90-95; P-in-c 95-97; C Elmsted w Hastingleigh 90-95; P-in-c 95-97; R Biddenden and Smarden 97-06; Bp's Officer for NSM 91-98; Dioc Dir of Reader Selection and Tr 98-00; Bp's Officer for OLM 00-06; Hon Can Cant Cathl 01-06; rtd 06. *31 Waldron Thorns, Heathfield TN21 0AB* Tel (01435) 868814 Mobile 07766-545341 E-mail pgcox@tiscali.co.uk

COX, Peter Allard. b 55. Univ of Wales (Lamp) BA76. Wycliffe Hall Ox 77. **d** 79 **p** 80. C Penarth All SS *Llan* 79-82; V Aberpergwm and Blaengwrach 82-86; V Bargoed and Deri w Brithdir 86-97; V Penarth All SS from 97. *All Saints' Vicarage, 2 Lower Cwrt-y-Vil Road, Penarth CF64 3HQ* Tel (029) 2070 8952 E-mail petercox6@virgin.net

COX, Philip Gordon. b 36. St Jo Coll Cam MA62 Lon Univ PGCE71. Dioc OLM tr scheme 99. **d** 02 **p** 03. OLM Charing w Charing Heath and Lt Chart *Cant* 02-10; Perm to Offic from 11. *Home Meadow, Little Chart Forstal, Little Chart, Ashford TN27 0PU* Tel (01233) 840274 E-mail philip@homemeadow.plus.com

COX, Miss Rosemary Jennifer. b 54. St Aid Coll Dur BA75 Lon Bible Coll BTh97 Trin Coll Bris MA99. Cranmer Hall Dur 01. **d** 03 **p** 04. C Leeds All SS w Osmondthorpe *Ripon* 03-05; C Ireland Wood 05-07. *7 The Paddock, Waterhouses, Durham DH7 9AW* Tel 0191-373 1539 E-mail rosemaryjcox@aol.com

COX, Mrs Sheila Margaret. b 54. Nottm Univ BA76 Reading Univ PGCE77. SEITE 00. **d** 03 **p** 04. NSM Cranbrook *Cant* 03-08; NSM Mersham w Hinxhill and Sellindge from 08; NSM Smeeth w Monks Horton and Stowting and Brabourne from 08; Asst Dir of Ords from 08. *The Rectory, Bower Road, Mersham, Ashford TN25 6NN* Tel 07985-003095 (mobile) E-mail sheila.m.cox@btopenworld.com

COX, Mrs Sheila Stuart. b 41. Aber Coll of Educn CertEd63. Edin Dioc NSM Course 85. **d** 88 **p** 94. NSM Livingston LEP *Edin* 88-93; Asst Chapl St Jo and Bangour Hosps W Lothian 89-93; Chapl 96-98; Hon C Edin St Mark 93-96; Missr Edin St Andr and St Aid 95-96; NSM Eyemouth 98-05; rtd 05; Lic to Offic *Edin* from 06. *5 Northfield Farm Cottages, St Abbs, Eyemouth TD14 5QF* Tel (01890) 771764

COX, Canon Simon John. b 53. Qu Mary Coll Lon BSc74 Liv Univ PhD81 Selw Coll Cam BA81 MA85 Lanc Univ MA87 MIBiol79 CBiol79. Ridley Hall Cam 79. **d** 82 **p** 83. C Livesey *Blackb* 82-85; C Cheadle Hulme St Andr *Ches* 85-89; V Disley 89-94; R Bispham *Blackb* from 94; P-in-c S Shore St Pet 05-07; AD Blackpool from 04; Hon Can Blackb Cathl from 07. *All Hallows Rectory, 86 All Hallows Road, Blackpool FY2 0AY* Tel (01253) 351886 E-mail drsjcox@yahoo.co.uk

COX, Stephen. b 38. Open Univ BA80. Bps' Coll Cheshunt 65. **d** 68 **p** 69. C Gaywood, Bawsey and Mintlyn *Nor* 68-72; Youth Chapl 72-82; C N Lynn w St Marg and St Nic 73-82; Chapl Guildf Coll of Tech 82-87; Chapl Surrey Univ 82-91; Tr and Development Manager Jas Paget Hosp Gorleston 91-93; Manager Medical Records 93-96; Consumer Relns and Litigation Manager 96-99; rtd 99. *56 Bately Avenue, Gorleston, Great Yarmouth NR31 6HN* Tel (01493) 662061

COX, Stephen John Wormleighton. b 54. New Coll Ox MA79 Fitzw Coll Cam BA79. Ridley Hall Cam 77. **d** 80 **p** 81. C Clapton Park All So *Lon* 80-85; TV Hackney Marsh 85-87; V Holloway St Mary w St Jas 87-88; P-in-c Barnsbury St Dav w St Clem 87-88; V Holloway St Mary Magd 88-97; AD Islington 95-99; TR Upper Holloway 97-10; Preb St Paul's Cathl 07-10; Local Miss Adv *Guildf* from 10. *17 Glenmount Road, Mytchett, Camberley GU16 6AY* E-mail stephenj.cox@virgin.net

COX, Mrs Susan. b 55. WEMTC 05. **d** 08 **p** 09. NSM Bourton-on-the-Water w Clapton etc *Glouc* from 08. *30 Lamberts Field, Bourton-on-the-Water, Cheltenham GL51 8LB* Tel (01451) 821641 Mobile 07903-451932 E-mail suemcox@yahoo.co.uk

COX, William John Francis. b 24. SWMTC. **d** 77 **p** 78. NSM Liskeard w St Keyne and St Pinnock *Truro* 77-82; NSM Liskeard w St Keyne, St Pinnock and Morval 82-86; NSM N Hill w Altarnon, Bolventor and Lewannick 86-87; TV Bolventor 87-92; P-in-c North Hill and Lewannick 92-94; rtd 94; Perm to Offic *Truro* from 94. *9 Trelawney Rise, Callington PL17 7PT* Tel (01579) 384347

COXHEAD, Mrs Margaret. b 40. S Dios Minl Tr Scheme 91. **d** 94 **p** 95. NSM High Hurstwood *Chich* 94-00; P-in-c High Hurstwood and Fairwarp 00-05; rtd 05. *Rock Hall, Chillies Lane, High Hurstwood, Uckfield TN22 4AD* Tel (01825) 733833

COYNE, John Edward. b 52. Cheadle Hulme S Th Coll BA79. **d** 79 **p** 80. C Cheadle Hulme St Andr *Ches* 79-81; C Macclesfield St Mich 81-83; V Stalybridge H Trin and Ch Ch

83-88; Chapl RAF 88-03; Command Chapl RAF 03-05; RAF Adv in Evangelism 93-98; Hon C Hemingford Grey *Ely* 96-98; Dean of Coll St Jo Coll Nottm 05-09; Dir Local and Regional Delivery CPAS from 09. *CPAS, Athena Drive, Tachbrook Park, Warwick CV34 6NG* Tel (01926) 458458 Fax 458459 E-mail jcoyne@cpas.org.uk or j2scoyne@hotmail.com

COYNE, Terence Roland Harry. b 37. Chich Th Coll 64. **d** 66 **p** 67. C Meir *Lich* 66-69; C Horninglow 69-72; V Walsall St Gabr Fulbrook 72-10; C Walsall St Mary and All SS Palfrey 97-02; C Caldmore w Palfrey 02-10; rtd 10. *20 Frame Lane, Doseley, Telford TF4 3BQ* Tel (01952) 503394

COZENS, Mrs Audrey Lilian. b 35. St Hugh's Coll Ox BA56 MA84. Gilmore Course 79. **dss** 82 **d** 87 **p** 94. Shenfield *Chelmsf* 82-87; Par Dn 87-89; Par Dn Westcliff St Andr 89-94; C 94-95; P-in-c Chelmsf St Andr 95-02; P-in-c The Chignals w Mashbury 95-02; rtd 02; Perm to Offic *Chelmsf* from 02. *56 Victoria Road, Writtle, Chelmsford CM1 3PA* Tel (01245) 420165 E-mail revacozens@supanet.com

COZENS, Daniel Harry. b 44. Oak Hill Th Coll. **d** 71 **p** 72. C St Paul's Cray St Barn *Roch* 71-74; C Deptford St Nic w Ch Ch S'wark 74-76; C Deptford St Nic and St Luke 76-78; Rees Missr *Ely* 78-09; rtd 09; Perm to Offic *Ely* from 09; Six Preacher Cant Cathl from 94. *Walnut Top, High Street, Bury, Ramsey, Huntingdon PE26 2NR*

COZENS, Canon Michael Graeme. b 59. Chich Th Coll 91. **d** 93 **p** 94. C Emscote *Cov* 93-96; C Prestbury *Glouc* 96-03; TV Prestbury and All SS 03-06; P-in-c 06-08; TR N Cheltenham from 08; Hon Can Glouc Cathl from 10. *The Vicarage, 66 All Saints' Road, Cheltenham GL52 2HA* Tel (01242) 523177 E-mail michael.cozens@northchelt.org.uk

CRABB, Paul Antony. b 58. St Chad's Coll Dur BSc79 Leeds Univ PGCE80. Qu Coll Birm 90. **d** 91 **p** 92. C Gomersal *Wakef* 91-95; V Drighlington 95-01; TV Dewsbury 01-09; P-in-c Hanging Heaton from 09; P-in-c Batley St Thos from 09. *The Vicarage, 96 Old Bank Road, Dewsbury WF12 7AJ* Tel (01924) 461917 Mobile 07946-530415 E-mail paulthepriest@yahoo.co.uk

CRABTREE, Derek. b 32. Leic Univ BSc(Econ)53. Cant Sch of Min 91. **d** 94 **p** 95. NSM Hackington *Cant* 94-02; Asst Chapl Kent Univ 94-02; rtd 02; Perm to Offic *Cant* from 02. *19 Monastery Street, Canterbury CT1 1NJ* Tel (01227) 471503

CRABTREE, Eric. b 30. Chelt & Glouc Coll of HE BA CACSS FCA68. Premontre Community (RC) 58. **d** 64 **p** 64. In RC Ch 64-90; Perm to Offic *Glouc* 00-04 and *Ox* from 04. *St Katharine's House, Ormond Road, Wantage OX12 8EA* Tel (01235) 769279

CRABTREE, Hazel. b 40. SRN82 Yorks & Humberside Assn for F&HE TCert89. **d** 07 **p** 08. OLM Went Valley *Wakef* 07-10; Perm to Offic from 10. *11 Hillcroft Close, Darrington, Pontefract WF8 3BD* Tel (01977) 793268 E-mail hazel@darringtonchurch.com

CRABTREE, Martine Charmaine. b 74. Glas Bible Coll BA96 St Jo Coll Nottm MTh02. **d** 02 **p** 03. C Kippax w Allerton Bywater *Ripon* 02-06; P-in-c Sowerby *Wakef* from 06; P-in-c Norland from 09. *The Vicarage, Towngate, Sowerby, Sowerby Bridge HX6 1JJ* Tel (01422) 832830 E-mail martinecrabtree@aol.com

CRABTREE, Stephen. See JONES-CRABTREE, Stephen

CRABTREE, Stephen John. b 62. Roehampton Inst BEd85 Surrey Univ MA93. SEITE 93. **d** 96 **p** 97. NSM N Farnborough *Guildf* 96-08; NSM Rowledge and Frensham from 08. *40 West Street, Farnham GU9 7DX* Tel (01252) 541873 E-mail thepecrab@aol.com

CRACKNELL, Heather Louise. b 76. UEA BSc97. ERMC 08. **d** 11. C Cringleford and Colney *Nor* from 11. *5 Poppy Close, Cringleford, Norwich NR4 7JZ* Tel (01603) 501364 E-mail heather.cracknell@gmail.com

CRACKNELL, Paul Allen. NTMTC. **d** 10 **p** 11. NSM Harlow St Mary Magd *Chelmsf* from 10. *135 Woodcroft, Harlow CM18 6YB*

CRADDOCK, Jeremy Graham. b 37. Lon Univ BSc64 Nottm Univ MPhil72. EAMTC 93. **d** 94 **p** 95. NSM Godmanchester *Ely* 94-99; Perm to Offic from 99. *8 Hall Close, Hartford, Huntingdon PE29 1XJ* Tel (01480) 458011 E-mail zen172463@zen.co.uk

CRADDUCK, Martin Charles. b 50. Hull Univ BSc71. St Jo Coll Nottm. **d** 79 **p** 80. C W Kilburn St Luke w St Simon and St Jude *Lon* 79-83; C Oxhey All SS *St Alb* 83-86; Asst Chapl HM Pris Man 86-87; Dep Chapl HM Young Offender Inst Glen Parva 87-89; Chapl HM Pris Stocken 89-95. *35 Worcester Road, Grantham NG31 8SF* Tel (01476) 571351

CRADDUCK, Stuart William. b 74. Bp Otter Coll Chich BA97. Ripon Coll Cuddesdon BTh00. **d** 00 **p** 01. C W Leigh *Portsm* 00-03; Min Can St Alb Abbey 03-07; R Whyke w Rumboldswhyke and Portfield *Chich* from 07. *St George's Rectory, 199 Whyke Road, Chichester PO19 7HQ* E-mail stuart@cradduckmail.freeserve.co.uk

CRAFER, Mrs Jeanette Angela. b 48. Keswick Hall Coll CertEd78. EAMTC 99. **d** 01 **p** 02. C Ashmanhaugh, Barton Turf etc *Nor* 01-05; P-in-c Martham and Repps with Bastwick,

Thurne etc 05-07; V from 07. *The Rectory, 68 Black Street, Martham, Great Yarmouth NR29 4PR* Tel (01493) 740240 E-mail jeanette.crafer@tesco.net

CRAFT, William Newham. b 46. Lon Univ BSc68 MCIPD70. Oak Hill Th Coll 87. **d** 89 **p** 90. C Werrington *Pet* 90-93; C-in-c Norfolk Park St Leonard CD *Sheff* 93-02; P-in-c Sheff St Jo 99-02; V 02-03; V Stapleford *S'well* 03-09; AD Beeston 07-09; rtd 09; Perm to Offic *Sheff* from 09. *435 Redmires Road, Sheffield S10 4LF* Tel 0114-230 2718 E-mail billncraft@gmail.com

✠**CRAGG, The Rt Revd Albert Kenneth.** b 13. Jes Coll Ox BA34 MA38 DPhil50 Huron Coll Hon DD63 Virginia Th Sem Hon DD85 Leeds Univ Hon DD93 Lambeth DD02. Tyndale Hall Bris 34. **d** 36 **p** 37 **c** 70. C Tranmere St Cath *Ches* 36-39; Lebanon 39-47; R Longworth *Ox* 47-51; USA 51-56; Can Res Jerusalem 56-59; St Aug Coll Cant 59-60; Sub-Warden 60-61; Warden 61-67; Hon Can Cant Cathl 61-80; Hon Can Jerusalem 65-73; Asst Bp Jerusalem 70-73; Bye-Fellow G&C Coll Cam 69-70; Asst Bp Chich 73-78; Asst Bp Wakef 78-81; V Helme 78-81; rtd 81; Hon Asst Bp Ox from 82. *3 Goring Lodge, White House Road, Oxford OX1 4QE* Tel (01865) 249895

CRAGG, Edward William Adrian. b 55. St Cath Coll Cam BA77 MA81. Cranmer Hall Dur 97. **d** 99 **p** 00. C Clifton *York* 99-02; R Skelton w Shipton and Newton on Ouse 02-09; Chapl York Hosps NHS Foundn Trust 02-09; R Bridlington Priory *York* from 09. *The Rectory, Church Green, Bridlington YO16 7JX* Tel (01262) 672221 *or* 601938 E-mail adrian@cragg.myzen.co.uk

CRAGG, Mrs Sandra Anne. b 45. St Hugh's Coll Ox BA67. SEITE 94. **d** 97 **p** 98. NSM Kingston All SS w St Jo *S'wark* from 97. *10 Lingfield Avenue, Kingston upon Thames KT1 2TN* Tel (020) 8546 1997 Fax 8541 5281 E-mail sandy@toadstool.co.uk

CRAGGS, Colin Frederick. b 41. Open Univ BA80. Sarum & Wells Th Coll 85. **d** 88 **p** 89. NSM Wilton *B & W* 88-90 and 93-06; NSM Taunton St Andr 90-93; Chapl Taunton and Somerset NHS Trust 90-06; rtd 06. *31 Highfield, Taunton TA1 5JG* Tel and fax (01823) 271989

CRAGGS, Michael Alfred. b 43. Open Univ BA79. St Mich Coll Llan 66. **d** 69 **p** 70. C Clee *Linc* 69-72; C Old Brumby 72-76; TV Kingsthorpe w Northampton St Dav *Pet* 76-83; P-in-c Gt w Lt Addington 83-89; RD Higham 88-89; TR Corby SS Pet and Andr w Gt and Lt Oakley 89-02; V Corby SS Pet and Andr 02-08; RD Corby 90-95; rtd 08. *1 Johnson Drive, Scotter, Gainsborough DN21 3HA* Tel (01724) 764200 E-mail mikeccorb@aol.com

CRAGO, Geoffrey Norman. b 44. Linc Th Coll 67. **d** 70 **p** 71. C Matson *Glouc* 70-75; V Dean Forest H Trin 75-80; Relig Progr Producer Radio Severn Sound 80-85; P-in-c Huntley 80-82; Perm to Offic 82-90; Dioc Communications Officer 84; Gen Syn Broadcasting Dept 85-88; Hon C Highnam, Lassington, Rudford, Tibberton etc 90-08; Relig Progr Producer BBC Radio Gloucestershire 94-03; Bp's Press Officer and Dioc Communications Officer 97-01; rtd 09. *Milestones, 2 Two Mile Lane, Highnam, Gloucester GL2 8DW* Tel (01452) 750575 Fax 08700-940404 E-mail g.crago@btinternet.com

CRAIG, Canon Alan Stuart. b 38. Leeds Univ BA59. Cranmer Hall Dur. **d** 61 **p** 62. C Newcastle w Butterton *Lich* 61-65; C Scarborough St Mary w Ch Ch, St Paul and St Thos *York* 65-67; V Werrington *Lich* 67-72; asst Chapl HM Pris Man 72-73; Chapl HM Borstal Hindley 73-78; Chapl HM Pris Acklington 78-84; V Longhirst *Newc* 84-90; R Morpeth 90-99; RD Morpeth 84-95; Hon Can Newc Cathl 90-02; Chapl St Geo and Cottage Hosp Morpeth 90-93; Chapl Northd Mental Health NHS Trust 93-99; Dir of Ords and Bp's Chapl *Newc* 99-02; Chapl to The Queen 95-08; rtd 02; Perm to Offic *Newc* from 02. *5 Springfield Meadows, Alnwick NE66 2NY* Tel (01665) 602806 Mobile 07779-519040

CRAIG, Andrew John. b 54. Selw Coll Cam BA76 MA80 PhD80 Dur Univ MBA92. NEOC 00. **d** 03 **p** 04. NSM Stranton *Dur* from 03. *25 Egerton Road, Hartlepool TS26 0BW* Tel (01429) 422461 E-mail andrewj.craig@ntlworld.com

CRAIG, David Paul. b 46. Univ of K Coll Halifax NS Hon DD94. ACT. **d** 84 **p** 85. Australia 84-88; P-in-c Innisfail 85; C St Jas Cathl Townsville 85-88; Miss to Seamen Halifax Canada 88-94; Chapl Immingham Seafarers' Cen 94-05; Gen Preacher *Linc* 97-05; P-in-c Denman Australia from 05. *33 Palace Street, Denman NSW 2328, Australia* Tel (0061) (2) 6547 2243 *or* tel and fax 6547 1149 Fax 6547 2249 Mobile 41-083 8089 E-mail denmanap@bigpond.net.au

CRAIG, Eric. b 39. Birm Univ BA62. Qu Coll Birm 62. **d** 64 **p** 65. C Todmorden *Wakef* 64-68; C Hurstpierpoint *Chich* 68-70; C Cobham *Guildf* 70-73; V Dawley St Jerome *Lon* 73-76; V Stainland *Wakef* 76-87; R Yarnton w Begbroke and Shipton on Cherwell *Ox* 87-04; rtd 04; Perm to Offic *Ox* 04-09. *17 Farmers Close, Witney OX28 1NN* Tel (01993) 704892

CRAIG, Gillean Weston. b 49. York Univ BA72 Qu Coll Cam BA76 MA80. Westcott Ho Cam 76. **d** 77 **p** 78. C St Marylebone Ch Ch *Lon* 77-82; C Ealing St Barn 82-88; P-in-c St Geo-in-the-East w St Paul 88-89; R 89-02; V Kensington St Mary Abbots w St Geo 02-06; V Kensington St Mary Abbots w Ch Ch and

St Phil from 06. *St Mary Abbots Vicarage, Vicarage Gate, London W8 4HN* Tel (020) 7937 6032 E-mail gillean.craig@stmaryabbotschurch.org

CRAIG, James Owen Maxwell. b 72. Open Univ BA98. Cranmer Hall Dur 99. **d** 02 **p** 03. C Ch the K *Dur* 02-05; Gateshead and Bensham Community Chapl to Arts from 05; TV Gateshead from 11. *St Columba House, Peterborough Close, Gateshead NE8 1NL* Tel 07918-659088 (mobile) E-mail rev.jim@btopenworld.com

CRAIG, Canon John Newcome. b 39. Selw Coll Cam BA63 MA67. Linc Th Coll 63. **d** 65 **p** 66. C Cannock *Lich* 65-71; V Gt Wyrley 71-79; TR Wednesfield 79-91; Prec Leic Cathl 91-03; Hon Can 93-03; Can Res Leic Cathl 03-04; rtd 04; Perm to Offic *Birm* from 04. *109 Kingsbury Road, Erdington, Birmingham B24 8QH* Tel 0121-373 2809 E-mail john.olivia.craig@lineone.net

CRAIG, Judy Howard. *See* CRAIG PECK, Judy Howard

CRAIG, Julie Elizabeth. *See* EATON, Mrs Julie Elizabeth

CRAIG, Julie Elizabeth. *See* LEAVES, Julie Elizabeth

CRAIG, Patrick Thomas. b 36. BA. St D Coll Lamp 59 Bps' Coll Cheshunt 59. **d** 61 **p** 62. C Belfast St Mary *Conn* 61-65; C Belfast St Pet 65-69; CF 69-88; R Hartfield w Coleman's Hatch *Chich* 88-01; rtd 01; P-in-c Six Pilgrims *B & W* 03-11. *Briars, Broadclose Way, Barton St David, Somerton TA11 6BS* Tel (01458) 850825 E-mail pat.craig092@btinternet.com

CRAIG, Richard Harvey. b 31. Em Coll Cam BA58. Linc Th Coll. **d** 60 **p** 61. C Bottesford *Linc* 60-65; Bp's Ind Chapl 65-69; Dioc Adv on Laity *Tr Bris* 69-74; V Whitchurch 74-86; TV N Lambeth *S'wark* 86-96; Bp's Ecum Adv 88-96; Ecum Officer 90-96; rtd 96; Perm to Offic *St Alb* 96-99 and *S'wark* from 01. *18 Holst Court, Westminster Bridge Road, London SE1 7JQ* Tel (020) 7928 0495

CRAIG, Robin Joseph. b 43. TCD BA65 Div Test66 Birm Univ CertEd70. **d** 66 **p** 67. C Carrickfergus *Conn* 66-69; Chapl Ld Wandsworth Coll Hants 75-85; Chapl K Sch Macclesfield 85-01; Lic to Offic *Ches* 85-01; rtd 01. *5 Winston Court, Lavant Road, Chichester PO19 5RG* Tel (01243) 778636

CRAIG PECK, Judy Howard. b 57. Lon Univ MB, BS81 MRCGP86. WMMTC 97. **d** 00 **p** 01. NSM Billing *Pet* 00-07; NSM Yardley Hastings, Denton and Grendon etc from 07; NSM Officer 03-10. *Dreamstead, 10 Sharplands, Grendon, Northampton NN7 1JL* Tel (01933) 665965 E-mail judy@peckc.fsnet.co.uk

CRAIG-WILD, Ms Dorothy Elsie (Dhoe). b 54. Birm Univ BA77. Qu Coll Birm 79. dss 81 **d** 87 **p** 94. Middleton St Mary *Ripon* 81-87; Par Dn Chapeltown *Sheff* 88-94; C 94-96; P-in-c Bruntcliffe *Wakef* 96-02; RD Birstall 98-08; Jt P-in-c Morley St Paul 00-02; P-in-c Roberttown w Hartshead 02-08; C Heckmondwike 05-08; C Liversedge w Hightown 05-08; TV Maltby *Sheff* from 08; C Thurcroft from 09. *The Rectory, 69 Blyth Road, Maltby, Rotherham S66 7LF* Tel (01709) 812684 E-mail dhoe@craig-wild.me.uk

CRAIG-WILD, Peter John. b 55. Leeds Univ BA77. Qu Coll Birm 77. **d** 80 **p** 81. C Rothwell w Lofthouse *Ripon* 80-83; C Beeston 83-87; V Chapeltown *Sheff* 87-96; RD Tankersley 93-96; V Mirfield *Wakef* 96-08; P-in-c Eastthorpe and Upper Hopton 03-07; Hon Can Wakef Cathl 03-08; RD Dewsbury 06-08; TR Maltby *Sheff* from 08; P-in-c Thurcroft from 09. *The Rectory, 69 Blyth Road, Maltby, Rotherham S66 7LF* Tel (01709) 812684 E-mail peter@craig-wild.me.uk

CRAIGHEAD, Mrs Patricia Anne. b 60. Northumbria Univ BSc02. NEOC 05. **d** 08 **p** 09. C Monkseaton St Pet *Newc* from 08. *23 Airedale, Wallsend NE28 8TL* Tel 07967-316615 (mobile) E-mail patcraighead@hotmail.co.uk

CRAM, Mrs Ruth Frances Isobel. b 52. Kingston Poly BA87 Poly Cen Lon MA92. NOC 94. **d** 97 **p** 98. C E Crompton *Man* 97-99; C Cirencester *Glouc* 99-02; C Broad Blunsdon *Bris* 02; V N Swindon St Andr 02-05; rtd 05. *52 Hague Street, Glossop SK13 8NS* Tel (01457) 868107 E-mail rc.cram@btinternet.com

CRAMERI, Mrs Mary Barbara. b 46. K Coll Lon BD65 AKC91 Lon Inst of Educn PGCE66. S Dios Minl Tr Scheme 86. **d** 88 **p** 94. C Whitton SS Phil and Jas *Lon* 88-91; Staff Member S Dios Minl Tr Scheme 91-97; Minl Development Officer STETS 97-98; Vice-Prin Sarum & Wells Th Coll 93-98; Par Dn Bemerton *Sarum* 91-92; TV Pewsey and Swanborough 98-00; TR Whitton 00-01; rtd 01; Perm to Offic *Sarum* 02-05 and *Ox* from 10; Hon C Chase *Ox* 05-10. *6 Browning Close, Stratford-upon-Avon CV37 7PF* Tel (01789) 296650 E-mail marymcrameri@freeserve.co.uk

CRAMP, Barry Leonard. b 46. St Luke's Coll Ex CertEd67 CChem76 MRSC76. **d** 04 **p** 05. OLM Ditchingham, Hedenham, Broome, Earsham etc *Nor* from 04. *Wyvern, The Street, Earsham, Bungay NR35 2TY* Tel (01986) 895535 E-mail sbcramp@waitrose.com

CRAMP, Susan Louise. b 53. Univ of Wales (Abth) BSc74 Leic Univ PGCE75. **d** 04 **p** 05. OLM Ditchingham, Hedenham, Broome, Earsham etc *Nor* from 04. *Wyvern, The Street, Earsham, Bungay NR35 2TY* Tel (01986) 895535 E-mail sbcramp@waitrose.com

CRAMPTON, John Leslie. b 41. CITC 64. **d** 67 **p** 68. C Lurgan Ch the Redeemer *D & D* 67-71; C Dundela St Mark 71-73; C Umtali Rhodesia 73-76; R Fort Victoria 73-76; I Killanne w Killegney, Rossdroit and Templeshanbo *C & O* 82-88; Preb Ferns Cathl 85-88; Chapl Wilson's Hosp Sch Multyfarnham *M & K* 88-91; C Mullingar, Portnashangan, Moyliscar, Kilbixy etc 89-91; I Athy w Kilberry, Fontstown and Kilkea *D & G* 91-01; Can Ch Ch Cathl Dublin 95-01; I Geashill w Killeigh and Ballycommon *M & K* 01-06; rtd 06. *41 Beech Avenue, The Paddock, Enniscorthy, Co Wexford, Republic of Ireland* Tel (00353) (53) 923 2589 Mobile 87-907 7981 E-mail cramptoj@gofree.indigo.ie

CRANE, John Walter. b 32. Chich Th Coll. **d** 58 **p** 59. C Forest Town *S'well* 58-60; C Primrose Hill St Mary w Avenue Road St Paul *Lon* 60-64; R Greenford H Cross 64-67; Min Can and Chapl Windsor 67-79; Chapl St Geo Sch Ascot 67-79; Warden Dioc Retreat Ho (Holland Ho) Cropthorne *Worc* 79-83; P-in-c Harvington and Norton and Lenchwick 84-87; rtd 87. *16 Allesborough Drive, Pershore WR10 1JH* Tel (01386) 556444

CRANE, Mrs Judith. b 53. Matlock Coll of Educn BCombStuds81. Cranmer Hall Dur 94. **d** 96 **p** 97. C Tadcaster w Newton Kyme *York* 96-99; TV Brayton 99-02; V Blackwell w Tibshelf *Derby* 02-08; Asst Dir of Ords 06-09; Perm to Offic from 09. *27 Highfield Road, Little Eaton, Derby DE21 5AG* Tel (01332) 833872 E-mail judithcrane@yahoo.co.uk

CRANFIELD, Nicholas William Stewart. b 56. Mert Coll Ox BA77 MA81 DPhil88 Leeds Univ BA81 Selw Coll Cam PhD95 FSA07. Coll of Resurr Mirfield 79 Union Th Sem (NY) STM84. **d** 86 **p** 87. C Ascot Heath *Ox* 86-89; Prin Berks Chr Tr Scheme 89-92; Hon C Reading St Mary w St Laur 89-92; Chapl and Fell Selw Coll Cam 92-99; Dean of Chpl 94-99; Chapl Newnham Coll Cam 92-99; V Blackheath All SS *S'wark* from 99; Chapl St Dunstan's Coll Catford 00-05. *All Saints' Vicarage, 10 Duke Humphrey Road, London SE3 0TY* Tel (020) 8852 4280 E-mail vicar@allsaintsblackheath.org

CRANIDGE, Mrs Wendy Ann. b 31. Sheff Univ CertEd52. Cant Sch of Min 81. **dss** 84 **d** 87 **p** 94. Roch 84-88; Hon Par Dn 87-88; Soc Resp Adv *Cant* and *Roch* 86-88; Hon C Washingborough w Heighington and Canwick *Linc* 88-92; Perm to Offic 92-93; C Farnborough *Roch* 94-96; rtd 96; Perm to Offic *Roch* 96-02 and *Wakef* from 04. *1 Fern Valley Chase, Todmorden OL14 7HB* Tel (01706) 815062

CRANKSHAW, Ronald. b 41. Coll of Resurr Mirfield 74. **d** 76 **p** 77. C Orford St Andr *Liv* 76; C N Meols 76-79; V Abram 79-85; V Wigan St Anne 85-99; AD Wigan W 94-99; V Heston *Lon* 99-07; rtd 07. *Orchard House, Westlinton, Carlisle CA6 6AA* Tel (01228) 791434 E-mail roncrankshaw@sky.com

CRANMER, Ms Elaine. b 56. Hockerill Coll Cam CertEd77. SEITE 97. **d** 00 **p** 01. C Charlton *S'wark* 00-03; P-in-c Eltham Park St Luke 03-10; V from 11; AD Eltham and Mottingham from 06. *St Luke's Vicarage, 107 Westmount Road, London SE9 1XX* Tel (020) 8850 3030 E-mail rev.elaine@virgin.net

CRANMER, John Abery. b 33. K Alfred's Coll Win CertEd56 Southn Univ MPhil69. **d** 94 **p** 00. NSM Crawley and Littleton and Sparsholt w Lainston *Win* 94-02; rtd 02; Perm to Offic *Win* from 02. *The Coach House, Crawley, Winchester SO21 2PU* Tel (01962) 776214

CRANSHAW, Trevor Raymond. b 58. Trin Coll Bris 00. **d** 03 **p** 04. C Westbury-on-Trym H Trin *Bris* 03-07; P-in-c Wheathill Priory Gp *B & W* from 07. *The Rectory, Church Street, Keinton Mandeville, Somerton TA11 6ER* Tel (01485) 223216 Mobile 07734-304116

CRANSTON, Andrew David. b 79. Ex Univ MEng02 PGCE04 Cam Univ BTh11. Ridley Hall Cam 08. **d** 11. C Stone Ch Ch and Oulton *Lich* from 11. *1 Navigation Loop, Stone ST15 8YU* E-mail acranston.ccstone@gmail.com

CRANSTON, Miss Margaret Elizabeth. b 56. Newnham Coll Cam BEd78 Ex Univ BTh10. SWMTC 04. **d** 07 **p** 08. NSM Heanton Punchardon w Marwood *Ex* from 07. *Broom Cottage, Middle Marwood, Barnstaple EX31 4EG* Tel (01271) 372426 E-mail mecranston@btinternet.com

CRANSWICK, James Harvard. b 22. Melbourne Univ BA47 St Cath Coll Ox BA50 MA54 Birm Univ MA76. Wycliffe Hall Ox 49. **d** 50 **p** 51. C Werneth *Man* 50-51; C St Pancras H Cross w St Jude and St Pet *Lon* 52-54; P-in-c Dartford St Alb *Roch* 54-56; Australia 56-66 and 68-88; C Raynes Park St Sav *S'wark* 68-70; rtd 88. *Rhodoglade Retirement Village, 3/1502 Mount Dandenong Tourist Road, Olinda Vic 3788 Australia* Tel (0061) (3) 9751 0021 Fax 9754 3518 E-mail jimcranswick@hotmail.com

CRANWELL, Brian Robert. b 32. Sheff Poly MSc Sheff Hallam Univ MPhil96. Cranmer Hall Dur. **d** 84 **p** 85. C Ecclesfield *Sheff* 84-86; V Handsworth Woodhouse 86-99; rtd 99; Perm to Offic *Sheff* from 99 and *Derby* from 00. *9 Westview Close, Totley, Sheffield S17 3LT* Tel 0114-262 1499 E-mail brian_cranwell@lineone.net

CRASKE, Leslie Gordon Hamilton. b 29. AKC54 Lambeth STh80. **d** 55 **p** 56. C Malden St Jo *S'wark* 55-58; C Streatham St Leon 58-60; S Rhodesia 60-65; Rhodesia 65-66; V Upper Norwood St Jo *Cant* 67-83; R Guernsey St Sav *Win* 83-97; rtd 97; Perm to Offic *Win* from 97. *La Gruterie, 3 Mount Row, St Peter Port, Guernsey GY1 1NS* Tel (01481) 716027

CRASTON (née FULLALOVE), Mrs Brenda Hurst. b 33. Open Univ BA75 Man Univ MPhil86. St Mich Ho Ox 58. **dss** 80 **d** 87 **p** 94. Bolton St Paul w Em *Man* 80-93; Par Dn 87-93; rtd 93; Perm to Offic *Man* from 94. *12 Lever Park Avenue, Horwich, Bolton BL6 7LE* Tel (01204) 699972

CRASTON, Canon Richard Colin. b 22. Bris Univ BA49 Lon Univ BD51 Lambeth DD92. Tyndale Hall Bris 46. **d** 51 **p** 52. C Dur St Nic 51-54; V Bolton St Paul *Man* 54-76; P-in-c Bolton Em 64-66; V 66-76; Hon Can Man Cathl 68-95; RD Bolton 72-92; V Bolton St Paul w Em 77-86; TR 86-93; Chapl to The Queen 85-92; rtd 93; Perm to Offic *Man* from 93. *12 Lever Park Avenue, Horwich, Bolton BL6 7LE* Tel (01204) 699972

CRAVEN, Miss Alison Ruth Miranda. b 63. Cen Sch Speech & Drama BSc86. Westcott Ho Cam 05. **d** 07 **p** 08. C Chelsea St Luke and Ch Ch *Lon* 07-11. *Address temp unknown*

CRAVEN, Canon Allan. b 35. LTCL77 Univ of Wales (Lamp) BA57 Lon Univ BD72. Chich Th Coll 57. **d** 59 **p** 60. C Blaenau Ffestiniog *Ban* 59-61; C Milford Haven St D 61-65; V Llwynhendy 65-68; R Nolton w Roch 68-00; RD Roose 85-99; Can St D Cathl from 91; rtd 00. *25 West Lane Close, Keeston, Haverfordwest SA62 6EW* Tel (01437) 710709

CRAVEN, Colin Peter. b 48. Dartmouth RN Coll. St Steph Ho Ox 83. **d** 85 **p** 86. C Holbeach *Linc* 85-88; Chapl Fleet Hosp 86-97; TV Grantham *Linc* 88-97; P-in-c Fairfield *Derby* 97-03; OCF 88-03; CF 03-06; Rtd Officer Chapl RAChD from 06. *c/o MOD Chaplains (Army)* Tel (01980) 615804 Fax 615800

CRAVEN, David Alex. b 80. Univ of Wales (Ban) BA01. Wycliffe Hall Ox BTh06. **d** 06 **p** 07. C Holme Eden and Wetheral w Warwick *Carl* 06-09; R from 09; C Croglin 06-09; P-in-c from 09. *The Rectory, Warwick Bridge, Carlisle CA4 8RF* E-mail dacraven@hotmail.com

CRAVEN, Janet Elizabeth. *See* CHAPMAN, Canon Janet Elizabeth

CRAVEN, Mrs Janet Mary. b 43. Bp Otter Coll TCert64. **d** 06 **p** 07. OLM Shelley and Shepley *Wakef* from 06. *70 Jenkyn Lane, Shepley, Huddersfield HD8 8AW* Tel (01484) 604107 E-mail jmcraven@btinternet.com

CRAVEN, Rebecca Clare. b 58. Bris Univ BDS80 Glas Univ MPH90 Man Univ PhD97 RCPS FDS97. **d** 01 **p** 02. OLM Reddish *Man* 01-06; NSM 06-07; NSM Salford Sacred Trin and St Phil from 07. *201 Thornton Road, Fallowfield, Manchester M14 7NS* Tel 0161-225 7336 E-mail rebecca.c.craven@manchester.ac.uk

CRAVEN, Archdeacon of. *See* SLATER, The Ven Paul John

CRAW, Jane Mary. **d** 10 **p** 11. NSM Sherborne w Castleton, Lillington and Longburton *Sarum* from 10. *Jubilee Cottage, Lower Kingsbury, Milborne Port, Sherborne DT9 5ED* Tel (01963) 251527

CRAWFORD, Mrs Anne Elizabeth. b 59. SAOMC 01. **d** 04 **p** 05. C Billington, Egginton, Hockliffe etc *St Alb* 04-08; R Toddington and Chalgrave from 08. *The Rectory, 41 Leighton Road, Toddington, Dunstable LU5 6AL* Tel (01525) 872298 E-mail annie.anselm@btinternet.com

CRAWFORD, Duncan Alexander. b 59. Newc Univ BA81 MA83 K Coll Lon CertEd83. St Jo Coll Nottm 86. **d** 89 **p** 90. C Hatcham St Jas *S'wark* 89-92; Perm to Offic 93-02. *Gortestraat 44, 2311 NM Leiden, The Netherlands*

CRAWFORD, Canon Ivy Elizabeth. b 50. Trin Coll Bris 83. **dss** 85 **d** 87 **p** 94. Collier Row St Jas *Chelmsf* 85; Collier Row St Jas and Havering-atte-Bower 86-89; Par Dn 87-89; Par Dn Harlow New Town w Lt Parndon 89-94; C Harlow Town Cen w Lt Parndon 94-95; V Blackmore and Stondon Massey 95-09; RD Ongar 06-09; P-in-c Broxted w Chickney and Tilty etc from 09; CME Adv from 09; Hon Can Chelmsf Cathl from 98. *The Rectory, Park Road, Little Easton, Dunmow CM6 2JJ* Tel (01371) 872509 E-mail ivycrawford@btinternet.com

CRAWFORD, James Robert Harry. b 55. Cumbria Univ BA09. CBDTI 00. **d** 03 **p** 04. NSM Lower Darwen St Jas *Blackb* 03-10; C Colne and Villages from 10. *St Mary's Vicarage, Burnley Road, Trawden, Colne BB8 8PN* Tel (01282) 864046 Mobile 07923-484785 E-mail jayjay644@btinternet.com

CRAWFORD, John William Rowland. b 53. Open Univ BA81 NUI MA95 PhD03 AKC75. CITC 75. **d** 76 **p** 77. C Dundela St Mark *D & D* 76-79; C Taney Ch Ch *D & G* 79-84; V Dublin St Patr Cathl Gp 84-09; Preb Tipperkevin St Patr Cathl Dublin 84-09; rtd 09. *9 Ashbrooke Manor, Moyne Hall, Cavan, Republic of Ireland* Tel (00353) (49) 433 2929 E-mail jwrcrawf@eircom.net

CRAWFORD, Kenneth Ian. b 48. Melbourne Univ BMus77 Columbia Univ MA79 MEd80 MACE84. Trin Coll Melbourne BD86. **d** 87 **p** 87. Australia 87-97; C Ringwood St Paul 87-89; C Cheltenham St Matt 89-90; P-in-c Vermont S H Name 90-93; Can Prec Melbourne Cathl 93-97; P-in-c Warndon St Nic *Worc* 97-03; V Pershore w Pinvin, Wick and Birlingham from 03. *The Abbey Vicarage, Church Street, Pershore WR10 1DT* Tel (01386) 552071 E-mail vicar@pershoreabbey.fsnet.co.uk

CRAWFORD, Michael Davis. b 45. Oak Hill Th Coll BA97 K Coll Lon PGCE98. **d** 00 **p** 01. NSM New Barnet St Jas *St Alb* 00-04; C Limassol St Barn Cyprus 04-08; Chapl SE Cyprus from 08. *39 Dionisou Street, Protaras, Paralimni 5296, Cyprus* Tel (00357) (2) 381 1045 Mobile 99-848164 E-mail rev.michael@cytanet.com.cy

CRAWFORD, Canon Robin. b 33. Pemb Coll Cam BA57 MA61. Roch Th Coll 66. **d** 67 **p** 80. Hd Master Navrongo Sch Ghana 67-69; Dep Sec Chrs Abroad 69-73; Dep Hd Priory Sch Lewes 74-76; Nigeria 77-79; Dep Sec Buttle Trust 79-86; Sec 86-90; Dir 90-92; Hon C Win H Trin 80-82; Hon C Notting Hill All SS w St Columb *Lon* 82-87; Hon C Westmr St Matt 87-11; Hon Can Tamale Ghana from 01. *5 Ponts Hill, Littleport, Ely CB6 1PZ*

CRAWFORD JONES, Neil. *See* JONES, Canon Neil Crawford

CRAWFORD-McCAFFERTY, Louise Dorothy Anita. b 60. Oak Hill Th Coll BA91 Princeton Th Sem MDiv00. Irish Sch of Ecum MPhil02. **d** 02 **p** 03. C Drumragh w Mountfield *D & R* 02-05; I Aghadowey w Kilrea from 05. *40 Brone Road, Garvagh, Coleraine BT51 5EQ* Tel (028) 7086 9277 E-mail anamchara00@yahoo.com

CRAWLEY, Alan John. b 58. Trin Coll Cam MA83. SAOMC 04. **d** 07 **p** 08. NSM Gt Marlow w Marlow Bottom, Lt Marlow and Bisham *Ox* 07-08; C Amersham on the Hill from 08. *Westfields, Church Lane, Ludgershall, Aylesbury HP18 9NU* Tel (01844) 239268 E-mail alan.crawley@btinternet.com

CRAWLEY, Canon David. b 47. TD. St Steph Ho Ox 75. **d** 78 **p** 79. C Solihull *Birm* 78-81; TV Newbury *Ox* 81-84; Lic to Offic 84-95; Chapl Stoke Mandeville Hosp Aylesbury 84-95; Distr Chapl 88-95; Hd Chapl Services W Suffolk Hosps NHS Trust 95-11; Bp's Adv on Hosp Chapl *St E* from 00; Hon Can St E Cathl from 05. *22 Westbury Avenue, Bury St Edmunds IP33 3QE* Tel (01284) 750526

CRAWLEY, John Lloyd Rochfort. b 22. Selw Coll Cam BA47 MA52. Cuddesdon Coll 47. **d** 49 **p** 50. C Newc H Cross 49-52; V Byker St Ant 52-59; V Longhoughton w Howick 59-69; Chapl Newc Univ 69-74; Master Newc St Thos Prop Chpl 69-74; P-in-c Cockermouth All SS w Ch *Carl* 74-77; TR Cockermouth w Embleton and Wythop 77-86; Perm to Offic *Arg* from 86; rtd 87. *Flat 15, Manormead, Tilford Road, Hindhead GU26 6RA*

CRAWLEY (*née* FELLOWS), **Lesley June.** b 70. Salford Univ BEng91 New Coll Ox DPhil01. Ox Min Course 04. **d** 07 **p** 08. C Bernwode *Ox* from 07. *Westfields, Church Lane, Ludgershall, Aylesbury HP18 9NU* Tel (01844) 239268 E-mail lesley.fellows@hotmail.co.uk

CRAWLEY, Nicholas Simon. b 58. Southn Univ BSc79 ACIB82 AIIM85. Wycliffe Hall Ox 85. **d** 88 **p** 89. C E Twickenham St Steph *Lon* 88-93; R Avondale Zimbabwe 93-99; P-in-c Netherthorpe St Steph *Sheff* 99-04; Network Miss P (Bris Adnry) from 04; P-in-c Clifton H Trin, St Andr and St Pet from 10. *27 Carnarvon Road, Bristol BS6 7DU* Tel 0117-944 1980 E-mail nick.crawley@blueyonder.co.uk

CRAWLEY, Simon Ewen. b 31. Em Coll Cam BA57 MA60. Ridley Hall Cam 56. **d** 58 **p** 59. C Denton Holme *Carl* 58-61; P-in-c Cinderford St Steph w Littledean *Glouc* 61-67; V Margate H Trin *Cant* 67-74; V Folkestone H Trin w Ch Ch 74-81; R Patterdale *Carl* 81-87; RD Penrith 83-86; R Culworth w Sulgrave and Thorpe Mandeville etc *Pet* 87-95; RD Brackley 89-95; rtd 95; Perm to Offic *Ex* 96-03 and *York* from 03. *The Old Vicarage, Main Street, Healaugh, Tadcaster LS24 8DB* Tel (01937) 830160

CRAWSHAW, Clinton. b 70. St Steph Ho Ox. **d** 02 **p** 03. C Hendon St Alphage *Lon* 02-04; rtd 04. *21 Beckmeadow Way, Mundesley, Norwich NR11 8LP* E-mail revcrawshaw@yahoo.com

CRAWTE, William Richard. b 30. TCD BA54. **d** 55 **p** 56. C Belfast St Aid *Conn* 55-57; C Newcastle *D & D* 57-59; CF 59-79. *38 Heath Estate, Great Waldingfield, Sudbury CO10 0TZ* Tel (01787) 377356

✠**CRAY, The Rt Revd Graham Alan.** b 47. Leeds Univ BA68. St Jo Coll Nottm 69. **d** 71 **p** 72 **c** 01. C Gillingham St Mark *Roch* 71-75; N Area Co-ord CPAS Youth Dept 75-78; C York St Mich-le-Belfrey 78-82; V 82-92; Prin Ridley Hall Cam 92-01; Six Preacher Cant Cathl 97-01; Suff Bp Maidstone 01-09; Abps' Missr and Team Ldr Fresh Expressions from 09; Hon Asst Bp Cant from 09. *The Rectory, Church Road, Harrietsham, Maidstone ME17 1AP*

CRAY, Mrs Jacqueline. b 49. Glos Coll of Educn CertEd70. SEITE 01. **d** 04 **p** 05. NSM Gt Chart Cant 04-08; P-in-c Maidstone St Faith from 08; Asst Dir of Ords from 09. *The Rectory, Church Road, Harrietsham, Maidstone ME17 1AP* Tel (01622) 851822 Mobile 07889-742973 E-mail jackiecray@hotmail.com

CREAN, Patrick John Eugene. b 38. TCD BA81 MA84. Edin Th Coll 82. **d** 84 **p** 85. C Perth St Jo *St And* 84-86; P-in-c Liv St Phil w St Dav 86-87; V 87-90; R Cupar and Ladybank *St And* 90-92; P-in-c Sefton *Liv* 92-93; Dioc Children's Officer 92-03; V Aintree St Giles 97-98; V Aintree St Giles w St Pet 98-03; rtd 03; Perm to Offic *Liv* from 03. *36 Lingfield Close, Netherton, Bootle L30 1BB* Tel 0151-525 8838

CREASER, Canon David Edward. b 35. St Cath Coll Cam BA58 MA62. Clifton Th Coll 59. **d** 61 **p** 62. C Cheadle *Ches* 61-67; V Weston *Bradf* 67-69; P-in-c Denton 67-69; V Weston w Denton 69-74 and 82-02; Dir Educn 73-96; V Frizinghall 74-82; V Weston w Denton 82-02; Hon Can Bradf Cathl 80-02; P-in-c Leathley w Farnley, Fewston and Blubberhouses 96-02; rtd 02; Perm to Offic *Bradf* from 03. *Rose Cottage, Pant Lane, Austwick, Lancaster LA2 8BH* Tel (01542) 51536 E-mail david.creaser@bradford.anglican.org

CREASEY, David John. b 46. Univ of Wales (Abth) BSc69. **d** 06 **p** 07. OLM Ringstone in Aveland Gp *Linc* from 06. *Hanthorpe Farm, 22 Stainfield Road, Hanthorpe, Bourne PE10 0RE* Tel (01778) 570553

CREASEY, Graham. *See* GOLDSTONE-CREASEY, Graham

CREBER, Preb Arthur Frederick. b 45. NOC 84. **d** 87 **p** 88. C Rickerscote *Lich* 87-91; V Gt Wyrley 91-99; RD Rugeley 94-98; P-in-c Newcastle w Butterton 99-07; R 07-08; Preb Lich Cathl 04-08; rtd 08. *22 Malvern Rise, Rhos-on-Sea, Colwyn Bay LL28 4RX* Tel (01492) 547761 E-mail arthur.creber@btinternet.com

CREDITON, Suffragan Bishop of. *See* EVENS, The Rt Revd Robert John Scott

CREE, John Renack. b 44. Open Univ BA74 Lanc Univ MA92. Coll of Resurr Mirfield. **d** 83 **p** 84. C Blackb St Jas 83-86; V Feniscowles 86-01; Chapl Blackb Coll 86-01; R Chorley St Laur *Blackb* 01-09; rtd 09; Perm to Offic *Bre* from 86 and *Blackb* from 09. *5 Bromley Green, Chorley PR6 8TX* Tel (01257) 263398 E-mail john.cree@tiscali.co.uk

CREER, Irene. *See* SIIAW, Mrs Irene

CREES, David Paul. b 68. Southn Univ BSc89. Trin Coll Bris BA99 MA00. **d** 00 **p** 01. C Patcham *Chich* 00-04; CF from 04. *clo MOD Chaplains (Army)* Tel (01264) 381140 Fax 381824

CREES, Geoffrey William. b 35. Open Univ BA85. Cranmer Hall Dur 65. **d** 67 **p** 68. C Hoddesdon *St Alb* 67-70; C Harwell and Chilton All SS *Ox* 70-73; V Greenham 73-82; TR Marfleet and AD E Hull *York* 82-88; TR Rodbourne Cheney *Bris* 88-99; rtd 99; Perm to Offic *Glouc* from 99. *The Thatch, New Road, Popes Hill, Newnham GL14 1JT* Tel (01452) 760843

CREGAN, Mark. b 59. Lon Bible Coll BA91. Wycliffe Hall Ox 95. **d** 97 **p** 98. C Chippenham St Pet *Bris* 97-01; P-in-c Stapleton 01-05; Asst Chapl Colston's Sch Bris 01-03; Chapl 03-05; Chapl Alexandria Egypt 05-07; P-in-c Casablanca *Eur* from 07. *7 Impasse Chasseur Jules Gros, Quartier Oasis, 20100 Casablanca, Morocco* Tel and fax (00212) (2) 257120 E-mail chaplain@stjohnscasablanca.org

CREGEEN, Gary Marshall. b 62. Oak Hill Th Coll BA00. **d** 00 **p** 01. C Carl St Jo 00-03; P-in-c Scotby and Cotehill w Cumwhinton 03-05; V from 06; RD Brampton from 09. *The Vicarage, Lambley Bank, Scotby, Carlisle CA4 8BX* Tel (01228) 513205 E-mail gary@gandjcregeen.co.uk

CREIGHTON, Canon Frederick David. b 50. TCD BTh88 ACII74. **d** 88 **p** 89. C Lisburn Ch Ch *Conn* 88-91; I Drumclamph w Lower and Upper Langfield *D & R* 91-00; I Glendermott from 00; Can Derry Cathl from 08. *Glendermott Rectory, 11 Church Brae, Altnagelvin BT47 2LS* Tel (028) 7134 3001

CREIGHTON, Mrs Judith. b 36. Reading Univ BSc57. Trin Coll Bris 80 Edin Th Coll 81. **dss** 83 **d** 87 **p** 94. Greenock *Glas* 83-85; Lawrence Weston *Bris* 85-87; Par Dn Kingswood 87-90; Chapl Stoke Park and Purdown Hosps Stapleton 90-93; Hon C Marshfield w Cold Ashton and Tormarton etc *Bris* 93-97; rtd 96; Perm to Offic *Bris* from 97. *Rose Cottage, West Littleton, Marshfield, Chippenham SN14 8JE* Tel (01225) 891021

CREIGHTON, Ms Rachel Margaret Maxwell. b 64. Br Is Nazarene Coll BTh86 BD87 Lon Bible Coll MA89. Cranmer Hall Dur 92. **d** 94 **p** 95. C Basford w Hyson Green S'well 94-96; C Nottingham All SS 96-98; P-in-c Broxtowe 98-02; Chapl HM Pris Bedf 02-04; Chapl HM Pris Wellingborough 04-09; I Belfast H Trin and St Silas *Conn* from 09. *The Rectory, 313 Ballysillan Road, Belfast BT14 6RD* Tel (028) 9071 3046 Mobile 07748-063770 E-mail rachel.creighton64@btinternet.com

CRELLIN, Howard Joseph. b 30. Magd Coll Cam BA52 MA56 Magd Coll Ox BA54 MA56. Wycliffe Hall Ox 53. **d** 55 **p** 56. C Dovercourt *Chelmsf* 55-58; R Theydon Garnon 58-70; Select Preacher Ox Univ 68; Perm to Offic *Ox* 70-82; Hon C High Wycombe 72-77; Asst Master K Chas I Sch Kidderminster 74-80; Caldicott Sch Farnham 80-82; Perm to Offic *Chelmsf* 82-91; Asst Master Fryerns Sch Basildon 82-88; St Anselm's Sch Basildon 88-91; P-in-c Whatfield w Semer, Nedging and Naughton *St E* 91-98; rtd 98; Perm to Offic *St E* from 98 and *Eur* from 02. *10 Green Willows, Lavenham, Sudbury CO10 9SP* Tel (01787) 247568

CREMIN (*née* LAKE), **Mrs Eileen Veronica.** b 58. Aston Tr Scheme 83 Sarum & Wells Th Coll 85. **d** 88 **p** 94. Par Dn Islington St Mary *Lon* 88-92; Asst Chapl Homerton Hosp Lon and Hackney Hosp Gp 92-94; P-in-c Brondesbury Ch Ch and St Laur 94-01; C Douglas Union w Frankfield *C, C & R* 01-06; Fermoy Union from 06. *The Rectory, Forglen Terrace, Fermoy,*

Co Cork, Republic of Ireland Tel (00353) (25) 31016 Mobile 86-333 0206 E-mail evcremin@eircom.net *or* ecremin@hotmail.com
CRESSALL, Paul Richard. b 51. UEA BA74. Ripon Coll Cuddesdon 86. **d** 88 **p** 89. C Stevenage H Trin *St Alb* 88-91; V Caldecote All SS 91-95; V Old Warden 91-95; V Rothwell *Ripon* 95-10; P-in-c Markington w S Stainley and Bishop Thornton from 10; P-in-c Ripley w Burnt Yates from 10. *The Vicarage, Westerns Lane, Markington, Harrogate HG3 3PB* Tel (01765) 677123 Mobile 07801-582503 E-mail paulcressall@talktalk.net
CRESSEY, Canon Roger Wilson. b 35. Chich Th Coll 72. **d** 74 **p** 75. C Pontefract St Giles *Wakef* 74-77; Hon C Dewsbury All SS 77-80; Chapl Pinderfields Gen Hosp Wakef 80-94; Chapl Carr Gate Hosp Wakef 80-94; Chapl Fieldhead Hosp Wakef 80-94; Chapl Pinderfields and Pontefract Hosps NHS Trust 94-00; Hon Can Wakef Cathl 98-00; rtd 00. *1 Wellhead Mews, Chapelthorpe, Wakefield WF4 3JG* Tel (01924) 258972 E-mail roger-cressey@supanet.com
CRESSWELL, Howard Rex. b 31. Ely Th Coll 56. **d** 59 **p** 60. C Dovercourt *Chelmsf* 59-61; C Victoria Docks Ascension 61-64; V 64-71; R E w W Harling *Nor* 71-72; TV Quidenham w Eccles and Snetterton 72-73; V Arminghall 75-82; R Caistor w Markshall 75-82; V Trowse 75-82; V Heigham St Barn w St Bart 82-91; rtd 91; Perm to Offic *Nor* from 91. *28 Penryn Close, Norwich NR4 7LY* Tel (01603) 458591 E-mail cresswellriol@hotmail.co.uk
CRESSWELL, Jane Stella. b 62. Bris Univ BA84. SEITE 04. **d** 07 **p** 08. C Sutton *S'wark* 07-11; P-in-c Nork *Guildf* from 11. *St Paul's Vicarage, Warren Road, Banstead SM7 1LG* Tel (01737) 353849 E-mail janescresswell@hotmail.com
CRESSWELL, Canon Jeremy Peter. b 49. St Jo Coll Ox BA72 MA78 K Coll Lon MA83. Ridley Hall Cam 73. **d** 75 **p** 76. C Wisley w Pyrford *Guildf* 75-78; C Weybridge 78-82; P-in-c E Clandon 82-83; P-in-c W Clandon 82-83; R E and W Clandon 83-90; V Oxshott from 90; RD Leatherhead 03-08; Hon Can Owerri from 01; Hon Can Guildf Cathl from 10. *The Vicarage, Steel's Lane, Oxshott, Leatherhead KT22 0QH* Tel (01372) 842071 E-mail vicar@oxshott.co.uk
CRETNEY, Mrs Antonia Lois. b 48. York Univ BA69 Bris Univ BA87 PGCE89. S Dios Minl Tr Scheme 92. **d** 94 **p** 95. NSM Bedminster *Bris* 94-96; C 96-97; P-in-c Beedon and Peasemore w W Ilsley and Farnborough *Ox* 97-99; R 99-04; Deanery P Wantage from 04; Bp's Adv for Women in Ord Min from 05. *8 Elm Farm Close, Grove, Wantage OX12 9FD* Tel (01235) 763192 E-mail antcret@aol.com
CREW, Ruan John. b 70. Bris Univ BSc92 PGCE93 All Nations Chr Coll BA99 Anglia Ruskin Univ MA10. ERMC 07. **d** 10 **p** 11. C Almondsbury and Olveston *Bris* from 10; C Pilning w Compton Greenfield from 10. *The Vicarage, The Glebe, Pilning, Bristol BS35 4LE* Tel (01454) 633067 E-mail ruancrew@gmail.com
CRIBB, Mrs Karen Elisabeth. b 63. Liv Univ BA85 Leeds Univ BA10. Yorks Min Course 97. **d** 10 **p** 11. NSM Sheff St Mary Bramall Lane from 10. *St Mary's Church, Bramall Lane, Sheffield S2 4QZ* Tel 0114-223 0237 E-mail revkaren@stmarys-church.co.uk
CRIBB, Robert John. b 22. Spurgeon's Coll 45. **d** 85 **p** 86. NSM Curry Rivel w Fivehead and Swell *B & W* 85-89; rtd 89; Perm to Offic *B & W* 89-04. *4 Heale Lane, Curry Rivel, Langport TA10 0PG* Tel (01458) 252333
CRICHTON, James Kenneth. b 35. Glouc Sch of Min 78. **d** 80 **p** 80. NSM Minchinhampton *Glouc* 80-83; NSM Nailsworth 83-86; Dep Chapl HM Pris Pentonville 86-87; Chapl HM Pris The Mount 87-97; rtd 97. *Pennant, Horeb, Llandysul SA44 4JG* Tel (01559) 362448
CRICK, Peter. b 39. Lon Univ BD68 NY Univ DMin84. Wells Th Coll 66. **d** 67 **p** 68. C Horsham *Chich* 67-71; Asst Dioc Youth Officer *Ox* 71-75; R Denham 75-88; Bp's Adv for CME *Dur* 88-97; P-in-c Coniscliffe 88-97; Hon Can Dur Cathl 93-97; R City of Bris 97-04; rtd 04. *7 Westfield Common, Hamble, Southampton SO31 4LB* Tel (023) 8045 7025 E-mail pandvcrick@btinternet.com
CRICK, Philip Benjamin Gordon (Ben). b 33. Bris Univ BA63. Clifton Th Coll 60. **d** 64 **p** 65. C Clerkenwell St Jas and St Jo w St Pet *Lon* 64-67; CF 67-72; C Southall Green St Jo *Lon* 72-73; P-in-c Southall H Trin 75-83; P-in-c Kidbrooke St Jas *S'wark* 83-85; TV 85-92; C E Acton St Dunstan w St Thos *Lon* 92-95; Sub-Chapl HM Pris Wormwood Scrubs 92-95; rtd 95; Perm to Offic *Cant* from 95; Sub-Chapl HM Pris Cant 97-06. *232 Canterbury Road, Birchington CT7 9TD* Tel (01843) 846049 Mobile 07818-040651 E-mail ben.crick@argonet.co.uk
CRIDLAND, Clarissa Rosemary Dorothea. b 55. STETS 03. **d** 06 **p** 07. NSM Coleford w Holcombe *B & W* from 06. *4 Rock Terrace, Church Street, Coleford, Radstock BA3 5NF* Tel (01373) 812705 Mobile 07800-578967 E-mail clarissacridland@hotmail.com
CRINKS, Kevin David. b 63. Aston Tr Scheme 86 Sarum & Wells Th Coll BTh91. **d** 93 **p** 94. C Aylesford *Roch* 93-96; C Hessle *York* 96-97; TV Upholland *Liv* 97-00; V Platt Bridge 00-09;

P-in-c Leigh St Mary *Man* from 09; Borough Dean Wigan from 10. *The Vicarage, Westleigh Lane, Leigh WN7 5NW* Tel (01942) 882883 Mobile 07947-807767 E-mail kcrinks@btinternet.com
CRIPPS, Keith Richard John. b 21. Trin Coll Cam BA43 MA47 Newc Univ PhD80. Ridley Hall Cam 43. **d** 45 **p** 47. Inter-Colleg Sec SCM (Man) 45-47; C Man Victoria Park 45-47; C Aston SS Pet and Paul *Birm* 47-50; R Chorlton upon Medlock *Man* 50-60; Chapl Man Univ 51-60; Lect 52-60; Chapl and Lect Ripon Coll of Educn 60-65; Sen Lect Kenton Lodge Coll of Educn 65-71; Sen Lect City of Newc Coll of Educn 71-84; Lect Newc Poly 74-79; Chapl Jes Coll Cam 84-88; rtd 88; Perm to Offic *Ely* 88-02. *24 Mowbray Court, Butts Road, Exeter EX2 5TQ*
CRIPPS, Martyn Cyril Rowland. b 46. Birm Univ LLB68 Solicitor 71. Wycliffe Hall Ox 80. **d** 82 **p** 83. C Canford Magna *Sarum* 82-86; V Preston St Cuth *Blackb* 87-94; Warden Les Cotils *Win* 94-96; V Gipsy Hill Ch Ch *S'wark* 96-00; R Ashmanhaugh, Barton Turf etc *Nor* 00-04; P-in-c Davenham *Ches* 04-06; R from 06. *The Rectory, Church Street, Davenham, Northwich CW9 8NF* Tel (01606) 42450 E-mail mandmc@btopenworld.com
CRIPPS, Michael Frank Douglas. b 28. Ch Ch Ox BA50 MA53. Ridley Hall Cam 58. **d** 59 **p** 60. C Cambridge Gt St Mary w St Mich *Ely* 59-62; Ceylon 62-66; C-in-c Swindon Covingham CD *Bris* 66-72; V Swindon St Paul 72-73; P-in-c Aldbourne and Baydon *Sarum* 73; TV Whitton 73-81; C Marlborough 81-94; 94; Chapl Pau *Eur* 94-96; Perm to Offic *Sarum* from 96. *1 Irving Way, Marlborough SN8 1UE* Tel (01672) 512748
CRISPIN, Martyn Bright. b 46. Stranmillis Coll TCert69 Open Univ BA75 Lon Sch of Th BA03. **d** 06 **p** 09. Peru 06-08; Perm to Offic *Lon* from 08. *47 Etchingham Park Road, London N3 2EB* Tel (020) 8346 8698 E-mail mavecrispin@yahoo.co.uk
CRITCHELL, Denise Eileen. b 49. SAOMC 96. **d** 99 **p** 00. C Flackwell Heath *Ox* 99-03; TV Risborough from 03. *The Vicarage, Church Lane, Lacey Green, Princes Risborough HP27 0QX* Tel (01844) 347741 E-mail denisecritchell@btconnect.com
CRITCHLEY, Colin. b 41. Dur Univ BA63 Liv Univ MA69 AFBPsS94. NW Ord Course 75. **d** 78 **p** 79. NSM Halewood *Liv* 78-06; Dioc Child Protection Adv 90-06; rtd 06. *53 Elwyn Drive, Halewood, Liverpool L26 0UX* Tel 0151-487 5710 Fax 280 4937
CRITCHLEY, Mrs Patsy Eva. b 49. Reading Univ CertEd70. ERMC 04. **d** 07 **p** 08. NSM Meppershall and Shefford *St Alb* 07-10; NSM Henlow and Langford from 10. *39 Rooktree Way, Haynes, Bedford MK45 3PT* Tel (01234) 381510 E-mail patsy@critchley04.plus.com
CRITCHLOW, Mrs Anne-Louise. b 51. Westf Coll Lon BA73 Qu Mary Coll Lon MA75 Leeds Univ MA05 Grenoble Univ MèsL74 Cam Univ PGCE76. NOC 03. **d** 05 **p** 06. C Eccles *Man* 05-08; TV Eccles from 08. *St Andrew's Vicarage, 11 Abbey Grove, Eccles, Manchester M30 9QN* Tel 0161-707 9996 E-mail mmcritchlow@btinternet.com
CRITCHLOW (née KHARITONOVA), Mrs Natalia (Tasha). b 74. St Petersburg State Univ MA98 Dallas Th Sem MTh04. Westcott Ho Cam 07. **d** 09 **p** 10. C Brondesbury Ch Ch and St Laur *Lon* from 09. *St Dunstan's Rectory, Rectory Square, London E1 3NQ* Tel (020) 7791 3545 Mobile 07540-588860 E-mail tasha.critchlow@googlemail.com
CRITCHLOW, Trevor Francis. b 61. Lanc Univ BA83 K Coll Lon MA96. Westcott Ho Cam 88. **d** 90 **p** 91. C Croydon St Jo *S'wark* 90-92; C Lewisham St Mary 92-94; Perm to Offic *Ely* 94-05; Development Dir Westmr St Matt *Lon* 95-99; TV Wembley Park *Lon* 05-11; CME Officer Willesden Area 06-10; R Stepney St Dunstan and All SS from 11. *St Dunstan's Rectory, Rectory Square, London E1 3NQ* Tel (020) 7791 3545 Mobile 07850-578193 Fax 07092-868327 E-mail trevor.critchlow@googlemail.com
CRITTALL, Richard Simon. b 47. Sussex Univ BA69 Linacre Coll Ox BA71. St Steph Ho Ox 69. **d** 72 **p** 73. C Oswestry H Trin *Lich* 72-75; C E Grinstead St Mary *Chich* 75-78; TV Brighton Resurr 78-83; R E Blatchington 83-95; V Heathfield St Rich 95-07; Dioc Ecum Officer *Ex* from 07; P-in-c Broadhembury, Payhembury and Plymtree from 07. *The Rectory, Broadhembury, Honiton EX14 3LT* Tel (01404) 841848 E-mail simoncrittall@breathmail.net
CROAD, Arthur Robert. b 35. Down Coll Cam BA58 MA61. Clifton Th Coll 58. **d** 61 **p** 62. C Sneinton St Chris w St Phil *S'well* 61-64; C Kinson *Sarum* 64-72; R Sherfield English *Win* 72-74; R Awbridge w Sherfield English 74-92; P-in-c Hinton Ampner w Bramdean and Kilmeston 92-01; rtd 01. *48 Woodfield Drive, Winchester SO22 5PU* Tel (01962) 851978
CROAD, David Richard. b 31. Reading Univ BSc55. Clifton Th Coll. **d** 57 **p** 58. C Iver *Ox* 57-60; C Rushden *Pet* 60-63; V Loudwater *Ox* 63-72; SW Area Sec CPAS 72-75; V Bovingdon *St Alb* 78-91; Min Hampstead St Jo Downshire Hill Prop Chpl *Lon* 91-94; rtd 94; Perm to Offic *Guildf* and *Win* from 97. *8 Compass Court, 42-44 Winn Road, Southampton SO17 1EZ*
CROCKER, Jeremy Robert. b 67. S Bank Univ BA94 Heythrop Coll Lon MA98 MCIM92. Westcott Ho Cam 94 CITC 96. **d** 97 **p** 98. C Stevenage H Trin *St Alb* 97-00; TV Bp's Hatfield 00-04;

TR Elstow from 04. *The Abbey Vicarage, Church End, Elstow, Bedford MK42 9XT* Tel (01234) 261477 E-mail jeremy.crocker@tesco.net
CROCKER, Keith Gwillam. b 49. Lanchester Poly Cov BSc70. Oak Hill Th Coll 74. **d** 77 **p** 78. C Whitnash *Cov* 77-80; C Gt Horton *Bradf* 80-83; C Grays SS Pet and Paul, S Stifford and W Thurrock *Chelmsf* 83-84; TV Grays Thurrock 84-88; TR Wreningham *Nor* 88-95; P-in-c New Catton Ch Ch 95-99; V from 99. *Christ Church Vicarage, 65 Elm Grove Lane, Norwich NR3 3LF* Tel (01603) 408332 E-mail keith.crocker@which.net
CROCKER, Peter James. b 56. Lon Univ MB, BS80 MRCGP. Mon Dioc Tr Scheme 93. **d** 96 **p** 97. NSM Bassaleg *Mon* 96-02; TV 02-06; P-in-c Bedwas and Rudry 06-07; R Bedwas w Machen w Rudry from 07. *1A Navigation Street, Trethomas, Caerphilly CF83 8DJ* Tel (029) 2088 5220
CROCKER, Richard Campbell. b 54. Nottm Univ BSc76. Wycliffe Hall Ox BA81 MA85. **d** 82 **p** 83. C Summerfield *Birm* 82-84; Chapl K Edw Sch Birm 84-91; R Council Bluffs USA 91-99; Assoc R Truro Episc Ch from 99. *10520 Main Street, Fairfax VA 22030, USA* Tel (001) (703) 273 1300 E-mail rcrocker@trurochurch.org
CROCKETT, Peter James Sinclair. b 44. Sarum & Wells Th Coll 74. **d** 77 **p** 78. C Heavitree *Ex* 77; C Heavitree w Ex St Paul 78-80; TV Ex St Thos and Em 80-87; V Countess Wear 87-09; Chapl St Loyes Tr Coll for the Disabled 87-09; Chapl W of England Sch for those w little or no sight 87-09; rtd 09; CF (TA) from 88. *The Old House, 7 Strete Ralegh House, London Road, Strete Ralegh, Whimple, Exeter EX5 2PT* Tel (01404) 823651
CROFT, James Stuart. b 57. K Coll Lon BD80 Leeds Univ MA95. Ripon Coll Cuddesdon 83. **d** 85 **p** 86. C Friern Barnet St Jas *Lon* 85-88; R Lea *Linc* 88-93; V Knaith 88-93; V Upton 88-93; R Gate Burton 88-93; R Lea Gp 93-97; Chapl N Lincs Coll 90-93; V Froyle and Holybourne *Win* 97-10; P-in-c Chesterfield St Aug *Derby* from 10. *St Augustine's Vicarage, 1 Whitecotes Lane, Chesterfield S40 3HJ* Tel (01246) 224423 E-mail jamescroft57@fsmail.net
CROFT, Jennifer Sara. b 69. Leeds Univ BSc94. Ripon Coll Cuddesdon 99. **d** 01 **p** 02. C Lillington *Cov* 01-05; Chapl Cov Univ 05-11; Chapl amongst Deaf People 03-08; V Over Tabley *Ches* from 11; V High Legh from 11; Sen Research Fell Warw Univ from 11. *St John's Vicarage, The Avenue, High Legh, Knutsford WA16 6ND* Tel (01925) 759132 E-mail j.croft@coventry.ac.uk
CROFT, Michael Peter. b 60. GradIPM MCIPD95 FCIPD08. Trin Coll Bris BA88. **d** 88 **p** 89. C Drypool *York* 88-91; P-in-c Sandal St Cath *Wakef* 91-95; V 95-07; Perm to Offic from 05. *5 College Terrace, Ackworth, Pontefract WF7 7LB* Tel (01977) 611251 Mobile 078139-59066 E-mail michael@michaelcroftlimited.co.uk
CROFT, Ronald. b 30. St Aid Birkenhead 61. **d** 63 **p** 64. C Lawton Moor *Man* 63-65; C Withington St Crispin 65-66; R 74-86; C Prestwich St Marg 66-67; V Oldham St Ambrose 67-71; P-in-c Oldham St Jas 67-68; V 68-71; V Prestwich St Hilda 71-74; P-in-c 96-00; R Heaton Norris St Thos 86-96; rtd 00; Perm to Offic *Man* from 00. *St Hilda's Vicarage, 55 Whittaker Lane, Prestwich, Manchester M25 5ET* Tel 0161-773 1642
CROFT, Simon Edward Owen. b 51. Ch Ch Coll Cant CertEd73. St Steph Ho Ox 75. **d** 78 **p** 79. C Heavitree w Ex St Paul 78-83; V Seaton 83-93; P-in-c Ex St Mark 93-96; P-in-c Ex St Sidwell and St Matt 96; R Ex St Mark, St Sidwell and St Matt 96-09; C Dawlish 09-10; P-in-c from 10. *The Vicarage, 13 West Cliff Road, Dawlish EX7 9EB* Tel (01626) 864569 E-mail simoncdevon@yahoo.co.uk
✠**CROFT, The Rt Revd Steven John Lindsey.** b 57. Worc Coll Ox BA80 MA83 St Jo Coll Dur PhD84. Cranmer Hall Dur 80. **d** 83 **p** 84 **c** 09. C Enfield St Andr *Lon* 83-87; V Ovenden *Wakef* 87-96; Dioc Miss Consultant 94-96; Warden Cranmer Hall Dur 96-04; Abps' Missr and Team Ldr Fresh Expressions 04-09; Bp Sheff from 09. *Bishopscroft, Snaithing Lane, Sheffield S10 3LG* Tel 0114-230 2170 Fax 263 0110 E-mail bishop@bishopofsheffield.org.uk
CROFT, Canon Warren David. b 36. ACT ThL62. **d** 61 **p** 62. Australia 61-69 and from 79; Papua New Guinea 69-77; C Mottingham St Andr w St Alban *S'wark* 77-78; Hon Can Dogura 86; C Hunters Hill 87; R Kogarah 87-01; rtd 01. *43 Sierra Avenue, PO Box 3078, Bateau Bay NSW 2261, Australia* Tel (0061) (2) 4333 3967 Mobile 425-206621 Fax 9553 8594 E-mail isandwas@bigpond.com
CROFT, Canon William Stuart. b 53. Trin Hall Cam BA76 MA79 K Coll Lon MTh88. Ripon Coll Cuddesdon BA80. **d** 80 **p** 81. C Friern Barnet St Jas *Lon* 80-83; Tutor Chich Th Coll 83-92; Vice-Prin 88-92; V Fernhurst *Chich* 92-98; Dir of Ords *Pet* 98-03; Prec and Min Can Pet Cathl 98-01; Can Res and Prec 01-04; Liturg Officer 03-04; Non-res Can from 04; P-in-c Longthorpe from 04; P-in-c Pet H Spirit Bretton from 11. *The Vicarage, 315 Thorpe Road, Longthorpe, Peterborough PE3 6LU* Tel (01733) 263016 E-mail williamsbill croft@hotmail.com
CROFTON, Edwin Alan. b 46. Univ Coll Ox BA68 MA72. Cranmer Hall Dur. **d** 73 **p** 74. C Hull St Jo Newland *York* 73-77;

C Worksop St Jo *S'well* 77-81; Chapl Kilton Hosp Worksop 80-81; V Scarborough St Mary w Ch Ch and H Apostles *York* 81-91; Miss to Seamen 81-91; Chapl St Mary's Hosp Scarborough 82-91; V Cheltenham Ch Ch *Glouc* 91-02; RD Cheltenham 95-00; Hon Can Glouc Cathl 01-02; TR Eccles *Man* from 02; P-in-c Hope St Jas 07-09; AD Eccles 05-11. *The Rectory, 12B Westminster Road, Eccles, Manchester M30 9EB* Tel 0161-281 5739 E-mail ea_crofton@msn.com
CROFTON, Robert Edwin. b 75. UEA BSc98. Ridley Hall Cam 03. **d** 06 **p** 07. C Churchdown *Glouc* 06-09; TV Cheltenham St Mark from 09. *St Barnabas' Vicarage, 152 Alstone Lane, Cheltenham GL51 8HL* Tel (01242) 575679 E-mail rob.crofton@tiscali.co.uk
CROFTS, David Thomas. b 47. Cheshire Coll of Educn CertEd68 Open Univ BA76. Dioc OLM tr scheme. **d** 99 **p** 00. OLM Bury St Edmunds St Mary *St E* from 99. *8 Linton Gardens, Bury St Edmunds IP33 2DZ* Tel (01284) 761801 Fax 765501 E-mail david@pandda.co.uk
CROFTS, Ian Hamilton. b 55. BSc. St Jo Coll Nottm 79. **d** 82 **p** 83. C Leamington Priors St Paul *Cov* 82-86; C Oadby *Leic* 86; TV 86-91; V Maidstone St Faith *Cant* 91-07; V Forty Hill Jes Ch *Lon* from 07. *The Vicarage, Forty Hill, Enfield EN2 9EU* Tel (020) 8363 1935 E-mail ian.crofts@gmail.com
CROFTS, Stephen Andrew. b 76. Ch Ch Coll Cant BA98 Ox Brookes Univ MA09. Ripon Coll Cuddesdon 07. **d** 09 **p** 10. C Birstall and Wanlip *Leic* from 09. *22 Oakfield Avenue, Birstall, Leicester LE4 3DQ*
CROISDALE-APPLEBY, Mrs Carolyn Elizabeth. b 46. Ch Ch Coll Cant CertEd68. SAOMC 01. **d** 04 **p** 05. NSM Amersham and Gt Coxwell w Buscot, Coleshill etc *Ox* 04-07; NSM Beaconsfield from 07. *Abbotsholme, Hervines Road, Amersham HP6 5HS* Tel (01494) 725194 Fax 725474 E-mail croisdaleappleby@aol.com
CROMARTY, Andrew Robert McKean. b 63. Newc Univ MB, BS86 Homerton Coll Cam PGCE89 St Jo Coll Dur BA04. Cranmer Hall Dur 02. **d** 06 **p** 07. NSM Crook *Dur* 06-10; C Upper Weardale from 10. *14 Burnfoot, St John's Chapel, Bishop Auckland DL13 1QH* E-mail andrew@cromarty4500.fsnet.co.uk
CROMPTON (*née* KILGOUR), **Mrs Christine Mary.** b 39. Newnham Coll Cam BA61 MA York Univ MA86 Lon Inst of Educn PGCE62. **d** 06 **p** 07. OLM Newc St Geo and St Hilda from 06. *11 South Bend, Newcastle upon Tyne NE3 5TR* Tel 0191-236 3679
CROMPTON, Canon Roger Martyn Francis. b 47. Sheff Univ BA69 PGCE73 St Jo Coll Dur BA84. Cranmer Hall Dur 82. **d** 85 **p** 86. C Woodford Wells *Chelmsf* 85-89; V Golcar *Wakef* from 89; P-in-c Longwood from 10; RD Huddersfield 99-09; Hon Can Wakef Cathl from 06. *The Vicarage, Church Street, Golcar, Huddersfield HD7 4PX* Tel (01484) 654647 E-mail rmf4vmc@btinternet.com
CROMPTON-BATTERSBY, Holly Jo. b 74. Bath Coll of HE BA95. Wycliffe Hall Ox BTh01. **d** 01 **p** 02. C Luton Lewsey St Hugh *St Alb* 01-04; Chapl Bennett Memorial Dioc Sch Tunbridge Wells 04-07; Chapl Bedgebury Sch Kent 05-06; Chapl St Bede's Sch Cam from 09. *St Bede's Inter-Church School, Birdwood Road, Cambridge CB1 3TD* Tel (01223) 568816 ext 210 Mobile 07761-628335 E-mail hollycrompton@hotmail.com *or* hcrompton@stbedes.cambs.sch.uk
CRONIN, Mrs Linda Nancy. b 61. NTMTC BA08. **d** 08 **p** 09. C Barrow St Mark *Carl* 08-10; C S Barrow from 10. *St Aidan's Vicarage, 31 Middle Hill, Barrow-in-Furness LA13 9HD* Tel (01229) 830445 Mobile 07817-678775 E-mail linda@thecronins.org.uk
CRONK, Simon Nicholas. b 59. CQSW85 Poly of Wales BA82. Wycliffe Hall Ox 89. **d** 92 **p** 93. C Cheltenham Ch Ch *Glouc* 92-96; V Cinderford St Steph w Littledean 96-02; V Hughenden *Ox* from 02. *The Vicarage, Valley Road, Hughenden Valley, High Wycombe HP14 4PF* Tel (01494) 563439
CROOK, Colin. b 44. JP78. Lon Univ BSc(Econ)74 ALA67 FLA93. S'wark Ord Course 87. **d** 90 **p** 91. NSM Dartford Ch Ch *Roch* 90-97; P-in-c Crockenhill All So 97-05; Dioc Ecum Officer 96-04; rtd 05; Perm to Offic *Chich* from 06. *11 Fulbourne House, 56 Blackwater Road, Eastbourne BN20 7DN* Tel (01323) 728477 E-mail revcolincrook@yahoo.co.uk
CROOK, David Creighton. b 37. Trin Coll Cam BA61 MA68. Cuddesdon Coll 61. **d** 63 **p** 64. C Workington St Mich *Carl* 63-66; C Penrith St Andr 66-70; V Barrow St Jas 70-78; V Maryport 78-81; TV Greystoke, Matterdale and Mungrisdale 81-87; TV Watermillock 84-87; V Hesket-in-the-Forest and Armathwaite 87-98; rtd 98; Perm to Offic *Carl* from 01. *11 Lowther Street, Penrith CA11 7UW* Tel (01768) 866773
CROOK, Mrs Diana Elizabeth. b 47. Hull Univ BA73 Open Univ BSc93 City Univ MSc97 Middx Univ BA03 RGN70 CPsychol. NTMTC 00. **d** 03 **p** 04. NSM Waltham H Cross *Chelmsf* 03-07; P-in-c Uley w Owlpen and Nympsfield *Glouc* from 07. *The Rectory, 2 The Green, Uley, Dursley GL11 5SN* Tel (01453) 861363 *or* 860249 E-mail revdiana@dianacrook.org

CROOK, Graham Leslie. b 49. Chich Th Coll 74. **d** 76 **p** 77. C Withington St Crispin *Man* 76-79; C Prestwich St Marg 79-82; V Nelson St Bede *Blackb* 82-92; Chapl Southend Health Care NHS Trust from 92; Bp's Adv for Hosp Chapl (Bradwell Area) *Chelmsf* 98-04; Perm to Offic from 09. *Ebenezer, 249 Woodgrange Drive, Southend-on-Sea SS1 2SQ* Tel (01702) 613429

✠**CROOK, The Rt Revd John Michael.** b 40. Univ of Wales (Lamp) BA62. Coll of Resurr Mirfield 62. **d** 64 **p** 65 **c** 99. C Horninglow *Lich* 64-66; C Bloxwich 66-70; R Inverness St Mich *Mor* 70-78; R Inverness St Jo 74-78; Dioc Youth Chapl *St And* 78-86; R Aberfoyle 78-87; R Doune 78-87; R Callander 78-87; Can St Ninian's Cathl Perth 85-99; R Bridge of Allan 87-99; Syn Clerk 97-99; Bp Mor 99-06; rtd 06; Lic to Offic *St And* from 07. *8 Buccleuch Court, Dunblane FK15 0AR* Tel (01786) 826872

CROOK, Malcolm Geoffrey. b 53. St Steph Ho Ox 88. **d** 90 **p** 91. C Pet St Jude 90-93; C Barrow St Matt *Carl* 93-96; TV Langley and Parkfield *Man* 96-97; R Man Apostles w Miles Platting 97-03; P-in-c Sneinton St Steph w St Alb *S'well* 03-04; P-in-c Sneinton St Matthias 03-04; V Sneinton St Steph w St Matthias 04-11; P-in-c Sculcoates from 03. *St Paul's Vicarage, Bridlington Avenue, Hull HU2 0DU* Tel (01482) 620341 E-mail malccrook@hotmail.com

CROOK, Marie Elizabeth. b 46. CBDTI 02. **d** 05 **p** 06. OLM Over Darwen St Jas *Blackb* 05-07; NSM from 07. *The Vicarage, Johnson New Road, Hoddlesden, Darwen BB3 3NN* Tel (01254) 702598 Mobile 07742-029757 E-mail mariecrook500@hotmail.com

CROOK, Rowland William. b 39. Tyndale Hall Bris 61. **d** 64 **p** 65. C Penn Fields *Lich* 64 68; C Lower Broughton St Clem w St Matthias *Man* 68-70; C Bucknall and Bagnall *Lich* 70-76; V New Shildon *Dur* 76-86; V Northwich St Luke and H Trin *Ches* 86-99; P-in-c Helsby and Dunham-on-the-Hill 99-04; rtd 04; Perm to Offic *Ches* from 04. *14 Bollington Avenue, Northwich CW9 8SB* Tel (01606) 45177 E-mail rowland.crook@talktalk.net

CROOK, Timothy Mark. b 68. Oak Hill Th Coll BA00. **d** 00 **p** 01. C Charles w Plymouth St Matthias *Ex* 00-03; C Harold Wood *Chelmsf* 03-09; V S w N Bersted *Chich* from 09. *121 Victoria Drive, Bognor Regis PO21 2EH* Tel (01243) 862018 E-mail timothycrook@hotmail.com

CROOKES, Keith John. b 54. Sheff Univ BA94 Leeds Univ PhD02. NOC 02. **d** 05 **p** 06. NSM Deepcar *Sheff* 05-09; NSM Sheff St Paul from 09. *219 High Greave, Sheffield S5 9GS* Tel 0114-240 3790 E-mail keith.crookes@sheffield.anglican.org

CROOKS, Canon Christopher John (Kip). b 53. St Bede's Coll Dur CertEd75. Trin Coll Bris BA90. **d** 90 **p** 91. C The Quinton *Birm* 90-93; V Ince Ch Ch *Liv* 93-03; R Much Woolton from 03; AD Liv S from 06; Hon Can Liv Cathl from 06. *The Rectory, 67 Church Road, Woolton, Liverpool L25 6DA* Tel 0151-428 1853

CROOKS, Canon David William Talbot. b 52. TCD BA75 MA78 BD83. **d** 77 **p** 78. C Glendermott *D & R* 77-81; C Edin Old St Paul 81-84; I Taughboyne, Craigadooish, Newtowncunningham etc *D & R* from 84; Bp's Dom Chapl 88-07; Can Raphoe Cathl from 91. *Taughboyne Rectory, Churchtown, Carrigans, Lifford, Co Donegal, Republic of Ireland* Tel (00353) (74) 914 0135 Mobile 86-212 5670 E-mail dcrooks@eircom.net

CROOKS, Eric. b 34. Oak Hill Th Coll 68. **d** 70 **p** 71. C Chadderton Ch Ch *Man* 70-73; C Bolton St Paul 73-75; C Lurgan Ch the Redeemer *D & D* 75-77; I Aghaderg w Donaghmore 77-80; I Dundonald 80-01; rtd 01. *17 Cumberland Close, Dundonald, Belfast BT16 2AW* Tel (028) 9048 0540

CROOKS, Mrs Jayne Barbara. b 52. Birm Univ BSc73 Avery Hill Coll PGCE74. WMMTC 01. **d** 04 **p** 05. NSM Kings Norton *Birm* 04-08; C from 08. *15 Chalgrove Avenue, Birmingham B38 8YP* Tel 0121-459 3733 E-mail jayne.crooks@blueyonder.co.uk

CROOKS, Kenneth Robert. b 36. CEng FIEE FCMI. S'wark Ord Course 80. **d** 83 **p** 84. NSM Wisley w Pyrford *Guildf* 83-92; Perm to Offic *Ex* from 98. *Foxes Corner, Peak Hill Road, Sidmouth EX10 0NW* Tel (01395) 577578

CROOKS, Kip. See **CROOKS, Canon Christopher John**

CROOKS, Peter James. b 50. MBE09. St Jo Coll Cam BA72. Cranmer Hall Dur. **d** 76 **p** 77. C Onslow Square St Paul *Lon* 76-77; C Brompton H Trin w Onslow Square St Paul 77-79; C Wembley St Jo 79-82; CMS 82-92; Lebanon 83-89; Syria 85-89; Dean Jerusalem 89-92; P-in-c Hunningham and Wappenbury w Weston under Wetherley *Cov* 92-01; P-in-c Offchurch 96-01; V Long Itchington and Marton 96-01; CMS Iran 01-02; TV Dolgellau w Llanfachreth and Brithdir etc *Ban* 02-04; Chapl Aden Ch Ch Yemen 04-09; Dir Ras Morbat Clinics 04-09; rtd 09; P-in-c Arthog w Fairbourne w Llangelynnin w Rhoslefain *Ban* 09-10. *Broneirian, Springfield Street, Dolgellau LL40 1LY* Tel (01341) 421155 Mobile 07866-276562 E-mail pncrooks@ukonline.co.uk

CROOS, John Princely. b 59. Madurai Univ BA82. Oak Hill Th Coll BA04. **d** 04 **p** 05. C Becontree St Mary *Chelmsf* 04-07; C E

Ham St Paul 07-08; Chapl Lon City Miss from 08. *103 Browning Road, London E12 6RB* Tel (020) 8472 4143 E-mail sprincecroos@hotmail.com

CROSBIE, Andrew. b 62. St Steph Ho Ox 96. **d** 98 **p** 99. C St Paul's Cathl St Helena 98-00; CF 00-03; Perm to Offic *Blackb* 03-11; Chantry P Shrine of Our Lady of Haddington from 08. *151 Ashley Gardens, London SW1P 1HW*, or *The Parsonage, 7 Gordon Street, Dumfries DG1 1EG* Tel (020) 7233 8240 Mobile 07791-540535 E-mail fathercrosbie@aol.com

CROSBIE, Timothy John. b 44. ACMA72. **d** 00 **p** 01. OLM Shotley *St E* 00-08. *27 Kitchener Way, Shotley Gate, Ipswich IP9 1RN* Tel (01473) 787316 E-mail tim@timcrosbie.fsnet.co.uk

CROSBY, Bernard Edward. b 47. Oak Hill Th Coll 86. **d** 88 **p** 89. C Springfield H Trin *Chelmsf* 88-91; C Penn Fields *Lich* 91-94; V St Leonards St Ethelburga *Chich* 94-02; R Fairlight, Guestling and Pett 02-10; rtd 10. *4 Willowbed Walk, Hastings TN34 2QL* Tel (01424) 435800 E-mail bernardcrosby@supanet.com

CROSBY, David Edward. b 48. SAOMC 96. **d** 99 **p** 00. NSM Newbury *Ox* 99-01; C The Bourne and Tilford *Guildf* 01-04; P-in-c Hurst Green and Mitton *Bradf* 04. *29 The Maltings, Gamlingay, Sandy SG19 3JN* E-mail david@kandy.f2s.com

CROSFIELD, Canon George Philip Chorley. b 24. OBE90. Selw Coll Cam BA50 MA55. Edin Th Coll 46. **d** 51 **p** 52. C Edin St Dav 51-53; C St Andrews St Andr *St And* 53-55; R Hawick *Edin* 55-60; Chapl Gordonstoun Sch 60-67; Can St Mary's Cathl 68-91; Vice-Provost 68-70; Provost 70-90; R Edin St Mary 70-90; rtd 90; Hon Can St Mary's Cathl from 91; Hon C Penicuik from 91; Hon C W Linton from 91. *21 Biggar Road, Silverburn, Penicuik EH26 9LQ* Tel (01968) 676607

CROSS, Alan. See **CROSS, Thomas Alan**

CROSS, Canon Alan. b 43. Chich Th Coll 68. **d** 70 **p** 71. C Bordesley St Oswald *Birm* 70; C S Yardley St Mich 70-73; C Colchester St Jas, All SS, St Nic and St Runwald *Chelmsf* 73-77; V Leigh-on-Sea St Jas 77-89; V Woodford St Barn 89-09; Hon Can Chelmsf Cathl 97-09; rtd 09; Perm to Offic *Chelmsf* from 09. *11 Grayling Drive, Colchester CO4 3EN* Tel (01206) 790984

CROSS, Preb Elizabeth Mary. b 46. Leeds Univ BA69 CertEd70. Sarum Th Coll 80. **dss** 83 **d** 87 **p** 94. Wootton Bassett *Sarum* 83-86; Westbury 86-87; Par Dn 87-89; C Glastonbury w Meare, W Pennard and Godney *B & W* 89-95; Asst Dir of Ords 89-95; Preb Wells Cathl 93-07; V Wedmore w Theale and Blackford 95-07; rtd 07. *7 Carpenters Close, Stratton, Dorchester DT2 9SR* Tel (01305) 260499

CROSS, Canon Greville Shelly. b 49. Sarum & Wells Th Coll 73. **d** 76 **p** 77. C Kidderminster St Mary *Worc* 76-80; P-in-c Worc St Mark 80-81; TV Worc St Martin w St Pet, St Mark etc 81-85; R Inkberrow w Cookhill and Kington w Dormston 85-98; RD Evesham 93-97; R Old Swinford Stourbridge 98-11; RD Stourbridge 01-04; NSM Upton-on-Severn, Ripple, Earls Croome etc from 11; NSM Hanley Castle, Hanley Swan and Welland from 11; Hon Can Worc Cathl from 05. *The Vicarage, 5 Westmere, Hanley Swan, Worcester WR8 0DG* Tel (01684) 310102 E-mail canon.cross@btinternet.com

CROSS, James Stuart. b 36. Magd Coll Ox BA65 MA71. Ripon Hall Ox 62. **d** 65 **p** 66. C Leckhampton SS Phil and Jas *Glouc* 65-66; CF 66-92; QHC 89-92; R Stretford St Pet *Man* 92-00; rtd 00. *St Davids, Redbrook Road, Monmouth NP25 3LY* Tel and fax (01600) 715977 E-mail jimcross1@aol.com

CROSS, Jeremy Burkitt. b 45. St Pet Coll Ox BA68 MA71. Wycliffe Hall Ox 83. **d** 69 **p** 70. C Mildenhall *St E* 69-72; C Lindfield *Chich* 72-77; V Framfield 77-89; R St Leonards St Leon 89-01; R Birling, Addington, Ryarsh and Trottiscliffe *Roch* 01-10; rtd 10. *Les Sapins Verts, Branla, 56140 Reminiac, France* Tel (0033) 2 97 93 25 63 E-mail jandscross@aol.com

CROSS, John Henry Laidlaw. b 30. Peterho Cam BA53 MA57. Ridley Hall Cam 53. **d** 55 **p** 56. C Ealing Dean St Jo *Lon* 55-58; C Gt Baddow *Chelmsf* 58-60; V Maidenhead St Andr and St Mary *Ox* 60-68; News Ed C of E Newspaper 68-71; Assoc Ed 71-72; Ed 72-75; Hon C St Pet Cornhill *Lon* 68-87; P-in-c 87-95; Hon C Chelsea All SS 76-93; rtd 95. *8 Pinetum Close, Devizes SN10 5EW* Tel (01380) 722997 E-mail revjhlcross@aol.com

CROSS, Kenneth James. b 69. Trin Coll Bris BA09. **d** 09 **p** 10. C Alcombe *B & W* from 09. *31 Manor Road, Minehead TA24 6EJ* Tel (01643) 706467 Mobile 07951-568703 E-mail kennethjcross@gmail.com

CROSS, Kingsley James. b 50. SWMTC 09. **d** 11. NSM N Creedy *Ex* from 11. *9 Church Close, Puddington, Tiverton EX16 8PJ* Tel (01884) 860382 E-mail kingsleycross@btinternet.com

CROSS, Mrs Linda Ann. b 57. St Jo Coll Dur BA79 Wye Coll Lon MSc80. **d** 10 **p** 11. OLM Wye w Brook and Hastingleigh etc *Cant* from 10. *Yew Tree House, The Street, Brook, Ashford TN25 5PF* Tel (01233) 813360 E-mail jandlcross@btinternet.com

CROSS, Canon Michael Anthony. b 45. Leeds Univ BA67 BA69. Coll of Resurr Mirfield 68. **d** 70 **p** 71. C Bloemfontein Cathl S Africa 70-73; C Adel *Ripon* 74-76; Chapl Birm Univ 76-81; V Chapel Allerton *Ripon* 81-92; V Headingley 92-04; AD Headingley 96-01; P-in-c Wetherby 04-10; Hon Can Ripon Cathl

06-10; rtd 11. *1 Angram Close, York YO30 5ZN* Tel (01904) 347051 E-mail mandacross@yahoo.co.uk

CROSS, Canon Michael Harry. b 28. Liv Univ BVSc50. Cuddesdon Coll 74. d 76 p 77. C Ledbury *Heref* 76-79; P-in-c Bosbury 79-82; P-in-c Coddington 79-82; P-in-c Wellington Heath 79-82; V Bosbury w Wellington Heath etc 82-83; V Bishop's Castle w Mainstone 83-84; P-in-c Snead 83-84; V Morland, Thrimby and Gt Strickland *Carl* 84-93; RD Appleby 91-93; Hon Can Carl Cathl 92-93; rtd 93; Perm to Offic *Carl* from 93. *Hollin Knowle, Kilmidyke Road, Grange-over-Sands LA11 7AQ* Tel (01539) 535908

CROSS, Stephanie. b 53. Essex Univ BSc74 Loughb Univ MSc76 Bris Univ BA01 Reading Univ PGCE93. Trin Coll Bris 99. d 01 p 02. C Lytchett Minster *Sarum* 01-05; TV Wheatley *Ox* from 05; R Aston-le-Walls, Byfield, Boddington, Eydon etc *Pet* from 11. *The Rectory, 55 Church Street, Byfield, Daventry NN11 6XH* E-mail crossstevie@hotmail.com

CROSS, Thomas Alan. b 58. CITC BTh05. d 05 p 06. C Drumglass w Moygashel *Arm* 05-08; I Lissan from 08; Hon V Choral Arm Cathl from 06; Dom Chapl to Abp Arm from 09. *Lissan Rectory, 150 Moneymore Road, Cookstown BT80 8PY* Tel (028) 8676 6112 Mobile 07795-436918

CROSSE, Mrs Anne-Marie. b 48. d 99 p 09. NSM W Worthing St Jo *Chich* 99-02; NSM Arundel w Tortington and S Stoke 02-05; Perm to Offic from 05. *25 Strathmore Close, Worthing BN13 1PQ* Tel (01903) 247706 E-mail amcrosse@talktalk.net

CROSSEY, Nigel Nicholas. b 59. Cam Univ BA. d 84 p 85. C Drumglass w Moygashel *Arm* 84-87; I Magheraculmoney *Clogh* 87-93; CF 93-09; Chapl St Columba's Coll Dub from 09. *St Columba's College, Whitechurch, Dublin 16, Republic of Ireland* Tel (00353) (1) 4906791

CROSSLAND, Felix Parnell. b 20. CEng MIMechE57 Univ of Wales (Swansea) BSc49. St Deiniol's Hawarden 73. d 75 p 76. Hon C Skewen *Llan* 75-78; Hon C Neath w Llantwit 78-85; rtd 85; Perm to Offic *Llan* from 85. *21 Cimla Road, Neath SA11 3PR* Tel (01639) 643560

CROSSLAND, June Marcia. b 44. d 01. OLM Monk Bretton *Wakef* from 01; OLM Staincross from 05. *16 Deacons Way, Barnsley S71 2HU* Tel (01226) 203895

CROSSLAND, Richard Henry. b 49. Ex Univ BA72. S'wark Ord Course 91. d 94 p 96. NSM Surbiton St Andr and St Mark *S'wark* 94-95; NSM Linc Cathl 95-98; NSM Spring Line Gp from 10; NSM Owmby Gp from 10. *Manor Farm, Brattleby, Lincoln LN1 2SQ* Tel (01522) 730000 E-mail rcrossland@voxhumana.co.uk

CROSSLEY, Mrs Charmain Janice. b 47. Sarum Th Coll 07. d 09 p 10. OLM Shaftesbury *Sarum* from 09. *Tanders, Elm Hill, Motcombe, Shaftesbury SP7 9HR* Tel (01747) 852545 E-mail jancrossley.may1594@mirpin.net

CROSSLEY, Dennis Thomas. b 23. AKC52 St Boniface Warminster. d 53 p 54. C Crofton Park St Hilda *S'wark* 53-56; C Beddington 56-59; C Talbot Village *Sarum* 59-62; R Finchampstead *Ox* 62-97; rtd 97; Perm to Offic *Ox* from 97. *1 Larkswood Close, Sandhurst, Camberley GU47 8QJ*

CROSSLEY, George Alan. b 34. St Jo Coll Dur BA56. Cranmer Hall Dur. d 60 p 61. C Blackb St Steph 60-63; C Ashton-on-Ribble St Andr 63-65; V Oswaldtwistle St Paul 65-72; R Dufton *Carl* 72-73; P-in-c Milburn w Newbiggin 72-73; R Long Marton w Dufton and w Milburn 73-76; P-in-c Beckermet St Jo 76-78; V Beckermet St Jo and St Bridget w Ponsonby 78-84; Chapl Furness Gen Hosp 84-89; TV Newbarns w Hawcoat *Carl* 84-89; Chapl Princess R Hosp Telford 89-97; rtd 95; P-in-c Bilsborrow *Blackb* 97-99; Perm to Offic from 00. *6 Eden Mount Way, Carnforth LA5 9XN* Tel (01524) 734568

CROSSLEY, George John. b 57. Bradf Univ BA81 PhD84. NOC 91. d 94 p 95. C Balderstone *Man* 94-98; V Branston w Tatenhill *Lich* 98-02; RD Tutbury 00-02; Chapl Burton Hosps NHS Trust from 04; P-in-c Burton St Chad *Lich* from 09. *St Chad's Vicarage, 113 Hunter Street, Burton-on-Trent DE14 2SS* (01283) 564044 Mobile 07976-979755 E-mail george@gcrossley.wanadoo.co.uk

CROSSLEY, James Salter Baron. b 39. Linc Th Coll 70. d 72 p 74. C Chesterfield St Mary and All SS *Derby* 72-75; Chapl Doncaster R Infirmary 75-92; Chapl Doncaster R Infirmary and Montagu Hosp NHS Trust 92-95; Chapl Asst Tickhill Road and St Cath Hosps 75-92; Hon C Doncaster Intake *Sheff* 78-95; rtd 95; Perm to Offic *Sheff* 95-99 and *Ripon* from 00. *The Gables, Low Row, Richmond DL11 6NH* Tel (01748) 886429

CROSSLEY, Janice. *See* CROSSLEY, Mrs Charmain Janice

CROSSLEY, Jeremy. *See* CROSSLEY, William Jeremy Hugh

CROSSLEY, Joan Winifred. b 57. Sussex Univ BA78 Leic Univ MA80 Univ Coll Lon PhD85. SAOMC 97. d 00 p 01. C Goldington *St Alb* 00-02; C Bedf St Mark 02-08; Asst Chapl Gt Ormond Street Hosp for Children NHS Trust 03-05; Asst Chapl Westmr Sch 08-10; Chapl K Coll Sch Wimbledon from 10; PV Westmr Abbey from 08. *King's College School, Southside Common, London SW19 4TT* Tel (020) 8255 5300 E-mail jwcrossley@aol.com

CROSSLEY, John Eric. b 51. St Martin's Coll Lanc BA92. Carl Dioc Tr Inst 92. d 94 p 95. C Westfield St Mary *Carl* 94-97; P-in-c Penrith w Newton Reigny and Plumpton Wall 97-02; Chapl Newton Rigg Coll of H&FE 97-02; TV Cartmel Peninsula *Carl* 02-09; rtd 09. *The Vicarage, Vicarage Road, Levens, Kendal LA8 8PY* Tel (01539) 560223 E-mail rjoncros@aol.com

CROSSLEY, Kenneth Ernest. b 38. NEOC 01. d 03 p 04. NSM Ripon Cathl from 03. *11 Station Drive, Ripon HG4 1JA* Tel (01765) 692499 E-mail kennethecrossley@aol.com

CROSSLEY, Canon Robert Scott. b 36. Lon Univ BSc61 BD68 PhD75. ALCD64. d 64 p 65. C Beckenham St Jo *Roch* 64-68; C Morden *S'wark* 68-72; Chapl Ridley Hall Cam 72-75; V Camberley St Paul *Guildf* 75-83; TR 83-98; RD Surrey Heath 81-84; Hon Can Guildf Cathl 89-98; rtd 98; Perm to Offic *Guildf* 98-01 and from 07; Hon C Camberley St Mich Yorktown 01-07. *20 Highbury Crescent, Camberley GU15 1JZ* Tel (01276) 500036 E-mail robertcrossley@ntlworld.com

CROSSLEY, Mrs Ruth Joy. b 54. Cranmer Hall Dur 00. d 02 p 03. C Cartmel Peninsula *Carl* 02-06; P-in-c Levens from 06; Bp's Adv for CME 06-11. *The Vicarage, Vicarage Road, Levens, Kendal LA8 8PY* Tel (01539) 560223 E-mail rcross3357@aol.com

CROSSLEY, William Jeremy Hugh. b 55. St Jo Coll Dur BA76. Cranmer Hall Dur 81. d 84 p 85. C Gillingham St Mark *Roch* 84-87; C Ches Square St Mich w St Phil *Lon* 87-94; V Westminster St Jas the Less 94-00; R St Marg Lothbury and St Steph Coleman Street etc from 00; AD The City 06-09; Dir Post-Ord Tr from 06; Dir of Ords from 08. *The Rectory, 1 St Olave's Court, London EC2V 8EX* Tel (020) 7600 2379 E-mail the.rector@stml.org.uk

CROSSMAN, Ms Sharon Margaret Joan. b 65. DipCOT87. Linc Th Coll BTh93. d 93 p 94. Par Dn Chippenham St Andr w Tytherton Lucas *Bris* 93-94; C 94-96; Chapl UWE 96-02; Hon C Almondsbury 97-98; Hon C Almondsbury and Olveston 98-02; Chapl Würzburg Univ Germany 02-03; TV Portishead *B & W* 03-10; V Highbridge from 10; Chapl MU from 05. *The Vicarage, 81A Church Street, Highbridge TA9 3HS* Tel (01278) 783671 E-mail sharon.crossman@btopenworld.com

CROSTHWAITE, George Roger. b 38. Dur Univ BSc62 Fuller Th Sem California DMin83. Ridley Hall Cam 62. d 65 p 66. C Bradf Cathl Par 65-67; C Ox St Aldate w H Trin 67-70; Youth Adv CMS 70-73; P-in-c Derby St Werburgh 73-78; V 78-82; C La Crescenta St Luke USA 77-78; V Anston *Sheff* 82-83; Registrar St Giles-in-the-Fields *Lon* 83-86; V Barnes St Mich *S'wark* 86-88; Perm to Offic *Guildf* 88-93; Dir Cen Essential Psychology from 92; Perm to Offic *Derby* 01-04 and *Chich* 04-07; P-in-c Findon w Clapham and Patching *Chich* 07-09; P-in-c Bexhill St Barn from 09; Hon C Bexhill St Pet from 09. *The Vicarage, Cantelupe Road, Bexhill-on-Sea TN40 1JG* Tel 07748-575592 (mobile) E-mail rogercrosthwaite@yahoo.com

CROSTHWAITE, Howard Wellesley. b 37. St Cuth Soc Dur BA59. St Steph Ho Ox 59. d 61 p 62. C Workington St Mich *Carl* 61-63; Grenada 63-64; C Barnsley St Mary *Wakef* 64-68; V Milnsbridge 68-70; V Thurgoland 70-79; rtd 99; Perm to Offic *Sheff* from 08. *50 Low Road West, Warmsworth, Doncaster DN4 9LE* Tel (01302) 811164 E-mail howard@yogadon.co.uk

CROTON, John Barry. b 43. d 09 p 10. NSM Reading Ch Ch *Ox* from 09. *35 Vine Crescent, Reading RG30 3LT* Tel 0118-954 3134 Mobile 07704-858928 E-mail revjohnc@virginmedia.com

CROUCH, Prof David Bruce. b 53. Univ of Wales (Cardiff) BA75 PhD84 FRHistS86. NEOC 95. d 98 p 99. NSM Scarborough St Martin *York* 98-01; NSM Scarborough St Columba 01-07. *Department of History, Hull University, Hull HU6 7RX* Tel (01482) 465613 E-mail d.crouch@hull.ac.uk

CROUCH, Keith Matheson. b 45. Whitelands Coll Lon CertEd71 Westhill Coll Birm BPhil00. K Coll Lon AKC70. d 72 p 73. C Hill *Birm* 72-75; C-in-c Woodgate Valley CD 75-77; V Bishop's Castle w Mainstone *Heref* 91-98; Vice-Prin WEMTC 98-04; TV Tenbury Wells 98-02; Public Preacher 02-04; Chapl Dorothy House Hospice Winsley 05-10; rtd 10; Perm to Offic *B & W* from 05. *166 Weymouth Road, Frome BA11 1HJ* Tel (01373) 453502

CROUCHER, Jonathan Edward. b 68. Trin Coll Cam BA90 MA93. SEITE 01. d 04 p 05. NSM Lee Gd Shep w St Pet *S'wark* 04-08; C Blackheath Park St Mich 08-11; C from 11. *14 Southbrook Road, London SE12 8LQ* Tel (020) 8852 6913 *or* 7300 4758 Fax 7300 7100 Mobile 07956-649902 E-mail revjec@hotmail.co.uk

CROUCHMAN, Eric Richard. b 30. Bps' Coll Cheshunt 64. d 66 p 67. C Ipswich H Trin *St E* 66-69; C Ipswich All Hallows 69-72; R Crowfield w Stonham Aspal and Mickfield 72-81; R Combs 81-90; RD Stowmarket 84-90; P-in-c Lydgate w Ousden and Cowling 90-95; R Wickhambrook w Lydgate, Ousden and Cowling 95-96; rtd 96; Perm to Offic *St E* from 97. *6 Mitre Close, Woolpit, Bury St Edmunds IP30 9SJ* Tel and fax (01359) 240070 E-mail erictheclerc@lineone.net

CROW, Arthur. b 26. St Chad's Coll Dur BA51. d 52 p 53. C Thornhill *Wakef* 52-54; C Holmfirth 54-57; V Shelley 57-63; V Flockton cum Denby Grange 63-91; rtd 91; Perm to Offic *York*

from 91. *2 Thatchers Croft, Copmanthorpe, York YO23 3YD* Tel (01904) 709861

CROW, Michael John. b. 35. AKC63. **d** 64 **p** 65. C Welwyn Garden City *St Alb* 64-67; C Sawbridgeworth 67-69; C Biscot 69-71; V Luton St Aug Limbury 71-79; TR Borehamwood 79-87; V Markyate Street 87-00; P-in-c Flamstead 98-00; rtd 00; Perm to Offic *Ex* from 00. *216 Pinhoe Road, Exeter EX4 7HH* Tel (01392) 424804

CROWDER, George Timothy. b. 74. Liv Univ MEng96. Oak Hill Th Coll MTh07. **d** 07 **p** 08. C Hartford *Ches* 07-11; V Over St Jo from 11. *St John's Vicarage, Delamere Street, Winsford CW7 2LY* Tel (01606) 594651 E-mail gtcrowder@yahoo.co.uk

CROWDER, The Ven Norman Harry. b. 26. St Jo Coll Cam BA48 MA52. Westcott Ho Cam 50. **d** 52 **p** 53. C Radcliffe-on-Trent *S'well* 52-55; Bp's Res Chapl *Portsm* 55-59; Asst Chapl Canford Sch 59-64; Chapl 64-72; V Oakfield St Jo *Portsm* 72-75; Can Res Portsm Cathl 75-85; Dir RE 75-85; Adn Portsm 85-93; rtd 93; Perm to Offic *Portsm* and *Sarum* from 94. *37 Rectory Road, Salisbury SP2 7SD* Tel (01722) 320052
E-mail pauleen@pcrowder.freeserve.co.uk

CROWE, Anthony Murray. b. 34. St Edm Hall Ox BA58 MA61. Westcott Ho Cam 57. **d** 59 **p** 60. C Stockingford *Cov* 59-62; C New Eltham All SS *S'wark* 62-66; V Clapham St Jo 66-73; R Charlton St Luke w H Trin 73-94; rtd 94; Sub-Chapl HM Pris Elmley 94-97; Sub-Chapl HM Pris Swaleside 94-99; Perm to Offic *Cant* from 94. *4 South Lodge Close, Whitstable CT5 2AD* Tel (01227) 273046 E-mail ailsaandtonyc@aol.com

CROWE, Brian David. QUB BA92 PhD95 TCD BA98. **d** 98 **p** 99. C Ballynure and Ballveaston *Conn* 98-01; I Galloon w Drumully *Clogh* 01-02. *Ulster Unionist Party, First Floor, 174 Albertbridge Road, Belfast BT5 4GS*
E-mail brian.crowe@uup.org

CROWE, Eric Anthony. b. 29. St Jo Coll Dur BA53 MA98. Cuddesdon Coll 53. **d** 55 **p** 56. C Huddersfield St Jo *Wakef* 55-58; C Barnsley St Pet 58-60; R High Hoyland w Clayton W 60-68; V Battyeford 68-74; P-in-c Pitminster w Corfe *B & W* 75-76; V 76-90; rtd 90; Perm to Offic *Ex* 95-01 and *B & W* 02-08. *15 Gracey Court, Woodland Road, Broadclyst, Exeter EX5 3GA* Tel (01392) 460759

CROWE, Grant Norman. b. 74. Keele Univ LLB96. Cranmer Hall Dur 00. **d** 03 **p** 04. C Burton All SS w Ch Ch *Lich* 03-07; TV Cen Telford from 07. *The Vicarage, 40 Church Road, Dawley, Telford TF4 2AS* Tel (01952) 501655

CROWE, Canon John Yeomans. b. 39. Keble Coll Ox BA62 MA66. Linc Th Coll 62. **d** 64 **p** 65. C Tettenhall Regis *Lich* 64-67; C Caversham *Ox* 67-71; V Hampton *Worc* 72-76; P-in-c Leek St Edw *Lich* 76-79; TR Leek 79-83; TR Leek and Meerbrook 83-87; RD Leek 82-87; TR Dorchester and V Warborough *Ox* 87-04; RD Aston and Cuddesdon 93-02; Hon Can Ch Ch 94-04; rtd 04. *9 Pierrepont Road, Leominster HR6 8RB* Tel (01568) 611081 E-mail john.crowe90@ntlworld.com

CROWE, Leonard Charles. b 25. S Dios Minl Tr Scheme 80. **d** 82 **p** 83. NSM Buxted and Hadlow Down *Chich* 82-84; NSM Fairlight 84-86; P-in-c 86-89; V 89-92; RD Rye 93-95; Perm to Offic 95-98; Hon C Ashburnham w Penhurst 98-99; rtd 99; Perm to Offic *Chich* from 99. *34 Peter House, Church Street, Bexhill-on-Sea TN40 2HF* Tel (01424) 218676

CROWE, Canon Philip Anthony. b. 36. Selw Coll Cam BA60 MA64. Ridley Hall Cam 60. **d** 62 **p** 63. Tutor Oak Hill Th Coll 62-67; C Enfield Ch Ch Trent Park *Lon* 62-65; Ed *C of E Newspaper* 67-71; Lect Birm St Martin 71-76; R Breadsall *Derby* 77-88; Prin and Tutor Sarum & Wells Th Coll 88-95; Can and Preb Sarum Cathl 91-95; R Overton and Erbistock and Penley *St As* 95-97; Dir St As and Ban Minl Tr from 96; rtd 97; Perm to Offic *Lich* from 01. *Alder Lea, Babbinswood, Whittington, Oswestry SY11 4PQ* Tel (01691) 671698

CROWE, Canon Sydney Ralph. b 32. Edin Th Coll 61. **d** 63 **p** 64. C Bingley H Trin *Bradf* 63-66; C Bierley 66-69; V Toller Lane St Chad from 69; Hon Can Bradf Cathl from 85; RD Airedale 95-99. *The Vicarage, St Chad's Road, Toller · Lane, Bradford BD8 9DE* Tel (01274) 543957
E-mail ralph.crowe@bradford.anglican.org

CROWE, Toby Nicholas. b. 70. Oriel Coll Ox BA94 Univ of Wales (Swansea) PGCE97 Cam Univ BTh09. Ridley Hall Cam 07. **d** 09 **p** 10. C Alperton *Lon* from 09. *19 Bowrons Avenue, Wembley HA0 4QS* E-mail toby.crowe@rocketmail.com

CROWHURST, Preb David Brian. b. 40. Qu Coll Birm 77. **d** 80 **p** 81. NSM Ribbesford w Bewdley and Dowles *Worc* 80-82; Hon Chapl Birm Cathl 81-82; C Kidderminster St Jo *Worc* 82-83; C-in-c Wribbenhall 83-84; P-in-c 84-87; V Oswestry St Oswald *Lich* 87-94; P-in-c Oswestry H Trin 93-94; V Oswestry 94-08; P-in-c Rhydycroesau 90-91; R 91-08; RD Oswestry 95-01; Preb Lich Cathl 00-08; rtd 08; Perm to Offic *Heref* and *Lich* from 08. *The Old Hall Coach House, Main Road, Dorrington, Shrewsbury SY5 7JD* Tel (01743) 718049 Mobile 07885-021878
E-mail d.crowhurst@btinternet.com

CROWIE, Hermon John. b 41. Kelham Th Coll 61. **d** 69 **p** 73. C Sneinton St Cypr *S'well* 69; C Balderton 72-75; V Basford St Aid

75-78; R Everton and Mattersey w Clayworth 78-84; St Helena 84-89; Chapl HM Pris Nor 89-91; Chapl HM Pris Cant 91-02; Bulgaria from 02. *Nova Mahala 6191, Municipality Nikolaevo, Stara Zagora, Bulgaria*

CROWLE, Sarah Ann. *See* BROUGH, Mrs Sarah Ann

CROWLEY, Mrs Jennifer Eileen. b 55. CITC 00. **d** 03 **p** 04. NSM Waterford w Killea, Drumcannon and Dunhill *C & O* 03-07; NSM New w Old Ross, Whitechurch, Fethard etc 07-10; Chapl Waterford Regional Hosp from 10. *Glen, Stradbally, Kilmacthomas, Co Waterford, Republic of Ireland* Tel (00353) (51) 293143 Mobile 87-780 0257
E-mail jcrowleyglen@gmail.com

CROWLEY, Melanie. b 55. **d** 10 **p** 11. NSM St Alb St Mich *St Alb* from 10. *14 Ravenscroft, Harpenden AL5 1ST* Tel (01582) 769234

CROWN, Ola. **d** 06 **p** 07. NSM Walworth St Jo *S'wark* from 06. *23 Dawes House, Orb Street, London SE17 1RE*

✠**CROWTHER, The Rt Revd Clarence Edward.** b 29. Leeds Univ BA50 LLB52 LLM53 California Univ PhD75. Cuddesdon Coll 55. **d** 56 **p** 57 **c** 65. C Ox SS Phil and Jas 56-59; Episc Chapl California Univ USA 59-64; Dean Kimberley S Africa 64-65; Bp Kimberley and Kuruman 65-67; Asst Bp California 70-84; Asst Bp Los Angeles from 84. *289 Moreton Bay Lane Nr 2, Goleta CA 93117, USA* Tel (001) (805) 683 1016 E-mail cctravel@west.net

CROWTHER, Donald James. b 23. Oak Hill NSM Course 80. **d** 82 **p** 83. NSM Seal St Lawr *Roch* 82-85; NSM Sevenoaks St Nic 85-87; P-in-c Sevenoaks Weald 87-90; Perm to Offic 90-08. *2 Summerhill Court, 9-11 South Park, Sevenoaks TN13 1DR* Tel (01732) 461179
E-mail djcrowther@btinternet.com

CROWTHER, Frank. b 28. Qu Coll Birm 68. **d** 69 **p** 70. C Bulwell St Mary *S'well* 69-72; TV Clifton 72-77; V Kirkby in Ashfield St Thos 77-85; rtd 86; Perm to Offic *Derby* 86-00 and *S'well* 86. *30 Bramley Court, Sutton-in-Ashfield NG17 4AT* Tel (01623) 443251

CROWTHER, Gordon Allan. b 63. Rhodes Univ BA85 LLB87. Spurgeon's Coll BD94 St Jo Coll Dur MA98. **d** 00 **p** 01. C Lancaster St Thos *Blackb* 00-03; Miss P Newcastle and Stoke *Lich* 03-08; C Kirstenhof H Spirit S Africa from 09. *38 Raapkraal Road, Kirstenhof, Cape Town, 7945 South Africa* Tel (0027) (21) 701 201

CROWTHER, Mrs Hildred Anne. b 49. ERMC 05. **d** 08 **p** 09. NSM Oakham, Ashwell, Braunston, Brooke, Egleton etc *Pet* from 08. *6 The Limes, Market Overton, Oakham LE15 7PX* Tel (01572) 767779 E-mail hildred.c@btinternet.com

CROWTHER, Stephen Alfred. b 59. **d** 87 **p** 88. C Willowfield *D & D* 87-89; I Belfast St Chris 89-92; I Kiltegan w Hacketstown, Clonmore and Moyne *C & O* 93-99; Philippines 99-00; C Kill *D & G* 00-01; I Lisnaskea *Clogh* 01-07. *128 Newcourt Road, Bray, Co Wicklow, Republic of Ireland* E-mail crowther@oceanfree.net

CROWTHER-ALWYN, Benedict Mark. b. 53. Kent Univ BA74. Qu Coll Birm 74. **d** 77 **p** 78. C Fenny Stratford and Water Eaton *Ox* 77-80; C Moulsecoomb *Chich* 80-81; TV 81-83; R Glas St Serf and Baillieston *Glas* 83-87; R Bassingham *Linc* 87-90; V Aubourn w Haddington 87-90; V Carlton-le-Moorland w Stapleford 87-90; R Thurlby w Norton Disney 87-90; V Elmton *Derby* 90-03; P-in-c Matlock 03-05; R from 05. *The Rectory, Church Street, Matlock DE4 3BZ* Tel (01629) 582199
E-mail mcrowther-alwyn@tiscali.co.uk

CROWTHER-GREEN, Michael Leonard. b 36. K Coll Lon 56. **d** 60 **p** 61. C Caterham *S'wark* 60-64; C Lewisham St Jo Southend 64-69; Chr Aid Area Sec (Berks, Oxon and Bucks) 69-78; Lic to Offic *Ox* 78-83; Dioc Stewardship Adv 83-92; rtd 92; Perm to Offic *Ox* from 92. *8 Egerton Road, Reading RG2 8HQ* Tel 0118-987 2502

CROYDON, Archdeacon of. *Vacant*

CROYDON, Area Bishop of. *Vacant*

CRUDDAS, Mrs Valerie Mary. b 52. Univ of Wales (Swansea) BSc73 St Mark & St Jo Coll Lon PGCE75. St Jo Coll Nottm 05 MA10. **d** 07 **p** 08. NSM Leatherhead and Mickleham *Guildf* 07-11; TV Schorne *Ox* from 11. *The Rectory, Rectory Drive, Waddesdon, Aylesbury HP18 0JQ* Tel (01296) 655069
E-mail marycruddas@yahoo.co.uk

CRUICKSHANK, Ian Morison. QUB BTh. **d** 04 **p** 05. C Bray *D & G* 04-07; I Kilcooley w Littleon, Crohane and Fertagh *C & O* from 07. *The Rectory, Grange, Barna, Thurles, Co Tipperary, Republic of Ireland* Tel and fax (00353) (56) 883 4147 Mobile 87-948 4408
E-mail ian.mcruickshank@btopendoor.com

CRUICKSHANK, Jonathan Graham. b 52. K Coll Lon BD74 AKC74 Keble Coll Ox PGCE75. St Aug Coll Cant 75. **d** 76 **p** 77. C Stantonbury *Ox* 76-79; C Burnham 79-82; Chapl RNR 80-83; C Burnham w Dropmore, Hitcham and Taplow *Ox* 82-83; Chapl RN 83-89; TV New Windsor *Ox* 89-01; R Itchen Valley *Win* 01-09; RD Alresford 01-09; P-in-c Newton Ferrers w Revelstoke *Ex* 09-11; P-in-c Holbeton 09-11; P-in-c St Peter-in-Thanet *Cant* from 11; Corps Chapl Sea Cadet Corps from 95. *St Peter's Vicarage, 14 Vicarage Street, Broadstairs CT10 2SG* E-mail jcruickshank@btclick.com

CRUICKSHANKS, Mrs Arlene Elizabeth Henderson. b 42. d 06 p 07. OLM Gt Finborough w Onehouse, Harleston, Buxhall etc *St E* from 06. *23 Ash Road, Onehouse, Stowmarket IP14 3HA* Tel (01449) 676123

CRUISE, Brian John Alexander. Bris Univ BA86 TCD BTh88. d 88 p 89. C Lurgan Ch the Redeemer *D & D* 88-92; I Kildress w Altedesert *Arm* from 92. *Kildress Rectory, 6 Rectory Road, Cookstown BT80 9RX* Tel (028) 7965 1215 E-mail brian@aonet.org.uk

CRUMPTON, Colin. b 38. AKC61 Sheff Univ Dip Leadership, Renewal & Miss Studies 97. d 64 p 65. C Billingham St Cuth *Dur* 64-66; C Shirley *Birm* 66-69; V Mossley *Ches* 69-75; Miss to Seamen 75-77; V Burslem St Paul *Lich* 77-82; V Edensor 82-97; V Llanrhaeadr-ym-Mochnant etc *St As* 97-00; Dir Accra Retreat Cen Ghana 00-01; rtd 02; Hon C Redmarley D'Abitot, Bromesberrow, Pauntley etc *Glouc* 02-03; Perm to Offic *Lich* from 03 and *Ches* from 04. *60 Craig Walk, Alsager ST7 2RJ* Tel (01270) 882666 Mobile 07799-183971 E-mail colin.crumpton@virgin.net

CRUSE, Jack. b 35. ARIBA67. Sarum & Wells Th Coll 76. d 79 p 80. NSM W Teignmouth *Ex* 79-85; C Ideford, Luton and Ashcombe 85-89; C Bishopsteignton 85-89; R Broadhempston, Woodland, Staverton etc 90-98; RD Totnes 94-98; rtd 98; Perm to Offic *Ex* from 98. *41 Butts Close, Honiton EX14 2FS* Tel (01404) 46567 E-mail jack@jcruse.freeserve.co.uk

CRUSE, John Jeremy. b 58. Univ of Wales (Lamp) BA79 Hughes Hall Cam CertEd87. Sarum & Wells Th Coll 81. d 82 p 83. C Newton St Pet *S & B* 82-84; P-in-c Newbridge-on-Wye and Llanfihangel Brynpabuan 84-86; Perm to Offic *Heref* 88-89; C Waltham H Cross *Chelmsf* 89-91; TV Yatton Moor *B & W* 91-00; V Shalford *Guildf* from 00. *The Vicarage, East Shalford Lane, Shalford, Guildford GU4 8AE* Tel and fax (01483) 562396 Mobile 07889-919928 E-mail john_cruse@stmary-shalford.org.uk

CRUSE, Mrs Susan Elizabeth. b 51. Middx Univ BA04. NTMTC 01. d 04 p 05. NSM Ingatestone w Fryerning *Chelmsf* 04-11; TV Halstead Area from 11. *The Vicarage, Church Road, Gosfield, Halstead CO9 1UD* Tel (01787) 273434 Mobile 07885-909837 E-mail sue.cruse@sky.com

CRUST, Mrs Erica Doreen. b 51. d 10 p 11. NSM Moulton *Linc* from 10. *3 St Guthlac's Close, Crowland, Peterborough PE6 0ES* Tel (01733) 210779

CRUTCHLEY, John Hamilton. b 62. Kingston Poly LLB85. Trin Coll Bris 99. d 01 p 02. C Barnstaple *Ex* 01-06; R Ardingly *Chich* from 06. *The Rectory, Church Lane, Ardingly, Haywards Heath RH17 6UR* Tel (01444) 892332 E-mail crutchleyfam@tesco.net

CRYER, Gordon David. b 34. St D Coll Lamp BA63. d 64 p 65. C Mortlake w E Sheen *S'wark* 64-67; C Godstone 67-70; Chapl St Dunstan's Abbey Sch Plymouth 71-02; R Stoke Damerel *Ex* 71-02; P-in-c Devonport St Aubyn 88-02; rtd 02; Perm to Offic *Truro* from 02. *9 St Stephens Road, Saltash PL12 4BG* Tel (01752) 510436

CRYER, Neville Barker. b 24. Hertf Coll Ox BA48 MA52. Ridley Hall Cam. d 50 p 51. C Derby St Werburgh 50-53; C Ilkeston St Mary 53-54; R Blackley St Pet *Man* 55-59; V Addiscombe St Mary *Cant* 59-67; Sec Conf Br Miss Socs 67-70; Gen Sec BFBS 70-86; rtd 86; Perm to Offic *York* from 90. *14 Carmires Road, Haxby, York YO32 3NN* Tel (01904) 763371

CUBA, Bishop of. *See* HURTADO, The Rt Revd Jorge A Perera

CUBITT, Paul. b 64. Sheff Univ BA86. Cranmer Hall Dur 95. d 97 p 98. C Bromyard *Heref* 97-01; V Elloughton and Brough w Brantingham *York* 01-07; R Blofield w Hemblington *Nor* from 07; RD Blofield from 08. *The Rectory, 10 Oak Wood, Blofield, Norwich NR13 4JQ* Tel (01603) 713160 E-mail revp@cubitt.karoo.co.uk

CUDBY, Paul Edward Frank. b 66. Hatf Poly BSc88. Ridley Hall Cam 99. d 02 p 03. C Bedford St Andr *St Alb* 02-06; V Tanworth *Birm* from 06. *The Vicarage, Vicarage Hill, Tanworth-in-Arden, Solihull B94 5EB* Tel (01564) 742565 E-mail paulcudby@ntlworld.com

CUFF, Gregor John. b 61. Keele Univ BSc82 LTCL07. Ridley Hall Cam 93. d 95 p 96. C Stanley *Liv* 95-99; V Waterloo Ch Ch and St Jo from 99; Hon Chapl Mersey Miss to Seafarers from 06. *The Vicarage, 22 Crosby Road South, Liverpool L22 1RQ* Tel and fax 0151-920 7791 E-mail gregor.cuff@btinternet.com

CUFF, Preb Pamela. b 47. MCSP68. S Dios Minl Tr Scheme 89. d 92 p 94. NSM Nether Stowey w Over Stowey *B & W* 92-93; NSM Quantoxhead 93-07; NSM Quantock Coast from 07; Asst Chapl Taunton Hosps 93-94; Asst Chapl Taunton and Somerset NHS Trust 94-05; Bp's Officer for Ord NSM (Taunton Adnry) *B & W* 06-09; Preb Wells Cathl from 08. *Millands, Kilve, Bridgwater TA5 1EA* Tel (01278) 741229 E-mail cuffings@hotmail.com

CULBERTSON, Eric Malcolm. b 54. Ch Ch Ox BA76 MA80 K Coll Lon PhD91. Edin Th Coll 78. d 80 p 81. C Edin St Thos

80-83; C Ealing St Mary *Lon* 83-87; R Clarkston *Glas* 87-89; Area Sec Crosslinks 89-94; I Tullaniskin w Clonoe *Arm* 94-09; Hon V Choral Arm Cathl from 07. *18 The Ash, Cookstown BT80 8TR* Tel (028) 8676 4870 E-mail ericmculbertson@yahoo.co.uk

CULL, John. b 31. Oak Hill Th Coll 56. d 59 p 60. C Radipole *Sarum* 59-66; Chapl Mariners' Ch Glouc 66-70; R Woodchester *Glouc* 70-90; RD Stonehouse 85-89; V Walton *St E* 90-94; rtd 94; Perm to Offic *Glouc* from 94. *Hillgrove Stables, Bear Hill, Woodchester, Stroud GL5 5DH* Tel (01453) 872145

CULLEN, Canon John Austin. b 43. Auckland Univ BA67 Otago Univ BD76 Keble Coll Ox DPhil86 FRSA89. St Jo Coll Auckland 66. d 69 p 70. C Papatoetoe New Zealand 69-73; Assoc P Mt Albert St Luke 73-75; P-in-c 74; Hon C Remuera St Aidan 75-78; Asst Chapl Keble Coll Ox 79-82; Perm to Offic *Lon* 82-84; Chapl and Lect Worc Coll Ox 84-86; C St Botolph Aldgate w H Trin Minories *Lon* 86-87; Dir Inst of Chr Studies 87-91; Hon C St Marylebone All SS 87-91; Dir of Tr *Win* 91-97; Dir of Min Development 97-01; Hon Can Win Cathl 96-02; Sen Asst to Bp Lon 02-04; P-in-c St Geo-in-the-East w St Paul 03-04; V Palmers Green St Jo from 05. *St John's Vicarage, 1 Bourne Hill, London N13 4DA* Tel (020) 8886 1348 E-mail john.cullen@ukgateway.net

CULLIFORD, Jane Margaret. b 48. Lon Univ MB, BS73. STETS 03. d 06 p 07. NSM Dorchester *Sarum* from 06; Bp's Adv for Wholeness and Healing from 10. *8 Grosvenor Road, Dorchester DT1 2BB* Tel (01305) 264360 E-mail janeculliford@aol.com

CULLIMORE, Jeremy Stuart. b 53. TD. Westcott Ho Cam. d 06 p 07. C New Sleaford *Linc* 06-10; P-in-c Linc St Pet-at-Gowts and St Andr from 10; P-in-c Linc St Botolph from 10; P-in-c Linc St Mary-le-Wigford w St Benedict etc from 10. *St Peter-at-Gowts Vicarage, 1 Sibthorpe Street, Lincoln LN5 7SP* Tel (01522) 530256 Mobile 07733-114280 E-mail jscullimore@btinternet.com

CULLING, Elizabeth Ann. *See* HOARE, Elizabeth Ann

CULLINGWORTH, Anthony Robert. b 42. BSc. Ox NSM Course. d 83 p 84. NSM Slough *Ox* 83-99; NSM Denham 99-02; NSM Morton St Luke *Bradf* 02-04; Perm to Offic from 04. *2 Thurleston Court, East Morton, Keighley BD20 5RG* Tel (01535) 601187 E-mail thecullies@aol.com

CULLINGWORTH (née CHAPMAN), Mrs Claire Louise. b 74. St Anne's Coll Ox BA96 St Jo Coll Dur BA08. Cranmer Hall Dur 06. d 08 p 09. C Tadcaster w Newton Kyme from 08. *83 Wighill Lane, Tadcaster LS24 8EY* Tel (01937) 830902 E-mail claire@secondmouse.co.uk

CULLIS, Andrew Stanley Weldon. b 48. Hertf Coll Ox BA69 LTh. St Jo Coll Nottm 70. d 73 p 74. C Reigate St Mary *S'wark* 73-78; C Yateley *Win* 78-82; V Dorking St Paul *Guildf* 82-00; RD Dorking 94-99; P-in-c Chilwell *S'well* 00-04; R Fisherton Anger *Sarum* from 04. *St Paul's Rectory, Fisherton Street, Salisbury SP2 7QW* Tel (01722) 334005

CULLWICK, Christopher John. b 53. Hull Univ BA75. Wycliffe Hall Ox BA80 MA85. d 81 p 82. C Nottingham St Jude *S'well* 81-84; C York St Mich-le-Belfrey 84-87; TV Huntington 87-02; Ind Chapl 02-10; Ldr York Community Chapl from 10. *64 Strensall Road, Huntington, York YO32 9SH* Tel (01904) 764608 Mobile 07792-565805 E-mail cullwick@lineone.net

CULLY, Miss Elizabeth Faith. b 46. SRN67 SCM69 RGN72. Trin Coll Bris BA88. d 88 p 94. Par Dn Filton *Bris* 88-92; Par Dn Fishponds St Jo 92-94; C 94-95; P-in-c Brinsley w Underwood *S'well* 95-98; V 98-02; P-in-c Farnsfield 02-08; P-in-c Kirklington w Hockerton 02-08; P-in-c Bilsthorpe 02-08; P-in-c Eakring 02-08; P-in-c Maplebeck 02-08; P-in-c Winkburn 02-08; rtd 08; Hon C Salcombe and Malborough w S Huish *Ex* from 08. *26 Weymouth Park, Hope Cove, Kingsbridge TQ7 3HD* Tel (01548) 561081 E-mail faith.cully@btinternet.com

CULROSS, James Fred. b 17. Lon Univ BD51. Bps' Coll Cheshunt 47. d 50 p 51. C Pateley Bridge *Ripon* 50-54; C Romaldkirk 54-55; V Middleton St Cross 55-62; R Glas St Jas 62-65; C Bramley and Grafham *Guildf* 65-67; Chapl R Wanstead Sch 67-71; Chapl Sir Roger Manwood's Sch Sandwich 71-79; R Barrowden and Wakerley w S Luffenham *Pet* 79-82; rtd 82; Perm to Offic *Pet* 77-09 and *B & W* from 82. *St Christopher's Home, Abington Park Crescent, Northampton NN3 3AE* Tel (01604) 234388

CULVERWELL, Martin Phillip. b 48. Sarum & Wells Th Coll 72. d 75 p 76. C Ashford St Hilda *Lon* 75-78; C Chelsea St Luke 78-80; Chapl RN 80-83; TV Yeovil *B & W* 83-87; P-in-c Sarratt *St Alb* 87-90; NSM Bradford w Oake, Hillfarrance and Heathfield *B & W* 90-92; R Rode Major 92-96; Perm to Offic *B & W* 07-09 and *Portsm* from 09. *8 Sandisplatt, Fareham PO14 3AG* Tel (01329) 841534 E-mail stbeon@gmail.com

CUMBERLAND, The Very Revd Barry John. b 44. Birm Univ BA67 Worc Coll Ox DipEd68. Trin Coll Singapore MDiv88. d 88 p 89. NSM Westmr St Matt *Lon* 88-90; Perm to Offic 90-96; Philippines 90-96, 98-01 and from 03; Dean Manila 92-96; Chapl Stockholm w Gävle and Västerås *Eur* 96-98; P-in-c Las Palmas

01-03; rtd 09. *85A Aurora Pijuan Street, BFRV, Las Pinas 1740, Metro Manila, Philippines* Tel (0063) (2) 875 3528 E-mail barrycumberland@yahoo.co.uk
CUMBERLAND, John Allan. b 51. Chu Coll Cam BA73 MA78. WEMTC 07. **d** 10. NSM Wenlock *Heref* from 10. *Priory Cottage, 5 The Bull Ring, Much Wenlock TF13 6HS* Tel (01952) 727386 E-mail jacumberland@btinternet.com
CUMBERLEGE, Francis Richard. b 41. AKC65. **d** 66 **p** 67. C Leigh Park St Fran CD *Portsm* 66-71; P-in-c Gona Papua New Guinea 71-75; Adn N Papua 74-81; R Popondetta 79-81; R Hastings St Clem and All SS *Chich* 81-86; V Broadwater Down 86-91; V Tunbridge Wells St Mark *Roch* 91-99; RD Tunbridge Wells 96-99; P-in-c Brockenhurst *Win* 99-03; V 03-06; rtd 06; P-in-c Ashburnham w Penhurst *Chich* from 09. *Faith Cottage, 5 The Byeway, Bexhill-on-Sea TN39 4PA* Tel (01424) 843728 E-mail cum.cum@littleoaks.net
CUMBERLIDGE, Anthony Wynne. b 49. ACIB75. Sarum & Wells Th Coll 79. **d** 82 **p** 83. C Llanrhos *St As* 82-85; R Llanfair Talhaearn and Llansannan etc 85-87; CF 87-04; P-in-c Lambourn *Ox* from 04; P-in-c Eastbury and E Garston from 04. *The Vicarage, Newbury Street, Lambourn, Hungerford RG17 8PD* Tel (01488) 71546 E-mail vicaratlambourn@aol.com
CUMBRAE, Provost of. *Vacant*
CUMINGS, Llewellyn Frank Beadnell. b 29. Natal Univ BA50 St Cath Coll Cam CertEd53. Ridley Hall Cam 65. **d** 67 **p** 68. C Leamington Priors St Mary *Cov* 67-70; V Lobley Hill *Dur* 70-74; R Denver *Ely* 74-82; V Ryston w Roxham 74-82; R St Leonards St Leon *Chich* 82-88, V Billinghay *Linc* 88-93, rtd 93. *Y Bwthyn, Coedllan, Llanfyllin SY22 5BP* Tel (01691) 648013
CUMMING, Canon Nigel Patrick. b 42. St Jo Coll Nottm 73. **d** 75 **p** 76. C Castle Hall *Ches* 75-77; C Stalybridge H Trin and Ch Ch 77-78; C Tadley St Pet *Win* 78-82; R Overton w Laverstoke and Freefolk 82-07; RD Whitchurch 89-98; Hon Can Win Cathl 99-07; rtd 07. *Pasture House, Whitsbury, Fordingbridge SP6 3QB* Tel (01725) 518248 E-mail nigel.cumming@btinternet.com
CUMMING, Paul James. b 79. Cliff Coll BA00. St Jo Coll Nottm 09. **d** 11. C Poynton *Ches* from 11. *18 Ivy Road, Poynton, Stockport SK12 1PE* E-mail cumming-no-s@hotmail.co.uk
CUMMING, Ms Susan Margaret. b 47. Man Univ BSc68 Makerere Univ Kampala DipEd69. EMMTC 82. **dss** 82 **d** 87 **p** 95. Cinderhill *S'well* 82-85; Dioc Adv in Adult Educn 85-92; Par Dn Nottingham St Mary and St Cath 93-95; Lect 95-97; Asst Chapl Qu Medical Cen Nottm Univ Hosp NHS Trust 97-03; Sen Chapl 03-07; rtd 07. *33 Upton Close, Millers Reach, Castle Donington, Derby DE74 2GN* Tel (01332) 858267
CUMMING-LATTEY, Mrs Susan Mary Ruth. b 47. Open Univ BA77 SRN69. STETS 00. **d** 03 **p** 04. NSM Ash Vale *Guildf* 03-07; NSM Cranleigh and Ewshot from 07. *38A Elms Road, Fleet GU51 3EQ* Tel (01252) 621295 Fax 815882 Mobile 07761-126354 E-mail suelattey@btinternet.com
CUMMINGS, Mrs Elizabeth. b 45. St Jo Coll Dur BA84. NEOC 85. **d** 87 **p** 94. NSM Dur St Giles 87-89; Chapl HM Pris Dur 89-90; Chapl HM Rem Cen Low Newton 90-95; Chapl HM Pris Stocken 95-96; Chapl HM Pris Frankland 96-05; rtd 05. *8 Bridgemere Drive, Framwellgate Moor, Durham DH1 5FG* Tel 0191-383 0832
CUMMINGS, John _Michael_. b 53. Ex Univ BTh07 Solicitor 87. SWMTC 02. **d** 05 **p** 06. NSM Langport Area *B & W* from 05; Chapl Yeovil Distr Hosp NHS Foundn Trust from 09. *32 Bishops Drive, Langport TA10 9HW* Tel (01458) 250449 Mobile 07966-416675 E-mail headways1@waitrose.com
CUMMINGS, Canon William Alexander Vickery. b 38. Ch Ch Ox BA62 MA64. Wycliffe Hall Ox 61. **d** 64 **p** 65. C Leytonstone St Jo *Chelmsf* 64-67; C Writtle 67-71; R Stratton St Mary w Stratton St Michael *Nor* 71-73; R Wacton Magna w Parva 71-73; R Stratton St Mary w Stratton St Michael etc 73-91; RD Depwade 81-91; Hon Can Nor Cathl 90-91; V Battle *Chich* 91-04; Dean Battle 91-04; rtd 04. *80 Samber Close, Lymington SO41 9LF* Tel (01590) 610426
CUMMINS, Ashley Wighton. b 56. St Andr Univ BD83. Coates Hall Edin 82. **d** 84 **p** 85. C Broughty Ferry *Bre* 84-87; P-in-c Dundee St Ninian 87-92; P-in-c Invergowrie from 92; Chapl Angl Students Dundee Univ 92-07. *27 Errol Road, Invergowrie, Dundee DD2 5AG* Tel (01382) 562525
CUMMINS, Daphne Mary. *See* GREEN, Daphne Mary
CUMMINS, James Ernest. b 32. Brasted Th Coll 56 Westcott Ho Cam 57. **d** 60 **p** 61. C Baswich *Lich* 60-64; V Hales w Heckingham *Nor* 64-70; V Raveningham 70-76; Perm to Offic *Heref* and *S & B* 76-08; rtd 97. *Skyborry, Knighton LD7 1TW* Tel (01547) 528369 Fax 640677
CUMMINS, Nicholas Marshall. b 36. CITC 65. **d** 67 **p** 68. C Ballymena *Conn* 67-70; C Belfast St Nic 70-73; I Buttevant *Union C, C & R* 73-78; I Mallow Union 78-83; I Kilmoe Union 83-96; Can Cork Cathl 90-96; Treas Cork Cathl 95-96; Preb Tymothan St Patr Cathl Dublin 95-01; Dean Killaloe and

Clonfert *L & K* 96-01; Dean Kilfenora and Provost Kilmacduagh 96-01; I Killaloe w Stradbally 96-01; rtd 01. *13 Borough Hill, Petersfield GU32 3LQ* Tel (01730) 269742
CUNDIFF, Mrs Margaret Joan. b 32. St Mich Ho Ox 51. **dss** 77 **d** 87 **p** 94. Broadcasting Officer *York* 75-99; Angl Adv Yorkshire TV 79-90; Selby St Jas *York* 77-01; Par Dn 87-94; Assoc Min 94-01; rtd 01; Perm to Offic *York* from 01. *37 Oaklands, Camblesforth, Selby YO8 8HH* Tel (01757) 618148
CUNDILL, David James. b 65. Leic Poly BEng88. St Jo Coll Nottm MTh05. **d** 05 **p** 06. C Leic Martyrs 05-09; Pioneer Min Leic City Cen from 09; Chapl De Montfort Univ from 10. *29 Holmfield Road, Leicester LE2 1SE* E-mail david.cundill@btinternet.com
CUNLIFFE, Anne. b 48. CBDTI 01. **d** 04 **p** 05. OLM Poulton-le-Sands w Morecambe St Laur *Blackb* 04-07; NSM from 04. *14 Coniston Road, Morecambe LA4 5PS* Tel (01524) 422509 E-mail revanne@gmail.com
CUNLIFFE, The Ven Christopher John. b 55. Ch Ch Ox BA77 MA81 DPhil81 Trin Coll Cam BA82 MA86 ARHistS94. Westcott Ho Cam 80. **d** 83 **p** 84. C Chesterfield St Mary and All SS *Derby* 83-85; Chapl Linc Coll Ox 85-89; Chapl City Univ and Guildhall Sch of Music and Drama *Lon* 89-91; Voc Officer and Selection Sec ABM 91-97; Dir Professional Min *Lon* 97-03; Chapl to Bp Bradwell *Chelmsf* 04-06; Adn Derby from 06; Can Res Derby Cathl 06-08. *1 Thatch Close, Derby DE22 1EA* Tel (01332) 553455 or 382233 Fax 552322 or 292969 E-mail archderby@talk21.com
CUNLIFFE, Harold. b 28. St Aid Birkenhead 57. **d** 60 **p** 61. C Hindley All SS *Liv* 60-64; V Everton St Chad w Ch Ch 64-69; V Golborne 70-93; rtd 93; Perm to Offic *Liv* from 93. *51 Greenfields Crescent, Ashton-in-Makerfield, Wigan WN4 8QY* Tel (01942) 202956 E-mail cunliffe@cableinet.co.uk
CUNLIFFE, The Ven Helen Margaret. b 54. St Hilda's Coll Ox BA77 MA78. Westcott Ho Cam 81. **dss** 83 **d** 87 **p** 94. Chesterfield St Mary and All SS *Derby* 83-85; Ox St Mary V w St Cross and St Pet 86-89; Par Dn 87-89; Chapl Nuff Coll Ox 86-89; TD Clapham Team *S'wark* 89-94; TV 94-96; Can Res S'wark Cathl 96-03; Chapl Welcare 96-03; Adn St Alb 03-07; rtd 08. *1 Thatch Close, Derby DE22 1EA* Tel (01332) 553455
CUNLIFFE, Peter Henry. b 54. SRN77 RSCN79 RCNT83 Univ of Wales MA93. Trin Coll Bris 92. **d** 94 **p** 95. C Carshalton Beeches *S'wark* 94-95; C Reigate St Mary 95-02; P-in-c Hemingford Grey *Ely* 02-04; V from 04; P-in-c Hemingford Abbots from 04. *The Vicarage, 6 Braggs Lane, Hemingford Grey, Huntingdon PE28 9BW* Tel (01480) 394378 E-mail peter@sjhg.org.uk
CUNNINGHAM, Arthur. b 48. Man Univ PhD95 Oak Hill Th Coll BA88 Lon Bible Coll MA89. NOC 92. **d** 93 **p** 94. C Walkden Moor *Man* 93; C Walkden Moor w Lt Hulton 93-96; Chapl Salford 93-96; C Camelot Par *B & W* 96-98; Chapl Yeovil Coll 96-97; R Berrow w Pendock, Eldersfield, Hollybush etc *Worc* 98-03; Dioc Warden of Readers and Moderator of Reader Tr 98-03; P-in-c Leigh St Mary *Man* 03-08; rtd 08. *7 Milnes Avenue, Leigh WN7 3JU* E-mail artcunningham@compuserve.com
CUNNINGHAM, Brian James. b 65. York Univ BA88. Ripon Coll Cuddesdon BA91. **d** 92 **p** 93. C Merrow *Guildf* 92-96; C Kennington St Jo w St Jas *S'wark* 96-99; Chapl Pangbourne Coll 99-11; Chapl Oundle Sch from 11. *Oundle School, New Street, Oundle, Peterborough PE8 4GH* Tel (01832) 277122
CUNNINGHAM, John James. b 50. TCD Div Sch BTh98. **d** 98 **p** 99. C Drumachose *D & R* 98-01; I Camus-juxta-Bann 01-06; I Ballymoney w Finvoy and Rasharkin *Conn* 06-11; I Ballynascarrett *D & D* from 11. *155 Upper Newtownards Road, Belfast BT4 3HX*
CUNNINGHAM, Philip John. b 52. St Jo Coll Dur BA74 PGCE75 MA85. NOC 93. **d** 95 **p** 96. NSM York St Luke 95-97; NSM York St Olave w St Giles 97-99; TV Haxby w Wigginton 99-02; V Gosforth St Nic *Newc* from 02; AD Newc Cen from 05. *The Vicarage, 17 Rectory Road, Gosforth, Newcastle upon Tyne NE3 1XR* Tel 0191-285 1326 E-mail philipcunningham@hotmail.com
CUNNINGHAM, Richard Martin. b 61. Goldsmiths' Coll Lon BEd84. SAOMC 95. **d** 98 **p** 99. NSM Kingham w Churchill, Daylesford and Sarsden *Ox* 98-01; NSM Chipping Norton 01-02; NSM Ox St Andr from 01. *Churchill Mill, Sarsden Halt, Churchill, Chipping Norton OX7 6NT* Tel (01608) 659426 Fax 659134 E-mail richard.cunningham@standrewsoxford.org.uk
CUNNINGHAM, Wendy. b 42. SAOMC 01. **d** 95. NSM Hook Norton w Gt Rollright, Swerford etc *Ox* from 04. *Dewlands, Church End, Great Rollright, Chipping Norton OX7 5RX* Tel (01608) 737135
CUNNINGTON, Andrew Thomas. b 56. Southn Univ BTh86. Sarum & Wells Th Coll 82. **d** 85 **p** 86. C Ifield *Chich* 85-89; TV Haywards Heath St Wilfrid 89-94; V Midhurst 94-06; R Woolbeding 94-06; RD Midhurst 03-06; V Redhill St Matt *S'wark* from 06; Jt Dir of IME Croydon Area from 09. *St Matthew's Vicarage, 27 Ridgeway Road, Redhill RH1 6PQ* Tel (01737) 761568

CUNNINGTON, Miss Averil. b 41. St Mary's Coll Chelt CertEd61 Man Univ BA68 MEd73. NOC 93. **d** 95 **p** 96. Hd Mistress Counthill Sch Oldham 84-96; NSM Milnrow *Man* 95-98; NSM Hey 98-02; Lic Preacher 02-05; Tutor NOC 98-05; Perm to Offic *Heref* 05-10 and *Man* from 10. *6 Summerhill View, Denshaw, Oldham OL3 5TB*

CUNNINGTON, Howard James. b 56. Southn Univ BA77 St Jo Coll Dur PGCE78. Trin Coll Bris 90. **d** 92 **p** 93. C Ex St Leon w H Trin 92-96; V Sandown Ch Ch and Lower Sandown St Jo *Portsm* 96-04; Perm to Offic from 04. *5 The Mall, Lake Hill, Sandown PO36 9ED* E-mail howard@cunnington.org.uk

CUPITT, Don. b 34. Trin Hall Cam BA55 MA58 Bris Univ Hon DLitt84. Westcott Ho Cam 57. **d** 59 **p** 60. C Salford St Phil w St Steph *Man* 59-62; Vice-Prin Westcott Ho Cam 62-66; Dean Em Coll Cam 66-91; Asst Lect Div Cam Univ 68-73; Lect 73-96; rtd 96; Life Fell Em Coll Cam from 96. *Emmanuel College, Cambridge CB2 3AP* Tel (01223) 334200

CURD, Preb Christine Veronica. b 51. Bris Univ BA Leic Univ MSc05. Oak Hill Th Coll 84 WMMTC 88. **d** 89 **p** 94. NSM Widecombe-in-the-Moor, Leusdon, Princetown etc *Ex* 89-93; NSM Bovey Tracey SS Pet, Paul and Thos w Hennock 94-97; Asst Chapl HM Pris Channings Wood 92-01; Chapl HM Pris Ex 01-10; Bp's Officer for Pris *Ex* from 10; Preb Ex Cathl from 05. *The Old Deanery, The Cloisters, Cathedral Close, Exeter EX1 1HS* E-mail christine.curd@exeter.anglican.org

CURD, Clifford John Letsom. b 45. SRN RNT. Oak Hill Th Coll 84. **d** 86 **p** 87. C Stone Ch Ch *Lich* 86-89; TV Widecombe-in-the-Moor, Leusdon, Princetown etc *Ex* 89-93; P-in-c Ilsington 93-04; rtd 05. *c/o Crockford, Church House, Great Smith Street, London SW1P 3AZ* E-mail cliff-chris@ccurd.freeserve.co.uk

CURL, Roger William. b 50. BA BD DPhil. Oak Hill Th Coll. **d** 82 **p** 83. C Cromer *Nor* 82-86; C Sevenoaks St Nic *Roch* 86-88; V Fulham St Mary N End *Lon* from 88. *St Mary's Vicarage, 2 Edith Road, London W14 9BA* Tel (020) 7602 1996 E-mail stmarys.westken@london.anglican.org

CURNEW, Brian Leslie. b 48. Qu Coll Ox BA69 DPhil77 MA77. Ripon Coll Cuddesdon 77. **d** 79 **p** 80. C Sandhurst *Ox* 79-82; Tutor St Steph Ho Ox 82-87; V Fishponds St Mary *Bris* 87-94; TR Ludlow *Heref* 94-09; P-in-c Bitterley w Middleton, Stoke St Milborough etc 09; Preb Heref Cathl 02-09; P-in-c Headcorn *Cant* 09-11; P-in-c Sutton Valence w E Sutton and Chart Sutton 09-11; V Headcorn and The Suttons from 11. *The Vicarage, 64 Oak Lane, Headcorn, Ashford TN27 9TB* Tel (01622) 860403 E-mail briancurnew@btinternet.com

CURNOCK, Canon Karen Susan. b 50. Nottm Univ BTh78. Linc Th Coll 74. **d** 95 **p** 97. NSM Graffoe Gp *Linc* 95-96; Dioc Sec *Sarum* 96-03; NSM Chalke Valley 96-03; V Buckland Newton, Cerne Abbas, Godmanstone etc 03-10; Can and Preb Sarum Cathl 02-10; RD Dorchester 06-09; rtd 10. *Stoneacre, Castle Hill, Seaton EX12 2QP* E-mail kcurnock@dsl.pipex.com

CURNOW, Terence Peter. b 37. Univ of Wales (Lamp) BA62. **d** 63 **p** 64. C Llanishen and Lisvane 63-71; Youth Chapl 67-71; Asst Chapl K Coll Taunton 71-74; Chapl Taunton Sch 74-84; Ho Master 84-98; Perm to Offic *B & W* from 84; rtd 02. *19 Stonegallows, Taunton TA1 5JW* Tel (01823) 330003

CURRAH, Michael Ewart. b 31. Down Coll Cam BA54 MA58. Sarum Th Coll 54. **d** 56 **p** 57. C Calne *Sarum* 56-60; V Southbroom 60-69; Perm to Offic 70-88; Asst Master Woodroffe Sch Lyme Regis 71-85; Hon C Taunton H Trin *B & W* 88-96; rtd 96; Perm to Offic *B & W* 96-06 and *Leic* from 06. *14 Latimer Crescent, Market Harborough LE16 8AP* Tel (01858) 433706

CURRAN, John Henry. b 77. Nottm Univ BA00. Wycliffe Hall Ox 00. **d** 02 **p** 03. C W Bridgford *S'well* 02-05; Perm to Offic 05-07; P-in-c Wollaton Park from 07; Chapl Nottm Univ from 07. *St Mary's Vicarage, Wollaton Hall Drive, Nottingham NG8 1AF* Tel 0115-978 4914 E-mail henry@curransonline.co.uk

CURRAN, The Ven Patrick Martin Stanley. b 56. K Coll (NS) BA80 Southn Univ AShed. Chich Th Coll 80. **d** 84 **p** 85. C Heavitree w Ex St Paul 84-87; Bp's Chapl to Students *Bradf* 87-93; Chapl Bonn w Cologne *Eur* 93-00; Chapl Vienna from 00; Can Malta Cathl from 00; Adn E Adnry from 02. *The British Embassy, Jaurèsgasse 12, A-1030 Vienna, Austria* Tel and fax (0043) (1) 714 8900 *or* 718 5902 E-mail office@christchurchvienna.org

CURRAN, Thomas Heinrich. b 49. Toronto Univ BA72 Dalhousie Univ Canada MA75 Hatf Coll Dur PhD91. Atlantic Sch of Th MTS80. **d** 78 **p** 79. Canada 77-81 and from 92; Chapl Hatf Coll Dur 88-92. *PO Box 28010 RPO Tacoma, Dartmouth NS B2W 6E2, Canada*

CURRELL, Linda Anne. See SCOTT, Mrs Linda Anne

CURRER, Caroline Mary. b 49. Keele Univ BA71 Warwick Univ PhD86 Anglia Ruskin Univ MA09 CQSW71. EAMTC 02. **d** 04 **p** 05. NSM Stansted Mountfitchet w Birchanger and Farnham *Chelmsf* 04-09; P-in-c Poynings w Edburton, Newtimber and Pyecombe *Chich* from 09. *The Rectory, The Street, Poynings, Brighton BN45 7AQ* Tel (01273) 857456 E-mail c.currer@btinternet.com

CURRIE, Alan Richard. b 58. St Andr Univ MA82 Aber Univ DipEd83. NEOC 97. **d** 00 **p** 01. NSM Haydon Bridge and Beltingham w Henshaw *Newc* 00-05; NSM St John Lee and Warden w Newbrough 05-08; NSM Hexham from 08. *35 Dotland Close, Eastwood Grange, Hexham NE46 1UF* Tel (01434) 607614

CURRIE, Daniel Robert. b 71. Trin Coll Bris 07. **d** 09 **p** 10. C Gorleston St Andr *Nor* from 09. *2 Elmgrove Road, Gorleston, Great Yarmouth NR31 7PP* E-mail revdcurrie@gmail.com

CURRIE, John Stuart. b 47. SEITE 94. **d** 97 **p** 98. C S Chatham H Trin *Roch* 97-01; TV from 01; Dioc Ecum Officer from 09. *The Team Vicarage, 18 Marion Close, Walderslade, Chatham ME5 9QA* Tel and fax (01634) 684888 Mobile 07803-283917 E-mail john.currie@diocese-rochester.org

CURRIE, Canon Stuart William. b 53. Hertf Coll Ox MA79 Fitzw Coll Cam BA85 CertEd. Westcott Ho Cam 82. **d** 85 **p** 86. C Whitley Ch Ch *Ox* 85-89; TV Banbury 89-94; V Barbourne *Worc* from 94; Hon Can Worc Cathl from 09. *St Stephen's Vicarage, 1 Beech Avenue, Worcester WR3 8PZ* Tel (01905) 452169 E-mail sw.currie@virgin.net

CURRIE, Walter. b 39. Tyndale Hall Bris 64. **d** 67 **p** 68. C Cromer *Nor* 67-70; C Macclesfield St Mich *Ches* 70-74; R Postwick *Nor* 74-87; Chapl Jas Paget Hosp Gorleston 87-94; Chapl Jas Paget Hosp NHS Trust Gorleston 94-01; rtd 01; Perm to Offic *Nor* from 01. *11 Langham Green, Blofield, Norwich NR13 4LD* Tel (01603) 713484 E-mail currie-w@tiscali.co.uk

CURRIN, John. b 56. Keele Univ CertEd78. St Jo Coll Nottm MA93. **d** 93 **p** 94. C Eastwood *S'well* 93-97; P-in-c Matlock Bath and Cromford *Derby* 97-02, V 02-06, R Dibden *Win* from 06. *The Rectory, Beaulieu Road, Dibden Purlieu, Southampton SO45 4PT* Tel (023) 8084 3204

CURRY, Anthony Bruce. b 31. St Edm Hall Ox BA53 MA56 ARCO49. Wells Th Coll 53. **d** 55 **p** 56. C Northfleet *Roch* 55-56; Chapl K Sch Cant 56-61; R Penshurst *Roch* 61-75; Dir Music Kelly Coll Tavistock 75-85; Hon C Calstock *Truro* 75-85; R Brasted *Roch* 85-93; rtd 93. *Monta Rosa, King Street, Gunnislake PL18 9JU* Tel and fax (01822) 834133

CURRY, Canon Bruce. b 39. Dur Univ BA61. Wells Th Coll 61. **d** 63 **p** 64. C Shepton Mallet *B & W* 63-67; C Cheam *S'wark* 67-71; R W Walton *Ely* 71-78; V St Neots 78-94; P-in-c Everton w Tetworth 94-98; P-in-c Abbotsley 94-99; P-in-c Waresley 94-99; P-in-c Gt w Lt Gransden 98-99; R Gt Gransden and Abbotsley and Lt Gransden etc 99-04; RD St Neots 90-02; Hon Can Ely Cathl 98-04; rtd 04; Perm to Offic *Ely* from 05. *10 Ravens Court, Ely CB6 3ED* Tel (01353) 661494 E-mail janeandbruce@waitrose.com

CURRY, David John. b 24. St Cath Coll Cam BA48 MA58. Oak Hill Th Coll 73. **d** 74 **p** 75. C Watford *St Alb* 74-77; V Whitehall Park St Andr Hornsey Lane *Lon* 77-82; R Heydon w Gt and Lt Chishill *Chelmsf* 82-88; rtd 89; Perm to Offic *Chich* from 89. *Little Compton, Compton Road, Lindfield, Haywards Heath RH16 2JZ* Tel (01444) 487206

CURRY, George Robert. b 51. JP90. Bede Coll Dur BA72 Newc Univ MA97. Cranmer Hall Dur Oak Hill Th Coll. **d** 76 **p** 77. C Denton Holme *Carl* 76-81; V Low Elswick *Newc* 81-06; P-in-c High Elswick St Paul 97-06; V Elswick from 06. *St Stephen's Vicarage, Clumber Street, Newcastle upon Tyne NE4 7ST* Tel 0191-273 4680 E-mail g.r.curry@btinternet.com

CURRY, James Sebastian. b 63. Hatf Coll Dur BA84. Ripon Coll Cuddesdon BTh93. **d** 93 **p** 94. C Four Oaks *Birm* 93-96; C Erdington St Barn 96-99; TV Jarrow *Dur* 99-06; R Aboyne from 06; R Ballater from 06; R Braemar from 06. *Glenmoriston, 7 Invercauld Road, Ballater AB35 5RP* Tel (01339) 755726 E-mail upper.deeside@virgin.net

CURRY, Thomas Christopher. b 47. Sarum & Wells Th Coll 71. **d** 74 **p** 75. C Bradford-on-Avon H Trin *Sarum* 74-78; Asst Chapl Hurstpierpoint Coll 78-82; P-in-c The Donheads *Sarum* 82-08; RD Chalke 87-92; rtd 08; Lic to Offic *Ex* 08-09; C Lifton, Broadwoodwidger, Stowford etc from 09. *The Rectory, Lewdon, Okehampton EX20 4DN*

CURTIS, Anthony Gordon. b 74. Selw Coll Cam BTh10. Westcott Ho Cam 07. **d** 10 **p** 11. C Morpeth *Newc* from 10. *23 Green Acres, Morpeth NE61 2AD* Tel (01670) 514724 Mobile 07969-737763 E-mail tony curtis@europe.com

CURTIS, Bert. b 20. Lon Univ BCom42 BA46. Ripon Hall Ox. **d** 46 **p** 47. C Moseley St Mary *Birm* 46-48; Perm to Offic *Carl* 74-07. *Greystones, Embleton, Cockermouth CA13 9YP* Tel (01768) 776503

CURTIS, Colin. b 47. Open Univ BA80 ALA69. St Jo Coll Nottm 83. **d** 93 **p** 94. NSM Clarkston *Glas* from 93. *78 Auldhouse Road, Glasgow G43 1UR* Tel 0141-569 4206 E-mail colin.curtis540@ntlworld.com

CURTIS, Canon Geoffrey John. b 35. Dur Univ BA57. Ripon Hall Ox 59. **d** 61 **p** 62. C Gosport Ch Ch *Portsm* 61-65; C Bedhampton 65-68; Producer Schs Broadcasting Dept BBC Lon 68-75; Dioc Communications Adv *Guildf* 75-00; P-in-c Grayswood 75-91; Dir Grayswood Studio 84-00; Hon Can Guildf Cathl 87-00; rtd 00; Perm to Offic *Guildf* from 00.

1 Clairville, Woodside Road, Chiddingfold, Godalming GU8 4QY Tel (01428) 685943

CURTIS, Gerald Arthur. b 46. Lon Univ BA69. Sarum & Wells Th Coll 85. d 87 p 88. C Allington and Maidstone St Pet *Cant* 87-90; TV Gt Grimsby St Mary and St Jas *Linc* 90-95; P-in-c Morton w Hacconby 95-96; R Ringstone in Aveland Gp 96-02; rtd 03. *Le Val, 61560 Saint-Germain-de-Martigny, France* E-mail gacurt@btinternet.com

CURTIS, Mrs Jacqueline Elaine. b 60. Sarum & Wells Th Coll 87. d 90 p 94. Par Dn Bridport *Sarum* 90-94; C 94-95; TV Melbury 95-00; TV Maltby *Sheff* 00-02; TR 02-08; TR Crosslacon *Carl* from 08. *The Vicarage, Trumpet Road, Cleator CA23 3EF* Tel (01946) 810510 E-mail j.curtis@dogcollar.org.uk

CURTIS, Canon Jane Darwent. b 64. Leic Univ BA86. Linc Th Coll BTh93. d 93 p 94. Par Dn Oadby *Leic* 93-94; C 94-96; Chapl De Montfort Univ 96-03; C Leic H Spirit 96-97; TV 97-03; TV Gilmorton, Peatling Parva, Kimcote etc 03-09; Bp's Adv for Women's Min from 04; V Whatborough Gp from 09; Officer for IME 4-7 from 09; Hon Can Leic Cathl from 06. *The Vicarage, Oakham Road, Tilton on the Hill, Leicester LE7 9LB* Tel 0116-259 7244 E-mail jcurtis@leicester.anglican.org

CURTIS, John Durston. b 43. Lich Th Coll 65. d 68 p 69. C Coseley Ch Ch *Lich* 68-71; C Sedgley All SS 71-74; CF 74-79; P-in-c Newton Valence *Win* 79-82; P-in-c Selborne 79-82; R Newton Valence, Selborne and E Tisted w Colemore 82-87; R Marchwood 87-09; AD Lyndhurst 05-08; rtd 09; Perm to Offic *Nor* from 09. *7 Pearce Road, Diss IP22 4YF* Tel (01379) 640036 E-mail john.curtis@care4free.net

CURTIS, Layton Richard. b 61. Leic Univ BSc84 PGCE85. Linc Th Coll BTh93. d 93 p 94. C Knighton St Mary Magd *Leic* 93-96; C Leic St Phil 96-01; P-in-c Wigston Magna from 01. *The Vicarage, Oakham Road, Tilton-on-the-Hill, Leicester LE7 9LB* Tel 0116-259 7244 Mobile 07855-746041 E-mail rcurtis@leicester.anglican.org

CURTIS, Mrs Marian Ruth. b 54. Nottm Univ BA75 CQSW80. Trin Coll Bris 03. d 05 p 06. C Blackheath Park St Mich *S'wark* 05-08; Asst Chapl Salisbury NHS Foundn Trust 08-09; P-in-c Slindon, Eartham and Madehurst *Chich* from 09. *The Rectory, Dyers Lane, Slindon, Arundel BN18 0RE* Tel (01243) 814725 E-mail mariancurtis@btinternet.com

CURTIS, Peter Bernard. b 35. St Pet Hall Ox BA60 MA64. Westcott Ho Cam 60. d 62 p 63. C Warsop *S'well* 62-65; Chapl Dur Univ 65-69; V Worle *B & W* 69-78; R Crewkerne w Wayford 78-00; rtd 00; Perm to Offic *B & W* from 01. *The Old Farmhouse, 28 Millstream Gardens, Wellington TA21 0AA* Tel (01823) 662638

CURTIS, Ronald Victor. b 47. SAOMC 98. d 01 p 02. NSM Shipton-under-Wychwood w Milton, Fifield etc *Ox* 01-05; P-in-c Stourbridge St Thos *Worc* from 05. *St Thomas's Vicarage, 34 South Road, Stourbridge DY8 3YB* Tel (01384) 392401

CURTIS, Mrs Susan Anne. b 51. Birm Univ CertEd72 Open Univ BA79. d 07 p 08. OLM Epsom Common Ch Ch *Guildf* from 07. *11 Epsom College, College Road, Epsom KT17 4JH* E-mail curtis-s@epsomcollege.org.uk

CURTIS, Thomas John. b 32. Pemb Coll Ox BA55 MA59 Lon Univ BD58. Clifton Th Coll 55. d 58 p 59. C Wandsworth All SS *S'wark* 58-61; Chile 61-71; R Saxmundham *St E* 71-77; V Cheltenham St Mark *Glouc* 77-84; TR 84-86; V Chipping Norton *Ox* 86-95; rtd 95; Hon Dioc Rep SAMS *St E* 95-01; Perm to Offic *Glouc* and *Worc* from 01. *60 Courtney Close, Tewkesbury GL20 5FB* Tel (01684) 295298 E-mail curtistomjon@aol.com

CURTIS, Timothy. d 08 p 09. NSM Cheltenham St Mary w St Matt *Glouc* from 08. *1 Benhall Avenue, Cheltenham GL51 6AF*

CURWEN, Canon David. b 38. St Cath Coll Cam BA62. Cuddesdon Coll 62. d 64 p 65. C Orford St Andr *Liv* 64-67; Ind Chapl *Cant* 67-77 and 83-84; C S'wark Ch Ch 78-83; Ind Chapl *S'wark* 78-83 and 85-88; Dioc Soc Resp Adv *St E* 88-93; Dioc Adv for CME 93-97; R Capel St Mary w Lt and Gt Wenham 97-03; Hon Can St E Cathl 97-03; rtd 03; Perm to Offic *St E* from 03. *41 Cuckfield Avenue, Ipswich IP3 8SA* Tel (01473) 272706

CURZEN, Prof Peter. b 31. Lon Univ BSc52 MB, BS55 MD66 MRCOG62 FRCOG70. Sarum & Wells Th Coll 93. d 94 p 95. NSM Bemerton *Sarum* 94-98; NSM Wylye and Till Valley 98-00; rtd 01; Perm to Offic *Sarum* 01-04. *The Meadows, Hindon Lane, Tisbury, Salisbury SP3 6PZ*

CUTCLIFFE, Canon Neil Robert. b 50. NUU BA72 TCD BA72. d 75 p 76. C Belfast St Mary *Conn* 75-78; C Lurgan Ch the Redeemer *D & D* 78-80; I Garrison w Slavin and Belleek *Clogh* 80-86; I Mossley *Conn* from 86; Can Belf Cathl from 02. *558 Doagh Road, Mossley, Newtownabbey BT36 6TA* Tel (028) 9083 2726 E-mail rathdune@hotmail.com

CUTHBERT, John. b 52. Edin Univ BSc76 PhD80. Coates Hall Edin BD92. d 92 p 93. Chapl St Mary's Cathl 92-98; C Edin St Mary 92-98; P-in-c Forres *Mor* 98-03; R Arbroath *Bre* from 04; R Auchmithie from 04. *St Mary's Rectory, 2 Springfield Terrace, Arbroath DD11 1EL* Tel (01241) 873392 E-mail john@cuth100.freeserve.co.uk

CUTHBERT, John Hamilton. b 34. Univ of Wales (Lamp) BA59. Coll of Resurr Mirfield 59. d 61 p 62. C Cov St Pet 61-64; Australia 64-69; C Willesden St Andr *Lon* 69-72; CMP from 72; C Sheff St Cecilia Parson Cross 72-74; V Lavender Hill Ascension *S'wark* 74-97; rtd 97; Perm to Offic *St Alb* from 97 and *Lon* from 99. *29 The Cloisters, Welwyn Garden City AL8 6DU* Tel (01707) 376748

CUTHBERT, Vernon John. b 66. Trin Coll Bris 02. d 04 p 05. C Alvaston *Derby* 04-08; P-in-c Cleadon *Dur* from 08. *The Vicarage, 5 Sunderland Road, Cleadon, Sunderland SR6 7UR* 0191-536 7147

CUTHBERT, Victor. b 46. d 01 p 02. OLM Surbiton St Matt *S'wark* 01-11. *4 St Thomas Close, Surbiton KT6 7TU* Tel (020) 8399 8722 E-mail victorcuthbert@btinternet.com

CUTHBERTSON, Mrs Amanda. b 54. K Coll Lon BD92 AKC92 Open Univ PGCE98 Loughb Univ MA00 ALCM85 LLCM87. EAMTC 98. d 00 p 01. C Northampton St Benedict *Pet* 00-03; V Wellingborough St Mark from 03. *St Mark's Vicarage, Queensway, Wellingborough NN8 3SD* Tel (01933) 673893 E-mail revacuthbertson@o2.co.uk

CUTHBERTSON, Raymond. b 52. AKC75. Coll of Resurr Mirfield 76. d 77 p 78. C Darlington St Mark w St Paul *Dur* 77-81; C Usworth 81-83; C Darlington St Cuth 83-86; V Shildon w Eldon 86-00; V Shildon 00-04; RD Auckland 94-96; Chapl N Tees and Hartlepool NHS Trust 04-07; Chapl Tees, Esk and Wear Valley NHS Trust from 07. *Tees, Esk and Wear Valley NHS Trust, County Hospital, North Road, Durham DH1 4ST* Tel 0191-333 3423 E-mail raymond.cuthbertson@cddps.nhs.uk

CUTLER, Robert Francis. b 37. Lon Univ BSc57. Clifton Th Coll 62. d 64 p 65. C Peckham St Mary Magd *S'wark* 64-68; C Rdhill H Trin 68-70; Travel Sec Inter-Coll Chr Fellowship of IVF 70-74; Hon C Selly Hill St Steph *Birm* 70-74; Interserve Internat Bangladesh 74-93; Internat Fellowship Evang Students 74-85; Bible Students Fellowship of Bangladesh 85-93; V Rochdale Deeplish St Luke *Man* 94-99; TV S Rochdale 00-02; rtd 02; Perm to Offic *St Alb* 03-10 and *Pet* from 11. *10 Troon Crescent, Wellingborough NN8 5WG* Tel (01933) 676322 E-mail rfcutler@zetnet.co.uk

CUTLER, Roger Charles. b 49. Liv Univ BSc70 Glas Univ MPhil98. Coll of Resurr Mirfield 86. d 88 p 89. C Walney Is *Carl* 88-91; Chapl RN 91-98; Perm to Offic *Glas* 91-95; Hon C Challoch w Newton Stewart 95-98; V Gosforth St Nic *Newc* 98-01; P-in-c St John Lee 01-04; R 05-08; P-in-c Warden w Newbrough 01-04; V 05-08; R Kirkcudbright *Glas* from 08; R Gatehouse of Fleet from 08. *The Rectory, 9 St Mary Street, Kirkcudbright DG6 4AA* Tel (01557) 330146 E-mail therectory@dsl.pipex.com

CUTMORE, Simon Giles. b 72. Trin Coll Bris BA95 St Jo Coll Dur MA00. Cranmer Hall Dur 97. d 99 p 00. C Biggleswade *St Alb* 99-03; TV Chambersbury 03-09; TV Langelei 09-11; P-in-c Mill End and Heronsgate w W Hyde from 11. *St Peter's Vicarage, Berry Lane, Rickmansworth WD3 7HQ* Tel (01923) 772785 E-mail simoncutmore@o2.co.uk

CUTT, Canon Samuel Robert. b 25. Selw Coll Cam BA50 MA54. Cuddesdon Coll 51. d 53 p 54. C W Hartlepool St Aid *Dur* 53-56; Tutor St Boniface Coll Warminster 56-59; Sub Warden 59-65; Tutor Chich Th Coll 65-71; PV Chich Cathl 66-71; Min Can St Paul's Cathl 71-79; Lect K Coll Lon 73-79; P in O 75-79; Can Res Wells Cathl 79-93; Chan 79-85; Treas 85-93; Dir of Ords 79-86; Warden CSD 87-93; rtd 93. *clo J C Cutt Esq, 37 Sallows Road, Peterborough PE1 4EX* Tel (01733) 562796

CUTTELL, Jeffrey Charles. b 59. Birm Univ BSc80 PhD83 Sheff Univ MA91. Trin Coll Bris 84. d 87 p 88. C Normanton *Wakef* 87-91; V 91-95; Producer Relig Progr BBC Radio Stoke 95-97; Presenter Relig Progr BBC 97-99; CF (TA) 97-06; R Astbury and Smallwood *Ches* 99-08; RD Congleton 04-08; Assoc Lect Th Univ of Wales (Cardiff) 01-06; Tutor St Mich Coll Llan 01-06; Dean Derby 08-10. *15 Henshall Drive, Sandbach CW11 1YN*

CUTTER, John Douglas. b 31. Lon Univ BD61. Chich Th Coll 56. d 59 p 60. C Blyth St Mary *Newc* 59-62; C Rugeley *Lich* 62-65; V Rocester 65-73; V Shrewsbury St Giles 73-83; R Yoxall and Dean's V Lich Cathl 83-91; rtd 91; Perm to Offic *Win* 91; Hon Chapl Win Cathl from 98. *Little Wykeham, 111 Teg Down Meads, Winchester SO22 5NN* Tel (01962) 852203

CUTTING, Alastair Murray. b 60. Westhill Coll Birm BEd83 Heythrop Coll Lon MA03. St Jo Coll Nottm 84. d 87 p 88. C Woodlands *Sheff* 87-88; C Wadsley 89-91; C Uxbridge *Lon* 91-96; Chapl to the Nave and Uxbridge Town Cen 91-96; V Copthorne *Chich* 96-10; R Henfield w Shermanbury and Woodmancote from 10. *Henfield Vicarage, Church Lane, Henfield BN5 9NY* Tel (01273) 492017 or 495532 Mobile 07736-676106 E-mail acutting@mac.com

CUTTS, Canon David. b 52. Van Mildert Coll Dur BSc73. St Jo Coll Nottm BA79. d 80 p 81. C Ipswich St Matt *St E* 80-82; Bp's Dom Chapl 82-85; R Coddenham w Gosbeck and Hemingstone w Henley 85-94; RD Bosmere 92-94; V Ipswich St Marg from 94; RD Ipswich 96-01; Hon Can St E Cathl from 00. *St Margaret's Vicarage, 32 Constable Road, Ipswich IP4 2UW* Tel (01473) 253906 Mobile 07733-406552 E-mail david.cutts3@ntlworld.com

D

CUTTS, Elizabeth Joan Gabrielle. *See* STRICKLAND, Mrs Elizabeth Joan Gabrielle
CUTTS, Nigel Leonard. b 57. Sheff Univ BA86 BTh. Linc Th Coll 83. d 87 p 88. C Old Brampton and Loundsley Green *Derby* 87-89; C Chesterfield St Mary and All SS 89-91; V Morecambe St Barn *Blackb* 91-99; V Colwyn *St As* 99-03; rtd 03. *2 Cwm Road, Dyserth, Rhyl LL18 6BB* Tel (01745) 571496
CYPRUS, Archdeacon of. *See* HOLDSWORTH, The Ven John Ivor
CZERNIAWSKA EDGCUMBE, Mrs Irena Christine. b 59. Trin Coll Ox BA82. Oak Hill Th Coll 93. d 95 p 96. NSM De Beauvoir Town St Pet *Lon* 95-99; Chapl Raines Foundn Sch Tower Hamlets 99-04; NSM Bow Common 00-04; P-in-c Hoxton St Anne w St Columba from 04; Min Development Adv Stepney Area 04-07; Dean of Women's Min Stepney Area from 07. *St Anne's Vicarage, 37 Hemsworth Street, London N1 5LF* Tel (020) 7729 1243
E-mail irenaczerniawskaedgcumbe@hotmail.com

DA SILVA, Carlos Alberto Tome. *See* TOME DA SILVA, Carlos Alberto
DABORN, Mark Henry. b 55. Magd Coll Cam BA76 MA80 Wolv Univ QTS01 MRICS82. WEMTC 99. d 05 p 06. NSM Cleobury Mortimer w Hopton Wafers etc *Heref* from 05. *Kinlet Hall, Kinlet, Bewdley DY12 3AY* Tel (01299) 841230 Fax 841444 Mobile 07808-840992 E-mail mhd@moffats.co.uk
DABORN, Robert Francis. b 53. Keble Coll Ox BA74 MA78 Fitzw Coll Cam BA77. Ridley Hall Cam 75. d 78 p 79. C Mortlake w E Sheen *S'wark* 78-81; Chapl Collingwood and Grey Coll *Dur* 82-86; V Lapley w Wheaton Aston *Lich* 86-91; P-in-c Blymhill w Weston-under-Lizard 89-91; P-in-c Tibberton w Bolas Magna and Waters Upton 91-99; Shropshire Local Min Adv 91-99; P-in-c Childs Ercall and Stoke upon Tern 92-95; Dir Local Min Development 99-05; Dir Past Studies WEMTC *Heref* from 05; Vice-Prin from 09. *The Vicarage, Orleton, Ludlow SY8 4HN* Tel (01568) 780881
E-mail robert.daborn@btinternet.com
DACK, Miss Margaret Patricia. b 39. Offley Teacher Tr Coll TCert61. Oak Hill NSM Course 91. d 93 p 94. NSM Letchworth St Paul w Willian *St Alb* from 93. *91 Penn Way, Letchworth Garden City SG6 2SH* Tel (01462) 634956
DACK, Paul Marven. K Coll Lon AKC51 BD51. St Boniface Warminster. d 52 p 53. C Leckhampton St Pet *Glouc* 52-55; R Bourton on the Hill 55-61; R Quedgeley 61-82; P-in-c Hasfield w Tirley and Ashleworth 82-90; rtd 90; Perm to Offic *Glouc* from 90. *19 Arle Gardens, Cheltenham GL51 8HP* Tel (01242) 697297
DADD, Alan Edward. b 50. St Jo Coll Nottm 77. d 78 p 79. C Bishopsworth *Bris* 78-81; V Springfield *Birm* 81-85; Chapl Poly Cen Lon 85-86; V Hanger Lane St Ann 86-93; rtd 93. *C14 Elizabeth Court, Grove Road, Bournemouth BH1 3DU*
DADD, Canon Peter Wallace. b 38. Sheff Univ BA59. Qu Coll Birm 59. d 61 p 62. C Grays Thurrock *Chelmsf* 61-65; C Grantham St Wulfram *Linc* 65-70; C Grantham w Manthorpe 70-72; TV 72-73; V Haxey 73-90; RD Is of Axholme 82-90; V Gainsborough All SS 90-98; Can and Preb Linc Cathl 91-08; P-in-c Flixborough w Burton upon Stather 98-00; V 00-08; rtd 08. *15 Southfields Rise, North Leverton, Retford DN22 0AY* Tel (01427) 884191 E-mail peterdadd@tiscali.co.uk
DADSON, Lawrence Michael (Mike). b 29. G&C Coll Cam MA56 Lon Univ BSc(Econ)64. St Deiniol's Hawarden 80. d 92 p 92. NSM Bramhall *Ches* 92-95; Perm to Offic from 97. *14 Yew Tree Park Road, Cheadle Hulme, Cheadle SK8 7EP* Tel 0161-485 2482
DADSWELL, David Ian. b 58. New Coll Ox BA80 MA83 Brunel Univ MPhil97. Westcott Ho Cam 80. d 83 p 84. C W Derby St Mary *Liv* 83-87; Chapl Brunel Univ 87-96; Perm to Offic *Lon* 96-04 and *Ox* 98-04; Hon C New Windsor *Ox* from 04. *243 St Leonards Road, Windsor SL4 3DR* Tel (01753) 864827
E-mail d.dadswell@mac.com
DADSWELL, The Ven Richard Edward. b 46. CITC BTh98. d 98 p 99. C Cork St Fin Barre's Union *C, C & R* 98-01; Min Can Cork Cathl 00-01; I Ballisodare w Collooney and Emlaghfad *T, K & A* 01-09; Dioc Dir of Ords 03-09; Adn Killala and Achonry 05-09; rtd 09. *8 Fox Ridge, Rathfriland, Newry BT34 5FR* Tel (028) 4063 1154
D'AETH, Mrs Emma Louise Alice. b 63. Portsm Univ BA03. STETS 04. d 07. NSM Portsea St Mary *Portsm* from 07.

CUTTS [right column start]

52 Belmont Street, Southsea PO5 1ND Tel (023) 9286 2108
E-mail emmadaeth@yahoo.co.uk
DAFFERN, Canon Adrian Mark. b 68. St Jo Coll Dur BA89 MA06 FRCO98 FRSA99. St Steph Ho Ox 90. d 92 p 93. C Lich St Chad 92-95; TV Stafford 95-00; V Walsall Wood 00-03; Treas V Lich Cathl 97-03; Can Res and Prec Cov Cathl 03-10; TR Blenheim *Ox* from 10. *The Rectory, Rectory Lane, Woodstock OX20 1UQ* Tel (01993) 811415
E-mail rectorblenheim@btinternet.com
DAFFERN, Mrs Megan Isobel Jane. b 80. Ex Coll Ox BA02 MA06 SS Coll Cam BA05 MA09. Westcott Ho Cam 03. d 06 p 07. C Rugby *Cov* 06-09; Chapl Jes Coll Ox from 09; Perm to Offic *Cov* from 09. *Jesus College, Oxford OX1 3DW* Tel (01865) 279757 E-mail chaplain@jesus.ox.ac.uk
DAGGETT, Michael Wayne. b 47. Portland State Univ BSc72. Ridley Hall Cam 84. d 86 p 87. C Tyldesley w Shakerley *Man* 86-90; V Swinton H Rood 90-02; Chapl Eccles Sixth Form Coll 90-02; rtd 02. *138 Elliott Street, Tyldesley, Manchester M29 8FJ* Tel (01942) 883437
DAGLEISH, John. b 38. Goldsmiths' Coll Lon MA01 ACIB74. S'wark Ord Course 75. d 78 p 79. NSM Riddlesdown *S'wark* 78-99; NSM All Hallows by the Tower etc *Lon* 79-89; Chapl Asst Guy's Hosp Lon 87-89. *42 Brancaster Lane, Purley CR8 1HF* Tel and fax (020) 8660 6060
DAGLISH, John David. b 44. RMCS BSc70. Cranmer Hall Dur 74. d 77 p 78. C Ormesby *York* 77-79; C Kirk Ella 79-82; V Hull St Cuth 82-97; NSM Beverley St Mary 00-01; P-in-c Thorpe Edge *Bradf* 01-05; V Gt Marsden w Nelson St Phil *Blackb* 05-09; rtd 09. *13 St Barnabas Close, Gloucester GL1 5LH*
E-mail john.daglish2@ntlworld.com
DAGNALL, Canon Bernard. b 44. K Coll Lon BSc65 AKC65 Ox Univ BA75 MA78 CChem MRSC MSOSc88 CSci04. St Steph Ho Ox 72. d 75 p 76. C Stanningley St Thos *Ripon* 75-76; C Lightbowne *Man* 76-78; C-in-c Grahame Park St Aug CD *Lon* 78-84; V Earley St Nic *Ox* 84-91; Ind Chapl 85-91; TR N Huddersfield *Wakef* 91-93; TV Newbury *Ox* 93-09; Chapl W Berks Priority Care Services NHS Trust 93-01; Chapl Newbury and Community Primary Care Trust 01-06; Chapl Berks W Primary Care Trust 06-09; Superior Soc of Retreat Conductors 00-05; rtd 09; Perm to Offic *Ox* from 10; Hon Can Ho Ghana from 04. *10 Windsor Street, Headington, Oxford OX3 7AP* Tel (01865) 751854 E-mail bernarddagnall@btinternet.com
DAILEY, Douglas Grant. b 56. Nottm Univ BTh88. Linc Th Coll 85. d 88 p 89. C Leominster *Heref* 88-91; Assoc R Hickory Ascension USA 91-93; R Statesville 93-02; R Gainesville Grace Ch from 02. *3603 Tradition Drive, Gainesville GA 30506-3600, USA* Tel (001) (770) 536 0126
E-mail ddailey@gracechurchgainesville.org
DAIMOND, John Ellerbeck. b 39. St Cuth Soc Dur BA61. Ripon Hall Ox 61. d 63 p 64. C Caverswall *Lich* 63-66; Chapl RAF 66-85; Asst Chapl-in-Chief RAF 85-91; QHC 89-91; V Shawbury *Lich* 91-95; R Moreton Corbet 91-95; V Stanton on Hine Heath 91-95; rtd 99; P-in-c Pattingham w Patshull *Lich* 02-08; Perm to Offic from 08. *The Hollies, Church Street, Uffington, Shrewsbury SY4 4SN* Tel (01743) 709034
DAINTREE, Canon Geoffrey Thomas. b 54. Bris Univ BSc77. Trin Coll Bris 78. d 81 p 82. C Old Hill H Trin *Worc* 81-85; C Tunbridge Wells St Jo *Roch* 85-89; V Framfield *Chich* 89-00; RD Uckfield 96-00; V Eastbourne St Jo 00-09; Chs Relns Manager Chr Aid from 09; Perm to Offic *Chich* from 09; Hon Can Cyangugu (Rwanda) from 97. *5 Upper Wish Hill, Eastbourne BN20 9HB* Tel (01323) 501102
E-mail geoff.daintree@googlemail.com
DAINTY, James Ernest. b 46. Open Univ BA86 ALBC68. Cranmer Hall Dur 71. d 73 p 74. C Normanton *Wakef* 73-76; C Gillingham St Mark *Roch* 76-78; V Barnsley St Geo *Wakef* 78-88; Chapl Barnsley Distr Gen Hosp 78-88; Chapl Seacroft Hosp Leeds 88-94; Chapl Killingbeck and Meanwood Park Hosps Leeds 88-94; P-in-c Turnham Green Ch Ch *Lon* 94-97; V 97-06; rtd 06; Perm to Offic *Ches* from 06; Chapl Maranatha Community Flixton from 08. *10 Albion Street, Wallasey CH45 9LF* Tel 0151-638 4425
E-mail jimdainty@dunelm.org.uk
DAKIN (née HOLLETT), Mrs Catherine Elaine. b 53. Qu Eliz Coll Lon BSc74. St Jo Coll Nottm 88. d 90 p 05. Par Dn Horley *S'wark* 90-93; NSM Heydon, Gt and Lt Chishill, Chrishall etc *Chelmsf* 93-97; NSM Gt and Lt Maplestead w Gestingthorpe 97-99; NSM Knights and Hospitallers Par 99-01; NSM Fulford w Hilderstone *Lich* from 01. *20 Tudor Hollow, Fulford, Stoke-on-Trent ST11 9NP* Tel (01782) 397073
DAKIN, Peter David. b 57. Wye Coll Lon BSc79. St Jo Coll Nottm 91. d 91 p 92. NSM Southgate *Chich* 91-93; C Heydon, Gt and Lt Chishill, Chrishall etc *Chelmsf* 93-97; P-in-c Gt and Lt Maplestead w Gestingthorpe 97-99; P-in-c Pebmarsh 99; V Knights and Hospitallers Par 99-01; P-in-c Fulford w Hilderstone *Lich* from 01; Rural Officer for Staffs from 01; RD Stone from 07. *20 Tudor Hollow, Fulford, Stoke-on-Trent ST11 9NP* Tel (01782) 397073 Fax (01780) 761764
E-mail pdakin@waitrose.com

DAKIN, Reginald James Blanchard. b 25. S'wark Ord Course 66. **d** 70 **p** 71. C Preston Ascension *Lon* 70-74; C Greenhill St Jo 74-76; P-in-c Littleton 76-80; R 80-95; CF (ACF) 78-95; Warden for Readers (Kensington Episc Area) 88-95; rtd 95; Perm to Offic *Nor* 95-00 and from 01; Chapl Malta 97-99. *22 Heywood Avenue, Diss IP22 4DN* Tel (01379) 641167

DAKIN, Mrs Sally. b 58. SRN79 SCM82 RHV85 K Coll Lon MSc89 TCert92. SAOMC 02. **d** 04 **p** 05. NSM Ruscombe and Twyford *Ox* from 04. *3 Highgrove Place, Ruscombe, Reading RG10 9LF* Tel 0118-934 3909 E-mail timsal@tinyworld.co.uk

DAKIN, Canon Stanley Frederick. b 30. CA52. Roch Th Coll 63. **d** 65 **p** 66. C Meole Brace *Lich* 65-68; V 68-72; R Sutton 68-72; Hosp Chapl Nairobi Kenya 72-75; P-in-c Nettlebed *Ox* 75-81; P-in-c Bix w Pishill 77-81; P-in-c Highmore 78-81; R Nettlebed w Bix and Highmore 81; V Ealing Dean St Jo *Lon* 81-84; V W Ealing St Jo w St Jas 84-92; Hon Can Mombasa from 89; Gen Sec CA Africa from 92; rtd 99; Perm to Offic *Lich* 99-02; *Ox* from 02. *71 Rectory Crescent, Middle Barton, Chipping Norton OX7 7BP* Tel (01869) 349983

DAKIN, Canon Timothy John. b 58. SS Mark & Jo Univ Coll Plymouth BA86 K Coll Lon MTh87. **d** 93 **p** 94. Prin Carlile Coll Kenya 93-00; C Nairobi Cathl 94-00; Gen Sec CMS from 00; Gen Sec SAMS from 09; Hon C Ruscombe and Twyford *Ox* from 00; Can Th Cov Cathl from 01. *3 Highgrove Place, Ruscombe, Reading RG10 9LF* Tel and fax 0118-934 3909 E-mail timsal@tinyworld.co.uk

DALAIS, Duncan John. b 56. St Paul's Coll Grahamstown. **d** 83 **p** 84. C Pinetown S Africa 83-87; C Chingford SS Pet and Paul *Chelmsf* 87-92; V Aldersbrook 92-02; P-in-c Leytonstone St Andr from 02; P-in-c Leytonstone H Trin and St Aug Harrow Green from 11; Asst Chapl Forest Healthcare NHS Trust Lon 02-09. *St Andrew's Vicarage, 7 Forest Glade, London E11 1LU* Tel (020) 8989 0942 Mobile 07714-760068 E-mail duncan.dalais@virgin.net

DALBY, The Ven John Mark Meredith. b 38. Ex Coll Ox BA61 MA65 Nottm Univ PhD77. Ripon Hall Ox 61. **d** 63 **p** 64. C Hambleden *Ox* 63-68; C Medmenham 66-68; V Birm St Pet 68-75; RD Birm City 73-75; Hon C Tottenham All Hallows *Lon* 75-80; Selection Sec and Sec Cttee for Th Educn ACCM 75-80; V Worsley *Man* 80-84; TR 84-91; AD Eccles 87-91; Adn Rochdale 91-00; rtd 00; Chapl Beauchamp Community 00-07. *St Christopher's, The Beauchamp Community, Newland, Malvern WR13 5AX* Tel and fax (01684) 899198 E-mail jmmdalby@btinternet.com

DALE, Miss Barbara. b 48. Cranmer Hall Dur 78. **dss** 81 **d** 87 **p** 94. N Wingfield, Pilsley and Tupton *Derby* 81-90; Par Dn 87-90; Par Dn N Wingfield, Clay Cross and Pilsley 90-94; TV 94-00; C Eckington and Ridgeway 00-04; TV E Scarsdale from 04. *The Vicarage, Main Street, Shirebrook, Mansfield NG20 8DN* Tel (01623) 740479

DALE, Charles William. b 49. **d** 02 **p** 03. OLM Uttoxeter Area *Lich* from 02. *Manor Court, Kingstone, Uttoxeter ST14 8QH* Tel (01889) 500428 E-mail charles.dale@tesco.net

DALE, Ms Christine. b 62. Trin Coll Bris BA94. **d** 94 **p** 95. C Thatcham *Ox* 94-98; TV Bracknell 98-02; R E Woodhay and Woolton Hill *Win* 02-09; R NW Hants from 09; RD Whitchurch from 08. *The Rectory, The Mount, Highclere, Newbury RG20 9QZ* Tel (01635) 253323 E-mail revdc@cdsm.wanadoo.co.uk

DALE, Eric Stephen. b 24. Roch Th Coll 63. **d** 65 **p** 66. C Kippax *Ripon* 65-67; C Fulford *York* 67-69; V Askham Bryan 69-70; V Askham Richard 69-70; V Askham Bryan w Askham Richard 70-78; Chapl HM Pris Askham Grange 69-78; Chapl HM Pris Wakef 78-79; Chapl HM Pris Gartree 79-82; Chapl HM Pris Leeds 82-89; rtd 89. *31 Kirkwood Lane, Leeds LS16 7EN* Tel 0113-230 0766

DALE, John Anthony. b 42. Open Univ BSc00. Qu Coll Birm 72. **d** 75 **p** 76. C Elmley Castle w Bricklehampton and Combertons *Worc* 75-81; P-in-c 81-83; R 83-88; Hon Can Worc Cathl 87-92; V Hallow 88-92; Dioc Registrar 92; P-in-c Michaelston-y-Fedw *Mon* 03-08; rtd 08. *5 Tan y Bryn, Machynlleth SY20 8TL* Tel (01654) 703758 E-mail jadale@onetel.com

DALE, Martin Nicholas. b 55. Chelsea Coll Lon BSc76 CPA83. Wycliffe Hall Ox 99. **d** 01 **p** 02. C Stiffkey and Cockthorpe w Morston, Langham etc *Nor* 01-03; C Stiffkey and Bale 03-04; P-in-c New Romney w Old Romney and Midley *Cant* 04-07; P-in-c St Mary's Bay w St Mary-in-the-Marsh etc 04-07; P-in-c Dymchurch w Burmarsh and Newchurch 05-07; P-in-c Upper Wreake *Leic* 07-10; P-in-c S Croxton Gp and Burrough Hill Pars 07-10; V E Marshland *Ely* from 10. *The Vicarage, 37 Church Road, Tilney St Lawrence, King's Lynn PE34 4QQ* Tel (01945) 880259 Mobile 07887-554761 E-mail mndale@aol.com

DALES, Douglas John. b 52. FRHistS90 Ch Ch Ox BA74 MA78 BD89. Cuddesdon Coll 74. **d** 77 **p** 78. C Shepperton *Lon* 77-81; C Ely 81-83; Chapl Marlborough Coll from 84; Hd of RE from 84. *Hillside, Bath Road, Marlborough SN8 1NN* Tel (01672) 514557

DALEY, David Michael. b 50. Oak Hill Th Coll BA90. **d** 92 **p** 92. C Enfield Ch Ch Trent Park *Lon* 92-94; V Chitts Hill St Cuth from 94. *St Cuthbert's Vicarage, 85 Wolves Lane, London N22 5JD* Tel (020) 8888 6178 E-mail ddaley24@btinternet.com

DALEY, Judith. b 54. Sheff Univ BA94 Leeds Univ PhD03. NOC 03. **d** 04 **p** 05. NSM Sheff St Leon Norwood from 04; Chapl Sheff Teaching Hosps NHS Foundn Trust from 02. *112 Broad Inge Crescent, Chapeltown, Sheffield S35 1RU* Tel 0114-246 8824 E-mail judith.daley@sth.nhs.uk

DALEY, Preb Victor Leonard. b 38. Chich Th Coll 76. **d** 78 **p** 79. C Durrington *Chich* 78-81; C Somerton w Compton Dundon, the Charltons etc *B & W* 81-87; P-in-c Cheddar 87-88; V 88-08; P-in-c Rodney Stoke w Draycott 02-03; RD Axbridge 91-03; rtd 08; Preb Wells Cathl from 97. *Barns, Cheddar Road, Wedmore BS28 4EJ* Tel (01934) 710404 E-mail victormrwoo@aol.com

DALGLISH, David John. b 45. Heriot-Watt Univ BSc70 Open Univ BA94 Edin Univ MBA97. TISEC 07. **d** 08. NSM Melrose *Edin* from 08. *The Birks, 14 Abbotsferry Road, Tweedbank, Galashiels TD1 3RX* Tel (01896) 758803 Mobile 07858-140200 E-mail david dalglish@btinternet.com

DALLAWAY, Philip Alan. b 48. Chich Th Coll 80. **d** 81 **p** 82. C Newbury *Ox* 81-83; C Newport Pagnell w Lathbury 83-85; V Stewkley w Soulbury and Drayton Parslow 85-92; P-in-c Didcot All SS 92-97; R 97-00; V Caversham St Jo 00-07; rtd 07. *20 Applehaigh Close, Bradford BD10 9DW* Tel (01274) 614803 E-mail p.dallaway@btinternet.com

DALLEN, Julia Anne. b 58. Matlock Coll of Educn TCert79 Ex Univ BTh10. SWMTC 07. **d** 10. NSM Brampford Speke, Cadbury, Newton St Cyres etc *Ex* from 10. *5 Prispen House, Prispen Drive, Silverton, Exeter EX5 4DR* Tel 07733-673842 (mobile) E-mail juliadallen@btinternet.com

DALLEY, Mrs Gail Margaret. b 53. Cranmer Hall Dur 05. **d** 07 **p** 08. NSM Pocklington Wold *York* 07-10; V Barmby Moor Gp from 10. *The Vicarage, St Helen's Square, Barmby Moor, York YO42 4HF* Tel (01759) 307490 E-mail gaildalley@btinternet.com

DALLING, Roger Charles. b 26. Lon Univ BSc53. S Dios Minl Tr Scheme 79. **d** 83 **p** 84. NSM Lewes St Jo sub Castro *Chich* 83-84; NSM Uckfield 84-98; NSM Isfield 84-98; NSM Lt Horsted 84-98; rtd 98; Perm to Offic *Chich* from 98. *1 Avis Close, Denton, Newhaven BN9 0DN* Tel (01273) 515970

DALLISTON, The Very Revd Christopher Charles. b 56. Ox Univ BA Cam Univ MA. St Steph Ho Ox 81. **d** 84 **p** 85. C Halstead St Andr w H Trin and Greenstead Green *Chelmsf* 84-87; Bp's Dom Chapl 87-91; V Forest Gate St Edm 91-95; P-in-c Boston *Linc* 95-97; V 97-03; RD Holland E 97-03; Dean Newc from 03. *The Cathedral Vicarage, 26 Mitchell Avenue, Jesmond, Newcastle upon Tyne NE2 3LA* Tel 0191-281 6554 or 232 1939 Fax 230 0735 E-mail dean@stnicnewcastle.co.uk

DALLISTON, Mrs Michelle Aleysha Caron. b 67. Qu Mary Coll Lon BSc89 St Jo Coll Dur 10. Cranmer Hall Dur 08. **d** 10 **p** 11. C Gosforth St Nic *Newc* from 10. *The Cathedral Vicarage, 26 Mitchell Avenue, Jesmond, Newcastle upon Tyne NE2 3LA* Tel 0191-281 6554 E-mail michelleacd@hotmail.co.uk

DALLOW, Gillian Margaret. b 45. Univ of Wales (Ban) BA66 DipEd67 Bris Univ MEd87. Oak Hill Th Coll 93. **d** 96 **p** 97. NSM W Ealing St Jo w St Jas *Lon* 96-99; P-in-c Barlestone and Dioc Children's Min Adv *Leic* 99-08; rtd 08; Perm to Offic *Leic* 08-09; NSM Gabalfa *Llan* from 09. *26 Baron's Court Road, Penylan, Cardiff CF23 9DF* Tel (029) 2046 3754 Mobile 07801-650187 E-mail g.dallow@btinternet.com

DALLY, Keith Richard. b 47. FCCA77. St Jo Coll Nottm 80. **d** 82 **p** 83. C Southend St Sav Westcliff *Chelmsf* 82-85; Ind Chapl 85-93; C Southend 85-86; TV 86-92; C Harold Hill St Geo 92-93; Cen Co-ord Langham Place All So Clubhouse *Lon* 97-02; Perm to Offic *Ox* 02-05 and Pet from 05. *44 Lindsay Avenue, Abington, Northampton NN3 2SJ* Tel (01604) 414453 E-mail keithdally@aol.com

DALRIADA, Archdeacon of. See FORDE, The Ven Stephen Bernard

DALRYMPLE, Wendy. b 75. Coll of Resurr Mirfield. **d** 07 **p** 08. C Mirfield *Wakef* 07-10; Chapl Sir Robert Woodard Academy Lancing from 10. *The Sir Robert Woodard Academy, Upper Boundstone Lane, Lancing BN15 9QG* Tel (01903) 755894 Mobile 07939-513561 E-mail pristwendy@btinternet.com

DALTON, Anthony Isaac. b 57. Em Coll Cam BA78 MA82 Leeds Univ BA82. Coll of Resurr Mirfield. **d** 82 **p** 83. C Carl St Aid and Ch Ch 82-86; C Caversham St Pet and Mapledurham etc *Ox* 86-88; P-in-c Accrington St Mary *Blackb* 88-91; V 91-92; Chapl Victoria Hosp Accrington 88-92; V Sheff St Cecilia Parson Cross 92-96; P-in-c Burnley St Cath w St Alb and St Paul *Blackb* 96-98; V 98-01; R Orton and Tebay w Ravenstonedale etc *Carl* 01-07; CF from 07. *c/o MOD Chaplains (Army)* Tel (01264) 381140 Fax 381824 E-mail tonydaltonuk@yahoo.co.uk

DALTON, Bertram Jeremy (Tod). b 32. ACIB64. Sarum & Wells Th Coll 81. **d** 83 **p** 84. C Ringwood *Win* 83-86; R Norton sub Hamdon, W Chinnock, Chiselborough etc *B & W* 86-97; rtd 97; Perm to Offic *B & W* from 97. *Meadow Cottage, 8 Woodbarton, Milverton, Taunton TA4 1LU* Tel (01823) 400302

D'ALTON, Craig William. b 68. Melbourne Univ BA90 MA94 PhD99. Melbourne Coll of Div BTheol98. **d** 00 **p** 00. C S Yarra

Ch Ch Australia 00-03; C Melbourne St Pet 03-07; C Ox St Mary V w St Cross and St Pet 07-10; P-in-c N Melbourne St Mary from 10. *St Mary's North Melbourne, 430 Queensberry St, North Melbourne, 3051 Australia* E-mail craig.stmarys@gmail.com

DALTON, Derek. b 40. NOC. **d** 84 **p** 85. NSM Pool w Arthington *Ripon* 84-87; P-in-c Thornton Watlass w Thornton Steward 87-90; C Bedale 87-90; R Wensley 90-95; V W Witton 90-95; R Romaldkirk w Laithkirk 95-97; rtd 97; Perm to Offic *Ripon* from 98. *North Wing, Thornton Watlass Hall, Ripon HG4 4AS* Tel (01677) 425302

DALTON, Kevin. b 32. TCD BA65. Ch Div Sch of the Pacific (USA) BD67 CITC 66. **d** 66 **p** 67. C Stillorgan *D & G* 66-72; I Dublin Drumcondra w N Strand 72-79; I Monkstown 79-07; rtd 07. *Norwood Lodge, Shanganagh Road, Ballybrack, Co Dublin, Republic of Ireland* Tel (00353) (1) 282 2778 Mobile 87-122 4807 E-mail kevinthehumble@gmail.com

DALTON, Tod. *See* DALTON, Bertram Jeremy

DALTRY, Canon Paul Richard. b 56. St Jo Coll Nottm 90. **d** 92 **p** 93. C Ipswich St Matt *St E* 92-96; P-in-c Needham Market w Badley 96-05; RD Bosmere 01-05; R Ipswich St Helen, H Trin, and St Luke 05-09; Min for Ch and Community Engagement from 09; Hon Can St E Cathl from 10. *264 Norwich Road, Ipswich IP1 4BT* E-mail paul@daltry.co.uk

DALY, Ms Bernadette Theresa. b 45. TCD BTh94. **d** 97 **p** 98. C Taney *D & G* 97-00 and 05-06; Dir Past Studies CITC 00-04; rtd 06. *27 Southmede, Ballinteer Road, Ballinteer, Dublin 16, Republic of Ireland* Tel (00353) 86-241 9009 (mobile) E-mail berdaly@live.com

DALY, Miss Dorothy Isabel. b 40. Vancouver Sch of Th BTh74. dss 64 **d** 77. Stepney St Aug w St Phil *Lon* 65-66; Hanworth St Geo 66-71; Canada from 71; rtd 00. *26 Farquhar Place, Elliot Lake ON P5A 3J3, Canada* E-mail didaly@onlink.net

DALY, Gary James. b 63. Wycliffe Hall Ox 07. **d** 09 **p** 10. C Muswell Hill St Jas w St Matt *Lon* from 09. *8 St James Lane, London N10 3DB* Tel (020) 8442 2902 Mobile 07957-154787 E-mail gazdaly@tinyonline.co.uk

DALY, Jeffrey. b 50. Bris Univ BA73 Jes Coll Cam PGCE74 Fitzw Coll Cam BA82 MA86 Westmr Coll Ox MTh03. Ridley Hall Cam 80. **d** 83 **p** 84. C Tilehurst St Mich *Ox* 83-89; P-in-c Steventon w Milton 89-92; Asst Chapl Sherborne Sch 92-96; Chapl St Pet Sch York 96-11; rtd 11; Perm to Offic *Eur* from 07. *3 Shotel Close, York YO30 5FY* Tel (01904) 630142 E-mail fatherj.daly@cantab.net

DALY, Martin Jonathan. b 48. Woolwich Poly BSc69. **d** 05 **p** 06. C Upton (Overchurch) *Ches* from 05. *Fairfield Lodge, 1 Columbia Road, Prenton CH43 6TU* Tel 0151-670 1461 Mobile 07710-242241 E-mail martin@stm-upton.org.uk

DALZELL, Donald Paul. b 52. Qld Agric Coll BAppSc74. Trin Coll Melbourne BD77 DMin03. **d** 80 **p** 81. C Geelong All SS Australia 80-82; Chapl Turana w Winlaton 82-89; P-in-c Bulleen 90-00; Lect St Fran Th Coll 00-03; P-in-c Alexandra 05-11; P-in-c Montreux w Anzere, Gstaad and Monthey *Eur* from 11. *avenue de Chillon 92, CH-1820 Territet, Montreux, Switzerland* Tel (0041) (21) 963 4354 Fax 963 4391 E-mail chaplain@stjohns-montreux.ch

DAMIAN, Brother. *See* KIRKPATRICK, Roger James

DANBY, Shirley Elizabeth. b 49. St Hugh's Coll Ox BA72 Portsm Univ PhD76. STETS 07. **d** 09 **p** 10. NSM Cricklade w Latton *Bris* from 09; NSM Ashton Keynes, Leigh and Minety from 09. *The Old Manse, 21 High Street, Cricklade, Swindon SN6 6AP* Tel (01793) 751463 Mobile 07980-548844 E-mail shirleydanby@tiscali.co.uk

DANCE, Peter Patrick. b 31. Em Coll Saskatoon 66. **d** 69 **p** 69. Canada 69-71; C Hednesford *Lich* 71-75; P-in-c Westcote Barton and Steeple Barton *Ox* 76-77; P-in-c Sandford St Martin 76-77; R Westcote Barton w Steeple Barton, Duns Tew etc 77-89; R Castle Douglas *Glas* 89-97; rtd 97. *Mannville, High Street, Adderbury, Banbury OX17 3NA* Tel (01295) 811989

DAND, Mrs Angela Jane. b 49. St Andr Univ BSc70 Newc Univ PGCE71. **d** 98 **p** 99. OLM Astley *Man* 98-06; OLM Astley, Tyldesley and Mosley Common from 06. *20 Acresfield, Astley, Tyldesley, Manchester M29 7NL* Tel (01942) 879608

DANDO, Ms Elaine Vera. b 53. Coll of Resurr Mirfield 94 NOC 98. **d** 00 **p** 01. C Luddenden w Luddenden Foot *Wakef* 00-03; C Halifax 03-04; Lic to Offic 04-05; Chapl Univ Coll *Lon* 05-08; C St Pancras w St Jas and Ch Ch 05-08; C Northwood H Trin 08-10; rtd 10. *St Lawrence's Vicarage, 2 Bridle Road, Pinner HA5 2SJ* Tel (020) 8866 1263 E-mail evd.macrina@btinternet.com

DANDO, Stephen. b 49. Goldsmiths' Coll *Lon* TCert70. Coll of Resurr Mirfield 81. **d** 83 **p** 84. C Wandsworth St Anne *S'wark* 83-87; V Stainland *Wakef* 87-99; V Illingworth 99-05; V Eastcote St Lawr *Lon* from 05. *St Lawrence's Vicarage, 2 Bridle Road, Pinner HA5 2SJ* Tel (020) 8866 1263 E-mail dandostephen@hotmail.com

DANE, John William. b 52. St Jo Coll Nottm 04. **d** 06 **p** 07. C Deddington w Barford, Clifton and Hempton *Ox* 06-09; Chapl Chich Univ from 09. *Chaplaincy, University of Chichester, Bishop Otter Campus, College Lane, Chichester PO19 6PE* Tel (01243) 816041 E-mail chaplain@chi.ac.uk *or* john@ausome.co.uk

DANES, Charles William. b 28. Chich Th Coll 54. **d** 56 **p** 57. C N Greenford All Hallows *Lon* 56-59; C Caversham *Ox* 59-63; V Walsgrave on Sowe *Cov* 63-65; P-in-c Hanworth All SS *Lon* 65-67; V 68-76; P-in-c Wick *Chich* 76-78; V Littlehampton St Jas 76-78; P-in-c Littlehampton St Mary 76-78; V W Worthing St Jo 78-87; Chapl Monte Carlo *Eur* 87-93; rtd 93; Perm to Offic *Chelmsf* and *Eur* from 93. *31 Oakley Road, Braintree CM7 5QS* Tel (01376) 324586

DANGERFIELD, Canon Andrew Keith. b 63. Univ of Wales (Ban) BD87. St Steph Ho Ox 87. **d** 89 **p** 90. C St Marychurch *Ex* 89-93; C-in-c Grahame Park St Aug CD *Lon* 93-96; V Tottenham St Paul 96-06; P-in-c Edmonton St Mary w St Jo 98-04; AD E Haringey 00-05; V Kensal Green St Jo from 06; Hon Can Cape Coast from 04. *St John's New Vicarage, Kilburn Lane, London W10 4AA* Tel (020) 8969 2615 Mobile 07767-687954

DANGERFIELD, Miss Sarah Ann. b 66. Ripon Coll Cuddesdon 09. **d** 11. C Badgeworth, Shurdington and Witcombe w Bentham *Glouc* from 11. *25 Blenheim Orchard, Shurdington, Cheltenham GL51 4TG* Tel (01242) 863979 E-mail s.dangerfield150@btinternet.com

DANIEL, Gaynor Elizabeth. *See* DANIEL-LOWANS, Mrs Gaynor Elizabeth

DANIEL, Canon Herrick Haynes. b 38. Open Univ BA81. Trin Coll Bris 73. **d** 75 **p** 76. C Harlesden St Mark *Lon* 75-78; C Livesey *Blackb* 78-81; V Blackb St Barn 81-08; Hon Can Blackb Cathl 98-08; rtd 08; Perm to Offic *Blackb* from 08. *40 Appletree Drive, Lancaster LA1 4QY* Tel (01524) 389764 E-mail herrickdaniel@hotmail.co.uk

DANIEL, Mrs Joy. b 44. Gilmore Course 81 Oak Hill Th Coll 82. dss 84 **d** 87 **p** 94. Luton St Fran *St Alb* 84-02; Par Dn 87-94; C 94-02; P-in-c Woodside 02-10; rtd 10; Perm to Offic *St Alb* from 10. *22 Rowelfield, Luton LU2 9HN* E-mail joydaniel1@btinternet.com

DANIEL, Pamela Olive. b 52. Middx Poly BEd86 K Coll Lon MA94 Westmr Coll Ox BTh98. Wycliffe Hall Ox 04. **d** 06 **p** 07. C Kennington St Mark *S'wark* 06-10; P-in-c W Bromwich St Phil *Lich* from 10. *The Vicarage, 33 Reform Street, West Bromwich B70 7PF* Tel 07771-633035 (mobile) E-mail pamdaniel8@hotmail.com

DANIEL, Philip Sharman. b 62. Man Univ BA83 Rob Coll Cam CertEd84. Wycliffe Hall Ox 84. **d** 86 **p** 87. C Macclesfield Team *Ches* 86-89; C Cheadle 89-94; V Disley 94-07; TR Mid Trent *Lich* from 07. *The Rectory, Stafford Road, Weston, Stafford ST18 0HX* Tel (01889) 271870 E-mail revpsdan@btinternet.com

DANIEL, Rajinder Kumar. b 34. St Steph Coll Delhi 55 Westcott Ho Cam 61. **d** 63 **p** 64. C Purley St Barn *S'wark* 63-66; C Battersea St Pet 66-67; C N Harrow St Alb *Lon* 67-72; TV Beaconsfield *Ox* 72-75; V Smethwick St Matt w St Chad *Birm* 75-87; Dioc Adv on Black Min 87-92; Chapl Birm Gen Hosp 91-92; TR Braunstone *Leic* 92-01; rtd 01; USPG and R Arima St Jude Trinidad and Tobago 03-04; Perm to Offic *Birm* from 04. *508 Chester Road, Kingshurst, Birmingham B36 0LG* Tel 0121-770 1066

DANIEL-LOWANS, Mrs Gaynor Elizabeth. b 46. Llan Ord Course 98. **d** 98 **p** 99. NSM St Brides Minor w Bettws *Llan* 98-01; C 01-02; C St Brides Minor w Bettws w Aberkenfig 02-04; C Llansantffraid, Bettws and Aberkenfig from 04. *36 Heol Crwys, Cwmavon, Port Talbot SA12 9NT* Tel (01639) 891871

DANIELL, Robert. b 37. **d** 87 **p** 88. C Camberwell St Giles w St Matt *S'wark* 90-92; V Lewisham St Swithun 92-07; rtd 07; Perm to Offic *S'wark* from 10. *4 Glenhouse Road, London SE9 1JQ* Tel (020) 8850 4594

DANIELS, Geoffrey Gregory. b 23. St Pet Coll Ox BA48 MA53 Lambeth STh60. Linc Th Coll 73. **d** 73 **p** 75. NSM Diss *Nor* 73-74; NSM Bexhill St Pet *Chich* 74-83; C Eastbourne St Andr 83-84; V Horam 84-88; rtd 88; Chapl Convent of Dudwell St Mary from 88; NSM Bexhill St Andr CD *Chich* 90-95; Perm to Offic from 95. *20 Richmond Grove, Bexhill-on-Sea TN39 3EQ* Tel (01424) 211719

DANIELS, John Wyn. b 60. Southn Univ BSc82 PhD87. Trin Coll Bris MA92. **d** 92 **p** 93. C Roundhay St Edm *Ripon* 92-95; India 96; C Ambleside w Brathay *Carl* 97-01; Chapl St Martin's Coll Lanc 97-01; Res Can Ban Cathl 01-05; Min Development Officer *Bradf* 05-10; C Embsay w Eastby and Skipton H Trin 05-10; Local Min Officer *Heref* from 10. *Diocese of Hereford, Unit 8-9, The Business Quarter, Eco Park Road, Ludlow SY8 1FD* Tel (01584) 871084 E-mail j.daniels@hereford.anglican.org *or* jd001@supanet.com

DANIELS, Lee Martin. b 61. Coll of Resurr Mirfield 99. **d** 01 **p** 02. C Toxteth Park St Agnes and St Pancras *Liv* 01-05; TV Staveley and Barrow Hill *Derby* 05-10; P-in-c Blackb St Thos w St Jude from 10; P-in-c Blackb St Mich w St Jo and H Trin from 10. *The Vicarage, Didsbury Street, Blackburn BB1 3JL* E-mail mazdaz@fsmail.net

DANKS, Alan Adam. b 41. Essex Univ MA01. Edin Th Coll 61. **d** 64 **p** 65. C Dumfries *Glas* 64-67; C Earl's Court St Cuth w St Matthias *Lon* 68-71; C St Steph Walbrook and St Swithun etc 71-74; C Brookfield St Mary 75-76; C Hendon St Mary 76-85. *327 Hanworth Road, Hampton TW12 3EJ* Tel (020) 8941 6055 E-mail luccas@btinternet.com

DANKS-FLOWER, Marilyn Clare. b 42. **d** 08 **p** 11. Chapl Barts and The Lon NHS Trust 08-10; NSM Egremont and Haile *Carl* from 11; Chapl N Cumbria Univ Hosps NHS Trust from 11. *18 Lamb Lane, Egremont CA22 2AH* Tel (01946) 822913 Mobile 07967-369103 E-mail kajori1@gmail.com

DANSIE, Bruce John. b 40. Woolwich Poly BSc67 Univ Coll Lon MSc71 CEng72. Linc Th Coll 92. **d** 92 **p** 93. C Ivybridge w Harford *Ex* 92-96; P-in-c Charleton w Buckland Tout Saints etc 96-01; rtd 01. *3 Second Avenue, Murrumbeena, Melbourne VIC 3163, Australia* Tel (0061) (3) 9563 2196

DAPLYN, Timothy James. b 52. Ripon Coll Cuddesdon 92. **d** 94 **p** 95. C Southmead *Bris* 94-97; P-in-c Abbots Leigh w Leigh Woods 97-99; Dioc Communications Officer 97-99; R Clutton w Cameley *B & W* 99-04; RD Chew Magna 03-04; P-in-c E w W Harptree and Hinton Blewett 04-08. *Coillegillie, Applecross, Strathcarron IV54 8LZ* Tel 07747-464833 (mobile) E-mail coillegillie@hotmail.com

DARBY, Canon Anthony Ernest. b 26. Linc Th Coll 74. **d** 76 **p** 77. C Chilvers Coton w Astley *Cov* 76-79; P-in-c Longford 79-81; V 81-84; V Cov St Mary 84-91; RD Cov S 88-91; rtd 91; Chapl Cov Cathl from 91; Hon Can Th 00; Perm to Offic *Cov* from 00. *53 Ivybridge Road, Coventry CV3 5PF* Tel (024) 7641 4174 E-mail darby@bushinternet.com

DARBY, George. b 48. SWMTC 06. **d** 09 **p** 10. NSM Egloskerry, N Petherwin, Tremaine and Tresmere *Truro* 09-10; NSM Egloskerry, N Petherwin, Tremaine, Tresmere etc from 10; NSM Lezant w Lawhitton and S Petherwin w Trewen 09-10; NSM Altarnon w Bolventor, Laneast and St Clether 10-11. *7 Culvers Meadow, Launceston PL15 8RR* Tel (01566) 774719 E-mail gdandpd@btinternet.com

DARBY, Michael Barwick. b 34. St D Coll Lamp BA61 Tyndale Hall Bris 61. **d** 63 **p** 64. C Islington St Andr w St Thos and St Matthias *Lon* 63-66; C Ealing Dean St Jo 66-68; V Broomfleet *York* 68-73; Area Sec CCCS *York* and *Sheff* 68-73; V Paddington Em Harrow Road *Lon* 73-78; Iran 78-79; Brazil 80-83; Perm to Offic *Cant* 80-84; from 01; V Maidstone St Faith 84-90; UAE 90-92; V Platt Bridge *Liv* 93-99; rtd 99. *Paqueta, 79 Sandwich Road, Cliffsend, Ramsgate CT12 5JA* Tel (01843) 597228 Mobile 07947-582469

DARBY, Nicholas Peter. b 50. Kent Univ BA82 Surrey Univ MSc02. Sarum & Wells Th Coll 71. **d** 74 **p** 75. C Walton-on-Thames *Guildf* 74-78; C Horsell 78-80; USA 82-84; Chapl Lon Univ 84-89; Chapl R Lon Hosp (Whitechapel) 90-91; V Kew St Phil and All SS w St Luke *S'wark* 91-04; Dean Gaborone Botswana 04-07; V Fenham St Jas and St Basil *Newc* from 09. *St James and St Basil Vicarage, Wingrove Road North, Newcastle upon Tyne NE4 9EJ* Tel 0191-274 5078

DARBY, Preb Philip William. b 44. Bede Coll Dur TCert66. Qu Coll Birm. **d** 70 **p** 71. C Kidderminster St Geo *Worc* 70-74; P-in-c Dudley St Jo 74-79; V 79-80; P-in-c Catshill 80-82; V Catshill and Dodford 82-88; V Ipplepen w Torbryan *Ex* 88-00; V Ipplepen, Torbryan and Denbury 01-02; RD Newton Abbot and Ipplepen 93-01; V Ashburton w Buckland in the Moor and Bickington 02-05; P-in-c Widecombe-in-the-Moor, Leusdon, Princetown etc 04-05; TR Ashburton, Bickington, Buckland in the Moor etc 05-10; Preb Ex Cathl 02-10; rtd 10. *3 Kellett Close, Ashburton, Newton Abbot TQ13 7FB* Tel (01364) 652844 Mobile 07814-272198 E-mail pwdarby@supanet.com

DARBYSHIRE, Brian. b 48. TD04. Oak Hill Th Coll BA83. **d** 83 **p** 84. C Enfield St Jas *Lon* 83-86; R Slaidburn *Bradf* 86-92; V Gt Harwood St Jo *Blackb* 92-02; V Douglas St Ninian *S & M* 02-08; CF (TA) 90-04; V Bingara Australia from 08. *St John's Vicaraage, 8 Frazer Street, Bingara NSW 2404, Australia* Tel (0061) (2) 7624 1668 E-mail darbyshirebrian@hotmail.com

DARCH, John Henry. b 52. Univ of Wales (Lamp) BA73 PhD97 Lon Univ PGCE74 MA77 FRHistS09 FHEA04. Trin Coll Bris 80. **d** 82 **p** 83. C Meole Brace *Lich* 82-85; C Hoole *Ches* 85-88; V Hyde St Geo 88-99; P-in-c Godley cum Newton Green 89-93; RD Mottram 91-99; Lect St Jo Coll Nottm 99-06; Chapl 03-06; Public Preacher *S'well* 99-06; Perm to Offic *Derby* 03-06; Dir of Ords and Dir IME 4-7 *Blackb* from 06. *24 Bosburn Drive, Mellor Brook, Blackburn BB2 7PA* Tel (01254) 813544 E-mail j.darch248@btinternet.com

DARK, Nicholas John. b 62. Leic Univ BA83 ACIB92. CITC BTh98. **d** 98 **p** 99. C Ballyholme *D & D* 98-05; I Magheragall *Conn* from 05. *Magheragall Rectory, 70 Ballinderry Road, Lisburn BT28 2QS* Tel (028) 9262 1273 E-mail magheragall@aol.com

DARKINS, Mrs Judith Rosemary. b 45. **d** 10 **p** 11. OLM Benenden and Smarden *Cant* from 10. *5 Pittlesden Place, High Street, Tenterden TN30 6HT* Tel (01580) 765475 E-mail judy.darkins@btinternet.com

DARLEY, Canon Shaun Arthur Neilson. b 36. Dur Univ BA61 Reading Univ MSc75. Cranmer Hall Dur 61. **d** 63 **p** 64. C Luton w E Hyde *St Alb* 63-67; Chapl Bris Tech Coll 67-69; Chapl Bris Poly 69-92; Sen Chapl UWE 92-01; Lect 69-75; Sen Lect 75-01; Dir Cen for Performing Arts 85-02; Bp's Cathl Chapl 69-76; Hon Can Bris Cathl 89-01; rtd 01; Perm to Offic *B & W* from 98 and *Bris* from 02. *Church Paddock, Winscombe Hill, Bristol BS25 1DE* Tel (01934) 843633

DARLING, David Francis. b 55. TISEC 93. **d** 96 **p** 97. SSF 88-05; Novice Guardian 99-05; NSM Edin St Ninian 96-98; Chapl W Gen Hosps NHS 96-98; Chapl Edin Sick Children's NHS Trust 96-98; Lic Preacher *Lon* 03-05. *8 Church Mead, 234 Camberwell Road, London SE5 0ET* Tel (020) 7703 9794

✠**DARLING, The Rt Revd Edward Flewett.** b 33. TCD BA55 MA58. CITC. **d** 56 **p** 57 **c** 85. C Belfast St Luke *Conn* 56-59; C Orangefield *D & D* 59-62; C-in-c Carnalea 62-72; Chapl Ban Hosp 63-72; I Belfast Malone St Jo *Conn* 72-85; Min Can Belf Cathl 78-85; Chapl Ulster Independent Clinic 81-85; Bp L & K 85-00. *15 Beechwood Park, Moira, Craigavon BT67 0LL* Tel (028) 9261 2982 E-mail darling-moira@utvinternet.com

DARLING, John. b 47. Sarum & Wells Th Coll 76. **d** 79 **p** 80. NSM Trowbridge St Thos *Sarum* 79-82; NSM Trowbridge St Thos and W Ashton 82-92; NSM Melksham from 01; NSM Atworth w Shaw and Whitley from 07; NSM Broughton Gifford, Gt Chalfield and Holt from 07. *43 Horse Road, Hilperton Marsh, Trowbridge BA14 7PF*

DARLINGTON, Paul Trevor. b 71. Imp Coll Lon BSc92 K Coll Lon PGCE93. Oak Hill Th Coll BA99 MPhil00. **d** 00 **p** 01. C Bispham *Blackb* 00-05; P-in-c Oswestry H Trin *Lich* 05-10; V from 10. *Holy Trinity Vicarage, 29 Balmoral Crescent, Oswestry SY11 2XQ* Tel (01691) 652184 E-mail paul.t.darlington@ntlworld.com

DARLISON, Geoffrey Stuart. b 49. MRTPI80. St Jo Coll Nottm 89. **d** 91 **p** 92. C Horncastle w Low Toynton *Linc* 91-95; P-in-c Welton and Dunholme w Scothern 95-97; V 97-08; RD Lawres 07-08; P-in-c Thorpe Edge *Bradf* from 08; P-in-c Greengates from 08. *The Vicarage, Northwood Crescent, Bradford BD10 9HX* Tel (01274) 405421 E-mail s.darlison@googlemail.com

DARMODY, Canon Richard Arthur. b 52. Lon Univ BD90. Linc Th Coll MDiv94. **d** 94 **p** 95. C Cherry Hinton St Jo *Ely* 94-97; I Belfast St Aid *Conn* 97-99; TR The Ramseys and Upwood *Ely* 99-10; R from 10; RD St Ives 02-06; Hon Can Ely Cathl from 08. *The Rectory, 16 Hollow Lane, Ramsey, Huntingdon PE26 1DE* Tel (01487) 813271 E-mail darmodyrichard@hotmail.com

DARRALL, Charles Geoffrey. b 32. Nottm Univ BA55 MA57. Qu Coll Birm. **d** 57 **p** 58. C Cockermouth All SS w Ch Ch *Carl* 57-63; Chapl Dioc Youth Cen 63-95; V St John's in the Vale w Wythburn 63-95; P-in-c Threlkeld 85-95; rtd 96; Perm to Offic *Carl* from 98. *Piper House, Naddle, Keswick CA12 4TF* Tel (01768) 774500

DARRALL, John Norman. b 34. Nottm Univ BA57. Ripon Hall Ox 57. **d** 60 **p** 61. C Nottingham St Mary *S'well* 60-65; Chapl Nottm Children's Hosp 64-65; V Bole w Saundby and Sturton w Littleborough *S'well* 65-66; Chapl Oakham Sch 84-99; rtd 99; Perm to Offic *Leic* from 01 and *Pet* from 05. *Grange Cottage, 99 Main Street, Cottesmore, Oakham LE15 7DH* Tel (01572) 812443 E-mail johndarrall@googlemail.com

DARRANT, Louis Peter. b 77. Aber Univ BD00 Leeds Univ MA03. Coll of Resurr Mirfield 01. **d** 03 **p** 04. C Kennington St Jo w St Jas *S'wark* 03-07; R Maldon St Mary w Mundon *Chelmsf* from 07. *St Mary's Rectory, Park Drive, Maldon CM9 5JG* Tel (01621) 857191 Mobile 07949-765523 E-mail louis.darrant@btinternet.com

DARROCH, Ronald Humphrey. b 45. Trin Coll Cam BA67 MA71 Ch Ch Ox BA67 MA71. Ripon Hall Ox 67. **d** 70 **p** 71. C Kingston upon Hull St Nic *York* 70-73; Hon C 73-74; Hon C Perth St Jo *St And* from 74; Chapl Stancliffe Hall Derby 84-87; Perm to Offic *Worc* 87-98; Chapl Old Swinford Hosp Sch *Worc* 89-98. *17 Viewlands Terrace, Perth PH1 1BN* Tel (01738) 628880

DART, John Peter. b 40. St Jo Coll Ox BA62. Cuddesdon Coll 62. **d** 64 **p** 65. C W Hartlepool St Aid *Dur* 64-67; C Alverthorpe *Wakef* 67-70; Lic to Offic 70-79; rtd 05. *3 Springhill Avenue, Crofton, Wakefield WF4 1HA* Tel (01924) 860374 E-mail mail@dart.eclipse.co.uk

DARVILL, Christopher Mark. b 61. Ox Univ BA83. St Steph Ho Ox 84. **d** 86 **p** 87. C Tottenham St Paul *Lon* 86-88; C Oystermouth *S & B* 88-90; Chapl Univ of Wales (Swansea) 90-94; Asst Dioc Warden of Ords from 92; V Llansamlet from 94. *The Vicarage, 61 Church Road, Llansamlet, Swansea SA7 9RL* Tel (01792) 771420

DARVILL, Canon George Collins. b 36. Kelham Th Coll 56. **d** 61 **p** 62. C Middlesbrough St Chad *York* 61-64; C Manston *Ripon* 64-66; V Kippax 66-79; V Catterick 79-88; RD Richmond 80-86; Chapl HM Pris Kirklevington Grange 88-89; Hon Can Ripon Cathl 91-01; rtd 01; Perm to Offic *Bradf* and *Ripon* from 01. *39 Woodlea Lane, Meanwood, Leeds LS6 4SX* Tel 0113-275 7973

✠**DARWENT, The Rt Revd Frederick Charles.** b 27. JP87. ACIB. Wells Th Coll 61. **d** 63 **p** 64 **c** 78. C Pemberton St Jo *Liv* 63-65; R Strichen *Ab* 65-71; R New Pitsligo 65-71; R Fraserburgh w New Pitsligo 71-78; Can St Andr Cathl 71-78; Dean Ab 73-78; Bp Ab 78-92; rtd 92; Lic to Offic *Ab* from 92. *107 Osborne Place, Aberdeen AB25 2DD* Tel (01224) 646497

DARWENT, Thomas James. b 74. Wycliffe Hall Ox. **d** 07 **p** 08. C Claygate *Guildf* 07-11; C Guildf St Sav from 11. *16 Cunningham Avenue, Guildford GU1 2PE*

DASH, Mrs Janet Eleanor Gillian. b 47. SRN69. Cant Sch of Min 89. **d** 93 **p** 94. C Morden *S'wark* 93-96; C S Croydon Em 96-98; P-in-c Borstal and Chapl HM Pris Cookham Wood 98-05; P-in-c Darenth *Roch* 05-10; rtd 10; Perm to Offic *Cant* from 11. *5 Edenfield, Birchington CT7 9DE* Tel (01843) 448846 Mobile 07853-844509 E-mail janet.dash@btinternet.com

DATCHLER, Colin Neil. b 72. Univ Coll Chich BA01. Ripon Coll Cuddesdon 07. **d** 09 **p** 10. C Hythe *Cant* from 09. *2 Palmarsh Avenue, Hythe CT21 6NT* E-mail colindatchler@hotmail.co.uk

DATE, Stephen James. b 69. LSE BA90 Dur Univ MA92. SEITE 99. **d** 02 **p** 03. NSM Brighton Gd Shep Preston *Chich* 02-08; C Uckfield from 08. *7 Park View Road, Uckfield TN22 1JP* Tel (01825) 762304 Mobile 07747-895213 E-mail heather.stephen@ntlworld.com

DATSON, Mrs Sheila Mary. b 24. CertEd67. S'wark Ord Course 76. **dss** 78 **d** 87 **p** 94. Bexleyheath Ch Ch *Roch* 78-91; Hon Par Dn 87-91; rtd 91; Perm to Offic *Worc* 91-94 and from 95; NSM Stourport and Wilden 94-95. *17 Moorhall Lane, Stourport-on-Severn DY13 8RB* Tel (01299) 823044

DAUBNEY, Howard. b 49. Woolwich Poly BA70. S'wark Ord Course 86. **d** 89 **p** 90. C Roch 89-04; V Strood St Fran from 04. *St Francis's Vicarage, Galahad Avenue, Rochester ME2 2YS* Tel and fax (01634) 717162 Mobile 07932-384823 E-mail howard.daubney@diocese-rochester.org

DAUGHTERY, Stephen John. b 61. Kent Univ BSc82. Trin Coll Bris BA94. **d** 96 **p** 97. C Guildf Ch Ch 96-98; C Guildf Ch Ch w St Martha-on-the-Hill 98-03; R Southover *Chich* from 03. *The Rectory, Southover High Street, Lewes BN7 1HT* Tel (01273) 472018 E-mail steve@daughtery.plus.com

DAULMAN, John Henry. b 33. Lich Th Coll 60. **d** 62 **p** 63. C Monkseaton St Mary *Newc* 62-65; Min Can Newc Cathl 65-67; Chapl Crumpsall and Springfield Hosp 67-73; V Tyldesley w Shakerley *Man* 73-81; V Turton 81-00; rtd 00; Perm to Offic *Blackb* from 01. *17 Higher Bank Street, Withnell, Chorley PR6 8SF* Tel (01254) 832597

DAUNTON-FEAR, Andrew. b 45. Univ of Tasmania BSc64 Qu Coll Cam BA67 MA72 St Andr Univ BPhil76 K Coll Lon PhD00. Ridley Hall Cam 67 ACT ThL68. **d** 68 **p** 70. C Thomastown Australia 68-71; P-in-c Islington H Trin Cloudesley Square *Lon* 71-75; Hon C Islington St Mary 71-75; C Stoke Bishop *Bris* 76-79; R Thrapston *Pet* 79-89; R Barming *Roch* 89-03; Lect St Andr Th Sem Philippines from 03. *PO Box 3167, 1099 Manila, Philippines* Tel (0063) (2) 722 2571 E-mail nothingdaunted@hotmail.com

DAVAGE, William Ernest Peter. b 50. MA94. St Steph Ho Ox 89. **d** 91 **p** 92. C Eyres Monsell *Leic* 91-94; P Lib Pusey Ho from 94. *Pusey House, St Giles, Oxford OX1 3LZ* Tel (01865) 288024 E-mail william.davage@stx.ox.ac.uk

DAVENPORT (née HALL), Elizabeth Jayne Louise. b 55. St Hugh's Coll Ox BA77 MA81 Univ of S California PhD03. Fuller Th Sem California ThM89 NOC 79. **dss** 82 **d** 87 **p** 91. Halliwell St Pet *Man* 82-83; Paris St Mich *Eur* 83-85; Lic to Offic *St Alb* 85-87; Hon Par Dn Chorleywood St Andr 87-89; USA from 89. *University of Southern California, University Religious Center, Los Angeles, CA 90089-0751, USA* Tel (001) (213) 740 1366 E-mail ejld@usc.edu

DAVENPORT, Canon Ian Arthan. b 54. Linc Th Coll 85. **d** 87 **p** 88. C Ches H Trin 87-91; V Newton 91-97; V Oxton 97-10; RD Birkenhead 05-10; R Malpas and Threapwood 10-11; R Malpas and Threapwood and Bickerton from 11; Hon Can Ches Cathl from 06. *The Rectory, Church Street, Malpas SY14 8PP* Tel (01948) 860922

DAVENPORT, Mrs Joy Gwyneth. b 46. Glam Coll of Educn TCert68. SEITE 01. **d** 04 **p** 07. NSM Rye *Chich* from 04; Asst Chapl E Sussex Hosps NHS Trust from 04. *2 The Oakfields, Rye Road, Rye TN31 7UA* Tel (01797) 224209

DAVENPORT, Ms Sally Elizabeth. b 59. Lon Bible Coll BA99. Ripon Coll Cuddesdon 99. **d** 01 **p** 02. C Bishop's Stortford St Mich *St Alb* 01-05; TV Bp's Hatfield, Lemsford and N Mymms 05-10; P-in-c Fareham H Trin *Portsm* from 11. *Bishopsgrove, 26 Osborn Road, Fareham PO16 7DQ* Tel (01329) 232688 Mobile 07500-775926 E-mail sally.davenport@portsmouth.anglican.org

DAVENPORT, Miss Sybil Ann. b 36. Nottm Univ CertEd57. EMMTC 85. **d** 89 **p** 94. NSM Thurgarton w Hoveringham and Bleasby etc *S'well* 89-94; NSM Collingham w S Scarle and Besthorpe and Girton 94-02; rtd 02; Perm to Offic *S'well* from 02. *Holmedale, North Muskham, Newark NG23 6HQ* Tel (01636) 701552

DAVEY, Andrew John. b 53. St Mich Coll Llan. **d** 77 **p** 78. C Gt Stanmore *Lon* 77-79; NSM Watford St Jo *St Alb* 87-92; C Potters Bar 92-95; P-in-c Clenchwarton *Ely* 95-96; P-in-c W Lynn 95-96; R Clenchwarton and W Lynn from 96. *The Rectory, Clenchwarton, King's Lynn PE34 4DT* Tel and fax (01553) 772089 E-mail postmaster@andrewdavey.plus.com

DAVEY, Andrew John. b 57. Magd Coll Ox BA78 MA83. Wycliffe Hall Ox 80. **d** 83 **p** 84. C Bermondsey St Jas w Ch Ch *S'wark* 83-87; Chapl Trin Coll Cam 87-92; Pilsdon Community 94-04. *Kingswood, North Street, Axminster EX13 5QF* Tel (01297) 33534

DAVEY, Andrew Paul. b 61. Southn Univ BA82 Sheff Univ DMinTh99. Westcott Ho Cam 85. **d** 87 **p** 88. C S'wark H Trin w St Matt 87-91; V Camberwell St Luke 91-96; Min Development Officer Woolwich Area Miss Team 96-98; Ho of Bps' Officer for UPAs 96-98; Asst Sec Abps' Coun Bd for Soc Resp from 98; Chapl S'wark Cathl from 01. *171 Waller Road, London SE14 5LX* Tel (020) 7277 9688 *or* 7898 1446 E-mail apd@clara.net *or* andrew.davey@churchofengland.org

DAVEY, Christopher Mark. b 64. EN(G)84 RGN89. St Steph Ho Ox 92. **d** 95 **p** 96. C Leeds Belle Is St Jo and St Barn *Ripon* 95-97; C-in-c Grahame Park St Aug CD *Lon* 97-01; V St Alb St Mary Marshalswick *St Alb* 01-08; P-in-c Leavesden from 08. *All Saints' Vicarage, Horseshoe Lane, Watford WD25 7HJ* Tel (01923) 672375 E-mail cdavey2776@aol.com

DAVEY, Colin Hugh Lancaster. b 34. Em Coll Cam BA56 MA60 PhD89. Cuddesdon Coll 59. **d** 61 **p** 62. C Moseley St Agnes *Birm* 61-64; Lic to Offic *Eur* 64-65; Sub Warden St Boniface Coll Warminster 66-69; C Bath Weston St Jo *B & W* 69-70; Asst Chapl Abp Cant's Cllrs on Foreign Relns 70-74; Angl Sec ARCIC 70-74; Hon C St Dunstan in the West *Lon* 71-73; Hon C Kennington St Jo *S'wark* 73-74; V S Harrow St Paul *Lon* 74-80; V Paddington St Jas 80-83; Sec Ecum Affairs BCC 83-90; Ch Life Sec CCBI 90-99; Perm to Offic *St Alb* from 97; rtd 00. *20 Honeysuckle Way, Bedford MK41 0TF* Tel (01234) 360851 E-mail colinandjane@davey8.freeserve.co.uk

DAVEY, Mrs Hilary Margaret. b 49. Bris Univ BSc70. EAMTC 98. **d** 01 **p** 02. NSM Saffron Walden w Wendens Ambo, Littlebury etc *Chelmsf* 01-07; P-in-c Debden and Wimbish w Thunderley from 07. *3 Springhill Road, Saffron Walden CB11 4AH* Tel (01799) 522616 E-mail hilarydavey@btopenworld.com

DAVEY, James Garland. b 21. **d** 75 **p** 76. C Liskeard w St Keyne and St Pinnock *Truro* 75-77; Perm to Offic *B & W* 77-80; TV S Molton w Nymet St George, High Bray etc *Ex* 80-86; rtd 86; Perm to Offic *B & W* 86-05. *43 Tree Field Road, Clevedon BS21 6JD* Tel (01275) 540648

DAVEY, John. b 35. Birkbeck Coll Lon BSc84 MPhil87 PhD91 FRSH94 CPsychol92 AFBPsS92. Chich Th Coll 67. **d** 69 **p** 70. C Eastbourne St Elisabeth *Chich* 69-72; C Eastbourne St Mary 72-74; V W Wittering 74-77; Min Can and Chapl Windsor 77-81; R The Rissingtons *Glouc* 81-85; R Alfriston w Lullington, Litlington and W Dean *Chich* 85-92; Chapl Bramshill Police Coll *Win* 92-96; rtd 97; P-in-c Amberley w N Stoke and Parham, Wiggonholt etc *Chich* 97-98; Perm to Offic 98-08. *20 Holly Avenue, Wilford, Nottingham NG11 7AF*

DAVEY, John Michael. b 31. St Chad's Coll Dur BA54. **d** 56 **p** 61. C Southwick H Trin *Dur* 56-57; C Harton 60-64; C Bawtry w Austerfield *S'well* 64-67; V Stillington *Dur* 67-70; Lic to Offic 70-78; Perm to Offic *Sheff* 78-93; rtd 96. *11 Darfield Close, Owlthorpe, Sheffield S20 6SW* Tel 0114-248 0917

DAVEY, Nathan Imberall. b 40. Jes Coll Ox BA62 MA65. Wells Th Coll 62. **d** 64 **p** 65. C Weston-super-Mare St Jo *B & W* 64-66; Perm to Offic *St Alb* 66-68; Chapl St Alb Sch 68-73; Chapl Merchant Taylors' Sch Crosby 73-82; Perm to Offic *Truro* 82-83; P-in-c Meavy w Sheepstor *Ex* 83-85; P-in-c Walkhampton 83-85; R Meavy, Sheepstor and Walkhampton 85; Chapl Warw Sch 86-89; P-in-c The Winterbournes and Compton Valence *Sarum* 89-94; TV Marshwood Vale 96-98; P-in-c St Gennys, Jacobstow w Warbstow and Treneglos *Truro* 98-02; rtd 02; Perm to Offic *Truro* from 02. *18 Pondfield Road, Latchbrook, Saltash PL12 4UA* Tel (01752) 840086

DAVEY, Julian Warwick. b 45. LRCPI70 LRCSI70. Qu Coll Birm 78. **d** 81 **p** 82. NSM Ipsley *Worc* 81-05; Perm to Offic *Cov* and *Worc* from 05. *The Field House, Allimore Lane, Alcester B49 5PR* Tel (01789) 764640 E-mail affgan1@yahoo.com

DAVEY, Kenneth William. b 41. Qu Coll Birm 84. **d** 86 **p** 87. C Baswich *Lich* 86-90; V Lostock Gralam *Ches* 90-96; P-in-c Thornton-le-Moors w Ince and Elton 96-07; rtd 07. *4 Firbank, Elton, Chester CH2 4LY* Tel (01928) 726166 E-mail kenzor@daveyk1.fsnet.co.uk

DAVEY, Nathan Paul. *See* PAINE DAVEY, Nathan Paul

DAVEY, Peter James. b 59. Bris Univ BSc81 Loughb Univ MBA91. Trin Coll Bris BA00. **d** 00 **p** 01. C Long Eaton St Jo *Derby* 00-04; V Cotmanhay from 04. *The Vicarage, 197 Heanor Road, Ilkeston DE7 8TA* Tel 0115-932 5670 E-mail petedavey@aol.com

DAVEY, Peter William. b 44. Culham Coll of Educn TCert65. Linc Th Coll 93. **d** 93 **p** 94. C Cheadle w Freehay *Lich* 93-96;

P-in-c Calton, Cauldon, Grindon and Waterfall 96-99; R Calton, Cauldon, Grindon, Waterfall etc 99-00; R Norton in the Moors 04-09; rtd 09. *24 rue des Vergers, Verdroux, 79120 St Coutant, France*

DAVEY, Piers Damer. b 57. Dur Univ BSc. Coll of Resurr Mirfield 80. **d** 83 **p** 84. C Heworth St Mary *Dur* 83-86; C Barnard Castle w Whorlton 86-89; V Aycliffe 89-95; V Chilton Moor 95-06; R Gawler St Geo Australia from 06. *26 Cowan Street, Gawler SA 5118, Australia* Tel (0061) (8) 8523 5677 E-mail stgeorgegawler@optusnet.com.au

DAVEY, Richard Henry. b 66. Man Univ BA88 Nottm Univ PhD06. Linc Th Coll BTh93. **d** 93 **p** 94. C Parkstone St Pet w Branksea and St Osmund *Sarum* 93-96; Chapl and Min Can St E Cathl 96-99; Can Res S'well Minster 99-04; Chapl Nottm Trent Univ from 04; C Clifton from 04; C Nottingham All SS, St Mary and St Pet from 10. *All Saints Vicarage, 16 All Saints Street, Nottingham NG7 4DP* Tel 0115-808 4149 E-mail rdavey1175@aol.com

DAVID, Brother. See JARDINE, Canon David John

DAVID, Faith Caroline. See CLARINGBULL, Canon Faith Caroline

DAVID, Gilbert. b 56. Ripon Coll Cuddesdon. **d** 11. C New Bury w Gt Lever *Man* from 11. *25 Reed Close, Farnworth, Bolton BL4 7EF* Tel (01204) 576053 Mobile 07880-710122 E-mail gildavid2u@hotmail.com

DAVID, Canon Kenith Andrew. b 39. Natal Univ BA(Theol)64. Coll of Resurr Mirfield 64. **d** 66 **p** 67. C Harpenden St Nic *St Alb* 66-69; R Chatsworth Epiphany S Africa 69-71; P-in-c Southwick St Mich *Chich* 71-72; Th Educn Sec Chr Aid 72-75; Project Officer India and Bangladesh 76-81; Hon C Kingston All SS *S'wark* 72-76; Hon C Kingston All SS w St Jo 76-81; Lic to Offic Botswana 81-83; Hon C Geneva *Eur* 83-95; Co-ord Urban Rural Miss WCC 83-94; Can Lundi Zimbabwe from 93; V Hessle York 95-05; rtd 05; Perm to Offic *Cant* from 05. *5 Randolph Close, Canterbury CT1 3AZ* Tel and fax (01227) 452009

DAVID, Michael Anthony Louis. b 29. AKC58. **d** 59 **p** 60. C Greenhill St Jo *Lon* 59-63; V Gravesend St Mary *Roch* 63-78; V Foremark *Derby* 78-81; V Repton 78-81; TV Buxton w Burbage and King Sterndale 81-85; R Warlingham w Chelsham and Farleigh *S'wark* 85-90; rtd 91; Perm to Offic *Sarum* from 91. *95 Lulworth Avenue, Hamworthy, Poole BH15 4DH* Tel (01202) 684475

DAVID, Philip Evan Nicholl. b 31. Jes Coll Ox BA53 MA57 Univ of Wales BA61 Nottm Univ MPhil86 Leic Univ MEd88. St Mich Coll Llan 56. **d** 57 **p** 58. C Llanblethian w Cowbridge 57-60; C Cardiff St Jo 60-64; Chapl Ch Coll Brecon 64-75; P-in-c Aberyscir and Llanfihangel Nantbran *S & B* 70-75; Chapl Loretto Sch Musselburgh 75-82; Chapl Trent Coll Nottm 83-91; R Llanfyllin and Bwlchycibau *St As* 91-96; P-in-c Llangynog 95-96; rtd 96; P-in-c Newbridge-on-Wye and Llanfihangel Brynpabuan etc *S & B* 98-00; P-in-c Llanwrtyd w Llanddulas in Tir Abad etc 05. *Woodside Cottage, The Bron, Cross Gates, Llandrindod Wells LD1 6RS* Tel (01597) 851401

DAVID, Wayne Aldwyn. b 74. Univ of Cen England in Birm BA97. St Mich Coll Llan 04. **d** 07 **p** 08. NSM Merthyr Tydfil St Dav *Llan* 07-10; NSM Rhydyfelin w Graig from 10. *16 St Illtyd's Road, Church Village, Pontypridd CF38 1DA* Tel (01443) 203422 E-mail wayneadavid@hotmail.com

DAVID, William John. b 57. Ban Univ BTh07. **d** 04 **p** 05. OLM Eltham St Barn *S'wark* 04-07; NSM 07-09; C Toowoomba St Luke Australia 09-11; NSM Eltham St Barn *S'wark* from 11. *Address temp unknown* E-mail williamdavid10@aol.com

DAVID FRANCIS, Brother. See DARLING, David Francis

DAVIDGE-SMITH, Mrs Margaret Kathleen. b 53. CQSW77. STETS 99. **d** 02 **p** 03. NSM E Acton St Dunstan w St Thos *Lon* 02-06; Asst Chapl Ealing Hosp NHS Trust 04-06; Asst Chapl Meadow House Hospice 04-06; Asst Chapl W Middx Univ Hosp NHS Trust 05-06; Asst Chapl W Lon Mental Health NHS Trust 05-06; Chapl Ealing Hosp NHS Trust from 06. *36 Newburgh Road, London W3 6DQ* Tel and fax (020) 8993 0868 E-mail mdavidge s@hotmail.com

DAVIDSON, Canon Charles Hilary. b 29. St Edm Hall Ox BA52 MA56 Leic Univ MPhil89. Lich Th Coll 52. **d** 54 **p** 55. C Abington *Pet* 54-59; C Pet St Jo 59-60; R Sywell w Overstone 60-66; P-in-c Lamport w Faxton 66-76; R Maidwell w Draughton and Scaldwell 67-76; R Maidwell w Draughton, Scaldwell, Lamport etc 77-80; RD Brixworth 77-79; V Roade 80-87; V Roade and Ashton w Hartwell 87-94; RD Towcester 91-94; Can Pet Cathl 79-94; rtd 94; Perm to Offic *Pet* from 94. *Croftside, Butlins Lane, Roade, Northampton NN7 2PU* Tel (01604) 863016

DAVIDSON, Christopher John. b 45. St Luke's Coll Ex CertEd67 St Martin's Coll Lanc BEd74. EAMTC. **d** 91 **p** 92. NSM Taverham w Ringland *Nor* 91-93; Dir of Educn 87-93; P-in-c Whixley w Green Hammerton *Ripon* 93-96; RE Adv 93-96; Dioc Dir of Educn *Ex* 97-01; Assoc P Exminster and Kenn 97-01; R Quidenham Gp *Nor* 01-08; P-in-c Guiltcross 04-08; rtd 08; P-in-c Pyworthy, Pancrasweek and Bridgerule *Ex* 08-11. *2 The Old School, Hinderclay Road, Rickinghall, Diss IP22 1HD* E-mail chris.davidson@virgin.net

DAVIDSON, Mrs Dawn Margaret. b 59. **d** 09 **p** 10. OLM Mulbarton w Bracon Ash, Hethel and Flordon *Nor* from 09. *8 Wild Radish Close, Mulbarton, Norwich NR14 8DB* Tel (01508) 570073 Mobile 07784-003432 E-mail davidsonhome1@btinternet.com

DAVIDSON, Donald. b 52. TISEC 00. **d** 05 **p** 06. C W Highland Region *Arg* from 05. *4 Kearan Road, Kinlochleven, Argyll PH50 4QU* Tel (01855) 831444 E-mail donaldd@btinternet.com

DAVIDSON, Graeme John. b 42. Victoria Univ Wellington BA64 BA66 Ox Univ MA70. St Steph Ho Ox 67. **d** 70 **p** 71. C Maidenhead St Luke *Ox* 70-73; New Zealand 73-77 and from 93; USA 77-88. *3 Tauroa Road, Havelock North, Hawke's Bay 4130, New Zealand* E-mail graeme.davidson@paradise.net.nz

DAVIDSON, Hilary. See DAVIDSON, Canon Charles Hilary

DAVIDSON, Ian George. b 32. LSE BSc(Econ)54. Linc Th Coll 55. **d** 58 **p** 59. C Waltham Cross *St Alb* 58-60; C St Alb Abbey 61-63; Hon PV S'wark Cathl 63-67; V Gt Cornard *St E* 67-72; R Lt Cornard 67-70; Lic to Offic 72-79; Student Counsellor Suffolk Coll 72-79; P-in-c Witnesham w Swilland and Ashbocking 79-83; Warden Scargill Ho 83-88; Chapl Chr Fellowship of Healing *Edin* 88-97; rtd 97. *28 Fox Spring Crescent, Edinburgh EH10 6NQ* Tel 0131-445 3381 E-mail iangill@foxspring.freeserve.co.uk

DAVIDSON, John Lindsay. b 27. LRCP51. St Steph Ho Ox. **d** 58 **p** 59. C Croydon St Mich *Cant* 58-61; P-in-c H Cross Miss 62-66; V Lewisham St Steph *S'wark* 67-70; V Croydon St Mich *Cant* 70-80; V Croydon St Mich w St Jas 80-81; TR N Creedy *Ex* 81-92; RD Cadbury 86-90; rtd 92; Perm to Offic *Ex* 92-09. *9 Redvers House, Union Road, Crediton EX17 3AW* Tel (01363) 775998

DAVIDSON, Ralph. b 38. **d** 01 **p** 02. OLM Birkenshaw w Hunsworth *Wakef* from 01. *Bedale, Moorhouse Lane, Birkenshaw, Bradford BD11 2BA* Tel (01274) 681955 E-mail ralphdavidson@bedale1938.wanadoo.co.uk

DAVIDSON, Trevor John. b 49. CertEd. Oak Hill Th Coll 80. **d** 85 **p** 86. C Drypool *York* 85-88; V Bessingby 88-97; V Carnaby 88-97; Chapl Bridlington and Distr Gen Hosp 88-94; Chapl E Yorks Community Healthcare NHS Trust 94-97; V Felling *Dur* from 97; CUF Projects Officer from 97. *The Vicarage, Carlisle Street, Felling, Gateshead NE10 0HQ* Tel 0191-420 3434 E-mail trevor@christchurch5.freeserve.co.uk

DAVIDSON, William Watkins. b 20. Wadh Coll Ox BA48 MA53. Westcott Ho Cam 49. **d** 50 **p** 51. C Radcliffe-on-Trent *S'well* 50-53; Chapl RN 53-57; R Esher *Guildf* 57-65; V Westmr St Steph w St Jo *Lon* 65-83; rtd 85. *62 Calmsden, Cirencester GL7 5ET* Tel (01285) 831823 E-mail sallyandbill62@talktalk.net

DAVIE (née JONES), Mrs Alyson Elizabeth. b 58. Ex Univ BA86. Wycliffe Hall Ox 86. **d** 88 **p** 94. Par Dn Ipswich St Fran *St E* 88-92; Perm to Offic *Ox* 92-93 and *St Alb* 93-94; NSM E Barnet *St Alb* 94-97; Asst Chapl Oak Hill Th Coll 94-96; P-in-c The Mundens w Sacombe *St Alb* 97-06; V St Paul's Cray St Barn *Roch* from 06. *The Vicarage, Rushet Road, Orpington BR5 2PU* Tel (01689) 825852 E-mail alyson.davie@btinternet.com

DAVIE, Peter Edward Sidney. b 36. LSE BSc57 Birm Univ MA73 K Coll Lon MPhil78 Kent Univ PhD90. Coll of Resurr Mirfield 57. **d** 60 **p** 61. C De Beauvoir Town St Pet *Lon* 60-63; C-in-c Godshill CD *Portsm* 63-67; R Upton St Leonards *Glouc* 67-73; Sen Lect Ch Ch Coll of HE Cant 73-98; Prin Lect Cant Ch Ch Univ Coll 98-01; rtd 01; Hon C Cant St Pet w St Alphege and St Marg etc 79-10; Perm to Offic from 10. *8 Brockenhurst Close, Canterbury CT2 7RX* Tel (01227) 451572 E-mail pedavie@dircon.co.uk

DAVIE, Stephen Peter. b 52. S Bank Poly BA75 MRTPI77. Oak Hill Th Coll BA93. **d** 93 **p** 94. C Luton Ch Ch *Roch* 93-97; R Cobham w Luddesdowne and Dode 97-04; P-in-c Horley *S'wark* 04-08; TR from 08. *4 Russells Crescent, Horley RH6 7DN* Tel (01293) 783509 E-mail steve.davie@btinternet.com

DAVIES, Adrian. See DAVIES, Glanmor Adrian

DAVIES, Adrian Paul. b 43. K Coll Lon. **d** 69 **p** 70. C Nottingham St Mary *S'well* 69-74; C Gt w Lt Billing *Pet* 74-75; P-in-c Marholm 75-82; R Castor 75; R Castor w Sutton and Upton 76-82; V Byker St Mich w St Lawr *Newc* 82-94; rtd 95. *27 Clougha Avenue, Halton, Lancaster LA2 6NR* Tel (01524) 811141

DAVIES, Alan. See DAVIES, James Alan

DAVIES, Alan Arthur. b 35. Sarum & Wells Th Coll 83. **d** 85 **p** 86. C Eastleigh *Win* 85-88; C Portsea N End St Mark *Portsm* 88-90; V Lydiate *Liv* 90-00; rtd 00; Perm to Offic *Sarum* from 01. *25 St Catherine's, Wimborne BH21 1BE* Tel (01202) 848233

DAVIES, Alan Douglas. b 49. ERMC 08. **d** 10 **p** 11. NSM Downham Market and Crimplesham w Stradsett *Ely* from 10. *The Lodge, Wallington Hall, Runcton Holme, King's Lynn PE33 0EP* Tel (01533) 810675

DAVIES, Alastair John. b 56. Nottm Univ BA MTh. Westcott Ho Cam. **d** 84 **p** 85. C Eltham St Jo *S'wark* 84-87; C Dulwich St Barn 87-89; Chapl RAF 89-07; P-in-c Lyneham w Bradenstoke *Sarum* 01-03; Sen Chapl R United Hosp Bath NHS

Trust from 07. *Royal United Hospital, Combe Park, Bath BA1 3NG* Tel (01225) 428331 E-mail alastair.davies@ruh-bath.swest.nhs.uk

DAVIES, Albert Brian. b 37. Worc Coll of Educn CertEd60. Wycliffe Hall Ox 03. **d** 04 **p** 05. C Poitou-Charentes *Eur* 04-07; P-in-c The Vendée 07-10; Asst Chapl Aquitaine from 11. *La Basse Coussaie, 85140 Les Essarts, France* Tel (0033) 2 51 62 96 32 E-mail briandpam@free.fr

DAVIES, Mrs Alison Margaret. b 57. Nottm Univ BA78. STETS 96. **d** 99 **p** 00. NSM Win St Barn 99-04; Perm to Offic *Win* 04-07 and *Nor* 07-10; Chapl King's Lynn and Wisbech Hosps NHS Trust from 10. *The Vicarage, 12B Church Lane, Heacham, King's Lynn PE31 7HJ* Tel (01485) 570125

DAVIES, Andrew James. b 53. Univ of Wales (Cardiff) BD00. St Mich Coll Llan 01. **d** 03 **p** 04. C Caerphilly *Llan* 03-06; P-in-c Rhondda Fach Uchaf from 06. *Ty Nant, Margaret Street, Pontygwaith, Ferndale CF43 3EH* Tel (01443) 732321 Mobile 07931-370054 E-mail daviesaj8@yahoo.co.uk

DAVIES, Andrew John. b 54. Univ of Wales (Abth) BMus76 St Martin's Coll Lanc PGCE78 FRCO75 FTCL76 LRAM75. Sarum & Wells Th Coll 79. **d** 81 **p** 82. C Tenby w Gumfreston *St D* 81-84; C Llanelli 84-86; V Monkton 86-91; V Fairfield *Derby* 91-96; P-in-c Barlborough 96-01; R Barlborough and Renishaw 01-03; V Pembroke Dock *St D* 03-04; TR Carew 04-08; TR Tenby from 08. *The Rectory, Church Park, Tenby SA70 7EE* Tel (01834) 842068 E-mail andrewdavies19@aol.com

DAVIES, Anthony. *See* DAVIES, The Ven Vincent Anthony

DAVIES, Anthony. *See* DAVIES, David Anthony

DAVIES, Anthony Paul. b 56. JP02. Univ of Wales (Swansea) BSc76 CEng85. St Mich Coll Llan 03. **d** 06 **p** 07. NSM Penllergaer *S & B* 06-07; NSM Gorseinon from 07. *142 Bolgoed Road, Pontarddulais, Swansea SA4 8JP* Tel (01792) 883157 Mobile 07855-237866 E-mail anthonypdavies@yahoo.com

DAVIES, Arthur Gerald Miles. b 29. Univ of Wales (Ban) BA51. St Mich Coll Llan 51. **d** 53 **p** 54. C Shotton *St As* 53-60; R Nannerch 60-63; V Llansilin and Llangadwaladr 63-68; V Llansilin w Llangadwaladr and Llangedwyn 68-71; V Llanfair Caereinion w Llanllugan 71-75; TV Wrexham 75-83; V Hanmer, Bronington, Bettisfield, Tallarn Green 83-94; rtd 94. *Elland, School Lane, Bronington, Whitchurch SY13 3HN* Tel (01948) 780296

DAVIES, Arthur Lloyd. *See* LLOYD-DAVIES, Arthur

DAVIES, Barry Lewis. b 46. Boro Road Teacher Tr Coll CertEd69 Lon Inst of Educn DipEd84 MA86. STETS 02. **d** 05 **p** 06. NSM Hardington Vale *B & W* 05-08; rtd 08; Perm to Offic *B & W* from 09 and *Bris* from 10; Chapl Avon and Somerset Constabulary *B & W* from 10; Chapl Partis Coll Bath from 10. *3 The Lays, Googse Street, Beckington, Frome BA11 6RS* Tel (01373) 831344 E-mail bandkdavies@msn.com

DAVIES, Miss Belinda Jane. b 68. Ox Poly BSc91. STETS BA08. **d** 08 **p** 10. C Yateley *Win* 08-09; C Salisbury St Thos and St Edm *Sarum* from 10. *11 Albany Road, Salisbury SP1 3YQ* E-mail belindajdavies@googlemail.com

DAVIES, Benjamin John. b 27. Glouc Sch of Min 80 Trin Coll Bris 87. **d** 88 **p** 89. NSM Cinderford St Steph w Littledean *Glouc* 88-98; Perm to Offic 98-00. *22 Withy Park, Bishopston, Swansea SA3 3EY* Tel (01792) 232352

DAVIES, Canon Bernard. b 34. Lon Univ BD63. Oak Hill Th Coll 59. **d** 63 **p** 64. C Rawtenstall St Mary *Man* 63-69; Sec Rwanda Miss 69-71; R Widford *Chelmsf* 71-78; V Braintree 78-00; RD Braintree 87-95; Hon Can Chelmsf Cathl 92-00; rtd 00; Perm to Offic *Nor* from 00 and *St E* from 01. *3 Brookwood Close, Worlingham, Beccles NR34 7RJ* Tel (01502) 719739

DAVIES, Sister Beverley. b 55. **d** 11. NSM Leic Presentation from 11. *St Matthew's House, 25 Kamloops Crescent, Leicester LE1 2HX* Tel 0116-253 9158

DAVIES, Brian. *See* DAVIES, Albert Brian

DAVIES, Carol Ann. b 52. Bp Otter Coll 94. **d** 96 **p** 98. NSM Oakfield St Jo *Portsm* 96-00; NSM Bonchurch 00-04; NSM Ventnor St Cath 00-04; NSM Ventnor H Trin 00-04; TR Upper Kennet *Sarum* 04; R 04-07; rtd 08. *La Salle, 16350 Le Bouchage, France* Tel (0033) 5 45 85 58 94 E-mail caroldaviesfrance@orange.fr

DAVIES, Catharine Mary. *See* FURLONG, Mrs Catharine Mary

DAVIES, Mrs Catherine Olive Sarah Skeel. b 61. Univ of Wales (Cardiff) BA84. WMMTC 03. **d** 06 **p** 07. NSM Wootton Wawen and Claverdon w Preston Bagot *Cov* 06-09; NSM Barford w Wasperton and Sherbourne from 09; NSM Hampton Lucy w Charlecote and Loxley from 09. *3 Wilkins Close, Barford, Warwick CV35 8EX* E-mail davieshchl@aol.com

DAVIES, Ceri John. b 61. Univ of Wales (Lamp) BA91 Univ of Wales (Abth) PGCE92 Univ of Wales (Cardiff) BTh00. St Mich Coll Llan 97. **d** 00 **p** 01. C Carmarthen St Dav *St D* 00-03; TV Llanelli 03-11; C Cynwyl Elfed w Newchurch and Trelech a'r Betws from 11. *The Vicarage, Cynwyl Elfed, Carmarthen SA33 6TH* Tel (01267) 281552 E-mail cdavies465@btinternet.com

DAVIES, Chris. *See* DAVIES, Canon David Christopher

DAVIES, Christopher. b 51. NE Lon Poly BA72. SEITE 99. **d** 02 **p** 03. NSM Peckham St Sav *S'wark* 02-07. *Address temp unknown* E-mail christopherscott@tinyworld.co.uk

DAVIES, Christopher Edward. b 72. **d** 03 **p** 04. OLM Bilston *Lich* from 03. *10 Wroxham Glen, Willenhall WV13 3HU* Tel (01902) 655305 Mobile 07952-196204

DAVIES, Christopher John. b 55. St Alb Minl Tr Scheme 83. **d** 86 **p** 87. C Tooting All SS *S'wark* 86-90; V Malden St Jas 90-96; RD Kingston 92-96; TR Wimbledon 96-06; Hon Can S'wark Cathl 06; V Wymondham *Nor* from 06; RD Humbleyard from 08. *The Vicarage, 5 Vicar Street, Wymondham NR18 0PL* Tel (01953) 602269 E-mail revd@christopherdavies.fsnet.co.uk

DAVIES, Canon Clifford Thomas. b 41. Glouc Th Course. **d** 83 **p** 84. NSM Dean Forest H Trin *Glouc* 83-87; C Huntley and Longhope 87; R Ruardean 87-06; Hon Can Glouc Cathl 02-06; rtd 06. *Purbeck, 13 Park View, Ruardean GL17 9YW*

DAVIES, David Anthony (Tony). b 57. Thames Poly BSc81 MRICS84. Coll of Resurr Mirfield 85. **d** 88 **p** 89. C Stalybridge *Man* 88-91; C Swinton and Pendlebury 91-92 and 01-02; TV 92-01; V Tonge Moor from 02. *St Augustine's Vicarage, Redthorpe Close, Bolton BL2 2PQ* Tel and fax (01204) 523899 Mobile 07866-359864 E-mail tony@davieses.co.uk

DAVIES, David Barry Grenville. b 38. St Jo Coll Dur BA60 MA77. Sarum Th Coll 61. **d** 63 **p** 64. C Aberystwyth St Mich *St D* 63-66; Min Can St D Cathl 66-72; R Stackpole Elidor w St Petrox 72-83; V Laugharne w Llansadwrnen and Llandawke 83-03; rtd 03. *3 Clos y Drindod, Buarth Road, Aberystwyth SY23 1LR* Tel (01970) 626289

DAVIES, David Berwyn. b 42. St Mich Coll Llan 95. **d** 96 **p** 97. C Llanelli *St D* 96-98; R Llanerch Aeron w Ciliau Aeron and Dihewyd etc 98-07; rtd 07; Perm to Offic *St D* from 07. *56 Tyisha Road, Llanelli SA15 1RW* Tel (01554) 774391 E-mail taddavid@aol.com

DAVIES, Canon David Christopher (Chris). b 52. Lon Univ BSc73 UWE MSc11. Coll of Resurr Mirfield 73. **d** 76 **p** 77. C Bethnal Green St Jo w St Simon *Lon* 76-78; C Bethnal Green St Jo w St Bart 78-80; C-in-c Portsea St Geo CD *Portsm* 80-81; V Portsea St Geo 81-87; Relig Affairs Producer Radio Victory 81-86; Chapl Ham Green Hosp Bris 87-94; Chapl Southmead Hosp Bris 87-94; Chapl Southmead Health Services NHS Trust 94-99; Chapl N Bris NHS Trust 99-05; Hd Spiritual and Past Care from 05; Hd Spiritual and Past Care Univ Hosps Bris NHS Foundn Trust from 05; Perm to Offic *B & W* from 94; Hon Can Bris Cathl from 99. *Southmead Hospital, Westbury-on-Trym, Bristol BS10 5NB* Tel 0117-342 0610 E-mail chris.davies@nbt.nhs.uk

DAVIES, David Geoffrey George. b 24. Univ of Wales (Ban) BA49 Lon Univ BD55 Chorley Coll of Educn PGCE75. St Mich Coll Llan 49. **d** 51 **p** 52. C Brecon St Mary w Battle and Llanhamlach *S & B* 51-55; Min Can Brecon Cathl 53-55; C Oystermouth 55-59; V Cwm *St As* 59-63; Warden of Ords 62-70; V Ruabon 63-70; Hon Can St As Cathl 66-69; Cursal Can 69-70; Hon C W Derby St Jo *Liv* 70-81; Chapl to Welsh Speaking Angl in Liv 74-81 and from 96; TV Bourne Valley *Sarum* 81-87; TR 87-89; Bp's Chapl to Schs 83-89; RD Alderbury 86-89; rtd 89; Hon Chapl Liv Cathl 89-04; Sub-Chapl HM Pris Risley 90-96. *1 Sinclair Drive, Liverpool L18 0HN* Tel 0151-722 1415

DAVIES, Canon David Islwyn. b 42. St Deiniol's Hawarden 83. **d** 85 **p** 86. C Llangiwg *S & B* 85-87; C Swansea St Pet 87-89; Chapl Schiedam Miss to Seamen *Eur* 89-92; Chapl Milford Haven Miss to Seamen 92-94; V Pontyates and Llangyndeyrn *St D* 94-99; R Ystradgynlais *S & B* from 99; AD Cwmtawe from 06; Can Res Brecon Cathl from 06. *The Rectory, 2 Heol Eglwys, Ystradgynlais, Swansea SA9 1EY* Tel (01639) 843200

DAVIES, Canon David Jeremy Christopher. b 46. CCC Cam BA68 MA72. Westcott Ho Cam 68. **d** 71 **p** 72. C Stepney St Dunstan and All SS *Lon* 71-74; Chapl Qu Mary Coll 74-78; Chapl Univ of Wales (Cardiff) *Llan* 78-85; Can Res Sarum Cathl from 85. *Hungerford Chantry, 54 The Close, Salisbury SP1 2EL* Tel (01722) 555179 Fax 555117 E-mail jeremydavies@waitrose.com *or* precentor@salcath.co.uk

DAVIES, Canon David Michael Cole. b 44. St D Coll Lamp. **d** 68 **p** 69. C Carmarthen St Pet *St D* 68-72; R Dinas 72-77; V Ty-Croes w Saron 77-80; V Llanedi w Tycroes and Saron 80-90; RD Dyffryn Aman 85-90; V Dafen and Llwynhendy 90-94; V Dafen 94-08; Hon Can St D Cathl 00-08; rtd 08. *30 Bro'r Dderwen, Clynderwen SA66 7NR* E-mail dcmcd@aol.com

DAVIES, Prof David Protheroe. b 39. CCC Cam BA62 MA66 CCC Ox MA69 BD69. Ripon Hall Ox 62. **d** 64 **p** 65. C Swansea St Mary w H Trin *S & B* 64-67; Lect Th Univ of Wales (Lamp) 67-75; Sen Lect 75-86; Dean Faculty of Th 75-77 and from 81; Hd Th and Relig Studies from 84; Prof Th Univ of Wales (Trin St Dav) from 86; Pro Vice-Chan from 88; Bp's Chapl for Th Educn *S & B* from 79. *University of Wales, Lampeter SA48 7ED* Tel (01570) 422351

DAVIES, David Vernon. b 14. AFBpS68 Univ of Wales (Swansea) BA35 BD38 St Cath Coll Ox MA40 K Coll Lon PhD56. St D Coll Lamp 41. **d** 41 **p** 42. C Llanelli Ch Ch *St D*

41-46; Chapl St John's Coll Nassau Bahamas 46-50; Chapl Cane Hill Hosp Coulsdon 50-61; Lect St Luke's Coll Ex 61-65; Lic to Offic *Ex* 61-68; Sen Lect St Luke's Coll Ex 65-68; Lic to Offic *Llan* from 68; Prin Lect Llan Coll of Educn 68-77; Sen Lect Univ of Wales (Cardiff) 77-79; rtd 79. *41 Cefn Coed Avenue, Cyncoed, Cardiff CF23 6HF* Tel (029) 2075 7635

DAVIES, David William. b 64. d 90 p 91. C Newton St Pet *S & B* 90-93; V Llywel and Traean-glas w Llanulid 93-97; CF from 97. *c/o MOD Chaplains (Army)* Tel (01264) 381140 Fax 381824

DAVIES, Derek George. b 47. UWIST BEng74 Univ of Wales (Lamp) BD03. St Mich Coll Llan 03. d 05 p 06. NSM Steynton *St D* from 05. *Ty Llosg, Clarbeston Road, Pembroke SA63 4SG* Tel (01437) 563560 E-mail derekgeorgedavies@hotmail.com

DAVIES, Dewi Gwynfor. b 56. Univ of Wales (Abth) BD92 MTh98 RIBA81. d 98 p 99. C Llangunnor w Cwmffrwd *St D* 98-99; P-in-c Elerch w Penrhyncoch w Capel Bangor and Goginan 99-00; P-in-c Cil-y-Cwm and Ystrad-ffin w Rhandirmwyn etc 00-01; V Llanedi w Tycroes and Saron 03-09; V Pen-bre from 09. *The Vicarage, Ar-y-bryn, Pembrey, Burry Port SA16 0AJ* Tel (01554) 832403

DAVIES, Dillwyn. b 30. St Mich Coll Llan 52. d 54 p 55. C Laugharne w Llansadwrnen and Llandawke *St D* 54-57; Lic to Offic *Dur* 57-58; Miss to Seamen 57-58; Ceylon 58-62; R Winthorpe *S'well* 62-71; V Langford w Holme 62-71; V Mansfield Woodhouse 71-85; R Gedling 85-92; RD Gedling 85-90; Hon Can S'well Minster 90-92; rtd 92. *7 Norbury Drive, Mansfield NG18 4HT* Tel (01623) 458594

DAVIES, Canon Dorrien Paul. b 64. Univ of Wales (Lamp) BA95. Llan Dioc Tr Schøme 86. d 88 p 89. C Llanelli *St D* 88-91; V Llanfihangel Ystrad and Cilcennin w Trefilan etc 91-99; V St Dogmael's w Moylgrove and Monington 99-10; TV Dewisland from 10; Can St D Cathl from 07. *The Archdeaconry, The Close, St Davids, Haverfordwest SA62 6PE* Tel (01437) 720456 E-mail davies.vicarage1@virgin.net

DAVIES, Prof Douglas James. b 47. St Jo Coll Dur BA69 St Pet Coll Ox MLitt72 Nottm Univ PhD80 DLitt04 Uppsala Univ Hon DTh98. Cranmer Hall Dur 71. d 75 p 76. Lect Nottm Univ 75-97; Sen Lect 90-97; Hon C Wollaton *S'well* 75-83; Hon C Attenborough 83-85; Hon C E Leake 85-91; Hon C Daybrook 91-97; Prof RS Nottm Univ 93-97; Prin SS Hild and Bede Coll Dur 97-00; Prof Th Dur Univ from 97; Prof Study of Relig Dur Univ from 00. *Department of Theology and Religion, Abbey House, Palace Green, Durham DH1 3RS* Tel 0191-375 7697 E-mail douglas.davies@durham.ac.uk

DAVIES, Canon Douglas Tudor. b 20. Univ of Wales (Ban) BA44. Coll of Resurr Mirfield 44. d 46 p 47. C Swansea Ch Ch *S & B* 46-52; C Oystermouth 52-57; R Llangynllo and Bleddfa 57-63; C-in-c Treboeth CD 63-65; V Treboeth 65-90; RD Penderi 78-90; Hon Can Brecon Cathl 82-83; Can 83-90; rtd 90. *245A Swansea Road, Waunarlwydd, Swansea SA5 4SN* Tel (01792) 879587

DAVIES, Edward Earl. b 40. Llan Dioc Tr Scheme 88. d 90 p 91. C Pontypridd St Cath w St Matt *Llan* 90-93; V Ferndale w Maerdy 93-00; V Cardiff Ch Ch Roath Park 00-09; rtd 09. *4 St Augustine Road, Heath, Cardiff CF14 4BD*

DAVIES, Edward Trevor. b 37. MRSC62 MInstE74 CEng78. NOC 92. d 95 p 96. Hon Asst Chapl Countess of Chester Hosp NHS Foundn Trust 95-02; Chapl 02-05; NSM Waverton *Ches* 95-99; NSM Hargrave 99-00; C Bunbury and Tilstone Fearnall 00-02; NSM 02-03; Perm to Offic 05-10; C Waverton w Aldford and Bruera 10-11; rtd 11. *Athergreen, 5 Allansford Avenue, Waverton, Chester CH3 7QH* Tel (01244) 332106 E-mail etdavies1@btinternet.com

DAVIES, Canon Edward William Llewellyn. b 51. St Jo Coll Nottm BTh77. d 78 p 79. C Southsea St Jude *Portsm* 78-81; C Alverstoke 81-84; R Abbas and Templecombe w Horsington *B & W* 84-89; Perm to Offic *Ches* 89-99; V Sutton St Jas from 99; Asst Warden of Readers from 02; RD Macclesfield from 05; Hon Can Ches Cathl from 10. *St James's Vicarage, Church Lane, Sutton, Macclesfield SK11 0DS* Tel (01260) 252228 E-mail taffy@parishpump.co.uk

DAVIES, Eileen. See DAVIES, Mrs Rachel Hannah Eileen

DAVIES, Ms Elizabeth Jane. b 58. Man Univ BA97 RGN82 RSCN88. Qu Coll Birm MA01. d 01 p 02. C Spotland *Man* 01-04; Chapl Pennine Acute Hosps NHS Trust 04-05; Chapl Bolton Hospice 05-08; P-in-c Ladybarn *Man* from 08. *St Chad's Rectory, 1 St Chad's Road, Manchester M20 4WH* Tel 0161-445 1185

DAVIES, Mrs Elizabeth Jean. b 39. Lon Univ MB, BS63 MRCS63 LRCP63. Chich Th Coll 86. d 89 p 95. Par Dn Southwick St Mich *Chich* 89-91; Par Dn Littlehampton and Wick 91-95; C Seaford w Sutton 95-97; NSM E Preston w Kingston 97-04; rtd 99; P-in-c Everton and Mattersey w Clayworth *S'well* 04-05; Perm to Offic from 06. *Mayfield, Bone Mill Lane, Welham, Retford DN22 9NL* Tel (01777) 703717

DAVIES, Mrs Emma Louise. b 67. St Andr Univ MA89. Ripon Coll Cuddesdon 05. d 07 p 08. C Market Harborough and The Transfiguration etc *Leic* 07-10; TV Gilmorton, Peatling Parva,

Kimcote etc from 10. *The Rectory, Church Lane, Gilmorton, Lutterworth LE17 5LU* Tel (01455) 553475 E-mail emmydavies@aol.com

DAVIES, Eric Brian. b 36. St Jo Coll Nottm. d 87 p 89. NSM Castle Donington and Lockington cum Hemington *Leic* 87-88; Hon C Hathern, Long Whatton and Diseworth 89-90; Hon C Hathern, Long Whatton and Diseworth w Belton etc 90-93; C Minster-in-Sheppey *Cant* 93-00; rtd 00; NSM Walsall St Gabr Fulbrook *Lich* 00-03; NSM Caldmore 00-02; NSM Caldmore w Palfrey 02-03; NSM Kinver and Enville 03-08. *1 White Cottages, Gospel Ash Road, Bobbington, Stourbridge DY7 5EF* E-mail reverend.ericdavies@kirion.net

DAVIES, Evelyn Dorothy. MBE99. BEd72 Liv Univ CertEd56. d 96 p 97. NSM Llangynog *St As* 96-00; P-in-c Aberdaron w Rhiw and Llanfaelrhys etc *Ban* 00-04; R 04-07; rtd 07. *Edmund V Bungalow, Lon Ednyfed, Criccieth LL52 0AG* E-mail melangell@pennant1.demon.co.uk

DAVIES, Mrs Felicity Ann. b 58. Wycliffe Hall Ox. d 11. C Wadhurst *Chich* from 11. *The Vicarage, Bardown Road, Stonegate, Wadhurst TN5 7EJ* Tel (01580) 201855 E-mail fadavies58@gmail.com

DAVIES, Frances Elizabeth. b 38. BA CertEd. Moray Ord Course. d 95. Hon C Thurso *Mor* from 95; Hon C Wick from 95. *22 Granville Crescent, Thurso, Caithness KW14 7NP* Tel (01847) 892386 E-mail reallyfed@yahoo.co.uk

✠**DAVIES, The Rt Revd Francis James Saunders.** b 37. Univ of Wales (Ban) BA60 Selw Coll Cam BA62 MA66 Bonn Univ 63. St Mich Coll Llan 62. d 63 p 64 c 00. C Holyhead w Rhoscolyn *Ban* 63-67; Chapl Ban Cathl 67-69; R Llanllyfni 69-75; Can Missr Ban Cathl 75-78; V Gorseinon *S & B* 78-86; RD Llwchwr 83-86; V Cardiff Dewi Sant *Llan* 86-93; R Criccieth w Treflys *Ban* 93-99; Adn Meirionnydd 93-99; Bp Ban 99-04; rtd 04. *Ger-y-Nant, 5 Maes-y-Coed, Cardigan SA43 1AP* Tel (01239) 615664

DAVIES, Gareth Rhys. b 51. Oak Hill Th Coll. d 83 p 84. C Gt Warley Ch Ch *Chelmsf* 83-86; C Oxhey All SS *St Alb* 86-90; C Aldridge *Lich* 90-99; V Colney Heath St Mark *St Alb* 99-00; V Sneyd Green *Lich* from 00; Bp's Adv on Healing from 09. *St Andrew's Vicarage, 42 Granville Avenue, Sneyd Green, Stoke-on-Trent ST1 6BH* Tel (01782) 215139

DAVIES, Geoffrey. See DAVIES, David Geoffrey George

✠**DAVIES, The Rt Revd Geoffrey Francis.** b 41. Cape Town Univ BA62 Em Coll Cam BA67 MA71. Cuddesdon Coll 67. d 69 p 70 c 87. C W Brompton St Mary *Lon* 69-72; C Serowe St Aug Botswana 72-76; R Kalk Bay H Trin S Africa 77-80; Dir Dept of Miss 81-87; Suff Bp St John 88-91; Bp Umzimvubu 91-03; rtd 03. *Waterfall Cottage, 7 Upper Quarterdeck Road, Kalk Bay, 7990 South Africa* Tel and fax (0027) (21) 788 6591 E-mail geoffd@intermail.co.za

DAVIES, Geoffrey Michael. b 43. St D Coll Lamp. d 70 p 71. C Brynmawr *S & B* 70-73; Coll of Ascension Selly Oak 73-74; S Africa 74-91 and from 99; C Claremont St Sav 74-76; R Strand 76-82; R E London St Sav 82-84; Assoc R Constantia Ch Ch 90-91; C Roath *Llan* 91-95; V Llanishen w Trellech Grange and Llanfihangel etc *Mon* 95-99; R Graaff-Reinet St Jas 03-09. *PO Box 13, Herold, 6615 South Africa*

DAVIES, George Vivian. b 21. CCC Cam BA47 MA49. Ely Th Coll. d 49 p 50. C Maidstone St Martin *Cant* 49-51; C Folkestone St Mary and St Eanswythe 51-56; V Leysdown w Harty 56-59; R Warehorne w Kenardington 59-74; R Rounton w Welbury *York* 74-86; rtd 86; Perm to Offic *Derby* 86-99. *c/o R P Davies Esq, Beech House, Cannonsfield, Hathersage, Hope Valley S32 1AG* Tel (01433) 659132

DAVIES, George William. b 51. Open Univ BA74 MPhil89 MCIPD. Sarum & Wells Th Coll 83. d 85 p 86. C Mansfield SS Pet and Paul *S'well* 85-89; Chapl Cen Notts HA 86-89; P-in-c Fobbing and Ind Chapl *Chelmsf* 89-96; Chapl Thurrock Lakeside Shopping Cen 93-96; R Mottingham St Andr w St Alban *S'wark* 96-04; V Lamorbey H Trin *Roch* from 04; Chapl Rose Bruford Coll from 04. *Holy Trinity Vicarage, 1 Hurst Road, Sidcup DA15 9AE* Tel (020) 8309 7886 *or* 8300 8231 E-mail george@daviesgeorge.wanadoo.co.uk

DAVIES, Glanmor Adrian. b 51. St D Coll Lamp. d 73 p 75. C Llanstadwel *St D* 73-78; R Dinas w Llanllawer and Pontfaen w Morfil etc 78-84; V Lamphey w Hodgeston 84-85; V Lamphey w Hodgeston and Carew 85-03; V Borth and Eglwys-fach w Llangynfelyn 03-06. *Bayford, Freshwater East Road, Lamphey, Pembroke SA71 5JX*

✠**DAVIES, The Rt Revd Glenn Naunton.** b 50. Sydney Univ BSc72 Sheff Univ PhD88. Westmr Th Sem (USA) BD78 ThM79. d 81 p 81 c 01. Australia 81-85; Hon C Fulwood *Sheff* 85-87; Hon C Lodge Moor St Luke 86-87; Australia from 87; Lect Moore Th Coll 83-95; R Miranda 95-01; Bp N Sydney from 01. *PO Box Q190, Queen Victoria Building, Sydney NSW 1230, Australia* Tel (0061) (2) 9265 1527 *or* 9419 6761 Fax 9265 1543

DAVIES, Glyn Richards. b 28. Solicitor 52. Mon Dioc Tr Scheme 76. d 79 p 80. NSM Michaelston-y-Fedw and Rudry *Mon* 79-88; NSM St Mellons and Michaelston-y-Fedw 88-96; NSM St Mellons 96-07. *Narnia, 4 Pilgrim's Way, Guildford GU4 8AB*

DAVIES, Glyndwr George. b 36. Glouc Sch of Min 88. **d** 91 **p** 92. NSM Clodock and Longtown w Craswall, Llanveynoe etc *Heref* 91-02; rtd 02; Perm to Offic *Heref* from 02. *White House Farm, Llanfihangel Crucorney, Abergavenny NP7 8HW* Tel (01873) 890251

DAVIES, The Ven Graham James. b 35. Univ of Wales BD72 St D Coll Lamp BA56. St Mich Coll Llan 56 Episc Th Sch Cam Mass 58. **d** 59 **p** 60. C Johnston w Steynton *St D* 59-62; C Llangathen w Llanfihangel Cilfargen 62-64; Min Can St D Cathl 64-66; R Burton 66-71; R Hubberston 71-74; Hon C Lenham w Boughton Malherbe *Cant* 74-80; V Cwmdauddwr w St Harmon and Llanwrthwl *S & B* 80-86; V Cydweli and Llandyfaelog *St D* 86-97; Can St D Cathl 92-02; Adn St D 96-02; V Steynton 97-02; rtd 02. *16 Freshwater East Road, Lamphey, Pembroke SA71 5JX*

DAVIES, Canon Henry Joseph. b 38. Univ of Wales (Cardiff) BSc61. St Mich Coll Llan 75. **d** 76 **p** 77. C Griffithstown *Mon* 76-79; TV Cwmbran 79-85; V Newport St Andr 85-03; Can St Woolos Cathl 98-03; rtd 03; Perm to Offic *Mon* 03-11; P-in-c Bettws from 11. *14 Morden Road, Newport NP19 7EU*

DAVIES, Herbert John. b 30. Cheltenham & Glouc Coll of HE BA97. Glouc Sch of Min 84. **d** 87 **p** 88. NSM Cheltenham St Mark *Glouc* 87-01; Perm to Offic from 01. *45 Farmington Road, Benhall, Cheltenham GL51 6AG* Tel (01242) 515996

DAVIES, Huw. See DAVIES, Philip Huw

DAVIES, Huw. See DAVIES, Peter Huw

DAVIES, Hywel John. b 45. Univ of Wales (Abth) BA67 Univ of Wales (Ban) DipEd68 Univ of Wales (Cardiff) MA90 Univ of Wales (Ban) BTh99. St Mich Coll Llan 94 Qu Coll Birm 96. **d** 97 **p** 98. Min Can Ban Cathl 97-98; C Llandudno 98-99; Lic to Offic *Llan* 99-03; NSM Canton Cardiff 03-04; P-in-c Llanarthne and Llanddarog *St D* 04-07; Chapl Coleg Sir Gâr 04-07; rtd 07; P-in-c Cardiff Dewi Sant *Llan* 08-10. *68 Glas y Gors, Cwmbach, Aberdare CF44 0BQ* Tel (01685) 378457
E-mail hywel33@btinternet.com

DAVIES, Ian. b 45. Man Coll of Educn TCert74 Open Univ BA79. Carl Dioc Tr Inst 88. **d** 91 **p** 92. NSM Harraby *Carl* 91-95; C Barrow St Jo 95-96; P-in-c 96-00; P-in-c Beetham and Youth and Sch Support Officer 00-05; V Marown *S & M* from 05. *Marown Vicarage, Main Road, Crosby, Isle of Man IM4 4BH* Tel (01624) 851378 E-mail reviand@manx.net

DAVIES, Ian. b 54. Sheff Hallam Univ BA80 Univ of Wales (Cardiff) MSc(Econ)86 MBA92 Bris Univ PhD01 CQSW80. Wycliffe Hall Ox 02. **d** 04 **p** 05. C Swansea St Pet *S & B* 04-06; C Waunarllwydd 06-07; P-in-c 07-10; V from 10. *The New Vicarage, 59A Victoria Road, Waunarlwydd, Swansea SA5 4SY* Tel (01792) 874286 Mobile 07779-145267
E-mail iandavies12@hotmail.com

DAVIES, Ian Charles. b 51. Sarum & Wells Th Coll 78. **d** 81 **p** 82. C E Bedfont *Lon* 81-84; C Cheam *S'wark* 84-87; V Merton St Jas 87-96; RD Merton 91-96; Chapl Tiffin Sch Kingston 96-97; P-in-c Kingston St Luke *S'wark* 96-98; V S Beddington St Mich 98-99. *111 Milton Road, London W7 1LG* Tel (020) 8621 4450

DAVIES, Ian Elliott. b 64. Univ of Wales (Ban) BD85. Ridley Hall Cam 86. **d** 88 **p** 89. C Baglan *Llan* 88-90; C Skewen 90-96; C St Marylebone All SS *Lon* 96-01; R Hollywood St Thos USA from 02. *St Thomas's Church, 7501 Hollywood Boulevard, Hollywood CA 90046, USA* Tel (001) (323) 876 2102 Fax 876 7738 E-mail frdavies@saintthomashollywood.org

DAVIES, Ion. See DAVIES, Johnston ap Llynfi

DAVIES, Islwyn. See DAVIES, Canon David Islwyn

DAVIES, Canon Ivor Llewellyn. b 35. Univ of Wales BA56 St Cath Soc Ox BA58 MA63. Wycliffe Hall Ox 56. **d** 62 **p** 63. C Wrexham *St As* 62-64; India 65-71; V Connah's Quay *St As* 71-79; P-in-c Gorsley w Cliffords Mesne *Glouc* 79-84; P-in-c Hempsted 84-90; Dir of Ords 84-90; Hon Can Glouc Cathl 89-01; V Parkend 90-01; P-in-c Viney Hill 97-01; rtd 01; Perm to Offic *Glouc* from 01 and *Heref* from 04. *Rose Cottage, Church Walk, Parkend, Lydney GL15 4HQ* Tel (01594) 564512

DAVIES, James Alan. b 38. Lambeth STh95. St Jo Coll Nottm. **d** 83 **p** 84. C Fletchamstead *Cov* 83-87; P-in-c Hartshill 87-89; V 89-93; V E Green 93-03; rtd 03; Hon C Mickleton, Willersey, Saintbury etc *Glouc* 04-05; Perm to Offic *Cov* from 05. *5 Margetts Close, Kenilworth CV8 1EN* Tel (01926) 854337
E-mail alan.davies@ukonline.co.uk

DAVIES, Canon James Trevor Eiddig. b 17. St D Coll Lamp BA39 AKC41. **d** 41 **p** 42. C Rhymney *Mon* 41-44; C Newport St Andr 44-47; P-in-c 47-51; P-in-c Nash 50-51; R Bettws Newydd w Trostrey and Kemeys Commander 51-58; V Blaenavon w Capel Newydd 58-68; V Llantarnam 68-71; TR Cwmbran 71-86; Hon Can St Woolos Cathl 83-86; rtd 86; Lic to Offic *Mon* from 86. *34 Rockfield Road, Monmouth NP25 5BA* Tel (01600) 716649

DAVIES, James William. b 51. Trin Hall Cam BA72 MA76 St Jo Coll Dur BA79. Cranmer Hall Dur 77. **d** 80 **p** 81. C Croydon Ch Ch Broad Green *Cant* 80-83; CMS 83-86; Chapl Bethany Sch Goudhurst 86-90; P-in-c Parkstone St Luke *Sarum* 90-00; Hon C Bournemouth St Andr *Win* from 05. *8 Newton Road, Swanage BH19 2DZ* Tel (01929) 475770
E-mail jameswdavies@btopenworld.com

DAVIES, Preb Jane Ann. b 58. Coll of Ripon & York St Jo MA97. Aston Tr Scheme 91 WMMTC 93 NOC 94. **d** 96 **p** 97. NSM Heref S Wye 96-97; C 97-00; P-in-c Bishop's Frome w Castle Frome and Fromes Hill 00-08; P-in-c Acton Beauchamp and Evesbatch w Stanford Bishop 00-08; P-in-c Stoke Lacy, Moreton Jeffries w Much Cowarne etc 00-08; V Frome Valley from 09; Preb Heref Cathl from 10. *The Vicarage, Bishop's Frome, Worcester WR6 5AP* Tel (01885) 490204
E-mail jane@davies4771.fsnet.co.uk

DAVIES, Mrs Jaqueline Ann. b 42. Bris Univ BA64 CertEd65 Univ of Wales (Lamp) MA99. EMMTC 84 St As Minl Tr Course 97. **d** 98 **p** 99. NSM Llanfair DC, Derwen, Llanelidan and Efenechtyd *St As* 98-00; Perm to Offic from 00. *Sisial y Llyn, 3 Glannau Tegid, Bala LL23 7DZ* Tel (01678) 520636

DAVIES, Jeffrey William. b 45. St Cath Coll Cam BA66 MA69 LLM67 Liv Univ MTh07 Solicitor 69. NOC 01. **d** 04 **p** 05. NSM Ramsbottom St Andr *Man* 04-05; NSM Ramsbottom and Edenfield 05-11; NSM Heaton Ch Ch w Halliwell St Marg from 11. *44 Higher Dunscar, Egerton, Bolton BL7 9TF* Tel and fax (01204) 412503 E-mail jeffdavies1@ntlworld.com

DAVIES, Jeremy. See DAVIES, Canon David Jeremy Christopher

DAVIES, Joanna. b 65. NTMTC. **d** 10 **p** 11. C Onslow Square and S Kensington St Aug *Lon* from 10. *54 Mayford Road, London SW12 8SN* E-mail jo.davies@htb.org

DAVIES, John. See DAVIES, Herbert John

DAVIES, John. See DAVIES, Benjamin John

DAVIES, John. See PAGE DAVIES, David John

DAVIES, John. See DAVIES, Kenneth John

DAVIES, John. b 62. Univ of Wales (Cardiff) BA88. Ridley Hall Cam 98. **d** 00 **p** 01. C Wavertree H Trin *Liv* 00-04; P-in-c W Derby Gd Shep 04-09; V 09-10; TV Okehampton w Inwardleigh, Bratton Clovelly etc *Ex* from 10. *The Rectory, Lydford, Okehampton EX20 4BH* Tel (01822) 820564
E-mail john@johndavies.org

DAVIES, John Atcherley. b 27. St Jo Coll Dur BA55. Wycliffe Hall Ox 55. **d** 57 **p** 58. C Eastbourne St Jo *Chich* 57-61; Chapl RN 61-82; V Hyde Common *Win* 82-92; rtd 92; Perm to Offic *Win* from 98. *6 Durlston Crescent, Christchurch BH23 2ST* Tel (01202) 484398

DAVIES, John Barden. b 47. St D Coll Lamp 70. **d** 71 **p** 72. C Rhosllannerchrugog *St As* 71-75; R Llanbedr-y-Cennin *Ban* 75-86; Adult Educn Officer 86-93; V Betws-y-Coed and Capel Curig w Penmachno etc 86-93; R Llanfwrog and Clocaenog and Gyffylliog *St As* 93-09; AD Dyffryn Clwyd 95-09. *183 Station Road, Deganwy, Conwy LL31 9EX* Tel (01492) 583045 Mobile 07590-465052 E-mail jbdrtn@hotmail.co.uk

DAVIES, John Daniel Lee. b 55. Trin Coll Carmarthen BEd79. **d** 00 **p** 00. C Leverburgh *Arg* 00-01; P-in-c Harris Ch Ch from 01. *3A Cluer, Isle of Harris HS3 3EP* Tel (01859) 530344

✠**DAVIES, The Rt Revd John David Edward.** b 53. Southn Univ LLB74 Univ of Wales (Cardiff) LLM95. St Mich Coll Llan 82. **d** 84 **p** 85 **c** 08. C Chepstow *Mon* 84-86; C-in-c Michaelston-y-Fedw and Rudry 86-89; R Bedwas and Rudry 89-95; V Maindee Newport 95-00; Dean Brecon and V Brecon St Mary w Llanddew *S & B* 00-08; P-in-c Cynog Honddu 05-08; Bp *S & B* from 08. *Ely Tower, Castle Square, Brecon LD3 9DJ* Tel (01874) 622008 E-mail bishop.swanbrec@churchinwales.org.uk

✠**DAVIES, The Rt Revd John Dudley.** b 27. Trin Coll Cam BA51 MA63. Linc Th Coll 52. **d** 53 **p** 54 **c** 87. C Leeds Halton St Wilfrid *Ripon* 53-56; C Yeoville S Africa 57; R Evander 57-61; R Empangeni 61-63; Chapl Witwatersrand Univ 63-71; Sec Chapls in HE Gen Syn Bd of Educn 71-74; P-in-c Keele *Lich* 74-76; Chapl Keele Univ 74-76; Prin USPG Coll of the Ascension Selly Oak 76-81; Preb Lich Cathl 76-87; Can Res, Preb and Sacr St As Cathl 82-85; Dioc Missr 82-87; V Llanrhaeadr-ym-Mochnant, Llanarmon, Pennant etc 85-87; Suff Bp Shrewsbury *Lich* 87-92; Area Bp 92-94; rtd 94; Perm to Offic *Lich* from 05. *Nyddfa, By-Pass Road, Gobowen, Oswestry SY11 3NG* Tel and fax (01691) 653434
E-mail sddjdd@sddjdd.free-online.co.uk

DAVIES, John Edwards Gurnos. b 18. Ch Coll Cam BA41 MA45. Westcott Ho Cam 40. **d** 42 **p** 43. C Portwood St Paul *Ches* 42-44; CF (EC) 44-46; CF 46-73; Asst Chapl Gen 70; QHC 72; R Monk Sherborne and Pamber *Win* 73-76; P-in-c Sherborne 76; R The Sherbornes w Pamber 76-83; rtd 83. *3 Parsonage Lane, Edington, Westbury BA13 4QS* Tel (01380) 830479

DAVIES, John Gwylim. b 27. Ripon Hall Ox 67. **d** 70 **p** 71. C Ox St Mich 70-71; C Ox St Mich w St Martin and All SS 71-72; TV New Windsor 73-77; R Hagley *Worc* 77-83; TV Littleham w Exmouth 83-92; Asst Dioc Stewardship Adv 83-92; rtd 92; Perm to Offic *Ex* from 92. *5 The Retreat, The Retreat Drive, Topsham, Exeter EX3 0LS* Tel (01392) 876995

DAVIES, The Very Revd John Harverd. b 57. Keble Coll Ox BA80 MA84 CCC Cam MPhil82 Lanc Univ PhD. Westcott Ho Cam 82. **d** 84 **p** 85. C Liv Our Lady and St Nic w St Anne 84-87; C Pet St Jo 87-90; Min Can Pet Cathl 88-90; V Anfield St Marg *Liv* 90-94; Chapl, Fell and Lect Keble Coll Ox 94-99; V Melbourne *Derby* 99-10; P-in-c Ticknall, Smisby and Stanton by Bridge etc 07-10; V Melbourne, Ticknall, Smisby and Stanton 10; Dioc Dir of Ords 00-09; Hon Can Derby Cathl 10; Dean Derby from 10. *Derby Cathedral Centre, 18-19 Iron Gate, Derby DE1 3GP* Tel (01332) 341201 E-mail dean@derbycathedral.org

DAVIES, Canon John Howard. b 29. St Jo Coll Cam BA50 MA54 Nottm Univ BD62. Westcott Ho Cam 54. **d** 55 **p** 56. Succ Derby Cathl 55-58; Chapl Westcott Ho Cam 58-63; Lect Th Southn Univ 63-81; Lic to Offic *Win* 63-81; Sen Lect 74-81; Dir Th and RS Southn Univ 81-94; Can Th Win Cathl 81-91; Hon C Southampton St Alb 88-91; Hon C Swaythling 91-94; rtd 94. *13 Glen Eyre Road, Southampton SO16 3GA* Tel (023) 8067 9359

DAVIES, Canon John Howard. b 35. Brasted Th Coll 60 Ely Th Coll 62. **d** 64 **p** 65. C Bromsgrove All SS *Worc* 64-67; C Astwood Bank w Crabbs Cross 67-70; R Worc St Martin 70-74; P-in-c Worc St Pet 72-74; R Worc St Martin w St Pet 74-79; RD Worc E 77-79; TR Malvern Link w Cowleigh 79-93; Hon Can Worc Cathl 81-00; RD Malvern 83-92; V Bromsgrove St Jo 93-00; rtd 00; Perm to Offic *Worc* from 00. *10 Baveney Road, Worcester WR2 6DS* Tel (01905) 428086 E-mail jjhd39@aol.com

DAVIES, John Howard. b 51. EAMTC 98. **d** 01 **p** 02. NSM Walsingham, Houghton and Barsham *Nor* 01-04; NSM Holt w High Kelling 04-06; P-in-c Lake *Portsm* from 06; P-in-c Shanklin St Sav from 06. *The Vicarage, 46 Sandown Road, Lake, Sandown PO36 9JT* Tel (01983) 401121 Mobile 07870-509439 E-mail john@apostle.co.uk

DAVIES, John Hugh Conwy. b 42. Bris Univ BSc64 PhD67 CEng72 MICE72. Linc Th Coll 84. **d** 86 **p** 87. C Limber Magna w Brocklesby *Linc* 86-89; R Walesby Gp 89-94; R Denbigh and Nantglyn *St As* 94-99; R Denbigh 99-00; V Llanrhaeadr-ym-Mochnant etc 01 07; rtd 07. *Sisial y Llyn, 3 Glanrau Tegid, Bala LL23 7DZ* Tel (01678) 520636

DAVIES, Canon John Hywel Morgan. b 45. St D Coll Lamp BA71 LTh73. **d** 73 **p** 74. C Milford Haven *St D* 73-77; V 89-11; R Castlemartin w Warren and Angle etc 77-82; R Walton W w Talbenny and Haroldston W 82-89; Can St D Cathl 03-11; rtd 11. *6 Waterloo Road, Hakin, Milford Haven SA73 3PB* Tel (01646) 692766 E-mail johnmorgandavies@talk21.com

DAVIES, John Ifor. b 20. ACP DipEd. **d** 80 **p** 81. Hon C Allerton *Liv* 80-84; Hon C Ffynnongroew *St As* 84-87; Hon C Whitford 87-88. *Hafan Deg, Ffordd-y-Graig, Lixwm, Holywell CH8 8LY* Tel (01352) 781151

DAVIES, John Keith. b 33. St Mich Coll Llan 80. **d** 82 **p** 83. C Llanbadarn Fawr w Capel Bangor and Goginan *St D* 82-84; V Llandygwydd and Cenarth w Cilrhedyn etc 84-89; V Abergwili w Llanfihangel-uwch-Gwili etc 89-98; RD Carmarthen 93-98; rtd 98. *Tanyfron, 81 Hafod Cwnin, Carmarthen SA31 2AS* Tel (01267) 223931

DAVIES, John Melvyn George. b 37. Wycliffe Hall Ox 68. **d** 71 **p** 72. C Norbury *Ches* 71-75; C Heswall 76-78; V Claughton cum Grange 78-83; R Waverton 83-02; RD Malpas 90-97; rtd 02; Perm to Offic *Ches* from 03. *15 Tattenhall Road, Tattenhall, Chester CH3 9QQ* Tel (01829) 770184

DAVIES, Canon John Oswell. b 27. St D Coll Lamp 74. **d** 75 **p** 76. C Henfynyw w Aberaeron and Llanddewi Aberarth *St D* 75-76; P-in-c Eglwysnewydd w Ysbyty Ystwyth 76-77; V 77-83; R Maenordeifi and Capel Colman w Llanfihangel etc 83-93; RD Cemais and Sub-Aeron 87-93; Hon Can St D Cathl 92-93; rtd 93. *Hafod, Carregwen, Llechryd, Cardigan SA43 2PJ* Tel (01239) 682568

✠**DAVIES, The Rt Revd John Stewart.** b 43. Univ of Wales BA72 Qu Coll Cam MLitt74. Westcott Ho Cam 72. **d** 74 **p** 75 **c** 99. C Hawarden *St As* 74-78; Tutor St Deiniol's Lib Hawarden 76-83; V Rhosymedre *St As* 78-87; Dir Dioc Minl Tr Course 83-93; Warden of Ords 83-91; Hon Can St As Cathl 86-91; V Mold 87-92; Adn St As 91-99; R Llandyrnog and Llangwyfan 92-99; Bp St As 99-08; rtd 09. *17 Pont y Bedol, Llanrhaeadr, Denbigh LL16 4NF*

DAVIES, Johnston ap Llynfi (Ion). b 28. St D Coll Lamp BA51 St Mich Coll Llan 51. **d** 53 **p** 54. C Swansea Ch Ch *S & B* 53-55; C Sketty 55-57; Nigeria 57-61; R Whittington *Derby* 61-64; Chapl Broadmoor Hosp Crowthorne 64-66; Perm to Offic *Ox* 67-72; Perm to Offic *York* 72-86; R Creeksea w Althorne, Latchingdon and N Fambridge *Chelmsf* 86-88; rtd 88; Asst Chapl Costa Blanca *Eur* 89-92; Chapl 92-93; Lic to Offic 93-95. *Calle Ponent 1, Apartamentos Esmeralda 41A, 03710 Calpe (Alicante), Spain* Tel (0034) 965 838 063

DAVIES, Jonathan Byron. b 69. Univ of Wales (Cardiff) BTh95. St Mich Coll Llan 94. **d** 96 **p** 97. C Betws w Ammanford and Dioc Youth Chapl *St D* 96-99; C Newton St Pet *S & B* 99-00; P-in-c Swansea St Luke 03-05; V Manselton and Cwmbwrla from 05; Chapl Mid and W Wales Fire and Rescue Service from 05. *The Vicarage, Manor Road, Manselton, Swansea SA5 9PA* Tel (01792) 464595 Mobile 07760-210975 E-mail rev.jbd@sky.com

DAVIES, Judith. b 54. Man Univ BA75. WEMTC 97. **d** 00 **p** 01. C Harlescott *Lich* 00-04; Chapl Shrewsbury and Telford NHS Trust 04-05; Asst Chapl Severn Hospice Shrewsbury 05-06; Perm to Offic *Heref* 05-06; TV Wenlock from 06. *The Vicarage, Harley Road, Cressage, Shrewsbury SY5 6DF* Tel (01952) 510417

DAVIES, Prof Julia Mary. b 44. Ex Univ BA65 FCIPD00. **d** 04 **p** 05. OLM Deane *Man* from 04; Hon Assoc Dioc Dir of Ords from 10. *15 Newland Drive, Bolton BL5 1DS* Tel (01204) 660260 Mobile 07966-528877

DAVIES, Julian Edward. b 60. Jes Coll Ox BA82 MA86 DPhil87 Selw Coll Cam BA92 MA96. Ridley Hall Cam 90. **d** 94 **p** 95. C Hucknall Torkard *S'well* 94-96; C Eglwysilan *Llan* 96-99; Assoc R St Marylebone w H Trin *Lon* 99-03; Assoc R St Giles-in-the-Fields 03-08; TR Southampton (City Cen) *Win* from 08. *The Rectory, 32B Morris Road, Southampton SO15 2BR* Tel (023) 8023 5716 E-mail jed-ihs@o2.co.uk

DAVIES, Mrs Karen Elizabeth. Univ of Wales (Abth) BA66 Univ of Wales (Ban) MEd85. **d** 11. OLM Criftins w Dudleston and Welsh Frankton *Lich* from 11. *Horseshoe Cottage, Horseshoe Lane, Eastwick, Ellesmere SY12 9JT* Tel (01691) 690346 Mobile 07787-324953 E-mail karendavies2000@btinternet.com

DAVIES, Keith. See DAVIES, John Keith

DAVIES, Keith. See BERRY-DAVIES, Charles William Keith

DAVIES, Kenneth John. b 42. Ripon Coll Cuddesdon 79. **d** 80 **p** 81. C Buckingham *Ox* 80-83; V Birstall *Wakef* 83-91; TV Crookes St Thos *Sheff* 91-94; TR Huntington *York* 94-07; rtd 07. *18 Hall Rise, Haxby, York YO32 3LP* Tel (01904) 768211 E-mail johnsuedavies@aol.com

DAVIES, Leonard Hamblyn Kenneth. b 57. Birm Univ MA03 Dur Univ MA06. Sierra Leone Bible Coll 84. **d** 93 **p** 94. C St Geo Cathl Freetown Lierra Leone 93-96; C Freetown St Jo 96-98; P-in-c Freetown H Spirit 98-01; Perm to Offic *Worc* 01-02; *Birm* 02-03; *Chelmsf* 03-08; Lic to Offic from 08; Asst Chapl E Lon Univ 08-09; Asst Chapl London SW YMCA from 09; C Forest Gate All SS and St Edm from 10. *281 Central Park Road, London E6 3AF* Tel (020) 8471 7193 Mobile 07834-971467 E-mail kendavies90@hotmail.com

DAVIES, The Ven Lorys Martin. b 36. JP78. Univ of Wales (Lamp) BA57 ALCM52. Wells Th Coll 57. **d** 59 **p** 60. C Tenby w Gumfreston *St D* 59-62; Asst Chapl Brentwood Sch Essex 62-66; Chapl Solihull Sch 66-68; V Moseley St Mary *Birm* 68-81; Can Res Birm Cathl 81-92; Dioc Dir of Ords 82-90; Adn Bolton *Man* 92-01; Bp's Adv Hosp Chapl 92-01; Warden of Readers 94-01; rtd 02; Perm to Offic *Birm* and *Worc* from 04. *Heol Cerrig, 28 Penshurst Road, Bromsgrove B60 2SN* Tel (01527) 577337

DAVIES (née ROACH), Mrs Lynne Elisabeth. b 44. WMMTC 95. **d** 98 **p** 99. NSM Snitterfield w Bearley *Cov* 98-01; NSM Salford Priors from 01; NSM Exhall w Wixford from 01; NSM Temple Grafton w Binton from 01. *19 Garrard Close, Salford Priors, Evesham WR11 8XG* Tel (01789) 773711 Fax 490231

DAVIES, Malcolm. b 35. St Mich Coll Llan 82. **d** 84 **p** 85. C Roath *Llan* 84-88; C Pentre 88-94; V Llancarfan w Llantrithyd 94-02; rtd 02. *141 Fontygary Road, Rhoose, Barry CF62 3DU* Tel (01446) 710509

DAVIES, Malcolm Thomas. b 36. Open Univ BA81. St Mich Coll Llan 71. **d** 73 **p** 74. C Betws w Ammanford *St D* 73-76; V Cil-y-Cwm and Ystrad-ffin w Rhandir-mwyn etc 76-80; V Llangyfelach *S & B* 80-85; V Loughor 85-94; V Llanelli St Paul *St D* 94-95; V Llanelli St Pet 95-01; rtd 01. *25 Walters Road, Llanelli SA15 1LR* Tel (01554) 770295

DAVIES, Mrs Margaret Adelaide. b 45. Weymouth Coll of Educn CertEd67. S Dios Minl Tr Scheme 92. **d** 95 **p** 96. NSM Westbury Sarum 95-02; NSM White Horse 02-11; TV 07-11; rtd 11. *Address temp unknown*

DAVIES, Mrs Margot Alison Jane. b 55. SWMTC 02. **d** 05 **p** 06. C St Ives *Truro* 05-09; C Halsetown 05-09; TV Saltash from 09. *35 Lower Port View, Saltash PL12 4BY* Tel (01752) 841698

✠**DAVIES, The Rt Revd Mark.** b 62. Leeds Univ BA85. Coll of Resurr Mirfield 86. **d** 89 **p** 90 **c** 08. C Barnsley St Mary *Wakef* 89-95; R Hemsworth 95-06; Dioc Vocations Adv and Asst Dir of Ords 98-06; RD Pontefract 00-06; Hon Can Wakef Cathl 02-06; Adn Rochdale *Man* 06-08; Suff Bp Middleton from 08. *The Hollies, Manchester Road, Rochdale OL11 3QY* Tel (01706) 358550 Fax 354851 E-mail markdavies62@bigfoot.com

DAVIES, Martin. See DAVIES, William Martin

DAVIES, Martyn John. b 60. Chich Th Coll 82. **d** 85 **p** 86. C Llantrisant 85-87; C Whitchurch 87-90; V Porth w Trealaw 90-01; R Merthyr Tydfil St Dav 01-10; R Merthyr Tydfil St Dav and Abercanaid from 10; AD Merthyr Tydfil from 04. *The Rectory, Bryntirion Road, Merthyr Tydfil CF47 0ER* Tel (01685) 722992 E-mail fr.martyn@sky.com

DAVIES, Melvyn. See DAVIES, John Melvyn George

DAVIES, Canon Mervyn Morgan. b 25. Univ of Wales BA49. Coll of Resurr Mirfield 49. **d** 51 **p** 52. C Pennarth w Lavernock *Llan* 51-58; Lic to Offic *Wakef* 58-60; C Port Talbot St Theodore *Llan* 60-63; V Pontycymer and Blaengarw 63-69; V Fairwater 69-95; RD Llan 81-95; Jt Ed *Welsh Churchman* 82-95; Can Llan Cathl 84-89; Prec 89-95; rtd 95; Perm to Offic *Llan* from 95. *20 Palace Avenue, Llandaff, Cardiff CF5 2DW* Tel (029) 2057 5327

DAVIES, Michael. See DAVIES, Canon David Michael Cole

DAVIES, Miss Moira Kathleen. b 41. Cant Sch of Min. **d** 88 **p** 94. Par Dn Walmer *Cant* 88-94; C 94-96; P-in-c Somercotes and

Grainthorpe w Conisholme *Linc* 96-99; R 99-06; rtd 06. *9 Amanda Drive, Louth LN11 0AZ* Tel (01507) 609960
DAVIES, Canon Mostyn David. b 37. AKC64. **d** 65 **p** 66. C Corby St Columba *Pet* 65-69; Ind Chapl 69-03; P-in-c Pet St Barn 80-03; Can Pet Cathl 95-03; rtd 03; Perm to Offic *Pet* from 03. *92 West End, Langtoft, Peterborough PE6 9LU* Tel (01778) 342838 E-mail mostyn@zetnet.co.uk
DAVIES, Canon Myles Cooper. b 50. Sarum & Wells Th Coll 71. **d** 74 **p** 75. C W Derby St Mary *Liv* 74-77; C Seaforth 77-80; V 80-84; V Stanley 84-07; P-in-c Liv St Paul Stoneycroft 05-07; V Stanley w Stoneycroft St Paul 07-11; Chapl Rathbone Hosp Liv 84-92; Chapl N Mersey Community NHS Trust 92-05; Dir of Ords *Liv* 94-05; Hon Can Liv Cathl 01-05; Can Res Liv Cathl from 06; Prec from 08. *2 Cathedral Close, Liverpool L1 7BZ* Tel 0151-702 7203 E-mail myles.davies@liverpoolcathedral.org
DAVIES, Neil Anthony Bowen. b 52. Ex Univ BSc74. Westcott Ho Cam 75. **d** 78 **p** 79. C Llanblethian w Cowbridge and Llandough etc 78-80; C Aberdare 80-82; V Troedyrhiw w Merthyr Vale 82-88; Min Lower Earley LEP *Ox* 88-92; V Earley Trin 92-95; P-in-c Reading St Luke w St Bart 95-99; Perm to Offic 99-02. *Address temp unknown*
DAVIES, Nicholas Duff. b 67. Sheff Univ BA88 Edin Univ MTh89 Anglia Ruskin Univ MA09 FRSA01. Westcott Ho Cam 06. **d** 08 **p** 09. C S Dulwich St Steph *S'wark* from 08. *18 Talisman Square, London SE26 6XY* Tel (020) 8768 4273 Mobile 07801-336144 E-mail nickduffdavies@gmail.com
DAVIES, Mrs Nicola Louise. b 55. Birm Univ BA77 Lon Inst of Educn PGCE78. STETS 02. **d** 05. NSM Rowledge and Frensham *Guildf* 05-06. *1 Little Austins, Farnham GU9 8JR* Tel (01252) 714640 E-mail nicoladavies27@hotmail.com
DAVIES, Canon Nigel Lawrence. b 55. Lanc Univ BEd77. Sarum & Wells Th Coll 84. **d** 87 **p** 88. C Heywood St Luke w All So *Man* 87-91; V Burneside *Carl* 91-07; P-in-c Crosscrake 04-06; P-in-c Skelsmergh w Selside and Longsleddale 06-07; V Beacon from 07; RD Kendal 03-08; Hon Can Carl Cathl from 06. *St Oswald's Vicarage, The Main Road, Burneside, Kendal LA9 6QX* Tel (01539) 722015 Fax 07974-448370 E-mail vicar_stoswald@hotmail.com *or* ruraldean kendal@hotmail.com
DAVIES, Noel Paul. b 47. Chich Th Coll 83. **d** 85 **p** 86. C Milford Haven *St D* 85-89; R Jeffreyston w Reynoldston and E Williamston etc 89-09; R Jeffreyston w Reynoldston and Loveston etc from 09. *The Rectory, Jeffreyston, Kilgetty SA68 0SG* Tel (01646) 651269
DAVIES, Mrs Pamela Elizabeth. b 55. Oak Hill Th Coll 09. **d** 11. C Berechurch St Marg w St Mich *Chelmsf* from 11. *3 Helen Ewing Place, Colchester CO2 8WS* Tel (01206) 657697 Mobile 07866-600304
DAVIES, Canon Patricia Elizabeth. b 36. Westf Coll Lon BA58 Hughes Hall Cam CertEd59 Leeds Univ MA74. NEOC 83. dss 86 **d** 87 **p** 94. Killingworth *Newc* 86-90; Hon C 87-90; Hon C Newc H Cross 91-96; NSM Newc Epiphany 96-99; NSM Gosforth St Hugh 99-00; P-in-c 00-01; Hon Can Newc Cathl 00-01; rtd 01; Perm to Offic *York* from 01. *Applegarth, Middlewood Lane, Fylingthorpe, Whitby YO22 4TT* Tel (01947) 881175
DAVIES, Patrick Charles Steven. b 59. RGN86 RMN92 RHV94 Leeds Univ BA99. Coll of Resurr Mirfield 97. **d** 99 **p** 00. C Reddish *Man* 99-04; P-in-c Withington St Crispin from 04. *St Crispin's Rectory, 2 Hart Road, Manchester M14 7LE* Tel 0161-224 3452 E-mail fatherpat@btinternet.com
DAVIES, Paul. *See* DAVIES, Richard Paul
DAVIES, Paul Lloyd. b 46. Bris Univ LLB68 Solicitor 71. Trin Coll Carmarthen 84. **d** 87 **p** 88. NSM Newport w Cilgwyn and Dinas w Llanllawer *St D* 87-97; P-in-c Mathry w St Edren's and Grandston etc 97-01; V 01-08; rtd 08. *Treetops, Osborn Park, Neyland, Milford Haven SA73 1SX* Tel (01646) 602919
DAVIES, Paul Martin. b 35. Lon Univ BD75. Sarum & Wells Th Coll 73. **d** 75 **p** 76. C Walthamstow St Mary w St Steph *Chelmsf* 75-79; Kenya 79-86; R Leven w Catwick *York* 86-95; RD N Holderness 90-95; rtd 95; Perm to Offic *York* from 95. *54 The Meadows, Cherry Burton, Beverley HU17 7SD* Tel (01964) 551739
DAVIES, Paul Scott. b 59. Cranmer Hall Dur 85. **d** 88 **p** 89. C New Addington *S'wark* 88-91; C Croydon H Sav 91-94; P-in-c Norton in the Moors *Lich* 94-99; R 99-03; V Sunbury *Lon* from 03. *The Vicarage, Thames Street, Sunbury-on-Thames TW16 6AA* Tel (01932) 779431 E-mail paul@zippor.com
DAVIES, Peter. b 67. Lon Bible Coll BA97 Cardiff Univ MTh08. St Mich Coll Llan 06. **d** 07 **p** 08. C Llanelli *St D* 07-10; TV E Carmarthen 10-11. *153 Gabalfa Avenue, Cardiff CF14 2PB*
DAVIES, Peter Huw. b 57. Crewe & Alsager Coll BEd79. Wycliffe Hall Ox 87. **d** 89 **p** 90. C Moreton *Ches* 89-93; V Weston-super-Mare St Paul *B & W* 93-05; P-in-c Chesham Bois *Ox* 05-08; R from 08. *The Rectory, Glebe Way, Amersham HP6 5ND* Tel (01494) 726139 E-mail daviesp5@aol.net
DAVIES, Peter Richard. b 32. St Jo Coll Ox BA55 MA58. Westcott Ho Cam 56. **d** 58 **p** 59. C Cannock *Lich* 58-62; Kenya 63-76; Chapl Bedford Sch 76-85; V Dale and St Brides w

Marloes *St D* 85-92; rtd 92. *Canthill Cottage, Dale, Haverfordwest SA62 3QZ* Tel (01646) 636535
DAVIES, Peter Timothy William. b 50. Leeds Univ BSc74. Oak Hill Th Coll 75. **d** 78 **p** 79. C Kingston Hill St Paul *S'wark* 78-81; C Hove Bp Hannington Memorial Ch *Chich* 81-88; V Audley *Lich* from 88; P-in-c Alsagers Bank from 06. *The Vicarage, 1 Wilbrahams Walk, Audley, Stoke-on-Trent ST7 8HL* Tel (01782) 720392
DAVIES, Philip Huw. b 64. Aston Univ BSc86 MRPharmS87. St Mich Coll Llan 00. **d** 02 **p** 03. C Llangynwyd w Maesteg 02-03; C Betws w Ammanford *St D* 03-07; P-in-c Slebech and Uzmaston w Boulston 07-10; V from 10; P-in-c Llawhaden w Bletherston and Llancyefn 07-10; V from 10. *The Vicarage, Maenclochog, Clynderwen SA66 7LD* Tel (01437) 532925
DAVIES, Philip James. b 58. UEA BA79 Keswick Hall Coll PGCE80 K Coll Lon MA92. Ridley Hall Cam 86. **d** 89 **p** 90. C Rainham *Roch* 89-90; C Gravesend St Geo and Rosherville 90-95; V Rosherville 95-98; Dioc Schs Development Officer *Pet* from 98; P-in-c King's Cliffe 98-10; C Bulwick, Blatherwycke w Harringworth and Laxton 07-10; R King's Cliffe, Bulwick and Blatherwycke etc from 10. *The Rectory, 3 Hall Yard, King's Cliffe, Peterborough PE8 6XQ* Tel (01780) 470314 E-mail p.j.davies@tesco.net
DAVIES, Philip Simon. b 65. Trin Coll Ox BA87 MA91. Aston Tr Scheme 93 Ridley Hall Cam 95. **d** 97 **p** 98. C Burntwood *Lich* 97-00; TV Cheswardine, Childs Ercall, Hales, Hinstock etc 00-03; TR 03-04; P-in-c Olney *Ox* 04-08; P-in-c Banbury St Hugh from 08. *St Hugh's Vicarage, 4 Longfellow Road, Banbury OX16 9LB* Tel (01295) 256513 E-mail revdavies@btinternet.com
DAVIES, Philip Wyn. b 50. Univ of Wales BA72 MA82. St D Dioc Tr Course 93 St Mich Coll Llan BD96. **d** 96 **p** 97. C Llandysul *St D* 96-98; V Tregaron w Ystrad Meurig and Strata Florida from 98; P-in-c Blaenpennal 01-07; V from 07; Dioc Archivist from 04; AD Lampeter and Ultra-Aeron from 11. *The Vicarage, Tregaron SY25 6HL* Tel (01974) 299010
DAVIES, Mrs Rachel Hannah Eileen. b 64. St Mich Coll Llan 01. **d** 04 **p** 05. NSM Lampeter and Llanddewibrefi Gp *St D* 04-06; NSM Bro Teifi Sarn Helen 06-08; P-in-c Llanerch Aeron w Ciliau Aeron and Dihewyd etc from 08. *Gwndwn, New Inn, Pencader SA39 9BE* Tel and fax (01559) 384248 Mobile 07814-272998
DAVIES, Raymond Emlyn Peter. b 25. St Mich Coll Llan 51. **d** 53 **p** 54. C Llangeinor 53-58; C Llanishen and Lisvane 58-62 and 65-68; R Glyncorrwg w Afan Vale and Cymmer Afan 62-65; V Penrhiwceiber w Matthewstown and Ynysboeth 68-72; C Whitchurch 72-73; V Childs Ercall *Lich* 73-81; R Stoke upon Tern 73-81; P-in-c Hamstall Ridware w Pipe Ridware 81-82; P-in-c Kings Bromley 81-82; P-in-c Mavesyn Ridware 81-82; R The Ridwares and Kings Bromley 83-90; rtd 90; Perm to Offic *B & W* from 95. *51 Vereland Road, Hutton, Weston-super-Mare BS24 9TH* Tel (01934) 814680
DAVIES, Rebecca Jane. b 75. Clare Coll Cam MA96. St Mich Coll Llan 01. **d** 03 **p** 04. C Llandeilo Fawr and Taliaris *St D* 03-05; C Llandybie 05-07; P-in-c Maenclochog and New Moat etc 07-10; V from 10. *The Vicarage, Maenclochog, Clynderwen SA66 7LD* Tel (01437) 532925
DAVIES, Reginald Charles. b 33. Tyndale Hall Bris 58. **d** 64 **p** 65. C Heywood St Jas *Man* 64-66; C Drypool St Columba w St Andr and St Pet *York* 66-69; V Denaby Main *Sheff* from 69. *The Vicarage, Church Road, Denaby Main, Doncaster DN12 4AD* Tel (01709) 862297
DAVIES, Rendle Leslie. b 29. St Chad's Coll Dur BA52. **d** 54 **p** 55. C Monmouth 54-58; V Llangwm Uchaf w Llangwm Isaf w Gwernesney etc 58-63; V Usk and Monkswood w Glascoed Chpl and Gwehelog 63-99; Chapl HM YOI Usk and Prescoed 63-94; rtd 99; Perm to Offic *Heref* from 08. *12 Ridgeway, Wyesham, Monmouth NP25 3JX* Tel (01600) 714189
DAVIES, Rhiannon Mary Morgan. *See* JOHNSON, Rhiannon Mary Morgan
DAVIES, Richard Paul. b 48. Wycliffe Hall Ox 72. **d** 75 **p** 76. C Everton St Sav w St Cuth *Liv* 75-78; Chapl Asst Basingstoke Distr Hosp 78-80; TV Basingstoke *Win* 80-85; V Southampton Thornhill St Chris 85-94; V Eastleigh from 94. *The Vicarage, 1 Cedar Road, Eastleigh SO50 9NR* Tel (023) 8061 2073
DAVIES, Richard Paul. b 73. Univ of Wales (Lamp) BA94 Ox Univ MTh98. Ripon Coll Cuddesdon 94. **d** 97 **p** 98. Min Can St D Cathl 97-00; Succ 00-06; TV Dewisland 01-06; V Burry Port and Pwll from 06; Dioc Ecum Officer 02-07; OCF 05-07; Dioc Warden Ords *St D* from 11. *The Vicarage, Cae Ffwrnes, Burry Port SA16 0FW* Tel (01554) 832936 E-mail plgllddavies@btinternet.com
DAVIES, Robert Emlyn. b 56. N Staffs Poly BA79. Coll of Resurr Mirfield 83. **d** 86 **p** 87. C Cardiff St Jo *Llan* 86-90; V Cwmparc 90-97; V Aberdare from 97; AD Cynon Valley 02-08. *The Vicarage, 26 Abernant Road, Aberdare CF44 0PY* Tel (01685) 884769
DAVIES, Robert Gwynant. **d** 08 **p** 09. NSM Canwell *Lich* from 08; NSM Drayton Bassett from 08; NSM Fazeley from 08.

Middleton House Farm, Tamworth Road, Middleton, Tamworth B78 2BD Tel (01827) 873474 E-mail rob.jane@tinyonline.co.uk
DAVIES, Roger Charles. b 46. Univ of Wales BD72. St Mich Coll Llan 67. **d** 73 **p** 74. C Llanfabon 73-75; C Llanblethian w Cowbridge and Llandough etc 75-78; CF 78-84; TV Halesworth w Linstead, Chediston, Holton etc St E 84-87; R Claydon and Barham 87-91; R Lavant and Chapl Lavant Ho Sch 91-94; TV Gt Aycliffe and Chilton Dur 04-08; P-in-c Wheatley Hill and Wingate w Hutton Henry from 08. The Old Rectory, The Village, Castle Eden, Hartlepool TS27 4SL Tel (01429) 836846 Mobile 07866-649300 E-mail r876davies@btinternet.com
✠**DAVIES, The Rt Revd Ross Owen.** b 55. Melbourne Univ BA77 LLB79. ACT ThL81. **d** 81 **p** 82 **c** 02. Australia 81-91 and from 97; P-in-c Mundford w Lynford Nor 91-94; P-in-c Ickburgh w Langford 91-94; P-in-c Cranwich 91-94; C Somerton w Compton Dundon, the Charltons etc B & W 94-97; R Hindmarsh 97-00; Vic Gen and Adn The Murray 00-02; Bp from 02. 23 Ellendale Avenue, PO Box 269, Murray Bridge SA 5253, Australia Tel (0061) (8) 8532 2270 Fax 8532 5760 Mobile 42-889 1850 E-mail r.davies@murray.anglican.org
DAVIES, Miss Rowan. b 55. Univ of Wales (Swansea) BA78 PGCE79. WMMTC 00. **d** 03 **p** 04. NSM Wigginton Lich from 03. 16 Queen's Way, Tamworth B79 8QD Tel (01827) 69651 E-mail rowan.davies1@ukonline.co.uk
DAVIES, Preb Roy Basil. b 34. Bris Univ BA55. Westcott Ho Cam 57. **d** 59 **p** 60. C Ipswich St Mary le Tower St E 59-63; C Clun w Chapel Lawn Heref 63-70; V Bishop's Castle w Mainstone 70-83; RD Clun Forest 72-83; Preb Heref Cathl 82-99; P-in-c Billingsley w Sidbury 83-86; P-in-c Chelmarsh 83-86; P-in-c Chetton w Deuxhill and Glazeley 83-86; P-in-c Middleton Scriven 83-86; R Billingsley w Sidbury, Middleton Scriven etc 86-89; RD Bridgnorth 87-89; TR Wenlock 89-99; rtd 99; Perm to Offic Heref from 00. 13 Courtnay Rise, Hereford HR1 1BP Tel (01432) 341154
✠**DAVIES, The Rt Revd Roy Thomas.** b 34. St D Coll Lamp BA55 Jes Coll Ox BLitt59. St Steph Ho Ox 57. **d** 59 **p** 60 **c** 85. C Llanelli St Paul St D 59-64; V Llanafan y Trawscoed and Llanwnnws 64-67; Chapl Univ of Wales (Abth) 67-73; C Aberystwyth 67-69; TV 70-73; Sec Ch in Wales Prov Coun for Miss and Unity 73-79; V Carmarthen St Dav St D 79-83; Adn Carmarthen 82-85; V Llanegwad w Llanfynydd 83-85; Bp Llan 85-99; rtd 99. 25 Awel Tywi, Llangunnor, Carmarthen SA31 2NL Tel (01267) 230654
DAVIES, Mrs Sally Jane. b 63. Linc Coll Ox BA86. Trin Coll Bris BA92. **d** 92 **p** 94. C E Molesey St Paul Guildf 92-96; C Chalfont St Peter Ox 96-99; Chapl RN Coll Greenwich and Trin Coll of Music 99-06; Hon C Greenwich St Alfege S'wark 99-06; P-in-c Shamley Green Guildf 06-11; V from 11. The Vicarage, Church Hill, Shamley Green, Guildford GU5 0UD Tel (01483) 892030 E-mail vicar@shamleygreen.net
DAVIES, Canon Sarah Isabella. b 39. Llan Dioc Tr Scheme 87. **d** 91 **p** 97. NSM Pontypridd St Cath w St Matt Llan 91-93; C Ferndale w Maerdy 93-00; Chapl Univ Hosp of Wales and Llandough NHS Trust 98-00; Chapl Pontypridd and Rhondda NHS Trust 98-00; C Cardiff Ch Ch Roath Park Llan 00-09; Dioc Child Protection Officer 02-09; Hon Can Llan Cathl 06-09; rtd 09. 4 St Augustine Road, Heath, Cardiff CF14 4BD
DAVIES, Saunders. See DAVIES, The Rt Revd Francis James Saunders
DAVIES, Scott Lee. b 73. St Jo Coll Nottm. **d** 06 **p** 07. C Childwall All SS Liv 06-10; V Carr Mill from 10. St David's Vicarage, 27 Eskdale Avenue, St Helens WA11 7EN Tel (01744) 732330
DAVIES, Simon Stanley Miles. b 65. Cranfield Univ BEng88 MSc95 Greenwich Univ PGCE00. Seabury-Western Th Sem 97 Westcott Ho Cam 98. **d** 00 **p** 01. C Llanrhos St As 00-03; R Alberton Canada 03-05; Hon C Win St Cross w St Faith from 07. 7 St Cross Mede, Mead Road, Winchester SO23 9RF Tel (01962) 843989
DAVIES, Stephen. b 56. Nottm Univ BSc77. Wycliffe Hall Ox 01. **d** 03 **p** 04. C Crawley and Littleton and Sparsholt w Lainston Win 03-07; V Heacham Nor from 07; RD Heacham and Rising from 11. The Vicarage, 12B Church Lane, Heacham, King's Lynn PE31 7HJ Tel (01485) 570268 E-mail heacham.vicar@gmail.com
DAVIES, Stephen John. b 55. Bp Otter Coll Chich BA01 IEng77. St Steph Ho Ox 96. **d** 98 **p** 99. C Leigh Park and Warren Park Portsm 98-02; C Durrington Chich 02-05; P-in-c Earnley and E Wittering 05-08; R from 08; Chapl Chich Cathl from 02. The Rectory, Church Road, East Wittering, Chichester PO20 8PS Tel (01243) 672260
DAVIES, Stephen John. b 65. Nottm Univ BA86 Reading Univ MPhil88 MRICS90. Wycliffe Hall Ox BTh97. **d** 97 **p** 98. C Barton Seagrave w Warkton Pet 97-01; P-in-c Enderby w Lubbesthorpe and Thurlaston Leic 01-09. Address temp unknown
DAVIES, Mrs Susan Anne. b 48. N Co Coll Newc CertEd69. St Mich Coll Llan 98. **d** 01 **p** 02. NSM Monmouth w Overmonnow etc 01-05; NSM Goetre w Llanover 05; TV Rossendale Middle Valley Man from 05; Dioc Rural Officer from

07. The Rectory, 539 Newchurch Road, Rossendale BB4 9HH Tel (01706) 219768 E-mail susannanedavies@aol.com
DAVIES, Taffy. See DAVIES, Canon Edward William Llewellyn
DAVIES, Canon Thomas Philip. b 27. Univ of Wales (Ban) BEd73. St Mich Coll Llan 55. **d** 56 **p** 57. C Ruabon St As 56-59; C Prestatyn 59-62; V Penley 62-69; V Bettisfield 66-69; V Holt and Isycoed 69-77; Dioc Dir of Educn 76-92; Dioc RE Adv 76-92; RD Wrexham 76-77; TR Hawarden 77-92; Can St As Cathl 79-92; rtd 93. 53 Muirfield Road, Buckley CH7 2NN Tel (01244) 547099
DAVIES, Canon Timothy Robert. b 64. Bradf Univ BSc87. Wycliffe Hall Ox BTh93. **d** 93 **p** 94. C Eynsham and Cassington Ox 93-97; C Fulwood Sheff 97-03; Crosslinks Assoc Ch Ch Cen from 03; Hon Can Nairobi Cathl from 08. Egerton Hall, Fitzwilliam Street, Sheffield S1 4JR Tel 0114-273 9750 E-mail tim.davies@christchurchcentral.co.uk
DAVIES, Trevor. See DAVIES, Edward Trevor
DAVIES, Canon Trevor Gwesyn. b 28. Univ of Wales (Ban) BEd73. St Mich Coll Llan 55. **d** 56 **p** 57. C Holywell St As 56-63; V Cwm 63-74; V Colwyn Bay 74-95; Can St As Cathl from 79; rtd 95. Dalkeith, 37 Brompton Avenue, Rhos on Sea, Colwyn Bay LL28 4TF Tel (01492) 548044
DAVIES, The Ven Vincent Anthony (Tony). b 46. Brasted Th Coll 69 St Mich Coll Llan 71. **d** 73 **p** 74. C Owton Manor CD Dur 73-76; C Wandsworth St Faith S'wark 76-78; P-in-c 78-81; V Walworth St Jo 81-94; RD S'wark and Newington 88-93; Adn Croydon from 94; Bp's Adv for Hosp Chapl 00-11; P-in-c Sutton New Town St Barn 04-06; rtd 11. Flat 5, 46 Palmeira Avenue, Hove BN3 3GF E-mail v.a.davies@hotmail.com
DAVIES, William Martin. b 56. Univ of Wales (Cardiff) BSc78. Wycliffe Hall Ox 78. **d** 81 **p** 82. C Gabalfa Llan 81-84; P-in-c Beguildy and Heyope S & B 84-85; V 85-87; V Swansea St Thos and Kilvey 87-93; V Belmont Lon 93-03; Asst Chapl Miss to Seafarers 87-03; Area Co-ord Leprosy Miss for Wales 04-07; Area Co-ord Lon and Essex 07-11; V Harefield Lon from 11. The Vicarage, 28 Countess Close, Harefield, Uxbridge UB9 6DL Tel (01895) 825960 Mobile 07050-042586
DAVIES-COLE, Charles Sylester. b 38. New Coll Dur BA BD. Edin Th Coll 66. **d** 66. Hon C Edin Old St Paul from 66; Prin Teacher Jas Gillespie's High Sch 82-03. 121 Mayburn Avenue, Loanhead EH20 9ER Tel 0131-440 4190
DAVIES-HANNEN, Robert John. b 65. W Glam Inst of HE BEd89. St Mich Coll Llan BTh92. **d** 92 **p** 93. C Gorseinon S & B 92-95; P-in-c Swansea St Luke 95-02; V Llangyfelach from 02. The Vicarage, 64 Heol Pentrefelin, Morriston, Swansea SA6 6BY Tel (01792) 774120
DAVIES-JAMES, Mrs Roxana Ruth de la Tour. b 56. **d** 05 **p** 06. OLM Cusop w Blakemere, Bredwardine w Brobury etc Heref from 05. Brickleys, Dorstone, Hereford HR3 6BA Tel (01497) 831567 Mobile 07870-929040 E-mail rana.james@virgin.net
DAVILL, Robin William. b 51. SS Paul & Mary Coll Cheltenham CertEd73 BEd74 Leic Univ MA79. Westcott Ho Cam 86. **d** 88 **p** 89. C Broughton Blackb 88-91; C Howden York 91-93; NSM Crayke w Brandsby and Yearsley 93-97; P-in-c 97-03; P-in-c Thirkleby w Kilburn and Bagby 03-09; P-in-c Topcliffe, Baldersby w Dishforth, Dalton etc from 09. Leyland House, 44 Uppleby, Easingwold, York YO61 3BB Tel (01347) 823472 E-mail robin@davill.eclipse.co.uk
DAVINA, Sister. See WILBY, Mrs Jean
DAVIS, Alan. b 34. Birm Univ BSc56. Ox NSM Course. **d** 75 **p** 76. NSM Chesham St Mary Ox 75-80; NSM Gt Chesham 80-00; rtd 00; Perm to Offic Ox from 00. 18 Cheyne Walk, Chesham HP5 1AY Tel (01494) 782124
DAVIS, Alan John. b 33. St Alb Minl Tr Scheme 77. **d** 80 **p** 81. NSM Goldington St Alb 80-84; C Benchill Man 84-86; R Gt Chart Cant 86-02; rtd 02; Perm to Offic Cant from 02. 8 Roberts Road, Greatstone, New Romney TN28 8RL Tel (01797) 361917
DAVIS, The Ven Alan Norman. b 38. Open Univ BA75. Lich Th Coll 63. **d** 65 **p** 66. C Kingstanding St Luke Birm 65-68; C-in-c Ecclesfield St Paul CD Sheff 68-73; V Sheff St Paul 73-75; V Shiregreen St Jas and St Chris 75-80; R Maltby 80-81; TR 81-89; Abp's Officer for UPA 90-92; P-in-c Carl St Cuth w St Mary 92-96; Dioc Communications Officer 92-96; Adn W Cumberland and Hon Can Carl Cathl 96-04; RD Solway 98-99; rtd 04; Perm to Offic Cov and Leic from 05; RD Sparkenhoe W Leic 07-08. 71 North Street, Atherstone CV9 1JW Tel (01827) 718210 E-mail alannorman@aol.com
DAVIS, Preb Andrew Fisher. b 46. St Chad's Coll Dur BA67 K Coll Lon MA99 MPhil06. St Steph Ho Ox 68. **d** 70 **p** 71. C Beckenham St Jas Roch 70-74; C Kensington St Mary Abbots w St Geo Lon 74-80; V Sudbury St Andr 80-90; AD Brent 85-90; V Ealing Ch the Sav from 90; Preb St Paul's Cathl from 07. The Clergy House, The Grove, London W5 5DX Tel and fax (020) 8567 1288 E-mail fr.a@btopenworld.com
DAVIS, Andrew George. b 63. Bath Univ BSc Edin Univ BD. Edin Th Coll. **d** 89 **p** 90. C Alverstoke Portsm 89-92; C Portsea N End St Mark 92-96; Bp's Dom Chapl 96-98; R Bishop's Waltham and Upham 98-07; V Gosport H Trin from 07; V Gosport Ch Ch

from 07. *9 Britannia Way, Gosport PO12 4FZ* Tel (023) 9258 0173
DAVIS, Anne. See DAVIS, Canon Maureen Anne
DAVIS, Arthur Vivian. b 24. Clifton Th Coll 60. **d** 62 **p** 63. C Derby St Chad 62-65; C Cambridge St Andr Less *Ely* 65-68; V 68-75; V Kirtling 75-86; V Wood Ditton w Saxon Street 75-86; P-in-c Cheveley 83-86; P-in-c Ashley w Silverley 83-86; rtd 86; Perm to Offic *St E* from 93. *408 Studland Park, Newmarket CB8 7BB* Tel (01638) 661709
DAVIS, Canon Bernard Rex. b 33. OAM05. Sydney Univ BA55 Gen Th Sem (NY) MDiv60 Newc Univ MA67 FRSA87. Coll of Resurr Mirfield 55. **d** 57 **p** 58. C Guildf St Nic 57-59; USA 59-61; R Wickham Australia 62-66; Studies Sec ACC 66-68; Exec Sec Unit 3 WCC Geneva 68-77; Warden Edw K Ho 77-03; Can Res and Subdean Linc Cathl 77-03; rtd 03; Perm to Offic *Lon* and *Eur* from 06. *425 Bromyard House, Bromyard Avenue, London W3 7BY* Tel (020) 8743 0181 E-mail subdean@aol.com
DAVIS, Canon Brian. b 40. AKC69 BD69. St Aug Coll Cant 69. **d** 70 **p** 71. C Humberstone *Leic* 70-73; C Kirby Muxloe 73-74; V Countesthorpe w Foston 74-91; RD Guthlaxton I 90-91; V Hinckley St Mary 91-10; RD Sparkenhoe W 92-02; Hon Can Leic Cathl 94-10; Bp's Adv for Wholeness and Healing 04-10; rtd 10. *62 Lubenham Hill, Market Harborough LE16 9DQ* Tel (01858) 431843 E-mail revbdavis@aol.com
DAVIS, Mrs Bryony Elizabeth. b 64. DipCOT86. EAMTC 99. **d** 02 **p** 03. C Beccles St Mich *St E* 02-05; P-in-c Ottershaw *Guildf* 05-08; rtd 08. *2 Hammond Road, Woking GU21 4TQ* E-mail bryony.davis@tiscali.co.uk
DAVIS, Christopher James. b 63. Worc Coll Ox BA85. Cranmer Hall Dur 88. **d** 91 **p** 92. C Margate H Trin *Cant* 91-94; C Cambridge H Sepulchre *Ely* 94-00; C Wimbledon Em Ridgway Prop Chpl *S'wark* 00-04; R Tooting Graveney St Nic from 04. *The Rectory, 20A Rectory Lane, London SW17 9QJ* Tel (020) 8672 7691 E-mail cjd-stnicholas@ukonline.co.uk or cjandmary@ukonline.co.uk
DAVIS, Clinton Ernest Newman. b 46. Solicitor 71. Wycliffe Hall Ox 78. **d** 80 **p** 81. C Margate H Trin *Cant* 80-84; C St Laur in Thanet 84-87; V Sandgate St Paul 87-92; P-in-c Folkestone St Geo 92; V Sandgate St Paul w Folkestone St Geo 92-97; Chapl HM Pris Standford Hill 97-08; rtd 08; Perm to Offic *Cant* from 08. *Springfield, 39 Ashford Road, Maidstone ME14 5DP* Tel (01622) 682330 E-mail clintonendavis@btinternet.com
DAVIS, Colin Anthony John. b 65. St Jo Coll Nottm. **d** 99 **p** 00. C Bletchley *Ox* 99-02; C S Molton w Nymet St George, High Bray etc *Ex* 02-03; TV 03-10; I Carrowdore w Millisle *D & D* from 10. *The Rectory, 2 Castle Meadows Drive, Carrowdore, Newtownards BT22 2TT* Tel (028) 9186 1802 E-mail revcol23@btinternet.com
DAVIS, David John. b 35. St Steph Ho Ox 79. **d** 81 **p** 82. C Reading St Mark *Ox* 81-84; C Gt Grimsby St Mary and St Jas *Linc* 84-85; TV 85-89; V Caistor w Clixby 89-94; TV Louth 98-01; rtd 01; Perm to Offic *Linc* from 03 and *Nor* from 04. *34 Park Road, Hunstanton PE36 5BY* Tel (01485) 534700
DAVIS, David Cyril. b 26. Open Univ BA79. NTMTC 94. **d** 96 **p** 97. NSM N Greenford All Hallows *Lon* from 96. *33 Sherwood Avenue, Greenford UB6 0PG* Tel (020) 8864 1060 E-mail donald.davis07@ntlworld.com
DAVIS, Donald Richard. b 59. Oak Hill Th Coll 92. **d** 94 **p** 95. C Plymouth St Jude *Ex* 94-99; C Devonport St Boniface and St Phil 99-08; V W Norwood St Luke *S'wark* from 08. *The Vicarage, 6 Chatsworth Way, London SE27 9HR* Tel (020) 8265 5139 E-mail dondavis@blueyonder.co.uk
DAVIS, Edward Gabriel Anastasius. b 75. R Holloway Coll Lon BA97. Trin Coll Bris BA02. **d** 03 **p** 04. C Boldmere *Birm* 03-06; Chapl Aston Univ 06; Chapl Bris Univ from 07; NSM Inner Ring Partnership from 07. *67 Waverley Road, Bristol BS6 6ET* Tel 0117-942 5390 E-mail ed.davis@bris.ac.uk
DAVIS, Mrs Elizabeth Jane. b 42. S'wark Ord Course 91. **d** 94 **p** 95. NSM Plaistow St Mary *Roch* 94-99; NSM Bromley St Andr from 99. *11 Park Avenue, Bromley BR1 4EF* Tel (020) 8460 4672 E-mail elizabeth.davis@diocese-rochester.org
DAVIS, Felicity Ann. See SMITH, Felicity Ann
DAVIS, Geoffrey. See DAVIS, Ronald Geoffrey
DAVIS, George Shaun. b 75. Middx Univ BA01 Lon Inst of Educn PGCE02 Leeds Univ BA10. Coll of Resurr Mirfield 08. **d** 10 **p** 11. C W Bromwich All SS *Lich* from 10. *50 Wilford Road, West Bromwich B71 1QN* Tel 0121-588 4353 E-mail fr.georgedavis@hotmail.com
DAVIS, Canon Herbert Roger. b 36. Kelham Th Coll 60. **d** 65 **p** 66. C Barkingside St Fran *Chelmsf* 65-69; C Harpenden St Nic *St Alb* 69-73; P-in-c Eaton Bray 73-75; V Eaton Bray w Edlesborough 75-81; RD Dunstable 77-81; R St Berkhamsted 81-95; Hon Can St Alb 93-95; rtd 99. *6 St Thomas Terrace, St Thomas Street, Wells BA5 2XG* Tel (01749) 677195
DAVIS, Ian Andrew. b 58. Sheff Univ BSc79 PGCE80 MIBiol85 CBiol85. St Jo Coll Nottm 87. **d** 90 **p** 91. C Hatfield *Sheff* 90-92; C Beighton 92-95; R Thurnscoe St Helen 95-99; P-in-c Chesterfield St Aug *Derby* 99-01; V 01-05; P-in-c Hope,

Castleton and Bradwell from 05. *The Vicarage, Church Street, Bradwell, Hope Valley S33 9HJ* Tel (01433) 620485 E-mail reviandavis@aol.com
DAVIS, Jack. b 35. LRSC63 CChem80 MRSC80 Sheff Univ MSc88. Oak Hill Th Coll 86. **d** 88 **p** 89. C Owlerton *Sheff* 88-91; V Manea *Ely* 91-93; R Wimblington 91-93; P-in-c Walsoken 93-94; R 94-00; rtd 00; Perm to Offic *Sheff* from 00. *5 Pinfold Court, Barnby Dun, Doncaster DN3 1RQ* Tel and fax (01302) 888065 E-mail revjackdavis@aol.com
DAVIS, Mrs Jacqueline. b 47. Cant Ch Ch Univ Coll BA01. **d** 05 **p** 06. OLM Upchurch w Lower Halstow *Cant* from 05. *Mill House, The Street, Lower Halstow, Sittingbourne ME9 7DY* Tel (01795) 842557 E-mail jackytd@dsl.pipex.com
DAVIS, Jennifer Anne Stanway. b 38. SWMTC 04. **d** 05 **p** 06. NSM Cullompton, Willand, Uffculme, Kentisbeare etc *Ex* 06-08; rtd 08. *36 Church Acre, Bradford-on-Avon BA15 1RL* Tel (01225) 865777
DAVIS, Mrs Joanna Helen. b 82. Ex Univ BA04 K Coll Lon PGCE05. St Jo Coll Nottm MTh10. **d** 10 **p** 11. C Inglewood Gp *Carl* from 10. *The Rectory, Skelton, Penrith CA11 9SE* E-mail joannahelendavis@hotmail.com
DAVIS, John Brian. b 33. Linc Th Coll 72. **d** 75 **p** 76. Hon C Bungay H Trin w St Mary *St E* 75-84; P-in-c Barrow 84-85; P-in-c Denham St Mary 84-85; R Barrow w Denham St Mary and Higham Green 85-98; rtd 98; Perm to Offic *Nor* and *St E* from 98. *Cherry Tree House, 4 Outney Road, Bungay NR35 1DY* Tel (01986) 895574
DAVIS, John George. b 65. Roehampton Inst BSc87 S Glam Inst HE PGCE88. St Steph Ho Ox BTh96. **d** 96 **p** 97. C Newton Nottage *Llan* 96-00; V Tredegar *Mon* from 00. *St George's Vicarage, Church Street, Tredegar NP22 3DU* Tel (01495) 722672
DAVIS, John Harold. b 54. St Jo Coll Dur BSc76 MA86. Cranmer Hall Dur 76. **d** 79 **p** 80. C Marske in Cleveland *York* 79-82; C Pocklington w Yapham-cum-Meltonby, Owsthorpe etc 82-83; TV Pocklington Team 84-86; V Carlton and Drax 86-95; P-in-c Sessay 95-98; R 98-03; V Sowerby 95-03; Ind Chapl 88-97; Sen Chapl Selby Coalfield Ind Chapl 03-11; Chapl Askham Bryan Coll 04-11; rtd 11; Perm to Offic *York* from 11. *46 Sandsacre Avenue, Bridlington YO16 6UG* Tel (01262) 228427 E-mail revjhdavis@gmail.com
DAVIS, John James. b 48. MBE08. Keele Univ MA93 Staffs Univ PGCE98. Qu Coll Birm BA05. **d** 05 **p** 06. NSM Baswich *Lich* 05-08; NSM Bradeley, Church Eaton, Derrington and Haughton 08-09; NSM Stafford from 09; RD Stafford from 11; CF (ACF) from 06. *Stockton Croft, 87 Weeping Cross, Stafford ST17 0DQ* Tel (01785) 661382 E-mail revjohndavis@talktalk.net
DAVIS, John Stephen. b 51. N Staffs Poly BSc75. Wycliffe Hall Ox 75. **d** 78 **p** 79. C Meole Brace *Lich* 78-81; C Bloxwich 81-85; V Walsall St Paul 85-96; Development Officer Prince's Trust 96-01; Hospice Development Manager Walsall Primary Care Trust 01-06; Hon C Halas *Worc* 98-07. *57 Moss Lane, Burscough, Ormskirk L40 4AL*
DAVIS, Miss Judith Alison. b 88. Cam Univ BTh11. Ridley Hall Cam 08. **d** 11. C Doncaster St Geo *Sheff* from 11. *278 Thorne Road, Doncaster DN2 5AJ* E-mail judedavis1@yahoo.co.uk
DAVIS, Mrs Kathleen Mary. b 37. Derby Coll of Educn TCert58. **d** 07 **p** 08. OLM Morley *Wakef* from 07. *13 New Park Street, Morley, Leeds LS27 0PT* Tel 0113-253 4521
DAVIS, Margaret Ann. b 59. Kingston Poly BA81 Liv Univ MSc93 RGN85. Westcott Ho Cam 06. **d** 08 **p** 09. C Abbots Langley *St Alb* from 08; P-in-c Clavering and Langley w Arkesden etc *Chelmsf* from 11. *The Vicarage, 54 Pelham Road, Clavering, Saffron Walden CB11 4PQ* Tel 07941-691544 (mobile) E-mail m.a.davis.merle@googlemail.com
DAVIS, Martin John. b 59. Van Mildert Coll Dur BSc80. Ox Min Course 07. **d** 09 **p** 10. C Colnbrook and Datchet *Ox* from 09. *Linna, Park Street, Colnbrook, Slough SL3 0JF* Tel (01753) 680586 Mobile 07909-976637 E-mail martindavis26@tiscali.co.uk
DAVIS, Matthias. See DAVIS, Peter Langdon
DAVIS, Canon Maureen Anne. b 59. St Hilda's Coll Ox BA80 MA84. NOC 96. **d** 99 **p** 00. NSM Plemstall w Guilden Sutton *Ches* 99-01; C Ches St Mary 01-03; R Woodchurch from 03; Hon Can Ches Cathl from 11. *The Rectory, Church Lane, Upton, Wirral CH49 7LS* Tel 0151-677 5352 Mobile 07974-816390 E-mail revannedavis@uwclub.net
DAVIS, Michael James Burrows. b 36. ED JP87. St Deiniol's Hawarden Ridley Hall Cam. **d** 72 **p** 72. Bermuda from 72. *PO Box SN 74, Southampton SN BX, Bermuda* Tel (001441) 238 0236 Fax 238 3767
DAVIS, Nicholas Anthony Wylie. b 56. Univ of Wales (Lamp) BA80. Chich Th Coll 82. **d** 84 **p** 85. C N Lambeth *S'wark* 84-88; TV Catford (Southend) and Downham 88-94; C Camberwell St Phil and St Mark 94-04; V Shrub End *Chelmsf* from 04. *All Saints' Vicarage, 270 Shrub End Road, Colchester CO3 4RL* Tel (01206) 570922 E-mail nicholas a.davis@virgin.net

DAVIS, Nicholas Edward. b 75. Univ of Wales (Ban) BD96. Coll of Resurr Mirfield 98. **d** 00 **p** 01. C Darwen St Cuth w Tockholes St Steph *Blackb* 00-05; P-in-c Tarleton 05-11; P-in-c Rufford 07-11; P-in-c Rufford and Tarleton from 11; P-in-c Hesketh w Becconsall from 07. *The Rectory, 92 Blackgate Lane, Tarleton, Preston PR4 6UT* Tel and fax (01772) 812614
E-mail httarleton@hotmail.com

DAVIS, Canon Norman. b 38. FCII66. Oak Hill Th Coll 77. **d** 79 **p** 80. C Walton *St E* 79-82; P-in-c Grundisburgh w Burgh 82-91; P-in-c Bredfield w Boulge 86-91; R Boulge w Burgh and Grundisburgh 91-03; P-in-c Hasketon 01-03; R Boulge w Burgh, Grundisburgh and Hasketon 03-04; RD Woodbridge 90-96; Hon Can *St E* Cathl 01-04; rtd 04; Perm to Offic *St E* from 04. *The Randalls, Front Street, Orford, Woodbridge IP12 2LN* Tel (01394) 459469

DAVIS, Norman John. b 41. Oak Hill Th Coll 63. **d** 66 **p** 67. C Wellington w Eyton *Lich* 66-70; C Higher Openshaw *Man* 70-72; R S Levenshulme 72-79; P-in-c Berrow w Pendock and Eldersfield *Worc* 79-81; V 81-87; R Churchill-in-Halfshire w Blakedown and Broome 87-07; rtd 07. *48 Waterside Grange, Kidderminster DY10 2LA* Tel (01562) 750079
E-mail n.davis@sky.com

DAVIS, Peter Langdon (Matthias). b 51. Univ of Wales (Cardiff) BD99 PGCE00. Westcott Ho Cam 03. **d** 05 **p** 06. C Daventry, Ashby St Ledgers, Braunston etc *Pet* 05-08; R Aylmerton, Runton, Beeston Regis and Gresham *Nor* 08-10; TV Wolstanton *Lich* from 10. *The Rectory, Knutton Road, Newcastle ST5 0HU* Tel (01782) 717561 E-mail plmd@hotmail.co.uk

DAVIS, Peter Thomas. b 61. Flinders Univ Aus BTh87 MThSt02. St Barn Coll Adelaide 83. **d** 87 **p** 87. C Modbury and Dioc Youth Chapl Adelaide 87-89; C Port Lincoln 89-91; TV G1 and Lt Coates w Bradley *Linc* 91-92; Dioc Youth Officer Adelaide 92-94; P-in-c Parafield Gardens St Barbara 94-98; R Elizabeth H Cross 98-01; Chapl Anglicare S Australia 98-01; V Satley, Stanley and Tow Law *Dur* 01-04. *21 Winwick Place, Peterborough PE3 7HJ* Tel 07795-417337 (mobile)
E-mail montedog2000@yahoo.co.uk

DAVIS, Rex. *See* DAVIS, Canon Bernard Rex

DAVIS, Roger. *See* DAVIS, Canon Herbert Roger

DAVIS, Ronald Frank. b 26. Oak Hill Th Coll 62. **d** 64 **p** 65. C Bilton *Ripon* 64-67; V N and S Otterington *York* 67-77; C Rainham *Chelmsf* 77-82; V Hainault 82-88; rtd 88; Perm to Offic *Bradf* 90-04. *Home View, Westview Grove, Keighley BD20 6JJ* Tel (01535) 681294

DAVIS, Ronald Geoffrey. b 47. St Jo Coll Nottm 79. **d** 81 **p** 81. C Maidstone St Luke *Cant* 81-84; P-in-c Lostwithiel *Truro* 84-86; P-in-c Lanhydrock 84-86; Asst Dioc Youth Officer 84-86; P-in-c Boughton Monchelsea *Cant* 86-88; V from 88; Six Preacher Cant Cathl 94-99; C-in-c Parkwood CD 95-98; AD N Downs 99-02. *The Vicarage, Church Hill, Boughton Monchelsea, Maidstone ME17 4BU* Tel and fax (01622) 743321
E-mail stpeters.church@btinternet.com

DAVIS, Ruth Elizabeth. *See* TAIT, Canon Ruth Elizabeth

DAVIS, Simon Charles. b 63. Plymouth Poly BSc86 Univ of Wales (Lamp) MTh08 MIET. Trin Coll Bris BA92. **d** 92 **p** 93. C Bollington St Jo *Ches* 92-96; P-in-c Abbots Bromley w Blithfield *Lich* 96-10; P-in-c Colton, Colwich and Gt Haywood 05-10; R Abbots Bromley, Blithfield, Colton, Colwich etc from 11. *The Vicarage, Market Place, Abbots Bromley, Rugeley WS15 3BP* Tel (01283) 840422
E-mail revdsimon@davisfamily.waitrose.com

DAVIS, Stephen Charles. b 19. AKC48 St Cath Soc Ox BA50 MA54. Wycliffe Hall Ox 48. **d** 50 **p** 51. C Slough *Ox* 50-52; Chapl Witwatersrand Univ S Africa 53-57; R Brixton and Newlands 53-57; V Leic H Trin 58-64; Chapl HM Pris Leic 58-64; R Dur St Marg 64-87; rtd 87; Perm to Offic *Worc* from 87. *10 Spencer Avenue, Bewdley DY12 1DB* Tel (01299) 409014

DAVIS, Thomas Henry. b 60. OLM course 97 Coll of Resurr Mirfield 05. **d** 99 **p** 00. OLM Sudbury and Chilton *St E* 99-03; NSM Preston St Jo and St Geo *Blackb* 03-05; C Torrisholme 05-08; C Blackpool St Steph 08-09; Perm to Offic 09-10; C Morecambe St Barn from 10. *St Barnabas' Vicarage, 101 Regent Road, Morecambe LA3 1AG4* Tel (01524) 415216 Mobile 07854-770360 E-mail father.tom@live.co.uk

DAVIS, Timothy Alwyn. b 74. Trin Coll Bris BTh. **d** 01 **p** 02. C Crich and S Wingfield *Derby* 01-05; V Leyton St Mary w St Edw and St Luke *Chelmsf* 05-10; V Clifton w Newton and Brownsover *Cov* from 10. *The Vicarage, 43 Bow Fell, Rugby CV21 1JF* Tel (01788) 573696
E-mail timandjo.davis@ntlworld.com

DAVIS, Timothy Charles. b 59. Reading Univ BA81 Homerton Coll Cam PGCE82. Trin Coll Bris 89. **d** 91 **p** 92. C Normanton *Wakef* 91-95; C Fisherton Anger *Sarum* 95-99; TV Abingdon *Ox* from 99. *69 Northcourt Road, Abingdon OX14 1NR* Tel (01235) 520115 *or* 539172 Fax 539179 E-mail chch@clara.net

DAVIS, Trevor Lorenzo. b 45. Simon of Cyrene Th Inst 92. **d** 94 **p** 95. NSM Upper Norwood St Jo *S'wark* 94-00. *Address temp unknown*

DAVIS, Mrs Yvonne Annie. b 30. CQSW75. **d** 96 **p** 97. OLM Purley St Barn *S'wark* 96-00; Perm to Offic from 00. *Address temp unknown*

DAVISON, Andrew Paul. b 74. Mert Coll Ox BA96 MA99 DPhil00 CCC Cam BA02 MA08. Westcott Ho Cam 00 Ven English Coll Rome 02. **d** 03 **p** 04. C Bellingham St Dunstan *S'wark* 03-06; Tutor St Steph Ho Ox 06-10; Jun Chapl Mert Coll Ox 06-10; Tutor Westcott Ho Cam from 10. *Jesus Lane, Cambridge CB5 8BP* Tel (01223) 741000 Fax 741002

DAVISON, Deborah Karin Mary. b 56. Ex Univ BA79 SRN83 RHV85. Ripon Coll Cuddesdon 09. **d** 11. C Boyne Hill *Ox* from 11. *All Saints' Church, Church Close, Maidenhead SL6 4HE* Tel 07833-935901 (mobile)

DAVISON, George Thomas William. b 65. St Andr Univ BD88. Oak Hill Th Coll 88 CITC BTh92. **d** 92 **p** 93. C Portadown St Mark *Arm* 92-95; I Kinawley w H Trin *K, E & A* 95-09; Dir of Ords 97-09; Preb Kilmore Cathl 02-09; Adn Kilmore 04-09; I Carrickfergus *Conn* from 09. *The Rectory, 12 Harwood Gardens, Carrickfergus BT38 7US* Tel and fax (028) 9336 3244 *or* 9336 0061 Mobile 07771-812844
E-mail carrickfergus@connor.anglican.org

DAVISON, Philip Anthony. b 66. Magd Coll Cam BA88 MA93. Cuddesdon Coll BA98. **d** 98 **p** 99. C Lancaster St Mary w St John and St Anne *Blackb* 98-02; P-in-c Feniscowles 02-08; R Finchley St Mary *Lon* from 08. *St Mary's Rectory, Rectory Close, London N3 1TS* Tel (020) 8346 4600 *or* tel and fax 8248 3818 E-mail rector@stmaryatfinchley.org.uk

DAVISON, Canon Richard Ireland. b 42. St Chad's Coll Dur BSc63. Linc Th Coll 64. **d** 66 **p** 67. C Cockerton *Dur* 66-70; C Houghton le Spring 70-73; V Heworth St Alb 73-80; Ascension Is 80-82; V Dunston *Dur* 82-85; V Bishopwearmouth Ch Ch 85-98; AD Wearmouth 94-99; P-in-c Dur St Giles 99-00; V 00-08; P-in-c Shadforth and Sherburn 03-08; Hon Can Dur Cathl 97-08; AD Dur 06-08; rtd 08. *16 Loraine Crescent, Darlington DL1 5TF*

DAVISON, Canon Roger William. b 20. Kelham Th Coll 46. **d** 51 **p** 52. C Tonge Moor *Man* 51-55; V 55-65; Hon Can Man Cathl 63-65; V Higham Ferrers w Chelveston *Pet* 65-88; rtd 88; Perm to Offic *Roch* 88-05. *The College of St Barnabas, Blackberry Lane, Lingfield RH7 6NJ* Tel (01342) 872819

DAVOLL, Ivan John (Snowy). b 33. LNSM course 87. **d** 88 **p** 90. NSM Bermondsey St Jas w Ch Ch *S'wark* 88-93; C 93-98; rtd 98; Perm to Offic *S'wark* 98-03 and *Heref* from 03. *42 Ecroyd Park, Credenhill, Hereford HR4 7EL*

DAVY, Mrs Helen Mary. b 44. **d** 05 **p** 06. NSM Kirton w Falkenham *St E* 05-06; NSM Nacton and Levington w Bucklesham etc from 06. *9 Roman Way, Felixstowe IP11 9NJ* Tel (01394) 270703

DAVY, Mrs Judith Ann. b 60. SRN82. STETS 01. **d** 04 **p** 05. NSM Jersey St Brelade *Win* from 04. *Brookvale House, Les Grupieaux, St Peter, Jersey JE3 7YW* Tel (01534) 507800 Mobile 07797-730983 E-mail judithdavy@jerseymail.co.uk

DAVY, Peter Geoffrey. b 31. St Pet Coll Saltley TCert54. SWMTC 93. **d** 94 **p** 94. NSM St Columb Minor and St Colan *Truro* 94-99; rtd 99; Perm to Offic *Truro* from 00. *9 Tredour Road, Newquay TR7 2EY* Tel (01637) 872241

DAVYS, Mark Andrew. b 66. St Cath Coll Ox BA87 MA97 Keele Univ MA01 Qu Coll Birm BA04 Solicitor 90. WMMTC 01. **d** 04 **p** 05. NSM Colton, Colwich and Gt Haywood *Lich* 04-10; NSM Abbots Bromley, Blithfield, Colton, Colwich etc from 11. *Deer's Leap, Meadow Lane, Little Haywood, Stafford ST18 0TT* Tel (01889) 882855 E-mail revmdavys@deersleap.org.uk

DAW, Geoffrey Martin. b 57. Oak Hill Th Coll 81. **d** 84 **p** 85. C Hollington St Leon *Chich* 84-87; C Seaford w Sutton 87-90; V Iford w Kingston and Rodmell from 90; RD Lewes and Seaford from 08. *The Rectory, 14 Lockitt Way, Kingston, Lewes BN7 3LG* Tel (01273) 473665 E-mail geoffrey.daw@btinternet.com

DAWE, David Fife Purchas. b 20. Keble Coll Ox BA41 MA45. Wells Th Coll 41. **d** 43 **p** 44. C Wolstanton *Lich* 43-46; C Meole Brace 46-47; C Leek All SS 47-50; C Tardebigge *Worc* 50-52; R Stoke Bliss w Kyre Wyard 52-54; R Jackfield *Heref* 54-61; V Criftins *Lich* 61-77; V Dudleston 63-77; P-in-c Alkmonton w Yeaveley *Derby* 77-81; P-in-c Cubley w Marston Montgomery 77-81; R Alkmonton, Cubley, Marston Montgomery etc 81-85; rtd 85; Perm to Offic *Derby* and *Lich* 85-94; *Pet* 94-07. *11 Coaching Walk, Northampton NN3 3EU* Tel (01604) 414083

DAWES, Dori Katherine. b 37. ARCM. Oak Hill Th Coll 85. **d** 88 **p** 94. Par Dn Watford St Luke *St Alb* 88-90; Par Dn Watford 90-94; C 94-96; P-in-c Dunton w Wrestlingworth and Eyeworth 96-01; rtd 01; Perm to Offic *B & W* from 05. *Orchard House, Upway, Porlock, Minehead TA24 8QE* Tel (01643) 862474

DAWES, Mrs Helen Elizabeth. b 74. Trin Coll Cam BA96 MA00. Westcott Ho Cam 99. **d** 02 **p** 03. C Chesterton St Andr *Ely* 02-05; P-in-c Sandon, Wallington and Rushden w Clothall *St Alb* 05-09; Dep Public Affairs Sec to Abp Cant from 09. *Lambeth Palace, London SE1 7JU* Tel (020) 7898 1200
E-mail helen.dawes@churchofengland.org

DAWES, Hugh William. b 48. Univ Coll Ox BA71 MA76. Cuddesdon Coll 71. **d** 74 **p** 75. C Purley St Mark *S'wark* 74-77;

Chapl G&C Coll Cam 77-82; Chapl Em Coll Cam 82-87; V Cambridge St Jas *Ely* 87-00; Dir Focus Chr Inst Cambridge 87-00; V N Dulwich St Faith *S'wark* 00-10; rtd 10; Perm to Offic *S'wark* from 10. *8 The Wells, Lower Street, Haslemere GU27 2PA* Tel (01428) 652466 E-mail hugh@hughdawes.com

DAWES, Julian Edward. b 27. RAF Coll Cranwell 49. Bps' Coll Cheshunt 58. **d** 59 **p** 60. C Whitton St Aug *Lon* 59-62; Chapl RAF 62-65; V Overbury w Alstone, Teddington and Lt Washbourne *Worc* 65-70; V Cropthorne w Charlton 70-76; Chapl Dioc Conf Cen 70-76; Chapl Exe Vale Hosp Gp 76-84; Chapl Bromsgrove and Redditch Distr Gen Hosp 84-86; rtd 91; Perm to Offic *Ex* 91-09. *Maranatha, Exeter Road, Rewe, Exeter EX5 4EU* Tel (01392) 841877 Fax 841577

✠**DAWES, The Rt Revd Peter Spencer.** b 28. Hatf Coll Dur BA52. Tyndale Hall Bris 53. **d** 54 **p** 55 **c** 88. C Whitehall Park St Andr Hornsey Lane *Lon* 54-57; C Ox St Ebbe 57-60; Tutor Clifton Th Coll 60-65; V Romford Gd Shep *Chelmsf* 65-80; Hon Can Chelmsf Cathl 78-80; Adn W Ham 80-88; Dioc Dir of Ords 80-86; Bp Derby 88-95; rtd 95; Hon Asst Bp Ely from 95. *45 Arundell, Ely CB6 1BQ* Tel (01353) 661241

DAWKES, Peter. b 31. Roch Th Coll 64. **d** 66 **p** 67. C Newbold w Dunston *Derby* 66-69; C Buxton 69-72; V Somercotes 72-93; rtd 93; Hon C Kenton, Mamhead, Powderham, Cofton and Starcross *Ex* from 93. *115 Exeter Road, Dawlish EX7 0AN* Tel (01626) 862593

DAWKIN, Peter William. b 60. Nottm Univ BTh88 Open Univ BA91. St Jo Coll Nottm 85. **d** 88 **p** 89. C Birkdale St Jo *Liv* 88-91; C Netherton 91-93; V Liv Ch Ch Norris Green 93-03; Assoc Min Wigan Deaneries 03-06; V Hough Green St Basil and All SS from 06. *339 Ditchfield Road, Widnes WA8 8XR* Tel 0151-420 4963 Mobile 07947-164207 E-mail peter.dawkin@blueyonder.co.uk

DAWKINS, Canon Alan Arthur Windsor. b 26. St Aid Birkenhead 53. **d** 55 **p** 56. C Preston Em *Blackb* 55-57; C S Shore H Trin 57-59; V Slade Green *Roch* 59-61; V St Mary Cray and St Paul's Cray 61-63; V White Colne *Chelmsf* 63-66; R Pebmarsh 63-66; P-in-c Mt Bures 65-66; V Westgate St Jas *Cant* 66-74; V Herne Bay Ch Ch 74-83; Hon Can Cant Cathl 79-91; P-in-c Chilham 83-85; Adv for Miss and Unity 85-91; rtd 91; Chapl St Jo Hosp Cant 96-07; Perm to Offic *Cant* 96-10. *44 Columbia Avenue, Whitstable CT5 4EH*

DAWKINS, John Haswell. b 47. NEOC 98. **d** 01 **p** 02. NSM Barmby Moor Gp *York* from 01. *9 Fossbeck Close, Wilberfoss, York YO41 5PR* Tel (01759) 388144

DAWKINS, Michael Howard. b 44. Bris Univ BTh68 Man Univ MA96. Tyndale Hall Bris 67. **d** 69 **p** 69. C Drypool St Columba w St Andr and St Pet *York* 69-73; CF 74-80; P-in-c Bulford *Sarum* 80-81; P-in-c Figheldean w Milston 80-81; R Meriden *Cov* 93-09; rtd 09. *60 Wassell Road, Wollescote, Stourbridge DY9 9DB* Tel (01384) 893299 E-mail mhdawkins@aol.com

DAWKINS, Nigel Jonathan. b 72. St Jo Coll Ox BA94 MA97 Univ Coll Lon MSc97 Peterho Cam BA05. Westcott Ho Cam 03. **d** 06 **p** 07. C Caterham *S'wark* 06-09; Chapl Aden Ch Ch and Yemen from 09. *PO Box 1319, Tawahi, Aden, Yemen* Tel (00967) (2) 201204 Mobile 73-376 2704 E-mail chaplain@christchurchaden.org

DAWN, Maggi Eleanor. b 59. Fitzw Coll Cam MA96 Selw Coll Cam PhD02. Ridley Hall Cam 96. **d** 99 **p** 00. C Ely 99-01; Chapl K Coll Cam 01-03; Chapl Rob Coll Cam from 03. *Robinson College, Cambridge CB3 9AN* Tel (01223) 339140 Mobile 07743-351467 E-mail med1000@cam.ac.uk

DAWSON, Alan. b 28. St Jo Coll Dur BA54 Liv Univ MA67. Clifton Th Coll 54. **d** 56 **p** 57. C Bowling St Steph *Bradf* 56-59; C Attenborough w Bramcote *S'well* 59-62; V Everton St Jo *Liv* 62-69; V Birkdale St Pet 69-91; rtd 91; NSM Kirkcudbright and Gatehouse of Fleet *Glas* 98-06; Perm to Offic *Ches* from 07. *The Bungalow, Church Lane, Guilden Sutton, Chester CH3 7EW* Tel (01244) 301685

DAWSON, Alan David Hough. b 67. St Jo Coll Dur BA09 ACIB92. Cranmer Hall Dur 07. **d** 09 **p** 10. C Hale and Ashley *Ches* from 09. *152 Hale Road, Hale, Altrincham WA15 8SQ* Tel 0161-941 2206 Mobile 07919-278104 E-mail alan.dawson21@btinternet.com

DAWSON, Andrew. *See* DAWSON, Canon William James Andrew

DAWSON, Andrew. *See* DAWSON, Francis Andrew Oliver Duff

DAWSON, Miss Anne. b 54. Nottm Univ BA76 Hull Coll of Educn PGCE77. NEOC 03. **d** 06 **p** 07. NSM Market Weighton *York* 06-09; P-in-c Sigglesthorne w Nunkeeling and Bewholme 10-11; rtd 11. *23 Sloe Lane, Beverley HU17 8ND* Tel (01482) 862940 E-mail andaw@andaw.karoo.co.uk

DAWSON, Barry. b 38. Oak Hill Th Coll 63. **d** 66 **p** 67. C Fulham St Mary N End *Lon* 66-69; C St Marylebone All So w SS Pet and Jo 69-73; Bp's Chapl *Nor* 73-76; Gen Sec CEMS 76-81; V Rye Park St Cuth *St Alb* 81-89; V Attenborough *S'well* 89-98; rtd 98; Perm to Offic *S'well* from 98. *27 Orlando Drive, Carlton, Nottingham NG4 3FN*

DAWSON, Brian. b 33. Leeds Univ BA54 Man Univ MA84 Newc Univ MPhil01. Coll of Resurr Mirfield 56. **d** 58 **p** 59. C

Hollinwood *Man* 58-62; C Rawmarsh w Parkgate *Sheff* 62-63; V Royton St Anne *Man* 63-75; V Urswick *Carl* 75-86; V Bardsea 75-86; R Skelton and Hutton-in-the-Forest w Ivegill 86-98; RD Penrith 91-96; Hon Can Carl Cathl 94-98; rtd 98; Perm to Offic *Carl* from 98. *Apple Croft, High Hesket, Carlisle CA4 0HS* Tel (01697) 473069

DAWSON, Christopher John Rowland. b 26. OBE QPM. S'wark Ord Course 82. **d** 86 **p** 87. NSM Sevenoaks St Jo *Roch* 86-98; Perm to Offic 98-99. *Craggan House, 58 Oak Hill Road, Sevenoaks TN13 1NT* Tel (01732) 458037

DAWSON, Miss Claire Louise. b 68. Nottm Poly BA92 CQSW92 Nottm Univ MA04. EMMTC 01. **d** 04 **p** 05. C Mansfield Woodhouse *S'well* 04-05; C Sutton in Ashfield St Mary 05-08; C Orrell Hey St Jo and St Jas *Liv* 08-11; P-in-c from 11. *20 Mount Avenue, Bootle L20 6DT* Tel 0151-284 1359 E-mail claire.dawson1@virgin.net

DAWSON, Canon Cyril. b 34. St Chad's Coll Dur BA58. **d** 59 **p** 60. C Honicknowle *Ex* 59-63; C Paignton St Jo 63-66; V Heptonstall *Wakef* 66-71; V Todmorden 71-82; RD Calder Valley 75-82; Can Res Wakef Cathl 82-92; Vice-Provost 86-92; Hon Can 92-99; V Darrington 92-99; rtd 99; Perm to Offic *York* and *Linc* from 00. *24 Beacon Road, Bridlington YO16 6UX* Tel (01262) 672911

DAWSON, David. b 57. TISEC 99. **d** 99 **p** 00. NSM Kirkwall *Ab* from 99; P-in-c from 05. *St Olaf's Rectory, Dundas Crescent, Kirkwall, Orkney KW15 1JQ* Tel (01856) 872024 Mobile 07881-932657 E-mail frdave 473@hotmail.com

DAWSON, Edward. **d** 81 **p** 83. NSM Newington St Paul *S'wark* 81-85; NSM Walworth St Jo 85-00; Chapl Asst Maudsley Hosp Lon from 87. *3 Ethel Street, London SE17 1NH* Tel (020) 7701 8923

DAWSON, Francis Andrew Oliver Duff. b 48. Keble Coll Ox BA70 MA74. St Jo Coll Nottm 74. **d** 76 **p** 77. C Billericay St Mary *Chelmsf* 76-77; C Billericay and Lt Burstead 77-80; C Childwall All SS *Liv* 80-84; Chapl St Kath Coll 80-84; V Shevington *Blackb* 84-97; Internat Officer and Team Ldr for Evang Affairs *Man* 97-03; P-in-c Werneth from 03. *St Thomas's Vicarage, 3 Regency Close, Oldham OL8 1SS* Tel 0161-678 8926 Fax 832 2869 E-mail andrewdawson51@hotmail.com

DAWSON, Frederick William. b 44. St Chad's Coll Dur BA66 Nottm Univ MTh74. Linc Th Coll 67. **d** 69 **p** 70. C Caversham *Ox* 69-72; C Ranmoor *Sheff* 72-79; R Kibworth Beauchamp *Leic* 79-82; R Kibworth and Smeeton Westerby and Saddington 82-94; R Tilehurst St Mich *Ox* 94-07; P-in-c Mickleton, Willersey w Saintbury etc *Glouc* from 07. *The Rectory, Weston-sub-Edge, Chipping Campden GL55 6QH* Tel (01386) 840292

DAWSON, Hilary. b 64. Univ of Wales (Lamp) BA85 UWE PGCE89 Ex Univ MA08. SWMTC 05. **d** 08. C Thorverton, Cadbury, Upton Pyne etc *Ex* 08-10; C Brampford Speke, Cadbury, Newton St Cyres etc 10-11; P-in-c Colyton, Musbury, Southleigh and Branscombe from 11. *The Vicarage, Vicarage Street, Colyton EX24 6LJ* Tel (01297) 553180 E-mail hilary.dawson2@btinternet.com

DAWSON, Ian Douglas. b 52. Liv Univ BSc73. NOC 83. **d** 86 **p** 87. NSM Southport SS Simon and Jude *Liv* 86-93; NSM Birkdale St Jas 93-95; NSM Southport St Phil and St Paul 96-01; Perm to Offic *Linc* from 01. *18 Park View, Barton-upon-Humber DN18 6AX* Tel (01652) 637554

DAWSON, John William Arthur. b 43. EMMTC. **d** 95 **p** 96. NSM Breedon cum Isley Walton and Worthington *Leic* 95-05; NSM Ashby-de-la-Zouch and Breedon on the Hill from 05. *Orchard House, 2 Manor Drive, Worthington, Ashby-de-la-Zouch LE65 1RN* Tel (01530) 222673 E-mail johndawson@benefice.org.uk

DAWSON, Miss Mary. b 51. Loughb Coll ALA73. EMMTC 85. **d** 90 **p** 94. Par Dn Braunstone *Leic* 90-92; Par Dn Shrewsbury H Cross *Lich* 92-94; C 94-95; P-in-c Glentworth Gp *Linc* 95-97; V 97-10; rtd 10. *20 Newbolt Close, Caistor, Market Rasen LN7 6NY* Tel (01472) 859802 E-mail fenellacoughdrop@btinternet.com

DAWSON, Neil. b 49. Ripon Hall Ox 71. **d** 74 **p** 75. C Putney St Mary *S'wark* 74-78; C Camberwell St Giles 78-80; TV N Lambeth 84-86; V E Dulwich St Clem 86; V Dulwich St Clem w St Pet 86-89; Hon C Wilton Place St Paul *Lon* 92-06; P-in-c Madeira *Eur* from 06. *The Parsonage, 18 rua do Quebra Costas, 9000 Funchal, Madeira* Tel (00351) (291) 220674 Fax 220161 E-mail neil.dawson6@btinternet.com *or* holytrinity@netmadeira.com

DAWSON, Nicholas Anthony. b 52. St Jo Coll Nottm 88. **d** 90 **p** 91. C Mortomley St Sav High Green *Sheff* 90-95; V Owlerton from 95; P-in-c Hillsborough and Wadsley Bridge 06-09. *Owlerton Vicarage, Forbes Road, Sheffield S6 2NW* Tel 0114-234 3560 E-mail nick.dawson@sheffield.anglican.org

DAWSON, Canon Norman William. b 41. MBE99. K Coll Lon BD63 AKC63. **d** 65 **p** 66. C Salford St Phil w St Steph *Man* 65-68; C Heaton Ch Ch 68-70; R Longsight St Jo 70-75; R Longsight St Jo w St Cypr 75-82; R Withington St Paul 82-99; Chapl Christie Hosp *Man* 81-91; AD Withington 91-99; P-in-c

Davyhulme St Mary 99-04; Hon Can Man Cathl 98-04; rtd 04; Perm to Offic *Blackb* and *Man* from 04. *Well House, Lowgill, Lancaster LA2 8RA* Tel (01524) 262936

DAWSON, Paul Christopher Owen. b 61. Leeds Univ BA82. Ripon Coll Cuddesdon 83. **d** 85 **p** 86. C Dovecot *Liv* 85-89; V Westbrook St Phil 89-94; Bp's Dom Chapl 94-98; V Witton *Ches* 98-06; R Ches St Mary from 06. *10 Lower Park Road, Chester CH4 7BB* Tel (01244) 675199 E-mail comet411@tiscali.co.uk

DAWSON, Paul Richard. b 67. Bris Univ BSc89. Oak Hill Th Coll 99. **d** 01 **p** 02. C Wimbledon Em Ridgway Prop Chpl *S'wark* 01-09; V Chelsea St Jo w St Andr *Lon* from 09. *The Vicarage, 43 Park Walk, London SW10 0AU* Tel (020) 7352 1675 E-mail paul@standrewschelsea.org

DAWSON, The Ven Peter. b 29. Keble Coll Ox BA52 MA56. Ridley Hall Cam 52. **d** 54 **p** 55. C Morden *S'wark* 54-59; R 68-77; V Barston *Birm* 59-63; R Higher Openshaw *Man* 63-68; RD Merton *S'wark* 75-77; Adn Norfolk 77-93; rtd 93; Perm to Offic *Nor* from 93 and *Carl* from 98. *The Coach House, Harmony Hill, Milnthorpe LA7 7QA* Tel (01539) 562020

DAWSON, Peter John. b 44. Local Minl Tr Course. **d** 06 **p** 07. NSM Heckmondwike *Wakef* from 06; NSM Liversedge w Hightown from 06; NSM Robetttown w Hartshead from 06. *10 Meadow Drive, Liversedge WF15 7QF* Tel (01924) 404311 E-mail manxpeter@yahoo.co.uk

DAWSON, Peter Rodney. b 44. **d** 98 **p** 99. OLM Ashtead *Guildf* 98-05; Asst Chapl Pau *Eur* 05-06; Perm to Offic 06-08; P-in-c Biarritz 08-11. *Le Bosquet, 64400 Poey d'Oloron, France* Tel (0033) 5 59 27 63 14 E-mail peter.dawson@free.fr

DAWSON, Ronald Eric John. b 27. St Mark & St Jo Coll Lon TCert54 Lon Univ BD64. Bps' Coll Cheshunt 62. **d** 62 **p** 63. C Dartford H Trin *Roch* 62-66; C Fulham St Etheldreda *Lon* 66-74; V Brentford St Faith 74-80; rtd 92. *13 Birkbeck Road, London W5 4ES* Tel (020) 8560 3564

DAWSON, Stephen Charles. b 62. LCTP 08. **d** 10 **p** 11. NSM Bentham *Bradf* from 10. *16 Mount Pleasant, Bentham LA2 7LB* Tel (01524) 262242 Fax 242027 E-mail scudawson@hotmail.com

DAWSON, Thomas Douglas. b 52. Newc Univ BA. St Steph Ho Ox. **d** 80 **p** 82. C N Gosforth *Newc* 80-81; C Leic St Chad 82-85; TV Catford (Southend) and Downham *S'wark* 85-88; V Chevington *Newc* 88-94; V Cowgate 94-96; P-in-c Cresswell and Lynemouth 96-98; C Blyth St Mary 98-01; rtd 01; Perm to Offic *Newc* from 02. *Iona, 2 Hillside, Lesbury, Alnwick NE66 3NR* Tel (01665) 830412 Mobile 07763-122259 E-mail fr_tom_dawson@hotmail.com

DAWSON (*formerly* CORY), **Mrs Valerie Ann.** b 44. CertEd65 Nottm Univ BEd85. EMMTC 85. **d** 88 **p** 94. Area Sec CMS *Linc* and *Pet* 87-91; NSM Grantham *Linc* 88-91; Par Dn Ealing St Mary *Lon* 91-94; Chapl NW Lon Poly 91-92; Chapl Thames Valley Univ 92-96; C Ealing St Mary 94-96; Chapl Birm Cathl 96-99; C Surbiton St Andr and St Mark *S'wark* 99-08; rtd 08. *15A Greengate Close, Chesterfield S40 3SJ* Tel (01246) 550445 E-mail valcory@blueyonder.co.uk

DAWSON, Canon William James Andrew. b 48. TCD MA72. CITC 88. **d** 88 **p** 89. NSM Killyman *Arm* 88-91; NSM Pomeroy from 91; Can Arm Cathl from 98; Preb 98-01. *Tamlaght, Coagh, Cookstown BT80 0AB* Tel (028) 8673 7151 *or* tel and fax 8676 2227

DAWSON-CAMPBELL, Olive Sheila. b 37. ACIB70. WEMTC 99. **d** 00 **p** 01. OLM Longden and Annscroft w Pulverbatch *Heref* from 00. *Sheaves, Lyth Bank, Lyth Hill, Shrewsbury SY3 0BE* Tel (01743) 872071

DAWSWELL, Jonathan Andrew. b 65. Jes Coll Cam BA86. Wycliffe Hall Ox BA91. **d** 92 **p** 93. C Childwall All SS *Liv* 92-96; C Leyland St Andr *Blackb* 96-99; V Knypersley *Lich* 99-09; P-in-c Biddulph Moor 05-09; R Biddulph Moor and Knypersley from 09. *St John's Vicarage, 62 Park Lane, Knypersley, Stoke-on-Trent ST8 7AU* Tel (01782) 512240 E-mail andrew@dawswell.freeserve.co.uk

DAWTRY, Canon Anne Frances. b 57. Westf Coll Lon BA79 PhD85. Ripon Coll Cuddesdon 91. **d** 93 **p** 94. C Corfe Mullen *Sarum* 93-96; C Parkstone St Pet w Branksea and St Osmund 96-97; Chapl Bournemouth Univ and Bournemouth and Poole Coll of FE 97-99; Prin OLM and Integrated Tr 99-03; Dir Tr and Prin Dioc OLM Scheme *Man* 03-06; Course Dir SNWTP 06-08; C Chorlton-cum-Hardy St Werburgh 06-08; P-in-c 08-09; R from 09; Hon Can Man Cathl from 06. *St Werburgh's Rectory, 388 Wilbraham Road, Manchester M21 0UH* Tel 0161-881 1642 Mobile 07834-390380 E-mail adawtry@aol.com

DAXTER, Preb Gregory. b 42. Chelmer Inst of HE PGCE76. Oak Hill Th Coll 64. **d** 68 **p** 69. C Paignton St Paul Preston *Ex* 68-72; C Woodford Wells *Chelmsf* 72-75; Hon C Harold Hill St Paul 75-77; Hon C Wilmington *Roch* 77-87; PV Ex Cathl and Chapl Ex Cathl Sch 87-03; Preb Ex Cathl from 02; rtd 03. *36 Lyncombe Crescent, Higher Lincombe Road, Torquay TQ1 2HP*

DAY, Audrey. b 34. Ex Cathl IDC57. **d** 88 **p** 94. Par Dn Mildenhall *St E* 88-91; Dioc Officer for the Care of the Elderly 91-95; NSM Blackbourne 94-95; rtd 95; Perm to Offic *St E* 95-04

and *Glouc* from 04. *25 Capel Court, The Burgage, Prestbury, Cheltenham GL52 3EL* Tel (01242) 576494

DAY, Charles George. b 28. Keble Coll Ox BA51 MA63. Cuddesdon Coll 51. **d** 53 **p** 54. C Hythe *Cant* 53-56; C S Norwood St Alb 56-59; R Stisted *Chelmsf* 59-65; V Brenchley *Roch* 65-75; rtd 93. *Flat 4, The Gatehouse, Mote Park, Maidstone ME15 8NQ* Tel (01622) 843248 Fax 844298

DAY, Charles Ian. b 48. Univ of Wales (Ban) BA72. St Mich Coll Llan 73. **d** 75 **p** 76. C Llanrhos *St As* 75-79; V Mochdre 79-83; CF 80-91; V Minera *St As* 83-92; Dioc Soc Resp Officer 89-94; V Mold from 92; AD Mold 03-11. *The Vicarage, Church Lane, Mold CH7 1BW* Tel and fax (01352) 752960 Mobile 07977-001692 E-mail moldciw01@spamex.com

DAY, Christine Audrey. b 63. K Alfred's Coll Win BTh01 Univ of Wales (Lamp) MA(Theol)06. STETS 02. **d** 04 **p** 05. NSM N Stoneham *Win* 04-08; NSM Swaythling from 08; Chapl Southn Univ from 11. *86 Copperfield Road, Southampton SO16 3NY* Tel (023) 8058 2042 *or* 8059 4623 Mobile 07580-968215 E-mail revchrisday@gmail.com *or* c.a.day@soton.ac.uk

DAY, Canon Colin Michael. b 40. Lon Univ BSc62 AKC62 Em Coll Cam BA66 MA71. Ridley Hall Cam 65. **d** 67 **p** 68. C Heworth w Peasholme St Cuth *York* 67-70; C Ox St Clem 70-76; V Kidsgrove *Lich* 76-86; Exec Officer Angl Evang Assembly and C of E Coun 86-90; Adv on Miss and Evang *Sarum* 90-95; P-in-c Branksome Park All SS 95-01; V 01-05; Can and Preb Sarum Cathl 94-05; Dioc Tr in Evang 95-05; rtd 05. *113 Archery Grove, Southampton SO19 9ET* Tel (023) 8043 9854 E-mail colin.day1@tiscali.co.uk

DAY, David John. b 44. CEng72 MICE72. Trin Coll Bris. **d** 90 **p** 91. C Stratton St Margaret w S Marston etc *Bris* 90-94; Perm to Offic from 94; Manager SA Addictions Rehab Cen Highworth 98-09; rtd 09. *56 Beechcroft Road, Swindon SN2 7PX* Tel (01793) 725721 E-mail davidjday1@hotmail.co.uk

DAY, David Vivian. b 36. Lon Univ BA57 Nottm Univ MEd73 MTh77. **d** 99 **p** 00. NSM Dur St Nic from 99. *35 Orchard Drive, Durham DH1 1LA* Tel 0191-386 6909 E-mail dv.day@virgin.net

DAY, Canon David William. b 37. St Andr Univ MA58 BD61 CertEd73. St And Dioc Tr Course 74. **d** 76 **p** 77. C St Andrews All SS *St And* 76-77; P-in-c Dundee St Ninian *Bre* 77-84; Itinerant Priest *Arg* 84-02; R Duror 84-02; P-in-c Gruline 84-02; P-in-c Kentallen 84-02; P-in-c Kinlochleven 84-02; P-in-c Kinlochmoidart 84-96; P-in-c Lochbuie 84-96; P-in-c Portnacrois 84-02; P-in-c Strontian 84-96; Can St Jo Cathl Oban 99-02; rtd 02; Hon Can Cumbrae *Arg* from 02; Hon C St Andrews All SS *St And* from 03. *10 Doocot Road, St Andrews KY16 8QP* Tel (01334) 476991 E-mail david@arkville.freeserve.co.uk

DAY, George Chester. b 45. Ex Univ BA66 Lon Univ BD70. Clifton Th Coll 67. **d** 71 **p** 72. C Reading St Jo *Ox* 71-75; C Morden *S'wark* 75-81; Sec for Voc and Min CPAS 81-86; Hon C Bromley Ch *Roch* 83-86; V St Paul's Cray St Barn 86-05; RD Orpington 01-05; V Joydens Wood St Barn 05-10; rtd 10. *5 Abbey Grange Close, Buckfast, Buckfastleigh TQ11 0EU* E-mail revgeorgeday@ntlworld.com

DAY, Canon James Alfred. b 23. DFC44. AKC49. **d** 50 **p** 51. C Wembley Park St Aug *Lon* 50-52; Mauritius 52-57; V E and W Ravendale w Hatcliffe *Linc* 57-60; R Beelsby 57-60; PC Gt Grimsby St Paul 60-66; V Tattershall 66-80; R Coningsby 66-80; RD Horncastle 73-80; V Heckington 80-89; Can and Preb Linc Cathl 77-05; rtd 89. *22 Ancaster Drive, Sleaford NG34 7LY* Tel (01529) 305318

DAY, Prof James Meredith. b 55. Oberlin Coll (USA) AB77 Harvard Univ EdM81 Univ of Penn PhD87. Westcott Ho Cam 01. **d** 03 **p** 04. C Ostend and Antwerp St Boniface *Eur* 03-06; Asst Chapl Brussels from 06. *Mooiboslaan 20, 1170 St Pieters Woluwe, Belgium* Tel (0032) 486-141323 (mobile) E-mail james.day@psp.ucl.ac.be

DAY, Jennifer Ann. See BRADSHAW, Mrs Jennifer Ann

DAY, John Cuthbert. b 36. Sarum Th Coll 66. **d** 68 **p** 69. C Bedhampton *Portsm* 68-72; V Froxfield 72-73; V Froxfield w Privett 73-77; V Warminster Ch Ch *Sarum* 77-81; R Pewsey 81-90; Chapl Pewsey Hosp 81-90; P-in-c Sturminster Newton and Hinton St Mary *Sarum* 90-01; P-in-c Stock and Lydlinch 90-01; rtd 01; Perm to Offic *B & W* and *Sarum* from 01. *Kingfisher Cottage, Clements Lane, Mere, Warminster BA12 6DF* Tel (01347) 860984

DAY, John Kenneth. b 58. Hull Univ BA85. Cranmer Hall Dur 85. **d** 87 **p** 88. C Thornbury *Bradf* 87-90; V 90-96; V Whitkirk *Ripon* 96-01; V Fendalton New Zealand from 01. *7 Makora Street, Fendalton, Christchurch 8041, New Zealand* Tel (0064) (3) 351 7392 *or* 351 7064 E-mail thedays@clear.net.nz

DAY, Martyn John. b 69. Univ Coll Lon BSc90. St Jo Coll Nottm 07. **d** 09 **p** 10. C Horwich and Rivington *Man* from 09; C Blackrod from 11. *36 Greenstone Avenue, Horwich, Bolton BL6 5SJ* Tel (01204) 468555 E-mail martyn.day9@btinternet.com

DAY, Canon Mary Elizabeth. b 57. Leic Poly BEd79. St Jo Coll Nottm 93. **d** 93 **p** 94. C Newbarns w Hawcoat *Carl* 93-98; P-in-c

Allonby 98-03; P-in-c Cross Canonby 98-03; P-in-c Dearham 02-03; V Allonby, Cross Canonby and Dearham from 03; Adv for Women in Min from 07; RD Solway from 08; Hon Can Carl Cathl from 08. *The Vicarage, Crosscanonby, Maryport CA15 6SJ* Tel (01900) 814192 E-mail mary.day1@tesco.net

DAY, Michael. b 37. AKC61 RCA(Lon) MA75. d 62 p 63. C Hulme St Phil *Man* 62-65; Asst Chapl Newc Univ 65-70; Chapl Chelsea Coll *Lon* 70-85; Chapl R Coll of Art 70-90; Chapl Cen, Chelsea and St Martin's Schs of Art *Lon* 85-90; P-in-c Bloomsbury St Geo w Woburn Square Ch Ch 91-95; C St Pancras w St Jas and Ch Ch 95-02; Chapl Lon Art Colls 95-02; rtd 02. *40 Thistlewaite Road, London E5 0QQ* Tel (020) 8985 8568

DAY, Paul Geoffrey. b 51. Dur Univ BEd75. Trin Coll Bris 76. d 78 p 79. C Roxeth Ch Ch *Lon* 78-82; TV Barking St Marg w St Patr *Chelmsf* 82-87; V Barrow St Mark *Carl* 87-00; V Eccleston St Luke *Liv* 00-07; TV Eccleston from 07. *St Luke's Vicarage, Mulberry Avenue, St Helens WA10 4DE* Tel (01744) 21173 E-mail paulgday@btinternet.com

DAY, Peter. b 50. BPharm71. Coll of Resurr Mirfield 85. d 87 p 88. C Eastcote St Lawr *Lon* 87-91; C Wembley Park St Aug 91-94; V Glen Parva and S Wigston *Leic* from 94. *9 Hindoostan Avenue, Wigston LE18 4UD* E-mail peterday@leicester.anglican.org

DAY, Peter Andrew. b 67. Westmr Coll Ox BTh98 Bris Univ PhD03. Ripon Coll Cuddesdon 07. d 10 p 11. C Wokingham St Paul *Ox* from 10. *13 Brook Close, Wokingham RG41 1ND* Tel 0118-978 7658 Mobile 07702-043857 E-mail fr.peterday@virginmedia.com

DAY, Peter Maurice. b 43. d 04 p 05. OLM Dover St Martin *Cant* from 04. *42 Elms Vale Road, Dover CT17 9NT* Tel (01304) 201966 E-mail peterm.day@ntlworld.com

DAY, Roy Frederick. b 24. S'wark Ord Course 63. d 67 p 68. C Newington St Paul *S'wark* 67-70; C Radlett *St Alb* 70-72; P-in-c Ponsbourne 72-76; R Campton 76-82; V Shefford 76-82; R Shenley 82-89; rtd 89; Perm to Offic *St Alb* from 89. *11 Hill End Lane, St Albans AL4 0TX* Tel (01727) 845782

DAY, Miss Sally Ann. b 43. d 07 p 08. OLM Shifnal and Sheriffhales *Lich* from 07. *11 Cherry Tree Hill, Coalbrookdale, Telford TF8 7EF* Tel and fax (01952) 433213 Mobile 07831-101361 E-mail sallyannday@hotmail.com

DAY, Stephen Michael. b 60. Down Coll Cam BA82 MA85 Open Univ BA00. Ridley Hall Cam 02. d 05 p 06. C Waltham H Cross *Chelmsf* 05-09; TV Papworth *Ely* from 09. *The Rectory, 1 Barons Way, Papworth Everard, Cambridge CB23 3QJ* Tel (01480) 831915 E-mail revdsmday@tesco.net *or* stephen.day@ely.anglican.org

DAY, Timothy Robert. b 63. WMMTC 07. d 10 p 11. NSM Leic H Apostles from 10. *11 Jarrett Close, Enderby, Leicester LE19 4PJ* Tel 0116-286 1335 Mobile 07989-549450 E-mail day.timothy@siemens.com

DAY, William Charles. b 47. Portsm Poly BEd86. Ripon Coll Cuddesdon 88. d 90 p 91. C Bishop's Waltham *Portsm* 90-93; P-in-c Greatham w Empshott and Hawkley w Prior's Dean 93-95; R 95-98; V Titchfield 98-09; RD Fareham 04-08; C-in-c Whiteley CD 08-09; rtd 09; Perm to Offic *Portsm* from 09. *19 Peter's Road, Locks Heath, Southampton SO31 6EB* Tel (01489) 564035 E-mail carolday@frmail.net

DAYKIN, Mrs Jean Elizabeth. b 43. d 04 p 05. NSM Cawthorne *Wakef* from 04. *13 Maltkiln Road, Cawthorne, Barnsley S75 4HH* Tel (01226) 793804 Mobile 07967-767839 E-mail rev.jeand@btinternet.com

DAYKIN, Timothy Elwin. b 54. R Holloway Coll Lon BSc75 St Jo Coll Dur MA81 K Coll Lon MPhil93 MEHS89 FRSA02. Cranmer Hall Dur 75. d 78 p 79. C Bourne *Guildf* 78-81; Chapl K Alfred Coll *Win* 82-87; C-in-c Valley Park CD 87-91; V Valley Park 91-92; P-in-c Fordingbridge 92-98; V 98-01; P-in-c Hale w S Charford 94-01; P-in-c Breamore 99-01; TR Fordingbridge and Breamore and Hale etc 01-05; TV Southampton (City Cen) from 05; Producer/Presenter Relig Progr BBC Radio Solent from 05. *St Michael's Vicarage, 55 Bugle Street, Southampton SO14 2AG* E-mail vicar@buglestreet.co.uk

DAYNES, Andrew John. b 47. Jes Coll Cam BA69 MA73. Westcott Ho Cam 69. d 72 p 73. C Radlett *St Alb* 72-76; Chapl St Alb Abbey 76-80; Chapl Bryanston Sch 80-08; rtd 08. *20 Liddington Crescent, Blandford Forum DT11 7RP*

DAZELEY, Mrs Lorna. b 31. CertEd53 New Hall Cam BA82 MA86. EAMTC 82. dss 84 d 87 p 94. Chesterton St Andr *Ely* 84-87; C 87-97; rtd 97; Perm to Offic *Ely* from 01. *Chesterton House, Church Street, Chesterton, Cambridge CB4 1DT* Tel (01223) 356243 E-mail lornadazeley@mac.com

DE ALMEIDA FEITAL, Peterson. b 75. Cliff Coll BA05 MA09. Ridley Hall Cam 09. d 11. C Muswell Hill St Jas w St Matt *Lon* from 11. *5 Woodland Rise, London N10 3UP* Tel 07791-581745 (mobile) E-mail petersonfeital@hotmail.com

DE ALWIS, Anthony Clarence. b 39. Nottm Univ MA99. EAMTC 96. d 99 p 00. NSM Carrington *S'well* 99-04; NSM Basford St Leodegarius 04-06; rtd 06. *85 Marlborough Road, Beeston, Nottingham NG9 2HL* Tel 0115-967 8097 Mobile ˜74-084514 E-mail tonydealwis270@hotmail.com

de BERRY, Andrew Piers. b 44. St Jo Coll Dur BA66. Ripon Hall Ox 70. d 74 p 75. C Aylesbury *Ox* 74-77; USA 78; TV Clyst St George, Aylesbeare, Clyst Honiton etc *Ex* 78-80; Asst Chapl HM Pris Wormwood Scrubs 80-82; Chapl HM Pris Sudbury 82-84; V Blackwell *Derby* 84-91; V Thurgarton w Hoveringham and Bleasby etc *S'well* 91-10; rtd 10; Perm to Offic *S'well* from 10. *The Vicarage, Church Road, Clipstone Village, Mansfield NG21 9DG* Tel (01623) 623916 E-mail adeberry@tiscali.co.uk

de BERRY, Barnabas John de la Tour. b 75. Heythrop Coll Lon BA99. Wycliffe Hall Ox 99. d 01 p 02. C Derby St Alkmund and St Werburgh 01-04; C Cambridge H Trin *Ely* 04-10; V Cant St Mary Bredin from 10. *St Mary Bredin Vicarage, 57 Nunnery Fields, Canterbury CT1 3JN* Tel (01227) 453777 Mobile 07968-728840 E-mail barney.deberry@btinternet.com

DE BERRY, Robert Delatour. b 42. Qu Coll Cam BA64 MA68. Ridley Hall Cam 65. d 67 p 68. C Bradf Cathl 67-70; Youth Worker CMS Uganda 71-75; V Attercliffe *Sheff* 75-83; V W Kilburn St Luke w St Simon and St Jude *Lon* 83-97; Gen Sec Mid-Africa Min (CMS) 97-99; P-in-c Kennington St Mark *S'wark* 99-01; V 01-08; rtd 08. *27 Cossor Road, Pewsey SN9 5HX*

de BOWEN, Alfred William. b 24. St Paul's Coll Grahamstown 76. d 78 p 86. NSM Port Alfred S Africa 78-86; NSM Cil-y-Cwm and Ystrad-ffin w Rhandir-mwyn etc *St D* 86-88; Lic to Offic *Linc* 88-92; rtd 90. *Elmham House, Bay Hill, Ilminster TA19 0AT* Tel (01460) 52694

DE CHAIR LADD, Anne. See LADD, Mrs Anne de Chair

de COSTOBADIE, James Palliser. b 72. G&C Coll Cam BA94 MA98. Oak Hill Th Coll BA01. d 02 p 03. C Mayfair Ch Ch and St Helen Bishopsgate w St Andr Undershaft etc *Lon* 02-05; P-in-c Sydenham w Beckenham New Zealand from 05. *8A Roxburgh Street, Sydenham, Christchurch 8023, New Zealand* Tel (0064) (3) 332 3432 E-mail jdecostobadie@hotmail.com

de GARIS, Jean Helier Thomson. b 60. K Alfred's Coll Win BA82 PGCE83. Sarum & Wells Th Coll BTh93. d 93 p 94. C Chandler's Ford *Win* 93-98; P-in-c Lytchett Minster *Sarum* 98-10; TR The Lytchetts and Upton from 10; RD Poole from 09. *The Vicarage, New Road, Lytchett Minster, Poole BH16 6JQ* Tel (01202) 622253 E-mail jean@degaris.freeserve.co.uk

de GAY, Sandra Jane. NOC. d 08 p 09. NSM Potternewton *Ripon* from 08. *48 Vesper Way, Leeds LS5 3LN* Tel 0113-258 2673 E-mail j.degay@leedstrinity.ac.uk

de GREY-WARTER, Philip. b 67. Leeds Univ BEng89. Ridley Hall Cam BA94. d 94 p 95. C Bromley Ch Ch *Roch* 94-97; C Sevenoaks St Nic 97-02; P-in-c Fowey *Truro* from 02; P-in-c St Sampson from 02; Chapl Cen Cornwall Primary Care Trust 02-07; Hon Chapl Miss to Seafarers 04-07. *The Vicarage, Church Avenue, Fowey PL23 1BU* Tel (01726) 833535 E-mail pdgw@btinternet.com

de la BAT SMIT, Reynaud. b 50. St Edm Hall Ox BA80 MA86 Dur Univ PhD94 FRSA94. Ripon Coll Cuddesdon. d 82 p 83. C Headington Ox 82-85; Chapl St Hild and St Bede Coll *Dur* 85-96; Chapl Cheltenham Coll 96-11; rtd 11; Sec Chs' Peace Forum CTBI from 97. *Address temp unknown* E-mail reynaud@ukonline.co.uk

de la HOYDE, Canon Denys Ralph Hart. b 33. G&C Coll Cam BA57 MA61. Westcott Ho Cam 57. d 59 p 60. C Moss Side Ch Ch *Man* 59-60; Chapl G&C Coll Cam 60-64; P-in-c Naini Tal etc India 64-68; C Eltham H Trin *S'wark* 68-69; Chapl Bromsgrove Sch 69-71; Asst Master Harrogate High Sch 71-78; Lic to Offic *Ripon* 71-78; V Pool w Arthington 86-98; Dioc Dir of Ords 86-98; Hon Can Ripon Cathl 92-98; rtd 98; Perm to Offic *Ripon* from 00. *36 Hookstone Chase, Harrogate HG2 7HS* Tel (01423) 548146 E-mail denys.delahoyde@ntlworld.com

de la MOUETTE, Norman Harry. b 39. Southn Univ BEd73 MA98. Sarum & Wells Th Coll 76. d 79 p 80. NSM Win St Lawr and St Maurice w St Swithun 79-99; Deputation Appeals Org CECS *Win* and *Portsm* 83-96; Chapl St Jo Win Charity 96-99; NSM Win St Lawr and St Maurice w St Swithun 99-04; rtd 04. *146 Greenhill Road, Winchester SO22 5DR* Tel (01962) 853191

de MELLO, Gualter Rose. b 34. MBE96. Ridley Hall Cam 63. d 64 p 65. C S Hackney St Jo w Ch Ch *Lon* 64-66; Toc H Chapl (Hackney) 66-72; Hon C All Hallows by the Tower etc *Lon* from 73; Dir Friends Anonymous Service from 73; Dir Community of Reconciliation and Fellowship from 88; rtd 99. *Prideaux House, 10 Church Crescent, London E9 7DL*

de POMERAI, David Ian Morcamp. b 50. Edin Univ BSc72 Univ Coll Lon PhD75. EMMTC 90. d 93 p 94. NSM Sutton in Ashfield St Mary *S'well* 93-96; NSM Clifton 96-02; NSM Walton-on-Trent w Croxall, Rosliston etc *Derby* from 02. *The Rectory, 2 Station Lane, Walton-on-Trent, Swadlincote DE12 8NA* Tel (01283) 711350 E-mail david.depomerai@nottingham.ac.uk

de POMERAI, Mrs Lesley Anne. b 60. ACIPD82. St Jo Coll Nottm BTh90. d 92 p 94. Par Dn Sutton in Ashfield St Mary *S'well* 92-94; C 94-96; TV Clifton 96-02; R Walton-on-Trent w Croxall, Rosliston etc *Derby* from 02; RD Repton from 09. *The Rectory, 2 Station Lane, Walton-on-Trent, Swadlincote DE12 8NA* Tel (01283) 711350 E-mail ddepomerai@aol.com

DE PURY, Andrew Robert. b 28. K Coll Lon BD57 AKC57. **d** 58 **p** 59. C Epping St Jo *Chelmsf* 58-60; C Loughton St Jo 60-65; V Harold Hill St Geo 65-72; Missr Swan Par Gp *Ox* 72-76; TR Swan 76-85; R Worminghall w Ickford, Oakley and Shabbington 85-95; rtd 95; Perm to Offic *B & W* 95-06. *8 Russell Pope Avenue, Chard TA20 2JN* Tel (01460) 66714

de QUIDT, Mrs Fiona Margaret Munro. b 53. St Andr Univ MTheol76. NTMTC 97. **d** 00 **p** 01. NSM Kingston Hill St Paul S'wark from 00. *10 Norbiton Avenue, Kingston-upon-Thames KT1 3QS* Tel (020) 8549 4175

de QUIDT, Mrs Marion Elizabeth. b 59. STETS. **d** 11. C Fetcham *Guildf* from 11. *5 Oswald Close, Fetcham, Leatherhead KT22 9UA* E-mail marion@stmarysfetcham.org.uk

DE ROBECK, Fiona Caroline. See GIBBS, Mrs Fiona Caroline

DE SAUSMAREZ, Canon John Havilland Russell. b 26. Lambeth MA81 Wells Th Coll 54. **d** 56 **p** 57. C N Lynn w St Marg and St Nic *Nor* 56-58; C Hythe *Cant* 58-61; V Maidstone St Martin 61-68; V St Peter-in-Thanet 68-81; RD Thanet 74-81; Hon Can Cant Cathl 78-81; Can Res Cant Cathl 81-94; rtd 94; Perm to Offic *Cant* from 94. *9 St Peter's Court, Broadstairs CT10 2UU* Tel (01843) 867050

DE SILVA, David Ebenezer Sunil. b 48. **d** 72 **p** 73. Sri Lanka 72-84; C Elm Park St Nic Hornchurch *Chelmsf* 84-87; R Mistley w Manningtree and Bradfield 87-90; TR Stanground and Farcet *Ely* 90-01; V Stanground 01-05; rtd 05. *52 Spring Avenue, Hampton Vale, Peterborough PE7 8HW* Tel (01733) 240319

DE SMET, Andrew Charles. b 58. Ex Univ BSc79 Southn Univ BTh88. Sarum & Wells Th Coll 85. **d** 88 **p** 89. C Portsea St Mary *Portsm* 88-93; R Shipston-on-Stour w Honington and Idlicote *Cov* 93-00; Warden Offa Retreat Ho and Dioc Spirituality Adv 00-07; P-in-c Kirkdale w Harome, Nunnington and Pockley *York* from 07; Dioc Adv in Past Care from 07. *Kirkdale Vicarage, Main Road, Nawton, York YO62 7ST* Tel (01439) 770760 E-mail andrewdesmet@btinternet.com

DE VERNY, David Dietrich Schuld. b 55. Trier Univ MTh81. **d** 83 **p** 83. Asst Chapl Bonn *Eur* 83; C Henfield w Shermanbury and Woodmancote *Chich* 84-86; C Westmr St Sav and St Jas Less *Lon* 86-88; P-in-c Cheddington w Mentmore and Marsworth *Ox* 88-90; Gen Sec Fellowship of St Alb and St Sergius 90-92; Chapl for Migrant Workers *Linc* 06-08; Dioc Link Person for Ethnic Minority Anglicans 06-08; Hon C Boston 05-08; Chapl Hull Univ 08-10; P-in-c Swineshead *Linc* from 10; P-in-c Bicker from 10; P-in-c Donington from 10; P-in-c Sutterton and Wigtoft from 10. *The Vicarage, Church Lane, Swineshead, Boston PE20 3JA* Tel (01205) 820771 Mobile 07761-469456 E-mail david.deverny129@btinternet.com

de VIAL, Raymond Michael. b 39. Oak Hill Th Coll 77. **d** 80 **p** 81. NSM Beckenham St Jo *Roch* 80-84; C Morden *S'wark* 84-88; TV 88-94; V Kingston Hill St Paul 94-04; rtd 04; Perm to Offic *S'wark* 04-05 and *Carl* from 05. *39 Helme Drive, Kendal LA9 7JB* Tel (01539) 729396 E-mail revray@btinternet.com

de WAAL, Victor Alexander. b 29. Pemb Coll Cam BA49 MA53 Nottm Univ Hon DD83. Ely Th Coll 50. **d** 52 **p** 53. C Isleworth St Mary *Lon* 52-56; Chapl Ely Th Coll 56-59; Chapl K Coll Cam 59-63; Hon C Nottingham St Mary *S'well* 63-69; Chapl Nottm Univ 63-69; Can Res and Chan Linc Cathl 69-76; Dean Cant 76-86; Perm to Offic *Heref* 88-99; rtd 90; Chapl Soc of Sacred Cross Tymawr 90-00; Lic to Offic *Mon* 90-02; Perm to Offic from 02. *St James Close, Bishop Street, London N1 8PH* Tel (020) 7354 2741 E-mail victordewaal@aol.com

DE WIT, The Ven John. b 47. Oriel Coll Ox BA69 MA73 Clare Coll Cam BA78 MA84. Westcott Ho Cam 75. **d** 78 **p** 79. C The Quinton *Birm* 78-81; TV Solihull 81-85; V Kings Heath 85-94; RD Moseley 91-94; P-in-c Hampton in Arden 94-04; Chapl Utrecht w Zwolle *Eur* from 04; Adn NW Eur from 08. *Van Hogendorpstraat 26, 3581KE Utrecht, The Netherlands* Tel (0031) (30) 251 3424 Fax 254 1580 E-mail chaplain@holytrinityutrecht.nl

DE WOLF, Mark Anthony. b 32. BA55. Ely Th Coll 56. **d** 59 **p** 60. C Hackney Wick St Mary of Eton w St Aug *Lon* 59-64; P-in-c Brooklyn St Jo and Sheepshead Bay Em USA 64-66; R Amityville St Mary 67-75; R Stamford St Andr 75-06; rtd 06. *9 Weetamoe Farm Drive, Bristol RI 02809-5199, USA*

DEACON, Charles Edward. b 57. Westf Coll Lon BSc78. Ridley Hall Cam 92. **d** 94 **p** 95. C Ex St Jas 94-98; V Shiphay Collaton from 98. *St John's Vicarage, 83 Cadewell Lane, Torquay TQ2 7HP* Tel (01803) 401316

DEACON, Donald (Brother Angelo). Chich Th Coll 66. **d** 68 **p** 69. SSF from 63; Lic to Offic *Man* 69-70; USA 70-72; C Kennington St Jo *S'wark* 72-74; C Wilton Place St Paul *Lon* 74-75; Angl-Franciscan Rep Ecum Cen Assisi *Eur* 75; Franciscanum Sem 76-78; Perm to Offic *Sarum* 78-82; Lic to Offic *Chelmsf* 82-90; *Birm* 90-93; *Linc* 94-97; rtd 98; Lic to Offic *Lon* 98-07 and *Chich* from 07. *Bishop's House, 21 Guildford Road, Horsham RH12 1LU*

DEACON, Frederick George Raymond. b 15. Tyndale Hall Bris 63. **d** 65 **p** 66. C Knowood *Bris* 65-69; C Leckhampton SS Phil and Jas *Glouc* 69-71; V Longcot *Ox* 71-72; V Longcot w Fernham and Bourton 72-77; Zambia 77-80; P-in-c Cressage w

Sheinton *Heref* 80-81; P-in-c Harley w Kenley 80-81; TV Wenlock 81-85; rtd 85; Perm to Offic *Heref* 85-90; *Glouc* from 1986 and *Worc* from 90. *29 Robinson Meadow, Ledbury HR8 1SU* Tel (01531) 634500

DEACON, John. b 37. Arm Aux Min Course 87. **d** 90 **p** 91. NSM Enniscorthy w Clone, Clonmore, Monart etc *C & O* 90-05; rtd 05. *The Rectory, Creagh, Gorey, Co Wexford, Republic of Ireland* Tel (00353) (53) 942 0354

DEACON, Mrs Selina Frances. b 52. SRN74. Ripon Coll Cuddesdon 01. **d** 03 **p** 04. C White Horse *Sarum* 03-07; P-in-c Studley from 07. *The Vicarage, 340 Frome Road, Studley, Trowbridge BA14 0ED* Tel (01225) 753162 Mobile 07867-521909 E-mail selinadeacon@hotmail.com

DEACON, Timothy Randall. b 55. Ex Univ BA78. Chich Th Coll 79. **d** 80 **p** 81. C Whitleigh *Ex* 80-83; P-in-c Devonport St Aubyn 83-88; P-in-c Newton Ferrers w Revelstoke 88-94; R 94-07; P-in-c Holbeton 93-07; TR Brixham w Churston Ferrers and Kingswear from 07; RD Ivybridge 98-03. *The Rectory, 16 Holwell Road, Brixham TQ5 9NE* Tel and fax (01803) 851570 E-mail revtimdeacon@hotmail.co.uk

DEADMAN, Richard George Spencer. b 63. Ex Univ BA85. Coll of Resurr Mirfield 86. **d** 88 **p** 89. C Grangetown *York* 88-91; P-in-c 91-93; V 93-96; V Wallsend St Luke *Newc* 96-01; V Newc St Phil and St Aug and St Matt w St Mary from 01. *St Matthew's Vicarage, 10 Winchester Terrace, Newcastle upon Tyne NE4 6EY* Tel 0191-232 9039 E-mail richardgsd@aol.com

DEAKIN, Christopher Harold. b 49. ARMCM72. Qu Coll Birm 02. **d** 04 **p** 05. C Wrockwardine Deanery *Lich* 04-07; P-in-c Bicton, Montford w Shrawardine and Fitz from 07; P-in-c Leaton and Albrighton w Battlefield from 07. *The Rectory, 15 Brookside, Bicton, Shrewsbury SY3 8EP* Tel (01743) 851310 E-mail deaks@fsmail.net

DEAKIN, John David. b 58. Qu Coll Birm BA03. **d** 03 **p** 04. C Blakenall Heath *Lich* 03-07; TV Willenhall H Trin 07-11; TV Bentley Em and Willenhall H Trin from 11. *129 Essington Road, Willenhall WV12 5DT* Tel (01922) 409460

DEAKIN, Preb John Hartley. b 27. K Coll Cam BA50 MA63. Cranmer Hall Dur. **d** 65 **p** 66. C Newcastle St Geo *Lich* 65-70; V Cotes Heath 70-84; RD Eccleshall 82-92; R Standon and Cotes Heath 84-95; Preb Lich Cathl 88-02; Sub-Chapl HM Pris Drake Hall 89-95; rtd 95; Hon C Kinver and Enville *Lich* 95-02; Perm to Offic *Heref* from 04. *8C Cliff Road, Bridgnorth WV16 4EY* Tel (01746) 762574

DEAMER, Mrs Carylle. b 40. SAOMC 96. **d** 99 **p** 00. OLM Riverside *Ox* 99-05; rtd 05; Perm to Offic *Ox* 05-08 and *B & W* from 09. *7 Coombe Close, Castle Cary BA7 7HJ* Tel (01963) 359243 E-mail rev.carylle@deamer.me.uk

DEAN, The Ven Alan. b 38. Hull Univ BA61. Qu Coll Birm. **d** 63 **p** 64. C Clitheroe St Mary *Blackb* 63-67; C Burnley St Pet 67-68; CF 68-93; Dep Chapl Gen and Adn for the Army 93-95; QHC 93-95; rtd 96; Perm to Offic *York* from 95. *1 Midway Avenue, Nether Poppleton, York YO26 6NT* Tel (01904) 785305

DEAN, Andrew James. b 40. FCII ACIArb. WEMTC 92. **d** 95 **p** 96. NSM Rodbourne Cheney *Bris* 95-05; rtd 05; Perm to Offic *Bris* from 05. *Koinonia, 2 Wicks Close, Haydon Wick, Swindon SN25 1QH* Tel (01793) 725526

DEAN, Canon Arthur. b 32. Southn Univ CQSW80. Wesley Coll Leeds 55 S Dios Minl Tr Scheme 89. **d** 90 **p** 90. NSM Eastney *Portsm* 90-96; P-in-c Portsea St Alb 96-02; Hon Can Portsm Cathl from 02; rtd 02; Perm to Offic *Portsm* from 02. *9 Kingsley Road, Southsea PO4 8HJ* Tel (023) 9273 5773 Mobile 07855-146929 E-mail annenarthur.dean@btopenworld.com

DEAN, Benjamin Timothy Frederic. b 70. Lon Bible Coll BA93 K Coll Lon MA94 Selw Coll Cam MPhil02 PhD06. Ridley Hall Cam 04. **d** 07. C Georgeham *Ex* 07-08; Lect Geo Whitefield Coll S Africa from 08. *George Whitefield College, PO Box 64, Muizenberg, 7950 South Africa* Tel (0027) (21) 788 1652 E-mail btfd@mac.com

DEAN, John Milner. b 27. S'wark Ord Course 68. **d** 72 **p** 73. C Lewisham St Mary *S'wark* 72-75; C Merton St Mary 75-77; V S Beddington St Mich 77-97; rtd 97. *69 Groveside Close, Carshalton SM5 2ER* Tel (020) 8669 9369

DEAN, Jonathan Charles. b 57. St Cath Coll Cam MA83. NEOC 04. **d** 07 **p** 08. NSM Gt Ayton w Easby and Newton under Roseberry *York* from 07. *The White House, 2 Dikes Lane, Great Ayton, Middlesbrough TS9 6HJ* Tel (01642) 722649

DEAN, Mrs Linda Louise. b 39. **d** 04 **p** 05. NSM Primrose Hill St Mary w Avenue Road St Paul *Lon* from 04. *52 Lanchester Road, London N6 4TA* Tel (020) 8883 5417 E-mail linda@lindadean52.wanadoo.co.uk

DEAN, Lucas John William. b 57. St Jo Coll Nottm 05. **d** 07 **p** 08. C St Laur in Thanet *Cant* from 07. *1 Warwick Drive, Ramsgate CT11 0JP* Tel (01843) 588385 Mobile 07712-834472 E-mail ljwdean@hotmail.com

DEAN, Malcolm. b 34. Tyndale Hall Bris 67. **d** 69 **p** 70. C Daubhill *Man* 69-73; P-in-c Constable Lee 73-74; V 74-79; P-in-c Everton St Sav w St Cuth *Liv* 79-86; P-in-c Anfield SS Simon and Jude 81-86; V Walton Breck Ch Ch 86-89; rtd 89; Perm to

Offic *Man* from 89. *40 Grasmere Road, Haslingden, Rossendale BB4 4EB* Tel (01706) 215953

DEAN, Margaret Heath. b 50. Newton Park Coll Bris BEd72. STETS 05. **d** 07 **p** 08. C Farncombe *Guildf* 07-11; R Reepham, Hackford w Whitwell, Kerdiston etc *Nor* from 11. *The Rectory, 26 Station Road, Reepham, Norwich NR10 4LJ* Tel (01603) 879275 E-mail margaretdean@cnet.org

DEAN, Mark William John. **d** 10 **p** 11. NSM N Greenford All Hallows *Lon* from 10. *76 Essendine Road, London W9 2LY* Tel (020) 7289 7900 Mobile 07960-793683 E-mail md@tailbiter.com

DEAN, Simon Timothy Michael Rex. b 62. Liv Univ BEng83. Ridley Hall Cam 86. **d** 89 **p** 90. C St German's Cathl 89-92; V Castletown 92-05; Perm to Offic *Cant* 08-11. *11 Viking Court, St Stephen's Close, Canterbury CT2 7HZ*

DEAN, Stuart Peter. b 75. Cant Ch Ch Univ Coll BA97. Oak Hill Th Coll 03. **d** 06 **p** 07. C Lindfield *Chich* 06-10. *Address temp unknown*

DEAN, Timothy Charles Painter. b 50. STETS MA08. **d** 07 **p** 08. NSM Godalming *Guildf* 07-11; Continuing MinI Development Officer *Nor* from 11; NSM Reepham, Hackford w Whitwell, Kerdiston etc from 11. *The Rectory, 26 Station Road, Reepham, Norwich NR10 4LJ, or 65 The Close, Norwich NR1 4DH* Tel (01603) 871062 *or* 729817 E-mail timdean@cnet.org *or* tim.dean@norwich.anglican.org

DEAN, Trevor Stephen. b 58. Lon Hosp MB, BS81. Trin Coll Bris BA03. **d** 10 **p** 11. NSM Nailsea H Trin *B & W* from 10. *3 Ilminster Close, Nailsea, Bristol BS48 4YU* Tel (01275) 851218 Mobile 07905-757649 E-mail trevor.dean@blueyonder.co.uk

DEAN-REVILL, David Frank. b 68. Univ Coll Ches BA06. NOC 03. **d** 06 **p** 07. C Dinnington w Laughton and Throapham *Sheff* 06-09; P-in-c Shiregreen from 09. *The Vicarage, 510 Bellhouse Road, Sheffield S5 0RG* Tel 0114-245 6526 E-mail daviddeanrevill@hotmail.com

DEANE, Mrs Angela Christine. b 52. WEMTC 00. **d** 04 **p** 05. NSM Credenhill w Brinsop and Wormsley etc *Heref* from 04. *The Oak, Mansel Lacy, Hereford HR4 7HQ* Tel (01981) 590615 E-mail angiestutheoak@lineone.net

DEANE, John. **d** 02 **p** 03. NSM Stranorlar w Meenglas and Kilteevogue *D & R* 02-06; NSM Derg w Termonamongan 06-07; NSM Urney w Sion Mills 07-08; Bp's C Ardara w Glencolumbkille, Inniskeel etc from 08. *The Rectory, Ardara, Co Donegal, Republic of Ireland* Tel (00353) (74) 954 1124 E-mail revjohndeane@yahoo.ie

DEANE, Nicholas Talbot Bryan. b 46. Bris Univ BA69. Clifton Th Coll 70. **d** 72 **p** 73. C Accrington Ch Ch *Blackb* 72-75; OMF Korea 75-89; P-in-c Newburgh *Liv* 90-93; P-in-c Westhead 90-93; V Newburgh w Westhead 93-97; R Chadwell *Chelmsf* 97-11; rtd 11; C Waverton w Aldford and Bruera *Ches* from 11. *The Rectory, Green Lake Lane, Aldford, Chester CH3 6HW* Tel (01244) 620281 E-mail nic@ntbd.uklinux.net

DEANE, Canon Robert William. b 52. CITC. **d** 85 **p** 86. C Raheny w Coolock *D & G* 85-88; I Clonsast w Rathangan, Thomastown etc *M & K* 88-00; Can Kildare Cathl 97-00; Can Meath Cathl 98-00; I Swords w Donabate and Kilsallaghan *D & G* from 00; Can Ch Ch Cathl Dublin from 08. *The Rectory, Church Road, Swords, Co Dublin, Republic of Ireland* Tel (00353) (1) 840 2308 E-mail rwdeane@eircom.net

DEANE, Stuart William. b 45. Sarum & Wells Th Coll 86. **d** 88 **p** 89. C Bromyard *Heref* 88-92; V Astley, Clive, Grinshill and Hadnall *Lich* 92-95; TV Cen Telford 98-00; TR 00-05; rtd 05; Perm to Offic *Heref* from 07. *38 Crest Court, Hereford HR4 9QD* Tel (01432) 351937

DEANS, Bruce Gibson. b 64. MCIBS86. Wycliffe Hall Ox 02. **d** 04 **p** 05. C Hartley Wintney, Elvetham, Winchfield etc 04-08; V Shedfield and Wickham *Portsm* from 08. *The Vicarage, 52 Brooklynn Close, Waltham Chase, Southampton SO32 2RZ* Tel (01489) 896637 E-mail brucedeans@thebearsden.fsnet.co.uk

DEAR, Graham Frederick. b 44. St Luke's Coll Ex CertEd66. Wycliffe Hall Ox 67. **d** 70 **p** 71. C Chigwell *Chelmsf* 70-73; C Chingford SS Pet and Paul 73-75; V Southchurch Ch Ch 75-82; CF 82-89; P-in-c The Cowtons *Ripon* 89-94; RE Adv 89-94; V Startforth and Bowes and Rokeby w Brignall 94-97; Chapl HM Pris Garth 97-01; rtd 09; Perm to Offic *Ripon* from 01. *1 The Old Wynd, Bellerby, Leyburn DL8 5QJ* Tel (01969) 623960

DEAR, Neil Douglas Gauntlett. b 35. Linc Th Coll 87. **d** 89 **p** 90. C Framlingham w Saxtead *St E* 89-92; P-in-c Eyke w Bromeswell, Rendlesham, Tunstall etc 92-98; Chapl Local Health Partnerships NHS Trust 98-02; Chapl Cen Suffolk Primary Care Bedfield etc *St E* 02-05; rtd 05; Perm to Offic *St E* from 05. *Peacehaven, Duke Street, Stanton, Bury St Edmunds IP31 2AB* Tel (01359) 252001

DEARDEN, Geoffrey. b 36. Salford Univ MSc74. CBDTI 05. **d** 06 **p** 07. NSM Hurst Green and Mitton *Bradf* from 06. *14 Church Close, Waddington, Clitheroe BB7 3HX* Tel (01200) 427380 E-mail elizabeth.dearden@virgin.net

DEARDEN, James Varley. b 22. Wycliffe Hall Ox 61. **d** 62 **p** 63. C ˇrypool St Columba w St Andr and St Pet *York* 62-66; V

Newington Transfiguration 66-75; V Huddersfield H Trin *Wakef* 75-87; rtd 87; Perm to Offic *Wakef* from 87. *26 Sycamore Avenue, Meltham, Holmfirth HD9 4EE* Tel (01484) 852519

DEARDEN, Canon Philip Harold. b 43. AKC65. **d** 66 **p** 67. C Haslingden w Haslingden Grane *Blackb* 66-69; C Burnley St Pet 69-71; V Langho Billington 71-78; TR Darwen St Pet w Hoddlesden 78-91; RD Darwen 86-91; V Altham w Clayton le Moors 91-97; RD Accrington 95-97; V Clitheroe St Mary 97-08; Hon Can Blackb Cathl 96-08; rtd 08; Perm to Offic *Blackb* from 08. *16 Sun Street, Ulverston LA12 7BX* Tel (01229) 480155 E-mail philip.dearden@btinternet.com

DEARING, Henry Ernest. b 26. Lon Univ BD53. St Deiniol's Hawarden 55. **d** 55 **p** 56. C Skerton St Chad *Blackb* 55-57; V Huncoat 57-60; rtd 95. *St David's Rest Home, 49 Llandudno Road, Penrhyn Bay, Llandudno LL30 3EP* Tel (01492) 545402

DEARING, Trevor. b 33. Lon Univ BD58. Qu Coll Birm MA63. **d** 61 **p** 62. C Todmorden *Wakef* 61-63; V Silkstone 63-66; V Northowram 66-68; C Harlow New Town w Lt Parndon *Chelmsf* 68-70; V Hainault 70-75; Dir Healing Miss 75-79; Hon C Gt Ilford St Andr 75-79; Perm to Offic *Linc* 80-81; 90-02; USA 81-83; rtd 83. *4 Rock House Gardens, Radcliffe Road, Stamford PE9 1AS* Tel (01780) 751680

DEARNLEY, Miss Helen Elizabeth. b 77. De Montfort Univ LLB98 Cam Univ BTh02. Westcott Ho Cam 99. **d** 02 **p** 03. C Knighton St Mary Magd *Leic* 02-06; Co-ord Chapl HM Pris Leic from 06. *HM Prison, Welford Road, Leicester LE2 7AJ* Tel 0116-228 3000 Fax 228 3001 E-mail helen.dearnley@ukgateway.net

DEARNLEY, John Wright. b 37. Open Univ BA81. **d** 99 **p** 05. NSM Llandogo w Whitebrook Chpl and Tintern Parva *Mon* from 99; P-in-c from 07. *2 Greenbanks, Llandogo, Monmouth NP25 4TG* Tel (01594) 530080

DEARNLEY, Mark Christopher. b 59. Cranmer Hall Dur 84. **d** 87 **p** 88. C Purley Ch Ch *S'wark* 87-91; C Addiscombe St Mary 91-93; C Addiscombe St Mary Magd w St Martin 93-94; V Hook 94-02; R Wendover and Halton *Ox* from 02; AD Wendover from 04. *The Vicarage, 34 Dobbins Lane, Wendover, Aylesbury HP22 6DH* Tel (01296) 622230 E-mail dearnley@ukgateway.net

DEARNLEY, Preb Patrick Walter. b 34. Nottm Univ BA55 LTh75. ALCD64. **d** 64 **p** 65. C New Malden and Coombe *S'wark* 64-68; C Portswood Ch Ch *Win* 68-71; C Leeds St Geo *Ripon* 71-74; Hon C Nottingham St Nic *S'well* 74-77; P-in-c Holloway Em w Hornsey Road St Barn *Lon* 77-85; AD Islington 80-85; Abp's Officer for UPA 85-90; Preb St Paul's Cathl 86-91; P-in-c Waterloo St Jo *Liv* 91-99; rtd 99; Perm to Offic *Bradf* from 00. *14 Beanlands Parade, Ilkley LS29 8EW* Tel (01943) 603927 E-mail gilrea@blueyonder.co.uk

DEAS, Leonard Stephen. b 52. New Coll Ox BA75 CertEd76 MA78. St Mich Coll Llan 81. **d** 82 **p** 83. C Dowlais *Llan* 82-84; Chapl St Mich Coll Llan 84-85; Chapl Univ of Wales (Cardiff) *Llan* 85-86; V Newbridge *Mon* 86-93; Can Res St Woolos Cathl 92-96; Master Charterhouse Hull from 96. *The Charterhouse, Charterhouse Lane, Hull HU2 8AF* Tel (01482) 329307

DEAVE, Mrs Gillian Mary. b 31. EMMTC 79. **dss** 82 **d** 87 **p** 94. Nottingham St Pet and St Jas *S'well* 82-87; Par Dn 87-91; rtd 91; Perm to Offic *Pet* and *S'well* from 91. *Greensmith Cottage, 8 City Road, Stathern, Melton Mowbray LE14 4HE* Tel (01949) 860340 E-mail g.deave@leicester.anglican.org

DEAVES, Mrs Hannah Claire. b 73. York Univ BSc94 Bp Grosseteste Coll PGCE95 Univ of Wales (Ban) BTh06. 4 E OLM Triangle, St Matt and All SS *St E* from 11. *2 Exeter Road, Ipswich IP3 8JL* Tel (01473) 399635 Mobile 07906-372733 E-mail hannahdeaves@yahoo.co.uk

DEBENHAM, Peter Mark. b 68. Nottm Univ BSc89 PhD94. EAMTC 98. **d** 01 **p** 03. NSM Burwell *Ely* 01-02; NSM Swaffham Bulbeck and Swaffham Prior w Reach 01-02; Perm to Offic 02-03; NSM Fordham St Pet 03-08; NSM Kennett 03-08; NSM Three Rivers Gp from 08. *23 Burleigh Rise, Burwell, Cambridge CB25 0RS* Tel (01638) 603142 E-mail peter.debenham@ely.anglican.org

DEBNEY, Canon Wilfred Murray. b 26. ACA48 FCA60. Wycliffe Hall Ox 58. **d** 60 **p** 61. C Leic H Apostles 60-65; V Thorpe Edge *Bradf* 65-69; TV Wendy w Shingay *Ely* 69-75; R Brampton 75-94; Offg Chapl RAF 75-94; RD Huntingdon *Ely* 81-94; Hon Can Ely Cathl 85-94; rtd 94; Lic to Offic *Eur* 94-01; Chapl Lugano 98-02; Perm to Offic *Ely* 02-10. *10 Montague Walk, Upper Poppleton, York YO26 6JG* Tel (01904) 783119

DEBOO, Canon Alan John. b 45. Qu Coll Cam BA73 MA77. Westcott Ho Cam 72. **d** 74 **p** 75. C Brackley St Pet w St Jas 74-77; Perm to Offic *Sarum* 85-94; NSM Wexcombe 94-02; NSM Savernake 02-09; Bp's Officer for NSMs 03-09; Bp's Adv for Assoc Min from 09; Can and Preb Sarum Cathl from 05. *Mayzells Cottage, Collingbourne Kingston, Marlborough SN8 3SD* Tel (01264) 850683 E-mail alandeboo@aol.com

DEBOYS, David Gordon. b 54. QUB BD76 Wolfs Coll Ox MLitt. Ridley Hall Cam 90. **d** 92 **p** 93. C Ipswich St Aug *St E* 92-93; C Whitton and Thurleston w Akenham 93-95; R Hardwick *Ely* 95-00; R Toft w Caldecote and Childerley 95-00; V Cambridge

St Jas 00-07; Dir Focus Chr Inst Cambridge 00-07; V Ealing St Barn Lon from 07. *St Barnabas' Vicarage, 66 Woodfield Road, London W5 1SH* Tel (020) 8998 0826 E-mail daviddeboys@btconnect.com

DEDMAN, Canon Roger James. b 45. Oak Hill Th Coll 68. **d** 71 **p** 72. C Gresley *Derby* 71-74; C Ipswich St Fran *St E* 74-79; P-in-c Bildeston w Wattisham 79-92; P-in-c Bramford 92-10; P-in-c Somersham w Flowton 94-02; P-in-c Lt Blakenham, Baylham and Nettlestead 02-10; RD Bosmere 96-01 and 05-07; Hon Can St E Cathl 01-10; rtd 10; Perm to Offic *St E* from 10. *10 St Martin's Field, Otley LS21 2FN* E-mail roger.dedman@talktalk.net

DEE, Clive Hayden. b 61. Ripon Coll Cuddesdon 86. **d** 89 **p** 90. C Bridgnorth, Tasley, Astley Abbotts, etc *Heref* 89-93; P-in-c Wellington w Pipe-cum-Lyde and Moreton-on-Lugg 93-96. *Ross Cottage, Crumpton Hill Road, Storridge, Malvern WR13 5HE* Tel (01886) 832639

DEED, Michael James. b 77. **d** 04 **p** 05. C Notting Dale St Clem w St Mark and St Jas *Lon* 04-07; C Burlington St Chris Canada from 07. *662 Guelph Line, Burlington ON L7R 3M8, Canada* Tel (001) (905) 320 6034 E-mail michael.deed@googlemail.com

DEEDES, Canon Arthur Colin Bouverie. b 27. Bede Coll Dur BA51. Wells Th Coll 51. **d** 53 **p** 54. C Milton *Portsm* 53-58; C Worplesdon *Guildf* 58-60; V Weston 60-66; V Fleet 66-73; RD Aldershot 69-73; TR Bournemouth St Pet w St Swithun, H Trin etc *Win* 73-80; RD Bournemouth 74-80; Hon Can Win Cathl 78-92; Master Win St Cross w St Faith 80-92; rtd 92; Perm to Offic *Win* from 92; Hon Chapl Win Cathl from 97. *Dolphins, 17 Chesil Street, Winchester SO23 0HU* Tel (01962) 861617

DEEDES, Ms Rosemary Anne. b 66. Birm Univ BA87 City Univ 90. Westcott Ho Cam 94. **d** 96 **p** 97. C St Botolph Aldgate w H Trin Minories *Lon* 96-99; Asst Chapl HM Pris Holloway 99-02; Chapl HM Pris Downview 02-10; Chapl HM Pris Is of Wight from 10. *HM Prison Isle of Wight, Clissold Road, Newport PO30 5RS* Tel (01983) 556300 E-mail rosie.deedes@hmps.gsi.gov.uk

DEEGAN, Arthur Charles. b 49. CertEd71 Birm Univ BEd86. Qu Coll Birm 86. **d** 88 **p** 89. C Leic St Jas 88-91; C Melton St Framland 91-92; TV 92-93; TV Melton Mowbray 93-96; R Barwell w Potters Marston and Stapleton 96-08; P-in-c Braunstone Town from 08; CF (TA) from 95; Chapl ACF Leics, Northants, and Rutland from 95. *The Vicarage, 36 Woodcote Road, Leicester LE3 2WD* Tel 0116-224 8346 E-mail ac.deegan@ntlworld.com

DEEGAN, Michael Joseph. b 54. Ripon Coll Cuddesdon. **d** 09 **p** 10. Dir Soc Justice Sarum Cathl from 09. *36B The Close, Salisbury SP1 2EL* Tel 07502-216607 (mobile) E-mail mdeegan01@aol.com

DEELEY, Mrs Elke Christiane. b 58. Birm Univ BA81. SWMTC 99. **d** 02 **p** 03. NSM Roche and Withiel *Truro* from 02; NSM St Columb Major w St Wenn from 09; Chapl Cornwall Partnership NHS Trust from 09. *44 Duporth Bay, St Austell PL26 6AQ* Tel (01726) 63083 E-mail elke1@tinyonline.co.uk

DEEMING, Paul Leyland. b 44. CA Tr Coll 65 CMS Tr Coll Selly Oak 70. **d** 80 **p** 80. CMS Pakistan 71-82; R E and W Horndon w Lt Warley *Chelmsf* 83-89; V Gt Ilford St Andr 89-01; Co-ord Chapl Heatherwood and Wexham Park Hosp NHS Trust 01-09; rtd 09. *10 Glenthorn Road, Bexhill-on-Sea TN39 3QH* Tel (01424) 222287 E-mail deeming346@btinternet.com

DEENY, David Anthony. b 61. Waterrsrand Univ BA81. ERMC 03. **d** 06 **p** 07. NSM Alresford *Chelmsf* 06-11; Chapl John Wollaston Angl Community Sch Australia from 11. *John Wollaston Anglican Community School, Lake Road, Kelmscott WA 6111, Australia* Tel (0061) (8) 9495 8100 E-mail davedeeny@aol.com

DEER, Diane Antonia. See JOHNSON, Mrs Diane Antonia

DEES, Miss Marilyn Monica (Mandy). b 34. Nottm Univ BSc65 PGCE56. WEMTC 94. **d** 96 **p** 97. NSM Fownhope w Mordiford, Brockhampton etc *Heref* from 96. *Hazelbank, 24 Nover Wood Drive, Fownhope, Hereford HR1 4PN* Tel (01432) 860369

DEETH, William Stanley. b 38. St Pet Coll Ox BA59 MA67. St Steph Ho Ox 66. **d** 68 **p** 69. C Eastbourne St Mary *Chich* 68-71; C Benwell St Jas *Newc* 71-75; C-in-c Byker St Martin CD 75-76; P-in-c Byker St Martin 76; V 76-89; P-in-c Bothal 89-91; R Bothal and Pegswood w Longhirst 91-94; rtd 94; Perm to Offic *Newc* 94-08. *2 All Saints Square, Ripon HG4 1FN* Tel (01765) 690366

DEGG, Miss Jennifer Margaret. b 39. Open Univ BA85 Rolle Coll CertEd64. NOC. **d** 06 **p** 07. NSM Saddleworth *Man* 06-09; Perm to Offic from 09. *2 Lowerfields, Dobcross, Oldham OL3 5NW* E-mail jennydegg@onetel.com

DEHOOP, Brother Thomas Anthony. b 38. Bp's Univ Lennox BA63 LTh63. **d** 68 **p** 69. Canada 68-79; C Fort George w Painthills 68-70; I Mistassini 70-72; R La Tuque 72-75; Assoc P Pierrefonds 75-79; SSF from 79; Perm to Offic *Sarum* 79-80; C Toxteth St Marg *Liv* 80-85; Chapl Newsham Gen Hosp Liv 82-85; P-in-c Cambridge St Benedict *Ely* 85-88; V 88-92; Perm to

Offic *Liv* 92-94 and *Eur* from 94. *Glasshampton Monastery, Shrawley, Worcester WR6 6TQ* Tel (01299) 896345 E-mail glasshamptonssf@franciscans.org.uk

DEIGHTON, Ian Armstrong. b 19. Glas Univ MA40. Edin Th Coll 40. **d** 43 **p** 44. C Paisley H Trin *Glas* 43-45; Bp's Dom Chapl *Arg* 45-47; P-in-c Nether Lochaber 45-47; P-in-c Kinlochleven 45-47; P-in-c Glas St Mark 47-52; R Clydebank *Glas* 52-57; R Musselburgh *Edin* 57-84; P-in-c Prestonpans 76-84; rtd 84. *6 Duddingston Park South, Edinburgh EH15 3PA* Tel 0131-669 5108

DEIGHTON, William John. b 44. Plymouth Poly CQSW74. K Coll Lon AKC68 St Boniface Warminster 68. **d** 69 **p** 70. C Kenwyn *Truro* 69-72; Hon C Winterbourne *Bris* 90-04. *22 Salem Road, Winterbourne, Bristol BS36 1QF* Tel (01454) 778847

DEIMEL, Margaret Mary. b 49. CertEd71. WMMTC 91. **d** 94 **p** 95. NSM Bidford-on-Avon *Cov* 94-97; NSM Studley 97-10; NSM Spernall, Morton Bagot and Oldberrow 07-10; Dioc Adv on New Relig Movements 02-10; NSM Escomb *Dur* from 10; NSM Etherley from 10; NSM Witton Park from 10; NSM Hamsterley and Witton-le-Wear from 10. *The Vicarage, Escomb, Bishop Auckland DL14 7ST* Tel (01388) 602861

DEIMEL, Richard Witold. b 49. Lon Univ BA84. Cranmer Hall Dur 86. **d** 88 **p** 89. C Bilton *Cov* 88-93; P-in-c Studley 93-97; V 97-10; P-in-c Spernall, Morton Bagot and Oldberrow 07-10; RD Alcester 08-10; Dioc Adv on New Relig Movements 02-10; P-in-c Escomb *Dur* from 10; P-in-c Etherley from 10; P-in-c Witton Park from 10; P-in-c Hamsterley and Witton-le-Wear from 10; Dioc Adv on New Spiritual Movements from 10. *The Vicarage, Escomb, Bishop Auckland DL14 7ST* Tel (01388) 602861

DEKKER, Denise Rosemary Irene. b 43. Th Ext Educn Coll 90. **d** 95 **p** 96. C Stutterheim S Africa 96-99; P-in-c 99-04; P-in-c Kokstad 04-09; Perm to Offic *Win* 09-11; P-in-c Guernsey St Andr from 11. *St Andrew's Rectory, Route de St André, St Andrew, Guernsey GY6 8XN* Tel (01481) 238568 Mobile 07781-469241 E-mail dekkerd1@hotmail.com

del RIO, Michael Paul Juan. b 73. Univ of Wales (Cardiff) BScEcon94 PGCE00. Oak Hill Th Coll MTh05. **d** 05 **p** 06. NSM Ealing St Mary *Lon* 05-10. *Apartment 19, 21 Whitestone Way, Croydon CR0 4WJ* Tel (020) 8840 2208 E-mail michael@didasko.org.uk

DELAFORCE, Stephen Robert. b 52. Middx Poly BSc80 Cranfield Inst of Tech MSc88 Nottm Univ MA03 CEng MIMechE83. EMMTC 04. **d** 07 **p** 08. NSM Woodhouse, Woodhouse Eaves and Swithland *Leic* 07-10; NSM Beaumont Leys from 10. *10 Silverbirch Way, Loughborough LE11 2DH* Tel (01509) 240496 E-mail steve.delaforce@googlemail.com

DELAMERE, Allen Stephen. BTh. **d** 90 **p** 91. C Bangor Abbey *D & D* 90-93; I Saintfield 93-03; P-in-c Cumbernauld *Glas* 05-07; I Killinchy w Kilmood and Tullynakill *D & D* from 07. *Killinchy Rectory, 11 Whiterock Road, Killinchy, Newtownards BT23 6PR* E-mail allen@sonow.com

DELAMERE, Isaac George. b 71. CITC BTh02. **d** 02 **p** 03. C Newtownards *D & D* 02-05; I Narraghmore and Timolin w Castledermot etc *D & G* from 05. *The Rectory, Timolin, Co Kildare, Republic of Ireland* Tel (00353) (59) 862 4278 E-mail delamereisaac@hotmail.com

DELANEY, Anthony. b 65. St Jo Coll Nottm BTh95. **d** 95 **p** 96. C Cullompton *Ex* 95-98; C Maidstone St Luke *Cant* 98-01; P-in-c W Horsley *Guildf* 01-03; R 03-08; Perm to Offic *Man* from 09. *97 Barlow Moor Road, Didsbury, Manchester M20 2GP* Tel 07881-902966 (mobile) E-mail antidal@tiscali.co.uk

DELANEY, Janet. b 50. STETS. **d** 07 **p** 08. C Wootton Bassett *Sarum* 07-11; R Askerswell, Loders, Powerstock and Symondsbury from 11. *The Vicarage, Loders, Bridport DT6 3SA* Tel (01308) 538118 E-mail reverendjan@thedelaneys.me.uk

DELANEY, The Ven Peter Anthony. b 39. MBE01. AKC65. **d** 65 **p** 67. C St Marylebone w H Trin *Lon* 66-70; Chapl Nat Heart Hosp Lon 66-70; Res Chapl Univ Ch Ch the K 70-73; Can Res and Prec S'wark Cathl 73-77; V All Hallows by the Tower etc *Lon* 77-04; P-in-c St Kath Cree 98-02; Can Cyprus and the Gulf from 88; Preb St Paul's Cathl 95-99; Adn Lon 99-09; P-in-c St Steph Walbrook and St Swithun etc from 04. *29 Portland Square, London E1W 2QR* Tel (020) 7481 1786

DELANY, Michael Edward. b 34. Lon Univ BSc55 PhD58. S'wark Ord Course 80. **d** 83 **p** 84. NSM Hampton St Mary *Lon* 83-87; R Copythorne and Minstead *Win* 87-94; rtd 94; Perm to Offic *Win* 94-00. *Littlecott, Tytherley Road, Winterslow, Salisbury SP5 1PZ* Tel (01980) 862183

DELAP, Ms Dana Lurkse. b 65. St Jo Coll Dur BA87 MA93 MATM11. Cranmer Hall Dur 09. **d** 11. C Fenham St Jas and St Basil *Newc* from 11. *9 Wanless Terrace, Durham DH1 1RU* Tel 0191-384 3854 Mobile 07952-096789 E-mail dana@delap.org.uk

DELFGOU, John. b 35. Oak Hill Th Coll 81. **d** 84 **p** 85. NSM Loughton St Mary and St Mich *Chelmsf* 84-90; NSM Loughton St Jo 90-93; C 93-94; TV 94-00; rtd 00; Perm to Offic *Chelmsf* from 01. *20 Carroll Hill, Loughton IG10 1NN* Tel (020) 8508 6333 E-mail john@delfgou.freeserve.co.uk

DELFGOU, Jonathan Hawke. b 63. Aston Tr Scheme 89 Linc Th Coll BTh94. **d** 94 **p** 95. C Greenstead *Chelmsf* 94-98; TV Wickford and Runwell from 98; Chapl Southend Community Care Services NHS Trust 98-99; Chapl S Essex Mental Health & Community Care NHS Trust from 00. *St Mary's Vicarage, Church End Lane, Runwell, Wickford SS11 7JQ* Tel (01268) 732068

DELIGHT, The Ven John David. b 25. Liv Univ CSocSc48 Open Univ BA75. Oak Hill Th Coll 49. **d** 52 **p** 53. C Tooting Graveney St Nic *S'wark* 52-55; C Wallington 55-58; Lic to Offic *Man* 58-61; Travelling Sec IVF 58-61; C-in-c Leic St Chris CD 61-68; Chapl HM Pris Leic 64-67; V Leic St Chris 68-69; R Aldridge *Lich* 69-82; Preb Lich Cathl 80-90; RD Walsall 81-82; Adn Stoke 82-90; Dir Th Educn Machakos Kenya 90-94; Hon Can Machakos 90-94; Perm to Offic *Lich* 99-04 and *Ches* from 99. *Karibuni, 17 Hillside Drive, Macclesfield SK10 2PL* Tel (01625) 428117

DELINGER, Ian Michael. b 70. Truman State Univ (USA) BSc02 SS Coll Cam BTh04. Westcott Ho Cam 01. **d** 04 **p** 05. C Chorlton-cum-Hardy St Clem *Man* 04-07; Chapl Ches Univ from 08. *University of Chester, Warrington Campus, Crab Lane, Warrington WA2 0DB* Tel (01925) 534361 E-mail i.delinger@chester.ac.uk

DELL, Murray John. b 31. Cape Town Univ BA51 BSc54 Edin Univ MB, ChB59. Westcott Ho Cam 63. **d** 65 **p** 65. C Kloof S Africa 65-70; Dean Windhoek 71-80; V Lyme Regis *Sarum* 80-96; Chapl Lyme Regis Hosp 80-96; rtd 96. *2 Charles House, Ward Royal, Windsor SL4 1SR* Tel (01753) 832424

DELMEGE, Andrew Mark. b 68. Essex Univ BA91 Southn Univ MTh98. SWMTC 94. **d** 97 **p** 98. C Kings Heath *Birm* 97-01; V Brandwood from 01; Chapl to Deaf People from 01; P-in-c Weoley Castle from 10. *The Vicarage, 77 Doversley Road, Birmingham B14 6NN* Tel 0121-693 0217, 246 6100 or 456 1535 Fax 246 6125 E-mail andydelmege@hotmail.com

DELVE, Eric David. b 42. Trin Coll Bris. **d** 89 **p** 90. NSM Bris St Matt and St Nath 89-92; P-in-c Kirkdale St Lawr *Liv* 93-96; V Maidstone St Luke *Cant* from 96; AD Maidstone 99-03; Six Preacher Cant Cathl from 99. *The Vicarage, 24 Park Avenue, Maidstone ME14 5HN* Tel (01622) 754856 E-mail ericdelve@stlukes.org.uk

DELVES, Canon Anthony James. b 47. Birm Univ BSocSc70 Hull Univ PhD94. St Steph Ho Ox 83. **d** 85 **p** 86. C Cantley *Sheff* 85-90; V Goldthorpe w Hickleton 90-07; Hon Can Sheff Cathl 98-07; AD Wath 00-06; rtd 07; Perm to Offic *Sheff* and *Wakef* from 07. *4 Balmoral Street, Hebden Bridge HX7 8BJ* Tel (01422) 843948 E-mail ajd@delwood.plus.com

DELVES (formerly MANHOOD), Canon Phyllis. b 32. Aston Tr Scheme 78 Qu Coll Birm 79. **dss** 82 **d** 87 **p** 94. Harwich *Chelmsf* 82-83; Dovercourt and Parkeston 83-85; Fawley *Win* 85-87; Par Dn 87-92; P-in-c Bournemouth St Aug 92-99; Hon Can Win Cathl 96-99; rtd 99; Perm to Offic *Win* from 01. *11 Rhyme Hall Mews, Fawley, Southampton SO45 1FX* Tel (023) 8089 4450

DELVES BROUGHTON, Simon Brian Hugo. b 33. Ex Coll Ox BA56 MA64. Kelham Th Coll 56. **d** 59 **p** 60. Ox Miss to Calcutta 60-64; C Skirbeck St Nic *Linc* 64-67; E Pakistan/Bangladesh 67-74; Chapl Chittagong 67-69; V St Thos Cathl Dhaka 69-74; V Northampton Ch Ch *Pet* 74-95; Chapl Northn Gen Hosp 77-87; rtd 95; Perm to Offic *Ox* 95-00. *71A Observatory Street, Oxford OX2 6EP* Tel (01865) 515463

DEMAIN, Peter James. b 64. Salford Univ BA85. SNWTP 07. **d** 10 **p** 11. OLM Middleton and Thornham *Man* from 10. *3 St Gabriel's Close, Rochdale OL11 2TG* Tel (01706) 522985 Mobile 07747-398012 E-mail peterdemain@tiscali.co.uk

DEMERY, Rupert Edward Rodier. b 72. Trin Hall Cam BA94 MA01 BTh01. Ridley Hall Cam 98. **d** 01 **p** 02. C New Borough and Leigh *Sarum* 01-05; Lower Chapl Eton Coll from 05. *136A High Street, Eton, Windsor SL4 6AR* Tel (01753) 441629 Mobile 07801-825671 E-mail r.demery@etoncollege.org.uk

DEMPSEY, Miss Denise Susan. St Mich Coll Llan. **d** 11. C Gorseinon *S & B* from 11. *28 Bryneithin Road, Gorseinon, Swansea SA4 4XA* Tel (01792) 229223

DEMPSTER, Adrian. b 49. Newc Univ BSc70. EMMTC 05. **d** 08 **p** 09. NSM Kirkby in Ashfield *S'well* from 08. *105 Nottingham Road, Selston, Nottingham NG16 6BU* Tel (01773) 811846 Fax 0115-950 4646 Mobile 07971-142829 E-mail adrian@dempstera.freeserve.co.uk

den HAAN, Peter Albert Percy. b 67. Wycliffe Hall Ox BA07. **d** 08 **p** 09. C Bedworth *Cov* from 08. *132 Heath Road, Bedworth CV12 0BH* Tel (024) 7664 4663 E-mail peter@denhaan.co.uk

DENBY, Canon Paul. b 47. NW Ord Course 73. **d** 76 **p** 77. C Stretford All SS *Man* 76-80; V Stalybridge 80-87; Chapl Tameside Distr Gen Hosp Ashton-under-Lyne 82-87; Dir of Ords *Man* 87-95; LNSM Officer 91-95; Hon Can Man Cathl 92-95; Bp's Dom Chapl 94-95; Can Admin and Prec Man Cathl 95-07; rtd 07; Perm to Offic *Man* 07-08. *14 Cranberry Drive, Bolton BL3 3TB* Tel (01204) 655157 E-mail paul@denby94.wanadoo.co.uk

DENCH, Canon Christopher David. b 62. RGN83. Aston Tr Scheme 86 Sarum & Wells Th Coll 88. **d** 91 **p** 92. C Crayford

Roch 91-94; P-in-c Leybourne 94-98; R 98-05; Dioc Lay Tr Adv 01-05; Tr Officer for CME 03-10; Min Development Officer 05-10; Bp's Officer for Min and Tr from 10; Hon Can Roch Cathl from 11. *340 New Hythe Lane, Larkfield, Aylesford ME20 6RZ* Tel (01732) 220245 E-mail chris.dench@rochester.anglican.org

DENERLEY, John Keith Christopher. b 34. Qu Coll Ox BA58 MA61. St Steph Ho Ox 58. **d** 61 **p** 62. C Airedale w Fryston *Wakef* 61-64; Chapl Sarum Th Coll 64-68; Min Can Cov Cathl 68-76; Chapl Lanchester Poly 70-76; Chapl The Dorothy Kerin Trust Burrswood 76-85; V Trellech and Cwmcarvan *Mon* 85-87; V Penallt 85-87; V Penallt and Trellech 87-99; Chapl Ty Mawr Convent (Wales) 85-90; RD Monmouth 93-99; rtd 99; Perm to Offic *Glouc* from 00. *1 The Pales, English Bicknor, Coleford GL16 7PQ* Tel (01594) 860028

DENFORD, Keith Wilkie. b 35. AKC62. **d** 63 **p** 64. C Gunnersbury St Jas *Lon* 63-66; C Brighton St Pet *Chich* 66-71; Min Can Cant Cathl 71-75; R W Tarring *Chich* 75-85; V Burgess Hill St Jo 85-90; R Pulborough 90-96; rtd 96; Perm to Offic *Chich* from 96. *1 Bowline Point, Broad Reach Mews, Shoreham-by-Sea BN43 5ED* Tel (01273) 464251

DENGATE, Richard Henry. b 39. Cant Sch of Min 82. **d** 85 **p** 86. NSM Wittersham w Stone and Ebony *Cant* 85; R Sandhurst w Newenden 90-01; rtd 01; Perm to Offic *Cant* from 01. *Apuldram, Main Street, Peasemarsh, Rye TN31 6UL* Tel (01797) 230980

DENHAM, Anthony Christopher. b 43. Keble Coll Ox BA65 MA70. Oak Hill Th Coll 91. **d** 93 **p** 94. C Hythe *Cant* 93-97; V Haddenham w Cuddington, Kingsey etc *Ox* 97-08; rtd 08; Perm to Offic *Guildf* from 08. *3 The Larches, Woking GU21 4RE* Tel (01483) 823310 E-mail a.chris.denham@googlemail.com

DENHAM, Nicholas Philip. b 50. Salford Univ BSc72 Birm Univ CertEd74. Wycliffe Hall Ox 87. **d** 89 **p** 90. C Bishopwearmouth St Gabr *Dur* 89-90; C Chester le Street 90-92; TV Rushden w Newton Bromswold *Pet* 92-95; R Teigh w Whissendine and Market Overton 95-02; P-in-c Thistleton 01-02; RD Rutland 01-02; TR Bedworth *Cov* 02-05; V Escomb *Dur* 05-08; R Etherley 05-08; V Witton Park 05-08; V Hamsterley and Witton-le-Wear 05-08; rtd 08; Perm to Offic *Ox* from 09. *13 Yarnton Court, Kidlington OX5 1AU* Tel (01865) 370294 E-mail nickden@btinternet.com

DENHOLM, Robert Jack. b 31. Edin Th Coll 53. **d** 56 **p** 57. C Dundee St Mary Magd *Bre* 56-59; C Edin St Pet 59-61; R Bridge of Allan *St And* 61-69; Chapl Stirling Univ 67-69; R N Berwick *Edin* 69-80; R Gullane 76-80; R Edin St Mark 80-90; Can St Mary's Cathl 88-90; rtd 90. *15 Silverknowes, Midway, Edinburgh EH4 5PP* Tel 0131-312 6462 E-mail jackdenholm@blueyonder.co.uk

DENIS LE SEVE, Hilary. See LE SEVE, Mrs Jane Hilary

DENISON, Canon Keith Malcolm. b 45. Down Coll Cam BA67 MA71 PhD70. Westcott Ho Cam 70. **d** 71 **p** 72. C Chepstow *Mon* 71-72; C Bassaleg 72-75; Post-Ord Tr Officer 75-85; V Mathern and Mounton 75-80; V Mathern and Mounton w St Pierre 80-85; RD Chepstow 82-85; V Risca 85-91; V Goldcliffe and Whitson and Nash 91-96; Dioc Dir of Educn from 91; Hon Can St Woolos Cathl 91-94; Can from 94; Can Res from 96. *Canon's House, Stow Hill, Newport NP20 4EA* Tel (01633) 264919

DENISON, Philip. b 55. York Univ BA77 CertEd. St Jo Coll Nottm 83. **d** 86 **p** 87. C Barnoldswick w Bracewell *Bradf* 86-88; P-in-c Basford St Leodegarius *S'well* 88-91; C Basford w Hyson Green 91-94; V Nether Stowey w Over Stowey *B & W* 94-04; R Aisholt, Enmore, Goathurst, Nether Stowey etc 05; RD Quantock 01-05; Perm to Offic 06-10; C Alfred Jewel from 10. *15 Sylvan Way, Monkton Heathfield, Taunton TA2 8PH* Tel (01823) 410021 E-mail denisonphil15@hotmail.com

DENLEY, Trevor Maurice. b 47. **d** 06 **p** 07. OLM Bristol St Aid w St Geo from 06. *31 Dundridge Gardens, Bristol BS5 8SZ* Tel 0117-961 4468 Mobile 07960-329127

DENMAN, Frederick George. b 46. Chich Th Coll 67. **d** 70 **p** 71. C Stafford St Mary *Lich* 70-72; C Ascot Heath *Ox* 72-75; P-in-c Culham 75-77; P-in-c Sutton Courtenay w Appleford 75-77; TV Dorchester 78-81; Chapl Henley Memorial Hosp 81-82; P-in-c W Hill *Ex* 82; TV Ottery St Mary, Alfington and W Hill 82-87; V Sparkwell from 87; V Shaugh Prior 87-93; P-in-c Cornwood from 98. *The Vicarage, Sparkwell, Plymouth PL7 5DB* Tel (01752) 837218 E-mail freddie@sparkwell.fsnet.com

DENNEN, Lyle. b 42. Harvard Univ LLB67 Trin Coll Cam BA70 MA75. Cuddesdon Coll 70. **d** 72 **p** 73. C S Lambeth St Ann *S'wark* 72-75; C Richmond St Mary 75-78; P-in-c Kennington St Jo 78-79; V Kennington St Jo w St Jas 79-99; P-in-c Brixton Road Ch Ch 81-89; RD Brixton 90-99; Hon Can S'wark Cathl 99; Adn Hackney *Lon* 99-10; V St Andr Holborn from 99. *St Andrew's Vicarage, 5 St Andrew's Street, London EC4A 3AB* Tel (020) 7353 3544 Fax 7583 2750

DENNER-BROWN, Sarah. See BROWN, Mrs Sarah Romilly Denner

DENNESS, Mrs Linda Christine. b 51. Portsm Dioc Tr Course 88. **d** 89 **p** 01. NSM Milton Portsm 89-93; Chapl Asst Portsm Hosps NHS Trust 89-91; NSM Portsea St Mary *Portsm* 93-96; NSM Wymering 96-06; P-in-c Cosham 06-09; P-in-c Wymering

07-09; Perm to Offic 09-10; NSM Portsea N End St Mark from 10. *19 Fourth Avenue, Cosham, Portsmouth PO6 3HX* Tel (023) 9232 6885 E-mail linda@ldenness.wanadoo.co.uk

DENNETT, John Edward. b 36. Tyndale Hall Bris 66. **d** 68 **p** 69. C Chell *Lich* 68-71; C Bispham *Blackb* 71-73; C Cheltenham Ch Ch *Glouc* 73-75; V Coppull *Blackb* 75-79; P-in-c Parkham, Alwington and Buckland Brewer *Ex* 79-80; R 80-84; V Blackpool St Thos *Blackb* 84-92; rtd 92; Chapl Trin Hospice in the Fylde from 88; Perm to Offic *Blackb* from 92. *37 Village Way, Bispham, Blackpool FY2 0AH* Tel (01253) 358039 E-mail johned.dennett@btinternet.com

DENNIS, Mrs Barbara Christine. b 56. NTMTC 94. **d** 97 **p** 98. NSM Romford St Edw *Chelmsf* 97-01; C 01-11; P-in-c Upper Colne from 11. *The Rectory, Church Road, Great Yeldham, Halstead CO9 4PT* Tel (01787) 237138 E-mail revbarbara8@btinternet.com

DENNIS, David Alan. b 46. St Luke's Coll Ex BSc90. **d** 05 **p** 06. OLM Alderholt *Sarum* from 05. *18 Oak Road, Alderholt, Fordingbridge SP6 3BL* Tel (01425) 655230 E-mail david@dennisd.fsnet.co.uk

DENNIS, Miss Drucilla Lyn. b 49. Ox Univ BEd71 Southn Univ MA(Ed)82 Win Univ MA10. S Dios Minl Tr Scheme 92. **d** 95 **p** 96. NSM Cowes H Trin and St Mary *Portsm* 95-01; TV Dorchester *Sarum* 01-08; Hon C Brighstone and Brooke w Mottistone *Portsm* from 08; Hon C Shorwell w Kingston from 08; Hon C Chale from 08; Chapl Isle of Wight NHS Primary Care Trust from 09. *The Vicarage, 5 Northcourt Close, Newport PO30 3LD* Tel (01983) 740522 E-mail drucilladennis@hotmail.com

✠**DENNIS, The Rt Revd John.** b 31. St Cath Coll Cam BA54 MA59. Cuddesdon Coll 54. **d** 56 **p** 57 **c** 79. C Armley St Bart *Ripon* 56-60; C Kettering SS Pet and Paul 60-62; V Is of Dogs Ch Ch and St Jo w St Luke *Lon* 62-71; V Mill Hill Jo Keble Ch 71-79; RD W Barnet 73-79; Preb St Paul's Cathl 77-79; Suff Bp Knaresborough *Ripon* 79-86; Dioc Dir of Ords 80-86; Bp St E 86-96; rtd 96; Perm to Offic *St E* from 96; Hon Asst Bp Win from 99. *7 Conifer Close, Winchester SO22 6SH* Tel (01962) 868881 E-mail johndor_dennis@onetel.com

DENNIS, Keith Aubrey Lawrence. b 55. City of Lon Poly BA79. Cranmer Hall Dur 88. **d** 90 **p** 91. C Bushbury *Lich* 90-94; P-in-c Newcastle St Geo 94-99; TV Kirby Muxloe *Leic* 99-03; C Ashby-de-la-Zouch St Helen w Coleorton 03; C Breedon cum Isley Walton and Worthington 03; Chapl HM Pris Glouc from 04. *The Chaplaincy, HM Prison Gloucester, Barrack Square, Gloucester GL1 2JN* Tel (01452) 529551

DENNIS, Robert Franklin. b 51. St Paul's Coll Grahamstown 91. **d** 94 **p** 94. C Kuils River S Africa 94-96; C Matroosfontein 96-99; R Maitland 99-03; TR Bredasdorp 03-05; P-in-c Crumpsall *Man* 06-09; Min Can St Woolos Cathl 09-11; P-in-c Llantilio Pertholey w Bettws Chpl etc from 11. *The New Vicarage, 10 The Pines, Mardy, Abergavenny NP7 6HQ* Tel (01873) 859881 E-mail robert.dennis2@virginmedia.com

DENNIS, Samuel James. b 85. Westcott Ho Cam. **d** 11. C Catford (Southend) and Downham S'wark from 11. *59 Southend Lane, London SE6 3AB* E-mail samuel.j.dennis@gmail.com

DENNIS, Canon Trevor John. b 45. St Jo Coll Cam BA68 MA71 PhD74. Westcott Ho Cam 71. **d** 72 **p** 73. C Newport Pagnell *Ox* 72-74; Chapl Eton Coll 75-82; Tutor Sarum & Wells Th Coll 82-94; Vice-Prin 89-94; Can Res Ches Cathl 94-10; rtd 10. *11 Anne's Way, Chester CH4 7BA*

DENNISON, Philip Ian. b 52. Nottm Univ BTh81. St Jo Coll Nottm 77. **d** 81 **p** 82. C Stalybridge H Trin and Ch Ch *Ches* 81-84; C Heswall 84-91; TV Bushbury *Lich* 91-04; V Shevington *Blackb* from 04. *St Anne's Vicarage, Gathurst Lane, Shevington, Wigan WN6 8HW* Tel (01257) 252136 E-mail stannepc.office@googlemail.com

DENNISS, Mrs Amanda Jane. b 57. Univ Coll Lon LLB78. Oak Hill Th Coll 98 NTMTC 00. **d** 03 **p** 04. C Turnham Green Ch Ch *Lon* 03-06; Perm to Offic 06-08; C Westwood Cov from 08. *3 Bronze View, Coventry CV4 8HR* Tel (024) 7646 1353 E-mail amandadenniss@aol.com

DENNISTON, James Keith Stuart. b 49. Down Coll Cam MA70 Barrister-at-Law 70. Oak Hill Th Coll DipEd92. **d** 93 **p** 94. C Harborne Heath *Birm* 93-97; Chapl Lee Abbey 97-02; Perm to Offic *Ex* 02-03; TV Chippenham St Paul w Hardenhuish etc *Bris* 03-07. *Rectory Cottage, King's Nympton, Umberleigh EX37 9SS* Tel (01769) 581326 E-mail j-denniston@tiscali.co.uk

DENNISTON, Robin Alastair. b 26. Ch Ch Ox MA48 Edin Univ MSc92 Univ Coll Lon PhD96. **d** 78 **p** 79. NSM Clifton upon Teme *Worc* 78-81; NSM Clifton-on-Teme, Lower Sapey and the Shelsleys 81-85; NSM S Hinksey *Ox* 85-87; NSM Gt w Lt Tew 87-90; NSM Aberdour *St And* 90-94; NSM W Fife Team Min 90-94; NSM Marylebone St Mark Hamilton Terrace *Lon* 94-95; P-in-c Gt w Lt Tew and Over w Nether Worton *Ox* 95-02; rtd 02. *112 Randolph Avenue, London W9 1PQ* Tel (020) 7286 0880

DENNO, Basil. b 52. Dundee Univ BSc74. Oak Hill Th Coll BA81. **d** 81 **p** 83. C Chaddesden St Mary *Derby* 81-83; Hon C

83-84. *21 Parkside Road, Chaddesden, Derby DE21 6QR* Tel (01332) 672687

DENNO, Elizabeth (Skye). b 79. Derby Univ BA00. St Jo Coll Nottm BA08. **d** 08 **p** 09. C Dursley *Glouc* from 08. *1 Riversmill Walk, Dursley GL11 5GL* Tel (01453) 542404 Mobile 07720-768684 E-mail jaskso@yahoo.co.uk

DENNY, John Peter Sekeford. b 43. RIBA69. Chich Th Coll 90. **d** 91 **p** 92. C Aylmerton w Runton *Nor* 91-95; P-in-c Barney, Fulmodeston w Croxton, Hindringham etc 95-96; R 96-98; rtd 98; Perm to Offic *Truro* 98-04 and *Nor* 04-06. *Little Folly, Mutton Dingle, New Radnor, Presteigne LD8 2TL* Tel (01544) 350568

DENNY, Lorne Robert. b 58. Pemb Coll Ox MA84 Lon Inst of Educn PGCE84. SAOMC 98. **d** 01 **p** 02. NSM Ox St Barn and St Paul 01-04; NSM Cowley St Jo 04-07; P-in-c Milton next Sittingbourne *Cant* from 07. *The Vicarage, Vicarage Road, Sittingbourne ME10 2BL* Tel (01795) 472016

DENNY, Michael Thomas. b 47. Kelham Th Coll 68 St Jo Coll Nottm 71. **d** 73 **p** 74. C Gospel Lane St Mich *Birm* 73-77; P-in-c Frankley 77-82; R 82-07; rtd 07; Perm to Offic *Birm* from 07. *Orchard Cottage, Green Lane, Yarpole, Leominster HR6 0BE* Tel (01568) 780874 E-mail michael@revdenny1.freeserve.co.uk

DENT, Canon Christopher Mattinson. b 46. K Coll Lon BA68 AKC68 MTh69 Jes Coll Cam BA72 MA76 New Coll Ox MA76 DPhil80. Westcott Ho Cam 70. **d** 72 **p** 73. C Chelsea St Luke *Lon* 72-76; Asst Chapl New Coll Ox 76-79; Fell Chapl and Dean Div 79-84; V Hollingbourne and Hucking w Leeds and Broomfield *Cant* 84-93; V Bedford St Andr *St Alb* from 93; Hon Can St Alb from 01; RD Bedford 05-10. *St Andrew's Vicarage, 1 St Edmond Road, Bedford MK40 2NQ* Tel (01234) 354234 *or* 216881 E-mail dent@tinyworld.co.uk

DENT, Joseph Michael. b 73. Jes Coll Cam BA94. Wycliffe Hall Ox 96. **d** 99 **p** 00. C Plymouth St Andr and Stonehouse *Ex* 99-03; Hon C Sevenoaks St Nic *Roch* from 03. *6 Sackville Close, Sevenoaks TN13 3QD* Tel (01732) 779140 E-mail joe.dent@diocese-rochester.org

DENT, Marie Penelope. b 46. K Coll Lon BA88. Westcott Ho Cam 02. **d** 04 **p** 05. C N Walsham and Edingthorpe *Nor* 04-08; TV Redditch H Trin *Worc* 08-10; rtd 10; Perm to Offic *Nor* from 10. *1 Stirling Road, Norwich NR6 6GE* Tel (01603) 487938 Mobile 07799-220357 E-mail penelopedent@live.co.uk

DENT, Michael Leslie. b 54. Leeds Univ BEd76. St Steph Ho Ox 93. **d** 95 **p** 96. C Cockerton *Dur* 95-98; V Escomb 98-03; R Etherley 98-03; V Witton Park 98-03; Chapl Dur Constabulary 02-03; TR E Darlington from 03. *30 Smithfield Road, Darlington DL1 4DD* Tel (01325) 244430

DENT, Raymond William. b 47. TD03. Open Univ BA84 Birm Coll of Educn CertEd68. Ridley Hall Cam 70. **d** 73 **p** 74. C Hyde St Geo *Ches* 73-76; C Eastham 76-79; TV E Runcorn w Halton 79-80; V Hallwood 80-83; V New Brighton Em 83-94; V Willaston from 94. *The Vicarage, 13 Hooton Road, Willaston, Neston CH64 1SE* Tel 0151-327 4737 E-mail raymond@raydent.freeserve.co.uk

DENT, Richard William. b 32. Down Coll Cam BA56 MA LLB59. Bris Sch of Min 73. **d** 77 **p** 78. NSM Southmead *Bris* 77-81; NSM Henleaze 81-85; V Highworth w Sevenhampton and Inglesham etc 85-88; TV Oldland 88-91; V Longwell Green 91-93; C Bedminster St Mich 93-94; C 94-97; Chapl Asst Frenchay Healthcare NHS Trust *Bris* 94-97; rtd 97; Perm to Offic *Bris* from 99 and *B & W* 03-06. *1 Bakers Buildings, Wrington, Bristol BS40 5LQ* Tel (01934) 861070

DENTON, Peter Brian. b 37. Kelham Th Coll 57. **d** 62 **p** 63. C Ellesmere Port *Ches* 62-66; Chapl HM Borstal Hollesley Bay 66-69; CF 69-89; Warden Bridge Cen and C Hounslow H Trin w St Paul *Lon* 89-92; V Northolt Park St Barn 92-94; P-in-c Perivale 97-01; P-in-c N Greenford All Hallows 00-04; rtd 04; Perm to Offic *Ely* from 05 and *Pet* 05-10; P-in-c Pet All SS from 10. *52 Lornas Field, Hampton Hargate, Peterborough PE7 8AY* Tel (01733) 552353 E-mail revddenton@aol.com

DENTON, Peter Charles. b 54. St Jo Coll Dur BA52. Oak Hill Th Coll 49. **d** 52 **p** 53. C Ushaw Moor *Dur* 52-54; C-in-c Throckley St Mary CD *Newc* 54-58; V Long Horsley 58-67; Lect City of Newc Coll of Educn 67-75; Sen Lect Newc Poly 75-90; rtd 90. *Avalon, High Street, Low Pittington, Durham DH6 1BE* Tel 0191-372 2494

DENYER, Alan Frederick. b 31. Wycliffe Hall Ox 80. **d** 82 **p** 83. C Rodbourne Cheney *Bris* 82-84; P-in-c Garsdon w Lea and Cleverton 84-87; R Garsdon, Lea and Cleverton and Charlton 87-91; R Lydbury N w Hopesay and Edgton *Heref* 91-97; Asst Dioc Soc Resp Officer 91-97; rtd 97; Hon C Long Preston w Tosside *Bradf* 97-02; Perm to Offic *Ripon* from 03. *25 Lupton Close, Glasshouses, Harrogate HG3 5QX* Tel (01423) 712307

DENYER, Canon Paul Hugh. b 46. Lon Univ BA68. Ripon Coll Cuddesdon 74. **d** 77 **p** 78. C Horfield H Trin *Bris* 77-82; TV Yate New Town 82-88; V Bris Lockleaze St Mary Magd w St Fran 88-95; Dioc Dir of Ords 95-02; Hon Can Bris Cathl from 99; R Warmley, Syston and Bitton from 02. *The Rectory, Church Avenue, Warmley, Bristol BS30 5JJ* Tel 0117-967 3965 E-mail paul@denyer03.freeserve.co.uk

DENYER, Samuel. b 74. Ripon Coll Cuddesdon 07. **d** 09 **p** 10. C Lostwithiel, St Winnow w St Nectan's Chpl etc *Truro* from 09; C Lanreath, Pelynt and Bradoc from 09; C Lanlivery from 09. *Woodpeckers, Cott Road, Lostwithiel PL22 0EU* Tel (01208) 871619 Mobile 07827-013808

DEO, Paul. b 60. Coll of Ripon & York St Jo CertEd81. St Jo Coll Nottm 95. **d** 97 **p** 98. C Tong *Bradf* 97-00; P-in-c Laisterdyke 00-02; V 02-07; C Baildon from 07. *93 Hoyle Court Road, Baildon, Shipley BD17 6EL* Tel (01274) 586080 E-mail pauldeo@sky.com

DERBY, Archdeacon of. See CUNLIFFE, The Ven Christopher John

DERBY, Bishop of. See REDFERN, The Rt Revd Alastair Llewellyn John

DERBY, Dean of. See DAVIES, The Very Revd John Harverd

DERBYSHIRE, Mrs Anne Margaret. b 31. Open Univ BA87 Lon Univ CertEd75. SWMTC. **dss** 84 **d** 87 **p** 01. NSM Tiverton St Pet *Ex* 87-90; Perm to Offic 90-01 and from 02; NSM Washfield, Stoodleigh, Withleigh etc 01-02. *6 Devenish Close, Weymouth DT4 8RU* Tel (01305) 750909

DERBYSHIRE, Douglas James. b 26. **d** 81 **p** 82. NSM Heald Green St Cath *Ches* 81-86; NSM Stockport St Geo 86-89; C 89-91; rtd 91; Perm to Offic *Man* 92-95 and 00-06; *Ches* from 92. *91 East Avenue, Heald Green, Cheadle SK8 3BR* Tel 0161-437 3748

DERBYSHIRE, Philip Damien. b 50. Leic Poly LLB71. Sarum & Wells Th Coll 80. **d** 82 **p** 83. C Chatham St Wm *Roch* 82-86; R Melfort Zimbabwe 86-88; TV Burnham w Dropmore, Hitcham and Taplow *Ox* 88-92; Chapl HM Pris Reading 92-97; Chapl HM Pris Holloway 97-00; Chapl HM Pris Bullingdon 00-04; C Buckingham *Ox* 04-11; AD Buckingham 10-11; P-in-c Stewkley w Soulbury from 11. *The Vicarage, High Street North, Stewkley, Leighton Buzzard LU7 0HH* Tel (01525) 240287 E-mail revphil5@btinternet.com

DERHAM, Miss Hilary Kathlyn. b 50. Nottm Univ BPharm71 MRPharmS71. Chich Th Coll 89. **d** 91 **p** 95. Par Dn Stevenage H Trin *St Alb* 91-94; C 94-98; P-in-c London Colney St Pet 98-03; rtd 03; Perm to Offic *St Alb* from 03. *Maryland Care Home, 29 Townsend Drive, St Albans AL3 5RF* Tel (01727) 842089 E-mail h.derham@btopenworld.com

DEROSAIRE, Leslie John. b 50. Univ of Wales BA85 Univ of Wales Coll Newport MA03. St Mich Coll Llan 01. **d** 04 **p** 05. NSM Govilon w Llanfoist w Llanelen *Mon* 04-07; NSM Llanddewi Rhydderch w Llangattock-juxta-Usk etc 07-09; P-in-c from 09. *Elmgrove, Hereford Road, Mardy, Abergavenny NP7 6HU* Tel (01873) 857256 E-mail derosaire@tiscali.co.uk

DEROY-JONES, Philip Antony (Tony). b 49. St Mich Coll Llan 92. **d** 92 **p** 93. C Neath w Llantwit 92-95; V Caerau St Cynfelin 95-98; V Pontlottyn w Fochriw from 98. *The Vicarage, Picton Street, Pontlottyn, Bargoed CF81 9PS* Tel and fax (01685) 841322 E-mail curate@deroy-jones.freeserve.co.uk

DERRICK, David John. b 46. S'wark Ord Course. **d** 84 **p** 85. NSM Angell Town St Jo *S'wark* 84-98; NSM St Mary le Strand w St Clem Danes *Lon* 86-93. *Weavers Cottage, 8 Bellvue Place, London E1 4UG* Tel (020) 7791 2943

DERRICK, Mrs Dorothy Margaret. b 41. St Mary's Coll Chelt CertEd63. Ox Min Course 89. **d** 92 **p** 94. NSM Gt Missenden w Ballinger and Lt Hampden *Ox* 92-98; P-in-c Drayton St Pet (Berks) 98-04; rtd 04. *33 Parkland Avenue, Carlisle CA1 3GN* Tel (01228) 593159 E-mail dorothyderrick@aol.com

DERRIMAN, Canon Graham Scott. b 39. Bps' Coll Cheshunt 63. **d** 66 **p** 67. C Wandsworth St Mich *S'wark* 66-70; C Merton St Mary 70-74; P-in-c Earlsfield St Andr 74-79; V 79-81; V Camberwell St Luke 81-90; V Croydon St Aug 90-04; Voc Adv Croydon Adnry 93-04; RD Croydon Cen 95-04; Hon Can S'wark Cathl 01-04; rtd 04; Perm to Offic *S'wark* from 04. *15 Goodwood Close, Morden SM4 5AW* Tel (020) 8648 1550 Mobile 07952-471515 E-mail gsd.24@virginmedia.com

DERRY AND RAPHOE, Bishop of. See GOOD, The Rt Revd Kenneth Raymond

DERRY, Archdeacon of. See McLEAN, The Ven Donald Stewart

DERRY, Dean of. See MORTON, The Very Revd William Wright

DESERT, Thomas Denis. b 31. Bps' Coll Cheshunt 54. **d** 56 **p** 57. C Goldington *St Alb* 56-60; C-in-c Luton St Hugh Lewsey CD 60-63; C St Alb St Sav 63-65; C Cheshunt 65-68; V Bedford All SS 68-89; R Northill w Moggerhanger 89-96; rtd 96; Perm to Offic *St Alb* from 96. *2 Phillpotts Avenue, Bedford MK40 3UJ* Tel (01234) 211413 E-mail denisdesert@ntlworld.com

DESHPANDE, Lakshmi Anant. See JEFFREYS, Mrs Lakshmi Anant

DESICS, Robert Anthony. b 77. Bp Grosseteste Coll BA99 Open Univ MA00. St Jo Coll Nottm 99. **d** 01 **p** 02. C Potters Bar *St Alb* 01-04; C Rainham w Wennington *Chelmsf* 04-05; V Hemlington *York* from 05. *St Timothy's House, 31 Coatham Close, Hemlington, Middlesbrough TS8 9JW* Tel (01642) 590496 E-mail rob desics@hotmail.com

DESMOND, Mrs Margaret Elspeth. b 49. S Dios Minl Tr Scheme 90. **d** 93 **p** 95. NSM Filton *Bris* from 93; Asst Chapl HM Pris Bris 98-09. *14 Kenmore Crescent, Bristol BS7 0TN* E-mail ian.desmond@lineone.net

DESON, Rolston Claudius. b 39. Qu Coll Birm 85. **d** 84 **p** 85. NSM Saltley *Birm* 84-86; C Edgbaston SS Mary and Ambrose 86-90; V W Bromwich St Phil *Lich* 90-08; rtd 08. *97 Cardington Avenue, Birmingham B42 2PB*

DESROSIERS, Jacques Thomas Maurice. b 55. Qu Univ Kingston Ontario BCom77. S'wark Ord Course 91. **d** 94 **p** 95. NSM Benenden *Cant* 94-97; C Maidstone All SS and St Phil w Tovil 97-01; TV Pewsey and Swanborough *Sarum* 01-04; P-in-c Rolvenden *Cant* 04-10; P-in-c Newenden and Rolvenden from 10; AD Tenterden from 07. *The Vicarage, Rolvenden, Cranbrook TN17 4ND* Tel (01580) 241235 E-mail vicarage1965@btinternet.com

d'ESTERRE, Mrs Jennifer Ann. b 48. Coll of St Matthias Bris BEd77. WEMTC 01. **d** 04 **p** 05. NSM Sharpness, Purton, Brookend and Slimbridge *Glouc* 04-11; C Cromhall, Tortworth, Tytherington, Falfield etc from 11. *Gossington Cottage, Gossington, Slimbridge, Gloucester GL2 7DN* Tel (01453) 890384 Mobile 07855-243264 E-mail revdjenny@gmail.com

DETTMER, Douglas James. b 64. Univ of Kansas BA86 Yale Univ MDiv90. Berkeley Div Sch 90. **d** 90 **p** 91. C Ilfracombe, Lee, Woolacombe, Bittadon etc *Ex* 90-94; Bp's Dom Chapl 94-98; P-in-c Thorverton, Cadbury, Upton Pyne etc 98-10; P-in-c Stoke Canon, Poltimore w Huxham and Rewe etc 06-10; P-in-c Brampford Speke, Cadbury, Newton St Cyres etc from 10. *The Rectory, School Lane, Thorverton, Exeter EX5 5NR* Tel (01392) 860332

DEUCHAR, Canon Andrew Gilchrist. b 55. Southn Univ BTh86. Sarum & Wells Th Coll 81. **d** 84 **p** 85. C Alnwick *Newc* 84-88; TV Heref St Martin w St Fran 88-90; Adv to Coun for Soc Resp *Roch* and *Cant* 90-94; Sec for Angl Communion Affairs 94-00; Hon Prov Can Cant Cathl from 95; R Nottingham St Pet and St Jas *S'well* 00-02; R Nottingham St Pet and All SS 02-07; P-in-c Nottingham St Mary and St Cath 04-07; P-in-c Nottingham All SS, St Mary and St Pet 07-08; Chapl to The Queen 03-08; Dioc Audit Officer *Mor* from 08. *Address temp unknown*

DEUCHAR de MELLO, Bridget Dorothea. b 55. Sussex Univ BA77 Leic Univ PGCE78. SEITE BA08. **d** 08 **p** 09. NSM Gt Ilford St Luke *Chelmsf* from 08. *3 Lennox Gardens, Ilford IG1 3LF* Tel (020) 8518 1746 E-mail bridget@demello.co.uk

DEVADASON, Mrs Abraham Jasmine Jebakani. b 67. Kakatiya Univ India BA91 Tamilnadu Th Sem BD96 United Th Coll Bangalore MTh99. SNWTP. **d** 08 **p** 09. C W Didsbury and Withington St Chris *Man* from 08. *St Martin's Vicarage, 2 Blackcarr Road, Wythenshawe, Manchester M23 1LX* Tel 0161-998 3408 Mobile 07515-726923 E-mail jasdevadason@yahoo.co.uk

DEVAL, Mrs Joan Margaret. b 38. Southlands Coll Lon TDip58. SAOMC 95. **d** 98 **p** 99. OLM Chinnor, Sydenham, Aston Rowant and Crowell *Ox* 98-10; Perm to Offic from 10. *3 Orchard Way, Chinnor OX39 4UD* Tel (01844) 353404

DEVALL, Elizabeth Jane. b 70. SNWTP. **d** 10 **p** 11. C Royton St Anne *Man* from 10. *136 Denbydale Way, Royton, Oldham OL2 5TE* Tel 0161-628 9886 Mobile 07725-739506 E-mail lizdevall@btinternet.com

DEVARAJ, Jacob Devadason. b 61. Madras Bible Sem BTh Serampore Univ BTh Annamalai Univ MA United Th Coll Bangalore MTh. Tamilnadu Th Sem BD NOC. **d** 06 **p** 07. C Man Clayton St Cross w St Paul 06-09; TV Wythenshawe from 09. *St Martin's Vicarage, 2 Blackcarr Road, Wythenshawe, Manchester M23 1LX* Tel 0161-998 3408 E-mail jacob_devadason@yahoo.co.uk

DEVENISH, Nicholas Edward. b 64. Ridley Hall Cam 02. **d** 04 **p** 05. C Huntingdon *Ely* 04-07; C Farcet Hampton from 07. *105 Eagle Way, Hampton Vale, Peterborough PE7 8EL* Tel (01733) 248764 E-mail nickdevenish@mac.com

DEVENNEY, Raymond Robert Wilmont. b 47. TCD BA69 MA73. CITC 70. **d** 70 **p** 71. C Ballymena *Conn* 70-75; C Ballyholme *D & D* 75-81; I Killinchy w Kilmood and Tullynakill 81-00; I Drumbeg from 00. *The Rectory, 64 Drumbeg Road, Dunmurry, Belfast BT17 9LE* Tel (028) 9061 0255 E-mail raydev@hotmail.com

✠DEVENPORT, The Rt Revd Eric Nash. b 26. Open Univ BA74. Kelham Th Coll 46. **d** 51 **p** 52 **c** 80. C Leic St Mark 51-54; C Barrow St Matt *Carl* 54-56; Succ Leic Cathl 56-59; V Shepshed 59-64; R Oadby 64-73; Hon Can Leic Cathl 73-80; Dioc Missr 73-80; Suff Bp Dunwich *St E* 80-92; rtd 92; Chapl Adn Italy and Malta *Eur* 92-97; Florence w Siena 92-97; Asst Bp Eur 93-97; Perm to Offic *Nor* from 97; Hon PV Nor Cathl from 98; Hon Asst Bp Nor from 00. *6 Damocles Court, Norwich NR2 1HN* Tel (01603) 664121

DEVER, Paul. b 71. BSc. Wycliffe Hall Ox. **d** 06 **p** 07. C Fair Oak *Win* 06-10; TV Horwich and Rivington *Man* from 10; Dioc Young Adults Missr from 10; C Blackrod from 11. *St Elizabeth's Vicarage, Cedar Avenue, Horwich, Bolton BL6 6HT* E-mail pauldever@btinternet.com

DEVERELL, Clive David. b 61. Anglia Ruskin Univ BA09. CA Tr Coll 83 ERMC 04. **d** 07 **p** 08. C Paston *Pet* 07-10; TV W Swindon and the Lydiards *Bris* from 10. *26 The Bramptons, Shaw, Swindon SN5 5SL* Tel (01793) 877111
E-mail clive.deverell@btinternet.com

DEVERELL, William Robert Henry. b 61. CITC 88 St Jo Coll Nottm 90. **d** 92 **p** 93. C Agherton *Conn* 92-95; I Sixmilecross w Termonmaguirke *Arm* 95-99; I Tallaght *D & G* from 99. *St Maelruain's Rectory, 6 Sally Park, Firhouse Road, Tallaght, Dublin 24, Republic of Ireland* Tel (00353) (1) 462 1044 *or* 462 6006 Fax 462 1044 Mobile 86-803 0239
E-mail tallaghtparish@ireland.com

DEVEREUX, Canon John Swinnerton. b 32. Lon Univ BSc53. Wells Th Coll. **d** 58 **p** 59. C Wigan St Mich *Liv* 58-60; C Goring-by-Sea *Chich* 60-69; Ind Chapl 69-97; Can and Preb Chich Cathl 90-97; rtd 97; Perm to Offic *Chich* from 97. *4 Pony Farm, Findon, Worthing BN14 0RS* Tel (01903) 873638

DEVERILL, Jennifer. b 40. Auckland Medical Sch MSR62. **d** 96 **p** 97. OLM Battersea St Luke *S'wark* 96-05; Chapl St Geo Healthcare NHS Trust Lon 96-05; P-in-c Le Gard *Eur* from 08. *8 rue de l'Eglise, 30140 Bagard, France* Tel (0033) 4 6 25 17 63
E-mail jennifer.deverill@wanadoo.fr

DEVINE, Margaret Rose. b 50. Sunderland Poly BEd76. NEOC 00. **d** 03 **p** 04. NSM E Boldon *Dur* from 03. *13 Rectory Green, West Boldon NE36 0QD* Tel 0191-537 2129

DEVINE, Maureen Mary. b 37. Cheltenham & Glouc Coll of HE TCert74. SAOMC 95. **d** 98 **p** 99. NSM Reading St Jo *Ox* 98-01; NSM Beech Hill, Grazeley and Spencers Wood 01-05; NSM Loddon Reach 05-08; Perm to Offic from 08. *33 Radstock Lane, Earley, Reading RG6 5RX* Tel 0118-921 2767
E-mail julmar99@aol.com

DEVONISH, Clive Wayne. b 51. Ridley Hall Cam. **d** 96 **p** 97. C Meole Brace *Lich* 96-05; V Greenside *Dur* from 05. *The Vicarage, Greenside, Ryton NE40 4AA* Tel 0191-413 8281
E-mail revclivedevo@talktalk.net

DEVONSHIRE, Canon Roger George. b 40. AKC62. **d** 63 **p** 64. C Rotherhithe St Mary w All SS *S'wark* 63-67; C Kingston Hill St Paul 67-71; Chapl RN 71-95; QHC 92-95; R Pitlochry and Kilmaveonaig *St And* 95-05; Syn Clerk and Can St Ninian's Cathl Perth 00-05; rtd 05; Perm to Offic *Portsm* 05-07 and from 10; Chapl QinetiQ 07-10. *4 Chiltern Court, 27 Florence Road, Southsea PO5 2NX* Tel (023) 9287 3397 Mobile 07769-680922
E-mail rdevonshire@btinternet.com

DEVONSHIRE JONES, Thomas Percy Norman. See JONES, Thomas Percy Norman Devonshire

DEW, Glyn. b 55. Worc Coll of Educn BEd90. St Jo Coll Nottm MA97. **d** 97 **p** 98. C Beoley *Worc* 97-01; TV Redditch, The Ridge 01-05; P-in-c Tardebigge 04-05; Perm to Offic from 09. *St Luke's Rectory, 69 Evesham Road, Redditch B97 4JX* Tel (01527) 545521

DEW, Lindsay Charles. b 52. Wilson Carlile Coll 76 Cranmer Hall Dur 85. **d** 86 **p** 86. C Knottingley *Wakef* 86-89; V Batley St Thos 89-97; R Thornhill and Whitley Lower 97-09; RD Dewsbury 96-06; Hon Can Wakef Cathl 05-09; P-in-c Dunton w Wrestlingworth and Eyeworth *St Alb* from 09. *22 Angell's Meadow, Ashwell, Baldock SG7 5QS* Tel (01462) 743617 Mobile 07545-878082 E-mail lindsaydew@aol.com

DEW, Martin John. b 49. CBDTI 00. **d** 04 **p** 05. NSM Natland *Carl* 04-09; NSM Shap w Swindale and Bampton w Mardale from 09. *The Vicarage, Shap, Penrith CA10 3LB* Tel (01931) 716232

DEW, Mrs Maureen. b 51. Univ of Wales MA98. Qu Coll Birm BA99. **d** 99 **p** 00. C Inkberrow w Cookhill and Kington w Dormston *Worc* 99-02; C Redditch, The Ridge 02-05; TV Redditch Ch the K from 05. *St Luke's Rectory, 69 Evesham Road, Redditch B97 4JX* Tel (01527) 545521
E-mail modew@thesharpend33.freeserve.co.uk

DEW, Robert David John. b 42. St Pet Coll Ox BA63. St Steph Ho Ox 63. **d** 65 **p** 66. C Abington *Pet* 65-69; Chapl Tiffield Sch Northants 69-71; Ind Chapl *Pet* 71-79; Ind Chapl *Liv* 79-87; Sen Ind Missr 88-91; V Skelsmergh w Selside and Longsleddale *Carl* 91-06; Bp's Research Officer 91-95; Bp's Adv for CME 95-06; rtd 06. *Tither Crag Barn, Crook, Kendal LA8 8LE* Tel (01539) 568680 E-mail bob.dew@virgin.net

DEWAR, Francis John Lindsay. b 33. Keble Coll Ox BA56 MA59. Cuddesdon Coll 58. **d** 60 **p** 61. C Hessle *York* 60-63; C Stockton St Chad *Dur* 63-66; V Sunderland St Chad 66-81; Org Journey Inward, Journey Outward Project 82-07; rtd 07; Perm to Offic *B & W* from 01. *Wellspring, Church Road, Wookey, Wells BA5 1JX* Tel (01749) 675365 E-mail dewar@waitrose.com

DEWAR, Ian John James. b 61. Kingston Poly BA83. Cranmer Hall Dur 89. **d** 92 **p** 93. C Blackb St Gabr 92-95; C Darwen St Cuth w Tockholes St Steph 95-97; V Appley Bridge 97-05; Chapl St Cath Hospice Preston from 05. *St Catherine's Hospice, Lostock Lane, Lostock Hall, Preston PR5 5XU* Tel (01772) 629171 Fax 620982 E-mail ian.dewar@stcatherines.co.uk *or* ijjdewar@hotmail.com

DEWAR, John. b 32. Chich Th Coll 58. **d** 61 **p** 62. C Leeds St Hilda *Ripon* 61-65; C Cullercoats St Geo *Newc* 65-69; V

Newsham 69-76; V Kenton Ascension 76-86; R Wallsend St Pet 86-92; V Longhorsley and Hebron 92-96; rtd 96; Perm to Offic *S'well* from 04. *51 Bonner Lane, Calverton, Nottingham NG14 6FU* Tel 0115-965 2599
E-mail jandmedewar@ntlworld.com

DEWES, Ms Deborah Mary. b 59. Homerton Coll Cam BEd81 St Jo Coll Dur BA90 MA93. Cranmer Hall Dur 88. **d** 92 **p** 94. C Stockton St Pet *Dur* 92-96; C Knowle *Birm* 96-03; C Bath Abbey w St Jas *B & W* 03-08; Chapl R United Hosp Bath NHS Trust 03-08; P-in-c Brislington St Luke from 08. *The Vicarage, 9 St Luke's Gardens, Bristol BS4 4NW* Tel 0117-977 7633

DEWEY, David Malcolm. b 43. Lon Univ BA72 LSE MSc(Econ)87 Fitzw Coll Cam MPhil94. Westcott Ho Cam 76. **d** 78 **p** 79. Sen Lect Middx Poly 72-92; Sen Lect Middx Univ 92-01; Hon C Enfield St Mich *Lon* 78-79; Hon C Bush Hill Park St Steph 79-84; Hon C Palmers Green St Jo 84-90; Perm to Offic *Lon* 90-95 and *St Alb* 95-98; Hon C Hertford All SS *St Alb* 98-01; P-in-c St Paul's Walden 01-08; rtd 08; Perm to Offic *St Alb* from 09. *44 The Elms, Hertford SG13 7UX* Tel (01992) 551968 Mobile 07813-439463 E-mail daviddewey8566@fsmail.net

DEWEY, Peter Lewis. b 38. Wycliffe Hall Ox 69. **d** 71 **p** 72. C Hammersmith St Sav *Lon* 71-73; Chapl to Bp Kensington 73-75; C Isleworth All SS 75-81; TV Dorchester *Ox* 81-91; CF (TA) 86-91; Chapl Gordonstoun Sch 92-97; TR St Laur in Thanet *Cant* 97-03; rtd 03; P-in-c Sulhamstead Abbots and Bannister w Ufton Nervet *Ox* 03-10; Hon C from 10; AD Bradfield from 10. *The Rectory, Sulhamstead Road, Ufton Nervet, Reading RG7 4DH* Tel 0118-983 2328

DEWEY, Sanford Dayton. b 44. Syracuse Univ AB67 MA72. Gen Th Sem (NY) MDiv79. **d** 79 **p** 80. Assoc Chapl Roosevelt Hosp New York USA 80-81; Assoc Dir Relig Services 81-86; C St Mary le Bow w St Pancras Soper Lane etc *Lon* 87-92; C Hampstead St Steph w All Hallows 92-94; Co-Dir Hampstead Counselling Service 94-00; Dir from 00; NSM Hampstead Ch Ch 94-96; Hon C Grosvenor Chpl from 96; Prov Past Consultant URC from 96; Perm to Offic from 97. *B908 New Providence Wharf, 1 Fairmont Avenue, London E14 9PJ*
E-mail daytondewey@gmail.com

DEWHIRST, Janice. b 50. EMMTC 99. **d** 02 **p** 03. NSM Forest Town *S'well* 02-04; NSM Mansfield SS Pet and Paul 04-06; P-in-c Ladybrook 06-09; rtd 09. *26 King Street, Mansfield Woodhouse, Mansfield NG19 9AU* Tel (01623) 454471
E-mail revd.jan.d@ntlworld.com

DEWHURST, Gabriel George. b 30. **d** 59 **p** 60. In RC Ch 60-69; C Darlington St Jo *Dur* 70; C Bishopwearmouth St Nic 71-73; C-in-c Stockton St Mark CD 73-81; V Harton 81-86; R Castle Eden w Monkhesleden 86-97; rtd 97; Perm to Offic *York* from 98. *9 Knott Lane, Easingwold, York YO61 3LX* Tel (01347) 823526

DEWHURST, Russell James Edward. b 77. Magd Coll Ox MPhys99 Selw Coll Cam BTh03. Westcott Ho Cam 00. **d** 03 **p** 04. C Blewbury, Hagbourne and Upton *Ox* 03-05; P-in-c St Frideswide w Binsey 05-09; Web Pastor i-church 05-07; Asst Chapl Ex Coll Ox 06-09; V Ewell *Guildf* from 09. *St Mary's Vicarage, 14 Church Street, Ewell, Epsom KT17 2AQ* Tel (020) 8393 2643 E-mail rdewhurst@mac.com

DEWICK, David Richard. b 36. SAOMC 96. **d** 99 **p** 00. NSM Risborough *Ox* 99-10; rtd 10. *Russets, Peters Lane, Monks Risborough, Princes Risborough HP27 0LQ* Tel (01844) 343016

DEWING, Robert Mark Eastwood. b 68. Bris Univ BA90 PGCE91. Ridley Hall Cam BA98. **d** 99 **p** 00. C Alverstoke *Portsm* 99-03; V Sheet 03-11; AD Petersfield 09-11; Past Dir Lee Abbey from 11. *Lee Abbey Fellowship, Lee Abbey, Lynton EX35 6JJ* Tel (01598) 752621 E-mail robdewing@hotmail.com

DEWING, William Arthur. b 52. NEOC 99. **d** 02 **p** 03. NSM Middlesbrough St Oswald *York* 02-06; NSM Stainton w Hilton from 06. *19 Monarch Grove, Marton, Middlesbrough TS7 8QQ* Tel (01642) 321074 Fax 500661 Mobile 07966-191640
E-mail bill@revd.me.uk

DEWSBURY, Michael Owen. b 31. St Aid Birkenhead 54. **d** 57 **p** 58. C Hellesdon *Nor* 57-60; C Speke All SS *Liv* 60-62; R Gt and Lt Glemham *St E* 62-67; R W Lynn *Nor* 67-68; R Dongara Australia 69-71; R Nollamara 71-76; Chapl R Perth Hosp 76-79; Chapl Fremantle Hosp 79-99; rtd 99. *8 Thomas Street, South Fremantle WA 6162, Australia* Tel (0061) (8) 9335 6852
E-mail dewsbury@iinet.net.au

DEXTER, Canon Frank Robert. b 40. Cuddesdon Coll 66. **d** 68 **p** 69. C Newc H Cross 68-71; C Whorlton 71-73; V Pet Ch Carpenter 73-80; V High Elswick St Phil *Newc* 80-85; RD Newc W 81-85; V Newc St Geo 85-05; Hon Can Newc Cathl 94-05; P-in-c Newc St Hilda 95-98; rtd 05. *8 Tynedale Terrace, Hexham NE46 3JE* Tel (01434) 601759
E-mail frank.dexter@talk21.com

DEY, Canon Charles Gordon Norman. b 46. Lon Coll of Div. **d** 71 **p** 72. C Almondbury *Wakef* 71-76; V Mixenden 76-85; TR Tong *Bradf* 85-11; C Laisterdyke 08-11; Hon Can Bradf Cathl 00-11; rtd 11. *30 Bartle Close, Bradford BD7 4QH*
E-mail thedeyteam@blueyonder.co.uk

DEY, John Alfred. b 33. ALCD57 ALCM57. **d** 57 **p** 58. C Man Albert Memorial Ch 57-60; C Pennington 60-62; V Mosley Common 62-69; V Chadderton Em 69-79; V Flixton St Jo 79-96; rtd 96; Perm to Offic *Man* from 96. *8 Woodlands Avenue, Urmston, Manchester M41 6NE*

DI CASTIGLIONE, James Alexander. b 81. St Jo Coll Nottm. **d** 08 **p** 09. C Mid-Sussex Network Ch *Chich* from 08. *22 Marchants Road, Hurstpierpoint, Hassocks BN6 9UU* Tel (01273) 835262 Mobile 07796-945662

DI CASTIGLIONE, Nigel Austin. b 57. St Jo Coll Dur BA78. St Jo Coll Nottm MA94. **d** 94 **p** 95. C Tamworth *Lich* 94-97; P-in-c Trentham 97-01; V 02-10; V Hanford 02-10; V Harborne Heath *Birm* from 10. *St John's Vicarage, 99 Wentworth Road, Birmingham B17 9ST* Tel 0121-428 2093 Mobile 07770-697240 E-mail nigeldicastiglione@stjohns-church.co.uk

DI CHIARA, Miss Alessandra Maddalena. b 59. Univ of Wales (Swansea) BA80. Wycliffe Hall Ox 00. **d** 02 **p** 03. C Hooton *Ches* 02-05; P-in-c Millbrook from 05. *11 Standrick Hill Rise, Stalybridge SK15 3RT* Tel 0161-304 0281 E-mail rev.alessandra@stjamesmillbrook.org.uk

DIALI, The Ven Daniel Chukwuma. b 47. Portsm Univ BA80 Surrey Univ MA04. Basic Ord Course by Ext 85. **d** 84 **p** 86. Nigeria 84-01; V Lagos St Bart 86-92; V Bp Tugwell Cn 92-96; Can Lagos W 96-99; Adn St Paul's 00-01; Perm to Offic *S'wark* from 02. *36 Arnold Estate, Druid Street, London SE1 2DU* Tel (020) 7231 5357 E-mail dcdvnd@yahoo.com

DIAMOND, Canon Michael Lawrence. b 37. St Jo Coll Dur BA60 MA74 Sussex Univ DPhil84. ALCD62. **d** 62 **p** 63. C Wandsworth St Mich *S'wark* 62-64; C Patcham *Chich* 64-69; R Hamsey 70-75; P-in-c Cambridge St Andr Less *Ely* 75-86; V 86-04; Hon Can Ely Cathl 94-04; RD Cambridge 96-04; rtd 04; Perm to Offic *S'well* from 04. *16 St Michael's Square, Beeston, Nottingham NG9 3HG* Tel 0115-925 4452

DIAMOND, Capt Richard Geoffrey Colin. b 49. MBE00. CA Tr Coll. **d** 93 **p** 93. Miss to Seafarers Kenya 90-01; rtd 01; Perm to Offic *Win* from 02. *209A Priory Road, Southampton SO17 2LR* Tel (02380) 678558 E-mail rgcdiamond@ic24.net

DIANA, Sister. *See* MORRISON, Diana Mary

DIAPER, James Robert. b 30. Portsm Dioc Tr Course 84. **d** 85. NSM Portsea St Sav *Portsm* 85-89 and 91-95; NSM Milton 89-91; rtd 95; Perm to Offic *Portsm* from 95. *48 Wallington Road, Portsmouth PO2 0HB* Tel (023) 9269 1372

DIAZ BUTRON, Marcos Máximo. b 72. St Steph Ho Ox 06. **d** 08. C Wantage *Ox* 08-10. *Address temp unknown* E-mail maxdiazbutron@yahoo.es

DIBB SMITH, John. b 29. Ex & Truro NSM Scheme 78. **d** 81 **p** 82. NSM Carbis Bay *Truro* 81-82; NSM Carbis Bay w Lelant 82-84; Warden Trelowarren Fellowship Helston 84-89; Chapl 89-91; NSM Halsetown *Truro* 91-97; rtd 98; Perm to Offic *Truro* from 00. *Cargease Cottage, Cockwells, Penzance TR20 8DG* Tel (01736) 740707

DIBBENS, Canon Hugh Richard. b 39. Lon Univ BA63 MTh67 St Pet Coll Ox BA65 MA74. Oak Hill Th Coll 60. **d** 67 **p** 68. C Holborn St Geo w H Trin and St Bart *Lon* 67-72; CMS 73-74; Japan 74-77; TR Chigwell *Chelmsf* 78-92; V Hornchurch St Andr 92-06; RD Havering 98-04; Hon Can Chelmsf Cathl 01-06; rtd 06; Perm to Offic *Chelmsf* from 07. *9 Stonehill Road, Roxwell, Chelmsford CM1 4PF* Tel (01245) 248173 E-mail hughandruth@dibbens10.freeserve.co.uk

DIBDEN, Alan Cyril. b 49. Hull Univ LLB70 Fitzw Coll Cam BA72 MA76. Westcott Ho Cam 70 Virginia Th Sem 73. **d** 73 **p** 74. C Camberwell St Luke *S'wark* 73-77; TV Walworth 77-79; TV Langley Marish *Ox* 79-84; C Chalfont St Peter 84-90; TV Burnham w Dropmore, Hitcham and Taplow 90-08; V Taplow and Dropmore from 08. *The Rectory, Rectory Road, Taplow, Maidenhead SL6 0ET* Tel (01628) 661182 E-mail alan.dibden@btinternet.com

DICK, Canon Angela. b 62. Sheff Univ BA92. St Jo Coll Nottm MA94. **d** 96 **p** 97. C Mixenden *Wakef* 96-97; C Mount Pellon 97-99; P-in-c Bradshaw 99-00; P-in-c Holmfield 99-00; V Bradshaw and Holmfield 00-10; P-in-c Sowerby Bridge from 10; Hon Can Wakef Cathl from 10. *The Vicarage, 62 Park Road, Sowerby Bridge HX6 2BJ* Tel (01422) 831253 E-mail angedix110@talktalk.net

DICK, Canon Caroline Ann. b 61. Nottm Univ BTh88. Linc Th Coll 85. **d** 88 **p** 94. Par Dn Houghton le Spring *Dur* 88-93; Par Dn Hetton le Hole 93-94; C 94-96; Asst Chapl Sunderland Univ 94-98; C Harton 96-09; Development Officer Dioc Bd of Soc Resp 98-09; Adv for Women's Min 02-09; TV Dur N from 09; Hon Can Dur Cathl from 03. *Harton Vicarage, 182 Sunderland Road, South Shields NE34 6AH* Tel 0191-454 3804 E-mail bsr.development.officer@durham.anglican.org

DICK, Cecil Bates. b 42. TD97. Selw Coll Cam BA68 MA72. EMMTC 73. **d** 76 **p** 78. NSM Cinderhill *S'well* 76-79; Chapl Dame Allan's Schs Newc 79-85; C Gosforth All SS *Newc* 85-87; Chapl HM Pris Dur 88-89; Chapl HM Pris Hull 89-04; rtd 04; Perm to Offic *Newc* from 01 and *York* from 04. *11 Juniper Chase, Beverley HU17 8GD* Tel (01482) 862985

DICK, Malcolm Gordon (Mac). b 40. SWMTC 10. **d** 11. NSM Ottery St Mary, Alfington, W Hill, Tipton etc *Ex* from 11. *Green Hollow, Lower Broad Oak Road, West Hill, Ottery St Mary EX11 1XH* Tel (01404) 812494 E-mail macdick1@aol.com

DICK, Norman MacDonald. b 32. ACIB. Ox NSM Course 87. **d** 90 **p** 91. NSM Bedgrove *Ox* 90-95; NSM Ellesborough, The Kimbles and Stoke Mandeville 95-01; Perm to Offic from 01. *21 Camborne Avenue, Aylesbury HP21 7UH* Tel (01296) 485530 E-mail norman.dick@care4free.net

DICK, Raymond Owen. b 53. Edin Univ BD77. Edin Th Coll 73. **d** 77 **p** 78. C Glas St Mary 77-84; Perm to Offic *St Alb* 84-85; P-in-c Edin St Paul and St Geo 85; Edin St Phil 85-86; P-in-c Edin St Marg 85-87; TV Edin Old St Paul 87-88; R Hetton le Hole *Dur* 88-96; V Harton from 96; P-in-c Cleadon Park from 09. *Harton Vicarage, 182 Sunderland Road, South Shields NE34 6AH* Tel and fax 0191-427 5538 E-mail rodick182@aol.com *or* raymond.dick@durham.anglican.org

DICKENS, Adam Paul. b 65. Man Univ BA89 Nottm Univ MDiv93. Linc Th Coll 91. **d** 93 **p** 94. C Pershore w Pinvin, Wick and Birlingham *Worc* 93-98; C Portsea St Mary *Portsm* 98-04; Pilsdon Community from 04. *Pilsdon Manor, Pilsdon, Bridport DT6 5NZ* Tel (01308) 868308

DICKENS, Timothy Richard John. b 45. Leeds Univ BSc68. Westcott Ho Cam 68. **d** 71 **p** 72. C Meole Brace *Lich* 71-74; C-in-c Stamford Ch Ch CD *Linc* 74-80; V Anlaby St Pet *York* 80-91; V Egg Buckland *Ex* 91-10; P-in-c Estover 04-10; RD Plymouth Moorside 03-09; rtd 10. *52 Budshead Road, Plymouth PL5 2RA* E-mail timothy.vicar@tiscali.co.uk

DICKENSON, Charles Gordon. b 29. Bps' Coll Cheshunt 53. **d** 56 **p** 57. C Ellesmere Port *Ches* 56-61; R Egremont St Columba 61-68; V Latchford Ch Ch 68-74; P-in-c Hargrave 74-79; Bp's Chapl 75-79; V Birkenhead St Jas w St Bede 79-83; R Tilston and Shocklach 83-94; rtd 94; Perm to Offic *Ches* from 94. *58 Kingsway, Crewe CW2 7ND* Tel (01270) 560722 E-mail cg.dickenson@talktalk.net

DICKENSON, Canon Robin Christopher Wildish. b 44. Lon Univ CertEd67 Ex Univ BPhil81 MA98. SWMTC 94. **d** 97 **p** 98. NSM Week St Mary w Poundstock and Whitstone *Truro* 97-98; P-in-c 98-06; P-in-c St Gennys, Jacobstow w Warbstow and Treneglos 02-06; R Week St Mary Circle of Par from 06; RD Stratton 05-11; Hon Can Truro Cathl from 07. *The Rectory, The Glebe, Week St Mary, Holsworthy EX22 6UY* Tel and fax (01288) 341134 E-mail parsonrob@aol.com

DICKER, Ms Jane Elizabeth. b 64. Whitelands Coll Lon BA87 Anglia Ruskin Univ MA08. Linc Th Coll 87. **d** 89 **p** 94. Par Dn Merton St Jas *S'wark* 89-93; C Littleham w Exmouth 93-97; Chapl Plymouth Univ 93-97; Ecum Chapl for F&HE Grimsby *Linc* 97-02; Chapl Univ of Greenwich *Roch* 02-05; Chapl Kent Inst of Art and Design 02-05; Hon PV Roch Cathl 03-05; P-in-c Waltham Cross *St Alb* 05-08; TV Cheshunt from 08. *The Vicarage, 5 Longlands Close, Cheshunt, Waltham Cross EN8 8LW* Tel (01992) 633243 Mobile 07843-667971 E-mail mthr jane@yahoo.co.uk

DICKER, Miss Mary Elizabeth. b 45. Girton Coll Cam BA66 MA70 Sheff Univ MSc78. Cranmer Hall Dur 83. **dss** 85 **d** 87 **p** 94. Mortlake w E Sheen *S'wark* 85-88; Par Dn 87-88; Par Dn Irlam *Man* 88-92; Par Dn Ashton Ch Ch 92-94; C 94-97; P-in-c Hopwood 97-98; TV Heywood 98-05; rtd 05; Perm to Offic *Man* from 05. *32 Souchay Court, 1 Clothorn Road, Manchester M20 6BR* Tel 0161-434 7634

DICKERSON, Richard Keith. b 31. Sir Geo Williams Univ Montreal BA60 McGill Univ Montreal BD60. Montreal Dioc Th Coll. **d** 60 **p** 60. Canada 60-69 and from 78; C Hampstead St Matt 60-63; R Waterloo St Luke 63-69; Perm to Offic *Cant* 72; C Canvey Is *Chelmsf* 73-75; Perm to Offic Montreal 75-78; C Georgeville St Geo 78-82; P-in-c 82-91; R Lennoxville St Geo 91-01; rtd 96. *172 McGowan Road, Georgeville QC J0B 1T0, Canada*

DICKIE, James Graham Wallace. b 50. Worc Coll Ox BA72 MA BLitt77. Westcott Ho Cam 78. **d** 81 **p** 82. C Bracknell *Ox* 81-84; Lic to Offic *Ely* 84-89; Chapl Trin Coll Cam 84-89; Chapl Clifton Coll Bris 89-96; Sen Chapl Marlborough Coll 96-10; rtd 10. *Address temp unknown*

DICKIN (née LENTON), Mrs Patricia Margarita. b 72. STETS MA08. **d** 08 **p** 09. C Epsom Common Ch Ch *Guildf* 08-10; C Oxshott from 10. *278 The Greenway, Epsom KT18 7JF*

DICKINSON, Albert Hugh. b 34. Trin Coll Connecticut AB55. Episc Th Sch Harvard STB58. **d** 58 **p** 59. USA 58-97; C Portarlington w Cloneyhurke and Lea *M & K* 97-99; USA from 99. *802 Seashore Road, Cold Spring NJ 08204, USA* E-mail husan@avaloninternet.net

DICKINSON, Canon Anthony William. b 48. New Coll Ox BA71 MA74. Linc Th Coll 80. **d** 82 **p** 83. C Leavesden *St Alb* 82-86; TV Upton cum Chalvey *Ox* 86-94; P-in-c Terriers 94-99; V from 99; Chapl Bucks New Univ from 03; Hon Can Ch Ch *Ox* from 05. *St Francis's Vicarage, Amersham Road, High Wycombe HP13 5AB* Tel (01494) 520676 E-mail tony.dickinson@ukonline.co.uk *or* sainsw01@bcuc.ac.uk

DICKINSON, David Charles. b 58. BA79 Lanc Univ MA97. CBDTI. **d** 99 **p** 00. NSM Ewood *Blackb* 99-04; NSM Blackb Redeemer 04-05; P-in-c Hoghton from 05. *The Vicarage, Chapel Lane, Hoghton, Preston PR5 0RY* Tel (01254) 852529 E-mail dickinsonrev@aol.com

DICKINSON, Dyllis Annie. b 52. **d** 01 **p** 02. OLM Stalmine w Pilling *Blackb* 01-07; NSM from 07. *Springfield, Moss Side Lane, Stalmine, Poulton-le-Fylde FY6 0JP* Tel (01253) 700011 E-mail dyllisdickinson@talktalk.net

DICKINSON, Gareth Lee. b 69. Ridley Hall Cam 06. **d** 08 **p** 09. C Bryanston Square St Mary w St Marylebone St Mark *Lon* 08-10; NSM Cheltenham H Trin and St Paul *Glouc* from 10. *17 Sissinghurst Grove, Up Hatherley, Cheltenham GL51 3FA* Tel 07788-742700 (mobile) E-mail garethdickinson@me.com

DICKINSON, Henry. b 29. St Deiniol's Hawarden 84. **d** 86 **p** 87. NSM Blackb St Mich w St Jo and H Trin 86-89; NSM Burnley St Cath w St Alb and St Paul 89-95; Perm to Offic from 98. *22 Notre Dame Gardens, Blackburn BB1 5EF* Tel (01254) 693414

DICKINSON, The Very Revd the Hon Hugh Geoffrey. b 29. Trin Coll Ox BA53 MA56. Cuddesdon Coll 54. **d** 56 **p** 57. C Melksham *Sarum* 56-58; Chapl Trin Coll Cam 58-63; Chapl Win Coll 63-69; P-in-c Milverton *Cov* 69-77; V St Alb St Mich *St Alb* 77-86; Dean Sarum 86-96; rtd 96. *5 St Peter's Road, Cirencester GL7 1RE* Tel (01285) 657710 E-mail hughanjean@aol.com

DICKINSON, Canon Robert Edward. b 47. Nottm Univ BTh74. St Jo Coll Nottm 70. **d** 74 **p** 75. C Birm St Martin 74-78; P-in-c Liv St Bride w St Sav 78-81; TV St Luke in the City 81-86; Chapl Liv Poly 86-92; Chapl Liv Jo Moores Univ 92-08; Hon Can Liv Cathl 03-08; rtd 08. *3 Wightman Avenue, Newton-Le-Willows WA12 0LS* Tel (01925) 271124 E-mail bobdicko@blueyonder.co.uk

DICKINSON, Simon Braithwaite Vincent. b 34. SAOMC 93. **d** 97 **p** 98. OLM Waddesdon w Over Winchendon and Fleet Marston *Ox* 97-02; OLM Schorne 02-04; Perm to Offic from 04. *12A Croft Road, Thame OX9 3JF* Tel (01844) 212408 E-mail dickinson@whitehousewaddesdon.freeserve.co.uk

DICKINSON, Stephen Paul. b 54. SRN75. NOC 85. **d** 88 **p** 89. NSM Purston cum S Featherstone *Wakef* 88-91; C Goldthorpe w Hickleton *Sheff* 91-94; V New Bentley 94-05; P-in-c Arksey 04-05; V New Bentley w Arksey from 05. *The Vicarage, Victoria Road, Bentley, Doncaster DN5 0EZ* Tel (01302) 875266

DICKINSON, Victor Tester. b 48. Univ of Wales (Cardiff) BSc70. St Steph Ho Ox 70. **d** 73 **p** 74. C Neath w Llantwit 73-76; Asst Chapl Univ of Wales (Cardiff) 76-79; TV Willington *Newc* 79-86; V Kenton Ascension 86-97; V Lowick and Kyloe w Ancroft from 97; R Ford and Etal from 97. *The Vicarage, 1 Main Street, Lowick, Berwick-upon-Tweed TD15 2UD* Tel (01289) 388229

DICKSON, Brian John. b 19. Reading Univ BSc41. Qu Coll Birm 49. **d** 51 **p** 52. C S Wimbledon H Trin *S'wark* 51-53; C Golders Green St Alb *Lon* 53-55; Sec SCM Th Colls Dept 53-55; Chapl Hulme Gr Sch Oldham 55-59; Chapl K Sch Worc 60-67; Min Can Worc Cathl 60-67; Chapl Colston's Sch Bris 67-74; V Bishopston *Bris* 74-85; RD Horfield 80-85; rtd 85; Perm to Offic Worc 85-05 and *Heref* from 05. *2 Coach House Fields, Livesey Road, Ludlow SY8 1AZ* Tel (01584) 874018

DICKSON, Colin James. b 74. St Andr Univ MA96 MPhil00 Leeds Univ BA01. Coll of Resurr Mirfield 99. **d** 02 **p** 03. C Tottenham St Paul *Lon* 02-05; C Croydon St Mich w St Jas *S'wark* 05-10; SSF from 10. *The Friary of St Francis, Alnmouth, Alnwick NE66 3NJ* E-mail josephemmanuelssf@franciscans.org.uk

DICKSON, Colin Patrick Gavin. b 56. **d** 96 **p** 97. C Grays Thurrock *Chelmsf* 96-00; V Glantawe *S & B* from 00. *The Vicarage, 122 Mansel Road, Bonymaen, Swansea SA1 7JR* Tel (01792) 652839

DICKSON, Samuel Mervyn James. b 41. CITC. **d** 66 **p** 67. C Ballyholme *D & D* 66-70; C Knockbreda 70-75; I Clonallon w Warrenpoint 75-84; I Down H Trin w Hollymount 84-06; Bp's C Rathmullan 00-05; Bp's C Tyrella 00-06; Bp's C Loughinisland 01-06; Can Down Cathl 91-06; Treas 98-00; Prec 00-01; Chan 01-06; rtd 06. *Apartment 1, 40A Main Street, Dundrum, Newcastle BT33 0LY* Tel (028) 4375 1112

DIDUK, Sergiy. b 74. Ukranian Nat Academy BA08. St Jo Coll Nottm MA11. **d** 11. C Hucknall Torkard *S'well* from 11. *149 Beardall Street, Hucknall, Nottingham NG15 7HA* Tel 07817-488425 (mobile) E-mail sergius nd@hotmail.co.uk

DIETZ, Matthew Paul Richard. b 70. Magd Coll Cam MA95. Wycliffe Hall Ox 05. **d** 07 **p** 08. C Win Ch Ch 07-08; C Throop 08-11; Chapl Monkton Combe Sch Bath from 11. *Monkton Combe School, Church Lane, Monkton Combe, Bath BA2 7HG* Tel (01225) 721102 Mobile 07751-454993 E-mail matthew.dietz@btinternet.com

DIFFEY, Margaret Elsie. b 39. MCSP. **d** 02 **p** 03. OLM Nor St Geo Tombland 02-10; rtd 10; Perm to Offic *Nor* from 10. *45 Welsford Road, Norwich NR4 6QB* Tel and fax (01603) 457248 E-mail maggiediffey@tiscali.co.uk

DIGGLE, Judith Margaret. See BROWN, Prof Judith Margaret

DIGGLE, Richard James. b 47. Lon Inst BA69 Man Poly CertEd73. **d** 01 **p** 02. OLM Chorlton-cum-Hardy St Werburgh *Man* 01-05; NSM Bickerton, Bickley, Harthill and Burwardsley *Ches* 05-08; V Antrobus, Aston by Sutton, Lt Leigh etc from 08. *The Vicarage, Street Lane, Lower Whitley, Warrington WA4 4EN* Tel (01925) 730158 Mobile 07749-849783 E-mail diggle163@btinternet.com

DIGGORY, Mrs Susan. b 51. SEITE BA09. **d** 09 **p** 10. NSM Tunbridge Wells St Mark *Roch* from 09. *Oakdene, 8 Glenmore Park, Tunbridge Wells TN2 5NZ* Tel (01892) 531941 E-mail sue.diggory@oakdene.eclipse.co.uk

DIGMAN (née BUTTERFIELD), Mrs Amanda Helen. b 73. Derby Univ BA96. St Jo Coll Nottm 07. **d** 09 **p** 10. C Sutton in Ashfield St Mary *S'well* from 09; C Huthwaite from 09. *10 Huthwaite Road, Sutton-in-Ashfield NG17 2GW* Tel 07803-625049 (mobile) E-mail amanda.digman@ntlworld.com

DILKES, Nigel Bruce. b 58. Univ of Wales (Ban) BSc97 Lanc Univ PhD01. Ridley Hall Cam 03. **d** 05 **p** 06. C Llandudno *Ban* 05-07; C Holyhead 07-09; TV Barnstaple *Ex* from 09. *The Rectory, 4 Northfield Lane, Barnstaple EX31 1QB* Tel (01271) 343225 E-mail nigeldilkes@aol.com

DILL, Nicholas Bayard Botolf. b 63. Toronto Univ BA86 Lon Univ LLB89 Barrister 91. Wycliffe Hall Ox 96. **d** 98 **p** 99. C Lindfield *Chich* 98-05; R Pembroke St Jo Bermuda from 05. *St John's Rectory, 15 Langton Hill, Pembroke HM 13, Bermuda* Tel (001) (441) 292 5308 Fax 296 9173 E-mail nickdill@logic.bm

DILL, Peter Winston. b 41. ACP66 K Coll Lon BD72 AKC72. St Aug Coll Cant 72. **d** 73 **p** 74. C Warsop *S'well* 73-75; C Rhyl w St Ann *St As* 75-77; C Oxton *Ches* 77-78; V Newton in Mottram 78-82; P-in-c Shelton and Oxon *Lich* 82-84; V 84-87; Chapl Clifton Coll Bris 87-00; C Thorverton, Cadbury, Upton Pyne etc *Ex* 00-01; Perm to Offic *Bris* 02-03; Past Co-ord St Monica Trust Westbury Fields 03-06; rtd 06. *85B Pembroke Road, Clifton, Bristol BS8 3EB* Tel 0117-973 9769

DILNOT, Canon John William. b 36. Selw Coll Cam BA60 MA64. Cuddesdon Coll 60. **d** 62 **p** 63. C Stafford St Mary *Lich* 62-66; C Stoke upon Trent 66-67; V Leek All SS 67-74; V Leeds w Broomfield *Cant* 74-79; P-in-c Aldington 79-81; P-in-c Bonnington w Bilsington 79-81; P-in-c Fawkenhurst 79-81; R Aldington w Bonnington and Bilsington 81-87; RD N Lympne 82-87; Hon Can Cant Cathl 85-99; V Folkestone St Mary and St Eanswythe 87-99; rtd 99; Perm to Offic *Cant* from 99. *Underhill Cottage, The Undercliff, Sandgate, Folkestone CT20 3AT* Tel (01303) 248000

DILWORTH, Anthony. b 41. St Deiniol's Hawarden 87. **d** 90 **p** 91. NSM Gt Saughall *Ches* 90-93; P-in-c Cwmcarn *Mon* 93-95; V 95-99; V Abercarn and Cwmcarn 99-01; TV Upholland *Liv* 01-06; rtd 06; P-in-c Llansilin w Llangadwaladr and Llangedwyn *St As* from 10. *The Vicarage, Llansilin, Oswestry SY10 7PX* Tel (01691) 791209 Mobile 07773-389179 E-mail anthonydilworth536@btinternet.com

DIMERY, Richard James. b 76. CCC Cam MA98 Leeds Univ MA99. Wycliffe Hall Ox MA03. **d** 04 **p** 05. C Upper Armley *Ripon* 04-08; P-in-c Woodside from 08. *St James's Vicarage, 1 Scotland Close, Horsforth, Leeds LS18 5SG* Tel 0113-228 2902 E-mail richard@dimery.com

DIMES, Stuart Christopher Laurence. b 60. Warwick Univ BSc81. St Jo Coll Nottm 99. **d** 01 **p** 02. C Branksome St Clem *Sarum* 01-05; P-in-c W Heath *Birm* 05-10; V from 10. *The Vicarage, 54A Lilley Lane, Birmingham B31 3JT* Tel 0121-476 7776 E-mail revsdimes@live.com

DIMMICK, Kenneth Ray. b 55. Texas A&M Univ BA77. Nashotah Ho MDiv84. **d** 84 **p** 84. C Shreveport St Matthias USA 84-86; P-in-c 86-87; R St Francisville Grace Ch 87-00; Assoc R Houston Palmer Memorial Ch 00-05; V Anahuac Trin 05-06; P-in-c Stuttgart *Eur* from 06. *Lorenzstaffel 8, 70182 Stuttgart, Germany* Tel (0049) (711) 787 8783 Mobile 151-5798 9140 E-mail vicar@stcatherines-stuttgart.de

DIMMICK, Mrs Margaret Louisa. b 44. Keswick Hall Coll TCert65 Open Univ BA75. SAOMC 97. **d** 00 **p** 02. OLM Caversham St Pet and Mapledurham etc *Ox* 00-03; OLM Emmer Green w Caversham Park from 03. *12 Lowfield Road, Caversham, Reading RG4 6PA* Tel 0118-947 0258 E-mail margaret@dimmick33.freeserve.co.uk

DIMOLINE, Keith Frederick. b 22. Clifton Th Coll 48. **d** 51 **p** 52. C Watford Ch Ch *St Alb* 51-54; C Corsham *Bris* 54-59; C-in-c Swindon St Jo Park CD 59-62; V Swindon St Jo 62-65; V Coalpit Heath 65-74; V Hanham 74-83; C Cudworth w Chillington *B & W* 83-84; P-in-c Dowlishwake w Chaffcombe, Knowle St Giles etc 83-84; R Dowlishwake w Chaffcombe, Knowle St Giles etc 84-88; rtd 88; Perm to Offic *B & W* from 88. *16 Exeter Road, Weston-super-Mare BS23 4DB* Tel (01934) 635006

DIMOND, Mark James. **d** 11. C Penarth All SS *Llan* from 11. *Address temp unknown*

DINES, Edward Paul Anthony. b 73. Chelt & Glouc Coll of HE BEd96. Trin Coll Bris BA11. **d** 11. C Knight's Enham and

Smannell w Enham Alamein *Win* from 11. *2 Madrid Road, Andover SP10 1JR* Tel 07507-184150 (mobile) E-mail dines@inbox.com

DINES, The Very Revd Philip Joseph (Griff). b 59. Univ Coll Lon BScEng80 Clare Coll Cam PhD84 Man Univ MA(Theol)93. Westcott Ho Cam 83. d 86 p 87. C Northolt St Mary *Lon* 86-89; C Withington St Paul *Man* 89-91; V Wythenshawe St Martin 91-98; P-in-c Newall Green St Fran 95-98; R Glas St Mary and Provost St Mary's Cathl 98-05; Lic to Offic 05-08. *Address temp unknown* Tel 07974-611438 (mobile) E-mail griff@dines.org

DINNEN, John Frederick. b 42. TCD BA65 BD72 QUB MTh91. CITC. d 66 p 67. C Belfast All SS *Conn* 66-68; ICM Dub 69-71; C Carnmoney 71-73; Asst Dean of Residences QUB 73-74; Dean 74-84; I Hillsborough *D & D* 84-07; Preb Down Cathl 93-96; Dir of Ords 96-98; Dean Down 96-06; rtd 08. *74 Demesne Road, Ballynahinch BT24 8NS* Tel (028) 4481 1148 E-mail jdinnen@btinternet.com

DINNEN, Mrs Judith Margaret. b 48. Open Univ BA87 Univ of Wales (Cardiff) MA00 Goldsmiths' Coll Lon TCert71. WEMTC 01. d 05 p 06. NSM Madley w Tyberton, Peterchurch, Vowchurch etc *Heref* from 05. *The Hawthorns, Madley, Hereford HR2 9LU* Tel (01981) 251866 E-mail judy@dinnen.plus.com

DINSMORE, Ivan Ernest. b 71. TCD BTh01. CITC 98. d 01 p 02. C Glendermott *D & R* 01-04; I Balteagh w Carrick from 04; I Tamlaghtard w Aghanloo from 04. *Balteagh Rectory, 115 Drumsurn Road, Limavady BT49 0PD* Tel (028) 7776 3069 E-mail ivandinsmore@hotmail.com

DINSMORE, Stephen Ralph. b 56. Wye Coll Lon BSc78 Man Univ MA06. Cranmer Hall Dur 82. d 85 p 86. C Haughton le Skerne *Dur* 85-88; C Edgware *Lon* 88-93; V Plymouth St Jude *Ex* 93-05; RD Plymouth Sutton 96-01; Dioc Adv for Miss and Par Development *Chelmsf* 05-07; Hon C Cranham Park 05-07; Nat Dir SOMA UK from 07. *SOMA UK, PO Box 69, Merriott TA18 9AP* Tel (01460) 279737 E-mail stephen.dinsmore@somauk.org

DINWIDDY SMITH, Emma Ruth. b 67. d 10 p 11. C Hampstead St Jo *Lon* from 10. *50 Minster Road, London NW2 3RE* Tel (020) 7435 7016

DISLEY, Mrs Edith Jennifer. b 51. Sheff Univ BSc72 Man Univ BD79. NOC 99. d 01 p 02. NSM Man Victoria Park 01-10; NSM Withington St Paul 02-10; NSM Wythenshawe from 10. *49 Broadstone Hall Road North, Heaton Chapel, Stockport SK4 5LA* Tel 0161-432 5114 E-mail sisteredith@priest.com

DITCH, David John. b 45. St Cath Coll Cam BA67 MA70 Leeds Univ PGCE68. WMMTC 88. d 91 p 92. C Biddulph *Lich* 91-94; V Hednesford 94-02; V Chasetown 02-08; rtd 09; Perm to Offic *Derby* from 09. *6 Redwing Croft, Derby DE23 1WF* Tel (01332) 271767

DITCHBURN, Hazel. b 44. NEOC 82. dss 84 d 87 p 94. Scotswood *Newc* 84-86; Ind Chapl *Dur* 86-95; TV Gateshead 95-98; AD Gateshead 92-98; P-in-c Stella 98-04; P-in-c Swalwell 01-04; R Blaydon and Swalwell 04-06; AD Gateshead W 98-00; Hon Can Dur Cathl 94-06; P-in-c Freshwater Australia 06-09. *2 Woburn Way, Westerhope, Newcastle upon Tyne NE5 5JD* Tel 0191-286 0553

DITCHFIELD, Timothy Frederick. b 61. CCC Cam BA83. Cranmer Hall Dur 85. d 88 p 89. C Accrington St Jo *Blackb* 88-89; C Accrington St Jo w Huncoat 89-91; C Whittle-le-Woods 91-95; Chapl K Coll Lon from 95. *19 Maunsel Street, London SW1P 2QN, or King's College, London WC2R 2LS* Tel (020) 7828 1772 *or* 7848 2373 Fax 7848 2344 E-mail tim.ditchfield@kcl.ac.uk

DIVALL, David Robert. b 40. New Coll Ox BA64 Sussex Univ DPhil74. Sarum & Wells Th Coll 75. d 77 p 78. Hon C Catherington and Clanfield *Portsm* 77-92; Hon C Rowlands Castle 92-93; Perm to Offic from 01. *17 Pipers Mead, Clanfield, Waterlooville PO8 0ST* Tel (023) 9259 4845

DIVALL, Stephen Robert. b 70. Pemb Coll Ox MA92. Ridley Hall Cam 95. d 98 p 99. C Cheadle *Ches* 98-01; Team Ldr UCCF 01-06; V Kensington St Helen w H Trin *Lon* from 06. *St Helen's Vicarage, St Helen's Gardens, London W10 6LP* Tel (020) 8968 7807

DIX, Edward Joseph. b 77. Goldsmiths' Coll Lon BMus00. Wycliffe Hall Ox BTh09. d 09 p 10. C Shadwell St Paul w Ratcliffe St Jas *Lon* from 09. *53 Prospect Place, Wapping Wall, London E1W 3TJ* Tel 07899-075935 (mobile) E-mail edjdix@gmail.com

DIXON, Ms Anne Elizabeth. b 56. Leeds Univ LLB77 Solicitor 80. Westcott Ho Cam. d 01 p 02. C Guildf H Trin w St Mary 01-05; Chapl HM Pris Bullwood Hall 06-09; Perm to Offic *Guildf* from 05 and *Blackb* from 10. *2 Highcroft Court, Bookham, Leatherhead KT23 3QU* Tel (01372) 450643

DIXON, Bruce Richard. b 42. Lon Univ BScEng63. Sarum Th Coll 66. d 68 p 69. C Walton St Mary *Liv* 68-70; C Harnham *Sarum* 70-73; C Streatham St Leon *S'wark* 73-77; R Cranborne w Boveridge, Edmondsham etc *Sarum* 83-02; rtd 07. *East Heddon, Filleigh, Barnstaple EX32 0RY* Tel (01598) 760513 E-mail bandk2d@hotmail.com

DIXON, Bryan Stanley. b 61. St Jo Coll Nottm BTh93. d 93 p 94. C Beverley Minster *York* 93-96; C Kingston upon Hull St Aid Southcoates 96-97; Asst Chapl HM Pris Dur 97-98; R Mid Marsh Gp *Linc* 98-03; R Brandesburton and Leven w Catwick *York* 03-10; P-in-c Patrick Brompton and Hunton *Ripon* from 10; P-in-c Crakehall from 10; P-in-c Hornby from 10; AD Wensley from 11. *The Vicarage, Patrick Brompton, Bedale DL8 1JN* E-mail tdogcollar3@tdogcollar3.yahoo.co.uk

DIXON, Campbell Boyd. d 07 p 08. NSM Jordanstown *Conn* from 07. *10 Meadowbank, Newtownabbey BT37 0UP* E-mail campbelldixon@hotmail.co.uk

DIXON, Charles William. b 41. NW Ord Course 78. d 81 p 82. C Almondbury *Wakef* 81-82; C Almondbury w Farnley Tyas 82-84; P-in-c Shelley 84-88; P-in-c Shepley 84-88; V Shelley and Shepley 88-89; V Rippondea 89-94; V Barkisland w W Scammonden 89-94; P-in-c Thornes 94-98; Chapl among Deaf People *Chelmsf* 98-06; rtd 06; Chapl among Deaf People *Ely* 06-10; Perm to Offic from 10. *9 The Paddock, Huntingdon PE29 1BY* Tel (01480) 451109 Mobile 07749-702924 E-mail c.dixon4@btinternet.com

DIXON, Canon David. b 19. Lich Th Coll 57. d 58 p 59. C Barrow St Luke *Carl* 58-61; V Westfield St Mary 61-68; Warden Rydal Hall 68-84; P-in-c Rydal 78-84; rtd 84; Perm to Offic *Carl* from 84; Hon Can Carl Cathl 84-85. *Rheda, The Green, Millom LA18 5JA* Tel (01229) 774300

DIXON, David Hugh. b 40. Chich Th Coll 90. d 92 p 93. C Launceston *Truro* 92-95; TV Probus, Ladock and Grampound w Creed and St Erme 95-06; rtd 06. *1 Rectory Close, Old Village, Willand, Cullompton EX15 2RH* Tel (01884) 839984

DIXON, David Michael. b 58. Preston Poly BA82 Barrister 83. Coll of Resurr Mirfield BA98. d 98 p 99. C Goldthorpe w Hickleton *Sheff* 98-01; P-in-c W Kirby St Andr *Ches* 01-07; V 07-10; P-in-c Scarborough St Sav w All SS *York* from 10; P-in-c Scarborough St Martin from 10. *St Martin's Vicarage, Craven Street, Scarborough YO11 2BY* E-mail standvic@aol.com

DIXON, Edward Michael. b 42. St Chad's Coll Dur BA64 Newc Univ MA93. d 66 p 67. C Hartlepool H Trin *Dur* 66-70; C Howden *York* 70-73; Chapl HM Pris Liv 73; Chapl HM Pris Onley 74-82; Chapl HM Pris Frankland 82-87; Chapl HM Pris Dur 87-97; Chapl HM Pris Acklington 97-98; Asst Chapl 98-02; P-in-c Shilbottle *Newc* 98-07; P-in-c Chevington 03-07; rtd 07. *2 Crowley Place, Newton Aycliffe DL5 4JH* Tel (01325) 312872

DIXON, Eric. b 31. MPS. EMMTC 78. d 81 p 82. NSM Kirk Langley *Derby* 81-96; NSM Mackworth All SS 81-96; Perm to Offic from 96. *5 Wentworth Close, Mickleover, Derby DE3 9YE* Tel (01332) 516546

DIXON, Mrs Francesca Dorothy. b 52. Cam Univ MA73. Qu Coll Birm 81. dss 84 d 87 p 94. W Bromwich All SS *Lich* 84-94; Par Dn 87-94; C 94; Chapl Burrswood Chr Cen *Roch* 95; Perm to Offic *Chich* 97-04; Lic to Offic from 04. *46 Arun Vale, Coldwaltham, Pulborough RH20 1LP* Tel (01798) 872177

DIXON, John Kenneth. b 40. Linc Th Coll 79. d 81 p 82. C Goldington *St Alb* 81-85; V Cardington 85-94; RD Elstow 89-94; R Clifton 94-95; P-in-c Southill 94-95; R Clifton and Southill 95-05; RD Shefford 95-01; rtd 05. *7 Milton Fields, Brixham TQ5 0BH* Tel (01803) 854396 E-mail eidyn@cainnech.fsworld.co.uk

DIXON, John Scarth. b 69. Aber Univ MA92. Westcott Ho Cam 95. d 98 p 99. C Walney Is *Carl* 98-01; R Harrington 01-06; V Hawkshead and Low Wray w Sawrey and Rusland etc from 06. *The Vicarage, Vicarage Lane, Hawkshead, Ambleside LA22 0PD* Tel (015394) 36301 E-mail jjcdixon@btinternet.com

DIXON, Karen Belinda. See BEST, Miss Karen Belinda

DIXON, Kenneth. See DIXON, John Kenneth

DIXON, Lorraine. b 65. Leeds Univ BA96. Qu Coll Birm BD98. d 98 p 99. C Potternewton *Ripon* 98-01; Chapl Ches Univ 01-05; Min Can Ches Cathl 04-05; Deanery Missr to Young Adults Yardley & Bordsley *Birm* from 05. *26-28 Lincoln Street, Birmingham B12 9EX* Tel 0121-440 1221 E-mail l.dixon6@btopenworld.com

DIXON, Margaret Innes Goodwin. b 58. Reading Univ BA01. Ox Min Course 08. d 11. NSM Ellesborough, The Kimbles and Stoke Mandeville *Ox* from 11. *Norvic, Ballinger Road, South Heath, Great Missenden HP16 9QH* Tel (01494) 862438 Mobile 07773-017636 E-mail margaretigdixon@tinyworld.co.uk

DIXON, Michael. See DIXON, Edward Michael

DIXON, Nicholas Scarth. b 30. G&C Coll Cam BA54 MA63. Westcott Ho Cam 55. d 56 p 57. C Walney Is *Carl* 56-59; CF 59-62; V Whitehaven Ch Ch w H Trin *Carl* 62-70; R Blofield w Hemblington *Nor* 70-77; P-in-c Bowness *Carl* 77-79; R 79-81; V Frizington and Arlecdon 81-87; V Barton, Pooley Bridge and Martindale 87-95; rtd 95; Perm to Offic *Carl* from 95. *7 Mayburgh Avenue, Penrith CA11 8PA* Tel (01768) 892864

DIXON, Canon Peter. b 36. Qu Coll Ox BA58 MA62 Birm Univ BD65 PhD75. Qu Coll Birm. d 60 p 61. C Mountain Ash *Llan* 60-63; C Penrhiwceiber w Matthewstown and Ynysboeth 63-68; P-in-c 68-70; V Bronllys w Llanfilo *S & B* 70-02; Bp's Chapl for Readers 80-02; Bp's Chapl for Th Educn 83-02; Warden of Readers 92-02; RD Hay 90-02; Can Res Brecon Cathl 98-02; rtd

02. *22 The Caerpound, Hay-on-Wye, Hereford HR3 5DU* Tel (01497) 820775
DIXON, Peter. b 70. Ex Univ BTh08. SWMTC 04. **d** 07 **p** 08. C Redruth w Lanner and Treleigh *Truro* 07-10; V Wisborough Green *Chich* from 10. *The Vicarage, Glebe Way, Wisborough Green, Billingshurst RH14 0DZ* Tel (01403) 700339
E-mail peter.dixon@btinternet.com
DIXON, Peter David. b 48. Edin Univ BSc71 MIMechE. Edin Dioc NSM Course 75. **d** 79 **p** 80. NSM Prestonpans *Edin* 79-89; NSM Musselburgh 79-89; NSM Edin St Luke 90; P-in-c Edin St Barn from 91. *8 Oswald Terrace, Prestonpans EH32 9EG* Tel (01875) 812985
DIXON, Philip. b 48. Leeds Univ BSc69 Open Univ BA91. St Jo Coll Nottm 77. **d** 80 **p** 81. C Soundwell *Bris* 80-82; C Stoke Bishop 82-84; TV Hemel Hempstead *St Alb* 84-85; Chapl Westonbirt Sch from 85; Perm to Offic *Bris* from 86. *East Lodge, Westonbirt, Tetbury GL8 8QE* Tel (01666) 880345
E-mail pdnovenove@yahoo.com
DIXON, Philip Roger. b 54. CCC Ox BA77 MA80. Oak Hill Th Coll BA80. **d** 80 **p** 81. C Droylsden St Mary *Man* 80-84; TV Rochdale 84-91; V Audenshaw St Steph from 91; AD Ashton-under-Lyne 03-08. *St Stephen's Vicarage, 176 Stamford Road, Audenshaw, Manchester M34 5WW* Tel 0161-370 1863
E-mail ssaudenshaw@aol.com
DIXON, Robert. b 50. Univ of Wales (Lamp) BA80 Sussex Univ MA04. Chich Th Coll 80. **d** 81 **p** 82. C Maidstone St Martin *Cant* 81-84; Chapl HM Youth Cust Cen Dover 84-88; C All Hallows by the Tower etc *Lon* 88-90; P-in-c Southwick H Trin *Dur* 90-97; R 97; R Etchingham *Chich* 97-10; V Hurst Green 97-10; V Bedford Leigh *Man* from 10. *St Thomas's Vicarage, 121 Green Lane, Leigh WN7 2TW* Tel (01942) 673519 Mobile 07779-121169 E-mail sussexrob@aol.com
DIXON, Roger John. b 33. Magd Coll Cam BA58 MA61. EAMTC 78. **d** 79 **p** 80. NSM Fakenham w Alethorpe *Nor* 79-82; C Brandeston w Kettleburgh *St E* 82-84; P-in-c 84-99; Asst Chapl Framlingham Coll 82-99; RD Loes *St E* 97-98; rtd 99; Perm to Offic *Nor* 99-05 and *Llan* from 05. *9 The Crescent, Fairwater, Cardiff CF5 3DF* Tel (029) 2056 6031
DIXON, Ms Sheila. b 46. Open Univ BA78 Trent Poly CertEd79. St Jo Coll Nottm 93. **d** 93 **p** 94. Par Dn Ordsall *S'well* 93-94; C 94-97; P-in-c Sutton w Carlton and Normanton upon Trent etc 97-11; P-in-c Norwell w Ossington, Cromwell and Caunton 05-11; rtd 11. *8 Cherry Avenue, Malton YO17 7DE*
E-mail sdixonrev@btinternet.com
DIXON, Stephen William. b 53. Nottm Univ BA75 Man Metrop Univ PGCE88 Liv Univ MTh00. NOC 96. **d** 99 **p** 00. NSM Meltham *Wakef* 99-02; NSM Upper Holme Valley from 02; Lic Preacher *Man* from 01. *83 Totties, Holmfirth HD9 1UJ* Tel (01484) 687376 E-mail familymasondixon@uwclub.net
DIXON, Mrs Teresa Mary. b 61. Southn Univ BSc82 Ball Coll Ox PGCE83. EAMTC 99. **d** 02 **p** 03. NSM Sutton and Witcham w Mepal *Ely* 02-04; C Littleport 04-06; NSM Witchford w Wentworth from 06. *Ash Tree Farm, A Furlong Drove, Little Downham, Ely CB6 2EW* Tel (01353) 699552
E-mail revteresa@googlemail.com
DNISTRIANSKYJ, Stefan Myron. b 61. Leic Univ BSc82 Ches Coll of HE BTh02. NOC 99. **d** 02 **p** 03. C Halliwell St Luke *Man* 02-06; TV New Bury w Gt Lever 06-09; P-in-c Anchorsholme *Blackb* from 09. *The Vicarage, 36 Valeway Avenue, Thornton-Cleveleys FY5 3RN* Tel (01253) 823904 Mobile 07931-785598
E-mail dnists@gmail.com
DOARKS, Andrew John. b 68. Leic Univ BA91 De Montfort Univ MSc92. St Mellitus Coll BA08. **d** 11. C Brislington St Luke from 11. *119 Birchwood Road, Bristol BS4 4RB* Tel 0117-908 5715 Mobile 07970-495654 E-mail adoarks@gmail.com
DOBB, Christopher. b 46. Dur Univ BA68. Cuddesdon Coll 68. **d** 70 **p** 71. C Portsea St Mary *Portsm* 70-73; Lic to Offic *S'wark* 73-77; Perm to Offic *Bris* 77-79; Lic to Offic 79-81; V Swindon St Aug 81-98; rtd 98. *Kingsbury Hall, The Green, Calne SN11 8DG* Tel (01249) 821521 Fax 817246
E-mail kingsburyhallcd@aol.com
DOBBIE, Charles William Granville. b 49. OBE92. Wycliffe Hall Ox 94. **d** 96 **p** 97. C Morriston *S & B* 96-00; Asst Chapl Morriston Hosp/Ysbyty Treforys NHS Trust 97-00; V Lyonsdown H Trin *St Alb* from 00. *Holy Trinity Vicarage, 18 Lyonsdown Road, Barnet EN5 1JE* Tel (020) 8216 3786
E-mail charles@holytrinitylyonsdown.org.uk
DOBBIE, Gary William. b 51. St Andr Univ MA75 BD77 Magd Coll Cam CertEd80 FRSA98 FSAScot. Coll of Resurr Mirfield 83. **d** 83 **p** 83. Kimbolton Sch 83-84; Hon C Kimbolton *Ely* 83-84; Sen Chapl Ch Hosp Horsham 86-96; Asst Chapl 96-03; Housemaster 93-03; Chapl Shrewsbury Sch from 03. *Shrewsbury School, Kingsland, Shrewsbury SY3 7BA* Tel (01743) 280550 Mobile 07879-426056 E-mail chaplain@shrewsbury.org.uk
DOBBIN, Canon Charles Philip. b 51. Jes Coll Cam BA73 MA77 Oriel Coll Ox BA75 MA88. St Steph Ho Ox 74. **d** 76 **p** 77. C New Addington *Cant* 76-79; C Melton Mowbray w Thorpe Arnold *Leic* 79-83; V Loughb Gd Shep 83-89; V Ashby-de-la-Zouch St Helen w Coleorton 89-00; RD Akeley W 93-00; Hon

Can *Leic* Cathl 94-00; TR Moor Allerton *Ripon* 00-09; TR Moor Allerton and Shadwell from 09; Dioc Interfaith Relns Officer from 09. *St John's Rectory, 1 Fir Tree Lane, Leeds LS17 7BZ* Tel 0113-268 4598 E-mail cdobbin@aol.com
DOBBIN, Harold John. b 47. Liv Univ BSc69. St Steph Ho Ox 70. **d** 73 **p** 74. C Newbold w Dunston *Derby* 73-77; C Leckhampton SS Phil and Jas w Cheltenham St Jas *Glouc* 77-80; V Hebburn St Cuth *Dur* 80-86; R Barlborough *Derby* 86-95; P-in-c Alfreton 95-00; V 00-04; RD Alfreton 02-04; P-in-c Clifton 04-08; P-in-c Norbury w Snelston 04-08; rtd 08. *21 Dale Close, Fritchley, Belper DE56 2HZ* E-mail harolddobbin@yahoo.co.uk
DOBBIN, Miss Penelope Jane. b 59. GRSC88. SAOMC 96. **d** 99 **p** 00. C Bideford, Northam, Westward Ho!, Appledore etc *Ex* 99-05; TV from 05; V Minehead *B & W* from 11. *7 Paganel Road, Minehead TA24 5ET*
E-mail penelopedobbin@btinternet.com
DOBBINS, Lorraine Sharon. b 72. Ripon Coll Cuddesdon BTh01. **d** 01 **p** 02. C Talbot Village *Sarum* 01-05; TV Preston w Sutton Poyntz and Osmington w Poxwell from 05. *2 Primula Close, Weymouth DT3 6SL*
E-mail lorrainedobbins@hotmail.com
DOBBS, George Christopher. b 43. Linc Th Coll 66. **d** 68 **p** 69. C Hykeham *Linc* 68-71; Asst Master Heneage Sch Grimsby 71-78; Perm to Offic *S'well* 78-80; TV Chelmsley Wood *Birm* 80-84; TV Rochdale *Man* 84-99; V Sudden St Aidan and C Castleton Moor 00-08; rtd 08; Perm to Offic *Man* from 08. *9 Highlands, Littleborough OL15 0DS* Tel (01706) 377688
E-mail g3rjv@gqpr.demon.co.uk
DOBBS, Matthew Joseph. b 62. St Mich Coll Llan BTh04. **d** 04 **p** 05. C Llantwit Major 04-08; TV Monkton *St D* 08-09. *42 Llanmead Gardens, Rhoose, Barry CF62 3HX*
E-mail matthew@mdobbs.freeserve.co.uk
DOBBS, Michael John. b 48. Linc Th Coll 74. **d** 77 **p** 78. C Warsop *S'well* 77-82; V Worksop St Paul 82-89; P-in-c Mansfield St Mark 89-03; V Kirk Hallam *Derby* 03-05; rtd 05; Perm to Offic *S'well* from 06. *30 Waverley Road, Mansfield NG18 5AG* E-mail mjdmjd@ntlworld.com
DOBELL (née PRICE), Mrs Alison Jane. b 63. Aston Tr Scheme 91 Westcott Ho Cam 93. **d** 95 **p** 96. C Upper Norwood All SS *S'wark* 95-99; V Mitcham St Barn 99-07. *74 Radway Road, Southampton SO15 7PJ* Tel (023) 8077 3631
E-mail alisonjane.price@btinternet.com
DOBLE, Dominic Julian Anderson. b 71. Wye Coll Lon BSc92 Univ of Wales (Ban) MSc99 Leeds Univ BA10. Coll of Resurr Mirfield 08. **d** 10. C Crediton, Shobrooke and Sandford etc *Ex* from 10. *50 Beech Park, Crediton EX17 1HW* Tel (01363) 777924 Mobile 07743-554955
E-mail dominic.doble@thephone.coop
DOBLE, Mrs Maureen Mary Thompson. b 44. RGN65. S Dios Minl Tr Scheme 90. **d** 93 **p** 94. NSM Kingston St Mary w Broomfield etc *B & W* 93-07; Chapl Taunton and Somerset NHS Trust 03-07; rtd 07; Perm to Offic *B & W* from 07. *Rosebank, Lyngford Lane, Taunton TA2 7LL* Tel (01823) 286772
DOBLE, Peter. b 29. Univ of Wales (Cardiff) BA51 Fitzw Coll Cam BA54 MA58 St Edm Hall Ox MA68 Leeds Univ PhD92. Wesley Ho Cam 52. **d** 55 **p** 58. In Ch of S India 55-60; In Meth Ch 60-64; Hd of RE Qu Mary Sch Lytham St Annes *Blackb* 64-67; Lect RS Culham Coll Abingdon *Ox* 67-69; Sen Lect 69-74; Prin Lect and Hd Relig Studies 74-80; Perm to Offic *York* from 80; Dir York RE Cen 80-94; Sen Fell Th and RS Leeds Univ 95-98; Hon Lect from 98. *6 Witham Drive, Huntington, York YO32 9YD* Tel (01904) 761288
E-mail peter.doble@btinternet.com
DOBSON, Catherine Heather. b 71. ERMC. **d** 09 **p** 10. NSM Broughton w Loddington and Cransley etc *Pet* 09-11; C from 11; C Rothwell w Orton, Rushton w Glendon and Pipewell from 11. *6A Kipton Close, Rothwell, Kettering NN14 6DR* Tel (01536) 357945 E-mail catherine.dobson2@virgin.net
DOBSON, Christopher John. b 62. Univ of Wales (Abth) BA83. Wycliffe Hall Ox BA88. **d** 89 **p** 90. C Biggin Hill *Roch* 89-92; C Tunbridge Wells St Jas w St Phil 92-95; USPG Zimbabwe 95-99; V Paddock Wood *Roch* 00-08; Dioc Ecum and Global Partnership Officer *Bris* from 08; Hon C Downend from 09. *St John's Vicarage, Mayfield Park, Bristol BS16 3NW* Tel 0117-965 0878 Mobile 07904-831829
E-mail chris.j.dobson@gmail.com
or chris.dobson@bristoldiocese.org
DOBSON, Geoffrey Norman. b 46. Leeds Univ CertEd68 Open Univ BA77 MA05 ACP70. Wells Th Coll 71. **d** 74 **p** 75. C Wanstead H Trin Hermon Hill *Chelmsf* 74-76; Colchester Adnry Youth Chapl 76-78; C Halstead St Andr w H Trin and Greenstead Green 76-78; Asst Dir Educn (Youth) *Carl* 78-82; P-in-c Kirkandrews-on-Eden w Beaumont and Grinsdale 78-82; V Illingworth *Wakef* 82-86; V Roxton w Gt Barford *St Alb* 86-93; Chapl N Man Health Care NHS Trust 93-98; P-in-c Newton Heath St Wilfrid and St Anne *Man* 93-97; C Newton Heath 97-98; P-in-c Alconbury cum Weston *Ely* 98-00; P-in-c Buckworth 98-00; P-in-c Gt w Lt Stukeley 98-00; Perm to Offic

from 02. *30 Lees Lane, Southoe, St Neots PE19 5YG* Tel (01480) 475474 E-mail geoffreyndobson@aol.com

DOBSON, Mrs Joanna Jane Louise. b 61. Coll of Ripon & York St Jo BEd83. NEOC 98. **d** 01 **p** 02. NSM Scalby *York* 01-04; V Bridlington Em 04-08; P-in-c Skipsea w Ulrome and Barmston w Fraisthorpe 04-08; Pioneer Min Retford Deanery *S'well* 08-10; P-in-c Mitford and Hebron *Newc* from 10. *The Vicarage, Stable Green, Mitford, Morpeth NE61 3PZ* Tel (01670) 511468 Mobile 07828-181506 E-mail revjoannadobson@yahoo.co.uk

DOBSON, Canon John Richard. b 64. Van Mildert Coll Dur BA87. Ripon Coll Cuddesdon 87. **d** 89 **p** 90. C Benfieldside *Dur* 89-92; C Darlington St Cuth 92-96; C-in-c Blackwell All SS and Salutation CD 96-98; V Blackwell All SS and Salutation from 98; P-in-c Coniscliffe from 04; AD Darlington from 01; Hon Can Dur Cathl from 08. *104 Blackwell Lane, Darlington DL3 8QQ* Tel (01325) 354503 E-mail john.dobson@durham.anglican.org

DOBSON, Owen James. b 83. Ex Univ BA04. Westcott Ho Cam 08. **d** 10 **p** 11. C St John's Wood *Lon* from 10. *3 Cochrane Street, London NW8 7PA* Tel 07891-890837 (mobile) E-mail owenjamesdobson@hotmail.com

DOBSON, Philip Albert. b 52. Lanc Univ BA73 CertEd74. Trin Coll Bris 89. **d** 90. C Grenoside *Sheff* 89-92; C Cove St Jo *Guildf* 92-93; TV 93-96; V Camberley St Martin Old Dean 96-07; TR Bushbury *Lich* from 07. *The Rectory, 382 Bushbury Lane, Wolverhampton WV10 8JP* Tel (01902) 787688 E-mail philipdobson1@tiscali.co.uk

DOBSON, Stuart Joseph. b 51. Westmr Coll Ox BA85. Chich Th Coll 86. **d** 88 **p** 89. C Costessey *Nor* 88-90; C Chaddesden St Phil *Derby* 90-92; C Friern Barnet St Jas *Lon* 92-93; TV Plymouth Em, Efford and Laira *Ex* 93-96; P-in-c Laira 96; R Withington St Crispin *Man* 96-98; P-in-c Beguildy and Heyope *S & B* 98-00; P-in-c Llangynllo and Bleddfa 99-00; TV Bruton and Distr *B & W* 00-01; Community Chapl *Linc* from 09. *The Vicarage, Station Road, Sutterton, Boston PE20 2JH* Tel (01205) 461294 E-mail stuart.dobson@btinternet.com

DOCHERTY, William Sales Hill. b 54. Open Univ BA96 Callendar Park Coll of Educn Falkirk DipEd75. TISEC 98. **d** 05 **p** 06. C Broughty Ferry *Bre* 05-09; C Heswall *Ches* 09-11; V Grange St Andr from 11. *The Vicarage, 37 Lime Grove, Runcorn WA7 5JZ* Tel (01928) 574411 E-mail therevdoc@btinternet.com

✠**DOCKER, The Rt Revd Ivor Colin.** b 25. Birm Univ BA46 St Cath Soc Ox BA49 MA52. Wycliffe Hall Ox 46. **d** 49 **p** 50 **c** 75. C Normanton *Wakef* 49-52; C Halifax St Jo Bapt 52-54; Area Sec (Dios Derby Linc and S'well) CMS 54-58; Metrop Sec (S) 58-59; V Midhurst *Chich* 59-64; RD Midhurst 61-64; R Woolbeding 61-64; V Seaford w Sutton 64-71; RD Seaford 64-71; Can and Preb Chich Cathl 66-91; V Eastbourne St Mary 71-75; RD Eastbourne 71-75; Suff Bp Horsham 75-84; Area Bp Horsham 84-91; rtd 91; Asst Bp Ex from 91. *Braemar, Bradley Road, Bovey Tracey, Newton Abbot TQ13 9EU* Tel (01626) 832468

DOCKREE, Peter Martin. b 74. Keele Univ BA96 Ox Univ MSc00. Ox Min Course 07. **d** 10 **p** 11. C Wolverton *Ox* from 10. *62 Anson Road, Wolverton, Milton Keynes MK12 5BP* Tel (01908) 315338 Mobile 07972-439865 E-mail peter.dockree@yahoo.co.uk

DODD, Alan Henry. b 42. Man Univ BA70 MA79. Chich Th Coll 82. **d** 82 **p** 83. C Fareham H Trin *Portsm* 82-84; TV 84-89; V Osmotherley w Harlsey and Ingleby Arncliffe *York* 89-05; RD Mowbray 02-04; Chapl Northallerton Health Services NHS Trust 92-05; rtd 06; Perm to Offic *Ripon* from 06. *3 Nightingale Close, Brompton on Swale, Richmond DL10 7TR* Tel (01748) 810147 E-mail thedodds178@btinternet.com

DODD, Andrew Patrick. b 68. Hatf Poly BEng91 Selw Coll Cam BTh00. Westcott Ho Cam 97. **d** 00 **p** 01. C New Addington *S'wark* 00-04; R Newington St Mary from 04; AD S'wark and Newington from 07. *The Rectory, 57 Kennington Park Road, London SE11 4JQ* Tel (020) 7735 2807 or 7735 1894 E-mail rector@stmarynewington.org.uk

DODD, Miss Denise Kate. b 72. Cranmer Hall Dur 07. **d** 09 **p** 10. C Porchester *S'well* from 09. *127A Digby Avenue, Nottingham NG3 6DT* Tel 0115-987 7938 E-mail denisekdodd@yahoo.co.uk

DODD, Jane. b 33. Loughb Univ ALA51 FLA51. **d** 98 **p** 99. OLM Wroxham w Hoveton and Belaugh *Nor* 98-08; Perm to Offic from 08. *Locheil, Tunstead Road, Hoveton, Norwich NR12 8QN* Tel (01603) 782509

DODD, Mrs Jean. b 47. **d** 98 **p** 99. OLM Irlam *Man* from 98; OLM Cadishead from 09. *75 Harewood Road, Manchester M44 6DL* Tel 0161-775 9125

DODD, John Stanley. b 24. Huron Coll Ontario 46. **d** 50 **p** 51. C Kitchener Canada 50-52; Leeds St Jo Ev *Ripon* 52-54; C High Harrogate Ch Ch 54-58; V Stainburn 58-65; V Weeton 58-64; V Meanwood 65-89; rtd 89; Perm to Offic *Ripon* from 89. *3 Shawdene, Burton Crescent, Leeds LS6 4DN* Tel 0113-278 9069

DODD, Malcolm Ogilvie. b 46. Dur Univ BSc67 Loughb Univ MSc90. Edin Th Coll 67. **d** 70 **p** 71. C Hove All SS *Chich* 70-73;

C Crawley 73-78; P-in-c Rusper 79-83; Chapl Brighton Coll Jun Sch 83; Chapl Stancliffe Hall Sch 84-97; rtd 01. *210 chemin des Villecrozes, 26170 Buis-les-Baronnies, France* Tel (0033) 4 75 28 05 99 E-mail m.et.j.dodd@wanadoo.fr

DODD, Michael Christopher. b 33. Ch Coll Cam BA55 MA59. Ridley Hall Cam 57. **d** 59 **p** 60. C Stechford *Birm* 59-62; V Quinton Road W St Boniface 62-72; TV Paston *Pet* 72-77; TR Hodge Hill *Birm* 77-89; rtd 90; Perm to Offic *Birm* from 90. *39 Regency Gardens, Birmingham B14 4JS* Tel 0121-474 6945

DODD, Canon Peter Curwen. b 33. St Jo Coll Cam BA57 FRSA93. Linc Th Coll 58 Wm Temple Coll Rugby 59. **d** 60 **p** 61. C Eastwood *Sheff* 60-63; Ind Chapl 63-67; Ind Chapl *Newc* 67-98; RD Newc E 78-83 and 92-95; Hon Can Newc Cathl 82-98; rtd 98; Perm to Offic *Newc* from 98. *Glenesk, 26 The Oval, Benton, Newcastle upon Tyne NE12 9PP* Tel 0191-266 1293

DODDS, Alan Richard. b 46. Greenwich Univ BA92 K Coll Lon MA94. **d** 95 **p** 96. C Deal St Geo *Cant* 95-99; C-in-c Deal, The Carpenter's Arms 98-99; Prin OLM Course 99-01; TV Cullompton, Willand, Uffculme, Kentisbeare etc *Ex* 02-07; rtd 07. *Green Pastures, Smithincott Farm, Uffculme, Cullompton EX15 3EF* Tel (01884) 841801 E-mail alan.and.chris@tesco.net

DODDS, Brian Martin. b 37. AKC62. **d** 63 **p** 64. C Morpeth *Newc* 63-67; C Georgetown Cathl Guyana 67-69; V Morawhanna 69-71; V Willington 71-74; TV Brayton *York* 75-79; V Gravelly Hill *Birm* 79-83; V Winterton *Linc* 83-85; V Winterton Gp 85-90; V Gainsborough St Jo 90-96; V Morton 95-96; R Walesby 96-00; rtd 00; Perm to Offic *Linc* from 01. *69 Pennell Street, Lincoln LN5 7TD* Tel (01522) 512593 E-mail bmdodds@talk21.com

DODDS, Canon Graham Michael. b 58. Liv Univ MA01 Bris Univ PhD08 LTCL80 GTCL80 York Univ PGCE81. Trin Coll Bris 84. **d** 84 **p** 85. C Reigate St Mary *S'wark* 84-91; P-in-c Bath Walcot *B & W* 91-93; R 93-96; Dir Reader Studies from 96; Lay Tr Adv 96-01; Asst Dir Min Development 01-04; Prin Sch of Formation 04-10; Dir of Learning Communities from 10; Preb Wells Cathl from 03; Can Res and Treas Wells Cathl from 10. *2 The Liberty, Wells BA5 2SU* Tel (01749) 670607 or 670777 Fax 674240 Mobile 07702-658687 E-mail graham.dodds@bathwells.anglican.org

DODDS, Linda. b 54. **d** 08 **p** 09. OLM Bishop Auckland Woodhouse Close CD *Dur* from 08. *30 Low Etherley, Bishop Auckland DL14 0EU* Tel (01388) 832756 E-mail linda_dodds@yahoo.co.uk

DODDS, The Ven Norman Barry. b 43. Open Univ BA. CITC 73. **d** 76 **p** 77. C Ballynafeigh St Jude *D & D* 76-80; I Belfast St Mich *Conn* from 80; Chapl HM Pris Belfast from 84; Can Belf Cathl from 98; Adn Belfast *Conn* from 07. *5 Sunningdale Park, Belfast BT14 6RU* Tel and fax (028) 9071 5463 Mobile 07763-935160 E-mail doddscavehill@yahoo.com

DODDS, Peter. b 35. WMMTC 88 Qu Coll Birm 88. **d** 91 **p** 92. NSM Hartshill *Cov* 91-93; NSM Nuneaton St Mary 94-95; Hon Chapl Geo Eliot Hosp NHS Trust Nuneaton from 95; Hon Chapl Mary Ann Evans Hospice from 95; NSM Camp Hill w Galley Common *Cov* 99-01; Perm to Offic from 02. *Wem House, 51 Magyar Crescent, Nuneaton CV11 4SQ* Tel (024) 7638 4061

DODGE, Robin Dennis. b 58. Cornell Univ NY BA80 Boston Univ JD83. Virginia Th Sem MDiv99. **d** 98 **p** 99. C Arlington St Mary USA 98-02; C Bris St Mary Redcliffe w Temple etc 02-05; R Washington St Dav USA from 05. *5150 Macomb Street NW, Washington DC 20016, USA* Tel (001) (202) 966 2093 Fax 966 3437 E-mail robindodge@starpower.net

DODHIA, Hitesh Kishorilal. b 57. Cranmer Hall Dur 85. **d** 88 **p** 89. C Leamington Priors All SS *Cov* 88-91; Chapl HM YOI Glen Parva 91-92; Asst Chapl 94-98; Chapl HM Pris Roch 92-94; The Mount 98-01; Perm to Offic St Alb from 02. *Address withheld by request* E-mail dodhias@hotmail.com

DODSON, Canon Gordon. b 31. Em Coll Cam BA54 MA58 LLB55 LLM01 Barrister 56. Ridley Hall Cam 57. **d** 59 **p** 60. C Belhus Park *Chelmsf* 59-60; C Barking St Marg 60-63; CMS 63-67; C New Malden and Coombe *S'wark* 67-69; V Snettisham *Nor* 69-81; RD Heacham and Rising 76-81; P-in-c Reepham and Hackford w Whitwell and Kerdiston 81-83; P-in-c Salle 81-83; P-in-c Thurning w Wood Dalling 81-83; R Reepham, Hackford w Whitwell, Kerdiston etc 83-94; Hon Can Nor Cathl 85-94; rtd 94; Perm to Offic *Nor* from 94. *Poppygate, 2 The Loke, Cromer NR27 9DH* Tel (01263) 511811

DODSON, James Peter. b 32. Lich Th Coll 58. **d** 61 **p** 62. C Chasetown *Lich* 61-63; C Hednesford 63-68; V Halifax St Hilda *Wakef* 68-76; V Upperthong 76-85; TV York All SS Pavement w St Crux and St Martin etc 85-90; rtd 92; Perm to Offic *Ripon* from 92. *Roseville, Studley Road, Ripon HG4 2QH* Tel (01765) 602053

DODSWORTH, George Brian Knowles. b 34. Open Univ BSc94. St Mich Coll Llan 59. **d** 62 **p** 63. C Kidderminster St Mary *Worc* 62-67; Asst Chapl HM Pris Man 67-68; Chapl HM Pris Eastchurch 68-70; Chapl HM Pris Wakef 70-74; Chapl HM Pris Wormwood Scrubs 74-83; Asst Chapl Gen of Pris (SE) 83-90; Asst Chapl Gen of Pris (HQ) 90-94; Chapl HM Pris Brixton 94-95; rtd 95; Perm to Offic *S'wark* from 95. *19 Farnsworth*

Court, West Parkside, London SE10 0QF Tel and fax (020) 8305 0283 E-mail briandodsworth611@btinternet.com

DODWELL, Andrew. b 75. Man Univ BSc96 MSc98. SWMTC 06. **d** 08. C Barnstaple *Ex* from 08. *28 Old School Road, Barnstaple EX32 9DP* Tel (01271) 371068 E-mail andyandcarolyn.dodwell@virgin.net

DOE, Martin Charles. b 54. Lon Univ BSc(Econ)75 PGCE87 MA95. St Steph Ho Ox 89. **d** 91 **p** 92. C Portsea St Mary *Portsm* 91-94; Chapl Abbey Grange High Sch Leeds 94-00; Sen Angl Chapl Scarborough and NE Yorks Healthcare NHS Trust from 00. *Scarborough Hospital, Woodlands Drive, Scarborough YO12 6QL* Tel (01723) 342500 E-mail martin.doe@acute.sney.nhs.uk

✠**DOE, The Rt Revd Michael David.** b 47. St Jo Coll Dur BA69 Bath Univ Hon LLD02. Ripon Hall Ox 69. **d** 72 **p** 73 **c** 94. C St Helier *S'wark* 72-76; Youth Sec BCC 76-81; C-in-c Blackbird Leys CD *Ox* 81-88; V Blackbird Leys 88-89; RD Cowley 86-89; Soc Resp Adv *Portsm* 89-94; Can Res Portsm Cathl 89-94; Suff Bp Swindon *Bris* 94-04; Gen Sec USPG 04-11; rtd 11; Preacher Gray's Inn from 11; Hon Asst Bp S'wark from 04. *405 West Carriage House, Royal Carriage Mews, London SE18 6GA* Tel (020) 3259 3841 E-mail michaeldd@btinternet.com

DOE, Mrs Priscilla Sophia. b 41. LRAM61. SEITE 97. **d** 00 **p** 01. NSM Maidstone All SS and St Phil w Tovil *Cant* 00-11; Perm to Offic from 11. *Mount St Laurence, High Street, Cranbrook TN17 3EW* Tel (01580) 712330

DOEL, Patrick Stephen. b 71. Peterho Cam BA92 MA97. Wycliffe Hall Ox BA01 MA06 MSt03. **d** 03 **p** 04. C Blackheath St Jo *S'wark* 03-06; P-in-c Deptford St Nic and St Luke 06-08; V 08-10; V Walmley *Birm* from 10. *The Vicarage, 2 Walmley Road, Sutton Coldfield B76 1QN* E-mail steve@doel.org

DOERR, Mrs Anne. b 55. Man Univ BA76. SEITE 06. **d** 09 **p** 10. NSM Belmont *S'wark* from 09. *14 Central Way, Carshalton SM5 3NF* Tel (020) 8669 2494 Mobile 07811-908731 E-mail aedoerr@btinternet.com

DOGGETT, Margaret Ann. b 36. Open Univ BA78 Homerton Coll Cam PGCE79. **d** 96 **p** 97. OLM Pulham Market, Pulham St Mary and Starston *Nor* 96-99; OLM Dickleburgh and The Pulhams 99-01; rtd 02; Perm to Offic *Nor* from 02. *Antares, Station Road, Pulham St Mary, Diss IP21 4QT* Tel and fax (01379) 676662 Mobile 07710-621547 E-mail john.doggett@btinternet.com

DOHERTY, Mrs Christine. b 46. SEN72. STETS 97. **d** 00 **p** 01. NSM Framfield *Chich* 00-03; C Seaford w Sutton from 03. *St Luke's House, 16 Saltwood Road, Seaford BN25 3SP* Tel (01323) 892969 E-mail chris.doh@virgin.net

DOHERTY, Deana Rosina Mercy. b 21. St Aid Coll Dur BA55. dss 82 **d** 87 **p** 94. Sutton St Jas and Wawne *York* 82-95; Par Dn 87-94; C 94-95; Perm to Offic 95-99; rtd 98. *Alana, Chapel Street, Lismore, Co Waterford, Republic of Ireland* Tel (00353) (58) 54418

DOHERTY, Sean William. d 07 **p** 08. C Cricklewood St Gabr and St Mich *Lon* 07-10; Lect St Paul's Th Cen 08-10; Tutor from 10. *20 Bramley House, Bramley Road, London W10 6SX* Tel (020) 8960 8986 Mobile 07710-515800 E-mail sean.doherty@theology.ox.ac.uk

DOHERTY, Thomas Alexander. b 48. Chich Th Coll 73. **d** 76 **p** 77. V Choral Derry Cathl 76-79; C Llandaff w Capel Llanilltern 79-80; PV Llan Cathl 80-84; V Penmark w Porthkerry 84-90; R Merthyr Dyfan 90-02; V Margam from 02. *Margam Vicarage, 59A Bertha Road, Margam, Port Talbot SA13 2AP* Tel (01639) 891067

DOICK, Paul Stephen James. b 70. Chich Univ BA10. Ripon Coll Cuddesdon 03. **d** 05 **p** 06. C Hove *Chich* 05-09; TV 09-10; V Hove St Jo from 10. *The Vicarage, 119 Holland Road, Hove BN3 1JS* Tel (01273) 725811 Mobile 07542-868602 E-mail p.doick@btinternet.com

DOIDGE, Charles William. b 44. Univ Coll Lon BSc65 MSc65 PhD72. EMMTC 93. **d** 93 **p** 94. NSM Blaby *Leic* 93-96; P-in-c Willoughby Waterleys, Peatling Magna etc 96-04; rtd 04. *21 Brunel Mews, Solsbro Road, Torquay TQ2 6QA* Tel (01803) 690548 E-mail doidge@dmu.ac.uk

DOIDGE, Valerie Gladys. b 49. STETS 98. **d** 01 **p** 02. C St Leonards St Ethelburga *Chich* 01-07; C Hollington St Leon from 07. *6 Collinswood Drive, St Leonards-on-Sea TN38 0NU* Tel (01424) 425651 E-mail valrod@rdoidge.freeserve.co.uk

DOIG, Allan George. b 51. Univ of BC BA69 K Coll Cam BA73 MA80 PhD82 FSA98. Ripon Coll Cuddesdon 86. **d** 88 **p** 89. C Abingdon *Ox* 88-91; Chapl LMH Ox from 91; Fell from 96; Select Preacher *Ox* 95-96. *Lady Margaret Hall, Oxford OX2 6QA* Tel (01865) 274300 Fax 511069 E-mail allan.doig@lmh.ox.ac.uk

DOLAN, Miss Louise. b 68. St Paul's Coll Chelt BA89 Reading Univ PGCE90. Aston Tr Scheme 92 Linc Th Coll 94 Westcott Ho Cam MA95. **d** 96 **p** 97. C N Stoneham *Win* 96-99. *19 Ipswich Grove, Norwich NR2 2LU* Tel (01603) 469865

DOLBY, Mrs Christine Teresa. b 54. Nottm Univ MA01 SRN80. EMMTC 98. **d** 01 **p** 02. C Cropwell Bishop w Colston Bassett, Granby etc *S'well* 01-05; P-in-c Ancaster Wilsford Gp *Linc*

05-08; Chapl Qu Medical Cen Nottm Univ Hosp NHS Trust from 08. *16 Morley's Close, Lowdham, Nottingham NG14 7HN* Tel 0115-966 5890 Mobile 07738-851181 E-mail c.dolby263@btinternet.com

DOLL, Canon Peter Michael. b 62. Yale Univ BA84 Ch Ch Ox DPhil89. Cuddesdon Coll BA94. **d** 95 **p** 96. C Cowley St Jo *Ox* 95-99; Chapl Worc Coll Ox 98-02; TV Abingdon *Ox* 02-09; Can Res Nor Cathl from 09. *56 The Close, Norwich NR1 4EG* Tel (01603) 218336 E-mail canonlibrarian@cathedral.org.uk

DOLLERY, Anne Mary Elizabeth. b 55. Hull Univ BA78. Ridley Hall Cam 02. **d** 04. C Thundersley *Chelmsf* 04-09; V Walthamstow St Andr from 09. *St Andrew's Vicarage, 37 Sutton Road, London E17 5QA* Tel (020) 8527 3969 E-mail annedollery@yahoo.co.uk

DOLMAN, Derek Alfred George Gerrit. b 40. ALCD64. **d** 65 **p** 66. C St Alb St Paul *St Alb* 65-68; C Bishopwearmouth St Gabr *Dur* 68-72; R Jarrow Grange 72-80; V New Catton St Luke *Nor* 80-98; V New Catton St Luke w St Aug 98-00; R S Croxton Gp *Leic* 00-06; rtd 06; Perm to Offic *Derby* and *Lich* from 07. *17 Kestrel Way, Burton-on-Trent DE15 0DJ* Tel (01283) 845330 E-mail derekdolman@uwclub.net

DOLMAN, William Frederick Gerrit. b 42. JP. K Coll Lon MB, BS65 Lon Univ LLB87 MRCS65 LRCP65. SEITE 04. **d** 06 **p** 07. NSM Beckley and Peasmarsh *Chich* from 06. *Little Bellhurst Cottage, Hobbs Lane, Beckley, Rye TN31 6TT* E-mail hmcwd@aol.com

DOLPHIN, Mark Patrick (Pads). b 58. Man Univ BSc81. St Jo Coll Nottm 06. **d** 08 **p** 09. C Reading Greyfriars *Ox* 08-11; P-in-c Reading St Matt from 11. *St Matthew's Vicarage, 205 Southcote Lane, Reading RG30 3AX* Tel 0118-957 3755 Mobile 07866-754770

DOMINIAK, Paul Anthony. b 78. Univ of the S (USA) BA05 SS Coll Cam BA07 MPhil08. Westcott Ho Cam 05. **d** 08 **p** 09. C Ingleby Barwick *York* 08-11. *Address temp unknown* Tel 07972-761831 (mobile) E-mail pdominiak@gmail.com

DOMINIC MARK, Brother. *See* IND, Dominic Mark

DOMINY, Canon Peter John. b 36. Qu Coll Ox BA60 MA64 Aber Univ MLitt83. Oak Hill Th Coll 60. **d** 62 **p** 63. C Bedworth *Cov* 62-66; Nigeria 66-67; Sudan United Miss 67-72; V Jos St Piran 72-84; R Broadwater St Mary *Chich* 84-92; TR Broadwater 92-98; P-in-c Danehill 98-99; V 99-03; Can and Preb Chich Cathl 93-03; RD Uckfield 00-03; rtd 03; Perm to Offic *Sarum* from 03. *5 St Nicholas Gardens, Durweston, Blandford Forum DT11 0QH* Tel (01258) 450975

DOMMETT, Canon Richard Radmore. b 19. St Jo Coll Ox BA41 MA45. Wells Th Coll 41. **d** 43 **p** 44. C E Dulwich St Jo *S'wark* 43-48; C Peckham St Jo 48-52; V Clapham St Pet 52-60; R Caister *Nor* 60-81; P-in-c Saxthorpe and Corpusty 81-85; P-in-c Oulton SS Pet and Paul 81-85; P-in-c Blickling w Ingworth 81-85; P-in-c Heydon w Irmingland 82-85; Hon Can Nor Cathl 77-85; rtd 85; Perm to Offic *Nor* and *St E* from 85. *14 Norwich Road, Halesworth IP19 8HN* Tel (01986) 873778

DOMMETT, Simon Paul. b 58. Warwick Univ BSc79. St Jo Coll Nottm MA99. **d** 99 **p** 00. C Weston Favell *Pet* 99-02; P-in-c Gt w Lt Harrowden and Orlingbury 02-06; P-in-c Isham w Pytchley 05-06; R Gt w Lt Harrowden and Orlingbury and Isham etc from 06. *The Vicarage, 18 Kings Lane, Little Harrowden, Wellingborough NN9 5BL* Tel (01933) 678225 E-mail rev.simon@virgin.net

DOMONEY, Canon Lynette May (Lyndy). b 44. Th Ext Educn Coll 90. **d** 92 **p** 93. S Africa 92-06; P-in-c Kessingland, Gisleham and Rushmere *Nor* 06-08; R from 08. *The Rectory, 1 Wash Lane, Kessingland, Lowestoft NR33 7QZ* Tel (01502) 740256 E-mail l.domoney@btinternet.com

DONAGHEY, Thomas Alfred. b 67. Trin Coll Bris 06. **d** 08 **p** 09. C Whittle-le-Woods *Blackb* from 08. *16 Carr Meadow, Bamber Bridge, Preston PR5 8HS* Tel (01772) 497687 Mobile 07974-457544 E-mail tdonaghey@hotmail.com

DONAGHY, Paul Robert Blount. b 56. **d** 00 **p** 01. OLM Goldsworth Park *Guildf* from 00. *5 Knightswood, Woking GU21 3PU* Tel (01483) 835503 E-mail p.donaghy@hotmail.co.uk

DONALD, Andrew William. b 19. St Jo Coll Morpeth 47 ACT ThL50. **d** 49 **p** 50. C Claremont Australia 49-50; C Perth Cathl 50-52; R Wyalkatchem 52-56; Perm to Offic *Lon* 57-58; Chapl Gothenburg *Eur* 58-65; Chapl Lausanne 65-68; Asst P Mt Lawley Australia 68-70; R Bellevue and Darlington 70-79; R Toodyay and Goomalling 79-84; rtd 84. *Eriswell, 18A Cobham Way, Camillo WA 6111, Australia* Tel (0061) (8) 9390 8425

DONALD, Brother. *See* GREEN, Donald Pentney

DONALD, Dennis Curzon. b 38. Oak Hill Th Coll 68. **d** 70 **p** 71. C Carl St Jo 70-73; Lic to Offic 73-77; Warden Blaithwaite Ho Chr Conf Cen Wigton 73-90; Chapl Cumberland Infirmary 85-92; Chapl Eden Valley Hospice Carl 92-98; rtd 98; Perm to Offic *Carl* from 77. *5 The Old Bakery, Gretna DG16 5FZ* Tel (01461) 338053

DONALD, Mrs Philippa Jane. b 58. Bath Univ BA79 Moray Ho Edin DipEd80. WEMTC 08. **d** 11. NSM Churchdown St Jo and

Innsworth *Glouc* from 11. *8 Seabroke Road, Gloucester GL1 3JH*
Tel (01452) 528569 E-mail talk2philippa@hotmail.com
DONALD, Robert Francis. b 49. St Jo Coll Nottm BTh75 LTh.
d 75 p 76. C New Barnet St Jas *St Alb* 75-79; C St Alb St Paul
79-86; C St Alb St Mary Marshalswick 86-87; Lic to Offic from
87; Dir Chr Alliance Housing Assn Ltd 87-98. *24 Meadowcroft,*
St Albans AL1 1UD Tel (01727) 841647 Mobile 07973-208289
DONALD, Rosemary Anne. b 52. STETS 99. d 02 p 03. NSM
Blendworth w Chalton w Idsworth *Portsm* 02-07; P-in-c from 07.
1A Havant Road, Horndean, Waterlooville PO8 0DB Tel (023)
9259 1719 E-mail rosemary.donald@virgin.net
DONALD, Steven. b 55. CertEd76 Hull Univ MA99. Oak Hill Th
Coll BA88. d 88 p 89. C Cheadle All Hallows *Ches* 88-91; C
Ardsley *Sheff* 91; V Kendray 92-99; P-in-c Chadderton Ch Ch
Man 99-03; V 03-05; V Carl St Jo from 05. *St John's Vicarage,*
London Road, Carlisle CA1 2QQ Tel (01228) 521601
E-mail stevedon1@aol.com
DONALD, William. b 30. Tyndale Hall Bris 58. d 61 p 62. C
Stapenhill w Cauldwell *Derby* 61-63; Perm to Offic *Ox* 63-66; Lic
to Offic *Bris* 66-70; C Cheltenham St Mark *Glouc* 70-77; C
Glouc St Jas 77-82; Lic to Offic 82-95; rtd 95; Perm to Offic
Glouc from 95. *82 Forest View Road, Gloucester GL4 0BY* Tel
(01452) 506993
DONALDSON, Miss Elizabeth Anne. b 55. Univ of Wales (Ban)
BSc76 Surrey Univ MSc80 Nottm Univ BA82. St Jo Coll Nottm
80. dss 83 d 87 p 94. Guildf Ch Ch 83-86; Cuddington 86-90; C
87-90; C Keresley and Coundon *Cov* 90-99; V Gt Amwell w
St Margaret's and Stanstead Abbots *St Alb* from 00. *The*
Vicarage, 25 Hoddesdon Road, Stanstead Abbotts, Ware
SG12 8EG Tel (01920) 870115 Pager 07666-545248
E-mail vicar@3churches.net *or* anne.donaldson@ntlworld.com
DONALDSON, Mrs Janet Elizabeth. b 53. GTCL74 Whitelands
Coll Lon CertEd75. EAMTC 95. d 98 p 99. NSM Tolleshunt
Knights w Tiptree and Gt Braxted *Chelmsf* 98-02; V Knights
and Hospitallers Par 02-11; P-in-c Deeping St James *Linc* from
11. *50 Spalding Road, Deeping St James, Peterborough PE6 8UJ*
Tel (01778) 343750 E-mail janet@amdonaldson.freeserve.co.uk
DONALDSON, Malcolm Alexander. b 48. Cranmer Hall Dur 84.
d 86 p 87. C Heworth H Trin *York* 86-89; Chapl York Distr Hosp
86-89; C Marfleet *York* 89-90; TV 90-96; R Collyhurst *Man*
96-05; rtd 05. *12 Clove Court, Tweedmouth, Berwick-upon-Tweed*
TD15 2FJ
DONALDSON, Canon Roger Francis. b 50. Jes Coll Ox BA71
MA75. Westcott Ho Cam 72. d 74 p 75. C Mold *St As* 74-78; V
Denio w Abererch *Ban* 78-95; TR Llanbeblig w Caernarfon and
Betws Garmon etc from 95; AD Arfon 04-09; Hon Can Ban
Cathl from 04. *The Rectory, 4 Ffordd Menai, Caernarfon*
LL55 1LF Tel (01286) 673750
DONALDSON, William Richard. b 56. St Cath Coll Cam BA78
MA81. Ridley Hall Cam 79. d 82 p 83. C Everton St Sav w
St Cuth *Liv* 82-85; C Reigate St Mary *S'wark* 85-89; V Easton H
Trin w St Gabr and St Lawr and St Jude *Bris* 89-99; V W Ealing
St Jo w St Jas *Lon* 99-07; Dir of Ords Willesden Area 06-07; Dir
Chr Leadership Wycliffe Hall Ox from 07. *Wycliffe Hall, 54*
Banbury Road, Oxford OX2 6PW Tel (01865) 274200
E-mail will.donaldson@wycliffe.ox.ac.uk
DONCASTER, Archdeacon of. *See* FITZHARRIS, The Ven
Robert Aidan
DONCASTER, Suffragan Bishop of. *Vacant*
DONE, Mrs Margaret. b 43. LNSM course 84 Linc Th Coll 91.
d 92 p 94. OLM Coningsby w Tattershall *Linc* 92-06; OLM Bain
Valley Gp from 06. *43 Park Lane, Coningsby, Lincoln LN4 4SW*
Tel (01526) 343013
DONE, Nigel Anthony. b 68. Wye Coll Lon BSc89. St Jo Coll Dur
BA98. d 98 p 99. C Pilton w Croscombe, N Wootton and Dinder
B & W 98-02; R Hardington Vale from 02. *The Rectory, Vicarage*
Lane, Norton St Philip, Bath BA2 7LY Tel (01373) 834447
E-mail nigel.done@btinternet.com
DONE, Roy Edward. b 46. d 11. NSM Bain Valley Gp *Linc* from
11. *43 Park Lane, Coningsby, Lincoln LN4 4SW* Tel (01526)
343013 E-mail roy.done@btinternet.com
DONEGAN-CROSS, Guy William. b 68. St Aid Coll Dur BA90.
Trin Coll Bris BA98. d 99 p 00. C Swindon Ch Ch *Bris* 99-03; V
Saltburn-by-the-Sea *York* 03-10; V Harrogate St Mark *Ripon*
from 10. *St Mark's Vicarage, 15 Wheatlands Road, Harrogate*
HG2 8BB Tel (01423) 504959
E-mail guydonegancross@yahoo.co.uk
DONELLA, Sister. *See* MATHIE, Patricia Jean
DONEY, Malcolm Charles. b 50. Lon Univ BA71 Middx Univ
BA05. NTMTC 02. d 05 p 06. NSM Tufnell Park St Geo and All
SS *Lon* 05-07; NSM W Holloway St Luke 07; NSM All Hallows
Lon Wall from 07; Perm to Offic *St E* from 10. *26 Womersley*
Road, London N8 9AN Tel (020) 8340 2060 Mobile
07812-566520 E-mail malcolmdoney@blueyonder.co.uk
DONKERSLEY, Mrs Christine Mary. b 44. K Alfred's Coll Win
CertEd65. STETS 98. d 01 p 02. NSM Baltonsborough w
Butleigh, W Bradley etc *B & W* 01-06; P-in-c Fosse Trinity from
06. *The Rectory, Folly Drive, Ditcheat, Shepton Mallet BA4 6QH*
Tel (01749) 860345 E-mail cm.donkersley@btinternet.com

DONKIN, Canon Robert. b 50. St Mich Coll Llan 71. d 74 p 75. C
Mountain Ash *Llan* 74-77; C Coity w Nolton 77-79; V Oakwood
79-84; V Aberaman and Abercwmboi 84-91; V Aberaman and
Abercwmboi w Cwmaman 91-99; R Penarth w Lavernock 99-04;
R Penarth and Llandough 04-08; AD Penarth and Barry 04-08;
R Caerphilly from 08; AD Caerphilly from 10; Hon Can Llan
Cathl from 06. *2 Clos Cae'r Wern, Caerphilly CF83 1SQ* Tel
(029) 2088 8442 E-mail robert.donkin@sky.com
DONN, Mrs Julie. b 61. Lincs & Humberside Univ BA98 Hull
Univ BA07. EMMTC 08. d 10 p 11. C Skegness Gp *Linc* from
10. *18 Danial Close, Skegness PE25 1RQ* Tel (01754) 766877
Mobile 07885-843207 E-mail revjulie.donn@btinternet.com
DONNE, Miranda. d 04 p 05. NSM Whitchurch *Ex* from 04.
Whitchurch House, Whitchurch, Tavistock PL19 9EL Tel (01822)
614552
DONNELLY, Ms Juliet Ann. b 70. K Coll Lon BD92 AKC92
PGCE93. Ripon Coll Cuddesdon 01. d 05 p 06. C Bexley St Jo
Roch 05-07; C Sidcup St Jo 07-08; Chapl Bp Justus C of E Sch
Bromley from 09. *The Vicarage, 40 Dartmouth Row, London*
SE10 8AP Tel 07910-166491 (mobile)
E-mail juliet.blessed@virgin.net
DONNELLY, Trevor Alfred. b 71. K Coll Lon BA93 AKC93.
Cuddesdon Coll 94. d 97 p 98. C Southgate Ch Ch *Lon* 97-01; V
Hinchley Wood *Guildf* 01-05; Sen Chapl Medway Secure Tr Cen
06-09; TV Deptford St Jo w H Trin and Ascension *S'wark* from
09. *The Vicarage, 40 Dartmouth Row, London SE10 8AP* Tel
(020) 8694 1074 E-mail trevordonnelly@mac.com
DONOHOE, Olive Mary Rose. b 58. TCD BA79 BTh94 MA95
CPA83. CITC 91. d 95 p 96. C Bandon Union *C, C & R* 95-98; I
Mountmellick w Coolbanagher, Rosenallis etc *M & K* 98-10;
P-in-c Stradbally w Ballintubbert, Coraclone etc *C & O* from 10.
The Rectory, 1 The Glebe, Stradbally, Co Laois, Republic of
Ireland Tel (00353) (57) 862 5173 Mobile 87-220 9945
E-mail revol@elive.ie
DONOVAN, Mrs Rosalind Margaret. b 48. Birm Univ LLB69
Bedf Coll Lon DASS73. SAOMC 95. d 98 p 99. NSM Seer
Green and Jordans *Ox* 98-03; P-in-c Wexham from 03. *The*
Rectory, 7 Grangewood, Wexham, Slough SL3 6LP Tel (01753)
523852 E-mail rosdonovan@tiscali.co.uk
DONOVAN, Mrs Rosemary Ann. b 71. La Sainte Union Coll
BTh92 Birm Univ PGCE93. Qu Coll Birm MA01. d 01. C Kings
Heath *Birm* 01-04; C Moseley St Mary and St Anne 04-11; V
Epsom Common Ch Ch *Guildf* from 11. *Christ Church Vicarage,*
20 Christ Church Road, Epsom KT19 8NE Tel (01372) 720302
E-mail rosemary.donovan@o2.co.uk
DONSON, Miss Helen Cripps. b 32. Somerville Coll Ox DipEd55
MA58. Dalton Ho Bris 58 Gilmore Ho 69. dss 79 d 87. Staines
St Pet *Lon* 80-83; Staines St Mary and St Pet 83-90; Par Dn
87-90; Par Dn Herne Bay Ch Ch *Cant* 90-92; rtd 93; Hon Par Dn
Bexhill St Aug *Chich* 93-97; Perm to Offic 97-07. *Flat 27,*
Manormead, Tilford Road, Hindhead GU26 6RA Tel (01428)
601527
DOODES, Peter John. b 45. STETS 98. d 01. NSM Ninfield and
Hooe *Chich* 01-02; NSM Hastings H Trin 02-07. *Catslide, The*
Common, Hooe, Battle TN33 9ET Tel (01424) 892329 Mobile
07718-302115 E-mail pjdoodes@hotmail.com
DOOGAN, Simon Edward. b 70. Univ of Wales (Abth) LLB93
Univ of Wales (Cardiff) LLM01 TCD BTh97. CITC 94. d 97
p 98. C Cregagh *D & D* 97-01; Dom Chapl to Bp Horsham
Chich 01-04; I Aghalee *D & D* 04-08; I Ballyholme from 08; Dioc
Registrar from 07. *Ballyholme Rectory, 3 Ward Avenue, Bangor*
BT20 5JW Tel (028) 9127 4901 *or* 9127 4912 Fax 9146 6357
E-mail simon doogan@hotmail.com
DOOLAN, Canon Leonard Wallace. b 57. St Andr Univ MA79
Ox Univ BA82 MA88. Ripon Coll Cuddesdon 80. d 83 p 84. C
High Wycombe *Ox* 83-85; C Bladon w Woodstock 85-88; C
Wootton by Woodstock 85-88; P-in-c 88-90; C Kiddington w
Asterleigh 85-88; P-in-c 88-90; P-in-c Glympton 88-90; R
Wootton w Glympton and Kiddington 90-91; TR Halesworth w
Linstead, Chediston, Holton etc *St E* 91-98; RD Halesworth
95-98; TR Ifield *Chich* 98-08; V Cirencester *Glouc* from 08; Hon
Can Douala Cameroon from 09. *The Vicarage, 1 Dollar Street,*
Cirencester GL7 2AJ Tel (01285) 653142
E-mail vicarcirencester@hotmail.com
DOOR, Hazel Lesley. b 48. Open Univ BSc99. EAMTC 01. d 04
p 05. C Poitou-Charentes *Eur* 05-07; P-in-c Brittany 07-10; Asst
Chapl Poitou-Charentes from 10. *Fortran, 86400 Linzay, France*
Tel (0033) 5 49 87 71 45 E-mail rev.hazel@wanadoo.fr
DOORES, Jennifer Mary. *See* McKENZIE, Jennifer Mary
DOORES, Canon Peter George Herbert. b 46. Hull Univ BSc67
Birm Univ PGCE68. Linc Th Coll 92. d 92 p 93. C N Stoneham
Win 92-96; V St Leonards and St Ives 96-03; P-in-c Alton
St Lawr 03-09; V Alton from 10; Hon Can Win Cathl from 09.
St Lawrence's Vicarage, Church Street, Alton GU34 2BW Tel
(01420) 83234
DORAN, Clive. b 58. St Jo Coll Nottm 99. d 01 p 02. C Maghull
Liv 01-05; V Huyton St Geo from 05; Bp's Adv on Children and

Communion from 06. *St George's Vicarage, 46 Primrose Drive, Liverpool L36 8DW* Tel 0151-489 1997
E-mail revclivedoran@yahoo.co.uk

DORAN, Edward Roy. b 47. St Jo Coll Nottm. **d** 85 **p** 86. C Roby *Liv* 85-88; V Ravenhead 88-07; TV Eccleston 07-09; V Knotty Ash St Jo from 09. *St John's Vicarage, Thomas Lane, Liverpool L14 5NR* Tel 0151-228 2396

DORANS, Robert Marshall. b 47. Open Univ BA82 Ex Univ MEd85 Dur Univ MA96. **d** 01 **p** 02. OLM Longhorsley and Hebron *Newc* 01-05. *Address temp unknown*

DORBER, The Very Revd Adrian John. b 52. St Jo Coll Dur BA74 K Coll Lon MTh91. Westcott Ho Cam 76. **d** 79 **p** 80. C Easthampstead *Ox* 79-85; P-in-c Emmer Green 85-88; Chapl Portsm Poly 88-92; Chapl Portsm Univ 92-97; Lect 91-97; Public Orator 92-97; Hon Chapl Portsm Cathl 92-97; P-in-c Brancepeth *Dur* 97-01; Dir Min and Tr 97-05; Hon Can Dur Cathl 97-05; Dean Lich from 05. *The Deanery, 16 The Close, Lichfield WS13 7LD* Tel (01543) 306250 Fax 306109
E-mail adrian.dorber@lichfield-cathedral.org

DORCHESTER, Area Bishop of. *See* FLETCHER, The Rt Revd Colin William

DORÉ, Eric George. b 47. S Dios Minl Tr Scheme 87. **d** 90 **p** 91. NSM Hove Bp Hannington Memorial Ch *Chich* 90-92; C Burgess Hill St Andr 92-95; R Frant w Eridge 95-00; V Framfield 00-07; rtd 07; Perm to Offic *St E* from 08. *Oak House, 86A Southwold Road, Wrentham, Beccles NR34 7JF* Tel (01502) 675777 E-mail ericdore@onetel.com

DOREY, Miss Alison. b 77. Sheff Univ BA98 Sheff Hallam Univ PGCE01 St Jo Coll Dur MA08. Cranmer Hall Dur 05. **d** 07 **p** 08. C Askern *Sheff* 07-11; Miss Development Co-ord N Sheff Estates from 11. *85 Malton Street, Sheffield S4 7EA* Tel 0114-272 6855 E-mail ali.dorey@sheffield.anglican.org

DOREY, Trevor Eric. b 30. ACIS53. S Dios Minl Tr Scheme 87. **d** 90 **p** 91. NSM E Woodhay and Woolton Hill *Win* 90-96; P-in-c Manaccan w St Anthony-in-Meneage and St Martin *Truro* 96-99; rtd 99; Perm to Offic *Sarum* 01-05 and *Ox* from 07. *6 Marshall Court, Speen Lane, Newbury RG14 1RY* Tel (01635) 551956 E-mail tandvdorey@btinternet.com

DORGU, Woyin Karowei. b 58. MB, BS85. Lon Bible Coll BA93 Oak Hill Th Coll 93. **d** 95 **p** 96. C Tollington Lon 95-98; C Upper Holloway 98-00; TV from 00. *St John's Vicarage, 51 Tytherton Road, London N19 4PZ* Tel and fax (020) 7272 5309
E-mail karmos.timsim@virgin.net

DORKING, Archdeacon of. *See* HENDERSON, The Ven Julian Tudor

DORKING, Suffragan Bishop of. *See* BRACKLEY, The Rt Revd Ian James

DORLING, Philip Julian. b 69. Edin Univ BSc90. Ripon Coll Cuddesdon 03. **d** 05 **p** 06. C Ulverston St Mary w H Trin *Carl* 05-09; R Vryheid St Pet S Africa from 10. *The Rectory, St Peter's Church, 166 Hoog Street, Vryheid, 3100 South Africa*
E-mail philipdorling123@btinternet.com

DORMANDY, Richard Paul. b 59. Univ Coll Lon BA81 St Edm Ho Cam BA88. Ridley Hall Cam 86. **d** 89 **p** 90. C Sydenham H Trin *S'wark* 89-93; V 93-01; V Westminster St Jas the Less *Lon* 01-09; V Tulse Hill H Trin and St Matthias *S'wark* from 09. *Holy Trinity Vicarage, 49 Trinity Rise, London SW2 2QP* Tel (020) 8674 6721 E-mail richard@dormandy.co.uk

DORMOR, Duncan James. b 67. Magd Coll Ox BA88 Lon Univ MSc89. Ripon Coll Cuddesdon BA94. **d** 95 **p** 96. C Wolverhampton *Lich* 95-98; Chapl St Jo Coll Cam 98-02; Fell and Dean from 02. *St John's College, Cambridge CB2 1TP* Tel (01223) 338633 E-mail djd28@cam.ac.uk

DORMOR, Preb Duncan Stephen. b 36. St Edm Hall Ox BA60. Cuddesdon Coll 60. **d** 62 **p** 63. C Headington *Ox* 62-66; USA 66-72; R Hertford St Andr *St Alb* 72-88; RD Hertford 77-83; TR Tenbury Wells *Heref* 88-01; R Burford I, Nash and Boraston 88-01; R Whitton w Greete and Hope Bagot 88-01; R Burford III w Lt Heref 88-01; V Tenbury St Mich 94-01; RD Ludlow 96-01; Preb Heref Cathl 99-02; C Tenbury Wells 01-02; C Burford I, Nash and Boraston 01-02; C Whitton w Greete and Hope Bagot 01-02; C Burford III w Lt Heref 01-02; C Tenbury St Mich 01-02; rtd 02; Perm to Offic *Heref* from 02. *Brantwood, Hereford Road, Leominster HR6 8JU* Tel (01568) 610897

DORNAN, Michael. CITC. **d** 09 **p** 10. C Hillsborough *D & D* from 09. *2 Beechgrove, Ballynahinch BT24 8NQ* Tel (028) 9756 5685 E-mail mikedornan@gmail.com

DORRELL, Martin Christopher. b 57. STETS. **d** 09 **p** 10. NSM Portsea St Alb *Portsm* from 09; NSM Portsea St Sav from 09. *284B Allaway Avenue, Portsmouth PO6 4QR* Tel (023) 9238 8689 E-mail martin.dorrell1@ntlworld.com

DORRIAN, Adrian Terence Warren. b 82. QUB BA03 TCD BTh06. CITC 04. **d** 06 **p** 07. C Newtownards *D & D* 06-09; I Belfast St Pet and St Jas *Conn* from 09. *St Peter's Rectory, 17 Waterloo Park South, Belfast BT15 5HX* Tel (028) 9077 7053 Mobile 07760-664337 E-mail adriandorrian@gmail.com

DORRINGTON, Brian Goodwin. b 32. Leeds Univ CertEd55. St Deiniol's Hawarden 65. **d** 66 **p** 67. C Poynton *Ches* 66-71; Perm to Offic *Truro* 71-78; Hd Master Veryan Sch Truro 71-84;

Hon C Veryan *Truro* 78-84; C N Petherwin 84-87; C Boyton w N Tamerton 84-87; TV Bolventor 87-90; R Kilkhampton w Morwenstow 90-97; RD Stratton 92-97; rtd 97; Perm to Offic *Truro* from 00. *Southcroft, 18 Elm Drive, Bude EX23 8EZ* Tel (01288) 352467

DORRINGTON, Richard Bryan. b 48. Linc Th Coll 79. **d** 81 **p** 82. C Streetly *Lich* 81-84; C Badger 84-85; R 85-88; C Ryton 84-85; R 85-88; C Beckbury 84-85; R 85-88; V Geddington w Weekley *Pet* 88-98; P-in-c Bradworthy *Ex* 98-00; P-in-c Abbots Bickington and Bulkworthy 98-00; R Bradworthy, Sutcombe, Putford etc from 00; RD Holsworthy from 99. *The Rectory, St Peterswell Lane, Bradworthy EX22 7TQ* Tel (01409) 241411 E-mail therector@bradworthy.co.uk

DORSET, Archdeacon of. *See* WAINE, The Ven Stephen John

DORSETT, Mark Richard. b 63. Univ of Wales (Lamp) BA84 MTh86 Birm Univ PhD90. Ripon Coll Cuddesdon 91. **d** 93 **p** 94. C Yardley St Edburgha *Birm* 93-96; Chapl K Sch Worc from 96; Min Can Worc Cathl from 96. *12A College Green, Worcester WR1 2LH* Tel (01905) 25837

DOSE, Lara Ellen. b 70. De Pauw Univ USA BA92 Trin Hall Cam BTh08. Westcott Ho Cam 06. **d** 09 **p** 10. C Birch-in-Rusholme St Agnes w Longsight St Jo etc *Man* from 09. *58 Reynell Road, Manchester M13 0PT* Tel 07801-789802 (mobile) E-mail lara@stagneslongsight.org

DOSSOR, John Haley. b 41. Leeds Univ BA62. EAMTC 87. **d** 90 **p** 91. NSM Hadleigh *St E* 90-01; P-in-c Ipswich St Mary at the Elms 01-07; rtd 07; Perm to Offic *Chelmsf* and *St E* from 07. *Butley Barn, 1 Struston Mead, Kirton, Felixstowe IP10 0QH* Tel (01394) 448188 E-mail haley@dossor.org

DOSSOR, Timothy Charles. b 70. Birm Univ BEng94. Ridley Hall Cam BTh99. **d** 99 **p** 00. C Ipswich St Jo *St E* 99-03; Asst Ldr Iwerne Holidays Titus Trust from 03; Perm to Offic *Ox* from 08. *31 Southdale Road, Oxford OX2 7SE* Tel (01865) 553226 *or* 310513 Mobile 07748-184503 E-mail tim@dossor.org

DOTCHIN, Andrew Steward. b 56. Federal Th Coll S Africa. **d** 84 **p** 85. S Africa 84-01; C Standerton w Evender 84-87; Asst P St Martin's-in-the-Veld 87-89; R Belgravia St Jo the Divine 89-94; Chapl St Martin's Sch Rosettenville 94-01; TV Blyth Valley *St E* 01-04; P-in-c Whitton and Thurleston w Akenham 04-09; R from 09. *The Rectory, 176 Fircroft Road, Ipswich IP1 6PS* Tel (01473) 741389 Mobile 07814-949828 E-mail andrew.dotchin@ntlworld.com

DOTCHIN, Canon Joan Marie. b 47. NEOC 84. **d** 87 **p** 94. C Newc St Gabr 87-92; TD Willington 92-94; TV 94-95; TR 95-03; V Fenham St Jas and St Basil 03-08; Hon Can Newc Cathl 01-08; rtd 08. *22 Astley Gardens, Seaton Sluice, Whitley Bay NE26 4JJ* Tel 0191-237 3030
E-mail revj.dotchin@goldserve.net

DOUBLE, Richard Sydney (Brother Samuel). b 47. K Coll Lon BD69 AKC69. St Aug Coll Cant 69. **d** 70 **p** 71. C Walton St Mary *Liv* 70-74; SSF from 75; Guardian Hilfield Friary Dorchester 92-01; Can and Preb Sarum Cathl 95-01 and from 09; V Cambridge St Benedict *Ely* 01-05. *The Friary, Hilfield, Dorchester DT2 7BE* Tel (01300) 341345

DOUBTFIRE, Canon Barbara. b 39. LMH Ox BA61 MA65. **d** 91 **p** 94. Par Development Adv *Ox* 88-04; NSM Kidlington w Hampton Poyle 91-04; Hon Can Ch Ch 98-04; rtd 04. *6 Meadow Walk, Woodstock OX20 1NR* Tel (01993) 812095
E-mail spidir@oxford.anglican.org

DOUBTFIRE, Samuel. b 33. Edin Th Coll 63. **d** 66 **p** 66. C Knottingley *Wakef* 66-68; V Ripponden 68-76; V Crosthwaite Keswick *Carl* 76-81; V Barrow St Matt 81-87; R N Reddish *Man* 87-92; rtd 92; Perm to Offic *Bradf* 92-06. *21 Lichfield Lane, Mansfield NG18 4RA* Tel (01623) 633266

DOUGAL, Stephen George. b 62. FICS. **d** 06 **p** 07. OLM Lyminge w Paddlesworth, Stanford w Postling etc *Cant* from 06. *Bereforstal Farm Bungalow, Canterbury Road, Elham, Canterbury CT4 6UE* Tel (01303) 840750

DOUGHTY, The Ven Andrew William. b 56. K Coll Lon BD AKC. Westcott Ho Cam 80. **d** 82 **p** 83. C Alton St Lawr *Win* 82-85; TV Basingstoke 85-91; V Chilworth w N Baddesley 91-95; R Warwick St Mary V Bermuda from 95; Adn Bermuda from 04. *PO Box WK 530, Warwick WK BX, Bermuda* Tel (001) (441) 236 5744 Fax 236 3667 E-mail adoughty@ibl.bm

DOUGLAS, Ann Patricia. b 49. Lon Univ CertEd71. Oak Hill NSM Course 83. **d** 88 **p** 94. Par Dn Chorleywood Ch Ch *St Alb* 88-94; V Oxhey All SS 94-02; TR Woodley *Ox* 02-06; rtd 06; Development Officer Li Tim-Oi Foundn from 06; Perm to Offic *Sarum* from 07. *Heather Cottage, 9A Cauldron Crescent, Swanage BH19 1QL* Tel (01929) 421691 Mobile 07885-022155 E-mail anni@weymouthandportlandchurch.org

DOUGLAS, Anthony Victor. b 51. St Jo Coll Nottm 74. **d** 76 **p** 77. C Gt Crosby St Luke *Liv* 76-79; TV Fazakerley Em 79-84; TR Speke St Aid 84-90; TR Gt and Lt Coates w Bradley *Linc* 90-97; TR E Ham w Upton Park *Chelmsf* 97-02; R Holkham w Egmere w Warham, Wells and Wighton *Nor* from 02. *The Rectory, Church Street, Wells-next-the-Sea NR23 1JB* Tel (01328) 710107

DOUGLAS, Gavin Allan. b 52. OBE00. Cardiff Univ BTh08. St Mich Coll Llan 03. **d** 05 **p** 06. C Week St Mary Circle of Par

Truro 05-08; R Castle Bromwich SS Mary and Marg *Birm* from 08. *67 Chester Road, Castle Bromwich, Birmingham B36 9DP* Tel 0121-747 8546 E-mail gavinadouglas@yahoo.co.uk

DOUGLAS, Miss Janet Elizabeth. b 60. SS Paul & Mary Coll Cheltenham BEd83. Cranmer Hall Dur 88. **d** 90 **p** 94. Par Dn Yardley St Edburgha *Birm* 90-93; Par Dn Hamstead St Paul 93-94; C 94-00; Perm to Offic 00-04; C Birm St Martin w Bordesley St Andr 04-11; Perm to Offic from 11. *6 Baxter Court, 96 School Road, Moseley, Birmingham B13 9TP* Tel 0121-449 3763

DOUGLAS, Jonathan William Dixon. b 75. QUB BSc96 K Coll Lon MA01 Keele Univ MBA03 Spurgeon's Coll MTh09. **d** 11. C Spitalfields Ch Ch w All SS *Lon* from 11. *Flat D, 35 Buxton Street, London E1 5EH* Tel 07799-072845 (mobile) E-mail revjohnnydouglas@gmail.com

DOUGLAS, Michael Williamson. b 51. Birm Univ BSc72 Liv Univ PGCE74. Trin Coll Bris 00. **d** 02 **p** 03. C Macclesfield Team *Ches* 02-06; TV Hawarden *St As* 06-10. *46 Far Meadow Lane, Wirral CH61 4XW* E-mail mikedougie@yahoo.co.uk

DOUGLAS, Pamela Jean. *See* WELCH, Pamela Jean

DOUGLAS, Peter Melvyn. b 47. **d** 96 **p** 97. NSM Prestwick *Glas* 96-01; Chapl HM Pris Dovegate 01-03; P-in-c Kilmarnock *Glas* from 07. *The Parsonage, 1 Dundonald Road, Kilmarnock KA1 1EQ* Tel (01563) 523577

DOUGLAS, Richard Norman Henry. b 37. SAOMC 94. **d** 97 **p** 98. NSM Watercombe *Sarum* 97-02; Perm to Offic *Sarum* 02-04 and *Ox* 04-06; NSM Grove *Ox* 06-07; rtd 07; Perm to Offic *Ox* from 07. *6 Vale Avenue, Grove, Wantage OX12 7LU* Tel (01235) 767753 E-mail dickandnan@talktalk.net

DOUGLAS, Simon Alexander. b 70. Nottm Univ BEng92. Qu Coll Birm 09. **d** 11. C Tettenhall Regis *Lich* from 11. *7 Camden Close, Birmingham B36 9BY* Tel 0121-748 3781 Mobile 07946-440464 E-mail simon@sadbuttrue.co.uk

DOUGLAS LANE, Charles Simon Pellew. b 47. BNC Ox MA71 MCIPD79. Oak Hill Th Coll 91. **d** 94 **p** 95. C Whitton St Aug *Lon* 94-97; P-in-c Hounslow W Gd Shep 97-02; V 02-05; TV Riverside *Ox* 05-08; V Horton and Wraysbury from 08. *The Vicarage, 55 Welley Road, Wraysbury, Staines TW19 5ER* Tel (01784) 481258 E-mail simondouglaslane@tiscali.co.uk

DOUGLAS-PENNANT, Oliver Andrew. b 79. Edin Univ MA06. Trin Coll Bris 08. **d** 10 **p** 11. C Kidderminster St Geo *Worc* from 10. *107 Shakespeare Drive, Kidderminster DY10 3QX* Tel 07870-270514 (mobile) E-mail olidpennant@gmail.com

DOUGLASS, Michael Crone. b 49. Open Univ BA96. NEOC 02. **d** 05 **p** 06. NSM Gosforth St Nic *Newc* from 05. *44 Regent Road, Newcastle upon Tyne NE3 1ED* Tel and fax 0191-285 0977 E-mail m.douglass@blueyonder.co.uk

DOUGLASS, Preb Philip. b 48. Open Univ BA88. St Steph Ho Ox 87. **d** 89 **p** 90. C Peterlee *Dur* 89-92; V Crowan w Godolphin *Truro* 92-97; V Crowan and Treslothan from 98; P-in-c Penponds from 01; Preb St Endellion from 02. *Crowan Vicarage, 37 Trethannas Gardens, Praze, Camborne TR14 0LL* Tel and fax (01209) 831009 E-mail philip@thedouglasses.freeserve.co.uk

DOULL, Canon Iain Sinclair. b 43. St Mich Coll Llan 86. **d** 88 **p** 89. C Malpas *Mon* 88-91; P-in-c Newport All SS 91-98; V 98-02; V Newport Ch Ch from 02; Hon Can St Woolos Cathl from 11. *The Vicarage, Christchurch, Newport NP18 1JJ* Tel (01633) 420701

DOULTON, Dick. b 32. St Cath Coll Cam BA60 MA64. Ridley Hall Cam 61. **d** 63 **p** 64. C Gedling *S'well* 63-65; C Danbury *Chelmsf* 65; Lic to Offic *Ox* 88-90; Lic to Offic *L & K* from 90. *Ballygriffin, Kenmare, Killarney, Co Kerry, Republic of Ireland* Tel (00353) (64) 41743

DOULTON, Roderick John. b 55. Oak Hill Th Coll 91. **d** 93 **p** 94. C Hoddesdon *St Alb* 93-96; P-in-c Caldecote All SS 96-98; P-in-c Old Warden 97-98; V Caldecote, Northill and Old Warden 98-99; TV Macclesfield Team *Ches* 99-07; Chapl W Park Hosp Macclesfield 99-07; P-in-c Heydon, Gt and Lt Chishill, Chrishall etc *Chelmsf* 07-08. *7A Doddington Road, Chatteris PE16 6UA*

DOVE, Giles Wilfred. b 62. St Andr Univ MA85 MPhil88 FSAScot FRSA. TISEC 03. **d** 05 **p** 06. NSM Dunblane *St And* 05-07; Chapl Glenalmond Coll from 07. *The Chaplain's House, Glenalmond College, Glenalmond, Perth PH1 3RY* Tel (01738) 880479 E-mail gilesdove@glenalmondcollege.co.uk

DOVE, Lionel John. b 38. **d** 06 **p** 07. OLM N Bradley, Southwick, Heywood and Steeple Ashton *Sarum* from 06. *Chobham Cottage, Acreshot Lane, Steeple Ashton, Trowbridge BA14 6HD* Tel (01380) 870013 E-mail lionel@dove8569.freeserve.co.uk

DOVE, Richard. b 54. EMMTC. **d** 09 **p** 10. NSM Dronfield w Holmesfield *Derby* from 09. *29 Hollins Spring Avenue, Dronfield S18 1RN* Tel (01246) 412502 E-mail rdove1553@aol.com *or* dick.dove@dwhparish.org.uk

DOVER, Suffragan Bishop of. *See* WILLMOTT, The Rt Revd Trevor

DOVEY, Andrew Michael Stanley. b 59. SEITE 00. **d** 06 **p** 07. NSM Selsdon St Jo w St Fran *S'wark* 06-10; Perm to Offic from 10. *6 Stokes Road, Croydon CR0 7SD* Tel (020) 8656 9911 E-mail kdoveys@tiscali.co.uk

DOW, Canon Andrew John Morrison. b 46. Univ Coll Ox BA67 MA71. Oak Hill Th Coll 69. **d** 71 **p** 72. C Watford St Luke *St Alb* 71-74; C Chadderton Ch Ch *Man* 75-78; V Leamington Priors St Paul *Cov* 78-88; V Knowle *Birm* 88-97; RD Solihull 95-97; V Clifton Ch Ch w Em *Bris* 97-04; P-in-c Cheltenham St Mary, St Matt, St Paul and H Trin *Glouc* 04-07; R Cheltenham St Mary w St Matt 07-10; AD Cheltenham 06-10; Hon Can Glouc Cathl 08-10; rtd 10. *17 Brownlow Drive, Stratford-upon-Avon CV37 9QS* Tel (01789) 417852 E-mail andrewdow@blueyonder.co.uk

✠**DOW, The Rt Revd Geoffrey Graham.** b 42. Qu Coll Ox BA63 MA68 BSc65 MSc81 Nottm Univ MPhil82. Clifton Th Coll 66. **d** 67 **p** 68 **c** 92. C Tonbridge SS Pet and Paul *Roch* 67-72; Chapl St Jo Coll Ox 72-75; Lect St Jo Coll Nottm 75-81; V Cov H Trin 81-92; Can Th Cov Cathl 88-92; Area Bp Willesden *Lon* 92-00; Bp Carl 00-09; rtd 09; Hon Asst Bp Ches from 09. *34 Kimberley Avenue, Romiley, Stockport SK6 4AB* Tel 0161-494 9148 E-mail graham@gdow.co.uk

DOWD, Garfield George. b 60. QUB BSc. **d** 86 **p** 87. C Monkstown *D & G* 86-90; I Carlow w Urglin and Staplestown *C & O* 90-05; Can Ossory Cathl 96-05; I Glenageary *D & G* from 05. *St Paul's Vicarage, Silchester Road, Glenageary, Co Dublin, Republic of Ireland* Tel and fax (00353) (1) 280 1616 Mobile 87-926 6558 E-mail glenageary@dublin.anglican.org

DOWDESWELL, Anne Marjory. b 68. **d** 06 **p** 07. C Leckhampton St Pet *Glouc* 06-10; TV Ex St Thos and Em from 10. *The Vicarage, 78 Queens Road, Exeter EX2 9EW* E-mail anne.dowdeswell@hotmail.co.uk

DOWDING, Ms Clare Alice Elizabeth. b 74. Ch Ch Coll Cant BA98 Greenwich Univ PGCE99. Westcott Ho Cam BA02. **d** 03 **p** 05. USA 03-04; C Longsight St Luke *Man* 04-07; Chapl Man HE Institutions from 07. *St Peter's House, Precinct Centre, Oxford Road, Manchester M13 9GH* Tel 0161-275 2894 Fax 275 0890 Mobile 07903-553113 E-mail caedowding@hotmail.com

DOWDING, Canon Edward Brinley. b 47. St Mich Coll Llan 70 St D Coll Lamp BA71. **d** 72 **p** 73. C Canton St Cath *Llan* 72-75; C Aberdare 75-78; V Aberavon H Trin 78-85; R Sully from 85; R Wenvoe and St Lythans from 10; RD Penarth and Barry 98-04; Hon Can Llan Cathl from 11. *The Rectory, 26 South Road, Sully, Penarth CF64 5TG* Tel (029) 2053 0221 E-mail edward.dowding@btinternet.com

DOWDING, Mrs Elizabeth Jean. b 43. Bath Coll of HE TCert67. SAOMC 00. **d** 04 **p** 05. NSM Goring w S Stoke *Ox* 04-07; NSM Goring and Streatley w S Stoke from 07. *30 Milldown Avenue, Goring, Reading RG8 0AS* Tel (01491) 873140 E-mail elizdowding@aol.com

DOWDING, Jeremy Charles. b 51. St Steph Ho Ox 89. **d** 91 **p** 92. C Newport St Steph and H Trin *Mon* 91-94; C Risca 94-96; P-in-c Whitleigh *Ex* 96-05; P-in-c Thorpe-le-Soken *Chelmsf* from 05. *The Vicarage, Mill Lane, Thorpe-le-Soken, Clacton-on-Sea CO16 0ED* Tel (01255) 861234

DOWDLE, Canon Cynthia. b 48. Cranmer Hall Dur 88. **d** 90 **p** 94. C Allerton *Liv* 90-94; TR Halewood 94-00; V Knowsley 00-11; Hd Spiritual Care Adelaide Ho Probation Hostel from 11; Dean of Women's Min from 01; Hon Can Liv Cathl 01-10; Can Res from 10. *19 Belvedere Road, 2-4 Ullet Road, Liverpool L8 3SR* Tel 0151-727 5766 E-mail cynthiadowdle@hotmail.com

DOWDY, Simon Mark Christopher. b 67. Trin Hall Cam BA89 MA93. Wycliffe Hall Ox 93. **d** 96 **p** 97. C Beckenham Ch Ch *Roch* 96-00; C St Helen Bishopsgate w St Andr Undershaft etc *Lon* 00-05; P-in-c St Botolph without Aldersgate from 02. *45 Woodwarde Road, London SE22 8UN* Tel (020) 8299 1631 E-mail mail@stbotolphsaldersgate.org.uk

DOWER, Frances Helen. b 45. Lon Univ MB, BS69. **d** 09 **p** 10. OLM Kirkwhelpington, Kirkharle, Kirkheaton and Cambo *Newc* from 09. *Cambo House, Front Row, Cambo, Morpeth NE61 4AY* Tel (01670) 774297 E-mail frances.dower@dower.org.uk

DOWIE, Canon Winifred Brenda McIntosh. b 57. Callendar Park Coll of Educn Falkirk DipEd78. Trin Coll Bris BA91. **d** 92 **p** 94. Par Dn Downend *Bris* 92-94; C 94-95; Chapl Asst Southmead Health Services NHS Trust 95-98; Chapl St Pet Hospice Bris 98-10; Hon Can Bris Cathl from 02. *Address temp unknown*

DOWLAND, Martin John. b 48. Lon Univ BD70 Southn Univ PGCE71. Wycliffe Hall Ox 75. **d** 77 **p** 78. C Jesmond Clayton Memorial *Newc* 77-80; C Chadderton Ch Ch *Man* 80-85; R Haughton St Mary from 85. *Haughton Green Rectory, Meadow Lane, Denton, Manchester M34 7GD* Tel and fax 0161-336 4529 E-mail m.dowland@ntlworld.com

DOWLAND-OWEN, Edward Farrington. b 73. St D Coll Lamp BA95 Trin Coll Carmarthen PGCE96 FVCM99. S Wales Ord Course 00. St Mich Coll Llan 03. **d** 04 **p** 05. C Llandaff 04-08; P-in-c Llandyfodwg and Cwm Ogwr 08-10; C Penarth and Llandough from 10. *153 Windsor Road, Penarth CF64 1JF* Tel (029) 2140 2180 E-mail revedward@dowlandowen.co.uk

DOWLAND-PILLINGER, Catherine Louise. b 60. New Hall Cam BA82 MA86 PhD89. SEITE 05. **d** 08 **p** 09. C Addington

S'wark from 08. *56 Viney Bank, Courtwood Lane, Croydon CR0 9JT* Tel (020) 8657 4603 Mobile 07768-065301 E-mail rev.catherine1@googlemail.com

DOWLEN, Isabella McBeath. b 45. Man Univ CertEd86 Edin Univ MTh06 RGN67 SCM68 HVCert69. STETS 96. **d** 99 **p** 01. NSM Branksome St Clem *Sarum* 99-04; NSM Clarkston *Glas* 04-06; P-in-c Glas St Oswald 06-08; R Elie and Earlsferry *St And* from 10; R Pittenweem from 10. *The Great House, Priory Court, Pittenweem, Anstruther KY10 2LJ* Tel 07974-084657 (mobile) E-mail isabel.dowlen@tesco.net

DOWLER, Robert Edward Mackenzie. b 67. Ch Ch Ox BA89 Selw Coll Cam BA93 Dur Univ PhD07. Westcott Ho Cam 91. **d** 94 **p** 95. C Southgate Ch Ch *Lon* 94-97; C Somers Town 97-01; Tutor and Dir Past Th St Steph Ho Ox 01-09; Vice Prin 03-09; Asst Chapl Malvern Coll 09-10; V Clay Hill St Jo and St Luke *Lon* from 10. *St Luke's Vicarage, 92 Browning Road, Enfield EN2 0HG* Tel (020) 8363 6055

DOWLING, Donald Edward. b 43. St Andr Univ MA66. Cranmer Hall Dur. **d** 74 **p** 75. C Thame w Towersey *Ox* 74-77; C Norton *St Alb* 77-80; V Wilbury 81-99; V Stevenage St Nic and Graveley 99-10; rtd 10. *56 Caslon Way, Letchworth Garden City SG6 4QL* E-mail don@btinternet.com

DOWLING, Graham Paul. b 62. NTMTC BA09. **d** 09 **p** 10. C Rainham w Wennington *Chelmsf* from 09. *260 Upminster Road North, Rainham RM13 9JL* Tel 07889-286308 (mobile) E-mail graham@pdowling.freeserve.co.uk

DOWLING, Kingsley Avery Paul. b 60. Open Univ BA. Aston Tr Scheme 93 Ripon Coll Cuddesdon 95. **d** 97 **p** 98. C Headingley *Ripon* 97-99; C Far Headingley St Chad 99-01; V Wortley de Leeds from 01; P-in-c Farnley from 10; AD Armley from 08. *Wortley Vicarage, Dixon Lane Road, Leeds LS12 4RU* Tel 0113-263 8867 E-mail kingsleydowling@talktalk.net

DOWMAN, Jonathan Robert. b 76. Westmr Coll Ox BEd00. Trin Coll Bris 04. **d** 07 **p** 08. C Anglesey Gp *Ely* 07-10; Deanery Missr *Birm* from 10. *117 Metchley Lane, Birmingham B17 0JH* E-mail dowman@tiscali.co.uk

DOWMAN, Peter Robert. b 52. City Univ BSc76. Wycliffe Hall Ox 82. **d** 84 **p** 85. C Cheltenham Ch Ch *Glouc* 84-87; C Danbury *Chelmsf* 87-90; R Woodham Ferrers and Bicknacre 90-95; Consultant E England CPAS 95-03; R Warboys w Broughton and Bury w Wistow *Ely* from 03. *The Rectory, 15 Church Road, Warboys, Huntingdon PE28 2RJ* Tel (01487) 824612 E-mail pdowman@bigfoot.com

DOWN, Martin John. b 40. Jes Coll Cam BA62 MA68. Westcott Ho Cam 63. **d** 65 **p** 66. C Bury St Mary *Man* 65-68; C Leigh St Mary 68-70; R Fiskerton *Linc* 70-75; V Irnham w Corby 75-79; RD Beltisloe 76-84; P-in-c Swayfield and Creeton w Swinstead 78-79; V Corby Glen 79-84; Good News Trust 84-88; Perm to Offic *Linc* 84-88 and *Pet* 86-88; P-in-c Ashill w Saham Toney *Nor* 88-94; R 94-00; C Watton w Carbrooke and Ovington 00-05; rtd 05; Perm to Offic *Nor* from 05. *22 Lee Warner Road, Swaffham PE37 7GD* Tel and fax (01760) 336492

DOWN, Peter Michael. b 54. K Coll Lon BD78 AKC. Coll of Resurr Mirfield 78. **d** 79 **p** 80. C Swindon Ch Ch *Bris* 79-82; C Southmead 82-84; TV Cannock *Lich* 84-92; V Coleford w Holcombe *B & W* 92-01; Hon C Westfield 01-02; Perm to Offic 07-11; P-in-c Tintinhull w Chilthorne Domer, Yeovil Marsh etc from 11. *The Rectory, Vicarage Street, Tintinhull, Yeovil BA22 8PY* Tel (01935) 822655 E-mail peterdown836@btinternet.com

DOWN, The Ven Philip Roy. b 53. Hull Univ MA93. Melbourne Coll of Div BTh82 MTh88. **d** 89 **p** 89. C Gt Grimsby St Mary and St Jas *Linc* 89-91; TV 91-95; R Hackington *Cant* 95-02; AD Cant 99-02; Adn Maidstone 02-11; Adn Ashford from 11. *The Archdeaconry, Pett Lane, Charing, Ashford TN27 0DL* Tel (01233) 712649 E-mail pdown@archdeacashford.org

✠**DOWN, The Rt Revd William John Denbigh.** b 34. St Jo Coll Cam BA57 MA61 FNI91. Ridley Hall Cam 57. **d** 59 **p** 60 **c** 90. C Fisherton Anger *Sarum* 59-63; Miss to Seamen 63-90; Australia 71-74; Dep Gen Sec Miss to Seamen 75; Gen Sec 76-90; Hon C Gt Stanmore *Lon* 75-90; Chapl St Mich Paternoster Royal 76-90; Perm to Offic *St Alb* 78-90; Hon Can Gib Cathl 85-90; Hon Can Kobe Japan from 87; Bp Bermuda 90-95; Asst Bp *Leic* 95-01; P-in-c Humberstone 95-01; P-in-c Thurnby Lodge 01; rtd 01; Hon Asst Bp Ox from 01. *54 Dark Lane, Witney OX28 6LX* Tel (01993) 706615 E-mail bishbill@aol.com

DOWN AND DROMORE, Bishop of. See MILLER, The Rt Revd Harold Creeth

DOWN, Archdeacon of. See PATTERSON, The Ven Philip Fredrick

DOWN, Dean of. See HULL, The Very Revd Thomas Henry

DOWNER, Barry Michael. b 58. STETS 99. **d** 02 **p** 07. NSM Lake and Shanklin St Sav *Portsm* 02-05; NSM Bonchurch 05-08; NSM Ventnor H Trin 05-08; NSM Ventnor St Cath 05-08; NSM Oakfield St Jo 09-10. *Address temp unknown*

DOWNER, Cuthbert John. b 18. S'wark Ord Course 60. **d** 74 **p** 75. Hon C Kirdford *Chich* 74-76; C Halesworth w Linstead and Chediston *St E* 76-79; P-in-c Knodishall w Buxlow 79-80; P-in-c Friston 79-80; R Bacton w Wyverstone 80-83; P-in-c Cotton and

Wickham Skeith 80-83; R Bacton w Wyverstone and Cotton 83-84; rtd 84; Perm to Offic *St Alb* 84-87; *B & W* 88-95 and from 97. *Cote House, Cote Drive, Westbury-on-Trym, Bristol BS9 3UP*

DOWNES, Gregory Charles. b 69. Roehampton Inst BSc91 Hughes Hall Cam PGCE92. Wycliffe Hall Ox BA95. **d** 96 **p** 97. C Hazlemere *Ox* 96-99; Chapl HM Pris Ashfield 99-01; Lect Lon Sch of Th 01-04; Chapl Pemb Coll Ox 04-05; Chapl Ox Pastorate 05-06. *Address temp unknown*

DOWNES, Richard John. b 63. Cranmer Hall Dur 91. **d** 94 **p** 95. C Bishopwearmouth St Gabr *Dur* 94-97; CF from 97. *c/o MOD Chaplains (Army)* Tel (01264) 381140 Fax 381824

DOWNEY, Canon John Stewart. b 38. QUB CertEd60 Open Univ BA76. Oak Hill Th Coll 63. **d** 66 **p** 67. C Londonderry St Aug *D & R* 66-71; I Dungiven w Bovevagh 71-82; Bp's Dom Chapl 75-82; V Bishopwearmouth St Gabr *Dur* 82-91; V New Malden and Coombe *S'wark* 91-06; Hon Can S'wark Cathl 97-06; rtd 06; Perm to Offic *S'wark* from 08. *33A Queen's Road, Kingston upon Thames KT2 7SF* Tel (020) 8974 5074

DOWNHAM, Canon Peter Norwell. b 31. Man Univ BA52. Ridley Hall Cam 54. **d** 56 **p** 57. C Cheadle *Ches* 56-62; V Rawtenstall St Mary *Man* 62-68; Chapl Rossendale Gen Hosp 62-68; V Denton Holme *Carl* 68-79; V Reading Greyfriars *Ox* 79-95; Hon Can Ch Ch 90-95; rtd 95; Hon C Cotehill and Cumwhinton *Carl* 95-00; Perm to Offic *Carl* 98-07 and *Ox* from 07. *17 Grange Close, Goring, Reading RG8 9DY* Tel (01491) 875983

DOWNHAM, Simon Garrod. b 61. K Coll Lon LLB84 Solicitor 87. Wycliffe Hall Ox BA93. **d** 94 **p** 95. C Brompton H Trin w Onslow Square St Paul *Lon* 94-99; P-in-c Hammersmith St Paul 00-06; V from 06. *14 Lena Gardens, London W6 7PZ* Tel (020) 7603 9662 or 8748 3855 E-mail simon.downham@sph.org.uk

DOWNING, Francis Gerald. b 35. Qu Coll Ox BA56 MA60. Linc Th Coll. **d** 58 **p** 59. C Filwood Park CD *Bris* 58-60; Tutor Linc Th Coll 60-64; V Unsworth *Man* 64-80; Tutor NOC 80-82; Vice-Prin 82-90; V Bolton SS Simon and Jude *Man* 90-97; rtd 97; Perm to Offic *Blackb* from 97. *33 Westhoughton Road, Chorley PR7 4EU* Tel (01257) 474240

DOWNS, Caroline Rebecca. b 58. UWIST BA80 Univ of Wales (Cardiff) PGCE81. St Mich Coll Llan 98. **d** 02 **p** 03. C Roath *Llan* 02-07; P-in-c Cathays from 07. *6 Newminster Road, Roath, Cardiff CF23 5AP* Tel (029) 2049 5699 E-mail carolinerebecca.downs@btinternet.com

DOWNS, Miss Geinor. b 47. UEA BA72 Southn Univ BTh89 Birm Univ MA05. Chich Th Coll 85. **d** 87 **p** 94. Par Dn Wellingborough All SS *Pet* 87-89; Development Officer Chich Th Coll 89-92; C Durrington *Chich* 92-95; Chapl City Hosp NHS Trust Birm 95-02; Chapl Sandwell and W Birm Hosps NHS Trust 02-06. *35 Fairmead Rise, Northampton NN2 8PP* Tel (01604) 842554

DOWNS, John Alfred. b 58. Leic Univ BSc79 PGCE80 CBiol80 MIBiol80. EMMTC 90. **d** 93 **p** 94. NSM Barlestone *Leic* 93-96; NSM Markfield, Thornton, Bagworth and Stanton etc 96-11; NSM Newbold de Verdun, Barlestone and Kirkby Mallory from 11. *29 Meadow Road, Barlestone, Nuneaton CV13 0JG* Tel (01455) 290195

DOWNS, Mrs Lynsay Marie. b 75. Hull Univ BA98. Ripon Coll Cuddesdon BTh05. **d** 05 **p** 06. C Tettenhall Wood and Perton *Lich* 05-09; TV Brereton and Rugeley from 09. *The Vicarage, 14 Peakes Road, Rugeley WS15 2LY* Tel (01889) 582809

DOWSE, Ivor Roy. b 35. ARHistS MRSL. St Deiniol's Hawarden 66. **d** 68 **p** 70. C Harrow St Pet *Lon* 68-69; C Sudbury St Andr 69-71; C Weeke *Win* 71-73; Min Can Ban Cathl 73-78; V Hollym w Welwick and Holmpton *York* 78-81; R Bearwood *Ox* 81-82; P-in-c Rothesay *Arg* 83-86; C Boxmoor St Jo *St Alb* 86-92; Hon C Cowes H Trin and St Mary *Portsm* 92-94; Perm to Offic 94-98; P-in-c St Hilary w Perranuthnoe *Truro* 98-00; rtd 01; Perm to Offic *Win* from 06; Hon Chapl Win Cathl from 06; Hon Asst Chapl St Jo Win Charity from 09. *10 St Mary Magdalen Almshouses, Colebrook Street, Winchester SO23 9LR* Tel (01962) 890877

DOWSETT, Alan Charles. b 27. Selw Coll Cam BA51 MA55 Bris Poly CQSW76. Cuddesdon Coll 51. **d** 53 **p** 54. C Portsea St Mary *Portsm* 53-57; C Wokingham All SS *Ox* 57-60; V Water Orton *Birm* 60-64; Chapl Colston's Sch Bris 64-65; C Stoke Bishop *Bris* 65-68; Lic to Offic 69-89; rtd 89. *23 Upper Cranbrook Road, Bristol BS6 7UW* Tel 0117-924 3227

DOWSETT, Andrew Christopher. b 72. Sheff Univ BA95 PhD99. St Jo Coll Nottm 07. **d** 09. C Clubmoor *Liv* 09-11; C Birkdale St Jas from 11; C Birkdale St Pet from 11. *St Peter's Vicarage, 2 St Peters Road, Southport PR8 4BY* Tel (01704) 568448 Mobile 07783-760012 E-mail andrew@dowsetts.net

DOWSETT, Ian Peter. b 71. Liv Univ BA95 Lon Inst of Educn PGCE96. Wycliffe Hall Ox BA01. **d** 02. C Kensington St Helen w H Trin *Lon* 02-09; V S Harrow St Paul from 09. *St Paul's Vicarage, Findon Close, Harrow HA2 8NJ* Tel (020) 8864 0362 Mobile 07985-726465 E-mail ianpeter@talk21.com

DOWSETT, Canon Marian Ivy Rose. b 40. **d** 88 **p** 97. NSM Rumney *Mon* 88-94; C St Mellons and Michaelston-y-Fedw 94-96; C St Mellons 96-03; V Llanrumney 03-10; rtd 10; P-in-c

Llanrumney *Mon* from 10; Hon Can St Woolos Cathl 09-11. *114 Ridgeway Road, Rumney, Cardiff CF3 4AB* Tel (029) 2079 2635

DOWSON, Simon Paul. b 63. Bris Univ BSc85 Cam Univ PGCE89. Cranmer Hall Dur 95. **d** 97 **p** 98. C Bradf St Aug Undercliffe 97-99; C Werrington *Pet* 99-04; V Skirbeck H Trin *Linc* from 04. *Holy Trinity Vicarage, 64 Spilsby Road, Boston PE21 9NS* Tel (01205) 363657 E-mail sifi@dowzim.fsnet.co.uk

DOXSEY, Canon Roy Desmond. b 41. St D Coll Lamp 64. **d** 67 **p** 68. C Pembroke St Mary w St Mich *St D* 67-70; C Milford Haven 70-73; C Loughton *Ox* 73-75; Chapl Llandovery Coll 75-81 and 92-96; Zambia 81-86; Chapl Epsom Coll 86-92; V Roath St German *Llan* 96-11; Hon Can Llan Cathl 09-11. *St Anne's Clergy House, 3 Snipe Street, Cardiff CF24 3RB*

DOYE, Andrew Peter Charles. b 64. BNC Ox BA85. Trin Coll Bris BA93. **d** 93 **p** 94. C Surbiton St Matt *S'wark* 93-96; C Bourne *Guildf* 96-99; C The Bourne and Tilford 99-00; R Wheathampstead *St Alb* 00-09; RD Wheathampstead 07-09. *Address temp unknown* E-mail andrewdoye@hotmail.com

DOYLE, Andrew Michael. b 63. K Coll Lon BD85 AKC85. Ripon Coll Cuddesdon 86. **d** 88 **p** 89. C Lytchett Minster *Sarum* 88-92; TV Kirkby *Liv* 92-97; V Rotherhithe H Trin *S'wark* 97; AD Bermondsey 00-08. *Holy Trinity Vicarage, Bryan Road, London SE16 5HF* Tel (020) 7237 4098

DOYLE, Edward Michael. b 70. St Mich Coll Llan BTh93. **d** 94 **p** 95. C Sketty *S & B* 94-96; C Llwynderw 96-00; R Rogate w Terwick and Trotton w Chithurst *Chich* from 00. *The Vicarage, Fyning Lane, Rogate, Petersfield GU31 5EE* Tel (01730) 821576 E-mail edwarddoyle@freenet5.freeserve.co.uk

DOYLE, Eileen Ann. b 53. SEITE 08. **d** 11. NSM Coxheath, E Farleigh, Hunton, Linton etc *Roch* from 11. *63 Felderland Close, Maidstone ME15 9YD* Tel (01622) 236170 E-mail eileen@leedoyle.co.uk

DOYLE, Graham Thomas. b 48. St Barn Coll Adelaide ThL73 ThSchol77 Worc Coll Ox BA85 MA90. **d** 73 **p** 74. Australia 73-83; Perm to Offic *Ox* 83-85; C Cobbold Road St Sav w St Mary *Lon* 86; P-in-c Bradf St Oswald Chapel Green 86-91; Chapl Belgrade w Zagreb *Eur* 91-93; Chapl Belgrade 93-97; Taiwan 97-00; I Killeshandra w Killegar and Derrylane *K, E & A* 00-03; I Athlone w Benown, Kiltoom and Forgney *M & K* from 03. *St Mary's Rectory, Killion Hill Street, Bonavalley, Athlone, Co Westmeath, Republic of Ireland* Tel and fax (00353) (90) 647 8350 E-mail gtdoyleathlone@eircom.net

DOYLE, Michael Christopher. b 64. St Jo Coll Nottm 06. **d** 08 **p** 09. C Ashbourne w Mapleton *Derby* from 08. *12 Meynell Rise, Ashbourne DE6 1RU* Tel (01335) 346474 E-mail mike c doyle@hotmail.co.uk

DOYLE, Nigel Paul. b 55. MHort(RHS)82. St Mich Coll Llan 00. **d** 03 **p** 04. NSM Landore w Treboeth *S & B* 03-09; NSM Gower Deanery from 09. *3 Ael-y-Bryn, Penclawdd, Swansea SA4 3LF* Tel (01792) 850659 E-mail tadnigel@yahoo.co.uk

DOYLE, Robin Alfred. b 43. Dur Univ BA65. Westcott Ho Cam 66. **d** 68 **p** 69. C Edgbaston St Geo *Birm* 68-70; C Erdington St Barn 70-73; P-in-c Oldbury 73-81; R Maker w Rame *Truro* 81-11; rtd 11. *9 Camperknowle Close, Millbrook, Torpoint PL10 1QB*

DOYLE, Mrs Tracey Elizabeth. b 58. Open Univ BA00. SAOMC 94. **d** 97 **p** 98. OLM Winslow w Gt Horwood and Addington *Ox* 97-99; C 00-04; P-in-c Ivinghoe w Pitstone and Slapton 04-08; V Ivinghoe w Pitstone and Slapton and Marsworth from 08. *The Vicarage, Station Road, Ivinghoe, Leighton Buzzard LU7 9EB* Tel (01296) 668260 Mobile 07814-538208 E-mail mick.doyle@virgin.net

DRACKLEY, John Oldham. b 36. Em Coll Cam BA57 MA61. Wells Th Coll 57. **d** 59 **p** 60. C Eckington *Derby* 59-62; C Lee Gd Shep w St Pet *S'wark* 62-63; C Derby St Thos 63-67; C Matlock and Tansley 67-77; P-in-c Radbourne 77-82; P-in-c Dalbury, Long Lane and Trusley 77-82; P-in-c Longford 77-82; Sec Dioc Cttee for Care of Chs 82-98; rtd 95; Perm to Offic *Derby* from 98. *26 Highfield Drive, Matlock DE4 3FZ* Tel (01629) 55902

DRAFFAN, Canon Ian William. b 42. Aston Univ BSc65 MSc66 FBCS77 CEng83. NOC 83. **d** 86 **p** 87. NSM Millhouses H Trin *Sheff* 86-04; NSM Endcliffe 04-10; P-in-c 08-10; Hon Can Sheff Cathl from 05; Perm to Offic from 10. *13 Bocking Lane, Sheffield S8 7BG* Tel 0114-236 4523 E-mail ian.draffan@sheffield.anglican.org

DRAIN, Walter. b 39. JP75. Open Univ BA76 ACP66. NW Ord Course 76. **d** 79 **p** 80. NSM Cheadle *Ches* 79-81; C 81-84; V Chatburn *Blackb* 84-02; Sub Chapl HM Pris Preston 94-02; rtd 02; Perm to Offic *Blackb* from 02. *Angels, 28 The Croft, Euxton, Chorley PR7 6LH* Tel (01257) 249646

DRAKE, Frances Maud. b 43. Brentwood Coll of Educn TCert67 Sussex Univ BEd74. S'wark Ord Course 90. **d** 93 **p** 94. NSM Fryerning w Margaretting *Chelmsf* 93-01; P-in-c Margaretting w Mountnessing and Buttsbury 01-07; rtd 07; Perm to Offic *Chelmsf* from 07. *Little Pump House, Ongar Road, Kelvedon Hatch, Brentwood CM15 0LA* Tel and fax (01277) 364383 E-mail revfrances.drake@tiscali.co.uk

DRAKE, Graham. b 46. Linc Th Coll 81. **d** 83 **p** 85. C Alford w Rigsby *Linc* 83-84; Perm to Offic *Wakef* 84-85; Hon C Purston cum S Featherstone 85-89; NSM Castleford All SS 89-92; C Cudworth 92-95; rtd 11. *8A Broomhill, Castleford WF10 4QP* Tel (01977) 518407 E-mail alison-drake@btinternet.com

DRAKE, Canon Graham Rae. b 45. Fitzw Coll Cam BA68 MA72. Qu Coll Birm 70. **d** 73 **p** 74. C New Windsor *Ox* 73-77; TV 77-78; P-in-c Bath Ascension *B & W* 78-81; TV Bath Twerton-on-Avon 81-86; P-in-c Buxton w Oxnead *Nor* 86-90; P-in-c Lammas w Lt Hautbois 86-90; R Buxton w Oxnead, Lammas and Brampton 90-95; RD Ingworth 88-94; P-in-c Cockley Cley w Gooderstone 95-01; P-in-c Gt and Lt Cressingham w Threxton 95-01; P-in-c Didlington 95-01; P-in-c Hilborough w Bodney 95-01; P-in-c Oxborough w Foulden and Caldecote 95-01; P-in-c Mundford w Lynford 99-01; P-in-c Ickburgh w Langford 99-01; P-in-c Cranwich 99-01; V Thorpe St Matt 01-10; Hon Can Nor Cathl 99-10; rtd 10; Perm to Offic *Nor* from 10. *13 Needham Place, St Stephen's Square, Norwich NR1 3SD* Tel (01603) 886084 E-mail grahamrdrake@btinternet.com

DRAKE, John Paul. b 19. Qu Coll Ox BA41 MA44. Cuddesdon Coll 46. **d** 47 **p** 48. C Stepney St Dunstan and All SS *Lon* 47-54; V Brighton All So *Chich* 54-59; Chapl St Edw Sch Ox 59-69; V Stewkley *Ox* 69-75; V Stewkley w Soulbury and Drayton Parslow 75-85; RD Mursley 77-83; rtd 85; Perm to Offic *St Alb* from 85. *c/o Mrs C E Grace, Tythe Cottage, 1 School Lane, Stewkley, Leighton Buzzard LU7 0HL*

DRAKE, Leslie Sargent. b 47. Boston Univ BA69 MTh72 Hull Univ BPhil74 Anglia Poly Univ MSc93. Coll of Resurr Mirfield 78. **d** 78 **p** 79. C Oldham *Man* 78-81; TV Rochdale 81-83; V Palmers Green St Jo *Lon* 83-89; St Mary's Sch Cheshunt 89-91; Hd RE St Mary's Sch Hendon 91-99; TV Wimbledon *S'wark* 99-03; V Clay Hill St Jo and St Luke *Lon* 03-09; V Aiken St Aug USA from 09. *184 Kline Street, Aiken SC 29801, USA* Tel (001) (803) 514 2486

DRAKELEY, Stephen Richard Francis. b 51. Aston Univ BSc73. Chich Th Coll 76. **d** 76 **p** 77. C Yardley Wood *Birm* 76-79; V Rednal 79-89; TV Bodmin w Lanhydrock and Lanivet *Truro* 89-99; P-in-c Falmouth All SS from 99. *All Saints' Vicarage, 72 Dracaena Avenue, Falmouth TR11 2EN* Tel and fax (01326) 317474 E-mail srfd@compuserve.com

DRAPER, Canon Alfred James. b 23. Natal Univ BA50. St Aug Coll Cant St Paul's Coll Grahamstown. **d** 54 **p** 54. C Durban St Paul 54-58; V Umkomaas 60-63; V Tile Cross *Birm* 63-72; V Olton 72-75; R Durban St Paul 75-87; Adn Durban 79-87; R S Ferriby *Linc* 87-93; V Horkstow 87-93; R Saxby All Saints 87-93; rtd 93; Perm to Offic *Ches* from 93. *13 St James Avenue, Gawsworth, Macclesfield SK11 9RY* Tel (01625) 619033

DRAPER, Charles James. b 59. Dur Univ BSc80 Cam Univ BA86. Ridley Hall Cam 84. **d** 87 **p** 88. C Wareham *Sarum* 87-90; C Maltby *Sheff* 90-93; R The Claydons *Ox* 93-99; R Chinnor w Emmington and Sydenham etc 99-02; P-in-c Gt Faringdon w Lt Coxwell 02-07; V *The Vicarage, Coach Lane, Faringdon SN7 8AB* Tel (01367) 240106 E-mail 6drapers@cdraper.fslife.co.uk

DRAPER, Christine. b 46. **d** 06 **p** 07. OLM Newburgh w Westhead *Liv* from 06. *Arenal, 38 Hoscar Moss Road, Lathom, Ormskirk L40 4BQ* Tel (01704) 893081

DRAPER, Derek Vincent. b 38. Linc Th Coll 65. **d** 68 **p** 69. C Orpington All SS *Roch* 68-72; C Bramley *Guildf* 72-74; P-in-c Kempston All SS *St Alb* 74-76; Min Kempston Transfiguration CD 77-79; V Kempston Transfiguration 79-84; RD Bedford 79-84; V Bromham w Oakley 84-88; P-in-c Stagsden 84-88; V Bromham w Oakley and Stagsden 88-03; RD Elstow 00-02; Chapl Bromham Hosp 84-03; rtd 03; Perm to Offic *Ely* from 03. *24 Wilkinson Close, Eaton Socon, St Neots PE19 8HJ* Tel (01480) 384031 E-mail drapers24@ntlworld.com

DRAPER, Elizabeth Ann. See BRADLEY, Mrs Elizabeth Ann

DRAPER, Ivan Thomas. b 32. Aber Univ MB, ChB56 FRCP FRCPGlas. St Jo Coll Nottm 87. **d** 90 **p** 91. NSM Glas St Bride from 90; P-in-c 96-99. *1311 Whistlefield Court, 2 Canniesburn Road, Bearsden, Glasgow G61 1PX* Tel 0141-943 0954

DRAPER, James. See DRAPER, Canon Alfred James

DRAPER, Jean Margaret. b 31. **d** 80 **p** 97. NSM Pontnewydd *Mon* 80-83; BRF 82-83; NSM Llantilio Pertholey w Bettws Chpl etc *Mon* 83-94; NSM Newport St Andr 94-03. *Govilon House, Merthyr Road, Govilon, Abergavenny NP7 9PT* Tel (01873) 830380

DRAPER, John William. b 54. Qu Coll Birm 88. **d** 90 **p** 91. C Stepney St Dunstan and All SS *Lon* 90-94; C Leigh Park and Warren Park *Portsm* 94-96; R Rowner from 96; V Bridgemary 04-08; AD Gosport from 09. *The Rectory, 174 Rowner Lane, Gosport PO13 9SU* Tel (023) 9258 1834 Fax 9258 7934 Mobile 07966-559970 E-mail stmrowner174@btinternet.com

DRAPER, Canon Jonathan Lee. b 52. Gordon Coll Mass BA76 St Jo Coll Dur BA78 PhD84. Ripon Coll Cuddesdon 83. **d** 83 **p** 84. C Baguley *Man* 83-85; Dir Academic Studies Ripon Coll Cuddesdon 85-92; V Putney St Mary *S'wark* 92-00; Can Res

York Minster from 00. *3 Minster Court, York YO1 7JJ* Tel (01904) 625599 *or* 557211 Fax 672022 *or* 557215
E-mail jonathan.draper3@btinternet.com

DRAPER, Canon Martin Paul. b 50. OBE98. Birm Univ BA72 Southn Univ BTh79. Chich Th Coll 72. **d** 75 **p** 76. C Primrose Hill St Mary w Avenue Road St Paul *Lon* 75-78; C Westmr St Matt 79-84; Chapl Paris St Geo *Eur* 84-02; Adn France 94-02; Can Gib Cathl 94-02. *112 Bolanachi Building, Enid Street, London SE16 3EX* E-mail martin.draper@sfr.fr

DRAPER, Patrick Hugh. b 43. S Dios Minl Tr Scheme 91. **d** 94 **p** 95. NSM Boscombe St Jo *Win* 94-99; P-in-c Southbourne St Chris 99-02; rtd 02; Perm to Offic *Win* from 02. *82 Tuckton Road, Bournemouth BH6 3HT* Tel (01202) 420190

DRAPER, The Very Revd Paul Richard. b 64. Glas Univ MA87 TCD BTh90. **d** 90 **p** 91. C Drumragh w Mountfield *D & R* 90-94; I Ballydehob w Aghadown *C, C & R* 94-09; Can Cork and Ross Cathls 98-09; Bp's Dom Chapl 99-09; Dean Lismore *C & O* from 09; I Lismore w Cappoquin, Kilwatermoy, Dungarvan etc from 09; Dioc Dir of Ords from 10. *The Deanery, The Mall, Lismore, Co Waterford, Republic of Ireland* Tel (00353) (58) 54105 E-mail dean@lismore.anglican.org

DRAPER (née TRIMMER), Mrs Penelope Marynice. b 65. STETS 01. **d** 04 **p** 05. C Talbot Village *Sarum* 04-08; TV Dunstable *St Alb* from 08. *St Augustine's Vicarage, 83 Halfmoon Lane, Dunstable LU5 4AE* Tel (01582) 668019 Mobile 07733-172460 E-mail p.trimmer1@ntlworld.com

DRAPER, Peter Raymond. b 57. Leeds Poly BSc86 Leeds Univ CertEd88 Hull Univ PhD94 SRN80. NEOC 01. **d** 04 **p** 05. NSM S Cave and Ellerker w Broomfleet *York* from 04. *2 East Dale Road, Melton, North Ferriby HU14 3HS* Tel (01482) 632470 Mobile 07956-531002 E-mail p.r.draper@hull.ac.uk

DRAPER, Raymond James. b 48. Ex Coll Ox BA70 MA75 Em Coll Cam BA73 MA78. Ridley Hall Cam 71. **d** 74 **p** 75. C Sheff Manor 74-78; Ind Chapl 78-82; R Wickersley 82-00; V Leytonstone St Jo *Chelmsf* from 00. *St John's Vicarage, 44 Hartley Road, London E11 3BL* Tel (020) 8257 2792

DRAPER, Mrs Sylvia Edith. b 39. ARCM60. NOC 86. **d** 89 **p** 94. C Aughton St Mich *Liv* 89-92; Par Dn Wigan St Jas w St Thos 92-94; Asst Chapl Wigan and Leigh Health Services NHS Trust 92-97; C Wigan St Jas w St Thos *Liv* 94-97; TV Walton-on-the-Hill 97-02; rtd 02; Perm to Offic *Liv* from 03. *6 Brookfield Lane, Aughton, Ormskirk L39 6SP* Tel (01695) 422138

DRAX, Elizabeth Margaret. *See* ANSON, Mrs Elizabeth Margaret

DRAY, John. b 66. St Chad's Coll Dur BSc87. St Steph Ho Ox BTh95. **d** 95 **p** 96. C Byker St Ant *Newc* 95-98; C Cullercoats St Geo 98-01; P-in-c Platt *Roch* 01-05; Chapl to the Deaf 01-05. *51 Widmere Lodge Road, Bromley BR1 2QE* E-mail john.dray@bigfoot.com

DRAYCOTT, John. b 53. Sheff Univ BA84. Linc Th Coll 85. **d** 85 **p** 86. In Wesleyan Reform Union 77-82; C Wombwell *Sheff* 85-87; V W Bessacarr 87-92; V Erith Ch Ch *Roch* from 92; P-in-c Erith St Jo 92-95. *Christ Church Vicarage, Victoria Road, Erith DA8 3AN* Tel and fax (01322) 334729

DRAYCOTT, John Edward. b 54. EMMTC 99. **d** 01 **p** 02. Calverton, Epperstone, Gonalston etc *S'well* 01-05; TV Parr *Liv* from 05. *St Philip's Vicarage, 459 Fleet Lane, St Helens WA9 2NQ* Tel (01744) 21213

DRAYCOTT, Philip John. b 27. Sarum & Wells Th Coll. **d** 83 **p** 84. C Bishop's Cleeve *Glouc* 83-86; V Chedworth, Yanworth and Stowell, Coln Rogers etc 86-93; rtd 94; Perm to Offic *B & W* from 94. *April Cottage, Newton Road, North Petherton, Bridgwater TA6 6NA* Tel (01278) 662487

DRAYCOTT, Tina. b 57. Win Univ BA11. STETS 08. **d** 11. NSM Avon Valley *Sarum* from 11; NSM Durrington from 11. *27 Vicarage Gardens, Netheravon, Salisbury SP4 9RW* Tel (01980) 670649 Mobile 07747-033585 E-mail tina_draycott@hotmail.com

✠**DRAYSON, The Rt Revd Nicholas James Quested.** b 53. Keble Coll Ox BA75 MA83. Wycliffe Hall Ox 82. **d** 79 **p** 79 **c** 09. SAMS Argentina 79-82 and 92-00; Pastor Tartagal and Chapl to Chorote Indians 79-82; P-in-c Seville Ascension Spain 83-91; Adn Andalucia 89-91; Translations Co-ord 92-98; Pastor Salta St Andr 98-00; C Beverley Minster *York* 00-09; Suff Bp N Argentina from 09. *Casilla 187, 4400 Salta, Argentina* Tel (0054) (387) 431 1718 E-mail diaan.epi@gmail.com *or* nicobispo@gmail.com

DRAYTON, James Edward. b 30. St Deiniol's Hawarden 81. **d** 84 **p** 86. Hon C Heald Green St Cath *Ches* 84-88; C Bollington St Jo 88-92; P-in-c Lt Leigh and Lower Whitley 92-96; P-in-c Aston by Sutton 92-96; P-in-c Antrobus 92-96; rtd 96; Perm to Offic *York* from 96. *87 Wharfedale, Filey YO14 0DP* Tel (01723) 512662

DREDGE, David John. b 32. Cranmer Hall Dur 69. **d** 71 **p** 72. C Goole *Sheff* 71-74; P-in-c Eastoft 74-77; V Whitgift w Adlingfleet 74-77; V Whitgift w Adlingfleet and Eastoft 77-78; V Walkley 78-81; TV Bicester w Bucknell, Caversfield and Launton *Ox* 81-86; V N Brickhill and Putnoe *St Alb* 86-90; P-in-c Sarratt 90-95; rtd 95; Perm to Offic *Lich* from 95.

19 Waterdale, Wombourne, Wolverhampton WV5 0DH Tel (01902) 897467

DREDGE, David Julian. b 36. ALA74 Sheff Univ BA59. Cranmer Hall Dur 61 Ban Ord Course 85. **d** 87 **p** 88. NSM Dwygyfylchi *Ban* 87-92; R Llanllechid 92-97; rtd 97; Perm to Offic *Ban* from 97. *Westfield, Treforris Road, Penmaenmawr LL34 6RH* Tel (01492) 623439 Mobile 07721-941861 Fax 0870-056 7258 E-mail david@djdredge.plus.com

DREW, Gerald Arthur. b 36. Bps' Coll Cheshunt 59. **d** 61 **p** 62. C Lyonsdown H Trin *St Alb* 61-67; C Tring 67-71; R Bramfield w Stapleford and Waterford 71-78; V Langleybury St Paul 78-90; P-in-c Hormead, Wyddial, Anstey, Brent Pelham etc 90-95; V 95-01; rtd 01; Perm to Offic *St Alb* and *St E* from 01. *33 The Glebe, Lavenham, Sudbury CO10 9SN* Tel (01787) 248133

DREW (née ROY), Mrs Jennifer Pearl. b 53. SRN75 CSS91. Cranmer Hall Dur. **d** 01 **p** 02. C Hebburn St Jo and Jarrow Grange *Dur* 01-05; NSM Broom Leys *Leic* 05-08; Perm to Offic 08-11; NSM Loughborough Em and St Mary in Charnwood from 11. *5 Balmoral Road, Coalville LE67 4RF* Tel (01530) 836329 E-mail bobandjennied@o2.co.uk

DREW, Jo Ann. b 57. Ripon Coll Cuddesdon 09. **d** 11. C Milton next Gravesend Ch Ch *Roch* from 11. *18 Brenchley Avenue, Gravesend DA11 7RQ* Tel (01474) 356221 E-mail jodrew9@hotmail.co.uk

DREW, Michael Edgar Cecil. b 31. Oriel Coll Ox BA55 MA59. St Steph Ho Ox 55. **d** 57 **p** 58. C Plymouth St Pet *Ex* 57-63; Missr Pemb Coll Cam Miss Walworth 63-67; Asst Chapl All Hallows Sch Rousdon 67-75; Chapl 80-81; Chapl Ex Sch 81-83; V Scraptoft *Leic* 83-97; V Hungarton 83-87; P-in-c Leic St Eliz Neither Hall 87-97, ltd 97. *28 St Mary's Paddock, Wellingborough NN8 1HJ* Tel (01933) 277407

DREW, Canon Rosemary. b 43. SRN64. EAMTC 90. **d** 93 **p** 94. NSM Gt Dunmow *Chelmsf* 93-96; NSM Gt Dunmow and Barnston from 96; Hon Can Chelmsf Cathl from 01; Area Adv for Healing and Deliverance Min from 04. *The Bowling Green, 8 The Downs, Dunmow CM6 1DT* Tel and fax (01371) 872662 E-mail bruce.drew@btinternet.com

DREW, Simon Mark. b 68. Liv Univ BEng89 CEng94 MICE94. St Jo Coll Nottm MA98. **d** 99 **p** 00. C Torquay St Matthias, St Mark and H Trin *Ex* 99-03; V Marshfield w Cold Ashton and Tormarton etc *Bris* 03-11; V Middlewich w Byley *Ches* from 11. *The Rectory, Poplar Fell, Nantwich Road, Middlewich CW10 9HG* Tel (01606) 833124 E-mail revsdrew@btinternet.com

DREWETT, Mrs Susan. b 06 **p** 07. NSM Bemerton *Sarum* from 06. *Melford House, 36 Bulford Road, Durrington, Salisbury SP4 8DJ* Tel (01980) 652751 E-mail susandrewett@hotmail.net

DREYER, Rodney Granville. b 55. Lon Univ MPhil91 AKC91. St Paul's Coll Grahamstown 79. **d** 81 **p** 82. S Africa 81-84 and 94-98; NSM Headstone St Geo *Lon* 84-86; NSM Northolt St Mary 86-87; C Portsea St Mary *Portsm* 87-90; V Sudbury St Andr *Lon* 90-94; Adn W and S Free State 94-95; V Hawkhurst *Cant* from 98. *The Vicarage, Moor Hill Road, Hawkhurst, Cranbrook TN18 4QB* Tel (01580) 753397 E-mail rodneydreyer@sky.com

DRISCOLL, Canon David. b 42. Lon Univ BSc64. Linc Th Coll 68. **d** 71 **p** 72. C Walthamstow St Jo *Chelmsf* 71-76; Chapl NE Lon Poly 71-79; C-in-c Plaistow St Mary 76-79; P-in-c Stratford St Jo and Ch Ch w Forest Gate St Jas 79-89; V Theydon Bois 89-01; RD Epping Forest 92-00; Hon Can Chelmsf Cathl 01; C All Hallows by the Tower etc *Lon* 01-07; rtd 07; Educn Tutor R Foundn of St Kath in Ratcliffe 05-10; Exec Officer Miss in London's Economy 07-10; Perm to Offic *Chelmsf* and *Lon* 07-10; *Sarum* from 11. *24 Baileys Barn, Bradford-on-Avon BA15 1BX* Tel (01225) 865314 E-mail daviddriscoll42@gmail.com

DRIVER, Arthur John Roberts. b 44. SS Coll Cam MA70 FCIPA73. Linc Th Coll 73. **d** 76 **p** 77. C S'wark H Trin w St Matt 76-80; TV N Lambeth 80-85; CMS Sri Lanka 86-92; V Putney St Mary *S'wark* 92-97; V Streatham St Paul 97-09; rtd 09; Perm to Offic *Chelmsf* from 09. *91 Ernest Road, Wivenhoe, Colchester CO7 9LJ* Tel (01206) 822135 E-mail ajrdriver@gmail.com

DRIVER, Bruce Leslie. b 42. Lon Univ LLB73. Linc Th Coll 76. **d** 78 **p** 79. C Dunstable *St Alb* 78-81; TV 81-86; V Rickmansworth 86-98; RD Rickmansworth 91-98; V Northwood Hills St Edm *Lon* 98-08; rtd 08. *7 Bromley College, London Road, Bromley BR1 1PE* Tel (020) 8290 0366 E-mail bldriver@tiscali.co.uk

DRIVER, Mrs Deborah Jane. b 59. **d** 10. OLM Poringland *Nor* from 10. *50 Rectory Lane, Poringland, Norwich NR14 7SL* Tel (01508) 494641 Fax 494948 Mobile 07719-281531 E-mail debbie.driver@virgin.net

DRIVER, Geoffrey. b 41. Chich Th Coll 86. **d** 88 **p** 89. C Pontefract St Giles *Wakef* 88-91; V Glass Houghton 91-97; Chapl Pontefract Hosps NHS Trust 97-99; R Southwick H Trin *Dur* 99-03; TR N Wearside 03-11; rtd 11. *115 Killingworth Drive, High Barnes, Sunderland SR4 8QX* Tel 0191-528 5142 E-mail geoffreydriver@msn.com

DRIVER, Geoffrey Lester. b 59. Liv Poly BA83. Chich Th Coll 86. **d** 89 **p** 90. C Walton St Mary *Liv* 89-92; C Selsey *Chich* 92-95;

V Cowfold 95-07; Lic to Offic from 07; Chapl St Mich Hospice from 08. *1 Belvedere Court, 12 St Anne's Road, Eastbourne BN21 2HH* Tel (01323) 439669 Mobile 07871-488224

DRIVER, Gordon Geoffrey. b 32. Garnett Coll Lon Dip Teaching59. Trin Coll Bris. **d** 95 **p** 96. NSM Radipole and Melcombe Regis *Sarum* 95-03; rtd 03; Perm to Offic *Sarum* from 03. *11 Greenway Close, Weymouth DT3 5BQ* Tel (01305) 812784

DRIVER (née FRENCH), Janet Mary. b 43. Leeds Univ BA65 PGCE66 Surrey Univ BA98. Linc Th Coll 74. **dss** 80 **d** 92 **p** 94. St Paul's Cathl 80-82; N Lambeth *S'wark* 80-85; CMS Sri Lanka 86-92; NSM Putney St Marg *S'wark* 92-97; Hon C Streatham St Paul 97-09; rtd 09; Perm to Offic *Chelmsf* from 11. *91 Ernest Road, Wivenhoe, Colchester CO7 9LJ* Tel (01206) 822135
E-mail janet@janetdriver.co.uk

DRIVER, Jennifer. b 63. SEITE 05. **d** 08 **p** 09. NSM Farnborough *Roch* from 08. *3 Starts Hill Road, Orpington BR6 7AR* Tel (01689) 858766 Mobile 07974-722736
E-mail driverjen1@aol.com

DRIVER, John. *See* DRIVER, Arthur John Roberts

DRIVER, The Ven Penelope May. b 52. NOC. **d** 87 **p** 94. Dioc Youth Adv *Newc* 86-88; C Cullercoats St Geo 87-88; Youth Chapl *Ripon* 88-96; Dioc Adv Women's Min 91-06; Asst Dir of Ords 96-98; Dioc Dir of Ords 98-06; Min Can Ripon Cathl 96-06; Hon Can 98-06; Adn Ex from 06; P-in-c Dawlish 09-10. *Emmanuel House, Station Road, Ide, Exeter EX2 9RS* Tel (01392) 420972 *or* 425577
E-mail archdeacon.of.exeter@exeter.anglican.org

DRIVER, Canon Roger John. b 64. Liv Univ MA08. Trin Coll Bris BA88. **d** 90 **p** 91. C Much Woolton *Liv* 90-93; C Fazakerley Em 93-94; TV 94-00; P-in-c Bootle St Matt 00-03; P-in-c Bootle St Leon 00-03; P-in-c Litherland St Andr 00-03; TR Bootle from 04; AD Bootle from 07; Hon Can Liv Cathl from 07. *The Vicarage, 70 Merton Road, Bootle L20 7AT* Tel 0151-922 3316
E-mail rogerdriver@btinternet.com

DROBIG, Marion. *See* WOOD, Mrs Marion

DROMORE, Archdeacon of. *Vacant*

DROMORE, Dean of. *See* LOWRY, The Very Revd Stephen Harold

DROWLEY, Arthur. b 28. Oak Hill Th Coll 54. **d** 56 **p** 57. C Longfleet *Sarum* 56-59; C Wallington *S'wark* 59-62; V Taunton St Jas *B & W* 62-73; RD Taunton N 72-73; V Rodbourne Cheney *Bris* 73-87; R Bigbury, Ringmore and Kingston *Ex* 87-94; rtd 94; Perm to Offic *Ex* 94-02; *Man* 03-08; *Lich* from 05. *4 Inglis Road, Park Hall, Oswestry SY11 4AN* Tel (01691) 671994

DROWN, Richard. b 19. BNC Ox BA41 MA43. Wycliffe Hall Ox 41. **d** 42 **p** 43. C St Helens St Helen *Liv* 42-45; Chapl K Coll Budo Uganda 46-65; Hd Master St Andr Sch Turi Kenya 65-73; Hd Master Edin Ho Sch New Milton 73-84; rtd 84; Hon C Brockenhurst *Win* from 85. *3 Waters Green Court, Brockenhurst SO42 7QR* Tel (01590) 624038

DRUCE, Brian Lemuel. b 31. MRICS55. Bps' Coll Cheshunt 58. **d** 60 **p** 61. C Whitton St Aug *Lon* 60-63; C Minehead *B & W* 63-66; R Birch St Agnes *Man* 66-70; V Overbury w Alstone, Teddington and Lt Washbourne *Worc* 70-81; Ind Chapl 81-91; rtd 91; Perm to Offic *Worc* from 91. *Park Cottage, Elmley Castle, Pershore WR10 3HU* Tel (01386) 710577
E-mail brian.druce@talk21.com

DRUCE, John Perry. b 34. Em Coll Cam BA57 MA61 Lambeth STh97 ALCM86. Wycliffe Hall Ox 57. **d** 59 **p** 60. C Wednesbury St Bart *Lich* 59-62; C Bushbury 62-64; V Walsall Wood 64-74; R Farnborough *Roch* 74-87; R E Bergholt *St E* 87-99; P-in-c Bentley w Tattingstone 95-99; rtd 99. *9 Fullers Close, Hadleigh, Ipswich IP7 5AS* Tel (01473) 827242
E-mail jgdruce@realemail.co.uk

DRUMMOND, Canon Christopher John Vaughan. b 26. Magd Coll Ox MA51 Magd Coll Cam MA56. Ridley Hall Cam 51. **d** 53 **p** 54. C Barking St Marg *Chelmsf* 53-56; Tutor Ridley Hall Cam 56-59; Lic to Offic *Ely* 57-62; Chapl Clare Coll Cam 59-62; Nigeria 63-69; V Walthamstow St Jo *Chelmsf* 69-74; P-in-c Stantonbury *Ox* 74-75; R 75-84; P-in-c Ducklington 84-88; Dioc Ecum Officer 84-88; Can Ibadan from 87; Home Sec Gen Syn Bd for Miss and Unity 88-91; rtd 91; P-in-c Colton *Lich* 91-94; Perm to Offic *Lich* 94-99 and *Guildf* from 97. *77 Markham Road, Capel, Dorking RH5 5JT* Tel (01306) 712637 Mobile 07966-518681

DRUMMOND, John Malcolm. b 44. Nottm Univ CertEd65. Edin Th Coll 68. **d** 71 **p** 72. C Kirkholt *Man* 71-74; C Westleigh St Pet 74-76; Hd of RE Leigh High Sch from 76; Lic Preacher 76-84; Hon C Leigh St Jo 84-90; Hon C Tonge Moor 90-10; Perm to Offic from 10. *14 Bull's Head Cottages, Tottington Road, Turton, Bolton BL7 0HS* Tel (01204) 852232
E-mail rev.m.drummond@btinternet.com

DRUMMOND, Josceline Maurice Vaughan. b 29. Lon Univ BD70. Wycliffe Hall Ox 55. **d** 58 **p** 59. C Tunbridge Wells St Jo *Roch* 58-60; C Walthamstow St Mary *Chelmsf* 60-62; V Oulton *Lich* 62-68; V Leyton St Cath *Chelmsf* 71-85; Gen Dir CMJ 85-94; Public Preacher *St Alb* 88-94; rtd 94; Perm to Offic *St Alb* from 94. *3 Fryth Mead, St Albans AL3 4TN* Tel (01727) 857620

DRUMMOND, Ms Judi. b 74. Cranmer Hall Dur. **d** 06 **p** 07. C Kirkby *Liv* 06-09; C Rainhill from 09; Chapl E Lon Univ from 11. *The Rectory, Navarre Road, London E6 3AQ* Tel (020) 8470 7803 Mobile 07748-965856 E-mail drummondjudi@gmail.com

DRURY, Anthony Desmond. b 42. NOC. **d** 99 **p** 00. NSM New Ferry *Ches* from 99. *61 Church Road, Bebington, Wirral CH63 3DZ* Tel 0151-334 4797
E-mail des@stmarksnewferry.org.uk

DRURY, Mrs Carol. b 61. SRN83. Trin Coll Bris BA02. **d** 01 **p** 02. NSM Soundwell *Bris* 01-03; CMS Uganda 04-05; C Motueka New Zealand from 06. *St Thomas's Church, 101 High Street, Motueka, New Zealand* Tel (0064) (3) 528 8825

DRURY, Mrs Caroline Nora. b 60. SAOMC 00. **d** 03 **p** 04. C Leavesden *St Alb* 03-09; C Bushey from 09. *466 Bushey Mill Lane, Bushey WD23 2AS* Tel (01923) 220340
E-mail caroline.drury@btinternet.com

DRURY, Desmond. *See* DRURY, Anthony Desmond

DRURY, The Very Revd John Henry. b 36. Trin Hall Cam MA66. Westcott Ho Cam 61. **d** 63 **p** 64. C St John's Wood *Lon* 63-66; Chapl Down Coll Cam 66-69; Chapl Ex Coll Ox 69-73; Can Res Nor Cathl 73-79; Vice-Dean 78-79; Lect Sussex Univ 79-81; Dean K Coll Cam 81-91; Dean Ch Ch Ox 91-03; rtd 03; Chapl and Fell All So Coll Ox from 03. *All Souls College, Oxford OX1 4AL* Tel (01865) 279379 Fax 279299

DRURY, Michael Dru. b 31. Trin Coll Ox BA55 MA59. Wycliffe Hall Ox. **d** 58 **p** 59. C Fulham St Mary N End *Lon* 58-62; C Blackheath St Jo *S'wark* 62-64; Chapl and Asst Master Canford Sch Wimborne 64-80; Chapl and Teacher Fernhill Manor Sch New Milton 80-81; P-in-c Stowe *Ox* 82-92; Asst Master Stowe Sch Bucks 82-92; R Rampton w Laneham, Treswell, Cottam and Stokeham *S'well* 92-96; rtd 96; Perm to Offic *Sarum* from 96. *Tanfield, Giddylake, Wimborne BH21 2QT* Tel (01202) 881246
E-mail michaeldrury@talktalk.net

DRURY, Richard Alexander. b 63. Lon Univ BD85 Avery Hill Coll PGCE86 ACII91. Trin Coll Bris MA00. **d** 00 **p** 01. C Kingswood *Bris* 00-03; CMS Uganda 04-05; V Motueka New Zealand from 06. *St Thomas's Church, 101 High Street, Motueka, New Zealand* Tel (0064) (3) 528 8825

DRURY, Stephen Roger. b 45. Univ Coll Lon LLB66 Solicitor 70. Coll of Resurr Mirfield 06. **d** 07 **p** 08. NSM Seamer w East Ayton *York* from 07. *74 Garth End Road, West Ayton, Scarborough YO13 9JH* Tel (01723) 862044 E-mail stephen drury@hotmail.com

DRURY, Valerie Doreen. b 40. Univ of Wales (Cardiff) BA62 K Coll Lon PGCE63 Lon Inst of Educn ADEDC80 MBATOD80. Oak Hill Th Coll 85. **d** 87 **p** 94. NSM Becontree St Alb *Chelmsf* 87-89; NSM Becontree S 89-02; rtd 02; Perm to Offic *Chelmsf* from 02. *37 Blunts Hall Road, Witham CM8 1ES* Tel (01376) 517330 E-mail vdrury@tiscali.co.uk

DRYDEN, Barry Frederick. b 44. Ches Coll of HE BTh00. NOC 97. **d** 00 **p** 01. C Formby St Pet *Liv* 00-03; V Woolston 03-10; rtd 10. *5 Briton Lodge Close, Moira, Swadlincote DE12 6DD*
E-mail revbarrydryden@ntlworld.com

DRYDEN, Martin John. b 57. Loughb Univ BA80 Univ of Wales (Lamp) MA09. STETS 07. **d** 09 **p** 10. NSM Jersey St Clem *Win* from 09. *Mont Ubé House, La rue de la Blinerie, St Clement, Jersey JE2 6QT* Tel (01534) 874668 Mobile 07797-729525
E-mail martin@mont-ube.net

DRYE, Douglas John. b 37. Man Univ BSc61. Clifton Th Coll. **d** 63 **p** 64. C Whalley Range St Edm *Man* 63-66; C Drypool St Columba w St Andr and St Pet *York* 66-68; V Worsbrough Common *Sheff* 68-86; R Armthorpe 86-92; rtd 92; Perm to Offic *Pet* from 92. *25 Willow Crescent, Oakham LE15 6EQ* Tel (01572) 770429 E-mail ddrye@supanet.com

D'SOUZA, Derek Emile. b 54. Trin Coll Bris. **d** 07 **p** 08. C Edgbaston St Germain *Birm* 07-11; P-in-c Prince's Park *Roch* from 11. *6 Thrush Close, Chatham ME5 7TG* Tel (01634) 685828
E-mail helennderek@yahoo.co.uk

du SAIRE, Ms Michele Marie. b 55. Leeds Poly BSc78. ERMC 06. **d** 09 **p** 10. C Leavesden *St Alb* from 09. *St Hilda's House, 49 Ross Crescent, Watford WD25 0DA* Tel (01923) 673129
E-mail micheledusaire@googlemail.com

DUBLIN (Christ Church), Dean of. *See* DUNNE, The Very Revd Dermot Patrick Martin

DUBLIN (St Patrick's), Dean of. *See* MacCARTHY, The Very Revd Robert Brian

DUBLIN, Archbishop of, and Bishop of Glendalough. *See* JACKSON, The Most Revd Michael Geoffrey St Aubyn

DUBLIN, Archdeacon of. *See* PIERPOINT, The Ven David Alfred

DUBREUIL, Yann. b 70. Birm Univ BA04. Wycliffe Hall Ox 05. **d** 07 **p** 08. C Four Marks *Win* 07-11; R Bentley, Binsted and Froyle from 11. *Holy Cross Vicarage, Church Street, Binsted, Alton GU34 4NX* Tel 07777-684533 (mobile)
E-mail yann@benbinfro.org

DUCKERS, Miss Linda Jean. b 62. Univ of Wales (Abth) BSc84 PGCE85 Rob Coll Cam BTh06. Ridley Hall Cam 04. **d** 06 **p** 07. C Leek and Meerbrook *Lich* 06-10; TV Warwick *Cov* from 10.

St Nicholas' Vicarage, 184 Myton Road, Warwick CV34 6PS Tel (01926) 496209 E-mail linda.duckers@googlemail.com
DUCKERS, Paul Gerrard. b 42. Qu Coll Birm 07. **d** 09 **p** 10. NSM Sutton Coldfield H Trin *Birm* from 09. *5 Moor Meadow Road, Sutton Coldfield B75 6BU* Tel 0121-378 1835 E-mail paulduckers@talktalk.net
DUCKETT, Canon Brian John. b 45. ALCD70. **d** 70 **p** 71. C S Lambeth St Steph *S'wark* 70-73; C Norwood St Luke 73-75; C Bushbury *Lich* 75-77; TV 77-79; V Dover St Martin *Cant* 79-92; TR Swindon Dorcan *Bris* 92-00; RD Highworth 95-99; V Clifton H Trin, St Andr and St Pet 00-09; Vulnerable Adults Policy Officer 07-09; Hon Can Bris Cathl 98-09; rtd 09. *52 The Fieldings, Southwater, Horsham RH13 9LZ* Tel (01403) 733417
DUCKETT, Ms Helen Lorraine. b 71. Keble Coll Ox BA92 Sheff Univ MA94 Birm Univ MPhil98. Qu Coll Birm 95. **d** 98 **p** 99. C Cannock *Lich* 98-01; TV Wednesfield 01-10; TV Cen Wolverhampton from 10. *St Chad's Vicarage, Manlove Street, Wolverhampton WV3 0HG* Tel (01902) 710173 E-mail duckett.h@tinyworld.co.uk
DUCKETT, John Dollings. b 41. Nottm Univ BA62 BTh81. Linc Th Coll 79. **d** 81 **p** 82. C Boston *Linc* 81-84; V Baston 84-86; V Langtoft Gp 86-88; V Sutterton and Wigtoft 88-89; R Sutterton w Fosdyke and Algarkirk 89-92; P-in-c Chapel St Leonards w Hogsthorpe 92-97; V 97-00; V Bracebridge 00-06; rtd 06. *Old Post Office, Faldingworth Road, Spridlington, Market Rasen LN8 2DF* Tel (01673) 860116
DUCKETT, Keith Alexander. b 69. Worc Coll of Educn BA93. Qu Coll Birm BD97 MA98. **d** 98 **p** 99. C Willenhall H Trin *Lich* 98-01; TV Blakenall Heath 01-03; Asst Chapl Sandwell and W Birm Hosps NHS Trust 03-06; Chapl from 06. *Sandwell General Hospital, Lyndon, West Bromwich B71 4HJ* Tel 0121-507 3552 *or* (01902) 710173 E-mail keith.duckett@swbh.nhs.uk *or* duckettk@fish.co.uk
DUCKETT, Lee Christopher James. b 67. Wycliffe Hall Ox BTh04. **d** 04 **p** 05. C Cranham Park *Chelmsf* 04-08; C Purley Ch Ch *S'wark* from 08. *72 Riddlesdown Road, Purley CR8 1DB* Tel 07782-171320 (mobile) E-mail leeduckett@ymail.com
DUCKETT, Matthew Robert. b 64. UEA BSc85 PGCE88. NTMTC BA09. **d** 09 **p** 10. NSM Old St Pancras *Lon* from 09. *Little Ilford Rectory, 124 Church Road, London E12 6HA* Tel (020) 8478 2182 E-mail m.duckett@ucl.ac.uk
DUCKETT, Raphael Thomas Marie James. b 65. N Staffs Poly BA87. Cranmer Hall Dur 01. **d** 03 **p** 04. C Madeley *Heref* 03-06; V Bradley St Martin *Lich* from 06. *St Martin's Vicarage, 7 King Street, Bradley, Bilston WV14 8PQ* Tel (01902) 650101 E-mail revraphael@blueyonder.co.uk
DUCKWORTH, Mrs Angela Denise. b 58. SRN95 RM98. Ripon Coll Cuddesdon 05. **d** 07 **p** 08. C Malvern H Trin and St Jas *Worc* 07-10; Perm to Offic *Roch* from 10. *Address temp unknown*
DUCKWORTH, Annette Jacqueline. b 54. Univ of Wales (Ban) BSc75 PGCE76. **d** 00 **p** 01. OLM Moxley *Lich* from 00; Chapl Blue Coat Comp Sch Walsall 07-10. *1 Sutton Road, Wednesbury WS10 8SG* E-mail annette.duckworth@hotmail.co.uk
DUCKWORTH, Brian George. b 47. Edin Th Coll 85. **d** 87 **p** 88. C Sutton in Ashfield St Mary *S'well* 87-95; C Sutton in Ashfield St Mich 89-95; P-in-c 95-98; TV Hucknall Torkard 98-03; R S Ockendon and Belhus Park *Chelmsf* from 03. *The Vicarage, 121 Foyle Drive, South Ockendon RM15 5HF* Tel and fax (01708) 853246 E-mail brian288@btinternet.com
DUCKWORTH, Patrick Richard Stephen. b 52. **d** 77 **p** 77. C Bendigo Australia 77-79; C Swan Hill 80; R Ouyen 80-83; Chapl Launceston Ch Gr Sch 88-98; Chapl St Pet Coll Adelaide 99-10; P-in-c Barnsley St Mary *Wakef* from 10. *22 Elmwood Way, Barnsley S75 1EY* Tel (01226) 208780 Mobile 07762-245229 E-mail duckworth52@btinternet.com
DUDLEY, Mrs Janet Carr. b 36. EMMTC 86. **d** 89 **p** 94. NSM Countesthorpe w Foston *Leic* 89-94; NSM Arnesby w Shearsby and Bruntingthorpe 94-01; rtd 01; Perm to Offic *Leic* 01-02; NSM Market Harborough and The Transfiguration etc from 02. *13 The Broadway, Market Harborough LE16 7LZ* Tel (01858) 467619
DUDLEY, John Donald Swanborough. b 34. Ox Univ BTh95. SAOMC 96. **d** 97 **p** 98. NSM Emmer Green *Ox* 97-02; Perm to Offic from 02. *26 Russet Glade, Emmer Green, Reading RG4 8UJ* Tel and fax 0118-954 6664
DUDLEY, Ms Josephine. b 52. ERMC 04. **d** 06 **p** 07. NSM Tolleshunt Knights w Tiptree and Gt Braxted *Chelmsf* 06-11; P-in-c Laxey *S & M* from 11; P-in-c Lonan from 11. *The Vicarage, 56 Ard Reayrt, Ramsey Road, Laxey, Isle of Man IM4 7QQ* Tel 07704-431790 (mobile) E-mail jo@dudley.plus.com
DUDLEY, Martin Raymond. b 53. K Coll Lon BD77 AKC72 MTh78 PhD94 City Univ MSc07 FRHistS95 FSA97 FRSA06. St Mich Coll Llan 78. **d** 79 **p** 80. C Whitchurch *Llan* 79-83; V Weston *St Alb* 83-88; P-in-c Ardeley 87-88; V Owlsmoor *Ox* 88-95; Lect Simon of Cyrene Th Inst 92-95; R Smithfield St Bart from 95. *The Parish Office, 6 Kinghorn Street, London EC1A 7HW* Tel (020) 7606 5171 *or* 7628 3644 Fax 7600 6909 E-mail rector@greatstbarts.com

DUDLEY, Miss Wendy Elizabeth. b 46. City of Sheff Coll CertEd68. Cranmer Hall Dur 79. **dss** 81 **d** 87 **p** 94. Cumnor *Ox* 81-89; Par Dn 87-89; Par Dn Hodge Hill *Birm* 89-94; C 94-95; TV 95-98; TV Bucknall *Lich* 98-06; rtd 06; Perm to Offic *Lich* from 08. *26 Swallow Croft, Lichfield WS13 7HF* Tel (01543) 306509 E-mail wed.btm@tinyworld.co.uk
DUDLEY-SMITH, James. b 66. Fitzw Coll Cam BA89 MA92. Wycliffe Hall Ox BTh94. **d** 97 **p** 98. C New Borough and Leigh *Sarum* 97-01; C Hove Bp Hannington Memorial Ch *Chich* 01-06; R Yeovil w Kingston Pitney *B & W* from 06. *The Rectory, 41 The Park, Yeovil BA20 1DG* Tel (01935) 475352
✠**DUDLEY-SMITH, The Rt Revd Timothy.** b 26. OBE03. Pemb Coll Cam BA47 MA51 Lambeth MLitt91 Dur Univ Hon DD09. Ridley Hall Cam 48. **d** 50 **p** 51 **c** 81. C Erith St Paul *Roch* 50-53; Lic to Offic *S'wark* 53-62; Hd of Cam Univ Miss Bermondsey 53-55; Chapl 55-60; Ed Sec Evang Alliance and Ed *Crusade* 55-59; Asst Sec CPAS 59-65; Gen Sec 65-73; Adn Nor 73-81; Suff Bp Thetford 81-91; rtd 92. *9 Ashlands, Ford, Salisbury SP4 6DY* Tel (01722) 326417
DUDLEY, Archdeacon of. *See* TRETHEWEY, The Ven Frederick Martyn
DUDLEY, Suffragan Bishop of. *See* WALKER, The Rt Revd David Stuart
DUERDEN, Martin James. b 55. Liv Poly BA77. Oak Hill Th Coll 86. **d** 88 **p** 89. C Tunbridge Wells St Jas *Roch* 88-92; V Southport SS Simon and Jude *Liv* 92-98; P-in-c Maghull 98-02; TR 02-07; P-in-c Marsh Green w Newtown 07; V from 08. *65 Plane Avenue, Wigan WN5 9PT* Tel (01942) 211545 E-mail martinduerden@hotmail.com
DUERR, Robert Kenneth. b 54. Univ of S California BMus77 MMus80. Ridley Hall Cam 99. **d** 04 **p** 06. NSM Cambridge Gt St Mary w St Mich *Ely* 04-05; C Marton-in-Cleveland *York* 06-07; C Scarborough St Martin and Scarborough St Sav w All SS 07-10. *258 Christiana Street, North Tonawanda NY 14120, USA* Tel (001) (904) 671 2916 (mobile) E-mail robert@robertduerr.com
DUFF, James. *See* FINCH, Mrs Alison
DUFF, Andrew John. b 57. Open Univ BSc07. Sarum & Wells Th Coll 92. **d** 92 **p** 93. C Banbury *Ox* 92-95; C Bracknell 95-96; TV 96-98; CF 98-04; Chapl RN from 04. *Royal Naval Chaplaincy Service, Mail Point 1-2, Leach Building, Whale Island, Portsmouth PO2 8BY* Tel (023) 9262 5055 Fax 9262 5134
DUFF, Garden Ian. b 34. Imp Coll Lon BScEng56. Sarum & Wells Th Coll 92. **d** 93 **p** 94. NSM Ashton Gifford *Sarum* 93-97; TV Upper Wylye Valley 97-03; rtd 03. *Trinity Trees Cottage, 58 Upton Lovell, Warminster BA12 0JP* Tel and fax (01985) 850291
DUFF, Jeremy. b 71. MA DPhil. **d** 06 **p** 07. NSM Toxteth St Philemon w St Gabr and St Cleopas *Liv* 06-10; Dir Lifelong Learning and Can Liv Cathl 04-10; TV S Widnes from 10. *St Paul's Vicarage, Victoria Square, Widnes WA8 7QU* E-mail jeremy.duff@liverpool.anglican.org
DUFF, Jillian Louise Calland. b 72. Ch Coll Cam BA93 MA97 Worc Coll Ox DPhil96. Wycliffe Hall Ox BA02. **d** 03. C Litherland St Phil *Liv* 03-05; Lic to Adn Liv from 05. *St Paul's Vicarage, Victoria Square, Widnes WA8 7QU*
DUFF, John Alexander. b 57. York Univ BA78. EMMTC 91. **d** 94 **p** 95. NSM Linc St Geo Swallowbeck 94-00; Perm to Offic *Ripon* from 02. *37 Mornington Crescent, Harrogate HG1 5DL* Tel (01423) 549987 Mobile 07788-432009 E-mail ffudnhoj@hotmail.com
DUFF, Michael Ian. b 63. Ox Univ BA85. Trin Coll Bris BA98 MA99. **d** 99 **p** 00. C Southsea St Jude *Portsm* 99-03; CMS Bandung Indonesia 03-07; V Southsea St Jude *Portsm* from 07. *St Jude's Vicarage, 7 Hereford Road, Southsea PO5 2DH* Tel (023) 9234 9622 E-mail all@theduffs.me.uk
DUFF, Timothy Cameron. b 40. G&C Coll Cam BA62 LLM63 MA66 Solicitor 65. NEOC 90. **d** 93 **p** 94. NSM Tynemouth Priory *Newc* 93-96; NSM N Shields 96-00; Hon TV 00-05; rtd 05; Perm to Offic *Newc* from 05. *24A Percy Gardens, Tynemouth, North Shields NE30 4HQ* Tel 0191-257 1463 E-mail timothy@timothyduff.co.uk
DUFFETT, Canon Paul Stanton. b 33. Keble Coll Ox BA55 MA59. Ripon Hall Ox. **d** 59 **p** 60. C Portsea St Cuth *Portsm* 59-63; C Inhlwathi S Africa 63-65; R Inandhlwana 65-68; Chapl Nqutu Hosp 68-70; R Vryheid 71-79; Hon Can Zululand from 87; Accredited Rep Zululand and Swaziland Assn from 89; P-in-c Greatham w Empshott *Portsm* 80-85; R 85-88; R Papworth Everard *Ely* 88-98; Chapl Papworth Hosps 88-98; rtd 98; Hon Chapl MU from 97; Perm to Offic *Ely* from 99. *11 Roman Hill, Barton, Cambridge CB23 7AX* Tel (01223) 262831 E-mail duffett@ifightpoverty.com
DUFFETT-SMITH (née RUSHTON), Ms Patricia Mary. b 54. Lon Univ BPharm76 Anglia Poly Univ MA99 MRPharmS77. EAMTC 94. **d** 97 **p** 98. NSM Haddenham and Wilburton *Ely* 97-00; Asst Chapl Hinchingbrooke Health Care NHS Trust from 99. *Holme House, 4B The Avenue, Godmanchester, Huntingdon PE29 2AF* Tel 07788-668900 (mobile) E-mail trishads@googlemail.com

DUFFIELD, Ian Keith. b 47. K Coll Lon BD71 AKC71 MTh73. NY Th Sem DMin84. **d** 73 **p** 74. C Broxbourne *St Alb* 73-77; C Harpenden St Nic 77-81; TV Sheff Manor 81-87; V Walkley 87-02; V Sheff St Leon Norwood from 02. *St Leonard's Vicarage, 93 Everingham Road, Sheffield S5 7LE* Tel 0114-243 6689

DUFFIELD, John Ernest. b 55. BA86. Oak Hill Th Coll 83. **d** 86 **p** 87. C Walton Breck Ch Ch *Liv* 86-89; TV Fazakerley Em 89-00; Chapl N Cheshire Hosps NHS Trust from 00. *Warrington Hospital, Lovely Lane, Warrington WA5 1QG* Tel (01925) 662146 Fax 662048 E-mail john.duffield@nch.nhs.uk

DUFFIELD, Ronald Bertram Charles. b 26. Hull Univ Coll BA49 TCert50. Sarum & Wells Th Coll 91. **d** 92 **p** 93. NSM E Knoyle, Semley and Sedgehill *Sarum* 92-94; P-in-c 94-95; rtd 95; Perm to Offic *York* 95-99 and from 01; P-in-c Isfield *Chich* 99-01. *16 Wylies Road, Beverley HU17 7AP* Tel (01482) 880983

DUFFUS, Barbara Rose. *See* HOBBS, Mrs Barbara Rose

DUGDALE, Angela Marion. b 33. MBE06 DL92. ARCM52 GRSM54 UEA Hon MA89. **d** 97 **p** 98. OLM Weybourne Gp *Nor* 97-03; rtd 03; Perm to Offic *Nor* from 03. *The Old Carpenter's Shop, Kelling, Holt NR25 7EL* Tel (01263) 588389 Fax 588594 E-mail dugdale@freeuk.com

DUGMORE, Barry John. b 61. STETS. **d** 01 **p** 02. C Cowplain *Portsm* 01-04; C-in-c Whiteley CD and Dioc Ecum Officer 04-07; P-in-c Tiverton St Geo and St Paul *Ex* from 07. *St Paul's Vicarage, Bakers Hill, Tiverton EX16 5NE* Tel (01884) 255705 E-mail b.dugmore@ukgateway.net

DUGUID, Alison Audrey. b 52. STETS 99. **d** 02 **p** 03. C Appledore w Brookland, Fairfield, Brenzett etc *Cant* 02-06; P-in-c The Brents and Davington w Oare and Luddenham from 06; P-in-c Ospringe from 06; Dir Dioc Poverty and Hope Appeal from 07. *The Vicarage, Brent Hill, Faversham ME13 7EF* Tel (01795) 533272 Mobile 07880-711202 E-mail ali@dogooders.co.uk

DUGUID, Reginald Erskine. b 29. S'wark Ord Course. **d** 88 **p** 89. NSM Notting Hill All SS w St Columb *Lon* 88-99; Perm to Offic from 99. *53 Sandbourne, Dartmouth Close, London W11 1DS* Tel (020) 7221 4436

DUKE, Canon Alan Arthur. b 38. Tyndale Hall Bris 59. **d** 64 **p** 65. C Whalley Range St Marg *Man* 64-67; C Folkestone H Trin w Ch Ch *Cant* 67-71; V Queenborough 71-76; V Bearsted w Thurnham 76-86; P-in-c Torquay St Luke *Ex* 86-91; R Barham w Bishopsbourne and Kingston *Cant* 91-00; Dioc Communications Officer 91-95; Hon Can Cant Cathl 99-03; Chapl to Bp Dover 00-03; Bp's Media Link Officer 00-03; rtd 03; Perm to Offic *Cant* from 03. *Roundways, Derringstone Hill, Barham, Canterbury CT4 6QD* Tel (01227) 831817 Fax 784985 Mobile 07751-833670

DUKE, David Malcolm. b 40. Ch Ch Ox BA61 MA65 Newc Poly MPhil80 CQSW81. Cuddesdon Coll 63. **d** 65 **p** 66. C Sunderland Pennywell St Thos *Dur* 65-68; C Dur St Oswald 68-70; C Harton 70-74; Perm to Offic 85-96; Hon C Hedworth from 96. *43 Coquet Street, Jarrow NE32 5SW* Tel 0191-430 1200 Fax 537 4409 Mobile 07979-036977

DUKE, Miss Judith Mary. b 47. Leeds Univ LLB68. Cranmer Hall Dur 03. **d** 04 **p** 05. NSM Buckrose Carrs *York* 04-07; R from 07. *2 High Street, Rillington, Malton YO17 8LA* Tel (01944) 758305

DULFER, John Guidi. b 37. Lich Th Coll 62. **d** 64 **p** 65. C Fenny Stratford and Water Eaton *Ox* 64-67; C Cheshunt *St Alb* 67-68; C Kennington Cross St Anselm *S'wark* 68-74; C N Lambeth 74-76; P-in-c Kensington St Phil Earl's Court *Lon* 76-79; V 79-84; V Jersey City St Jo and Jersey City St Matt USA 84-85; R New York Resurr 00-01; P-in-c Castleton 02-06. *110 West 15 Street, Apartment 1, New York NY 10011-6724, USA* E-mail johndulfer@hotmail.com

DULLEY, Arthur John Franklyn. b 32. Mert Coll Ox BA54 MA57. St Jo Coll Nottm 69. **d** 71 **p** 72. Lect St Jo Coll Nottm 71-96; Hon C Attenborough w Chilwell *S'well* 71-73; C Penn Fields *Lich* 73-74; Chapl Aldenham Sch Herts 74-79; Chapl HM Pris Ashwell 79-87; V Langham *Pet* 79-96; rtd 96; Perm to Offic *Ely* 96-98. *2 St Augustines Close, Bexhill-on-Sea TN39 3AZ* Tel (01424) 733020

DUMAT, Mrs Jennifer. b 42. ARCM62. Qu Coll Birm 80 EMMTC 82. **dss** 83 **d** 87 **p** 94. Chapl Asst Pilgrim Hosp Boston 83-94; P-in-c Friskney *Linc* 94-04; rtd 04. *11 Sea Lane, Butterwick, Boston PE22 0EY* Tel (01205) 760883

✠**DUMPER, The Rt Revd Anthony Charles.** b 23. Ch Coll Cam BA45 MA48. Westcott Ho Cam. **d** 47 **p** 48 **c** 77. C E Greenwich Ch Ch w St Andr and St Mich *S'wark* 47-49; Malaya 49-63; Malaysia 63-64; Dean Singapore 64-70; V Stockton St Pet *Dur* 70-77; P-in-c Stockton H Trin 76-77; RD Stockton 70-77; Suff Bp Dudley *Worc* 77-93; rtd 93; Hon Asst Bp Birm from 93. *John Wills House, Jessop Crescent, Bristol BS10 6TU* Tel 0117-377 3801

DUNBAR, Peter Lamb. b 46. Bede Coll Dur DipEd68. Lambeth STh77 NOC 78. **d** 81 **p** 82. NSM Knaresborough *Ripon* 81-82; C Knaresborough 82-84; R Farnham w Scotton, Staveley, Copgrove etc 84-92; V Upper Nidderdale from 92; Chapl St Aid

Sch Harrogate 86-94. *The Vicarage, Church Street, Pateley Bridge, Harrogate HG3 5LQ* Tel (01423) 711414 E-mail lion.lamb@virgin.net

DUNCAN, Mrs Amanda Jayne. b 58. Balls Park Coll Hertford BEd79. ERMC 08. **d** 11. C Harpenden St Jo *St Alb* from 11. *2 Linwood Road, Harpenden AL5 1RR* Tel 07506-715026 (mobile) E-mail amanda.duncan2387@o2.co.uk

DUNCAN, Canon Bruce. b 38. MBE93. Leeds Univ BA60 FRSA. Cuddesdon Coll 65. **d** 67 **p** 68. C Armley St Bart *Ripon* 67-69; Dir Children's Relief Internat 69-71; Hon C Cambridge St Mary Less *Ely* 69-70; Chapl OHP and St Hilda's Sch Whitby 70-71; Chapl Vienna w Budapest and Prague *Eur* 71-75; V Crediton *Ex* 75-82; R Crediton and Shobrooke 82-86; RD Cadbury 76-81 and 84-86; Can Res Man Cathl 86-95; Prin Sarum Coll and Can and Preb Sarum Cathl 95-02; rtd 02; Perm to Offic *Ex* 02-08 and *Sarum* from 08; Chapl Ex Univ 03-04. *92 Harnham Road, Salisbury SP2 8JW* Tel (01722) 502227 Mobile 07851-737230 E-mail churchpath1@ntlworld.com

DUNCAN, Christopher Robin. b 41. AKC71. **d** 72 **p** 73. C Allington *Cant* 72-77; P-in-c Wittersham 77-82; R Wittersham w Stone and Ebony 82-85; V Chilham 85-92; P-in-c Challock w Molash 87-92; RD W Bridge 92-95 and 02-03; V Chilham w Challock and Molash from 92. *The Vicarage, 3 Hambrook Close, Chilham, Canterbury CT4 8EJ* Tel (01227) 730235 E-mail chris.duncan@chil-vic.co.uk

DUNCAN, Colin Richard. b 34. SS Coll Cam BA58 MA60. Ripon Coll Cuddesdon 83. **d** 85 **p** 86. C Stafford *Lich* 85-89; C Wednesfield 89-90; TV 90-99; rtd 99; Perm to Offic *Glouc* from 99. *Fir Tree Cottage, Union Road, Bakers Hill, Coleford GL16 7QB*

DUNCAN, Graham Charles Dewar. b 65. Sheff Univ BSc87. NTMTC 95. **d** 98 **p** 99. NSM Dawley St Jerome *Lon* 98-00; NSM Sheff St Mary Bramall Lane from 00; Manager St Mary's Ch Community Cen from 00. *11 Coverdale Road, Sheffield S7 2DD* Tel 0114-258 7275 *or* 272 5596 Fax 275 3892

✠**DUNCAN, The Rt Revd Gregor Duthie.** b 50. Glas Univ MA72 Clare Coll Cam PhD77 Oriel Coll Ox BA83. Ripon Coll Cuddesdon 81. **d** 83 **p** 84 **c** 10. C Oakham, Hambleton, Egleton, Braunston and Brooke *Pet* 83-86; Chapl Edin Th Coll 87-89; R Largs *Glas* 89-99; Dean Glas 96-10; R Glas St Ninian 99-10; Bp Glas from 10. *Bishop's Office, Diocesan Centre, 5 St Vincent Place, Glasgow G1 2DH* Tel 0141-221 6911 Fax 221 7014 E-mail bishop@glasgow.anglican.org

DUNCAN, John. b 22. Open Univ BA. Roch Th Coll 64. **d** 66 **p** 67. C Gainsborough All SS *Linc* 66-68; C Boultham 68-71; V W Pinchbeck 72-76; Miss at Fort Smith Canada 76-81; R Ridgewell w Ashen, Birdbrook and Sturmer *Chelmsf* 81-88; rtd 88; Perm to Offic *Pet* 91-09. *20 Westcott Way, Northampton NN3 3BE* Tel (01604) 630797

DUNCAN, The Ven John Finch. b 33. Univ Coll Ox BA57 MA63. Cuddesdon Coll 57. **d** 59 **p** 60. C S Bank *York* 59-61; SSF 61-62; C Birm St Pet 62-65; Chapl Birm Univ 65-76; V Kings Heath 76-85; Hon Can Birm Cathl 83-85; Adn Birm 85-01; rtd 01; Perm to Offic *Birm* and *Pet* from 01. *66 Glebe Rise, King's Sutton, Banbury OX17 3PH* Tel (01295) 812641 E-mail jfduncan66@googlemail.com

DUNCAN, Thomas James. b 37. **d** 97 **p** 98. NSM Poplar *Lon* from 97. *1 Chardwell Close, London E6 5RR* Tel (020) 7474 9965 *or* 7538 9198 Mobile 07732-666434

DUNCAN, The Ven William Albert. b 30. TCD BA53 MA61 BD66. CITC 54. **d** 54 **p** 55. C Bangor Abbey *D & D* 54-57; C Larne and Inver *Conn* 57-61; Hd of Trin Coll Miss Belf 61-66; I Rasharkin w Finvoy 66-78; I Ramoan w Ballycastle and Culfeightrin 78-96; Adn Dalriada 93-96; rtd 96. *8 Beech Hill, Ballymoney BT53 6DB* Tel (028) 7066 4285

DUNCANSON, Derek James. b 47. TD93. AKC69 Open Univ BA80 Lon Univ MA(Ed)93 FCollP94. St Aug Coll Cant 69. **d** 70 **p** 71. C Norbury St Oswald *Cant* 70-72; CF (TAVR) 71-76 and 79-95; C Woodham *Guildf* 72-76; CF 76-79; V Burneside *Carl* 79-84; R Coppull St Jo *Blackb* 84-86; Chapl Bloxham Sch 86-99; V Pet St Mary Boongate 99-04; RD Pet 01-04; Chapl Pet Regional Coll 00-04; Chapl Heathfield St Mary's Sch Ascot 04-08; rtd 08; Perm to Offic *Cant* from 08; rtd 08. *Old Forge Cottage, 235 Canterbury Road, Birchington CT7 9TB* Tel (01843) 843289 E-mail dmduncanson@btinternet.com

DUNCOMBE, Maureen Barbara. *See* WHITE, Mrs Maureen Barbara

DUNDAS, Edward Paul. b 67. NUU BSc88. TCD Div Sch BTh91. **d** 91 **p** 92. C Portadown St Mark *Arm* 91-95; I Ardtrea w Desertcreat 95-00; Dioc Youth Adv to Abp Armagh 99-00; I Belfast St Aid *Conn* 00-05; I Lisburn Ch Ch from 05. *Christ Church Rectory, 27 Hillsborough Road, Lisburn BT28 1JL* Tel (028) 9266 2163 *or* 9267 3271 Mobile 07740-589465 E-mail paul dundas@yahoo.com

DUNDAS, Edward Thompson. b 36. TCD BA63. **d** 64 **p** 65. C Conwall *D & R* 64-67; I Kilbarron 67-78; I Donaghady 78-84; I Kilmore St Aid w St Sav *Arm* 84-00; rtd 04. *114 Brownstown Road, Portadown, Craigavon BT62 3PZ* Tel (028) 3833 4474 Mobile 07989-842709

DUNDAS, Gary Walter. b 56. EMMTC 04. **d** 07 **p** 08. NSM Stanton-by-Dale w Dale Abbey and Risley *Derby* from 07. *17-19 Victoria Road, Draycott, Derby DE72 3PS* Tel (01332) 872893 Fax 875371 Mobile 07971-783083 E-mail gwdundas@aol.com

DUNDEE, Provost of. See AULD, The Very Revd Jeremy Rodger

DUNFORD, Malcolm. b 34. FCA74. EMMTC 73. **d** 76 **p** 77. NSM Frodingham *Linc* from 76. *57 Rowland Road, Scunthorpe DN16 1SP* Tel (01724) 840879

DUNGAN, Hilary Anne. b 46. TCD BA98 ARCM68. CITC 98. **d** 00 **p** 01. C Arm St Mark 00-03; I Maryborough w Dysart Enos and Ballyfin *C & O* 03-11; Chapl Midlands Portlaoise Pris 03-11; rtd 11. *Address temp unknown*

DUNGAN, Ivan. CITC. **d** 09 **p** 10. NSM Bunclody w Kildavin, Clonegal and Kilrush *C & O* from 09. *Address temp unknown*

DUNHAM, Angela Mary. See CHEESEMAN, Mrs Angela Mary

DUNK, Mrs Carol Ann. b 65. EMMTC 08. **d** 11. NSM Retford Area *S'well* from 11. *42 Whitehall Road, Retford DN22 6HX* Tel (01777) 709092 Mobile 07527-081388 E-mail dunkavicar@hotmail.co.uk

DUNK, Carolyn Margaret. b 55. Wycliffe Hall Ox 04. **d** 06 **p** 07. C Uxbridge *Lon* 06-09; C W Ealing St Jo w St Jas from 09. *23A Culmington Road, London W13 9NJ* Tel (020) 8566 3459 E-mail cazdunk@yahoo.co.uk *or* caz.dunk@stjamesealing.org.uk

DUNK, Michael Robin. b 43. Oak Hill Th Coll BA82. **d** 82 **p** 83. C Northampton All SS w St Kath *Pet* 82-86; Ind Chapl *Birm* 86-96; P-in-c Warley Woods 96; V 96-08; AD Warley 01-06; rtd 08; Hon C Shepshed and Oaks in Charnwood *Leic* 08-10. *271 Monument Road, Edgbaston B16 8XF* Tel 0121-448 4734 E-mail michael.dunk@talk21.com

DUNK, Peter Norman. b 43. Sarum Th Coll 67. **d** 69 **p** 70. C Sheff St Mary w St Simon w St Matthias 69-71; C Margate St Jo *Cant* 71-74; Dioc Youth Officer *Birm* 74-78; R Hulme Ascension *Man* 78-83; V E Farleigh and Coxheath *Roch* 83; P-in-c Linton w Hunton 83; R Coxheath w E Farleigh, Hunton and Linton 83-88; R Swanbourne Australia 88-99; rtd 00. *7 Raffan View, Gwelup WA 6018, Australia* Tel and fax (0061) (8) 9447 8877

DUNKERLEY, James Hobson. b 39. Seabury-Western Th Sem BD69 STh70. **d** 64 **p** 65. C Stirchley *Birm* 64-66; C Perry Barr 66-70; R Chicago St Pet USA from 70. *6033 N Sheridan Road, Unit 44B, Chicago IL 60660-3059, USA* Tel (001) (772) 275 2773

DUNKLEY, Canon Christopher. b 52. Edin Univ MA74 Ox Univ BA77 MA81. St Steph Ho Ox 75. **d** 78 **p** 79. C Newbold w Dunston *Derby* 78-82; C Chesterfield St Mary and All SS 82; Chapl Leic Univ 83-85; TV Leic Ascension 85-92; Chapl Leics Hospice 85-87; V Leic St Aid 92-97; V Holbrooks *Cov* from 97; Hon Can Cov Cathl from 07. *St Luke's Vicarage, Rotherham Road, Coventry CV6 4FE* Tel (024) 7668 8604 E-mail kitdunkley@tiscali.co.uk

DUNKLING, Miss Judith Mary. b 77. Westcott Ho Cam 01 Bossey Ecum Inst Geneva 03. **d** 04 **p** 05. C Holbeach *Linc* 04-07; TV Maryport, Netherton and Flimby *Carl* 07-08; TV Tenbury *Heref* 08-11; P-in-c Sutton Bridge *Linc* from 11; P-in-c The Suttons w Tydd from 11. *The Vicarage, 79 Bridge Road, Sutton Bridge, Spalding PE12 9SD* Tel (01406) 351503 E-mail j.dunkling@btinternet.com

DUNLOP, Andrew James. b 76. Collingwood Coll Dur BSc97 PGCE98. Wycliffe Hall Ox BTh07. **d** 07. C Plymouth St Andr and Stonehouse *Ex* 07-10; Pioneer Min Gtr Northampton Deanery *Pet* from 10. *22 Berrywood Drive, Duston, Northampton NN5 6GB* E-mail ajdunlop@tiscali.co.uk

DUNLOP, Brian Kenneth Charles. b 49. Ex Univ BSc73. WEMTC 07. **d** 10 **p** 11. NSM S Cheltenham *Glouc* from 10. *31 Pickering Road, Cheltenham GL53 0LF* Tel (01242) 580731 E-mail dogcollar@quinweb.net

DUNLOP, Mrs Frances Jane. b 57. New Hall Cam MA82 ACA84. STETS 06. **d** 09 **p** 10. NSM Clarendon *Sarum* from 09. *Little Paddock, Romsey Road, Whiteparish, Salisbury SP5 2SD* Tel (01794) 884793 Mobile 07795-836653 E-mail fjdunlop@hotmail.com

DUNLOP, Canon Ian Geoffrey David. b 25. New Coll Ox BA48 MA56 FSA65. Linc Th Coll 54. **d** 56 **p** 57. C Bp's Hatfield *St Alb* 56-60; Chapl Westmr Sch 60-62; C Bures *St E* 62-72; Can Res and Chan Sarum Cathl 72-92; Dir Post-Ord Tr 72-92; Dir of Ords 73-92; Lect Sarum & Wells Th Coll 76-92; rtd 92; Hon C Selkirk *Edin* 99-04; Lic to offic from 04. *Gowanbrae, The Glebe, Selkirk TD7 5AB* Tel (01750) 20706

DUNLOP, Neil Stuart. b 78. Qu Coll Birm. **d** 11. C Lighthorne *Cov* from 10; C Newbold Pacey w Moreton Morrell from 10; C Chesterton from 10. *5 Chestnut Grove, Moreton Morrell, Warwick CV35 9DG* Tel (01926) 650094

DUNLOP, Peter John. b 44. TCD BA68 MA72 Dur Univ CertEd71. Cranmer Hall Dur. **d** 71 **p** 72. C Barking St Marg w St Patr *Chelmsf* 71-75; C Gt Malvern Ch Ch *Worc* 75-78; Chapl K Sch Tynemouth 78-89; R Monkseaton St Pet *Newc* 90-96; rtd 96; Perm to Offic *Newc* from 96. *19 Cliftonville Gardens, Whitley Bay NE26 1QJ* Tel 0191-251 0983

DUNN, Canon Alastair Matthew Crusoe. b 40. Lon Univ LLB64 AKC64. Wycliffe Hall Ox 78. **d** 80 **p** 81. C Yardley St Edburgha *Birm* 80-83; R Bishop's Sutton and Ropley and W Tisted *Win* 83-90; V Milford 90-04; Hon Can Win Cathl 03-04; C Harrogate St Mark *Ripon* 04-05; Hon C 05-07; rtd 05; Perm to Offic *York* from 08. *13 Littlefield Close, Nether Poppleton, York YO26 6HX* Tel (01904) 798487 E-mail asdunn@talk21.com

DUNN, Mrs Anne. b 36. **d** 03 **p** 04. OLM Weymouth H Trin *Sarum* from 03. *6 Ilchester Road, Weymouth DT4 0AW* Tel (01305) 770066 E-mail annedunn@uk2.net

DUNN, Mrs Barbara Anne. b 42. Man Univ BA72 Sheff Univ CQSW76. NOC 92. **d** 95 **p** 96. NSM Stretford St Matt *Man* 95-02; Perm to Offic from 02. *36 Alcester Road, Sale M33 3QP* E-mail bnsdunn@btinternet.com

DUNN, Brian. b 40. St Aid Birkenhead 66. **d** 69 **p** 70. C Over Darwen H Trin *Blackb* 69-71; C Burnley St Pet 71-74; V Darwen St Barn 74-84; V S Shore H Trin 84-02; Chapl Arnold Sch Blackpool 84-02; rtd 02; Perm to Offic *Blackb* from 02. *11 Kingsway, Blackpool FY4 2DF*

DUNN, Christopher George Hunter. b 28. Pemb Coll Cam BA49 MA53. Oak Hill Th Coll 51. **d** 53 **p** 54. C Tunbridge Wells H Trin *Roch* 53-54; C Broadwater St Mary *Chich* 54-58; R Garsdon w Lea and Cleverton *Bris* 59-74; Chapl Marie Curie Foundn (Tidcombe Hall) 74-95; V Tiverton St Geo *Ex* 74-01; RD Tiverton 84-91; rtd 01; Perm to Offic *Sarum* from 02. *8 Counter Close, Blandford Forum DT11 7XJ* Tel (01258) 456843

DUNN, David James. b 47. Leeds Univ CertEd79 BA82. Trin Coll Bris 88. **d** 90 **p** 91. C Magor w Redwick and Undy *Mon* 90-92; Chapl Toc H from 90; C St Mellons and Michaelston-y-Fedw *Mon* 92-93; V Pontnewydd from 93. *The Vicarage, 44 Church Road, Pontnewydd, Cwmbran NP44 1AT* Tel (01633) 482300

DUNN, David Michael. b 47. AKC70. St Aug Coll Cant 70. **d** 71 **p** 72. C Padgate *Liv* 71-74; C Halliwell St Marg *Man* 74-76; V Lever Bridge 76-84; V Bradshaw 84-01; TR Turton Moorland Min from 01. *10 Sweetstone Gardens, Bolton BL1 7GE* Tel and fax (01204) 304240

DUNN, Derek William Robert. b 48. Open Univ BA81 MA01. Stranmillis Coll CertEd70 AMusTCL74 LTCL75. **d** 85 **p** 87. Aux Min Carnalea *D & D* 85-97; Aux Min Bangor Abbey 97-05; C Ballymena w Ballyclug *Conn* 05-09; Bp's C Acton and Drumbanagher *Arm* from 09. *Drumbanagher Vicarage, 128 Tandragee Road, Newry BT35 6LW* Tel (028) 3082 1556 E-mail derek@mambolo.freeserve.co.uk

DUNN, Florence Patricia. b 37. Ches Coll of HE BTh02. NOC 99. **d** 02 **p** 03. NSM Basford *Lich* from 02. *213 Newcastle Road, Trent Vale, Stoke-on-Trent ST4 6PU* Tel (01782) 846417 E-mail rev.patdunn@tesco.net

DUNN, John Frederick. b 44. Trin Coll Bris 71. **d** 74 **p** 75. C Carl St Jo 74-77; C Tooting Graveney St Nic *S'wark* 77-82; V Attleborough *Cov* 85; Perm to Offic *Cant* 86-02; V Tipton St Martin and St Paul *Lich* from 02. *St Martin's Vicarage, 1 Dudley Port, Tipton DY4 7PR* Tel 0121-557 1902

DUNN, Julian. b 46. Open Univ BA84. K Coll Lon 67 St Aug Coll Cant 70. **d** 71 **p** 72. C Hanworth All SS *Lon* 71-74; C Kidlington *Ox* 74-76; C-in-c Cleethorpes St Fran CD *Linc* 76-77; TV Cleethorpes 77-85; Chapl Friarage and Distr Hosp Northallerton 85-88; Chapl Broadmoor Hosp Crowthorne 88; Ind Chapl *York* 88-89; P-in-c Micklefield 88-89; Perm to Offic *Ox* from 91. *timbles brewery (sic), 1 Lewington Close, Great Haseley, Oxford OX44 7LS* Tel (01844) 279687

DUNN, Kevin Lancelot. b 62. Newc Univ BSc83. St Steph Ho Ox 89. **d** 92 **p** 93. C Tynemouth Cullercoats St Paul *Newc* 92-95; C Newc St Matt w St Mary 95-97; P-in-c Kirkholt *Man* 97-00; Chapl Rochdale Healthcare NHS Trust 00-02; Chapl Pennine Acute Hosps NHS Trust 02-07; Chapl Christie Hosp NHS Trust Man from 07. *Christie Hospital, Wilmslow Road, Manchester M20 4BX* Tel 0161-446 3000

DUNN (née LEE), Mrs Mary Elizabeth. b 49. Open Univ BA81 Bp Grosseteste Coll CertEd78. St Mich Coll Llan 08. **d** 09 **p** 10. NSM Malpas *Mon* from 09. *The Vicarage, 44 Church Road, Pontnewydd, Cwmbran NP44 1AT* Tel (01633) 482300 E-mail ourmarylou@googlemail.com

DUNN, Michael Henry James. b 34. Em Coll Cam BA56 MA62. Cuddesdon Coll 57 and 62. **d** 62 **p** 63. C Chatham St Steph *Roch* 62-66; C Bromley SS Pet and Paul 66-70; V Roch St Justus 70-83; P-in-c Malvern Wells and Wyche *Worc* 83-85; P-in-c Lt Malvern, Malvern Wells and Wyche 85-97; rtd 97; Perm to Offic *Worc* from 97. *253 Oldbury Road, Worcester WR2 6JT* Tel (01905) 429938

DUNN, Nicholas Roger (Jack). b 78. New Coll Ox DPhil07. Ripon Coll Cuddesdon 09. **d** 11. C Chelsea St Luke and Ch Ch *Lon* from 11. *27 Paradise Walk, London SW3 4JL* Tel 07960-512433 (mobile) E-mail jackdunn@hotmail.com

DUNN, Pat. See DUNN, Florence Patricia

DUNN, Paul James Hugh. b 55. Dur Univ PhD93. Ripon Coll Cuddesdon. **d** 83 **p** 84. C Wandsworth St Paul *S'wark* 83-87; C Richmond St Mary w St Matthias and St Jo 88-92; TV Wimbledon 92-98; V Ham St Rich from 98. *The Vicarage,*

Ashburnham Road, Ham, Richmond TW10 7NL Tel (020) 8948 3758 E-mail revpdunn@aol.com

DUNN, Reginald Hallan. b 31. Oak Hill NSM Course 79. **d** 82 **p** 83. NSM Enfield St Andr *Lon* 82-88; NSM Forty Hill Jes Ch 88-92; NSM Enfield Chase St Mary 92-97; rtd 97; Perm to Offic *Lon* from 97. *3 Conway Gardens, Enfield EN2 9AD* Tel (020) 8366 3982

DUNN, Sharon Louise. *See* GOBLE, Mrs Sharon Louise

DUNN, Simon David. b 69. Trin Coll Bris BA08. **d** 08 **p** 09. C Stoke Gifford *Bris* from 08. *18 Marjoram Place, Bradley Stoke, Bristol BS32 0DQ* Tel (01454) 616864 Mobile 07904-733141 E-mail dunnsimonann@aol.com

DUNN, Canon Struan Huthwaite. b 43. Ch Coll Hobart 66 Moore Th Coll Sydney 67 Clifton Th Coll 68. **d** 70 **p** 71. C Orpington Ch Ch *Roch* 70-74; C Cheltenham St Mary *Glouc* 74-76; C Welling *Roch* 76-79; Chapl Barcelona w Casteldefels *Eur* 79-83; R Addington w Trottiscliffe *Roch* 83-89; P-in-c Ryarsh w Birling 83-89; P-in-c S Gillingham 89-90; TR 90-96; RD Gillingham 91-96; R Meopham w Nurstead 96-08; Hon Can Roch Cathl 97-08; rtd 08; Perm to Offic *Cant* and *Roch* from 08; Chapl HM Pris Standford Hill from 09. *18 Blenheim Avenue, Faversham ME13 8NR* Tel (01795) 531700

DUNNAN, Donald Stuart. b 59. Harvard Univ AB80 AM81 Ch Ch Ox BA85 MA90 DPhil91. Gen Th Sem (NY) 86. **d** 86 **p** 87. USA 86-87; Lib Pusey Ho 87-89; Lic to Offic *Ox* 87-92; Perm to Offic *Cant* 87-92; Chapl Linc Coll Ox 90-92; USA from 92. *St James School, 17641 College Road, St James MD 21781-9900, USA* E-mail dsdunnan@stjames.edu

DUNNE, The Very Revd Dermot Patrick Martin. b 59. Dub City Univ BA04. St Patr Coll Maynooth 78 CITC 98. **d** 83 **p** 84. In RC Ch 83-95; Dean's V Ch Ch Cathl Dublin 99-01; I Crosspatrick Gp *C & O* 01-08; Prec Ferns Cathl 04-08; Adn Ferns 07-08; Dean Ch Ch Cathl Dublin from 08. *19 Mountainview Road, Ranelagh, Dublin 6, Republic of Ireland* Tel (00353) (1) 498 3608 *or* 677 8099 Fax 679 8991 Mobile 87-986 5073 E-mail dean@cccclub.ie

DUNNE, Kevin Headley. b 43. Cranmer Hall Dur 85. **d** 87 **p** 88. C Chester le Street *Dur* 87-90; V S Hetton w Haswell 90-94; P-in-c Oxclose 94-02; R Chester le Street 02-08; AD Chester-le-Street 97-02 and 04-08; rtd 08; Chapl Sherburn Hosp Dur from 09. *Shincliffe House, Sherburn Hospital, Durham DH1 2SE* Tel 0191-372 4993 E-mail revdunne@btopenworld.com

DUNNE, The Very Revd Nigel Kenneth. b 66. TCD BA88 BTh90 MA00 MPhil00. **d** 90 **p** 91. C Dublin St Bart w Leeson Park *D & G* 90-93; C Taney 93-95; I Blessington w Kilbride, Ballymore Eustace etc 95-03; Can Ch Ch Cathl Dublin 01-03; I Bandon Union *C, C & R* 03-07; Dean Cork from 07; I Cork St Fin Barre's Union from 07. *The Deanery, Gilabbey Street, Cork, Republic of Ireland* Tel (00353) (21) 431 8073 E-mail dean@cork.anglican.org

DUNNETT, John Frederick. b 58. SS Coll Cam MA84 Worc Coll Ox MSc83 CQSW82. Trin Coll Bris BA87. **d** 88 **p** 89. C Kirkheaton *Wakef* 88-93; V Cranham Park *Chelmsf* 93-06; Gen Dir CPAS from 06. *39 Crescent Road, Warley, Brentwood CM14 5JR* Tel (01277) 221419 *or* (01926) 458427 E-mail jd@johndunnett.co.uk *or* jdunnett@cpas.org.uk

DUNNETT, Keith Owen. b 66. Cranfield Inst of Tech BSc87. Trin Coll Bris BA00. **d** 00 **p** 01. C Walton and Trimley *St E* 00-03; V Clayton *Bradf* 03-11; C Abingdon *Ox* from 11. *102 Gibsons Close, Abingdon OX14 1XT* Tel (01235) 209145 Mobile 07974-081354 E-mail keith.dunnett@btinternet.com

DUNNETT, Nigella. *See* YOUNGS-DUNNETT, Elizabeth Nigella

DUNNETT, Robert Curtis. b 31. SS Coll Cam BA54 MA58. Oak Hill Th Coll 56. **d** 58 **p** 59. C Markfield *Leic* 58-60; C Bucknall and Bagnall *Lich* 60-73; Perm to Offic *Birm* from 72; Chapl and Tutor Birm Bible Inst 72-79; Vice-Prin 84-92; Hon Vice-Prin 92-05; rtd 96. *30 Station Road, Harborne, Birmingham B17 9LY* Tel 0121-428 3945 Fax 428 3370

DUNNILL, Canon John David Stewart. b 50. UEA BA72 Ox Univ CertEd76 Birm Univ PhD88. Ripon Coll Cuddesdon 86. **d** 88 **p** 89. C Tupsley *Heref* 88-92; Lect Glouc Sch for Min 89-91; Sen Lect Murdoch Univ Australia from 92; Dir Bibl and Th Studies Angl Inst of Th from 92; Can Perth from 99. *School of Social Inquiry, Murdoch University, Murdoch WA 6150, Australia* Tel (0061) (8) 9360 6369 *or* 9383 4403 Fax 9360 6480 E-mail j.dunnill@murdoch.edu.au

DUNNING, Adam Jonathan. b 73. Regent's Park Coll Ox BA95 MA99 Birm Univ PhD00 Wolv Univ CertEd05. Westcott Ho Cam 97. **d** 99 **p** 00. C Evesham w Norton and Lenchwick *Worc* 99-02; C Hamstead St Paul *Birm* 02-03; Hon C Moseley St Mary and Moseley St Anne 03-05; The Ortons, Alwalton and Chesterton *Ely* 06-10; V Orton Longueville w Bottlebridge 10-11; Chapl Cheltenham Coll from 11. *Cheltenham College, Bath Road, Cheltenham GL53 7LD* Tel (01242) 265600 E-mail adamdunning@btinternet.com

DUNNING, Martyn Philip. b 51. Reading Univ MSc79 Dur Univ MA95 MRTPI77. St Jo Coll Dur 89. **d** 92 **p** 93. C Beverley Minster *York* 92-96; P-in-c Brandesburton 96-97; P-in-c Leven w

Catwick 96-97; R Brandesburton and Leven w Catwick 97-02; RD N Holderness 97-02; P-in-c Scarborough St Mary w Ch Ch and H Apostles 02-04; V from 04; RD Scarborough from 04. *St Mary's Vicarage, 1 North Cliff Gardens, Scarborough YO12 6PR* Tel (01723) 371354 E-mail parish.office@scarborough-stmarys.org.uk

DUNNINGS, Reuben Edward. b 36. Clifton Th Coll 62. **d** 66 **p** 67. C Longfleet *Sarum* 66-70; C Melksham 70-73; TV 73-78; R Broughton Gifford w Gt Chalfield 78-84; V Holt St Kath 78-84; R Broughton Gifford, Gt Chalfield and Holt 85-86; V Salisbury St Fran 86-99; P-in-c Stratford sub Castle 98-99; V Salisbury St Fran and Stratford sub Castle 99-01; rtd 01; Perm to Offic *Sarum* from 01. *11 Cornbrash Rise, Hilperton, Trowbridge BA14 7TS* Tel (01225) 768834

DUNSETH, George William. b 52. Multnomah Sch of the Bible Oregon BRE79. Oak Hill Th Coll BA85. **d** 85 **p** 86. C Cheadle All Hallows *Ches* 85-88; C New Borough and Leigh *Sarum* 88-91; V Thurnby w Stoughton *Leic* 91-06; Perm to Offic 07-08; P-in-c Leic St Leon CD from 08. *46 Brading Road, Leicester LE3 9BG* E-mail g52e0@btinternet.com

DUNSTAN, Canon Gregory John Orchard. b 50. Cam Univ MA75 TCD BTh90. CITC 87. **d** 90 **p** 91. C Ballymena w Ballyclug *Conn* 90-93; I Belfast St Matt from 93; Preb Swords St Patr Cathl Dublin from 07. *Shankill Rectory, 51 Ballygomartin Road, Belfast BT13 3LA* Tel and fax (028) 9071 4325

DUNSTAN, Kenneth Ian. b 40. Goldsmiths' Coll Lon BEd71 ACP. Oak Hill NSM Course 86. **d** 88 **p** 89. NSM Creeksea w Althorne, Latchingdon and N Fambridge *Chelmsf* 88-94; P-in-c Woodham Mortimer w Hazeleigh 94-98; P-in-c Woodham Walter 94-98; NSM Bradwell on Sea 99-05; rtd 05; Perm to Offic *Chelmsf* from 05. *35 Ely Close, Southminster CM0 7AQ* Tel (01621) 772199 E-mail kandk@wclub.net

DUNSTAN, Mark Philip. b 70. Middx Univ BSc93. Oak Hill Th Coll BA03. **d** 03 **p** 04. C Stranton *Dur* 03-06; P-in-c Hunsdon w Widford and Wareside *St Alb* from 06. *The Rectory, Acorn Street, Hunsdon, Ware SG12 8PB* Tel (01920) 877276 E-mail dunstan mark@hotmail.com

DUNSTAN-MEADOWS, Victor Richard. b 63. Chich Th Coll BTh90. **d** 90 **p** 91. C Clacton St Jas *Chelmsf* 90-93; C Stansted Mountfitchet 93-95; CF 95-00; Chapl RAF 00-10; P-in-c Up Hatherley *Glouc* from 10. *The Vicarage, Hatherley Road, Cheltenham GL51 6HX* Tel (01242) 210673 Mobile 07712-050629 E-mail bramleyend@yahoo.com

DUNTHORNE, Paul. b 63. K Coll Lon LLB85 St Jo Coll Dur BA90 Dur Univ MA98. Cranmer Hall Dur 88. **d** 91 **p** 92. C Heacham and Sedgeford *Nor* 91-95; C Eastbourne H Trin *Chich* 95-98; P-in-c Preston and Ridlington w Wing and Pilton *Pet* 98-00; Local Min Officer 98-00; CME Officer *Heref* 00-06; TR Ledbury from 06. *The Rectory, Worcester Road, Ledbury HR8 1PL* Tel (01531) 632571 E-mail p.dunthorne@btinternet.com

DUNWICH, Suffragan Bishop of. *See* YOUNG, The Rt Revd Clive

DUNWOODY, Stephen John Herbert. b 71. Glam Univ BA92. St Steph Ho Ox BTh96. **d** 96 **p** 97. C Skewen *Llan* 96-98; C Roath 98-99; C Stanley *Liv* 99-02; TV Colyton, Southleigh, Offwell, Widworthy etc *Ex* 02-03; V Offwell, Northleigh, Farway, Cotleigh etc 03-05; CF from 05. *c/o MOD Chaplains (Army)* Tel (01264) 381144 Fax 381824 E-mail stephendunwoody@hotmail.com

DUNWOODY, Thomas Herbert Williamson. b 35. TCD BA58 MA64. TCD Div Sch Div Test59. **d** 59 **p** 60. C Newcastle *D & D* 59-61; Asst Missr Ballymacarrett St Martin 61-63; C Lurgan Ch the Redeemer 63-66; I Ardglass w Dunsford 66-74; Offg Chapl RAF 66-74; V Urmston *Man* 74-85; I Wexford w Ardcolm and Killurin *C & O* 85-93; Can Ferns Cathl 88-93; I Newry *D & D* 93-02; rtd 02. *36 Godfrey Avenue, Bangor BT20 5LS* Tel (028) 9145 3918 E-mail tha@tiscali.co.uk

DUPLOCK, Canon Peter Montgomery. b 16. OBE76. Qu Coll Cam BA38 MA42. Ridley Hall Cam 38. **d** 40 **p** 41. C Anston *S'wark* 40-43; CF (EC) 43-47; R Nottingham St Nic *S'well* 47-52; R Loddington w Harrington *Pet* 52-55; V Kettering St Andr 55-64; Chapl Geneva *Eur* 64-71; Chapl Brussels w Charleroi, Liège and Waterloo 71-81; Chan Brussels Cathl 81; Adn NW Eur 81; rtd 81; Hon Can Brussels Cathl from 81; R Breamore *Win* 81-86; Perm to Offic 86-95; Perm to Offic *Sarum* 86-98. *Room 36, Manormead, Tilford Road, Hindhead GU26 6RA*

DUPRÉ, Robin Charles. b 50. Nottm Univ BA72 Worc Coll of Educn PGCE76. SWMTC 08. **d** 11. NSM Jersey Grouville *Win* from 11. *Le Picachon, 4 Le Clos Royale, La Rue de la Ville es Renauds, Grouville, Jersey JE3 9DF* Tel (01534) 856378 Mobile 07829-936250 E-mail dupre@freeuk.com

DUPREE, Hugh Douglas. b 50. Univ of the South (USA) BA72 Virginia Th Sem MDiv75 Ch Ch Ox MA86 Ball Coll Ox DPhil88. **d** 75 **p** 76. USA 75-80; Hon C Ox St Mich w St Martin and All SS 80-87; Asst Chapl Ball Coll Ox 84-87; Chapl from 87; Dean from 07; Chapl HM Pris Ox 88-97. *Balliol College, Oxford OX1 3BJ* Tel (01865) 277777 E-mail douglas.dupree@balliol.ox.ac.uk

DUPUY, Alan Douglas William. b 48. SEITE 98. **d** 00 **p** 01. NSM Forest Hill St Aug *S'wark* 00-01; NSM S Dulwich St Steph 01-04; NSM Perry Hill St Geo w Ch Ch and St Paul from 04. *16 Dominic Court, 43 The Gardens, London SE22 9QR* Tel (020) 8695 5769 Fax 8693 4175 Mobile 07960-226518
E-mail alandupuy1@aol.com

DURAND, Noel Douglas. b 33. Jes Coll Cam BA57 MA61 BD76. Westcott Ho Cam 72. **d** 74 **p** 75. C Eaton *Nor* 74-78; V Cumnor *Ox* 78-01; rtd 01; Perm to Offic *Nor* from 01. *21 Nelson Road, Sheringham NR26 8BU* Tel (01263) 822388

DURAND, Stella Evelyn Brigid, Lady. b 42. TCD BA64 Sorbonne Univ Paris DèS65. CITC BTh99. **d** 00. C Kiltegan w Hacketstown, Clonmore and Moyne *C & O* 00-03; I from 03. *The Rectory, Kiltegan, Co Wicklow, Republic of Ireland* Tel and fax (00353) (59) 647 3368 E-mail stelladurand@eircom.net

DURANT, Robert-Ashton. b 23. St D Coll Lamp BA47. Bp Burgess Hall Lamp. **d** 48 **p** 49. C Brynmawr *S & B* 48-49; C Fleur-de-Lis *Mon* 49-51; C Bassaleg 51-56; CF (TA) 53-55; V Trellech and Cwmcarvan *Mon* 56-69; Priest Tymawr Convent 56-69; V Slapton *Ex* 69-81; V Strete 69-81; R E Allington, Slapton and Strete 81-92; rtd 92; Perm to Offic *Ex* 92-09. *Fairfield, Hynetown Road, Strete, Dartmouth TQ6 0RS*

DURANT, William John Nicholls. b 55. K Coll Lon BA76. St Jo Coll Nottm 77. **d** 80 **p** 81. C Norwood St Luke *S'wark* 80-83; C Morden 83-88; TV 88-92; V Frindsbury w Upnor *Roch* 92-00; CF from 00. *c/o MOD Chaplains (Army)* Tel (01264) 381140 Fax 381824

DURANT-STEVENSEN, Mrs Helen Mary. b 53. Saffron Walden Coll TCert74. Trin Coll Bris BA04. **d** 04 **p** 05. C S Croydon Em *S'wark* 04-08; C New Malden and Coombe from 08. *2 California Road, New Malden KT3 3RU* Tel (020) 8942 0544

DURBIN, Roger. b 41. Bris Sch of Min 83. **d** 85 **p** 86. NSM Bedminster *Bris* 85-91; NSM Henbury 91-94; NSM Clifton All SS w St Jo from 94. *13 Charbury Walk, Bristol BS11 9UU* Tel 0117-985 8404

DURELL, Miss Jane Vavasor. b 32. Bedf Coll Lon BSc55 Lambeth STh64. Gilmore Ho 61. **dss** 86 **d** 87 **p** 94. Banbury *Ox* 86-92; Par Dn 87-92; rtd 92; Perm to Offic *Nor* 92-94 and from 02; NSM Norwich St Mary Magd w St Jas 94-02. *38 Brakendon Close, Norwich NR1 3BX* Tel (01603) 627949

DURHAM, Miss Bethany Helen. b 58. Cranmer Hall Dur 86. **d** 89 **p** 94. C Newark *S'well* 89-93; rtd 93; Perm to Offic *S'well* from 93. *c/o Crockford, Church House, Great Smith Street, London SW1P 3AZ*

DURHAM, Mrs Eleanore Jane. b 62. St Andr Univ MTheol84. Trin Coll Bris MA01. **d** 01 **p** 02. C Childwall All SS *Liv* 01-05; P-in-c Hunts Cross from 05. *The Vicarage, 7 Kingsmead Drive, Liverpool L25 0NG* Tel 0151-486 1220
E-mail jane.durham@dsl.pipex.com

DURHAM, Archdeacon of. See JAGGER, The Ven Ian

DURHAM, Bishop of. See WELBY, The Rt Revd Justin Portal

DURHAM, Dean of. See SADGROVE, The Very Revd Michael

DURIE, David James. b 63. Em Lancs Univ BA93 St Martin's Coll Lanc MA99. CBDTI 97. **d** 99 **p** 00. C Briercliffe *Blackb* 99-01; P-in-c Edin St Dav from 02. *33 Lamberton Shiels, Lamberton, Berwick-upon-Tweed TD15 1XB* Tel (01890) 781542 E-mail patricia.durie@btinternet.com

DURING, Arthur Christopher. b 59. Sierra Leone Th Hall 80. **d** 83 **p** 85. C Freetown H Trin Sierra Leone 83-85; C St Geo Cathl 85-86; Perm to Offic *S'wark* 00-05. *22 Challice Way, London SW2 3RD* Tel (020) 8671 7678

DURKAN, Barbara Isobel Mary. b 43. Kent Univ BSc71 MPhil00 Ch Ch Coll Cant MA95 Sarum Dioc Tr Coll CertEd65. SEITE 99. **d** 01 **p** 02. Aux Chapl HM Pris Standford Hill 01-08; Perm to Offic *Cant* 08-09; Hon C Minster-in-Sheppey from 09. *69 Darlington Drive, Minster-on-Sea, Sheerness ME12 3LG*

DURKIN, Anthony Michael. b 45. Sarum & Wells Th Coll 87. **d** 89 **p** 90. C Faversham *Cant* 89-92; V St Margarets-at-Cliffe w Westcliffe etc 92-09; rtd 09. *Church Cottage, Leigh, Sherborne DT9 6HL* Tel (01935) 872117
E-mail tony.durkin6595.freeserve.co.uk

DURKIN, Mrs Derath May. b 52. N Staffs Poly LLB87. SAOMC 01. **d** 02 **p** 03. C Harlington Ch Ch Lon 02-06; TV Brentford from 06. *St Faith's Vicarage, 122 Windmill Road, Brentford TW8 9NA* Tel (020) 8560 3782 Mobile 07962-168440
E-mail derath.durkin@parishofbrentford.org.uk

DURLEY, Jonathan Richard Hall. b 66. Wolv Univ BA97 Ch Ch Coll Cant MA01. S Wales Ord Course 04. **d** 05 **p** 06. C Canton Cardiff *Llan* 05-07; C Newton Nottage 07-10; P-in-c Kenfig Hill from 10. *The Vicarage, 5 Redman Close, Kenfig Hill, Bridgend CF33 6BF* Tel (01656) 670148
E-mail fatherjon@btinternet.com

DURNDELL, Miss Irene Frances. b 43. Trin Coll Bris 84. **dss** 86 **d** 87 **p** 94. Erith Ch Ch *Roch* 86-93; Par Dn 87-93; Par Dn Erith St Paul 93-94; C 94-98; Asst Dir of Tr 93-98; V Falconwood 98-07; rtd 07. *17A Buxton Drive, Bexhill-on-Sea TN39 4BA* Tel (01424) 810477 E-mail renee.durndell@btinternet.com

DURNELL, John. b 32. St Aid Birkenhead 64. **d** 66 **p** 67. C Newport w Longford *Lich* 66-69; P-in-c Church Aston 69-72; R 72-77; V Weston Rhyn 77-82; P-in-c Petton w Cockshutt and Weston Lullingfield etc 82-83; R Petton w Cockshutt, Welshampton and Lyneal etc 83-97; rtd 97; Perm to Offic *Lich* 97-09. *Fronlwyd, Hirnant, Penybontfawr, Oswestry SY10 0HP* Tel (01691) 870686

DURNFORD, Canon Catherine Margaret. b 36. St Mary's Coll Dur BA57. Gilmore Course 78 NW Ord Course 77. **d** 87 **p** 94. Area Sec USPG *York* and *Ripon* 82-89; Par Dn Whitby *York* 89-92; Par Dn Redcar 92-94; C Selby Abbey 94-97; V New Marske and Wilton 97-03; Can and Preb York Minster 01-03; rtd 03; Perm to Offic *York* from 03. *18 Canongate, Cottingham HU16 4DG* Tel (01482) 844868
E-mail cmdurnford@tiscali.co.uk

DURNFORD, John Edward. b 30. CCC Cam BA53 MA61. Linc Th Coll 53. **d** 55 **p** 56. C Selby Abbey *York* 55-58; C Newland St Jo 58-62; C Umtali S Rhodesia 62-64; R Mazoe Valley 64-76; V Hebden Bridge *Wakef* 76-84; RD Calder Valley 82-84; P-in-c Blanchland w Hunstanworth *Newc* 84-90; P-in-c Edmundbyers w Muggleswick *Dur* 84-90; R Blanchland w Hunstanworth and Edmundbyers etc *Newc* 90-94; RD Corbridge 88-93; rtd 94; Perm to Offic *Newc* 94-05 and *Cant* 06-09. *19 Sunburst Close, Marden, Tonbridge TN12 9TS*

DURRAN, Ms Margaret. b 47. Surrey Univ MSc96 Lady Spencer Chu Coll of Educn CertEd70. S'wark Ord Course 88. **d** 91 **p** 94. Par Dn Brixton St Matt *S'wark* 91-94; C Streatham St Leon 94-95; V Walworth St Chris 95-99; Hon C S'wark St Geo w St Alphege and St Jude 99-09; Hist Churches Project Officer *Lon* 99-07; rtd 08; Perm to Offic *Ox* from 09. *8 Bath Terrace, Victoria Road, Bicester OX26 6PR* Tel 07739-988742 (mobile)
E-mail maggie.durran@virginmedia.com

DURRANS, Mrs Janet. b 58. Westcott Ho Cam 09. **d** 11. C Chislehurst St Nic *Roch* from 11. *Southbeech, Old Perry Street, Chislehurst BR7 6PP* Tel (020) 8295 4111 Mobile 07585-660621
E-mail jandurrans@googlemail.com

DURRANT, Melvyn Richard Bloomfield. b 59. Leeds Univ BA82 St Luke's Coll Ex PGCE86. Trin Coll Bris 01. **d** 03 **p** 04. C Watercombe *Sarum* 03-06; C Moreton and Woodsford w Tincleton 03-06; P-in-c Sixpenny Handley w Gussage St Andrew etc from 06; C Chase from 06. *The Vicarage, 60 High Street, Sixpenny Handley, Salisbury SP5 5ND* Tel (01725) 552608
E-mail durrant@talktalk.net

DURSTON, Canon David Michael Karl. b 36. Em Coll Cam BA60 MA64. Clifton Th Coll 61. **d** 63 **p** 64. C Wednesfield Heath *Lich* 63-66; Project Officer Grubb Inst 67-78; Ind Chapl *Lich* 78-84; P-in-c W Bromwich St Paul 78-82; V 82-84; Adult Educn Officer 84-92; Preb Lich Cathl 89-92; Can Res and Chan Sarum Cathl 92-03; Can and Preb 03-06; TR Wylye and Till Valley 03-06; rtd 06. *26 Mill Road, Salisbury SP2 7RZ* Tel (01722) 334017

DURWARD, Rosemary. **d** 10 **p** 11. NSM Notting Hill St Jo *Lon* from 10. *St John's Parish Office, Lansdowne Crescent, London W11 2NN* E-mail rdurward@msn.com

DUSSEK, Jeremy Neil James Christopher. b 70. St Jo Coll Dur BA92. Westcott Ho Cam 96. **d** 97 **p** 98. C Whickham *Dur* 97-00; C Fareham H Trin *Portsm* 00-01; TV 01-07; V Moseley St Mary and St Anne *Birm* from 07. *St Mary's Vicarage, 18 Oxford Road, Moseley, Birmingham B13 9EH* Tel 0121-449 1459 Fax 449 2243
E-mail jeremy@dussek.fsnet.co.uk

DUST, Simon Philip. b 63. Oak Hill Th Coll BA95. **d** 95 **p** 96. C Chesham Bois *Ox* 95-00; C-in-c Bushmead CD *St Alb* 00-04; V Bushmead 04-08; TV High Wycombe *Ox* from 08. *15 The Brackens, High Wycombe HP11 1EB* Tel (01494) 529668
E-mail simon@sac-hw.org.uk

DUTFIELD, Canon Alan. b 20. Linc Th Coll 54. **d** 55 **p** 56. C Kimberworth *Sheff* 55-60; V New Rossington 60-71; R Old Brumby *Linc* 71-77; TR 77-86; Can and Preb Linc Cathl 81-86; RD Manlake 82-86; rtd 86; Perm to Offic *Linc* 89-94 and from 01; Perm to Offic *S'well* from 03. *30 Barnes Green, Scotter, Gainsborough DN21 3RW* Tel (01724) 764220

DUTHIE, Elliot Malcolm. b 31. Clifton Th Coll 63. **d** 66 **p** 67. C Eccleston St Luke *Liv* 66-69; Malaysia 70-75; P-in-c Bootle St Leon *Liv* 76-78; V 78-81; V Charlton Kings H Apostles *Glouc* 81-94; rtd 94; Perm to Offic *Glouc* 94-00; *Ex* 02-05; *Derby* from 07. *11 Fairisle Close, Oakwood, Derby DE21 2SJ* Tel (01332) 668238 E-mail emduthie@btinternet.com

DUTHIE, John. b 39. **d** 04 **p** 05. NSM Aberdeen St Pet 04-07; Chapl Grampian Healthcare NHS Trust from 06. *Moraine, Inchmarlo, Banchory AB31 4BR* Tel (01330) 824108
E-mail johnduthie@nhs.net

DUTTON, Andrew Rivers George. b 49. Bris Univ BSc71 PGCE72 Reading Univ MSc79. EAMTC 98. **d** 98 **p** 99. NSM Kettering SS Pet and Paul 98-03; NSM Broughton w Loddington and Cransley etc 04-09; P-in-c Kettering All SS from 09; Chapl Bp Stopford Sch 99-10. *10 Beardsley Gardens, Kettering NN15 5UB* Tel (01536) 392401
E-mail andrew.allsaints@gmail.com

DUTTON, Leonard Arthur. b 35. Bps' Coll Cheshunt 63. **d** 66 **p** 67. C Knighton St Jo *Leic* 66-70; C Chilvers Coton w Astley *Cov* 70-73; R Hathern *Leic* 73-79; V Ashby-de-la-Zouch H Trin 79-04; rtd 04; Perm to Offic *Leic* from 04. *8 Merganser Way, Coalville LE67 4QA* Tel (01530) 815420
E-mail lenmeg@dutton8.wanadoo.co.uk

DUTTON, Sandra Rosemary. b 50. Ripon Coll Cuddesdon 03. **d** 04 **p** 05. NSM Chatham St Steph *Roch* 04-08; TV Hartshill, Penkhull and Trent Vale *Lich* from 08. *The Vicarage, 214 Queens Road, Penkhull, Stoke-on-Trent ST4 7LG* Tel (01782) 744224
E-mail sandydutton@hotmail.com

DUVAL, Canon Philip Ernest. b 18. MBE45. Mert Coll Ox BA45 MA45. Westcott Ho Cam 47. **d** 47 **p** 48. C Tooting All SS *S'wark* 47-51; C Raynes Park St Sav 51-55; V Balham St Mary 55-66; R Merstham and Gatton 66-86; Hon Can S'wark Cathl 78-86; rtd 86; Perm to Offic *Cant* 88-06 and *B & W* from 07. *7 George & Crown Cottages, Hinton St George TA17 8SD* Tel (01460) 75369

DUVALL, Michael James. b 31. **d** 79 **p** 80. Hon C Kings Langley *St Alb* 79-89; Hon C Selworthy and Timberscombe and Wootton Courtenay *B & W* 89-95; Hon C Luccombe 89-95; Hon C Selworthy, Timberscombe, Wootton Courtenay etc 95-97; rtd 97; Perm to Offic *B & W* from 97. *Dovery Edge, 19 Hawkcombe View, Porlock, Minehead TA24 8NB* Tel (01634) 862834

DUXBURY, Clive Robert. b 49. Open Univ BA(ThM)06. St Jo Coll Nottm 90. **d** 92 **p** 93. C Horwich and Rivington *Man* 92-96; P-in-c Bury St Paul and Bury Ch King 98-00; P-in-c Freethorpe, Wickhampton, Halvergate w Tunstall *Nor* 00-02; P-in-c Reedham w Cantley w Limpenhoe and Southwood 00-02; R Freethorpe, Wickhampton, Halvergate etc 02-05; RD Blofield 04-05; R High Ongar w Norton Mandeville *Chelmsf* 05-08; Chapl HM Pris Everthorpe from 08; Hon C Elloughton and Brough w Brantingham *York* from 11. *HM Prison Everthorpe, Beck Road, Everthorpe, Brough HU15 1RB* Tel (01430) 426500 Mobile 07777-602980 E-mail duxbury@duxbury.karoo.co.uk

DUXBURY, Canon James Campbell. b 33. Tyndale Hall Bris 58. **d** 61 **p** 62. C Southport SS Simon and Jude *Liv* 61-65; V Tittensor *Lich* 65-70; V W Bromwich Gd Shep w St Jo 70-75; P-in-c Wellington w Eyton 75-80; V 80-85; V Padiham *Blackb* 85-01; Hon Can Blackb Cathl 97-01; rtd 01; Perm to Offic *Blackb* from 01. *1 Gills Croft, Clitheroe BB7 1LJ* Tel (01200) 429261
E-mail theduxburys@talktalk.net

DUXBURY, Miss Margaret Joan. b 30. JP81. DipEd52. St Jo Coll Nottm 83. **dss** 84 **d** 87 **p** 94. Thornthwaite w Thruscross and Darley *Ripon* 84-86; Middleton St Cross 86-90; C 87-90; Par Dn Dacre w Hartwith and Darley w Thornthwaite 90-94; C 94-96; rtd 97; NSM Bishop Monkton and Burton Leonard *Ripon* 97-02; Perm to Offic from 01. *Scot Beck House, Low Lane, Darley, Harrogate HG3 2QN* Tel (01423) 780451

DYAS, Stuart Edwin. b 46. Lon Univ BSc67. Ridley Hall Cam 78. **d** 80 **p** 81. C Bath Weston St Jo w Kelston *B & W* 80-83; C Tunbridge Wells St Jas *Roch* 83-90; V Nottingham St Jude *S'well* 90-99; AD Nottingham Cen 93-98; V Long Eaton St Jo *Derby* 99-05; rtd 05; Perm to Offic *Derby* from 05. *179 Bye Pass Road, Beeston, Nottingham NG9 5HR* Tel 0115-922 5844

DYAS, Sylvia Denise (Dee). b 51. Bedf Coll Lon BA72 Nottm Univ PhD99. St Jo Coll Nottm 98. **d** 00 **p** 01. Tutor St Jo Coll Nottm from 00; Perm to Offic *Derby* from 00. *179 Bye Pass Road, Beeston, Nottingham NG9 5HR* Tel 0115-922 5844
E-mail d.dyas@stjohns-nottm.ac.uk

DYBLE, Ian Hugh. b 64. Anglia Poly LLB85 Leic Univ MSc98. Ridley Hall Cam 08. **d** 10 **p** 11. C Onslow Square and S Kensington St Aug *Lon* from 10. *St Augustine's Flat, 117 Queen's Gate, London SW7 5LP* Tel 07770-592733 (mobile)
E-mail iandyble@live.co.uk

DYE, Mrs Margaret Mary. b 48. NOC 95. **d** 98 **p** 99. C Morley St Pet w Churwell *Wakef* 98-02; TV Morley 02-08; TR from 08. *St Andrew's Vicarage, 4 Lewisham Street, Morley, Leeds LS27 0LA* Tel 0113-252 3783 E-mail rev.m.dye@ntlworld.com

DYE, Stephen. b 49. NOC 01. **d** 04 **p** 05. C Gildersome *Wakef* 04-08; Chapl St Geo Crypt Leeds *Ripon* from 08; Chapl to the Homeless from 10. *St Andrew's Vicarage, 4 Lewisham Street, Morley, Leeds LS27 0LA* Tel 0113-252 3783 Mobile 07720-975688 E-mail rev.s.dye@ntlworld.com

DYER, Adrian Louis. b 67. Cant Univ (NZ) BA02 Auckland Univ BTheol03. **d** 04 **p** 05. C Methven New Zealand 04-06; V Ellesmere 06-09; Chapl RAF from 09. *Chaplaincy Services, Valiant Block, HQ Air Command, RAF High Wycombe HP14 4UE* Tel (01494) 496800 Fax 496343

DYER, Canon Anne Catherine. b 57. St Anne's Coll Ox MA80 Lon Univ MTh89. Wycliffe Hall Ox 84. **d** 87 **p** 94. NSM Beckenham St Jo *Roch* 87-88; NSM Beckenham St Geo 88-89; Hon Par Dn Luton Ch Ch 89-94; Chapl for Evang 93-98; NSM Istead Rise 94-98; Min Development Officer 98-04; Hon Can Roch Cathl 00-04; Warden Cranmer Hall Dur 05-11; Hon Can Dur Cathl 08-11; R Haddington *Edin* from 11. *The Rectory, 6 Church Street, Haddington EH41 3EX* Tel (01620) 824158
E-mail adyer82120@aol.com

DYER, Ms Catherine Jane. b 46. Westf Coll Lon BA68. Ox NSM Course 85. **d** 88 **p** 94. NSM Wokingham All SS *Ox* 88-90; C 90-95; TV W Slough 95-01; P-in-c Linslade 01-07; AD Mursley 03-06; rtd 07. *45 Shady Bower, Salisbury SP1 2RG*
E-mail catherine.dyer46@hotmail.co.uk

DYER, Canon Christine Anne. b 53. Nottm Univ BEd75 MA97. EMMTC 81. **dss** 84 **d** 87 **p** 94. Mickleover St Jo *Derby* 85-90; Par Dn 87-90; Dioc Voc Adv 86-90; Par Educn Adv 90-98; Dioc Youth Officer 91-98; P-in-c Morton and Stonebroom 98-99; P-in-c Shirland 98-99; R Morton and Stonebroom w Shirland 99-06; P-in-c Allestree 06-10; P-in-c Darley Abbey 06-10; V Allestree St Edm and Darley Abbey from 10; Hon Can Derby Cathl from 02. *The Vicarage, Kings Croft, Allestree, Derby DE22 2FN* Tel (01332) 551404
E-mail c.a.dyer.t21@btinternet.com *or* c.a.dyer@talk21.com

DYER, Fraser Colin. b 65. SEITE. **d** 09 **p** 10. C De Beauvoir Town St Pet *Lon* from 09. *Studio 3, 96 De Beauvoir Road, London N1 4EN* Tel (020) 7683 1609 E-mail fraserdyer@mac.com

DYER, Mrs Gillian Marie. b 50. Sheff Univ BA71 Leic Univ PGCE72. S Dios Minl Tr Scheme 81. **dss** 84 **d** 87 **p** 94. Witney *Ox* 84-85; Carl St Cuth w St Mary 86-89; Par Dn 87-89; Dioc Communications Officer 86-89; Par Dn Kirkbride w Newton Arlosh 89-91; Par Dn Carl H Trin and St Barn 91-94; TV 94-97; P-in-c Arbroath *Bre* 01-03; P-in-c Lower Darwen St Jas *Blackb* 03-10; P-in-c Whalley from 10; P-in-c Sabden and Pendleton from 10. *The Vicarage, 40 The Sands, Whalley, Clitheroe BB7 9TL* Tel (01254) 824679
E-mail revvygilly141@btinternet.com

DYER, Canon James Henry. b 14. ALCD39. **d** 39 **p** 40. C S Hackney St Jo w Ch Ch *Lon* 39-43; C New Malden and Coombe *S'wark* 43-50; New Zealand from 50; V Murchison 50-56; V Collingwood 56-59; V Spring Creek 59-67; V Amuri 67-70; V Motupiko 70-77; Hon Can Nelson Cathl 85. *7 Talbot Street, Richmond, Nelson, New Zealand* Tel (0064) (3) 554 8638
E-mail james.dyer@xtra.co.nz

DYER, Janet. b 35. LNSM course 77. **dss** 85 **d** 86 **p** 94. Balerno *Edin* 85-86; NSM 86-93; Chapl Edin R Infirmary 88-93; Dn-in-c Roslin (Rosslyn Chpl) *Edin* 93-94; P-in-c 94-97; NSM Livingston LEP 97-00; Angl Chapl Livingstone St Jo Hosp 97-00; NSM Dalmahoy from 02. *499 Lanark Road West, Balerno EH14 7AL* Tel 0131-449 3767 E-mail adrian@dyer499.freeserve.co.uk

DYER, Ronald Whitfield. b 29. Solicitor 51. Guildf Dioc Min Course 91. **d** 95 **p** 96. NSM Fleet *Guildf* 95-99; rtd 99; Perm to Offic *Guildf* from 99. *7 Dukes Mead, Fleet GU51 4HA* Tel (01252) 621457

DYER, Stephen Roger. b 57. Brunel Univ BSc. Wycliffe Hall Ox 83. **d** 86 **p** 87. C Beckenham St Jo *Roch* 86-89; C Luton Ch Ch 89-94; V Istead Rise 94-01; V Frindsbury w Upnor 01-04; Hon C Easington, Easington Colliery and S Hetton *Dur* 05-09. *The Rectory, 6 Church Street, Haddington EH41 3EX* Tel (01620) 824158 E-mail revrogdyer@aol.com

DYER, Miss Sylvia Mary. b 30. Westf Coll Lon BA66. Ab Dioc Tr Course 90. **d** 95 **p** 98. NSM Turriff *Ab* 95-06; NSM Cuminestown 95-06; rtd 06; Perm to Offic *Bre* from 07. *Lily Cottage, 19 Long Row, Westhaven, Carnoustie DD7 6BE* Tel (01241) 856652 E-mail sylviadyer@blueyonder.co.uk

DYER, Terence Neville. b 50. Sheff Univ BEng71 Leic Univ PGCE72. Carl Dioc Tr Course 86. **d** 89 **p** 90. NSM Kirkbride w Newton Arlosh *Carl* 89-91; NSM Carl H Trin and St Barn 91-97; NSM Arbroath *Bre* 01; P-in-c Monifieth 01-03; P-in-c Over Darwen St Jas *Blackb* from 03; C Darwen St Pet w Hoddlesden 08-10; C Hoddlesden 08-10. *The Vicarage, 40 The Sands, Whalley, Clitheroe BB7 9TL* Tel (01254) 824679 Mobile 07919-543475 E-mail terry255dyer@btinternet.com

DYKE, Mrs Elizabeth Muriel. b 55. St Mary's Coll Dur BSc77 St Martin's Coll Lanc PGCE78. Oak Hill Th Coll 92. **d** 94 **p** 95. C High Wycombe *Ox* 94-95; C W Wycombe w Bledlow Ridge, Bradenham and Radnage 95-97; TV Bedworth *Cov* 97-02; V Dunchurch 02-09; R Kidman Park and Mile End Australia from 09. *2 Elgar Court, Fulham Gardens SA 5024, Australia* Tel (0061) (8) 8353 0049 E-mail elizabeth@dykefamily.plus.com

DYKE, George Edward. b 22. TCD BA78 BCom65 MA80. CITC. **d** 79 **p** 80. NSM Dublin St Geo *D & G* 79-82; NSM Tallaght 83-89; NSM Killiney Ballybrack 89-90; Bp's C Dublin St Geo and St Thos and Finglas 90-95; Bp's C Dublin St Geo and St Thos 95-96; Chapl Mountjoy Pris 90-96; Chapl Arbour Hill Pris 90-96; rtd 96. *45 Thornhill Road, Mount Merrion, Co Dublin, Republic of Ireland* Tel (00353) (1) 288 9376

DYKES, John Edward. b 33. Trin Coll Bris 82. **d** 84 **p** 85. C Rushden w Newton Bromswold *Pet* 84-87; R Heanton Punchardon w Marwood *Ex* 87-97; rtd 97; Perm to Offic *Guildf* 98-01 and *B & W* from 02. *42 Ashley Road, Taunton TA1 5BP* Tel (01823) 282507 E-mail johnandvickyd@tiscali.co.uk

DYKES, Mrs Katrina Mary. b 66. Trin Coll Bris BA90. Guildf Dioc Min Course 03. **d** 04 **p** 05. NSM Windlesham *Guildf* 04-07; Chapl St Swithun's Sch Win from 08. *St Swithun's School, Alresford Road, Winchester SO21 1HA* Tel (01962) 835700 E-mail dykesk@stswithuns.com

DYKES, Philip John. b 61. Loughb Univ BSc83. Trin Coll Bris 88. **d** 91 **p** 92. C Morden *S'wark* 91-95; C St Helier 95-98; TV Camberley St Paul *Guildf* 98-99; V Camberley Heatherside 99-08; Chapl Win Univ from 08. *University of Winchester, Sparkford Road, Winchester SO22 4NR* Tel (01962) 827063 E-mail phil.dykes@ntlworld.com

DYMOND, Rosemary Carmen. b 70. Ox Univ MEng94 Aber Univ MSc95 Bremen Univ Dr rer nat 99. Wycliffe Hall Ox BA02. **d** 03 **p** 04. C The Hague *Eur* 03-06; Asst Chapl 06-07; V Bedwellty w New Tredegar *Mon* from 07. *The Rectory, Church Street, Aberbargoed, Bargoed CF81 9FF* Tel (01443) 829555 E-mail rosiedymond@yahoo.com

DYSON, Mrs Clare Louise. b 63. WMMTC 02. **d** 05 **p** 06. C Tupsley w Hampton Bishop *Heref* 05-08; P-in-c Kingstone w Clehonger, Eaton Bishop etc 08-10; R Cagebrook from 10. *The Rectory, Kingstone, Hereford HR2 9EY* Tel (01981) 250350

DYSON, Mrs Debra Anne. b 62. **d** 08 **p** 09. C Lich St Mich w St Mary and Wall from 08. *19 Mawgan Drive, Lichfield WS14 9SD* Tel (01543) 411694 E-mail debdyson@btinternet.com

DYSON, Frank. b 28. Oak Hill Th Coll 60. **d** 62 **p** 63. C Parr *Liv* 62-65; V Newchapel *Lich* 65-77; R Bunwell w Carleton Rode *Nor* 77-79; P-in-c Tibenham 78-80; R Bunwell w Carleton Rode and Tibenham 80-81; R Pakefield 81-93; rtd 93; Perm to Offic *Nor* from 93. *12 Viburnum Green, Lowestoft NR32 2SN* Tel (01502) 574898

DYSON, Peter Whiteley. b 51. Man Univ BA73 LLB75. Qu Coll Birm 77. **d** 81 **p** 82. C Swindon Ch Ch *Bris* 81-84; P-in-c Brislington St Luke 84-91; V Bourne *Guildf* 91-92; Perm to Offic 02-04; P-in-c Herriard w Winslade and Long Sutton etc 04-08; P-in-c Newnham w Nately Scures w Mapledurwell etc 04-08; R N Hants Downs from 08; RD Odiham from 11. *The Vicarage, Church Street, Upton Grey, Basingstoke RG25 2RB* Tel (01256) 861750 E-mail pwdyson@onetel.com

DYSON, Steven John. b 79. Univ of Wales (Ban) BSc00. Trin Coll Bris BA11. **d** 11. C Pinhoe and Broadclyst *Ex* from 11; C Aylesbeare, Rockbeare, Farringdon etc from 11. *The Rectory, Grove Road, Whimple, Exeter EX5 2TP* Tel (01404) 822000 Mobile 07779-594037 E-mail revstevedyson@gmail.com

DYTHAM, Linda Alison. b 52. STETS 02. **d** 05 **p** 06. NSM Savernake *Sarum* 05-07; Chapl Fitzwarren Ho and Standon Lodge from 07. *Fitzwarren House, Kingsdown Road, Swindon SN3 4TD* Tel (01793) 836920 Mobile 07921-123422 E-mail ladytham@btinternet.com

E

EADE, John Christopher. b 45. Ch Coll Cam BA68 MA72. Linc Th Coll 68. **d** 70 **p** 71. C Portsea N End St Mark *Portsm* 70-73; C Henleaze *Bris* 73-77; V Slad *Glouc* 77-82; V N Bradley, Southwick and Heywood *Sarum* 82-91; R Fovant, Sutton Mandeville and Teffont Evias etc 91-08; C Nadder Valley 06-08; TR 08-11; rtd 11. *Odd Acre, Ryall Road, Ryall, Bridport DT6 6EG* Tel (01297) 489633 E-mail john@thames.me.uk

EADES, David Julian John. b 74. Univ of Wales BA95 St Jo Coll Dur BA99. Cranmer Hall Dur. **d** 00 **p** 01. C Walbrook Epiphany *Derby* 00-04; Chapl Essex Univ 04-06. *Address temp unknown* E-mail julian eades@yahoo.co.uk

EADES, Preb Jonathan Peter. b 51. Dundee Univ MA74 Edin Univ BD77. Coates Hall Edin 74. **d** 77 **p** 78. Chapl St Paul's Cathl Dundee 77-88; Chapl Dundee Univ 79-88; TV Leek and Meerbrook *Lich* 88-96; RD Leek 93-96; TR Wolstanton 96-08; P-in-c Ashley and Mucklestone 08-09; C Broughton w Croxton and Cotes Heath w Standon 08-09; R Ashley and Mucklestone and Broughton and Croxton from 09; Preb Lich Cathl from 08. *The Rectory, Charnes Road, Ashley, Market Drayton TF9 4LQ* Tel (01630) 672210

EADON, Benjamin Myles. b 85. Univ Coll Dur BA07 Clare Coll Cam BA10. Westcott Ho Cam 08. **d** 11. C Sunderland St Chad *Dur* from 11. *12 Meadow Drive, East Herrington, Sunderland SR3 3RD* Tel 0191-528 6729 E-mail ben.eadon@btinternet.com

EADY, David Robert. b 43. Salford Univ BSc. Glouc Th Course 82. **d** 85 **p** 86. NSM Highnam, Lassington, Rudford, Tibberton etc *Glouc* 85-95; NSM Stratton, N Cerney, Baunton and Bagendon 95-99; P-in-c Swindon and Elmstone Hardwicke w Uckington 99-08; P-in-c N Cheltenham 08-10; rtd 10; Perm to Offic *Glouc* from 10. *117 Sussex Gardens, Hucclecote, Gloucester GL3 3SP* E-mail davideady@hotmail.com

EADY, Timothy William. b 57. Open Univ BA. Cranmer Hall Dur 82. **d** 85 **p** 86. C Boulton *Derby* 85-88; C Portchester *Portsm* 88-92; R Brighstone and Brooke w Mottistone 92-07; Relig Progr Adv Ocean Sound Radio 88-07; V Iver *Ox* from 07. *The Vicarage, Delaford Close, Iver SL0 9JX* Tel (01753) 653131 E-mail timothy eady@yahoo.co.uk

EAGER, Ms Rosemary Anne McDowall. b 65. St Andr Univ MA87 Strathclyde Univ 88. Ridley Hall Cam 92. **d** 95 **p** 96. C Walthamstow St Mary w St Steph *Chelmsf* 95-98; C Walthamstow 98-01; TV Bushbury *Lich* 01-05; Perm to Offic 05-07. *37 Park Dale East, Wolverhampton WV1 4TD* Tel (01902) 710340 *or* 553945 E-mail revdrosie@yahoo.co.uk

EAGGER, Mrs Christine Mary. b 32. **d** 94 **p** 95. NSM Upper w Lower Gravenhurst *St Alb* 94-03; Perm to Offic *St Alb* 03-05 and *S'well from* 05. *27 Lancaster Road, Coddington, Newark NG24 2TA* Tel (01636) 643885

EAGLE, Canon Julian Charles. b 32. Qu Coll Cam BA56 MA60. Westcott Ho Cam. **d** 58 **p** 59. C Billingham St Aid *Dur* 58-61; C Eastleigh *Win* 61-65; Ind Chapl 65-97; Hon Can Win Cathl 83-97; rtd 97; Perm to Offic *Win* from 97. *123 Cranleigh Road, Bournemouth BH6 5JY* Tel (01202) 429639

EAGLES, The Ven Peter Andrew. b 59. K Coll Lon BA82 AKC82 Ox Univ BA88. St Steph Ho Ox 86. **d** 89 **p** 90. C Ruislip St Martin *Lon* 89-92; CF from 92; Chapl Guards Chpl Lon 07-08; Asst Chapl Gen from 08; Adn for the Army from 11. *c/o MOD Chaplains (Army)* Tel (01264) 381841 Fax 381824 E-mail peter.eagles330@mod.uk

EALES, Geoffrey Pellew. b 50. Trin Coll Bris 95. **d** 97 **p** 98. C Uphill *B & W* 97-00; C Weston super Mare Em 00-05; Chapl Weston Area Health Trust 00-05, V Milton *B & W* 05-09, P-in-c Kewstoke w Wick St Lawrence 08-09; V Milton and Kewstoke from 09. *St Peter's Vicarage, Baytree Road, Weston-super-Mare BS22 8HG* Tel (01934) 624247 E-mail geoffeales@aol.com

EALES, Canon Howard Bernard. b 46. Sarum & Wells Th Coll 73. **d** 76 **p** 77. C Timperley *Ches* 76-78; C Stockport St Thos 78-82; V Wythenshawe Wm Temple Ch *Man* 82-95; V Cheadle Hulme All SS *Ches* from 95; RD Cheadle 02-09; Hon Can Ches Cathl from 06. *All Saints' Vicarage, 27 Church Road, Cheadle Hulme, Cheadle SK8 7JL* Tel 0161-485 3455

EAMAN, Michael Leslie. b 47. Ridley Hall Cam 87. **d** 89 **p** 90. C Wharton *Ches* 89-93; V Buglawton 93-98; TV Congleton 98-10; rtd 10; Hon C Alcester and Arrow w Oversley and Weethley *Cov* from 10; Hon C Kinwarton w Gt Alne and Haselor from 10. *Kinwarton Rectory, Spernall Lane, Great Alne, Alcester B49 6HY* Tel (01789) 488072 E-mail revmike@btopenworld.com

EAMES, Charles George. b 69. CITC 05. **d** 08 **p** 09. NSM Magheracross *Clogh* from 08. *79 The Limes, Drumlyon, Enniskillen BT74 5NB* Tel 07792-191565 (mobile) E-mail charles@charleseames.orangehome.co.uk

EAMES, David John. b 80. Liv Hope Univ Coll BA01 MA04 St Jo Coll Dur MA08. Cranmer Hall Dur 06. **d** 08 **p** 09. C Brigg, Wrawby and Cadney cum Howsham *Linc* from 08. *5 Winston Way, Brigg DN20 8UA* Tel (01652) 652396

✠**EAMES, The Most Revd and Rt Hon Lord (Robert Henry Alexander).** b 37. OM07. QUB LLB60 PhD63 Hon LLD89 TCD Hon LLD92 Cam Univ Hon DD94 Lanc Univ Hon LLD94 Aber Univ Hon DD97 Ex Univ Hon DD99 Hon FGCM88. TCD Div Sch Div Test 60. **d** 63 **p** 64 c 75. C Bangor St Comgall *D & D* 63-66; I Gilnahirk 66-74; Bp's Dom Chapl 70-72; I Dundela St Mark 74-75; Bp D & R 75-80; Bp D & D 80-86; Abp Arm 86-06; rtd 06. *3 Downshire Crescent, Hillsborough BT26 6DD* Tel (028) 9268 9913

EARDLEY, John. b 38. Ch Coll Cam BA61. Ridley Hall Cam 60. **d** 62 **p** 63. C Barnston *Ches* 62-65; C Wilmslow 65-67; V Hollingworth 67-75; V Leasowe 75-91; Chapl Leasowe Hosp 75-82; RD Wallasey 86-91; V Church Hulme and Chapl Cranage Hall Hosp 91-03; rtd 03; Perm to Offic *Ches* from 03. *7 Banks Road, Heswall, Wirral CH60 9JS* Tel 0151-342 9537

EARDLEY, Canon John Barry. b 35. MBE97. MEd87. AKC62. **d** 63 **p** 64. C Merton St Jas *S'wark* 63-66; C St Helier 66-69; C Bilton *Cov* 69-70; C Canley *Cov* 70-74; P-in-c Church Lawford w Newnham Regis 74-80; P-in-c Leamington Hastings and Birdingbury 82-88; Dioc Educn Officer 82-00; Hon Can Cov Cathl 87-00; rtd 01; Perm to Offic *Cov* from 01. *8 Margetts Close, Kenilworth CV8 1EN* Tel 024-7630 2345 *or* 7667 3467 E-mail johnbarry.eardley@ntlworld.com

EARDLEY, Robert Bradford. b 44. St Alb Minl Tr Scheme 90. **d** 93 **p** 94. NSM Digswell and Panshanger *St Alb* 93-96; NSM Wheathampstead 97-98; NSM Tewin 98-05; P-in-c 98-04; rtd 05; Perm to Offic *St Alb* 05-07. *Bridge Cottage, Martin, Fordingbridge SP6 3LD* Tel (01725) 519423 Mobile 07941-345895 E-mail rob.eardley@virgin.net

EARDLEY, William Robert. b 56. Oak Hill Th Coll 94. **d** 96 **p** 97. C Whitfield *Derby* 96-99; TV Dronfield w Holmesfield from 99. *The Vicarage, Vicarage Close, Holmesfield, Dronfield S18 7WZ* Tel 0114-289 1425 E-mail william.eardley@dhwparish.org.uk

EAREY, Mark Robert. b 65. Loughb Univ BSc87 St Jo Coll Dur BA91. Cranmer Hall Dur 88. **d** 91 **p** 92. C Glen Parva and S Wigston *Leic* 91-94; C Luton Ch Ch *Roch* 94-97; Praxis Nat

Educn Officer Sarum Coll 97-02; TR Morley *Wakef* 02-07; Tutor Qu Foundn Birm from 07. *The Queen's Foundation, Somerset Road, Edgbaston, Birmingham B15 2QH* Tel 0121-452 2667 E-mail m.earey@queens.ac.uk

EARIS, Canon Stanley Derek. b 50. Univ Coll Dur BA71 BCL80. Ripon Hall Ox BA73 MA80. **d** 74 **p** 75. C Sutton St Jas and Wawne *York* 74-77; C Acomb St Steph 77-81; V Skelmanthorpe *Wakef* 81-87; R Market Deeping *Linc* 87-02; V N Walsham and Edingthorpe *Nor* from 02; C Bacton w Edingthorpe w Witton and Ridlington 04-07; Hon Can Nor Cathl from 10. *The Vicarage, 28A Yarmouth Road, North Walsham NR28 9AT* Tel (01692) 406380 E-mail derek@earis.fsnet.co.uk

EARL, Andrew John. b 61. Huddersfield Univ CertEd01 Ches Coll of HE BTh04. NOC. **d** 04 **p** 05. NSM Barnsley St Mary *Wakef* from 04; Chapl W Yorks Police from 04. *The Chines, 22 Faith Street, South Kirkby, Pontefract WF9 3AL* Tel (01977) 658925 Mobile 07919-048689 E-mail aj sc earl@hotmail.com

EARL, David Arthur. b 34. Hartley Victoria Coll 63 Coll of Resurr Mirfield. **d** 83 **p** 83. In Meth Ch 67-83; P-in-c Paddock *Wakef* 83-84; C Huddersfield St Pet and All SS 84-99; rtd 99; Perm to Offic *Wakef* from 99. *2 Clifton Court, Cleveland Road, Huddersfield HD1 4PU* Tel (01484) 535608

EARL, The Very Revd David Kaye Lee. b 28. TCD BA54. **d** 55 **p** 56. C Chapelizod *D & G* 55-58; I Rathkeale *L & K* 58-65; I Killarney 65-79; Prec Limerick Cathl 77-79; Dean Ferns *C & O* 79-94; I Ferns w Kilbride, Toombe, Kilcormack etc 79-94; rtd 94. *Random, Seafield, Tramore, Co Waterford, Republic of Ireland* Tel (00353) (51) 390503

EARL, Simon Robert. b 50. Culham Coll of Educn CertEd71 Open Univ BA82. Linc Th Coll 94. **d** 96 **p** 97. C Bexhill St Aug *Chich* 96-99; R Ninfield from 99; V Hooe from 99. *The Rectory, Church Lane, Ninfield, Battle TN33 9JW* Tel and fax (01424) 892308 E-mail srearl@btopenworld.com

EARL, Stephen Geoffrey Franklyn. b 53. Lon Univ BA76 Goldsmiths' Coll Lon PGCE77. Ridley Hall Cam 91. **d** 93 **p** 94. C Sawston *Ely* 93-96; V Burwell w Reach 96-10; RD Fordham and Quy 02-10; Hon Can Ely Cathl 07-10; P-in-c Lavenham w Preston *St E* from 10. *The Rectory, Church Street, Lavenham, Sudbury CO10 9SA* Tel and fax (01787) 247244 E-mail searl@toucansurf.com

EARLE, Mrs Sylvia. b 51. St Aid Coll Dur BA72. Cranmer Hall Dur 05. **d** 07 **p** 08. C Whitkirk *Ripon* from 07. *12 Darnley Lane, Leeds LS15 9EX* Tel 0113-260 0382 E-mail sylvia.earle@tesco.net

EARLEY, Stephen John. b 48. Trin Coll Bris 91. **d** 93 **p** 94. C Stroud H Trin *Glouc* 93-98; C Leckhampton SS Phil and Jas w Cheltenham St Jas 98-02; V Nailsworth w Shortwood, Horsley etc from 02. *The Vicarage, Avening Road, Nailsworth, Stroud GL6 0BS* Tel (01453) 832181 E-mail stevearl@earleys.f9.co.uk

EARNEY, Preb Graham Howard. b 45. AKC67. **d** 68 **p** 69. C Auckland St Helen *Dur* 68-72; C Corsenside Newc 72-76; P-in-c 76-79; TV Willington 79-83; TR 83-87; Dioc Soc Resp Officer *B & W* 87-95; Dir Bp Mascall Cen *Heref* 95-02; Hon TV Ludlow, Ludford, Ashford Carbonell etc 95-02; Dioc Development Rep 93-06; Preb Heref Cathl 02-10; rtd 10. *The Coppice, Castle Pulverbatch, Pulverbatch, Shrewsbury SY5 8DS* Tel (01743) 718930 E-mail gandsearney@btinternet.com

EARNSHAW, Alan Mark. b 36. CQSW81. Lon Coll of Div LTh60. **d** 60 **p** 61. C Fazakerley Em *Liv* 60-65; V Ovenden *Wakef* 65-79; NSM Halifax St Jude 79-90; V Coley 90-99; rtd 99; Perm to Offic *Wakef* from 00. *67 Smithy Clough Lane, Ripponden, Sowerby Bridge HX6 4LG* Tel (01422) 822833

EARNSHAW, Robert Richard. b 42. NOC 78. **d** 81 **p** 82. NW Area Sec Bible Soc 78-85; NSM Liv All So Springwood 81-85; R Hinton Ampner w Bramdean and Kilmeston *Win* 85-87; Chapl HM YOI Huntercombe and Finnamore 87-92; Chapl HM YOI Finnamore Wood Camp 87-92; R Spaxton w Charlynch, Goathurst, Enmore etc *B & W* 92-98; R Old Cleeve, Leighland and Treborough 98-03; rtd 03; Perm to Offic *Cov* 03-10 and *Portsm* from 10. *11 Chesterton Place, Whiteley, Fareham PO15 7EZ* Tel (01489) 886687 E-mail bobjen@sagainternet.co.uk

EARP, John William. b 19. Jes Coll Cam BA42 MA45. Ridley Hall Cam 42. **d** 43 **p** 44. C Portman Square St Paul *Lon* 43-46; Tutor Ridley Hall Cam 46-48; Chapl 48-51; Vice-Prin 51-56; Chapl Eton Coll 56-62; V Hartley Wintney and Elvetham 62-77; RD Odiham 76-83; V Hartley Wintney, Elvetham, Winchfield etc 77-88; rtd 88; Perm to Offic *Nor* from 89. *3 The Driftway, Sheringham NR26 8LD* Tel (01263) 825487

EARWAKER, John Clifford. b 36. Keble Coll Ox BA59 MA63 Man Univ MEd71. Linc Th Coll 59. **d** 61 **p** 62. C Ecclesall *Sheff* 61-64; Succ St Mary's Cathl 64-65; Lic to Offic *Man* 65-69 and *Sheff* 69-93; Chapl and Lect Sheff Poly 81-92; Chapl and Lect Sheff Hallam Univ 92-93; rtd 93; Perm to Offic *Sheff* from 93. *89 Dransfield Road, Crosspool, Sheffield S10 5RP* Tel 0114-230 3487

EASEMAN, Robert Leslie. b 44. **d** 00 **p** 01. OLM Hunstanton St Mary w Ringstead Parva etc *Nor* 00-09; rtd 09; Perm to Offic

Nor from 09. *5 Lighthouse Close, Hunstanton PE36 6EL* Tel and fax (01485) 535258 Mobile 07941-323218 E-mail robert.easeman@virgin.net

EAST, Bryan Victor. b 46. Oak Hill Th Coll 91. **d** 93 **p** 94. C Waltham Cross *St Alb* 93-96; C Wotton St Mary *Glouc* 96-99; V Humberston *Linc* from 99. *The Vicarage, 34 Tetney Road, Humberston, Grimsby DN36 4JF* Tel (01472) 813158 E-mail bryan.east@ntlworld.com

EAST, Mark Richard. b 57. Trin Coll Bris BA89. **d** 89 **p** 90. C Dalton-in-Furness *Carl* 89-93; TV Bucknall and Bagnall *Lich* 93-00; P-in-c Church Coniston *Carl* from 00; P-in-c Torver from 00. *St Andrew's Vicarage, Yewdale Road, Coniston LA21 8DX* Tel (01539) 441262 E-mail mark.east@lineone.net

EAST, Martin James. STETS. **d** 10 **p** 11. NSM N Hants Downs *Win* from 10. *North Lodge, Farnham Road, Odiham, Hook RG29 1HR* Tel (01256) 703887 Mobile 07740-025263 E-mail martineast@btinternet.com

EAST, Peter Alan. *See* OSTLI-EAST, Peter Alan

EAST, Canon Richard Kenneth. b 47. Oak Hill Th Coll 86. **d** 88 **p** 89. C Necton w Holme Hale *Nor* 88-92; R Garsdon, Lea and Cleverton and Charlton *Bris* from 92; P-in-c Gt Somerford, Lt Somerford, Seagry, Corston etc from 10; C Brinkworth w Dauntsey from 10; RD Malmesbury 93-99; Hon Can Bris Cathl from 10. *The Rectory, The Street, Lea, Malmesbury SN16 9PG* Tel (01666) 823861 E-mail lea.rectory@btinternet.com

EAST, Stuart Michael. b 50. Chich Th Coll 86. **d** 88 **p** 89. C Middlesbrough St Martin *York* 88-92; R Upper Ryedale 92-97; V Macclesfield St Paul *Ches* 97-01; C Maidstone St Luke *Cant* 01-03; R Peopleton and White Ladies Aston w Churchill etc *Worc* 03-10; V Nunthorpe *York* from 10. *St Mary's Vicarage, Church Lane, Nunthorpe, Middlesbrough TS7 0PD* Tel (01642) 316570 Mobile 07754-244929 E-mail stuart@the-rectory.fsnet.co.uk

EAST KERALA, Bishop of. *See* SAMUEL, The Most Revd Kunnumpurathu Joseph

EAST RIDING, Archdeacon of. *See* BUTTERFIELD, The Ven David John

EASTELL, Jane Rosamund. b 47. Sheff Univ BA68 Univ of Wales (Lamp) MA08 RIBA73. Trin Coll Bris BA99. **d** 99 **p** 00. C Backwell w Chelvey and Brockley *B & W* 99-03; C Chew Stoke w Nempnett Thrubwell 03-08; C Chew Magna w Dundry and Norton Malreward 03-08; Hon C Taunton St Jo from 09; Dioc Adv in Prayer and Spirituality from 04. *Meadowside, Wild Oak Lane, Trull, Taunton TA3 7JT* Tel (01823) 321069 E-mail jane.eastell@bathwells.anglican.org

EASTER, Canon Ann Rosemarie. SRN68 Univ of E Lon MBA94. Gilmore Ho 78. **dss** 80 **d** 87 **p** 94. Stratford St Jo and Ch Ch w Forest Gate St Jas *Chelmsf* 80-89; Par Dn 87-89; Chapl Asst Newham Gen Hosp 80-89; Perm to Offic *Chelmsf* 89-08; C Chief Exec Officer The Renewal Programme from 95; AD Newham 97-07; NSM W Ham 08-10; NSM E Ham w Upton Park from 11; Hon Can Chelmsf Cathl from 00; Chapl to The Queen from 07. *The Renewal Programme, 66B Sebert Road, London E7 0NJ* Tel (020) 8221 4420 Mobile 07889-799290 E-mail ann@renewalprogramme.org.uk

EASTERN ARCHDEACONRY, Archdeacon of the. *See* CURRAN, The Ven Patrick Martin Stanley

EASTGATE, Canon John. b 30. Kelham Th Coll 47. **d** 54 **p** 55. C Ealing St Pet Mt Park *Lon* 54-58; C-in-c Leic St Gabr CD 58-64; V Leic St Gabr 64-69; V Glen Parva and S Wigston 69-74; V Woodley St Jo the Ev *Ox* 74-83; V Hughenden 83-94; RD Wycombe 87-90; Hon Can Ch Ch 90-94; rtd 94; Perm to Offic *Sarum* from 05. *12A Mowlem Court, Rempstone Road, Swanage BH19 1DR* Tel (01929) 421558 E-mail john@eastgate1702.fsnet.co.uk

EASTOE, Canon Robin Howard Spenser. b 53. Lon Univ BD75 AKC75. Coll of Resurr Mirfield 77. **d** 78 **p** 79. C Gt Ilford St Mary *Chelmsf* 78-81; C Walthamstow St Sav 81-84; V Barkingside St Fran 84-92; V Leigh-on-Sea St Marg 92-08; RD Hadleigh 00-08; Chapl Southend Health Care NHS Trust 96-08; Hon Can Chelmsf Cathl 06-08; P-in-c Heavitree and St Mary Steps *Ex* from 08. *The Rectory, 10 Victoria Park Road, Exeter EX2 4NT* Tel (01392) 677150 E-mail theeastoes@btinternet.com

EASTON, Christopher Richard Alexander. b 60. TCD BA81. **d** 84 **p** 85. C Belfast St Donard *D & D* 84-89; I Inishmacsaint *Clogh* 89-95; I Magheralin w Dollingstown *D & D* 95-01; I Coleraine *Conn* 01-09; P-in-c Belfast Whiterock from 09. *5 Millbrooke Manor, Ballymoney BT53 7HX* Tel (028) 2766 9852 E-mail stpat@btinternet.com

EASTON, Donald Fyfe. b 48. St Edm Hall Ox BA69 MA85 Nottm Univ CertEd72 Univ Coll Lon MA76 PhD90 Clare Hall Cam MA85. Westcott Ho Cam 89. **d** 90 **p** 91. NSM Fulham St Andr *Lon* 90-97; Lic Preacher from 97. *12 Weltje Road, London W6 9TG* Tel (020) 8741 0233

EASTON, John. b 34. St Cath Soc Ox BA59 MA63. Chich Th Coll 59. **d** 61 **p** 62. C Rugeley *Lich* 61-64; TR 72-87; C Shrewsbury All SS 64-66; Ind Chapl *Sheff* 66-72; V Bolsover *Derby* 87-99; RD Bolsover and Staveley 93-98; rtd 99; Perm to

Offic *Derby* from 99. *71 Wythburn Road, Chesterfield S41 8DP* Tel (01246) 555610
EASTON, John. b 41. Nor City Coll 71. **d** 97. OLM New Catton Ch Ch *Nor* 97-11; Perm to Offic from 11. *14 Carterford Drive, Norwich NR3 4DW* Tel (01603) 412589
E-mail jejo@waitrose.com
EASTON, Robert Paul Stephen. b 62. Bris Univ BA84. St Steph Ho Ox BTh00. **d** 00 **p** 01. C Stoke Newington St Mary *Lon* 00-03; Chapl Brighton Coll from 03. *The Chaplaincy, Brighton College, Eastern Road, Brighton BN2 2AL* Tel (01273) 606524
E-mail roberteaston1@onetel.com
EASTON-CROUCH, Jonathan Brian. b 65. SEITE 96. **d** 99 **p** 00. C Mitcham SS Pet and Paul *S'wark* 99-02; Hon C S Wimbledon H Trin and St Pet 03-06; C New Addington 06-09; P-in-c Merton St Jas from 09. *St James's Vicarage, Beaford Grove, London SW20 9LB* Tel 07939-121252 (mobile)
E-mail jonathan.ec@virgin.net
EASTWOOD, Colin Foster. b 34. Leeds Univ BA56 MA66. Linc Th Coll 65. **d** 67 **p** 68. C Cottingham *York* 67-70; C Darlington St Cuth *Dur* 70-75; V Eighton Banks 75-81; V Sutton St Jas *Ches* 81-99; rtd 99; Perm to Offic *Glouc* from 00. *14 Ross Close, Chipping Sodbury, Bristol BS37 6RS* Tel (01454) 317594
EASTWOOD, David Dean. b 54. Newc Univ LLB77. Ridley Hall Cam 06. **d** 08 **p** 09. C Westbrook St Phil *Liv* 08-10; P-in-c St Helens St Helen 10; TR St Helens Town Cen from 10. *The Rectory, 51A Rainford Road, Dentons Green, St Helens WA10 6BZ* Tel (01744) 27446 Mobile 07785-542594
E-mail davideastwood86@googlemail.com
EASTWOOD, Harry. b 26. Man Univ BSc48. Ridley Hall Cam 81. **d** 82 **p** 83. NSM Barton Seagrave w Warkton *Pet* 82-00; Perm to Offic from 00. *22 Poplars Farm Road, Kettering NN15 5AF* Tel (01536) 513271 E-mail harry.eastwood@virginmedia.com
EASTWOOD, Canon Janet. b 54. Wycliffe Hall Ox 83. **dss** 86 **d** 87 **p** 94. Ainsdale *Liv* 86-90; Par Dn 87-90; TD Kirkby Lonsdale *Carl* 90-94; TV 94-95; Dioc Youth Officer 90-94; R Wavertree H Trin *Liv* from 95; P-in-c Wavertree St Thos 95-97; Hon Can Liv Cathl from 06; Chapl Blue Coat Sch Liv from 96. *Wavertree Rectory, Hunters Lane, Liverpool L15 8HL* Tel 0151-733 2172
E-mail janet@holytrinitywavertree.co.uk
EASTWOOD, Canon Martin Russell. b 66. Edin Univ BMus88 LRSM02. Ripon Coll Cuddesdon BTh05. **d** 03 **p** 04. C Wymondham *Nor* 03-06; P-in-c Fulham St Andr *Lon* 06-07; V 07-11; Can Res St E Cathl from 11. *1 Abbey Precincts, The Great Churchyard, Bury St Edmunds IP33 1RS* Tel (01284) 761982
E-mail precentor@stedscathedral.org
EASTWOOD, Mrs Nicola. b 63. **d** 11. C Upton (Overchurch) *Ches* from 11. *34 Birch Road, Prenton CH43 5UA* Tel 0151-653 3910
EATOCK, John. b 45. Lanc Univ MA82. Lich Th Coll 67. **d** 70 **p** 71. C Crumpsall St Mary *Man* 70-73; C Atherton 73-74; C Ribbleton *Blackb* 74-77; V Ingol 77-83; V Laneside 83-92; RD Accrington 90-92; Perm to Offic *Blackb* 92-08 and *Truro* from 08. *29 Wellington Road, Camborne TR14 7LH* Tel (01209) 714899 E-mail john.eatock@tiscali.co.uk
EATON, Barry Anthony. b 50. St Martin's Coll Lanc MA98. CBDTI 94. **d** 97 **p** 98. C W Burnley All SS *Blackb* 97-99; Dep Chapl HM Pris Leeds 99-00; Chapl HM Pris Buckley Hall 00-07; Chapl HM Pris Styal 07-10; Chapl HM Pris Preston from 10. *HM Prison Preston, 2 Ribbleton Lane, Preston PR1 5AB* Tel (01772) 444550
EATON, Benjamin. See EATON, Canon Oscar Benjamin
EATON, David Andrew. b 58. MBE06. Man Univ BSc79 ACA83 FCA. Trin Coll Bris BA89. **d** 89 **p** 90. C Barking St Marg w St Patr *Chelmsf* 89-92; C Billericay and Lt Burstead 92-95; P-in-c Vange 95-05; TV Sole Bay *St E* 05-10; Perm to Offic *St E* from 10. *The Cedars, School Lane, Great Barton, Bury St Edmunds IP31 2RQ* Tel (01284) 787718 Mobile 07841-215182 E-mail davideaton@lineone.net
EATON, Canon David John. b 45. Nottm Univ LTh BTh74. St Jo Coll Nottm 70. **d** 74 **p** 75. C Headley All SS *Guildf* 74-77; Ind Chapl *Worc* 77-82; TV Halesowen 82-87; V Rowledge *Guildf* 82-89; V Leatherhead 89-01; R Leatherhead and Mickleham 01-09; RD Leatherhead 93-98; Hon Can Guildf Cathl 02-09; rtd 09. *Two Way House, Wheelers Lane, Brockham, Betchworth RH3 7LA* Tel (01737) 843915
E-mail rev_davideaton@hotmail.com
✠EATON, The Rt Revd Derek Lionel. b 41. MA78. Trin Coll Bris. **d** 71 **p** 71 **c** 90. C Barton Hill St Luke w Ch Ch *Bris* 71-72; Chapl Br Emb Tunisia 72-78; Provost All SS Cathl Cairo and Chapl Br Emb 78-83; Hon Can 85; Assoc P Papanui St Paul New Zealand 84; V Sumner-Redcliffs 85-90; Bp Nelson 90-06; rtd 06. *67 Grove Street, The Wood, Nelson 7010, New Zealand* Tel (0064) (3) 545 6998
✠EATON (née CRAIG), Mrs Julie Elizabeth. b 57. Open Univ BA08 SEN81. Trin Coll Bris 87. **d** 89 **p** 94. Par Dn Gt Ilford St Andr *Chelmsf* 89-92; NSM Billericay and Lt Burstead 92-95; C 95-96; TV 96-01; Chapl Thameside Community Healthcare NHS Trust 92-95; Perm to Offic *Chelmsf* 01-05; TV Sole Bay

St E 05-10. *The Cedars, School Lane, Great Barton, Bury St Edmunds IP31 2RQ* Tel (01284) 787718
E-mail juliecraigeaton@tiscali.co.uk
EATON, Mrs Margaret Anne. b 44. Ab Dioc Tr Course 82. **dss** 84 **d** 86 **p** 94. NSM Ellon and Cruden Bay *Ab* 84-95; C Bridge of Don 95-00; Co-ord Scottish Episc Renewal Fellowship 00-04; C Ellon 01-03; C Elgin w Lossiemouth *Mor* 03-04 and 06-09; C Aberlour 06-09; C Dufftown 06-09. *Address temp unknown*
E-mail maggie-e@hotmail.co.uk
EATON, Canon Oscar Benjamin. b 37. Puerto Rico Th Coll STB66. **d** 66 **p** 67. Ecuador 66-69; C Wandsworth St Anne *S'wark* 69-71; C Aldrington *Chich* 71-73; TV Littleham w Exmouth 74-79; R Alphington 79-84; Chapl Barcelona w Casteldefels *Eur* 84-88; Chapl Maisons-Laffitte 88-02; rtd 02; P-in-c St Raphaël *Eur* 02-10; Can Malta Cathl 96-10. *62 Hameau de Valescure, 83600 Fréjus, France* Tel (0033) 4 94 40 48 61 *or* tel and fax 4 94 95 45 78 E-mail revbeaton@aol.com
EATON, The Very Revd Peter David. b 58. K Coll Lon BA82 AKC82 Qu Coll Cam BA85 MA89 Magd Coll Ox MA90. Westcott Ho Cam 83. **d** 86 **p** 87. C Maidstone All SS and St Phil w Tovil *Cant* 86-89; Fells' Chapl Magd Coll Ox 89-91; Lic to Offic *Ox* 89-96; Assoc R Salt Lake City St Paul USA 91-95; Hon Can Th Utah 91-01; R Lancaster St Jas Penn 95-01; Dean St Jo Cathl Denver from 02. *St John's Cathedral, 1350 Washington Street, Denver CO 80203-2008, USA* Tel (001) (303) 831 7115 *or* 295 0956 Fax 831 7119 E-mail deansadmin@sjc-den.org
EATON, Miss Phyllis Mary. b 42. SRD Qu Eliz Coll Lon BSc63 UNISA BA79. WMMTC 87. **d** 90 **p** 94. NSM Washwood Heath *Birm* 90-91; NSM Edgbaston SS Mary and Ambrose 91-95; Perm to Offic 93-03; NSM Oldbury, Langley and Londonderry from 05. *26 Blackthorne Road, Smethwick, Warley B67 6PZ* Tel 0121-552 4904 *or* 507 4085
EAVES, Alan Charles. b 37. Tyndale Hall Bris 62. **d** 65 **p** 66. C Southport SS Simon and Jude *Liv* 65-66; C Eccleston Ch Ch 66-70; V Earlestown 70-79; V Orpington Ch Ch *Roch* 79-02; rtd 02; Perm to Offic *Ely* from 03. *4 Chervil Close, Folksworth, Peterborough PE7 3SZ* Tel (01733) 241644 Mobile 07904-357476 E-mail vaeaves@talktalk.com
EAVES, Brian Maxwell. b 40. Tyndale Hall Bris 66. **d** 69 **p** 70. C Wolverhampton St Jude *Lich* 69-72; C Fazeley 72-75; TV Ipsley *Worc* 75-79; Chapl Amsterdam *Eur* 79-86; Chapl Bordeaux w Riberac, Chatres, Duras etc 86-91; Monaco 91-93; TV Buckhurst Hill *Chelmsf* 93-96; R Culworth w Sulgrave and Thorpe Mandeville etc *Pet* 96-03; rtd 03. *13 Blenheim Drive, Newent GL18 1TU* Tel (01531) 822760
EBBSFLEET, Suffragan Bishop of (Provincial Episcopal Visitor). See BAKER, The Rt Revd Jonathan Mark Richard
EBELING, Mrs Barbara. b 44. Hull Univ BA67. St Alb Minl Tr Scheme 87. **d** 94 **p** 95. C Stevenage St Hugh and St Jo *St Alb* 94-99; R Riversmeet 99-08; rtd 08; Perm to Offic *St Alb* 08-09 and *Chelmsf* from 09. V High Cross *St Alb* from 10; V Thundridge from 10. *7 Wicklands Road, Hunsdon, Ware SG12 8PD* Tel (01279) 842086
E-mail barbara.ebeling@sky.com
ECCLES, James Henry. b 30. DipEd. Wycliffe Hall Ox 86. **d** 87 **p** 88. NSM Llandudno *Ban* 87-91; rtd 91; NSM Llanrhos *St As* 94-00; Perm to Offic *Ban* from 97. *Lowlands, 7 St Seiriol's Road, Llandudno LL30 2YY* Tel (01492) 878524
ECCLES, Mrs Vivien Madeline. b 92 **p** 94. OLM Old Trafford St Bride *Man* from 92. *479 Barton Road, Stretford, Manchester M32 9TA* Tel 0161-748 9795
ECCLESTON, Mrs Frances Mary. b 61. Jes Coll Cam BA83 York St Jo Coll MA05 CQSW88. NOC 00. **d** 03 **p** 04. C Ranmoor *Sheff* 03-06; C Sheff St Leon Norwood 06-09; P-in-c Crosspool from 09; Dioc Ecum Officer from 10. *The Vicarage, 1 Barnfield Road, Sheffield S10 5TD* Tel 0114-230 2531
E-mail frances.eccleston@sheffield.anglican.org
ECCLESTONE, Gary Edward. b 73. Ex Univ BA95 PGCE96. Cuddesdon Coll BTh99. **d** 99 **p** 00. C Salisbury St Martin and Laverstock *Sarum* 99-03; P-in-c Hanslope w Castlethorpe *Ox* 03-09; V from 09. *The Vicarage, Park Road, Hanslope, Milton Keynes MK19 7LT* Tel (01908) 337936
ECHOLS, Mrs Janet Lyn Roberts. b 58. Coll of Charleston (USA) BA. Trin Episc Sch for Min Penn MDiv. **d** 95 **p** 96. Asst R Mt Pleasant Ch Ch USA 95-02; P-in-c Stapleford *Ely* 02-07; Tutor Past Studies Ridley Hall Cam 05-07. *Address temp unknown* E-mail janetechols@yahoo.com
ECKERSLEY, Mrs Nancy Elizabeth. b 50. York Univ BA72 Leeds Univ CertEd73. NEOC 86. **d** 89 **p** 94. C Clifton *York* 89-00; Chapl York Distr Hosp 90-93; Lay Tr Officer *York* 93-00; V Heslington 00-11; rtd 11. *The Vicarage, School Lane, Heslington, York YO10 5EE*
E-mail nancyeckersley@yahoo.com
ECKERSLEY, Canon Richard Hugh. b 25. Trin Coll Cam BA48 MA50. Chich Th Coll 49. **d** 51 **p** 52. C Portsea St Jo Rudmore *Portsm* 51-57; C Portsea N End St Mark 57-62; V Paulsgrove 62-73; V Brighton St Nic *Chich* 73-84; Can Res Portsm Cathl 84-92; rtd 92; Perm to Offic *Portsm* from 92. *136 Kensington Road, Portsmouth PO2 0QY* Tel (023) 9265 3512

ECKHARD, Robert Leo Michael. b 60. Middx Poly BA87 Open Univ MA96 La Sainte Union Coll PGCE88. NTMTC BA05. **d** 05 **p** 06. C Ealing St Paul *Lon* 05-08; C Hounslow H Trin w St Paul 08-10. *Address temp unknown* E-mail bob.eckhard@ukonline.co.uk

EDDY, Paul Anthony. b 67. St Jo Coll Nottm 07. **d** 09 **p** 10. C Grove *Ox* from 09. *2 Edington Place, Grove, Wantage OX12 0BX* Tel 07958-905716 (mobile) E-mail paul@pauleddy.org

EDE, The Ven Dennis. b 31. Nottm Univ BA55 Birm Univ MSocSc73. Ripon Hall Ox 55. **d** 57 **p** 58. C Sheldon *Birm* 57-60; C Castle Bromwich SS Mary and Marg 60-64; Chapl E Birm Hosp 60-76; C-in-c Hodge Hill CD *Birm* 64-70; V Hodge Hill 70-72; TR 72-76; Chapl Sandwell Distr Gen Hosp 76-90; V W Bromwich All SS *Lich* 76-90; P-in-c W Bromwich Ch Ch 76-79; RD W Bromwich 76-90; Preb Lich Cathl 83-90; Adn Stoke 90-97; rtd 97; Hon C Tilford *Guildf* 97-99; Hon C The Bourne and Tilford 99-02; Perm to Offic *Guildf* and *S'wark* from 03. *Tilford, 13 Park Close, Carshalton SM5 3EU* Tel (020) 8647 5891 E-mail dennisangelaede@aol.co.uk

EDEN, Grenville Mervyn. b 37. Bris Univ BA58 Lon Univ MPhil78. Ox Min Course 88. **d** 95 **p** 96. NSM Burnham w Dropmore, Hitcham and Taplow *Ox* 95-06; Perm to Offic from 06. *Langdale, Grays Park Road, Stoke Poges, Slough SL2 4JG* Tel (01753) 525962

EDEN, Henry. b 36. G&C Coll Cam BA59 MA64. Ox NSM Course. **d** 87 **p** 88. NSM Abingdon w Shippon *Ox* 87-88; Chapl Brentwood Sch Essex 88-95; TV Beaconsfield *Ox* 95-00; Perm to Offic *St E* from 01 and *Ely* from 03. *Ely Cottage, Denham, Bury St Edmunds IP29 5EQ* Tel (01284) 811884 E-mail heden@btinternet.com

EDEN, Mrs Lesley Patricia. b 54. Liv Univ MTh99. NOC 93. **d** 96 **p** 97. C Wallasey St Hilary *Ches* 96-98; C Oxton 98-01; V Whitegate w Lt Budworth from 01; Min Review Officer 01-07; RD Middlewich from 10. *The Vicarage, Cinder Hill, Whitegate, Northwich CW8 2BH* Tel and fax (01606) 882151 E-mail lesley_eden88@hotmail.com

EDEN, Leslie Thomas Ernest. b 19. ACII55. S'wark Ord Course. **d** 69 **p** 70. NSM Kidbrooke St Jas *S'wark* 69-94; rtd 94; Perm to Offic *S'wark* from 94. *47 Begbie Road, London SE3 8DA* Tel (020) 8856 3088

EDEN, Mervyn. See EDEN, Grenville Mervyn

EDEN, Michael William. b 57. Nottm Univ BTh86. Linc Th Coll 83. **d** 86 **p** 87. C Daventry *Pet* 86-89; TV Northampton Em 89-92; V Corby St Columba 92-03; P-in-c Stowmarket *St E* from 03. *The Vicarage, 7 Lockington Road, Stowmarket IP14 1BQ* Tel (01449) 678623 *or* 774652 Fax 774652 E-mail theedens@talk21.com

EDGAR, David. b 59. Newc Univ BA81. Linc Th Coll BTh86. **d** 86 **p** 87. C Wednesbury St Paul Wood Green *Lich* 86-91; V Winterton Gp *Linc* 91-00; C Linc St Swithin 00-01; P-in-c Linc All SS from 06; Chapl N Lincs Coll from 00. *1 St Giles Avenue, Lincoln LN2 4PE* Tel (01522) 528199 E-mail david.edgar1@tesco.net

EDGCUMBE, Irena Christine. *See* CZERNIAWSKA EDGCUMBE, Mrs Irena Christine

EDGE, John Nicholson. b 53. **d** 99 **p** 00. OLM Flixton St Jo *Man* from 99. *5 Devon Road, Flixton, Manchester M41 6PN* Tel 0161-748 4736

EDGE, Michael MacLeod. b 45. St Andr Univ BSc68 Qu Coll Cam BA70 MA74. Westcott Ho Cam 68. **d** 72 **p** 73. C Allerton *Liv* 72-76; R Bretherton *Blackb* 76-82; P-in-c Kilpeck *Heref* 82-84; P-in-c St Devereux w Wormbridge 82-84; TR Ewyas Harold w Dulas, Kenderchurch etc 82-93; RD Abbeydore 84-90; V Enfield St Andr *Lon* from 93. *Enfield Vicarage, Silver Street, Enfield EN1 3EG* Tel (020) 8363 8676

EDGE, Philip John. b 54. Ripon Coll Cuddesdon 77. **d** 80 **p** 81. C N Harrow St Alb *Lon* 80-83; C St Giles Cripplegate w St Bart Moor Lane etc 83-86; P-in-c Belmont 86-88; V 88-92; V Ellesmere and Welsh Frankton *Lich* 92-97; V Ellesmere from 97; RD Ellesmere from 10. *The Vicarage, Church Hill, Ellesmere SY12 0HB* Tel (01691) 622571

EDGE, Ms Renate Erika. b 50. Cranmer Hall Dur 86. **d** 88. Par Dn Leic H Spirit 88-89; Asst Chapl Leic and Co Miss for the Deaf 88-89; Par Dn Leic H Apostles 89-94. *Flat 3, 1 Stuart Court, Stuart Square, Edinburgh EH12 8UU* E-mail mail@renata.org.uk *or* renata.edge@hotmail.co.uk

EDGE, Timothy Peter. b 55. Brighton Poly BSc80 K Coll Lon MA10 CEng85 MIET85 FRAS80. Westcott Ho Cam 85. **d** 88 **p** 89. C Norton *Ches* 88-91; C Bedworth *Cov* 91-96; TV Witney *Ox* 96-02; Asst Chapl HM Pris Bullingdon 02-04; Chapl 04-09; NSM Cogges and S Leigh *Ox* from 03. *27 Burford Road, Witney OX28 6DP* Tel (01993) 773438 E-mail tim.edge@talk21.com

EDGELL, Hugh Anthony Richard. b 31. ARHistS84. AKC57. **d** 58 **p** 59. C N Lynn w St Marg and St Nic *Nor* 58-64; R S Walsham 64-74; V Upton w Fishley 64-74; R Hingham 74-81; R Hingham w Woodrising w Scoulton 81-85; V Horning 85-89; P-in-c Beeston St Laurence w Ashmanhaugh 85-89; R Horning w Beeston St Laurence and Ashmanhaugh 89-95; Prior St Benet's Abbey Horning 87-95; rtd 95; Perm to Offic *Nor* from

95. *Brambles, Brimbelow Road, Hoveton, Norwich NR12 8UJ* Tel (01604) 782206

EDGERTON, Ms Hilary Ann. b 66. R Holloway & Bedf New Coll Lon BSc88. Wycliffe Hall Ox BTh93. **d** 93 **p** 94. Par Dn S Cave and Ellerker w Broomfleet *York* 93-94; C 94-97; TV Howden 97-00; V Hayfield and Chinley w Buxworth *Derby* from 00. *8 Bluebell Close, Hayfield, High Peak SK22 2PG* Tel (01663) 743350 E-mail hilaryedgerton@freeola.net

EDIE, Jennifer Mary. b 40. Edin Univ MA62 Hong Kong Univ PGCE77. **d** 03 **p** 04. NSM Eyemouth *Edin* 03-09; P-in-c 06-09; rtd 09. *Burnbank House, Foulden, Berwick-upon-Tweed TD15 1UH* Tel (01289) 386338 E-mail rev.jennifer@gmail.com

EDINBOROUGH, David. b 36. Nottm Univ BA58 MEd74. EMMTC 79. **d** 82 **p** 83. NSM Bramcote *S'well* 82-01; P-in-c 94-01; Dioc Officer for NSMs 89-94; rtd 01; Perm to Offic *S'well* 01-02; P-in-c Radford St Pet 02-04; Perm to Offic from 04; Bp's Chapl for Rtd Clergy from 09. *105A Derby Road, Beeston, Nottingham NG9 3GZ* Tel 0115-925 1066 E-mail david.edinborough@btopenworld.com

EDINBURGH, Bishop of. *See* SMITH, The Rt Revd Brian Arthur

EDINBURGH, Dean of. *See* ARMES, The Very Revd John Andrew

EDINBURGH, Provost of. *See* FORBES, The Very Revd Graham John Thompson

EDIS, John Oram. b 26. Open Univ BA81 ACIS50 ACP52 FCollP89. Ox NSM Course 85. **d** 88 **p** 89. Hon Warden and Chapl E Ivor Hughes Educn Foundn from 88; NSM Gt Chesham *Ox* 88-96; Perm to Offic *Lon* 96-03 and *Ox* from 96. *2 Meades Lane, Chesham HP5 1ND* Tel (01494) 774242

EDLIN-WHITE, Glenys Rowena Dexter. b 48. **d** 11. NSM Lowdham w Caythorpe, and Gunthorpe *S'well* from 11. *Willow House, 11 Frederick Avenue, Carlton, Nottingham NG4 1HP* Tel 0115-987 3135 E-mail ro@edlin-white.net

EDMANS, Mrs Jennifer. b 56. **d** 07 **p** 08. OLM Bernwode *Ox* 07-10; C from 10. *2 The Bungalow, Coldharbour Farm, Brill, Aylesbury HP18 9UA* Tel (01844) 237855 Mobile 07808-347276 E-mail jennyedmans@aol.com

EDMEADS, Andrew. b 53. Linc Th Coll 84. **d** 86 **p** 87. C Sholing *Win* 86-89; R Knights Enham 89-97; rtd 97; Perm to Offic *Win* 97-99; Chapl St Mich Hospice Basingstoke from 00. *10 Altona Gardens, Andover SP10 4LG* Tel (01264) 391464

EDMONDS (*née* HARRIS), Mrs Catherine Elizabeth. b 52. Leic Coll of Educn CertEd73 ACP79. S Dios Minl Tr Scheme 91. **d** 95 **p** 96. NSM Basing *Win* 95-99; C Yeovil H Trin w Barwick B & W 99-01; Chapl Coll of SS Mark and Jo Plymouth *Ex* 01-06; TV Ottery St Mary, Alfington, W Hill, Tipton etc from 06; C Broadhembury, Payhembury and Plymtree from 09; Dioc Youth Adv from 06. *The Rectory, Station Road, Feniton, Honiton EX14 3DF* Tel (01404) 851401 E-mail pauledmonds@lineone.net

EDMONDS, Clive Alway. b 42. ACII. S'wark Ord Course 78. **d** 81 **p** 82. C Horsell *Guildf* 81-85; R Bisley and W End 85-92; RD Surrey Heath 90-92; R Haslemere 92-00; Chapl Wispers Sch Haslemere 92-00; P-in-c Westbury-on-Severn w Flaxley and Blaisdon *Glouc* 00-02; V Westbury-on-Severn w Flaxley, Blaisdon etc 03-06; rtd 06; Perm to Offic *Heref* from 07. *3 Church Road, Longhope GL17 0LH* Tel (01452) 831545 E-mail alwayedmonds@hotmail.com

EDMONDS, Michelle Kay. b 70. S Bank Univ BSc98. Ripon Coll Cuddesdon BTh08. **d** 06 **p** 07. C Croydon St Matt *S'wark* 06-09; TV Warlingham w Chelsham and Farleigh from 09. *The Vicarage, 2 Chelsham Road, Warlingham CR6 9EQ* Tel (01883) 623011 Mobile 07799-713957 E-mail revmichelle@btinternet.com

EDMONDS (*née* MAGUIRE), Mrs Sarah Alison. b 65. Univ Coll Lon BSc87 Southn Univ MSc93. STETS 95. **d** 98 **p** 99. C Warwick St Paul *Cov* 98-02; P-in-c Hampton Lucy w Charlecote and Loxley 02-06. *39 Hammond Green, Wellesbourne, Warwick CV35 9EY* E-mail sedmonds@informs.co.uk

EDMONDS, Stephen Harry James. b 77. SS Hild & Bede Coll Dur BA99 Leeds Univ MA08. Coll of Resurr Mirfield 06. **d** 08 **p** 09. C Hendon *Dur* from 08. *2 Bennett Court, Sunderland SR2 9QZ* Tel 07882-443025 (mobile) E-mail sedmonds@mirfield.org.uk

EDMONDS, Tony Ernest. b 50. R Holloway Coll Lon BSc71 Imp Coll Lon MSc73 PhD75 Nottm Univ MA05. EMMTC 02. **d** 05 **p** 06. NSM Barrow upon Soar w Walton le Wolds *Leic* 05-10; TV Kegworth, Hathern, Long Whatton, Diseworth etc from 10; Warden of Readers from 10. *The Vicarage, Present Lane, Belton, Loughborough LE12 9UN* Tel (01530) 223447 Mobile 07837-009147 E-mail t.e.edmonds@btconnect.com

EDMONDS-SEAL, John. b 34. FFARCS63 Lon Univ MB, BS58. Ox NSM Course. **d** 90 **p** 91. NSM Ox St Aldate w St Matt 90-94; NSM Wheatley from 95. *Otway, Woodperry Road, Oxford OX3 9UY* Tel (01865) 351582 E-mail edmondsseal@doctors.org.uk

✠**EDMONDSON, The Rt Revd Christopher Paul.** b 50. St Jo Coll Dur BA71 MA81. Cranmer Hall Dur 71. **d** 73 **p** 74 **c** 08. C

Kirkheaton *Wakef* 73-79; V Ovenden 79-86; Bp's Adv on Evang 81-86; Dioc Officer for Evang *Carl* 86-92; P-in-c Bampton w Mardale 86-92; V Shipley St Pet *Bradf* 92-02; Warden Lee Abbey 02-08; Suff Bp Bolton *Man* from 08. *Bishop's Lodge, Walkden Road, Worsley, Manchester M28 2WH* Tel 0161-790 8289 Fax 703 9157 E-mail bishopchrisedmondson@manchester.anglican.org

EDMONDSON, The Very Revd John James William. b 55. St Jo Coll Dur BA83 MA91 PhD04. Cranmer Hall Dur 80. d 83 p 84. C Gee Cross *Ches* 83-86; C Camberley St Paul *Guildf* 86-88; TV 88-90; Chapl Elmhurst Ballet Sch 86-90; V Foxton w Gumley and Laughton and Lubenham *Leic* 90-94; R Bexhill St Mark *Chich* 94-05; V Battle from 05; Dean Battle from 05; P-in-c Sedlescombe w Whatlington 05-08; Dioc Voc Adv 98-02; Asst Dir of Ords from 02. *The Deanery, Caldbec Hill, Battle TN33 0JY* Tel and fax (01424) 772693 E-mail dean@johnedmondson.org.uk

EDMONDSON, Paul. Qu Coll Birm. d 10 p 11. NSM Shottery St Andr *Cov* from 10. *Shakespeare Centre, Henley Street, Stratford-upon-Avon CV37 6QW*

EDMONTON, Area Bishop of. See WHEATLEY, The Rt Revd Peter William

EDMUND, Brother. See BLACKIE, Richard Footner

EDMUNDS, Andrew Charles. b 57. Whitelands Coll Lon BEd80 CQSW83. Oak Hill NSM Course 87. d 89 p 90. NSM Hawkwell *Chelmsf* 89-95; C Torquay St Matthias, St Mark and H Trin *Ex* 95-97; V Ripley *Derby* 97-09; RD Heanor 06-09; Perm to Offic 09-11; R Yateley *Win* from 11. *The Vicarage, 99 Reading Road, Yateley GU46 7LR* Tel (01252) 873133 Mobile 07715 377225 E-mail andy.ed@msn.com

EDMUNDS, Eric John. b 39. Univ of Wales TCert60. WMMTC 87. d 90 p 91. NSM Brewood *Lich* 90-93; Chapl St Pet Colleg Sch Wolv 91-93; R Llanerch Aeron w Ciliau Aeron and Dihewyd etc *St D* 93-97; R Aberporth w Tremain w Blaenporth and Betws Ifan 97-02; Bp's Adv on Tourism 95-02; Asst Dioc Dir of Educn 95-97 and 97-02; rtd 02. *15 Cwrt y Gloch, Peniel, Carmarthen SA32 7HW* Tel (01267) 221426

EDSON, John Benedict. b 73. Wolv Univ BSc95 York St Jo Coll MA02. NOC 06. d 08 p 09. C Brunswick *Man* 08-11; TV Didsbury St Jas and Em from 11. *453 Parrswood Road, East Didsley, Manchester M20 5NE* Tel 07951-170511 (mobile) E-mail ben@benedson.co.uk

EDSON, The Ven Michael. b 42. Birm Univ BSc64 Leeds Univ BA71. Coll of Resurr Mirfield 69. d 72 p 73. C Barnstaple St Pet w H Trin *Ex* 72-77; TV Barnstaple and Goodleigh 77-79; TV Barnstaple, Goodleigh and Landkey 79-82; V Roxbourne St Andr *Lon* 82-89; AD Harrow 85-89; P-in-c S Harrow St Paul 86-89; Warden Lee Abbey 89-94; Lic to Offic *Ex* 89-94; Adn Leic 94-02; Bp's Insp of Par Registers and Records 94-02; TR Bideford, Northam, Westward Ho!, Appledore etc *Ex* 02-09; rtd 09. *43 Old Torrington Road, Barnstaple EX31 3AS* Tel (01271) 327917 E-mail ven.mike.edson@googlemail.com

EDWARDS, Aled. b 55. OBE06. Univ of Wales (Lamp) BA77. Trin Coll Bris 77. d 79 p 80. C Glanogwen *Ban* 79-82; V Llandinorwig w Penisa'r-waen 82-85; R Botwnnog 85-92; V Cardiff Dewi Sant *Llan* 93-99; Nat Assembly Liaison Officer from 99; Hon Chapl Llan Cathl from 99. *20 Hilltop Avenue, Cilfynydd, Pontypridd CF37 4HZ* Tel (01443) 407310 E-mail aled@globalnet.co.uk

EDWARDS, Allen John. b 50. Univ of Wales (Cardiff) BSc72 Imp Coll Lon PhD81 CEng81 EurIng88 FIMechE93 FNucI95 MCMI95 MAPM95. SAOMC 00. d 02 p 03. NSM Didcot All SS *Ox* from 02; Perm to Offic *Eur* from 10. *23 North Bush Furlong, Didcot OX11 9DY* Tel (01235) 519090

EDWARDS, Andrew Colin. b 55. ACA81 Pemb Coll Cam BA77 MA80. St Mich Coll Llan BD89. d 89 p 90. C Newport St Paul *Mon* 89-91; C Newport St Woolos 91-93; Min Can St Woolos Cathl 91-93; P-in-c Ynysddu 93-95; TV Mynyddislwyn 95-97; rtd 97. *197 Heritage Park, St Mellons, Cardiff CF3 0DU* Tel (029) 2079 2715

EDWARDS, Canon Andrew David. b 42. Tyndale Hall Bris 67. d 70 p 71. C Blackpool Ch Ch *Blackb* 70-73; C W Teignmouth *Ex* 73-76; P-in-c Ilfracombe SS Phil and Jas 76-85; C-in-c Lundy Is 79-89; V Ilfracombe SS Phil and Jas w W Down 85-89; TV Canford Magna *Sarum* 89-98; R Moresby *Carl* 98-07; RD Calder 02-07; Hon Can Carl Cathl 05-07; rtd 07; Perm to Offic *Carl* from 07. *Kiln Brow Cottage, High Ireby, Wigton CA7 1HF* Tel (01697) 371618 E-mail a.edwards@btinternet.com

EDWARDS, Andrew James. b 54. York Univ BA76. Wycliffe Hall Ox 77. d 80 p 81. C Beckenham St Jo *Roch* 80-83; C Luton Ch Ch 83-87; V Skelmersdale Ch at Cen *Liv* 87-95; V Netherton 95-02; V Southport St Phil and St Paul from 02; C Southport All SS from 03. *37 Lethbridge Road, Southport PR8 6JA* Tel (01704) 531615 E-mail andrew@ajedwards.freeserve.co.uk

EDWARDS, Andrew Jonathan Hugo (Joe). b 56. Ex Univ BA78. Sarum & Wells Th Coll BTh93. d 93 p 94. C Honiton, Gittisham, Combe Raleigh, Monkton etc *Ex* 93-97; P-in-c Queen Thorne *Sarum* 97-01; Chapl Claysmore Sch Blandford 01-10; P-in-c

Bridge Par *Sarum* from 11; Chapl Qu Eliz Sch Wimborne from 11. *The Vicarage, Newton Road, Sturminster Marshall, Wimborne BH21 4BT* Tel (01258) 857620 E-mail bridgeparishes@gmail.com

EDWARDS, Anita Carolyn. See COLPUS, Mrs Anita Carolyn

EDWARDS, Mrs Anne Joan. b 67. Lanc Univ BA89. NOC 97. d 00 p 01. C Elton All SS *Man* 00-04; Chapl Bolton Hosps NHS Trust 02-04; Chapl Team Ldr Wrightington Wigan and Leigh NHS Trust from 04. *9 Stocks Courts, 2 Harriet Street, Worsley, Manchester M28 3JW* E-mail anna.edwards@dsl.pipex.com or anne.j.edwards@wwl.nhs.uk

EDWARDS, Canon Arthur John. b 42. Qu Mary Coll Lon BA64 MPhil66. St Mich Coll Llan 66. d 68 p 69. C Newport St Woolos *Mon* 68-71; V Llantarnam 71-74; Chapl Bp of Llan High Sch 74-78; V Griffithstown *Mon* 78-86; Dioc Dir RE 86-91; TR Cwmbran 86-95; Hon Can St Woolos Cathl 88-91; Can from 91; V Caerleon 95-02; V Caerleon w Llanhennock 02-09; V Caerleon and Llanfrechfa from 09; AD Newport 98-09. *The Vicarage, High Street, Caerleon, Newport NP18 1AZ* Tel (01633) 420248

EDWARDS, Carl Flynn. b 63. Cranmer Hall Dur 03. d 05 p 06. C Scartho *Linc* 05-09; P-in-c Fairfield *Derby* from 09; C Buxton w Burbage and King Sterndale from 09. *The Vicarage, North Road, Fairfield, Buxton SK17 7EA* Tel (01298) 23629 E-mail carl.mara@tiscali.co.uk

EDWARDS, Miss Carol Rosemary. b 46. Trin Coll Bris 74. dss 81 d 87 p 94. Hengrove *Bris* 81-82; Filton 82-85; Brislington St Chris 85-99; Dn-in-c 87-94; P-in-c 94-99; P-in-c Brislington St Chris and St Cuth 99-00; Hon Can Bris Cathl 93-00; P in o California *Ox* 00-10; rtd 10. *44 Godwin Drive, Nailsea, Bristol BS48 2XF* Tel (01275) 858168 E-mail caroledwards@tiscali.co.uk

EDWARDS, Charles Grayson. b 37. Macalester Coll (USA) BSc59. Ripon Hall Ox 64. d 66 p 67. C Bletchley *Ox* 66-68; C Ware St Mary *St Alb* 68-73; TV Basingstoke *Win* 73-80; P-in-c Sandford w Upton Hellions *Ex* 80-82; R 82-94; Perm to Offic from 95; rtd 97. *The Peak, Higher Road, Crediton EX17 2EU* Tel (01363) 772530

EDWARDS, Christopher. b 61. ACT BTh92. Moore Th Coll Sydney 90. d 94 p 94. C Engandine Australia 94-95; C Adelaide H Trin 95-07; Chapl Tervuren *Eur* from 07. *Parklaan 49, 3080 Tervuren, Belgium* Tel (0032) (2) 767 3435 Fax 688 0989

EDWARDS, Christopher Alban. b 27. Hertf Coll Ox. Th Ext Educn Coll. d 89 p 92. C Pietersburg Ch Ch S Africa 89; C Montagu 90-96; C Harare Cathl Zimbabwe 96-01; Perm to Offic *Ripon* 01 and *York* from 01. *1 Hastings House, Holywood Lane, Ledsham, South Milford, Leeds LS25 5LL* Tel (01977) 682117 Mobile 07780-543114 E-mail chrisalban@btopenworld.com

EDWARDS, David Arthur. b 26. Wadh Coll Ox BA50 MA51. Wycliffe Hall Ox 50. d 52 p 53. C Didsbury St Jas and Em *Man* 52-55; Liv Sec SCM 55-58; Chapl Liv Univ 55-58; R Burnage St Nic *Man* 58-65; V Yardley St Edburgha *Birm* 65-73; Org Sec CECS *Blackb*, *Carl* and *Man* 73-78; R Man Resurr 78-81; V Lorton and Loweswater w Buttermere *Carl* 81-87; USPG 87-92; Malaysia 87-92; rtd 92; Perm to Offic *Carl* from 00. *Wood Close, 11 Springs Road, Keswick CA12 4AQ* Tel (01768) 780274

EDWARDS, David John. b 60. Loughb Univ BA81 Homerton Coll Cam PGCE82 Kent Univ MA95. CA Tr Coll 86 EAMTC 94. d 95 p 96. C High Ongar w Norton Mandeville *Chelmsf* 95-98; Prin Taylor Coll Saint John Canada 98-05; P-in-c Saint John St Jas 98-00; R Saint John St Mark (Stone Ch) from 00. *31 Carlile Crescent, Saint John NB E2J 5C3, Canada* Tel (001) (506) 634 1474 E-mail david.edwards@anglican.nb.ca

EDWARDS, The Very Revd David Lawrence. b 29. OBE95. Magd Coll Ox BA52 MA56 Lambeth DD90. Westcott Ho Cam 53. d 54 p 55. Fell All So Coll Ox 52-59; Tutor Westcott Ho Cam 54-55; SCM Sec 55-58; C Hampstead St Jo *Lon* 55-58; C St Martin-in-the-Fields 58-66; Ed SCM Press 59-66; Gen Sec SCM 65-66; Dean K Coll Cam 66-70; Six Preacher Cant Cathl 69-76; Can Westmr Abbey 70-78; R Westmr St Marg 70-78; Chapl to Speaker of Ho of Commons 72-78; Sub Dean Westmr 74-78; Chmn Chr Aid 71-78; Dean Nor 78-83; Provost S'wark 83-94; rtd 94; Perm to Offic *Win* from 95; Hon Chapl Win Cathl from 95. *4 Morley College, Market Street, Winchester SO23 9LF*

EDWARDS, Canon Diana Clare. b 56. Nottm Univ BTh86 SRN77 RSCN81. Linc Th Coll 83. dss 86 d 87 p 94. S Wimbledon H Trin and St Pet *S'wark* 86-90; Par Dn 87-90; Par Dn Lingfield and Crowhurst 90-94; C 94-95; Chapl St Piers Hosp Sch Lingfield 90-95; R Bletchingley *S'wark* 95-04; RD Godstone 98-04; Hon Can S'wark Cathl 01-04; Dean of Women's Min 03-04; Can Res Cant Cathl from 04. *22 The Precincts, Canterbury CT1 2EP* Tel (01227) 865227 E-mail canonclare@canterbury-cathedral.org

EDWARDS (née DALLISON), Canon Frances Mary. b 39. RSCN61 SRN64. Cranmer Hall Dur IDC71. d 92 p 94. NSM Skerton St Chad *Blackb* 92-97; Asst Chapl R Albert Hosp Lanc 92-94; Chapl 94-96; Regional Co-ord (NW) Ch Action on Disability 96-04; Hon Can Blackb Cathl 00-04; rtd 04; Perm to

Offic *Blackb* from 04. *9 Rochester Avenue, Morecambe LA4 4RH* Tel (01524) 421224 Fax 413661
E-mail frances@floray.fsnet.co.uk
EDWARDS, Canon Geraint Wyn. b 47. Univ of Wales (Ban) BTh93. St D Coll Lamp. **d** 71 **p** 72. C Llandudno *Ban* 71-73; C Ban St Mary 73-74; V Penisarwaen and Llanddeiniolen 74-77; V Llandinorwig w Penisarwaen and Llanddeiniolen 77-78; R Llanfechell w Bodewryd w Rhosbeirio etc from 78; RD Twrcelyn 94-01; AD from 01; Hon Can Ban Cathl 97-99; Prec from 99. *The Rectory, Penbodeistedd Estate, Llanfechell, Amlwch LL68 0RE* Tel (01407) 710356
E-mail geraintedwards@fsmail.net
EDWARDS, Canon Gerald Lalande. b 30. Bris Univ MEd72. Glouc Th Course 75. **d** 76 **p** 76. NSM Pittville All SS *Glouc* 76-79; NSM Cheltenham St Mich 79-96; Hon Can Glouc Cathl 91-96; rtd 96; Perm to Offic *Glouc* 96-97. *26 Monica Drive, Cheltenham GL50 4NQ* Tel (01242) 516863
EDWARDS, Canon Graham Arthur. b 32. St D Coll Lamp 56. **d** 61 **p** 62. C Betws w Ammanford *St D* 61-65; V Castlemartin and Warren 65-69; R Castlemartin w Warren and Angle etc 69-77; V St Clears w Llangynin and Llanddowror 77-83; CF (TAVR) 78-96; V St Clears w Llangynin and Llanddowror etc *St D* 83-94; Can St D Cathl 90-94; rtd 94. *Caswell, Station Road, St Clears, Carmarthen SA33 4BX* Tel (01994) 230342
EDWARDS, Graham Charles. b 40. Qu Coll Birm 80. **d** 82 **p** 83. C Baswich *Lich* 82-86; C Tamworth 86-88; R Hertford St Andr *St Alb* 88-05; RD Hertford and Ware 96-99; rtd 05; Perm to Offic *Lich* from 06. *2 The Old Forge, Main Road, Great Haywood, Stafford ST18 0RZ* Tel (01889) 882868
EDWARDS, Guy. See EDWARDS, Jonathan Guy
EDWARDS, Harold James. b 50. Lon Univ CertEd72. Ridley Hall Cam 84 Qu Coll Birm 78. **d** 81 **p** 82. NSM The Quinton *Birm* 81-84; C Highters Heath 84-85; V Llanwddyn and Llanfihangel-yng-Nghwynfa etc *St As* 85-88; V Ford *Heref* 88-97; V Alberbury w Cardeston 88-97; Chapl Team Ldr Severn Hospice from 96. *Severn Hospice, Bicton Heath, Shrewsbury SY3 8HS* Tel (01743) 236565 Mobile 07713-639447
E-mail harrye@severnhospice.org.uk
EDWARDS, Harry Steadman. b 37. St Aid Birkenhead 64. **d** 66 **p** 67. Hon C Handsworth St Jas *Birm* 66-83; Hon C Curdworth w Castle Vale 83-85; P-in-c Small Heath St Greg 85-88; V High Crompton *Man* 88-98; rtd 98; Perm to Offic *Man* from 99. *42 Manor Road, Shaw, Oldham OL2 7JJ* Tel (01706) 672820
EDWARDS, Helen. See HINGLEY, Mrs Helen
EDWARDS (*née* BENNETT), **Helen Anne.** b 69. Coll of Ripon & York St Jo BEd91 Bris Univ BA01. Trin Coll Bris 99. **d** 01 **p** 02. C Beverley Minster *York* 01-05; P-in-c Liv Ch Ch Norris Green 05-09; V from 09. *4 Christchurch Close, Liverpool L11 3EN* Tel 0151-474 1444 E-mail helenedwards@ymail.com
EDWARDS, Helen Glynne. See WEBB, Mrs Helen Glynne
EDWARDS, The Ven Henry St John. b 30. Southn Univ DipEd. Ripon Hall Ox. **d** 59 **p** 60. C Wickford *Chelmsf* 59-62; R Woodburn Australia 62-65; Educn Officer Dio Grafton 65-69; Dean Grafton 69-78; V Mt Waverley St Steph 78-83; R Chelmer 83-89; Adn Moreton 85-89; Abp's Chapl 89-90; R Tamborine Mountain 90-95; Adn W Moreton 91-93; Adn Gold Coast 93-95; rtd 95. *24 Kooya Road, Mitchelton Qld 4053, Australia*
EDWARDS, Canon Henry Victor. b 48. AKC71 Open Univ BA85 Middx Univ MSc00. St Aug Coll Cant 72. **d** 73 **p** 74. C W Leigh CD *Portsm* 73-77; V Cosham 77-84; V Reydon *St E* 84-86; V Blythburgh w Reydon 86-96; Chapl St Felix Sch Southwold 86-96; Chapl Blythburgh Hosp 86-96; P-in-c Campsea Ashe w Marlesford, Parham and Hacheston *St E* 96-00; R from 00; P-in-c Brandeston w Kettleburgh and Easton from 07; Dioc Adv for Counselling and Past Care from 96; Hon Can St E Cathl from 00. *The Rectory, Marlesford, Woodbridge IP13 0AT* Tel (01728) 746747 Fax 748175 Mobile 07748-986022
E-mail harry@psalm23.demon.co.uk
EDWARDS, Herbert Joseph. b 29. Nottm Univ BA51. Wells Th Coll 54. **d** 56 **p** 57. C Leic St Pet 56-61; C-in-c Broom Leys CD 61-65; V Broom Leys 65-68; Lect Lich Th Coll 68-71; Rhodesia 71-79; Botswana 74-75; V Bloxwich *Lich* 80-84; R Asfordby *Leic* 84-92; R N w S Kilworth and Misterton 92-96; rtd 96; Perm to Offic *Leic* from 97 and *Lich* from 00. *Beechfields Nursing Home, 1 Wissage Road, Lichfield WS13 6EJ* Tel (01543) 418351 or 418354
EDWARDS, Canon James Frederick. b 36. ALCD62. **d** 62 **p** 63. C Kenwyn *Truro* 62-68; V Tuckingmill 68-76; V St Columb Minor and St Colan 76-01; RD Pydar 84-93; Hon Can Truro Cathl 92-01; rtd 01; Perm to Offic *Truro* from 01. *45 Tretherras Road, Newquay TR7 2TF* Tel (01637) 870967
EDWARDS, Jane. See EDWARDS, Wendy Jane
EDWARDS, Janet Margaret. b 41. TCert62 Lon Bible Coll BD73. WEMTC 98. **d** 01 **p** 02. NSM Coalbrookdale, Iron-Bridge and Lt Wenlock *Heref* from 01. *2 Madeley Wood View, Madeley, Telford TF7 5TF* Tel (01952) 583254
EDWARDS, Mrs Jill Kathleen. b 48. Man Univ BA69 CQSW72. S'wark Ord Course 90. **d** 93 **p** 95. NSM Grays Thurrock and Ind Chapl *Chelmsf* 93-07; Asst Dioc Soc Resp Officer *Truro* from 07;

Public Preacher 07-08; P-in-c Gerrans w St Anthony-in-Roseland and Philleigh from 08. *Trelowen, Rosevine, Portscatho, Truro TR2 5EW* Tel (01872) 580117
E-mail jill@jilledwards.com
EDWARDS, Joe. See EDWARDS, Andrew Jonathan Hugo
EDWARDS, John Ralph. b 50. Bris Univ BSc71 FCA74. SAOMC 98. **d** 01 **p** 02. NSM California *Ox* 01-06; NSM Finchampstead from 06. *Green Hedges, 25 St John's Street, Crowthorne RG45 7NJ* Tel (01344) 774586 Fax 774056 Mobile 07850-602488
EDWARDS, Jonathan Guy. b 63. Bris Univ BA85. Ridley Hall Cam BA93 MA96. **d** 94 **p** 95. C Preston Plucknett *B & W* 94-98; C Clevedon St Andr and Ch 98-02; V Farrington Gurney 02-06; V Paulton 02-06; P-in-c High Littleton 05-06; V Paulton w Farrington Gurney and High Littleton from 07. *The Vicarage, Church Street, Paulton, Bristol BS39 7LG* Tel (01761) 416581
E-mail guyedwards455@btinternet.com
EDWARDS, Joseph. See EDWARDS, Herbert Joseph
EDWARDS, Judith Sarah. See McARTHUR-EDWARDS, Mrs Judith Sarah
EDWARDS (*née* EVANS), **Mrs Linda Mary.** b 49. Univ of Wales (Cardiff) BA71 K Coll Lon BD74 AKC74. Yale Div Sch STM76. **dss** 76 **d** 80 **p** 99. Llanishen and Lisvane 76-78; Wrexham *St As* 78-80; C 80-82; Chapl Maudsley Hosp Lon 82-84; Chapl Bethlem R Hosp Beckenham 82-84; Chapl Lon Univ 84-87; NSM Llanfair-pwll and Llanddaniel-fab etc *Ban* 99-03; P-in-c Llangynog *St As* 03-06; C Llanrhaeadr ym Mochnant etc 07-10; rtd 10. *15 The Meadows, Llandudno Junction LL31 9LP* Tel (01492) 585063
E-mail eleme@tiscali.co.uk
EDWARDS, Lynda. Qu Coll Birm. **d** 11. NSM Allesley *Cov* from 11. *3 Torbay Road, Coventry CV5 9JY* Tel (024) 7671 3235
EDWARDS, Malcolm Ralph. b 27. Man Univ 49. Cranmer Hall Dur 57. **d** 59 **p** 60. C Withington St Paul *Man* 59-62; C Chadderton Em 62-64; R Longsight St Jo 64-70; V Halliwell St Thos 70-81; V Milnrow 81-92; rtd 92; Perm to Offic *Man* from 92. *20 Upper Lees Drive, Westhoughton, Bolton BL5 3UE* Tel (01942) 813279
EDWARDS, Mrs Marie. b 73. NEOC 06. **d** 09 **p** 10. NSM Middlesbrough St Agnes *York* from 09. *76 Hesleden Avenue, Middlesbrough TS5 8RN* Tel (01642) 509381 Mobile 07908-608605 E-mail medwards15@ntlworld.com
EDWARDS, Mark Anthony. b 61. MBE10. Cranmer Hall Dur 91. **d** 95 **p** 97. C Ulverston St Mary w H Trin *Carl* 95-97; C Barrow St Jo 97-00; TV Barrow St Matt 00-08; TV Ch the King *Newc* from 08; Chapl Northumbria Police from 08. *The Vicarage, 2 East Acres, Dinnington, Newcastle upon Tyne NE13 7NA* Tel (01661) 872320 E-mail hayden@fox9411.freeserve.co.uk
EDWARDS, Mrs Mary. b 47. St Jo Coll York CertEd69 Birkbeck Coll Lon BSc74 New Coll Edin BD93. S Dios Minl Tr Scheme 96. **d** 96 **p** 97. NSM Avon Valley *Sarum* 96-00; TV Wexcombe 00-02; TV Savernake from 02; RD Pewsey from 10. *The Vicarage, Church Street, Collingbourne Ducis, Marlborough SN8 3EL* Tel (01264) 852692 E-mail mary avonvalley@hotmail.com
EDWARDS, Michael Norman William. b 34. Bp Gray Coll Cape Town 61 St Paul's Coll Grahamstown 62. **d** 63 **p** 65. S Africa 63-81; C Woodstock 63-66; C Plumstead 66-69; P-in-c Lansdowne All SS 69-72; R Hoetjes Bay 73-78; R Parow St Marg 78-80; Chaplain Tristan da Cunha 81-83; R Aston-on-Trent and Weston-on-Trent *Derby* 84-87; V Derby St Thos 87-95; P-in-c Blackwell 95-01; rtd 01; Perm to Offic *Win* from 02. *16 Hailey Close, Holbury, Southampton SO45 2NR* Tel (023) 8089 2924 E-mail mnwedwards.novaforest@googlemail.com
EDWARDS, Nicholas John. b 53. UEA BA75 Fitzw Coll Cam BA77 MA80. Westcott Ho Cam 75. **d** 78 **p** 79. C Kirkby *Liv* 78-81; V Cantril Farm 81-87; V Hale 87-94; R Chingford SS Pet and Paul *Chelmsf* 94-04; R Colyton, Musbury, Southleigh and Branscombe *Ex* 04-10; P-in-c Ex St Thos and from 10. *Emmanuel Vicarage, 49 Okehampton Road, Exeter EX4 1EL* Tel (01392) 202583 E-mail nicholas.edwards@ntlworld.com
EDWARDS, Mrs Nita Mary. b 50. Univ of Wales (Ban) BD72 Nottm Univ PGCE73. Cranmer Hall Dur 93. **d** 93 **p** 94. C Ormesby *York* 93-95; C Billingham St Aid *Dur* 95-97; V 97-02; V Clayton *Lich* from 02. *The Vicarage, Clayton Lane, Newcastle ST5 3DW* Tel and fax (01782) 614500
E-mail nita.edwards@ntlworld.com
EDWARDS, Mrs Patricia Anne. b 52. EMMTC 76. **dss** 79 **d** 87 **p** 94. Hon Par Dn Clifton *S'well* 87-91; NSM Edwalton from 91. *Le Petit Champ, Widmerpool Road, Wysall, Nottingham NG12 5QW* Tel (01509) 880385
EDWARDS, Peter Clive. b 50. Lon Univ BA72. St Steph Ho Ox 83. **d** 85 **p** 86. C Lee St Aug *S'wark* 85-90; V Salfords 90-97; R Newington St Mary 97-03; Chapl Costa Blanca *Eur* 04-09; Sen Chapl from 09. *Apdo Correos 158, 03420 Castalla, Alicante, Spain* Tel (0034) 966 560 716 E-mail pce11@yahoo.com
EDWARDS, Peter Daniel. b 81. St Aid Coll Dur BA02 Peterho Cam BA09. Ridley Hall Cam 07. **d** 10 **p** 11. C Gt Malvern

St Mary *Worc* from 10. *107 Court Road, Malvern WR14 3EF* Tel (01684) 563077 E-mail peter.edwards@cantab.net
EDWARDS, Peter Richard Henderson. b 65. Nottm Univ BA86. St Steph Ho Ox 03. **d** 05 **p** 06. C Uppingham w Ayston and Wardley w Belton *Pet* 05-08; TV Bridport *Sarum* from 08. *Allington Vicarage, Parsonage Road, Bridport DT6 5ET* Tel (01308) 456588 E-mail frpeteredwards@sky.com
EDWARDS, Canon Philip John. b 28. Lon Univ MRCS51 LRCP51. Chich Th Coll 58. **d** 60 **p** 61. C Orpington St Andr *Roch* 60-67; C Mayfield *Chich* 67-71; V Haywards Heath St Rich 71-91; Can and Preb Chich Cathl 84-91; rtd 91; Perm to Offic *Chich* from 91. *22 Hamsey Road, Sharpthorne, East Grinstead RH19 4PA* Tel (01342) 810210
EDWARDS, Phillip Gregory. b 52. Lon Univ BSc73 Imp Coll Lon ARCS73 MSOSc90. Qu Coll Birm 78. **d** 81 **p** 82. C Lillington *Cov* 81-85; P-in-c Cov St Alb 85-86; TV Cov E 86-01; C Bury St Paul and Bury Ch King *Man* 01-03; Chapl Bolton Univ from 03; C Westhoughton and Wingates 04-05; C Leverhulme 05-07. *St Stephen and All Martyrs Vicarage, Radcliffe Road, Bolton BL2 1NZ* Tel (01204) 528300 E-mail phil@edwards.clara.co.uk
EDWARDS, Raymond Lewis. Keble Coll Ox BA46 MA47 TCert48. St Deiniol's Hawarden 69. **d** 70 **p** 71. Prin Educn Cen Penmaenmawr 56-81; Hon C Dwygyfylchi *Ban* 70-81; P-in-c Llandwrog 81-82; R 82-90; Dioc Dir of Educn 84-92; rtd 90; Perm to Offic *Ban* from 90. *Bryn Llwyd, St Davids Road, Caernarfon LL55 1EL* Tel 07789-566370 (mobile)
EDWARDS, Richard John. b 47. Univ of Qld BA85. St Fran Coll Brisbane 83. **d** 85 **p** 85. C St Lucia Australia 85-87; C Olveston *Bris* 87-88; R N Pine Australia 88-96; R Kingston St Mary w Broomfield etc *B & W* 96-10; rtd 10. *PO Box 181, Franklin Tas 7113, Australia*
EDWARDS, Robert James. b 52. Chich Univ BA07. Cranmer Hall Dur 01. **d** 03 **p** 04. C Broadwater *Chich* 03-08; TV Southgate from 08. *Holy Trinity House, Titmus Drive, Crawley RH10 5EU* Tel (01293) 618214 E-mail rev.rob@ctlconnect.co.uk
EDWARDS, Roger Brian. b 41. Sarum & Wells Th Coll 87. **d** 89 **p** 90. C Wellington and Distr *B & W* 89-92; V Hursley and Ampfield *Win* 92-06; rtd 06. *34 Heatherstone Avenue, Dibden Purlieu, Southampton SO45 4LH* Tel (023) 8087 9689
EDWARDS, Canon Rowland Thomas. b 62. Univ of Wales BTh91. St Mich Coll Llan 85. **d** 88 **p** 89. C Llangiwg *S & B* 88-90; C Morriston 90-91; V Llangorse, Cathedine, Llanfihangel Talyllyn etc 91-01; V Llyn Safaddan 01-06; V Talgarth w Bronllys w Llanfilo from 06; AD Hay from 06; Can Res Brecon Cathl from 08. *The Vicarage, Bronllys, Brecon LD3 0HS* Tel (01874) 711200
EDWARDS, Rupert Quintin. b 67. Bris Univ LLB89. Wycliffe Hall Ox BTh94. **d** 97 **p** 98. C Bromley Ch Ch *Roch* 97-00; C Hammersmith St Paul *Lon* 00-02; Hon C from 06. *342 Bluewater House, Smugglers Way, London SW18 1ED* E-mail rupert.edwards@arqiva.com
EDWARDS, Canon Ruth Blanche. b 39. Girton Coll Cam BA61 MA65 PhD68 Aber Coll of Educn PGCE75. Ab Dioc Tr Course 77. **d** 87 **p** 94. Lect Aber Univ 77-90; Sen Lect 90-96; NSM Aberdeen St Jas 87-88; NSM Aberdeen St Jo 88-96; Lect Ripon Coll Cuddesdon 96-99; Hon Can St Andr Cathl from 97; rtd 00; NSM Aberdeen St Jas from 00. *99 Queen's Den, Aberdeen AB15 8BN* Tel (01224) 312688
EDWARDS, Mrs Sandra May. b 48. STETS 96. **d** 99 **p** 01. NSM Denmead *Portsm* 99-05; P-in-c 05-06; V from 06. *The Vicarage, Ludcombe, Waterlooville PO7 6TL* Tel (023) 9225 5490 E-mail sandra@pinoy.fsnet.co.uk
EDWARDS, Scott. b 71. Wolv Univ LLB93 St Jo Coll Dur BA00. Cranmer Hall Dur 97. **d** 00 **p** 01. C Halas *Worc* 00-03; V Frimley Green and Mytchett *Guildf* from 03. *The Vicarage, 37 Sturt Road, Frimley Green, Camberley GU16 6HY* Tel (01252) 835179 E-mail scott.edwards@btopenworld.com
EDWARDS, Stephen. b 44. S'wark Ord Course. **d** 82 **p** 83. C Benhilton *S'wark* 82-86; P-in-c Clapham Ch Ch and St Jo 86-87; TV Clapham Team 87-94; Chapl HM Pris Wormwood Scrubs 94-96; Chapl HM Pris Maidstone 96-01; Chapl HM Pris Wandsworth 01-04; rtd 04; Perm to Offic *S'wark* from 04. *12 Bucharest Road, London SW18 3AR* Tel (020) 8870 1991
EDWARDS, Stephen David. b 67. Univ of Wales (Lamp) BA06 MTh10. St Mich Coll Llan 09. **d** 11. C Henfynyw w Aberaeron and Llanddewi Aberarth etc *St D* from 11. *Dyffryn, Lampeter Road, Aberaeron SA46 0ED* Tel (01545) 574864 E-mail stephen.edwards67@gmail.com
EDWARDS, Stephen Michael. b 72. Lanc Univ BSc93 Anglia Poly Univ MA99. Westcott Ho Cam 93. **d** 96 **p** 97. C Colwyn Bay *St As* 96-02; P-in-c Brynmaen 99-02; P-in-c Birch-in-Rusholme St Agnes w Longsight St Jo etc *Man* from 02. *St Agnes's Rectory, Slade Lane, Manchester M13 0GN* Tel 0161-224 2596 E-mail stephen@stagneslongsight.org
EDWARDS, Steven Charles. b 58. Lanc Univ BSc82 PhD86. Linc Th Coll 94. **d** 94 **p** 95. C Bradshaw *Man* 94-98; P-in-c Bolton Breightmet St Jas 98-04; TR Walkden and Lt Hulton 04-10; rtd 10; Perm to Offic *Man* from 10. *9 Stocks Courts, 2 Harriet Street, Worsley, Manchester M28 3JW* E-mail steve@sajm.net

EDWARDS, Stuart. b 46. Lanc Univ BA73. Kelham Th Coll 66. **d** 71 **p** 72. C Skerton St Luke *Blackb* 71-76; C Ribbleton 76-80; TV 80-82; V Blackb St Mich w St Jo and H Trin 82-91; V Blackpool H Cross from 91; RD Blackpool 93-94; P-in-c S Shore St Pet 00-05. *Holy Cross Vicarage, Central Drive, Blackpool FY1 6LA* Tel (01253) 341263
EDWARDS, Mrs Susan. b 54. R Holloway Coll Lon BSc75 SS Hild & Bede Coll Dur PGCE76. Qu Coll Birm 78. **dss** 81 **d** 87 **p** 94. Lillington *Cov* 81-85; Cov E 85-01; Par Dn 87-94; C 94-01; P-in-c Woolfold *Man* 01-07; TV Leverhulme from 07. *St Stephen and All Martyrs Vicarage, Radcliffe Road, Bolton BL2 1NZ* Tel (01204) 528300 E-mail sue@edwards.clara.co.uk
EDWARDS, Mrs Susan Diane. b 48. St Alb Minl Tr Scheme 86 Cranmer Hall Dur 91. **d** 92 **p** 94. Par Dn Borehamwood *St Alb* 92-94; C 94-96; V Arlesey w Astwick from 96. *The Vicarage, 77 Church Lane, Arlesey SG15 6UX* Tel (01462) 731227 E-mail susan.d.edwards@ntlworld.com
EDWARDS, Wendy Jane. b 49. Bingley Coll of Educn CertEd71 Kent Univ BA07. SEITE 03. **d** 06 **p** 07. C Riverhead w Dunton Green *Roch* 06-11; P-in-c Belvedere All SS from 11. *c/o Crockford, Church House, Great Smith Street, London SW1P 3AZ* Tel 07858-483652 (mobile) E-mail edwards23@supanet.com
EDWARDSON, David Roger Hately. b 54. Stirling Univ BSc79 DipEd79 Edin Univ BD91. Edin Th Coll 88. **d** 91 **p** 92. C Edin St Jo 91-93; R Kelso 93-98; Asst Chapl Oundle Sch 98-09. *Address temp unknown*
EDWARDSON, Joseph Philip. b 28. Dur Univ BA52 Leeds Univ PGCE53. Wells Th Coll 61. **d** 63 **p** 64. C Macclesfield St Mich *Ches* 63-66, V Egremont St Jo 66-72, V Eastham 72-81, V Poulton 81-94; rtd 94; Perm to Offic *Ches* from 94. *Keppler, 38 Hazel Grove, Irby, Wirral CH61 4UZ* Tel 0151-648 2661
EDY, Robert James. b 48. Southn Univ BA70 CertEd71. Ox Min Course 90. **d** 93 **p** 94. Dep Hd Master Henry Box Sch Witney from 90; NSM Ducklington *Ox* 93-99; P-in-c from 99. *The Rectory, 6 Standlake Road, Ducklington, Witney OX29 7XG* Tel (01993) 776625 E-mail bobedy21@hotmail.com
EDYE, Ian Murray. b 21. K Coll Lon BD AKC. S'wark Ord Course 66. **d** 69 **p** 70. NSM E Grinstead St Swithun *Chich* 69-00; Perm to Offic 00-02. *Bramcote House, Town Street, Bramcote, Nottingham NG9 3DP* Tel 0115-925 7316
EFEMEY, Raymond Frederick. b 28. Ball Coll Ox BA51 MA64. Cuddesdon Coll 51. **d** 53 **p** 54. C Croydon St Mich *Cant* 53-57; C Hendford *B & W* 57-60; V Upper Arley *Worc* 60-66; Ind Chapl 60-66; P-in-c Dudley St Jas 66-69; V Dudley St Thos 66-69; V Dudley St Thos and St Luke 69-75; Hon C Stretford All SS *Man* 76-82; SSF from 81; P-in-c Weaste *Man* 82-87; V 87-93; rtd 93. *20 Groby Road, Chorlton-cum-Hardy, Manchester M21 1DD* Tel 0161-860 5416
EFIRD, David Hampton. b 74. Duke Univ (USA) BA94 Princeton Th Sem MDiv98 Edin Univ MSc99 Ox Univ DPhil02. Yorks Min Course 08. **d** 10 **p** 11. NSM York Minster from 10. *1 Bleachfield, Heslington, York YO10 5DB* Tel (01904) 323226 Mobile 07930-754045 E-mail de5@york.ac.uk
EGAR, Miss Judith Anne. b 57. Somerville Coll Ox BA79 MA84 Solicitor 83. STETS 01. **d** 04 **p** 05. NSM Brighton St Nic *Chich* 04-07; Lic to Offic from 09; Perm to Offic *Lon* from 08. *15 St Peter's Place, Lewes BN7 1YP* Tel (020) 7898 1722 E-mail judith.egar@churchofengland.org
EGERTON, George. b 28. S'wark Ord Course 70. **d** 73 **p** 74. NSM Shere *Guildf* 73-94; Perm to Offic from 94. *Weyside, Lower Street, Shere, Guildford GU5 9HX* Tel (01483) 202549
EGERTON, Mrs Susan Doreen. b 52. MCSP75. **d** 09 **p** 10. OLM Surrey Weald *Guildf* from 09. *Hollington, Horsham Road, Capel, Dorking RH5 5LF* Tel (01306) 711299
EGGERT, Max Alexander. b 43. AKC67 Birkbeck Coll Lon BSc74 Poly Cen Lon MA87 CPsychol90. **d** 67 **p** 68. C Whitton St Aug *Lon* 67-69; Hon C Hackney 72-74; Hon C Llantwit Major 74-76; NSM Haywards Heath St Rich *Chich* 78-93. *Address temp unknown*
EGGLESTON, Hugh Patrick. b 60. LSE BSc(Econ)82 Leeds Univ BA10. Coll of Resurr Mirfield 03. **d** 10 **p** 11. C E Dulwich St Jo *S'wark* from 10. *11 Hinckley Road, London SE15 4HZ* Tel (020) 7787 9654 Mobile 07788-563253 E-mail peggleston@ymail.com
EGGLETON, Michael John. b 50. SAOMC 96 ERMC 06. **d** 07 **p** 08. NSM Northchurch and Wigginton *St Alb* from 07. *St Bartholomew's Vicarage, Vicarage Road, Wigginton, Tring HP23 6DZ* Tel (01442) 823273 Mobile 07962-145398 E-mail mikeeggleton7@btopenworld.com
EGLIN, Ian Charles. b 55. St Jo Coll Dur BA76. Coll of Resurr Mirfield 77. **d** 79 **p** 80. C Cov St Mary 79-83; TV Kingsthorpe w Northampton St Dav *Pet* 83-87; P-in-c Pitsford w Boughton 85-87; Chapl RN 87-03; V Ipplepen, Torbryan and Denbury *Ex* from 03; RD Newton Abbot and Ipplepen from 07. *The Rectory, Paternoster Lane, Ipplepen, Newton Abbot TQ12 5RY* Tel and fax (01803) 812215 E-mail ianeglin@talktalk.net
EJIAKU, Sebastian Chidozie. b 58. Herts Univ MSc95. NTMTC 02. **d** 05 **p** 06. NSM Hoxton St Jo w Ch Ch *Lon* 05-09; NSM

St John-at-Hackney from 09. *116 Cann Hall Road, London E11 3NH* Tel (020) 8519 2555 Mobile 07952-950681 E-mail ejiakuo@aol.com

EJINKONYE, Prorenata Emeka. b 52. **d** 08 **p** 09. OLM Victoria Docks St Luke *Chelmsf* 08-10; Hon C from 10. *26 Boreham Avenue, London E16 3AG* E-mail emeka12@hotmail.com

EKIN, Tom Croker. b 29. Linc Th Coll 59. **d** 60 **p** 61. C Leamington Priors All SS *Cov* 60-63; R Ilmington w Stretton-on-Fosse 63-72; S Africa 72-77; R Moreton-in-Marsh w Batsford *Glouc* 77-83; R Moreton-in-Marsh w Batsford, Todenham etc 83-94; rtd 95; Hon C Theale and Englefield *Ox* 96-04; Perm to Offic *B & W* from 04. *6 Old Bell Court, Wrington, Bristol BS40 5QH* Tel (01934) 862398

ELBOURNE, Keith Marshall. b 46. Nottm Univ BTh74 Lon Univ BD76. St Jo Coll Nottm 70. **d** 74 **p** 75. C Romford Gd Shep *Chelmsf* 74-78; C Victoria Docks St Luke 78-81; P-in-c 81-92; V Walthamstow St Pet 92-02; TR Tettenhall Wood and Perton *Lich* 02-10; rtd 10; Perm to Offic *Lich* from 10. *33 Princes Gardens, Codsall, Wolverhampton WV8 2DH* E-mail keith.elbourne@dsl.pipex.com

ELBOURNE, Canon Timothy. b 60. Selw Coll Cam BA81 MA85 PGCE82. Westcott Ho Cam 84. **d** 86 **p** 87. C Tottenham H Trin *Lon* 86-88; Chapl York Univ 88-94; P-in-c Thorp Arch w Walton 94-98; Dir of Educn *Ely* from 98; Hon Can Ely Cathl from 99. *19 The Oaks, Soham, Ely CB7 5FF* Tel and fax (01353) 723867 *or* tel 652711 Fax 652745 Pager (04325) 320796 E-mail tim.elbourne@ely.anglican.org

ELCOCK, Jonathan. b 64. Westcott Ho Cam 07. **d** 09 **p** 11. C Aberavon *Llan* 09; C Salford All SS *Man* from 10. *32 Laburnum Street, Salford M6 5LZ* Tel 0161-925 0801

ELDER, Andrew John. b 49. Sunderland Poly BSc72 MSc76. NEOC 91. **d** 94 **p** 95. NSM Wallsend St Luke *Newc* 94-02; NSM Wallsend St Pet and St Luke 02-03; C Monkseaton St Pet 03-06; V Blyth St Mary from 06. *St Mary's Vicarage, 51 Marine Terrace, Blyth NE24 2JP* Tel (01670) 353417 E-mail andy.elder@btinternet.com

ELDER, David. b 28. Brechin NSM Ord Course 75. **d** 79 **p** 80. NSM Dundee St Salvador *Bre* 79-93; rtd 93; P-in-c Dundee St Martin *Bre* from 93. *Thistlemount, 21 Law Road, Dundee DD3 6PZ* Tel (01382) 827844

ELDER, Nicholas John. b 51. Hatf Poly BA73. Cuddesdon Coll 73. **d** 76 **p** 77. C Mill End and Heronsgate w W Hyde *St Alb* 76-79; TV Borehamwood 79-85; V Bedford St Mich 85-90; V Bedford All SS 90-00; V Camberwell St Geo *S'wark* from 00; Warden Trin Coll Cen Camberwell from 00. *St George's Vicarage, 115 Wells Way, London SE5 7SZ* Tel (020) 7703 2895 *or* 7703 9855 E-mail nicholas.elder@virgin.net

ELDRID, John Gisborne Charteris. b 25. OBE97. AKC52. **d** 53 **p** 54. C St Geo-in-the-East w Ch Ch w St Jo *Lon* 53-56; C E Grinstead St Mary *Chich* 56-58; C St Steph Walbrook and St Swithun etc *Lon* 58-64 and 72-81; V Portsea All SS *Portsm* 64-71; P-in-c Portsea St Jo Rudmore 69-71; V Portsea All SS w St Jo Rudmore 71-72; Gen Consultant Cen Lon Samaritans 72-74; Dir The Samaritans 74-87; Gen Consultant-Dir 87-99; Consultant from 99; Lic to Offic *Lon* from 82; rtd 90; Perm to Offic *Portsm* from 90. *46 Marshall Street, London W1V 1LR* Tel (020) 7439 1406 Fax 7439 1233

ELDRIDGE, John Frederick. b 48. Loughb Univ BSc70 Golden Gate Sem (USA) MDiv83 Fuller Th Sem California DMin96. Oak Hill Th Coll 90. **d** 92 **p** 93. C Maidstone St Luke *Cant* 92-97; Min Prince's Park CD *Roch* 97-02; P-in-c Wickham Market w Pettistree *St E* 02-07; V from 07. *The Vicarage, Crown Lane, Wickham Market, Woodbridge IP13 0SA* Tel (01728) 746026 E-mail jeldridge@supanet.com

ELDRIDGE, John Kenneth Tristan. b 59. St Steph Ho Ox 90. **d** 92 **p** 93. C Brighton Resurr *Chich* 92-96; C Hangleton 96-98; TR Moulsecoomb 98-05; V W Worthing St Jo from 05; Chapl Sussex Beacon Hospice from 00. *St John's Vicarage, 15 Reigate Road, Worthing BN11 5JY* Tel (01903) 247340

ELDRIDGE, Stephen William. b 50. Open Univ BA98. Chich Th Coll 87. **d** 89 **p** 90. C Stroud and Uplands w Slad *Glouc* 89-92; C Glouc St Mary de Crypt w St Jo and Ch Ch 92-95; C Glouc St Mary de Lode and St Nic 92-95; Bp's Chapl 92-93; P-in-c Kingswood w Alderley and Hillesley 95-00; P-in-c Cheltenham St Pet 00-08; TV N Cheltenham from 08. *St Peter's Vicarage, 375 Swindon Road, Cheltenham GL51 9LB* Tel and fax (01242) 524369 E-mail stephen.eldridge@northchelt.org.uk

ELEY, John Edward. b 49. Sarum & Wells Th Coll 74. **d** 77 **p** 78. C Sherborne w Castleton and Lillington *Sarum* 77-80; Min Can Carl Cathl 80-84; V Bromsgrove All SS *Worc* 84-88; Perm to Offic *St E* 90-98; V Stourhead 98-10; rtd 10. *5 Church Walks, Bury St Edmunds IP33 1NJ* Tel (01284) 763564 Mobile 07783-584651 E-mail john.eley5@btopenworld.com

ELFICK, Brian Richard. b 76. Ex Coll Ox BA98 Selw Coll Cam BA04 MPhil05. Ridley Hall Cam 02. **d** 06 **p** 07. C Cambridge H Sepulchre *Ely* from 06. *9 Victoria Street, Cambridge CB1 1JP* Tel (01223) 518352 *or* 518218 E-mail brian.elfick@stag.org

ELFORD, Keith Anthony. b 59. Em Coll Cam BA80 MA84. Wycliffe Hall Ox 87. **d** 90 **p** 91. C Chertsey *Guildf* 90-94; P-in-c Ockham w Hatchford 94-98; Bp's Chapl 94-98; Perm to Offic 98-00; Lic to Offic from 01. *15 Canford Drive, Addlestone KT15 2HH* Tel (01932) 885137 E-mail keith.elford@lineone.net

ELFORD, Canon Robert John. b 39. Man Univ MA71 Ex Univ PhD74. Brasted Th Coll 64 Ridley Hall Cam 66. **d** 68 **p** 69. C Denton St Lawr *Man* 68-71; P-in-c Gwinear *Truro* 71-74; R Phillack w Gwithian and Gwinear 74-78; Lect Man Univ 78-87; Hon C Withington St Paul *Man* 79-83; Warden St Anselm Hall 82-87; Lic to Offic 84-87; Pro-R Liv Inst of HE 88-99; Can Th Liv Cathl 92-04; rtd 04. *1 North Quay, Wapping Quay, Liverpool L3 4BU* Tel 0151-709 0461

ELFRED, Michael William. b 48. BA76 MPhil. Linc Th Coll 77. **d** 79 **p** 80. C Boultham *Linc* 79-82; C Croydon H Sav *Cant* 82-84; C Upper Norwood All SS *S'wark* 84-88; V Sanderstead St Mary 88-01; P-in-c Tadworth 01-11; V from 11. *The Vicarage, 1 The Avenue, Tadworth KT20 5AS* Tel (01737) 813152 Mobile 07931-463661 E-mail michael.elfred@talk21.com

ELGAR, Richard John. b 50. Charing Cross Hosp Medical Sch MB, BS73 LRCP73 MRCS73 MRCGP80. St Jo Coll Nottm 92. **d** 92 **p** 93. NSM Derby St Alkmund and St Werburgh 92-96; P-in-c Derby St Barn 96-01; V 01-08; RD Derby N 05-06; rtd 08. *38 Holborn Drive, Derby DE22 4DX* Tel (01332) 342553 E-mail relgar1015@aol.com

ELIZABETH, The Ven Danny Rollan Henry. b 67. Seychelles Poly DipEd87 Edith Cowan Univ (Aus) BEd93 Rhodes Univ BTh00. Coll of Transfiguration Grahamstown 97. **d** 99 **p** 00. R St Paul's Cathl Seychelles 00-05; Perm to Offic *Lon* 05-06; NSM Hanwell St Mellitus w St Mark 06-08; V Hayes St Anselm 08-10; Adn Seychelles from 10. *PO Box 44, Victoria, Mahe, Seychelles* E-mail dannyelizabeth@btinternet.com

ELIZABETH, Sister. *See* WEBB, Marjorie Valentine

ELIZABETH MARY, Sister. *See* NOLLER, Hilda Elizabeth Mary

ELKINGTON, The Ven Audrey Anne. b 57. St Cath Coll Ox BA80 ALU PhD83. St Jo Coll Nottm 85 EAMTC 86. **dss** 88 **d** 92 **p** 94. Monkseaton St Mary *Newc* 88-91; Ponteland 91-93; Par Dn 92-93; C Prudhoe 93-02; RD Corbridge 99-02; Bp's Adv for Women in Min 01-11; Bp's Chapl 02-11; Dir of Ords 02-11; Hon Can Newc Cathl 06-11; Adn Bodmin *Truro* from 11. *Archdeacon's House, Cardinham, Bodmin PL30 4BL* Tel (01208) 821614 E-mail audrey@truro.anglican.org

ELKINGTON, Canon David John. b 51. Nottm Univ BTh76 Leic Univ MEd81 Dur Univ MATM05. St Jo Coll Nottm 73. **d** 76 **p** 77. C Leic Martyrs 76-78; C Kirby Muxloe 78-80; Asst Chapl Leic Univ 80-82; Hon C Leic H Spirit 82; Chapl UEA *Nor* 82-88; TV Newc Epiphany 88-91; TR 91-93; P-in-c Prudhoe 93-98; V 98-02; Can Res Newc Cathl 02-11; rtd 11. *Archdeacon's House, Cardinham, Bodmin PL30 4BL* Tel (01208) 821614 E-mail djelk@btinternet.com

ELKINGTON-SLYFIELD, John David. *See* SLYFIELD, John David

ELKINS, Alan Bernard. b 47. Sarum & Wells Th Coll 70. **d** 73 **p** 74. C Wareham *Sarum* 73-77; P-in-c Codford, Upton Lovell and Stockton 77-79; P-in-c Boyton w Sherrington 77-79; C Ashton Gifford 79; R Bishopstrow and Boreham 79-92; R Corfe Mullen 92-03; V W Byfleet *Guildf* 03-08; P-in-c from 08; Bp's Adv for Spirituality from 08. *The Vicarage, 5 Dartnell Avenue, West Byfleet KT14 6PJ* Tel (01932) 345270 E-mail alan-elkins@lineone.net

ELKINS, Mrs Joy Kathleen. b 45. S Tr Scheme 93. **d** 96 **p** 97. NSM Corfe Mullen *Sarum* 96-03; NSM W Byfleet *Guildf* 03-08; C from 08. *The Vicarage, 5 Dartnell Avenue, West Byfleet KT14 6PJ* Tel (01932) 345270 E-mail joy-elkins@lineone.net

ELKINS, Canon Patrick Charles. b 34. St Chad's Coll Dur BA57 DipEd58. **d** 60 **p** 61. C Moordown *Win* 60-63; C Basingstoke 64-67; V Bransgore 67-04; Hon Can Win Cathl 89-04; rtd 04; Perm to Offic *Win* from 04. *1 Tyrrells Court, Bransgore, Christchurch BH23 8BU* Tel (01425) 673103

ELKS, Roger Mark. b 60. Imp Coll Lon BSc83. Wycliffe Hall Ox 89. **d** 92 **p** 93. C St Austell *Truro* 92-95; V Carbis Bay w Lelant 95-01; I Holywood *D & D* from 01. *The Vicarage, 156 High Street, Holywood BT18 9HT* Tel (028) 9042 2069 *or* 9042 3622 E-mail vicarroger@ntlworld.com

ELLACOTT, Alan Gren. b 58. Ripon Coll Cuddesdon 02. **d** 04 **p** 05. C Crewkerne w Wayford *B & W* 04-07; C Wulfric Benefice 07-09; R Llandysilio and Penrhos and Llandrinio etc *St As* from 09. *The Rectory, Rhos Common, Four Crosses, Llanymynech SY22 6RW* Tel (01691) 830533 Mobile 07989-299063 E-mail alkatch@tiscali.co.uk

ELLACOTT, David Alfred. b 35. SWMTC 95. **d** 97 **p** 98. NSM Fremington *Ex* 97-02; Perm to Offic from 02. *2 Coppice Close, Fremington, Barnstaple EX31 2QE* Tel (01271) 373270

ELLAM, Stuart William. b 53. Westcott Ho Cam. **d** 85 **p** 86. C Ditton St Mich *Liv* 85-88; C Greenford H Cross *Lon* 88-91; Perm to Offic from 91-94. *243 St Leonards Road, Windsor SL4 3DR* Tel (01753) 864827

ELLEM, Peter Keith. b 58. Nottm Univ BTh90 Leeds Univ MA99 CQSW. St Jo Coll Nottm 87. **d** 90 **p** 91. C Islington

St Mary *Lon* 90-94; C Leeds St Geo *Ripon* 94-99; Australia from 99; R Yagoona from 00. *211 Auburn Road, Yagoona NSW 2199, Australia* Tel (0061) (2) 9790 6281 Fax 9796 6201 E-mail prellem@bigfoot.com

ELLENS, Gordon Frederick Stewart. b 26. Columbia Univ (NY) MPhil62 PhD68 FRAS. K Coll Lon BD52 AKC52 St Boniface Warminster 52. **d** 53 **p** 54. C Old Street St Luke w St Mary Charterhouse etc *Lon* 53-55; C Chiswick St Mich 55-57; Canada 57-60; USA 62-66 and from 88; Japan 70-88; Asst Prof Relig St Sophia Univ Tokyo 70-75; Rikkyo Women's Univ 75-84; Prof Humanities Ueno Gakueu 84-88; rtd 92. *4 Bennetts Close, West Wittering, Chichester PO20 8EP* Tel (01243) 671313

ELLERTON, Mrs Mary Diane. b 45. RGN67 Southn Univ RHV68. NOC 90. **d** 93 **p** 94. NSM Upper Holme Valley *Wakef* from 93; TV from 10; Chapl Calderdale and Huddersfield NHS Trust from 01. *13 Liphill Bank Road, Holmfirth, Huddersfield HD9 2LQ* Tel (01484) 684207, 482266 *or* 343437 E-mail diane.ellerton@btopenworld.com

ELLERY, Arthur James Gabriel. b 28. St Jo Coll Dur BSc49. Linc Th Coll 51. **d** 53 **p** 54. C Milton next Sittingbourne *Cant* 53-56; C St Laur in Thanet 56-58; C Darlington St Cuth *Dur* 58-62; V Tanfield 62-70; Chapl St Olave's Sch York 70-78; V St Ayton w Easby and Newton-in-Cleveland *York* 78-81; Chapl Bancroft's Sch Woodford Green 81-86; V Chipperfield St Paul *St Alb* 86-93; rtd 93; Perm to Offic *Pet* 93-05. *7 Church Drive, Orton Waterville, Peterborough PE2 5EX* Tel (01733) 231800

ELLERY, Ian Martyn William. b 56. K Coll Lon BD AKC. Chich Th Coll. **d** 82 **p** 83. C Hornsey St Mary w St Geo *Lon* 82-85; V Choral York Minster 85-89; Subchanter 86-89; R Patrington w Hollym, Welwick and Winestead 89-97; TR Howden 97-05; RD Howden 97-02; P-in-c Cawood w Ryther and Wistow 05-11; R from 11. *Cawood Vicarage, Rythergate, Cawood, Selby YO8 3TP* Tel (01757) 268273 E-mail ellerys@tiscali.co.uk

ELLIN, Lindsey Jane. *See* GOODHEW, Mrs Lindsey Jane Ellin

ELLINGTON, David John. b 39. Oriel Coll Ox BA63 MA. Cuddesdon Coll 63. **d** 65 **p** 66. C Sheff St Mark Broomhall 65-68; C Timperley *Ches* 68-72; P-in-c Altrincham St Jo 72-74; V 74-80; P-in-c Ashley 82-86; rtd 86; Perm to Offic *Ches* 87-00. *Flat 1, 46 High Street, Woodstock OX20 1TG* Tel (01993) 815808

ELLIOT, Neil Robert Minto. b 63. Hatf Poly BEng87 Herts Univ CertEd93 Kingston Univ PhD11. St Jo Coll Nottm 94. **d** 96 **p** 97. C Walbrook Epiphany *Derby* 96-00; Chapl Univ of Cen England in Birm 00-05; V Trail SS Andr and Geo Canada from 05. *St Andrew's Church, 1347 Pine Avenue, Trail BC V1R 4E7, Canada* Tel (001) (250) 368 5581 E-mail rev.nelli@virgin.net

ELLIOT, William. b 33. Glouc Sch of Min 84. **d** 87 **p** 88. C Kington w Huntington, Old Radnor, Kinnerton etc *Heref* 87-90; C Heref H Trin 90-92; Chapl Corfu *Eur* 92-98; rtd 98; P-in-c Barlavington, Burton w Coates, Sutton and Bignor *Chich* 98-06. *2 Lawn Road, Guildford GU2 4DE* Tel (01483) 574540

ELLIOT, William Brunton. b 41. Edin Dioc NSM Course 81. **d** 84 **p** 85. NSM Lasswade *Edin* 84-92; NSM Dalkeith 84-92; Assoc P Edin St Pet 92-94; R Selkirk 94-06; rtd 06; Lic to Offic *Edin* from 06. *157 Newbattle Abbey Crescent, Dalkeith EH22 3LR* Tel 0131-663 1369 E-mail bille157@aol.com

ELLIOT-NEWMAN, Christopher Guy. b 43. Bede Coll Dur TCert67 Hull Univ BTh83 MEd87. Westcott Ho Cam 67. **d** 70 **p** 71. C Ditton St Mich *Liv* 70-73; C Hazlemere *Ox* 73-77; R Stockton-on-the-Forest w Holtby and Warthill *York* 77-87; Dir of Educn *Cant* 87-94; P-in-c Warden w Newbrough *Newc* 99-01; Perm to Offic 95-99 and from 02. *15 Hextol Terrace, Hexham NE46 2DF* Tel (01434) 600547 Mobile 07951-471189 E-mail christopher@firststandardltd.co.uk

ELLIOTT, Anne. *See* ELLIOTT, Mrs Elizabeth Anne

ELLIOTT, Ben. *See* ELLIOTT, William Henry Venn

ELLIOTT, Brian. b 49. Dur Univ BA73. Coll of Resurr Mirfield 73. **d** 75 **p** 76. C Nunthorpe *York* 75-77; CF 77-09; Dep Asst Chapl Gen 96-09; rtd 09; Perm to Offic Dio Cyprus and the Gulf and *Win* from 09. *St Paul's Cathedral, PO Box 22014, 1516 Nicosia, Cyprus* Tel (01904) 898941 E-mail brian@newpost.org

ELLIOTT, Christopher John. b 44. Sarum Th Coll 66. **d** 69 **p** 70. C Walthamstow St Pet *Chelmsf* 69-71; C Witham 71-74; P-in-c Gt and Lt Bentley 74-80; R Colchester Ch Ch w St Mary V 80-85; R Sible Hedingham 85-93; V Leigh-on-Sea St Aid 93-98; P-in-c Thornton Gp *Linc* 98-01; RD Horncastle 98-01; P-in-c Gt Leighs *Chelmsf* 01-05; P-in-c Lt Leighs 01-05; P-in-c Lt Waltham 01-05; R Gt and Lt Leighs and Lt Waltham 05-06; RD Chelmsf N 04-06; rtd 06; Perm to Offic *Chelmsf* 06-10; P-in-c Middleton-in-Teesdale w Forest and Frith *Dur* from 10. *The Rectory, Hude, Middleton-in-Teesdale, Barnard Castle DL12 0QW* Tel (01833) 641013 E-mail christopher@celliott1.wanadoo.co.uk

ELLIOTT, Christopher John. b 67. Southn Univ 93. Chich Th Coll 94. **d** 94 **p** 95. C Alton St Lawr *Win* 94-97; Perm to Offic *Guildf* 99-02. *77 Wickham Place, Church Crookham, Fleet GU52 6NQ* Tel 07788-195548 (mobile)

ELLIOTT, Colin David. b 32. AKC55. **d** 56 **p** 57. C W Wickham St Jo *Cant* 56-59; C Dover St Mary 59-64; V Linton 64-66; V Gillingham H Trin *Roch* 66-81; V Belvedere All SS 81-88; V Bromley St Jo 88-97; rtd 97; Perm to Offic *S'wark* from 98 and

Roch 99-03. *Flat 3, 160 George Lane, London SE13 6JF* Tel (020) 8698 4901

ELLIOTT, David Reed. b 62. Lon Bible Coll BA91. Oak Hill Th Coll 91. **d** 93 **p** 94. C Luton Lewsey St Hugh *St Alb* 93-98; Dioc Communications Dept 98-00; Chapl W Herts Hosps NHS Trust 07-10; Chapl Bucks Hosps NHS Trust from 10. *Wycombe Hospital, Queen Alexandra Road, High Wycombe HP11 2TT* Tel (01494) 526161

ELLIOTT, Derek John. b 26. Pemb Coll Cam BA50 MA55. Oak Hill Th Coll 48. **d** 51 **p** 53. C Ealing Dean St Jo *Lon* 51-53; C New Milverton *Cov* 53-55; C Boscombe St Jo *Win* 55-57; V Biddulph *Lich* 57-63; R Rushden w Newton Bromswold *Pet* 63-68; RD Higham 66-68; Chapl Bedford Modern Sch 68-83; V Potten End w Nettleden *St Alb* 83-91; rtd 91; Hon C Twickenham St Mary *Lon* from 91; Perm to Offic *Guildf* from 99. *Westwinds, Ridgeway Lane, Dorking RH4 3AT* Tel (01306) 876655

ELLIOTT, Mrs Elizabeth Anne. b 52. Lon Bible Coll BA03. STETS 09. **d** 11. NSM Pennington *Win* from 11. *19 Heron Close, Sway, Lymington SO41 6ET* Tel (01590) 683778 Mobile 07895-004134 E-mail anne.elliott@uwclub.net

ELLIOTT, Miss Eveline Mary. b 39. Bedf Coll Lon BA60 Cam Univ 92 ALA63. EAMTC 92. **d** 95 **p** 96. NSM Bury St Edmunds St Mary *St E* 95-97; NSM Lark Valley 97-07; rtd 07; Perm to Offic *St E* from 07. *4 St Michael's Close, Northgate Street, Bury St Edmunds IP33 1HT* Tel (01284) 753592 E-mail me@larkvalley57.fsnet.co.uk

ELLIOTT, Gordon. b 25. St Aid Birkenhead 63. **d** 65 **p** 66. C Latchford St Jas *Ches* 65-68; C Bollington St Jo 68-70; V Dukinfield St Mark 70-73; TV Tenbury Wells *Heref* 74-78; V Bromfield 78-82; R Culmington w Onibury 78-82; V Stanton Lacy 78-82; P-in-c Withybrook w Copston Magna *Cov* 82-83; P-in-c Wolvey, Burton Hastings and Stretton Baskerville 82-83; V Wolvey w Burton Hastings, Copston Magna etc 83-90; rtd 90; Perm to Offic *Worc* from 90; Perm to Offic *Heref* 90-95. *12 Handbury Road, Malvern WR14 1NN* Tel (01684) 569388

ELLIOTT, Ian David. b 40. Qu Coll Cam BA61 MA65. Tyndale Hall Bris 64. **d** 66 **p** 67. C Halewood *Liv* 66-71; C Gt Crosby St Luke 71-74; C-in-c Dallam CD 74-80; V Dallam 80-83; TV Fazakerley Em 83-92; V Warrington H Trin 92-05; rtd 05. *High Bank, 1 West End Road, Orton, Penrith CA10 3RT* Tel (015396) 24441 E-mail ian@ianandronelliott.freeserve.co.uk

ELLIOTT, Jane. d 08 p 09. NSM Hatcham St Cath *S'wark* from 08. *13 Seymour Gardens, London SE4 2DN* Tel (020) 7277 7968 E-mail jane.elliott@kcl.ac.uk

ELLIOTT, Mrs Joanna Margaret. b 64. Bris Univ BA85. STETS 03. **d** 06 **p** 07. NSM Haywards Heath St Wilfrid *Chich* from 06. *20 Courtlands, Haywards Heath RH16 4JD* Tel (01444) 413799 Mobile 07710-273299 E-mail joanna@ctsn.co.uk

ELLIOTT, John Andrew. b 44. ACIB68. SAOMC 95. **d** 98 **p** 99. NSM Bedgrove *Ox* 98-01; C Modbury, Bigbury, Ringmore w Kingston etc *Ex* 01-09; rtd 09; Perm to Offic *Ex* from 10. *Little Cumery, Aveton Gifford, Kingsbridge TQ7 4NN* Tel (01548) 830688

ELLIOTT, John Philip. b 37. MIChemE61 MBIM Salford Univ CEng. Glouc Th Course 79. **d** 80 **p** 80. NSM Brimscombe *Glouc* 80-86; C Caverswall *Lich* 86-91; R Tredington and Darlingscott w Newbold on Stour *Cov* 91-97; rtd 97; Perm to Offic *Glouc* from 97. *Pipers Barn, 69 Bownham Park, Stroud GL5 5BZ*

ELLIOTT, Kathryn Georgina. b 50. **d** 08. NSM Manston *Ripon* from 08. *19 Roper Avenue, Leeds LS8 1LG* Tel 0113-217 7805 Mobile 07979-954472 E-mail kelliott@ntlworld.com

ELLIOTT, Capt Keith Alcock. b 51. CA Tr Coll 83 Cranmer Hall Dur 94. **d** 95 **p** 96. C Chulmleigh, Chawleigh w Cheldon, Wembworthy etc *Ex* 95-99; TV Barnstaple and C-in-c Roundswell CD 99-08; V Thorpe Acre w Dishley *Leic* from 08. *The Vicarage, Thorpe Acre Road, Loughborough LE11 4LF* Tel (01509) 211656 E-mail elliottkeith@btinternet.com

ELLIOTT (née JUTSUM), Mrs Linda Mary. b 56. St Pet Coll Birm CertEd77. WMMTC 92. **d** 95 **p** 96. NSM Longthorpe *Pet* 95-99; P-in-c Etton w Helpston and Maxey 99-04; Chapl Thorpe Hall Hospice 04-09; Perm to Offic *Pet* from 09. *68 Bradwell Road, Longthorpe PE3 9PZ* Tel (01733) 261793 E-mail rev_linda@lycos.co.uk

ELLIOTT, Marilyn Elizabeth. b 53. Ex Univ BTh10. SWMTC 05. **d** 08 **p** 09. C Stoke Climsland *Truro* 08-10; C Linkinhorne from 08. *23 Woodland Rise, Rilla Mill, Callington PL17 7NZ* Tel (01579) 363307

ELLIOTT, Mary. *See* ELLIOTT, Miss Eveline Mary

ELLIOTT, Maurice John. b 65. St Andr Univ MA87 TCD BTh92 MPhil93 QUB PhD01. CITC 89. **d** 93 **p** 94. C Coleraine *Conn* 93-98; I Greenisland 98-02; I Lurgan Ch the Redeemer *D & D* 02-08; Dir Ch of Ireland Th Inst from 08. *7 Coolgraney, Nutgrove Park, Clonskeagh, Dublin 14, Republic of Ireland* Tel (00353) (1) 260 5737 *or* 492 3506 Fax 492 3082 Mobile 87-968 5218 E-mail mauriceelliott@theologicalinstitute.ie

ELLIOTT, Canon Michael Cowan. b 38. Auckland Univ BA63 Episc Th Sch Mass MDiv66 Massey Univ (NZ) MPhil82. St Jo Coll Auckland LTh61. **d** 61 **p** 62. New Zealand 61-65; C New

Lynn 61-64; C Thames 65; USA 65-66; Warden Pemb Coll Miss Walworth *S'wark* 66-70; Dir St Luke's Cen Haifa Jerusalem 70-74; BCC 74-75; C Amersham *Ox* 74-75; Ecum Secretariat on Development NZ 76-84; Dir Chr Action NZ 84-87; Chapl City of Lon Poly 87-89; Dir Inner City Aid 89-91; Tutor Westmr Coll Ox 91-98; Dir Ox Educn Trust 99-02; Dir Taught Progr Ox Cen for Miss Studies 00-02; rtd 03; Lect Univ of Wales (Lamp) 03-09. *PO Box 69, Warkworth 0941, New Zealand* E-mail canonmcelliott@aol.com

ELLIOTT, Michael James. b 58. St Jo Coll Nottm 80. **d** 83 **p** 84. C Pontypridd St Cath *Llan* 83-86; C Leamington Priors St Paul *Cov* 86-89; Chapl RAF 89-06 and from 07; Chapl Kimbolton Sch 06-07. *Chaplaincy Services, HQ Air Command, RAF High Wycombe HP14 4UE* Tel (01494) 496800 Fax 496343

ELLIOTT, Nigel Harvey. b 55. St Jo Coll Nottm 90. **d** 92 **p** 93. C Radcliffe *Man* 92-95; V Kilnhurst *Sheff* 95-08; R Wombwell from 08; AD Wath from 06. *The Rectory, 1 Rectory Close, Wombwell, Barnsley S73 8EY* Tel (01226) 211100 E-mail nell199076@aol.com

ELLIOTT, The Ven Peter. b 41. Hertf Coll Ox BA63 MA68. Linc Th Coll 63. **d** 65 **p** 66. C Gosforth All SS *Newc* 65-68; C Balkwell 68-72; V High Elswick St Phil 72-80; V N Gosforth 80-87; V Embleton w Rennington and Rock 87-93; RD Alnwick 89-93; Hon Can Newc Cathl 90-93; Adn Northd and Can Res Newc Cathl 93-05; rtd 05. *56 King Street, Seahouses NE68 7XS* Tel (01665) 721133

ELLIOTT, Peter Wolstenholme. b 31. CChem MRSC. NEOC 78. **d** 81 **p** 82. NSM Yarm *York* 81-02; Perm to Offic from 02. *48 Butterfield Drive, Eaglescliffe, Stockton-on-Tees TS16 0EZ* Tel (01642) 652698 E-mail revdpeter@hotmail.com

ELLIOTT, Philip. See ELLIOTT, John Philip

ELLIOTT, Philip. b 58. Westcott Ho Cam. **d** 11. C Bradford-on-Avon H Trin *Sarum* from 11. *15 Mythern Meadow, Bradford-on-Avon BA15 1HF* Tel 07990-604890 (mobile) E-mail philipelliottra@yahoo.co.uk

ELLIOTT, Richard David Clive. b 53. Portsm Poly BSc74 MICE79 MIStructE. STETS 03. **d** 06 **p** 07. NSM Sway *Win* from 06. *19 Heron Close, Sway, Lymington SO41 6ET* Tel (01590) 683778 Mobile 07836-760150 E-mail richard.elliott3@tesco.net

ELLIOTT, Mrs Rosemary Miriam. b 37. Toronto Univ BPaed62 Birm Univ BPhil86. **d** 04 **p** 05. Asst Chapl Birm Specialist Community Health NHS Trust 04-05; rtd 06. *10 Homethwaite House, Erskin Street, Keswick CA12 4DG* Tel (017687) 72513 Mobile 07721-855007 E-mail rosemary.elliott@btinternet.com

ELLIOTT, Simon Mark. b 76. Liv Hope Univ Coll BA97. Ridley Hall Cam 05. **d** 08. C Gt Crosby St Luke *Liv* from 08. *69 York Road, Crosby, Liverpool L23 5TT* E-mail sielliott76@btinternet.com

ELLIOTT, Simon Richard James. b 66. Lon Univ BSc88. Cranmer Hall Dur BA95. **d** 95 **p** 96. C Hendon St Paul Mill Hill *Lon* 95-99; V Hull St Martin w Transfiguration *York* from 99. *St Martin's Vicarage, 942 Anlaby Road, Hull HU4 6AH* Tel (01482) 352995 Mobile 07776-143084 E-mail stmartinshull@hotmail.co.uk

ELLIOTT, Stuart. b 75. Univ of Wales (Ban) BTh98 MTh00. St Mich Coll Llan 05. **d** 07 **p** 08. C Holywell *St As* 07-10; V Llanasa and Ffynnongroew from 10. *The Vicarage, Llanasa Road, Gronant, Prestatyn LL19 9TL* Tel (01745) 888797 E-mail stu@stubiedoo.co.uk

ELLIOTT, William. b 20. Lon Univ BA56. Ripon Hall Ox 60. **d** 61 **p** 62. C Kidderminster St Mary *Worc* 61-70; V Bewdley Far Forest 70-78; V Rock w Heightington w Far Forest 78-82; V Mamble w Bayton, Rock w Heightington etc 82-85; rtd 85; Perm to Offic *Heref* and *Worc* from 85. *8 Lea View, Cleobury Mortimer, Kidderminster DY14 8EE* Tel (01299) 270993

ELLIOTT, William Henry Venn (Ben). b 34. K Coll Cam BA55 MA59. Wells Th Coll 59. **d** 61 **p** 62. C Almondbury *Wakef* 61-66; V Bramshaw *Sarum* 66-81; P-in-c Landford w Plaitford 77-81; V Mere w W Knoyle and Maiden Bradley 81-99; rtd 99. *3 St George's Close, Salisbury SP2 8HA* Tel (01722) 338409

ELLIOTT, William James. b 38. Jes Coll Cam BA62 MA66 Birm Univ MA69 PhD74. Qu Coll Birm 62. **d** 64 **p** 65. C Hendon St Paul Mill Hill *Lon* 64-67; C St Pancras w St Jas and Ch Ch 67-69; P-in-c Preston St Paul *Blackb* 69-74; Chapl Preston R Infirmary 69-74; R Elstree *St Alb* 74-00; Research Fell Birm Univ 00-03; rtd 03; Perm to Offic *Nor* from 00. *23 Neil Avenue, Holt NR25 6TG* Tel and fax (01263) 713853 E-mail bill.elliott@akainternet.co.uk

ELLIOTT DE RIVEROL, Mrs Jennifer Kathleen. b 52. St Pet Coll Birm CertEd75 UEA MA88. ERMC 09. **d** 11. C Puerto de la Cruz Tenerife *Eur* from 11. *El Bho, Calle Tamarahoya 1, El Paso, 38750 La Palma, Canary Islands* Tel (0034) 922 497 446 Mobile 670 813 599 E-mail jkelliottderiverol@hotmail.com

ELLIS, Anthony. See ELLIS, Canon John Anthony

ELLIS, Anthony Colin. b 56. Keble Coll Ox BA77 Man Univ PhD80. Linc Th Coll 80. **d** 81 **p** 82. C Mill Hill Jo Keble Ch *Lon* 81-83; Staff Tutor in RS Man Univ from 83; Dir Cen for

Continuing Educn from 99; C Stretford St Pet *Man* 83-87; NSM Shore 87-89; Lic Preacher from 89. *2 Crowther Terrace, Blackshaw, Hebden Bridge HX7 6DE* Tel (01422) 844242 *or* 0161-275 3302

ELLIS, Brian Eric James. b 50. STETS 05. **d** 08 **p** 09. NSM Preston w Sutton Poyntz and Osmington w Poxwell *Sarum* from 08. *27 Fisherbridge Road, Preston, Weymouth DT3 6BT* Tel (01305) 832427 Mobile 07533-941686 E-mail brian-ellis@talktalk.net

ELLIS, Canon Bryan Stuart. b 31. Qu Coll Cam BA54 MA58. Ridley Hall Cam 55. **d** 57 **p** 58. C Ramsgate St Luke *Cant* 57-59; C Herne Bay Ch Ch 59-62; V Burmantofts St Steph and St Agnes *Ripon* 62-81; RD Wakef 81-96; V Wakef St Andr and St Mary 81-00; Hon Can Wakef Cathl 89-00; rtd 00; Perm to Offic *Ripon* from 01. *302 Oakwood Lane, Leeds LS8 3LE* Tel 0113-240 3122

ELLIS, Charles Harold. b 50. NOC 78. **d** 81 **p** 82. C Davyhulme St Mary *Man* 81-85; V Tonge w Alkrington 85-91; P-in-c Radcliffe St Thos and St Jo 91; P-in-c Radcliffe St Mary 91; TR Radcliffe 91-99; AD Radcliffe and Prestwich 96-99; P-in-c Newchurch 99-00; TR Rossendale Middle Valley 00-04; AD Rossendale 00-04; V Ingleton w Chapel le Dale *Bradf* from 04. *St Mary's Vicarage, Main Street, Ingleton, Carnforth LA6 3HF* Tel (015242) 41440 E-mail chasellis@btinternet.com

ELLIS, Christopher Charles. b 55. Edin Univ BD78 Hull Univ MA80. Edin Th Coll 76 Irish Sch of Ecum 78. **d** 79 **p** 80. C Selby Abbey *York* 79-82; C Fulford 82-85; Dioc Ecum Officer 81-98; Dioc Ecum Adv 90-98; Lect Ecum Th Hull Univ from 84; P-in-c Kexby w Wilberfoss *York* 85-90; Ecum Officer S Cleveland and N Yorks Ecum Coun 88-98; P-in-c Bulmer w Dalby, Terrington and Welburn 98-01; R Howardian Gp 01-05; P-in-c Sheriff Hutton, Farlington, Stillington etc 05-06; V Forest of Galtres from 06. *The Vicarage, Main Street, Sutton-on-the-Forest, York YO61 1DW* Tel (01347) 810251 E-mail benefice.admin@googlemail.com

ELLIS, Christopher Duncan. b 67. Anglia Ruskin Univ BA09. ERMC 05. **d** 08 **p** 09. C Thorpe St Andr *Nor* from 08; V Thorpe St Matt from 11. *St Matthew's Vicarage, Albert Place, Norwich NR1 4JL* E-mail chris.ellis23@btinternet.com

ELLIS, Canon David Craven. b 34. Man Univ BA56 MA57. St Aid Birkenhead 59. **d** 61 **p** 62. C Gt Crosby St Luke *Liv* 61-65; Hong Kong 65-69; P-in-c Sawrey *Carl* 69-74; Dioc Youth Officer 69-74; V Halifax St Aug *Wakef* 74-84; R Greystoke, Matterdale and Mungrisdale *Carl* 84-87; R Watermillock 84-87; TR Greystoke, Matterdale, Mungrisdale etc 88-91; RD Penrith 87-91; TR Carl H Trin and St Barn 91-96; Hon Can Carl Cathl 91-96; rtd 96; Perm to Offic *Carl* 97-02 and from 04; NSM Cartmel Peninsula 02-04. *Calderstones, 5 Fellside, Allithwaite, Grange-over-Sands LA11 7RN* Tel (01539) 533974

ELLIS, Dorothy Pearson. b 43. Sheff Univ BA66 MA67. Dioc OLM tr scheme 05. **d** 07 **p** 08. NSM Oakenshaw, Wyke and Low Moor *Bradf* from 07. *2 Woodrow Drive, Low Moor, Bradford BD12 0JU* Tel (01274) 679048

ELLIS, Mrs Emma Louise. b 79. Coll of Ripon & York St Jo BA00 Heythrop Coll Lon MTh03. Ridley Hall Cam 05. **d** 07 **p** 08. C Addiscombe St Mary Magd w St Martin *S'wark* 07-10; TV Limpsfield and Tatsfield from 10. *The Rectory, Ricketts Hill Road, Tatsfield, Westerham TN16 2NA* Tel 07949-697075 (mobile) E-mail rev.louiseellis@googlemail.com

ELLIS, Gay Winifred. b 48. Oak Hill Th Coll 94. **d** 96 **p** 97. NSM Nazeing *Chelmsf* 96-99; C 99-00; P-in-c Chingford St Anne 00-02; V 02-04; P-in-c Lambourne w Abridge and Stapleford Abbotts 04-10; Ind Chapl 04-10; rtd 10; Perm to Offic *Chelmsf* from 11. *16 Church Ponds, Castle Hedingham, Halstead CO9 3BZ* Tel (01787) 461575 E-mail gayellis@aol.com

ELLIS, Gillian Patricia. **d** 99 **p** 00. OLM Blymhill w Weston-under-Lizard *Lich* 99-00; OLM Lapley w Wheaton Aston 00-09; OLM Watershed from 09. *18 Ashleigh Crescent, Wheaton Aston, Stafford ST19 9PN* Tel (01785) 840925 E-mail gellis3011@toucansurf.com

ELLIS, Hugh William. b 54. Sussex Univ BSc76. Ridley Hall Cam 88. **d** 90 **p** 91. C Reading St Jo *Ox* 90-93; P-in-c Bradfield and Stanford Dingley 93-97; R 97-03; TR Langport Area *B & W* from 03. *The Rectory, Huish Episcopi, Langport TA10 9QR* Tel (01458) 250480 E-mail hughelli@aol.com

ELLIS, Canon Ian Morton. b 52. QUB BD75 MTh82 TCD PhD89. CITC. **d** 77 **p** 78. C Portadown St Columba *Arm* 77-79; C Arm St Mark 79-85; Chapl Arm R Sch 79-85; Hon V Choral Arm Cathl 82-93; I Mullavilly 85-93; Dom Chapl to Abp Arm 86-93; Tutor for Aux Min (*Arm*) 90-93; Dioc Adv on Ecum 92-93; I Newcastle *D & D* from 93; Can Belf Cathl from 00; Ed *The Church of Ireland Gazette* from 01; Preb Newcastle St Patr Cathl Dublin from 16. *The Rectory, 1 King Street, Newcastle BT33 0HD* Tel (028) 4372 2439 Fax 4372 5977 E-mail ian.m.ellis@btinternet.com

ELLIS, Ian William. b 57. QUB BSc78 CertEd79 TCD BTh89. CITC 86. **d** 89 **p** 90. C Arm St Mark w Aghavilly 89-91; V Loughgall w Grange 91-02; Sec Gen Syn Bd of Educn from 02.

Church of Ireland House, 61-67 Donegall Street, Belfast BT1 2QH Tel (028) 9023 1202 Fax 9023 7802 E-mail edunorth@ireland.anglican.org

ELLIS, Jean Miriam. b 35. St Mich Coll Llan 92. **d** 95 **p** 97. NSM Llanelli *S & B* 95-98; NSM Rockfield and St Maughen's w Llangattock etc *Mon* 99-04; NSM Rockfield and Dingestow Gp 05-09. *2 Watery Lane, Monmouth NP25 5AT* Tel (01600) 719562

ELLIS, Jenny Susan. b 56. Bp Grosseteste Coll BEd80. STETS 08. **d** 11. NSM Martock w Ash *B & W* from 11. *The Rectory, Huish Episcopi, Langport TA10 9QR* Tel (01458) 250480 E-mail ellisjene@aol.com

ELLIS, Canon John Anthony. b 47. Open Univ BA80. Coll of Resurr Mirfield 70. **d** 72 **p** 73. C Sketty *S & B* 72-75; C Duston *Pet* 75-80; R Lichborough w Maidford and Farthingstone 80-85; V Stratfield Mortimer *Ox* 85-98; P-in-c Mortimer W End w Padworth 85-98; TR Kidlington w Hampton Poyle from 98; AD Ox from 04; Hon Can Ch Ch from 07. *St Mary's Rectory, 19 Mill Street, Kidlington OX5 2EE* Tel and fax (01865) 372230 E-mail churchkid@tesco.net

ELLIS, John Beaumont. b 45. Univ of Wales (Lamp) BA67 LTh69. Bp Burgess Hall Lamp. **d** 69 **p** 70. C Abergavenny St Mary w Llanwenarth Citra *Mon* 69-72; C Swansea St Gabr *S & B* 72-75; V Llanbister and Llanbadarn Fynydd w Llananno 75-77; V Newport St Andr *Mon* 77-80; V Risca 80-84; V Cheadle Heath *Ches* 84-94. *12 Upper Hibbert Lane, Marple, Stockport SK6 7HX* Tel 0161-427 1963

ELLIS, John Franklyn. b 34. Leeds Univ BA58. Linc Th Coll 58. **d** 60 **p** 61. C Ladyharn *Man* 60-63; C Stockport St Geo *Ches* 63-66; V High Lane 66-81; V Chelford w Lower Withington 81-99; rtd 99; Perm to Offic *Ches* from 00. *3 Millers Croft, Adlington Street, Macclesfield SK10 1BD*

ELLIS, John Keith Randolph. b 44. Univ of Wales MEd Man Univ CertEd. Westcott Ho Cam 98. **d** 01 **p** 02. C Glanogwen w St Ann's w Llanllechid *Ban* 01-04; Min Can Ban Cathl 04-09; rtd 09. *Glan Arthur, Penisarwaun, Caernarfon LL55 3PW* Tel (01286) 873623 E-mail randolph@afoncejin.freeserve.co.uk

ELLIS, John Raymond. b 63. St Steph Ho Ox 95. **d** 97 **p** 98. C Clare w Poslingford, Cavendish etc *St E* 97-00; P-in-c Bury St Edmunds St Jo 00-02; P-in-c Bury St Edmunds St Geo 00-02; TV Bury St Edmunds All SS w St Jo and St Geo 02-04; Chapl RAF from 04. *Chaplaincy Services, Valiant Block, HQ Air Command, RAF High Wycombe HP14 4UE* Tel (01494) 496800 Fax 496343

ELLIS, John Roland. b 32. Wells Th Coll 67. **d** 69 **p** 70. C Kettering SS Pet and Paul 69-71; C Kingsthorpe 71-73; TV 73-74; TV Ebbw Vale *Mon* 74-76; V Llanddewi Rhydderch w Llanvapley etc 76-83; Miss to Seamen 79-86; V New Tredegar *Mon* 83-86; V Llanelli *S & B* 86-98; RD Crickhowell 91-98; rtd 99; P-in-c Rockfield and St Maughen's w Llangattock etc *Mon* 99-05; Hon C Rockfield and Dingestow Gp 05-07. *2 Watery Lane, Monmouth NP25 5AT* Tel (01600) 719562

ELLIS, Canon John Wadsworth. b 42. MBE98. TCD BA64. **d** 66 **p** 67. C Lisburn Ch Ch Cathl 66-69; C Norbiton *S'wark* 69-72; C New Clee *Linc* 72-85; V from 85; RD Grimsby and Cleethorpes 94-99; Can and Preb Linc Cathl from 98. *120 Queen Mary Avenue, Cleethorpes DN35 7SZ* Tel and fax (01472) 696521 *or* 329922 E-mail jwellis@ntlworld.com

ELLIS, Kevin Stuart. b 67. Newc Univ BA91 Lon Bible Coll PhD97. Qu Coll Birm 99. **d** 01 **p** 02. C Matson *Glouc* 01-04; TV Maryport, Netherton and Flimby *Carl* 04-07; TR 07-09; V Bartley Green *Birm* from 09. *The Vicarage, 96 Romsley Road, Birmingham B32 3PS* Tel 0121-475 1508

ELLIS, Sister Lilian. b 44. Keswick Hall Coll TCert66. Oak Hill Th Coll 95. **d** 96 **p** 97. C Vange *Chelmsf* 96-00; C Pitsea w Nevendon 00-02; rtd 02; Perm to Offic *Chelmsf* from 02. *9 The Poplars, Basildon SS13 2ER* Tel (01268) 551018 E-mail lilian.ellis@tesco.net

ELLIS, Malcolm Railton. b 35. LTCL71 Univ of Wales (Lamp) BA56. Sarum Th Coll 56. **d** 58 **p** 59. C Llangynwyd w Maesteg 58-61; C Llantrisant 61-67; V Troedrhiwgarth 67-70; PV Truro Cathl 70-73; V Egloshayle 73-81; V Margam *Llan* 81-87; V Cardiff St Jo 87-00; TR Cen Cardiff 00-02; Prec and Can Llan Cathl 96-02; rtd 02. *41 Wendron Street, Helston TR13 8PT* Tel (01326) 574000

ELLIS, Preb Mark Durant. b 39. Ex Univ BA62. Cuddesdon Coll 62. **d** 64 **p** 65. C Lyngford *B & W* 64-67; V Weston-super-Mare St Andr Bournville 67-76; TV Yeovil 76-88; V Yeovil St Mich 88-09; Preb Wells Cathl 90-09; RD Yeovil 94-04; rtd 09; Hon C Bruton and Distr *B & W* from 09. *The Parsonage, Gold Hill, Batcombe, Shepton Mallet BA4 6HF* Tel (01749) 850074

ELLIS, Paul. b 49. **d** 07 **p** 08. NSM Wakef St Jo from 07. *98 Bradford Road, Wakefield WF1 2AH* Tel (01924) 367976

ELLIS, Paul. b 56. Aston Tr Scheme 88 Trin Coll Bris 92. **d** 92 **p** 93. C Pennington *Man* 92-96; TV Deane 96-06; P-in-c Grassendale *Liv* from 06; P-in-c Liv All So Springwood from 11. *St Mary's Vicarage, 22 Eaton Road, Cressington, Liverpool L19 0PW* Tel 0151-427 1474

ELLIS, Peter Andrew. b 46. St D Coll Lamp 65. **d** 69 **p** 70. C Milford Haven *St D* 69-71; R Walwyn's Castle w Robeston W 71-74; Miss to Seafarers 74-11; Hong Kong 74-75 and 92-11; Singapore 75-82; The Tees and Hartlepool 82-92; rtd 11. *26 The Grove, Marton-in-Cleveland, Middlesbrough TS7 8AA*

ELLIS, John Keith Randolph. *See* ELLIS, John Keith Randolph

ELLIS, Richard. b 47. **d** 02 **p** 03. OLM Leiston *St E* from 02. *9 Kings Road, Leiston IP16 4DA* Tel (01728) 832168 Mobile 07759-349057 E-mail us@rellis41.freeserve.co.uk

ELLIS, Robert Albert. b 48. K Coll Lon BD70 AKC70. St Aug Coll Cant 70. **d** 72 **p** 73. C Liv Our Lady and St Nic w St Anne 72-76; P-in-c Meerbrook *Lich* 76-80; Producer Relig Progr BBC Radio Stoke 76-80; V Highgate All SS *Lon* 80-81; P-in-c Longdon *Lich* 81-87; Dioc Communications Officer 81-01; Chapl Palma de Mallorca *Eur* from 01; Perm to Offic *Lich* from 11. *Nuñez de Balboa 6, Son Armadans, 07014 Palma de Mallorca, Spain* Tel (0034) 971 737 279 Fax 971 454 492 E-mail anglicanpalma@terra.es

ELLIS, Roger Henry. b 40. Natal Univ BA61 Selw Coll Cam BA64 MA68 Linacre Coll Ox BLitt69. **d** 66 **p** 67. C Ox St Mich 66-68; Sen Lect Univ of Natal S Africa 68-76; Hon C Pietermaritzburg Cathl 68-76; P-in-c Wortham *St E* 77; V Wheatley Hills *Sheff* 77-84; Chapl St Edm Sch Cant 84-00; P-in-c Dymchurch w Burmarsh and Newchurch *Cant* 00-04; AD Romney 01-03; rtd 05. *5 Bishops Reach, Wyndham Lane, Allington, Salisbury SP4 0BB* Tel (01980) 610757 E-mail ellisrhdm@yahoo.co.uk

ELLIS, Susannah Margaret. b 44. Open Univ BA82 New Coll Dur CertEd88. EAMTC 93. **d** 96 **p** 97. NSM S Elmham and Ilketshall *St E* 96-98; Warden Quiet Waters Chr Retreat Ho 96-98; C Worlingham w Barnby and N Cove *St E* 98-01; C Beccles St Mich 98-01; P-in-c Worlingham w Barnby and N Cove 01-03; R from 03. *27 Lowestoft Road, Worlingham, Beccles NR34 7DZ* Tel (01502) 715403

✠**ELLIS, The Rt Revd Timothy William.** b 53. AKC75 York Univ DPhil98. St Aug Coll Cant 75. **d** 76 **p** 77 **c** 06. C Old Trafford St Jo *Man* 76-80; V Pendleton St Thos 80-87; Chapl Salford Coll of Tech 80-87; V Sheff St Leon Norwood 87-01; P-in-c Shiregreen St Hilda 94-01; RD Ecclesfield 94-99; Hon Can Sheff Cathl 00-01; Adn Stow *Linc* 01-06; Suff Bp Grantham from 06; Dean Stamford 05-11; Can and Preb Linc Cathl from 01. *Saxonwell Vicarage, Church Street, Long Bennington, Newark NG23 5ES* Tel (01400) 283344 Fax 283321 E-mail bishop.grantham@lincoln.anglican.org

ELLISDON, Patrick Leon Shane. b 61. St Jo Coll Nottm 99. **d** 01 **p** 02. C Margate St Phil *Cant* 01-04; P-in-c Cliftonville from 04. *St Paul's Vicarage, 18 Devonshire Gardens, Margate CT9 3AF* Tel (01843) 226832 Mobile 07932-734932 E-mail panddellisdon@tesco.net

ELLISON, John. b 37. FCA64. Qu Coll Birm. **d** 04 **p** 05. NSM Northanger *Win* from 04. *High Candovers, Hartley Mauditt, Alton GU34 3BP* Tel (01420) 511346 E-mail revjohnellison@hotmail.com

✠**ELLISON, The Rt Revd John Alexander.** b 40. ALCD67. **d** 67 **p** 68 **c** 88. C Woking St Paul *Guildf* 67-70; SAMS from 71; C Belgrano St Sav Argentina 80-83; R Aldridge *Lich* 83-88; Bp Paraguay 88-07; rtd 07. *The Furrow, Evingar Road, Whitchurch RG28 7EU* Tel (01256) 892126

ELLISON, Mrs Margaret Helen. b 50. Edin Univ BSc77 RN72. Yorks Min Course 07. **d** 09 **p** 10. NSM York St Hilda from 09; NSM York St Lawr w St Nic from 09. *17 Foresters Walk, Stamford Bridge, York YO41 1BB* Tel (01759) 372696 E-mail maggs.ellison@googlemail.com

ELLISON, Ms Sandra Anne. b 53. Anglia Poly Univ BA96 RMN74. EAMTC 99. **d** 02 **p** 03. C Hunstanton St Mary w Ringstead Parva etc *Nor* 02-05; R Ashmanhaugh, Barton Turf etc from 05. *11 Pinewood Drive, Horning, Norwich NR12 8LZ* Tel (01692) 630216

ELLISON, Simon John. b 51. SEITE 99. **d** 02 **p** 03. NSM Caterham *S'wark* 02-08; Asst Chapl Newcastle upon Tyne Hosps NHS Foundn Trust 08-09; Chapl Epsom and St Helier Univ Hosps NHS Trust from 09. *Trust Headquarters, St Helier Hospital, Wrythe Lane, Carshalton SM5 1AA* Tel (020) 8296 2000 E-mail simon.ellison@epsom-sthelier.nhs.uk

ELLISTON, John Ernest Nicholas. b 37. ALCD61. **d** 61 **p** 62. C Gipsy Hill Ch Ch *S'wark* 61-64; C Whitton and Thurleston w Akenham *St E* 64-68; P-in-c New Clee *Linc* 68-71; V 75-76; V Grimsby St Steph 71-75; P-in-c Mildenhall *St E* 77-79; RD Mildenhall 81-84; R Barton Mills, Beck Row w Kenny Hill etc 80-84; V Ipswich St Aug 84-96; R Guernsey St Peter Port *Win* 96-02; Chapl Princess Eliz Hosp Guernsey 96-02; rtd 02; Perm to Offic *St E* from 03. *27 Wyvern Road, Ipswich IP3 9TJ* Tel (01473) 726617 *or* 720036

ELLMORE, Peter Robert. b 44. Portsm Univ MA. Sarum & Wells Th Coll 84. **d** 86 **p** 87. C Bridgemary *Portsm* 86-89; C Portsea N End St Mark 89-91; Asst Chapl St Mary's Hosp Portsm 91-92; Chapl Qu Alexandra Hosp Portsm 91-93; Chapl Team Ldr Portsm Hosps NHS Trust 93-97; P-in-c Cosham *Portsm* 97-99; Angl Chapl Univ Coll Lon Hosps NHS Trust

99-01; Chapl Team Ldr United Bris Healthcare NHS Trust 01-04; Lead Chapl (S) *Caring for the Spirit* NHS Project 04-07; Chapl St Pet Hospice Bris 07-09; rtd 09. *2 Westover Drive, Bristol BS9 3LX* Tel 0117-950 2927 E-mail peter.ellmore@lineone.net

ELLOR, Preb Michael Keith. b 52. St Jo Coll Nottm 92. **d** 94 **p** 95. C Stafford St Jo and Tixall w Ingestre *Lich* 94-97; TV Bucknall and Bagnall 97-03; TR Bucknall 03-09; RD Stoke 02-06; V Branston from 09; Local Min Adv (Stafford) from 09; Local Par Development Adv Stafford Area from 10; Preb Lich Cathl from 09. *The Vicarage, Church Road, Branston, Burton-on-Trent DE14 3ER* Tel (01283) 567017 E-mail ellors@bucknall12.fsnet.co.uk

ELLSON, Montague Edward. b 33. Birm Univ BA56 Cam Univ CertEd67 Univ of Wales (Lamp) MA08. EAMTC 84. **d** 87 **p** 88. Hon C Freethorpe w Wickhampton, Halvergate etc *Nor* 87-90; C Gaywood, Bawsey and Mintlyn 90-92; Miss to Seafarers from 90; R Pulham *Nor* 92-94; P-in-c Starston 93-94; Dioc NSM Officer 94-97; R Pulham Market, Pulham St Mary and Starston 94-97; RD Redenhall 95-97; rtd 97; Perm to Offic *Nor* from 97. *Barn Cottage, Neatishead Road, Horning, Norwich NR12 8LB* Tel (01692) 630251

ELLSWORTH, Lida Elizabeth. b 48. Columbia Univ (NY) BA70 Girton Coll Cam PhD76. EMMTC 85. **d** 88 **p** 94. NSM Bakewell *Derby* 88-07; Perm to Offic 04-11; NSM Longstone, Curbar and Stony Middleton from 11. *Apple Croft, Granby Gardens, Bakewell DE45 1ET* Tel and fax (01629) 814255

ELLWOOD, Mrs Ethney. **d** 06 **p** 07. OLM Uttoxeter Area *Lich* 06-11; rtd 11. *42 Jacks Lane, Marchington, Uttoxeter ST14 8LW* Tel (01283) 820459 E-mail revethneyellwood@hotmail.co.uk

ELLWOOD, Keith Brian. b 36. Curwen Coll Lon BA58 MMus65 Bede Coll Dur CertEd58 Hon DD99 AIGCM58 FRSA64 ACP66 FCollP83. Bps' Coll Cheshunt 64. **d** 64 **p** 65. Asst Master R Wanstead Sch 60-66; Chapl 64-66; C Wanstead St Mary *Chelmsf* 64-66; CF 66-70; OCF 70-71 and 76-79; Chapl St Paul's Coll Hong Kong 70-71; P-in-c Bicknoller *B & W* 71-73; Chapl Roedean Sch Brighton 73-76; Chapl Windsor Boys' Sch Hamm W Germany 76-79; Chapl Trin Coll Glenalmond 79-81; Hd Master St Chris Sch Burnham-on-Sea 82-86; Hon C Burnham *B & W* 82-86; R Staple Fitzpaine, Orchard Portman, Thurlbear etc 86-89; P-in-c Hugill and Dioc Educn Adv *Carl* 89-93; P-in-c Coldwaltham and Hardham *Chich* 93-95; rtd 96; Perm to Offic *Chich* 96-04 and *Sheff* from 04. *21 Fiddlers Drive, Armthorpe, Doncaster DN3 3TS* Tel (01302) 834031 E-mail k.b.e@btinternet.com

ELMAN, Simon Laurie. b 57. NTMTC. **d** 99 **p** 00. C Loughton St Jo *Chelmsf* 99-01; C Tye Green w Netteswell 01-07; Perm to Offic from 08. *26 Pakes Way, Theydon Bois, Epping CM16 7NA* Tel (01992) 813057 E-mail simon.elman@btinternet.com

ELMES, Amanda Jane. b 53. Lon Univ BDS76 RCS LDS77 Herts Univ PhD04. ERMC 06. **d** 08 **p** 09. NSM W w E Mersea *Chelmsf* 08-10; NSM W w E Mersea, Peldon, Gt and Lt Wigborough from 10. *Deoban, 171 Lexden Road, Colchester CO3 3TE* Tel (01206) 543516 E-mail amanda@deoban.co.uk

ELMES, Sister Evelyn Sandra. b 61. **d** 97 **p** 98. CA from 89; C Southchurch H Trin *Chelmsf* 97-00; Perm to Offic *Win* 01-08. *Address temp unknown* E-mail eveelmes@tesco.net

ELMES, Ruth Katherine. b 65. TCD BTh09 RGN83. CITC 06. **d** 09 **p** 10. C Stillorgan w Blackrock *D & G* from 09. *97 Wedgewood, Sandyford, Dublin 16, Republic of Ireland* Tel (00353) (1) 295 4870 E-mail relmes@eircom.net

ELMQVIST, Gunilla. *See* AQUILON-ELMQVIST, Mrs Gunilla

ELMS, Christian Grant. b 71. Salford Univ BSc04. Trin Coll Bris 07. **d** 09 **p** 10. C Pennington *Man* from 09. *11 Ruby Grove, Leigh WN7 4JW* Tel (01942) 607695 Mobile 07796-988907 E-mail christian.elms@virgin.net

ELPHICK, Robin Howard. b 37. ALCD63. **d** 64 **p** 65. C Clapham Common St Barn *S'wark* 64-67; C Woking St Pet *Guildf* 67-71; R Rollesby w Burgh w Billockby *Nor* 71-80; P-in-c Ashby w Oby, Thurne and Clippesby 79-80; R Rollesby w Burgh w Billockby w Ashby w Oby etc 80-84; R Frinton *Chelmsf* 84-94; P-in-c W w E Mersea and Peldon w Gt and Lt Wigborough 94-02; rtd 02; Perm to Offic *Nor* from 02. *1 Barn Cottages, Dodma Road, Weasenham, King's Lynn PE32 2TJ* Tel (01328) 838340 E-mail robin@relphick.fsnet.co.uk

ELPHICK, Canon Vivien Margaret. b 53. Kent Univ BA74 Solicitor 77. Trin Coll Bris BA90. **d** 90 **p** 94. C Oulton Broad *Nor* 90-94; P-in-c Burlingham St Edmund w Lingwood, Strumpshaw etc 94-06; RD Blofield 98-04; Hon Can Nor Cathl 03-06; P-in-c Measham *Leic* 06-08; P-in-c Packington w Normanton-le-Heath 06-08; P-in-c Donisthorpe and Moira w Stretton-en-le-Field 06-08; TR Woodfield from 08. *The Vicarage, High Street, Measham, Swadlincote DE12 7HZ* Tel (01530) 270354 E-mail vivien@rectorybarn.wanadoo.co.uk

ELPHIN AND ARDAGH, Archdeacon of. *Vacant*

ELPHIN AND ARDAGH, Dean of. *See* WILLIAMS, The Very Revd Arfon

ELSDON, Bernard Robert. b 29. Roch Th Coll 65. **d** 67 **p** 68. C Wallasey St Hilary *Ches* 67-71; C Liv Our Lady and St Nic w

St Anne 71-72; V Anfield St Marg 73-89; Dioc Exec Dir for Chr Resp 80-83; rtd 89; Perm to Offic *Man* 89-08 and *Ches* from 89. *31 Douglas Road, Hazel Grove, Stockport SK7 4JE* Tel 0161-292 1858 E-mail bernard.hillcrest@ntlworld.com

ELSDON, Mrs Janice Margaret. b 49. CITC 92. **d** 95 **p** 96. NSM Cloughfern *Conn* 95-99; NSM Ahoghill w Portglenone 99-02; NSM Belfast St Thos from 02. *St Bartholomew's Rectory, 16 Mount Pleasant, Belfast BT9 5DS* Tel (028) 9066 9995

ELSDON, Ronald. b 44. St Jo Coll Cam BA66 Trin Hall Cam PhD69 K Coll Lon BD86 Milltown Inst Dub PhD. CITC 97. **d** 99 **p** 00. C Ballymena w Ballyclug *Conn* 99-02; I Belfast St Bart from 02. *St Bartholomew's Rectory, 16 Mount Pleasant, Belfast BT9 5DS* Tel (028) 9066 9995 E-mail elsdon.rj@nireland.com *or* stbartholomew@connor.anglican.org

ELSMORE, Guy Charles. b 66. Edin Univ BSc88. Ridley Hall Cam 93. **d** 93 **p** 94. C Huyton St Mich *Liv* 93-98; V Hough Green St Basil and All SS 98-05; AD Widnes and Hon Can Liv Cathl 03-05; P-in-c St Luke in the City 05-10; TR from 10. *31 Mount Street, Liverpool L1 9HD* Tel 0151-709 2788 Mobile 07787-848229

ELSMORE (née HANOVA), Ms Petra. b 70. Chas Univ Prague BA97. Ridley Hall Cam 00. **d** 03 **p** 04. C Toxteth St Philemon w St Gabr and St Cleopas *Liv* 03-06; P-in-c Everton St Geo 06-09. *31 Mount Street, Liverpool L1 9HD* Tel 0151-709 2788 E-mail petra.elsmore@yahoo.co.uk

ELSON, Christopher John. b 52. K Coll Lon BD75 AKC75. St Aug Coll Cant. **d** 76 **p** 77. C New Haw *Guildf* 76-79; C Guildf H Trin w St Mary 79-82; C Hale 85-87; V Ripley from 87; Sub Chapl HM Pris Send 88-92. *The Vicarage, 8 Grove Heath North, Ripley, Woking GU23 6EN* Tel (01483) 211798 Mobile 07956-103289 E-mail chris@elsons.org.uk

ELSON, John Frederick. Roch Th Coll 62. **d** 64 **p** 65. C Tenterden St Mildred w Smallhythe *Cant* 64-68; P-in-c Chart next Sutton Valence 68-71; V Fletching *Chich* 71-93; Chapl Wivelsfield Green Hospice 91-93; rtd 93; Perm to Offic *Chich* from 93. *1 Manor House Court, Regency Close, Uckfield TN22 1DS* Tel (01825) 764735

ELSON, Sharon Anne. b 50. WEMTC 99. **d** 00 **p** 01. OLM Heref St Pet w St Owen and St Jas from 00. *100 Green Street, Hereford HR1 2QW* Tel (01432) 370417 Mobile 07718-481318 E-mail upinalms@btinternet.com

ELSTOB, Stephen William. b 57. Sarum & Wells Th Coll. **d** 86 **p** 87. C Sunderland Springwell w Thorney Close *Dur* 86-88; C Upholland *Liv* 88-89; TV 89-96; V Cinnamon Brow 96-07; TV N Wearside *Dur* from 07. *The Vicarage, Bootle Street, Sunderland SR5 4EY* Tel 0191-537 3744

ELSTON, Mrs Anthea Elizabeth Lynne. b 64. **d** 10 **p** 11. NSM Berrow w Pendock, Eldersfield, Hollybush etc *Worc* from 10. *The Plough, Eight Oaks, Castlemorton, Malvern WR13 6BU*

ELSTON, James Ian. b 70. City Univ BSc95. SEITE 01. **d** 04 **p** 05. NSM Old St Pancras *Lon* from 04. *8 Mansfield Road, London NW3 2HN* Tel (020) 7482 4056 E-mail jamesielston@aol.com

ELSTON, Philip Herbert. b 35. RD80 and Bar 90. Leeds Univ MA76 K Coll Lon AKC63 Leic Coll of Educn CertEd67. St Boniface Warminster 63. **d** 64 **p** 65. C Thurnby Lodge *Leic* 64-66; Hon C Far Headingley St Chad *Ripon* 75-79; V Knowl Hill w Littlewick *Ox* 79-84; Chapl RN Sch Haslemere 85-89; C Felpham w Middleton *Chich* 89-90; Asst S Regional Dir Miss to Seamen 91-93; Dep S Regional Dir 93-97; S Regional Dir 97-00; Perm to Offic *Win* from 93; *Cant* 94-00; *Chich* from 97; Corps Chapl Sea Cadet Corps 83-95; rtd 00; Hon C Witchampton, Stanbridge and Long Crichel etc *Sarum* 00-04; Hon Chapl Miss to Seafarers from 00. *East Farm Cottage, Dinton Road, Wylye, Warminster BA12 0RE* Tel (01985) 248598

ELSWORTH, Mrs Teresa Karen. b 60. Cape Town Univ BSc82. SEITE 03. **d** 06 **p** 07. NSM Yalding w Collier Street *Roch* 06-10; Perm to Offic *Cant* 07-10; NSM Goudhurst w Kilndown from 10. *10 Lurkins Rise, Goudhurst, Cranbrook TN17 1ED* Tel (01580) 211550 E-mail karenelsworth@hotmail.com

ELTON, Canon Derek Hurley. b 31. Lon Univ BSc52. Wycliffe Hall Ox 53. **d** 55 **p** 56. C Ashton-on-Ribble St Andr *Blackb* 55-57; India 58-70; R Wickmere w Lt Barningham and Itteringham *Nor* 71-79; R Lt w Gt Ellingham 79-83; P-in-c Rockland All SS and St Andr w St Pet 81-83; R Lt w Gt Ellingham w Rockland 83-88; Chapl Wayland Hosp Norfolk 84-88; Miss to Seamen 89-98; Algeria 89-94; Eritrea 94-98; rtd 96; Perm to Offic *Nor* from 00. *22 Alfred Road, Cromer NR27 9AN* Tel (01263) 511730 E-mail jedclef@paston.co.uk

ELTRINGHAM, Anna. b 74. St Jo Coll Dur BA96. SEITE 05. **d** 08 **p** 09. C S Norwood H Innocents *S'wark* from 08. *2 Roman Pleasant View, Dalmally Road, Croydon CR0 6LU* Tel (020) 8656 4548 Mobile 07826-524038 E-mail revd.anna@gmail.com

ELTRINGHAM, Mrs Fiona Ann. b 48. Bp Grosseteste Coll CertEd69. NEOC 86. **d** 89 **p** 94. Par Dn Willington *Newc* 89-92; Chapl HM YOI Castington 92-95; Chapl HM Pris Dur 95-07; rtd 07; Perm to Offic *Dur* from 07. *Granary Cottage, Stockley House Farm, Oakenshaw, Crook DL15 0TJ* Tel (01388) 746058 E-mail davefi@tiscali.co.uk

ELVERSON, Ronald Peter Charles. b 50. St Edm Hall Ox BA73 MA86. St Jo Coll Nottm 84. **d** 86 **p** 87. C Whitnash *Cov* 86-90; V Dunchurch 90-01; R Dersingham w Anmer and Shernborne *Nor* 01-05; P-in-c Ore Ch Ch *Chich* 05-08; V 08-11; rtd 11. *Address temp unknown* E-mail ronelverson@theelversons.fsnet.co.uk

ELVEY, Ms Charlotte Evanthia. b 44. St Anne's Coll Ox BA66 Bris Univ CertEd67. S'wark Ord Course 91. **d** 94 **p** 95. C Sydenham St Bart *S'wark* 94-98; P-in-c Worcester Park Ch Ch w St Phil 98-03; V from 03. *The Vicarage, 1E Lindsay Road, Worcester Park KT4 8LF* Tel (020) 8337 1327 E-mail c.elvey@btinternet.com

ELVIDGE, Joanna. b 55. FCIPD84. STETS BA06. **d** 06 **p** 07. NSM Horsham *Chich* from 06. *2 Garden Cottages, Forest Grange, Horsham RH13 6HX* Tel (01293) 852105 Fax 852187 E-mail joanna.elvidge@ukonline.co.uk

ELVIN, Jonathan Paul Alistair. b 65. Bris Univ BSc90 Fitzw Coll Cam BA94. Ridley Hall Cam 92. **d** 95 **p** 96. C Gravesend St Geo *Roch* 95-98; C Ex St Leon w H Trin 98-07; Min Ex Trin CD from 07. *23 Couper Meadows, Exeter EX2 7TF* Tel (01392) 363627 E-mail jonny@trinityexeter.com

ELVY, Canon Peter David. b 38. Lon Univ BA62 Fitzw Ho Cam BA64 MA68 Edin Univ PhD95. Ridley Hall Cam. **d** 65 **p** 66. C Herne Cam 65-66; C New Addington 66-68; C Addiscombe St Mildred 69-71; Youth Chapl *Chelmsf* 71-80; V Gt Burstead 75-92; Can Chelmsf Cathl 80-92; V Chelsea All SS *Lon* 92-05; Can Ughelli from 98; Preb St Paul's Cathl from 05; rtd 05; Perm to Offic *Lon* from 05. *2 Honiton Mansions, Flood Street, London SW3 5TU* Tel (020) 7795 0084 E-mail peterelvy@googlemail.com

ELWIN, Ernest John. b 31. Selw Coll Cam BA54 MA58. Ridley Hall Cam 54. **d** 56 **p** 57. C Wandsworth All SS *S'wark* 56-59; C Harlow New Town w Lt Parndon *Chelmsf* 59-61; Asst Teacher Tidworth Down Sch Dorset 61-63; V Soundwell *Bris* 63-66; Asst Teacher Seldown Sch Dorset 66-68; Wareham Modern Sch 68-69; Perm to Offic *Sarum* from 67; Lect S Dorset Tech Coll Weymouth 70-85; Weymouth Coll 85-88; Sub Chapl HM Youth Cust Cen Portland from 93. *4 Portesham Hill, Portesham, Weymouth DT3 4EU* Tel (01305) 871358

ELWIS, Malcolm John. b 42. Melbourne Univ DipEd74. St Jo Coll Morpeth 69. **d** 70 **p** 72. C Bentleigh St Jo Australia 70-72; C St Paul's Cathl Sale 72-73; Perm to Offic Brisbane 73-80; Perm to Offic *Chich* from 80; Chapl Hellingly and Amberstone Hosps 88-93; Chapl Eastbourne and Co Healthcare NHS Trust 93-02; Chapl E Sussex Co Healthcare NHS Trust from 02; Sub Chapl HM Pris Lewes 92-04; Chapl 04-06. *Puddledock, Boreham Lane, Wartling, Hailsham BN27 1RS* Tel (01323) 833233 E-mail malcolmelwis21@yahoo.co.uk

ELWOOD, Alan Roy. b 54. Sarum & Wells Th Coll 90. **d** 92 **p** 93. C Street w Walton *B & W* 92-96; V Kingsbury Episcopi w E Lambrook, Hambridge etc from 96. *The Vicarage, Folly Road, Kingsbury Episcopi, Martock TA12 6BH* Tel (01935) 824605

ELY, Nigel Patrick. b 62. Thames Poly BA83 Southn Univ BTh92. Chich Th Coll 89. **d** 92 **p** 93. C Rustington *Chich* 92-93; C Bexhill St Pet 93-96; Chapl St Geo Post 16 Cen *Birm* 96-99; Perm to Offic from 02. *57 Cherry Orchard Road, Birmingham B20 2LD* Tel 0121-554 6340

ELY, Bishop of. See CONWAY, The Rt Revd Stephen David

ELY, Dean of. See CHANDLER, The Very Revd Michael John

EMBLIN, Canon Richard John. b 48. BEd71 MA81. S Dios Minl Tr Scheme 83. **d** 86 **p** 87. C S w N Hayling *Portsm* 86-89; P-in-c Wootton 89-95; V Cowes H Trin and St Mary from 95; RD W Wight 01-07; Hon Can Portsm Cathl from 05. *The Vicarage, Church Road, Cowes PO31 8HA* Tel (01983) 292509 E-mail cowesvic@yahoo.com

EMERSON, Arthur Edward Richard. b 24. Lich Th Coll 69. **d** 72 **p** 73. C Barton upon Humber *Linc* 72-74; V Chapel St Leonards 75-88; P-in-c Hogsthorpe 77-88; V Chapel St Leonards w Hogsthorpe 88-91; rtd 91; Perm to Offic *Linc* 91-09. *119 Folkestone Road, Southport PR8 5PH* Tel (01704) 514778

EMERSON, Mrs Jan Vivien. b 44. S Dios Minl Tr Scheme 89. **d** 92 **p** 95. NSM Chich St Paul and St Pet 92-94; NSM Bosham 94-02; Asst Chapl R W Sussex NHS Trust from 02. *Lea-Rig, 3 Elm Park, Bosham, Chichester PO18 8PD* Tel (01243) 574948 E-mail janvemerson@aol.com

EMERTON, Andrew Neil. b 72. York Univ BSc93 Qu Coll Ox DPhil96 Down Coll Cam BTh05. Ridley Hall Cam 02. **d** 05 **p** 06. C Brompton H Trin w Onslow Square St Paul *Lon* 05-07; Dir St Paul's Th Cen from 08. *70 Archel Road, London W14 9QP* Tel (020) 7052 0755 *or* 7381 0506 Mobile 07815-498162 E-mail andy.emerton@htb.org.uk

EMERTON, David Mark. b 78. Edin Univ MA01 K Coll Lon MA11. St Mellitus Coll BA11. **d** 11. C E Twickenham St Steph *Lon* from 11. *94 Kenley Road, Twickenham TW1 1JU* Tel 07951-602102 (mobile) E-mail davidemerton@st-stephens.org.uk

EMERTON, Prof John Adney. b 28. CCC Ox BA50 MA54 CCC Cam MA55 BD60 St Jo Coll Cam DD73 Edin Univ Hon DD77 FBA79. Wycliffe Hall Ox 50. **d** 52 **p** 53. C Birm Cathl 52-53; Asst Lect Th Birm Univ 52-53; Lect Hebrew and Aramaic Dur Univ 53-55; Lect Div Cam Univ 55-62; Fell St Pet Coll Ox 62-68; Reader in Semitic Philology Ox Univ 62-68; Regius Prof Hebrew Cam Univ 68-95; Fell St Jo Coll Cam from 70; Hon Can Jerusalem from 84; Perm to Offic *Ely* from 98. *34 Gough Way, Cambridge CB3 9LN* Tel (01223) 363219

EMERY, Karen Maureen. See BECK, Ms Karen Maureen

EMERY, Sandra Faith. **d** 10 **p** 11. NSM Minchinhampton w Box and Amberley *Glouc* from 10. *The Old Carriage House, Edge, Stroud GL6 6PQ* Tel (01452) 814148 E-mail emery31@btinternet.com

EMINSON, Mark Franklin. b 79. Mert Coll Ox BA01 MSt03 MA06 Trin Coll Cam BA07. Westcott Ho Cam 05. **d** 08 **p** 09. C E Grinstead St Swithun *Chich* from 08. *21 Bourg de Peage Avenue, East Grinstead RH19 3YD* Tel (01342) 311021 Mobile 07816-273452 E-mail eminsons@btinternet.com

EMM, Robert Kenneth. b 46. K Coll Lon BD68 AKC68. **d** 69 **p** 70. C Hammersmith SS Mich and Geo White City Estate CD *Lon* 69-72; C Keynsham *B & W* 72-75; C Yeovil 75-80; TV Gt Grimsby St Mary and St Jas *Linc* 80-85; R N Thoresby 85-94; R Grainsby 85-94; V Waithe 85-94; R The North-Chapel Parishes from 94. *The Rectory, Church Lane, North Thoresby, Grimsby DN36 5QG* Tel and fax (01472) 840029 E-mail bob@bobemm.demon.co.uk

EMMEL, Canon Malcolm David. b 32. Qu Coll Birm. **d** 58 **p** 59. C Hessle *York* 58-62; Canada 62-66; V Catterick *Ripon* 66-73; V Pateley Bridge and Greenhow Hill 73-77; P-in-c Middlesmoor w Ramsgill 76-77; V Upper Nidderdale 77-88; RD Ripon 79-86; Hon Can Ripon Cathl 84-97; R Bedale 88-97; P-in-c Leeming 88-97; rtd 97; Perm to Offic *Bradf* from 98. *29 Greystone Close, Burley in Wharfedale, Ilkley LS29 7RS* Tel (01943) 865047

EMMETT, Kerry Charles. b 46. St Jo Coll Dur BA68. St Jo Coll Nottm 71. **d** 73 **p** 74. C Attenborough w Chilwell *S'well* 73-75; C Chilwell 75-76; C Wembley St Jo *Lon* 76-79; V Hanworth St Rich 79-89; R Ravenstone and Swannington *Leic* 89-04; RD Akeley S 97-03; P-in-c Mountsorrel Ch Ch and St Pet from 04. *Christ Church Vicarage, 4 Rothley Road, Mountsorrel, Loughborough LE12 7JU* Tel 0116-230 2235

EMMOTT, David Eugene. b 41. St Chad's Coll Dur BA63. **d** 66 **p** 67. C Bingley H Trin *Bradf* 66-69; C Anfield St Marg *Liv* 69-70; C Kirkby 70-75; Chapl Newc Poly 75-78; Hon C Toxteth Park St Marg *Liv* 78-80; TV Upholland 80-88; V Southfields St Barn *S'wark* 88-99; TV Liv Our Lady and St Nic w St Anne 99-06; rtd 06. *6A Eastern Drive, Liverpool L19 0NB* Tel 0151-281 5493 E-mail davidemmott@mac.com

EMMOTT, Douglas Brenton. b 45. K Coll Lon BD78 AKC78 York Univ MA97. Linc Th Coll 79. **d** 80 **p** 81. C Kingston upon Hull St Alb *York* 80-83; V Scarborough St Sav w All SS 83-91; V York St Chad 91-99; V Leeds All So *Ripon* 99-07; rtd 07. *Le Moulin de Vernay, 72500 Dissay-sous-Courcillon, France* Tel (0033) 2 43 46 53 82 Mobile 6 37 79 26 45 E-mail douglas.emmott@mac.com

EMMOTT, John Charles Lionel. b 32. SEITE 96. **d** 96 **p** 97. NSM Tenterden St Mich *Cant* 96-02; Perm to Offic *Cant* from 02. *58 Grange Crescent, St Michaels, Tenterden TN30 6DZ* Tel (01580) 762092 E-mail emmott@connectfree.co.uk

EMPEY, Clement Adrian. b 42. TCD BA64 MA68 PhD71. CITC. **d** 74 **p** 75. C Dublin St Ann *D & G* 75-76; I Kells-Inistioge Gp *C & O* 76-84; I Clane w Donadea and Coolcarrigan *M & K* 84-88; Hon Chapl Miss to Seafarers from 88; Sen Chapl Miss to Seamen (Irish Republic) 97-08; I Dublin St Ann and St Steph *D & G* 88-01; Preb Tassagard St Patr Cathl Dublin 82-89; Treas 89-91; Chan 91-96; Prec 96-01; Chapl Rotunda Hosp 98-08; Prin CITC 01-08; Prec Ch Ch Cathl Dublin 01-08; rtd 08. *40 Thorncliffe Park, Orwell Road, Dublin 14, Republic of Ireland* Tel (00353) (1) 405 5056 Mobile 87-902 2169 E-mail adrianempey@gmail.com

✠**EMPEY, The Rt Revd Walton Newcome Francis.** b 34. TCD BA57 Hon FGCM02. K Coll (NS) BD68. **d** 58 **p** 59 **c** 81. C Glenageary *D & G* 58-60; Canada 60-66; Bp's C Grand Falls New Brunswick 60-63; I Madawaska 63-66; I Stradbally *C & O* 66-71; Dean Limerick *L & K* 71-81; I Limerick St Mich 71-81; Preb Taney St Patr Cathl Dublin 73-81; Bp *L & K* 81-85; Bp *M & K* 85-96; Abp Dublin *D & G* 96-02; Preb Cualaun St Patr Cathl Dublin 96-02; rtd 02. *Rathmore Lodge, Rathmore, Tullow, Co Carlow, Republic of Ireland* Tel (00353) (59) 916 1891 E-mail louempey@hotmail.com

EMTAGE, Miss Susan Raymond. b 34. St Mich Ho Ox 63. dss 79 **d** 87 **p** 94. SW Area Sec CPAS Women's Action 75-82; Leic St Chris 82-86; Bramerton w Surlingham *Nor* 86-88; C 87-88; C Rockland St Mary w Hellington, Bramerton etc 88-89; Par Dn W Bromwich St Jas and St Paul 89-94; C 94; rtd 94; Hon C Stapleton *Bris* 96-04. *23 Capel Court, The Burgage, Prestbury, Cheltenham GL52 3EL* Tel (01242) 577535 E-mail sue.emtage@ukonline.co.uk

ENDALL, Peter John. b 38. Linc Th Coll 83. **d** 85 **p** 86. C Burley in Wharfedale *Bradf* 85-88; V Thwaites Brow 88-03; RD S Craven 92-02; rtd 03; Hon C Tamworth *Lich* 04-08; Perm to Offic from 08. *19 Cordwell Close, Castle Donington, Derby DE74 2JL* Tel (01332) 390863

ENDEAN, Michael George Devereux. b 33. Ox NSM Course. **d** 84 **p** 85. NSM Wantage Downs *Ox* 84-93. *87 Brookmead Drive, Wallingford OX10 9BH* Tel (01491) 824231

ENDICOTT, Michael John. b 45. **d** 97. NSM Pontnewydd *Mon* 97; NSM The Well Cen from 97. *The Well Centre, Station Road, Pontnewydd, Cwmbran NP44 1NZ* Tel (01633) 483660

ENEVER, John William. b 44. MBE92. Open Univ BA80. NTMTC 94. **d** 97 **p** 98. NSM Waltham H Cross *Chelmsf* 97-02; NSM Gt Ilford St Andr 02-08; Asst Chapl Gt Ormond Street Hosp for Children NHS Trust 08-10. *197 Pinhoe Road, Exeter EX4 8AB* Tel (01392) 200510 E-mail johnenever@gmail.com

ENEVER, Canon Rosemary Alice Delande. b 45. Oak Hill Th Coll 86. **d** 88 **p** 94. NSM Gt Ilford St Jo *Chelmsf* 88-94; TV Waltham H Cross 94-02; Asst Area Dean Epping Forest 00-01; V Gt Ilford St Andr 02-10; RD Redbridge 06-08; Hon Can Chelmsf Cathl 06-10; rtd 10. *197 Pinhoe Road, Exeter EX4 8AB* Tel (01392) 200510 E-mail rosemaryenever@googlemail.com

ENEVER, Mrs Susan Elizabeth. b 33. WMMTC 87. **d** 92 **p** 94. NSM Rugby *Cov* 92-97; Perm to Offic 97-05; Pet 98-05; Worc from 00. *7 Rocheberie Way, Rugby CV22 6EG* Tel (01788) 813135

ENEVER, Vivian John. b 61. Collingwood Coll Dur BA82 Cam Univ PGCE85 Man Univ BPhil97. Westcott Ho Cam 88. **d** 91 **p** 92. C Gt Crosby St Faith *Liv* 91-95; C Cantril Farm 95-97; TV Halas *Worc* 97-03; TR Newark w Coddington *S'well* from 03. *The Rectory, 6 Bede House Lane, Newark NG24 1PY* Tel (01636) 704513

ENGEL, Jeffrey Davis. b 38. Man Univ BA59 Liv Univ PGCE60 Aston Univ MSc82 FCP83. St Deiniol's Hawarden 86. **d** 89 **p** 90. NSM Formby St Pet *Liv* 89-92; C Prescot 92-94; P-in-c Hale 94-03; Dioc Adv for Past Care and Counselling 94-03; rtd 04; Chapl MU from 05. *Church View, West Street, Prescot L34 1LQ*

ENGELSEN, Christopher James. b 57. Nottm Univ BTh86. Linc Th Coll 83. **d** 86 **p** 87. C Sprowston *Nor* 86-89; C High Harrogate Ch Ch *Ripon* 89-92; TV Seacroft 92-95; P-in-c Foulsham w Hindolveston and Guestwick *Nor* 95-01; P-in-c Hevingham w Hainford and Stratton Strawless 01-05; R Coltishall w Gt Hautbois, Frettenham etc from 05. *The Rectory, Rectory Road, Coltishall, Norwich NR12 7HL* Tel (01603) 737255 E-mail christopher.engelsen@btinternet.com

ENGLAND (formerly LEFROY), Mrs Kathleen Christine. b 33. Newton Park Coll Bris TCert53. St Mich Ho Ox 56 Trin Coll Bris 90. **d** 90 **p** 02. Personnel Sec SAMS 83-91; Asst Gen Sec 87-92; rtd 92; NSM Eastbourne H Trin *Chich* 90-02; NSM Eastbourne St Jo 02-08; Perm to Offic from 08. *11 Holywell Close, Eastbourne BN20 7RX* Tel (01323) 640294 E-mail katieengland8@gmail.com

ENGLAND, Richard Alan. b 74. Sheff Univ BA97 Dur Univ MA07. Wycliffe Hall Ox 06. **d** 08 **p** 09. C Whitfield *Derby* from 08. *12 Rushmere, Glossop SK13 8TH* Tel (01457) 855993 E-mail richard@glossop.org

ENGLAND-SIMON, Haydn Henry. b 57. Llan Dioc Tr Scheme 92. **d** 96 **p** 97. NSM Penydarren *Llan* 96-97; C Caerphilly 97-01; V Pentre 01-07; V Ystradyfodwg from 07. *The Vicarage, 7 Llewellyn Street, Pentre CF41 7BY* Tel (01443) 433651

ENGLER, Mrs Margaret Dorothy. b 44. Lon Univ TCert77. S'wark Ord Course 90. **d** 93 **p** 94. NSM Harlesden All So *Lon* 93-97; Dep Chapl HM Pris Wandsworth 97; Acting Chapl HM Pris Wormwood Scrubs 97-98; Chapl HM Pris High Down 98-04; rtd 04; Perm to Offic *Lon* 04-07; NSM Harlesden All So from 07. *33 Sheppard's Colleges, London Road, Bromley BR1 1PE* Tel 07929-300048 (mobile) E-mail margaretengler@waitrose.com

ENGLISH, Peter Gordon. b 31. Edin Univ MA55. Ripon Hall Ox 59. **d** 61 **p** 62. C Bingley All SS *Bradf* 61-64; V Cottingley 64-66; Uganda 66-72; rtd 86; Perm to Offic *Sarum* from 96. *9 Carlton Row, Trowbridge BA14 0RJ* Tel (01225) 752243

ENGLISH, Philip Trevor. b 37. Dur Univ BSc60 FLIA81 MITPA84. Cranmer Hall Dur 60. **d** 62 **p** 63. C Hall Green Ascension *Birm* 62-66; Chapl St Jo Cathl Hong Kong 66-67; V Dorridge *Birm* 67-72; Perm to Offic *Ox* from 04. *Churchlands, Appletree Road, Chipping Warden, Banbury OX17 1LN* Tel (01295) 660222 Fax 660725 Mobile 07831-446421 E-mail pteifs@aol.com

ENNION, Peter. b 56. Aston Tr Scheme 85 Coll of Resurr Mirfield 87. **d** 89 **p** 90. C Middlewich w Byley *Ches* 89-91; C Aylestone St Andr w St Jas *Leic* 91-92; C Coppenhall *Ches* 92-94; P-in-c Newton in Mottram 94-99; P-in-c Tranmere St Paul w St Luke 99-04; V Torrisholme *Blackb* from 04. *The Ascension Vicarage, 63 Michaelson Avenue, Morecambe LA4 6SF* Tel (01524) 413144 E-mail ennipet@aol.com

ENNIS, Mrs Lesley. b 47. Bp Lonsdale Coll CertEd68 Open Univ BA84. OLM course 97. **d** 99 **p** 00. NSM Sowerby *Wakef* 99; NSM Norland from 99. *26 Springfield, Sowerby Bridge HX6 1AD* Tel (01422) 832747 Mobile 07703-628897 Fax 842747 E-mail lesleyennis@hotmail.co.uk

ENNIS, Martin Michael. b 58. Man Univ BSc80 MCollP84. Sarum & Wells Th Coll 87. **d** 89 **p** 90. C Newquay *Truro* 89-92; C Tewkesbury w Walton Cardiff *Glouc* 92-95; P-in-c Brockworth

95-96; V 96-03; Hon C Wotton St Mary 09-10; V Tividale *Lich* from 10. *26 View Point, Tividale, Oldbury B69 1UU* Tel (01384) 257888 E-mail frmennis@gmail.com

ENOCH, William Frederick Palmer. b 30. EMMTC 76. **d** 79 **p** 80. NSM Ilkeston St Mary *Derby* 79-85; P-in-c Ilkeston H Trin 85-95; rtd 95; Perm to Offic *Derby* from 95. *82 Derby Road, Ilkeston DE7 5EZ* Tel 0115-944 3003

ENSOR, Paul George. b 56. Ripon Coll Cuddesdon. **d** 82 **p** 83. C Newington St Mary *S'wark* 82-87; TV Croydon St Jo 87-91; P-in-c Brandon and Santon Downham *St E* 91-92; R Brandon and Santon Downham w Elveden 92-95; V Mitcham St Olave *S'wark* from 95. *St Olave's Vicarage, 22 Church Walk, London SW16 5JH* Tel (020) 8764 2048 E-mail pedrazzini@ukgateway.net

ENSOR, Canon Terence Bryan. b 45. K Coll Lon BD78 AKC78. Westcott Ho Cam 78. **d** 79 **p** 80. C Bermondsey St Hugh CD *S'wark* 79-82; Seychelles 82-85; V Northampton St Benedict *Pet* 85-90; Uruguay 90-93; Fieldworker USPG *Blackb, Bradf, Carl* and *Wakef* 93-96; V Blackb St Jas 96-02; Assoc P Caracas Venezuela 02-03; Hon Can Venezuela and Curazao from 02; TV Ribbleton *Blackb* 03-06; C Standish 06-11; rtd 11; Perm to Offic *Blackb* from 11. *7 Rectory Lane, Standish, Wigan WN6 0XA* Tel (01257) 421265 E-mail ensor@hotmail.co.uk

ENTICOTT, Ian Peter. b 59. Sheff Univ BA82 St Jo Coll Dur MA00. Cranmer Hall Dur 97. **d** 99 **p** 00. C Higher Bebington *Ches* 99-02; P-in-c Kelsall 02-10; Dir African Pastors' Fellowship from 10; Perm to Offic *Cov* from 10. *African Pastors' Fellowship, The Vicarage, Budbrooke, Warwick CV35 8QL* Tel and fax (01926) 402926 E-mail director@africanpastors.org *or* ian.enticott@dunelm.org.uk

ENTWISLE, George Barry. b 43. St Jo Coll Ox BA66 MA72 Massey Univ (NZ) MEd99. Linc Th Coll 73. **d** 75 **p** 76. C Rawmarsh w Parkgate *Sheff* 75-78; C Ashburton New Zealand 78-80; V Upper Clutha 80-84; V Gore 84-94; Can St Paul's Cathl Dunedin 87-94; Hon C Upper Clutha 01-06; rtd 08. *5 Bruce Street, Cromwell 9310, New Zealand* Tel and fax (0064) (3) 445 1797 Mobile 27-426 5539 E-mail b.entwistle@xtra.co.nz

ENTWISTLE, Christopher John. b 47. NOC 79. **d** 82 **p** 83. NSM Colne H Trin *Blackb* 82-84; C Poulton-le-Fylde 84-87; V Blackpool St Paul 87-96; RD Blackpool 94-96; P-in-c Overton 96-01; V Ashton-on-Ribble St Andr 01-06; TV W Preston 06-10; AD Preston 04-09; rtd 10; Perm to Offic *Blackb* from 10. *9 Chatsworth Avenue, Warton, Preston PR4 1BQ* Tel (01772) 460435 E-mail revcjentwistle@yahoo.co.uk

ENTWISTLE, Frank Roland. b 37. Dur Univ BA59. Cranmer Hall Dur 59. **d** 61 **p** 62. C Harborne Heath *Birm* 61-65; S Area Sec BCMS 65-66; Educn Sec 66-73; Hon C Wallington *S'wark* 68-73; UCCF 73-02; Hon C Ware Ch Ch *St Alb* 73-76; Hon C Leic H Trin w St Jo 76-02; rtd 02. *Three Gables, Tews Lane, Bickington, Barnstaple EX31 2JU* Tel (01271) 321861 E-mail entwistles@cwcom.net

ENTWISTLE, Howard Rodney. b 36. Ball Coll Ox BA61. Linc Th Coll 61. **d** 63 **p** 64. C Langley St Aid CD *Man* 63-66; C Langley All SS and Martyrs 64-66; V Wythenshawe St Martin 66-73; R Stretford St Matt 73-99; rtd 99; Perm to Offic *Ches* from 03. *3 Coombes Avenue, Marple, Stockport SK6 7BW* Tel 0161-427-6294

ENWUCHOLA, Canon Benjamin Ameh. b 56. Lon Bible Coll BA94. **d** 95 **p** 98. NSM S Tottenham St Ann *Lon* 96-99; NSM W Kilburn St Luke w St Simon and St Jude from 99; Chapl Nigerian Congregation from 99; Hon Can Ondo from 02. *St Marylebone Church, 17 Marylebone Road, London NW1 5LR* Tel (020) 7935 9478 Fax 7486 5493 *or* Tel and fax 8969 2379 E-mail benwuchola@yahoo.com *or* nigerianchaplaincy@yahoo.co.uk

EPPS, Christopher Derek. b 54. ACII79. Linc Th Coll 95. **d** 95 **p** 96. C Clevedon St Jo *B & W* 95-98; R St John w Millbrook *Truro* 98-03; P-in-c Truro St Geo and St Jo from 03; P-in-c Truro St Paul and St Clem from 03. *St George's Vicarage, St George's Road, Truro TR1 3NR* Tel (01872) 272630 Fax 823559 E-mail frdepps@btinternet.com

EPPS, Gerald Ralph. b 31. Open Univ BA79. Oak Hill Th Coll 52 K Coll Lon 54. **d** 57 **p** 58. C Slade Green *Roch* 57-60; V Freethorpe w Wickhampton *Nor* 60-70; P-in-c Halvergate w Tunstall 62-67; V 67-70; R Pulham St Mary Magd 70-80; P-in-c Alburgh 76-77; P-in-c Denton 76-77; P-in-c Pulham St Mary V 76-80; R Pulham 80-91; rtd 91; Perm to Offic *Nor* from 91. *10 Lime Close, Harleston IP20 9DG* Tel (01379) 854532

EPTON, John Alan. b 47. EMMTC 08. **d** 10 **p** 11. NSM Morton and Stonebroom w Shirland *Derby* from 10. *Phare, 22 Fernwood Close, Shirland, Alfreton DE55 6BW* Tel (01773) 834153

EQUEALL, Canon David Edward Royston. b 41. Open Univ BA. St Mich Coll Llan 68. **d** 71 **p** 72. C Mountain Ash *Llan* 71-74; C Gabalfa and Chapl Asst Univ Hosp of Wales Cardiff 74-77; Chapl 77-79; Chapl N Gen Hosp Sheff 79-94; Chapl N Gen Hosp NHS Trust Sheff 94-02; Chapl Manager Sheff Teaching Hosps NHS Trust 02-06; Hon Can Sheff Cathl 98-06; rtd 06. *4 Riverside Court, Dinnington, Sheffield S25 3PH* Tel (01909) 655355

ERIKSSON, Olaf Lennart. b 62. Ridley Hall Cam 03. **d** 05 **p** 06. C Cockerton *Dur* 05-09; P-in-c Millfield St Mark and Pallion St Luke from 09. *The Vicarage, St Mark's Terrace, Sunderland SR4 7BN* Tel 0191-565 1789

ERLEBACH, Jonathan Bartholomew (Bart). b 77. York Univ BSc99. Oak Hill Th Coll BA05. **d** 05 **p** 06. C Hove Bp Hannington Memorial Ch *Chich* 05-09; C Surbiton Hill Ch Ch *S'wark* from 09. *181 Elgar Avenue, Surbiton KT5 9JX* Tel (020) 8399 1503 Mobile 07714-379836 E-mail bartbev@erlebach.org.uk

✠**ERNEST, The Most Revd Gerald James Ian.** b 54. **p** 85 **c** 01. Bp Mauritius from 01; Abp Indian Ocean from 08. *Bishop's House, Nalletamby Avenue, Phoenix, Mauritius* Tel (00230) 686 5158 Fax 697 1096 E-mail dioang@intnet.mu

ERRIDGE, David John. b 45. Tyndale Hall Bris 66. **d** 69 **p** 70. C Bootle St Matt *Liv* 69-72; C Horwich H Trin *Man* 72-77; R Blackley St Andr 77-00; AD N Man 85-94; V Acomb St Steph *York* 00-10; rtd 10; Perm to Offic *York* from 11. *2 Nidderdale Close, Bridlington YO16 6FS* Tel (01262) 608036 E-mail djerridge@tiscali.co.uk

ERRIDGE, Timothy John. b 65. Wye Coll Lon BSc86 Croydon Coll CertEd90. St Jo Coll Nottm 08. **d** 10 **p** 11. C Congresbury w Puxton and Hewish St Ann *B & W* from 10. *7 Weetwood Road, Congresbury, Bristol BS49 5BN* Tel (01934) 833126 E-mail revtimerridge@gmail.com

ERRINGTON, Mrs Sarah. b 67. UEA BA90. Wycliffe Hall Ox BTh94. **d** 97 **p** 98. C Gateacre *Liv* 97-02; TV Halewood 02-10; TV Wrexham *St As* from 10. *The Vicarage, 160 Borras Road, Wrexham LL13 9ER* Tel (01978) 266018 E-mail sarah.errington@wrexhamparish.org.uk

ESAU, John Owen. b 39. St Mich Coll Llan 93. **d** 95 **p** 96. Min Can St D Cathl 95-97; V Llanpumsaint w Llanllawddog 97-01; V Cydweli and Llandyfaelog 01-03; R Aberporth w Tremain w Blaenporth and Betws Ifan 03-04; rtd 04. *28 Cwrt y Gloch, Peniel, Carmarthen SA32 7HW* Tel (01267) 220549

ESCOLME, Miss Doreen. b 29. St Jo Coll Nottm 82. **dss** 83 **d** 87 **p** 94. Hunslet Moor St Pet and St Cuth *Ripon* 83-87; C 87-88; Par Dn Wyther 88-94; C 94; rtd 94; Perm to Offic *Ripon* from 94. *6 Heather Gardens, Leeds LS13 4LF* Tel 0113-257 9055

ESCRITT, Canon Margaret Ruth. b 37. Selly Oak Coll IDC62. **d** 87 **p** 94. Dioc Adv for Diaconal Mins *York* 85-91; Hon C Selby Abbey 87-90; C Kexby w Wilberfoss 93-94; Asst Chapl HM Pris Full Sutton 92-94; Chapl HM Pris Everthorpe 95-98; Can and Preb York Minster 95-01; rtd 97; Perm to Offic *York* from 01. *73 Heslington Lane, York YO10 4HN* Tel (01904) 639444

ESDAILE, Canon Adrian George Kennedy. b 35. Mert Coll Ox BA57 MA61. Wells Th Coll 59. **d** 61 **p** 62. C St Helier *S'wark* 61-64; C Wimbledon 64-68; V Hackbridge and N Beddington 68-80; RD Sutton 76-80; TR Chipping Barnet w Arkley *St Alb* 80-01; RD Barnet 89-94; Hon Can St Alb 94-01; rtd 01; Perm to Offic *S'wark* from 01 and *Guildf* from 02. *29 Hereford Close, Epsom KT18 5DZ* Tel (01372) 723770 E-mail esdaileadrian@yahoo.co.uk

ESHUN, Daniel Justice. b 69. Cape Coast Univ Ghana BA93 K Coll Lon MA97 PhD00 St Jo Coll Dur MA03. Cranmer Hall Dur 00. **d** 03 **p** 04. C Staines *Lon* 03-06; C Kensal Town St Thos w St Andr and St Phil 06-07; Chapl Surrey Univ Roehampton from 07. *Whitelands College, Holybourne Avenue, London SW15 4JD* Tel (020) 8392 3500 E-mail daniel.eshun@yahoo.co.uk

ESPIN-BRADLEY, Richard John. b 61. Lanc Univ BSc84. Oak Hill Th Coll 93. **d** 95 **p** 96. C Brundall w Braydeston and Postwick *Nor* 95-98; C St Helier *S'wark* 98-02; V Wolverhampton St Luke *Lich* from 02. *St Luke's Vicarage, 122 Goldthorn Hill, Wolverhampton WV2 3HU* Tel (01902) 340261 E-mail richardeb@blueyonder.co.uk

ESSER, Lindsay Percy David. b 53. BA. Oak Hill Th Coll. **d** 84 **p** 85. C Barnsbury St Andr and H Trin w All SS *Lon* 84-87; Chapl Paris St Mich *Eur* 87-90; C Spring Grove St Mary *Lon* 90-95; Mauritius from 95. *The Rectory, St Barnabas Church, Royal Road, Pamplemousses, Mauritius* Tel (00230) 243 3549 E-mail st.barnabas@intnet.mu

ESSEX, Mary Rose. b 50. **d** 02 **p** 03. NSM E and W Leake, Stanford-on-Soar, Rempstone etc *S'well* 02-08; P-in-c Kirkby Woodhouse from 08. *The Vicarage, 57 Skegby Road, Kirkby-in-Ashfield, Nottingham NG17 9JE* Tel (01623) 759094 E-mail rev.maryessex@btopenworld.com

ETCHELLS, Peter. b 26. Kelham Th Coll 48. **d** 52 **p** 53. C Chesterton St Geo *Ely* 52-55; C Leic St Marg 55-58; R Willoughby Waterleys, Peatling Magna etc 58-96; rtd 96. *29 Upperfield Drive, Felixstowe IP11 9LS*

ETCHES, Haigh David. b 45. St Jo Coll Dur BA71. Cranmer Hall Dur. **d** 73 **p** 74. C Whitnash *Cov* 73-77; C Wallingford w Crowmarsh Gifford etc *Ox* 77-83; P-in-c Bearwood 83-86; R 86-11; rtd 11. *Silver Birches, 6 Chelmick Drive, Church Stretton SY6 7BP* Tel (01694) 723266 E-mail haigh.etches@btinternet.com

ETHERIDGE, Alastair. **d** 10 **p** 11. NSM Woking Ch Ch *Guildf* from 10. *110 Rydens Way, Woking GU22 9DJ* Tel (01483) 773728 E-mail ali.etheridge@christchurchwoking.org

ETHERIDGE, Canon Richard Thomas. b 32. Lon Univ BD62. ALCD61. **d** 62 **p** 63. C Wilmington *Roch* 62-65; C Rainham 65-69; V Langley St Jo *Birm* 69-01; P-in-c Oldbury 83-01; P-in-c Langley St Mich 95-01; Hon Can Birm Cathl 97-01; rtd 01; Perm to Offic *Birm* from 01 and *Worc* from 02. *23 Scobell Close, Pershore, Worcester WR10 1QJ* Tel (01386) 554745

ETHERIDGE, Terry. b 44. Wells Th Coll 68. **d** 70 **p** 71. C Barrow St Jo *Carl* 70-73; C Wilmslow *Ches* 73-76; V Knutsford St Cross 76-85; R Malpas and Threapwood 85-10; rtd 10. *12 School Road North, Rudheath, Northwich CW9 7TX* Tel (01606) 352343

ETHERINGTON (née SMITH), Mrs Elizabeth Anne. b 68. Keele Univ BA95. Ridley Hall Cam 04. **d** 06 **p** 07. C E Twickenham St Steph *Lon* from 06. *61 Elizabeth Gardens, Isleworth TW7 7BD* Tel 07903-112082 (mobile) E-mail libbyjesha@hotmail.com

ETHERINGTON, Mrs Ferial Mary Gould. b 44. Open Univ BA. St Alb Minl Tr Scheme 86. **d** 93 **p** 94. NSM Luton St Chris Round Green *St Alb* 93-04; Selection Sec and Co-ord for OLM Min Division 97-04; rtd 04; Perm to Offic *Carl* from 04; Dioc Min Review Officer 05-10; TV Cartmel Peninsula from 10. *The Vicarage, Station Road, Flookburgh, Grange-over-Sands LA11 7JY* Tel (015395) 58751 E-mail ferial.etherington@talktalk.net

ETHERINGTON, Robert Barry. b 37. Man Univ BA62. Linc Th Coll 62. **d** 64 **p** 65. C Linc St Jo 64-67; C Frodingham 67-69; V Reepham 69-78; Ind Chapl 70-78; Ind Chapl *St Alb* 78-88; V Luton St Chris Round Green 88-04; RD Luton 98-02; rtd 04; Perm to Offic *Carl* from 05. *The Vicarage, Station Road, Flookburgh, Grange-over-Sands LA11 7JY* Tel (015395) 58751

ETHERTON, Christopher Charles. b 47. UMIST BSc68. STETS 04. **d** 07 **p** 08. NSM Lower Sandown St Jo and Sandown Ch Ch *Portsm* 07-10; P-in-c Binstead from 10; P-in-c Havenstreet St Pet from 10. *The New Rectory, Pitts Lane, Ryde PO33 3SU* Tel (01983) 562890 Mobile 07906-238368 E-mail revd.etherton@uwclub.net

ETHERTON, Geoffrey Robert. b 74. Univ of Cen England in Birm BMus96. Trin Coll Bris BA01. **d** 02 **p** 03. C Trentham and Hanford *Lich* 02-03; C Hanley H Ev 03-06; Pioneer Min 04-06. *c/o Crockford, Church House, Great Smith Street, London SW1P 3AZ*

ETTERLEY, Peter Anthony Gordon. b 39. Kelham Th Coll 63 Wells Th Coll 66. **d** 68 **p** 69. C Gillingham St Aug *Roch* 68-71; Papua New Guinea 71-80; V Cleeve w Chelvey and Brockley *B & W* 80-84; V Seaton Hirst *Newc* 84-86; TR 86-96; P-in-c Longframlington w Brinkburn 96-00; V 00-04; P-in-c Felton 96-00; V 00-04; rtd 04. *4 Clive Terrace, Alnwick NE66 1LQ* Tel (01665) 606252 E-mail peter.etterley@tiscali.co.uk

EUNSON, Ms Lisa Kei. b 54. San Francisco State Univ BA78. Ch Div Sch of the Pacific (USA) MDiv01. **d** 01 **p** 02. C Burlingame USA 01-06; R Banchory *Ab* from 06; R Kincardine O'Neil from 06. *The Rectory, High Street, Banchory AB31 5TB* Tel (01330) 826045 Mobile 07917-886672 E-mail rev_lisa_eunson@yahoo.com

EUROPE, Bishop of Gibraltar in. *See* ROWELL, The Rt Revd Douglas Geoffrey

EUROPE, Suffragan Bishop in. *See* HAMID, The Rt Revd David

EUSTICE, Peter Lafevre. b 32. AKC56. **d** 57 **p** 58. C Finsbury Park St Thos *Lon* 57-60; C Redruth *Truro* 60-63; V Treslothan 63-71; V Falmouth All SS 71-76; R St Stephen in Brannel 76-97; rtd 97; Perm to Offic *Truro* from 97. *21 Gloucester Avenue, Carlyon Bay, St Austell PL25 3PT* Tel (01726) 817343

EVANS, Miss Alison Jane. b 66. Sheff Univ BSc87 Bris Univ PGCE93. Trin Coll Bris BA04. **d** 04 **p** 05. C Finham *Cov* 04-08; V Cov St Geo from 08. *St George's Vicarage, 101 Moseley Avenue, Coventry CV6 1HR* Tel (024) 7659 1994 E-mail aevans@talktalk.net

EVANS, The Ven Alun Wyn. b 47. Down Coll Cam BA70 MA73. Cuddesdon Coll 70. **d** 72 **p** 73. C Bargoed w Brithdir Llan 72-74; C Bargoed and Deri w Brithdir 74-75; C Coity w Nolton 75-77; V Cwmavon 77-81; Warden of Ords 80-81; V Llangynwyd w Maesteg 81-86; Prov Officer for Soc Resp w Cardiff Ch Ch 93-99; V Swansea St Mary w H Trin *S & B* 90-00; TR Cen Swansea 00-04; Can Res Brecon Cathl 00-04; V Cynwil Elfed and Newchurch *St D* 04-07; V Cynwyl Elfed w Newchurch and Trelech a'r Betws 07-09; P-in-c Llanarthne and Llanddarog from 09; Adn Carmarthen from 04. *The Vicarage, Llanddarog, Carmarthen SA32 8PA* Tel (01267) 275268 E-mail archdeacon.carmarthen@churchinwales.org.uk

EVANS, Mrs Amanda Jane. b 49. Rachel McMillan Teacher Tr Coll Lon CertEd70 Cant Ch Ch Univ Coll MA01. STETS 94. **d** 97 **p** 98. C Faversham *Cant* 97-01; TV Whitstable 01-06; Dioc Co-ord for Healing and Wholeness from 07. *The Vicarage, Vicarage Lane, Nonington, Dover CT15 4JT* Tel (01304) 842847 E-mail amanda.livingwell@btinternet.com

EVANS, Andrew. *See* EVANS, John Andrew

EVANS, Andrew. b 57. Southn Univ BEd80. S Dios Minl Tr Scheme 88. d 91 p 92. NSM Cricklade w Latton *Bris* 91-97; C Yatton Keynell 97-99; TV By Brook 99-00; R Hullavington, Norton and Stanton St Quintin 00-09; P-in-c Sherston Magna, Easton Grey, Luckington etc 06-09; Bp's Adv for Rural Min 00-09; Hon Can Bris Cathl 05-09; AD N Wilts 06-09; TR Bridport *Sarum* from 09; OCM from 00. *The Rectory, 84 South Street, Bridport DT6 3NW* Tel (01308) 422138 Mobile 07931-616329 E-mail canonandrewevans@gmail.com

EVANS, Andrew Eric. b 58. Sheff Univ LLB80 Solicitor 83. Trin Coll *Bris* 01. d 03 p 04. C Gt Bookham *Guildf* 03-06; P-in-c Broughton Gifford, Gt Chalfield and Holt *Sarum* from 06; C Atworth w Shaw and Whitley from 07; C Melksham 07-10; TR from 10; RD Bradford from 08. *The Rectory, Ham Green, Holt, Trowbridge BA14 7PZ* Tel (01225) 782289 E-mail goodevansitsandrew@tiscali.co.uk

EVANS, Anne. b 47. Ches Coll of HE MTh99. d 05 p 06. Broughton *Lich* from 05; OLM Myddle from 05; OLM Loppington w Newtown from 05. *The Fields, Welshampton, Ellesmere SY12 0NP* Tel (01948) 710206

EVANS, Canon Anthony Nigel. b 53. Nottm Univ BA74 Fitzw Coll Cam BA76. Westcott Ho Cam 74. d 77 p 78. C Sneinton St Cypr *S'well* 77-80; C Worksop Priory 80-83; V Nottingham St Geo w St Jo 83-88; R Ordsall 88-95; P-in-c Sutton in Ashfield St Mary 95-07; AD Newstead 01-05; Bp's Dom Chapl from 07; Hon Can S'well Minster 04-11. *8 Raysmith Close, Southwell NG25 0BG* Tel (01636) 816764 E-mail frtony@care4free.net

EVANS, Ashley Francis. b 58. Birm Univ BA79. WEMTC 00. d 03 p 04. C Kington w Huntington, Old Radnor, Kinnerton etc *Heref* 03-07; P-in-c Ewyas Harold w Dulas, Kenderchurch etc 07-10; R from 11; RD Abbeydore from 09. *The Rectory, Ewyas Harold, Hereford HR2 0EZ* Tel (01981) 240079 Mobile 07763-070177 E-mail ashley@castlefrome.freeserve.co.uk

EVANS, Brian. b 34. Open Univ BA86. St Deiniol's Hawarden 70. d 71 p 72. C Porthkerry *Llan* 71-72; C Barry All SS 72-75; V Abercynon 75-82; V Pendoylan w Welsh St Donats 82-87; R Maentwrog w Trawsfynydd *Ban* 87-99; rtd 99; Perm to Offic *Ban* from 99. *Madryn, 46 Glan Ysgethin, Talybont LL43 2BB* Tel (01341) 247965

EVANS, Caroline Mary. b 46. Ban Coll CertEd69. St Jo Coll Nottm. d 86 p 97. C Llanbeblig w Caernarfon and Betws Garmon etc *Ban* 86-88; Dn-in-c Bodedern w Llechgynfarwy and Llechylched etc 88-97; V 97; RD Llifon and Talybolion 96-97; R Llanfairfechan w Aber from 97. *The Rectory, Aber Road, Llanfairfechan LL33 0HN* Tel (01248) 680591

EVANS, Prof Christopher Francis. b 09. CCC Cam BA32 MA38 Ox Univ MA48 Southn Univ Hon DLitt77 Glas Univ Hon DD85 FBA91 FKC70. Linc Th Coll 33. d 34 p 35. C Southampton St Barn *Win* 34-38; Tutor Linc Th Coll 38-44; Chapl and Lect Linc Dioc Tr Coll 44-48; Chapl and Fell CCC Ox 48-58; Select Preacher Ox Univ 55-57; Select Preacher Cam Univ 59-60; Lightfoot Prof Div Dur Univ 58-62; Can Res Dur Cathl 58-62; Prof NT Studies K Coll Lon 62-77; rtd 77. *23 The Court, Fen End Road West, Knowle, Solihull B93 0AN* Tel (01564) 776233

EVANS, Christopher Idris. b 51. Chich Th Coll 74. d 77 p 78. C Gelligaer *Llan* 77-80; C St Andrews Major w Michaelston-le-Pit 80-81; V Llangeinor 81-87; V Watlington w Pyrton and Shirburn *Ox* 87-97; R Icknield from 97. *The Vicarage, Hill Road, Watlington OX49 5AD* Tel (01491) 612494 E-mail icknield@aol.com

EVANS, Christopher James Catherall. b 75. Oak Hill Th Coll. d 11. C Chadderton Ch Ch *Man* from 11. *23 Lindale Avenue, Chadderton, Oldham OL9 9DW* Tel 0161-628 1366

EVANS, Christopher Jonathan. b 43. AKC67 and 88. d 68 p 69. C Wednesfield St Thos *Lich* 68-71; C Dorridge *Birm* 71-74; V Marston Green 74-81; V Acocks Green 81-86; RD Yardley 84-86; V Hill 86-88; Area Officer COPEC Housing Trust 88-91; V Harborne St Pet 91-08; rtd 08; Perm to Offic *Heref* from 08. *5 The Square, Clun, Craven Arms SY7 9EY* Tel (01588) 640439 E-mail jo@evansj84.fsnet.co.uk

EVANS, Clive Richard. b 49. WEMTC 99. d 00 p 01. OLM Heref S Wye from 00. *14 St Vincents Cross, Lower Bullingham, Hereford HR2 6EL* Tel (01432) 270838 or 353717 E-mail clivelinda@clivevans11.wanadoo.co.uk

EVANS, Canon Clive Roger. b 59. Worc Coll Ox BA80 MA84. St Jo Coll Nottm 94. d 94 p 95. C Barton Seagrave w Warkton *Pet* 94-97; V Long Buckby w Watford 97-11; P-in-c W Haddon w Winwick and Ravensthorpe 03-11; V Long Buckby w Watford and W Haddon w Winwick from 11; RD Brixworth 01-09; Can Pet Cathl from 09. *The Vicarage, 10 Hall Drive, Long Buckby, Northampton NN6 7QU* Tel and fax (01327) 842909 E-mail cliverevans@tiscali.co.uk

EVANS, Canon Colin Rex. b 24. Reading Univ BA49. Linc Th Coll. d 57 p 58. C Boultham *Linc* 57-59; C Linc St Nic w St Jo Newport 59-62; V Linc St Mary-le-Wigford w St Martin 62-66; P-in-c Linc St Faith 63-66; R Bassingham 66-74; V Aubourn w Haddington 66-74; V Carlton-le-Moorland w Stapleford 66-74; R Skinnand 66-74; R Thurlby w Norton Disney 66-74; RD

EVANS, Daniel Barri. b 70. St Steph Ho Ox 01. d 03 p 04. C Weymouth H Trin *Sarum* 03-07; V Llwynderw *S & B* from 07. *Llwynderw Vicarage, Fairwood Road, West Cross, Swansea SA3 5JP* Tel (01792) 401903 Mobile 07948-692927 E-mail vicar.llwynderw@virgin.net

EVANS, Miss Daphne Gillian. b 41. Bible Tr Inst Glas 67 Trin Coll Bris IDC75. dss 83 d 87. Wenlock *Heref* 83-88; TD 87-88; rtd 88. *33 Light Oaks Avenue, Light Oaks, Stoke-on-Trent ST2 7NF* Tel (01782) 541218

EVANS, Canon David. b 37. Keble Coll Ox BA60 MA65 Lon Univ BD64. Wells Th Coll 62. d 64 p 65. Min Can Brecon Cathl 64-68; C Brecon w Battle 64-68; C Swansea St Mary and H Trin 68-71; Chapl Univ of Wales (Swansea) 68-71; Bp's Chapl for Samaritan and Soc Work *Birm* 71-75; Jt Gen Sec Samaritans 75-84; Gen Sec 84-89; R Heyford w Stowe Nine Churches *Pet* 89-96; R Heyford w Stowe Nine Churches and Flore etc 96-01; Chapl Northants Police 89-01; RD Daventry 96-00; Can Pet Cathl 97-01; rtd 01; Perm to Offic *Ex* from 01. *Curlew River, The Strand, Starcross, Exeter EX6 8PA* Tel (01626) 891712

EVANS, David. b 37. Open Univ BA73 FRSA95. St Mich Coll Llan 65. d 67 p 68. C Swansea St Pet *S & B* 67-70; C St Austell *Truro* 70-75; R Purley *Ox* 75-90; RD Bradfield 85-90; R Bryanston Square St Mary w St Marylebone St Mark *Lon* 90-99; P-in-c St Marylebone St Cypr 90-91; R Nuthurst and Mannings Heath *Chich* 99-07; P-in-c 07-11; rtd 11. *10 Eastgate Mews, Brighton, Horsham RH13 5AW* Tel (01403) 581394

EVANS (*or* BURTON), David Burton. b 35. Open Univ BA87 Goldsmiths' Coll Lon BMus93. K Coll Lon 58 Edin Th Coll 60. d 62 p 63. C Leeds St Hilda *Ripon* 62-63; C Cross Green St Sav and St Hilda 63-67; Min Can Dur Cathl 67-71; PV Chich Cathl and Chapl Prebendal Sch 71-74; R Lynch w Iping Marsh *Chich* 74-79; V Easebourne 79-86; Chapl K Edw VII Hosp Midhurst 77-86; R St Mich Cornhill w St Pet le Poer etc *Lon* 86-96; rtd 96; Pau *Eur* 96-01; Perm to Offic from 05. *128 Little Breach, Chichester PO19 5UA* Tel (01243) 773266 Mobile 07795-662991 E-mail evtherev7@btinternet.com

EVANS, David Elwyn. b 43. St Mich Coll Llan 71. d 73 p 74. C Llandybie *St D* 73-75; C Llanelli 75-78; V Tre-lech a'r Betws w Abernant and Llanwinio 78-02; rtd 02. *8 Ger y Llan, The Parade, Carmarthen SA31 1LY*

EVANS, David Frederick Francis. b 35. Univ of Wales BSc59. Wells Th Coll 59. d 61 p 62. C Eltham St Jo *S'wark* 61-64; C Banbury *Ox* 64-69; V Brize Norton and Carterton 69-73; V Tilehurst St Geo 73-84; V Lydney w Aylburton *Glouc* 84-95; V Lydney 95-02; RD Forest S 90-95; Chapl Severn NHS Trust 94-02; rtd 02. *2 Bodforis, Braichmelyn, Bethesda, Bangor LL57 3PU* Tel (01248) 601994

EVANS, David John. b 49. Univ of Wales (Ban) BSc72 Bath Univ CertEd73. Coll of Resurr Mirfield 75. d 78 p 79. C Wandsworth St Anne *S'wark* 78-81; C Angell Town St Jo 81-82; TV Catford (Southend) and Downham 82-90; P-in-c Broughton *Ely* 90-91; P-in-c Somersham w Pidley and Oldhurst 90-91; R 91-98; R Hilgay from 98; R Southery from 98; RD Fincham and Feltwell from 09. *The Rectory, Church Road, Hilgay, Downham Market PE38 0JL* Tel (01366) 384418 E-mail cofe1@btinternet.com

EVANS, David Julian James. b 65. Rob Coll Cam BA87. Westcott Ho Cam 03. d 05 p 06. C W Hackney St Barn *Lon* 05-08; C St John-at-Hackney 08-10; V Walworth St Chris *S'wark* from 10; Warden Pemb Coll Miss Walworth from 10. *76 Tatum Street, London SE17 1QR* Tel (020) 7740 6382 E-mail davidjjevans@me.com

EVANS, David Leslie Bowen. b 28. Univ of Wales (Lamp) BA52 LTh54. d 54 p 55. C Cardigan *St D* 54-57; C Llangathen w Llanfihangel Cilfargen 57-58; C Betws w Ammanford 58-60; V Betws Ifan 60-64; V Burry Port and Pwll 64-76; V Cardiff Dewi Sant *Llan* 76-86; Asst Chapl HM Pris Cardiff 76-86; V Llan-llwch w Llangain and Llangynog *St D* 86-95; Can St D Cathl 89-90; rtd 96. *35 Ger y Capel, Llangain, Carmarthen SA33 5AQ* Tel (01267) 241916

EVANS, David Richard. b 47. St Steph Ho Ox 68. d 72 p 73. C Cardiff St Jo *Llan* 72-76; PV Llan Cathl 76-80; V Cleeve Prior and The Littletons *Worc* from 80. *The Vicarage, South Littleton, Evesham WR11 8TJ* Tel and fax (01386) 830397 E-mail father.richard@tesco.net

✠EVANS, The Rt Revd David Richard John. b 38. G&C Coll Cam BA63 MA66. Clifton Th Coll 63. d 65 p 66 c 78. C Enfield Ch Ch Trent Park *Lon* 65-68; SAMS Argentina 69-77; Peru 77-88; Bp Peru 78-88; Bp Bolivia 82-88; Asst Bp Bradf 88-93; Gen Sec SAMS 93-03; Hon Asst Bp Chich 94-97; Hon Asst Bp Roch 95-97; Hon Asst Bp Birm 97-03; rtd 03; Hon Asst Bp Cov from 03; Hon C Alderminster and Halford 03-07; Hon C Butlers Marston and the Pillertons w Ettington 03-07; Hon C Stourdene Gp 07-10. *30 Charles Street, Warwick CV34 5LQ* Tel (01926) 258791 E-mail bishop.drjevans@virgin.net

EVANS, David Russell. b 36. Liv Univ BA57. Ripon Hall Ox 59. d 61 p 62. C Netherton CD *Liv* 61-65; Chapl Canon Slade Sch Bolton 65-93; Lic Preacher *Man* 65-09; Perm to Offic from 09. *2 Rushford Grove, Bolton BL1 8TD* Tel (01204) 592981

EVANS, Derek. b 38. St As Minl Tr Course 93. d 97 p 98. NSM Llangollen w Trevor and Llantysilio *St As* 97-00; NSM Corwen and Llangar w Gwyddelwern and Llawrybetws 00-02; NSM Betws Gwerful Goch w Llangwm, Gwyddelwern etc 02-05; P-in-c Gwyddelwern 05-08; rtd 09. *Fern Mount, 68 Berwyn Street, Llangollen LL20 8NA* Tel (01978) 861893

EVANS, Canon Derek. b 45. St D Coll Lamp. d 68 p 69. C Pembroke Dock *St D* 68-74; V Ambleston, St Dogwells, Walton E and Llysyfran 74-78; V Wiston w Ambleston, St Dogwells and Walton E 78-81; V Wiston w Ambleston, St Dogwells, Walton E etc 81-85; R Haverfordwest St Mary and St Thos w Haroldston 85-09; Dep Dioc Dir of Educn 92-97; Dir 97-09; Can St D Cathl 99-09; RD Roose 00-04; rtd 09. *Thimble Cottage, Milford Road, Haverfordwest SA61 1PJ* E-mail derek.evans0@talk21.com

EVANS, Desmond. b 26. Univ of Wales (Lamp) BA48 St Cath Soc Ox BA50 MA54. St Steph Ho Ox 48. d 51 p 52. C Clydach *S & B* 51-54; V 82-87; Chapl Cranleigh Sch Surrey 54-59; Lic to Offic *Ban* 59-78; St Mary's Coll Ban 59-78; V Llanwrtyd w Llanddulas in Tir Abad etc *S & B* 78-82; RD Builth 79-82; V Abercraf and Callwen 87-95; rtd 95. *26 Palleg Road, Lower Cwmtwrch, Swansea SA9 2QE* Tel (01639) 845839

EVANS, Canon Edward John. b 47. St Mich Coll Llan 67. d 71 p 72. C Llantwit Fardre 71-77; R Eglwysilan 77-88; V Laleston w Tythegston and Merthyr Mawr 88-09; V Laleston and Merthyr Mawr from 09; RD Bridgend 94-04; Hon Can Llan Cathl from 07. *The Vicarage, Rogers Lane, Laleston, Bridgend CF32 0LD* Tel and fax (01656) 654254 Mobile 07968-044583 E-mail edward@laleston.org.uk

EVANS, Elaine. See EVANS, Jennifer Elaine

EVANS, Ms Elaine. b 63. St Mich Coll Llan BTh02. d 02 p 03. C Llantwit Major 02-05; C Penarth All SS 05-09; P-in-c Pontypridd St Matt and Cilfynydd w Llanwynno from 09. *The Vicarage, 40 Heol-y-Plwyf, Ynysybwl, Pontypridd CF37 3HU* Tel (01443) 790340

EVANS, Elwyn David. b 36. Keble Coll Ox BA58 MA62. St Steph Ho Ox 58 St Mich Coll Llan 60. d 61 p 62. C Aberystwyth H Trin *St D* 61-63; C Llanelli St Paul 63-66; C Roath St German *Llan* 66-69; V Crynant 69-78; R Llanilid w Pencoed 79-95; rtd 95; Perm to Offic *Llan* and *S & B* from 95. *23 Christopher Rise, Pontlliw, Swansea SA4 9EN* Tel (01792) 891961

EVANS, Ernest Maurice. b 28. JP70. MIMechE66. St As Minl Tr Course 84. d 86 p 87. NSM Hope *St As* 86-89; P-in-c Corwen and Llangar w Gwyddelwern and Llawrybetws 89-90; R 90-95; rtd 95; Perm to Offic *Ban* from 97. *43 Cil-y-Graig, Llanfairpwllgwyngyll LL61 5NZ* Tel (01248) 712169 E-mail e.mauriceevans@btinternet.com

EVANS, Ms Freda Christine. b 48. MBE89. NTMTC 96. d 99 p 00. C Hampton Hill *Lon* 99-02; V Kingshurst *Birm* 02-08; TR Erdington from 08. *The Vicarage, 26 Church Road, Birmingham B24 9AX* Tel 0121-373 0884

EVANS, Mrs Freda Mary Ann (Frieda). b 54. St D Coll Lamp 95. d 00 p 05. OLM Malpas *Mon* 00-09; OLM Caerleon and Llanfrechfa from 09. *3 The Firs, Malpas, Newport NP20 6YD* Tel (01633) 850600 Mobile 0411-650088 E-mail frieda@evafirs.freeserve.co.uk

EVANS, Frederick James Stephens. b 21. Qu Coll Cam BA42 MA46. St D Coll Lamp LTh44. d 44 p 45. C Shirley *Birm* 44-47; R Scotter w E Ferry *Linc* 47-65; CF (TA) 48-51; R Chalfont St Peter *Ox* 65-78; V Rustington *Chich* 78-86; rtd 86; Perm to Offic *Chich* from 86. *45 Falmer Avenue, Goring-by-Sea, Worthing BN12 4SY* Tel (01903) 503905

EVANS, Canon Frederick John Margam. b 31. Magd Coll Ox BA53 MA57. St Mich Coll Llan 53. d 54 p 55. C New Tredegar *Mon* 54-58; C Chepstow 58-60; Asst Chapl United Sheff Hosps 60-62; Chapl Brookwood Hosp Woking 62-70; V Crookham *Guildf* 70-98; RD Aldershot 78-83; Hon Can Guildf Cathl 89-98; rtd 98; Perm to Offic *Guildf* from 98. *4 Radford Close, Farnham GU9 9AB* Tel and fax (01252) 710594 E-mail johnjunee@btinternet.com

EVANS, Gareth Rae. b 48. MCIPD. Ripon Coll Cuddesdon 96. d 98 p 99. C Chepstow *Mon* 98-00; TV Cwmbran 00-07; Hon C Torquay St Martin Barton *Ex* from 07. *4 Froude Avenue, Torquay TQ2 8NS*

EVANS, Genevieve Sarah. b 62. Univ of Wales (Cardiff) BA04. St Mich Coll Llan 02. d 04 p 05. C Whalley Range St Edm and Moss Side etc *Man* 04-08; V Walsall Pleck and Bescot *Lich* from 08; C Walsall St Matt from 08; C Walsall St Paul from 08. *St John's Vicarage, Vicarage Terrace, Walsall WS2 9HB* Tel (01922) 639805 E-mail rev.gen@tiscali.co.uk

EVANS, Canon Geoffrey Bainbridge. b 34. Lambeth MA94. St Mich Coll Llan 56. d 58 p 59. C Llan All SS CD 58-60; C Llandaff N 60-67; Guyana 67-73; Chapl Izmir (Smyrna) w Bornova *Eur* 73-94; Adn Aegean 78-94; Can Malta Cathl 78-00; Chapl Ankara 85-91; Chapl Istanbul 87-89; Chapl Rome 94-99; Chapl Moscow 99; P-in-c Ankara 00-11. *Sehit Ersan Caddesi*

32/12, Cankaya, Ankara 06680, Turkey Tel (0090) (312) 467 8276 or 455 3285 Fax 455 3352 E-mail gb evans@hotmail.com

EVANS, Geoffrey David. b 44. Ex Univ PGCE74. K Coll Lon BD69 AKC69 St Aug Coll Cant 69. d 70 p 71. C Lawrence Weston *Bris* 70-73; Chapl Grenville Coll Bideford 74-79; Chapl Eastbourne Coll 79-82; Chapl Taunton and Somerset Hosp 83-91; Chapl Musgrove Park Hosp 83-91; Chapl Taunton Sch 92-04; rtd 09. *Milton House, 75 Wellsway, Bath BA2 4RU* Tel (01225) 335632 E-mail bidabid@yahoo.co.uk

EVANS, Mrs Gillian. b 39. Imp Coll Lon BSc61. Mon Dioc Tr Scheme 84. d 88 p 94. NSM Penallt and Trellech *Mon* 88-89; NSM Overmonnow w Wonastow and Michel Troy 89-92; Dioc Ecum Officer and C Ludlow, Ludford, Ashford Carbonell etc *Heref* 92-95; Pakistan 95-96; Perm to Offic *Heref* 96-06; Hon C Dawlish *Ex* 97-98; TV Golden Cap Team *Sarum* 98-01; rtd 01; Perm to Offic *Cov* and *Mon* 01-06; Hon C Wolford w Burmington *Cov* 06-08; Hon C Cherington w Stourton 06-08; Hon C Barcheston 06-08; Hon C Long Compton, Whichford and Barton-on-the-Heath 06-08; Hon C S Warks Seven Gp from 08. *16 The Long Close, Stourton, Shipston-on-Stour CV36 5HT* Tel (01608) 685773

EVANS, Glyn. b 59. Nene Coll Northn BA80 Leic Univ BA80 Ch Ch Coll Cant CertEd82 Kent Univ PGCE82. Qu Coll Birm 85. d 88 p 89. C Denton *Newc* 88-92; V Choppington 92-97; P-in-c Longhorsley and Hebron 97-01; Chapl HM Pris Acklington 97-01; P-in-c Newc St Andr and St Luke from 01; City Cen Chapl from 01. *12 The Glebe, Stannington, Morpeth NE61 6HW* Tel 0191-232 7935 or 232 0259

EVANS, Canon Glyn Peter. b 54. Leeds Univ BA75. Ripon Coll Cuddesdon 76. d 77 p 78. C Binley *Cov* 77-80; C Clifton upon Dunsmore w Brownsover 80-84; P-in-c Lacock w Bowden Hill *Bris* 84-89; P-in-c Lt Compton w Chastleton, Cornwell etc *Ox* 89-00; Agric Chapl 89-00; Dioc Rural Officer from 00; Hon Can Ch Ch from 05. *Upper Chelmscote Cottage, Brailes, Banbury OX15 5JJ* Tel (01608) 686749 Mobile 07581-491713 E-mail glynevansrro@tiscali.co.uk *or* glynevans@goldserve.net

EVANS, Godfrey. See EVANS, Joseph Henry Godfrey

EVANS, Canon Gwyneth Mary. b 43. Gilmore Ho 69 Linc Th Coll 70. dss 74 d 87 p 94. Stamford Hill St Thos *Lon* 74-79; Chapl Asst R Free Hosp Lon 79-89; Chapl Salisbury Health Care NHS Trust 89-01; Can and Preb Sarum Cathl 96-01; rtd 01; Perm to Offic *Sarum* from 01. *39 The Close, Salisbury SP1 2EL* Tel (01722) 412546

EVANS, Canon Henry Thomas Platt. b 28. Selw Coll Cam BA51 MA55. Linc Th Coll 51. d 53 p 54. C Lt Ilford St Barn *Chelmsf* 53-56; C-in-c Stocking Farm CD *Leic* 56-58; V Stocking Farm 58-67; R Stretford St Matt *Man* 67-73; V Knighton St Mary Magd *Leic* 73-83; Hon Can Leic Cathl 76-93; RD Christianity S 81-83; Warden Launde Abbey 83-93; P-in-c Loddington 83-92; rtd 93; Perm to Offic *Leic* from 93. *157 Avenue Road, Leicester LE2 3ED*

EVANS (née TAYLOR), Mrs Hilary Elizabeth. b 57. d 03 p 04. OLM Reddish *Man* 03-11; NSM Hulme Ascension from 11. *13 Lindfield Road, Stockport SK5 6SD* Tel 0161-442 3023 E-mail hilary@mojomusica.freeserve.co.uk

EVANS, Hilary Margaret. b 49. Redland Coll of Educn TDip71 Ches Coll of HE BTh97. NOC 94. d 97 p 98. C Heald Green St Cath *Ches* 97-00; P-in-c Davyhulme Ch Ch *Man* 00-03; P-in-c Blackley St Pet 03-09; AD N Man 06-08; rtd 09; Hon C SW Gower *S & B* from 09. *The Rectory, Church Meadow, Reynoldston, Swansea SA3 1AF* Tel (01792) 392963 E-mail hilary@evanses.plus.com

EVANS, Huw David. b 68. Sheff Univ BEng90 PGCE91. Trin Coll Bris BA98. d 98 p 02. C Sherborne w Castleton and Lillington *Sarum* 98-99; NSM Martock w Ash *B & W* 01-04; CF from 04. *c/o MOD Chaplains (Army)* Tel (01264) 381140 Fax 381824

EVANS, Mrs Jane. b 59. W Midl Coll of Educn BEd81. d 03 p 04. OLM Lilleshall and Muxton *Lich* from 03. *5 Collett Way, Priorslee, Telford TF2 9SL* Tel (01952) 291340 E-mail revjane@talktalk.net

EVANS, Mrs Jennifer. b 41. Ilkley Coll DipEd62. Sarum Th Coll 88. d 88. Par Dn Bramshott *Portsm* 88-91; Par Dn Bramshott and Liphook 91-92; Par Dn Whippingham w E Cowes 92-95; Par Dn Sarisbury 95-05; Hon C Llawhaden w Bletherston and Llanycefn *St D* 08-10; Hon C Slebech and Uzmaston w Boulston 08-10; Hon C Chaffcombe, Cricket Malherbie etc *B & W* from 10. *34 Tansee Hill, Thorncombe, Chard TA20 4LQ* Tel (01460) 30844 E-mail jennie.honeycombs@virgin.net

EVANS, Mrs Jennifer. b 43. d 01. NSM New Tredegar *Mon* 01-05; NSM Bedwellty w New Tredegar from 05. *4 Glynsifi, Elliots Town, New Tredegar NP24 6DE* Tel (01443) 836798

EVANS, Jennifer Elaine. b 59. Wolv Univ BA92. Qu Coll Birm 00. d 02 p 03. C Stafford St Jo and Tixall w Ingestre *Lich* 02-06; TV Stafford from 06. *St Bertelin's Vicarage, 36 Holmcroft Road, Stafford ST16 1JF* Tel (01785) 252874

EVANS, Jill. See EVANS, Mrs Gillian

EVANS, Mrs Joan. b 36. Nor Tr Coll TCert57 UEA BEd94. d 02 p 03. OLM Loddon, Sisland, Chedgrave, Hardley and Langley

Nor 02-06; rtd 06; Perm to Offic *Nor* from 06. *13 Drury Lane, Loddon, Norwich NR14 6LB* Tel (01508) 528656
E-mail joanevans936@btinternet.com

EVANS, John. See EVANS, Canon Frederick John Margam

EVANS, John Andrew. b 53. Hull Univ BSc74 Univ of Wales MSc75 Bris Univ BA96. Trin Coll Bris 94. **d** 96 **p** 97. C Walton H Trin *Ox* 96-98; C Caversham St Pet and Mapledurham etc 98-01; R Bradford Abbas and Thornford w Beer Hackett *Sarum* 01-09; V N Hayes St Nic *Lon* from 09. *St Nicholas' Vicarage, Raynton Drive, Hayes UB4 8BG* Tel (020) 8573 4122 Mobile 07725-805437 E-mail j_andrew_evans@btconnect.com

EVANS, John David Vincent. b 41. CQSW78. Lich Th Coll 66. **d** 68 **p** 70. C Kingsthorpe *Pet* 68-69; C Corby Epiphany w St Jo 69-72; Bp's Adv in Children's Work 72-74; Probation Officer 74-90; Perm to Offic 88-90; R Green's Norton w Bradden 90-91; R Greens Norton w Bradden and Lichborough 91-96; V Northampton Ch Ch 96-06; rtd 06; Perm to Offic *Pet* 06-09. *Ivy Cottage, Creaton Road, Hollowell, Northampton NN6 8RP* Tel (01604) 743878 E-mail revjohnwenevans@yahoo.co.uk

EVANS, Canon John Griffiths. b 37. Glouc Th Course 76. **d** 77 **p** 77. Hd Master Corse Sch Glos 86-90; C Hartpury w Corse and Staunton *Glouc* 77-79; P-in-c 79-09; P-in-c Maisemore 01-09; Hon Can Glouc Cathl 96-09; rtd 09. *Elm House, Gadfield Elms, Staunton, Gloucester GL19 3PA* Tel (01452) 840302

EVANS, John Laurie. b 34. Pretoria Univ BSc54 Imp Coll Lon BSc55 Rhodes Univ BA59. Ripon Coll Cuddesdon 84. **d** 86 **p** 87. C Bruton and Distr *B & W* 86-89; P-in-c Ambrosden w Merton and Piddington *Ox* 89-91; C Pet St Mary Boongate 91-93; V Michael *S & M* 93-96; R Ballaugh 93-96; rtd 96; Chapl Allnutt's Hosp Goring Heath 96-99; P-in-c Fochabers *Mor* 99-00; P-in-c Strathnairn St Paul 00-03; TV Langtree *Ox* 03-07; Hon C Kelso *Edin* from 07; Hon C Coldstream from 07. *The Cottage, Pressen Farm, Cornhill-on-Tweed TD12 4RS* Tel (01890) 850309 Mobile 07909-986369 E-mail jonevansscotland@btinternet.com

EVANS, John Miles. b 39. Yale Univ BA61 JD67 St Cath Coll Cam BA64 MA68. NY Th Sem MDiv93. **d** 95 **p** 95. Chapl St Jo Cathl Oban 95-97; USA from 97; Interim R Lynbrook Ch Ch 98-99; R Davidsonville All Hallows 99-05. *PO Box 1272, Portsmouth NH 03802-1272, USA*

EVANS, John Rhys. b 45. Hull Univ BSc66. Sarum & Wells Th Coll 77. **d** 79 **p** 80. C Alton St Lawr *Win* 79-82; C Tadley St Pet 82-85; V Colden 85-91; V Bitterne Park 91-01; C Ringwood 01-11; Chapl R Bournemouth and Christchurch Hosps NHS Trust 01-11; rtd 11. *The Cottage, Alderley, Wotton-under-Edge GL12 7QT* E-mail johnrhyevans@yahoo.co.uk

EVANS, John Ronald. b 16. Univ of Wales BA40. St Mich Coll Llan 41. **d** 42 **p** 44. C Rhosllannerchrugog *St As* 42-45; C Holywell 45-54; V Glyndyfrdwy 54-81; RD Edeyrnion 64-81; Dioc Sec SPCK 66-81; rtd 81. *22 Glebe Avenue, Hardingstone, Northampton NN4 6DG*

EVANS, John Stuart. b 57. Univ of Wales (Abth) BA78 Bretton Hall Coll PGCE81. Trin Coll Bris BA98. **d** 98 **p** 99. C Connah's Quay *St As* 98-02; V Rhosllannerchrugog 02-10; AD Llangollen 05-10; R Ruthin w Llanrhydd and Llanfwrog from 10. *The Cloisters, School Road, Ruthin LL15 1BL* Tel (01824) 702068 E-mail jsevans@surfaid.org

EVANS, Canon John Thomas. b 43. St Mich Coll Llan 66. **d** 67 **p** 68. C Connah's Quay *St As* 67-71; C Llanrhos 71-74; Chapl Rainhill Hosp Liv 74-78; TV Wrexham *St As* 78-83; V Holywell 83-96; RD Holywell 95-96; V Colwyn Bay 96-99; V Colwyn Bay w Brynymaen 99-02; RD Rhos 00-02; R Caerwys and Bodfari 02-08; Can Cursal St As Cathl 96-08; rtd 08. *25 Everard Road, Rhos-on-Sea, Colwyn Bay LL28 4EY* Tel (01492) 540506 Mobile 07905-861174 E-mail johnbethevans@btinternet.com

✠**EVANS, The Rt Revd John Wyn.** b 46. FSA88 FRHistS94 Univ of Wales (Cardiff) BA68 BD71. St Mich Coll Llan 68. **d** 71 **p** 72 **c** 08. C St D Cathl 71-72; Min Can St D Cathl 72-75; Perm to Offic *Ox* 75-77; Dioc Archivist *St D* 76-82; R Llanfallteg w Clunderwen and Castell Dwyran etc 77-82; Warden of Ords 78-83; Dioc Dir of Educn 82-92; Chapl Trin Coll Carmarthen 82-90; Dean of Chpl 90-94; Hd Th and RS 91-94; Hon Can St D Cathl 88-90; Can St D Cathl 90-94; Dean St D 94-08; V St D Cathl 94-01; TR Dewisland 01-08; Bp St D from 08. *Llys Esgob, Abergwili, Carmarthen SA31 2JG* Tel (01267) 236597 E-mail bishop.stdavids@churchinwales.org.uk

EVANS, Jonathan Alan. b 53. Fitzw Coll Cam BA75 PGCE77 MA79. St Jo Coll Nottm MA95. **d** 95 **p** 96. C Drypool *York* 95-98; V Beverley St Nic from 98. *St Nicholas' Vicarage, 72 Grovehill Road, Beverley HU17 0ER* Tel (01482) 881458 E-mail evansfamily@macunlimited.net

EVANS, Joseph Henry Godfrey. b 31. Univ of Wales (Lamp) BA50 St Mary's Coll Chelt CertEd75 Kingston Poly 89. Qu Coll Birm 53. **d** 55 **p** 56. C Hackney St Jo *Lon* 55-58; C Stonehouse *Glouc* 58-60; V Selsley 60-65; V Cheltenham St Pet 65-74; R Willersey w Saintbury 74-77; Chapl Tiffin Sch Kingston 74-94; rtd 95; Perm to Offic *S'wark* from 01. *300 Raeburn Avenue, Surbiton KT5 9EF* Tel (020) 8390 0936

EVANS, Mrs Judith Ann. b 55. SEITE 99. **d** 02 **p** 03. C Crayford *Roch* 02-06; P-in-c Kells *Carl* from 06; Chapl N Cumbria Univ

Hosps NHS Trust from 06. *St Peter's Vicarage, Cliff Road, Whitehaven CA28 9ET* Tel (01946) 692496 Mobile 07929-978523 E-mail revdjudyevans@btopenworld.com

EVANS, Canon Keith. b 57. Trin Coll Carmarthen CertEd81 BEd82. St D Coll Lamp BA84 Sarum & Wells Th Coll 84. **d** 85 **p** 86. C Swansea St Thos and Kilvey *S & B* 85-87; C Gorseinon 87-89; V Oxwich w Penmaen and Nicholaston 89-94; Dir Post-Ord Tr from 93; R Ystradgynlais 94-98; V Oystermouth from 98; Hon Can Brecon Cathl from 04. *The Vicarage, 9 Western Close, Mumbles, Swansea SA3 4HF* Tel (01792) 369971

EVANS, Kenneth. b 50. Bp Burgess Hall Lamp. **d** 74 **p** 75. C Llanaber w Caerdeon *Ban* 74-79; C Upper Clapton St Matt *Lon* 79-82; P-in-c Tottenham St Phil 82-95; V from 95. *St Philip's Vicarage, 226 Philip Lane, London N15 4HH* Tel and fax (020) 8808 4235 E-mail fr kenmjd@tiscali.co.uk

EVANS, Kenneth Roy. b 47. Lon Univ BSc FRSA96. Ridley Hall Cam 79. **d** 81 **p** 81. C Stratford-on-Avon w Bishopton *Cov* 81-82; C Trunch *Nor* 82-85; Chapl Mapperley Hosp Nottm 85-89; Chapl Nottm Mental Illness and Psychiatric Unit 85-94; Chapl Notts Healthcare NHS Trust from 94; Lic to Offic *S'well* from 85; Dir Scarborough Psychotherapy Tr Inst from 03. *117 Columbus Ravine, Scarborough YO12 7QU* Tel (01723) 376246 E-mail ken@kenevans.fsnet.co.uk

EVANS, Kevin Stuart. b 56. Bris Poly CQSW80. Qu Coll Birm 93. **d** 95 **p** 96. C Madeley *Heref* 95-98; P-in-c Wombridge *Lich* from 98; TV Cen Telford from 05. *Wombridge Vicarage, Wombridge Road, Telford TF2 6HT* Tel (01952) 613334

EVANS, Mrs Linda Joyce. b 54. Trin Coll Bris BA06. **d** 06 **p** 07. NSM Weston super Mare Ch Ch and Em *B & W* 06-10; P-in-c Dale and St Brides w Marloes *St D* from 10; P-in-c Herbrandston and Hasguard w St Ishmael's from 10. *The Vicarage, Castle Way, Dale, Haverfordwest SA62 3RN* Tel (01646) 636966 E-mail landevans79@aol.com

EVANS, Linda Mary. See EDWARDS, Mrs Linda Mary

EVANS, Miss Madeleine Thelma Bodenham. b 30. K Coll Lon BD76 AKC76. Gilmore Course 80. dss 85 **d** 87 **p** 94. Chapl Pipers Corner Sch 85-91; Par Dn Calne and Blackland *Sarum* 91-94; C 94-00; Chapl St Mary's Sch Calne 91-99; rtd 00; Perm to Offic *Sarum* from 00. *11 Fairway, Rookery Park, Calne SN11 0LB* Tel and fax (01249) 814755

EVANS, Ms Margaret Elizabeth. b 48. Leeds Univ BA69 Lon Inst of Educn CertEd70. Oak Hill Th Coll 91. **d** 94 **p** 95. NSM Canonbury St Steph *Lon* from 94. *St Stephen's Canonbury, 17 Canonbury Road, London N1 2DF* Tel (020) 7226 7526 or 7359 4343 E-mail margareteevans@hotmail.com

EVANS, Mark Roland John. b 55. St Cath Coll Cam MA81 Bris Univ PGCE78. WEMTC 01. **d** 04 **p** 05. NSM Frenchay and Winterbourne Down *Bris* 04-08; NSM Frampton Cotterell and Iron Acton 08; NSM Winterbourne 08. *60 High Street, Thornbury, Bristol BS35 2AN* Tel (01454) 414101 Mobile 07702-289385 E-mail mark.evans@bathwells.anglican.org

EVANS, Martin Lonsdale. b 69. Man Univ BA91. Ripon Coll Cuddesdon 93. **d** 95 **p** 96. C Morpeth *Newc* 95-98; Chapl RN from 98. *Royal Naval Chaplaincy Service, Mail Point 1-2, Leach Building, Whale Island, Portsmouth PO2 8BY* Tel (023) 9262 5055 Fax 9262 5134

EVANS, Matthew Scott. b 72. Grey Coll Dur BA93. Cranmer Hall Dur 96. **d** 98 **p** 99. C Fountains Gp *Ripon* 98-03; P-in-c Dacre w Hartwith and Darley w Thornthwaite from 03; Jt AD Ripon from 09. *The Vicarage, Dacre Banks, Harrogate HG3 4ED* Tel (01423) 780262

EVANS, Michael. b 49. St Jo Coll Nottm 88. **d** 90 **p** 91. C Beeston *S'well* 90-93; P-in-c Kirkby in Ashfield St Thos 93-97; V 97-08; Chapl Notts Healthcare NHS Trust 93-08; rtd 08. *2 Westminster Avenue, Kirkby-in-Ashfield, Nottingham NG17 7HY* Tel (01623) 759537 Mobile 07825-223189 E-mail munnamonk@aol.com

EVANS, Michael John. b 53. **d** 00 **p** 01. OLM Longnor, Quarnford and Sheen *Lich* 00-04; OLM Ipstones w Berkhamsytch and Onecote w Bradnop 04-11; P-in-c from 11. *The Vicarage, Church Lane, Ipstones, Stoke-on-Trent ST10 2LF* Tel (01538) 266313 E-mail revdmjevans@btinternet.com

EVANS, Neil Robert. b 54. Lon Univ MA93 K Coll Lon DMin10. Coll of Resurr Mirfield. **d** 84 **p** 85. C Bethnal Green St Jo w St Bart *Lon* 84-86; C St Jo on Bethnal Green 87-88; P-in-c Stoke Newington Common St Mich 88-95; V 95-98; V Twickenham All Hallows 98-05; Kensington Area CME Officer 98-05; Par Min Development Adv Willesden Area 05-07; Dir Tr and Development from 07. *23 St Albans Avenue, London W4 5LL* Tel (020) 8987 7332 E-mail neil.evans@london.anglican.org

EVANS, Nicholas Anthony Paul. b 60. Sheff Univ BA81 Liv Univ PGCE86. Qu Coll Birm 84. **d** 84 **p** 87. C Ludlow *Heref* 84-85; C Sunbury *Lon* 86-92; Hd RE Guildf Co Sch 93-99; NSM Crookham *Guildf* 94-99; CF 99-02; V Shenley Green *Birm* from 02. *St David's Vicarage, 49 Shenley Green, Birmingham B29 4HH* Tel 0121-475 4874 Mobile 07769-550204 E-mail evansnick@aol.com

EVANS, Nigel William Reid. b 70. Sheff Hallam Univ BEd96. Ridley Hall Cam BTh01. **d** 01 **p** 02. C Ossett and Gawthorpe *Wakef* 01-05; V Loddon, Sisland, Chedgrave, Hardley and

Langley *Nor* 05-10; RD Loddon 06-10; TR Bucknall *Lich* from 10. *The Rectory, 151 Werrington Road, Bucknall, Stoke-on-Trent ST2 9AQ* Tel (01782) 280661 E-mail nigel.evans4@tesco.net

EVANS, Norman Cassienet. b 30. Keble Coll Ox MA54. Guildf Dioc Min Course 91. **d** 95 **p** 96. OLM Seale, Puttenham and Wanborough *Guildf* 95-00; Perm to Offic from 00. *Hoplands, Riversmeet, Tilford, Farnham GU10 2BW* Tel (01252) 782933 E-mail norman@thereverend.fsnet.co.uk

EVANS, Mrs Patricia Rosemary. b 47. **d** 01 **p** 05. Par Dn Panteg *Mon* 01-03; Par Dn Panteg w Llanfihangel Pontymoile from 03. *Pentwyn Farm, Glascoed, Pontypool NP4 0TX* Tel and fax (01495) 785285 Mobile 07814-783714

EVANS, The Ven Patrick Alexander Sidney. b 43. Linc Th Coll 70. **d** 73 **p** 74. C Lyonsdown H Trin *St Alb* 73-76; C Royston 76-78; V Gt Gaddesden 78-82; V Tenterden St Mildred w Smallhythe *Cant* 82-89; Adn Maidstone 89-02; Hon Can Cant Cathl 89-02; Dir of Ords 89-93; Adn Cant and Can Res Cant Cathl 02-07; rtd 07. *1 Streamside, Main Road, Tolpuddle, Dorchester DT2 7FD* Tel (01305) 849484 E-mail patrickevans120@hotmail.co.uk

EVANS, Peter. b 35. St Aid Birkenhead 57. **d** 60 **p** 61. C Higher Bebington *Ches* 60-63; C W Kirby St Bridget 63-66; P-in-c Lower Tranmere 66-68; V Flimby *Carl* 68-74; V Kirkby Ireleth 74-79; P-in-c Kirkbride w Newton Arlosh 79-80; R 80-85; V Beckermet St Jo and St Bridget w Ponsonby 85-97; rtd 97; Perm to Offic *Carl* from 98. *26 Gelt Close, Carlisle CA3 0HJ*

EVANS, Peter. b 40. S'wark Ord Course 75. **d** 75 **p** 76. C Welling S'wark 75-78; C Sutton New Town St Barn 78-81; C Kingston All SS w St Jo 81-87; V Croydon Woodside 87-99; TV Sanderstead All SS 99-03; rtd 03. *174 Main Street, Stanton-under Bardon, Markfield LE67 9TP* Tel (01530) 243470

EVANS, Peter Anthony. b 36. Imp Coll Lon BScEng57. St Steph Ho Ox 58. **d** 60 **p** 61. C Surbiton St Mark *S'wark* 60-63; Asst Chapl Lon Univ 63-64; C S Kensington St Luke 64-68; C Surbiton St Andr and St Mark *S'wark* 68-69; C Loughton St Jo *Chelmsf* 69-74; P-in-c Becontree St Geo 74-82; Perm to Offic 82-89; NSM Romford St Alb 89-93; NSM Coopersale 93-95; NSM Epping Distr 95-96; rtd 97; Perm to Offic *Chelmsf* from 97. *6 Woodhall Crescent, Hornchurch RM11 3NN* Tel (01708) 509399

EVANS, Peter Gerald. b 41. Man Univ BA71. AKC65. **d** 65 **p** 66. C Kidbrooke St Jas *S'wark* 65-68; C Fallowfield *Man* 68-71; C Brockley Hill St Sav *S'wark* 71-73; P-in-c Colchester St Botolph w H Trin and St Giles *Chelmsf* 74-79; V 79-92; Perm to Offic from 93. *97 Northgate Street, Colchester CO1 1EY* Tel (01206) 543297

EVANS, Peter Kenneth Dunlop. b 38. Ch Coll Cam BA60. St D Coll Lamp 72. **d** 74 **p** 75. C Roath *Llan* 74-77; V Buttington and Pool Quay *St As* 77-87; V Llanfair Caereinion w Llanllugan 87-03; rtd 03. *Stepaside, Llanfair Caereinion, Welshpool SY21 0HU* Tel (01686) 627076

EVANS, Richard. *See* EVANS, David Richard

EVANS, Richard Edward Hughes. b 14. Univ of Wales BA44. St Mich Coll Llan. **d** 45 **p** 46. C Nantymoel *Llan* 45-48; C Pontyberem *St D* 48-50; C Llandeilo Fawr 50-53; V Ysbyty Cynfyn 53-64; V Llanybydder and Llanwenog w Llanwnnen 64-72; V Llanychaiarn 72-79; rtd 79. *23 Gwarfelin, Llanilar, Aberystwyth SY23 4PE* Tel (01974) 241357

EVANS, Richard Gregory. b 50. St Mich Coll Llan 69. **d** 73 **p** 74. C Oystermouth *S & B* 73-76; C Clydach 76-79; CF 78-81; V Llanddew and Talachddu *S & B* 79-83; Youth Chapl 79-83; Hon Min Can Brecon Cathl 79-83; Chapl Huntley Sch New Zealand 83-87; Chapl Nga Tawa Sch 83-90; Chapl Wanganui Sch from 90. *Wanganui Collegiate School, Private Bag 3002, Wanganui 4540, New Zealand* Tel (0064) (6) 349 0281 ext 8750 Fax 348 8302 E-mail rgevans@collegiate.school.nz

EVANS, Richard Trevor. b 33. Jes Coll Ox MA58 DipEd58. St And Dioc Tr Course 73. **d** 76 **p** 76. NSM Leven *St And* 76-95; NSM St Andrews St Andr from 95. *33 Huntingtower Park, Whinnyknowe, Glenrothes KY6 3QF* Tel and fax (01592) 741670 E-mail revans9973@blueyonder.co.uk

EVANS, Robert. *See* EVANS, Simon Robert

EVANS, Canon Robert Arthur. b 24. Univ of Wales (Cardiff) BA48. St Mich Coll Llan 48. **d** 50 **p** 51. C Aberdare St Fagan *Llan* 50-52; C Roath 52-57; C Llandaff w Capel Llanilltern 57-61; Asst Chapl Mersey Miss to Seamen 61-62; Chapl Supt Mersey Miss to Seamen 62-74 and 79-89; Chapl RNR 67-89; V Rainhill *Liv* 74-79; Perm to Offic *Ches* 79-91; Hon Can Liv Cathl 88-92; rtd 89; Perm to Offic *Liv* 89-05. *1 Floral Wood, Riverside Gardens, Liverpool L17 7HR* Tel 0151-727 3608

EVANS, Robert Charles. b 55. K Coll Lon BA77 AKC77 MA78 MTh89 Qu Coll Cam BA80 MA83 CertEd85. Westcott Ho Cam 79. **d** 81 **p** 87. C St Breoke *Truro* 81-83; C St Columb Minor and St Colan 83-84; Chapl Rob Coll Cam 87-92; Lect Ches Univ from 92. *University of Chester, Parkgate Road, Chester CH1 4BJ* Tel (01244) 510000

EVANS, Robert George Roger. b 49. Cam Univ MA. Trin Coll Bris 74 St Jo Coll Nottm 94. **d** 77 **p** 78. C Bispham *Blackb* 77-80; C Chadwell *Chelmsf* 80-84; V Ardsley *Sheff* 84-09; P-in-c Kendray 04-09; Chapl Barnsley Community & Priority Services

NHS Trust 98-00; rtd 09. *73 High Street, Wombwell, Barnsley S73 8HS* Tel (01226) 345635 E-mail rgrevans@gmail.com

EVANS, Robert Stanley. b 51. Univ of Wales (Lamp) BA72 Univ of Wales (Cardiff) PGCE73. St Mich Coll Llan 90. **d** 92 **p** 93. C Penarth All SS *Llan* 92-95; R Gelligaer 95-99; V Roath 99-04; R Coychurch, Llangan and St Mary Hill 04-06; rtd 06. *13 Priory Gardens, Barry CF63 1FH* Tel (01446) 407606

EVANS, Ronald. b 47. St Mich Coll Llan 85. **d** 87 **p** 88. C Flint *St As* 87-91; TV Wrexham 91-97; V Rhosymedre 97-99; V Rhosymedre w Penycae 99-05; PV Connah's Quay from 05. *8 Eurgain Avenue, Connah's Quay, Deeside CH5 4PW* Tel (01244) 812101 E-mail godshelp2002@yahoo.com

EVANS, Ronald Wilson. b 47. Windsor Univ Ontario BA69 Dalhousie Univ MA83. Trin Coll Toronto MDiv73. **d** 72 **p** 73. Canada 72-98; R Springhill 73-76; Chapl Univ of Prince Edw Is 76-79; Lect 82-85; Chapl King's-Edgehill Sch 85-87; R Clements 87-98; Lect Bilgi Univ Istanbul 98-00; Asst Chapl Izmir (Smyrna) w Bornova *Eur* 00-03; P-in-c 03-04; Chapl from 04. *PK 1005, Pasaport, Izmir 35120, Turkey* Tel (0090) (232) 463 7263 *or* tel and fax 464 5753 E-mail seljuk85@hotmail.com

EVANS, Roy Clifford. b 39. Qu Coll Birm 04. **d** 05 **p** 05. Chapl Univ Hosp Birm NHS Foundn Trust 05-07; NSM Billesley Common *Birm* 05-07; Chapl Countess of Chester Hosp NHS Foundn Trust 07-11; Perm to Offic *Lich* from 08; Clergy Widows Visitor from 11. *Hawthorn Cottage, Llandrinio, Llanymynech SY22 6SB* Tel (01691) 831389 Mobile 07791-398923 E-mail brother.evans@tesco.net

EVANS, Rupert Alexander. b 81. St Cath Coll Cam BA02. Wycliffe Hall Ox MTh10. **d** 10 **p** 11. C Crowborough *Chich* from 10. *1 Croft Cottages, Church Road, Crowborough TN6 1ED* Tel (01892) 652513 E-mail rupertaevans@gmail.com

EVANS, Mrs Sarah Rosemary. b 64. Trevelyan Coll Dur BA85. STETS 05. **d** 08 **p** 09. NSM Hullavington, Norton and Stanton St Quintin *Bris* from 08; NSM Sherston Magna, Easton Grey, Luckington etc from 08. *The Deanery Office, The Old Squash Court, Holloway, Malmesbury SN16 9BA* Tel (01666) 818228 E-mail sarah.evans@deanery.org.uk

EVANS, Sheila Jean. *See* ROBERTSON, Mrs Sheila Jean

EVANS, Canon Simon. b 55. Newc Univ BA77 Heythrop Coll Lon MA06. St Steph Ho Ox 78. **d** 80 **p** 81. C Pet St Jude 80-84; Chapl Asst Pet Distr Hosp 80-84; C Wantage *Ox* 84-87; V W Leigh *Portsm* 87-96; Chapl E Hants Primary Care Trust 88-96; V Ruislip St Martin *Lon* from 96; AD Hillingdon from 08; Can Wiawso Ghana from 08. *The Vicarage, 13 Eastcote Road, Ruislip HA4 8BE* Tel (01895) 633040 *or* 625456 E-mail frsimon@waitrose.com

EVANS, Simon Andrew. b 59. Sarum & Wells Th Coll 81. **d** 84 **p** 85. C Norbury St Steph and Thornton Heath *S'wark* 84-88; C Putney St Mary 88-92; P-in-c Telford Park St Thos 92-94; V 94-04; V Ensbury Park *Sarum* from 04. *St Thomas's Vicarage, 42 Coombe Avenue, Bournemouth BH10 5AE* Tel (01202) 519735 E-mail simon@evansonline.info

EVANS, Simon Robert. b 58. Reading Univ BSc79. NOC 99. **d** 02 **p** 03. C Pudsey St Lawr and St Paul *Bradf* 02-04; P-in-c Low Moor 04-05; TV Oakenshaw, Wyke and Low Moor 06-07; TR 07-10; P-in-c Harden and Wilsden from 10; P-in-c Denholme from 10; P-in-c Cullingworth from 10. *The Vicarage, Wilsden Old Road, Harden, Bingley BD16 1JD* Tel (01535) 273758 E-mail vicarbob@talktalk.net *or* bob.evans@bradford.anglican.org

EVANS, Stanley George. b 43. CITC 00. **d** 03 **p** 04. Aux Min Killaloe w Stradbally *L & K* 03-04; P-in-c Killarney w Aghadoe and Muckross 04-05; Aux Min Leighlin w Grange Sylvae, Shankill etc *C & O* 05-09; Perm to Offic *L & K* from 09. *Killernan, Milltown Malbay, Co Clare, Republic of Ireland* Tel (00353) (65) 708 4970 Mobile 87-636 9473 E-mail stanevans@eircom.net

EVANS, Stanley Munro. b 30. AKC53. **d** 54 **p** 55. C Norbury St Oswald *Cant* 54-57; C St Laur in Thanet 57-63; V Bredgar 63-71; V Bredgar w Bicknor and Huckinge 71-72; V Westgate St Sav 72-01; rtd 01; Perm to Offic *Cant* from 01. *40 Queen Bertha Road, Ramsgate CT11 0ED* Tel (01843) 594459

EVANS, Stephen John. b 60. Dartmouth RN Coll 81 St Steph Ho Ox BA85 MA89 Aber Univ MPhil94. **d** 86 **p** 87. Prec St Andr Cathl Inverness 86-89; R Montrose and P-in-c Inverbervie *Bre* 89-91; Miss to Seamen 89-91; V Northampton St Paul *Pet* 91-98; Continuing Minl Educn Officer 94-00; Liturg Officer 96-03; P-in-c Ecton and Warden Ecton Ho 98-00; R Uppingham w Ayston and Wardley w Belton *Pet* 00-10; Can Pet Cathl 03-10; RD Rutland 03-10; R St Marylebone w H Trin *Lon* from 10. *21 Beaumont Street, London W1G 6DQ* Tel (020) 7935 8965 E-mail stephen@stephenjevans.wanadoo.co.uk

EVANS, Steven Edward. b 52. CBDTI 97. **d** 00 **p** 01. NSM Caton w Littledale *Blackb* 00-05; NSM Hornby w Claughton and Whittington etc 05-06; NSM Slyne w Hest and Halton w Aughton 06-08; Perm to Offic from 08. *Brookhouse Hall, Brookhouse Road, Brookhouse, Lancaster LA2 9PA* Tel (01524) 771827

EVANS, Stuart. *See* EVANS, John Stuart

EVANS, Ms Susan Mary. b 55. St Jo Coll Dur BA76 CertEd77 Nottm Univ BCombStuds84. Linc Th Coll 81. **dss** 84 **d** 87 **p** 94. Weaste *Man* 84-88; Par Dn 87-88; Par Dn Longsight St Luke 88-92; Par Dn Claydon and Barham *St E* 92-94; C 94-99; P-in-c Henley 95-99; Chapl HM YOI Hollesley Bay Colony 99-02; NSM Henley, Claydon and Barham *St E* 02-06; Chapl HM Pris Whatton 06-09. *The Rectory, 15 Hillview Road, South Witham, Grantham NG33 5QW* Tel (01572) 767240

EVANS, Terence. b 35. St Mich Coll Llan 67. **d** 69 **p** 70. C Loughor *S & B* 69-73; C Gowerton w Waunarlwydd 73-77; V Llanbister and Llanbadarn Fynydd w Llananno 77-82; V Llanyrnewydd 82-01; rtd 01. *28 Orchard Court, New Orchard Street, Swansea SA1 5EN*

EVANS, Terence Robert. b 45. NOC 82. **d** 85 **p** 86. C Warrington St Elphin *Liv* 85-88; V Cantril Farm 88-94; V Rainhill 94-03; R Odd Rode *Ches* 03-10; rtd 10. *65 Harpur Crescent, Alsager, Stoke-on-Trent ST7 2SX* Tel (01270) 878209 E-mail evans338@btinternet.com

EVANS, Timothy Simon. b 57. York Univ BA79 Sussex Univ MA81 Fitzw Coll Cam BA85 MA88. Ridley Hall Cam 83. **d** 87 **p** 88. C Whitton St Aug *Lon* 87-90; C Ealing St Steph Castle Hill 90-93; P-in-c Shireshead *Blackb* 93-97; Asst Chapl Lanc Univ 93-97; Vice Prin LCTP 97-09; P-in-c Natland *Carl* 97-09; C Old Hutton and New Hutton 06-09; RD Kendal 00-03; Hon Can Carl Cathl 00-09; Dir Past Studies and Tutor Yorks Min Course from 09. *The Yorkshire Ministry Course, The Mirfield Centre, Stocks Bank Road, Mirfield WF14 0BW* Tel (01924) 481926 E-mail tim@ymc.org.uk

EVANS, Trevor Owen. b 37. Univ of Wales BSc59. Coll of Resurr Mirfield 59. **d** 61 **p** 62. C Llanaber w Caerdeon *Ban* 61-64; C Llandudno 64-70; TV 70-75; V Llanidloes w Llangurig 75-89; RD Arwystli 75-89; Can and Preb Ban Cathl 82-98; Dioc Adv on Spirituality 84-03; R Trefdraeth 89-90; Dir of Min 89-98; R Llanfairpwll w Penmynydd 90-98; Dean Ban 98-03; RD Ogwen 99-03; rtd 03. *Hafan, 3 Coed y Castell, Bangor LL57 1PH* Tel (01248) 352855

EVANS, Mrs Wendy Nicola. b 59. St Jo Coll Dur BA11. Cranmer Hall Dur 09. **d** 11. C Oulton Broad *Nor* from 11. *3 Windward Way, Lowestoft NR33 9HF* Tel (01502) 580637 Mobile 07971-082603 E-mail wendy.evans2009@gmail.com

EVANS, William James Lynn. b 30. St D Coll Lamp 73. **d** 75 **p** 76. P-in-c Penbryn and Blaenporth *St D* 75-77; V Penbryn and Betws Ifan w Bryngwyn 77-79; V Penrhyncoch and Elerch 79-83; V Cynwil Elfed and Newchurch 83-87; V Llandybie 87-95; rtd 95. *5 Dolau Tywi, Manordeilo, Llandeilo SA19 7BL* Tel (01550) 777944

EVANS, Wyn. See EVANS, The Rt Revd John Wyn

EVANS-HILLS, Ms Bonnie Jean. b 57. Westcott Ho Cam. **d** 09 **p** 10. C Leic Resurr 09-10; C Oadby from 10. *11 Fludes Court, Oadby, Leicester LE2 4QQ* Tel (0116) 271 8177

EVANS-PUGHE, Thomas Goronwy. b 29. TCD. Wycliffe Hall Ox 59. **d** 61 **p** 62. C Grassendale *Liv* 61-63; P-in-c Mossley Hill St Matt and St Jas 63-64; C 64-65; Prec Chelmsf Cathl 65-69; R Birchanger 69-94; rtd 94; Perm to Offic *Glouc* from 94. *Bath Orchard, Blockley, Moreton-in-Marsh GL56 9HU* Tel (01386) 701223

EVANS-SMITH, Brian George. b 49. **d** 02 **p** 03. OLM S Ramsey St Paul *S & M* 02-06; P-in-c Lezayre from 06. *41 Barrule Park, Ramsey, Isle of Man IM8 2BR* Tel (01624) 817322

EVASON, Stuart Anthony. b 44. Salford Univ BSc. Chich Th Coll 79. **d** 81 **p** 82. C Heref St Martin 81-85; TV Cleethorpes *Linc* 85-87; TV Howden *York* 87-92; V Heywood St Jas *Man* 92-03; P-in-c Barrow St Jas *Carl* 03-10; TR Barrow St Matt 06-09; rtd 10; Perm to Offic *Man* from 10. *17 Drake Hall, Westhoughton, Bolton BL5 2RA* Tel (01942) 810128 E-mail s.evason@gmail.com

EVE, David Charles Leonard. b 45. AKC74. St Aug Coll Cant 74. **d** 75 **p** 76. C Hall Green Ascension *Birm* 75-79; TV Kings Norton 79-84; V Rowley Regis 84-93; Perm to Offic *Heref* 94-98 and from 01; *Worc* from 05; NSM Hallow and Grimley w Holt *Worc* 98-05. *14 Orchard End, Cleobury Mortimer, Kidderminster DY14 8BA* Tel (01299) 270510 E-mail gabrielle.davideve@btinternet.com

EVE, Hilary Anne. See FIFE, Hilary Anne

EVE, Canon Ian Halliday. b 33. St Paul's Coll Grahamstown LTh59. **d** 59 **p** 60. S Africa 59-80 and from 81; P-in-c Salcombe *Ex* 80-81; Can Cape Town from 86. *Christ Church Rectory, Main Road, Constantia, 7800 South Africa* Tel (0027) (21) 794 6352 or 794 5051 Fax 794 1065

EVELEIGH, Raymond. b 36. Univ of Wales (Cardiff) BSc58. NW Ord Course 73. **d** 76 **p** 77. NSM S Cave and Ellerker w Broomfleet *York* 76-79; P-in-c Kingston upon Hull St Mary 79-82; Chapl Hull Coll of FE 79-01; V Anlaby Common St Mark *York* 82-94; V Langtoft w Foxholes, Butterwick, Cottam etc 94-01; rtd 01; Perm to Offic *York* from 04. *Pasture Lodge, West End, Kilham, Driffield YO25 4RR* Tel (01262) 420060 E-mail rev@revray.co.uk

EVENS, Jonathan Adrian Harvey. b 63. Middx Poly BA84 Middx Univ BA03 ACIPD90. NTMTC 00. **d** 03 **p** 04. C Barking

St Marg w St Patr *Chelmsf* 03-06; V Gt Ilford St Jo from 06. *St John's Vicarage, 2 Regent Gardens, Ilford IG3 8UL* Tel (020) 8590 5884 E-mail jonathan.evens@btinternet.com

EVENS, Robert Alan. b 51. **d** 00 **p** 01. NSM Sharnbrook and Knotting w Souldrop *St Alb* 00-03; P-in-c Wymington w Podington 03-05; R Sharnbrook, Felmersham and Knotting w Souldrop from 05. *The Rectory, 81 High Street, Sharnbrook, Bedford MK44 1PE* Tel (01234) 782000 E-mail robert.evens@lineone.net

✠**EVENS, The Rt Revd Robert John Scott.** b 47. ACIB74. Trin Coll Bris 74. **d** 77 **p** 78 **c** 04. C Southsea St Simon *Portsm* 77-79; C Portchester 79-83; V Locks Heath 83-96; RD Fareham 93-96; Adn Bath and Preb Wells Cathl 96-04; Suff Bp Crediton *Ex* from 04. *32 The Avenue, Tiverton EX16 4HW* Tel (01884) 250002 Fax 258454 E-mail bishop.of.crediton@exeter.anglican.org

EVENSON, Bruce John. b 46. Wittenberg Univ Ohio BA68. Lutheran Sch of Th Chicago MDiv72. **d** 98 **p** 98. C Charleston Grace Ch USA 98-02; Chapl Porter-Gaud Sch Charleston 01-02; Chapl Stockholm w Gävle and Västerås *Eur* 02-05. *Bovikvagen 547, AX-22240 Hammarland, Aland, Finland* Tel (00358) (18) 37754 E-mail ebruceven@gmail.com

EVEREST, Canon John Cleland. b 45. Sarum Th Coll 66. **d** 68 **p** 69. C Moulsecoomb *Chich* 68-71; C Easthampstead *Ox* 71-74; C Southwick St Mich *Chich* 74-77; Dioc Soc Services Adv *Worc* 77-84; Ind Chapl 84-93; R Worc City St Paul and Old St Martin etc 84-93; RD Worc E 89-93; TR Halas 93-10; RD Dudley 95-98; Hon Can Worc Cathl 90-10; rtd 10. *18 Tunnel Hill, Worcester WR4 9RP* Tel (01905) 723305 E-mail cleland@tunnelhill.plus.com

EVERETT, Alan Neil. b 57. St Cath Coll Ox BA79 DPhil96 SS Coll Cam BA84. Westcott Ho Cam 82. **d** 85 **p** 86. C Hindley All SS *Liv* 85-88; Chapl Qu Mary Coll *Lon* 88-91; V S Hackney St Mich w Haggerston St Paul 94-10; V Notting Dale St Clem w St Mark and St Jas from 10. *12 St Anns Villas, London W11 4RS* Tel (020) 7221 3548 E-mail alan@n16.org.uk

EVERETT, Anthony William. b 60. S Bank Poly BA82. Oak Hill Th Coll BA89. **d** 89 **p** 90. C Hailsham *Chich* 89-92; C New Malden and Coombe *S'wark* 92-97; V Streatham Park St Alb 97-02; V Herne Bay Ch Ch *Cant* from 02; Asst Dir of Ords 05-09. *Christ Church Vicarage, 38 Beltinge Road, Herne Bay CT6 6BU* Tel (01227) 374906 or 366640 E-mail anthony@fayland.freeserve.co.uk

EVERETT, Mrs Christine Mary. b 46. St Osyth Coll of Educn CertEd67. Westcott Ho Cam 90. **d** 92 **p** 94. Par Dn Ipswich St Fran *St E* 92-94; C 94-95; C Gt and Lt Bealings w Playford and Culpho 96; P-in-c 96-02; P-in-c Creeting St Mary, Creeting St Peter etc from 02; rtd 11. *35 Chainhouse Road, Needham Market, Ipswich IP6 8TB* Tel (01449) 720319 Mobile 07980-023236 E-mail chrstevr@aol.com

EVERETT, Colin Gerald Grant. b 44. Open Univ BA77 Keswick Hall Coll CertEd. Ripon Coll Cuddesdon 79. **d** 81 **p** 82. C Aston cum Aughton *Sheff* 81-84; R Fornham All SS and Fornham St Martin w Timworth *St E* 84-92; P-in-c Old Newton w Stowupland 92-94; C Ipswich All Hallows 94-95; TV Ipswich St Fran 95-97; TV Ipswich St Mary at Stoke w St Pet and St Fran 97-09; rtd 09; Perm to Offic *St E* from 09. *35 Chainhouse Road, Needham Market, Ipswich IP6 8TB* Tel (01449) 720319 E-mail revcolin@btinternet.com

EVERETT, David Gordon. b 45. Pemb Coll Ox BA67 MA. Lon Coll of Div 68. **d** 70 **p** 71. C Hatcham St Jas *S'wark* 70-73; C Reading St Jo *Ox* 73-77; TV Fenny Stratford and Water Eaton 77-82; Hon C Bletchley 82-87; C Loughton 84-85; NSM Stantonbury and Willen 87-92; Chapl Ox Brookes Univ 92-96; NSM Iffley 93-96; C Treslothan *Truro* 96-97; C Crowan and Treslothan 98-02; Chapl Camborne Pool Redruth Coll 98-02; R Ketton, Collyweston, Easton-on-the-Hill etc *Pet* 03-10; rtd 10. *35 Lower Pengegon, Pengegon, Camborne TR14 7UJ*

EVERETT, David John. b 51. Leeds Univ BA07. NOC 04. **d** 07 **p** 08. NSM Moor Allerton and Shadwell *Ripon* 07-11; V Market Weighton *York* from 11; R Goodmanham from 11; V Sancton from 11. *The Vicarage, 38 Cliffe Road, Market Weighton, York YO43 3BN* Tel (01430) 872808 E-mail david.j.everett51@gmail.com

EVERETT, Canon John Wilfred. b 37. Qu Coll Cam BA61 MA65. Cuddesdon Coll 64. **d** 66 **p** 67. C St Helier *S'wark* 66-69; C Yeovil St Jo w Preston Plucknett *B & W* 69-73; R Wincanton 73-82; R Pen Selwood 80-82; V Ashford *Cant* 82-02; Hon Can Cant Cathl 90-02; rtd 02; Perm to Offic *Cant* from 02. *Stream Cottage, 17 Gladstone Road, Willesborough, Ashford TN24 0BY* Tel (01233) 640736

EVERETT, Robert Henry. b 60. Em Coll Cam BA82 MA86 Ox Univ BA85 MA90 Ex Univ MPhil95. St Steph Ho Ox 83. **d** 86 **p** 87. C Ex St Thos and Em 86-88; C Plymstock 88-91; R St Dominic, Landulph and St Mellion w Pillaton *Truro* 91-96; P-in-c Reading All SS *Ox* 96-98; V 98-07; P-in-c Paddington St Mary Magd *Lon* 07-09; P-in-c Paddington St Pet 07-09; V Paddington St Mary Magd and St Pet from 09. *The Vicarage, 2 Rowington Close, London W2 5TF* Tel (020) 7289 1818 or 7289 2011 E-mail frhenry@btinternet.com

EVERETT, Robin Nigel. b 34. Dur Univ BA55. Cranmer Hall Dur 57. d 59 p 60. C New Humberstone *Leic* 59-62; C Humberstone 62-66; V Quorndon 66-74; V Castle Donington 74-82; P-in-c Lockington w Hemington 81-82; V Castle Donington and Lockington cum Hemington 82-86; Antigua 86-87; R Ibstock w Heather *Leic* 87-98; rtd 98; Perm to Offic *Derby* 98-01 and *Leic* 99-01. *90 Sevenlands Drive, Boulton Moor, Derby DE24 5AQ* Tel (01332) 751879

EVERETT, Canon Simon Francis. b 58. Oak Hill Th Coll BA89. d 89 p 90. C Wroughton *Bris* 89-93; TV Wexcombe *Sarum* 93-98; P-in-c The Iwernes, Sutton Waldron and Fontmell Magna 98-01; V Iwerne Valley from 01; RD Milton and Blandford from 01; Can and Preb Sarum Cathl from 09. *The Vicarage, Iwerne Minster, Blandford Forum DT11 8NF* Tel and fax (01747) 811291 E-mail reveveretti@btinternet.com

EVERETT-ALLEN, Canon Clive. b 47. AKC70. St Aug Coll Cant 69. d 70 p 71. C Minera *St As* 70-72; C Hatcham St Cath *S'wark* 72-75; TV Beaconsfield *Ox* 75-83; R Southwick St Mich *Chich* 83-98; V E Grinstead St Swithun from 98; Can and Preb Chich Cathl from 98; RD E Grinstead 05-10; Chapl Qu Victoria Hosp NHS Trust East Grinstead from 98. *St Swithun's Vicarage, Church Lane, East Grinstead RH19 3AZ* Tel (01342) 323307 E-mail clive47@gmail.com

EVERINGHAM, Georgina Wendy (formerly WALLACE, Godfrey Everingham). b 32. Tyndale Hall Bris BA57. d 58 p 59. C Broadwater St Mary *Chich* 58-61; V Shipton Bellinger w S Tidworth *Win* 61-70; V Bournemouth St Paul 70-84; V Throop 84-95; rtd 95; Perm to Offic *Worc* from 96. *3 Harlech Close, Berkeley Alford, Worcester WR4 0JU* Tel (01905) 754394 E-mail gina@wordoflife.uk.com

EVERITT, Mrs Jane. b 57. St Jo Coll Nottm 08. d 10 p 11. C Poulton Carleton and Singleton *Blackb* from 10. *29 Mossbourne Road, Poulton-le-Fylde FY6 7DU* Tel (01253) 884298 Mobile 07762-811170 E-mail jane.everitt@yahoo.co.uk

EVERITT, Mark. b 34. Linc Coll Ox BA58 MA62. Wells Th Coll. d 60 p 61. C Hangleton *Chich* 60-63; Chapl Mert Coll Ox 63-02; rtd 02. *48 Annandale Avenue, Bognor Regis PO21 2EX* Tel (01243) 823852

EVERITT, The Ven Michael John. b 68. K Coll Lon BD90 AKC90. Qu Coll Birm 90 English Coll Rome 91. d 92 p 93. C Cleveleys *Blackb* 92-95; Succ Bloemfontein Cathl S Africa 95-98; Prec 96-98; Chapl and Asst Lect Univ of Orange Free State 96-98; Sen Chapl St Martin's Coll *Blackb* 98-02; Asst Dir of Ords 00-02; R Standish 02-11; P-in-c Appley Bridge 06-09; AD Chorley 04-11; Adn Lancaster from 11; Hon Can Blackb Cathl from 10. *6 Eton Park, Fulwood, Preston PR2 9NL* Tel (01772) 700337 E-mail michael.everitt@blackburn.anglican.org

EVERITT, William Frank James. b 38. Dur Univ BA68 FCA63. Cranmer Hall Dur 65. d 69 p 70. C Leic St Phil 69-73; P-in-c Prestwold w Hoton 73-77; R Settrington w N Grimston and Wharram *York* 77-84; RD Buckrose 80-84; V Cheltenham St Pet *Glouc* 84-99; rtd 99; Perm to Offic *Ripon* from 03. *27 Lark Hill Crescent, Ripon HG4 2HN* Tel (01765) 603683 E-mail reveveritt@yahoo.com

EVES, Barry. b 51. Cranmer Hall Dur 86. d 88 p 89. C Tadcaster w Newton Kyme *York* 88-91; C York St Paul 91-93; V Bubwith w Skipwith 93-04. *8 Marina Avenue, Sunderland SR6 9AL* Tel 0191-549 1742

EVETTS-SECKER, Ms Josephine. b 42. Univ Coll Lon BA63 MPhil65. Coll of Resurr Mirfield 06. d 07 p 08. NSM Hinderwell, Roxby and Staithes etc *York* from 07. *Lidgate, Victoria Square, Lythe, Whitby YO21 3RW* Tel and fax (01947) 893338 Mobile 07717-061343 E-mail revj@evetts-secker.co.uk

EWART, John. b 66. QUB BA89. CITC BTh02. d 02 p 03. C Derryloran *Arm* 02-05; China 05-07; I Bright w Ballee and Killough *D & D* from 07; Min Can Down Cathl from 10. *Bright Rectory, 126 Killough Road, Downpatrick BT30 8LL* Tel (028) 4484 2229 E-mail ewartj@btinternet.com

EWBANK, Mark Robert. b 59. Qu Coll Ox MA86 Heythrop Coll Lon MTh05. Westcott Ho Cam 84. d 86 p 87. Zimbabwe 86-00; Asst P N End St Marg Balswaye 87-88; P-in-c Pumula St Luke 88-96; R Famona St Mary 96-00; C Chalfont St Peter *Ox* 00-06; V Englefield Green *Guildf* from 06; CF (ACF) from 01; CF (TA) from 05. *The Vicarage, 21 Willow Walk, Englefield Green, Egham TW20 0DQ* Tel (01784) 432553 E-mail v.ewbank@btinternet.com

EWBANK, The Very Revd Robert Arthur Benson. b 22. Qu Coll Ox BA45 MA48. Cuddesdon Coll 46. d 48 p 49. C Boston *Linc* 48-52; Chapl Uppingham Sch 52-56; Zimbabwe 57-00; Prin Cyrene Secondary Sch Bulawayo 57-62; P-in-c Figtree CD 60-82; Can Bulawayo 64-80; Can Th 80-82; Dean Bulawayo 82-90; rtd 97; Perm to Offic *Ely* 01-05. *14 Chapel Street, Ely CB6 1AD* Tel (01353) 645981 E-mail rabewbank@hotmail.com

EWBANK, Canon Robin Alan. b 42. Ex Coll Ox BA64 MA88 Lon Univ BD68. Clifton Th Coll 66. d 69 p 70. C Woodford Wells *Chelmsf* 69-72; Warden Cam Univ Miss Bermondsey 72-76; TV Sutton St Jas and Wawne *York* 76-82; R Bramshott *Portsm* 82-91; R Bramshott and Liphook 91-99; Hon Can Koforidua

from 96; P-in-c Hartley Wintney, Elvetham, Winchfield etc 99-02; V from 02; RD Odiham 04-11. *The Vicarage, Church Lane, Hartley Wintney, Basingstoke RG27 8DZ* Tel (01252) 842670 Fax 08707-052123 E-mail robin ewbank@lineone.net or robin.ewbank@stjohnshw.co.uk

EWBANK, The Ven Walter Frederick. b 18. Ball Coll Ox BA45 MA45 BD52. Bps' Coll Cheshunt. d 46 p 47. C Windermere St Martin *Carl* 46-49; V Hugill 49-52; V Casterton H Trin 52-62; V Raughton Head w Gatesgill 62-66; Hon Can Carl Cathl 66-78 and 83-84; V Carl St Cuth 66-71; Adn Westmorland and Furness 71-77; V Winster 71-78; Adn Carl 78-84; Can Res Carl Cathl 78-82; rtd 84; Perm to Offic *Carl* 84-94. *10 Castle Court, Castle Street, Carlisle CA3 8TP* Tel (01228) 810293

EWEN, Ralph John McGregor. b 43. Sarum & Wells Th Coll 77. d 79 p 80. C Kington w Huntington *Heref* 79-82; C Kington w Huntington, Old Radnor, Kinnerton etc 82-83; P-in-c Culmington w Onibury 83-89; P-in-c Bromfield 83-89; P-in-c Stanton Lacy 83-89; R Culmington w Onibury, Bromfield etc 90-01; R Llangenni and Llanbedr Ystrad Yw w Patricio *S & B* 01-08; rtd 08. *Ty Goleuddydd, 5 Goylands Close, Llandrindod Wells LD1 5RB* Tel (01597) 825183

EWER, Edward Sydney John (Jonathan). b 36. Univ of New England BA69 Lanc Univ MPhil91 Ch Div Sch of the Pacific (USA) DMin02. St Mich Th Coll Crafers ThL63. d 62 p 63. Australia 62-83; SSM from 68; Perm to Offic *Blackb* 83-84; Lic to Offic *Dur* 84-98; Prior SSM Priory Dur 85-98; Dioc Dir of Ords 94-98; Perm to Offic *S'wark* 00-05; Hon C Pimlico St Mary Bourne Street *Lon* 05-06; Perm to Offic *Lon* from 06 and *Ox* from 09. *The Well, Newport Road, Willen, Milton Keynes MK15 9AA* Tel (01908) 242741 Mobile 07915377554 E-mail j_ewer@yahoo.com

EWINGTON, John. b 43. MRICS65. Chich Th Coll 74. d 78 p 79. C Walthamstow St Jo *Chelmsf* 78-81; Papua New Guinea 81-87; V Southend St Sav Westcliff *Chelmsf* 87-96; TV Bideford, Northam, Westward Ho!, Appledore etc *Ex* from 96. *The Vicarage, Meeting Street, Appledore, Bideford EX39 1RJ* Tel (01237) 470469 E-mail sarah.e@talktalk.net

EXCELL, Robin Stanley. b 41. AKC64. St Boniface Warminster 64. d 65 p 66. C Ipswich St Mary Stoke *St E* 65-68; C Melton Mowbray w Thorpe Arnold *Leic* 68-70; TV 70-71; R Gt and Lt Blakenham w Baylham *St E* 71-76; R Gt and Lt Blakenham w Baylham and Nettlestead 76-86; RD Bosmere 84-86; NSM Sproughton w Burstall 91-94; R Rattlesden w Thorpe Morieux, Brettenham etc 94-05; rtd 05; Perm to Offic *St E* from 05. *Hollywater, Upper Street, Baylham, Ipswich IP6 8JR* Tel (01473) 830228 E-mail robin.excell@tesco.net

EXELL, Ernest William Carter. b 28. Qu Coll Cam BA52 MA53. Tyndale Hall Bris 49. d 52 p 53. C Sydenham H Trin *S'wark* 52-54; C E Ham St Paul *Chelmsf* 54-57; Uganda 57-65; Tanzania 66-70; R Abbess and Beauchamp Roding *Chelmsf* 70-71; P-in-c White Roding w Morrell Roding 70-71; R Abbess Roding, Beauchamp Roding and White Roding 71-94; RD Roding 75-79; rtd 94; Perm to Offic *St E* from 94. *8 Ickworth Drive, Bury St Edmunds IP33 3PX* Tel (01284) 724726

EXELL, Michael Andrew John. b 45. FHCIMA MRIPHH67 MICA70. Sarum & Wells Th Coll 87. d 89 p 90. C Ryde H Trin *Portsm* 89-93; C Swanmore St Mich w Havenstreet 89-92; C Swanmore St Mich 92-93; P-in-c Carisbrooke St Mary 93-99; V 99-10; P-in-c Carisbrooke St Nic 93-99; V 99-10; rtd 10; Perm to Offic *Portsm* from 10. *3 Glossop Close, East Cowes PO32 6PD* Tel (01983) 293686 E-mail mikeexell@aol.com

EXETER, Archdeacon of. See DRIVER, The Ven Penelope May

EXETER, Bishop of. See LANGRISH, The Rt Revd Michael Laurence

EXETER, Dean of. *Vacant*

EXLEY, Malcolm. b 33. Cranmer Hall Dur. d 67 p 68. C Sutton St Jas *York* 67-73; V Mappleton w Goxhill 73-77; V Market Weighton 77-90; P-in-c Goodmanham 77-78; R 78-90; V Bridlington Em 90-98; rtd 98; Perm to Offic *York* from 00. *11 The Chase, Driffield YO25 7FJ* Tel (01377) 272312

EXLEY-STIEGLER, Canon George Ebdon. b 16. Syracuse Univ BS51. Berkeley Div Sch STM53. d 53 p 54. R Camden Trin USA 53-57; R Brockport St Luke 57-64; R Rochester Calvary-St Andr 64-79; rtd 79; Hon C Knowsley *Liv* 80-81; Hon C Upholland 81-89; Lect Upholland N Inst 80-84; USA from 89. *168 Dalaker Drive, Rochester NY 14624, USA* E-mail geoes@frontiernet.net

EXON, Helier John Philip. b 44. MBE87. BSc70 CEng87 MIET87. STETS 96. d 99 p 00. NSM Milton Abbas, Hilton w Cheselbourne etc *Sarum* 99-05; NSM Piddletrenthide w Plush, Alton Pancras etc 02-05; NSM Piddle Valley, Hilton, Cheselbourne etc from 05. *The Monk's House, Hilton, Blandford Forum DT11 0DG* Tel (01258) 880396 E-mail helier@exon.demon.co.uk

EYDEN, Christopher David. b 59. RSAMD BA81. St Steph Ho Ox 88. d 91 p 92. C Tottenham St Paul *Lon* 91-93; C Ealing St Pet Mt Park 93-96; TV Wimbledon *S'wark* 96-04; Perm to Offic 04-05; C Putney St Mary 05-10; TV from 10. *All Saints'*

Vicarage, 70 Fulham High Street, London SW6 3LG Tel (020) 7384 0115 Mobile 07951-600924 E-mail chriseyden@talk21.com

EYEONS, Keith James. b 70. Clare Coll Cam BA92 MA96 Down Coll Cam PhD10 Lon Inst of Educn PGCE95. St Jo Coll Nottm MA(MM)03. **d** 01 **p** 02. C Iffley *Ox* 01-03; Chapl Down Coll Cam from 03. *Downing College, Cambridge CB2 1DQ* Tel (01223) 334810 E-mail kje11@cam.ac.uk

EYERS, Frederick Thomas Laurence. b 12. Ridley Coll Melbourne LTh39. **d** 39 **p** 40. C S Yarra Australia 39-42; Chapl Aus Mil Forces 42-46; C E Malvern St Jo 46; Perm to Offic *York* 46-50; C Sheff St Cecilia Parson Cross 48-50; SSM from 50; Australia 50-73 and from 82. *Broughton Hall, 2 Berwick Street, Camberwell Vic 3124, Australia* Tel (0061) (3) 9813 4053 E-mail ssm1@bigpond.com

EYLES, Anthony John. b 34. Bris Univ BSc57. Sarum Th Coll 61. **d** 63 **p** 64. C Wellington w W Buckland *B & W* 63-67; C Wilton 67-74; Ind Chapl *Dur* 74-85; Ind Chapl *Worc* 85-90; P-in-c Bickenhill w Elmdon *Birm* 90; P-in-c Bickenhill 90-00; Chapl Birm Airport 90-00; rtd 00; Perm to Offic *Ex* from 00. *5 Kersbrook Lane, Kersbrook, Budleigh Salterton EX9 7AD* Tel (01395) 446084

EYNON, John Kenneth. b 56. Nottm Univ BA77 BArch80. **d** 96 **p** 97. OLM Croydon Ch Ch *S'wark* 96-05. *21 Rye Close, Saltdean, Brighton BN2 8PP* Tel (01273) 308397 Mobile 07789-877541 E-mail johneynon@btinternet.com

EYNSTONE, Ms Sarah Francesca Louise. b 75. Univ Coll Lon BA96 Fitzw Coll Cam BA04. Westcott Ho Cam 02. **d** 05 **p** 06. C Hampstead St Jo *Lon* 05-09; Min Can and Chapl St Paul's Cathl from 10. *7B Amen Court, London EC4M 7BU* E-mail sarah.eynstone@cantab.net

EYRE, The Very Revd Richard Montague Stephens. b 29. Oriel Coll Ox BA53 MA56. St Steph Ho Ox 53. **d** 56 **p** 57. C Portsea N End St Mark *Portsm* 56-59; Tutor Chich Th Coll 59-61; Chapl 61-62; Chapl Eastbourne Coll 62-65; V Arundel w Tortington and S Stoke *Chich* 65-73; V Bramley Gd Shep Preston 73-75; Dir of Ords 75-79; Adn Chich 75-81; Can Res and Treas Chich Cathl 78-81; Dean Ex 81-95; rtd 95; Perm to Offic *B & W* 95-00 and 04-10; P-in-c Pau *Eur* 01-03. *32 Exe Vale Road, Exeter EX2 6LF* Tel (01392) 221082

EYRE, Canon Richard Stuart. b 48. Bris Univ BEd81 Nottm Univ MTh86. Linc Th Coll 74. **d** 77 **p** 78. C Henbury *Bris* 77-81; C Bedminster 81-82; TV 82-84; Chapl Bp Grosseteste Coll Linc 84-95; Sen Tutor 89-95; P-in-c Long Bennington w Foston *Linc* 95; P-in-c Saxonwell 95-97; R 97-01; RD Grantham 96-01; TR Hykeham from 01; RD Graffoe 02-09; Can and Preb Linc Cathl from 03. *The Rectory, Mill Lane, North Hykeham, Lincoln LN6 9PA* Tel (01522) 882880 Fax 883100 E-mail richard.eyre3@ntlworld.com

EZE, Geoffrey Ejike. b 73. Trin Coll Bris 06. **d** 08 **p** 09. C Gt Ilford St Jo *Chelmsf* from 08. *53 Friars Close, Ilford IG1 4AZ* Tel (020) 8553 9898 E-mail geoffj-e-eze@yahoo.fr

F

FACCINI (née LEGG), Sandra Christine. b 55. Surrey Univ BSc78 PhD82 Univ of Wales (Ban) BTh07. **d** 04 **p** 05. OLM Howell Hill w Burgh Heath *Guildf* 04-09; P-in-c Ottershaw from 09. *50 Slade Road, Ottershaw, Chertsey KT16 0HZ* Tel (01932) 873160 Mobile 07743-675633 E-mail sandra@faccinis.freeserve.co.uk

FACER, Miss Rosemary Jane. b 44. Hull Univ BA65 Reading Univ CertEd66 LTCL72. Trin Coll Bris 78. **dss** 80 **d** 87 **p** 98. St Paul's Cray St Barn *Roch* 80-88; Par Dn 87-88; C Cheltenham St Mark *Glouc* 88-01; C Clifton *York* 01-09; rtd 09. *16 Garborough Close, Crosby, Maryport CA15 6RZ* Tel (01900) 810776 E-mail r.rj.facer@talk21.com

FACEY, Andrew John. b 57. Trin Coll Cam BA79 MA83 Barrister-at-Law 80. Trin Coll Bris BA92. **d** 92 **p** 93. C Egham *Guildf* 92-96; P-in-c E Molesey St Paul 96-01; P-in-c Epsom Common Ch Ch 01-02; V 02-10; Dioc Inter Faith Adv 96-10. *Address temp unknown* E-mail andrew.facey@virgin.net

FACEY, Jane (BJ). b 54. EMMTC 05. **d** 07 **p** 08. NSM W Hallam and Mapperley w Stanley *Derby* from 07. *2 George Street, Langley Mill, Nottingham NG16 4DJ* Tel (01773) 531057 E-mail bjfacey@btinternet.com

FAGAN, Jeremy David. b 75. Qu Coll Ox BA98. Wycliffe Hall Ox 99. **d** 01 **p** 02. C Chell *Lich* 01-04; TV Kirkby *Liv* from 04. *27 Shakespeare Avenue, Liverpool L32 9SH* Tel 0151-547 2133 E-mail faganj@mac.com

FAGAN, John Raymond. b 32. Lon Univ BD69. Ripon Hall Ox 71. **d** 72 **p** 73. C Stalybridge *Man* 72-74; C Madeley *Heref* 74-79; V Amington *Birm* 79-91; P-in-c Stonnall *Lich* 91-97; Chapl HM YOI Swinfen Hall 91-97; rtd 97; C Stonnall *Lich* 97; Res Min Elford 98-07. *19 Homewelland House, Leicester Road, Market Harborough LE16 7BT* Tel (01858) 419988

FAGAN, Thomas. b 27. MCIOB67 Man Univ CertEd70. NW Ord Course 78. **d** 81 **p** 82. NSM Rainhill *Liv* 81-90; NSM Prescot 90-97; rtd 97; Perm to Offic *Liv* 97-03. *4 Wensleydale Avenue, Prescot L35 4NR* Tel 0151-426 4788

FAGBEMI, Olubunmi Ayobami (Bunmi). b 57. Lagos Univ LLB78 LSE LLM81 Qu Mary Coll Lon PhD91 Solicitor 79. Ripon Coll Cuddesdon 95. **d** 97 **p** 98. C Enfield St Andr *Lon* 97-01; V Tottenham H Trin from 01; AD E Haringey from 11. *Holy Trinity Vicarage, Philip Lane, London N15 4GZ* Tel (020) 8801 3021 E-mail bunmif@btinternet.com

FAGBEMI, The Ven Stephen Ayodeji Akinwale. b 67. St Jo Coll Nottm BTh96 Kent Univ PhD04. Immanuel Coll Ibadan 87. **d** 90 **p** 91. C Iyere St Jo Nigeria 90-91; C Owo St Patr 91-92; P-in-c Wakajaye-Etile Ch 92-93; V Ebenezer-Ile St Sav 96-00; Can Owo from 99; Perm to Offic *Cant* 00-03; Hon C Murston w Bapchild and Tonge 03-05; Co-ord Chapl Sunderland Univ and Hon C Sunderland Minster 05-11; Dean Abp Vining Coll of Th Nigeria from 11. *Abp Vining College of Theology, Oke-Emeso, PMB 727, Akure, Ondo State, Nigeria* E-mail saaf95@hotmail.com *or* saaf90@yahoo.co.uk

FAGERSON, Joseph Leonard Ladd. b 35. Harvard Univ BA57. Ridley Hall Cam 61. **d** 63 **p** 64. C Tonbridge SS Pet and Paul *Roch* 63-67; Afghanistan 67-74; P-in-c Marbury *Ches* 74-75; P-in-c Kinloch Rannoch *St And* 75-00; Chapl Rannoch Sch Perthshire 75-00; rtd 00; Hon C Killin *St And* from 00. *Westgarth, Tomnacroich, Fortingall, Aberfeldy PH15 2LJ* Tel (01887) 830569

FAHIE, Mrs Stephanie Bridget. b 48. St Jo Coll Nottm 85. **d** 87 **p** 94. Par Dn Leic St Chris 87-90; Chapl Scargill Ho 90-95; P-in-c Hickling w Kinoulton and Broughton Sulney *S'well* 95-00; R 00-10; rtd 11. *61 Monkmoor Avenue, Shrewsbury SY2 5ED* Tel (01743) 588307

FAINT, Paul Edward. b 38. Qu Coll Birm 85. **d** 87 **p** 88. C Cradley *Worc* 87-90; V Hanley Castle, Hanley Swan and Welland 90-94; V Northwood H Trin *Lon* 94-97; Miss to Seafarers from 97; Chapl Larnaca Cyprus 97-01; rtd 01; Perm to Offic *Ox* from 01; Hon Chapl Miss to Seafarers from 02. *17 Priory Orchard, Wantage OX12 9EL* Tel (01235) 772297 E-mail thefaints@lineone.net

FAIR, Dorothy Enid. b 48. **d** 11. OLM Swinton H Rood *Man* from 11. *375 Worsley Road, Swinton, Manchester M27 0EJ* Tel 0161-794 0010 E-mail de.fair@uwclub.net

FAIRALL, Hannah Marie. *See* MEARS, Mrs Hannah Marie

FAIRALL, Michael John. b 45. SWMTC 88. **d** 90 **p** 91. NSM Southway *Ex* 90-00; NSM Bickleigh and Shaugh Prior from 00. *25 Buzzard Road, Whitchurch, Tavistock PL19 9FZ* Tel (01822) 610926 E-mail m.j.fairall@talk21.com

FAIRBAIRN, Andrew Graham. b 48. SEITE 06. **d** 09 **p** 10. NSM Surbiton Hill Ch Ch *S'wark* from 09. *Christ Church, 8 Christ Church Road, Surbiton KT5 8JL* Tel (020) 8390 7215 Mobile 07789-992843 E-mail graham.fairbairn@ccsurbiton.org

FAIRBAIRN, Francis Stephen. b 41. **d** 98 **p** 99. OLM Orrell *Liv* from 98. *27 Greenslate Road, Billinge, Wigan WN5 7BQ* Tel (01695) 623127 *or* (01722) 812176 Fax (01722) 815398

FAIRBAIRN, John Alan. b 46. Trin Coll Cam BA67 MA72. Wycliffe Hall Ox 84. **d** 86 **p** 87. C Boscombe St Jo *Win* 86-89; C Edgware *Lon* 89-95; R Gunton St Pet *Nor* 95-11; Chapl Jas Paget Healthcare NHS Trust 96-08; rtd 11. *28 Clifton Road, Bournemouth BH6 3PA* Tel (01202) 424466 E-mail jfairbairn@fsmail.net

FAIRBAIRN, Stella Rosamund. **d** 87 **p** 94. NSM Banbury *Ox* 87-99; Perm to Offic *Pet* 88-94. *Hillside, Overthorpe, Banbury OX17 2AF* Tel (01295) 710648

FAIRBAIRN, Stephen. *See* FAIRBAIRN, Francis Stephen

FAIRBANK, Brian Douglas Seeley. b 53. AKC75. St Steph Ho Ox 77. **d** 78 **p** 79. C Newton Aycliffe *Dur* 78-81; C Stocking Farm *Leic* 81-84; TV Ratby cum Groby 84-91; Chapl RN 91-04; R Bramfield, Stapleford, Waterford etc *St Alb* from 04. *The Rectory, Church Lane, Watton-at-Stone, Hertford SG14 3RD* Tel (01920) 830575

FAIRBROTHER, Robin Harry. b 44. Ho of Resurr Mirfield 64 Wells Th Coll 68. **d** 69 **p** 70. C Wrexham *St As* 69-74; C Welshpool w Castle Caereinion 74-77; V Bettws Cedewain and Tregynon 77-80; V Betws Cedewain and Tregynon and Llanwyddelan 80-92; TR Marshwood Vale *Sarum* 92-98; TR Golden Cap Team 98-05; rtd 06. *30 Résidence des Deux Mers, 11700 Capendu, France* E-mail robin.fairbrother2356@freeserve.co.uk

FAIRCLOUGH, Miss Amanda Ann Catherine. b 68. Man Univ BSc89. St Jo Coll Nottm 06 SNWTP 08. **d** 10 **p** 11. NSM Orford St Marg *Liv* from 10. *7 Time Park, Whiston, Prescot L35 7NU* Tel 0151-426 6114 Mobile 07788-101178 E-mail a.fairclough@amandafairclough.co.uk

FAIRCLOUGH, Clive Anthony. b 54. TISEC 01. **d** 04 **p** 05. C Nadder Valley *Sarum* 04-08; R Abberton, The Flyfords, Naunton Beauchamp etc *Worc* from 08; P-in-c Fladbury, Hill and Moor, Wyre Piddle etc from 11; C Peopleton and White Ladies Aston w Churchill etc from 11. *The Rectory, Church End, Bishampton, Pershore WR10 2LT* Tel (01386) 462648 Mobile 07962-023882

FAIRCLOUGH, John Frederick. b 40. St Jo Coll Dur BA63 MA68 MBIM. Coll of Resurr Mirfield 81. **d** 83 **p** 84. C Horninglow *Lich* 83-87; V Skerton St Luke *Blackb* 87-94; V Thornton-le-Fylde 94-00; rtd 00; Perm to Offic *Blackb* from 01. *18 Crossfield Avenue, Bury BL9 5NX* Tel (01706) 825664

FAIREY, Michael. b 51. NEOC. **d** 08 **p** 10. NSM York St Hilda from 08. *Boston Gates, Whinns Lane, Thorp Arch, Wetherby LS23 7AL* Tel (01937) 844794 Fax 845385 E-mail mike.fairey@bostongates.co.uk

FAIRHURST, John Graham. b 39. Linc Th Coll 86. **d** 88 **p** 89. C Whiston *Sheff* 88-91; V Elsecar 91-04; AD Tankersley 01-04; Chapl Barnsley Community & Priority Services NHS Trust 98-04; rtd 04; Perm to Offic *Sheff* from 04. *30 Barberry Way, Ravenfield, Rotherham S65 4RE* Tel (01709) 548206

FAIRHURST, Ms Rosemary Anne. b 63. Newnham Coll Cam BA85 MA85 Lon Inst of Educn PGCE86. Wycliffe Hall Ox BA92. **d** 93 **p** 94. C Hackney Marsh *Lon* 93-97; C Islington St Mary 97-02; Dir Miss and Min Ripon Coll Cuddesdon 02-06; Organizational Analyst Grubb Inst from 07; Perm to Offic *Lon* from 07. *The Grubb Institute, Cloudesley Street, London N1 0HU* Tel (020) 7278 8061 E-mail r.fairhurst@grubb.org.uk

FAIRLAMB, Neil. b 49. Univ of Wales (Ban) BA71 Jes Coll Ox BPhil75 Pemb Coll Cam CertEd74 Univ of Wales (Abth) MTh00. S'wark Ord Course 90. **d** 93 **p** 94. Hon C Dulwich St Barn S'wark 93-95; P-in-c Elerch w Penrhyncoch w Capel Bangor and Goginan *St D* 95-96; V 96-98; R Arthog w Fairbourne w Llangelynnin w Rhoslefain *Ban* 98-03; R Beaumaris from 03. *The Rectory, 5 Tros yr Afon, Beaumaris LL58 8BN* Tel and fax (01248) 811402 E-mail rheithor@aol.com

FAIRLESS (*née* **CARTER), Mrs Elizabeth Jane.** b 57. Derby Univ BSc00. St Jo Coll Nottm MTh02. **d** 02 **p** 03. C Leek and Meerbrook *Lich* 02-05; C Harlescott and Chapl Shropshire Co Primary Care Trust 05-11; R Darlaston St Lawr *Lich* from 11. *The Rectory, 1 Victoria Road, Darlaston, Wednesbury WS10 8AA* Tel 07968-033489 (mobile) E-mail liz.fairless@btinternet.com

FAIRWEATHER, David James. b 35. Keele Univ BEd79. Wycliffe Hall Ox 70. **d** 72 **p** 73. C Trentham *Lich* 72-76; C Cheddleton 76; C Hanley H Ev 77-79; C Rugeley 79-86; V Brown Edge 86-03; rtd 03; Perm to Offic *Lich* from 09. *7 Lockwood Close, Kingsley Holt, Stoke-on-Trent ST10 2BN* Tel (01538) 267054 E-mail father.david222@googlemail.com

FAIRWEATHER, John. b 39. K Coll Lon AKC66 BD72. **d** 67 **p** 68. C Plymouth St Jas Ham *Ex* 67-69; C Townstal w St Sav and St Petrox w St Barn 69-73; R Corringham w Springthorpe *Linc* 73-78; P-in-c Blyborough 76-78; P-in-c Heapham 76-78; P-in-c Willoughton 76-78; V Pinchbeck 78-82; V Exwick 82-04; rtd 04. *52 Woodman's Crescent, Honiton EX14 2DY* Tel (01404) 549711 E-mail john.fairweather6@btinternet.com

FAIRWEATHER, Sally Helen. *See* ROSS, Mrs Sally Helen

FALASCHI-RAY, Sonia Ofelia. Surrey Univ BSc79 Wolfs Coll Cam BA02 MA06 CEng86. Ridley Hall Cam 03. **d** 05 **p** 06. NSM Fowlmere, Foxton, Shepreth and Thriplow *Ely* 05-09; Perm to Offic *Ely* from 09 and *St Alb* 09-10; NSM Barkway, Reed and Buckland w Barley *St Alb* from 10. *27 Church Lane, Barkway, Royston SG8 8EJ* Tel (01763) 849057 Mobile 07747-844265 E-mail sonia.falaschi-ray@virgin.net

FALCONER, Ian Geoffrey. b 40. BNC Ox BA62 Newc Univ MA93. Cuddesdon Coll 62. **d** 64 **p** 65. C Chiswick St Nic w St Mary *Lon* 64-68; C-in-c Hounslow Gd Shep Beavers Lane CD 68-76; P-in-c Hammersmith St Matt 76-84; P-in-c Byker St Silas *Newc* 84-93; V 93-95; P-in-c Newc St Phil and St Aug 95-98; P-in-c Newc St Matt w St Mary 95-98; P-in-c Newc St Phil and St Aug and St Matt w St Mary 98-00; V Seghill 00-06; rtd 06. *70 Lowgates, Staveley, Chesterfield S43 3TU* Tel (01246) 471913 E-mail frianfalc@aol.com

FALKINGHAM (*née* **MOORE), Mrs Caroline Judith.** b 57. Coll of Ripon & York St Jo BA78 Leeds Univ MA07. NOC 05. **d** 07 **p** 08. C Bilton *Ripon* from 07. *64 Knox Lane, Harrogate HG1 3DA* Tel (01423) 505372 E-mail caroline@falkingham.fslife.co.uk

FALKNER, Canon Jonathan Michael Shepherd. b 47. Open Univ BA74. Cranmer Hall Dur. **d** 79 **p** 80. C Penrith w Newton Reigny *Carl* 79-81; C Penrith w Newton Reigny and Plumpton Wall 81-82; C Dalton-in-Furness 82-84; V Clifton 84-90; P-in-c Dean 85-89; R 89-90; P-in-c Rumburgh w S Elmham w the Ilketshalls *St E* 90-92; R S Elmham and Ilketshall 92-99; RD Beccles and S Elmham 94-99; Hon Can St E Cathl 98-99; P-in-c W Newton and Bromfield w Waverton *Carl* 99-02; P-in-c Holme Cultram St Mary and St Cuth 00-02; TR Solway Plain 02-05;

P-in-c Gosforth w Nether Wasdale and Wasdale Head from 05. *The Rectory, Gosforth, Seascale CA20 1AZ* Tel (01946) 725251 E-mail southcaplan@falconfleet.org.uk

FALLA, Miles. b 43. MCIM. EAMTC 93. **d** 96 **p** 97. NSM Buckden *Ely* 96-98; P-in-c Gretton w Rockingham *Pet* 98-99; V Gretton w Rockingham and Cottingham w E Carlton 99-04; RD Corby 01-02; rtd 04; Perm to Offic *Ely* from 05. *Bowlings, Silver Street, Buckden, St Neots PE19 5TS* Tel (01480) 811335 E-mail miles@falla.ndo.co.uk

FALLON, James Anthony. b 62. Qu Coll Birm. **d** 11. C Chard St Mary w Combe St Nicholas, Wambrook etc *B & W* from 11. *83 Brutton Way, Chard TA20 2HB*

FALLONE, Christopher. b 55. Aston Tr Scheme 85 Oak Hill Th Coll 87. **d** 90 **p** 91. C Rochdale *Man* 90-93; P-in-c Thornham w Gravel Hole 93-94; TV Middleton w Thornham 94-08; P-in-c Collyhurst from 08. *The Rectory, Eggington Street, Collyhurst, Manchester M10 7RN* Tel 0161-205 2808 Mobile 07976-624124 E-mail chrisfallone@bigfoot.com

FALLOWS, Stuart Adrian. b 50. Moray Ho Edin 75. **d** 78 **p** 79. Hon C Forres w Nairn *Mor* 78-81; Hon C Elgin w Lossiemouth 81-86; Hon Dioc Chapl 86; C Brighton St Geo w St Anne and St Mark *Chich* 86-89; V Wivelsfield 89-98; P-in-c Kieth, Huntly and Aberchirder *Mor* 98-02; P-in-c Ringwould w Kingsdown *Cant* 02-04; R Ringwould w Kingsdown and Ripple etc 05-09; R W Highland Region *Arg* from 09. *The Rectory, Carnoch, Glencoe, Ballachulish PH49 4HP* Tel (01855) 811987 E-mail afallows222@aol.co.uk

FALSHAW, Simon Meriadoc. b 60. Leeds Univ BSc82. Oak Hill Th Coll BA93. **d** 93 **p** 94. C Stapleford *S'well* 93-99; Miss Partner Crosslinks 99-00; P-in-c The Lye and Stambermill *Worc* from 01; RD Stourbridge 04-07. *Christ Church Vicarage, High Street, Lye, Stourbridge DY9 8LF* Tel (01384) 423142 *or* 894948 E-mail christchurchlye@classicfm.net

FALUDY, Alexander Raban Spencer. b 83. Peterho Cam BA01 MA05 Linc Coll Ox MSt04. Coll of Resurr Mirfield 05. **d** 08 **p** 09. C Tynemouth Cullercoats St Paul *Newc* from 08. *14 Naters Street, Whitley Bay NE26 2PG* Tel 0191-289 5135 Mobile 07806-459374 E-mail alexander.faludy@lincoln.oxon.net

FANCOURT, Graeme. b 77. St Jo Coll Dur BA00 DThM11. Ripon Coll Cuddesdon 09. **d** 10 **p** 11. C Caversham Thameside and Mapledurham *Ox* from 10. *18 St Peter's Avenue, Caversham, Reading RG4 7DD* Tel 0118-947 8450 E-mail fancourt@gmail.com

FANTHORPE, Robert Lionel. b 35. Open Univ BA80 CertEd63 FCMI81 FCP90. Llan Dioc Tr Scheme. **d** 87 **p** 88. NSM Roath St German *Llan* 87-00; Lic to Offic from 00. *Rivendell, 48 Claude Road, Roath, Cardiff CF24 3QA* Tel (029) 2049 8368 Fax 2049 6832 Mobile 07767-207289 E-mail fanthorpe@aol.com

FARADAY, John. b 49. Leeds Univ BSc71 MICE78. Oak Hill Th Coll 81. **d** 83 **p** 84. C Sutton *Liv* 83-86; C Rainhill and Chapl Whiston Hosp 86-89; V Over Darwen St Jas *Blackb* 89-02; TR S Rochdale *Man* 02-08; TR Gorton and Abbey Hey from 08. *Emmanuel Rectory, 35 Blackwin Street, Manchester M12 5LD* Tel 0116-223 3510 E-mail john.faraday@sky.com

FARAH, Mones Anton. b 64. Trin Coll Bris BA88. **d** 88 **p** 89. C Aberystwyth *St D* 88-91; Chapl St D Coll Lamp 91-98; TV Gt Baddow *Chelmsf* from 98. *The Vicarage, 42 Riffhams Drive, Great Baddow, Chelmsford CM2 7DD* Tel (01245) 471516 E-mail monesf@yahoo.com

FARBRIDGE, Nicholas Brisco. b 33. FCA. Sarum & Wells Th Coll 75. **d** 77 **p** 78. C Gt Bookham *Guildf* 77-80; C Ewell 80-83; V Addlestone 83-89; R Shere 89-95; rtd 96; Perm to Offic *Guildf* from 96. *55 Curling Vale, Guildford GU2 7PH* Tel (01483) 531140

FARDON, Raymond George Warren. b 30. St Pet Hall Ox BA52 MA56. Ridley Hall Cam 54. **d** 59 **p** 60. C High Wycombe All SS *Ox* 59-63; Chapl Bedford Secondary Modern Sch 63-68; Dep Hd Dunstable Secondary Modern Sch 68-72; Hd Master K Sch Grantham 72-82; Travelling Ev from 82; Hon C Longfleet *Sarum* 82-83; Perm to Offic *Sarum* 83-05 and *S'well* from 05; rtd 95. *9 Somerby Court, Bramcote, Nottingham NG9 3NB* Tel 0115-928 0810

FAREY, David Mark. b 56. St Jo Coll Dur BA85. Cranmer Hall Dur 82. **d** 86 **p** 87. C Brackley St Pet w St Jas 86-89; TV Kingsthorpe w Northampton St Dav 89-96; R Laughton w Ripe and Chalvington *Chich* 96-10; Chapl to Bp Lewes 96-10; Dioc Communications Officer from 10. *6 Gundreda Road, Lewes BN7 1PX* Tel (01273) 425691 Mobile 07899-828787 E-mail david.farey@diochi.org.uk

FARGUS, Gavin James Frederick. b 30. AKC54. K Coll Lon. **d** 55 **p** 57. C Salisbury St Mark *Sarum* 55-57; C Wareham w Arne 57-60; C Marlborough 60-63; P-in-c Davidstow w Otterham *Truro* 63-65; R Nether Lochaber *Arg* 65-81; R Kinlochleven 65-81; rtd 81; Lic to Offic *Arg* 82-94. *61 Loan Fearn, Ballachulish, Argyll PH49 4JB* Tel (01855) 811851

FARISH, Alan John. b 58. Lanc Univ BA. St Jo Coll Nottm 83. **d** 86 **p** 87. C Bishopwearmouth St Gabr *Dur* 86-89; C Fatfield 89-98; P-in-c Preston on Tees 98-03; V Preston-on-Tees and

Longnewton 03-10; P-in-c Stockton from 08. *12 Pennypot Lane, Eaglescliffe, Stockton-on-Tees TS16 0BN* Tel (01642) 782961

FARLEY, Claire Louise. See MADDOCK, Mrs Claire Louise

FARLEY, David Stuart. b 53. Univ Coll Dur BA75 Westmr Coll Ox MTh00. St Jo Coll Nottm. **d** 84 **p** 85. C Bath Weston All SS w N Stoke *B & W* 84-87; Chapl Scargill Ho 87-90; Min Hedge End N CD *Win* 90-94; V Hedge End St Luke 94-00; Dep Chapl HM Pris Belmarsh 00; Chapl HM Pris Shrewsbury from 00. *HM Prison, The Dana, Shrewsbury SY1 2HR* Tel (01743) 352511 ext 325

FARLEY, Ian David. b 56. Linc Coll Ox BA78 MA87 Dur Univ PhD88. Cranmer Hall Dur 84. **d** 87 **p** 88. C Thorpe Acre w Dishley *Leic* 87-92; V S Lambeth St Steph *S'wark* 92-99; V Bacton w Edingthorpe w Witton and Ridlington *Nor* 99-03; Ind Chapl 99-03; TR Buckhurst Hill *Chelmsf* from 03. *St John's Rectory, High Road, Buckhurst Hill IG9 5RX* Tel (020) 8504 1931 E-mail parish-office@buckhursthill.free-online.co.uk

FARLEY, James Trevor. b 37. IEng MIET FRSA. EMMTC 80. **d** 82 **p** 83. NSM Grantham *Linc* from 82. *Highfield Cottage, Station Road, Bottesford, Nottingham NG13 0EN* Tel (01949) 843646 Fax 843860 Mobile 07768-360592 E-mail jimandroma@highfield40.fsnet.co.uk

FARLEY, Ronald Alexander. b 30. Oak Hill NSM Course. **d** 79 **p** 80. NSM Stoke Newington St Faith, St Matthias and All SS *Lon* 79-97; NSM Upper Clapton St Matt 99-04; rtd 04; Perm to Offic *Lon* from 04. *2 St James Close, Bishop Street, London N1 8PH* Tel (020) 7354 2231

FARLEY-MOORE, Peter James. b 72. Sheff Univ BA94 UEA MA00. Ridley Hall Cam. **d** 00 **p** 01. C Chapeltown *Sheff* 00-03; Miss Cell Adv CMS 04-05; Asst Min Kowloon St Andr Hong Kong 05-07; V Blackheath St Jo *S'wark* from 07. *146 Langton Way, London SE3 7JS* E-mail peter@stjohnsblackheath.org.uk

FARMAN, Joanne Margaret. b 46. Birkbeck Coll Lon BA81 Leeds Univ MA08 Southlands Coll Lon PGCE82. SEITE 97. **d** 00 **p** 01. NSM Limpsfield and Titsey *S'wark* 00-04; Chapl St Geo Healthcare NHS Trust Lon 00-10; Lead Chapl R Hosp for Neuro-Disability 05-07; Perm to Offic *S'wark* from 10. *10 Detillens Lane, Limpsfield, Oxted RH8 0DJ* Tel (01883) 713086 *or* (020) 8725 3070 E-mail joanne.farman@stgeorges.nhs.uk

FARMAN, Robert Joseph. b 54. Ridley Hall Cam 86. **d** 88 **p** 89. C Sutton St Nic *S'wark* 88-90; C Cheam Common St Phil 90-92; R Wootton w Glympton and Kiddington *Ox* 92-00; TV Kings Norton *Birm* 00-04; Chapl St Mary's Hospice from 04; Chapl R Orthopaedic Hosp NHS Trust 05-06; Chapl Birm and Solihull Mental Health Trust from 06. *58 Station Road, Kings Norton, Birmingham B30 1DA* Tel 0121-451 1234, 472 1191 *or* 678 2000 Mobile 07766-054137 E-mail robfarman@evemail.net

FARMAN, Mrs Roberta. b 48. Aber Univ MA70 Cam Univ CertEd72. Qu Coll Birm 78. **dss** 82 **d** 87 **p** 01. Ovenden *Wakef* 80-82; Scargill Ho 83-84; Coulsdon St Jo *S'wark* 85-86; Hon Par Dn Cambridge St Mark *Ely* 86-88; Hon Par Dn Sutton St Nic *S'wark* 88-92; Hon Par Dn Wootton w Glympton and Kiddington *Ox* 92-00; NSM Kings Norton *Birm* 01-04; Chapl Univ Hosp Birm NHS Foundn Trust from 01. *58 Station Road, Kings Norton, Birmingham B30 1DA* Tel 0121-451 1234 *or* 627 1627 E-mail bj@robfarman.evesham.net

FARMBOROUGH, James Laird McLelland (Mac). b 22. MBE90. Magd Coll Cam BA49 MA54. Tyndale Hall Bris. **d** 52 **p** 53. C Wolverhampton St Luke *Lich* 52-55; C Holloway St Mary w St Jas *Lon* 55-56; C Broadwater St Mary *Chich* 56-58; Chapl All SS Niteroi Brazil 58-64; Org Sec SAMS 65-70; V Marple All SS *Ches* 70-80; Chapl Vina del Mar St Pet Chile 80-92; Miss to Seamen 80-92; rtd 92. *Flat 8, Manormead, Tilford Road, Hindhead GU26 6RA*

✠**FARMBROUGH, The Rt Revd David John.** b 29. Linc Coll Ox BA51 MA53. Westcott Ho Cam 51. **d** 53 **p** 54 **c** 81. C Bp's Hatfield *St Alb* 53-57; P-in-c 57-63; V Bishop's Stortford St Mich 63-74; RD Bishop's Stortford 73-74; Adn St Alb 74-81; Suff Bp Bedford 81-93; rtd 94; Hon Asst Bp St Alb from 94. *St Michael Mead, 110 Village Road, Bromham, Bedford MK43 8HU* Tel (01234) 825042 E-mail david@farmbrough.com

FARMER, Mrs Anne Louise. b 61. Warwick Univ BEd84. Trin Coll Bris 04. **d** 06 **p** 07. NSM Stoke Bishop *Bris* 06-09; TV Worle *B & W* from 09. *21 Westmarch Way, Weston-super-Mare BS22 7JY* Tel (01934) 515610 E-mail annefarmer21@o2.co.uk

FARMER, Diane Marcia (Diana). b 61. Warwick Univ BSc82 PGCE83. WMMTC 97 Cranmer Hall Dur 00. **d** 01 **p** 02. C Allesley Park and Whoberley *Cov* 01-05; Hd Tr and Development Rethink from 05; Hon C Pennsett *Worc* 05-07; Perm to Offic 07-09; Hon C Wollaston from 09. *13 Rectory Street, Stourbridge DY8 5QT* Tel (01384) 295205 E-mail diana@farmerfamilyuk.fsnet.co.uk *or* diana.farmer@rethink.org

FARMER, Lorelie Joy. Southn Univ BA65 MA68 Univ of Mass EdD88. Cranmer Hall Dur 97. **d** 99 **p** 00. C Newbury *Ox* 99-03; C Stratford-upon-Avon, Luddington etc *Cov* 03-05; C Warmington w Shotteswell and Radway w Ratley 05-06; rtd 08;

Hon C Witchampton, Stanbridge and Long Crichel etc *Sarum* 08-10. *27 Norman Crescent, Budleigh Salterton EX9 6RB* E-mail loreliefarmer@dunelm.org.uk

FARMER, Robert James. b 65. WMMTC 03. **d** 06 **p** 07. C Lich St Chad 06-10; C Longdon 08-10; P-in-c Longdon and C Heath Hayes 10-11; V Shelfield and High Heath from 11. *Church House, 25 Green Lane, Shelfield, Walsall WS4 1RN* Tel (01922) 692550 E-mail robert@farmer2181.freeserve.co.uk

FARMER, Robert John Thayer. b 62. Kent Univ BA84. St Steph Ho Ox 91. **d** 93 **p** 94. C Leigh St Clem *Chelmsf* 93-96; P-in-c Wellingborough St Mary *Pet* 96-00; V from 00; Chapl Northants Healthcare NHS Trust from 99. *St Mary's Vicarage, 193 Midland Road, Wellingborough NN8 1NG* Tel (01933) 225626 E-mail robert@farmer17.freeserve.co.uk

FARMER, Simon John. b 60. Birm Univ BSc82. St Jo Coll Nottm 86. **d** 89 **p** 90. C Ulverston St Mary w H Trin *Carl* 89-92; CF 92-97; Chapl HM Pris Lowdham Grange 97-00; CF (TA) from 99; Perm to Offic *S'well* from 00; Operations Dir (Africa) ACCTS Mil Min Internat from 00. *26 Halloughton Road, Southwell NG25 0LR* Tel (01636) 813599 E-mail farmer@f2s.com

FARMILOE, Preb Trevor James. b 42. Sarum & Wells Th Coll. **d** 82 **p** 82. C S Petherton w the Seavingtons *B & W* 82-85; R Norton St Philip w Hemington, Hardington etc 85-93; Chapl Rural Affairs Wells Adnry 87-92; RD Frome 89-93; V Martock w Ash 93-07; RD Ivelchester 95-01 and 04-07; Preb Wells Cathl 96-07; rtd 07; Perm to Offic *B & W* 07-11; C Yeovil St Mich from 11. *38 Ashmead, Yeovil BA20 2SQ* Tel (01935) 428952 E-mail revtrev.martock@btinternet.com

FARNHAM, Douglas John. b 30. SS Mark & Jo Univ Coll Plymouth TCert52 Ex Univ MEd75. S Dios Minl Tr Scheme 80. **d** 83 **p** 84. Lect Bp Otter Coll Chich 70-78; Sen Lect W Sussex Inst of HE 78-92; NSM Barnham and Eastergate *Chich* 83-85; NSM Aldingbourne, Barnham and Eastergate 85-92; R 92-96; rtd 96; Perm to Offic *Chich* from 96. *12 Summersdale Court, The Drive, Chichester PO19 5RF* Tel (01243) 532251

FARNWORTH, Ms Joanna Helen. b 66. Jes Coll Cam BA88 MA92. St Jo Coll Nottm BTh98 MA99. **d** 99 **p** 00. C Middleton w Thornham *Man* 99-03; C Ashton 03-05; TV 05-11; P-in-c Droylsden St Martin from 11. *St James's Vicarage, Union Street, Aston-under-Lyne OL6 9NQ* Tel 0161-330 4925 E-mail joannafarnworth@aol.com

FARNWORTH, Roger. b 60. Man Univ BSc81. St Jo Coll Nottm MA99. **d** 99 **p** 00. C Tonge w Alkrington *Man* 99-03; TV Ashton 03-05; TR from 05; AD Ashton-under-Lyne from 08. *St James's Vicarage, Union Street, Ashton-under-Lyne OL6 9NQ* Tel 0161-330 2771 E-mail rogerfarnworth@aol.com

FARQUHAR, Iain. b 45. **d** 05 **p** 06. OLM Catford St Laur *S'wark* from 05. *18 Birkhall Road, London SE6 1TE* Tel (020) 8698 7438 E-mail iain@thefarquhars.freeserve.co.uk

FARQUHAR, Preb Patricia Ann. b 42. **dss** 78 **d** 87 **p** 94. S Hackney St Jo w Ch Ch *Lon* 80-01; Par Dn 87-94; C 94-01; Preb St Paul's Cathl 97-01; rtd 01. *5A Coronation Close, Norwich NR6 5HF* Tel (01603) 417554

FARQUHARSON, The Very Revd Hunter Buchanan. b 58. ALAM LLAM. Edin Th Coll 85. **d** 88 **p** 89. C Dunfermline *St And* 88-91; R Glenrothes 91-97; R Leven 95-97; R Dunfermline from 97; Provost St Ninian's Cathl Perth from 99. *St Ninian's Cathedral, North Methven Street, Perth PH1 5PP* Tel and fax (01738) 850987 *or* tel 632053 E-mail huntfar@gmail.com *or* stninians.cathedral@btinternet.com

FARR, Arthur Ronald. b 24. JP77. Llan Dioc Tr Scheme 77. **d** 81. NSM Penarth All SS *Llan* 80-90; rtd 90; Perm to Offic *Llan* from 90. *3 Cymric Close, Ely, Cardiff CF5 4GR* Tel (029) 2056 1765

FARR, John. See FARR, William John

FARR, John. b 44. ACIOB68. NOC 04. **d** 06 **p** 07. C Wallasey St Hilary *Ches* 06-10. *41 Knaresborough Road, Wallasey CH44 2BQ* Tel 0151-639 1367 Fax 637 1777 Mobile 07966-665402 E-mail johnfarr@talktalk.net

FARR (née ROSE), Margaret. b 37. Man Univ BDS, LDS60 Birm Univ MB, ChB69 MD85. WMMTC 99. **d** 02 **p** 03. NSM Handsworth St Jas *Birm* from 02; Hon Chapl Sandwell and W Birm Hosps NHS Trust from 07. *35 West Drive, Handsworth, Birmingham B20 3ST* Tel 0121-554 0909

FARR, Richard William. b 55. Ridley Hall Cam. **d** 83 **p** 84. C Enfield Ch Ch Trent Park *Lon* 83-87; C Eastbourne H Trin *Chich* 87-90; P-in-c Henham and Elsenham w Ugley *Chelmsf* 90-91; V 91-09; C Tunbridge Wells St Jo *Roch* from 09. *112 Stephens Road, Tunbridge Wells TN4 9QA* Tel (01892) 540897 E-mail dickthevic@btopenworld.com

FARR, William John. b 66. QUB BTh05 MTh07. **d** 08 **p** 09. NSM Muckamore and Killead w Gartree *Conn* 08-11; P-in-c Stoneyford from 11. *1 Ballyvannon Road, Ballinderry Upper, Lisburn BT28 2LB* Tel (028) 9442 2158 Mobile 07808-399579 E-mail j20far@hotmail.com

FARRAN, Canon George Orman. b 35. Worc Coll Ox BA58 MA62. Wycliffe Hall Ox 58. **d** 60 **p** 61. C Tyldesley w Shakerley

Man 60-62; Tutor Wycliffe Hall Ox 62-64; V Netherton *Liv* 64-73; R Sefton 69-73; R Credenhill w Brinsop, Mansel Lacey, Yazor etc *Heref* 73-83; RD Heref Rural 81-83; R Ditcheat w E Pennard and Pylle *B & W* 83-94; Dir of Ords 86-89; Can and Chan Wells Cathl 85-97; rtd 97; Perm to Offic *B & W* 97-00 and from 01. *6 The Empire, Grand Parade, Bath BA2 4DF* Tel (01225) 339365

FARRANT, David Stuart. b 38. Ripon Coll Cuddesdon 82. **d** 84 **p** 85. C Woodford St Mary w St Phil and St Jas *Chelmsf* 84-87; R Clymping and Yapton w Ford *Chich* 87-92; Dioc Schs Admin Officer 92-95; Chapl Qu Alexandra Hosp Home Worthing 95-04; P-in-c Amberley w N Stoke and Parham, Wiggonholt etc *Chich* 04-10; rtd 10. *3 Fairlands, East Preston, Littlehampton BN16 1HS*

FARRANT, Canon Martyn John. b 38. AKC61. **d** 62 **p** 63. C Hampton St Mary *Lon* 62-65; C Shere *Guildf* 65-67; V Stoneleigh 67-75; V Addlestone 75-83; V Dorking w Ranmore 83-98; RD Dorking 89-94; Hon Can Guildf Cathl 96-98; rtd 98; Perm to Offic *Guildf* from 98; Chapl Phyllis Tuckwell Hospice Farnham 98-01. *42 Hampstead Road, Dorking RH4 3AE* Tel (01306) 740916

FARRAR, Canon James Albert. b 27. TCD BA55 MA57. CITC 56. **d** 56 **p** 57. C Dublin Drumcondra w N Strand *D & G* 56-59; C Dublin Rathmines 59-61; I Ballinaclash 61-72; I Dunganstown w Redcross 72-79; Warden Ch Min of Healing 79-95; Hon Clerical V Ch Ch Cathl Dublin 79-92; Can Ch Ch Cathl Dublin from 92; rtd 95. *12 Ailtanoir, Upper Glenageary Road, Dun Laoghaire, Co Dublin, Republic of Ireland* Tel (00353) (1) 284 1060

FARRAR, Prof Roy Alfred. b 39. Imp Coll Lon BSc60 PhD67 FWeld85. Wycliffe Hall Ox 99. **d** 00 **p** 01. NSM Portswood St Denys *Win* 00-04; P-in-c Lille *Eur* 04-06; Perm to Offic *Bris* from 07. *20 Orchard Court, Arches Lane, Malmesbury SN16 0ED* Tel (01666) 826700

FARRAR, Ruth. b 43. Matlock Coll of Educn CertEd64. **d** 04 **p** 05. OLM Leesfield *Man* from 04. *Belvoir, 43 Coverhill Road, Grotton, Oldham OL4 5RE* Tel 0161-633 0374

FARRELL, Mrs Joanna Susan Elizabeth. b 53. Southn Univ LLB95. STETS 03. **d** 06 **p** 07. NSM Steep and Froxfield w Privett *Portsm* from 06. *Hurst Farm Cottage, Hurst Lane, Privett, Alton GU34 3PL* Tel (01730) 828450
E-mail joanna@hurstfarmcottage.co.uk

FARRELL, Miss Katherine Lucy Anne. b 61. Westcott Ho Cam 00. **d** 02 **p** 03. C Forest Gate Em w Upton Cross *Chelmsf* 02-03; C Lt Ilford St Mich 03-07; V Bellingham St Dunstan *S'wark* 07-11; C Croydon St Jo from 11. *48 Northampton Road, Croydon CR0 7HT* Tel (020) 8662 0894
E-mail k.farrell916@btinternet.com

FARRELL, Ms Margaret Ruth. b 57. Linc Inst Melbourne BAppSc(OT)78. **d** 02 **p** 03. C Bury St Edmunds All SS w St Jo and St Geo *St E* 02-06; P-in-c Woolpit w Drinkstone 06-08; R from 08. *The Rectory, Rectory Lane, Woolpit, Bury St Edmunds IP30 9QP* Tel (01359) 242244

FARRELL, Peter Godfrey Paul. b 39. Sarum & Wells Th Coll 72. **d** 74 **p** 75. C St Just in Roseland *Truro* 74-77; C Kenwyn 77-80; V Knighton St Jo *Leic* 80-86; TR Clarendon Park St Jo w Knighton St Mich 86-89; V Woodham *Guildf* 89-99; V Wells St Cuth w Wookey Hole *B & W* 99-09; rtd 09. *The Rectory, Bath Road, West Harptree, Bristol BS40 6HB* Tel (01761) 221239
E-mail peter.farrell2@tiscali.co.uk

FARRELL, Robert Edward. b 54. Univ of Wales (Abth) BA74 Jes Coll Ox BA77 MA81. Qu Coll Birm 83. **d** 86 **p** 87. C Llanrhos *St As* 86-88; C Prestwich St Marg *Man* 89-91; V Moulsham St Luke *Chelmsf* 91-98; V Thorpe Bay 98-08; R Ardleigh and The Bromleys from 08. *The Rectory, Hall Road, Great Bromley, Colchester CO7 7TS* Tel (01206) 230344
E-mail robert_farrell21@hotmail.com

FARRELL, Ronald Anthony. b 57. Edin Univ BD84 Birm Univ MA86. Qu Coll Birm 84. **d** 86 **p** 87. C Shard End *Birm* 86-87; C Shirley 87-89; Bp's Officer for Schs and Young People 89-93; V Kingstanding St Mark 93-01; TR Swinton and Pendlebury *Man* 01-05; P-in-c Lower Broughton Ascension 02-05; V W Bromwich St Fran *Lich* from 05. *Friar Park Vicarage, Freeman Road, Wednesbury WS10 0HJ* Tel 0121-556 5823

FARRELL, Stephen Andrew. b 84. Jes Coll Ox BA05. CITC BTh08. **d** 08 **p** 09. C Taney *D & G* 08-11; I Dublin Zion Ch from 11. *Zion Rectory, 18 Bushy Park Road, Rathgar, Dublin 6, Republic of Ireland* Tel (00353) (1) 492 2365 or 406 4730
E-mail zion@dublin.anglican.org

FARRELL, Thomas Stanley. b 32. Lon Univ BD71. Ridley Hall Cam 69. **d** 71 **p** 72. C Much Woolton *Liv* 71-73; C Gt Sankey 73-74; Asst Chapl Dulwich Coll 74-76; Chapl 76-81; P-in-c Wonersh *Guildf* 81-86; V 86-90; RD Cranleigh 87-90; R St Marg Lothbury and St Steph Coleman Street etc *Lon* 90-00; P-in-c St Botolph without Aldersgate 90-97; rtd 00; Hon C Burford w Fulbrook, Taynton, Asthall etc *Ox* 00-04; Perm to Offic from 04. *Candle Cottage, 23 Frogmore Lane, Long Crendon, Aylesbury HP18 9DZ* Tel (01844) 208683

FARRER, Canon Carol Elizabeth. b 47. Open Univ BA88. Cranmer Hall Dur 81. **dss** 83 **d** 87 **p** 94. Newbarns w Hawcoat *Carl* 83-86; Egremont and Haile 86-91; Par Dn 87-91; TD Penrith w Newton Reigny and Plumpton Wall 91-94; TV 94-01; Dioc Lay Min Adv 87-88; Assoc Dir of Ords 88-97; Dir of Ords 97-00; Dioc OLM Officer 00-05; TV S Barrow 01-07; Hon Can Carl Cathl 01-07; rtd 08. *3 Marlow Terrace, Mold CH7 1HH* Tel (01352) 756011

FARRER, Canon Michael Robert Wedlake. b 22. St Pet Hall Ox BA52 MA57. Tyndale Hall Bris 47. **d** 52 **p** 53. C Ox St Ebbe 52-56; Tutor Clifton Th Coll 56-65; R Barton Seagrave *Pet* 65-73; R Barton Seagrave w Warkton 73-78; V Cambridge St Paul *Ely* 78-92; RD Cambridge 84-89; Hon Can Ely Cathl 88-92; rtd 92; Bp's Sen Chapl *Ely* 92-95; Perm to Offic 92-03. *2 Houghton Gardens, Ely CB7 4JN* Tel (01353) 665654

✠FARRER, The Rt Revd Ralph David. b 44. St Barn Coll Adelaide ThL68. **d** 68 **p** 69 **c** 98. C Plympton w Richmond Australia 68-71; P-in-c Hillcrest 71-73; C Melbourne St Pet 73-75; V Brunswick 75-90; V Melbourne St Pet 90-98; Can La Trobe 85-98; Adn La Trobe 94-96; Adn Melbourne 96-98; Bp Wangaratta 98-08; V Arundel w Tortington and S Stoke *Chich* from 08; Hon Asst Bp Chich from 09. *The Vicarage, 26 Maltravers Street, Arundel BN18 9BU* Tel (01903) 885209
E-mail stnicholasvicar@tiscali.co.uk

FARRINGTON, Canon Christine Marion. b 42. Birkbeck Coll Lon BA65 Nottm Univ DASS66 Middx Poly MA75. St Alb Minl Tr Scheme 79. **dss** 82 **d** 87 **p** 94. Redbourn *St Alb* 82-87; Dir Past Studies Linc Th Coll 86-87; HM Pris Linc 86-87; Dir Sarum Chr Cen 87-93; Dn Sarum Cathl 87-93; Co-Dir of Ords and Dir of Women's Min *Ely* 93-02, Hon Can Ely Cathl 93-02; C Cambridge Gt St Mary w St Mich 93-96; V Cambridge St Mark 96-02; Chapl Wolfs Coll Cam 97-02; Perm to Offic *St Alb* 97-04; Chapl to The Queen from 98; rtd 02; RD Wheathampstead *St Alb* 04-07. *42 East Common, Redbourn, St Albans AL3 7NQ* Tel (01582) 793409

FARRINGTON, Mrs Lynda June. b 59. WMMTC. **d** 01 **p** 02. NSM Cannock *Lich* 01-07; NSM Abbots Bromley w Blithfield 07-10; NSM Abbots Bromley, Blithfield, Colton, Colwich etc from 11; Officer for NSMs 06-08. *Blithford Farm, Blithbury, Rugeley WS15 3JB* Tel (01283) 840253 or 502131
E-mail revmumlynda@aol.com

FARROW, Edward. b 38. Sarum Th Coll 69. **d** 71 **p** 72. C Parkstone St Pet w Branksea *Sarum* 71-74; R Tidworth 74-79; P-in-c W and E Lulworth 79-80; P-in-c Winfrith Newburgh w Chaldon Herring 79-80; R The Lulworths, Winfrith Newburgh and Chaldon 80-83; V Ensbury Park 83-03; Chapl Talbot Heath Sch Bournemouth 83-97; rtd 03; P-in-c Marseille w Aix-en-Provence *Eur* 05-08. *21 Avenue de Bourgogne, 13600 La Ciotat, France* Tel (0033) 4 42 83 03 20

FARROW, Elizabeth Maura. b 43. Edin Th Coll. **d** 91 **p** 96. NSM Glas H Cross 91-96; TV Bearsden w Milngavie 96-00 and 03-05. *5 Campsie Road, Strathblane G63 9AB* Tel (01360) 770936

FARROW, Ian Edmund Dennett. b 38. S'wark Ord Course 70. **d** 72 **p** 73. C Tunbridge Wells St Jo *Roch* 72-78; Chapl N Cambs Gen Hosp Gp 78-92; P-in-c Walsoken *Ely* 78-80; R 80-92; V Bisley, Oakridge, Miserden and Edgeworth *Glouc* 92-04; rtd 04. *Wellspring, Brook Lane, Stonesfield, Witney OX29 8PR* Tel (01993) 891293

FARROW, Keith. b 59. Leeds Univ BA05. NOC 02. **d** 05 **p** 06. C Sprotbrough *Sheff* 05-07; C Hillsborough and Wadsley Bridge 07-09; P-in-c from 09. *Christ Church Vicarage, 218 Fox Hill Road, Sheffield S6 1HJ* Tel 0114-231 1576
E-mail keith.farrow@sheffield.anglican.org

FARROW, Peter Maurice. b 44. St Chad's Coll Dur BSc65. **d** 68 **p** 69. C Gt Yarmouth *Nor* 68-71; C N Lynn w St Marg and St Nic 71-75; P-in-c Sculthorpe w Dunton and Doughton 75-77; Perm to Offic 78-89; TV Lowestoft and Kirkley 89-94; Ind Miss 89-94; Sen Ind Chapl 94-99; TV Gaywood 95-02; P-in-c Mundford w Lynford, Cranwich and Ickburgh w Langford 02-09; rtd 09; Perm to Offic *Nor* from 09. *129 Carlton Road, Lowestoft NR33 0LZ* Tel (01502) 521817
E-mail farrpm@dialstart.net

FARTHING, Michael Thomas. b 28. St Cuth Soc Dur 48 Lambeth STh81 CertHE08. St Steph Ho Ox. **d** 58 **p** 59. C St Marylebone St Mark w St Luke *Lon* 58-61; C Newport Pagnell *Ox* 63-69; R Standlake 69-76; R Yelford 69-76; R Lower Windrush 76-82; V Wheatley w Forest Hill and Stanton St John 82-95; rtd 95. Perm to Offic *Ox* from 95. *32 Falstaff Close, Eynsham, Oxford OX29 4QA* Tel (01865) 883805

FARTHING, Paul Andrew. b 58. McGill Univ Montreal BA80 STM82. Montreal Dioc Th Coll. **d** 83 **p** 84. C Montreal W St Phil Canada 83-85; R Montreal St Jo Divine 85-96; R Montreal St Jo Ev 96-99; P-in-c Burton *Lich* 99-05; V Burton St Aid and St Paul from 05. *The Vicarage, Rangemore Street, Burton-on-Trent DE14 2ED* Tel (01283) 544054
E-mail paul@pafarthing.clara.co.uk

FARTHING, Ronald Edward. b 27. Oak Hill Th Coll. **d** 58 **p** 59. C Tollington Park St Anne *Lon* 58-61; C Tollington Park St Mark 58-61; V Clodock and Longtown w Craswell and Llanveyno

Heref 61-67; R Langley *Cant* 67-72; V Bapchild w Tonge and Rodmersham 72-80; TV Widecombe, Leusden and Princetown etc *Ex* 80-84; P-in-c Riddlesworth w Gasthorpe and Knettishall *Nor* 84-87; P-in-c Garboldisham w Blo' Norton 84-87; P-in-c Brettenham w Rushford 84-87; R Garboldisham w Blo' Norton, Riddlesworth etc 88-92; rtd 92; Perm to Offic *Nor* and *St E* from 92. *23 Home Close, Great Ellingham, Attleborough NR17 1HW* Tel (01953) 456750

FASS, Michael John. b 44. Trin Coll Cam MA75. Edin Dioc NSM Course 89. **d** 95 **p** 95. NSM Penicuik *Edin* 95-97; NSM W Linton 95-97; NSM Roslin (Rosslyn Chpl) 97-06; Bp's Officer for Min from 03. *Royal Scots Club, 29 Abercromby Place, Edinburgh EH3 6QE* E-mail michael.fass@btinternet.com

FATHERS, Jeremy Mark. b 54. Crewe & Alsager Coll BEd78. WMMTC 93. **d** 96 **p** 97. NSM Baxterley w Hurley and Wood End and Merevale etc *Birm* 96-00; C Sheldon 00-03; Chapl N Warks NHS Trust 00-02; R Chelmsley Wood *Birm* from 03. *The Vicarage, Pike Drive, Birmingham B37 7US* Tel 0121-770 5155 or 770 1511 Mobile 07769-780306 E-mail j.fathers@virgin.net

FAUCHON-JONES, Susan Gurmito. b 61. **d** 06 **p** 07. NSM Eynsford w Farningham and Lullingstone *Roch* 06-08; NSM Southborough St Pet w Ch Ch and St Matt etc from 08. *1 Springfield Cottages, Glebe Road, Weald, Sevenoaks TN14 6RD* Tel (01732) 463289

FAULDS, Ian Craig. b 48. **d** 03 **p** 04. NSM Maughold *S & M* from 03. *The Lynague, Ramsey Road, Lynague, Peel, Isle of Man IM5 2AQ* Tel (01624) 842045

FAULDS, John Parker. b 33. Edin Th Coll 55. **d** 57 **p** 58. C Edin St Dav 57-58; C Edin St Jo 58-60; Chapl Dundee Hosps 60-63; Chapl Qu Coll Dundee 60-63; Dioc Supernumerary *Bre* 60-63; Lic to Offic *Birm* 65-66; P-in-c Aston Brook 66-69; V Handsworth St Pet 69-87; Perm to Offic 87-98; rtd 99. *Address withheld by request*

FAULKES, Edmund Marquis. See MARQUIS-FAULKES, Edmund

FAULKNER, Mrs Anne Elizabeth. b 38. Bp Otter Coll BA58. **d** 00 **p** 01. NSM Aylesbury w Bierton and Hulcott *Ox* 00-04; Chapl to Bp Buckingham 02-04; rtd 04; Hon C Wroxall *Portsm* 04-05; P-in-c from 05; P-in-c St Lawrence 08-10. *13 Western Road, Shanklin PO37 7NF* Tel and fax (01983) 862291 E-mail anne.faulkner@dsl.pipex.com

FAULKNER, Brian Thomas. b 48. S Dios Minl Tr Scheme. **d** 84 **p** 85. C W Leigh *Portsm* 84-88; R Foulsham w Hindolveston and Guestwick *Nor* 88-93; P-in-c Erpingham w Calthorpe, Ingworth, Aldborough etc 93-94; R from 94; RD Ingworth from 10. *The Rectory, School Road, Erpingham, Norwich NR11 7QX* Tel (01263) 768073 E-mail brian-faulkner@lineone.net

FAULKNER, Bruce Stephen. b 63. Trin Coll Bris BA97 St Jo Coll Dur MA08. Cranmer Hall Dur 06. **d** 08 **p** 09. C Somerton w Compton Dundon, the Charltons etc *B & W* from 08. *6 Northfield Way, Somerton TA11 6ST* Tel 07796-283766 (mobile) E-mail bsfaulkner1@aol.com

FAULKNER, Mrs Catherine Evelyn. b 43. Man Poly RHV82. **d** 01 **p** 02. OLM Urmston *Man* from 01. *5 Barnfield, Urmston, Manchester M41 9EW* Tel 0161-748 3226 E-mail cath@northwood1.freeserve.co.uk

FAULKNER, David Ernest. b 43. St Mich Coll Llan 65. **d** 66 **p** 67. C Aberystwyth St Mich *St D* 66-68; C Tenby and Gumfreston 68-69; C Burry Port and Pwll 69-73; R Jeffreyston w Reynalton and E Williamston 73-79; R Jeffreyston w Reynoldston and E Williamston etc 79-89; V Whitland w Cyffig and Henllan Amgoed etc 89-96; V Llawhaden w Bletherston and Llanycefn 96-06; rtd 06. *Littledean, Maes Abaty, Whitland SA34 0HQ* Tel (01994) 241464

FAULKNER, Henry Odin. b 35. G&C Coll Cam BA56 MA59. St Jo Coll Nottm 70. **d** 74 **p** 75. C Heigham H Trin *Nor* 74-76; C Heeley *Sheff* 76-80; TV Netherthorpe 80-84; Perm to Offic *St Alb* from 84; rtd 00. *69 Holywell Hill, St Albans AL1 1HF* Tel (01727) 854177 Mobile 07719-642479

FAULKNER, (née RITCHIE), Ms June. b 41. UCD BA64. **d** 05 **p** 06. OLM New Windsor *Ox* from 05. *69 Springfield Road, Windsor SL4 3PR* Tel (01753) 622808

FAULKNER, Margaret Evelyn. See WHITFORD, Mrs Margaret Evelyn

FAULKNER, Martin Trevor. b 62. Salford Univ BSc83 Bretton Hall Coll PGCE88 Leeds Univ BA10. Coll of Resurr Mirfield 09. **d** 11. C Spilsby Gp *Linc* from 11. *3 Woodlands View, Spilsby PE23 5GD* Tel (01790) 755615 E-mail rev.martin@hotmail.co.uk

FAULKNER, Peter Graham. b 47. Lon Univ CertEd69. Oak Hill Th Coll BA87. **d** 82 **p** 83. C Crofton *Portsm* 87-89; R Mid Marsh Gp *Linc* 89-98; V S Cave and Ellerker w Broomfleet *York* from 98; P-in-c N Cave w Cliffe from 09; P-in-c Hotham from 09; RD Howden 05-10. *The Vicarage, 10 Station Road, South Cave, Brough HU15 2AA* Tel (01430) 423693 E-mail peter@faulkner.go-plus.net

FAULKNER, Canon Roger Kearton. b 36. AKC62. **d** 63 **p** 64. C Oxton *Ches* 63-67; C Ellesmere Port 67-69; V Runcorn H Trin 69-73; TV E Runcorn w Halton 73-76; V Altrincham St Geo

76-90; Chapl Altrincham Gen Hosp 80-96; Hon Can Ches Cathl 88-96; V Higher Bebington 90-96; rtd 96; Perm to Offic *Ches* 96-98. *58 Albermarle Road, Wallasey, Wirral CH44 6LX*

FAULKNER, Ms Susan Ann. b 70. Lanc Univ BA96. Ripon Coll Cuddesdon 97. **d** 99 **p** 00. C Scotswood *Newc* 99-03; P-in-c Byker St Silas 03-10; P-in-c Badby w Newham and Charwelton w Fawsley etc *Pet* from 10. *The Vicarage, 24A High Street, Silverstone, Towcester NN12 8US* Tel (01327) 857996 Mobile 07786-265422 E-mail revsuefaulkner@aol.com

FAULKS, David William. b 45. EMMTC 82. **d** 86 **p** 87. C Market Harborough *Leic* 86-88; C Wootton Bassett *Sarum* 88-96; R Clipston w Naseby and Haselbech w Kelmarsh *Pet* from 90. *The Rectory, 18 Church Lane, Clipston, Market Harborough LE16 9RW* Tel and fax (01858) 525342 E-mail david.faulks@btinternet.com

FAULKS, Simon George. b 73. Moorlands Th Coll BA99 St Jo Coll Nottm 09. **d** 11. C Warminster Ch Ch *Sarum* from 11. *19 Ashley Coombe, Warminster BA12 9QU* Tel 07795-154222 (mobile) E-mail revsimon@notashamed.co.uk

FAULL, The Very Revd Cecil Albert. b 30. TCD BA52 MA87. **d** 54 **p** 55. C Dublin Zion Ch *D & G* 54-57; C Dublin St Geo 57-59; Hon Clerical V Ch Ch Cathl Dublin 58-63; C Dun Laoghaire 59-63; I Portarlington w Cloneyhurke and Lea *M & K* 63-71; I Dublin St Geo and St Thos *D & G* 71-80; I Clondalkin w Rathcoole 81-91; Can Ch Ch Cathl Dublin 90-91; I Dunleckney w Nurney, Lorum and Kiltennel *C & O* 91-96; Dean Leighlin 91-96; P-in-c Leighlin w Grange Sylvae, Shankill etc 91-96; rtd 96. *1 Mageough Home, Cowper Road, Rathmines, Dublin 6, Republic of Ireland* Tel (00353) (1) 497 2377

FAULL, Mrs Janet. b 60. SS Paul & Mary Coll Cheltenham PGCE86 LGSM82. WEMTC 05. **d** 08 **p** 09. C Cheltenham Ch Ch *Glouc* from 08. *26 Eldorado Road, Cheltenham GL50 2PT* Tel (01242) 519183 Mobile 07986-650459 E-mail martin.faull@btinternet.com

FAULL, The Very Revd Vivienne Frances. b 55. St Hilda's Coll Ox BA77 MA82 Clare Coll Cam MA90. St Jo Coll Nottm BA81. dss 82 **d** 87 **p** 94. Mossley Hill St Matt and St Jas *Liv* 82-85; Chapl Clare Coll Cam 85-90; Chapl Glouc Cathl 90-94; Can Res Cov Cathl 94-00; Vice-Provost 95-00; Provost Leic 00-02; Dean Leic from 02. *The Cathedral Centre, 21 St Martin's, Leicester LE1 5DE* Tel 0116-248 7456 Fax 248 7470 E-mail viv@leccofe.org

FAULL, William Baines. b 29. FRCVS70 Lon Univ BSc51. NW Ord Course 77. **d** 79 **p** 80. NSM Willaston *Ches* 79-80; NSM Neston 80-82; P-in-c Harthill and Burwardsley 82-86; Perm to Offic 87-91; from 96; Sen Fell Liv Univ from 89; V Ashton Hayes *Ches* 91-96; Chapl Hospice of the Good Shepherd Backford 99-06. *Tioman, Briardale Road, Willaston, Neston CH64 1TD* Tel 0151-327 4424

FAULTLESS, Mrs Patricia Doreen. b 53. **d** 05 **p** 06. OLM Glascote and Stonydelph *Lich* from 05. *40 Stephenson Close, Glascote, Tamworth B77 2DQ* Tel (01827) 287171 Mobile 07980-434897 E-mail patfaultless@hotmail.com

FAURE WALKER, Edward William. b 46. DL01. SAOMC 01. **d** 04 **p** 05. NSM Stevenage All SS Pin Green *St Alb* from 04. *Sandon Bury, Sandon, Buntingford SG9 0QY* Tel and fax (01763) 287753 Mobile 07801-175009 E-mail e.faure.walker@farming.me.uk

FAUX, Steven Paul. b 58. UEA BA79. Trin Coll Bris BA07. **d** 07 **p** 08. C Bath St Mich w St Paul *B & W* from 07. *Fleetlands, Weston Park, Bath BA1 4AL* Tel (01225) 313145 E-mail steven@stevenfaux.com

FAWCETT, Mrs Diane Elizabeth. b 49. Cant Univ (NZ) BA72 Kent Univ MA03. Westcott Ho Cam 03. **d** 04 **p** 05. C Egerton w Pluckley *Cant* 04-08; Perm to Offic 08-10; Hon C St Margarets-at-Cliffe w Westcliffe etc from 10. *The Vicarage, Sea Street, St Margarets-at-Cliffe, Dover CT15 6AR* Tel (01304) 852179 E-mail fawcett38@hotmail.com

FAWCETT, Mrs Joanna Mary. b 45. SRN67 SCM69. EAMTC 01. **d** 04 **p** 05. NSM Blakeney w Cley, Wiveton, Glandford etc *Nor* from 04. *14 The Cornfields, Langham, Holt NR25 7DQ* Tel (01328) 830415 E-mail jofawcett@btinternet.com

FAWCETT, Canon Pamela Margaret. b 29. Univ Coll Lon BA51 DipEd75. EAMTC 83. dss 86 **d** 87 **p** 94. Stiffkey and Cockthorpe w Morston, Langham etc *Nor* 86-90; Hon C 87-90; Hon Asst Min Repps Deanery 91-92; Hon C Trunch 92-01; Asst Dir of Ords 93-99; Bp's Consultant for Women's Min 93-01; Hon Can Nor Cathl 94-01; Perm to Offic from 01. *Seekings, 47A High Street, Mundesley, Norwich NR11 8JL* Tel (01263) 721752 E-mail pam.seekings@tinyworld.co.uk

FAWCETT, Timothy John. b 44. K Coll Lon BD66 AKC67 PhD71. St Boniface Warminster 66. **d** 67 **p** 68. C Blackpool St Steph *Blackb* 67-70; Hon C St Marylebone All SS *Lon* 68-70; C Southgate St Mich 70-72; Sacr Dur Cathl 72-75; V Wheatley Hill 75-79; V Torrisholme *Blackb* 79-84; V Thaxted *Chelmsf* 84-89; NSM Holt Deanery *Nor* 09-12; C Stiffkey and Bale 06-09; rtd 09; Perm to Offic *Nor* from 09. *Dowitchers, 14 The Cornfield, Langham, Holt NR25 7DQ* Tel (01328) 830415 E-mail tjfawcett@btinternet.com

FAWNS, Lynne. b 56. Thames Valley Univ BA95. NTMTC 97. **d** 00 **p** 01. C Hillingdon All SS *Lon* 00-03; V London Colney St Pet *St Alb* from 03. *The Vicarage, Riverside, London Colney, St Albans AL2 1QT* Tel (01727) 769797 E-mail lynne@ffamily.freeserve.co.uk

FAYERS, Robert Stanley. b 48. St Steph Ho Ox 82. **d** 84 **p** 85. C Deptford St Paul *S'wark* 84-88; V Beckenham St Mich w St Aug *Roch* 88-00; V Brighton St Mich *Chich* from 00; P-in-c Brighton St Paul from 06. *St Michael's Vicarage, 6 Montpelier Villas, Brighton BN1 3DH* Tel (01273) 727362 E-mail fatherobertfayersssc@gmail.com

FAYLE, David Charles Wilfred. b 51. Sarum & Wells Th Coll. **d** 83 **p** 84. C Parkstone St Pet w Branksea and St Osmund *Sarum* 83-87; TV Dorchester 87-96; P-in-c Taunton All SS *B & W* 96-97; V from 97. *All Saints' Vicarage, Roman Road, Taunton TA1 2DE* Tel (01823) 324730 E-mail dfayle@freeserve.co.uk

FAZZANI, Keith. b 47. Portsm Poly BSc70. Cant Sch of Min 93. **d** 96 **p** 97. NSM Appledore w Brookland, Fairfield, Brenzett etc *Cant* 96-01 and from 05; Chapl Team Ldr E Kent Hosps NHS Trust from 01. *Oakhouse Farm, Appledore, Ashford TN26 2BB* Tel (01233) 758322 *or* (01227) 766877 ext 74212 E-mail kfazzani@btinternet.com

FEAK, Christopher Martin. b 52. Keele Univ BA75. Trin Coll Bris 92. **d** 94 **p** 95. C Handsworth St Mary *Birm* 94-97; P-in-c Perry Common 97-00; V 00-05; AD Aston 01-05; P-in-c Sandown Ch Ch *Portsm* from 05; P-in-c Lower Sandown St Jo from 05. *10 Elmbank Gardens, Sandown PO36 9SA* Tel (01983) 402548 E-mail chris.feak@ukonline.co.uk

FEAR, Mrs Susan. b 59. **d** 11. NSM Werrington *Pet* from 11. *21 Riverside, Deeping Gate, Peterborough PE6 9AJ* Tel (01778) 348857 E-mail sue.fear@googlemail.com

FEARN, Anthony John. b 34. Lich Th Coll 58. **d** 61 **p** 62. C Redditch St Steph *Worc* 61-64; C Bladon w Woodstock *Ox* 64-66; V Ruscombe and Twyford 67-85; P-in-c Westmill w St Munden *St Alb* 85-87; Asst Dioc Stewardship Adv 85-87; Chr Giving Adv *Heref* 87-99; rtd 99; Perm to Offic *Heref* from 99. *8 St Mary's Close, Madley, Hereford HR2 9DP* Tel and fax (01981) 250320 E-mail john fearn@bigfoot.com

FEARN, Michael Wilfred. b 47. Sarum & Wells Th Coll 92. **d** 94 **p** 95. C Blandford Forum and Langton Long *Sarum* 94-98; TV Wylye and Till Valley 98-04; R Flint *St As* 04-08; rtd 09. *22 Hesketh Road, Old Colwyn, Colwyn Bay LL29 8AT* Tel (01492) 512723 E-mail fearn m@sky.com

FEARNLEY, Jeffrey Malcolm. b 46. Newc Univ BSc69. St Jo Coll Nottm 90. **d** 92 **p** 93. C Bispham *Blackb* 92-95; C Bolton w Ireby and Uldale *Carl* 95-00; TV Binsey 00-02; C 02-07; rtd 07; Perm to Offic *Blackb* from 07. *32 Chestnut Court, Leyland PR25 3GN* Tel (01772) 458696

FEARNSIDE, Mary Ingrid. b 44. OLM course 98. **d** 98 **p** 99. OLM Shelton and Oxon *Lich* from 98; Chapl R Shrewsbury Hosps NHS Trust 98-04; Chapl Shrewsbury and Telford NHS Trust from 04. *23 Eastwood Road, Shrewsbury SY3 8YJ* Tel (01743) 353290 Pager 01743-261000 E-mail mary.fearnside@fsmail.net

FEARON, Mrs Doris Ethel Elizabeth. b 26. Gilmore Ho 66. **dss** 72 **d** 87. Lingfield *S'wark* 68-75; Farnborough *Roch* 75-77; Bitterne *Win* 78-86; rtd 86; Bexhill St Pet *Chich* 86-87; Hon Par Dn 87-89; Perm to Offic 89-95; New Zealand from 96; Hon Asst Dn One Tree Hill St Oswald 99-02. *Waiatarua Mercy Parklands, 12 Umere Crescent, Ellerslie, Auckland 1051, New Zealand*

FEARON, Mrs Irene. b 51. CBDTI 00. **d** 03 **p** 04. NSM Maryport, Netherton and Flimby *Carl* 03-08; NSM Camerton, Seaton and W Seaton from 08. *Kirkborough Lodge, Ellenborough, Maryport CA15 7RD* Tel (01900) 813108 E-mail irene@kirklodge.com

FEATHERSTON, Margery. *See* GRANGE, Mrs Alice Margery

FEATHERSTONE, Canon Andrew. b 53. St Chad's Coll Dur BA74 MA93. Sarum & Wells Th Coll 78. **d** 80 **p** 81. C Newc H Cross 80-83; C Seaton Hirst 83-86; TV 86-87; R Crook *Dur* 87-99; V Stanley 87-99; AD Stanhope 94-99; V Stockton 99-05; Can and Chan Wells Cathl from 05. *8 The Liberty, Wells BA5 2SU* Tel (01749) 679587 E-mail andrew.featherstone@btinternet.com

FEATHERSTONE, Gray. b 42. Stellenbosch Univ BA62 LLB64. Cuddesdon Coll 65. **d** 67 **p** 68. C Woodstock S Africa 67-70; Asst Master Waterford Sch Swaziland 70-72; P-in-c Maputo St Steph and St Lawr Mozambique 73-76; Miss to Seamen 73-80; V Upper Clapton St Matt *Lon* 80-83; V Stamford Hill St Thos 80-89; Chr Aid Area Sec (N & W Lon) 89-06; (Lon) 06-07; rtd 07; Perm to Offic *Lon* from 97. *137 Leslie Road, London N2 8BH* Tel (020) 8444 1975

FEATHERSTONE, John. b 32. Man Univ BA53 St Cath Soc Ox MTh59 Dur Univ DipEd66. Wycliffe Hall Ox 57. **d** 60 **p** 61. C Newland St Aug *York* 60-62; C Kidderminster St Jo and All Innocents *Worc* 62-65; Hd RE Co Gr Sch St Pet 66-70; Hd RE Qu Anne Gr Sch *York* 70-85; Chapl Tangier *Eur* 86-87 and 90-93; Chapl Pau w Biarritz 87-88; C Mexborough *Sheff* 88-90; rtd 93; Perm to Offic *York* from 93. *39 Cambridge Avenue, Marton-in-Cleveland, Middlesbrough TS7 8EH* Tel (01642) 318181

FEATHERSTONE, Robert Leslie. b 54. Leeds Univ MA04 LLCM74 Lon Univ CertEd75. Chich Th Coll 84. **d** 86 **p** 87. C Crayford *Roch* 86-89; V Belvedere St Aug 89-94; V Crowborough St Jo *Chich* 94-01; P-in-c New Brompton St Luke *Roch* 01-06; Hon Succ Roch Cathl 03-06; Perm to Offic 07-08; P-in-c Hastings St Clem and All SS *Chich* from 09. *The Rectory, 7 High Street, Hastings TN34 3EY* Tel (01424) 422023 Mobile 07878-237312 E-mail frrobertf@live.co.uk

FEAVER, Nigel Conway McDonald. b 51. Leeds Univ BA73 Brunel Univ MA76 CQSW76. Ripon Coll Cuddesdon 03. **d** 05 **p** 06. C Oxton *Ches* 05-08; R Wincanton *B & W* from 08; R Pen Selwood from 08. *The Oaks, 3 Bayford Court, Bayford Hill, Wincanton BA9 9GY* Tel (01963) 31507 E-mail revnigelfeaver@googlemail.com

FEENEY, Damian Prescott Anthony. b 62. Grey Coll Dur BA83 PGCE84 ALCM81. Chich Th Coll BTh94. **d** 94 **p** 95. C Harrogate St Wilfrid *Ripon* 94-96; C Preston St Jo and St Geo *Blackb* 96-99; Bp's Miss P to Longsands 99-01; TR Ribbleton 01-04; V Woodplumpton 04-09; Vice-Prin St Steph Ho Ox from 09. *St Stephen's House, 16 Marston Street, Oxford OX4 1JX* Tel (01865) 613515 E-mail damian.feeney@ssho.ox.ac.uk

FEIST, Canon Nicholas James. b 45. Solicitor 70. St Jo Coll Nottm. **d** 76 **p** 77. C Didsbury St Jas *Man* 76-80; TV Didsbury St Jas and Em 80; V Friarmere 80-88; R Middleton 88-94; TR Middleton w Thornham 94-10; R Middleton and Thornham from 10; AD Heywood and Middleton 99-07; Hon Can Man Cathl from 98. *Middleton Rectory, Mellalieu Street, Middleton, Manchester M24 5DN* Tel and fax 0161-643 2693 E-mail nickjfeist@ntlworld.com

FELL, Michael John. b 24. FICE68 FIStructE68. S'wark Ord Course. **d** 69 **p** 71. C Feltham *Lon* 69-76; C Ashford St Matt 76-78; C Hykeham *Linc* 78-81; V Cranwell 81-85; R Leasingham 81-85; R Bishop Norton, Wadingham and Snitterby 85-90; rtd 90; Hon C Surrey Epiphany Canada from 91. *162-10659 150th Street, Surrey BC V3R 4B9, Canada* Tel (001) (604) 582 5889

FEITAL, Peterson. *See* DE ALMEIDA FEITAL, Peterson

FELCE, Brian George. b 30. Jes Coll Ox BA54 MA57. Oak Hill Th Coll. **d** 58 **p** 59. C E Twickenham St Steph *Lon* 58-60; C Ramsgate St Luke *Cant* 60-64; R Bedingfield w Southolt *St E* 64-73; V Preston All SS *Blackb* 73-86; rtd 86. *11 St Barnabas Road, Sutton SM1 4NL* Tel (020) 8642 7885

FELIX, Canon David Rhys. b 55. Univ of Wales (Cardiff) LLB76 Solicitor 81. Ripon Coll Cuddesdon 83. **d** 86 **p** 87. C Bromborough *Ches* 86-89; V Grange St Andr 89-99; Chapl Halton Gen Hosp NHS Trust 95-99; P-in-c Runcorn H Trin *Ches* 96-99; RD Frodsham 98-99; V Daresbury from 99; Sen Ind Chapl from 00; Hon Can Ches Cathl from 06. *All Saints' Vicarage, Daresbury Lane, Daresbury, Warrington WA4 4AE* Tel (01925) 740348 Fax 740799 E-mail david.felix@btinternet.com

FELL, Canon Alan William. b 46. Ball Coll Ox BA69. Coll of Resurr Mirfield 68. **d** 71 **p** 72. C Woodchurch *Ches* 71-74; C Man Clayton St Cross w St Paul 74-75; C Prestwich St Marg 75-77; V Hyde St Thos *Ches* 77-80; R Tattenhall and Handley 80-86; V Sedbergh, Cautley and Garsdale *Bradf* from 86; Hon C Firbank, Howgill and Killington 86-06; P-in-c from 06; Hon Can Bradf Cathl from 96; RD Ewecross 00-05. *The Vicarage, Loftus Hill, Sedbergh LA10 5SQ* Tel (015396) 20283 *or* 20559 E-mail alan.fell@bradford.anglican.org *or* vixed@btopenworld.com

FELL, David Edward. b 61. Bradf Univ BSc84 Brunel Univ BA05. ERMC 05. **d** 07 **p** 08. C Wootton *St Alb* 07-11; TV Barnsbury *Lon* from 11. *2 Brooksby Street, London N1 1HA* Tel (020) 7697 4400 Mobile 07989-203429 E-mail ted fell@hotmail.com

FELLINGHAM, Wendy Margaret. b 48. St Mich Coll Sarum BEd70. STETS 03. **d** 06 **p** 07. NSM Swanage and Studland *Sarum* from 06. *47 Bay Crescent, Swanage BH19 1RB* Tel (01929) 426454 E-mail wendy.fellingham@btinternet.com

FELLOWS, Grant. b 56. K Coll Lon BD77 AKC77. Coll of Resurr Mirfield 79. **d** 80 **p** 81. C Addington *Cant* 80-84; C S Gillingham *Roch* 84-86; V Heath and Reach *St Alb* 86-94; V Radlett 94-03; RD Aldenham 98-03; V Leighton Buzzard w Eggington, Hockliffe etc 03-05; TR Billington, Egginton, Hockliffe etc 06-08; TR Ouzel Valley from 08. *The Vicarage, Pulford Road, Leighton Buzzard LU7 1AB* Tel (01525) 373217 E-mail grantfellows@btinternet.com

FELLOWS, Ian Christopher. b 73. Univ Coll Ox BA94 MA98 St Jo Coll Dur BA99. Cranmer Hall Dur 96. **d** 99 **p** 00. C Bucknall and Bagnall *Lich* 99-03; TV Broughton *Man* 03-07; P-in-c Blackley St Andr from 07. *St Andrew's Vicarage, Churchdale Road, Higher Blackley, Manchester M9 8NE* Tel 0161-740 2961 E-mail ianfellows@yahoo.co.uk

FELLOWS, John Lambert. b 35. LTCL67 SS Mark & Jo Coll Chelsea CertEd58. Portsm Dioc Tr Course 86. **d** 88. NSM Portsea St Cuth *Portsm* 88-94; NSM Farlington 94-05; Perm to Offic from 05. *7 Court Lane, Portsmouth PO6 2LG* Tel (023) 9237 7270

FELLOWS, John Michael. b 46. Oriel Coll Ox MA77. Coll of Resurr Mirfield 74. **d** 77 **p** 78. C Kings Heath *Birm* 77-80; TV E Ham w Upton Park *Chelmsf* 80-85; P-in-c Wormingford 85-90;

P-in-c Mt Bures 85-90; P-in-c Lt Horkesley 85-90; V Wormingford, Mt Bures and Lt Horkesley 90; R Compton w Shackleford and Peper Harow *Guildf* from 90; RD Godalming from 07; Chapl Prior's Field Sch from 90. *The Rectory, The Street, Compton, Guildford GU3 1ED* Tel (01483) 810328 E-mail csph.office@btinternet.com

FELLOWS, Lesley June. See CRAWLEY, Lesley June

FELLOWS, Peter William. b 48. CertEd70 DipEd79. Chich Th Coll 86. d 88 p 89. C Westmr St Steph w St Jo *Lon* 88-93; R Deptford St Paul *S'wark* 93-05; TV Redruth w Lanner and Treleigh *Truro* from 05. *The Vicarage, Pencoys, Four Lanes, Redruth TR16 6LR* Tel (01209) 215035

FELLOWS, Mrs Susan Elizabeth. b 46. ATCL65 LTCL66 GTCL82. SAOMC 99. d 02 p 03. NSM Weston Turville *Ox* from 02. *65 Craigwell Avenue, Aylesbury HP21 7AG* Tel (01296) 424982 Mobile 07712-226999 E-mail susan@sefellows.freeserve.co.uk

FELTHAM, Keith. b 40. d 75 p 76. In Bapt Ch 66-75; C Plympton St Mary *Ex* 75-79; TV Northam w Westward Ho! and Appledore 79-82; TR Lynton, Brendon, Countisbury, Lynmouth etc 82-85; P-in-c Bickleigh (Plymouth) 85-86; TR 86-91; Chapl R Bournemouth Gen Hosp 91-95; P-in-c Whimple, Talaton and Clyst St Lawr *Ex* 95-00; rtd 00; Perm to Offic *Ex* from 00. *16 Jefferson Walk, Plymouth PL3 4HN* Tel (01792) 254383

FELTHAM-WHITE, Antony James. b 67. Ox Brookes Univ BSc92 Reading Univ MA94. Wycliffe Hall Ox 99. d 01 p 02. C Bernwode *Ox* 01-05; CF from 05. *c/o MOD Chaplains (Army)* Tel (01264) 381140 Fax 381824

FENBY, Andrew Robert. b 66. Loughb Univ BSc88. St Steph Ho Ox 03. d 05 p 06. C Leigh-on-Sea St Marg *Chelmsf* 05-09; V Barkingside St Fran from 09. *St Francis's Vicarage, 144 Fencepiece Road, Ilford IG6 2LA* Tel (020) 8500 2970 E-mail frandrew@mac.com

FENBY, Mrs Sarah Louise. b 66. Kent Univ BA88 Lon Bible Coll BA96. Trin Coll Bris MA00. d 00 p 01. C Stoke Gifford *Bris* 00-04; C S Croydon Em *S'wark* 04-10; Min Selsdon St Fran CD 07-10; P-in-c Lydney *Glouc* from 10; P-in-c Woolaston w Alvington and Aylburton from 10. *5 Raglan Gardens, Lydney GL15 5GZ* Tel (01594) 842321 E-mail revfenby@live.co.uk

FENN, Norman Alexander. b 20. Kelham Th Coll 37. d 43 p 44. C Tunstall Ch Ch *Lich* 43-47; C Leek St Edw 47-51; V Tilstock 51-55; V Milton 55-61; V Ellesmere 61-85; V Welsh Frankton 62-85; RD Ellesmere 70-85; rtd 85; Perm to Offic *Lich* from 85. *1 Larkhill Road, Oswestry SY11 4AW* Tel (01691) 659411

FENNELL, Anthony Frederick Rivers. b 26. Pemb Coll Cam BA50 MA55 York Univ BPhil76 Leic Univ PGCE51. Ab Dioc Tr Course 90. d 90 p 91. NSM Braemar *Ab* 90-96; NSM Ballater 90-96; NSM Aboyne 90-96; rtd 96; Lic to Offic *Ab* from 01. *19 Craigendarroch Circle, Ballater AB35 5ZA* Tel (01339) 755048

FENNELL (née PAVYER), Mrs Jennifer Elizabeth. b 75. Ex Univ BSc96 Cam Univ BTh02 Lon Univ MA05. Westcott Ho Cam 99. d 02 p 03. C Stevenage St Andr and St Geo *St Alb* 02-05; C Harpenden St Nic 05-10; P-in-c Welwyn Garden City from 10. *The Vicarage, 48 Parkway, Welwyn Garden City AL8 6HH* Tel (01707) 320960 E-mail jennyfennell@virginmedia.com

FENNELL, Julian. b 56. d 08 p 09. NSM Ipswich St Mary at Stoke w St Pet and St Fran *St E* from 08. *70 Wellesley Road, Ipswich IP4 1PH* Tel (01473) 212818 E-mail julianfennell@hotmail.com

FENNEMORE, Canon Nicholas Paul. b 53. Wycliffe Hall Ox 76. d 79 p 80. C N Mymms *St Alb* 79-82; C Chipping Barnet w Arkley 82-83; TV 83-84; TV Preston w Sutton Poyntz and Osmington w Poxwell *Sarum* 84-86; Chapl St Helier Hosp Carshalton 86-90; Chapl Jo Radcliffe Hosp Ox 90-94; Chapl Ox Radcliffe Hosp NHS Trust 94-96; Sen Chapl Ox Radcliffe Hosps NHS Trust 96-06; Hon Can Ch Ch *Ox* 03-06; Hd Chapl Services Portsm Hosps NHS Trust from 06. *Queen Alexandra Hospital, Southwick Hill Road, Cosham, Portsmouth PO6 3LY* Tel (023) 9232 1554 E-mail nick@npfennemore.fsnet.co.uk

FENSOME, Canon Anthony David. b 49. Open Univ BA89. Sarum & Wells Th Coll 82. d 84 p 85. C Gtr Corsham *Bris* 84-88; P-in-c Lyddington w Wanborough 88-91; P-in-c Bishopstone w Hinton Parva 88-91; V Lyddington and Wanborough and Bishopstone etc 91-93; V Chippenham St Pet 93-08; RD Chippenham 94-99; AD 06-08; Hon Can Bris Cathl 98-08; rtd 08. *42 Francis Crescent, Tiverton EX16 4EP* E-mail tonyfens@aol.com

FENTIMAN, David Frank. b 43. RIBA74 Roehampton Inst PGCE94. S Dios Minl Tr Scheme 90. d 93 p 94. NSM Hastings St Clem and All SS *Chich* 93-98; P-in-c Blacklands Hastings Ch Ch and St Andr 98-01; V 01-05; rtd 05. *4 Barnfield Close, Hastings TN34 1TS* Tel (01424) 421821 E-mail xxblacklands@tiscali.co.uk

FENTON, Ms Allison Jane. b 66. Grey Coll Dur BA87 Dur Univ PGCE90 St Jo Coll Dur MATM08. Cranmer Hall Dur 06. d 08 p 09. C Newc St Geo and St Hilda 08-10; C Newc Ch Ch w

St Ann from 10. *63 Rosebery Crescent, Newcastle upon Tyne NE2 1EX* Tel 0191-281 5639 E-mail allison@fentonius.net

FENTON, Canon Barry Dominic. b 59. Leeds Univ BA85. Coll of Resurr Mirfield 85. d 87 p 88. C Leigh Park *Portsm* 87-90; Chapl and Prec Portsm Cathl 90-95; Min Can and Prec Westmr Abbey 95-02; Chapl N Middx Hosp NHS Trust from 02; PV Westmr Abbey from 04; P-in-c Grosvenor Chpl *Lon* from 11. *North Middlesex Hospital, Sterling Way, London N18 1QX* Tel (020) 8887 2000 or 8887 2724 E-mail dominic.fenton@nmh.nhs.uk

FENTON, Christopher Miles Tempest. b 28. Qu Coll Cam BA50 LLB51 MA55 LLM. Ridley Hall Cam 52. d 54 p 55. C Welling *Roch* 54-57; Chapl Malsis Prep Sch Keighley 57-63; C Hove Bp Hannington Memorial Ch *Chich* 63-65; V Ramsgate Ch Ch *Cant* 65-71; Hd Dept of Gp Studies Westmr Past Foundn 71-83; P-in-c Mottingham St Andr w St Alban *S'wark* 71-73; Sen Tutor Cambs Consultancy in Counselling 73-85; Co-ord of Tr St Alb Past Foundn 80-88; Dir St Anne's Trust for Psychotherapy Ledbury from 85; Perm to Offic *Heref* from 85; rtd 93. *The Leys, Aston, Kingsland, Leominster HR6 9PU* Tel (01568) 708632

FENTON, David Frank. b 43. Open Univ BA79 Matlock Coll of Educn CertEd67. Wycliffe Hall Ox 07. d 08 p 09. NSM Win Ch Ch from 08. *5 Glenwood Avenue, Southampton SO16 3PY* Tel (023) 8076 9574 Mobile 07967-419169 E-mail dave.fenton1@btinternet.com

FENTON, Geoffrey Eric Crosland. b 54. St Jo Coll Ox BA75 MSc76. WEMTC 98. d 01 p 02. NSM Wedmore w Theale and Blackford *B & W* 01-05; NSM Greinton and W Poldens 05-08; C Mark w Allerton 08-10; P-in-c from 10. *Grove Cottage, Redmans Hill, Blackford, Wedmore BS28 4NG* Tel (01934) 713083 or 710224 E-mail geoffrey.fenton@wildyeast.co.uk

FENTON, Heather. b 48. Trin Coll Bris. d 87 p 97. C Corwen and Llangar *St As* 87-89; C Corwen and Llangar w Gwyddelwern and Llawrybetws 89-98; Dioc Rural Min Co-ord 87-98; Lic to Offic 98-01; C Penllyn Deanery 01-03; P-in-c Bryneglwys from 03; P-in-c Gwyddelwern from 09; AD Penllyn and Edeirnion from 10. *Coleg y Groes, The College, London Road, Corwen LL21 0DR* Tel (01490) 412169 E-mail colegygroes@btconnect.com

FENTON, Ian Christopher Stuart. b 40. AKC62. d 63 p 64. C Banstead *Guildf* 63-67; V N Holmwood 67-84; RD Dorking 80-84; V Witley 84-00; Perm to Offic *Ex* from 00; rtd 05. *The Barn, Kingsford Farm, Longdown, Exeter EX6 7SB* Tel (01392) 811887

FENTON, Keith John. b 54. Coll of Resurr Mirfield 01. d 03 p 04. C St Annes St Anne *Blackb* 03-07; TV Ribbleton from 07. *140 Teil Green, Fulwood, Preston PR2 9PE* Tel (01772) 791147 Mobile 07773-630784 E-mail keithjfenton@yahoo.co.uk

FENTON, Michael John. b 42. Linc Th Coll 67. d 69 p 70. C Guiseley *Bradf* 69-72; C Heswall *Ches* 72-75; TV Birkenhead Priory 75-81; V Alvanley 81-91; Chapl Crossley Hosp Cheshire 82-91; V Holbrook and Lt Eaton *Derby* 91-03; V Allenton and Shelton Lock 03-07; rtd 07; Perm to Offic *Derby* from 07. *11 Nethercroft Lane, Danesmoor, Chesterfield S45 9DE* Tel (01246) 250071 E-mail michaeljfenton@yahoo.co.uk

FENTON, Miss Penelope Ann. b 41. Leic Univ BSc64. Cant Sch of Min 92. d 95 p 96. NSM Eastling w Ospringe and Stalisfield w Otterden *Cant* 95-00; P-in-c 00-05; Asst to Bp's Officer for NSM 99-05; rtd 05; Perm to Offic *Cant* from 05. *9 Brogdale Road, Faversham ME13 8SX* Tel (01795) 536366 E-mail penny@lineone.net

FENTON, Vincent Thompson. b 52. Cranmer Hall Dur 94. d 96 p 97. C Heworth St Mary *Dur* 96-99; C-in-c Bishop Auckland Woodhouse Close CD 99-06; Chapl S Durham Healthcare NHS Trust 01-05; P-in-c Crook *Dur* from 06; AD Stanhope from 07. *The Rectory, 14 Hartside Close, Crook DL15 9NH* Tel (01388) 766129 E-mail vincent.fenton@durham.anglican.org

FENTON, Canon Wallace. b 32. TCD. d 64 p 65. C Glenavy *Conn* 64-67; I Tullaniskin w Clonoe *Arm* 67-87; Bp's C Sallaghy *Clogh* 87-96; Warden of Readers 91-96; Preb Clogh Cathl 95-96; I Kilwarlin Upper w Kilwarlin Lower *D & D* 96-99; rtd 99. *2 Beech Green, Doagh, Ballyclare BT39 0QB* Tel (028) 9334 0576

FENWICK, The Very Revd Jeffrey Robert. b 30. Pemb Coll Cam BA53 MA57. Linc Th Coll 53. d 55 p 56. C Upholland *Liv* 55-58; P-in-c Daramombe S Rhodesia 58-64; Area Sec USPG *Ox* 64-65; R Gatooma All SS Rhodesia 65-67; R Salisbury E 67-75; P-in-c Mabvuku 68-70; Adn Charter 73-75; Dean and Adn Bulawayo 75-78; Can Res Worc Cathl 78-89; R Guernsey St Peter Port *Win* 89-95; Dean Guernsey 89-95; Hon Can Win Cathl 89-95; Pres Guernsey Miss to Seamen 89-95; rtd 95; Zimbabwe 95-04; S Africa from 04. *3 Suid Street, Alexandria, 6185 South Africa*

FENWICK, Canon Malcolm Frank. b 38. Cranmer Hall Dur 62. d 65 p 66. C Tynemouth Cullercoats St Paul *Newc* 65-68; C Bywell 68-73; V Alnmouth 73-75; CF (TAVR) 75-83; V Lesbury w Alnmouth *Newc* 75-80; V Delaval 80-91; RD Bedlington 83-88; V Riding Mill 91-01; P-in-c Whittonstall 91-01; Chapl Shepherd's Dene Retreat Ho from 91; RD Corbridge 93-99; P-in-c Slaley 97-99; P-in-c Healey 99-01; Hon Can Newc Cathl

97-01; rtd 01; Perm to Offic *Newc* from 01. *21 Welburn Close, Ovingham, Prudhoe NE42 6BD* Tel (01661) 835565

✠**FENWICK, The Rt Revd Richard David.** b 43. Univ of Wales (Lamp) BA66 MA86 TCD MusB79 MA92 Univ of Wales (Lamp) PhD95 FLCM68 FTCL76 Hon FGCM04. Ridley Hall Cam 66. d 68 p 69 c 11. C Skewen *Llan* 68-72; C Penarth w Lavernock 72-74; PV, Succ and Sacr Roch Cathl 74-78; Min Can St Paul's Cathl 78-79; Min Can and Succ 79-83; Warden Coll Min Cans 81-83; PV Westmr Abbey 83-90; V Ruislip St Martin *Lon* 83-90; Can Res and Prec Guildf Cathl 90-97; Sub-Dean 96-97; Dean Mon 97-11; V Newport St Woolos 97-11; Warden Guild of Ch Musicians 98-11; Bp St Helena from 11. *Bishopsholme, PO Box 62, St Helena, South Atlantic Ocean* Tel (00290) 4471 Fax 4728 E-mail richard.d.fenwick@googlemail.com

FEREDAY, Harold James Rodney. b 46. St Jo Coll Nottm 87. d 89 p 90. C Rastrick St Matt *Wakef* 89-92; V Siddal 92-99; Dir Chr Care from 99; rtd 01; Perm to Offic *Wakef* and *York* from 01. *311 Filey Road, Scarborough YO11 3AF*

FERGUS, David. b 52. Imp Coll Lon BSc74. St Jo Coll Nottm 00. d 02 p 03. C Ilkeston St Mary *Derby* 02-06; P-in-c Kirk Hallam from 06. *The Vicarage, 71 Ladywood Road, Ilkeston DE7 4NF* Tel 0115-932 2402 E-mail revdave.fergus@ntlworld.com

FERGUSON, Aean Michael O'Shaun. b 39. CITC 87. d 90 p 91. NSM Kilmallock w Kilflynn, Kilfinane, Knockaney etc *L & K* 90; NSM Killaloe w Stradbally 90-94; NSM Adare and Kilmallock w Kilpeacon, Croom etc 94-97; C Killala w Dunfeeny, Crossmolina, Kilmoremoy etc *T, K & A* 97-00; 1 Skreen w Kilmacshalgan and Dromard 00-08; Can Killala Cathl 05-08, rtd 08, Dioc Information Officer *T, K & A* 04-09. *Ruhlee, Easkey, Co Sligo, Republic of Ireland* Tel (00353) (96) 49865 Mobile 87-812 1020 E-mail amferguson@iol.ie

FERGUSON, Alastair Stuart. b 45. Lon Univ MB, BS69 Ball Coll Ox BA78 MA82 LRCP69 MRCS69. St Steph Ho Ox 80. d 82 p 83. NSM Dengie w Asheldham *Chelmsf* 82-86; NSM Mayland 86-89; NSM Steeple 86-89; Perm to Offic 89-91; R Mvurwi St Andr Zimbabwe 91-00; V Lastingham w Appleton-le-Moors, Rosedale etc *York* from 00. *The Vicarage, Lastingham, York YO62 6TN* Tel (01751) 417344 Mobile 07967-588776 E-mail vicarage@lastinghamchurch.org.uk

FERGUSON, David Edward. d 04 p 05. NSM Antrim All SS *Conn* 04-11; I Ramoan w Ballycastle and Culfeightrin from 11. *12 Novally Road, Ballycastle BT54 6HB* Tel (028) 2076 2010 E-mail davidedwardferguson@gmail.com

FERGUSON, Edith Constance May (Joy). b 37. Ch of Ireland Tr Coll DipEd60. CITC 99. d 02 p 03. NSM Bandon Union *C, C & R* from 02. *Telkador, Kinure, Oysterhaven, Co Cork, Republic of Ireland* Tel (00353) (21) 477 0663 Mobile 86-350 3138

FERGUSON, Canon Ian John. b 51. Aber Univ BD77. Trin Coll Bris 77. d 78 p 79. C Foord St Jo *Cant* 78-82; C Bieldside *Ab* 82-86; Dioc Youth Chapl 82-86; P-in-c Westhill 86-96; R from 96; Can St Andr Cathl from 01. *1 Westwood Drive, Westhill, Skeene AB32 6WW* Tel (01224) 740007 E-mail ianferguson@freenet.co.uk

FERGUSON, John Aitken. b 40. Glas Univ BSc64 Strathclyde Univ PhD74 CEng MICE ARCST64. Linc Th Coll 79. d 81 p 82. C Morpeth *Newc* 81-85; V Whittingham and Edlingham w Bolton Chapel 85-96; rtd 06. *Cold Harbour Cottage, Cold Harbour, Berwick-upon-Tweed TD15 2TQ*

FERGUSON, Joy. See *Edith Constance May*

FERGUSON, Mrs Kathleen. b 46. LMH Ox BA68 MA72 ALA76. St As Minl Tr Course 86. d 88 p 97. NSM Llanidloes w Llangurig *Ban* 88-01; P-in-c Llandinam w Trefeglwys w Penstrowed 01-02; V 02-04; AD Arwystli 02-04; NSM Shelswell *Ox* 04-07; rtd 07; Perm to Offic *Ban* from 11. *Oerle, Trefeglwys, Caersws SY17 5QX* Tel (01686) 430666 E-mail kathy@oerle.co.uk

FERGUSON, Marie Dorothy Michelle. b 58. Ottawa Univ BA78. Cranmer Hall Dur 93. d 95 p 96. NSM Gt Aycliffe *Dur* 95-97; Chapl Asst HM Pris Holme Ho 97-98; NSM Heighington *Dur* 99-04; R Hurworth 04-09; R Dinsdale w Sockburn 04-09; Chapl Ian Ramsey Sch Stockton 10-11. *27A Millbank, Heighington Village, Newton Aycliffe DL5 6RY* Tel (01325) 320510

FERGUSON, The Ven Paul John. b 55. New Coll Ox BA76 MA80 K Coll Cam BA84 MA88 FRCO75. Westcott Ho Cam 82. d 85 p 86. C Ches St Mary 85-88; Sacr and Chapl Westmr Abbey 88-92; Prec 92-95; Can Res and Prec York Minster 95-01; Adn Cleveland from 01; Can and Preb York Minster from 01; Warden of Readers from 04. *48 Langbaurgh Road, Hutton Rudby, Yarm TS15 0HL* Tel (01642) 706095 Fax 706097 E-mail archdeacon.of.cleveland@yorkdiocese.org

FERGUSON, Peter. d 10. C Carrickfergus *Conn* from 10. *1 Coates Gardens, Carrickfergus BT38 7XA* Tel (028) 9332 9741 E-mail peteferg50@hotmail.com

FERGUSON, Richard Archie. b 39. Dur Univ BA62. Linc Th Coll 62. d 64 p 65. C Stretford St Matt *Man* 64-68; Bp's Dom Chapl *Dur* 68-69; C Newc St Geo 69-71; V Glodwick *Man* 71-77; V Tynemouth Ch Ch *Newc* 77-82; V Tynemouth Ch Ch w H Trin

82-87; P-in-c Tynemouth St Aug 82-87; TR N Shields 87-90; TR Upton cum Chalvey *Ox* 90-95; V Kirkwhelpington, Kirkharle, Kirkheaton and Cambo *Newc* 95-04; AD Morpeth 95-04; rtd 04. *6 Green Close, Stannington, Morpeth NE61 6PE* Tel (01670) 789795 E-mail frgsno@aol.com

FERGUSON, Robert Garnett Allen. b 48. Leeds Univ LLB70 Clare Coll Cam. Cuddesdon Coll 71. d 73 p 74. C Wakef Cathl 73-76; V Lupset 76-83; Chapl Cheltenham Coll 83-87; Sen Chapl Win Coll 87-05; Perm to Offic *S & M* from 09. *Follaton, Highfield Drive, Baldrine, Isle of Man IM4 6EE*

FERGUSON, Robin Sinclair. b 31. Worc Coll Ox BA53 MA57 Lon Univ CertEd63. ALCD55 Wycliffe Coll Toronto 55. d 57 p 58. C Brompton H Trin *Lon* 57-60; C Brixton St Matt *S'wark* 60-63; Hon C Framlingham w Saxtead *St E* 63-65; Hon C Haverhill 65-67; Chapl St Mary's Sch Richmond 65-75; C Richmond St Mary *S'wark* 68-76; P-in-c Shilling Okeford *Sarum* 76-87; Chapl Croft Ho Sch Shillingstone 76-87; R Milton Abbas, Hilton w Cheselbourne etc *Sarum* 87-96; rtd 96; Perm to Offic *Sarum* from 98. *Durnovria, East Walls, Wareham BH20 4NJ* Tel (01929) 551340

FERGUSON, Ronald Leslie. b 36. Open Univ BA86 BA89. Chich Th Coll 65. d 68 p 69. C Toxteth Park St Marg *Liv* 68-72; C Oakham w Hambleton and Egleton *Pet* 72-74; Asst Chapl The Dorothy Kerin Trust Burrswood 74-76; V Castleside *Dur* 76-96; C Washington 96-99; P-in-c Eighton Banks 99-06; Chapl Gateshead Health NHS Trust 96-06; rtd 06. *2 Lapwing Court, Burnopfield, Newcastle upon Tyne NE16 6LP* Tel (01207) 271559

FERGUSON (née PAMPLIN), Mrs Samantha Jane. b 71. St Andr Univ MTheol06. TISEC 06. d 08 p 09. C Aberdeen St Pet and Aberdeen St Jo 08-10, P-in-c Aberdeen St Ninian from 10. *696 King Street, Aberdeen AB24 1SJ* Tel 07971-231709 (mobile) E-mail samferguson@fsmail.net

FERGUSON, The Very Revd Wallace Raymond. b 47. Qu Coll Birm BTheol CITC 76. d 78 p 79. C Lurgan Ch the Redeemer *D & D* 78-80; I Newtownards w Movilla Abbey 80-84; I Mullabrack w Markethill and Kilcluney *Arm* 84-00; I Carnteel and Crilly 00-05; Hon V Choral Arm Cathl 86-05; Dioc Chapl to Rtd Clergy 92-05; Dean Kilmore *K, E & A* from 05; I Kilmore w Ballintemple from 05. *The Deanery, Danesfort, Kilmore, Cavan, Republic of Ireland* Tel and fax (00353) (49) 433 1918 Mobile 87-127 1658 E-mail dean@kilmore.anglican.org

FERGUSON-STUART, Hamish. b 51. Open Univ BA92 RGN. St Mich Coll Llan MTh10. d 99 p 00. OLM Burton St Chad *Lich* 99-05; Asst Chapl Rotherham NHS Foundn Trust from 05. *13 Oakwood Hall Drive, Rotherham S60 3AQ* Tel (01709) 837503 E-mail hamish.ferguson-stuart@rothgen.nhs.uk

FERGUSSON, Mrs Norma. b 52. St Hugh's Coll Ox BA73 MA83. d 11. NSM Rowde and Bromham *Sarum* from 11. *Carpenters Cottage, 12 High Street, Bromham, Chippenham SN15 2EX* Tel (01380) 850811 Mobile 07799-545035 E-mail norma.fergusson@tiscali.co.uk

FERMER, Michael Thorpe. b 30. Lon Univ BSc52 ARCS52 St Cath Soc Ox BA54. Wycliffe Hall Ox 52. d 54 p 55. C Upper Holloway All SS *Lon* 54-57; C Plymouth St Andr *Ex* 57-59; V Tamerton Foliot 59-63; Asst Chapl United Sheff Hosps 63-64; Chapl 64-66; Lic to Offic *Sheff* 66-73; V Holmesfield *Derby* 73-79; TR Old Brampton and Loundsley Green 79-83; V Brightside w Wincobank *Sheff* 83-89; V Loscoe *Derby* 89-94; rtd 94; Perm to Offic *Derby* from 94. *123 Bacons Lane, Chesterfield S40 2TN* Tel (01246) 555793

FERMER, Richard Malcolm. b 71. St Pet Coll Ox BA94 K Coll Lon MA95 PhD02 Surrey Univ PGCE96. Coll of Resurr Mirfield 00. d 02 p 03. C Palmers Green St Jo *Lon* 02-05; USPG Brazil 05-09; Asst Chapl Paris St Geo *Eur* from 09. *St George, 7 rue Auguste-Vacquerie, 75116 Paris, France* Tel (0033) 1 47 20 22 51 E-mail richard.fermer@tiscali.co.uk

FERN, John. b 36. Nottm Univ BA88. Coll of Resurr Mirfield 57. d 59 p 60. C Carlton *S'well* 59-61; C Hucknall Torkard 61-68; V Rainworth 68-97; rtd 97; Perm to Offic *S'well* from 03. *Fosbrooke House, 8 Clifton Drive, Lytham St Annes FY8 5RQ*

FERNANDES, Sheila Maud. Punjab Univ MB, BS69. NTMTC 05. d 08 p 09. NSM Leyton Em *Chelmsf* from 08. *33 Markmanor Avenue, London E17 8HJ* E-mail fernandesgideon@aol.com

FERNANDEZ, Mrs Valerie Anne. b 48. WMMTC 03. d 05 p 06. C Mile Cross *Nor* 05-08; P-in-c Doddington w Benwick and Wimblington *Ely* 08-11; rtd 11. *51 Glyn Bedw, Llanbradach, Caerphilly CF83 3PF* Tel (029) 2088 2725 E-mail revval@btinternet.com

FERNANDEZ-VICENTE, Lorenzo Michel Manuel. b 68. Louvain Univ BA92 MA97 STL97. d 97 p 97. C Battersea St Mary *S'wark* 04-08; V Malden St Jas from 08. *St James's Vicarage, 7 Bodley Road, New Malden KT3 5QD* Tel (020) 8942 5070 Mobile 07780-914434 E-mail lorenzo.fernandez@mac.com

FERNANDO, Percy Sriyananda. b 49. St And Dioc Tr Course 85. d 88 p 89. NSM Blairgowrie *St And* 88-93; NSM Alyth and Coupar Angus 89-93. *Gowrie Cottage, Perth Road, Blairgowrie PH10 6QB*

FERNELEY, Alastair John. b 69. Roehampton Inst BA93 K Coll Lon MA94 Birm Univ MPhil98 St Jo Coll Dur MA02. Cranmer Hall Dur 00. **d** 02 **p** 03. C Skipton Ch Ch *Bradf* 02-05; P-in-c Scalby *York* from 05; P-in-c Scarborough St Luke from 05. *The Vicarage, 48 High Street, Scalby, Scarborough YO13 0PS* Tel (01723) 362740 E-mail irreverend@btinternet.com

FERNS, Stephen Antony Dunbar. b 61. St Chad's Coll Dur BA84 MA94. Ripon Coll Cuddesdon BA87 MA91. **d** 88 **p** 89. C Billingham St Cuth *Dur* 88-90; Chapl Dur Univ 91; Chapl Van Mildert and Trevelyan Colls Dur 91-95; V Norton St Mary 95-97; Bp's Dom Chapl *Blackb* 97-01; Voc Officer and Selection Sec Min Division 01-06; Sen Selection Sec from 06. *Ministry Division, Church House, Great Smith Street, London SW1P 3AZ* Tel (020) 7898 1399 Fax 7898 1421 E-mail stephen.ferns@churchofengland.org

FERNS, Archdeacon of. *See* LONG, The Ven Christopher William

FERNS, Dean of. *See* MOONEY, The Very Revd Paul Gerard

FERNYHOUGH, Timothy John Edward. b 60. Leeds Univ BA81. Linc Th Coll 81. **d** 83 **p** 84. C Daventry *Pet* 83-86; Chapl Tonbridge Sch 86-92; Chapl Dur Sch 92-02; Hd RS and Asst Chapl Radley Coll from 02. *Radley College, Radley, Abingdon OX14 2HR* Tel (01235) 543000 Fax 543106

FERRAR, Andrew Nicholas. b 46. Em Coll Cam MA70 Liv Univ PhD70. **d** 06 **p** 07. NSM St Alb St Sav *St Alb* from 06. *The Jolly Gardener, 2 Church End, Redbourn, St Albans AL3 7DU* Tel (01582) 794265 Mobile 07818-446720 E-mail andrewferrar@btinternet.com

FERRIS, Amanda Jane. b 61. RGN83. SAOMC 00. **d** 03 **p** 04. NSM Letchworth St Paul w Willian *St Alb* from 03; Chapl E and N Herts NHS Trust from 07. *Rivendell, 33B Stotfold Road, Arlesey SG15 6XL* Tel (01462) 834627 *or* (01438) 781518 Mobile 07780-670651 E-mail amanda.ferris@btinternet.com

FERRIS, Robert Joseph. b 82. Ulster Univ BSc05 QUB PGCE06. CITC BTh09. **d** 09 **p** 10. C Knock *D & D* from 09. *3 Sandown Park South, Belfast BT5 6HE* Tel (028) 9065 3370 E-mail rferris281@gmail.com

FERRIS, Samuel Albert. b 41. Open Univ BA80. S & M Dioc Tr Inst 98. **d** 99 **p** 00. OLM Douglas All SS and St Thos *S & M* from 99. *27 Hillberry Meadows, Governors Hill, Douglas, Isle of Man IM2 7BJ* Tel and fax (01624) 619631

FERRIS, Samuel Christopher. b 77. Univ of Wales (Lamp) BA98. Trin Coll Bris 02. **d** 04 **p** 05. C Tunbridge Wells St Mark *Roch* 04-07; TV S Gillingham from 07. *26 Pear Tree Lane, Hempstead, Gillingham ME7 3PT* Tel (01634) 322711 Mobile 07910-077885 E-mail chris.ferris@diocese-rochester.org

FERRITER, Felicity Eunicé Myfanwy. b 54. Sheff Univ BA76 Nottm Univ MA98. EMMTC 95. **d** 98 **p** 99. NSM Retford S'well 98-03; Asst Chapl Rampton Hosp Retford 99-01; Asst Chapl Notts Healthcare NHS Trust 01-02; Chapl 02-03; Asst to AD Retford 03-04; C Rampton w Laneham, Treswell, Cottam and Stokeham S'well 04-11; C N and S Leverton 04-11; TV Retford Area from 11. *The Gables, Treswell Road, Rampton, Retford DN22 0HU* Tel (01777) 248580 E-mail felicityferriter@yahoo.com

FERRY, Canon David Henry John. b 53. TCD BTh88. **d** 88 **p** 89. C Enniskillen *Clogh* 88-90; I Leckpatrick w Dunnalong *D & R* 90-01; Bp's Dom Chapl from 96; I Donagheady from 01; Can Derry Cathl from 05. *Earlsgift Rectory, 33 Longland Road, Dunamanagh, Strabane BT82 0PH* Tel (028) 7139 8017

FERRY, Malcolm Ronald Keith. b 66. QUB BEd88. CITC BTh96. **d** 96 **p** 97. C Agherton *Conn* 96-99; I Kilwaughter w Cairncastle and Craigy Hill 99-03; I Castlerock w Dunboe and Fermoyle *D & R* 03-08; I Clooney w Strathfoyle from 08. *All Saints' Rectory, 20 Limavady Road, Londonderry BT47 6JD* Tel (028) 7134 4306 *or* 7134 9348 E-mail allsaintsclooney@btinternet.com

FESSEY, Mrs Annis Irene. b 40. St Mary's Coll Chelt CertEd60. Ripon Coll Cuddesdon 88. **d** 90 **p** 94. Par Dn Bris St Andr Hartcliffe 90-94; C The Lydiards 94-95; C Penhill 95-00; rtd 00; Perm to Offic *Bris* 00-03 and from 03. *Tintern, 17 Mayfield Road, Ryde PO33 3PR* Tel (01983) 616466

FESSEY, Canon Brian Alan. b 39. Bris Univ CertEd61 Leeds Univ DipEd71. Ripon Coll Cuddesdon 88. **d** 90 **p** 91. Hon C Bishopsworth *Bris* 90; C Withywood CD 91-94; V Purton 94-03; Hon Can Bris Cathl 01-03; rtd 03; Perm to Offic *Portsm* 03. *Tintern, 17 Mayfield Road, Ryde PO33 3PR* Tel (01983) 616466

FEWKES, Jeffrey Preston. b 47. Derby Univ MA99 DMin04. Wycliffe Hall Ox 72. **d** 75 **p** 76. C Chester le Street *Dur* 75-78; C Kennington St Mark S'wark 78-81; V Bulwell St Jo S'well 81-98; V Stapleford 98-02; Victim Support Nottinghamshire from 02; Perm to Offic *Derby* from 06. *3 Monks Close, Ilkeston DE7 5EY* Tel 0115-930 2482 E-mail j.fewkes@btopenworld.com

FFRENCH (*née* WILLIAMS), Mrs Janet Patricia (Trish). b 59. Bradf Univ BTech81. Trin Coll Bris BA02. **d** 02 **p** 03. C Quinton Road W St Boniface *Birm* 02-05; C Mamble w Bayton, Rock w Heightington etc *Worc* 05-07; C Elmsett w Aldham, Hintlesham, Chattisham etc *St E* from 07. *The Rectory, Hadleigh Road,*

Elmsett, Ipswich IP7 6ND Tel (01473) 658803 Mobile 07801-257959 E-mail revsff@btinternet.com

FFRENCH, Timothy Edward. b 58. Ball Coll Ox MA86. Trin Coll Bris BA01 MA03. **d** 03 **p** 04. C Pedmore *Worc* 03-07; R Elmsett w Aldham, Hintlesham, Chattisham etc *St E* from 07. *The Rectory, Hadleigh Road, Elmsett, Ipswich IP7 6ND* Tel (01473) 658803 Mobile 07801-492126 E-mail revsff@btinternet.com

FICKE, Michael John. b 46. **d** 97 **p** 98. OLM Marnhull *Sarum* 97-07; rtd 07; Perm to Offic *Sarum* from 07. *13 Plowman Close, Marnhull, Sturminster Newton DT10 1LB* Tel (01258) 820509

FIDDIAN-GREEN, Anthony Brian. b 39. Sussex Univ MA88 Birm Univ CertEd60 ACP66. Bps' Coll Cheshunt 62. **d** 64 **p** 65. C Batheaston w St Cath *B & W* 64-67; Chapl Aiglon Coll and Chapl Villars *Eur* 67-71; Hd Master Battisborough Sch Holbeton 71-81; Chapl R Gr Sch *Worc* 81-83; Hd Master Frewen Coll Rye 83-96; P-in-c New Groombridge *Chich* 97-11; rtd 11. *21 Chatham Green, Eastbourne BN23 5PQ* Tel (01323) 478553 E-mail revtfg@googlemail.com

FIDDYMENT, Alan John. b 40. Cant Sch of Min 91. **d** 94 **p** 95. NSM Chatham St Wm *Roch* 94-96; NSM Spalding *Linc* 96-99; R Barkston and Hough Gp 99-07; rtd 07. *5 Ascot Close, Spalding PE11 3BZ* Tel (01775) 712837 Mobile 07930-434126 E-mail alan.fiddyment@tiscali.co.uk

FIDLER, John Harvey. b 49. Hatf Poly BSc72. St Alb Minl Tr Scheme 84. **d** 87 **p** 88. NSM Royston *St Alb* from 87; Perm to Offic *Ely* from 00. *8 Stamford Avenue, Royston SG8 7DD* Tel (01763) 241886

FIELD, Brian Hedley. b 31. St Jo Coll York CertEd53 ACP66 FCP84. **d** 99 **p** 00. NSM Maidstone St Luke *Cant* 99-04; Hon C 06-10; Perm to Offic 04-05 and from 11. *Shebri, 21 Fauchons Close, Bearsted, Maidstone ME14 4BB* Tel (01622) 730117 Fax 663109 Mobile 07785-156606

FIELD, David Hibberd. b 36. K Coll Cam BA58. Oak Hill Th Coll 58. **d** 60 **p** 61. C Aldershot H Trin *Guildf* 60-63; C Margate H Trin *Cant* 63-66; Sec Th Students Fellowship 66-68; Tutor Oak Hill Th Coll 68-93; Vice Prin 79-93; Dean Minl Tr Course 88-93; Dir Professional Min Div CPAS 94-00; Patr Sec CPAS 94-00; Perm to Offic *Cov* from 94; rtd 00. *25 Field Barn Road, Hampton Magna, Warwick CV35 8RX* Tel (01926) 410291

FIELD, Geoffrey Alder. b 13. Ely Th Coll. **d** 47 **p** 48. C King Cross *Wakef* 47-50; C Ely 50-54; V Whittlesey St Andr 54-75; V Foxton 75-80; rtd 81; Perm to Offic *Ely* 81-02. *14 Poplar Close, Great Shelford, Cambridge CB22 5LX* Tel (01223) 842099

FIELD, Canon Gerald Gordon. b 54. K Coll Lon BD75 AKC75. Coll of Resurr Mirfield 76. **d** 77 **p** 78. C Broughton *Blackb* 77-79; C Blackpool St Steph 79-82; V Skerton St Luke 82-86; NSM Westleigh St Pet *Man* 92-93; V Shap w Swindale and Bampton w Mardale *Carl* 93-97; P-in-c Netherton 97; V 98-01; I Tullamore w Durrow, Newtownfertullagh, Rahan etc *M & K* from 01; Can Meath from 10; Can Kildare Cathl from 10. *St Catherine's Rectory, Church Avenue, Tullamore, Co Offaly, Republic of Ireland* Tel and fax (00353) (57) 932 1731 E-mail tullamore@meath.anglican.org

FIELD, James Lewis. b 46. Open Univ BSc96. SEITE 94. **d** 97 **p** 98. NSM Chatham St Mary w St Jo *Roch* 97-00; R Gravesend H Family w Ifield 00-08; P-in-c New Romney w Old Romney and Midley *Cant* from 08. *The Vicarage, North Street, New Romney TN28 8DR* Tel (01797) 362308 Mobile 07749-591496 E-mail revjimfield@googlemail.com

FIELD, Jeremy Mark. b 75. St Jo Coll Dur BA96. Ridley Hall Cam 10. **d** 10 **p** 11. C Onslow Square and S Kensington St Aug *Lon* from 10. *54 Bushy Park Road, Teddington TW11 9DG* Tel (020) 8943 4233 Mobile 07767-784011 E-mail jerryfield@hotmail.com

FIELD, Martin Richard. b 55. Keswick Hall Coll CertEd76 Leic Univ MA87. St Jo Coll Nottm BTh82. **d** 82 **p** 83. C Gaywood, Bawsey and Mintlyn *Nor* 82-85; Perm to Offic *Leic* 85-87; Hon C S'well Minster 87-88; Hon C Stand *Man* 88-89; Dioc Press and Communications Officer 88-91; CUF 91-95; Perm to Offic *Cant* 96-99; Fundraising and Campaigns Dir Children's Soc 04-09; UK Dir of Fundraising Barnardo's from 09. *40 Elm Grove Road, Salisbury SP1 1JW* Tel (01722) 502910 *or* (020) 8498 7647 E-mail martin.field@barnardos.org.uk

FIELD, Preb Olwen Joyce. b 53. St Jo Coll Nottm 86. **d** 88 **p** 94. Par Dn Kensal Rise St Mark and St Martin *Lon* 88-91; Par Dn Northwood H Trin 91-94; C 94-95; Chapl Mt Vernon Hosp 91-99; P-in-c W Drayton 99-03; V from 03; Dean of Women's Min Willesden Area from 01; AD Hillingdon 03-08; Preb St Paul's Cathl from 10. *The Vicarage, 4 Beaudesert Mews, West Drayton UB7 7PE* Tel (01895) 442194 E-mail olwen@swanroad.go-plus.net

FIELD, Richard Colin. b 33. St Cath Soc Ox BA54 MA63. Clifton Th Coll 63. **d** 65 **p** 66. C Highbury Ch Ch *Lon* 65-70; V Hanger Lane St Ann 70-85; V Leytonstone St Jo *Chelmsf* 85-98; rtd 98; Perm to Offic *Chich* from 99. *21 Rufus Close, Lewes BN7 1BG* Tel (01273) 472884

FIELD, Canon Susan Elizabeth. b 59. York Univ BA80 Birm Univ CertEd81 Ox Univ MTh98. Qu Coll Birm 84. **d** 87 **p** 94. C Coleshill *Birm* 87-90; Chapl Loughb Univ 91-98; TV

Loughborough Em and St Mary in Charnwood from 98; Dir Post-Ord Tr 95-04; Bp's Adv for Women's Min 97-04; Dir of Ords from 04; Hon Can Leic Cathl from 04. *134 Valley Road, Loughborough LE11 3QA* Tel (01509) 234472 E-mail sue.field1@tesco.net

FIELDEN, Elizabeth Ann. b 42. TCert63. **d** 99 **p** 00. OLM Broughton Gifford, Gt Chalfield and Holt *Sarum* from 99; OLM Atworth w Shaw and Whitley from 07; OLM Melksham from 07. *393 Ham Green, Holt, Trowbridge BA14 6PX* Tel (01255) 782509 Fax 783152 E-mail winesource@saqnet.co.uk

FIELDEN, Hugh. b 66. BNC Ox BA88 Birm Univ PGCE90. Qu Coll Birm 91. **d** 93 **p** 94. C Sholing *Win* 93-97; TV Bramley *Ripon* 97-02; TV Bingley All SS *Bradf* 02-07; P-in-c Earby 07; P-in-c Kelbrook 07; V Earby w Kelbrook from 08. *The Vicarage, 40 Brookfield Way, Earby, Barnoldswick BB18 6YQ* Tel (01282) 844877 E-mail hugh.fielden@bradford.anglican.org

FIELDEN, Mrs Janice. b 46. Warwick Univ BEd82 MEd89. SAOMC 99. **d** 02 **p** 03. NSM Chipping Norton *Ox* 02-05; NSM Charlbury w Shorthampton from 05. *The Vicarage, Church Lane, Charlbury, Chipping Norton OX7 3PX* Tel and fax (01608) 810286 E-mail jan@cnfogies.co.uk

FIELDEN, Robert. b 32. Linc Th Coll 65. **d** 67 **p** 68. C Bassingham *Linc* 67-72; R Anderby w Cumberworth 72-88; P-in-c Huttoft 72-88; P-in-c Mumby 77-88; R Fiskerton 88-90; rtd 90; Perm to Offic *Carl* 91-99 and *Linc* from 91. *Woodlands, 8 Fiskerton Road, Reepham, Lincoln LN3 4EB* Tel (01522) 750480 E-mail robert@rfielden.freeserve.co.uk

FIELDER, Joseph Neil. b 67. Univ of Wales BSc89. Wycliffe Hall Ox 93. **d** 96 **p** 97. C Cheadle All Hallows *Ches* 96-00; V Preston St Steph *Blackb* 00-09; P-in-c Baxenden from 09. *The Vicarage, Langford Street, Baxenden, Accrington BB5 2RF* Tel (01254) 384179 E-mail vicarjoe.baxenden@gmail.com

FIELDGATE, John William Sheridan. b 44. St Jo Coll Dur BA68. Ox NSM Course 75. **d** 79 **p** 80. NSM Haddenham w Cuddington, Kingsey etc *Ox* 79-90; C Northleach w Hampnett and Farmington *Glouc* 90-92; C Cold Aston w Notgrove and Turkdean 90-92; P-in-c Upper and Lower Slaughter w Eyford and Naunton 92-01; P-in-c The Guitings, Cutsdean and Farmcote 92-01; V Acton w St Waldingfield *St E* 01-09; rtd 09; Perm to Offic *St E* and *Chelmsf* from 09. *Patmos, 23 Woodfield Drive, West Mersea, Colchester CO5 8PX* Tel (01206) 386851 E-mail jandjfieldgate@tiscali.co.uk

FIELDING, John Joseph. b 29. TCD BA53 MA65 QUB DipEd57. TCD Div Sch Div Test 54. **d** 54 **p** 55. C Belfast St Luke *Conn* 54-57; C Belfast St Mary Magd 57-60; Chapl Windsor Boys' Sch Hamm W Germany 61-69; Chapl St Edw Sch Ox 69-73; V Highgate St Mich *Lon* 73-95; rtd 95; Perm to Offic *Guildf* from 95 and *S'wark* from 06. *30 Sackville Mews, Sackville Road, Sutton SM2 6HS* E-mail j.j.fielding@btinternet.com

FIELDING, Mrs Pamela Florence. b 46. **d** 10 **p** 11. OLM Sherington w Chicheley, N Crawley, Astwood etc *Ox* from 10. *4 Griggs Orchard, Sherington, Newport Pagnell MK16 9PL* Tel (01908) 616763 E-mail john_fielding@hotmail.com

FIELDING, Robert David. b 67. Liv Univ BA89 St Jo Coll Dur BA08. Cranmer Hall Dur 07. **d** 08. C Formby St Pet *Liv* 08-10; Chapl Mersey Care NHS Trust from 10. *Mersey Care NHS Trust, 8 Princes Parade, Liverpool L3 1DL* Tel 07951-173434 (mobile) E-mail rfielding@homecall.co.uk

FIELDING, Stephen Aubrey. b 67. Ulster Univ BSc89 TCD BTh93. CITC 90. **d** 93 **p** 94. C Bangor Abbey *D & D* 93-97; I Templepatrick w Donegore *Conn* 97-07; I Agherton from 07. *The Rectory, 59 Strand Road, Portstewart BT55 7LU* Tel (028) 7083 2538 *or* 7083 3277 E-mail agherton@connor.anglican.org

FIELDING, Stephen Lister. b 52. Ch Ch Ox BA73 MA77 Barrister 74. SAOMC 04. **d** 07 **p** 08. NSM Welwyn *St Alb* from 07. *The Rectory, Brookbridge Lane, Datchworth, Knebworth SG3 6SU* Tel (01438) 811593 Mobile 07760-287614 E-mail slfielding@hotmail.com

FIELDSEND, John Henry. b 31. Nottm Univ BSc54 Lon Univ BD61. Lon Coll of Div ALCD59. **d** 61 **p** 62. C Pennington *Man* 61-64; C Didsbury Ch Ch 64-66; P-in-c Bayston Hill *Lich* 66-67; V 67-88; UK Dir CMJ 89-91; Dir and Min at Large CMJ 91-96; rtd 96; Perm to Offic *St Alb* 96-00; Hon C Thame *Ox* from 01. *58 Cedar Crescent, Thame OX9 2AU* Tel (01844) 212559 E-mail john@tehillah.freeserve.co.uk

FIELDSON, Robert Steven. b 56. Qu Coll Cam BA78 MA81 Wye Coll Lon MSc79. St Jo Coll Nottm BA86. **d** 87 **p** 88. C Walmley *Birm* 87-90; Chapl Protestant Ch in Oman 90-95; P-in-c Cofton Hackett w Barnt Green *Birm* 95-98; V from 98; AD Kings Norton 00-06. *The Vicarage, 8 Cofton Church Lane, Barnt Green, Birmingham B45 8PT* Tel 0121-445 1269 E-mail rob@fieldson.co.uk

FIFE (née EVE), Hilary Anne. b 57. Lon Univ BEd80. Ripon Coll Cuddesdon 89. **d** 91 **p** 94. Par Dn Coulsdon St Andr *S'wark* 91-94; C 94-95; Chapl Croydon Coll 92-94; Asst Chapl Mayday Healthcare NHS Trust Thornton Heath 94-02; Sen Chapl from 02; Chapl Harestone Marie Curie Cen Caterham 94-98; Hon C Shirley St Geo *S'wark* from 08. *19 Greenview Avenue, Croydon CR0 7QW* Tel (020) 8654 8685 *or* 8401 3105

FIFE, Janet Heather. b 53. Sussex Univ BA77 Man Univ MPhil98. Wycliffe Hall Ox 84. **d** 87 **p** 94. Chapl Bradf Cathl 87-89; Par Dn York St Mich-le-Belfrey 89-92; Chapl Salford Univ 92-00; Hon TV Pendleton St Thos w Charlestown 92-95; Hon TV Pendleton 95-96; V Upton Priory *Ches* 00-10; P-in-c Marske in Cleveland *York* from 10. *The Vicarage, 6 Windy Hill Lane, Marske-by-the-Sea, Redcar TS11 7BN* Tel (01642) 482896 E-mail j.fife@virgin.net

FIGG, Robin Arthur Rex. b 62. RN Eng Coll Plymouth BScEng84. Westcott Ho Cam 91. **d** 94 **p** 95. C Old Cleeve, Leighland and Treborough *B & W* 94-97; C Gt Berkhamsted *St Alb* 97-01; V Kildwick *Bradf* from 01. *The Vicarage, Kildwick, Keighley BD20 9BB* Tel (01535) 633307 E-mail robin.figg@bradford.anglican.org

FILBERT-ULLMANN, Mrs Clair. b 44. Leuven Univ Belgium BTh94 MA94. Virginia Th Sem 95. **d** 94 **p** 96. USA 94-95; Asst Chapl Charleroi *Eur* 95-00; P-in-c Leuven 99-02; Asst Chapl Tervuren w Liège 99-01; Perm to Offic from 02. *Muhlbach am Hochkonig 437, A-5505, Austria* Tel (0043) (6467) 20107 E-mail crullmann2001@yahoo.com

FILLERY, William Robert. b 42. Univ of Wales (Swansea) BA65 St D Coll Lamp BD69 PGCE72 Surrey Univ MA96. Bp Burgess Hall Lamp 65. **d** 68 **p** 69. C Llangyfelach and Morriston *S & B* 68-71; C Morriston 71-72; Lic to Offic *Ox* 73-76; Chapl Windsor Girls' Sch Hamm W Germany 76-81; OCF 79-81; Chapl Reed's Sch Cobham 81-86; V Oxshott *Guildf* 86-89; P-in-c Seale 89-91; P-in-c Puttenham and Wanborough 89-91; Hd RE Streatham Hill & Clapham Sch for Girls 91-03; V Llanybydder and Llanwenog w Llanllwni *St D* 03-10; rtd 10. *Afon Del, Falcondale Drive, Lampeter SA48 7SB* Tel (01570) 421425 Mobile 07971-007336 E-mail billfill@btinternet.com

FILLINGHAM, Richard James. b 58. Man Univ BA80 Sheff Univ MA03 ACA83. All Nations Chr Coll Wycliffe Hall Ox. **d** 98 **p** 99. C Brinsworth w Catcliffe and Treeton *Sheff* 98-01; C Ecclesall 01-05. *92 Greystones Road, Sheffield S11 7BQ* Tel 0114-266 1804

FILMER, Paul James. b 58. Open Univ BA88. Aston Tr Scheme 93 Oak Hill Th Coll 95. **d** 97 **p** 98. C Petham and Waltham w Lower Hardres etc *Cant* 97-00; P-in-c Patrixbourne w Bridge and Bekesbourne 00-06; P-in-c Lower Hardres w Nackington 00-06; Chapl Univ of Greenwich *Roch* 06-09; Chapl Univ for the Creative Arts 06-09; V Yalding w Collier Street from 09. *The Vicarage, Vicarage Road, Yalding, Maidstone ME18 6DR* Tel (01622) 814182 Mobile 07595-176797 E-mail revpfilmer@mac.com

FILTNESS, Trevor Moshe. b 50. MNI MInstD. STETS 05. **d** 08 **p** 09. NSM Farlington *Portsm* 08-11; NSM Rowlands Castle from 11. *Manor Cottage, 1 Lower Road, Havant PO9 3LH* Tel 07785-568056 (mobile) E-mail trevor@filtness.org *or* trevor@farlingtonparish.co.uk

FINCH, Alan James. b 51. **d** 06 **p** 07. OLM Orrell Hey St Jo and St Jas *Liv* from 06. *1 Kirkstone Road North, Liverpool L21 7NP* Tel 0151-928 3919 E-mail alan@chesed.freeserve.co.uk

FINCH, Mrs Alison. b 59. SEN79. Sarum & Wells Th Coll 90. **d** 92 **p** 94. Par Dn Banbury *Ox* 92-94; C 94-95; C Wokingham All SS 95-98; C Binfield 98-99; C St Peter-in-Thanet *Cant* 99-02; R Kirkwall and P-in-c Stromness *Ab* 02-05; Ind Chapl *Chelmsf* from 05; C Colchester St Pet and St Botolph from 05. *St Botolph's Vicarage, 50B Priory Street, Colchester CO1 2QB* Tel (01206) 868043 Mobile 07762-744977

FINCH, Barry Marshall. See PALMER FINCH, Barry Marshall

FINCH, Christopher. b 41. Lon Univ BA63 AKC63 BD69. Sarum Th Coll 63. **d** 65 **p** 66. C High Wycombe *Ox* 65-69; Prec Leic Cathl 69-73; R Lt Bowden St Nic 73-81; V Evington 81-99; P-in-c Leic St Phil 95-99; P-in-c Lower Dever Valley *Win* 99-01; R 00-07; rtd 07; Perm to Offic *Portsm* from 07. *7 Arundel Drive, Fareham PO16 7NP* Tel (01329) 829015

FINCH, Canon David Walter. b 40. Cam Univ MA74 FIBMS69. Ridley Hall Cam. **d** 91 **p** 92. C Ixworth and Bardwell *St E* 91-92; C Blackbourne 92-94; P-in-c Stoke by Nayland w Leavenheath 94-00; P-in-c Polstead 95-00; P-in-c Fressingfield, Mendham etc 00-08; C Hoxne w Denham, Syleham and Wingfield 06-08; RD Hoxne 00-07; Hon Can St E Cathl 05-08; rtd 08; Perm to Offic *St E* from 08; Lic to Offic *Ab* from 08. *Mayfield House, Seafield Place, Cullen, Buckie AB56 4TE* Tel (01542) 840098

FINCH, Frank. b 33. Qu Coll Birm 72. **d** 74 **p** 75. C Bilston St Leon *Lich* 74-78; R Sudbury and Somersal Herbert *Derby* 78-87; Chapl HM Pris Sudbury 78-87; HM Det Cen Foston Hall 80-87; V Lilleshall and Sheriffhales *Lich* 87-90; R The Ridwares and Kings Bromley 90-98; rtd 98; Perm to Offic *Lich* from 00. *11 Ferrers Road, Yoxall, Burton-on-Trent DE13 8PS* Tel (01543) 472065

FINCH, Jeffrey Walter. b 45. Man Univ BA(Econ)66 Liv Univ DASE80. Linc Th Coll 82. **d** 84 **p** 85. C Briercliffe *Blackb* 84-87; P-in-c Brindle and Asst Dir of Educn 87-93; V Laneside 93-00; TV Fellside Team 00-08; TR from 08. *The Vicarage, Church Lane, Bilsborrow, Preston PR3 0RL* Tel (01995) 640269 E-mail teamvicar@fellside@btinternet.com

FINCH, John. b 20. Bps' Coll Cheshunt 59. d 61 p 62. C Middlesbrough St Paul *York* 61-64; V Easington w Skeffling and Kilnsea 64-68; V Habergham Eaves St Matt *Blackb* 68-75; V Garstang St Helen Churchtown 75-86; rtd 86; Perm to Offic *Blackb* from 86. *Bushells House Retirement Home, Mill Lane, Goosnargh, Preston PR3 2BJ* Tel (01772) 865225

FINCH, Morag Anne Hamilton. b 64. EAMTC 97. d 00 p 01. C Cranham *Chelmsf* 00-05; V Gidea Park from 05. *St Michael's Vicarage, Main Road, Romford RM2 5EL* Tel (01708) 741084 E-mail moragandrichard.finch@ukonline.co.uk

FINCH, Paul William. b 50. Oak Hill Th Coll Lon Bible Coll. d 75 p 76. C Hoole *Ches* 75-78; C Charlesworth *Derby* 78-87; C Charlesworth and Dinting Vale 87-88; TV Radipole and Melcombe Regis *Sarum* 88-01; V Malvern St Andr and Malvern Wells and Wyche *Worc* from 01. *St Andrew's Vicarage, 48 Longridge Road, Malvern WR14 3JB* Tel (01684) 573912 E-mail paul@finchnest.freeserve.co.uk

FINCH, Richard William. b 62. Westcott Ho Cam 95. d 97 p 98. C Saffron Walden w Wendens Ambo and Littlebury *Chelmsf* 97-00; C Elm Park St Nic Hornchurch 00-01; V 01-10; Chapl and Faith Support Officer Forest YMCA from 10; OLM Gidea Park *Chelmsf* from 11. *Forest YMCA, 642 Forest Road, London E17 3EF* Tel (020) 8509 4646 E-mail rfinch@forestymca.org.uk

FINCH, Ronald. b 15. Qu Coll Birm 79. d 80 p 80. Hon C Welford w Weston and Clifford Chambers *Glouc* 80-85; Perm to Offic *Ches* 85-03 and *Sheff* from 03. *55 Folds Crescent, Sheffield S8 0EP* Tel 0114-249 9029

FINCH, Miss Rosemary Ann. b 39. Leeds Univ CertEd60. d 93 p 94. OLM S Elmham and Ilketshall *St E* 93-00; Asst Chapl Ipswich Hosp NHS Trust 00-11; rtd 11; Perm to Offic *St E* from 11. *Grace House, 15 Weston Park, Weston under Penyard, Ross-on-Wye HR9 7FR* Tel (01989) 565019 E-mail rosie.finch@virgin.net

FINCH, Canon Stanley James. b 31. Mert Coll Ox BA55 MA58. Wells Th Coll 55. d 57 p 58. C Lancaster St Mary *Blackb* 57-61; C Leeds St Pet *Ripon* 61-65; V Habergham All SS *Blackb* 65-73; V S Shore H Trin 73-84; V Broughton 84-98; RD Preston 86-92; Hon Can Blackb Cathl 91-98; rtd 98; P-in-c Alderton, Gt Washbourne, Dumbleton etc *Glouc* 98-02; Perm to Offic from 02. *14 Bellflower Road, Walton Cardiff, Tewkesbury GL20 7SB* Tel (01684) 850544

FINCH, Thomas. b 20. Lon Univ BD57. Edin Th Coll 48. d 51 p 51. Chapl St Andr Cathl 51-55; C St Marylebone St Cypr *Lon* 55-58; V Warmington Pet 58-67; RD Oundle 62-67; V Wellingborough St Mary 67-88; rtd 88; Perm to Offic *Blackb* from 88. *18 Royal Avenue, Leyland, Preston PR25 1BQ* Tel (01772) 433780

FINCHAM, Nicholas Charles. b 56. St Jo Coll Dur BA78 MA80. Westcott Ho Cam 80 Bossey Ecum Inst Geneva 81. d 82 p 83. C Seaham w Seaham Harbour *Dur* 82-85; C Lydney w Aylburton *Glouc* 85-87; C Isleworth All SS *Lon* 87-95; P-in-c Chiswick St Mich 95-10; rtd 10. *7 Harding Avenue, Eastbourne BN22 8PH* Tel (01323) 638273 E-mail nicholas.fincham@talk21.com

FINDLAY, Brian James. b 42. Wellington Univ (NZ) BA62 MA63 BMus66 Magd Coll Ox MA75. Qu Coll Birm. d 72 p 73. C Deptford St Paul *S'wark* 72-75; Chapl and Dean of Div Magd Coll Ox 75-84; V Tonge Moor *Man* 84-02; Hon Can Man Cathl 00-03; R Monks Eleigh w Chelsworth and Brent Eleigh etc *St E* from 03; rtd 11. *The Bull Pen, Hallthwaites, Millom LA18 5HP* Tel (01229) 770049

FINDLAY, James. b 68. Bp Otter Coll BA90 Westmr Coll Ox PGCE92. Wycliffe Hall Ox 02. d 04 p 05. C Gillingham St Mark *Roch* 04-07; P-in-c Salisbury St Mark *Sarum* from 07. *St Mark's Vicarage, 62 Barrington Road, Salisbury SP1 3JD* Tel (01722) 323767 Mobile 07854-510569 E-mail jim.magsfindlay@btinternet.com

FINDLAYSON, Roy. b 44. Man Univ MA89 CQSW69. Sarum & Wells Th Coll 80. d 82 p 83. C Benwell St Jas *Newc* 82-83; Hon C 83-85; C Morpeth 85-88; C N Gosforth 88; TV Ch the King 88-94; V Newc St Fran 94-98; Asst Chapl Newcastle upon Tyne Hosps NHS Trust 98-06; Chapl Marie Curie Cen Newc 98-06; rtd 06. *3 Balmoral Terrace, Stockton-on-Tees TS18 4DD* Tel (01642) 601702

FINDLEY, Peter. b 55. Trin Coll Ox BA77 MA80 Barrister-at-Law (Gray's Inn) 78. Trin Coll Bris 90. d 92 p 93. C Yateley *Win* 92-97; V Westwood *Cov* from 97; P-in-c Canley from 09. *St John's Vicarage, Featherbed Lane, Coventry CV4 7DD* Tel (024) 7647 0515 or 7669 5026 E-mail peterfindley@stjohnswestwood.freeserve.co.uk

FINDON, John Charles. b 50. Keble Coll Ox BA71 MA75 DPhil79. Ripon Coll Cuddesdon. d 77 p 78. C Middleton *Man* 77-80; Lect Bolton St Pet 80-83; V Astley 83-91; V Baguley 91-98; P-in-c Bury St Mary 98-05; R from 05. *St Mary's Rectory, Tithebarn Street, Bury BL9 0JR* Tel 0161-764 2452 E-mail bpc.office@tiscali.co.uk

FINKENSTAEDT, Harry Seymour. b 23. Yale Univ BA49 Univ of Mass MA68. Episc Th Sch Cam Mass BD50. d 53 p 54. USA 53-71; C Hazlemere *Ox* 71-73; C Huntingdon St Mary w St Benedict *Ely* 73-75; R Castle Camps 75-84; R Shudy Camps

75-84; P-in-c W Wickham 79-84; P-in-c Horseheath 79-81; P-in-c Gt w Lt Stukeley 84-88; rtd 88; Perm to Offic *Ely* 88-01. *13761 Charismatic Way, Gainesville VA 20155-3119, USA* Tel (001) (703) 743 5787

FINLAY, Alison Mary. See CAW, Alison Mary

FINLAY, Canon Christopher John. b 46. FCII71. WMMTC 95. d 98 p 99. NSM Coln St Aldwyns, Hatherop, Quenington etc *Glouc* 98-08; NSM Fairford Deanery from 09; Hon Can Glouc Cathl from 09. *Coombe House, Calcot, Cheltenham GL54 3JZ* Tel (01285) 720806 E-mail coombehousecalcol@tiscali.co.uk

FINLAY, Canon Hueston Edward. b 64. TCD BA85 BAI85 BTh89 MA92 Cam Univ MA98 Lon Univ PhD98. CITC 86. d 89 p 90. C Kilkenny w Aghour and Kilmanagh *C & O* 89-92; Bp's Dom Chapl 89-92; Bp's V and Lib Kilkenny Cathl 90-92; Chapl Girton Coll Cam 92-95; C Cambridge Gt St Mary w St Mich *Ely* 92-95; Chapl and Fell Magd Coll Cam 95-99; Dean of Chpl 99-04; Can Windsor from 04. *8 The Cloisters, Windsor Castle, Windsor SL4 1NJ* Tel (01753) 867094 Fax 833806 E-mail hueston.finlay@stgeorges-windsor.org

FINLAY, Canon Michael Stanley. b 45. NOC 78. d 81 p 82. C Padgate *Liv* 81-85; V Newton-le-Willows 85-90; V Orford St Marg 90-98; P-in-c Warrington St Elphin 98-00; R from 00; Hon Can Liv Cathl from 07. *The Rectory, Church Street, Warrington WA1 2TL* Tel (01925) 635020

FINLAY, Nicholas. b 47. Regent Coll Vancouver MCS00. St Jo Coll Nottm 01. d 02 p 03. C Haydock St Mark *Liv* 02-03; C Bootle 03-04; Lic to Adn Warrington 04-05; V Sittingbourne St Mary and St Mich *Cant* 05-09; rtd 09; C Upper Ithon Valley *S & B* from 09; C Lower Ithon Valley from 09. *The Vicarage, Llanbister, LLandrindod Wells LD1 6TN* Tel (01597) 840468 E-mail nick.finlay047@btinternet.com

FINLAYSON, Duncan. b 24. d 76 p 76. NSM Bridge of Allan *St And* 76-94; NSM Alloa 77-94; NSM Dollar 77-94; Hon AP Hillfoots Team 80-87; rtd 94. *29 Cawder Road, Bridge of Allan, Stirling FK9 4JJ* Tel (01786) 833074

FINLAYSON, Mrs Gladys Victoria. b 49. TCert67. ERMC 05. d 09 p 10. NSM Luton St Anne w St Chris *St Alb* 09-11. *St Andrew's Vicarage, 11 Blenheim Crescent, Luton LU3 1HA* Tel (01582) 732380 E-mail gladysfinlayson@sky.com

FINLAYSON, Grantley Adrian. b 55. Wilson Carlile Coll 74 Chich Th Coll 87. d 89 p 90. C Watford St Mich *St Alb* 89-92; TV W Slough *Ox* 92-97; Dioc Officer for Race Relations *Glouc* 97-02; V Luton St Andr *St Alb* from 02. *St Andrew's Vicarage, 11 Blenheim Crescent, Luton LU3 1HA* Tel and fax (01582) 481711 E-mail grantley@gfinlayson.fsworld.co.uk

FINLINSON, Paul. b 58. St Chad's Coll Dur BA79 St Martin's Coll Lanc PGCE81. Carl Dioc Tr Course 86. d 89 p 90. NSM Kirkby Lonsdale *Carl* 89-99; Chapl Worksop Coll Notts from 99; Chapl Ranby Ho Sch Retford from 11. *Worksop College, Sparken Hill, Worksop S80 3AP* Tel (01909) 537109 or (01524) 69652 E-mail paul@worksopcollege.notts.sch.uk

FINN, Gordon Frederick. b 33. Dur Univ BA60. Ely Th Coll 60. d 62 p 63. C Kingswinford St Mary *Lich* 62-65; C Northampton St Mary *Pet* 65-67; Chapl Barnsley Hall Hosp and Lea Hosp Bromsgrove 67-71; C Swanage *Sarum* 71-73; P-in-c Ford End *Chelmsf* 73-79; V S Shields St Oswin *Dur* 79-98; rtd 98. *58 Hutton Lane, Guisborough TS14 8AW* Tel (01287) 619132

FINN, Ian Michael. b 58. AKC. Chich Th Coll 81. d 82 p 83. C Habergham All SS *Blackb* 82-83; C W Burnley All SS 83-85; C Torrisholme 85-87; V Lancaster Ch Ch w St Jo and St Anne 87-91; P-in-c Tillingham and Dengie w Asheldham *Chelmsf* 91-97; Chapl R Gr Sch Worc 97-99; P-in-c Denston w Stradishall and Stansfield *St E* 99-01; P-in-c Wickhambrook w Lydgate, Ousden and Cowlinge 00-01; R Bansfield 02-07; V Haverhill w Withersfield from 07; RD Clare from 06. *The Rectory, 10 Hopton Rise, Haverhill CB9 7FS* Tel (01440) 708768 E-mail ian.finn1@btinternet.com

FINN, Miss Sheila. b 30. LMH Ox BA68 MA69. Gilmore Ho 68. dss 78 d 87 p 94. Tettenhall Wood *Lich* 78-86; Dioc Ecum Officer 86-95; The Ridwares and Kings Bromley 86-87; Par Dn 87-94; C 94-95; rtd 95; Perm to Offic *Lich* from 97. *15 Leacroft Road, Penkridge, Stafford ST19 5BU* Tel (01785) 716018

FINNEMORE, James Christopher. b 59. Pemb Coll Cam BA81 MA85. Coll of Resurr Mirfield. d 85 p 86. C Manston *Ripon* 85-88; C Hessle *York* 88-92; R Bishop Wilton w Full Sutton, Kirby Underdale etc 92-99; R Garrowby Hill from 99; RD S Wold from 07. *The Rectory, Bishop Wilton, York YO42 1SA* Tel (01759) 368230 E-mail j.c.finnemore@btinternet.com

FINNEMORE, Thomas John. b 79. Hull Univ BA01. Wycliffe Hall Ox 05. d 07 p 08. C Crookes St Thos *Sheff* 07-11; C Cambridge St Barn *Ely* from 11. *80 St Barnabas Road, Cambridge CB1 2DE*

FINNERTY, Cynthia Ann. b 46. d 05 p 06. OLM E Greenwich *S'wark* from 05. *33 Ruthin Road, London SE3 7SJ* Tel (020) 8858 2883 E-mail cynthiafin@hotmail.com

FINNEY, Canon David. b 41. St Mich Coll Llan 68. d 70 p 71. C Wythenshawe Wm Temple Ch *Man* 70-73; C Bedford Leigh 73-75; V Royton St Anne 75-81; V Dearnley 81-94; TV Rochdale

94-07; Hon Can Man Cathl 04-07; rtd 07; Perm to Offic *Man* from 09. *59 Knowl Road, Rochdale OL1 4BB* Tel (01706) 346384
FINNEY, Canon Fred. b 17. Bris Univ BA38 DipEd39. Wycliffe Hall Ox 61. **d** 62 **p** 63. C Gt Crosby St Luke *Liv* 62-66; V Ashton-in-Makerfield St Thos 66-86; Hon Can Liv Cathl 83-86; rtd 86; Perm to Offic *Blackb* and *Liv* 86-08. *c/o Mrs B J Nuttall, 2 Barelees Farm Cottages, Cornhill-on-Tweed TD12 4SF*
FINNEY, Canon John Thomas. b 27. Sheff Univ BA51 DipEd52. Ripon Hall Ox 60. **d** 62 **p** 63. C Leigh St Mary *Man* 62-65; V 83-97; V Peel 65-69; Chapl Hockerill Coll Bishop's Stortford 69-74; V Astley *Man* 74-83; AD Leigh 85-93; Hon Can Man Cathl 87-97; rtd 97; Perm to Offic *Man* from 97. *36 Station Road, Blackrod, Bolton BL6 5BW* Tel (01204) 698010
✠**FINNEY, The Rt Revd John Thornley.** b 32. Hertf Coll Ox BA55. Wycliffe Hall Ox 56. **d** 58 **p** 59 **c** 93. C Highfield *Ox* 58-61; C Weston Turville 61-65; R Tollerton *S'well* 65-71; V Aspley 71-80; Bp's Adv on Evang 80-89; Bp's Research Officer 88-89; Hon Can S'well Minster 84-89; Officer for Decade of Evang in C of E 90-93; Suff Bp Pontefract *Wakef* 93-98; rtd 98; Hon Asst Bp S'well and Nottm from 98. *Greenacre, Crow Lane, South Muskham, Newark NG23 6DZ* Tel and fax (01636) 679791 E-mail john.finney2@ntlworld.com
FINNEY, Ms Melva Kathleen. b 24. LTh76. St Jo Coll Auckland 47 Gilmore Ho 56. **dss** 57 **d** 78. E Dulwich St Jo *S'wark* 56-59; Community of Sisters of the Love of God Ox 59-61; New Zealand from 61; Asst Chapl Christchurch 61-62; Fendalton St Barn 62-63; Asst Chapl Womens and Templeton Hosp 63-72; Asst Chapl Princess Marg Hosp Christchurch 63-72; Chapl 72-86; rtd 86. *22 Gunns Crescent, Cashmere, Christchurch 8022, New Zealand* Tel (0064) (3) 332 7100
FINNIMORE, Keith Anthony. b 36. AKC59. **d** 60 **p** 61. C Wanstead H Trin Hermon Hill *Chelmsf* 60-63; C Kingswood *S'wark* 63-65; V Bolney *Chich* 65-67; V Elmstead *Chelmsf* 67-73; R Pentlow, Foxearth, Liston and Borley 73-77; NSM Cockfield w Bradfield St Clare, Felsham etc *St E* 89-91; R Hawstead and Nowton w Stanningfield etc 91-96; P-in-c 96-01; rtd 96; Perm to Offic *St E* 01-09 and *Chelmsf* from 09. *52B Summerhill Road, Saffron Walden CB11 4AJ* Tel (01799) 521763
FIRBANK, Michael John. b 73. R Holloway Coll Lon BA94 St Mary's Coll Twickenham PGCE94. St Jo Coll Nottm MTh05. **d** 05 **p** 06. C St Illogan *Truro* 05-07; P-in-c Camborne from 07. *The Rectory, Rectory Gardens, Camborne TR14 7DN* Tel (01209) 613020 Mobile 07888-711645 E-mail mjfirbank@hotmail.com
FIRMIN, Canon Dorrie Eleanor Frances. b 19. LNSM course. **d** 88 **p** 94. NSM Ellon *Ab* 88-99; NSM Cruden Bay 88-99; Hon Can St Andr Cathl from 97; rtd 99. *Airdlin Croft, Ythanbank, Ellon AB41 7TS* Tel (01358) 761360
FIRMIN, Paul Gregory. b 57. ACIB80. Trin Coll Bris BA87. **d** 87 **p** 88. C Swindon Ch Ch *Bris* 87-91; V Shrewsbury H Trin w St Julian *Lich* 91-99; V Astley, Clive, Grinshill and Hadnall 99-01; V Southampton St Mary Extra *Win* 01-10; V Shrewsbury H Cross *Lich* from 10. *1 Underdale Court, Underdale Road, Shrewsbury SY2 5DD* E-mail nimrifs@btinternet.com
FIRMSTONE, Ian Harry. b 44. Qu Coll Birm. **d** 82 **p** 83. C Warminster St Denys *Sarum* 82-84; C N Stoneham *Win* 84-88; R Freemantle 88-90; V Littleport *Ely* 90-91; TV Stanground and Farcet 91-97; P-in-c Holme w Conington 95-96; rtd 97. *Cotswold Cottage, School Lane, Alvechurch, Birmingham B48 7SA* Tel 0121-445 1318
FIRTH, Mrs Ann Neswyn. b 40. St As Minl Tr Course 95. **d** 98 **p** 99. NSM Llanidloes w Llangurig *Ban* 98-05; Perm to Offic from 05. *Springfield, Westgate Street, Llanidloes SY18 6HJ* Tel (01686) 413098 E-mail davidandneswyn@firth19.freeserve.co.uk
FIRTH, Christopher John Kingsley. b 37. St Mich Coll Llan. **d** 66 **p** 67. C Sutton in Ashfield St Mary *S'well* 66-70; V Langold 70-74; C Falmouth K Chas *Truro* 74-77; P-in-c Mabe 77-81; V 81-95; RD Carnmarth S 90-94; rtd 99. *1 Boscawen, Cliff Road, Falmouth TR11 4AW* Tel (01326) 316734
FIRTH, Geoffrey David. b 74. Lincs & Humberside Univ BA96. Oak Hill Th Coll BA08. **d** 06 **p** 07. C Poynton *Ches* 06-10; Chapl RAF from 10. *Chaplaincy Services, Valiant Block, HQ Air Command, RAF High Wycombe HP14 4UE* Tel (01494) 496800 Fax 496343 E-mail geoffreyfirth@aol.com
FIRTH, Mrs Jennifer Anne. b 52. Goldsmiths' Coll Lon BMus75 Kingston Poly PGCE83. **d** 07 **p** 08. OLM Dorking St Paul *Guildf* from 07. *33 Downsview Gardens, Dorking RH4 2DX* Tel (01306) 887189 Mobile 07970-102987 E-mail jennyafirth@aol.com
FIRTH, Matthew Paul. b 83. Magd Coll Cam BA04 MA08. Wycliffe Hall Ox BTh09. **d** 09 **p** 10. C Triangle, St Matt and All SS *St E* from 09. *43 Clarkson Street, Ipswich IP1 2JN* Tel (01473) 212661 Mobile 07932-482929 E-mail mpf1983@hotmail.com
FIRTH, Neswyn. *See* FIRTH, Mrs Ann Neswyn
✠**FIRTH, The Rt Revd Peter James.** b 29. Em Coll Cam BA52 MA63. St Steph Ho Ox 53. **d** 55 **p** 56 **c** 83. C Barbourne *Worc* 55-58; C Malvern Link St Matthias 58-62; R Abbey Hey *Man*

62-66; Asst Network Relig Broadcasting BBC Man 66-67; Sen Producer/Org Relig Progr TV & Radio BBC Bris 67-83; Hon Can Bris Cathl 74-83; Suff Bp Malmesbury 83-94; Angl Adv HTV West 84-94; rtd 94; Hon Asst Bp Glouc from 03; Hon Asst Bp Bris from 09. *Mill House, Silk Mill Lane, Winchcombe, Cheltenham GL54 5HZ* Tel (01242) 603669 E-mail peter@firth7.fsbusiness.co.uk
FIRTH, Peter William Simpson. b 39. **d** 11. NSM New Romney w Old Romney and Midley *Cant* from 11. *114 Leonard Road, Greatstone, New Romney TN28 8RZ* Tel (01797) 367296 E-mail firth166@btinternet.com
FIRTH, Mrs Rachel Naomi. b 73. Huddersfield Univ BA97 Leeds Univ BA08. NOC 05. **d** 08 **p** 09. C Halifax *Wakef* from 08. *27 Central Park, Halifax HX1 2BT* Tel (01422) 361942 Mobile 07793-709988 E-mail rnfirth@hotmail.com
FIRTH, Richard Geoffrey. b 48. **d** 06 **p** 07. OLM Dur St Marg and Neville's Cross St Jo 06-08; Perm to Offic *York* from 08. *6 Vicarage Close, Seamer, Scarborough YO12 4QS* Tel (01723) 867957 E-mail afirth9819@aol.com
FISH, Mrs Jacqueline Wendy. b 42. NTMTC 02. **d** 04 **p** 05. NSM Enfield Chase St Mary *Lon* from 04. *41 Churchbury Lane, Enfield EN1 3TX* Tel (020) 8366 2235 E-mail jacquiefishie@aol.com
FISH, Michael. b 61. Lanc Univ BA05. CBDTI 01. **d** 04 **p** 05. NSM Blackb St Mich w St Jo and H Trin 04-07; NSM Blackb St Thos w St Jude 04-07; P-in-c Cen Buchan *Ab* 07-08; P-in-c Shrewsbury All SS w St Mich *Lich* from 08. *All Saints' Vicarage, 5 Lingen Close, Shrewsbury SY1 2UN* Tel (01743) 244879 Mobile 07867-760110 E-mail fr.michaelfish@btinternet.com
FISH, Winthrop. b 40. Dalhousie Univ Canada BA63 BEd Birm Univ BPhil76 MEd78. K Coll (NS) 62. **d** 64 **p** 65. I Arichat Canada 64-66; I Neil's Harbour and Baddock 66-67; I Cut Knife 68-70; Perm to Offic Nova Scotia 70-74; Perm to Offic *Birm* 74-77; Asst Chapl Solihull Sch 77-79; Chapl Wroxall Abbey Sch 79-82; C Newquay *Truro* 82-84; V Highertown and Baldhu 84-89; P-in-c Newlyn St Newlyn 89-97; Dioc Children's Adv 89-97; Dioc Adv in RE 95-97; rtd 98; Perm to Offic *Ex* from 98. *4 Dukes Close, Otterton, Budleigh Salterton EX9 7EY* Tel (01395) 568331
FISHER, Adrian Charles Proctor. b 24. TCD BA48 MA62. TCD Div Sch Div Test47. **d** 49 **p** 50. C Carlow *C & O* 49-52; C Tintern and Killesk 49-52; CF 52-57 and 62-69; I Fethard w Killesk, Tintern and Templetown *C & O* 57-62; P-in-c N Stoke w Mongewell and Ipsden *Ox* 70-83; V 83-92; Chapl Oratory Prep Sch 73-80; rtd 92; Perm to Offic *Ox* from 99. *Pitt House, 25 New Street, Henley-on-Thames RG9 2BP* Tel (01491) 636 008
FISHER, Mrs Alison. b 48. Cranmer Hall Dur 04. **d** 05 **p** 06. NSM The Thorntons and The Otteringtons *York* 05-11; rtd 11; Perm to Offic *York* from 11. *31 Church Close, Marske-by-the-Sea, Redcar TS11 7AW* Tel (01642) 488682 E-mail ali@endican.gotads1.co.uk
FISHER, Andrew John. b 72. St Jo Coll Nottm BA02. **d** 02 **p** 03. C Ilkeston St Jo *Derby* 02-05; P-in-c Hodge Hill *Birm* 05-08; Chapl Worcs Acute Hosps NHS Trust from 08. *Department of Spiritual and Pastoral Care, The Alexandra Hospital, Woodrow Drive, Redditch B98 7UB* Tel (01527) 505723 E-mail andrew.fisher@worcsacute.nhs.uk
FISHER, Brian Robert. b 36. **d** 02 **p** 03. OLM Sole Bay *St E* 02-07; rtd 07; Perm to Offic *St E* from 07. *Green Gates, The Street, Walberswick, Southwold IP18 6UH* Tel (01502) 723023 Mobile 07766-216111 E-mail fishell@btopenworld.com
FISHER, David Stephen. b 66. Ripon Coll Cuddesdon BTh98. **d** 98 **p** 99. C Stockport SW *Ches* 98-01; V Gatley 01-06; V Gt Sutton from 06. *St John's Vicarage, 1 Church Lane, Great Sutton, Ellesmere Port CH66 4RE* Tel 0151-339 9916 E-mail daifisher@aol.com
FISHER, Eric Henry George. b 48. NTMTC 94. **d** 97 **p** 98. NSM Heydon, Gt and Lt Chishill, Chrishall etc *Chelmsf* 97-03; P-in-c Gt Oakley w Wix and Wrabness 03-08; rtd 08; Perm to Offic *Chelmsf* and *St E* from 09. *Sheldon, 12 Joseph Close, Hadleigh, Ipswich IP7 5FH* Tel (01473) 832626 E-mail eric.fisher@ukgateway.net
FISHER, Eric William. b 30. Birm Univ BA53. Coll of Resurr Mirfield 70. **d** 72 **p** 73. C Styvechale *Cov* 72-75; C Chesterfield St Mary and All SS *Derby* 75-78; Chapl Buxton Hosps 78-84; TV Buxton w Burbage and King Sterndale *Derby* 78-84; R Shirland 84-89; V Sheff St Matt 89-95; rtd 95; Perm to Offic *Lich* from 95. *6 Wickstead Row, Main Road, Betley, Crewe CW3 9AB* Tel (01270) 820621
FISHER, Frank. *See* FISHER, Canon Kenneth Francis McConnell
FISHER, George Arnold. b 54. Lon Univ BD75. NOC 81. **d** 84 **p** 85. C Conisbrough *Sheff* 84-92; V Blackpool St Thos *Blackb* 92-07; Dir Par Miss *Lich* from 07; Hon C Walsall St Matt from 07. *14 Gorway Gardens, Walsall WS1 3BJ* Tel (01922) 650063 Mobile 07814-166951 E-mail george.fisher@lichfield.anglican.org
FISHER, Gordon. b 44. NW Ord Course 74. **d** 77 **p** 78. NSM Airedale w Fryston *Wakef* 77-81; C Barkisland w W

Scammonden 81-84; C Ripponden 81-84; V Sutton St Mich *York* 84-87; V Marton-in-Cleveland 87-96; R Kettering SS Pet and Paul 96-02; rtd 02. *8 Mount Pleasant Avenue, Marske-by-the-Sea, Redcar TS11 7BW* Tel (01642) 489489 E-mail gandgmf@tiscali.co.uk

FISHER, Humphrey John. b 33. Harvard Univ AB55 Ox Univ DPhil59. Heythrop Coll Lon MA. d 91 p 92. NSM Bryngwyn and Newchurch and Llanbedr etc *S & B* 91-06; Perm to Offic from 06. *Rose Cottage, Newchurch, Kington, Hereford HR5 3QF* Tel (01544) 370632

FISHER, Ian St John. b 59. Down Coll Cam BA80 MA84 Leic Univ PhD84. St Steph Ho Ox BA88. d 88 p 89. C Colwall w Upper Colwall and Coddington *Heref* 88-91; Chapl Surrey Univ 92-97; V Hurst *Man* 97-04; V N Shoebury *Chelmsf* from 04. *The Vicarage, 2 Weare Gifford, Shoeburyness, Southend-on-Sea SS3 8AB* Tel (01702) 584053 E-mail ian.fisher@btclick.com

FISHER, Mrs Joan. b 52. d 00 p 01. NSM Blackpool St Mark *Blackb* 00-04; NSM Blackpool St Thos 04-07; C Aldridge *Lich* from 08. *14 Gorway Gardens, Walsall WS1 3BJ* Tel (01922) 650063

FISHER, John Andrew. b 63. Bath Univ BSc85 MA97. Wycliffe Hall Ox BA93. d 94 p 95. C Rayleigh *Chelmsf* 94-98; V Burton Joyce w Bulcote and Stoke Bardolph *S'well* 98-09; AD Gedling 00-05; Regional Leadership Adv (Midl) CPAS from 09; Perm to Offic *Sheff* from 10. *CPAS, Athena Drive, Tachbrook Park, Warwick CV34 6NG* Tel (01926) 458457 E-mail jfisher@cpas.org.uk

FISHER, Canon Kenneth Francis McConnell (Frank). b 36. K Coll Lon 57. d 61 p 62. C Sheff St Geo and St Steph 61-63; Chapl Sheff Univ 64-69; Chapl Lon Univ 69-75; P-in-c Dean *Carl* 75-80; Soc Resp Officer 75-80; TR Melksham *Sarum* 80-90; P-in-c Stapleford *Ely* 90-01; Dioc Ecum Officer 90-01; RD Shelford 94-03; Hon Can Ely Cathl 98-06; rtd 01; P-in-c Grantchester *Ely* 01-06; Perm to Offic *B & W* from 06. *Hollybrook, Station Road, Castle Cary BA7 7BU* Tel (01963) 351304 E-mail frankfisher@waitrose.com

FISHER, Mark Simon. b 52. K Coll Lon BD76 AKC76 Trin Coll Ox MA82 DPhil83. Kelham Th Coll 70 Perkins Sch of Th (USA) 76. d 78 p 78. SSF 78-80; Hon C Victoria Docks Ascension *Chelmsf* 78-79; Lic to Offic *Eur* and *Lon* 78-80; *Ox* 78-87; Chapl LMH Ox 80-86; R Glas St Matt 87-89; Hon Asst P W Derby St Jo *Liv* 97-05. *29A Rodney Street, Liverpool L1 9EH* Tel 0151-707 9748

FISHER, Mary Christine. b 43. Bris Univ BA64. LCTP 07. d 08 p 09. NSM Heaton St Barn *Bradf* from 08. *423 Toller Lane, Bradford BD9 5NN* Tel (01274) 541238

FISHER, Canon Michael Harry. b 39. Ex Univ BA61. St Steph Ho Ox 61. d 63 p 64. C Wolverhampton St Pet *Lich* 63-67; C Newquay *Truro* 67-70; V Newlyn St Pet 70-75; P-in-c Launceston St Steph w St Thos 75-82; V Carbis Bay w Lelant 82-95; V Newquay 95-99; Hon Can Truro Cathl 85-99; RD Penwith 88-93; Chapl Costa del Sol W *Eur* 99-00; rtd 00; Perm to Offic *Truro* from 00 and *Eur* from 04. *Chymedda, Southway, Windmill, Padstow PL28 8RN* Tel (01841) 521544 Mobile 07970-865049 E-mail mfisher39@aol.com

FISHER, Michael John. b 43. Leic Univ BA64 Keele Univ MA67. Qu Coll Birm 71. d 78 p 79. NSM Stafford St Mary and St Chad *Lich* 78-79; NSM Stafford from 79. *35 Newland Avenue, Stafford ST16 1NL* Tel (01785) 245069

FISHER, Nicholas. b 48. Newc Univ BA71 MLitt87 Man Univ MA98 Leeds Univ PhD04 Birm Univ BA09. Qu Coll Birm 06. d 08 p 09. NSM Northleach w Hampnett and Farmington etc *Glouc* from 08. *Providence House, High Street, Northleach, Cheltenham GL54 3EU* Tel (01451) 861195 E-mail nick@5fishers.co.uk

FISHER, Paul Vincent. b 43. Worc Coll Ox BA66 MA70 ARCM73. Qu Coll Birm. d 70 p 71. C Redditch St Steph *Worc* 70-73; C Chorlton upon Medlock *Man* 73-79; Chapl Man Univ 73-79; Exec Sec Community Affairs Division BCC 79-81; Asst Dir of Tr and Dir of Lay Tr *Carl* 81-86; P-in-c Raughton Head w Gatesgill 81-85; Lay Tr Team Ldr *S'wark* 86-90; Dir of Tr 90-94; V Kingswood *S'wark* 90; rtd 00; Perm to Offic *Bradf* from 01. *3 Buxton Park, Langcliffe, Settle BD24 9NQ* Tel (01729) 824058 E-mail paul.fisher@ukonline.co.uk

FISHER, Peter Francis Templer. b 36. CCC Cam BA60 MA. Wells Th Coll 62. d 63 p 64. C Gt Ilford St Mary *Chelmsf* 63-67; C Colchester St Mary V 67-70; C-in-c Basildon St Andr CD 70-72; P-in-c Edstaston *Lich* 83-87; P-in-c Whixall 83-87; P-in-c Tilstock 84-87; V Shelton and Oxon 87-97; rtd 97; Perm to Offic *Derby* from 07 and *Sheff* from 10. *1 Cherry Tree Close, Sheffield S11 9AF* Tel 0114-327 4718

FISHER, Canon Peter Timothy. b 44. Dur Univ BA68 MA75. Cuddesdon Coll 68. d 70 p 71. C Bedford St Andr *St Alb* 70-74; Chapl Surrey Univ 74-78; Sub-Warden Linc Th Coll 78-83; R Houghton le Spring *Dur* 83-94; RD Houghton 87-92; Prin Qu Coll Birm 94-02; V Maney *Birm* 02-10; Hon Can Birm Cathl 00-10; rtd 10. *Eden, Unicorn View, Bowes, Barnard Castle DL12 9HW* Tel (01833) 628001 E-mail peter.fisher@onetel.net

FISHER, Richard John. b 60. K Coll Lon BA82 AKC82 Selw Coll Cam BA87 MA95. Ridley Hall Cam 85. d 88 p 89. C Woodley St Jo the Ev *Ox* 88-91; C Acomb St Steph *York* 91-95; Chapl Preston Acute Hosps NHS Trust 98-02; Chapl Lancs Teaching Hosps NHS Trust 02-06; Perm to Offic *Blackb* 08-09; NSM Rufford and Tarleton 09; C Loughton St Jo *Chelmsf* from 09. *24 The Summit, Loughton IG10 1SW* Tel (020) 8281 1389 E-mail reverendrichard@virginmedia.com

FISHER, Roy Percy. b 22. SS Mark & Jo Coll Chelsea TCert50 Univ of Wales MTh00. Linc Th Coll 51. d 53 p 54. C Lewisham St Jo Southend *S'wark* 53-56; Clare Coll Miss Rotherhithe 56-59; V Boughton under Blean *Cant* 59-66; V Westgate St Sav 66-71; R Staplegrove *B & W* 71-79; TR Eckington w Handley and Ridgeway *Derby* 79-87; rtd 87; Perm to Offic *Llan* from 87. *258 New Road, Porthcawl CF36 5BA* Tel (01656) 788682

FISHER, Mrs Sheila Janet. b 50. WEMTC 01. d 04 p 05. NSM Cam w Stinchcombe *Glouc* from 04. *1 Ashmead Court, Ashmead, Cam, Dursley GL11 5EN* Tel (01453) 544656 E-mail ashmead.fishers@btinternet.com

FISHER, Simon John Plumley. b 80. St Jo Coll Dur BA01. Ripon Coll Cuddesdon BA04. d 05 p 06. C Bath Bathwick *B & W* 05-09; P-in-c Brigstock w Stanion and Lowick and Sudborough *Pet* 09-11; P-in-c Weldon w Deene 09-11; P-in-c W Derby St Jo *Liv* from 11. *The Vicarage, 1A Snaefell Avenue, Liverpool L13 7HA* Tel 0151-228 2023 Mobile 07525-617067

FISHER, Stephen Newson. b 46. Univ of Wales (Swansea) BSc67 CEng82 MIET82. Linc Th Coll 84. d 86 p 87. C Nunthorpe *York* 86-89; P-in-c Middlesbrough St Oswald 89-90; V 90-94; V Redcar 94-02; P-in-c The Thorntons and The Otteringtons 02-11; Chapl N Yorks Police 01-11; rtd 11; Perm to Offic *Bradf* from 02 and *York* from 11. *31 Church Close, Marske-by-the-Sea, Redcar TS11 7AW* Tel (01642) 488682 E-mail stephen.fisher913@btinternet.com

FISHER, Stuart Frederick. d 11. OLM Swindon Dorcan *Bris* from 11. *30 Blakeney Avenue, Swindon SN3 3NL* Tel (01793) 497169 Mobile 07774-205640 E-mail sfisher111@btinternet.com

FISHER, Susan. b 49. Yorks Min Course 09. d 11. NSM Gomersal *Wakef* from 11. *275 Cliffe Lane, Gomersal, Cleckheaton BD19 4SB* Tel (01274) 875956 Mobile 07756-069635 E-mail suefisher21@yahoo.co.uk

FISHER, Thomas Andrew. b 35. Sarum & Wells Th Coll 84. d 86 p 87. C Win Ch Ch 86-89; Chapl Salisbury Coll of Tech *Sarum* 89-94; Chapl Salisbury Coll of FE 89-94; Perm to Offic *Sarum* 94-99; rtd 00; NSM Salisbury St Mark *Sarum* from 99. *Mombasa, Manor Farm Road, Salisbury SP1 2RR* Tel (01722) 335155

FISHER, Thomas Ruggles. b 20. Cranmer Hall Dur 58. d 60 p 61. C Melton Mowbray w Thorpe Arnold *Leic* 60-63; R Husbands Bosworth 63-74; R Husbands Bosworth w Mowsley and Knaptoft etc 74-82; Perm to Offic *Leic* 82-96 and *Pet* 83-04; rtd 85. *12 The Dell, Oakham LE15 6JG* Tel (01572) 757630

FISHER-BAILEY, Mrs Carol. b 56. d 96 p 97. C Eccleshill *Bradf* 96-99; TV Sutton St Jas and Wawne *York* from 99. *Wawne Vicarage, 50 Main Street, Wawne, Hull HU7 5XH* Tel (01482) 370414 E-mail ladyvicar@googlemail.com

FISHLOCK, Christopher Douglas. b 70. Anglia Poly BA91. Oak Hill Th Coll BA06. d 07. C St Helen Bishopsgate w St Andr Undershaft etc *Lon* from 07. *St Helen's Church Office, Great St Helens, London EC3A 6AT* E-mail c.fishlock@st-helens.org.uk

FISHLOCK, Mrs Margaret Winifred (Peggy). b 28. Cant Sch of Min 87. d 97 p 98. NSM Deal St Leon and St Rich and Sholden *Cant* 97-04; Perm to Offic from 04. *58 Gilford Road, Deal CT14 7DQ* Tel (01304) 365841

FISHWICK, Alan. b 48. Chich Th Coll 87. d 89 p 90. C Laneside *Blackb* 89-92; C Accrington 92-93; TV 93-96; V Blackb St Aid 96-02; V Scorton and Barnacre and Calder Vale 02-05; P-in-c Coppull St Jo 05-09; rtd 09. *3 Burnside Cottages, Rye Hill Road, Flimby, Maryport CA15 8PJ*

FISHWICK, Mrs Ann. b 40. St Barn Coll Adelaide 91 Trin Coll Melbourne 93. d 91 p 94. Chapl Charters Towers Hosp and Home Australia 91-94; Dn Charters Towers St Paul 91-94; Asst P 94-97; Perm to Offic *Heref* 98-99; NSM Worthen 99-02; NSM Hope w Shelve 99-02; NSM Middleton 99-02; Asst P Weipa Australia 02-04; Asst P Innisfail 04-08. *217 Edward Road, Meru WA 6530, Australia* Tel (0061) (8) 9921 5537 E-mail rayannf@bigpond.com

FISHWICK, Ian Norman. b 54. Lanc Univ BEd E Lon Univ MA99. d 82 p 83. C High Wycombe *Ox* 82-87; V Walshaw Ch Ch *Man* 87-93; Area Voc Adv 88-93; V W Ealing St Jo w St Jas *Lon* 93-98; Dir of Ords Willesden Area 94-98; E Region Area Co-ord for CA 98-99; Operations Dir 99-04; Par Development Adv *Ox* 05-07; Lead Org Consultant S Lon and Maudsley NHS Foundn Trust from 07. *89 Carver Hill Road, High Wycombe HP11 2UB* Tel (01494) 538775

FISHWICK, Raymond Allen. b 42. St Fran Coll Brisbane 93 N Queensland Coll of Min ACP96. d 91 p 92. P-in-c Charters Towers Australia 92-94; R 94-97; P-in-c Worthen *Heref* 98-02;

P-in-c Hope w Shelve 98-02; P-in-c Middleton 98-02; P-in-c Weipa Australia 02-04; P-in-c Innisfail 04-08; CF 02-08; rtd 08. *217 Edward Road, Geraldton WA 6530, Australia* Tel (0061) (8) 9921 5537 E-mail rfi64412@bigpond.net.au

FISKE, Paul Francis Brading. b 45. St Jo Coll Dur BA68 PhD72. Wycliffe Hall Ox 72. **d** 73 **p** 74. C Sutton *Liv* 73-76; TV Cheltenham St Mary, St Matt, St Paul and H Trin *Glouc* 76-80; C-in-c Hartplain CD *Portsm* 80-84; Hd of Miss UK CMJ 84-86; Hon C Edgware *Lon* 84-86; R Broughton Gifford, Gt Chalfield and Holt *Sarum* 86-95; TV Bourne Valley 95-97; Adv Chr Action 95-97; P-in-c Princes Risborough w Ilmer *Ox* 97-98; TR Risborough 98-08; rtd 08. *30 Elmdene Road, Kenilworth CV8 2BX* Tel (01926) 857118 E-mail paulfiske@live.co.uk

FISON, Geoffrey Robert Martius. b 34. Dur Univ BA59. Ely Th Coll 59. **d** 61 **p** 62. C Heavitree *Ex* 61-64; Australia 64-69; BSB 64-69; C Southampton Maybush St Pet *Win* 70-73; TV Strood *Roch* 73-79; TV Swindon Dorcan *Bris* 79-83; P-in-c Islington St Cuth 83-99; rtd 99; Perm to Offic *Glouc* and *Bris* from 99. *88 Oakleaze Road, Thornbury, Bristol BS35 2LP* Tel (01454) 850678

FITCH, Capt Alan John. b 45. Open Univ BA82 Warwick Univ MA84. Wilson Carlile Coll 64 Qu Coll Birm 92. **d** 92 **p** 93. CA from 66; C Glouc St Jas and All SS 92-97; NSM Wotton St Mary 93-97; V Douglas All SS and St Thos *S & M* 97-02; Chapl HM Pris Is of Man 97-02; TR Walbrook Epiphany *Derby* 02-09; Dioc Adv on Racial Justice from 02; rtd 09. *16 Nether Slade Road, Ilkeston DE7 8ET* E-mail a.fitch@virgin.net

FITCH, Canon John Ambrose. b 22. CCC Cam BA44 MA48. Wells Th Coll 45. **d** 47 **p** 48. C Newmarket All SS *St E* 47-50; Chapl St Felix Sch Southwold 51-69, V Reydon *St E* 51-70, R Brandon and Santon Downham 70-80; Hon Can St E Cathl 75-87; RD Mildenhall 78-80; R Monks Eleigh w Chelsworth and Brent Eleigh etc 80-87; rtd 87; Perm to Offic *St E* and *Chelmsf* 87-10. *1 Ramsay Hall, 9-13 Byron Road, Worthing BN11 3HN*

FITTER, Matthew Douglas. b 59. City of Lon Poly BSc81. Trin Coll Bris MA03. **d** 03 **p** 04. C Purley Ch Ch *S'wark* 03-07; C Beckenham Ch Ch *Roch* 07-10; TR Anerley from 10. *The Vicarage, 234 Anerley Road, London SE20 8TJ* Tel (020) 8778 4800 E-mail matthewfitter@hotmail.com

FITTER, Mrs Ruth Patricia. b 69. Chelt & Glouc Coll of HE BEd99. WEMTC 08. **d** 11. C S Cheltenham *Glouc* from 11. *341 Old Bath Road, Cheltenham GL53 9AH* Tel (01242) 222345 Mobile 07876-170964 E-mail ruthfitter@yahoo.co.uk

FITZGERALD, John Edward. b 44. Leic Univ MSc98. Oak Hill Th Coll. **d** 76 **p** 77. C Rainham *Chelmsf* 76-79; C Cambridge St Andr Less *Ely* 79-86; Min Cambridge St Steph CD 79-86; V Holmesfield *Derby* 86-88; Chapl HM Pris Wakef 88-90; Whatton 90-93; Nottm 90-98; Chapl HM YOI Glen Parva 98-05; Chapl Leic Constabulary 05-10; rtd 11. *288A Derby Road, Bramcote, Nottingham NG9 3JN* Tel 0115-939 9664 Mobile 07768-507883

FITZGERALD, Miss Melanie Anne. b 52. Sheff Univ BMus75. Westcott Ho Cam 96. **d** 98 **p** 99. C Rotherham *Sheff* 98-01; C Stannington 01-02; P-in-c Walkley 02-05; V from 05. *St Mary's Vicarage, 150 Walkley Road, Sheffield S6 2XQ* Tel 0114-234 5029 E-mail melanie.fitzgerald@zen.co.uk

FITZGERALD, Sarah. b 65. DipCOT87. St Jo Coll Nottm 06. **d** 08 **p** 09. C Folkestone Trin *Cant* from 08. *St George's Vicarage, 133 Shorncliffe Road, Folkestone CT20 3PB* Tel (01303) 248675 E-mail sarah.vicar@googlemail.com

FITZGERALD CLARK, Mrs Diane Catherine. b 54. Rhode Is Univ BA76. Gen Th Sem NY MDiv86. **d** 86 **p** 87. USA 86-95; NSM Hampstead Em W End *Lon* 96-99; Chapl St Alb High Sch for Girls from 98; Assoc Min St Alb Abbey from 98. *13 Eleanor Avenue, St Albans AL3 5TA* Tel (01727) 860099

FITZGIBBON, Kevin Peter. b 49. St Jo Coll Nottm BTh81. **d** 81 **p** 82. C Corby St Columba *Pet* 81-85; V Newborough 85-99; V Eaton Socon *St Alb* 99-07; P-in-c Christchurch and Manea and Welney *Ely* from 07; Min Consultant CPAS from 07. *The Rectory, 49 Charlemont Drive, Manea, March PE15 0GD* Tel (01354) 680969 E-mail k.fitzgibbon@care4free.net

FITZHARRIS, Barry. b 47. Lon Univ BA69 W Ontario Univ MA70 K Coll Lon BD72 AKC72. St Aug Coll Cant 72. **d** 73 **p** 74. C Whitstable All SS *Cant* 73-75; C Whitstable All SS w St Pet 75-76; Hon C Clapham Old Town *S'wark* 77-79; Asst Chapl Abp Tenison's Sch Kennington 78-84; Chapl and Hd RS 87-89; Hon C Streatham Ch Ch *S'wark* 80-84; R Radwinter w Hempstead *Chelmsf* 84-87; Hon C Streatham St Pet *S'wark* 87-89 and 97-98. *8 Holmlea Court, Chatsworth Road, Croydon CR0 1HA*

FITZHARRIS, The Ven Robert Aidan. b 46. Sheff Univ BDS71. Linc Th Coll 87. **d** 89 **p** 90. C Dinnington *Sheff* 89-92; V Bentley 92-01; RD Adwick 95-01; Hon Can Sheff Cathl 98-01; Adn Doncaster from 01. *Fairview House, 14 Armthorpe Lane, Doncaster DN2 5LZ* Tel (01302) 325787 *or* (01709) 309110 Mobile 07767-355357 Fax (01709) 309107 E-mail archdeacons.office@sheffield.anglican.org

FITZMAURICE, Arthur William John. b 65. AGSM89 Lon Inst of Educn PGCE92 Leeds Univ BA99 Heythrop Coll Lon

MA04. Coll of Resurr Mirfield 97. **d** 99 **p** 00. C Spondon *Derby* 99-02; P-in-c Emscote *Cov* 02-03; TV Warwick from 03. *All Saints' Vicarage, Vicarage Fields, Warwick CV34 5NJ* Tel (01926) 492073 E-mail john@fmaurice.freeserve.co.uk

FITZPATRICK, Paul Kevin. b 60. Open Univ BA99 Univ of Wales (Lamp) MTh05 Plymouth Univ PGCE07. Cuddesdon Coll 96. **d** 98 **p** 99. C Okehampton w Inwardleigh, Bratton Clovelly etc *Ex* 98-02; P-in-c Whipton 02-04; V 04-07; RD Christianity 05-07; Chapl Univ of Wales Inst Cardiff *Llan* from 07. *The Student Centre, UWIC, Western Avenue, Cardiff CF5 2YB* Tel (029) 2041 7252

FITZPATRICK, Victor Robert Andrew. b 75. Milltown Inst Dub BA00 Pontifical Univ Maynooth BD03 Cant Ch Ch Univ MA04. CITC 08. **d** 03 **p** 04. Chapl Cork Univ Hosp 03; C Bray *D & G* 04-07; C Dublin St Ann and St Steph 09-10; C Castleknock and Mulhuddart w Clonsilla from 10. *Kilbride, Main Street, Castleknock, Dublin 15, Republic of Ireland* Tel (00353) (1) 821 2218 Mobile 86-397 4035 E-mail prayspot@live.ie

FITZSIMONS, Canon Kathryn Anne. b 57. Bedf Coll of Educn CertEd78. NEOC 87. **d** 90. NSM Bilton *Ripon* 90-01; Soc Resp Development Officer Richmond Adnry 92-99; Urban Min Officer from 99; Hon Can Ripon Cathl from 04. *52 Newton Court, Leeds LS8 2PM* Tel 0113-248 5011 E-mail kathrynfitzsimons@hotmail.com

FLACH (née ROLLINS), Canon Deborah Mary Rollins. b 54. Sarum & Wells Th Coll 88. **d** 94 **p** 97. C Chantilly *Eur* 94-96; C Maisons-Laffitte 96-04; Asst Chapl 04-07; P-in-c Lille from 07; Can Gib Cathl from 07. *Christ Church, 14 rue Lyderic, 59000 Lille, France* Tel and fax (0033) 3 28 52 66 36 E-mail debbieflach@gmail.com

FLACK, Miss Heather Margaret. b 47. **d** 95 **p** 96. C Shenley Green *Birm* 95-00; TV Kings Norton 00-07; rtd 07; Perm to Offic *Birm* from 07. *23 Stourport Road, Bewdley DY12 1BB*

✠**FLACK, The Rt Revd John Robert.** b 42. Leeds Univ BA64. Coll of Resurr Mirfield 64. **d** 66 **p** 67 **c** 97. C Armley St Bart *Ripon* 66-69; C Northampton St Mary *Pet* 69-72; V Chapelthorpe *Wakef* 72-81; V Ripponden and Barkisland w W Scammonden 81-85; Chapl Rishworth Sch Ripponden 81-85; V Brighouse *Wakef* 85-88; TR Brighouse St Martin 88-92; RD Brighouse and Elland 86-92; Hon Can Wakef Cathl 89-92; Adn Pontefract 92-97; Suff Bp Huntingdon and Hon Can Ely Cathl 97-03; Abp's Rep H See and Dir Angl Cen Rome 03-08; P-in-c Nassington w Yarwell and Woodnewton w Apethorpe *Pet* from 08; Hon Asst Bp Pet and Eur from 03; Can Pet Cathl from 04. *The Vicarage, 34 Station Road, Nassington, Peterborough PE8 6QB* Tel (01780) 782271 E-mail johnrobertflack@hotmail.com

FLAGG, David Michael. b 50. CCC Cam BA71 MA75. St Jo Coll Nottm BA76. **d** 77 **p** 78. C Hollington St Leon *Chich* 77-80; C Woodley St Jo the Ev *Ox* 80-86; Chapl The Dorothy Kerin Trust Burrswood 86-94; R Knockholt w Halstead *Roch* 94-99; Dir Chapl Services Mildmay UK 99-02; Hd Chapl Services Qu Eliz Hosp NHS Trust 02-11; Hd Chapl Services S Lon Healthcare NHS Trust from 11. *Queen Elizabeth Hospital, Stadium Road, London SE18 4QH* Tel (020) 8836 6831 *or* 8836 6000 bleep 370 E-mail david.flagg@nhs.net

FLAHERTY, Jane Venitia. See ANDERSON, Mrs Jane Venitia

FLAHERTY, Ms Mandy Carol. b 63. Ches Coll of HE BA86 Leic Univ PGCE87. St Jo Coll Nottm MTh04. **d** 04 **p** 05. C Oadby *Leic* 04-08; Perm to Offic *Ely* 09-10; NSM Alconbury cum Weston from 10. *5 Bramble End, Alconbury, Huntingdon PE28 4EZ* Tel (01480) 896541 E-mail heddamand@aol.com

FLANAGAN, Kevin Joseph. b 60. Middx Poly BA87 Newman Coll Birm PGCE80. St Jo Coll Nottm 04. **d** 06 **p** 07. C Allesley Park and Whoberley *Cov* 06-09; V Wolston and Church Lawford from 09. *The Vicarage, Brook Street, Wolston, Coventry CV8 3HD* Tel (024) 7654 0778 *or* 7654 2722 E-mail kevandjayne@yahoo.co.uk

FLANAGAN, Miss Vivienne Lesley. b 66. Liv Poly BA89 Nottm Univ PGCE90. St Jo Coll Nottm BA98. **d** 98 **p** 99. C Huthwaite *S'well* 98-02; P-in-c Lenton Abbey 02-08; Chapl Bp Bell Sch from 08. *Bishop Bell Church of England School, 16 Priory Road, Eastbourne BN23 7EJ* Tel (01323) 465400 E-mail vflanagan@bishopbell.e-sussex.sch.uk

FLASHMAN, Stephen. b 49. Spurgeon's Coll Lon 69. **d** 08 **p** 10. NSM Chich St Paul and Westhampnett from 08. *70 Winterbourne Road, Chichester PO19 6PB* Tel (01243) 539129 Mobile 07950-000910 E-mail steve@ontheboxmission.com

FLATHER, Peter George. b 29. Sarum Th Coll. **d** 59 **p** 60. C Fordingbridge w Ibsley *Win* 59-63; C Lyndhurst 63-65; R E w W Bradenham *Nor* 65-72; P-in-c Speke All SS *Liv* 72-73; R Gunthorpe w Bale *Nor* 73-87; P-in-c Sharrington 73-87; P-in-c Gt w Lt Snoring 77-83; R Gunthorpe w Bale w Field Dalling, Saxlingham etc 87-89; rtd 89; Perm to Offic *Nor* 89-99. *9 Lloyd Court, High Kelling, Holt NR25 6AE* Tel (01263) 713936

FLATT, Stephen Joseph. b 57. SRN79 RSCN81. Sarum & Wells Th Coll 92. **d** 92 **p** 93. C Limpsfield and Titsey *S'wark* 92-96; TV Pewsey *Sarum* 96-97; Staff Nurse R Free Hampstead NHS Trust

97-99; Charge Nurse 99-00; Asst Chapl Univ Coll Lon Hosps NHS Trust 00-01; Chapl 01-03; Perm to Offic *S'wark* 98-99; NSM Clapham H Trin and St Pet 99-02; Lead Chapl St Mary's NHS Trust Paddington 03-10; Hd Spiritual and Past Care Imp Coll Healthcare NHS Trust from 10. *Chaplain's Office, St Mary's Hospital, Praed Street, London W2 1NY* Tel (020) 7886 1508 E-mail stephen.flatt@st-marys.nhs.uk

FLATTERS, Clive Andrew. b 56. Sarum & Wells Th Coll 83. **d** 86 **p** 88. C Weston Favell *Pet* 86-87; C Old Brumby *Linc* 88-91; C Syston *Leic* 91-93; TV 93-99; V Knottingley *Wakef* 99-02; TR Knottingley and Kellington w Whitley from 02. *The Vicarage, Chapel Street, Knottingley WF11 9AN* Tel (01977) 672267

FLAVELL, Paul William Deran. b 44. St Mich Coll Llan 67. **d** 68 **p** 69. C W Cairns Australia 68-71; C Blaenavon w Capel Newydd *Mon* 71-74; V Ynysddu 74-84; R Llanaber w Caerdeon *Ban* 84-00; V Llanstadwel *St D* 00-10; rtd 10. *14 Rhiw Grange, Colwyn Bay LL29 7TT* Tel (01492) 532601

FLEET, Daniel James Russell. b 60. Wye Coll Lon BSc84 Keele Univ PGCE02. St Jo Coll Nottm 86. **d** 89 **p** 90. C Boldmere *Birm* 89-92; C Caverswall and Weston Coyney w Dilhorne *Lich* 92-95; V Alton w Bradley-le-Moors and Oakamoor w Cotton 95-01; rtd 01; Perm to Offic *Lich* 01-10. *124 Byrds Lane, Uttoxeter ST14 7NB* Tel (01889) 560214 E-mail byrdfleet@tiscali.co.uk

FLEETNEY, Colin John. b 33. Cant Sch of Min. **d** 83 **p** 84. NSM Upper Hardres w Stelling *Cant* 83-85; Chapl Asst St Aug Hosp Cant 85-86; NSM Petham and Waltham w Lower Hardres etc *Cant* 85-86; V Lezayre *S & M* 86-90; rtd 98; Perm to Offic *S & M* from 10. *43 Magherchirrym, Port Erin, Isle of Man IM9 6DB* Tel (01624) 835249

FLEMING (formerly LOOKER), Miss Clare Margaret. b 55. Liv Univ CertEd78. Westcott Ho Cam 85. **d** 87 **p** 02. Par Dn Prestwood and Gt Hampden *Ox* 87-90; Hon C Olney w Emberton 90-92; Hon C Blunham, Gt Barford, Roxton and Tempsford etc *St Alb* 01-03; P-in-c Welford w Sibbertoft and Marston Trussell *Pet* 03-04; Perm to Offic *St Alb* 04-05; Hon C Wilden w Colmworth and Ravensden 05-08. *16 Carisbrooke Way, Eynesbury, St Neots PE19 2SP* Tel 07519-590767

FLEMING, The Ven David. b 37. Kelham Th Coll 58. **d** 63 **p** 64. C Walton St Marg Belmont Road *Liv* 63-67; Chapl HM Borstal Gaynes Hall 68-76; V Gt Staughton *Ely* 68-76; RD St Neots 72-76; V Whittlesey 76-85; RD March 77-82; Hon Can Ely Cathl 82-01; P-in-c Ponds Bridge 83-85; Adn Wisbech 84-97; V Wisbech St Mary 85-89; Chapl Gen of Pris 93-01; Chapl to The Queen 95-07; Perm to Offic *Ely* from 01. *Fair Haven, 123 Wisbech Road, Littleport, Ely CB6 1JJ* Tel (01353) 862498 E-mail davidfleming@hotmail.com

FLEMING, Elizabeth Julie. b 57. Westhill Coll Birm CertEd79 Ches Coll of HE BTh00. NOC 97. **d** 00 **p** 01. C Widnes St Jo *Liv* 00-03; P-in-c Walton Breck Ch Ch 03-04; V Walton Breck 04-08; V Becontree St Mary *Chelmsf* from 08. *The Vicarage, 191 Valence Wood Road, Dagenham RM8 3AH* Tel (020) 8592 2822 E-mail jooolz57@hotmail.com

FLEMING, George. b 39. CITC. **d** 78 **p** 79. C Donaghcloney w Waringstown *D & D* 78-80; C Newtownards 80; I Movilla 80; C Heref St Pet w St Owen and St Jas 80-85; V Holmer w Huntington 85-96; P-in-c Worfield 96-98; V 98-04; rtd 04; Perm to Offic *Truro* 05-08. *The Vicarage, South Marston, Swindon SN3 4SR* Tel (01793) 827021

FLEMING, Mrs Kathryn Claire. b 60. Trin Coll Cam BA82 MA91 Montessori TDip92. WEMTC 01. **d** 04 **p** 05. C Charlton Kings St Mary *Glouc* 04-08; P-in-c Cainscross w Selsley from 08. *The Vicarage, 58 Cashes Green Road, Stroud GL5 4RA* Tel (01453) 750949 Mobile 07775-630922 E-mail revkathryn@googlemail.com

FLEMING (formerly JOHNSTON), Mrs Patricia Anne. b 42. Qu Coll Birm 05. **d** 06 **p** 07. NSM Rubery *Birm* 06-09; P-in-c Allens Cross from 09. *9 Dowles Close, Birmingham B29 4LE* Tel 0121-475 6190

FLEMING, Penelope Rawling. See SMITH, Penelope Rawling

FLEMING, Ronald Thorpe. b 29. Codrington Coll Barbados 52. **d** 56 **p** 57. Barbados 56-61; C Delaval *Newc* 61-64; V Cambois 64-69; V Ancroft w Scremerston 69-81; V Longhirst 81-84; Chapl Preston Hosp N Shields 84-94; Chapl N Tyneside Hosps 84-94; rtd 94; Perm to Offic *Newc* 94-04; Lic to Offic *Mor* from 04. *49 Woodside Drive, Forres IV36 2UF* Tel (01309) 671101

FLEMING, Victoria Rosalie. b 58. WEMTC 01. **d** 04 **p** 05. NSM St Breoke and Egloshayle *Truro* 04-08; TV Stratton St Margaret w S Marston etc *Bris* from 08. *The Vicarage, South Marston, Swindon SN3 4SR* Tel (01793) 827021 E-mail revs.fleming@tiscali.co.uk

FLEMING, William Edward Charlton. b 29. TCD BA51 MA65. CITC 52. **d** 52 **p** 53. C Dublin Santry *D & G* 52-56; C Arm St Mark 56-61; I Tartaraghan 61-80; Prov Registrar 79-96; I Tartaraghan w Diamond 80-96; Can Arm Cathl 86-96; Treas Arm Cathl 88-92; Chan Arm Cathl 92-96; rtd 96. *65 Annareagh Road, Drumorgan, Richhill, Armagh BT61 9JT* Tel (028) 3887 9612

FLENLEY, Benjamin Robert Glanville. b 50. Sarum & Wells Th Coll 86. **d** 88 **p** 89. C Eastleigh *Win* 88-92; V Micheldever and E

Stratton, Woodmancote etc 92-03; R Bentworth, Lasham, Medstead and Shalden from 03. *The Rectory, Bentworth, Alton GU34 5RB* Tel and fax (01420) 563218 E-mail flenbenley@aol.com

FLETCHER, Mrs Angela. b 59. EMMTC 04. **d** 07 **p** 08. C Edwinstowe and Perlethorpe *S'well* 07-10; P-in-c Warsop from 10. *The Rectory, Church Road, Warsop, Mansfield NG20 0SL* E-mail angela.fletcher43@hotmail.com

FLETCHER, Anthony. See FLETCHER, James Anthony

FLETCHER, Anthony Peter Reeves. b 46. Bede Coll Dur CertEd Nottm Univ BTh78. Ridley Hall Cam 71. **d** 74 **p** 75. C Luton St Mary *St Alb* 74-78; Chapl RAF 78-00; P-in-c Lyneham w Bradenstoke *Sarum* 98-99; P-in-c Kyrenia St Andr and Chapl N Cyprus 00-04; P-in-c Lyneham w Bradenstoke *Sarum* 04-07; rtd 07. *Glentworth House, Giles Avenue, Cricklade, Swindon SN6 6HS* Tel (01793) 751333

FLETCHER, Barbara. b 41. ALAM79. WMMTC 93. **d** 96 **p** 97. NSM Smethwick *Birm* 96-97; C 97-02; rtd 02; Perm to Offic *Birm* from 02. *231 Abbey Road, Smethwick B67 5NN* Tel 0121-429 9354

FLETCHER, Bryce Clifford. ACIB. Cranmer Hall Dur. **d** 08 **p** 09. NSM Arle Valley *Win* from 08. *Robinia House, 23 Rosebery Road, Alresford SO24 9HQ*

FLETCHER, Colin John. b 46. Chich Th Coll. **d** 83 **p** 84. C Lt Ilford St Mich *Chelmsf* 83-86; C Hockerill *St Alb* 86-89; V New Cantley *Sheff* 89-95; C Kenton *Lon* 95-01; C Heavitree w Ex St Paul 01-02; C Heavitree and St Mary Steps 02-09; C Exwick 05-09; rtd 09. *8 Belvedere Court, High Street, Dawlish EX7 9ST* E-mail abcon@kenton62.freeserve.co.uk

✠**FLETCHER, The Rt Revd Colin William.** b 50. OBE00. Trin Coll Ox BA72 MA76. Wycliffe Hall Ox 72. **d** 75 **p** 76 **c** 00. C Shipley St Pet *Bradf* 75-79; Tutor Wycliffe Hall Ox 79-84; Hon C Ox St Andr 79-84; V Margate H Trin *Cant* 84-93; RD Thanet 88-93; Abp's Chapl 93-00; Hon Can Dallas from 93; Area Bp Dorchester *Ox* from 00. *Arran House, Sandy Lane, Yarnton, Kidlington OX5 1PB* Tel (01865) 375541 Fax 379890 E-mail bishopdorchester@oxford.anglican.org

FLETCHER, David Clare Molyneux. b 32. Worc Coll Ox BA55 MA59. Wycliffe Hall Ox 56. **d** 58 **p** 59. C Islington St Mary *Lon* 58-62; Hon C 62-83; Field Worker Scripture Union 62-86; R Ox St Ebbe w H Trin and St Pet 86-98; rtd 98; Perm to Offic *Ox* from 06. *32 Linkside Avenue, Oxford OX2 8JB* Tel (01865) 552420

FLETCHER, David Ernest. b 53. Worc Coll of Educn BEd76 Open Univ MTh01. St Jo Coll Nottm 99. **d** 01 **p** 02. C Mixenden *Wakef* 01-04; P-in-c 04-10; V Mixenden and Illingworth from 10; Dioc Urban Officer from 08. *37 Hops Lane, Halifax HX3 5FB* Tel (01422) 349844 Mobile 07702-385885 E-mail de.fletcher@btopenworld.com

FLETCHER, David Mark. b 56. Chich Th Coll 84. **d** 87 **p** 88. C Taunton St Andr *B & W* 87-91; P-in-c Chard, Furnham w Chaffcombe, Knowle St Giles etc 91-95; P-in-c Tiverton St Andr *Ex* 95-11; RD Tiverton 02-11; Chapl Mid Devon Primary Care Trust 95-11; TV Barnstaple *Ex* from 11. *The Vicarage, Sowden Lane, Barnstaple EX32 8BU* Tel (01271) 373837 E-mail davidfletcher56@btinternet.com

FLETCHER, Douglas. b 40. Coll of Resurr Mirfield 67. **d** 68 **p** 69. C Notting Hill St Jo *Lon* 68-73; C Cambridge St Mary Less *Ely* 73-74; C Fulham St Jo Walham Green *Lon* 74-76; C Walham Green St Jo w St Jas 76-84; P-in-c Kensal Town St Thos w St Andr and St Phil 84-92; V 92-06; rtd 06; Perm to Offic *Lon* from 07. *68 Clarendon Road, London W11 2HW* Tel (020) 7229 8146

FLETCHER, Capt Frank. b 40. Wilson Carlile Coll 71 EAMTC 94. **d** 96 **p** 96. Asst Chapl HM Pris Highpoint 90-97; Chapl HM Pris Wealstun 97-05; rtd 05; Perm to Offic *York* from 05. *6 Kingsclere, Huntington, York YO32 9SF* Tel (01904) 758453

FLETCHER, Gordon Wolfe (Robin). b 31. Edin Th Coll. **d** 62 **p** 63. C Eston *York* 62-65; C Harton Colliery *Dur* 65-68; V Pelton 68-81; V Ryhope 81-96; rtd 96. *23 Swinburne Road, Darlington DL3 7TD* Tel (01325) 265994 E-mail gordon.fletcher@btinternet.com

FLETCHER, Ian Paul. b 76. **d** 09 **p** 10. C Holdenhurst and Iford *Win* from 09. *19 Colemore Road, Bournemouth BH7 6RZ* E-mail ianpaulfletcher@googlemail.com

FLETCHER, James Anthony. b 36. St Edm Hall Ox BA60 MA66. St Steph Ho Ox 60. **d** 62 **p** 63. C Streatham St Pet *S'wark* 62-65; C Hobs Moat CD *Birm* 65-68; C Cowley St Jo *Ox* 68-77; V Hanworth All SS *Lon* 77-02; P-in-c Hanworth St Geo 89-91; rtd 02; Perm to Offic *Cant* from 02. *19 Strand Street, Sandwich, Kent CT13 9OX* Tel (01304) 620506

FLETCHER, James Arthur. b 79. Reading Univ BA99. Trin Coll Bris 03. **d** 05 **p** 06. C Bexleyheath Ch Ch *Roch* 05-08; R Fawkham and Hartley from 08. *The Rectory, 3 St John's Lane, Hartley, Longfield DA3 8ET* Tel (01474) 703819 E-mail rector@fawkhamandhartley.org.uk

FLETCHER, James John Gareth. b 79. Aber Univ MA02 Cam Univ BA08. Ridley Hall Cam 06. **d** 09 **p** 10. C Tooting Graveney

St Nic *S'wark* from 09. *48 Ashvale Road, London SW17 8PW* Tel 07880-552660 (mobile) E-mail james.fletcher@cantab.net
FLETCHER, Miss Janet. b 59. Lanc Univ MA07. Cranmer Hall Dur. **d** 00 **p** 01. C Ainsdale *Liv* 00-04; TV Walton-on-the-Hill and Hon Chapl Liv Cathl 04-09; C Prescot from 09. *56 Park Road, Prescot L34 3LR* Tel 0151-426 2325 E-mail jan.f.nathanael@btinternet.com
FLETCHER, Jeremy James. b 60. Dur Univ BA81. St Jo Coll Nottm 85. **d** 88 **p** 89. C Stranton *Dur* 88-91; C Nottingham St Nic *S'well* 91-94; P-in-c Skegby 94-00; P-in-c Teversal 96-00; Bp's Dom Chapl 00-02; Can Res and Prec York Minster 02-09; V Beverley Minster from 09; P-in-c Routh from 09. *The Minster Vicarage, Highgate, Beverley HU17 0DN* Tel (01482) 881434 *or* 868540 E-mail vicar@beverleyminster.org.uk *or* jeremy@jjfletcher.co.uk
FLETCHER, Canon John Alan Alfred. b 33. Oak Hill Th Coll 58. **d** 61 **p** 62. C Erith St Paul *Roch* 61-64; C Rushden *Pet* 64-67; R Hollington St Leon *Chich* 67-86; V Chadwell Heath *Chelmsf* 86-00; RD Barking and Dagenham 91-00; Chapl Chadwell Heath Hosp Romford 86-93; Chapl Redbridge Health Care NHS Trust 93-00; Hon Can Chelmsf Cathl 99-00; rtd 00; Perm to Offic *Chich* from 01. *87 Hoads Wood Road, Hastings TN34 2BB* Tel (01424) 712345 Mobile 07860-128912 E-mail jaaf@btinternet.com
FLETCHER, Jonathan James Molyneux. b 42. Hertf Coll Ox BA66 MA68. Wycliffe Hall Ox 66. **d** 68 **p** 69. C Enfield Ch Ch Trent Park *Lon* 68-72; C Cambridge St Sepulchre *Ely* 72-76; C St Helen Bishopsgate w St Martin Outwich *Lon* 76-81; Min Wimbledon Em Ridgway Prop Chpl *S'wark* from 82. *Emmanuel Parsonage, 8 Sheep Walk Mews, London SW19 4QL* Tel (020) 8946 4728
FLETCHER, Keith. b 47. Chich Th Coll 79. **d** 80 **p** 81. C Hartlepool St Paul *Dur* 80-82; V Eighton Banks 82-85; V Haydon Bridge *Newc* 85-96; RD Hexham 93-96; P-in-c Beltingham w Henshaw 93-96; R Ashmanhaugh, Barton Turf etc *Nor* 96-99; rtd 99. *2 Churchill Terrace, Sherburn Hill, Durham DH6 1PF* Tel 0191-372 0362
FLETCHER, Ms Linda. b 72. Man Univ BA93. Trin Coll Bris BA09. **d** 09 **p** 10. C Coulsdon St Jo *S'wark* from 09. *8 Waddington Avenue, Coulsdon CR5 1QE* Tel 07852-911598 (mobile) E-mail lindaandarun@tiscali.co.uk
FLETCHER, Linden Elisabeth. b 50. Lon Univ BEd73 MA80. St Jo Coll Nottm 87. **d** 89 **p** 94. C Fakenham w Alethorpe *Nor* 89-93; C Cumnor *Ox* 93-02; P-in-c Ringshall w Battisford, Barking w Darmsden etc *St E* 02-08; P-in-c Somersham w Flowton and Offton w Willisham 02-08; V Llanfair Caereinion, Llanllugan and Manafon *St As* 08-11; rtd 11. *Tanrallt, Cwrtnewydd, Llanybydder SA40 9YJ*
FLETCHER, Mrs Margaret. b 44. **d** 04 **p** 05. NSM Thurstaston *Ches* 04-07; V Thornton-le-Moors w Ince and Elton from 07. *The Vicarage, Ince Lane, Elton, Chester CH2 4QB* Tel (01928) 724028
FLETCHER, Mark. b 72. Staffs Poly BSc93. Oak Hill Th Coll BA00. **d** 00 **p** 01. C Paddington Em Harrow Road *Lon* 00-03; C W Kilburn St Luke w St Simon and St Jude 00-03; C Barnsbury from 04. *43 Matilda Street, London N1 0LA* Tel (020) 7278 5208 E-mail mark@midwinter.org.uk
FLETCHER, Martin. b 60. Bradf Univ BEng83 CEng MIMechE. Ripon Coll Cuddesdon. **d** 00 **p** 01. C Oatlands *Guildf* 00-04; R Tolleshunt Knights w Tiptree and Gt Braxted *Chelmsf* 04-10; V Hersham *Guildf* from 10. *The Vicarage, 5 Burwood Road, Walton-on-Thames KT12 4AA* Tel (01932) 227445 E-mail fletcher martin@yahoo.co.uk
FLETCHER, Martin James. b 48. Ex Univ BA03 MIFA89. SWMTC 99. **d** 02 **p** 03. NSM Wolborough and Ogwell *Ex* 02-05; NSM Chudleigh w Chudleigh Knighton and Trusham from 05. *11 Troarn Way, Chudleigh, Newton Abbot TQ13 0PP* Tel (01626) 853998 E-mail m.fletcher@uwclub.net
FLETCHER, Maurice. See FLETCHER, Ralph Henry Maurice
FLETCHER, Mrs Patricia. b 34. K Alfred's Coll Win CertEd74. Chich Th Coll 94. **d** 94. NSM Droxford *Portsm* 94-97; NSM Meonstoke w Corhampton cum Exton 94-97; Perm to Offic 97-00; NSM Blendworth w Chalton w Idsworth 00-04; rtd 04; Perm to Offic *Portsm* from 04. *17 Maylings Farm Road, Fareham PO16 7QU* Tel (01329) 311489 E-mail patfletch2004@yahoo.co.uk
FLETCHER, Paul Gordon MacGregor. b 61. St Andr Univ MTheol84. Edin Th Coll 84. **d** 86 **p** 87. C Cumbernauld *Glas* 86-89; C-in-c Glas H Cross 89-93; P-in-c Milngavie 93-99; R Clarkston 99-07; Lic to Offic *Arg* from 08. *Corriecravie Moor Farm, Sliddery, Isle of Arran KA27 8PE* Tel (01770) 870234 E-mail paulmcgregorfletcher@hotmail.com
FLETCHER, Ralph Henry Maurice. b 43. St Luke's Coll Ex CertEd65. St Steph Ho Ox 71. **d** 74 **p** 75. C Chislehurst Annunciation *Roch* 74-77; Chapl Quainton Hall Sch Harrow *Lon* 94-00; Perm to Offic Lon 94-00; C Hillingdon All SS *Lon* 87-94; Perm to Offic *Lon* 94-00; *Roch* 00-02; *Wakef* from 05. *6 Joseph Court, Joseph Street, Barnsley S70 1LJ* Tel (012260) 779928

FLETCHER, Robert Alexander. b 52. Ridley Hall Cam. **d** 84 **p** 85. C Chalfont St Peter *Ox* 84-88; C Bushey *St Alb* 88-93; TV Digswell and Panshanger 93-00; P-in-c Aldenham 00-05; TV Aldenham, Radlett and Shenley from 05. *The Vicarage, Church Lane, Aldenham, Watford WD25 8BE* Tel and fax (01923) 854209 E-mail r.a.fletcher@btinternet.com
FLETCHER, Robin. See FLETCHER, Gordon Wolfe
FLETCHER, Canon Robin Geoffrey. b 32. Nottm Univ BA57. Ridley Hall Cam 57. **d** 59 **p** 60. C S Mimms Ch Ch *Lon* 59-64; V Wollaton Park *S'well* 64-71; V Clifton *York* 71-97; Chapl Clifton Hosp York 71-88; RD City of York 86-97; Can and Preb York Minster 89-00; rtd 98; Perm to Offic *York* 00-04 and *Wakef* from 04. *14 South Avenue, Fartown, Huddersfield HD2 1BY* Tel (01484) 510266 E-mail rgfletcher@tiscali.co.uk
FLETCHER, Mrs Sheila Elizabeth. b 35. Nottm Univ BA57 CertEd58. NEOC 84. **d** 87 **p** 94. NSM Dringhouses *York* 87-90; Par Dn 90-94; C 94-97; P-in-c Sutton on the Forest 97-02; rtd 02; Perm to Offic *York* from 02. *68 Huntsman's Walk, York YO24 3LA* Tel (01904) 796876 E-mail rgeoff@soo.co.uk
FLETCHER, Stephen. b 57. Man Univ BA79 MA84. St Jo Coll Nottm 82. **d** 84 **p** 85. C Didsbury St Jas and Em *Man* 84-88; R Kersal Moor 88-01; TR Horwich and Rivington from 01; C Blackrod from 11. *The Rectory, Chorley Old Road, Horwich, Bolton BL6 6AX* Tel and fax (01204) 468263 E-mail stephen@fletchers.freeserve.co.uk
FLETCHER, Stephen William. b 62. Wolv Poly BA84. Qu Coll Birm 85. **d** 88 **p** 89. C Rainham *Roch* 88-91; C Shottery St Andr *Cov* 91-97; Min Bishopton St Pet 91-97; V Llanrumney *Mon* 97-02; V Adderbury w Milton *Ox* from 02. *11 Walton Avenue, Adderbury, Banbury OX17 3JY* Tel (01295) 810309
FLETCHER, Timothy John. b 63. Sheff Univ BA88 St Jo Coll Dur MA04. Cranmer Hall Dur 01. **d** 03 **p** 04. C Four Marks *Win* 03-06; V Walton le Soken *Chelmsf* from 06. *The Vicarage, Martello Road, Walton on the Naze CO14 8BP* Tel (01255) 675452 E-mail tim@fletcherchester.fsnet.co.uk
FLEWKER, David William. b 53. Birm Univ BA75. Wycliffe Hall Ox 76. **d** 78 **p** 79. C Netherton *Liv* 78-82; C Prescot 82-84; V Seaforth 84-88; TV Whitstable *Cant* 88-96; Miss to Seamen 88-96; V Bethersden w High Halden *Cant* 96-08; Asst Dir of Ords 02-06; P-in-c Deal St Leon w St Rich and Sholden etc from 08. *St Leonard's Rectory, Addelam Road, Deal CT14 9BZ* Tel (01304) 374076 E-mail d.flewker@btinternet.com
FLEWKER-BARKER, Miss Linda. b 68. Redcliffe Coll BA02 St Jo Coll Dur MA04. Cranmer Hall Dur 02. **d** 04 **p** 05. C Cheltenham Ch Ch *Glouc* 04-07; Chapl RAF from 07. *Chaplaincy Services, Valiant Block, HQ Air Command, RAF High Wycombe HP14 4UE* Tel (01494) 496800 Fax 496343 E-mail lindafbarker@yahoo.com
FLIGHT, Michael John. b 41. Sarum Th Coll 68. **d** 71 **p** 72. C Wimborne Minster *Sarum* 71-75; R Tarrant Gunville, Tarrant Hinton etc 75-78; P-in-c Tarrant Rushton, Tarrant Rawston etc 77-78; R Tarrant Valley 78-80; V Westbury 80-00; RD Heytesbury 83-87 and 96-00; R Broad Town, Clyffe Pypard, Hilmarton etc 00-07; RD Calne 03-06; rtd 07. *11 Nursteed Close, Devizes SN10 3EU* Tel (01380) 738493 E-mail flightvic@aol.com
FLINN, Canon John Robert Patrick. b 30. CITC. **d** 65 **p** 66. C Dublin Rathfarnham *D & G* 65-67; I Baltinglass w Ballynure etc *C & O* 67-76; I Castlepollard and Oldcastle w Loughcrew etc *M & K* 76-84; rtd 84; Treas Ossory and Leighlin Cathls 90-92; Chan Ossory and Leighlin Cathls 96-01. *The Old School House, Kells, Co Kilkenny, Republic of Ireland* Tel (00353) (56) 772 8297
FLINT, Edward Benedict William. b 80. **d** 08 **p** 09. C Bryanston Square St Mary w St Marylebone St Mark *Lon* from 08. *25 Bloemfontein Avenue, London W12 7BJ* Tel (020) 8743 1508 E-mail edflint@gmail.com
FLINT, Howard Michael. b 59. Edge Hill Coll of HE BEd81. Cranmer Hall Dur 95. **d** 97 **p** 98. C Chipping Campden w Ebrington *Glouc* 97-00; V Upper Wreake *Leic* 00-06; RD Framland 02-06; V Tunbridge Wells H Trin w Ch Ch *Roch* from 06. *The Vicarage, 63 Claremont Road, Tunbridge Wells TN1 1TE* Tel (01892) 526644 *or* 522323 Fax 529300 E-mail rev4howard@hotmail.com
FLINT, Nicholas Angus. b 60. Chich Th Coll 84. **d** 87 **p** 88. C Aldwick *Chich* 87-91; Bp's Asst Chapl for the Homeless *Lon* 91-92; TV Ifield *Chich* 92-96; R Rusper w Colgate from 96. *The Rectory, High Street, Rusper, Horsham RH12 4PX* Tel (01293) 871251 E-mail nick.flint@totalise.co.uk
FLINT, Toby. b 76. Wycliffe Hall Ox BA08. **d** 08 **p** 09. C Brompton H Trin w Onslow Square St Paul *Lon* 08-11; C Onslow Square and S Kensington St Aug from 11. *Holy Trinity Brompton, Brompton Road, London SW7 1JA* Tel 08456-447533 E-mail tobyflint@hotmail.com
FLINTHAM, Alan Jenkinson. b 45. Leeds Univ BSc66 PGCE67 MEd74. WEMTC 98. **d** 00 **p** 01. NSM Melbourne *Derby* 00-10; NSM Melbourne, Ticknall, Smisby and Stanton from 10. *50 Burlington Way, Mickleover, Derby DE3 9BD* Tel (01332) 512293 E-mail flintham@flinthams.org.uk

FLINTOFT, Ian Hugh. b 74. Pemb Coll Cam BA97 MA99 MPhil98. Westcott Ho Cam 01. d 04 p 05. C Newc St Geo 04-06; C Newc St Geo and St Hilda 06-07; C Ch the King 07-08; TV 08-11; Bp's Chapl and Dioc Dir of Ords from 11. St Luke's Vicarage, 15 Claremont Street, Newcastle upon Tyne NE2 4AH Tel 0191-221 0256 E-mail ianflintoft@hotmail.com
FLINTOFT-CHAPMAN, Margaret. See CHAPMAN, Mrs Margaret
FLINTOFT-CHAPMAN, Mrs Margaret. b 47. Leeds Univ BA68. NTMTC 03. d 05 p 06. NSM Barkingside St Cedd Chelmsf from 05. 84 Roding Lane North, Woodford Green IG8 8NG Tel (020) 8504 6750
FLIPPANCE, Kim Sheelagh May. See STEPHENS, Mrs Kim Sheelagh May
FLIPSE, Miss Adriana Maria (Marja). b 82. Leiden Univ MA05. St Mich Coll Llan 07. d 08 p 09. C Roath Llan 08-11; C Newton Nottage from 11. Ty Dewi Sant, 5B West End Avenue, Porthcawl CF36 3NE Tel (01656) 772595 E-mail marjaflipse@btinternet.com
FLOATE, Herbert Frederick Giraud. b 25. Keble Coll Ox BA50 MA54. Qu Coll Birm 50. d 61 p 62. Seychelles 61; Hon C Quarrington w Old Sleaford Linc 63-65; P-in-c Mareham le Fen 65-66; Australia 66-72; R Stroxton Linc 72-74; R Harlaxton w Wyville and Hungerton 72-74; Lect Shenston New Coll Worcs 74-78; P-in-c Redditch St Geo Worc 78-79; Lic to Offic 80-84; R Upton Snodsbury and Broughton Hackett etc 84-89; Chapl Mojácar Eur 89-91; rtd 91; Perm to Offic Heref from 97. 15 Progress Close, Ledbury HR8 2QZ Tel (01531) 635509
FLOATE, Miss Rhona Cameron. b 59. Univ of Wales (Cardiff) BA80. Trin Coll Bris 01. d 03 p 04. C Lighthorne Cov 03-07; C Chesterton 03-07; C Newbold Pacey w Moreton Morrell 03-07; P-in-c Wool and E Stoke Sarum from 07. The Vicarage, Vicarage Close, Wool, Wareham BH20 6EB Tel (01929) 462215 E-mail vicar@holyroodwool.org.uk
FLOCKHART, Mrs Ruth. b 56. TISEC 96. d 99 p 00. NSM Strathpeffer Mor from 99; NSM Dingwall from 99. Kilmuir Farm Cottage, North Kessock, Inverness IV1 3ZG Tel (01463) 731580 E-mail kilmuirseabreeze@btinternet.com
FLOOD, Mrs Jean Anne. b 51. Liv Hope Univ MEd00 Liv Univ CertEd95. NOC 06. d 08. NSM Fazakerley Em Liv 08-11; Co-ord Miss in the Economy from 11; NSM Walton-on-the-Hill from 11. 19 Palm Close, Liverpool L9 1JD Tel 0151-525 0304 E-mail floods@merseymail.com
FLOOD, John Leslie. b 45. Yorks Min Course 10. d 11. NSM Todmorden Wakef from 11. 52 Stansfield Street, Todmorden OL14 5EB Tel (01706) 813539 Mobile 07976-209480 E-mail aestus@talk21.com
FLOOD, Kenneth. b 75. St Chad's Coll Dur BSc96. St Steph Ho Ox BTh01. d 01 p 02. C Hulme Ascension Man 01-05; C Wokingham St Paul Ox 05-08; P-in-c Chorlton-cum-Hardy St Clem Man 08-09; R from 09. The Rectory, 6 Edge Lane, Manchester M21 9JF Tel 0161-881 3063 E-mail ken@mightyflood.org.uk
FLOOD, Nicholas Roger. b 42. FCA. Ripon Hall Ox 71. d 92 p 93. NSM Romsey Win 92-94; Chapl Win and Eastleigh Healthcare NHS Trust 94-08; rtd 08. Forest View, Salisbury Road, Plaitford, Romsey SO51 6EE Tel (01794) 323731
FLORANCE, James Andrew Vernon. b 44. MCIOB. Linc Th Coll 84. d 86 p 87. C Lt Ilford St Mich Chelmsf 86-90; TV Becontree S 90-93; R Orsett and Bulphan and Horndon on the Hill 93-97; P-in-c Liscard St Mary w St Columba Ches 97-02; RD Wallasey 99-02; Chapl St D Foundn Hospice Care Newport 02-03; P-in-c Abersychan and Garndiffaith Mon 03-08; rtd 08; Perm to Offic Heref and Mon 08-10; St E from 10. 3 Waterloo Mews, Leiston IP16 4GX Tel (01728) 635588 E-mail jandp.florance@talktalk.net
FLORANCE (née WAINWRIGHT), Mrs Pauline Barbara. b 40. St Deiniol's Hawarden 83. dss 84 d 87 p 94. New Ferry Ches 84-90; Par Dn 87-90; Par Dn Hallwood 90-94; C 94-00; rtd 00; Perm to Offic Ches 00-03; Mon 04-08; Heref 08-10; Bp's Adv in Past Care and Counselling Mon 07-10; Perm to Offic St E from 10. 3 Waterloo Mews, Leiston IP16 4GX Tel (01728) 635588 E-mail jandp.florance@talktalk.net
FLORENTINUS, Erik. ERMC. d 09 p 10. C Amsterdam w Den Helder and Heiloo Eur from 09. 0Z Achterburgwal 100, NL-1012 DS Amsterdam, The Netherlands
FLORY, John Richard. b 35. Clare Coll Cam BA59 MA63. Westcott Ho Cam 69. d 71 p 72. C Shirehampton Bris 71-74; V Patchway 74-82; R Lydiard Millicent w Lydiard Tregoz 82-86; TR The Lydiards 86-93; R Box w Hazlebury and Ditteridge 93-01; rtd 01; Perm to Offic Derby from 02. Beechbank, 3 Ivonbrook Close, Darley Bridge, Matlock DE4 2JX Tel (01629) 734707
FLOWERDAY, Andrew Leslie. b 53. Imp Coll Lon BSc75. St Jo Coll Nottm. d 90 p 91. C Farnborough Guildf 90-95; TV Morden S'wark from 95. 140 Stonecot Hill, Sutton SM3 9HQ Tel (020) 8330 6566 or 8337 6421
FLOWERDEW, Martin James. b 56. Herts Coll CertEd78 Pemb Coll Cam BEd79. Sarum & Wells Th Coll 89. d 91 p 92. C

Leagrave St Alb 91-95; C Radlett 95-99; TV Wilford Peninsula St E 99-01; V St Osyth Chelmsf 01-09; V Hoylake Ches from 09. The Vicarage, 1 Stanley Road, Hoylake, Wirral CH47 1HL Tel 0151-632 3897 E-mail theblacksheep@tinyworld.co.uk
FLOWERS, John Henry. b 33. Qu Coll Birm 63. d 65 p 66. C Aberdare St Fagan Llan 65-68; C Llantrisant 68-72; V Nantymoel w Wyndham 72-76; Asst Chapl HM Pris Wormwood Scrubs 76-78; Chapl HM Pris Birm 78-80; Chapl HM Pris Albany 80-93; rtd 93; Perm to Offic Portsm from 93. 1 Ulster Crescent, Newport PO30 5RU Tel (01983) 525493
FLUX, Brian George. b 39. Oak Hill Th Coll 68. d 71 p 72. C Chadderton Ch Ch Man 71-74; C Preston All SS Blackb 74-76; Min Preston St Luke 76-81; CF (TA) from 78; R Higher Openshaw Man 81-88; Chapl HM Pris Haverigg 88-92; rtd 92. 65 Crosby Street, Maryport CA15 6DR Tel (01900) 810635
FLYNN, Alexander Victor George. b 45. d 90 p 91. C Kilsaran w Drumcar, Dunleer and Dunany Arm 90-91; P-in-c 91-94; I 94-98; I Clonenagh w Offerlane, Borris-in-Ossory etc C & O 98-00; I Aughrim w Ballinasloe etc L & K from 08. The Rectory, Aughrim, Ballinasloe, Co Galway, Republic of Ireland Tel (00353) (90) 967 3735 Mobile 87-2074739 E-mail georgeandgwyn@eircom.net
FLYNN, Mrs Diane. b 62. Yorks Min Course. d 09 p 10. C Roundhay St Edm Ripon from 09. 15 Talbot Court, Leeds LS8 1LT Tel 0113-266 9243 E-mail dianeflynn888@btinternet.com
FLYNN, Peter Murray. b 35. Oak Hill Th Coll 76. d 79 p 80. NSM Finchley St Mary Lon 79-83; NSM Mill Hill Jo Keble Ch 84-86; C Mill End and Heronsgate w W Hyde St Alb 86-92; V Chessington Guildf 92-05; rtd 05; Perm to Offic Roch from 05. 16 The Street, Plaxtol, Sevenoaks TN15 0QQ Tel (01732) 811304 E-mail revpeterflynn@yahoo.co.uk
FOALE, Rosemary. See MASON, Sheila Rosemary
FOBISTER, Mrs Wendy Irene. b 44. Lon Inst of Educn TCert65. d 07 p 08. OLM Charminster and Stinsford Sarum 07-11; NSM from 11. 44 Meadow View, Charminster, Dorchester DT2 9RE Tel (01305) 251681 E-mail wenfob@gmail.com
FODEN, Eric. Local Minl Tr Course. d 93 p 94. OLM New Bury Man 93-96. 45 Stetchworth Drive, Worsley, Manchester M28 1FU Tel 0161-790 4627
FODEN, Mrs Janice Margaret. b 54. Sheff Univ BA76 Sheff City Poly PGCE77. NOC 98. d 01 p 02. NSM Kimberworth Sheff 01-05; P-in-c Barnby Dun from 05; AD Doncaster from 10. The Vicarage, Stainforth Road, Barnby Dun, Doncaster DN3 1AA Tel (01302) 882835 E-mail janfoden@hotmail.com or jan.foden@sheffield.anglican.org
FODEN-CURRIE, Mary Agnes. b 43. Bp Grosseteste Coll BEd64. St Jo Coll Nottm MA97. d 98 p 99. NSM Skegby S'well 98-02; NSM Skegby w Teversal 02-03; rtd 03; Perm to Offic S'well from 03. 40 Harvey Road, Mansfield NG18 4ES Tel (01623) 479838
FOGDEN, Canon Elizabeth Sally. b 40. MBE04. MCSP61. Qu Coll Birm 76. dss 78 d 87 p 94. Chevington w Hargrave and Whepstead w Brockley St E 78-84; Honington w Sapiston and Troston 84-92; Par Dn 87-92; Par Dn Euston w Barnham, Elvedon and Fakenham Magna 90-92; TD Blackbourne 92-94; TV 94-06; Chapl Center Parc Elvedon from 90; Dioc Adv Women's Min 90-06; Hon Can St E Cathl 92-06; rtd 06; Perm to Offic St E from 06. Meadow Farm, Coney Weston Road, Sapiston, Bury St Edmunds IP31 1RX Tel (01359) 268923 Mobile 07860-101980
FOGDEN, Mrs Patricia Lily Margaret. b 51. SRN73. d 03 p 04. OLM Orlestone w Snave and Ruckinge w Warehorne etc Cant 03-10; NSM 10-11; NSM Appledore w Brookland, Fairfield, Brenzett etc from 11; NSM Wittersham w Stone and Ebony from 11. Harewood, Wey Street, Snave, Ashford TN26 2QH Tel (01233) 733862 Mobile 07885-285636
FOGG, Cynthia Mary (Sister Mary Clare). b 34. Bp Grosseteste Coll TCert54. LNSM course 94. d 95 p 96. NSM Westgate Common Wakef 95-09; rtd 09. St Peter's Convent, Dovecote Lane, Horbury, Wakefield WF4 6BD Tel (01924) 272181 Fax 261225
FOGG, Mrs Margaret. b 37. CBDTI 04. d 05 p 06. NSM Allonby, Cross Canonby and Dearham Carl from 05. Green Pastures, 59 Sycamore Road, Maryport CA15 7AE Tel (01900) 816203 E-mail margaret.fogg@btinternet.com
FOLEY, Geoffrey Evan. b 30. Univ of New England BA71 DipEd73 MEd79. St Jo Coll Morpeth 51. d 53 p 54. C Murwillumbah Australia 53-59; R Mallanganee 59-65; R Woodburn 65-72; P-in-c Lismore 84-85; P-in-c Bangalow 87-88; P-in-c Alstonville 88-89; Perm to Offic S'wark 90-91; Chapl Hamburg w Kiel Eur 91; C Stoke-upon-Trent Lich 91; rtd 93; Perm to Offic Grafton from 93; Dioc Archivist from 97. 198 Dawson Street, Lismore NSW 2480, Australia Tel (0061) (2) 6621 4684 E-mail gefoley@bigpond.net.au
FOLEY, James Frank. b 50. MBE91. Reading Univ BSc72. STETS 95. d 99 p 00. C St Illogan Truro 99-03; P-in-c Droxford and Meonstoke w Corhampton cum Exton Portsm 03-08; C Balham Hill Ascension S'wark 09-11; rtd 11. Flat 1, 4 Eastern

Terrace, Brighton BN2 1DJ Tel (01273) 278330 Mobile 07545-831961 E-mail jim.ffoley@yahoo.co.uk

✠**FOLEY, The Rt Revd Ronald Graham Gregory.** b 23. St Jo Coll Dur BA49. **d** 50 **p** 51 **c** 82. C S Shore H Trin *Blackb* 50-54; V Blackb St Luke 54-60; Dir RE *Dur* 60-71; R Brancepeth 60-71; Hon Can Dur Cathl 65-71; Hon Can Ripon Cathl 71-82; V Leeds St Pet 71-82; Chapl to The Queen 77-82; Suff Bp Reading *Ox* 82-87; Area Bp Reading 87-89; rtd 89; Hon Asst Bp York from 95. *3 Poplar Avenue, Kirkbymoorside, York YO62 6ES* Tel (01751) 432439

FOLKARD, Oliver Goring. b 41. Nottm Univ BA63. Lich Th Coll 64. **d** 66 **p** 67. C Carlton *S'well* 66-67; C Worksop Priory 67-68; C Brewood *Lich* 68-71; C Folkingham w Laughton *Linc* 72-75; P-in-c Gedney Hill 77-84; V Whaplode Drove 76-84; V Sutton St Mary 84-94; RD Elloe E 89-94; P-in-c Scotter w E Ferry 94-99; R 99-06; R Scotton w Northorpe 99-06; rtd 06; Perm to Offic *Nor* from 06. *1 Barons Close, Fakenham NR21 8BE* Tel (01328) 851468

FOLKS, Andrew John. b 42. St Jo Coll Dur BA65. Cranmer Hall Dur. **d** 69 **p** 70. C Stranton *Dur* 69-72; Chapl Sandbach Sch 73-80; Chapl Casterton Sch Lancs 80-85; Hd Master Fernhill Manor Sch New Milton 85-97; NSM Langdale *Carl* 97-07; rtd 07; Perm to Offic *Bradf* from 09. *10 Winfield Road, Sedbergh LA10 5AZ* Tel (01539) 621314
E-mail folksandrew@yahoo.co.uk

FOLKS, Peter William John. b 30. FRCO56 ARCM. Launde Abbey 72. **d** 72 **p** 73. C Leic St Aid 72-76; V Newfoundpool 76-84; V Whetstone 84-94; rtd 94; Perm to Offic *Leic* from 94. *4 Beaufort Close, Desford, Leicester LE9 9HS* Tel (01455) 828090 E-mail peterfolks@hotmail.com

FOLLETT, Jeremy Mark. b 60. Jes Coll Cam BA82. St Jo Coll Nottm 90. **d** 91 **p** 92. C Newark *S'well* 91-95; C Hellesdon *Nor* 95-01; V St Alb Ch Ch St Alb from 01. *Christ Church Vicarage, 5 High Oaks, St Albans AL3 6DJ* Tel (01727) 855759

FOLLETT, Neil Robert Thomas. b 50. RMCS BSc75 Open Univ BA85. EAMTC 86. **d** 89 **p** 90. C Godmanchester *Ely* 89-92; V 92-00; V Wilton Place St Paul *Lon* 00; rtd 00. *Address withheld by request*

FOLLIN, Michael Stuart. b 62. UMIST BSc84. St Jo Coll Nottm MTh02. **d** 02 **p** 03. C Aughton Ch Ch *Liv* 02-06; TV Maghull 06-09; TV Maghull and Melling from 09. *St Peter's Vicarage, 1 St Peter's Row, Liverpool L31 5LU* Tel 0151-526 3434 Mobile 07813-794252 E-mail michael.follin@tiscali.co.uk

FOLLIS, Bryan Andrew. b 61. Ulster Poly BA83 QUB PhD90 TCD BA98. CITC 95. **d** 98 **p** 99. C Portadown St Mark *Arm* 98-01; I Belfast All SS *Conn* from 01. *All Saints' Rectory, 25 Rugby Road, Belfast BT7 1PT* Tel (028) 9032 3327 or 9031 4114 Mobile 07758-289936 E-mail b.a.follis@hotmail.co.uk

FOLLIS, Raymond George Carlile. b 23. DFC45. Lich Th Coll 63. **d** 65 **p** 66. C Walsall Wood *Lich* 65-69; R New Fishbourne *Chich* 69-88; P-in-c Appledram 84-88; rtd 88; Perm to Offic *Chich* 88-10. *The College of St Barnabas, Blackberry Lane, Lingfield RH7 6NJ*

FONTAINE, Mrs Marion Elizabeth. b 39. RN61 RM62. SAOMC 96. **d** 99 **p** 00. OLM Thatcham *Ox* from 99. *33 Druce Way, Thatcham RG19 3PF* Tel (01635) 827746

FOOKS, George Edwin. b 25. Trin Hall Cam BA49 MA52 Reading Univ AdDipEd70. Linc Th Coll 49. **d** 51 **p** 52. C Portsea St Cuth *Portsm* 51-53; C Fareham SS Pet and Paul 53-55; Chapl Earnseat Sch Carl 55-59; V Sheff St Cuth 59-64; Hd Careers Fairfax Gr Sch Bradf 64-66; Hd RE/Careers Buttershaw Comp Sch Bradf 66-70; Counsellor Ifield Sch Crawley 70-73; Hd Guidance Hengrove Sch Bris 73-78; Counsellor w Hearing Impaired Children (Avon) 78-89; Chapl Southmead Hosp Bris 89-90; Chapl Qu Eliz Hosp Bris 90-96; Chapl Thornbury Hosp from 90; rtd 90; Perm to Offic *Glouc* 90-97. *26 Rudgeway Park, Rudgeway, Bristol BS35 3RU* Tel (01454) 614072

FOOT, Adam Julian David. b 58. Thames Poly BSc80 Garnett Coll Lon CertEd87. Trin Coll Bris 93. **d** 97 **p** 98. C Luton Ch Ch *Roch* 97-00; V Welling from 00. *St John's Vicarage, Danson Lane, Welling DA16 2BQ* Tel (020) 8303 1107
E-mail adam.foot@diocese-rochester.org

FOOT, Daniel Henry Paris. b 46. Peterho Cam BA67 MA74. Ridley Hall Cam 77. **d** 79 **p** 80. C Werrington *Pet* 79-82; P-in-c Cranford w Grafton Underwood 82; R Cranford w Grafton Underwood and Twywell from 83; P-in-c Slipton from 94. *The Rectory, Rectory Hill, Cranford, Kettering NN14 4AH* Tel (01536) 330231

FOOT, Elizabeth Victoria Anne. b 55. St Mich Coll Sarum BEd77. Trin Coll Bris BA04. **d** 04 **p** 05. C Linkinhorne and Stoke Climsland *Truro* 04-07; C Godrevy 07-08; TV 08-11; V Halsetown from 11; P-in-c Zennor from 11; P-in-c Towednack from 11. *St John's in the Fields, Hellesvean, St Ives TR26 2HG* Tel (01736) 794899 E-mail godrevyvic@hotmail.co.uk

FOOT, Jeremy Michael. b 67. Qu Mary Coll Lon BSc88. St Mellitus Coll 07. **d** 10 **p** 11. NSM Enfield St Jas *Lon* from 10. *24 St Andrews Road, Enfield EN1 3UB* Tel (020) 8366 1456 Mobile 07725-474769 E-mail jeremy@thefeet.net

FOOT, Keith George. b 45. Surrey Univ BSc70 Lon Univ PhD73 MRSC CChem. NTMTC 96. **d** 99 **p** 00. C New Thundersley *Chelmsf* 99-03; Min Prince's Park CD *Roch* 03-07; V Prince's Park 07-10; rtd 10. *51 Elmshurst Gardens, Tonbridge TN10 3QT* Tel (01732) 365185 E-mail rev.keith.foot@btinternet.com

FOOT, Lynda. b 43. Reading Univ BEd75 Loughb Univ MSc82 Nottm Univ MA00. EMMTC 97. **d** 00 **p** 01. NSM Coalville and Bardon Hill *Leic* 00-03; NSM Hickling w Kinoulton and Broughton Sulney *S'well* 04-05; NSM Bingham 05-08; rtd 08. *34 White Furrows, Cotgrave, Nottingham NG12 3LD* Tel 0115-989 9724 Mobile 07799-662852
E-mail lyndafoot@btinternet.com

FOOT, Paul. b 41. Lon Univ BA64. Chich Th Coll 65. **d** 67 **p** 68. C Portsea St Mark *Portsm* 67-72; C Grimsbury *Ox* 72-74; V Cury w Gunwalloe *Truro* 74-80; P-in-c Port Isaac 80-83; P-in-c St Kew 80-83; V St Day 83-91; rtd 95. *Aeaea, 39 New Road, Llandovery SA20 0EA* Tel (01550) 720140

FOOTE, Desmond. b 46. S Dios Minl Tr Scheme. **d** 82 **p** 83. NSM Furze Platt *Ox* 82-88; NSM Ruscombe and Twyford 88-05; NSM Woolhampton w Midgham and Beenham Valance 05-08; NSM Aldermaston w Wasing and Brimpton 05-08; NSM Aldermaston and Woolhampton from 08. *The Rectory, Birds Lane, Midgham, Reading RG7 5UL* Tel 0118-971 2186
E-mail des@foote2fsnet.co.uk

✠**FOOTTIT, The Rt Revd Anthony Charles.** b 35. K Coll Cam BA57 MA70. Cuddesdon Coll 59. **d** 61 **p** 62 **c** 99. C Wymondham *Nor* 61-64; C Blakeney w Lt Langham 64-67; P-in-c Hindringham w Binham and Cockthorpe 67-71; P-in-c Yarlington *B & W* 71-76; R N Cadbury 71-75; P-in-c S Cadbury w Sutton Montis 73-76; TR Camelot Par 76-81, RD Cary 79-81, Dioc Missr *Linc* 81-87; Can and Preb Linc Cathl 86-87; Dioc Rural Officer *Nor* 87; Adn Lynn 87-99; Suff Bp Lynn 99-03; rtd 03; Hon Asst Bp Nor from 04; Dioc Environmental Officer 04-09. *Ivy House, Whitwell Street, Reepham, Norwich NR10 4RA* Tel (01603) 870340

FORAN, Andrew John. b 55. Aston Tr Scheme 84 Linc Th Coll 86. **d** 88 **p** 89. C Epping St Jo *Chelmsf* 88-92; TV Canvey Is 92-97; C Dorking w Ranmore *Guildf* 97-99; Chapl HM Pris Send 97-09; Chapl HM Pris Bullingdon from 09. *HM Prison Bullingdon, PO Box 50, Bicester OX25 1PZ* Tel (01869) 353100
E-mail andrew.foran@hmps.gsi.gov.uk

FORBES, Mrs Angela Laura. b 47. Ox Min Course 91. **d** 94 **p** 96. NSM Cowley St Jo *Ox* 94-04; Perm to Offic from 04. *6 Elm Crescent, Charlbury, Chipping Norton OX7 3PZ* Tel (01608) 819121

FORBES, The Very Revd Graham John Thompson. b 51. CBE04. Aber Univ MA73 Edin Univ BD76. Edin Th Coll 73. **d** 76 **p** 77. C Edin Old St Paul 76-82; Can St Ninian's Cathl Perth 82-90; R Stanley 82-88; Provost St Ninian's Cathl Perth 82-90; R Perth St Ninian 82-90; Provost St Mary's Cathl from 90; R Edin St Mary from 90. *8 Lansdowne Crescent, Edinburgh EH12 5EQ* Tel 0131-225 2978 *or* 225 6293 Mobile 07711-199297 Fax 0131-226 1482 *or* 225 3181 E-mail provost@cathedral.net

FORBES, Iain William. b 56. Ex Univ BA81. Chich Th Coll 83. **d** 85 **p** 86. C Upper Norwood St Jo *S'wark* 85-88; C Lewisham St Mary 88-90; Chapl St Martin's Coll of Educn *Blackb* 90-94; P-in-c Woodplumpton 94-99; Dioc Voc Adv 94-99; V Woodham *Guildf* from 99. *The Vicarage, 25 Woodham Waye, Woking GU21 5SW* Tel (01483) 762857
E-mail fatheriainforbes@aol.com

FORBES, Canon John Francis. b 29. CITC 85. **d** 88 **p** 90. Aux Min Ferns w Kilbride, Toombe, Kilcormack etc *C & O* 88-04; Treas Ferns Cathl 98-03; rtd 04. *Ballinabarna House, Enniscorthy, Co Wexford, Republic of Ireland* Tel (00353) (53) 923 3353 Mobile 87-237 9319

FORBES, Canon John Franey. b 33. AKC57. **d** 58 **p** 59. C Darlington H Trin *Dur* 58-62; C St Geo Cathl Cape Town S Africa 62-65; R Hoedjies Bay 65-69; Warden Zonnebloem Coll Cape Town 69-75; Dean Pietermaritzburg 76-03; rtd 03. *PO Box 481, Noordhoek, 7979 South Africa* Tel and fax (0027) (21) 789 2227

FORBES, Joyce Brinella. b 52. **d** 03 **p** 04. OLM Norbury St Steph and Thornton Heath *S'wark* from 03. *36 Dalmeny Avenue, London SW16 4RT* Tel (020) 8240 0283 *or* 7525 7982
E-mail petnard36@aol.com

FORBES, Patrick. b 38. Open Univ BA82. Linc Th Coll 64. **d** 66 **p** 67. C Yeovil *B & W* 66-69; C Plumstead Wm Temple Ch Abbey Wood CD *S'wark* 69-70; Thamesmead Ecum Gp 70-73; TV Thamesmead 73-78; Dioc Communications Officer *St Alb* 78-90; P-in-c Offley w Lilley 78-82; Info Officer Communications Dept Ch Ho Lon 91-95; Press Officer Miss to Seamen 95-99; rtd 99; Perm to Offic *St Alb* from 04. *18 Francis Road, Hinxworth, Baldock SG7 5HL* Tel (01462) 742015
E-mail fool1@patrickforbes.plus.com

FORBES, Raymond John. b 34. ALCD58. **d** 58 **p** 59. C Wandsworth St Steph *S'wark* 58-61; C Kewstoke *B & W* 61-63; V Fordcombe *Roch* 63-73; R Ashurst 64-73; P-in-c Morden w Almer and Charborough *Sarum* 73-76; P-in-c Bloxworth 73-76; V Red Post 76-84; P-in-c Hamworthy 84-92; P-in-c

Symondsbury and Chideock 92-96; rtd 96; Perm to Offic *Sarum* from 96. *3 Shelley Court, Library Road, Ferndown BH22 9JZ* Tel (01202) 897567

FORBES, Stuart. b 33. Lon Univ BD59. Oak Hill Th Coll 56. **d** 61 **p** 62. C Halliwell St Pet *Man* 61-64; P-in-c Wicker w Neepsend *Sheff* 64-69; V Stainforth 69-77; V Salterhebble All SS *Wakef* 77-89; V Toxteth Park St Mich w St Andr *Liv* 89-98; rtd 98; Perm to Offic *Lich* from 00. *29 Firbeck Gardens, Wildwood, Stafford ST17 4QR* Tel (01785) 663658

FORBES, Susan Margaret. See VAN BEVEREN, Mrs Susan Margaret

FORBES ADAM, Stephen Timothy Beilby. b 23. Ball Coll Ox. Chich Th Coll 59. **d** 61 **p** 62. C Guisborough *York* 61-64; R Barton in Fabis *S'well* 64-70; V Thrumpton 65-70; P-in-c S Stoke *B & W* 74-81; C Combe Down w Monkton Combe and S Stoke 81-83; Perm to Offic *B & W* 83-86; *Ox* 86-87; *York* from 88; NSM Epwell w Sibford, Swalcliffe and Tadmarton *Ox* 87-92; rtd 88. *Woodhouse Farm, Escrick, York YO19 6HT* Tel (01904) 878827

FORBES STONE, Elizabeth Karen. b 61. Birm Univ MB, BCh85 MRCGP89. Ridley Hall Cam BA99. **d** 00 **p** 01. C Brentford *Lon* 00-02; C Shaw cum Donnington *Ox* 02-10. *55 Cotswold Drive, Coventry CV3 6EZ* Tel 07980-431710 (mobile) E-mail buff@dandb.org.uk

FORCE-JONES, Graham Roland John. b 41. Sarum Th Coll 65. **d** 68 **p** 69. C Calne and Blackland *Sarum* 68-73; TV Oldbury 73-78; R 78-80; TR Upper Kennet 80-94; RD Marlborough 90-94; P-in-c Atworth w Shaw and Whitley 94-06; Chapl Stonar Sch Melksham 01-06; rtd 06. *Le Petit Cormy, 86700 Vaux-en-Couche, France*

FORD, Adam. b 40. Lanc Univ MA72 K Coll Lon BD63 AKC63. **d** 65 **p** 65. C Cirencester *Glouc* 65-70; V Hebden Bridge *Wakef* 70-76; Chapl St Paul's Girls' Sch Hammersmith 77-01; Lic to Offic *Lon* 77-98; P in O 84-91; rtd 05. *Bramble, Weaver's Lane, Alfriston BN26 5TH* E-mail adamfordspgs@hotmail.com

FORD, Alun James. b 73. Ex Univ BA94 MA96 Man Univ PhD09 St Jo Coll Cam BA11. Westcott Ho Cam 08. **d** 11. C Newc St Geo and St Hilda from 11. *Close House, St George's Close, Newcastle upon Tyne NE2 2TF* Tel 0191-281 2556 E-mail alun.ford@gmail.com

FORD, Ms Amanda Kirstine. b 61. Middx Univ BA83 Open Univ MA97. St Steph Ho Ox 98. **d** 00 **p** 01. C Leic Resurr 00-05; P-in-c Beaumont Leys 05-09; V from 09; P-in-c Stocking Farm from 11; AD City of Leic from 11; Dioc CUF Officer from 04. *The Vicarage, 10 Parkside Close, Leicester LE4 1EP* Tel 0116-235 2667 E-mail mandyford@btinternet.com

FORD, Anthony. b 60. Oak Hill Th Coll 06. **d** 08 **p** 09. C Chadderton Ch Ch *Man* 08-11; P-in-c Balderstone from 11. *St Mary's Vicarage, The Sett, Badger Lane, Rochdale OL16 4RQ* Tel (01706) 649886 Mobile 07816-596878 E-mail tonyford227@btinternet.com

FORD, Mrs Avril Celia. b 43. St Mary's Coll Dur BSc64 Chelsea Coll Lon PGCE65. **d** 92 **p** 94. OLM Horncastle w Low Toynton *Linc* 92-98; NSM 98-06; OLM High Toynton 92-98; NSM 98-06; OLM Greetham w Ashby Puerorum 92-98; NSM 98-06; NSM Horncastle Gp from 06. *Frolic, Reindeer Close, Horncastle LN9 5AA* Tel (01507) 526234 or 525600

FORD, Brian. b 40. OBE89. Imp Coll Lon BSc62 Nottm Univ MSc66 PhD74 Ox Univ MA74 Open Univ MA74 Chath FIMA ARCS. SAOMC 96. **d** 99 **p** 00. NSM Witney *Ox* 99-02; NSM Forest Edge from 02. *Ramsden Farmhouse, Ramsden, Oxford OX7 3AU* Tel (01993) 868343 Fax 868322 E-mail brian@nag.co.uk

FORD (née HARRISON-WATSON), Mrs Carole. b 44. Reading Univ BSc66 St Martin's Coll Lanc PGCE79. Carl Dioc Tr Inst 92. **d** 95 **p** 96. NSM Windermere *Carl* 95-98; NSM Borrowdale 98-01; NSM Thornthwaite cum Braithwaite, Newlands etc 01-05; rtd 05; Perm to Offic *Carl* from 05. *Croft View, Low Lorton, Cockermouth CA13 9UW* Tel (01900) 85519

FORD, Canon Christopher Simon. b 51. Leeds Univ MPhil86 PhD91. AKC74. **d** 75 **p** 76. C Wythenshawe Wm Temple Ch *Man* 75-77; C New Bury 77-80; R Old Trafford St Jo 80-94; R Moston St Jo 94-05; P-in-c Davyhulme St Mary 05-09; V from 09; Bp's Adv on Archives from 93; AD N Man 94-00; Hon Can Man Cathl from 04; Borough Dean Trafford from 11. *St Mary's Vicarage, 13 Vicarage Road, Urmston, Manchester M41 5TP* Tel 0161-748 2210 E-mail christopher.ford5@btinternet.com

FORD, David John. b 38. Lon Coll of Div BD68. **d** 69 **p** 70. C Blackheath St Jo *S'wark* 69-71; C Westlands St Andr *Lich* 71-75; V Sheff St Steph w St Phil and St Ann 75-77; R Netherthorpe 77-80; TR 80-84; R Thrybergh 82-84; R Thrybergh w Hooton Roberts 84-94; Ind Chapl 86-87; TV Parkham, Alwington, Buckland Brewer etc *Ex* 94-01; rtd 03; Hon C Knaresborough *Ripon* 01-05; Perm to Offic *York* from 07. *10 Grove Hill Road, Filey YO14 9NL* Tel (01723) 518292 E-mail shielandavid@4afairworld.co.uk

FORD, David Stuart. b 61. City of Lon Poly BA82 Qu Coll Birm MA09. WMMTC 06. **d** 09 **p** 10. C Bramhope and Ireland Wood *Ripon* 09-10; C Leeds City from 10; Chapl Chapl Abbey Grange

High Sch from 09. *Holy Trinity Vicarage, 28 Hawkswood Avenue, Leeds LS5 3PN* Tel 07973-412625 (mobile) E-mail davidford09@googlemail.com

FORD, Mrs Deborah Perrin. b 59. Leeds Univ BA81 Birm Univ MSocSc85 Univ of Wales (Ban) BTh CQSW85. EAMTC 00. **d** 03 **p** 04. NSM Cambridge St Benedict *Ely* from 03; Chapl Cam Univ Hosps NHS Foundn Trust from 03. *102 Millington Lane, Cambridge CB3 9HA* Tel (01223) 329321 or 363113 E-mail debbie.ford@addenbrookes.nhs.uk

FORD, Derek Ernest. b 32. St Mich Coll Llan 56. **d** 58 **p** 59. C Roath St Martin *Llan* 58-61; C Newton Nottage 61-67; V Abercanaid 67-70; Perm to Offic *Win* 70-80; SSF from 72; Lic to Offic *Sarum* 73-80 and *Newc* 75-80; USA from 80; Min Prov American Province SSF 02-05; P-in-c Siparia Trinidad and Tobago 06-09. *PO Box 399, Mount Sinai NY 11766-0399, USA* E-mail broderekssf@aol.com

FORD, Canon Henry Malcolm. b 33. Em Coll Cam BA54 MA58. Ely Th Coll 58. **d** 59 **p** 69. C Ipswich St Matt *St E* 59-61; Hon C Bury St Edmunds St Jo 66-76; Hon C Hawstead and Newton w Stanningfield etc 76-89; Hon Can St E Cathl 86-97; NSM Cockfield w Bradfield St Clare, Felsham etc 89-98; Perm to Offic from 99. *Thatch on the Green, Cross Green, Cockfield, Bury St Edmunds IP30 0LG* Tel (01284) 828479

FORD, John. See FORD, William John

✠**FORD, The Rt Revd John Frank.** b 52. Chich Univ MA06. Chich Th Coll 76. **d** 79 **p** 80 **c** 05. C Forest Hill Ch Ch *S'wark* 79-82; V Lee St Aug 82-91; V Lower Beeding and Dom Chapl to Bp Horsham *Chich* 91-94; Dioc Missr 94-00; Can and Preb Chich Cathl 97-00; Can Res and Prec 00-05; Suff Bp Plymouth *Ex* from 05; Asst Bp Truro from 11. *31 Riverside Walk, Tamerton Foliot, Plymouth PL5 4AQ* Tel (01752) 769836 Fax 769818 E-mail bishop.of.plymouth@exeter.anglican.org

FORD, Jonathan Laurence. See ALDERTON-FORD, Canon Jonathan Laurence

FORD, Joyce. b 42. Qu Coll Birm 97. **d** 00 **p** 01. NSM Bentley *Lich* 00-04; NSM Wednesfield 04-06; Perm to Offic from 07. *33 Bowness Grove, Willenhall WV12 5DB* Tel (01922) 408420

FORD, Mrs Kimberley Kaye. b 65. St Jo Coll Nottm 09. **d** 11. C Market Harborough and The Transfiguration etc *Leic* from 11. *69 Tymecrosse Gardens, Market Harborough LE16 7US* Tel (01858) 680264 E-mail kimberleykford@aim.com

FORD, Nancy Celia. b 48. Open Univ BA02 FCIPD00. STETS 98. **d** 01 **p** 02. NSM Crookham *Guildf* 01-04; NSM Aldershot St Mich 04-07; Asst Dioc Dir of Ords 04-05; Bp's Chapl 05-10; rtd 10. *34 Rowhill Avenue, Aldershot GU11 3LS* Tel (01252) 677995 E-mail nancy.ford@sky.com

FORD, Peter. b 46. York Univ MA96 Bede Coll Dur TCert72 ACP75. Linc Th Coll 76. **d** 78 **p** 79. OGS from 72; C Hartlepool H Trin *Dur* 78-81; Dioc Youth Officer *Wakef* 81-84; C Mirfield Eastthorpe St Paul 82-84; C Upper Hopton 82-84; V Dodworth 84-88; Chapl and Hd RS Rishworth Sch Ripponden 88-97; Ho Master 94-97; P-in-c Accrington St Mary *Blackb* 97-99; C Torrisholme 99-01; V Warton St Paul 01-08; Dioc Ecum Officer 01-08; Germany 08-09; P-in-c Las Palmas *Eur* from 09. *Calle Montevideo 2-7, 35007 Las Palmas de Gran Canaria (Las Palmas), Spain* Tel (0034) 928 267 202 E-mail pford@ogs.net

FORD, Canon Peter Hugh. b 43. St Cath Coll Cam BA65 MA69. Cuddesdon Coll 65. **d** 67 **p** 68. C Is of Dogs Ch Ch and St Jo w St Luke *Lon* 67-70; C Tillsonburg St Jo Canada 70-71; St Catharine's St Thos 71-73; P-in-c Thorold South Resurr 71-73; R Port Colborne St Brendan 73-78; R Milton Grace Ch 78-80; Can Pastor Ch Ch Cathl Hamilton 80-86; Adn Lincoln 86-91; R Niagara-on-the-Lake St Mark 86-91; Hon Can Niagara from 91; Hon C Montserrat St Geo 91; R Saba 92-98; Perm to Offic *Chich* 98-99; V Newchurch and Arreton *Portsm* 99-07; rtd 07. *11 Vokins Rise, Esplanade, Ryde PO33 2AX* Tel (01983) 568286 E-mail islandpeter@btinternet.com

FORD, Richard. b 47. Grey Coll Dur BA69 PGCE70 FRSA94. SEITE 06. **d** 09 **p** 10. NSM Sanderstead *S'wark* from 09. *7 Sylvan Way, West Wickham BR4 9HA* Tel (020) 8289 2432 Mobile 07706-998272 E-mail richard.ford73@ntlworld.com

FORD, Richard Graham. b 39. AKC65 Open Univ BA96. **d** 66 **p** 67. C Morpeth *Newc* 66-71; C Fordingbridge w Ibsley *Win* 71-73; TV Whorlton *Newc* 73-80; Chapl RNR 75-92; V Choppington *Newc* 80-92; V Tynemouth Priory 92-04; rtd 04. *43 Farriers Rise, Shilbottle, Alnwick NE66 2EN* Tel (01665) 581115

FORD, Roger James. b 33. Sarum & Wells Th Coll 81. **d** 83 **p** 84. C Sidcup St Jo *Roch* 83-86; V Darenth 86-98; rtd 98; Perm to Offic *Cov* 02-04. *21 Hawthorn Way, Shipston-on-Stour CV36 4FD* Tel (01608) 664875 E-mail margaretandroger@hotmail.com

FORD, Roger Lindsay. b 47. Ex Univ LLB68. Llan Dioc Tr Scheme 87. **d** 91 **p** 92. NSM Fairwater *Llan* 91-96; NSM Llandaff 96-01. *93 Cardiff Road, Caerphilly CF83 1WS* Tel (029) 2088 2441

FORD, Mrs Shirley Elsworth. b 40. AIMLS67. Sarum & Wells Th Coll 89. **d** 91 **p** 94. C Farnham *Guildf* 91-96; V Wrecclesham 96-04; rtd 04; Perm to Offic *Chich* from 05. *North House, Queen's*

Park Mews, Queen's Park Rise, Brighton BN2 9YY Tel (01273) 674061
FORD, Simone Louise. *See* BENNETT, Ms Simone Louise
FORD, William John. b 50. Linc Th Coll 89. **d** 91 **p** 92. C Marton-in-Cleveland *York* 91-94; V Whorlton w Carlton and Faceby 94-02; P-in-c Stainton w Hilton from 02; RD Stokesley from 03; P-in-c Brookfield from 11. *The Vicarage, 21 Thornton Road, Stainton, Middlesbrough TS8 9DS* Tel (01642) 288131
E-mail revjohn.ford@ntlworld.com
FORD-WHITCOMBE, William. *See* WHITCOMBE, William Ashley
FORDE, Barry George. **d** 07 **p** 08. C Coleraine *Conn* 07-10; Chapl and Dean of Residence QUB from 10. *20 Elmwood Avenue, Belfast BT9 6AY* Tel (028) 9066 7844 *or* 9066 7754
E-mail barry@csmforde.co.uk
FORDE, The Ven Stephen Bernard. b 61. Edin Univ BSc. TCD Div Sch. **d** 86 **p** 87. C Belfast St Mary *Conn* 86-89; Chapl QUB 89-95; Min Can Belf Cathl 89-91; Bp's Dom Chapl *Conn* 90-95; I Dublin Booterstown *D & G* 95-99; Dean of Res UCD 95-99; I Larne and Inver *Conn* from 99; I Glynn w Raloo from 99; Adn Dalriada from 06. *The Rectory, 8 Lower Cairncastle Road, Larne BT40 1PQ* Tel (028) 2827 2788 *or* 2827 4633
E-mail stephenforde@btinternet.com
FORDHAM, Mrs June Erica. b 28. Oak Hill Th Coll 83. **dss** 86 **d** 87 **p** 94. Digswell and Panshanger *St Alb* 86-87; Par Dn 87-90; TD 91-93; rtd 93; NSM Lemsford *St Alb* 93-01; Perm to Offic from 01. *22 Crossway, Welwyn Garden City AL8 7EE* Tel (01707) 326997
FORDHAM, Richard George. b 34. AIMarF60. TEng(CEI)71 FBIM74. **d** 91 **p** 92. NSM Cookham *Ox* 91-94; NSM Hedsor and Bourne End 94-01; Perm to Offic *Ox* 01-03 and *Ely* from 03. *6 Sorrel Way, Downham Market PE38 9UD* Tel (01366) 384271
E-mail richardfordham939@btinternet.com
FORDYCE, Andrew Ian. b 70. K Alfred's Coll Win BA94 Southn Univ PGCE96. Trin Coll Bris BA03. **d** 03 **p** 04. C Bramshott and Liphook *Portsm* 03-07; V Berechurch St Marg w St Mich *Chelmsf* from 07. *The Vicarage, 348 Mersea Road, Colchester CO2 8RA* Tel (01206) 576859 Mobile 07884-010376
E-mail revdyce@googlemail.com
FOREMAN, Joseph Arthur. b 26. ACIB. S Dios Minl Tr Scheme 83. **d** 86 **p** 87. NSM Win St Bart 86-96; Perm to Offic from 96. *4 Denham Close, Winchester SO23 7BL* Tel (01962) 852138
FOREMAN, Canon Patrick Brian. b 41. CertEd. St Jo Coll Nottm 77. **d** 79 **p** 80. C Gainsborough All SS *Linc* 79-83; V Thornton St Jas *Bradf* 83-91; R Hevingham w Hainford and Stratton Strawless *Nor* 91-99; RD Ingworth 94-99; V Heacham 99-06; Hon Can Nor Cathl 03-06; rtd 06; Perm to Offic *Nor* from 06; Bp's Officer for Rtd Clergy and Widows from 08. *Seorah, 7 Mallard Close, Fakenham NR21 8PU* Tel (01328) 853691
E-mail patrick@pandmforeman.eclipse.co.uk
FOREMAN, Mrs Penelope. b 47. Lon Inst of Educn TCert68 Ch Ch Coll Cant BEd90 MA93. SEITE 04. **d** 06 **p** 07. NSM Roch St Justus from 06. *28 Kingsway, Chatham ME5 7HT* Tel (01634) 571220 E-mail penny.foreman@btinternet.com
FOREMAN, Roy Geoffrey Victor. b 31. Oak Hill Th Coll 62. **d** 64 **p** 65. C Chitts Hill St Cuth *Lon* 64-67; C Rodbourne Cheney *Bris* 67-70; C Walthamstow St Mary w St Steph *Chelmsf* 71-92; TV 92-96; rtd 96; Perm to Offic *S'wark* 97-05. *c/o E C Foreman Esq, 7 Netherne Lane, Coulsdon CR5 1NR* Tel (01737) 557456
FOREMAN, Timothy. b 56. K Coll Lon BD77. SEITE 97. **d** 99 **p** 00. C Camberwell St Giles w St Matt *S'wark* 99-02; R Buckland-in-Dover *Cant* from 02; Hon Min Can Cant Cathl from 04. *St Andrew's Rectory, London Road, Dover CT17 0TF* Tel (01304) 201324 E-mail fr.tim@ntlworld.com
FOREMAN, Vanessa Jane. *See* LAWRENCE, Mrs Vanessa Jane
FORGAN, Eleanor. b 44. St Andr Univ MA66 Aber Univ DipEd67. St And Dioc Tr Course. **d** 89 **p** 95. NSM Alloa *St And* from 89. *18 Alexandra Drive, Alloa FK10 2DQ* Tel (01259) 212836
FORMAN, Alastair Gordon. b 48. St Jo Coll Nottm 78. **d** 80 **p** 81. C Pennycross *Ex* 80-83; C Woking St Jo *Guildf* 83-88; V Luton Lewsey St Hugh *St Alb* 88-95; P-in-c Jersey Millbrook St Matt *Win* 95-01; P-in-c Jersey St Lawr 95-01. *Address temp unknown*
FORMAN, Carolyn Dawn. b 45. SEITE. **d** 07 **p** 08. NSM Meopham w Nurstead *Roch* from 07. *Aysgarth, White Hill Road, Meopham, Gravesend DA13 0NZ* Tel (01474) 812373
E-mail acform@btinternet.com
FORMAN, Deborah Jayne. b 56. LMH Ox BA78 MA83 PGCE79 Lambeth STh07. STETS 05. **d** 08 **p** 09. C Churchdown St Jo and Innsworth *Glouc* from 08; P-in-c Pebworth, Dorsington, Honeybourne etc from 11. *The Vicarage, Stratford Road, Honeybourne, Evesham WR11 5PP* Tel (01386) 830302 Mobile 07985-943371
E-mail deborah.forman2@btinternet.com
FORMAN, Miss Diana Blanche Grant. b 19. Edin Dioc NSM Course 79. **dss** 83 **d** 86 **p** 94. Edin St Jo 83-91; NSM 86-91; rtd 91. *Strathmore House, 4/3 Church Hill, Edinburgh EH10 4BQ* Tel 0131-447 4463

FORRER, Michael Dennett Cuthbert. b 34. St Pet Hall Ox BA59 MA63. Wycliffe Hall Ox 59. **d** 60 **p** 61. C Westwood *Cov* 60-63; C Cov Cathl 63-71; Ind Chapl 63-69; Sen Ind Chapl 69-71; Hon C All Hallows by the Tower etc *Lon* 76-99; Asst P Bangkok Ch Ch Thailand 81-89; Perm to Offic *Sarum* from 99 and *Ox* 01-02; Hon C Sonning *Ox* from 02; rtd 04. *6 Park View Drive South, Charvil, Reading RG10 9QX* Tel 0118-934 1989
FORREST, Antony William. b 60. Imp Coll Lon BSc82 Sussex Univ PGCE83 Leic Univ MBA06 ARCS82 FCollP08. STETS 08. **d** 11. C Portsea N End St Mark *Portsm* from 11. *St Francis House, 186 Northern Parade, Portsmouth PO2 9LU*
E-mail curate.netm@btinternet.com
FORREST, The Very Revd Leslie David Arthur. b 46. TCD BA68 MA86. CITC 70. **d** 70 **p** 71. C Conwall *D & R* 70-73; I Tullyaughnish 73-80; I Galway w Kilcummin *T, K & A* 80-95; Dir of Ords 84-95; Can Tuam Cathl 86-95; Provost Tuam 91-95; Dean Ferns *C & O* 95-11; I Ferns w Kilbride, Toombe, Kilcormack etc 95-11; Preb Tassagard St Patr Cathl Dublin 91-11; rtd 11. *Tassagard, Coolamurry, Davidstown, Enniscorthy, Co Wexford, Republic of Ireland* Tel (00353) (53) 923 0651
E-mail ldaforrest@eircom.net
FORREST, Michael Barry Eric. b 38. Lon Univ BA87 MA89. NZ Bd of Th Studies LTh62 Chich Th Coll 64. **d** 66 **p** 67. C Beckenham St Jas *Roch* 66-70; P-in-c Cape Vogel Papua New Guinea 70-73; P-in-c Alotau 74; R Lae 74-76; C Altarnon and Bolventor *Truro* 76-78; TV N Hill w Altarnon, Bolventor and Lewannick 78-79; R St Martin w E and W Looe 79-84; V Kensington St Phil Earl's Court *Lon* 84-04; rtd 04; Perm to Offic *Chich* from 04, *12 Rilev Road, Brighton BN2 4AH* Tel (01273) 690231
FORREST, Canon Robin Whyte. b 33. Edin Th Coll 58. **d** 61 **p** 62. C Glas St Mary 61-66; R Renfrew 66-70; R Motherwell 70-79; R Wishaw 75-79; R Forres *Mor* 79-98; R Nairn 79-92; Can St Andr Cathl Inverness 88-98; Hon Can from 98; Syn Clerk 91-92; Dean Mor 92-98; rtd 98. *Landeck, Cummingston, Elgin IV30 5XY* Tel and fax (01343) 835539
FORREST-REDFERN, Mrs Susan Michéle. b 57. S Bank Poly BEd86. St Jo Coll Nottm 01. **d** 03 **p** 04. C Lostock St Thos and St Jo *Man* 03-06; C Bolton St Bede 05-06; Ch/Sch Missr E Bolton from 06; C Tonge Fold 07-10; Chapl St Cath Academy Bolton from 11. *St Chad's Vicarage, 9 Tonge Fold Road, Bolton BL2 6AW* Tel (01204) 528159 E-mail revsuefr@yahoo.co.uk
FORRESTER, Ian Michael. b 56. Chich Th Coll. **d** 82 **p** 83. C Leigh-on-Sea St Marg *Chelmsf* 82-84; Min Can, Succ and Dean's V Windsor 84-86; Prec and Chapl Chelmsf Cathl 86-91; Chapl Lancing Coll 91-99; P-in-c Boxgrove *Chich* from 99; Dioc Liturgy and Music Consultant from 95. *The Vicarage, Boxgrove, Chichester PO18 0ED* Tel (01243) 774045
E-mail iforrester@hotmail.com
FORRESTER, James Oliphant. b 50. SS Coll Cam BA72 MA76. Wycliffe Hall Ox 73. **d** 76 **p** 77. C Hull St Jo Newland *York* 76-80; C Fulwood *Sheff* 80-87; V Lodge Moor St Luke 87-90; V Ecclesfield 90-01; AD Ecclesfield 99-01; P-in-c Kingston upon Hull H Trin *York* 01-02; V and Lect 02-09; V Longnor, Quarnford and Sheen *Lich* from 09. *The Vicarage, Gauledge Lane, Longnor, Buxton SK17 0PA* Tel (01298) 83742
FORRESTER, Mrs Joyce. b 33. Thornbridge Hall Coll of Educn TCert53 ACP84 DACE85 Crewe & Alsager Coll MSc88. St Jo Coll Nottm 94. **d** 94 **p** 95. NSM Endon w Stanley *Lich* 94-00; NSM Stonnall 00-06; rtd 06; Perm to Offic *Lich* from 06. *Daisybank Bungalow, The Village, Endon, Stoke-on-Trent ST9 9EX* Tel (01782) 504990
FORRESTER, Matthew Agnew. b 31. Univ of Wales (Cardiff) BA64. Trin Coll Bris 70. **d** 72 **p** 73. C Tonbridge SS Pet and Paul *Roch* 72-77; Chapl Elstree Sch Woolhampton 77-78; Chapl Duke of York's R Mil Sch Dover 78-96; rtd 96; Perm to Offic *Cant* from 96. *4 Abbots Place, Canterbury CT1 2AH* Tel (01227) 458882
FORRESTER, Robin William. b 43. Kent Univ MA84 Aston Univ MSc90. All Nations Chr Coll 64. **d** 04 **p** 05. NSM Wharton *Ches* 04-06; P-in-c Moulton 06-11; rtd 11. *66 Jack Lane, Moulton, Northwich CW9 8NR* Tel (01606) 593355
E-mail robin.forrester@tiscali.co.uk
FORRYAN, Thomas Quested. b 64. Pemb Coll Cam BA85. Wycliffe Hall Ox 87. **d** 90 **p** 91. C Cheadle Hulme St Andr *Ches* 90-93; C Aberavon *Llan* 93-94; UCCF 94-98. *1 Grosvenor Road, Watford WD1 2QS*
FORSDIKE, Alan William. b 55. **d** 05 **p** 06. NSM Westerfield and Tuddenham w Witnesham *St E* from 05. *Hill House, 2 Henley Road, Ipswich IP1 3SF* Tel (01473) 252904
E-mail alan.forsdike@btinternet.com
FORSDIKE, Mrs Catherine Agnes. b 57. **d** 10 **p** 11. OLM Westerfield and Tuddenham w Witnesham *St E* from 10. *2 Henley Road, Ipswich IP1 3SF* Tel (01473) 252904
FORSE, Reginald Austin. b 43. Oak Hill Th Coll 77. **d** 79 **p** 80. C Crofton *Portsm* 79-84; NSM Gosport Ch Ch 91-96; NSM Alverstoke from 96. *40 Osprey Gardens, Lee-on-the-Solent PO13 8LJ* Tel (023) 9255 3395 E-mail regforse@yahoo.co.uk

FORSHAW, David Oliver. b 27. Trin Coll Cam BA50 MA52. Qu Coll Birm. **d** 53 **p** 54. C Glen Parva and S Wigston *Leic* 53-55; Singapore 55-59; V Heptonstall *Wakef* 59-66; V Whitehaven St Nic *Carl* 66-76; P-in-c Whitehaven Ch Ch w H Trin 73-76; V Benchill *Man* 76-89; C Elton All SS 89-92; rtd 92; Perm to Offic *Carl* from 92. *Tynashee, Church Street, Broughton-in-Furness LA20 6HJ* Tel (01229) 716068

FORSHAW, Mrs Frances Ann. b 52. Edin Univ BSc74 Glas Univ MN91 RGN76 SCM78. Moray Ord Course 91. **d** 98 **p** 02. NSM Elgin w Lossiemouth *Mor* 98-01; NSM Perth St Jo *St And* 01-05; P-in-c Pitlochry and Kilmaveonaig 05-09. *1 Cairnies House, Glenalmond College, Glenalmond, Perth PH1 3RY* Tel (01738) 880777 E-mail jandfforshaw@tiscali.co.uk

FORSTER, Andrew James. QUB BA89. CITC BTh92. **d** 92 **p** 93. C Willowfield *D & D* 92-95; Dean of Res QUB 95-02; C of I Adv Downtown Radio Newtownards 96-02; I Drumcliffe w Lissadell and Munninane *K, E & A* 02-07; Adn Elphin and Ardagh 02-07; I Drumglass w Moygashel *Arm* from 07. *The Rectory, 26 Circular Road, Dungannon BT71 6BE* Tel (028) 8772 2614 E-mail drumglass@armagh.anglican.org

FORSTER, Gregory Stuart. b 47. Worc Coll Ox BA69 MA73. Wycliffe Hall Ox. **d** 72 **p** 73. C Bath Walcot *B & W* 72-74; C Bolton Em *Man* 74-76; C Bolton St Paul w Em 77-79; R Northenden from 79. *The Rectory, Ford Lane, Northenden, Manchester M22 4NQ* Tel 0161-998 2615 E-mail gsfm22@tiscali.co.uk

FORSTER, Ian Duncan. b 51. St Mich Coll Llan 95. **d** 97 **p** 98. C Lampeter Pont Steffan w Silian *St D* 97-00; C Llandysul w Bangor Teifi w Henllan etc 00-03; V Llangrannog w Llandysiliogogo w Penbryn 03-10; TV Hawarden *St As* from 10. *St Mary's Vicarage, Church Road, Broughton, Chester CH4 0QG* Tel (01244) 520148

FORSTER, Kenneth. b 27. St Jo Coll Cam BA50 MA52 Salford Univ MSc77 PhD80. NEOC 83. **d** 86 **p** 87. NSM Hessle *York* 86-92; Chapl Humberside Univ 87-92; rtd 92; NSM Hull St Mary Sculcoates *York* 92-95; Perm to Offic *York* 95-09; Ox 04-09; Portsm from 09. *3 Ventnor Way, Fareham PO16 8RU* Tel 07542-527466 (mobile)

✠**FORSTER, The Rt Revd Peter Robert.** b 50. Mert Coll Ox MA73 Edin Univ BD77 PhD85. Edin Th Coll 78. **d** 80 **p** 81 **c** 96. C Mossley Hill St Matt and St Jas *Liv* 80-82; Sen Tutor St Jo Coll Dur 83-91; V Beverley Minster *York* 91-96; C Routh 91-96; Bp Ches from 96. *Bishop's House, 1 Abbey Street, Chester CH1 2JD* Tel (01244) 350864 Fax 314187 E-mail bpchester@chester.anglican.org

FORSTER, Thomas Shane. b 72. QUB BA93. CITC BTh93. **d** 96 **p** 97. C Drumglass w Moygashel *Arm* 96-99; Hon V Choral Arm Cathl 97-99; I Donaghmore w Upper Donaghmore 99-06; I Ballymore from 06; Sen Dom Chapl to Abp Arm from 06; Dioc Communications Officer 02-09; Asst Dioc and Prov Registrar from 09. *Ballymore Rectory, 10 Glebe Hill Road, Tandragee, Craigavon BT62 2DP* Tel (028) 3884 0234 E-mail ballymore@armagh.anglican.org or dco@armagh.anglican.org

FORSTER, William. b 50. NOC 92. **d** 95 **p** 96. C Ashton-in-Makerfield St Thos *Liv* 95-00; TR Fazakerley Em 00-08; TV Eccleston from 08. *The Vicarage, Chapel Lane, Eccleston, St Helens WA10 5DA* Tel (01744) 22698 E-mail william.forster1@btopenworld.com

FORSYTH, Jeanette Mary Shaw. b 48. Aber Coll of Educn ACE78. St Jo Coll Nottm 85. **d** 89. NSM Old Deer 89-92; NSM Longside 89-92; NSM Strichen 89-92; NSM Fraserburgh 92-94; Tanzania 95-96, 97-98 and 99-00. *Moss-side of Strichen, Bogensourie, Strichen AB43 7TU* Tel (01771) 637230 E-mail jeanetteforsyth@hotmail.com

FORSYTH, John Warren. b 38. Univ of W Aus BA62 Princeton Th Sem DMin98. St Mich Th Coll Crafers 65. **d** 65 **p** 66. C Busselton Australia 65-68; R Kondinin 68-72; C Warwick St Mary *Cov* 72-74; C Eden St Pet 74-76; R E Fremantle and Palmyra Australia 76-79; Chapl Abp Perth and Warden Wollaston 79-82; R Midland 82-89; Sen Angl Chapl R Perth Hosp 89-06; rtd 06; Perm to Offic Dio Perth from 06. *40B Cookham Road, Lathlain WA 6100, Australia* Tel (0061) (8) 9472 1893 Mobile 89-472 1893 E-mail forsyth@iinet.net.au

FORSYTHE, John Leslie. b 27. CITC. **d** 65 **p** 66. C Cloughfern *Conn* 65-67; C Carnmoney 67-71; I Mossley 71-80; I Antrim All SS 80-95; Preb Conn Cathl 94-95; rtd 95. *96 Hopefield Road, Portrush BT56 8HF* Tel (028) 7082 2623

FORTNUM, Brian Charles Henry. b 48. Hertf Coll Ox MA Imp Coll Lon MSc. Wycliffe Hall Ox 82. **d** 84 **p** 85. C Tonbridge St Steph *Roch* 84-87; V Shorne 87-94; P-in-c Speldhurst w Groombridge and Ashurst 94-98; R 98-01; V Tunbridge Wells St Mark from 01. *The Vicarage, 1 St Mark's Road, Tunbridge Wells TN2 5LT* Tel (01892) 526069 E-mail brian.fortnum@diocese-rochester.org

FORWARD, Canon Eric Toby. b 50. Nottm Univ BEd72 Hull Univ MA93. Cuddesdon Coll 74. **d** 77 **p** 78. C Forest Hill Ch Ch *S'wark* 77-80; Chapl Goldsmiths' Coll Lon 80-84; Chapl Westwood Ho Sch Pet 84-86; V Brighton St Aug and St Sav

Chich 86-90; Perm to Offic *York* 90-95; V Kingston upon Hull St Alb 95-05; Can Res and Prec Liv Cathl 05-07; rtd 07. *2 Kingsway, Liverpool L22 4RQ* Tel 0151-928 0681

FORWARD, Miss Frances Mary. b 43. Bp Otter Coll Chich TCert64. SEITE 96. **d** 99 **p** 00. NSM Ham St Andr *S'wark* 99-09; NSM Ham St Rich from 09; NSM Petersham from 09. *66 Tudor Drive, Kingston upon Thames KT2 5QF* Tel (020) 8546 1833

FORWARD, Canon Ronald George. b 25. Selw Coll Cam BA50 MA54. Ridley Hall Cam 50. **d** 52 **p** 53. C Denton Holme *Carl* 52-55; C-in-c Mirehouse St Andr CD 55-61; V Mirehouse 61-66; V Kendal St Thos 66-90; V Crook 78-90; Hon Can Carl Cathl 79-90; rtd 90; Perm to Offic *Carl* from 90. *51 Mayo Park, Cockermouth CA13 0BJ* Tel (01900) 824359

FORWARD, Toby. See FORWARD, Canon Eric Toby

FOSBUARY, David Frank. b 32. Leeds Univ BA63. Coll of Resurr Mirfield 63. **d** 65 **p** 66. C Fleetwood St Pet *Blackb* 65-68; Lesotho 69-76; C Dovercourt *Chelmsf* 76-78; TV 78-79; TV Basildon St Martin w H Cross and Laindon etc 79-82; R Colsterworth *Linc* 82-84; R Colsterworth Gp 84-90; RD Beltisloe 89-90; R Lawshall w Shimplingthorne and Alpheton *St E* 90-96; rtd 96; Perm to Offic *St E* from 96. *56 Lindisfarne Road, Bury St Edmunds IP33 2EH* Tel (01284) 767687

FOSKETT, Canon John Herbert. b 39. St Cath Coll Cam BA62 Lambeth MA04. Chich Th Coll 62. **d** 64 **p** 65. C Malden St Jo *S'wark* 64-70; P-in-c Kingston St Jo 70-76; Chapl Maudsley Hosp Lon 76-94; Chapl Bethlem R Hosp Beckenham 76-94; Hon Can S'wark Cathl 88-94; rtd 94; Perm to Offic *B & W* 95-01 and from 06. *Victoria Cottage, 8 Cornwall Road, Dorchester DT1 1RT* Tel (01305) 751572

FOSS, David Blair. b 44. Bris Univ BA65 Dur Univ MA66 Fitzw Coll Cam BA68 MA72 K Coll Lon PhD86. St Chad's Coll Dur 68. **d** 69 **p** 70. C Barnard Castle *Dur* 69-72; Sierra Leone 72-74; Chapl St Jo Coll York 74-75; Chapl Ch Ch Coll of HE Cant 75-80; Chapl Elmslie Girls' Sch Blackpool 80-83; Tutor Coll of Resurr Mirfield 83-88; V Battyeford *Wakef* 88-99; V Ryde All SS *Portsm* 99-01; TR Rochdale *Man* 01-09; R 09-10; rtd 10; Perm to Offic *Man* from 10. *11 Sims Close, Ramsbottom, Bury BL0 9NT* Tel (01706) 828248

FOSS, Esther Rose. b 79. Regent's Park Coll Ox BA00 MA04 Clare Hall Cam MPhil04. Westcott Ho Cam 03. **d** 05 **p** 06. C Altrincham St Geo *Ches* 05-07; C Bramhall 07-09; TV Knaresborough *Ripon* from 09. *4 Greengate Drive, Knaresborough HG5 9EN* Tel (01423) 797260 E-mail esther.foss@live.co.uk

FOSSETT, Michael Charles Sinclair. b 30. Dur Univ BSc54 CEng59 MIMechE59. NEOC 82. **d** 90 **p** 91. NSM Nether w Upper Poppleton *York* from 90. *20 Fairway Drive, Upper Poppleton, York YO26 6HE* Tel (01904) 794712

FOSSEY (née HIRST), Margaret. b 52. Huddersfield Univ BA96. NOC 06. **d** 09 **p** 10. NSM Birkby and Birchencliffe *Wakef* from 09. *103 Kirkstone Avenue, Dalton, Huddersfield HD5 9ES* Tel (01484) 301242 E-mail m.fossey@ntlworld.com

FOSTEKEW, Dean James Benedict. b 63. Bulmershe Coll of HE BEd86. Chich Th Coll 89. **d** 92 **p** 93. C Boyne Hill *Ox* 92-95; P-in-c Lockerbie and Annan *Glas* 95-97; P-in-c Dalmahoy *Edin* 97-02; TV Edin St Mary 02-09; R Edin Gd Shep from 09; Dioc Miss 21 Co-ord 97-11; Prov Miss 21 Co-ord 01-11. *9 Upper Coltbridge Terrace, Edinburgh EH12 6AD* Tel 0131-346 4127 Mobile 07968-099470 E-mail therector@uwclub.net or mission21@edinburgh.anglican.org

FOSTER, Anthony Stuart. b 47. K Coll Lon BD69 Peterho Cam BA72 MA74 Lon Inst of Educn PGCE70. Pontifical Beda Coll Rome 82. **d** 85 **p** 86. In RC Ch 85-98; NSM Leighton-cum-Minshull Vernon *Ches* 05-07; rtd 07; Perm to Offic *Ches* from 07 and *Ban* from 10. *10 Uppergate Street, Conwy LL32 8RF* Tel (01492) 562658 E-mail revtonyfoster@btinternet.com

FOSTER, Antony John. b 39. Down Coll Cam BA61 MA65. Ridley Hall Cam 65. **d** 66 **p** 67. C Sandal St Helen *Wakef* 66-69; Uganda 69-74; V Mount Pellon *Wakef* 74-92; rtd 92; Perm to Offic *Wakef* from 92. *32 Savile Drive, Halifax HX1 2EU* Tel (01422) 344152

✠**FOSTER, The Rt Revd Christopher Richard James.** b 53. Univ Coll Dur BA75 Man Univ MA77 Trin Hall Cam BA79 MA83 Wadh Coll Ox MA83. Westcott Ho Cam 78. **d** 80 **p** 81 **c** 01. C Tettenhall Regis *Lich* 80-82; Chapl Wadh Coll Ox 82-86; C Ox St Mary V w St Cross and St Pet 82-86; V Southgate Ch Ch *Lon* 86-94; CME Officer 88-94; Can Res and Sub-Dean St Alb 94-01; Suff Bp Hertford 01-10; Bp Portsm from 10. *Bishopsgrove, 26 Osborn Road, Fareham PO16 7DQ* Tel (01329) 280247 Fax 231538 E-mail bishports@portsmouth.anglican.org

FOSTER, David Brereton. b 55. Selw Coll Cam BA77 MA81 Ox Univ BA80. Wycliffe Hall Ox 78. **d** 81 **p** 82. C Luton St Mary *St Alb* 81-84; C Douglas St Geo and St Barn *S & M* 84-87; V S Ramsey St Paul 87-91; Dir Dioc Inst 88-91; Asst Dir Buckingham Adnry Chr Tr Progr *Ox* 91-95; Dir 95-97; C W Wycombe w Bledlow Ridge, Bradenham and Radnage 91-97; TV High Wycombe 97-07; Tr Officer CME and Laity

Development *Man* from 07. *109 Ascot Avenue, Sale M33 4GT* Tel 0161-976 1693 E-mail rev.dbf@ntlworld.com

FOSTER, Edward James Graham. b 12. St Jo Coll Cam BA34 MusBac35 MA38. Wells Th Coll 35. **d** 37 **p** 38. C Kidderminster St Mary *Worc* 37-43; C Feckenham w Astwood Bank 43-45; Chapl and Lect Dioc Tr Coll Chester 45-51; V Balby w Hexthorpe *Sheff* 51-67; V Ashford w Sheldon *Derby* 67-78; rtd 78; Perm to Offic *Derby* from 78. *Beckside, Baslow Road, Ashford-in-the-Water, Bakewell DE45 1QA* Tel (01629) 812868

FOSTER, Edward Philip John. b 49. Trin Hall Cam BA70 MA74. Ridley Hall Cam 76. **d** 79 **p** 80. C Finchley Ch Ch *Lon* 79-82; C Marple All SS *Ches* 82-86; P-in-c Cambridge St Matt *Ely* 86-90; V 90-07; rtd 07. *1 Barnfield, Common Lane, Hemingford Abbots, Huntingdon PE28 9AX* Tel (01480) 399098

FOSTER, Frances Elizabeth. *See* TYLER, Mrs Frances Elizabeth

FOSTER, Canon Gareth Glynne. b 44. Open Univ BA. Chich Th Coll 66. **d** 69 **p** 70. C Fairwater *Llan* 69-71; C Merthyr Tydfil and Cyfarthfa 71-76; TV 76-87; P-in-c Abercanaid and Dioc Soc Resp Officer 87-10; Exec Officer Dioc Bd Soc Resp 95-10; Can Llan Cathl 00-10; rtd 10. *19 The Walk, Merthyr Tydfil CF47 8RW* Tel (01685) 722375 Mobile 07850-823038

FOSTER, Gavin Richard. b 76. Regent's Park Coll Ox BA97 MA01 Barrister-at-Law (Gray's Inn) 98. Wycliffe Hall Ox BTh09. **d** 09 **p** 10. C Radipole and Melcombe Regis *Sarum* from 09. *130B Belgrave, Southill Garden Drive, Weymouth DT4 9SN*

FOSTER, Mrs Geraldine. b 55. SAOMC 00. **d** 03 **p** 04. C Flackwell Heath *Ox* 03-07; C Ashton-upon-Mersey St Mary Magd *Ches* from 07. *109 Ascot Avenue, Sale M33 4GT* Tel 0161-976 1693 E-mail gf@virgin net

FOSTER, Mrs Gillian Susan. b 62. Leeds Univ BA09. NOC 06. **d** 09 **p** 10. C Frankby w Greasby *Ches* from 09. *35 Hillfield Drive, Wirral CH61 6UJ* Tel 0151-342 8412 Mobile 07970-522365 E-mail stephen@foster5344.fsnet.co.uk

FOSTER, Graham Paul. b 66. Univ of W Aus BSc86 DipEd87 BEd88 Murdoch Univ Aus BD99 Qu Coll Ox MSt00 DPhil02. **d** 04 **p** 05. Lect NT Edin Univ from 03; NSM Edin St Mary from 04. *University of Edinburgh, Mound Place, Edinburgh EH1 2LX*

FOSTER, James. b 29. Man Univ BA52 MA55 Lon Univ CertEd53 Leeds Univ MEd74. NEOC 82. **d** 85 **p** 86. NSM Aldborough w Boroughbridge and Roecliffe *Ripon* 85-91; P-in-c Kirby-on-the-Moor, Cundall w Norton-le-Clay etc 91-97; rtd 97; Perm to Offic *Ripon* from 97. *Shippen Bower, Marton, Marton cum Grafton, York YO51 9QY* Tel (01423) 323133

FOSTER, Mrs Joan Alison. b 46. ARMCM67. NOC 95. **d** 98 **p** 99. NSM Blundellsands St Nic *Liv* 98-02; Asst Chapl Southport and Ormskirk NHS Trust 98-02; V N Harrow St Alb *Lon* from 02. *St Alban's Vicarage, Church Drive, Harrow HA2 7NS* Tel (020) 8868 6567 Mobile 07713-819012 E-mail revjoanfoster@yahoo.co.uk

FOSTER, Jonathan Guy Vere. b 56. Goldsmiths' Coll Lon BA78. Wycliffe Hall Ox 83. **d** 86 **p** 87. C Hampreston *Sarum* 86-90; Chapl Chantilly *Eur* 90-97; V Branksome St Clem *Sarum* from 97. *The Vicarage, 7 Parkstone Heights, Branksome, Poole BH14 0QE* Tel (01202) 748058

FOSTER, Mrs Julia. b 58. RGN RSCN. STETS 03. **d** 06 **p** 07. NSM Chilworth w N Baddesley *Win* 06-10; NSM Ampfield 07-10; NSM Ampfield, Chilworth and N Baddesley 10-11; NSM N Waltham and Steventon, Ashe and Deane from 11. *11 West Lane, North Baddesley, Southampton SO52 9GB* Tel (023) 8041 0682 E-mail juliafoster58@hotmail.com

FOSTER, Leslie. b 49. Linc Th Coll 89. **d** 91 **p** 92. C Coseley Ch Ch *Lich* 91-93; C Coseley Ch Ch *Worc* 93-95; V Firbank, Howgill and Killington *Bradf* 95-00; Hon C Sedbergh, Cautley and Garsdale 95-00; Dioc Rural Adv 96-00; P-in-c Ruyton XI Towns w Gt and Lt Ness *Lich* from 00; RD Ellesmere 08-10. *The Vicarage, The Village, Ruyton Eleven Towns, Shrewsbury SY4 1LQ* Tel (01939) 261234 E-mail lesfoster@lunevic.freeserve.co.uk

FOSTER, Luke Richard. b 78. St Anne's Coll Ox MA00. Oak Hill Th Coll MTh11. **d** 11. C Banbury St Paul *Ox* from 11. *10 Hardwick Park, Banbury OX16 1YD* Tel (01295) 270692 E-mail lukerichardfoster@gmail.com

FOSTER, Michael John. b 52. St Steph Ho Ox 76. **d** 79 **p** 80. C Wood Green St Mich *Lon* 79-82; TV Clifton *S'well* 82-85; P-in-c Aylesbury *Ox* 85-87; Dep Warden Durning Hall Chr Community Cen 87-89; V Lydbrook *Glouc* 89-97; R Hemsby, Winterton, E and W Somerton and Horsey *Nor* 97-99; P-in-c Tarrant Valley *Sarum* 99-01; P-in-c Tollard Royal w Farnham, Gussage St Michael etc 99-01; R Chase from 01; C Sixpenny Handley w Gussage St Andrew etc from 06. *The Rectory, Church Hill, Tarrant Hinton, Blandford Forum DT11 8JB* Tel (01258) 830764 E-mail drmike@church.prestel.co.uk

FOSTER, Paul. *See* FOSTER, Graham Paul

FOSTER, Paul. b 60. MAAT80. Oak Hill Th Coll 91. **d** 93 **p** 94. C New Clee *Linc* 93-96; P-in-c Aldington w Bonnington and Bilsington *Cant* 96-02; P-in-c Lympne w W Hythe 00-02; Chapl HM Pris Aldington 96-02; Chapl HM YOI Feltham from 02.

HM Young Offender Institution, Bedfont Road, Feltham TW13 4ND Tel (020) 8890 0061 *or* 8844 5325 E-mail pfozzy@hotmail.com *or* paul.foster01@hmps.gsi.gov.uk

FOSTER, Philip. *See* FOSTER, Edward Philip John

FOSTER, Ronald George. b 25. Bris Univ BSc51 AKC51. **d** 52 **p** 53. C Lydney w Aylburton *Glouc* 52-54; C Leighton Buzzard *St Alb* 54-60; Chapl Bearwood Coll Wokingham 60-83; R Wantage Downs *Ox* 83-91; rtd 91; RD Wantage *Ox* 92-95; Perm to Offic from 92. *Ascension Cottage, Horn Lane, East Hendred, Wantage OX12 8LD* Tel (01235) 820790 E-mail ronfos@ukgateway.net

FOSTER, Miss Samantha. b 80. Sunderland Univ BA01 St Jo Coll Dur BA04. Cranmer Hall Dur 01. **d** 04 **p** 05. C Fulford *York* 04-08; Pioneer Min Scarborough Deanery from 08. *9 Green Lane, Scarborough YO12 6HL* Tel (01723) 503809 E-mail samantha.foster7@btinternet.com

FOSTER, Simon John Darby. b 57. Qu Mary Coll Lon BSc78. Wycliffe Hall Ox 85. **d** 88 **p** 89. C Bedgrove *Ox* 88-92; C Glyncorrwg w Afan Vale and Cymmer Afan *Llan* 92-94; R Breedon cum Isley Walton and Worthington *Leic* 94-98; R Anstey 98-06; R Anstey and Thurcaston w Cropston 06-10; V Croydon St Matt *S'wark* from 10. *The Vicarage, 7 Brownlow Road, Croydon CR0 5JT* Tel (020) 8688 5055 E-mail revsimonfoster@ntlworld.com

FOSTER, Stephen. b 47. Leeds Univ CertEd69. NEOC 83. **d** 86 **p** 87. NSM Kingston upon Hull St Nic *York* 86-87; NSM Aldbrough, Mappleton w Goxhill and Withernwick 87-98; TV Howden 98-05; RD Howden 02-05; Chapl HM Pris Wolds 03-05; rtd 05; Perm to Offic *York* from 05. *Wycliffe, 6 Victoria Terrace, Robin Hoods Bay, Whitby YO22 4RJ* Tel (01947) 880055 E-mail sf@rhbay.com

FOSTER, Stephen. b 52. **d** 06 **p** 07. OLM Halliwell *Man* 06-08; OLM Turton Moorland from 08; Chapl Bolton Hosps NHS Trust from 07. *68 Adrian Road, Bolton BL1 3LQ* Tel (01204) 841382

FOSTER, Canon Stephen Arthur. b 54. Lon Univ BMus75 BA78 Potchefstroom Univ PhD98. Coll of Resurr Mirfield 75. **d** 78 **p** 79. C Ches H Trin 78-82; C Tranmere St Paul w St Luke 82-83; V Grange St Andr 83-88; V Cheadle Hulme All SS 88-94; P-in-c Stockport St Matt 94-00; Asst Dir of Ords 96-04; V Sale St Anne 00-04; Can Res Leic Cathl 04-10; Prec Leic Cathl 04-10; Chapl Leic Univ from 10; Hon Can Leic Cathl from 11. *290 Victoria Park Road, Leicester LE2 1XE* E-mail stephen.foster@leccofe.org

FOSTER, Steven. b 52. Wadh Coll Ox BA75 MA80. Ridley Hall Cam 76. **d** 79 **p** 80. C Ipsley *Worc* 79-83; TV Woughton *Ox* 83-94; V Walshaw Ch Ch *Man* from 94. *Christ Church Vicarage, 37 Gisburn Drive, Walshaw, Bury BL8 3DH* Tel 0161-763 1193 Fax 08707-052490 E-mail mail@alimus.plus.com

FOSTER, Steven Francis. b 55. Lon Univ BD76 AKC76 Open Univ BA91 FRSA90. Coll of Resurr Mirfield 77. **d** 78 **p** 79. C Romford St Edw *Chelmsf* 78-80; C Leigh St Clem 80-83; Ed Mayhew McCrimmon Publishers 84-86; Hon C Southend 85-86; P-in-c Sandon 86-90; R 90-91; R Wanstead St Mary 91-93; R Wanstead St Mary w Ch Ch 93-00; Perm to Offic 00-05; Asst to Master R Foundn of St Kath in Ratcliffe 00-04; P-in-c Brighton Annunciation *Chich* 05-09; rtd 10; Perm to Offic *Chich* from 11. *45 Holland Mews, Hove BN3 1JG* Tel (01273) 206478 Mobile 07901-554866 E-mail stevenffoster@aol.com

FOSTER, Stuart Jack. b 47. Oak Hill Th Coll BA80 Lambeth STh86. **d** 80 **p** 81. C Worting *Win* 80-84; C-in-c Kempshott CD 84-88; R Hook 88-95; Chapl and Warden Bp Grosseteste Coll Linc 95-99; R Grayingham and Kirton in Lindsey w Manton *Linc* 99-05; P-in-c Vale of Belvoir *Leic* 05-09; OCF 99-04; Chapl ATC 04-09; rtd 09. *Sans Souci, 3 Marigold Close, Lincoln LN2 4SZ* Tel (01522) 524918 Mobile 07887 701876

FOSTER, Susan. b 58. Nottm Univ BMedSci80 BM, BS82. WEMTC 00. **d** 03 **p** 06. NSM Tenbury *Heref* from 03; Chapl Kemp Hospice Kidderminster from 07. *Little Oaks Cottage, Hope Bagot, Ludlow SY8 3AE* Tel (01584) 891200 E-mail thefosters@littleoakshb.fsnet.uk

FOSTER, Susan Anne. b 53. Trin Coll Bris BA97. **d** 98 **p** 99. C Watton w Carbrooke and Ovington *Nor* 98-02; Min S Wonston CD *Win* 02-07; P-in-c Micheldever and E Stratton, Woodmancote etc 05-07; V Upper Dever from 07. *The Rectory, Micheldever, Winchester SO21 3DA* Tel (01962) 774379

FOSTER, Thomas Andrew Hayden. b 43. CITC 70. **d** 73 **p** 74. C Dublin Clontarf *D & G* 73-78; I Drumcliffe w Clare Abbey and Kildysart *L & K* 78-80; P-in-c Polstead *St E* 78; I Kilscoran w Killinick and Mulrankin *C & O* 80-85; I Fanlobbus Union *C, C & R* 85-86; R Lasswade and Dalkeith *Edin* 86-87; C Woodford St Mary w St Phil and St Jas *Chelmsf* 87-88; I New w Old Ross, Whitechurch, Fethard etc *C & O* 89-91; Dioc Info Officer (Ferns) 90-91; I Whitehouse *Conn* 03-10; rtd 10. *18 Marguerite Park, Belfast BT10 0HF* Tel (028) 9062 0471 Mobile 07595-348856 E-mail hfoster@ireland.com

FOSTER-CLARK, Mrs Sarah Hazel. b 75. Man Univ BA97 Heythrop Coll Lon MA99. Wycliffe Hall Ox 98. **d** 00 **p** 01. C Walmsley *Man* 00-01; C Turton Moorland Min 01; C Horwich and Rivington 01-04; C Halliwell 04-07; Perm to Offic 07-08. *Address temp unknown* Tel 07909-916741 (mobile) E-mail revdf-c@xalt.co.uk

FOTHERBY, Miss Doreen. b 41. d 05 p 06. OLM Shipdham w E and W Bradenham *Nor* from 05. *6 Pound Green Lane, Shipdham, Thetford IP25 7LF* Tel (01362) 821481 E-mail d.fotherby@btinternet.com

FOTHERGILL, Richard Patrick. b 61. Newc Univ BA83. Trin Coll Bris 91. d 95 p 96. C E Twickenham St Steph *Lon* 95-97; Assoc R Kirstenhof S Africa 97-04; Network Miss P *Bris* 04-06; Hon C Peasedown St John w Wellow and Foxcote etc *B & W* from 09. *Flossie Cottage, South Stoke, Bath BA2 7ED* Tel (01225) 832804

FOUHY, Giles. b 71. Oak Hill Th Coll. d 07 p 08. C Shoreditch St Leon w St Mich *Lon* from 07. *16 Albion Drive, London E8 4ET* E-mail gilesfouhy@hotmail.com

FOULDS, John Stuart. b 64. Lanc Univ BA87 Southn Univ BTh91. Chich Th Coll 88. d 91 p 92. C Eastcote St Lawr *Lon* 91-95; C Wembley Park 95-99; P-in-c Meir *Lich* 99-07. *Address temp unknown*

FOULGER, Wendy. b 43. St D Coll Lamp BA90. St Jo Coll Nottm 04. d 11. NSM Cil-y-Cwm and Ystrad-ffin w Rhandirmwyn etc *St D* from 11. *The Vicarage, Cilycwm, Llandovery SA20 0SP* Tel (01550) 721109 E-mail defld6@aol.com

FOULIS BROWN, Canon Graham Douglas. b 50. JP87. St Steph Ho Ox 80. d 82 p 83. C Hungerford and Denford *Ox* 82-84; Chapl Hungerford Hosp 83-84; C Bicester w Bucknell, Caversfield and Launton *Ox* 84-85; TV 85-90; V Kidmore End and Sonning Common 90-03; P-in-c Rotherfield Peppard 02-03; R Rotherfield Peppard and Kidmore End etc from 03; AD Henley from 06; Hon Can Ch Ch from 11. *The Rectory, Kidmore End, Reading RG4 9AY* Tel 0118-972 3987 E-mail gdfb.vicarage@lineone.net

FOULKES, Chan Meurig. b 21. St D Coll Lamp BA46. St Mich Coll Llan 46. d 47 p 48. C Llanbeblig w Caernarfon *Ban* 47-55; Bp's Private Chapl 55-58; V Harlech and Llanfair juxta Harlech 58-66; RD Ardudwy 64-76; R Llanaber w Caerdeon 66-76; Can Ban Cathl 71-89; Treas 74-83; Chan 83-89; R Llandegfan and Beaumaris w Llanfaes w Penmon etc 76-89; rtd 90; Perm to Offic *Ban* from 90. *Llanaber, 11 Gogarth Avenue, Penmaenmawr LL34 6PY* Tel (01492) 623011

FOULKES, Simon. b 58. Ox Poly BA81. Oak Hill Th Coll BA89. d 89 p 90. C St Austell *Truro* 89-92; C Boscombe St Jo *Win* 92-94; P-in-c Portswood St Denys 94-99; Par Evang Adv *Wakef* 99-04; TR Almondbury w Farnley Tyas 02-05; Perm to Offic *Cant* 07-09; P-in-c Bethersden w High Halden 09-11; Asst Dir of Educn from 11. *53 Littlestone Road, Littlestone, New Romney TN28 8LN* Tel (01797) 364517 E-mail vicar@idnet.co.uk

FOUNTAIN, David Roy (Brother Malcolm). b 48. Qu Coll Birm 85. d 87 p 88. SSF from 72; NSM Handsworth St Mich *Birm* 87-92; Lic to Offic *Sarum* 92-95; Perm to Offic *Worc* 95-00, Newc 00-02, *Lon* 02-03; V Bentley *Sheff* from 03. *The Vicarage, 3A High Street, Bentley, Doncaster DN5 0AA* Tel (01302) 876272

FOUNTAIN, John Stephen. b 43. RAF Coll Cranwell 65 Solicitor 80. LNSM course 91. d 93 p 94. NSM Nacton and Levington w Bucklesham and Foxhall *St E* 93-03; NSM Taddington, Chelmorton and Flagg, and Monyash *Derby* 03-11; NSM Taddington, Chelmorton and Monyash etc from 11. *The Old School, Chelmorton, Buxton SK17 9SG* Tel (01298) 85009

FOUNTAIN, Miss Stephanie Ann Cecilia. b 58. Lon Univ BMus81 Roehampton Inst PGCE88. Westcott Ho Cam 00. d 02 p 03. C Tadworth *S'wark* 02-06; TV Boston *Linc* 07-10; P-in-c Bishop's Castle w Mainstone, Lydbury N etc *Heref* from 10. *The Vicarage, Church Lane, Bishops Castle SY9 5AF* Tel (01588) 638095 E-mail stephaniefountain@yahoo.co.uk

FOUTS, Arthur Guy. b 44. Washington Univ BA72 Seabury-Western Th Sem DMin98. Ridley Hall Cam 78. d 81 p 82. C Alperton *Lon* 81-84; R Pinxton *Derby* 84-87; R Dublin St Patr USA 88-89; Pastor Warren St Mark 90-91; R Silver Spring St Mary Magd 91-99; Chapl St Andr Sch 99-00; P-in-c Point of Rocks St Paul 01-08. *12304 Guinevere Road, Glenn Dale MD 20769-8938, USA* Tel (001) (301) 860 1551 E-mail rubberduck301@yahoo.com

FOWELL, Preb Graham Charles. b 48. Southn Univ BTh85. Chich Th Coll. d 82 p 83. C Clayton *Lich* 82-86; C Uttoxeter w Bramshall 86-90; V Oxley 90-95; P-in-c Shifnal 95-07; V Shifnal and Sheriffhales 07-08; RD Edgmond and Shifnal 06-08; TR Stafford from 08; Preb Lich Cathl from 08. *The Rectory, 32 Rowley Avenue, Stafford ST17 9AG* Tel (01785) 258511

FOWLER, Anthony Lewis. b 57. Oak Hill Th Coll BA93. d 93 p 94. C Walton *St E* 93-96; P-in-c Combs 96-00; P-in-c Hitcham w Lt Finborough 98-00; R Combs and Lt Finborough 00-04; Chapl Suffolk Coll 00-04; Chapl HM Pris Coldingley 04-05; Chapl HM Pris Blundeston 05-07; Chapl HM Pris Swinfen Hall 07-09; Chapl HM Pris Highpoint from 09. *HM Prison Highpoint, Stradishall, Newmarket CB8 9YG* Tel (01440) 743232 E-mail tony.fowler@hmps.gsi.gov.uk *or* alfowler@supanet.com

FOWLER, Canon Colin. b 40. Linc Th Coll 80. d 82 p 83. C Barbourne *Worc* 82-85; TV Worc St Martin w St Pet, St Mark

etc 85-86; TV Worc SE 86-92; P-in-c Moulton *Linc* 92-95; Chapl Puerto de la Cruz Tenerife *Eur* 95-01; Hon Can Madrid Cathl from 99; R Tangmere and Oving *Chich* 01-05; rtd 05; Perm to Offic *Nor* from 07. *10 Drakes Heath, Lowestoft NR32 2QQ* Tel (01502) 564707

FOWLER, Canon David Mallory. b 51. Ian Ramsey Coll Brasted 74 Trin Coll Bris 75. d 78 p 79. C Rainhill *Liv* 78-81; C Houghton *Carl* 81-84; P-in-c Grayrigg 84-89; P-in-c Old Hutton w New Hutton 84-89; V Kirkoswald, Renwick and Ainstable 89-99; P-in-c Gt Salkeld w Lazonby 98-99; R Kirkoswald, Renwick, Gt Salkeld and Lazonby from 00; RD Penrith 99-06; Hon Can Carl Cathl from 99. *The Vicarage, Kirkoswald, Penrith CA10 1DQ* Tel (01768) 898176 E-mail revdmf@aol.com

FOWLER, Mrs Janice Karen Brenda. b 56. Middx Univ BA97. Oak Hill Th Coll 91. d 93 p 94. NSM Walton *St E* 93-96; Chapl Ipswich Hosp NHS Trust 94-00; NSM Combs *St E* 96-00; NSM Combs and Lt Finborough 98-00; C 00-04; P-in-c 04; C S Hartismere 04-07; Perm to Offic *Lich* 08-09; C Lich St Chad 09-10; P-in-c Worlingworth, Southolt, Tannington, Bedfield etc *St E* 10-11; Perm to Offic from 11. *Willowbrook Cottage, Church Road, Bacton, Stowmarket IP14 4LW* Tel 07709-921385 (mobile) E-mail jan.fowler@tesco.net

FOWLER, John Ronald. b 30. Ely Th Coll 55. d 58 p 59. C Surbiton St Andr *S'wark* 58-61; C St Sidwell Lodge Guyana 61-62; V Morawhanna 62-65; R Plaisance 65-70 and 83-89; V Sydenham All SS 70-81; V Wood End *Cov* 81-83; Adn Demerara and Can St Geo Cathl 86-89; V Bedford St Mich *St Alb* 90-95; rtd 95. *12 St Marys Paddock, Wellingborough NN8 1HL* Tel (01933) 228691

FOWLER, John Thomas. b 42. EAMTC. d 01 p 02. NSM Stoke by Nayland w Leavenheath and Polstead *St E* 01-11; rtd 11; Perm to Offic *St E* from 11. *Warners, Thorington Street, Stoke by Nayland, Colchester CO6 4SP* Tel and fax (01206) 337229 E-mail twam.johnf@googlemail.com

FOWLES, Canon Christopher John. b 31. Lich Th Coll 54. d 58 p 59. C Englefield Green *Guildf* 58-63; C Worplesdon 63-69; V Chessington 69-77; V Horsell 77-95; RD Woking 92-94; Hon Can Guildf Cathl 94-95; rtd 95; Perm to Offic *Guildf* from 95. *78 St Jude's Road, Egham TW20 0DF* Tel (01784) 439457

FOX, Mrs Carole Ann. b 36. TISEC 98. d 99 p 00. NSM Ellon *Ab* from 99. *4 Mavis Bank, Newburgh, Ellon AB41 6FB* Tel (01358) 789693 E-mail charlesandcarole@btinternet.com

FOX, Charles Edward. b 36. Lich Th Coll 62. d 66 p 67. C S Bank *York* 66-69; C Stokesley 69-72; V Egton w Grosmont 72-82; P-in-c Ugthorpe 72-82; P-in-c Newbold Verdon *Leic* 82-83; R Newbold de Verdun and Kirkby Mallory 84-04; rtd 04; Perm to Offic *Leic* from 04. *White Rose Cottage, 6 Brascote Lane, Newbold Verdon, Leicester LE9 9LF* Tel (01455) 822103

FOX, Christopher. b 79. UWE BSc01. Trin Coll Bris BA10. d 11. C Ealing St Paul *Lon* from 11. *2 Nightingale Road, London W7 1DG* Tel 07974-320324 (mobile) E-mail chrispfox@gmail.com

FOX, Colin George. b 46. TD. Sarum & Wells Th Coll 73. d 75 p 76. C N Hammersmith St Kath *Lon* 75-79; CF (TA) 76-90; C Heston *Lon* 79-81; TV Marlborough *Sarum* 81-90; P-in-c Pewsey 90-91; TR 91-98; TR Pewsey and Swanborough 98-03; Chapl Pewsey Hosp 90-95; P-in-c Avon Valley *Sarum* 03-11; C Durrington 08-11; rtd 11. *The Pightle, The Street, Teffont, Salisbury SP3 5QP* Tel (01722) 716010 E-mail foxy.col@talk21.com

FOX, Harvey Harold. b 27. Lich Th Coll 58. d 60 p 61. C Birchfield *Birm* 60-62; C Boldmere 62-65; V Sparkbrook Em 65-71; V Dordon 71-77; V Four Oaks 77-82; V Packwood w Hockley Heath 82-90; rtd 90; Perm to Offic *Cov* from 90. *37 Meadow Road, Henley-in-Arden B95 5LB* Tel (01564) 795302

FOX, Canon Herbert Frederick. b 26. Leeds Univ BA50. Coll of Resurr Mirfield 50. d 52 p 53. C Bury St Thos *Man* 52-55; V Unsworth 55-61; V Turton 61-72; V Farnworth and Kearsley 72-78; RD Farnworth 77-84; TR E Farnworth and Kearsley 78-84; Hon Can Man Cathl 81-84; V Ashford Hill w Headley *Win* 84-91; rtd 91; Perm to Offic *Man* from 91. *9 Highfield Road, Blackrod, Bolton BL6 5BP* Tel (01204) 669368

FOX, Canon Ian James. b 44. Selw Coll Cam BA66 MA70. Linc Th Coll 66. d 68 p 69. C Salford St Phil w St Steph *Man* 68-71; C Kirkleatham *York* 71-73; TV Redcar w Kirkleatham 73-77; V Bury St Pet *Man* 77-85; V Northallerton w Kirby Sigston *York* 85-03; RD Northallerton 85-91; Chapl Friarage and Distr Hosp Northallerton 88-92; Chapl Northallerton Health Services NHS Trust 92-03; P-in-c Barlby w Riccall *York* 03-09; P-in-c Hemingbrough 06-09; rtd 09; Can and Preb York Minster from 95; Perm to Offic from 10. *21 Springfield Close, Thirsk YO7 1FH* Tel (01845) 526889 E-mail ianfox321@btinternet.com

FOX, Preb Jacqueline Frederica. b 43. Harper Adams Coll of Educn CertEd66 Leeds Univ BEd74 MEd84 HonRCM85. S Dios Minl Tr Scheme 83. dss 85 d 87 p 94. RCM *Lon* 85-86; Dioc FE Officer 87-96; Hon C Acton St Mary 87-96; R 96-08; Dean of Women's Min 96-08; Dir of Ords Willesden Area 01-08; Preb St Paul's Cathl 01-08; rtd 08. *52 North Street, Ripon HG4 1EN* Tel (01765) 603698 E-mail jackie@actonfox.co.uk

FOX, Mrs Jane. b 47. Open Univ BA91 Bp Otter Coll Chich CertEd75 ALA70. S Dios Minl Tr Scheme 92. **d** 95 **p** 96. NSM W Blatchington *Chich* 95-98; C Peacehaven and Telscombe Cliffs 98-01; C Telscombe w Piddinghoe and Southease 98-01; TV Hitchin *St Alb* 01-08; P-in-c Harrold and Carlton w Chellington from 08. *Church House, 3 The Moor, Carlton, Bedford MK43 7JR* Tel (01234) 720262 E-mail janefox 1@btinternet.com

FOX (née COULDRIDGE), Mrs Janice Evelyn. b 49. Bognor Regis Coll of Educn CertEd71. Glouc Sch of Min 89. **d** 92 **p** 94. C Tupsley w Hampton Bishop *Heref* 92-96; P-in-c Orleton w Brimfield 96-01; Dioc Ecum Officer 96-01; TV Worc SE 01-05; rtd 05. *70 Woodstock Road, Worcester WR2 5NF* Tel (01905) 423637 E-mail janfox7@netscape.net

FOX, Jeremy Robin. b 68. St Chad's Coll Dur BA89 MA92 Leeds Univ BA94. Coll of Resurr Mirfield 92. **d** 95 **p** 96. C S Shields All SS *Dur* 95-99; C Tottenham St Paul *Lon* 99-04; C Edmonton St Mary w St Jo 99-04; Chapl Belgrade *Eur* from 04. *c/o FCO (Belgrade), King Charles Street, London SW1A 2AH* Tel (00381) (11) 402315 E-mail robin.fox@fco.gsi.gov.yu

FOX, John Brian. b 38. **d** 94 **p** 95. NSM Phillack w Gwithian and Gwinear *Truro* 94-96; NSM Godrevy 96-03; Chapl St Mich Mt from 04. *Abbeydale, 26 Tresdale Parc, Connor Downs, Hayle TR27 5DX* Tel (01736) 753935

FOX, Jonathan Alexander. b 56. St Jo Coll Nottm LTh77 BTh78. **d** 81 **p** 82. C Chasetown *Lich* 81-85; TV Fazakerley Em *Liv* 85-89; NSM Swanwick and Pentrich *Derby* 89-92; Miss Aviation Fellowship Kenya 92-96; TV Madeley *Heref* 97-02; Co-ord Chapl HM Pris Onley from 04. *HM Prison Onley, Willoughby, Rugby CV23 8AP* Tel (01788) 523530 E mail jonathan.fox@hmpa.gsi.gov.uk

FOX, Leonard. b 41. AKC66. **d** 67 **p** 68. C Salford Stowell Memorial *Man* 67-68; C Hulme St Phil 68-72; C Portsea All SS w St Jo Rudmore *Portsm* 72-75; V Oakfield St Jo 75-92; P-in-c Portsea All SS 92-06; V 06; Dir All SS Urban Miss Cen 92-06; rtd 06; Perm to Offic *Portsm* from 07. *Middle Reach, Ashlake Farm Lane, Wootton Bridge, Ryde PO33 4LF* Tel (01983) 880138

FOX, Linda Margaret. b 58. **d** 08 **p** 09. NSM S Croydon St Pet and St Aug *S'wark* from 08. *67 Kingsdown Avenue, South Croydon CR2 6QJ*

FOX, Maurice Henry George. b 24. Lon Univ BD58. St Aid Birkenhead 47. **d** 49 **p** 50. C Ecclesihill *Bradf* 49-52; C Bingley All SS 52-56; V Cross Roads cum Lees 56-62; V Sutton 62-79; V Grange-over-Sands *Carl* 79-88; rtd 89. *7 Manor Close, Topcliffe, Thirsk YO7 3RH* Tel (01845) 578322

FOX, Michael Adrian Orme. b 47. Bris Univ BSc68 PhD72. WMMTC 01. **d** 04 **p** 05. NSM Codsall *Lich* from 04; Ind Chapl Black Country Urban Ind Miss from 04. *30 Bromley Gardens, Codsall, Wolverhampton WV8 1BE* Tel (01902) 843442 E-mail mike@maofox.me.uk

FOX, The Ven Michael John. b 42. Hull Univ BSc63. Coll of Resurr Mirfield 64. **d** 66 **p** 67. C Becontree St Elisabeth *Chelmsf* 66-70; C Wanstead H Trin Hermon Hill 70-72; V Victoria Docks Ascension 72-76; V Chelmsf All SS 76-88; P-in-c Chelmsf Ascension 85-88; RD Chelmsf 86-88; R Colchester St Jas, All SS, St Nic and St Runwald 88-93; Hon Can Chelmsf Cathl 91-93; Adn Harlow 93-95; Adn W Ham 95-07; rtd 07; Perm to Offic *Chelmsf* from 08. *17A Northgate Street, Colchester CO1 1EZ* Tel (01206) 710701

FOX, Michael John Holland. b 41. Lon Univ BD68. Oak Hill Th Coll 64. **d** 69 **p** 70. C Reigate St Mary *S'wark* 69-73; NSM 76-01; C Guildf St Sav 73-76; Asst Chapl Reigate Gr Sch 76-81; Chapl 81-01; NSM Reigate St Pet CD *S'wark* 96-01; P-in-c Reigate St Luke w Doversgreen 01-09; rtd 09; Hon C Reigate St Mary *S'wark* from 09. *71 Blackborough Road, Reigate RH2 7BU* Tel (01737) 226616 E-mail mikejh.fox@virgin.net

FOX, Norman Stanley. b 39. Wolv Univ LLB97 Birm Univ LLM09. St Mich Coll Llan 61. **d** 64 **p** 65. C Brierley Hill *Lich* 64-67; C Tettenhall Regis 67-70; V Cradley *Worc* 70-73; Asst Chapl HM Pris Wakef 73-74; Chapl HM Pris The Verne 74-76; R Clayton W w High Hoyland *Wakef* 76-81; R Cumberworth 81-84; C Tettenhall Wood *Lich* 85-89; TV 89-91; V Pensnett 91-93; rtd 99. *54 Lyndon Road, Solihull B92 7RQ* Tel 0121-707 8216 E-mail nsfox390@hotmail.co.uk

✠**FOX, The Rt Revd Peter John.** b 52. AKC74. St Aug Coll Cant 74. **d** 75 **p** 76 **c** 02. C Wymondham *Nor* 75-79; Miss P Papua New Guinea 79-85; R Gerehu 80-85; Dioc Sec Port Moresby 84-85; P-in-c E w W Rudham *Nor* 85-88; P-in-c Syderstone w Barmer and Bagthorpe 85-88; P-in-c Tatterford 85-88; P-in-c Tattersett 85-88; P-in-c Houghton 85-88; R Coxford Gp 88-89; TR Lynton, Brendon, Countisbury, Lynmouth etc *Ex* 89-95; RD Shirwell 92-95; P-in-c Harpsden *Ox* 95-02; Gen Sec Melanesian Miss 95-02; Bp Port Moresby Papua New Guinea 02-06; Hon Asst Bp Nor from 06; P-in-c Nor Lakenham St Jo and All SS and Tuckswood 06-07; V from 07. *The Vicarage, Harwood Road, Norwich NR1 2NG* Tel (01603) 625679 E-mail peterandangiefox@yahoo.co.uk

FOX, Raymond. b 46. QUB BSc69. CITC 71. **d** 71 **p** 72. C Holywood *D & D* 71-75; C Min Can Down Cathl 75-78; I Killinchy w Kilmood and Tullynakill 78-81; I Belfast St Mary

Conn 81-88; I Killaney w Carryduff *D & D* 88-02; Can Down Cathl 98-02; Chapter Clerk and V Choral Belf Cathl 00-02; I Donegal w Killymard, Lough Eske and Laghey *D & R* 02-10; Can Raphoe Cathl 09-10; rtd 10. *10 Garden Avenue, Portstewart BT55 7AW* Tel (028) 7083 4623 Mobile 07511-752160 E-mail canonfox@btinternet.com

FOX, Robert. b 54. Man Univ BEd76. NOC 89. **d** 91 **p** 92. NSM Stalybridge *Man* 91; NSM Ashton 91-08; NSM Ashton from 08. *36 Norman Road, Stalybridge SK15 1LY* Tel 0161-338 8481 E-mail rob.foxesbridge@tiscali.co.uk

FOX, Robin. See FOX, Jeremy Robin

FOX, Sidney. b 47. Nottm Univ BTh79 PhD93. Linc Th Coll 75. **d** 79 **p** 80. C Middlesbrough St Oswald *York* 79-81; P-in-c 81-86; V 86-87; V Newby 87-92; R Brechin and Tarfside *Bre* 92-05; P-in-c Auchmithie 92-00; Can St Paul's Cathl Dundee 98-05; V Broughton *Blackb* from 05. *The Vicarage, 410 Garstang Road, Broughton, Preston PR3 5JB* Tel (01772) 862330 E-mail revsfox@yahoo.co.uk

FOX, Timothy William Bertram. b 37. CCC Cam BA61. Qu Coll Birm 66. **d** 68 **p** 69. C Cannock *Lich* 68-72; C Bilston St Leon 72-75; V Essington 75-81; R Buildwas and Leighton w Eaton Constantine etc 81-92; RD Wrockwardine 88-92; R Beadeley, Church Eaton and Moreton 92-04; rtd 04; Hon C Hanbury, Newborough, Rangemore and Tutbury *Lich* 04-08; Perm to Offic *Bradf* from 09. *40 Lakeber Avenue, High Bentham, Lancaster LA2 7JN* Tel (01524) 262575

FOX-WILSON, Francis James. b 46. Nottm Univ BTh73. Linc Th Coll 69. **d** 73 **p** 74. C Eastbourne St Elisabeth *Chich* 73-76; C Seaford w Sutton 76-78; P-in-c Hellingly 78-79; P-in-c Upper Dicker 78 79; V Hellingly and Upper Dicker 79 85; V Goring by-Sea 85-93; R Alfriston w Lullington, Litlington and W Dean 93-08; rtd 08; Hon C Isfield *Chich* from 08. *The Parsonage, Station Road, Isfield, Uckfield TN22 5EY* Tel (01825) 750247

FOXWELL, Rupert Edward Theodore. b 54. Magd Coll Cam BA76 MA80 Solicitor 79. Wycliffe Hall Ox 91. **d** 93 **p** 94. C Tonbridge SS Pet and Paul *Roch* 93-98. *24 Cheviot Close, Tonbridge TN9 1NH* Tel and fax (01732) 358535 E-mail foxwell@harvester.org.uk

FOY, Malcolm Stuart. b 48. Univ of Wales (Lamp) BA71 Magd Coll Cam CertEd72 K Coll Lon MA89 ACP80 FCollP FRSA. Ox NSM Course 84. **d** 87 **p** 88. NSM Tilehurst St Mich *Ox* 87-90; C Ireland Wood *Ripon* 90-96; Adv RE Leeds Adnry 90-96; Dir Educn *Bradf* 96-99; C Otley 99; Perm to Offic 00-05; Hon C Keighley All SS from 05. *45 The Chase, Keighley BD20 6HU* Tel (01535) 665112

FOY, Peter James. b 59. **d** 08 **p** 09. NSM Warminster Ch Ch *Sarum* from 08. *122 High Street, Chapmanslade, Westbury BA13 4AW* Tel (01373) 832088

FRAIS, Jonathan Jeremy. b 65. Kingston Poly LLB87. Oak Hill Th Coll BA92. **d** 92 **p** 93. C Orpington Ch Ch *Roch* 92-96; Asst Chapl Moscow *Eur* 96-99; Chapl Kiev 99-05; R Bexhill St Mark *Chich* from 05. *St Mark's Rectory, 11 Coverdale Avenue, Bexhill-on-Sea TN39 4TY* Tel and fax (01424) 843733 E-mail frais@tiscali.co.uk

FRAMPTON, Miss Marcia Ellen. b 36. SRN65 SCM66. Ripon Coll Cuddesdon 86. **d** 88 **p** 95. Par Dn Paston *Pet* 88-89; Par Dn Burford w Fulbrook and Taynton *Ox* 90-92; Par Dn Witney 92-93; NSM Heref S Wye 94-01; rtd 01; Perm to Offic *Heref* from 02. *15 Waterfield Road, Hereford HR2 7DD* Tel (01432) 278955

FRAMPTON-MORGAN, Anthony Paul George. See MORGAN, Anthony Paul George

FRANCE, Alistair. See FRANCE, Robert Alistair

FRANCE, Andrew. See FRANCE, John Andrew

FRANCE, Charles Malcolm. b 48. ACA71 FCA76. EAMTC 94. **d** 97 **p** 98. C Gt Grimsby St Mary and St Jas *Linc* 97-02; P-in-c Skegness and Winthorpe 02-04; P-in-c Ingoldmells w Addlethorpe 02-04; R Skegness Gp from 04. *20 Drake Road, Skegness PE25 3BH* Tel (01754) 612079 E-mail malcolmfrance@aol.com

FRANCE (née PIERCY), Mrs Elizabeth Claire. b 66. Qu Mary Coll Lon BSc87. Wycliffe Hall Ox 97. **d** 99 **p** 00. C Dronfield w Holmesfield *Derby* 99-03; V Allestree 03-05; P-in-c Etchingham Chich from 11. *The Rectory, Rectory Close, Etchingham Road, Burwash, Etchingham TN19 7BH* Tel (01435) 882301 E-mail lizcfrance@tiscali.co.uk

FRANCE, Evan Norman Lougher. b 52. Jes Coll Cam BA74 MA78. Wycliffe Hall Ox 76. **d** 79 **p** 80. C Hall Green Ascension *Birm* 79-82; CMS 82-84; C Bexhill St Pet *Chich* 84-87; V Westfield 87-11; R Buxted and Hadlow Down from 11. *The Rectory, Church Road, Buxted, Uckfield TN22 4LP* Tel (01825) 722103 E-mail enlfrance@gmail.com

FRANCE, Geoffrey. b 37. S Dios Minl Tr Scheme 87. **d** 90 **p** 91. NSM Uckfield *Chich* 90-92; C 92-94; R Warbleton and Bodle Street Green 94-02; rtd 02. *Little Croft, 19 James Avenue, Herstmonceux, Hailsham BN27 4PB* Tel (01323) 831840

FRANCE, John Andrew. b 68. Edin Univ MA90 Leeds Univ BA00 Dur Univ MA09. Coll of Resurr Mirfield 98. **d** 00 **p** 01. C Hartlepool H Trin *Dur* 00-04; Co-ord Chapl HM Pris Low

Newton 04-05; V Earsdon and Backworth *Newc* from 05. *The Vicarage, 5 Front Street, Earsdon, Whitley Bay NE25 9JU* Tel 0191-252 9393 E-mail andrewfrance1968@hotmail.com

FRANCE, Malcolm. See FRANCE, Charles Malcolm

FRANCE, Malcolm Norris. b 28. Ch Ch Ox BA53 MA57 Essex Univ PhD75. Westcott Ho Cam 53. **d** 55 **p** 56. C Ipswich St Mary le Tower *St E* 55-58; V Esholt *Bradf* 58-64; Chapl Essex Univ 64-73; Perm to Offic *Chich* 77-87; P-in-c Starston *Nor* 87-93; rtd 93; Perm to Offic *Nor* from 93. *The Old Swan, Townsend, Wylye, Warminster BA12 0RZ* Tel (01985) 248189

FRANCE, Canon Richard Thomas. b 38. Ball Coll Ox BA60 MA63 Lon Univ BD62 Bris Univ PhD67. Tyndale Hall Bris 60. **d** 66 **p** 67. C Cambridge St Matt *Ely* 66-69; Nigeria 69-73 and 76-77; Hon Can Ibadan from 94; Lib Tyndale Ho Cam 73-76; Warden 78-81; Vice-Prin Lon Bible Coll 81-88; Prin Wycliffe Hall Ox 89-95; R Wentnor w Ratlinghope, Myndtown, Norbury etc *Heref* 95-99; rtd 99; Perm to Offic *Ban* from 00. *Tyn-y-twll, Llwyngwril LL37 2QL* Tel (01341) 250596 E-mail dick@tynytwll.co.uk

FRANCE, Robert Alistair. b 71. Ox Poly BA92. Oak Hill Th Coll BA97. **d** 97 **p** 98. C Hartford *Ches* 97-02; P-in-c Stokenchurch and Ibstone *Ox* from 02. *The Vicarage, Wycombe Road, Stokenchurch, High Wycombe HP14 3RG* Tel (01494) 483384 E-mail revalistair@aol.com

FRANCE, Stephen Mark. b 66. Wycliffe Hall Ox BTh00. **d** 00 **p** 01. C Newbold w Dunston *Derby* 00-03; P-in-c Darley Abbey 03-05; Dioc Duty Press Officer 03-04; P-in-c Burwash *Chich* 05-06; R from 06. *The Rectory, Rectory Close, Etchingham Road, Burwash, Etchingham TN19 7BH* Tel (01435) 882301 E-mail revfrance@tiscali.co.uk

FRANCE, William Michael. b 43. Sydney Univ BA68 Lon Univ BD72 Chas Sturt Univ NSW MEd96. Moore Th Coll Sydney LTh70. **d** 73 **p** 73. C Turramurra Australia 73-75; C Barton Seagrave w Warkton *Pet* 76-78; R Dundas Australia 79-82; Chapl The K Sch 83-94; Chapl Syndey C of E Girls' Gr Sch 94-99; Assoc Chapl St Andr Cathl Sch 99-04; R Murchison 04-08; rtd 08. *6 Wesson Road, West Pennant Hills NSW 2125, Australia* Tel (0061) (2) 9945 0939 E-mail billandjackie@optusnet.com.au *or* wfrance@sacs.nsw.edu.au

FRANCE-WILLIAMS, Andrew David Azariah. b 75. Man Univ BA97 Sheff Univ MA04. Trin Coll Bris 08. **d** 10 **p** 11. C Onslow Square and S Kensington St Aug *Lon* from 10. *30A Eynham Road, London W12 0HA* Tel 07818-422586 (mobile) E-mail azariah10@gmail.com

FRANCE, Archdeacon of. See LETTS, The Ven Kenneth John

FRANCES, Nicolas Francis. b 61. MBE98. NOC 92. **d** 95 **p** 96. NSM Anfield St Columba *Liv* 95-98; Australia from 98; Acting Dir Health and Welfare Chapls Melbourne 98-99; Exec Dir Brotherhood of St Laur from 99. *15 Traill Street, Northcote Vic 3070, Australia* Tel (0061) (3) 9481 7373 *or* 9483 1347 Fax 9486 9724 E-mail nic@bsl.org.au

FRANCES ANNE, Sister. See COCKER, Mrs Frances Rymer

FRANCIS, Miss Annette. b 44. Trin Coll Bris 91. **d** 93 **p** 94. NSM Belmont *Lon* 93; C 94-97; C Swansea St Pet *S & B* 97-99; V Llanelli 99-11; rtd 11. *58 Garden City, Rhymney, Tredegar NP22 5JZ* Tel (01685) 840465 E-mail rev.a.francis@btinternet.com

FRANCIS, Claude Vernon Eastwood. b 15. Univ of Wales BA38. Ripon Hall Ox 38. **d** 40 **p** 41. C Cilybebyll *Llan* 40-44; C Treorchy 44-46; C Whitchurch 46-49; C Winscombe *B & W* 49-55; R E Pennard w Pylle 55-75; R Ditcheat w E Pennard and Pylle 75-81; rtd 81; Perm to Offic *B & W* from 81. *The Garden Flat, Sexey's Hospital, Bruton BA10 0AS* Tel (01749) 812147

FRANCIS, David Carpenter. b 45. Southn Univ BSc66 Loughb Univ MSc71 Sussex Univ MA83. Westcott Ho Cam 85. **d** 87 **p** 88. C Ealing St Mary *Lon* 87-90; Chapl Ealing Coll of HE 87-90; Chapl Clayponds Hosp Ealing 88-90; P-in-c Wembley St Jo *Lon* 90-93; Chapl Wembley Hosp 90-93; V Platt *Roch* 93-01; Post Ord Tr Officer 93-98; RD Shoreham 99-01; R Stow on the Wold, Condicote and The Swells *Glouc* from 01; AD Stow 04-09; rtd 11. *The Rectory, Sheep Street, Stow on the Wold, Cheltenham GL54 1AA* Tel (01451) 830607 Fax 830903 Mobile 07799-410370

FRANCIS, David Everton Baxter. b 45. St Deiniol's Hawarden 76. **d** 77 **p** 78. C Llangyfelach *S & B* 77-78; C Llansamlet 78-80; V Llanrhaeadr-ym-Mochnant, Llanarmon, Pennant etc *St As* 80-85; V Penrhyncoch and Elerch *St D* 85-93; V Borth and Eglwys-fach w Llangynfelyn 93-02; V Garthbeibio w Llanerfyl w Llangadfan etc *St As* from 02; AD Caereinion from 02. *Ty'r Eglwys, Pont Robert, Meifod SY22 6HY* Tel (01938) 500361

FRANCIS, Miss Gillian Cartwright. b 40. CertEd61. Dalton Ho Bris 69. **dss** 85 **d** 87 **p** 94. Blackheath *Birm* 86-94; Par Dn 87-94; P-in-c Stechford 94-03; rtd 03; Perm to Offic *Glouc* from 03. *22 Ince Castle Way, Gloucester GL1 4DT* Tel (01452) 503059

FRANCIS, Canon Graham John. b 45. St Mich Coll Llan 66. **d** 70 **p** 71. C Llanblethian w Cowbridge and Llandough etc 70-76; V Penrhiwceiber w Matthewstown and Ynysboeth 76-02; V Cardiff St Mary and St Steph w St Dyfrig etc from 02; V

Grangetown from 05; Can Llan Cathl from 02. *St Mary's Vicarage, 2 North Church Street, Cardiff CF10 5HB* Tel and fax (029) 2048 7777 E-mail fathergraham@aol.com

FRANCIS, Canon James More MacLeod. b 44. Edin Univ MA65 BD68 PhD74 Yale Univ STM69. New Coll Edin 65. **d** 87 **p** 87. Sen Lect RS Sunderland Univ from 82; NSM Sunderland St Chad 87-98; TV Sunderland 98-07; NSM Sunderland Minster 07-09; Tutor NEOC 89-98; Bp's Adv for NSM *Dur* from 99; Prin Dioc OLM Course 02-09; Hon Can Dur Cathl from 00. *Woodside, David Terrace, Bowburn, Durham DH6 5EF* Tel 0191-377 9215 E-mail jamesfrancis@mac.com

FRANCIS, James Stephen. b 66. FInstD97 FRSA99. SEITE 95. **d** 99 **p** 07. NSM St Botolph Aldgate w H Trin Minories *Lon* 99-02; NSM Soho St Anne w St Thos and St Pet 02-05; Chapl RNR 05-07; NSM St Mary le Strand w St Clem Danes *Lon* 07; Chapl RN from 07. *Royal Naval Chaplaincy Service, Mail Point 1-2, Leach Building, Whale Island, Portsmouth PO2 8BY* Tel (023) 9262 5055 Fax 9262 5134 Mobile 07961-123811 E-mail james.francis118@hotmail.co.uk

FRANCIS, Canon James Woodcock. b 28. OBE97. Wilberforce Univ Ohio AB57 Payne Th Sem Ohio BD58. Bexley Hall Div Sch Ohio 59. **d** 59 **p** 60. USA 59-84; Bermuda from 85; Can Res Bermuda 85-99; R Devonshire Ch Ch from 99. *PO Box HM 627, Hamilton HM CX, Bermuda* Tel (001809) 295 1125 Fax 292 5421

FRANCIS, Jeffrey Merrick. b 46. Bris Univ BSc69. Qu Coll Birm 72. **d** 76 **p** 77. C Bris Ch the Servant Stockwood 76-79; C Bishopston 79-82; V Bris St Andr Hartcliffe 82-93; TV Bris St Paul's 93-00; P-in-c Barton Hill St Luke w Ch Ch and Moorfields 00-02; Perm to Offic from 02. *32 Burfoot Gardens, Stockwood, Bristol BS14 8TE* Tel (01275) 831020

FRANCIS, Jennifer Anne Harrison. b 45. JP. Southn Univ BSc67 Brunel Univ MA74 CQSW73. WEMTC 07. **d** 07 **p** 08. NSM Stow on the Wold, Condicote and The Swells *Glouc* from 07. *The Rectory, Sheep Street, Stow on the Wold, Cheltenham GL54 1AA* Tel (01451) 830607 Fax 830903 Mobile 07881-953769 E-mail jennyfrancis1@btinternet.com

FRANCIS, Jeremy Montgomery. b 31. BNC Ox BA53 MA56. Glouc Sch of Min 84. **d** 87 **p** 88. NSM Chedworth, Yanworth and Stowell, Coln Rogers etc *Glouc* 87-90; NSM Coates, Rodmarton and Sapperton etc 90-01; NSM Daglingworth w the Duntisbournes and Winstone 95-97; NSM Brimpsfield w Birdlip, Syde, Daglingworth etc 97-00; Perm to Offic from 01. *Old Barnfield, Duntisbourne Leer, Cirencester GL7 7AS* Tel (01285) 821370

FRANCIS, John. b 56. Bris Poly BA78 MCIH81. **d** 98 **p** 99. OLM Hatcham Park All SS *S'wark* from 98. *Flat 2, 133 Deptford High Street, London SE8 4NS* Tel (020) 8691 3145 *or* 8875 5942 E-mail franci@threshold.org.uk

FRANCIS, John Sims. b 25. Fitzw Ho Cam BA54 MA58. St D Coll Lamp BA47 LTh49. **d** 49 **p** 50. C Swansea St Barn *S & B* 49-52; C Chesterton St Andr *Ely* 52-54; C Swansea St Mary and H Trin *S & B* 54-58; V Newbridge-on-Wye w Llanfihangel Brynpabuan 58-65; R Willingham *Ely* 65-82; RD N Stowe 78-82; R Rampton 82; P-in-c Buckden 82-85; V 85-91; rtd 91; Perm to Offic *Linc* 92-01. *3 The Brambles, Bourne PE10 9TF* Tel (01778) 426396

FRANCIS, Julian Montgomery. b 60. Selw Coll Cam BA83 MA83. S'wark Ord Course 88. **d** 91 **p** 92. C S Wimbledon H Trin and St Pet *S'wark* 91-95; V Cottingley *Bradf* 95-99; Minority Ethnic Angl Concerns Officer *Lich* 99-02; C W Bromwich St Andr w Ch Ch 99-02; TR Coventry Caludon 02-08; Nat Tr Co-ord for Minority Ethnic Anglicans 08-11; V Edgbaston St Geo *Birm* from 11. *The Vicarage, 3 Westbourne Road, Birmingham B15 3TH* Tel 0121-454 4204 E-mail j.francis@queens.ac.uk

FRANCIS, Miss Katherine Jane. b 67. St Jo Coll Dur BA08 RGN88 RM92. Cranmer Hall Dur 06. **d** 08 **p** 09. C Sprotbrough *Sheff* 08-10; Chapl Newcastle upon Tyne Hosps NHS Foundn Trust from 10. *The Freeman Hospital, High Heaton, Newcastle upon Tyne NE7 7DN* Tel 0191-244 8680 E-mail katherine.francis@nuth.nhs.uk

FRANCIS, Kenneth. b 30. Em Coll Cam BA56 MA60. Coll of Resurr Mirfield. **d** 58 **p** 59. C De Beauvoir Town St Pet *Lon* 58-61; Zambia 62-70; V Harlow St Mary Magd *Chelmsf* 70-76; V Felixstowe St Jo *St E* 76-97; rtd 98. *33 Cordy's Lane, Trimley, Felixstowe IP10 0UD*

FRANCIS, Kenneth Charles. b 22. Oak Hill Th Coll 46. **d** 50 **p** 51. C Wandsworth All SS *S'wark* 50-53; V Deptford St Nic w Ch Ch 53-61; V Summerstown 61-77; R Cratfield w Heveningham and Ubbeston etc *St E* 77-87; rtd 87; Perm to Offic *Truro* from 87. *Wheal Alfred, Chapel Hill, Bolingey, Perranporth TR6 0DQ* Tel (01872) 571317

FRANCIS, Prof Leslie John. b 47. Pemb Coll Ox BA70 MA74 BD90 DD01 Nottm Univ MTh76 Qu Coll Cam PhD76 ScD97 Lon Univ MSc77 Univ of Wales (Ban) DLitt07 FBPsS88 FCP94. Westcott Ho Cam 70. **d** 73 **p** 74. C Haverhill *St E* 73-77; P-in-c Gt Bradley 78-82; P-in-c Lt Wratting 79-82; Research Officer Culham Coll Inst 82-88; P-in-c N Cerney w Bagendon

Glouc 82-85; Perm to Offic 85-95; Fell Trin Coll Carmarthen 89-99; Dean of Chpl 95-99; Prof Th Univ of Wales (Lamp) 92-99; Prof Practical Th Univ of Wales (Ban) 99-07; Prof Religions and Educn Warw Univ from 07; Perm to Offic *Ox* 95-01 and *Ban* 99-06; Hon C Llanfair-pwll and Llanddaniel-fab etc *Ban* from 06; Hon Can St D Cathl 98-99; Hon Can and Can Th *Ban* Cathl from 06. *Llys Onnen, Abergwyngregyn, Llanfairfechan LL33 0LD* Tel (01248) 681877

FRANCIS, Mark Simon. b 77. Dur Univ BSc98. Oak Hill Th Coll BA10. **d** 10 **p** 11. C Egham *Guildf* from 10. *33 Grange Road, Egham TW20 9QP* Tel (01784) 475305
E-mail mark@stjohnsegham.com

FRANCIS, Martin Rufus. b 37. Pemb Coll Ox BA60 MA64. Linc Th Coll 60. **d** 63 **p** 64. C W Hartlepool St Paul *Dur* 63-67; C Yeovil St Jo w Preston Plucknett *B & W* 67-69; Chapl Tonbridge Sch 69-83; Chapl and Dep Hd St Jo Sch Leatherhead 83-94; R Herstmonceux and Wartling *Chich* 94-01; rtd 01; Perm to Offic *Sarum* from 02. *50 Lower Bryanston, Blandford Forum DT11 0DR* Tel (01258) 488619

FRANCIS, Canon Paul Edward. b 52. Southn Univ BTh84. Sarum & Wells Th Coll 78. **d** 81 **p** 82. C Biggin Hill *Roch* 81-85; R Fawkham and Hartley 85-90; V Aylesford 90-99; V Riverhead w Dunton Green from 99; Chapl Dioc Assn of Readers 01-11; RD Sevenoaks 05-11; R Beckenham St Geo from 11; Hon Can Roch Cathl from 10. *The Rectory, 14 The Knoll, Beckenham BR3 3JW* Tel (020) 8650 0983
E-mail paul.francis@diocese-rochester.org

FRANCIS, Peter Alan. b 73. Wycliffe Hall Ox. **d** 09 **p** 10. C Horsham *Chich* from 09. *18 Queensway, Horsham RH13 5AY* Tel (01403) 230329

FRANCIS, Peter Brereton. b 53. St Andr Univ MTheol77. Qu Coll Birm 77. **d** 78 **p** 79. C Hagley *Worc* 78-81; Chapl Qu Mary Coll *Lon* 81-87; R Ayr *Glas* 87-92; Miss to Seamen 87-92; Provost St Mary's Cathl 92-96; R Glas St Mary 92-96; Warden and Lib Gladstone's Lib Hawarden from 97; Visiting Prof Glyndwr Univ from 09. *Gladstone's Library, Church Lane, Hawarden, Deeside CH5 3DF* Tel (01244) 532350
E-mail peter.francis@gladlib.org

FRANCIS, Peter Philip. b 48. St Jo Coll Dur BA73. Wycliffe Hall Ox 73. **d** 75 **p** 76. C Foord St Jo *Cant* 75-78; C Morden *S'wark* 78-83; P-in-c Barford St Martin, Dinton, Baverstock etc *Sarum* 83-88; P-in-c Fovant, Sutton Mandeville and Teffont Evias etc 83-86; R Newick *Chich* from 88. *The Rectory, Church Road, Newick, Lewes BN8 4JX* Tel (01825) 722692
E-mail pnfrancis@btinternet.com

FRANCIS, Philip Thomas. b 58. TD03. St D Coll Lamp BA81 Regent's Park Coll Ox MTh99. Chich Th Coll 81. **d** 82 **p** 83. C Llanelli St Paul *St D* 82-84; C Barnsley St Mary *Wakef* 84-87; V Burton Dassett *Cov* 87-10; V Gaydon w Chadshunt 87-10; P-in-c Avon Dassett w Farnborough and Fenny Compton 07-10; CF (TA) 88-10; CF from 10. *c/o MOD Chaplains (Army)* Tel (01264) 381140 Fax 381824
E-mail philip.francis@regents.ox.ac.uk

FRANCIS, Mrs Sharon. b 57. Westmr Coll Ox BTh99. SEITE 98. **d** 08 **p** 09. NSM Langton Green *Roch* from 08. *Mill Cottage, Mill Lane, Lamberhurst, Tunbridge Wells TN3 8EG* Tel (01892) 890109 E-mail sharon.francis@ukonline.co.uk

FRANCIS, Younis. b 66. **d** 95 **p** 95. C Addington *S'wark* 05-07; TV Cheam 07-11; P-in-c Norbury St Phil from 11. *39 Pollards Hill South, London SW16 4LW* Tel 07504-721294 (mobile)
E-mail younis francis@hotmail.com

FRANCIS-DEHQANI, Gulnar Eleanor (Guli). b 66. Nottm Univ BA89 Bris Univ MA94 PhD99. SEITE 95. **d** 98 **p** 99. C Mortlake w E Sheen *S'wark* 98-02; Chapl R Academy of Music *Lon* 02-04; Chapl St Marylebone C of E Sch 02-04; Perm to Offic *Pet* 04-11; C Tr Officer from 11. *Bouverie Court, 6 The Lakes, Bedford Road, Northampton NN4 7YD* Tel 07771-948190 (mobile) E-mail guli.fd@btinternet.com

FRANCIS-DEHQANI, Canon Lee Thomas. b 67. Nottm Univ BA89. Sarum & Wells Th Coll 92 Trin Coll Bris BA95. **d** 95 **p** 96. C Putney St Mary *S'wark* 95-98; TV Richmond St Mary w St Matthias and St Jo 98-04; P-in-c Oakham, Hambleton, Egleton, Braunston and Brooke *Pet* 04-10; P-in-c Langham 04-10; C Teigh w Whissendine and Market Overton 04-10; C Cottesmore and Barrow w Ashwell and Burley 04-10; TR Oakham, Ashwell, Braunston, Brooke, Egleton etc from 11; RD Rutland from 10. *The Vicarage, Vicarage Lane, Oakham LE15 6EG* Tel and fax (01572) 722108 Mobile 07827-668169 E-mail lee.fd@btinternet.com

FRANK, Derek John. b 49. Imp Coll Lon BScEng70 Warwick Univ MSc71. Cranmer Hall Dur 83. **d** 85 **p** 86. C Clay Cross *Derby* 85-87; C Crookes St Thos *Sheff* 87-90; TV 90-93; Chapl Vevey w Château d'Oex and Villars *Eur* 93-02; rtd 02. *702 rue des Allobroges, 74140 Saint-Cergues, France* Tel (0033) 4 50 94 26 22
E-mail derek@ebeg.ch

FRANK, Penelope Edith. b 45. WMMTC 96. **d** 99 **p** 00. NSM Edgbaston St Geo *Birm* 99-02; Perm to Offic *Cov* 03-04; NSM Stoneleigh w Ashow 04-10; CPAS 87-06; rtd 06; Asst Chapl

Vevey w Château d'Oex Eur from 10. *All Saints, avenue de la Prairie 40, 1800 Vevey, Switzerland*
E-mail pennyfrank@mail.com

FRANK, Canon Richard Patrick Harry. b 40. St Chad's Coll Dur BA66. **d** 68 **p** 69. C Darlington H Trin *Dur* 68-72; C Monkwearmouth St Andr 72-74; C-in-c Harlow Green CD 74-79; R Skelton and Hutton-in-the-Forest w Ivegill *Carl* 79-86; V Carl St Luke Morton 86-92; RD Carl 88-89; P-in-c Thursby 89-90; P-in-c Kirkbride w Newton Arlosh 89-92; TR Greystoke, Matterdale, Mungrisdale etc 92-98; P-in-c Patterdale 95-98; TR Gd Shep TM 98-99; RD Penrith 96-99; Hon Can Carl Cathl 97-99; rtd 99; Perm to Offic *Carl* 00-02; *York* from 02. *8 Taylors Rise, Walkington, Beverley HU17 8SF* Tel (01482) 872262
E-mail richardandann.frank@virgin.net

FRANK, Richard Stephen. b 70. Keble Coll Ox MEng93 Fitzw Coll Cam MA98. Ridley Hall Cam 96. **d** 99 **p** 00. C Cranham Park *Chelmsf* 99-04; P-in-c St Margaret's-on-Thames *Lon* 05-11; V from 11. *295 St Margarets Road, Twickenham TW1 1PN* Tel (020) 8891 3504 Mobile 07973-719730
E-mail richardfrank@allsoulschurch.org.uk

FRANKLAND, Angela Tara. b 69. Lon Bible Coll BA96 MA98. EAMTC 97. **d** 99 **p** 00. C Hornchurch St Andr *Chelmsf* 99-03; TV Wickford and Runwell 03-11; P-in-c Aveley and Purfleet from 11. *The Vicarage, Mill Road, Aveley, South Ockendon RM15 4SR* Tel (01708) 891471
E-mail tfrankland@btinternet.com

FRANKLIN, David John. b 67. Selw Coll Cam BA88 MA92. St Jo Coll Nottm MTh06. **d** 06 **p** 07. C Windermere *Carl* 06-10; Hon C Bramley *Sheff* from 10. *122 Green Arbour Road, Thurcroft, Rotherham S66 9ED* Tel (01709) 542791
E-mail david@franklind.freeserve.co.uk

FRANKLIN, Hector Aloysius. b 32. NOC 94. **d** 97 **p** 98. NSM Chapeltown *Sheff* 97-99; P-in-c Sheff St Paul 99-02; rtd 02; Perm to Offic *Sheff* from 04. *108 Mackenzie Crescent, Burncross, Sheffield S35 1US* Tel 0114-245 7160

FRANKLIN, Mrs Janet. b 67. Selw Coll Cam VetMB91 MA92 Cumbria Univ BA10. LCTP 06. **d** 10 **p** 11. C Maltby *Sheff* from 10; C Thurcroft from 10. *122 Green Arbour Road, Thurcroft, Rotherham S66 9ED* Tel (01709) 542791
E-mail janet@franklind.freeserve.co.uk

FRANKLIN, Canon Lewis Owen. b 46. Natal Univ BSc67. S'wark Ord Course 68. **d** 73 **p** 74. C Durban St Paul S Africa 74-75; R Newcastle H Trin 76-79; Dir St Geo Cathl Cen Cape Town 80-83; Chapl St Geo Gr Sch 84-86; R Sea Pt H Redeemer 87-89; R Cape Town St Paul 89-90; Subdean and Prec Kimberley Cathl 91-94 and 96-99; Hon Can from 93; Dioc Sec Kimberley and Kuruman 94-96; C Altrincham St Geo *Ches* 99-00; P-in-c Newcastle St Paul *Lich* 00-05; R Bryanston St Mich S Africa 05-09; rtd 08. *414 Carlingford, Randjes Estate, PO Box 565, Highlands North, 2037 South Africa* Tel and fax (0027) (11) 440 1857 E-mail fr.owen@gmail.com

FRANKLIN, Miss Ola. b 55. Balls Park Coll Hertford CertEd76 Open Univ BA92 Birkbeck Coll Lon MA95. NTMTC BA09. **d** 09 **p** 10. C Harlow St Mary and St Hugh w St Jo the Bapt *Chelmsf* from 09. *9 Longacre, Harlow CM17 0TA* Tel (01279) 450204 E-mail ofrank@btinternet.com

FRANKLIN, Canon Richard Charles Henry. b 48. Ch Ch Coll Cant CertEd70 Heythrop Coll Lon MA08. Sarum & Wells Th Coll 75. **d** 78 **p** 79. C Pershore w Pinvin, Wick and Birlingham *Worc* 78-80; Educn Chapl 80-85; V Wollescote 85-92; V Fareham SS Pet and Paul *Portsm* 92-98; V Luton All SS w St Pet *St Alb* from 98; RD Luton 02-07; Hon Can St Alb from 09. *All Saints' Vicarage, Shaftesbury Road, Luton LU4 8AH* Tel (01582) 720129 E-mail richardfranklin@mail2world.com

FRANKLIN, Canon Richard Heighway. b 54. Southn Univ BA75 MPhil83. Sarum & Wells Th Coll 75. **d** 78 **p** 79. C Thame w Towersey *Ox* 78-81; Asst Chapl Southn Univ 81-83; Dir of Studies Chich Th Coll 83-89; P-in-c Stalbridge *Sarum* 89-94; V Weymouth H Trin from 94; Can and Preb Sarum Cathl from 02; RD Weymouth 04-08. *Holy Trinity Vicarage, 7 Glebe Close, Weymouth DT4 9RL* Tel (01305) 760354 *or* 774597
E-mail richardfranklin@btinternet.com

FRANKLIN (née WESTMACOTT), Mrs Rosemary Margaret. b 41. WEMTC 03. **d** 05 **p** 06. NSM Cirencester *Glouc* from 05. *Waterton Farm House, Ampney Crucis, Cirencester GL7 5RR* Tel (01285) 654282 E-mail revrmf@btinternet.com

FRANKLIN, Preb Simon George. b 54. Bris Univ BA75. Ridley Hall Cam 77. **d** 79 **p** 80. C Woodmansterne *S'wark* 79-83; C St Peter-in-Thanet *Cant* 83-86; R Woodchurch 86-96; P-in-c Ottery St Mary, Alfington, W Hill, Tipton etc *Ex* 96-99; TR from 99; P-in-c Feniton and Escot from 07; Preb Ex Cathl from 07. *The Vicar's House, 7 College Road, Ottery St Mary EX11 1DQ* Tel (01404) 812062
E-mail stpaul church@lineone.net
or safranklin@btopenworld.com

FRANKLIN, Stephen Alaric. b 58. Lon Univ BD87. Sarum & Wells Th Coll 87. **d** 89 **p** 90. C Chenies and Lt Chalfont, Latimer and Flaunden *Ox* 89-93; CF from 93. *c/o MOD Chaplains (Army)* Tel (01264) 381140 Fax 381824

FRANKS, John Edward. b 29. d 61 p 62. C Plymouth St Matthias *Ex* 61-66; V Upton Grey w Weston Patrick and Tunworth *Win* 66-77; V Upton Grey, Weston Patrick, Tunworth etc 77-79; P-in-c Wolverton cum Ewhurst and Hannington 79-80; R Baughurst, Ramsdell, Wolverton w Ewhurst etc 81-94; rtd 94. *Victoria, 57 Triq Santa Lucija, Naxxar, NXR 1507, Malta GC* Tel (00356) 2143 7006

FRANKS, John William. b 45. K Alfred's Coll Win BEd87 DAES94 MISM89. STETS 97. d 00 p 01. NSM Fareham H Trin *Portsm* 00-03; Hon Chapl Pitmore Sch Chandler's Ford 00; Hon Chapl Fareham Coll of F&HE 01-03; C Rowner *Portsm* 03-07; C Bridgemary 05-07; P-in-c Banwell *B & W* from 08. *Park House, East Street, Banwell BS29 6BW* Tel (01934) 822320

FRANKUM, Matthew David Hyatt. b 65. Leic Poly BSc87. Trin Coll Bris 97. d 99 p 00. C Bath St Luke *B & W* 99-03; TV Worle 03-08; P-in-c Bath St Luke from 08. *St Luke's Vicarage, Hatfield Road, Bath BA2 2BD* Tel (01225) 311904

FRANSELLA, Cortland Lucas. b 48. Trin Hall Cam BA70 MA74 Heythrop Coll Lon MA00 Open Univ BSc05. NTMTC 95. d 98 p 99. NSM Palmers Green St Jo *Lon* 98-03; NSM Hornsey St Mary w St Geo 03-08; Perm to Offic from 08. *17 Warner Road, London N8 7HB* Tel (020) 8340 7706 E-mail fransella@btinternet.com

FRANZ, Kevin Gerhard. b 53. Edin Univ MA74 BD79 PhD92. Edin Th Coll 76. d 79 p 80. C Edin St Martin 79-83; R Selkirk 83-90; Provost St Ninian's Cathl Perth 90-99; R Perth St Ninian 90-99; Gen Sec Action of Churches Together in Scotland 99-07; Hon Can St Ninian's Cathl Perth 00-05. *Address temp unknown*

FRASER, Alan Richard. b 69. Leeds Univ BA91 MA94. WMMTC 04. d 07 p 08. NSM Gravelly Hill *Birm* from 07. *41 Hobhouse Close, Birmingham B42 1HB* E-mail alan-fraser@blueyonder.co.uk

FRASER, Andrew Thomas. b 52. Newc Univ Aus BA81. St Jo Coll (NSW) ThL79. d 81 p 82. Australia 81-87; C Prestbury *Glouc* 87-91; C Wotton St Mary 91-92. *79 Victoria Street, Gloucester GL1 4EP* Tel (01452) 381082

FRASER, Beverly. b 49. d 10 p 11. NSM Sutton *S'wark* from 10. *53 Sherwood Park Road, Sutton SM1 2SG* Tel (020) 8661 7448 or 7735 8338 Mobile 07799-580570 E-mail beverly.fraser1@googlemail.com

FRASER, Charles Ian Alexander. Ex Univ BA Cam Univ PGCE Open Univ MA MCMI. ERMC. d 10 p 11. NSM Cherry Hinton St Jo *Ely* from 10; Asst Master The Leys Sch from 10. *The Leys School, Fen Causeway, Cambridge CB2 7AD* Tel (01223) 508952 Mobile 07889-019157 E-mail ciaf@theleys.net or revd.charlesfraser@gmail.com

FRASER, Christine Nancy. b 61. TISEC 98. d 02 p 03. NSM St Ninian's Cathl Perth from 02. *9 Balvaird Place, Perth PH1 5EA* Tel (01738) 623827 E-mail cnfraser@btinternet.com

FRASER, Darren Anthony. b 71. Wilson Carlile Coll 02. d 08 p 09. C Bucknall *Lich* from 08. *The Vicarage, 161A Dawlish Drive, Stoke-on-Trent ST2 0ET* Tel (01782) 260876 Mobile 07766-198455

FRASER, David Ian. b 32. Em Coll Cam BA54 MA58. Oak Hill Th Coll 56. d 58 p 59. C Bedford St Jo *St Alb* 58-61; C Cheadle Hulme St Andr *Ches* 61-64; R Fringford w Hethe and Newton Purcell *Ox* 64-67; V Preston St Luke *Blackb* 67-71; V Surbiton Hill Ch Ch *S'wark* 71-91; rtd 91; Perm to Offic *Ox* from 97. *7 Godwyn Close, Abingdon OX14 1DU* Tel (01235) 532049 E-mail david@ab-frasers.freeserve.co.uk

FRASER, Mrs Elizabeth Ann. b 44. d 07 p 08. OLM Witley *Guildf* from 07. *Oakwood, Petworth Road, Milford, Godalming GU8 5BS* Tel (01483) 417190 Mobile 07966-513450 E-mail ann.fraser@btinternet.com

FRASER, Geoffrey Michael. b 29. Sarum Th Coll. d 59 p 60. C Thames Ditton *Guildf* 59-63; C Shere 63-65; C Dunsford and Doddiscombsleigh *Ex* 65-70; V Uffculme 70-92; rtd 92; Perm to Offic *Worc* from 92. *46 Priory Road, Malvern WR14 3DB* Tel (01684) 576302

FRASER, Canon Giles Anthony. b 64. Newc Univ BA84 Ox Univ BA92 MA97 Lanc Univ PhD99. Ripon Coll Cuddesdon. d 93 p 94. C Streetly *Lich* 93-97; C Ox St Mary V w St Cross and St Pet 97-00; Chapl Wadh Coll Ox 97-00; V Putney St Mary *S'wark* 00-04; TR 04-09; Can Res and Chan St Paul's Cathl from 09; Hon Can Sefwi-Wiawso Ghana from 09. *6 Amen Court, London EC4M 7BU* Tel (020) 7248 2559 E-mail chancellor@stpaulscathedral.org.uk

FRASER, Mrs Helen Jane. b 77. Man Univ LLB98. Trin Coll Bris BA11. d 11. C Chipstead *S'wark* from 11. *42 Blue Leaves Avenue, Coulsdon CR5 1NU* Tel (01737) 557654 E-mail fraserhj@gmail.com

FRASER, Canon Jane Alicia. b 44. Man Univ BA. Glouc Sch of Min 86. d 89 p 94. NSM Upton on Severn *Worc* 89-00; NSM Ripple, Earls Croome w Hill Croome and Strensham 97-00; Faith Adv Dept of Health's Adv Gp on Teenage Pregnancy from 00; NSM Upton-on-Severn, Ripple, Earls Croome etc *Worc* from 00; Hon Can Worc Cathl from 05. *The Campanile, Church Lane, Stoulton, Worcester WR7 4RE* Tel (01905) 840266 E-mail ministry@revjane.demon.co.uk

FRASER, Jeremy Stuart. b 58. d 08 p 09. NSM E Greenwich *S'wark* 08-09; C from 09. *185 Charlton Church Lane, London SE7 7AA* Tel 07970-139881 (mobile) E-mail jeremy@fraserwireless.co.uk

FRASER, Leslie. b 34. ALCD62. d 62 p 63. C St Helens St Matt Thatto Heath *Liv* 62-64; C Fazakerley Em 64-67; R Collyhurst St Oswald and St Cath *Man* 67-72; P-in-c Collyhurst St Jas 67-72; R Collyhurst 72-74; RNLI 75-92; rtd 95; Hon C Bispham *Blackb* 95-98; Perm to Offic 98-00; P-in-c Bridekirk *Carl* 99-04. *Bridesbeck Cottage, Dovenby, Cockermouth CA13 0PG* Tel (01900) 821282

FRASER, Leslie John. b 60. d 99 p 00. NSM Thamesmead *S'wark* 99-04; Perm to Offic 05-07. *4 Goldcrest Close, London SE28 8JA* Tel (020) 8473 4736 E-mail les.fraser@virgin.net

FRASER, Mark Adrian. b 69. Warwick Univ BSc90 Birm Univ MSc91. St Jo Coll Nottm MTh04. d 05 p 06. C Astley Bridge *Man* 05-08; P-in-c Gamston and Bridgford *S'well* from 08. *10 Scafell Close, West Bridgford, Nottingham NG2 6RJ* Tel 07963-397688 (mobile) E-mail mark.fraser@tiscali.co.uk

FRASER-SMITH, Keith Montague. b 48. St Jo Coll Dur BA70. Trin Coll Bris. d 73 p 74. C Bishopsworth *Bris* 73-75; CMS 76-84; Egypt 76-80; Jerusalem 80-84; Asst Chapl Marseille w St Raphaël, Aix-en-Provence etc *Eur* 84-90; Media Dir Arab World Min 84-92; E Area Dir 92-97; Dep Internat Dir 97-98; NSM Worthing Ch the King *Chich* 90-93; Cyprus 93-97; NSM Tranmere St Cath *Ches* 97-98; P-in-c Barnton 98-03; Dir Global Mobilisation Arab World Min from 03; Perm to Offic *Ches* from 03. *33 Lord Street, Crewe CW2 7DH* Tel (01270) 214212 E-mail kieth.fraser-smith@tiscali.co.uk

FRAY, Bernard Herbert. b 44. Worc Coll of Educn CertEd65 Open Univ BA73 LTCL67. Cranmer Hall Dur 02. d 03 p 04. NSM Long Marston *York* 03-06; NSM Rufforth w Moor Monkton and Hessay 03-06; NSM Healaugh w Wighill, Bilbrough and Askham Richard 03-06; NSM Tockwith and Bilton w Bickerton 03-06; P-in-c Aberford w Micklefield 06-11; rtd 11; Perm to Offic *York* and *Eur* from 11. *Address temp unknown* Tel 07967-232535 (mobile) E-mail fraybernard985@gmail.com

FRAY, Vernon Francis. b 41. FCIOB79. *S'wark* Ord Course 91. d 94 p 95. NSM Heston *Lon* 94-96; NSM Twickenham All Hallows 96-02; NSM Teddington St Mark and Hampton Wick 02-08; NSM Whitton SS Phil and Jas from 08. *11 Paget Lane, Isleworth TW7 6ED* Tel (020) 8587 1386 E-mail v.fray@btinternet.com

FRAY, Vivienne Jane. *See* KERNER, Vivienne Jane

FRAYLING, The Very Revd Nicholas Arthur. b 44. Ex Univ BA69 Liv Univ Hon LLD01. Cuddesdon Coll 69. d 71 p 72. C Peckham St Jo *S'wark* 71-74; V Tooting All SS 74-83; Can Res and Prec Liv Cathl 83-87; R Liv Our Lady and St Nic w St Anne 87-90; TR 90-02; Hon Can Liv Cathl 89-02; Dean Chich from 02. *The Deanery, Canon Lane, Chichester PO19 1PX* Tel (01243) 812485 or 812494 Fax 812499 E-mail dean@chichestercathedral.org.uk

FRAYNE, The Very Revd David. b 34. St Edm Hall Ox BA58 MA62. Qu Coll Birm 58. d 60 p 61. C E Wickham *S'wark* 60-63; C Lewisham St Jo Southend 63-67; V N Sheen St Phil and All SS 67-73; R Caterham 73-83; RD Caterham 80-83; Hon Can *S'wark* Cathl 82-83; V Bris St Mary Redcliffe w Temple etc 83-92; RD Bedminster 86-92; Hon Can Bris Cathl 91-92; Provost Blackb 92-00; Dean Blackb 00-01; rtd 01; Perm to Offic *Sarum* from 02. *Newlands Cottage, Peacemarsh, Gillingham SP8 4HD* Tel (01747) 824065

FRAZER, David. b 60. QUB BSSc. TCD Div Sch. d 84 p 85. C Taney *D & G* 84-87; C Dublin Ch Ch Cathl Gp 87-88; I Clane w Donadea and Coolcarrigan *M & K* 88-05; Dioc P and Soc Officer from 05. *3 The Glen, Inse Bay, Laytown, Co Meath, Republic of Ireland* Tel (00353) (41) 981 3897 Mobile 87-383 6215 E-mail dublinblackdog@yahoo.ie

FRAZER, Deborah. b 58. Open Univ BA90 PGCE96. Th Ext Educn Coll 89. d 92 p 95. C Pretoria St Fran S Africa 92-93; Perm to Offic *S'wark* 93-94; NSM Merton St Mary 94-96; Asst Chapl HM Pris Brixton 96-97; P-in-c Barton Hill St Luke w Ch Ch and Moorfields *Bris* from 02; AD City 06-10. *41 Birchall Road, Bristol BS6 7TT* Tel 07817-567215 (mobile) E-mail rev.d.frazer@btinternet.com

FRAZER, Ian Martin. b 44. QUB BTh. d 91 p 93. Lic to Offic *D & D* 91-98; Aux Min Orangefield w Moneyreagh 98-04; Aux Min Ballymacarrett from 04. *The Stacks, Deramore Park South, Belfast BT9 5JY* Tel (028) 9066 7100

FRAZER, Canon James Stewart. b 27. TCD Div Sch. d 57 p 58. C Belfast Whiterock *Conn* 57-59; C Belfast St Matt 59-61; I Lack *Clogh* 61-64; I Mullaglass *Arm* 64-65; I Milltown 65-70; Australia 70-74; I Heathcote w Axedale 70-72; I Kangaroo Par w Marong, Lockwood and Ravenswood 72-74; I Dromore *Clogh* 74-82; Bp Dom Chapl 82; I Derryvullen S w Garvary 82-90; Can Clogh Cathl 83-85; Preb 85-94; I Clogh w Errigal Portclare 90-94; Glebes Sec 91-94; Chan Clogh Cathl 93-94; rtd 94. *8 Carsons Avenue, Ballygowan, Newtownards BT23 5GD* Tel (028) 9752 1562

FREAR, Canon Philip Scott. b 45. Univ of Wales (Lamp) BA66. Bris & Glouc Tr Course 77. **d** 80 **p** 81. Hon C Purton *Bris* 80-81; C Rodbourne Cheney 81-85; V Hengrove 85-95; V Braddan *S & M* from 95; Chapl Isle of Man Dept of Health and Social Security from 98; Can St German's Cathl from 04. *The Vicarage, Saddle Road, Braddan, Isle of Man IM4 4LB* Tel (01624) 675523

FREARSON, Andrew Richard. b 57. Wolv Univ BA80. Wycliffe Hall Ox. **d** 83 **p** 84. C Acocks Green *Birm* 83-86; C Moseley St Mary 86-89; P-in-c Holme *Blackb* 89-96; P-in-c Norcross Ch Ch USA 97-06; TV Bracknell *Ox* 06-10; R Dollar *St And* from 10. *St James's Rectory, 12 Harviestown Road, Dollar FK14 7HF* E-mail andrewfrearsontron@hotmail.co.uk

FREATHY, Nigel Howard. b 46. Lon Univ BA68 CertEd. Sarum & Wells Th Coll 79. **d** 81 **p** 82. C Crediton *Ex* 81-82; C Crediton and Shobrooke 82-84; TV Ex St Thos and Em 84-86; V Beer and Branscombe 86-01; P-in-c Stockland, Dalwood, Kilmington and Shute 01-03; V Kilmington, Stockland, Dalwood, Yarcombe etc 03-08; RD Honiton 96-99; rtd 08. *5 Mill Lane, Branscombe, Seaton EX12 3DS* Tel (01297) 680424 E-mail nigelfreathy@hotmail.co.uk

FREDERICK, David George. b 68. Birm Univ BSc92. Ridley Hall Cam 08. **d** 10 **p** 11. C Cromer *Nor* from 10. *18 Vicarage Road, Cromer NR27 9DQ* Tel 07766-051948 (mobile) E-mail dgfrederick@hotmail.com

FREDERICK, John Bassett Moore. b 30. Princeton Univ BA51 Birm Univ PhD73. Gen Th Sem (NY) MDiv54. **d** 54 **p** 55. C Cheshire St Pet USA 54-56; C All Hallows Barking *Lon* 56-58; C Ox SS Phil and Jas 58-60; R New Haven St Jo USA 61-71; R Bletchingley *S'wark* 74-95; Reigate Adnry Ecum Officer 90-95; RD Godstone 92-95; rtd 95. *32 Chestnut Street, Princeton NJ 08542-3806, USA* Tel (001) (609) 924 7590 Fax 924 1694 E-mail jf9642@netscape.net

FREDERICK, Warren Charles. b 47. Illinois Univ BSc. Qu Coll Birm 86. **d** 88 **p** 89. C W Leigh *Portsm* 88-91; V N Holmwood *Guildf* 91-00; R Cumberland H Cross USA from 00. *612 Brookfield Avenue, Cumberland 21502-3712, USA* Tel (001) (301) 759 2688

FREDRIKSEN, Martin. b 47. St Chad's Coll Dur BA69 Univ of Wales (Lamp) MA03. **d** 70 **p** 71. C Bideford *Ex* 70-73; C Guildf St Nic 73-76; R Cossington *B & W* 76-82; V Woolavington 76-82; Asst Chapl K Coll Taunton 82-84; C Bp's Hatfield *St Alb* 84-94; P-in-c Broadstone *Sarum* 94; V from 94. *St John's Vicarage, Macaulay Road, Broadstone BH18 8AR* Tel (01202) 694109 E-mail fr.martin1@eggconnect.net

FREE, Canon James Michael. b 25. K Coll Lon BD50 AKC50. **d** 51 **p** 52. C Corsham *Bris* 51-54; Trinidad and Tobago 54-62; PC Knowle St Barn *Bris* 62-67; V Pilning 67-75; P-in-c Lydiard Millicent w Lydiard Tregoz 75-82; Hon Can Bris Cathl 76-82; Can Res, Prec and Sacr Bris Cathl 82-83; Can Treas 83-90; Bp's Adv for Miss 82-87; Bp's Officer for Miss and Evang 87-89; rtd 90; Perm to Offic *B & W* 90-03 and from 06; *Bris* from 90; P-in-c Haselbury Plucknett, Misterton and N Perrott 03-05. *Well House, Silver Street, Misterton, Crewkerne TA18 8NG* Tel (01460) 271133 E-mail jamesfree05@aol.com

FREEBAIRN-SMITH, Canon Jane. b 36. St Chris Coll Blackheath IDC60. **d** 88 **p** 94. NSM Uddingston *Glas* 88-91; NSM Cambuslang 88-91; Dioc Missr 88-92; Dioc Past Cllr 92-95; NSM Baillieston 91-92; C St Mary's Cathl 92-95; TV Hykeham *Linc* 95-03; Can and Preb Linc Cathl 02-03; rtd 04. *12 Bell Grove, Lincoln LN6 7PL* Tel (01522) 705421

FREEBORN, John Charles Kingon. b 30. G&C Coll Cam BA52 MA56. Ridley Hall Cam 53. **d** 55 **p** 56. C Doncaster St Geo *Sheff* 55-57; Tutor Wycliffe Hall Ox 57-61; R Flixton St Mich *Man* 61-72; C Leic H Apostles 72-73; C E Crompton *Man* 73-74; Teacher Greenacres Sch Oldham 73-75; Hon C Ashton St Mich 74-76; Teacher St Jo Sch Ellesmere 75-79; Perm to Offic 77-80; Hd Master H Trin Sch Halifax 80-88; Hon C Sowerby *Wakef* 83-94; Teacher St Chad's Sch Hove Edge Wakef 88-91; NSM Halifax All SS from 94; Perm to Offic *Bradf* from 01. *27 Crossley Hill, Halifax HX3 0PL* Tel (01422) 342489

FREELAND, Nicolas John Michell. b 65. FNMSM99 FCMI10. STETS 07. **d** 10 **p** 11. NSM Jersey St Pet *Win* from 10. *Le Vieux Ménage, Rue de la Ville au Neveu, St Ouen, Jersey JE3 2DU* Tel (01534) 618284 Mobile 07797-736023 E-mail nicolas.freeland@jerseymail.co.uk

FREEMAN, Canon Alan John Samuel. b 27. SS Coll Cam BA48 MA52. Sarum Th Coll 50. **d** 52 **p** 53. C Tottenham Ch Ch W Green *Lon* 52-55; C Harpenden St Nic *St Alb* 55-60; R Aspley Guise 60-75; RD Fleete 67-70; RD Ampthill 70-75; Hon Can St Alb 74-92; V Boxmoor St Jo 75-92; Chapl Hemel Hempstead Gen Hosp (W Herts Wing) 75-92; RD Berkhamsted *St Alb* 85-92; rtd 92; Perm to Offic *St Alb* from 00. *3A Queen Street, Leighton Buzzard LU7 1BZ* Tel (01525) 384799

FREEMAN, Anthony John Curtis. b 46. Ex Coll Ox BA68 MA72. Cuddesdon Coll 70. **d** 72 **p** 73. C Worc St Martin 72-74; C Worc St Martin w St Pet 74-75; Bp's Dom Chapl *Chich* 75-78; C-in-c Parklands St Wilfrid CD 78-82; V Durrington 82-89; P-in-c Staplefield Common 89-94; Bp's Adv on CME 89-93; Asst Dir

of Ords 89-93. *4 Godolphin Close, Newton St Cyres, Exeter EX5 5BZ* Tel and fax (01392) 851453 E-mail anthony@imprint.co.uk

FREEMAN, Mrs Dorothy Lloyd (Dee). b 54. Lon Inst of Educn BEd76. EMMTC 06. **d** 09 **p** 10. NSM Linc St Geo Swallowbeck from 09. *Bethany, 69 Lincoln Road, Bassingham, Lincoln LN5 9JR* Tel (01522) 788942 E-mail freemn@btinternet.com

FREEMAN, Gordon Bertie. b 37. CITC BTh95. **d** 95 **p** 96. C Lecale Gp *D & D* 95-98; I Ardara w Glencolumbkille, Inniskeel etc *D & R* 98-07; Bp's Dom Chapl 06-07; rtd 07. *3 Leyland Meadow, Ballycastle BT54 6JX* Tel (028) 2076 8458

FREEMAN, Canon Jane. b 54. Dur Univ BA75 PhD80. Qu Coll Birm BD00. **d** 00 **p** 01. C Waterloo St Jo w St Andr *S'wark* 00-03; TV E Ham w Upton Park *Chelmsf* 03-11; TR Wickford and Runwell from 11; Hon Can Chelmsf Cathl from 09. *8 Friern Walk, Wickford SS12 0HZ* Tel (01268) 734077 Mobile 07702-922818 E-mail email@janefreeman.fsnet.co.uk

FREEMAN, Mrs Karen Lynn. b 62. San Diego State Univ USA BS86 Leeds Univ BA09. NOC 06. **d** 09 **p** 10. C New Brighton St Jas w Em *Ches* from 09. *86 Bayswater Road, Wallasey CH45 8ND* Tel 0151-638 8672 E-mail k.freeman62@gmail.com

FREEMAN, Karl Fredrick. b 57. St Luke's Coll Ex BEd80. **d** 90 **p** 91. C Plymouth St Andr w St Paul and St Geo *Ex* 90-95; TV Plymouth St Andr and Stonehouse 95-96; Chapl Coll of SS Mark and Jo Plymouth 96-01; TR Plymouth Em, St Paul Efford and St Aug from 01. *The Rectory, 9 Seymour Drive, Plymouth PL3 5BG* Tel (01752) 248601 or 260317 E-mail revkarl@aol.com

FREEMAN (formerly MARSHALL), Kirstin Heather. b 64. St Jo Coll Nottm 90 TISEC 95. **d** 93 **p** 95. NSM Glas St Marg 93-96; Hon Asst P Glas St Mary 96-99; P-in-c E Kilbride from 99. *6 Kelvin Crescent, East Kilbride, Glasgow G75 0TY* Tel (01355) 261232 E-mail revkirstin@freemanhome.co.uk

FREEMAN, Malcolm Robin. b 48. Master Mariner 78. St And NSM Tr Scheme 85. **d** 88 **p** 89. NSM Kirkcaldy *St And* 88-94; NSM Westbury *Sarum* 99-02; R Tidworth, Ludgershall and Faberstown from 02. *The Rectory, 10 St James's Street, Ludgershall, Andover SP11 9QF* Tel (01264) 791202 Mobile 07810-862740 E-mail fgmastermariner@aol.com

FREEMAN (née ADAMS), Mrs Margaret Anne. b 27. AKC48. Gilmore Ho. dss 82 **d** 87 **p** 94. Gt Yarmouth *Nor* 80-87; rtd 87; Hon Par Dn Malborough w S Huish, W Alvington and Churchstow *Ex* 87-94; Hon C 94-96; Perm to Offic *Nor* 97-04 and *Portsm* from 07. *4 Beamond Court, Lindisfarne Close, Portsmouth PO6 2SB* Tel (023) 9237 6128

FREEMAN, Martin. *See* FREEMAN, Philip Martin

FREEMAN, Michael. *See* FREEMAN, Philip Michael

FREEMAN, Michael Charles. b 36. Magd Coll Cam BA61 MA68 Lon Univ BD69 PhD93. Clifton Th Coll 67. **d** 69 **p** 70. C Bedworth *Cov* 69-72; C Morden *S'wark* 72-77; P-in-c Westcombe Park St Geo 77-85; V Kingston Vale St Jo 85-94; rtd 99. *6 Wristland Road, Watchet TA23 0DH* Tel (01984) 634378 E-mail FreemMic@aol.com

FREEMAN, Michael Curtis. b 51. Lanc Univ BA72 Liv Hope Univ Coll MA96 PhD05. Cuddesdon Coll 72. **d** 75 **p** 76. C Walton St Mary *Liv* 75-78; C Hednesford *Lich* 78-81; TV Solihull *Birm* 81-86; V Yardley Wood 86-90; V Farnworth *Liv* 90-03; AD Widnes 02-03; P-in-c Blundellsands St Mich from 03; P-in-c Gt Crosby All SS from 05. *St Michael's Vicarage, 41 Downhills Road, Liverpool L23 8SJ* Tel 0151-924 9905 E-mail mcfreem@btinternet.com

FREEMAN, Michael Raymond. b 58. Chu Coll Cam BA80 MA84 Ox Univ BA87. St Steph Ho Ox 85. **d** 88 **p** 89. C Clifton All SS w St Jo *Bris* 88-92; TV Elland *Wakef* 92-01; V Horninglow *Lich* from 01; RD Tutbury from 10. *Horninglow Vicarage, 14 Rolleston Road, Burton-on-Trent DE13 0JZ* Tel (01283) 568613 E-mail cft-rfreeman@supanet.com

FREEMAN, Preb Pamela Mary. b 45. WMMTC 83. dss 86 **d** 87 **p** 94. Cannock *Lich* 86-88; Par Dn 87-88; Min for Deaf (Salop Adnry) 88-95; Par Dn Shelton and Oxon 88-94; C 94-95; V Stafford 95-00; P-in-c High Offley and Norbury 00-02; R Adbaston, High Offley, Knightley, Norbury etc 02-10; Preb Lich Cathl 07-10; rtd 10; Perm to Offic *Lich* from 11; Chapl Severn Hospice from 11. *14 Meadow Close, Trentham Road, Wem, Shrewsbury SY4 5HP* Tel (01939) 234672 E-mail p.m.freeman@btinternet.com

FREEMAN, Peter Cameron Jessett. b 41. **d** 05 **p** 06. OLM Sturry w Fordwich and Westbere w Hersden *Cant* 05-11; rtd 11; Perm to Offic *Cant* from 11. *29 Cedar Road, Sturry, Canterbury CT2 0HZ*

FREEMAN, Philip Martin. b 54. Westcott Ho Cam 76. **d** 79 **p** 80. C Stanley *Liv* 79-82; C Bromborough *Ches* 82-84; V Runcorn H Trin and Chapl Halton Gen Hosp 84-91; R Ashton-upon-Mersey St Martin 91-96; SSF 96-06; Perm to Offic *Sarum* 96-99; *Birm* 98-99; *Lon* 99-02; *Ely* 02-05; *S'wark* 05-07; Asst Chapl HM Pris Birm 98-99; Chapl Barts and The Lon NHS Trust 00-02 and 05-08; Chapl Guy's and St Thos' NHS Foundn Trust 05-08; Chapl Univ Coll Lon Hosps NHS Foundn Trust from 08; Hon C

Smithfield St Bart Gt *Lon* from 06. *Flat 1, 48 Huntley Street, London WC1E 6DD* Tel (020) 7419 9095 Mobile 07985-512436 E-mail martin.freeman@uclh.nhs.uk

FREEMAN, Philip Michael. b 25. Jes Coll Cam BA50 MA54. Qu Coll Birm 50. **d** 52 **p** 53. C Gainsborough All SS *Linc* 52-58; V Messingham 58-65; V Goxhill 65-66; P-in-c Bottesford w Ashby 66-73; TR 73-75; P-in-c Warwick St Nic *Cov* 75-76; TV Warwick 77-87; P-in-c Claverdon w Preston Bagot 87-90; rtd 90; Perm to Offic *Cov* from 90. *38 Cocksparrow Street, Warwick CV34 4ED* Tel (01926) 411431 E-mail p.m.freeman@btinternet.com

FREEMAN, Richard Alan. b 52. Ripon Coll Cuddesdon. **d** 83 **p** 84. C Crayford *Roch* 83-86; V Slade Green 86-94; R Eynsford w Farningham and Lullingstone 94-01; P-in-c Shoreham from 01; Chapl St Mich Sch Otford from 01. *The Vicarage, Station Road, Shoreham, Sevenoaks TN14 7SA* Tel (01959) 522363 E-mail richard.freeman@diocese-rochester.org

✠**FREEMAN, The Rt Revd Robert John.** b 52. St Jo Coll Dur BSc74 Fitzw Coll Cam BA76 MA. Ridley Hall Cam 74. **d** 77 **p** 78 **c** 11. C Blackpool St Jo *Blackb* 77-81; TV Chigwell *Chelmsf* 81-85; V Leic Martyrs 85-99; Hon Can Leic Cathl 94-03; RD Christianity S 95-98; Nat Adv in Evang 99-03; Lic to Offic *Leic* 99-03; Adn Halifax *Wakef* 03-11; Suff Bp Penrith *Carl* from 11. *Holm Croft, 13 Castle Road, Kendal LA9 7AU* Tel (01539) 727836 Fax 734380 E-mail bishop.penrith@carlislediocese.org.uk

FREEMAN, Rodney. *See* FREEMAN, William Rodney

FREEMAN, Rosemary. b 47. **d** 03 **p** 04. NSM Madeley *Heref* from 03. *5 Rowley Close, Madeley, Telford TF7 5RR* Tel (01952) 583460

FREEMAN, Terence. b 40. Wells Th Coll 67. **d** 70 **p** 71. C Hanham *Bris* 70-75; C Cockington *Ex* 75-77; R Sampford Spiney w Horrabridge 77-89; V Wembury 89-08; rtd 08. *85 Blackstone Close, Plymouth PL9 8UW* E-mail revkarl.freeman@lineone.net

FREEMAN, William Rodney. b 35. Ch Coll Cam MA63 FCA73. **d** 95 **p** 96. OLM Chelmondiston and Erwarton w Harkstead *St E* 95-05; rtd 05; Perm to Offic *St E* from 05. *Lavender Cottage, Harkstead, Ipswich IP9 1BN* Tel (01473) 328381 E-mail revrod@lavcot.freeserve.co.uk

FREESTONE, Anne Elizabeth. b 52. Bp Otter Coll Chich CertEd73 Coll of Ripon & York St Jo MA00. NEOC 04. **d** 07 **p** 08. NSM Middleton-in-Teesdale w Forest and Frith *Dur* from 07. *22 Birch Road, Barnard Castle DL12 8JR* Tel (01833) 631018 Mobile 07939-964011 E-mail silverbirch22@hotmail.com

FREETH, Barry James. b 35. Birm Univ BA60. Tyndale Hall Bris 60. **d** 62 **p** 64. C Selly Hill St Steph *Birm* 62-63; C Birm St Jo Ladywood 63-71; Chapl RAF 71-75; P-in-c Crudwell w Ashley *Bris* 75-81; P-in-c Lanreath *Truro* 81-84; R 84-87; P-in-c Pelynt 81-84; V 84-87; R Harvington and Norton and Lenchwick *Worc* 87-93; V Ramsden, Finstock and Fawler, Leafield etc *Ox* 93-99; rtd 99; Perm to Offic *Derby* 99-03 and *Ox* from 08. *The Vicarage, High Street, Cropredy, Banbury OX17 1NG* Tel (01295) 750980

FREETH, John Stanton. b 40. Selw Coll Cam BA62 MA66. Ridley Hall Cam 64. **d** 66 **p** 67. C Gillingham St Mark *Roch* 66-72; TV Heslington *York* 72-80; Chapl York Univ 72-80; TR Wynberg St Jo S Africa 83-93; Adn Athlone 88-93. *15 Wellington Road, Wynberg, 7800 South Africa* Tel (0027) (21) 761 0908 E-mail jill@pdg.co.za

FREETH, Mrs Patricia. b 48. Wycliffe Hall Ox BTh95. **d** 95 **p** 96. NSM Ramsden, Finstock and Fawler, Leafield etc *Ox* 95-99; TV Buxton w Burbage and King Sterndale *Derby* 99-03; V Shires' Edge *Ox* from 03; AD Deddington from 10. *The Vicarage, High Street, Cropredy, Banbury OX17 1NG* Tel (01295) 750980 Mobile 07947-436751 E-mail patfreeth@objn.freeserve.co.uk

FREMMER, Ludger. b 56. Ridley Hall Cam 02. **d** 04 **p** 05. C Mattishall w Mattishall Burgh, Welborne etc *Nor* 04-07; P-in-c Kibworth and Smeeton Westerby and Saddington *Leic* from 07. *The Rectory, 25 Church Road, Kibworth, Leicester LE8 0NB* Tel 0116-279 2294 Mobile 07753-213145 E-mail ludger.fremmer@tesco.net

FRENCH, Basil Charles Elwell. b 19. Edin Th Coll LTh44. **d** 45 **p** 46. C Falkirk *Edin* 45-46; C Bris St Aid 46-49; C Hendford *B & W* 49-51; V Ash 51-58; P-in-c Long Load 57-58; C Ndola N Rhodesia 59-60; Chapl Rhodesia and Nyasaland Railway Miss 60-61; P-in-c Arcadia and Cranbourne S Rhodesia 61-69; R Umvukwes 69-85; Adn Gt Dyke 80-85; rtd 85; Hon C Wrington w Butcombe *B & W* 85-88; Perm to Offic *B & W* 88-92 and *Ex* from 92. *9 Elmbridge Gardens, Exeter EX4 4AE* Tel (01392) 215933

FRENCH, Mrs Christine. b 68. Nottm Trent Univ PGCE05. EMMTC MA08 Qu Coll Birm MPhil09. **d** 09 **p** 10. C Keyworth and Stanton-on-the-Wolds and Bunny etc *S'well* from 09. *The Vicarage, 10 Moor Lane, Bunny, Nottingham NG11 6QX* Tel 0115-984 2407 E-mail clayton-french@live.com

FRENCH, Canon Clive Anthony. b 43. AKC70. St Aug Coll Cant 70. **d** 71 **p** 72. C Monkseaton St Mary *Newc* 71-73; Dio Youth Adv 73-76; Chapl RN 76-97; Dir of Ords RN 85-90; Chapl RN Coll Greenwich 95-97; R Cheam *S'wark* 97-06; TR Catford (Southend) and Downham 06-09; Hon Can S'wark Cathl 08-09;

rtd 09; Perm to Offic *S'wark* from 10. *17 Kingslea, Leatherhead KT22 7SN* Tel (01372) 375418

FRENCH, Daniel Alain. b 68. Kent Univ BSc91. St Jo Sem Wonersh BTh97. **d** 97 **p** 98. In RC Ch 97-01; P-in-c Aberdeen St Clem 03-08; V Salcombe and Malborough w S Huish *Ex* from 08. *The Vicarage, Devon Road, Salcombe TQ8 8HJ* Tel (01548) 842853

FRENCH, Canon Dendle Charles. b 29. Lon Univ BD56. ALCD55. **d** 56 **p** 57. C Gt Yarmouth *Nor* 56-63; Jamaica 63-66; V Sedgeford w Southmere *Nor* 66-71; P-in-c Gt Ringstead 66-67; R 67-71; TV Thetford 71-74; Chapl Hockerill Coll Bishop's Stortford 74-78; P-in-c St Paul's Walden *St Alb* 78-85; V 85-94; RD Hitchin 84-89; Hon Can St Alb 91-94; rtd 94; Chapl Glamis Castle 94-10. *4 Curtis Close, Collingham, Newark NG23 7QW* Tel (01636) 892217 E-mail dendle.french@talk21.com

FRENCH, Derek John. b 47. Man Univ BA03. Ripon Coll Cuddesdon 93. **d** 95 **p** 96. C Stand *Man* 95-98; TV E Farnworth and Kearsley 98-00; P-in-c Halliwell St Marg 00-09; P-in-c Ringley w Prestolee 06-09; P-in-c Elton St Steph 09-11; V from 11. *St Stephen's Vicarage, 44 Peers Street, Bury BL9 2QF* Tel 0161-764 9894 E-mail rev.delboy@talktalk.net

FRENCH, George Leslie. b 47. AIFST NE Lon Poly BSc70. S'wark Ord Course 86. **d** 89 **p** 90. NSM Reading St Barn *Ox* 89-99. *Hawthorne House, 2 Cutbush Close, Lower Earley, Reading RG6 4XA* Tel 0118-986 1886

FRENCH, Janet. b 54. Anglia Poly Univ MA05. EAMTC 99. **d** 02 **p** 03. C Thetford *Nor* 02-06; R Thrybergh *Sheff* 06-11; V Heaton Ch Ch w Halliwell St Marg *Man* from 11. *The Vicarage, 2 Towncroft Lane, Bolton BL1 5EW* Tel (01204) 840430 E-mail frenchrevj@hotmail.com

FRENCH, Janet Mary. *See* DRIVER, Janet Mary

FRENCH, Jonathan David Seabrook. b 60. Westcott Ho Cam 84. **d** 87 **p** 88. C Loughton St Jo *Chelmsf* 87-90; Chapl St Bede's Ch for the Deaf Clapham 90-92; C Richmond St Mary w St Matthias and St Jo *S'wark* 92-95; TV 96-03; V Downham St Barn 03-10; Chapl RAD 92-03; Dioc Adv for Min of Deaf and Disabled People *S'wark* 03-10; R Southwick *Chich* from 10. *The Rectory, 22 Church Lane, Southwick, Brighton BN42 4GB* Tel (01273) 592389 E-mail jo.nathan@btinternet.com

FRENCH, Ms Judith Karen. b 60. St D Coll Lamp BA89. St Steph Ho Ox 89. **d** 91 **p** 94. Par Dn Botley *Portsm* 91-94; C Bilton *Cov* 94-97; V Charlbury w Shorthampton *Ox* from 97; AD Chipping Norton from 07. *The Vicarage, Church Lane, Charlbury, Chipping Norton OX7 3PX* Tel (01608) 810286 E-mail vicar@stmaryscharlbury.co.uk

FRENCH, Julia. **d** 06 **p** 07. NSM Plympton St Maurice *Ex* from 06. *45 Lotherton Close, Plymouth PL7 1QQ*

FRENCH, Michael Anders. b 61. Ch Coll Cam BA83 MA87 Ridley Hall Cam BA91 Man Univ MA(Econ)96. **d** 92 **p** 93. C Norbury *Ches* 92-96; Chapl Univ Coll Ches 96-01; Chapl Geneva *Eur* 01-08; Dir Advocacy World Vision UK from 08; Perm to Offic *Ox* and *St Alb* from 09. *175 route de la Douane, F-01220 Sauverny, France* Tel (0041) (79) 668 7592 *or* 207 6814 E-mail m.french@bluewin.ch

FRENCH, Michael John. b 37. WEMTC 92. **d** 95 **p** 96. OLM Cheltenham St Pet *Glouc* 95-01; NSM 01-08; NSM N Cheltenham from 08. *8 Alexandria Walk, Cheltenham GL52 5LG* Tel (01242) 236661

FRENCH, Peter Robert. b 65. Man Univ BTh87. Qu Coll Birm 88. **d** 90 **p** 91. C Unsworth *Man* 90-93; C Bury Ch King w H Trin 93-95; V Bury Ch King 95-98; V Handsworth St Andr *Birm* 98-06; Sch Support Officer from 06. *Diocesan Office, 175 Harborne Park Road, Birmingham B17 0BH* Tel 0121-426 0400 E-mail pfrench@birmingham.anglican.org *or* peterfrench55@aol.com

FRENCH, Philip Colin. b 50. Sarum & Wells Th Coll 81. **d** 83 **p** 84. C Llansamlet *S & B* 83-86; P-in-c Waunarllwydd 86-87; V 87-97; P-in-c Swansea St Barn 97-98; V 98-07; rtd 08. *17 Corrymore Mansions, Sketty Road, Swansea SA2 0LQ* Tel (01792) 423984

FRENCH, Richard John. b 34. Open Univ BA82. Tyndale Hall Bris 62. **d** 64 **p** 65. C Rustington *Chich* 64-68; C Walton H Trin *Ox* 68-72; V Grove 72-99; rtd 99; Perm to Offic *Chich* from 01. *5 Green Meadows, The Welkin, Haywards Heath RH16 2PE* Tel (01444) 487842

FRENCH, Stephen Robert James. b 52. St Jo Coll Nottm. **d** 87 **p** 88. C Chell *Lich* 87-91; TV 91-94; V Wednesfield Heath 94-01; TV Hemel Hempstead *St Alb* 01-06; P-in-c Bugbrooke w Rothersthorpe *Pet* 06-10; P-in-c Kislingbury and Harpole 06-10; R Bugbrooke, Harpole, Kislingbury etc from 10. *The Rectory, Church Lane, Bugbrooke, Northampton NN7 3PB* Tel (01604) 830373 E-mail srjfrench@hotmail.co.uk

FRENCH, William Stephen. b 49. STETS 07. **d** 10 **p** 11. NSM Verwood *Sarum* from 10. *Hollow Tree House, Chalbury, Wimborne BH21 7ER* Tel (01258) 841061 Mobile 07771-560128 E-mail william.french4@btinternet.com

FRERE, Christopher Michael Hanbury. b 21. Roch Th Coll 65. **d** 67 **p** 68. C Spilsby w Hundleby *Linc* 67-71; V N Kelsey 71-76; V Cadney 71-76; P-in-c Aisthorpe w W Thorpe and Scampton

75-79; P-in-c Brattleby 75-79; R Fillingham 76-78; V Ingham w Cammeringham 76-78; RD Lawres 78-84; V Ingham w Cammeringham w Fillingham 79-86; R Aisthorpe w Scampton w Thorpe le Fallows etc 79-86; rtd 86; Perm to Offic *Linc* from 86. *164 Newark Road, North Hykeham, Lincoln LN6 8LZ* Tel (01522) 806326 E-mail cmh.frere@ntlworld.com

FRESHNEY, June. b 46. EMMTC 95. **d** 98 **p** 99. NSM Washingborough w Heighington and Canwick *Linc* 98-05; Asst Chapl St Barn Hospice Linc 03-05; P-in-c Caythorpe *Linc* from 05. *The Rectory, 45B Old Lincoln Road, Caythorpe, Grantham NG32 3EJ* Tel (01400) 272728 Mobile 07798-840015 E-mail revjune@supanet.com

FRESTON, John Samuel Kern. b 28. Lich Th Coll 70. **d** 72 **p** 73. C Walsall *Lich* 72-75; TV Trunch w Swafield *Nor* 75-77; TV Trunch 77-82; R W Winch 82-91; Chapl St Jas Hosp King's Lynn 82-85; Chapl Qu Eliz Hosp King's Lynn 85-90; rtd 91; Perm to Offic *Ely* and *Nor* from 91. *71 Howdale Road, Downham Market PE38 9AH* Tel (01366) 385936

FRETT, Daniel Calvin. b 60. Univ of S Carolina 85. NTMTC 95 Oak Hill Th Coll BA99. **d** 98 **p** 99. NSM Clerkenwell St Jas and St Jo w St Pet *Lon* 98-00; NSM Chelsea St Jo w St Andr 00-05; NSM Tulse Hill H Trin and St Matthias *S'wark* 05-08; NSM Cranleigh *Guildf* from 09. *3 Edgefield Close, Cranleigh GU6 8PX* Tel (01483) 275861 E-mail frettd@netscape.net

FRETWELL, Brian George. b 34. TD. CEng MIMechE. Chich Th Coll 79. **d** 81 **p** 82. C Bude Haven *Truro* 81-82; C Saltash 82-85; C Walthamstow St Sav *Chelmsf* 85-87; V Doncaster Intake *Sheff* 87-97; rtd 99. *55 Bankside, Woking GU21 3DZ* Tel (01483) 721182

FRETWELL, Cynthia Mary. b 37. EMMTC 90. **d** 91 **p** 94. Chapl Asst Doncaster R Infirmary 91-92; Chapl Asst Tickhill Road and St Cath Hosps 91-92; Chapl Asst Doncaster R Infirmary and Montagu Hosp NHS Trust 92-95; Chapl 95-96; rtd 96. *55 Bankside, Woking GU21 3DZ* Tel (01483) 721182

FREWIN, William Charles. b 46. Trin Coll Bris 84. **d** 86 **p** 87. C Southchurch H Trin *Chelmsf* 86-89; C Shrub End 89-91; R W Bergholt 91-00; P-in-c Gt Wakering w Foulness 00-07; P-in-c Barling w Lt Wakering 06-07; rtd 07. *95 Windermere Avenue, Ramsgate CT11 0QD*

FREY, Christopher Ronald. b 44. AKC69 Uppsala Univ BD73 MTh77. St Aug Coll Cant 69. **d** 70 **p** 71. C Addington *Ox* 70-72; Lic to Offic *Eur* 73-78; Chapl Stockholm w Uppsala 78-85; Can Brussels Cathl 81-85; Chapl Casterton Sch Lancs 85-89; Chapl Epsom Coll 89-91; Chapl Worksop Coll Notts 91-94; rtd 96. *Koriandergatan 42, 261 61 Landskrona, Sweden* Tel (0046) (418) 20953

FRIARS, Ian Malcolm George. b 50. Sarum & Wells Th Coll 83. **d** 85 **p** 86. C Norton *St Alb* 85-88; C Ramsey *Ely* 88-90; TV The Ramseys and Upwood 90-93; P-in-c Cottenham 93-94; R 94-01; P-in-c Long Melford *St E* 01-02; R Chadbrook from 02. *The Rectory, The Green, Long Melford, Sudbury CO10 9DT* Tel (01787) 310845 E-mail ianfriars@btinternet.com

FRIDD, Nicholas Timothy. b 53. Ch Ch Ox BA74 MA78. STETS 05. **d** 08 **p** 09. NSM Wells St Thos w Horrington *B & W* from 08. *Manor Farm, East Horrington, Wells BA5 3EA* Tel (01749) 679832 Mobile 07831-209240

FRIEND, Adam Lyndon David. b 76. St Martin's Coll Lanc BA98. Cranmer Hall Dur 99. **d** 02 **p** 03. C Witton *Ches* 02-05; V Over St Chad 05-10; Chapl St Luke's Cheshire Hospice 06-10; V Tarvin *Ches* from 10. *St Andrew's Vicarage, Church Street, Tarvin, Chester CH3 8EB* Tel (01829) 740354 E-mail friendie@talk21.com

FRIEND, Frederick James. b 41. BA. Oak Hill NSM Course. **d** 82 **p** 83. NSM Hughenden *Ox* 82-11; Perm to Offic from 11. *The Chimes, Cryers Hill Road, High Wycombe HP15 6JS* Tel (01494) 563168

FRIENDSHIP, Roger Geoffrey (John-Francis). b 46. ACII72. WMMTC 90. **d** 93 **p** 94. SSF 76-02; NSM Harborne St Faith and St Laur *Birm* 93-94; Asst Novice Guardian Hilfield Friary 94-97; Novice Guardian 97-99; Gen Sec SSF 99-01; C Clerkenwell H Redeemer and St Mark *Lon* 00-01; R Romford St Andr *Chelmsf* from 01; rtd 11. *22 The Old Fire Station, Eaglesfield Road, London SE18 3BT* Tel 07808-500717 (mobile) E-mail jff2209@yahoo.com

FRIGGENS, Canon Maurice Anthony. b 40. Sheff Univ BA65. Westcott Ho Cam 65. **d** 67 **p** 68. C Stocksbridge *Sheff* 67-70; C St Buryan, St Levan and Sennen *Truro* 70-72; R 72-84; RD Penwith 82-84; R St Columb Major w St Wenn 84-91; Dioc Dir of Ords 87-93; Hon Can Truro Cathl 87-00; V St Cleer 91-00; rtd 00; Perm to Offic *Ban* from 00; *Eur* from 01. *Tŷ Cernyw, Rhiw, Pwllheli LL53 8AF* Tel (01758) 780365

FRISWELL, Caroline Anne. b 52. St Mary's Coll Chelt BEd78 Sunderland Poly MA90 Dur Univ PhD99. Cranmer Hall Dur 06. **d** 09 **p** 10. NSM Greenside *Dur* from 09. *Westholme, Durham Moor, Durham DH1 5AH* Tel 0191-384 0191 E-mail caroline.friswell@btinternet.com

FRITH, Canon Christopher John Cokayne. b 44. Ex Coll Ox BA65 MA69. Ridley Hall Cam 66. **d** 68 **p** 69. C Crookes St Thos *Sheff* 68-71; C Rusholme H Trin *Man* 71-74; R Haughton

St Mary 74-85; R Brampton St Thos *Derby* 85-02; V Alvaston 02-09; Hon Can Derby Cathl 99-09; rtd 09. *Cover Point, Back Lane, Bredon, Tewkesbury GL20 7LH* Tel (01684) 773164 E-mail cjcfrith@gmail.com

FRITH, Mrs Gillian. b 43. EAMTC 99. **d** 02 **p** 03. NSM Chipping Ongar w Shelley *Chelmsf* 02-06; P-in-c Doddinghurst from 06. *The Rectory, Church Lane, Doddinghurst, Brentwood CM15 0NJ* Tel (01277) 821366 Mobile 07890-376779 E-mail g.frith@waitrose.com

FRITH, Jonathan Paul (Jonty). b 72. Jes Coll Cam BA94 MA97. Wycliffe Hall Ox 95. **d** 97 **p** 98. C Houghton *Carl* 97-00; Chapl Cranleigh Sch Surrey 00-04; C Crowborough *Chich* from 04. *1 Mardens, Myrtle Road, Crowborough TN6 1EY* Tel (01892) 662909 E-mail jp@jpfrith.freeserve.co.uk

FRITH, Richard John. b 77. Warwick Univ BA98 Sheff Univ MA99 Trin Hall Cam PhD04. Ripon Coll Cuddesdon BA10. **d** 11. C Ox St Mary Magd from 11. *24 Salford Road, Marston, Oxford OX3 0RY* Tel (01865) 791509 Mobile 07754-524206 E-mail richard.frith@ymail.com

✠**FRITH, The Rt Revd Richard Michael Cokayne.** b 49. Fitzw Coll Cam BA72 MA76. St Jo Coll Nottm 72. **d** 74 **p** 75 **c** 98. C Mortlake w E Sheen *S'wark* 74-78; TV Thamesmead 78-83; TR Keynsham *B & W* 83-92; Preb Wells Cathl 91-98; Adn Taunton 92-98; Suff Bp Hull *York* from 98. *Hullen House, Woodfield Lane, Hessle HU13 0ES* Tel (01482) 649019 Fax 647449 E-mail richard@bishop.karoo.co.uk

FRITZE-SHANKS, Miss Annette. Sydney Univ BA86 DipEd87 LLB89 Solicitor. SEITE 01. **d** 04 **p** 05. NSM Kilburn St Mary w All So and W Hampstead St Jas *Lon* 04-08; Perm to Offic from 08. *21A Kylemore Road, London NW6 2PS* Tel 07771-544201 (mobile) E-mail annettefritze-shanks@campbellhooper.com

FROGGATT, Mrs Alison. b 35. Dur Univ BA56 Bradf Univ MA79. NOC 96. **d** 98 **p** 98. NSM Bingley H Trin *Bradf* 98-02; rtd 02; Perm to Offic *Bradf* from 02. *2 Gilstead Hall, Bingley BD16 3NP* Tel (01274) 565716 E-mail alison.froggatt@bradford.anglican.org

FROGGATT, Mrs Elaine Muriel. b 43. **d** 00 **p** 01. OLM Skirwith, Ousby and Melmerby w Kirkland *Carl* 00-04; NSM Cross Fell Gp 04-10; rtd 10. *The Old Corn Mill, Blencarn, Penrith CA10 1TX* Tel (01768) 88757

FROGGATT, Peter Michael. b 65. St Hild Coll Dur BA86 PGCE88. Wycliffe Hall Ox BTh95. **d** 95 **p** 96. C Bebington *Ches* 95-00; V Rock Ferry from 00; RD Birkenhead from 10. *The Vicarage, St Peter's Road, Birkenhead CH42 1PY* Tel 0151-645 1622 or 643 1042 E-mail peter@froggatt.org.uk

FRONDIGOUN, Mrs Marjorie Elizabeth. b 46. Open Univ BA87 MSc94. **d** 08 **p** 09. OLM Cannock *Lich* 08-09; OLM Cannock and Huntington from 09. *12 Adamson Close, Cannock WS11 1TJ* Tel (01543) 571199 Mobile 07889-359358 E-mail elizabeth.frondigoun@btinternet.com

FROOM, Ian Leonard John. b 42. Sarum Th Coll 69. **d** 71 **p** 72. C Gillingham and Fifehead Magdalen *Sarum* 71-75; C Parkstone St Pet w Branksea and St Osmund 75-78; V Sedgley St Mary *Lich* 78-85; TV Weston-super-Mare Cen Par *B & W* 85-94; Perm to Offic 94-97; V Truro St Geo and St Jo 97-03; rtd 03; Perm to Offic *Truro* from 03. *11 Marlborough Crescent, Falmouth TR11 2RJ* Tel (01326) 311760

FROST, Alan Sydney. b 26. K Coll Lon BD50 AKC50. **d** 51 **p** 52. C Folkestone St Sav *Cant* 51-56; C Sneinton St Steph *S'well* 56-59; C Croydon Woodside *Cant* 60-63; Asst Chapl Mersey Miss to Seamen 63-66; rtd 91. *Address withheld by request*

FROST, David John. b 48. **d** 86 **p** 87. Hon C Upper Norwood All SS *S'wark* 86-89; C Battersea St Luke 90-94; V Shirley St Geo from 94. *St George's Vicarage, The Glade, Croydon CR0 7QJ* Tel (020) 8654 8747 Fax 8654 1102 E-mail revdfrost1@btinternet.com

FROST, Canon David Richard. b 54. Ridley Hall Cam 84. **d** 86 **p** 87. C Burgess Hill St Andr *Chich* 86-90; TV Rye 90-94; V Bexhill St Steph 94-10; RD Battle and Bexhill 06-10; TR Rye from 10; Can and Preb Chich Cathl from 10. *The Rectory, Gungarden, Rye TN31 7HH* Tel (01797) 222430 Mobile 07970-746545 E-mail david@drfrost.org.uk

FROST, Derek Charles. b 47. Lich Th Coll 69. **d** 71 **p** 72. C Woodley St Jo the Ev *Ox* 71-76; V Bampton w Clanfield 76-81; V Minster Lovell and Brize Norton 81-88; TV Upper Kennet *Sarum* 88-92; P-in-c Seend and Bulkington 92-97; P-in-c Poulshot 95-97; V Seend, Bulkington and Poulshot 97-01; V Derry Hill w Bremhill and Foxham 01-10; rtd 10. *Windrush House, 2 Church Corner, Whistley Road, Potterne, Devizes SN10 5LZ* Tel (01380) 736472

FROST, The Ven George. b 35. Dur Univ BA56 MA61. Linc Th Coll 57. **d** 60 **p** 61. C Barking St Marg *Chelmsf* 60-64; C-in-c Marks Gate CD 64-70; V Tipton St Matt *Lich* 70-77; V Penn 77-87; RD Trysull 84-87; Preb Lich Cathl 85-87; Adn Salop 87-98; V Tong 87-98; P-in-c Donington 97-98; Adn Lich and Can Res and Treas Lich Cathl 98-00; rtd 00; Perm to Offic *Lich* from 00. *23 Darnford Lane, Lichfield WS14 9RW* Tel (01543) 415109 E-mail frost151@btinternet.com

FROST, Jeremy James. b 74. New Coll Ox BA96 MA99. Wycliffe Hall Ox BA99. **d** 00 **p** 01. C Wellington All SS w Eyton *Lich* 00-04; Min Can and Prec Cant Cathl 04-09; Chapl Greenwich Univ from 09; Chapl RN Coll Greenwich from 09; Chapl Trin Coll of Mus from 09. *40 Vanburgh Park, London SE3 7AA* Tel (020) 8853 1969 E-mail jeremy@jamesfrost.fsnet.co.uk

✠**FROST, The Rt Revd Jonathan Hugh.** b 64. Aber Univ BD88 Nottm Univ MTh99 MSSTh91 FRSA06. Ridley Hall Cam 91. **d** 93 **p** 94 **c** 10. C W Bridgford *S'well* 93-97; Police Chapl Trent Division 94-97; R Ash *Guildf* 97-02; Tutor Local Min Progr 99-10; Can Res Guildf Cathl 02-10; Chapl Surrey Univ 02-10; Co-ord Chapl 08-10; Bp's Adv Inter-Faith Relns 07-10; Suff Bp Southampton *Win* from 10. *Bishop's House, St Mary's Church Close, Southampton SO18 2ST* Tel (023) 8067 2684 E-mail bishop.jonathan@winchester.anglican.org

FROST, Canon Julian. b 36. Bris Univ BA61 MA65 Lon Univ CertEd70 Solicitor 57. Clifton Th Coll 64. **d** 65 **p** 66. C Welling *Roch* 65-69; Hon C 70-73; Dep Dir Schs Coun RE Project Lanc Univ 73-78; V New Beckenham St Paul 78-01; Hon Can Roch Cathl 00-01; rtd 01; Perm to Offic *Blackb* from 01. *93 Scotforth Road, Lancaster LA1 4JN* Tel (01524) 841967 E-mail julian@canonfrost.plus.com

FROST, Michael John. b 42. Westmr Coll Ox TCert64. **d** 95 **p** 96. OLM Harwood *Man* from 95. *86 Harden Drive, Harwood, Bolton BL2 5BX* Tel (01204) 413596

FROST, Paul William. b 75. Sheff Univ BA97 Ox Univ PGCE98. Wycliffe Hall Ox MTh08. **d** 08 **p** 09. C Kettering Ch the King *Pet* from 08. *9 Churchill Way, Kettering NN15 5DP* Tel (01536) 485772 Mobile 07979-547279 E-mail p-frost@bigfoot.com *or* paul.frost@ctk.org.uk

FROST, Richard John. b 49. Ch Ch Coll Cant CertEd71 BA00. SWMTC 95. **d** 97 **p** 98. NSM Bideford, Northam, Westward Ho!, Appledore etc *Ex* 97-00; C 00-03; TV 03-09; rtd 09. *PO Box 171, Girne, Mersin, Turkey* Tel (0090) (392) 815 4329 E-mail richard.frost@talktalk.net

FROST, Ronald Andrew. b 48. Univ of S Carolina BTh81. Ridley Hall Cam 86. **d** 87 **p** 88. C Gt Wilbraham *Ely* 87-89; P-in-c Kimbolton 89-91; V 91-10; P-in-c Stow Longa 89-91; V 91-10; P-in-c Covington and Tilbrook 07-10; rtd 10. *41 Botany Road, Broadstairs CT10 3SA* Tel (01843) 869788 Mobile 07866-648493 E-mail ronfrostis@gmail.com

FROST, Stanley. b 37. Univ of Wales BSc61 Liv Univ MSc65 PhD68 MIBiol66 CBiol66 FAEB82. NOC 79. **d** 82 **p** 83. NSM Lower Kersal *Man* 82-87; NSM Patricroft 87-89; NSM Convenor *Man* 87-95; Lic Preacher 89-03; P-in-c Pittenweem and Elie and Earlsferry *St And* 03-04; rtd 04; Perm to Offic *Derby* from 04. *25 Somersall Park Road, Chesterfield S40 3LD* Tel (01246) 567184 E-mail stan.frost@homecall.co.uk

FROST, Preb William Selwyn. b 29. Wells Th Coll 61. **d** 62 **p** 63. C Cheddleton *Lich* 62-67; V Longdon-upon-Tern 67-81; R Rodington 67-81; RD Wrockwardine 77-84; Preb Lich Cathl 81-96; R Longdon-upon-Tern, Rodington, Uppington etc 81-84; R Whittington St Jo 84-86; C Trysull 86-89; TV Wombourne w Trysull and Bobbington 89-96; rtd 96; Perm to Offic *Heref* from 96. *Ty Ffos, Dilwyn, Hereford HR4 8HZ* Tel (01544) 318703

FROSTICK, Canon John George. b 23. Wells Th Coll 52. **d** 54 **p** 55. C Loughborough St Pet *Leic* 54-57; C Knighton St Mary Magd 57-58; V Frisby-on-the-Wreake w Kirby Bellars 58-71; V Shepshed 71-83; R Kirton w Falkenham *St E* 83-90; Hon Can Leic Cathl 80-83; rtd 90; Perm to Offic *Leic* from 91. *68 Melton Road, Barrow-upon-Soar, Loughborough LE12 8NX* Tel (01509) 620110

FROSTICK, Paul Andrew. b 52. Stockwell Coll of Educn CertEd73. Ripon Hall Ox 74. **d** 77 **p** 78. C Shepton Mallet *B & W* 77-80; TV Barton Mills, Beck Row w Kenny Hill etc *St E* 80-85; TV Mildenhall 85-86; TV Raveningham *Nor* 86-89; V Bottisham and P-in-c Lode and Longmeadow *Ely* 89-90; V Bottisham and Lode w Long Meadow 90-94; Hd RE Brittons Sch Romford 94-97; Hd RE The Grove Sch St Leonards 97-00; rtd 00; Assoc P Bexhill St Aug *Chich* from 99. *18 The Ridings, Bexhill-on-Sea TN39 5HU* Tel (01424) 218126 E-mail paul@frostickrev.freeserve.co.uk

FROUD, Andrew William. b 65. Mansf Coll Ox BA87 St Cath Coll Cam MPhil92. Westcott Ho Cam 90. **d** 93 **p** 94. C Almondbury w Farnley Tyas *Wakef* 93-96; P-in-c Wootton *Portsm* 96-00; R 00-01; V Thornton-le-Fylde *Blackb* 01-05; Chapl St Geo C of E Sch Blackpool 05-09; P-in-c Clitheroe St Mary from 09. *The Vicarage, Church Street, Clitheroe BB7 2DD* Tel (01253) 764467 E-mail andyfroud@googlemail.com

FROUDE (née WOOLCOCK), The Ven Christine Ann. b 47. ACIB73. S Dios Minl Tr Scheme 92. **d** 95 **p** 96. NSM Stoke Bishop *Bris* 95-99; Chapl United Bris Healthcare NHS Trust 99-01; P-in-c Shirehampton *Bris* 01-11; Dean Women's Min 00-11; Hon Can Bris Cathl 01-11; Adn Malmesbury from 11. *1 Orchard Close, Winterbourne, Bristol BS36 1BF* Tel (01454) 778366 E-mail christinefroude@lineone.net

FROWLEY, Peter Austin. b 32. CEng61 MIMechE61. WMMTC 82. **d** 84 **p** 85. NSM Tardebigge *Worc* 84-87; P-in-c 87-88; NSM Redditch St Steph 84-87; Hong Kong 88-92; V St Minver *Truro* 92-96; rtd 96; Perm to Offic *Ex* 96-07. *40 Sandhills Lane, Barnt Green, Birmingham B45 8NX* E-mail peter.frowley@virgin.net

FRY, Alison Jacquelyn. b 65. Newnham Coll Cam BA86 MA90 Hertf Coll Ox DPhil90 St Jo Coll Dur BA95. Cranmer Hall Dur 93. **d** 96 **p** 97. C Milton *B & W* 96-00; V Batheaston w St Cath from 00. *Batheaston Vicarage, Bannerdown Road, Batheaston, Bath BA1 7ND* Tel (01225) 858192 E-mail revajfry@tiscali.co.uk

FRY, Canon Barry James. b 49. K Alfred's Coll Win MA03 ACIB. Ripon Coll Cuddesdon 81. **d** 83 **p** 84. C Highcliffe w Hinton Admiral *Win* 83-87; V Southampton St Barn from 87; Hon Can Ruvuma Cathl Tanzania from 02. *St Barnabas' Vicarage, 12 Rose Road, Southampton SO14 6TE* Tel (023) 8022 3107

FRY, David William. b 51. St Jo Coll Nottm. **d** 08 **p** 09. C Heeley and Gleadless Valley *Sheff* 08-10; V Ardsley from 10. *Christ Church Vicarage, Doncaster Road, Barnsley S71 5EF* Tel (01226) 785069 E-mail davefry@talktalk.net

FRY, Mrs Florence Marion. b 24. WMMTC 87. **d** 88 **p** 94. Chapl and Welfare Officer to the Deaf 70-94; Chapl Cov Cathl 88-94; Chmn Cov Coun of Chs 88-91; rtd 94; Perm to Offic *St Alb* from 96. *37 Grace Gardens, Bishop's Stortford CM23 3EU* Tel (01279) 652315

FRY, Canon James Reinhold. b 30. St Cuth Soc Dur BSc53 MA70 Kent Univ MA04 Lambeth STh90. Oak Hill Th Coll 55. **d** 57 **p** 58. C Bromley St Jo *Roch* 57-60; V Deptford St Luke *S'wark* 60-66; V Chalk *Roch* 66-97; RD Gravesend 81-91; Hon Can Roch Cathl 87-97; rtd 97; Perm to Offic *Roch* from 99 and *Cant* from 00. *67 Park Lane, Birchington CT7 0AU* Tel (01843) 843423 Fax 845376 E-mail j.fry3@btinternet.com

FRY, Lynn Jane. b 60. **d** 03 **p** 04. OLM A W Harling, Bridgham w Roudham, Larling etc *Nor* from 03. *40 White Hart Street, East Harling, Norwich NR16 2NE* Tel (01953) 717423 E-mail fryfam@talktalk.net

FRY, Marion. *See* FRY, Mrs Florence Marion

FRY, Michael John. b 59. Nottm Univ BA80 Sheff Univ CQSW83 Cam Univ BA85. Westcott Ho Cam 83. **d** 86 **p** 87. C Upholland *Liv* 86-89; C Dovecot 89-91; TV St Luke in the City from 91. *2 Minster Court, Liverpool L7 3QB* Tel 0151-709 9665

FRY, Nigel. b 49. Kent Univ BA95 Cant Ch Ch Univ MA06. SEITE 97. **d** 00 **p** 01. NSM Len Valley *Cant* 00-03; C Hollingbourne and Hucking w Leeds and Broomfield 03-11; P-in-c from 11; Chapl HM Pris E Sutton Park 02-10. *The Vicarage, Upper Street, Hollingbourne, Maidstone ME17 1UJ* Tel (01622) 880243 Mobile 07768-053400 E-mail nigel.fry1@btinternet.com

FRY, Nigel Edward. b 57. St Jo Coll Nottm 91. **d** 93 **p** 94. C Wellingborough All Hallows *Pet* 93-96; R Peakirk w Glinton and Northborough 96-05; V Pet Ch Carpenter from 05. *The Vicarage, Chestnut Avenue, Peterborough PE1 4PE* Tel (01733) 567140 E-mail enfrys@gmail.com

FRY, Roger Joseph Hamilton. b 29. Em Coll Cam BA52 MA56. Clifton Th Coll 52. **d** 54 **p** 55. C Walcot *B & W* 54-57; C Grassley *Derby* 57-61; P-in-c Bowling St Bart and St Luke *Bradf* 61-65; V Bowling St Jo 61-87; V Ingleton w Chapel le Dale 87-95; rtd 95; Perm to Offic *Bradf* from 95. *5 Margerison Crescent, Ilkley LS29 8QZ* Tel (01943) 608738

FRYDAY, Canon Barbara Yvonne. b 47. Ch of Ireland Tr Coll TCert67. CITC 90. **d** 92 **p** 93. NSM Cashel w Magorban, Tipperary, Clonbeg etc *C & O* 93-96; C Kilcooley w Littleon, Crohane and Fertagh 96-99; I 99-07; I Clonmel w Innislounagh, Tullaghmelan etc from 07; Can Ossory Cathl from 03; Warden of Readers from 08. *The Rectory, 7 Linden Lea, Silversprings, Clonmel, Co Tipperary, Republic of Ireland* Tel and fax (00353) (52) 618 7464 Mobile 86-275 0735 E-mail frydayb@gmail.com

FRYER, Alison Jane. *See* BOWNASS, Alison Jane

FRYER, Mrs Jenifer Anne. b 43. NOC 89. **d** 92 **p** 94. Par Dn Ecclesfield *Sheff* 92-94; C 94-95; Asst Chapl Cen Sheff Univ Hosps NHS Trust 93-96; Chapl Weston Park Hosp Sheff 94-96; Chapl Asst N Gen Hosp NHS Trust Sheff 96-04; Chapl Asst Sheff Teaching Hosps NHS Foundn Trust 04-07; rtd 07; Perm to Offic *Sheff* from 07. *5 Nursery Drive, Ecclesfield, Sheffield S35 9XU* Tel 0114-246 1027 E-mail jeni fryer@talktalk.net

FRYER, Michael Andrew. b 56. St Jo Coll Nottm 88. **d** 90 **p** 91. C Hull St Martin w Transfiguration *York* 90-95; V Kingston upon Hull St Aid Southcoates from 95; AD E Hull from 06. *St Aidan's Vicarage, 139 Southcoates Avenue, Hull HU9 3HF* Tel (01482) 374403 E-mail mick@staidans.org.uk

FRYER-SPEDDING, Mrs Clare Caroline. b 47. St Aid Coll Dur BA69. LCTP 06. **d** 09 **p** 10. NSM Binsey *Carl* from 09. *West Mirehouse, Underskiddaw, Keswick CA12 4QE* E-mail cfs@mirehouse.com

FUDGE, Prof Erik Charles. b 33. Ch Coll Cam BA55 MA59 Southn Univ CertEd58 Cam Univ PhD68. Ox Min Course 91. **d** 93 **p** 94. NSM Wokingham St Sebastian *Ox* from 93. *4 South Close, Wokingham RG40 2DJ* Tel 0118-978 6081

FUDGER, David John. b 53. Sheff Univ MMin96. K Coll Lon 73 Coll of Resurr Mirfield 76. **d** 77 **p** 78. C Sutton in Ashfield St Mary *S'well* 77-80; P-in-c Duston *Pet* 80-82; V Radford All So w Ch Ch and St Mich *S'well* 82-91; Min Bermondsey St Hugh CD *S'wark* 91-97; P-in-c Blackheath Ascension 97-04; Hon PV S'wark Cathl 91-01; P-in-c Mansfield SS Pet and Paul *S'well* from 04. *The Vicarage, Lindhurst Lane, Mansfield NG18 4JE* Tel (01623) 642546 *or* tel and fax 640250 E-mail revfudger@mistral.co.uk

FUDGER, Michael Lloyd. b 55. K Coll Lon BD77 AKC77. Coll of Resurr Mirfield 77. d 78 p 79. C Weston Favell *Pet* 78-82; C Pet H Spirit Bretton 82-84; V Irchester 84-90; TV Darnall-cum-Attercliffe *Sheff* 90-96; TV Attercliffe, Darnall and Tinsley 96-97; TR 97-03; TR Attercliffe and Darnall 03-05; V 05-06; Chapl Nine o'Clock Community 04-06; RD Attercliffe 91-96; Hon Can Sheff Cathl 00-06; R Bedford St Pet w St Cuth *St Alb* from 06. *St Peter's Rectory, 36 De Parys Avenue, Bedford MK40 2TP* Tel (01234) 354543 E-mail fudgerml@yahoo.co.uk

FULFORD, Stephen James. b 79. CCC Cam BA00 MA04. Ridley Hall Cam 01. d 04 p 05. C Old Catton *Nor* 04-07; Hon Chapl St Jo Coll Nottm from 08. *1 Peache Way, Chilwell Lane, Bramcote, Nottingham NG9 3DX* Tel 0115-922 0064 E-mail alisonfulford 1@hotmail.com

FULFORD, Susan Yvonne. b 61. d 03. OLM Pemberton St Mark Newtown *Liv* 03-07; OLM Marsh Green w Newtown from 08. *13 Mitchell Street, Wigan WN5 9BY* Tel (01942) 242369 E-mail sueandmike2003@yahoo.co.uk

FULHAM, Suffragan Bishop of. *Vacant*

FULKER, Lois Valerie. b 42. Keele Univ BA64. Cranmer Hall Dur 03. d 04 p 05. NSM Egremont and Haile *Carl* from 04. *3 Mill Farm, Calderbridge, Seascale CA20 1DN* Tel (01946) 841475 E-mail m.l.fulker@btinternet.com

FULLAGAR, Michael Nelson. b 35. SS Coll Cam BA57 MA61. Chich Th Coll 57. d 59 p 60. C Camberwell St Giles *S'wark* 59-61; C Northolt Park St Barn *Lon* 61-64; C Hythe *Cant* 64-66; R Chipata Zambia 66-70; P-in-c Livingstone 70-75; P-in-c Chingola 75-78; R Freemantle *Win* 78-87; P-in-c Westbury w Turweston, Shalstone and Biddlesden *Ox* 87-94; Chapl S Bucks NHS Trust 94-96; P-in-c Burwash Weald *Chich* 97-04; Perm to Offic from 04. *1 Roffrey Avenue, Eastbourne BN22 0AE* Tel (01323) 503212 E-mail michaelfullagar@aol.com

FULLALOVE, Brenda Hurst. *See* CRASTON, Mrs Brenda Hurst

FULLARTON, Mrs Heather Mary. b 42. Whitelands Coll Lon TCert63. Qu Coll Birm 90. d 92 p 94. Par Dn Colwich w Gt Haywood *Lich* 92-94; C 94-97; P-in-c Swindon and Himley 97-01; V Prees and Fauls 01-02; rtd 02; Perm to Offic *Sarum* from 03. *3 Rivers Arms Close, Sturminster Newton DT10 1DL* Tel (01258) 471895 Mobile 07703-379684 E-mail hfullarton@aol.com

FULLER, Alison Jane. b 61. St Andr Univ MTheol84. Edin Th Coll 85. d 87 p 94. C Selkirk *Edin* 87-89; C Melrose 87-89; C Galashiels 87-89; C Edin H Cross 89-92; Dn-in-c Edin St Columba 92-94; R 94-10; Chapl Edin Univ 96-00; P-in-c Leic Presentation from 10. *254 Kimberley Road, Leicester LE2 1LJ* Tel 0116-212 2973

FULLER, Christopher John. b 53. Chich Th Coll 85. d 87 p 88. C Swinton and Pendlebury *Man* 87-90; C Chiswick St Nic w St Mary *Lon* 90-92; V Hounslow W Gd Shep 92-96; V Stoke Newington St Faith, St Matthias and All SS 96-05; V Enfield St Geo from 05. *St George's Vicarage, 706 Hertford Road, Enfield EN3 6NR* Tel (01992) 762581

FULLER, Canon Graham Drowley. b 33. AKC58. d 59 p 60. C E Grinstead St Swithun *Chich* 59-62; C Coulsdon St Andr *S'wark* 62-64; Chapl RN 64-68; V Battersea St Luke *S'wark* 68-75; V S Stoneham *Win* 75-90; R Eversley 90-96; Bp's Ecum Officer 84-95; Hon Can Win Cathl 93-96; rtd 96; Perm to Offic *Portsm* from 03. *Brookside Dairy, Nunnery Lane, Newport PO30 1YR* Tel (01983) 525976 E-mail teazle@metronet.co.uk

FULLER, Canon John James. b 38. SS Coll Cam BA63 SS Coll Cam MA66. Chich Th Coll 63 Union Th Sem (NY) STM64. d 65 p 66. C Westmr St Steph w St Jo *Lon* 65-71; Tutor Cuddesdon Coll 71-75; Tutor Ripon Coll Cuddesdon 75-77; Prin S Dios Minl Tr Scheme 77-96; Can and Preb Sarum Cathl 83-96; V Wheatley w Forest Hill and Stanton St John *Ox* 96-97; TR Wheatley 97-03; rtd 03. *11 Ratcliffs Garden, Shaftesbury SP7 8HJ* Tel (01747) 850079

FULLER, Matthew John. b 74. Birm Univ BA95 PGCE96. Oak Hill Th Coll BA05. d 05 p 06. C St Helen Bishopsgate w St Andr Undershaft etc *Lon* from 05. *61 Monkton Street, London SE11 4TX* Tel (020) 7735 2494 Mobile 07903-045667 E-mail matt@thebibletalks.org

FULLER, Michael George. b 46. Chich Th Coll 90. d 92 p 93. C Fulham All SS *Lon* 92-94; C Kensington St Mary Abbots w St Geo 94-06; V Holland Park from 06; Dir Post-Ord Tr Kensington Area 94-99; Bp Kensington's Liaison Officer to Metrop Police from 99. *2 Aubrey Walk, London W8 7JG* Tel 020-7727 9486 Mobile 07980-932403 E-mail frmichael@stgeorgescampdenhill.co.uk

FULLER, Canon Michael Jeremy. b 63. Worc Coll Ox BA85 MA89 DPhil89 Qu Coll Cam BA91. Westcott Ho Cam 89. d 92 p 93. C High Wycombe *Ox* 92-95; C Edin St Jo 95-00; Prin

TISEC 00-02; Min Development Officer from 02; Can St Mary's Cathl from 00. *28 Blackford Avenue, Edinburgh EH9 2PH* Tel 0131-667 7273 *or* 220 2272 Fax 220 2294 E-mail michaelf@scotland.anglican.org

FULLER, Canon Terence James. b 30. Bris Univ BA55. Clifton Th Coll 55. d 56 p 57. C Uphill *B & W* 56-60; V Islington St Jude Mildmay Park *Lon* 60-67; V Southgate *Chich* 67-80; R Stoke Climsland *Truro* 80-95; RD Trigg Major 85-91; P-in-c Lezant w Lawhitton and S Petherwin w Trewen 93-95; Hon Can Truro Cathl 94-96; rtd 96; Perm to Offic *Truro* from 96. *9 Westover Road, Callington PL17 7EW* Tel (01579) 384958

FULLERTON, Hamish John Neville. b 45. Ball Coll Ox BA68 MA73. S'wark Ord Course 76. d 79 p 80. Hd English Abp Tenison's Sch Kennington 79-88; Hon C Clapham Old Town *S'wark* 79-82; Perm to Offic 82-89; Hon C Brixton Road Ch Ch 89-91; C Streatham Ch Ch 91-96; C Purley St Mark 96-98; Asst P Tooting St Aug 98-01; Perm to Offic from 03. *Flat 4, 21 Offerton Road, London SW4 0DJ* Tel (020) 7622 7890

FULLJAMES, Mrs Janet Kathleen Doris. b 43. Open Univ BA79 Birm Univ MA93. Qu Coll Birm 85. d 87 p 94. Par Dn Harborne St Pet *Birm* 87-93; Par Dn Smethwick SS Steph and Mich 93-94; C 94-95; C Smethwick Resurr 95-98; P-in-c Dudley St Thos and St Luke *Worc* 98-04; P-in-c Dudley St Jo 98-04; rtd 04; Perm to Offic *B & W* from 04. *12 Obridge Road, Taunton TA2 7PX* Tel (01823) 333585

FULLJAMES, Michael William. b 36. OBE94. K Coll Lon AKC60. St Boniface Warminster 60. d 61 p 62. C Armley St Bart *Ripon* 63-64; C E Wells *B & W* 64-67; Chapl Mendip Hosp Wells 64-67; R Stanningley St Thos *Ripon* 67-73; Chapl St Aug Hosp Cant 73-88; St Martin's Hosp 82-88; RD W Bridge *Cant* 87-88; Chapl Rotterdam *Eur* 88-94; Sen Chapl Rotterdam Miss to Seamen 88-94; Sen Chapl Burrswood Chr Cen *Roch* 94-01; rtd 01; Perm to Offic *Cant* and *Roch* from 01. *40 Somner Close, Canterbury CT2 8LJ* Tel (01227) 766950 E-mail m.fulljames@gmail.com

FULLJAMES, Peter Godfrey. b 38. BNC Ox BA60 MA64 Birm Univ PhD91. Qu Coll Birm. d 62 p 63. C Mexborough *Sheff* 62-65; Chapl Union Chr Coll India 65-69; Asst Master Wednesfield High Sch Wolverhampton 69-71; Asst Master Moorside High Sch Werrington 71-79; NSM Nairobi St Mark Kenya 80-85; Asst Master Nairobi High Sch 80-85; Research Fell Qu Coll Birm 85-87; Tutor WMMTC 87-90; Vice-Prin 90-93; Tutor Qu Coll Birm 93-94; Tutor Crowther Hall CMS Tr Coll Selly Oak 94-00; Hon Lect Th Birm Univ 97-03; rtd 00; Perm to Offic *B & W* from 04. *12 Obridge Road, Taunton TA2 7PX* Tel (01823) 333585

FULTON, Miss Ann Elizabeth. b 47. SWMTC 01. d 04 p 05. NSM Kingston St Mary w Broomfield etc *B & W* 04-11; NSM W Monkton 10-11; NSM W Monkton w Kingston St Mary, Broomfield etc from 11. *The Vicarage, Kingston St Mary, Taunton TA2 8HW* Tel (01823) 451257 E-mail annfulton29@yahoo.co.uk

FULTON, John William. b 49. Ex Coll Ox BA71 BPhil72 MA75 MPhil79. Wycliffe Hall Ox 72. d 76 p 77. C Bexleyheath Ch Ch *Roch* 76-79; C Ealing Dean St Jo *Lon* 79-83; V Aldborough Hatch *Chelmsf* 83-87; Chapl Chantilly *Eur* 87-90; R Hepworth, Hinderclay, Wattisfield and Thelnetham *St E* from 90; RD Ixworth from 09. *The Rectory, Church Lane, Hepworth, Diss IP22 2PU* Tel and fax (01359) 250285

FUNNELL, Preb Norman Richard James. b 40. Univ of Wales (Lamp) BA64. Ripon Hall Ox 64. d 66 p 67. C Hackney *Lon* 66-70; Hon C 71-85; TV 85-93; R S Hackney St Jo w Ch Ch 93-08; Chapl St Joseph's Hospice 93-08; Preb St Paul's Cathl 05-08; rtd 08. *37 Brunel Quays, Great Western Village, Lostwithiel PL22 0JB* Tel (01208) 873867 Mobile 07966-238934 E-mail jamesfunnell@btinternet.com

FURBER, Mrs Jennifer Margaret. b 50. WEMTC 98. d 01 p 02. NSM Malvern Link w Cowleigh *Worc* 01-08; rtd 09. *3 Ravenswood, 23 Wimborne Road, Bournemouth BH2 6LZ* Tel (01202) 296886 E-mail jenny@furber.me.uk

FURBER, Peter. b 43. Ex Univ BA. Sarum & Wells Th Coll 83. d 85 p 86. C Stanmore *Win* 85-88; TV Basingstoke 88-95; C Ringwood 95-98; P-in-c Gt Malvern Ch Ch *Worc* 98-99; V 99-08; rtd 09. *3 Ravenswood, 23 Wimborne Road, Bournemouth BH2 6LZ* Tel (01202) 296886 E-mail peter@furber.me.uk

FURBEY, Mrs Linda Alice. b 49. Hockerill Coll of Educn CertEd70 Wolfs Coll Cam BEd71 Coll of Ripon & York St Jo MA03. NOC 00. d 03 p 04. NSM Crosspool *Sheff* 03-07 and from 08; Perm to Offic 07-08; Chapl Sheff Children's NHS Foundn Trust 08-10. *20 Crimicar Avenue, Sheffield S10 4EQ* Tel 0114-230 6356 E-mail linda.furbey1@btinternet.com

FURBY, Penelope. b 51. Middx Univ 06. NTMTC BA03. d 06 p 07. NSM Leigh-on-Sea St Aid *Chelmsf* from 06. *72A Cliffsea Grove, Leigh-on-Sea SS9 1NQ* Tel (01702) 711067 Mobile 07817-766513 E-mail penny.furby@btinternet.com

FURLONG, Andrew William Ussher. b 47. TCD BA69 Jes Coll Cam BA71. Westcott Ho Cam 70 CITC 72. d 72 p 73. C Dundela St Mark *D & D* 72-76; C Dublin St Ann w St Mark and

St Steph *D & G* 76-83; Zimbabwe 83-94; Adn W Harare 88-89; Can Harare 89-94; Asst Chapl Leeds Teaching Hosps NHS Trust 94-97; Dean Clonmacnoise *M & K* 97-02; I Trim and Athboy Gp 97-02; Prec Kildare Cathl 98-02. *12 Tubbermore Road, Dalkey, Co Dublin, Republic of Ireland* Tel (00353) (1) 285 9817 E-mail tiripo@gofree.indigo.ie

FURLONG (*née* **DAVIES**)**, Mrs Catharine Mary.** b 48. Philippa Fawcett Coll CertEd73. EMMTC 85. **d** 88 **p** 95. C Spalding *Linc* 88-92; Zimbabwe 92-94; C Gt w Lt Gidding and Steeple Gidding *Ely* 94-96; P-in-c 96-06; P-in-c Brington w Molesworth and Old Weston 96-06; P-in-c Leighton Bromswold 96-06; P-in-c Winwick 96-06; P-in-c Gt Gransden and Abbotsley and Lt Gransden etc from 06; Asst Chapl Hinchingbrooke Health Care NHS Trust from 06. *The Vicarage, 4 Webb's Meadow, Great Gransden, Sandy SG19 3BL* Tel (01767) 677227 E-mail catherinemfurlong@tiscali.co.uk

FURNESS, Barry Keith. b 47. Open Univ BSc93. **d** 04 **p** 05. OLM High Oak, Hingham and Scoulton w Wood Rising *Nor* 04-09; P-in-c Smallburgh w Dilham w Honing and Crostwight from 09; R from 11. *The Rectory, The Street, Honing, North Walsham NR28 9AB* Tel (01692) 536812 E-mail barry.furness@norwich.anglican.org

FURNESS, Christine Anne. b 51. Leic Coll of Educn CertEd73 Open Univ BA76 Man Univ MEd84 PhD91 Ches Coll of HE MTh02. NOC 99. **d** 02 **p** 03. C Offerton *Ches* 02-06; V Brinnington w Portwood from 06. *St Luke's Vicarage, Brinnington Road, Stockport SK5 8BS* Tel 0161-430 4164 Mobile 07771-601615 E-mail anne@afurness.co.uk

FURNESS, Dominic John. b 53. Bris Univ BA76. Ridley Hall Cam 82. **d** 84 **p** 85. C Downend *Bris* 84-88; V Stoke Hill *Guildf* 88-05; V Milford *Win* from 05; AD Lyndhurst from 08. *The Vicarage, Lymington Road, Milford on Sea, Lymington SO41 0QN* Tel (01590) 643289 E-mail dominic.furness@tiscali.co.uk

FURNESS, Edward Joseph. b 41. S'wark Ord Course 74. **d** 77 **p** 78. NSM S Lambeth St Steph *S'wark* 77-81; Warden Mayflower Family Cen Canning Town *Chelmsf* 82-96; P-in-c Aston St Jas *Birm* 96-00; V 00-05; rtd 05; Perm to Offic *Birm* from 05. *304 New Oscott Village, 25 Fosseway Drive, Birmingham B23 5GP* Tel 0121-377 5304

FURSE, Adrian Thomas. b 76. Bris Univ BA99 Univ of Wales (Swansea) MA01 Leeds Univ PhD06. St Steph Ho Ox 08. **d** 10 **p** 11. C Wistow *Leic* from 10. *2 Furnival Close, Fleckney, Leicester LE8 8DZ* Tel (0116) 240 3131 Mobile 07890-020849 E-mail adrian.t.furse@gmail.com

FURST, John William. b 41. Bris Sch of Min 81 Ripon Coll Cuddesdon. **d** 84 **p** 85. C Bris Ch the Servant Stockwood 84-88; V Hanham 88-94; Perm to Offic *Llan* 98-99; V Gosberton, Gosberton Clough and Quadring *Linc* 99-05; P-in-c Hasfield w Tirley and Ashleworth *Glouc* 05-06; rtd 06. *10 Wetherby Crescent, Lincoln LN6 8SX* Tel (01522) 684910 E-mail sandj.furst@btinternet.com

FUTCHER, Christopher David. b 58. Edin Univ BD80 Lon Univ MTh04. Westcott Ho Cam 80. **d** 82 **p** 83. C Borehamwood *St Alb* 82-85; C Stevenage All SS Pin Green 85-88; V 88-96; V St Alb St Steph 96-00; R Harpenden St Nic from 00. *The Rectory, 9 Rothamsted Avenue, Harpenden AL5 2DD* Tel (01582) 712202 *or* 765524 Fax 713646 E-mail cfutcher@toucansurf.com

FUTERS, Michael Roger. b 58. Trin & All SS Coll Leeds BEd80. St Jo Coll Nottm 82. **d** 85 **p** 86. C Narborough and Huncote *Leic* 85-87; C Spondon *Derby* 87-90; P-in-c Derby St Jas 90-95; TV Walbrook Epiphany 95-99; Hon C Derby St Mark 99-09; Community Development Officer Home Housing from 99; Hon C Chaddesden St Phil w Derby St Mark from 09. *3 St Pancras Way, Derby DE1 3TH* Tel (01332) 203075 E-mail michaelf@derwentliving.com

FYFE, Mrs Deirdre Bettina. b 44. STETS 05. **d** 07 **p** 08. NSM S Petherton w the Seavingtons *B & W* from 07. *The Beeches, Water Street, Seavington, Ilminster TA19 0QH* Tel (01460) 241977 E-mail d.alastairf@virgin.net

FYFE, Gordon Boyd. b 63. Aber Univ BD93 Edin Univ MTh95. TISEC 94. **d** 96 **p** 97. C Ayr *Glas* 96-99; C Maybole 96-99; C Girvan 96-99; R Airdrie and Coatbridge 99-09; Chapl to Primus 06-09; R Largs *Glas* from 09. *St Columba's Rectory, Aubrey Crescent, Largs KA30 8PR* Tel (01475) 673143 Mobile 07523-128493 E-mail gordon.fyfe@virginmedia.com

FYFE, Stewart John. b 69. City Univ BSc91. Ridley Hall Cam 03. **d** 05 **p** 06. C Barony of Burgh *Carl* 05-07 and 08-10; P-in-c Bolton from 10; P-in-c Crosby Ravensworth from 10; P-in-c Morland, Thrimby, Gt Strickland and Cliburn from 10. *The Vicarage, Morland, Penrith CA10 3AX* Tel (01931) 714620 Mobile 07985-900477 E-mail stewart.fyfe@btinternet.com

FYFFE, Robert Clark. b 56. Dundee Univ BD78 Napier Univ Edin MBA98. Edin Th Coll 74. **d** 79 **p** 80. C Edin St Jo 79-83; Youth Chapl *B & W* 83-87; Prov Youth Officer Scottish Episc Ch 87-92; R Perth St Jo *St And* 93-06; Co-ord Internat Angl Youth Network 88-92; Can St Ninian's Cathl Perth 96-06; Gen Sec CTBI from 06. *Bastille Court, 2 Paris Garden, London SE1 8ND* Tel (020) 7654 7254 Fax 7654 7222 E-mail gensec@ctbi.org.uk

FYFFE, Timothy Bruce. b 25. New Coll Ox MA54. Westcott Ho Cam 54. **d** 56 **p** 57. C Lewisham St Mary *S'wark* 56-60; Nigeria 60-68; TV Lowestoft St Marg *Nor* 69-80; Chapl HM Pris Blundeston 70-78; TV Tettenhall Regis *Lich* 80-85; Chapl Compton Hospice 85-87; rtd 90; NSM Wolverhampton St Andr *Lich* 88-10; Perm to Offic from 10. *40 Glentworth Gardens, Wolverhampton WV6 0SG* Tel (01902) 716510 E-mail tim@timfyffe.plus.com

FYLES, Gordon. b 39. Trin Coll Bris 76. **d** 77 **p** 78. C Islington St Mary *Lon* 77-81; Ext Sec BCMS 81-88; C Wimbledon Em Ridgway Prop Chpl *S'wark* 88-97; I Crinken *D & G* 97-04; rtd 04. *7 Shore Street, Hilton, Tain IV20 1XD* Tel (01862) 832131 E-mail gordonandyvonne@yahoo.co.uk

FYSH, Leslie David. b 35. Glouc Sch of Min 88. **d** 91 **p** 92. NSM Stonehouse *Glouc* 91-95; Asst Chapl Wycliffe Coll Glos 91-95; NSM W Walton *Ely* 95-00; Perm to Offic *Ely* from 00 and *Nor* from 08; PV Ely Cathl 03-06. *2 Waldens Barn, Chapel Road, Dersingham, King's Lynn PE31 6PN* Tel (01485) 542785

G

GABB-JONES, Adrian William Douglas. b 43. MRICS. Ripon Coll Cuddesdon 79. **d** 81 **p** 82. C Northolt Park St Barn *Lon* 81-84; C Ruislip St Martin 84-89; V Minster Lovell and Brize Norton *Ox* 89-03; V Minster Lovell from 03. *The Vicarage, Burford Road, Minster Lovell, Oxford OX29 0RA* Tel (01993) 776492

GABBADON, Kenneth Fitz Arthur. b 53. NOC 97. **d** 99 **p** 00. C Burnage St Marg *Man* 99-01; C Bury St Jo w St Mark 01-03; P-in-c Newton Heath 03-08; R 08-09; Chapl HM Pris Leeds from 09; P-in-c Clifford *York* from 09. *The Chaplaincy Department, HM Prison, Armley Jail, Gloucester Terrace, Armley, Leeds LS12 2TJ* Tel 0113-203 2704/5 *or* (01937) 541165 E-mail ken.gabbadon@hmps.gsi.gov.uk *or* kgabba7036@aol.com

GABLE, Michael David. b 70. Poly of Wales BEng92. St Mich Coll Llan BTh95. **d** 95 **p** 96. C Newton Nottage *Llan* 95-99; V Aberavon H Trin 99-01; TV Aberavon 01-05; P-in-c Rhydyfelin w Graig from 05; AD Pontypridd from 11. *St John's Vicarage, 28 Llantrisant Road, Graig, Pontypridd CF37 1LW* Tel (01443) 650336 E-mail michaelgable@hotmail.com

GABRIEL, Michael Hunt. b 29. BA. **d** 57 **p** 58. C Waterford Ch Ch *C & O* 57-60; C New Windsor H Trin *Ox* 60-62; C Albany Street Ch Ch *Lon* 62-63; R W and E Shefford *Ox* 63-67; C Hillingdon St Jo *Lon* 67-86; C Kingston Buci *Chich* 86-94; rtd 94. *Flat 1, 6 Dittons Road, Eastbourne BN21 1DN*

GADD, Alan John. b 44. Imp Coll Lon BSc65 PhD69 FRMetS67. S'wark Ord Course 68. **d** 71 **p** 72. Asst Chapl Lon Univ 71-72; Perm to Offic *S'wark* 73-91; C Battersea Park All SS 91-95; P-in-c 95-96; C Battersea Fields 96-05; rtd 05; Perm to Offic *S'wark* from 05. *24 Holmewood Gardens, London SW2 3RS* Tel (020) 8678 9977

GADD, Brian Hayward. b 33. Hatf Coll Dur BA54 DipdEd55. Glouc Sch of Min 82. **d** 85 **p** 87. NSM Cleobury Mortimer w Hopton Wafers etc *Heref* 85-98; rtd 98; Perm to Offic *Heref* from 99. *34 Lower Street, Cleobury Mortimer, Kidderminster DY14 8AB* Tel (01299) 270758

GADD, Bryan Stephen Andrew. b 56. Dur Univ BA Ox Univ CertEd. Chich Th Coll. **d** 81 **p** 82. C Newlyn St Pet *Truro* 81-86; R St Mawgan w St Ervan and St Eval 86-90; Chapl Summer Fields Sch Ox 90-02; Perm to Offic *Truro* 90-00; Chapl Southport Sen Sch Australia from 02. *Southport School, Winchester Street, Southport Qld 4215, Australia* Tel (0061) (7) 5531 9956 *or* 5531 9935 E-mail bsag@tss.qld.edu.au

GADEN, Timothy John. b 64. Melbourne Univ BA86 Monash Univ Aus PhD96. Melbourne Coll of Div BD90. **d** 91 **p** 91. Australia 91-96 and from 01; C Battersea St Mary *S'wark* 97; V 97-01; Dir Post-Ord Tr Kingston Area 99-01; R Camberwell St Jo from 01. *15 The Grove, Camberwell Vic 3124, Australia* Tel (0061) (3) 9889 6456 *or* 9882 4851 Fax 9882 0086 Mobile 41-911 4697 E-mail gaden@stjohnscamberwell.org.au

GADSBY, Julian Timothy David Moritz. b 74. K Coll Lon BA96 AKC96. Oak Hill Th Coll 02. **d** 04 **p** 05. C Chadwell *Chelmsf* 04-09; P-in-c Bucklebury w Marlston *Ox* from 09. *The Vicarage, Burdens Heath, Upper Bucklebury, Reading RG7 6SX* Tel (01635) 874441 E-mail j_gadsby@tiscali.co.uk

GAFFIN, Jennifer Clare. b 78. Mansf Coll Ox BA99 Man Univ MA00 Win Univ PhD06. Ripon Coll Cuddesdon 07. **d** 09 **p** 10. C Parkstone St Pet and St Osmund w Branksea *Sarum* from 09. *61 Felton Road, Poole BH14 0QR* Tel 07855-024789 (mobile) E-mail jennygaffin@hotmail.com

GAGE, Alan William. b 52. Univ of Wales (Cardiff) BMus72 PGCE73 Bris Univ MEd90. WEMTC 98. **d** 00 **p** 01. NSM Tuffley *Glouc* 00-08; NSM Hardwicke and Elmore w Longney 08-09. *Chadburn, 83 Dinglewell, Hucclecote, Gloucester GL3 3HT* Tel (01452) 614892
E-mail curatealan@blueyonder.co.uk

GAGE, Aëlla Rupert Fitzehardinge Berkeley. b 66. Reading Univ BEd92. Oak Hill Th Coll 98. **d** 00. C Muswell Hill St Jas w St Matt *Lon* 00-05; C Hadley Wood St Paul Prop Chpl 05-08; C Highgate Australia 08-10; C Fordham *Chelmsf* from 10. *The Rectory, Wood Lane, Fordham Heath, Colchester CO3 9TR* Tel (01206) 242112 Mobile 07796-475130
E-mail aella.gage@gmail.com

GAGE, Jennifer Anne. b 50. Girton Coll Cam MA75 Open Univ BA85 PhD05 Keele Univ PGCE86. ERMC 07. **d** 09 **p** 10. NSM Three Rivers Gp *Ely* from 09. *51 Henley Way, Ely CB7 4YH* Tel (01353) 664626 E-mail jennygage3@talktalk.net

GAGE, Canon Robert Edward. b 47. Whitman Coll Washington BA69. Cuddesdon Coll BA75 MA81. **d** 76 **p** 77. C Cheshunt *St Alb* 76-79; C Harpenden St Nic 79-81; V S Mymms 81-82; P-in-c Ridge 81-82; V S Mymms and Ridge 82-97; Prec and Can Res Wakef Cathl 97-05; Can Res Newc Cathl 05-09; rtd 09. *44 Warkworth Avenue, Whitley Bay NE26 3PS*
E-mail robertgage1@yahoo.co.uk

GAGEN, Mrs Valerie Elizabeth. b 52. Ripon Coll of Educn BEd75. NTMTC BA10. **d** 10 **p** 11. NSM N Hinckford *Chelmsf* from 10. *7 Raleigh Close, Sudbury CO10 1YF* Tel (01787) 371787 Mobile 07874-067371 E-mail valgagen@hotmail.com

GAINER, Canon Jeffrey. b 51. Jes Coll Ox BA73 MA77 Univ of Wales LLM94. Wycliffe Hall Ox 74. **d** 77 **p** 78. C Baglan *Llan* 77-81; V Cwmbach 81-85; V Tonyrefail w Gilfach Goch and Llandyfodwg 85-87; Dir NT Studies and Dir Past Studies St Mich Coll Llan 87-92; V Meidrim and Llanboidy and Merthyr *St D* from 92; AD St Clears from 03; P-in-c Abernant from 07; Cursal Can St D Cathl from 11. *The Vicarage, Meidrim, Carmarthen SA33 5QF* Tel (01994) 231378

GAINSBOROUGH, Jonathan Martin. b 66. SOAS Lon MA91 MSc95 PhD01. STETS MA10. **d** 10 **p** 11. NSM Barton Hill St Luke w Ch Ch and Moorfields *Bris* from 10. *21 Cotham Lawn Road, Bristol BS6 6DS*
E-mail martin.gainsborough@virgin.net

GAIR, Andrew Kennon. b 62. Westcott Ho Cam 88. **d** 91 **p** 92. C Clare w Poslingford, Cavendish etc *St E* 91-95; R Debden and Wimbish w Thunderley *Chelmsf* 95-06. *18-20 High Street, Wrentham, Beccles NR34 7HB*
E-mail andrew.gair@btinternet.com

✠**GAISFORD, The Rt Revd John Scott.** b 34. St Chad's Coll Dur BA59 MA76. **d** 60 **p** 61 **c** 94. C Audenshaw St Hilda *Man* 60-62; C Bramhall *Ches* 62-65; V Crewe St Andr 65-86; RD Nantwich 74-85; Hon Can Ches Cathl 80-86; Adn Macclesfield 86-94; Suff Bp Beverley (PEV) *York* 94-00; Asst Bp Ripon and Leeds 96-00; rtd 00; Perm to Offic *Ches* from 00 and *Man* from 04. *5 Trevone Close, Knutsford WA16 9EJ* Tel (01565) 633531 Mobile 07855-615469 E-mail jandg.gaisford@tiscali.co.uk

GAIT, Canon David James. b 48. BNC Ox BA71 BSc72 MA77 MSc83. Ridley Hall Cam 71. **d** 74 **p** 75. C Litherland St Paul Hatton Hill *Liv* 74-77; C Farnworth 77-80; V Widnes St Jo from 80; Chapl Widnes Maternity Hosp 86-90; Hon Can Liv Cathl from 05; AD Widnes from 07. *St John's House, Greenway Road, Widnes WA8 6HA* Tel 0151-424 3134
E-mail dave.gait@btinternet.com

GALANZINO, Diego. b 80. St Steph Ho Ox BTh11. **d** 11. C St Ives *Truro* from 11; C Halsetown from 11. *Mount Pleasant, Trerice Place, St Ives TR26 1AT*
E-mail diego@anotheranglicanblog.com

GALBRAITH, Alexander Peter James. b 65. Qu Coll Ox BA86 MA90. Wycliffe Hall Ox 87. **d** 90 **p** 91. C Southport Em *Liv* 90-94; C Mossley Hill St Matt and St Jas 94-97; V Kew from 97; Chapl Southport and Ormskirk NHS Trust 97-11. *20 Markham Drive, Kew, Southport PR8 6XR* Tel (01704) 547758

GALBRAITH, Jane Alexandra. **d** 95 **p** 96. NSM Kildare w Kilmeague and Curragh *M & K* 95-97; NSM Newbridge w Carnalway and Kilcullen 97-99; C Limerick *L & K* from 03. *50 Ballinvoher, Father Russell Road, Dooradoyle, Limerick, Republic of Ireland* Tel and fax (00353) (61) 302038
E-mail janeg@iolfree.ie

GALBRAITH, John Angus Frame. b 44. Sarum Th Coll 68. **d** 71 **p** 72. C Richmond St Mary *S'wark* 71-74; Chapl W Lon Colls 74-79; R S'wark H Trin w St Matt 79-95; V New Addington 95-02; Asst Chapl HM Pris Wandsworth 02-04; Chapl 04-09; rtd 09; Perm to Offic *S'wark* from 09. *35 Joseph Hardcastle Close, London SE14 5RN* Tel (020) 7635 3607
E-mail angus.galbraith@talktalk.net

GALBRAITH, Peter John. b 59. QUB BA MTh. CITC. **d** 85 **p** 86. C Knockbreda *D & D* 85-88; C Ballynafeigh St Jude 88-91; I Broomhedge *Conn* from 91. *Broomhedge Rectory, 30 Lurganure Road, Broughmore, Lisburn BT28 2TR* Tel (028) 9262 1229

GALE, Ms Charlotte. b 70. Leeds Univ BEng92 Nottm Univ MA00. St Jo Coll Nottm 98. **d** 01 **p** 02. C Whitnash *Cov* 01-05;

P-in-c Potters Green 05-08; P-in-c Lillington and Old Milverton from 08; C Leamington Spa H Trin from 08. *The Vicarage, Vicarage Road, Lillington, Leamington Spa CV32 7RH* Tel (01926) 424674 *or* 470449 E-mail charlotte.gale@tiscali.co.uk

GALE, Canon Christopher. b 44. ALCD67. **d** 68 **p** 69. C Balderton *S'well* 68-72; C Bilborough St Jo 72-75; P-in-c Colwick 75-78; V Radford St Pet 78-84; V Sherwood 84-98; AD Nottingham N 90-98; P-in-c Bulwell St Mary 98-02; R 02-07; Hon Can S'well Minster 03-07; rtd 08. *11 Cliff Road, Carlton, Nottingham NG4 1BS* Tel 0115-844 0209
E-mail rev.chrisgale@gmail.com

GALE, Colin Edward. b 49. Lon Univ PGCE74. St Jo Coll Nottm BTh73. **d** 79 **p** 80. C Hoole *Ches* 79-82; C Woodley St Jo the Ev *Ox* 82-87; V Clapham St Jas *S'wark* 87-96; V Sutton Ch Ch 96-05; R Burstow w Horne from 05. *The Rectory, 5 The Acorns, Smallfield, Horley RH6 9QJ* Tel (01342) 842224
E-mail revceg@aol.com

GALE, The Ven John. b 34. Univ of Wales (Lamp) 67. **d** 69 **p** 70. C Aberdare *Llan* 69-71; C Merthyr Dyfan 71-74; S Africa 74-00; R Walmer St Sav 74-82; R Knysna St Geo 82-00; Adn Knysna 93-00; Lic to Offic *St D* from 00. *3 Connacht Way, Pembroke Dock SA72 6FB* Tel and fax (01646) 622219

GALE, Keith George. b 44. St Jo Coll Lusaka 68 Sarum Th Coll 69. **d** 70 **p** 71. C Sheff St Cuth 70-77; P-in-c Brightside All SS 72-77; C Birm St Martin 77-81; C Dwangwa Malawi 81-83; R Lilongwe St Pet 83-93; Adn Lilongwe 89-92; TV Sampford Peverell, Uplowman, Holcombe Rogus etc *Ex* 94-09; rtd 09. *101 Chapel Street, Tiverton EX16 6BU* Tel (01884) 821879
E-mail keith@gale5.eclipse.co.uk

GALE, Ms Lucille Catherine. b 67. Sarum & Wells Th Coll 92. **d** 94 **p** 95. C Welling *S'wark* 94-97; Chapl Greenwich Univ 97-00; V Welling 00-09; Officer Lay Min and Miss from 09. *The Vicarage, 2 The Grove, West Wickham BR4 9JS*
E-mail lugale2@gmail.com *or* lu.gale@southwark.anglican.org

GALE, Peter Simon. b 56. Welsh Coll of Music & Drama 73 K Alfred's Coll Win PGCE78. St Mich Coll Llan BD83. **d** 83 **p** 84. C Caerphilly *Llan* 83-89; Chapl RN 89-93; V Ystrad Rhondda w Ynyscynon *Llan* 93-07; V Pont Rhondda from 07. *St Stephen's Vicarage, Ystrad, Pentre CF41 7RR* Tel (01443) 434426

GALES, Alan. b 29. Sarum Th Coll 56. **d** 59 **p** 60. C Greenside *Dur* 59-60; C Peterlee 60-63; Ind Chapl 60-70; V Marley Hill 63-94; Asst Chapl HM Pris *Dur* 74-81; rtd 94. *46 Corsair, Whickham, Newcastle upon Tyne NE16 5YA* Tel 0191-488 7352

GALES, Bernard Henry. b 27. Lon Univ BSc(Econ)51 Open Univ BA02. Wells Th Coll 62. **d** 64 **p** 65. C Sholing *Win* 64-67; C Fordingbridge w Ibsley 67-71; C S Molton w Nymet St George *Ex* 71-73; C Thelbridge 73-77; P-in-c 77-78; P-in-c Creacombe 77-78; P-in-c W w E Worlington 77-78; P-in-c Meshaw 77-78; P-in-c Witheridge 77-78; C Witheridge, Thelbridge, Creacombe, Meshaw etc 79-80; R Bow w Broad Nymet 80-93; V Colebrooke 80-93; R Zeal Monachorum 80-93; RD Cadbury 90-93; rtd 93; Perm to Offic *Ex* from 93. *8 Old Rectory Gardens, Morchard Bishop, Crediton EX17 6PF* Tel (01363) 877601

GALES, Simon Richard. b 59. CEng87 MICE87 Jes Coll Cam BA81 MA84. Wycliffe Hall Ox 91. **d** 93 **p** 94. C Houghton *Carl* 93-97; V Lindow *Ches* from 97. *St John's Vicarage, 137 Knutsford Road, Wilmslow SK9 6EL* Tel (01625) 583251 *or* 586329
E-mail simon@srgales.freeserve.co.uk

GALILEE, Canon George David Surtees. b 37. Oriel Coll Ox BA60 MA64. Westcott Ho Cam 61. **d** 62 **p** 63. C Knighton St Mary Magd *Leic* 62-67; V Stocking Farm 67-69; Tutor Westcott Ho Cam and Homerton Coll 69-71; V Sutton *Ely* 71-80; P-in-c Addiscombe St Mildred *Cant* 80-81; V 81-84; V Addiscombe St Mildred *S'wark* 85-95; Can Res and Chan Blackb Cathl 95-04; rtd 04; Perm to Offic *Blackb* from 04. *Ivy Hatch, 25 Ryburn Avenue, Blackburn BB2 7AU* Tel (01254) 671540 Fax 689666

GALLAGHER, Adrian Ian. b 43. CITC 89. **d** 92 **p** 93. C Drumachose *D & R* 92-96; I Camus-juxta-Bann 96-00; TV Langley and Parkfield *Man* 00-09; rtd 09; Perm to Offic *Man* from 09. *22 Ashness Drive, Middleton, Manchester M24 5PJ* Tel 0161-654 9470 Mobile 07749-719028

GALLAGHER, Mrs Barbara Jean. b 53. Ex Univ BA73 Coll of Ripon & York St Jo PGCE76 Open Univ MA99. **d** 08 **p** 09. OLM Creeting St Mary, Creeting St Peter etc *St E* from 08. *Primrose Cottage, Forward Green, Stowmarket IP14 5HJ* Tel (01449) 711337 E-mail barbarajg@btopenworld.com

GALLAGHER, Canon Ian. BTh. **d** 90 **p** 91. C Annagh w Drumgoon, Ashfield etc *K, E & A* 90-93; I Drumcliffe w Lissadell and Munninane 93-01; Can Elphin Cathl 97-01; Dioc Sec (Elphin and Ardagh) 97-01; Preb Mulhuddart St Patr Cathl Dublin 98-01; I Stillorgan w Blackrock *D & G* from 01. *The Rectory, St Brigid's Church Road, Stillorgan, Blackrock, Co Dublin, Republic of Ireland* Tel (00353) (1) 288 1091 Fax 278 1833 Mobile 86-811 9544
E-mail stillorgan@dublin.anglican.org

GALLAGHER, Ian Míceál. b 71. Oberlin Coll (USA) BMus93 Duke Univ (USA) MA95. Westcott Ho Cam 06. **d** 08. C Walton-on-the-Hill *Liv* from 08. *Curate's House, 7 Walton Village, Liverpool L4 6TJ* Tel 0151-523 6626 E-mail imgall@gmx.net

GALLAGHER, Mrs Margaret. b 60. SRN82 RM84. Westcott Ho Cam 09. **d** 11. C Carrington *S'well* from 11. *65 Osborne Grove, Nottingham NG5 2HE* Tel 0115-960 3733 E-mail margot gl@hotmail.com

GALLAGHER, Matthew Edward. b 51. Glas Univ BSc75. EAMTC. **d** 00 **p** 01. NSM Northampton St Jas *Pet* 00-02. *11 Penfold Gardens, Great Billing, Northampton NN3 9PG* Tel (01604) 416972 E-mail me.gallagher@virgin.net

GALLAGHER, Michael Collins. b 48. St Jo Coll Dur BA70. Sarum Th Coll 79. **d** 82 **p** 83. C Bridport *Sarum* 82-86; V Downton 86-01; RD Alderbury 93-99; R Crewkerne w Wayford *B & W* 01-07; R Wulfric Benefice from 07. *The Rectory, Gouldsbrook Terrace, Crewkerne TA18 7JA* Tel (01460) 271188 Fax 271194 E-mail mcfgallagher@lineone.net

GALLAGHER, Neville Roy. b 45. Birm Univ CertEd66 K Coll Lon AKC70 BD76 Open Univ BA97. **d** 71 **p** 72. C Folkestone St Mary and St Eanswythe *Cant* 71-74; Hon C Sutton Valence w E Sutton and Chart Sutton 74-76; TV Cen Telford *Lich* 76-78; P-in-c Gt Mongeham *Cant* 78-80; P-in-c Ripple 78-80; R Gt Mongeham w Ripple and Sutton by Dover 80-83; V Kennington 83-88; Chapl and Dep Hd Bedgebury Sch Kent 88-05; P-in-c Appledore w Brookland, Fairfield, Brenzett etc *Cant* 05-11; P-in-c Woodchurch 06-11; P-in-c Wittersham w Stone and Ebony 08-11; AD Romney 08-10; rtd 11. *1 Church Cottages, Church Road, Kilndown, Cranbrook TN17 2SF* E-mail nrwg45@aol.com

GALLAGHER, Padraig Francis Majella. b 52. **d** 81 **p** 82. P-in-c Caereithin *S & B* 05-09; V from 09. *Caereithin Vicarage, 64 Cheriton Close, Portmead, Swansea SA5 5LA* Tel (01792) 583646

GALLAGHER, Robert. b 43. St Chad's Coll Dur BSc65. **d** 67 **p** 68. C Crosland Moor *Wakef* 67-69; C Huddersfield SS Pet and Paul 69-71; Chapl Huddersfield Poly 72-79; Min Coulby Newham LEP *York* 79-90; V Toxteth St Marg *Liv* from 90. *St Margaret's Vicarage, 3 Princes Road, Liverpool L8 1TG* Tel 0151-709 1526

GALLAGHER, Canon Stephen. b 58. Southn Univ BTh89. Chich Th Coll 86. **d** 89 **p** 90. C S Shields All SS *Dur* 89-92; C Hartlepool St Paul and Chapl Hartlepool Gen Hosp 92-94; R Loftus and Carlin How w Skinningrove *York* 94-97; P-in-c Lower Beeding and Dioc Youth Officer *Chich* 97-09; Shrine P and Youth Missr Shrine of Our Lady of Walsingham from 09. *The Shrine of Our Lady of Walsingham, The College, Knight Street, Walsingham NR22 6EF* Tel (01328) 824203 E-mail shrine.pr@olw-shrine.org.uk

GALLANT, Mrs Joanna-Sue Sheena. b 62. SAOMC 99. **d** 02 **p** 03. C Amersham on the Hill *Ox* 02-05; NSM Gt Missenden w Ballinger and Lt Hampden 06-10; NSM Chenies and Lt Chalfont, Latimer and Flaunden from 10. *The Rectory, Latimer, Chesham HP5 1UA* Tel (01494) 763430 Mobile 07813-886805

GALLEY, Giles Christopher. b 32. Qu Coll Cam BA56 MA60. Linc Th Coll 56. **d** 58 **p** 59. C Gt Yarmouth *Nor* 58-62; C Lynn w St Marg and St Nic 62-66; C Leeds St Pet *Ripon* 66-69; V N Hull St Mich *York* 70-79; V Strensall 79-00; RD Easingwold 82-97; rtd 00; Perm to Offic *York* from 00. *19 St John's Road, Stamford Bridge, York YO41 1PH* Tel (01759) 371592

✠**GALLIFORD, The Rt Revd David George.** b 25. Clare Coll Cam BA49 MA51. Westcott Ho Cam. **d** 51 **p** 52 **c** 75. C Newland St Jo *York* 51-54; C Eton w Boveney *Ox* 54-56; Min Can Windsor 54-56; V Middlesbrough St Oswald *York* 56-61; R Bolton Percy 61-71; Dioc Adult Tr Officer 61-71; Can and Preb York Minster 69-70; Can Res and Treas 70-75; Suff Bp Hulme *Man* 75-84; Suff Bp Bolton 84-91; rtd 91; Hon Asst Bp *York* from 95. *10 St Mary's Mews, Greenshaw Drive, Wigginton, York YO32 2SE* Tel (01904) 761489

GALLIGAN, Ms Adrienne. TCD BA81 HDipEd82. CITC BTh03. **d** 03 **p** 04. C Seapatrick *D & D* 03-08; I Dublin Crumlin w Chapelizod *D & G* from 08. *St Mary's Rectory, 118 Kimmage Road West, Dublin 12, Republic of Ireland* Tel (00353) (1) 455 5639

GALLON, Mrs Audrey Kay. b 41. SEITE 94. **d** 97 **p** 98. NSM Gt Mongeham w Ripple and Sutton by Dover *Cant* 97-98; NSM Eastry and Northbourne w Tilmanstone etc 97-98; NSM Walmer 98-04; Perm to Offic *Cant* 04-05 and *Roch* from 07. *12 Arne Close, Tonbridge TN10 4DH* Tel (01732) 355633

GALLOWAY, Canon Charles Bertram. b 41. Lon Univ BA62. Qu Coll Birm 64. **d** 64 **p** 65. C Darlington H Trin *Dur* 64-68; Ind Chapl Teesside 68-77; Sen Ind Chapl *Liv* 77-87; Team Ldr and Convener Lon Ind Chapl 87-93; P-in-c Gosforth w Nether Wasdale and Wasdale Head *Carl* 93-98; R 98-04; Chapl Sellafield 94-04; Hon Can Carl Cathl from 03; rtd 04. *27 Oakfield Close, Sunderland SR3 3RT* Tel 0191-528 8459 E-mail bert.galloway@btinternet.com

GALLOWAY, Michael Edward. b 41. Chich Th Coll 72. **d** 74 **p** 75. C Aldwick *Chich* 74-77; C Bournemouth St Clem w St Mary *Win* 78-82; V S Benfleet *Chelmsf* 83-06; rtd 06; Perm to Offic *B & W* from 06. *3 Church Street, Chard TA20 2DW* Tel (01460) 65026 E-mail ceag@dialstart.net

GALLOWAY, Prof Peter John. b 54. OBE96 JP89. Goldsmiths' Coll Lon BA76 K Coll Lon PhD87 Brunel Univ Hon DLitt09 FRSA88 FSA00. St Steph Ho Ox 80. **d** 83 **p** 84. C St John's Wood *Lon* 83-86; C St Giles-in-the-Fields 86-90; Warden of Readers (Lon Episc Area) 87-92; P-in-c Hampstead Em W End 90-95; V 95-08; AD N Camden 02-07; Chapl to RVO and Qu Chpl of the Savoy from 08; Hon Fell Goldsmiths' Coll Lon from 99; Visiting Prof Brunel Univ from 08. *The Queen's Chapel of the Savoy, Savoy Hill, London WC2R 0DA* Tel (020) 7379 8088 E-mail peter.galloway@sja.org.uk

GALSWORTHY, Colin. b 44. St Mich Coll Llan 95. **d** 00 **p** 01. NSM Skewen *Llan* 00-01; NSM Resolven w Tonna 01-04; NSM Tonna and Cadoxton-juxta-Neath 04-08; rtd 08. *29 Woodlands Park Drive, Cadoxton, Neath SA10 8DE* Tel (01639) 636128

GALT, Ian Ross. b 34. Leeds Univ BSc56. **d** 76 **p** 77. NSM Newport St Julian *Mon* 76-87; NSM Newport St Teilo 87-98. *47 Brynglas Avenue, Newport NP20 5LR* Tel (01633) 821494

GALWAY, Gary Ford. **d** 04 **p** 07. C Donaghadee *D & D* 04-06; C Portadown St Mark *Arm* 06-08; I Drumcree from 08. *78 Drumcree Road, Portadown, Craigavon BT62 1PE* Tel (028) 3833 2503 E-mail ggalway@drumcree.org

GAMBLE, Bronwen. *See* GAMBLE, Mrs Edana Bronwen

GAMBLE, David Lawrence. b 34. AKC61. **d** 62 **p** 63. C-in-c Shrub End All SS CD *Chelmsf* 62-65; C Colchester St Jas, All SS, St Nic and St Runwald 65-69; V Chelmsf St Andr 69-73; P-in-c Hatfield Heath 69-73; C 74-77; TV Hemel Hempstead *St Alb* 77-82; P-in-c Renhold 82-90; Chapl HM Pris Bedf 82-90; P-in-c Petersham *S'wark* 90-96; Chapl HM Pris Latchmere Ho 90-96; P-in-c Portsea St Geo *Portsm* 96-99; rtd 99; Hon C Yarmouth and Freshwater *Portsm* 99-04. *35 Kings Chase, Andover SP10 3TH* Tel (01264) 338017

GAMBLE, Diane Mary. b 36. BSc. **d** 00 **p** 01. NSM Sanderstead *S'wark* 00-07; Perm to Offic from 07. *14 Barnfield Road, Sanderstead CR2 0EY* Tel (020) 8651 0700

GAMBLE, Donald William. b 67. NUU BSc88. TCD Div Sch BTh91. **d** 91 **p** 92. C Belfast St Mich *Conn* 91-95; I Dromore Clogh 95-00; P-in-c Renewal and Outreach in the City *Conn* from 00; Chapl Belfast Health and Soc Care Trust from 09. *5 Fernridge Road, Newtownabbey BT36 5SP* Tel (028) 9084 2171 or 9074 1099 Mobile 07876-361653 E-mail don.gamble@rocbelfast.com

GAMBLE, Mrs Edana Bronwen. b 56. Hull Univ BSc(Econ)78 Nottm Univ MA02 FCA82. EMMTC 99. **d** 02 **p** 03. NSM Nuthall *S'well* 02-06; R Cropwell Bishop w Colston Bassett, Granby etc from 06. *The Rectory, 2 Dobbin Close, Cropwell Bishop, Nottingham NG12 3GR* Tel 0115-989 3172

GAMBLE, Ian Robert. b 66. Ulster Univ BA90 MA98 TCD BTh93. **d** 93 **p** 94. C Bangor St Comgall *D & D* 93-96; C Bangor Primacy 93-96; Bp's C Belfast Whiterock *Conn* 96-99; R Donaghadee *D & D* from 99. *The Rectory, 3 The Trees, New Road, Donaghadee BT21 0EJ* Tel (028) 9188 2594

GAMBLE, Kenneth Wesley. b 52. Ulster Univ BA81. CITC 04. **d** 07 **p** 08. NSM Ballymacash *Conn* from 07. *21 Dalboyne Park, Lisburn BT28 3BU* Tel (028) 9267 7498 E-mail ken_gamble@talktalk.net

GAMBLE, Norman Edward Charles. b 50. TCD BA72 HDipEd73 PhD78. CITC 76. **d** 79 **p** 80. C Bangor St Comgall *D & D* 79-83; I Dunleckney w Nurney, Lorum and Kiltennel *C & O* 83-90; Warden of Readers 84-90; P-in-c Leighlin w Grange Sylvae, Shankill etc 89-90; Can Leighlin Cathl 89-90; Preb Ossory Cathl 89-90; I Malahide w Balgriffin *D & G* from 90; Abp's Dom Chapl 95-03. *The Rectory, Church Road, Malahide, Co Dublin, Republic of Ireland* Tel and fax (00353) (1) 845 4770 Mobile 86-815 3277 E-mail normanegamble@iol.ie

GAMBLE, Robin Philip. b 53. Oak Hill Th Coll 74. **d** 77 **p** 78. C Kildwick *Bradf* 77-78; C Laisterdyke 78-80; C York St Paul 80-82; V Bradf St Aug Undercliffe 82-95; Dioc Adv in Evang 93-01; Can Ev Man Cathl 01-08; P-in-c Idle *Bradf* from 08; Dioc Ev from 08. *The Vicarage, 470 Leeds Road, Idle, Bradford BD10 9AA* Tel (01274) 419754 or 615411 Mobile 07748-943541 E-mail robinp.gamble@blueyonder.co.uk

GAMBLE, Ronald George. b 41. Cant Sch of Min 92. **d** 95 **p** 96. NSM Loose 95-00; P-in-c Boxley w Detling 00-07; Chapl NHS Ambulance Trust 99-07; rtd 07; Perm to Offic *Cant* from 07. *18 Copper Tree Court, Maidstone ME15 9RW* Tel (01622) 744455 E-mail r-gamble@sky.com

GAMBLE, Stanley Thomas Robert. b 82. QUB BA03 MTh05. CITC 05. **d** 07 **p** 08. C Knockbreda *D & D* from 07. *28 Church Road, Newtownbreda, Belfast BT8 7AQ* Tel (028) 9064 1339 E-mail stanleygamble@gmail.com

GAMBLE, Stephen Robert. b 69. York Univ BA91. Cranmer Hall Dur 07. **d** 08 **p** 09. C Loughborough All SS w H Trin *Leic* from 08. *60 Brush Drive, Loughborough LE11 1LT* Tel (01509) 219545

GAMBLE, Thomas Richard. b 42. K Coll Lon BA64 AKC. **d** 65 **p** 66. C Gt Ilford St Jo *Chelmsf* 65-68; Hon C 68-73; Asst Master Pettits Sec Sch Romford 68-73; Hall Mead Sch Upminster 73-75; Tabor High Sch Braintree 75-77; Chapl Warminster Sch 77-80; Norway from 80. *Holmen 35, 4842 Arendal, Norway* Tel (0047) 3701 6811 or 9974 7494 E-mail gamble@c2i.net

GAMBLES, Una Beryl. b 33. Man Univ BEd78. St Chris Coll Blackheath 59. d 87 p 94. NSM Upton Priory *Ches* 87-01; Chapl Parkside Hosp Ches 87-93; Chapl E Cheshire NHS Trust 93-01; Chapl HM Pris Styal 94-98; Perm to Offic *Ches* from 01. *23 Grangelands, Upton, Macclesfield SK10 4AB* Tel (01625) 421691

GAMBLING, Paul Anthony. b 62. Middx Univ BA06. NTMTC 03. d 06 p 07. C Warley Ch Ch and Gt Warley St Mary *Chelmsf* 06-10; TV Billericay and Lt Burstead from 10. *The Vicarage, 7A Horace Road, Billericay CM11 1AA* Tel (01277) 656266 E-mail paul.gambling@btinternet.com

GAMESTER, Sidney Peter. b 27. SS Coll Cam BA51 MA55. Oak Hill Th Coll 56. d 58 p 59. C Surbiton Hill Ch Ch *S'wark* 58-61; C Worthing H Trin *Chich* 61-69; R Silverhill St Matt 69-86; R Bexhill St Mark 86-93; rtd 93; Perm to Offic *Chich* from 93. *18 Crofton Park Avenue, Bexhill-on-Sea TN39 3SE* Tel (01424) 842276

GAMLEN, Laurence William. b 59. STETS BA07. d 07 p 08. NSM Chertsey, Lyne and Longcross *Guildf* from 07. *9 Redwood, Egham TW20 8SU* Tel (01932) 561503 Fax 570299 Mobile 07939-094851 E-mail lgamlen@cpas.org.uk

GAMMON, Elizabeth Angela Myfanwy. b 47. SWMTC 06. d 09 p 10. NSM Sidmouth, Woolbrook, Salcombe Regis, Sidbury etc *Ex* from 09. *Tracey Mill, Tracey Road, Honiton EX14 3SL* Tel (01404) 45114 E-mail angie@traceymill.co.uk *or* angiegammon@hotmail.com

GAMMON, William Paul Lachlan. b 60. SS Hild & Bede Coll Dur BA82. St Steph Ho Ox 89. d 91 p 92. C Chalfont St Peter *Ox* 91-94; Lect Bolton St Pet *Man* 94-98; R Woodston *Ely* from 98, P-in-c Fletton from 98. *The Rectory, 2 Rectory Gardens, Peterborough PE2 8HN* Tel (01733) 562786

✠**GANDIYA, The Rt Revd Chad Nicholas.** b 53. Nottm Univ BTh80 Univ of Zimbabwe MA84 DPhil06 Michigan State Univ MA95. St Jo Coll Nottm 77. d 80 p 81 c 09. C Avondale Zimbabwe 80-83; R Mabelreigh St Pet 83-85; Chapl Michigan Univ USA 86-87; Asst P Harare Cathl 88; Warden Bp Gaul Coll 88-91; USA 92-95; R Marlborough St Paul 95-96; Prin Bp Gaul Coll 96-01; Tutor United Coll of Ascension Selly Oak 01-05; Regional Desk Officer USPG 05-09; Tanzania and Cen Africa 05-06; Africa and Indian Ocean 06-09; Bp Harare from 09. *Bishopsmount Close, PO Box UA7, Harare, Zimbabwe* Tel (00263) (4) 702253 *or* 702254 Fax 700419

GANDIYA, Leonard Farirayi (Lee). b 64. Boston Coll (USA) MA92. Gordon-Conwell Th Sem 90 Ridley Hall Cam 92. d 94 p 95. NSM Camberwell St Luke *S'wark* 94-95; C Lowestoft St Marg *Nor* 95-98; Dioc Rep for Black Anglican Concerns 96-98; CF from 98. *clo MOD Chaplains (Army)* Tel (01264) 381140 Fax 381824

GANDON, Andrew James Robson. b 54. St Jo Coll Dur BA76. Ridley Hall Cam 76. d 78 p 79. C Aston SS Pet and Paul *Birm* 78-82; CMS 82-95; Zaïre 82-88; Kenya 89-94; V Harefield *Lon* 95-10; Chapl R Brompton and Harefield NHS Trust 95-05; V Exhall *Cov* from 10. *36 St Giles Road, Coventry CV7 9HA* Tel (024) 7767 7461

GANDON, James Philip. b 31. ALCD56. d 56 p 57. C Westcliff St Mich *Chelmsf* 56-58; Canada from 58; rtd 92. *62 Cambria Road North, Goderich ON N7A 2P3, Canada* E-mail phil.gandon@odyssey.on.ca

GANDY, Nicholas John. b 53. Westf Coll Lon BSc75 Reading Univ MSc76 Ex Coll Ox CertEd78 CBiol79 MIBiol. St Steph Ho Ox 86. d 88 p 89. C Crowthorne *Ox* 88-89; C Tilehurst St Mary 89-93; P-in-c Didcot St Pet 93-97; V 97-03; V Brackley St Pet w St Jas from 03; OGS from 96. *The Vicarage, Old Town, Brackley NN13 7BZ* Tel (01280) 702767 E-mail nicholas.gandy@btinternet.com

GANE, Canon Christopher Paul. b 33. Qu Coll Cam BA57 MA61. Ridley Hall Cam 57. d 59 p 60. C Rainham *Chelmsf* 59-62; C Farnborough *Guildf* 62-64; V Erith St Paul *Roch* 64-71; V Ipswich St Marg *St E* 71-88; Hon Can St E Cathl 82-98; R Hopton, Market Weston, Barningham etc 88-98; rtd 98; Perm to Offic *St E* from 98. *1 Post Office Lane, Thurston, Bury St Edmunds IP31 3RW* Tel (01359) 271152

GANE, Nicholas. b 57. St Jo Coll Nottm 93. d 95 p 96. C Keynsham *B & W* 95-99; TV 99-02. *10 Ludlow Court, Willsbridge, Bristol BS30 6HB* E-mail nick.gane@virgin.net

GANGA, Jeremy Franklin. b 62. Cape Town Univ BSocSc86 Lon Bible Coll BA92 St Jo Coll Nottm MA93. Ridley Hall Cam 93. d 95 p 96. C St Peter-in-Thanet *Cant* 95-98; Chapl Felsted Sch 98-00; Past Chapl St Paul's Sch Barnes 00-02; NSM Fulham St Pet *Lon* 00-02; P-in-c Fulham St Pet 02-06; Tutor Reader Min Tr from 03; Tutor and Registrar NTMTC from 06. *The Crypt, St George-in-the-East, 16 Cannon Street Road, London E1 0BH* Tel (020) 7481 9477 Fax 7481 8907 E-mail jeremy.ganga@btinternet.com *or* admissions@ntmtc.org.uk

GANJAVI, John Farhad. b 57. Imp Coll Lon BSc79. Ridley Hall Cam 79. d 82 p 83. C Yardley St Edburgha *Birm* 82-85; C Knowle 85-89; P-in-c Beaudesert and Henley-in-Arden w Ullenhall *Cov* 89-92; R from 92; RD Alcester 92-99. *The Rectory,*

Beaudesert Lane, Henley-in-Arden B95 5JY Tel (01564) 792570 E-mail bdesert@btinternet.com

GANN, Canon Anthony Michael. b 37. TCD BA60 MA64 BD64. d 62 p 63. V Choral Derry Cathl 62-66; Lesotho 66-74; Dioc Officer for Miss and Unity *Carl* 75-80; P-in-c Bampton and Mardale 75-80; TV Cen Telford *Lich* 80-89; TR Wolvercote w Summertown *Ox* 89-02; RD Ox 95-99; rtd 02; Perm to Offic *Worc* from 02. *Avalon, 84 Pickersleigh Road, Malvern WR14 2RS* Tel (01684) 568114

GANN, John West. b 29. Ex Coll Ox BA55 MA59. Wells Th Coll 55. d 57 p 58. C Wendover *Ox* 57-59; C Walton St Mary *Liv* 59-62; R Didcot *Ox* 62-70; R Newbury St Nic 70-78; TR Newbury 73-78; V Twickenham St Mary *Lon* 78-87; Dir of Ords 81-87; TR Bridport *Sarum* 87-94; RD Lyme Bay 89-92; rtd 94; Perm to Offic *Glouc* from 94 and *Bris* from 96. *3 Buttercross Lane, Prestbury, Cheltenham GL52 5SF* Tel (01242) 220787 E-mail jandhgann@btinternet.com

GANNEY (*née* **CHAMBERS**), **Mrs Rachel Jill.** b 73. Hull Univ BSc94 MSc96 Selw Coll Cam BTh04. Ridley Hall Cam 01. d 04 p 05. C Sutton St Jas and Wawne *York* 04-10; TV Plaistow and N Canning Town *Chelmsf* from 10. *34 St Martin's Avenue, London E6 3DX* Tel (020) 3532 8437 E-mail rachel@ganney.net

GANNON, James Dub. b 75. W Sydney Univ BComm98 BAppSc(Agric)98. Moore Th Coll Sydney BTheol08. d 10 p 11. NSM Henham and Elsenham w Ugley *Chelmsf* from 10. *Church Office, Henham Cottage, High Street, Henham, Bishop's Stortford CM22 6AS* Tel (01279) 850805 E-mail dubgannon@o2.co.uk

GANT, Canon Brian Leonard. b 45. Ox Univ MTh01. K Coll Lon 72. d 73 p 74. C Hillmorton *Cov* 73-75; C Cov St Geo 76; P-in-c Maldon St Mary *Chelmsf* 76-79; R Muthill, Crieff and Comrie *St And* 79-81; V Walsall St Paul *Lich* 81-84; Chapl K Sch Worc and Min Can Worc Cathl 84-89; V Tunbridge Wells K Chas *Roch* 89-95; Hon Can Kumasi from 94; V Wymondham *Nor* 95-01; P-in-c York All SS N Street 01-03; TV Haxby and Wigginton 03-09; CME Officer York Adnry 01-07; rtd 09; Perm to Offic *York* from 09. *7 Slessor Road, York YO24 3JJ* Tel (01904) 790799 Mobile 07800-922985 E-mail brianlgant@aol.com

GANT, Peter Robert. b 38. BNC Ox BA60 MA64 G&C Coll Cam BA62 MA67. Ridley Hall Cam 61. d 63 p 64. C Portsea St Mary *Portsm* 63-67; V Blackheath *Birm* 67-73; Asst Master Harold Malley Gr Sch Solihull 73-75; Perm to Offic *Birm* 73-75 and *Guildf* from 75; rtd 93. *8 Sandon Close, Esher KT10 8JE* Tel (020) 8398 5107

GANT, Trevor Malcolm. b 56. Leeds Univ BSc97. NEOC 05. d 08 p 09. NSM York St Luke from 08. *6 Lumley Road, York YO30 6DB* Tel (01904) 654784 E-mail t.gant@st-peters.york.sch.uk

GANZ, Timothy Jon. b 36. Univ Coll Ox BA58 MA62 ARCM63. St Steph Ho Ox 58. d 61 p 62. C Shrewsbury H Cross *Lich* 61-65; Asst Chapl Hurstpierpoint Coll 65-69; Chapl 69-73; Chapl Univ of Wales (Swansea) *S & B* 74-75; P-in-c Hanley All SS *Lich* 75-80; TV Stoke-upon-Trent 80-81; V Tutbury 81-04; rtd 04. *3 Warren Close, Stretton, Burton-on-Trent DE13 0DD* Tel (01283) 749171

GARBETT, Capt Phillip Ronald. b 52. EAMTC 95. d 97 p 98. CA from 80; C Ipswich St Mary at Stoke w St Pet and St Fran *St E* 97-00; TV Walton and Trimley 00-09; TR Blackbourne from 09. *The Vicarage, Comminster Lane, Ixworth, Bury St Edmunds IP31 2HE* Tel (01359) 234415 Mobile 07884-212218 E-mail philip.garbett@ntlworld.com

GARBUTT, Gerald. b 41. St Aid Birkenhead 65. d 67 p 68. C Stretford All SS *Man* 67-70; Lic to Offic 70-72; R Salford St Bart 72-74; V Lower Kersal 74-79; TR Bethnal Green St Jo w St Bart *Lon* 79-90; P-in-c Stepney St Pet w St Benet 85-87; Chapl Furness Gen Hosp 90-94; Chapl S Cumbria HA 90-94; Hosp Services Chapl Furness Hosps NHS Trust 94-98; Chapl Westmorland Hosps NHS Trust 94-98; Chapl Morecambe Bay Hosps NHS Trust 98-06; rtd 03; P-in-c Beetham *Carl* 06-07. *20 Highbury Road, Stockport SK4 5AZ* Tel 0161-975 9110

GARBUTT, Mrs Mary Yvonne. b 45. Ridley Hall Cam 00. d 02 p 03. C Desborough, Brampton Ash, Dingley and Braybrooke *Pet* 02-05; P-in-c Arthingworth, Harrington w Oxendon and E Farndon 05-07; R from 07; P-in-c Maidwell w Draughton, Lamport w Faxton 05-07; R from 07; RD Brixworth from 09. *The Rectory, 35 Main Street, Great Oxendon, Market Harborough LE16 8NE* Tel (01858) 461992 E-mail mary@familygarbutt.plus.com

GARDEN, Robert Andrew (Robin). b 26. Edin Univ BSc49 Kent Univ MA95 MInstP58 FIMA72. Cant Sch of Min 87. d 90 p 91. NSM Sandwich *Cant* 90-97; Chapl St Bart Hosp Sandwich 91-00; Perm to Offic *Cant* from 97. *Naini, 164 St George's Road, Sandwich CT13 9LD* Tel (01304) 612116

GARDHAM, Mrs Linda Elizabeth. b 49. Leeds Univ BA70 Warwick Univ PGCE71. Cranmer Hall Dur 04. d 05 p 06. NSM Monkseaton St Pet *Newc* 05-08; NSM Cornhill w Carham from 08; NSM Branxton from 08. *The Vicarage, Old School House,*

Branxton, Cornhill-on-Tweed TD12 4SW Tel (01890) 820308
E-mail leg@lgardham.freeserve.co.uk
GARDINER, Anthony Reade. b 35. Univ of NZ BA59.
Cuddesdon Coll 60. d 62 p 63. C Gosforth All SS Newc 62-65; V
Waikohu New Zealand 65-69; V Edgecumbe 69-74; V Eltham
74-78; V Trentham 78-81; V Waipukurau 81-88; Chapl Nelson
Cathl 88-92; C Highcliffe w Hinton Admiral Win 93-94; TV N
Creedy Ex 94-00; rtd 00; Perm to Offic Wellington from 00.
1 Puriri Street, Eastbourne, Lower Hutt 5013, New Zealand Tel
(0064) (4) 562 6177 E-mail nantony2@paradise.net.nz
GARDINER, Mrs Cathrine Leigh. b 64. STETS 05. d 08 p 09. C
Bedminster Bris from 08; TV Anerley Roch from 11. St Paul's
Vicarage, Hamlet Road, London SE19 2AW Tel (020) 8653 0978
E-mail cathrinegardiner@gmail.com
GARDINER, Charles Graham. b 18. AKC49. St Boniface
Warminster. d 50 p 51. C Clapham H Trin S'wark 50-54; S Africa
from 54. 55 Weltevreden Avenue, Rondebosch, 7700 South Africa
Tel (0027) (21) 689 1111
GARDINER, David Andrew. b 81. Surrey Univ BA03 Fitzw Coll
Cam BTh08. Westcott Ho Cam 05. d 08 p 09. C N Cheltenham
Glouc from 08. 8 Boulton Road, Cheltenham GL50 4RZ Tel
(01242) 238601 E-mail david.gardiner@northchelt.org.uk
GARDINER, Gerald. See GARDINER, Preb William Gerald
Henry
GARDINER, James Carlisle. b 18. Tyndale Hall Bris. d 49 p 50. C
Blackpool Ch Ch Blackb 49-52; C Rushen S & M 52-56; R
Ditton Roch 56-83; rtd 83; Perm to Offic Roch 83-04. Rosset Holt
Care Home, Pembury Road, Tunbridge Wells TN2 3RB Tel
(01892) 526077
GARDINER (née SAYERS), Mrs Karen Jane. b 69. Sheff Univ
BMus90. Ripon Coll Cuddesdon 00. d 02 p 03. C Dunstable
St Alb 02-05; TV Elstree and Borehamwood from 05. The
Rectory, St Nicholas Close, Elstree, Borehamwood WD6 3EW
Tel (020) 8953 1411
E-mail revdkarengardiner@googlemail.com
GARDINER, Canon Kenneth Ashton. b 27. S'wark Ord Course
60. d 63 p 64. C Sydenham H Trin S'wark 63-67; C Macclesfield
St Mich Ches 67-70; V Chatham St Phil and St Jas Roch 70-93;
RD Roch 88-93; Hon Can Roch Cathl 88-93; rtd 93; Perm to
Offic Roch from 93. 44 Trevale Road, Rochester ME1 3PA Tel
(01634) 844524 E-mail ken.gardiner@diocese-rochester.org
GARDINER, Preb William Gerald Henry. b 46. Lon Univ BD72.
Oak Hill Th Coll 68. d 72 p 73. C Beckenham St Jo Roch 72-75;
C Cheadle Ches 75-81; P-in-c Swynnerton Lich 81-83; P-in-c
Swynnerton and Tittensor 81-83; R Swynnerton and Tittensor
83-86; V Westlands St Andr 86-11; RD Newcastle 97-11; Preb
Lich Cathl 05-11; rtd 11. 4 The Lindens, Stone ST15 0BD
GARDINER, Canon Anthony Brian. b 32. Lon Coll of Div 62. d 64
p 65. C Stoke Cov 64-68; R Whitnash 68-98; RD Leamington
78-79; RD Warwick and Leamington 79-87; Hon Can Cov Cathl
83-98; rtd 98; Perm to Offic Cov from 99. 4 Mark Antony Drive,
Heathcote, Warwick CV34 6XA Tel (01926) 832690
GARDINER, Brian Charles. b 46. FIBMS71. d 04 p 05. OLM
Bodicote Ox from 04. 11 Farm Way, Banbury OX16 9TB Tel
(01295) 253309 Mobile 07967-859457
E-mail bri.jen@btopenworld.com
GARDNER, Christine. See GARDNER, Mary Christine
GARDNER, Clive Bruce. b 67. Selw Coll Cam BA89 MA93.
Wycliffe Hall Ox BA95 MA01. d 96 p 97. C Beverley Minster
York 96-98; Bp's Dom Chapl Liv 98-01; V Cumnor Ox 01-06; TV
Wimbledon S'wark from 11. 55 Alwyne Road, London
SW19 7AE Tel (020) 8944 0184 E-mail clivegardner@tesco.net
GARDNER, David. b 57. Oak Hill Th Coll BA87. d 87 p 88. C
Ogley Hay Lich 87-91; TV Mildenhall St E 91-98; P-in-c
Woodbridge St Jo 98-00; V 00-03; P-in-c Bredfield 01-03; V
Woodbridge St Jo and Bredfield from 03. St John's Vicarage,
St John's Hill, Woodbridge IP12 1HS Tel (01394) 382083 or tel
and fax 383162 E-mail stjohns.woodbridge@btinternet.com
GARDNER, Elizabeth Mary. b 47. Nottm Univ BA01. Trin Coll
Bris 72 St Jo Coll Nottm 00. d 01 p 02. C Swindon Dorcan Bris
01-04; P-in-c Runcorn St Jo Weston Ches 04-09; V from 09; Dioc
Clergy Widows and Retirement Officer from 07. The Vicarage,
225 Heath Road South, Weston, Runcorn WA7 4LY Tel (01928)
573798 E-mail beth47@btopenworld.com
GARDNER, Geoffrey Maurice. b 28. Hull Coll BA51 Lon Inst
of Educn PGCE52 Bris Univ DipEd74. Cranmer Hall Dur. d 59
p 60. C Bowling St Jo Bradf 59-62; Nigeria 62-72; Hon C Bath
St Luke B & W 72-73; Perm to Offic 73-90; and 94-99; NSM
Bath Widcombe 90-94; rtd 94; Perm to Offic Ex from 99.
15 Bramley Gardens, Whimple, Exeter EX5 2SJ Tel (01404)
823235
GARDNER, Mrs Helen Elizabeth. b 56. ERMC 05. d 08 p 09. C
Sunnyside w Bourne End St Alb from 08. 3 Broadwater,
Berkhamsted HP4 2AH Tel (01442) 862512
E-mail helerevg@aol.com
GARDNER, Helen Jane. b 39. Man Univ BSc61 PGCE62.
WEMTC 93. d 96 p 97. NSM Stow on the Wold Glouc 96-00;
NSM Stow on the Wold, Condicote and The Swells 00-02; NSM
The Guitings, Cutsdean, Farmcote and Upper and Lower

Slaughter w Eyford and Naunton 03-04; Perm to Offic 04-07;
NSM Stow on the Wold, Condicote and The Swells from 07.
6 St Mary's Close, Lower Swell, Cheltenham GL54 1LJ Tel
(01451) 832553 E-mail gardner269@btinternet.com
GARDNER, Ian Douglas. b 34. St Pet Hall Ox BA58 MA62. Oak
Hill Th Coll 58. d 60 p 61. C Biddulph Lich 60-63; C Weston
St Jo B & W 64; Nigeria 65-76; P-in-c Hurstbourne Tarrant and
Faccombe Win 77-79; V Hurstbourne Tarrant, Faccombe,
Vernham Dean etc 79-85; R Nursling and Rownhams 85-99; rtd
99. Wilderness Cottage, Haroldston Hill, Broad Haven,
Haverfordwest SA62 3JP Tel (01437) 781592
GARDNER, Ian Norman. b 52. Open Univ BSc96. WEMTC 03.
d 05 p 06. NSM Dursley Glouc from 05. 9 Chestal Lodge,
Chestal, Dursley GL11 5AA Tel (01453) 546895 Mobile
07960-287403 E-mail ian@chestal.freeserve.co.uk
GARDNER, Mrs Jacqueline Anne. b 49. WEMTC 95. d 98 p 99.
NSM Fairford and Kempsford w Whelford Glouc 98-02; NSM
Cirencester 02-05; Perm to Offic Ox 05-07; NSM Hanborough
and Freeland from 07. 15 Oakdale Road, Witney OX28 1AX Tel
(01993) 866110
GARDNER, Jane. See GARDNER, Helen Jane
GARDNER, Canon John Phillip Backhouse. b 21. St Aid
Birkenhead 49. d 52 p 53. C Ashtead Guildf 52-55; C Bromley SS
Pet and Paul Roch 55-57; V New Hythe 57-63; V Roch St Justus
63-69; R Wisley w Pyrford Guildf 70-87; RD Woking 82-87; Hon
Can Guildf Cathl 86-87; rtd 87; Perm to Offic Pet 87-98 and
Guildf from 98. 42 Godley Road, Byfleet, West Byfleet KT14 7ER
Tel (01932) 347431
GARDNER, Mrs Marian Elizabeth. b 50. Ripon Coll of Educn
DipEd71. WMMTC 00. d 03 p 04. NSM Kirkleatham York
03-07; P-in-c Easington w Liverton from 07. The Rectory,
Grinkle Lane, Easington, Saltburn-by-the-Sea TS13 4NT Tel
(01287) 641348 Mobile 07736-350643
E-mail marian@thegardners.org.uk
GARDNER, Canon Mark Douglas. b 58. TCD BA80 MA83. d 83
p 84. C Ballymacarrett St Patr D & D 83-87; C Belfast St Steph w
St Luke Conn 87-89; C Hendon and Sunderland Dur 89-90; TV
Sunderland 90-95; I Dublin Santry w Glasnevin and Finglas
D & G 95-01; PV and Chapter Clerk Ch Ch Cathl Dublin from
96; Min Can St Patr Cathl Dublin 96; Treas V 96-01; Can Ch Ch
Cathl Dublin from 08; V Dublin St Patr Cathl Gp from 10; Preb
Tipperkevin St Patr Cathl Dublin from 10. 248 South Circular
Road, Dolphin's Barn, Dublin 8, Republic of Ireland Tel (00353)
(1) 454 2274 Mobile 87-266 0228
E-mail markgardner@eircom.net
GARDNER, Mary Christine. b 42. SRN64 SCM66. St Jo Coll
Nottm 80. dss 82 d 85 p 94. Ches St Paul 82-87; Macclesfield
St Mich 84-85; Macclesfield Team 85-87; Par Dn 87; Chapl Asst
Nottm City Hosp 87-93; Chapl St Chris Hospice Lon 93-01; V
Over St Jo Ches 01-03; rtd 03. Pot Shop Cottage, Main Street,
Farnsfield, Newark NG22 8EF Tel (01623) 884116
GARDNER, Michael Ronald. b 53. Trin Coll Bris 95. d 97 p 98.
CA 86-00; C Stanmore Win 97-01; V from 01. St Luke's
Vicarage, Mildmay Street, Winchester SO22 4BX Tel (01962)
865240
GARDNER, Neil Kenneth. b 65. Univ of Wales (Swansea) BA92
Peterho Cam BA00 Univ of Wales (Cardiff) PhD01. Westcott
Ho Cam 98. d 01 p 02. C Wisbech SS Pet and Paul Ely from 01;
C Wisbech St Aug 03-04; P-in-c from 04. The Rectory, 35
Gorefield Road, Leverington, Wisbech PE13 5AS Tel and fax
(01945) 581486 Mobile 07855-111794
E-mail n.gardner952@btinternet.com
GARDNER, Richard Beverley Twynam. b 11. Chich Th Coll 33.
d 36 p 37. C Gainsborough St Jo Linc 36-38; C Linc St Giles
38-39; C Horsell Guildf 39-42; Chapl RNVR 42-47; C York
Town St Mich Guildf 47-48; V E Molesey St Paul 48-54; V
Botleys and Lyne 54-71; V Long Cross 56-71; V Ewshott 71-76;
rtd 76; Perm to Offic Guildf 81-93. Manormead, Tilford Road,
Hindhead GU26 6RA Tel (01428) 602500
GARDNER (née JAMES), Mrs Sandra Kay. b 66. Westcott Ho
Cam 97. d 99 p 00. C Whittlesey, Pondersbridge and Coates Ely
99-02; R Leverington 02-04; V Southea w Murrow and Parson
Drove 02-04; R Leverington, Newton and Tydd St Giles from
05. The Rectory, 35 Gorefield Road, Leverington, Wisbech
PE13 5AS Tel (01945) 585850
E-mail sandra.gardner@ely.anglican.org
GARDNER, Stephen John. b 70. Southn Univ MEng92. St Jo
Coll Nottm 00. d 02 p 03. C Brinsworth w Catcliffe and Treeton
Sheff 02-03; C Rivers Team 03-05; V Woodlands from 05; AD
Adwick from 11. All Saints' Vicarage, 9 Great North Road,
Woodlands, Doncaster DN6 7RB Tel (01302) 339618 Mobile
07740-200942 E-mail stephen.gardner@sheffield.anglican.org
GARDNER, Susan Carol. See CLARKE, Mrs Susan Carol
GARDNER, Vincent Lyndon. b 62. St Luke Coll Ex MA98 Robert
Gordon Univ Aber BFA90. St Steph Ho Ox 02. d 04 p 05. C
Carew St D 04-07; V Reading St Jo Ox from 08. The Vicarage,
5A Alexandra Road, Reading RG1 5PE Tel (0118-926 9906
Mobile 07901-737649 E-mail vincent gardner@hotmail.com
GARDOM, Francis Douglas. b 34. Trin Coll Ox BA55 MA59.

Wells Th Coll 58. **d** 60 **p** 61. C Greenwich St Alfege w St Pet *S'wark* 60-68; C Lewisham St Steph and St Mark 68-76; Hon C from 76. *79 Maze Hill, London SE10 8XQ* Tel (020) 8858 7052 *or* 8852 1474 E-mail francisgardom@aol.com

GARDOM, James Theodore Douglas. b 61. St Anne's Coll Ox BA83 K Coll Lon PhD92. Ripon Coll Cuddesdon 88. **d** 90 **p** 91. C Witney *Ox* 90-92; Dean of Studies Bp Gaul Coll Harare Zimbabwe 93-97; V Chesterton St Andr *Ely* 97-06; Dean and Chapl Pemb Coll Cam from 06. *Pembroke College, Cambridge CB2 1RF* Tel (01223) 338147 Fax 338163 E-mail jtdg2@cam.ac.uk

GARLAND, Christopher John. b 47. Ex Univ BA69 PhD72. Qu Coll Birm 78. **d** 80 **p** 81. C Beckenham St Jas *Roch* 80-82; C Roch 82-84; Papua New Guinea 85-93; Australia 94-95; R Copford w Easthorpe and Messing w Inworth *Chelmsf* from 95. *The Vicarage, Kelvedon Road, Messing, Colchester CO5 9TN* Tel (01621) 815434 E-mail garlandc79@aol.com

GARLAND, Michael. b 50. Sarum & Wells Th Coll 72. **d** 73 **p** 74. C Swansea St Thos and Kilvey *S & B* 73-76; C Boldmere *Birm* 76-79; V Kingshurst 79-88; P-in-c Curdworth w Castle Vale 88-90; R Curdworth 90-03; P-in-c Wishaw 99-00; V Charlton Kings St Mary *Glouc* from 03. *The Vicarage, 63 Church Street, Charlton Kings, Cheltenham GL53 8AT* Tel (01242) 253402 Mobile 07974-066929 E-mail michaelgarland368@btinternet.com

GARLAND, Peter Stephen John. b 52. Univ Coll Lon BA73 Univ of W Ontario MA74 St Jo Coll Dur MA09 Dur Univ PGCE75 ALA79. Ripon Coll Cuddesdon 88. **d** 90 **p** 91. C Crookham Guildf 90-94; V Tongham 94-99; Chapl Farnborough Coll of Tech 94-99; V Spalding St Jo w Deeping St Nicholas *Linc* from 99; Chapl Lincs Teaching Primary Care Trust from 07. *St John's Vicarage, 66A Hawthorn Bank, Spalding PE11 1JQ* Tel and fax (01775) 722816 E-mail peter@stjohnsspalding.org

GARLICK, Canon David. b 37. Nottm Univ BA62. St Steph Ho Ox 62. **d** 64 **p** 65. C Kennington St Jo *S'wark* 64-66; Hon C Newington St Paul 66-68; P-in-c Vauxhall St Pet 68-79; V Lewisham St Mary 79-07; RD E Lewisham 92-99; Hon Can S'wark Cathl 93-07; rtd 07. *Limekilns Farmhouse, Braidley, Horsehouse, Leyburn DL8 4TX* Tel (01969) 640280 E-mail limekilnsfarm@yahoo.co.uk

GARLICK, Preb Kathleen Beatrice. b 49. Leeds Univ BA71 Birm Univ PGCE72. Glouc Sch of Min 87. **d** 90 **p** 94. NSM Much Birch w Lt Birch, Much Dewchurch etc *Heref* 90-03; P-in-c 03-07; R Wormelow Hundred 07-09; Chapl Heref Sixth Form Coll 96-03; Chapl Heref Cathl from 09; Preb Heref Cathl from 99. *Birch Lodge, Much Birch, Hereford HR2 8HT* Tel (01981) 540666 Mobile 07812-995442 E-mail kaygarlick@hotmail.com

GARLICK, Canon Peter. b 34. AKC57. **d** 58 **p** 59. C Swindon New Town *Bris* 58-63; St Kitts-Nevis 63-66; V Heyside *Man* 66-73; R Stretford All SS 73-79; RD Wootton *Pet* 79-88; V Duston 79-91 and 91-94; Can Pet Cathl 85-94; rtd 94; Perm to Offic *Pet* from 94. *120 Worcester Close, Northampton NN3 9GD* Tel (01604) 416511 E-mail pandcgarlick@tiscali.co.uk

GARLICK, William Frederick. b 51. **d** 98 **p** 99. OLM Bermondsey St Jas w Ch Ch and St Crispin *S'wark* 98-06. *33 Penfolds Place, Arundel BN18 9SA*

GARNER, Alistair Ross. b 58. Pemb Coll Ox BA81 MA86. St Jo Coll Nottm 90. **d** 92 **p** 93. C Ashton-upon-Mersey St Mary Magd *Ches* 92-96; P-in-c Bredbury St Mark 96-01; V 01-09; Miss Growth Team Ldr *Roch* from 09. *St Barnabas' Vicarage, 1 St Barnabas Close, Gillingham ME7 4BU* Tel (01634) 575598 E-mail revrossgarner@hotmail.com

GARNER, Canon Carl. b 42. Rhodes Univ BA62 Keble Coll Ox BA65 MA70. St Paul's Coll Grahamstown 66. **d** 67 **p** 68. C Pietersburg S Africa 67-71; R Louis Trichardt 71-75; Chapl St Paul's Coll Grahamstown 75-84; Dioc Missr *St Alb* 84-98; Can Res St Alb 84-98; P-in-c Digswell and Panshanger 98-06; TR from 06; Hon Can St Alb from 99; Jt RD Welwyn Hatfield from 01. *The Rectory, 354 Knightsfield, Welwyn Garden City AL8 7NG* Tel (01707) 326677 E-mail carl@stjohnsdigswell.freeserve.co.uk

GARNER, David Henry. b 40. Trin Coll Bris 70. **d** 73 **p** 74. C Tunstead *Man* 73-75; C Fazeley *Lich* 76-78; V Sparkhill St Jo *Birm* 78-85; V Blackheath 85-01; Deanery P Warley Deanery 01-05; rtd 05; Perm to Offic *Birm* from 05; Chapl Sandwell and W Birm Hosps NHS Trust from 06. *94 Honeybourne Road, Halesowen B63 3HD* Tel 0121-550 2498 Mobile 07779-948333

GARNER, Geoffrey Walter. b 40. Ripon Hall Ox 69. **d** 71 **p** 72. C Stoke *Cov* 71-76; V Tile Hill 76-80; TV Hackney *Lon* 80-89; V Bow w Bromley St Leon 89-06; rtd 06. *98 Wordsworth Road, Plymouth PL2 2JQ*

GARNER, John David. b 47. **d** 03. OLM Kirkdale St Lawr *Liv* from 03. *10 Doon Close, Liverpool L4 1XW* Tel 0151-284 0388

GARNER, John Howard. b 45. Univ of Wales (Swansea) BSc67 Univ of Wales (Ban) PhD75. SWMTC 95. **d** 98 **p** 99. NSM Upton *Ex* from 98; Sen Chapl S Devon Healthcare NHS Trust from 06. *Highgrove Lodge, Sunbury Hill, Upton, Torquay TQ1 3ED* Tel (01803) 293640 *or* 654186 E-mail johngarner@onetel.net.uk

GARNER, Canon Peter. b 35. Lon Univ BSc56 Leeds Univ MEd91. Wycliffe Hall Ox 56. **d** 58 **p** 59. C Walthamstow St Jo *Chelmsf* 58-61; V Hainault 61-70; R Theydon Garnon 70-73; P-in-c Kirby-le-Soken 73-74; V 74-82; P-in-c Fountains *Ripon* 82-88; P-in-c Kirkby Malzeard w Grewelthorpe and Mickley etc 82-88; Par Development Adv 88-93; P-in-c Birstwith 91-93; R Walkingham Hill 93-01; Hon Can Ripon Cathl 99-01; rtd 01; Perm to Offic *Ripon* from 02. *Firtops, 2 Shirley Avenue, Ripon HG4 1SP* Tel (01765) 601543 Mobile 07734-088521 E-mail peter@hellwath29.fsnet.co.uk

GARNER, Canon Rodney George. b 48. Lon Univ BA87 Hull Univ MPhil96 Man Univ PhD01 MCIPD75. Qu Coll Birm 75. **d** 78 **p** 79. C Tranmere St Paul w St Luke *Ches* 78-81; V Eccleston St Thos *Liv* 81-90; P-in-c Sculcoates St Paul w Ch St and St Silas *York* 90-95; Lay Tr Officer (E Riding Adnry) 90-95; P-in-c Southport H Trin *Liv* 95-96; V from 96; Dioc Th Consultant from 95; Hon Can Liv Cathl from 07. *24 Roe Lane, Southport PR9 9DX* Tel and fax (01704) 538560 E-mail anglican@garnerr.freeserve.co.uk

GARNER, Ross. See GARNER, Alistair Ross

GARNER, Mrs Selina Clare. b 69. Newnham Coll Cam BA90 K Coll Lon PGCE93. EAMTC 00. **d** 06 **p** 07. C Fulbourn *Ely* 06-09; C Gt Wilbraham 06-09; C Lt Wilbraham 06-09; C Cullompton, Willand, Uffculme, Kentisbeare etc *Ex* from 09; Pioneer Youth Min Cullompton Deanery from 09. *The Vicarage, Bridge Street, Uffculme, Cullompton EX15 3AX* Tel (01884) 841001 E-mail selina@thegarners.me.uk

GARNER, Thomas Richard. b 43. K Coll Lon. **d** 69 **p** 70. C Tynemouth Ch Ch *Newc* 69-73; C Fenham St Jas and St Basil 73-76; V Hamstead St Bernard *Birm* 76-80; V Greytown New Zealand 80-87; V Levin 87-96; Can Wellington 96-99; V Upper Riccarton w Yaldhurst 99-05; rtd 05. *267 Chester Road, RD 1, Carterton 5791, New Zealand*

GARNETT, The Ven David Christopher. b 45. Nottm Univ BA67 Fitzw Coll Cam BA69 MA73. Westcott Ho Cam 67. **d** 69 **p** 70. C Cottingham *York* 69-72; Chapl Selw Coll Cam 72-77; P-in-c Patterdale *Carl* 77-80; Dir of Ords 78-80; V Heald Green St Cath *Ches* 80-87; R Christleton 87-92; TR Ellesmere Port 92-96; Adn Chesterfield *Derby* 96-09; P-in-c Beeley and Edensor 07-10; Hon Can Derby Cathl 96-10; rtd 10. *The Vicarage, Edensor, Bakewell DE45 1PH* Tel (01246) 582130 E-mail davidcgarnett@yahoo.co.uk

GARNETT, Preb Ralph Henry. b 28. Cuddesdon Coll 58. **d** 60 **p** 61. C Broseley w Benthall *Heref* 60-64; V Leintwardine 64-69; P-in-c Downton w Burrington and Aston and Elton 66-69; RD Ludlow 72-75; R Whitton w Greete and Hope Bagot 69-87; R Burford III w Lt Heref 69-87; P-in-c Burford I, Nash and Boraston 72-74; R 74-87; V Tenbury Wells 69-74; TR 74-87; Preb Heref Cathl 82-93; P-in-c Fownhope 87-93; P-in-c Brockhampton w Fawley 87-93; RD Heref Rural 92-93; rtd 93; Perm to Offic *Heref* from 93. *5 Hampton Manor Close, Hereford HR1 1TG* Tel (01432) 274985

GARNSEY, George Christopher. b 36. Qu Coll Ox BA63. **d** 60 **p** 60. Lic to Offic *Wakef* 78-79; C Lupset 80; Australia from 80; Prin St Jo Coll Morpeth 80-91; R Gresford w Paterson 93-01; rtd 01; Lect St Jo Coll Morpeth from 01. *17 James Street, Morpeth NSW 2321, Australia* Tel (0061) (2) 4934 2658 Fax 4921 6898 E-mail jan@maths.newcastle.edu.au

GARRARD, Mrs Christine Ann. b 51. Open Univ BA86 LCST75. EAMTC 87. **d** 90 **p** 94. Par Dn Kesgrave *St E* 90-94; C 94-96; V Ipswich All Hallows 96-02; R Higham, Holton St Mary, Raydon and Stratford 02-08; Asst Dioc Dir of Ords 03-08; Sen Chapl Burrswood Chr Hosp from 08. *May Cottage, Burrswood, Groombridge, Tunbridge Wells TN3 9PY* Tel (01892) 860433 E-mail revdchris@aol.com

GARRARD, Canon James Richard. b 65. Dur Univ BA88 Keble Coll Ox DPhil92 Leeds Univ MA01. Westcott Ho Cam. **d** 94 **p** 95. C Elland *Wakef* 94-97; TV Brighouse and Clifton 98-01; P-in-c Balderstone *Blackb* 01-08; Warden of Readers 01-08; Can Res Ely Cathl from 08. *The Precentor's House, 32 High Street, Ely CB7 4JU* Tel (01353) 660335 *or* 660300 Fax 665658 E-mail j.garrard@cathedral.ely.anglican.org

GARRARD, Nicholas James Havelock. b 62. Leeds Univ BA83. Westcott Ho Cam 86. **d** 88 **p** 89. C Scotforth *Blackb* 88-91; C Eaton *Nor* 91-95; V Heigham St Thos 95-96; RD Nor S 03-06; R Ranworth w Panxworth, Woodbastwick etc from 06. *The Rectory, The Street, South Walsham, Norwich NR13 6DQ* Tel (01603) 270769 E-mail nickgarr39@aol.com

✠**GARRARD, The Rt Revd Richard.** b 37. K Coll Lon BD60 AKC60. **d** 61 **p** 62 **c** 94. C Woolwich St Mary w H Trin *S'wark* 61-66; C Cambridge Gt St Mary w St Mich *Ely* 66-68; Chapl Keswick Hall Coll of Educn 68-74; Prin Wilson Carlile Coll of Evang 74-79; Can Res and Chan S'wark Cathl 79-87; Dir of Tr 79-87; Can Res St E Cathl 87-94; Dioc Adv for CME 87-91; Adn Sudbury 91-94; Suff Bp Penrith *Carl* 94-01; Hon Can Carl Cathl 94-01; Abp's Rep H See and Dir Angl Cen Rome 01-03; Hon Asst Bp Eur from 01; rtd 03; Perm to Offic *Nor* from 03;

Hon Asst Bp Nor from 03. *26 Carol Close, Stoke Holy Cross, Norwich NR14 8NN* Tel (01508) 494165
E-mail garrard.r-a@tiscali.co.uk

GARRARD, Miss Valerie Mary. b 48. K Alfred's Coll Win TCert69 St Paul's Coll Chelt BEd84. **d** 03 **p** 04. OLM Wylye and Till Valley *Sarum* from 03. *Cowslip Cottage, Wylye Road, Hanging Langford, Salisbury SP3 4NW* Tel (01722) 790739
E-mail vmgarrard@btinternet.com

GARRATT, Alan. b 54. **d** 04 **p** 05. NSM Hazlemere *Ox* 04-08; TR Thame from 08. *The Rectory, 3 Fish Ponds Lane, Thame OX9 2BA* Tel (01844) 212225
E-mail alan.garratt@hotmail.co.uk

GARRATT, David John. b 66. Leic Poly BA98. Wycliffe Hall Ox 05. **d** 07 **p** 08. C Southover *Chich* from 07. *6 Verralls Walk, Southover, Lewes BN7 1LP* Tel (01273) 480114 Mobile 07963-988618 E-mail david.garratt@macmail.com

GARRATT, Mrs Helen Louise Fontana. b 66. Univ Coll Lon BSc88 MSc96. SEITE BA11. **d** 11. NSM Southover *Chich* from 11. *6 Verralls Walk, Lewes BN7 1LP* Tel (01273) 480114

GARRATT, Malcolm John. b 52. Nottm Univ BSc73. Trin Coll Bris 97. **d** 99 **p** 00. C Bawtry w Austerfield and Misson *S'well* 99-00; C Hucknall Torkard 00-03; P-in-c Clipstone 03-10; P-in-c Dunchurch *Cov* from 10. *The Vicarage, 11 Critchley Drive, Dunchurch, Rugby CV22 6PJ* Tel (01788) 810274
E-mail malcolm.garratt@ntlworld.com

GARRATT, Peter James. b 37. ALCD64. **d** 64 **p** 65. C Bingham *S'well* 64-67; C Mansfield SS Pet and Paul 67-69; V Purlwell *Wakef* 69-73; R Kirk Sandall and Edenthorpe *Sheff* 73-82; R Whippingham w E Cowes *Portsm* 82-87; V Soberton w Newtown 87-01; rtd 02; Perm to Offic *Portsm* from 02. *35 Fair Isle Close, Fareham PO14 3RT* Tel (01329) 661162

GARRATT, Roger Charles. b 50. St Jo Coll Dur BA72. Cranmer Hall Dur 72. **d** 74 **p** 75. C Leamington Priors St Paul *Cov* 74-77; Chapl Emscote Lawn Sch Warw 77-00; Chapl and Dep Hd Arden Lawn Sch 77-00; TV Warwick *Cov* 02-08; rtd 08. *8 Wasdale Close, Leamington Spa CV32 6NF* Tel (01926) 335474 E-mail roger.garratt@btinternet.com

GARRETT, Ms Celia Joy. b 60. RGN81 RM85. Cant Sch of Min 92. **d** 95. C S Ashford St Fran *Cant* 95-98; NSM 98-05. *Address withheld by request*

GARRETT, Christopher Hugh Ahlan. b 35. Sarum & Wells Th Coll 72. **d** 75 **p** 76. C Addiscombe St Mildred *Cant* 75-81; V Thornton Heath St Jude w St Aid *S'wark* 81-00; rtd 00; Perm to Offic *Glouc* from 01. *Edge View, 18 Gloucester Road, Painswick GL6 6RA* Tel (01452) 813688

GARRETT, Clive Robert. b 54. Sheff Univ BA75 PhD80 Ex Univ PGCE88. St Jo Coll Nottm MA98. **d** 98 **p** 99. C Bath Weston St Jo w Kelston *B & W* 98-02; R from 02. *The Rectory, 8 Ashley Avenue, Bath BA1 3DR* Tel (01225) 317323
E-mail crg@cix.co.uk

GARRETT, Miss Elizabeth Clare. b 46. Trin Coll Bris. **d** 94 **p** 95. C Ewyas Harold w Dulas, Kenderchurch etc *Heref* 94-96; C Tupsley w Hampton Bishop 96-00; TV Uttoxeter Area *Lich* 00-05; P-in-c Gt Canfield w High Roding and Aythorpe Roding *Chelmsf* from 05. *The Rectory, 3 Old Vicarage Close, High Easter, Chelmsford CM1 4RW* Tel (01245) 231429
E-mail claregarrett@aol.com

GARRETT, Geoffrey David. b 57. Oak Hill Th Coll 83. **d** 86 **p** 87. C Trentham *Lich* 86-90; V Rhodes *Man* 90-00; P-in-c Bardsley 00-05; V 05-08; V Watton *Nor* from 08; C Cockley Cley w Gooderstone from 10. *St Mary's Vicarage, Norwich Road, Watton, Thetford IP25 6DB* Tel (01953) 881439
E-mail garretts@talktalk.net

GARRETT, Ian Lee. b 60. MCSP81. Sarum & Wells Th Coll 86. **d** 89 **p** 90. C Maidstone St Martin *Cant* 89-95; P-in-c S Ashford St Fran 95-07; TV Bishopsworth and Bedminster Down *Bris* from 07; C Brislington St Chris and St Cuth 07-08; P-in-c Brislington St Cuth from 08. *St Oswald's Vicarage, Cheddar Grove, Bristol BS13 7EN* Tel 0117-964 2649
E-mail ian@ilgarrett.fsnet.co.uk

GARRETT, Kevin George. b 48. Oak Hill Th Coll BA86. **d** 86 **p** 87. C Hoddesdon *St Alb* 86-89; C Loughton St Mary and St Mich *Chelmsf* 89-90; TV 90-95; P-in-c Loughton St Mich 95-96; Public Preacher 97; V Dover St Martin *Cant* from 97. *St Martin's Vicarage, 339 Folkestone Road, Dover CT17 9JG* Tel (01304) 339273 E-mail kevin.garrett@nltworld.com

GARRETT (*née* KIRK), **Natalie Roberta.** b 71. Leeds Univ BA93. Wycliffe Hall Ox 03. **d** 05 **p** 06. C Gipsy Hill Ch Ch *S'wark* 05-06; Hon C Burford w Fulbrook, Taynton, Asthall etc *Ox* 06-10; Hon C Twickenham Common H Trin *Lon* from 10. *Holy Trinity Vicarage, 1 Vicarage Road, Twickenham TW2 5TS* Tel (020) 8898 1168

GARRETT, Timothy Michael. b 70. Univ of Wales (Abth) BA91. Wycliffe Hall Ox BA01. **d** 02 **p** 03. C Ox St Andr 02-06; C Burford w Fulbrook, Taynton, Asthall etc 06-10; V Twickenham Common H Trin *Lon* from 10. *Holy Trinity Vicarage, 1 Vicarage Road, Twickenham TW2 5TS* Tel (020) 8898 1168
E-mail revgaz@hotmail.com

GARRISH (*née* SMITH), **Elaine Joan.** b 46. NTMTC BA07. **d** 07 **p** 08. NSM Roxbourne St Andr *Lon* 07-10; Perm to Offic from 10. *33 Farthings Close, Pinner HA5 2QR* Tel (020) 8429 0659 Mobile 07780-904402
E-mail elainegarrish@blueyonder.co.uk

GARROD, Mrs Christine Anne. b 49. EAMTC. **d** 00 **p** 01. C N w S Wootton *Nor* 00-04; P-in-c Brinklow *Cov* 04-09; P-in-c Harborough Magna 04-09; P-in-c Monks Kirby w Pailton and Stretton-under-Fosse 04-09; P-in-c Churchover w Willey 04-09; R Gt and Lt Plumstead w Thorpe End and Witton *Nor* from 09. *The Rectory, 9 Lawn Crescent, Thorpe End, Norwich NR13 5BP* Tel (01603) 304432 E-mail cagarrod@hotmail.com

GARROW, Alan John Philip. b 67. Lon Bible Coll BA90 Wycliffe Hall Ox MPhil94 Jes Coll Ox DPhil00. **d** 93 **p** 94. C Waltham H Cross *Chelmsf* 93-97; C Akeman *Ox* 00-04; Tutor SAOMC 00-04; Dir Studies 04-05; Dir Studies Ox Min Course 05-06; C Bath Abbey w St Jas *B & W* from 06. *48 Devonshire Buildings, Bath BA2 4SU* Tel (01225) 464172
E-mail alan.garrow@ctrt.net

GARRUD, Christopher Charles. b 54. Cranmer Hall Dur. **d** 85 **p** 86. C Watford *St Alb* 85-89; C Ireland Wood *Ripon* 89-95; Chapl Cookridge Hosp Leeds 93-95; R Farnley 95-02. *75 Hill Court Drive, Leeds LS13 2AN*

GARSIDE, Geoffrey Malcolm. b 43. Huddersfield Poly CertEd Huddersfield Univ BEd. **d** 05 **p** 06. OLM Almondbury w Farnley Tyas *Wakef* 05-10; P-in-c Marsden from 10. *20A Station Road, Marsden, Huddersfield HD7 6DG* Tel (01484) 847864
E-mail ggarside@aol.com

GARSIDE, Canon Howard. b 24. Leeds Univ BA49. Coll of Resurr Mirfield 49. **d** 51 **p** 52. C Barnsley St Pet *Wakef* 51-53; C Linthorpe *York* 53-56; V Middlesbrough St Aid 56-64; V Manston *Ripon* 64-78; RD Whitkirk 70-78; Hon Can Ripon Cathl 78-89; V Harrogate St Wilfrid 78-80; P-in-c Harrogate St Luke 78-80; V Harrogate St Wilfrid and St Luke 80-89; RD Harrogate 83-88; rtd 89; Perm to Offic *Ripon* from 89. *73 Kirkby Road, Ripon HG4 2HH* Tel (01765) 690625 Mobile 07714-454829 E-mail hjgarside@aol.com

GARSIDE, Melvin. b 42. NOC 85. **d** 88 **p** 89. C Lindley *Wakef* 88-91; C Shelf *Bradf* 91-93; V Lundwood *Wakef* 93-97; V Hanging Heaton 97-01; V Woodhouse and Bp's Adv in Racial Justice 01-05; rtd 05. *5 Hawthorne Close, Nether Poppleton, York YO26 6HP* Tel 07803-250258 (mobile)
E-mail melgarside@melgarside.demon.co.uk

GARTLAND, Christopher Michael. b 49. Man Univ BA78 Leeds Univ MEd99 Univ Coll Lon MSc04. Coll of Resurr Mirfield 82. **d** 84 **p** 85. C Almondbury w Farnley Tyas *Wakef* 84-87; P-in-c Upperthong 87-89; TV Upper Holme Valley 89-91; Chapl Stanley Royd Hosp Wakef 91-94; Chapl Wakef HA (Mental Health Services) 91-95; Chapl Wakef and Pontefract Community NHS Trust 95-01; Hd Past/Spiritual Care SW Yorks Mental Health NHS Trust from 02. *2 Weirside, Marsden, Huddersfield HD7 6BU* Tel (01924) 327498
E-mail mike.gartland@swyt.nhs.uk
or michaelgartland4@aol.com

GARTON, Mrs Anne-Marie. b 48. BA MSW CQSW. **d** 02 **p** 03. NSM Caterham *S'wark* 02-10; Perm to Offic from 10. *51 Crescent Road, Caterham CR3 6LH* Tel (01883) 343188

GARTON, Capt Jeremy. b 56. Wilson Carlile Coll 78 SEITE 94. **d** 96 **p** 97. C Clapham Team *S'wark* 96-00; P-in-c Caterham Valley 00-03; TV Caterham from 03. *The Vicarage, 2 Churchview Close, Caterham CR3 6EZ* Tel (01883) 343188 Fax (020) 7863 4120 E-mail jerry@garton.com

✠**GARTON, The Rt Revd John Henry.** b 41. Worc Coll Ox BA67 MA. Cuddesdon Coll 67. **d** 69 **p** 70 **c** 96. CF 69-73; Lect Linc Th Coll 73-78; TR Cov E 78-86; V Cuddesdon and Prin Ripon Coll Cuddesdon 86-96; Hon Can Worc Cathl 87-96; Suff Bp Plymouth *Ex* 96-05; rtd 05; Hon Asst Bp Ox from 05. *clo P M Garton Esq, 68 Stapleton Road, Headington, Oxford OX3 7LU*

GARTSIDE, Philip Oswin. b 60. Pemb Coll Ox BA82 MA86 Leeds Univ BA92. Coll of Resurr Mirfield 93. **d** 93 **p** 94. C Walton-on-the-Hill *Liv* 93-97; CR from 97. *House of the Resurrection, Stocks Bank Road, Mirfield WF14 0BN* Tel (01924) 483327

GARVIE, Mrs Anna-Lisa Karen. b 48. Luton Univ BA99 Leeds Univ MA05. St Alb Minl Tr Scheme 89. **d** 96 **p** 97. NSM Caddington *St Alb* 96-99; NSM St Paul's Walden 99-01; Chapl Chelsea and Westmr Healthcare NHS Trust 98-01; Co-ord Chapl Hinchingbrooke Health Care NHS Trust 01-09; Chapl Thorpe Hall Hospice from 09. *Thorpe Hall Hospice, Thorpe Road, Longthorpe, Peterborough PE3 6LW* Tel (01733) 330060 Fax 269078 E-mail anna.garvie@suerydercare.org

GARVIE, Peter Francis. b 84. Univ Coll Dur BA08. St Steph Ho Ox 09. **d** 11. C Sunderland St Mary and St Pet *Dur* from 11. *113 Holborn Road, Sunderland SR4 8BJ*
E-mail ptrgarvie@gmail.com

GARWOOD, Simon Frederick. b 62. Reading Univ BA85 Lon Univ PGCE93 Birm Univ BD99. Qu Coll Birm MA00. **d** 00

p 01. C Chelmsf All SS 00-03; TV Witham from 03. *18 Witham Lodge, Witham CM8 1HG* Tel (01376) 519017
E-mail sgarwood@keme.co.uk

GASCOIGNE, Philip. b 27. Oak Hill Th Coll. **d** 62 **p** 63. C Blackpool Ch Ch *Blackb* 62-65; V Bootle St Leon *Liv* 65-71; Staff Evang CPAS 71-74; V St Helens St Mark *Liv* 74-77; V Blackpool Ch Ch *Blackb* 77-81; V Blackpool Ch Ch w All SS 81-97; rtd 98; Perm to Offic *Blackb* from 98. *18 Grange Road, Blackpool FY3 8EJ* Tel (01253) 315607

GASH, Christopher Alan Ronald. b 39. EMMTC 83. **d** 86 **p** 87. C Thurmaston *Leic* 86-89; P-in-c Stoke Golding w Dadlington 89-01; rtd 01; Perm to Offic *Cov* 01-03; *Sarum* 03-04; *Ox* 04-06; *St E* 06-09. *13 Warwick Lane, Market Bosworth, Nuneaton CV13 0JU* Tel (01455) 292998

GASH, Canon Wilfred John. b 31. St Aid Birkenhead 60. **d** 62 **p** 63. C St Mary Cray and St Paul's Cray *Roch* 62-65; C Bexley St Jo 65-67; R Levenshulme St Pet *Man* 67-72; V Clifton 72-94; AD Eccles 87-17; Hon Can Man Cathl 86-97; P-in-c Pendlebury Ch Ch and St Aug 86-87; TR Bolton St Paul w Em 94-96; C Urmston 96-97; Dioc Adv on Evang 89-97; rtd 98; Perm to Offic *Carl* 98-06 and *Blackb* from 08. *11 East Bank, Barrowford, Nelson BB9 6HD* Tel (01282) 611419

GASKELL, Barrie Stuart. b 56. SNWTP 07. **d** 10 **p** 11. NSM Bolton St Pet *Man* from 10; Chapl R Bolton Hosp NHS Foundn Trust from 10. *1 Old Vicarage Mews, Westhoughton, Bolton BL5 2EQ* Tel (01942) 818797 E-mail barrie.gaskell@rbh.nhs.uk

GASKELL, David. b 48. Lon Univ BD76. Trin Coll Bris 72. **d** 76 **p** 77. C Eccleston Ch Ch *Liv* 76-80; C Rainhill 80-83; V Over Darwen St Jas *Blackb* 83-88; V Livesey 88-95; V Preston St Cuth 95-01; V Copp w Inskip from 01. *St Peter's Vicarage, Preston Road, Inskip, Preston PR4 0TT* Tel (01772) 690316

GASKELL, Canon Ian Michael. b 51. Nottm Univ BTh81. Linc Th Coll 77. **d** 81 **p** 82. C Wakef St Jo 81-83; Ind Chapl *Sheff* 83-86; V Cleckheaton St Luke and Whitechapel *Wakef* 86-93; V Birkenshaw w Hunsworth 93-98; RD Birstall 96-98; Can Res Wakef Cathl 98-05; Hon Can from 05; Dioc Soc Resp Adv 98-06; V Chapelthorpe from 06. *21 Stoney Lane, Chapelthorpe, Wakefield WF4 3JN* Tel (01924) 255360

GASKELL, Preb John Bernard. b 28. Jes Coll Ox BA52 MA58. Chich Th Coll 59. **d** 60 **p** 61. C Beckenham St Jas *Roch* 60-64; C St Marylebone All SS *Lon* 64-68; C-in-c Grosvenor Chpl 68-79; Warden Liddon Ho Lon 68-79; V Holborn St Alb w Saffron Hill St Pet *Lon* 79-93; AD S Camden 81-86; Preb St Paul's Cathl 85-93; rtd 93; Perm to Offic *Lon* 93-02 and from 07; Hon C St Marylebone All SS 92-07. *12 Up The Quadrangle, Morden College, 19 St Germans Place, London SE3 0PW* Tel (020) 8858 9589

GASKELL, Marion Ingrid. b 52. Wilson Carlile Coll 74 NOC 96. **d** 99 **p** 00. C Thorpe Edge *Bradf* 99-02; TV Shelf w Buttershaw St Aid 02-04; TR from 04. *8 Redwing Drive, Bradford BD6 3YD* Tel (01274) 881701
E-mail marion.gaskell@bradford.anglican.org

GASKELL, Mary. b 50. Nottm Univ BTh81 Bradf and Ilkley Coll CertEd89. Linc Th Coll 77. **dss** 81 **d** 89 **p** 94. Wakef St Jo 81-83; NSM Cleckheaton St Luke and Whitechapel 89-93; NSM Birkenshaw w Hunsworth 93-95; Asst Chapl St Jas Univ Hosp NHS Trust Leeds 95-97; Chapl Rishworth Sch Ripponden 97-99; P-in-c Purlwell *Wakef* 00-01; Chapl Dewsbury Health Care NHS Trust 01-02; Chapl Mid Yorks Hosps NHS Trust 02-10; rtd 10. *21 Stoney Lane, Chapelthorpe, Wakefield WF4 3JN* Tel (01924) 255360

GASKELL, Peter John. b 70. Bris Univ MS93 ChB93. Oak Hill Th Coll BA03. **d** 03 **p** 04. NSM Poulton Lancelyn H Trin *Ches* 03-07; NSM Rusholme H Trin *Man* from 09. *47 Linden Park, Manchester M19 2PQ* Tel 07769-682142 (mobile)
E-mail peter@glod.co.uk

GASPER (*née* COHEN), **Mrs Janet Elizabeth.** b 47. Birm Univ CertEd70. WMMTC 93. **d** 96 **p** 97. NSM Leominster *Heref* 96-99; C Letton w Staunton, Byford, Mansel Gamage etc 99-01; Hon Chapl RAF 97-01; R Baxterley w Hurley and Wood End and Merevale etc *Birm* from 01; P-in-c Kingsbury from 04. *The Vicarage, Church Lane, Kingsbury, Tamworth B78 2LR* Tel (01827) 874252 E-mail mgasper1@tiscali.net

GASTON, Mrs Lydia Madeleine. b 79. St Andr Univ MA03 Rob Coll Cam BTh09. Ridley Hall Cam 06. **d** 09 **p** 10. C Erdington Ch the K *Birm* from 09. *144 Witton Lodge Road, Perry Common, Birmingham B23 5AP* Tel 07779-006178 (mobile)
E-mail lydgaston@hotmail.co.uk

GASTON, Raymond Gordon. b 62. Leeds Univ BA94. Linc Th Coll MTh94. **d** 96 **p** 97. C Leeds Gipton Epiphany *Ripon* 96-99; V Leeds St Marg and All Hallows 99-07; Tutor Qu Coll Birm from 08. *Flat 12, Queen's Foundation, Somerset Road, Birmingham B15 2QH* Tel 0121-454 1527 Fax 454 8171

GATENBY, Simon John Taylor. b 62. Nottm Univ BA83. St Jo Coll Nottm 84. **d** 87 **p** 88. C Haughton St Mary *Man* 87-90; C Newburn *Newc* 90-93; P-in-c Brunswick *Man* 93-96; R from 96; AD Hulme 99-05. *The Rectory, Hartfield Close, Brunswick, Manchester M13 9YX* Tel 0161-273 2470
E-mail simon@brunswickchurch.freeserve.co.uk

GATES, Alan Raymond. b 46. EAMTC 98. **d** 01 **p** 02. C W w E Mersea and Peldon w Gt and Lt Wigborough *Chelmsf* 01-05; P-in-c Gt Barton *St E* from 05; RD Thingoe from 08. *The Vicarage, Church Road, Great Barton, Bury St Edmunds IP31 2QR* Tel and fax (01284) 787274 Mobile 07974-020379 E-mail alan.gates@virgin.net

GATES, Mrs Frances Margaret. b 44. STETS 01. **d** 04 **p** 05. NSM Portsea St Mary, Portsea St Geo and Portsea All SS *Portsm* 04-11; rtd 11. *114 Kings Road, Southsea PO5 4DW* Tel (023) 9282 0326 Mobile 07951-062226

GATES, John Michael. b 35. Dur Univ BA56. Cranmer Hall Dur 58. **d** 60 **p** 61. C Felixstowe St Jo *St E* 60-67; R Boyton w Capel St Andrew and Hollesley 67-98; P-in-c Shottisham w Sutton 87-92; rtd 98. *9 Foxgrove Lane, Felixstowe IP11 7JS* Tel (01394) 276886

GATES, Richard James. b 46. BA85. Oak Hill Th Coll 82. **d** 85 **p** 86. C Heald Green St Cath *Ches* 85-89; V Norton 89-98; V Bunbury and Tilstone Fearnall from 98. *The Vicarage, Vicarage Lane, Bunbury, Tarporley CW6 9PE* Tel (01829) 260991 Mobile 07715-178750 E-mail rick@prayer.fsnet.co.uk

GATES, Simon Philip. b 60. St Andr Univ MA82 St Jo Coll Dur BA86. Cranmer Hall Dur 84. **d** 87 **p** 88. C Southall Green St Jo *Lon* 87-91; Assoc Min St Andr Ch Hong Kong 91-95; V Clapham Park St Steph *S'wark* 96-06; P-in-c Telford Park St Thos 05-06; V Telford Park from 06; AD Lambeth S from 06. *The Vicarage, 2 Thornton Road, London SW12 0JU* Tel (020) 8671 8276 E-mail sgates2207@aol.com

GATFORD, The Ven Ian. b 40. AKC65. **d** 67 **p** 68. C Clifton w Glapton *S'well* 67-71; TV Clifton 71-75; V Sherwood 75-84; Can Res Derby Cathl 84-99; Adn Derby and Hon Can Derby Cathl 93-05; rtd 05; Perm to Offic *Derby* from 05. *9 Poplar Nook, Allestree, Derby DE22 2DW* Tel (01332) 557567

GATISS, Lee. b 72. New Coll Ox BA96 MA01. Oak Hill Th Coll BA00. **d** 01 **p** 02. C Barton Seagrave w Warkton *Pet* 01-04; C St Helen Bishopsgate w St Andr Undershaft etc *Lon* 04-09; Perm to Offic *Ely* from 10. *Peterhouse, Cambridge CB2 1RD* E-mail editor@theologian.org.uk

GATLIFFE, David Spenser. b 45. Keble Coll Ox BA67 Fitzw Coll Cam BA69. Westcott Ho Cam 67. **d** 69 **p** 70. C Oxted *S'wark* 69-72; C Roehampton H Trin 72-75; C S Beddington St Mich 76-77; TV Clapham Old Town 78-87; P-in-c Clapham Ch Ch and St Jo 81-87; TV Clapham Team 87-89; V S Wimbledon H Trin and St Pet 89-01; R Lee St Marg 01-10; Ldr Post Ord Tr Woolwich Area 04-09; rtd 10. *47 Catherine Street, Frome BA11 1DA* Tel (01373) 228757

GATRILL, Adrian Colin. b 60. Southn Univ BTh82 FRSA99. Linc Th Coll 83. **d** 85 **p** 86. C W Bromwich St Andr *Lich* 85-88; C W Bromwich St Andr w Ch Ch 88-89; Chapl RAF from 89; Dir of Ords from 06; Perm to Offic *St D* 90-95 and *Ripon* from 00. *Chaplaincy Services, Valiant Block, HQ Air Command, RAF High Wycombe HP14 4UE* Tel (01494) 496800 Fax 496343 E-mail adrian.gatrill@tesco.net

GAU, Justin. b 65. **d** 11. NSM S Hackney St Jo w Ch Ch *Lon* from 11. *27 Arlington Square, London N1 7DP* Tel (020) 7359 1357

GAUGE, Canon Barrie Victor. b 41. St D Coll Lamp BA62 Selw Coll Cam BA64 MA74. Bp Burgess Hall Lamp. **d** 65 **p** 66. C Newtown w Llanllwchaiarn w Aberhafesp *St As* 65-68; C Prestatyn 68-73; R Bodfari and Dioc RE Adv 73-76; Perm to Offic *Ches* 76-84; V Birkenhead St Jas w St Bede 84-90; Dir of Resources 90-98; Hon Can Ches Cathl 94-98; C Lache cum Saltney 95-98; Par Development Adv *Derby* 98-06; Can Res Derby Cathl 99-06; Dioc Miss Adv 01-06; rtd 06. *40 Saxon Street, Wrexham LL13 7BD* Tel (01978) 353715 E-mail barrie.gauge@talk21.com

GAUNT, Adam. b 79. St Jo Coll Dur BA00 MA02. St Steph Ho Ox 03. **d** 05 **p** 06. C Middlesbrough Ascension *York* 05-09; R Loftus and Carlin How w Skinningrove from 09. *The Rectory, 11 Micklow Lane, Loftus, Saltburn-by-the-Sea TS13 4JE* Tel (01287) 644047 E-mail adamgaunt@btinternet.com

GAUNT (*née* COTTELL), **Mrs Avril Jane.** b 50. SRN72 SCM74. S Dios Minl Tr Scheme 92. **d** 95 **p** 97. NSM Yatton Moor *B & W* 95-96 and 97-02; NSM Bourne *Guildf* 96-97; Asst Chapl N Bris NHS Trust 02-05; Perm to Offic *B & W* from 05. *Myrtle Cottage, Ham Lane, Kingston Seymour, Clevedon BS21 6XE* Tel (01934) 832995

GAUNT, Eric Emmerson. b 33. Sarum Th Coll 65. **d** 67 **p** 68. C Hatch End St Anselm *Lon* 67-74; V Neasden cum Kingsbury St Cath 74-80; V Neasden St Cath w St Paul from 80. *St Catherine's Vicarage, Tanfield Avenue, London NW2 7RX* Tel (020) 8452 7322 E-mail dianachapman@madasafish.com

GAUNTLETT, Gilbert Bernard. b 36. Oriel Coll Ox BA59 MA62. Wycliffe Hall Ox 59. **d** 61 **p** 62. C Maidenhead St Andr and St Mary *Ox* 61-64; C Ox St Ebbe w St Pet 64-68; R Nottingham St Nic *S'well* 68-72; Asst Master Leys High Sch Redditch 73-79; Asst Master Stourport High Sch 79-85; rtd 97. *The Tower, Brynygwin Isaf, Dolgellau LL40 1YA* Tel (01341) 423481

GAUSDEN, Canon Peter James. b 32. Qu Coll Birm 57. **d** 60 **p** 61. C Battersea St Pet *S'wark* 60-63; C St Peter-in-Thanet *Cant* 63-68; V Sturry 68-74; R Sturry w Fordwich and Westbere w

Hersden 74-97; Dioc Ecum Officer 91-97; Hon Can Cant Cathl 96-97; rtd 97; Perm to Offic *Cant* 97-99 and from 04; Hon C St Nicholas at Wade w Sarre and Chislet w Hoath 99-04. *2 The Paddocks, Collards Close, Monkton, Ramsgate CT12 4JZ* Tel (01843) 825374 E-mail peter@pgausden.fsnet.co.uk

GAVED, Kenneth John Drew. b 31. **d** 95 **p** 96. OLM W Wickham St Jo *S'wark* 95-04 and from 07. *42 Queensway, West Wickham BR4 9ER* Tel (020) 8462 4326

GAVIGAN, Canon Josephine Katherine. b 49. Univ Coll Chich BA00. Sarum Th Coll 93. **d** 96. NSM Boxgrove *Chich* 96-00; C 00-03; Dn-in-c Maybridge from 03; RD Worthing 05-10; Can and Preb Chich Cathl from 07. *56 The Boulevard, Worthing BN13 1LA* Tel (01903) 249463 Mobile 07760-277262 E-mail ruraldean@worthingdeanery.org.uk

GAVIN, David Guy. b 63. Birm Univ BA85 St Jo Coll Dur BA90. Cranmer Hall Dur 88. **d** 91 **p** 92. C Parr *Liv* 91-95; TV Toxteth St Philemon w St Gabr and St Cleopas 95-02; P-in-c 02-06; TR 06-11; TV from 11. *St Cleopas' Vicarage, Beresford Road, Liverpool L8 4SG* Tel 0151-727 0633 E-mail gavins@uwclub.net

GAVIN (*née* GREGORY), **Mrs Judith Rosalind.** b 61. Open Univ BA97. St Jo Coll Nottm 99. **d** 01 **p** 02. C Moss Side St Jas w St Clem *Man* 01-04; C Whalley Range St Edm 01-04; C Rhyl w St Ann *St As* 04-05. *82 Grosvenor Avenue, Rhyl LL18 4HB* Tel (01745) 332224 E-mail judithanddarrell.gavin@btinternet.com

GAWITH, Canon Alan Ruthven. b 24. Lich Th Coll 54. **d** 56 **p** 57. C Appleby and Murton cum Hilton *Carl* 56-59; C Newton Aycliffe *Dur* 59-61; C-in-c Owton Manor CD 61-67; V Kendal St Geo *Carl* 67-74; Soc Resp Officer *Man* 74-89; Hon Can Man Cathl 82-89; Bp's Adv on AIDS 88-92; rtd 90; Perm to Offic *Man* from 90. *7 Redwaters, Leigh WN7 1JD* Tel (01942) 676641

GAWNE-CAIN, John. b 38. G&C Coll Cam BA61 MA66 CEng MICE. Cuddesdon Coll 74. **d** 76 **p** 77. C Cowley St Jas *Ox* 76-80; P-in-c Ox St Giles 80-85; V Ox St Giles and SS Phil and Jas w St Marg 85-92; P-in-c Uffington w Woolstone and Baulking 92-93; P-in-c Shellingford 92-93; R Uffington, Shellingford, Woolstone and Baulking 93-03; rtd 03; Perm to Offic *Ox* 04-08. *61 St Johns Street, Winchester SO23 0HF* Tel (01962) 851366 E-mail j.gawne-cain@ruralnet.org.uk

GAWTHROP-DORAN, Mrs Sheila Mary. b 37. Birm Univ CertEd. Dalton Ho Bris 68. **dss** 79 **d** 87. Halliwell St Paul *Man* 79-82; New Bury 82-89; Par Dn 87-89; Par Dn Tonge w Alkrington 89-94; rtd 94; Perm to Offic *York* from 95. *35 Swarthdale, Haxby, York YO32 3NZ* Tel (01904) 761247

GAWTHROPE, Julie Anne. b 57. **d** 10 **p** 11. C Cherry Hinton St Jo *Ely* from 10. *46 Hölmbrook Road, Cambridge CB1 7ST* Tel (01223) 244311 Mobile 07789-838084 E-mail julie.gawthrope@ntlworld.com

GAY, Adam Garcia Hugh. b 57. STETS 02. **d** 05 **p** 06. C Bitterne *Win* 05-09; V Hedge End St Luke from 09. *16 Elliot Rise, Hedge End, Southampton SO30 2RU* Tel (01489) 786765 E-mail adamgay@totalise.co.uk

GAY, Colin James. b 57. Univ of Wales (Lamp) BA63. Chich Th Coll 63. **d** 65 **p** 66. C W Hackney St Barn *Lon* 65-69; C Hitchin H Sav *St Alb* 69-74; P-in-c Apsley End 74-80; TV Chambersbury 80-85; V Barnet Vale St Mark 85-03; rtd 03; Perm to Offic *St Alb* from 03. *Colters, 14 Barleyfield Way, Houghton Regis, Dunstable LU5 5ER* Tel (01582) 862309

GAY, John Charles Nankervis. b 58. ERMC 03. **d** 06 **p** 07. C Wilton *B & W* 06-10; R Itchingfield w Slinfold *Chich* from 10. *The Rectory, The Street, Slinfold, Horsham RH13 0RR* Tel (01403) 790197 E-mail jlmd@surfree.co.uk

GAY, John Dennis. b 43. St Pet Coll Ox BA64 MA68 DPhil69 MSc78. Ripon Hall Ox 64. **d** 67 **p** 68. C Paddington St Jas *Lon* 67-71; P-in-c 71-72; Chapl Culham Coll Abingdon 72-79; Lect Ox Univ 78-80; Dir Culham Inst from 80. *Culham Institute, 15 Norham Gardens, Oxford OX2 6PY* Tel (01865) 284885 Fax 284886 E-mail john.gay@culham.ac.uk

GAY, Canon Perran Russell. b 59. St Cath Coll Cam BA81 MA85 Ex Univ PGCE82 FRGS97. Ripon Coll Cuddesdon BA86. **d** 87 **p** 88. C Bodmin w Lanhydrock and Lanivet *Truro* 87-90; Bp's Dom Chapl and Dioc Officer for Unity 90-94; Can Res and Chan Truro Cathl from 94; Prec from 01; Dir of Tr 94-99; Chapl Epiphany Ho from 06. *52 Daniell Road, Truro TR1 2DA* Tel (01872) 276782 *or* 276491 Fax 277788 E-mail perran@perrangay.com *or* perran@trurocathedral.org.uk

GAY, Stuart. b 66. Oak Hill Th Coll BA94. **d** 00 **p** 01. C Sunningdale *Ox* 00-04; V Margate St Phil *Cant* from 04. *St Philip's Vicarage, 82 Crundale Way, Margate CT9 3YH* Tel (01843) 221589 E-mail stuartgay@btinternet.com

GAYFORD, John. b 37. Lon Univ BDS61 MB, BS65 MD78 FDSRCS64 FRCPsych86 Heythrop Coll Lon MA05 Univ of Wales (Lamp) MTh09. St Jo Sem Wonersh 02. **d** 03 **p** 04. NSM E Grinstead St Mary *Chich* from 03. *Third Acre, 217 Smallfield Road, Horley RH6 9LR* Tel (01342) 842752

GAYLER, Canon Roger Kenneth. b 44. Lich Th Coll 68. **d** 70 **p** 71. C Chingford St Anne *Chelmsf* 70-75; P-in-c Marks Gate 75-81; V from 81; RD Barking and Dagenham from 00; Hon Can

Chelmsf Cathl from 09. *The Vicarage, 187 Rose Lane, Romford RM6 5NR* Tel (020) 8599 0415 E-mail rev@r-gayler.fsnet.co.uk

GAYNOR, Christopher Thomas. b 68. **d** 08 **p** 09. C Banbury St Fran *Ox* from 08. *26 Meadowsweet Way, Banbury OX16 1WE* Tel (01295) 271403 E-mail pheechris@yahoo.co.uk

GAYNOR, Mrs Mieke Aaltjen Cornelia. b 43. UEA BA79. St Jo Coll Nottm 02. **d** 03 **p** 04. NSM Hambleden Valley *Ox* 03-09; C Wollaton *S'well* from 09. *32 Deddington Lane, Bramcote, Nottingham NG9 3EW* Tel 0115-928 7765 E-mail mieke.gaynor@btopenworld.com

GAZE, Mrs Sally Ann. b 69. SS Coll Cam BA91 MA95 Birm Univ MPhil98 PGCE92. Qu Coll Birm 94. **d** 96 **p** 97. C Martley and Wichenford, Knightwick etc *Worc* 96-00; C Crickhowell w Cwmdu and Tretower *S & B* 00-02; TR Newton Flotman, Swainsthorpe, Tasburgh, etc *Nor* from 02; Dioc Fresh Expressions Facilitator from 09. *The Rectory, Church Road, Newton Flotman, Norwich NR15 1QB* Tel (01508) 470762 E-mail sally@tasvalley.org

GBEBIKAN, Angela Maria Abíke. b 56. Westcott Ho Cam 02. **d** 04 **p** 05. C Norbury St Steph and Thornton Heath *S'wark* 04-07; P-in-c S Beddington and Roundshaw 07-08; V from 08. *St Michael's Vicarage, Milton Road, Wallington SM6 9RP* Tel (020) 8647 1201 Mobile 07801-065472 E-mail gbebikan@cantab.net

GBONDA, Egerton Joe Fode. b 67. Univ of Sierra Leone BSc94 MSc03. **d** 06 **p** 08. Sierra Leone 06-09; Perm to Offic *S'wark* from 10. *36 Queensberry Place, London E12 6UN* Tel (020) 8470 8786 Mobile 07882-872830 E-mail father.egerton.gbonda@gmail.com

GEACH, Canon Michael Bernard. b 26. Qu Coll Cam BA51 MA56. Westcott Ho Cam 51. **d** 53 **p** 54. C Kenwyn *Truro* 53-56; C Bodmin 56-59; C Helland 56-59; R St Dominic 59-65; Chapl Cotehele Ho Chapl Cornwall 60-65; V Linkinhorne 65-84; R Veryan w Ruan Lanihorne 84-96; Hon Can Truro Cathl 92-96; rtd 96; Perm to Offic *Truro* from 96. *17 Paul's Row, Truro TR1 1HH* Tel (01872) 262927

GEACH, Mrs Sarah Jane. b 50. Trin Coll Carmarthen CertEd73. WEMTC 96. **d** 99 **p** 00. C Pill w Easton in Gordano and Portbury *B & W* 99-02; TV Ross *Heref* 02-07; P-in-c Begelly w Ludchurch and Crunwere *St D* 07-09; P-in-c Begelly w Ludchurch and E Williamston 09-10; R from 10. *The Rectory, New Road, Kilgetty SA68 0YG* Tel (01834) 812078 E-mail sgeach@btinternet.com

GEAR, John Arthur. b 37. St Aid Birkenhead 62. **d** 64 **p** 66. C Attleborough *Cov* 64-66; C Attercliffe *Sheff* 66-68; C Sheerness H Trin w St Paul *Cant* 68-73; Asst Youth Adv *S'wark* 73-78; Youth Chapl *Lich* 78-88; V Stafford St Jo and Tixall w Ingestre 88-92; Gen Sec NCEC 92-97; rtd 97; Perm to Offic *Lich* 01-02 and from 04; P-in-c Shrewsbury H Cross 02-03. *Greenside, Lime Kiln Bank, Telford TF2 9NU* Tel (01952) 613487 *or* (01743) 232723

✠**GEAR, The Rt Revd Michael Frederick.** b 34. Dur Univ BA59. Cranmer Hall Dur 59. **d** 61 **p** 62 **c** 93. C Bexleyheath Ch Ch *Roch* 61-64; C Ox St Aldate w H Trin 64-67; V Clubmoor *Liv* 67-71; Rhodesia 71-76; Tutor Wycliffe Hall Ox 76-80; V Macclesfield St Mich *Ches* 80-85; RD Macclesfield 84-88; TR Macclesfield Team 85-88; Adn Ches 88-93; Hon Can Ches Cathl 86-88; Suff Bp Doncaster *Sheff* 93-99; rtd 99; Hon Asst Bp Roch from 99; Hon Asst Bp Guarr from 00. *10 Acott Fields, Yalding, Maidstone ME18 6DQ* Tel (01622) 817388 E-mail mike.gear@rochester.anglican.org

GEARY, John Martin. b 52. LRSC77. **d** 08 **p** 09. OLM Heywood *Man* 08-10; OLM Heywood St Marg and Heap Bridge from 10. *30 Conway Close, Heywood OL10 4SG* Tel (01706) 622715 Mobile 07753-462460 E-mail john@johngeary.co.uk

GEARY, Mrs Paula June. b 48. NUI BSc69 HDipEd70. CITC 06. **d** 06 **p** 07. NSM Movildy Union *C, C & R* from 06. *Lehenaghbeg Farm, Lehenaghbeg, Togher, Cork, Republic of Ireland* Tel (00353) (21) 496 1391 E-mail pjgeary650@hotmail.com

GEBAUER, George Gerhart. b 25. Sarum & Wells Th Coll 71. **d** 73 **p** 74. C Portsdown *Portsm* 73-78; V Purbrook 78-91; rtd 91; Perm to Offic *Portsm* from 91. *52 St John's Road, Locks Heath, Southampton SO31 6NF* Tel (01489) 575172

GEDDES, Peter Henry. b 51. Trin Coll Bris 84. **d** 86 **p** 87. C Blackpool St Mark *Blackb* 86-88; C Barnston *Ches* 88-92; V Haslington w Crewe Green 92-04; V Partington and Carrington from 04. *St Mary's Vicarage, Manchester Road, Partington, Manchester M31 4FB* Tel 0161-775 3542

GEDDES, Roderick Charles. b 47. Man Univ DipEd78 MPhil85. NOC 88. **d** 91 **p** 93. C Alverthorpe *Wakef* 91-92; C S Ossett 92-94; R Andreas, V Jurby and V Andreas St Jude *S & M* 94-03; P-in-c Gargrave *Bradf* 03-09; P-in-c Gargrave w Coniston Cold from 09. *The Vicarage, Mill Hill Lane, Gargrave, Skipton BD23 3NQ* Tel (01756) 748548 E-mail roderick.geddes@bradford.anglican.org

GEDGE, Lloyd Victor. b 25. Cuddesdon Coll 54. **d** 57 **p** 58. C Headington *Ox* 57-60; P-in-c Virden Canada 60-63; V Riverton New Zealand 63-66; C All SS Cathl Edmonton Canada 66-68;

P-in-c Edmonton St Steph 68-72; I Edgerton 72-76; I Hanna 76-80; P-in-c N Creake *Nor* 82-83; P-in-c S Creake 82-83; R N and S Creake w Waterden 84-86; rtd 86. *Holden Lodge Box 370, Holden AB T0B 2C0, Canada*

GEDGE, Richard John Anthony. b 70. Bath Univ BEng92 CEng96 MIMechE96. St Jo Coll Nottm MTh09. **d** 09 **p** 11. C Much Woolton *Liv* from 09. *48 Babbacombe Road, Liverpool L16 9JW* E-mail rjagedge@googlemail.com

GEE, Anne Alison. b 43. OBE99. Man Univ MB, ChB66. STETS BA01. **d** 01 **p** 02. NSM Canford Magna *Sarum* 01-06; NSM Horton, Chalbury, Hinton Martel and Holt St Jas from 06; P-in-c from 11; NSM Witchampton, Stanbridge and Long Crichel etc from 06; P-in-c from 11. *The Rectory, Hinton Martell, Wimborne BH21 7HD* Tel (01258) 840256 E-mail a.gee@doctors.org.uk

GEE, Mrs Dorothy <u>Mary</u>. b 33. St Jo Coll Nottm 88. **d** 89 **p** 94. Chapl Asst Univ Hosp Nottm 89-95; NSM Plumtree *S'well* 95-97; P-in-c 97-01; rtd 01; Perm to Offic *S'well* from 01. *16 The Leys, Normanton-on-the-Wolds, Keyworth, Nottingham NG12 5NU* Tel 0115-937 4927 E-mail mary.gee@microhelpuk.net

GEE, Canon Edward. b 28. St Deiniol's Hawarden 59. **d** 61 **p** 62. C Hanging Heaton *Wakef* 61-65; V Brownhill 65-75; V Alverthorpe 75-84; R Castleford All SS 84-92; Hon Can Wakef Cathl 87-92; rtd 92; Perm to Offic *Bradf* and *Wakef* from 92. *1 Holme Ghyll, Colne Road, Glusburn, Keighley BD20 8RG* Tel (01535) 630060 E-mail edward@mandegee.plus.com

GEEN, James William. b 50. Chich Th Coll 76. **d** 79 **p** 80. C Brandon *Dur* 79-84; C Sunderland Red Ho 84-86; P-in-c N Hylton St Marg Castletown 86-89; V 89-91; Dep Chapl HM Pris Dur 91-92; Chapl HM YOI Lanc Farms 92-95; Chapl HM Pris Long Lartin 95-01; Chapl HM Pris Blakenhurst 01-06; Chapl HM Pris Kilmarnock from 07; CMP from 96. *HM Prison Kilmarnock, Bowhouse, Kilmarnock KA1 5AA* Tel (01563) 548800 E-mail jacobus@fsmail.net

GEERING, Preb Anthony Ernest. b 43. Columbia Pacific Univ BSc. Kelham Th Coll 62. **d** 68 **p** 69. C Cov St Mary 68-71; New Zealand 71-75; P-in-c Brinklow *Cov* 75-77; R 77-81; V Monks Kirby w Pailton and Stretton-under-Fosse 77-81; R Harborough Magna 77-81; V Pilton w Ashford *Ex* 81-86; P-in-c Shirwell w Loxhore 83-86; R Crediton and Shobrooke 86-01; P-in-c Sandford w Upton Hellions 00-01; R Crediton, Shobrooke and Sandford etc 01; RD Cadbury 93-97; R Chagford, Drewsteignton, Hittisleigh etc 01-09; P-in-c 09-10; RD Okehampton 02-05; Preb Ex Cathl 02-09; rtd 09. *20 Iter Park, Bow, Crediton EX17 6BY*

GEESON, Brian Alfred. b 30. Qu Coll Ox BA51 Trin & All SS Coll Leeds PGCE76. Qu Coll Birm 54. **d** 55 **p** 56. C Newbold w Dunston *Derby* 55-59; PC Calow 59-64; R Broughton *Bradf* 64-71; TV Seacroft *Ripon* 71-77; Hon C Hanging Heaton *Wakef* 77-87; Hon C Purlwell 87-94; rtd 94; Perm to Offic *Wakef* from 94. *32 Willerton Close, Dewsbury WF12 7SH* Tel (01924) 465621

GEILINGER, John Edward. b 27. Lon Univ BSc53 BD58 BA76 MPhil79. Tyndale Hall Bris. **d** 59 **p** 60. C Plymouth St Jude *Ex* 59-61; Lect Trin Th Coll Umuahia Nigeria 62-73; Lect Th Coll of N Nigeria 72-77; Perm to Offic *Portsm* from 79; rtd 92. *Emmaus House, Colwell Road, Freshwater PO40 9LY* Tel (01983) 753030

GEISOW, Hilary Patricia. b 46. Salford Univ BSc67 Warwick Univ PhD71 Nottm Univ PGCE94. St Jo Coll Nottm 01. **d** 03 **p** 04. C Linc St Faith and St Martin w St Pet 03-06; P-in-c Colsterworth Gp 06-08; P-in-c Peakirk w Glinton and Northborough *Pet* from 08; P-in-c Etton w Helpston and Maxey from 08. *The Rectory, 11 Lincoln Road, Glinton, Peterborough PE6 7JR* Tel (01733) 252265 E-mail hilary.geisow@btinternet.com

GELDARD, Preb Mark Dundas. b 50. Liv Univ BA71 Bris Univ MA75. Trin Coll Bris 73. **d** 75 **p** 76. C Aughton Ch Ch *Liv* 75-78; Tutor Trin Coll Bris 78-84; V Fairfield *Liv* 84-88; Dioc Dir of Ords *Lich* 88-07; C Lich St Mich w St Mary and Wall 95-07; P-in-c Wigginton 07-08; V 08-11; Preb Lich Cathl 00-11; rtd 11. *22 Parnell Avenue, Lichfield WS13 6NX* Tel (01543) 268398 E-mail mark.geldard2@btinternet.com

GELL, Anne Elizabeth. b 63. St Hugh's Coll Ox BA85 MA01 R Free Hosp Sch of Medicine MB, BS90 Surrey Univ BA01. STETS 98. **d** 01 **p** 02. C Headley All SS *Guildf* 01-05; V Wrecclesham from 05; RD Farnham from 11. *2 King's Lane, Wrecclesham, Farnham GU10 4QB* Tel (01252) 716431 E-mail annegell@lineone.net

GELL, Miss Margaret Florence. b 30. **d** 00 **p** 01. NSM Madeley *Lich* 00-04; rtd 04; Perm to Offic *Lich* from 04. *19 Pear Tree Drive, Madeley, Crewe CW3 9EN* Tel (01782) 750669

GELLI, Frank Julian. b 43. Birkbeck Coll Lon BA78 K Coll Lon MTh82. Ripon Coll Cuddesdon 84. **d** 86 **p** 87. C Chiswick St Nic w St Mary *Lon* 86-89; Chapl Ankara *Eur* 89-91; C Kensington St Mary Abbots w St Geo *Lon* 91-99; rtd 03. *58 Boston Gardens, Brentford TW8 9LP* Tel (020) 8847 4533 E-mail numapomp@talk21.com

GELSTON, Anthony. b 35. Keble Coll Ox BA57 MA60 DD85. Ridley Hall Cam 59. **d** 60 **p** 61. C Chipping Norton *Ox* 60-62; Lect Th Dur Univ 62-76; Sen Lect 76-88; Dean Div Faculty 77-79; Reader 89-95; Lic to Offic 62-95; rtd 95. *Lesbury, Hetton Road, Houghton le Spring DH5 8JW* Tel 0191-584 2256 E-mail anthony.gelston@durham.ac.uk

GEMMELL, Canon Ian William Young. b 52. ALAM. St Jo Coll Nottm. **d** 77 **p** 78. C Old Hill H Trin *Worc* 77-81; C Selly Park St Steph and St Wulstan *Birm* 81-83; V Leic St Chris 83-93; RD Christianity S 92-93; P-in-c Gt Bowden w Welham, Glooston and Cranoe 93-02; P-in-c Church Langton w Tur Langton, Thorpe Langton etc 93-99; P-in-c Church Langton cum Tur Langton etc 99-02; R Gt Bowden w Welham, Glooston and Cranoe etc 02-06; RD Gartree I 97-06; Hon Can Leic Cathl 03-06; P-in-c Welford w Sibbertoft and Marston Trussell *Pet* from 06. *The Vicarage, 35 The Leys, Welford, Northampton NN6 6HS* Tel (01858) 571101 E-mail bud.gemmell@btopenworld.com

GENDALL, Stephen Mark. b 63. **d** 89 **p** 90. Lundi St Apollos Zimbabwe 89-01; Youth Chapl 93-01; Can Cen Zimbabwe 00-01; V Lingfield and Crowhurst *S'wark* from 02. *The Vicarage, Vicarage Road, Lingfield RH7 6HA* Tel (01342) 832021 Mobile 07752-063150 E-mail steve@thegendalls.freeserve.co.uk

GENDERS, Nigel Mark. b 65. Oak Hill Th Coll BA92. **d** 92 **p** 93. C New Malden and Coombe *S'wark* 92-96; C Enfield Ch Ch Trent Park *Lon* 96-98; P-in-c Eastry and Northbourne w Tilmanstone etc *Cant* 98-03; P-in-c Woodnesborough w Worth and Staple 03-08; AD Sandwich 06-08; Min to Sandwich Secondary Schs 03-08; Dir of Educn *Cant* from 08; C Margate H Trin from 11. *31 Dover Road, Sandwich CT13 0BS* Tel (01304) 611084 E-mail nmg@f2s.com

GENEREUX, Patrick Edward. b 47. William Carey Coll BSc73 Univ of the South (USA) MDiv78. **d** 78 **p** 79. USA 78-81 and from 82; C Spalding *Linc* 81-82. *621 North 5th Street, Burlington IA 52601-0608, USA* Tel (001) (319) 754 6420 E-mail pgenereux@aol.com

GENOE, Simon Alfred. b 82. Stranmillis Coll BEd06 TCD BTh09. CITC 06. **d** 09 **p** 10. C Lisburn Ch Ch Cathl from 09. *82 Thornleigh Drive, Lisburn BT28 2DS* Tel (028) 9267 6499 Mobile 07501-288941 E-mail simon.genoe@gmail.com

GENT, David Robert. b 71. Surrey Univ BSc94. Qu Coll Birm BD97. **d** 98 **p** 99. C Wotton-under-Edge w Ozleworth and N Nibley *Glouc* 98-02; Chapl Yeovil Coll and C Yeovil H Trin w Barwick *B & W* 02-08; P-in-c Martock w Ash from 08. *The Vicarage, 10 Water Street, Martock TA12 6JN* Tel (01935) 826113 E-mail revdgent@aol.com

GENT, Mrs Miriam. b 29. Leeds Univ BA51. SWMTC 84. **d** 87 **p** 94. NSM Pinhoe and Broadclyst *Ex* 87-02; Dioc Adv in Adult Tr 96-99; Perm to Offic from 02. *Moss Hayne Cottage, West Clyst, Exeter EX1 3TR* Tel (01392) 467288 Fax 462980

GENT, Miss Susan Elizabeth. K Coll Lon LLB78 Brunel Univ BA95. Wycliffe Hall Ox MPhil96. **d** 97 **p** 98. C Notting Hill St Jo and St Pet *Lon* 97-00; Chapl to City law firms from 00; Hon Assoc P St Paul's Cathl from 00; Dioc Visitor from 01; P-in-c St Martin Ludgate from 05. *3B Amen Court, London EC4M 7BU* Tel (020) 7329 2702 Fax 7248 3104 E-mail susan.gent@ukgateway.net

GENTILELLA, Barbara Catherine. b 55. SEITE 05. **d** 08 **p** 09. NSM Shirley St Jo *S'wark* from 08. *42 Devonshire Way, Croydon CR0 8BR* Tel (020) 8777 4462 E-mail bb2ke@sky.com

GENTRY, Michael John. b 66. St Steph Ho Ox BTh95. **d** 98 **p** 99. C Bromley SS Pet and Paul *Roch* 98-02; V Langton Green from 02. *The Vicarage, The Green, Langton Green, Tunbridge Wells TN3 0JB* Tel and fax (01892) 862072 *or* tel 861889 E-mail michael.gentry@diocese-rochester.org

GEOGHEGAN, Prof Luke. b 62. SS Hild & Bede Coll Dur BA83 Bedf Coll Lon MSc87 CQSW87 FRSA93. SAOMC 87. **d** 00 **p** 01. NSM Spitalfields Ch Ch w All SS Lon 00-03; NSM Gt Berkhamsted *St Alb* 03-05; NSM Gt Berkhamsted, Gt and Lt Gaddesden etc from 05; Warden Toynbee Hall from 98. *16 Gravel Path, Berkhamsted HP4 2EF*

GEORGE, Alexander Robert. b 46. K Coll Lon BD69 AKC69. St Aug Coll Cant. **d** 70 **p** 71. C Newmarket St Mary w Exning St Agnes *St E* 70-74; C Swindon Ch Ch *Bris* 74-76; C Henbury 76-79; Lic to Offic 79-80; TV Oldland 80-88; C Ipswich St Aug *St E* 89; C Hadleigh w Layham and Shelley 89-90; P-in-c Assington 90-91; R Assington w Newton Green and Lt Cornard 91-00; P-in-c Hundon 00-03; Hon C 03-04; C Stour Valley 04-11; Dioc Moderator for Reader Tr 95-03; Asst Liturg Officer (Formation and Educn) 00-03; Nat Moderator for Reader Tr 04-08; rtd 11; Perm to Offic *St E* from 11. *The Vicarage, 5 Armstrong Close, Hundon, Sudbury CO10 8HD* Tel (01440) 786617 E-mail alecrg@btinternet.com

GEORGE, David. b 64. Wycliffe Hall Ox 01. **d** 03 **p** 04. C Inkberrow w Cookhill and Kington w Dormston *Worc* 03-07; P-in-c Dudley St Jo 07-10; TV Kidderminster St Jo and H Innocents from 10. *9 Sutton Park Road, Kidderminster DY11 6LB* Tel (01562) 637882 E-mail revdave.george@virgin.net

GEORGE, David Michael. b 45. Selw Coll Cam BA66 MA70. Chich Th Coll 70. **d** 73 **p** 74. C Chiswick St Nic w St Mary *Lon* 73-76; C Kensington St Mary Abbots w St Geo 76-78; C Northolt Park St Barn 78-81; Argentina from 81; R Martinez St Mich 82-00; R St Jo Cathl Buenos Aires 00-08; Adn River Plate 84-02; rtd 08. *Pje Dr Rodolfo Rivarola 112-4-10, C1015AAB Buenos Aires, Argentina* Tel (0054) (11) 4372 4596 E-mail davidmg@ciudad.com.ar

GEORGE, Mrs Elizabeth Ann. b 33. Westf Coll Lon BA56. S Dios Minl Tr Scheme 84. **d** 87 **p** 94. NSM Basingstoke *Win* 87-05; Perm to Offic from 05. *71 Camrose Way, Basingstoke RG21 3AW* Tel (01256) 464763 E-mail elizabethgeorge@compuserve.com

GEORGE, The Ven Frederick. b 39. St Luke's Coll Ex TCert61. Chich Th Coll 82. **d** 72 **p** 83. Australia 72-75; Brunei 75-80; The Gambia 80-82 and 83-88; Prin Angl Tr Cen Farafeni 85-88; P-in-c Ringsfield w Redisham, Barsham, Shipmeadow etc *St E* 89-92; R Wainford 92-97; V Jamestown St Helena 97-03; Adn St Helena 99-03; rtd 03; Perm to Offic *Chich* from 03; Perm to Offic St Helena from 04. *PO Box 87, Woody Ridge, St Helena, STHL 1ZZ, South Atlantic* Tel and fax (00290) 3140

GEORGE, Henderson Rudolph. b 44. Open Univ BA80 Chelsea Coll Lon MEd85. NTMTC BA07. **d** 07 **p** 08. NSM Clapton St Jas *Lon* from 07. *12 Cowland Avenue, Enfield EN3 7DX* Tel (020) 8804 9224

GEORGE, Nicholas Paul. b 58. St Steph Ho Ox 86. **d** 89 **p** 90. C Leeds St Aid *Ripon* 89-92; C Leeds Richmond Hill 92-96; Chapl Agnes Stewart C of E High Sch Leeds 93-96; V Leeds Halton St Wilfrid *Ripon* 96-02; V Camberwell St Giles w St Matt *S'wark* from 02. *St Giles's Vicarage, 200 Benhill Road, London SE5 7LL* Tel and fax (020) 7703 4504 Mobile 07771-603217 E-mail mail@nickgeorge.org.uk

✠**GEORGE, The Rt Revd Randolph Oswald.** b 24. Codrington Coll Barbados 46. **d** 50 **p** 51 **c** 76. Barbados 50-53; C Leigh *Lich* 53-55; C Ardwick St Benedict *Man* 55-57; C Bedford Park *Lon* 57-58; C Lavender Hill Ascension *S'wark* 58-60; Dom Chapl to Bp Trinidad and Chapl Colonial Hosp 60-62; R Couva 62-67; R Port of Spain All SS 67-71; Hon Can Trinidad 68-71; Dean Georgetown Guyana 71-76; Suff Bp Stabroek 76-80; Bp Guyana 80-08; rtd 08. *590 Republic Park, Peter's Hall, East Bank Demerara, Guyana* Tel (00592) (233) 6522

GEORGE, Robert Henry. b 45. FCCA73. WEMTC 99. **d** 01 **p** 02. OLM S Cerney w Cerney Wick and Down Ampney *Glouc* 01-05; NSM Brimpsfield w Birdlip, Syde, Daglingworth etc from 05. *Jedems, Berkeley Close, South Cerney, Cirencester GL7 5UN* Tel (01285) 860973 E-mail member@jedems.wanadoo.co.uk

GEORGE, Shuna. b 64. **d** 11. NSM Bridport *Sarum* from 11. Tel 07971-759997 (mobile) E-mail shuna@bridport-team-ministry.org

GEORGE-JONES, Canon Gwilym Ifor. b 26. K Coll (NS) 56. **d** 57 **p** 57. R Seaforth St Jas Canada 57-61; V Kirton in Lindsey *Linc* 61-71; R Grayingham 61-71; R Manton 61-71; V Alford w Rigsby 71-92; R Maltby 71-92; R Well 71-92; V Bilsby w Farlesthorpe 71-92; R Hannah cum Hagnaby w Markby 71-92; R Saleby w Beesby 71-92; RD Calcewaithe and Candleshoe 77-85 and 87-89; Can and Preb Linc Cathl 81-01; rtd 92. *42 Kelstern Road, Lincoln LN6 3NJ* Tel (01522) 691896

GEORGE-ROGERS, Gillian Jean Richeldis. b 47. St Mich Coll Llan. **d** 99 **p** 02. C Llanishen 99-05; P-in-c Rhondda Fach Uchaf 05; rtd 06. *Faith House, 82 King's Fee, Monmouth NP25 5BQ* Tel (01600) 716696 E-mail gillian@richeldis.fslife.co.uk

GEORGESTONE, Arthur Raymond William. b 51. K Coll Lon MA95. Sierra Leone Th Hall 78. **d** 82 **p** 83. C Freetown Bp Crowther Memorial Ch Sierra Leone 82-83; C St Geo Cathl Freetown 83-85; P-in-c Goderich St Luke 85-87; Perm to Offic *Chelmsf* 87-08 and *Ox* from 10. *117 Langcliffe Drive, Heelands, Milton Keynes MK13 7LD* Tel (01908) 315261 Mobile 07535-163379 E-mail georgestone93@gmail.com

GERARD, Patrick Hoare. b 64. Man Univ BSc86 MSc88. Qu Coll Birm 04. **d** 06 **p** 07. C Solihull *Birm* 06-10; R Baddesley Clinton from 10; R Lapworth from 10. *The Rectory, Church Lane, Lapworth, Solihull B94 5NX* Tel (01564) 782098 Mobile 07905-967930 E-mail patrick@gerard.net

GERARDO, Brother. *See* ROMO-GARCIA, Brother Gerardo

GERD, Sister. *See* SWENSSON, Sister Gerd Inger

GERMANY AND NORTHERN EUROPE, Archdeacon of. *See* LLOYD, The Ven Jonathan Wilford

GERRANS, Daniel. b 58. Em Coll Cam LLB80 MA83 Barrister-at-Law (Middle Temple) 81. SEITE 02. **d** 05 **p** 06. NSM De Beauvoir Town St Pet *Lon* 05-11; Chapl to Bp Stepney 07-11; V S Hackney St Mich w Haggerston St Paul from 11. *97 Lavender Grove, London E8 3LR* Tel (020) 7249 2627 E-mail daniel.gerrans@xxiv.co.uk

GERRARD, The Ven David Keith Robin. b 39. St Edm Hall Ox BA61. Linc Th Coll 61. **d** 63 **p** 64. C Stoke Newington St Olave *Lon* 63-66; C Primrose Hill St Mary w Avenue Road St Paul 66-69; V Newington St Paul *S'wark* 69-79; V Surbiton St Andr and St Mark 79-89; RD Kingston 84-88; Hon Can S'wark Cathl 85-89; Adn Wandsworth 89-04; rtd 05; Perm to Offic *Guildf* from

05. *15 Woodbourne Drive, Claygate, Esher KT10 0DR* Tel (01372) 467295 E-mail david.gerrard@gawab.com

GERRARD, Paul Christian Francis. b 58. St Steph Ho Ox 92. **d** 94 **p** 01. C Longton *Lich* 94-95; NSM New Radnor and Llanfihangel Nantmelan etc *S & B* 01-04; NSM Knighton, Norton, Whitton, Pilleth and Cascob 04-07; Perm to Offic 07-09. *The Old Vicarage, Norton, Presteigne LD8 2EN* Tel (01544) 260038

GERRISH, David Victor. b 38. St Jo Coll Dur BSc61 MA65. Oak Hill Th Coll 61. **d** 64 **p** 65. C Fareham St Jo *Portsm* 64-66; Asst Chapl K Sch Roch 67-71; Asst Chapl Bryanston Sch 71-73; Chapl 73-77; Chapl Mon Sch 77-86; Chapl Warminster Sch 86-89; R Portland All SS w St Pet *Sarum* 89-96; Chapl Aquitaine *Eur* 96-00; rtd 00; Perm to Offic *Sarum* from 01. *Flat 8, 6 Ricketts Close, Weymouth DT4 7UP* Tel (01305) 789319

GERRY, Brian John Rowland. b 38. Oak Hill Th Coll 69. **d** 71 **p** 72. C Hawkwell *Chelmsf* 71-74; C Battersea Park St Sav *S'wark* 74-77; C Battersea St Geo w St Andr 74-77; V Axmouth w Musbury *Ex* 77-86; R Upton 86-04; rtd 04. *49 Peasland Road, Torquay TQ2 8PA* Tel (01803) 322788

GERRY, Ulric James. b 67. Bris Univ BEng89. Wycliffe Hall Ox BA96. **d** 97 **p** 98. C Hemel Hempstead *St Alb* 97-00; Perm to Offic 01-02; Crosslinks Tanzania 02-11; R Glas St Oswald from 11. *4 Woodfarm Road, Thornliebank, Glasgow G46 7JJ* Tel 0141-563 5179 E-mail ulricgerry@yahoo.com

GHEORGHIU GOULD, Helen Elizabeth-Anne. b 65. Lanc Univ BA87. St Mellitus Coll BA10. **d** 10 **p** 11. C Epping Distr *Chelmsf* from 10. *76 The Plain, Epping CM16 6TW* Tel (01992) 560999 E-mail hsgheorghiu@btinternet.com

GHEST, Richard William Iliffe. b 31. Em Coll Cam BA53 MA57 Lon Univ BA66. Wells Th Coll 53. **d** 55 **p** 56. C Weston-super-Mare St Jo *B & W* 55-57; India 58-63; C Holborn St Geo w H Trin and St Bart *Lon* 63-67; Ceylon 67-68; C Combe Down *B & W* 68-73; C Combe Down w Monkton Combe 73-74; R Tickenham 74-96; rtd 96. *120 Cottrell Road, Roath, Cardiff CF24 3EX* Tel (029) 2048 1597

GHINN, Edward. b 45. Oak Hill Th Coll 71. **d** 74 **p** 75. C Purley Ch Ch *S'wark* 74-77; Chile 77-82; V Sevenoaks Weald *Roch* 82-86; Chapl HM Pris Hull 86-89; Chapl HM Pris Pentonville 89-91; Chapl HM Pris Maidstone 91-96; Brazil 96-98; Min Parkwood CD *Cant* 98-01; Chapl HM Pris Grendon and Spring Hill 01-03; Chapl HM Pris Stocken 03-11; rtd 11. *11 Burns Road, Stamford PE9 2XD* Tel (01780) 480111 E-mail e.ghinn@virgin.net

GHOSH, Dipen. b 43. St Jo Coll Nottm 71. **d** 74 **p** 75. C Bushbury *Lich* 74-77; Hon C 86-89; C Wednesfield Heath 89-91; TV Wolverhampton 91-98; TV Bushbury 98-02; Chapl Compton Hospice 98-02; V Wolverhampton St Matt *Lich* from 02. *St Matthew's Vicarage, 14 Sydenham Road, Wolverhampton WV1 2NY* Tel (01902) 453056

GIBB, David Richard Albert. b 68. Lon Bible Coll BA90 Cov Univ MPhil95. **d** 95 **p** 96. C Ox St Ebbe w H Trin and St Pet 95-01; V Leyland St Andr *Blackb* from 01. *St Andrew's Vicarage, 1 Crocus Field, Leyland PR25 3DY* Tel (01772) 621645 E-mail d.gibb@talktalk.net

GIBBARD, Roger. b 48. Southn Univ BA73. Cuddesdon Coll 73. **d** 75 **p** 76. C Portsea St Mary *Portsm* 75-79; P-in-c New Addington *Cant* 79-81; C Ditton St Mich *Liv* 81-82; TV 82-88; Asst Chapl HM Pris Liv 88-89; Chapl HM YOI Hindley 89-92; Chapl HM Pris Risley 92-00; V Wigan St Mich *Liv* 01-04. *97 Barnsley Street, Wigan WN6 7HB* Tel (01942) 233465 E-mail thegibbards@blueyonder.co.uk

GIBBENS, Gwyneth Andrea. b 52. Nottm Univ BA73 PhD78. WEMTC 07. **d** 10 **p** 11. NSM Kemble, Poole Keynes, Somerford Keynes etc *Glouc* from 10. *3 Wordings Mount, Church Hill, Sheepscombe, Stroud GL6 7RE* Tel (01452) 813666 E-mail gwyneth.gibbens@btinternet.com

GIBBINS, John Grenville. b 53. Aston Tr Scheme 89 Linc Th Coll 89. **d** 91 **p** 92. C Market Harborough *Leic* 91-95; P-in-c Blaby from 95. *The Rectory, Wigston Road, Blaby, Leicester LE8 4FU* Tel 0116-277 2588 E-mail jgibbins@leicester.anglican.org

GIBBON, Matthew. b 79. Trin Coll Carmarthen BA00. St Steph Ho Ox BTh03. **d** 03 **p** 04. C Caerau w Ely *Llan* 03-05; C Aberavon 05-08; P-in-c Treharris, Trelewis and Bedlinog from 08. *The Vicarage, 13 The Oaks, Quakers Yard, Treharris CF46 5HQ* Tel (01443) 410280 E-mail frmatthewgibbon@talktalk.net

GIBBONS, David Austen. b 63. York Univ BSc84. Ch Div Sch of Pacific 93 Ripon Coll Cuddesdon BA94. **d** 94 **p** 95. C Ryde H Trin *Portsm* 94-97; C Swanmore St Mich 94-97; C Gosport Ch Ch 97-01; R Havant 01-08; R Barrington Hills USA from 08. *337 Ridge Road, Barrington IL 60010-2331, USA* Tel (001) (847) 381 0596 E-mail d gibbons@talk21.com

GIBBONS, David Robin Christian. b 36. Chich Th Coll 82. **d** 84 **p** 85. C Seaford w Sutton *Chich* 84-87; R Harting 87-93; R Harting w Elsted and Treyford cum Didling 93-04; rtd 04. *Richmond Villas, 102 East Street, Selsey, Chichester PO20 0BX* Tel (01243) 602978

GIBBONS, Eric. b 47. Sarum & Wells Th Coll 69. d 72 p 73. C New Haw *Guildf* 72-76; C Hawley H Trin 76-79; P-in-c Blackheath and Chilworth 79-90; V 90-98; C Shere, Albury and Chilworth 98-99; P-in-c Tongham 99-04; rtd 04; Perm to Offic *Guildf* from 06. *38 Ambleside Close, Farnborough GU14 0LA* Tel (01252) 540586

GIBBONS, Harvey Lloyd. b 62. Ripon Coll Cuddesdon 97. d 99 p 00. C Verwood *Sarum* 99-00; C Gillingham 00-02; Dioc Voc Adv and P-in-c Upavon w Rushall and Charlton 02-07; R Warminster St Denys and Upton Scudamore from 07. *The Rectory, 5 Church Street, Warminster BA12 8PG* Tel (01985) 213456 E-mail revdharvey@btinternet.com

GIBBONS, The Ven Kenneth Harry. b 31. Man Univ BSc52. Cuddesdon Coll 54. d 56 p 57. C Fleetwood St Pet *Blackb* 56-60; NE Sch Sec SCM 60-62; Hon C Leeds St Pet *Ripon* 60-62; C St Martin-in-the-Fields *Lon* 62-65; V New Addington *Cant* 65-70; V Portsea St Mary *Portsm* 70-81; RD Portsm 73-79; Hon Can Portsm Cathl 76-81; Dir Post-Ord Tr *Blackb* 81-83; Acting Chapl HM Forces Weeton 81-85; Dir of Ords 82-90; Adn Lancaster 81-97; P-in-c Weeton 81-85; V St Michaels-on-Wyre 85-97; rtd 97; P-in-c St Magnus the Martyr w St Marg New Fish Street *Lon* 97-03; P-in-c St Clem Eastcheap w St Martin Orgar 99-08. *112 Valley Road, Kenley CR8 5BU* Tel (020) 8660 7502 E-mail margaret@gibbons440.fsnet.co.uk

GIBBONS, Mrs Lissa Melanie. b 58. Birm Univ BA79 PGCE80. SAOMC 98. d 01 p 02. C Risborough *Ox* 01-06; Chapl Bucks Hosps NHS Trust 05-07; TV Monkwearmouth *Dur* 07-11; P-in-c Heighington from 11; P-in-c Darlington St Matt and St Luke from 11. *The Vicarage, 15 East Green, Heighington, Newton Aycliffe DL5 6PP* Tel (01325) 312134 E-mail lissaandtom@btinternet.com

GIBBONS, Paul James. b 37. JP. Chich Th Coll 63. d 65 p 66. C Croydon St Mich *Cant* 65-72; V Maidstone St Mich from 72. *The Vicarage, 109 Tonbridge Road, Maidstone ME16 8JS* Tel (01622) 752710

GIBBONS, Mrs Susan Janet. b 51. St Mary's Coll Dur BA73 Birm Univ PGCE74. WMMTC 89. d 92 p 94. NSM Fladbury w Wyre Piddle and Moor etc *Worc* 92-00; Perm to Offic from 00. *The Old School, Bricklehampton, Pershore WR10 3HJ* Tel (01386) 710475

GIBBONS, Thomas Patrick. b 59. St Jo Coll Dur BA82. St Steph Ho Ox 88. d 90 p 91. C Whorlton *Newc* 90-94; C Gosforth St Nic 94-96; R Radley and Sunningwell *Ox* 96-04; P-in-c Lenborough 04-07; TV Monkwearmouth *Dur* from 07; Chapl Co Durham and Darlington NHS Foundn Trust from 07. *St Peter's Vicarage, St Peter's Way, Sunderland SR6 0DY* Tel 0191-567 3726 E-mail lissaandtom@tesco.net

GIBBONS, Mrs Valerie Mary Lydele. b 49. St Aid Coll Dur BA72 Solicitor 75. Wycliffe Hall Ox 98. d 03 p 04. OLM Cholsey and Moulsford *Ox* from 03. *Kilifi, Caps Lane, Cholsey, Wallingford OX10 9HF* Tel and fax (01491) 651377 E-mail val.gibbons@btinternet.com

GIBBONS, William Jacob. d 11. C E Carmarthen *St D* from 11. *St Peter's Clergy House, 10A The Parade, Carmarthen SA31 1LY* Tel (01267) 233316

GIBBONS, William Simpson. b 32. TCD BA60 MA64. d 61 p 62. C Londonderry Ch Ch *D & R* 61-65; I Drumholm and Rossnowlagh 65-70; C Dublin St Ann w St Steph *D & G* 70-72; I Kill 72-95; Can Ch Ch Cathl Dublin 91-95; rtd 95. *Muthaiga, 3 Glenageary Terrace, Dun Laoghaire, Co Dublin, Republic of Ireland* Tel and fax (00353) (1) 214 8699 Mobile 87-218 7771 E-mail wsgibbons@eircom.net

GIBBS, Colin Hugh. b 35. St Mich Coll Llan 82. d 84 p 85. C Bistre *St As* 84-87; V Penycae 87-92; rtd 92. *Asaph, 26 Cil y Coed, Ruabon, Wrexham LL14 6TA* Tel (01978) 823503

GIBBS, Colin Wilfred. b 39. Man Univ BA62 Birm Univ CertEd63. St Jo Coll Nottm 71. d 73 p 74. C Crowborough Chich 73-76; C Rodbourne Cheney *Bris* 76-77; C Bickenhill w Elmdon *Birm* 77-80; CF 80-96; Dir Ichthus Ho Homestay 96-06; Chapl Grenville Coll Bideford 99-02; P-in-c Cowden w Hammerwood Chich 06-10. *11 The Gorses, Bexhill-on-Sea TN39 3BE* Tel (01424) 845299 E-mail ichthushouse@tiscali.co.uk

GIBBS, Edmund. b 38. Fuller Th Sem California DMin81. Oak Hill Th Coll BD62. d 63 p 64. C Wandsworth All SS *S'wark* 63-66; SAMS Chile 66-70; Educn Sec SAMS 70-77; Ch Progr Manager Bible Soc 77-84; USA from 84; Assoc Prof Evang and Ch Renewal Fuller Th Sem 84-93; Prof Ch Growth from 96; Assoc R Beverly Hills All SS 93-96. *625 W Commonwealth Avenue, Apt 314, Alhambra CA 91801-3652, USA* E-mail eddgibbs@fuller.edu

GIBBS (née DE ROBECK), Mrs Fiona Caroline. b 74. St Martin's Coll Lanc BA96. St Jo Coll Nottm MA(TS)99. d 00 p 01. C Bitterne *Win* 00-05; C Chandler's Ford from 05. *45 Pantheon Road, Chandler's Ford, Eastleigh SO53 2PD* Tel (023) 8026 8433

GIBBS, Mrs Fiorenza Silvia Elisabetta. b 49. SRN71. St Alb Minl Tr Scheme 90. d 93 p 99. NSM Hitchin *St Alb* 93-96; NSM Pirton 97-99; Asst Chapl N Herts NHS Trust 99-00; Asst Chapl

E and N Herts NHS Trust 00-02; Chapl 02-10; NSM Hitchin *St Alb* from 10. *12 Bunyon Close, Pirton, Hitchin SG5 3RE* Tel (01462) 711846

GIBBS, Ian Edmund. b 47. Lon Univ BEd69. St Steph Ho Ox 72. d 75 p 76. C Stony Stratford *Ox* 75-79; V Forest Town *S'well* 79-83; R Diddlebury w Munslow, Holdgate and Tugford *Heref* from 83; R Abdon from 83. *The Rectory, Munslow, Craven Arms SY7 9ET* Tel (01584) 841688

GIBBS, James Millard. b 28. Univ of Michigan BSE51 Nottm Univ PhD68. Seabury-Western Th Sem BD57. d 57 p 57. USA 57-60; Lic to Offic *S'well* 61-62 and 65-66; C Brandon *Dur* 62-64; Vice-Prin Lich Th Coll 66-71; Lic to Offic *Lich* 66-71; India 72-77; Tutor Qu Coll Birm 78-84; V Stechford *Birm* 84-93; rtd 93; Perm to Offic *Birm* from 93. *13 Lingfield Court, 60 High Street, Harbourne, Birmingham B17 9NE* Tel 0121-426 2108 E-mail jmanddagibbs@aol.com

GIBBS, Jane Anne. b 46. W Midl Coll of Educn CertEd67. EMMTC 03. d 06 p 07. NSM Hinckley St Mary *Leic* from 06. *4 Kirfield Drive, Hinckley LE10 1SX* Tel (01455) 635934

GIBBS, Jonathan Robert. b 61. Jes Coll Ox MA89 Jes Coll Cam PhD90. Ridley Hall Cam 84. d 89 p 90. C Stalybridge H Trin and Ch Ch *Ches* 89-92; Chapl Basle w Freiburg-im-Breisgau *Eur* 92-98; R Heswall *Ches* from 98. *The Rectory, Village Road, Heswall, Wirral CH60 0DZ* Tel 0151-342 3471 Fax 342 2275 E-mail jgibbs@heswallparish.co.uk

GIBBS, Marcus Timothy. b 73. UMIST BSc95. Trin Coll Bris BA10. d 10 p 11. C Northampton St Giles *Pet* from 10. *18 The Avenue, Cliftonville, Northampton NN1 5BT* Tel (01604) 949479 E-mail revdmarcus@gmail.com

GIBBS, Michael Robin. b 42. Th Ext Educn Coll 74. d 83 p 84. NSM Malawi 83-04; Can Upper Shire from 03; Chapl Essex Chs Coun for Ind and Commerce *Chelmsf* from 05. *120 St John's Road, London E17 4JQ* Tel and fax (020) 8523 1375 E-mail micgibbs@talktalk.net

GIBBS, Mrs Patricia Louise. b 39. S'wark Ord Course 91. d 94 p 95. NSM Croydon H Sav *S'wark* 94-07; Chapl Asst Mayday Healthcare NHS Trust Thornton Heath 94-05; rtd 07. *41 Sandringham Road, Thornton Heath CR7 7AX* Tel (020) 8684 9720

GIBBS, Peter Winston. b 50. Ex Univ BA72 CQSW75. St Jo Coll Nottm. d 90 p 91. C Hampreston *Sarum* 90-94; P-in-c Ipswich St Matt *St E* 94-99; Assoc P Attenborough *S'well* 99-01; V Toton 01-08; TV N Poole Ecum Team *Sarum* from 08. *St Paul's Vicarage, 16 Rowbarrow Close, Poole BH17 9EA* Tel (01202) 565187 E-mail ladybird1@ntlworld.com

GIBBS, Canon Philip Roscoe. b 33. Codrington Coll Barbados 57. d 60 p 61. C St Jo Cathl Belize 61-63; P-in-c S Distr Miss 63-70; V Pomona St Matt 70-71; R Corozal 71-74; Hon Can Belize from 71; V Stoke Newington Common St Mich *Lon* 74-87; V Johnsonville New Zealand 87-96; rtd 96. *10 Gardener Street, Levin 5510, New Zealand* Tel (0064) (6) 367 9884 E-mail philip.g@actrix.co.nz

GIBBS, Raymond George. b 55. NTMTC 94. d 97 p 98. NSM Becontree S *Chelmsf* 97-99; C Dedham 99-04; C Colchester St Mich Myland 04-08; P-in-c from 08; Area Youth Officer 04-08. *352 Mill Road, Mile End, Colchester CO4 5JF* Tel (01206) 843926 E-mail raymond359gibbs@btinternet.com

GIBBS, Richard James. b 68. St Paul's Coll Chelt BSc90. St Jo Coll Nottm MTh01. d 01 p 02. C Southport Ch Ch *Liv* 01-05; Min Banks St Steph CD from 05. *33 Abington Drive, Banks, Southport PR9 8FL* Tel (01704) 546294

GIBBS, Stewart Henry. b 77. CCC Cam BA98 MA PGCE99 Anglia Poly Univ BTh05. Ridley Hall Cam 02. d 05 p 06. C Grays North *Chelmsf* 05-10; R Hatfield Heath and Sheering from 10. *The Vicarage, Broomfields, Hatfield Heath, Bishop's Stortford CM22 7EH* Tel (01279) 730288 Mobile 07899-753559 E-mail stewarthgibbs@hotmail.co.uk

GIBBS, Miss Valerie Edwina. b 47. Sussex Univ BEd78 Open Univ BA98. STETS 07. d 10. *Address withheld by request* Tel (01424) 814278 E-mail valeriegibbs@aol.com

GIBBS, Canon William Gilbert. b 31. Bps' Coll Cheshunt 55. d 58 p 59. C Wellington w W Buckland *B & W* 58-61; C Kensington St Mary Abbots w St Geo *Lon* 61-68; V Guilsborough *Pet* 68; V Guilsborough w Hollowell 68-74; V Guilsborough w Hollowell and Cold Ashby 74-98; Jt P-in-c Cottesbrooke w Gt Creaton and Thornby 83-98; Jt P-in-c Maidwell w Draughton, Lamport w Faxton 88-98; Can Pet Cathl 88-98; rtd 98; Perm to Offic *Pet* 98-01 and from 03; P-in-c W Haddon w Winwick and Ravensthorpe 01-03. *Paines Close, Maidwell, Northampton NN6 9JB* Tel (01604) 686424

GIBBS, William John Morris. b 71. Birm Univ BSc94. Ripon Coll Cuddesdon BTh00. d 00 p 01. C Staines St Mary and St Pet *Lon* 00-03; C Kensington St Mary Abbots w St Geo 03-06; V Redbourn *St Alb* from 06; RD Wheathampstead from 10. *The Vicarage, 49 Church End, Redbourn, St Albans AL3 7DU* Tel (01582) 791669

GIBLIN, Brendan Anthony. b 64. K Coll Lon BD86 AKC93 Leeds Univ MA95. Wycliffe Hall Ox 90. d 92 p 93. C Tadcaster w Newton Kyme *York* 92-96; R Stockton-on-the-Forest w Holtby and Warthill 96-02; P-in-c Middleham w Coverdale and E Witton etc *Ripon* 02-03; R from 03; AD Wensley 10-11. *The Rectory, Wensley, Leyburn DL8 4HS* Tel (01969) 623736 E-mail bgiblin@toucansurf.com

GIBLING, Derek Vivian. b 31. Wadh Coll Ox BA56 MA63. Wycliffe Hall Ox 70. **d** 72 **p** 73. C Fisherton Anger *Sarum* 72-74; C Yatton Keynell *Bris* 74-77; C Castle Combe 74-77; C Biddestone w Slaughterford 74-77; P-in-c Youlgreave *Derby* 77-82; P-in-c Stanton-in-Peak 77-82; V Youlgreave, Middleton, Stanton-in-Peak etc 82-88; P-in-c Hartington and Biggin 88-90; V Hartington, Biggin and Earl Sterndale 90-96; rtd 96; Perm to Offic *Linc* 96-02; RD Bolingbroke 00-02. *15 Howards Meadow, Glossop SK13 6PZ* Tel (01457) 851423

GIBRALTAR IN EUROPE, Bishop of. See ROWELL, The Rt Revd Douglas Geoffrey

GIBRALTAR, Archdeacon of. See SUTCH, The Ven Christopher David

GIBRALTAR, Dean of. See PADDOCK, The Very Revd John Allan Barnes

GIBSON, Alan. b 35. Birm Univ BSc56 Man Univ MSc72. NW Ord Course 71. **d** 74 **p** 75. C Sale St Anne *Ches* 74-77; V Runcorn St Mich 77-82; Educn Adv *Carl* 82-88; P-in-c Hugill 82-88; V Grange-over-Sands 88-97; rtd 97; Perm to Offic *Derby* from 01. *11 Ecclesbourne Drive, Buxton SK17 9BX* Tel (01298) 22621

GIBSON, Anthony Richard. b 43. Ridley Hall Cam 83. **d** 85 **p** 86. C Rushmere *St E* 85-88; R N Tawton, Bondleigh, Sampford Courtenay etc *Ex* 88-93; RD Okehampton 92-93; P-in-c Tiverton St Pet and Chevithorne w Cove 93-03; rtd 03. *Le Bourg, 82210 Fajolles, France* Tel (0033) 5 63 94 14 83

GIBSON, Brenda. b 55. St Mary's Coll Dur BSc77 PhD80 Hughes Hall Cam PGCE81 Surrey Univ BA04. STETS 01. **d** 04 **p** 05. NSM Wimborne Minster *Sarum* from 04. *12 Meadow Court, Leigh Road, Wimborne BH21 2BG* Tel (01202) 881472 E-mail brenda@p-b-gibson.demon.co.uk

GIBSON, Catherine Snyder. b 39. Parson's Sch of Design (NY) 57. Ab Dioc Tr Course 82 Edin Th Coll 92. **d** 86 **p** 94. Colombia 86-87; NSM Aberdeen St Marg 87-88; Dioc Hosp Chapl 89-92; C Aberdeen St Mary 93-94; Bp's Chapl for Tr and Educn 93-94; P-in-c Ballater 95-96; P-in-c Aboyne 95-96; R 96-98; P-in-c Braemar 95-97; Assoc P Fort Lauderdale USA 98-04; I Fermoy Union *C, C & R* 04-06; rtd 06; P-in-c Lugano *Eur* 06-07; Hon C Dayton St Matt USA from 09. *404 James Boulevard, Signal Mountain TN 37377-2218, USA* Tel (001) (423) 886 4748 *or* 775 3773 E-mail kategib@btinternet.com

GIBSON, Charles Daniel. b 48. **d** 03 **p** 04. OLM Wisley w Pyrford *Guildf* from 03. *The Corner Cottage, Send Marsh Road, Ripley, Woking GU23 6JN* Tel (01483) 225317 Fax 223681 E-mail charles@chasdi.freeserve.co.uk

GIBSON, Colin Taylor. b 54. Trin Coll Cam BA77. Oak Hill Th Coll 86. **d** 88 **p** 89. C Thrybergh w Hooton Roberts *Sheff* 88-91; P-in-c Tinsley 91-96; TV Attercliffe, Darnall and Tinsley 96-02; TR Walsall *Lich* 02-11; R Walsall St Matt from 11; Hon C Walsall St Paul from 05; Hon C Walsall Pleck and Bescot from 05. *St Matthew's Rectory, 48 Jesson Road, Walsall WS1 3AX* Tel (01922) 624012 E-mail c.t.gibson@btinternet.com

GIBSON, David Francis. b 36. Magd Coll Cam BA57 BChir60 MB61. SWMTC 84. **d** 90 **p** 91. NSM Newport, Bishops Tawton and Tawstock *Ex* 90-95; Chapl N Devon Healthcare NHS Trust 95-96; Perm to Offic *Ex* from 96. *Little Beara, Marwood, Barnstaple EX31 4EH* Tel (01271) 814876

GIBSON, David Innes. b 31. Oak Hill Th Coll 56. **d** 59 **p** 60. C S Croydon Em *Cant* 59-62; C Washfield *Ex* 62-63; Asst Master and Chapl Blundells Sch Tiverton 63-64; Chapl Sutton Valence Sch Maidstone 64-68; Chapl Dean Close Sch Cheltenham 68-75; Asst Chapl and Ho Master 75-85; Asst Master Brightlands Sch Newnham-on-Severn 85-90; C Cheltenham St Mary, St Matt, St Paul and H Trin *Glouc* 91-96; rtd 96; Perm to Offic *Glouc* 96-97; and from 01. *2 Withyholt Park, Charlton Kings, Cheltenham GL53 9BP* Tel (01242) 511612

GIBSON, Douglas Harold. b 20. Portsm Dioc Tr Course. **d** 87. NSM Portsea St Luke *Portsm* 87-92; Perm to Offic from 92. *83 Middle Street, Southsea PO5 4BW* Tel (023) 9282 9769

GIBSON, Mrs Fiona Ruth. b 70. Homerton Coll Cam BEd93. Oak Hill Th Coll MTh11. **d** 11. C Bedford Ch Ch *St Alb* from 11. *161 Dudley Street, Bedford MK40 3SY* Tel (01234) 301708 E-mail fiona.gibson@mac.com

GIBSON, Garry Stuart. b 36. Univ Coll Lon BA62 PhD75 Birkbeck Coll Lon BA79. Oak Hill Th Coll 62. **d** 64 **p** 65. C Watford St Mary *St Alb* 64-67; Lect Cambs Coll of Arts and Tech 67-69; Government of Israel Scholar Hebrew Univ 69-70; Asst Master Angl Sch Jerusalem 69-70; Sen Lect Middx Univ 70-97; Hon C Sidmouth, Woolbrook, Salcombe Regis, Sidbury etc *Ex* 96-99; C Stockland, Dalwood, Kilmington and Shute 99-03; C Kilmington, Stockland, Dalwood, Yarcombe etc 03-04. *14 Argus Close, Honiton EX14 1UT* Tel (01404) 44083 E-mail garrygib@yahoo.co.uk

GIBSON, The Ven George Granville. b 36. Cuddesdon Coll 69. **d** 71 **p** 72. C Tynemouth Cullercoats St Paul *Newc* 71-73; TV Cramlington 73-77; V Newton Aycliffe *Dur* 77-85; R

Bishopwearmouth St Mich w St Hilda 85-90; TR Sunderland 90-93; RD Wearmouth 85-93; Hon Can Dur Cathl 88-01; Adn Auckland 93-01; rtd 01. *12 West Crescent, Darlington DL3 7PR* Tel (01325) 462526 E-mail granville.gibson@durham.anglican.org

GIBSON, Canon Ian. b 48. Open Univ BA85 Wolv Univ MSc95 Liv Jo Moores Univ MA09 FCIPD. S Dios Minl Tr Scheme 82. **d** 85 **p** 86. NSM Uckfield *Chich* 85-88; NSM Lt Horsted 85-88; NSM Isfield 85-88; V Fairwarp 88-93; P-in-c 94-00; NSM 00-04; V High Hurstwood 88-93; P-in-c 94-00; RD Uckfield 03-04; Bp's Dom Chapl and Research Asst 04-09; Episc V for Min and Bp's Sen Chapl from 09; Can Res and Treas Chich Cathl from 09. *Caigers Cottage, Westergate Street, Woodgate, Chichester PO20 3SQ* Tel (01243) 544534 *or* 782161 Fax 531332 E-mail ian.gibson@diochi.org.uk

GIBSON, John Murray Hope. b 35. Dur Univ BA58. Cranmer Hall Dur 58. **d** 60 **p** 61. C Chester le Street *Dur* 60-63; C Stockton 63-68; V Denton and Ingleton 68-75; V Swalwell 75-00; Chapl Dunston Hill Hosp Gateshead 80-99; rtd 00; Perm to Offic *Dur* and *Newc* from 01. *50 Church Road, Gosforth, Newcastle upon Tyne NE3 1BJ* Tel 0191-285 2942

GIBSON, Canon John Noel Keith. b 22. MBE89. Ch Coll Cam MA48 Lon Univ BD59. Coll of Resurr Mirfield 45. **d** 47 **p** 48. C S Elmsall *Wakef* 47-51; Antigua 51-56; Virgin Is from 56; Can All SS Cathl 89-92; rtd 92. *PO Box 65, Virgin Gorda VG1 150, British Virgin Islands* Tel (001284) 495 5587

GIBSON, Kenneth George Goudie. b 54. Glas Univ MA83 Edin Univ BD87 Strathclyde Univ PGCE95. Edin Th Coll 83. **d** 88 **p** 89. C Glas St Marg 88-90; R E Kilbride 90-98; R Carnoustie *Bre* 98-07. *39 Durham Street, Monifieth, Dundee DD5 4PF* E-mail kenneth.gibson@homecall.co.uk

GIBSON, Laura Mary. See WILFORD, Laura Mary

GIBSON, Lynne Margaret. b 65. St Andr Univ MA88 TCD BTh10. CITC 08. **d** 10 **p** 11. C Dundela St Mark *D & D* from 10. *29 Marmont Park, Belfast BT4 2GR* Tel (028) 9076 1967

GIBSON, Nigel Stephen David. b 53. St Barn Coll Adelaide 84. **d** 87 **p** 87. C N Adelaide Ch Ch Australia 87-89; Lect Boston *Linc* 90-91; P-in-c Stamford St Mary and St Mich 91-92; P-in-c Stamford Baron 91-92; R Stamford St Mary and St Martin 92-98; Perm to Offic 98-00; V Kempston Transfiguration *St Alb* 00-04; Chapl Milan w Cadenabbia and Varese *Eur* 04-10. *Address temp unknown* E-mail frnigel@boxingkangaroo.org.uk

GIBSON, Mrs Patricia Elizabeth. b 57. Nottm Univ MA02. EMMTC 99. **d** 02 **p** 03. C Wigston Magna *Leic* 02-06; TV Gt Berkhamsted, Gt and Lt Gaddesden etc *St Alb* 06-10; Bp's Adv for Women in Min 07-10. *Venskab Barn, Morebath, Tiverton EX16 9AQ* E-mail revteg1@btinternet.com

GIBSON, Paul Saison. b 32. BA LTh Huron Coll Ontario Hon DD90. Coll of Em and St Chad Hon DD88 Vancouver Sch of Th Hon DD95 Montreal Dioc Th Coll Hon DD98 Trin Coll Toronto Hon DD99. **d** 56 **p** 57. C Bloomsbury St Geo w St Jo Lon 56-59; R Homer St Geo Canada 59-60; Chapl McGill Univ Montreal 60-66; Prin Hong Kong Union Th Coll 66-72; Consultant Angl Ch of Canada 72-82; Liturg Officer 82-98. *588 Millwood Road, Toronto ON M4S 1K8, Canada* Tel (001) (416) 487 2008

GIBSON, Philip Nigel Scott. b 53. St Jo Coll Dur BA78. Cranmer Hall Dur 79. **d** 79 **p** 80. C Yardley St Edburgha *Birm* 79-82; C Stratford-on-Avon w Bishopton *Cov* 82-84; Chapl SW Hosp Lon 84-91; Chapl St Thos Hosp Lon 84-91; Assoc P Newington St Paul *S'wark* 91-92; Chapl Charing Cross Hosp Lon 92-93; Chapl R Lon Hosp (Whitechapel) 93-94; Chapl Bedford Hosp NHS Trust 95-08. *Sillwood, 1 Wood Lane, Aspley Guise, Milton Keynes MK17 8EJ*

GIBSON, Raymond. b 23. Ely Th Coll 60. **d** 62 **p** 63. C Leic St Jas 62-67; Succ Leic Cathl 67-68; Chapl Leic R Infirmary 67-68; Chapl Nottm City Hosp 68-84; V Barlings *Linc* 84-88; rtd 88. *11 Cornell Drive, Nottingham NG5 8RF*

GIBSON, Raymond Frank. b 34. Toronto Bible Coll BTh61 Tyndale Hall Bris 62. **d** 64 **p** 65. C Gt Horton *Bradf* 64-67; C Otley 67-72; V Fairlight *Chich* 72-83; V Hallwood *Ches* 83-85; R Freethorpe, Wickhampton, Halvergate w Tunstall *Nor* 85-99; P-in-c Reedham w Cantley w Limpenhoe and Southwood 94-99; rtd 99; Perm to Offic *Nor* 99-09. *23 Ramsay Hall, 9-13 Byron Road, Worthing BN11 3HN* Tel (01903) 239957

GIBSON, Canon Robert Swinton. b 26. Wadh Coll Ox BA50 MA55. Wells Th Coll 50. **d** 53 **p** 54. C Greenwich St Alfege w St Pet *S'wark* 53-61; Ind Missr 55-62; Hon Chapl to Bp *S'wark* 56-67; Sen Chapl S Lon Ind Miss 62-67; Nigeria 67-69; R Guisborough *York* 69-83; RD Guisborough 73-83; TR Halifax *Wakef* 83-94; Hon Can Wakef Cathl 85-94; RD Halifax 86-92; rtd 94; Perm to Offic *Wakef* from 94 and *York* 94-11. *The Cottage, Main Street, Hutton Buscel, Scarborough YO13 9LL* Tel (01723) 862133

GIBSON, The Ven Terence Allen. b 37. Jes Coll Cam BA61 MA65. Cuddesdon Coll 61. **d** 63 **p** 64. C Kirkby *Liv* 63-66; TV 72-75; TR 75-84; Warden Cen 63 66-75; Youth Chapl 66-72; RD Walton 79-84; Adn Suffolk *St E* 84-87; Adn Ipswich 87-05; rtd

05; Perm to Offic *St E* from 05. *5 Berry Close, Purdis Farm, Ipswich IP3 8SP* Tel (01473) 714756
E-mail archdeaconterry@dsl.pipex.com
GIBSON, Thomas Thomson. b 23. Sarum Th Coll 62. **d** 63 **p** 64. C E w W Harnham *Sarum* 63-66; V Rowde 66-74; R Poulshot 67-74; V Badminton w Acton Turville *Glouc* 74-84; P-in-c Hawkesbury 81-84; V Badminton w Lt Badminton, Acton Turville etc 84-93; rtd 93; Perm to Offic *Glouc* 93-96 and from 01; *B & W* and *Sarum* from 95; *Eur* from 99. *9 Lansdown Place West, Bath BA1 5EZ* Tel (01225) 337903 Fax 483676
GIDDENS, Leslie Vernon. b 29. Bps' Coll Cheshunt 54. **d** 56 **p** 57. C Harrow St Pet *Lon* 56-58; C Tottenham St Benet Fink 58-63; C-in-c Hayes St Nic CD 63-94; rtd 94; Perm to Offic *Lon* from 94. *6 Ashdown Road, Uxbridge UB10 0HY* Tel (01895) 232406
GIDDINGS, Mrs Jacqueline Mary. b 44. St Aid Coll Dur BA67. SWMTC 91. **d** 94 **p** 95. C Plympton St Mary *Ex* 94-02; rtd 02. *Grange End, Harrowbeer Lane, Yelverton PL20 6EA* Tel (01822) 854825
GIFFORD, David Christopher. b 53. Lon Univ BEd75 Sussex Univ MA85 Ox Brookes Univ BA11. Ripon Coll Cuddesdon 08. **d** 11. NSM Benson *Ox* from 11; Chief Exec Coun of Chrs and Jews from 06. *13 High Street, Dorchester-on-Thames, Wallingford OX10 7HH* Tel (020) 7015 5160 Mobile 07720-555858 E-mail ceo@ccj.org.uk
GIFFORD, Ms Elizabeth Ann. b 47. St Kath Coll Liv CertEd72 Open Univ BSc96. STETS 99. **d** 02 **p** 09. NSM Trowbridge H Trin *Sarum* 02-09; NSM Studley from 09. *14 Innox Mill Close, Trowbridge BA14 9BA* Tel (01225) 752756 Mobile 07903-269587 E-mail revgif@aol.com
GIFFORD, Patricia Rose. **d** 10 **p** 11. NSM Glouc St Jas and All SS and Ch from 10. *49 Ducie Street, Gloucester GL1 4NZ* Tel (01452) 306746 E-mail patgifford@btopenworld.com
GIFFORD-COLE, David Henry. b 30. San Francisco Th Sem DMin87 ALCD56. **d** 56 **p** 57. C Ashtead *Guildf* 56-59; C Farnham 59-60; Canada from 60. *225 Hoylake Road West, Qualicum Beach BC V9K 1K5, Canada*
✠**GILBERD, The Rt Revd Bruce Carlyle.** b 38. CNZM02. Auckland Univ BSc59. St Jo Coll Auckland STh74. **d** 62 **p** 64 **c** 85. C Devonport New Zealand 62-64; C Ponsony and Grey Lynn 65; P Asst Panmure 66-68; V Avondale 68-71; Ind Chapl and C Eaglescliffe *Dur* 71-73; Dir Ind Miss Wellington New Zealand 73-79; Dir Th Educn by Ext 80-85; Bp Auckland 85-94; P-in-c Albany Greenhithe 95-00; P-in-c Tamaki St Thos 96-00; Chapl K Sch 97-00; rtd 00. *81 Manaia Road, Tairua 3508, New Zealand* Tel (0064) (7) 864 8727 Fax (0064) (7) 864 8240
GILBERT, Anthony John David. b 54. Open Univ BA91 LRSC83. Ripon Coll Cuddesdon 83. **d** 86 **p** 87. C Exning St Martin w Landwade *St E* 86-89; Chapl RAF from 89. *Chaplaincy Services, Valiant Block, HQ Air Command, RAF High Wycombe HP14 4UE* Tel (01494) 496800 Fax 496343
E-mail tngilbert@aol.com
GILBERT, Canon Barry. b 46. Leeds Univ BA67. Coll of Resurr Mirfield 67. **d** 69 **p** 70. C Malvern Link w Cowleigh *Worc* 69-73; P-in-c Bromsgrove All SS 73-81; V 81-83; P-in-c Lower Mitton 83-88; V 88-92; V Stourport and Wilden 92-06; RD Stourport 93-00 and 02-06; P-in-c Brierley Hill 06-07; TR 07-11; Hon Can Worc Cathl 09-11; rtd 11. *Allandale, High Street, New Galloway, Castle Douglas DG7 3RL* Tel (01644) 420665
E-mail barry_gilbert@talk21.com
GILBERT, Clive Franklyn. b 55. City of Liv Coll of HE CertEd76 BEd77. SEITE 01. **d** 02 **p** 03. C Paddock Wood *Roch* 02-06; V Dartford St Alb from 06. *St Alban's Vicarage, 51 Watling Street, Dartford DA1 1RW* Tel (01322) 224052 Mobile 07752-676663 E-mail clive.gilbert@diocese-rochester.org
GILBERT, Frederick Joseph. b 29. Lich Th Coll 58. **d** 59 **p** 60. C Westhoughton *Man* 59-62; V Goodshaw 62-68; R Crumpsall St Matt 68-75; RD Cheetham 70-74; RD N Man 74-75; V Rochdale St Aid 75-78; TV Rochdale 78-80; V Westhoughton 80-84; TR 84-87; AD Deane 85-87; R W Bowbrook *Worc* 87-89; R Bowbrook N 89-93; rtd 93; Perm to Offic *Worc* from 93. *Freshways, Main Road, Peopleton, Pershore WR10 2EG* Tel (01905) 841629
GILBERT, Howard Neil. b 73. Southn Univ BA96. Ripon Coll Cuddesdon BTh05. **d** 05 **p** 06. C Dulwich St Barn *S'wark* 05-08; C Cirencester *Glouc* from 09. *The Parsonage, 32 Watermoor Road, Cirencester GL7 1JR* Tel (01285) 885109 Mobile 07887-800478 E-mail father.howard@gmail.com
GILBERT, Mark. *See* GILBERT, Philip Mark
GILBERT, Ms Mary Rose. b 63. Ridley Hall Cam 94. **d** 97 **p** 97. C Walsall Wood *Lich* 97-00; TV Bilston 00-07; AD Wolverhampton 03-07; V Birm St Paul from 07. *71 Wellington Road, Edgbaston, Birmingham B15 2ET* Tel 0121-440 2337 E-mail mgdartford@aol.com
GILBERT, Michael Victor. b 61. Dur Univ BA84. Trin Coll Bris 92. **d** 94 **p** 95. C Chapeltown *Sheff* 94-97; V Brightside w Wincobank 97-07; adult Educator Wilson Carlile Coll of Evang from 07. *Wilson Carlile College of Evangelism, 50 Cavendish Street, Sheffield S3 7RZ* Tel 0114-278 7020 E-mail m.gilbert@churcharmy.org.uk

GILBERT, Philip Mark. b 62. Liv Univ BA84. Coll of Resurr Mirfield 84. **d** 87 **p** 88. C Frodsham *Ches* 87-89; C Stockton Heath 89-92; R Tangmere and Oving *Chich* 92-01; Chapl Seaford Coll and P-in-c Graffham w Woolavington 01-09; P-in-c Chich St Wilfrid 09-10; V from 10; Chapl Bp Luffa Sch Chich from 09. *St Wilfrid's House, 7 Durnford Close, Chichester PO19 3AG* Tel (01243) 783853 Mobile 07810-004062 E-mail frmark@mgilbert.clara.co.uk
GILBERT, Raymond. b 34. AKC61. **d** 62 **p** 63. C Newbold w Dunston *Derby* 62-66; PV and Succ S'wark Cathl 66-68; P-in-c Stuntney *Ely* 68-74; Prec and Sacr Ely Cathl 68-74; Min Can Cant Cathl 74-79; Hon Min Can from 79; P-in-c Patrixbourne w Bridge and Bekesbourne 79-81; V 81-00; RD E Bridge 92-98; rtd 00; Perm to Offic *Cant* from 09. *16 Green Acres, Eythorne, Dover CT15 4LX* Tel (01304) 831485
GILBERT, Raymond Frederick. b 44. **d** 93 **p** 94. OLM Stowmarket *St E* 93-10; rtd 10; Perm to Offic *St E* from 10. *3 Violet Hill Road, Stowmarket IP14 1NE* Tel (01449) 677700
GILBERT, Mrs Rebecca. b 76. Univ of Wales (Lamp) BA. Ridley Hall Cam. **d** 10 **p** 11. C Ely from 10. *44 Bentham Way, Ely CB6 1BS* Tel (01353) 665420 E-mail rebecca@elyparishchurch.co.uk
GILBERT, Robert John Crispin. b 74. Hatf Coll Dur BSc95 Leic Univ PhD99 Magd Coll Ox MA05. Ripon Coll Cuddesdon 09. **d** 11. NSM Wolvercote and Wytham *Ox* from 11. *Magdalen College, High Street, Oxford OX1 4AU* Tel (01865) 276070 E-mail gilbert@strubi.ox.ac.uk
GILBERT, Roger Charles. b 46. Ex Coll Ox BA69 MA74 Nottm Univ MEd81. St Steph Ho Ox 69. **d** 71 **p** 72. NSM Bridgwater St Mary w Chilton Trinity *B & W* 71-74; NSM Rugeley *Lich* 74-81; NSM Cannock 81-83; NSM Wednesbury St Jas and St Jo from 83; NSM Tividale 08-11; NSM W Bromwich St Pet from 11. *41 Stafford Road, Cannock WS11 4AF* Tel (01543) 570531 E-mail roger.gilbert@talk21.com
GILBERT, Canon Roger Geoffrey. b 37. K Coll Lon BD69 AKC69. **d** 70 **p** 71. C Walton-on-Thames *Guildf* 70-74; R St Mabyn and P-in-c Helland *Truro* 74-81; P-in-c Madron 81-86; R Falmouth K Chas 86-02; Hon Can Truro Cathl 94-02; RD Carnmarth S 94-00; Chapl to The Queen 95-02; rtd 02; Perm to Offic *Eur* from 98. *2 rue de Plouzon, 22690 Pleudihen-sur-Rance, France* Tel (0033) 2 96 88 28 69
GILBERT, Sidney Horace. b 34. Dur Univ BA58 MA69 Univ of Wales BD62 CertEd83. St Mich Coll Llan 58. **d** 61 **p** 62. C Colwyn Bay *St As* 61-63; C Llanrhos 63-69; R Penley and Bettisfield 69-78; V Brymbo and Bwlchgwyn 78-82; Univ of Wales (Swansea) *S & B* 82-83; R Beeston Regis *Nor* 84-97; Holiday Chapl 84-91; Sen Chapl 92-97; V Llanwddyn and Llanfihangel-yng-Nghwynfa etc *St As* 97-99; rtd 99; Perm to Offic *Ches* 01-04 and from 07; Hon C Odd Rode 04-06. *79 Latham Avenue, Helsby, Frodsham WA6 0EA*
GILBERTSON, The Ven Michael Robert. b 61. New Coll Ox BA82 MA92 Dur Univ PhD97. St Jo Coll Dur BA91. **d** 97 **p** 98. C Surbiton St Matt *S'wark* 97-00; V Stranton *Dur* 00-10; AD Hartlepool 02-10; Hon Can Dur Cathl 08-10; Adn Ches from 10. *Church House, Lower Lane, Aldford, Chester CH3 6HP* Tel (01244) 681973 Fax 620456 E-mail michael.gilbertson@chester.anglican.org
GILCHRIST, Mrs Alison Roxanne. b 62. Dur Univ BA05. Cranmer Hall Dur 02. **d** 04 **p** 05. C Preston St Cuth *Blackb* 04-06; C Fulwood Ch Ch 06-08; TV Marfleet *York* from 08. *St Hilda's House, 256 Annandale Road, Hull HU9 4JY* Tel (01482) 799100 E-mail twiggy256@twiggy256.karoo.co.uk
GILCHRIST, David John. b 51. Mert Coll Ox BA75 MA79 Maryvale Inst PGCE08. St Jo Coll Nottm. **d** 79 **p** 80. C Gt Ilford St Andr *Chelmsf* 79-81; C Buckhurst Hill 81-84; Chapl Dover Coll 84-95; Chapl Brentwood Sch Essex from 95. *Mitre House, 6 Shenfield Road, Brentwood CM15 8AA* Tel (01277) 244442 E-mail djgilx@btinternet.com
GILCHRIST, Gavin Frank. b 53. AKC74. Coll of Resurr Mirfield 76. **d** 77 **p** 78. C Newbold w Dunston *Derby* 77-80; C Addlestone *Guildf* 80-84; V Blackpool St Mary *Blackb* 84-92; P-in-c Carl St Herbert w St Steph 92-97; V 97-01; V Tynemouth Cullercoats St Paul *Newc* from 01. *The Vicarage, 53 Grosvenor Drive, Whitley Bay NE26 2JR* Tel and fax 0191-252 4916 E-mail gavingilchrist@btinternet.com
GILCHRIST, Lawrence Edward. b 29. Liv Univ BSc52. NW Ord Course 74. **d** 76 **p** 77. NSM Buxton w Burbage and King Sterndale *Derby* 76-83; V Chinley w Buxworth 83-94; rtd 94; Perm to Offic *St E* 94-03. *9 Santingley Lane, New Crofton, Wakefield WF4 1LG* Tel (01924) 860262
GILCHRIST, Spencer. b 66. QUB BA88. BTh. **d** 91 **p** 92. C Ballynafeigh St Jude *D & D* 91-97; I Connor w Antrim St Patr 97-09. *Address temp unknown*
GILDERSLEVE, Paul. Lon Univ BD. Ridley Hall Cam. **d** 06 **p** 07. NSM Papworth *Ely* from 06. *Manor Farm, 14 Alms Hill, Bourn, Cambridge CB23 2SH* Tel (01954) 713989 *or* 719318 E-mail paulg@miscom.co.uk
GILDING, James Peter. b 33. Leeds Univ BA64. Ely Th Coll 61. **d** 63 **p** 64. C Chorley St Pet *Blackb* 63-66; C Pemberton St Fran

Kitt Green *Liv* 66-69; P-in-c Terrington St John *Ely* 69-74; P-in-c Walpole St Andrew 69-74; V Elm 74-81; TR Stanground and Farcet 81-89; V Haslingfield 89-95; R Harlton 89-95; R Haslingfield w Harlton and Gt and Lt Eversden 95-96; rtd 96; Perm to Offic *York* from 98. *14 Main Street, Bishop Wilton, York YO42 1RX* Tel (01759) 368510

GILES, Anthony John. b 50. Aston Univ BSc71 Surrey Univ MSc78 Homerton Coll Cam PGCE86 CEng80 MIET80. SAOMC 01. d 04 p 05. NSM Stevenage H Trin *St Alb* 04-09; NSM Norton 09-11; P-in-c High Wych and Gilston w Eastwick from 11. *The Rectory, High Wych Road, High Wych, Sawbridgeworth CM21 0HX* Tel (01279) 600894 E-mail anthony.giles@ntlworld.com

GILES, Anthony Richard. b 68. St Jo Coll Nottm MA00. d 01 p 02. C Chellaston *Derby* 01-06; P-in-c Epperstone *S'well* 06-10; P-in-c Gonalston 06-10; P-in-c Oxton 06-10; P-in-c Woodborough 06-10; P-in-c Epperstone, Gonalston, Oxton and Woodborough from 10. *The Vicarage, 12 Lingwood Lane, Woodborough, Nottingham NG14 6DX* Tel 0115-965 3727 E-mail ant.dianne@btopenworld.com

GILES, Brother. See SPRENT, Michael Francis

GILES, Edward Alban. b 34. Bps' Coll Cheshunt. d 58 p 59. C Colne St Bart *Blackb* 58-61; C Warrington St Paul *Liv* 61-63; C Knysna S Africa 63-66; R Eersterus w Silverton 66-70; Chapl HM Pris Camp Hill 70-75; Chapl HM Pris Stafford 75-83; Chapl HM YOI Hollesley Bay Colony 83-94; rtd 94; Sub-Chapl HM Pris Blundeston from 94; Perm to Offic *Nor* 94-00 and *St E* from 94. *The Hollies, Ferry Farm Drive, Sutton Hoo, Woodbridge IP12 3DR* Tel (01394) 387486 E-mail eag1@onetel.net.uk

GILES, Canon Eric Francis. b 34. Sarum Th Coll 61. d 63 p 64. C Plympton St Mary *Ex* 63-71; R Dumbleton w Wormington *Glouc* 71-77; P-in-c Toddington w Stanley Pontlarge 71-77; R Dumbleton w Wormington and Toddington 77-79; V Churchdown St Jo 79-99; Hon Can Glouc Cathl 95-99; rtd 99; Perm to Offic *Glouc* and *Worc* from 99. *25 Station Road, Pershore WR10 1PN* Tel (01386) 554246

GILES, Gordon John. b 66. Lanc Univ BA88 Magd Coll Cam BA95 MLitt95. Ridley Hall Cam 92. d 95 p 96. C Chesterton Gd Shep *Ely* 95-98; Min Can and Succ St Paul's Cathl 98-03; V Enfield Chase St Mary from 03; Dir Post-Ord Tr Edmonton Area from 08. *St Mary Magdalene Vicarage, 30 The Ridgeway, Enfield EN2 8QH* Tel (020) 8363 1875 E-mail vicar@saintmarymagdalene.org.uk or gjg@ggiles.net

GILES, Graeme John. b 56. Linc Th Coll 82. d 85 p 86. C Prestbury *Glouc* 85-88; C Paulsgrove *Portsm* 88-96; V Friern Barnet St Pet le Poer *Lon* 96-04. *30A Vine Road, East Molesey KT8 9LF* Tel 07981-708606 (mobile) E-mail graeme@priest.com

GILES (née WILLIAMS), Mrs Gwenllian. b 34. RSCN55 SRN58 SCM60. WMMTC 88. d 92 p 94. NSM Bromsgrove St Jo *Worc* 92-00; Perm to Offic *Worc* 00-03 and *Ex* from 06; P-in-c Clifton-on-Teme, Lower Sapey and the Shelsleys 03-04. *4 Tidal View Close, Fore Street, Aveton Gifford, Kingsbridge TQ7 4LT* Tel (01548) 559164

GILES, Canon John Robert. b 36. Em Coll Cam BA60 MA65. Ripon Hall Ox 60. d 61 p 62. C Lowestoft St Marg *Nor* 61-65; Chapl UEA 65-72; R Kidbrooke St Jas *S'wark* 72-79; Sub-Dean Greenwich 74-79; V Sheff St Mark Broomhall 79-87; Ind Chapl 79-92; Can Res Sheff Cathl 87-92; V Lee Gd Shep w St Pet *S'wark* 92-98; rtd 98; Perm to Offic *St E* from 99. *25 The Terrace, Aldeburgh IP15 5HJ* Tel (01728) 452319

GILES, Kevin Norman. b 40. Lon Univ BD69 Dur Univ MA74. ACT ThL67 MTh78 ThD90. d 68 p 69. C Mosman St Clem Australia 68-69; C Wollongong 69; Chapl Wollongong Univ Coll 70-72; TV Chester le Street *Dur* 73-74; Chapl Tubingen Univ W Germany 75; Chapl Armidale Univ Australia 75-80; R Kensington 81-95; I Carlton N from 96. *44 Arnold Street, North Carlton Vic 3054, Australia* Tel (0061) (3) 9387 7214 or 9380 6387 Fax 9388 9050 E-mail giles@melbpc.org.au

GILES, Mrs Penelope Sylvia. b 61. SEITE 08. d 11. NSM Angmering *Chich* from 11. *4 The Chantrelles, Angmering, Littlehampton BN16 4GR* Tel (01903) 770567 Mobile 07717-152205 E-mail p.giles2@sky.com

GILES, Peter Michael Osmaston. b 40. Solicitor 65. S Dios Minl Tr Scheme 85. d 88 p 89. Hon C Wootton Bassett *Sarum* 88-90; Lic to RD Calne from 91; RD Calne 98-03; Chapl St Mary's Sch Calne from 00. *The Old Vicarage, Honeyhill, Wootton Bassett, Swindon SN4 7DY* Tel (01793) 852643 Fax 853191 E-mail gilesoldvic@talk21.com

GILES, The Very Revd Richard Stephen. b 40. Newc Univ BA63 MLitt88 MRTPI71. Cuddesdon Coll 64. d 65 p 66. C Higham Ferrers w Chelveston *Pet* 65-68; Perm to Offic *Ox* 69; C Oakengates *Lich* 70; C Stevenage St Geo *St Alb* 71-75; P-in-c Howdon Panns *Newc* 75-76; TV Willington 76-79; Bp's Adv for Planning *Pet* 79-87; V Pet St Jude 79-87; Par Development Officer *Wakef* 87-99; P-in-c Huddersfield St Thos 87-93; V 93-99; Hon Can Wakef Cathl 94-99; Can Th Wakef Cathl 98-99; Dean

Philadelphia USA 99-08; rtd 08. *5 Lovaine Row, North Shields NE30 4HF* Tel 0191-258 7621 E-mail tynegiles@talktalk.net

GILES, Sarah Jayne. See MORRIS, Ms Sarah Jayne

GILES, Susan Jane. b 58. BSc. dss 83 d 92 p 94. Balsall Heath St Paul *Birm* 83-85; Asst Chapl Southmead Hosp Bris 86-90; Asst Chapl HM Rem Cen Pucklechurch 90-96; Asst Chapl HM Pris Bris 92-98; Chapl HM Pris Shepton Mallet 98-01; P-in-c Stockton H Trin *Dur* 01-10; P-in-c Stockton H Trin w St Mark from 10; Chapl Ian Ramsey Sch Stockton 01-09. *4 Greymouth Close, Stockton-on-Tees TS18 5LF* Tel (01642) 585749

GILES, Canon Timothy David. b 46. FCA69. Oak Hill Th Coll 88. d 90 p 91. C Ipswich St Marg *St E* 90-94; C Reigate St Mary *S'wark* 94-99; P-in-c W Wickham St Jo 99-03; V 03-10; rtd 10; Hon Can Offa Nigeria from 06. *Lea Cottage, Hillhead Road, Kergilliack, Falmouth TR11 5PA* Tel (01326) 377094 E-mail timgiles04@googlemail.com

GILKES, Donald Martin. b 47. St Jo Coll Nottm 78. d 80 p 81. C Conisbrough *Sheff* 80-84; P-in-c Balne 84-86; P-in-c Hensall 84-86; TV Gt Snaith 86-88; V Whittle-le-Woods *Blackb* 88-02; V Normanton *Wakef* from 02. *The Vicarage, High Street, Normanton WF6 1NR* Tel and fax (01924) 893100 E-mail don.gilkes@allsaintsnormanton.org

GILKS, Peter Martin. b 51. Nottm Univ BMus72 SRN77. Ripon Coll Cuddesdon 82. d 84 p 85. C Bitterne Park *Win* 84-87; TV Basingstoke 87-93; R Abbotts Ann and Upper and Goodworth Clatford 93-98; V Boyatt Wood 98-06; V Chilworth w N Baddesley 06-10; P-in-c Ampfield 08-10; V Ampfield, Chilworth and N Baddesley from 10. *The Vicarage, 33 Crescent Road, North Baddesley, Southampton SO52 9HU* Tel (023) 8073 2393 E-mail peter.gilks@ntlworld.com

GILL, Canon Alan Gordon. b 42. Sarum & Wells Th Coll 73. d 75 p 76. C Wimborne Minster *Sarum* 75-78; R Winterbourne Stickland and Turnworth etc 78-86; V Verwood 86-00; TR Gillingham 00-04; V Gillingham and Milton-on-Stour 04-08; Can and Preb Sarum Cathl 99-08; rtd 09. *1 Cheshire Close, Salisbury SP2 9JT* Tel (01722) 325239 E-mail erznmine@houseofgill.org

GILL, Mrs Carol Ann. b 42. Lady Mabel Coll TCert71. NOC 96. d 99 p 00. NSM Hanging Heaton *Wakef* 99-07; P-in-c 02-07; rtd 07; Perm to Offic *Wakef* from 08. *6 Queen's Crescent, Ossett WF5 8AU* Tel (01924) 276821 Mobile 07946-038562 E-mail rev@cgill2.fsnet.co.uk

GILL, Christopher John Sutherland. b 28. Selw Coll Cam BA52 MA70. Ely Th Coll 52. d 54 p 55. C Portslade St Nic *Chich* 54-58; C Goring-by-Sea 58-60; Chapl St Edm Sch Cant 60-76; Chapl Bennett Memorial Dioc Sch Tunbridge Wells 76-92; Hon C Tunbridge Wells K Chas *Roch* 77-93; rtd 93; Perm to Offic *Roch* from 93. *Flat 1, Hurstleigh, Hurstwood Lane, Tunbridge Wells TN4 8YA* Tel (01892) 528409

GILL, David Alan. b 64. Coll of Resurr Mirfield 98. d 00 p 01. C Devizes St Jo w St Mary *Sarum* 00-04; P-in-c Brockworth *Glouc* 04-10; V from 10; P-in-c Abenhall w Mitcheldean from 11. *The Rectory, Hawkers Hill, Mitcheldean GL17 0BS* E-mail frdavid@houseofgill.org

GILL, David Brian Michael. b 55. Southn Univ BTh88. Sarum & Wells Th Coll 83. d 86 p 87. C Honiton, Gittisham, Combe Raleigh, Monkton etc *Ex* 86-89; C Teignmouth, Ideford w Luton, Ashcombe etc 89-91; TV Ex St Thos and Em 91-05; RD Christianity 03-05; P-in-c Tamerton Foliot from 05; C Southway from 06; RD Plymouth Moorside from 09. *The Vicarage, 53 Whitson Cross Lane, Tamerton Foliot, Plymouth PL5 4NT* Tel (01752) 771033 E-mail david@dbmg.freeserve.co.uk

GILL, Mrs Gabrielle Mary (Gay). d 90 p 94. NSM Timperley *Ches* 90-96; rtd 96; Perm to Offic *Ches* from 97. *The Croft, 3 Harrop Road, Hale, Altrincham WA15 9BU* Tel 0161-928 1800

GILL, Gary George. b 44. Culham Coll Ox CertEd70. Cant Sch of Min 85. d 87 p 88. C Addlestone *Guildf* 87-90; C Buckland in Dover w Buckland Valley *Cant* 90-98; Chapl Buckland Hosp Dover 90-94; Chapl S Kent Hosps NHS Trust 94-98; C Birchington w Acol and Minnis Bay *Cant* 98-99; rtd 04. *9 Tooting Bec Road, London SW17 8BS* Tel (020) 8672 2179

GILL, Miss Helen Barbara. b 61. K Alfred's Coll Win BEd87. Cranmer Hall Dur. d 99 p 00. C Newc St Gabr 99-04; P-in-c Tynemouth St Jo from 04. *St John's Vicarage, St John's Terrace, Percy Main, North Shields NE29 6HS* Tel 0191-257 1819 E-mail helen@gill1999.freeserve.co.uk

✠GILL, The Rt Revd Kenneth Edward. b 32. Lambeth MA04 Serampore Univ Hon DD06. Hartley Victoria Coll. d 58 p 60 c 72. In Ch of S India 58-80; Bp Karnataka Cen 72-80; Asst Bp Newc 80-98; rtd 99; Hon Asst Bp Newc from 99. *Kingfisher Lodge, 41 Long Cram, Haddington EH41 4NS* Tel (01620) 822113 E-mail k.gill@newcastle.anglican.org

GILL, Michael John. b 59. K Coll Lon BA81 AKC81 Univ of Wales (Cardiff) BD85. St Mich Coll Llan 82. d 85 p 86. Min Can St Woolos Cathl 85-90; Chapl St Woolos Hosp Newport 87-90; Succ Heref Cathl and C Heref St Jo 90-93; TV Ebbw Vale *Mon* 93-96; V Tonypandy w Clydach Vale *Llan* 96-09; R Cranford *Lon* from 09. *The Rectory, 34 High Street, Cranford, Hounslow TW5 9RG* Tel (020) 8897 8836

GILL, Paul Joseph. b 45. Melbourne Coll of Div MMin07. Ridley Coll Melbourne 73. **d** 74 **p** 74. C Applecross Australia 74-76; C Birm St Martin 77-79; V Pype Hayes 79-89; Perm to Offic Perth 89-93; R Perth St Paul 93-00; Sen Chapl HM Min of Justice 00-10; rtd 10; Hon C Heref S Wye from 11. *26 St Clares Court, Lower Bullingham, Hereford HR2 6PX* Tel 07765-660418 (mobile) E-mail pandagilli@gmail.com

GILL, Peter Stephen. b 48. FCA79. **d** 09 **p** 10. NSM Exning St Martin w Landwade *St E* from 09. *11 Isinglass Close, Newmarket CB8 8HX* Tel (01638) 660335 Mobile 07762-608031 E-mail petergill861@btinternet.com

GILL, Prof Robin Morton. b 44. K Coll Lon BD66 AKC66 Lon Univ PhD69 Birm Univ MSocSc72. **d** 68 **p** 69. C Rugby St Andr *Cov* 68-71; Papua New Guinea 71-72; Lect Th Edin Univ 72-86; Sen Lect 86-88; Assoc Dean Faculty of Div 85-88; P-in-c Edin SS Phil and Jas 73-75; P-in-c Ford *Newc* 75-87; P-in-c Coldstream *Edin* 87-92; Wm Leech Prof Applied Th Newc Univ 88-92; Mich Ramsey Prof Modern Th Kent Univ 92-11; Prof Th from 11; Hon Prov Can Cant Cathl from 92; AD N Downs 02-09; P-in-c Hollingbourne and Hucking w Leeds and Broomfield 03-11; Hon C from 11. *Hucking Court Barn, Church Road, Hucking, Maidstone ME17 1QT* Tel (01622) 884120 E-mail r.gill@kent.ac.uk

GILL, Mrs Ruth Montcrieff. b 48. CITC 01. **d** 04 **p** 05. NSM Cloughjordan w Borrisokane etc *L & K* 04-06; NSM Birr w Lorrha, Dorrha and Lockeen from 06. *Kilgolan House, Kilcormac, Birr, Co Offaly, Republic of Ireland* Tel (00353) (57) 913 5341 Mobile 87-948 4402 E-mail ruth gill40@hotmail.com

GILL, Miss Sandra Julie. b 67. N Riding Coll of Educn BEd90 Rolle Coll MEd01 Ex Univ BTh08. SWMTC 03. **d** 06 **p** 07. NSM Kingsteignton and Teigngrace *Ex* from 06. *58 Furze Cap, Kingsteignton, Newton Abbot TQ12 3TF* Tel (01626) 355287

GILL, Miss Sarah Siddique. b 77. Punjab Univ BA96 MA01. Qu Coll Birm 08. **d** 11. C Shipley St Paul *Bradf* from 11. *15 Caroline Street, Shipley BD18 4QA* Tel 07584-498390 (mobile) E-mail sarah_siddique_gill@yahoo.co.uk

GILL, Simon David. b 66. Southn Univ BSc87 PhD91. St Jo Coll Nottm BTh00. **d** 01 **p** 02. C Frinton *Chelmsf* 01-05; P-in-c Sudbury w Ballingdon and Brundon *St E* from 05. *5 Clermont Avenue, Sudbury CO10 1ZJ* Tel (01787) 375334 E-mail sallie.simon@tinyworld.co.uk

GILL, Stanley. b 34. Sarum Th Coll 66. **d** 68 **p** 69. C Ipswich St Mary at Stoke w St Pet etc *St E* 68-73 and 78-80; TV 80-82; V Bury St Edmunds St Geo 73-78; P-in-c Childe Okeford, Manston, Hammoon and Hanford *Sarum* 82-89; R The Lulworths, Winfrith Newburgh and Chaldon 89-94; R Hazelbury Bryan and the Hillside Par 94-99; rtd 99; Perm to Offic *Ex* 99-02 and *Sarum* 00-02. *11 White Lodge, 36 Holbeck Hill, Scarborough YO11 3BJ* Tel (01723) 362751

GILL, Timothy Charles. b 66. Newc Univ BA88 Jes Coll Cam MPhil93 Leeds Univ PhD08. Westcott Ho Cam 89. **d** 92 **p** 93. C N Hull St Mich *York* 92-96; P-in-c Sculcoates St Paul w Ch Ch and St Silas 96-98; P-in-c Hull St Mary Sculcoates 96-98; V York St Luke 98-02; R Adel *Ripon* 02-08; V Roby *Liv* from 08. *The Vicarage, 11 Church Road, Liverpool L36 9TL* Tel 0151-489 1438 E-mail ttimgill@aol.com

GILL, Wilson Ernest. b 55. SAOMC. **d** 05 **p** 06. C Walton H Trin *Ox* 05-09; V Southall Em *Lon* from 09. *37 Dormers Wells Lane, Southall UB1 3HX* Tel (020) 8843 9556 E-mail wilsongill37@gmail.com *or* vicar.ecs@googlemail.com

GILLARD, David John. b 66. Ridley Hall Cam 96. **d** 98 **p** 99. C Seaford w Sutton *Chich* 98-02; P-in-c Eastbourne St Elisabeth 02-06; V from 06. *The Vicarage, 11 Baldwin Avenue, Eastbourne BN21 1UJ* Tel (01323) 649728 E-mail djgillard@tiscali.co.uk

GILLARD-FAULKNER, Mrs Sarah Kate. b 80. Coll of Ripon & York St Jo BA01 Glos Univ PGCE02. St Mich Coll Llan BTh06. **d** 09. C Abertillery w Cwmtillery *Mon* 09-10; C Abertillery w Cwmtillery w Llanhilleth etc from 10. *St Paul's Vicarage, Church Lane, Cwmtillery, Abertillery NP13 1LS* Tel (01495) 212364 Mobile 07900-393358 E-mail sarah_gillard@hotmail.com

GILLESPIE, David Ivan. b 68. TCD BTh01. CITC 98. **d** 01 **p** 02. C Agherton *Conn* 01-04; I Moy w Charlemont *Arm* 04-09; I Dublin St Ann and St Steph *D & G* from 09. *88 Mount Anville Wood, Lower Kilmacud Road, Dublin 14, Republic of Ireland* Tel (00353) (1) 288 0663 *or* 676 6814 Mobile 86-026 7528 E-mail digillespie15@aol.com

GILLESPIE, Michael David. b 41. EMMTC 86. **d** 89 **p** 90. NSM Countesthorpe w Foston *Leic* from 89. *3 Penfold Drive, Countesthorpe, Leicester LE8 3TP* Tel 0116-278 1130 E-mail mick.gillespie@btinternet.com

GILLESPIE, Canon Nancy Gillian. b 41. TCD MA68. **d** 97 **p** 98. Bp's V and Lib Kilkenny Cathl and C Kilkenny w Aghour and Kilmanagh *C & O* 97-00; I Stradbally w Ballintubbert, Coraclone etc 00-09; P-in-c Maryborough w Dysart Enos and Ballyfin 02-03; Can Ossory Cathl 06-09; rtd 09; Hon C Carlow w Urglin and Staplestown *C & O* from 10. *1 Fisherman's Lock, Leighlinbridge, Co Carlow, Republic of Ireland* Tel (00353) (59) 972 2643 Mobile 87-232 2574 E-mail ngilles@iol.ie

GILLETT, Brian Alan Michael. b 42. MRICS73. Chich Th Coll. **d** 82 **p** 83. C Tupsley *Heref* 82-86; R Kingstone w Clehonger, Eaton Bishop etc 86-97; V Baltonsborough w Butleigh, W Bradley etc *B & W* 97-09; Sub-Warden of Readers Wells Adnry 00-02; rtd 09. *1 Barn Close, Somerton TA11 6PH* Tel (01458) 272738

✠**GILLETT, The Rt Revd David Keith.** b 45. Leeds Univ BA65 MPhil68. Oak Hill Th Coll 66. **d** 68 **p** 69. C Watford St Luke *St Alb* 68-71; Sec Pathfinders and CYFA N Area 71-74; Lect St Jo Coll Nottm 74-79; Ch of Ireland Renewal Cen 80-82; V Luton Lewsey St Hugh *St Alb* 82-88; Prin Trin Coll Bris 88-99; Hon Can Bris Cathl 91-99; Suff Bp Bolton *Man* 99-08; rtd 08; Hon Asst Bp Nor from 08; Dioc Interfaith Adv from 10. *10 Burton Close, Diss IP22 4YJ* Tel (01379) 640309 E-mail dkgillett@btinternet.com

GILLETT, Vincent. b 30. Lon Univ BSc55 UEA MSc72 Open Univ BA01 FCollP81. Chich Th Coll 59. **d** 61 **p** 62. C Blackpool St Mich *Blackb* 61-63; Chapl Adisadel Coll Ghana 63-66; Chapl Kumasi Univ 66-72; Asst Master St Marg C of E High Sch Aigburth Liv 72-75; Asst Master Halewood Comp Sch 75-79; Hd Master St Wilfrid's Sch Ex 79-84; R Atherington and High Bickington *Ex* 84-94; V Burrington 84-94; rtd 95. *Birchy Barton Lodge, 2 Honiton Road, Exeter EX1 3EA* Tel (01392) 436393 E-mail vincent.gillett@btinternet.com

GILLEY, Margaret Mary. b 54. St Andr Univ MTheol76 Dur Univ PhD97. NEOC 97. **d** 00 **p** 01. C Birtley *Dur* 00-03; P-in-c Stockton St Mark 03; V 03-09; V Elton 03-09; Assoc P Lanchester Deanery 09-11; V Bensham and Teams from 11. *St Chad's Vicarage, Dunsmuir Grove, Gateshead NE8 4QL* Tel 0191-478 6338 E-mail meg.gilley@durham.anglican.org

GILLHAM, Catherine Anne. b 73. Southn Univ BN95. Trin Coll Bris BA09. **d** 09 **p** 10. C Kempshott *Win* from 09. *1 Lark Close, Basingstoke RG22 5PX* Tel (01256) 361747 Mobile 07873-525602 E-mail catgillham@hotmail.com

GILLHAM, Martin John. b 45. Wilson Carlile Coll IDC66 Qu Coll Birm 72. **d** 75 **p** 76. C Whitley Ch Ch *Ox* 75-78; TV Crowmarsh Gifford w Newnham Murren 78-79; TV Wallingford w Crowmarsh Gifford etc 79-83; V Kintbury w Avington 83-94; Dioc Lay Min Adv and Warden of Readers 89-97; P-in-c W Wycombe w Bledlow Ridge, Bradenham and Radnage 94-00; R 00; Prov Chapl Third Order SSF 95-99; P-in-c Norham and Duddo *Newc* 00-04; V 04-09; P-in-c Cornhill w Carham 00-09; P-in-c Branxton 00-09; AD Norham 05-09; rtd 09. *Rose Cottage, 25 Rock Village, Rock, Alnwick NE66 3SD* Tel (01665) 579048 E-mail m.gillham@virgin.net

GILLHAM, Mrs Patricia Anne. b 40. Wilson Carlile Coll IDC66 Ox Min Course 90. **d** 93 **p** 94. Par Dn Kintbury w Avington *Ox* 93-94; C 94-95; C W Wycombe w Bledlow Ridge, Bradenham and Radnage 95-00; rtd 00; Perm to Offic *Newc* from 00. *Rose Cottage, 25 Rock Village, Rock, Alnwick NE66 3SD* Tel (01665) 579048

GILLHESPEY, Canon Clive. b 28. Lon Univ BD73. Cranmer Hall Dur 63. **d** 65 **p** 66. C Barrow St Geo w St Luke *Carl* 65-69; V Flookburgh 69-74; R Barrow St Geo w St Luke 74-81; TR 81-92; Hon Can Carl Cathl 84-92; rtd 92; Perm to Offic *Carl* from 92. *Canon's Court, 43 Holyoake Avenue, Barrow-in-Furness LA13 9LH* Tel (01229) 839041

GILLIAN, Ronald Trevor. b 57. Ulster Univ MTD78 QUB BEd89 TCD BTh93. CITC 90. **d** 93 **p** 94. C Belfast St Donard *D & D* 93-96; I Aghalurcher w Tattykeeran, Cooneen etc *Clogh* 96-11; Dir of Ords 04-11; Preb Donaghmore St Patr Cathl Dublin 05-11. *18 Garlaw Road, Clogher BT76 0TN* Tel (028) 8554 8547 Mobile 07977-157637 E-mail colebrooke_clogher@hotmail.com

GILLIBRAND, John Nigel. b 60. Ox Univ BA82 MA86 Lon Univ PGCE83. St Steph Ho Ox BTh87. **d** 88 **p** 89. C Dolgellau w Llanfachreth and Brithdir etc *Ban* 88-90; C Llanbeblig w Caernarfon and Betws Garmon etc 90-91; R Ffestiniog w Blaenau Ffestiniog 91-97; V Llandegfan w Llandysilio 97-02; Nat Co-ord (Wales) Nat Autistic Soc 02-04; P-in-c Llangeler w Pen-Boyr *St D* 04-10; V from 10. *The Vicarage, Llangeler, Llandysul SA44 5EX* Tel (01559) 371170

GILLIBRAND, Margaret Ann Jane. b 43. **d** 01 **p** 02. OLM Deal St Leon and St Rich and Sholden *Cant* 01-04; Perm to Offic *Eur* 04-07; Asst Chapl Poitou-Charentes 07-09; NSM Whitstable *Cant* from 11. *69 Swalecliffe Court Drive, Whitstable CT5 2NF* Tel (01227) 793432 E-mail cornerstone161@yahoo.co.uk

GILLIES, Mrs Jennifer Susan. b 63. Westmr Coll Ox BEd85. SNWTP 07. **d** 10 **p** 11. C Bidston *Ches* from 10. *10 Cavendish Road, Birkenhead CH41 8AX* Tel 0151-652 6280 E-mail revjennygillies@gmail.com

✠**GILLIES, The Rt Revd Robert Arthur.** b 51. Edin Univ BD77 St Andr Univ PhD91. Edin Th Coll 73. **d** 77 **p** 78 **c** 07. C Falkirk *Edin* 77-80; C Edin Ch Ch 80-84; Chapl Napier Coll 80-84; Chapl Dundee Univ 84-90; R St Andrews St Andr *St And* 91-07; Dioc Dir of Ords 96-07; Can St Ninian's Cathl Perth 97-07; Dean St Andr 07; Bp Aber from 07. *Diocesan Office, 39 King's Crescent, Aberdeen AB24 3HP* Tel (01224) 636653 *or* 208142 Fax 636186 *or* 312141 E-mail bishop@aberdeen.anglican.org

GILLIES, Miss Sheila Jennifer. St Martin's Coll Lanc TCert71. **d** 06 **p** 07. OLM Childwall All SS *Liv* from 06. *190 Thomas Drive, Liverpool L14 3LE* Tel 0151-228 4304

GILLINGHAM, John Bruce. b 48. Ch Ch Ox BA69 MA74. St Jo Coll Nottm BA73. **d** 73 **p** 74. C Plymouth St Andr w St Paul and St Geo *Ex* 73-77; C Ox St Aldate w H Trin 78; Chapl Jes Coll Ox 78-88; Chapl Ox Pastorate 79-88; Dioc Missr *Birm* 88-92; R Ox St Clem from 92; AD Cowley from 07. *St Clement's Rectory, 58 Rectory Road, Oxford OX4 1BW* Tel (01865) 248735

GILLINGHAM, Michael John. b 46. Hull Univ MA90. Chich Th Coll 68. **d** 71 **p** 72. C Llanharan w Peterston-super-Montem 71-73; C Skewen 73-76; Neath Deanery Youth Chapl 74-76; Perm to Offic 79-80; TV Kirkby *Liv* 76-77; Youth Chapl Woodchurch *Ches* 77-79; Sen Youth Worker (Bedfordshire) *St Alb* 80-83; Perm to Offic 80-83; TV Sheff Manor 83-88; R Frecheville from 88; Chapl Sheff Sea Cadets from 87; Chapl RNR 90-92; Chapl S Yorks Police *Sheff* from 93. *Frecheville Rectory, Brackenfield Grove, Sheffield S12 4XS* Tel 0114-239 9555 Mobile 07764-606456 E-mail mgillingham@talktalk.net

GILLINGHAM, Mrs Stephanie Ruth. b 60. W Lon Inst of HE CertEd82 Open Univ BA86 Man Univ MEd06. NTMTC BA09. **d** 09 **p** 10. C Galleywood Common *Chelmsf* from 09. *St Michael's House, 13 Roughtons, Chelmsford CM2 8PE* Tel (01245) 477818 E-mail stephanie@stmichaelsgalleywood.co.uk

GILLINGS, The Ven Richard John. b 45. St Chad's Coll Dur BA67. Linc Th Coll 68. **d** 70 **p** 71. C Altrincham St Geo *Ches* 70-75; P-in-c Stockport St Thos 75-77; R 77-83; P-in-c Stockport St Pet 78-83; TR Birkenhead Priory 83-93; V Bramhall 93-05; RD Birkenhead 85-93; Hon Can Ches Cathl 92-94; Adn Macclesfield 94-10; rtd 11. *Culvardie, Deshar Road, Boat of Garten PH24 3BN* Tel (01479) 831545

GILLION, Alan Robert. b 51. LRAM. Sarum & Wells Th Coll 81. **d** 83 **p** 84. C E Dereham *Nor* 83-86; C Richmond St Mary w St Matthias and St Jo *S'wark* 86-90; P-in-c Discovery Bay Ch Hong Kong 90-98; Chapl Shek Pik Pris 90-98; Bp Kensington's Officer for Evang *Lon* 98-01; P-in-c Upper Chelsea St Sav and St Simon 01-02; V 02-08; R Upper Chelsea H Trin from 08; AD Chelsea 04-11. *Upper Chelsea Rectory, 97A Cadogan Lane, London SW1X 9DU* Tel (020) 7730 7270 E-mail rob.gillion@london.anglican.org

GILLIONS, Michael George. b 37. Ch Ch Ox MA65 Keele Univ PGCE74. WEMTC 93. **d** 96 **p** 97. NSM Dorrington w Leebotwood, Longnor, Stapleton etc *Heref* 96-00; NSM Condover w Frodesley, Acton Burnell etc from 00. *The Maltsters, Dorrington, Shrewsbury SY5 7JD* Tel (01743) 718550

GILLON, Patrick. b 51. WMMTC 05. **d** 08 **p** 09. NSM Kingstanding St Mark *Birm* from 08. *161 Beacon Road, Great Barr, Birmingham B43 7DA* Tel 0121-605 2890 Mobile 07792-635831 E-mail patrick_gillon2000@yahoo.co.uk

GILLUM, Thomas Alan. b 55. Ex Univ BSc76. Cranmer Hall Dur 87. **d** 89 **p** 90. C Brompton H Trin w Onslow Square St Paul *Lon* 89-94; P-in-c Paddington St Steph w St Luke 94-04; P-in-c S Kensington St Jude 04-06; Warden Community of St Jude 06-11; P-in-c Isleworth St Jo from 11. *The New Vicarage, St John's Road, Isleworth TW7 6NY* Tel (020) 8560 2881

GILMARTIN, Frances. See CLARKE, Mrs Frances

GILMORE, David Samuel. b 70. Univ of Ulster BSc92 QUB MSSc95 Anglia Poly Univ MA05 CQSW92. EAMTC 01. **d** 03 **p** 04. C Basildon St Martin *Chelmsf* 03-04; C Danbury 04-08; R Soho St Anne w St Thos and St Pet *Lon* 08-10. *Address temp unknown* E-mail davidgilmore@btinternet.com

GILMORE, Canon Henry. b 51. Man Univ BA72 TCD BD82. CITC 75. **d** 75 **p** 76. C Arm St Mark w Aghavilly 75-78; C Dublin St Patr Cathl Gp 78-81; I Stranorlar w Meenglas and Kilteevogue *D & R* 81-84; I Achill w Dugort, Castlebar and Turlough *T, K & A* 84-91; I Moville w Greencastle, Donagh, Cloncha etc *D & R* 91-11; I Tullyaughnish w Kilmacrenan and Killygarvan from 11; Can Raphoe Cathl from 01. *The Rectory, Ramelton, Letterkenny, Co Donegal, Republic of Ireland* Tel (00353) (74) 915 1013 E-mail hgilmore@eircom.net

GILMOUR, Ian Hedley. b 57. Ex Univ LLB Lon Univ BD. Wycliffe Hall Ox 80. **d** 83 **p** 84. C Harold Wood *Chelmsf* 83-86; C Thame w Towersey *Ox* 86-91; V Streatham Vale H Redeemer *S'wark* from 91. *The Vicarage, Churchmore Road, London SW16 5UZ* Tel (020) 8764 5808

GILPIN, Jeremy David. b 59. Pemb Coll Ox BA80 CertEd82. Trin Coll Bris BA88. **d** 88 **p** 89. C Southsea St Jude *Portsm* 88-92; V Itchingfield w Slinfold *Chich* 92-96; Chapl St Hugh's Coll Ox 97-07. *Address temp unknown*

GILPIN, Canon Richard John. b 45. Lon Univ BSc66. Wells Th Coll 67. **d** 70 **p** 71. C Davyhulme Ch Ch *Man* 70-74; Pastor Gustav Adolf Berlin EKD 74-77; R Heaton Norris Ch w All SS 77-83; R Chorlton-cum-Hardy St Clem 83-99; AD Hulme 95-99; V Norley, Crowton and Kingsley *Ches* 99-07; RD Frodsham 03-06; Hon Can Ches Cathl 04-06; rtd 07. *4 Smithy Close, Shocklach, Malpas SY14 7BX* Tel (01829) 250413 E-mail dick@gilp.in

GILPIN, The Ven Richard Thomas. b 39. Lich Th Coll 60. **d** 63 **p** 64. C Whipton *Ex* 63-66; C Tavistock and Gulworthy 66-69; V

73-91; V Swimbridge 69-73; Preb Ex Cathl from 82; RD Tavistock 87-90; Dioc Dir of Ords 90-91; Adv for Voc and Dioc Dir of Ords 91-96; Sub Dean Ex Cathl 92-96; Adn Totnes 96-05; rtd 05. *7 The Strand, Shaldon, Teignmouth TQ14 0DL* Tel (01626) 873443 E-mail richard.gilpin2@btinternet.com

GILROY, Peter William. b 62. Univ of Wales (Ban) MTh09. Ridley Hall Cam 09. **d** 11. C Stapleford *S'well* from 11. *41 Perth Drive, Stapleford, Nottingham NG9 8PZ* Tel 0115-969 9958 E-mail peterwgilroy@gmail.com

GIMSON, Francis Herbert. b 54. Reading Univ BSc79. St Jo Coll Nottm 83. **d** 86 **p** 87. C Menston w Woodhead *Bradf* 86-89; C Barnoldswick w Bracewell 89-91; V Langleybury St Paul *St Alb* 91-02; P-in-c Downton *Sarum* 02-06; P-in-c Redlynch and Morgan's Vale 04-06; TR Forest and Avon from 06. *The Vicarage, Barford Lane, Downton, Salisbury SP5 3QA* Tel (01725) 510326 E-mail fgimson@nildram.co.uk

GINEVER, Paul Michael John. b 49. AKC71. **d** 72 **p** 73. C Davyhulme Ch Ch *Man* 72-75; Australia 76-77; C Tettenhall Wood *Lich* 77-80; C Halesowen *Worc* 80; TV 80-86; P-in-c Gt Malvern Ch Ch 86-98; V S Hayling *Portsm* from 98. *The Vicarage, 34 Church Road, Hayling Island PO11 0NT* Tel (023) 9246 2914 or 9263 7649 E-mail parishoffice@haylinganglicans.freeserve.co.uk

GINGELL, John Lawrence. b 27. Lon Univ BD55. ALCD55. **d** 55 **p** 56. C Normanton *Derby* 55-58; C Ilkeston St Bart CD 58-61; Toc H Staff Padre 61-70; Asst Chapl S Lon Ind Miss 61-64; Lic to Offic *S'wark* 61-66; Lic to Offic *Liv* 67-70; V Somercotes *Derby* 70-72; Bp's Ind Adv 72-80; rtd 92. *18 Bournville Road, London SE6 4RN* Tel (020) 8690 0148

GINGRICH, Dale Robert. b 64. Midland Lutheran Coll (USA) BSc86 Lutheran Th Sem Gettysburg MDiv93. EAMTC 03. **d** 04 **p** 05. NSM Shingay Gp *Ely* 04-08; TV Gaywood *Nor* from 08; Dioc Ecum Officer from 09. *Church Bungalow, Gayton Road, Gaywood, King's Lynn PE30 4DZ* Tel (01553) 765167 Mobile 07766-706773 E-mail dale.gingrich@norwich.anglican.org

GINN, Daniel Vivian. b 33. Univ of Wales (Cardiff) BSc55 DipEd56. Llan Dioc Tr Scheme 79. **d** 82 **p** 83. NSM Llantwit Major and St Donat's 82-83; NSM Llantwit Major 83-02; TV 88-02; RD Llantwit Major and Cowbridge 94-02; Perm to Offic from 02. *Chenet, 24 Voss Park Drive, Llantwit Major CF61 1YE* Tel (01446) 792774

GINN, Canon Richard John. b 51. Lon Univ BD77 Dur Univ MLitt05 ACIB73 Lambeth STh85. Oak Hill Th Coll 75 Cranmer Hall Dur 77. **d** 79 **p** 80. C Hornsey Ch Ch *Lon* 79-82; C Highgate St Mich 82-85; V Westleton w Dunwich *St E* 85-08; V Darsham 85-08; P-in-c Yoxford, Peasenhall and Sibton 01-08; P-in-c Middleton cum Fordley and Theberton w Eastbridge 01-08; V Yoxmere from 08; Hon Can St E Cathl from 01. *The Vicarage, Darsham Road, Westleton, Saxmundham IP17 3AQ* Tel (01728) 648271 E-mail r.ginn@btinternet.com

GINNO, Albert Charles. b 31. CA Tr Coll 51 Lon Coll of Div 66. **d** 68 **p** 69. C Kemp Town St Mark and St Matt *Chich* 68-72; P-in-c E Hoathly 72-83; V Westham 83-96; rtd 96; Perm to Offic *Chich* from 96. *106 Sorrel Drive, Eastbourne BN23 8BJ* Tel (01323) 761479 Fax 768920

GIRARD, Canon William Nicholas Charles. b 35. Coll of Resurr Mirfield 65. **d** 67 **p** 68. C Yate *Glouc* 67-70; C Westbury-on-Trym St Alb *Bris* 70-73; Chapl K Sch Ely 73-76; V Fenstanton and Hilton *Ely* 76-85; R Balsham and P-in-c W Wickham 85-99; P-in-c Horseheath 85-96; RD Linton 93-94 and 96-99; Hon Can Ely Cathl 97-03; C Alconbury cum Weston 99-00; Hon C 00-03; C Buckworth 99-00; Hon C 00-03; C Gt w Lt Stukeley 99-00; Hon C 00-03; rtd 00; P-in-c Hamerton *Ely* 00-04; RD Leightonstone 00-02; Perm to Offic *Ely* and *Pet* from 05. *Ferrar House, Little Gidding, Huntingdon PE28 5RJ* Tel (01832) 293083

GIRLING, Andrew Martin. b 40. Em Coll Cam BA63 MA67. Wycliffe Hall Ox 63. **d** 65 **p** 66. C Luton w E Hyde *St Alb* 65-69; Chapl Hull Univ 69-75; V Dringhouses 75-00; Can and Preb York Minster 97-00; P-in-c Thurlestone w S Milton *Ex* 00-02; R Thurlestone, S Milton, W Alvington etc 02-08; rtd 08. *2 Mead Drive, Thurlestone, Kingsbridge TQ7 3TA* E-mail sueand@talktalk.net

GIRLING, David Frederick Charles. b 33. Kelham Th Coll 49 Edin Th Coll 58. **d** 61 **p** 62. C Caister *Nor* 61-65; C Leigh St Clem *Chelmsf* 65-66; CF 66-83; V Prittlewell St Luke *Chelmsf* 83-98; rtd 98; Perm to Offic *Nor* from 98. *37 Dell Road East, Lowestoft NR33 9LA* Tel (01502) 567426

GIRLING, Francis Richard (Vincent). b 28. Worc Coll Ox BA52 MA56 Lon Univ BD65. Coll of Resurr Mirfield 55. **d** 57 **p** 59. CR from 57; rtd 98; Lic to Offic *Wakef* from 98. *House of the Resurrection, Stocks Bank Road, Mirfield WF14 0BN* Tel (01924) 494318

GIRLING, Ian John. b 53. Oak Hill Th Coll 03. **d** 05 **p** 06. C Hubberston *St D* 05-08; TV Aberystwyth from 08. *Holy Trinity Vicarage, Buarth Road, Aberystwyth SY23 1NB* Tel (01970) 617015 E-mail iangirling@yahoo.co.uk

GIRLING, Stephen Paul. b 61. Southn Univ BSc83. Trin Coll Bris BA91. **d** 91 **p** 92. C Ogley Hay *Lich* 91-95; TV S Molton w Nymet St George, High Bray etc *Ex* 95-01; RD S Molton 97-01;

V Crofton *Portsm* from 01; RD Fareham from 08. *The Vicarage, 40 Vicarage Lane, Stubbington, Fareham PO14 2JX* Tel and fax (01329) 662007 E-mail girlingsp@aol.com

GIRLING, Canon Timothy Havelock. b 43. St Aid Birkenhead 63. d 67 p 68. C Wickford *Chelmsf* 67-70; C Luton w E Hyde *St Alb* 70-74; C Luton All SS w St Pet 74-80; Chapl Luton and Dunstable Hosp 74-80; R Northill w Moggerhanger *St Alb* 80-89; Chapl Glenfield Hosp Leic 89-00; Chapl Glenfrith Hosp 89-93; Chapl Univ Hosps Leic NHS Trust 00-04; Hon Can Leic Cathl 97-04; rtd 04; Chapl Leics Partnership NHS Trust from 04; Perm to Offic Pet 04-08 and Leic from 04. *36 Winton Avenue, Leicester LE3 1DH* Tel 0116-291 3795 Mobile 07879-418721 E-mail tgirling@ntlworld.com

GIRLING, Vincent. *See* GIRLING, Francis Richard

GIRTCHEN, John Christopher. b 54. Linc Th Coll 94. d 96 p 97. C Bourne *Linc* 96-00; V Barrow and Goxhill from 00. *The Vicarage, Thornton Street, Barrow-upon-Humber DN19 7DG* Tel (01469) 530357 E-mail jcgirtchen@lineone.net

GISBOURNE, Michael Andrew. b 65. Leeds Univ BA87 St Martin's Coll Lanc MA09. St Jo Coll Nottm BTh91. d 92 p 93. C Gateacre *Liv* 92-95; C Marton *Blackb* 95-98; V Freckleton 98-03; V Garstang St Thos 03-10; Chapl Cumbria Univ from 10; V Scotforth from 11. *St Paul's Vicarage, 24 Scotforth Road, Lancaster LA1 4ST* Tel (01524) 32106 E-mail michael.gisbourne@phonecoop.coop

GISBY, Vivien Barbara. b 56. d 08 p 09. NSM Sutton St Jas *Ches* from 08. *1 Fearndown Way, Macclesfield SK10 2UF* Tel (01625) 501449 E-mail vivien.gisby@btinternet.com

✠**GITARI, The Most Revd David Mukuba.** b 37. K Coll Lon BA64 BD71 Ashland Univ (USA) Hon DD83 Kent Univ Hon DD98. Tyndale Hall Bris 68. d 71 p 72 c 75. Gen Sec Bible Soc Kenya 71-75; Bp Mt Kenya E 75-90; Bp Kirinyaga 90-97; Dean of Angl Ch of Kenya 94-97; Abp Kenya 96-02; rtd 02. *PO Box 607, 60100 Embu, Kenya* Tel (00254) (161) 30832 Fax 30824 E-mail davidgitari@insightkenya.com

GITTINGS, Graham. b 46. Qu Coll Birm 75. d 78 p 79. C Caverswall *Lich* 78-81; C Wolverhampton St Matt 81-82; C Walthamstow St Mary w St Steph *Chelmsf* 82-83; C Dagenham 83-89; V Earl Shilton w Elmesthorpe *Leic* from 89; rtd 11. *Address temp unknown* E-mail ggvicar@aol.com

GITTOES, Julie Anne. b 76. Trevelyan Coll Dur BA98 Graduate Soc Dur MA99 Selw Coll Cam PhD04. Westcott Ho Cam 99. d 03 p 04. C Hampton Hill *Lon* 03-06; V Hampton All SS from 06. *All Saints' Vicarage, 40 The Avenue, Hampton TW12 3RS* Tel (020) 8941 4424 Mobile 07941-871570 E-mail juliegittoes@googlemail.com

GIVEN, Harold Richard. b 54. Oak Hill Th Coll 75. d 78 p 79. C Belfast St Clem *D & D* 78-80; C Belfast St Donard 80-83; I Tamlaght O'Crilly Upper w Lower *D & R* 83-92; I Tamlaghtfinlagan w Myroe from 92. *Finlagan Rectory, 77 Ballykelly Road, Limavady BT49 9DS* Tel (028) 7176 2743

GLADSTONE, Canon Robert Michael. b 60. Ch Ch Ox BA82 MA86. Wycliffe Hall Ox 92. d 94 p 95. C Trentham *Lich* 94-97; C Heigham H Trin *Nor* 97-01; V Rothley *Leic* from 01; RD Goscote from 06; Hon Can Leic Cathl from 10. *The Vicarage, 128 Hallfields Lane, Rothley, Leicester LE7 7NG* Tel 0116-230 2241 E-mail rob.gladstone@btconnect.com

✠**GLADWIN, The Rt Revd John Warren.** b 42. Chu Coll Cam BA65 MA68. Cranmer Hall Dur. d 67 p 68 c 94. C Kirkheaton *Wakef* 67-71; Tutor St Jo Coll Dur 71-77; Dir Shaftesbury Project 77-82; Sec Gen Syn Bd for Soc Resp 82-88; Preb St Paul's Cathl 84-88; Provost Sheff 88-94; Angl Adv Yorkshire TV 88-94; Bp Guildf 94-03; Bp Chelmsf 03-09; rtd 09. *131A Marford Road, Wheathampstead, St Albans AL4 8NH* Tel (01582) 834223 E-mail johnwgladwin@hotmail.com

GLADWIN, Thomas William. b 35. St Alb Minl Tr Scheme 78. d 81 p 82. NSM Hertford St Andr *St Alb* 81-82; NSM Digswell and Panshanger 82-86; C 86-96; rtd 96; Perm to Offic *St Alb* from 96. *99 Warren Way, Welwyn AL6 0DL* Tel (01438) 714700

GLAISTER, James Richard. b 30. Oak Hill Th Coll 81. d 83 p 84. NSM Shrub End *Chelmsf* 83-85; NSM Lawshall w Shimplingthorne and Alpheton *St E* 85-87; NSM Lavenham 87-88; C Felixstowe St Jo 88-95; rtd 95; Perm to Offic *St E* 95-01; Carl 00-02; Blackb 02-05. *Les Planchettes, 61350 Saint-Roche-sur-Egrenne, France*

GLAISYER, Canon Hugh. b 30. Oriel Coll Ox BA51 MA55. St Steph Ho Ox 51. d 56 p 56. C Tonge Moor *Man* 56-62; C Sidcup St Jo *Roch* 62-64; V Milton next Gravesend Ch Ch 64-81; RD Gravesend 74-81; V Hove All SS *Chich* 81-91; Can and Preb Chich Cathl 82-91; RD Hove 82-91; P-in-c Hove St Jo 87-91; Adn Lewes and Hastings 91-97; rtd 97; Perm to Offic *Chich* 97-03; Lic to Offic from 03. *Florence Villa, Hangleton Lane, Ferring, Worthing BN12 6PP* Tel and fax (01903) 244688 Mobile 07712-317118 E-mail h.glaisyer@virgin.net

GLANVILLE-SMITH, Canon Michael Raymond. b 38. Leeds Univ MA95 AKC61. d 62 p 63. C St Marylebone St Mark w St Luke *Lon* 62-64; C Penzance St Mary *Truro* 64-68; R Worc St Andr and All SS w St Helen 68-74; Dioc Youth Chapl 68-74; V Catshill 74-80; P-in-c Worc St Martin w St Pet 80-81; TR Worc

St Martin w St Pet, St Mark etc 81-86; TR Worc SE 86-90; Hon Can Worc Cathl 83-90; Can Res Ripon Cathl 90-07; RD Ripon 96-97; rtd 07. *13 Ure Bank Terrace, Ripon HG4 1JG* Tel (01765) 609428 Mobile 07792-014055 E-mail mglansmith@hotmail.com

GLARE, Michael Francis. b 28. Southn Univ BA54. St Steph Ho Ox 56. d 57 p 58. C Withycombe Raleigh *Ex* 57-62; C-in-c Goodrington CD 62-65; C Tamerton Foliot 65-70; R Weare Giffard w Landcross 70-76; RD Hartland 74-76; P-in-c Babbacombe 76-80; V 80-87; V Ilsington 87-93; rtd 93; Perm to Offic *Ex* from 94. *Poplar Lodge, 23 Albion Street, Shaldon, Teignmouth TQ14 0DF* Tel (01626) 872679

GLASBY, Alan Langland. b 46. St Jo Coll Nottm 74. d 77 p 78. C Erith St Paul *Roch* 77-80; C Moor Allerton *Ripon* 80-81; TV 81-87; V Middleton St Mary 87-92; V Bilton 92-00; V Barton and Manfield and Cleasby w Stapleton 00-04; TR E Richmond 04-11; rtd 11. *23 Westwinn View, Leeds LS14 2HY* Tel 0113-265 5992 Mobile 07970-712484 E-mail alanglasby@btinternet.com

GLASGOW AND GALLOWAY, Bishop of. *See* DUNCAN, The Rt Revd Gregor Duthie

GLASGOW AND GALLOWAY, Dean of. *See* BARCROFT, The Very Revd Ian David

GLASGOW, Provost of. *See* HOLDSWORTH, The Very Revd Kelvin

GLASS, Caroline Mary. b 57. Southn Univ BSc79 Open Univ MA(Ed)01. Trin Coll Bris BA06. d 06 p 07. C Redhill H Trin S'wark 06-10; V Tunbridge Wells St Luke *Roch* from 10. *St Luke's Vicarage, 158 Upper Grosvenor Road, Tunbridge Wells TN1 2EQ* Tel (01892) 521374 Mobile 07910-066837 E-mail caroline.glass957@btinternet.com

GLASS, Mrs Yvonne Elizabeth. b 58. EMMTC 94. d 97 p 98. NSM Bingham *S'well* 97-00; Chapl Nottm City Hosp NHS Trust 00-11; rtd 11. *25 Valley Road, West Bridgford, Nottingham NG2 6HG* Tel 0115-846 2125

GLASSPOOL, John Martin. b 59. Kent Univ BA83 Heythrop Coll Lon MTh95 Leeds Univ MA05 RGN87. Westcott Ho Cam 88. d 90 p 91. C Forest Gate Em w Upton Cross *Chelmsf* 90-93; P-in-c Theydon Garnon 93-95; Chapl St Marg Hosp Epping 93-99; TV Epping Distr *Chelmsf* 95-99; Asst Chapl R Free Hampstead NHS Trust 99-02; Chapl Surrey and Sussex Healthcare NHS Trust from 02. *Chaplaincy Department, East Surrey Hospital, Canada Avenue, Redhill RH1 5RH* Tel (01737) 768511 ext 6120 E-mail john.glasspool@sash.nhs.uk

GLAZEBROOK, William Leng. b 29. Edin Th Coll 76. d 76 p 77. C Dollar *St And* 76-82; Dioc Supernumerary 83; Chapl Trin Coll Glenalmond 84; P-in-c Glencarse *Bre* 84-87; Dioc Sec 84-87; Chapl HM Pris Perth 85-87; V Broughton Poggs w Filkins, Broadwell etc *Ox* 87-94; rtd 94; Perm to Offic *Bre* 94-08 and *St And* from 98. *10 Rose Terrace, Perth PH1 5HA* Tel (01738) 624913

GLEADALL, John Frederick. b 39. Ripon Hall Ox 66 Sarum Th Coll 69. d 70 p 71. C S Ashford Ch Ch *Cant* 70-76; P-in-c Hothfield 76-83; P-in-c Westwell 81-83; P-in-c Eastwell w Boughton Aluph 81-83; V Westwell, Hothfield, Eastwell and Boughton Aluph 84-03; rtd 03; Hon C Old Leake w Wrangle *Linc* 03-07; Chapl HM Pris N Sea Camp 03-07. *2 Pinewood Gardens, North Cove, Beccles NR34 7PG* Tel (01502) 476483

GLEAVES, John. b 39. Alsager Coll of Educn CertEd60 Westmr Coll Ox BTh03. NOC 99. d 00 p 01. NSM Alsager St Mary *Ches* 00-03; P-in-c Alvanley 03-08; rtd 08. *46 Linley Grove, Alsager, Stoke-on-Trent ST7 2PS* Tel (01270) 878169 E-mail j.gleaves@btinternet.com

GLEDHILL, Alan. b 43. Lon Univ BSc(Econ)73. NOC 81. d 84 p 85. C Knaresborough *Ripon* 84-87; P-in-c Easby 87-88; P-in-c Bolton on Swale 87-88; V Easby w Brompton on Swale and Bolton on Swale 88-96; Teacher St Fran Xavier Sch Richmond 96-08; Perm to Offic *Ripon* 96-08; rtd 08; Hon C Gilling and Kirkby Ravensworth *Ripon* from 08. *The Vicarage, High Street, Gilling West, Richmond DL10 5JG* Tel (01748) 824466 Mobile 07906-195390 E-mail gledhill356@btinternet.com

✠**GLEDHILL, The Rt Revd Jonathan Michael.** b 49. Keele Univ BA72 Hon DUniv07 Bris Univ MA75. Trin Coll Bris 72. d 75 p 76 c 96. C Marple All SS *Ches* 75-78; C Folkestone H Trin w Ch Ch *Cant* 78-83; V Cant St Mary Bredin 83-96; Tutor Cant Sch of Min 83-96; RD Cant 88-94; Hon Can Cant Cathl 92-96; Suff Bp Southampton *Win* 96-03; Bp Lich from 03. *Bishop's House, 22 The Close, Lichfield WS13 7LG* Tel (01543) 306000 Fax 306009 E-mail bishop.lichfield@lichfield.anglican.org

GLEESON, Robert Godfrey. b 49. Man Univ CQSW74. Qu Coll Birm 83. d 85 p 86. C Hall Green St Pet *Birm* 85-88; Asst Chapl Mental Health & Elderly Care Services Birm HA 88-90; Chapl 90-94; Chapl Moseley Hall Hosp Birm 90-94; Chapl S Birm Mental Health NHS Trust 94-03; Perm to Offic *Birm* from 03. *180 Pineapple Road, Birmingham B30 2TY* Tel 0121-444 2793 *or* 678 2002 Mobile 07966-188006

GLEN, Mrs Dawn Andrea. b 64. Liv Univ BA86. Westcott Ho Cam 07. d 09 p 10. C Derby Cathl 09-11; C Kirk Langley from 11; C Mackworth All SS from 11; C Mugginton and Kedleston from 11. *54 Park Grove, Derby DE22 1HF* Tel (01332) 332535 E-mail dawn.glen@gmail.com

GLENDALOUGH, Archdeacon of. *See* ROUNTREE, The Ven Richard Benjamin

GLENFIELD, Samuel Ferran. b 54. QUB BA76 TCD MLitt90 MA94 Ox Univ MTh99. Wycliffe Hall Ox 88. **d** 91 **p** 92. C Douglas Union w Frankfield *C, C & R* 91-94; I Rathcooney Union 94-96; I Kill *D & G* from 96. *The Rectory, Kill o' the Grange, Blackrock, Co Dublin, Republic of Ireland* Tel (00353) (1) 280 1721 *or* tel and fax 289 6442 E-mail office@kotg.ie

GLENNON, James Joseph. b 37. St Mary's Coll Strawberry Hill TCert69 BA70. Franciscan Ho of Studies. **d** 62 **p** 63. C S Woodford *Chelmsf* 64-65; NSM Hadleigh w Layham and Shelley *St E* 88-95; C Hadleigh 95-02; rtd 02; Perm to Offic *St E* from 02. *5 Carlford Court, 112 Parliament Road, Ipswich IP4 5EL* Tel (01473) 721072

GLOUCESTER, Archdeacon of. *See* SIDAWAY, The Ven Geoffrey Harold

GLOUCESTER, Bishop of. *See* PERHAM, The Rt Revd Michael Francis

GLOUCESTER, Dean of. *See* LAKE, The Very Revd Stephen David

GLOVER, Alan. b 47. SWMTC 96. **d** 99 **p** 00. NSM Bideford, Northam, Westward Ho!, Appledore etc *Ex* from 99. *West Fordlands, Heywood Road, Northam, Bideford EX39 3QA* Tel (01237) 479542

GLOVER, David Charles. b 66. St Jo Coll Dur BA87 St Jo Coll Cam MPhil91. Ridley Hall Cam 87. **d** 90 **p** 91. C Wath-upon-Dearne w Adwick-upon-Dearne *Sheff* 90-92; Chapl Hatf Coll Dur 92-00; P-in-c Dur St Marg 95-00; R Dur St Marg and Neville's Cross St Jo 00-05; P-in-c Washington 05-08; R from 08; AD Chester-le-Street from 08. *27 Wroxton, Washington NE38 7NU* Tel 0191-418 7911 Mobile 07932-683745 E-mail david.glover17@btinternet.com

GLOVER, Mrs Diana Mary. b 50. Kent Univ BA73 MA75. SAOMC. **d** 01 **p** 02. C Aylesbury w Bierton and Hulcott *Ox* 01-05; P-in-c Amersham on the Hill 05-08; V from 08. *The Vicarage, 70 Sycamore Road, Amersham HP6 5DR* Tel (01494) 727553 E-mail diana.glover@btinternet.com

GLOVER, Elisabeth Ann. b 53. Univ Coll Ches BTh99. **d** 98 **p** 99. NSM Thurstaston *Ches* 98-99; C Stockton Heath 00-04; V Eastham from 04. *The Vicarage, 29 Ferry Road, Eastham, Wirral CH62 0AJ* Tel 0151-327 2182 E-mail beth.glover@tesco.net

GLOVER, Janet Mary. b 58. Natal Univ BSc79 UED80. EAMTC 98. **d** 01 **p** 02. NSM Cambridge St Phil *Ely* 01-04; NSM Histon from 04; NSM Impington from 04; Hon Asst Dir of Ords from 07. *139 Waterbeach Road, Landbeach, Cambridge CB25 9FA* Tel (01223) 864931 E-mail janet@theglovers.name

GLOVER, Canon John. b 48. Kelham Th Coll 67. **d** 71 **p** 72. C Foley Park *Worc* 71-75; TV Sutton *Ex* 75-79; P-in-c Churchill w Blakedown *Worc* 79-84; R 84-87; R Belbroughton w Fairfield and Clent 87-91; Chapl Children's Family Trust from 91; NSM Flint *St As* 92-93; R Halkyn w Caerfallwch w Rhesycae 93-97; V Rhyl w St Ann from 97; Can Cursal St As Cathl 02-08; Sacr from 08. *The Vicarage, 31 Bath Street, Rhyl LL18 3LU* Tel (01745) 353732 Fax 350075 E-mail gloverjohn@supanet.com

GLOVER, Canon Judith Rosalind. b 53. NEOC 93. **d** 95 **p** 96. C Glendale Gp *Newc* 95-99; P-in-c Alwinton w Holystone and Alnham 99-04; R Upper Coquetdale 04-09; R Alston Moor from 09; Hon Can Newc Cathl from 10. *The Parsonage House, Brampton Road, Alston CA9 3AA* Tel (01434) 382558 E-mail judy@alwinton.net

GLOVER, Michael John Myers. b 28. Lon Univ BSc48 CEng MICE MSAICE. Cuddesdon Coll 54. **d** 56 **p** 57. C Leic St Pet 56-60; S Africa 60-73 and from 86; TR Northampton Em *Pet* 74-86; Bp's Chapl E Area Northn 73-74; rtd 93. *PO Box 447, Nongoma, 3950 South Africa* Tel (0027) (358) 310044 Fax 310457

GLOVER, Richard John. b 47. Nottm Univ BTh77. Linc Th Coll 73. **d** 77 **p** 78. C Barrow St Geo w St Luke *Carl* 77-79; C Netherton 79-80; P-in-c Addingham 80-83; P-in-c Edenhall w Langwathby and Culgaith 80-83; V Addingham, Edenhall, Langwathby and Culgaith 83-84; V Bishops Hull *B & W* 84-89; V Shilbottle *Newc* 89-96; V Whittingham and Edlingham w Bolton Chapel 96-00; P-in-c Barton, Pooley Bridge and Martindale *Carl* 00-04; Dioc Adv for Spiritual Direction and Healing 00-04; R Lower Swale *Ripon* from 04. *The Rectory, Manor Lane, Ainderby Steeple, Northallerton DL7 9PY* Tel (01609) 773346 E-mail richard@richardglover.wanadoo.co.uk

GLOVER, Thomas Edward. b 85. Grey Coll Dur BA06 Clare Coll Cam BA09. Westcott Ho Cam 07. **d** 10 **p** 11. C Dur N from 10. *The Vicarage, 8 Woodland Close, Bearpark, Durham DH7 7EB* Tel 0191-373 3886 Mobile 07711-576522

GLYN, Aneirin. b 75. St Hugh's Coll Ox MMath98 DPhil02. Oak Hill Th Coll MTh09. **d** 09 **p** 10. C St Helen Bishopsgate w St Andr Undershaft etc *Lon* from 09. *15 Morgan Street, London E3 5AA* Tel 07905-288078 (mobile) E-mail aneirin@gmail.com

GLYN-JONES, Alun. b 38. JP. CCC Cam BA59 MA63. Bps' Coll Cheshunt 60. **d** 61 **p** 62. C Portsea St Mary *Portsm* 61-65; Chapl

Hampton Sch Middx 65-76; Hd Master Abp Tenison Gr Sch Croydon 76-88; V Twickenham St Mary *Lon* 88-01; rtd 01; Perm to Offic *B & W; Bris; Sarum* and *Eur* from 01. *23 Bainton Close, Bradford-on-Avon BA15 1SE* Tel (01225) 866874 E-mail acglynj@aol.com

GLYNN, Simon Adrian. b 59. Van Mildert Coll Dur BSc80 Univ Coll Ches BTh99. NOC 96. **d** 99 **p** 00. NSM Carr Mill *Liv* 99-04; C Burscough Bridge 04-09; P-in-c Douglas *Blackb* from 09; C Appley Bridge from 09. *The Vicarage, 5 Tan House Lane, Parbold, Wigan WN8 7HG* Tel (01257) 462350 E-mail simon@simonglynn.plus.com

GOALBY, George Christian. b 55. Leeds Univ BA77. St Jo Coll Nottm 79. **d** 81 **p** 82. C Wakef St Andr and St Mary 81-84; Asst Chapl HM Pris Wakef 84-85; Chapl HM Youth Cust Cen Deerbolt 85-87; Chapl HM Pris Frankland 87-89; V Swinderby *Linc* from 89; CF (ACF) from 04. *All Saints' Vicarage, 27 Station Road, Swinderby, Lincoln LN6 9LY* Tel and fax (01522) 868430

GOATCHER, Mrs Sara Jacoba Helena. b 46. Oak Hill NSM Course 86. **d** 89 **p** 94. NSM S Croydon Em *S'wark* 89-95; C 95-96; R Sutton St Nic 96-06; Asst Chapl Old Palace Sch Croydon 06-11; C Croydon St Jo *S'wark* from 07. *8 Hornchurch Hill, Whyteleafe CR3 0DA* Tel (020) 8660 6198 Mobile 07785-230983 E-mail sara.goatcher@btinternet.com

GOATER, Canon Michael Robert. b 46. York Univ BA MA. NOC 89. **d** 92 **p** 93. C Norton *Sheff* 92-94; V Endcliffe 94-99; Chapl Sheff Ind Miss 94-95; Assoc Chapl Sheff Hallam Univ 95-99; Asst Post-Ord Tr Officer 95-99; Dioc Voc Officer 96-99; C Stratford-upon-Avon, Luddington etc *Cov* 99-02; P-in-c Gt Shelford *Ely* 02-11; RD Shelford 04-09; RD Granta 09-11; Hon Can Ely Cathl 10-11; Master St Nic Hosp Salisbury from 11. *St Nicholas Hospital, 5 St Nicholas Road, Salisbury SP1 2SW* Tel (01722) 336874 E-mail michael@mickthevic.org.uk

GOATLY, Mrs Ruth Christine. b 50. Leic Univ LLB72 Herts Univ MA98 CQSW74. Westcott Ho Cam 08. **d** 09 **p** 10. NSM Boxmoor St Jo *St Alb* from 09. *23 Beechfield Road, Hemel Hempstead HP1 1PP* Tel (01442) 253102 Mobile 07961-980158 E-mail ruth@goatly.fsnet.co.uk

GOBBETT, Michael George Timothy. b 64. St Chad's Coll Dur BSc86. St Steph Ho Ox BA89 MA98. **d** 90 **p** 91. CMP from 91; C Hartlepool St Aid *Dur* 90-94; P-in-c Norton St Mich 94-95; V 95-05; TR Upper Skerne from 05. *The Rectory, 2 Durham Road, Sedgefield, Stockton-on-Tees TS21 3DW* Tel (01740) 620274 E-mail michael.gobbett@btinternet.com

GOBEY, Ian Clifford. b 48. WEMTC 94. **d** 96 **p** 97. NSM Whiteshill and Randwick *Glouc* 96-00; NSM Painswick, Sheepscombe, Cranham, The Edge etc 00-07; P-in-c Westbury-on-Severn w Flaxley, Blaisdon etc from 07. *The Vicarage, Adsett, Westbury-on-Severn GL14 1PH* Tel (01452) 760592 E-mail ian@gobey7818.fsnet.co.uk

GOBLE, Christopher. b 75. Univ of Wales (Lamp) BA96. Trin Coll Bris 96. **d** 98 **p** 99. C St Jo in Bedwardine *Worc* 98-01; P-in-c Worc St Clem 01-02; R Brington w Whilton and Norton etc *Pet* 02-08; P-in-c Ilmington w Stretton-on-Fosse etc *Cov* from 08; P-in-c Tredington and Darlingscott from 08. *The Rectory, Valenders Lane, Ilmington, Shipston-on-Stour CV36 4LB* Tel (01608) 682282 E-mail ilmingtonrectory@btinternet.com

GOBLE, Clifford David. b 41. Oak Hill Th Coll 69. **d** 72 **p** 73. C Erith St Paul *Roch* 72-76; C Tunbridge Wells St Jas 76-79; R Southfleet 79-05; RD Gravesend 94-05; Hon Can Roch Cathl 99-05; rtd 05; Perm to Offic *Cant* from 06. *15 Martindown Road, Whitstable CT5 4PX* Tel (01227) 263333

GOBLE, (née DUNN), Mrs Sharon Louise. b 71. Univ of Wales (Swansea) BA93 Fitzw Coll Cam BA97. Ridley Hall Cam 95. **d** 98 **p** 99. C Malpas *Mon* 98-01; C Cyncoed 01-02; R Heyford w Stowe Nine Churches and Flore etc *Pet* 02-04; Perm to Offic 04-08; Chapl Shakespeare Hospice from 08. *The Rectory, Valenders Lane, Ilmington, Shipston-on-Stour CV36 4LB* Tel (01608) 682282 *or* (01789) 266852 E-mail sharon.goble@btinternet.com

GODBER, Canon Francis Giles. b 48. Open Univ BA88. Ridley Hall Cam 72. **d** 75 **p** 76. C Blackheath *Birm* 75-78; C Wolverhampton St Matt *Lich* 78-80; TV Washfield, Stoodleigh, Withleigh etc *Ex* 80-85; R Shenley and Loughton *Ox* 85-88; TR Watling Valley 88-96; Chapl Heatherwood and Wexham Park Hosp NHS Trust 96-00; P-in-c Geddington w Weekley *Pet* from 00; Dioc Ecum Officer from 00; Can Pet Cathl from 03. *The Vicarage, 25 West Street, Geddington, Kettering NN14 1BD* Tel (01536) 742200 E-mail ecuman.gilbar@talktalk.net

GODDARD, Andrew John. b 67. St Jo Coll Ox BA88 MA93 DPhil96. Cranmer Hall Dur 94. **d** 96 **p** 97. C Cogges and S Leigh *Ox* 96-99; Tutor Wycliffe Hall Ox 99-08; Tutor Trin Coll Bris from 08. *Trinity College, Stoke Hill, Bristol BS9 1JP* Tel 0117-968 2803 E-mail andrew.goddard@trinity-bris.ac.uk

GODDARD, Canon Charles Douglas James. b 47. CITC 67. **d** 70 **p** 71. C Orangefield *D & D* 70-73; C Stormont 73-75; Miss to Seafarers from 75; Sen Chapl and Sec N Ireland 77-09; rtd 10; Can Belf Cathl from 05. *9 Governors Gate Manor, Hillsborough BT26 6FZ* Tel (028) 9268 3592 E-mail cdjgoddard@googlemail.com

GODDARD, Christopher. b 45. Sarum & Wells Th Coll 79. **d** 81 **p** 82. C Whitehaven *Carl* 81-83; C Barrow St Geo w St Luke 83-85; P-in-c Hayton St Mary 85-90; V Brigham 90-98; V Mosser 90-98; Perm to Offic 00-03; Hon C Cockermouth w Embleton and Wythop 03-05; TV Cockermouth Area 05-10; rtd 10. *5 Craig Drive, Whitehaven CA28 6JX*
E-mail chrisgoddardmail@gmail.com

GODDARD, Derek George. b 38. St Martin's Coll Lanc BA97 CEng FIMechE FIMarEST FCMI. Cranmer Hall Dur 94 CBDTI 95. **d** 97 **p** 98. NSM Windermere St Mary and Troutbeck *Carl* 97-01; P-in-c Leven Valley 01-06; P-in-c Palermo w Taormina *Eur* 06-09; Perm to Offic *Blackb* 09-10; Hon C Overton from 10. *3 Chapel Barn, Chapel View, Overton, Morecambe LA3 3EP* Tel (01524) 858739
E-mail d.d.goddard@hotmail.co.uk

GODDARD, Mrs Doris. b 48. St Mary's Coll Twickenham CertEd70 Open Univ BA80. S'wark Ord Course 93. **d** 96 **p** 97. Chapl John Nightingale Sch W Molesley 96-00; NSM Addlestone *Guildf* 96-98; NSM Botleys and Lyne 98-04; NSM Long Cross 98-04; NSM Chertsey, Lyne and Longcross 04-05; NSM Blackdown *B & W* 05-09; P-in-c Puriton and Pawlett from 09. *The Vicarage, 1 The Rye, Puriton, Bridgwater TA7 8BZ* Tel (01278) 683500 E-mail rev.doris.goddard@btinternet.com

GODDARD, Douglas. *See* GODDARD, Canon Charles Douglas James

GODDARD, Mrs Elaine Clare. b 53. K Alfred's Coll Win CertEd78. WEMTC 96. **d** 99 **p** 00. C Leominster *Heref* 99-04; P-in-c St Weonards 04-07; R from 07; RD Ross and Archenfield from 07. *The Vicarage, Mount Way, St Weonards, Hereford HR2 8NN* Tel (01981) 580307 E-mail email@ecgoddard.co.uk

GODDARD, Elisabeth Ann. b 64. St Hugh's Coll Ox BA89 MA99. Cranmer Hall Dur 94. **d** 96 **p** 97. C Cogges and S Leigh *Ox* 96-99; Chapl Jes Coll Ox 99-04; Tutor Wycliffe Hall Ox 04-08; Hon C Ox St Andr 04-08; Hon C Stoke Bishop *Bris* 09-10; V Westminster St Jas the Less *Lon* from 10. *56 Tachbrook Street, London SW1V 2NA* Tel (020) 7834 1343
E-mail goddardea@mac.com

GODDARD, Canon Giles William. b 62. Clare Coll Cam MA84. S'wark Ord Course 92. **d** 95 **p** 96. C N Dulwich St Faith *S'wark* 95-98; R Walworth St Pet 98-09; AD S'wark and Newington 02-07; P-in-c Waterloo St Jo w St Andr from 09; Hon Can S'wark Cathl from 07. *St John's Vicarage, 1 Secker Street, London SE1 8UF* Tel (020) 7633 9819
E-mail gileswgoddard@googlemail.com

GODDARD, Canon Harold Frederick. b 62. Keble Coll Ox BA63 MA69. Cuddesdon Coll 64. **d** 66 **p** 67. C Birm St Pet 66-70; Chapl Dudley Road Hosp Birm 66-70; Chapl HM Pris Birm 68-70; C Alverstoke *Portsm* 70-72; Chapl Gosport Cottage Hosp Portsm 70-72; Chapl HM Det Cen Haslar 70-72; P-in-c Portsea St Geo CD *Portsm* 72-76; Chapl Portsm Cathl 73-76; P-in-c Stoke Prior *Worc* 76-78; P-in-c Wychbold and Upton Warren 77-78; R Stoke Prior, Wychbold and Upton Warren 78-80; Chapl Forelands Orthopaedic Hosp Worc 77-80; Chapl R Marsden Hosp Lon and Surrey 80-83; R Martley and Wichenford *Worc* 83-88; P-in-c Knightwick w Doddenham, Broadwas and Cotheridge 85-88; R Martley and Wichenford, Knightwick etc 89-90; Bp's Adv on Min of Healing 84-99; Chapl St Richard's Hospice Worc 87-94; RD Martley and Worc W 88-90; Chapl Kidderminster Gen Hosp 90-92; P-in-c Hallow *Worc* 91-92; P-in-c Sedgeberrow w Hinton-on-the-Green 92-00; Chapl Evesham Community Hosp Worc 93-00; Chapl Worcs Community Healthcare NHS Trust 97-00; Co-ord W Midl Healing Advisers 94-99; RD Evesham *Worc* 97-00; TR Kidderminster St Jo and H Innocents 00-08; Hon Can Worc Cathl 03-08; rtd 08; Perm to Offic *Worc* from 08. *1 Springfield House, Como Road, Malvern WR14 2HS* Tel (01684) 563350 Mobile 07768-106287 E-mail hgoddard@hotmail.com

GODDARD, John David. b 42. Guy's Hosp Medical Sch MB, BS64 MRCP73. **d** 03 **p** 04. OLM Morden *S'wark* from 03. *58 Queen Mary Avenue, Morden SM4 4JR* Tel (020) 8540 5082 E-mail jdg13@blueyonder.co.uk

✠**GODDARD, The Rt Revd John William.** b 47. St Chad's Coll Dur BA69. **d** 70 **p** 71 **c** 00. C S Bank *York* 70-74; C Cayton w Eastfield 74-75; V Middlesbrough Ascension 75-82; RD Middlesbrough 81-87; V Middlesbrough All SS 82-88; Can and Preb York Minster 87-88; Vice-Prin Edin Th Coll 88-92; TR Ribbleton *Blackb* 92-00; Suff Bp Burnley from 00; Bp's Adv on Hosp Chapls from 01; Co-ord for Interfaith Work from 07. *All Saints' House, Padiham Road, Burnley BB12 6PA* Tel (01282) 688060 Fax 470361 E-mail bishop.burnley@googlemail.com

GODDARD, Mrs Margaret. b 50. **d** 01 **p** 02. NSM Cockermouth Area *Carl* 01-10; rtd 10. *5 Craig Drive, Whitehaven CA28 6JX*
E-mail margaret@cateam.org.uk

GODDARD, Ms Marion. b 54. Sarum & Wells Th Coll 87. **d** 89 **p** 94. Par Dn Lewisham St Swithun *S'wark* 89-94; C 94-95; TV Thamesmead 96-04; rtd 04. *1 Hollows Close, Salisbury SP2 8JU* Tel (01722) 338562

GODDARD, Matthew Francis. b 45. Kelham Th Coll 65. **d** 69 **p** 70. C Mansfield St Mark *S'well* 69-72; C Northolt Park

St Barn *Lon* 72-78; P-in-c Acton Green St Pet 78-87; R Norwood St Mary 87-96. *27 Hounslow Avenue, Hounslow TW3 2DZ* Tel (020) 8230 6591
E-mail mattandtrace@hotmail.com

GODDARD, Mrs Pamela Gay. b 53. LSE BSc(Econ)74 CQSW77. SAOMC 95 EAMTC 97. **d** 98 **p** 99. C New Catton St Luke w St Aug *Nor* 98-03; Perm to Offic 03-05; NSM Hamworthy *Sarum* 05-07; C Throop *Win* 07-08; C Hamworthy *Sarum* from 08. *The Rectory, 1 St Michael's Close, Poole BH15 4QT* Tel (01202) 674878 E-mail pam.goddard@googlemail.com

GODDARD, Mrs Rosemary Joy. b 48. Philippa Fawcett Coll CertEd69. EAMTC 00. **d** 03 **p** 04. C Linc St Nic w St Jo Newport 03-05; P-in-c Bicker 05-08; P-in-c Donington 08; P-in-c Fleet w Gedney from 08; P-in-c Holbeach Marsh from 08. *The Rectory, Church End, Fleet, Spalding PE12 8NN* Tel (01406) 420711 Mobile 07740-203149 E-mail rosemaryjg@aol.com

GODDARD, Stuart David. b 53. Cen Sch of Art Lon BA76 Middx Poly PGCE82. Trin Coll Bris 91. **d** 93 **p** 94. C Watling Valley *Ox* 93-97; P-in-c Bowthorpe *Nor* 97-00; TV 00-05; P-in-c Hamworthy *Sarum* 05-09; R from 09. *The Rectory, 1 St Michael's Close, Poole BH15 4QT* Tel (01202) 674878
E-mail goddard.stuart@gmail.com

GODDARD, Trevor Paul. b 63. NTMTC 03. **d** 06 **p** 07. NSM Kensal Rise St Mark and St Martin *Lon* 06-11; NSM Kensal Rise St Mark from 11. *17 Odessa Road, London NW10 5YJ* Tel (020) 8357 2731 Mobile 07957-482926
E-mail trevorgoddard@mac.com

GODDEN, Canon Peter David. b 47. Leeds Univ BA69 MA04 ARCO70. Linc Th Coll 85. **d** 87 **p** 88. C Bearsted w Thurnham *Cant* 87-90; C Hykeham *Linc* 90-91; TV 91-95; P-in-c Linc St Pet-at-Gowts and St Andr 95-99; Hon PV Linc Cathl 90-99; R Armthorpe *Sheff* 99-00; R Owmby Gp *Linc* from 00; RD Lawres 05-06 and from 09; P-in-c Spring Line Gp from 08; Can and Preb Linc Cathl from 10. *The Vicarage, Main Street, Hackthorn, Lincoln LN2 3PF* Tel (01673) 860856
E-mail peter@owmbygroup.co.uk

GODDEN, Timothy Richard James. b 62. Univ Coll Lon BA84. St Jo Coll Nottm 89. **d** 89 **p** 90. C Tulse Hill H Trin and St Matthias *S'wark* 89-93; TV Horsham *Chich* 93-01; TR Bishopsworth and Bedminster Down *Bris* from 01. *St Peter's Vicarage, 61 Fernsteed Road, Bristol BS13 8HE* Tel and fax 0117-964 2734 E-mail tim@cgodden.fsnet.co.uk

GODECK, John William George. b 30. Chich Th Coll 57. **d** 60 **p** 61. C Wadhurst *Chich* 60-62; C Tidebrook 60-62; C Eastbourne 62-63; R Bondleigh *Ex* 63-78; R Zeal Monachorum 63-78; P-in-c Broadwoodkelly 65-67; R 68-78; R Dunchideock and Shillingford St George w Ide 78-96; RD Kenn 83-89; rtd 96; Perm to Offic *Ex* 96-09. *Boxgrove, 6 Barley Lane, Exeter EX4 1TE* Tel (01392) 424224

GODFREY, Ann Veronica. *See* MacKEITH, Mrs Ann Veronica

GODFREY, Canon Brian Ernest Searles. b 37. Lon Univ BSc60 MSc63 PhD72. S'wark Ord Course 78. **d** 81 **p** 82. NSM Hayes *Roch* 81-86; C 86-88; R Kingsdown 88-93; R Sundridge w Ide Hill 93-02; RD Sevenoaks 95-00; Hon Can Roch Cathl 99-03; rtd 02; Perm to Offic *Sarum* from 03. *Rowans, Kingcombe Road, Toller Porcorum, Dorchester DT2 0DG* Tel (01300) 320833
E-mail godfrey@centrenet.co.uk

GODFREY, David Samuel George. b 35. CITC 64. **d** 66 **p** 67. C Londonderry Ch Ch *D & R* 66-68; I Tomregan w Drumlane *K, E & A* 68-72; I Cloonclare 72-79; I Templebreedy *C, C & R* 79-85; I Bray *D & G* 85-97; Can Ch Ch Cathl Dublin 95-97; Dean Kilmore *K, E & A* 97-04; I Kilmore w Ballintemple etc; Preb Mulhuddart St Patr Cathl Dublin 01-04; rtd 04. *37 Earlsfort Meadows, Earlsfort, Lucan, Co Dublin, Republic of Ireland* Tel (00353) (1) 624 1906 Mobile 86-238 9686
E-mail godfreyd@tcd.ie *or* dsggodfrey@gmail.com

✠**GODFREY, The Rt Revd Harold William.** b 48. AKC71. St Aug Coll Cant 71. **d** 72 **p** 73 **c** 87. C Warsop *S'well* 72-75; TV Hucknall Torkard 75-86; Dioc Ecum Officer 81-82; USPG from 86; R and Adn Montevideo and Can Buenos Aires 86-88; Asst Bp Argentina and Uruguay 87-88; Bp Uruguay 88-98; Bp Peru from 98. *Calle Alcalá 336, Urb la Castellana, Santiago de Surco, Lima 33, Peru* Tel and fax (0051) (1) 422 9160 *or* 448 4855
E-mail wgodfrey@amauta.rcp.net.pe

GODFREY, Ian. b 56. **d** 01 **p** 02. NSM Mill Hill Jo Keble Ch *Lon* 01-11; V Goostrey w Swettenham *Ches* from 11. *The Vicarage, Blackden Lane, Goostrey, Crewe CW4 8PG* Tel (01477) 532109 E-mail igodfrey@ukonline.co.uk

GODFREY, Jennifer Olwen. **d** 02 **p** 03. C Lasswade *Edin* 02-03; NSM from 03; C Dalkeith 02-03; NSM from 03. *131 Newbattle Abbey Crescent, Dalkeith EH22 3LP* Tel 0131-660 6145 Mobile 07812-923159 E-mail jenniegodfrey@fsmail.net

GODFREY, John Frederick. b 31. Lon Univ LLB53 AKC54 Solicitor 57. Cuddesdon Coll 59. **d** 61 **p** 62. C Battersea St Luke *S'wark* 61-65; Min Reigate St Phil CD 65-72; Public Preacher St Alb 73-03; Perm to Offic from 03. *3 Davidge Place, Knotty Green, Beaconsfield HP9 2SR* Tel (01494) 689925 Fax 672930

GODFREY, Kesari Freeda. b 73. Nesamony Memorial Chr Coll Marthandam BSc93 United Th Coll Bangalore BD99. Princeton

Th Sem ThM01. **p** 05. Perm to Offic *Birm* 05-07; C Bridlington Priory *York* 07-10; V Southwater *Chich* from 10. *The Vicarage, Church Lane, Southwater, Horsham RH13 9BT* Tel (01403) 730229 Mobile 07709-947056
E-mail revdgodfrey@yahoo.co.uk

GODFREY, Matthew Fenton. b 69. Univ Coll Dur BA91 K Coll Lon MA94. Ripon Coll Cuddesdon MTh04. **d** 04 **p** 05. C Bodmin w Lanhydrock and Lanivet *Truro* 04-09; Chapl RN from 09. *Royal Naval Chaplaincy Service, Mail Point 1-2, Leach Building, Whale Island, Portsmouth PO2 8BY* Tel (023) 9262 5055 Fax 9262 5134 E-mail nitrogen_narcosis@hotmail.com

GODFREY, Michael. b 49. K Coll Lon BD70 Wolv Univ PGCE97. St Aug Coll Cant AKC72. **d** 72 **p** 73. C Birtley *Dur* 72-75; Ind Chapl 76-79; TV Bilston *Lich* 79-86; TV Wolverhampton 86-93; Chapl Black Country Urban Ind Miss 79-86; Team Ldr 86-93; Preb Lich Cathl 87-93; Perm to Offic *Worc* 04-08 and *Cov* 05-08; R Newport Pagnell w Lathbury and Moulsoe *Ox* from 08. *The Rectory, 81 High Street, Newport Pagnell MK16 8AB* Tel (01908) 611145
E-mail rector_08@btinternet.com

GODFREY, Michael James. b 50. Sheff Univ BEd77. St Jo Coll Nottm 79. **d** 82 **p** 83. C Walton H Trin *Ox* 82-86; C Chadderton Ch Ch *Man* 86-91; V Woodlands *Sheff* 91-03; V Wythall *Birm* 03-11; TV Morley *Wakef* from 11. *The Vicarage, Rooms Lane, Morley, Leeds LS27 9PA* Tel 0113-252 6836
E-mail mikegodfrey@btinternet.com

GODFREY, Myles. *See* GODFREY, Rumley Myles

GODFREY, Nigel Philip. b 51. Ripon Coll Cuddesdon BA78 MA84 Lon Guildhall Univ MBA00 K Coll Lon MSc09 MRTPI76. Ripon Coll Cuddesdon 77. **d** 79 **p** 80. C Kennington St Jo w St Jas *S'wark* 79-89; Community of Ch the Servant 84-93; V Brixton Road Ch Ch *S'wark* 89-01; Prin OLM Scheme 01-07; Chapl S'wark Cathl 02-07; V German *S & M* from 07; P-in-c Patrick from 11; Vice-Dean St German's Cathl from 07. *4 The Net Loft, Mariners Wharf, Peel, Isle of Man IM5 1AR* Tel (01624) 844830 *or* 842608 E-mail vice-dean@sodorandman.im

GODFREY, Mrs Patricia Ann. b 54. SEITE 01. **d** 04 **p** 05. NSM Dover St Mary *Cant* from 04. *8 Longfield Road, Dover CT17 9QU* Tel (01304) 206019
E-mail trish@godfrey88.screaming.net

GODFREY (née ROGERS), Mrs Pauline Ann. b 58. LMH Ox BA79 MA83 Ox Univ Inst of Educn PGCE80. S Dios Minl Tr Scheme 89. **d** 92 **p** 94. NSM Headley All SS *Guildf* 92-96; C 96-99; Past Tutor Local Min Progr from 96; P-in-c Wyke 99-01; V from 01. *Wyke Vicarage, Guildford Road, Normandy, Guildford GU3 2DA* Tel (01483) 811332
E-mail pag@yerfdog1.screaming.net *or* p.a.g@talktalk.net

GODFREY, Rumley Myles. b 48. S'wark Ord Course. **d** 83 **p** 84. NSM Dorchester *Ox* 83-11; Perm to Offic from 11. *The Old Malt House, Warborough, Wallingford OX10 7DY* Tel (01865) 858627
E-mail myles@warborough.fsnet.co.uk

GODFREY, Mrs Sarah Joy. b 64. Southn Univ BSc85 Bath Univ PGCE86. STETS 02. **d** 05 **p** 06. NSM Puddletown, Tolpuddle and Milborne w Dewlish *Sarum* from 05. *Bankfield House, Pound Lane, Dewlish, Dorchester DT2 7LZ* Tel (01258) 839067 E-mail sarah.godfrey@tiscali.co.uk

GODFREY, Canon Simon Henry Martin. b 55. TD00. K Coll Lon BD80 AKC80. St Steph Ho Ox 80. **d** 81 **p** 82. C Kettering SS Pet and Paul 81-84; R Crick and Yelvertoft w Clay Coton and Lilbourne 84-89; V Northampton All SS w St Kath 89-98; R Northampton All SS w St Kath and St Pet 98-09; Sen Chapl Malta and Gozo *Eur* from 09; Can and Chan St Paul's Pro-Cathl Valetta from 09. *St Paul's Anglican Pro-Cathedral, Independence Square, Valetta VLT12, Malta GC* Tel (00356) 2122 5714 Fax 2122 5867 E-mail simonhmgodfrey@googlemail.com

GODFREY, Stanley William. b 24. CEng MIET67. Qu Coll Birm 71. **d** 74 **p** 74. C Sutton Coldfield St Chad *Birm* 74-78; Hon C Handsworth St Andr 78-86; Hon C Worc City St Paul and Old St Martin etc 86-89; Hon C Droitwich Spa 89-96; Perm to Offic from 96. *2 The Pippins, Eckington, Pershore WR10 3PY* Tel (01386) 751184

GODIN, Mrs Mary Louise. b 42. SRN64 QN66. Oak Hill Th Coll Course 89. **d** 92 **p** 94. NSM Surbiton Hill Ch Ch *S'wark* 92-97; Chapl Kingston and Distr Community NHS Trust 97-01; Team Chapl SW Lon and St George's Mental Health NHS Trust 01-03; Chapl Taunton and Somerset NHS Trust 03-11; NSM Beercrocombe w Curry Mallet, Hatch Beauchamp etc *B & W* from 11. *The Stables, Capland Court, Capland Lane, Hatch Beauchamp, Taunton TA3 6TP* Tel (01823) 480606

GODSALL, Canon Andrew Paul. b 59. Birm Univ BA81. Ripon Coll Cuddesdon 86. **d** 88 **p** 89. C Gt Stanmore *Lon* 88-91; C Ealing All SS 91-94; V Hillingdon All SS 94-01; Dir of Ords Willesden Area 99-01; Bp's Chapl and Asst *Ex* 01-06; Dioc Dir of Min from 06; PV Ex Cathl 04-06; Can Res and Chan Ex Cathl from 06. *12 The Close, Exeter EX1 1EZ* Tel (01392) 275756
E-mail andrew.godsall@exeter.anglican.org

GODSALL, Canon Ralph Charles. b 48. Qu Coll Cam BA71 MA75. Cuddesdon Coll 73. **d** 75 **p** 76. C Sprowston *Nor* 75-78; Chapl Trin Coll Cam 78-84; V Hebden Bridge *Wakef* 84-93; V

Westmr St Steph w St Jo *Lon* 93-01; Can Res Roch Cathl 01-08; rtd 08; PV Westmr Abbey from 08. *39 Vincent Square, London SW1P 2NP* Tel (020) 7976 5899 Mobile 07786-959540
E-mail canonralph@hotmail.co.uk

GODSELL, David Brian. b 40. Lon Univ BA62. Coll of Resurr Mirfield 65. **d** 67 **p** 68. C Middlesbrough All SS *York* 67-73; CMP from 69; C Stainton-in-Cleveland *York* 73-75; V Byker St Ant *Newc* 75-90; P-in-c Brandon *Dur* 90-94; V 94-04; V Brandon and Ushaw Moor 04-05; rtd 05; Hon C Brandon and Ushaw Moor *Dur* from 05; Chapl St Cuthb Soc Dur from 05. *The Clergy House, Sawmill Lane, Brandon, Durham DH7 8NS* Tel 0191-378 0845

GODSELL, Kenneth James Rowland. b 22. Birm Coll of Educn Dip Teaching50. Qu Coll Birm 75. **d** 76 **p** 77. Sen Lect Westhill Coll of HE Birm 74-85; Hon C Selly Hill St Steph *Birm* 76-81; Hon C Selly Park St Steph and St Wulstan 81-90; rtd 90; Lic to Offic *Birm* 90-96; Perm to Offic *Worc* from 96. *The Quest, Dock Lane, Tewkesbury GL20 7LN* Tel (01684) 772469

GODSON, Alan. b 31. Ch Coll Cam BA61 MA65. Clifton Th Coll 61. **d** 63 **p** 64. C Preston All SS *Blackb* 63-66; Lic to Offic *Man* 66-69; Asst Chapl Emb Ch Paris 69; Dioc Ev *Liv* 69-01; P-in-c Edge Hill St Mary 72-78; V 78-01; rtd 01; Perm to Offic *Liv* from 01. *28 Handley Court, Aigburth, Liverpool L19 3QS* Tel 0151-427 0255

GODSON, Mark Rowland. b 61. K Coll Lon BD83 AKC83 CertEd84. Linc Th Coll 84. **d** 86 **p** 87. C Hurst Green *S'wark* 86-88; C Fawley *Win* 88-90; TV Wimborne Minster and Holt *Sarum* 90-95; P-in-c Horton and Chalbury 90-95; P-in-c Stalbridge 95-96; Chapl Forest Healthcare NHS Trust Lon 96-00; P-in-c Bicton, Montford w Shrawardine and Fitz *Lich* 00-06; Chapl Shropshire Co Primary Care Trust 01-06; TR Fordingbridge and Breamore and Hale etc *Win* 06-10; R from 10; AD Christchurch from 10. *The Rectory, 71 Church Street, Fordingbridge SP6 1BB* Tel (01425) 650855
E-mail team.rector@gmail.com

GODWIN, Canon David Harold. b 45. Glos Univ BA09. Kelham Th Coll 67. **d** 71 **p** 72. C Camberwell St Phil and St Mark *S'wark* 71-75; Asst Chapl The Lon Hosp (Whitechapel) 75-79; Chapl R E Sussex Hosp Hastings 79-86; Chapl Over Hosp Glouc 86-92; Chapl Glos R Hosp 86-94; Chapl Glos R Hosp NHS Trust 94-02; Chapl Glos Hosps NHS Foundn Trust 02-05; Hon Can Glouc Cathl 03-05; rtd 05; Perm to Offic *Glouc* from 05. *Mews Two, Wallsworth Hall, Sandhurst Lane, Sandhurst, Gloucester GL2 9PA* Tel (01452) 730435 E-mail davidhgodwin@live.co.uk

GODWIN, Canon Michael Francis Harold. b 35. Nottm Univ BSc57. Ely Th Coll 59. **d** 61 **p** 62. C Farnborough *Guildf* 61-65; V Epsom St Barn 66-85; V Bramley and Grafham 85-98; Hon Can Guildf Cathl 89-98; rtd 00. *14 Lemmington Way, Horsham RH12 5JG* Tel (01403) 273411

GOFF, Philip Francis Michael. b 52. K Coll Lon BD73 AKC73 FBS00 FSA08. St Aug Coll Cant 74. **d** 75 **p** 76. C Ruislip St Martin *Lon* 75-79; Chapl Aldenham Sch Herts 79-82; V Tokyngton St Mich *Lon* 82-89; In RC Ch 89-91; Primary Care Cllr NHS 91-98; Perm to Offic *Lon* 99-00; Chapl to Bp Edmonton 00-04; P-in-c Highgate St Aug from 04; Asst Dir Post-Ord Tr Edmonton Area 03-06; AD W Haringey from 11. *St Augustine's Vicarage, Langdon Park Road, London N6 5QG* Tel (020) 8374 6985 Mobile 07768-920506
E-mail phildress@blueyonder.co.uk

GOFTON, Canon William Alder. b 31. Dur Univ BA54. Coll of Resurr Mirfield 59. **d** 61 **p** 62. C Benwell St Aid *Newc* 61-64; CN Gosforth 64-69; V Seaton Hirst 69-77; V Newc H Cross 77-89; RD Newc W 85-89; Hon Can Newc Cathl 88-96; R Bolam w Whalton and Hartburn w Meldon 89-96; P-in-c Nether Witton 89-95; V 95-96; Chapl Kirkley Hall Coll 90-96; rtd 96; Perm to Offic *Newc* from 96. *4 Crossfell, Ponteland, Newcastle upon Tyne NE20 9EA* Tel (01661) 820344 E-mail aggofton@yahoo.co.uk

GOGGIN, Philip Frederick de Jean. b 46. Rhodes Univ BA66 Lon Univ MA73 Keele Univ PhD89 Leeds Univ MA05. NOC 03. **d** 05 **p** 06. NSM Sandbach Heath w Wheelock *Ches* 05-07; P-in-c Leighton-cum-Minshull Vernon from 07. *The Vicarage, Middlewich Road, Minshull Vernon, Crewe CW1 4RD* Tel (01270) 522213 E-mail gail.philip@virgin.net

GOLD, Guy Alastair Whitmore. b 16. TD50. Trin Coll Cam BA38 MA48. Qu Coll Birm 55. **d** 55 **p** 56. C Prittlewell St Pet *Chelmsf* 55-57; Bp's Dom Chapl 58-61; R Wickham Bishops 62-69; R Hasketon *St E* 69-76; rtd 76; Perm to Offic *St E* 76-89. *Grove Court, Beech Way, Woodbridge IP12 4BW* Tel (01394) 383277

GOLDEN, Stephen Gerard. b 61. Lon Univ BA84. St Steph Ho Ox 84. **d** 86 **p** 87. C Reading St Luke w St Bart *Ox* 86-90; CF 90-94; Perm to Offic *Lon* from 07. *35 Lonsdale Road, London SW13 9JP* Tel (020) 8748 5306
E-mail sggolden@btinternet.com

GOLDENBERG, Ralph Maurice. b 45. City Univ FBCO67 FBOA67. Trin Coll Bris 88. **d** 90 **p** 91. C Kinson *Sarum* 90-93; C Edgware *Lon* 93-97; TV Roxeth 97-01; V Bayston Hill *Lich* 01-10; rtd 10. *2 Golf Links, Ferndown BH22 8BY*
E-mail r.goldenberg@btopenworld.com

GOLDER, Rebecca Marie. *See* ROGERS, Mrs Rebecca Marie

GOLDIE, Prof James Stuart. b 46. Lon Univ BTh73 Edin Univ BEd73 Hon MEd81. Lon Coll of Div BDQ66 ALCD69. **d** 69 **p** 70. C Blackpool St Paul *Blackb* 69-70; C-in-c Penketh CD *Liv* 70-73; Asst Chapl Greystone Heath Sch 70-73; Chapl Kilmarnock Academy 73-75; V Flixton St Jo *Man* 75-78; Chapl Friars Sch Man 75-78; V Skelmersdale St Paul *Liv* 78-80; Chapl Trin Sch Liv 78-80; Lect Man Bible Coll and Dir Man City Miss 80-83; Hon Prof from 81; Chapl Westbrook Hay Sch Hemel Hempstead 83-89; V Pennington w Lindal and Marton *Carl* 89-90; Chapl Bp Wand Sch *Lon* 90-95; Chapl Queenswood Sch Herts 96-97; Hd Master Westcliff Prep Sch 97-03; V Red Sea Area Egypt from 04; Prin El Gouna Internat Sch from 04; rtd 06. *23 Ffordd Naddyn, Glan Conway, Colwyn Bay LL28 4NH* Tel (01492) 593996

GOLDIE, Katrina Ruth. *See* SCOTT, Canon Katrina Ruth

GOLDING, Neil Christopher. b 47. Warwick Univ BA69. S'wark Ord Course 92. **d** 95 **p** 96. C Mitcham Ascension *S'wark* 95-00; P-in-c Croydon Woodside 00-05; V from 05. *St Luke's Vicarage, Portland Road, London SE25 4RB* Tel and fax (020) 8654 9841 E-mail rev_neil@btopenworld.com

GOLDING, Piers Edwin Hugh. b 26. RD76. St Aug Coll Cant 48 Edin Th Coll 50. **d** 53 **p** 54. C Guildf Ch Ch 53-55; C Enfield St Andr *Lon* 55-58; Chapl RN 58-62; Chapl RNR 62-93; V S Bermondsey St Aug *S'wark* 62-93; rtd 93; Perm to Offic *St E* and *S'wark* from 93. *6 White Lion House, Broad Street, Eye IP23 7AF* Tel (01379) 871253

GOLDING, The Ven Simon Jefferies. b 46. CBE02. Brasted Place Coll 70. Linc Th Coll 72. **d** 74 **p** 75. C Wilton *York* 74-77; Chapl RN 77-97; Chapl of the Fleet 97-98 and 00-02; Adn for the RN 97-02; Dir Gen Naval Chapl Service 00-02; QHC 97-02; Hon Can Gib Cathl 98-02; rtd 02; Perm to Offic *Ripon* 02-11; Dioc Adv for NSM 08-11; Hon C E Richmond from 11. *Arlanza, Hornby Road, Appleton Wiske, Northallerton DL6 2AF* Tel (01609) 881185 E-mail perce.2000@virgin.net

GOLDING, Stephen. b 57. Keele Univ BTh79 CertEd79 Lon Bible Coll BA86 Heythrop Coll Lon MA09. Cant Sch of Min 93. **d** 95 **p** 96. NSM Ramsgate St Luke *Cant* 95-98; Chapl St Lawr Coll Ramsgate 95-98; Chapl Berkhamsted Sch Herts 98-10; Chapl Ch Hosp Horsham from 10. *Cornerways, Christ's Hospital, Horsham RH13 0LD*

GOLDING, Trevor. b 58. Ridley Hall Cam 07. **d** 09 **p** 10. C Highbury Ch Ch w St Jo and St Sav *Lon* from 09. *7 Compton Terrace, Hermitage Road, London N4 1LS* Tel 07511-870694 (mobile) E-mail trevor.golding@googlemail.com

GOLDINGAY, Prof John Edgar. b 42. Keble Coll Ox BA64 Nottm Univ PhD83 Lambeth DD97. Clifton Th Coll 64. **d** 66 **p** 67. C Finchley Ch Ch *Lon* 66-69; Lect St Jo Coll Nottm 70-75; Dir Studies 76-79; Registrar 79-85; Vice-Prin 85-88; Prin 88-97; Prof OT Fuller Th Sem Pasadena from 97. *111 South Orange Grove Apt 108, Pasadena CA 91105-1756, USA* Tel (001) (626) 405 0626 E-mail johngold@fuller.edu

GOLDRING, Mrs Philippa Elizabeth Vincent. b 58. Southn Univ LLB79 Spurgeon's Coll BD05. SEITE BA10. **d** 10 **p** 11. C Wednesfield Heath *Lich* from 10. *2A Victoria Road, Wednesfield, Wolverhampton WV11 1RZ* Tel (01902) 732698

GOLDSMITH, Brian Derek. b 36. Leeds Univ BA64. Coll of Resurr Mirfield 64. **d** 66 **p** 67. C Littlehampton St Mary *Chich* 66-69; C Guildf St Nic 69-73; V Aldershot St Aug 73-81; C-in-c Leigh Park St Clare CD *Portsm* 82-85; C Rowner 85-96; rtd 97; C Catherington and Clanfield *Portsm* 97-01; Perm to Offic *Win* from 98. *27 White Dirt Lane, Catherington, Waterlooville PO8 0NB* Tel (023) 9259 9462

GOLDSMITH, Christopher David. b 54. York Univ BA76 DPhil79. NTMTC 97. **d** 00 **p** 01. NSM Pitsea w Nevendon *Chelmsf* 00-04; V Warley Ch Ch and Gt Warley St Mary from 04. *The Vicarage, 79 Mount Crescent, Warley, Brentwood CM14 5DD* Tel (01277) 220428 Mobile 07981-912576 E-mail c.goldsmith@btinternet.com

GOLDSMITH, Mrs Ellen Elizabeth. b 48. York Univ BA77 Middx Univ BA06. NTMTC 03. **d** 06 **p** 07. NSM Bentley Common, Kelvedon Hatch and Navestock *Chelmsf* 06-10; NSM Warley Ch Ch and Gt Warley St Mary from 10. *The Vicarage, 79 Mount Crescent, Warley, Brentwood CM14 5DD* Tel (01277) 220428 Mobile 07906-979321 E-mail ellen.goldsmith@btinternet.com

GOLDSMITH, John Oliver. b 46. K Coll Lon BD69 AKC69. St Aug Coll Cant 69. **d** 70 **p** 71. C Dronfield *Derby* 70-73; C Ellesmere Port *Ches* 73-74; TV Ellesmere Port 74-81; P-in-c Pleasley *Derby* 81-87; P-in-c Pleasley Hill *S'well* 83-87; V Matlock Bank *Derby* 87-97; RD Wirksworth 92-97; P-in-c Kirk Hallam 97-01; V 01-02; P-in-c Taddington, Chelmorton and Flagg, and Monyash 02-11; P-in-c Hartington, Biggin and Earl Sterndale 02-11; V Taddington, Chelmorton and Monyash etc from 11; RD Buxton from 02. *The Vicarage, Church Street, Monyash, Bakewell DE45 1JH* Tel (01629) 812234 E-mail goldsmith681@btinternet.com

GOLDSMITH, Lesley Anne. NTMTC 02. **d** 05 **p** 06. C E Ham w Upton Park *Chelmsf* 05-08; V Chingford St Edm from 08.

St Edmund's Vicarage, Larkswood Road, London E4 9DS Tel (020) 8529 5226 E-mail lesley.goldsmith@btinternet.com

GOLDSMITH, Canon Mary Louie. b 48. K Coll Lon BA70 AKC70. Qu Coll Birm 91. **d** 93 **p** 94. NSM Matlock Bank *Derby* 93-97; NSM Kirk Hallam 97-02; NSM Taddington, Chelmorton and Monyash etc from 00; Hon Can Derby Cathl from 05. *The Vicarage, Church Street, Monyash, Bakewell DE45 1JH* Tel (01629) 812234

GOLDSMITH, Mrs Pauline Anne. b 40. Linc Th Coll 82. **dss** 84 **d** 87 **p** 94. Waddington *Linc* 86-88; Par Dn 87-88; Par Dn Gt and Lt Coates w Bradley 88-94; TV 94-96; TV Kidderminster St Mary and All SS w Trimpley etc *Worc* 96-01; rtd 01; Perm to Offic *Derby* and *Sheff* from 01. *143 Ravencar Road, Eckington, Sheffield S21 4JR* Tel (01246) 430083

GOLDSMITH, Stephen. b 32. Edin Th Coll. **d** 76 **p** 77. SPCK Staff 53-97; Bookshops Regional Manager SPCK 87-97; NSM Penicuik *Edin* 76-81; NSM Linc St Nic w St Jo Newport 81-90; NSM Gt and Lt Coates w Bradley 90-96; NSM Kidderminster St Mary and All SS w Trimpley etc *Worc* 96-01; Perm to Offic *Derby* and *Sheff* from 01. *143 Ravencar Road, Eckington, Sheffield S21 4JR* Tel (01246) 430083

GOLDSPINK, David. b 35. Open Univ BA81. Lon Coll of Div 62. **d** 65 **p** 66. C Mile Cross *Nor* 65-68; C St Austell *Truro* 68-70; TV Bramerton w Surlingham *Nor* 70-73; Min Gunton St Pet 73-75; R Mutford w Rushmere w Gisleham w N Cove w Barnby 75-81; Asst Chapl HM Pris Man 81-82; Chapl HM Youth Cust Cen Hollesley Bay Colony 82-84; Chapl HM Pris Blundeston 84-88; Perm to Offic *St E* 87-01; rtd 88; Perm to Offic *Nor* from 88. *14 Deepdale, Carlton Colville, Lowestoft NR33 8TU* Tel (01502) 537769

GOLDSTONE-CREASEY, Graham. b 51. Trent Poly BA73. Cranmer Hall Dur 80. **d** 83 **p** 84. C Birstall and Wanlip *Leic* 83-87; C-in-c Wheatley Park St Paul CD *Sheff* 87-92; V Wheatley Park 92-95; P-in-c Gleadless Valley 95-98. *281 Fleetwood Road North, Thornton-Cleveleys FY5 4LE* Tel (01253) 862668 E-mail grahamgc10@gmail.com

GOLDTHORP, Ms Ann Lesley. b 59. Qu Coll Birm 08. **d** 11. C Harbury and Ladbroke *Cov* from 11. *7 Sutcliffe Drive, Harbury, Leamington Spa CV33 9LT* Tel (01926) 614868 E-mail anngoldthorp@yahoo.co.uk

GOLDTHORPE, Ms Shirley. b 42. Linc Th Coll 70. **dss** 76 **d** 87 **p** 94. Thornhill Lees *Wakef* 76-78; Birkenshaw w Hunsworth 78-80; Batley St Thos 80-85; Batley All SS 80-85; Purlwell 80-92; Par Dn 87-88; Dn-in-c 88-92; Dn-in-c Horbury Junction 92-94; P-in-c 94-01; rtd 02; Perm to Offic *Wakef* from 02. *10 Orchid View, Alverthorpe, Wakefield WF2 0FG* Tel (01924) 383181 Mobile 07885-462837

GOLLEDGE, Christopher John. b 66. St Mich Coll Llan 89. **d** 92 **p** 93. C Newton Nottage *Llan* 92-95; Perm to Offic *Chich* 95-00. *Address temp unknown*

GOLLEDGE, Miss Patricia Anne. b 55. Trin Coll Bris BA00. **d** 00 **p** 01. C Pontypool *Mon* 00-03; TV 03-09; V Griffithstown from 09. *St Hilda's Vicarage, 2 Sunnybank Road, Griffithstown, Pontypool NP4 5LT* Tel (01495) 763641 E-mail anne.golledge@virgin.net

GOLLOP, Michael John. b 58. Keble Coll Ox BA81 MA85. St Mich Coll Llan BD85. **d** 85 **p** 86. C Newport St Mark *Mon* 85-87; C Bassaleg 87-91; V St Hilary Greenway 91-93; V St Arvans w Penterry, Itton, Devauden etc from 93. *The Vicarage, St Arvans, Chepstow NP16 6EU* Tel (01291) 622664

GOLTON, Alan Victor. b 29. St Jo Coll Ox BA51 MA54 DPhil54. **d** 85 **p** 86. P-in-c Barston *Birm* 87-95; Perm to Offic 95-96; Hon C Grenoble *Eur* 97-00. *Chez du Matin, Les Michallons, 38250 St Nizier du Moucherotte, France* Tel (0033) 4 76 53 43 77 E-mail avgolton@hotmail.com

GOMERSALL, Canon Ian Douglass. b 56. Birm Univ BSc77 Fitzw Coll Cam BA80 MA85 Dur Univ MA94. Westcott Ho Cam 78. **d** 81 **p** 82. C Darlington St Mark w St Paul *Dur* 81-84; C Barnard Castle w Whorlton 84-86; Chapl HM YOI Deerbolt 85-90; P-in-c Cockfield *Dur* 86-88; R 88-90; Dep Chapl HM Pris Wakef 90-91; Chapl HM Pris Full Sutton 91-97; P-in-c Kexby w Wilberfoss *York* 93-97; TV Man Whitworth 97-03; P-in-c Man Victoria Park 98-09; R from 09; Chapl Man Metrop Univ 97-03; Hon Chapl from 03; AD Ardwick from 08; Hon Can Man Cathl from 11. *St Chrysostom's Rectory, 38 Park Range, Manchester M14 5HQ* Tel 0161-224 6971 Mobile 07711-670225 E-mail fatherian@priest.com

GOMERSALL, Richard. b 45. FCA68. NOC 90. **d** 93 **p** 94. NSM Thurcroft *Sheff* 93-96; NSM Sheff St Matt 96-03; Ind Chapl 98-03; C-in-c Southey Green St Bernard CD 03-11. *Dale View House, 14 Wignall Avenue, Wickersley, Rotherham S66 2AX* Tel (01709) 546441 Fax 701900 E-mail fr.gomersall@btinternet.com

GOMES, Canon Jules Francis Paulinus. b 66. Bombay Univ BA86 United Th Coll Serampore MTh97 Selw Coll Cam PhD04. Union Bibl Sem Serampore BD94. **d** 98 **p** 98. India 98-04; Co-ord Chapl Greenwich Univ 04-08; Lect Lon Sch of Th 08-10; NSM Harefield *Lon* 08-09; Can Res Liv Cathl from 11.

4 Cathedral Close, Liverpool L1 7BR Tel 0151-707 1931 Mobile 07981-570384

✠**GOMEZ, The Rt Revd Drexel Wellington.** b 37. Dur Univ BA59. Codrington Coll Barbados 55. **d** 59 **c** 72. Tutor Codrington Coll Barbados 64-68; Bp Barbados 72-93; Bp Coadjutor Nassau and Bahamas 95-96; Dioc Bp 96-01; Bp Bahamas and Turks and Caicos Is 01-08; Abp W Indies 98-08; rtd 09. *Address temp unknown*

GOMM, Timothy Frank. b 64. St Jo Coll Nottm 00. **d** 02 **p** 03. C Kinson *Sarum* 02-04; C Heatherlands St Jo and Community Chapl Rossmore Community Coll 04-10; C Longfleet *Sarum* from 10. *72 Alexandra Road, Poole BH14 9EW* Tel (01202) 770833 E-mail tim.gomm@ntlworld.com

GOMPERTZ, Helen Morey. b 40. **d** 06 **p** 07. NSM Kettering St Andr *Pet* from 06. *19 Grendon Drive, Barton Seagrave, Kettering NN15 6RW* E-mail morey.gompertz@btinternet.com

GOMPERTZ, Canon Peter Alan Martin. b 40. ALCD63. **d** 64 **p** 65. C Eccleston St Luke *Liv* 64-69; Scripture Union 69-73; C Yeovil *B & W* 73-75; V Northampton St Giles *Pet* 75-96; R Aynho and Croughton w Evenley etc 96-06; P-in-c Gt w Lt Addington and Woodford 06-10; Can Pet Cathl 88-10; rtd 10. *19 Grendon Drive, Barton Seagrave, Kettering NN15 6RW* Tel 07771-615364 (mobile) E-mail p.gompertz@btinternet.com

GONIN, Christopher Willett. b 33. Man Univ DACE87 MBA92. AKC59. **d** 60 **p** 61. C Camberwell St Geo *S'wark* 60-64; C Stevenage H Trin *St Alb* 64-69; C Bletchley *Ox* 70-73; R Newington St Mary *S'wark* 73-76; Perm to Offic *Bris* 76-77; Hon C Horfield H Trin 77-89; Hon C City of Bris 89-91; V Milton Ernest *St Alb* 92-97; V Thurleigh 92-97; rtd 97; Perm to Offic *St E* from 97. *15 The Gables, Leiston IP16 4UZ* Tel (01728) 635549 E-mail christopher@gonin.wanadoo.co.uk

GOOCH, John Ellerton. b 46. Natal Univ BEcon70. Trin Coll Bris 73. **d** 75 **p** 76. C Pinetown Ch Ch S Africa 75-77; P-in-c Escombe 77-79; P-in-c E London St Sav 80-81; R E London St Mich 81-82; TV Beacon Bay 82-83; P-in-c Casablanca *Eur* 98-07; Perm to Offic from 07. *109 rue Mozart/Kouttoubia, Amerchich 40000, Marrakech, Morocco* Tel (00212) (24) 311600 Mobile 63-203174 E-mail johnpen@swissmail.net

GOOCH, Michael Anthony. b 44. Nottm Coll of Educn TCert66. Cant Sch of Min 90. **d** 93 **p** 94. NSM New Romney w Old Romney and Midley *Cant* 93-97; P-in-c Teynham w Lynsted and Kingsdown 97-08; Bp's Officer for NSM 98-03; rtd 08; Perm to Offic *Cant* from 08. *Little Owls, Tookey Road, New Romney TN28 8ET* Tel (01797) 367858 E-mail mgooch@connectfree.co.uk

GOOD, Alan Raymond. b 39. Bris Sch of Min 83. **d** 85 **p** 86. NSM Horfield St Greg *Bris* 85-97; Chapl Asst Southmead Health Services NHS Trust 97-99; Chapl Asst N Bris NHS Trust from 99. *Southmead Hospital, Westbury-on-Trym, Bristol BS10 5NB* Tel 0117-959 5447, 950 5050 or (01454) 415778

GOOD, Andrew Ronald. b 60. Bris Univ BA82. Linc Th Coll 83. **d** 85 **p** 86. C Epping St Jo *Chelmsf* 85-88; C Cheshunt *St Alb* 88-91; R Spixworth w Crostwick and Frettenham *Nor* 91-04; Perm to Offic from 04; P-in-c Ashwellthorpe, Forncett, Fundenhall, Hapton etc from 11. *20 Ebbisham Drive, Norwich NR4 6HN* Tel (01603) 458501 E-mail andrewrgood@hotmail.com

GOOD, Anthony Ernest. b 28. ARIBA51 Heriot-Watt Univ MSc73. Wells Th Coll 54. **d** 56 **p** 57. C Maidstone All SS *Cant* 56-60; C Reading St Mary V *Ox* 60-62; R Sandhurst 62-70; Perm to Offic *Ex* 71-82; TR Wallingford w Crowmarsh Gifford etc *Ox* 82-92; RD Wallingford 85-91; rtd 92; Perm to Offic *Ex* from 92. *Cotts Weir Quay, Bere Alston, Yelverton PL20 7BX* Tel (01822) 840524

GOOD, David Howard. b 42. Glouc Sch of Min 84. **d** 87 **p** 88. NSM Bromyard *Heref* 87-92; C Pontesbury I and II 92-95; P-in-c Ditton Priors w Neenton, Burwarton etc 95-98; R Ditton Priors w Neenton, Burwarton etc 98-02; rtd 02; Perm to Offic *Heref* from 02. *26 Farjeon Close, Ledbury HR8 2FU* Tel (01531) 636474

GOOD, Geoffrey. b 27. St Aid Birkenhead. **d** 61 **p** 62. C Roby *Liv* 61-65; V Staincliffe *Wakef* 65-70; V Thornes 79-93; rtd 93; Perm to Offic *Wakef* from 93. *147 Thornes Road, Wakefield WF2 8QN* Tel (01924) 378273

GOOD, Preb John Hobart. b 43. Bps' Coll Cheshunt 66 Coll of Resurr Mirfield 68. **d** 69 **p** 70. C Ex St Jas 69-73; C Cockington 73-75; C Wolborough w Newton Abbot 75-78; P-in-c Exminster 78-80; P-in-c Kenn 78-80; R Exminster and Kenn 80-95; RD Kenn 89-95; TR Axminster, Chardstock, All Saints etc 95-09; Preb Ex Cathl 02-09; Chapl All Hallows Sch Rousdon 98-09; rtd 09; Hon C The Winterbournes and Compton Valence *Sarum* from 09; Hon C Dorchester from 09. *The Rectory, Martinstown, Dorchester DT2 9JZ* Tel (01305) 889466 E-mail jhgood_minster@hotmail.com

✠**GOOD, The Rt Revd Kenneth Raymond.** b 52. TCD BA74 Nottm Univ BA76 NUI HDipEd81 MEd84. St Jo Coll Nottm 75. **d** 77 **p** 78 **c** 02. C Willowfield *D & D* 77-79; Chapl Ashton Sch Cork 79-84; I Dungannon w Redcross and Conary *D & G* 84-90; I Lurgan Ch the Redeemer *D & D* 90-02; Adn Dromore

97-02; Bp D & R from 02. *The See House, 112 Culmore Road, Londonderry BT48 8JF* Tel (028) 7135 1206 *or* 7126 2440 Fax 7135 2554 E-mail bishop@derry.anglican.org

GOOD, The Ven Kenneth Roy. b 41. K Coll Lon BD66 AKC66. **d** 67 **p** 68. C Stockton St Pet *Dur* 67-70; Chapl Antwerp Miss to Seamen *Eur* 70-74; Chapl Kobe Japan 74-79; Asst Gen Sec Miss to Seamen and Asst Chapl St Mich Paternoster Royal *Lon* 79-85; Hon Can Kobe from 85; V Nunthorpe *York* 85-93; RD Stokesley 90-93; Adn Richmond *Ripon* 93-06; rtd 06; Perm to Offic *York* from 07. *18 Fox Howe, Coulby Newham, Middlesbrough TS8 0RU* Tel (01642) 594158 E-mail joken.good@ntlworld.com

GOOD, Stuart Eric Clifford. b 37. Wycliffe Hall Ox 63. **d** 64 **p** 65. C Walton H Trin *Ox* 64-67; Australia from 66; Dir Chapl Services Angl Homes Inc 85-05; rtd 05. *6 Enright Circuit, Stanford Gardens, Beeliar WA 6164, Australia* Tel (0061) 418-943337 (mobile) E-mail sbargood@bigpond.net.au

GOODACRE, Canon David Leighton. b 36. AKC59. **d** 60 **p** 61. C Stockton St Chad *Dur* 60-63; C Birtley 63-68; Chapl Sunderland Gen Hosp 69-74; P-in-c Ryhope *Dur* 75-81; V Ovingham *Newc* 81-01; Hon Can Newc Cathl 92-01; rtd 01; Perm to Offic *Newc* from 01. *9 Wilmington Close, Newcastle upon Tyne NE3 2SF* Tel 0191-271 4382

GOODACRE, Philip James. b 81. Ox Brookes Univ BA04 Birm Univ MA06. Ridley Hall Cam 09. **d** 11. C Brightside w Wincobank *Sheff* from 11. *15 Nursery Drive, Sheffield S35 9XU* Tel 07779-597752 (mobile) E-mail philipgoodacre@gmail.com

GOODAIR, Jan. b 59. K Coll Lon BA81 Leeds Univ PhD02 Roehampton Inst PGCE82. NEOC 97. **d** 00 **p** 01. NSM Tockwith and Bilton w Bickerton *York* 00-01; NSM York St Olave w St Giles 00-01; Chapl Harrogate Ladies' Coll 01-10; Chapl Haberdashers' Aske's Sch Elstree from 10. *Flat 3, First Floor, Aldenham House, Haberdashers' Aske's Boys' School, Butterfly Lane, Elstree WD6 3AF* Tel (020) 8266 1700 Mobile 07840-731137 E-mail jan.cheeseman@ntlworld.com

GOODALL, George. b 24. LCP. **d** 86 **p** 87. NSM Bretby w Newton Solney *Derby* 86-94; Perm to Offic *Derby* from 94 and Lich 06-10. *Brizlincote Farm, Middle Lane, Wythall, Birmingham B47 6LD*

GOODALL, James Richard. b 51. Reading Univ BA73 Ox Univ DPhil79 York St Jo Univ MA09. Coll of Resurr Mirfield 08. **d** 09 **p** 10. NSM Hurst Green and Mitton *Bradf* from 09. *Smithy Cottage, Walker Fold, Chaigley, Clitheroe BB7 3LU* Tel (01254) 826746 Mobile 07989-949743 E-mail jamesrgoodall@btinternet.com

GOODALL, Canon John William. b 45. Hull Univ BA69. Ripon Hall Ox 69. **d** 71 **p** 72. C Loughborough Em *Leic* 71-74; C Dorchester *Ox* 74-75; TV 75-80; Tutor Sarum & Wells Th Coll 80-88; Vice Prin S Dios Minl Tr Scheme 80-88; P-in-c Gt Wishford *Sarum* 80-83; P-in-c Colehill 88-96; V from 96; Dioc Dir of Readers 88-95; Can and Preb Sarum Cathl from 07. *The Vicarage, Smugglers Lane, Colehill, Wimborne BH21 2RY* Tel (01202) 883721

GOODALL, Canon Jonathan Michael. b 61. R Holloway Coll Lon BMus83. Wycliffe Hall Ox 86. **d** 89 **p** 90. C Bicester w Bucknell, Caversfield and Launton *Ox* 89-92; Asst Chapl HM Pris Bullingdon 90-92; Min Can, Chapl, and Sacr Westmr Abbey 92-98; Bp's Chapl and Research Asst *Eur* 98-05; Can Gib Cathl from 05; Abp's Chapl and Ecum Officer *Cant* 05-09; Abp's Personal Chapl and Ecum Sec from 09; Hon C Westmr St Matt *Lon* 99-03; PV Westmr Abbey from 04. *Lambeth Palace, London SE1 7JU* Tel (020) 7898 1200 E-mail jonathan.goodall@churchofengland.org

GOODALL, Malcolm. b 39. Newc Univ MA93. Carl Dioc Tr Course 80. **d** 85 **p** 86. NSM Allonby and Cross Canonby *Carl* 85-88; C Auckland St Andr and St Anne *Dur* 88-90; V Grindon and Stillington 90-98; P-in-c Wolsingham and Thornley 98-03; R 03-08; rtd 08. *West Wing, Eden Place, Kirkby Stephen CA17 4AP* Tel (017683) 72320 E-mail mg@malcolmgoodall.co.uk

GOODBODY, Ruth Vivien. b 68. Surrey Univ BA02. Wycliffe Hall Ox 96 STETS 00. **d** 03. C Bourne Valley *Sarum* 02-06; C Stebbing and Lindsell w Gt and Lt Saling *Chelmsf* 06-10; rtd 10. *The Vicarage, 7 Ruffels Place, Stebbing, Dunmow CM6 3TJ* Tel (01371) 856080 E-mail timandruthgoodbody@virgin.net

GOODBODY, Steven John. b 70. Univ of Wales (Cardiff) BD92. Wycliffe Hall Ox 00. **d** 02 **p** 03. C Tunbridge Wells St Jo *Roch* 02-05; C Ex St Leon w H Trin 05-10; TR Washfield, Stoodleigh, Withleigh etc from 10. *The Rectory, Withleigh, Tiverton EX16 8JQ* Tel (01884) 251132 Mobile 07768-645172

GOODBODY, Timothy Edward. b 66. York Univ BA89. Wycliffe Hall Ox BTh98. **d** 98 **p** 99. C Blandford Forum and Langton Long *Sarum* 98-02; NSM Bourne Valley 02-06; P-in-c Stebbing and Lindsell w Gt and Lt Saling *Chelmsf* from 06. *The Vicarage, 7 Ruffels Place, Stebbing, Dunmow CM6 3TJ* Tel (01371) 856080 E-mail the.goodbodies@virgin.net

GOODBURN, David Henry. b 41. S'wark Ord Course 73. **d** 76 **p** 77. NSM Enfield SS Pet and Paul *Lon* 76-82; Perm to Offic 83-85; NSM Potters Bar *St Alb* 85-88; Chapl RN 88-96; V Luton

St Sav *St Alb* 96-09; rtd 09. *6 Mount View, Enfield EN2 8LF* Tel (020) 8342 0161

GOODCHILD, Andrew Philip. b 55. CertEd80. Oak Hill Th Coll BA85. **d** 85 **p** 86. C Barnston *Ches* 85-88; C Hollington St Leon *Chich* 88-89; P-in-c Millbrook *Ches* 89-94; Chapl and Hd RE Kimbolton Sch 94-03. *Sand Pit Lodge, 72 Lynn Road, Dersingham, King's Lynn PE31 6LB* Tel (01485) 543743 Mobile 07748-815479 E-mail mel-andy@tiscali.co.uk

GOODCHILD, Canon John McKillip. b 42. Clare Coll Cam BA64 MA68 Oriel Coll Ox CertEd69. Wycliffe Hall Ox 67. **d** 69 **p** 70. C Clubmoor *Liv* 69-72; CMS Nigeria 72-83; Hon Can Aba from 74; V Ainsdale *Liv* 83-89; TR Maghull 89-98; Prin Dioc Minl Course and Dir OLM Tr *Nor* 98-06; rtd 06. *39 St Michael's Road, Aigburth, Liverpool L17 7AN*

GOODCHILD, Mrs Penelope Faith. Local Minl Tr Course. **d** 11. NSM Pinxton *Derby* from 11. *89 Market Street, South Normanton, Alfreton DE55 2AA* Tel (01773) 811460 E-mail pennygoodchild@btinternet.com

GOODDEN, John Maurice Phelips. b 34. Sarum & Wells Th Coll 70. **d** 72 **p** 75. C Weymouth H Trin *Sarum* 72-74; C Harlow New Town w Lt Parndon *Chelmsf* 74-78; Ind Chapl and Chapl Princess Alexandra Hosp Harlow 78-82; V Moulsham St Jo *Chelmsf* 86-90; R Chipstead and Adv Rural Min *S'wark* 90-04; rtd 04; Perm to Offic *B & W* from 05. *Easter Cottage, 64 Kingston Deverill, Warminster BA12 7HG* Tel (01985) 845318 E-mail goodden@msn.com

GOODDEN, Stephanie Anne. *See* NADARAJAH, Mrs Stephanie Anne

GOODE, Anthony Thomas Ryall. b 42. Ex Coll Ox BA64 MA71. Cuddesdon Coll 65. **d** 67 **p** 68. C Wolvercote *Ox* 67-71; P-in-c Edith Weston w Normanton *Pet* 72-74; Chapl RAF 71-91; Asst Chapl-in-Chief 91-97; Chapl to The Queen 95-97; Chapl Abu Dhabi St Andr UAE 97-00; V Hurstbourne Tarrant, Faccombe, Vernham Dean etc *Win* 00-07; rtd 07. *9 rue de la Gargoille, 79600 Marnes, France* Tel (0033) 5 49 66 79 14 E-mail spetroshbt@aol.com

GOODE, Claire Elizabeth. b 60. Nottm Univ BSc82. EMMTC 04. **d** 08 **p** 09. C S Notts Cluster of Par *S'well* from 08. *10 Lantern Lane, East Leake, Loughborough LE12 6QN* Tel (01509) 856532 E-mail goodepc@btinternet.com

GOODE, John Laurence. b 48. W Cheshire Coll of Tech TEng70 Federal Univ Minas Gerais Brazil Dip Teaching78. Chich Th Coll 81. **d** 83 **p** 84. C Crewe St Andr *Ches* 83-86; USPG 87-94; Brazil 91-94; TV Crawley *Chich* 83-93; TR Abingdon and V Shippon *Ox* 93-05; rtd 05. *13 Britannia Square, Worcester WR1 3DG* Tel (01235) 532722 E-mail jenny.goode@btinternet.com

GOODE, Jonathan. b 67. St Martin's Coll Lanc BA89. Qu Coll Birm. **d** 00 **p** 01. C Middleton St Mary *Ripon* 00-04; P-in-c Hartlepool St Hilda *Dur* 04-08; Chapl St Hilda's Sch 04-08; V Denton *Newc* from 08. *The Vicarage, Dunblane Crescent, Newcastle upon Tyne NE5 2BE* Tel 0191-267 2058 E-mail revjgoode@yahoo.com

GOODE, Michael Arthur John. b 40. K Coll Lon BD AKC63. **d** 64 **p** 65. C Sunderland Springwell w Thorney Close *Dur* 64-68; C Solihull *Birm* 68-70; R Fladbury, Wyre Piddle and Moor *Worc* 70-75; P-in-c Foley Park 75-81; V 81-83; RD Kidderminster 81-83; TR Crawley *Chich* 83-93; TR Abingdon and V Shippon *Ox* 93-05; rtd 05. *13 Britannia Square, Worcester WR1 3DG* Tel (01235) 532722 E-mail jenny.goode@btinternet.com

GOODE, Canon Peter William Herbert. b 23. Oak Hill Th Coll 60. **d** 62 **p** 63. C Woodford Wells *Chelmsf* 62-65; V Harold Hill St Paul 65-76; V Gt Warley Ch Ch 76-93; RD Brentwood 89-93; Hon Can Chelmsf Cathl 90-93; rtd 93; Perm to Offic *St Alb* from 93. *52 Slimmons Drive, St Albans AL4 9AP* Tel (01727) 852166

GOODE, Thomas. *See* GOODE, Anthony Thomas Ryall

GOODE, Timothy. b 69. Huddersfield Poly BA90 Roehampton Inst PGCE91. Ripon Coll Cuddesdon 07. **d** 09 **p** 10. C Croydon St Jo *S'wark* from 09. *37 Alton Road, Croydon CR0 4LZ* Tel (020) 8643 0192 E-mail musicgoode@hotmail.com

GOODER, Canon Martin Lee. b 37. Sheff Univ BSc58. Oak Hill Th Coll 58. **d** 60 **p** 61. C Barrow St Mark *Carl* 60-63; C Halliwell St Pet *Man* 63-66; R Chorlton on Medlock St Sav 66-71; R Brunswick 71-92; P-in-c Bacup Ch Ch 92-02; Hon Can Man Cathl 90-02; rtd 02; Perm to Offic *Man* from 02. *12 Walton Close, Bacup OL13 9RE* Tel (01706) 872418 E-mail gooder@btopenworld.com

GOODERHAM, Daniel Charles. b 24. St Fran Coll Brisbane 49. **d** 52 **p** 53. Australia 52-60; C Staveley *Derby* 60-61; C Ipswich St Thos *St E* 61-64; V Ipswich St Bart 64-71; R Drinkstone 71-78; R Rattlesden 71-78; RD Lavenham 75-78; V Beckenham St Mich w St Aug *Roch* 78-87; P-in-c Whiteparish *Sarum* 87-89; rtd 89; Perm to Offic *St E* from 89. *58 Millfield, Eye IP23 7DE* Tel (01379) 871589

GOODEY, Philip Julian Frank. b 61. Aston Tr Scheme 87 Trin Coll Bris 89. **d** 92 **p** 93. C Iver *Ox* 92-94; C Hornchurch St Andr *Chelmsf* 94-99; V Wickham Market w Pettistree *St E* 99-01; TR Parkham, Alwington, Buckland Brewer etc *Ex* 01-06; P-in-c Lundy Is 01-06; R Botley *Portsm* 06-11; V Curdridge 06-11; R

Durley 06-11; TR Drypool *York* from 11. *The Rectory, 139 Laburnum Avenue, Garden Village, Hull HU8 8PA* E-mail phil.goodey@me.com

GOODFELLOW, Ian. b 37. St Cath Coll Cam BA61 MA65 Lon Univ PGCE76 Dur Univ PhD83. Wells Th Coll 61. **d** 63 **p** 64. C Dunstable *St Alb* 63-67; Chapl Haileybury Coll 67-71; Asst Chapl St Bede Coll Dur 71-74; Lect and Tutor 71-75; Sen Lect and Tutor SS Hild and Bede Coll Dur 75-78; Sen Cllr Open Univ (SW Region) 78-97; Perm to Offic *Ex* from 89; rtd 02. *Crosslea, 206 Whitchurch Road, Tavistock PL19 9DQ* Tel (01822) 612069 E-mail goodfellow1@lineone.net

GOODFIELD, Dudley Francis. b 40. AKC65. **d** 66 **p** 67. C Bath Twerton-on-Avon *B & W* 66-69; C Lache cum Saltney *Ches* 69-71; C Portishead *B & W* 71-76; V Weston-super-Mare St Andr Bournville 76-82; V Ruishton w Thornfalcon 82-05; rtd 05; Perm to Offic *B & W* from 05. *4 Gillards Close, Rockwell Green, Wellington TA21 9DX* Tel (01823) 660533

GOODGER, Kenneth Andrew. b 67. Univ of Qld BA96. St Fran Coll Brisbane BTh97. **d** 93 **p** 96. C Milton Australia 93-96; C Caloundra 96-99; C Pimlico St Pet w Westmr Ch Ch *Lon* 99-02; R Moorooka and Salisbury Australia 02-06; R Caloundra from 06. *PO Box 52, Caloundra Qld 4551, Australia* Tel (0061) (7) 5491 1866 E-mail m.sanglican@uqconnect.net

GOODHAND, Richard. b 51. Sarum & Wells Th Coll 88. **d** 90 **p** 91. C Wollaton *S'well* 90-93; P-in-c Clarborough w Hayton 93-98; Sub-Chapl HM Pris Ranby 93-96; Asst Chapl 96-98; P-in-c Blidworth *S'well* 98-02; P-in-c Rainworth 98-02; V Blidworth w Rainworth 02-08; P-in-c Ollerton w Boughton from 08. *St Paulinus Vicarage, 65 Larch Road, New Ollerton, Newark NG22 9JX* Tel (01623) 836081 E-mail revrichard@goodhand.org.uk

GOODHEW, David John. b 65. Collingwood Coll Dur BA86 CCC Ox DPhil92 St Jo Coll Dur BA92. Cranmer Hall Dur 90. **d** 93 **p** 94. C Bedminster *Bris* 93-96; Chapl and Fell St Cath Coll Cam 96-01; V Fulford *York* 01-08; P-in-c York St Denys 01-04; Dir Minl Practice Cranmer Hall Dur from 08. *St John's College, 3 South Bailey, Durham DH1 3RJ* Tel 0191-334 3863 Fax 334 3501 E-mail d.j.goodhew@durham.ac.uk

GOODHEW, Mrs Lindsey Jane Ellin. b 66. UEA BA87 St Jo Coll Dur BA92. Cranmer Hall Dur 90. **d** 93 **p** 94. C Bishopsworth *Bris* 93-96; Perm to Offic *Ely* 96-97; Hon C Cambridge St Mark 97-01; Perm to Offic *York* 01-07; Hon C Fulford 07-08. *Address temp unknown*

GOODHEW, Roy William. b 41. Reading Univ BA Univ of Wales (Cardiff) PGCE. S Dios Minl Tr Scheme. **d** 89 **p** 90. C Southampton Maybush St Pet *Win* 89-94; V Hound 94-05; rtd 05; Perm to Offic *Lon* from 06. *121 Edgecot Grove, London N15 5HH* Tel (020) 8802 5101

GOODING, Canon Ian Eric. b 42. Leeds Univ BSc63 BCom65 CEng69 MIProdE68. St Jo Coll Nottm 70. **d** 73 **p** 74. C Wandsworth All SS *S'wark* 73-77; Bp's Ind Adv *Derby* from 77; P-in-c Stanton-by-Dale w Dale Abbey 77-87; R 87-00; P-in-c Risley 90-00; R Stanton-by-Dale w Dale Abbey and Risley from 00; RD Erewash from 98; Hon Can Derby Cathl from 02. *The Rectory, Stanhope Street, Stanton-by-Dale, Ilkeston DE7 4QA* Tel and fax 0115-932 4585 Mobile 07768-917385 E-mail ian.e.gooding@gmail.com

GOODING, Ian Peter Slade. b 56. Imp Coll Lon BScEng77 MBCS88. Qu Coll Birm 90. **d** 92 **p** 93. C Swindon Dorcan *Bris* 92-96; TV Langley Marish *Ox* 96-02; Internet Manager Scripture Union from 02; Hon C Woughton *Ox* from 09. *5 Pipston Green, Kents Hill, Milton Keynes MK7 6HT* Tel (01908) 673651 E-mail goodingip@clara.co.uk

GOODING, John Henry. b 47. St Jo Coll Nottm. **d** 84 **p** 85. C Charles w Plymouth St Matthias *Ex* 84-88; C Leeds St Geo *Ripon* 88-93; TV Liskeard, St Keyne, St Pinnock, Morval etc *Truro* 93-94; Lon and SE Consultant CPAS 94-00; Hon C Egham *Guildf* 96-00; Dioc Par Resource Officer 00-03; Dioc Dir Miss, Evang and Par Development from 03. *Diocesan House, Quarry Street, Guildford GU1 3XG* Tel (01483) 571826 ext 206 *or* (01932) 560407 E-mail john.gooding@cofeguildford.org.uk

GOODING, Ms Karen Ann. b 55. LRAM76 ARCM77. **d** 11. OLM Alford w Rigsby *Linc* from 11. *St Hildegard House, 71 South Street, Alford LN13 9AW* Tel (01507) 464934

GOODING, Paul David Buchanan. b 76. Pemb Coll Ox MA98 Green Coll Ox PGCE01. Ox Min Course 06. **d** 08. NSM Grove *Ox* from 08; Asst Chapl Abingdon Sch from 10. *c/o Crockford, Church House, Great Smith Street, London SW1P 3AZ* E-mail pdbgooding@hotmail.com

GOODLAD, Canon Martin Randall. b 39. Sheff City Coll of Educn TDip60. Linc Th Coll 63. **d** 66 **p** 67. C Bramley *Ripon* 66-69; TV Daventry *Pet* 69-71; Asst Dioc Youth Officer 69-71; Asst Dir of Educn *Wakef* 71-74; Youth Work Officer Gen Syn Bd of Educn 74-83; P-in-c Cheam Common St Phil *S'wark* 83-85; V 85-97; RD Sutton 90-97; Hon Chapl St Raphael's Hospice 87-97; V Coulsdon St Andr *S'wark* 97-05; Hon Can S'wark Cathl 96-05; rtd 05; Perm to Offic *S'wark* from 06. *3 Cromer Mansions, Cheam Road, Sutton SM1 2SR* Tel (020) 8915 0555 E-mail hornes27@aol.com

GOODLAND, Michael Eric. b 53. WEMTC 97. **d** 97 **p** 98. NSM Ilminster and Distr *B & W* 97-02; NSM Crewkerne w Wayford 02-07; Perm to Offic *Truro* 07-10; P-in-c Lanreath, Pelynt and Bradoc from 10. *Wesley House, Bay Tree Hill, Liskeard PL14 4BG* Tel (01579) 342127
E-mail michaelgoodland07@googlemail.com

GOODLEY, Christopher Ronald. b 47. K Coll Lon BD72 AKC72. **d** 73 **p** 74. C Shenfield *Chelmsf* 73-77; C Hanley H Ev *Lich* 77-78; TV 78-83; Chapl Whittington Hosp Lon 83-86; Chapl St Crispin's Hosp Northampton 88-94; Chapl Northampton Community Healthcare NHS Trust 94-01; Chapl Northants Healthcare NHS Trust from 01. *The Chaplaincy Centre, Berrywood Hospital, Berrywood Drive, Northampton NN5 6UD* Tel (01604) 596338 *or* 752323
E-mail christopher.goodley@nht.northants.nhs.uk

GOODMAN, Ms Alice Abigail. b 58. Harvard Univ BA80 Girton Coll Cam BA82 MA86 Boston Univ MDiv97. Ripon Coll Cuddesdon 00. **d** 01 **p** 03. C Redditch, The Ridge *Worc* 01-02; C Kidderminster St Mary and All SS w Trimpley etc 02-06; Chapl Trin Coll Cam 06-11; R Fulbourn *Ely* from 11; R Lt Wilbraham from 11; V Gt Wilbraham from 11. *The Rectory, 2 Apthorpe Street, Fulbourn, Cambridge CB21 5EY* Tel (01223) 880337
E-mail goodhill@apple.inter.net

GOODMAN, Andrew Francis Malby. b 56. Lon Univ BA79 Birm Univ MSocSc88 CQSW88. Qu Coll Birm 01. **d** 03 **p** 04. C Hamstead St Paul *Birm* 03-07; Co-ord Chapl Bedfordshire Univ from 07. *33 Felix Avenue, Luton LU2 7LE* Tel (01582) 432019
E-mail goodmanco@yahoo.co.uk

GOODMAN, Canon Derek George. b 34. Keble Coll Ox BA57 MA60. Ridley Hall Cam 59. **d** 61 **p** 62. C Attenborough *S'well* 61-65; R Eastwood 65-84; Dioc Insp of Schs 65-89; V Woodthorpe 84-89; Dioc Dir of Educn *Leic* 89-96; Hon Can Leic Cathl 90-96; rtd 96; Perm to Offic *Leic* from 96. *1 Brown Avenue, Quorn, Loughborough LE12 8RH* Tel (01509) 415692

GOODMAN, Garry Gordon. b 52. **d** 09 **p** 10. OLM Bure Valley *Nor* from 09. *Heath Farm House, Coltishall Road, Buxton, Norwich NR10 5JD* Tel (01603) 279393
E-mail garry.goodman@btinternet.com

GOODMAN, John. b 20. Selw Coll Cam BA42 MA46. Linc Th Coll 47. **d** 49 **p** 50. C Ashbourne St Jo *Worc* 49-53; C Marlborough *Sarum* 53-56; V Wootton Bassett 56-65; C Broad Town 56-65; C Salisbury St Mark 65-68; V 68-83; R Wool and E Stoke 83-88; Perm to Offic *Sarum* from 88. *141 Avon Road, Devizes SN10 1PY* Tel (01380) 721267

GOODMAN, John Dennis Julian. b 35. Sarum & Wells Th Coll 74. **d** 76 **p** 77. C Cotmanhay *Derby* 76-79; TV Old Brampton and Loundsley Green 79-86; R Finningley w Auckley *S'well* 86-96; rtd 96; Perm to Offic *Pet* from 96. *6 Mason Close, Thrapston, Kettering NN14 4UQ* Tel (01832) 731194

GOODMAN, Brother Kevin Charles. b 54. Surrey Univ BA06. STETS 03. **d** 06 **p** 07. NSM Buckland Newton, Cerne Abbas, Godmanstone etc *Sarum* 06-09; Perm to Offic *Cant* 09-10; C Cant St Dunstan w H Cross from 10. *The Master's Lodge, 58 St Peter's Street, Canterbury CT1 2BE* Tel (01227) 479364
E-mail kevinssf@franciscans.org.uk

GOODMAN, Mrs Mairion Kim (Mars). b 73. Leeds Univ BA95. Trin Coll Bris BA03. **d** 05 **p** 06. NSM Redland *Bris* 05-10. *6 Willoughby Road, Horfield, Bristol BS7 8QX* Tel 0117-989 2597 E-mail mars@redland.org.uk

GOODMAN, Mark Alexander Scott. b 61. Lanc Univ BA84 Nottm Univ BTh90 New Coll Edin MTh97. Linc Th Coll 87. **d** 90 **p** 91. C Denton St Lawr *Man* 90-93; R Dalkeith and Lasswade *Edin* 93-06; Dioc Communications Officer 96-06; Can St Mary's Cathl and Syn Clerk 02-06; Chapl Stamford Sch from 06. *Saddlers Cottage, 9A St Peter's Street, Stamford PE9 2PQ* Tel (01780) 763691 Mobile 07947-032739

GOODMAN, Mrs Penelope Jane. b 52. ERMC 06. **d** 09 **p** 10. OLM Bure Valley *Nor* from 09. *Heath Farm House, Coltishall Road, Buxton, Norwich NR10 5JD* Tel (01603) 279393
E-mail garry.goodman@btinternet.com

GOODMAN, Peter William (Bill). b 60. St Cath Coll Cam BA82 Sheff Univ MPhil98. St Jo Coll Nottm 85. **d** 89 **p** 90. C Stapenhill w Cauldwell *Derby* 89-92; C Ovenden *Wakef* 92-94; V Halifax St Aug 94-98; Crosslinks Ethiopia 98-05; C Leic H Trin w St Jo 05-08. *1 Reservoir View, Main Street, Saddington, Leicester LE8 0QH* E-mail goodmans@cooptel.net

GOODMAN, Veronica Mary. b 57. Newman Coll Birm BEd80. Qu Coll Birm 06. **d** 08 **p** 09. C Dunstable *St Alb* from 08. *33 Felix Avenue, Luton LU2 7LE* Tel (01582) 432019
E-mail ronigoodman@yahoo.co.uk

GOODMAN, Victor Terence. b 46. Liv Univ BSc67 CEng72 MBCS74. EMMTC 82. **d** 85 **p** 86. NSM Barwell w Potters Marston and Stapleton *Leic* 85-89; NSM Croft and Stoney Stanton 89-94; P-in-c Whetstone 94-03; TV Hugglescote w Donington, Ellistown and Snibston 03-07; C Coalville w Bardon Hill and Ravenstone 07-10; rtd 10. *21 New Inn Close, Broughton Astley, Leicester LE9 6SU* Tel (01455) 285410
E-mail victor.goodman@btinternet.com

GOODMAN, Mrs Victoria Elizabeth Stuart. b 51. RGN74. Trin Coll Bris. **d** 98 **p** 99. C Ilminster and Distr *B & W* 98-02; R Blagdon w Compton Martin and Ubley 02-10; Dioc Chapl MU 01-10; rtd 10. *Underhill, Castle Hill Lane, Mere, Warminster BA12 6JB* Tel (01747) 860070
E-mail vickieplum51@btinternet.com

GOODMAN, William. *See* GOODMAN, Peter William

GOODRICH, The Very Revd Derek Hugh. b 27. Selw Coll Cam BA48 MA54. St Steph Ho Ox 50. **d** 52 **p** 53. C Willesden St Andr *Lon* 52-57; V Lodge St Sidwell Guyana 57-67; V Port Mourant 67-71; R New Amsterdam All SS 71-84; Adn Berlice 81-84; V Gen Dio Guyana 82-94; Dean Georgetown 84-93; P-in-c St Aloysius 93-00; rtd 00; Perm to Offic *S'wark* from 03. *The College of St Barnabas, Blackberry Lane, Lingfield RH7 6NJ* Tel (01342) 872873

GOODRICH, Mrs Nancy Elisabeth. b 66. St Hilda's Coll Ox BA88 MA09 ACA93. WMMTC 06. **d** 09 **p** 10. C St Annes St Thos *Blackb* from 09. *4 The Boulevard, Lytham St Annes FY8 1EH* Tel (01253) 781119 Mobile 07974-250466
E-mail nancy@goodrich.myzen.co.uk

GOODRICH, Canon Peter. b 36. Dur Univ BA58. Cuddesdon Coll 60. **d** 62 **p** 63. C Walton St Jo *Liv* 62-66; C Prescot 66-68; V Anfield St Marg 68-72; V Gt Crosby St Faith 72-83; P-in-c Seaforth 76-80; RD Bootle 78-83; TR Upholland 83-94; R Halsall 94-02; Dir Dioc OLM Scheme 94-02; Hon Can Liv Cathl 89-02; rtd 03; Perm to Offic *Liv* from 03. *Dunelm, 16 Hillside Avenue, Ormskirk L39 4TD* Tel (01695) 573285

GOODRIDGE, Elizabeth Jane. b 57. SEITE 06. **d** 09 **p** 10. NSM S Beddington and Roundshaw *S'wark* from 09. *47 Chatsworth Road, Cheam SM3 8PL* Tel 07788-755752 (mobile)
E-mail elizabeth.goodridge1@btinternet.com

GOODRIDGE, John Francis James. b 49. Open Univ BA86. WEMTC 04. **d** 07 **p** 08. NSM Bristol St Aid w St Geo from 07; NSM E Bris St Ambrose and St Leon from 07; NSM Fishponds All SS from 07; NSM Fishponds St Jo from 07; NSM Fishponds St Mary from 07; NSM Two Mile Hill St Mich from 07. *153 Whittucks Road, Bristol BS15 3PY* Tel 0117-940 1508

GOODRIDGE, Paul Charles. b 54. Leic Univ MSc98 MCIPD88. **d** 04 **p** 05. OLM Cheam *S'wark* 04-08; C Beddington 08-10; R Godstone and Blindley Heath from 10. *The Rectory, 17 Ivy Mill Lane, Godstone RH9 8NH* Tel (01883) 742354
E-mail paul_goodridge1@btinternet.com

GOODRIDGE, Peter Warren. b 66. Liv Univ BA87. Wycliffe Hall Ox 07. **d** 09 **p** 10. C Tonbridge SS Pet and Paul *Roch* from 09. *14 Salisbury Road, Tonbridge TN10 4PB* Tel (01732) 355200
E-mail pwg@inbox.com

GOODSELL, Patrick. b 32. BA88. Linc Th Coll 62. **d** 64 **p** 65. C Thornton Heath St Jude *Cant* 64-65; C Croydon St Jo *S'wark* 65-70; V Tenterden St Mich *Cant* 70-78; P-in-c Sellindge w Monks Horton and Stowting 78-84; P-in-c Lympne w W Hythe 82-84; V Sellindge w Monks Horton and Stowting etc 84-92; V Nonington w Wymynswold and Goodnestone etc 92-98; rtd 98; Perm to Offic *Cant* from 98. *3 James Close, Lyminge, Folkestone CT18 8NL* Tel (01303) 863594 E-mail pat_goodsell@sky.com

GOODWIN, Barry Frederick John. b 48. Birm Univ BSc69 PhD77. St Jo Coll Nottm 86. **d** 88 **p** 89. C Ware Ch Ch *St Alb* 88-91; P-in-c Stanstead Abbots 91-96; P-in-c Gt Amwell w St Marg 95-96; V Gt Amwell w St Margaret's and Stanstead Abbots 96-99; RD Hertford and Ware 96-99; V Clapham Park All SS *S'wark* 99-05; RD Clapham 02-05; Soc Resp (Par Development) Adv Croydon Adnry 05-11; Hon C Addiscombe St Mildred from 09. *57 Southway, Croydon CR0 8RH*
E-mail barry.goodwin@southwark.anglican.org

GOODWIN, Bruce William. b 64. Univ of W Aus BA84 DipEd85. Trin Coll Bris 07. **d** 09 **p** 10. C Thornbury and Oldbury-on-Severn w Shepperdine *Glouc* from 09. *10 Meadowside, Thornbury, Bristol BS35 2EN* Tel 07720-772190 (mobile) E-mail goodwins07@gmail.com

GOODWIN, Daphne Mary. b 35. Lon Univ MB, BS60. STETS 94. **d** 97 **p** 98. NSM Ifield *Chich* from 97. *150 Buckswood Drive, Gossops Green, Crawley RH11 8JF* Tel (01293) 612906
E-mail dapheter.goodwin@ukgateway.net

GOODWIN, David Wayne. b 71. Univ of Wales BD95. Cranmer Hall Dur 95. **d** 97 **p** 98. C Ches H Trin 97-00; Dep Chapl HM Pris Dur 00-01; Chapl HM YOI Thorn Cross 01-04; Chapl HM Pris Liv 04-07; Chapl HM Pris Kennet from 07. *HM Prison Kennet, Parkbourn, Liverpool L31 1HX* Tel 0151-213 3000 Fax 213 3103

GOODWIN, Mrs Gillian Sheila. b 54. NOC MTh99. **d** 99 **p** 00. C Penkridge *Lich* 99-02; TV Wrockwardine Deanery from 02. *The Vicarage, Church Road, High Ercall, Telford TF6 6BE* Tel (01952) 770206

GOODWIN, Canon John Fletcher Beckles. b 20. Jes Coll Cam BA43 MA46. Ridley Hall Cam 42. **d** 45 **p** 46. C Southall H Trin *Lon* 45-48; C Drypool *York* 48-49; Niger 50-57; Vice-Prin Ripon Hall Ox 57-62; V Merton *Ox* 62-70; V Heanor *Derby* 70-74; V Hazlewood 74-85; V Turnditch 74-85; Adv for In-Service Tr and Chapl to Bp 74-88; Hon Can Derby Cathl 81-85; rtd 85; Perm to

Offic *Derby* 85-99. *1 Kirby Place, Oxford OX4 2RX* Tel (01865) 712356

GOODWIN, Ronald Victor. b 33. S'wark Ord Course. **d** 86 **p** 87. NSM Wickford and Runwell *Chelmsf* 86-98; Perm to Offic 98-01; NSM W Hanningfield 01-03; P-in-c 03-06; rtd 06; Perm to Offic *Chelmsf* from 06. *164 Southend Road, Wickford SS11 8EH* Tel (01268) 734447

GOODWIN, Stephen. b 58. Sheff Univ BA80. Cranmer Hall Dur 82. **d** 85 **p** 86. C Lytham St Cuth *Blackb* 85-87; C W Burnley All SS 88-90; TV Headley All SS *Guildf* 90-98; NSM Leek and Meerbrook *Lich* 98-03; Chapl Univ Hosp of N Staffs NHS Trust 03-08; Chapl Douglas Macmillan Hospice Blurton from 08. *2 Lordshire Mews, Armshead Road, Werrington, Stoke-on-Trent ST9 0HJ* Tel (01782) 302418 *or* 344300 E-mail stephen.goodwin@talktalk.net

GOODWIN, Mrs Susan Elizabeth. b 51. Leeds Poly BSc74 Leeds Univ MSc76. St Jo Coll Dur 82. **dss** 84 **d** 87 **p** 94. Norton Woodseats St Chad *Sheff* 84-87; Par Dn 87; Chapl Scargill Ho 87-89; NSM W Burnley All SS *Blackb* 89-90; NSM Headley All SS *Guildf* 90-98; Past Asst Acorn Chr Healing Trust 91-93; P-in-c Wetley Rocks *Lich* 98-09; P-in-c Werrington 08-09; V Werrington and Wetley Rocks from 09. *2 Lordshire Mews, Armshead Road, Werrington, Stoke-on-Trent ST9 0HJ* Tel (01782) 302418 E-mail revsgoodwinx2@talktalk.net

GOODWIN HUDSON, Brainerd Peter de Wirtz. b 34. K Coll Lon BD57 AKC57. Westcott Ho Cam 57. **d** 59 **p** 60. C Morden S'wark 59-60; Australia 61-65; Asst Sec CCCS 65-68; Chapl St Lawr Coll Ramsgate 68-74; Chapl Repton Sch Derby 74-94; Chapl Santiago Chile 94-01; rtd 99; Hon C Broadwell, Evenlode, Oddington, Adlestrop etc *Glouc* 02 06. *Brea Heights, Trebetherick, Wadebridge PL27 6SE* E-mail brainerd@freeuk.com

GOODWINS, Christopher William Hedley. b 36. St Jo Coll Cam BA58 MA62. Linc Th Coll 62. **d** 64 **p** 65. C Lowestoft Ch Ch *Nor* 64-69; V Tamerton Foliot *Ex* 69-98; P-in-c Southway 78-82; rtd 98; P-in-c Isleham *Ely* 99-04; Perm to Offic *Ely* from 05 and *St E* from 10. *102 The Causeway, Isleham, Ely CB7 5ST* Tel (01638) 780284 E-mail cwhgoodwins@gmail.com

GOODYEAR, Benjamin. b 76. LSE BSc98. Ridley Hall Cam 03. **d** 06 **p** 07. C Balham Hill Ascension *S'wark* 06-09; P-in-c Brixton St Paul w St Sav from 09. *73 Baytree Road, London SW2 5RR* Tel 07866-774354 (mobile) E-mail thegoodyears@gmail.com

GOODYER, Canon Edward Arthur. b 42. Witwatersrand Univ BA63 SS Coll Cam BA67 MA70 Rhodes Univ MTh91. St Paul's Coll Grahamstown 68. **d** 68 **p** 69. S Africa 69-92; Can Cape Town 80-84; R Alverstoke *Portsm* from 92; P-in-c Gosport Ch Ch 97-01; Hon Can Wusasa Nigeria from 99. *The Rectory, Little Anglesey Road, Alverstoke, Gosport PO12 2JA* Tel and fax (023) 9258 1979 *or* 9258 0551 Mobile 07952-194187 E-mail ego.lizg@virgin.net

GOOLD, Peter John. b 44. Lon Univ BD74. St Steph Ho Ox 67. **d** 70 **p** 71. C Chiswick St Nic w St Mary *Lon* 70-73; Chapl Asst R Masonic Hosp Lon 73-74; Chapl Asst Basingstoke Distr Hosp 74-77; Chapl R Marsden Hosp Lon and Surrey 77-80; Chapl N Hants Hosp 80-94; Chapl N Hants Hosps NHS Trust 94-00; Chapl N Hants Loddon Community NHS Trust 94-00; Perm to Offic *Guildf* 94-00; rtd 09. *Aepelford Acre, The Sands, Woodborough, Pewsey SN9 5PR* Tel (01672) 851942

GOOLJARY, Yousouf. b 59. Ex Univ BSc80 Man Poly PGCE82. SEITE 07. **d** 10 **p** 11. C Greenwich St Alfege *S'wark* from 10. *88 Ashburnham Grove, London SE10 8UJ* Tel (020) 8691 6670 Mobile 07734-284573 E-mail revgooljary@aol.com

GORDON, Alan Williamson. b 53. Strathclyde Univ BA75 MCIBS79. Wycliffe Hall Ox 98. **d** 98 **p** 99. C Win Ch Ch 98-02; R King's Worthy from 02; R Headbourne Worthy from 02; RD Win from 07. *The Rectory, 4 Campion Way, King's Worthy, Winchester SO23 7QP* Tel (01962) 882166 E-mail alan.gordon98@ntlworld.com

GORDON, The Very Revd Alexander Ronald. b 49. Nottm Univ BPharm71. Coll of Resurr Mirfield 74. **d** 77 **p** 78. C Headingley *Ripon* 77-80; C Fareham SS Pet and Paul *Portsm* 80-83; V Cudworth *Wakef* 83-85; P-in-c Tain *Mor* 85-87; P-in-c Lairg Miss 87-01; P-in-c Brora and Dornoch 88-01; Dioc Dir of Ords 89-01; Can St Andr Cathl Inverness 95-01; Hon Can 02-05; Chapl Strasbourg *Eur* 02-05; Provost St Andr Cathl Inverness from 05. *St Andrew's Lodge, 15 Ardross Street, Inverness IV3 5NS* Tel (01463) 233535 Mobile 07917-668918 E-mail canonalexgordon@btconnect.com

GORDON, Anne. *See* LE BAS, Mrs Jennifer Anne

✠**GORDON, The Rt Revd Archibald Ronald McDonald.** b 27. Ball Coll Ox BA50 MA52. Cuddesdon Coll 50. **d** 52 **p** 53 **c** 75. C Stepney St Dunstan and All Saints *Lon* 52-55; Chapl Cuddesdon Coll 55-59; Lic to Offic *Ox* 57-59; V Birm St Pet 59-68; Lect Qu Coll Birm 60-62; Can Res Birm Cathl 67-71; V Ox St Mary V w St Cross and St Pet 71-75; Bp Portsm 75-84; Bp at Lambeth (Hd of Staff) *Cant* 84-91; Asst Bp S'wark 84-91; Bp HM Forces 85-90; Can Res and Sub-Dean Ch Ch *Ox* 91-96; rtd 96; Hon Asst Bp *Ox* from 91. *Garden Flat B, St Katharine's House, Ormond Road, Wantage OX12 8EA* Tel (01235) 766766 E-mail ronaldgordon.ab@btinternet.com

GORDON, Mrs Avis Patricia. b 52. Man Univ BA73. **d** 08 **p** 09. OLM Clifton *Man* from 08. *47 Agecroft Road West, Prestwich, Manchester M25 9RF* Tel 0161-798 8018

GORDON, Bruce Harold Clark. b 40. Edin Univ MTh96. Cranmer Hall Dur 65. **d** 68 **p** 69. C Edin St Jas 68-71; C Blackheath St Jo *S'wark* 71-74; R Duns *Edin* 74-90; R Lanark and Douglas *Glas* 90-05; rtd 05. *52 Foxknowe Place, Livingston EH54 6TX* Tel (01506) 418466 E-mail brucehc.gordon@virgin.net

GORDON, Donald Ian. b 30. Nottm Univ BA52 PhD64. Westcott Ho Cam 71. **d** 71 **p** 72. NSM Newport *Chelmsf* 71-75; NSM Creeksea w Althorne, Latchingdon and N Fambridge 76-00; rtd 00; Perm to Offic *Chelmsf* from 01. *Holden House, Steeple Road, Latchingdon, Chelmsford CM3 6JX* Tel (01621) 740296 E-mail barbaragordon@tiscali.co.uk

GORDON, Edward John. b 32. Univ of Wales BA52. St Mich Coll Llan 52. **d** 55 **p** 56. C Baglan *Llan* 55-61; C Newcastle w Laleston and Tythegston 61-65; V Ynyshir 65-69; C Bramhall *Ches* 69-72; V Cheadle Hulme All SS 72-79; V Tranmere St Paul w St Luke 79-88; V Sandbach Heath 88-97; Chapl Arclid Hosp 90-93; RD Congleton *Ches* 92-97; P-in-c Wheelock 95-97; rtd 97; Perm to Offic *B & W* from 97. *55 Greenslade Gardens, Nailsea, Bristol BS48 2BJ* Tel (01275) 853404

GORDON, Jonathan Andrew. b 61. Keele Univ BA83 MPhil88 Southn Univ BTh88 Southn Inst MPhil04. Sarum & Wells Th Coll 84. **d** 87 **p** 88. C Wallingford w Crowmarsh Gifford etc *Ox* 87-91; C Tilehurst St Mich 91-93; TV Stoke-upon-Trent *Lich* 93-97; Chapl Southn Solent Univ 98-05; R Northchurch and Wigginton *St Alb* from 05. *St Mary's Rectory, 80 High Street, Northchurch, Berkhamstead HP4 3QW* Tel (01442) 871547 E-mail ebenezer@jonathangordon.wanadoo.co.uk

GORDON, Keith Adrian. b 49. Surrey Univ BSc71 Birm Univ MA02. Open Th Coll 95. **d** 98 **p** 99. Venezuela 98-03; C Caracas St Mary 98-99; Bp's Chapl Dioc Chpl 99-03; P-in-c Tenerife Sur *Eur* from 03. *Residencial Sonia #17, Calle El Mojon, Callao Salvaje, Adeje, 38678 Tenerife* Tel and fax (0034) 922 742 045 Mobile 679 660 277 E-mail kagordon40@hotmail.com

GORDON, Canon Kenneth Davidson. b 35. Edin Univ MA57 Univ of Wales MTh08. Tyndale Hall Bris 58. **d** 60 **p** 61. C St Helens St Helen *Liv* 60-66; V Daubhill *Man* 66-71; R Bieldside 71-01; Can St Andr Cathl 81-01; Syn Clerk 96-01; rtd 01; Hon Can St Andr Cathl from 01; Perm to Offic *Blackb* and *Liv* 01-07; Bp's Warrant *Ab* 07-10. *16 Reidford Gardens, Drumoak, Banchory AB31 5AW* Tel (01330) 810260 Mobile 07715-169548 E-mail canonken@btinternet.com

GORDON, Kristy. *See* PATTIMORE, Mrs Kristy

GORDON, Martin Lewis. b 73. Edin Univ MA97. Wycliffe Hall Ox BA09. **d** 10 **p** 11. C Stoke Gifford *Bris* from 10. *56 Simmonds View, Bristol BS34 8HL* E-mail martingordon2@gmail.com *or* martin@st-michaels-church.org.uk

GORDON, Noel. b 10. NSM Willowfield *D & D* from 10. *4 Falcon Drive, Newtownards BT23 4GH* Tel (028) 9182 0223

GORDON, Mrs Pamela Anne. b 48. Brighton Coll of Educn CertEd69 BEd70. SAOMC 99. **d** 02 **p** 03. NSM Wargrave w Knowl Hill *Ox* from 02. *Rebeny, 2A Hawthorn Road, Caversham, Reading RG4 6LY* Tel 0118-947 8676 Fax 954 3076 E-mail pam.gordon@ntlworld.com

GORDON, Sister Patricia Ann. b 44. SAOMC. **d** 00 **p** 01. CSMV from 80; NSM Didcot St Pet *Ox* 00-07; NSM Wantage Downs 07-11. *St Mary's Convent, Challow Road, Wantage OX12 9DJ* Tel (01235) 774084 Mobile 07884-196004 E-mail sisterpatriciaann@hotmail.co.uk

GORDON, Robert Andrew. b 42. Llan Dioc Tr Scheme 82. **d** 84 **p** 85. C Bargoed and Deri w Brithdir *Llan* 84-87; V Aberpergwm and Blaengwrach 87-94; R Johnston w Steynton *St D* 94-97; R Cosheston w Nash and Upton 97-04; TV Carew 04-07; rtd 07. *6 Oakridge Acres, Tenby SA70 8DB* Tel (01834) 844735

GORDON, Robert John. b 56. Edin Univ MA81. Wycliffe Hall Ox 87. **d** 89 **p** 90. C Wilnecote *Lich* 89-91; C Bideford *Ex* 91-95; P-in-c Feniton, Buckerell and Escot 95-05; P-in-c Tiverton St Pet and Chevithorne w Cove from 05. *St Peter's Vicarage, 29 Moorlands, Tiverton EX16 6UF* Tel (01884) 254079 E-mail robert.j.gordon@btopenworld.com

GORDON, Ronald. *See* GORDON, The Rt Revd Archibald Ronald McDonald

GORDON, The Very Revd Thomas William. b 57. QUB BEd80 Univ of Ulster MA86 TCD BTh89. CITC 85. **d** 89 **p** 90. C Ballymacash *Conn* 89-91; Min Can Belf Cathl 91-95; Chapl and Tutor CITC 91-96; Dir Extra-Mural Studies 96-10; Lect Past Th and Liturgy 01-10; Consultant Dir Past Formation and NSM 06-09; PV Ch Ch Cathl Dublin 96-10; Co-ord Relig Progr RTE 99-10; Dean Leighlin *C & O* from 10; 1 Leighlin w Grange Sylvae, Shankill etc from 10. *The Deanery, Old Leighlin, Co Carlow, Republic of Ireland* Tel (00353) (59) 972 1570 Mobile 87-276 7562 E-mail dean.leighlin@gmail.com

GORDON CLARK, John Vincent Michael. b 29. FCA. S'wark Ord Course 73. **d** 76 **p** 77. NSM Guildf H Trin w St Mary 76-81; NSM Albury w St Martha 81-91; Dioc Chapl to MU 92-95; Lic to Offic 95-99; Hon C Guildf Cathl 91-99; Perm to Offic from 99.

Hillfield, 8 Little Warren Close, Guildford GU4 8PW Tel (01483) 569027

GORDON-CUMMING, Henry Ian. b 28. Barrister-at-Law (Gray's Inn) 56. Oak Hill Th Coll 54. **d** 57 **p** 58. C Southsea St Jude *Portsm* 57-60; Chapl to Bp Ankole-Kigezi Uganda 61-65; Chapl Ntari Sch 65-67; V Virginia Water *Guildf* 68-78; R Busbridge 78-87; R Lynch w Iping Marsh and Milland *Chich* 87-94; rtd 94; Perm to Offic *Chich* from 94. *Bay Cottage, Brookside, Runcton, Chichester PO20 1PX* Tel (01243) 783395

GORDON-KERR, Canon Francis Alexander. b 39. Dur Univ BA64 MA67 Hull Univ PhD81 DipEd. Wycliffe Hall Ox 65. **d** 67 **p** 68. C Heworth St Mary *Dur* 67-70; Chapl Newc Poly 70-75; Chapl Hull Univ 75-82; V Welton w Melton 82-92; Clergy Tr Officer E Riding 82-92; AD W Hull 87-96; RD Hull 89-96; Can and Preb York Minster 89-98; V Anlaby St Pet 92-98; R Crowland *Linc* 98-04; rtd 04. *Alberic Cottage, Low Road, Barrowby, Grantham NG32 1DD* Tel (01476) 574961

GORDON-TAYLOR, Benjamin Nicholas. b 69. St Jo Coll Dur BA90 MA92 Leeds Univ BA94 Dur Univ PhD08 FRSA99. Coll of Resurr Mirfield 92. **d** 95 **p** 96. C Launceston *Truro* 95-97; C Northampton St Matt *Pet* 97-99; Fell and Chapl Univ Coll Dur 99-04; Lect and Tutor Coll of Resurr Mirfield from 05; Visiting Lect Leeds Univ from 05; Dir Mirfield Liturg Inst from 08. *College of the Resurrection, Stocks Bank Road, Mirfield WF14 0BW* Tel (01924) 490441
E-mail bgordon-taylor@mirfield.org.uk

GORDON-WALKER, Caroline. b 37. LMH Ox BA59. Cranmer Hall Dur 01. **d** 02 **p** 03. NSM Poitou-Charentes *Eur* 02-05; C Aquitaine 05-07; Asst Chapl from 07. *La Vieille Ferme, 24170 St Germain-de-Belvès, France* Tel (0033) 5 53 29 36 03
E-mail carolinegw@wanadoo.fr

GORE, Canon John Charles. b 29. Leeds Univ BA52. Coll of Resurr Mirfield 52. **d** 54 **p** 55. C Middlesbrough St Jo the Ev *York* 54-59; N Rhodesia 59-64; Zambia 64-75; Can Lusaka 70-75; R Elland *Wakef* 75-84; TR 84-86; RD Brighouse and Elland 77-86; V Wembley Park St Aug *Lon* 86-95; P-in-c Tokyngton St Mich 89-90; AD Brent 90-95; rtd 95; P-in-c Heptonstall *Wakef* 95-99; Perm to Offic *Bradf* from 99. *3 Navigation Square, Skipton BD23 1XB* Tel (01756) 792297

GORE, Canon John Harrington. b 24. Em Coll Cam BA49 MA52. Westcott Ho Cam 49. **d** 51 **p** 52. C Deane *Man* 51-54; C Whittstable All SS w St Pet *Cant* 54-59; CF 59-62; V Womenswold *Cant* 62-67; C-in-c Aylesham CD 62-67; R Deal St Leon 67-75; RD Sandwich 70-78; P-in-c Sholden 74-75; R Deal St Leon w Sholden 75-80; R Southchurch H Trin *Chelmsf* 80-90; RD Southend 84-89; Hon Can Chelmsf Cathl 86-90; rtd 90; Perm to Offic *St E* and *Chelmsf* from 90. *8 De Burgh Place, Clare, Sudbury CO10 8QL* Tel (01787) 278558

GORE, Mrs Margaret Lesley. b 44. Westf Coll Lon BA66. ERMC 05. **d** 07 **p** 08. NSM Cherry Hinton St Jo *Ely* 07-09; NSM Linton from 09. *38 Symonds Lane, Linton, Cambridge CB21 4HY* Tel (01223) 891970
E-mail lesley@lawngore.plus.com

GORHAM, Canon Andrew Arthur. b 51. Bris Univ BA73 Birm Univ MA87. Qu Coll Birm 77. **d** 79 **p** 80. C Plaistow St Mary *Roch* 79-82; Chapl Lanchester Poly *Cov* 82-87; TV Warwick 87-95; Chapl Birm Univ 95-00; Bp's Dom Chapl 00-11; Hon Can Birm Cathl 06-11; Master St Jo Hosp Lich from 11. *St John's Hospital, St John Street, Lichfield WS13 6PB* Tel (01543) 251884

GORHAM, The Ven Karen Marisa. b 64. Trin Coll Bris BA95. **d** 95 **p** 96. C Northallerton w Kirby Sigston *York* 95-99; P-in-c Maidstone St Paul *Cant* 99-07; Asst Dir of Ords 02-07; AD Maidstone 03-07; Hon Can Cant Cathl 06-07; Adn Buckingham *Ox* from 07. *The Rectory, Stone, Aylesbury HP17 8RZ* Tel (01865) 208264 Fax (01296) 747424
E-mail archdbuc@oxford.anglican.org

GORICK, David Charles. b 32. Reading Univ BA55 Nottm Univ DipEd72. EMMTC 81. **d** 84 **p** 85. NSM W Bridgford *S'well* 84-89; C Gotham 89-97; C Kingston and Ratcliffe-on-Soar 89-97; C Barton in Fabis 89-97; C Thrumpton 89-97; P-in-c Gotham 97-99; rtd 99; Perm to Offic *S'well* from 03. *11 Brookfields Way, East Leake, Loughborough LE12 6HD* Tel (01509) 856960

GORICK, Janet Margaret. b 30. Reading Univ BA54. EMMTC 84. **dss** 86 **d** 87 **p** 94. Hon Par Dn W Bridgford *S'well* 87-95; NSM Gotham 95-99; NSM Barton in Fabis 95-99; NSM Kingston and Ratcliffe-on-Soar 95-99; NSM Thrumpton 95-99; rtd 99; Perm to Offic *S'well* from 03. *11 Brookfields Way, East Leake, Loughborough LE12 6HD* Tel (01509) 856960

GORICK, Martin Charles William. b 62. Selw Coll Cam BA84 MA88. Ripon Coll Cuddesdon 85. **d** 87 **p** 88. C Birtley *Dur* 87-91; Bp's Dom Chapl *Ox* 91-94; V Smethwick *Birm* 94-01; AD Warley 97-01; R Stratford-upon-Avon, Luddington etc *Cov* from 01. *The Vicarage, 7 Old Town, Stratford-upon-Avon CV37 6BG* Tel (01789) 266022 or 266316
E-mail office@stratford-upon-avon.org

GORING, Charles Robert. b 60. Nottm Univ BA91. Linc Th Coll 91. **d** 93 **p** 94. C Thornbury *Glouc* 93-96; Perm to Offic *Chich*

97-98; C Mayfield 98-00; V The Hydneye 00-07; C Eastbourne Ch Ch and St Phil from 07; Asst Chapl E Sussex Hosps NHS Trust from 01. *St Philip's House, 10 St Philip's Place, Eastbourne BN22 8LW* Tel (01323) 749653
E-mail jc.goring@googlemail.com

GORRIE, Richard Bingham. b 27. Univ Coll Ox BA49 MA51. Ridley Hall Cam 49. **d** 51 **p** 52. C Ox St Clem 51-54; C Morden *S'wark* 54-56; Scripture Union Rep (Scotland) 56-92; Chapl Fettes Coll Edin 60-74; Dir Inter-Sch Chr Fellowship (Scotland) 74-80; rtd 92; Perm to Offic *Glas* from 92. *20 Auchlochan Courtyard, New Trows Road, Lesmahagow, Lanark ML11 0GS* Tel (01555) 895076 E-mail gorries@silas57.freeserve.co.uk

GORRINGE, Edward George Alexander. b 63. TD. QUB BA85 Strathclyde Univ MBA00 FCMA06. CITC 04. **d** 07 **p** 08. NSM Aghalee *D & D* 07-09; CF from 09. *c/o MOD Chaplains (Army)* Tel (01264) 381140 Fax 381824
E-mail edward.gorringe@virginmedia.com

GORRINGE, Prof Timothy Jervis. b 46. St Edm Hall Ox BA69 MPhil75. Sarum Th Coll 69. **d** 72 **p** 73. C Chapel Allerton *Ripon* 72-75; C Ox St Mary V w St Cross and St Pet 76-78; India 79-86; Chapl St Jo Coll Ox 86-96; Reader St Andr Univ from 96; Prof Th Ex Univ from 99. *Department of Theology, Exeter University, Queen's Building, The Queen's Drive, Exeter EX4 4QH* Tel (01392) 264242 E-mail t.j.gorringe@exeter.ac.uk

GORTON, Angela Deborah. *See* WYNNE, Mrs Angela Deborah

GORTON, Anthony David Trevor. b 39. Lon Univ BSc65. Oak Hill Th Coll 78. **d** 81 **p** 82. NSM Colney Heath St Mark *St Alb* 81-00; NSM Watford St Pet from 00. *Waterdell, Lane End, Hatfield AL10 9AG* Tel (01707) 263605
E-mail tonygorton@hotmail.com

GORTON, Ian Charles Johnson. b 62. Bp Otter Coll BA84. Sarum & Wells Th Coll 86. **d** 89 **p** 90. C Wythenshawe Wm Temple Ch *Man* 89-92; C Man Apostles w Miles Platting 92-95; P-in-c Abbey Hey 95-03; P-in-c Moston St Chad 03-11; P-in-c Moston St Jo 05-11; TV Salford All SS from 11. *The Vicarage, 43 Derby Road, Salford M6 5YD* Tel 0161-736 5819
E-mail charles.gorton@talk21.com

GORTON (née CARTER), Sarah Helen Buchanan. b 44. St Andr Univ BSc65 DipEd66. TISEC 93. **d** 96 **p** 98. NSM Lenzie *Glas* 96-01; P-in-c Alexandria from 01; Chapl Argyll and Clyde NHS from 01. *The Rectory, Queen Street, Alexandria G83 0AS* Tel (01389) 752633 E-mail shbgorton@btinternet.com

GOSDEN, Angela. b 50. Ox Min Course 07. **d** 11. NSM Stanford in the Vale w Goosey and Hatford *Ox* from 11. *Upper Bockhampton Farmhouse, Bockhampton Road, Lambourn, Hungerford RG17 7LS* Tel (01488) 73996 Fax 72517
E-mail angela gosden@btconnect.com

GOSDEN, Timothy John. b 50. Open Univ BA86. Chich Th Coll 74. **d** 77 **p** 78. C Cant All SS 77-81; Asst Chapl Loughb Univ 81-85; Lic to Offic *Cant* 85-87; Chapl Ch Ch Coll of HE Cant 85-87; Sen Chapl Hull Univ 87-94; V Taunton Lyngford *B & W* 94-98; V Harrow St Mary *Lon* from 98. *St Mary's Vicarage, Church Hill, Harrow HA1 3HL* Tel (020) 8422 2652
E-mail timgosden@tiscali.co.uk *or* stmaryharrow@aol.com

GOSHAI, Miss Veja Helena. b 32. SRN57 SCM59 City Univ BSc99. Trin Coll Bris 75. **d** 87 **p** 94. Asst Chapl St Barts Hosp Lon 87-97; rtd 92; Perm to Offic *S'wark* 99-03. *Grace, 26 Bilston Road, Crawford, Cape Town, 7780 South Africa*

GOSLING, David. b 27. SAOMC 95. **d** 98 **p** 99. OLM High Wycombe *Ox* 98-03; Perm to Offic *Ox* 02-09 and *Nor* from 10. *18 Parsons Mead, Norwich NR4 6PG* Tel (01603) 506025
E-mail greygoose@talktalk.net

GOSLING, David Lagourie. b 39. Man Univ MSc63 Fitzw Coll Cam MA69 Lanc Univ PhD74 MInstP69 CPhys84. Ridley Hall Cam 63. **d** 73 **p** 74. Hon C Lancaster St Mary *Blackb* 73-74; Hon C Kingston upon Hull St Matt w St Barn *York* 74-77; Hon C Cottingham 78-83; Asst Chapl Geneva *Eur* 84-89; C Cambridge Gt St Mary w St Mich *Ely* 89-90; C Dry Drayton 90-94; USPG India 95-99; Perm to Offic *York* from 95 and *Ely* from 01; Fell Clare Hall Cam from 01; Prin Edwardes Coll Peshawar Pakistan from 06. *Clare Hall, Herschel Road, Cambridge CB3 9AL* Tel (01223) 352450 Fax 332333 E-mail dlg26@cam.ac.uk

GOSLING, Ms Dorothy Grace. b 57. St Martin's Coll Lanc BA94 K Coll Lon MA06. SNWTP 07. **d** 10 **p** 11. NSM Ches Cathl from 10. *93 Station Road, Little Sutton, Ellesmere Port CH66 1HA* Tel 0151-339 9609 Mobile 07976-274459
E-mail d.gosling@chester.ac.uk

GOSLING, James Albert. b 41. Oak Hill Th Coll 81. **d** 84 **p** 85. NSM Victoria Docks St Luke *Chelmsf* 84-96; Hon C Gt Mongeham w Ripple and Sutton by Dover *Cant* 96-01; Hon C Eastry and Northbourne w Tilmanstone etc 96-01; C Kenton, Mamhead, Powderham, Cofton and Starcross *Ex* 01-02. *2 Wordsworth Close, Exmouth EX8 5SQ* Tel (01395) 225278
E-mail jimandjan@jimandjan.fsnet.co.uk

GOSLING, John William Fraser. b 34. St Jo Coll Dur BA58 MA71 Ex Univ PhD78. Cranmer Hall Dur 58. **d** 60 **p** 61. C Plympton St Mary *Ex* 60-68; V Newport 68-78; Org Sec CECS *St Alb* and *Ox* 78-82; C Stratford sub Castle *Sarum* 83-86; Adv on CME 83-86; Perm to Offic 86-91 and from 95; C Swindon

Ch Ch *Bris* 91-95; rtd 95. *1 Wiley Terrace, Wilton, Salisbury SP2 0HN* Tel (01722) 742788 E-mail jgosling@givemail.co.uk

GOSNEY, Jeanette Margaret. b 58. Bath Univ BA81 Univ Coll Ches MA05 Nottm Univ PGCE82. St Jo Coll Nottm BTh93 MPhil95. **d** 95 **p** 96. C Ipswich St Marg *St E* 95-98; Chapl Loughb Univ 98; Sen Chapl 98-01; Tutor Trin Coll Bris 01-04; Chapl Repton Sch Derby 04-05; TV Albury, Braughing, Furneux Pelham, Lt Hadham etc *St Alb* 06-10; Par Development Officer from 10. *1 Linden Glade, Hemel Hempstead HP1 1XB* Tel (01442) 239428 E-mail jgosney@stalbans.anglican.org

GOSS, David James. b 52. Nottm Univ BCombStuds York St Jo Univ MA10. Linc Th Coll. **d** 83 **p** 84. C Wood Green St Mich w Bounds Green St Gabr etc *Lon* 83-86; TV Gleadless Valley *Sheff* 86-89; TR 89-95; V Wheatley Hills from 95. *The Vicarage, 18 Central Boulevard, Doncaster DN2 5PE* Tel (01302) 342047 E-mail davidjamesgoss@gmail.com

GOSS, Kevin Ian. b 56. LRAM75 LTCL76 GRSM77 LGSM80 Hughes Hall Cam PGCE78 Heythrop Coll Lon MA08. S Dios Minl Tr Scheme 89. **d** 92 **p** 93. NSM Ardingly *Chich* 92-98; Asst Chapl Ardingly Coll 92-98; Min Can, Prec and Sacr Cant Cathl 98-03; P-in-c Hockerill *St Alb* from 04; Chapl Herts and Essex Community NHS Trust from 04. *Hockerill Vicarage, 4A All Saints Close, Bishop's Stortford CM23 2EA* Tel (01279) 506542 E-mail allsaintshockerill@btinternet.com

GOSS, Michael John. b 37. Chich Th Coll 62. **d** 65 **p** 66. C Angell Town St Jo *S'wark* 65-68; C Catford St Laur 68-71; P-in-c Lewisham St Swithun 71-81; V Redhill St Jo 81-88; V Dudley St Thos and St Luke *Worc* 88-98; C Small Heath *Birm* 98-02; rtd 02; Perm to Offic *Birm* from 02. *8 Mayland Road, Birmingham B16 0NG* Tel 0121-429 6022 E-mail michael.goss@tinyworld.co.uk

GOSSWINN, Nicholas Simon. b 50. Birm Poly FGA80. St D Coll Lamp. **d** 73 **p** 74. C Abergavenny St Mary *Mon* 73-74; C-in-c Bassaleg 74-80; TV Barrow St Geo w St Luke *Carl* 81-87; C Usworth *Dur* 89-90; TV 90-96; P-in-c Stockport St Matt *Ches* 02-03; rtd 10. *134 North Road, Barrow-in-Furness LA13 0HQ* E-mail gosswinn@hotmail.com

GOSTELOW (née THOMPSON), Mrs Ruth Jean. b 47. St Alb Minl Tr Scheme 85. **d** 90 **p** 94. Par Dn Stonebridge St Mich *Lon* 90-94; C Ealing St Paul 94-96; TV W Slough *Ox* 96-03; V New Haw *Guildf* from 03. *The Vicarage, 149 Woodham Lane, New Haw, Addlestone KT15 3NJ* Tel and fax (01932) 343187 E-mail rev.ruth@btinternet.com

GOSWELL, Geoffrey. b 34. SS Paul & Mary Coll Cheltenham CertEd68. Glouc Th Course 70. **d** 71 **p** 72. C Cheltenham Em *Glouc* 71-73; C Lydney w Aylburton 73-76; P-in-c Falfield w Rockhampton 76-79; Chapl HM Det Cen Eastwood Park 76-79; Area Sec CMS *Ely* 79-81; *Linc* and *Pet* 79-86; Dep Regional Sec (UK) CMS 86-97; P-in-c Orton Waterville *Ely* 90-96; TV The Ortons, Alwalton and Chesterton 96-97; rtd 97; Perm to Offic *Pet* 01-07. *8 Lapwing Close, Northampton NN4 0RT* Tel (01604) 701572 E-mail g.goswell@hotmail.co.uk

GOTHARD, Mrs Anne Marie. b 51. STETS. **d** 00 **p** 11. NSM E Meon and Langrish *Portsm* 00-04; NSM Catherington and Clanfield from 04. *27 Green Lane, Clanfield, Waterlooville PO8 0JU* Tel (023) 9259 6315 Mobile 07939-472796 E-mail rev_gothard@hotmail.com

GOTT, Stephen. b 61. St Jo Coll Nottm 92. **d** 94 **p** 95. C Mount Pellon *Wakef* 94-97; V Greetland and W Vale 97-06; TR Em TM from 06. *The Rectory, 12 Moor Close, Huddersfield HD4 7BP* Tel (01484) 652543 E-mail stephen.gott1@hotmail.co.uk

GOUGH, Andrew Stephen. b 60. Sarum & Wells Th Coll 83. **d** 86 **p** 87. C St Leonards Ch Ch and St Mary *Chich* 86-88; C Broseley w Benthall *Heref* 88-90; V Ketley and Oakengates *Lich* 90-93; TV Bickleigh (Plymouth) *Ex* 93; TV Bickleigh and Shaugh Prior 94; P-in-c St Day *Truro* 94-96; V Chacewater w St Day and Carharrack 96-09; P-in-c St Ives from 09; P-in-c Halsetown 09-11. *The Vicarage, St Andrew's Street, St Ives TR26 1AH* Tel (01736) 796404 Mobile 07590-695515 E-mail goughfr@hotmail.com

GOUGH, Andrew Walter. b 55. Bris Univ BA78. Trin Coll Bris 90. **d** 92 **p** 93. C Mossley Hill St Matt and St Jas *Liv* 92-94; C Wavertree H Trin 94-96; Chapl Warw Sch from 96. *9 Griffin Road, Warwick CV34 6QX* Tel (01926) 400533 or 776416 E-mail awg@warwickschool.org

GOUGH, Anthony Walter. b 31. Leic Univ MA76 Chicago Th Sem DMin81. Oak Hill Th Coll 57. **d** 60 **p** 61. C Southsea St Simon *Portsm* 60-64; R Peldon *Chelmsf* 64-71; V Rothley *Leic* 71-80; USA 80-81; Chapl St Jo Hosp Aylesbury 81-82; Perm to Offic *Leic* 82-96; rtd 96. *410 Hinckley Road, Leicester LE3 0WA* Tel 0116-285 4284 E-mail tg1@ntlworld.com

GOUGH, Canon Colin Richard. b 47. St Chad's Coll Dur BA69. Cuddesdon Coll 73. **d** 75 **p** 76. C Lich St Chad 75-78; C Codsall 78-84; V Wednesbury St Paul Wood Green 84-92; TR Tettenhall Wood 92-99; TR Tettenhall Wood and Perton 99-01; P-in-c Stannington *Newc* 01-10; Dioc Adv for CME 01-10; AD Morpeth 08-10; Hon Can Newc Cathl 06-10; rtd 10. *44 Tyelaw Meadows, Shilbottle NE66 2JJ* Tel (01665) 581100 E-mail colingough@onetel.com

GOUGH, David Kenneth. b 44. St Mark & St Jo Coll Lon TCert66 Open Univ BA93. **d** 07 **p** 08. OLM Kinnerley w Melverley and Knockin w Maesbrook *Lich* from 07. *Ainsdale House, Maesbrook, Oswestry SY10 8QP*

GOUGH, David Norman. b 42. Oak Hill Th Coll 70. **d** 70 **p** 71. C Penn Fields *Lich* 70-73; C Stapenhill w Cauldwell *Derby* 73-77; V Heath 77-86; P-in-c Derby St Chad 86-95; TV Walbrook Epiphany 95-03; P-in-c Codnor and Loscoe 03-07; rtd 07. *7 Mulberry Close, Belper DE56 1RQ* Tel (01773) 599013 E-mail thevic@dsl.pipex.com

GOUGH, David Richard. b 71. St Jo Coll Nottm 06. **d** 08 **p** 09. C Sheff St Jo 08-11; P-in-c Woodhouse St Jas from 11. *St James's Vicarage, 65 Cardwell Avenue, Sheffield S13 7XB* Tel 0114-348 4621 Mobile 07913-083656 E-mail david.gough@sheffield.anglican.org

GOUGH, Derek William. b 31. Pemb Coll Cam BA55 MA59. St Steph Ho Ox 55. **d** 57 **p** 58. C E Finchley All SS *Lon* 57-60; C Roxbourne St Andr 60-66; V Edmonton St Mary w St Jo 66-98; rtd 98; Perm to Offic *Chelmsf* 98-07 and *St Alb* 00-07. *43A Church Street, Market Deeping, Peterborough PE6 8AN* Tel (01778) 341421

GOUGH, Elizabeth. b 54. CBDTI 97. **d** 00 **p** 01. OLM Eden, Gelt and Irthing *Carl* 00-06; TV from 06. *Brackenside Barn, Brampton CA8 2QX* Tel (01697) 746252 E-mail elizabeth.gough3@btinternet.com

GOUGH, Canon Ernest Hubert. b 31. TCD BA53 MA57. TCD Div Sch Div Test 54. **d** 54 **p** 55. C Glenavy *Conn* 54-57; C Lisburn Ch Ch 57-61; P-in-c Belfast St Ninian 61-62; I 62-71; I Belfast St Bart 71-85; I Templepatrick w Donegore 85-97; Can Conn Cathl from 91; rtd 97. *The Caim, 15 Swilly Road, Portstewart BT55 7DJ* Tel (028) 7083 3253 E-mail ehg@thecaim.net

GOUGH, Frank Peter. b 32. Lon Coll of Div 66. **d** 68 **p** 69. C Weymouth St Mary *Sarum* 68-70; C Attenborough w Chilwell *S'well* 70-73; R Barrow *Ches* 73-77; P-in-c Summerstown *S'wark* 77-88; RD Tooting 80-88; Dioc Past Sec 88-93; Tutor and Chapl Whittington Coll Felbridge 93-98; rtd 98; Perm to Offic *Roch* 03-07. *24 Whittington College, London Road, Felbridge, East Grinstead RH19 2QU* Tel 07970-199135 (mobile) E-mail frank_gough@msn.com

GOUGH, Canon Jonathan Robin Blanning. b 62. Univ of Wales (Lamp) BA83 Westmr Coll Ox MTh96 FRSA03. St Steph Ho Ox 83. **d** 85 **p** 86. C Braunton *Ex* 85-86; C Matson *Glouc* 86-89; CF 89-01 and from 05; Chapl R Memorial Chpl Sandhurst from 08; Abp's Officer for Ecum *Cant* 01-05; Can Gib Cathl 02-05; Public Preacher *Win* from 02; Hon Can Nicosia from 06. *c/o MOD Chaplains (Army)* Tel (01264) 381140 Fax 381824 E-mail jonathan.gough443@mod.uk

GOUGH, Miss Lynda Elizabeth. b 54. SS Hild & Bede Coll Dur BA94 RGN83. Wycliffe Hall Ox 97. **d** 99 **p** 00. C Stranton *Dur* 99-03; V Spennymoor and Whitworth from 03. *The Vicarage, 30 Jubilee Close, Spennymoor DL16 6GA* Tel (01388) 815471

GOUGH, Martyn John. b 66. Univ of Wales (Cardiff) BTh87 Univ of Wales (Lamp) MA05 FRSA04. St Steph Ho Ox 88. **d** 90 **p** 91. C Port Talbot St Theodore *Llan* 90-92; C Roath 92-94; Asst Chapl Milan w Genoa and Varese *Eur* 95-98; Chapl RN from 98; Asst Dir of Ords RN and Voc Adv 07-09; Dir from 09. *Royal Naval Chaplaincy Service, Mail Point 1-2, Leach Building, Whale Island, Portsmouth PO2 8BY* Tel (023) 9262 5055 Fax 9262 5134

GOUGH, Stephen William Cyprian. b 50. Alberta Univ BSc71. Cuddesdon Coll BA80 MA. **d** 79 **p** 80. C Walton St Mary *Liv* 79-83; V New Springs 83-87; V Childwall St Dav 87-06; V Stoneycroft All SS 04-06; Co-ord Chapl HM Pris Risley 06-08; P-in-c Rainford *Liv* from 08; V from 11. *The Vicarage, 1 Tudor Close, Rainford, St Helens WA11 8SD* Tel (01744) 882200 Mobile 07965-554471 E-mail gough_stephen@btopenworld.com

GOULD, Alan Charles. b 26. **d** 62 **p** 63. C Bromborough *Ches* 62-67; V Audlem and Burleydam 67-80; V Knowbury and P-in-c Coreley w Doddington *Heref* 80-83; P-in-c Cound and Berrington w Betton Strange 83-91; rtd 91; Perm to Offic *Heref* and *Lich* from 91. *32 Mytton Oak Road, Shrewsbury SY3 8UD* Tel (01743) 244820

GOULD, Christine. b 52. **d** 10. NSM Darwen St Pet *Blackb* from 10. *10 King's Drive, Hoddlesden, Darwen BB3 3RB* Tel (01254) 773172 E-mail b.gould@yahoo.com

GOULD, David Robert. b 59. Cov Poly BA81. Cranmer Hall Dur 87. **d** 90 **p** 91. C Rugby *Cov* 90-93; CF 93-94; Perm to Offic *Cov* 01-05; TV Kings Norton *Birm* 05-08; V Smethwick Resurr from 08. *The Vicarage, 69 South Road, Smethwick, Warley B67 7BP* Tel 0121-558 0373 Mobile 07787-199998 E-mail davidgould1@btinternet.com

GOULD, Canon Douglas Walter. b 35. St Jo Coll Cam BA59 MA63. Ridley Hall Cam 59. **d** 61 **p** 62. C Clifton *York* 61-64; C Bridgnorth w Tasley *Heref* 64-67; C Astley Abbotts w Linley 64-67; R Acton Burnell w Pitchford 67-73; P-in-c Cound and Asst Dioc Youth Officer 68-73; P-in-c Frodesley 69-73; V Bromyard and P-in-c Stanford Bishop 73-00; P-in-c Ullingswick and Ocle Pychard 76-88; P-in-c Stoke Lacy, Moreton Jeffries w Much Cowarne etc 76-83; RD Bromyard 73-99; Chapl

Bromyard Community Hosp 73-92; Chapl Herefordshire Community Health NHS Trust 92-00; Preb Heref Cathl 83-00; rtd 00; Perm to Offic *Heref* from 00; Hon Can Dar-es-Salaam from 06. *Highwood Croft, Marden, Hereford HR1 3EW* Tel and fax (01432) 880084 E-mail waltergould@waitrose.com

GOULD, Helen Elizabeth-Anne. *See* GHEORGHIU GOULD, Helen Elizabeth-Anne

GOULD, Ms Janet. b 63. LTCL85. Westcott Ho Cam 92. **d** 95 **p** 96. C Pet St Mary Boongate 95-98; C Fleet *Guildf* 98-04; C St Mellons *Mon* 04-05; P-in-c Cardiff Ely *Llan* from 06. *St Michael and All Angels' College, 54 Cardiff Road, Llandaff, Cardiff CF5 2YJ* Tel (029) 2056 3116 E-mail jan.gould2@btinternet.com

GOULD, Jonathan George Lillico. b 58. Bris Univ LLB79. Wycliffe Hall Ox 86. **d** 89 **p** 91. Australia 89-93; Schs Worker Scripture Union Independent Schs 93-95; Perm to Offic *S'wark* 93-95; Min Hampstead St Jo Downshire Hill Prop Chpl *Lon* from 95. *The Parsonage, 64 Pilgrim's Lane, London NW3 1SN* Tel (020) 7794 8946 *or* tel and fax 7435 8404 E-mail jonathan@sjdh.org

GOULD, Mrs Pamela Rosemarie. b 41. **d** 01 **p** 02. NSM New Bilton *Cov* 01-03; Asst Chapl HM YOI Onley 01-03; NSM Clifton upon Dunsmore and Newton *Cov* 03-05; P-in-c 05-06; Perm to Offic from 07. *19 Church Road, Church Lawford, Rugby CV23 9EG* Tel (024) 7654 5745 E-mail revpamgould@aol.com

GOULD, Peter Richard. b 34. Univ of Wales BA57. Qu Coll Birm. **d** 62 **p** 63. C Rothwell *Ripon* 62-68; Chapl Agnes Stewart C of E High Sch Leeds 65-68; V Allerton Bywater *Ripon* 68-73; Asst Master S'well Minster Gr Sch 73-76; Chapl Lic Victuallers' Sch Ascot 76-93; V Aberavon H Trin *Llan* 93-99; rtd 99. *Amber Cottage, 1 Load Lane, Weston Zoyland, Bridgwater TA7 0EQ* Tel (01278) 691029

GOULD, Robert Ozburn. b 38. Williams Coll Mass BA59 St Andr Univ PhD63. **d** 78 **p** 83. NSM Edin St Columba 78-80; TV from 83; Hon Dioc Supernumerary 80-83; Hon Chapl Edin Univ 00-04. *33 Charterhall Road, Edinburgh EH9 3HS* Tel 0131-667 7230 E-mail gould@ed.ac.uk

GOULD, Susan Judith. *See* MURRAY, Mrs Susan Judith

GOULD, Walter. *See* GOULD, Canon Douglas Walter

GOULDER, Canon Catherine Helen. b 44. Hull Univ BA65 MA67 Ox Univ DipEd68. NEOC 96. **d** 98 **p** 99. NSM Sutton St Mich *York* 98-02; P-in-c Hotham and N Cave w Cliffe 02-08; Perm to Offic from 08; Can and Preb York Minster from 05. *5 Bishops Croft, Beverley HU17 8JY* Tel (01482) 880553

GOULDING, Amanda. b 53. STETS. **d** 07 **p** 08. NSM Upper Dever *Win* 07-08; NSM Win St Bart 08-10; NSM Win St Bart and St Lawr w St Swithun from 10. *Long Valley, Deane Down Drove, Littleton, Winchester SO22 6PP* Tel (01962) 884585 E-mail agoulding@btinternet.com

GOULDING, John Gilbert. b 29. Univ Coll Dur BA54 MA59. **d** 88 **p** 89. NSM Kemsing w Woodlands *Roch* 88-91; Hon Nat Moderator for Reader Tr ACCM 90-91; ABM 91-94; NSM Sevenoaks St Luke CD 91-96; Perm to Offic from 97. *Springwood, 50 Copperfields, Kemsing, Sevenoaks TN15 6QG* Tel (01732) 762558

GOULDING, Nicolas John. b 56. Southn Univ BSc78 PhD82. NTMTC 94. **d** 97 **p** 98. NSM St Bart Less *Lon* from 97; Chapl St Bart's and RLSMD Qu Mary and Westf Coll from 97; Perm to Offic *St Alb* from 99. *5 Greatfield Close, Harpenden AL5 3HP* Tel (01582) 461293 *or* (020) 7882 6128 Fax (020) 7982 6076 E-mail n.j.goulding@qmul.ac.uk

GOULDTHORPE, Rachel Carolyn. b 72. Bp Otter Coll 00. **d** 03 **p** 10. NSM Hove *Chich* 03-05; C Moulsecoomb 05-11; TV from 11. *The Vicarage, Selham Drive, Brighton BN1 9EL* Tel (01273) 601854 Mobile 07859-066557 E-mail rachelgouldthorpe@netbreeze.co.uk

GOULSTON, Jeremy Hugh. b 68. St Aid Coll Dur BA90. Ripon Coll Cuddesdon 01. **d** 03 **p** 04. C Henfield w Shermanbury and Woodmancote *Chich* 03-07; TV Wallingford *Ox* from 07. *The Vicarage, 34 Thames Mead, Crowmarsh Gifford, Wallingford OX10 8EY* Tel (01491) 837626 E-mail jgoulston@btinternet.com

GOULSTONE, Thomas Albert Kerry. b 36. Univ of Wales (Lamp) BA57. St Mich Coll Llan 57. **d** 59 **p** 60. C Llanbadarn Fawr *St D* 59-61; C Carmarthen St Pet 61-64; V 84-93; V Whitchurch w Solva and St Elvis 64-67; V Gors-las 67-76; V Burry Port and Pwll 76-84; Chapl W Wales Gen Hosp Carmarthen 84-93; Can St D Cathl 86-93; Hon Can St D Cathl from 93; RD Carmarthen 88-92; Adn Carmarthen 91-93; Dean and Lib St As Cathl 93-01; rtd 01. *25 Parc Tyisha, Burry Port SA16 0RR* Tel (01554) 832090

GOUNDREY-SMITH, Stephen John. b 67. Brighton Poly BSc88 MRPharmS89 City Univ MSc94. Aston Tr Scheme 96 Wycliffe Hall Ox BTh01. **d** 99 **p** 00. C Happisburgh, Walcott, Hempstead w Eccles etc *Nor* 99-01; Perm to Offic *Pet* 02-03; NSM Chenderit 03-08; Perm to Offic 09-11; P-in-c Chedworth, Yanworth and Stowell, Coln Rogers etc *Glouc* from 10; Hon C Northleach w Hampnett and Farmington etc from 10; Hon C Sherborne, Windrush, the Barringtons etc from 10. *The Vicarage, Cheap*

Street, Chedworth, Cheltenham GL54 4AA Tel (01285) 720392 Mobile 07771-741009 E-mail stephen@goundrey-smith.freeserve.co.uk

GOUNDRY, Canon Ralph Walter. b 31. St Chad's Coll Dur BA56. **d** 58 **p** 59. C Harton Colliery *Dur* 58-62; Prec Newc Cathl 62-65; V Sighill 65-72; V Long Benton 72-96; Hon Can Newc Cathl 94-96; rtd 96; Perm to Offic *York* 96-98. *16 Old Manor Way, Chislehurst BR7 5XS* Tel (020) 8249 9992

GOUPILLON, Mrs Jane Elizabeth. b 50. Univ of Wales (Lamp) BA92 Trin Coll Carmarthen PGCE94. St Mich Coll Llan. **d** 03 **p** 04. C Carmarthen St Dav *St D* 03-05; R Llangwm w Freystrop and Johnston from 05. *9 Cleddau Close, Llangwm, Haverfordwest SA62 4NQ* Tel (01437) 891317

GOURDIE, Mrs Janice Elizabeth. b 65. Univ of Wales (Ban) BTh04. **d** 04 **p** 05. C Botwnnog w Bryncroes w Llangwnnadl w Penllech *Ban* 04-05; C Llyn and Eifionydd 05-07; P-in-c Denio w Abererch 07-09; V from 09. *Y Ficerdy, Yr Ala, Pwllheli LL53 5BL* Tel (01758) 612305 Mobile 07969-655497 E-mail janicegourdie@hotmail.com

GOURLAY, Wendy Elizabeth. b 50. DipOT71. ERMC 08. **d** 11. NSM Boulge w Burgh, Grundisburgh and Hasketon *St E* from 11. *Tubric Cottage, The Street, Cretingham, Woodbridge IP13 7BL* Tel (01728) 685335 E-mail rev.gourlay@gmail.com

GOURLEY, Malcolm Samuel. b 37. MRPharmS58. NEOC 94. **d** 98 **p** 99. NSM Gt Smeaton w Appleton Wiske and Birkby etc *Ripon* 98-00; NSM Ainderby Steeple w Yafforth and Kirby Wiske etc 00-02; NSM Herrington, Penshaw and Shiney Row *Dur* from 02. *10 Weymouth Drive, Houghton le Spring DH4 7TQ* Tel 0191-385 4076

GOVAN, Kesh Rico. b 66. St Jo Coll Dur BA96. Cranmer Hall Dur 93. **d** 96 **p** 97. C Astley Bridge *Man* 96-00; TV Walkden and Lt Hulton 00-04; I Blessington w Kilbride, Ballymore Eustace etc *D & G* 04-07; C Uttoxeter Area *Lich* 07-10; C Rocester and Croxden w Hollington 07-10; V from 10; Chapl JCB Academy from 10. *The Vicarage, Church Lane, Rocester, Uttoxeter ST14 5JZ* Tel (01889) 590424 Mobile 07982-930384 E-mail revkesh@sky.com

GOVENDER, The Very Revd Rogers Morgan. b 60. Natal Univ BTh97. St Paul's Coll Grahamstown 83. **d** 85 **p** 86. C Overport Ch Ch S Africa 85-87; R Greyville St Mary 88-92; R Hayfields St Matt 93-98; Adn Pietermaritzburg 97-98; R Berea St Thos 99-00; P-in-c Didsbury Ch Ch *Man* 01-06; P-in-c Withington St Chris 03-06; AD Withington 04-06; Dean Man from 06. *1 Booth Clibborn Court, Salford M7 4PJ* Tel 0161-792 2801 *or* 833 2220 Fax 839 6218 E-mail dean@manchestercathedral.com

GOVIER, Howard Dudley. b 39. Wycliffe Hall Ox BA99 MA Solicitor 62. SWMTC 07. **d** 09 **p** 10. NSM Ottery St Mary, Alfington, W Hill, Tipton etc *Ex* from 09. *Ström House, 3 Seafield Avenue, Exmouth EX8 3NJ* Tel (01395) 265803 E-mail hdjg@govier.go-plus.net

GOW, Iain Douglas. b 60. Denver Univ USA BA83 MIM85. Trin Coll Bris MA94. **d** 94 **p** 95. C Kenilworth St Jo *Cov* 94-97; C Birm St Martin w Bordesley St Andr 97-05; AD Birm City Cen 02-04; New Zealand from 05. *2/82 Knights Road, Rothesay Bay, North Shore, Auckland 1311, New Zealand* Tel (0064) (9) 478 4894

GOW, Peter Draffin. b 52. Bede Coll Dur BEd76. St Jo Coll Nottm 83. **d** 85. C Kingston Hill St Paul *S'wark* 85-86; rtd 86. *Chatsworth Wing, Royal Hospital for Neuro-disability, London SW15 3SW* Tel (020) 8788 5158 E-mail petergow@waacis.edex.co.uk

GOWDEY, Michael Cragg. b 32. Oriel Coll Ox BA56 MA58 Keele Univ CertEd73. Qu Coll Birm. **d** 58 **p** 59. C Ashbourne w Mapleton and Clifton *Derby* 58-63; V Chellaston 63-69; Asst Chapl Ellesmere Coll 69-74; Chapl Trent Coll Nottm 74-81; Educn Chapl *Worc* 81-97; Chapl K Edw Sixth Form Coll Worc 81-97; rtd 97; P-in-c Beeley and Edensor *Derby* 97-02; Perm to Offic from 02. *18 Moorhall Estate, Bakewell DE45 1FP* Tel (01629) 814121

GOWEN, John Frank. b 30. **d** 87 **p** 89. Aux Min Lucale Gp and Cregagh *D & D* 87-91; Lic to Offic 89-99; Aux Min Stormont 99-01; Aux Min Knock 01-05; rtd 05. *36 Downshire Road, Belfast BT6 9JL* Tel (028) 9070 1640 Mobile 07815-301818 E-mail jgowen212@btinternet.com

GOWER, Canon Christopher Raymond. b 45. Nottm Univ BA73 Heythrop Coll Lon MA96 Univ of Wales MTh02 FRSA84. St Jo Coll Nottm 70. **d** 73 **p** 74. C Hounslow H Trin *Lon* 73-76; Hon C N Greenford All Hallows 76-77; P-in-c Willesden Green St Gabr 77-83; P-in-c Brondesbury St Anne w Kilburn H Trin 81-82; Perm to Offic 82-84; P-in-c Yiewsley 84-96; R St Marylebone w H Trin 97-09; C St Marylebone St Cypr 99-02; Preb St Paul's Cathl 07-09; rtd 09; Hon Can Ilesa from 04. *25 Newton Lane, Romsey SO51 8GX* Tel (01794) 514578

GOWER, Denys Victor. b 33. Cant Sch of Min 85. **d** 87 **p** 88. NSM Gillingham H Trin *Roch* 87-91; NSM Gillingham St Aug 89-91; C Perry Street 91-93; P-in-c Wateringbury w Teston and W Farleigh 93-96; R 96-00; rtd 00; Ind Chapl *Roch* from 02; Perm to Offic *Roch* from 00 and *Cant* 03-09; Hon Chapl Medway NHS Foundn Trust from 05; PV Roch Cathl from 07. *4 Locarno*

Avenue, Gillingham ME8 6ET Tel (01634) 375765 Mobile 07985-781161
GOWER, Nigel Plested. b 37. SS Coll Cam BA62 MA65 Lon Univ PGCE68. Ridley Hall Cam 61. **d** 63 **p** 64. C Walthamstow St Jo *Chelmsf* 63-66; CMS Nigeria 67-78; P-in-c Loscoe *Derby* 78-79; V 79-88; RD Heanor 84-88; R Bamford 88-98; Dioc World Development Officer 90-96; P-in-c Bradwell 96-98; Assoc P Alfreton Deanery 98-02; rtd 02; Perm to Offic *Heref* 02-08. *New Cottage, Llanbister Road, Llandrindod Wells LD1 5UW* Tel (01547) 550318
GOWER, Miss Patricia Ann. b 44. Wilson Carlile Coll IDC79 Sarum & Wells Th Coll 88. **d** 88 **p** 94. Chapl Bris Univ 88-91; Hon Par Dn Clifton St Paul 88-91; Par Dn Spondon *Derby* 91-94; C 94-95; P-in-c Hatton 95-98; Asst Chapl HM Pris Sudbury 95-98; Chapl 98-04; rtd 04; Perm to Offic *Derby* from 04. *19 Heronswood Drive, Spondon, Derby DE21 7AX* Tel (01332) 671031
GOWER, Miss Paulette Rose-Mary de Garis. b 70. Plymouth Univ BEd93. Cranmer Hall Dur 01. **d** 03 **p** 04. C Shrewsbury St Geo w Greenfields *Lich* 03-07; TV Hawarden *St As* from 07. *32 Well House Drive, Penymynydd, Chester CH4 0LB* Tel (01244) 540177 E-mail paulettegower@tiscali.co.uk
GOWER, Mrs Sarah Catherine. b 63. Ex Univ BA84 Cam Univ BTh09. Westcott Ho Cam 07. **d** 09 **p** 10. C St Neots *Ely* from 09. *56 Stone Hill, St Neots PE19 6AA* Tel (01480) 476739 E-mail sarahcgower@btinternet.com
GOWER, Archdeacon of. See WILLIAMS, The Ven Robert John
GOWERS, Nicholas Stephen. b 78. Jes Coll Cam MEng02 MA05. Oak Hill Th Coll MTh08. **d** 08. C Ex St Leon w H Trin from 08. *63 Cedars Road, Exeter EX2 1NB* Tel (01392) 286998 E-mail nick@stleonardsexeter.org.uk
GOWING, Wilfred Herbert. b 50. QUB BSc72. NEOC 03. **d** 06 **p** 07. NSM Ripon H Trin from 06. *Littlemead, 20 Springfield Rise, Great Ouseburn, York YO26 9SE* Tel (01423) 331177 Fax 331178 E-mail wilfgowing@btinternet.com
GOWING-CUMBER, Alexander John. b 72. Fitzw Coll Cam MA00 Moorlands Th Coll BA94. Ridley Hall Cam 98. **d** 00 **p** 03. C Vange *Chelmsf* 00-02; C Rayleigh 02-05; TV Grays Thurrock from 05. *The Vicarage, Clockhouse Lane, Grays RM16 6YW* Tel (01375) 482252 E-mail fralexgc@aol.com
GOYMOUR, Mrs Joanna Leigh. b 58. Reading Univ BA79. Dioc OLM tr scheme 99. **d** 02 **p** 03. OLM Bures w Assington and Lt Cornard *St E* from 02. *Dorking Tye House, Dorking Tye, Bures CO8 5JY* Tel (01787) 227494 E-mail jo@acgoymour.freeserve.co.uk
GOYMOUR, Michael Edwyn. b 29. Selw Coll Cam BA51 McGill Univ Montreal BD53. Montreal Dioc Th Coll 51 Wells Th Coll 53. **d** 53 **p** 54. C Bury St Edmunds St Jo *St E* 53-56; C Ipswich St Bart 56-60; R Gamlingay *Ely* 60-68; rtd 92; Perm to Offic *Ely* from 92 and *Pet* 92-06. *56 Church Drive, Orton Waterville, Peterborough PE2 5HE* Tel (01733) 231535
GRACE, Capt David Leonard. b 55. Wilson Carlile Coll 89 Ripon Coll Cuddesdon 97. **d** 99 **p** 00. CA from 92; C St Leonards and St Ives *Win* 99-04; V 04-09; Chapl Basingstoke and N Hants NHS Foundation Trust from 09; Chapl Hants Partnership NHS Trust from 09. *The North Hampshire Hospital, Aldermaston Road, Basingstoke RG24 9NA* Tel (01256) 473202
GRACE, Mrs Irene. b 36. Nottm Univ BSc58. Guildf Dioc Min Course 96. **d** 98 **p** 99. OLM Stoneleigh *Guildf* 98-06; Perm to Offic from 06. *33 Woodstone Avenue, Stoneleigh, Epsom KT17 2JS* Tel (020) 8393 7280
GRACE, Kenneth. b 24. Leeds Univ BA49. Wycliffe Hall Ox 62. **d** 63 **p** 64. C Tonge w Alkrington *Man* 63-66; R Thwing and V Wold Newton *York* 66-70; Chapl St Andr Sch Worthing 70-76; R Berwick w Selmeston and Alciston *Chich* 76-81; P-in-c Kingston Buci 81-85; R Westbourne 85-90; rtd 90; Perm to Offic *Chich* from 90. *5 Ramsay Hall, 11-13 Byron Road, Worthing BN11 3HN* Tel (01903) 230611
GRACE, Louise Sarah. b 68. Girton Coll Cam BA89. Ripon Coll Cuddesdon BA97 Ch Div Sch of Pacific 97. **d** 98 **p** 99. C Wordsley *Worc* 98-02; R Teme Valley N from 03; RD Stourport from 07. *The Rectory, Lindridge, Tenbury Wells WR15 8JQ* Tel (01584) 881331 E-mail revgrace@hotmail.co.uk
GRACE, Richard Maurice. b 29. St Chad's Coll Dur BA53. Chich Th Coll 53. **d** 55 **p** 56. C Toxteth Park St Agnes *Liv* 55-58; C Wolverhampton St Pet *Lich* 58-62; V W Bromwich St Fran 62-78; P-in-c Salt 78-84; P-in-c Sandon w Burston 82-84; V Salt and Sandon w Burston 84-93; rtd 94. *Little Owls, 1 Trinity Close, Crewe CW2 8FD* Tel (01270) 662221
GRACIE, Anthony Johnstone. b 25. Ch Coll Cam BA48 MA51. Linc Th Coll 57. **d** 59 **p** 60. C Edgbaston St Geo *Birm* 59-62; R Lyndon w Manton and Martinsthorpe *Pet* 62-76; R N Luffenham 66-76; V Odiham w S Warnborough and Long Sutton *Win* 76-85; Perm to Offic *Bris* 85-88; rtd 88. *Colt Corner, Horn Lane, East Hendred, Wantage OX12 8LD* Tel (01235) 821509 E-mail a.gracie@btconnect.com
GRACIE, Canon Bryan John. b 45. MBE06. Open Univ BA81. AKC67. **d** 68 **p** 69. C Whipton *Ex* 68-72; Chapl St Jo Sch Tiffield 72-73; Chapl HM Borstal Stoke Heath 74-78; Asst Chapl HM

Pris Liv 74; Chapl HM Youth Cust Cen Feltham 78-85; Chapl HM Pris Birm 85-10; Hon Can Birm Cathl 05-10; rtd 10. *346 Eachelhurst Road, Sutton Coldfield B76 1ER* Tel 0121-351 6532
GRAEBE, Canon Denys Redford. b 26. Qu Coll Cam BA48 MA51. Westcott Ho Cam 50. **d** 51 **p** 52. C Hitchin St Mary *St Alb* 51-57; R Gt Parndon *Chelmsf* 57-72; V Norton *St Alb* 72-83; R Kimpton w Ayot St Lawrence 83-92; RD Wheathampstead 87-92; Hon Can St Alb Abbey 90-92; rtd 92; Perm to Offic *St E* from 92. *5 Sancroft Way, Fressingfield, Eye IP21 5QN* Tel (01379) 588178
GRAESSER, Adrian Stewart. b 42. Tyndale Hall Bris 63. **d** 67 **p** 68. C Nottingham St Jude *S'well* 67-69; C Slaithwaite w E Scammonden *Wakef* 69-72; CF 72-75; V Earl's Heaton *Wakef* 75-81; R Norton Fitzwarren *B & W* 81-86; R Bickenhill w Elmdon *Birm* 86-90; R Elmdon St Nic 90-00; P-in-c Dolton *Ex* 00-05; P-in-c Iddesleigh w Dowland 00-05; P-in-c Monkokehampton 00-05; RD Torrington 02-05; rtd 05; Perm to Offic *Worc* from 09. *7 Mortlake Drive, Martley, Worcester WR6 6QU* Tel (01886) 888628 E-mail adrian.graesser@sky.com
GRAHAM, Alan Robert. b 44. St Edm Hall Ox BA67 MA71. St Steph Ho Ox BA70. **d** 70 **p** 71. C Clifton All SS *Bris* 70-74; C Tadley St Pet *Win* 74-77; P-in-c Upper Clatford w Goodworth Clatford 77-79; R Abbotts Ann and Upper and Goodworth Clatford 79-84; V Lyndhurst and Emery Down 84-92; P-in-c Over Wallop w Nether Wallop 92-02; rtd 02. *44 New Forest Drive, Brockenhurst SO42 7QW* Tel (01590) 622324 E-mail agwvgraham@waitrose.com
GRAHAM, Alexander. See GRAHAM, The Rt Revd Andrew Alexander Kenny
GRAHAM, Alfred. b 34. Bris Univ BA57. Tyndale Hall Bris. **d** 58 **p** 59. C Chaddesden St Mary *Derby* 58-61; C Bickenhill w Elmdon *Birm* 61-64; V Kirkdale St Lawr *Liv* 64-70; V Stapleford *S'well* 70-83; V Burton Joyce w Bulcote 83-95; V Burton Joyce w Bulcote and Stoke Bardolph 95-97; rtd 97; Perm to Offic *S'well* 03-11. *16 Meadow View, Clitheroe BB7 2NT* Tel (01200) 426805
GRAHAM, Alistair. See GRAHAM, Michael Alistair
✠GRAHAM, The Rt Revd Andrew Alexander Kenny (Alec). b 29. St Jo Coll Ox BA52 MA57 Lambeth DD95. Ely Th Coll 53. **d** 55 **p** 56 **c** 77. C Hove All SS *Chich* 55-58; Chapl, Lect Th, and Tutor Worc Coll Ox 58-70; Warden Linc Th Coll 70-77; Can and Preb Linc Cathl 70-77; Suff Bp Bedford *St Alb* 77-81; Bp Newc 81-97; Chmn ACCM 84-87; Chmn Doctrine Commn 87-95; rtd 97; Hon Asst Bp Carl from 97. *Fell End, Butterwick, Penrith CA10 2QQ* Tel (01931) 713147
GRAHAM, Canon Anthony Nigel. b 40. Univ of Wales (Abth) BA62 CertEd70. Ripon Hall Ox 62. **d** 64 **p** 65. C Heref H Trin 64-67; C Birm St Martin 67-69; C Selly Oak St Mary 71-75; V Edgbaston SS Mary and Ambrose 75-83; CMS Miss Partner Nigeria 84-88; Hon Can Jos from 88; V Highworth w Sevenhampton and Inglesham etc *Bris* 88-95; RD Highworth 93-95; P-in-c Coalpit Heath 95-99; V 99-00; rtd 00. *19 Dormer Road, Cheltenham GL51 0AX*
GRAHAM, Anthony Stanley David. b 34. SS Coll Cam BA56 MA60. Cuddesdon Coll 58. **d** 60 **p** 61. C Welwyn Garden City *St Alb* 60-64; Asst Chapl Ipswich Sch 64-65; C Margate St Jo Cant 65-68; Chr Aid Area Sec *Chich* 68-99; rtd 99; Perm to Offic *Chich* from 05. *48 Springfield Road, Crawley RH11 8AH* Tel (01293) 526279 E-mail tonygraham@dsl.pipex.com
GRAHAM, Bruce. See GRAHAM, William Bruce
GRAHAM, Christopher John. b 55. EMMTC. **d** 03 **p** 04. NSM Ripley *Derby* 03-08; NSM Ilkeston St Jo from 08. *41 Lathkill Drive, Ripley DE5 8HW* Tel (01773) 747223 E-mail chris@graham-family.freeserve.co.uk
GRAHAM, Clifton Gordon. b 53. ARCM72 GRSM74 FRCO75 Coll of Ripon & York St Jo PGCE76. St Steph Ho Ox 90. **d** 92 **p** 93. C Northfield *Birm* 92-93; C Perry Beeches 93-97; P-in-c S Yardley St Mich 97-00; V 00-06; Chapl Birm City Univ 06-10; Chapl Ex Univ from 10. *2 Velwell Road, Exeter EX4 4LE* Tel (01392) 411888 E-mail c.g.graham@blueyonder.co.uk *or* c.g.graham@exeter.ac.uk
GRAHAM, David. See GRAHAM, George David
GRAHAM, Canon Frederick Lawrence. b 35. TCD BA65. CITC 66. **d** 66 **p** 67. C Belfast St Matt *Conn* 66-69; TV Chelmsley Wood *Birm* 69-73; Ch of Ireland Youth Officer 73-78; Bp's C Stoneyford *Conn* 78-88; Bp's C Fahan Lower and Upper *D & R* 88-91; Can Raphoe Cathl 90-01; I Donagheady 91-01; Can Derry Cathl 95-01; rtd 01. *Thuma Mina, 80 Altnahinch Road, Loughguile, Ballymena BT44 9JS* Tel (028) 2764 1016 E-mail fredkate@btinternet.com
GRAHAM, Frederick Louis Roth. b 20. Selw Coll Cam BA47 MA49. Ridley Hall Cam 48. **d** 50 **p** 51. C Shirley *Win* 50-53; R Old Trafford St Jo *Man* 53-61; R Wombwell *Sheff* 61-71; V Thorne 71-77; P-in-c Chilton-super-Polden w Edington *B & W* 77-82; P-in-c Catcott 77-82; V W Poldens 82-86; rtd 86; Perm to Offic *Win* 86-08. *Flat 11, Manormead, Tilford Road, Hindhead GU26 6RA* Tel (01428) 602500

GRAHAM, George David. b 42. Jes Coll Cam BA64 MA68. St Jo Coll Nottm LTh Lon Coll of Div 66. **d** 71 **p** 72. C Corby St Columba *Pet* 71-74; C Deptford St Jo *S'wark* 74-77; P-in-c Deptford St Pet 77-82; C-in-c Wheatley Park St Paul CD *Sheff* 82-87; TV Dunstable *St Alb* 87-92; V Bromley Common St Luke *Roch* 92-02; R Hayes from 02. *The Rectory, Hayes Street, Bromley BR2 7LH* Tel (020) 8462 1373

GRAHAM, Canon George Edgar. b 55. QUB BA91. Sarum & Wells Th Coll 74 CITC 77. **d** 78 **p** 79. C Lisburn Ch Ch *Conn* 78-81; C Mossley 81-83; I Broomhedge 83-91; I Derriaghy w Colin 91-96; I Ballywalter 96-05; I Dunluce from 05; Can Conn Cathl from 05; Preb from 06. *Dunluce Rectory, 17 Priestland Road, Bushmills BT57 8QP* Tel (028) 2073 1221 *or* 2073 0537 E-mail rectordunluce@btconnect.com *or* adminoluce@btconnect.com

GRAHAM, George Gordon. b 17. OBE96. St Chad's Coll Dur BA48 MSc71. **d** 50 **p** 51. C Luton Ch Ch *St Alb* 50-53; C Bakewell *Derby* 53-56; P-in-c Wheatley Hill *Dur* 56-69; V Hunwick 69-88; Chapl Homelands Hosp Dur 80-94; Chapl Bishop Auckland Hospitals NHS Trust 94-98; Chapl S Durham Healthcare NHS Trust 98-02; rtd 88. *3 The Willows, Bishop Auckland DL14 7HH* Tel (01388) 602758

GRAHAM, George Gordon. b 34. Harvard Univ BA55 MDiv JD71. **d** 96 **p** 97. Aux Min Seapatrick *D & D* 97-99; Aux Min Lecale Gp 99-03; P-in-c Castlewellan w Kilcoo 03-06. *10 Castlebridge Court, Newcastle BT33 0RF* Tel (028) 4062 2612 *or* 4372 6175 E-mail gorbargrah@aol.com

GRAHAM, Gordon. *See* GRAHAM, Prof Lawrence Gordon

GRAHAM, Gordon Cecil. b 31. JP. Ch Coll Cam BA53 MA57. Ripon Hall Ox 53. **d** 55 **p** 56. C Didsbury St Jas and Em *Man* 55-58; C Rochdale 58-60; R Heaton Mersey 60-67; Chapl Hulme Gr Sch Oldham 67-74; Lic to Offic *Ches* 72-92; rtd 92. *21 The Crescent, Davenport, Stockport SK3 8SL* Tel 0161-483 6011

GRAHAM, Harry John. b 52. Magd Coll Cam BA75 MA86. Trin Coll Bris BA94. **d** 96 **p** 97. C Walkden and Lt Hulton *Man* 96-99; Chapl Salford Coll of Tech 96-99; P-in-c Edgeside *Man* 99-00; TV Rossendale Middle Valley 00-02; Gen Sec Miss without Borders (UK) Ltd from 02. *69 Eyre Court, Finchley Road, London NW8 9TX* Tel (020) 7586 8336 *or* 7940 1370 Fax 7403 7348 E-mail info u@mwbi.org

GRAHAM, Ian Maxwell. b 50. CertEd76. Chich Th Coll 86. **d** 88 **p** 89. C Middlesbrough St Thos *York* 88-90; C Stainton-in-Cleveland 90-93; V Hemlington 93-00; V Grangetown from 00. *The Vicarage, Clynes Road, Grangetown, Middlesbrough TS6 7LY* Tel (01642) 453704 E-mail casahild@hotmail.com

GRAHAM, James Hamilton. b 54. Trin Hall Cam BA76 MA80 Solicitor 78. Ripon Coll Cuddesdon BA83 MA87. **d** 84 **p** 85. C Harlescott *Lich* 84-88; C Adderley 88-93; C Drayton in Hales 88-93; C Moreton Say 88-93; R Hodnet w Weston under Redcastle 93-00; RD Hodnet 97-00; V Eccleshall from 00. *The Vicarage, Church Street, Eccleshall, Stafford ST21 6BY* Tel (01785) 850351

GRAHAM, John Galbraith. b 21. MBE05. K Coll Cam BA43 MA46. Ely Th Coll 46. **d** 48 **p** 49. C E Dulwich St Jo *S'wark* 48-49; Chapl St Chad's Coll *Dur* 49-52; C Aldershot St Mich *Guildf* 52-55; C-in-c Beaconsfield St Mich CD *Ox* 55-62; Chapl Reading Univ 62-72; C Pimlico St Pet w Westmr Ch Ch *Lon* 72-74; R Houghton w Wyton *Ely* 74-78; rtd 86; Lic to Offic *St E* from 86; Perm to Offic *Ely* from 93. *31 Rectory Lane, Somersham, Huntingdon PE28 3EL* Tel (01487) 842737 E-mail johngraham@waitrose.com

GRAHAM, Kevin. *See* GRAHAM, Terence Kevin Declan

GRAHAM, Prof Lawrence Gordon. b 49. OBE96. St Andr Univ MA Dur Univ MA PhD75 FRSE99. St Steph Ho Ox 90. **d** 05. Regius Prof Moral Philosophy Aber Univ 96-05; C Aberdeen St Mary 05-06; Prof Philosophy and Arts Princeton Th Sem USA from 06. *Princeton Theological Seminary, PO Box 821, Princeton NJ 08542, USA* Tel (001) (609) 497 7849

GRAHAM, Michael. b 51. CITC BTh95. **d** 95 **p** 96. C Cork St Fin Barre's Union *C, C & R* 95-98; Min Can Cork Cathl 97-98; I Drogheda w Ardee, Collon and Termonfeckin *Arm* from 98; Ch of Ireland Internet Co-ord 99-05; I Kilsaran w Drumcar, Dunleer and Dunany from 07. *St Peter's Rectory, Drogheda, Co Louth, Republic of Ireland* Tel (00353) (41) 987 0073 *or* 983 8791 E-mail office.drogheda@armagh.anglican.org

GRAHAM, Michael Alistair. b 47. CITC 67. **d** 70 **p** 71. C Dublin Clontarf *D & G* 71-75; C Ox St Mich w St Martin and All SS 76-78; P-in-c Dublin Sandymount *D & G* 80-86; I Stillorgan w Blackrock 86-00; Soc Worker E Health Bd Dub 00-09; I Mullingar, Portnashangan, Moyliscar, Kilbixy etc *M & K* from 09. *The Rectory, Jaol's Hill, Mullingar, Co Westmeath, Republic of Ireland* Tel (00353) (44) 934 8376 Mobile 87-787 0985 E-mail agkilliney@hotmail.com

GRAHAM, Nigel. *See* GRAHAM, Canon Anthony Nigel

GRAHAM, Ms Olivia Josephine. b 56. UEA BA84. SAOMC 94. **d** 97 **p** 98. NSM Wheatley *Ox* 97-98; C Risborough 98-01; TV Burnham w Dropmore, Hitcham and Taplow 01-07; Par Development Adv from 07. *Downs View, High Street, Long Wittenham, Abingdon OX14 4QD* Tel (01865) 407062 E-mail graham.glenny@virgin.net

GRAHAM, Peter. b 32. CEng MIMechE. **d** 86 **p** 87. NSM Minchinhampton *Glouc* 86-96; Perm to Offic 96-97; NSM Alderminster and Halford *Cov* 98-02; NSM Butlers Marston and the Pillertons w Ettington 98-02; rtd 02; Perm to Offic *Cov* 02-07. *21 Brick Meadow, Bishops Castle SY9 5DH* Tel (01588) 638176

GRAHAM, Richard William. b 63. Poly of Wales BA86 ACA91. Trin Coll Bris 03. **d** 05 **p** 06. C Savernake *Sarum* 05-09; TV Hemel Hempstead *St Alb* from 09. *St Barnabas Vicarage, Everest Way, Hemel Hempstead HP2 4HY* Tel (01442) 253681 E-mail randmgraham@hotmail.com

GRAHAM, Ronald Fleming. b 33. Edin Th Coll 67. **d** 69 **p** 69. Chapl St Andr Cathl 69-73; R Glas Gd Shep 73-75; R Glas Gd Shep and Ascension 75-76; CF (TA) 74-76; R Peterhead *Ab* 76-80; Chapl RAF 76-80; Bp's Dom Chapl *Arg* 80-84; Itinerant Priest 80-84; R Lanark *Glas* 84-89; R Douglas 84-89; rtd 89; Hon C Glas St Ninian 90-98. *Address temp unknown*

GRAHAM, Ronald Gaven. b 27. **d** 90 **p** 91. NSM Adare w Kilpeacon and Croom *L & K* 90-92; Dioc Info Officer (Limerick) 91-95; NSM Rathkeale w Askeaton and Kilcornan 92-96; NSM Wexford w Ardcolm and Killurin *C & O* 97-03; rtd 03. *8 Chestnut Grove, Fernyhill, Killinick, Co Wexford, Republic of Ireland* Tel (00353) (53) 915 8369 E-mail rvgraham@eircom.net

GRAHAM, Roy Richard Arthur. b 39. Lon Univ BD63 Open Univ BA78. ALCD62. **d** 63 **p** 64. C Southsea St Jude *Portsm* 63-66; C Morden *S'wark* 66-70; V Tittensor *Lich* 70-79; R Hurworth and Dinsdale w Sockburn *Dur* 79-02; rtd 02. *The School House, Eaglesfield, Lockerbie DG11 3PA* Tel (01461) 500499 E-mail rragraham@onenet.co.uk

GRAHAM, Stig. *See* GRAHAM, William Stig

GRAHAM, Mrs Susan Lochrie. b 46. Sheff Univ PhD01. Yale Div Sch MDiv90. **d** 90 **p** 91. Cow Head Par Canada 90-92; P-in-c Kingsway All SS, St Hilary, Bolton etc 92-96; NSM Ilminster and Distr *B & W* 96-97; Perm to Offic 97-03; NSM Glastonbury w Meare 03-08; NSM Combe Martin, Berrynarbor, Lynton, Brendon etc *Ex* from 08. *The Rectory, Lee Road, Lynton EX35 6BP* Tel (01598) 753251 E-mail s.l.graham@exeter.ac.uk

GRAHAM, Terence Kevin Declan. b 67. NUI BSc89 TCD BTh02. CITC 99. **d** 02 **p** 03. C Knock *D & D* 02-05; I Carrowdore w Millisle 05-09; I Movilla from 09. *34 Hollymount Road, Newtownards BT23 7DL* Tel (028) 9181 0787 *or* 9181 9794 Mobile 07964-663745 E-mail kevtherev@movilla-abbey.com

GRAHAM, Mrs Wendy. b 41. **d** 01 **p** 02. OLM Chalfont St Peter *Ox* from 01. *The Box, Hillfield Road, Chalfont St Peter, Gerrards Cross SL9 0DU* Tel (01753) 885066

GRAHAM, William Bruce. b 37. Univ of New Mexico BA60 Yale Univ MDiv90. **d** 90 **p** 91. Canada 90-97 and from 09; P-in-c W Poldens *B & W* 97-08; P-in-c Greinton 05-08; RD Glastonbury 03-08. *17635 Pierrefonds Boulevard Apt 5, Pierrefonds QC H9J 3L1, Canada* Tel (001) (514) 696 4797 E-mail wbg@bell.net

GRAHAM, William Stig. b 53. Newc Univ BSc75. NEOC. **d** 99 **p** 00. C W Acklam *York* 99-02; Chapl Myton Hamlet Hospice from 02. *2 Winyates Road, Lighthorne Heath, Leamington Spa CV33 9TU* Tel (01926) 640811 *or* 492518 E-mail stiggraham@netscape.net *or* stig.graham@mytonhospice.org

GRAHAM-BROWN, John George Francis. b 34. CA60. Wycliffe Hall Ox 63. **d** 63 **p** 64. C Darlington St Cuth *Dur* 63-67; C Rufforth w Moor Monkton and Hessay *York* 67-73; Sec York Dioc Redundant Chs Uses Cttee 69-89; Asst Sec DBF 73-84; Dioc Past Cttee 73-89; Hon C York St Barn 73-85; P-in-c 85-92; TV Marfleet 92-99; rtd 99; Perm to Offic *St Alb* from 00. *40 Hunters Oak, Hemel Hempstead HP2 7SW* Tel (01482) 402226 E-mail f.graham-brown@tinyonline.co.uk

GRAHAM-ORLEBAR, Ian Henry Gaunt. b 26. New Coll Ox BA49 MA56. Cuddesdon Coll 60. **d** 62 **p** 63. C Hemel Hempstead *St Alb* 62-70; R Barton-le-Cley w Higham Gobion 70-80; R Barton-le-Cley w Higham Gobion and Hexton 80-92; rtd 92; Perm to Offic *Ex* from 94. *Hole Farm, Bickington, Newton Abbot TQ12 6PE* Tel (01626) 821298

GRAINGER, Canon Bruce. b 37. Nottm Univ BA62 Hull Univ MA83. Cuddesdon Coll. **d** 64 **p** 65. C Bingley All SS *Bradf* 64-67; Chapl K Sch Cant 67-72; Hon Min Can Cant Cathl 69-72; V Baildon *Bradf* 72-88; V Oxenhope 88-04; Hon Can Bradf Cathl 84-04; Dir of Ords 88-96; Dioc Ecum Officer 96-04; Tutor Bradf Univ 99-03; RD S Craven 02-03; rtd 04; Perm to Offic *Bradf* from 04. *Aspen Lodge, Low Shann Farm, High Spring Gardens Lane, Keighley BD20 6LN* Tel (01535) 611989 E-mail bruce@graspen.gotadsl.co.uk

GRAINGER, Horace. b 34. Carl Dioc Tr Course 82. **d** 85 **p** 86. NSM Barrow St Matt *Carl* 85-89; C Carl St Herbert w St Steph 89-91; TV Penrith w Newton Reigny and Plumpton Wall 91-96; P-in-c Holme Cultram St Mary 96-00; P-in-c Holme Cultram St Cuth 96-00; rtd 00; NSM Barrow St Aid *Carl* 01-03; NSM S Barrow from 03. *15 Maylands Avenue, Barrow-in-Furness LA13 0AL* Tel (01229) 828603

GRAINGER, Ian. b 66. Cranmer Hall Dur 89. **d** 92 **p** 93. C Whitehaven *Carl* 92-94; C Walney Is 94-97; P-in-c Barrow St Aid 97-02; V Camerton, Seaton and W Seaton from 02. *The Vicarage, Ling Beck Park, Seaton, Workington CA14 1JQ* Tel (01900) 602162 E-mail revd.ian@grainger89.fsnet.co.uk

GRAINGER, Michael Noel Howard. b 40. Trin Coll Carmarthen. **d** 91 **p** 92. NSM Haverfordwest St Martin w Lambston *St D* 91-95; V Maenclochog and New Moat etc 95-05; rtd 05. *1 impasse Edith Piaf, Kerbregent, Plumeliau 56930, France* Tel (0033) 2 97 51 91 28 Mobile 8 79 39 24 61

GRAINGER, Prof Roger Beckett. b 34. Birm Univ MA70 Leeds Univ PhD79 Lon Univ BA80 DD90 Huddersfield Poly MPhil88 Bris Univ PhD92 Leeds Metrop Univ BSc98 PhD(Educ)01 Lambeth STh83 FRSA85 FRAI85 CPsychol96 AFBPsS99. Lich Th Coll 64. **d** 66 **p** 69. C W Bromwich All SS *Lich* 66-68; C Walsall 69-73; Chapl Stanley Royd Hosp Wakef 73-90; rtd 91; Hon C Wakef St Jo from 93; Dioc Drama Adv from 98; Prof Extraordinary Potchefstroom Univ S Africa from 01; Hon Chapl Wakef Cathl from 02. *7 Park Grove, Horbury, Wakefield WF4 6EE* Tel (01924) 272742

GRAINGER-SMITH, James Edward. b 71. Nottm Univ BA92. St Jo Coll Nottm MA02. **d** 02 **p** 03. C Hordle *Win* 02-07; R Beeford w Frodingham and Foston *York* from 07; P-in-c Brandesburton and Leven w Catwick from 11. *The Rectory, 11 Glebe Gardens, Beeford, Driffield YO25 8BF* Tel (01262) 488042 E-mail j.j.grainger-smith@lineone.net

GRANDEY, Frederick Michael. b 56. St Jo Coll Ox MA83 BM, BCh84 Newc Univ MSc98 MRCGP90 FFPH04. St Jo Coll Nottm 06. **d** 09 **p** 10. C Haxby and Wigginton *York* from 09. *5 Back Lane, Wigginton, York YO32 2ZH* Tel (01904) 765144 E-mail m.grandey@talk21.com

GRANGE (née FEATHERSTON), Mrs Alice Margery. b 55. Teesside Univ BA97. NEOC. **d** 99 **p** 00. C Pickering w Lockton and Levisham *York* 99-02; TV Crosslacon *Carl* 02-07; P-in-c Middlesbrough St Agnes *York* from 07; Chapl S Tees Hosps NHS Trust from 07. *St Agnes' Vicarage, 1 Broughton Avenue, Middlesbrough TS4 3PX* Tel (01642) 321770 E-mail margery-grange@sky.com

GRANNER, Mrs Linda. b 52. Westmr Coll Ox BTh00. WMMTC 01. **d** 03 **p** 04. NSM Bearwood *Birm* 03-06; C Edgbaston St Bart 06-08; C Edgbaston St Geo 06-08; P-in-c Hobs Moat from 08. *St Mary's House, 30 Hobs Meadow, Solihull B92 8PN* Tel 0121-743 4955 E-mail l.granner@sky.com

GRANT, Alistair Sims. b 25. SS Coll Cam BA49 MA53. Sarum Th Coll 49. **d** 51 **p** 52. C Northampton St Jas *Pet* 51-54; C Conisbrough *Sheff* 54-57; Org Sec (E Anglia) CECS 57-58; V Haddenham *Ely* 58-65; rtd 90; Perm to Offic *Ely* 90-00. *56 The Causeway, Burwell, Cambridge CB25 0DU* Tel (01638) 741670

GRANT, Amanda Rose Anna. b 63. Ripon Coll Cuddesdon 09. **d** 11. C N Hants Downs *Win* from 11. *Bartons, Weston Patrick, Basingstoke RG25 2NX* Tel 07745-130033 (mobile) E-mail amandagrant1@hotmail.com

GRANT, Andrew James. b 68. Cranmer Hall Dur 09. **d** 11. C Bramham *York* from 11. *The Vicarage, Church Causeway, Thorp Arch, Wetherby LS23 7AE* Tel (01937) 541272 Mobile 07519-423552 E-mail andygrant1968@btinternet.com

GRANT, Canon Andrew Richard. b 40. Univ of Wales BA62. Chich Th Coll 63. **d** 65 **p** 66. C Kennington St Jo *S'wark* 65-68; Hon C 70-72; Hon C Stockwell Green St Andr 68-70; V Nunhead St Antony 72-79; TR N Lambeth 79-92; USPG Ghana 92-99; Hon Can Kumasi from 02; C Paddington St Jo w St Mich *Lon* 99-01; P-in-c Stockwell St Mich *S'wark* 01-03; P-in-c Stockwell St Andr and St Mich 03-04; V 04-09; rtd 09; Perm to Offic *S'wark* from 09. *6 Bromley College, London Road, Bromley BR1 1PE* Tel (020) 8695 7348 Mobile 07903-369983

GRANT, Antony Richard Charles. b 34. Ch Ch Ox BA59 MA64. Coll of Resurr Mirfield 72. **d** 74 **p** 75. C St John's Wood *Lon* 74-77; Novice CR 77-79; CR from 79; Lic to Offic *Wakef* from 80; rtd 99. *House of the Resurrection, Stocks Bank Road, Mirfield WF14 0BN* Tel (01924) 483332 Fax 490489 E-mail agrant@mirfield.org.uk

GRANT, Arthur Glyndŵr Webber. b 28. St Luke's Coll Ex CertEd49. Wells Th Coll 52. **d** 54 **p** 55. C Cannock *Lich* 54-57; C Penhalonga St Aug Miss S Rhodesia 57-63; C Paignton St Jo *Ex* 63-68; C Brighton Gd Shep Preston *Chich* 68-76; C Moulsecoomb 76-80; Chapl HM Pris Northeye 80-83; P-in-c Wartling *Chich* 80-83; C Seaford w Sutton 83-87; Sub-Chapl HM Pris Lewes 86-92; rtd 92; Perm to Offic *Ex* 93-95 and 98-06. *The College of St Barnabas, Blackberry Lane, Lingfield RH7 6NJ* Tel (01342) 872328

GRANT, Eric. See GRANT, William Frederick

GRANT, Canon Geoffrey. b 27. Lich Th Coll 55. **d** 58 **p** 59. C Swindon New Town *Bris* 58-62; V Eastville St Thos 62-67; V Sherston Magna w Easton Grey 67-75; P-in-c Luckington w Alderton 71-75; P-in-c Woolcott Park 75-76; V Cotham St Mary 76-78; V Cotham St Sav w St Mary 78-81; TR Yate New Town 81-88; Hon Can Bris Cathl 82-92; Dir St Jo Home Bris 89-92; rtd 92; Perm to Offic *Bris* 92-97; Chapl Beaulieu-sur-Mer *Eur* 97-00.

GRANT, Canon Geoffrey Leslie. b 33. Trin Coll Cam BA57 MA61. Ridley Hall Cam 57. **d** 59 **p** 60. C Chelsea St Luke *Lon* 59-64; Chapl Orwell Park Sch Nacton from 64; R Nacton w Levington *St E* 64-78; P-in-c Bucklesham w Brightwell and Foxhall 75-76; R Nacton and Levington w Bucklesham and Foxhall 78-06; P-in-c Kirton w Falkenham 96-06; R Nacton and Levington w Bucklesham etc from 06; RD Colneys 86-11; Hon Can St E Cathl from 94. *The Rectory, Nacton, Ipswich IP10 0HY* Tel (01473) 659232 E-mail canon@nildram.co.uk

GRANT, Glyn. See GRANT, Arthur Glyndwr Webber

GRANT, James Neil. b 57. Toorak Coll of Educn BEd80. Trin Coll Melbourne BTh84. **d** 85 **p** 86. C E Frankston Australia 85-87; C Feltham *Lon* 87-89; Chapl Peninsula Sch Mt Eliza Melbourne 89-03; Assoc P Mt Eliza 99-03; Assoc P Richmond St Steph from 04. *21 Bent Street, East Malvern Vic 3145, Australia* Tel (0061) (3) 5976 1773 Mobile 425-721962 E-mail frjames.ststephens@keypoint.com.au

GRANT, James Nikolas. b 78. Glas Univ MA07 Anglia Ruskin Univ MA11. Westcott Ho Cam 09. **d** 11. C Chorlton-cum-Hardy St Clem *Man* from 11. *2 Ella Dene Park, Manchester M21 8PZ* Tel 07753-456210 (mobile) E-mail james_n_g@yahoo.de

GRANT, John Brian Frederick. b 47. Bris Univ BSc68 MB, ChB71 MD76 FRCS76. Coll of Resurr Mirfield 91. **d** 93 **p** 94. C Doncaster Ch Ch *Sheff* 93-95; C Doncaster H Trin 95-96; Chapl Asst Salford R Hosps NHS Trust 96-07; Hon C Man Victoria Park 08-10; Perm to Offic from 10. *179 Manley Road, Manchester M21 0GY* Tel 0161-860 7488

GRANT, Ms Kes. b 65. SEITE 00. **d** 03 **p** 04. NSM Eltham St Sav *S'wark* 03-09; C Bermondsey St Hugh CD 09-11; Chapl Lewisham Hosp NHS Trust 05-09; Chapl St Sav and St Olave's Sch Newington *S'wark* 09-11; Chapl St Aug Academy Maidstone from 11. *St Augustine Academy, Oakwood Road, Maidstone ME16 8AE* Tel (01622) 693789 Mobile 07805-482244 E-mail revkes@ntlworld.com

GRANT, Canon Malcolm Etheridge. b 44. Edin Univ BSc66 BD69. Edin Th Coll 66. **d** 69 **p** 70. C St Mary's Cathl 69-72; C Grantham w Manthorpe *Linc* 72; TV Grantham 72-78; P-in-c Invergordon St Ninian *Mor* 78-81; Provost St Mary's Cathl 81-91; R Glas St Mary 81-91; Provost St Andr Cathl Inverness 91-02; R Inverness St Andr 91-02; P-in-c Culloden St Mary-in-the-Fields 91-97; R Strathnairn St Paul 91-97; Hon Can St Andr Cathl Inverness from 02; V Eaton Bray w Edlesborough *St Alb* 02-09; RD Dunstable 04-09; rtd 09; Perm to Offic *Ox* and *St Alb* from 09. *13 Rock Lane, Leighton Buzzard LU7 2QQ* Tel (01525) 372771

GRANT, Murray William. b 36. Chich Th Coll 64. **d** 66 **p** 67. C Stanley *Liv* 66-70; C Munster Square St Mary Magd *Lon* 70-74; C Westmr St Sav and St Jas Less 74-82; P-in-c Albany Street Ch Ch 82; P-in-c Hammersmith H Innocents 83-94; V 94-99; Chapl Naples w Sorrento, Capri and Bari *Eur* 99-03; rtd 04. *12 Ashdown Crescent, London NW5 4QB* Tel (020) 7319 2519

GRANT, Patrick Iain Douglas. b 67. K Alfred's Coll Win BA88. Cuddesdon Coll BTh93. **d** 96 **p** 97. C Croydon Woodside *S'wark* 96-99; V S Beddington and Roundshaw 99-07; R Perth St Jo *St And* from 07. *23 Comely Bank, Perth PH2 7HU* Tel (01738) 634999 or 625394 E-mail rector@episcopal-perth.org.uk

GRANT, Canon Rodney Arthur. b 26. AKC52. K Coll Lon St Boniface Warminster. **d** 53 **p** 54. C Edin St Jas 53-56; C Musselburgh 56-59; P-in-c Prestonpans 59-60; P-in-c Edin St Aid Miss Niddrie Mains 60-72; R Edin St Jas 72-80; R Edin Ch Ch 72-80; R Edin Ch-St Jas 80-86; R Edin SS Phil and Jas 86-92; Chapl St Columba's Hospice Edin 86-92; Hon Can St Mary's Cathl from 91; rtd 92; P-in-c Edin St Vin from 98. *1F1, 29 Bruntsfield Gardens, Edinburgh EH10 4DY* Tel 0131-229 1857

GRANT, William Frederick (Eric). b 23. Fitzw Ho Cam BA48 MA50 Cam Univ CertEd50. Wycliffe Hall Ox 51. **d** 53 **p** 54. C Islington St Paul Ball's Pond *Lon* 53-57; V Islington All SS 57-60; Hd RE Therfield Sch Leatherhead 60-84; Perm to Offic *Guildf* from 66 and *S'wark* from 88. *Kingfishers, 24 The Avenue, Brockham, Betchworth RH3 7EN* Tel (01737) 842551

GRANTHAM, David George. b 70. Humberside Univ BA94. St Jo Coll Nottm. **d** 07 **p** 08. C Bury St Edmunds Ch Ch *St E* 07-10; V Jersey All SS *Win* from 11; V Jersey St Simon from 11. *All Saints' Vicarage, Savile Street, St Helier, Jersey JE2 3XF* Tel (01534) 768323 E-mail godistheguy@hotmail.com

GRANTHAM, Michael Paul. b 47. Linc Th Coll. **d** 84 **p** 85. C Gainsborough All SS *Linc* 84-87; R S Kelsey Gp 87-94; R Dunster, Carhampton and Withycombe w Rodhuish *B & W* 94-06; RD Exmoor 03-05; P-in-c Peakirk w Glinton and Northborough *Pet* 06-07; P-in-c Etton w Helpston and Maxey 06-07; rtd 07. *4 The Dovecote, Breedon-on-the-Hill, Derby DE73 8JD* Tel (01332) 864824

GRANTHAM, Suffragan Bishop of. See ELLIS, The Rt Revd Timothy William

GRASBY, Derek. b 56. Bris Univ BA80 MA82. Wesley Coll Bris 77 EAMTC 95. **d** 95 **p** 96. C Harlescott *Lich* 95-96; C W

Bromwich St Andr w Ch Ch 96-98; R Newton Heath *Man* 98-02; Chapl UWE *Bris* 02-03; R Farnley *Ripon* 03-09; rtd 09. *16 Stoneythorpe, Horsforth, Leeds LS18 4BN* Tel 07834-276382 (mobile) E-mail grasby@f2s.com

GRATTON, Patricia Margaret. *See* MAGUIRE, Canon Patricia Margaret

GRATY, Canon John Thomas. b 33. Univ Coll Ox BA58 MA60. Coll of Resurr Mirfield 58. **d** 60 **p** 61. C Cov St Mark 60-63; C Hitchin St Mary *St Alb* 63-67; R Cov St Alb 67-75; P-in-c Radway w Ratley 75-77; P-in-c Warmington w Shotteswell 75-77; RD Dassett Magna 76-79; R Warmington w Shotteswell and Radway w Ratley 77-84; Hon Can Cov Cathl 80-96; P-in-c Nuneaton St Mary 84-89; V 89-96; rtd 96; Perm to Offic *Cov* from 96. *10 Kendall Avenue, Stratford-upon-Avon CV37 6SG* Tel (01789) 298856

GRAVELL, Canon John Hilary. b 45. Univ of Wales (Abth) BA65 DipEd66. Bp Burgess Hall Lamp 66. **d** 68 **p** 69. C Aberystwyth *St D* 68-72; R Llangeitho w Blaenpennal 72-81; V Betws Leuci 73-81; V Llan-non 81-95; Can St D Cathl 92-09; V Llandybie 95-09; AD Dyffryn Aman 01-07; rtd 09. *16 Stewart Drive, Ammanford SA18 3BH* Tel (01269) 5943

GRAVES, John Ivan. b 44. **d** 10 **p** 11. OLM Romney Deanery from 10. *Gaynes House, St Andrews Road, Littlestone, New Romney TN28 8PZ* Tel (01797) 364011 E-mail jigbag@btinternet.com

GRAVES, Peter. b 33. EMMTC 78. **d** 81 **p** 82. NSM Roughey *Chich* 81-89; NSM Itchingfield w Slinfold 89-98; Perm to Offic *S'well* from 98. *5 Fletcher Court, The Woodlands, Farnsfield, Newark NG22 8LY* Tel (01623) 882987 E-mail gravespl@btinternet.com

GRAY, Alison Jane. b 63. New Hall Cam MB, BChir87 MA89 Birm Univ MMedSc01 MRCPsych95. Qu Coll Birm 07. **d** 10 **p** 11. NSM Malvern St Andr and Malvern Wells and Wyche *Worc* from 10. *42 Wyche Road, Malvern WR14 4EG* Tel (01684) 893637 E-mail a.j.gray@doctors.net.uk

GRAY, Andrew Stuart. b 70. LCTP. **d** 11. C Clitheroe St Jas *Blackb* from 11. *125 Henthorn Road, Clitheroe BB7 2QF* E-mail andyg@mrgiraffee.freeserve.co.uk

GRAY, Canon Angela Margery. b 46. St D Coll Lamp. **dss** 73 **d** 80 **p** 97. Aberystwyth *St D* 73-80; C Dafen and Llwynhendy 80-90; C-in-c 90-97; V Llwynhendy from 97; Hon Can St D Cathl from 01. *Clergy House, 10 Bryn Isaf, Llwynhendy, Llanelli SA14 9EX* Tel (01554) 774213

GRAY, Brett Christopher. b 71. Lon Bible Coll BA95 Selw Coll Cam MPhil04. Ridley Hall Cam 02. **d** 04 **p** 05. C Sunnyside w Bourne End *St Alb* 04-07; V St Alb St Mich 07-11; Asst Chapl Selw Coll Cam from 11. *Selwyn College, Cambridge CB3 9DQ* Tel (01223) 335846 E-mail bcgray@gmail.com

GRAY, Charles Malcolm. b 38. Lich Th Coll 67. **d** 69 **p** 70. C St Geo-in-the-East St Mary *Lon* 69-72; C Bush Hill Park St Mark 72-75; V Winchmore Hill H Trin 75-07; rtd 07; Perm to Offic *Lon* from 07. *16 Alpine Walk, Stanmore HA7 3HU* Tel (020) 8950 7860 E-mail frcmg.stanmore@btinternet.com

GRAY, Ms Christine Angela (Kit). b 46. Nottm Univ BA67 CertEd68. Cranmer Hall Dur 71. **dss** 80 **d** 87 **p** 94. Rawthorpe *Wakef* 74-81; Chapl Nottm Univ 81-88; C Rushmere *St E* 88-94; P-in-c Ringshall w Battisford, Barking w Darmsden etc 94-00; P-in-c Nayland w Wiston 00-10; rtd 10; Perm to Offic *St E* from 10. *16 Dyers Road, Stanway, Colchester CO3 0LG* E-mail kit.gray@keme.co.uk

GRAY, Dale Armitage. b 42. Edin Th Coll 62. **d** 92 **p** 93. Dioc Missr *Arg* 92-98; Chapl St Jo Cathl Oban 92-95; P-in-c Cumbrae (or Millport) 95-98; rtd 98; Perm to Offic *Edin* from 05. *The Dovecote, Duke Street, Coldstream TD12 4BN* Tel (01890) 883247

GRAY, David. b 55. Oak Hill Th Coll. **d** 00 **p** 01. C Bestwood Em w St Mark *S'well* 00-04; P-in-c Bulwell St Jo 04-06; V from 06. *St John's Vicarage, Snape Wood Road, Bulwell, Nottingham NG6 7GH* Tel 0115-927 8025 E-mail davidgray72@hotmail.com

GRAY, David Bryan. b 28. RD77. Roch Th Coll 59. **d** 61 **p** 62. C Linc St Giles 61-65; V Thurlby 65-67; P-in-c Ropsley 67-75; P-in-c Sapperton w Braceby 67-75; P-in-c Somerby w Humby 67-75; R Trimley *St E* 75-82; R Orford w Sudbourne, Chillesford, Butley and Iken 82-94; rtd 94; Perm to Offic *St E* 94-10. *The College of St Barnabas, Blackberry Lane, Lingfield RH7 6NJ* Tel (01342) 870260

GRAY, David Cedric. b 53. RMN77. **d** 97 **p** 98. OLM Gorton Em w St Jas *Man* 97-06; OLM Gorton and Abbey Hey 06-11. *39 Jessop Street, Gorton, Manchester M18 8TZ* Tel 0161-355 6605 Pager 017623-725682

GRAY, David Michael. b 57. St Jo Coll Dur BA99 ACIBS80. CA Tr Coll 90 Cranmer Hall Dur 97. **d** 99 **p** 00. C Newc H Cross 99-02; V Long Benton St Mary 02-11; V Killingworth from 11. *The New Vicarage, West Lane, Killingworth Village, Newcastle upon Tyne NE12 6BL* Tel 0191-268 3242 E-mail revdavegray@aol.com

GRAY, Canon Donald Cecil. b 24. Linc Th Coll 49. **d** 50 **p** 51. C Abington *Pet* 50-53; C Bedford St Paul *St Alb* 53-56; Chapl Bedf

Gen Hosp 53-56; C Wilton Place St Paul *Lon* 56-59; V N Holmwood *Guildf* 59-67; RD Dorking 63-67; R Farnham and Chapl Cobgates and Farnham Hosps 67-89; RD Farnham 69-74; Hon Can Guildf Cathl 71-89; rtd 89; Perm to Offic *Win* from 89. *13 Mallard Close, Alresford SO24 9BX* Tel (01962) 734371

GRAY, Canon Donald Clifford. b 30. CBE98 TD70. Liv Univ MPhil81 Man Univ PhD85 FRHistS88 FSA07. AKC55. **d** 56 **p** 57. C Leigh St Mary *Man* 56-60; CF (TA) 58-67; V Westleigh St Pet *Man* 60-67; V Elton All SS 67-74; CF (TAVR) 67-77; QHC 74-77; R Liv Our Lady and St Nic w St Anne 74-87; RD Liv 75-81; Hon Can Liv Cathl 82-87; Chapl to The Queen 82-00; Can Westmr Abbey 87-98; R Westmr St Marg 87-98; Chapl to Speaker of Ho of Commons 87-98; rtd 98; Perm to Offic *Linc* from 98. *3 Barn Hill Mews, Stamford PE9 2GN* Tel (01780) 765024

GRAY, Evan William. b 43. Oak Hill Th Coll 86. **d** 88 **p** 89. C Street w Walton *B & W* 88-92; V Blackpool St Mark *Blackb* 92-03; V Ellel w Shireshead 03-08; rtd 08; Perm to Offic *Blackb* from 08. *39 Boyes Avenue, Catterall, Preston PR3 0HB* Tel (01995) 604092 E-mail evan.gray@virgin.net

GRAY, James William. SAOMC. **d** 05 **p** 06. NSM Crich and S Wingfield *Derby* from 05. *Holmleigh, Market Place, Crich, Matlock DE4 5DD* Tel (01773) 857921

GRAY (née ROBERTS), Mrs Jennifer. b 55. R Holloway Coll Lon BA76 Somerville Coll Ox PGCE77. SAOMC 00. **d** 03 **p** 04. C Welwyn Garden City *St Alb* from 03. *62 Attimore Road, Welwyn Garden City AL8 6LP* Tel (01707) 321177 E-mail jennygraywgc@aol.com

GRAY, Joan. *See* BURKITT-GRAY, Mrs Joan Katherine

GRAY, John David Norman. b 38. Oak Hill Th Coll 84. **d** 86 **p** 87. C Portsdown *Portsm* 86-88; C Worthing St Geo *Chich* 88-91; TV Swanborough *Sarum* 91-98; rtd 98; Perm to Offic *Ex* 00-03 and *Portsm* from 03. *15 Charminster Court, 46 Craneswater Park, Southsea PO4 0NU* Tel (023) 9285 1299

GRAY, John Howard. b 39. St Aid Birkenhead 61. **d** 65 **p** 66. C Old Trafford St Cuth *Man* 65-68; C Urmston 68-74; V Oldham Moorside 74-08; rtd 08; Hon C Dulverton w Brushford, Brompton Regis etc *B & W* from 08. *The Vicarage, Brompton Regis, Dulverton TA22 9NL* Tel (01398) 371438

GRAY, Mrs Joy Dora. b 24. SRN46 SCM48. Gilmore Ho 79. **dss** 81 **d** 87 **p** 95. Newick *Chich* 81-94; Hon Par Dn 87-94; NSM Fletching 94-98; Perm to Offic from 98. *10 High Hurst Close, Newick, Lewes BN8 4NJ* Tel (01825) 722965

GRAY, Julian Francis. b 64. Univ of Wales (Lamp) BA86 MA09. Coll of Resurr Mirfield 86. **d** 88 **p** 89. Min Can St Woolos Cathl 88-91; C Bassaleg 91-93; V Overmonnow w Wonastow and Michel Troy 93-98; V King's Sutton and Newbottle and Charlton *Pet* 98-00; V Usk and Monkswood w Glascoed Chpl and Gwehelog 00-03; V Usk and Gwehelog w Llantrisant w Llanllowell from 03. *The Vicarage, 10 Cassia Drive, Usk NP15 1TZ* Tel (01291) 671032 E-mail usk.vicarage@btinternet.com

GRAY, Lindsay Doreen. b 50. Open Univ BA83 Leic Univ PhD87. Coll of Resurr Mirfield 05. **d** 06 **p** 07. NSM Firbank, Howgill and Killington *Bradf* 06-09; NSM Sedbergh, Cautley and Garsdale 06-09; Ind Chapl and TV Ergmont and Haile *Carl* from 09. *1 Bridge End Park, Egremont CA22 2RH* Tel (01946) 822051 E-mail lgray782@btinternet.com

GRAY, Malcolm. *See* GRAY, Charles Malcolm

GRAY, The Ven Martin Clifford. b 44. Westcott Ho Cam 78. **d** 80 **p** 81. C Gaywood, Bawsey and Mintlyn *Nor* 80-84; V Sheringham 84-94; TR Lowestoft St Marg 94-99; Chapl Lothingland Hosp 95-99; RD Lothingland *Nor* 97-99; Adn Lynn 99-09; rtd 09; Perm to Offic *Nor* from 09. *11 Canns Lane, Hethersett, Norwich NR9 3JE* Tel (01603) 812610 E-mail mandpgray@btinternet.com

GRAY, Melvyn Dixon. b 38. Lon Univ BD86 Dur Univ MA89 PhD07. NEOC 84. **d** 87 **p** 88. C Richmond w Hudswell *Ripon* 87-90; P-in-c Downholme and Marske 88-90; P-in-c Forcett and Aldbrough and Melsonby 90-91; R 91-00; R Mobberley *Ches* 00-04; rtd 04. *19 Windgroves, Chilton, Ferryhill DL17 0RS* Tel (01388) 721870 E-mail windgroves2004@talktalk.net

GRAY, Neil Kenneth. b 48. Kelham Th Coll 67. **d** 71 **p** 72. C Chorley St Laur *Blackb* 71-74; C S Shore H Trin 74-78; P-in-c Preston St Oswald 78-83; C Blackpool St Steph 83-87; Chapl Bolton HA from 87; Chapl Bolton Hosps NHS Trust from 90; Co-ord Spiritual and Cultural Care 90-03; Hd of Chapl from 04; Bp's Adv on Healthcare Chapl *Man* from 08. *The Chaplains' Office, Royal Bolton Hospital, Minerva Road, Farnworth, Bolton BL4 0JR* Tel (01204) 390770 *or* 390390 E-mail neil.gray@rbh.nhs.uk

GRAY, Neil Ralph. b 53. MA. St Steph Ho Ox. **d** 82 **p** 83. C Kennington St Jo w St Jas *S'wark* 82-85; C Somers Town *Lon* 85-88. *3 Parsonage Close, High Wycombe HP13 6DT* Tel (01494) 531875

GRAY, Mrs Patricia Linda. b 51. Univ of Wales (Swansea) BA73 Ches Coll of HE BTh02. NOC 99. **d** 02 **p** 03. C Glazebury w

Hollinfare *Liv* from 02. *10 Hesnall Close, Glazebury, Warrington WA3 5PB* Tel (01942) 603161 Mobile 07747-772345 E-mail pat.gray@virgin.net
GRAY, Patrick. *See* GRAY, Sidney Patrick
GRAY, Penelope Jane. *See* GRAYSMITH, Mrs Penelope Jane
GRAY, Percy. b 28. OBE94 TD71. Birkbeck Coll Lon BA53 St Cath Soc Ox BA55 MA59. Oak Hill Th Coll 50 Wycliffe Hall Ox 55. **d** 55 **p** 56. C Sutton *Liv* 55-58; C Chelsea Ch Ch *Lon* 58-59; V Bermondsey St Crispin w Ch Ch *S'wark* 59-99; CF (TA) 59-67; CF (TAVR) from 67; CF (ACF) from 76; rtd 99; Perm to Offic *S'wark* from 04; OCM from 04. *12 King Edward III Mews, Paradise Street, London SE16 4QH* Tel (020) 7394 7127 E-mail percylive@hotmail.com
GRAY, Canon Philip Charles. b 67. Nottm Univ BA91. St Steph Ho Ox 91. **d** 93 **p** 94. C Scarborough St Martin *York* 93-97; TV Leek and Meerbrook *Lich* 97-01; Bp's Dom Chapl *Blackb* 02-07; P-in-c Ilkley St Marg *Bradf* from 07; Pioneer Min Otley Deanery from 07; Hon Can Ho Ghana from 04. *St Margaret's Vicarage, Wells Road, Ilkley LS29 9JH* Tel (01943) 607015
GRAY, Philip Thomas. b 41. Lon Univ BA65. Chich Th Coll 66. **d** 68 **p** 69. C Leigh St Clem *Chelmsf* 68-74; P-in-c Wickham Skeith *St E* 86-97; V Mendlesham from 74. *The Vicarage, Old Station Road, Mendlesham, Stowmarket IP14 5RS* Tel (01449) 766359
GRAY, Canon Robert James. b 70. TCD BA92 HDipEd93 MA95 Irish Sch of Ecum MPhil97. CITC 94. **d** 96 **p** 97. C Glooney w Strathfoyle *D & R* 96-99; I Ardamine w Kiltennel, Glascarrig etc *C & O* from 99; Treas Ferns Cathl from 04. *Ardamine Rectory, Courtown Harbour, Gorey, Co Wexford, Republic of Ireland* Tel and fax (00353) (53) 942 5423 Mobile 86-684 7621 E-mail ardamine@ferns.anglican.org
GRAY, Sidney Patrick. b 19. Worc Ord Coll. **d** 63 **p** 63. C Skegness *Linc* 63-65; V Dunholme 65-71; R Cliffe at Hoo w Cooling *Roch* 72-78; V Gillingham St Aug 78-84; rtd 84; Perm to Offic *Cant* and *Roch* 84-08. *7 St Stephens Road, Retford DN22 7EZ*
GRAY, Stephen James Norman. b 66. Lon Univ BA89 Hughes Hall Cam PGCE91. Ridley Hall Cam MA00. **d** 00 **p** 01. C Cheltenham Ch Ch *Glouc* 00-03; Chapl RN 03-04; Chapl Sherborne Sch 04-10; Chapl Seaford Coll Petworth from 10; P-in-c Graffham w Woolavington *Chich* from 10. *The Rectory, Graffham, Petworth GU28 0NL*
GRAY, Mrs Susan Hazel. b 49. Kingston Univ BA06. **d** 09 **p** 10. OLM Hersham *Guildf* from 09. *39 Misty's Field, Walton-on-Thames KT12 2BG* Tel (01932) 242838 E-mail suehgray@btinternet.com
GRAY, Mrs Trudy Ann Jennifer. b 48. Univ of Wales (Abth) BSc69 Aston Univ MSc72. **d** 05 **p** 06. NSM Gt Finborough w Onehouse, Harleston, Buxhall etc *St E* 05-10; NSM Upper Coquetdale *Newc* from 10. *The Vicarage, Alwinton, Morpeth NE65 7BE* Tel (01669) 650203 E-mail tajgrayfin@aol.com
GRAY, Mrs Ursula Mary. b 33. K Coll Lon BD56 AKC91 Univ of Wales (Lamp) MA02. **d** 04 **p** 05. NSM Shaston *Sarum* 04-08; Perm to Offic 09. *Rowans, Chavenage Lane, Tetbury GL8 8JW* Tel (01666) 504548 E-mail umg@shaston.plus.com
GRAY-HAMMOND, Betsy. b 58. Ripon Coll Cuddesdon BA10. **d** 10 **p** 11. C Brighton St Nic *Chich* from 10. *30 Bigwood Avenue, Hove BN3 6AJ* Tel (01273) 327478 E-mail betsey.hammond@btopenworld.com
GRAY-STACK, Martha Mary Stewart. b 35. QUB BA57. **d** 90 **p** 91. NSM Limerick City *L & K* 90-93; Warden of Readers 90-93; NSM Clara w Liss, Moate and Clonmacnoise *M & K* 93-00; Chapl Kingston Coll Mitchelstown from 00. *16 Kingston College, Mitchelstown, Co Cork, Republic of Ireland* Tel and fax (00353) (25) 258 5975
GRAYSHON, Matthew Richard. b 47. St Jo Coll Nottm BTh81. **d** 81 **p** 82. C Beverley Minster *York* 81-85; V Hallwood *Ches* 85-93; R Hanwell St Mary w St Chris *Lon* from 93. *The Rectory, 91 Church Road, London W7 3BJ* Tel (020) 8567 6185 Fax 8579 8755 E-mail matthewgrayshon@tesco.net
GRAYSHON, Paul Nicholas Walton. b 50. St Jo Coll Dur 81. **d** 83 **p** 84. C Walkden Moor *Man* 83-87; V Radcliffe St Andr 87-07; P-in-c Matlock Bath and Cromford *Derby* from 07. *Holy Trinity Vicarage, 8 Derby Road, Matlock DE4 3PU* Tel (01629) 583924 E-mail nickgrayshon@btopenworld.com
GRAYSMITH (née GRAY), Mrs Penelope Jane. b 63. SS Hild & Bede Coll Dur BA85 Em Coll Cam MPhil88. Westcott Ho Cam 86. **d** 89 **p** 94. Par Dn Evington *Leic* 89-92; Par Dn Cannock *Lich* 92-94; C 94-96; Chapl Asst Mid Staffs Gen Hosps NHS Trust 96-07; Hd Chapl Services Mid Staffs NHS Foundn Trust from 07; Chapl Kath Ho Hospice Stafford from 96. *The Vicarage, 97 Baswich Lane, Stafford ST17 0BN* Tel (01785) 251057 *or* 230930 E-mail penny.graysmith@midstaffs.nhs.uk
GRAYSMITH, Peter Alexander. b 62. UEA BSc83. Westcott Ho Cam 85. **d** 88 **p** 89. C Tettenhall Regis *Lich* 88-89; C Cannock 89-92; TV 92-99; V Rocester and Croxden w Hollington 99-01; V Baswich from 01. *The Vicarage, 97 Baswich Lane, Stafford ST17 0BN* Tel (01785) 251057 E-mail petergraysmith@talktalk.net

GRAYSON, Jane Elizabeth. b 71. **d** 07 **p** 08. OLM Moston St Mary *Man* from 07. *296 St Mary's Road, Manchester M40 0BD* Tel 0161-688 7073 E-mail janegrayson@aol.com
GRAYSON, Robin John. b 53. Mert Coll Ox BA74 DPhil78. Wycliffe Hall Ox 00. **d** 02 **p** 03. C Beaconsfield *Ox* 02-06; P-in-c Langley Marish 06-08; TR from 08. *The Vicarage, 3 St Mary's Road, Slough SL3 7EN* Tel (01753) 542068 Mobile 07801-280475 E-mail r.j.grayson@btinternet.com
GREADY, Andrew John. b 63. Univ Coll Lon BSc84 Newc Univ MA93 Surrey Univ BSc05. St Jo Coll Nottm 86. **d** 89 **p** 90. C Monkwearmouth St Andr *Dur* 89-92; C Bramley St Cath S Africa 92-96; R Sunninghill St Steph 96-99; Chapl St Pet Prep Sch 99; V Shottermill *Guildf* 00-06; Chapl Amesbury Sch 01-06; P-in-c Wynberg St Jo S Africa 06-08; R from 08; Chapl W Prov Prep Sch from 07. *Barnabas House, 18 St John's Road, Wynberg 7800, South Africa* Tel (0027) (21) 797 7856 *or* 797 8968 Fax 762 5970 E-mail andrew@stjohns.org.za
GREANY, Canon Richard Andrew Hugh. b 44. Qu Coll Ox BA67 MA83. Coll of Resurr Mirfield 67. **d** 69 **p** 70. C Hartlepool St Oswald *Dur* 69-72; C Clifton All SS *Bris* 72-75; Tutor Coll of Resurr Mirfield 75-78; V Whitworth w Spennymoor *Dur* 78-83; P-in-c Byers Green 78-79; Asst Prin St Alb Minl Tr Scheme 83-88; V Flamstead *St Alb* 83-88; V Hessle *York* 88-94; V Cambridge St Mary Less *Ely* 94-11; Dioc Spirituality Officer 99-06; Hon Can Ely Cathl 05-11; RD Cambridge S 06-11; rtd 11; Chapl Laslett's *Worc* from 11; Hon C Worc City from 11. *Chaplain's House, Laslett's Almshouses, Union Street, Worcester WR1 2AS* Tel (01905) 734651 E-mail andrewgreany@btinternet.com
GREANY, Mrs Virginia Clare. b 52. Bris Univ BA74 PGCE75 Hull Univ MSc94. Westcott Ho Cam 96 EAMTC 97. **d** 98. Bp's Dn to Local Government *Ely* 98-99; Asst to Dean Trin Hall Cam 98-00. *Trinity Hall, Cambridge CB2 1TJ* Tel (01223) 332500
GREAR, Hugh Massey. b 60. Bris Univ LLB82. SEITE. **d** 00 **p** 01. C Warlingham w Chelsham and Farleigh *S'wark* 00-04; V Upper Tooting H Trin w St Aug 04-10; R Worplesdon *Guildf* from 10. *The Rectory, Perry Hill, Worplesdon, Guildford GU3 3RE* Tel and fax (01483) 234616 E-mail hugh.grear@sky.com
GREASLEY, James Kenneth. b 39. K Coll Lon BD66 AKC66. **d** 67 **p** 68. C Stoke upon Trent *Lich* 67-70; P-in-c Lusaka St Pet Zambia 70-76; V Gt Staughton *Ely* 76-81; Chapl HM Borstal Gaynes Hall 76-81; V Melbourn and Meldreth *Ely* 81-96; RD Shingay 82-96; R Chalfont St Peter *Ox* 96-04; rtd 04; Perm to Offic *Heref* from 05. *Bank Cottage, Norton, Presteigne LD8 2EN* Tel (01544) 267567 E-mail jk.greasley@btinternet.com
GREATOREX, Mrs Susan Kathleen. b 58. St Hilda's Coll Ox BA79 MA04 Univ of Wales (Cardiff) PGCE80. WEMTC 01. **d** 04 **p** 05. C Keynsham *B & W* 04-08; R Radstock w Writhlington from 08; R Kilmersdon w Babington from 08. *28 Wells Road, Radstock BA3 3RL* Tel (01761) 433917 E-mail susangreatorex@blueyonder.co.uk
GREATREX, Richard Quintin. b 65. K Coll Lon BD86 Surrey Univ BA02. STETS 99. **d** 02 **p** 03. NSM Westbury-on-Trym St Alb *Bris* 02-06; NSM Flax Bourton and Barrow Gurney *B & W* 06-09; NSM Long Ashton w Barrow Gurney and Flax Bourton from 09. *The Rectory, Main Road, Flax Bourton, Bristol BS48 3QJ* Tel (01275) 461179 E-mail rqg1@fsmail.net
GREAVES, Canon John Neville. b 29. Newc Univ MA96 Dur Univ MLitt03. St Aid Birkenhead 58. **d** 61 **p** 62. C Pendleton St Ambrose *Man* 61-62; P-in-c 62-63; C Benchill 63-65; C-in-c Wythenshawe St Rich CD 65-71; V Wythenshawe St Rich 71-73; R Sadberge *Dur* 73-78; V Dur St Cuth 78-94; Chapl New Coll Dur 78-92; Lect NEOC 79-84; Chapl Dur Co Fire Brigade 85-94; RD Dur 80-93; Dep Dir of Clergy Tr 91-94; Hon Can Dur Cathl 91-94; rtd 94; Perm to Offic *Ches* 94-97; P-in-c Salt and Sandon w Burston *Lich* 97-00; Past Aux Eccleshall Deanery 00-01; Perm to Offic *Lich* 01-02; *Heref* from 03; *S & B* from 10. *3 Sitwell Close, Bucknell SY7 0DD* Tel (01547) 530152
GREED, Frederick John. b 44. Trin Coll Bris 79. **d** 81 **p** 82. C Yateley *Win* 81-85; R Ore St Helen and St Barn *Chich* 85-95; R Street w Walton *B & W* 95-09; RD Glastonbury 08-09; rtd 09. *40 St Cleers Orchard, Somerton TA11 6QU* E-mail fj.greed@googlemail.com
GREEDY, Tegryd Joseph. b 31. St D Coll Lamp 59. **d** 61 **p** 62. C Newbridge *Mon* 61-64; C Bassaleg 64-66; V Newport St Teilo 66-74; Hon C Newport St Mark 80-83; V Goldcliffe and Whitson and Nash 83-90; Ind Chapl 83-90; V Marshfield and Peterstone Wentloog etc 90-96; rtd 96. *42 Churchward Drive, Newport NP19 4SB* Tel (01633) 282159
GREEN, Adrian Paul. b 66. Trin Coll Bris 06. **d** 08 **p** 09. NSM Willowfield *D & D* from 08. *122 Mount Merrion Avenue, Belfast BT6 0FS* Tel (028) 9029 4676 *or* 9045 7654 Mobile 07914-290193 E-mail adrian.familygreen@tiscali.co.uk
GREEN, Preb Alan John Enrique. b 56. Worc Coll Ox BA78 MA83. Linc Th Coll 83. **d** 85 **p** 86. C Kirkby *Liv* 85-88; TV 88-94; Chapl Knowsley Community Coll 87-90; Chapl Worc Coll and C Ox St Giles and SS Phil and Jas w St Marg 94-98; St Jo on Bethnal Green *Lon* from 98; AD Tower Hamlets from

06; Preb St Paul's Cathl from 10. *St John's Rectory, 30 Victoria Park Square, London E2 9PB* Tel and fax (020) 8980 1742 E-mail alan.green@virgin.net

GREEN, Alison Mary. b 51. Boro Road Teacher Tr Coll BEd74 Wesley Coll Bris MA03 Roehampton Univ PhD07. STETS 02. **d** 04 **p** 05. NSM Bath St Barn w Englishcombe *B & W* 04-06; NSM Monmouth w Overmonnow etc from 06. *Great Manson Hall, Manson Lane, Manson, Monmouth NP25 5RD* Tel (01600) 715538 E-mail alig9@btinternet.com

GREEN, Arthur Edward. b 27. Chich Th Coll 58. **d** 59 **p** 60. C Malden St Jas *S'wark* 59-62; C Caterham 62-67; R Burgh Parva w Briston *Nor* 67-75; V Middleton 75-76; V Middleton w E Winch 76-84; R Neatishead w Irstead 84-90; V Barton Turf 84-90; R Neatishead, Barton Turf and Irstead 90-92; rtd 92; Perm to Offic *Portsm* from 92. *10 James Butcher Court, 16 Eastern Villas Road, Southsea PO4 0TD* Tel (023) 9275 0701

GREEN, Barrie. b 51. SS Coll Cam BA72 MA76. Wycliffe Hall Ox 75. **d** 78 **p** 79. C Castle Vale *Birm* 78-81; V W Heath 81-96; RD Kings Norton 87-95; TR Dronfield w Holmesfield *Derby* 96-09; P-in-c Bris St Paul's from 09. *15 St Werburghs Park, Bristol BS2 9YT* Tel 0117-941 4217

GREEN, Benjamin Charles. b 83. Magd Coll Cam BA04 MA08. Wycliffe Hall Ox MTh08. **d** 08. C Stockton and Preston-on-Tees and Longnewton *Dur* 08-09. *8 High Church Wynd, Yarm TS15 9BQ* Tel (01642) 780950 E-mail bcgreen@me.com

GREEN, Brian Robert. b 31. Bris Univ BA55. Tyndale Hall Bris 52. **d** 56 **p** 57. C Toxteth Park St Philemon *Liv* 56-58; V Toxteth Park St Philemon w St Silas 58-69; P-in-c Toxteth Park St Gabr 64-69; P-in-c Toxteth Park St Jo and St Thos 64-69; P-in-c Toxteth Park St Jas and St Matt 68-69; V Elsenham *Chelmsf* 69-85; V Henham 69-85; P-in-c Ugley 84-85; V Henham and Elsenham w Ugley 85-89; RD Newport and Stansted 87-89; Perm to Offic *Ex* 90-91; V Tidenham w Beachley and Lancaut *Glouc* 91-97; RD Forest S 95-97; rtd 97; Perm to Offic *Ex* 97-11. *3 Crosbys, Burbage, Marlborough SN8 3TL* Tel (01672) 811655

GREEN, Brutus Zachary. b 78. Ex Univ BA99 PhD07 St Edm Coll Cam MPhil04. Westcott Ho Cam 07. **d** 09 **p** 10. C Paddington St Jo w St Mich *Lon* from 09. *23 Archery Close, London W2 2BE* Tel (020) 7402 9505 E-mail brutuszgreen@gmail.com

GREEN, Catherine Isabel. See HITCHENS, Mrs Catherine Isabel

GREEN, Christopher Frederick. b 46. Nottm Univ BTh75 Birm Univ DipEd85 Univ of Wales (Abth) MEd94. Bp Otter Coll CertEd69 Linc Th Coll 71. **d** 75 **p** 76. C Hodge Hill *Birm* 75-77; C S Lafford *Linc* 77-79; P-in-c Worc St Mich 79-82; Hd RS and Lib RNIB New Coll Worc 82-96; V Clipstone *S'well* 96-02; rtd 02; Perm to Offic *Linc* from 03. *Cobwebs, Middlefield Lane, Glentham, Market Rasen LN8 2ET* Tel (01673) 878633

GREEN, Christopher Martyn. b 58. New Coll Edin BD80. Cranmer Hall Dur 82. **d** 83 **p** 84. C Virginia Water *Guildf* 83-87; C Bromley Ch Ch *Roch* 87-91; Study Asst the Proclamation Trust 91-92; C Surbiton Hill Ch Ch *S'wark* 92-00; Vice Prin Oak Hill Th Coll from 00; Perm to Offic *Lon* from 02. *Oak Hill Theological College, Chase Side, London N14 4PS* Tel (020) 8449 0467 *or* 8441 0315

GREEN, Mrs Clare Noreen. b 30. SWMTC 84. **d** 88. NSM Bideford *Ex* 88-90; Perm to Offic 90-09. *30 Rosebarn Lane, Exeter EX4 5DX* Tel (01392) 272505

GREEN, Daphne Mary. b 55. K Coll Cam BA77 Bradf Univ MBA91 Leeds Univ PhD01 Lon Inst of Educn PGCE79. Cranmer Hall Dur 95. **d** 98 **p** 99. C Headingley *Ripon* 98-02; Chapl Leeds Metrop Univ 00-02; R Stanningley St Thos 02-08; Abp's Chapl and Researcher *York* from 08. *Bishopthorpe, York YO23 2GE* Tel (01904) 707021 Fax 709204 Mobile 07796-084264 E-mail daphne.green@archbishopofyork.org

GREEN, David Allen. b 61. Sheff City Poly BA90. Cranmer Hall Dur 00. **d** 02 **p** 03. C Huyton St Geo *Liv* 02-06; TV Walkden and Lt Hulton *Man* 06-10; P-in-c Thorne *Sheff* from 10. *The Vicarage, 2 Brooke Street, Thorne, Doncaster DN8 4AZ* Tel (01405) 814055 E-mail green426@btinternet.com

GREEN, Canon David John. b 54. SWMTC 82. **d** 85 **p** 86. C St Marychurch *Ex* 85-89; C Laira 89-90; V Maughold *S & M* from 90; RD Ramsey 98-08; Dioc Dir of Ords 05-08; Can St German's Cathl from 05. *The Vicarage, Maughold, Isle of Man IM7 1AS* Tel (01624) 812070 E-mail djgreen@mcb.net

GREEN, David Norman. b 37. Magd Coll Cam BA60. Clifton Th Coll 60. **d** 62 **p** 63. C Islington St Mary *Lon* 62-65; C Burley *Ripon* 65-68; Kenya 69-80; P-in-c Brimscombe *Glouc* 81-90; R Woodchester and Brimscombe 90-96; P-in-c Coberley w Cowley 96-97; P-in-c Colesborne 96-97; P-in-c Coberley, Cowley, Colesbourne and Elkstone 97-04; Dioc Rural Adv 96-04; rtd 04; Tanzania from 04. *Diocese of Tabora, PO Box 1408, Tabora, Tanzania*

GREEN, David Robert John. b 73. Sheff Univ BA96. Ridley Hall Cam 06. **d** 08 **p** 09. C Chatham St Phil and St Jas *Roch* from 08; P-in-c W Malling w Offham from 11. *The Vicarage, High Street, West Malling ME19 6NE* Tel (01732) 842245 E-mail mail@revdgreen.org.uk

GREEN, David William. b 53. CertEd75 Nottm Univ BCombStuds84. Linc Th Coll 81. **d** 84 **p** 85. C S Merstham *S'wark* 84-88; C Walton-on-Thames *Guildf* 88-91; V Gillingham H Trin and Chapl Lennox Wood Elderly People's Home *Roch* 91-99; V Strood St Nic w St Mary from 99. *The Vicarage, 3 Central Road, Strood, Rochester ME2 3HF* Tel (01634) 719052 E-mail david.green@diocese-rochester.org

GREEN, Denise Penelope. b 57. Bedf Coll of Educn BEd80 MPhil89. EMMTC 03. **d** 06 **p** 07. C Skirbeck H Trin *Linc* 06-10; P-in-c S Lawres Gp from 10. *The Vicarage, 14 Church Lane, Cherry Willingham, Lincoln LN3 4AB* Tel (01522) 595596 Mobile 07812-006295 E-mail revdpg@virginmedia.com

GREEN, Donald Henry. b 31. Selw Coll Cam BA54 Lon Inst of Educn PGCE55. Qu Coll Birm 81. **d** 83 **p** 84. C Dudley St Aug Holly Hall *Worc* 83-85; V Dudley St Barn 85-90; rtd 96. *The Cuckoo's Nest, 12 Mill Green, Knighton LD7 1EE* Tel (01547) 528289

GREEN, Donald Pentney (Brother Donald). b 25. Leeds Univ BA50. Coll of Resurr Mirfield 50. **d** 52 **p** 53. C Ardwick St Benedict *Man* 52-55; SSF from 55; Sec for Miss SSF 78-96; Lic to Offic *Chelmsf* 58-60 and 69-72; Papua New Guinea 60-63; Chapl HM Pris Kingston (Portsm) 72-76; Lic to Offic *Edin* 76-77; Org Sec Catholic Renewal 77; Lic to Offic *Lich* from 78; rtd 95. *85 Crofton Road, London E13 8QT* Tel (020) 7474 5863 E-mail donaldssf@aol.com

GREEN, Dorothy Mary. b 36. Westf Coll Lon BA58. Selly Oak Coll 60. **dss** 83 **d** 87 **p** 94. Ryde All SS *Portsm* 83-91; C 87-91; Hon C Hempnall *Nor* 91-96; rtd 96; Perm to Offic *B & W* 97-07. *2 Bramwell Lodge, Brighton Road, Woodmancote, Henfield BN5 9SX* Tel (01273) 495501 E-mail revdern17@yahoo.co.uk

GREEN, Douglas Edward. b 17. Sarum Th Coll 47. **d** 50 **p** 51. C Glouc St Paul 50-53; C Malvern Link St Matthias *Worc* 53-56; R Tolladine 56-58; V Bosbury *Heref* 58-78; R Coddington 59-79; V Wellington Heath 59-79; Hon C Minsterley 78-80; rtd 82; Perm to Offic *Worc* 83-08. *Adelaide Nursing Home, Park Road, Malvern WR14 4BJ*

GREEN, Canon Duncan Jamie. b 52. Sarum & Wells Th Coll 82. **d** 84 **p** 85. C Uckfield *Chich* 84-87; Dioc Youth Officer *Chelmsf* 87-96; Warden and Chapl St Mark's Coll Hen Cen 93-96; TR Saffron Walden w Wendens Ambo, Littlebury etc 96-07; RD Saffron Walden 05-07; C of E Olympic and Paralympic Co-ord from 07; Hon Can Chelmsf Cathl from 03. *86 Princes Road, Buckhurst Hill IG9 5DZ* E-mail cofeolympiccoordinator@greendj.co.uk

GREEN, Edward Bryan. b 75. Westcott Ho Cam 02. **d** 05 **p** 06. C Soham and Wicken *Ely* 05-09; TV Cherwell Valley *Ox* from 09. *The Rectory, Station Road, Lower Heyford, Bicester OX25 5PD* Tel (01869) 340562 Mobile 07974-107524 E-mail edward.green@cherwellvalleybenefice.org

GREEN, Edward John. b 35. Lich Th Coll. **d** 59 **p** 60. C Longford *Cov* 59-61; C Wigston Magna *Leic* 61-65; V 73-00; V Ellistown 65-73; rtd 00; Perm to Offic *Leic* 00-03 and from 05. *Holly Mount, 27 Greendale Road, Glen Parva, Leicester LE2 9HD* Tel 0116-277 2479

GREEN, Edward Marcus. b 66. Mert Coll Ox BA88 MA92. Wycliffe Hall Ox 90. **d** 94 **p** 95. C Glyncorrwg w Afan Vale and Cymmer Afan *Llan* 94-96; C Aberystwyth *St D* 96-99; P-in-c Pontypridd St Cath w St Matt *Llan* 00-01; V Pontypridd St Cath 01-11. *Address temp unknown* E-mail marcusgreen541@btinternet.com

GREEN, Canon Edward Michael Bankes. b 30. Ex Coll Ox BA53 MA56 Qu Coll Cam BA57 MA61 BD66 Toronto Univ DD92 Lambeth DD96. Ridley Hall Cam 55. **d** 57 **p** 58. C Eastbourne H Trin *Chich* 57-60; Lect Lon Coll of Div 60-69; Prin St Jo Coll Nottm 69-75; Can Th Cov Cathl 70-76; R Ox St Aldate w H Trin 75-82; R Ox St Aldate w St Matt 82-86; Prof Evang Regent Coll Canada 87-92; Abps' Adv Springboard for Decade of Evang 92-96; rtd 96; Six Preacher Cant Cathl 93-99; Sen Research Fell Wycliffe Hall Ox from 97; Perm to Offic *Ox* from 99. *7 Little Acreage, Marston, Oxford OX3 0PS* Tel (01865) 248387 Fax 792083 E-mail michael.green@wycliffe.ox.ac.uk

GREEN, Mrs Elizabeth Pauline Anne. b 29. Gilmore Ho 69. **dss** 76 **d** 87 **p** 94. Chorleywood Ch Ch *St Alb* 76-87; Par Dn 87-90; C Chipping Sodbury and Old Sodbury *Glouc* 90-95; Asst Dioc Missr 90-95; rtd 95; NSM Chipping Sodbury and Old Sodbury *Glouc* 95-99; Perm to Offic *Glouc*, *Bris* from 99. *The Old House, The Common, Chipping Sodbury, Bristol BS37 6PX* Tel (01454) 311936 E-mail p.green@care4free.net

GREEN, Eric Kenneth. b 18. Tyndale Hall Bris 40. **d** 45 **p** 47. C Heatherlands St Jo *Sarum* 45-48; C Radipole 48-49; C Bucknall and Bagnall *Lich* 49-50; V Halwell w Moreleigh *Ex* 50-53; V Wakef St Mary 53-55; R Peldon *Chelmsf* 55-57; P-in-c Leaden Roding 57-58; R 58-63; V Aythorpe Roding and High Roding 60-63; R All Cannings w Etchilhampton *Sarum* 63-75; V Over Kellet *Blackb* 75-83; rtd 83; Perm to Offic *Brady* 91-98. *Penlee Residential Care Home, 56 Morrab Road, Penzance TR18 4EB* Tel (01736) 364102

GREEN, Ernest James. b 31. Pemb Coll Cam BA55 MA62. Linc Th Coll 55. **d** 57 **p** 58. C Rawmarsh *Sheff* 57-60; Sec Th Colls Dept SCM 60-62; Prec and Sacr Bris Cathl 62-65; Min Can 62-65; V Churchill *B & W* 65-78; RD Locking 72-78; V Burrington and Churchill 78-82; Preb Wells Cathl 81-82; V Ryde All SS *Portsm* 82-91; P-in-c Ryde H Trin 82-86; RD E Wight 83-88; TR Hempnall *Nor* 91-96; rtd 96; Perm to Offic *B & W* 97-07. *2 Bramwell Lodge, Brighton Road, Woodmancote, Henfield BN5 9SX* Tel (01273) 495501 E-mail revdern17@yahoo.co.uk

GREEN, Ms Fiona Jenifer. b 67. Rob Coll Cam BA89 MA93. Ridley Hall Cam 02. **d** 05 **p** 06. C Highbury Ch Ch w St Jo and St Sav *Lon* 05-08; C St Jo on Bethnal Green from 08; Co-ord Reader Tr Stepney Area from 08. *The Rectory Flat, Hereford Street, London E2 6EX* Tel 07786-541559 (mobile) E-mail fionajgreen@yahoo.co.uk

GREEN, Fleur Estelle. b 72. Univ of Wales (Ban) BD94. Ripon Coll Cuddesdon 95. **d** 97 **p** 98. C Blackpool St Jo *Blackb* 97-00; C Lancaster St Mary w St John and St Anne 00-03; P-in-c Blackb St Luke w St Phil 03-04; P-in-c Witton 03-04; V Blackb Christ the King from 04; Asst Dir of Ords from 06. *St Mark's Vicarage, Buncer Lane, Blackburn BB2 6SY* Tel (01254) 676615 E-mail chauntry1@aol.com

GREEN, Frank Gilbert. b 23. Kelham Th Coll 46. **d** 50 **p** 51. C Sheff St Cecilia Parson Cross 50-56; SSM from 52; C Nottingham St Geo w St Jo *S'well* 56-58; Basutoland 59-62; S Africa 62-69 and 84-88; Lesotho 69-84; Lic to Offic *Ox* from 88; rtd 93. *Society of the Sacred Mission, 1 Linford Lane, Willen, Milton Keynes MK15 9DL* Tel (01908) 663749

GREEN, Gary Henry. b 64. Univ of Wales (Cardiff) BD87. St Mich Coll Llan 93. **d** 95 **p** 96. C Baglan *Llan* 95-97; C Neath w Llantwit 97-01; TV Neath 01-02; V Llangiwg *S & B* from 02. *The Vicarage, 10 Uplands Road, Pontardawe, Swansea SA8 4AH* Tel (01792) 862003

GREEN, George James. b 26. Cuddesdon Coll 69. **d** 69 **p** 70. C Handsworth St Mary *Birm* 69-76; R Croughton w Evenley *Pet* 76-88; R Aynho and Croughton w Evenley 88-95; rtd 95; Perm to Offic *Cov* from 95. *Dibbinsdale, Langley Road, Claverdon, Warwick CV35 8PU*

GREEN, Gillian. b 41. Balls Park Coll Hertford TCert61 Open Univ BA83. EAMTC 03. **d** 05 **p** 06. NSM Stour Valley *St E* from 05. *Lady's Green Cottage, Lady's Green, Ousden, Newmarket CB8 8TU* Tel (01284) 850605 E-mail gill@g-green.fsnet.co.uk

GREEN, Gloria. See SHERBOURNE, Gloria

GREEN, Gordon Sydney. b 33. Ridley Hall Cam 77. **d** 79 **p** 80. C Ipswich St Marg *St E* 79-83; TV Barton Mills, Beck Row w Kenny Hill etc 83-85; TV Mildenhall 85-86; rtd 86; Perm to Offic *St E* from 97. *28 Upton Close, Ipswich IP4 2QQ* Tel (01473) 252188

GREEN, Graham Reginald. b 48. Sarum & Wells Th Coll 71. **d** 74 **p** 75. C Chorley St Laur *Blackb* 74-76; C Padiham 76-79; V Osmondthorpe St Phil *Ripon* 79-94. *3 Northwood Gardens, Colton, Leeds LS15 9HH* Tel 0113-264 3558

GREEN, Imogen Elizabeth. See VIBERT, Imogen Elizabeth

GREEN, Mrs Janice Anne. b 48. NTMTC BA07. **d** 07 **p** 08. NSM Gt Hallingbury and Lt Hallingbury *Chelmsf* from 07; P-in-c from 09. *The Rectory, Wrights Green Lane, Little Hallingbury, Bishop's Stortford CM22 7RE* E-mail rev.janicegreen@btinternet.com

GREEN, Jeffrey. b 43. Chich Th Coll 76. **d** 78 **p** 79. C Crewkerne w Wayford *B & W* 78-81; C Cockington *Ex* 81-83; R Ripple, Earls Croome w Hill Croome and Strensham *Worc* 83-87; Perm to Offic *Glouc* 02-03; Hon C Boxwell, Leighterton, Didmarton, Oldbury etc 03-06; Hon C Nailsworth w Shortwood, Horsley etc 03-06; rtd 06. *7 Cherry Tree Close, Nailsworth, Stroud GL6 0DX* Tel (01453) 836910

GREEN, Miss Jennifer Mary. b 55. SEN78 SRN81 RM84. Trin Coll Bris 87. **d** 90 **p** 95. C Tong *Bradf* 90-93; Chapl Bradf Cathl 93; CMS from 94; Uganda from 94. *Muhabura Diocese, PO Box 22, Kisoro, Uganda*

GREEN, Jeremy Nigel. b 52. St Andr Univ MA. St Jo Coll Nottm 80. **d** 83 **p** 84. C Dorridge *Birm* 83-86; V Scrooby *S'well* 86-94; V Bawtry w Austerfield and Misson 94-06; AD Bawtry 01-06; P-in-c Haxey *Linc* from 06; P-in-c Owston from 06. *The Vicarage, Church Street, Haxey, Doncaster DN9 2HY* Tel (01427) 752351 E-mail jngreen@lineone.net

GREEN, John. See GREEN, Edward John

GREEN, The Ven John. b 53. CB10. Nottm Univ BCombStuds83. Linc Th Coll 80. **d** 83 **p** 84. C Watford St Mich *St Alb* 83-86; C St Alb St Steph 86-91; Chapl RN 91-06; Chapl of the Fleet and Adn for the RN from 06; Hon Can Portsm Cathl from 06. *Royal Naval Chaplaincy Service, Mail Point 1-2, Leach Building, Whale Island, Portsmouth PO2 8BY* Tel (023) 9262 5055 Fax 9262 5134

GREEN, John David. b 29. Lon Univ BD66. Roch Th Coll 63. **d** 66 **p** 66. C Roch St Pet w St Marg 66-72; V Oxshott *Guildf* 72-85; R Weybridge 85-94; rtd 94; Perm to Offic *Guildf* from 94. *103 Bitterne Drive, Woking GU21 3JX* Tel (01483) 727936

GREEN, John Francis Humphrey. b 44. Ex Univ BA65 Heythrop Coll Lon MA96. Westcott Ho Cam 91. **d** 93 **p** 94. C Tadworth *S'wark* 93-96; Chapl St Geo Sch Harpenden 96-01; P-in-c Flamstead *St Alb* from 01; P-in-c Markyate Street from 01; RD Wheathampstead 09-10. *The Vicarage, 50 Trowley Hill Road, Flamstead, St Albans AL3 8EE* Tel (01582) 842040 E-mail johnhumphreygreen@hotmail.com

GREEN, Canon John Henry. b 44. K Coll Lon BD72 AKC. **d** 73 **p** 74. C Tupsley *Heref* 73-77; Asst Chapl Newc Univ 77-79; V Stevenage St Hugh Chells *St Alb* 79-85; V St Jo in Bedwardine *Worc* 85-92; Dir of Ords 92-08; P-in-c Guarlford and Madresfield w Newland 92-99; C Fladbury w Wyre Piddle and Moor etc 99-08; P-in-c Bowbrook N from 08; P-in-c Bowbrook S from 08; Hon Can Worc Cathl from 94. *The Parsonage, Church Lane, Tibberton, Droitwich WR9 7NW* Tel (01905) 345242 E-mail jgreen@cofe-worcester.org.uk

GREEN, Julia Ann. See CARTWRIGHT, Julia Ann

GREEN, Canon Karina Beverley. b 61. Ripon Coll Cuddesdon 87. **d** 90 **p** 94. C Lee-on-the-Solent *Portsm* 90-93; Dioc Youth Officer *Guildf* 94-99; Youth and Children's Work Adv *Portsm* 99-03; P-in-c Portsea St Geo 03-05; V from 05; CME Officer from 03; Hon Can Portsm Cathl from 06. *The Vicarage, 8 Queen Street, Portsmouth PO1 3HL* Tel (023) 9283 8713 E-mail karina@stgeorgeschurch.freeserve.co.uk

GREEN, Miss Katharine Marisa. b 81. Bris Univ BA02 St Jo Coll Dur MA08. Cranmer Hall Dur 05. **d** 08 **p** 09. C Kidderminster St Mary and All SS w Trimpley etc *Worc* from 08. *201B Birmingham Road, Kidderminster DY10 2DB* Tel (01562) 825582 E-mail katharine.green@hotmail.com

✠**GREEN, The Rt Revd Laurence Alexander.** b 45. K Coll Lon BD68 AKC68. DMin82 NY Th Sem STM69 St Aug Coll Cant 70. **d** 70 **p** 71 **c** 93. C Kingstanding St Mark *Birm* 70-73; V Erdington St Chad 73-83; Prin Aston Tr Scheme 83-89; Hon C Birchfield *Birm* 84-89; TR Poplar *Lon* 89-93; Area Bp Bradwell *Chelmsf* 93-11; rtd 11. *Belclare, 86 Belle Hill, Bexhill-on-Sea TN40 2AP* Tel (01424) 217872

GREEN, Mrs Linda Anne. b 60. Westcott Ho Cam 84. **dss** 86 **d** 87 **p** 94. Borehamwood *St Alb* 86-89; Par Dn 87-89; Par Dn Sheff St Cuth 89-90; Chapl Asst N Gen Hosp Sheff 89-91; Chapl 91-95; Chapl Qu Mary's Sidcup NHS Trust 96-05; P-in-c Crockenhill All So *Roch* 06-10; P-in-c Brasted from 10. *The Rectory, Coles Lane, Brasted, Westerham TN16 1NR* Tel (01959) 565829 E-mail revlindagreen@aol.com

GREEN, Mrs Linda Jeanne. b 50. R Holloway Coll Lon BSc72 RGN74 RCNT79. SAOMC 01. **d** 04 **p** 05. C Headington Quarry *Ox* 04-09; P-in-c Banbury from 09. *The Vicarage, 89 Oxford Road, Banbury OX16 9AJ* Tel (01295) 262370 Mobile 07973-802863 E-mail linda@revgreen.wanadoo.co.uk

GREEN, Lucinda Jane. CITC. **d** 09. NSM Killaloe w Stradbally *L & K* from 09. *Address temp unknown*

GREEN, Marcus. See GREEN, Edward Marcus

GREEN, Mrs Margaret Elizabeth. b 34. St Mich Ho Ox 60. **dss** 84 **d** 87 **p** 94. Ecclesall *Sheff* 84-87; Par Dn 87-90; C Doncaster St Jas 90-94; rtd 95; Perm to Offic *Sheff* from 95. *91 Littemoor Lane, Doncaster DN4 0LQ* Tel (01302) 365884

GREEN, Martin Charles. b 59. Bris Univ BA81 MPhil86. Wycliffe Hall Ox 82. **d** 84 **p** 85. C Margate H Trin *Cant* 84-88; V Kingston upon Hull St Aid Southcoates *York* 88-94; P-in-c Bishop's Itchington *Cov* from 94; Dioc Children's Officer 94-05; P-in-c Radford Semele from 05. *The Vicarage, 1 Manor Road, Bishop's Itchington, Southam CV47 2QJ* Tel (01926) 613466 E-mail revmcg@aol.com

GREEN, Martyn. b 41. FCA. Ridley Hall Cam 78. **d** 80 **p** 81. C Wetherby *Ripon* 80-83; V Leeds St Cypr Harehills 83-90; V Ossett cum Gawthorpe *Wakef* 90-99; TR Haxby w Wigginton *York* 99-07; rtd 07. *29 Park Row, Knaresborough HG5 0BJ* Tel (01423) 797560

GREEN, Mrs Maureen. b 49. Avery Hill Coll CertEd70 Lon Univ BEd71. EAMTC 98. **d** 98 **p** 02. NSM Ipswich St Jo *St E* 98-10; Asst Chapl Ipswich Hosp NHS Trust 98-02; Asst Chapl Local Health Partnerships NHS Trust 98-02; Asst Chapl Cen Suffolk Primary Care Trust 02-05. *Address temp unknown* E-mail maureengreen@talk21.com

GREEN, Canon Maurice Paul. b 34. MCIMA60. Wells Th Coll 68. **d** 70 **p** 71. C Eaton *Nor* 70-74; R N w S Wootton 74-90; RD Lynn 83-89; Hon Can Nor Cathl 88-96; V Swaffham 90-96; rtd 96; Perm to Offic *St E* from 96. *6 Wimborne Avenue, Ipswich IP3 8QW* Tel (01473) 711061 E-mail m.green25@ntl.com

GREEN, Michael. See GREEN, Canon Edward Michael Bankes

GREEN, Muriel Hilda. b 38. SEITE 94. **d** 96 **p** 97. NSM Ealing St Barn *Lon* 96-98; C 98-00; Hon C Elmstead *Chelmsf* 00-04; P-in-c 04-06; rtd 06; Perm to Offic *Chelmsf* from 06. *3 Laurence Close, Elmstead Market, Colchester CO7 7EJ* Tel (01206) 820561 E-mail murielgreen@onetel.com

GREEN, Neil Howard. b 57. New Coll Ox BA80 PGCE81. Wycliffe Hall Ox 87. **d** 90 **p** 91. C Finchley St Paul and St Luke *Lon* 90-94; C Muswell Hill St Jas w St Matt 94-98; V Eastbourne All So *Chich* 98-10; Asst Master Eastbourne Coll from 10.

Eastbourne College, Old Wish Road, Eastbourne BN21 4JY Tel (01323) 452300 E-mail nhgreen@hotmail.co.uk

GREEN, Nicholas. b 67. Cranmer Hall Dur 07. **d** 08 **p** 09. C Marton-in-Cleveland *York* 08-11; C Brookfield from 11. *Brookfield Vicarage, 89 Low Lane, Middlesbrough TS5 8EF* Tel (01642) 284172 Mobile 07970-164175 E-mail greennick@live.co.uk

GREEN, Paul. b 25. RD. Sarum & Wells Th Coll 72. **d** 74 **p** 75. C Pinhoe *Ex* 74-77; P-in-c 77-79; V 79-85; P-in-c Bishopsteignton 85-88; P-in-c Ideford, Luton and Ashcombe 85-88; rtd 88; Perm to Offic *Ex* 88-08. *58 Maudlin Drive, Teignmouth TQ14 8SB* Tel (01626) 777312

GREEN, Paul John. b 48. Sarum & Wells Th Coll 72. **d** 73 **p** 74. C Tuffley *Glouc* 73-76; C Prestbury 76-82; P-in-c Highnam w Lassington and Rudford 82-83; P-in-c Tibberton w Taynton 82-83; R Highnam, Lassington, Rudford, Tibberton etc 84-92; Hon Min Can *Glouc* Cathl 85-96; V Fairford 92-96; RD Fairford 93-96; rtd 96; Perm to Offic *Glouc* from 98. *19 Prices Road, Abbeymead, Gloucester GL4 4PD* Tel (01452) 614259

GREEN, Pauline. *See* GREEN, Mrs Elizabeth Pauline Anne

GREEN, Penny. *See* GREEN, Denise Penelope

GREEN, Peter. b 38. Ex Univ BSc59. Sarum Th Coll 59. **d** 61 **p** 62. C Romford St Edw *Chelmsf* 61-66; Chapl Trin Coll Kandy Ceylon 66-70; V Darnall *Sheff* 71-80; TV Stantonbury *Ox* 80-87; TV Stantonbury and Willen 87-91; Dep Chapl HM Pris Belmarsh 91-92; Chapl HM Pris Woodhill 92-03; rtd 03; Perm to Offic *Ox* from 04. *34 North Twelfth Street, Milton Keynes MK9 3BT* Tel (01908) 240634 Fax 240635 Mobile 07808-556213 E-mail peter@pg34.eclipse.co.uk

GREEN, Peter Geoffrey. b 59. St Andr Univ MA83 Open Univ MA01 PhD10. Coll of Resurr Mirfield 85. **d** 89 **p** 89. C Pershore w Pinvin, Wick and Birlingham *Worc* 88-91; V Dudley St Barn 91-99; V W Bromwich St Fran *Lich* 99-04; RD W Bromwich 02-04; Chapl Abbots Bromley Sch from 04; P-in-c Hoar Cross w Newchurch *Lich* from 07. *Argyll Cottage, High Street, Abbots Bromley, Rugeley WS15 3BN* Tel (01283) 841978 E-mail peter@greenpeter8.orangehome.co.uk

GREEN, Peter Jamie. b 63. Aston Tr Scheme 87 Oak Hill Th Coll BA93. **d** 93 **p** 94. C Brigg *Linc* 93-97; C Brigg, Wrawby and Cadney cum Howsham 97; P-in-c Billinghay 97-01; V Carr Dyke Gp 01-02; R Kelsey Gp 02-09; P-in-c St Mark's Bermuda from 09. *The Rectory, 13 Mount Hope Lane, Smiths FL06, Bermuda* Tel (001) (441) 236 8360 E-mail peter.green 99@tiscali.co.uk

GREEN, Canon Philip Charles. b 53. NOC 91. **d** 94 **p** 95. C Southport Em *Liv* 94-98; P-in-c Crossens 98-03; TV N Meols 03-05; TR from 05; AD N Meols from 09; Hon Can Liv Cathl from 09. *St John's Vicarage, Rufford Road, Southport PR9 8JH* Tel (01704) 227662 E-mail revphilgreen@crossens1.freeserve.co.uk

GREEN, Canon Philip Harry. b 19. ALCD50. **d** 50 **p** 51. C Keighley *Bradf* 50-53; V Everton St Sav *Liv* 53-57; V Barnoldswick w Bracewell *Bradf* 57-64; V Shipley St Paul 64-77; V Gargrave 77-82; Hon Can Bradf Cathl 77-82; rtd 82; Perm to Offic *Bradf* 82-94 and *Carl* 82-09. *The Villa, Hornby, Northallerton DL6 2JQ* Tel (01609) 881288

GREEN, Richard Alistair. b 76. Ex Univ BA97. St Steph Ho Ox BA01. **d** 01 **p** 02. C Cockerton *Dur* 01-05; TV Ludlow *Heref* from 05; Chapl Shropshire Co Primary Care Trust from 05. *St Mary's Vicarage, Donkey Lane, Ashford Carbonel, Ludlow SY8 4DA* Tel (01584) 831113 E-mail richardgreen@ashfordcarbonell.co.uk

GREEN, Richard Charles. b 49. K Coll Lon 68 St Aug Coll Cant 73. **d** 74 **p** 75. C Broseley w Benthall *Heref* 74-79; TV Heref St Martin w St Fran 80-95; C Heref S Wye 95-99; rtd 99; Hon Chapl Heref S Wye 99-02; Chapl from 02. *5 Bardolph Close, Hereford HR2 7QA* Tel (01432) 354588 or 353717 Mobile 07976-910881 E-mail rghswtm@aol.com

GREEN, Robert Henry. b 57. K Coll Lon BD79. Wycliffe Hall Ox 81. **d** 83 **p** 84. C Norbury *Ches* 83-86 and from 91; C Knutsford St Jo and Toft 86-88; rtd 88. *122 Cavendish Road, Hazel Grove, Stockport SK7 6JH* Tel (01625) 858680 E-mail rob.green122@ntlworld.com

GREEN, Robert Leonard. b 44. Sarum & Wells Th Coll. **d** 84 **p** 85. C Battersea St Luke *S'wark* 84-89; CF 89-04; P-in-c Southwick w Boarhunt *Portsm* from 05. *The White House, High Street, Southwick, Fareham PO17 6EB* Tel (023) 9237 7568 E-mail revdbobgreen@talktalk.net

GREEN, Robert Stanley. b 42. Dur Univ BA65. Wells Th Coll 65. **d** 67 **p** 68. C Ashford *Cant* 67-73; R Otham 73-80; V Bethersden w High Halden 80-87; R Winterbourne Stickland and Turnworth etc *Sarum* 87-99; R Monkton Farleigh, S Wraxall and Winsley 99-05; rtd 05. *The Bungalow, Wootton Grove, Sherborne DT9 4DL* Tel (01935) 817066 E-mail albertgoat@aol.com

GREEN, Robin. b 47. St As Minl Tr Course. **d** 06 **p** 07. NSM Llangystennin St As 06-09; NSM Rhos-Cystennin from 09. *140 Queens Road, Landudno LL30 1UE* Tel (01492) 876451 E-mail rev.robin@tiscali.co.uk

GREEN, Robin Christopher William. b 43. Leeds Univ BA64 Fitzw Ho Cam BA67. Ridley Hall Cam 65. **d** 68 **p** 69. C S'wark H Trin 68-71; C Englefield Green *Guildf* 71-73; Chapl Whitelands Coll of HE *S'wark* 73-78; Team Ldr Dioc Lay Tr Team 78-84; V W Brompton St Mary w St Pet *Lon* 84-87; USPG 87-90; Perm to Offic *S'wark* 88-90; rtd 03. *The Catch, 53 Sandown Road, Deal CT14 6PE* Tel (01304) 389050

GREEN, Roderick. b 74. Reading Univ BA95 Brunel Univ MA99. Wycliffe Hall Ox MTh07. **d** 07 **p** 08. C Spitalfields Ch Ch w All SS *Lon* 07-11; C Shadwell St Paul w Ratcliffe St Jas from 11. *16 Mulberry Court, 1 School Mews, London E1 0EW* Tel 07957-247239 (mobile) E-mail rodeagreen@googlemail.com

GREEN, Rodney William. b 52. **d** 93 **p** 94. OLM Flixton St Jo *Man* from 93. *85 Arundel Avenue, Flixton, Manchester M41 6MG* Tel 0161-748 7238

GREEN, Roger Thomas. b 43. Oak Hill Th Coll. **d** 79 **p** 80. C Paddock Wood *Roch* 79-83; R High Halstow w All Hallows and Hoo St Mary 83-89; Chapl HM Pris Brixton 89-90; Standford Hill 90-94; Swaleside 94-99; Rochester 99-03; Blantyre Ho 03; Brixton 03-06; rtd 06. *4 Burnt House Close, Wainscott, Rochester ME3 8AU* Tel (01634) 730773 E-mail rogert.green@btinternet.com

GREEN, Preb Ronald Henry. b 27. Lambeth MA86 Bps' Coll Cheshunt 53. **d** 55 **p** 56. C St Marylebone Ch Ch w St Barn *Lon* 55-58; R 58-62; Dioc Youth Tr Officer 62-64; C St Andr Holborn 62-64; RE Adv 63-73; V Hampstead St Steph 64-73; RD N Camden 67-73; V Heston 73-80; Preb St Paul's Cathl 75-83; Jt Dir Lon and S'wark Bd of Educn 79-83; Dir of Educn *Sarum* 83-86; R Chiddingfold *Guildf* 86-91; rtd 91; Perm to Offic *Nor* 91-92; Master St Nic Hosp Salisbury 92-97; Perm to Offic *Sarum* from 98. *20 Ayleswade Road, Salisbury SP2 8DR* Tel (01722) 327660

GREEN (*née* JARMAN), **Mrs Rosemary Susan.** b 44. SAOMC 99. **d** 00 **p** 02. OLM Bradfield and Stanford Dingley *Ox* from 01. *1 Buscot Copse, Bradfield, Reading RG7 6JB* Tel 0118-974 4640 Fax 974 4910 E-mail rosemary.s.green@talk21.com

GREEN, Ruth. b 54. RGN76. New Coll Edin BD11. **d** 11. C Edin St Pet from 11. *10/2 Hope Park Crescent, Edinburgh EH8 9NA* Tel 0131-662 9171 Mobile 07941-552768

GREEN, Ruth Valerie. *See* JAGGER, Mrs Ruth Valerie

GREEN, Ryan Albert. b 77. Nottm Univ BA99. St Steph Ho Ox MTh05. **d** 05 **p** 06. C The Cookhams *Ox* 05-09; R Swanbourne w Mt Claremont Australia from 09. *The Rectory, Shenton Road, Swanbourne, Perth WA 6010, Australia* E-mail rev_green@hotmail.co.uk

GREEN, Sidney Leonard. b 44. K Coll Lon MTh86 Montessori DipEd84. Oak Hill Th Coll BD72. **d** 72 **p** 73. C Skelmersdale St Paul *Liv* 72-74; C Denton Holme *Carl* 74-76; In Bapt Min 76-85; Chapl Qu Eliz Gr Sch Blackb 85-91; Chapl Epsom Coll 91-01; P-in-c Sway *Win* 01-03; V 03-04; rtd 04; Australia from 04; Asst Min Adelaide H Trin 05; R Adelaide St Luke 06; Chapl Kensington St Matt from 07. *Bethany, 31 Maesbury Circuit, Sturt, Adelaide SA 5047, Australia* Tel (0061) (8) 8358 1406 E-mail sandjgreen@adam.com.au

GREEN, Ms Stella Louise. b 61. Kent Univ BA84 Cardiff Univ MTh05. St Mich Coll Llan 01. **d** 03 **p** 04. C Stamford Hill St Thos *Lon* 03-06; R Horsford, Felthorpe and Hevingham *Nor* 06-10; Chapl Norfolk and Nor Univ Hosp NHS Trust from 10. *41 Notykin Street, Norwich NR5 9DN* Tel (01603) 749836 *or* 287470 E-mail stella.green@nnuh.nhs.uk

GREEN, Steven Douglas. b 57. Univ of Wales BA97. Sarum & Wells Th Coll 81. **d** 82 **p** 83. C Hawarden *St As* 82-86; V Mostyn 86-93; V Ffynnongroew 86-93; V Mostyn w Ffynnongroyw 93-99; R Trefnant w Tremeirchion 99-01; R Cefn w Trefnant w Tremeirchion 01-07; V Shotton from 07; Warden of Readers from 10. *The Vicarage, Chester Road East, Shotton, Deeside CH5 1QD* Tel (01244) 836991 E-mail jackolad@talktalk.net

GREEN, Ms Susan Denise. b 66. TCD BA89 HDipEd90. **d** 92 **p** 93. C Antrim All SS *Conn* 92-95; Dioc Youth Officer (Cashel) *C & O* 95-00; Chapl Adelaide and Meath Hosp Dublin 00-09; Chapl Kilkenny Coll *C & O* from 10. *The Rectory, Tullow, Co Carlow, Republic of Ireland* Tel and fax (00353) (59) 915 1481 E-mail greens@iolfree.ie

GREEN, Mrs Susan Margaret. b 54. Univ of Wales (Abth) BSc75. SWMTC 92. **d** 95 **p** 96. NSM Wiveliscombe w Chipstable, Huish Champflower etc *B & W* 95-05; R Blackdown from 05; C Trull w Angersleigh from 05. *The Vicarage, Pitminster, Taunton TA3 7AZ* Tel (01823) 421232 E-mail suegreen@summit.me.uk

GREEN, Mrs Susannah Ruth. b 83. Jes Coll Cam BA05 MA09. Wycliffe Hall Ox MTh10. **d** 08 **p** 09. C Preston-on-Tees and Longnewton *Dur* from 08; C Stockton from 08. *61 Bishopton Road, Stockton-on-Tees TS18 4PD* Tel (01642) 617420

GREEN, Canon Trevor Geoffrey Nash. b 45. BA. Oak Hill Th Coll. **d** 84 **p** 85. C Stalybridge H Trin and Ch Ch *Ches* 84-89; V 89-96; V Lache cum Saltney 96-10; Hon Can Ches Cathl 08-10; rtd 10. *27 Winchester Road, Dukinfield SK16 5DH* Tel 0161-304 7796 Mobile 07837-424038 E-mail trevlaine10@aol.co.uk

GREEN, Trevor Howard. b 37. Sarum & Wells Th Coll 72. **d** 74 **p** 75. C Bloxwich *Lich* 74-77; C Willenhall St Steph 77-79; P-in-c 79-80; V 80-82; V Essington 82-90; V Bishopswood and Brewood 90-02; P-in-c Coven 00-02; RD Penkridge 94-01; rtd 02; Perm to Offic *Lich* from 02. *113 Stafford Street, Cannock WS12 2EN* Tel (01543) 271159

GREEN, William. b 44. Newc Univ BA66 DipEd67 MA77. NOC 87. **d** 90 **p** 91. NSM Utley *Bradf* 90-97; P-in-c Scarborough St Jas w H Trin York 97-00; V Thornton St Jas *Bradf* 00-06; rtd 07; Perm to Offic *Bradf* from 07. *105 Shann Lane, Keighley BD20 6DY* Tel (01535) 669360 E-mail billandagnes@tiscali.co.uk

GREEN OF HURSTPIERPOINT, Preb the Lord (Stephen Keith). b 48. Ex Coll Ox BA69 Mass Inst of Tech MSc75. NOC 84. **d** 87 **p** 88. NSM St Jo Cathl Hong Kong 87-93; Perm to Offic *Lon* from 93; Preb St Paul's Cathl from 07. *House of Lords, London SW1A 0PW*

GREENALL, Canon Ronald Gilbert. b 41. St Aid Birkenhead 61. **d** 64 **p** 65. C Adlington *Blackb* 64-67; C Ribbleton 67-69; R Coppull St Jo 69-84; V Garstang St Thos 84-99; RD Garstang 89-96; Hon Can Blackb Cathl 95-99; rtd 99; Perm to Offic *Blackb* from 99. *40 Duckworth Drive, Catterall, Preston PR3 1YS* Tel (01995) 606135

GREENE, Prof Colin John David. b 50. QUB BA73 Fitzw Coll Cam MA75 Nottm Univ PhD. St Jo Coll Nottm 78. **d** 80 **p** 81. NSM Sandiacre *Derby* 80-81; C Loughborough Em *Leic* 81-84; V Thorpe Acre w Dishley 84-89; Evang Tr Consultant Bible Soc 89-91; Tutor Trin Coll Bris 91-95; Th Consultant Bible Soc and Springdale Coll 95-96; Hd Th and Public Policy Bible Soc 96-03; Dean Th and Prof Seattle Pacific Univ USA 03-05. *Address temp unknown* E-mail cgreene@mhgs.edu

GREENE, John Howe. b 22. K Coll Lon AKC48 BD49. **d** 49 **p** 50. C Drayton in Hales *Lich* 49-52; C Stoke upon Trent 52-56; V Wilnecote 56-62; V Lodsworth and R Selham *Chich* 62-69; R Burwash 69-75; R Petworth 75-88; P-in-c Egdean 76-80; R 80-88; RD Petworth 76-88; rtd 88; Perm to Offic *Chich* from 88. *37 Wilderness Road, Hurstpierpoint, Hassocks BN6 9XD* Tel (01273) 833651

GREENE, Paul David O'Dwyer. b 53. Brunel Univ BSc78 Southn Univ DASS81 CQSW81. Oak Hill NSM Course 90. **d** 93 **p** 94. NSM Northwood Em *Lon* from 93. *50 The Drive, Northwood HA6 1HP* Tel (01923) 829605 Fax 828867 Mobile 07870-237104 E-mail paul@pgreene.demon.co.uk

GREENE, Ms Rachel Elizabeth. b 78. Virginia Univ BA01 Peterho Cam MPhil04. Westcott Ho Cam 05 Yale Div Sch 06. **d** 08 **p** 09. C Sturminster Newton, Hinton St Mary and Lydlinch *Sarum* 08-11; C Ox St Mary V w St Cross and St Pet from 11. *22 Stratford Street, Oxford OX4 1SW* E-mail rachelegreene@gmail.com

GREENE, Richard Francis. b 47. TCD BAI70 BA70 MA86 AMIMechE. CITC 03. **d** 06 **p** 07. NSM Waterford w Killea, Drumcannon and Dunhill *C & O* 06-10; NSM New w Old Ross, Whitechurch, Fethard etc 10-11; P-in-c from 11. *Shallon, 2 Pleasant Avenue, Mount Pleasant, Waterford, Republic of Ireland* Tel (00353) (51) 878477 Mobile 87-825 0418 E-mail rev.greene@gmail.com

GREENE, Valerie. b 45. Sheff Univ MA04. Linc Th Coll 09. **d** 11. OLM Kirkby Laythorpe *Linc* from 11. *68 Church Lane, Kirkby-la-Thorpe, Sleaford NG34 9NU* Tel (01529) 413148 E-mail val.greene@btinternet.com

GREENER, The Very Revd Jonathan Desmond Francis. b 61. Trin Coll Cam BA83 MA87. Coll of Resurr Mirfield 89. **d** 91 **p** 92. C S'wark H Trin w St Matt 91-94; Bp's Dom Chapl *Truro* 94-96; V Brighton Gd Shep Preston *Chich* 96-03; Adn Pontefract *Wakef* 03-07; Dean Wakef from 07. *The Deanery, 1 Cathedral Close, Wakefield WF1 2DP* Tel (01924) 239308 *or* 373923 Fax 215054 E-mail jonathan.greener@wakefield-cathedral.org.uk

GREENFIELD, Diana Marion. b 71. NTMTC. **d** 10 **p** 11. C Glastonbury w Meare *B & W* from 10. *25 Brookfield Way, Street BA16 0UE* E-mail dmgreenfield@me.com

GREENFIELD, Judith Frances. b 44. **d** 10. NSM Hove St Jo *Chich* from 10. *Flat 2, 117 St George's Road, Brighton BN2 1EA*

GREENFIELD, Canon Martin Richard. b 54. Em Coll Cam MA75. Wycliffe Hall Ox MA78. **d** 79 **p** 80. C Enfield Ch Ch Trent Park *Lon* 79-83; CMS 84-94; Nigeria 85-94; Hon Can Aba from 89; C Langdon Hills *Chelmsf* 94-95; R Brampton *Ely* from 95; RD Huntingdon 99-04. *The Rectory, 15 Church Road, Brampton, Huntingdon PE28 4PF* Tel (01480) 453341 E-mail m.greenfield@ntlworld.com

GREENFIELD, Norman John Charles. b 27. Leeds Univ BA51. Chich Th Coll 51. **d** 53 **p** 54. C Portsea St Cuth *Portsm* 53-56; C Whitley Ch Ch *Ox* 56-60; V Moorends *Sheff* 60-65; Asst Stewardship Adv *Ox* 65-70; V Littleworth 65-71; V New Marston 71-79; Dioc Stewardship Adv *Chich* 79-88; P-in-c Amberley w N Stoke 79-83; R Guestling and Pett 88-94; rtd 94; Perm to Offic *Chich* from 94. *5 Marlborough Close, Eastbourne BN23 8AN* Tel (01323) 769494

GREENHALGH, Harry. b 54. **d** 11. NSM Winwick *Liv* from 11. *13 Blair Avenue, Hindley Green, Wigan WN2 4HQ*

GREENHALGH, Ian Frank. b 49. Wycliffe Hall Ox 74. **d** 77 **p** 78. C Parr *Liv* 77-80; V Wigan St Barn Marsh Green 80-84; Chapl RAF 84-04; V Clapham-with-Keasden and Austwick *Bradf* from 04; RD Ewecross from 05. *The Vicarage, Clapham Road, Austwick, Lancaster LA2 8BE* Tel (01524) 251313 E-mail ian.greenhalgh@bradford.anglican.org

GREENHALGH, Philip Adrian. b 52. Dur Univ MA05. Ian Ramsey Coll Brasted 75 Wycliffe Hall Ox 76. **d** 79 **p** 80. C Gt Clacton *Chelmsf* 79-82; P-in-c Stalmine *Blackb* 82-86; Rep Leprosy Miss E Anglia 86-87; Area Org CECS 88-90; NSM Alston Team *Newc* 90-92; NSM Chulmleigh *Ex* 92-93; NSM Chawleigh w Cheldon 92-93; NSM Wembworthy w Eggesford 92-93; P-in-c Gilsland w Nether Denton *Carl* 93-95; V Millom 95-00; P-in-c Heathercleugh *Dur* 00-04; P-in-c Westgate 00-04; P-in-c St John in Weardale 00-04; P-in-c Stanhope w Frosterley 02-04; P-in-c Eastgate w Rookhope 02-04; R Upper Weardale 04-07; AD Stanhope 00-07; R Bewcastle, Stapleton and Kirklinton etc *Carl* from 07. *Stapleton Rectory, Roweltown, Carlisle CA6 6LD* Tel (01697) 748660

GREENHALGH, Stephen. b 53. Man Univ MA99. Lon Bible Coll BA81. **d** 81 **p** 82. C Horwich H Trin *Man* 81-84; C Horwich 84-85; Chapl RAF 85-89; Perm to Offic *Blackb* 96-01; *Carl* 01-07; Hon Min from 07. *2 Old Chapel Lane, Levens, Kendal LA8 8PX* Tel (01539) 737856

GREENHAM (née MORTIMER), Mrs Helen Teän. b 69. Leeds Univ BA91 Univ of Wales (Swansea) PGCE92. Ripon Coll Cuddesdon 06. **d** 08 **p** 09. C Bridgnorth, Tasley, Astley Abbotts, etc *Heref* from 08; TV Solihull *Birm* from 11. *St Helen's House, 6 St Helen's Road, Solihull B91 2DA* Tel 0121-704 2878 Mobile 07720-543885 E-mail helen.greenham@gmail.com

GREENHILL, Anthony David. b 39. Bris Univ BSc59. Tyndale Hall Bris 61. **d** 63 **p** 64. C Southsea St Jude *Portsm* 63-65; India 65-78; C Kinson *Sarum* 78-81; V Girlington *Bradf* 81-97; C Platt Bridge *Liv* 97-00; rtd 00; Perm to Offic *Bradf* from 01 and *Man* from 05. *65 Lymbridge Drive, Blackrod, Bolton BL6 5TH* Tel (01204) 696509 E-mail admp@greenhill.me.uk

GREENHOUGH, Alan Kenneth. b 40. St D Coll Lamp. **d** 66 **p** 67. C Allestree *Derby* 66-70; C Ilkeston St Mary 70-73; V Bradwell 73-85; R Twyford w Guist w Bintry w Themelthorpe etc *Nor* 85-95; P-in-c Stibbard 94-95; R Twyford, Guist, Bintree, Themelthorpe etc 95-05; rtd 05. *10 Newton Close, Metheringham, Lincoln LN4 3EQ* Tel (01526) 328642

GREENHOUGH, Andrew Quentin. b 68. E Lon Poly BSc89. Wycliffe Hall Ox BTh94. **d** 94 **p** 95. C Partington and Carrington *Ches* 94-98; C Davenham 98-05; P-in-c Moulton 01-05; V New Ferry from 05. *St Mark's Vicarage, New Chester Road, Wirral CH62 1DG* Tel 0151-645 2638 E-mail andy@macvicar.org.uk

GREENHOUGH, Arthur George. b 30. Fitzw Ho Cam BA52 MA56. Tyndale Hall Bris 53. **d** 57 **p** 58. C Wakef St Andr 57-63; R Birkin w Haddlesey *York* 63-85; RD Selby 77-84; P-in-c Hambleton 84-85; R Haddlesey w Hambleton and Birkin 85-00; rtd 01; Perm to Offic *York* from 01. *4 Sandway Drive, Camblesforth, Selby YO8 8JX* Tel (01757) 617347

GREENHOUGH, Geoffrey Herman. b 36. Sheff Univ BA57 Lon Univ BD71. St Jo Coll Nottm 74. **d** 75 **p** 76. C Cheadle Hulme St Andr *Ches* 75-78; R Tilston and Shocklach 78-82; V Hyde St Geo 82-87; V Pott Shrigley 87-00; rtd 00; Perm to Offic *Ches* from 01. *9 Spey Close, Winsford CW7 3BP* Tel (01606) 556275 E-mail geoffrey@greenhough.freeserve.co.uk

GREENISH, Brian Vivian Isitt. b 20. LRCP MRCS Lon Univ MB BS. **d** 89 **p** 89. NSM Bedford St Pet w St Cuth *St Alb* 89-91; Perm to Offic from 91. *69 Chaucer Road, Bedford MK40 2AL* Tel (01234) 352498

GREENLAND, Martin. b 65. Warwick Univ BSc87. Westcott Ho Cam 94. **d** 97 **p** 98. C Scarborough St Martin *York* 97-00; V Bramley and Ravenfield w Hooton Roberts etc *Sheff* 00-04; V Ravenfield, Hooton Roberts and Braithwell 04-08; R Acle w Fishley, N Burlingham, Beighton w Moulton *Nor* from 08. *The Rectory, Norwich Road, Acle, Norwich NR13 3BU* Tel (01493) 750393 E-mail martin@s-lidster.fsnet.co.uk

GREENLAND, Paul Howard. b 59. Bath Univ BA80 ACA85. Trin Coll Bris 98. **d** 00 **p** 01. C Caverswall and Weston Coyney w Dilhorne *Lich* 00-03; P-in-c Chelmsf St Andr 03-05; V from 05. *The Vicarage, 88 Chignal Road, Chelmsford CM1 2JB* Tel and fax (01245) 496722 Mobile 07811-539328 E-mail paulhgreenland@care4free.net

GREENLAND, Roy Wilfrid. b 37. St Steph Ho Ox 71. **d** 73 **p** 74. C Wanstead St Mary *Chelmsf* 73-76; V Harlow St Mary Magd 76-83; P-in-c Huntingdon All SS w St Jo *Ely* 83-84; P-in-c Huntingdon St Barn 83-84; P-in-c Huntingdon St Mary w St Benedict 83-84; Bermuda 84-89; V Northampton St Alb *Pet* 89-92; R Waldron *Chich* 92-02; rtd 02; Perm to Offic *Pet* 05-07. *7 Margetts Close, Kenilworth CV8 1EN* Tel (01926) 852560

GREENMAN, David John. b 35. Lon Univ BA59. Oak Hill Th Coll 57. **d** 61 **p** 62. C Wandsworth St Steph *S'wark* 61-63; C Bishopwearmouth St Gabr *Dur* 63-66; C-in-c Bedgrove CD *Ox* 66-74; P-in-c Macclesfield Ch Ch *Ches* 74-77; V 77-81; P-in-c Glouc All SS 81-85; V Glouc St Jas 81-85; V Bare *Blackb* 85-91; V Market Lavington and Easterton *Sarum* 91-99; rtd 99; Perm to

Offic *Sarum* and *Win* from 00. *3 Bure Lane, Christchurch BH23 4DJ* Tel (01425) 241034

GREENMAN (*née* **CHESTER), Mrs Irene Mary.** b 51. Dioc OLM tr scheme 97. **d** 99 **p** 00. OLM Cornholme *Wakef* 99-00; OLM Cornholme and Walsden from 00. *8 Glenview Street, Cornholme, Todmorden OL14 8LT* Tel and fax (01706) 817296 E-mail revgreenman@aol.com

GREENSLADE, Canon Gillian Carol. b 43. Leic Univ BA64 Essex Univ MA78 Nottm Univ PGCE65. EAMTC 93. **d** 96 **p** 97. NSM Dovercourt and Parkeston w Harwich *Chelmsf* 96-00; NSM Colchester, New Town and The Hythe 00-02; R Broxted w Chickney and Tilty etc 02-08; Hon Can Chelmsf Cathl 07-08; rtd 08; Adv for Women's Min (Colchester Area) 05-08; Perm to Offic *Chelmsf* from 08. *24 Quayside Court, The Quay, Harwich CO12 3HH* Tel (01255) 552055

GREENSLADE, Timothy Julian. b 63. St Jo Coll Ox BA86. Oak Hill Th Coll BA95. **d** 95 **p** 96. C Broadwater *Chich* 95-99; TV Radipole and Melcombe Regis *Sarum* from 99. *The Vicarage, 106 Spa Road, Weymouth DT3 5ER* Tel (01305) 771938

GREENSTREET, Mark George. b 68. St Jo Coll Dur BA97. Cranmer Hall Dur 94. **d** 97 **p** 98. C St Alb St Pet *St Alb* 97-99; C Stevenage St Hugh and St Jo 99-01; C Dorridge *Birm* 01-04; V Halton *Ches* 04-09; I Seapatrick *D & D* from 09. *26 Larchwood Avenue, Banbridge BT32 3XH* Tel (028) 4066 9086 E-mail mark-greenstreet@lineone.net

GREENWAY, John. b 32. Bps' Coll Cheshunt 68 Qu Coll Birm 69. **d** 69 **p** 70. C Luton Ch Ch *St Alb* 69-74; C Pulloxhill w Flitton 75-76; P-in-c Marston Morteyne 76-79; P-in-c Lidlington 77-79; P-in-c Marston Mortcyne w Lidlington 80-81; R 81-97; rtd 97; Perm to Offic *Portsm* from 98. *73 Northmore Road, Locks Heath, Southampton SO31 6ZW* Tel (01489) 886791

GREENWAY, John Michael. b 34. **d** 96 **p** 97. OLM Gt Yarmouth *Nor* 96-04; Perm to Offic from 04. *17 Hamilton Road, Great Yarmouth NR30 4ND* Tel (01493) 853558

GREENWELL, Christopher. b 49. Linc Th Coll 79. **d** 81 **p** 82. C Scarborough St Martin *York* 81-84; V S Bank 84-89; R Bolton by Bowland w Grindleton *Bradf* 89-92; V Nether Hoyland St Andr *Sheff* 92-96; V Kirkleatham *York* 96-07; rtd 07. *79 Hillshaw Park Way, Ripon HG4 1JU* Tel (01765) 600467 E-mail chris.h@greenwell49.wanadoo.co.uk

GREENWELL, Canon Paul. b 60. Magd Coll Ox BA81 MA85. St Steph Ho Ox 82. **d** 85 **p** 86. C Hendon and Sunderland *Dur* 85-88; Min Can and Prec Ripon Cathl 88-93; Chapl Univ Coll of Ripon and York St Jo 88-93; V Hunslet St Mary *Ripon* 93-02; Chapl Harrogate and Distr NHS Foundn Trust 02-08; Chapl St Mich Hospice Harrogate 02-08; Convenor Dioc Adv Gp for Chr Healing *Ripon* 03-08; Can Res Ripon Cathl from 08. *St Wilfrid's House, Minster Close, Ripon HG4 1QP* Tel (01765) 600211 E-mail canonpaul@riponcathedral.org.uk

GREENWOOD, Claire. *See* GREENWOOD, Helen Claire

GREENWOOD, David. *See* GREENWOOD, Canon Norman David

GREENWOOD, Elizabeth. *See* GREENWOOD, Mrs Margaret Elizabeth

GREENWOOD, Canon Gerald. b 33. Leeds Univ BA57 Sheff Poly MSc81 Surrey Univ Hon MA93. Linc Th Coll 57. **d** 59 **p** 60. C Rotherham *Sheff* 59-62; V Elsecar 62-70; V Wales 70-77; P-in-c Thorpe Salvin 74-77; Dioc Sch Officer 77-84; P-in-c Bramley and Ravenfield 77-78; P-in-c Hooton Roberts 77-78; R 78-84; Hon Can Sheff Cathl 80-84; Dioc Dir of Educn 84-97; Hon Can S'wark Cathl 84-97; Dir of Educn 84-97; rtd 97; Perm to Offic *Cant* from 97. *Home Farm Cottage, Westmarsh, Canterbury CT3 2LW* Tel (01304) 812160

GREENWOOD, Canon Gordon Edwin. b 44. Trin Coll Bris 78. **d** 80 **p** 81. C Bootle St Matt *Liv* 80-83; V Hunts Cross 83-93; V Skelmersdale St Paul 93-10; P-in-c Skelmersdale Ch at Cen 02-10; AD Ormskirk 06-10; Hon Can Liv Cathl 06-10; rtd 10. *53 Redwood Drive, Ormskirk L39 3NS* Tel (01695) 570951 E-mail gordon757greenwood@btinternet.com

GREENWOOD, Helen Claire. b 54. Cranmer Hall Dur 05. **d** 06 **p** 07. C Willington *Newc* 06-10; V Marden w Preston Grange from 10; V Billy Mill from 10. *St Aidan's Vicarage, 29 Billy Mill Lane, North Shields NE29 8BZ* Tel 0191-257 6595 E-mail hcgreenwood@yahoo.com

GREENWOOD, Ian Richard. b 74. Liv Hope BEd96. St Jo Coll Nottm MTh09. **d** 09. C Burscough Bridge *Liv* from 09. *3 Thistle Court, Burscough, Ormskirk L40 4AW* Tel 07840-829956 (mobile) E-mail iang.nicg@btinternet.com

GREENWOOD, James Peter. b 61. Univ Coll Lon BSc83 St Jo Coll Dur BA90 RIBA87. Cranmer Hall Dur 88. **d** 91 **p** 92. C Belper *Derby* 91-94; CMS Pakistan 95-01; V Islamabad St Thos 95-00; V Silsden *Bradf* 01-09; Dioc Spirituality Adv 05-09; RD S Craven 07-09; P-in-c Gillingham and Milton-on-Stour *Sarum* from 09. *The Rectory, High Street, Gillingham SP8 4AJ* Tel (01747) 822435 *or* 821598

GREENWOOD, John Newton. b 44. St Chad's Coll Dur BA66. **d** 70 **p** 71. C Hartlepool H Trin *Dur* 70-72; Lic to Offic from 72; Hd Master Archibald Primary Sch Cleveland 84-97; Asst Chapl

HM Pris Holme Ho from 99. *1 Brae Head, Eaglescliffe, Stockton-on-Tees TS16 9HP* Tel (01642) 783200

GREENWOOD, Leslie. b 37. Dur Univ BA59. St Jo Coll Dur. **d** 61 **p** 62. C Birstall *Wakef* 61-63; C Illingworth 64-70; Chapl H Trin Sch Halifax 64-89; V Charlestown 70-91; TV Upper Holme Valley 91-97; Perm to Offic from 97; rtd 00. *2 Trenance Gardens, Greetland, Halifax HX4 8NN* Tel and fax (01422) 373926 E-mail kyandles@aol.com

GREENWOOD, Mrs Margaret Elizabeth. b 34. St Mary's Coll Chelt TCert65 Surrey Univ MA93. St Mich Ho Ox 60. **d** 00. NSM Shepperton *Lon* 00-01; NSM Whitton SS Phil and Jas 01-04; Perm to Offic from 04. *Bundoran Cottage, Vicarage Lane, Staines TW18 1UE* Tel (01784) 458115 E-mail elizabethgreenwood@btinternet.com

GREENWOOD, Canon Michael Eric. b 44. Oak Hill Th Coll 78. **d** 80 **p** 81. C Clubmoor *Liv* 80-83; V Pemberton St Mark Newtown 83-94; V Grassendale 94-00; V Ashton-in-Makerfield St Thos 00-09; Hon Can Liv Cathl 08-09; rtd 09. *1 Fardon Close, Wigan WN3 6SN* E-mail mikeg@tinyonline.co.uk

GREENWOOD, Canon Norman David. b 52. Edin Univ BMus74 Lon Univ BD78 Nottm Univ MPhil90. Oak Hill Th Coll 76. **d** 78 **p** 79. C Gorleston St Andr *Nor* 78-81; SAMS 81-83; C Cromer *Nor* 83-84; R Appleby Magna and Swepstone w Snarestone *Leic* 84-94; P-in-c Chesterfield H Trin *Derby* 94-95; P-in-c Chesterfield Ch Ch 94-95; R Chesterfield H Trin and Ch Ch 95-99; V S Ramsey St Paul *S & M* from 99; Dir of Ords from 01; RD Ramsey from 08; Chapl HM Pris Is of Man from 05; Hon Can St German's Cathl from 09. *St Paul's Vicarage, Walpole Drive, Ramsey, Isle of Man IM8 1NA* Tel (01624) 812275

GREENWOOD, Peter. *See* GREENWOOD, James Peter

GREENWOOD, Canon Robin Patrick. b 47. St Chad's Coll Dur BA68 MA71 Birm Univ PhD92. **d** 70 **p** 71. C Adel *Ripon* 70-73; Min Can and Succ Ripon Cathl 73-78; V Leeds Halton St Wilfrid 78-86; Dioc Can Res Glouc Cathl 86-95; Dioc Missr and Dir Lay and Post-Ord Tr 86-95; Dir of Min and Hon Can Chelmsf Cathl 95-00; Prov Officer for Min Ch in Wales 01-05; Hon C Canton St Jo *Llan* 02-05; V Monkseaton St Mary *Newc* from 05. *St Mary's Vicarage, 77 Holywell Avenue, Whitley Bay NE26 3AG* Tel 0191-252 2484

GREENWOOD, Roy Douglas. b 27. Tyndale Hall Bris 58. **d** 60 **p** 61. C Ox St Matt 60-62; V Ulpha *Carl* 62-63; V Seathwaite w Ulpha 63-72; P-in-c Haverthwaite 72-74; C Ulverston St Mary w H Trin 74-78; V Egton w Newland 78-86; Assoc Chapl Palma de Mallorca and Balearic Is *Eur* 86-93; Assoc Chapl Palma de Mallorca 93-95; rtd 95. *La Finquita, Apartado 78, 07460 Pollenca (Illes Balears), Spain* Tel (0034) 971 530 966

GREENWOOD, Sharon. **d** 07 **p** 08. NSM Welling *S'wark* from 07. *44 Honiton Road, Welling DA16 3LE* Tel (020) 8854 3541 E-mail sharon.greenwood44@tiscali.co.uk

GREER, Eric Gordon. b 52. Pepperdine Univ BA74. Princeton Th Sem MDiv80. **d** 93 **p** 94. C Southgate St Andr *Lon* 93-96; C Camden Square St Paul 96-00; V Grange Park St Pet from 00. *The Vicarage, Langham Gardens, London N21 1DN* Tel (020) 8360 2294 E-mail egreer@talk21.com

GREETHAM, Canon William Frederick. b 40. Bede Coll Dur CertEd. Cranmer Hall Dur 63. **d** 66 **p** 67. C Heyhouses on Sea *Blackb* 66-69; C Ashton-on-Ribble St Andr 69-71; Chapl Aysgarth Sch 71-82; C Bedale *Ripon* 72-75; V Crakehall, Hornby and Patrick Brompton and Hunton 75-82; V Kirkby Stephen *Carl* 82-90; R Kirkby Stephen w Mallerstang etc 90-96; RD Appleby 86-91; P-in-c Crosthwaite Kendal 96-05; P-in-c Cartmel Fell 96-05; P-in-c Winster 96-05; P-in-c Witherslack 96-05; Hon Can Carl Cathl 89-05; rtd 05; Perm to Offic *Blackb* and *Carl* from 05. *2 Crosslands, Whittington, Carnforth LA6 2NX* Tel (015242) 71521 E-mail canonbill@hotmail.co.uk

GREEVES, Roger Derrick. b 43. TCD BA66 MA70 Fitzw Coll Cam BA68 MA73. Westcott Ho Cam 98. **d** 98 **p** 99. In Methodist Ch 68-98; NSM Cam St Edw *Ely* 98-00; Chapl Oakington Immigration Reception Cen 00-01; Chapl Peterho Cam 00-01; Dean Clare Coll Cam 01-08; rtd 08; Perm to Offic *Ely* from 08. *28 Bateman Street, Cambridge CB2 1NB* Tel (01223) 571699 Mobile 07817-032301 E-mail rdg20@cam.ac.uk

GREGG, David William Austin. b 37. Lon Univ BD66 Bris Univ MA69. Tyndale Hall Bris 63. **d** 68 **p** 69. C Barrow St Mark *Carl* 68-71; P-in-c Lindal w Marton 71-75; Communications Sec Gen Syn Bd for Miss and Unity 76-81; Prin Romsey Ho Coll Cam 81-88; V Haddenham w Cuddington, Kingsey etc *Ox* 88-96; P-in-c Newton Longville w Stoke Hammond and Whaddon 96-02; rtd 03; Perm to Offic *Carl* from 03. *Lowick Farm House, Lowick Green, Ulverston LA12 8DX* Tel (01229) 885258

GREGORY, Alan Paul Roy. b 55. K Coll Lon BD77 MTh78 Emory Univ Atlanta PhD94 AKC77. Ripon Coll Cuddesdon 78. **d** 79 **p** 80. C Walton-on-Thames *Guildf* 79-82; Lect Sarum & Wells Th Coll 82-88; Asso R Atlanta St Patr USA 88-94; R Athens Em 94-95; Assoc Prof Ch Hist Episc Th Sem of the SW 95-04; Academic Dean and Prof Ch Hist from

04. *800 West 5th Street #702, Austin TX 78703, USA* Tel (001) (512) 364 3888 Fax 472 3098 E-mail agregory@ssw.edu

GREGORY, Andrew Forsythe. b 71. St Jo Coll Dur BA92. Wycliffe Hall Ox BA96 MA00 DPhil01. d 97 p 98. C E Acton St Dunstan w St Thos *Lon* 97-99; Asst Chapl Keble Coll Ox 97-99; Chapl Linc Coll Ox 99-03; Research Fell Keble Coll Ox 03-05; Chapl and Fell Univ Coll Ox from 05. *University College, High Street, Oxford OX1 4BH* Tel (01865) 276663 E-mail andrew.gregory@theology.ox.ac.uk

GREGORY, Brian. b 43. Trin Coll Bris. d 82 p 83. C Burscough Bridge *Liv* 82-85; V Platt Bridge 85-92; V Ben Rhydding *Bradf* 92-06; rtd 06; Perm to Offic *Bradf* from 07. *9 Strawberry Street, Silsden, Keighley BD20 0AT* Tel (01535) 653056 E-mail brian.gregory@bradford.anglican.org

✠GREGORY, The Rt Revd Clive Malcolm. b 61. Lanc Univ BA84 Qu Coll Cam BA87 MA89 Warwick Univ Hon MA99. Westcott Ho Cam 85. d 88 p 89 c 07. C Margate St Jo *Cant* 88-92; Chapl Warw Univ 92-98; TR Cov E 98-07; Area Bp Wolverhampton *Lich* from 07. *61 Richmond Road, Wolverhampton WV3 9JH* Tel (01902) 824503 Fax 824504 E-mail bishop.wolverhampton@lichfield.anglican.org

GREGORY, Graham. b 36. Open Univ BA78. Tyndale Hall Bris 63. d 66 p 67. C Wandsworth St Mich *S'wark* 66-71; C Hastings Em and St Mary in the Castle *Chich* 71-75; V Douglas St Ninian *S & M* 75-91; Dioc Youth Officer 78-88; Chapl HM Pris Douglas 82-86; R/D Douglas *S & M* 86-91; V Wollaton Park *S'well* 91-95; V Lenton Abbey 91-95; rtd 95; Perm to Offic *York* 98-09. *15 Keble Drive, Bishopthorpe, York YO23 2TA* Tel (01904) 701679

GREGORY, Ian Peter. b 45. Open Univ BA82 Rolle Coll PGCE92. Bernard Gilpin Soc Dur 66 Chich Th Coll 67. d 70 p 71. C Tettenhall Regis *Lich* 70-73; C Shrewsbury H Cross 73-76; P-in-c Walsall St Mary and All SS Palfrey 76-80; R Petrockstowe, Petersmarland, Merton, Meeth etc *Ex* 80-87; TV Ex St Thos and Em 87-91; Hon C S Wimbledon All SS *S'wark* 94-00; rtd 10. *20 Etonhurst Close, Exeter EX2 7QZ* Tel (01392) 447548 Mobile 07598-984623 E-mail revipg@btinternet.com

GREGORY, John Frederick. b 33. Glouc Sch of Min 75. d 78 p 78. NSM S Cerney w Cerney Wick *Glouc* 78-81; NSM Coates, Rodmarton and Sapperton etc 81-88; P-in-c Kempsford w Welford 88-98; rtd 98; Perm to Offic *B & W* from 99. *2 Jury Road, Dulverton TA22 9DU* Tel (01398) 323587

GREGORY, Judith Rosalind. *See* GAVIN, Mrs Judith Rosalind

GREGORY, Mary Emma. b 70. Birm Univ BA92 St Jo Coll Dur BA04 MA06. Cranmer Hall Dur 02. d 05 p 06. C Hatfield *Sheff* 05-08; R Kirk Sandall and Edenthorpe from 08. *The Rectory, 31 Doncaster Road, Kirk Sandall, Doncaster DN3 1HP* Tel (01302) 882861 Mobile 07734-052524 E-mail maryegregory@tiscali.co.uk

GREGORY, Nathan James. b 82. Wycliffe Hall Ox. d 11. C Fair Oak *Win* from 11. *Windfall, Chapel Drove, Horton Heath, Eastleigh SO50 7DL* E-mail n.j.gregory@talk21.com

GREGORY, Peter. b 35. Cranmer Hall Dur 59. d 62 p 63. C Pennington *Man* 62-65; C N Ferriby *York* 65-68; V Tonge Fold *Man* 68-72; V Hollym w Welwick and Holmpton *York* 72-77; P-in-c Foston w Flaxton 77-80; P-in-c Crambe w Whitwell and Huttons Ambo 77-80; R Whitwell w Crambe, Flaxton, Foston etc 81-94; rtd 94. *6 High Terrace, Northallerton DL6 1BG* Tel (01609) 776956

GREGORY, Richard Branson. b 33. Fitzw Ho Cam BA58 MA62. Sarum Th Coll 58 Ridley Hall Cam 59. d 60 p 61. C Sheff St Cuth 60-62; Asst Chapl Leeds Univ 62-64; V Yeadon St Jo *Bradf* 64-71; R Keighley 71-74; TR Keighley St Andr 74-82; Hon Can Bradf Cathl 71-82; RD S Craven 71-73 and 78-82; P-in-c Broadmayne, W Knighton, Owermoigne etc *Sarum* 82-85; R 85-98; rtd 98; Perm to Offic *Sarum* from 98. *2 Huish Cottages, Sydling, Dorchester DT2 9NS* Tel (01300) 341835

GREGORY, Canon Stephen Simpson. b 40. Nottm Univ BA62 CertEd63. St Steph Ho Ox. d 68 p 69. C Aldershot St Mich *Guildf* 68-71; Chapl St Mary's Sch Wantage 71-74; R Edgefield *Nor* 74-88; R Holt 74-94; R Holt w High Kelling 94-95; RD Holt 79-84 and 93-95; Hon Can Nor Cathl 94-95; V Prestbury *Glouc* 95-03; P-in-c Pittville All SS 99-03; TR Prestbury and All SS 03-06; RD Cheltenham 00-05; Hon Can Glouc Cathl 04-06; rtd 06; Perm to Offic *Nor* from 08. *Mulberry Cottage, Balfour Road, West Runton, Cromer NR27 9QJ* Tel (01263) 838049

GREGORY, Timothy Stephen. b 48. Sheff City Coll of Educn CertEd70. NOC 96. d 99 p 00. NSM Deepcar *Sheff* 99-06; NSM Ecclesfield Deanery from 06. *33 St Margaret Avenue, Deepcar, Sheffield S36 2TE* Tel 0114-288 4198 E-mail t.gregory@tiscali.co.uk

GREGORY-SMITH, Hew Quentin. b 69. Univ of Wales (Abth) BSc93. St Mich Coll Llan 98. d 01 p 02. C Pembroke Gp *St D* 01-04; C Henfynyw w Aberaeron and Llanddewi Aberarth etc 04-07; P-in-c Llanllwchaearn and Llanina 07-10. *Brynawelon, New Cross, Aberystwyth SY23 4LY*

GREGSON, Gillian Amy. b 33. Westmr Coll Ox BTh02 CQSW78. d 98 p 99. OLM Coulsdon St Jo *S'wark* 98-05; Perm

to Offic from 05. *3 Coulsdon Road, Coulsdon CR5 2LG* Tel (020) 8660 0304 E-mail gillgregson@waitrose.com

GREGSON, Peter John. b 36. Univ Coll Dur BSc61. Ripon Hall Ox 61. d 63 p 64. C Radcliffe St Thos *Man* 63-65; C Baguley 65-67; Chapl RN 68-91; V Ashburton w Buckland in the Moor and Bickington *Ex* 91-01; RD Moreton 95-98; rtd 01; Perm to Offic *Sarum* 01-11 and *Blackb* from 11. *26 Astley Road, Chorley PR7 1RR* Tel (01257) 247999

GREIFF, Andrew John. b 64. Huddersfield Univ BA98 Leeds Univ PGCE99 St Jo Coll Dur BA05. Cranmer Hall Dur 03. d 05 p 06. C Pudsey St Lawr and St Paul *Bradf* 05-08; P-in-c Thornton St Jas from 08; P-in-c Fairweather Green from 08. *The Vicarage, 300 Thornton Road, Thornton, Bradford BD13 3AB* Tel (01274) 833200 E-mail thegoof@hotmail.com

GREIG, George Malcolm. b 28. CA53 St Andr Univ BD95. LNSM course 75. d 81 p 82. NSM Dundee St Mary Magd *Bre* 81-84; NSM Dundee St Jo 82-84; P-in-c Dundee St Ninian 84-85; Chapl St Paul's Cathl Dundee 85-98; rtd 98; Hon C Dundee St Salvador *Bre* from 98. *61 Charleston Drive, Dundee DD2 2HE* Tel (01382) 566709 E-mail gmg28@btinternet.com

GREIG, John Kenneth. b 38. Natal Univ BA57. d 61 p 62. C Durban St Thos S Africa 61-65; C Sheldon 65-66; C Friern Barnet St Jas *Lon* 66-69; C Kenton 69-71; Asst Chapl Dioc Coll Rondebosch S Africa 71-76; Chapl 76-78; Chapl Whitelands Coll of HE *S'wark* 78-84; V Purley St Swithun 84-04; Area Ecum Officer (Croydon) 84-04; rtd 04; Perm to Offic *S'wark* from 05. *29 Clive Road, London SW19 2JA* Tel (020) 8715 2784 E-mail jkgreig@hotmail.com

GREIG, Martin David Sandford. b 45. Dris Univ DSc67. St Jo Coll Nottm 72. d 75 p 76. C Keresley and Coundon Cov 75-79; C Rugby 79-83; TV 83-86; V Cov St Geo 86-93; TV Southgate *Chich* 93-01; R Maresfield 01-06; P-in-c Nutley 01-06; rtd 06. *Bodawen, Llangrannog, Llandysul SA44 6SH* Tel (01239) 654257 E-mail mg@bodawen.org.uk

GREIG, Michael Lawrie Dickson. b 48. All Nations Chr Coll 78 St Jo Coll Nottm 94. d 96 p 97. C Hunningham *Cov* 96-00; C Wappenbury w Weston under Wetherley 96-00; C Offchurch 96-00; C Long Itchington and Marton 96-00; P-in-c Napton-on-the-Hill, Lower Shuckburgh etc from 00; P-in-c Priors Hardwick, Priors Marston and Wormleighton from 09. *The Vicarage, Butt Hill, Napton, Rugby CV47 8NE* Tel (01926) 812383 E-mail mg@biggles99.freeserve.co.uk

GREIG, Phil. b 76. Ox Brookes Univ BA02. Ridley Hall Cam 09. d 11. C Chartham *Cant* from 11. *79 Rentain Road, Chartham, Canterbury CT4 7JJ* Tel (01227) 732473 Mobile 07411-936354 E-mail revphilgreig@me.com

GRENFELL, James Christopher. b 69. Qu Coll Ox BA93 MA96 MPhil95 Ox Univ DPhil00. Westcott Ho Cam 98. d 00 p 01. C Kirkby *Liv* 00-03; P-in-c Sheff Manor 03-06; TR 06-09; P-in-c Ranmoor from 09. *The Vicarage, 389A Fulwood Road, Sheffield S10 3GA* Tel 0114-230 1671 *or* 230 1199 E-mail james.grenfell@sheffield.anglican.org

GRENFELL, Canon Joanne Woolway. b 72. Oriel Coll Ox BA93 DPhil97 Univ of BC MA94. Westcott Ho Cam 98. d 00 p 01. C Kirkby *Liv* 00-03; St P-in-c Sheff Manor 03-06; Can Res Sheff Cathl from 06; Dioc Dir of Ords from 06; Dean of Women's Min from 08. *Sheffield Cathedral, Church Street, Sheffield S1 1HA* Tel 0114-263 6064 Mobile 07775-868259 E-mail joanne.grenfell@sheffield-cathedral.org.uk

GRENHAM-TOZE, Mrs Sharon Carmel. b 66. Reading Univ LLB87 Solicitor 92. Trin Coll Bris 94 SAOMC 96. d 98 p 00. C Buckingham *Ox* 98-00; C Milton Keynes 00-02; Miss Adv USPG *Lon, Ox* and *St Alb* 02-03; NSM Wilshamstead and Houghton Conquest *St Alb* 03-04; Chapl Oakhill Secure Tr Cen 04-05; Perm to Offic *St Alb* from 04; Asst Chapl HM Pris Woodhill 08-11; Chapl HM Pris Bedf from 11. *HM Prison Bedford, St Loyes Street, Bedford MK40 1HG* Tel (01234) 373000 E-mail sgtoze@btopenworld.com

GRESHAM, Karen Louise. *See* SMEETON, Mrs Karen Louise

GRETTON, Tony Butler. b 29. St Jo Coll Dur BA53. d 54 p 55. C W Teignmouth *Ex* 54-57; R Norton Fitzwarren *B & W* 57-68; rtd 68; Chapl Glouc Docks Mariners' Ch 73-92; P-in-c Brookthorpe w Whaddon 79-82; Hon C The Edge, Pitchcombe, Harescombe and Brookthorpe 82-89; Perm to Offic from 89. *18 Cover Drive, Hardwicke, Gloucester GL2 4TG* Tel (01452) 721505

GREW, Nicholas David. b 52. Surrey Univ BSc74 MSc75. Wycliffe Hall Ox 93. d 95 p 96. C Biddulph *Lich* 95-99; P-in-c Knaphill *Guildf* 99-00; V Knaphill w Brookwood from 00. *Trinity House, Trinity Road, Knaphill, Woking GU21 2SY* Tel (01483) 473489 E-mail nickthevic@talktalk.net

GREW, Richard Lewis. b 32. Clare Coll Cam BA54 MA58. Wycliffe Hall Ox 67. d 68 p 69. C Repton *Derby* 68-73; Asst Chapl Repton Sch Derby 74-93; Lic to Offic *Derby* 73-93; rtd 93; Perm to Offic *Sarum* 94-07. *5 Priory Gardens, Spetisbury, Blandford Forum DT11 9DS* Tel (01258) 857613

GREW, Timothy Richard. b 65. SS Coll Cam MA88. WEMTC 03. d 06 p 07. NSM Cheltenham H Trin and St Paul *Glouc* 06-10;

TV from 10. *7 Clarence Square, Cheltenham GL50 4JN* Tel (01242) 519709 E-mail tim.grew@trinitycheltenham.com
GREY, Andrew James. b 76. St Chad's Coll Dur BA99 MA00. Oak Hill Th Coll 03. **d** 08 **p** 09. C Harold Wood *Chelmsf* from 08. *48 Harold Court Road, Romford RM3 0YX* Tel (01708) 331684 E-mail andrew@stpetersharoldwood.org
GREY, Richard Thomas. b 50. QVRM06 TD94. St D Coll Lamp BA73 Ripon Hall Ox 73. **d** 75 **p** 76. C Blaenavon w Capel Newydd *Mon* 75-77; Ind Chapl 77-02; C Newport St Paul 77-80; CF (TA) from 78; Chapl Aberbargoed Hosp 80-88; V Bedwellty *Mon* 80-88; R Llanwenarth Ultra 88-92; R Govilon w Llanfoist w Llanelen 92-02; RD Abergavenny 98-02; V Brynmawr *S & B* 02-09. *Address temp unknown*
GREY, Canon Roger Derrick Masson. b 38. AKC61. **d** 62 **p** 63. C Darlington H Trin *Dur* 62-63; C Bishopwearmouth St Mich 63-67; V Mabe *Truro* 67-70; Dioc Youth Chapl 67-70; Youth Chapl *Glouc* 70-77; V Stroud H Trin 77-82; Dioc Can Res Glouc Cathl 82-03; Dir of Educn 82-94; Bp's Chapl 94-03; rtd 03; Clergy Widows' Officer (Glouc Adnry) from 03; Perm to Offic from 04. *12 Buckingham Close, Walton Cardiff, Tewkesbury GL20 7QB* Tel (01684) 275742
GREY, Stephen Bernard. b 56. Linc Th Coll 86. **d** 88 **p** 89. C Worsley *Man* 88-93; V Bamford 93-04; P-in-c Rochdale St Geo w St Alb 99-04; P-in-c Preesall *Blackb* 04-05; P-in-c Hambleton w Out Rawcliffe 04-05; V Waterside Par 05-10; P-in-c Garstang St Thos from 10. *St Thomas's Vicarage, Church Street, Garstang, Preston PR3 1PA* Tel (01995) 602192 Mobile 07910-854911 E-mail revsbgrey@btinternet.com
GREY-SMITH, Donald Edward. b 31. ACT ThL64. **d** 64 **p** 65. Australia 64-68 and from 71; W Germany 68-69; C Weeke *Win* 69-71; rtd 96. *6/317 Military Road, Semaphore Park SA 5019, Australia* Tel (0061) (8) 8449 4420
GRIBBEN, John Gibson. b 44. K Coll Lon BD75 QUB MTh81. CITC 73. **d** 75 **p** 76. C Dunmurry *Conn* 75-78; CR from 79; Lic to Offic *Wakef* from 83; rtd 09. *House of the Resurrection, Stocks Bank Road, Mirfield WF14 0BN* Tel (01924) 483339 E-mail jgribben@mirfield.org.uk
GRIBBIN, Canon Bernard Byron. b 35. Bradf Univ MPhil84. St Aid Birkenhead 58. **d** 60 **p** 61. C Maghull *Liv* 60-63; C Prescot 63-65; V Denholme Gate *Bradf* 65-71; V Bankfoot 71-79; Dioc Stewardship Adv 79-86; Prec and Chapl Choral Ches Cathl 86-91; V Ringway 91-96; Dioc Tourism Officer 91-96; Hon Can Ches Cathl 91-96; rtd 96; Perm to Offic *Bradf* from 96. *5 Heather Court, Ilkley LS29 9TZ* Tel (01943) 816253
GRIBBLE, Malcolm George. b 44. Chu Coll Cam BA67 MA71. Linc Th Coll 79. **d** 81 **p** 82. C Farnborough *Roch* 81-84; V Bostall Heath 84-90; V Bexleyheath Ch Ch 90-02; P-in-c Hever, Four Elms and Mark Beech 02-06; R 06-09; rtd 10. *26 Neville Road, Tewkesbury GL20 5ED* Tel (01684) 290641 E-mail m@griblog.net
GRICE, Charles. b 24. MBE83. **d** 58 **p** 59. C Stocksbridge *Sheff* 58-61; R Armthorpe 61-66; Ind Missr 66-69; Ind Chapl 69-76; V Tinsley 69-73; V Oughtibridge 73-76; Gen Sec Ch Lads' and Ch Girls' Brigade 77-91; R Braithwell w Bramley *Sheff* 88-91; rtd 89; Perm to Offic *Sheff* from 89. *57 Deepdale Road, Rotherham S61 2NR* Tel (01709) 557551
GRICE, Canon David Richard. b 32. Keble Coll Ox BA55 MA59. St Steph Ho Ox 55. **d** 57 **p** 58. C Leeds St Aid *Ripon* 57-61; C Middleton St Mary 61-62; V Woodlesford 62-69; V Leeds St Wilfrid 69-78; TR Seacroft 78-93; Hon Can Ripon Cathl 92-99; P-in-c Thorner 93-95; V 95-99; rtd 99; Perm to Offic *Ripon* from 00. *15 Mead Road, Leeds LS15 9JR* Tel 0113-260 4371 E-mail david@grice12.freeserve.co.uk
GRIDLEY, Miss Susan Mary. b 49. EAMTC 94. **d** 97 **p** 98. NSM Doddinghurst and Mountnessing *Chelmsf* 97-03; Perm to Offic *Bradf* 03-04 and *Chelmsf* from 06. *7 Thracian Close, Colchester CO2 9RN* Tel (01206) 548766
GRIER, James Emerson. b 74. St Pet Coll Ox BA95 MA01. Wycliffe Hall Ox 96. **d** 98 **p** 99. C Ox St Andr 98-02; C Harborne Heath *Birm* 02-07; TV Pinhoe and Broadclyst *Ex* from 07; Dioc Youth Adv from 07. *The Vicarage, Rockbeare, Exeter EX5 2EG* Tel (01404) 822883 E-mail james.grier@exeter.anglican.org
GRIERSON, Peter Stanley. b 42. Lon Univ BD68 Leeds Univ MPhil74. Linc Th Coll 68. **d** 69 **p** 70. C Clitheroe St Mary *Blackb* 69-71; C Aston cum Aughton *Sheff* 71-74; V Preston St Jude w St Paul *Blackb* 74-81; V Blackb St Luke w St Phil 89-97; RD Blackb 91-97; V Burnley St Matt w H Trin 97-02; Perm to Offic *Bradf* from 03. *2 Spindle Mill, Skipton BD23 1NY* Tel (01756) 797175
GRIEVE, David Campbell. b 51. St Jo Coll Dur BA74. Wycliffe Hall Ox 74. **d** 76 **p** 77. C Upton (Overchurch) *Ches* 76-80; C Selston *S'well* 80-82; V Pelton *Dur* 82-89; rtd 89. *The Rectory, 107 Front Street, Cockfield, Bishop Auckland DL13 5AA* Tel (01388) 718447 E-mail davidgrieve@cix.co.uk
GRIEVE (née PIERSSENÉ), Canon Frances Jane. b 55. St Jo Coll Dur BA76. Cranmer Hall Dur 99. **d** 01 **p** 02. C Barnard Castle w Whorlton *Dur* 01-05; P-in-c Cockfield from 05; P-in-c Lynesack from 05; P-in-c Evenwood from 09; Adv for Women's Min from 10; Hon Can Dur Cathl from 10. *The Rectory, 107*

Front Street, Cockfield, Bishop Auckland DL13 5AA Tel (01388) 718447 E-mail jane.grieve@durham.anglican.org
GRIEVE, Mrs Judith Margaret. b 52. Goldsmiths' Coll Lon CertEd73. NEOC 91. **d** 94 **p** 96. NSM Choppington *Newc* 94-99; P-in-c Woodhorn w Newbiggin 99-06; V 06-10; V Whorlton from 10; Chapl All SS Coll Newc from 10. *St John's Vicarage, Whorlton, Westerhope, Newcastle upon Tyne NE5 1NN* Tel 0191-286 9648
GRIEVES, Anthony Michael. b 47. St Alb Minl Tr Scheme 81. **d** 84 **p** 85. NSM Stevenage St Mary Shephall *St Alb* 84-86; NSM Stevenage St Mary Shephall w Aston 86-95; Perm to Offic from 95. *27 Falcon Close, Stevenage SG2 9PG* Tel (01438) 727204
GRIEVES, Ian Leslie. b 56. Bede Coll Dur CertEd77 BEd78. Chich Th Coll 82. **d** 84 **p** 85. C Darlington St Mark w St Paul *Dur* 84-87; C Whickham 87-89; V Darlington St Jas from 89. *St James's Vicarage, Vicarage Road, Darlington DL1 1JW* Tel (01325) 465980 E-mail father grieves@lineone.net
GRIFFIN, Alan Howard Foster. b 44. TCD BA66 MA69 Peterho Cam PhD71. Sarum & Wells Th Coll 75. **d** 78 **p** 79. Lect Ex Univ 78-01; Asst to Lazenby Chapl 78-92; Sub-Warden Duryard Halls 78-81; Warden 81-84; Sen Warden 84-98; Perm to Offic *Ex* 92-98; C Heavitree w Ex St Paul 98-01; Ex Campus Chapl Plymouth Univ 98-01; R St Andr-by-the-Wardrobe w St Ann, Blackfriars *Lon* 01-11; R St Jas Garlickhythe w St Mich Queenhithe etc 01-11; CME Officer Two Cities Area 01-08; rtd 11. *24 Cinnamon Street, London E1W 3NJ* E-mail a.h.f.griffin@gmail.com
GRIFFIN, Christopher Donald. b 59. Reading Univ BA80 CertEd81. Wycliffe Hall Ox 82. **d** 85 **p** 86. C Gerrards Cross *Ox* 85-88; Chapl Felsted Sch 88-98; Chapl Sedbergh Sch 98-06; Ho Master from 00. *Sedburgh School, Sedburgh LA10 5HG* Tel (01539) 620535
GRIFFIN, Gerald Albert Francis. b 31. Qu Coll Birm 74. **d** 77 **p** 78. NSM Bushbury *Lich* 77-83; Ind Chapl *Dur* 83-88; Chapl HM Pris Man 88-89; Chapl HM Pris Featherstone 89-93; C Toxteth St Philemon w St Gabr and St Cleopas *Liv* 93-96; rtd 96; NSM W Bromwich Deanery *Lich* 00-10. *7 Chartwell Drive, Bushbury, Wolverhampton WV10 8JL* Tel (01902) 836414 E-mail revgerrygriffinhome@msn.com
GRIFFIN, Harold Rodan Bristow. b 12. Jes Coll Cam BA33 LLB34 MA43. Ridley Hall Cam 43. **d** 45 **p** 46. C Kirby Moorside w Gillamoor *York* 45-49; C Linthorpe 49-52; C Boylestone *Derby* 52; R Hulland, Atlow and Bradley 52-61; V Framsden *St E* 61-71; R Helmingham 61-71; rtd 77; Perm to Offic *Ely* 91-99. *Highlands, Fitzgerald Road, Woodbridge IP12 1EN* Tel (01394) 383090
GRIFFIN, Joan Angela. b 35. Qu Coll Birm 82. dss 85 **d** 92 **p** 94. Moseley St Mary *Birm* 85-05; NSM 92-05; Chapl Univ Hosp Birm NHS Trust 95-02; Chapl Priory Hosp Birm from 02. *389 Wake Green Road, Birmingham B13 0BH* Tel 0121-777 8772
GRIFFIN, Canon Joseph William. b 48. St Mich Coll Llan 70. **d** 74 **p** 75. C Killay *S & B* 74-78; C Swansea St Thos and Kilvey 78-81; V Troedrhiwgarth *Llan* 81-91; V Llanrhidian w Llanmadoc and Cheriton *S & B* 91-99; RD Gower 94-99; V Swansea St Nic 99-04; RD Swansea 02-04; P-in-c SW Gower 04-06; V from 06; AD Gower from 11; Hon Can Brecon Cathl from 98. *The Rectory, Port Eynon, Swansea SA3 1NL* Tel (01792) 390456 E-mail joe.griffin@virgin.net
GRIFFIN, Keith. b 66. Nottm Trent Univ BA88. Cranmer Hall Dur BA94. **d** 95 **p** 96. C Gedling *S'well* 95-98; V Barkingside St Geo *Chelmsf* 99-02; TV Upper Holme Valley *Wakef* from 02. *The Vicarage, 3 Vicarage Meadows, Holmfirth HD9 1DZ* Tel (01484) 682644 E-mail revdkg@tiscali.co.uk
GRIFFIN, Kenneth Francis. b 21. Lon Univ BSc64. St Jo Coll Nottm 72. **d** 73 **p** 74. C Bexleyheath Ch Ch *Roch* 73-77; R Kingsdown 77-82; rtd 86. *Woodlands, Palmers Cross Hill, Rough Common, Canterbury CT2 9BL* Tel (01227) 457314
GRIFFIN, Mark Richard. b 68. Trin Coll Bris BA93. Westcott Ho Cam 94. **d** 96 **p** 97. C Walmer *Cant* 96-00; V Wingham w Elmstone and Preston w Stourmouth 00-07; V Sevenoaks St Luke *Roch* from 07. *St Luke's House, 30 Eardley Road, Sevenoaks TN13 1XT* Tel (01732) 452462 E-mail revd.mark.griffin@talk21.com
GRIFFIN, Michael. b 59. **d** 01 **p**. C Kirkdale St Lawr *Liv* 01-02; P-in-c 02-05; V from 05. *81 Rawcliffe Road, Liverpool L9 1AN* Tel 0151-523 6968 E-mail mike.j.griffin@amserve.net
GRIFFIN, Niall Paul. b 37. TCD BA61 Div Test61. **d** 61 **p** 62. C Newtownards *D & D* 61-63; C Arm St Mark 63-64; C Cross Roads Jamaica 64-66; C Lurgan Ch the Redeemer *D & D* 66-69; Chapl RAF 69-84; Missr Chr Renewal Cen *D & D* 84-89; Nat Dir (Ireland) SOMA UK 89-07; rtd 07. *7 Cloughmore Park, Rostrevor, Newry BT34 3AX* Tel and fax (028) 4173 8959 E-mail nandg@griffin.go-plus.net
GRIFFIN, Nicholas Philip. b 84. Moorlands Coll BA06. Wycliffe Hall Ox 09. **d** 11. C Frome H Trin *B & W* from 11. *23 Westover, Frome BA11 4ET* Tel (01373) 471890 Mobile 07947-672547 E-mail ngriffin84@gmail.com
GRIFFIN, Nigel Robert. b 50. Univ of Wales (Lamp) BA71. Ripon Hall Ox 71. **d** 73 **p** 74. C Burry Port and Pwll *St D* 73-77; C Carmarthen St Pet 77-79; Youth Chapl 79-86; V Whitland and

Kiffig 80-89; Warden of Ords 86-91; V Llangunnor w Cwmffrwd 89-92; RD Carmarthen 91-92; R Aberporth w Tremain and Blaenporth 92-95; R Aberporth w Tremain w Blaenporth and Betws Ifan 95-96; Chapl Morriston Hosp/Ysbyty Treforys NHS Trust 96-99; Chapl Swansea NHS Trust from 99. *Morriston Hospital, Heol Maes Eglwys, Cwmrhydyceirw, Swansea SA6 8EL* Tel (01792) 702222

GRIFFIN, Canon Rutland Basil. b 16. ALCD41. **d** 41 **p** 42. C Aylesbury *Ox* 41-45; C Bp's Hatfield *St Alb* 45-50; V Biggleswade 50-61; V Dartford H Trin *Roch* 61-84; RD Dartford 64-84; Hon Can Roch Cathl 70-84; rtd 84; Perm to Offic *Roch* and *Cant* 84-95; Cov from 97. *c/o Mrs C Kent, 39 Paddockhall Road, Haywards Heath RH16 1HN* Tel (01444) 440642 Fax 08701-334347

GRIFFIN, The Very Revd Victor Gilbert Benjamin. b 24. MRIA TCD BA46 MA57 Hon DD92. CITC 47. **d** 47 **p** 48. C Londonderry St Aug *D & R* 47-51; C Londonderry Ch Ch 51-57; I 57-68; Preb Howth St Patr Cathl Dublin 62-68; Dean St Patr Cathl Dublin 68-91; rtd 91. *7 Tyler Road, Limavady BT49 0DW* Tel (028) 7176 2093

GRIFFISS, Helen Mary. b 48. Univ of Wales (Ban) CertEd69 K Alfred's Coll Win MA98. STETS 97. **d** 00 **p** 01. Miss Adv USPG *Bris, Sarum* and *Win* 00-03; NSM Bransgore *Win* 00-03; C Milton 04-06; P-in-c Mudeford 06-09; V from 09. *All Saints' Vicarage, 22 Kestrel Drive, Christchurch BH23 4DE* Tel (01425) 276267 E-mail revhelen@4afairworld.co.uk

GRIFFITH, Benedict Lloyd. b 64. Trin Coll Carmarthen BA86. Ripon Coll Cuddesdon 04. **d** 06 **p** 07. C Kempston Transfiguration *St Alb* 06-09; V Upper Wye *S & B* from 09. *The Vicarage, 2 Highbury Fields, Llanyre, Llandrindod Wells LD1 6NF* Tel (01597) 823321 Mobile 07960-947137 E-mail rev.ben.griffith@btinternet.com

GRIFFITH, Brian Vann. b 34. Univ Sch Th Abth & Lamp BTh91 MTh94 St D Dioc Tr Course 81. **d** 82 **p** 83. NSM C Aberystwyth *St D* 82-87; NSM Llanfihangel w Llanafan and Llanwnnws etc 87-88; NSM C Llanbadarn Fawr w Capel Bangor and Goginan 88-93; Public Preacher 93-96; NSM Machynlleth w Llanwrin and Penegoes *Ban* 97-99; rtd 99; Perm to Offic *St D* from 00. *14 Ystwyth Close, Penparcau, Aberystwyth SY23 3RU*

GRIFFITH, The Ven David Vaughan. b 36. St D Coll Lamp BA60. Lich Th Coll 60. **d** 62 **p** 63. C Llanfairfechan *Ban* 62-66; C Dolgellau 66-70; R Llanfair Talhaiarn *St As* 70-82; R Llanfairtalhaiarn and Llansannan 82-85; P-in-c Llangernyw, Gwytherin and Llanddewi 77-85; V Colwyn 85-98; Warden of Readers 91-99; Can Cursal St As Cathl 95-98; P-in-c Berriew and Manafon 98-99; V 99-02; Preb St As Cathl and Adn Montgomery 98-02; rtd 02. *1 Bishop's Walk, St Asaph LL17 0SU* Tel (01745) 582903

GRIFFITH, Donald Bennet. b 17. Dur Univ LTh40. St Aid Birkenhead 36. **d** 40 **p** 41. C Collyhurst St Oswald *Man* 40-43; C Pendlebury St Jo 43-45; P-in-c Pendleton 45-47; V Everton St Cuth *Liv* 47-52; V Lathom 52-58; R Frating w Thorrington *Chelmsf* 58-66; R Lawford 66-73; R Theydon Garnon 73-77; P-in-c Bradfield 77-82; rtd 82; Perm to Offic *Chelmsf* from 82. *Don Thomson House, Low Road, Harwich CO12 3TS* Tel (01255) 503235

GRIFFITH, Frank Michael. b 24. Bris Univ BSc50. St Aid Birkenhead 58. **d** 60 **p** 61. C Leamington Priors H Trin *Cov* 60-63; C Stratford-on-Avon w Bishopton 63-67; V Rounds Green *Birm* 67-70; R Barford *Cov* 70-78; V Wasperton 70-78; RD Stratford-on-Avon 77-79; R Barford w Wasperton and Sherbourne 78-89; RD Fosse 79-87; rtd 90; Perm to Offic *Cov* from 90. *Wusi, Armscote Road, Tredington, Shipston-on-Stour CV36 4NP* Tel (01608) 661621 E-mail michaelgriffith1@btinternet.com

GRIFFITH, Glyn Keble Gethin. b 37. St D Coll Lamp BA59. Ridley Hall Cam 67. **d** 69 **p** 70. C Derby St Aug 69-72; C Coity w Nolton *Llan* 72-75; P-in-c Heage *Derby* 75-81; V Allestree St Nic 81-92; R Wilne and Draycott w Breaston 92-01; rtd 01; Perm to Offic *Mon* from 02; *Heref* 02-08; *Glouc* from 04. *3 Cornford Close, Osbaston, Monmouth NP25 3NT* Tel (01600) 719740

GRIFFITH, Canon John Vaughan. b 33. St D Coll Lamp 53. **d** 58 **p** 59. C Holyhead w Rhoscolyn *Ban* 58-63; R Maentwrog w Trawsfynydd 63-68; Chapl RAF 68-72; V Winnington *Ches* 72-76; V Northwich St Luke and H Trin 76-81; V Sandiway 81-98; Dioc Communications Officer 84-86; Ed Ches Dioc News 84-92; Hon Can Ches Cathl 89-98; rtd 98; Perm to Offic *Ches* from 99. *41 Moss Lane, Cuddington, Northwich CW8 2PT*

GRIFFITH, Justin David. b 48. Imp Coll Lon BScEng74 Cranfield Inst of Tech MSc89. NEOC 03. **d** 06 **p** 07. NSM N Ferriby *York* 06-09; NSM Broad Blunsdon and Highworth w Sevenhampton and Inglesham etc *Bris* 10-11; CF (ACF) from 09. *My Home, Highworth Road, South Marston, Swindon SN3 4SF* Tel (01793) 828638 Mobile 07973-937162 E-mail j@swanland.co.uk

GRIFFITH, Michael. *See* GRIFFITH, Frank Michael

GRIFFITH, Canon Peter Malcolm. b 43. FRICS71. EAMTC 94. **d** 97 **p** 98. NSM Stilton w Denton and Caldecote etc *Ely* 97-99; R Sawtry and Glatton 00-11; rtd 11; RD Yaxley *Ely* from 07;

Hon Can Ely Cathl from 08. *40 Chisenhale, Orton Waterville, Peterborough PE2 5FP* Tel (01733) 686042 Mobile 07837-927526 E-mail rev.griffith@tiscali.co.uk

GRIFFITH, Sandra. b 44. Open Univ BA94. EAMTC 01. **d** 04 **p** 05. NSM The Ortons, Alwalton and Chesterton *Ely* 04-06; NSM Sawtry and Glatton 06-11; Asst Chapl Hinchingbrooke Health Care NHS Trust from 05. *40 Chisenhale, Orton Waterville, Peterborough PE2 5FP* Tel (01733) 686042 E-mail sandra@revgriffith.com

GRIFFITH, Stephen. *See* GRIFFITH, William Stephen

GRIFFITH, Steven Ellsworth. b 63. Univ of Wales BTh91. St Steph Ho Ox. **d** 87 **p** 88. C Holyhead w Rhoscolyn w Llanfair-yn-Neubwll *Ban* 87-90; CF 90-08; Sen CF from 08. *c/o MOD Chaplains (Army)* Tel (01980) 615804 Fax 615800

GRIFFITH, Mrs Wendy Margaret. b 41. **d** 01 **p** 02. NSM Sixpenny Handley w Gussage St Andrew etc *Sarum* 01-08; NSM Somerton w Compton Dundon, the Charltons etc *B & W* from 08. *The Parsonage, George Street, Charlton Adam, Somerton TA11 7AS* Tel (01458) 224087 Mobile 07720-942996

GRIFFITH, William Stephen. b 50. MBE02. Univ of Wales (Ban) BA71 FRAS92. Westcott Ho Cam 71. **d** 73 **p** 74. C Llandudno *Ban* 73-76; C Calne and Blackland *Sarum* 76-78; P-in-c Broadwindsor w Burstock and Seaborough 78-79; TV Beaminster Area 79-81; Perm to Offic 81-83; Chapl St Pet Sch York 83-87; C Leeds St Pet *Ripon* 87; Chapl Bearwood Coll Wokingham 87-92; CMS Jordan 92-95; Sen Chapl Univ of Wales (Cardiff) *Llan* 95-96; Chapl Damascus 96-02; P-in-c Yerevan, Baku and Tbilisi *Eur* 03; V Denton *Newc* 04-08; TV Mortlake w E Sheen *S'wark* from 09. *17 Sheen Gate Gardens, London SW14 7PD* Tel (020) 8876 5002 Mobile 07729-278294 E-mail haywales@hotmail.com

GRIFFITH-JONES, Robin Guthrie. b 56. New Coll Ox BA78 Ch Coll Cam BA88. Westcott Ho Cam 86. **d** 89 **p** 90. C Cantril Farm *Liv* 89-92; Chapl Linc Coll Ox 92-99; Master of The Temple from 99. *The Master's House, Temple, London EC4Y 7BB* Tel (020) 7353 8559 E-mail master@templechurch.com

GRIFFITHS, Ainsley. *See* GRIFFITHS, John Mark Ainsley

GRIFFITHS, Alan Charles. b 46. Dur Univ BA67. Cranmer Hall Dur 66. **d** 69 **p** 70. C Leic H Apostles 69-72; Lic to Offic *York* 73-77; V Lea Hall *Birm* 77-87; Asst Dir of Educn *Sheff* 87-92; V W Bessacarr 92-02; V Conisbrough from 02. *The Vicarage, 8 Castle Avenue, Conisbrough, Doncaster DN12 3BT* Tel (01709) 864695 E-mail alan.c.griffiths@virgin.net

GRIFFITHS, Alec. b 42. St Chad's Coll Dur BA63. **d** 65 **p** 66. C Glas St Ninian 65-68; C Greenock 68-72; R Glas H Cross 72-79; V Birchencliffe *Wakef* 79-83; Chapl Kingston Hosp Surrey 83-99; rtd 99; Perm to Offic *S'wark* 99-00; Hon C W Acton St Martin and Ealing All SS *Lon* 00-10. *29 Hollywood, Largs KA30 8SR* Tel 07903-372561 (mobile) E-mail alec.griffiths@btopenworld.com

GRIFFITHS, Andrew Taylor. b 68. Jes Coll Ox BA92 MA96. Cranmer Hall Dur 98. **d** 00 **p** 01. C Paris St Mich *Eur* 00-04; C Galleywood Common *Chelmsf* 04-05; V from 05; RD Chelmsf S from 07. *Galleywood Vicarage, 450 Beehive Lane, Chelmsford CM2 8RN* Tel (01245) 353922 Mobile 07969-605059 E-mail andygr.iffiths@yahoo.co.uk

GRIFFITHS, Beatrice Mary. b 29. Chelsea Coll Lon CertEd60. Westcott Ho Cam 85. **dss** 86 **d** 87 **p** 94. W Bridgford *S'well* 86-87; NSM Wilford Hill 87-99; rtd 99; Perm to Offic *S'well* from 99. *7 Stella Avenue, Tollerton, Nottingham NG12 4EX* Tel 0115-937 4155

GRIFFITHS, Brian John. b 45. Brunel Univ PhD82. **d** 05 **p** 06. OLM Iver *Ox* from 05. *12 Saxon Court, High Street, Iver SL0 9PW* Tel (01753) 654768 E-mail brian.griffiths@iverparish.co.uk

GRIFFITHS, Caroline. *See* PRINCE, Caroline Heidi Ann

GRIFFITHS, (née MITCHELL), Mrs Clare Elizabeth. b 68. **d** 01 **p** 02. C Caerleon w Llanhennock *Mon* 01-03; Chapl Malvern Girls' Coll 03-06; C Gt Malvern Ch Ch *Worc* from 06. *St Mary's House, 137 Madresfield Road, Malvern WR14 2HD* Tel (01684) 564494

GRIFFITHS, Colin Lindsay. b 50. ACT 75. **d** 79 **p** 80. C Adelaide St Jo Australia 79-81; C Masite Lesotho 82-83; P-in-c Maseru St Jo 84; Chapl St Mich Priory Melbourne 85-87; Prior 87-90; P-in-c Port Augusta 90-95; P-in-c Point Pearce Min Distr 95-96; Assoc P Thornbury 97-98; R Alice Springs and Can Ch Ch Cathl Darwin 99-05; Dioc Admin N Territory 00-05; Perm to Offic *Ox* from 06; Prov SSM in Eur from 10. *The Well, Newport Road, Willen, Milton Keynes MK15 9AA* Tel (01908) 231986 E-mail colin.griffiths@hotmail.com

GRIFFITHS, Canon David. b 38. St Mich Coll Llan. **d** 67 **p** 68. C Llangollen *St As* 67-71; C Rhyl 71-74; V Kerry 74-77; V Kerry and Llanmerewig 77-82; R Caerwys and Bodfari 82-87; V Gresford 87-97; V Gresford w Holt 97-01; RD Wrexham 97-01; RD Gresford 01-03; Can St As Cathl 98-03; rtd 03. *16 Heol-y-Wal, Bradley, Wrexham LL11 4BY* Tel (01978) 751416

GRIFFITHS, David Bruce. b 44. Sussex Univ BA69 Hull Univ MA83. Linc Th Coll. **d** 82 **p** 83. C Springfield All SS *Chelmsf*

82-84; TV Horwich *Man* 84-92; V Heaton Ch Ch 92-03; P-in-c Ainsworth 03-09; rtd 09; Perm to Offic *Man* from 09. *Woodford, Mill Lane, Horwich, Bolton BL6 6AQ* Tel (01204) 469621 E-mail dandbgriffiths@googlemail.com

GRIFFITHS, David John. b 53. St Jo Coll Nottm BTh93. **d** 94 **p** 95. C Retford St Sav *S'well* 94-96; NSM Thwaites Brow *Bradf* 96-98; P-in-c Oakenshaw cum Woodlands 98-03; V Buttershaw St Paul 03-10; V Silsden from 10; Asst Chapl Airedale NHS Trust from 96. *The Vicarage, Briggate, Silsden, Keighley BD20 9JS* Tel (01535) 652204 E-mail david.griffiths@bradford.anglican.org

GRIFFITHS, David Mark. b 41. Univ of Wales (Cardiff) BA67 CertEd71. St Mich Coll Llan 92. **d** 94 **p** 95. C Llwynderw *S & B* 94-96; R Llanbadarn Fawr, Llandegley and Llanfihangel etc 96-02; P-in-c Slebech and Uzmaston w Boulston *St D* 02-06; rtd 06. *17 Catherine's Gate, Merlins Bridge, Haverfordwest SA61 1NB* Tel (01437) 783950 Mobile 07811-647910 E-mail markgriffiths16@btopenworld.com

GRIFFITHS, David Mark. b 59. Kent Univ BA80. Chich Th Coll 81. **d** 83 **p** 84. C Clydach *S & B* 83-84; C Llwynderw 84-88; V Swansea St Nic 88-98; Chapl Swansea Inst of HE 88-98; V Swansea St Gabr from 98; Chapl Swansea NHS Trust from 98. *St Gabriel's Vicarage, Bryn Road, Brynmill, Swansea SA2 0AP* Tel (01792) 464011

GRIFFITHS, The Ven David Nigel. b 27. RD77. Worc Coll Ox BA52 MA56 Reading Univ PhD91 FSA. Linc Th Coll 56. **d** 58 **p** 59. C Northampton St Matt *Pet* 58-61; SPCK HQ Staff 61-67; Chapl RNR 63-77; Hon C Bromley St Andr *Roch* 65-67; V Linc St Mich 67-73; R Linc St Mary Magd w St Paul 67-73; Vice Chan and Lib Linc Cathl 67-73; TR New Windsor *Ox* 73-87; RD Maidenhead 77-82 and 84-87; Chapl to The Queen 77-97; Hon Can Ch Ch *Ox* 83-87; Adn Berks 87-92; rtd 92; Chapl St Anne's Bede Houses Linc 93-00; Perm to Offic *Linc* from 00. *2 Middleton's Field, Lincoln LN2 1QP* Tel (01522) 525753 E-mail bibliophile@britishlibrary.net

GRIFFITHS, David Percy Douglas. b 25. St Mich Coll Llan. **d** 78 **p** 79. C Betws w Ammanford *St D* 78-80; V Llanarth w Mydroilyn, Capel Cynon, Talgarreg etc 80-84; V Llanarth and Capel Cynon w Talgarreg etc 84-86; V Newcastle Emlyn w Llandyfriog and Troed-yr-aur 86-95; rtd 95. *The Poplars, Ebenezer Street, Newcastle Emlyn SA38 9BS* Tel (01239) 711448

GRIFFITHS, David Rowson Hopkin. b 38. Oak Hill Th Coll 59. **d** 62 **p** 63. C Barrow St Mark *Carl* 62-65; OMF Internat 66-09; Japan 66-88; Philippines 88-09; rtd 03. *4 Warwick Place, West Cross, Swansea SA3 5JG* Tel (01792) 402885

GRIFFITHS, Ms Elizabeth Leigh. b 61. St Hugh's Coll Ox BA83 MA87 Warwick Univ PGCE84. Ripon Coll Cuddesdon 96. **d** 98 **p** 99. C Bettws *Mon* 98-99; C Maindee Newport 99-01; TV Cen Swansea and Dioc Chapl Tertiary Educn *S & B* 01-03; C St Martin-in-the-Fields *Lon* 03-09; Dir Past Studies ERMC and Nor Dioc Min Course 09-10; Dir Past Studies and Vice Prin ERMC 10-11; V Cardiff City Par *Llan* from 11. *The Vicarage, 16 Queen Anne Square, Cardiff CF10 3ED* Tel (029) 2022 9991 E-mail cfcitysjb.vicar@btinternet.com

GRIFFITHS, Eric. b 33. **d** 02 **p** 04. NSM St Andr-by-the-Wardrobe w St Ann, Blackfriars *Lon* 02-08; NSM St Jas Garlickhythe w St Mich Queenhithe etc 02-08; rtd 08. *The Charterhouse, Charterhouse Square, London EC1M 6AN* Tel (020) 7490 1025 E-mail egcharterhouse@yahoo.co.uk

GRIFFITHS, Garrie Charles. b 53. St Jo Coll Nottm. **d** 77 **p** 78. Canada 77-81; C Stalybridge H Trin and Ch Ches 78-81; C Moreton 81-84; V Godley cum Newton Green 84-89; V Bayston Hill *Lich* 89-01; TR Mildenhall *St E* 01-04; V Hadfield *Derby* 04-10; RD Glossop 06-10; V Youlgreave, Middleton, Stanton-in-Peak etc from 10. *The New Vicarage, Conksbury Lane, Youlgrave, Bakewell DE45 1WL* Tel (01629) 630409 E-mail ggriffiths787@btinternet.com

GRIFFITHS, Gerald Brian. b 41. Open Univ BA88. SEITE 97. **d** 00 **p** 01. NSM Cliftonville *Cant* 00-03; TV St Laur in Thanet 04-09; rtd 09; Chapl Costa Blanca *Eur* from 10. *Buzon 3, La Cometa 18, 03729 Senija, Benissa (Alicante), Spain* E-mail griffiths brian@hotmail.com

GRIFFITHS, Gerald Lewis. b 38. Westmr Coll Ox MTh97. Qu Coll Birm. **d** 88 **p** 89. C Wrexham *St As* 88-91; TV 91-95; R Hope 95-00; rtd 00. *10 Ryder Close, Wrexham LL13 9GS* Tel (01978) 355244

GRIFFITHS, Gordon John. b 31. Univ of Wales (Cardiff) BA53. S'wark Ord Course 72. **d** 75 **p** 76. NSM Sutton St Nic *S'wark* 75-78; Asst Chapl Eastbourne Coll 78-81; Perm to Offic *Chich* from 81. *15 Buckhurst Close, Willingdon, Eastbourne BN20 9EF* Tel (01323) 505547

GRIFFITHS, Griff. *See* GRIFFITHS, Stephen David

GRIFFITHS, Harvey Stephen. b 35. Linc Coll Ox BA58 MA62. Linc Th Coll 62. **d** 62 **p** 63. C Frodingham *Linc* 62-65; C Darlington St Cuth *Dur* 65-70; Chapl RN 70-92; P-in-c Southwick w Boarhunt *Portsm* 92-05; rtd 05; Perm to Offic *Portsm* from 05. *27 Burnham Wood, Fareham PO16 7UD* Tel (01329) 232915 Mobile 07747-093365 E-mail harvey@hsgriffiths.fsnet.co.uk

GRIFFITHS, Hugh. b 44. Nottm Univ BEd78. Clifton Th Coll 69. **d** 71 **p** 72. C Mansfield SS Pet and Paul *S'well* 71-77; NSM Stockport St Geo *Ches* from 08. *1 Heath Crescent, Stockport SK2 6JN* Tel 0161-285 9772 E-mail hughgriffiths@hotmail.co.uk

GRIFFITHS, Mrs Jean Rose. b 36. Avery Hill Coll TCert56. S'wark Ord Course 93. **d** 95 **p** 96. NSM Charlton *S'wark* 95-03; Asst Chapl HM Pris Brixton 95-03; Chapl 03-04; rtd 04; Perm to Offic *S'wark* from 04. *32 Weyman Road, London SE3 8RY* Tel (020) 8319 8676 *or* 8588 6051

GRIFFITHS, John Alan. b 48. CPsychol AFBPsS Univ of Wales BSc72 Cape Town Univ MSc76. St Mich Coll Llan 87. **d** 89 **p** 90. C Neath w Llantwit 89-93; V Roath St German 93-95. *All Pine Grange, Bath Road, Bournemouth BH1 2PF* Tel (01202) 314120

GRIFFITHS, John Gareth. b 44. Lich Th Coll 68. **d** 71 **p** 72. C Shotton *St As* 71-73; C Rhyl w St Ann 73-76; V Llanasa 76-95; RD Holywell 89-95; V Rhuddlan 95-10; rtd 10. *13 Llwyn Harlech, Bodelwyddan, Rhyl LL18 5WG* Tel (01745) 539955

GRIFFITHS, John Mark Ainsley. b 68. Man Univ BSc90 MSc91 PGCE92. Ripon Coll Cuddesdon BA97. **d** 98 **p** 99. Min Can Bangor 98-01; P-in-c Denio w Abererch 01-02; V 02-05; Chapl Univ of Wales (Trin St Dav) from 05. *University of Wales Trinity St David, Carmarthen Campus, Carmarthen SA31 3EP* Tel (01267) 676607 E-mail ainsley.griffiths@trinitysaintdavid.ac.uk

GRIFFITHS, Mrs Linda Betty. b 48. Trin Coll Carmarthen CertEd69 Gwent Coll of HE BEd96 Open Univ MA97. Mon Dioc Tr Scheme 05. **d** 06. NSM Newbridge *Mon* 06-10; NSM Risca from 10. *19 Cromwell Road, Risca, Newport NP11 7AF* Tel (01495) 270455 E-mail griff.l@btinternet.com

GRIFFITHS, Malcolm. b 47. St Alb Minl Tr Scheme. **d** 82 **p** 83. NSM Hemel Hempstead *St Alb* 82-86; C 86-87; TV Liskeard, St Keyne, St Pinnock, Morval etc *Truro* 87-96; V Landrake w St Erney and Botus Fleming from 96. *The Vicarage, School Road, Landrake, Saltash PL12 5EA* Tel (01752) 851801

GRIFFITHS, Margaret. *See* MacLACHLAN, Mrs Margaret

GRIFFITHS, Mrs Margarett. b 29. ATCL47 LRAM48. CA Tr Coll 50. **dss** 81 **d** 87. Hackington *Cant* 81-83; Ashford 84-89; Par Dn 87-89; rtd 89. *39 Newington Way, Craven Arms SY7 9PS* Tel (01588) 673848

GRIFFITHS, Mark. *See* GRIFFITHS, David Mark

GRIFFITHS, Mark. b 68. Nottm Univ PhD09. St Jo Coll Nottm 04. **d** 07 **p** 08. C Stoke Poges *Ox* 07-10; P-in-c Warfield from 10. *The Vicarage, Church Lane, Warfield, Bracknell RG42 6EE* Tel (01344) 882228 E-mail revmarkgriff@sky.com

GRIFFITHS, Canon Martyn Robert. b 51. Nottm Univ BTh74 St Martin's Coll Lanc PGCE75. Kelham Th Coll 70. **d** 74 **p** 75. C Kings Heath *Birm* 74-77; C-in-c Elmdon Heath CD 77-79; TV Solihull 79-81; Asst Admin Shrine of Our Lady of Walsingham 81-85; V Oldham St Steph and All Martyrs *Man* 85-89; TR Swinton and Pendlebury 89-98; Hon Can Man Cathl 96-98; R Preston St Jo and St Geo *Blackb* 98-05; Hon Can Blackb Cathl 00-05; R Henley w Remenham *Ox* from 05. *St Mary's Rectory, Hart Street, Henley-on-Thames RG9 2AU* Tel and fax (01491) 577340 E-mail rector.hwr@lineone.net

GRIFFITHS, Meirion. b 38. Clifton Th Coll 63. **d** 66 **p** 67. C Upper Holloway St Pet *Lon* 66-68; C Taunton St Jas *B & W* 68-70; C Radipole *Sarum* 70-74; R Chich St Pancras and St Jo 74-82; R Corwen and Llangar *St As* 82-88; RD Edeyrnion 82-88; C Albany Australia 88; R Collie 89-93; P-in-c Maddington 97-00; rtd 00. *27 Coachwood Way, Maddington WA 6109, Australia* Tel (0061) (8) 9459 2920 Fax 9452 2720 E-mail meirion4@aol.com

GRIFFITHS, Mervyn Harrington. b 15. Ripon Hall Ox 53. **d** 54 **p** 55. C Aigburth *Liv* 54-56; C Grassendale 56-58; C Findon Chich 58-59; R Bighton *Win* 59-78; V Bishop's Sutton 59-78; rtd 80; Perm to Offic *Ex* from 80. *c/o Smith and Williamson Investment, 25 Moorgate, London EC2R 6AY*

GRIFFITHS, Neville. b 39. Univ of Wales BA63. St D Coll Lamp LTh66. **d** 66 **p** 67. C Newport St Mark *Mon* 66-68; C Cardiff St Jo *Llan* 68-70; Chapl Greystoke Coll Carl 70-76; C Greystoke w Matterdale *Carl* 70-75; TV Greystoke, Matterdale and Mungrisdale 75-76; Chapl Grey Coll Dur 76-81; C Croxdale *Dur* 76-81; R Didsbury Ch Ch *Man* 81-83; P-in-c Lowther and Askham *Carl* 83-84; R 84-88; V Guernsey St Matt *Win* 88-93; R Guernsey St Pierre du Bois 93-02; R Guernsey St Philippe de Torteval 93-02; Vice-Dean Guernsey 99-02; rtd 03. *6 Howlcroft Villas, Neville's Cross, Durham DH1 4DU* Tel (0191-386 4778

GRIFFITHS, Mrs Pamela Verley. b 07 **p** 10. NSM Ebbw Vale *Mon* from 07. *3 Ivy Close, Rassau, Ebbw Vale NP23 5SJ* Tel (01495) 303926 Fax 210433

GRIFFITHS, Paul Edward. b 48. St Jo Coll Nottm 86. **d** 88 **p** 89. C Ipswich St Andr *St E* 88-92; P-in-c Tollerton *S'well* 92-00; P-in-c Plumtree 95-97; Ind Chapl and Dioc Adv on Ind Soc 97-00; V Hellesdon *Nor* from 00. *The Vicarage, Broom Avenue, Hellesdon, Norwich NR6 6LG* Tel (01603) 426902

GRIFFITHS, Ms Paula Whitmore Llewellyn. b 49. LMH Ox BA71 MA75 Anglia Ruskin Univ BA09. Westcott Ho Cam 08. **d** 09 **p** 10. NSM Saffron Walden w Wendens Ambo, Littlebury etc *Chelmsf* from 09. *Greatford Cottage, Stocking Green, Radwinter, Saffron Walden CB10 2SS* E-mail paula.greatford@btinternet.com

GRIFFITHS, Percy. See GRIFFITHS, David Percy Douglas

GRIFFITHS, Richard Barré Maw. b 43. CCC Ox BA65 MA69 St Jo Coll Dur BA71. Cranmer Hall Dur. **d** 71 **p** 72. C Fulwood *Sheff* 71-74; Hon C Sheff St Jo 74-76; Fell Dept of Bibl Studies Sheff Univ 74-76; C Fulham St Matt *Lon* 76-78; P-in-c 78-83; R Chich St Pancras and St Jo 83-09; rtd 09. *24 Beechcroft, Humshaugh, Hexham NE46 4ON* E-mail richardgriff@clara.co.uk

GRIFFITHS, Prof Richard Mathias. b 35. K Coll Cam BA57 MA61 PhD62 BNC Ox MA66 FIL91 FKC95. Ox Min Course 89 SAOMC 96. **d** 97 **p** 98. Prof French K Coll Lon 90-00; NSM W Woodhay w Enborne, Hampstead Marshall etc *Ox* 97-00; NSM Llantrisant 01-02; NSM Penarth and Llandough from 03. *Waltham House, Bradford Place, Penarth CF64 1AG* Tel (029) 2070 7828 Fax 2070 9699

GRIFFITHS, Canon Robert Herbert. b 53. Chich Th Coll 75. **d** 76 **p** 77. C Holywell *St As* 76-80; CF (TA) 79-87; P-in-c Gyffylliog *St As* 80-84; V Llanfair Dyffryn Clwyd 80-84; V Llanfair DC, Derwen, Llanelidan and Efenechtyd 84-88; Asst Dioc Youth Chapl 81-86; Dioc Youth Chapl 86-91; PV St As and Tremeirchion w Cefn 88-97; Chapl H M Stanley Hosp 88-97; Bp's Visitor and Dioc RE Adv *St As* 88-93; Chapl Glan Clwyd Distr Gen Hosp 93-97; V Llanrhos *St As* 97-09; TR Rhos-Cystennin from 09; Can St As Cathl from 98; AD Llanrwst 01-09; Chapl NW Wales NHS Trust from 97. *Llanrhos Vicarage, 2 Vicarage Road, Llandudno LL30 1PT* Tel (01492) 876152 E-mail robert@griffithsr0.fsnet.co.uk

GRIFFITHS, Robert James. b 52. Nottm Univ BTh82. St Jo Coll Nottm 79. **d** 82 **p** 83. C Kettering St Andr *Pet* 82-85; C Collier Row St Jas and Havering-atte-Bower *Chelmsf* 86-89; R High Ongar w Norton Mandeville 89-97; R Ilmington w Stretton-on-Fosse etc *Cov* 97-99; V Newport *Chelmsf* 99-03; V Newport and Widdington 03-06; Perm to Offic *Ely* 09-10; R Horringer *St E* from 10. *The Rectory, Manor Lane, Horringer, Bury St Edmunds IP29 5PY* Tel (01284) 735946 E-mail r.griffiths45@btinternet.com

GRIFFITHS, Canon Roger. b 46. Trin Coll Bris 70. **d** 74 **p** 75. C Normanton *Derby* 74-77; C Bucknall and Bagnall *Lich* 77-80; TV 80-83; TV Aberystwyth *St D* 83-86; R Letterston w Llanfair Nant-y-Gof etc from 86; AD Dewisland and Fishguard from 01; Hon Can St D Cathl from 10. *The Rectory, 9 Nant y Ffynnon, Letterston, Haverfordwest SA62 5SX* Tel (01348) 840336 E-mail groger6@aol.com

GRIFFITHS, Roger Michael. b 47. Wycliffe Hall Ox 83. **d** 86 **p** 87. Min Can St D Cathl 86-88; V Pen-boyr 88-94; V Fishguard w Llanychar and Pontfaen w Morfil etc 94-03. *Trebover Farmhouse, Llanychaer, Fishguard SA65 9SA* Tel (01348) 873963 E-mail roger@rogriff.freeserve.co.uk

GRIFFITHS, Sarah. See BICK, Mrs Sarah

GRIFFITHS, Shane Owen. b 63. Ripon Coll Cuddesdon 01. **d** 04 **p** 04. C Icknield *Ox* 04-07; P-in-c Mullion *Truro* from 07; P-in-c Cury and Gunwalloe from 07. *The Vicarage, Nansmellyon Road, Mullion, Helston TR12 7DH* Tel (01326) 240325 E-mail shaneowengriffiths@yahoo.co.uk

GRIFFITHS, The Ven Shirley Thelma. b 48. Univ of Wales (Ban) CertEd69 Open Univ BA83 Coll of Ripon & York St Jo MA01. St Deiniol's Hawarden 79. **d** 82 **p** 95. NSM Dyserth and Trelawnyd and Cwm *St As* 82-91; RE Officer 89-95; Min Can St As Cathl 91-95; P-in-c The Cowtons *Ripon* 95-02; RE Adv 95-02; V Abergele *St As* 02-08; V Abergele and St George 08-10; Adn Wrexham from 10; R Llandegla from 10. *The Rectory, Llandegla, Wrexham LL11 3AW* Tel (01978) 790362 E-mail archdeacon.wrexham@churchinwales.org.uk

GRIFFITHS, Simon Mark. b 62. Ch Ch Coll Cant BA84 Kent Univ MA95. Chich Th Coll. **d** 87 **p** 88. C Cardiff St Jo *Llan* 87-91; Sub-Chapl HM Pris Cardiff 87-91; Chapl and Succ Roch Cath 91-96; Chapl Univ Coll Chich 96-01; V Sheff St Matt from 01. *St Matthew's Vicarage, 29 Winchester Road, Sheffield S10 4EE* Tel 0114-230 5641

GRIFFITHS, Canon Stanley Arthur. b 17. Lon Univ BSc38. Cuddesdon Coll 46. **d** 47 **p** 48. C Southsea St Matt *Portsm* 47-48; C Southsea H Spirit 48-51; C Cowley St Jas *Ox* 51-55; V Northbourne 55-65; V St Neots *Ely* 65-77; RD St Neots 76-82; Hon Can Ely Cathl 76-82; V Buckden 77-82; rtd 82; Perm to Offic *Ely* 82-96 and *York* from 82. *9 Parkway, St Neots PE19 1EB* Tel (01480) 393372

GRIFFITHS, Stephen David (Griff). b 70. Oak Hill Th Coll BA96 Trin Coll Bris. **d** 00 **p** 01. C Cranleigh *Guildf* 00-04; TV Thetford *Nor* 04-10; Chapl Cam Univ Hosps NHS Foundn Trust from 10. *89 Sycamore Drive, Bury St Edmunds IP32 7PW* Tel (01842) 755769 Mobile 07592-800259 E-mail revgriff@sky.com

GRIFFITHS, Stephen Mark. b 67. Nottm Univ BTh93 PhD00. St Jo Coll Nottm 90. **d** 93 **p** 94. C Glascote and Stonydelph *Lich* 93-96; P-in-c Stratford New Town St Paul *Chelmsf* 96-02; P-in-c Steeple Bumpstead and Helions Bumpstead 02-05; Tutor Ridley Hall Cam 01-09; TR Linton *Ely* from 09. *The Rectory, 11A*

Joiners Road, Linton, Cambridge CB21 4NP Tel (01223) 891291 Mobile 07905-861234 E-mail smg48@cam.ac.uk

GRIFFITHS, Stephen Robert. b 78. Oak Hill Th Coll BA00 Anglia Poly Univ MA05. Ridley Hall Cam 02. **d** 04 **p** 05. C Normanton *Derby* 04-08; P-in-c Moresby *Carl* from 08. *The Rectory, Low Moresby, Whitehaven CA28 6RR* Tel (01946) 693970 E-mail steph78griff@hotmail.com

GRIFFITHS, Mrs Susan Angela. b 61. St Jo Coll Nottm BTh94. **d** 94 **p** 95. C Ingrow w Hainworth *Bradf* 94-98; V Wyke 98-03; C Buttershaw St Paul 03-10; C Silsden from 10; RD S Craven from 10. *The Vicarage, Briggate, Silsden, Keighley BD20 9JS* Tel (01535) 652204 E-mail susan.griffiths@bradford.anglican.org

GRIFFITHS, Canon Sylvia Joy. b 50. Gipsy Hill Coll of Educn CertEd71. St Jo Coll Nottm 85. **dss** 86 **d** 87 **p** 94. Woodthorpe *S'well* 86-90; Par Dn 87-90; Min Bestwood/Rise Park LEP 90-94; TD Bestwood 90-94; TR 94-99; P-in-c Sherwood 99-01; V from 01; Hon Can S'well Minster 04-11. *St Martin's Vicarage, Trevose Gardens, Sherwood, Nottingham NG5 3FU* Tel 0115-960 7547 E-mail sylvia.griffiths@homecall.co.uk

GRIFFITHS, Tudor Francis Lloyd. b 54. Jes Coll Ox BA76 MA81 Wycliffe Hall Ox BA78 MA81 Leeds Univ PhD99. Wycliffe Hall Ox 76. **d** 79 **p** 80. C Brecon w Battle *S & B* 79-81; Min Can Brecon Cathl 79-81; C Swansea St Mary w H Trin 81-83; R Llangattock and Llangynidr 83-88; CMS Uganda 89-95; C Newton St Pet *S & B* 96; Dioc Missr *Mon* 96-03; V Goldcliffe and Whitson and Nash 96-98; TV Magor 98-03; TR Hawarden *St As* 03-11; Can Cursal St As Cathl 05-08; Chan 08-11; R Cheltenham St Mary w St Matt *Glouc* from 11; AD Cheltenham from 11. *38 Sydenham Villas Road, Cheltenham GL52 6DZ* Tel (01242) 234470 Mobile 07718-906066 E-mail tudorg@stmstm.org.uk

GRIFFITHS, Canon William David Aled. b 52. Univ of Wales (Abth) BA74 Man Univ AHA77. St Mich Coll Llan. **d** 83 **p** 84. C Carmarthen St Pet *St D* 83-87; Asst Warden of Ords 84-91; Warden of Ords 91-07; V Llansadwrn w Llanwrda and Manordeilo 87-92; V Llangunnor w Cwmffrwd from 92; Can St D Cathl from 01. *The Vicarage, Llangunnor Road, Carmarthen SA31 2HY* Tel (01267) 236435

GRIFFITHS, William David Maldwyn. b 23. St D Coll Lamp BA47. **d** 50 **p** 51. C Cardigan *St D* 50-54; C Henfynyw w Aberaeron 54-57; P-in-c Llechryd 57-59; V Mathri, St Edrens and Llanrheithan 59-67; V Llanfihangel Genau'r Glyn 67-89; RD Llanbadarn Fawr 87-89; rtd 89. *Bro Enlli, Lower Regent Street, Aberaeron SA46 0HZ* Tel (01545) 570176

GRIFFITHS, William Thomas Gordon. b 48. York Univ BA70 Fitzw Coll Cam BA79. Ridley Hall Cam 78. **d** 80 **p** 81. C Dulwich St Barn *S'wark* 80-83; C Egglescliffe *Dur* 83-85; Ind Chapl 85-90; V Stockton St Jas 90-98; NSM Leamington Hastings and Birdingbury *Cov* 98-03; NSM Grandborough w Willoughby and Flecknoe 98-03; NSM Leam Valley 03-06; Perm to Offic from 06. *24 Park Road, Rugby CV21 2QH* Tel (01788) 547815

GRIGG, Robin Harold. b 44. **d** 07 **p** 08. NSM St Mewan w Mevagissey and St Ewe *Truro* from 07; Chapl R Cornwall Hosps Trust 07-11. *Higher Polstreath, School Hill, Mevagissey, St Austell PL26 6TH* Tel (01726) 843708 E-mail robingrigg124@btinternet.com

GRIGG, Simon James. b 61. Warwick Univ BA82 MA83 Southn Univ BTh90. Chich Th Coll 87. **d** 90 **p** 91. C Cowley St Jas *Ox* 90-94; C W Hampstead St Jas *Lon* 94-95; V Munster Square Ch Ch and St Mary Magd 95-06; R Covent Garden St Paul from 06. *Flat 3, 35 Craven Street, London WC2N 5NF* Tel (020) 7836 5221 Mobile 07958-472568 E-mail simon.grigg@btopenworld.com

GRIGG, Canon Terence George. b 34. Kelham Th Coll 54. **d** 59 **p** 60. C Brookfield St Anne, Highgate Rise *Lon* 59-62; Chapl Lee Abbey 63-66; Chapl and Lect St Luke's Coll Ex 66-70; V Stainton-in-Cleveland *York* 70-83; R Cottingham 83-04; rtd 04; Can and Preb York Minster from 90; Hon Can Koforidua from 84; Hon Can Ho from 06. *The Canon's House, 14 Grove Street, Norton, Malton YO17 9BG* Tel (01653) 691157

GRIGGS, Canon Alan Sheward. b 33. Trin Hall Cam BA56 MA60. Westcott Ho Cam 58. **d** 60 **p** 61. C Arnold *S'well* 60-63; Succ S'wark Cathl 63-66; Ind Chapl 66-71; C Leeds H Trin *Ripon* 71-81; V 81-91; Soc and Ind Adv 71-81; Hon Can Ripon Cathl 84-98; Soc Resp Officer 91-98; rtd 98; Perm to Offic *Ripon* from 98. *32 St Chad's Avenue, Leeds LS6 3QF* Tel 0113-275 8100 E-mail alan@griggs32.freeserve.co.uk

GRIGGS, Mrs Anthea Mary. b 37. Homerton Coll Cam TCert57 New Coll Edin BA86. SAOMC. **d** 00 **p** 01. NSM Sunningdale *Ox* 00-05; Lic to Offic *Edin* from 06. *8/1 Rattray Drive, Edinburgh EH10 5TH* Tel 0131-447 2448 E-mail amgriggs@freenetname.co.uk

✠**GRIGGS, The Rt Revd Ian Macdonald.** b 28. Trin Hall Cam BA52 MA56. Westcott Ho Cam. **d** 54 **p** 55 **c** 87. C Portsea St Cuth *Portsm* 54-59; Dioc Youth Chapl *Sheff* 59-64; Bp's Dom Chapl 59-64; V Sheff St Cuth 64-71; V Kidderminster St Mary *Worc* 71-82; Hon Can Worc Cathl 77-84; TR Kidderminster St Mary and All SS, Trimpley etc 82-84; Preb Heref Cathl 84-94;

Adn Ludlow 84-87; P-in-c Tenbury St Mich 84-87; Suff Bp Ludlow 87-94; rtd 94; Hon Asst Bp Carl from 94. *Rookings, Patterdale, Penrith CA11 0NP* Tel (01768) 482064 E-mail ian.griggs@virgin.net

GRIGOR, Miss Alice Moira (Tirsh). b 49. Ripon Coll Cuddesdon 94. **d** 96 **p** 97. C Curry Rivel w Fivehead and Swell *B & W* 96-98; C Nailsea Ch Ch w Tickenham 98-00; TV Ross *Heref* 00-06; P-in-c Quinton and Welford w Weston *Glouc* from 06. *The Rectory, Church Lane, Welford on Avon, Stratford-upon-Avon CV37 8EL* Tel (01789) 751576 E-mail tirshgrigor@hotmail.co.uk

GRIGOR, David Alexander. b 29. St Aid Birkenhead 51. **d** 54 **p** 55. C Hengrove *Bris* 54-57; C Marshfield w Cold Ashton 57-60; V Newport *Ex* 60-67; V Paignton St Paul Preston 67-73; R Rio de Janeiro Ch Ch Brazil 73-74; Hon C Heavitree *Ex* 74-77; Chapl Ex Sch 74-77; Chapl Brighton Coll 77-89; Chapl Warminster Sch 89-93; rtd 93; Perm to Offic *Win* 02-06 and *Portsm* 03-06. *42 Russell Crescent, Wollaton, Nottingham NG8 2BQ* Tel 0115-928 9036

GRIGSBY, Peter Edward. b 31. Magd Coll Cam MA56 CertEd56. NEOC 85. **d** 88 **p** 89. NSM Haxby w Wigginton *York* 88-90; C Brayton 90-92; TV 92-97; rtd 97; Perm to Offic *Chich* 98-01 and from 04: *4 The Hop Garden, South Harting, Petersfield GU31 5QL* Tel (01730) 825295

GRIGSON, Preb Richard John Stephen. b 60. Man Univ BA83. Qu Coll Birm 86. **d** 88 **p** 89. C W Bromwich St Fran *Lich* 88-92; V Smallthorne from 92; P-in-c Brown Edge from 05; Preb Lich Cathl from 11. *St Saviour's Vicarage, Ford Green Road, Stoke-on-Trent ST6 1NX* Tel (01782) 835941 Fax (07092) 214726 E-mail richard.grigson@lichfield.anglican.org

GRIMASON, The Very Revd Alistair John. b 57. CITC 76. **d** 79 **p** 80. C Belfast H Trin *Conn* 79-82; C Dublin Drumcondra w N Strand *D & G* 82-84; I Navan w Kentstown, Tara, Slane, Painestown etc *M & K* 84-91; Dioc Youth Officer (Meath) 90-94; Dioc Info Officer (Meath) 90-96; I Tullamore w Durrow, Newtownfertullagh, Rahan etc 91-00; Preb Tipper St Patr Cathl Dublin 92-00; Can Meath *M & K* 92-00; Chan Kildare Cathl 98-00; Dean Tuam *T, K & A* from 00; I Tuam w Cong and Aasleagh from 00; Dioc Communications Officer from 10. *Deanery Place, Cong, Claremorris, Co Mayo, Republic of Ireland* Tel and fax (00353) (94) 954 6017 E-mail deantuam@hotmail.com

GRIME, Arthur Michael. b 28. Kelham Th Coll 48. **d** 52 **p** 53. Basutoland 52-55; C Ealing St Barn *Lon* 55-57; C Pimlico St Gabr 57-59; C Greenford H Cross 59-62; V Fulham St Pet 62-66; V Chiswick St Paul Grove Park 66-88; rtd 89; Perm to Offic *Chich* 89-01. *29 Eton Close, Datchet, Slough SL3 9BE* Tel (01753) 545802

GRIME, William John Peter. b 38. St Jo Coll Ox BA60 MA66. Cuddesdon Coll 69. **d** 70 **p** 71. C Blackb St Jas 70-74; Chapl St Martin's Coll of Educn 74-77; V Seascale *Carl* 77-78; P-in-c Irton w Drigg 77-78; V Seascale and Drigg 78-05; rtd 05; Perm to Offic *York* 05-08. *Bridge House, Snape, Bedale DL8 2SZ* Tel (01677) 470077 E-mail wjpgrime@gmail.com

GRIMLEY, The Very Revd Robert William. b 43. Ch Coll Cam BA66 MA70 Wadh Coll Ox BA68 MA76 UWE Hon DLitt04 Bris Univ Hon LLD09. Ripon Hall Ox 66. **d** 68 **p** 69. C Radlett *St Alb* 68-72; Chapl K Edw Sch Birm 72-84; Hon C Moseley St Mary *Birm* 72-84; V Edgbaston St Geo 84-97; Dean Bris 97-09; rtd 09; Perm to Offic *Ox* from 10. *88 Old High Street, Headington, Oxford OX3 9HW* Tel (01865) 308219 E-mail robertgrimley88@gmail.com

GRIMSBY, Suffragan Bishop of. See ROSSDALE, The Rt Revd David Douglas James

GRIMSDALE, Mrs Margaret. b 24. SRN48. Gilmore Course 80. **dss** 82 **d** 87. Stoke Poges *Ox* 82-88; Hon Par Dn 87-88; Hon Par Dn Burrington and Churchill *B & W* 88-90; rtd 90; Perm to Offic *B & W* 90-94. *Widecombe House, Barrington Road, Torquay TQ1 2QJ* Tel (01803) 298692

GRIMSHAW, Eric Fenton Hall. b 34. Bris Univ BA57. Tyndale Hall Bris 54. **d** 58 **p** 59. C Moss Side St Jas *Man* 58-61; C Leyland St Andr *Blackb* 61-64; V Preston St Mark 64-72; V Mirehouse *Carl* 72-91; Hon Can Carl Cathl 86-91; V Knowsley *Liv* 91-99; rtd 99; Perm to Offic *Liv* from 99. *22 Lynwood Avenue, Aughton, Ormskirk L39 5BB* Tel (01695) 424864

GRIMSTER, Barry John. b 49. Ex Univ BA70. Trin Coll Bris 72. **d** 74 **p** 75. C S Lambeth St Steph *S'wark* 74-77; C New Malden and Coombe 77-82; P-in-c Deptford St Jo 82-84; V Deptford St Jo w H Trin 84-89; V Woking St Pet *Guildf* 89-01; TR from 02. *The Rectory, 28 High Street, Old Woking, Woking GU22 9ER* Tel (01483) 762707 E-mail bjay1@onetel.com

GRIMWADE, Canon John Girling. b 20. Keble Coll Ox BA48 MA52. Cuddesdon Coll 48. **d** 50 **p** 51. C Kingston All SS *S'wark* 50-53; C Ox St Mary V 53-56; PC Londonderry *Birm* 56-62; R Caversham *Ox* 62-81; Hon Can Ch Ch 73-90; Chapl to The Queen 80-90; R Caversham St Pet and Mapledurham etc *Ox* 81-83; P-in-c Stonesfield 83-89; rtd 89; Perm to Offic *Glouc* and *Ox* from 89. *88 Alexander Drive, Cirencester GL7 1UJ* Tel (01285) 885767

GRIMWOOD, Andrew Stuart. b 68. Ex Univ BA89. St Mich Coll Llan BD97. **d** 98 **p** 99. C Llangynwyd w Maesteg 98-01; P-in-c Rhyl w St Ann *St As* 01-04; R Llanllwchaiarn and Newtown w Aberhafesp from 04; AD Cedewain from 08. *The Rectory, 3 Old Barn Lane, Newtown SY16 2PT* Tel (01686) 622260 E-mail andygrimwood@live.co.uk

GRIMWOOD, Canon David Walter. b 48. Lon Univ BA70 K Coll Lon BD73 AKC73. **d** 74 **p** 75. C Newc St Geo 74-78; C Whorlton 78-80; TV Totton *Win* 80-93; Adv to Coun for Soc Resp *Roch* and *Cant* 93-02; Chief Exec Ch in Soc *Roch* and *Cant* 02-09; Hon Can Roch Cathl 97-09; Perm to Offic *Cant* from 09. *56 Postley Road, Maidstone ME15 6TR* Tel (01622) 764625 Mobile 07960-369681 E-mail d.grimwood@zedakah.co.uk

GRINDELL, James Mark. b 43. Nottm Univ BA66 Bris Univ MA69. Wells Th Coll 66. **d** 68 **p** 69. C Bushey Heath *St Alb* 68-72; C Ex St Dav 72-74; Chapl St Audries Sch W Quantoxhead 74-83; Chapl Berkhamsted Colleg Sch Herts 83-86; Chapl Denstone Coll Uttoxeter 86-91; Chapl Portsm Gr Sch and Hon Chapl Portsm Cathl 91-03; rtd 03. *6A Victoria Place, Ryde PO33 2PX* E-mail jmgrindell@yahoo.co.uk

GRINHAM, Julian Clive. b 39. Birkbeck Coll Lon BA65. Oak Hill Th Coll 79. **d** 81 **p** 82. C Blackb Ch Ch w St Matt 81-83; Nat Sec Pathfinders CPAS 83-89; Dir CYPECS 89-94; V Normanton *Derby* 94-00; rtd 00; Perm to Offic *Nor* from 01. *85 Gwyn Crescent, Fakenham NR21 8NE* Tel (01328) 853068

GRINSELL, Robert Paul. b 62. Ch Ch Coll Cant BA86 PGCE89. Trin Coll Bris MA03. **d** 03 **p** 04. C Foord St Jo *Cant* 03-07; P-in-c Hawkinge w Acrise and Swingfield from 07. *The Rectory, 78 Canterbury Road, Hawkinge, Folkestone CT18 7BP* Tel (01303) 893215 E-mail robgrinsell@tiscali.co.uk

GRINSTED, Richard Anthony. b 43. Leic Univ BSc65. Oak Hill Th Coll 67. **d** 70 **p** 71. C Egham *Guildf* 70-73; C Woodford Wells *Chelmsf* 73-76; P-in-c Havering-atte-Bower 76-84; R Ditton *Roch* 84-94; R Chulmleigh *Ex* 94-96; R Chawleigh w Cheldon 94-96; R Wembworthy w Eggesford 94-96; R Chulmleigh, Chawleigh w Cheldon, Wembworthy etc 96-00; rtd 00. *Stonehouse, Christow, Exeter EX6 7NE* Tel (01647) 252653

GRISCOME, David. b 47. Oak Hill Th Coll BA88 TCD Div Sch 89. **d** 89 **p** 90. C Glendermott *D & R* 89-91; I Clondehorkey w Cashel 91-95; I Mevagh w Glenalla 91-95; Bp's C Calry *K, E & A* 95-97; I 97-00; Dean Elphin and Ardagh 99-04; I Sligo w Knocknarea and Rosses Pt 99-04; Perm to Offic *Cant* 04-06; I Convoy w Monellan and Donaghmore *D & R* from 06; Bp's Dom Chapl from 07. *The Rectory, Convoy, Co Donegal, Republic of Ireland* Tel (00353) (74) 910 1898 E-mail keida@eircom.net

✠**GRISWOLD, The Most Revd Frank Tracy.** b 37. Harvard Univ AB59 Oriel Coll Ox BA62 MA66. Gen Th Sem NY 59 Hon DD85 Seabury-Western Th Sem Hon DD85. **d** 62 **p** 63 **c** 85. C Bryn Mawr Redeemer 63-67; R Yardley St Andr 67-74; R Philadelphia St Martin-in-the-Fields 74-85; Bp Coadjutor Chicago 85-87; Bp Chicago 87-97; Presiding Bp 98-06; rtd 06. *Episcopal Church Center, 815 Second Avenue, New York, NY 10017, USA* Tel (001) (212) 716 6276 *or* 867 8400 Fax 490 3298 E-mail pboffice@episcopalchurch.org

GROARKE, Ms Nicola Jane. b 62. Lanc Univ BA84. Ridley Hall Cam. **d** 00 **p** 01. C Balham Hill Ascension *S'wark* 00-08; V Canonbury St Steph *Lon* from 08. *St Stephen's Vicarage, 9 River Place, London N1 2DE* Tel (020) 7359 4164 *or* tel and fax 7226 7526 E-mail nikki@stsc.org.uk

GROEPE, Canon Thomas Matthew Karl. b 51. St Pet Coll Natal 76. **d** 78 **p** 79. S Africa 78-83 and from 88; Hon C Waterloo St Jo w St Andr *S'wark* 83-88. *PO Box 1932, Cape Town, 8000 South Africa* Tel and fax (0027) (21) 465 4946 *or* tel 461 9566 E-mail karlgroepe@mweb.co.za

GROOCOCK, Christopher John. b 59. St Jo Coll Nottm 89. **d** 92 **p** 93. C Shawbury *Lich* 92-95; V Hengoed w Gobowen 95-00; CF from 00. *clo MOD Chaplains (Army)* Tel (01264) 381140 Fax 381824

GROOCOCK, Craig Ronald. WMMTC 03. **d** 05 **p** 06. C Kenilworth St Nic *Cov* 05-08; P-in-c Harbury and Ladbroke from 08. *The Rectory, 2 Vicarage Lane, Harbury, Leamington Spa CV33 9HA* Tel (01926) 612377 Mobile 07811-395169 E-mail craiggroocock@aol.com

GROOM, Mrs Susan Anne. b 63. Univ of Wales BA85 Hughes Hall Cam MPhil86 Lon Bible Coll MA94 Open Univ MPhil00. St Jo Coll Nottm 94. **d** 96 **p** 97. C Harefield *Lon* 96-99; C Eastcote St Lawr 99-01; P-in-c Yiewsley 01-03; V 03-07; Dir Lic Min Kensington Area 07-09; P-in-c Henlow and Langford *St Alb* from 09. *The Vicarage, 65 Church Street, Langford, Biggleswade SG18 9QT* Tel (01462) 700248 E-mail sgroom28@googlemail.com

GROSSCURTH, Stephen. b 55. Sarum & Wells Th Coll 81. **d** 84 **p** 85. C Southport H Trin *Liv* 84-87; C Amblecote *Worc* 87-89; V Walton St Jo *Liv* 89-95; Chapl S Man Univ Hosps NHS Trust from 95. *Wythenshawe Hospital, Southmoor Road, Manchester M23 9LT* Tel 0161-291 2298 *or* (01925) 821124 Fax 0161-946 2603

GROSSE, Anthony Charles Bain. b 30. Oak Hill Th Coll 58. **d** 61 **p** 62. C Chislehurst Ch Ch *Roch* 61-65; C Washfield *Ex* 65-71;

TV Washfield, Stoodleigh, Withleigh etc 71-73; R Hemyock 73-86; P-in-c Clayhidon 76-86; R Hemyock w Culm Davy and Clayhidon 87-93; R Hemyock w Culm Davy, Clayhidon and Culmstock 93-96; rtd 96; Perm to Offic *Ex* from 98. *17 Frog Street, Bampton, Tiverton EX16 9NT* Tel (01398) 331981
E-mail acgrosse@btinternet.com

GROSSE, Peter George. b 43. St Steph Ho Ox 02. **d** 03 **p** 04. NSM Reading St Matt *Ox* 03-06; NSM Tilehurst St Mary from 06; NSM Tilehurst St Geo from 06. *18 Rangewood Avenue, Reading RG30 3NN* Tel 0118-959 4573
E-mail petergrosse@supanet.com

GROSSE, Richard William. b 52. Solicitor 77 Mid Essex Tech Coll LLB73. Ridley Hall Cam 86. **d** 88 **p** 89. C Soham *Ely* 88-91; C Bedale *Ripon* 91-93; P-in-c Thornton Watlass w Thornton Steward 91-93; V Barton and Manfield w Cleasby 93-95; V Barton and Manfield and Cleasby w Stapleton 95-99; R Keelby Gp *Linc* 99-04; R Callander *St And* from 04; R Aberfoyle from 04. *St Mary's Rectory, Main Street, Aberfoyle, Stirling FK8 3UJ* Tel and fax (01877) 382887 E-mail richard.grosse@hotmail.com

GROSU, Iosif. b 60. Iasi Univ BTh92. RC Inst Iasi. **d** 89 **p** 89. In RC Ch 89-93; C Darlington St Cuth *Dur* 96-99; C Stockton St Jo and Stockton St Jas 99-02; TV Ch the K 02-08; P-in-c Purston cum S Featherstone *Wakef* 08-09; P-in-c Featherstone 08-09; V from 09. *The Vicarage, Victoria Street, Featherstone, Pontefract WF7 5EZ* Tel (01977) 792280
E-mail iosifgrosu@btinternet.com

GROSVENOR, Royston Johannes Martin. b 47. K Coll Lon BD70 AKC. **d** 71 **p** 72. C Pontesbury I and II *Heref* 71-75; C Bishopston *Bris* 75-79; P-in-c Croydon St Pet S End *Cant* 79-81; V Croydon St Pet 81-84; V Croydon St Pet *S'wark* 85-87; R Merstham and Gatton 87-97; V Tidenham w Beachley and Lancaut *Glouc* from 97; P-in-c St Briavels w Hewelsfield from 05; AD Forest S 04-09; rtd 11. *75 King's Drive, Bishopston, Bristol BS7 8JQ* Tel 0117-924 7919
E-mail royston.grosvenor@hotmail.co.uk

GROVE, Lynn. b 43. Lon Univ MB, BS67. Cranmer Hall Dur 03. **d** 04 **p** 05. NSM Pickering w Lockton and Levisham *York* from 04. *37 Eastgate, Pickering YO18 7DU* Tel (01751) 477574
E-mail lynngrove43@hotmail.com

GROVER, Wilfrid John. b 29. Lich Th Coll 55. **d** 58 **p** 59. C Northampton St Alb *Pet* 58-61; C Boyne Hill *Ox* 61-65; V Cookham 65-85; RD Maidenhead 82-85; Warden Christchurch Retreat Ho *Glouc* 85-93; rtd 89; Hon C Jedburgh *Edin* from 93. *5 The Stables, Buccleuch Chase, St Boswells, Melrose TD6 0HE* Tel (01835) 824435

GROVES, Caroline Anne. b 41. **d** 05 **p** 06. OLM Norbiton *S'wark* from 05. *16 Beaufort Road, Kingston upon Thames KT1 2TQ* Tel (020) 8549 1585 E-mail sicaro@blueyonder.co.uk

GROVES, Elizabeth Ann. Bp Otter Coll 94. **d** 97 **p** 09. NSM Soberton w Newtown *Portsm* 97-01; NSM Botley, Durley and Curdridge 01-06; NSM Wickham 06; NSM Shedfield and Wickham from 07. *The Rectory, Southwick Road, Wickham, Fareham PO17 6HR* Tel (01329) 832134
E-mail akeagroves@aol.com

GROVES, James Alan. b 32. CCC Cam BA58 MA62. Wells Th Coll 58. **d** 60 **p** 61. C Milton next Gravesend Ch Ch *Roch* 60-64; C Beckenham St Jas 64-66; V Orpington St Andr 66-98; rtd 98; Perm to Offic *Chich* from 98. *9 Wykeham Road, Hastings TN34 1UA* Tel (01424) 200839

GROVES, Preb Jill. b 61. Univ Coll Lon BSc82. St Jo Coll Nottm MA93. **d** 93 **p** 94. C Tenbury Wells *Heref* 93-98; P-in-c Hope Bowdler w Eaton-under-Heywood from 98; P-in-c Cardington from 98; P-in-c Rushbury from 98; Preb Heref Cathl from 98. *The Rectory, Hope Bowdler, Church Stretton SY6 7DD* Tel (01694) 722918 E-mail jill@grovesfamily.org.uk

GROVES, Justin Simon James. b 69. Lon Bible Coll BA93. Ridley Hall Cam 00. **d** 02 **p** 03. C Glouc St Cath 02-05; C Newport St Paul *Mon* 05-07; P-in-c from 07. *52 Oakfield Road, Newport NP20 4LX* Tel (01633) 419775

GROVES, Margaret Ann. b 49. Nottm Univ BEd71 BPhil88. EMMTC 95. **d** 98 **p** 99. NSM Farnsfield *S'well* from 98; NSM Bilsthorpe from 98. *Churchill House, Church Hill, Bilsthorpe, Newark NG22 8RU* Tel (01623) 870679

GROVES, Peter John. b 70. New Coll Ox BA92 MA96 DPhil96. Westcott Ho Cam 95. **d** 97 **p** 98. C Leigh-on-Sea St Marg *Chelmsf* 97-99; Lib Pusey Ho 99-01; Asst Chapl and Tutor Keble Coll Ox 01-02; Chapl and Fell BNC Ox 02-06; Hon C Ox St Mary Magd 01-04; P-in-c from 05. *15 Beaumont Street, Oxford OX1 2NA* Tel (01865) 247836
E-mail peter.groves@theology.ox.ac.uk

GROVES, Canon Philip Neil. b 62. Man Univ BA84 Birm Univ PhD10. St Jo Coll Nottm 86. **d** 88 **p** 89. C Holbeck *Ripon* 88-91; CMS 91-99; Lect St Phil Th Coll Kongwa Tanzania 93-98; Hon Can Mpwapwa from 98; TV Melton Mowbray *Leic* 99-05; Listening Process Facilitator on Human Sexuality Angl Communion 06-09; Project Dir for Continuing Indaba from 09. *Anglican Communion Office, 16 Tavistock Crescent, London W11 1AP* Tel (020) 7313 3917
E-mail phil.groves@anglicancommunion.org
or rev.phil@ntlworld.com

GROVES, Robert John. b 42. Trin Coll Bris 74. **d** 76 **p** 77. C Norwood St Luke *S'wark* 76-79; P-in-c Clapham Park All SS 79-86; V Anerley *Roch* 86-95; TV Canford Magna *Sarum* 95-98; TR Tollington *Lon* 98-02; rtd 02; Perm to Offic *Cant* 02-09 and *Roch* from 02. *15 Mulberry Close, Tunbridge Wells TN4 9XR* E-mail bob.groves@lineone.net

GROWNS, John Huntley. b 28. Chich Th Coll 57. **d** 60 **p** 61. C Hayes St Mary *Lon* 60-64; C Addlestone *Guildf* 64-67; C-in-c Kempston Transfiguration CD *St Alb* 67-74; R Stevenage St Geo 74-82; R Felpham w Middleton *Chich* 82-88; P-in-c Westmill w Gt Munden *St Alb* 88-89; P-in-c Westmill 89-93; Dioc Stewardship Adv 88-93; rtd 93; Perm to Offic *Chich* 93-04; *St Alb* 93-00; *Ely* from 10. *5 Little London Gardens, Ely CB6 1BF* Tel (01353) 772794

GRUBB, Greville Alexander (Alex). b 36. Saltley Tr Coll Birm CertEd60. St Jo Coll Nottm 72. **d** 74 **p** 75. C Rushden w Newton Bromswold *Pet* 74-77; Chapl St D Coll Llandudno 77-89; Chapl Casterton Sch Lancs 90-96; rtd 96; Perm to Offic *Blackb* from 96 and *Bradf* from 02. *Beckstones, 21 Littledale Road, Brookhouse, Lancaster LA2 9PH* Tel (01524) 770512

GRUMBALL, Kevin. St Steph Ho Ox. **d** 11. NSM Temple Grafton w Binton *Cov* from 11; NSM Exhall w Wixford from 11; NSM Salford Priors from 11. *Stone Croft, Ardens Grafton, Alcester B49 6DR*

GRUNDY, Anthony Brian. b 36. Pemb Coll Cam BA62 MA87. Ridley Hall Cam 61. **d** 63 **p** 64. C Hatcham St Jas *S'wark* 63-66; C Margate H Trin *Cant* 66-68; C Brixton Hill St Sav *S'wark* 68-70; V Assington *St E* 70-76; TV Much Wenlock w Bourton *Heref* 76-81; TV Wenlock 81-82; TR 82-88; RD Condover 86-88; C Burghfield *Ox* 88-02; rtd 02; Perm to Offic *Chich* from 03. *29 Gerald Road, Worthing BN11 5QQ* Tel (01903) 507213

GRUNDY, Christopher John. b 49. ACA72. Trin Coll Bris 74. **d** 77 **p** 78. C Maidstone St Luke *Cant* 77-81; Argentina 81-82; Chile 82-84; Perm to Offic *Guildf* 84-96; NSM Guildf Ch Ch w St Martha-on-the-Hill 96-99; C Shere, Albury and Chilworth 99-06; TV Drypool *York* from 06. *St John's Vicarage, 383 Southcoates Lane, Hull HU9 3UN* Tel (01482) 781090
E-mail chris@grundy.org.uk

GRUNDY, David. *See* GRUNDY, Julian David

GRUNDY, Jocelyn Pratchitt. b 22. Trin Coll Cam MA. Westcott Ho Cam 64. **d** 66 **p** 67. C Guildf H Trin w St Mary 66-68; R Shere 68-73; V Fleet 73-83; C Aldershot St Mich 83-87; rtd 87; Perm to Offic *Guildf* from 87. *Richmond Cottage, School Hill, Seale, Farnham GU10 1HY* Tel (01252) 782238

GRUNDY, Judith Michal Towers Mynors. b 54. Lady Spencer Chu Coll of Educn CertEd76 Ox Univ BEd77. Trin Coll Bris 85. **d** 93 **p** 94. NSM Kensal Rise St Mark and St Martin *Lon* 93-95; NSM Snettisham w Ingoldisthorpe and Fring *Nor* 95-04; R Denver and Ryston w Roxham and W Dereham etc *Ely* from 04. *The Rectory, Ryston Road, Denver, Downham Market PE38 0DP* Tel (01366) 383226 E-mail judith.grundy@ely.anglican.org

GRUNDY, Julian David. b 60. St Andr Univ MA83. Trin Coll Bris BA88. **d** 89 **p** 90. C Lancaster St Thos *Blackb* 89-92; C Kensal Rise St Mark and St Martin *Lon* 92-95; R Snettisham w Ingoldisthorpe and Fring *Nor* 95-03; Perm to Offic *Ely* from 08. *The Rectory, Ryston Road, Denver, Downham Market PE38 0DP* Tel (01366) 383226 E-mail david@grundyd.fslife.co.uk

GRUNDY, Canon Malcolm Leslie. b 44. Open Univ BA76. St Boniface Warminster AKC68. **d** 69 **p** 70. C Doncaster St Geo *Sheff* 69-72; Ind Chapl 72-80; Dir of Educn *Lon* 80-86; TR Huntingdon *Ely* 86-91; Hon Can Ely Cathl 88-94; Dir Avec 91-94; Adn Craven *Bradf* 94-05; Dir Foundn for Ch Leadership 05-09; rtd 09; Perm to Offic *York* from 09. *4 Portal Road, York YO26 6BQ* Tel (01904) 787387 Mobile 07950-816641
E-mail malcolm.grundy@live-wires.org

GRUNDY, Paul. b 55. BD77 AKC. Linc Th Coll 79. **d** 80 **p** 81. C Ryhope *Dur* 80-82; C Ferryhill 82-85; TV Cramlington *Newc* 85-87; TV Swinton and Pendlebury *Man* 87-90; V Wingate Grange *Dur* 90-95; R Willington and Sunnybrow 95-07; P-in-c Usworth 07-09; R from 09. *Usworth Rectory, 14 Prestwick Close, Washington NE37 2LP* Tel 0191-416 7604

GRÜNEBERG, Keith Nigel. *See* BEECH-GRÜNEBERG, Keith Nigel

GRUNEWALD, Gottfried Johannes. b 38. Loyola Univ Chicago MPS92. Th Faculty Frankfurt 66. **d** 69 **p** 69. Denmark 70-95; C Dunbar *Edin* 95-97; R Dollar *St And* 98-05; rtd 05. *Teglparken 8, 8860 Ulstrup, Denmark* Tel (0045) 864 6341
E-mail grunewald@email.dk

GRYLLS, Ms Catherine Anne. b 70. **d** 00 **p** 01. C Hall Green St Pet *Birm* 00-04; P-in-c Balsall Heath St Paul 04-07; P-in-c Edgbaston SS Mary and Ambrose 04-07; P-in-c Balsall Heath and Edgbaston SS Mary and Ambrose 07-08; V from 08. *St Ambrose Vicarage, 15 Raglan Road, Birmingham B5 7RA* Tel 0121-440 2196

GRYLLS, Canon Michael John. b 38. Qu Coll Cam BA62 MA66. Linc Th Coll 62. **d** 64 **p** 65. C Sheff Gillcar St Silas 64-67; C-in-c Dunscroft CD 67-70; V Herringthorpe 70-78; V Amport, Grateley, Monxton and Quarley *Win* 78-89; RD Andover 85-89;

V Whitchurch w Tufton and Litchfield 89-03; Hon Can Win Cathl 01-03; rtd 03; Perm to Offic *Worc* from 04. *41 Church Street, Evesham WR11 1DY* Tel (01386) 442086

GUBBINS, Andrew Martin. b 65. York Univ BA86 Keele Univ 93. St Jo Coll Nottm LTh93. **d** 96 **p** 97. C Harrogate St Mark *Ripon* 96-00; P-in-c Osmondthorpe St Phil 00-03; V Leeds All SS w Osmondthorpe 03-09; P-in-c Chippenham St Pet *Bris* from 09. *St Peter's Vicarage, 32 Lords Mead, Chippenham SN14 0LL* Tel (01249) 448530 E-mail gubbinsrevs@sky.com

GUBBINS (*née* O'BRIEN), Mrs Mary. b 68. Leeds Univ BSc90. St Jo Coll Nottm BTh93. **d** 94 **p** 95. C Middleton St Mary *Ripon* 94-96; C Bilton 96-99; Perm to Offic 99-09. *St Peter's Vicarage, 32 Lords Mead, Chippenham SN14 0LL* Tel (01249) 448530

GUDGEON, Canon Michael John. b 40. Qu Coll Cam BA63 MA67. Chich Th Coll 65. **d** 66 **p** 67. C Kings Heath *Birm* 66-72; Asst Chapl K Edw Sch Birm 69-72; Chapl and Tutor Cuddesdon Coll 72-75; V Hawley H Trin *Guildf* 75-80; V Minley 75-80; Adult Educn Adv *Chich* 80-87; Can Res Portsm Cathl 87-90; Dioc Dir of Educn 87-90; V Hove St Thos *Chich* 90-93; TV Hove 93-94; Bp's Chapl *Eur* 94-98; Dir of Ords 94-97; Can Gib Cathl 96-06; P-in-c Worthing St Andr *Chich* 98-05; rtd 05. *11 Gloucester Road, Littlehampton BN17 7BT* Tel (01903) 739682 E-mail michaelgudgeon@aol.com

GUERNSEY, Dean of. See MELLOR, The Very Revd Kenneth Paul

✠**GUERRERO, The Rt Revd Orlando.** b 45. Episc Sem of Ecuador. **p** 80 **c** 95. P Puerto la Cruz H Trin 80-93; Interim P Caracas St Mary 80-84; Bp Venezuela from 95. *Apartado 49-143, Avenida Caron 100, Colinas de Bello Monte, Caracas 1042-A, Venezuela* Tel (0058) (2) 753 0723 Fax 751 3180

GUEST, David. b 41. Dur Univ BA62. Coll of Resurr Mirfield 70. **d** 72 **p** 73. C Horsforth *Ripon* 72-75; C Richmond 75-76; C Richmond w Hudswell 76-78; R Middleham 78-81; R Middleham and Coverham w Horsehouse 81-86; V V W Rainton and E Rainton *Dur* 86-03; RD Houghton 92-94 and 96-97; rtd 03; Perm to Offic *Ripon* from 03. *Lindisfarne, 3 New Croft, Horsforth, Leeds LS18 4TD* Tel 0113-258 0521

GUEST, David Andrew. b 61. Chich Th Coll BTh92. **d** 92 **p** 93. C Prenton *Ches* 92-94; C Ches H Trin 94-97; Assoc P Douglas All SS and St Thos *S & M* 97-00; Dioc Communications Officer 97-00; Relig Adv Manx Radio 97-00; Bp's Dom Chapl 98-00; Dioc Communications Officer *Chich* 00-09; C Hove 00-03; C Southwick 03-09; P-in-c Heathfield from 09. *The Vicarage, Old Heathfield, Heathfield TN21 9AB* Tel (01435) 862457 E-mail davidguest731@btinternet.com

GUEST, Derek William. b 55. NOC 90. **d** 93 **p** 94. C Cheadle Hulme St Andr *Ches* 93-99; V from 99. *2 Orrishmere Road, Cheadle Hulme, Cheadle SK8 5HP* Tel 0161-486 9306 E-mail redhatguest@yahoo.co.uk

GUEST, Ernest Anthony. b 64. NTMTC 99. **d** 02 **p** 03. C Gt Ilford St Jo *Chelmsf* 02-05; V Barkingside St Laur from 05. *St Laurence's Vicarage, Donington Avenue, Ilford IG6 1AJ* Tel (020) 8518 3113 Mobile 07810-516356 E-mail ernie@eguest.fsnet.co.uk

GUEST, Mrs Helen. b 54. Totley Thornbridge Coll CertEd75 Nottm Univ MA02. EMMTC 99. **d** 02 **p** 03. NSM Brimington *Derby* 02-05; C Hatton 05-07; P-in-c Killamarsh from 07; C Barlborough and Renishaw from 07; RD Bolsover and Staveley from 11. *The Rectory, Sheepcote Road, Killamarsh, Sheffield S21 1DU* Tel 0114-248 2769 E-mail revsguest@btinternet.com

GUEST, John. b 36. Trin Coll Bris 59. **d** 61 **p** 62. C Barton Hill St Luke w Ch Ch *Bris* 61-64; C Liv St Sav 65-66; USA from 66; rtd 01. *30 Myrtle Hill Road, Sewickley PA 15143-8700, USA* Tel (001) (412) 741 6445

GUEST, John Andrew Kenneth. b 55. Univ of Wales (Lamp) BA78. Wycliffe Hall Ox 78. **d** 80 **p** 81. C Eastwood *S'well* 80-84; TV Toxteth St Philemon w St Gabr and St Cleopas *Liv* 84-89; C Cranham Park *Chelmsf* 89-93; P-in-c Stanford-le-Hope w Mucking 93-03; R from 03. *The Rectory, The Green, Stanford-le-Hope SS17 0EP* Tel (01375) 672271 E-mail gof4god@aol.com

GUEST, Michael. b 52. EMMTC. **d** 99 **p** 00. NSM Heath *Derby* 99-07; NSM Killamarsh from 07; NSM Barlborough and Renishaw from 07. *The Rectory, Sheepcote Road, Killamarsh, Sheffield S21 1DU* Tel 0114-248 2769 E-mail revsguest@btinternet.com

GUEST, Simon Llewelyn. b 56. Univ of Wales (Lamp) BA78 CertEd79. St Mich Coll Llan 83. **d** 85 **p** 86. C Bassaleg *Mon* 85-88; C Cwmbran 88-89; TV 89-91; V Raglan w Llandenny and Bryngwyn 91-05; V Rockfield and Dingestow Gp from 05; AD Raglan-Usk 01-05; AD Monmouth from 06. *The Vicarage, Dingestow, Monmouth NP25 4DY* Tel (01600) 740206

GUEST-BLOFELD, Thomas. b 35. St D Coll Lamp BA59. Cranmer Hall Dur 59. **d** 62 **p** 63. C Maltby *Sheff* 62-63; C Goole 63-66; C Pocklington w Yapham-cum-Meltonby, Owsthorpe etc *York* 67-68; C Ely 68-70; C Pemberton St Jo *Liv* 70-72; V Walton St Jo 72-74; V Barkisland w W Scammonden *Wakef* 74-80; V Smallbridge *Man* 80-82; C Irlam 83-86; rtd 87. *234 M005, Tambon Maesai, Amphoe Mueang, Phayao 56000, Thailand* Tel (0066) (8) 7184 3624

GUILDFORD, Bishop of. See HILL, The Rt Revd Christopher John

GUILDFORD, Dean of. See STOCK, The Very Revd Victor Andrew

GUILFORD, John Edward. b 50. S & M Dioc Tr Inst 94. **d** 99 **p** 00. OLM Lonan *S & M* from 99; OLM Laxey from 99. *Tremissary House, Strathallan Road, Douglas, Isle of Man IM2 4PN* Tel and fax (01624) 672001 Mobile 07624-494274 E-mail revjohnnyg@manx.net

GUILLAN, Miss Barbara Doris. b 19. S'wark Ord Course 45. **d** 87. NSM St Stythians w Perranarworthal and Gwennap *Truro* 87-89; rtd 89; Perm to Offic *Truro* 89-94. *St Cecilia's Nursing Home, 1 Hitchen Lane, Shepton Mallet BA4 5TZ* Tel (01749) 342809

GUILLE, The Very Revd John Arthur. b 49. Southn Univ BTh79. Sarum & Wells Th Coll 73. **d** 76 **p** 77. C Chandler's Ford *Win* 76-80; P-in-c Bournemouth St Jo *Bris* 80-84; P-in-c Bournemouth St Mich 83-84; V Bournemouth St Jo w St Mich 84-89; R Guernsey St Andr 89-99; Adn Win 99-07; Can Res Win Cathl 99-07; Dean S'well from 07. *The Residence, Southwell NG25 0HP* Tel (01636) 812593 *or* 817282 E-mail dean@southwellminster.org.uk

GUILLEBAUD, Mrs Jette Margaret. b 48. Ex Univ BA70 UWE Hon MA98 FRSA95. Ripon Coll Cuddesdon 03. **d** 05 **p** 06. NSM Sarum Cathl 05-10; Asst Chapl Sarum Coll from 10. *Dovecot, Mount Sorrel, Broad Chalke, Salisbury SP5 5HQ* Tel (01722) 781281 Mobile 07985-576739

GUILLEBAUD, Canon Margaret Jean. b 43. MBE03. Edin Univ BSc66. Cranmer Hall Dur 79. **dss** 80 **d** 87 **p** 94. New Malden and Coombe *S'wark* 80-84; Carlton Colville w Mutford and Rushmere *Nor* 84-91; Par Dn 87-91; Par Dn Rodbourne Cheney *Bris* 91-94; C 94-95; CMS Rwanda 95-08; rtd 08; Perm to Offic *Birm* from 08; Can Res Byumba from 10. *7 Poplar Road, Dorridge, Solihull B93 8DD* Tel (01564) 770113 E-mail mguillebaud@gmail.com

GUILLEMIN, Thierry Jean-Louis. b 62. Coll of Resurr Mirfield 08. **d** 01 **p** 01. In RC Ch 01-07; Perm to Offic *Wakef* 08-09; C Heckmondwike 09-11; C Liversedge w Hightown 09-11; P-in-c Buttershaw St Paul *Bradf* from 11; C Shelf w Buttershaw St Aid from 11. *St Paul's Vicarage, 42A Wibsey Park Avenue, Bradford BD6 3QA* Tel (01274) 690832 Mobile 07778-577008 E-mail t.guillemin@btinternet.com

GUINNESS, Alexander. See GUINNESS, Graham Alexander

GUINNESS, Christopher Paul. b 43. Lon Coll of Div 64. **d** 67 **p** 68. C Farnborough *Guildf* 67-70; C Tulse Hill H Trin *S'wark* 70-74; C Worting *Win* 74-78; P-in-c S Lambeth St Steph *S'wark* 78-89; V 89-91; RD Lambeth 86-90; C Ches Square St Mich w St Phil *Lon* 91-97; Living Waters Trust 98-00; Chapl Ealing Hosp NHS Trust 00-01; Chapl Hammersmith Hosps NHS Trust 01-08; Chapl Imp Coll Healthcare NHS Trust from 08. *14 Goldsboro Road, London SW8 4RR* Tel (020) 7720 2301 E-mail christopherguinness@live.co.uk

GUINNESS, Canon Garry Grattan. b 40. Em Coll Cam BA64 MA68. Ridley Hall Cam 64. **d** 66 **p** 67. C Wallington *S'wark* 66-69; C St Marylebone All So w SS Pet and Jo *Lon* 69-72; P-in-c Clifton H Trin, St Andr and St Pet *Bris* 72-79; V Watford St Luke *St Alb* 79-90; TR Worthing Ch the King *Chich* 90-05; Hon Can Kigeme from 02; rtd 05. *37 Stowell Crescent, Wareham BH20 4PT* Tel (01929) 550215

GUINNESS, Graham Alexander. b 60. Edin Th Coll 82. **d** 85 **p** 86. Dioc Youth Chapl *Mor* 85-88; C Elgin w Lossiemouth 85-88; Asst P Glas St Ninian 88-90; R Tighnabruaich *Arg* 90-91 and 94-99; R Dunoon 90-99; Miss to Seamen 90-99; R Fort William *Arg* from 99. *St Andrew's Rectory, Parade Road, Fort William PH33 6BA* Tel and fax (01397) 702979 E-mail ftwilliam@argyll.anglican.org

GUINNESS, Peter Grattan. b 49. Man Univ BSc71 CertEd73. St Jo Coll Nottm 80. **d** 82 **p** 83. C Normanton *Wakef* 82-87; V Fletchamstead *Cov* 87-91; V Lancaster St Thos *Blackb* 91-10; Hon Can Blackb Cathl 04-10; P-in-c Gillingham St Mark *Roch* from 10. *St Mark's Vicarage, 173 Canterbury Street, Gillingham ME7 5TU* Tel (01634) 570489 E-mail peter.guinness@yahoo.co.uk

GUINNESS, Canon Robin Gordon. b 38. St Jo Coll Cam MA61. Ridley Hall Cam 63. **d** 63 **p** 64. C Bedworth *Cov* 63-66; CMS 66-68; Canada from 68. *1243-109 Front Street East, Toronto ON M5A 4P7, Canada* E-mail rguinnness@primus.ca

GUISE, John Christopher. b 29. Cheltenham & Glouc Coll of HE MA94 MRPharmS51. WMMTC 80. **d** 83 **p** 84. NSM Alfrick, Lulsley, Suckley, Leigh and Bransford *Worc* 83-94; NSM Martley and Wichenford, Knightwick etc 94-00; Perm to Offic from 00. *Marsh Cottage, Leigh, Worcester WR6 5LE* Tel (01886) 832336

GUISE, Stephen. b 48. Win Sch of Art BA75. Chich Th Coll 85. **d** 87 **p** 88. C Bexhill St Pet *Chich* 87-90; TV Haywards Heath St Wilfrid 90-94; V Knighton *Leic* 94-97; Chapl Community of Servants of the Cross 97-01; P-in-c Amberley w N Stoke and Parham, Wiggonholt etc *Chich* 99-03; TV Bridport *Sarum* 03-07; rtd 07; Perm to Offic *Chich* 07-09; P-in-c Sidlesham from 09. *The*

Vicarage, Church Farm Lane, Sidlesham, Chichester PO20 7RE Tel (01243) 641237

GUITE, Ayodeji Malcolm. b 57. Pemb Coll Cam BA80 MA84 Newc Poly PGCE82 Dur Univ PhD93. Ridley Hall Cam 88. **d** 90 **p** 91. C Ely 90-93; TV Huntingdon 93-98; Chapl Anglia Poly Univ 98-03; Chapl Girton Coll Cam from 03. *Girton College, Cambridge CB3 0JG* Tel (01223) 338999 E-mail mg320@cam.ac.uk

GUITE, Mrs Frances Clare. b 56. Leeds Univ BA08. Coll of Resurr Mirfield 06. **d** 08 **p** 09. C Westleigh St Pet *Man* 08-11; C Westleigh St Paul 09-11; P-in-c Castleton Moor from 11. *St Martin's Vicarage, Vicarage Road North, Rochdale OL11 2TE* Tel (01706) 632353 Mobile 07791-328624 E-mail francesguite@yahoo.co.uk

GUITE, Canon Margaret Ann. b 53. Girton Coll Cam BA74 MA78 St Jo Coll Dur PhD81. Cranmer Hall Dur 75. dss 79 **d** 87 **p** 94. Warlingham w Chelsham and Farleigh *S'wark* 79-82; Cherry Hinton St Jo *Ely* 82-86; Tutor Westcott Ho Cam 82-90; Tutor Wesley Ho Cam 87-90; NSM Ely 90-93; NSM Chettisham 90-93; NSM Prickwillow 90-93; NSM Huntingdon 93-99; V Fenstanton 99-06; V Hilton 99-06; RD Huntingdon 05-06; P-in-c Cambridge St Mark from 06; Hon Can Ely Cathl from 04. *St Mark's Vicarage, 13 Barton Road, Cambridge CB3 9JZ* Tel (01223) 327621 E-mail vicar@stmarksnewnham.org

GUIVER, Paul Alfred (George). b 45. St Chad's Coll Dur BA68. Cuddesdon Coll 71. **d** 73 **p** 74. C Mill End and Heronsgate w W Hyde *St Alb* 73-76; P-in-c Bishop's Frome *Heref* 76-82; P-in-c Castle Frome 76-82; P-in-c Acton Beauchamp and Evesbatch 76 82; CR from 85; Superior from 02; Lic to Offic *Wakef* from 85. *House of the Resurrection, Stocks Bank Road, Mirfield WF14 0BN* Tel (01924) 483301 Fax 490489 E-mail gguiver@mirfield.org.uk

GUIVER, Roger William Antony. b 53. Edin Univ MA75 St Chad's Coll Dur BA78. Coll of Resurr Mirfield. **d** 82 **p** 83. C Rekendyke *Dur* 82-85; Chapl Middlesbrough Gen Hosp 85-93; P-in-c Middlesbrough St Columba w St Paul *York* 85-94; V Acomb Moor 94-97; V Middlesbrough St Thos 97-00. *Swang Farm, Glaisdale, Whitby YO21 2QZ* Tel (01947) 897210

GULL, William John. b 42. Ripon Hall Ox 63. **d** 65 **p** 66. C Worksop Priory *S'well* 65-69; C Newark St Mary 69-71; P-in-c Mansfield St Lawr 71-77; V 77-78; Chapl HM YOI Lowdham Grange 78-90; R Lambley *S'well* 78-91; V Sneinton St Cypr 91-99; rtd 99; Perm to Offic *S'well* from 03. *37 Hazel Grove, Mapperley, Nottingham NG3 6DQ* Tel 0115-920 8071 E-mail wjgull@btopenworld.com

GULLAND, John Robertson. b 46. Open Univ BA76 Chelsea Coll Lon MA82 Avery Hill Coll CertEd70 ACIB. Oak Hill Th Coll 88. **d** 90 **p** 91. NSM Woodside Park St Barn *Lon* 90-92; Lic to Offic *S & M* 93-09; NSM Castletown 92-09; Chapl K W m Coll 92-09; P-in-c Corfu *Eur* from 09. *21 L Mavili Street, Kerkyra, Corfu 491 00, Greece* Tel and fax (0030) (2661) 031467 E-mail holytrin@otenet.gr

GULLIDGE, Philip Michael Nowell. b 60. Univ of Wales (Swansea) BSc82 Univ of Wales (Cardiff) BD93. St Mich Coll Llan 90. **d** 93 **p** 94. C Neath w Llantwit 93-97; V Treharris w Bedlinog 97-03; V Treharris, Trelewis and Bedlinog 04-08; V Llantwit Fardre from 08. *The Vicarage, Church Village, Pontypridd CF38 1EP* Tel (01443) 202538 E-mail philipgullidge@aol.com

GULLIFORD, Mrs Susan Diane. b 49. W Midl Coll of Educn BEd86. WMMTC 97. **d** 00 **p** 01. NSM Tettenhall Regis *Lich* 00-02; C Wednesfield 02-04; Perm to Offic from 04. *2 James Street, Willenhall WV13 1SS* E-mail sue.gulliford@btinternet.com

GULLIFORD, William Douglas FitzGerald. b 69. Selw Coll Cam BA91 MA95. Westcott Ho Cam. **d** 94 **p** 95. C Banstead *Guildf* 94-97; C Wilton Place St Paul *Lon* 97-00; Chapl Guildhall Sch of Music and Drama 97-01; P-in-c St Dunstan in the West 00-08; V from 08; Gen Sec Angl and E Churches Assn 00-05; Bp's Chapl *Lon* 00-02; R St Mary le Strand w St Clem Danes 02-08; Dioc Bp's Chapl for E Orthodox Affairs from 02; Dir of Ords *Eur* from 03. *184A Fleet Street, London EC4A 2HD* Tel and fax (020) 7405 1929 E-mail william.gulliford@london.anglican.org

GULLY, Mrs Carol Glenys. b 57. Coll of Ripon & York St Jo BEd79. NOC 02. **d** 05 **p** 06. NSM Castleton Moor *Man* 05-09; NSM Kirkholt 09-10; Perm to Offic *Portsm* 10-11; NSM Portsea St Cuth from 11. *The Rectory, 27 Farlington Avenue, Cosham, Portsmouth PO6 1DF* Tel (023) 9237 5145 E-mail revdcarolggully@gmail.com

GULLY, Paul David. b 59. Shoreditch Coll Lon BEd81. Trin Coll Bris BA95. **d** 95 **p** 96. C Radcliffe *Man* 95-99; TV New Bury 99-05; V Oakenrod and Bamford 05-10; R Farlington *Portsm* from 10. *The Rectory, 27 Farlington Avenue, Cosham, Portsmouth PO6 1DF* Tel (023) 9237 5145 E-mail paul@farlingtonparish.co.uk

GULVIN, Philip Christopher. b 53. BSc76. St Jo Coll Nottm 82. **d** 85 **p** 86. C Northwood H Trin *Lon* 85-89; TV Sanderstead All SS *S'wark* 89-96; V Croydon St Matt 96-99; C W Wickham

St Fran 99-02; C W Wickham St Fran and St Mary 02-04; rtd 04. *2 Ellis Close, Five Oak Green, Tonbridge TN12 6PQ* E-mail gulvins@tiscali.co.uk

GUMBEL, Jonathan Philip. b 82. Oriel Coll Ox BA05. NTMTC 07. **d** 09 **p** 10. C Brighton St Pet *Chich* from 09. *Flat 2, 87 Trafalgar Street, Brighton BN1 4ER* E-mail jonny@stpetersbrighton.org

GUMBEL, Nicholas Glyn Paul. b 55. Trin Coll Cam MA76. Wycliffe Hall Ox MA86. **d** 86 **p** 87. C Brompton H Trin w Onslow Square St Paul *Lon* 86-05; V 05-11; V Onslow Square and S Kensington St Aug from 11. *Holy Trinity Vicarage, 73 Princes Gate Mews, London SW7 2PP* Tel (020) 7052 0263 *or* 7052 0264 Fax 7589 3390 E-mail roslyn.dehaan@htb.org.uk

GUMMER, Dudley Harrison. b 28. Roch Th Coll 61. **d** 63 **p** 64. C Deptford St Paul *S'wark* 63-65; C Melton Mowbray w Thorpe Arnold *Leic* 65-68; C-in-c E Goscote CD 68-75; V E Goscote 75-78; V Luton St Anne *St Alb* 78-88; R Albury w St Martha *Guildf* 88-95; rtd 95; Perm to Offic *Chich* from 95 and *Portsm* 03-09. *Wyndham House, The Gardens, West Ashling, Chichester PO18 8DX* Tel (01243) 573002

GUNASEKERA, Nilanka Keith (Kit). b 72. Ridley Hall Cam 04. **d** 06 **p** 07. C Brentford *Lon* 06-09; P-in-c Clapham St Jas *S'wark* from 09. *The Vicarage, 8A West Road, London SW4 7DN* Tel 07968-591695 (mobile) E-mail kit_gunasekera@yahoo.co.uk

GUNN, Jeffrey Thomas. b 47. St Chad's Coll Dur BA77 Kent Univ MA95. Coll of Resurr Mirfield 77. **d** 79 **p** 80. C Prestbury *Glouc* 79-82; P-in-c Coldham, Elm and Friday Bridge *Ely* 82-87; V Larkfield *Roch* 87-94; P-in-c Leybourne 87-94; V Petts Wood 94 99; Dean Ballarat Australia 99 04; V Eastbourne St Sav and St Pet *Chich* from 05; RD Eastbourne from 10. *St Saviour's Vicarage, Spencer Road, Eastbourne BN21 4PA* Tel (01323) 722317

GUNN, Robert. b 35. Oak Hill Th Coll 59. **d** 62 **p** 63. C Upper Holloway St Jo *Lon* 62-66; C Woking St Jo *Guildf* 66-69; Scripture Union 69-71; R Necton w Holme Hale *Nor* 71-77; V Tottenham St Jo *Lon* 77-81; V Gt Cambridge Road St Jo and St Jas 82-85; V Luton St Fran *St Alb* 85-90; Chapl Luton Airport 90-95; rtd 95; Perm to Offic *St Alb* from 95. *95 Edgewood Drive, Luton LU2 8ER* Tel (01582) 416151

GUNN-JOHNSON, The Ven David Allan. b 49. Lambeth STh85 MA95. St Steph Ho Ox 79. **d** 81 **p** 82. C Oxhey St Matt *St Alb* 81-84; C Cheshunt 84-88; TR Colyton, Southleigh, Offwell, Widworthy etc *Ex* 88-03; RD Honiton 90-96; Preb Ex Cathl 99-03; Adn Barnstaple from 03; Dioc Warden of Readers from 04. *Stage Cross, Sanders Lane, Bishops Tawton, Barnstaple EX32 0BE* Tel (01271) 375475 Fax 377934 E-mail archdeacon.of.barnstaple@exeter.anglican.org

GUNNER, Canon Laurence François Pascal. b 36. Keble Coll Ox BA59 MA63. Wells Th Coll 59. **d** 61 **p** 62. C Charlton Kings St Mary *Glouc* 61-65; C Hemel Hempstead *St Alb* 65-69; Hd RE Adeyfield Secondary Modern Sch 67-69; Chapl Bloxham Sch 69-86; Chapl Tudor Hall Sch 70-84; Sen Chapl Marlborough Coll 86-96; Can Windsor 96-06; Can Steward 97-06; rtd 06. *Contin Mains, Contin, Strathpeffer IV14 9ES* Tel and fax (01997) 421996 Mobile 07836-369729 E-mail laurence@gunner.co.uk

GUNNER, Mrs Susanna Mary. b 58. St Jo Coll Dur BA80 SS Coll Cam PGCE81. ERMC 05. **d** 08 **p** 09. C N Walsham and Edingthorpe *Nor* from 08; Dioc Lay Development Co-ord from 07. *36 Vicarage Street, North Walsham NR28 9DQ* Tel (01692) 405501 E-mail susanna.ainsworth@ukonline.co.uk

GUNSTONE, Canon John Thomas Arthur. b 27. St Chad's Coll Dur BA48 MA55. Coll of Resurr Mirfield 50. **d** 52 **p** 53. C Walthamstow St Jas Gt *Chelmsf* 52-53; C Forest Gate St Edm 53-58; C-in-c Rush Green St Aug CD 58-71; Chapl Barn Fellowship Winterborne Whitechurch 71-75; Tutor Sarum & Wells Th Coll 71-75; Sec Gtr Man Co Ecum Coun 75-92; Lic to Offic *Man* 75-80; Hon Can Man Cathl 80-92; rtd 92; Perm to Offic *Man* from 03. *12 Deneford Road, Didsbury, Manchester M20 2TD* Tel 0161-434 8351

GUNTER, Timothy Wilson. b 37. Leeds Univ BA59 St Jo Coll Cam BA62 MA66. Ridley Hall Cam 59. **d** 62 **p** 63. C Beverley Minster *York* 62-65; C Hornsea and Goxhill 65-70; V Silsden *Bradf* 70-80; V Sunninghill *Ox* 80-03; rtd 03; Perm to Offic *Worc* from 04. *2 Hillstone Court, Victoria Road, Malvern WR14 2TE* Tel (01684) 899377 E-mail gunters@gmail.com

GURD, Brian Charles (Simon). b 44. Sarum & Wells Th Coll 72. **d** 74 **p** 75. OSP from 67; Lic to Offic *Win* 74-82; Prior Alton Abbey 79-82; C Shepherd's Bush St Steph w St Thos *Lon* 82-84; NSM Willesborough *Cant* 85-87; V Bethersden w High Halden 87-95; R Etchingham and V Hurst Green *Chich* 95-97; V Langney 97-01; R Yarm *York* 01-10; rtd 10. *Barley Cottage, Main Street, Beckley, Rye TN31 6RS* Tel (01797) 260244 E-mail simongurd@btinternet.com

GURDON, Mrs June Mary. b 38. Sarum Th Coll 83. dss 85 **d** 87 **p** 94. Jersey St Sav *Win* 85-86; Jersey St Mary 86-88; Par Dn 87-88; Par Dn Jersey St Brelade 88-94; C 94-00; rtd 00; Perm to Offic *Win* from 00. *Dower House Alfriston, La Route d'Ebenezer,*

Trinity, Jersey JE3 3EH   Tel (01534) 863245   Mobile 07797-736280

GURNER *(formerly RAVEN)*, **Mrs Margaret Ann.** b 54. Westmr Univ BSc76 City Univ MSc87. Ridley Hall Cam 03. **d** 05 **p** 06. C Woodhall Spa Gp *Linc* 05-08; P-in-c Cheveley *Ely* from 08; P-in-c Wood Ditton w Saxon Street from 08; P-in-c Kirtling from 08; P-in-c Ashley w Silverley from 08. *The Rectory, 132 High Street, Cheveley, Newmarket CB8 9DG*   Tel (01638) 730770   E-mail revgurner@btinternet.com

GURNEY, Miss Ann. b 27. Lambeth STh92. Gilmore Ho 45. **dss** 54 **d** 87 **p** 94. Lewisham St Jo *Southend S'wark* 54-56; Warden Berridge Ho Coll of Educn 56-59; Prin Gilmore Ho 59-70; Bp's Adv for Lay Min *Lon* 70-87; rtd 87; Hon C Eltham H Trin *S'wark* 94-98; Perm to Offic from 98. *3 Brecon Court, Greenacres, London SE9 5BG*   Tel (020) 8850 4083

GURNEY, Canon Dennis Albert John. b 31. OBE02. Lon Coll of Div. **d** 67 **p** 68. C Boscombe St Jo *Win* 67-69; V Hurstbourne Tarrant and Faccombe 70-77; R Jersey St Ouen w St Geo 77-84; Hon Chapl Miss to Seafarers from 84; Chapl ICS UAE 84-01; Can Bahrain from 98; rtd 01; Perm to Offic *Ex* and *B & W* from 02. *3 Stevens Cross Close, Sidford, Sidmouth EX10 9QJ*   Tel (01395) 515362   Mobile 07789-111226   E-mail dennis.gurney@.virgin.net

GURNEY, Nicholas Peter. b 69. St Jo Coll Nottm 09. **d** 11. C Ashby-de-la-Zouch and Breedon on the Hill *Leic* from 11. *5 Ulleswater Crescent, Ashby-de-la-Zouch LE65 1FH*   Tel 07841-842540 (mobile)   E-mail nick.gurney@ntlworld.com

GURR, Mrs Mary Sandra. b 42. SAOMC 95. **d** 98 **p** 99. C Easthampstead *Ox* 98-02; TV High Wycombe 02-09; rtd 09; Chapl Pipers Corner Sch from 04; Chapl to the Homeless *Ox* from 11. *12 Navigation Way, Oxford OX2 6XW*   Tel (01865) 552010   E-mail mary.gurr1@btinternet.com

GURR, Stephen John. b 72. Kent Univ BA94. Trin Coll Bris MLitt97. **d** 97 **p** 98. C Ore St Helen and St Barn *Chich* 97-00; C Goring-by-Sea 00-03; V Findon w Clapham and Patching 03-06; Chapl St Barn Ho Worthing from 07; Chapl Chestnut Tree Ho Arundel from 07. *St Barnabas House, Columbia Drive, Worthing BN13 2QF*   Tel (01903) 534030

GUSSMAN, Canon Robert William Spencer Lockhart. b 50. Ch Ch Ox BA72 MA76. Coll of Resurr Mirfield BA74. **d** 75 **p** 76. C Pinner *Lon* 75-79; C Northolt St Jos 79-81; P-in-c Sutton *Ely* 81-82; V 82-89; P-in-c Witcham w Mepal 81-82; R 82-89; RD Ely 86-89; V Alton St Lawr *Win* 89-02; Hon Can Win Cathl 99-02; rtd 02; Perm to Offic *Win* 02-10. *6A Patrick's Close, Liss GU33 7ER*   Tel (01730) 893545

GUTHRIE, Adrian Malcolm. b 57. Goldsmiths' Coll Lon BEd80. Wycliffe Hall Ox 01. **d** 03 **p** 04. C Ickenham *Lon* 03-05; R from 05. *St Giles's Rectory, 38 Swakeley's Road, Ickenham, Uxbridge UB10 8BE*   Tel (01895) 622970   E-mail am.guthrie@virgin.net

GUTHRIE, Preb Nigel. b 60. Bris Univ BA82 LRAM78 ARCO80 ARCM81. Ripon Coll Cuddesdon BA87 MA91. **d** 88 **p** 89. C Cov St Jo 88-91; Chapl Cov Cathl 91-94; V Chellaston *Derby* 94-02; RD Melbourne 99-02; R Crediton, Shobrooke and Sandford etc *Ex* from 02; Preb Ex Cathl from 10. *The Rectory, Church Street, Crediton EX17 2AQ*   Tel (01363) 772669 *or* 773226   E-mail rev.guthrie@btinternet.com

GUTSELL, Canon David Leonard Nicholas. b 35. Sheff Univ BA59. ALCD61. **d** 61 **p** 62. C Clapham Common St Barn *S'wark* 61-65; V Upper Tulse Hill St Matthias 65-76; RD Clapham and Brixton 74-75; V Patcham *Chich* 76-93; Can and Preb Chich Cathl 89-00; V Polegate 93-00; rtd 00; C Peacehaven and Telscombe Cliffs *Chich* 01-05; C Southease 01-05; C Piddinghoe 01-05; Perm to Offic from 05. *6 Solway Avenue, Brighton BN1 8UJ*   Tel (01273) 554434   E-mail davidgutsell@googlemail.com

GUTSELL, Eric Leslie. b 44. Goldsmiths' Coll Lon TCert65. Ox NSM Course 79. **d** 82 **p** 83. NSM Gt Faringdon w Lt Coxwell *Ox* 82-88; NSM Shrivenham w Watchfield and Bourton 82-99; Asst Chapl HM Pris Wormwood Scrubs 99-00; Chapl HM Pris Coldingley 00-03; Chapl HM Pris Erlestoke 03-04; rtd 04; Perm to Offic *Ox* from 05. *54 Folly View Road, Faringdon SN7 7DH*   Tel (01367) 240886   E-mail ericgutsell@virgin.net

GUTTERIDGE, David Frank. b 39. Man Univ BSc61 Lon Inst of Educn PGCE62 DipEd67 Birkbeck Coll Lon MSc73. WMMTC 82. **d** 85 **p** 87. NSM Droitwich *Worc* 85-87; NSM Droitwich Spa 87-93; C Shrawley, Witley, Astley and Abberley 93-98; Chapl Abberley Hall Sch *Worc* 93-97; Dioc Tertiary Educn Officer *Worc* 97-99; NSM Ombersley w Doverdale 98-99; TV Malvern Link w Cowleigh 99-02; rtd 02. *79 Tan House Lane, Malvern WR14 1LQ*   Tel (01886) 833578   E-mail dgutteridge@cofe-worcester.org.uk

GUTTERIDGE, John. b 34. Oak Hill Th Coll 60. **d** 63 **p** 64. C Deptford St Luke *S'wark* 65-70; C Southgate *Chich* 66-70; P-in-c Brixton Road Ch Ch *S'wark* 70-73; P-in-c Manuden w Berden *Chelmsf* 73-76; Distr Sec (N Lon, Herts and Essex) BFBS 76-82; Hon C Walthamstow St Gabr 79-82; V 82-95; Chapl Thorpe Coombe Psycho-Geriatric Hosp 83-95; rtd 95; Perm to Offic *Chelmsf* from 95. *52 Hatch Road, Pilgrims Hatch, Brentwood CM15 9PX*   Tel (01277) 375401   E-mail john_gutteridge@hotmail.com

GUTTERIDGE, John Philip. b 52. QUB BA74. Chich Th Coll 75. **d** 78 **p** 79. C Leeds St Aid *Ripon* 78-82; C Manston 82-85; P-in-c Beeston Hill H Spirit 85-00; Perm to Offic from 03. *4 Amberton Garth, Leeds LS8 3JW*

GUTTRIDGE *(née EVANS)*, **Mrs Frances Margaret Bethan.** b 54. Reading Univ BSc75 Univ of Wales (Cardiff) PGCE76. STETS. **d** 00 **p** 01. C Weston-super-Mare St Andr Bournville *B & W* 00-04; V 04-09; C Watchet and Williton from 09. *The Vicarage, 47A Brendon Road, Watchet TA23 0HU*   Tel (01984) 631103   Mobile 07778-137454   E-mail bethanguttridge@hotmail.com

GUTTRIDGE, John Arthur. b 26. Trin Hall Cam BA51 MA55. Westcott Ho Cam 51. **d** 53 **p** 54. C Rugby St Andr *Cov* 53-59; Lect Wells Th Coll 59-61; Chapl 61-63; Vice-Prin 63-66; Bp's Dom Chapl *Wakef* 66-68; Dir Post-Ord Tr 66-68; Dir of Further Tr *Dur* 68-74; Dir Studies Sarum & Wells Th Coll 74-78; C Bilston St Leon *Lich* 78-79; TV Bilston 80-84; V Wall 84-90; V Stonnall 84-90; rtd 91. *The Charterhouse, Charterhouse Square, London EC1M 6AN*   Tel (020) 7251 6357

GUTTRIDGE, John William. b 54. Surrey Univ BSc75 Cardiff Coll of Educn PGCE76 MRSC95. STETS 08. **d** 11. NSM Aisholt, Enmore, Goathurst, Nether Stowey etc *B & W* from 11. *The Vicarage, 47A Brendon Road, Watchet TA23 0HU*   Tel (01984) 631228   Mobile 07813-350710   E-mail jwguttridge@hotmail.com

GUY, Mrs Alison. b 43. CQSW69. WMMTC 95. **d** 98 **p** 99. NSM Minchinhampton *Glouc* 98-04; C Bisley, Chalford, France Lynch, and Oakridge 04-08. *7 Tooke Road, Minchinhampton, Stroud GL6 9DA*   Tel (01453) 883906   E-mail alisonguy@metronet.co.uk

GUY, Ian Towers. b 47. Newc Univ MB, BS70 MSc89 MRCGP. NEOC. **d** 83 **p** 84. NSM Saltburn-by-the-Sea *York* 83-88; NSM Skelton w Upleatham 88-92; Perm to Offic from 92. *14 North Terrace, Skelton-in-Cleveland, Saltburn-by-the-Sea TS12 2ES*   Tel (01287) 650309   Mobile 07092-298033   E-mail iantguy@mac.com

GUY, John Richard. *See* MORGAN-GUY, John Richard

GUY, Kate Anne. b 26. **d** 88 **p** 94. OLM Welton *Linc* 88-92; OLM Welton and Dunholme w Scothern 92-96; Perm to Offic 96-02. *2 Eastfield Close, Welton, Lincoln LN2 3NB*   Tel (01673) 860285

GUY, Peter-John. b 71. Bournemouth Univ BA93. Oak Hill Th Coll BA03. **d** 03 **p** 04. C Eastbourne All So *Chich* 03-07; C Lindfield 07-11; V Horam from 11. *The Vicarage, Horebeech Lane, Horam, Heathfield TN21 0DT*   E-mail pjgerdaguy@hotmail.com

GUY, Simon Edward Walrond. b 39. St Andr Univ MA61. St D Coll Lamp LTh67. **d** 67 **p** 68. C Bris St Mary Redcliffe w Temple etc 67-68; C Knowle St Martin 68-71; C Bishopston 71-75; V Westwood *Sarum* 75-81; TV Melksham 81-82; TV Wednesfield *Lich* 82-90; R Heaton Moor *Man* 90-02; P-in-c Heaton Norris Ch w All SS 99-01; TV Heatons 02-04; rtd 04. *1 Holley Close, Exminster, Exeter EX6 8SS*   Tel (01392) 823084   E-mail sewguy@supanet.com

GUYMER, Canon Raymond John. b 41. AKC64. St Boniface Warminster. **d** 65 **p** 66. C W Bromwich All SS *Lich* 65-70; Chapl HM Pris Wormwood Scrubs 70-71 and 84-93; Chapl HM Borstal Portland 71-78; Chapl HM Youth Cust Cen Hollesley Bay Colony 78-84; Chapl HM Pris Win 93-01; Hon C Upper Itchen *Win* 02-06; Hon Can Win Cathl 99-06; rtd 06. *16 St Mary's Gardens, Hilperton Marsh, Trowbridge BA14 7PG*   Tel (01225) 751063

GUZEK, Mrs Bridget Louise. b 47. York Univ BA70 Keswick Hall Coll PGCE79. STETS 05. **d** 08 **p** 09. NSM E Clevedon w Clapton in Gordano etc *B & W* from 08. *16 Woodlands Road, Clevedon BS21 7QD*   E-mail bridgetguzek@blueyonder.co.uk

GWILLIAM, Christopher. b 44. St Chad's Coll Dur BA65. **d** 67 **p** 68. C Chepstow *Mon* 67-70; C Risca 70-72; V Cwmtillery 72-75; V Hartlepool St Oswald *Dur* 75-82; Relig Progr Producer Radio Tees 82-87; C Stockton w St Jo 82-83; R Longnewton w Elton 83-87; Relig Progr Producer Radio Nottm *S'well* 87-93; Relig Progr Producer BBC Network Radio 93-95; rtd 04. *Les Perreaux, 71140 Maltat, France*   Tel (0033) 3 85 84 87 57   E-mail christopher.gwilliam@googlemail.com

GWILLIAMS, Canon Dianna Lynn. b 57. California Univ BA78 K Coll Lon MA01. S'wark Ord Course 89. **d** 92 **p** 94. NSM Peckham St Sav *S'wark* 92-97; C Dulwich St Barn 97-99; V from 99; P-in-c Peckham St Sav from 07; AD Dulwich from 05; Hon Can S'wark Cathl from 06; Dean of Women's Min from 09; Chapl Alleyn's Foundn Dulwich from 99. *St Barnabas's Vicarage, 38 Calton Avenue, London SE21 7DG*   Tel (020) 8693 1524 *or* 8693 2936   Fax 8693 0203   E-mail dianna.gwilliams@stbarnabasdulwich.org

GWILLIM, Allan John. b 54. Coll of Resurr Mirfield 87. **d** 89 **p** 90. C Skerton St Luke *Blackb* 89-94; P-in-c Ellel 94-98; V Fleetwood St Pet 98-06; V Leyland St Jas 06-08; V Ocker Hill *Lich* from 08. *St Mark's Vicarage, Ocker Hill Road, Tipton DY4 0UT*   Tel 0121-556 0678   E-mail allan.gwillim@btinternet.com

GWILT, Stephen Gary. b 59. **d** 88 **p** 89. S Africa 88-94; Chapl Glouc Docks Mariners' Ch 95-00; C Moreton *Ches* 00-03; R High Halstow w All Hallows and Hoo St Mary *Roch* from 03. *The Rectory, 2 Cooling Road, High Halstow, Rochester ME3 8SA* Tel (01634) 250637

GWINN, Brian Harvey. b 35. MIQA75. St Alb Minl Tr Scheme 83. **d** 86 **p** 87. NSM Wheathampstead *St Alb* 86-88; Ind Chapl 88-95; RD Hatfield 93-95; P-in-c Watton at Stone 95-99; P-in-c Bramfield w Stapleford and Waterford 96-99; R Bramfield, Stapleford, Waterford etc 99-01; rtd 01; Perm to Offic *St Alb* from 01. *32 Wick Avenue, Wheathampstead, St Albans AL4 8QB* Tel (01582) 629903 Mobile 07966-469754 E-mail gwinns@ntlworld.com

GWINNETT, Clifton Harry. b 57. Cranmer Hall Dur 08. **d** 10 **p** 11. C Golcar *Wakef* from 10. *24 Banks Avenue, Golcar, Huddersfield HD7 4LZ* Tel (01484) 520078 Mobile 07817-526342 E-mail harry@johns4u.org

GWYNN, Phillip John. b 57. Univ of Wales BA87. St Mich Coll Llan 87. **d** 89 **p** 90. C Clydach *S & B* 89-93; V Swansea St Thos and Kilvey 93-00; Hon Chapl Miss to Seafarers 93-00; V Tycoch *S & B* from 00; Chapl Swansea NHS Trust from 00. *The Vicarage, 26 Hendrefoilan Road, Swansea SA2 9LS* Tel and fax (01792) 204476 Mobile 07946-351787 E-mail rev.gwynn@virgin.net

GWYNNE, Robert Durham. b 44. Qu Coll Birm 67. **d** 70 **p** 72. C N Hammersmith St Kath *Lon* 70-75; C Ramsey *Ely* 76-78; TV Old Brumby *Linc* 78-81; P-in-c Goxhill and Thornton Curtis 81-83; C Edmonton All SS w St Mich *Lon* 83-84; rtd 86. *127 Eastfield Road, Louth LN11 7AS* Tel (01507) 600966

GWYTHER, Canon Geoffrey David. b 51. St D Coll Lamp. **d** 74 **p** 75. C Pembroke Dock *St D* 74-77; C Milford Haven 77-81; V Llawhaden w Bletherston and Llanycefn 81-88; R Prendergast w Rudbaxton from 88; AD Daugleddau from 01; Can St D Cathl from 01. *Prendergast Rectory, 5 Cherry Grove, Haverfordwest SA61 2NT* Tel (01437) 762625

GWYTHER, Ronald Lloyd. b 23. Lon Univ BA85 Southn Univ MA97. St Fran Coll Brisbane ThL47. **d** 47 **p** 48. Australia 48-50; Perm to Offic *Ox* 50-51; Australia 51-56; C Broadstairs *Cant* 56-60; R Pinxton *Derby* 60-73; CF (TA) 71-88; V Swanley St Mary *Roch* 73-89; rtd 89; Perm to Offic *Portsm* from 89. *St Helen's, 20 Maylings Farm Road, Fareham PO16 7QU* Tel (01329) 230990

GYLE, Alan Gordon. b 65. Aber Univ MA87 Ox Univ BA91 Univ of E Lon MA09 FRSA99. St Steph Ho Ox. **d** 92 **p** 93. C Acton Green *Lon* 92-94; Min Can, Succ and Dean's V Windsor 94-99; Chapl Imp Coll and R Coll of Art 99-04; P-in-c Wilton Place St Paul *Lon* 01-03; V from 03; PV Westmr Abbey from 07; Dir Development Two Cities Area *Lon* from 08. *St Paul's Vicarage, 32 Wilton Place, London SW1X 8SH* Tel and fax (020) 7201 9990 *or* tel 7201 9999 E-mail alan@stpaulsknightsbridge.org

GYLES, Ms Sonia. b 76. TCD BTh01. CITC 98. **d** 01 **p** 02. C Taney *D & G* 01-04; I Dublin Sandford w Milltown from 04. *The Rectory, Sandford Close, Ranelagh, Dublin 6, Republic of Ireland* Tel (00353) (1) 497 2983 Fax 496 4789 E-mail sandford@dublin.anglican.org

H

HAARHOFF, Preb Robert Russell. b 46. St Paul's Coll Grahamstown 89 Th Ext Educn Coll 91. **d** 90 **p** 91. Zimbabwe 91-02; Harare Cathl 91-94; I Makonde 94-02; P-in-c Astley, Clive, Grinshill and Hadnall *Lich* from 02; RD Wem and Whitchurch from 08; Preb Lich Cathl from 11. *The Vicarage, Shrewsbury Road, Hadnall, Shrewsbury SY4 4AG* Tel (01939) 210241 E-mail robhaarhoff@tiscali.co.uk

HABERMEHL, Canon Kenneth Charles. b 22. Em Coll Cam BA46 MA48. Chich Th Coll 47. **d** 49 **p** 50. C Luton St Chris Round Green CD *St Alb* 49-53; C Luton Ch 53-56; V Caddington 56-65; V Kempston All SS 65-87; Hon Can St Alb 81-87; rtd 87; Perm to Offic *St Alb* 87-93 and from 00. *34 Bedford Road, Aspley Guise, Milton Keynes MK17 8DH* Tel (01908) 584710

HABERSHON, Kenneth Willoughby. b 35. MBE01. New Coll Ox BA57 MA60. Wycliffe Hall Ox 57. **d** 59 **p** 60. C Finchley Ch Ch *Lon* 59-66; Sec CYFA 66-74; CPAS Staff 74-90; Hon C Slaugham *Chich* 84-10; Hon C Slaugham and Staplefield Common from 10; Ldr Mayfield CYFA 90-00; rtd 00; Sec Ch Patr Trust 90-07; Sec Peache Trustees 90-11. *Truckers Ghyll, Horsham Road, Handcross, Haywards Heath RH17 6DT* Tel (01444) 400274 E-mail kandmhab@btopenworld.com

✠**HABGOOD, The Rt Revd and Rt Hon Lord (John Stapylton).** b 27. PC83. K Coll Cam BA48 MA51 PhD52 Dur Univ Hon DD75 Cam Univ Hon DD84 Aber Univ Hon DD88 Huron Coll Hon DD90. Cuddesdon Coll 53. **d** 54 **p** 55 **c** 73. C Kensington St Mary Abbots w St Geo *Lon* 54-56; Vice-Prin Westcott Ho Cam 56-62; R Jedburgh *Edin* 62-67; Prin Qu Coll Birm 67-73; Hon Can Birm Cathl 71-73; Bp Dur 73-83; Abp York 83-95; rtd 95. *18 The Mount, Malton YO17 7ND*

HABGOOD, Simon. See LAWRENCE, Simon Peter

HABGOOD, Stephen Roy. b 52. Open Univ MBA95 Fitzw Coll Cam MSt01. St Mich Coll Llan 75. **d** 77 **p** 78. C Whitchurch *Llan* 77-80; Perm to Offic *Worc* 85-91. *Yew Tree Cottage, Wharf Road, Gnosall, Stafford ST20 0DA* Tel (01785) 824244

HABIBY, Canon Samir Jamil. b 33. Phillips Univ BA55 MA56. Ch Div Sch of Pacific MDiv58 Episc Th Sem Kentucky DD. **d** 58 **p** 59. R Hinesville St Phil USA 58-98 and from 04; P-in-c Lausanne *Eur* 98-04; rtd 04. *24 Sawyers Crossing Road, Swanzey NH 03446, USA* Tel and fax (001) (603) 357 8778

HACK, Arthur John. b 52. Bris Univ BEd75 St Paul's Coll Chelt CertEd74. **d** 08 **p** 09. NSM Alstonfield, Butterton, Ilam etc *Lich* from 08; Warden Dovedale Ho from 89. *Dovedale House, Ilam, Ashbourne DE6 2AZ* Tel (01335) 350365 Mobile 07749-294386 E-mail warden@dovedalehouse.org.uk

HACK, Canon Rex Hereward. b 28. ACA56 FCA67 Pemb Coll Cam BA50 MA56. Ripon Hall Ox 58. **d** 59 **p** 60. C Ashton-upon-Mersey St Mary Magd *Ches* 59-62; C Ellesmere Port 62-65; V Norton Cuckney *S'well* 65-69; V Bramhall *Ches* 69-93; RD Cheadle 87-92; Hon Can Ches Cathl 90-93; rtd 93; Perm to Offic *Ches* from 93. *Marshmead, 8A Pownall Avenue, Bramhall, Stockport SK7 2HE* Tel 0161-439 0300

✠**HACKER, The Rt Revd George Lanyon.** b 28. Ex Coll Ox BA52 MA56. Cuddesdon Coll 52. **d** 54 **p** 55 **c** 79. C Bris St Mary Redcliffe w Temple 54-59; Chapl St Boniface Coll Warminster 59-64; V Bishopwearmouth Gd Shep *Dur* 64-71; R Tilehurst St Mich *Ox* 71-79; Suff Bp Penrith *Carl* 79-94; Hon Can Carl Cathl 79-94; Episc Adv for the Angl Young People's Assn 87-94; rtd 94; Hon Asst Bp Carl from 94. *Keld House, Milburn, Penrith CA10 1TW* Tel (01768) 361506 E-mail bishhack@btopenworld.com

HACKER HUGHES, Katherine Lucy. b 60. York Univ BA81. Westcott Ho Cam 90. **d** 92 **p** 94. Par Dn S Woodham Ferrers *Chelmsf* 92-94; C 94-95; NSM Maldon All SS w St Pet 95-98; Chapl Chelmsf Cathl 98-01; P-in-c Gt Waltham w Ford End 01-05; Adv relationship and family issues (Bradwell Area) 01-03; Perm to Offic from 05; Chapl Mid-Essex Hosp Services NHS Trust 06-07; Chapl Farleigh Hospice from 07. *1 Swiss Avenue, Chelmsford CM1 2AD* Tel (01245) 600969 *or* 457300 E-mail katyhh@lineone.net

HACKETT, Bryan Malcolm. b 66. Magd Coll Ox BA88 MA93 Cam Univ BA92 MA03. Westcott Ho Cam 90. **d** 93 **p** 94. C Willington *Newc* 93-97; TV Radcliffe *Man* 97-03; P-in-c Prestwich St Mary from 03; C Prestwich St Marg from 10; C Prestwich St Gabr from 10. *The Rectory, Church Lane, Prestwich, Manchester M25 1AN* Tel 0161-773 2912 E-mail bryan.hackett@btinternet.com

HACKETT, Canon Frank James. b 33. Birm Univ MA77 AMIMechE68 MBIM72 MIIM79. Bps' Coll Cheshunt 62. **d** 64 **p** 65. C Feltham *Lon* 64-69; Ind Chapl *Lich* 69-73; Ind Chapl Port of Lon *Chelmsf* 73-98; P-in-c N Ockendon 79-93; Hon Can Chelmsf Cathl 93-98; Ind Chapl 93-98; rtd 98; Perm to Offic *Lon* 98-02 and from 05; *Chelmsf* from 99. *11 Fairfield Avenue, Upminster RM14 3AZ* Tel (01708) 221461

HACKETT, Glyndwr. See HACKETT, The Ven Ronald Glyndwr

HACKETT, John Nigel. b 32. Trin Hall Cam BA55 MA59. Ely Th Coll. **d** 59 **p** 60. C Handsworth St Mary *Birm* 59-66; V Handsworth St Jas 66-82; P-in-c Balsall Common 82-83; V 83-95; Perm to Offic *B & W* from 96; rtd 97. *Honeymead, Duck Lane, Kenn, Clevedon BS21 6TP* Tel (01275) 876591

HACKETT, Peter Edward. b 25. Magd Coll Ox BA48 MA51 ALCD60. **d** 60 **p** 61. C Lenton *S'well* 60-62; C Attenborough w Bramcote 62-63; V Lenton Abbey 63-67; R Acton Beauchamp and Evesbatch w Stanford Bishop *Heref* 67-71; V Choral Heref Cathl 72-76; P-in-c St Weonards w Orcop 76-79; P-in-c Tretire w Michaelchurch and Pencoyd 76-79; P-in-c Garway 76-79; P-in-c Welsh Newton w Llanrothal 77-79; V Rounds Green *Birm* 79-87; C Sutton Coldfield H Trin 87-90; rtd 90; NSM Shipton Moyne w Westonbirt and Lasborough *Glouc* 91-94; Perm to Offic *Birm* and *Worc* 94-99; *Heref* 00-09. *31 Capel Court, The Burgage, Prestbury, Cheltenham GL52 3EL* Tel (01242) 520348

HACKETT, The Ven Ronald Glyndwr. b 47. Hatf Coll Dur BA70. Cuddesdon Coll 70. **d** 72 **p** 73. C Pembroke St Mary w St Mich *St D* 72-75; C Bassaleg *Mon* 75-78; V Blaenavon w Capel Newydd 78-84; Chapl R Gwent Hosp 84-90; V Newport St Paul *Mon* 84-90; V Newport Ch Ch 90-01; Adn Mon 01-08; R Mamhilad and Llanfihangel Pontymoile 01-03; R Mamhilad w Monkswood and Glascoed Chapel 03-08; Adn Newport from 08. *The Archdeaconry, 93 Stow Hill, Newport NP20 4EA* Tel (01633) 215012 E-mail archdeacon.newport@churchinwales.org.uk

HACKETT, Victoria Anne. b 52. St Gabr Coll Lon CertEd73 Open Univ BA91. SEITE 97. **d** 00 **p** 01. NSM Earlsfield St Andr *S'wark* from 00. *40 Freshford Street, London SW18 3TF* Tel (020) 8947 3755 E-mail v.ah@btopenworld.com

HACKING, Philip Henry. b 31. St Pet Hall Ox BA53 MA57. Oak Hill Th Coll 53. **d** 55 **p** 56. C St Helens St Helen *Liv* 55-58; C-in-c Edin St Thos 59-68; V Fulwood *Sheff* 68-97; rtd 97; Perm to Offic *Sheff* from 98. *61 Sefton Court, Sefton Road, Sheffield S10 3TP* Tel 0114-230 4324 E-mail philiphacking@fulwood-s10.me.uk

HACKING, Rodney Douglas. b 53. K Coll Lon BD74 AKC74 Man Univ MA83. St Aug Coll Cant 75. **d** 76 **p** 78. C Byker St Mich *Newc* 76-77; C Eltham St Jo *S'wark* 77-79; Ind Chapl Ripon 80-85; R Upwell St Pet and Outwell *Ely* 85-88; Vice Prin S Dios Minl Tr Scheme 89-93; V Bolton-le-Sands *Blackb* 93-97; R The Wainfleet Gp *Linc* 03-06; rtd 06. *16 Eskrigge Court, Lancaster LA1 2LA* Tel (01524) 32884 E-mail rdnyhacking@aol.com

HACKING, Stuart Peter. b 60. St Pet Coll Ox BA82 MA. Oak Hill Th Coll 83. **d** 85 **p** 86. C Shipley St Pet *Bradf* 85-88; C Darfield *Sheff* 88-91; V Thornton St Jas *Bradf* 91-00; P-in-c Frizinghall St Marg from 00; Chapl Immanuel Coll from 00. *7 Redbeck Vale, Shipley BD18 3BN* Tel (01274) 580166 E-mail stuart.hacking@bradford.anglican.org

HACKL, Aileen Patricia. b 41. Wycliffe Hall Ox 00. **d** 01 **p** 02. C Vienna *Eur* 01-09; NSM 09-11; rtd 11. *Hardtmuthgasse 28/3/20, A-1100 Vienna, Austria* Tel and fax (0043) (1) 600 3083 E-mail aileen_hackl@hotmail.com

HACKNEY, Archdeacon of. See TREWEEK, The Ven Rachel

HACKSHALL, Brian Leonard. b 33. K Coll Lon BD53 AKC53. **d** 57 **p** 58. C Portsea St Mary *Portsm* 57-62; C Westbury-on-Trym St Alb *Bris* 62-64; V Avonmouth St Andr 64-71; Miss to Seamen 71-79; C Crawley *Chich* 79; TV 79-98; Ind Chapl 89-98; rtd 98. *5 St Michael Street, Brecon LD3 9AB* Tel (01874) 611319

HACKWOOD, Canon Paul Colin. b 61. Huddersfield Poly BSc84 Bradf Univ MBA05. Qu Coll Birm 86. **d** 89 **p** 90. C Horton *Bradf* 89-93; Soc Resp Adv *St Alb* 93-97; V Thornbury *Bradf* 97-05; Adn Loughborough *Leic* 05-09; Can Res Leic Cathl from 07. *110 Main Street, Kirby Muxloe, Leicester LE9 2AP* Tel 0116-239 6533 E-mail paul.hackwood@leccofe.org

HADDEN, Timothy. b 48. Brighton Poly BSc72 Surrey Univ MSc75. **d** 05 **p** 06. OLM Watling Valley *Ox* from 05. *13 Willets Rise, Shenley Church End, Milton Keynes MK5 6JW* Tel (01908) 507794 Mobile 07889-614386 E-mail tim@willets13.freeserve.co.uk

HADDLETON, Peter Gordon. b 53. UEA BA74 Southn Univ BTh80. Sarum & Wells Th Coll 76. **d** 79 **p** 80. C Thamesmead *S'wark* 79-83; TV Bridgnorth, Tasley, Astley Abbotts, etc *Heref* 83-91; TV Heref S Wye 91-98; TR 98-07; TR Worc St Barn w Ch Ch from 07. *St Barnabas' Vicarage, Church Road, Worcester WR3 8NX* Tel (01905) 23785 Fax 352142 E-mail peter.haddleton@talktalk.net

HADDOCK, Malcolm George. b 27. Univ of Wales (Cardiff) BA56 CertEd73. St Deiniol's Hawarden 87. **d** 80 **p** 81. NSM Newport Ch Ch *Mon* 80-85; NSM Risca 85-87; C 87-89; C Caerleon 89-96; rtd 96; Lic to Offic *Mon* from 96. *48 Cambria Close, Caerleon, Newport NP18 1LF* Tel (01633) 422960

HADDON-REECE (née STREETER), Mrs Christine Mary. b 50. St Jo Coll Nottm BTh81 LTh81. dss 83 **d** 87 **p** 94. Monkwearmouth St Andr *Dur* 83-85; Stranton 85-87; Par Dn 87-90; Par Dn Lastingham w Appleton-le-Moors, Rosedale etc *York* 90-94; C w NSM *York* 94; V Topcliffe, Baldersby w Dishforth, Dalton etc 94-08; V Middle Esk Moor from 08. *St Hilda's Vicarage, Egton, Whitby YO21 1UT* Tel (01947) 895315 E-mail c.haddonreece@btinternet.com

HADFIELD, Prof Brigid. b 50. Edin Univ LLB72 QUB LLM77 Essex Univ PhD03. EAMTC 02. **d** 03 **p** 04. NSM Wivenhoe *Chelmsf* 03-06; NSM Shrub End 06-11; NSM Harston w Hauxton and Newton *Ely* from 11. *The Vicarage, Church Street, Harston, Cambridge CB2 5NP*

HADFIELD, Christopher John Andrew Chad. b 39. Jes Coll Cam BA61. Wells Th Coll 63. **d** 65 **p** 66. C Wigton w Waverton *Carl* 65-68; Teacher Newlands Sch Seaford 70-06; Lic to Offic *Mor* from 92; Perm to Offic *Chich* from 96. *15 The Fridays, East Dean, Eastbourne BN20 0DH* Tel (01323) 422050

HADFIELD, Derek. b 34. **d** 01 **p** 02. OLM Folkestone H Trin w Ch Ch *Cant* 01-04; OLM Sandgate St Paul w Folkestone St Geo 01-04; rtd 04; Perm to Offic *Cant* from 04. *135 Capel Court, Capel-le-Ferne, Folkestone CT18 7AZ* Tel (01303) 244862 E-mail dhaddy49@tiscali.co.uk

HADFIELD, Douglas. b 22. K Coll Cam BA44 MA49. St Jo Coll Nottm 84. **d** 88 **p** 89. NSM Lenzie *Glas* 88-92; rtd 92; Perm to Offic *Glas* from 92 and *Pet* from 94. *8 Church Street, Helmdon, Brackley NN13 5QJ* Tel (01295) 760679 E-mail douglas.hadfield@firelight.co.uk

HADFIELD, Graham Francis. b 48. Bris Univ BSc69. Cranmer Hall Dur 69. **d** 73 **p** 74. C Blackpool St Thos *Blackb* 73-76; CF 76-99; Asst Chapl Gen 99-04; QHC 02-04; P-in-c Nottingham

St Jude *S'well* from 04. *St Jude's Vicarage, Woodborough Road, Nottingham NG3 5HE* Tel 0115-960 4102 E-mail graham@hadf48.fsnet.co.uk

HADFIELD, Jonathan Benedict Philip John. b 43. Lon Univ BA64 Jes Coll Cam BA67 MA72. Edin Th Coll 66. **d** 68 **p** 69. C Fort William *Arg* 68-70; Chapl K Sch Glouc and Hon Min Can Glouc Cathl 70-03; rtd 03. *36 Corsend Road, Hartpury, Gloucester GL19 3BP*

HADFIELD, Norman. b 39. Doncaster Coll of Educn TEng78. St Mich Coll Llan 89 Llan Dioc Tr Scheme 83. **d** 86 **p** 87. NSM Ferndale w Maerdy *Llan* 86-90; C Llanblethian w Cowbridge and Llandough etc 90-92; V Resolven w Tonna 92-04; RD Neath 01-03; rtd 04. *42 Lakeside, Cwmdare, Aberdare CF44 8AX* Tel (01685) 872764

HADJIOANNOU, John. b 56. Ch Coll Cam BA78 MA81. SAOMC 95. **d** 97 **p** 98. C Linslade *Ox* 97-00; V Kinsley w Wragby *Wakef* from 00; P-in-c Felkirk from 05. *Kinsley Vicarage, Wakefield Road, Fitzwilliam, Pontefract WF9 5BX* Tel (01977) 610497 E-mail john@minster.co.uk

HADLEY, Ann. See HADLEY, Preb Elizabeth Ann

HADLEY, Charles Adrian. b 50. Trin Coll Cam BA71 MA75. Cuddesdon Coll 73. **d** 75 **p** 76. C Hadleigh w Layham and Shelley *St E* 75-78; C Bracknell *Ox* 78-82; R Blagdon w Compton Martin and Ubley *B & W* 82-92; RD Chew Magna 88-92; R Somerton w Compton Dundon, the Charltons etc 92-04; Chapl Ex Univ 04-10; Chemin Neuf Community Israel from 10. *Chemin Neuf UK, St Gildas Christian Centre, The Hill, Langport TA10 9QF* Tel (01458) 250496 E-mail charles.felicity@gmail.com

HADLEY, David Charles. b 42. **d** 02 **p** 03. NSM Kenley *S'wark* from 02; NSM Purley St Barn from 08. *21 Park Road, Kenley CR8 5AQ* Tel (020) 8763 6206

HADLEY, Preb Elizabeth Ann. b 33. St Jo Coll Nottm 80. dss 81 **d** 87 **p** 94. Aspley *S'well* 81-85; Stone St Mich w Aston St Sav *Lich* 85-92; Par Dn 87-92; P-in-c Waddle 92-97; R 97-99; P-in-c Broughton 92-97; V 97-99; Dioc Voc Officer 92-99; Preb Lich Cathl 97-99; rtd 99; P-in-c Harvington *Worc* 99-00; Perm to Offic from 00. *6 Peninsular Road, Norton, Worcester WR5 2SE* Tel (01905) 353710

HADLEY, John Spencer Fairfax. b 47. Ch Ch Ox BA70 MA73. Coll of Resurr Mirfield BA72. **d** 73 **p** 74. C Stoke Newington St Mary *Lon* 73-77; C High Wycombe *Ox* 77-81; TV 82-87; P-in-c Clifton St Paul *Bris* 87-91; Sen Chapl Bris Univ 87-91; Chapl Hengrave Hall Ecum Cen 91-94; Ecum Assoc Min Chelsea Methodist Ch 94-97; Hon C Chelsea St Luke and Ch Ch *Lon* 94-97; Chapl Westcott Ho Cam 97-02; P-in-c Horfield H Trin *Bris* from 02. *Horfield Rectory, Wellington Hill, Bristol BS7 8ST* Tel 0117-924 6185 E-mail john-hadley@tiscali.co.uk

HADLEY, Stuart James. b 55. K Coll Lon BD76 AKC76. St Steph Ho Ox 77. **d** 78 **p** 79. C Mansfield St Mark *S'well* 78-82; V Cowbit *Linc* 82-86; Perm to Offic 86-88; NSM W w E Allington and Sedgebrook 88-95; NSM Saxonwell 95-96; NSM Hough and Dough Gp from 99. *35 Wensleydale Close, Grantham NG31 8FH* Tel (01476) 575854 E-mail hadleystuart@hotmail.com

HADLOW, Mrs Jennifer Lesley. b 48. **d** 01 **p** 02. OLM Herne *Cant* from 01; OLM Reculver and Herne Bay St Bart from 04. *2 Hicks Forstal Cottages, Hicks Forstal Road, Hoath, Canterbury CT3 4NA* Tel (01227) 711516 E-mail jennyhadlow@hotmail.com

HAGAN, Canon Kenneth Raymond. b 40. Fairfax Univ Australia BA97. St Jo Coll Morpeth 62. **d** 64 **p** 65. C Charlestown Australia 64-69; C Cessnock 69-70; R E Pilbara 70-75; C Portsea St Mary *Portsm* 75-78; P-in-c Wolvey, Burton Hastings and Stretton Baskerville *Cov* 78-81; P-in-c Withybrook w Copston Magna 78-81; P-in-c Shilton w Ansty 78-81; OCF 78-81; Dir St Mungo Community 82-88; R Hamilton Australia 89-98; R Portland 98-05; Can Ballarat from 99; rtd 05; P-in-c Heveningham *St E* 04-07. *35B Narrunga Avenue, Buff Point NSW 2262, Australia* Tel (0061) (2) 4399 3523

HAGAN, Matthew Henry. b 59. TCD MPhil09. CITC. **d** 06 **p** 07. NSM Derryloran *Arm* 06-10; P-in-c Tynan w Middletown and Aghavilly from 10. *10 Kingarve Road, Dungannon BT71 6LQ* (028) 8772 4356 Mobile 07778-038454 E-mail mhhagan@hotmail.com

HAGENBUCH, Mrs Andrea. b 63. STETS 05. **d** 08 **p** 09. C Corfe Castle, Church Knowle, Kimmeridge etc *Sarum* from 08. *Springbrook Cottage, Springbrook Close, Corfe Castle, Wareham BH20 5HS* Tel (01929) 481105 E-mail stephenhagenbuch@hotmail.com

HAGGAN, David Anthony. b 25. QUB LLB49 Barrister-at-Law 70. S'wark Ord Course 87. **d** 89 **p** 90. NSM Reigate St Mary *S'wark* 89-05; Perm to Offic from 05. *2 Fairford Close, Reigate RH2 0EY* Tel (01737) 246197

HAGGAR, Keith Ivan. b 38. MRPharmS61. Cant Sch of Min 87. **d** 90 **p** 91. NSM Woodnesborough w Worth and Staple *Cant* 90-98; Perm to Offic from 98; Chapl St Bart Hosp Sandwich

00-03. *Burtree Cottage, The Street, Worth, Deal CT14 0DE* Tel (01304) 613599

HAGGER, Jonathan Paul. b 59. St Jo Coll Nottm BTh95. **d** 95 **p** 96. C Newsham *Newc* 95-97; C Newc St Gabr 97-00; P-in-c Cresswell and Lynemouth 00-02; C Newc St Fran 02-10. *Address temp unknown*

HAGGIS, Richard. b 66. Ch Ch Ox BA88 MA95 Nottm Univ MA95. Linc Th Coll. **d** 95 **p** 96. C Romford St Edw *Chelmsf* 95-98; Chapl Trin Coll Cam 98-00; C St Giles-in-the-Fields *Lon* 00-03; C Upper Chelsea H Trin 04-06. *26 Bampton Close, Littlemore, Oxford OX4 6NN* Tel (01865) 749520 Mobile 07788-704044 E-mail rh.giles@btopenworld.com

HAGGIS, Timothy Robin. b 52. New Coll Ox BA75 MA79. St Jo Coll Nottm. **d** 82 **p** 83. C Chilwell *S'well* 82-86; TV Hucknall Torkard 86-94; Chapl Trent Coll Nottm 94-11; rtd 11. *86 Trowell Grove, Long Eaton, Nottingham NG10 4BB* Tel 0115-972 9589 E-mail timhaggis@hotmail.co.uk

HAGON, Roger Charles. b 58. Nottm Univ BA80. St Steph Ho Ox 82. **d** 85 **p** 86. C Charlton St Luke w H Trin *S'wark* 85-88; C St Helier 88-95; V Kenley 95-10; P-in-c Purley St Barn 01-10; V Addiscombe St Mildred from 10. *St Mildred's Vicarage, Sefton Road, Croydon CR0 7HR* Tel (020) 8676 1569 E-mail vicar@stmildredschurch.org.uk

HAGUE, David Hallett. b 59. Univ Coll Lon BScEng81 MSc82. Ridley Hall Cam 91. **d** 93 **p** 94. C Luton St Mary *St Alb* 93-96; V Stevenage St Pet Broadwater 96-09; P-in-c Romford Gd Shep *Chelmsf* from 09. *Good Shepherd Vicarage, 97 Collier Row Lane, Romford RM5 3BA* Tel (01708) 726423

HAHNEMAN, Geoffrey Mark. b 54. Baylor Univ (USA) BA77 Virginia Th Sem MDiv80 Ox Univ DPhil87. **d** 80 **p** 80. C Boston Advent USA 80-84; Hon C Ox St Mary Magd 85-87; Asst Chapl Brussels *Eur* 87-90; Can Minneapolis Cathl USA 90-94; R Portsmouth Trin Ch 95-00; R Bridgeport St Jo from 05. *154 Jackman Avenue, Fairfield CT 06825-1724, USA* Tel (001) (203) 362 0890 *or* 335 2528 E-mail rector@saintjohnbridgeport.org

HAIG, Alistair Matthew. b 39. K Coll Lon BD63 AKC63. **d** 64 **p** 65. C Forest Gate St Edm *Chelmsf* 64-67; C Laindon w Basildon 67-71; V S Woodham Ferrers 71-78; P-in-c Bath H Trin *B & W* 78-83; R 83-89; R Bocking St Mary *Chelmsf* 89-95; Dean Bocking 89-95; rtd 00. *17 Maidenburgh Street, Colchester CO1 1UB* Tel (01206) 795275

HAIG, Canon Andrew Livingstone. b 45. Keble Coll Ox BA67. Coll of Resurr Mirfield 67. **d** 69 **p** 70. C Elton All SS *Man* 69-75; R Brantham *St E* 75-76; R Brantham w Stutton 76-82; RD Samford 81-82; P-in-c Haverhill 82; TR Haverhill w Withersfield, the Wrattings etc 82-90; RD Clare 84-87; Chapl Qu Eliz Hosp King's Lynn 90-10; Hon Can Nor Cathl 07-10; rtd 10; Perm to Offic *Nor* from 10. *46 Elvington, King's Lynn PE30 4TA* Tel (01553) 761389

HAIG, Canon Murray Nigel Francis. b 39. Univ of Wales (Lamp) BA62. Kelham Th Coll 62. **d** 66 **p** 67. C Felixstowe St Jo *St E* 66-72; C Morpeth *Newc* 72-74; V Byker St Mich 74-79; V Byker St Mich w St Lawr 79-81; I Benwell St Jas 81-85; TR Benwell 85-91; TR Cramlington 91-97; Hon Can Newc Cathl 95-05; P-in-c Alnwick 97-98; V 98-05; rtd 05. *4 Farm Well Place, Prudhoe NE42 5FB* Tel (07801) 495616 E-mail d.haig@abbeyfield.com

HAIGH, Alan Bernard. b 42. NEOC 87. **d** 90 **p** 91. NSM Thorner *Ripon* from 90. *4 The Paddock, Thorner, Leeds LS14 3JB* Tel 0113-289 2870

HAIGH, Nicholas James. b 71. Sheff Univ BA00 St Jo Coll Dur MA04. Cranmer Hall Dur 02. **d** 04 **p** 05. C Bredbury St Mark *Ches* 04-06; P Missr Huddersfield *Wakef* 06-09; C Crookes St Thos *Sheff* from 09. *41 Ryegate Road, Sheffield S10 5FB* Tel 07876-782888 (mobile) E-mail nickhaigh@breathemail.net

HAIGH, Nicolas Peter. b 57. Teesside Poly BEd84. Ripon Coll Cuddesdon 07. **d** 09 **p** 10. C Eastbourne St Mary *Chich* from 09. *6 Bay Pond Road, Eastbourne BN21 1HX* Tel (01323) 641536 or 07966-187349 E-mail nickhaigh95@hotmail.com

HAIGH, Richard Michael Fisher. b 30. Dur Univ BA57. Cranmer Hall Dur 57. **d** 59 **p** 60. C Stanwix *Carl* 59-62; CMS India 63-67 and 68-70; R Salford St Clem w St Cypr Ordsall *Man* 71-75; R Holcombe 75-85; V Unsworth 85-93; R Brough w Stainmore, Musgrave and Warcop *Carl* 93-97; rtd 97; Perm to Offic *Carl* from 98. *21 Templand Park, Allithwaite, Grange-over-Sands LA11 7QS* Tel (01539) 532312

HAIGH, Samuel Edward. b 85. Anglia Ruskin Univ BA11. Ridley Hall Cam 08. **d** 11. C Wootton *St Alb* from 11. *9 Studley Road, Wootton, Bedford MK43 9DL* Tel (01234) 766317 Mobile 07429-022977 E-mail haigh22k@hotmail.com

HAILES, Derek Arthur. b 38. Coll of Resurr Mirfield. **d** 82 **p** 83. C Sneinton St Cypr *S'well* 82-84; V Kneesall w Laxton 84-85; P-in-c Wellow 84-85; V Kneesall w Laxton and Wellow 85-88; V Sneinton St Steph w St Alb 88-95; P-in-c Bury H Trin *Man* 95-03; rtd 03; Perm to Offic *S'well* from 05. *14 Manor Road, Carlton, Nottingham NG4 3AY* Tel 0115-987 3314

HAILS, Canon Brian. b 33. JP71. ACMA62 FCMA76. NEOC 77. **d** 81 **p** 82. NSM Harton *Dur* 81-87; Ind Chapl 87-99; Hon

Can Dur Cathl 93-99; TR Sunderland 96-99; rtd 99. *The Coach House, Church Lane, Whitburn, Sunderland SR6 7JL* Tel 0191-529 5297 E-mail canon-hails@ukonline.co.uk

HAINES, Andrew Philip. b 47. LSE BSc68. Oak Hill Th Coll 84. **d** 87 **p** 88. C Enfield Ch Ch Trent Park *Lon* 87-91; V Hillmorton *Cov* from 91. *The Vicarage, Hoskyn Close, Rugby CV21 4LA* Tel (01788) 576279 E-mail revaph@btinternet.com *or* andrew@haines.uk.com

HAINES, Daniel Hugo. b 43. TD89. Lon Univ BDS68 MRCS73. **d** 79 **p** 84. Hon C Bhunya Swaziland 79-80; Hon C Falkland Is 80-82; Hon C Hatcham St Cath *S'wark* 84-99; Perm to Offic from 99. *56 Vesta Road, London SE4 2NH* Tel (020) 7635 0305 E-mail 113270.506@compuserve.com

HAINES, Canon Robert Melvin. b 31. Coll of Resurr Mirfield 71. **d** 73 **p** 74. C Derringham Bank *York* 73-76; P-in-c Newport St Steph 76-79; TV Howden 80-82; R Turriff *Ab* 82-97; R Cuminestown 82-97; R Banff 82-97; P-in-c Portsoy 94-97; P-in-c Buckie 94-97; rtd 97; NSM Turriff *Ab* from 97; Hon Can St Andr Cathl from 01. *Ceol-na-Mara, 11 Scotstown, Banff AB45 1LA* Tel (01261) 818258

HAINES, Stephen Decatur. b 42. Freiburg Univ MA68 Fitzw Coll Cam BA70 MA74. **d** 71 **p** 72. C Fulham St Dionis *Lon* 71-76; C Finchley St Mary 76-78; Hon C Clapham Old Town *S'wark* 83-87; Hon C Clapham Team 87-88; Hon C Camberwell St Giles w St Matt 88-94; Hon Chapl S'wark Cathl from 92. *3 Lyndhurst Square, London SE15 5AR* Tel (020) 7703 4239

HAINSWORTH, Richard John. b 79. Jes Coll Cam BA01 MA03. St Mich Coll Llan 04. **d** 06 **p** 07. C Newtown w Llanllwchaiarn w Aberhafesp *St As* 06-07; C Llanllwchaiarn and Newtown w Aberhafesp 07-08; C Wrexham 08-09; TV from 09. *The Vicarage, 37 Acton Gate, Wrexham LL11 2PW* Tel (01978) 266685 Mobile 07886-117922 E-mail rich_hainsworth@yahoo.co.uk

HAIR, James Eric. b 48. Lon Univ BA69 MPhil92. St Steph Ho Ox 69. **d** 72 **p** 73. C Fishponds St Jo *Bris* 72-75; C Bushey *St Alb* 75-79; P-in-c Lake *Portsm* 79-81; V 81-88; P-in-c Shanklin St Sav 79-81; V 81-88; TV Totton *Win* 88-95; C Portchester *Portsm* 96-97; Community Mental Health Chapl Portsm Health Care NHS Trust 97-02; Community Mental Health Chapl Hants Partnership NHS Trust from 02; Chapl Team Ldr E Hants Primary Care Trust from 99; Asst to RD Fareham *Portsm* 97-98 and 99. *219 West Street, Fareham PO16 0ET* Tel (01329) 825231

HAITH, James Rodney. b 69. Ex Univ BA. Ridley Hall Cam 02. **d** 04 **p** 05. C Brompton H Trin w Onslow Square St Paul *Lon* 04-11; C Onslow Square and S Kensington St Aug from 11. *23 Pooles Lane, London SW10 0RH* Tel 08456-447533 Mobile 07833-705271 E-mail jamie.haith@htb.org.uk

HAKE, Darren Mark. b 73. Plymouth Univ BSc01 Lanc Univ MRes02 FGS01. Wycliffe Hall Ox 09. **d** 11. C Wembdon *B & W* from 11. *60 Moravia Close, Bridgwater TA6 3SN* Tel (01278) 457159 Mobile 07545-379112 E-mail markh@sgw.org.uk

HAKE *(née* JACKSON*),* **Mrs Ruth Victoria.** b 78. Univ Coll Dur BA99 Fitzw Coll Cam BA01 MA05. Ridley Hall Cam 99. **d** 02 **p** 03. C York St Mich-le-Belfrey 02-05; CF(V) 04-05; Chapl RAF from 05. *Chaplaincy Services, HQ Personnel and Training Command, RAF High Wycombe HP14 4UE* Tel (01494) 496800 Fax 496343

HALAHAN, Maxwell Crosby. b 30. Lon Univ BSc52 Southn Univ CertEd78. Westcott Ho Cam 54. **d** 56 **p** 57. C Forton *Portsm* 56-60; C Liv Our Lady and St Nic 60-62; Dom Chapl to Bp Nassau and the Bahamas 62-64; C Widley w Wymering *Portsm* 64-66; C-in-c Cowes St Faith CD 66-70; V Cowes St Faith 70-77; Hon C Portsea St Sav 77-84; rtd 84; Perm to Offic *Portsm* 84-94. *4 Coach House Mews, Old Canal, Southsea PO4 8HD*

HALBERT, Mrs Elizabeth Mary. b 58. Liv Hope BA97 PGCE98. **d** 06 **p** 07. OLM Sefton and Thornton *Liv* from 06. *15 Third Avenue, Crosby, Liverpool L23 5SA* Tel 0151-281 1390 E-mail lizhalbert1000@msn.com

HALE, Antony Jolyon (Jon). b 56. Newc Univ BA79 MRTPI89. Sarum & Wells Th Coll 86. **d** 88 **p** 89. C Monkseaton St Mary *Newc* 88-92; P-in-c Tandridge *S'wark* 92-97; C Oxted 92-97; C Oxted and Tandridge 97-98; V Crawley Down All SS *Chich* from 98. *The Vicarage, Vicarage Road, Crawley Down, Crawley RH10 4JJ* Tel (01342) 714922 E-mail aj@jkcahale.plus.com

HALE, David Nigel James. b 43. SEITE 00. **d** 03 **p** 04. NSM Aylesham w Adisham *Cant* from 03; NSM Nonington w Wymynswold and Goodnestone etc from 03. *Chilton House, 43 The Street, Ash, Canterbury CT3 2EN* Tel (01304) 813161 *or* (01843) 862991 E-mail halenigelval@hotmail.com

HALE, Jon. See HALE, Antony Jolyon

HALE, Canon Keith John Edward. b 53. Sheff Poly BSc75. St Jo Coll Nottm MA94. **d** 91 **p** 92. C Greasbrough *Sheff* 91-94; P-in-c Tankersley 94-95; R Tankersley, Thurgoland and Wortley from 95; Ind Chapl 96-01; Bp's Rural Adv from 01; AD Tankersley from 07; Hon Can Sheff Cathl from 10. *The Rectory, 9 Chapel Road, Tankersley, Barnsley S75 3AR* Tel (01226) 744140 E-mail revkeith.hale@virgin.net

HALE *(née* McKAY*),* **Mrs Margaret McLeish (Greta).** b 37. RN76. WEMTC 92. **d** 95 **p** 96. OLM Bream *Glouc* 95-01; NSM

01-04; NSM Newland and Redbrook w Clearwell 04-06; NSM Coleford, Staunton, Newland, Redbrook etc from 06. *1 The Bungalow, High Street, Clearwell, Coleford GL16 8JS* Tel (01594) 832400 E-mail gretahale@hotmail.com
HALE, Nigel. *See* HALE, David Nigel James
HALE, Roger Anthony. b 41. MCIH85. Brasted Th Coll 68 Oak Hill Th Coll 70. **d** 72 **p** 73. C Blackb Sav 72-75; C Burnley St Pet 75-77; Chapl Burnley Gen Hosp 75-77; V Fence in Pendle *Blackb* 77-82; Chapl Lancs Ind Miss 77-82; NSM Tottenham St Mary *Lon* 88-91; R Cheddington w Mentmore and Marsworth *Ox* 91-06; rtd 06; Perm to Offic *Ox* from 06. *Chiltern House, 12 High Street, Cheddington, Leighton Buzzard LU7 0RQ* Tel (01296) 668114 E-mail rogertherector@yahoo.co.uk
HALES, Peter John. b 45. Open Univ BSc02. ERMC 08. **d** 08 **p** 09. Chapl Coutances *Eur* from 08. *4 rue le Mascaret, 50220 Précey, France* Tel (0033) 2 33 58 86 76 Fax 6 87 53 20 13 E-mail halesphx2@aol.com
HALES, Sandra Louise. Lon Univ BSc94 Univ Coll Lon MSc96 TCD BTh02 RGN. CITC. **d** 02 **p** 03. C Lucan w Leixlip *D & G* 02-06; I Celbridge w Straffan and Newcastle-Lyons from 06. *The Rectory, Maynooth Road, Celbridge, Co Kildare, Republic of Ireland* Tel (00353) (1) 628 8231 E-mail slhales@eircom.net
HALEY, Thomas Arthur. b 52. NTMTC 98. **d** 98 **p** 99. NSM Old Ford St Paul and St Mark *Lon* 98-02; NSM Hackney Marsh from 02; TV from 07. *All Souls' Vicarage, 44 Overbury Street, London E5 0AJ* Tel (020) 8525 2863 E-mail tomarcie@aol.com
HALFORD, David John. b 47. JP84. Didsbury Coll Man CertEd69 Open Univ BA75 DipEd86 Man Univ MEd79 ACP72. **d** 96 **p** 97. OLM Royton St Anne *Man* from 96. *33 Broadway, Royton, Oldham OL2 5DD* Tel and fax 0161-633 4650
HALFPENNY, Brian Norman. b 36. CB90. St Jo Coll Ox BA60 MA64. Wells Th Coll 60. **d** 62 **p** 63. C Melksham *Sarum* 62-65; Chapl RAF 65-83; Sen Chapl RAF Coll Cranwell 82-83; Asst Chapl-in-Chief RAF 83-88; Chapl-in-Chief RAF 88-91; QHC 85-91; Can and Preb Linc Cathl 89-91; TR Redditch, The Ridge *Worc* 91-01; rtd 01; Perm to Offic *Glouc* from 02. *80 Roman Way, Bourton-on-the-Water, Cheltenham GL54 2EW* Tel (01451) 821589
HALIFAX, Archdeacon of. *Vacant*
HALKES, Canon John Stanley. b 39. SWMTC 87. **d** 90 **p** 91. NSM St Buryan, St Levan and Sennen *Truro* 90-92; P-in-c Lanteglos by Fowey 92-04; P-in-c Lansallos 03-04; Hon Can Truro Cathl 03-08; rtd 04. *Reading Room Cottage, Mixton Farm, Lerryn, Lostwithiel PL22 0QE*
HALL, Alan Maurice Frank. b 28. FCCA. Sarum & Wells Th Coll 86. **d** 89 **p** 90. NSM Winterbourne Stickland and Turnworth etc *Sarum* 89-97; Perm to Offic *Sarum* 97-00 and *St Alb* from 00. *2 Barnes Road, Wooton, Bedford MK43 9FA* Tel (01234) 764676
✠**HALL, The Rt Revd Albert Peter.** b 30. St Jo Coll Cam BA53 MA56. Ridley Hall Cam 53. **d** 55 **p** 56 **c** 84. C Birm St Martin 55-60; S Rhodesia 60-65; Rhodesia 65-70; R Birm St Martin 70-84; Hon Can Birm Cathl 75-84; Suff Bp Woolwich *S'wark* 84-91; Area Bp Woolwich 91-96; Chmn ACUPA 90-96; rtd 96; Asst Bp Birm from 96. *27 Jacey Road, Birmingham B16 0LL* Tel 0121-455 9240
HALL, Canon Alfred Christopher. b 35. Trin Coll Ox BA58 MA61. Westcott Ho Cam 58. **d** 61 **p** 62. C Frecheville *Derby* 61-64; C Dronfield 64-67; V Smethwick St Matt *Birm* 67-70; V Smethwick St Matt w St Chad 70-75; Can Res Man Cathl 75-83; Hon Can 83-90; Dioc Adult Educn Officer 75-83; Dioc World Development Officer 76-88; V Bolton St Pet 83-90; Co-ord Chr Concern for One World 90-00; rtd 96; Hon Can Ch Ch *Ox* 00-01; Perm to Offic from 03. *The Knowle, Philcote Street, Deddington, Banbury OX15 0TB* Tel (01869) 338225 Fax 337766 E-mail achall@globalnet.co.uk
HALL, Mrs Ann Addington. b 34. Ex Univ CertEd71. SWMTC 82. **dss** 85 **d** 87 **p** 94. SS St Mark 85-90; Hon Par Dn 87-90; Perm to Offic 90-92; NSM Cen Ex from 92. *5 Harringcourt Road, Exeter EX4 8PQ* Tel (01392) 278717
HALL, Arthur John. b 23. Bris Univ BSc48. Sarum & Wells Th Coll 74. **d** 76 **p** 77. NSM Portishead *B & W* 76-88; Perm to Offic from 88; Chapl St Brandon's Sch Clevedon 86-91. *34 Beechwood Road, Portishead, Bristol BS20 8EP* Tel (01275) 842603
HALL, Barry George. b 38. Solicitor 62. Oak Hill Th Coll 78. **d** 81 **p** 82. NSM Stock Harvard *Chelmsf* 81-90; NSM W Hanningfield 90-02; P-in-c 93-02; Perm to Offic from 02. *Harvard Cottage, Swan Lane, Stock, Ingatestone CM4 9BQ* Tel (01277) 840387
HALL, Brian. b 59. Aston Tr Scheme 90 Oak Hill Th Coll 92. **d** 94 **p** 95. C Mansfield St Jo *S'well* 94-96; C Skegby 96-99; P-in-c Sutton in Ashfield St Mich 99-04; R Carlton-in-the-Willows from 04. *St Paul's Rectory, Church Street, Nottingham NG4 1BJ* Tel 0115-961 1644 E-mail revbhall@aol.com
HALL, Canon Brian Arthur. b 48. Ex Univ BEd70. Cuddesdon Coll 73. **d** 75 **p** 76. C Hobs Moat *Birm* 75-79; V Smethwick 79-93; R Handsworth St Mary from 93; AD Handsworth 99-05

and 06-08; Hon Can Birm Cathl from 05. *Handsworth Rectory, 288 Hamstead Road, Birmingham B20 2RB* Tel 0121-554 3407 E-mail brian.a.hall@btinternet.com
HALL, Mrs Carolyn Ruth. **d** 08 **p** 09. NSM Builth and Llanddewi'r Cwm w Llangynog etc *S & B* from 08. *The Vicarage, 1 North Road, Builth Wells LD2 3BT* Tel (01982) 552355 E-mail nigeldhall@hotmail.com
HALL, Ms Christine Beryl. b 52. Southn Univ BSc73 Leeds Univ MA06. NTMTC BA08. **d** 08 **p** 09. NSM Stepney St Dunstan and All SS *Lon* from 08; Chapl Guy's and St Thos' NHS Foundn Trust from 08; Chapl Lon Fire Brigade from 08. *6 Arbour Square, London E1 0SH* Tel (020) 7790 9961 E-mail christine.b.hall@btinternet.com
HALL, Christine Mary. b 45. K Coll Lon BD67 MPhil86. **d** 87. NSM Bickley *Roch* 87-92; Vice-Prin Chich Th Coll 92-94; Lic to Offic *Chich* 95-03. *The Old School, East Marden, Chichester PO18 9JE* Tel (01243) 535244 E-mail dcnchall@eastmarden.net
HALL, Christopher. *See* HALL, Canon Alfred Christopher
HALL, Darryl Christopher. b 69. Cranmer Hall Dur 07. **d** 09 **p** 10. C Knaresborough *Ripon* from 09. *9 Castle Yard, Knaresborough HG5 8AS* Tel (01423) 869845 Mobile 07930-177337 E-mail horlix@aol.com
HALL, David Anthony. b 43. Reading Univ BA66. Qu Coll Birm 79. **d** 81 **p** 82. C Norton *St Alb* 81-85; TV Hitchin 85-93; P-in-c Bidford-on-Avon *Cov* 93; V 93-08; RD Alcester 05-08; rtd 08. *Holyoake Farm Cottage, Little Alne, Wooton Wawen, Henley-in-Arden B95 6HW* E-mail davidahall@onetel.com
HALL, David Martin. b 66. Avery Hill Coll BA89. Oak Hill Th Coll BA00. **d** 00 **p** 01. C Bebington *Ches* 00-03; P-in-c Danehill *Chich* 03-05; V from 05; RD Uckfield from 11. *The Vicarage, Lewes Road, Danehill, Haywards Heath RH17 7ER* Tel (01825) 790269
HALL, Denis. b 43. Lon Coll of Div 65. **d** 69 **p** 70. C Netherton *Liv* 69-71; C Roby 72-75; V Wigan St Steph 75-90; V Newton-le-Willows from 90. *The Vicarage, 243 Crow Lane East, Newton-le-Willows WA12 9UB* Tel (01925) 290545 E-mail allsaints@3tc4u.net
HALL, Derek. *See* HALL, Canon John Derek
HALL, Derek Guy. b 26. Tyndale Hall Bris 50. **d** 51 **p** 52. C Preston All SS *Blackb* 51-54; C Halliwell St Pet *Man* 54-56; C-in-c Buxton Trin Prop Chpl *Derby* 56-58; V Blackb St Jude 58-67; R Fazakerley Em *Liv* 67-74; TR 74-81; V Langdale *Carl* 81-86; rtd 86; Perm to Offic *Carl* from 86. *14 Gale Park, Ambleside LA22 0BN* Tel (01539) 433144
HALL, Elaine Chegwin. b 59. Liv Univ MTh01 RGN82. NOC 94. **d** 97 **p** 98. C Frankby w Greasby *Ches* 97-01; V Stretton and Appleton Thorn from 01; RD Gt Budworth 03-10. *The Vicarage, Stretton Road, Stretton, Warrington WA4 4NT* Tel (01925) 730276 E-mail petera.hall@care4free.net
HALL, Fiona Myfanwy Gordon. b 63. Regents Th Coll BA95 Roehampton Inst PGCE96 Anglia Ruskin Univ MA04. Ridley Hall Cam 02. **d** 04 **p** 05. C Southampton Maybush St Pet *Win* 04-06; C Maybush and Southampton St Jude 06-07; Asst Chapl R Berks NHS Foundn Trust from 08. *St John's Convent, Linden Hill Lane, Kiln Green, Reading RG10 9XP* Tel 0118-940 4311
HALL, Frances. *See* SHOESMITH, Mrs Judith Frances
HALL, Geoffrey Hedley. b 33. Bris Univ BA55. St Steph Ho Ox 63. **d** 65 **p** 66. C Taunton H Trin *B & W* 65-67; CF 67-80; Sen CF 80-86; P-in-c Ambrosden w Arncot and Blackthorn *Ox* 72-75; V Barnsley St Edw *Wakef* 86-98; rtd 98; Perm to Offic *St And* from 98 and *Bre* from 99. *Montana Villa, 39 Haston Crescent, Perth PH2 7XD* Tel (01738) 636802 Mobile 07803-578499 E-mail geoffreyhall@blueyonder.co.uk
HALL, George Richard Wyndham. b 49. Ex Univ LLB71. Wycliffe Hall Ox BA74 MA78. **d** 75 **p** 76. C Walton H Trin *Ox* 75-79; C Farnborough *Guildf* 79-84; Bp's Chapl *Nor* 84-87; R Saltford w Corston and Newton St Loe *B & W* from 87; Chapl Bath Coll of HE 88-90; RD Chew Magna *B & W* 97-03. *The Rectory, 12 Beech Road, Saltford, Bristol BS31 3BE* Tel and fax (01225) 872275 E-mail richardhall@blueyonder.co.uk
HALL, Canon George Rumney. b 37. LVO99 CVO03. Westcott Ho Cam 60. **d** 62 **p** 63. C Camberwell St Phil *S'wark* 62-65; C Waltham Cross *St Alb* 65-67; R Buckenham w Hassingham and Strumpshaw *Nor* 67-74; Chapl St Andr Hosp Thorpe 67-72; Chapl HM Pris *Nor* 72-74; V Wymondham *Nor* 74-87; RD Humbleyard 86-87; R Sandringham w W Newton 87-94; P-in-c Flitcham 87-94; P-in-c Wolferton w Babingley 87-94; R Sandringham w W Newton and Appleton etc 95-03; P-in-c Castle Rising 87-03; P-in-c Hillington 87-03; Hon Can Nor Cathl 87-03; RD Heacham and Rising 89-01; Dom Chapl to The Queen 87-03; Chapl to The Queen 89-07; rtd 03; Perm to Offic *Nor* from 03. *Town Farm Cottage, Lynn Road, Bircham, King's Lynn PE31 6RJ* Tel (01485) 576134
HALL, Mrs Gillian Louise. b 45. Univ of Wales (Ban) MPhil06. NOC 89. **d** 90 **p** 94. NSM Earby *Bradf* 90-96; NSM Gisburn 96-01; NSM Hellifield 96-01; Perm to Offic 01-02; Chapl Airedale NHS Trust 02-04; Hon C Sutton w Cowling and

Lothersdale *Bradf* from 05. *Mitton House, Lothersdale, Keighley BD20 8HR*   Tel (01535) 636144
E-mail gill@hesslelodge.freeserve.co.uk
HALL, Harry. b 41. Open Univ BA93. Chich Th Coll 91. **d** 91 **p** 92. C Boston *Linc* 91-92; C Bourne 92-94; P-in-c Sutterton w Fosdyke and Algarkirk 94-97; R Sutterton, Fosdyke, Algarkirk and Wigtoft 97-99; V Barnsley St Edw *Wakef* 99-05; Chapl ATC 99-05; I Ardstraw w Baronscourt, Badoney Lower etc *D & R* 05-10; rtd 10. *18 Kings Road, Metheringham, Lincoln LN4 3HT* Tel (01526) 320308 E-mail slk248@hotmail.com
HALL, Miss Helen Constance Patricia Mary. b 77. Peterho Cam BA99 MA03 St Jo Coll Dur BA05 Solicitor 02. Cranmer Hall Dur 03. **d** 06 **p** 07. C Maindee Newport *Mon* 06-09; P-in-c Newport St Andr from 09. *The Vicarage, 1 Brookfield Close, Newport NP19 4LA*   Tel (01633) 677775 Mobile 07919-538077 E-mail bititt@yahoo.co.uk
HALL, Canon Hubert William Peter. b 35. Ely Th Coll 58. **d** 60 **p** 61. C Louth w Welton-le-Wold *Linc* 60-62; C Gt Grimsby St Jas 62-69; C Gt Grimsby St Mary and St Jas 69-71; Hon Chapl Miss to Seafarers 71-01; V Immingham *Linc* 71-01; RD Haverstoe 86-01; Can and Preb Linc Cathl 89-01; rtd 01; Perm to Offic *Linc* from 01. *6 Abbey Rise, Barrow-upon-Humber DN19 7TF*   Tel (01469) 531504 E-mail hwphall@talktalk.net
HALL, Ian Alfred. b 60. Sheff Univ BA96. Ushaw Coll Dur 81 NOC 98. **d** 85 **p** 86. In RC Ch 86-98; C Whitkirk *Ripon* 99-02; TV Swinton and Pendlebury *Man* 02-09; P-in-c Winton from 09. *Winton Vicarage, Albany Road, Eccles, Manchester M30 8FE* Tel 0161-788 8991 E-mail carolian86@yahoo.co.uk
HALL, James. b 28. Wollongong Univ BA78. CITC 53. **d** 56 **p** 57. C Belfast St Mich *Conn* 56-59; I Cleenish *Clogh* 59-62; R Openshaw *Man* 63-68, C-in-c Figtree Australia 68-71; R 72-79; Lic to Offic Dio Sydney 81-89 and 93-03; R Morley w Deopham, Hackford, Wicklewood etc *Nor* 89-92; R High Oak 92-93; rtd 93. *319/2 Huntley Road, St Luke's Retirement Village, Dapto NSW 2530, Australia*   Tel (0061) (2) 4262 7881
E-mail jmhall@ihug.com.au
HALL, Canon James Robert. b 24. TCD BA48 MA54. **d** 49 **p** 50. C Seagoe *D & D* 49-51; C Lisburn Ch Ch *Conn* 51-59; I Belfast St Mich 59-66; I Finaghy 66-89; Can Belf Cathl 82-89; rtd 89. *3 Coachman's Way, Hillsborough BT26 6HQ*   Tel (028) 9268 9678
HALL, Mrs Jane Daphne. b 60. Trent Poly BA92 Solicitor 93. **d** 09 **p** 10. NSM Clopton w Otley, Swilland and Ashbocking *St E* from 09. *Countryside, Gibraltar Road, Otley, Ipswich IP6 9LL* Tel (01473) 785251 E-mail allthealls@tiscali.co.uk
HALL, Jeffrey Ernest. b 42. Linc Th Coll 73. **d** 75 **p** 76. C Brampton St Thos *Derby* 75-78; C Whittington and New Whittington 78-81; TV Riverside *Ox* 81-90; Ind Chapl Slough Deanery 81-89; R Anstey *Leic* 90-97; TR Hugglescote w Donington, Ellistown and Snibston 97-08; rtd 08; Perm to Offic *Sarum* from 10. *21 Woodsage Drive, Gillingham SP8 4UE* Tel (01747) 823480 Mobile 07876-540343
E-mail jeffreyhall123@btinternet.com
HALL, The Ven John Barrie. b 41. Sarum & Wells Th Coll 82. **d** 84 **p** 85. Chapl St Edward's Hosp Cheddleton 84-88; C Cheddleton *Lich* 84-88; V Rocester 88-94; V Rocester and Croxden w Hollington 94-98; RD Uttoxeter 91-98; Adn Salop 98-11; V Tong 98-11; P-in-c Donington 98-00; rtd 11; Perm to Offic *Lich* from 11. *16 Mill House Drive, Cheadle, Stoke-on-Trent ST10 1XL*   Tel (01538) 750628
E-mail j.hall182@btinternet.com
HALL, John Bruce. b 33. Covenant Th Sem St Louis MTh80 DMin85. ALCD60. **d** 60 **p** 61. C Kingston upon Hull H Trin *York* 60-67; C Beverley Minster 67-68; V Clapham Park St Steph *S'wark* 68-76; R Tooting Graveney St Nic 76-03; rtd 03; Perm to Offic *S'wark* from 03. *44 Mayford Road, London SW12 8SD* Tel (020) 8673 6869 E-mail jbewhall@johnbhall.plus.com
HALL, John Charles. b 46. Hull Univ BA71 Spurgeon's Coll MTh05. Ridley Hall Cam 71. **d** 73 **p** 74. C Bromley Common St Aug *Roch* 73-77; C Westbury-on-Trym St Alb *Bris* 78-80; Oman 80-82; C-in-c Bishop Auckland Woodhouse Close CD *Dur* 82-90; P-in-c Gt and Lt Glemham, Blaxhall etc *St E* 90-91; P-in-c Rodney Stoke w Draycott *B & W* 91-01; Dioc Ecum Officer 91-01; V Southmead *Bris* from 01. *St Stephen's Vicarage, Wigton Crescent, Bristol BS10 6DR* Tel 0117-950 7164 Mobile 07811-316249 E-mail sarasgarden@blueyonder.co.uk
HALL, John Curtis. b 39. CEng73 MIMechE73. Coll of Resurr Mirfield 80. **d** 82 **p** 83. C Pet Ch Carpenter 82-86; TV Heavitree w Ex St Paul 86-93; R Bow w Broad Nymet 93-04; V Colebrooke 93-04; R Zeal Monachorum 93-04; RD Cadbury 97-02; rtd 04. *37 Lawn Drive, Chudleigh, Newton Abbot TQ13 0LS* Tel (01626) 853245
HALL, Canon John Derek. b 25. St Cuth Soc Dur BA50. Linc Th Coll 50. **d** 52 **p** 53. C Redcar *York* 52-54; C Newland St Jo 54-57; V Boosbeck w Moorsholm 57-61; V Middlesbrough St Oswald 61-68; Chapl St Luke's Hosp Middlesbrough 61-67; V York St Chad 68-90; Chapl Bootham Park Hosp 68-85; Can and Preb York Minster 85-90; rtd 90; Chapl Castle Howard 90-02; Perm to Offic *York* from 98. *25 Fairfields Drive, Skelton, York YO30 1YP* Tel (01904) 470978

HALL, Canon John Edmund. b 49. Open Univ BA84 Birm Univ MPhil05 Warwick Univ PhD06 CQSW76. Trin Coll Bris BA89. **d** 89 **p** 90. C Winchmore Hill St Paul *Lon* 89-92; V Edmonton St Aldhelm 92-01; Dir Soc Resp *Cov* 01-10; Dir Interfaith Relns and Dir St Phil Cen *Leic* from 10; Hon Can Leic Cathl from 10. *15 Ratcliffe Road, Leicester LE2 3TE* Tel 0116-270 6766
HALL, Canon John Kenneth. b 32. Qu Coll Birm 61. **d** 63 **p** 64. C Ilminster w Whitelackington *B & W* 63-66; P-in-c Mackworth St Fran *Derby* 66-69; V Blackford *B & W* 69-76; R Chapel Allerton 76-79; New Zealand from 77; Can St Pet Cathl Waikato 85-91; rtd 93. *24 Pohutukawa Drive, RD 1, Katikati 3177, New Zealand* Tel and fax (0064) (7) 863 4465
E-mail gee.jay@paradise.net.nz
HALL, John MacNicol. b 44. Glas Univ BSc65 MB, ChB69 St Jo Coll Cam BA73 MA76 Nottm Univ MTh88 MSc93 MRCGP75. Westcott Ho Cam 71. **d** 86 **p** 86. NSM Clarendon Park St Jo w Knighton St Mich *Leic* 86-89; Perm to Offic *Ely* 89-91; St Alb 90-92; *Birm* from 91. *85 Galton Road, Smethwick B67 5JX* Tel 0121-434 3957
HALL, John Michael. b 47. BD. Oak Hill Th Coll 68. **d** 73 **p** 74. C Walthamstow St Mary w St Steph *Chelmsf* 73-76; C Rainham 76-79; P-in-c Woodham Mortimer w Hazeleigh 79-93; P-in-c Woodham Walter 79-93; Ind Chapl 79-93; R Fairstead w Terling and White Notley etc from 93; RD Witham 01-07. *The Rectory, New Road, Terling, Chelmsford CM3 2PN* Tel (01245) 233256 E-mail rev.john.hall@tinyworld.co.uk
HALL, Canon John Michael. b 62. Leeds Univ BA. Coll of Resurr Mirfield 83. **d** 86 **p** 87. C Ribbleton *Blackb* 86-89; C Carnforth 89-92; V Lt Marsden 92-98; V Lt Marsden w Nelson St Mary 98; V Warton St Oswald w Yealand Conyers 98-08; AD Tunstall 05-08; P-in-c Fleetwood St Pet 08-11; V from 11; P-in-c Fleetwood St Dav from 08; Hon Can Bloemfontein Cathl from 01; Hon Can Blackb Cathl from 09. *The Vicarage, 49 Mount Road, Fleetwood FY7 6QZ* Tel (01253) 876176
E-mail johnbloem@aol.com
HALL, The Very Revd John Robert. b 49. St Chad's Coll Dur BA71. Cuddesdon Coll 73. **d** 75 **p** 76. C Kennington St Jo *S'wark* 75-78; P-in-c S Wimbledon All SS 78-84; V Streatham St Pet 84-92; Dioc Dir of Educn *Blackb* 92-98; Hon Can Blackb Cathl 92-94 and 98-00; Can Res 94-98; Gen Sec Nat Soc 98-06; Gen Sec C of E Bd of Educn 98-02; Chief Educn Officer and Hd Educn Division Abps' Coun 03-06; Hon C S Norwood St Alb *S'wark* 03-06; Dean Westmr from 06. *The Deanery, Dean's Yard, London SW1P 3PA* Tel (020) 7654 4801 Fax 7654 4883
E-mail john.hall@westminster-abbey.org
HALL, Canon John Terence Peter. b 67. St Jo Coll Dur BA98. Cranmer Hall Dur. **d** 98 **p** 99. C Towcester w Easton Neston *Pet* 98-01; P-in-c Blakesley w Adstone and Maidford etc 01-07; C Greens Norton w Bradden and Lichborough 06-07; R Lambfold 07-11; P-in-c Irthlingborough from 11; P-in-c Gt w Lt Addington and Woodford from 11; Can Pet Cathl from 10. *The Rectory, 79 Finedon Road, Irthlingborough, Wellingborough NN9 5TY* E-mail fr-john@lambfold.org.uk
HALL, Jonathan. b 62. Ch Ch Coll Cant BA83 MCIPD94. STETS BTh99. **d** 99 **p** 00. C Weymouth H Trin *Sarum* 99-03; R Whippingham w E Cowes *Portsm* 03-10; RD W Wight 07-10; Chapl Burrswood Chr Hosp *Roch* from 10. *Burrswood Hospital, Burrswood, Groombrdige, Tunbridge Wells TN3 9PY* Tel (01892) 863637
HALL, The Very Revd Kenneth Robert James. b 59. St Jo Coll Nottm 95. **d** 98 **p** 99. NSM Derryloran *Arm* 98-02; C Drumglass w Moygashel 02-03; C Brackaville w Donaghendry and Ballyclog 03-04; I 04-10; Dean Clogh from 10; I Enniskillen from 10. *The Deanery, 13 Church Street, Enniskillen BT74 7DW* Tel (028) 6632 2465 *or* 6632 2917 E-mail krjhall@btinternet.com
HALL, Keven Neil. b 47. Auckland Univ BSc PhD74. K Coll Lon BD AKC79. **d** 79 **p** 80. New Zealand 79-87; NSM Shepherd's Bush St Steph w St Thos *Lon* 91-95 and 98-00; NSM W Acton St Martin 96-98; Asst Chapl NW Lon Hosp NHS Trust 00-07; Chapl Nat Soc for Epilepsy 91-03. *Flat B, Rutland House, 30 Greencroft Gardens, London NW6 3LT* Tel 07930-353717 (mobile) E-mail kevenhall@hotmail.com
HALL, Leslie. b 37. Man Univ BSc59. EMMTC 83. **d** 86 **p** 87. NSM Freiston w Butterwick and Benington *Linc* 86-02; Perm to Offic 02-05; Dioc NSM Officer 94-97. *29 Brand End Road, Butterwick, Boston PE22 0ET* Tel (01205) 760375
HALL, Mrs Lilian Evelyn Mary. b 42. SWMTC 02. **d** 05 **p** 06. NSM Ludgvan, Marazion, St Hilary and Perranuthnoe *Truro* 05-11; C Barkston and Hough Gp *Linc* from 11. *The Rectory, Barkston Road, Marston, Grantham NG32 2HN* Tel (01400) 251590 E-mail johnandlily.hall@btinternet.com
HALL, Mrs Linda Charlotte. b 50. Cam Inst of Educn CertEd72. St Alb Minl Tr Scheme 85 Oak Hill Th Coll 91. **d** 92 **p** 94. NSM St Alb St Steph *St Alb* 92-98; NSM Sandridge 98-99; C Ipswich All Hallows *St E* 99-00; Perm to Offic 01; TV Cwmbran *Mon* 01-08; P-in-c Maesglas and Duffryn from 08. *The Vicarage, Old Cardiff Road, Newport NP20 3AT* Tel (01633) 815738
HALL, Mrs Marigold Josephine. b 29. Linc Th Coll 81. dss 83 **d** 87. Chapl Asst Hellesdon Hosp Nor 83-94; Nor St Pet

Parmentergate w St Jo 83-87; C 87-94; rtd 90; Perm to Offic *Nor* from 94. *36 Cavendish House, Recorder Road, Norwich NR1 1BW* Tel (01603) 625933

HALL, Ms Melanie Jane. b 55. Ex Univ BA78. Ripon Coll Cuddesdon 01. **d** 03 **p** 04. C Stepney St Dunstan and All SS *Lon* 03-06; rtd 06. *28 St Gabriel's Manor, 25 Cormont Road, London SE5 9RH* Tel (020) 7587 1766
E-mail melanie.jh@btopenworld.com

HALL, Michael Alan. b 76. Univ of Wales (Lamp) BA98. Ripon Coll Cuddesdon 99. **d** 01 **p** 02. C Wellington Ch Ch *Lich* 01-05; V Chelmsf All SS from 05. *All Saints' Vicarage, 76A Kings Road, Chelmsford CM1 4HP* Tel (01245) 281706
E-mail revd.michael@btinternet.com

HALL, Canon Michael Anthony. b 41. St Paul's Coll Grahamstown LTh64. **d** 64 **p** 65. S Africa 64-01; C E London St Alb 65-67; C Queenstown St Mich 67-69; R Port Elizabeth All SS 70-78; R E London All SS 78-81; R Queenstown St Mich w Tarkastad St Mary 81-91; Adn Aliwal N 81-01; R Barkly E St Steph and P-in-c Dordrecht St Aug 91-01; Hon Can Grahamstown from 01; P-in-c Lapford, Nymet Rowland and Coldridge *Ex* 01-03; TV N Creedy 03-11; rtd 11. *10 Blagdon Rise, Crediton EX17 1EN* Tel (01363) 774023 Mobile 07751-798670 E-mail micsandhall@btopenworld.com

HALL, Michael Edward. b 32. Fitzw Ho Cam BA57 MA61. Ridley Hall Cam 68. **d** 69 **p** 70. C Aspley *S'well* 69-73; P-in-c Bulwell St Jo 73-75; V 75-81; P-in-c Tyler's Green *Ox* 81-90; V 90-00; rtd 00. *5 Hawkings Meadow, Marlborough SN8 1UR* Tel (01672) 511713

HALL, Murray. b 34. K Coll Lon. **d** 61 **p** 62. C Eaton *Nor* 61-64; C Shalford *Guildf* 64-67; V Oxshott 67-72; P-in-c Runham *Nor* 72-80; R Filby w Thrigby w Mautby 72-80; P-in-c Stokesby w Herringby 72-80; R Filby w Thrigby, Mautby, Stokesby, Herringby etc 80-94; rtd 94; Perm to Offic *Nor* 94-07. *64 Nursery Close, Acle, Norwich NR13 3EH* Tel (01493) 751287

HALL, Nicholas Charles. b 56. **d** 86 **p** 87. C Hyde St Geo *Ches* 86-89; C Cheadle 89-91; NSM from 91. *58 Warren Avenue, Cheadle SK8 1ND* Tel 0161-491 6758 Fax 491 0285
E-mail nick@domini.org

HALL, Canon Nigel David. b 46. Univ of Wales (Cardiff) BA67 BD76 Lon Univ CertEd68. St Mich Coll Llan 73. **d** 76 **p** 77. C Cardiff St Jo *Llan* 76-81; R Llanbadarn Fawr, Llandegley and Llanfihangel etc *S & B* 81-95; RD Maelienydd 89-95; V Builth and Llanddewi'r Cwm w Llangynog etc 95-11; Can Brecon Cathl 94-11; Prec 99-00; Treas 00-04; Chan 04-11; AD Builth 04-11; rtd 11. *Coedmor, Broadway, Llandrindod Wells LD1 5HT* Tel (01597) 829637

HALL (née WANSTALL), Canon Noelle Margaret. b 53. Wolfs Coll Cam BEd76. Sarum & Wells Th Coll 84. **dss** 86 **d** 87 **p** 94. Hythe *Cant* 86-89; Par Dn 87-89; Par Dn Reculver and Herne Bay St Bart 89-94; C 94-95; Dioc Adv in Women's Min 92-99; Asst Dir Post-Ord Tr 94-97; P-in-c Sittingbourne St Mary 95-00; P-in-c Cant St Martin and St Paul 00-02; R from 02; P-in-c Blean 07-09; Hon Can Cant Cathl from 96; AD Cant 05-11. *The Rectory, 13 Ersham Road, Canterbury CT1 3AR* Tel (01227) 462686 *or* tel and fax 768072
E-mail noelle@thinker117.freeserve.co.uk

HALL, Peter. See HALL, Canon Hubert William Peter

HALL, Peter. See HALL, The Rt Revd Albert Peter

HALL, Peter Douglas. b 60. Oak Hill Th Coll BA92. **d** 92 **p** 93. C Bromyard *Heref* 92-96; C Dorridge *Birm* 96-01; V Fareham St Jo *Portsm* from 01. *St John's Vicarage, 3A Upper St Michael's Grove, Fareham PO14 1DN* Tel (01329) 284203 *or* 280762
E-mail revpdhall@btinternet.com

HALL, Philip Edward Robin. b 36. Oak Hill Th Coll 64. **d** 67 **p** 68. C Ware Ch Ch *St Alb* 67-70; C Rayleigh *Chelmsf* 70-73; R Leven w Catwick *York* 73-85; P-in-c Mayfield *Lich* 85-95; P-in-c Ilam w Blore Ray and Okeover 89-95; Res Min Canwell, Hints and Drayton Bassett 95-01; rtd 01; Perm to Offic *Sheff* from 01 and *Derby* from 02. *45 St Alban's Road, Sheffield S10 4DN* Tel 0114-229 5032

HALL, Richard. See HALL, George Richard Wyndham

HALL, Richard Alexander Bullock. b 71. Ex Univ BA93 Edin Univ MTh95 BD98. TISEC 95. **d** 98 **p** 99. C Boxmoor St Jo *St Alb* 98-01; CF 01-09; Hon Min Can Ripon Cathl 06-09; P-in-c Kirkby Stephen w Mallerstang etc *Carl* 09-11; CF from 11. *c/o MOD Chaplains (Army)* Tel (01264) 381140 Fax 381824
E-mail richard.moonhall@btinternet.com

HALL, Robert Arthur. b 35. Lon Univ BSc66. NW Ord Course 74. **d** 77 **p** 78. C York St Paul 77-79; R Elvington w Sutton on Derwent and E Cottingwith 79-82; Chapl Tiffield Sch Northants 82-84; V Bessingby and Carnaby *York* 84-88; V Fulford 88-00; P-in-c York St Denys 97-00; rtd 00; Perm to Offic *York* from 00. *11 Almond Grove, Filey YO14 9EH* Tel (01723) 518355
E-mail robertandjune@cwctv.net

HALL, Robert Stainburn. b 72. Qu Coll Cam BA93. St Steph Ho Ox 96. **d** 98 **p** 99. C Worc SE 98-01; TV Halas 01-10; P-in-c from 10. *St Margaret's Vicarage, 55 Quarry Lane, Halesowen B63 4PD* Tel 0121-550 8744

HALL, Roger John. b 53. MBE97. Linc Th Coll. **d** 84 **p** 85. C Shrewsbury St Giles w Sutton and Atcham *Lich* 84-87; CF 87-07; Warden Amport Ho 98-01; Chapl Guards Chpl *Lon* 01-03; Asst Chapl Gen 03-07; Dir Ords 98-02 and Warden of Readers 98-07; QHC 06-07; Dep P in O from 07; Chapl St Pet-ad-Vincula at HM Tower of Lon from 07; Chapl Bacon's Coll from 07. *The Chaplain's Residence, HM Tower of London, London EC3N 4AB* Tel (020) 3166 6796
E-mail roger.hall@hrp.org.uk

HALL, Ronald Cecil. b 20. St Aid Birkenhead 63. **d** 65 **p** 66. C Tamworth *Lich* 65-69; R Talke 69-74; V Birstwith *Ripon* 74-90; P-in-c Thornthwaite w Thruscross and Darley 76-77; rtd 90. *Wickham House, Kingsmead, Farm Road, Bracklesham Bay, Chichester PO20 8JU* Tel (01243) 671190

HALL, Mrs Rosalyn. b 58. NEOC 04. **d** 07 **p** 08. C Washington *Dur* 07-11; V Hartlepool H Trin from 11. *Holy Trinity Vicarage, Davison Drive, Hartlepool TS24 9BX* Tel (01429) 869618 Mobile 07985-134577 E-mail rosalyn44@hotmail.com

HALL, Sandra June. b 58. Westcott Ho Cam. **d** 10 **p** 11. C Cuckfield *Chich* from 10. *70 Glebe Road, Cuckfield RH17 5BQ* Tel (01444) 616978

HALL, Sonia Winifred. See RUDD, Mrs Sonia Winifred

HALL, Stephen Philip. b 56. Ripon Coll Cuddesdon. **d** 84 **p** 85. C Camberwell St Giles *S'wark* 84-88; Chapl Brighton Poly *Chich* 88-92; TV Bicester w Bucknell, Caversfield and Launton *Ox* 92-02; Sub Chapl HM Pris Bullingdon 92-02; TV Southampton (City Cen) *Win* from 02. *The Deanery, 100 Chapel Road, Southampton SO14 5GL* Tel and fax (023) 8063 3134

HALL, Prof Stuart George. b 28. New Coll Ox BA52 MA55 BD72. Ripon Hall Ox 53. **d** 54 **p** 55. C Newark w Coddington *S'well* 54-58; Tutor Qu Coll Birm 58-62; Lect Th Nottm Univ 62-73; Sen Lect 73-78; Prof Ecclesiastical Hist K Coll Lon 78-90; Perm to Offic *St Alb* 80-86 and *S'wark* 86-90; R Pittenweem *St And* 90-98; R Elie and Earlsferry 90-98; rtd 93. *Hopedene, 15 High Street, Elie, Leven KY9 1BY* Tel and fax (01333) 330145 E-mail sgh1@st-andrews.ac.uk

HALL, Thomas Bartholomew Berners. b 39. St Fran Coll Brisbane 63 ThL65. **d** 65 **p** 66. Australia 65-75 and from 82; C Townsville Cathl 65-66; C Rockhampton Cathl 66-69; P-in-c Emerald 69-70; R 70-75; P-in-c Whitehawk *Chich* 75-82; V Inglewood and Texas 82-89; V Pine Rivers S 85-89; R Strathpine from 89. *2 Lindale Court, Cashmere Qld 4500, Australia* Tel (0061) (7) 3882 0880 *or* 3881 2090 Mobile 428-711719 E-mail tombbhall@aanet.com.au

HALL, Timothy Patrick. b 65. Bucks Coll of Educn BSc87 Oak Hill Th Coll BA93. Trin Coll Bris 99. **d** 01 **p** 02. C Kingsnorth and Shadoxhurst *Cant* 01-04; P-in-c Crowfield w Stonham Aspal and Mickfield *St E* from 04; P-in-c Coddenham w Gosbeck and Hemingstone w Henley from 04; RD Bosmere 07-08. *The Rectory, The Street, Stonham Aspal, Stowmarket IP14 6AQ* Tel (01449) 711409 E-mail tph@tesco.net

HALL, Timothy Robert. b 52. Dur Univ BA74. St Jo Coll Nottm LTh87. **d** 87 **p** 88. C Hawarden *St As* 87-89; Chapl St D Coll Llandudno from 90. *Woodpecker Cottage, St David's College, Llandudno LL30 1RD* Tel (01492) 581224

HALL, William. b 34. Hull Univ BSc(Econ)56. NEOC 89. **d** 92 **p** 93. NSM Bishopwearmouth St Nic *Dur* 92-01; rtd 01. *31 Nursery Road, Silksworth Lane, Sunderland SR3 1NT* Tel 0191-528 4843

HALL, Canon William Cameron. b 40. K Coll Lon 60. **d** 65 **p** 66. C Thornaby on Tees St Paul *York* 65-68; Chapl to Arts and Recreation *Dur* 68-05; V Grindon 71-80; Hon Can Dur Cathl from 84; Sen Chapl Actors' Ch Union 89-04; Hon Sen Research Fell Sunderland Univ from 98; Hon Fell St Chad's Coll Dur from 09. *41 Ellerby Mews, Thornley, Durham DH6 3FB* Tel (01429) 820869 E-mail billhalluk@yahoo.co.uk

HALL-MATTHEWS, Preb John Cuthbert Berners. b 33. Univ of Qld BA55 K Coll Lon PGCE65. Coll of Resurr Mirfield 58. **d** 60 **p** 61. C Woodley St Jo the Ev *Ox* 60-63; C Is of Dogs Ch Ch and St Jo w St Luke *Lon* 63-65; Asst Chapl Ch Hosp Horsham 65-72; Chapl R Hosp Sch Holbrook 72-75; V Tupsley *Heref* 75-90; P-in-c Hampton Bishop and Mordiford w Dormington 77-90; RD Heref City 84-90; Preb Heref Cathl 85-90; TR Wolverhampton *Lich* 90-98; TR Cen Wolverhampton 98-02; Preb Lich Cathl 01-02; rtd 02. *Hillcrest, Corvedale Road, Halford, Craven Arms SY7 9BT* Tel (01588) 672706
E-mail jotricia@hall-matthews.freeserve.co.uk

HALL-THOMPSON, Colin Lloyd. b 51. JP. TCD. **d** 84 **p** 85. C Dublin Rathfarnham *D & G* 84-86; Bp's C Clonmel Union *C, C & R* 86-91; Chapl Fort Mitchel Pris 86-91; Chapl Port of Cork 86-89; I Kilbride *Conn* 91-03; I Ballymacarrett *D & D* 03-09; Hon Chapl Miss to Seafarers 91-09; Sen Chapl from 09. *7A Wilshere Drive, Belmont, Belfast BT4 2GP* Tel (028) 9022 3910 *or* 9075 1131 Mobile 07984-571220
E-mail colin.hall-thompson@ntlworld.com

HALLAM, Mrs Janet Kay. b 59. EN(G)79 RGN01. STETS 05. **d** 08. NSM Newport St Jo *Portsm* from 08; NSM Newport

St Thos from 08. *Maranatha, 10 Broadwood Lane, Newport PO30 5NE* Tel (01983) 529973 Mobile 07955-381319 E-mail jezjanet@btinternet.com

HALLAM, Lawrence Gordon. b 31. Lich Th Coll 61. **d** 63 **p** 64. C Brighton St Martin *Chich* 63-68; R Cocking w Bepton 68-71; V Eastbourne Ch Ch 71-84; V Bexhill St Barn 84-87; rtd 87; Perm to Offic *Chich* 87-92. *18 Eaton Court, Eaton Gardens, Hove BN3 3PL* Tel (01273) 772328

HALLAM, Mrs Marilyn. d 03 p 04. NSM Hayes *Roch* from 03. *83 Pickhurst Rise, West Wickham, Bromley BR4 0AE* Tel (020) 8777 2246 E-mail lyn.hallam@diocese-rochester.org

HALLAM, Nicholas Francis. b 48. Univ Coll Ox BA71 MA81 Glas Univ PhD76 MB, ChB81 FRCPath00. Ox NSM Course 84. **d** 87 **p** 88. NSM Ox St Clem 87-93; NSM Balerno *Edin* 93-05; NSM Hawkshead and Low Wray w Sawrey and Rusland etc *Carl* from 06; NSM Ambleside w Brathay 06-10; NSM Loughrigg from 10. *Wetherlam, Hawkshead, Ambleside LA22 0NR* Tel (01539) 436069 E-mail nick.hallam@uwclub.net

HALLAM, Canon Peter Hubert. b 33. MBE98. Trin Hall Cam BA56 MA60. Westcott Ho Cam 56. **d** 58 **p** 59. C Heyhouses on Sea *Blackb* 58-62; Asst Chapl and Tutor St Bede Coll Dur 62-67; V Briercliffe *Blackb* 67-98; Hon Can Blackb Cathl 92-98; rtd 98; Perm to Offic *Blackb* from 02. *174 Briercliffe Road, Burnley BB10 2NZ* Tel (01282) 441070

HALLAM, Stuart Peter. b 66. St Martin's Coll Lanc BA92 Wolfs Coll Cam BTh99. Westcott Ho Cam 96. **d** 99 **p** 00. C Battersea St Mary *S'wark* 99-02; Chapl RN from 02. *Royal Naval Chaplaincy Service, Mail Point 1-2, Leach Building, Whale Island, Portsmouth PO2 8BY* Tel (023) 9262 5055 Fax 9262 5134 E-mail revhallam@aol.com

✠**HALLATT, The Rt Revd David Marrison.** b 37. Southn Univ BA59 St Cath Coll Ox BA62 MA66. Wycliffe Hall Ox 59. **d** 63 **p** 64 **c** 94. C Maghull *Liv* 63-67; PC Totley *Derby* 67-75; R Didsbury St Jas *Man* 75-80; R Barlow Moor 76-80; TR Didsbury St Jas and Em 80-89; Adn Halifax *Wakef* 89-94; Area Bp Shrewsbury *Lich* 94-01; Asst Bp Sheff 01-10; rtd 02; Hon Asst Bp Sarum from 11. *10 St Nicholas Hospital, St Nicholas Road, Salisbury SP1 2SW* Tel (01722) 413360 E-mail david.hallatt@btopenworld.com

HALLATT, John Leighton. b 34. St Pet Coll Ox BA58 MA62. Wycliffe Hall Ox 58. **d** 60 **p** 61. C Ipswich St Jo *St E* 60-63; C Warrington St Paul *Liv* 63-66; V Wadsley *Sheff* 66-72; V Hindley St Pet *Liv* 72-75; Area Sec (Scotland and Dios Newc and Dur) CMS 75-83; N Sec CMS 78-83; TR Cramlington *Newc* 83-90; V Monkseaton St Mary 90-99; rtd 99; Perm to Offic *Newc* from 99. *16 Eastfield Avenue, Whitley Bay NE25 8LT* Tel 0191-252 9454

HALLETT, Miss Caroline Morwenna. b 51. Nottm Univ BSc72 PGCE74 Univ of Wales (Ban) BTh05. EAMTC 03. **d** 05 **p** 06. C Sole Bay *St E* 05-09; P-in-c Acton w Gt Waldingfield from 09. *The Vicarage, Melford Road, Acton, Sudbury CO10 0BA* Tel (01787) 377287 E-mail challett@myself.com

HALLETT, Howard Adrian. b 43. Man Univ MPhil90. Oak Hill Th Coll BA81. **d** 81 **p** 82. C Walshaw Ch Ch *Man* 81-84; V Stoke sub Hamdon *B & W* 84-99; RD Ivelchester 91-95; V Kea *Truro* 99-05; rtd 05; Perm to Offic *Truro* from 05. *Tremanda, La Vague, Feock, Truro TR3 6RQ* Tel (01872) 862564

HALLETT, Keith Philip. b 37. Tyndale Hall Bris 61. **d** 64 **p** 65. C Higher Openshaw *Man* 64-68; C Bushbury *Lich* 68-71; P-in-c Drayton Bassett 71-72; R 72-90; V Fazeley 71-90; P-in-c Hints 78-83; V 83-90; C-in-c Canwell CD 78-83; V Canwell 83-90; RD Tamworth 81-90; P-in-c Buckhurst Hill *Chelmsf* 90-93; TR 93-02; rtd 02; Perm to Offic *B & W* from 03. *46 Balmoral Way, Worle, Weston-super-Mare BS22 9AL* Tel (01934) 413711 E-mail kph@webtribe.net

HALLETT, Peter. b 49. Bath Univ BSc72. Oak Hill Th Coll. **d** 76 **p** 77. C Brinsworth w Catcliffe *Sheff* 76-79; P-in-c Doncaster St Jas 80-81; V 81-86; R Henstridge and Charlton Horethorne w Stowell *B & W* 86-07; P-in-c Abbas and Templecombe w Horsington 06-07; R Abbas and Templecombe, Henstridge and Horsington from 07. *The Vicarage, Church Street, Henstridge, Templecombe BA8 0QE* Tel and fax (01963) 362266 E-mail halatvic@btinternet.com

HALLETT, Peter Duncan. b 43. CCC Cam BA66 MA68. Westcott Ho Cam 69. **d** 71 **p** 72. C Sawston *Ely* 71-73; C Lyndhurst and Emery Down *Win* 73-78; C Skegness and Winthorpe *Linc* 78-80; P-in-c Samlesbury *Blackb* 80-91; Asst Dir RE 80-00; C Leyland St Ambrose 91-94; V Lostock Hall 00-09; P-in-c Farington Moss 03-09; V Lostock Hall and Farington Moss 09; rtd 09; Perm to Offic *Blackb* from 09. *31 Southworth House, Larmenier Retirement Village, Preston New Road, Blackburn BB2 7AL*

HALLETT, Raymond. b 44. EMMTC 85. **d** 88 **p** 89. NSM Hucknall Torkard *S'well* 88-01; NSM Basford St Leodegarius 01-03. *26 Nursery Close, Hucknall, Nottingham NG15 6DQ* Tel 0115-953 7677

HALLIDAY, Christopher Norton Robert. b 48. Bradf Univ PhD99. NOC 82. **d** 85 **p** 86. C Davyhulme St Mary *Man* 85-87; Lect Bolton St Pet 87-90; I Rathdrum w Glenealy, Derralossary

and Laragh *D & G* 90-00; R Valley Lee St Geo USA 00-05; Perm to Offic *Man* 07-08; TR Saddleworth from 08. *Lydgate Vicarage, Stockport Road, Lydgate, Oldham OL4 4JJ* Tel (01457) 872117 E-mail christopher@olg.com

HALLIDAY, Mrs Diana Patricia. b 40. ALA66. NOC 89. **d** 92 **p** 94. NSM Burley in Wharfedale *Bradf* 92-95; NSM Harden and Wilsden 95-97; P-in-c Cullingworth 97-05; Chapl Airedale NHS Trust from 04. *7 Kirkstall Gardens, Keighley BD21 5PN* Tel (01535) 606048 E-mail di.halliday@bradford.anglican.org

HALLIDAY, Edwin James. b 35. NW Ord Course 70. **d** 73 **p** 74. C New Bury *Man* 73-76; V Bolton St Phil 76-82; Dioc Communications Officer 82-88; V Radcliffe St Thos and St Jo 82-90; R Gt Lever 90-02; rtd 02; Perm to Offic *Man* from 02. *8 Oxford Close, Farnworth, Bolton BL4 0NF* Tel (01204) 792347

HALLIDAY, Geoffrey Lewis. b 40. Lon Coll of Div LTh66. **d** 66 **p** 67. C W Bridgford *S'well* 66-72; V Woodborough 72-78; P-in-c St Dav Bermuda 78-80; V Rampton *S'well* 80-81; P-in-c Laneham 80-81; P-in-c Treswell and Cottam 80-81; V Rampton w Laneham, Treswell and Cottam 81-85; V Attenborough 85-88; Perm to Offic *Derby* 91-92; NSM Ilkeston St Mary 92-03; rtd 03; Perm to Offic *Derby* from 03. *Frog Hollow, 323 Heanor Road, Ilkeston DE7 8TN* Tel 0115-930 8607 Mobile 07799-111093 E-mail fayandgeoff@froghollow.f9.co.uk

HALLIDAY, Jean Douglas. b 47. NTMTC 99. **d** 01 **p** 02. NSM Forest Gate Em w Upton Cross *Chelmsf* 01-02; NSM E Ham w Upton Park 02-05; NSM Becontree S 05-09; P-in-c Margaretting w Mountnessing and Buttsbury from 09; Dioc Child Protection Adv from 05. *The Vicarage, Penny's Lane, Margaretting, Ingatestone CM4 0HA* Tel (01277) 356277 E mail jhalliday@chelmsford.anglican.org

HALLIDAY, Louisa. b 42. Open Univ BA77 BA94. STETS. **d** 00 **p** 01. NSM Wylye and Till Valley *Sarum* 00-09; rtd 09. *Station House, Great Wishford, Salisbury SP2 0PA* Tel (01722) 790618 E-mail greatwishford@yahoo.co.uk

HALLIDAY, Paula Patricia. *See* ROBINSON, Paula Patricia

✠**HALLIDAY, The Rt Revd Robert Taylor.** b 32. Glas Univ MA54 BD57. Edin Th Coll 55. **d** 57 **p** 58 **c** 90. C St Andrews St Andr *St And* 57-60; C Glas St Marg 60-63; Lect NT Edin Th Coll 63-74; R Edin H Cross 63-83; Tutor Edin Univ 69-71; Can St Mary's Cathl 73-83; R St Andrews St Andr *St And* 83-90; Tutor St Andr Univ 84-90; Bp Bre 90-96; rtd 96; Lic to Offic *Edin* from 97. *28 Forbes Road, Edinburgh EH10 4ED* Tel 0131-221 1490

HALLIGAN, Adrian Ronald. b 69. Ulster Univ MSc96 PGCE05. CITC 06. **d** 11. NSM Antrim All SS *Conn* from 11. *35 Castle Manor, Ballynure, Ballyclare BT39 9GW* Tel (028) 9334 2572 Mobile 07846-451932 E-mail adrian.halligan@sky.com

HALLING, William Laurence. b 43. Linc Coll Ox BA64 MA68 Lon Univ BD68. Tyndale Hall Bris 66. **d** 68 **p** 69. C Beckenham St Jo *Roch* 68-72; C Walton H Trin *Ox* 72-78; V Barrow St Mark *Carl* 78-86; R Kirkheaton *Wakef* 86-04; Chapl Mill Hill Hosp Huddersfield 86-95; rtd 04; Perm to Offic *Wakef* from 04; Dioc Adv on Environmental Issues from 08. *56 Westborough Drive, Halifax HX2 7QL* Tel (01422) 320829 E-mail halling@uwclub.net

HALLIWELL, Christopher Eigil. b 57. Newc Univ BA78. Trin Coll Bris 89. **d** 91 **p** 92. C Mildenhall *St E* 91-94; R Wrentham w Benacre, Covehithe, Frostenden etc 94-97; TV Sileby, Cossington and Seagrave *Leic* 97-01; V Preston St Cuth *Blackb* from 01. *St Cuthbert's Vicarage, 20 Black Bull Lane, Fulwood, Preston PR2 3PX* Tel (01772) 717346 E-mail vicarstcuthberts@btinternet.com

HALLIWELL, Ivor George. b 33. St Cath Coll Cam BA57 MA60. Wells Th Coll 58. **d** 60 **p** 60. C Hanworth St Geo *Lon* 60-62; C Willenhall *Cov* 62-65; C-in-c Whitley St Jas CD 65-68; V Whitley 68-72; V Corton *Nor* 72-77; P-in-c Hopton 72-74; V 74-77; Asst Chapl HM Pris Pentonville 77; Chapl HM Pris Ex 77-83; Chapl HM Pris Wakef 83-85; P-in-c Bickington *Ex* 85-87; P-in-c Ashburton w Buckland-in-the-Moor 85-87; V Ashburton w Buckland in the Moor and Bickington 87-90; Chapl HM Pris Channings Wood 90-97; Lic to Offic *Ex* 90-97; rtd 97; Perm to Offic *Ex* from 97. *Anastasis, Avenue Road, Bovey Tracey, Newton Abbot TQ13 9BQ* Tel (01626) 834899 E-mail ivor@ivorhalliwell.com

HALLIWELL, Canon Michael Arthur. b 28. St Edm Hall Ox BA50 MA53. Ely Th Coll 52. **d** 54 **p** 55. C Welling *S'wark* 54-57; C Bournemouth St Alb *Win* 57-59; Asst Gen Sec C of E Coun on Foreign Relns 59-62; C St Dunstan in the West *Lon* 60-62; Chapl Bonn w Cologne *Eur* 62-67; Chapl RAF 66-67; V Croydon St Andr *Cant* 67-71; R Jersey St Brelade *Win* 71-96; Chapl HM Pris Jersey 75-80; Vice-Dean Jersey *Win* 85-99; Tutor S Dios Minl Tr Scheme 92-96; rtd 96; Hon C Jersey Grouville *Win* 96-99; Hon Can Win Cathl 98-99; Perm to Offic from 99. *1 Alliance Cottages, Awbridge Hill, Romsey SO51 0HF* Tel (01794) 830395 E-mail halliwells@jerseymail.co.uk

HALLOWS, John Martin. b 50. Birm Univ BA78 Lon Univ PGCE82 E Lon Univ MSc93. Oak Hill Th Coll 92. **d** 94 **p** 95. C Boxmoor St Jo *St Alb* 94-98; TV Bracknell *Ox* 98-01; V Barrowford and Newchurch-in-Pendle *Blackb* from 01.

St Thomas's Vicarage, Wheatley Lane Road, Barrowford, Nelson BB9 6QS Tel and fax (01282) 613206 E-mail jhallows@tiscali.co.uk

HALLS, Canon Peter Ernest. b 38. Bris Univ BA62. Tyndale Hall Bris 59. **d** 64 **p** 65. C Blackb St Barn 64-67; C Bromley Ch Ch Roch 67-70; V Halvergate w Tunstall Nor 70-79; V Freethorpe w Wickhampton 71-79; P-in-c Beighton and Moulton 77-79; V Tuckswood 79-90; RD Nor S 86-90; R Brooke, Kirstead, Mundham w Seething and Thwaite 90-03; RD Depwade 91-97 and 01-03; Hon Can Nor Cathl 99-03; rtd 03; Perm to Offic Nor from 03. 1 Church Farm Close, Weston Longville, Norwich NR9 5JY Tel (01603) 880835

HALLS, Susan Mary. See HEMSLEY HALLS, Susan Mary

HALMSHAW, Mrs Stella Mary. b 36. Brighton Coll of Educn TCert57. St Alb Minl Tr Scheme 81. **dss** 84 **d** 87 **p** 96. Radlett St Alb 84-01; Par Dn 87-93; Hon C 93-01; Chapl Herts Univ 93-96; rtd 96; NSM Wittersham w Stone and Ebony Cant from 01. The Rectory, The Street, Wittersham, Tenterden TN30 7EA Tel (01797) 270142

HALSALL, Graham. b 61. Sheff Univ BA82 Westmr Coll Ox PGCE84. St Steph Ho Ox MTh00. **d** 00 **p** 01. C Preston St Jo and St Geo Blackb 00-02; C Torrisholme 02-04; P-in-c Bamber Bridge St Sav from 04. St Saviour's Vicarage, Church Road, Bamber Bridge, Preston PR5 6AJ Tel (01772) 335374 E-mail graham@halsall4461.freeserve.co.uk

HALSALL, Mrs Isobel Joan. b 47. Liv Univ CertEd71. Local Minl Tr Course 91. **d** 94 **p** 95. OLM Walshaw Ch Ch Man 94-05; NSM Cockermouth Area Carl from 05. The Vicarage, Bridekirk, Cockermouth CA13 0PE Tel (01900) 826557 E-mail stbridgets@tiscali.co.uk

HALSEY, Anthony Michael James. b 35. K Coll Cam BA56 MA62 Solicitor 64. St Jo Coll Nottm 73. **d** 75 **p** 76. C Derby St Werburgh 75-77; Chapl Canford Sch 78-87; TV Sanderstead All SS S'wark 87-89; Perm to Offic Portsm from 89; rtd 00. Woodlands, South Road, Liphook GU30 7HS Tel (01428) 724549 E-mail halseys@southroad.fsbusiness.co.uk

HALSEY, Brother John Walter Brooke. b 33. Cam Univ BA57. Westcott Ho Cam 61. **d** 61 **p** 62. C Stocksbridge Sheff 61-65; Community of the Transfiguration Midlothian from 65; Ind Chapl Edin 65-69. Hermitage of the Transfiguration, 23 Manse Road, Roslin EH25 9LF

HALSON, Bryan Richard. b 32. Jes Coll Cam BA56 MA60 Liv Univ MA72 Geneva Univ 59. Ridley Hall Cam 57. **d** 59 **p** 60. C Coulsdon St Andr S'wark 59-62; Lic to Offic Ches 63-68; Tutor St Aid Birkenhead 63-65; Sen Tutor 65-68; Vice-Prin 68-69; Lect Alsager Coll of Educn 69-72; Prin Lect Crewe and Alsager Coll of HE 72-90; Perm to Offic Ches from 97. 1 Victoria Mill Drive, Willaston, Nantwich CW5 6RR

HALSTEAD, James. b 74. Nottm Univ BA97. Oak Hill Th Coll MTh09. **d** 09 **p** 10. C Gee Cross Ches from 09. 121 Dowson Road, Hyde SK14 5HJ Tel 0161-366 5083 E-mail jameshalstead@mac.com

HALSTEAD, Stuart. NTMTC 02. **d** 05 **p** 06. C Houghton Regis St Alb 05-08; C Kilburn St Aug w St Jo Lon 08-10; V Gt Ilford St Alb Chelmsf from 10. The Vicarage, 99 Albert Road, Ilford IG1 1HS Tel (020) 8478 2031 E-mail stuart.halstead@btinternet.com

HALTON, Tony James. b 66. Dundee Univ BSc88 City Univ MSc01 RGN94. NTMTC BA06. **d** 06 **p** 07. NSM W Hendon St Jo Lon from 06. 29 Pageant Road, St Albans AL1 1NB Tel (01727) 893229 E-mail tonyjhalton@hotmail.com

✠**HAMBIDGE, The Most Revd Douglas Walter.** b 27. Lon Univ BD58. ALCD53 Angl Th Coll (BC) DD70. **d** 53 **p** 54 **c** 69. C Dalston St Mark w St Bart Lon 53-56; Canada 56-93 and from 95; R Cassiar 56-58; R Smithers 58-64; R Fort St John 64-69; Can Caledonia 65-69; Bp Caledonia 69-80; Bp New Westmr 80; Abp New Westmr and Metrop BC 81-93; Prin St Mark's Th Coll Dar es Salaam 93-95; Asst Bp Dar-es-Salaam 93-95; Chan Vancouver Sch of Th from 95. 1621 Golf Club Drive, Delta BC V4M 4E6, Canada Tel (001) (604) 948 1931 E-mail hambidge@vst.edu

HAMBIDGE, John Robert. b 29. Birm Univ MA02. Sarum Th Coll. **d** 55 **p** 56. C Tynemouth H Trin W Town Newc 55-57; C Middlesbrough St Jo the Ev York 58-63; C Clerkenwell H Redeemer w St Phil Lon 63-64; C Richmond St Mary S'wark 64-66; V Richmond St Jo 66-76; R Swanscombe Roch 76-84; V Aberedw w Llandeilo Graban and Llanbadarn etc S & B 84-91; P-in-c Sibson w Sheepy and Ratcliffe Culey Leic 91-94; P-in-c Orton-on-the-Hill w Twycross etc 92-94; R The Sheepy Gp 95-97; rtd 97; Perm to Offic Lich from 99. 99 Elizabeth Drive, Tamworth B79 8DE Tel (01827) 61526 E-mail john@hambidge.com

HAMBLEN, John William Frederick. b 24. Sarum Th Coll 64. **d** 65 **p** 66. C Weymouth H Trin Sarum 66-68; C Marlborough 68-70; V Chardstock 70-77; P-in-c Lytchett Matravers 77-83; P-in-c Burpham Chich 83-89; Dioc Stewardship Adv 83-89; rtd 89; Perm to Offic Ex 89-09. 2 Woodridge Mead, Bishops Lydeard, Taunton TA4 3PQ

HAMBLIN, Derek Gordon Hawthorn. b 35. SWMTC 94. **d** 96 **p** 97. NSM S Brent and Rattery Ex 96-01; Chapl Larnaca Cyprus 01-02; Asst Chapl Dubai UAE 03-04; Perm to Offic Ex and Cyprus and the Gulf from 04. 2 Brookwood Close, South Brent TQ10 9DH Tel (01364) 72388 or (00357) (24) 620455 E-mail derekthecleric1@aol.com

HAMBLIN, Mrs Karen Elizabeth. b 59. St Mary's Coll Dur BA80 Homerton Coll Cam PGCE82. St Jo Coll Nottm 05. **d** 07 **p** 08. C Long Eaton St Jo Derby 07-11; TV N Wingfield, Clay Cross and Pilsley from 11. The New Vicarage, Morton Road, Pilsley, Chesterfield S45 8EF Tel 07711-664649 (mobile) E-mail andrew.hamblin1@virgin.net

HAMBLIN, Canon Roger Noel. b 42. Ripon Hall Ox 67. **d** 70 **p** 71. C Scotforth Blackb 70-73; C Altham w Clayton le Moors 73-76; V Cockerham w Winmarleigh 76-87; V Cockerham w Winmarleigh and Glasson 87-00; P-in-c Wray w Tatham and Tatham Fells 00-03; V E Lonsdale 03-09; Agric Chapl 01-09; Hon Can Blackb Cathl 04-09; rtd 09; Perm to Offic Blackb from 09. Wycoller, School Lane, Pilling, Preston PR3 6AA Tel (01253) 790555 E-mail rogerhamblin@yahoo.co.uk

HAMBLING, Paul Gary. b 73. St Steph Ho Ox 05. **d** 07 **p** 08. C Woodbridge St Mary St E 07-10; TV Merton Priory S'wark from 10. St John's Vicarage, 135 High Path, London SW19 2JY Tel (020) 8542 7969 E-mail vicarpaul@yahoo.co.uk

HAMBORG, Graham Richard. b 52. Bris Univ BSc73 Nottm Univ BA76 MTh77. St Jo Coll Nottm 74. **d** 77 **p** 78. C Tile Cross Birm 77-80; C Upton cum Chalvey Ox 80-82; TV 82-86; V Ruscombe and Twyford 86-04; AD Sonning 03-04; CME Adv Chelmsf from 04; C Gt Baddow from 04; C Lt Baddow from 05. The Rectory, Colam Lane, Little Baddow, Chelmsford CM3 4SY Tel (01245) 222454 E-mail revghamborg@hotmail.com

HAMBORG, Peter Graham. b 79. BMus00. Trin Coll Bris BA09. **d** 10 **p** 11. C Fulwood Ch Ch Blackb from 10. 24 Greystock Avenue, Fulwood, Preston PR2 9QL Tel (01772) 497213 Mobile 07771-993004 E-mail christchurchcurate@hotmail.co.uk

HAMBROOK, Peter John. b 37. **d** 01 **p** 02. OLM Gt Mongeham w Ripple and Sutton by Dover Cant 01-04; OLM Deal St Leon w St Rich and Sholden etc 04-10; OLM Ringwould w Kingsdown and Ripple etc 05-10; Perm to Offic from 11. 4 Brewery Cottages, Northbourne Road, Great Mongeham, Deal CT14 0HA Tel (01304) 364457 E-mail peter@4brewerycotts.fsnet.co.uk

HAMEL COOKE, Ian Kirk. b 17. Birm Univ BA39. Chich Th Coll 39. **d** 41 **p** 42. C Bedminster St Fran Bris 41-43; C Alton All SS Win 43-48; V N Baddesley 48-55; R Hartest w Boxted St E 55-63; V Addlestone Guildf 63-75; R Tittleshall w Godwick and Wellingham Nor 75-76; R Tittleshall w Godwick, Wellingham and Weasenham 76-82; rtd 82; Perm to Offic Nor 82-09. Millfield, Norton Road, Great Ashfield, Bury St Edmunds IP31 3HJ Tel (01359) 244453

HAMER, David Handel. b 41. Cape Town Univ BA61 Trin Coll Ox BA66. Coll of Resurr Mirfield 62. **d** 66 **p** 67. S Africa 66-73; C Claremont 66-70; Chapl St Paul's Coll Grahamstown 70-73; Chapl Blundell's Sch Tiverton 73-01; rtd 01. Jaspers Green, Uplowman, Tiverton EX16 7DP Tel (01884) 829130

HAMER, Irving David. b 59. **d** 84 **p** 85. C Newton Nottage Llan 84-88; C Roath 88-90; V Llansawel, Briton Ferry 90-00; V Roath St Martin from 00; Miss to Seafarers from 90. St Martin's Vicarage, Strathnairn Street, Roath, Cardiff CF24 3JL Tel (029) 2048 2295 E-mail fr.irving.hamer@ntlworld.com

HAMER, Penelope Ann. See WEST, Penelope Ann

HAMER, Canon Val. b 52. Leeds Univ BA74. S'wark Ord Course 83. **dss** 86 **d** 87 **p** 94. Warlingham w Chelsham and Farleigh S'wark 86-88; Par Dn 87-88; Par Dn Caterham 88-94; C 94-96; RD Caterham 95-96; Sub Chapl HM Pris Wandsworth 98-99; V Addiscombe St Mildred S'wark 96-02; Ldr Post Ord Tr Croydon Area 94-99; Can Res and Chan Heref Cathl 02-08; Dioc Missr and P-in-c Coychurch, Llangan and St Mary Hill from 08. The Rectory, 9 Heol Cae Tyla, Coychurch, Bridgend CF35 5HR Tel (01656) 656313 E-mail valhamer@churchinwales.org.uk

✠**HAMID, The Rt Revd David.** b 55. McMaster Univ Ontario BSc78. Trin Coll Toronto MDiv81 Hon DD05. **d** 81 **p** 82 **c** 02. C Burlington St Chris Canada 81-83; R Burlington St Jo 83-87; Miss Co-ord Gen Syn of Angl Ch of Canada 87-96; Hon Can Santo Domingo 93-02; Dir Ecum Affairs ACC 96-02; Suff Bp Eur from 02; Hon Asst Bp Roch from 03; Hon C Orpington St Andr from 03. 14 Tufton Street, London SW1P 3QZ Tel (020) 7898 1160 Fax 7898 1166 E-mail david.hamid@churchofengland.org

HAMIL, Sheila. b 49. Northd Coll of Educn TCert71. NEOC 92. **d** 95 **p** 98. NSM Wallsend St Luke Newc 95-97; NSM Long Benton St Mary 97-02; NSM Willington 02-06; rtd 06; Perm to Offic Newc from 06. 5 Kings Road, Wallsend NE28 7QT Tel 0191-287 3449 E-mail sheila@sheilahamil.co.uk

HAMILL-STEWART, Simon Francis. b 32. Pemb Coll Cam BA56. NOC 77. **d** 80 **p** 81. NSM Neston Ches 80-83; C 83-86; V Over St Jo 86-00; Dioc Ecum Officer 92-00; rtd 00; Perm to Offic Ches 00-01 and from 04; C Middlewich w Byley 01-03.

87 Warmingham Lane, Middlewich CW10 0DJ Tel (01606)
737329
HAMILTON, Graham. *See* HAMILTON, William Graham
HAMILTON, John Frederick. b 57. Leeds Univ BA78. Edin Th
Coll 78. **d** 80 **p** 81. C Whitkirk *Ripon* 80-83; C Leeds Belle Is
St Jo and St Barn 83-86; V Oulton w Woodlesford 86-94; V
Cookridge H Trin from 94. *Cookridge Vicarage, 53 Green Lane,
Cookridge, Leeds LS16 7LW* Tel 0113-267 4921 Fax 261 2102
Mobile 07780-677341 E-mail sulaco57@btopenworld.com
HAMILTON, John Hans Patrick. b 44. K Coll Lon BD66
AKC67 Lon Univ DipAdEd76 FCMI96. St Boniface
Warminster 66. **d** 67 **p** 68. C Cleobury Mortimer w Hopton
Wafers *Heref* 67-69; C Sanderstead All SS *S'wark* 69-73; V
Battersea St Mary-le-Park 73-75; Perm to Offic *Ely* 75-90; Dir of
Educn *Derby* 90-95; P-in-c Cliddesden and Ellisfield w Farleigh
Wallop etc *Win* 95-00; Perm to Offic 00-03; P-in-c Dungeon Hill
and The Caundles w Folke and Holwell *Sarum* 03-07; TR Wylye
and Till Valley 07-11; rtd 11. *Hopper Cottage, Wylye Road,
Hanging Langford, Salisbury SP3 4NW* Tel (01722) 790117
E-mail johnhamilton365@gwa.1.com
HAMILTON, John Nicholas. b 49. Trin Coll Cam BA71 MA75.
Ridley Hall Cam 72. **d** 75 **p** 76. C Ealing Dean St Jo *Lon* 75-79; C
Stoughton *Guildf* 79-83; R Denton St Lawr *Man* 83-88; R The
Sherbornes w Pamber *Win* from 88. *The Rectory, Vyne Road,
Sherborne St John, Basingstoke RG24 9HX* Tel (01256) 850434
E-mail jnh@btinternet.com
HAMILTON, Nigel John. *See* TABER-HAMILTON, Nigel John
HAMILTON, Canon Noble Ridgeway. b 23. TD66. TCD BA45
MA49. **d** 47 **p** 48. C Dundela St Mark *D & D* 47-51; C
Holywood 51-55; I Belfast St Clem 55-61; I Seapatrick 61-89;
Can Dromore Cathl 84-89; Prec 75-84; Chan 84-89; rtd 89; Lic to
Offic *D & D* from 90. *67 Meadowvale, Waringstown, Craigavon
BT66 7RL* Tel (028) 3888 2064
HAMILTON, Paul Stuart. b 69. Univ of Wales (Ban) BTh02.
EAMTC. **d** 02 **p** 03. C Hawkwell *Chelmsf* 02-06; V Ingrave
St Nic and St Steph from 06. *The Rectory, Thorndon Gate,
Ingrave, Brentwood CM13 3RG* Tel (01277) 812190
E-mail pshamilton@btinternet.com
HAMILTON, Richard Alexander. *See* HAMILTON, Ryszard
Janusz
HAMILTON, Ryszard Janusz. b 46. Pemb Coll Cam BA67
MA87 Brunel Univ PGCE97. G Dios Minl Tr Scheme 82. **d** 85
p 86. NSM Guernsey St Sampson *Win* 85-89; C Highgate
St Mich *Lon* 89-91; P-in-c Tottenham H Trin 91-96; Master
Denbigh High Sch Luton 96-98; TV The Ortons, Alwalton and
Chesterton *Ely* 98-10; V Orton Waterville from 10. *The Rectory,
67 Church Drive, Orton Waterville, Peterborough PE2 5HE* Tel
(01733) 238877 Mobile 07958-317512 E-mail hamvic@aol.com
HAMILTON, William Graham. b 63. New Coll Ox BA86.
Wycliffe Hall Ox BA95. **d** 95 **p** 96. C Ivybridge w Harford *Ex*
95-99; V Bovey Tracey SS Pet, Paul and Thos w Hennock from
99. *The Vicarage, Coombe Cross, Bovey Tracey, Newton Abbot
TQ13 9EP* Tel (01626) 833813 E-mail pptbovey@mac.com
HAMILTON, William Joseph Taylor. b 40. Univ Coll Ches
MTh00. **d** 97 **p** 98. NSM Ches 97-02; C Thurlestone, S Milton,
W Alvington etc *Ex* 02-07; rtd 07; Perm to Offic *Ches* from 07.
51 Vincent Drive, Chester CH4 7RQ Tel (01244) 428457
E-mail william-hamilton3@sky.com
HAMILTON-BROWN, James John. b 35. Lon Univ BSc63.
Ridley Hall Cam 59. **d** 61 **p** 62. C Attenborough w Bramcote
S'well 61-67; V Bramcote 67-76; R and D Officer Abps' Coun on
Evang 76-79; Lic to Offic *Sarum* 76-81 and 91-95; TR
Dorchester 81-91; Sec Par and People 91-95; P-in-c Tarrant
Valley 95-99; C Tollard Royal w Farnham, Gussage St Michael
etc 99-00; rtd 00; Perm to Offic *Sarum* from 00. *April Cottage,
West Street, Winterborne Stickland, Blandford Forum DT11 0NT*
Tel (01258) 880627 E-mail jumperhb@btinternet.com
HAMILTON-MANON, Phillip Robert Christian. b 49. BA88.
St Steph Ho Ox 89. **d** 90 **p** 91. C Norton St Mary *Dur* 90-94;
P-in-c Cleadon Park 94-95; V 95-97; TV Lewes All SS, St Anne,
St Mich and St Thos *Chich* 97-00; R Lewes St Anne 00-10; R
Lewes St Anne and St Mich and St Thos etc from 10. *St Anne's
Rectory, 57 St Anne's Crescent, Lewes BN7 1SD* Tel (01273)
472545 E-mail hamilton-manon@aol.com
HAMLET, Paul Manning. b 42. Open Univ BA81 Ex Univ
MEd96 Univ of Wales (Lamp) MTh04 Lambeth STh84
FCollP96. Kelham Th Coll 61. **d** 66 **p** 67. C Rumboldswyke
Chich 66-69; C Ely 69-73; Hon C Ipswich St Bart *St E* 73-84;
Chapl Wellington Sch Somerset 84-94; Chapl Ipswich Sch 94-02;
CF (TAVR) 88-99; CF (ACF) from 99; rtd 02; Perm to Offic *St E*
from 02. *5 Wincanton Close, Ipswich IP4 3EE* Tel (01473)
724413 E-mail paul.hamlet@btopenworld.com
HAMLEY, Mrs Isabelle Maryvonne. b 75. Orléans Univ BA95
MA96 Birm Univ BA03. St Jo Coll Nottm 09. **d** 11. C W
Bridgford *S'well* from 11. *7 South Road, West Bridgford,
Nottingham NG2 7AG* Tel 07850-402321 (mobile)
E-mail isabellehamley@yahoo.co.uk
HAMMERSLEY, Peter Angus Ragsdale. b 35. Linc Th Coll 74.
d 76 **p** 77. C Stafford *Lich* 76-79; P-in-c W Bromwich St Andr

79-83; V 83-88; P-in-c W Bromwich Ch Ch 85-88; V Streetly
88-98; RD Walsall 90-98; C Ledbury *Heref* 98-00; Team Chapl
W Heref 98-00; rtd 01; Assoc TV Ledbury *Heref* 01-04; Perm to
Offic from 04. *15 Pound Close, Tarrington, Hereford HR1 4AZ*
Tel (01432) 890609
HAMMERSLEY, Susan. b 67. Nottm Univ BA90. Ripon Coll
Cuddesdon BA07. **d** 07 **p** 08. C Ecclesfield *Sheff* 07-10; C Sheff
St Mark Broomhill from 10. *9 Betjeman Gardens, Sheffield
S10 3FW* Tel 0114-327 6908
E-mail suehammersley@tiscali.co.uk
HAMMETT, The Ven Barry Keith. b 47. CB06. Magd Coll Ox
BA71 MA74. St Steph Ho Ox 71. **d** 74 **p** 75. C Plymouth St Pet
Ex 74-77; Chapl RN 77-02; Chapl of the Fleet and Adn for the
RN 02-06; Dir Gen Naval Chapl Service 02-06; QHC from 99;
Hon Can Portsm Cathl from 02; Can Gib Cathl from 03; rtd 06;
Perm to Offic *Portsm* from 07. *1 de Port Heights, Corhampton,
Southampton SO32 3DA*
HAMMILL, Anthony Lawrence. b 71. Linc Coll Ox BA92 MA97
Univ Coll Lon MSc95 Anglia Ruskin Univ MA08 Fitzw Coll
Cam MPhil08. Ridley Hall Cam 05. **d** 08 **p** 09. C Chalk *Roch*
from 08. *6 Dene Holm Road, Northfleet, Gravesend DA11 8LE*
E-mail anthony.hammill@diocese-rochester.org
HAMMON, David Edward. b 48. St Mich Coll Llan 99. **d** 01 **p** 02.
C Pembroke Dock *St D* 01-04; Perm to Offic 04-08; P-in-c
Lampeter Velfrey and Llanddewi Velfrey from 10; Dioc Officer
for Soc Resp from 10. *St David's, Church Street,
Templeton, Narberth SA67 8RT* Tel (01834) 861142 Mobile
07779-711239 E-mail revdavid.hammon@btinternet.com
HAMMOND, Andrew Charles Raphael. b 63. Clare Coll Cam
BA86 K Coll Cam MPhil07 LRAM91. Westcott Ho Cam 05.
d 07 **p** 08. C St John's Wood *Lon* 07-09; Min Can and Succ
St Paul's Cathl from 09. *7A Amen Court, London EC4M 7BU*
Tel (020) 7248 6151 Mobile 07884-185207
E-mail andrewch007@hotmail.com
HAMMOND, Mrs Barbara Watson. b 33. Lanc Univ MA79 Bp
Otter Coll TCert53 ACP70. S'wark Ord Course 89. **d** 92 **p** 94.
NSM Upper Norwood St Jo *S'wark* 92-94; Hon C Spring Park
All SS 94-97; Perm to Offic *S'wark* 97-02 and *Portsm* from 98.
27 Maisemore Gardens, Emsworth PO10 7JU Tel (01243)
370531 E-mail barbara@br2811.demon.co.uk
HAMMOND, Canon Brian Leonard. b 31. Bris Univ BSc54.
Wells Th Coll 56. **d** 58 **p** 59. C Clapham H Trin *S'wark* 58-62; V
Walworth All SS and St Steph 62-72; V S Merstham 72-87; RD
Reigate 80-86; Hon Can S'wark Cathl 83-97; V Spring Park All
SS 87-97; rtd 97; Perm to Offic *S'wark* 97-02; *Portsm* from 98;
Chich from 05. *27 Maisemore Gardens, Emsworth PO10 7JU* Tel
(01243) 370531 Mobile 07802-482974
E-mail brian@br2811.demon.co.uk
HAMMOND, Carolyn John-Baptist. b 64. St Jo Coll Ox MA90
Univ Coll Ox DPhil93 CCC Cam BA97 MA02. Westcott Ho
Cam 95. **d** 98 **p** 99. C Gamlingay w Hatley St George and E
Hatley *Ely* 98-99; C Gamlingay and Everton 99-01; R 01-05;
Dean G&C Coll Cam from 05. *Gonville and Caius College,
Trinity Street, Cambridge CB2 1TA* Tel (01223) 332400 Fax
332336 E-mail cjbh2@cam.ac.uk
HAMMOND, David Geoffrey. b 80. Glos Univ BA02. Cranmer
Hall Dur 02. **d** 04 **p** 05. NSM Preston-on-Tees and Longnewton
Dur 04-06; C 06-08; Pioneer Missr and P-in-c Nottingham St Sav
S'well from 08. *St Saviour's Vicarage, Arkwright Walk,
Nottingham NG2 2JU* Tel 0115-952 4860 Mobile 07939-464095
E-mail dave@saviours.org.uk
HAMMOND, Diana Mary. b 46. **d** 99 **p** 00. OLM Bishopstrow
and Boreham *Sarum* 99-04; OLM Upper Wylye Valley from 04.
123A Park Lane, Heytesbury, Warminster BA12 0HE Tel
(01985) 841185 E-mail roger.hammond12@virginmedia.com
HAMMOND, Kathryn Mary. b 49. JP. LCTP 07. **d** 08 **p** 09. NSM
Linton in Craven and Burnsall w Rylstone *Bradf* 08-11; NSM
Adbaston, High Offley, Knightley, Norbury etc *Lich* from 11.
Church House, Newport Road, Woodseaves, Stafford ST20 0NP
Tel (01785) 284648 E-mail ckham@tiscali.co.uk
HAMMOND, Canon Lindsay John. b 57. Southn Univ BA83.
Sarum & Wells Th Coll 84. **d** 86 **p** 87. C Ashford *Cant* 86-90; V
Appledore w Brookland, Fairfield, Brenzett etc 90-03; P-in-c
Stone-in-Oxney 95-03; RD S Lympne 95-01; P-in-c Westwell and
Hothfield 03-11; P-in-c Charing w Charing Heath and Lt Chart
06-11; AD Ashford 09-11; V Tenterden and Smallhythe from 11;
Hon Min Can Cant Cathl 93-08; Hon Can from 08. *The
Vicarage, Church Road, Tenterden TN30 6AT* Tel (01580) 761951
E-mail lindsayhammond@hotmail.co.uk
HAMMOND, Martin James. b 62. St Jo Coll Nottm 03. **d** 05
p 06. C Walmley *Birm* 05-08; C Erdington 08-09; TV Bedworth
Cov from 09. *2 Bryony Close, Bedworth CV12 0GG* Tel (024)
7664 4693 E-mail revmartinh@blueyonder.co.uk
HAMMOND, Michael John. b 36. St Jo Coll Dur BA57 MA65.
NW Ord Course 73. **d** 76. NSM Formby St Pet *Liv* 76-80; Sen
Lect Nor City Coll 86-01; Lect Guon Inst of HE Italy 01-06; rtd
06; Perm to Offic *Nor* from 09. *7 Friars Quay, Norwich NR3 1ES*
Tel (01603) 614969

HAMMOND, Peter Clark. b 27. Linc Coll Ox BA49 MA53. Wells Th Coll 51. d 52 p 53. C Willesborough *Cant* 52-55; C Croydon St Jo 55-59; R Barham 60-66; V Walmer 66-85; V Rolvenden 85-89; rtd 89; Perm to Offic *Ely* from 89. *19 Hardwick Street, Cambridge CB3 9JA* Tel (01223) 467425

HAMPEL, Canon Michael Hans Joachim. b 67. Univ Coll Dur BA89 St Chad's Coll Dur MA02 FRSA02. Westcott Ho Cam 90. d 93 p 94. C Whitworth w Spennymoor *Dur* 93-97; Min Can, Prec and Sacr Dur Cathl 97-02; Sen Tutor St Chad's Coll Dur 02-04; Can Res St E Cathl 04-11; Sub Dean 08-11; Can Res and Prec St Paul's Cathl from 11. *1 Amen Court, London EC4M 7BU* Tel (020) 7248 1817 Fax 7246 3104 E-mail michael.hampel@dunelm.org.uk

HAMPSON, Claude Eric. b 25. Rhodes Univ BA49. St Paul's Coll Grahamstown LTh50. d 50 p 51. C Pietermaritzburg Cathl S Africa 50-54; C Greenford H Cross *Lon* 54-58; Sec Fellowship of SS Alb and Sergius 58-60; Brotherhood of St Barn Australia 60-66; R Mt Isa and Adn of the W 67-74; priest-in-charge Mekong Vietnam 74-75; V Kilburn St Aug w St Jo *Lon* 75-77; R Branxton Australia 77-82; rtd 85. *17/250 Jersey Road, Woollahra NSW 2025, Australia* Tel (0061) (2) 9327 8215

HAMPSON, David. b 46. Chich Th Coll 69. d 72 p 73. C Penrith *Carl* 72-78; V Crosscrake 78-95; V Crosscrake and Preston Patrick 95; priest-in-charge Arnside 95-97; rtd 97. *81 Rectory Road, North Ashton, Wigan WN4 0QD* Tel (01942) 728760

HAMPSON, Miss Judith Elizabeth. b 50. I M Marsh Coll of Physical Educn Liv BEd72 Open Univ BA89. Ripon Coll Cuddesdon 90. d 92 p 94. C Alnwick *Newc* 92-96; R Allendale w Whitfield 96-05; V Haydon Bridge and Beltingham w Henshaw from 05. *The Vicarage, Haydon Bridge, Hexham NE47 6LL* Tel (01434) 684307 E-mail rev.jude@dsl.pipex.com

HAMPSON, Michael John. b 67. Jes Coll Ox BA88. Ripon Coll Cuddesdon 88. d 91 p 92. C W Burnley All SS *Blackb* 91-93; C Harlow St Mary Magd *Chelmsf* 93-00; V Church Langley 00-04; Perm to Offic *Blackb* from 10. *Station House, Arkholme, Carnforth LA6 1AZ* Tel (015242) 21712 Mobile 07712-477003 E-mail michael.hampson.mobile@googlemail.com

HAMPSON, Robert Edward. b 58. LSE BSc80 Heythrop Coll Lon BA91 MTh93. Ridley Hall Cam. d 97 p 98. C Chingford SS Pet and Paul *Chelmsf* 97-01; V Wanstead H Trin Hermon Hill from 01. *Holy Trinity Vicarage, 185 Hermon Hill, London E18 1QQ* Tel (020) 8530 3029 E-mail robertthampson@btopenworld.com

HAMPSTEAD, Archdeacon of. See MILLER, The Ven Luke Jonathan

HAMPTON, Alison Jean. b 61. St Mary's Coll Twickenham BA98. SEITE 98. d 01 p 02. C Notting Dale St Clem w St Mark and St Jas *Lon* 01-04; priest-in-charge Burrough Hill Pars *Leic* 04-06; Chapl Brooksby Melton Coll 04-06; priest-in-charge Husbands Bosworth w Mowsley and Knaptoft etc *Leic* 06-09; R Hexagon 09-10. *67 Lodge Road, Stratford-upon-Avon CV37 9DN* E-mail gladthatilive@hotmail.com

HAMPTON, Canon Carla Irene. b 47. ARCM67 GRSM68. NTMTC 96. d 99 p 00. Asst Chapl Mid-Essex Hosp Services NHS Trust 98-02; Chapl Team Ldr 02-04; NSM Chelmsf St Andr 99-04; NSM Gt and Lt Leighs and Lt Waltham 04-06; priest-in-charge Gt Waltham w Ford End 06-10; V from 10; RD Chelmsf N from 07; Hon Can Chelmsf Cathl from 08. *1 Glebe Meadow, Great Waltham, Chelmsford CM3 1EX* Tel (01245) 364081 E-mail carla@hamptonc.freeserve.co.uk

HAMPTON, Canon John Waller. b 28. Linc Coll Ox BA51 MA58. Westcott Ho Cam 51. d 53 p 54. C Rugby St Andr *Cov* 53-56; Chapl St Paul's Sch Hammersmith 56-65; Chapl St Paul's Girls' Sch Hammersmith 60-65; V Gaydon w Chadshunt *Cov* 65-69; Asst Dir RE 65-70; C-in-c Warwick St Nic 69-75; Fell Qu Coll Birm 75-76; priest-in-charge Wetton *Lich* 76-82; priest-in-charge Alstonfield 76-82; priest-in-charge Sheen 76-80; RD Alstonfield 80-82; priest-in-charge Butterton 80-82; priest-in-charge Warslow and Elkstones 80-82; priest-in-charge Broadway *Worc* 82-91; V 91-93; RD Evesham 87-93; Hon Can Worc Cathl 89-93; rtd 93; Perm to Offic *Ab* from 93. *87 Ruthrieston Crescent, Aberdeen AB10 7JS* Tel (01224) 593532

HAMPTON, Stephen William Peter. b 72. Magd Coll Cam BA93 MA97 Ex Coll Ox MSt99 DPhil02. Wycliffe Hall Ox BA95 MA98. d 96 p 97. C St Neots *Ely* 96-98; Chapl and Fell Ex Coll Ox 98-03; Sen Tutor St Jo Coll Dur 04-07; Hon Min Can Dur Cathl 05-07; Fell and Dean Peterho Cam from 07. *Peterhouse, Cambridge CB2 1RD* Tel (01223) 338217 Fax 337578 E-mail swph2@cam.ac.uk

HANAWAY, Peter Louis. b 47. Open Univ BA85 Middx Univ BA02. NTMTC 99. d 02 p 03. NSM Westmr St Matt *Lon* from 02. *St Matthew's House, 20 Great Peter Street, London SW1P 2BU* Tel (020) 7222 3704 Mobile 07947-722219 E-mail peter.hanaway@cwctv.com *or* fr.peter@stmw.org

HANCE, Mrs Joy. b 47. Cam Inst of Educn. SAOMC 99. d 02 p 03. NSM Cherbury w Gainfield *Ox* from 02. *The Vicarage, Buckland, Faringdon SN7 8QN* Tel (01367) 870618 Mobile 07752-187014 E-mail joysmail@talk21.com

HANCE, Mrs Marion. b 49. d 01 p 02. OLM Cheddington w Mentmore and Marsworth *Ox* 01-08; NSM Quantock Coast *B & W* from 08. *Shardloes, Staple Lane, West Quantoxhead, Taunton TA4 4DE* E-mail marion2212.hance@virgin.net

HANCE, Stephen John. b 66. Portsm Poly BSc89 Nottm Univ BTh92 MA93. St Jo Coll Nottm 90. d 93 p 94. C Southsea St Jude *Portsm* 93-96; TV Tollington *Lon* 96-99; V Balham Hill Ascension *S'wark* from 99. *Ascension Vicarage, 22 Malwood Road, London SW12 8EN* Tel (020) 8673 7666 *or* 8675 8626 Fax 8516 9429 *or* 8673 3796 E-mail stephen.hance@virgin.net

HANCOCK, Mrs Barbara. b 40. TCert60. EMMTC 93. d 96 p 04. NSM Caythorpe *Linc* 96-08; Perm to Offic from 08. *Fulbeck Cottage, Sudthorpe Hill, Fulbeck, Grantham NG32 3LE* Tel (01400) 272644 E-mail bchancock@lincone.net

HANCOCK, Christopher David. b 54. Qu Coll Ox BA75 MA80 St Jo Coll Dur BA78 PhD84. Cranmer Hall Dur. d 82 p 83. C Leic H Trin w St Jo 82-85; Chapl Magd Coll Cam 85-88; USA 88-94; V Cambridge H Trin *Ely* 94-02; Dean Bradf 02-04. *3 College Farm Cottages, Garford, Abingdon OX13 5PF* Tel (01865) 392804 E-mail chancock@btinternet.com

HANCOCK, Mrs Eleanor Mary Catherine. b 55. Huddersfield Univ CertEd91. CBDTI. d 05 p 06. C Carl H Trin and St Barn 05-08; priest-in-charge from 08. *104 Housesteads Road, Carlisle CA2 7XG* Tel and fax (01228) 527106 Mobile 07763-482542 E-mail emhancock@hartington.fsworld.co.uk

HANCOCK, Miss Gillian. b 59. St Jo Coll Nottm 05. d 07 p 08. C Iffley *Ox* 07-11; Chapl Mary Ann Evans Hospice from 11. *Mary Ann Evans Hospice, Eliot Way, Nuneaton CV10 7QL* Tel (024) 7686 5440 Mobile 07919-064612 E-mail gillhancock@btinternet.com

HANCOCK, Mrs Helen Margaret. b 62. Rob Coll Cam MA85. SEITE 06. d 09 p 10. NSM New Malden and Coombe *S'wark* from 09. *29 Rosebery Avenue, New Malden KT3 4JR* Tel (020) 8942 6987 E-mail helenhancock@ccnm.org

HANCOCK, Ivor Michael. b 31. Lon Univ BD60. Linc Th Coll 65. d 66 p 67. C Havant *Portsm* 66-69; V Gosport Ch Ch 69-76; priest-in-charge Southend St Alb *Chelmsf* 76-80; V Hawley H Trin *Guildf* 80-96; V Minley 80-96; RD Aldershot 83-88; rtd 96; Perm to Offic *Ox* from 98. *Assisi, 15 Whaley Road, Wokingham RG40 1QA* Tel 0118-962 9976

HANCOCK, Canon John Clayton. b 36. Dur Univ BA58. Cranmer Hall Dur. d 60 p 61. C Newbarns w Hawcoat *Carl* 60-65; V Church Coniston 65-76; R Torver 66-76; priest-in-charge Heversham 76-77; V 77-93; V Heversham and Milnthorpe 93-05; rtd 05; Hon Can Carl Cathl from 98; Hon C Levens from 05. *Fairfield, Sandside, Milnthorpe LA7 7HW* Tel (01539) 563659

HANCOCK, John Martin. b 55. Ealing Coll of Educn BA78. Wycliffe Hall Ox 97. d 99 p 00. C Bedford St Jo and St Leon *St Alb* 99-04; V Old Hill H Trin *Worc* from 04. *The Vicarage, 58 Wrights Lane, Cradley Heath B64 6RD* Tel (01384) 412987

HANCOCK, Canon John Mervyn. b 38. St Jo Coll Dur BA61 MA70 Hertf Coll Ox BA63 MA66. Cranmer Hall Dur 63. d 64 p 65. C Bishopwearmouth St Gabr *Dur* 64-67; V Hebburn St Jo 67-87; RD Jarrow 83-92; V S Westoe 87-03; C-in-c S Shields St Aid w St Steph 92-95; Hon Can Dur Cathl 88-03; rtd 03; C Chilton Moor *Dur* 07-08. *9 Railway Cottages, Dubmire, Houghton le Spring DH4 6LE* Tel 0191-385 7491 E-mail kda77@dial.pipex.com

HANCOCK, Malcolm James. b 50. Leeds Univ MA02 AGSM73. Sarum & Wells Th Coll 85. d 87 p 88. C Sandhurst *Ox* 87-90; priest-in-charge Bradbourne and Brassington *Derby* 90-92; TV Wirksworth 92-95; V Tunbridge Wells K Chas *Roch* 95-02; R Beckenham St Geo 02-10; Asst Chapl Lewisham Healthcare NHS Trust 10-11; Chapl from 11. *University Hospital Lewisham, Lewisham High Street, London SE13 6LH* Tel (020) 8333 3000 E-mail malcolm.j.hancock@btinternet.com

HANCOCK, Martin. See HANCOCK, John Martin

HANCOCK, Mrs Mary. b 52. Imp Coll Lon BSc73 ARCS73. Ridley Hall Cam 04. d 07 p 08. C Fen Orchards *Ely* 07-11; priest-in-charge Sutton from 11; priest-in-charge Witcham w Mepal from 11. *The Vicarage, 7 Church Lane, Sutton, Ely CB6 2RQ* E-mail mhancock@waitrose.com

HANCOCK, Ms Mary Joy. b 40. Auckland Univ BA61 Auckland Teachers' Coll PGCE62 Man Univ CQSW69. S'wark Ord Course 91. d 94 p 95. NSM Merton St Mary *S'wark* 94-01; NSM Colliers Wood Ch Ch 01-06; NSM Upper Tooting H Trin w St Aug from 06. *55 Huntspill Street, London SW17 0AA* Tel (020) 8946 8984

HANCOCK, Nigel John. b 35. K Coll Cam BA63 MA67. EAMTC 86. d 89 p 91. NSM Cambridge St Mary Less *Ely* 89-00; PV St Jo Coll Cam 95-99; Perm to Offic from 00. *5 Atherton Close, Cambridge CB4 2BE* Tel (01223) 355828

HANCOCK, Preb Paul. b 43. AKC66. d 67 p 68. C Wednesbury St Paul Wood Green *Lich* 67-70; C Rugeley 70-73; V Rickerscote 73-75; R Blisland w St Breward *Truro* 75-78; V Mansfield St Lawr *S'well* 78-82; priest-in-charge Charleton *Ex* 82-83; priest-in-charge E Portlemouth, S Pool and Chivelstone 82-83; R Charleton w Buckland Tout Saints etc 83-95; RD Woodleigh 88-95; priest-in-charge Plymouth Crownhill Ascension 95-99; V 99-09; Preb Ex Cathl

03-09; rtd 09. *27 Paddock Drive, Ivybridge PL21 0UB* Tel (01752) 690655 E-mail hazelnut33@aol.com
HANCOCK, Paul David. Oak Hill Th Coll. **d** 10 **p** 11. C Buxton Trin Prop Chpl *Derby* from 10. *24 Bath Road, Buxton SK17 6HH* Tel (01298) 23104 *or* 767551 Mobile 07816-409476 E-mail paulhancock2001@hotmail.com
✠**HANCOCK, The Rt Revd Peter.** b 55. Selw Coll Cam BA76 MA79. Oak Hill Th Coll BA80. **d** 80 **p** 81 **c** 10. C Portsdown *Portsm* 80-83; C Radipole and Melcombe Regis *Sarum* 83-87; V Cowplain *Portsm* 87-99; Adn The Meon 99-10; RD Havant 93-98; Hon Can Portsm Cathl 97-10; Dioc Dir Miss 03-06; Suff Bp Basingstoke *Win* from 10. *Bishop's Lodge, Colden Lane, Old Alresford, Alresford SO24 9DH* Tel (01962) 737330
HANCOCK, Peter Ernest. b 33. Man Univ BA54. Qu Coll Birm 54. **d** 56 **p** 57. C Wigston Magna *Leic* 56-59; C Hucknall Torkard *S'well* 59-61; V Sutton in Ashfield St Mich 61-65; Dioc Youth Officer *Portsm* 65-73; R Broughton Astley *Leic* 73-86; Dioc Adv for Min of Health and Healing *B & W* 86-93; rtd 94; Perm to Offic *B & W* from 98. *24 Mulberry Road, Congresbury, Bristol BS49 5HD* Tel (01934) 838920
HANCOCK, Peter Thompson. b 31. G&C Coll Cam BA54 MA58. Ridley Hall Cam 54. **d** 56 **p** 57. C Beckenham Ch Ch *Roch* 56-59; Chapl St Lawr Coll Ramsgate 59-62; Chapl Stowe Sch 62-67; Asst Chapl and Lect Br Embassy Ch Paris *Eur* 67-70; V Walton H Trin *Ox* 70-80; Canada 80-84; V Northwood H Trin *Lon* 84-94; rtd 94; Perm to Offic *Ox* 99-07 and *Guildf* from 07. *High Lawns, Woodhouse Lane, Holmbury St Mary, Dorking RH5 6NN* Tel (01483) 203548
HANCOCK, Reginald Legassicke (Rex). b 28. Trin Coll Cam BA51 MA57. Clifton Th Coll 60. **d** 61 **p** 62. C Finchley Ch Ch *Lon* 61-63; CF 63-82; R Quantoxhead *B & W* 82-93; rtd 93; Perm to Offic *B & W* from 94. *Stowleys, Bossington Lane, Porlock, Minehead TA24 8HD* Tel (01643) 862327
HANCOCK, Richard Manuel Ashley. b 69. LRPS02. Linc Th Coll 94 Westcott Ho Cam 95. **d** 97 **p** 98. C Didcot St Pet *Ox* 97-00; P-in-c Shrivenham w Watchfield and Bourton 00-03; V Shrivenham and Ashbury from 03; AD Vale of White Horse from 05. *St Andrew's Vicarage, Shrivenham, Swindon SN6 8AN* Tel (01793) 780183
E-mail vicar@standrews-shrivenham.fsnet.co.uk
HANCOCK, Mrs Vittoria Ruth. b 74. Univ of Wales (Ban) BSc95 BD99. Cranmer Hall Dur 91. **d** 01 **p** 02. C Llanberis w Llanrug *Ban* 01-04; C Dolgellau w Llanfachreth and Brithdir etc 04-05; Chapl St As Cathl and Dioc Evang Officer from 06. *Richmond, Upper Denbigh Road, St Asaph LL17 0RR* Tel (01745) 539992
HANCOCKS, Graeme. b 58. Univ of Wales (Ban) BD79 Oslo Univ 87. Linc Th Coll 79. **d** 81 **p** 82. C Denbigh and Nantglyn *St As* 81-84; Asst Chapl Oslo St Edm *Eur* 84-88; Chapl Stockholm 88-89; Chapl Marseille w St Raphaël, Aix-en-Provence etc 89; Chapl Gothenburg w Halmstad, Jönköping etc 90-93; Chapl Southn Univ Hosps NHS Trust 93-98; Chapl Trafford Healthcare NHS Trust 98-02; Chapl Leeds Teaching Hosps NHS Trust 02-09; rtd 09. *7 Woodfield Road, Cullingworth, Bradford BD13 5JL* Tel (01535) 271551
HANCOX, Ms Sarah Anne. b 85. Edin Univ BD07. Cranmer Hall Dur 09. **d** 11. C Kirk Sandall and Edenthorpe *Sheff* from 11. *8 Lichen Close, Edenthorpe, Doncaster DN3 2LF* Tel (01302) 884245 E-mail s.hancox@gmail.com
HAND, Michael. See HAND, Peter Michael
HAND, Michael Anthony (Tony). b 63. SROT York Univ BA84 DipCOT88. St Jo Coll Nottm MA95. **d** 95 **p** 96. C Lutterworth w Cotesbach *Leic* 95-98; C Lutterworth w Cotesbach and Bitteswell 99-01; V Acomb H Redeemer *York* from 01; Chapl Manor Sch from 01. *The Vicarage, 108 Boroughbridge Road, York YO26 6AB* Tel (01904) 798593
E-mail tony@holyredeemeryork.co.uk
HAND, Canon Nigel Arthur. b 54. St Jo Coll Nottm. **d** 84 **p** 85. C Birm St Luke 84-88; C Walton H Trin *Ox* 88-89; TV 89-97; C Selly Park St Steph and St Wulstan *Birm* 97-04; P-in-c Selly Park Ch Ch 04-08; AD Moseley 04-07; Can Res Birm Cathl from 08. *12 Nursery Drive, Handsworth, Birmingham B20 2SW* E-mail n.hand1@btinternet.com
HAND, Peter Michael. b 42. Univ Coll Ox BA63 Lon Univ BSc75. Sarum & Wells Th Coll 77. **d** 80 **p** 81. NSM Shaston *Sarum* 80-81; C Tisbury 81-83; C Glastonbury St Jo w Godney *B & W* 83-84; C Glastonbury w Meare, W Pennard and Godney 84-87; V High Littleton 87-99; RD Midsomer Norton 92-98; R Winford w Felton Common Hill 99-07; Warden of Readers Bath Adnry 98-06; rtd 07; TV Winchcombe *Glouc* from 11. *27 Stancombe View, Winchcombe, Cheltenham GL54 5LE* Tel (01242) 609575 E-mail anne_michael_hand@yahoo.co.uk
HAND, Philip Ronald. b 53. Spurgeon's Coll BA78. **d** 03 **p** 04. NSM Southampton (City Cen) *Win* from 03. *52 Cranbury Avenue, Southampton SO14 0LT* Tel (023) 8049 4490
✠**HANDFORD, The Rt Revd George Clive.** b 37. CMG07. Hatf Coll Dur BA61. Qu Coll Birm 61. **d** 63 **p** 64 **c** 90. C Mansfield SS Pet and Paul *S'well* 63-67; Chapl Beirut Lebanon 67-74; Dean Jerusalem 74-78; UAE 78-83; Adn Gulf 78-83; V Kneesall w Laxton *S'well* 83-84; P-in-c Wellow 83-84; RD Tuxford and Norwell 83-84;

Adn Nottingham 84-90; Suff Bp Warw *Cov* 90-96; Bp Cyprus and the Gulf 96-07; Pres Bp Episc Ch Jerusalem and Middle E 02-07; rtd 07; Hon Asst Bp Ripon and Leeds from 07. *Wayside, 1 The Terrace, Kirby Hill, Boroughbridge, York YO51 9DQ* Tel (01423) 325406 E-mail gchandford@gmail.com
HANDFORD, John Richard. b 32. Sydney Univ BSc52 Univ Coll Lon MSc58 Surrey Univ MA84 Heythrop Coll Lon MTh96 Lon Univ PhD04. Lon Coll of Div 68. **d** 69 **p** 70. Asst Chapl Wellington Coll Berks 69-87; Hon C Windlesham *Guildf* 87-92; Perm to Offic 92-02. *Desiderata, 33 Chertsey Road, Windlesham GU20 6EW* Tel (01276) 472397
HANDFORD, Maurice. b 25. Oak Hill Th Coll 48. **d** 52 **p** 53. C Dublin Miss Ch *D & G* 52-55; Org and Deputation Sec ICM (N and Midl) 55-58; C-in-c Buxton Trin Prop Chpl *Derby* 58-87; I Clondevaddock w Portsalon and Leatbeg *D & R* 87-90; Bp's Dom Chapl 88-90; rtd 90; Perm to Offic *Ches* 90-10 and *Derby* from 92. *21 Stuart Court, High Street, Kibworth, Leicester LE8 0LR* Tel 0116-279 6810
HANDFORTH, Canon Richard Brereton. b 31. St Pet Coll Ox BA55 MA60. Westcott Ho Cam 63. **d** 64 **p** 65. C Hornchurch St Andr *Chelmsf* 64-65; Warden St Steph Coll Hong Kong 65-73; Chapl CMS Fellowship Ho Chislehurst 73-75; Hon C Chislehurst St Nic *Roch* 73-75; Home Educn Sec CMS 75-83; V Biggin Hill *Roch* 83-88; Inter-change Adv CMS 88-96; Hon C Plaistow St Mary *Roch* 95-04; Hon Can Lagos from 95; rtd 96; Perm to Offic *Roch* from 01. *40 Sheppard's College, London Road, Bromley BR1 1PF* Tel (020) 8460 0238
E-mail richardhandforth@virgin.net
HANDLEY, The Ven Anthony Michael. b 36. Selw Coll Cam BA60 MA64. Chich Th Coll 60. **d** 62 **p** 63. C Thorpe St Andr *Nor* 62-66; C Gaywood, Bawsey and Mintlyn 66-72; V Hellesdon 72-81; RD Nor N 80-81; Adn Nor 81-93; Adn Norfolk 93-02; rtd 02; Perm to Offic *Nor* from 02. *25 New Street, Sheringham NR26 8EE* Tel (01263) 820928
HANDLEY, Dennis Francis. b 57. MIE79 TEng(CEI)80. Coll of Resurr Mirfield 82. **d** 85 **p** 86. C Headingley *Ripon* 85-88; C Rothwell 88-92; V Liversedge *Wakef* 92-97; V Ripponden and Barkisland w W Scammonden 97-06; TR Almondbury w Farnley Tyas from 06; Dioc Rural Officer from 04. *The Rectory, 2 Westgate, Almondbury, Huddersfield HD5 8XE* Tel (01484) 309469 E-mail dennis@ntlworld.com
HANDLEY, John. b 38. Oak Hill Th Coll. **d** 83 **p** 84. C Witton w Brundall and Braydeston *Nor* 83-86; R Reedham w Cantley w Limpenhoe and Southwood 86-93; P-in-c E w W Harling and Bridgham w Roudham 93-95; R E w W Harling, Bridgham w Roudham, Larling etc 95-05; P-in-c Garboldisham w Blo' Norton, Riddlesworth etc 94-96; RD Thetford and Rockland 95-98; rtd 05. Perm to Offic *Nor* from 05. *6 Barton Close, Swaffham PE37 7SB* Tel (01760) 336328
E-mail john.handley@hotmail.co.uk
HANDLEY, Michael. See HANDLEY, The Ven Anthony Michael
HANDLEY, Neil. b 40. St Aid Birkenhead 64. **d** 67 **p** 68. C Ashton Ch Ch *Man* 67-70; C Stretford All SS 70-73; C Tonge 73; C-in-c Bolton St Jo Breightmet CD 74-79; V Bolton St Jo 79-80; R Broughton St Jo 80-87; Perm to Offic *Eur* from 90. *La Taire du Grel, 24250 Domme, France* Tel (0033) 5 53 28 23 42
HANDLEY, Timothy John. b 63. St Steph Ho Ox 94. **d** 96 **p** 97. C St Marychurch *Ex* 96-98; Perm to Offic *Cant* 06-10. *All Saints' House, Churchview Road, Twickenham TW2 5BX* Tel (020) 8894 3580
HANDLEY MACMATH, Terence. b 59. Goldsmiths' Coll Lon BA80 K Coll Cam MA98. Westcott Ho Cam 91. **d** 94 **p** 95. NSM Southwold *St E* 94-95; Perm to Offic *St Alb* 96-99; C St Alb St Pet 99-05; V Harrow Weald All SS *Lon* 05-07; Chapl R Free Hampstead NHS Trust 07-09; Chapl R Brompton and Harefield NHS Trust from 09. *Harefield Hospital, Hill End Road, Harefield, Uxbridge UB9 6JH* Tel (01895) 823737
E-mail terencehandleymacmath@googlemail.com
HANDY, Thomas. b 79. Ex Univ BA02 Bris Univ PGCE05. Trin Coll Bris MA09. **d** 09 **p** 10. C Shepton Mallet w Doulting *B & W* from 09. *24 Walnut Grove, Shepton Mallet BA4 4HX* E-mail thomashandy100@hotmail.com
HANFORD, Canon William Richard. b 38. Keble Coll Ox BA60 MA64 Lon BD66 Univ of Wales LLM95. St Steph Ho Ox 60. **d** 63 **p** 64. C Roath St Martin *Llan* 63-66; C Llantwit Major 67-68; PV Llan Cathl 68-72; Chapl RN 72-76; Hon Chapl Gibraltar Cathl 74-76; Hon C Eastbourne St Sav and St Pet *Chich* 76-77; C Brighton St Pet 77-78; Can Res and Prec Guildf Cathl 78-83; Hon Can 03-09; V Ewell 83-09; Tutor and Lect Chich Th Coll 79-86; rtd 09; Perm to Offic *Guildf* and *Llan* from 09. *15 Austin Avenue, Laleston, Bridgend CF32 0LG* Tel (01656) 656892 *or* (020) 8786 0552 E-mail wrhanford@btinternet.com
HANKE, Canon Hilary Claire. b 53. Qu Coll Birm BTheol93. **d** 93 **p** 94. C Kempsey and Severn Stoke w Croome d'Abitot *Worc* 93-97; TV Wordsley 97-99; Convenor for Women's Min 98-05; P-in-c Reddal Hill St Luke 01-08; V from 08; Hon Can Worc Cathl from 98; RD Dudley 04-10. *St Luke's Vicarage,*

Upper High Street, Cradley Heath B64 5HX Tel and fax (01384) 569940 E-mail hchanke@btinternet.com

HANKEY, Miss Dorothy Mary. b 38. CertEd65. Trin Coll Bris 75. dss 78 **d** 87 **p** 94. Wigan St Jas w St Thos *Liv* 78-84; Middleton *Man* 84-85; Litherland Ch Ch *Liv* 85-89; Par Dn 87-89; Par Dn Blackpool St Mark *Blackb* 89-94; C 94-95; C Blackpool St Paul 95-98; rtd 98; Perm to Offic *Blackb* from 98. *89 Rutland Avenue, Poulton-le-Flyde FY6 7RX* Tel (01253) 890635

HANKEY, Rupert Christopher Alers. b 60. Sheff Univ LLB82. Wilson Carlile Coll 86 St Jo Coll Nottm MTh06. **d** 07 **p** 08. C Bedford St Jo and St Leon *St Alb* 07-11; V Sidcup St Andr *Roch* from 11. *The Vicarage, St Andrew's Road, Sidcup DA14 4SA* Tel (020) 8300 4712 Mobile 07539-319545 E-mail rupert3@tesco.net

HANKINS, Clifford James. b 24. Chich Th Coll 70. **d** 72 **p** 73. C Henfield *Chich* 72-76; V Fernhurst 76-84; V Mithian w Mount Hawke *Truro* 84-89; rtd 89; Hon C W Wittering and Birdham w Itchenor *Chich* from 90. *2 Kestrel Close, East Wittering, Chichester PO20 8PQ* Tel (01243) 672164

HANLEY, Máirt Joseph. b 74. Univ Coll Ches BA95. CITC BTh03. **d** 03 **p** 04. NSM Tralee w Kilmoyley, Ballymacelligott etc *L & K* 03-11; Bp's C Kilcolman w Kiltallagh, Killorglin, Knockane etc from 11. *20 Knocklyne, Sunhill, Killorglin, Co Kerry, Republic of Ireland* Tel (00353) 87-619 4733 (mobile) E-mail mairtjhanley@hotmail.com

HANLON, Michael James. b 50. St Jo Coll Nottm 96. **d** 98 **p** 99. C Tamworth *Lich* 98-00; C Melbourne St Jo Australia from 00. *25 The Eyrie, Lilydale Vic 3140, Australia* Tel (0061) (3) 9739 5235 *or* 9739 3541 E-mail mikeruth@alphalink.com.au

HANLON, Thomas Kyle. b 72. QUB BA94 TCD BTh97. **d** 97 **p** 98. C Bangor St Comgall *D & D* 97-00; I Dromore *Clogh* 00-06; I Fivemiletown from 06; Chapl to Bp Clogh from 03. *Fivemiletown Rectory, 160 Ballagh Road, Fivemiletown BT75 0QP* Tel (028) 8952 1030 *or* 8952 2422 E-mail tkhanlon@btinternet.com

HANMER, Sister Phoebe Margaret. b 31. Edin Univ MA54. **d** 96 **p** 97. NSM Brakpan S Africa 96-00; NSM Actonville 00-03; Perm to Offic *Ox* 99-00 and *Birm* from 04. *366 High Street, Smethwick B66 3PD* Tel and fax 0121-558 0004

HANMER, Canon Richard John. b 38. Peterho Cam BA61 MA65. Linc Th Coll 62. **d** 64 **p** 65. C Sheff St Swithun 64-69; Bp's Chapl *Nor* 69-73; V Cinderhill *S'well* 73-81; V Eaton *Nor* 81-94; Dioc Chapl MU 91-04; Hon Can Nor Cathl 93-94; Can Res Nor Cathl 94-04; P-in-c Nor St Mary in the Marsh 94-04; rtd 04; Perm to Offic *Nor* from 04. *18 Quebec Road, Dereham NR19 2DR* Tel (01362) 655092

HANNA, Miss Elizabeth. b 50. QUB BA73 Lon Bible Coll BA79 Milltown Inst Dub MA01. CITC 99. **d** 01 **p** 02. C Bangor Abbey *D & D* 01-04; I Magherally w Annaclone 04-08; I Belfast St Nic Conn from 08. *St Nicolas' Rectory, 15 Harberton Park, Belfast BT9 6TW* Tel (028) 9066 7753 Mobile 07801-946909 E-mail hannamanor15@btinternet.com

HANNA, Isaac James. b 70. York St Jo Coll MA03. CITC 07. **d** 08 **p** 09. Bp's C Dungiven w Bovevagh *D & R* 08-10; I Maghera w Killelagh from 10. *The Rectory, 20 Church Street, Maghera BT46 5EA* Tel (028) 7964 2252 *or* 7954 9290 E-mail issac17@btinternet.com *or* rector@magheraparish.co.uk

HANNA, John. b 44. Lon Bible Coll BA83. Westcott Ho Cam 86. **d** 87 **p** 88. C Denton Ch Ch *Man* 87-91; V Higher Walton *Blackb* 91-98; C Marple All SS *Ches* 98-02; TV Burrington, Chawleigh, Cheldon, Chulmleigh etc *Ex* 02-09; RD S Molton 03-09; rtd 09. *Victoria House, Victoria Road, Knighton LD7 1BD* Tel (01547) 529296

HANNA, Patricia Elizabeth. TCD BA HDipEd QUB BD NUU MA. **d** 99 **p** 00. Aux Min Nenagh *L & K* from 99; Aux Min Drumcliffe w Kilnasoolagh from 00. *St Columba's Rectory, Bindon Street, Ennis, Co Clare, Republic of Ireland* Tel (00353) (65) 682 0109 Mobile 87-660 6003 E-mail patricia.hanna@ul.ie

HANNA, Peter Thomas. b 45. ACII66 GIFireE75. CITC 85. **d** 88 **p** 89. NSM Cork St Fin Barre's Union *C, C & R* 88-95; Min Can Cork Cathl from 92; Dioc Info 94-95; Aux Min Cork St Luke Union 95-00; Aux Min Kinsale Union 00-04; Aux Min Douglas Union w Frankfield from 04. *Mount Windsor, Farnahoe, Inishannon, Co Cork, Republic of Ireland* Tel and fax (00353) (21) 477 5470 E-mail hanna7@ofive.indigo.ie

HANNA, Canon Robert Charles. b 49. Oak Hill Th Coll 75. **d** 77 **p** 78. C Coleraine *Conn* 77-82; I Convoy w Monellan and Donaghmore *D & R* 82-94; Can Raphoe Cathl 88-94; I Drumcliffe w Kilnasoolagh *L & K* from 94; Can Limerick, Killaloe and Clonfert Cathls from 00; Chan from 04. *St Columba's Rectory, Bindon Street, Ennis, Co Clare, Republic of Ireland* Tel (00353) (65) 682 0109 Mobile 86-356 0864 E-mail bobhanna@eircom.net

HANNA, Steven John. b 70. Oak Hill Th Coll BA02. **d** 02 **p** 03. C Dagenham *Chelmsf* 02-07; V Becontree St Elisabeth from 07. *St Elisabeth's Vicarage, Hewett Road, Dagenham RM8 2XT* Tel (020) 8517 0355 E-mail stevenhanna@yahoo.com

HANNAFORD, Prof Robert. b 53. Ex Univ BEd76 MA78 PhD87. St Steph Ho Ox 78. **d** 80 **p** 81. C Ex St Jas 80-83; Chapl

Ex Univ 83-88; Tutor St Steph Ho Ox 89-92; Sen Lect Ch Ch Coll Cant 92-99; Prof Chr Th Univ Coll Chich 99-01; Hon C Bury w Houghton and Coldwaltham and Hardham *Chich* 99-01; Th Consultant Bp Horsham 99-01; Can and Preb Chich Cathl from 00; Prof Th St Martin's Coll Lanc 02-05; Dean of Faculty 05-07; Dean of Faculty Cumbria Univ from 07; Hon C Tunstall w Melling and Leck *Blackb* 02-03; Hon C E Lonsdale from 03. *The Vicarage, Church Lane, Tunstall, Carnforth LA6 2RQ* Tel (015242) 74376 E-mail rhannaford@ucsm.ac.uk

HANNAH, Darrell Dale. b 62. Grand Canyon Univ BA85 S Bapt Th Sem MDiv89 Regent Coll Vancouver ThM92 Magd Coll Cam PhD96. WMMTC 00. **d** 03 **p** 03. NSM Edgbaston St Geo *Birm* 03-04; NSM Iffley *Ox* 04-07; NSM Earley St Pet 07-08; R Ascot Heath from 08. *All Saints' Rectory, London Road, Ascot SL5 8DQ* Tel (01344) 621200 E-mail drddhannah@yahoo.co.uk

HANNAH, Kimberley Victoria. See WILLIAMS, Mrs Kimberley Victoria

HANNAM, Robert Stephen. b 46. CertEd69. **d** 05 **p** 06. NSM Rastrick St Matt *Wakef* 05-08; NSM Rastrick from 08. *33 Lyndhurst Road, Brighouse HD6 3RX* Tel (01484) 716053 E-mail stephenr.hannam@btinternet.com

HANNEN, Robert John. See DAVIES-HANNEN, Robert John

✠**HANNON, The Rt Revd Brian Desmond Anthony.** b 36. TCD BA59 MA62. TCD Div Sch Div Test61. **d** 61 **p** 62 **c** 86. C Clooney *D & R* 61-64; I Desertmartin 64-69; I Londonderry Ch Ch 69-82; I Enniskillen *Clogh* 82-86; Preb Clogh Cathl 82-84; Dean Clogh 85-86; Bp Clogh 86-01; rtd 01. *Drumconnis Top, 202 Mullaghmeen Road, Ballinamallard, Enniskillen BT94 2DZ* Tel (028) 6638 8557 Fax 6638 8086 E-mail bdah@btinternet.com

HANNY, Mrs Annette Elizabeth. b 49. Keele Univ MA95. WMMTC 02. **d** 05 **p** 06. NSM Oldbury, Langley and Londonderry *Birm* from 05; Chapl Sandwell Mental Health NHS and Social Care Trust from 10. *93 St Mary's Road, Smethwick B67 5DG* Tel 0121-420 2858 Mobile 07970-841662 E-mail annette.hanny@hobtpct.nhs.uk

HANOVA, Petra. See ELSMORE, Ms Petra

HANSELL, Anupama. See KAMBLE-HANSELL, Anupama

HANSELL, Peter Michael. b 76. Selw Coll Cam BA97 MA01 MPhil99 PhD02. Qu Coll Birm 03. **d** 05 **p** 06. C Moseley St Mary *Birm* 05-07; C Moseley St Mary and St Anne 07-09; Reader Initial Tr Adv *Cov* 09-10; R Bure Valley *Nor* from 10. *The Vicarage, Back Lane, Buxton, Norwich NR10 5HD* Tel (01603) 279394 Mobile 07875-640575 E-mail revd.pmh@btinternet.com

HANSEN, Mrs Moira Jacqueline. b 55. K Coll Lon BSc76. Oak Hill Th Coll BA88. **d** 88 **p** 96. Par Dn Finchley Ch Ch *Lon* 88-91; Par Dn Broadwater *Chich* 91-94; Chapl Oak Hill Th Coll 94-00; P-in-c Stanton *St E* 00-04; P-in-c Hopton, Market Weston, Barningham etc 00-04; R Stanton, Hopton, Market Weston, Barningham etc 04-06; rtd 06. *49 Turnstone Drive, Bury St Edmunds IP32 7GT* Tel (01284) 717191 E-mail moira@hansenj.fsnet.co.uk

HANSFORD, Gordon John. b 40. Southn Univ BSc61. Trin Coll Bris 77. **d** 79 **p** 80. C Ex St Leon w H Trin 79-82; C Shirley *Win* 82-87; R Landcross, Littleham, Monkleigh etc *Ex* 87-96; TV Bideford, Northam, Westward Ho!, Appledore etc 96-99; P-in-c Monkleigh 96-99; RD Hartland 96-99; V Paul *Truro* 99-07; rtd 07. *14 Chilpark, Fremington, Barnastaple EX31 3BY* E-mail hansford@tinyworld.co.uk

HANSFORD, Ruth Patricia. b 68. K Coll Lon BSc90 Surrey Univ MSc96 Sch of Pharmacy Lon PhD00. Trin Coll Bris BA02. **d** 03 **p** 04. C Parkham, Alwington, Buckland Brewer etc *Ex* 03-07; P-in-c Hatherleigh, Meeth, Exbourne and Jacobstowe from 07. *The Rectory, Hatherleigh, Okehampton EX20 3JY* Tel (01837) 810314 Mobile 07718-765936 E-mail maggiethecat@waitrose.com

HANSON, Christopher. b 48. Ox Univ BTh02. Wycliffe Hall Ox 87. **d** 89 **p** 90. C Heref St Pet w St Owen and St Jas 89-91; C Plymouth St Andr w St Paul and St Geo *Ex* 91-93; C Devonport St Mich 93-94; TV Shebbear, Buckland Filleigh, Sheepwash etc 94-97; TV Langley Marish *Ox* 97-08; V Victoria Docks Ascension *Chelmsf* from 08. *The Vicarage, 5 Broadgate Road, London E16 3TL* Tel (020) 7476 5999 E-mail revhansonctwcc@aol.com

HANSON, Dale Robert. b 57. Fitzw Coll Cam BA78 MA81 Univ of BC MA80. Ridley Hall Cam 81. **d** 84 **p** 85. C Much Woolton *Liv* 84-87; Assoc Min Kowloon St Andr Hong Kong 87-91; TV Billingham St Aid *Dur* 91-95; C Dur St Nic 95-98; V 98-07; C Kowloon St Andr Hong Kong from 07. *Shatin Anglican Church, PO Box 1627, Shatin Central PO, Shatin, NT, Hong Kong, China* Tel (00852) 2694 9928 Fax 2695 0580 E-mail standrew@pacific.net.hk

HANSON, Edward William. b 51. Salem State Coll (USA) BA73 Tufts Univ MA78 Boston Coll PhD92 Episc Div Sch MDiv00. Ripon Coll Cuddesdon 00. **d** 01 **p** 02. C Linc St Botolph and Linc St Pet-at-Gowts and St Andr 01-04; P-in-c Orsett and Bulphan and Horndon on the Hill *Chelmsf* 04-06; R from 06;

RD Thurrock 08-11. *The Rectory, School Lane, Orsett, Grays RM16 3JS* Tel (01375) 891254 E-mail rector@hobnob.org.uk
HANSON, Keith. b 59. Cranmer Hall Dur 99. **d** 01 **p** 02. C Armley w New Wortley *Ripon* 01-04; C Whitkirk 04-06; P-in-c Illingworth *Wakef* 06-09; Chapl H Trin Sch Halifax 06-09; P-in-c Harlaxton Gp *Linc* from 09. *The Rectory, 6 Rectory Lane, Harlaxton, Grantham NG32 1HD* Tel (01476) 594608 E-mail revkeef@hotmail.com
HANSON, Mrs Margaret Patricia. b 45. Ripon Coll Cuddesdon 04. **d** 05 **p** 06. NSM Ifield *Chich* from 05. *Birch Cottage, 7 Barnwood, Crawley RH10 7TH* Tel (01293) 535569 E-mail margaret.hanson1@tesco.net
HANSON, Michael Beaumont. b 49. Univ Coll Ox MA70 PGCE71. NOC 81. **d** 84 **p** 85. Chapl Leeds Gr Sch and NSM Leeds St Geo *Ripon* 84-99; rtd 99; Perm to Offic *Carl* from 99. *5 The Crofts, Crosby, Maryport CA15 6SP* Tel (01900) 816630 E-mail mikeandchristinehanson@sky.com
HANSON, Peter Richard. b 45. ARCM. Chich Th Coll 72. **d** 75 **p** 76. C Forest Gate St Edm *Chelmsf* 75-79; C Chingford SS Pet and Paul 79-81; V Leytonstone H Trin and St Aug Harrow Green 81-86; Dep Chapl HM Pris Wandsworth 86-88; Chapl HM Pris Lewes 88-91; rtd 91; Perm to Offic *Chich* from 91. *Flat 2, 39 St Anne's Crescent, Lewes BN7 1SB* Tel (01273) 471714
HANSON, Robert Arthur. b 35. Keele Univ BA57. St Steph Ho Ox 57 St Mich Coll Llan 59. **d** 60 **p** 61. C Longton St Mary and St Chad *Lich* 60-65; Chapl St Mary's Cathl *Edin* 65-69; R Glas St Matt 69-79; R Paisley H Trin 79-87; V Walsall St Andr *Lich* 87-93; Perm to Offic *Worc* 94-97; C Kentish Town *Lon* 97-01; Hon C 02-06; rtd 02; Perm to Offic *Lon* from 06. *7B Fraser Regnart Court, Southampton Road, London NW5 4HU* Tel (020) 7284 3634 Mobile 07951-154384 E-mail bob.hanson@tiscali.co.uk
HANSON, Timothy David. b 68. Oak Hill Th Coll BA95. **d** 95 **p** 96. C Boscombe St Jo *Win* 95-00; V Wharton *Ches* from 00. *The Vicarage, 165 Crook Lane, Winsford CW7 3DR* Tel (01606) 593215 *or* 861860 E-mail tiohanson@aol.com
HANWELL, David John. b 46. Leic Univ CertEd74 UEA BEd94. **d** 98 **p** 99. OLM Mundford w Lynford, Cranwich and Ickburgh w Langford *Nor* 98-04; OLM Cockley Cley w Gooderstone 99-04; P-in-c from 04; OLM Gt and Lt Cressingham w Threxton 99-04; C from 04; OLM Hilborough w Bodney 99-04; C from 04; OLM Oxborough w Foulden and Caldecote 99-04; C from 04. *The Rectory, Elm Place, Gooderstone, King's Lynn PE33 9BX* Tel (01366) 328856 E-mail david.hanwell@btopenworld.com
HAOKIP (*formerly* **YAM**), **Canon David Tongkhoyam.** b 60. Serampore Univ BTh89 Madras Univ MDiv92. H Cross Coll Rangoon. **d** 84 **p** 85. Burma 83-93; Hon Can Sittwe from 09; India 93-95; Korea 96-97; Perm to Offic *S'wark* 99; TV Southampton (City Cen) *Win* 00-05; V E Ham St Geo *Chelmsf* from 05. *The Vicarage, Buxton Road, London E6 3NB* Tel (020) 8472 2111 Mobile 07817-702358 E-mail dthaokip1@yahoo.co.uk
HAPGOOD-STRICKLAND, Canon Peter Russell. b 57. St Steph Ho Ox BA83. **d** 83 **p** 84. C Ashford *Cant* 83-86; C Sheerness H Trin w St Paul 86-90; V Blackb St Thos w St Jude 90-97; P-in-c Burnley St Andr w St Marg 97; V Burnley St Andr w St Marg and St Jas from 98; Hon Can Blackb Cathl from 05. *St Andrew's Vicarage, 230 Barden Lane, Burnley BB10 1JD* Tel (01282) 423185 E-mail hapgoodstrickland@btinternet.com
HARARE, Bishop of. See GANDIYA, The Rt Revd Chad Nicholas
HARBIDGE, The Ven Adrian Guy. b 48. St Jo Coll Dur BA70. Cuddesdon Coll 73. **d** 75 **p** 76. C Romsey *Win* 75-80; V Bournemouth St Andr 80-86; V Chandler's Ford 86-99; RD Eastleigh 93-99; Adn Bournemouth 99-10; P-in-c Seale, Puttenham and Wanborough *Guildf* from 10. *The Rectory, Elstead Road, Seale, Farnham GU10 1JA* Tel (01252) 783057 E-mail rector@spw.org.uk
HARBORD, Canon Paul Geoffrey. b 56. JP99. Keble Coll Ox BA78 MA86. Chich Th Coll 81. **d** 83 **p** 84. C Rawmarsh w Parkgate *Sheff* 83-86; C Doncaster St Geo 86-90; C-in-c St Edm Anchorage Lane CD 90-95; V Masbrough 95-03; Bp's Chapl from 03; Hon Can Sheff Cathl from 07. *4 Clarke Drive, Sheffield S10 2NS* Tel 0114-266 1932 *or* 230 2170 Mobile 07898-485428 E-mail geoffrey.harbord@sheffield.anglican.org
HARBORD, Philip James. b 56. St Cath Coll Ox BA77. Cranmer Hall Dur 78. **d** 80 **p** 81. C Enfield St Andr *Lon* 80-83; CMS Pakistan 84-88; C Clay Hill St Jo and St Luke *Lon* 88-91; Chapl Wexham Park Hosp Slough 91-92; Chapl Upton Hosp Slough 91-92; Chapl Heatherwood and Wexham Park Hosp NHS Trust 92-95; Chapl Leic Gen Hosp NHS Trust 95-98; Chapl Fosse Health NHS Trust 98-99; P-in-c Cosby *Leic* 01-07; P-in-c Whetstone 03-07; rtd 07. *47 Maple Avenue, Blaby, Leicester LE8 4AT* Tel 0116-277 6522 E-mail philipjharbord@btinternet.com
HARBRIDGE, Philip Charles Anthony. b 65. K Coll Lon LLB88 AKC88 Ch Coll Cam BA98 MA02. Westcott Ho Cam. **d** 99 **p** 00. C Hampton All SS *Lon* 99-02; Chapl Ch Coll Cam 02-07;

Chapl Millfield Sch Somerset from 07. *Millfield School, Street BA16 0YD* Tel (01458) 442291 E-mail pch@millfieldschool.com
HARCOURT, Canon Giles. b 36. Westcott Ho Cam 68. **d** 71 **p** 72. C Bishopwearmouth St Mich w St Hilda *Dur* 71-73; C Fishponds St Mary *Bris* 73-75; Bp's Dom Chapl *S'wark* 75-78; Lic to Offic 78-79; V S Wimbledon H Trin and St Pet 79-88; V Greenwich St Alfege 88-04; Hon Chapl RN Coll Greenwich 89-99; RD Greenwich Thameside *S'wark* 94-98; Boro Dean Greenwich 94-98; Hon Can S'wark Cathl 96-04; rtd 05; Perm to Offic *Chich* from 05. *1A Trinity Trees, Eastbourne BN21 3LA* Tel (01323) 638790
HARCOURT, Paul George. b 67. Em Coll Cam BA88 MA92. Wycliffe Hall Ox BA91. **d** 92 **p** 93. C Moreton *Ches* 92-95; C Woodford Wells *Chelmsf* 95-00; V from 00; AD Redbridge from 10. *All Saints' Vicarage, 4 Inmans Row, Woodford Green IG8 0NH* Tel (020) 8504 0266 Fax 8504 9640 E-mail pharcourt@btconnect.com
HARCOURT-NORTON, Michael Clive. See NORTON, Michael Clive Harcourt
HARDACRE (*née* **BROOKFIELD**), **Mrs Patricia Anne.** b 50. St Mary's Coll Dur BA72 St Jo Coll Dur MA74. Cranmer Hall Dur. dss 84 **d** 87 **p** 94. Kingston upon Hull St Nic *York* 84-86; Acomb St Steph 86-96; Par Dn 87-94; C 94-96; TV Preston Risen Lord *Blackb* 96-07; rtd 07; Perm to Offic *Blackb* from 07. *17 Fairfield Drive, Clitheroe BB7 2PE* Tel (01200) 429341 E-mail anne@hipporiage.fsnet.co.uk
HARDCASTLE, Ian Kenneth Dalton. b 56. Auckland Univ BE78 ME80. St Jo Coll Nottm MTh04. **d** 04 **p** 05. C Denton Holme *Carl* 04-09; V Whangaparaoa Peninsular New Zealand from 09. *3/19 Wade River Road, Whangaparaoa 0932, New Zealand* Tel (0064) (9) 424 0939 E-mail vicar@ststephenswgp.org.nz
HARDCASTLE, Nigel John. b 47. Reading Univ BSc68. Qu Coll Birm. **d** 72 **p** 73. C Weoley Castle *Birm* 72-75; C Handsworth St Andr 75-78; V Garretts Green 78-86; Exec Sec Ch Computer Project BCC 86-89; R Emmer Green *Ox* 89-99; V Reading St Luke w St Bart from 99. *The Vicarage, 50 London Road, Reading RG1 5AS* Tel 0118-931 3740 E-mail nigel@hardcastle33.fsnet.co.uk
HARDCASTLE, Roger Clive. b 52. Southn Univ BSc73. Qu Coll Birm. **d** 78 **p** 79. C Walton St Mary *Liv* 78-82; V Pemberton St Fran Kitt Green 82-94; TV Padgate 94-96; V Birchwood 96-06; rtd 06. *15 Ullswater Avenue, Orrell, Wigan WN5 8PF* Tel (01942) 513568 E-mail rhardcastle@btopenworld.com
HARDIE, John Blair. b 16. MBE46. LDS FDS MRCS38 MRCSE66. Edin Th Coll 73. **d** 76 **p** 76. Chapl St Paul's Cathl Dundee 76-86; rtd 86; Hon C Carnoustie *Bre* from 86. *4 Lammerton Terrace, Dundee DD4 7BW* Tel (01382) 860836
HARDIE, Canon Stephen. b 41. AKC67. **d** 68 **p** 69. C Roxbourne St Andr *Lon* 68-73; C Colchester St Mary V *Chelmsf* 73-76; R Wivenhoe 76-92; TR Dovercourt and Parkeston 92-96; P-in-c Harwich 92-96; R Dovercourt and Parkeston w Harwich 96-04; TR Harwich Peninsula 04-05; P-in-c Ramsden Crays w Ramsden Bellhouse 02-05; RD Harwich 97-04; Hon Can Chelmsf Cathl 02-05; rtd 05; Perm to Offic *St E* from 06 and *Nor* from 09. *The Croft, 2 Lowestoft Road, Worlingham, Beccles NR34 7EH* Tel (01502) 711625
HARDING, Alan. b 45. St Jo Coll Ox BA67 MA73 Pemb Coll Ox DPhil92. Oak Hill NSM Course 89. **d** 93 **p** 94. NSM Lt Heath *St Alb* 93-09; P-in-c S Mymms and Ridge Hill *St Alb* 99-05; Perm to Offic *St E* 05-08 and *St Alb* from 05; NSM S Hartismere *St E* from 08. *The Old Guildhall, Mill Street, Gislingham, Eye IP23 8JT* Tel (01379) 783361
HARDING, Alec James. b 61. St Andr Univ MA83 DTh. Cranmer Hall Dur 86. **d** 89 **p** 90. C Thirsk *York* 89-93; TV Heref St Martin w St Fran 93-95; TV Heref S Wye 95-00; V Barnard Castle w Whorlton *Dur* from 00; AD Barnard Castle from 03. *The Vicarage, Parson's Lonnen, Barnard Castle DL12 8ST* Tel (01833) 637018 E-mail aleckim@barney16.fsnet.co.uk
HARDING, Andrew Barry. b 66. Westcott Ho Cam 97. **d** 99 **p** 00. C Rainham *Roch* 99-03; V Hoo St Werburgh 03-11; CF from 11. *c/o MOD Chaplains (Army)* Tel (01264) 381140 Fax 381824 E-mail ardy@abh123.freeserve.co.uk
HARDING, Benjamin Lee. b 75. Bris Univ BA97. Trin Coll Bris BA07. **d** 07. C Cullompton, Willand, Uffculme, Kentisbeare etc *Ex* from 07. *16 Gravel Walk, Cullompton EX15 1DA* Tel (01884) 34585 E-mail curate@cullompton.org
HARDING, Canon Brenda Kathleen. b 39. Bedf Coll Lon BA60 K Coll Lon BD62 Lon Inst of Educn PGCE65. St Deiniol's Hawarden 91. **d** 92 **p** 94. NSM Lancaster Ch Ch *Blackb* from 92; Acting Vice-Prin CBDTI 04-05; Hon Can Blackb Cathl from 05. *14 Ascot Close, Lancaster LA1 4LT* Tel (01524) 66071 E-mail brenda.harding@cumbria.ac.uk
HARDING, Canon Brian Edward. b 38. ALCD65. **d** 65 **p** 66. C Chislehurst Ch Ch *Roch* 65-68; P-in-c Baxenden *Blackb* 68-70; V 70-88; V Douglas 88-07; Hon Can Blackb Cathl 96-07; rtd 07. *8 Lon Eirlys, Prestatyn LL19 9JZ* Tel (01745) 851615 E-mail bnbharding@tiscali.co.uk

HARDING, Mrs Christine Joan. St Mellitus Coll. **d** 11. NSM Chadwell Heath *Chelmsf* from 11. *69 Eric Road, Romford RM6 6JH* Tel (020) 8599 6174

HARDING, Clifford Maurice. b 22. Leeds Univ BA47. Coll of Resurr Mirfield 46. **d** 48 **p** 49. C Tonge Moor *Man* 48-54; Nyasaland 54-56; CF 56-59; V Oldham St Jo *Man* 59-65; Lic to Offic *Blackb* 65-87; rtd 87; Perm to Offic *Blackb* from 87. *31 Riley Avenue, Lytham St Annes FY8 1HZ* Tel (01253) 725138

HARDING, Colin Ronald Stansby. b 32. RGN71 FVCM92. Bp Otter Coll. **d** 97. NSM Aldingbourne, Barnham and Eastergate *Chich* from 97. *Spindle Trees, 67 Elm Grove, Barnham, Bognor Regis PO22 0HJ* Tel (01243) 552579

HARDING, Mrs Elise. b 44. RGN65. STETS 07. **d** 10 **p** 11. NSM Wimborne Minster *Sarum* from 10. *The Beaches, 22 Middlehill Road, Wimborne BH21 2SD* Tel (01202) 884775 E-mail fur_elise_h@yahoo.co.uk

HARDING, James. b 77. Liv Univ BA01 MA02 PhD06. SNWTP 09. **d** 11. Chapl Liv Univ from 11; Chapl Liv Jo Moores Univ from 11. *71 Woodlands Road, Aigburth, Liverpool L17 0AL* Tel 07545-451542 (mobile) E-mail james@liverpool-anglican-chaplaincy.org

HARDING, James Alexander. b 78. Trin Coll Bris BA11. **d** 11. C Fulham Ch Ch *Lon* from 11. *55 Clancarty Road, London SW6 3AH* Tel 07956-222940 (mobile) E-mail hardingjamesa@gmail.com

HARDING, James Owen Glyn. b 42. Sussex Univ BA65. NEOC 04. **d** 06 **p** 07. NSM Acomb H Redeemer *York* from 06. *63 Station Road, Upper Poppleton, York YO26 6PZ* Tel (01904) 784495 E-mail jim2sal65@yahoo.co.uk

HARDING, John Stuart Michael. b 45. St Jo Coll Nottm 79. **d** 81 **p** 82. C Clifton *S'well* 81-87; V Broxtowe 87-98; Perm to Offic *Chelmsf* 98-01 and *M & K* 01-02; rtd 01. *Greystone Farm, 9 Liscable Road, Newtownstewart BT78 4EF*

HARDING, John William Christopher. b 31. St Jo Coll Dur BA55. **d** 58 **p** 59. C Wigan St Cath *Liv* 58-60; C Much Woolton 60-63; V Whiston 63-73; V Birkdale St Jo 73-97; rtd 97; Perm to Offic *Liv* from 98. *17 Baytree Close, Southport PR9 8RE* Tel (01704) 507654

HARDING, Ms Lesley Anne. b 58. Westcott Ho Cam 98 SEITE 99. **d** 01 **p** 02. C Walmer *Cant* 01-03; C Broadstairs 03-04; Perm to Offic 05-07; NSM Barkston and Hough Gp *Linc* 07-10; P-in-c Hattersley *Ches* from 10. *St Barnabas' Vicarage, Hattersley Road East, Hyde SK14 3EQ* Tel 0161-368 2795 E-mail lesley@revlesleyanne.plus.com

HARDING, Mrs Marion. b 33. Gilmore Course 75. **dss** 85 **d** 87 **p** 94. Hertford St André *St Alb* 85-87; Par Dn 87-93; rtd 93; NSM Lt Amwell *St Alb* 93-97; Perm to Offic from 97. *41 Calton Avenue, Hertford SG14 2ER*

HARDING, Mrs Mary Elizabeth. b 46. SRN67. STETS 97. **d** 00 **p** 01. NSM Shaftesbury *Sarum* from 00; Chapl Westmr Memorial Hosp Shaftesbury from 02. *21 Brionne Way, Shaftesbury SP7 8SL* Tel (01747) 850464 E-mail mary.harding3@virgin.net

HARDING, Michael Anthony John. b 37. Brasted Th Coll 67 Sarum Th Coll 68. **d** 71 **p** 72. C Forest Hill Ch Ch *S'wark* 71-72; C Catford St Laur 72-74; C Leominster *Heref* 74-77; R Neenton and V Ditton Priors 77-86; P-in-c Aston Botterell w Wheathill and Loughton 77-86; P-in-c Burwarton w N Cleobury 77-86; R Ditton Priors w Neenton, Burwarton etc 86-94; V E Budleigh w Bicton and Otterton *Ex* 94-03; rtd 03; Perm to Offic *Sarum* from 03. *The Beaches, 22 Middlehill Road, Wimborne BH21 2SD* Tel (01202) 884775 E-mail michaelharding@talktalk.net

HARDING, Preb Michael David. b 38. Man Univ BA61. Lich Th Coll 61. **d** 63 **p** 64. C Hednesford *Lich* 63-67; C Blurton 67-70; V Newcastle St Paul 70-99; RD Newcastle 87-97; Preb Lich Cathl 89-99; rtd 99; Perm to Offic *Lich* from 00. *7 Staines Court, Stone ST15 8XF* Tel (01785) 811737 E-mail mdharding@argonet.co.uk

HARDING, Peter Gordon. b 45. Lon Univ BA70 Open Univ BA88 MA90. Cranmer Hall Dur 77. **d** 79 **p** 80. C Kirkheaton *Wakef* 79-82; NSM New Sleaford *Linc* 90-00. *67 The Drove, Sleaford NG34 7AS* Tel (01529) 307231 E-mail peter@harding67.plus.com

HARDING, Mrs Ren Elaine Lois. b 56. Glos Univ BA05. Trin Coll Bris MA07. **d** 07 **p** 08. C Rainham *Roch* 07-11; V Joydens Wood St Barn from 11. *The Vicarage, 6 Tile Kiln Lane, Bexley DA5 2BB* Tel (01322) 528923 Mobile 07836-644782 E-mail renharding@hotmail.co.uk

HARDING, Richard Michael. b 42. St Alb Minl Tr Scheme 80. **d** 83 **p** 84. C Pershore w Pinvin, Wick and Birlingham *Worc* 83-86; V Longdon, Castlemorton, Bushley, Queenhill etc 86-95; P-in-c Catshill and Dodford 95-97; V 97-02; P-in-c Stokenham w Sherford and Beesands, and Slapton *Ex* 02-05; R 05-09; R Stokenham, Slapton, Charleton w Buckland etc 09-10; rtd 10; Perm to Offic *Portsm* from 10. *7 West View, Victoria Road, Yarmouth PO41 0QW*

HARDING, Richard Warrington. b 60. Trin Coll Bris 05. **d** 07 **p** 08. C Broadway w Wickhamford *Worc* 07-09; C Old Hill H Trin 09-11; TV Ipsley from 11. *Matchborough Vicarage, Winward Road, Redditch B98 0SX* Tel (01527) 523768

HARDING, Rolf John. b 22. Oak Hill Th Coll 41 Lon Coll of Div 46. **d** 49 **p** 50. C Sydenham H Trin *S'wark* 49-52; C Harold Wood *Chelmsf* 52-53; Min Harold Hill St Paul CD 53-61; V Coopersale 61-91; Chapl St Marg Hosp Epping 73-91; Chapl W Essex HA 86-91; rtd 91; Perm to Offic *B & W* 91-05; Asst Chapl R United Hosp Bath NHS Trust 92-94. *11 Westbrook Park, Weston, Bath BA1 4DP* Tel (01225) 484968

HARDING, Miss Sylvia. b 23. St Mich Ho Ox 55. **dss** 64 **d** 87. Rodbourne Cheney *Bris* 57-66; Midl Area Sec CPAS 66-71; Patchway 71-78; Sec Coun of Women's Min Bris 77-84; rtd 84; Westbury-on-Trym St Alb *Bris* 86-92; Hon Par Dn 87-92; Perm to Offic *Bris* and *B & W* from 92. *53 Brampton Way, Portishead, Bristol BS20 6YW* Tel (01275) 847046 or 848638

HARDINGHAM, Paul David. b 52. Lon Univ BSc74 Fitzw Coll Cam BA77. Ridley Hall Cam 75. **d** 78 **p** 79. C Cambridge St Martin *Ely* 78-81; C Jesmond Clayton Memorial *Newc* 81-88; C Harborne Heath *Birm* 88-91; R Ipswich St Matt *St E* 91-04; V Halliwell St Pet *Man* from 04. *St Peter's Vicarage, 1 Sefton Road, Bolton BL1 6HT* Tel (01204) 848567 E-mail paul@hardingham60.freeserve.co.uk

HARDINGHAM, Paul Ernest. b 57. **d** 06 **p** 07. OLM Gosberton, Gosberton Clough and Quadring *Linc* from 06; OLM Glen Gp from 07. *The Red House, 97 High Street, Gosberton, Spalding PE11 4NA* Tel (01775) 840803

HARDINGHAM, Timothy Kenneth. b 49. G&C Coll Cam BA70. ERMC 08. **d** 11. NSM Saffron Walden w Wendens Ambo, Littlebury etc *Chelmsf* from 11. *Steading, West End, Wendens Ambo, Saffron Walden CB11 4UJ* Tel (01799) 542874 Mobile 07894-537990 E-mail tim@hardingham.net

HARDISTY, Gloria. b 10 **p** 11. NSM Thornton St Jas *Bradf* from 10. *1 Wembley Avenue, Thornton, Bradford BD13 3BY* Tel (01274) 833280

HARDMAN, Bryan Edwin. b 29. Lon Univ BD60 Selw Coll Cam PhD64 K Coll Lon MTh75. Moore Th Coll Sydney. **d** 55 **p** 55. C Hurstville Australia 55-60; Perm to Offic *Ely* 60-65; V Cambridge St Andr Less 65-68; Prin Bible Coll of S Australia 68-83; Prin Karachi Dioc Sem Pakistan 83-86; Prin Discipleship Tr Cen Singapore 87-94; Nat Dir Interserve Korea 94-97; Visiting Prof Tyndale Univ Canada 99-00; rtd 01; Lic to Offic Adelaide from 06. *197 Kappler Court, 1215 Grand Junction Rd, Hope Valley, SA 5090, Australia* Tel (0061) (8) 8265 6494 E-mail hardmanbryan@gmail.com

HARDMAN, The Ven Christine Elizabeth. b 51. Lon Univ BSc(Econ)73. St Alb Minl Tr Scheme 81. **dss** 84 **d** 87 **p** 94. Markyate Street *St Alb* 84-88; Par Dn 87-88; Tutor St Alb Minl Tr Scheme 88-91; Course Dir 91-96; C Markyate Street 94-96; V Stevenage H Trin 96-01; RD Stevenage 99-01; Adn Lewisham *S'wark* 01-08; Adn Lewisham and Greenwich from 08. *129A Honor Oak Park, London SE23 3LD* Tel (020) 8699 8207 *or* 7939 9408 Fax 8699 9259 *or* 7939 9465 E-mail christine.hardman@southwark.anglican.org

HARDMAN, Geoffrey James. b 41. Birm Univ BA63. NOC 77. **d** 80 **p** 81. NSM Latchford St Jas *Ches* 80-93; NSM Haydock St Jas *Liv* from 94. *48 Denbury Avenue, Stockton Heath, Warrington WA4 2BW* Tel (01925) 264064 E-mail geoff@ghardman.freeserve.co.uk

HARDMAN, Mrs Pamela. b 39. **d** 01 **p** 02. NSM Bramhall *Ches* 01-07; NSM Prestbury from 07. *38 Deva Close, Poynton, Stockport SK12 1HH* Tel (01625) 877936 E-mail pamela.prestbury@yahoo.co.uk

HARDMAN, Canon Peter George. b 35. Man Univ BSc56. Ridley Hall Cam 58. **d** 60 **p** 61. C Oldham St Paul *Man* 60-63; NW England Area Sec SCM 63-64; NW England Area Sec CEM 64-67; Asst Chapl Marlborough Coll 67-72; Chapl 72-79; P-in-c Wareham *Sarum* 79-80; TR 80-00; Chapl Wareham Hosp 80-92; Chapl Dorset Health Care NHS Trust 92-00; Can and Preb Sarum Cathl 87-00; RD Purbeck 89-99; rtd 00; Perm to Offic *Sarum* from 00 and *B & W* from 02. *55 Palairet Close, Bradford-on-Avon BA15 1US* Tel (01225) 867198 E-mail peterhardman@onetel.com

HARDS, Mrs Valerie Joy. STETS. **d** 08 **p** 09. NSM Whippingham w E Cowes *Portsm* from 08. *Dallimores, Barton Estate, East Cowes PO32 6NR* Tel (01983) 883943

HARDWICK, The Very Revd Christopher George. b 57. Open Univ BA94 Birm Univ MA96 PhD00 ACIB79. Ripon Coll Cuddesdon 90. **d** 92 **p** 93. C Worc SE 92-95; R Ripple, Earls Croome w Hill Croome and Strensham 95-00; R Upton-on-Severn, Ripple, Earls Croome etc 00-05; RD Upton 97-05; Hon Can Worc Cathl 03-05; Dean Truro from 05; R Truro St Mary from 05. *The Deanery, The Avenue, Truro TR1 1HR* Tel (01872) 272661 *or* 276782 Fax 277788 E-mail dean@trurocathedral.org.uk

HARDWICK, Dennis Egerton. b 27. St Deiniol's Hawarden. **d** 82 **p** 83. NSM Lache cum Saltney *Ches* 82-85; P-in-c Backford 85-88; P-in-c Capenhurst 87-88; R Backford and Capenhurst 88-93; rtd 93; Perm to Offic *Chich* from 93. *11 Prime Close, Walberton, Arundel BN18 0PL* Tel (01243) 551379

HARDWICK, Canon Graham John. b 42. Qu Coll Birm 68. **d** 70 **p** 71. C Watford St Mich *St Alb* 70-73; C N Mymms 73-75; Youth Officer Cov Cathl 75-81; Chapl Lanchester Poly 76-81; V Nuneaton St Nic 81-95; Ind Chapl and P-in-c New Bilton 95-07; Hon Can Cov Cathl 04-07; rtd 08. *150 Pytchley Road, Rugby CV22 5NG* Tel (01788) 544011 Fax 333256 E-mail revgjh@btinternet.com

HARDWICK, John Audley. b 28. Em Coll Cam BA51 MA55. Westcott Ho Cam 51. **d** 53 **p** 54. C Selby Abbey *York* 53-56; Chapl St Edm Sch Hindhead 56-60; Chapl Aysgarth Sch 60-62; Chapl St Edm Sch Hindhead 62-86; Asst Hd Master 73-90; rtd 93; Perm to Offic *Ches* 95-09. *St Margarets, Little London, Chichester PO19 1PH* Tel (01243) 775002

HARDWICK, The Ven Robert. b 56. St Jo Coll Nottm 91. **d** 93 **p** 94. C Beeston *S'well* 93-97; V Scawby, Redbourne and Hibaldstow *Linc* 97-01; RD Yarborough 00-01; R Swift Current Canada from 01; Adn Swift Current from 02. *731 North Hill Drive, Swift Current SK S9H 1X4, Canada* Tel (001) (306) 773 8871 E-mail rob.hardwick@shaw.ca

HARDWICK, Canon Susan Frances. b 44. Warwick Univ BA81. Qu Coll Birm 82. **dss** 85 **d** 87 **p** 94. Chilvers Coton w Astley *Cov* 85-91; C 87-91; Dioc Disabilities Officer 91-96; Chapl Hereward Coll 91-96; Chapl FE Colls 94-09; Hon C New Bilton 96-98; FE Field Officer Team Co-ord (W Midl) 97-09; Chapl Rainsbrook Secure Tr Cen 99-09; Hon Can Cov Cathl 04-09; rtd 09. *150 Pytchley Road, Rugby CV22 5NG* Tel (01788) 544011 Fax 333256 E-mail revgjh@btinternet.com

HARDWICKE, Stephen Michael. b 57. Herts Coll BA85 Lon Bible Coll MA87 K Coll Lon MTh92. Westcott Ho Cam 93. **d** 95 **p** 96. C Leagrave *St Alb* 95-01, P-in-c Cowley *Lon* 01-03, R from 03. *St Laurence Rectory, Church Road, Cowley, Uxbridge UB8 3NB* Tel and fax (01895) 232728 E-mail stevehardwicke660@hotmail.com

HARDY, Ms Alison Jane. b 61. St Anne's Coll Ox BA82 MA96. NOC 92. **d** 95 **p** 96. C Flixton St Mich *Man* 95-98; Lect Bolton St Pet 98-00; P-in-c Irlam 00-05; R Stand from 05. *Stand Rectory, 32 Church Lane, Whitefield, Manchester M45 7NF* Tel 0161-766 2619 E-mail alisonhardy@fsmail.net

HARDY, Anthony. b 36. **d** 86 **p** 87. NSM Malden St Jas *S'wark* 86-06; Perm to Offic from 06. *48 Blake's Lane, New Malden KT3 6NR* Tel (020) 8949 0703 E-mail aehardy@waitrose.com

HARDY, Canon Anthony William. b 56. Man Univ BEd79 MEd86 Open Univ BSc00. St Jo Coll Nottm LTh88. **d** 88 **p** 89. C Pennington *Man* 88-91; V Eccleston St Luke *Liv* 91-00; Min Consultant CPAS 00-09; Dioc Evang *Liv* 00-02; Can Ev Man Cathl from 09. *30 Rathen Road, Manchester M20 4GH* Tel 0161-438 2834 E-mail canon.evangelist@manchestercathedral.org

HARDY, Canon Brian Albert. b 31. St Jo Coll Ox BA54 MA58. Westcott Ho Cam 55. **d** 57 **p** 58. C Rugeley *Lich* 57-62; Chapl Down Coll Cam 62-66; C-in-c Livingston Miss *Edin* 66-74; Preb Heref Cathl 74-78; Ch Planning Officer Telford 74-78; RD Telford Severn Gorge 75-78; Chapl Edin Th Coll 78-82; Chapl Edin R Infirmary 82-86; R Edin St Columba 82-91; Dean Edin 86-91; Hon Can St Mary's Cathl from 91; R St Andrews All SS *St And* 91-96; rtd 96. *3/3 Starbank Road, Edinburgh EH5 3BN* Tel 0131-551 6783

HARDY, Christopher Richard. b 52. R Holloway Coll Lon BMus77 Southn Univ BTh90. Chich Th Coll 87. **d** 90 **p** 91. C Kenton *Lon* 90-95; V E Finchley All SS from 95. *All Saints' Vicarage, Twyford Avenue, London N2 9NH* Tel and fax (020) 8883 9315 Mobile 07785-728272 E-mail christopherhardy@btinternet.com

HARDY, Miss Janet Frances. b 56. Newc Univ BA81 CertEd82. Trin Coll Bris 87. **d** 89 **p** 94. Par Dn Sheff St Paul 89-92; TD Gt Snaith 92-94; TV 94-96; V Pitsmoor Ch Ch 96-01; V Thorpe Hesley from 01; Asst Dioc Ecum Officer from 11. *The Vicarage, 30 Barnsley Road, Thorpe Hesley, Rotherham S61 2RR* Tel 0114-246 3487 E-mail jan.hardy@sheffield.anglican.org

HARDY, John Christopher. b 61. St Jo Coll Dur BA83 Dur Univ MA95 New Coll Edin BD92 Ox Univ MLitt00. Aston Tr Scheme 87 Coates Hall Edin 89. **d** 92 **p** 93. C Walker *Newc* 92-95; Fell Chapl Magd Coll Ox 95-98; TV Benwell *Newc* 98-03; R Alston Moor 03-08; R Newmarket St Mary w Exning St Agnes *St E* from 08. *The Rectory, 21 Hamilton Road, Newmarket CB8 0NY* Tel (01638) 660729

HARDY, Canon John Lewis Daniel. b 26. St Chad's Coll Dur BA51. **d** 52 **p** 53. C Hucknall Torkard *S'well* 52-58; V Harworth 58-65; V Sutton in Ashfield St Mary 65-85; R Keyworth 85-93; P-in-c Stanton-on-the-Wolds 85-93; RD S Bingham 91-93; Hon Can S'well Minster 92-93; rtd 93; Perm to Offic *S'well* from 93. *10 Redhill Lodge Drive, Nottingham NG5 8JH* Tel 0115-926 7370

HARDY, Joseph. b 42. RMN64. CA Tr Coll 68. **d** 05 **p** 05. C Tralee w Kilmoyley, Ballymacelligott etc *L & K* from 05. *18 Monavale, Monavally, Tralee, Co Kerry, Republic of Ireland* Tel (00353) (66) 712 6733

HARDY, Mrs Lesley Anne. b 53. Nottm Univ BA75 St Luke's Coll Ex PGCE76. **d** 05 **p** 06. OLM Lydd *Cant* 05-09; NSM

Barham w Bishopsbourne and Kingston from 09. *The Rectory, The Street, Barham, Canterbury CT4 6PA* Tel (01227) 831340

HARDY, Michael Frederick Bryan. b 36. Selw Coll Cam BA60 MA64. Linc Th Coll 60. **d** 62 **p** 63. C Pontefract St Giles *Wakef* 62-66; C Lightcliffe 66-69; V Highburn 69-78; V Birkby 78-85; C Boultham *Linc* 88-89; V Misterton and W Stockwith *S'well* 89-01; rtd 01; Perm to Offic *S'well* from 01. *23 Anderson Way, Lea, Gainsborough DN21 5EF* Tel (01427) 614468

HARDY, Michael Henry. b 33. Qu Coll Birm 85. **d** 86 **p** 87. C Leic St Jas 86-88; R Arnesby w Shearsby and Bruntingthorpe 88-94; RD Guthlaxton I 91-94; TV Bradgate Team 94-99; rtd 99; Perm to Offic *Leic* and *Pet* from 99. *14 Dean's Street, Oakham LE15 6AF* Tel (01572) 722591

HARDY, Michael John. b 35. Keble Coll Ox BA58 MA66. Cuddesdon Coll 59. **d** 61 **p** 62. C Dalton-in-Furness *Carl* 61-64; C Harborne St Pet *Birm* 64-68; Min Can Ripon Cathl 68-73; Appt and Tr Sec USPG 73-80; R Stretford St Pet *Man* 80-91; P-in-c Newton Hall *Dur* 91-96; TR Keighley St Andr *Bradf* 96-00; rtd 00; Perm to Offic *Wakef* from 01. *5 Dean Avenue, Netherthong, Holmfirth HD9 3UJ* Tel (01484) 687987

HARDY, Canon Paul Richard. b 30. K Coll Cam BA52 MA56. St Steph Ho Ox 57. **d** 59 **p** 60. C Corringham *Chelmsf* 59-61; C Prittlewell All SS 61-64; USPG Tanzania 64-95; Can Dar-es-Salaam 74-88; Can Zanzibar and Tanga 88-95; Hon Can from 95; rtd 95; Perm to Offic *Roch* from 95. *22 Bromley College, London Road, Bromley BR1 1PE* Tel (020) 8290 1289 E-mail paul@prhardy.co.uk

HARDY, Miss Pauline. b 41. CertEd. Linc Th Coll 85. **d** 87 **p** 88. Par Dn Walsall Wood *Lich* 87-89; Par Dn Buckingham *Ox* 89-93; C Buckingham w Radclive cum Chackmore 93-97; C Nash w Thornton, Beachampton and Thornborough 96-97; C Buckingham 97-03; C Watling Valley 03-06; rtd 06. *32 Campbell Road, Plymouth PL9 8UE* E-mail pauline@revhardy.plus.com

✠**HARDY, The Rt Revd Robert Maynard.** b 36. CBE01. Clare Coll Cam BA60 MA64 Hull Univ Hon DD92. Cuddesdon Coll 60. **d** 62 **p** 63 **c** 80. C Langley St Aid CD *Man* 62-64; C Langley All SS and Martyrs 64-65; Chapl and Tutor Th Selw Coll Cam 65-72; V Boreham Wood All SS *St Alb* 72-75; Dir St Alb Minl Tr Scheme 75-80; P-in-c Aspley Guise *St Alb* 75-79; P-in-c Husborne Crawley w Ridgmont 76-79; R Aspley Guise w Husborne Crawley and Ridgmont 80; Suff Bp Maidstone *Cant* 80-87; Bp Linc 87-01; Bp HM Pris 85-01; rtd 01; Hon Asst Bp Carl from 01. *Carleton House, Back Lane, Langwathby, Penrith CA10 1NB* Tel (01768) 881210

HARDY, Sam Richard Ian. b 71. Wall Hall Coll Aldenham BEd95 Open Univ MA00. Wycliffe Hall Ox BTh04. **d** 04. C Parr *Liv* 04-05. *Knarrside, Woodhead Road, Tintwistle, Glossop SK13 1JX* E-mail sam.hardy@tiscali.co.uk

HARDY, Stephen John Arundell. b 49. SEITE 95. **d** 97 **p** 98. NSM Marden *Cant* 97-00; P-in-c Lydd 00-09; AD Romney 03-08; P-in-c Barham w Bishopsbourne and Kingston from 09; C Nonington w Wymynswold and Goodnestone etc from 11; AD E Bridge from 11; AD W Bridge from 11. *The Rectory, The Street, Barham, Canterbury CT4 6PA* Tel (01227) 831340 E-mail stephenhardy1@mac.com

HARE, Christopher Sumner. b 49. Solicitor 73. WEMTC 92. **d** 95 **p** 96. NSM Saltford w Corston and Newton St Loe *B & W* 95-01; P-in-c Timsbury and Priston 01-10; R Timsbury w Priston, Camerton and Dunkerton from 10; Bp's Officer for Ord NSM (Bath Adnry) 07-08; RD Midsomer Norton from 07. *The Rectory, South Road, Timsbury, Bath BA2 0EJ* Tel (01761) 479660 E-mail chrishare@stmarystimsbury.org

HARE, David. b 46. Qu Coll Birm 81. **d** 83 **p** 83. SSF 67-94; Bp's Dom Chapl *Birm* 83-87; V Handsworth St Mich 87-97; R Newton Regis w Seckington and Shuttington 97-03; rtd 03; Perm to Offic *Birm* from 03. *118 Southam Road, Birmingham B28 0AD* Tel 0121-777 3493 E-mail dandjhare@hallgreen118.fsnet.co.uk

HARE, Douglas Stewart. b 27. Bris Univ BA51 Lon Inst of Educn PGCE52. Wycliffe Hall Ox 82. **d** 96 **p** 97. NSM Margate H Trin *Cant* 96-99; rtd 99; Perm to Offic *Sarum* from 00. *8 Lady Down View, Tisbury, Salisbury SP3 6LL* Tel (01747) 871544

HARE, Frank Richard Knight. b 22. Trin Hall Cam BA46 MA48. Cuddesdon Coll 46. **d** 48 **p** 49. C Dennington *St E* 48-51; C Eastbourne St Mary *Chich* 51-54; R Rotherfield 54-62; C Steyning 62-70; R Ashurst 62-70; TV Raveningham *Nor* 70-71; TR Barnham Broom 71-79; V Buxton w Oxnead 79-86; R Lammas w Lt Hautbois 79-86; rtd 86; Perm to Offic *St E* from 86. *14 Lee Road, Aldeburgh IP15 5HG* Tel (01728) 453372

HARE, Michael John. b 41. Lon Univ MD71 Cam Univ MA77. EAMTC 00. **d** 02 **p** 03. NSM E Leightonstone *Ely* 02-06; NSM Buckworth and Alconbury cum Weston 04-06; Perm to Offic *St E* 06-09; NSM Woodbridge St Mary from 09. *The Q Tower, 14 South Hill, Felixstowe IP11 2AA* Tel (01394) 670264 E-mail hare@waitrose.com

HARE, Richard William. b 66. Bris Univ BSc88 PhD94. Cranmer Hall Dur BA95. **d** 95 **p** 96. C Coulsdon St Jo *S'wark* 95-98; C Coventry Caludon 98-99; TV 99-07; AD Cov E 01-07; TR Bedworth from 07. *The Rectory, 1 Linden Lea, Bedworth CV12 8UD* Tel (024) 7631 0219 E-mail thehares@ic24.net

✠**HARE DUKE, The Rt Revd Michael Geoffrey.** b 25. Trin Coll Ox BA49 MA51 St Andr Univ Hon DD94. Westcott Ho Cam 50. **d** 52 **p** 53 **c** 69. C St John's Wood *Lon* 52-56; V Bury St Mark *Man* 56-62; Past Dir Clinical Th Assn Nottm 62-64; Past Consultant 64-69; V Daybrook *S'well* 64-69; Bp St And 69-94; rtd 94. *2 Balhousie Avenue, Perth PH1 5HN* Tel (01738) 622642 E-mail bishmick@blueyonder.co.uk

HARES, David Ronald Walter. b 40. Qu Coll Cam BA63 MA67 CertEd. Westcott Ho Cam 64. **d** 66 **p** 67. C Cannock *Lich* 66-69; Chapl Peterho Cam 69-72; Asst Master Chesterton Sch Cam 72-74; V Kesgrave *St E* 74-98; R Lt Barningham, Blickling, Edgefield etc *Nor* 98-05; rtd 05; Perm to Offic *Nor* from 05. *17 Trory Street, Norwich NR2 2RH* Tel (01603) 626392 E-mail dh@davidhares.freeserve.co.uk

HAREWOOD, John Rupert. b 24. Man Univ BA48. Sarum & Wells Th Coll 76. **d** 79 **p** 80. NSM Taunton St Jas *B & W* 79-82; TV Camelot Par 82-89; rtd 89; Perm to Offic *Ex* from 92. *19 Swains Road, Budleigh Salterton EX9 6HU* Tel (01395) 445802

HARFORD, Julian Gray. b 29. Univ Coll Ox BA52 MA59 Lon Univ PGCE58. Qu Coll Birm. **d** 64 **p** 65. C W End *Win* 64-67; C Chearsley w Nether Winchendon *Ox* 67-77; C Chilton All SS 72-77; R Westbury w Turweston, Shalstone and Biddlesden 77-86; C Chenies and Lt Chalfont 86-87; C Chenies and Lt Chalfont, Latimer and Flaunden 87-95; rtd 95; Perm to Offic *Sarum* from 95 and *Ox* from 11. *49 Dove Court, Faringdon SN7 7AB* Tel (01367) 243790

HARFORD, The Ven Michael Rivers Dundas. b 26. Trin Coll Cam BA49 MA51. Westcott Ho Cam 50. **d** 52 **p** 53. C Ashton-on-Ribble St Andr *Blackb* 52-55; Perm to Offic *Edin* 55-56; C Singapore Cathl and Chapl Univ of Malaya 56-60; C Kuala Lumpur St Mary 60-62; V 62-66; V Childwall St Dav *Liv* 66-71; R Katanning Australia 71-76; Adn Albany 76-79; R Bicton and Attadale 79-86; R Guildford 86-91; Adn Swan 86-89; Adn Mitchell 90-91; rtd 91. *Unit 12, 18 Bridges Road, Melville WA 6156, Australia* Tel (0061) (8) 9319 1538 Mobile 410-566896 E-mail venmike@optusnet.com.au

HARFORD, Paul Roger. b 83. York Univ BA04 Selw Coll Cam BA09. Ridley Hall Cam 07. **d** 10 **p** 11. C Stokesley w Seamer *York* from 10. *18 Station Road, Stokesley, Middlesbrough TS9 5AH* E-mail revharford@gmail.com

HARFORD, Timothy William. b 58. Nottm Univ BTh89. Linc Th Coll 86. **d** 89 **p** 90. C Minehead *B & W* 89-93; R Knebworth *St Alb* 93-03; Children's Soc 03-09; Perm to Offic *Bradf* from 04. *Address temp unknown*

HARGER, Robin Charles Nicholas. b 49. BTh. Sarum & Wells Th Coll 78. **d** 81 **p** 82. C Charlton Kings St Mary *Glouc* 81-85; C Folkestone St Mary and St Eanswythe *Cant* 85-89; TV Langley and Parkfield *Man* 89-95; TV Bournemouth Town Cen *Win* from 95. *The Vicarage, 2A St Anthony's Road, Bournemouth BH2 6PD* Tel (01202) 554355 E-mail robin.harger2@btopenworld.com

HARGRAVE, Canon Alan Lewis. b 50. Birm Univ BSc73 PhD77. Ridley Hall Cam 87. **d** 89 **p** 90. C Cambridge H Trin w St Andr Gt *Ely* 89-92; C Cambridge H Trin 92-93; C-in-c Fen Ditton 93-94; V Cambridge H Cross 94-04; Can Res Ely Cathl from 04. *Powchers Hall, The College, Ely CB7 4DL* Tel (01353) 660304 *or* 660300 Fax 665658 E-mail alan.hargrave@cathedral.ely.anglican.org

HARGRAVES, Mrs Christobel Mary Kathleen. b 58. Man Poly BSc79 Open Univ MBA RGN83. SAOMC 03. **d** 06 **p** 07. C Goring and Streatley w S Stoke *Ox* 06-09; R Shelswell from 09. *The Rectory, Water Stratford Road, Finmere, Buckingham MK18 4AT* Tel (01280) 847184 E-mail chris.hargraves@psaconnect.com

HARGREAVE, James David. b 44. K Coll Lon BA66 Lon Univ PGCE68 ALCM89 LTCL90. Coll of Resurr Mirfield 70. **d** 73 **p** 74. C Houghton le Spring *Dur* 73-77; C Gateshead St Cuth w St Paul 77-79; V Trimdon 79-87; C-in-c Stockton Green Vale H Trin CD 87-94; V Hedon w Paull *York* 94-02; rtd 02. *1 The Avenue, Crescent Street, Cottingham HU16 5QT* Tel (01482) 844297

HARGREAVES, Andrew David. b 74. Homerton Coll Cam BEd97. Trin Coll Bris BA08. **d** 08 **p** 09. C Shirley *Win* from 08. *16 Radway Road, Southampton SO15 7PW* Tel (023) 8077 0474 Mobile 07801-062986 E-mail adhargreaves@btinternet.com

HARGREAVES, Arthur Walsh. b 34. Man Univ MB, ChB FRCSE FRCS FRCSGlas. St Deiniol's Hawarden 89. **d** 90 **p** 91. NSM Baguley *Man* 90-04; rtd 04; Perm to Offic *Man* 04-08. *33 Chelford Road, Knutsford WA16 8NN* Tel (01565) 654343

HARGREAVES, John. b 43. St Jo Coll Nottm 86. **d** 88 **p** 89. C Werneth *Man* 88-91; TV Rochdale 91-96; C Man Gd Shep 96-97; Perm to Offic *Liv* 96-97; C Manchester Gd Shep and St Barn 97-98; rtd 98; Perm to Offic *Man* 06-08. *Penola, Wyebank, Bakewell DE45 1BH*

HARGREAVES, John Rodney. b 36. Open Univ BA74. Didsbury Methodist Coll 59 St Deiniol's Hawarden 74. **d** 75 **p** 75. In Methodist Ch 63-74; C Pontypool *Mon* 75-77; C Llandeyrn 77-79; Chapl HM Pris Aylesbury 79-83; Sen Chapl HM Pris

Stafford 83-88; Asst Chapl Gen of Pris (N) 88-90; Asst Chapl Gen of Pris 90-96; R Stone St Mich and St Wulfad w Aston St Sav *Lich* 96-01; rtd 01; Master St Jo Hosp Lich 01-04; Perm to Offic from 04. *217 Newcastle Road, Stone ST15 8LF* Tel (01785) 814765 E-mail jrhargreaves@easynet.co.uk

HARGREAVES, John Wilson. b 46. Aber Univ BScFor67. Westcott Ho Cam 84. **d** 86 **p** 87. C Rugby *Cov* 86-90; TV Daventry, Ashby St Ledgers, Braunston etc *Pet* 90-97; Chapl Daventry Tertiary Coll 94-97; P-in-c Pinxton *Derby* 97-01; R 01-02; TR E Scarsdale from 02. *The Rectory, Rectory Road, Upper Langwith, Mansfield NG20 9RE* Tel (01623) 748505

HARGREAVES, Julia Gay. b 61. EMMTC 04. **d** 07 **p** 08. NSM Glenfield *Leic* 07-08; NSM Upper Soar 08-11; TV Bosworth and Sheepy Gp from 11; C Nailstone and Carlton w Shackerstone from 11. *The Rectory, Church Lane, Sheepy Magna, Atherstone CV9 3QS* Tel (01827) 881389 E-mail julia.hargreaves@btinternet.com

HARGREAVES, Ms Marise. b 60. Leeds Univ BA81. Cranmer Hall Dur 82. **dss** 85 **d** 94 **p** 95. Yeadon St Jo *Bradf* 85-87; NSM Bradf St Clem 94-96; NSM Buttershaw St Paul 96-00; C Eccleshill 00-03; Perm to Offic 03-09; Chapl Derby Hosps NHS Foundn Trust from 09. *Chaplaincy, Royal Derby Hospital, Uttoxeter Road, Derby DE22 3NE* Tel (01332) 340131

HARGREAVES, Mark Kingston. b 63. Oriel Coll Ox BA85 MA89 Rob Coll Cam PhD91 W Lon Inst of HE PGCE86. Ridley Hall Cam 87. **d** 91 **p** 92. C Highbury Ch Ch w St Jo and St Sav *Lon* 91-94; C Ealing St Steph Castle Hill 94-97; C Notting Hill St Jo and St Pet 97-02; V Notting Hill St Pet from 03; AD Kensington 06-11. *48 Ladbroke Road, London W11 3NW* Tel (020) 7221 9841 E-mail mark@nottinghillchurch.org.uk

HARGREAVES-STEAD, Terence Desmond. b 32. Edin Th Coll 60. **d** 63 **p** 64. C Walney Is *Carl* 63-66; Chapl Withington Hosp Man 66-72; V Westleigh St Paul *Man* 72-06; Chapl Wigan and Leigh Health Services NHS Trust 96-01; Chapl Wrightington Wigan and Leigh NHS Trust 01-06; rtd 07; Perm to Offic *Man* from 08. *4 Hartford Green, Westhoughton, Bolton BL5 2GL* Tel (01942) 859929

HARINGTON, Roger John Urquhart. b 48. Trin Hall Cam BA70 MA71. Coll of Resurr Mirfield 72. **d** 75 **p** 76. C Liv Our Lady and St Nic w St Anne 75-78; Asst Chapl Leeds Univ and Poly 78-81; TV Moor Allerton 81-86; Dioc Drama Adv (Jabbok Theatre Co) 86-95; V Leeds Gipton Epiphany 95-02. *21 Spencer Place, Leeds LS7 4DQ* Tel 0113-240 0769 E-mail jabbok@gn.apc.org

HARKER, Harold Aidan. b 35. **d** 82 **p** 83. OSB from 53; C Reading St Giles *Ox* 82-83; Lic to Offic 83-87; C Halstead St Andr w H Trin and Greenstead Green *Chelmsf* 87-89; P-in-c Belchamp St Paul 89-97; R Belchamp Otten w Belchamp Walter and Bulmer etc 97-00; rtd 00; Lic to Offic *Chelmsf* from 00. *38 Sheppard's College, London Road, Bromley BR1 1PE* Tel (020) 8464 1206

HARKER, Ian. b 39. Dur Univ BA61. Lich Th Coll Moray Ho Edin 66. **d** 63 **p** 64. C Knottingley *Wakef* 63-66; Perm to Offic 66-70; C Notting Hill *Lon* 70-75; Chapl Newc Univ 75-83; Master Newc St Thos Prop Chpl 75-83; Perm to Offic *Chelmsf* 99-01; C Plaistow and N Canning Town 01; C Loughton St Jo 01-02; V Leytonstone H Trin and St Aug Harrow Green 02-11; rtd 11; Perm to Offic *Chelmsf* from 11. *Holy Trinity Vicarage, 4 Holloway Road, London E11 4LD* Tel (020) 8539 6067 E-mail harkatvic@aol.com

HARKER, John Hadlett. b 37. Dur Univ BSc59 Newc Univ PhD67 CEng MIChemE64 MInstE64 CChem MRSC65 FIChemE80. NEOC 81. **d** 84 **p** 85. C Earsdon *Newc* 84-87; P-in-c Long Horsley 87-91; V Bassenthwaite, Isel and Setmurthy *Carl* 91-94; TR Howden *York* 94-96; P-in-c Willerby w Ganton and Folkton 96-98; rtd 98; Perm to Offic *Newc* 98-01 and from 04; Hon C Newc St Andr and St Luke 01-04. *30 Station Road, Kenton Bank Foot, Newcastle upon Tyne NE13 8AG* Tel 0191-286 3206 E-mail harker@thestell.freeserve.co.uk

HARKER, Stephan John. b 47. Em Coll Cam BA68 MA72. Westcott Ho Cam 70. **d** 72 **p** 73. C Marton *Blackb* 72-76; C Preston St Matt 76-79; C Fleetwood St Pet 79-80; Sen Chapl Charterhouse Sch Godalming 81-07; Chapl from 07. *Firview, 63 Peperharow Road, Godalming GU7 2PL* Tel (01483) 422155 E-mail sjh@charterhouse.org.uk

HARKIN, Canon John Patrick. b 53. Oak Hill Th Coll 87. **d** 89 **p** 90. C Wisley w Pyrford *Guildf* 89-93; P-in-c Mickleham 93-98; Chapl Box Hill Sch Surrey 93-98; R Jersey St Ouen w St Geo *Win* 98-10; Vice-Dean Jersey 01-10; P-in-c Andover from 10; RD Andover from 10; Hon Can Win Cathl from 09. *St Mary's Vicarage, Church Close, Andover SP10 1DP* Tel (01264) 362268 E-mail harkin12@btinternet.com

HARKIN, Terence James. b 46. Lon Bible Coll BA82 New Coll Edin MTh94. **d** 95 **p** 96. In Bapt Min 86-95; C Edin H Cross 95-96; C S Queensferry 95-96; P-in-c from 96. *6 Wellhead Close, South Queensferry EH30 9WA* Tel 0131-319 1099 *or* 331 1958 E-mail tjharkin@priorychurch.com

HARKINS, James Robert. b 27. Minnesota Univ BA49. Seabury-Western Th Sem MTh53. **d** 52 **p** 52. USA 52-60, 72-79 and

91-93; Colombia 60-72; Dominica 79-85; Venezuela 85-91; Chapl Venice w Trieste *Eur* 94-99; P-in-c Menton 99-01; rtd 01. *69 Main Street Apt 201, North Adams MA 01247-3427, USA*

HARKNETT, David Philip. b 74. St Pet Coll Ox BA97. Oak Hill Th Coll BA03. **d** 03 **p** 04. C Radipole and Melcombe Regis *Sarum* 03-07; TV Melbury from 07. *The Vicarage, Corscombe, Dorchester DT2 0NU* Tel (01935) 891247 E-mail davidharknett@hotmail.com

HARKNETT, Linda. b 48. Open Univ BA81 Croydon Coll CertEd92. SEITE 97. **d** 00 **p** 01. NSM Sutton St Nic *S'wark* 00-03; Chapl Epsom and St Helier NHS Trust 00-03; Chapl Whitelands Coll Surrey Univ Roehampton 03-07; Dioc FE and HE Chapl Officer 03-07; P-in-c Headley w Box Hill *Guildf* from 07. *The Rectory, Church Lane, Headley, Epsom KT18 6LE* Tel (01372) 377327 Mobile 07796-903167

HARLAND, Brenda. **d** 08. NSM Thatcham *Ox* from 08. *St Mary's Church Office, Church Gate, Thatcham RG19 3PN* Tel (01635) 862277 E-mail brenda.harland@ntlworld.com

HARLAND, Canon Harold William James. b 35. Hertf Coll Ox BA59 MA63. Clifton Th Coll 59. **d** 61 **p** 62. C Reigate St Mary *S'wark* 61-64; C Farnborough *Guildf* 64-68; V Walmley *Birm* 68-74; V Bromley Ch Ch *Roch* 74-86; V Foord St Jo *Cant* 86-00; Dir Post-Ord Tr 93-97; Hon Can Cath 94-00; rtd 00; Perm to Offic *Cant* from 00. *121 Station Road West, Canterbury CT2 8DE* Tel (01227) 764699 E-mail harlandh992@aol.com

HARLE, Michael Richardson. b 58. BA80 Man Univ MBM91. **d** 11. NSM Claygate *Guildf* from 11. *1 The Green, Claygate, Esher KT10 0JL* Tel (01372) 463898 Mobile 07788-160040 E-mail mikeharle@btinternet.com

HARLEY, Brother Brian Mortimer. b 25. K Coll Lon 48. **d** 53 **p** 54. C Bris St Agnes w St Simon 53-56; Lic to Offic *Sarum* 56-62; SSF from 56; Chapl St Fran Sch Hooke 58-61; Papua New Guinea 61-79; Australia from 87; Min Gen SSF from 91. *The Hermitage of St Bernadine, PO Box 46, Stroud NSW 2425, Australia* Tel (0061) (2) 4994 5372

HARLEY, Canon Brian Nigel. b 30. Clare Coll Cam BA53 MA57. Cuddesdon Coll 53. **d** 55 **p** 56. C Basingstoke *Win* 55-60; TV 71-73; TR 73-80; C W End 60-61; C-in-c Southn St Chris Thornhill CD 61-71; V Eastleigh 80-93; RD Eastleigh 85-93; rtd 93; Perm to Offic *Win* from 93; Bp's Dom Chapl 94-96. *18 Phillimore Road, Southampton SO16 2NR* Tel (023) 8055 1049

HARLEY, Mrs Carol Anne. b 46. **d** 00 **p** 01. OLM Tettenhall Wood and Perton *Lich* from 00. *27 Tyrley Close, Compton, Wolverhampton WV6 8AP* Tel (01902) 755316 E-mail allynharley@lineone.net

HARLEY, Christopher David. b 41. Selw Coll Cam BA63 MA69 Bris Univ PGCE64 Columbia Bible Sem DMin92 Utrecht Univ PhD02. Clifton Th Coll 64. **d** 66 **p** 67. C Finchley Ch Ch *Lon* 66-69; Hon C 75-78; Ethiopia 70-75; Hd of UK Miss CMJ 75-78; Lect All Nations Chr Coll Ware 78-85; Prin 85-93; Chmn Lon Inst of Contemporary Christianity 88-89; Chmn CMJ 89-90; Crosslinks 93-06; Gen Dir OMF Internat 93-05; NSM Bromley Ch Ch *Roch* 93-96; NSM Singapore 96-06; rtd 06. *6 Michigan Way, Exeter EX4 5EU* Tel (01392) 207190 E-mail harleydavid@omf.net

HARLEY, David Bertram. b 22. Down Coll Cam BA50 MA55. Westcott Ho Cam 55. **d** 56 **p** 58. Asst Master Bedford Sch 50-58; C Biddenham *St Alb* 56-58; Chapl Stamford Sch 58-87; rtd 87; Confrater Browne's Hosp Stamford 87-11; Lic to Offic *Linc* 59-94; Perm to Offic from 94. *Beggars' Roost, Priory Road, Stamford PE9 2ES* Tel (01780) 763403

HARLEY, The Ven Michael. b 50. AKC73 Ch Ch Coll Cant CertEd74 Lambeth STh92 Kent Univ MPhil95. St Aug Coll Cant 74. **d** 75 **p** 76. C Chatham St Wm *Roch* 75-78; C-in-c Weeke *Win* 78-81; V Southampton St Mary Extra 81-86; V Hurstbourne Tarrant, Faccombe, Vernham Dean etc 86-99; ACORA Link Officer 91-94; Dioc Rural Officer 95-97; RD Andover 95-99; V Chandler's Ford 99-09; Tutor STETS 03-06; Hon Can Win Cathl 06-09; Adn Win from 09; Master St Cross Hosp 09-11; P-in-c Win St Cross w St Faith 09-11. *22 St John's Street, Winchester SO23 8HF* Tel (01962) 869442 E-mail michael.harley@winchester.anglican.org

HARLEY, Nigel. *See* HARLEY, Canon Brian Nigel

HARLEY, Peter David. b 59. Sheff Univ BSc82 Warwick Univ MBA86. **d** 09 **p** 10. OLM Horwich and Rivington *Man* from 09; OLM Blackrod from 11. *6 Barford Grove, Lostock, Bolton BL6 4NQ* Tel (01204) 694611 E-mail peter.harley@talktalk.net

HARLEY, Canon Robert Patterson. b 52. St Andr Univ MA75 Cam Univ CertEd76 Glas Univ PhD89 Edin Univ BD97. **d** 97 **p** 98. C Edin St Thos 97-00; Chapl Lothian Univ Hosps NHS Trust 98-00; P-in-c Kirriemuir *St And* from 00; Can St Ninian's Cathl Perth from 08. *128 Glengate, Kirriemuir DD8 4JG* Tel (01575) 575515 E-mail robert.harley@virgin.net

HARLEY, Roger Newcomb. b 38. Ely Th Coll 61. **d** 64 **p** 65. C Plymouth St Pet *Ex* 64-66; C Heston *Lon* 66-69; C Maidstone All SS w St Phil and H Trin *Cant* 69-73; R Temple Ewell w Lydden 73-79; P-in-c Shirley St Geo 79-81; V 81-85; V Croydon H Sav *S'wark* 85-95; V Forest Row *Chich* 95-03; rtd 03; Perm to

Offic *Cant* from 03. *7 Roman Way, St Margarets-at-Cliffe, Dover CT15 6AH* Tel (01304) 851720 E-mail rnharley@tesco.net

HARLING, Timothy Charles. b 80. Fitzw Coll Cam BA04. Westcott Ho Cam 02. **d** 05 **p** 06. C Romsey *Win* 05-09; Chapl HM Pris Peterborough from 09. *HM Prison Peterborough, Saville Road, Peterborough PE3 7PD* Tel (01733) 217500

HARLOW, Antony Francis. b 24. Pemb Coll Cam BA50 MA55. Oak Hill Th Coll 84. **d** 85 **p** 86. NSM Watford St Luke *St Alb* 85-86; CMS 86-91; Uganda 86-91; NSM Watford St Pet *St Alb* 92-96; Perm to Offic *St Alb* 90-98 and *B & W* from 98. *16 Derham Court, High Street, Yatton, Bristol BS49 4DW* Tel (01934) 832651

HARLOW, Canon Derrick Peter. b 30. St Jo Coll Cam BA53 MA57. Ridley Hall Cam 53. **d** 55 **p** 56. C Barking St Marg *Chelmsf* 55-58; V Leyton Em 58-63; V Goodmayes All SS 63-75; R Thundersley 76-83; TR Saffron Walden w Wendens Ambo and Littlebury 83-95; Hon Can Chelmsf Cathl 84-95; rtd 95; Perm to Offic *Ely* from 95 and *Chelmsf* from 98. *26 Kintbury, Duxford, Cambridge CB22 4RR* Tel (01223) 721405

HARLOW, Mrs Elizabeth Gilchrist. b 27. MSc50. Oak Hill Th Coll 85. **d** 91 **p** 94. NSM St Alb St Luke *St Alb* 91-94; NSM Watford St Luke 94-96; Perm to Offic *St Alb* 96-98 and *B & W* 98-10. *16 Derham Court, High Street, Yatton, Bristol BS49 4DW* Tel (01934) 832651

HARLOW, Kathryn. b 78. Southn Univ BSc99. Wycliffe Hall Ox BTh07. **d** 07 **p** 08. C Foord St Jo *Cant* from 07. *2 Chalk Close, Folkestone CT19 5TD* Tel (01303) 256356 E-mail rev_kathryn@hotmail.co.uk

HARLOW-TRIGG, Richard John St Clair. b 63. Cam Univ BA85 MA88. Cranmer Hall Dur 87. **d** 89 **p** 90. C Hyson Green *S'well* 89-91; C Basford w Hyson Green 91-94; C Mansfield SS Pet and Paul 94-97; TV Newark 97-01; Chapl Mid Sussex NHS Trust 01-02; Chapl Brighton and Sussex Univ Hosps NHS Trust from 02; Chapl St Pet and St Jas Hospice N Chailey 02-05. *The Princess Royal Hospital, Lewes Road, Haywards Heath RH16 4EX* Tel (01444) 441881 ext 4232 E-mail richard.harlow-trigg@bsuh.nhs.uk

HARLOW, Archdeacon of. *See* WEBSTER, The Ven Martin Duncan

HARMAN, Karin. *See* VOTH HARMAN, Karin

HARMAN, Kathleen Joyce. b 49. **d** 03 **p** 04. C Llangynwyd w Maesteg 03-08; R Dowlais and Penydarren from 08. *The Rectory, Gwernllwyn Road, Dowlais, Merthyr Tydfil CF48 3NA* Tel (01685) 722118

HARMAN, Canon Leslie Davies. b 46. Nottm Univ BTh76. St Jo Coll Nottm LTh75. **d** 76 **p** 77. C Wandsworth All SS *S'wark* 76-78; C Godstone 78-82; V Thorncombe w Winsham and Cricket St Thomas *B & W* 82-87; TV Hitchin *St Alb* 87-95; V Royston from 95; RD Buntingford 96-01; Hon Can St Alb from 09. *The Vicarage, 20 Palace Gardens, Royston SG8 5AD* Tel (01763) 243145 *or* 788933

HARMAN, Michael John. b 48. Chich Th Coll 71. **d** 74 **p** 75. C Blackpool St Steph *Blackb* 74-79; Chapl RN 79-06; rtd 06; Perm to Offic *Ex* and *Truro* from 06; P-in-c Wembury *Ex* from 08. *18 Furzeacre Close, Plymouth PL7 5DZ* Tel (01752) 338910 Mobile 07836-377820 E-mail revmikeharman@blueyonder.co.uk

HARMAN, Theodore Allan. b 27. Linc Coll Ox BA52 MA56 Hatf Coll Dur MA90. Wells Th Coll 52. **d** 54 **p** 55. C Hawkshead and Low Wray *Carl* 54-55; C Kirkby Stephen w Mallerstang 55-57; Asst Chapl Sedbergh Sch 57-84; Sen Chapl 84-87; Tutor Hatf Coll Dur from 88; Admissions Tutor 89-90; Lib and Coll Officer 91-02; Acting Chapl 99-00; Fell from 00; Perm to Offic *Dur* from 88. *Flat D1, Hatfield College, North Bailey, Durham DH1 3RQ* Tel 0191-334 2626 Fax 334 3101 E-mail t.a.harman@durham.ac.uk

HARMER, Timothy James. b 47. Birm Univ CertEd68. St Jo Coll Nottm BA95. **d** 95 **p** 96. C Studley *Cov* 95-98; V Tanworth *Birm* 98-05; P-in-c Helsington *Carl* from 05; P-in-c Underbarrow from 05; RD Kendal from 08. *Sunnybank, Underbarrow, Kendal LA8 8HG* Tel (01539) 568865 E-mail revtim.harmer@virgin.net

HARMSWORTH, Canon Roger James. b 46. Univ of W Ontario BA87. Huron Coll Ontario MDiv90. **d** 90 **p** 90. Canada 90-96; I Maryborough w Dysart Enos and Ballyfin *C & O* 96-01; I Killanne w Killegney, Rossdroit and Templeshanbo from 01; Treas Ferns Cathl 03-04; Chan from 04. *The Rectory, Clonroche, Enniscorthy, Co Wexford, Republic of Ireland* Tel and fax (00353) (53) 924 4180 E-mail precentor.1@hotmail.com

HARNDEN, Peter John. b 63. Coll of Resurr Mirfield 96. **d** 98 **p** 99. C Staplehurst *Cant* 98-02; V Tokyngton St Mich *Lon* from 02; P-in-c Benhilton *S'wark* from 11. *All Saints' Vicarage, All Saints' Road, Sutton SM1 3DA* E-mail phamden@tiscali.co.uk

HARNEY, Janice. b 56. **d** 02 **p** 03. OLM Pennington *Man* 02-06; NSM Leigh Deanery 06-11; NSM Astley, Tyldesley and Mosley Common from 11. *29 Green Lane, Leigh WN7 2TL* Tel and fax (01942) 671481 Mobile 07811-764355 E-mail jan.harney@btinternet.com

HARNISH, Robert George. b 64. Univ of Ottawa BSc87 Worc Coll Ox DPhil90 MA92. Wycliffe Hall Ox 90. **d** 93 **p** 94. C Chinnor w Emmington and Sydenham etc Ox 93-95; Chapl and Dean of Div New Coll Ox 96-01; Chapl Eliz Coll Guernsey from 01. *11 Saumarez Street, St Peter Port, Guernsey GY1 2PT* Tel (01481) 713298 *or* 726544

HARONSKI, Boleslaw. b 46. Pemb Coll Ox BA68 MA72 DPhil73. St Mich Coll Llan 80 Westcott Ho Cam 82. **d** 82 **p** 83. C Maindee Newport *Mon* 82-85; V Llanishen w Trellech Grange and Llanfihangel etc 85-89; V Blackwood 89-92; rtd 11. *Tir Llandre, Llanarthney, Carmarthen SA32 8JE*

✠**HARPER, The Most Revd Alan Edwin Thomas.** b 44. OBE96. Leeds Univ BA65. CITC 75. **d** 78 **p** 79 **c** 02. C Ballywillan *Conn* 78-80; I Moville w Greencastle, Upper Moville etc *D & R* 80-82; I Londonderry Ch Ch 82-86; I Belfast Malone St Jo *Conn* 86-02; Preb St Audoen St Patr Cathl Dublin 90-01; Adn *Conn* 96-02; Prec Belf Cathl 96-02; Bp *Conn* 02-07; Abp Arm from 07. *Diocesan Office, Church House, 46 Abbey Street, Armagh BT61 7DZ* Tel (028) 3752 2858
E-mail archbishop@armagh.anglican.org

HARPER, Alan Peter. b 50. Man Univ BA73 FCA83. Ripon Coll Cuddesdon 86. **d** 88 **p** 89. C Newport w Longford and Chetwynd *Lich* 88-91; P-in-c Wilnecote 91-94; V 94-98; V Codsall 98-07; Preb Lich Cathl 02-07; RD Penkridge 06-07; Bp's Dom Chapl *Derby* 07-11; P-in-c Mackworth All SS from 11; P-in-c Kirk Langley from 11; P-in-c Mugginton and Kedleston from 11. *The Vicarage, 4 Church Lane, Kirk Langley, Ashbourne DE22 4NG* Tel (01332) 825667 E-mail revd.alan8@btinternet.com

HARPER, Barry. *See* HARPER, Canon Malcolm Barry

HARPER, Brian John. b 61. Liv Univ BA82. CITC. **d** 85 **p** 86. C Portadown St Columba *Arm* 85-88; C Drumglass 88-89; I Errigle Keerogue w Ballygawley and Killeshil 89-93; I Mullavilly from 93. *89 Mullavilly Road, Tandragee, Craigavon BT62 2LX* Tel (028) 3884 0221 *or* 3884 1918
E-mail mullavilly@btinternet.com

HARPER, Clive Stewart. b 35. FCIS71. Ridley Hall Cam 80. **d** 82 **p** 83. C Bromyard *Heref* 82-85; P-in-c Bredenbury and Wacton w Grendon Bishop 85-89; P-in-c Edwyn Ralph and Collington w Thornbury 85-89; P-in-c Pencombe w Marston Stannett and Lt Cowarne 85-89; R Bredenbury w Grendon Bishop and Wacton etc 89-92; R Bilton *Cov* 92-02; rtd 02; Hon C Churchover w Willey *Cov* 02-05; Perm to Offic from 05. *Kairos, 18 Whimbrel Close, Rugby CV23 0WG* Tel (01788) 541041
E-mail harper@clival.freeserve.co.uk

HARPER, David Laurence. b 51. Qu Coll Cam BA73 MA77 PhD78. Wycliffe Hall Ox BA80. **d** 80 **p** 81. C Mansfield SS Pet and Paul *S'well* 80-84; C Wollaton 84-87; V Brinsley w Underwood 87-94; R Bingham from 94; AD Bingham 00-03; AD E Bingham 03-07. *The Rectory, Bingham, Nottingham NG13 8DR* Tel (01949) 837335
E-mail dl.harper@btopenworld.com

HARPER, Canon Geoffrey Roger. b 57. Jes Coll Cam BA79 MA83. St Jo Coll Nottm 81. **d** 84 **p** 85. C Belper *Derby* 84-87; C Birstall and Wanlip *Leic* 87-90; TV Tettenhall Regis *Lich* 90-97; C Aldridge 97-02; Perm to Offic 02-07; Chapl Douglas MacMillan Hospice Stoke-on-Trent 04-07; C W Bromwich Gd Shep w St Jo *Lich* 07-09; Perm to Offic *Derby* 09-10; P-in-c Burton Joyce w Bulcote and Stoke Bardolph *S'well* from 10; Hon Can W Ankole from 05. *The Vicarage, 9 Chestnut Grove, Burton Joyce, Nottingham NG14 5DP* Tel 0115-931 2109 Mobile 07954-409635 E-mail harperrog@googlemail.com

HARPER, Gordon. b 32. Oak Hill Th Coll 64. **d** 66 **p** 67. C Halliwell St Pet *Man* 66-71 and 84-99; P-in-c Brinsworth *Sheff* 71-75; V Brinsworth w Catcliffe 76-84; rtd 99; Perm to Offic *Man* from 99. *15 New Church Road, Bolton BL1 5QP* Tel (01204) 849413

HARPER, Gordon William Robert. b 48. Wellington Univ (NZ) BA70 St Chad's Coll Dur BA74 Nottm Univ PhD89. Coll of Resurr Mirfield 74. **d** 75 **p** 76. C Battyeford *Wakef* 75-76; New Zealand 76-80; P-in-c Byers Green *Dur* 80-83; V Evenwood 83-89; R Wolviston 89-00; V Billingham St Mary 97-01; P-in-c Winlaton from 01. *The Rectory, Winlaton, Blaydon-on-Tyne NE21 6PL* Tel and fax 0191-414 3165
E-mail drgwr&jharper@westbill.freeserve.co.uk

HARPER, Ian. b 51. AKC78. Oak Hill Th Coll 79. **d** 80 **p** 81. C Sidcup St Jo *Roch* 80-83; C Bushey *St Alb* 83-87; TV Thamesmead *S'wark* 87-92; TR N Lambeth 92-00; V Homerton St Luke *Lon* 00-10; AD Hackney 04-09; V Ladywood St Jo and St Pet *Birm* from 10. *St John's Vicarage, Darnley Road, Birmingham B16 8TF* Tel 0121-218 5530
E-mail harper-il@sky.com

HARPER, James. b 35. St Luke's Coll Ex TDip57. SWMTC. **d** 90 **p** 91. NSM Pendeen w Morvah *Truro* 90-97. *1 Millstream Mews, 50 Beaconsfield Road, Christchurch BH23 1QT* Tel (01202) 477138

HARPER, John Anthony. b 46. AKC69. **d** 70 **p** 71. C Pet St Mary Boongate 70-73; C Abington 73-75; V Grendon w Castle Ashby 75-82; Asst Dioc Youth Chapl 75-82; R Castor w Sutton and Upton 82-94; TV Riverside *Ox* 94-04; V Meppershall and

Shefford *St Alb* from 04; RD Shefford 08-11; rtd 11. *Address temp unknown* E-mail j.harper@ukgateway.net

HARPER, Joseph Frank. b 38. Hull Univ BA60 MA86 MPhil98 Dur Univ PhD10. Linc Th Coll 80. **d** 81 **p** 82. C Preston St Cuth *Blackb* 81-83; C Lancaster St Mary 83-87; V Bamber Bridge St Aid 87-92; V Kinsley w Wragby *Wakef* 92-99; R Newhaven *Chich* 99-04; rtd 04. *30 Greenways, Consett DH8 7DE* Tel (01207) 590962 E-mail joseph@josephharper.wanadoo.co.uk

HARPER, Canon Malcolm Barry. b 37. Dur Univ BSc59. Wycliffe Hall Ox 59. **d** 61 **p** 62. C Harold Wood *Chelmsf* 61-65; C Madeley *Heref* 65-68; V Slaithwaite w E Scammonden *Wakef* 68-75; V Walmley *Birm* 75-03; Hon Can Birm Cathl 96-03; rtd 03; Perm to Offic *Birm* from 03. *1 Welcombe Drive, Sutton Coldfield B76 1ND* Tel 0121-351 3990
E-mail canonbarryharper@tiscali.co.uk

HARPER, Mrs Margaret. b 51. Nottm Coll of Educn TCert73 Nottm Univ BEd74. SAOMC 98. **d** 01 **p** 02. C Slough *Ox* 01-05; P-in-c Leeds St Cypr Harehills *Ripon* 05-09; P-in-c Burmantofts St Steph and St Agnes 05-09; TV Ely from 09. *20 Barton Road, Ely CB7 4DE* Tel (01353) 645128
E-mail margaretharper@waitrose.com

HARPER, Martin Nigel. b 48. FRICS88 Cant Ch Ch Univ Coll PGCE95. S Dios Minl Tr Scheme 82. **d** 85 **p** 86. NSM St Leonards Ch Ch and St Mary *Chich* 85-93; NSM Rye 94-95; R Brede w Udimore from 08. *21 The Hawthorns, Brede TN31 6EN* Tel (01424) 883408 Mobile 07760-197954
E-mail martin.harper@tiscali.co.uk

HARPER, Canon Maurice. b 20. St Steph Ho Ox 60. **d** 62 **p** 63. C Upminster *Chelmsf* 62-67; V Gt Ilford St Mary 67-71; R Upminster 71-85; RD Havering 80-85; Hon Can Chelmsf Cathl 84-85; rtd 85; Perm to Offic *Chelmsf* and *Nor* from 85; *Chich* from 05. *30 Cookham Dene, Buckhurst Road, Bexhill-on-Sea TN40 1RU* Tel (01424) 222189
E-mail canonmauriceharper@o2.co.uk

HARPER, Michael Sydney. b 36. Portsm Dioc Tr Course 86. **d** 87. NSM Leigh Park St Clare CD *Portsm* 87-88; NSM Warren Park 88-05; NSM Leigh Park 96-05; rtd 05; Perm to Offic *Portsm* from 07. *17 Hampage Green, Warren Park, Havant PO9 4HJ* Tel (023) 9245 4275 E-mail michael harper06@tiscali.co.uk

HARPER, Richard Michael. b 53. Lon Univ BSc75 Univ of Wales PhD78. St Steph Ho Ox BA80 MA87. **d** 81 **p** 82. C Holt *Nor* 81-84; C-in-c Grahame Park St Aug CD *Lon* 84-88; Sub-Warden and Dir Studies St Mich Coll Llan 88-93; Lect Ch Hist Univ of Wales (Cardiff) 88-93; R St Leonards Ch Ch and St Mary *Chich* 94-03; RD Hastings 02-03; V Weymouth St Paul *Sarum* from 03. *St Paul's Vicarage, 58 Abbotsbury Road, Weymouth DT4 0BJ* Tel (01305) 778821
E-mail frrharper@btinternet.com

HARPER, Roger. *See* HARPER, Canon Geoffrey Roger

HARPER, Roger. b 43. Man Univ BSc64 FCA80. Local Minl Tr Course 84. **d** 87 **p** 88. NSM Onchan *S & M* 87-97; NSM Douglas St Geo 97-06. *The Barns, Strawberry Fields, Croit-e-Caley, Colby, Isle of Man IM9 4BZ* Tel (01624) 842466

HARPER, Canon Rosemary Elizabeth. b 55. Birm Univ BA76 ARCM75 LRAM78. NTMTC 96. **d** 99 **p** 00. C Amersham *Ox* 99-03; P-in-c Gt Missenden w Ballinger and Lt Hampden 03-07; V from 07; Chapl to Bp Buckingham from 06; Hon Can Ch Ch from 11. *The Rectory, Church Street, Amersham HP7 0BD* Tel (01494) 728988 E-mail rosie51619@aol.com

HARPER, Thomas Reginald. b 31. Dur Univ BA57 MA67. **d** 58 **p** 59. C Corbridge w Halton *Newc* 58-60; C Byker St Mich 60-62; V Ushaw Moor *Dur* 62-67; Asst Chapl HM Pris Dur 62-67; N Sec CMS 67-74; V Thornthwaite *Carl* 74-75; V Thornthwaite cum Braithwaite and Newlands 76-90; TV Bellingham/Otterburn Gp *Newc* 90-91; TV N Tyne and Redesdale 91-92; TR 92-98; RD Bellingham 93-98; rtd 98; Perm to Offic *Carl* from 98. *Dunelm, Old Lake Road, Ambleside LA22 0DH* Tel (01539) 433556

HARPER, Timothy James Lincoln. b 54. Lon Univ BMus76 MA96 CertEd LRAM. Wycliffe Hall Ox 84. **d** 86 **p** 87. C Morden *S'wark* 86-90; V Deptford St Pet 90-97; R Amersham *Ox* from 97. *The Rectory, Church Street, Amersham HP7 0DB* Tel (01494) 724426 *or* 729380 Fax 08701-639596
E-mail tjlharper@aol.com

HARPHAM, Mrs Diana Joan. b 44. MCSP66. St Alb Minl Tr Scheme 94. **d** 98 **p** 99. NSM Harrold and Carlton w Chellington *St Alb* 98-01; NSM Bromham w Oakley and Stagsden from 01. *The Old Police House, 40 Stagsden Road, Bromham, Bedford MK43 8PT* Tel (01234) 823222 Fax 825577
E-mail di@harpham.com

HARRATT, Philip David. b 56. Magd Coll Ox BA79 MA83. Ripon Coll Cuddesdon 82. **d** 85 **p** 86. C Ewyas Harold w Dulas, Kenderchurch etc *Heref* 85-88; V Chirbury 88-09; V Marton 88-09; V Trelystan 88-09; P-in-c Middleton 02-09; RD Pontesbury 01-08; Preb Heref Cathl 03-09; V Embleton w Rennington and Rock *Newc* from 09. *The Vicarage, Embleton, Alnwick NE66 3UW* Tel (01665) 576660
E-mail philipharratt@mypostoffice.co.uk

HARREX, Canon David Brian. b 54. Trin Coll Bris 87. **d** 89 **p** 90. C Bedminster St Mich *Bris* 89-93; V Pilning w Compton Greenfield 93-00; RD Westbury and Severnside 97-99; AD Bris W 99-00; TR Yate New Town from 00; C Frampton Cotterell and Iron Acton from 07; Hon Can Bris Cathl from 10. *The Rectory, 97 Canterbury Close, Yate, Bristol BS37 5TU* Tel (01454) 311483 E-mail davidharrex@hotmail.com

HARRIES, Henry Rayner Mackintosh. b 30. MBE67. Chich Th Coll 53. **d** 55 **p** 56. C Hastings H Trin *Chich* 55-58; Chapl RAF 58-79; Asst Chapl-in-Chief RAF 79-84; QHC 83-84; P-in-c Gt Brickhill w Bow Brickhill and Lt Brickhill *Ox* 84-86; R 86-94; RD Mursley 91-94; rtd 95; Perm to Offic *Chelmsf* from 94. *1A Shakletons, Ongar CM5 9AT* Tel (01277) 362783 E-mail raynerharries@hotmail.com

HARRIES, John Edward. b 60. Bris Univ BSc81 PhD84. Wycliffe Hall Ox 94. **d** 96 **p** 97. C Hyde St Geo *Ches* 96-00; P-in-c Walton from 00; C Latchford St Jas from 00; Chapl Sir Thos Boteler High Sch from 03. *13 Hillfoot Crescent, Stockton Heath, Warrington WA4 6SB* Tel (01925) 262939 E-mail stjohnswalton@btinternet.com

HARRIES, Mrs Judith Janice. b 43. SRN67 Trin Coll Bris BA93 Bris Univ PGCE94. WEMTC 99. **d** 01 **p** 02. NSM Bath St Sav w Swainswick and Woolley *B & W* 01-03; Hon C Farmborough, Marksbury and Stanton Prior 03-08. *19 Victoria Buildings, Bath BA2 3EH* Tel (01225) 332418 E-mail judithharries@hotmail.com

HARRIES, Malcolm David. b 44. BA99. Oak Hill Th Coll 94. **d** 96 **p** 97. C Rock Ferry *Ches* 96-00; P-in-c Godley cum Newton Green from 00. *The Vicarage, 43 Sheffield Road, Hyde SK14 2PR* Tel 0161-368 2159 E-mail liberteharries@aol.com

HARRIES, Rayner. See HARRIES, Henry Rayner Mackintosh

✠**HARRIES OF PENTREGARTH, The Rt Revd Lord (Richard Douglas).** b 36. Selw Coll Cam BA61 MA65 Lon Univ Hon DD94 FKC83 FRSL96. Cuddesdon Coll 61. **d** 63 **p** 64 **c** 87. C Hampstead St Jo *Lon* 63-69; Chapl Westf Coll Lon 67-69; Tutor Wells Th Coll 69-71; Warden Sarum & Wells Th Coll 71-72; V Fulham All SS *Lon* 72-81; Dean K Coll Lon 81-87; Consultant to Abps Cant and York on Inter-Faith Relns 86-06; Bp Ox 87-06; rtd 06; Asst Bp S'wark from 06; Hon Prof Th K Coll Lon from 06. *House of Lords, London SW1A 0PW* E-mail harriesr@parliament.uk

HARRINGTON, Christopher Robert. b 57. Wilson Carlile Coll 99 ERMC 06. **d** 08 **p** 09. C Middle Rasen Gp *Linc* from 08. *5 The Orchards, Middle Rasen, Market Rasen LN8 3TL* Tel (01673) 844657 E-mail c.r.harrington@btinternet.com

HARRINGTON, John Christopher Thomas. b 43. Qu Coll Birm 71. **d** 74 **p** 75. C Northampton St Mich *Pet* 74-76; C Paston 76-79; R Doddington *Ely* 79-82; R Benwick St Mary 79-82; R Doddington w Benwick 82-83; CF (TA) 75-85; Chapl Doddington Co Hosp 79-83; V Eastbourne St Mich *Chich* 83-02; R Selsey 02-11; Chapl RNLI 03-11; rtd 11; Custos St Mary's Hosp Chich from 11. *12 St Martin's Square, Chichester PO19 1NR* Tel (01243) 778987 E-mail jctharrington@tiscali.co.uk

HARRINGTON, William Harry. b 33. AKC57. **d** 58 **p** 59. C Childwall All SS *Liv* 58-60; C Sutton 60-64; V Ditton St Mich 64-76; V Mossley Hill St Barn 76-83; V Highfield 83-01; rtd 01; Perm to Offic *Liv* from 03. *4 Crowther Drive, Winstanley, Wigan WN3 6LY* Tel (01942) 225021

HARRIS, Mrs Alison Ann. b 54. Univ of Wales (Abth) BA75 Westmr Coll Ox PGCE76 Ches Univ MTh07. Qu Coll Birm 07. **d** 08 **p** 09. C Neston *Ches* from 08. *The Vicarage, Church Road, Saughall, Chester CH6 1EN* Tel (01244) 880213 Mobile 07969-005978 E-mail alisonannharris@hotmail.co.uk

HARRIS, Arthur Emlyn Dawson. b 27. Ex Univ BSc47. S'wark Ord Course 83. **d** 86 **p** 87. NSM Frant w Eridge *Chich* 86-87; P-in-c Withyham St Mich 87-95; rtd 95; Perm to Offic *Sarum* 96-07. *53A The Close, Salisbury SP1 2EL* Tel (01722) 339886 E-mail closecelts@aol.com

HARRIS, Bernard Malcolm. b 29. Leeds Univ BA54. Coll of Resurr Mirfield 54. **d** 56 **p** 57. C Shrewsbury St Chad *Lich* 56-60; C Porthill 60-61; V Birches Head 61-66; V W Bromwich St Jas 66-78; V Sedgley All SS 78-93; rtd 93; Perm to Offic *Worc* from 93 and *Lich* from 09. *6 Beacon Lane, Sedgley, Dudley DY3 1NB* Tel (01902) 663134 E-mail bernard.harris@care4free.co.uk

HARRIS, Brian. See HARRIS, The Ven Reginald Brian

HARRIS, Brian. b 33. Man Univ BSc. Qu Coll Birm 79. **d** 80 **p** 81. C Lich St Chad 80-81; Perm to Offic *Ches* 82-87; NSM Warburton 87-88; P-in-c 88-92; R Gt and Lt Casterton w Pickworth and Tickencote *Pet* 92-98; R Barnack 94-98; rtd 98; Perm to Offic *Pet* 99-07 and *St Alb* 06-07. *16 Westminster Green, Chester CH4 7LE* Tel (01244) 675824 E-mail meadowbrook@waitrose.com

HARRIS, Brian William. b 38. K Coll Lon BD61 AKC61. St Boniface Warminster 61. **d** 62 **p** 63. C Liversedge *Wakef* 62-65; C Kirkby *Liv* 65-70; V Dalton 70-79; V Aberford w Saxton *York* 79-91; V Hemingbrough 91-95; rtd 95; Perm to Offic *York* from 95; Dom Chapl to Bp Selby 95-03; Rtd Clergy

and Widows Officer (York Adnry) from 99. *2 Furness Drive, Rawcliffe, York YO30 5TD* Tel (01904) 638214 E-mail harrischap@ntlworld.com

HARRIS, Catherine Elizabeth. See EDMONDS, Mrs Catherine Elizabeth

HARRIS, Charles Edward. b 20. Roch Th Coll 63. **d** 65 **p** 66. C Hertford St Andr *St Alb* 65-71; R Sywell w Overstone *Pet* 71-90; rtd 90; Perm to Offic *Chich* from 92. *The College of St Barnabas, Blackberry Lane, Lingfield RH7 6NJ* Tel (01342) 870607

HARRIS, Cyril Evans. b 30. Linc Th Coll 61. **d** 63 **p** 64. C Beaconsfield *Ox* 63-68; V Stoke Poges 68-98; rtd 98; Perm to Offic *Ox* 99-07 and *St Alb* from 98. *The Gables, 8 De Parys Avenue, Bedford MK40 2TW* Tel (01234) 344927

HARRIS, David Anthony. b 68. **d** 96. Canada 96-11; R Reading St Giles *Ox* from 11. *St Giles's Rectory, Church Street, Reading RG1 2SB* Tel 0118-957 2831 E-mail sgiles.vicar@gmail.com

HARRIS, David Rowland. b 46. Ch Ch Ox BA69 MA72. Wycliffe Hall Ox 70. **d** 73 **p** 74. C Virginia Water *Guildf* 73-76; C Clifton Ch Ch w Em *Bris* 76-79; Scripture Union 79-85; V Bedford Ch Ch *St Alb* 85-99; R Ex St Leon w H Trin from 99. *St Leonard's Rectory, 27 St Leonard's Road, Exeter EX2 4LA* Tel (01392) 255681 *or* 255449 E-mail rector@stleonardsexeter.org.uk *or* dandsharris@hotmail.com

HARRIS, Derrick William. b 21. **d** 63 **p** 64. C Birkdale St Jo *Liv* 63-67; V Billinge 67-81; V Walton *Ches* 81-87; rtd 88; Perm to Offic *Ches* and *Liv* from 88. *3 Melrose Avenue, Southport PR9 9UY* Tel (01704) 213828

HARRIS, Mrs Elaine Sarah b 43. SWMTC 02. **d** 03 **p** 04. NSM Dyffryn *Llan* 03-06; P-in-c Penyfai from 06. *The Vicarage, Pen-y-fai, Bridgend CF31 4LS* Tel (01656) 651719 E-mail revel07@hotmail.com

HARRIS, Ernest John. b 46. QUB BD75. **d** 75 **p** 76. C Lisburn Ch Ch *Conn* 75-78; C Coleraine 78-83; I Belfast St Kath 83-90; I Ballinderry 90-11; Preb Conn Cathl 06-11; rtd 11. *10 Little Wenham, Moira, Cragavon BT67 0NN* Tel 07842-114854 (mobile)

HARRIS, Geoffrey Daryl. b 39. Open Univ BA83. St Aid Birkenhead 63. **d** 66 **p** 67. C Eston *York* 66-70; C Iffley *Ox* 70-75; V Bubwith *York* 75-78; V Bubwith w Ellerton and Aughton 78-79; P-in-c Stillingfleet w Naburn 79-80; R Escrick and Stillingfleet w Naburn 80-95; Chapl Qu Marg Sch York 83-94; Hon C Okehampton w Inwardleigh, Bratton Clovelly etc *Ex* 96-99; P-in-c Ashwater, Halwill, Beaworthy, Clawton etc 99-01; R 01-03; rtd 03; C Okehampton w Inwardleigh, Bratton Clovelly etc *Ex* from 07. *St Bridget's House, Bridestowe, Okehampton EX20 4ER* Tel (01837) 861644 E-mail the.harrisclan1@tinyonline.co.uk

HARRIS, George. b 36. Sarum Th Coll 66. **d** 68 **p** 69. C Shildon *Dur* 68-70; CF 70-74; P-in-c Doddington *Ely* 74-75; R 75-78; R Benwick St Mary 74-78; V Shotton *Dur* 78-86; V Stockton St Mark 86-87; V Chilton Moor 87-94; P-in-c Lyons 96; R 96-99; rtd 99. *49 Dunelm Drive, Houghton le Spring DH4 5QQ* Tel 0191-584 8608

HARRIS, Harriet Anne. b 68. Oriel Coll Ox BA90 New Coll Ox DPhil94. St Steph Ho Ox. **d** 00 **p** 01. C Ox St Mary V w St Cross and St Pet 00-06; Chapl Wadham Coll 00-10; Chapl Edin Univ from 10. *33 Manor Place, Edinburgh EH3 7EB* Tel 0131-225 7054

HARRIS, James. b 54. CITC 99. **d** 02 **p** 03. Aux Min Ballybeen *D & D* 02-05; C Belfast St Brendan from 05. *8 Grangewood Avenue, Dundondald, Belfast BT16 1GA* Tel (028) 9050 6074 Mobile 07761-066421 E-mail harrisj639@aol.com

HARRIS, Canon James Nigel Kingsley. b 37. St D Coll Lamp BA60. Sarum Th Coll. **d** 62 **p** 63. C Painswick *Glouc* 62-65; C Glouc St Paul 65-67; V Slad 67-77; V Cam 77-78; P-in-c Stinchcombe 77-78; V Cam w Stinchcombe 78-82; V Stonehouse 82-02; Chapl Glos R Hosp NHS Trust 92-02; rtd 02; Hon Can Antsiranana Madagascar from 00; Perm to Offic *Glouc* from 03. *14 Shalford Close, Cirencester GL7 1WG* Tel (01285) 885641

HARRIS, James Philip. b 59. Westf Coll Lon BA82 Univ of Wales PGCE97. St Mich Coll Llan BD86. **d** 86 **p** 87. C Newport St Paul *Mon* 86-89; C Bedwellty 89-91; V Newport St Matt 91-96; Chapl Univ of Wales Inst Cardiff *Llan* 97-99; Chapl Glam Univ 99-03; V Gwernaffield and Llanferres *St As* 03-09; V Bwlchgwyn and Minera 09-10; V Minera w Coedpoeth and Bwlchgwyn from 10. *The Vicarage, Church Road, Minera, Wrexham LL11 3DA* Tel (01978) 753133 E-mail jharris3@glam.ac.uk

HARRIS, Jeremy David. b 63. Leeds Metrop Univ MA00 Univ of Wales (Lamp) BA04 Cardiff Univ MPhil07 FCCA92. St Mich Coll Llan 05. **d** 07 **p** 08. C Monmouth w Overmonnow etc 07-09; C Magor 09-10; TV from 10. *The Vicarage, 6 Old Barn Court, Undy, Caldicot NP26 3TE* Tel (01633) 882551 Mobile 07710-410950 E-mail jeremydharris@hotmail.com

HARRIS, Jeremy Michael. b 64. St Steph Ho Ox BTh93. **d** 93 **p** 94. C Newport St Julian *Mon* 93-95; C Ebbw Vale 95-97; TV 97-98; Dioc Youth Chapl 96-98; TV Bracknell *Ox* 98-05; V

Boyne Hill from 05. *The Vicarage, Westmorland Road, Maidenhead SL6 4HB* Tel (01628) 626921 E-mail jeremy m harris@compuserve.com

HARRIS, The Very Revd John. b 32. Univ of Wales (Lamp) BA55. Sarum Th Coll 55. **d** 57 **p** 58. V Pontnewynydd *Mon* 57-60; C Bassaleg 60-63; V Penmaen 63-69; V Newport St Paul 69-84; RD Newport 77-93; V Maindee Newport 84-93; Can St Woolos Cathl 84-93; Dean Brecon *S & B* 93-98; V Brecon St Mary and Battle w Llanddew 93-98; rtd 98; Lic to Offic *Mon* from 98. *40 Mounton Drive, Chepstow NP16 5EH* Tel (01291) 621233

HARRIS, Canon John. b 45. St Steph Ho Ox 72. **d** 75 **p** 76. C Wanstead St Mary *Chelmsf* 75-84; V Penponds *Truro* 84-91; V St Gluvias from 91; RD Carnmarth S from 00; Hon Can Truro Cathl from 01. *The Vicarage, St Gluvias, Penryn TR10 9LQ* Tel (01326) 373356

HARRIS, John. b 54. Leeds Univ BSc75. St Jo Coll Nottm LTh86. **d** 86 **p** 87. C S Ossett *Wakef* 86-90; V Moldgreen 90-97; P-in-c S Ossett 97-04; V 04-10; P-in-c Luddenden w Luddenden Foot from 10. *The Vicarage, 50 Carr Field Drive, Luddenden, Halifax HX2 6RJ* Tel (01422) 884421

HARRIS, John Brian. b 53. Hertf Coll Ox BA76. Ripon Coll Cuddesdon 87. **d** 89 **p** 90. C Witton *Ches* 89-93; R Thurstaston 93-99; V Stockton Heath 99-04; P-in-c Gt Saughall from 04. *The Vicarage, Church Road, Saughall, Chester CH1 6EN* Tel (01244) 880213 E-mail brian@jbharris.fsnet.co.uk

HARRIS, John Stuart. b 29. Hertf Coll Ox BA52 MA56. Wells Th Coll 52. **d** 54 **p** 55. C Epsom St Martin *Guildf* 54-58; C Guildf H Trin w St Mary 58-63; R Bentley 63-72; V Milford 72-87; R Walton-on-the-Hill 87-98; Dioc Ecum Officer 87-92; rtd 98; Perm to Offic *Roch* from 98. *6 Pearse Place, Lamberhurst, Tunbridge Wells TN3 8EJ* Tel (01892) 890582

HARRIS, Mrs Judith Helen. b 42. Chelsea Coll Lon TCert64 Westmr Coll Ox MTh03. St Alb Minl Tr Scheme 83. **d**s 86 **d** 87 **p** 94. Leagrave *St Alb* 86-87; Hon Par Dn 87-91; TD Dunstable 91-94; TV 94-03; rtd 03; Perm to Offic *Truro* from 03. *Belmont, Fore Street, Porthleven, Helston TR13 9HN* Tel (01326) 563090 E-mail revdjhharris@ntlworld.com

HARRIS, Canon Kenneth. b 28. NW Ord Course 70. **d** 72 **p** 73. NSM Upton Ascension *Ches* 72-77; NSM Eccleston and Pulford 77-80; P-in-c Hargrave 80-81; V 81-94; Exec Officer Dioc Bd for Soc Resp 84-94; Hon Can Ches Cathl 91-94; rtd 94; Perm to Offic 94-96 and from 00; P-in-c Ashton Hayes 96-98; P-in-c Alvanley 98-99. *Delsa, Willington Road, Willington, Tarporley CW6 0ND* Tel (01829) 751880

HARRIS, Lawrence Rex Rowland. b 35. St Cath Coll Cam BA59 MA63. Ely Th Coll. **d** 61 **p** 62. C Carrington *S'well* 61-63; Chapl Rampton Hosp Retford 63-66; V Sturton w Littleborough *S'well* 66-71; V Bole w Saundby 66-71; R Clowne *Derby* 71-04; RD Bolsover and Staveley 81-86; rtd 04; Perm to Offic *Derby* from 04. *131 North Road, Clowne, Chesterfield S43 4PQ*

HARRIS, Leslie Gerald Conley Eyre. b 44. Culham Coll of Educn CertEd66 St Jo Coll Nottm LTh00 FRGS83. Wycliffe Hall Ox 71. **d** 75 **p** 76. Kenya 75-99; Chapl Banda Sch Nairobi 75-99; NSM Karen St Fran 75-99; NSM Kiambu St Paul 84-99; NSM Limuru All SS 90-99; C Sawley *Derby* 00-03; R Pinxton from 03. *The Rectory, 49 Town Street, Pinxton, Nottingham NG16 6HH* Tel (01773) 580024

HARRIS, Linda Margaret. b 55. Man Univ BSc76 UMIST MSc78 Birkbeck Coll Lon MSc98. Wycliffe Hall Ox 03. **d** 05 **p** 06. C Cannock *Lich* 05-08; P-in-c Hatch Warren and Beggarwood *Win* from 08. *Immanuel House, 29 Lapin Lane, Basingstoke RG22 4XH* Tel (01256) 472632 E-mail revlinda@btinternet.com

HARRIS, Margaret Claire (Sister Margaret Joy). b 53. RGN85 Homerton Coll Cam BEd78. Ridley Hall Cam 90. **d** 92. Par Dn Stevenage All SS Pin Green *St Alb* 92-93; CSMV 95-99; OSB from 99. *St Mary's Abbey, 52 Swan Street, West Malling ME19 6JX* Tel (01732) 843309

HARRIS, Mark Andrew. b 69. Heythrop Coll Lon BD92 K Coll Lon MA05. Ridley Hall Cam 06. **d** 10 **p** 11. C Meopham w Nurstead *Roch* from 10. *18 Hadley Close, Meopham, Gravesend DA13 0NX* Tel 07958-008189 (mobile) E-mail marknzharris@gmail.com

HARRIS, Canon Mark Jonathan. b 66. St Cath Coll Cam BA88 MA92 PhD92. Ripon Coll Cuddesdon BA01 MA05. **d** 02 **p** 03. C Cowley St Jas *Ox* 02-04; Chapl Oriel Coll Ox 04-10; Can and Vice Provost St Mary's Cathl Edin from 10. *33 Manor Place, Edinburgh EH3 7EB* Tel 0131-225 7054 E-mail viceprovost@cathedral.net

HARRIS, Martin John. b 54. Trin Coll Cam BA76 MA. Wycliffe Hall Ox 82. **d** 85 **p** 86. C Lindfield *Chich* 85-88; C Galleywood Common *Chelmsf* 88-91; V Southchurch Ch Ch 91-08; RD Southend 00-05; TR Harlow Town Cen w Lt Parndon from 08; RD Harlow from 09. *The Rectory, 43 Upper Park, Harlow CM20 1TW* Tel (01279) 411100 or 434243 E-mail martinharris@martinharris.messages.co.uk

HARRIS, Michael. b 34. St Mark & St Jo Coll Lon CertEd56 ACP65 MIL76. Qu Coll Birm. **d** 83 **p** 84. NSM Bournville *Birm*

83-90; NSM Stirchley 90-96; Chapl Univ of Cen England in Birm 92-99; Dean NSMs 96-99; rtd 00; Perm to Offic *Birm* and *Cov* from 00. *33 Bosley Close, Shipston-on-Stour CV36 4QA* Tel and fax (01608) 661672 Mobile 07811-489713 E-mail revmichael@harrisann.fsnet.co.uk

HARRIS, Michael Andrew. b 53. Ian Ramsey Coll Brasted 74 Trin Coll Bris 75. **d** 78 **p** 79. C St Paul's Cray St Barn *Roch* 78-82; C Church Stretton *Heref* 82-87; Res Min Penkridge w Stretton *Lich* 87-90; Res Min Penkridge Team 90-92; V Amington *Birm* from 92; AD Polesworth from 07. *The Vicarage, 224 Tamworth Road, Amington, Tamworth B77 3DE* Tel (01827) 62573 E-mail mike.harris26@ntlworld.com

HARRIS, Nicholas Bryan. b 60. Down Coll Cam BA81 MA85. Ridley Hall Cam 82. **d** 85 **p** 86. C Walney Is *Carl* 85-88; C S'wark Ch Ch 88-92; Perm to Offic *Chich* 92-08. *Wheelwrights, High Street, Fairwarp, Uckfield TN22 3BP* E-mail box534@yahoo.co.uk

HARRIS, Owen. b 50. Univ of Wales (Swansea) BSc(Econ)71 PGCE72. St Mich Coll Llan. **d** 94 **p** 95. C Bassaleg *Mon* 94-98; TV Cwmbran 98-01; V Maindee Newport 01-02; rtd 02. *5 Williams Terrace, Burry Port SA16 0PG* Tel (01554) 832479

✠HARRIS, The Rt Revd Patrick Burnet. b 34. Keble Coll Ox BA58 MA63. Clifton Th Coll 58. **d** 60 **p** 61 **c** 73. C Ox St Ebbe w St Pet 60-63; SAMS 63-81; Adn N Argentina 70-73; Bp 73-80; R Kirkheaton *Wakef* 81-85; Asst Bp Wakef 81-85; Sec C of E Partnership for World Miss 86-88; Asst Bp Ox 86-88; Bp S'well 88-99; rtd 99; Asst Bp Linc 99-05 and Eur from 99; Hon Asst Bp Glouc from 05. *Apartment B, Ireton House, Pavilion Gardens, Cheltenham GL50 2SR* Tel (01242) 231376 E-mail pandvharris@blueyonder.co.uk

HARRIS, Canon Paul. b 55. St Paul's Coll Chelt BEd79. Oak Hill Th Coll 82. **d** 84 **p** 85. C Billericay and Lt Burstead *Chelmsf* 84-87; TV Cheltenham St Mary, St Matt, St Paul and H Trin *Glouc* 87-93; V Bitterne *Win* 93-97; UK Evang Co-ord Evang Alliance 97-02; C Portswood Ch Ch *Win* 02-04; TR Cheltenham St Mark *Glouc* 04-11; Hon Can Glouc Cathl 09-11; rtd 11. *Flat 4, 4 Fisherman's Avenue, Bournemouth BH6 3SQ* Tel (01242) 690007 E-mail harrisrevpaul@blueyonder.co.uk

HARRIS, Paul Ian. b 45. MSc. Qu Coll Birm. **d** 82 **p** 83. C The Quinton *Birm* 82-86; V Atherstone *Cov* from 86. *40 Holte Road, Atherstone CV9 1HN* Tel (01827) 713200 E-mail paulih@ntlworld.com

HARRIS, Paul Michael. b 58. Chelsea Coll Lon BSc79 Oak Hill Th Coll BA89 Bath Coll of HE CertEd82 Open Univ BA04. **d** 89. C Finchley Ch Ch *Lon* 89-90; Asst Master St Luke's Sch W Norwood 90-91; Master and Asst Chapl Brent Internat Sch Manila 91-92; Volunteer Miss Movement Sunningdale 93-94; Past Asst St Joseph's RC Ch Dorking 94-95; Form Master Merton Court Prep Sch Sidcup 95-97; Asst Master Clewborough Ho Prep Sch Camberley 98-01; Teacher St Nic Sch for Girls Church Crookham 01-02; Teacher Culford Prep Sch Bury St Edmunds 02-04; Teacher St Marg Prep Sch Calne 05-07. *Maes-yr-Haf, 4 Penllain, Penparc, Cardigan SA43 1RJ* Tel (01239) 613797 E-mail paul.harris.007@hotmail.co.uk

HARRIS, Peter Frank. b 43. WMMTC 89. **d** 92 **p** 93. NSM Lich Ch Ch 92-96; NSM Ogley Hay 96-00; NSM Rushall 00-03; Perm to Offic from 03. *94 Ogley Hay Road, Burntwood WS7 2HU* Tel (01543) 319163

HARRIS, Peter Malcolm. b 52. Em Coll Cam BA74 MA79. Trin Coll Bris. **d** 80 **p** 81. C Upton (Overchurch) *Ches* 80-83; Crosslinks from 83; Portugal 93-97; France from 97. *rue de Meunier 4, Ribet, 13990 Fontvieille, France* Tel (0033) 8 77 35 61 53 (mobile) E-mail harris@crosslinks.org

HARRIS, Peter Samuel. b 68. Dundee Univ BA98 St Jo Coll Dur BA04. Cranmer Hall Dur 02. **d** 04 **p** 05. C Walton and Trimley *St E* 04-07; R Dalkeith *Edin* from 07; R Lasswade from 07. *The Rectory, 7 Ancrum Bank, Dalkeith EH22 3AY* Tel 0131-663 7000 E-mail revpharris@googlemail.com

HARRIS, Raymond. b 36. Nottm Univ BA58. Lich Th Coll 58. **d** 60 **p** 61. C Clifton St Fran *S'well* 60-63; C Davyhulme St Mary *Man* 63-66; V Bacup Ch Ch 66-82; R Dunsby w Dowsby *Linc* 82-87; R Rippingale 82-87; R Rippingale Gp 87-94; rtd 94. *2 The Bungalow, Swaton Lane, Swaton, Sleaford NG34 0JU* Tel (01529) 421343

HARRIS, Canon Raymond John. b 29. Leeds Univ BA51. Coll of Resurr Mirfield 51. **d** 53 **p** 54. C Workington St Mich *Carl* 53-59; V New Swindon St Barn Gorse Hill *Bris* 59-94; Hon Can Bris Cathl 80-94; RD Cricklade 82-88; rtd 94; Perm to Offic *Glouc* from 94. *c/o P Goodchild Esq, 20 Rodney Road, West Bridgford, Nottingham NG2 6JJ*

HARRIS, Rebecca Jane. See SWYER, Mrs Rebecca Jane

HARRIS (*née* LEE), Mrs Rebecca Susan. b 62. Man Univ BA85. Trin Coll Bris 93. **d** 95 **p** 96. C Cirencester *Glouc* 95-99; TV Gt Chesham *Ox* 99-11; C Creech St Michael and Ruishton w Thornfalcon *B & W* from 11. *The Rectory, Creech St Michael, Taunton TA3 5PP* E-mail harrisrs@tiscali.co.uk

HARRIS, The Ven Reginald Brian. b 34. Ch Coll Cam BA58 MA61. Ridley Hall Cam. **d** 59 **p** 60. C Wednesbury St Bart *Lich* 59-61; C Uttoxeter w Bramshall 61-64; V Bury St Pet *Man* 64-70;

V Walmsley 70-80; RD Walmsley 70-80; Adn Man 80-98; Can Res Man Cathl 80-98; rtd 98; Perm to Offic *Derby* from 98. *9 Cote Lane, Hayfield, Stockport SK22 2HL* Tel (01663) 746321

HARRIS, Robert. *See* WYNFORD-HARRIS, Robert William

HARRIS, Robert Douglas. b 57. Ex Univ BEd80 Bris Univ MEd96. Chich Th Coll 80. **d** 82 **p** 83. C Portsea St Mary *Portsm* 82-87; V Clevedon St Jo *B & W* 87-92; R Felpham w Middleton *Chich* 92-99; R Felpham 99-04; RD Arundel and Bognor 98-04; P-in-c Southwick 04-06; R 06-10; RD Hove 09-10; P-in-c Ilfracombe, Lee, Woolacombe, Bittadon etc *Ex* from 10. *The Vicarage, St Brannock's Road, Ilfracombe EX34 8EG* Tel (01271) 863467 E-mail robdharris@btinternet.com

HARRIS, Robert James. b 45. Nottm Univ MA02 ALCD73. St Jo Coll Nottm 69. **d** 72 **p** 73. C Sheff St Jo 72-76; C Goole 76-78; V Bramley and Ravenfield 78-91; P-in-c Boulton *Derby* 91-99; RD Melbourne 96-99; P-in-c Hazlewood 99-02; P-in-c Hazlewood and Milford 02-05; V Hazlewood, Holbrook and Milford 05-10; rtd 10. *13 Mill Lane, Findern, Derby DE65 6AP* Tel (01283) 703024 E-mail robert@kneetinnit.fsnet.co.uk

HARRIS, Mrs Ruth. b 60. Hull Univ BA82 Liv Univ MArAd84. NOC 01. **d** 04 **p** 05. C Kinsley w Wragby *Wakef* 04-07; C Felkirk 05-07; P-in-c Wrenthorpe from 07. *The Vicarage, 121 Wrenthorpe Road, Wrenthorpe, Wakefield WF2 0JS* Tel (01924) 373758 E-mail ruth.harris1@btinternet.com

HARRIS, Sian Elizabeth. b 54. Kingston Poly BSocSc75. WEMTC 03. **d** 06 **p** 07. NSM Leominster *Heref* 06-09; C Llanbadarn Fawr, Llandegley and Llanfihangel etc *S & B* 09; C Llanbister w Llanbadarn Fynydd w Llananno etc 09; Chapl St Mich Hospice Hereford from 10. *St Michael's Hospice, Bartestree, Hereford HR1 4HA* Tel (01432) 851000 E-mail sianharris@f2s.com

HARRIS, Stephen Mark. b 63. Mansf Coll Ox BA85 Lon Business Sch MBA95 Cam Univ BTh11 Solicitor 86. Ridley Hall Cam 09. **d** 11. NSM Trumpington *Ely* from 11. *6 Aberdeen Square, Cambridge CB2 8BZ* Tel 07971-818394 (mobile) E-mail steve16copperfields@msn.com

HARRIS, Suzanne Sarah. CITC. **d** 09 **p** 10. NSM Dublin Booterstown *D & G* from 09. *Caneel, 3 Belmont Green, Blackrock, Co Dublin, Republic of Ireland* Tel (00353) 87-935 4869 (mobile) E-mail curate.booterstown@dublin.anglican.org

HARRIS, Thomas William. b 54. Univ of Wales (Lamp) MA04 AKC76. Linc Th Coll 77. **d** 78 **p** 79. C Norton Woodseats St Chad *Sheff* 78-81; V Barnby Dun 81-91; P-in-c Kirk Bramwith and Fenwick 81-85; Chapl RN 91-94; R Draycot Bris 94-02; P-in-c Cawston w Booton and Brandiston etc *Nor* from 02; Chapl Norfolk and Nor Univ Hosp NHS Trust 02-07; Chapl Cawston Park Hosp from 07. *The Rectory, Ames Court, Cawston, Norwich NR10 4AN* Tel (01603) 871282 E-mail tomwharris@tiscali.co.uk

HARRIS, William Edric Mackenzie. b 46. Sarum & Wells Th Coll 72. **d** 75 **p** 76. C Langney *Chich* 75-79; C Moulsecoomb 80-81; TV 81-85; R W Grinstead from 85. *The Rectory, Steyning Road, West Grinstead, Horsham RH13 8LR* Tel (01403) 710339 E-mail williamem.harris@virgin.net

HARRIS, William Fergus. b 36. CCC Cam BA59 MA63 Edin Univ DipEd70. Yale Div Sch 59 Westcott Ho Cam 60. **d** 62 **p** 63. C St Andrews St Andr *St And* 62-64; Chapl Edin Univ 64-71; R Edin St Pet 71-83; R Perth St Jo *St And* 83-90; Hon C 90-08; rtd 90; Prov Archivist 91-02; Lic to Offic *St And* from 08. *35 St Mary's Drive, Perth PH2 7BY* Tel (01738) 621379

HARRIS-DOUGLAS, John Douglas. b 34. Ripon Hall Ox 65. **d** 66 **p** 67. C Ringwood *Win* 66-67; C Baswich *Lich* 67-71; R St Tudy *Truro* 71-74; R St Tudy w Michaelstow 74-76; Adv in Children's Work and Asst Dir Educn 71-76; R Fiskerton *Linc* 76-79; Dir of Educn and Adv RE 76-79; P-in-c Thormanby *York* 79-84; V Brafferton w Pilmoor and Myton-on-Swale 79-84; V Brafferton w Pilmoor, Myton-on-Swale etc 84-97; rtd 97; Perm to Offic *York* from 97. *Tanglewood Cottage, Newton-upon-Ouse, York YO30 2BN* Tel (01347) 848219

HARRIS-EVANS, William Giles. b 46. AKC68. Bangalore Th Coll. **d** 70 **p** 71. C Clapham H Trin *S'wark* 70-74; Sri Lanka 75-78; V Benhilton *S'wark* 78-86; TR Cov E 86-93; TR Brighouse and Clifton *Wakef* 93-99; V Petersfield and R Buriton *Portsm* 99-10; rtd 10; Perm to Offic *Portsm* from 11. *11 Great Southsea Street, Southsea PO5 3BY* E-mail wgh-evans12@tiscali.co.uk

HARRIS-WHITE, John Emlyn. b 34. St Aid Birkenhead 59. **d** 62 **p** 63. C Cricklade w Latton *Bris* 62-63; C Kingswood 63-66; C Ashton-on-Ribble St Andr *Blackb* 66-69; V Heyhouses 69-71; Chapl Roundway Hosp Devizes 71-77; Chapl R Variety Children's Hosp 77-89; Chapl K Coll and Belgrave Hosps Lon 77-89; Regional Community Relns Co-ord 89-93; rtd 94; Hon C Folkestone St Pet *Cant* 97-01. *40 Tippet Knowes Road, Winchburgh, Broxburn EH52 6UL*

HARRISON, Alastair Lee. b 22. ALCD51. **d** 51 **p** 52. C Stoke Damerel Ex 51-54; Chapl RAF 54-67; Chapl Miss to Seamen 67-77; Lic to Offic *D & G* 77-83; Lic to Offic *M & K* 77-83; C Dublin St Ann w St Mark and St Steph *D & G* 83-92; rtd 92.

8 Grosvenor Place, Rathgar, Dublin 6, Republic of Ireland Tel (00353) (1) 497 6053

HARRISON, Alison Edwina. *See* HART, Mrs Alison Edwina

HARRISON, Mrs Barbara Ann. b 41. Man Univ BA63 Leic Univ CertEd64. EMMTC 85. **d** 88 **p** 94. C Immingham *Linc* 88-94; P-in-c Habrough Gp 94-99; V 99-01; rtd 02; Perm to Offic *Linc* from 02. *3 Windsor Mews, Louth LN11 9AY* Tel (01507) 610015

HARRISON, Canon Barbara Anne. b 34. Westf Coll Lon BA56 CertEd57 Hull Univ MA85. Linc Th Coll 76. **dss** 79 **d** 87 **p** 94. Lakenham St Jo *Nor* 79-80; Chapl York Univ 80-88; TD Sheff Manor 88-93; Par Dn Holts CD *Man* 93-94; C-in-c 94-98; Dioc UPA Officer 93-98; Chapl Rochdale Healthcare NHS Trust 98-04; C Bury Ch King *Man* 98-01; C Bury St Paul 98-04; P-in-c Kirkholt 01-04; Hon Can Man Cathl 02-04; rtd 04; Perm to Offic *Man* from 04. *66 Gainsborough Drive, Rochdale OL11 2QT* Tel (01706) 639872

HARRISON, Bernard Charles. b 37. St Mich Coll Llan 61. **d** 64 **p** 65. C Toxteth Park St Marg *Liv* 64-69; C Hindley All SS 69-71; V Wigan St Geo 71-02; rtd 02. *66 Brookhouse Street, Wigan WN1 3FY* Tel (01942) 244500

HARRISON, Brian John. b 35. FCP. Glouc Sch of Min 83. **d** 86 **p** 89. NSM Broseley w Benthall *Heref* 86-93; Perm to Offic 94-97. *17 Hafren Road, Little Dawley, Telford TF4 3HJ* Tel (01952) 591891

HARRISON, Bruce. b 49. Linc Th Coll 86. **d** 88 **p** 89. C Syston Leic 88-90; C Whitby *York* 90-93; V Glaisdale 93-99; R Brotton Parva 99-04; V Coatham and Dormanstown 04-08; Chapl Tees and NE Yorks NHS Trust 04-07; rtd 08; Perm to Offic *York* from 08. *The Vicarage, 10 Allendale Tee, New Marske, Redcar TS11 8HN* Tel (01642) 484833 E-mail br218@hotmail.com

HARRISON, Bruce Mountford. b 49. AKC71. **d** 72 **p** 73. C Hebburn St Cuth *Dur* 72-75; C Bethnal Green St Jo w St Simon *Lon* 75-77; P-in-c Bethnal Green St Bart 77-78; TV Bethnal Green St Jo w St Bart 78-80; C-in-c Pennywell St Thos and Grindon St Oswald CD *Dur* 80-85; V Sunderland Pennywell St Thos 85-90; V Gateshead St Helen from 90. *The Vicarage, 7 Carlton Terrace, Gateshead NE9 6DE* Tel 0191-487 6510

HARRISON, Christine Amelia. b 47. STETS 94. **d** 98 **p** 99. NSM Goldsworth Park *Guildf* from 98. *2 Abercorn Way, Woking GU21 3NY* Tel (01483) 750645 E-mail revchrissie@btinternet.com

HARRISON, Christopher Dennis. b 57. Clare Coll Cam BA79 BA86. Westcott Ho Cam 84. **d** 87 **p** 88. C Camberwell St Geo *S'wark* 87-92; V Forest Hill 92-96; P-in-c Fenny Bentley, Kniveton, Thorpe and Tissington *Derby* 96-98; P-in-c Parwich w Alsop-en-le-Dale 96-98; R Fenny Bentley, Thorpe, Tissington, Parwich etc 98-09; RD Ashbourne 98-09; P-in-c Nottingham All SS, St Mary and St Pet *S'well* from 09. *2 Tennis View, Tattershall Drive, Nottingham NG7 1AD* Tel 0115-941 8927 E-mail christopher.d.harrison@btinternet.com

HARRISON, Christopher Joseph. b 38. AKC61 Hull Univ CertEd68 Bris Univ BEd75. **d** 62 **p** 63. C Bottesford *Linc* 62-67; C Elloughton *York* 67-68; Asst Master Bishop's Cleeve Primary Sch 68-74; Sen Master 74-78; Dep Hd 78-86; P-in-c Farmington *Glouc* 69-73; C Tredington w Stoke Orchard and Hardwicke 74-86; rtd 96; Perm to Offic *Glouc* from 87. *Appledore, 93 Stoke Road, Bishops Cleeve, Cheltenham GL52 8RP* Tel (01242) 673452

HARRISON, Crispin. *See* HARRISON, Michael Burt

HARRISON, Sister Cécile. b 29. Bp Lonsdale Coll TCert51. St Steph Ho Ox 97. **d** 97 **p** 97. CGA from 66; Lic to Offic *Eur* from 97. *Prasada, Quartier Subrane, Montauroux, 83440 Fayence, France* Tel and fax (0033) 4 94 47 74 26 E-mail cga.prasada@wanadoo.fr

HARRISON, David Daniel. b 62. St Paul's Coll Chelt BA84 Leeds Univ MA85 Westmr Coll Ox PGCE88. Westcott Ho Cam 03. **d** 05 **p** 06. C Beckenham St Geo *Roch* 05-09; P-in-c Woodnesborough w Worth and Staple *Cant* from 09. *The Vicarage, The Street, Woodnesborough, Sandwich CT13 0NQ* Tel (01304) 613056

HARRISON, David Henry. b 40. Tyndale Hall Bris 65. **d** 68 **p** 69. C Bolton St Paul *Man* 68-72; V Bircle 72-83; V Southport SS Simon and Jude *Liv* 83-91; TR Fazakerley Em 91-99; V Toxteth Park Ch Ch and St Mich w St Andr 99-05; rtd 05; Perm to Offic *Blackb* from 06. *55 The Oval, Shevington, Wigan WN6 8EN* Tel (01257) 400084 E-mail getrevdave@hotmail.com

HARRISON, David Samuel. b 44. Univ of Wales (Ban) BSc67. St Mich Coll Llan 67. **d** 70 **p** 71. C Canton St Jo *Llan* 70-74; C Witton *Ches* 74-78; V Sutton St Geo 78-96; P-in-c Henbury 96-01; V 01-06; rtd 06. *50 Cherryfields Road, Macclesfield SK11 8RF* Tel (01625) 268460

HARRISON, Dawn Michelle. b 78. Edge Hill Coll of HE BSc99 St Jo Coll Dur BA St Martin's Coll Lanc PGCE01. Cranmer Hall Dur 07. **d** 10 **p** 11. C S Widnes *Liv* from 10. *24 Dock Street, Widnes WA8 0QX* Tel 07786-365193 (mobile) E-mail dawnmharrison@hotmail.com

HARRISON, Miss Doreen. b 32. Leeds Univ BA53 PGCE54 Lanc Univ MLitt78 MA(Ed)79. **d** 92 **p** 94. C Ambleside w Brathay *Carl* 92-96; Asst P Colton 96-01; P-in-c 01-02; Asst P

Rusland 96-01; P-in-c 01-02; Asst P Satterthwaite 96-01; P-in-c 01-02; rtd 02; Perm to Offic *Carl* 02-07. *Fox How, Ambleside LA22 9LL* Tel (01539) 433021

HARRISON, Fred Graham. b 41. Lon Univ BSc62. Ridley Hall Cam 80. **d** 82 **p** 83. C Lenton *S'well* 82-85; V Ruddington 85-04; rtd 04; Perm to Offic *Ches* from 05. *18 Holly Bank, Hollingworth, Hyde SK14 8QL* Tel (01457) 765955 E-mail fg.harrison@virgin.net

HARRISON, Guy Patrick. b 58. Ox Univ MTh99 MBACP04. Sarum & Wells Th Coll 92. **d** 94 **p** 95. C Wimborne Minster and Holt *Sarum* 94-96; C Wimborne Minster 96-97; Chapl Dorothy House Hospice Winsley 97-01; Chapl Stoke Mandeville Hosp NHS Trust 01-02; Chapl Team Ldr 02-05; Team Ldr and Bereavement Service Manager Bucks Hosps NHS Trust 05-07; Hd Spiritual and Past Care W Lon Mental Health NHS Trust from 07. *The Chaplaincy Department, West London Mental Health NHS Trust, Uxbridge Road, Southall UB1 3EU* Tel (020) 8354 8864 E-mail guy.harrison@wlmht.nhs.uk

HARRISON, Herbert Gerald. b 29. Oak Hill Th Coll 53. **d** 56 **p** 57. C Chesterfield H Trin *Derby* 56-59; C Cambridge St Andr Less *Ely* 59-64; Miss to Seamen 64-74; Kenya 64-68; Port Chapl Ipswich 68-74; V Ipswich All SS *St E* 74-81; P-in-c Elmsett w Aldham 81-88; P-in-c Kersey w Lindsey 81-88; R Horringer cum Ickworth 88-94; rtd 94; Perm to Offic *St E* from 94. *15 Lynwood Avenue, Felixstowe IP11 9HS* Tel (01394) 283764

HARRISON, Ian David. b 45. Imp Coll Lon BSc66. Oak Hill Th Coll 93. **d** 96 **p** 97. NSM Tunbridge Wells St Jo *Roch* 96-99; P-in-c Chiddingstone w Chiddingstone Causeway 99-10; rtd 10. *3 Brunswick Terrace, Tunbridge Wells TN1 1TR* Tel (01892) 871639

HARRISON, Joanne Elizabeth. SAOMC. **d** 05 **p** 06. NSM Wokingham St Paul *Ox* 05-10; Perm to Offic from 10. *25 Harvard Road, Owlsmoor, Sandhurst GU47 0XB* Tel (01276) 34409

HARRISON, John. See HARRISON, Steven John

HARRISON, Canon John. b 49. Fitzw Coll Cam BA71 MA74. Westcott Ho Cam 74. **d** 77 **p** 78. C Nunthorpe *York* 77-81; C Acomb St Steph 81-83; C-in-c St Aid 81-83; V Heptonstall *Wakef* 83-91; R Stamford Bridge Gp *York* 91-02; V Easingwold w Raskelf from 02; RD Easingwold from 05; Can and Preb York Minster from 10. *The Vicarage, Church Hill, Easingwold, York YO61 3JT* Tel (01347) 821394 E-mail vicar.easingwold@hotmail.co.uk

HARRISON, John Christopher. b 69. Liv Univ BA90 MSc98 Liv Jo Moores Univ PhD06. SNWTP 07. **d** 10 **p** 11. NSM Hoylake *Ches* from 10. *St Hildeburgh's Church, Stanley Road, Hoylake, Wirral CH47 1HL* Tel 07834-262166 (mobile) E-mail j.c.harrison@ljmu.ac.uk

HARRISON, John Northcott. b 31. St Jo Coll Cam BA54. Westcott Ho Cam 54. **d** 56 **p** 57. C Moor Allerton *Ripon* 56-59; C Bedale 59-61; V Hudswell w Downholme 61-64; Youth Chapl *Dur* 64-68; V Auckland St Andr and St Anne 68-76; Community Chapl Stockton-on-Tees 76-83; TR Southampton (City Cen) *Win* 83-88; V Bris Ch the Servant Stockwood 88-96; RD Brislington 89-95; Chapl St Brendan's Sixth Form Coll 90-96; rtd 96; Perm to Offic *B & W* and *Bris* from 96. *8 Moorham Road, Winscombe BS25 1HS* Tel (01934) 844403

HARRISON, Josephine Mary. b 42. **d** 97 **p** 98. NSM Yatton Keynell *Bris* 97-99; NSM By Brook 99-01; Perm to Offic *B & W* 01-02 and from 07; NSM Wellington and Distr 02-07. *Pippins, 18 Cox Road, Wellington TA21 9RD* Tel and fax (01823) 669525

HARRISON, Keith. See HARRISON, Peter Keith

HARRISON, Lyndon. b 47. St Mich Coll Llan 91. **d** 93 **p** 94. C Ebbw Vale *Mon* 93-96; TV 96-01; TV Caldicot 01-05; TR from 05. *St Mary's Rectory, 39 Church Road, Caldicot NP26 4HN* Tel (01291) 420221

HARRISON, Mrs Marion Jeanne. b 56. SAOMC 04. **d** 07 **p** 08. C Watercombe *Sarum* from 07; P-in-c Lt Barningham, Blickling, Edgefield etc *Nor* from 11. *The Rectory, The Street, Itteringham, Norwich NR11 7AX* Tel 07932-521176 (mobile)

HARRISON, Martin. b 58. Bris Univ BA89. Trin Coll Bris 86. **d** 89 **p** 90. C Heworth H Trin *York* 89-94; Chapl York Distr Hosp 89-94; P-in-c Skelton w Shipton and Newton on Ouse *York* 94-95; R 95-01; V Strensall from 01; RD Easingwold 00-05. *The Vicarage, 10 York Road, Strensall, York YO32 5UN* Tel (01904) 490683 E-mail martinharrison2@btinternet.com

HARRISON, Matthew Henry. b 64. Univ Coll Dur BA85 Union Th Sem (NY) STM93. St Steph Ho Ox BA88 MA92. **d** 89 **p** 90. C Whickham *Dur* 89-92; C Owton Manor 93-95; USA 92-93; Asst Chapl Paris St Geo *Eur* 95-02; Perm to Offic 02-04; C Paddington St Jas Lon 04-07; Chapl Paris St Geo *Eur* from 07. *St George, 7 rue Auguste-Vacquerie, 75116 Paris, France* Tel (0033) (1) 47 20 22 51 E-mail office@stgeorgesparis.com

HARRISON, Maureen. b 48. OLM Sutton *Liv* from 08. *89 Farndon Avenue, Sutton Manor, St Helens WA9 4DN* E-mail maureen.harrison@talktalk.net

HARRISON, Michael Anthony. b 48. Westhill Coll Birm CertCYW72 Huddersfield Poly CertEd88 Leeds Poly BA91 Leeds Univ MA98. NOC 94. **d** 97 **p** 98. NSM Thornhill and

Whitley Lower *Wakef* 97-99; TV Wrexham *St As* 99-03; V Ruabon from 03. *The Vicarage, Park Street, Ruabon, Wrexham LL14 6LF* Tel (01978) 810176 E-mail whernside@aol.com

HARRISON, Michael Burt (Crispin). b 36. Leeds Univ BA59 Trin Coll Ox BA62 MA66. Coll of Resurr Mirfield 59. **d** 63 **p** 64. C W Hartlepool St Aid *Dur* 63-64; C Middlesbrough All SS *York* 64-66; Lic to Offic *Wakef* 67-69 and 78-87; CR from 68; S Africa 69-77 and 87-97; Registrar Coll of the Resurr Mirfield 78-84; Vice-Prin 84-87; Superior CR 97-02. *St Peter's Priory, PO Box 991, Southdale, 2135 South Africa* Tel (0027) (11) 434 2504 Fax 434 4556 E-mail crpriory@acenet.co.za

HARRISON, Canon Michael Robert. b 63. Selw Coll Cam BA84 K Coll Lon PhD97 Bradf Univ MA99. Ripon Coll Cuddesdon BA89 Union Th Sem (NY) STM90. **d** 90 **p** 91. C S Lambeth St Anne and All SS *S'wark* 90-94; Bp's Chapl to Students *Bradf* 94-98; Chapl Bradf Univ 94-98; Chapl Bradf and Ilkley Community Coll 94-98; V Eltham H Trin *S'wark* 98-06; RD Eltham and Mottingham 05-06; Dir Min and Miss *Leic* from 06; Hon Can Leic Cathl from 06. *11 Paterson Drive, Woodhouse Eaves, Loughborough LE12 8RL* Tel (01509) 891670 E-mail mikeharrison7@hotmail.com

HARRISON, Canon Noel Milburn. b 27. Leeds Univ MPhil75 PhD80. St Aid Birkenhead 54. **d** 57 **p** 58. C Doncaster St Jas *Sheff* 57-60; Chapl Yorkshire Res Sch for Deaf Doncaster 60-68; C Woodlands *Sheff* 60-62; Chapl to the Deaf 60-68; Hd Master Elmete Hall Sch Leeds 68-84; Hon C Whitgift w Adlingfleet and Eastoft 83-84; Hon C Abbeydale St Jo 84-86; Dioc Dir of Educn 84-94; R Tankersley 86-94; Hon Can Sheff Cathl 88-94; rtd 94; Perm to Offic *Sheff* from 94 and *Linc* 95-99. *Aidan House, 118 High Street, Crowle, Scunthorpe DN17 4DR*

HARRISON, Mrs Nona Margaret. b 50. Open Univ BA80. S Dios Minl Tr Scheme 92. **d** 95 **p** 96. NSM E w W Wellow and Sherfield English *Win* 95-99; NSM Barton Stacey and Bullington etc 99; NSM Hurstbourne Priors, Longparish etc 00-08. *5 Chichester Close, East Wellow, Romsey SO51 6EY* Tel (01794) 323154

HARRISON, Oliver. b 71. SS Paul & Mary Coll Cheltenham BA93. St Jo Coll Nottm MA95. **d** 97 **p** 98. Asst Chapl The Hague *Eur* 97-00; C Walmley *Birm* 00-04; C-in-c Grove Green LEP *Cant* 04-08; V Wilnecote *Lich* from 08. *The Vicarage, 64 Glascote Lane, Wilnecote, Tamworth B77 2PH* Tel (01827) 260560 E-mail oliver.harrison@tiscali.co.uk

HARRISON, Miss Patricia Mary. b 35. St Kath Coll Lon CertEd65 Open Univ BA74. St Mich Ho Ox IDC59. **dss** 85 **d** 87 **p** 94. NSM Nunthorpe *York* 85-98; rtd 98; Perm to Offic *York* from 98. *22 Lamonby Close, Nunthorpe, Middlesbrough TS7 0QG* Tel (01642) 313524

HARRISON, Paul Graham. b 53. Sarum & Wells Th Coll 76. **d** 79 **p** 80. C Brixham w Churston Ferrers *Ex* 79-82; C Portsea N End St Mark *Portsm* 82-87; V Tiverton St Andr *Ex* 87-94; Chapl Tiverton and Distr Hosp 90-94; P-in-c Astwood Bank *Worc* 94-05; TV Redditch Ch the K 05-08; P-in-c Churchill-in-Halfshire w Blakedown and Broome from 08; Chapl to the Deaf from 94; Perm to Offic *Cov* from 94. *The Rectory, 5 Mill Lane, Blakedown, Kidderminster DY10 3ND* Tel (01562) 700144 E-mail p.g.harrison@btinternet.com *or* dda@cofe-worcester.org.uk

HARRISON, Paul Thomas. b 57. Nor Sch of Art BA80 Leic Poly PGCE88 Coll of Ripon & York St Jo MA99. Qu Coll Birm 95. **d** 97 **p** 98. C Northallerton w Kirby Sigston *York* 97-01; TV Usworth *Dur* 01-05; V Dalton le Dale and New Seaham from 05. *The Vicarage, 269 Station Road, Seaham SR7 0BH* Tel 0191-581 3270

HARRISON, Mrs Penelope Ann. b 58. St Andr Univ MA79. Qu Coll Birm MA09. **d** 09 **p** 10. C Hamstead St Paul *Birm* from 09. *119 Lechlade Road, Birmingham B43 5NE* Tel 0121-357 1428 Mobile 07722-446222 E-mail penny h123@hotmail.com

HARRISON, Peter. See HARRISON, Robert Peter

HARRISON, Peter Keith. b 44. Open Univ BA85. St Aid Birkenhead. **d** 68 **p** 69. C Higher Bebington *Ches* 68-71; C Walmsley *Man* 71-74; V Lumb in Rossendale 74-79; V Heywood St Marg 79-87; V Hey 87-95; AD Saddleworth 93-95; Chapl Athens w Kifissia *Eur* 95-98; V Aston Cantlow and Wilmcote w Billesley *Cov* 98-02; V W Burnley All SS *Blackb* 02-09; rtd 09; Perm to Offic *Blackb* from 09. *57 West Cliffe, Lytham St Annes FY8 5DR* Tel (01253) 735128 E-mail harrison.ssc@virgin.net

HARRISON, The Ven Peter Reginald Wallace. b 39. Selw Coll Cam BA62. Ridley Hall Cam 62. **d** 64 **p** 65. C Barton Hill St Luke w Ch Ch *Bris* 64-69; Chapl Greenhouse Trust 69-77; Dir Northorpe Hall Trust 77-84; TR Drypool *York* 84-98; AD E Hull 88-98; Adn E Riding 98-06; Can and Preb York Minster 94-06; rtd 06; Perm to Offic *York* from 06. *10 Priestgate, Sutton-on-Hull, Hull HU7 4QR* Tel (01482) 797110 E-mail peter@harrisons.karoo.co.uk

HARRISON, Canon Philip Hubert. b 37. Sarum & Wells Th Coll 77. **d** 79 **p** 80. C Wymondham *Nor* 79-83; V Watton w Carbrooke and Ovington 83-92; R Drayton w Felthorpe 92-99; Hon Can Nor Cathl 99-02; rtd 02; Perm to Offic *Nor* from 02.

The Fairstead, 1 Back Street, Horsham St Faith, Norwich NR10 3JP Tel (01603) 893087
E-mail harrison-thewarren@talktalk.net

HARRISON, Mrs Rachel Elizabeth. b 53. NEOC 98. **d** 01 **p** 02. C Skelton w Upleatham *York* 01-04; P-in-c New Marske 04-06; V from 06; P-in-c Wilton 04-06; V from 06; Ind Chapl from 04. *The Vicarage, 10 Allendale Tee, New Marske, Redcar TS11 8HN* Tel (01642) 484833 E-mail rachelhere@hotmail.com

HARRISON, Richard Kingswood. b 61. Linc Coll Ox BA83 MA88 Leeds Univ BA90. Coll of Resurr Mirfield 88. **d** 91 **p** 92. C Reading St Giles *Ox* 91-93; Asst Chapl Merchant Taylors' Sch Northwood 93-96; Chapl Ardingly Coll 96-02; R Shill Valley and Broadshire *Ox* 02-04; Chapl Uppingham Sch 04-09; Chapl Lancing Coll from 09. *Ladywell House, Lancing College, Lancing BN15 0RW* Tel (01273) 465961

HARRISON, Robert Peter. b 28. Chich Th Coll. **d** 60 **p** 61. C Ealing Ch the Sav *Lon* 60-64; C Hammersmith SS Mich and Geo White City Estate CD 64-66; P-in-c Fulham St Pet 66-73; V 73-94; rtd 94; Perm to Offic *Chich* from 94. *8 Broadwater Way, Worthing BN14 9LP* Tel (01903) 217073

HARRISON, Robert William. b 62. Mansf Coll Ox BA84. Qu Coll Birm 87. **d** 89 **p** 90. C Sholing *Win* 89-93; Communications Adv to Bp Willesden *Lon* 93-97; C Cricklewood St Gabr and St Mich 93-97; V Hillingdon St Jo from 97. *St John's Vicarage, Royal Lane, Uxbridge UB8 3QR* Tel (01895) 461945
E-mail rob.harrison@london.anglican.org

HARRISON, Rodney Lovel Neal. b 46. MBE87. Dur Univ BA67. Ripon Coll Cuddesdon 93. **d** 95 **p** 96. C N w S Wootton *Nor* 95-98; P-in-c Gt and Lt Bedwyn and Savernake Forest *Sarum* 98-02; TV Savernake from 02. *The Vicarage, Church Street, Great Bedwyn, Marlborough SN8 3PF* Tel (01672) 870779
E-mail rodney@rlnh-ejhh.demon.co.uk

HARRISON, Rosemary Jane. b 53. Bradf Coll of Educn CertEd76. Trin Coll Bris 83. **d** 87 **p** 94. NSM Southway *Ex* 87-89; NSM Kinson *Sarum* 89-96. *28 First Avenue, Havant PO9 2QN* Tel (023) 9245 5226

HARRISON, Roy. *See* HARRISON, Canon William Roy

HARRISON, Miss Ruth Margaret. b 33. BEM85. FRSA94. Ripon Coll Cuddesdon 02. **d** 02 **p** 03. NSM Baddiley and Wrenbury w Burleydam *Ches* from 02. *2 Heywood Cottages, Heywood Lane, Audlem, Crewe CW3 0EX* Tel (01270) 812010

HARRISON, Shirley Ann. b 56. Leic Univ BA76. NOC 02. **d** 05 **p** 06. C Saddleworth *Man* 05-08; P-in-c Denton Ch Ch from 08. *Christ Church Rectory, 1 Windmill Lane, Denton, Manchester M34 3RN* Tel 0161-336 4456 Mobile 07584-416903
E-mail revdsah@yahoo.co.uk

HARRISON, Steven John. b 47. Univ of Wales (Aberth) BSc68 PhD74 FRMetS74. St And Dioc Tr Course 87. **d** 90 **p** 91. NSM Alloa *St And* 90-94; NSM Bridge of Allan 94-02; NSM Spittal *Newc* 02-10; NSM Scremerston 02-10; P-in-c 06-10; rtd 10. *East Cottage, Plunderheath, Haydon Bridge, Hexham NE47 6JU* Tel (01434) 684994 E-mail johnandaveril@aol.com

HARRISON, Canon William Roy. b 34. Dur Univ BA58. Cranmer Hall Dur 57. **d** 59 **p** 60. C Kingswood *Bris* 59-62; Kenya 62-65; P-in-c Gt Somerford *Bris* 66; V Soundwell 66-99; Hon Can Bris Cathl 92-99; rtd 99; Perm to Offic *Bris* from 99. *20 Pool Road, Bristol BS15 1XL* Tel 0117-967 9802

HARRISON-SMITH, Ms Fiona Jane. b 74. Huddersfield Univ BMus96 Ox Brookes Univ BA03 Leeds Univ MA07. Coll of Resurr Mirfield 05. **d** 07 **p** 08. C Redcar *York* 07-11; TV Seacroft *Ripon* from 11. *St James Vicarage, 47 St James Approach, Leeds LS14 6JJ* Tel 07709-914786 (mobile)
E-mail fharrisonsmith@btinternet.com

HARRISON-WATSON, Carole. *See* FORD, Mrs Carole

HARRISON, John Anthony Lomax. b 47. Ex Univ BA72. Qu Coll Birm 72. **d** 74 **p** 75. C Loughton St Jo *Chelmsf* 74-81; V Chingford St Anne 81-98; TV Aldrington *Chich* 98-04; TV Golden Cap Team *Sarum* 04-09; rtd 09. *82 Chestnut Way, Honiton EX14 2XF* E-mail john@jharrisson.wanadoo.co.uk

HARROLD, Canon Jeremy Robin. b 31. Hertf Coll Ox BA54 BSc56 MA58. Wycliffe Hall Ox. **d** 59 **p** 60. C Rushden *Pet* 59-61; Bp's Chapl *Lon* 61-64; Australia 64-67; V Harlesden St Mark *Lon* 67-72; V Hendon St Paul Mill Hill 72-84; V Stowmarket *St E* 84-96; RD Stowmarket 90-96; Hon Can St E Cathl 94-96; rtd 96; Perm to Offic *St E* from 96. *18 Wilkinson Way, Woodbridge IP12 1SS* Tel (01394) 380127

HARRON, Gareth Andrew. b 71. QUB BA92. CITC BTh95. **d** 95 **p** 96. C Willowfield *D & D* 95-98; C Dromore Cathl 98-02; I Magheralin w Dollingstown from 02. *The Rectory, 12 New Forge Road, Magheralin, Craigavon BT67 0QJ* Tel (028) 9261 1273
E-mail gareth@gharron.freeserve.co.uk

HARRON, James Alexander. b 37. GIMechE61. St Aid Birkenhead 63. **d** 65 **p** 66. C Willowfield *D & D* 65-69; I Desertmartin *D & R* 69-80; Dep Sec BCMS (Ireland) 80-84; I Aghalee *D & D* 84-03; Preb Dromore Cathl 02-03; Chapl HM Pris Magaberry 86-03; rtd 03. *8 Churchill Avenue, Lurgan, Craigavon BT66 7BW* Tel and fax (028) 3834 6543

HARROP, Stephen Douglas. b 48. St Jo Coll York CertEd74 Nan Univ DipAdEd90. Edin Th Coll 77. **d** 79 **p** 82. C Middlesbrough

St Martin *York* 79-80; C Cayton w Eastfield 80-81; C Oldham *Man* 82-84; V Oldham St Barn 84-89; P-in-c Em Ch Hong Kong 89-93; Ind Chapl and TV Kidderminster St Mary and All SS w Trimpley etc *Worc* 93-95; Chapl Kidderminster Coll 93-95; Sandwell Chs Link Officer *Birm* 95-96; Dep Chapl HM Pris Brixton 96-97; Chapl Taichung St Jas Taiwan 97-98; R Lower Merion St Jo USA 98-99; R Essington St Jo 99-03; Perm to Offic *Man* 03-04; C Elton St Steph 04-05; P-in-c 05-08; Chapl HM Pris Forest Bank from 08. *HM Prison Forest Bank, Agecroft Road, Pendlebury, Manchester M27 8FB* Tel 0161-925 7037
E-mail esharrop@aol.com

HARRY, Bruce David. b 40. JP77. Culham Coll Ox CertEd60. NOC 83. **d** 86 **p** 87. NSM Liscard St Thos *Ches* 86-91; NSM Eastham 91-94; C New Brighton St Jas 94-96; C New Brighton Em 94-96; C New Brighton St Jas w Em 96-98; NSM 98-02; NSM New Brighton All SS 98-02; P-in-c 02-03; Perm to Offic from 03. *21 Sandymount Drive, Wallasey CH45 0LJ* Tel 0151-639 7232

HART (formerly HARRISON), Mrs Alison Edwina. b 53. Newc Univ BEd75. Linc Th Coll 84. **dss** 86 **d** 87 **p** 94. Loughborough Em *Leic* 86-89; Par Dn 87-89; C Stockton *Dur* 89-92; P-in-c Lynesack and Cockfield 92-95; P-in-c Ebchester 95-96; R 96-97; V Medomsley 96-97; V Newc H Cross 97-01; P-in-c Ulgham and Widdrington 01-06; P-in-c Beckermet St Jo and St Bridget w Ponsonby *Carl* 06-10; rtd 10. *208 Newbiggin Road, Ashington NE63 0TN* Tel (01670) 812559
E-mail coolingstreams@yahoo.co.uk

HART, Allen Sydney George. b 38. Chich Th Coll 64. **d** 67 **p** 68. C N Wembley St Cuth *Lon* 67-71; C W Bromwich All SS *Lich* 71-74; TV Hucknall Torkard *S'well* 74-80; V Annesley Our Lady and All SS 80-86; V Bilborough St Jo 86-99; RD Nottingham W 94-99; P-in-c Clarborough w Hayton 99-03; Asst Chapl HM Pris Ranby 99-03; rtd 03; Perm to Offic *S'well* from 03. *3 Castleton Close, Hucknall, Nottingham NG15 6TD* Tel 0115-955 2067
E-mail a.hart557@ntlworld.com

HART, André Hendrik. b 62. Cape Town Univ BA86. St Steph Ho Ox 89. **d** 91 **p** 92. C Newbold w Dunston *Derby* 91-95; P-in-c Clifton and Norbury w Snelston 95-02; Chapl S Derbyshire Community Health Services NHS Trust 95-02; V Westbury-on-Trym H Trin *Bris* from 02. *Holy Trinity Vicarage, 44 Eastfield Road, Westbury-on-Trym, Bristol BS9 4AG* Tel 0117-962 1536 or 950 8644

HART, Anthony. b 35. St Mich Coll Llan 77. **d** 79 **p** 80. NSM Jersey St Helier *Win* 79-81; C Heref All SS 81-82; C Kingstone 82-84; C Eaton Bishop 82-84; C Clehonger 82-84; R Sutton St Nicholas w Sutton St Michael 84-88; R Withington w Westhide 84-88; R Jersey St Mary *Win* 88-01; rtd 01; Perm to Offic *Win* from 02. *Villa Rapallo, Mont de la Trinite, St Helier, Jersey JE2 4NJ* Tel (01534) 739146 Mobile 07797-750435
E-mail hart@localdial.com

HART, Colin Edwin. b 45. Leeds Univ BA66 PGCE67 MPhil89 Fitzw Coll Cam BA73 MA77 K Coll Lon MTh76 Man Univ PhD98. Trin Coll Bris 74. **d** 74 **p** 75. C Ware Ch Ch *St Alb* 74-78; TV Sheff Manor 78-80; V Wombridge *Lich* 80-87; Lect St Jo Coll Nottm 87-01; Public Preacher *S'well* 87-01; Hon C Chilwell 87-91; Hon C Trowell 91-01; Perm to Offic *Ches* from 01. *47 Deveraux Drive, Wallasey CH44 4DG* Tel 0151-630 0749
E-mail hart206@btinternet.com

HART, Dagogo. b 50. Birm Bible Inst 77. **d** 82 **p** 83. C Niger Delta St Cypr 82-88; V 93-96; Chapl to Bp Niger Delta 83-88; Res Min Niger Delta Ch Ch 89-92; Can Res St Steph Cathl Niger Delta 97-00; C W Bromwich St Jas w St Paul *Lich* 01-06; V from 06. *3 Tiverton Drive, West Bromwich B71 1DA* Tel 0121-553 0601

HART, David. b 48. Edge Hill Coll of HE BEd80 Liv Univ MEd87 Ches Coll of HE BPhil94. NOC 91. **d** 94 **p** 95. NSM Ashton-in-Makerfield St Thos *Liv* 94-02; NSM Wigan W Deanery 02-05. *12 Ratcliffe Road, Aspull, Wigan WN2 1YE* Tel (01942) 832918

HART, David Alan. b 54. Rhodes Univ BTh86 MTh89 PhD92 Bournemouth Univ DEd08. **d** 81 **p** 82. R Auckland Park St Pet S Africa 82-86; Sub Dean Kimberley Cathl 86-90; Chapl Cape Town Univ 90-94; NSM Cape Town Cathl 94-98; Chapl Bournemouth and Poole Coll of FE *Sarum* 99-06; Co-ord of IME 07-11; Vice Prin Sarum OLM Scheme 07-11; Asst Dioc Dir of Ords 07-11. *6 Wilton House, 4 Alum Chine Road, Bournemouth BH4 8DY* Tel 07521-741534 (mobile)

HART, David John. b 58. K Coll Lon BD80. St Mich Coll Llan 83. **d** 85 **p** 86. C Denbigh and Nantglyn *St As* 85-88; Chapl RAF 88-89; C Llanrhos *St As* 89-91; V Rhosllannerchrugog 91-01; Perm to Offic *Lich* from 11. *11 Cilcoed, Chirk, Wrexham LL14 5BX*

HART, David Maurice. b 35. Univ Coll Dur BSc57. Clifton Th Coll 59. **d** 61 **p** 62. C Bolton St Paul *Man* 61-64; C Hamworthy *Sarum* 64-70; R W Dean w E Grimstead 70-81; R Farley w Pitton and W Dean w E Grimstead 81-90; V Steeple Ashton w Semington and Keevil 90-03; rtd 03. *9 Field Close, Westbury BA13 3AG* Tel (01373) 827912

HART, Ms Debbie. b 56. d 11. NSM St Marylebone St Paul *Lon* from 11. *18C Chesham Flats, Brown Hart Gardens, London W1K 6WP* Tel 07985-649120 (mobile) E-mail debs.hart@rocketmail.com

HART, Canon Dennis Daniel. b 22. Linc Th Coll 45. d 48 p 49. C Abbots Langley *St Alb* 48-49; C Bedford St Paul 49-53; CF 53-55; V St Alb St Sav *St Alb* 55-92; Hon Can St Alb 74-92; RD St Alb 84-90; rtd 92. *Grace Muriel House, 104 Tavistock Avenue, St Albans AL1 2NW* Tel (01727) 815829

HART, Dennis William. b 30. JP. Open Univ BA. Oak Hill Th Coll 75. d 78 p 79. NSM Clacton St Paul *Chelmsf* 78-04; Perm to Offic 04-07. *Maranatha, 15 Albert Gardens, Clacton-on-Sea CO15 6QN* Tel (01255) 431794

HART, Edwin Joseph. b 21. Oak Hill Th Coll 56. d 58 p 59. C Harlow New Town w Lt Parndon *Chelmsf* 58-60; C Leyton 60-61; C-in-c Cranham Park St Luke CD 61-69; V Cranham Park 69-71; R Markfield *Leic* 71-89; rtd 89; Perm to Offic *Leic* from 89. *c/o Ms G Gordon, 1 Meadow Lane, Markfield LE67 9WT*

HART, Geoffrey Robert. b 49. TISEC 93. d 95 p 96. P-in-c Edin St Salvador 96-98; C Edin St Cuth 96-98; Lic to Offic 98-00; TV Edin St Marg 00-04; NSM Edin St Dav 04-09; P-in-c Edin St Marg from 09. *27 Links View, Port Seton, Prestonpans EH32 0EZ* Tel (01875) 811147 Mobile 07963-463551 E-mail geoff@lovehart.demon.co.uk

HART, Canon Gillian Mary. b 57. Sheff City Poly BA79. Carl Dioc Tr Inst 92. d 95 p 96. C Burgh-by-Sands and Kirkbampton w Kirkandrews etc *Carl* 95-99; C Aikton 95-99; C Orton St Giles 95-99; Dioc Youth Officer 99-03; Chapl St Martin's Coll Carl 99-03; R Barony of Burgh *Carl* 03-10; TR Maryport, Netherton and Flimby from 10; Adv for Women in Min from 08; Hon Can Carl Cathl from 10. *The Vicarage, Church Terrace, Maryport CA15 7PS* Tel (01900) 813077 E-mail hart.gill@btopenworld.com

HART, Graham Cooper. b 36. S Dios Minl Tr Scheme 88. d 91 p 92. NSM Filton *Bris* 91-93; NSM Downend 93-01. *11 West Hill, Portishead, Bristol BS20 6LQ* Tel (01275) 840363

HART, Canon Graham Merril (Merry). b 23. Ridley Coll Melbourne 65. d 77 p 77. Tanzania 69-84; CMS 72-83; Can Musoma from 85; Chapl Ostend w Knokke and Bruges *Eur* 84-93; Miss to Seamen 84-93; rtd 93; Perm to Offic *S'wark* from 93. *8 Alexander Court, 57 Kidbrooke Grove, London SE3 0LH* Tel (020) 8858 3731

HART, James. b 53. Dur Univ BA75 DipEd76 Lon Univ BD96 MIL84. Oak Hill Th Coll 86. d 88 p 89. C Starbeck *Ripon* 88-90; SAMS Argentina 90-96; R Buenos Aires St Sav 91-95; Chapl Bishop's Stortford Coll 96-00; Chapl Felsted Sch 00-06; Dioc FE Officer *Chelmsf* from 00; P-in-c Steeple Bumpstead and Helions Bumpstead from 06. *The Vicarage, 3 Church Street, Steeple Bumpstead, Haverhill CB9 7DG* Tel (01440) 730914 E-mail james@harthome.org

HART, John Peter. b 39. Bris Sch of Min 80. d 84 p 85. NSM Malmesbury w Westport and Brokenborough *Bris* 84-88; C Yatton Moor *B & W* 89-90; V Bridgwater H Trin 90-96; Chapl HM Pris The Mount 96-01; P-in-c Sarratt *St Alb* 96-04; P-in-c Chipperfield St Paul 01-04; rtd 04; Perm to Offic *Pet* from 05. *4 Waverley Gardens, Stamford PE9 1BH* Tel (01780) 754756

HART, Julia Lesley. b 43. d 08 p 09. NSM Nettleham *Linc* from 08. *Shrewsbury Cottage, Nettleham Lane, Scothern, Lincoln LN2 2TY* Tel (01673) 862426 E-mail jldf.hart@btinternet.com

HART, Mark. b 61. Chu Coll Cam BA82 Cam Univ MA86 PhD86. Trin Coll Bris BA98. d 98 p 99. C Bromborough *Ches* 98-02; V Plemstall w Guilden Sutton from 02; RD Ches from 09. *The Vicarage, Wicker Lane, Guilden Sutton, Chester CH3 7EL* Tel (01244) 300306 E-mail markhart61@googlemail.com

HART, Merril. See HART, Canon Graham Merril

HART, Canon Michael Anthony. b 50. AKC71. St Aug Coll Cant 72. d 73 p 74. C Southwick St Columba *Dur* 73-76; C Hendon St Alphage *Lon* 76-78; P-in-c Eltham Park St Luke *S'wark* 78-83; V 83-85; R Newington St Mary 85-96; P-in-c Camberwell St Mich w All So w Em 85-96; RD S'wark and Newington 93-96; P-in-c Chaldon 96-97; P-in-c Caterham 96-97; TR 98-05; RD Caterham 98-05; Hon Can S'wark Cathl 01-05 and from 10; Can Missr 05-10; TR Catford (Southend) and Downham from 10. *St John's Rectory, 353 Bromley Road, London SE6 2RP* Tel (020) 8697 3220 E-mail michael.hart@southwark.anglican.org

HART, Preb Michael Stuart. b 39. Univ of Wales (Lamp) BA61 Lanc Univ MA72. Wycliffe Hall Ox 61. d 63 p 64. C W Bromwich St Jas *Lich* 63-66; C Tarrington w Stoke Edith *Heref* 66-67; C Putney St Mary *S'wark* 67-70; V Accrington St Mary *Blackb* 70-82; RD Accrington 76-82; Hon Can Blackb Cathl 81-91; V Walton-le-Dale 82-91; TR Heavitree w Ex St Paul 91-02; P-in-c Ex St Mary Steps 01-02; TR Heavitree and St Mary Steps 02-07; P-in-c Exwick 05-07; Preb Ex Cathl 02-07; rtd 07; P-in-c Bath H Trin *B & W* from 09. *20 The Grove, Hallatrow, Bristol BS39 6ES* Tel (01761) 451359 Mobile 07786-516076 E-mail m.hart254@btinternet.com

HART, Mrs Mildred Elizabeth. b 49. d 10 p 11. OLM Len Valley *Cant* from 10. *15 Mercer Drive, Harrietsham ME17 1AY* Tel (01622) 859753 E-mail millie.hart@uwclub.net

HART, Peter. See HART, John Peter

HART, Peter Osborne. b 57. St Jo Coll Nottm. d 92 p 93. C Shipley St Pet *Bradf* 92-97; TV Walsall *Lich* 97-03; TV Cannock 03-10; V Cannock and Huntington from 10; V Hatherton from 10. *The Rectory, 11 Sherbrook Road, Cannock WS11 1HJ* Tel (01543) 579660

HART, Peter William. b 60. Liv Univ BA82 Université de Haute Normandie MèsL84 Univ of Wales (Swansea) MPhil92. Sarum & Wells Th Coll 86. d 88 p 89. C Llansamlet *S & B* 88-89; C Sketty 89-92; P-in-c Warndon St Nic *Worc* 92-97; R Berkhamsted St Mary *St Alb* 97-04; V Kew St Phil and All SS w St Luke *S'wark* from 04; Ecum Adv Kingston Area from 05. *St Philip's Vicarage, 70 Marksbury Avenue, Richmond TW9 4JF* Tel (020) 8392 1425 *or* 8332 1324 E-mail pwhart1@aol.com

HART, Robert William. b 76. R Holloway & Bedf New Coll Lon BSc97 Leeds Univ BA01 MA04. Coll of Resurr Mirfield 99. d 02 p 03. C Haydock St Jas *Liv* 02-06; R Hemsworth *Wakef* from 06. *The Rectory, 3 Church Close, Hemsworth, Pontefract WF9 4SJ* Tel (01977) 610507 E-mail frrobert@parishofhemsworth.org.uk

HART, Ronald George. b 46. BSc CQSW77. Sarum & Wells Th Coll. d 85 p 86. C Sittingbourne St Mich *Cant* 85-88; C Walton H Trin *Ox* 88-89; TV 89-96; R Broughton Gifford, Gt Chalfield and Holt *Sarum* 96-05; Chapl UWE *Bris* 05-07; C Mangotsfield 06-07; R Vale of White Hart *Sarum* from 07. *The Rectory, Holwell, Sherborne DT9 5LF* Tel (01963) 23035 E-mail ronhart1@yahoo.co.uk

HART, Mrs Sheila Elizabeth. b 49. ERMC. d 08 p 09. NSM Whinlands *St E* from 08. *3 Keats Close, Saxmundham IP17 1WJ* Tel (01728) 602456 E-mail sheila.hart@tesco.net

HART, Tony. b 36. CCC Cam BA59 MA63. Cuddesdon Coll 59. d 61 p 62. C Middlesbrough All SS *York* 61-64; Bp's Dom Chapl *Dur* 64-67; Hon Chapl 67-72; C Owton Manor CD 67-70; V Harton Colliery 70-71; TR S Shields All SS 71-83; RD Jarrow 77-83; Can Res Dur Cathl 83-92; V Easingwold w Raskelfe *York* 92-97; V 97-01; RD Easingwold 97-00; rtd 01; Perm to Offic *Newc* from 02. *13 Stobhill Villas, Morpeth NE61 2SH* Tel (01670) 519017

HART, Prof Trevor Andrew. b 61. St Jo Coll Dur BA82 Aber Univ PhD89. d 88 p 88. NSM Bieldside *Ab* 88-95; NSM St Andrews St Andr *St And* from 95; Prof Div St Mary's Coll St Andr Univ from 95; Prin St Mary's Coll from 01. *St Mary's College, South Street, St Andrews KY16 9JU* Tel (01334) 462864 E-mail tah@st-andrews.ac.uk

HART, Mrs Valerie Mary. b 44. Sheff Univ MEd89 Wolv Univ MSc95 Nottm Univ MA08 RSCN. EMMTC 06. d 08 p 09. NSM Derby St Andr w St Osmund from 08. *4 Kingswood Avenue, Belper DE56 1TU* Tel (01773) 821417

HARTE, Frederick George. b 25. AKC53. d 54 p 55. C Lewisham St Jo Southend *S'wark* 54-57; C Eltham H Trin 57-60; V Bellingham St Dunstan 60-73; V Plumstead St Nic 73-84; V Sutton Bridge *Linc* 84-90; rtd 90; Master St Jo Hosp Bath and P-in-c of Chpl 90-00; Perm to Offic *Guildf* from 00. *Heartsease, 5 Vale Road, Claygate, Esher KT10 0NJ* Tel and fax (01372) 802548 E-mail f.harte@gmx.net

HARTE, The Ven Matthew Scott. b 46. TCD BA70 MA74. CITC 71. d 71 p 72. C Bangor Abbey *D & D* 71-74; C Ballynafeigh St Jude 74-76; I Ardara w Glencolumbkille, Inniskeel etc *D & R* 76-98; I Dunfanaghy, Raymunterdoney and Tullaghbegley from 98; Adn Raphoe from 83; Preb Howth St Patr Cathl Dublin from 07. *The Rectory, Horn Head Road, Dunfanaghy, Letterkenny, Co Donegal, Republic of Ireland* Tel (00353) (74) 913 6187 Fax 913 6051 E-mail archdeacon@raphoe.anglican.org

HARTERINK, Mrs Joy Frances. b 49. Essex Univ BA71 Hughes Hall Cam CertEd72 Lon Univ MSc87. Oak Hill NSM Course 89. d 92 p 94. NSM Richmond H Trin and Ch Ch *S'wark* 92-05 Chapl Richmond Coll 97-01; Perm to Offic *Guildf* from 05. *9 Eastmead, Woking GU21 3BP* Tel (01483) 751179 E-mail joyharterink@yahoo.com

HARTLAND, Ian Charles. b 49. K Coll Lon BD72 AKC72 PGCE73 MTh76. Sarum & Wells Th Coll 83. d 84 p 85. C Orpington All SS *Roch* 84-87; Sen Lect Ch Ch Coll Cant 87-95 Adv RE Kent Coun 96-04; HMI of Schs from 04. *Ivy Lodge 4 The Terrace, Canterbury CT2 7AJ* Tel (01227) 472836 E-mail ian.hartland@ofsted.gov.uk

HARTLAND, Michael. d 08. NSM Sutton *S'wark* 08-10; Perm to Offic from 10. *63 Park Lane, Carshalton SM5 3EE* Tel (020) 8401 6706 E-mail mandjhartland@blueyonder.co.uk

HARTLESS, Mrs Berengaria Isabella de la Tour. b 52. Univ of Wales (Cardiff) BSc74 Goldsmiths' Coll Lon PGCE76 Liv Univ MA03. Ox Min Course 90. d 93 p 94. Par Dn High Wycombe *Ox* 93-94; C 94-97; P-in-c Seer Green and Jordans 97-00; SHM T Officer (Bucks) 97-00; Dioc Prin of OLM from 00. *Lloyd's House, Banbury Street, Kineton, Warwick CV35 0JS* Tel (01926) 642975

HARTLEY, Mrs Anne Theresa. b 52. St Cuth Soc Dur BSc74 Worc Coll of Educn PGCE75. d 03 p 04. OLM Shipton-under

Wychwood w Milton, Fifield etc *Ox* from 03. *The Old House, Upper Milton, Milton-under-Wychwood, Chipping Norton OX7 6EX* Tel (01993) 830160 Mobile 07976-025101 E-mail annethartley@hotmail.com

HARTLEY, Brian. b 41. NOC 82. **d** 85 **p** 86. NSM Royton St Paul *Man* 85-91; NSM Oldham St Steph and All Martyrs 91-94; TV E Farnworth and Kearsley 94-97; TR New Bury 97-06; P-in-c Gt Lever 03-06; AD Farnworth 98-05; rtd 06; Perm to Offic *Man* from 06. *21 Penryn Avenue, Royton, Oldham OL2 6JR* Tel (01706) 849132 E-mail brian.hartley@tiscali.co.uk

HARTLEY, Christopher Neville. b 56. Hull Univ BA82 SS Paul & Mary Coll Cheltenham PGCE84. SNWTP 08. **d** 10 **p** 11. OLM Man Victoria Park from 10. *8 Bronte Street, Manchester M15 6QL* Tel 0161-232 1432 Mobile 07783-932386 E-mail christopherhartley@ymail.com

HARTLEY, Colin Redfearn. b 60. Cant Ch Ch Univ Coll BA98. Ridley Hall Cam 02. **d** 04 **p** 05. C Herne Bay Ch Ch *Cant* 04-08; TV Langley Marish *Ox* from 08. *Christ the Worker Vicarage, Parlaunt Road, Slough SL3 8BB* Tel (01753) 596722 E-mail rev.hartley@btinternet.com

HARTLEY, Daniel George. b 73. Leeds Univ BA95. Coll of Resurr Mirfield 96. **d** 99 **p** 00. C Richmond w Hudswell *Ripon* 99-03; Chapl HM YOI Deerbolt 03-10; V Ecclesfield *Sheff* from 11. *The Vicarage, 230 The Wheel, Ecclesfield, Sheffield S35 9ZB* Tel 0114-257 0002 E-mail daniel@danielhartleyfsnet.co.uk

HARTLEY, Denis. b 54. NTMTC BA02. AT 07. NSM Wood Green St Mich w Bounds Green St Gabr etc *Lon* from 07. *33 Stanmore Road, London N15 3PR* Tel (020) 8374 0915 Mobile 07957-227764 E-mail dhart74802@blueyonder.co.uk

HARTLEY, Dianna Lynn. *See* GWILLIAMS, Canon Dianna Lynn

HARTLEY, Graeme William. b 68. Ripon Coll Cuddesdon 05. **d** 07 **p** 08. C Sherborne w Castleton, Lillington and Longburton *Sarum* 07-10; V Milborne Port w Goathill etc *B & W* from 10. *The Vicarage, Bathwell Lane, Milborne Port, Sherborne DT9 5AN* Tel (01963) 250248 E-mail revd.graeme@gmail.com

HARTLEY, Helen-Ann Macleod. b 73. St Andr Univ MTheol95 Princeton Th Sem ThM96 Worc Coll Ox MPhil00 DPhil05. SAOMC 03. **d** 05 **p** 06. C Wheatley *Ox* 05-07; C Littlemore from 07; Lect Ripon Coll Cuddesdon from 05; Tutor from 09. *43 Fairfax Gate, Holton, Oxford OX33 1QE* Tel (01865) 874466 Mobile 07981-914832 E-mail helen-ann.hartley@ripon-cuddesdon.ac.uk

HARTLEY, John Peter. b 56. Cam Univ BA78 Leeds Univ PhD82 Dur Univ BA84. Cranmer Hall Dur 82. **d** 85 **p** 86. C Spring Grove St Mary *Lon* 85-88; C Bexleyheath St Pet *Roch* 88-91; P-in-c Hanford *Lich* 91-00; Faith in the City Officer (Potteries) 91-00; V Eccleshill *Bradf* from 00. *The Vicarage, 2 Fagley Lane, Bradford BD2 3NS* Tel (01274) 636403 Mobile 07811-915320 E-mail john.hartley@bradford.anglican.org

HARTLEY, Canon John William. b 47. St Jo Coll Dur BA69. Linc Th Coll 70. **d** 72 **p** 73. C Poulton-le-Fylde *Blackb* 72-76; C Lancaster St Mary 76-79; V Barrowford 79-87; V Salesbury from 87; AD Whalley from 01; Hon Can Blackb Cathl from 09. *St Peter's Vicarage, 49A Ribchester Road, Blackburn BB1 9HU* Tel (01254) 248072 E-mail john@salesbury49a.freeserve.co.uk

HARTLEY, Julian John. b 57. Oak Hill Th Coll BA85. **d** 85 **p** 86. C Eccleston Ch Ch *Liv* 85-89; V Goose Green 89-00; P-in-c Mosley Common *Man* 00-06; TV Astley, Tyldesley and Mosley Common from 06. *St John's Vicarage, Mosley Common Road, Worsley, Manchester M28 1AN* Tel 0161-790 2957 Fax 799 0314 E-mail rev.hartley@hartley.me.uk

HARTLEY, Michael Leslie. b 56. Leeds Univ BSc77. Ripon Coll Cuddesdon 87. **d** 89 **p** 90. C Standish *Blackb* 89-93; V Bamber Bridge St Aid 93-98; TR Colne and Villages 98-08; P-in-c Warton St Paul from 08; Dioc Ecum Officer from 08. *The Vicarage, Church Road, Warton, Preston PR4 1BD* Tel (01772) 632227 E-mail blackburndeo@googlemail.com

HARTLEY, Canon Nigel John. b 48. Portsm Poly BA. St Jo Coll Nottm. **d** 83 **p** 84. C Ipswich St Marg *St E* 83-86; P-in-c Hintlesham w Chattisham 86-95; Dioc Radio Officer 86-95; P-in-c Gt Finborough w Onehouse, Harleston, Buxhall etc 95-04; RD Stowmarket 96-99; V Aldeburgh w Hazlewood from 04; RD Saxmundham from 05; Hon Can St E Cathl from 10. *The Vicarage, Church Walk, Aldeburgh IP15 5DU* Tel (01728) 452223 E-mail nigel.hartley@stedmundsbury.anglican.org

HARTLEY, Paul. b 51. Nottm Univ BTh88. Linc Th Coll 85. **d** 88 **p** 89. C Clitheroe St Mary *Blackb* 88-91; TV Guiseley w Esholt *Bradf* 91-97; R Ackworth *Wakef* from 97. *The Rectory, Cross Hill, Ackworth, Pontefract WF7 7EJ* Tel (01977) 602751 E-mail rev.paulhartley@yahoo.co.uk

HARTLEY, Canon Peter. b 44. St Cath Coll Cam BA66 MA69 Avery Hill Coll PGCE67. Sarum & Wells Th Coll 77. **d** 78 **p** 79. Hon C Freemantle *Win* 78-79; Chr Educn Officer *Pet* 79-81; Dir of Educn 81-90; Dir Coun of Educn and Tr *Chelmsf* 90-09; Hon Can Chelmsf Cathl 92-09; rtd 09; Perm to Offic *Nor* from 04. *3 St Mary's Lane, Langham, Holt NR25 7AF* Tel (01328) 830624

HARTLEY, Peter Mellodew. b 41. Qu Coll Cam BA63 MA66 Lon Univ MSc71 FICE. S'wark Ord Course 80. **d** 83 **p** 84. NSM Salfords *S'wark* 83-97; Chapl Surrey and Sussex Healthcare NHS Trust 97-02; rtd 02; Perm to Offic *Chich* from 00 and S'wark from 02. *Old Timbers, North Lane, West Hoathly, East Grinstead RH19 4QF* Tel (01342) 811238 E-mail petermhartley@btinternet.com

HARTLEY (née ARCHER), Sarah Elizabeth. b 66. Charing Cross Hosp Medical Sch MB, BS89 Heythrop Coll Lon MA03 MRCGP95. Ripon Coll Cuddesdon BA99 MA07. **d** 00 **p** 01. C Dulwich St Barn *S'wark* 00-03; C Shepherd's Bush St Steph w St Thos *Lon* 03-07; PV Westmr Abbey from 07; Perm to Offic *Lon* 07-08 and *B & W* 08-11; NSM Bath Abbey w St Jas *B & W* from 11. *Glen Gilda, St Saviour's Road, Bath BA1 6RN* Tel 07717-718569 (mobile) E-mail searcher@doctors.org.uk

HARTLEY, Stephen William Mark. b 50. St Chad's Coll Dur BA71. Westcott Ho Cam 72. **d** 74 **p** 75. C Holbrooks *Cov* 74-76; C Styvechale 76-79; P-in-c Snitterfield w Bearley 79-81; V 81-83; V Exhall 83-88; V Tilehurst St Cath *Ox* 88-95; TR Cowley St Jas 95-06; TR Hermitage 06-08; TR Cov E from 08. *St Peter's Rectory, Charles Street, Coventry CV1 5NP* Tel (024) 7622 8383 E-mail stephen.hartley@btinternet.com

HARTLEY, Stewart John Ridley. b 47. St Jo Coll Nottm 78. **d** 80 **p** 81. C Altham w Clayton le Moors *Blackb* 80-84; P-in-c Nelson St Phil 84-91; V 91-98; V Gt Marsden w Nelson St Phil 99-03; Hon Can Blackb Cathl 99-03; V Bermondsey St Anne and St Aug *S'wark* from 03; V Bermondsey St Jas w Ch Ch and St Crispin from 03. *St Anne's Vicarage, 10 Thorburn Square, London SE1 5QH* Tel (020) 7237 3950

HARTLEY, Susan Mary. b 49. Newc Univ MB, BS73 MRCGP77. SEITE 99. **d** 02 **p** 03. NSM Spitalfields Ch Ch w All SS *Lon* 02-07; NSM Hainault *Chelmsf* from 07; Asst Chapl St Joseph's Hospice Hackney from 06. *272 New North Road, Ilford IG6 3BT* Tel (020) 8500 4592 E-mail suemhartley@btinternet.com

HARTMAN, Mrs Jill Norma. b 57. Cen Sch of Art Lon BA80. SEITE 08. **d** 11. NSM Upper St Leonards St Jo *Chich* from 11. *21 Nelson Road, Hastings TN34 3RX* Tel (01424) 716126 Mobile 07952-950316

HARTNELL, Canon Bruce John. b 42. Ex Univ BA64 Linacre Coll Ox BA66 MA. Ripon Hall Ox 64. **d** 66 **p** 67. C S Stoneham *Win* 66-69; Chapl and Tutor Ripon Hall Ox 69-74; V Knowl Hill w Littlewick *Ox* 74-78; Chapl Southn Univ 78-83; V Sholing 83-07; AD Southampton 93-01; Hon Can Win Cathl 93-07; rtd 07. *9 Ash Close, Southampton SO19 5SD* Tel (023) 8090 5420 E-mail bruce.hartnell@ukgateway.net

HARTNELL, Graham Philip. b 50. **d** 08 **p** 08. NSM Flackwell Heath *Ox* from 08. *36 Whinneys Road, Loudwater, High Wycombe HP10 9RL* Tel (01494) 521783 E-mail g.hartnell@talktalk.net

HARTOPP, Mrs Penelope Faye. b 55. Ripon Coll Cuddesdon. **d** 03 **p** 04. C Studley *Cov* 03-04; C Cov E 04-07; TV Godalming *Guildf* 07-11; V Over St Chad *Ches* from 11. *The Vicarage, 1 Over Hall Drive, Winsford CW7 1EY* Tel (01606) 593222 Mobile 07884-314752 E-mail penniehartopp@googlemail.com

HARTREE, Steven John. b 45. FFA78. WEMTC 96. **d** 99 **p** 00. NSM Highbridge *B & W* 99-03; P-in-c Tintinhull w Chilthorne Domer, Yeovil Marsh etc 03-09; rtd 09. *60 Vereland Road, Hutton, Weston-super-Mare BS24 9TL* Tel (01934) 812013 E-mail stevenhartree194@btinternet.com

HARTRIDGE, James Bernard Robertson. b 44. Open Univ BSc01. S Dios Minl Tr Scheme 89. **d** 92 **p** 93. C Portsea St Cuth *Portsm* 92-95; In RC Ch 96-09; Perm to Offic *Portsm* from 10. *15 Hundred Acres, Wickham, Fareham PO17 6JB* Tel (01329) 833206 E-mail revjhartridge@rocketmail.com

HARTROPP, Andrew James. b 59. Southn Univ BSc80 PhD85 K Coll Lon PhD03. Oak Hill Th Coll BA95. **d** 98 **p** 99. C Watford St Alb 98-01; C Watford Ch Ch 01-08; Teacher Henrietta Barnett Sch 01-05; NSM White Waltham w Shottesbrooke *Ox* from 08; NSM Waltham St Lawrence from 08. *The Parsonage, School Road, Waltham St Lawrence, Reading RG10 0NU* Tel 0118-934 4841 E-mail a.hartropp@btinternet.com

HARTWELL, Mrs Jeanette May. b 65. Aston Univ BSc88. Qu Coll Birm BA07. **d** 07 **p** 08. C Brereton and Rugeley *Lich* 07-10; TV Smestow Vale from 10. *The Vicarage, School Road, Trysull, Wolverhampton WV5 7HR* Tel (01902) 896650

HARVEY, Alan Douglas. b 25. FRSH82. Melbourne Coll of Div 78. **d** 79 **p** 81. Australia 79-86; Perm to Offic *Ely* 86-87; V Wiggenhall St Germans and Islington 88-95; V Wiggenhall St Mary Magd 88-95; rtd 95; Perm to Offic *Cant* from 95. *17 Bay View Road, Broadstairs CT10 2EA* Tel (01843) 862794

HARVEY, Alison Christine Vera. b 57. Open Univ BA97 Nottm Univ MA03. EMMTC 01. **d** 03 **p** 04. C Horncastle Gp *Linc* 03-07; P-in-c Mablethorpe w Trusthorpe from 07; P-in-c Sutton, Huttoft and Anderby from 09. *The Rectory, 88 Wellington Road, Mablethorpe LN12 1HT* Tel (01507) 473159 Mobile 07789-835039 E-mail harvey524@btinternet.com

HARVEY, Canon Anthony Ernest. b 30. Worc Coll Ox BA53 MA56 DD83. Westcott Ho Cam 56. **d** 58 **p** 59. C Chelsea Ch Ch *Lon* 58-62; Ch Ch Ox 62-69; Warden St Aug Coll Cant 69-75; Lect Th Ox Univ 76-82; Chapl Qu Coll Ox 77-82; Can and Lib Westmr Abbey 82-99; Sub-Dean and Adn Westmr 87-99; rtd 99; Perm to Offic *Glouc* from 00. *Mendelssohn Cottage, Broadway Road, Willersey, Broadway WR12 7BH* Tel (01386) 859260

HARVEY, Anthony Peter. b 42. Birm Univ BSc63 MSc64. Wycliffe Hall Ox 79. **d** 81 **p** 82. C Stoke Damerel *Ex* 81-84; Canada 84-90; Chapl HM YOI Deerbolt 91-92; Chapl HM Pris Wakef 92-95; Chapl HM Pris Kirkham 95-01; rtd 07. *570-20th Avenue #5, Deux Montagnes QC J7R 7E9, Canada* Tel (001) (450) 974 4358

HARVEY, Brian. b 51. Hatf Poly BA74. St As Minl Tr Course 02. **d** 05 **p** 06. NSM Cilcain and Nannerch and Rhydymwyn *St As* 05-09; P-in-c 06-09; R Flint from 09. *The Rectory, Allt Goch, Flint CH6 5NF* Tel (01352) 733274
E-mail brianharvey@mac.com

HARVEY, Carol Richmond. b 47. NUU BA89. CITC 03. **d** 06 **p** 07. NSM Carnmoney *Conn* from 06. *26 Larne Road, Carrickfergus BT38 7DX* Tel (028) 9335 1654
E-mail carolrharvey@hotmail.com

HARVEY, Christopher John Alfred. b 41. S'wark Ord Course 66. **d** 69 **p** 70. C Grays Thurrock *Chelmsf* 69-73; C Gt Baddow 73-75; V Berechurch St Marg w St Mich 75-94; R Tendring and Lt Bentley w Beaumont cum Moze 94-00; P-in-c Alresford 00-08; rtd 08; Perm to Offic *Chelmsf* from 08. *Bethel, 9 Laburnum Crescent, Kirby Cross, Frinton-on-Sea CO13 0QQ* Tel (01255) 678649 E-mail chris.anne@tiscali.co.uk

HARVEY, The Ven Cyril John. b 30. Univ of Wales (Lamp) BA51. Coll of Resurr Mirfield 51. **d** 53 **p** 54. C Caerau w Ely *Llan* 53-57; C Milford Haven *St D* 57-61; V Castlemartin and Warren 61-65; R Begelly w Kilgetty 65-73; V Haverfordwest St Martin w Lambston 73-88; Can St D Cathl from 85; R Tenby 88-96; Adn St D 91-96; rtd 96. *10 Oakwood Grove, Slade Lane, Haverfordwest SA61 2HF* Tel (01437) 768036

HARVEY, Canon Debra Eileen. b 54. SWMTC. **d** 94 **p** 95. NSM Camborne *Truro* from 94; Chapl w Deaf People from 94; Hon Can Truro Cathl from 03. *Ankorva Salow, Tehidy Road, Camborne TR14 0NA* Tel (01209) 716282 Mobile 07774-975268
Fax and minicom as telephone
E-mail hippo@ankorva.freeserve.co.uk

HARVEY, Desmond Victor Ross. b 37. QUB BA59. Princeton Th Sem ThM63 Fuller Th Sem California DMin93 St Mich Coll Llan 95. **d** 95 **p** 96. Presbyterian Min 65-95; C Cwmbran *Mon* 95-97; TV 97; Perm to Offic from 97; OCM from 98. *Mallory, Llanmaes, Llantwit Major CF61 2XR* Tel and fax (01446) 792753

HARVEY, Ian Malcolm. b 51. **d** 03 **p** 04. NSM Burnie Australia 03-07; NSM Filwood Park *Bris* 07-09; C S Barrow *Carl* from 09. *98A Roose Road, Barrow-in-Furness LA13 9RL*
E-mail ian_harvey@blueyonder.co.uk

HARVEY, John. b 30. S'wark Ord Course. **d** 65 **p** 66. C Lewisham St Jo Southend *S'wark* 65-73; V Bellingham St Dunstan 73-78; TV Bourne Valley *Sarum* 78-81; TR 81-87; R Kilkhampton w Morwenstow *Truro* 87-90; rtd 90; Perm to Offic *Roch* 90-99. *18 Ramsay Hall, 11-13 Byron Road, Worthing BN11 3HN*

HARVEY, John Christopher. b 65. Univ of Wales (Lamp) BA86 Nottm Univ BTh89. Linc Th Coll 86. **d** 89 **p** 90. C Dwygyfylchi *Ban* 89-93; V Llangrannog w Llandysiliogogo w Penbryn *St D* 93-02; RD Glyn Aeron 99-02; P-in-c Llangystennin *St As* 02-04; R 04-09; V Meliden and Gwaenysgor from 09; Dioc Voc Adv from 08. *The Vicarage, Ffordd Penrhwylfa, Prestatyn LL19 8HN* Tel (01745) 856220

HARVEY, John Mark. b 64. QUB BEd87 TCD BTh93. CITC 90. **d** 93 **p** 94. C Portadown St Columba *Arm* 93-96; I Monaghan w Tydavnet and Kilmore *Clogh* 96-01; Dioc Communications Officer 97-00; Miss Officer (Ireland) CMS 01-05; I Ballybeen *D & D* from 05. *1 Grahamsbridge Road, Dundonald, Belfast BT16 2DB* Tel (028) 9048 0834 Mobile 07966-332310
E-mail rector@stmarysballybeen.com

HARVEY, Lt Col John William Arthur. b 43. Guildf Dioc Min Course 98. **d** 01 **p** 02. OLM Aldershot St Aug *Guildf* from 01. *59 Knoll Road, Fleet GU51 4PT* Tel (01252) 622793
E-mail father.john@talktalk.net

HARVEY, Lance Sydney Crockford. b 25. Ridley Hall Cam 67. **d** 69 **p** 70. C Mortlake w E Sheen *S'wark* 69-74; P-in-c Woolwich St Thos 75-86; V Lee Gd Shep w St Pet 86-92; RD E Lewisham 87-91; rtd 92; Perm to Offic *Truro* 92-06. *17 Lariggan Road, Penzance TR18 4NJ*

HARVEY, Lincoln. b 69. Univ of Wales (Swansea) BA92 K Coll Lon MA01 PhD08. SEITE. **d** 09 **p** 10. NSM St John-at-Hackney *Lon* from 09; Tutor SEITE 06-10; Tutor St Mellitus Coll *Lon* from 10. *St Mellitus College, St Paul's Church, Onslow Square, London SW7 3NX* Tel 07855-866823 (mobile)
E-mail lincoln.harvey@stmellitus.org

HARVEY, Margaret Claire. b 41. Univ of Wales (Abth) BA62 DipEd63 Lon Univ BD68. Dalton Ho Bris 66. **dss** 68 **d** 80 **p** 97. Flint *St As* 68-74; Lect Trin Coll Bris 74-80; Connah's Quay

St As 79-80; C 80-86; Bp's Adv for Continuing Clerical Educn 86-98; Hon C Corwen and Llangar 86-87; Dn-in-c Bryneglwys 87-97; P-in-c 97-02; rtd 02. *Coleg y Groes, The College, Corwen LL21 0AU* Tel (01490) 412169 E-mail colegygroes@talk21.com

HARVEY, Mark. See HARVEY, John Mark

HARVEY, Murray Alexander. b 63. Univ of Qld BA85 Deakin Univ Australia DHSc03 MAPsS87. St Fran Coll Brisbane BTh91. **d** 91 **p** 92. C Milton Australia 92-93; C Stafford 94-95; P-in-c Tamborine Mt St Geo 95-02; V Glen Gp *Linc* 02-11; R Clayfield Australia from 11. *The Rectory, 56 Bellevue Terrace, Clayfield QLD 4011, Australia* Tel (0061) (7) 3862 1411
E-mail revmharvey@stmarksclayfield.org

HARVEY, Canon Norman Roy. b 43. Nottm Univ DipAE86. Wycliffe Hall Ox 66. **d** 69 **p** 70. C Clay Cross *Derby* 69-72; C Dronfield 72-76; TV 76-79; P-in-c Rowsley 79-89; Dioc Youth Officer 79-83; Dioc Adv in Adult and Youth Educn 83-89; TR Eckington w Handley and Ridgeway 89-01; R Eckington and Ridgeway 01-08; RD Bolsover and Staveley 00-05; Hon Can Derby Cathl 00-08; rtd 08. *62 Parklands View, Aston, Sheffield S26 2GW* Tel 0114-287 2243
E-mail norman.harvey2@btopenworld.com

HARVEY, Oliver Paul. b 33. Magd Coll Ox BA55 MA59. Cuddesdon Coll 57. **d** 59 **p** 60. C S Norwood St Mark *Cant* 59-61; C Hythe 61-64; Zambia 64-71; Chapl Cant Coll of Tech 71-77; Hon C Cant St Martin and St Paul 73-77; Chapl K Sch Roch 77-88; C Roch 88-90; V Gillingham St Mary 90-00; RD Gillingham 98-00; rtd 00; Perm to Offic *Roch* 00-03 and *B & W* from 05. *11 Henley Road, Taunton TA1 5BN* Tel (01823) 272825

HARVEY, Miss Pamela Betty. b 33. Dalton Ho Bris IDC59. **dss** 68 **d** 87 **p** 95. Nottingham St Ann *S'well* 68-72; Bestwood St Matt 72-76; CPAS Staff 76-93; Dir Consultants Division CPAS 93-99; rtd 99; Hon C Glenfield *Leic* 95-04; Perm to Offic from 04. *72 Chestnut Road, Glenfield, Leicester LE3 8DB* Tel 0116-232 2959 E-mail pam.harvey@ukgateway.net

HARVEY, Mrs Patricia Ann. b 45. Qu Coll Birm. **dss** 82 **d** 87 **p** 94. Gospel Lane St Mich *Birm* 82-85; Exhall *Cov* 85-89; C 87-89; TD Droitwich Spa *Worc* 89-94; TV 94-97; P-in-c Finstall 97-00; V 00-02; rtd 02; Perm to Offic *Heref* from 02 and *Worc* from 04. *15 Mount Orchard, Tenbury Wells WR15 8DW* Tel (01584) 819444 E-mail patricia.harvey3@virgin.net

HARVEY, Canon Patrick Arnold. b 58. TCD BA MA. CITC 82. **d** 85 **p** 86. C Bandon Union *C, C & R* 85-88; Dean's V Limerick St Mich *L & K* 88-91; Dioc Info Officer 88-91; I Abbeyleix w Ballyroan etc *C & O* from 91; Can Ossory Cathl from 97. *The Rectory, Abbeyleix, Portlaoise, Co Laois, Republic of Ireland* Tel and fax (00353) (57) 873 1243
E-mail abbeyleix@leighlin.anglican.org

HARVEY, Paul. See HARVEY, Oliver Paul

HARVEY, Robert Martin. b 30. S'wark Ord Course 69. **d** 70 **p** 71. C Sutton New Town St Barn *S'wark* 70-75; C Leatherhead *Guildf* 76-78; V Wadworth w Loversall *Sheff* 78-96; RD W Doncaster 94-97; rtd 96; Perm to Offic *Sheff* from 96. *58 Thomson Avenue, Doncaster DN4 0NU*

HARVEY, Robin Grant. b 43. Clare Coll Cam BA64 MA68 Univ of NSW PhD74. Linc Th Coll 85. **d** 87 **p** 88. C Keynsham *B & W* 87-91; R E w W Harptree and Hinton Blewett 91-97; Chapl Surrey Univ 98-02; P-in-c Cuddington 02-07; V 07-08; rtd 08. *21 St Cadoc House, Temple Street, Keynsham, Bristol BS31 1HD* Tel 0117-986 2295
E-mail rgharvey.194@btinternet.com

HARVEY, Roland. b 68. St Jo Coll Nottm 99. **d** 01 **p** 02. C Skelmersdale St Paul *Liv* 01-05; P-in-c Pemberton St Fran Kitt Green from 05. *The Vicarage, 42 Sherborne Road, Orrell, Wigan WN5 0JA* Tel (01942) 213227 Mobile 07817-901455

HARVEY, Simon John. b 63. Trin Coll Bris BA00. **d** 00 **p** 01. C Walsall St Paul *Lich* 00-03; TV Oadby and Warden of Reader Leic 05-10; V Islington St Mary *Lon* from 10. *St Mary Vicarage, 302 Upper Street, London N1 2TX* Tel (020) 7226 8981
E-mail simon@sjharvey.org.uk

HARVEY, Steven Charles. b 58. Reading Univ BA79 Cam Univ PGCE80 Ox Univ BA83 MA88. Ripon Coll Cuddesdon 81. **d** 84 **p** 85. C Oldham *Man* 84-87; Chapl and Hd RS St Pet Sch York 87-96; Sen Dep Hd Kingswood Sch Bath 96-03; Sen Provost and Educn Officer Woodard Corp 03-06; Hd Master Bury Gr Sch from 06; Perm to Offic *Blackb* and *Man* from 06. *41 Bury New Road, Ramsbottom, Bury BL0 0AR* Tel (01706) 822690

HARVEY, Mrs Susan Esther. b 44. **d** 11. OLM Sherston Magna, Easton Grey, Luckington etc *Bris* from 11. *55 The Tarters, Sherston, Malmesbury SN16 0NT* Tel (01666) 840696

HARVEY, Thomas James. b 71. Nottm Univ BA92 Leic Univ MA96 DipSW96. Cranmer Hall Dur 09. **d** 11. C Cramlington *Newc* from 11. *24 Lindsey Close, Cramlington NE23 8EJ* Tel 07722-405253 (mobile) E-mail james.harvey@live.com

HARVEY, Mrs Verity Margaret. b 48. Bris Univ BA69 Saltley Tr Coll Birm DipEd70. SAOMC 99. **d** 02 **p** 03. NSM Radlett *St Alb* 02-05; NSM Bushey 05-11; Chapl Herts Partnership NHS Foundn Trust from 10. *28 Field Road, Watford WD19 4DR* Tel (01923) 492863

ARVEY, Wendy Marion. b 46. SEITE 06. **d** 09 **p** 10. NSM Hurst Green *S'wark* from 09. *Surrey Beeches West, Westerham Road, Westerham TN16 2EX* Tel (01959) 562340 Mobile 07973-428683 E-mail wendyharvey@talktalk.net

ARVEY-NEILL, Nicola Lisa Jane. b 69. QUB BD91 TCD MPhil95. CITC BTh94. **d** 95 **p** 96. Dioc C *T, K & A* 95-96; C Galway w Kilcummin 96-97; Dioc Youth Adv (Limerick) *L & K* 97-01; Chapl Villier's Sch Limerick 98-01; Chapl Limerick Univ 98-01; Perm to Offic from 01. *Modreeny Rectory, Cloughjordan, Co Tipperary, Republic of Ireland* Tel and fax (00353) (505) 42183 Mobile 87-250 0570 E-mail nickihn@eircom.net *or* smneill@iol.ie

ARVIE, Robert. b 53. **d** 04 **p** 05. OLM Godalming *Guildf* from 04. *7 Ockford Ridge, Godalming GU7 2NP* Tel (01483) 415931 E-mail rhl.swift@ukonline.co.uk *or* robbie.harvie@godalming.org.uk

ARWOOD, Ann Jane. *See* CLARKE, Mrs Ann Jane

ARWOOD, Anna Charlotte. b 75. Ripon Coll Cuddesdon. **d** 11. C Ruscombe and Twyford *Ox* from 11. *Hurst Vicarage, Church Hill, Hurst, Reading RG10 0SJ* E-mail harwoodanna@yahoo.co.uk

ARWOOD (formerly SOUTH), Mrs Gillian. b 51. NEOC 87. **d** 90 **p** 94. C Rothbury *Newc* 90-93; C Morpeth 93-97; V Amble 97-06; Chapl Northumbria Healthcare NHS Trust from 06. *Wansbeck General Hospital, Woodhorn Lane, Ashington NE63 9JJ* Tel (01670) 521212 E-mail gillysouth@btopenworld.com

ARWOOD, Canon John Rossiter. b 26. Selw Coll Cam BA51 MA55. Wycliffe Hall Ox 51. **d** 53 **p** 54. C Handsworth St Mary *Birm* 53-55; Tutor Trin Coll Umuahia Nigeria 57-64; Warden Minl Tr Cen Freetown Sierra Leone and Bp's Dom Chapl 64-67; Home Educn Sec CMS 67-75; V Cheltenham Ch *Glouc* 75-91; RD Cheltenham 84-89; Hon Can Glouc Cathl 85-91; rtd 91; Perm to Offic *Ex* 91-99; *Chich* and *Portsm* from 00. *8 Kingsey Avenue, Emsworth PO10 7HP* Tel (01243) 372215

ARWOOD, Mary Ann. b 46. Cam Inst of Educn CertEd68. Ox Min Course 04. **d** 07 **p** 08. NSM Burghfield *Ox* 07-10; NSM W Downland from 10. *The Rectory, Main Street, Chaddleworth, Newbury RG20 7EW* Tel (01488) 638566 Mobile 07721-437316 E-mail maryh@globalnet.co.uk

ARWOOD, Peter James. b 64. Birm Univ MB88 ChB88. Wycliffe Hall Ox BA93. **d** 94 **p** 95. C Cov H Trin 94-97; C Kensington St Barn *Lon* 97-02; V Woking Ch Ch *Guildf* from 02; Chapl Woking Hospice from 06. *Christ Church Vicarage, 10 Russetts Close, Woking GU21 4BH* Tel (01483) 762100 E-mail peter.harwood@christchurchwoking.org

ASELHURST (née STERLING), Mrs Anne. b 51. Macalester Coll (USA) BA73. EAMTC 89. **d** 92 **p** 94. Par Dn Bury St Edmunds St Jo *St E* 92-94; C 94-95; V Fordham St Pet *Ely* 95-06; P-in-c Kennett 95-06; P-in-c Isleham 05-06; R Cupar *St And* from 06; R Ladybank from 06. *13 Robertson Road, Cupar KY15 5YR* Tel (01334) 652982 E-mail annehaselhurst@talktalk.net

ASELOCK, Canon Jeremy Matthew. b 51. York Univ BA73 BPhil74. St Steph Ho Ox BA82 MA86. **d** 83 **p** 84. C Pimlico St Gabr *Lon* 83-86; C Paddington St Jas 86-88; Bp's Dom Chapl *Chich* 88-91; P-in-c Boxgrove 91-94; V 94-98; Dioc Adv on Liturgy 91-98; Can and Preb Chich Cathl 94-98; Can Res and Prec Nor Cathl from 98. *34 The Close, Norwich NR1 4DZ* Tel (01603) 619169 Fax 766032

ASKETT, Mrs Fiona Ann. b 55. SEITE 01. **d** 04 **p** 05. NSM Leigh *Roch* 04-09; V Whittington w Weeford *Lich* from 09; V Hints from 09. *5 Bramley Way, Lichfield WS14 9SB* Tel (01543) 432233 E-mail fiona.haskett@btopenworld.com

ASKEY, Alyn Rex. b 51. EMMTC 02. **d** 04 **p** 05. NSM Sneinton St Chris w St Phil *S'well* from 04; NSM Nottingham St Sav from 04; NSM Nottingham St Nic from 04; Dioc Ev from 09. *Flat 1, 6 Vickers Street, Nottingham NG3 4LD* Tel 0115-960 5489 E-mail alynhaskey@freedomministries.freeserve.co.uk

ASKINS, Thomas. b 41. TCD BA72. CITC 71. **d** 73 **p** 74. C Larne and Inver *Conn* 73-78; C Antrim All SS 78-83; I Belfast St Mark 83-90; I Dublin Clontarf *D & G* 90-02; I Dublin St Ann and St Steph 02-08; Can Ch Ch Cathl Dublin 99-08; rtd 08. *7 Gorse Haven, Coolboy, Tinahely, Co Wicklow, Republic of Ireland* Tel (00353) (402) 34997

ASLAM, Andrew James. b 57. Univ Coll Dur BSc78 Coll of Ripon & York St Jo PGCE79 Lambeth STh84. Trin Coll Bris 80. **d** 83 **p** 84. C Leyland St Andr *Blackb* 83-86; C Hartford *Ches* 86-88; V Grimsargh *Blackb* 88-98; V St Helens St Mark *Liv* 98-05; V Birkenhead Ch Ch *Ches* from 05. *Christ Church Vicarage, 7 Palm Grove, Prenton CH43 1TE* Tel 0151-652 5647 E-mail vicar@christchurch.birkenhead.net

ASLAM, Canon Frank. b 26. Bris Univ BA50. Tyndale Hall Bris 49. **d** 51 **p** 52. C Halliwell St Paul *Man* 51-55; Uganda 56-60; C Wednesfield Heath *Lich* 60-61; V Wolverhampton St Matt 61-65; V Blackpool Ch Ch *Blackb* 65-70; V Macclesfield St Mich *Ches* 71-80; Dir of Resources 80-91; Hon Can Ches Cathl 81-91; rtd 91; Perm to Offic *Ches* from 91; P-in-c Bistre St As 99-00. *Brackendale, Chester Road, Buckley CH7 3AH* Tel (01244) 549291

ASLAM, James Robert. b 31. Open Univ BA74. Bps' Coll Cheshunt 55. **d** 57 **p** 58. C Penwortham St Mary *Blackb* 57-63; V Cockerham 63-74; V Cockerham w Winmarleigh 74-76; V Gt Harwood St Bart 76-88; V Fairhaven 88-95; rtd 95; Perm to Offic *Blackb* from 95. *5 Willow Trees Drive, Blackburn BB1 8LB* Tel (01254) 697092

ASLAM, Mrs Jane. b 70. Leeds Poly BA92. Trin Coll Bris BA97. **d** 97 **p** 98. C Minehead *B & W* 97-00; Perm to Offic *Newc* 00-03; C Balkwell 03-04; P-in-c Purton *Bris* 04-10; R Alfred Jewel *B & W* from 10. *The New Rectory, Cliff Road, North Petherton, Bridgwater TA6 6NY* Tel (01278) 662429 E-mail revjane.haslam@hotmail.co.uk

ASLAM, John Gordon. b 32. Birm Univ LLB53. Qu Coll Birm 75. **d** 77 **p** 77. Hon C Bartley Green *Birm* 77-79; Hon C Moseley St Mary 79-96; Chapl to The Queen 89-02; Perm to Offic *Heref* from 97. *16 Mill Street, Ludlow SY8 1BE* Tel and fax (01584) 876663

ASLAM, Michael Henry. b 72. Buckingham Univ BA93. Trin Coll Bris BA94 MA94. **d** 97 **p** 98. C Minehead *B & W* 97-00; Chapl Newc Univ 00-04; C Purton and Dioc Ecum Officer *Bris* 04-06; P-in-c N Swindon St Andr 06-09; NSM Alfred Jewel *B & W* from 10. *The New Rectory, Cliff Road, North Petherton, Bridgwater TA6 6NY* Tel (01278) 662429 Mobile 07530-677493 E-mail mike.haslam@hotmail.co.uk

ASLAM, Robert John Alexander. b 34. CCC Cam BA58. Coll of Resurr Mirfield 58. **d** 60 **p** 61. C Rawmarsh w Parkgate *Sheff* 60-66; Perm to Offic *Edin* 66-73 and *Carl* 73-77; P-in-c Peebles *Edin* 77-81; V Darnall *Sheff* 81-85; Hon C Bermondsey St Hugh CD *S'wark* 86-88; R Clydebank *Glas* 88-98; Chapl Málaga *Eur* 98-03. *Flat 1/1, 134 Fergus Drive, Glasgow G20 6AT* Tel 0141-945 4132

ASLER, Canon John Joseph. b 45. Univ of Wales (Cardiff) MPhil99. Qu Coll Birm 89. **d** 90 **p** 91. C Horfield H Trin *Bris* 90-93; V Bris St Andr Hartcliffe 93-01; V Bris Lockleaze St Mary Magd w St Fran from 01; AD City 03-06; Hon Can Bris Cathl from 08. *The Vicarage, Copley Gardens, Bristol BS7 9YE* Tel 0117-951 2516

ASLER, Kevin John. b 56. RGN80 RMN80. St Mich Coll Llan 03. **d** 06 **p** 07. NSM Raglan w Llandenny and Bryngwyn *Mon* 06-08; NSM Llangwm Uchaf and Llangwm Isaf w Gwernesney etc from 08. *The Steps, Old Abergavenny Road, Brynglyn, Raglan, Usk NP15 2AA* Tel (01291) 690163 Mobile 07592-822022 E-mail kevin@hasler.org.uk *or* kevin@llangwm-parishes.org.uk

ASSALL, Mrs Elizabeth Claire. b 80. R Holloway Coll Lon BSc01. Trin Coll Bris BA08. **d** 09 **p** 10. C Bempton w Flamborough, Reighton w Speeton *York* from 09. *Briel Cottage, Bridlington Road, Flamborough, Bridlington YO15 1PW* Tel (01262) 851385 E-mail lizthecurate@trundlebug.co.uk

ASSALL, William Edwin. b 41. St Jo Coll Nottm 75. **d** 77 **p** 78. C Wellington w Eyton *Lich* 77-80; C Farewell 80-82; V 82-93; C Gentleshaw 80-82; V 82-93; P-in-c Cheddleton 93-94; Asst Chapl Birm Heartlands and Solihull NHS Trust 98-01; Chapl Team Ldr 01-06; rtd 06; Perm to Offic *Lich* 97-09 and *Birm* from 06; C Hatherton Lich from 09. *17 Bradwell Lane, Rugeley WS15 4RW* Tel (01543) 670739

ASSAN, Brian Joseph. b 67. CITC 05. **d** 08 **p** 09. NSM Clooney w Strathfoyle *D & R* 08-09; NSM Faughanvale from 09. *96 Castle Park, Limavady BT49 0SB* Tel (028) 7776 6281 Mobile 07828-668342 E-mail brian.hassan@btinternet.com

ASSELL, David Edwin. b 38. WMMTC 87. **d** 90 **p** 91. NSM Worc SE 90-93; C Abberton, Naunton Beauchamp and Bishampton etc 93-94; P-in-c 94; R Abberton, The Flyfords, Naunton Beauchamp etc 94-04; rtd 04; Perm to Offic *Worc* from 04. *14 Napleton Lane, Kempsey, Worcester WR5 3PT* Tel (01905) 828096

ASTE, James Victor William. b 36. St Mich Th Coll Crafers 64. **d** 68 **p** 70. C Ormond Australia 68-69; C Roehampton H Trin *S'wark* 70-72; P-in-c Boroko Papua New Guinea 72-76; Sec ABM Vic Australia 76-81; I Armadale w Hawksburn 81-86; I Vermont S 86-89; Inter-Ch Trade and Ind Chapl 89-99; rtd 01; Lic to Offic The Murray 99-05; Perm to Offic Melbourne from 05. *17 Park View Drive, Aspendale Vic 3195, Australia* Tel (0061) (3) 9588 2805 Mobile 407-044086 E-mail baha@picknowl.com.au

ASTED, Marcus Arthur David. b 35. Qu Coll Birm 63. **d** 66 **p** 67. C Woodchurch *Ches* 66-69; C W Kirby St Bridget 69-72; V Farndon 72-76; V Farndon and Coddington 76-79; Perm to Offic 98-00 and from 02; NSM Liscard St Mary w St Columba 00-02. *62 South Road, West Kirby, Wirral CH48 3HQ* Tel 0151-625 0428

ASTE, Erle. b 44. St Mich Coll Llan 66. **d** 68 **p** 69. C Pontefract St Giles *Wakef* 68-71; C Almondbury 71-74; V Purlwell 74-79; P-in-c Batley Carr 76-79; V Ynyshir *Llan* 79-86; V Tylorstown w Ynyshir 86-87; V Tonyrefail w Gilfach Goch 87-97; P-in-c Llandyfodwg 87-97; V Tonyrefail w Gilfach Goch and Llandyfodwg 97-99; V Pyle w Kenfig 99-04; rtd 04. *2 Cambray Close, Porthcawl CF36 3PY* Tel (01656) 783935

HASTIE-SMITH, Timothy Maybury. b 62. Magd Coll Cam MA84. Wycliffe Hall Ox 85. **d** 88 **p** 89. C Ox St Ebbe w H Trin and St Pet 88-91; Chapl Stowe Sch 91-98; Hd Master Dean Close Sch Cheltenham 98-08; TV Fairford Deanery *Glouc* from 08. *The Parsonage, High Street, Kempsford, Fairford GL7 4ET* Tel (01285) 810773 E-mail tim.hastie-smith@hotmail.com

HASTINGS, David Kerr. b 40. St Luke's Coll Ex CertEd63. NSM Course 84. **d** 87 **p** 88. Hd Master St Edburg's Sch Bicester 82-89; Asst Chapl HM Pris Grendon and Spring Hill 87-89; NSM Bicester w Bucknell, Caversfield and Launton *Ox* 87-89; Chapl HM Pris Reading 90-92; P-in-c Gt Wishford *Sarum* 92; P-in-c S Newton 92; P-in-c Stapleford w Berwick St James 92; P-in-c Winterbourne Stoke 92; R Lower Wylye and Till Valley 92-95; Chapl HM Pris Ex 96-01; Perm to Offic *Ex* from 01; rtd 01. *26 Hoopern Street, Exeter EX4 4LY* Tel (01392) 498233

HASTINGS, The Ven Gary Lea. b 56. NUU BA82 MA87 TCD BTh93. CITC 90. **d** 93 **p** 94. C Galway w Kilcummin *T, K & A* 93-95; I Aughaval w Achill, Knappagh, Dugort etc 95-09; I Galway w Kilcummin from 09; Dom Chapl to Bp Tuam from 94; Can Tuam Cathl from 00; Adn Tuam from 06; Can St Patr Cathl Dublin from 10. *The Rectory, Taylor's Hill, Galway, Republic of Ireland* Tel (00353) (91) 521914 E-mail gryhastings@iol.ie

HASTROP, Paul. b 39. Wells Th Coll 70. **d** 72 **p** 73. C Parkstone St Osmund *Sarum* 72-76; C Penzance St Mary w St Paul *Truro* 76-79; V St Blazey 79-87; TV Bournemouth St Pet w St Swithun, H Trin etc *Win* 87-94; TV Thornaby on Tees *York* 94-96; P-in-c Portsea St Sav *Portsm* 96-03; rtd 03; Hon C Paignton St Jo *Ex* 05-06; Perm to Offic *Portsm* from 08. *23 Chawton Close, Winchester SO22 6HY* Tel (01962) 883061

HASTWELL, James Sydney. b 37. Roch Th Coll 67. **d** 69 **p** 70. C Croydon St Aug *Cant* 69-73; C Hurstpierpoint *Chich* 73-75; P-in-c Twineham 76; P-in-c Sayers Common 76; P-in-c Albourne 76; R Albourne w Sayers Common and Twineham 76-88; V Forest Row 88-94; rtd 94; Perm to Offic *Chich* 97-09 and *Nor* from 11. *36 Broad Reaches, Ludham, Great Yarmouth NR29 5PD* Tel (01692) 678574 E-mail jen-jim@hotmail.co.uk

HASWELL, Jeremy William Drake. b 60. Ridley Hall Cam. **d** 08 **p** 09. C St Alb St Paul *St Alb* from 08. *46 Brampton Road, St Albans AL1 4PT* Tel (01727) 847236 Mobile 07717-762539 E-mail jeremy@haswells.fsnet.co.uk

HATCH, Canon George Andrew. b 29. Leeds Univ BA. Coll of Resurr Mirfield 51. **d** 53 **p** 54. C S Farnborough *Guildf* 53-55; Windward Is 55-63; Barbados from 63; R St Mary Barbados 63-73; Assoc Dir Chr Action Development in Caribbean 73-83; R St Jas Barbados 83-94; rtd 94. *St James, Barbados* (001809) 432 0700

HATCH, Richard Francis. b 36. Qu Coll Cam BA60 MA64. Cuddesdon Coll 60. **d** 62 **p** 63. C Leigh St Mary *Man* 62-66; PC Peel Green 66-71; V Barton w Peel Green 71-75; Dioc Broadcasting Officer 73-85; R Birch St Jas and Fallowfield 75-78; Lic Preacher 78-08; rtd 01. *c/o Mr P A Macniven, 15 Faircross Way, St Albans AL1 4RT*

HATCHETT, Michael John. b 49. Enfield Coll BSc72 K Coll Lon BD77 AKC77. Linc Th Coll 77. **d** 78 **p** 79. C Halstead St Andr *Chelmsf* 78-79; C Halstead St Andr w H Trin and Greenstead Green 79-81; C Greenstead 81-85; V Gt Totham 85-01; R Gt Totham and Lt Totham w Goldhanger 01-06; RD Witham 96-01; Dioc Chapl MU 04-06; R Melton and Ufford *St E* from 06. *The Vicarage, 6 Rectory Road, Hollesley, Woodbridge IP12 3JS* Tel (01394) 412052 E-mail mikehatchett2004@yahoo.com

HATCHETT, Mrs Ruth Merrick. b 54. K Coll Lon BD77 AKC77 Open Univ BA92. EAMTC 03. **d** 05 **p** 06. NSM Tolleshunt Knights w Tiptree and Gt Braxted *Chelmsf* 05-06; NSM Melton and Ufford *St E* 06-10; TV Wilford Peninsula from 10. *The Vicarage, 6 Rectory Road, Hollesley, Woodbridge IP12 3JS* Tel (01394) 412052 E-mail ruth.hatchett@yahoo.com

HATCHMAN, Ms Elizabeth Mary. b 63. St Andr Univ MA85. Selly Oak Coll Qu Coll Birm BD92. **d** 93 **p** 94. C Aston SS Pet and Paul *Birm* 93-96; C Rowley Regis 96-00; Chapl St Geo Post 16 Cen 00-04; Perm to Offic from 05. *21 Westfield Road, Birmingham B14 7SX* Tel 0121-441 2711

HATFIELD, Rebecca Alison. See LUMLEY, Rebecca Alison

HATHAWAY, Canon David Alfred Gerald. b 48. St Mich Coll Llan. **d** 72 **p** 73. C Newport St Julian *Mon* 72-74; P-in-c Oakham w Hambleton and Egleton *Pet* 74-77; V Newport St Matt *Mon* 77-83; CF (TA) from 78; V Abertillery *Mon* 83-88; V Rumney from 88; Hon Can St Woolos Cathl 91-05; Can from 05. *The Vicarage, 702 Newport Road, Rumney, Cardiff CF3 4DF* Tel (029) 2079 7882

HATHAWAY, John Albert. b 24. Sarum Th Coll 59. **d** 60 **p** 61. C Fleet *Guildf* 60-64; C Cowley St Jas *Ox* 64-66; V Holmwood *Guildf* 66-71; V Westborough 71-74; V Newmarket All SS *St E* 74-82; V Acton w Gt Waldingfield 82-85; R W Downland *Sarum* 85-90; rtd 90; Perm to Offic *Sarum* 94-10. *The College of St Barnabas, Blackberry Lane, Lingfield RH7 6NJ* Tel (01342) 872825

HATHAWAY, Martin Charles. b 48. St Jo Coll Nottm 93. **d** 95 **p** 96. C Weddington and Caldecote *Cov* 95-99; V Potters Green 99-04; C The Heyfords w Rousham and Somerton *Ox* 04-05; C Fritwell w Souldern and Ardley w Fewcott 04-05; TV Dunstable *St Alb* from 05. *20 Friars Walk, Dunstable LU6 3JA* Tel (01582) 668996 E-mail revd.martinhathaway@tiscali.co.uk

HATHAWAY, Vivienne Ann. b 57. Bucks Chilterns Univ Coll BSc96. Westcott Ho Cam 00. **d** 02 **p** 03. C Bp's Hatfield *St Alb* 02-05; C Bp's Hatfield, Lemsford and N Mymms 05-07; P-in-c Stevenage St Mary Shephall w Aston from 07. *St Mary's Vicarage, 148 Hydean Way, Shephall, Stevenage SG2 9YA* Tel (01438) 351963 E-mail vivienne@vhathaway.freeserve.co.uk

HATHERLEY, Peter Graham. b 46. Univ of Wales (Cardiff) BSc67 PhD70. St Mich Coll Llan 70. **d** 72 **p** 73. C Ystrad Mynach *Llan* 72-75; Hon C Tonyrefail 75-88; Perm to Offic from 88. *Treetops, The Derwen, Bridgend CF35 6HD* Tel (01656) 662196

HATHORNE (née MARSH), Mrs Carol Ann. b 44. W Midl Coll of Educn BA83. WMMTC 88. **d** 91 **p** 94. Par Dn Wednesbury St Paul Wood Green *Lich* 91-93; NSM Pensnett *Worc* 93-97; TV Cannock *Lich* 97-01; NSM Willenhall H Trin 05-11; NSM Bentley Em and Willenhall H Trin from 11. *Holy Trinity Vicarage, 20 Church Road, Willenhall WV12 5PT* Tel (01922) 476416 E-mail hathorne@btinternet.com

HATHORNE, Mark Stephen. b 51. Boston Univ MDiv76. **d** 00 **p** 00. C Willenhall H Trin *Lich* 00-01; TV 01-06; TR 06-11; P-in-c Bentley 06-09; TR Bentley Em and Willenhall H Trin from 11 Holy Trinity Vicarage, 20 Church Road, Willenhall WV12 5PT Tel (01922) 476416 E-mail m.s.hathorne@virgin.net

HATHWAY, Ross Arthur. b 56. Moore Th Coll Sydney BTh86. **d** 86 **p** 87. C Tamworth St Pet Australia 87-88; C Corby St Columba *Pet* 89-92; R Trull w Angersleigh *B & W* 92-02; R Kellyville St Steph Australia from 03. *45 President Road Kellyville NSW 2155, Australia* Tel (0061) (2) 9629 6255 E-mail kellyvilleanglican@bigpond.com

HATREY, David Nigel. b 57. SS Mark & Jo Univ Coll Plymouth CertEd79 BEd90 Ex Univ MA01. SWMTC 90. **d** 93 **p** 94. NSM S Hill w Callington *Truro* 93-01; Hon C Street w Walton *B & W* from 01. *Pilgrims Way, Chilton Polden Hill, Edington, Bridgwater TA7 9AL* Tel (01278) 723616 E-mail hatreys@micehouse.fsnet.co.uk

HATTAN, Jeffrey William Rowland. b 49. Cranmer Hall Dur 83. **d** 85 **p** 86. C Eston w Normanby *York* 85-89; TV 89-95; V Hunmanby w Muston from 95. *The Vicarage, 6 Northgate, Hunmanby, Filey YO14 0NT* Tel (01723) 890294 E-mail jeff@all-saints.freeserve.co.uk

HATTAWAY, Judith Helen Alison. b 53. Kent Univ BA79 PGCE80 Liv Univ MA02 MBACP00. STETS 07. **d** 10 **p** 11. NSM Hurst *Ox* from 10; Asst Chapl Broadmoor Hosp Crowthorne 10-11; Asst Chapl Frimley Park Hosp NHS Foundr Trust from 11. *15 Rayner Drive, Arborfield, Reading RG2 9FE* Tel 0118-976 1197 Mobile 07798-723232 E-mail judihattaway@mac.com

HATTON, Jane Elizabeth. b 53. SAOMC 95. **d** 98 **p** 99. NSM Stevenage St Pet Broadwater *St Alb* 98-04; Asst Chapl E and N Herts NHS Trust from 04. *2 Dancote, Park Lane, Knebworth SG3 6PB* Tel (01438) 811039 E-mail janehatton@dial.pipex.com

HATTON, Jeffrey Charles. b 49. K Coll Lon BD70 Bris Univ MA72. Westcott Ho Cam 72 Episc Th Sch Cam Mass 73. **d** 74 **p** 75. C Nor St Pet Mancroft 74-78; C Earlham St Anne 78-79 Relig Broadcasting Asst IBA 79-82; Hon C Kensington St Barn *Lon* 79-84; Hon C Fulham All SS 85-89; R Win All SS w Chilcomb and Chesil 89-94; Dioc Communications Office 89-94; P-in-c Salisbury St Thos and St Edm *Sarum* 94-99; R 99-05; rtd 05; Hon C Chalke Valley *Sarum* 06-11; Hon C Coker w Sutton Bingham and Closworth *B & W* from 11; Hon C W Coker w Hardington Mandeville, E Chinnock etc from 11. *The Vicarage, East Coker, Yeovil BA22 9JG* Tel (01935) 862125 E-mail harles.hatton51@btinternet.com

HATTON, Michael Samuel. b 44. St Jo Coll Dur BA72. Cranmer Hall Dur. **d** 74 **p** 75. C Dudley St Jas *Worc* 74-75; C N Lynn w St Marg and St Nic *Nor* 75-77; C Walsall Wood *Lich* 78-79; Mi Shelfield St Mark CD 79-89; V Middleton St Cross *Ripon* 89-97 V Ingol *Blackb* 97-11; rtd 11. *7 Laurel Avenue, Euxton, Chorley PR7 6AY* Tel (01257) 274584 E-mail midoha76@waitrose.com

HATTON, Trevor. b 55. Oak Hill Th Coll BA86. **d** 86 **p** 87. C Chilwell *S'well* 86-90; R Trowell 90-95; Chapl Nottm Trent Univ 95-99; P-in-c Nottingham St Nic 99-02; R 02-07; rtd 07 *53 Ashchurch Drive, Nottingham NG8 2RB* E-mail trev_ali@tiscali.co.uk

HATTON, Mrs Vivienne Gloria. b 57. Birm Univ BA03. St Jo Coll Nottm MA06. **d** 06 **p** 07. C Wednesfield Heath *Lich* 06-09 V Chasetown from 09. *The Vicarage, 158A High Street, Chasetown, Burntwood WS7 3XG* Tel (01543) 686276 E-mail viviennehatton@blueyonder.co.uk

HATWELL, Timothy Rex. b 53. Oak Hill Th Coll BA85. **d** 8 **p** 86. C Tonbridge St Steph *Roch* 85-90; V Cudham and Down 90-07; V Falconwood from 07. *The Vicarage, The Green, Welling, DA16 2PD* Tel (020) 8298 0065 Mobile 07799-601546 E-mail tim.hatwell@diocese-rochester.org

HAUGHTON, Peter Steele. b 57. K Coll Lon BD84 MA90. Westcott Ho Cam 84. **d** 86 **p** 87. C Cheam Common St Phil *S'wark* 86-90; Chapl Lon Univ Medical Schs 90-94; Educn Adv Lon Univ Medical Schs 94-95; P-in-c Kingston Vale St Jo 95-03; Adv in Ethics and Law K Coll Lon from 03. *95 Bullar Road, Southampton SO18 1GT* Tel 07815-803920 (mobile) E-mail peter.haughton@btinternet.com

HAUGHTY, Miss Rebecca Mary. b 69. Coll of Resurr Mirfield 09. **d** 11. C Pocklington Wold *York* from 11. *110 Wold Road, Pocklington, York YO42 2QG* Tel 07518-412149 (mobile)

HAVARD, Alan Ernest. b 27. Qu Coll Birm 79. **d** 81 **p** 82. NSM Rugby St Matt *Cov* 81-84; C Portishead *B & W* 84-86; V Mickleover All SS *Derby* 86-96; rtd 96; Perm to Offic *Derby* from 96. *7 Headingley Court, Littleover, Derby DE3 6XS*

HAVARD, David William. b 56. Man Univ BA84. Qu Coll Birm 84. **d** 85. C Man Clayton St Cross w St Paul 85-88; Canada 88-02; Perm to Offic *Sheff* from 03. *35 Roe Lane, Sheffield S3 9AL* Tel 0114-272 9695 E-mail deacondave@onetel.com

HAVELL, Edward Michael. b 38. Dur Univ BA65. Ridley Hall Cam 66. **d** 68 **p** 69. C Ecclesall *Sheff* 68-71; C Roch St Justus 71-74; P-in-c Holbeach Hurn *Linc* 74-75; C Hollington St Jo *Chich* 75-85; TV Rye 85-92; C E Dereham and Scarning *Nor* 92; rtd 93; Perm to Offic *Chich* from 99. *4 Gammons Way, Sedlescombe, Battle TN33 0RQ* Tel (01424) 870864

HAVENS, Mrs Anita Sue. b 44. Univ of Mass BSEd67 Clark Univ (USA) MA72 Hughes Hall Cam BA79. Cranmer Hall Dur MA83. **dss** 84 **d** 87 **p** 94. Gateshead Hosps 84-87; Par Dn Cen Telford *Lich* 87-90; Ind Chapl 87-90; Ind Chapl *Lich* 90-96; TV Man Whitworth 96-99; Chapl Man Univ 96-99; R Birch St Agnes w Longsight St Jo w St Cypr 99-01; rtd 01; Perm to Offic *Carl* from 03. *Stone Cottage, Kirkby Thore, Penrith CA10 1UE* Tel (01768) 362682 E-mail sue.havens@lineone.net

HAVEY, Kenneth Richard. b 61. St Steph Ho Ox 95. **d** 97 **p** 98. C Corringham *Chelmsf* 97-98; C Leigh St Clem 98-02; R from 02. *St Clement's Rectory, 80 Leigh Hill, Leigh-on-Sea SS9 1AR* Tel (01702) 475967 E-mail frkenneth@leighhill.plus.com

HAVILAND, Andrew Mark James. b 65. Leeds Univ BEd87. STETS 02. **d** 05 **p** 06. NSM N Holmwood *Guildf* 05-08; Chapl Bryanston Sch from 08. *Bryanston School, Blandford DT11 0PX* Tel (01258) 452411 Mobile 07855-823255 E-mail amjh@talktalk.net

HAVILAND, Edmund Selwyn. b 24. K Coll Cam BA49 MA51. Wells Th Coll 49. **d** 51 **p** 52. C St Helier *S'wark* 51-55; C-in-c Bermondsey St Hugh CD 55-58; V Ockbrook *Derby* 58-68; V E Peckham *Roch* 68-78; R E Peckham and Nettlestead 78-84; S Africa 84-85; Dep Chapl HM Pris Brixton 85-89; rtd 89; Perm to Offic *Guildf* from 89. *Hill Farm, Thursley, Godalming GU8 6QQ* Tel (01252) 702115

HAWES, Canon Andrew Thomas. b 54. Sheff Univ BA77 Em Coll Cam MA79. Westcott Ho Cam 77. **d** 80 **p** 81. C Gt Grimsby St Mary and St Jas *Linc* 80-84; P-in-c Gedney Drove End 84-86; P-in-c Sutton St Nicholas 84-86; V Lutton w Gedney Drove End, Dawsmere 86-89; V Edenham w Witham on the Hill 89-00; V Edenham w Witham on the Hill and Swinstead from 00; RD Beltisloe from 97; Can and Preb Linc Cathl from 09. *The Vicarage, Church Lane, Edenham, Bourne PE10 0LS* Tel and fax (01778) 591358

HAWES, The Ven Arthur John. b 43. UEA BA86. Chich Th Coll 65. **d** 68 **p** 69. C Kidderminster St Jo *Worc* 68-72; P-in-c Droitwich 72-76; R Alderford w Attlebridge and Swannington *Nor* 76-92; Chapl Hellesdon and David Rice Hosps and Yare Clinic 76-92; RD Sparham *Nor* 81-91; Mental Health Act Commr 86-94; Hon Can Nor Cathl 88-95; TR Gaywood 92-95; Adn Linc and Can and Preb Linc Cathl 95-08; rtd 08; Perm to Offic *S'wark* from 10. *49 Thamespoint, Fairways, Teddington TW11 9PP* Tel (020) 8274 2635 Mobile 07803-249834 E-mail arthur.hawes@yahoo.co.uk

HAWES, Joseph Patricius. b 65. St Chad's Coll Dur BA87. St Steph Ho Ox 88. **d** 91 **p** 92. C Clapham Team *S'wark* 91-96; P-in-c Barnes St Mich 96-97; TV Barnes 97-03; V Fulham All SS *Lon* from 03. *All Saints' Vicarage, 70 Fulham High Street, London SW6 3LG* Tel (020) 7371 5202 *or* 7736 6301 E-mail vicarasfulham@aol.com

HAWES, Mary Elizabeth. b 56. SEITE 94. **d** 00 **p** 01. Dioc Children's Adv *Lon* 98-06; Nat Children's Adv Abps' Coun from 06; NSM Streatham St Leon *S'wark* 00-11; NSM Teddington St Mary w St Alb *Lon* from 11. *32 Burnell Avenue, Richmond TW10 7YE* Tel (020) 8549 8868 E-mail mary.hawes@churchofengland.org

HAWES, Michael Rowell. b 31. AKC61. **d** 62 **p** 63. C Epsom St Martin *Guildf* 62-65; Chapl RAF 65-86; R Newnham w Nately Scures w Mapledurwell etc *Win* 86-97; rtd 97; Perm to Offic *Win* from 97. *7 Holly Lane, Ashley, New Milton BH25 5RF* Tel (01425) 620698

HAWES, Ms Rachel. b 54. St Hugh's Coll Ox BA76 MA80. STETS 05. **d** 07 **p** 08. NSM Kensington St Mary Abbots w Ch Ch and St Phil *Lon* 07-10; NSM Notting Hill St Jo from 10. *26 Talbot Road, London W2 5LJ* Tel (020) 7792 3909 Mobile 07768-875590 E-mail rachel.hawes@lawcol.co.uk

HAWKEN, Andrew Robert. b 58. K Coll Lon BD81 AKC81. St Steph Ho Ox 83. **d** 85 **p** 86. C Ex St Dav 85-88; TV Witney *Ox* 88-93; V Benson 93-10; AD Aston and Cuddesdon 02-07; Hon Can Ch Ch 09-10; Chapl Midi-Pyrénées and Aude *Eur* from 10. *Le Presbytère, St Gervais, 82190 Touffailles, France* Tel (0033) (5) 63 95 78 24 E-mail andrew.hawken@ntlworld.com

HAWKEN, Rosalind Mary. b 56. York Univ BA77 Univ of Wales (Cardiff) BTh02. St Mich Coll Llan 99. **d** 02 **p** 03. C Swansea St Thos and Kilvey *S & B* 02-03; C Gorseinon 03-07. *Society of the Sacred Cross, Tymawr Convent, Lydart, Monmouth NP25 4RN* Tel (01600) 860244

HAWKER, The Ven Alan Fort. b 44. Hull Univ BA65. Clifton Th Coll 65. **d** 68 **p** 69. C Bootle St Leon *Liv* 68-71; C Fazakerley Em 71-73; V Goose Green 73-81; TR Southgate *Chich* 81-98; Can and Preb Chich Cathl 91-98; RD E Grinstead 94-98; Hon Can Bris Cathl 98-10; Adn Swindon 98-99; Adn Malmesbury 99-10; rtd 10. *21 Paddocks Close, Wolston, Coventry CV8 3GW* Tel (024) 7654 4021 E-mail alanandjen68@gmail.com

HAWKER, Alan John. b 53. BD76 AKC76. Sarum & Wells Th Coll 77. **d** 78 **p** 79. C Coleford w Staunton *Glouc* 78-81; C Up Hatherley 81-84; V Plymouth St Jas Ham *Ex* 84-92; TV Worc SE 92-99; TR Leic Presentation 99-03; P-in-c Leic St Chad 02-03; Perm to Offic 09-10; NSM Eyres Monsell 10-11; R Narborough and Huncote from 11. *The Rectory, 15 Church View, Narborough, Leicester LE9 5GY*

HAWKER, Brian Henry. b 34. AKC61 St Boniface Warminster 61. **d** 62 **p** 63. C Hemel Hempstead *St Alb* 62-66; R Stone w Hartwell w Bishopstone *Ox* 66-69; Chapl St Jo Hosp Stone 66-69; V W Wycombe 69-72; Past Consultant Clinical Th Assn 72-83, Past Consultant 83-94, Public Preacher *S'well* 72-76, rtd 94; Perm to Offic *B & W* 76-83; Truro 83-90; and Leic from 99. *12 Burfield Avenue, Loughborough LE11 3AZ* Tel (01509) 261439

HAWKER, Canon Peter John. b 37. OBE96. Ex Univ BA59. Wycliffe Hall Ox 69. **d** 70 **p** 71. Asst Chapl Berne *Eur* 70-76; Chapl Berne w Neuchâtel 76-89; past Switzerland 86-04; Chapl Zürich w St Gallen, Baden and Zug 90-00; Can Brussels Cathl 86-04; rtd 04. *Schulgasse 10, 3280 Murten, Switzerland* Tel (0041) (26) 670 6221 Fax 670 6219 E-mail phawker@anglican.ch

HAWKES, Mrs Cecilia Mary (Cilla). b 48. Reading Univ BSc69 Canley Coll of Educn DipEd71. EAMTC 99. **d** 02 **p** 03. NSM Takeley w Lt Canfield *Chelmsf* 02-10; NSM Stebbing and Lindsell w Gt and Lt Saling from 10; Voc Officer Colchester Area from 08; RD Dunmow and Stansted from 10. *Greenfields, Felsted, Dunmow CM6 3LF* Tel and fax (01371) 856480 E-mail cilla@hawkesfarming.co.uk

HAWKES, Mrs Elisabeth Anne. b 56. GRNCM78 PGCE80 Kent Univ MA97. Linc Th Coll 86. **d** 88 **p** 97. Hon Par Dn Finham *Cov* 88-90; Hon Par Dn Bexhill St Pet *Chich* 90-97; Asst to RD Oundle *Pet* 97-98; NSM Oundle 98-00; NSM Benefield and Southwick w Glapthorn 99-00; Perm to Offic *Cant* 00-04; Hon Min Can Cant Cathl from 03; NSM Reculver and Herne Bay St Bart from 04; NSM Hoath H Cross from 04; Dioc Adv in Liturgy from 04. *The Vicarage, 25 Dence Park, Herne Bay CT6 6BQ* Tel and fax (01227) 360948 E-mail liz@hawkes48.freeserve.co.uk

HAWKES, Mrs Helen Vanda. b 50. Surrey Univ BA01. STETS 98. **d** 01 **p** 02. NSM N Hayling St Pet and Hayling Is St Andr *Portsm* 01-05; NSM Bedhampton 05-11; rtd 11; Perm to Offic *Portsm* from 11. *67 East Lodge Park, Farlington, Portsmouth PO16 1BZ* Tel (023) 9221 9005 Mobile 07719-828113 E-mail vanda.hawkes@btinternet.com

HAWKES, Keith Andrew. b 28. Oak Hill Th Coll 72. **d** 74 **p** 75. C Gt Yarmouth *Nor* 74-77; C-in-c Bowthorpe CD 77; Chapl Düsseldorf *Eur* 77-83; TV Quidenham *Nor* 83-88; TR 88-90; RD Thetford and Rockland 86-90; R Wickmere w Lt Barningham, Itteringham etc 90-96; Dioc Rural Officer 90-94; P-in-c Saxthorpe w Corpusty, Blickling, Oulton etc 94-96; R Lt Barningham, Blickling, Edgefield etc 96-98; Bp's Chapl 98; rtd 98; Perm to Offic *Nor* 98-00 and from 04; P-in-c Guiltcross 00-03; Chapl Norwich Primary Care Trust 00-02; Chapl Riddlesworth Hall Sch Nor from 04. *Peel Cottage, West Church Street, Kenninghall, Norwich NR16 2EN* Tel and fax (01953) 888533 E-mail revkahawkes@aol.com

HAWKES, Martyn John. b 71. Nottm Univ BA94 St Jo Coll Dur BA01. Cranmer Hall Dur 99. **d** 02 **p** 03. C Is of Dogs Ch Ch and St Jo w St Luke *Lon* 02-05; C Brownswood Park and Stoke Newington St Mary 05-11; V Aldersbrook *Chelmsf* from 11. *St Gabriel's Vicarage, 12 Aldersbrook Road, London E12 5HH* Tel (020) 8989 0315 E-mail mj_hawkes@yahoo.co.uk

HAWKES, Nigel Anthony Robert. b 59. UEA BSc80 Edin Univ MSc82. Ripon Coll Cuddesdon 00. **d** 02 **p** 03. C Chase *Ox* 02-04; C Chipping Norton 04-05; TV Dorchester from 05. *The Vicarage, 49 The Green North, Warborough, Wallingford OX10 7DW* Tel (01865) 858381

HAWKES, Ronald Linton. b 54. St Jo Coll York CertEd75 Leeds Univ BEd76 Kent Univ MA96. Linc Th Coll 85. **d** 87 **p** 88. C Finham *Cov* 87-90; TV Bexhill St Pet *Chich* 90-97; V Oundle *Pet*

97-00; P-in-c Benefield and Southwick w Glapthorn 99-00; Dir Post-Ord Tr 98-00; Chapl St Edm Sch Cant 00-03; V Reculver and Herne Bay St Bart *Cant* from 03; P-in-c Hoath H Cross from 04; Hon Min Can Cant Cathl from 01; AD Reculver from 06. *The Vicarage, 25 Dence Park, Herne Bay CT6 6BQ* Tel and fax (01227) 360948 E-mail revronald@hotmail.com

HAWKES, Vanda. See HAWKES, Mrs Helen Vanda

HAWKETT, Graham Kenneth. b 20. Bps' Coll Cheshunt 61. **d** 63 **p** 64. C Farncombe *Guildf* 63-67; V Wyke 67-85; rtd 85; Perm to Offic *Guildf* from 85. *Bede House, Beech Road, Haslemere GU27 2BX* Tel (01428) 656430

HAWKEY, James Douglas Thomas. b 79. Girton Coll Cam BA01 MA05 Selw Coll Cam MPhil02 PhD08. Westcott Ho Cam 03 St Thos Aquinas Pontifical Univ Rome 06. **d** 07 **p** 08. C Portsea St Mary *Portsm* 07-10; Min Can Westmr Abbey from 10. *The Chapter Office, 20 Dean's Yard, London SW1P 3PA* Tel (020) 72225152 Mobile 07810-356617
E-mail jamiehawkey@googlemail.com

HAWKINS, Timothy Denison. b 55. Ex Univ BA78. St Jo Coll Nottm BA80. **d** 81 **p** 82. C Penn *Lich* 81-85; TV Stafford 85-94; TR Stratton St Margaret w S Marston etc *Bris* 94-05; P-in-c Axbridge w Shipham and Rowberrow *B & W* 05-11; R from 11; P-in-c Mark w Allerton 08-10; RD Axbridge from 08. *The Rectory, Cheddar Road, Axbridge BS26 2DL* Tel (01934) 732261 E-mail revhawkings@googlemail.com

HAWKINS, The Very Revd Alun John. b 44. K Coll Lon BA66 AKC66 Univ of Wales (Ban) BD81. St Deiniol's Hawarden 78. **d** 81 **p** 82. C Dwygyfylchi *Ban* 81-84; R Llanberis 84-89; Tutor Ban Dioc NSM Course 85-90; Dir of Ords *Ban* 86-90; V Knighton and Norton *S & B* 89-93; Chapl Knighton Hosp 89-93; TR Bangor 93-06; Adult Educn Officer 93-11; Sec Dioc Bd of Miss 93-11; Can Res and Can Missr Ban Cathl 93-00; Adn Ban 00-04; Dean Ban 04-11; rtd 11; Perm to Offic *Ban* from 11. *9 Cil y Craig, Llanfairpwllgwyngyll LL61 5NZ* Tel (01248) 717403

HAWKINS, Andrew Robert. b 40. St Andr Univ BSc64. St Chad's Coll Dur BA68. **d** 69 **p** 70. C Sutton St Nic *S'wark* 69-73; C Wimbledon 73-77; TV Cramlington *Newc* 77-81; R Clutton w Cameley *B & W* 81-89; Chapl City of Bath Coll of FE from 89; Perm to Offic *B & W* from 90. *18 Wally Court Road, Chew Stoke, Bristol BS40 8XN* Tel (01275) 332422
E-mail andrewr.hawkins@virgin.net

HAWKINS (née BRAZIER), Mrs Annette Michaela. b 59. Brighton Univ BEd95 Homerton Coll Cam BTh. Ridley Hall Cam 07. **d** 09 **p** 10. C Ore St Helen and St Barn *Chich* from 09. *225 Harley Shute Road, St Leonards-on-Sea TN38 9JJ* Tel (01424) 423859 Mobile 07900-332791
E-mail annette@jhbd.co.uk

HAWKINS, Canon Bruce Alexander. b 44. Qu Coll Ox BA66 MA71. Sarum Th Coll 66. **d** 68 **p** 69. C Epsom St Martin *Guildf* 68-71; Dioc Youth Chapl *Cant* 72-81; Hon Min Can Cant Cathl 75-99; Dep Dir of Educn 81-86; V Walmer 86-05; RD Sandwich 94-00; Hon Can Cant Cathl 99-05; rtd 05; Perm to Offic *Cant* from 05. *88 The Gateway, Dover CT16 1LQ* Tel (01304) 240820

HAWKINS, Canon Clive Ladbroke. b 53. St Pet Coll Ox BA76 MA79. Trin Coll Bris 80. **d** 82 **p** 83. C Win Ch Ch 82-86; R Eastrop from 86; AD Basingstoke 00-08; Hon Can Win Cathl from 05. *Eastrop Rectory, 2A Wallis Road, Basingstoke RG21 3DW* Tel (01256) 355507 *or* 464249
E-mail clive.hawkins@stmarys-basingstoke.org.uk

✠**HAWKINS, The Rt Revd David John Leader.** b 49. Nottm Univ BTh73. St Jo Coll Nottm 69 ALCD73. **d** 73 **p** 74. c 02. C Bebington *Ches* 73-76; Nigeria 76-82; C Ox St Aldate w St Matt 83-86; V Leeds St Geo *Ripon* 86-99; TR 99-02; Area Bp Barking *Chelmsf* from 02. *Barking Lodge, 35A Verulam Avenue, London E17 8ES* Tel (020) 8509 7377 Fax 8521 4097
E-mail b.barking@chelmsford.anglican.org

HAWKINS, David Kenneth Beaumont. b 36. Em Coll Saskatoon LTh63. **d** 63 **p** 64. C Northminster Canada 63-69; C Belleville Ch Ch 69-71; I Wellington 71-79; I Barriefield w Pittsburgh 80-85; C St Alb St Paul *St Alb* 85-87; C Hednesford *Lich* 87-92; R Buildwas and Leighton w Eaton Constantine etc 92-95; TV Wrockwardine Deanery 95-01; rtd 01. *PO Box 454, 131 Westwood Crescent, Wellington ON K0K 3L0, Canada* Tel (001) (613) 399 5666 E-mail rowenadavid@sympatico.ca

HAWKINS, Canon Francis John. b 36. Ex Coll Ox BA61 MA63. Chich Th Coll 59. **d** 61 **p** 62. C Tavistock and Gulworthy *Ex* 61-64; Lect Chich Th Coll 64-73; Vice-Prin 73-75; V E Grinstead St Mary *Chich* 75-81; Can Res and Treas Chich Cathl 81-01; V Sidlesham 81-89; Dir of Ords 89-01; rtd 01; Perm to Offic *Chich* from 01; Custos St Mary's Hosp Chich 01-11. *6 Priory Road, Chichester PO19 1NS* Tel (01243) 771921

HAWKINS, James Reginald. b 39. Ex Univ BA61 Hull Univ MA00. Westcott Ho Cam 61. **d** 63 **p** 64. C Cannock *Lich* 63-66; C Wem 66-67; C Cheddleton 67-69; R Yoxall 69-77; R The Quinton *Birm* 77-84; V Bosbury w Wellington Heath etc *Heref* 84-96; P-in-c Ancaster Wilsford Gp *Linc* 96-99; R 99-04; RD Loveden 97-03; rtd 04. *14 Pound Pill, Corsham SN13 9JA* Tel (01249) 715353 E-mail james.hawkins39@btopenworld.com

HAWKINS, John Colin. b 50. SEITE 97. **d** 00 **p** 01. NSM W Wickham St Jo *S'wark* 00-04; P-in-c Burwash Weald *Chich* 04-11. *Address temp unknown*
E-mail john.c.hawkins@btinternet.com

HAWKINS, John Edward Inskipp. b 63. K Coll Lon BD85. Qu Coll Birm 86. **d** 88 **p** 89. C Birchfield *Birm* 88-92; C Poplar *Lon* 92-93; TV 93-99; V W Hendon St Jo from 99; P-in-c Colindale St Matthias from 07; AD W Barnet 04-09. *St John's Vicarage, Vicarage Road, London NW4 3PX* Tel and fax (020) 8202 8606
E-mail jeih.stj@aladdinscave.net

HAWKINS, Jonathan Desmond. b 53. FRICS93. Ox Min Cours 04. **d** 07 **p** 08. NSM Walton H Trin *Ox* 07-09; NSM Southcour 09-10; NSM Haddenham w Cuddington, Kingsey etc from 10 *22 Limes Avenue, Aylesbury HP21 7HA* Tel (01296) 428631 Fa 339239 Mobile 07976-281699 E-mail jon@jdhawkins.co.uk

HAWKINS, Nicholas Milner. b 45. Univ of Wales (Swansea) BA MSc. **d** 01. Par Dn Dingestow and Llangovan w Penyclawdd etc *Mon* 01-02; Perm to Offic *Ban* 02-03; NSM Nefyn w Tudweilio w Llandudwen w Edern 03-08; P-in-c Botwnnog w Bryncroes w Llangwnnadl w Penllech from 08. *Bryn Mor, Llangwnadl Pwllheli LL53 8NS* Tel (01758) 770582 Fax 770228 Mobil 07870-264385 E-mail nick.hawkins@btinternet.com

HAWKINS, Noel. b 46. St Jo Coll Nottm 82. **d** 84 **p** 85. C Worksop St Jo *S'well* 84-86; C Wollaton Park 86-89; TV Billericay and Lt Burstead *Chelmsf* 89-95; TV Keynsham *B & W* 95-00; V Brislington St Chris and St Cuth 00-08; V Brislington St Chris from 08; P-in-c Hengrove from 06. *The Vicarage, 3 Wick Crescent, Bristol BS4 4HG* Tel 0117-977 6351
E-mail noel-lynda@hawkins99.freeserve.co.uk

HAWKINS, Preb Patricia Sally. b 59. LMH Ox BA80 MA84 E Univ BPhil85 Ox Univ BTh04 CQSW85. St Steph Ho Ox 99 **d** 01 **p** 02. C Stafford *Lich* 01-04; V Oxley from 04; AI Wolverhampton from 08; Preb Lich Cathl from 09. *The Vicarage Lymer Road, Oxley, Wolverhampton WV10 6AA* Tel (01902 783342 E-mail pathawkins@btinternet.com

HAWKINS, Paul Henry Whishaw. b 46. Ex Coll Ox BA68 MA7 SS Coll Cam MA84. St Steph Ho Ox 70. **d** 72 **p** 73. C Fawle *Win* 72-75; C Ealing St Steph Castle Hill *Lon* 75-77; P-in-Dorney *Ox* 77-78; TV Riverside 78-81; Chapl SS Coll Cam 82-87; V Plymstock *Ex* 87-97; RD Plymouth Sutton 91-96; TF Plymstock and Hooe 97-00; Preb Ex Cathl 98-00; P-in-St Pancras w St Jas and Ch Ch *Lon* 00-02; V from 02. *St Pancra Vicarage, 6 Sandwich Street, London WC1H 9PL* Tel (020) 738: 1630 *or* tel and fax 7388 1461
E-mail vicar@stpancraschurch.com

HAWKINS, Peter Edward. b 35. Leeds Univ BA60. Coll o Resurr Mirfield 60. **d** 62 **p** 63. C Forest Gate St Edm *Chelms* 62-65; C Sevenoaks St Jo *Roch* 65-68; Chapl Metrop Polic Cadet Corps Tr Sch 68-73; P-in-c Knowle H Nativity *Bris* 73; T Knowle 73-79; V Westbury-on-Trym H Trin 79-87; TR Solihu *Birm* 79-96; Hon Can Birm Cathl 92-96; rtd 00. *Back Stree Cottage, 15 St Andrew's Road, Stogursey, Bridgwater TA5 1T.* Tel and fax (01278) 733635 E-mail peh.stogursey@tiscali.uk

HAWKINS, Peter Michael. b 38. Kelham Th Coll 58. **d** 63 **p** 6 India 63-69; Ox Miss to Calcutta 63-64; C Calcutta Cathl 64-6 C-in-c Kidderpore 66-68; V Asansol w Burnpur 68-69; C Manningham St Paul and St Jude *Bradf* 70-72; C Bradf Catl 72-75; V Allerton 75-90; V Pet H Spirit Bretton 90-07; P-in-Marholm 90-95; rtd 07. *Belle Vue Nord, Mane Guelo, 5669! Landaul, France* Tel (0033) 2 97 59 90 83
E-mail peter.hawkins@orange.fr

HAWKINS, Mrs Rachel Ann. b 76. Trin Coll Bris 09. **d** 11. C Long Eaton St Jo *Derby* from 11. *5 Mendip Close, Long Eaton Nottingham NG10 4NY* Tel 0115-946 3893 Mobi 07930-827203 E-mail revrach@hotmail.co.uk

HAWKINS, Richard Randal. b 39. **d** 65 **p** 66. C Bushbury *Lic* 65-68; C Woodford St Mary *Chelmsf* 68-71; S Africa from 71; rt 04. *7 Chapter Close, 6 Taunton Road, Pietermaritzburg, 320 South Africa*

✠**HAWKINS, The Rt Revd Richard Stephen.** b 39. Ex Coll O BA61 MA65 Ex Univ BPhil76. St Steph Ho Ox 61. **d** 63 **p** 6 c 88. C Ex St Thos 63-66; C Clyst St Mary 66-75; TV Clys St George, Aylesbeare, Clyst Honiton etc 75-78; TV Cen E 78-81; Bp's Officer for Min and Jt Dir Ex and Truro NSM Scheme 78-81; Dioc Dir of Ords 79-81; Adn Totnes 81-88; P-in Oldridge and Whitestone 81-87; Suff Bp Plymouth 88-96; Su Bp Crediton 96-04; rtd 04; Hon Asst Bp Ex from 0: *3 Westbrook Close, Exeter EX4 8BS* Tel (01392) 462622

HAWKINS, Richard Whishaw. b 51. Coll of Resurr Mirfield 9 **d** 95 **p** 96. C Weymouth H Trin *Sarum* 95-99; P-in-c Hey *Ma* 99-06; TR Medlock Head from 06; AD Rochdale 03-0! *St John's Vicarage, 1 Owen Fold, Oldham OL4 3DT* Tel 0161-62 3630 E-mail richard.hawkins107@ntlworld.com

HAWKINS, Roger David William. b 33. K Coll Lon BD5 AKC58. **d** 59 **p** 60. C Twickenham St Mary *Lon* 59-61; C Hesto 61-64; C Dorking w Ranmore *Guildf* 64-65; V Mitcham St Mar *S'wark* 65-74; V Redhill St Matt 74-91; P-in-c Warlingham v Chelsham and Farleigh 91-97; TR 97-98; rtd 98. *2 Grove Cour Falkland Grove, Dorking RH4 3DL* Tel (01306) 885817

HAWKINS, Roger Julian. b 32. Ripon Hall Ox 59. **d** 61 **p** 62. C-in-c Newall Green CD *Man* 61-63; Chapl RAF 63-67; R Mawgan in Pyder *Truro* 67-75; R Lanteglos by Camelford w Advent 75-78; R Newmarket St Mary w Exning St Agnes *St E* 78-85; P-in-c Coltishall w Gt Hautbois *Nor* 85-87; R Coltishall w Gt Hautbois and Horstead 87-90; Chapl Whiteley Village *Guildf* 90-94; rtd 97; Perm to Offic *Win* 01-02; *Sarum* 02-08; *Nor* from 10. *3 Norman Cockaday Court, Holt NR25 6JA* Tel (01263) 710004

HAWKINS, Steven Andrew. b 51. Nottm Univ BEd75 Open Univ BSc91 Bris Poly ADEd90. STETS 95. **d** 98 **p** 99. C Horfield H Trin *Bris* 98-02; V Brislington St Anne 02-08; P-in-c Knowle St Martin from 08. *St Martin's Vicarage, 46 St Martin's Road, Bristol BS4 2NG* Tel 0117-977 6275 Mobile 07929-485006 E-mail fr.stevenhawkins@googlemail.com

HAWKINS, Susan. b 47. Doncaster Coll of Educn CertEd69 Ches Coll of HE BTh99. NOC 95. **d** 99 **p** 00. NSM Prestbury *Ches* 99-02; P-in-c Marthall and Chapl David Lewis Cen for Epilepsy 02-09; rtd 09; Perm to Offic *Ches* from 09. *3 Thorne Close, Prestbury, Macclesfield SK10 4DE* Tel (01625) 829833 E-mail dvs.hawkins@btinternet.com

HAWKINS, Timothy St John. b 59. CCC Ox BA82. Trin Coll Bris BA87. **d** 87 **p** 88. C Cheltenham St Mary, St Matt, St Paul and H Trin *Glouc* 87-90; C Cowplain *Portsm* 90-94; V Pennycross *Ex* 94-96; P-in-c St Keverne *Truro* 96-05; P-in-c Gulval and Madron from 05. *The Vicarage, Church Road, Madron, Penzance TR20 8SW* Tel (01736) 360992 E-mail revtimhawkins@hotmail.co.uk

HAWKSWORTH, Maldwyn Harry. b 45. Aston Univ CertEd74 St Jo Coll Nottm 87. **d** 89 **p** 90. C Penn *Lich* 89-94; TV Bloxwich 94-09; P-in-c Yoxall from 09; Local Min Adv (Wolverhampton) from 09; Local Par Development Adv Wolverhampton Area from 10. *The Rectory, Savey Lane, Yoxall, Burton-on-Trent DE13 8PD* Tel (01543) 473202

HAWKSWORTH, Peter John Dallas. b 54. St Jo Coll Ox BA75 MA79 Solicitor 79. Sarum & Wells Th Coll 89. **d** 91 **p** 92. C Warminster St Denys, Upton Scudamore etc *Sarum* 91-95; P-in-c Salisbury St Mark 95-99; V 99-05; RD Salisbury 03-05; Perm to Offic from 07. *Little Acre, Tytherley Road, Winterslow, Salisbury SP5 1PY* E-mail onehundredkilos@btinternet.com

HAWLEY, Canon Anthony Broughton. b 41. St Pet Coll Ox BA67 MA71. Westcott Ho Cam 67. **d** 69 **p** 70. C Wolverhampton St Pet *Lich* 69-72; C-in-c Bermondsey St Hugh CD *S'wark* 73-84; Hon PV S'wark Cathl 83-84; TR Kirkby *Liv* 84-02; AD Walton 93-02; Hon Can Liv Cathl 96-02; Can Res Liv Cathl 02-11; rtd 11. *Pimlico Cottage, Black Lane, Lover, Salisbury SP5 2PQ* Tel (01794) 390607 E-mail anthony@hawley77.freeserve.co.uk

HAWLEY, Georgina. b 45. **d** 01 **p** 02. Australia 01-02 and from 07; NSM Chippenham St Pet *Bris* 02-03; Perm to Offic 03-07. *32A Wishart Street, Gwelup WA 6018, Australia* Tel (0061) (8) 9446 4021 E-mail georginahawley@hotmail.co.uk

HAWLEY, The Ven John Andrew. b 50. K Coll Lon BD71 AKC71. Wycliffe Hall Ox 72. **d** 74 **p** 75. C Kingston upon Hull H Trin *York* 74-77; C Bradf Cathl Par 77-80; V Woodlands *Sheff* 80-91; TR Dewsbury *Wakef* 91-02; Hon Can Wakef Cathl 98-02; Adn Blackb from 02. *19 Clarence Park, Blackburn BB2 7FA* Tel (01254) 262571 Fax 263394 Mobile 07980-945035 E-mail john.hawley@blackburn.anglican.org

HAWLEY, William David Llewellyn. b 41. Univ of W Aus BCom77 Murdoch Univ Aus BD94. **d** 92 **p** 95. Hon C Bullcreek w Bateman Australia 92-94; Hon C Kwinana 94-95; Dioc Registrar and Assoc P Spearwood w Hilton 95-98; R Hilton 98-00; TV By Brook *Bris* 01-07; C Colerne w N Wraxall 06-07; rtd 07. *32A Wishart Street, Gwelup WA 6018, Australia* Tel (0061) (8) 9446 4021

HAWNT, John Charles Frederick. b 30. Westwood Cen Zimbabwe 72. **d** 75 **p** 76. Zimbabwe 75-81; C Rugby *Cov* 81-85; R Lydeard St Lawrence w Brompton Ralph etc *B & W* 85-00; rtd 00. *39 St Andrew Road, Houghton, Johannesburg, 2198 South Africa* Tel (0027) (11) 487 3259

HAWORTH (née ARMSTRONG), Fiona Heather. b 65. Reading Univ BSc86 Nottm Univ PhD90. St Jo Coll Nottm BTh94. **d** 97 **p** 98. C Sutton in Ashfield St Mary *S'well* 97-02; TV Kidderminster St Mary and All SS w Trimpley etc *Worc* 02-09; Chapl Worc Univ from 09. *University of Worcester, Henwick Grove, Worcester WR2 6AJ* Tel (01905) 542327 E-mail f.haworth@worc.ac.uk

HAWORTH, Julie. b 50. St Mich Coll Llan. **d** 09. C Wigan All SS and St Geo *Liv* from 09. *63 Kendal Street, Wigan WN6 7DJ* Tel (01942) 733209

HAWORTH, Mark Newby. b 50. Aber Univ BSc73 MICFor81. Westcott Ho Cam 88. **d** 90 **p** 91. C Cherry Hinton St Andr *Ely* 90-93; C Teversham 90-93; P-in-c Swaffham Bulbeck and Swaffham Prior w Reach 93-94; V 94-02; Sub Warden of Readers 95-02; RD Fordham 96-02; Chapl Framlingham Coll and Brandeston Hall Sch 03; Chapl to Bp Pet 03-05; TR Pendleton *Man* 05-09; P-in-c Lower Kersal 06-09; TR Salford All SS from 09; Borough Dean Salford from 10. *The Rectory, 92*

Fitzwarren Street, Salford M6 5RS Tel 0161-745 7608 Mobile 07932-160009 E-mail father.mark@virgin.net

HAWORTH, Paul. b 47. G&C Coll Cam BA68 MA72. Westcott Ho Cam 75. **d** 78 **p** 79. C Hornchurch St Andr *Chelmsf* 78-81; C Loughton St Mary and St Mich 81-88; TV Waltham H Cross 88-92; TR Becontree S 92-00; P-in-c S Woodham Ferrers from 00; rtd 11. *17 Ember Way, Burnham-on-Crouch CM0 8TJ* E-mail preacherman@pewend.org

HAWORTH, Stanley Robert. b 48. St Jo Coll Dur BA69. Sarum & Wells Th Coll 71. **d** 73 **p** 74. C Skipton H Trin *Bradf* 73-76; C Bradf Cathl 76-78; C Grantham *Linc* 78; TV 78-82; V Deeping St James 82-96; V Middlewich w Byley *Ches* 96-01; P-in-c Forcett and Aldbrough and Melsonby *Ripon* from 01; AD Richmond from 08. *The Vicarage, 1 Appleby Close, Aldbrough St John, Richmond DL11 7TT* Tel (01325) 374634 E-mail stantherevman@hotmail.com

HAWORTH, Stuart. b 43. **d** 94 **p** 95. OLM Bradshaw *Man* 94-01; OLM Turton Moorland Min 01-08; rtd 08; Perm to Offic *Man* from 08. *39 Patterdale Road, Bolton BL2 3LX* Tel (01204) 384006

HAWRISH, Mary-Beth Louise Ladine. **d** 09 **p** 10. OLM Oxshott *Guildf* from 09. *Cedar House, Sandy Lane, Cobham KT11 2EP* Tel (01932) 864695 E-mail mhawrish@yahoo.co.uk

HAWTHORN, The Ven Christopher John. b 36. Qu Coll Cam BA60 MA64. Ripon Hall Ox 60. **d** 62 **p** 63. C Sutton St Jas *York* 62-66; V Kingston upon Hull St Nic 66-72; V E Coatham 72-79; V Scarborough St Martin 79-91; RD Scarborough 82-91; Can and Preb York Minster 87-01; Adn Cleveland 91-01; rtd 01; Perm to Offic *York* from 01. *4J Burley Rise, Strensall, York YO32 5AB* Tel (01904) 492060

HAWTHORN, David. b 63. Chich Th Coll 87. **d** 90 **p** 91. C Hartlepool H Trin *Dur* 90-94; C Middlesbrough All SS *York* 94-95; P-in-c Thornaby on Tees 95-96; V S Thornaby 96-02; P-in-c Brighton Annunciation *Chich* 02-04; V Hollinwood and Limeside *Man* from 04. *St Margaret's Vicarage, 61 Chapel Road, Oldham OL8 4QQ* Tel and fax 0161-681 4541 E-mail hawthorn@supanet.com

HAWTHORN, Philip Alan. b 58. Essex Univ BSc79. Ripon Coll Cuddesdon 05. **d** 07 **p** 08. C Hardington Vale *B & W* 07-10; P-in-c Charlcombe w Bath St Steph from 10. *The Rectory, Richmond Place, Bath BA1 5PZ* Tel (01225) 466114 Mobile 07973-350560 E-mail philiphawthorn@btinternet.com

HAWTHORN, Thomas Russell. b 18. MBE90. Imp Coll Lon BSc48. **d** 82 **p** 82. Mexico 82-84; Perm to Offic *Nor* from 84; Sub Chapl HM Pris Blundeston 86-94. *82 Wollaston Road, Lowestoft NR32 2PF* Tel (01502) 518741

HAWTHORNE, Canon Andrew. b 68. Jes Coll Ox BA89 MA93 K Coll Lon PhD04. Chich Th Coll BTh93. **d** 93 **p** 94. C Christchurch *Win* 93-97; TV Dorchester *Sarum* 97-00; rtd 00; Hon Can Kinkizi from 04; V Christchurch *Win* from 05. *68 Arnewood Road, Southbourne, Bournemouth BH6 5DN* Tel (01202) 569163 E-mail andrewahawthorne@aol.com

HAWTHORNE, John William. b 32. St Aug Coll Cant 74. **d** 77 **p** 78. C Boxley *Cant* 77-80; P-in-c Otham 80-82; P-in-c Langley 80-82; R Otham w Langley 82-83; TR Preston w Sutton Poyntz and Osmington w Poxwell *Sarum* 83-87; R Tetbury w Beverston *Glouc* 87-01; rtd 01; Perm to Offic *Ex* from 02. *19 Long Street, Devizes SN10 1NN* Tel (01380) 728056 E-mail honitonhawthorne@aol.com

HAWTHORNE, Canon William James (Jim). b 46. MBE01. TCD 66 Ch of Ireland Tr Coll 66. **d** 69 **p** 70. C Gilnahirk *D & D* 69-72; Asst Chapl Miss to Seamen 72-76; C Boultham *Linc* 76-78; C Bracebridge Heath 78-90; Dioc Adv for Relig Broadcasting 80-90; Chapl Palma de Mallorca and Balearic Is *Eur* 90-93; Chapl Palma de Mallorca 93-01; P-in-c Menorca 97-98; Can Gib Cathl 97-01; rtd 01. *16-08 Victoria Centre, Milton Street, Nottingham NG1 3PL* Tel 0115-840 7913 E-mail williamjameshawthorne@hotmail.com

HAWTIN, The Rt Revd David Christopher. b 43. Keble Coll Ox BA65 MA70. Wm Temple Coll Rugby 65 Cuddesdon Coll 66. **d** 67 **p** 68 **c** 99. C Pennywell St Thos and Grindon St Oswald CD *Dur* 67-71; C Stockton St Pet 71-74; C-in-c Leam Lane CD 74-79; R Washington 79-88; Dioc Ecum Officer 88-91; Adn Newark *S'well* 92-99; Suff Bp Repton *Derby* 99-06; rtd 06; Hon Asst Bp Sheff from 07. *162 Greenhill Avenue, Sheffield S8 7TF* Tel 0114-274 0006

HAY, David Frederick. b 38. MA67. Qu Coll Birm 82. **d** 84 **p** 85. C Prenton *Ches* 84-88; V Stockport St Sav 88-96; P-in-c Gt Saughall 96-03; rtd 03; Perm to Offic *Ches* from 04; Hon Min Can Ches Cathl from 04. *2 Moel View Road, Buckley CH7 2BT* Tel (01244) 541342

HAY, Ian Gordon. b 52. Dundee Univ MA73 Edin Univ BD76 CertEd84. Edin Th Coll 73. **d** 76 **p** 77. C Dumfries *Glas* 76-79; Dioc Chapl *Bre* 79-81; R Brechin 81-85; Asst Chapl H Trin Sch Halifax 85-88; Dioc Youth Officer *Carl* 89-98; Sen Development Worker Youth Link Scotland from 98. *The Ross House, Pittendreich, Kinross KY13 9HD* Tel (01592) 840820 E-mail youthlink-scot@sol.co.uk

HAY, Jack Barr. b 31. Bps' Coll Cheshunt 57. d 60 p 61. C Byker St Ant Newc 60-63; C Killingworth 63-68; V Cowgate 68-77; V Woodhorn w Newbiggin 77-96; rtd 96; Perm to Offic Newc from 96. 7 Glebelands, Corbridge NE45 5DS Tel (01434) 632979

HAY, Joanna Jane Louise. See DOBSON, Mrs Joanna Jane Louise

HAY, John. b 43. St D Coll Lamp 63. d 67 p 68. C Ynyshir Llan 67-70; C Cardiff St Mary and St Steph w St Dyfrig etc 70-74; V Llanwynno 74-78; P-in-c Weston-super-Mare All SS B & W 78-80; TV Weston-super-Mare Cen Par 80-85; P-in-c Handsworth St Mich Birm 85-86; NSM Eastbourne St Sav and St Pet Chich 88-91; V Buckley St As 91-96; P-in-c Ardwick St Benedict Man 96-99; C Hollinwood and Oldham St Chad Limeside 99-01; rtd 01; Hon C Hampden Park and The Hydnye Chich from 09. St Peter's House, The Hydneye, Eastbourne BN22 9BY Tel (01323) 504392

HAY, The Very Revd John. b 45. CITC 77. d 79 p 80. C Newtownards D & D 79-81; I Galloon w Drummully Clogh 81-89; I Donacavey w Barr 89-03; Can Clogh Cathl 91-03; Dean Raphoe D & R from 03; I Raphoe w Raymochy and Clonleigh from 03. Maranatha, The Deanery, Raphoe, Lifford, Co Donegal, Republic of Ireland Tel (00353) (74) 914 5226 or (028) 8284 0377 E-mail dean@raphoe.anglican.org or johnhayraphoe@eircom.net

HAY, Miss Lesley Jean Hamilton. b 48. St Andr Univ MA71. Westcott Ho Cam 04 Yale Div Sch 05. d 06 p 07. C Shrivenham and Ashbury Ox 06-08; C Bethany USA 08; Asst R Hamden from 08. Address temp unknown E-mail lesleyhay@yahoo.co.uk

HAY, Margaret Ann. b 47. Brunel Univ BTech71 W Sussex Inst of HE PGCE95. STETS 02. d 05 p 06. NSM Elson Portsm from 05. Bodinnick, 12 Longwater Drive, Gosport PO12 2UP Tel (023) 9234 3303

HAY, Canon Nicholas John. b 56. Sheff Poly BSc85. St Jo Coll Nottm 85. d 88 p 89. C Blackb Redeemer 88-91; C Hellesdon Nor 91-95; R Widford Chelmsf 95-01; Sen Chapl HM Pris Ashfield 01-09; C Bedminster Bris from 09; C Whitchurch from 09; Hon Can Bris Cathl from 09. St Paul's Vicarage, 2 Southville Road, Bristol BS3 1DG Tel 07534-249338 (mobile) E-mail nickthevichay@googlemail.com

HAY, Richard. b 42. CMG92. Ball Coll Ox BA63. Cranmer Hall Dur 94. d 96 p 97. C Hastings St Clem and All SS Chich 96-99; V Addlestone Guildf 99-07; RD Runnymede 02-07; rtd 07; Perm to Offic Guildf from 07. 15 Fox Close, Woking GU22 8LP Tel (01932) 343585 E-mail richard.hay3@btinternet.com

HAYCOCK, Edward. d 09 p 10. OLM Adbaston, High Offley, Knightley, Norbury etc Lich from 09. 390 New Inn Lane, Stoke-on-Trent ST4 8BW Tel (01782) 641867

HAYCRAFT, Roger Brian Norman. b 43. Oak Hill Th Coll 69. d 73 p 74. C Belsize Park Lon 73-76; C Yardley St Edburgha Birm 76-79; V Hornchurch H Cross Chelmsf 79-03; rtd 03; Perm to Offic Chelmsf from 04. 12 Hannards Way, Hainault IG6 3TB Tel (020) 8501 1718

HAYDAY, Canon Alan Geoffrey David. b 46. Kelham Th Coll 65. d 69 p 70. C Evington Leic 69-72; C Spalding Linc 72-78; V Cherry Willingham w Greetwell 78-86; RD Lawres 84-86; TR Brumby 86-02; RD Manlake 93-99; Can and Preb Linc Cathl 00-02; Dean St Chris Cathl Bahrain 02-09; Hon Can Bahrain from 09; rtd 09. 22 Kestral Drive, Louth LN11 0GE Tel (01507) 600877 Mobile 07709-873224 E-mail windhover22@live.co.uk

HAYDEN, Carol Toni. b 64. Leeds Univ BA05. NOC 02. d 05 p 06. NSM Ainsworth Man 05-09; NSM Bury SE 09-11; TV Radcliffe from 11. 38 Launceston Road, Radcliffe, Manchester M26 3UN Tel 0161-725 9283 Mobile 07866-995567 E-mail c_hayden1@sky.com

HAYDEN, The Ven David Frank. b 47. Lon Univ BD71. Tyndale Hall Bris 67. d 71 p 72. C Silverhill St Matt Chich 71-75; C Galleywood Common Chelmsf 75-79; R Redgrave cum Botesdale w Rickinghall St E 79-84; RD Hartismere 81-84; V Cromer Nor 84-02; P-in-c Gresham 84-98; Chapl Cromer and Distr Hosp Norfolk 84-94; Chapl Norfolk and Nor Health Care NHS Trust 94-00; Chapl Fletcher Hosp Norfolk 85-00; RD Repps Nor 95-02; Hon Can Nor Cathl from 96; Adn Norfolk from 02. 8 Boulton Road, Thorpe St Andrew, Norwich NR7 0DF Tel and fax (01603) 702477 E-mail archdeacon.norfolk@4frontmedia.co.uk

HAYDEN, Eric Henry Ashmore. b 26. ACII65. Sarum & Wells Th Coll 71. d 73 p 74. C Horsham Chich 73-78; V Cuckfield 78-92; rtd 92; P-in-c Tilshead, Orcheston and Chitterne Sarum 92-97; Perm to Offic Sarum and Ox 98-08; Chich from 09. 3 Heather Bank, Haywards Heath RH16 1HY Tel (01444) 412510

✠HAYDEN, The Rt Revd John Donald. b 40. Lon Univ BD62. Tyndale Hall Bris 63. d 65 p 66 c 04. C Macclesfield Ch Ch Ches 65-68; C H Spirit Cathl Dodoma Tanzania 68-69; V Moshi 70-77; Home Sec USCL 77-83; TV Ipswich St Mary at Stoke w St Pet St E 83-94; P-in-c Bury St Edmunds St Mary 94-99; V 99-04; Asst Bp mt Kilimanjaro from 04; Hon Asst Bp Ches from 08. 45 Birkenhead Road, Meols, Wirral CH47 5AF Tel 0151-632 0448 E-mail johndhayden@talktalk.net

HAYDEN, Canon Mark Joseph James. b 68. St Thos Aquinas Pontifical Univ Rome BD93. H Cross Coll Clonliffe 86. d 92 p 93. In RC Ch 92-99; C Monkstown D & G 99-01; I Gorey w Kilnahue, Leskinfere and Ballycanew C & O from 01; Can Treas Ferns Cathl from 07. The Rectory, The Avenue, Gorey, Co Wexford, Republic of Ireland Tel and fax (00353) (53) 942 1383 E-mail gorey@ferns.anglican.org

HAYDOCK, Canon Alan. b 41. Kelham Th Coll 60. d 65 p 66. C Rainworth S'well 65-68; C Hucknall Torkard 68-71; TV 71-74; V Bilborough St Jo 74-80; R E Bridgford 80-82; R E Bridgford and Kneeton 82-06; RD Bingham 84-94; Hon Can S'well Minster 86-06; rtd 06. 29 The Teasels, Bingham, Nottingham NG13 8TY Tel (01949) 875805 Mobile 07944-569661

HAYDON, Keith Frank. b 46. Cuddesdon Coll 73. d 75 p 76. C De Beauvoir Town St Pet Lon 75-77; C Wells St Thos w Horrington B & W 77-80; TV Weston-super-Mare Cen Par 80-84; TV Cowley St Jas Ox 84-87; TR 87-95; V Walsingham, Houghton and Barsham Nor 95-96; P-in-c 96-99; rtd 01; C Sutton on Plym Ex from 09; C Plymouth St Simon and St Mary from 09. Address withheld by request

HAYE, Alfred Kirby. b 40. Lon Univ BA67 Saltley Tr Coll Birm TCert65. d 05 p 06. OLM Delaval Newc 05-09; Hon C Salcombe and Malborough w S Huish Ex from 09. The Vicarage, Malborough, Kingsbridge TQ7 3RR Tel (01548) 561234 E-mail kirby.haye@btinternet.com

HAYES, Brian Richard Walker. b 33. Qu Coll Birm 81. d 83 p 84. C Cheadle Hulme All SS Ches 83-87; C Sheff St Cecilia Parson Cross 87-88; C Sheff St Leon Norwood 88-91; V Gazeley w Dalham, Moulton and Kentford St E 91-02; P-in-c Higham Green 98-02; rtd 02; Hon C W Felton Lich 02-07; Perm to Offic 07-10. 8 Lutton Close, Oswestry SY11 2GZ E-mail brianhayes@cwcom.net

HAYES, Bruce John. b 75. UCD BA97 TCD BTh01. CITC 98. d 01 p 02. C Cregagh D & D 01-04; I Abbeystrewry Union C, C & R from 04; Warden of Readers from 08. The Rectory, Coronea Drive, Skibbereen, Co Cork, Republic of Ireland Tel (00353) (28) 21234 E-mail abbeystrewryunion@eircom.net

HAYES, Carmen Miranda. b 61. TCD BTh08. d 08 p 09. C Portadown St Mark Arm from 08. 4 Killycomain Drive, Portadown, Craigavon BT63 5JJ Tel (028) 3833 5813 Mobile 07907-579913 E-mail carmenmirandahayes@hotmail.com

HAYES, Christopher John. b 64. Univ of Wales BN Leeds Univ MA RGN. Cranmer Hall Dur. d 96 p 97. C Burton Fleming w Fordon, Grindale etc York 96-99; R Buckrose Carrs 99-06; P-in-c Weaverthorpe w Helperthorpe, Luttons Ambo etc 03-06; C Heworth Ch Ch 06-07; Perm to Offic from 11. 1 Poplars, West Knapton, Malton YO17 6RW Tel (01944) 753777 E-mail chris@gileadbooks.com

HAYES, David Malcolm Hollingworth. b 42. K Coll Lon BD68 AKC68 MPhil97. d 69 p 70. C Upper Teddington SS Pet and Paul Lon 69-70; C Ruislip St Martin 70-75; P-in-c Ludford Heref 75-80; P-in-c Ashford Carbonell w Ashford Bowdler 75-80; V Eastcote St Lawr Lon 80-90; R Cant St Pet w St Alphege and St Marg etc 90-07; P-in-c Blean 03-07; Master Eastbridge Hosp 90-07; Guardian of the Greyfriars 97-07; rtd 07; Perm to Offic Sarum from 07. Forge Cottage, 3 North Row, Warminster BA12 9AD Tel (01985) 212929 E-mail dmhforge@btinternet.com

HAYES, David Roland Payton. b 37. Hertf Coll Ox BA62 MA66. Coll of Resurr Mirfield 62. d 64 p 65. C Woodley St Jo the Ev Ox 64-67; C Emscote Cov 67-69; C Farnham Royal Ox 69-75; P-in-c 75-78; P-in-c Lathbury 78-79; P-in-c Newport Pagnell 78-79; R Newport Pagnell w Lathbury 79-85; RD Newport 80-85; Chapl Renny Lodge Hosp 85-87; R Newport Pagnell w Lathbury and Moulsoe Ox 85-86; P-in-c 86-87; P-in-c Bucknell w Buckton, Llanfair Waterdine and Stowe Heref 87-91; V Bucknell w Chapel Lawn, Llanfair Waterdine etc 91-94; RD Clun Forest 91-94; P-in-c Presteigne w Discoed, Kinsham and Lingen 94-00; P-in-c Knill 97-00; R Presteigne w Discoed, Kinsham, Lingen and Knill 00-01; rtd 01; Perm to Offic Heref from 01. 3 Redcar Avenue, Hereford HR4 9TJ Tel (01432) 261466

HAYES, David Thomas. b 70. Yorks Min Course. d 09 p 10. NSM Leeds Belle Is St Jo and St Barn Ripon from 09. 15 Windsor Mount, Leeds LS15 7DD Tel 0113-232 6588 Mobile 07739-364755 E-mail dandh.whitkirk.uk@lineone.net

HAYES, Denise Angela. b 62. NOC 02. d 05 p 06. C Ashton-in-Makerfield St Thos Liv 05-10; P-in-c Litherland St Phil from 10. St Philip's Vicarage, Orrell Road, Litherland, Liverpool L21 8NG Tel 0151-928 7334 Mobile 07736-523168 E-mail denisehayes4@aol.com

HAYES, Helen. d 10 p 11. NSM Bradgate Team Leic from 10. 32 Hawthorne Drive, Thornton, Leicester LE67 1AW Tel (01530) 231401

HAYES, Canon John Henry Andrew. b 52. BSc. Wycliffe Hall Ox 82. d 84 p 85. C Moreton Ches 84-87; R Barrow 87-94; Bp's Chapl 87-94; P-in-c Runcorn St Mich 94-04; P-in-c Runcorn All SS 94-05; P-in-c Runcorn H Trin 04-05; V Runcorn All SS w H

Trin from 05; Hon Can Ches Cathl from 08. *The Vicarage, 1 Highlands Road, Runcorn WA7 4PS* Tel (01928) 572417 E-mail revjohnhayes@ntlworld.com

HAYES, Mrs Marion Anne. b 51. Leeds Univ BA05 Liv Inst of Educn CertEd72. NOC 02. **d** 05 **p** 06. NSM Runcorn All SS w H Trin *Ches* from 05. *The Vicarage, 1 Highlands Road, Runcorn WA7 4PS* Tel (01928) 572417 E-mail marion.hayes@ntlworld.com

HAYES, Michael Gordon William. b 48. St Cath Coll Cam BA69 MA73 PhD73. Ridley Hall Cam 73. **d** 75 **p** 76. C Combe Down w Monkton Combe *B & W* 75-78; C Cambridge H Trin *Ely* 78-81; V Bathampton *B & W* 81-88; V Clevedon St Andr and Ch Ch 88-95; C Belper *Derby* 95-00; P-in-c Drayton in Hales *Lich* 00-07; RD Hodnet 01-06; P-in-c Chilton Cantelo, Ashington, Mudford, Rimpton etc *B & W* from 07. *The New Rectory, Camel Street, Marston Magna, Yeovil BA22 8DD* Tel (01935) 850536 E-mail mhhayes@freeuk.com

HAYES, Michael John. b 52. Lanc Univ BA73. Coll of Resurr Mirfield 75. **d** 78 **p** 79. C Notting Hill *Lon* 78-81; C-in-c Hammersmith SS Mich and Geo White City Estate CD 81-88; Perm to Offic 98-00; NSM Norwood St Mary 00-03; Chapl Heart of Kent Hospice from 05. *22 Ridley Road, Rochester ME1 1UL* Tel (01622) 792200 E-mail mike.hayes@diocese-rochester.org

HAYES, Mrs Miranda Jane. b 57. STETS BA06. **d** 06 **p** 07. C Dorking w Ranmore *Guildf* 06-10; P-in-c Earls Barton *Pet* from 10. *The Vicarage, 7 High Street, Earls Barton, Northampton NN6 0JG* Tel (01604) 810447 E-mail mail@mirandahayes.org

HAYES, Richard. b 39. K Coll Lon DD68 AKC68. **d** 69 **p** 70. C Dartford H Trin *Roch* 69-72; C S Kensington St Steph *Lon* 72-76; V Ruislip Manor St Paul 76-82; V Ealing St Pet Mt Park 82-91; R St Edm the King and St Mary Woolnoth etc 91-99; rtd 99; Perm to Offic *Lich* 99-04 and *Heref* from 00; Hon C Shrewsbury St Alkmund *Lich* 04-07; Hon C Shrewsbury St Chad, St Mary and St Alkmund from 07; OCM from 09. *26 St John's Hill, Shrewsbury SY1 1JJ* Tel (01743) 244668 E-mail l.r.hayes@btinternet.com

HAYES, Richard Henry. b 65. St Jo Coll Nottm 89. **d** 92 **p** 93. C Southborough St Pet w Ch Ch and St Matt *Roch* 92-95; C Downend *Bris* 95-97; V Gravesend St Mary *Roch* 97-02; R Clymping and Yapton w Ford *Chich* from 02. *The Rectory, St Mary's Meadow, Yapton, Arundel BN18 0EE* Tel (01243) 552962 Mobile 07944-804933 E-mail hayesrev@supanet.com

HAYES, Canon Rosemarie Eveline. b 51. Brighton Coll of Educn CertEd72. NOC 88. **d** 91 **p** 94. Par Dn Manston *Ripon* 91-94; C 94-95; C Beeston 95-00; V Horsforth 00-11; P-in-c Kirkstall 06-11; TR Abbeylands from 11; Hon Can Ripon Cathl from 10. *St Margaret's Vicarage, Hall Park Avenue, Horsforth, Leeds LS18 5LY* Tel 0113-258 2481 E-mail rosemarie@hayes2482.fsnet.co.uk

HAYES, Sarah Caroline. b 61. Man Univ BA84 Solicitor 90. St Jo Coll Nottm 05 Qu Coll Birm 07. **d** 09 **p** 10. NSM Hall Green St Pet *Birm* from 09. *25 Valentine Road, Birmingham B14 7AN* Tel 0121-441 1264 Mobile 07891-136654 E-mail stitchsarah@yahoo.co.uk

HAYES, Sarah Elizabeth. b 63. Ch Coll Cam BA85 MA89. Wycliffe Hall Ox 08. **d** 10 **p** 11. C Chipping Campden w Ebrington *Glouc* from 10. *Moreton House, High Street, Chipping Campden GL55 6AG* Tel (01386) 849056 E-mail curate@stjameschurchcampden.co.uk

HAYES, Stephen Anthony. b 57. St Jo Coll Dur BA80 S Bank Univ PGCE96. SAOMC 97. **d** 99 **p** 00. NSM Kingham w Churchill, Daylesford and Sarsden *Ox* 99-01; NSM Chipping Norton 01-06; Chapl Kingham Hill Sch Oxon 99-06; Teacher Arnold Lodge Sch Leamington Spa from 06. *9 Hastings Hill, Churchill, Chipping Norton OX7 6NA* Tel (01608) 658267 E-mail hayesfamily@freeuk.com

HAYES, Timothy James. b 62. **d** 89 **p** 90. C Lache cum Saltney *Ches* 89-94; P-in-c Dukinfield St Jo 94-99; V from 99. *37 Harold Avenue, Dukinfield SK16 5NH* Tel 0161-308 4708

HAYHOE, Geoffrey John Stephen. b 57. Portsm Univ BSc00. Qu Coll Birm 01. **d** 03 **p** 04. C Felixstowe St Jo *St E* 03-06; V Geraldine New Zealand from 06. *The Parish Office, 77 Talbot Street, Geraldine 7930, New Zealand* Tel (0064) (3) 693 9691 E-mail john@hayhoe.net

HAYLER, Peter John. b 65. R Holloway Coll Lon BSc87 Univ of Wales (Cardiff) MPhil01. Wilson Carlile Coll 89 St Mich Coll Llan 99. **d** 00 **p** 04. Ind Chapl *Mon* 95-03; C Pontnewydd 00-03; C Magor 03-06; TV Magor 06-09; C Cambridge Gt St Mary w St Mich *Ely* from 09; Chapl Univ Staff Cam from 09. *35 Pakenham Close, Cambridge CB4 1PW* Tel (01223) 510595 *or* 741718 E-mail pjhayler@virginmedia.com

HAYLES, Graham. b 39. Clifton Th Coll 64. **d** 67 **p** 68. C Gipsy Hill Ch Ch *S'wark* 67-70; C Heatherlands St Jo *Sarum* 70-74; V W Streatham St Jas *S'wark* 74-90; TR Hinckley H Trin *Leic* 90-03; rtd 03; Perm to Offic *S'wark* from 04. *19 Park Road, Redhill RH1 1BT* Tel (01737) 761732

HAYLETT, David William. b 44. **d** 05 **p** 06. OLM Dorchester *Ox* from 05. *8 Westfield Road, Long Wittenham, Abingdon OX14 4RF* Tel (01865) 407382 E-mail familyhaylett@yahoo.com

HAYMAN, Mrs Audrey Doris. b 41. St Mary's Coll Chelt 61 Bris Univ CertEd61 Cov Coll of Educn 65. Glouc Sch of Min 88. **d** 91 **p** 94. NSM Matson *Glouc* 91-98; P-in-c Falfield w Rockhampton 98-02; P-in-c Oldbury-on-Severn 98-02; Perm to Offic 02-04; NSM Barnwood from 04. *32 Corncroft Lane, Matson, Gloucester GL4 6XU* Tel (01452) 411786 E-mail adhayman@yahoo.co.uk

HAYMAN, Canon Robert Fleming. b 31. Princeton Univ BA53. Gen Th Sem (NY) MDiv56. **d** 56 **p** 56. USA 56-88; I Drumcliffe w Lissadell and Munninane *K, E & A* 88-92; Preb Elphin Cathl 88-92; rtd 92. *1102 East Boston Street, Seattle WA 98102-4128, USA* Tel (001) (206) 860 7565

HAYNES, Anthony. See HAYNES, Michael Anthony Richard

HAYNES, Miss Catherine Mary. b 68. Man Univ BA90. St Mich Coll Llan BD95. **d** 96 **p** 97. C Llantwit Major 96-99; C Coity w Nolton 99-01; P-in-c Llangammarch w Llanganten and Llanlleonfel etc *S & B* 01-03; P-in-c Irfon Valley 03-06; R 06-10; V Blaenau Irfon 06-10. *East Lyn, Lazonby, Penrith CA10 1BX* Tel (01768) 897018 E-mail cmhaynes@compuserve.com

HAYNES, Clifford. b 33. Cam Univ MA60. Linc Th Coll 80. **d** 82 **p** 83. C Lightcliffe *Wakef* 82-85; V Bradshaw 85-98; rtd 98; Perm to Offic *Carl* from 98. *East Lyn, Lazonby, Penrith CA10 1BX* Tel (01768) 897018

HAYNES (née RYDER), Mrs Jennifer Ann. b 40. Bath Spa Univ Coll BSc99. **d** 04 **p** 06. OLM Potterne w Worton and Marston *Sarum* 04-06; OLM Southbroom from 06. *9 Cranesbill Road, Devizes SN10 2TJ* Tel (01380) 738536 E-mail jennifer.a.haynes@hotmail.com

HAYNES, Canon John Richard. b 35. Ely Th Coll 60. **d** 63 **p** 64. C Bollington St Jo *Ches* 63-67; C Ches St Jo 67-68; C Davenham 68-70; Rhodesia 70-80; Zimbabwe 80-90; Sub-Dean Bulawayo Cathl 78-83; Hon Can Matabeleland from 90; V Bishop's Stortford St Alb 90-00; rtd 00; Perm to Offic *B & W* 01-10 and *York* from 11. *33 Dulverton Hall, Esplanade, Scarborough YO11 2AR* Tel (01723) 341530

HAYNES, John Stanley. b 30. WMMTC. **d** 82 **p** 83. NSM Westwood *Cov* 82-84; C Radford Semele and Ufton 84-85; V 85-95; rtd 95; Perm to Offic *Cov* from 95. *64 Rugby Road, Cubbington, Leamington Spa CV32 7JF* Tel (01926) 330016

HAYNES, Michael Anthony Richard (Tony). b 47. Heythrop Coll Lon MA95 Univ of Wales (Cardiff) LLM03. NTMTC 98. **d** 00 **p** 01. NSM Tottenham St Paul *Lon* 00-05; Hon C W Green Ch Ch w St Pet from 05. *Christ Church Vicarage, Waldeck Road, London N15 3EP* Tel (020) 8889 9677

HAYNES, Canon Michael Thomas Avery. b 32. AKC61. St Boniface Warminster 61. **d** 62 **p** 63. C Hebden Bridge *Wakef* 62-64; C Elland 64-68; V Thornhill Lees 68-82; V Lindley 82-97; Hon Can Wakef Cathl 82-97; rtd 97; Perm to Offic *Wakef* from 97. *Longwood Edge Cottage, 86 Lamb Hall Road, Huddersfield HD3 3TJ*

HAYNES, The Very Revd Peter. b 25. Selw Coll Cam BA49 MA54. Cuddesdon Coll 50. **d** 52 **p** 53. C Stokesley *York* 52-54; C Hessle 54-58; V Drypool St Jo 58-63; Asst Dir RE *B & W* 63-70; Youth Chapl 63-70; V Glastonbury St Jo 70-72; V Glastonbury St Jo w Godney 72-74; Adn Wells, Can Res and Preb Wells Cathl 74-82; Dean Heref and V Heref St Jo 82-92; rtd 92; Perm to Offic *B & W* 92-04 and *Heref* 05-09. *Dove Barn, Longworth Lane, Bartestree, Hereford HR1 4DA* Tel (01432) 850398

HAYNES, Peter Nigel Stafford. b 39. Hertf Coll Ox BA62 MA66. Cuddesdon Coll 62. **d** 64 **p** 65. C Norwood All SS *Cant* 64-68; C Portsea N End St Mark *Portsm* 68-72; Asst Chapl Brussels *Eur* 72-76; TV Banbury *Ox* 76-80; Asst Sec (Internat Affairs) Gen Syn Bd Soc Resp 80-85; P-in-c E Peckham and Nettlestead *Roch* 85-92; R Bredgar w Bicknor and Frinsted w Wormshill etc *Cant* 92-99; rtd 99. *1 Vesper Cottage, Cage Lane, Smarden, Ashford TN27 8QD* Tel (01233) 770367

HAYNES, Spencer Malcolm. b 46. Sarum & Wells Th Coll 93. **d** 93 **p** 94. C Devonport St Budeaux *Ex* 93-96; TV Tedburn St Mary, Whitestone, Oldridge etc 96-97; rtd 11. *Leander, 23 Silverdale, Silverton, Exeter EX5 4JF* Tel (01392) 860885 E-mail mhaynes@allotment.eclipse.co.uk

HAYNES, Stuart Edward. b 69. Edge Hill Coll of HE BA91. SNWTP 07. **d** 10 **p** 11. NSM Ormskirk *Liv* from 10. *11 Fairfield Close, Ormskirk L39 1RN* Tel 07534-218122 (mobile) E-mail stuart.haynes@liverpool.anglican.org

HAYNES, Valerie Elizabeth Mary-Benedict. b 53. Cant Ch Ch Univ BA00. St Steph Ho Ox 03. **d** 05 **p** 06. C Sheerness H Trin w St Paul *Cant* 05-09; Perm to Offic 09-10; P-in-c Boosbeck and Lingdale *York* from 10; P-in-c Skelton w Upleatham from 10. *The Vicarage, Church Drive, Boosbeck, Saltburn-by-the-Sea TS12 3AY* Tel (01287) 654040 Mobile 07803-798475 E-mail revhaynes@btinternet.com

HAYNS, Mrs Clare Julia Yates. b 69. Warwick Univ BA91 R Holloway Coll Lon MSc95 DipSW95. Ripon Coll Cuddesdon 08. **d** 11. NSM Blenheim *Ox* from 11. *11 Gidley Way, Horspath,*

Oxford OX33 1RQ Tel (01865) 876439 Mobile 07801-930702 E-mail clare@hayns.com

HAYSMORE, Geoffrey Frederick. b 39. Bps' Coll Cheshunt 63. **d** 66 **p** 67. C St Marylebone St Mark w St Luke *Lon* 66-69; C Stockton St Chad *Dur* 69-72; C-in-c Town End Farm CD 72-77; Perm to Offic *York* from 95; rtd 01. *139 Lambton Road, Middlesbrough TS4 2ST* Tel (01642) 275259

HAYTER, Mary Elizabeth. See BARR, Mary Elizabeth

HAYTER, Raymond William. b 48. Oak Hill Th Coll 74. **d** 77 **p** 78. C Bermondsey St Jas w Ch Ch *S'wark* 77-80; C Sydenham H Trin 81-83; Asst Chapl HM Pris Brixton 83-84; Chapl HM Youth Cust Cen Stoke Heath 84-88; Chapl HM Pris Maidstone 88-91; CF 91-08; Chapl HM Pris Standford Hill 08-11; Min Can St Woolos Cathl from 11. *10 Clifton Road, Newport NP20 4EW* Tel (01633) 263741

HAYTER, Sandra. See RAILTON, Sandra

HAYTON, John Anthony. b 45. TD81. Heythrop Coll Lon MA00 ACII70. Oak Hill Th Coll 93. **d** 96 **p** 97. NSM St Alb St Mich *St Alb* from 96; OLF 02-08. *89 Harpenden Road, St Albans AL3 6BY* Tel (01727) 761719 or 835037 Fax 811744 E-mail john.hayton@ntlworld.com

HAYTON, Mark William. b 59. St Steph Ho Ox 85. **d** 88 **p** 89. C Sittingbourne St Mich *Cant* 88-91; C Kennington 91-94; R Broadstairs 94-07; RD Thanet 96-01; P-in-c Folkestone Trin from 07. *Holy Trinity Vicarage, 21 Manor Road, Folkestone CT20 2SA* Tel (01303) 253831 E-mail markhayton@supanet.com

HAYTON, Norman Joseph Patrick. b 32. MRICS57. Sarum Th Coll 69. **d** 71 **p** 72. C Lytham St Cuth *Blackb* 71-74; V Wesham 74-79; V Chorley St Geo 79-80; NSM Kells *Carl* 84-85; P-in-c Flimby 85-90; V Barrow St Jas 90-94; TV Egremont and Haile 94-97; P-in-c Distington 97-00; rtd 00; P-in-c Charnock Richard *Blackb* 01-05; Perm to Offic *Ches* 05-11. *28 Stuart Court, High Street, Kibworth, Leicester LE8 0LR* Tel 0116-279 1568 E-mail normanhayton@hotmail.com

HAYWARD, Canon Alan Richard. b 25. Open Univ BA72. Wycliffe Hall Ox 54. **d** 56 **p** 57. C Dudley St Fran *Worc* 56-59; C-in-c Wollescote CD 59-65; V Wollescote 65-85; Hon Can Worc Cathl 85-91; R Alvechurch 85-91; rtd 91; Perm to Offic *Worc* 91-01. *2 St Kenelm's Court, St Kenelm's Road, Romsley, Halesowen B62 0NF* Tel (01562) 710749

HAYWARD, Canon Christopher Joseph. b 38. TCD BA63 MA67. Ridley Hall Cam 63. **d** 65 **p** 66. C Hatcham St Jas *S'wark* 65-69; Warden Lee Abbey Internat Students' Club Kensington 69-74; Chapl Chelmsf Cathl 74-77; P-in-c Darlaston All SS *Lich* 77-83; Ind Chapl 77-83; Can Res Bradf Cathl 83-92; Sec Bd Miss 83-92; R Linton in Craven 92-03; P-in-c Burnsall w Rylstone 97-03; RD Skipton 93-98; Hon Can Bradf Cathl 92-03; rtd 03; Perm to Offic *Bradf* from 04. *12 Ron Lawton Crescent, Burley in Wharfedale, Ilkley LS29 7ST* Tel (01943) 865261 E-mail chris.hayward@bradford.anglican.org

HAYWARD, Jane. See HAYWARD, Ms Pamela Jane

HAYWARD, Jeffrey Kenneth. b 47. St Jo Coll Nottm BTh74. **d** 74 **p** 75. C Stambermill *Worc* 74-77; C Woking St Jo *Guildf* 77-83; V Springfield H Trin *Chelmsf* 83-98; Chapl HM Pris Chelmsf 86-00; Area RD Chelmsf 86-88; RD Chelmsf 88-93; RD Chelmsf N 93-95; Hon Can Chelmsf Cathl 93-98; Chapl HM Pris Wakef 00-05; Chapl HM Pris Long Lartin from 05. *HM Prison Long Lartin, South Littleton, Evesham WR11 8TZ* Tel (01386) 835100 Fax 835101

HAYWARD, Mrs Jennifer Dawn. b 38. WMMTC 85. **d** 88 **p** 94. NSM Gt Malvern St Mary *Worc* 88-90; NSM Gt Malvern Ch Ch 88-90; Par Dn 90-94; C 94-96; TV Wirksworth *Derby* 96-04; rtd 04; Perm to Offic *Worc* from 04. *26 Barley Crescent, Long Meadow, Worcester WR4 0HW* Tel (01905) 29545

HAYWARD, John Andrew. b 63. Nottm Univ BTh89 MHCIMA83. Linc Th Coll 86. **d** 89 **p** 90. C Seaford w Sutton *Chich* 89-92; C St Pancras H Cross w St Jude and St Pet *Lon* 92-95; V Kentish Town St Martin w St Andr 95-08; AD S Camden 05-08; V Merton St Mary *S'wark* from 08. *The Vicarage, 3 Church Path, London SW19 3HJ* Tel (020) 8543 6192 E-mail vicar@stmarysmerton.org.uk

HAYWARD, Preb John Talbot. b 28. Selw Coll Cam BA52 MA56. Wells Th Coll 52. **d** 54 **p** 55. C S Lyncombe *B & W* 54-58; R Lamyatt 58-71; V Bruton w Wyke Champflower and Redlynch 58-71; RD Bruton 62-71; R Weston-super-Mare St Jo 71-75; Preb Wells Cathl from 73; TR Weston-super-Mare Cen Par 75-92; rtd 92; Perm to Offic *B & W* from 92. *5 Chelswood Avenue, Weston-super-Mare BS22 8QP* Tel (01934) 628431

HAYWARD, Martin. b 45. WMMTC 07. **d** 07 **p** 08. Dir Internat Min *Cov* from 07; NSM Cov St Fran N Radford from 07. *47 Benedictine Road, Coventry CV3 6GW* Tel (024) 7652 1205 Mobile 07917-182579 E-mail martin.hayward@coventrycathedral.org.uk

HAYWARD, Ms Pamela Jane. b 52. RGN82. Westcott Ho Cam 84. **d** 87 **p** 94. Par Dn Northampton St Mary *Pet* 87-90; Par Dn Bris St Mary Redcliffe w Temple etc 90-94; C 94-96; V Eastville St Anne w St Mark and St Thos from 96. *266 Glenfrome Road, Bristol BS5 6TS* Tel and fax 0117-952 0202

HAYWARD, Peter Noel. b 26. Leeds Univ BA48 BD78. Coll of Resurr Mirfield 48. **d** 50 **p** 51. C S Elmsall *Wakef* 50-56; C Sheldon *Birm* 56-60; C-in-c Garretts Green CD 60-69; V Garretts Green 69-70; V N Cave w Cliffe *York* 70-00; R Hotham 70-00; RD Howden 78-86; P-in-c Newbald 97-00; rtd 00; Perm to Offic *Carl* from 00; Hon C Solway Plain from 02. *The Old Chapel, Allonby, Maryport CA15 6QH* Tel (01900) 881466

HAYWARD, Mrs Sarah. b 77. St Mary's Coll Strawberry Hill BA99. St Jo Coll Nottm MTh06. **d** 08 **p** 09. C Dibden *Win* from 08. *Church House, 2 Corsair Drive, Dibden, Southampton SO45 5UF* Tel 07828-046193 (mobile) E-mail curate@dibdenchurches.org

HAYWARD, Timothy David Mark. b 78. St Andr Univ MTheol00. Westcott Ho Cam 07. **d** 09 **p** 10. C Buckden w the Offords *Ely* from 09. *19 Church Street, Buckden, St Neots PE19 5SJ* Tel (01480) 819665 Mobile 07988-994481 E-mail timhayward@hotmail.co.uk

HAYWARD-WRIGHT, Mrs Diane. b 51. WEMTC 06. **d** 09 **p** 10. NSM Inkberrow w Cookhill and Kington w Dormston *Worc* from 09. *1 Church Drive, Cookhill, Alcester B49 5JH* Tel (01527) 892727 Mobile 07815-520107 E-mail diane@shopwright.co.uk

HAYWOOD, James William. b 36. Chich Th Coll 69. **d** 73 **p** 74. C Leeds Halton St Wilfrid *Ripon* 73-76; C Workington St Jo *Carl* 76-78; V Clifton 78-84; P-in-c Barrow St Jas 84-85; V 85-89; V Crosby Ravensworth 89-94; R Asby 89-94; V Bolton 89-94; rtd 98. *19 Bramham Road, Whitwood, Castleford WF10 5PA*

HAYWOOD, Preb Keith Roderick. b 48. Oak Hill Th Coll 84. **d** 86 **p** 87. C Fazeley *Lich* 86-90; TV Leek and Meerbrook 90-01 Acting TR Hanley H Ev 01-03; TR from 03; Preb Lich Cath from 07. *Hanley Rectory, 35 Harding Road, Hanley, Stoke-on-Trent ST1 3BQ* Tel (01782) 266066 E-mail keithhaywood@talktalk.net

HAZEL, Sister. See SMITH, Sister Hazel Ferguson Waide

HAZELL, The Ven Frederick Roy. b 30. Fitzw Ho Cam BA53 MA59. Cuddesdon Coll 54. **d** 56 **p** 57. C Ilkeston St Mary *Derby* 56-59; C Heanor 59-62; V Marlpool 62-63; Chapl Univ of W Indies 63-66; C St Martin-in-the-Fields *Lon* 66-68; V Croydon H Sav *Cant* 68-84; RD Croydon 72-78; Hon Can Cant Cathl 73-84 P-in-c Croydon H Trin 77-80; Adn Croydon *S'wark* 84-93; rtc 93; P-in-c Chard, Furnham w Chaffcombe, Knowle St Giles etc *B & W* 95-99; P-in-c Tardebigge *Worc* 00-03; Perm to Offic *Birm* 00-11 and *Worc* 04-11. *27 Ramsay Hall, 9-13 Byron Road Worthing BN11 3HN* Tel (01903) 217108

HAZELL, Thomas Jeremy. b 35. Bris Univ LLB56 PhD01. St D Coll Lamp 56. **d** 58 **p** 59. C Newport St Paul *Mon* 58-61; C Derby St Jo 61-64; V Arksey *Sheff* 64-69; Sen Student Cllr Univ of Wales (Cardiff) *Llan* 69-89; rtd 95. *Castlewood Barn, Ponde Llandefalle, Brecon LD3 0NR* Tel (01874) 754030

HAZELTON, John. b 35. St Cath Coll Cam BA56 MA60 Bris Univ MLitt74 Newc Univ BPhil80. Wells Th Coll 59. **d** 61 **p** 62 C Twerton *B & W* 61-65; V Pitcombe w Shepton Montagu 65-72; Lect SS Hild and Bede Dur 72-79; Asst Master Dame Allan's Schs Newc 79-88; Chapl 88-95; rtd 95; Perm to Offic *Du* 97-09. *30 Pahiatua Street, Palmerston North, New Zealand* Te (0064) (6) 357 6469

HAZELTON, Michael John. b 53. UEA BA76 Bedf Coll Lon PhD81 Heythrop Coll Lon BD89. **d** 90 **p** 91. Asst Chap Helsinki *Eur* 94-95; Asst Chapl Zürich w Winterthur 95-98; R Mablethorpe w Trusthorpe *Linc* 98-02; R Saxonwell 02-05; V Danby w Castleton and Commondale *York* from 05; V Westerdale from 05; V Moorsholm from 09. *The Vicarage, Ya Flats Lane, Danby, Whitby YO21 2NQ* Tel (01287) 660388 E-mail mjh_uk@hotmail.com

HAZELTON, Robert Henry Peter. b 22. Wells Th Coll 65. **d** 6 **p** 68. C Eastover *B & W* 67-69; C Milton 69-76; V Peasedown St John 76-80; V Peasedown St John w Wellow 80-89; rtd 9C Perm to Offic *B & W* 90-06. *37 High Meadows, Midsome Norton, Bath BA3 2RY* Tel (01761) 419675

HAZELWOOD, Ms Jillian. b 32. Bp Otter Coll CertEd52 St Alt Minl Tr Scheme 82. **d** 87 **p** 94. NSM Wheathampstead *St Al* 87-02; Perm to Offic from 02. *14 Butterfield Roac Wheathampstead, St Albans AL4 8PU* Tel and fax (01582 833146

HAZELDINE, Basil William. b 18. St Pet Hall Ox BA42 MA45 Wycliffe Hall Ox 42. **d** 43 **p** 44. C Highfield *Ox* 43-46; C Gerrard Cross 46-51; V Barking St Patr *Chelmsf* 51-55; R Twineham an V Sayers Common *Chich* 55-60; V Stoughton *Guildf* 60-70; V Westlands St Andr *Lich* 70-77; P-in-c Whatfield w Semer *St* 77-78; R 78-81; P-in-c Nedging w Naughton 77-81; R Whatfiel w Semer, Nedging and Naughton 81-84; rtd 84. *4 Abbeyfiel House, 48 Rowley Bank, Stafford ST17 9BA* Tel (01785) 24862

HAZLEHURST, Anthony Robin. b 43. Man Univ BSc64 Tyndale Hall Bris 65. **d** 68 **p** 69. C Macclesfield Ch Ch *Che* 68-71; C Bushbury *Lich* 71-75; P-in-c New Clee *Linc* 75-85; TV Deane *Man* 85-96; V Harwood 96-07; rtd 07; Perm to Offic *Ma* from 07. *1 Maybury Close, Ramsbottom, Bury BL0 9WG* Te (01706) 281661 E-mail robinhaz@btinternet.com

HAZLEHURST, David. b 32. Liv Univ BSc54. St Steph Ho Ox 55. **d** 57 **p** 58. C Sheff Arbourthorne 57-59; C Doncaster Ch C

59-61; C W Wycombe *Ox* 61-63; P-in-c Collyhurst St Jas *Man* 66-67; V Blackrod 67-79; V Halliwell St Marg 79-84; R Sutton St Nic *S'wark* 84-94; rtd 94; Perm to Offic *S'wark* from 95; Perm to Offic *Guildf* 95-99. *3 Up The Quadrangle, Morden College, 19 St Germans Place, London SE3 0PW* Tel (020) 8853 1180

HAZLEHURST, David John Benedict (Benny). b 63. Trin Coll Bris 88. **d** 91 **p** 92. C Plumstead St Jo w St Jas and St Paul *S'wark* 91-98; Estates Outreach Worker (S'wark Adnry) 98-02; V Brixton Road Ch Ch 02-05; R Puddletown, Tolpuddle and Milborne w Dewlish *Sarum* 05-11; Perm to Offic from 11. *Carriers Cottage, Cheselbourne, Dorchester DT2 7NJ* Tel (01258) 839294 Mobile 07973-498590 E-mail benny@somail.it

HAZLEHURST, Robin. *See* HAZLEHURST, Anthony Robin

HAZLETT, Stephen David. b 56. TCD BTh88. CITC. **d** 88 **p** 89. C Ballywillan *Conn* 88-90; I Rathcoole 90-95; I Dunluce 95-00; Ind Chapl *Dur* from 00; TV Sunderland 00-07; Chapl Sunderland Minster from 07. *14 The Oaks West, Sunderland SR2 8HZ* Tel 0191-565 4121 E-mail stephen.hazlett@lineone.net

HAZLEWOOD, Canon Andrew Lord. b 54. Essex Univ BSc76. Wycliffe Hall Ox. **d** 82 **p** 83. C Leckhampton SS Phil and Jas w Cheltenham St Jas *Glouc* 82-85; C Waltham H Cross *Chelmsf* 85-89; R Pedmore *Worc* from 89; P-in-c Wollaston from 09; RD Stourbridge from 07; Hon Can Worc Cathl from 10. *The Rectory, Pedmore Lane, Stourbridge DY9 0SW* Tel (01562) 884856 or 887287 E-mail andrewhazlewood@gmail.com

HAZLEWOOD, David Paul. b 47. Sheff Univ MB, ChB70 Campion Hall Ox BA72 MA77. Wycliffe Hall Ox 70. **d** 73 **p** 74. C Chapeltown *Sheff* 73-75; Singapore 76; Indonesia 76 88; R Ipswich St Helen *St E* 88-97; V Shirley *Win* 97-11; rtd 11. *Address temp unknown* E-mail david.hazlewood@ukgateway.net

HAZLEWOOD, William Peter Guy. b 71. De Montfort Univ BA97. St Steph Ho Ox BTh01. **d** 01 **p** 02. C Knowle H Nativity and Easton All Hallows *Bris* 01-04; P-in-c Iver Heath *Ox* 04-08; R 08-11; P-in-c Dartmouth and Dittisham *Ex* from 11. *The Vicarage, 79 Seymour Drive, Dartmouth TQ6 9GE* Tel (01803) 414767 E-mail frwill@hazlewoodhq.co.uk

HEAD, David Nicholas. b 55. Pemb Coll Cam BA77 MA81 Westmr Coll of Educn MTh01. Westcott Ho Cam 78. **d** 81 **p** 82. C Surbiton St Andr and St Mark *S'wark* 81-84; C St Marylebone w H Trin *Lon* 84-89; TV Clapham Team *S'wark* 89-96; Chapl Trin Hospice Lon 89-96; Chapl Princess Alice Hospice Esher 96-03; R Lyng, Sparham, Elsing, Bylaugh, Bawdeswell etc *Nor* from 03. *The Rectory, Rectory Road, Lyng, Norwich NR9 5RA* Tel and fax (01603) 872381 E-mail david@davidhead.plus.com

HEAD, Canon Derek Leonard Hamilton. b 34. ALCD58. **d** 58 **p** 59. C Bexleyheath Ch Ch *Roch* 58-61; C Wisley w Pyrford *Guildf* 61-66; C-in-c Ewell St Paul Howell Hill CD 66-73; R Headley All SS 73-81; TR 81-82; RD Farnham 80-82; V Chertsey 82-99; Hon Can Guildf Cathl 83-99; RD Runnymede 88-93; Dir Post-Ord Tr 90-94; rtd 99; Perm to Offic *Win* from 00. *9 Tangmere Close, Mudeford, Christchurch BH23 4LZ* Tel (01425) 276545 E-mail headd@onetel.com

HEAD, Canon Ivan Francis. b 53. Univ of W Aus BA75 Glas Univ PhD85. Melbourne Coll of Div BD78. **d** 79 **p** 79. Australia 79-81 and from 85; C Uddingston *Glas* 81-85; C Cambuslang 81-85; Dir Angl Inst Theol Perth 85-91; Warden Ch Coll Tasmania Univ 91-94; Warden St Paul's Coll Sydney Univ from 95. *St Paul's College, University of Sydney NSW 2006, Australia* Tel (0061) (2) 9550 7444 or 9557 1447 Fax 9519 7246 E-mail ihead@mail.usyd.edu.au

HEAD, Peter Ernest. b 38. Lon Univ BSc59. Ridley Hall Cam 61. **d** 63 **p** 64. C Fulwood *Sheff* 63-66; C Belper *Derby* 66-68; Hd RE Shoeburyness Sch Southend-on-Sea 69-74; Hd RE Bilborough Coll 74-79; Public Preacher *S'well* 74-79; NSM Bramcote 74-79; Vice-Prin Totton Coll Southn 79-93; Hon C Hordle *Win* 94-02; rtd 03; Perm to Offic *Win* from 02. *44 Lentune Way, Lymington SO41 3PF* Tel and fax (01590) 678097 E-mail peter_head@bigfoot.com

HEADING, Margaret Anne. b 66. Leeds Univ BSc88 Man Univ PhD91 Aston Univ PGCE99. Wycliffe Hall Ox BA01. **d** 02 **p** 03. C Fletchamstead *Cov* 02-05; V Ingleby Greenhow, Bilsdale Priory etc *York* from 05. *3 Holmemead, Great Broughton, Middlesbrough TS9 7HQ* Tel (01642) 710045 E-mail anne.heading@tesco.net

HEADING, Canon Richard Vaughan. b 43. Lon Univ BSc65 ARCS65. Coll of Resurr Mirfield 66. **d** 68 **p** 69. C Heref St Martin 68-75; P-in-c Birches Head and Northwood *Lich* 75-77; TV Hanley H Ev 77-82; V Heref H Trin 82-92; TR Bedminster *Bris* 92-08; AD Bris S 01-06; Hon Can Bris Cathl 01-08; rtd 08. *18 Timberdine Avenue, Worcester WR5 2BD* Tel (01905) 360998 E-mail richard.heading@gmx.com

HEADLAND, James Frederick. b 20. Clifton Th Coll 51. **d** 53 **p** 54. C Barnsbury St Andr *Lon* 53-55; C Spitalfields Ch Ch w All SS 55-57; V Upper Tulse Hill St Matthias *S'wark* 57-65; R Church Pulverbatch *Heref* 65-81; P-in-c Smethcott w Woolstaston 65-81; R Reedham w Cantley w Limpenhoe and

Southwood *Nor* 81-86; rtd 86; Perm to Offic *Heref* from 86 and *Lich* 88-00. *3 Ashford Avenue, Pontesbury, Shrewsbury SY5 0QN* Tel (01743) 790565

HEADLEY, Miss Carolyn Jane. b 50. K Coll Lon MA94 MCSP71. Oak Hill Th Coll BA83. **dss** 83 **d** 87 **p** 94. Kensal Rise St Mark and St Martin *Lon* 83-87; Par Dn Uxbridge 87-90; TD 90-92; Warden of Readers (Willesden Area) 88-92; Tutor Wycliffe Hall Ox 94-05; P-in-c W Meon and Warnford *Portsm* 05-07; Chapl Portsm Hosps NHS Trust from 07. *31 Canal Wharf, Chichester PO19 8EY* Tel (01243) 774558 Mobile 07777-617516 E-mail carolynheadley@btinternet.com

HEADS, John. b 27. Bps' Coll Cheshunt 60. **d** 62 **p** 63. C Beamish *Dur* 61-64; C Monkwearmouth St Andr 64-65; C Stockton St Chad 65-70; rtd 94. *18 Green Crescent, Golcar, Huddersfield HD7 4RF* Tel (01484) 651232

HEAGERTY, Alistair John. b 42. MBE86. Oriel Coll Ox BA63 MA67. Lon Coll of Div BD68. **d** 68 **p** 69. C Margate H Trin *Cant* 68-72; CF 72-97; Chapl R Memorial Chpl Sandhurst 92-97; TV Kingswood *Bris* 97-08; rtd 08. *44 Ferney Road, East Barnet, Barnet EN4 8LF* Tel (020) 3234 1003 E-mail alistair@heagerty.freeserve.co.uk

HEAK, Philip George. b 70. QUB BA92. CITC BTh95. **d** 95 **p** 96. C Ballymacash *Conn* 95-98; C Galway w Kilcummin *T, K & A* 98-00; Dioc Youth Officer (Cashel) *C & O* 00-06; I Naas w Kill and Rathmore *M & K* from 06. *15 Spring Gardens, Naas, Co Kildare, Republic of Ireland* Tel (00353) (45) 897206 Mobile 86-817 2356 E-mail pheak@eircom.net

HEAL, David Walter. b 37. Ox Univ MA63. Trin Coll Carmarthen 87. **d** 90 **p** 91. NSM Llanfynyw w Aberaeron and Llanddewi Aberarth *St D* 90-96; Hon Asst Chapl Algarve *Eur* 96-98; Chapl Madeira 98-03; rtd 03; Perm to Offic *St D* from 04. *Cae Gwair Bach, Llanon SY23 5LZ* Tel (01974) 202596

HEAL, Miss Felicity Joan. b 42. Portsm Dioc Tr Course 89. **d** 92. NSM Bramshott and Liphook *Portsm* 92-95; NSM Blendworth w Chalton w Idsworth 95-97; Perm to Offic from 97. *40 Rushes Road, Petersfield GU32 3BW* Tel (01730) 260410 Mobile 07712-249608 E-mail fj.heal@ntlworld.com

HEALD, William Roland. b 40. St Jo Coll Auckland 72. **d** 74 **p** 75. C Howick New Zealand 74; C Kaitaia 75; C Auckland St Paul Symonds Street 76-78; C Bournville *Birm* 78-79; V Henderson New Zealand 79-82; V Auckland St Paul Symonds Street 84-93; V S Kensington St Luke *Lon* 93-07; rtd 07; V Kaitaia New Zealand from 07. *47 Church Street, Kaitaia 0441, New Zealand* Tel (0064) (9) 408 0524 E-mail bill.heald@virgin.net

HEALE, Nicholas James. b 67. St Cath Coll Ox BA89 DPhil95 Leeds Univ BA94. Coll of Resurr Mirfield 95. **d** 95 **p** 96. C Syston *Leic* 95-99; V Blackpool St Mich *Blackb* 99-10; P-in-c Skerton St Chad from 10. *St Chad's Vicarage, 1 St Chad's Drive, Lancaster LA1 2SE*

HEALE, Walter James Grenville. b 40. Wycliffe Hall Ox 77. **d** 79 **p** 80. C Walsall *Lich* 79-82; TV Marfleet *York* 82-89; TR 89-94; R Easington w Skeffling, Kilnsea and Holmpton 94-05; P-in-c Owthorne and Rimswell w Withernsea 00-05; rtd 05; P-in-c Easington w Skeffling, Kilnsea and Holmpton *York* 05-06; Perm to Offic from 06. *18 Sloe Lane, Beverley HU17 8ND* Tel (01482) 865915

HEALES, Canon John. b 48. K Coll Lon BD71 AKC71 PGCE72. St Mich Coll Llan 75. **d** 76 **p** 77. C Cwmbran *Mon* 76-78; Chapl Rendcomb Coll Cirencester 78-82; Chapl Mon Sch 84-88; V Penhow, St Brides Netherwent w Llandavenny etc *Mon* from 88; Hon Can St Woolos Cathl from 11. *The New Rectory, Llanvaches, Newport NP26 3AY* Tel (01633) 400901

HEALEY, James Christopher. b 44. Linc Th Coll 84. **d** 86 **p** 87. C Boultham *Linc* 86-90; TV Gt Grimsby St Mary and St Jas 90-91; I Narraghmore and Timolin w Castledermot etc *D & G* 91-93; I New Ross *C & O* 93-97; Dean Lismore 97-99; I Lismore w Cappoquin, Kilwatermoy, Dungarvan etc 97-99; Chan Cashel Cathl 97-99; Prec Waterford Cathl 97-99; Can Ossory Cathl 97-99; I Arvagh w Carrigallen, Gowna and Columbkille *K, E & A* 99-02; P-in-c Winthorpe and Langford w Holme *S'well* 02-03; R Coddington and Winthorpe and Langford w Holme 03-05; rtd 05. *12 Ridgeway, Nettleham, Lincoln LN2 2TL* Tel (01522) 753622

HEALEY, Michael Harry Edmund. b 74. Mansf Coll Ox MA01 Leeds Univ BA03. Coll of Resurr Mirfield 01. **d** 04 **p** 05. C Norton *Sheff* 04-07; P-in-c Beighton from 07. *The Vicarage, 27 Tynker Avenue, Beighton, Sheffield S20 1DX* Tel 0114-248 7635 E-mail mhehealey@hotmail.com

HEALY (née THOROLD), Mrs Alison Susan Joy. b 59. St Jo Coll Dur BA80. Ripon Coll Cuddesdon 97 SEITE 03. **d** 06 **p** 07. NSM Shooters Hill Ch Ch *S'wark* from 06. *68 Charlton Lane, London SE7 8LA* Tel (020) 8858 1736 Mobile 07962-318728 E-mail vicardancer@supanet.com

HEANEY, Eileen. b 59. **d** 11. NSM Burscough Bridge *Liv* from 11. *473 Southport Road, Scarisbrick, Ormskirk L40 9RF*

HEANEY, Canon James Roland. b 59. **d** 85 **p** 86. C Ballynafeigh St Jude *D & D* 85-88; C Lisburn Ch Ch Cathl 88-90; I Dunganstown w Redcross and Conary *D & G* from 90; Can

Ch Ch Cathl Dublin from 05. *The Rectory, Redcross, Co Wicklow, Republic of Ireland* Tel and fax (00353) (404) 41637 E-mail heaneyr@indigo.ie
HEANEY, Michael Roger. b 43. TCD BA66 HDipEd67 MA69. CITC 74. **d** 76 **p** 77. Chapl St Columba's Coll Dub 76-09; rtd 09. *Montana, Scholarstown Road, Dublin 16, Republic of Ireland* Tel (00353) (1) 493 1167 *or* 493 2219 E-mail mheaney@iol.ie
HEANEY, Robert Stewart. **d** 01 **p** 02. C Dunboyne Union *M & K* 01-04; Perm to Offic *Ox* from 05. *46 Court Place Gardens, Iffley, Oxford OX4 4EW* Tel (01865) 715996 E-mail robert.heaney@theology.ox.ac.uk
HEANEY, Samuel Stewart. b 44. Open Univ BA79 Ulster Univ BEd83 Lon Univ BD93 QUB MPhil99. St Deiniol's Hawarden 92. **d** 92 **p** 93. In Presbyterian Ch 85-92; C Knockbreda *D & D* 92-96; I Belfast H Trin and St Silas *Conn* 96-02; I Ballyrashane w Kildollagh 02-09; rtd 09. *3 Edgewood Court, Antrim BT41 4PG* Tel (028) 9446 1076
HEANEY, Timothy Daniel. b 59. Trin Coll Bris BA04. **d** 04 **p** 05. C Dursley *Glouc* 04-08; P-in-c Paul *Truro* from 08. *The Vicarage, 1 St Pol-de-Leon View, Paul, Penzance TR19 6US* Tel (01736) 731261 E-mail tim@heaney.org.uk *or* timheaney@paulchurch.co.uk
HEANEY, Wendy Anne. b 42. St Alb Minl Tr Scheme 90. **d** 95 **p** 96. NSM Clifton and Southill *St Alb* 95-99; Asst Chapl HM Pris Bedf 95-99; Chapl 99-02; Lic to Offic *St Alb* 99-02; rtd 02; Perm to Offic *St Alb* from 03. *34 Meadow Way, Letchworth Garden City SG6 3JB* Tel (01462) 641303
HEAP, David Leonard. b 58. Man Univ BA79. Cranmer Hall Dur 82. **d** 85 **p** 86. C Clitheroe St Jas *Blackb* 85-88; C Blackb St Gabr 88-92; V Bare from 92. *St Christopher's Vicarage, 12 Elm Grove, Morecambe LA4 6AT* Tel (01524) 411363 E-mail davidheap@readingroom.freeserve.co.uk
HEAPS, Richard Peter. b 35. Bernard Gilpin Soc Dur 58 Qu Coll Birm 58. **d** 61 **p** 62. C Castle Bromwich SS Mary and Marg *Birm* 61-65; C-in-c Erdington St Chad CD 65-70; V Nechells 70-81; RD Aston 75-81; V Marston Green 81-86; P-in-c Shrawley and Witley w Astley *Worc* 86-92; R Shrawley, Witley, Astley and Abberley 92-01; rtd 01; Perm to Offic *Worc* from 01. *9 Timberdyne Close, Rock, Kidderminster DY14 9RT* Tel (01299) 832376
HEARD, Charles. b 19. S'wark Ord Course 62. **d** 65 **p** 66. C Plumstead St Nic *S'wark* 65-71; C Blackheath All SS 71-72; V Barnes H Trin 72-84; rtd 84; Hon C E Wickham *S'wark* 84-07; Perm to Offic from 07. *5 Elmfield Court, Wickham Street, Welling DA16 3DF* Tel (020) 8855 9809
HEARD, James Barrie. b 66. Brunel Univ BA98 K Coll Lon MA01. Ridley Hall Cam 03. **d** 06 **p** 07. C Fulham All SS *Lon* 06-09; C Chelsea St Luke and Ch Ch from 09. *29 Burnsall Street, London SW3 3SR* Tel 07867-508919 (mobile)
HEARD, Richard Adrian. b 72. Univ of Wales (Swansea) BSc94 Hull Univ PGCE96. St Jo Coll Nottm 06. **d** 08 **p** 09. C Hackenthorpe *Sheff* from 08; V W Bessacarr from 11. *The Vicarage, 39 Sturton Close, Doncaster DN4 7JG* Tel 07818-850347 (mobile) E-mail rev.richardheard@yahoo.co.uk
HEARD, Stephen Edward. b 53. NTMTC 02. **d** 04 **p** 08. NSM Bush Hill Park St Mark *Lon* from 04; Parliamentary Chapl to Bp Lon from 07. *43 Speed House, Barbican, London EC2Y 8AT, or Old Deanery, Dean's Yard, London EC4V 5AA* Tel (020) 7638 9501 *or* 7248 6233 Mobile 07939-263657 E-mail stephen.heard3@btinternet.com
HEARL, Maria Christina. b 47. New Hall Cam BA69 Ex Univ MA98 PhD07 PGCE70. SWMTC 03. **d** 07 **p** 08. NSM Ex St Dav from 07. *16 Twyford Place, Tiverton EX16 6AP* Tel (01884) 256380 E-mail rev.maria@stdavidschurchexeter.org.uk
HEARN, John Henry. b 49. Trin Coll Bris. **d** 82 **p** 83. C Epsom Common Ch Ch *Guildf* 82-85; C Ringwood *Win* 85-88; Chapl Basingstoke Distr Hosp 88-91; Chapl Luton and Dunstable Hosp 91-96; C Ampthill w Millbrook and Steppingley *St Alb* 96-99; P-in-c Wymington w Podington 99-03; V W Acklam *York* from 03. *St Mary's Vicarage, 50 Church Lane, Middlesbrough TS5 7EB* Tel (01642) 814701 E-mail john.hearn@tesco.net
HEARN, Jonathan. b 58. Leeds Univ BA81 GradIPM85. Westcott Ho Cam 89. **d** 91 **p** 92. C Tuffley *Glouc* 91-94; C Milton *Win* 94-02; P-in-c Warwick St Paul *Cov* 02-03; TV Warwick from 03. *St Paul's Vicarage, 33 Stratford Road, Warwick CV34 6AS* Tel (01926) 419814
HEARN, Canon Peter Brian. b 31. St Jo Coll Dur 52. **d** 55 **p** 56. C Frodingham *Linc* 55-59; R Belton SS Pet and Paul 59-64; PC Manthorpe w Londonthorpe 59-64; V Billingborough 64-73; V Sempringham w Pointon and Birthorpe 64-73; V Flixborough w Burton upon Stather 73-96; RD Manlake 87-93; Can and Preb Linc Cathl 92-01; rtd 96; Perm to Offic *Linc* from 01. *7 St Andrews Drive, Burton-upon-Stather, Scunthorpe DN15 9BY* Tel (01724) 720510
HEARN, Stephen Isaac Raphael. b 79. Linc Coll Ox BA04 MA08. St Steph Ho Ox 06 Ven English Coll Rome 08. **d** 09 **p** 10. C Market Deeping *Linc* from 09. *16 Church Street, Deeping St James, Peterborough PE6 8HD* Tel (01778) 344516 E-mail stephen.hearn@lincoln.oxon.org

HEARN, Thomas Peter. b 18. Selw Coll Cam BA40 MA45. Linc Th Coll 40. **d** 42 **p** 43. C Oxhey St Matt *St Alb* 42-45; C Cirencester *Glouc* 45-52; V Childswyckham 52-62; R Aston Somerville 52-62; RD Winchcombe 60-62; R Stratton w Baunton 62-75; V France Lynch 75-83; rtd 84; Perm to Offic *Glouc* from 84. *9 Cotswold Close, Cirencester GL7 1XP* Tel (01285) 655627 E-mail hearn.petvon@amserve.net
HEARN, Trevor. b 36. Sarum Th Coll 61. **d** 64 **p** 65. C Hounslow St Steph *Lon* 64-67; Miss to Seafarers 67-01; UAE 92-01; rtd 01; Perm to Offic *Bris* from 01. *37 Elberton Road, Bristol BS9 2PZ* Tel 0117-983 6526 E-mail tandv@hearn3136.fsnet.co.uk
HEARTFIELD, Canon Peter Reginald. b 27. Chich Th Coll 61. **d** 63 **p** 64. C Hurstpierpoint *Chich* 63-67; V Brighton St Alb Preston 67-73; Chapl Kent and Cant Hosp 73-92; Chapl Nunnery Fields Hosp Cant 73-92; Six Preacher Cant Cath 79-84; Hon Can Cant Cathl 84-92; rtd 92; Perm to Offic *Can* from 00; Chapl St Jo Hosp Cant from 10. *1 St John's House, 40 Northgate, Canterbury CT1 1BE* Tel (01227) 451621 E-mail prheartfield@btinternet.com
HEASLIP, Eoghan. b 76. St Mellitus Coll. **d** 11. C Worc City from 11. *160 Bath Road, Worcester WR5 3EP*
HEASLIP, William John (Jack). b 44. TCD BA66 HDipEd CITC 79. **d** 80 **p** 81. Chapl Mt Temple Sch Dub 80-86; Bp's C Aughaval w Burrishoole, Knappagh and Louisburgh *T, K & A* 86-88; I Aughaval w Achill, Knappagh, Dugort etc 88-95; Radio Officer (Tuam) 90-95; I Cork St Luke Union *C, C & R* 95-98 Colann Renewal Min *T, K & A* 98-09; rtd 09; Lic to Offic *D & C* from 09. *Cloghadockan, Turlough, Castlebar, Co Mayo, Republic of Ireland* Tel (00353) (94) 902 5282 E-mail jackheaslip@me.com
HEATH, Mrs Cynthia Grace. b 46. St Mark & St Jo Coll Lon TCert68 Open Univ BA85 ARCM66 GRSM68. WMMTC 94. **d** 97 **p** 98. NSM Penkridge *Lich* 97-00; TV 00-07. *2 Hall Farm Road, Brewood, Stafford ST19 9EZ* Tel (01902) 850175
HEATH, Henry. b 40. FCII77. Oak Hill Th Coll 77. **d** 80 **p** 81 NSM Lexden *Chelmsf* 80-86; C Colne Engaine 86; NSM Halstead St Andr w H Trin and Greenstead Green 86-90; NSM W w E Mersea 90-95; R Stanway 95-02; rtd 02; Perm to Offic *Chelmsf* 02-05; P-in-c Wormingford, Mt Bures and Lt Horkesley from 05. *The Vicarage, Church Road, Wormingford, Colchester CO6 3AZ* Tel and fax (01787) 227398 E-mail heathatquayside@aol.com
HEATH, Mrs Janet. b 45. EMMTC 89. **d** 91 **p** 94. Par Dn Rainworth *S'well* 91-94; C 94-96; C Mansfield Woodhouse 96-99; rtd 00; Perm to Offic *S'well* from 00. *17 The Hollies, Sherwood Park, Rainworth, Mansfield NG21 0FZ* Tel (01623 490422 E-mail janheath@supanet.com
HEATH, John Henry. b 41. Chich Th Coll 69. **d** 71 **p** 72. C Crediton *Ex* 71-74; C Tavistock and Gulworthy 74-76; C Brixham 76-77; C Brixham w Churston Ferrers 77-79; R Ber Ferrers 79-85; P-in-c Moretonhampstead, N Bovey an Manaton 85-88; R 88-93; P-in-c Lifton 93-99; P-in-c Kelly v Bradstone 93-99; C Broadwoodwidger 93-99; R Lifton Broadwoodwidger, Coryton, Stowford etc 99-01; V Lifton Broadwoodwidger, Stowford etc 01-03; rtd 03; Perm to Offi *Heref* 04-10. *30 Wye Way, Hereford HR1 2NP*
HEATH, Julie Ann. b 62. EMMTC. **d** 06 **p** 07. NSM Kegworth Hathern, Long Whatton, Diseworth etc *Leic* 06-08. *Fairmount House, 87 Leicester Road, Ashby-de-la-Zouch LE65 1DD* E-mail jaheath@globalnet.co.uk
HEATH, Martin Jonathan. b 68. St Jo Coll Nottm 07. **d** 09 **p** 10. C Gt Wyrley *Lich* from 09. *6 Clover Ridge, Cheslyn Hay, Walsa WS6 7DP* Tel 07847-370572 (mobile) E-mail martinjheath@talktalk.net
HEATH, Mrs Wendy Hillary. b 47. WMMTC 95. **d** 98 **p** 99. NSM Rugeley *Lich* 98-99; C 00-01; P-in-c Brereton 01-06; TV Brereto and Rugeley from 06. *The Vicarage, 72 Main Road, Brereton Rugeley WS15 1DU* Tel (01889) 582466 E-mail wen_heath@hotmail.com
HEATH-WHYTE, David Robert. b 68. Fitzw Coll Cam BA89 Wycliffe Hall Ox BTh98. **d** 98 **p** 99. C Gt Chesham *Ox* 98-02; V Frogmore *St Alb* from 02. *Holy Trinity Vicarage, 39 Frogmore St Albans AL2 2JU* Tel (01727) 872172 E-mail david@hotfrog.info
HEATHCOTE, Warwick Geoffrey. b 46. Th Ext Educn Coll 97 **d** 00 **p** 01. C Grahamstown Cathl S Africa 00-03; C Cirenceste *Glouc* 03-09; P-in-c Stratton, N Cerney, Baunton and Bagendo from 09. *The Rectory, 94 Gloucester Road, Cirencester GL7 2L* Tel (01285) 653359 E-mail warwick.heathcote@sky.com
HEATHER, Dennis Eric. b 34. **d** 98 **p** 99. OLM Hook *S'war* from 98. *276 Hook Road, Chessington KT9 1PF* Tel (020) 839 0063
HEATHER, Mark Duncan Grainger. b 62. Leic Poly LLB8 Leeds Univ BA99. Coll of Resurr Mirfield 97. **d** 99 **p** 00. C Leed St Aid *Ripon* 99-03; V Leeds Halton St Wilfrid 03-10; Bp's Chap Guildf from 10. *59 Brookside, Jacob's Well, Guildford GU4 7N* Tel (01483) 566082 *or* 590500 Fax 590501 E-mail mark.heather@cofeguildford.org.uk

HEATHER, Mrs Sally Patricia. b 51. Avery Hill Coll BEd73. STETS 99. d 02 p 03. NSM Michelmersh and Awbridge and Braishfield etc *Win* 02-06; TV Basingstoke from 06. *75 Cumberland Avenue, Basingstoke RG22 4BQ* Tel (01256) 422665 E-mail spheather@gmail.com

HEATHFIELD, Simon David. b 67. Birm Univ BMus88 Fitzw Coll Cam BTh99. Ridley Hall Cam 96. d 99 p 00. C Heswall *Ches* 99-02; Voc and Min Adv CPAS 02-05; TR Walthamstow *Chelmsf* from 06. *St Mary's Rectory, 117 Church Hill, London E17 3BD* Tel (020) 8520 4281 *or* 8520 1430 E-mail simonh@walthamstowchurch.org.uk

HEATLEY, Cecil. See HEATLEY, Canon William Cecil

HEATLEY, David Henry. b 50. Kent Univ BA72. Qu Coll Birm 86. d 88 p 89. C Liss *Portsm* 88-91; V Newchurch and Arreton 91-99; R Greatham w Empshott and Hawkley w Prior's Dean from 99; Dioc Rural Officer from 98. *The Vicarage, Hawkley, Liss GU33 6NF* Tel (01730) 827459 E-mail dhheatley@aol.com

HEATLEY, Canon William Cecil. b 39. QUB BA61. Ridley Hall Cam 62. d 64 p 65. C Ballymacarrett St Patr *D & D* 64-69; C Herne Hill St Paul *S'wark* 69-74; TV Sanderstead All SS 75-82; P-in-c Peckham St Sav 82-87; V 87-07; RD Dulwich 97-02; Hon Can S'wark Cathl 01-07; rtd 07; Perm to Offic *S'wark* from 07. *37 Bromley College, London Road, Bromley BR1 1PE* Tel (020) 8460 9505 E-mail cecilheatley@yahoo.com

HEATON, Alan. b 36. K Coll Lon BD64 AKC64 Nottm Univ MTh76. d 65 p 66. C Stockton St Chad *Dur* 65-68; C Englefield Green *Guildf* 68-70; C Winlaton *Dur* 70-74; Chapl Derby Lonsdale Coll 74-79; V Alfreton 79-87; RD Alfreton 81-86; TR Clifton *S'well* 87-93; P-in-c Rolleston w Fiskerton, Morton and Upton 93-96; rtd 97; Perm to Offic *Liv* from 97. *29 The Parchments, Newton-le-Willows WA12 0DX* Tel (01925) 292209 E-mail a.ms-heaton@tiscali.co.uk

HEATON, Sister Elizabeth Ann. b 65. Bath Coll of HE BSc87. Ripon Coll Cuddesdon 98. d 00 p 01. C Lostwithiel, St Winnow w St Nectan's Chpl etc *Truro* 00-03; CSF from 03; Perm to Offic *B & W* 03-10 and *Linc* from 10. *San Damiano, 38 Drury Street, Metheringham, Lincoln LN4 3EZ* Tel (01526) 321115 E-mail lizcsf@franciscans.org.uk

HEATON, Joseph Anthony Turnley. b 70. Univ of Wales (Abth) BSc91 PhD95 St Jo Coll Dur BA08. Cranmer Hall Dur 06. d 08 p 09. C Ribbesford w Bewdley and Dowles *Worc* from 08. *18 Brook Vale, Bewdley DY12 1BQ* Tel (01299) 401425

HEATON, Julian Roger. b 62. LSE BSc(Econ)83. St Steph Ho Ox BA86 MA92. d 87 p 88. C Stockport St Thos w St Pet *Ches* 87-90; Chapl Asst Qu Medical Cen and Univ Hosp Nottm 90-92; V Knutsford St Cross 92-01; P-in-c Altrincham St Jo 01-05; Voc Officer (Macclesfield Adnry) 01-05; V Sale St Anne from 05. *St Anne's Vicarage, Church Road West, Sale M33 3GD* Tel 0161-973 4145 E-mail julian.heaton@talktalk.net

HEATON, Nicholas Mark. b 70. Leeds Metrop Univ BEd92 Ches Coll of HE BTh04. NOC 01. d 04 p 05. C Linthorpe *York* 04-08; TV Morley *Wakef* 08-10; TV Upper Holme Valley from 10. *The Vicarage, Ashgrove Road, Holmfirth HD9 3JR* Tel (01484) 683593 E-mail nickheaton2@sky.com

HEATON, Timothy. b 59. STETS 08. d 08 p 10. NSM Upper Stour *Sarum* 08-11; NSM Gillingham and Milton-on-Stour from 11. *Grange Cottage, Chaffeymoor, Bourton, Gillingham SP8 5BY* Tel (01747) 841076

HEAVER, Derek Cyril. b 47. St Jo Coll Nottm BTh69. d 73 p 74. C Win Ch Ch 73-77; CF 77-02; rtd 02. *Orchard Cottage, 2 Myrtle Close, Puncknowle, Dorchester DT2 9EH* Tel and fax (01308) 898466 E-mail delsaun@eurobell.co.uk

HEAVISIDES, Canon Neil Cameron. b 50. Selw Coll Cam BA72 MA76 Ox Univ BA74 MA85. Ripon Hall Ox 72. d 75 p 76. C Stockton St Pet *Dur* 75-78; Succ S'wark Cathl 78-81; V Seaham w Seaham Harbour *Dur* 81-88; P-in-c Edington and Imber, Erlestoke and E Coulston *Sarum* 88-89; R 89-93; Can Res Glouc Cathl from 93. *7 College Green, Gloucester GL1 2LX* Tel (01452) 523987 E-mail nheavisides@gloucestercathedral.org.uk

HEAWOOD, Canon Alan Richard. b 32. G&C Coll Cam BA54 MA58. Union Th Sem (NY) BD56 Ripon Hall Ox 56. d 57 p 58. C Horwich H Trin *Man* 57-59; C Weaste 59-60; C Beverley Minster *York* 60-62; Chapl and Lect St Pet Coll Saltley 62-65; R Hockwold w Wilton *Ely* 65-72; R Weeting 65-72; V Melbourn 72-80; V Meldreth 72-80; P-in-c Teversham 80-90; Adult Educn Sec 80-89; Dir of Educn 80-98; Hon Can Ely Cathl 80-98; rtd 98; Perm to Offic *Ely* from 98. *10 Westberry Court, Grange Road, Cambridge CB3 9BG* Tel (01223) 460088

HEAZELL, Pamela Fletcher. b 50. NEMTC 96. d 99 p 00. NSM Hayes St Nic CD *Lon* 99-01; NSM N Greenford All Hallows 01-04; P-in-c 04-08; V from 08. *72 Horsenden Lane North, Greenford UB6 0PD* Tel (020) 8933 7700 E-mail pfheazell@aol.com

EBBERN, Geoffrey Alan. b 43. MBE98. d 05 p 06. NSM Radipole and Melcombe Regis *Sarum* from 05; Asst Chapl HM Pris The Verne from 05. *11 Hawthorn Close, Weymouth DT4 9UG* Tel and fax (01305) 772205 E-mail ghebbern@hotmail.com

HEBBLETHWAITE, Canon Brian Leslie. b 39. Magd Coll Ox BA61 MA67 Magd Coll Cam BA63 MA68 BD84. Westcott Ho Cam 62. d 65 p 66. C Elton All SS *Man* 65-68; Chapl Qu Coll Cam 68; Dean of Chpl and Fell 69-94; Asst Lect Div Cam Univ 73-77; Lect 77-99; Can Th Leic Cathl 82-00; rtd 99; Perm to Offic *Ely* from 02. *The Old Barn, 32 High Street, Stretham, Ely CB6 3JQ* Tel (01353) 648279 Mobile 07740-307568 E-mail blh1000@cam.ac.uk

HEBBLEWHITE, David Ernest. b 52. Hull Univ BA81 Nottm Univ MA82 CQSW82. St Jo Coll Nottm MA95. d 97 p 98. C Melton Mowbray *Leic* 97-00; TV Cannock *Lich* 00-07; P-in-c Countesthorpe w Foston *Leic* from 07; Warden of Ev from 10. *The Vicarage, 102 Station Road, Countesthorpe, Leicester LE8 5TB* Tel 0116-278 4442 *or* 277 8643

HEBBORN, Roy Valentine Charles. S Dios Minl Tr Scheme 83. d 86 p 87. NSM Lewes All SS, St Anne, St Mich and St Thos *Chich* 86-00; NSM Lewes St Anne 00-01; rtd 01; Perm to Offic *Chich* from 03. *27 Greater Paddock, Ringmer, Lewes BN8 5LH* Tel (01273) 812005 E-mail roy.hebborn@connectfree.co.uk

HEBDEN, Mrs Cynthia Margaret. b 47. Univ of Wales (Ban) BTh94. d 94 p 97. NSM Llanfairpwll w Penmynydd *Ban* 94-95; C Twrcelyn Deanery 95-96; C Knighton St Mary Magd *Leic* 96-99; P-in-c Higham-on-the-Hill w Fenny Drayton and Witherley 99-02; P-in-c Stoke Golding w Dadlington 01-02; R Fenn Lanes Gp 02-03; V Shepshed and Oaks in Charnwood from 03; RD Akeley E 06-11. *1 Charles Hall Close, Shepshed, Loughborough LE12 9UP* Tel (01509) 508550 E-mail cynthia.hebden@talktalk.net

HEBDEN, John Percy. b 18. Sheff Univ 46 Lon Univ 67. St Aid Birkenhead 58. d 60 p 60. C Skipton H Trin *Brad* 60-62; R Kirby Misperton *York* 63-67; V Laxey *S & M* 70-83; V Lonan 80-83; rtd 84; Hon C Douglas St Geo and St Barn *S & M* 84-95. *Begra, Clayhead Road, Baldrine, Isle of Man IM4 6DN* Tel (01624) 861296

HEBDEN, Keith Oliver. b 76. Univ of Wales (Ban) BD98 MTh00 Warwick Univ PGCE01 Birm Univ PhD08. Qu Coll Birm 07. d 09 p 10. C Matson *Glouc* from 09. *58 Haycroft Drive, Matson, Gloucester GL4 6XX* Tel (01452) 311041

HEBER, Andrew John. b 63. Nottm Univ BA86 MA89 CQSW89. Trin Coll Bris BA99. d 99 p 00. C Parr *Liv* 99-03; TV Kirkby from 03. *St Andrew's Vicarage, 9 Redwood Way, Liverpool L33 4DU* Tel 0151-548 7969 E-mail gill.heber@bigfoot.com

HEBER PERCY, Canon Christopher John. b 41. St Jo Coll Cam BA64 MA68. Wells Th Coll 66. d 68 p 69. C Leigh St Mary *Man* 68-71; Asst Ind Chapl 71-80; P-in-c Oldham St Andr 75-78; TV Oldham 78-80; Ind Chapl *Win* 80-90; N Humberside Ind Chapl *York* 90-06; AD E Hull 98-06; Can and Preb York Minster 05-06; rtd 06. *59 Swarcliffe Road, Harrogate HG1 4QZ* Tel (01423) 884076 E-mail percy@lindisandchris.karoo.co.uk

HECTOR, Noel Antony. b 61. Sheff Univ LLB83 Barrister-at-Law 84. Oak Hill Th Coll BA91. d 91 p 92. C Rodbourne Cheney *Bris* 91-92; C Bris St Mary Redcliffe w Temple etc 92-95; R Wrington w Butcombe *B & W* 95-03; R E Clevedon w Clapton in Gordano etc from 03; Chapl N Bris NHS Trust from 03; RD Portishead *B & W* from 10. *The Rectory, All Saints' Lane, Clevedon BS21 6AU* Tel and fax (01275) 873257 E-mail eastcleveub@blueyonder.co.uk

HEDDERLY, Katherine. b 63. St Hugh's Coll Ox BA85 MA94. NTMTC BA06. d 06 p 07. C Bedford Park *Lon* 06-09; C St Martin-in-the-Fields from 09. *Flat 2, 6 St Martin's Place, London WC2N 4JH*

HEDDLE, Duncan. b 34. Wadh Coll Ox BA57 MA61 DPhil60. d 86 p 86. Chapl Aber Univ from 86; P-in-c Bucksburn from 90. *2 Douglas Place, High Street, Aberdeen AB24 3EA* Tel (01224) 485975 *or* 272888 E-mail d.heddle@abdn.ac.uk

HEDGECOCK, Jonathan James. b 64. Imp Coll Lon BScEng85 CEng MIET89. d 07 p 08. OLM Guildf H Trin w St Mary from 07. *8 Foxglove Gardens, Guildford GU4 7ES* Tel (01483) 502199 Mobile 07785-766631 E-mail jonathan.hedgecock@powerplanning.com

HEDGER, Canon Graham. b 57. Lon Bible Coll BA79. Ridley Hall Cam 81. d 83 p 84. C Walton *St E* 83-86; TV Mildenhall 86-91; R Swainsthorpe w Newton Flotman *Nor* 91-94; Dioc Evang Officer 91-94; Perm to Offic *St E* 95-99; Bp's Chapl and Liaison Officer 99-07; Bp's Policy and Liaison Officer from 07; P-in-c Clopton w Otley, Swilland and Ashbocking from 09; Hon Can St E Cathl from 04; Asst Dioc Sec from 10. *14 St Peter's Close, Charsfield, Woodbridge IP13 7RG* Tel (01473) 277042 E-mail graham@stedmundsbury.anglican.org

HEDGES, Mrs Anne Violet. b 53. Ripon Coll Cuddesdon 87. d 89 p 94. C Thetford *Nor* 89-94; P-in-c Garboldisham w Blo' Norton, Riddlesworth etc 94-97; R Guiltcross 97-00; Chapl Riddlesworth Hall Sch Nor 93-00; Dep Chapl HM Pris Leeds 00-01; Chapl HM Pris Leic 01-05; Chapl HM Pris Highpoint 05-09; Chapl HM Pris Bure from 09. *HM Prison Bure, Jaguar Drive, Scottow, Norwich NR10 5GB* Tel (01603) 326180 E-mail anne.hedges@hmps.gsi.gov.uk

HEDGES, Canon Dennis Walter. b 29. Sarum Th Coll. d 62 p 63. C Walton-on-Thames *Guildf* 62-66; C Westborough 66-69; V

Blackheath and Chilworth 69-79; R Farncombe 79-94; RD Godalming 84-89; Hon Can Guildf Cathl 92-94; rtd 94; Perm to Offic *Guildf* 94-07; *Win* from 94; *Portsm* from 99. *21 Lincoln Green, Alton GU34 1SX* Tel and fax (01420) 542624 Mobile 07989-110454 E-mail dennisw.hedges@lineone.net

HEDGES, Ian Charles. b 55. Sarum & Wells Th Coll 79. **d** 82 **p** 83. C Chessington *Guildf* 82-85; C Fleet 85-90; Dioc Adv on Homelessness from 87; V S Farnborough from 90; Tr Officer for Past Assts 91-00. *The Vicarage, 1 St Mark's Close, Farnborough GU14 6PP* Tel (01252) 544711 E-mail smarksfbro@btinternet.com

HEDGES, Canon Jane Barbara. b 55. St Jo Coll Dur BA78. Cranmer Hall Dur 78. **dss** 80 **d** 87 **p** 94. Fareham H Trin *Portsm* 80-83; Southampton (City Cen) *Win* 83-87; Par Dn 87-88; Dioc Stewardship Adv *Portsm* 88-93; Can Res Portsm Cathl 93-01; P-in-c Honiton, Gittisham, Combe Raleigh, Monkton etc *Ex* 01-03; TR 03-06; RD Honiton 03-06; Can Steward Westmr Abbey from 06. *2 Little Cloister, London SW1P 3PL* Tel (020) 7654 4867 *or* 7654 4815 Fax 7654 4811 E-mail jane.hedges@westminster-abbey.org

HEDGES, Mrs Jane Rosemary. b 44. RGN65. S Dios Minl Tr Scheme 86. **d** 89 **p** 94. NSM Gillingham *Sarum* 89-04; NSM Gillingham and Milton-on-Stour 04-08; Lic to RD Blackmore Vale from 08. *Dene Hollow, Wyke Road, Gillingham SP8 4NG* Tel (01747) 822812 E-mail denehollow@msn.com

HEDGES, John Michael Peter. b 34. Leeds Univ BA60. Ripon Hall Ox 60. **d** 61 **p** 62. C Weaste *Man* 61-65; V Ashton St Pet 65-74; C Easthampstead *Ox* 74-85; V Tilehurst St Geo 85-91; C Thatcham 91-94; TV 94-99; rtd 99; Perm to Offic *Ox* from 99. *39 Mallard Way, Grove, Wantage OX12 0QG* Tel (01235) 766834

HEDGES, Leslie Norman. b 26. Bris Univ BA51 Lon Univ BD56. Clifton Th Coll 48. **d** 53 **p** 54. C Summerstown *S'wark* 53-55; C Wolverhampton St Luke *Lich* 55-56; C Reigate St Mary *S'wark* 56-59; V Clapham Park All SS 59-70; V Findern *Derby* 70-82; V Willington 70-82; V Trowbridge St Thos and W Ashton *Sarum* 82-91; rtd 91; Perm to Offic *Truro* from 91. *16 Penwerris Road, Truro TR1 3QS* Tel (01872) 279858

HEDLEY, Charles John Wykeham. b 47. R Holloway Coll Lon BSc69 PhD73 Fitzw Coll Cam BA75 MA79. Westcott Ho Cam 73. **d** 76 **p** 77. C Chingford St Anne *Chelmsf* 76-79; C St Martin-in-the-Fields *Lon* 79-84 and 85-86; P-in-c 84-85; Chapl Ch Coll Cam 86-90; TR Gleadless *Sheff* 90-99; R Westmr St Jas *Lon* 99-09; rtd 09. *8 Clydesdale Avenue, Chichester PO19 7PW* E-mail chequal@googlemail.com

HEDLEY, Mrs Julia Margaret. b 56. Goldsmiths' Coll Lon BA78 Bedf Coll Lon MSc85 Liv Univ MTh03 SRN80. NOC 97. **d** 00 **p** 01. C Altrincham St Geo *Ches* 00-04; P/V Ches Cathl 04-07; Bps' Dom Chapl *B & W* from 07. *The Palace, Wells BA5 2PD* Tel (01749) 672341 Fax 679355 E-mail julia.hedley@bathwells.anglican.org

HEDLEY, William Clifford. b 35. Tyndale Hall Bris 65. **d** 67 **p** 68. C Hensingham *Carl* 67-69; C Rainhill *Liv* 69-71; C St Helens St Helen 71-73; V Low Elswick *Newc* 73-81; V Kingston upon Hull St Aid Southcoates *York* 81-87; TV Heworth H Trin 87-94; V Norton juxta Malton 94-97; C Newburn *Newc* 97-01; rtd 01. *21 Laburnum Grove, Sunniside, Newcastle upon Tyne NE16 5LY* Tel 0191-488 2908

HEDWORTH, Paul Simon James. b 56. Worc Coll of Educn BEd78. Qu Coll Birm BA(Theol)84. **d** 04 **p** 05. NSM Bacup and Stacksteads *Man* 04-06; Chapl Qu Eliz Gr Sch Blackb 98-06; Chapl Bromsgrove Sch from 06. *Bromsgrove School, Worcester Road, Bromsgrove B61 7DU* Tel (01527) 579679 Mobile 07966-503194 E-mail hedworthfamily@yahoo.co.uk

HEELEY, Mrs Janet. b 45. **d** 00 **p** 01. OLM Lich St Chad 00-10; rtd 10; Perm to Offic *Lich* from 10. *43 High Grange, Lichfield WS13 7DU* Tel (01543) 251600 E-mail janet.heeley@talktalk.net

HEELEY, Robert Francis. b 54. NOC 06. **d** 08 **p** 09. NSM Hadfield *Derby* from 08. *3 Chesham Close, Hadfield, Glossop SK13 1QX* Tel (01457) 855541 E-mail rob.heeley@uwclub.net

HEELEY, Mrs Ruth Mary. b 41. Qu Coll Birm 04. **d** 06 **p** 07. NSM Halas *Worc* 06-11; rtd 11; Perm to Offic *Worc* from 11. *4 Cherry Tree Lane, Halesowen B63 1DU* Tel 0121-550 7622 E-mail ruthmh@hotmail.co.uk

HEENAN, Vivienne Mary. b 48. Univ of Wales (Abth) BA70 SS Paul & Mary Coll Cheltenham PGCE90. STETS 03. **d** 06 **p** 07. NSM Whitwell and Niton *Portsm* 06-11; NSM Ventnor St Cath from 11; NSM Ventnor H Trin from 11; NSM Bonchurch from 11. *Dolphins House, Boxers Lane, Niton, Ventnor PO38 2BH* Tel and fax (01983) 730352 Mobile 07740-780767 E-mail vivienne.heenan@tiscali.co.uk

HEFFER, Thomas Patrick Peter. b 69. K Coll Lon BD90 AKC90 Univ of Wales (Cardiff) LLM03. Ripon Coll Cuddesdon 94. **d** 96 **p** 97. C Sprowston w Beeston *Nor* 96-98; Bp's Chapl and Press Officer 98-01; Min Sec Miss to Seafarers 01-05; Dir Chapl 05-09; Sec Gen from 09; Lic to Offic *Lon* and Perm to Offic *St Alb* from 01. *The Mission to Seafarers, St Michael Paternoster Royal, College Hill, London EC4R 2RL* Tel (020) 7248 5202 Fax 7248 4761 E-mail secgen@missiontoseafarers.org

HEFFER, William John Gambrell. b 30. AKC55. **d** 56 **p** 57. C Biggleswade *St Alb* 56-59; C Clacton St Jas *Chelmsf* 59-61; V Langford *St Alb* 61-67; V Luton All SS 67-73; P-in-c Eato Socon 73-75; V 75-77; Lic to Offic 78-81; R Wingrave w Rowsham, Aston Abbotts and Cublington *Ox* 81-88; R Wilder w Colmworth and Ravensden *St Alb* 88-91; C Leighton Buzzard w Eggington, Hockliffe etc 91-94; rtd 94; Perm to Offic *St Alb* 94-00 and from 01; *Ox* 97-01; P-in-c Empingham and Exton w Horn w Whitwell *Pet* 00-01. *Domus, 35 Pebblemoor, Edlesborough, Dunstable LU6 2HZ* Tel (01525) 220618

HEFFERNAN, Anna Elizabeth. *See* LINDSEY, Anna Elizabeth

HEGARTY, Ms Bernadette Grace. b 58. Man Poly BA81 Leeds Univ BA11 CQSW90. Coll of Resurr Mirfield 09. **d** 11. C High Harrogate St Pet *Ripon* from 11. *14 Christ Church Oval, Harrogate HG1 5AJ* E-mail bhgrace@hotmail.co.uk

HEGEDUS, Frank Michael. b 48. St Louis Univ BA71 Michigan State Univ MA76 Univ of St Thos St Paul MBA84. Colgate Rochester Div Sch DMin80. **d** 74. In RC Ch 74-87; R Northfields All SS and Dundas H Cross USA 88-90; R Farmington Advent 89-96; Asst P Orange Trin Ch 97-98; P-in-c Norwalk St Fran 98-99; NSM Budapest *Eur* 99-01; Asst P Huntington Beach St Wilfrid USA 01-02; R Redlands Trin Ch 02-03; R Plymouth St Jo 04-05; P-in-c El Cajon St Alb 05-08; R Del Mar St Pet 08-09; P-in-c Budapest from 11. *The Rectory, 2092 Budakeszi, Pf 25, Hungary* Tel (0036) (23) 452023 E-mail frankhegedus@hotmail.com

HEIGHT (formerly WATKINS), Susan Jane. b 58. Qu Coll Birm. **d** 01 **p** 02. C Edgbaston St Germain *Birm* 01-05; TV Salter Street and Shirley from 05. *18 Widney Lane, Solihull B91 3LS* Tel 0121-705 6586 E-mail sue-watkins@blueyonder.co.uk

HEIGHTON, George. b 55. Qu Coll Birm 08. **d** 11. NSM Bilton *Cov* from 11. *21 Dalkeith Avenue, Rugby CV22 7NN* Tel and fax (01788) 815514 Mobile 07766-478004 E-mail heighton@ntlworld.com

HEIGHTON, Miss Janet Elizabeth. b 67. Leeds Poly BSc92. Ripon Coll Cuddesdon. **d** 00 **p** 01. C Leeds Gipton Epiphany *Ripon* 00-04; P-in-c 04-07; TV Upholland *Liv* from 07. *158 Back Lane, Birleywood, Skelmersdale WN8 9BX* Tel (01695) 728091 E-mail janet@christtheservantchurch.org.uk

HEIL, Janet. b 53. Liv Univ BEd75 St Jo Coll Dur BA84 Cranmer Hall Dur. **dss** 85 **d** 87 **p** 94. Ashton Ch Ch *Man* 85-91; Par Dn 87-91; Par Dn Scotforth *Blackb* 91-94; C 94-95; V G Harwood St Bart 95-06; P-in-c Gt Harwood St Jo 02-06; Hon Can Blackb Cathl 04-06; Chapl Oslo w Bergen, Trondheim and Stavanger *Eur* from 06. *Harald Hårfagres Gate 2 (L512), 036 Oslo, Norway* Tel (0047) 2269 2214 Fax 2269 2163

HEINZE, Canon Rudolph William. b 31. Concordia Coll (USA) BSc56 CertEd56 De Paul Univ (USA) MA59 Univ of Iowa PhD65. **d** 86 **p** 87. NSM London Colney St Pet *St Alb* 86-98; Lect Oak Hill Th Coll 86-98; Sen Tutor 88-94; Vice-Prin 94-97; Visiting Scholar from 99; Hon Can Port Sudan from 94; Hon Prof Middx Univ from 98. *1714D Lakecliffe Drive, Wheaton IL 60187-8368, USA* Tel (001) (630) 588 8954 E-mail revrudi@aol.com

HELEN, Sister. *See* LODER, Sister Helen

HELEY, John. b 28. Lon Univ BA72. Bps' Coll Cheshunt 54. **d** 56 **p** 57. C Claremont St Sav S Africa 57-61; C Wimborne Minster *Sarum* 61-62; V Narborough w Narford *Nor* 62-67; R Pentney St Mary Magd w W Bilney 62-67; V Catton 67-69; Lic to Offic *Ox* 69-72; R E w W Rudham *Nor* 72-75; P-in-c Houghton 72-74; V 74-75; V Hunstanton St Edm 75-82; V Hunstanton St Edm w Ringstead 82-83; rtd 88. *24 Kestrel Close, Burnham Market, King's Lynn PE31 8EF* Tel (01328) 730036

HELFT, Gunter. b 23. Lon Univ BA48. Ely Th Coll 46. **d** 48 **p** 49. Chapl Essex Home Sch Chelmsf 48-52; C Chelmsf Ascension 48-49; C Billesley Common *Birm* 52-53; Miss to Seamen 53-62; Japan 53-57; Sudan 57; Sec HQ 57-62; Bp's Youth Officer *Ox* 62-65; Tr Officer C of E Youth Coun 65-67; Hd Master Abbey Temple's Sch Lambeth 67-71; Hd Master Don Valley High Sch Yorkshire 71-80; rtd 80; Perm to Offic *Worc* from 87. *7 Cripplegate House, St Clement's Close, Worcester WR2 5BA* Tel (01905) 421496 E-mail ghelft@btinternet.com

HELLARD, Dawn Yvonne Lorraine. b 47. St Mich Coll Llan 88. **d** 91 **p** 97. C Llantwit Major 91-95; TV Cowbridge 95-05; rtd 05. *10 Maes Lloi, Aberthin, Cowbridge CF71 7HA* Tel (01446) 772460

HELLEWELL, John. b 63. Bris Univ BSc86 BTh93 Nottm Univ MA94. St Jo Coll Nottm 93. **d** 94 **p** 95. C Greasbrough *Sheff* 94-98; P-in-c High Hoyland, Scissett and Clayton W Wake 98-04; V Mount Pellon 04-09; V Halifax St Aug and Mount Pellon from 09; Warden of Readers from 04. *The Vicarage, Church Lane, Halifax HX2 0EF* Tel (01422) 365027 E-mail revjhell@blueyonder.co.uk

HELLICAR, Hugh Christopher. b 37. Qu Coll Birm 69. **d** 70 **p** 71. C Bromyard *Heref* 70-73; C Bishop's Castle w Mainstone 73-77; Perm to Offic *S'wark* 77-85 and *Chich* 83-93; NSM Hove Chic 93-98; rtd 02. *74 Marina, St Leonards-on-Sea TN38 0BJ* Tel (01424) 444072

HELLIER, Jeremy Peter. b 53. K Coll Lon BD75 AKC75 QTS01. St Aug Coll Cant 75. **d** 76 **p** 77. C Walton *St E* 76-79; C Ipswich St Fran 79-80; C Wolborough w Newton Abbot *Ex* 80-82; CF 82-84; R Pendine w Llanmiloe and Eglwys Gymyn w Marros *St D* 84-89; TR Widecombe-in-the-Moor, Leusdon, Princetown etc *Ex* 89-94; CF (TAVR) 90-03; RD Moreton *Ex* 91-94; Chapl and Hd RE Wellington Sch Somerset from 94; Hon Chapl Miss to Seafarers from 02. *Wellington School, Wellington TA21 8NT* Tel (01823) 668827 *or* 668837 Fax 668844 Mobile 07971-588184 E-mail jeremyhellier@hotmail.com

HELLINGS, Mrs Tara Charmian Lashmar. b 68. Ch Ch Ox MA90. STETS 06. **d** 09 **p** 10. NSM Alton *Win* from 09; Chapl Alton Coll from 11. *Serendib, 1 Poacher's Field, South Warnborough, Hook RG29 1RB* Tel (01256) 862810 Mobile 07932-184873 E-mail tartzhellings@yahoo.co.uk

HELLIWELL, Mrs Judith Hazel. b 46. Dioc OLM tr scheme 99. **d** 01 **p** 02. OLM Meltham *Wakef* from 01. *3 Upper Wilshaw, Meltham, Holmfirth HD9 4EA* Tel (01484) 851158

HELLMUTH, Miss Lynn. b 61. Lon Bible Coll BA82 Birm Univ PGCE83. Wycliffe Hall Ox 00. **d** 02 **p** 03. C Twickenham Common H Trin *Lon* 02-05; TV Crawley *Chich* 05-08; V Stoneleigh *Guildf* from 08. *The Vicarage, 59 Stoneleigh Park Road, Epsom KT19 0QU* Tel (020) 8393 3738 E-mail lynnhellmuth@yahoo.co.uk

HELLYER, Stephen John. b 56. St Cath Coll Cam BA77 MA81. Wycliffe Hall Ox 82. **d** 84 **p** 85. C Plymouth St Andr w St Paul and St Geo *Ex* 84-88; Chapl Lee Abbey 88-89; Lon and SE Consultant CPAS 90-94; C Nottingham St Nic *S'well* 94-98; P-in-c Ox St Matt 98-10; R from 10. *St Matthew's Vicarage, Marlborough Road, Oxford OX1 4LW* Tel (01865) 243434 E-mail steve@hellyers.fsworld.co.uk

HELM, Alistair Thomas. b 53. Aston Univ BSc75. EAMTC 88. **d** 91 **p** 92. NSM Leic St Jas 91-95; NSM Humberstone 95-03; NSM Ascension TM 03-04; NSM Emmaus Par Team 04-09; NSM Giggleswick and Rathmell w Wigglesworth *Bradf* from 09. *The Vicarage, Bankwell Road, Giggleswick, Settle BD24 0AP* E-mail alistair.helm@btinternet.com

HELM, Catherine Mary. b 64. St Martin's Coll Lanc BEd86. St Jo Coll Nottm 03. **d** 05 **p** 06. C Heswall *Ches* 05-09; V Burton and Shotwick from 09. *The Vicarage, Vicarage Lane, Burton, Neston CH64 5TJ* Tel 0151-353 0453

HELM, Nicholas. b 57. Surrey Univ BSc81. St Jo Coll Nottm 85. **d** 88 **p** 89. C Old Ford St Paul w St Steph and St Mark *Lon* 88-92; TV Netherthorpe *Sheff* 92-93; V Sheff St Bart 93-98; Bp's Chapl 99-03; Bp's Adv in Spirituality 99-09; Chapl Whirlow Grange Conf Cen Sheff 99-09; Continuing Minl Development Officer *Heref* from 10. *Address temp unknown*

HELMS, David Clarke. b 50. Boston Univ BA72. Yale Div Sch MDiv77. **d** 77 **p** 77. USA 77-88; Ind Chapl *Worc* 88-97; Ind Chapl Teesside *York* 97-02; Dir Workplace Min for Ch in Soc *Roch* from 05. *3 Royal Oak Terrace, Gravesend DA12 1JU* Tel (01474) 321593 Mobile 07957-193816 E-mail davidh@churchinsociety.org

HELYER, Patrick Joseph Peter. b 15. ALCD39 FRGS83. Wycliffe Hall Ox 38. **d** 38 **p** 39. C Maidstone St Paul *Cant* 38-41; Asst Chapl Miss to Seamen 41-42; Chapl RNVR 42-46; V St Nicholas at Wade w Sarre *Cant* 46-50; Chapl RAN Australia 51-61; V Rolvenden *Cant* 62-66; R Frome St Quintin w Evershot and Melbury Bubb *Sarum* 66-71; R Ch Ch Cathl Falkland Is 71-75; Hon Can Port Stanley 72-75; R Streat w Westmeston *Chich* 75-78; P-in-c Tristan da Cunha 78-81; rtd 81; Perm to Offic *Heref* 84-00; *Glouc* from 84. *c/o C J A Helyer Esq, Eight Bells, South Embankment, Dartmouth TQ6 9BB*

HEMINGRAY, Raymond. b 47. Leeds Univ LLB68 Solicitor 71. ERMC 04. **d** 07 **p** 08. Dioc Registrar *Pet* from 74; NSM Castor w Sutton and Upton w Marholm from 07; Perm to Offic *Ely* from 11. *4 Holywell Way, Peterborough PE3 6SS* Tel (01733) 262523 Fax 330280 Mobile 07860-227354 E-mail rh@raymondhemingray.co.uk

HEMINGWAY, Peter. b 32. S'wark Ord Course 72. **d** 75 **p** 76. NSM Belmont *S'wark* 75-79; C Herne Hill St Paul 79-81; V Headstone St Geo *Lon* 81-92; V N Harrow St Alb 87-02; rtd 02. *Chelmerton, 138 Winthrope Road, Bury St Edmunds IP33 3XW* Tel (01284) 705070

HEMMING, Andrew Martyn. b 56. Bath Univ BSc78. STETS 08. **d** 11. NSM Axbridge w Shipham and Rowberrow *B & W* from 11. *Eleuthera, Garston Lane, Blagdon, Bristol BS40 7TF* Tel (01761) 462582 Mobile 07584-124198 E-mail andrewhemming@btinternet.com

HEMMING, Terry Edward. b 47. Calvin Coll Michigan MA84. S Dios Minl Tr Scheme 88. **d** 90 **p** 91. NSM E Win 90-09; Chapl St Swithun's Sch Win 95-07; NSM Hurstbourne Priors, Longparish etc *Win* from 09. *St Nicholas House, Longparish, Andover SP11 6PG* Tel (01264) 720215 E-mail revhemm@yahoo.co.uk

HEMMING-CLARK, Stanley Charles. b 29. Peterho Cam BA52 MA56. Ridley Hall Cam 52. **d** 54 **p** 55. C Redhill H Trin *S'wark* 54-56; C Woking St Jo *Guildf* 56-59; V Crockenhill All So *Roch*

59-97; rtd 97; Perm to Offic *Guildf* from 97. *St Anthony's, 22 Ashcroft, Shalford, Guildford GU4 8JT* Tel (01483) 568197

HEMMINGS, Ms Jane Marie. b 68. Lon Univ BD91 AKC91 Heythrop Coll Lon MTh95 Southn Univ PGCE08. NTMTC 01. **d** 03 **p** 04. C Bishop's Waltham and Upham *Portsm* 03-08; NSM 07-08; NSM Akeman *Ox* from 08. *The Rectory, Troy Lane, Kirtlington, Kidlington OX5 3HA* Tel (01869) 350224 E-mail dauphin.jg@btinternet.com

HEMMINGS, Keith. b 43. **d** 97. Par Dn Bedwellty *Mon* 97-05; Par Dn Bedwellty w New Tredegar 05-06; Perm to Offic from 06. *Penydarren, Park Drive, Bargoed CF81 8PJ* Tel (01443) 830662

HEMMINGS, Roy Anthony. b 48. Univ of Wales (Cardiff) BD85 MTh00. St Mich Coll Llan 82. **d** 86 **p** 87. C Rhyl w St Ann *St As* 86-90; CF 90-08; V Maybush and Southampton St Jude *Win* from 08. *Maybush Vicarage, Sedbergh Road, Southampton SO16 9HJ* Tel (023) 8070 3443 Mobile 07710-774431 E-mail padreroy48@aol.com

HEMPHILL, John James. b 44. TCD BA68 MA72. Oak Hill Th Coll 71. **d** 73 **p** 74. C Dundonald *D & D* 73-78; I Balteagh w Carrick *D & R* 78-02; I Ballyhalbert w Ardkeen *D & D* from 02. *Ballyeasboro Rectory, 187 Main Road, Portavogie, Newtownards BT22 1DA* Tel (028) 4277 1234 Mobile 07890-012843

HEMSLEY, David Ridgway. b 36. AKC61. **d** 61 **p** 62. C Penhill *Bris* 61-64; C Highworth w Sevenhampton and Inglesham etc 64-66; C Surbiton St Andr *S'wark* 67-70; P-in-c Tingewick w Water Stratford *Ox* 70-75; P-in-c Radclive 72-75; PM N Marston w Granborough etc 75-81; P-in-c Quainton 75-81; TV Schorne 81-90; P-in-c Lt Missenden 90-93; V 93-01; rtd 01; Perm to Offic *Ox* from 03; AD Buckingham 09-10. *27 Green Avenue, Buckingham MK18 1LG* Tel (01280) 814636

HEMSLEY HALLS, Susan Mary. b 59. Cranmer Hall Dur 93. **d** 95 **p** 96. C Wilnecote *Lich* 95-00; P-in-c Attenborough *S'well* from 00; Dioc Chapl amongst Deaf People from 00. *Vale Cottage, 19 Church Lane, Attenborough, Beeston NG9 6AS* Tel 0115-925 9602 E-mail mail@smca.fsworld.co.uk

HEMSTOCK, Julian. b 51. Trent Poly BSc74 CEng MIProdE. Sarum & Wells Th Coll 89. **d** 91 **p** 92. C Carrington *S'well* 91-94; C Basford St Aid 94-97; Asst Chapl Qu Medical Cen Nottm Univ Hosp NHS Trust 97-03; Chapl from 03. *Queen's Medical Centre University Hospital, Derby Road, Nottingham NG7 2UH* Tel 0115-924 9924 ext 43799 E-mail julian.hemstock@qmc.nhs.uk

HEMSTOCK, Mrs Pat. b 51. Sarum & Wells Th Coll 89. **d** 91 **p** 95. Par Dn Carrington *S'well* 91-94; Par Dn Basford St Aid 94-95; C 95-97; P-in-c 97-05; V Calverton from 05. *The Vicarage, Crookdole Lane, Calverton, Nottingham NG14 6GF* Tel 0115-965 2552 E-mail pat.hemstock@btinternet.com

HEMSWORTH, John Alan. b 45. FGA67. **d** 02 **p** 03. OLM Droylsden St Andr *Man* 02-10; P-in-c from 10. *St Andrew's Rectory, Merton Drive, Droylsden, Manchester M43 6BH* Tel 0161-370 3242 E-mail john.hemsworth@ntlworld.com

HENDERSON, Canon Alastair Roy. b 27. BNC Ox BA51 MA54. Ridley Hall Cam 52. **d** 54 **p** 55. C Ex St Leon w H Trin 54-57; Travelling Sec IVF 57-60; C St Mary le Bow w St Pancras Soper Lane etc *Lon* 58-60; V Barton Hill St Luke w Ch Ch *Bris* 60-68; P-in-c Bris St Phil and St Jacob w Em 67-68; V Stoke Bishop 68-92; Lect Clifton Th Coll 69-71; Lect Trin Coll Bris 71-73; RD Westbury and Severnside *Bris* 73-79; Hon Can Bris Cathl 80-92; rtd 92; Perm to Offic *Ex* from 92. *3 Garden Court, Cricketfield Lane, Budleigh Salterton EX9 6PN* Tel (01395) 446147

HENDERSON, Andrew Douglas. b 36. Trin Coll Cam BA60 MA64 Liv Univ DASS65 MBASW. Cuddesdon Coll 60. **d** 62 **p** 63. C Newington St Paul *S'wark* 62-64; Hon C Camberwell St Luke 65-80; Perm to Offic *Lon* 85-06 and *Chich* from 06. *4 Western Terrace, Brighton BN1 2LD* Tel (01273) 327829

HENDERSON, Ashley. *See* HENDERSON, Peter Ashley

HENDERSON, Colin. *See* HENDERSON, Francis Colin

HENDERSON, Daniel Thomas. b 81. Nottm Univ BSc03. Oak Hill Th Coll BTh10. **d** 10 **p** 11. C Hailsham *Chich* from 10. *19 St Wilfred's Green, Hailsham BN27 1DR* Tel (01323) 843261 Mobile 07734-928877 E-mail dan-henderson@hotmail.co.uk

HENDERSON, David. *See* HENDERSON, Robert David Druitt

HENDERSON, David. b 35. Oak Hill NSM Course. **d** 83 **p** 84. NSM Rush Green *Chelmsf* 83-00; Perm to Offic from 00. *Le Strange Cottages, 2-8 Hunstanton Road, Heacham, King's Lynn PE31 7HH* Tel (01485) 572150

HENDERSON, Mrs Elizabeth. b 42. CITC 96. **d** 99 **p** 00. C Ballymacash *Conn* 99-00; C Finaghy from 00; Asst Chapl Belfast City Hosp Health and Soc Services Trust 99-05; Asst Chapl Down Lisburn Health and Soc Services Trust from 05. *39 Garvey Court, Lisburn BT27 4DG* Tel (028) 9260 7146 E-mail hclerics@msn.com

HENDERSON, Francis Colin. b 35. St Cath Coll Cam BA59 MA63. Cuddesdon Coll 60. **d** 62 **p** 63. C Croydon St Jo *Cant* 62-67; V Westwood *Cov* 67-75; V Chilvers Coton w Astley 75-80; P-in-c Wolston 80; P-in-c Church Lawford w Newnham Regis 80; V Wolston and Church Lawford 80-85; USA from 85; rtd 00. *1364 Katella Street, Laguna Beach CA 92651-3247, USA* Tel (001) (949) 497 2239 E-mail echenderson@earthlink.net

HENDERSON, The Ven Janet. b 57. St Jo Coll Dur BA88 RGN82. Cranmer Hall Dur 85. **d** 88 **p** 94. Par Dn Wisbech SS Pet and Paul *Ely* 88-90; Par Dn Bestwood *S'well* 90-93; Tutor St Jo Coll Nottm 92-97; Lect Worship 93-97; NSM Bramcote *S'well* 94-97; Lect Worship and Tutor Ridley Hall Cam 97-01; Dir Studies 00-01; P-in-c Nuthall *S'well* 01-07; Dean of Women's Min 01-07; AD Beeston 06-07; Hon Can S'well Minster 03-07; Adn Richmond *Ripon* from 07; Hon Can Ripon Cathl from 11; Dioc Adv for NSM from 11. *Hoppus House, Hutton Conyers, Ripon HG4 5DX* Tel and fax (01765) 601316
E-mail janeth@riponleeds-diocese.org.uk

HENDERSON, Mrs Janet Elizabeth. b 53. N Lon Poly BSc75. Ripon Coll Cuddesdon 05. **d** 06 **p** 07. NSM Ellesborough, The Kimbles and Stoke Mandeville *Ox* 06-09; R from 09. *The Rectory, 28A Risborough Road, Stoke Mandeville, Aylesbury HP22 5UT* Tel (01296) 612855
E-mail brook-farm@supanet.com

HENDERSON, Judith Ann. b 37. **d** 89 **p** 94. NSM Sheringham *Nor* 89-92; NSM Brampton St Thos *Derby* 92-00; Perm to Offic *Sarum* from 00. *Blackmore House, Stone Lane, Wimborne BH21 1HD* Tel (01202) 881422

HENDERSON, The Ven Julian Tudor. b 54. Keble Coll Ox BA76 MA81. Ridley Hall Cam 77. **d** 79 **p** 80. C Islington St Mary *Lon* 79-83; V Hastings Em and St Mary in the Castle *Chich* 83-92; V Claygate *Guildf* 92-05; RD Emly 96-01; Adn Dorking from 05; Hon Can Guildf Cathl from 02. *The Old Cricketers, Portsmouth Road, Ripley, Woking GU23 6ER* Tel (01483) 479300
E-mail julian.henderson@cofeguildford.org.uk

HENDERSON, Nicholas Paul. b 48. Selw Coll Cam BA73 MA77 Univ of Wales (Lamp) PhD09. Ripon Hall Ox 73. **d** 75 **p** 76. C St Alb St Steph *St Alb* 75-78; Warden J F Kennedy Ho Cov Cathl 78-79; C Bow w Bromley St Leon *Lon* 79-85; P-in-c W Acton St Martin 85-96; V from 96; P-in-c Ealing All SS 89-95; V from 96. *The Parishes Office, 25 Birch Grove, London W3 9SP* Tel (020) 8992 2333 *or* 8248 0608 Fax 8993 5812
E-mail nicholashenderson@btinternet.com

HENDERSON, Olive Elizabeth. b 48. St Jo Coll Nottm. **d** 97 **p** 98. Aux Min Tallaght *D & G* 97-99; P-in-c Moviddy Union *C, C & R* 99-01; P-in-c Rathdrum w Glenealy, Derralossary and Laragh *D & G* 01-04; C 04-07; I 07-08; I Killeshin w Cloydagh and Killabban *C & O* 08-10; Chapl Kingston Coll Mitchelstown from 10. *31 Kingston College, Mitchelstown, Co Cork, Republic of Ireland* Tel (00353) 87-218 1891 (mobile)
E-mail oliveernest@hotmail.com

HENDERSON, Patrick James. b 57. R Holloway Coll Lon BA78 Surrey Univ PGCE01. St-Steph Ho Ox 83. **d** 86 **p** 87. C Hornsey St Mary w St Geo *Lon* 86-90; V Whetstone St Jo 90-95; In RC Ch 95-01; Perm to Offic *Lon* 01-02; C Hornsey H Innocents 02-07; C Stroud Green H Trin 02-04; P-in-c 04-07; V from 07; C Hornsey H Innocents from 07; C Harringay St Paul from 10; Chapl Greig City Academy from 02. *Holy Trinity Vicarage, Granville Road, London N4 4EL* Tel (020) 8340 2051 Mobile 07947-714893
E-mail pjhenderson2001@yahoo.co.uk

HENDERSON, Peter Ashley. b 59. St Martin's Coll Lanc PGCE00. CBDTI 02. **d** 05 **p** 06. NSM Arnside *Carl* 05-08; NSM Kendal H Trin from 08. *2 Lowther Park, Kendal LA9 6RS* Tel (01539) 736079 E-mail janash@btinternet.com

HENDERSON, Richard. b 69. St Jo Coll Nottm 04. **d** 06 **p** 07. C Beccles St Mich and St Luke *St E* 06-09; TV Sole Bay from 09. *The Rectory, 45 Wangford Road, Reydon, Southwold IP18 6PZ* Tel (01502) 722192 E-mail richhenderson@btinternet.com

✠**HENDERSON, The Rt Revd Richard Crosbie Aitken.** b 57. Magd Coll Ox MA84 DPhil84. St Jo Coll Nottm 83. **d** 86 **p** 87 **c** 98. C Chinnor w Emmington and Sydenham etc *Ox* 86-89; I Abbeystrewry Union *C, C & R* 89-95; I Ross Union 95-98; Dean Ross 95-98; Chan Cork Cathl 95-98; Bp T, K & A 98-11; TV Heart of Eden *Carl* from 11; Hon Asst Bp Carl from 11. *The Vicarage, Appleby-in-Westmorland CA16 6QW* Tel (017683) 51461 E-mail richardhenderson589@btinternet.com

HENDERSON, Robert. b 43. TCD 66 Lambeth STh94. **d** 69 **p** 70. C Drumglass *Arm* 69-72; Chapl Miss to Seamen 72-77; Sen Chapl Mombasa Kenya 77-78; I Mostrim w Granard, Clonbroney, Killoe etc *K, E & A* 78-82; I Belfast St Matt *Conn* 82-92; I Kilroot and Templecorran 92-98; rtd 98. *39 Garvey Court, Lisburn BT27 4DG* Tel (028) 9260 7146
E-mail hclerics@tesco.net

HENDERSON, Robert David Druitt. b 41. St Edm Hall Ox MA64 Brunel Univ MA77 K Alfred's Coll Win PGCE88. **d** 03 **p** 04. OLM Wylye and Till Valley *Sarum* 03-10; rtd 10. *Orchard House, Salisbury Road, Steeple Langford, Salisbury SP3 4NQ* Tel (01722) 790388 E-mail henderson.family@virgin.net

HENDERSON, Mrs Shirley Claire. b 49. Surrey Univ BA02. Bp Otter Coll 94. **d** 96 **p** 02. NSM Gatcombe, Chale and Shorwell w Kingston *Portsm* 96-00; NSM Whitwell, Niton and St Lawrence 00-03; P-in-c Shedfield 03-06; R Shedfield and Wickham 07; TV Parkham, Alwington, Buckland Brewer etc *Ex* from 07; RD Hartland from 09. *The Vicarage, Hartland, Bideford EX39 6BP* Tel (01237) 440229 E-mail shirley.1949@hotmail.co.uk

HENDERSON, Terry James. b 45. St Deiniol's Hawarden 76. **d** 77 **p** 77. C Wrexham *St As* 77-79; Wilson Carlile Coll of Evang 79-81; TV Langtree *Ox* 81-87; P-in-c Aston Cantlow and Wilmcote w Billesley *Cov* 87-90; V 90-97; V St Peter-in-Thanet *Cant* 97-02; R Elmley Castle w Bricklehampton and Combertons *Worc* from 02; C Overbury w Teddington, Eaton etc from 09. *The Rectory, 22 Parkwood, Elmley Castle, Pershore WR10 3HT* Tel (01386) 710394
E-mail terryhenderson@onetel.com

HENDERSON, William Ernest. b 53. CEng81 MICE81 Southn Univ BSc75. St Jo Coll Nottm 87. **d** 89 **p** 90. C Win Ch Ch 89-93; V Stanley *Wakef* from 93. *The Vicarage, 379 Aberford Road, Stanley, Wakefield WF3 4HE* Tel (01924) 822143 *or* 835746
E-mail billh@stpeters-stanley.org.uk

HENDERSON, William Ralph. b 32. Oak Hill Th Coll 65. **d** 67 **p** 68. C Littleover *Derby* 67-68; C Nottingham St Sav *S'well* 68-74; V Alne *York* 75-92; Chapl York Distr Hosp 86-92; rtd 92; Perm to Offic *York* 92-11. *15 Drakes Close, Huntington, York YO32 9GN* Tel (01904) 761741

HENDERSON SMITH, Mrs Judith Hazel. b 55. De Montfort Univ BSc00 Nottm Univ MA11. EMMTC 08. **d** 11. NSM Alvaston *Derby* from 11. *91 Nottingham Road, Long Eaton, Nottingham NG10 2BU* Tel and fax 0115-946 0395 Mobile 07810-580340 E-mail jhhs91@hotmail.com

HENDRICKSE, Canon Clarence David. b 41. Nottm Univ PGCE73 CEng MIMechE71. St Jo Coll Nottm 71. **d** 74 **p** 75. C St Helens St Helen *Liv* 74-76; C Netherley Ch Ch CD 76-77; TV 78-87; V Liv Ch Ch Norris Green 87-93; V Eccleston Ch Ch 93-06; Hon Can Liv Cathl 96-06; rtd 06. *Highfield, 17 Meadow Road, Windermere LA23 2EU* Tel (015394) 43058
E-mail canon.clarence.hendrickse@talktalk.net

HENDRY, Felicity Ann. b 65. **d** 10 **p** 11. NSM Crawley *Chich* from 10. *21 East Park, Crawley RH10 6AN*

HENDRY, Mrs Helen Clare. b 58. Lanc Univ BA79 Cam Univ PGCE80. Reformed Th Sem Mississippi MA85 Oak Hill Th Coll 94. **d** 95. Lect Oak Hill Th Coll 86-08; NSM Muswell Hill St Jas w St Matt *Lon* from 95. *44 The Grove, London N13 5JR* Tel (020) 8882 2186 *or* 8883 6277
E-mail clare.hendry@st-james.org.uk

HENDRY, Leonard John. b 34. St D Coll Lamp 65. **d** 68 **p** 69. C Minchinhampton *Glouc* 68-71; C Bishop's Cleeve 71-74; V Cheltenham St Mich 74-78; V Horsley and Newington Bagpath w Kingscote 78-82; Chapl Salonika *Eur* 82-91; rtd 94. *Stratigi 34, Pilea, 543 52 Salonika, Greece* Tel (0030) (31) 281193

HENDY, Canon Graham Alfred. b 45. St Jo Coll Dur BA67 MA75 Fitzw Coll Cam CertEd Univ of Wales (Lamp) MTh03 MPhil07. Sarum Th Coll 67. **d** 70 **p** 71. C High Wycombe *Ox* 70-75; TV 75-78; R Upton cum Chalvey 78-83; TR 83-90; R S Walsham and Upton *Nor* 90-97; Dioc Lay Tr Officer 90-97; Can Res S'well Minster 97-02; R Upper Itchen *Win* 02-08; rtd 08. *74 Bath Road, Wells BA5 3LJ* Tel (01749) 677003

HENEY, William Butler. b 22. Potchefstroom Univ BA99. CITC. **d** 60 **p** 61. C Seagoe *D & D* 60-63; I Carrickmacross *Clogh* 64-73; I Newbridge w Carnalway and Kilcullen *M & K* 73-95; Treas Kildare Cathl 81-86; Can Kildare Cathl 81-95; Adn Kildare 86-94; rtd 95; Chapl Mageough Home *D & G* from 96. *14 Trees Road, Mount Merrion, Blackrock, Co Dublin, Republic of Ireland* Tel (00353) (1) 288 9773

HENGIST, Barry. b 59. N Lon Poly BA88. Ripon Coll Cuddesdon 07. **d** 09 **p** 10. C Weybridge *Guildf* from 09. *87 Greenlands Road, Weybridge KT13 8PS* Tel (01932) 821196 Mobile 07947-068209 E-mail barryhengist@f2s.com

HENIG, Martin Edward. b 42. St Cath Coll Cam BA63 MA66 Worc Coll Ox DPhil72 DLitt98 FSA75. St Steph Ho Ox 08. **d** 10 **p** 11. NSM Osney *Ox* from 10. *16 Alexandra Road, Oxford OX2 0DB* Tel (01865) 241118
E-mail martin.henig@arch.ox.ac.uk

HENLEY, Claud Michael. b 31. Keble Coll Ox BA55 MA59. Chich Th Coll 55. **d** 57 **p** 58. C Cowley St Jas *Ox* 57-60; C Wetherby *Ripon* 60-63; C Brighton St Pet *Chich* 63-69; V Brighton St Jo 69-75; V New Groombridge 75-96; rtd 96; Perm to Offic *Chich* from 97. *12 Barn Stables, De Montfort Road, Lewes BN7 1ST* Tel (01273) 472467

HENLEY, David Edward. b 44. Sarum & Wells Th Coll 69. **d** 72 **p** 73. C Fareham H Trin *Portsm* 72-76; C-in-c Leigh Park St Clare CD 76-78; R Freshwater 78-87; RD W Wight 83-87; R Meonstoke w Corhampton cum Exton 87-02; R Droxford 87-02; RD Bishop's Waltham 93-98; Hon Can Portsm Cathl 96-02; TR Chalke Valley *Sarum* from 02; RD Chalke from 07. *The Vicarage, Newtown, Broad Chalke, Salisbury SP5 5DS* Tel (01722) 780262 E-mail david.henley257@btinternet.com

HENLEY, Dean. b 64. St Chad's Coll Dur BA93. Westcott Ho Cam 95. **d** 96 **p** 97. C Farncombe *Guildf* 95-99; TV Hale w Badshot Lea 99-06; R Campton, Clophill and Haynes *St Alb* from 06. *The Rectory, 4A North Lane, Haynes, Bedford MK45 3PW* Tel (01234) 381235
E-mail deanhenley@waitrose.com

HENLEY, John Francis Hugh. b 48. SS Mark & Jo Coll Chelsea CertEd69. St Mich Coll Llan. **d** 82 **p** 83. C Griffithstown *Mon*

82-85; V St Hilary Greenway 85-90; P-in-c Fulham St Etheldreda w St Clem *Lon* from 90. *St Etheldreda's Vicarage, Doneraile Street, London SW6 6EL* Tel (020) 7736 3809

HENLEY, Michael. *See* HENLEY, Claud Michael

✠**HENLEY, The Rt Revd Michael Harry George.** b 38. CB91. Lon Coll of Div. **d** 61 **p** 62 **c** 95. C St Marylebone w H Trin *Lon* 61-64; Chapl RN 64-68 and 74-89; Chapl of the Fleet and Adn for the RN 89-93; Dir Gen Naval Chapl Services 92-93; Chapl St Andr Univ 68-72; Chapl R Hosp Sch Holbrook 72-74; QHC 89-93; Hon Can Gib Cathl 89-93; P-in-c Pitlochry *St And* 94-95; Bp St And 95-04; rtd 04. *West Chattan, Mavis Haugh, 108 Hepburn Gardens, St Andrews KY16 9LT* Tel (01334) 473167

HENLY, Francis Michael. b 25. Sarum Th Coll. **d** 67 **p** 68. C E w W Harnham *Sarum* 67-70; P-in-c Stour Provost w Todbere 70-75; P-in-c Rowde 75-79; V 79-83; R Poulshot 79-83; V Bishop's Cannings, All Cannings etc 83-92; rtd 92; Perm to Offic *Sarum* from 92. *Oldbury View, Middle Lane, Cherhill, Calne SN11 8XX* Tel (01249) 815191

HENNING, Mrs Judy. b 49. Portsm Univ MSc99. S Dios Minl Tr Scheme 85. **d** 88 **p** 97. C Catherington and Clanfield *Portsm* 88-91; C Leigh Park 91-92; Perm to Offic 94-96; Min in Whiteley and Asst to RD Fareham 96-99; C-in-c Whiteley CD 99-04; P-in-c Old Cleeve, Leighland and Treborough *B & W* 04-06; R 06-11; P-in-c Rainham *Roch* from 11. *The Vicarage, 80 Broadview Avenue, Gillingham ME8 9DE* Tel (01634) 231538 E-mail judy.henning@btinternet.com

HENNINGS, John Richard (Brother John). b 58. Sheff Univ BA80. Spurgeon's Coll BA87. **d** 07 **p** 08. SSF from 05; Perm to Offic *Ripon* 09-10 and *Sheff* 10-11. *The Friary, Hilfield, Dorchester DT2 7BE* Tel (01300) 341345 E-mail johnssf@franciscans.org.uk

HENRY, Cornelius Augustus. b 70. K Coll NY BA92 Heythrop Coll Lon MA06. NTMTC 07. **d** 09 **p** 10. C Hornchurch St Andr *Chelmsf* from 09. *49 Burnway, Hornchurch RM11 3SN* Tel (01708) 442868 E-mail cahenry70@yahoo.com

HENRY, Miss Jacqueline Margaret. b 40. Open Univ BA82. Trin Coll Bris 77. **dss** 83 **d** 87 **p** 94. Deptford St Jo *S'wark* 79-82; Catshill and Dodford *Worc* 83-86; The Lye and Stambermill 86-87; Par Dn 87-89; Educn Chapl 89-93; C Tolleshunt Knights w Tiptree and Gt Braxted *Chelmsf* 94-97; Chapl amongst Deaf People 94-97; TV Stantonbury and Willen *Ox* 97-02; rtd 02; Perm to Offic *Cant* 02-09. *114 Maidstone Road, Rochester ME1 3DT* Tel (01634) 829183

HENRY, Peter. b 49. BTh. St Jo Coll Nottm. **d** 84 **p** 85. C Sinfin Moor and Blagreaves St Andr CD *Derby* 84-89; V Guernsey St Jo *Win* 89-97; P-in-c Sawley *Derby* 97-01; R 01-06; rtd 06. *5 Les Casquets, Amherst Road, St Peter Port, Guernsey GY1 2DH* Tel (01481) 715609

HENRY, Canon Stephen Kenelm Malim. b 37. Brasted Th Coll 58 Bps' Coll Cheshunt 60. **d** 62 **p** 63. C Leic St Phil 62-67; CF 67-70; V Woodhouse *Wakef* 70-01; Hon Can Wakef Cathl 00-01; rtd 01; Perm to Offic Wakef from 01. *1 Yorkstone, Crosland Moor, Huddersfield HD4 5NQ* Tel (01484) 644807 E-mail mandsmalim64@btinternet.com

HENSHALL, Keith. *See* HENSHALL, Ronald Keith

✠**HENSHALL, The Rt Revd Michael.** b 28. St Chad's Coll Dur BA54. **d** 56 **p** 57 **c** 76. C Sewerby w Marton *York* 56-59; C Bridlington Quay H Trin 56-59; C-in-c Micklehurst CD *Ches* 59-62; V Micklehurst 62-63; V Altrincham St Geo 63-76; Hon Can Ches Cathl 72-76; Suff Bp Warrington *Liv* 76-96; rtd 96; Perm to Offic *Liv* 96-03 and *York* 96-99; Hon Asst Bp York from 99. *28 Hermitage Way, Sleights, Whitby YO22 5HG* Tel (01947) 811233

HENSHALL, Nicholas James. b 62. Wadh Coll Ox BA84 MA88. Ripon Coll Cuddesdon 85. **d** 88 **p** 89. C Blyth St Mary *Newc* 88-92; V Scotswood 92-02; Can Res Derby Cathl 02-08; V High Harrogate Ch Ch *Ripon* from 08. *Christ Church Vicarage, 11 St Hilda's Road, Harrogate HG2 8JX* Tel (01423) 883390

HENSHALL, Ronald Keith. b 54. Loughb Coll of Educn CertEd76. Chich Th Coll 87. **d** 89 **p** 90. C Ribbleton *Blackb* 89-92; TV 95-98; P-in-c Charlestown and Lowlands Nevis 92-95; V Ellel w Shireshead 98-02; Cyprus 02-05; Chapl R Alexandra and Albert Sch Reigate 05-06; P-in-c Lerwick and Burravoe *Ab* 06-10; V Holme-in-Cliviger w Worsthorne *Blackb* from 10. *The Vicarage, Gorple Road, Worsthorne, Burnley BB10 3NN* Tel (01282) 428478 E-mail keithhenshall@btinternet.com

HENSHAW, Nicholas Newell. b 49. Rhodes Univ BA72. Cuddesdon Coll 73. **d** 75 **p** 76. C Beaconsfield *Ox* 75-78; Chapl Wellington Coll Berks 78-80; C Pimlico St Pet w Westmr Ch Ch *Lon* 80-82; Chapl Sevenoaks Sch from 82; Hon C Sevenoaks St Nic *Roch* from 82; Perm to Offic *St E* from 08. *Sevenoaks School, High Street, Sevenoaks TN13 1HU* Tel (01732) 455133

HENSON, Carolyn. b 44. Bedf Coll Lon BA65 Nottm Univ MTh88 PhD97 Solicitor 75. EMMTC 82. **dss** 85 **d** 87 **p** 94. Braunstone *Leic* 85-89; Par Dn 87-89; Adult Educn and Tr Officer *Ely* 89-91; NSM Sutton and Witcham w Mepal 89-95; NSM Cainscross w Selsley *Glouc* 96-97; Vice Prin EMMTC *S'well* 97-01; R Morley w Smalley and Horsley Woodhouse

Derby 02-05; rtd 05; Chapl St Mich Hospice Harrogate from 09. *Ryedale View, Scagglethorpe, Malton YO17 8DY* E-mail carolyn.henson@virgin.net

HENSON, Joanna. b 06 **p** 07. NSM Egton-cum-Newland and Lowick and Colton *Carl* from 06. *Woodside Cottage, Colton, Ulverston LA12 8HE* Tel (01229) 861800 E-mail joannahenson@aol.com

HENSON, John David. b 49. EMMTC. **d** 00 **p** 01. NSM Beckingham w Walkeringham *S'well* 00-02; NSM Gringley-on-the-Hill 00-02; NSM Misterton and W Stockwith 02-05; C 06-07; C Beckingham w Walkeringham and Gringley 06-07; P-in-c Beckingham and Walkeringham and Misterton etc from 07; Asst Chapl HM Pris Whatton 00-05; Sen Police Chapl *S'well* from 03. *The Vicarage, 4 Church Lane, Misterton, Doncaster DN10 4AL* Tel (01427) 890270 E-mail jd.henson@btinternet.com

HENSON, Canon John Richard. b 40. Selw Coll Cam BA62 MA66. Ridley Hall Cam 62. **d** 65 **p** 66. C Ollerton *S'well* 65-68; Univs Sec CMS 68-73; Chapl Scargill Ho 73-78; V Shipley St Paul *Bradf* 78-83; TR Shipley St Paul and Frizinghall 83-91; V Ilkeston St Mary *Derby* 91-99; V Mickleover St Jo 99-05; Dioc Ecum Officer 96-05; Hon Can Derby Cathl 00-05; rtd 05; Perm to Offic *Derby* from 05. *6 Ganton Close, Nottingham NG3 3ET* E-mail john.henson3@ntlworld.com

HENSON, Shaun Christopher. b 64. E Nazarene Coll (USA) BA94 Duke Univ (USA) MDiv98 Regent's Park Coll Ox DPhil07. Wycliffe Hall Ox 03. **d** 04 **p** 05. C Blenheim *Ox* from 04; Chapl St Hugh's Coll Ox from 07. *St Hugh's College, St Margarets Road, Oxford OX2 6LE, or 19 Park Close, Bladon, Woodstock OX20 1RN* Tel (01865) 274955 Mobile 07795-547555 E-mail shaun.henson@st-hughs.ox.ac.uk

HENSTRIDGE, Edward John. b 31. Ex Coll Ox BA55 MA59 FCIPD77. Wells Th Coll 55. **d** 57 **p** 58. C Milton *Portsm* 57-62; V Soberton w Newtown 62-69; Lic to Offic *Derby* 69-71; Perm to Offic *Guildf* 72-84 and from 02; Lic to Offic 84-02; Bp's Officer for NSMs 97-01. *Hunters Moon, Lower Ham Lane, Elstead, Godalming GU8 6HQ* Tel (01252) 702272 E-mail johnhn@globalnet.co.uk

HENTHORNE, Thomas Roger. b 30. EAMTC. **d** 79 **p** 80. Hd Master St Mary's Sch St Neots 67-93; NSM St Neots *Ely* 79-04; Perm to Offic from 04. *Stapeley, 45 Berkley Street, Eynesbury, St Neots PE19 2NE* Tel (01480) 472548 E-mail roger.henthorne@tesco.net

HENTON, John Martin. b 48. AKC71 St Luke's Coll Ex DipEd72. St Aug Coll Cant 74. **d** 74 **p** 75. C Woolwich St Mary w H Trin *S'wark* 74-77; C Cotham St Mary *Bris* 77-78; C Cotham St Sav w St Mary 78-80; R Filton 80-87; Chapl Ex Sch and St Marg Sch 87-91; V Ex St Dav 91-09; rtd 09. *Upexe Cottage, Upexe, Exeter EX5 5ND* Tel (01392) 860038 E-mail j.henton@tesco.net

HENWOOD, Mrs Gillian Kathleen. b 56. ABIPP81 Lanc Univ MA97. CBDTI 94. **d** 97 **p** 98. NSM Whitechapel w Admarsh-in-Bleasdale *Blackb* 97-01; Rural Chapl 00-03; Bp's Adv for Leisure and Tourism 01-03; C Westmr St Jas *Lon* 03-04; V Nunthorpe *York* 04-09; P-in-c Riding Mill *Newc* 09-10; Chapl Shepherd's Dene Retreat Ho 09-10; Adv for Spirituality and Spiritual Direction 09-10; P-in-c Ribchester w Stidd *Blackb* 10-11; R from 11. *The Rectory, Riverside, Ribchester, Preston PR3 3XS* Tel (01254) 878352 E-mail gillhenwood@hotmail.com

HENWOOD, Martin John. b 58. DL05. Glas Univ BD81. Ripon Coll Cuddesdon. **d** 85 **p** 86. C Dartford H Trin *Roch* 85-88; C St Martin-in-the-Fields *Lon* 89-93; V Dartford H Trin *Roch* from 93. *The Vicarage, High Street, Dartford DA1 1RX* Tel (01322) 222782

HENWOOD, Canon Peter Richard. b 32. St Edm Hall Ox BA55 MA69. Cuddesdon Coll 56. **d** 57 **p** 58. C Rugby St Andr *Cov* 57-62; C-in-c Gleadless Valley CD *Sheff* 62-71; V Plaistow St Mary *Roch* 71-97; RD Bromley 79-96; Hon Can Roch Cathl 88-97; rtd 97. *Wayside, 1 Highfield Close, Sandling Road, Saltwood, Hythe CT21 4QP* Tel (01303) 230039

HENWOOD (née OAKLEY), Mrs Susan Mary. b 55. Salford Univ BSc76. St Jo Coll Nottm 84. **d** 87 **p** 94. Par Dn Armthorpe *Sheff* 87-91; C Howell Hill *Guildf* 91-96; Perm to Offic *Cov* 02-04; NSM Bidford-on-Avon from 04. *24 High Street, Bidford-on-Avon, Alcester B50 4BU* Tel (01789) 490630

HEPPER, Christopher Michael Alan. b 55. St Jo Coll Nottm 90. **d** 92 **p** 93. C High Harrogate Ch Ch *Ripon* 92-95; Bp's Dom Chapl 95-99; P-in-c Poitou-Charentes *Eur* 99-11; P-in-c Leyburn w Bellerby *Ripon* from 11. *The Vicarage, I'Anson Close, Leyburn DL8 5LF* Tel (01969) 622251 E-mail lepuitsduchapelain@wanadoo.fr

HEPPER, William Raymond. b 62. Kingston Poly BA83. Trin Coll Bris BA98. **d** 98 **p** 99. C Spring Grove St Mary *Lon* 98-01; CMS Egypt 01-04; NSM Greenford H Cross *Lon* 05-08; Perm to Offic from 08. *12A Medway Drive, Perivale, Greenford UB6 8LN* Tel (020) 8997 4953 E-mail williamhepper@hotmail.com

HEPPLE, Gordon. b 32. Edin Th Coll. **d** 63 **p** 68. C Billingham St Cuth *Dur* 63-64; C Ryhope 64; Perm to Offic 66-68; C Wingate Grange 68-69; C Heworth St Mary 69; C Gateshead

St Mary 69-71; P-in-c Low Team 71-72; R Lyons 72-79; V Basford St Aid *S'well* 79-84; V Blackhill *Dur* 84-95; rtd 97; Perm to Offic *Win* from 97. *66B Ringwood Road, Christchurch BH23 5RE* Tel (01425) 279068

HEPTINSTALL, Mrs Lillian. b 49. EMMTC 99. **d** 02 **p** 03. NSM Chilwell *S'well* from 02. *8 Cranston Road, Bramcote, Nottingham NG9 3GU* Tel 0115-916 4588 E-mail heptinstall@ntlworld.com

HEPTINSTALL, Mrs Susan Margaret. b 56. Yorks Min Course 08. **d** 10 **p** 11. NSM Halifax St Aug and Mount Pellon *Wakef* from 10. *26 Sandbeds Road, Pellon, Halifax HX2 0JF* Tel (01422) 341436 Mobile 07510-510359 E-mail paulsue.heptinstall@talktalk.net

HEPWORTH, Canon Ernest John Peter. b 42. K Coll Lon BD65 AKC65 Hull Univ MA87. **d** 66 **p** 67. C Headingley *Ripon* 66-69; Asst Chapl St Geo Hosp Lon 69-71; C Gt Grimsby St Mary and St Jas *Linc* 71-72; TV 72-74; V Crosby 74-80; V Barton upon Humber 80-04; RD Yarborough 86-92; Can and Preb Linc Cathl 94-04; rtd 04. *63 Ferriby Road, Barton-upon-Humber DN18 5LQ* Tel (01652) 661363 E-mail ehep01@aol.com

HEPWORTH, Michael David Albert. b 37. Em Coll Cam BA59 MA63 Lon Inst of Educn PGCE60. Ridley Hall Cam 65. **d** 67 **p** 68. C Eastbourne All SS *Chich* 67-69; Teacher Eastbourne Coll 67-69; Asst Chapl Bedford Sch 69-72; Chapl 72-83; Hd Master Birkdale Sch 83-98; Perm to Offic *Derby* and *Sheff* 83-09. *6 Elm Gardens, Claygate, Esher KT10 0JS* Tel (01372) 466651 E-mail michaelhepworth@talktalk.net

HEPWORTH, Michael Edward. b 29. Leeds Univ BA51. NW Ord Course 74. **d** 77 **p** 78. NSM Timperley *Ches* 77-98; Perm to Offic from 00. *56 Ridgeway Road, Timperley, Altrincham WA15 7HD* Tel 0161-980 5104

HERAPATH, Jonathan James. b 67. Westmr Coll Ox BTh96 Ox Brookes Univ PGCE02. St Steph Ho Ox MTh06. **d** 05 **p** 06. C Cowley St Jo *Ox* 05-07; Chapl SS Helen and Kath Sch Abingdon 07-10; Chapl Wadh Coll Ox from 10. *Wadham College, Oxford OX1 3PN* Tel 07745-405150 (mobile) E-mail jonathanherapath@o2.co.uk

HERBERT, Christopher John. b 37. Dur Univ BA60. Cranmer Hall Dur 60. **d** 62 **p** 63. C Huyton Quarry *Liv* 62-65; C Rainford 65-68; V Impington *Ely* 68-78; RD N Stowe 76-78; V Gt Shelford 78-97; RD Shelford 80-85; rtd 97. *North Place, Crown Street, Great Bardfield, Braintree CM7 4ST* Tel (01371) 810516

✠**HERBERT, The Rt Revd Christopher William.** b 44. Univ of Wales (Lamp) BA65 Bris Univ PGCE65 Leic Univ MPhil02 PhD08 Herts Univ Hon DLitt03. Wells Th Coll 65. **d** 67 **p** 68 **c** 95. C Tupsley *Heref* 67-71; Dioc RE Adv 71-76; Dioc Dir RE 76-81; Preb Heref Cathl 76-81; V Bourne *Guildf* 81-90; Hon Can Guildf Cathl 85-95; Adn Dorking 90-95; Bp St Alb 95-09; rtd 09; Hon Asst Bp Guildf from 09. *1 Beacon Close, Wrecclesham, Farnham GU10 4PA* Tel (01252) 795600 E-mail cherbert@threeabbeys.org.uk

HERBERT, Clair Geoffrey Thomas. b 36. Tyndale Hall Bris 61. **d** 64 **p** 65. C Nottingham St Sav *S'well* 64-67; C Harwell *Ox* 67-70; C Chilton All SS 67-70; V Bucklebury w Marlston 70-80; Chapl Brighton Coll Jun Sch 80-83; Hon C Upton (Overchurch) *Ches* 85-86; C 86-88; V Collier Row St Jas and Havering-atte-Bower *Chelmsf* 88-01; rtd 01; Perm to Offic *Ripon* from 01. *24 Birstwith Grange, Birstwith, Harrogate HG3 3AH* Tel (01423) 771315 E-mail geoffnval@vwclub.net

HERBERT, Clare Marguerite. b 54. St Hild Coll Dur BA76 New Coll Edin MTh78. Linc Th Coll 79. **dss** 81 **d** 87 **p** 94. Clifton St Paul and Asst Chapl Bris Univ 81-84; Hon Par Dn Bris St Mary Redcliffe w Temple etc 87-92; Dioc Past Care Adv *Lon* 92-95; Hon C Clapham Team *S'wark* 94-96; C St Martin-in-the-Fields *Lon* 96-98; R Soho St Anne w St Thos and St Pet 98-07; Dean of Women's Min Two Cities Area 01-07; Nat Co-ord Inclusive Ch 07-10; Lect St Martin-in-the-Fields from 10. *37 Sydenham Hill, London SE26 6SH* Tel 07504-577210 (mobile) E-mail clare.herbert@smitf.com

HERBERT, Canon David Alexander Sellars. b 39. Bris Univ BA60. St Steph Ho Ox 65. **d** 67 **p** 68. C St Leonards Ch in *Chich* 67-81; V Bickley *Roch* 81-09; Hon Can Roch Cathl 92-09; rtd 09. *Flat 2, 52 High Street, Chislehurst BR7 5AQ* Tel (020) 8467 5230 Mobile 07748-997586 E-mail fatherdavidherbert@btinternet.com

HERBERT, Canon David Roy. b 51. K Coll Lon BD73 AKC73. **d** 74 **p** 75. C Sheff St Aid w St Luke 74-76; C Sheff Manor 76-78; TV Gleadless Valley 78-83; TV Ellesmere Port *Ches* 83-93; V Tarvin 93-09; Continuing Minl Tr Officer 03-09; Clergy Development Officer from 09; Hon Can Ches Cathl from 08. *25 Blackstairs Road, Ellesmere Port CH66 1TX* Tel 0151-356 4554 E-mail david.herbert@chester.anglican.org

HERBERT, Mrs Denise Bridget Helen. b 42. SRN72 SCM74. Ripon Coll Cuddesdon. **d** 95 **p** 96. C Ocean View S Africa 95-97; C Grahamstown Cathl 97-99; Sub-Dean 99-00; R Jedburgh *Edin* 00-08; rtd 08; R Newport-on-Tay *St And* from 09. *60 Riverside Road, Wormit, Newport-on-Tay DD6 8LJ* Tel (01382) 541571

HERBERT, Geoffrey. See HERBERT, Clair Geoffrey Thomas

HERBERT, Geoffrey William. b 38. Ox Univ MA62 Birm Univ PhD72. Qu Coll Birm 80. **d** 82 **p** 83. C Hall Green Ascension

Birm 82-85; R Sheldon 85-95; rtd 95; Perm to Offic *Birm* from 95; Co-ord for Spiritual Direction 00-05. *28 Lulworth Road, Birmingham B28 8NS* Tel 0121-777 2684 E-mail gandjherbert@tesco.net

HERBERT, Graham Victor. b 61. St Jo Coll Nottm BA02. **d** 02 **p** 03. C Strood St Nic w St Mary *Roch* 02-06; P-in-c Grain w Stoke 06-09; R Milton next Gravesend w Denton from 09. *The Rectory, Church Walk, Gravesend DA12 2QU* Tel (01474) 533434 E-mail graham.herbert@diocese-rochester.org

HERBERT, Jonathan Patrick. b 62. Bris Univ BA86. Linc Th Coll 86. **d** 88 **p** 89. C Kirkby *Liv* 88-91; TV Blakenall Heath *Lich* 91-96; Pilsdon Community 96-10. *Address temp unknown*

HERBERT, Malcolm Francis. b 53. K Coll Lon BD74 AKC74 St Mary's Coll Chelt CertEd75. Trin Coll Bris 76. **d** 77 **p** 78. C Wotton-under-Edge w Ozleworth and N Nibley *Glouc* 77-79; C Milton *B & W* 79-80; C Worle 80-85; V Woking Ch Ch *Guildf* 86-02; RD Woking 94-99; Dioc Dir of Ords *Bris* 02-07; C Kington St Michael and Chippenham St Paul w Hardenhuish etc 02-05; C Chippenham St Pet 05-07; Hon Can Bris Cathl 05-07; V Hounslow H Trin w St Paul *Lon* from 07. *14 Lampton Park Road, Hounslow TW3 4HS* Tel (020) 8570 3066

HERBERT, Michael. b 35. Nottm Univ BA57. St D Coll Lamp 59. **d** 61 **p** 62. C Paston *Pet* 61-65; C Northampton All SS w St Kath 65-67; R Sutton w Upton 67-72; Asst Youth Chapl 67-72; Ind Chapl 72-84; P-in-c Pitsford 79-84; Ind Chapl *Worc* 84-01; TV Redditch, The Ridge 84-01; Chapl NE Worcs Coll 86-01; rtd 01; Perm to Offic *Worc* from 01. *33 Abbey Road, Redditch B97 4BL* Tel and fax (01527) 69975

HERBERT, Canon Ronald. b 53. Worc Coll Ox BA75 MA80 Lon Univ BD78 W Kentucky Univ MA79. Oak Hill Th Coll 75. **d** 79 **p** 80. C Welling *Roch* 79-89; V Falconwood 89-90; V Becontree St Mary *Chelmsf* 90-07; Hon Can Chelmsf Cathl 02-07; V Stonebridge St Mich *Lon* from 07. *St Michael's Vicarage, Hillside, London NW10 8LB* Tel (020) 8965 7443 E-mail ronald.herbert@virgin.net

HERBERT, Mrs Rosemary. b 44. Westf Coll Lon BSc65. Qu Coll Birm 81. **dss** 85 **d** 87. Malvern Link w Cowleigh *Worc* 85-91; Hon Par Dn 87-91; NSM Malvern H Trin and St Jas from 91. *4 Cedar Avenue, Malvern WR14 2SG* Tel (01684) 572497

HERBERT, Stephen Edward. b 54. Hastings Coll Nebraska BA76 Bemidji State Univ MA81. Seabury-Western Th Sem MDiv87. **d** 87 **p** 87. V Lake City Grace Ch USA 87-90; Asst P Vancouver St Jas Canada 90-00; TV Wythenshawe *Man* 00-06; TR 06-09; P-in-c Byker St Martin *Newc* from 09; P-in-c Byker St Mich w St Lawr from 09. *St Martin's Vicarage, 152 Roman Avenue, Newcastle upon Tyne NE6 2RJ* Tel 0191-265 5931 E-mail stephenherbert152@btinternet.com

HERBERT, Canon Timothy David. b 57. Man Univ BA78 MPhil88 PhD04. Ridley Hall Cam 79. **d** 81 **p** 82. C Macclesfield St Mich *Ches* 81-85; V Wharton 85-93; Asst CME Officer 90-93; P-in-c Thanington *Cant* 93-98; Dir of Ords 93-98; Dir Dioc Tr Inst *Carl* from 99; C Cotehill and Cumwhinton 99-00; C Scotby and Cotehill w Cumwhinton from 00; Hon Can Carl Cathl from 99. *The Vicarage, Cotehill, Carlisle CA4 0DY* Tel (01228) 561745 Fax 562366 E-mail therbert@globalnet.co.uk

✠**HERD, The Rt Revd William Brian.** b 31. Clifton Th Coll 53. **d** 58 **p** 59 **c** 76. C Wolverhampton St Luke *Lich* 58-61; Uganda 61-77; Adn Karamoja 70-75; Bp Karamoja 76-77; Deputation Sec (Ireland) BCMS 77-89; C Harrow Trin St Mich *Lon* 89-93; V Gresley *Derby* 93-98; rtd 98; Perm to Offic *Sarum* from 98. *Karibu, 13 Ambleside, Weymouth DT3 5HH* Tel (01305) 770257

HEREFORD, Archdeacon of. See BENSON, The Ven George Patrick

HEREFORD, Bishop of. See PRIDDIS, The Rt Revd Anthony Martin

HEREFORD, Dean of. See TAVINOR, The Very Revd Michael Edward

HEREWARD, John Owen. b 53. Lon Univ MB, BS77 FRCSE82. Ridley Hall Cam 89. **d** 91 **p** 92. C W Ealing St Jo w St Jas *Lon* 91-95; P-in-c Hanwell St Mellitus w St Mark 95-10; V from 10; Dir Post-Ord Tr 97-05; AD Ealing 98-03. *St Mellitus Vicarage, 1 Church Road, London W7 3BA* Tel (020) 8567 6535 E-mail john@jhereward.fsnet.co.uk

HEREWARD-ROTHWELL, Canon Michael John. b 46. MA Tulane Univ (USA) DPhil03. Chich Th Coll 74. **d** 78 **p** 79. C Chelmsf All SS 78-82; C Clacton St Jas 82-85; V Thorpe *Guildf* 85-09; Hon Can Guildf Cathl 99-09; rtd 09. *Nashdom Lodge, 19A Langham Place, Egham TW20 9EB*

HERITAGE, Barry. b 35. Clifton Th Coll 59. **d** 61 **p** 62. C Wolverhampton St Jude *Lich* 61-65; C Chaddesden St Mary *Derby* 65-67; V Kidsgrove Holl 67-76; NE Area Sec CPAS 76-89; V Elloughton and Brough w Brantingham *York* 89-93; C York St Paul 93-00; rtd 00; Perm to Offic *York* from 00. *32 St Swithins Walk, York YO26 4UF* Tel (01904) 786077

HERKES, Richard Andrew. b 54. Kent Univ BA75. STETS 99. **d** 02 **p** 03. NSM Polegate *Chich* from 02. *31 Wannock Lane, Eastbourne BN20 9SB* Tel (01323) 488328 E-mail rherkes@hotmail.com

HERKLOTS, Canon John Radu. b 31. Trin Hall Cam BA53 MA61. Westcott Ho Cam 54. **d** 55 **p** 56. C Attercliffe w Carbrook *Sheff* 55-60; C Stoke Damerel *Ex* 60-65; V Devonport St Bart 65-72; V Denmead *Portsm* 72-97; RD Havant 82-87; Hon Can Portsm Cathl 86-97; rtd 97; Perm to Offic *Heref* 97-02 and *Portms* from 03. *14 Derwent Road, Lee-on-the-Solent PO13 8JG* Tel (023) 9255 2652

HERON, David George. b 49. AKC72. **d** 73 **p** 74. C Stockton St Chad *Dur* 73-77; C Beamish 77-81; R Willington and Sunnybrow 81-95; V Dipton and Leadgate from 95. *The Vicarage, St Ives Road, Leadgate, Consett DH8 7SN* Tel (01207) 503918 E-mail frdavidheron@aol.com

HERON, George Dobson. b 34. TD. Cranmer Hall Dur 58. **d** 61 **p** 62. C Benfieldside *Dur* 61-65; C Winlaton 65-68; V Dunston St Nic 68-77; P-in-c Dunston Ch Ch 74-77; V Dunston 77-82; V Gateshead St Helen 82-89; rtd 94; Perm to Offic *Dur* 94-96 and *Newc* from 94. *36 Woodlands Road, Shotley Bridge, Consett DH8 0DE* Tel (01207) 507733

HERON, Nicholas Peter. b 60. Man Univ BA81 Southn Univ BTh86. Sarum & Wells Th Coll. **d** 84 **p** 85. C Brinnington w Portwood *Ches* 84-87; Chapl RAF from 87. *Chaplaincy Services, Valiant Block, HQ Air Command, RAF High Wycombe HP14 4UE* Tel (01494) 496800 Fax 496343

HERON, Simon Alexander. b 68. Ridley Hall Cam 05. **d** 07 **p** 08. C Frindsbury w Upnor and Chattenden *Roch* 07-11; P-in-c Lawford *Chelmsf* from 11. *The Rectory, Church Hill, Lawford, Manningtree CO11 2JX* Tel 07768-525512 (mobile) E-mail simon.heron@mac.com

HERRICK, Andrew Frederick. b 58. Univ of Wales (Lamp) BA80. Wycliffe Hall Ox 80. **d** 82 **p** 83. C Aberystwyth *St D* 82-85; P-in-c Llangeitho and Blaenpennal w Betws Leucu etc 85-86; R 86-88; Youth Chapl 86-88; R Aberporth w Tremain and Blaenporth 88-91; Succ St D Cathl 91-94; V Betws w Ammanford 94-00; TV Aberystwyth from 00. *The Vicarage, Piercefield Lane, Penparcau, Aberystwyth SY23 1RX* Tel (01970) 617732

HERRICK, David William. b 52. Middx Poly BSc73. St Jo Coll Nottm 79. **d** 82 **p** 83. C Ipswich St Matt *St E* 82-85; C Nor St Pet Mancroft w St Jo Maddermarket 85-88; V Bury St Edmunds St Geo *St E* 88-96; P-in-c Gt Barton 96-99; Dir Studies Dioc Min Course from 99; Vice Prin from 04. *24 Cromwell Road, Ely CB6 1AS* Tel (01353) 662909 Fax 662056

HERRICK (formerly COWLEY), Mrs Jean Louie Cameron. b 39. Sarum Dioc Tr Coll CertEd59. SAOMC 94. **d** 96 **p** 97. NSM Chorleywood Ch Ch *St Alb* 96-02; NSM Hermitage *Ox* 02-05; Perm to Offic *Glouc* from 05. *52 Cambrian Road, Walton Cardiff, Tewkesbury GL20 7RP* Tel (01684) 295598 E-mail jean.herrick@tesco.net

HERRICK (née RENAUT), Canon Vanessa Anne. b 58. York Univ BA80 Fitzw Coll Cam MA96 LTCL75. St Jo Coll Nottm 80 Ridley Hall Cam 94. **d** 96 **p** 97. C St E Cathl Distr 96-99; Chapl Fitzw Coll Cam 99-02; Fell 01-02; Tutor Ridley Hall Cam 99-02; Dir Min and Vocation *Ely* from 03; Hon Can Ely Cathl from 03. *24 Cromwell Road, Ely CB6 1AS* Tel (01353) 662909 Fax 662056 Mobile 07778-496340 E-mail vanessa.herrick@ely.anglican.org

HERROD, Canon Kathryn. b 59. Warwick Univ BSc80 Matlock Coll of Educn PGCE81. St Jo Coll Nottm MA97. **d** 97 **p** 98. C Wollaton *S'well* 97-01; R Warsop 01-10; TR Hucknall Turkard from 10; Hon Can S'well Minster from 11. *The Rectory, Annesley Road, Hucknall, Nottingham NG15 7DE* Tel 0115-964 1499 E-mail revkathryn@aol.com

HERRON, Robert Gordon John. b 36. MCIPD75. Wycliffe Hall Ox 65. **d** 77 **p** 78. C Ditton St Mich *Liv* 77-80; C W Kirby St Bridget *Ches* 80-82; R Gorton Our Lady and St Thos *Man* 82-00; rtd 00. *The Gables, 13 West Road, Bowden, Altrincham WA14 2LD*

HERSCHEL, Richard James. b 27. Villanova Univ USA MA72. **d** 57 **p** 57. USA 57-81 and 84-97; TV Cannock *Lich* 82-84; rtd 92. *80B King Street, Norwich NR1 1PG* Tel (01603) 614873

HERTFORD, Archdeacon of. *See* JONES, The Ven Trevor Pryce

HERTFORD, Suffragan Bishop of. *See* BAYES, The Rt Revd Paul

HERTH, Daniel Edwin. b 36. Xavier Univ Cincinnati BS58. Ch Div Sch of Pacific MDiv83. **d** 83 **p** 84. C Oakland St Paul USA 83-86; R Alameda Ch Ch 86-97; NSM Gt and Lt Ouseburn w Marton cum Grafton etc *Ripon* 98-01; Chapl HM YOI Wetherby from 99. *The Garden House, 32 Mallorie Park Drive, Ripon HG4 2QF* Tel and fax (01765) 602558 Mobile 07779-379420 E-mail danieleherthsr@hotmail.com

HERVÉ, Canon John Anthony. b 49. TD94. Open Univ BA81 Wolv Univ PGCE95. Lich Th Coll 70. **d** 73 **p** 74. C Middlesbrough All SS *York* 73-76; CF 76-81; P-in-c Handsworth St Andr *Birm* 81-86; Hon C Cowley St Jo *Ox* 86-90; Tutor St Steph Ho Ox 86-90; V Sparkbrook St Agatha w Balsall Heath St Barn *Birm* from 90; P-in-c Highgate 05-10; Hon Can Birm Cathl from 09. *The Clergy House, 288A Ladypool Road, Birmingham B12 8JU* Tel 0121-449 2790 E-mail fr.john@saintagathas.org.uk

HERVEY, Mrs Mary Diana. b 41. St Hugh's Coll Ox BA63. St And Dioc Tr Course 83 TISEC 96. **d** 92 **p** 94. Par Dn Cupar *St And* 92-94; Asst Chapl St Andr Univ 94-97; Asst P Cen Fife Team 94-97; C Ulverston St Mary w H Trin *Carl* 97-00; P-in-c Barrow St Jo 00-06; rtd 06. *21 Rossefield Road, Heaton, Bradford BD9 4DD* Tel (01274) 497044 E-mail revdih@aol.com

HESELTINE, Mrs Barbara Joan. b 42. Keele Univ BA65. S'wark Ord Course 85. **d** 88 **p** 94. NSM Addington *S'wark* 88-98; Perm to Offic *Truro* 98-02; NSM Feock from 02. *The Lodge, Penpol, Devoran, Truro TR3 6NA* Tel and fax (01872) 870039 Mobile 07767-264060 E-mail barbara.heseltine@tiscali.co.uk

HESELWOOD, Eric Harold. b 43. Oak Hill Th Coll 84. **d** 86 **p** 87. C Farnborough *Roch* 86-88; V Biggin Hill 88-96; V Orpington All SS 96-98; V Bromley Common St Aug 98-05; rtd 05; Perm to Offic *Roch* 06-08; P-in-c Cudham and Downe from 08. *34 Victoria Gardens, Biggin Hill, Westerham TN16 3DJ* Tel and fax (01959) 509131 E-mail eric.heselwood@ntlworld.com

HESELWOOD, Mrs Hilda. b 39. CA Tr Coll 61. dss 85 **d** 87 **p** 94. CA from 63; Bromley Common St Luke *Roch* 85-00; Par Dn 87-94; C 94-00; rtd 00; Perm to Offic *Roch* from 00. *34 Victoria Gardens, Biggin Hill, Westerham TN16 3DJ* Tel and fax (01959) 509131

HESFORD-LOCKE, Richard Nigel. b 61. Coll of Resurr Mirfield 92. **d** 94 **p** 95. C Middlesbrough Ascension *York* 94-97; C Paignton St Jo *Ex* 97-98; rtd 98. *2 Windyhill Drive, Bolton BL3 4TH*

HESKETH, Canon Philip John. b 64. K Coll Lon BD86 AKC86 PhD94. Ripon Coll Cuddesdon 92. **d** 94 **p** 95. C Bearsted w Thurnham *Cant* 94-98; V Chatham St Steph *Roch* 98-05; Can Res Roch Cathl from 05. *East Canonry, Kings Orchard, Rochester ME1 1TG* Tel (01634) 841491 *or* 843366

HESKETH, The Ven Ronald David. b 47. CB04. Bede Coll Dur BA68 FRGS02. Ridley Hall Cam 69 St Mich Coll Llan 71. **d** 71 **p** 72. C Southport H Trin *Liv* 71-74; Asst Chapl Miss to Seamen 74-75; Chapl RAF 75-98; Command Chapl RAF 98-01; Chapl-in-Chief RAF 01-06; Can and Preb Linc Cathl 01-06; Voc Officer *Worc* from 06; Co-ord Chapl W Mercia Police from 09; QHC from 01. *The Old Police Station, Bredon Road, Tewkesbury GL20 5BZ* Tel (01684) 299773 E-mail vera&ron.hesketh@dunelm.org.uk

HESKINS, Georgiana Mary. b 48. K Coll Lon BD81 AKC81 MTh93. Westcott Ho Cam 81. dss 83 **d** 87 **p** 94. Cobbold Road St Sav w St Mary *Lon* 83-85; St Botolph Aldgate w H Trin Minories 85-87; Par Dn 87; Perm to Offic *S'wark* 88-93; Par Dn Kidbrooke St Jas 93-95; Tutor S'wark Ord Course 93-94; Tutor SEITE 94-98; Teacher Eltham Coll 98-02; Asst Chapl Qu Eliz Hosp NHS Trust 03-11; Asst Chapl S Lon Healthcare NHS Trust from 11; Hon Chapl S'wark Cathl from 95. *4 Roupell Street, London SE1 8SP* Tel (020) 7642 1161 Mobile 07776-122350 E-mail georgiana@lineone.net

HESKINS, Canon Jeffrey George. b 55. Heythrop Coll Lon MA94 Princeton Th Sem DMin00 AKC78. Chich Th Coll 80. **d** 81 **p** 82. C Primrose Hill St Mary w Avenue Road St Paul *Lon* 81-85; Enfield Deanery Youth Officer 85-88; C Enfield Chase St Mary 85-88; TV Kidbrooke St Jas *S'wark* 88-95; R Charlton St Luke w H Trin 95-02; P-in-c Old Charlton St Thos 02; R Charlton 02-07; Dioc Dir of Ords *Linc* from 07; Min Can and Preb Linc Cathl from 10. *Church House, The Old Palace, Lincoln LN2 1PU* Tel (01522) 504029 Fax 504051 E-mail jeffrey.heskins@lincoln.anglican.org

HESLAM, Peter Somers. b 63. Hull Univ BA89 Keble Coll Ox DPhil94 Trin Coll Cam BA96 MA01. Ridley Hall Cam 93. **d** 96 **p** 97. C Huntingdon *Ely* 96-99; Min Stukeley Meadows LEP 99; Dir Studies EAMTC 99-00; Tutor Ridley Hall Cam from 99; Dir Capitalism Project Lon Inst of Contemporary Chr 00-04; Hon C Cherry Hinton St Jo *Ely* from 00; Fell Faculty of Div Cam Univ from 05. *Glebe House, 64A Glebe Road, Cambridge CB1 7SZ* Tel (01223) 722822 E-mail psh20@cam.ac.uk

HESLOP, Alan. *See* HESLOP, James Alan

HESLOP, Andrew James. b 66. Man Univ BA87 PGCE88. **d** 03 **p** 04. OLM Turton Moorland Min *Man* from 03; Chapl Wrightington Wigan and Leigh NHS Trust from 07; Perm to Offic *Blackb* from 07. *The Chaplaincy, Royal Albert Edward Infirmary, Wigan Lane, Wigan WN1 2NN* Tel (01942) 244000

HESLOP, David Anthony. b 45. BSc DipEd MTh Birm Univ MLitt97. St Jo Coll Nottm 81. **d** 83 **p** 84. C Willenhall H Trin *Lich* 83-86; V Gresley *Derby* 86-92; V Marston on Dove w Scropton 92-95; Chapl Derby Univ 95-99; V Castle Donington and Lockington cum Hemington *Leic* 99-03; Chapl E Midl Airport 99-03; Prin OLM and Integrated Tr *Sarum* 03-07; Co-ord for Learning and Discipleship 07-10; rtd 11; Dir of Ords (Berks) *Ox* from 11. *23A High Street, Sutton Courtenay, Abingdon OX14 4AW* Tel (01235) 847962 E-mail revdave@heslops.co.uk

HESLOP, Harold William. b 40. Leeds Univ BA62 Open Univ BA72. Ox NSM Course 75. **d** 78 **p** 79. NSM Stoke Mandeville *Ox* 78-91; NSM Wendover 82-00; NSM Ellesborough, The Kimbles and Stoke Mandeville 91-94. *Farmside House, 42 Beechburn Park, Crook DL15 8NA* Tel (01388) 765903

HESLOP, James Alan. b 37. Codrington Coll Barbados 61. **d** 64 **p** 65. C Bartica Guyana 64-68; P-in-c Long Is Nassau 68-71; C Ch Ch Cathl 71-72; C Haxby w Wigginton *York* 72-74; TV 74-76; V York St Olave w St Giles 76-87; V Northampton All SS w St Kath *Pet* 87-88; R Felpham w Middleton *Chich* 88-92; TR Howden *York* 92-94; Warden Coll of St Barn Lingfield 94-95; Warden Morley Retreat and Conf Ho Derby 95-98; R Kirkbride and V Lezayre St Olave Ramsey *S & M* 98-99; P-in-c Woburn w Eversholt, Milton Bryan, Battlesden etc *St Alb* 99-03; rtd 03; Chapl Soc of St Marg 04-05; P-in-c Pau *Eur* 05-06. *1 Coniston Close, Bognor Regis PO22 8ND* Tel (01243) 869499

HESLOP, Michael Andrew. b 47. Trin Coll Bris 73. **d** 76 **p** 77. C Burmantofts St Steph and St Agnes *Ripon* 76-80; V Thorpe Edge *Bradf* 80-87; TV Penrith w Newton Reigny and Plumpton Wall *Carl* 87-91; V Silloth 91-01; V Kettlewell w Conistone, Hubberholme etc *Bradf* 01-07; Perm to Offic *Carl* from 07. *8 Lowscales Drive, Cockermouth CA13 9DR* Tel (01900) 829542

HESS, Paul Austin. b 67. Cape Town Univ BA89. St Bede's Coll Umtata. **d** 93 **p** 93. C Matroosfontein S Africa 92-94; NSM Eythorne and Elvington w Waldershare etc *Cant* 95-96; C Storrington *Chich* 96-99; Chapl Hurstpierpoint Coll 99-05; Chapl Eton Coll from 05. *Eton College, Windsor SL4 6DW* Tel (01753) 671161 E-mail pahess@tiscali.co.uk

HETHERINGTON, Andrew. b 50. Sheff Univ BSc71. Wycliffe Hall Ox 71. **d** 74 **p** 75. C Leic H Trin w St Jo 74-78; C Leic H Apostles 78-82; V Bootle St Mary w St Paul *Liv* 82-93; TR W Swindon and the Lydiards *Bris* 93-01; P-in-c Chebsey, Ellenhall and Seighford-with-Creswell *Lich* 01-06; V Chebsey, Creswell, Ellenhall, Ranton etc from 06. *The Vicarage, The Green, Seighford, Stafford ST18 9PQ* Tel (01785) 282829 E-mail andrewhetherington@btinternet.com

HETHERINGTON, Mrs Charlotte Elizabeth. b 52. Girton Coll Cam BA74 Maria Grey Coll Lon PGCE75 Heythrop Coll Lon MA02. SAOMC 95. **d** 98 **p** 99. NSM Stratfield Mortimer and Mortimer W End etc *Ox* 98-04; C Portsea St Mary *Portsm* from 04. *Flat 10, 1 Bill Sargent Crescent, Portsmouth PO1 4JP* Tel (023) 9282 6892 E-mail charlottehetherington@hotmail.com

HETHERINGTON, Mrs Glynis Catherine. b 48. EMMTC 93. **d** 93 **p** 94. NSM E and W Leake, Stanford-on-Soar, Rempstone etc *S'well* 93-99; R from 99. *The Rectory, 3 Bateman Road, East Leake, Loughborough LE12 6LN* Tel (01509) 852228

HETHERINGTON, John Carl. b 52. Hull Univ BTh93. Linc Th Coll 82. **d** 84 **p** 85. C Crosby *Linc* 84-88; TV Cleethorpes 88-93; Chapl RAF 93-07; R Monk Fryston and S Milford *York* from 07. *The Rectory, Main Street, Hillam, Leeds LS25 5HH* Tel and fax (01977) 682357 Mobile 07903-450542 E-mail hetherington556@btinternet.com

HETHERINGTON, Mrs Rachel Marie. b 65. ERMC 05. **d** 08. NSM Northampton Ch Ch *Pet* 08-11; NSM Northampton H Sepulchre w St Andr and St Lawr 08-11; NSM Northampton St Mich w St Edm 08-11; NSM Northampton H Trin and St Paul 08-11; Asst Chapl St Andr Healthcare from 11. *13 Woodrush Way, Moulton, Northampton NN3 7HU* Tel (01604) 459864 E-mail rh10@ntlworld.com

HETLING, William Maurice. b 37. AKC61. **d** 62 **p** 63. C Eltham St Barn *S'wark* 62-66; C Horley 66-71; C Kingston Jamaica 71-72; R Highgate 72-73; P-in-c Porus 74-75; C-in-c Farnham Royal S CD *Ox* 75-78; TV Slough 78-80 and 88-91; TR 80-88; TV Parkstone St Pet w Branksea and St Osmund *Sarum* 91-96; P-in-c Reading St Barn *Ox* 96-99; rtd 99; Perm to Offic *Chich* 99-06. *12 Manor Close, Storrington, Pulborough RH20 4LF*

HEWES, John. b 29. Nottm Univ BA50. Chich Th Coll 79. **d** 81 **p** 82. C Buckland in Dover w Buckland Valley *Cant* 81-84; P-in-c Elmsted w Hastingleigh 84-89; P-in-c Crundale w Godmersham 84-89; RD W Bridge 88-89; R Lydd 89-95; RD S Lympne 89-95; rtd 95; Perm to Offic *Cant* from 95. *Brambledown, Tamley Lane, Hastingleigh, Ashford TN25 5HW* Tel (01233) 750214

HEWES, Timothy William. b 50. Sheff Univ BDS74. SAOMC 98. **d** 01. NSM Abingdon *Ox* from 01. *55 Lower Radley, Abingdon OX14 3AY* Tel (01235) 523963 Mobile 07771-880117 E-mail tim@rdlf.uninet.co.uk

HEWETSON, The Ven Christopher. b 37. Trin Coll Ox BA60 MA64. Chich Th Coll 67. **d** 69 **p** 70. C Leckhampton St Pet *Glouc* 69-71; C Wokingham All SS *Ox* 71-73; V Didcot St Pet 73-82; R Ascot Heath 82-90; RD Bracknell 86-90; P-in-c Headington Quarry 90-94; Hon Can Ch Ch 92-94; RD Cowley 94; Adn Ches 94-02; rtd 02; Bp's Adv for Spirituality *Ex* 03-07; Perm to Offic *Ches* from 05. *The Old Estate House, The Square, North Molton, South Molton EX36 3HP* Tel (01598) 740573 E-mail cahewetson@tiscali.co.uk

HEWETSON, David Geoffrey. b 31. S'wark Ord Course 71. **d** 74 **p** 75. NSM Brighton St Mich *Chich* 74-06; rtd 06; Perm to Offic *Chich* from 07. *Flat 1, 166 Dyke Road, Brighton BN1 5PU* Tel (01273) 275776

HEWETSON, Canon Robin Jervis. b 39. AKC63 K Coll Lon MA93. **d** 64 **p** 65. C Thorpe St Andr *Nor* 64-67; C E Dereham w Hoe 67-69; TV Mattishall w Mattishall Burgh 69-72; R Ingham w Sutton 72-78; R Catfield 75-78; R Taverham w Ringland 78-89; P-in-c Marsham 89-92; P-in-c Burgh 89-92; Dioc Ecum Officer 89-04; Exec Officer Norfolk Ecum Coun 89-04; R Marsham w Burgh-next-Aylsham 92-04; Hon Can Nor Cathl 01-04; rtd 04; Perm to Offic *Nor* from 04. *83 Soame Close, Aylsham, Norwich NR11 6JF* Tel (01263) 734325

HEWETSON, Canon Valerie Patricia. b 44. St Mary's Coll Dur BSc66 MSc70 Leeds Univ MA75. Linc Th Coll 89. **d** 91 **p** 94. C Kingston upon Hull St Nic *York* 91-94; V Barmby Moor w Allerthorpe, Fangfoss and Yapham 94-98; V Barmby Moor Gp 98-10; RD S Wold 01-06; Can and Preb York Minster 01-10; rtd 10. *27 Briarsfield, Barmby Moor, York YO24 4HN* Tel (01759) 303816 E-mail hewetson@ajustworld.co.uk

HEWETT, Andrew David. b 63. Univ of Wales (Lamp) BA. Chich Th Coll 84. **d** 86 **p** 87. C Caldicot *Mon* 86-90; Chapl RAF from 90. *Chaplaincy Services, Valiant Block, HQ Air Command, RAF High Wycombe HP14 4UE* Tel (01494) 496800 Fax 496343

HEWETT, Maurice Gordon. b 28. Lon Univ BA53. Oak Hill Th Coll 49. **d** 54 **p** 55. C Gipsy Hill Ch Ch *S'wark* 54-57; C Maidstone St Faith *Cant* 57-60; R Chevening *Roch* 60-95; rtd 95; Perm to Offic *Roch* and *Cant* from 95; Hon Wing Chapl ATC 96-04. *Rosings, 12 The Thicketts, Sevenoaks TN13 3SZ* Tel and fax (01732) 464734

HEWETT, Canon Roger Leroy. b 45. St Mich Coll Llan 93. **d** 95 **p** 96. C Whitchurch *Llan* 95-98; R Blaina and Nantyglo *Mon* 98-10; AD Blaenau Gwent 05-10; Can St Woolos Cathl 08-10; rtd 10. *27 Maenor Helig, Burry Port SA16 0TU* Tel (01554) 834595 E-mail roger.hewett@tiscali.co.uk

HEWISH, Mrs Lesley Gillian. b 60. Trin Coll Bris 08. **d** 10 **p** 11. C Tetbury, Beverston, Long Newnton etc *Glouc* from 10. *The Bungalow, Lower House Lane, North Nibley, Dursley GL11 6DN* Tel (01453) 542742 Mobile 07876-775290 E-mail lesley.hewish1@virgin.net

HEWISON, Alan Stuart. b 30. SS Mark & Jo Univ Coll Plymouth BEd82. K Coll Lon. **d** 57 **p** 58. C S Mymms K Chas *Lon* 57-60; C Bourne *Guildf* 60-63; Chapl RN 63-79; Perm to Offic *Ex* from 79; rtd 95. *8 Hazelwood Crescent, Plymouth PL9 8BL*

HEWITSON, John Kenneth. b 48. Curtin Univ Aus BA Flinders Univ Aus MA96. Adelaide Coll of Div ThL70 ACT ThSchol83. **d** 71 **p** 72. C Swindon Ch Ch *Bris* 71-74; Australia from 74; C Spearwood 74-76; R Balga 76-77; Chapl Royal Perth Hosp 79-83; R Lockridge 83-86; R Eliz 92-97; Chapl Trin Coll 93-98; Chapl Kormilda Coll Darwin from 99; R Freds Pass from 00. *PO Box 346, Humpty Doo NT 0836, Australia* Tel (0061) (8) 8983 3947 Fax 8983 3951 E-mail jah@octa4.net.au

HEWITT, Christopher James Chichele (Chich). b 45. Witwatersrand Univ BSc68 UNISA BA78 MTh92 LTCL69. St Paul's Coll Grahamstown. **d** 78 **p** 79. S Africa 78-99; Chapl St Paul's Coll Grahamstown 84-86; Warden 86-92; Can Grahamstown Cathl 88-93; Chan 92; Sub-Dean 93; Dean and Adn Grahamstown 93-98; USA 99; TR Radcliffe *Man* 00-09; AD Radcliffe and Prestwich 02-09; P-in-c Swinton H Rood from 09. *Holy Rood Vicarage, 33 Moorside Road, Swinton, Manchester M27 3EL* Tel 0161-794 2464 E-mail chich@rink-hewitt.co.uk

HEWITT, Colin Edward. b 52. Man Poly BA80 Em Coll Cam BA82 MA86 Maryvale Inst PGCE08. Westcott Ho Cam 81. **d** 83 **p** 84. C Radcliffe St Thos and St Jo *Man* 83-84; C Langley and Parkfield 84-86; R Byfield w Boddington *Pet* 86-89; R Byfield w Boddington and Aston le Walls 89-91; Chapl RAF 91-09; V Brentwood St Thos *Chelmsf* from 09. *The Vicarage, 91 Queen's Road, Brentwood CM14 4EY* Tel (01277) 225700 Mobile 07704-495001 E-mail fathercolin@live.co.uk

HEWITT, David Warner. b 33. Selw Coll Cam BA56 MA60. Wells Th Coll 57. **d** 59 **p** 60. C Longbridge *Birm* 59-61; C Sheldon 61-64; V Smethwick Old Ch 64-70; V Smethwick 70-78; P-in-c Littlehampton St Jas *Chich* 78-85; P-in-c Wick 78-85; V Littlehampton St Mary 78-85; TR Littlehampton and Wick 86-89; Perm to Offic *Eur* from 95; rtd 98; Hon Asst Chapl Gtr Athens *Eur* 00-03; Perm to Offic *Chelmsf* from 07. *18 Orchard Close, Weaverhead Lane, Thaxted, Dunmow CM6 2JX* Tel (01371) 830591 E-mail tangulls@the.forthnet.gr

HEWITT, Canon Francis John Adam. b 42. St Chad's Coll Dur BA64. **d** 66 **p** 67. C Dewsbury Moor *Wakef* 66-69; C Huddersfield St Jo 69-73; V King Cross 73-81; V Lastingham w Appleton-le-Moors, Rosedale etc *York* 81-94; RD Helmsley 85-94; V Pickering 94-95; V Pickering w Lockton and Levisham 95-07; RD Pickering 94-06; rtd 07; Perm to Offic *York* from 07; Can and Preb York Minster from 97. *Michaelmas Cottage, 3 Lime Chase, Kirkbymoorside, York YO62 6BX* Tel (01751) 430322 E-mail fandb.michaelmas1@btinternet.com

HEWITT, Canon Garth Bruce. b 46. St Jo Coll Dur BA68. Lon Coll of Div LTh70. **d** 70 **p** 71. C Maidstone St Luke *Cant* 70-73; Staff Evang CPAS 73-79; Hon C W Ealing St Jo w St Jas *Lon* 73-81; Dir Amos Trust 88-96; World Affairs Adv *Guildf* 94-96; Regional Co-ord (Lon and SE) Chr Aid from 96; Perm to Offic *S'wark* 96-04; P-in-c All Hallows Lon Wall 97-99; V from 99; Hon Can Jerusalem from 06. *Christian Aid, All Hallows on the Wall, 83 London Wall, London EC2M 5ND* Tel (020) 7496 1680 or 7588 2638 Fax 7496 1684 E-mail ghewitt@christian-aid.org

HEWITT, Geoffrey Williams. b 48. Leeds Univ BA69. Wells Th Coll 70. **d** 72 **p** 73. C Heywood St Luke *Man* 72-74; Ind Chapl 74-77; P-in-c Hulme St Geo 74-77; R Mamhilad and Llanfihangel Pontymoile *Mon* 77-80; Ind Chapl 77-80; V Arthog w Fairbourne *Ban* 80-89; R Llangelynnin w Rhoslefain 87-89; TV Bangor 89-94; Dioc Soc Resp Officer 89-02; P-in-c Pentir 94-02; Hon Can Ban Cathl 99-02; RD Ogwen 00-02; P-in-c Draycot *Bris* from 02. *Draycot Rectory, Seagry Road, Sutton Benger, Chippenham SN15 4RY* Tel and fax (01249) 720070 Mobile 07950-497580
E-mail geoffrey@revhewitt.freeserve.co.uk

HEWITT, Guy Arlington Kenneth. b 67. Univ of W Indies BSc92 MSc94. SEITE 00. **d** 04 **p** 05. C Ch Ch Barbados 04-06 and 07-08; P-in-c Ruby H Trin 06-07. *33 Tino Terrace, Warners, Christ Church BB15104, Barbados* Tel (001) (246) 437 6569 Mobile 435 6052 E-mail guyhewitti@gmail.com

HEWITT, John Kaffrell. b 34. St Aid Birkenhead 60. **d** 63 **p** 64. C Woking Ch Ch *Guildf* 63-66; P-in-c Sudbury w Ballingdon and Brundon *St E* 66-70; V 70-80; V Portsdown *Portsm* 80-96; rtd 96; Perm to Offic *Win* from 97. *45 Knowland Drive, Milford-on-Sea, Lymington SO41 0RH* Tel (01590) 644473

HEWITT, Kenneth Victor. b 30. Lon Univ BSc49 CertEd51 MSc53. Cuddesdon Coll 60. **d** 62 **p** 63. C Maidstone St Martin *Cant* 62-64; C Croydon St Mich 64-67; P-in-c S Kensington St Aug *Lon* 67-73; V 73-95; Asst Chapl Lon Univ 67-73; rtd 95; Perm to Offic *Roch* from 95. *41 Bromley College, London Road, Bromley BR1 1PE* Tel (020) 8464 0014

HEWITT, Michael David. b 49. K Coll Lon BD79 AKC79 CertEd. Qu Coll Birm 79. **d** 80 **p** 81. C Bexleyheath Ch Ch *Roch* 80-84, C Buckland in Dover w Buckland Valley *Cant* 84-89, R Ridgewell w Ashen, Birdbrook and Sturmer *Chelmsf* from 89. *The Rectory, Church Lane, Ridgewell, Halstead CO9 4SA* Tel (01440) 785355

HEWITT, Patrick. See HEWITT, Canon William Patrick

HEWITT, Paul Stephen Patrick. b 59. TCD BA82 MA87. CITC 83. **d** 86 **p** 87. C Ballymacash *Conn* 86-89; C Ballymena w Ballyclug 89-91; I Glencraig *D & D* from 91. *The Parish Office, 6 Seahill Road, Craigavad, Holywood BT18 0DA* Tel (028) 9042 3903 *or* 9042 1847 E-mail glencraigoffice@btconnect.com

HEWITT, Peter. See HEWITT, Thomas Peter James

HEWITT, Robert Samuel. b 51. QUB BSc73. CITC 77. **d** 80 **p** 81. C Dundela St Mark *D & D* 80-84; R Donaghadee 84-92. *3 The Trees, New Road, Donaghadee BT21 0EJ* Tel (028) 9188 2594

HEWITT, Stephen Wilkes. b 49. Fitzw Coll Cam MA71. St Jo Coll Nottm 88. **d** 90 **p** 91. C Eaton *Nor* 90-93; V Warwick St Paul *Cov* 93-01; Perm to Offic *Newc* 01-02; P-in-c High Spen and Rowlands Gill *Dur* 02-05; V 05-09; TR Cramlington *Newc* from 09. *33 Twyford Close, Cramlington NE23 1PH* E-mail sandshewitt@hotmail.com

HEWITT, Thomas Peter James. b 24. St Andr Univ MA50. St Steph Ho Ox 50. **d** 52 **p** 53. C Ellesmere Port *Ches* 52-56; C Leytonstone St Marg w St Columba *Chelmsf* 56-60; V Barlby *York* 60-65; V Godshill *Portsm* 65-93; rtd 93. *c/o C L Wiggins Esq, Jerome and Co Solicitors, 98 High Street, Newport PO30 1BD*

HEWITT, Timothy James. b 67. St D Coll Lamp BD88. Ripon Coll Cuddesdon 89. **d** 91 **p** 92. C Milford Haven *St D* 91-94; C Llanelli 94-96; P-in-c Llan-non 96-97; V Clydach *S & B* 98-07; V Ystalyfera from 07; Dioc Voc Adv from 07. *The Vicarage, Glan yr Afon Road, Ystalyfera, Swansea SA9 2EP* Tel (01639) 842257

HEWITT, Canon William Patrick. b 48. Nottm Univ BTh79. Linc Th Coll 75. **d** 79 **p** 80. C Workington St Jo *Carl* 79-83; V Flookburgh 83-87; V Barrow St Matt 87-90; V Lowick and Kyloe w Ancroft *Newc* 90-96; R Ford and Etal 90-96; RD Norham 91-96; I Fanlobbus Union *C, C & R* 96-07; I Bandon Union 07-10; I Youghal Union from 10; Can Cork Cathl from 00; Can Cloyne Cathl from 00. *The Pines, Knocknacally, Youghal, Co Cork, Republic of Ireland* Tel (00353) (24) 92350 E-mail youghal@cloyne.anglican.org

HEWLETT, Mrs Caroline Joan. b 68. Coll of Ripon & York St Jo BEd92 St Jo Coll Dur BA01. Cranmer Hall Dur 99. **d** 01 **p** 02. C Leeds St Geo *Ripon* 01-04; C Aldborough w Boroughbridge and Roecliffe 04-06; Chapl Leeds Combined Court Cen 03-06; V Swaledale from 06. *The Vicarage, Reeth, Richmond DL11 6TR* Tel (01748) 886429 Mobile 07866-750211 E-mail carolinehewlett@hotmail.com

HEWLETT, David Bryan. b 49. Bris Univ BEd72. Qu Coll Birm 77. **d** 79 **p** 80. C Ludlow *Heref* 79-81; TV 81-84; V Marden w Amberley and Wisteston 84-92; Lect Glouc Sch for Min 84-92; Field Officer for Lay Min *Heref* 84-91; CME Officer 86-92; Dir Post-Ord Tr 91-92; Hd Master St Fran Sch Pewsey 92-94; Co-ord Chapl Frenchay Healthcare NHS Trust Bris 94-00; Dir Past Studies OLM Scheme and CME *Linc* 00-04; Par Development Adv (South) 00-04; R Pontesbury I and II *Heref* 04-08; V Corbridge w Halton and Newton Hall *Newc* from 08; AD Corbridge from 09. *The Vicarage, Greencroft Avenue, Corbridge NE45 5DW* Tel (01434) 632128 E-mail david.hewlett3@btopenworld.com

HEWLETT, David Jonathon Peter. b 57. Dur Univ BA79 PhD83. Ridley Hall Cam 82. **d** 83 **p** 84. C New Barnet St Jas *St Alb* 83-86; Lect CITC 86-90; P-in-c Feock *Truro* 91-95; Jt Dir SWMTC 91-95; Prin 95-03; Adv Local Ord Min 91-95; Hon Can Truro Cathl 01-03; Prin Qu Coll Birm from 03. *71 Farquhar Road, Edgbaston, Birmingham B15 2QP* Tel 0121-452 2612 *or* 452 2603 Fax 454 8171 E-mail d.hewlett@queens.ac.uk

HEWLETT, Guy Edward. b 59. Thames Poly CertEd89 Open Univ BA90. Oak Hill Th Coll 96. **d** 96 **p** 97. NSM Sudbury St Andr *Lon* 96-99; C Harrow Trin St Mich 99-05; V Harrow Weald St Mich from 05. *74 Bishop Ken Road, Harrow HA3 7HR* Tel (020) 8861 1710 E-mail guy.saintmikes@gmail.com

HEWLETT-SMITH, Peter Brian. b 40. OBE87. Ripon Coll Cuddesdon 06. **d** 06. NSM Heckfield w Mattingley and Rotherwick *Win* 06-07; NSM Whitewater from 07. *10 Winchfield Court, Pale Lane, Winchfield, Hook RG27 8SP* Tel (01252) 842163 Mobile 07709-404046 E-mail peter.hewlettsmith@gmail.com

HEWLINS, Pauline Elizabeth. See SEAMAN, Mrs Pauline Elizabeth

HEWSON, Mrs Mandy Carol. b 61. Anglia Ruskin Univ BSc05. St Mellitus Coll BA11. **d** 11. NSM E Springfield *Chelmsf* from 11. *33 Meon Close, Chelmsford CM1 7QG* Tel (01245) 287710 E-mail mandy@hewson67.fsnet.co.uk

HEWSON, Mrs Rose Raylene. b 47. SAOMC 96. **d** 99 **p** 00. NSM High Wycombe *Ox* 99-02; NSM Burnham w Dropmore, Hitcham and Taplow 02-08; NSM Hitcham 08-10; rtd 10. *11 Hammerwood Road, Ashurst Wood, East Grinstead RH19 3TJ* Tel (01342) 319027 E-mail rosie@hewsons.net

HEWSON, Thomas Robert. b 45. Man Univ BA66. S'wark Ord Course 85. **d** 89 **p** 90. C Chinnor w Emmington and Sydenham etc *Ox* 89-92; TV Burnham w Dropmore, Hitcham and Taplow 92-08; V Hitcham 08-10; rtd 10. *11 Hammerwood Road, Ashurst Wood, East Grinstead RH19 3TJ* Tel (01342) 319027 E-mail trh@hewsons.net

HEYCOCKS, Christian John. b 71. Univ of Wales (Ban) BA93 MA96. Westcott Ho Cam 94 CITC 97. **d** 97 **p** 98. C Rhyl w St Ann *St As* 97-00; Chapl RN 00-06; Chapl Univ Staff Cam and C Cambridge Gt St Mary w St Mich *Ely* 06-09; V Sheringham *Nor* from 09. *The Vicarage, 10 North Street, Sheringham NR26 8LW* Tel (01263) 822089 E-mail rev.heycocks15@btinternet.com

HEYES, Andrew Robin. b 61. Man Univ BA93. St Steph Ho Ox 93. **d** 95 **p** 96. C Tonge Moor *Man* 95-00; V Glodwick 00-06; R Tampa St Clem USA from 06. *3817 Beneraid Street, Land o' Lakes FL 34638, USA* Tel (001) (813) 995 5364 E-mail aheyes@tampabay.rr.com

HEYES, Robert John. b 46. STETS 00. **d** 03 **p** 04. NSM Bramley and Grafham *Guildf* 03-08; NSM Shamley Green 08-11; rtd 11. *Juniper Cottage, 22 Eastwood Road, Bramley, Guildford GU5 0DS* Tel (01483) 893706 Fax 894001 E-mail bobheyes@onetel.com

HEYGATE, Stephen Beaumont. b 48. Loughb Univ BSc71 CQSW73 PhD89. St Jo Coll Nottm 86. **d** 88 **p** 89. C Aylestone St Andr w St Jas *Leic* 88-90; V Cosby 90-00; V Evington from 00; P-in-c Leic St Phil 00-04; Bp's Adv for Healing and Deliverance from 04. *Evington Vicarage, Stoughton Lane, Stoughton, Leicester LE2 2FH* Tel 0116-271 2032 E-mail stephenheygate@btinternet.com

HEYHOE, Jonathan Peter. b 53. Man Univ BA75. Trin Coll Bris 77. **d** 80 **p** 81. C Woking St Pet *Guildf* 80-83; C Heatherlands St Jo *Sarum* 83-91; Chr Renewal Cen Rostrevor 91-95; Perm to Offic *D & D* 91-97; I Ballybay w Mucknoe and Clontibret *Clogh* 98-11; Preb Clogh Cathl 06-11; rtd 11. *11 Rowallon, Warrenpoint, Newry BT34 3TR* E-mail jheyhoe@esatclear.ie

HEYN, Lucinda Jane. b 68. Ripon Coll Cuddesdon 07. **d** 10 **p** 11. C Goring and Streatley w S Stoke *Ox* from 10. *7 The Bull Meadow, Streatley, Reading RG8 9QD* Tel (01491) 871970 E-mail luci_heyn@hotmail.co.uk

HEYWARD, Daniel James. b 74. Ex Univ BA97 MCIPD. Wycliffe Hall Ox 09. **d** 11. C Reading Greyfriars *Ox* from 11. *26 Prospect Street, Reading RG1 7YG* Tel 0118-958 7850 Mobile 07508-346550 E-mail dan.heyward@greyfriars.org.uk

HEYWOOD, Mrs Anne Christine. b 44. Sarum Th Coll. **d** 97 **p** 98. C Talbot Village *Sarum* 97-01; TV Shaston 01-09; rtd 10. *26 Casterbridge Way, Gillingham SP8 4FG* Tel (01747) 825259 E-mail ac.heywood@virgin.net

HEYWOOD, Anthony. See HEYWOOD, Richard Anthony

HEYWOOD, David Stephen. b 55. Selw Coll Cam BA76 MA80 SS Hild & Bede Coll Dur PhD89. St Jo Coll Dur 80. **d** 86 **p** 87. C Cheltenham St Luke and St Jo *Glouc* 86-90; TV Sanderstead All SS *S'wark* 90-98; V Edensor *Lich* 98-03; Deanery and Min Development Officer 03-06; Lect Past Th Ripon Coll Cuddesdon from 06. *3 College Field, Cuddesdon, Oxford OX44 9HL* Tel (01865) 874974 *or* 877444 E-mail david.heywood@ripon-cuddesdon.ac.uk

HEYWOOD, Deiniol John Owen. See KEARLEY-HEYWOOD, Deiniol John Owen

HEYWOOD, Geoffrey Thomas. b 26. St Mich Coll Llan 60. **d** 62 **p** 63. C Porthmadog *Ban* 62-64; C Llandudno 64-67; V Caerhun w Llangelynin 67-74; Asst Chapl HM Pris Liv 74-75; Chapl HM

Pris Ex 75-77; Chapl HM Pris Wakef 77-79; Chapl HM YOI Eastwood Park 79-90; Chapl HM Pris Leyhill 79-90; rtd 90; Perm to Offic *Glouc* 94-05. *5 Meadow Road, Leyhill, Wotton-under-Edge GL12 8HW*

HEYWOOD, Mrs Margaret Anne (Meg). b 52. Luton Coll of HE BSc81. EMMTC 04. **d** 07 **p** 07. Chapl Ox Min Course from 06; NSM Ox St Clem 07-08; NSM Thame 09-10; Perm to Offic from 10. *3 College Field, Cuddesdon, Oxford OX44 9HL* Tel (01865) 874974 E-mail meg.heywood@hotmail.com

HEYWOOD, Michael Herbert. b 41. Liv Univ BSc63. Clifton Th Coll 63. **d** 65 **p** 66. C Low Elswick *Newc* 65-68; C St Helens St Mark *Liv* 68-75; Leprosy Miss Area Org NE and Cumbria 75-85; S Lon, Surrey and Berks 85-91; Internat Publicity and Promotional Co-ord 91-01; Hon C New Malden and Coombe *S'wark* 01-06; rtd 06. *9 Dryburn Road, Durham DH1 5AJ* Tel 0191-386 0087 E-mail biddyandmike@lineone.net

HEYWOOD, Peter. b 46. Cranmer Hall Dur 72. **d** 75 **p** 76. C Blackley St Andr *Man* 75-78; C Denton Ch Ch 78-80; V Constable Lee 80-01; rtd 01; Perm to Offic *Man* from 01. *3 Brockclough Road, Rossendale BB4 9LG* Tel (01706) 212297

HEYWOOD, Richard Anthony. b 77. St Jo Coll Dur BA99. Oak Hill Th Coll 04. **d** 07 **p** 08. C Lt Shelford *Ely* 07-11; TV Thetford *Nor* from 11. *44 Nunsgate, Thetford IP24 3EL* Tel 07804-671405 (mobile) E-mail tony.heywood@talk21.com

HEZEL, Adrian. b 43. Chelsea Coll Lon BSc64 PhD67. NOC 78. **d** 81 **p** 82. NSM Mirfield *Wakef* 81-89; C 89-90; V Shelley and Shepley 90-99; V Hoylake *Ches* 99-08; rtd 08. *14 John Yeoman Close, Little Neston, Neston CH64 4BF* Tel 0151-336 3773 E-mail ahezel@btinternet.com

HIBBARD, John. b 42. **d** 03 **p** 04. NSM Stewkley w Soulbury and Drayton Parslow *Ox* 03-06; Perm to Offic 06-08 and from 11; NSM Fenny Stratford 08-11. *Chapel Side, 6 Nearton End, Swanbourne, Milton Keynes MK17 0SL* Tel (01296) 720449

HIBBERD, Brian Jeffery. b 35. Fitzw Coll Cam MA62 Southn Univ MA84. Ridley Hall Cam 58. **d** 60 **p** 61. C Cambridge H Trin *Ely* 60-63; C Doncaster St Mary *Sheff* 63-66; Asst Master Price's Sch Fareham 66-69; Warblington Sch Havant 69-71; Hd Soc and RS Carisbrooke High Sch 71-84; Distr Health Promotion Officer Is of Wight 84-88; SW Herts 88-90; Hd RS Goffs Sch Cheshunt 90-95; rtd 95; Teacher Qu Sch Bushey 95-97; Teacher R Masonic Sch for Girls Rickmansworth 97-00; Hon C Abbots Langley *St Alb* 00-01; Perm to Offic from 01. *50 Rosehill Gardens, Abbots Langley WD5 0HF* Tel (01923) 267391

HIBBERD, John. b 60. Wadh Coll Ox MA82. Trin Coll Bris BA89. **d** 89 **p** 90. C Northolt St Mary *Lon* 89-92; C-in-c Southall Em CD 92-94; Min of Miss Through Faith Miss *Ely* from 95. *Celandine, 1 School Lane, Swavesey, Cambridge CB24 4RL* Tel (01954) 200285 E-mail john.hibberd3@ntlworld.com

HIBBERD, John Charles. b 38. Bernard Gilpin Soc Dur 62 Chich Th Coll 63. **d** 66 **p** 67. C W Drayton *Lon* 66-70; C Noel Park St Mark 70-72; C Ealing St Steph Castle Hill 72-75; V Gunnersbury St Jas 75-84; V Whitton SS Phil and Jas 84-86; Finance and Trust Sec Lon Dioc Fund 87-98; Perm to Offic 87-98; rtd 98. *18 Pursley Close, Sandown PO36 9QP* Tel (01983) 401036

HIBBERT, Miss Anne Mary Elizabeth. Southn Univ BA81. Trin Coll Bris 81. dss 83 **d** 87 **p** 94. Muswell Hill St Jas w St Matt *Lon* 83-86; Lee H Trin w St Jo 86-87; Par Dn 87-90; Perm to Offic *Cov* from 90; Evang Co-ord and Adv CPAS 90-98; Churches Millennium Exec 98-99; Miss & Spirituality Adv BRF 99-03; Dir Well Chr Healing Cen from 03. *The Well Christian Healing Centre, PO Box 3407, Leamington Spa CV32 6ZH* Tel (01926) 888003 Mobile 07973-563667 E-mail anne@wellhealing.org

HIBBERT, Charles Dennis. b 24. Linc Th Coll 69. **d** 70 **p** 71. C Radcliffe-on-Trent *S'well* 70-73; P-in-c Ladybrook 73-77; V 77-79; V Boughton 79-85; V Ollerton 79-85; R Nuthall 85-89; rtd 89; Perm to Offic *S'well* from 89. *27 Nottingham Road, Kimberley, Nottingham NG16 2NB* Tel 0115-938 6302

HIBBERT, Canon Peter John. b 43. Hull Univ BA71 Lon Univ CertEd72 MA79. Sarum & Wells Th Coll 85. **d** 88 **p** 89. C Newsome and Armitage Bridge *Wakef* 88-92; P-in-c Newton Flowery Field *Ches* 92-00; P-in-c Hyde St Thos 97-00; V Handsworth St Jas *Birm* 00-08; P-in-c Altarnon w Bolventor, Laneast and St Clether *Truro* 08-09; P-in-c Micklehurst *Ches* from 09; P-in-c Hyde St Thos from 10; Hon Can Ches Cathl from 11. *The Vicarage, Church Lane, Mossley, Ashton-under-Lyne OL5 9HY* E-mail hibbert631@btinternet.com

HIBBERT, Prof Peter Rodney. b 53. Man Univ LLB74 Nottm Univ MA99 Solicitor 77. EMMTC 96. **d** 99 **p** 00. C Knighton St Mary Magd *Leic* 99-01; Perm to Offic *Leic* from 01 and *Birm* from 03. *Grange Cottage, 37 Rushes Lane, Lubenham, Market Harborough LE16 9TN* Tel (01858) 433174

HIBBERT, Richard Charles. b 62. Trin Coll Bris BA93. **d** 96 **p** 97. C Luton St Mary *St Alb* 96-00; V Bedford Ch Ch from 00; RD Bedford from 10. *Christ Church Vicarage, 115 Denmark Street, Bedford MK40 3TJ* Tel and fax (01234) 359342 E-mail vicar@christchurchbedford.org.uk

HIBBINS, Neil Lance. b 60. St Anne's Coll Ox BA82 MA87. St Mich Coll Llan 83. **d** 85 **p** 86. C Griffithstown *Mon* 85-87; C Pontypool 87-88; TV Pontypool 88-92; Walsall Hosps NHS

Trust 92-96; Asst Chapl Manor Hosp Walsall 92-96; R Norton Canes *Lich* from 96. *The Rectory, 81 Church Road, Norton Canes, Cannock WS11 9PQ* Tel (01543) 278969 E-mail neil_hibbins@lycos.com

HIBBS, Peter Wilfred. b 56. NOC 05. **d** 08 **p** 09. NSM Gt Snaith *Sheff* from 08. *Peveril, High Street, Snaith, Goole DN14 9HJ* Tel (01405) 862517 Mobile 07885-348498

HICHENS, Anthony. b 29. AKC59. **d** 60 **p** 61. C Ashford St Hilda *Lon* 60-64; C Leeds St Wilfrid *Ripon* 64-66; V Waramuri Guyana 67-75; P-in-c Stratton Audley w Godington *Ox* 76-83; P-in-c Finmere w Mixbury 76-78; P-in-c Fringford w Hethe and Newton Purcell 78-83; R Stratton Audley and Godington, Fringford etc 83-95; rtd 95; Perm to Offic *Pet* 95-07. *9 Brookside Mews, 666 Town Bush Road, Oak Park, Pietermaritzburg, 3201 South Africa* Tel (0027) (33) 347 3762

HICKES, Roy Edward. b 31. St Aid Birkenhead 56. **d** 59 **p** 60. C New Bury *Man* 59-63; C Wyther *Ripon* 63-65; R Oldham St Andr *Man* 65-69; V Smallbridge 69-79; R Winford *B & W* 79-81; R Winford w Felton Common Hill 81-88; RD Chew Magna 85-88; Chapl Costa Blanca *Eur* 88-92; rtd 92; Perm to Offic *B & W* and *Bris* from 92; Hon C Wrington w Butcombe *B & W* 97-98. *17 Haycombe, Bristol BS14 0AJ* Tel (01275) 544750 E-mail royhickes@blueyonder.co.uk *or* randwhickes@blueyonder.co.uk

HICKFORD, Canon Michael Francis. b 53. Edin Th Coll 84. **d** 86 **p** 87. Chapl St Jo Cathl Oban 86-89; R Alexandria *Glas* 89-95; P-in-c Dingwall and Strathpeffer *Mor* 95-03; Dean Mor 98-03; R Inverness St Andr and Provost St Andr Cathl Inverness 03-04; Chapl NHS Highland from 04; Hon Can St Andr Cathl Inverness from 07. *New Craigs Hospital, 8 Leachkin Road, Inverness IV3 8NP* Tel (01463) 704000 ext 2426 Mobile 07795-238928 E-mail michael.hickford@nhs.net

HICKLING, John. b 34. Handsworth Coll Birm 56. Launde Abbey 69. **d** 69 **p** 70. In Methodist Ch 59-69; C Melton Mowbray w Thorpe Arnold *Leic* 69-71; TV 71-75; R Waltham on the Wolds w Stonesby and Saltby 75-84; R Aylestone St Andr w St Jas 84-93; R Husbands Bosworth w Mowsley and Knaptoft etc 93-96; rtd 96; Perm to Offic *Leic* from 99. *28 Oxford Drive, Melton Mowbray LE13 0AL* Tel (01664) 560770

HICKMAN, John William. b 38. Barrister-at-Law (Middle Temple) 69 Qu Coll Cam LLM81. Oak Hill Th Coll 92. **d** 95 **p** 96. NSM Sevenoaks St Nic *Roch* 95-98; P-in-c Stedham w Iping *Chich* 98-04; rtd 04; Perm to Offic *Chich* from 05. *Bywood, Selham Road, West Lavington, Midhurst GU29 0EG* Tel (01730) 810821

HICKS, Miss Barbara. b 42. Cranmer Hall Dur BA71. dss 85 **d** 87 **p** 94. Norton Woodseats St Paul *Sheff* 85-87; Par Dn Sheff St Jo 87-94; C 94-02; Chapl Shrewsbury Hosp 96-02; rtd 02; Perm to Offic *Sheff* from 06. *87 Underwood Road, Sheffield S8 8TG* Tel 0114-255 8087

HICKS, Clive Anthony. b 58. Man Univ BA79 Bris Univ PhD88. Coll of Resurr Mirfield 09. **d** 11. C Budbrooke *Cov* from 11. *29 Rogers Way, Chase Meadow, Warwick CV34 6PY* Tel (01926) 400263 Mobile 07804-792307 E-mail cliveahicks@gmail.com

HICKS, Ms Eunice. b 41. Trin Coll Bris BA00. WEMTC 01. **d** 01 **p** 02. NSM Chew Magna w Dundry and Norton Malreward *B & W* 01-06; NSM Rowledge and Frensham *Guildf* 06-10; rtd 10. *The Vicarage, The Street, Frensham, Farnham GU10 3DT* Tel (01252) 792137

HICKS, Francis Fuller. b 28. Sarum & Wells Th Coll 71. **d** 74 **p** 75. C Broadstone *Sarum* 74-78; P-in-c Kington Magna and Buckhorn Weston 78-79; TV Gillingham 79-86; P-in-c Portland St Jo 86-89; V 89-93; rtd 93; Perm to Offic *B & W* and *Sarum* from 93. *Windyridge, 21 Castle Road, Sherborne DT9 3RW* Tel (01935) 814837

HICKS, Hazel Rebecca. b 54. Open Univ BA92. CITC 05. **d** 08 **p** 09. NSM Annagh w Drumaloor, Cloverhill and Drumlane *K, E & A* 08-11; P-in-c Arvagh w Carrigallen, Gowna and Columbkille from 11. *Garvary Lodge, 49 Teemore Road, Derrylin, Enniskillen BT92 9QB* Tel (028) 6774 8422 Mobile 07770-852362 E-mail hazel6004@yahoo.co.uk

HICKS, Miss Joan Rosemary. b 60. Homerton Coll Cam BEd83. Westcott Ho Cam 87. **d** 90 **p** 94. C Wendover *Ox* 90-95; C Earley St Pet 95-98; P-in-c Beech Hill, Grazeley and Spencers Wood 98-05; P-in-c Cox Green from 05. *The Vicarage, 9 Warwick Close, Maidenhead SL6 3AL* Tel (01628) 622139 E-mail joanhicks@compuserve.com

HICKS, John Michael. b 67. Crewe & Alsager Coll BA89 K Coll Lon MA01 K Alfred's Coll Win PGCE90. NTMTC 02. **d** 05 **p** 06. NSM Grosvenor Chpl *Lon* 05-09; NSM Westmr St Steph w St Jo from 09. *167 John Ruskin Street, London SE5 0PQ* Tel (020) 7641 5930 Mobile 07971-670092 E-mail jnhx@hotmail.com

HICKS (née HODGSON), Julia Ruth. b 66. Somerville Coll Ox BA88 UEA PGCE89. Westcott Ho Cam 06. **d** 08 **p** 09. C Bridgwater St Mary and Chilton Trinity *B & W* from 08; R Merriott w Hinton, Dinnington and Lopen from 11. *The Rectory, Church Street, Merriott TA16 5PS* Tel 07812-179381 (mobile) E-mail juliahicks1@googlemail.com

HICKS, Richard Barry. b 32. Dur Univ BA55. Sarum Th Coll 59. **d** 61 **p** 62. C Wallsend St Luke *Newc* 61-64; C Tynemouth Ch Ch 64-69; V Tynemouth St Jo 69-75; V Prudhoe 75-82; TV Swanborough *Sarum* 82-86; R Hilperton w Whaddon and Staverton etc 86-97; rtd 97; Perm to Offic *Newc* from 97 and *Carl* from 98. *Lane House, Sawmill Lane, Brampton CA8 1DA* Tel (01697) 72156

HICKS, Robert Buxton. b 66. Ex Univ BSc90. Westcott Ho Cam 06. **d** 08 **p** 09. C Bridgwater St Fran *B & W* from 08; C Merriott w Hinton, Dinnington and Lopen from 11. *The Rectory, Church Street, Merriott TA16 5PS* Tel 07968-153988 (mobile) E-mail bobhicks66@googlemail.com

HICKS, Stuart Knox. b 34. Univ of W Ontario BA56 Huron Coll LTh59 Ox Univ DipEd67. **d** 58 **p** 60. Canada 58-65; C Allerton *Liv* 65-66; Hon C Rye Park St Cuth *St Alb* 68-72; Lic to Offic *B & W* 72-87 and 88-95; Chapl Magdalen Chpl Bath 80-86; Chapl Partis Coll Bath 88-90; rtd 99. *Folly Orchard, The Folly, Saltford, Bristol BS31 3JW* Tel (01225) 873391

HICKS, Mrs Valerie Joy. b 47. SRN69. Cant Sch of Min 82. **dss** 85 **d** 87 **p** 94. Roch 85-89; Hon Par Dn 87-89; Par Dn Thatcham *Ox* 89-93; TD Aylesbury w Bierton and Hulcott 93-94; TV 94-00; P-in-c Dordon *Birm* 00-09; V 09-10; Dioc Chapl MU 01-06; rtd 10; Perm to Offic *Lich* from 11. *12 Rocklands Crescent, Lichfield WS13 6DH* E-mail val@hicksres.plus.com

HICKS, Canon William Trevor. b 47. Hull Univ BA68 Fitzw Coll Cam BA70 MA74. Westcott Ho Cam 68. **d** 70 **p** 71. C Cottingham *York* 70-73; C Elland *Wakef* 73-76; V Walsden 76-81; V Knottingley 81-92; R Castleford All SS 92-96; P-in-c Womersley and Kirk Smeaton 96-00; RD Pontefract 94-99; V Bolsover *Derby* 00-11; RD Bolsover and Staveley 05-11; Hon Can Derby Cathl 07-11; rtd 11. *18 Spittal Green, Bolsover, Chesterfield S44 6TP* E-mail trevorhicks1@aol.com

HICKSON, Gordon Crawford Fitzgerald. b 51. CCC Cam MA76. **d** 06 **p** 07. NSM Ox St Aldate 06-10; Perm to Offic from 10. *31 Orchard Road, Oxford OX2 9BL* Tel (01865) 862981 Mobile 07713-688079

HIDE, Timothy John. b 71. Roehampton Inst BA95. St Steph Ho Ox 97. **d** 99 **p** 00. C Woodford St Mary w St Phil and St Jas *Chelmsf* 99-01; C Upminster 01-05; Asst P Forest Gate Em w Upton Cross 05-06; Perm to Offic 06-08; TV Canvey Is from 08. *St Anne's House, 51 St Anne's Road, Canvey Island SS8 7LS* Tel (01268) 514412 Fax 08707-622402 E-mail frtimhide@btinternet.com

HIDER, David Arthur. b 46. Lon Univ BSc67. Sarum & Wells Th Coll 86. **d** 89 **p** 90. NSM Southbourne w W Thorney *Chich* 89-91; C Goring-by-Sea 91-94; P-in-c Peacehaven and Telscombe Cliffs 94-99; V 99-09; P-in-c Telscombe w Piddinghoe and Southease 94-99; V Telscombe Village 99-09; V Piddinghoe 99-09; V Southease 99-09; rtd 09. *4 Guildford Close, Emsworth PO10 8LW* Tel (01243) 377636 E-mail revd_d_hider@msn.com

HIDER, Mrs Melanie Anne. b 53. UEA BA91 Homerton Coll Cam PGCE92. **d** 06 **p** 07. OLM Nor Lakenham St Alb and St Mark from 06. *10 Brian Avenue, Norwich NR1 2PH* Tel (01603) 622373 E-mail melaniehider@beemerz.co.uk

HIGGINBOTTOM, Richard. b 48. Lon Univ BD74. Oak Hill Th Coll. **d** 74 **p** 75. C Kenilworth St Jo *Cov* 74-77; C Finham 77-79; P-in-c Attleborough 79-81; V 81-84; Asst Chapl HM Pris Brixton 84-85; Chapl HM Pris Roch 85-92; Camp Hill 92-00; HM YOI Dover 00-03; rtd 03; Perm to Offic *Cant* 03-07. *c/o Crockford, Church House, Great Smith Street, London SW1P 3AZ* Tel 07779-775081 (mobile)

HIGGINBOTTOM, Richard William. b 51. Man Univ BA73 MA75. Edin Th Coll 83. **d** 85 **p** 86. C Knighton St Mary Magd *Leic* 85-87; C Northleach w Hampnett and Farmington *Glouc* 87-89; V Hayfield *Derby* 89-93; CPAS Min Adv for Scotland 93-08; Community Development Officer Tulloch NET from 08. *2 Highfield Place, Bankfoot, Perth PH1 4AX* Tel (01738) 787429 Mobile 07548-209922 E-mail richardh@tullochnet.org.uk

HIGGINS, Anthony Charles. b 46. **d** 97 **p** 98. OLM Swanage and Studland *Sarum* from 97. *The Old School House, School Lane, Studland, Swanage BH19 3AJ* Tel (01929) 450691 E-mail revtonyhiggins@btinternet.com

HIGGINS, Bernard. b 42. Leic Poly BPharm63 PhD66 MRPharmS68. St Jo Coll Nottm 89. **d** 91 **p** 92. C Stockport St Geo *Ches* 91-94; C Stockport SW 94-95; P-in-c Dunham Massey St Marg and St Mark 95-98; V 98-00; rtd 00; Perm to Offic *Blackb* and *Carl* from 01. *16 Inglemere Close, Arnside, Carnforth LA5 0AP* Tel (01524) 761000 E-mail bclhigg@btinternet.com

HIGGINS, Canon Godfrey. b 39. St Chad's Coll Dur BA61 DipEd63. **d** 63 **p** 64. C Brighouse *Wakef* 63-66; C Huddersfield St Jo 66-68; R High Hoyland w Clayton W 68-75; V Marsden 75-83; V Pontefract St Giles 83-04; Hon Can Wakef Cathl 93-04; rtd 04; Perm to Offic *Bradf* from 07. *2 Holme View, Ilkley LS29 9EL* Tel (01943) 603861 E-mail godfreyhiggins@yahoo.co.uk

HIGGINS, John. b 44. Lon Bible Coll MTh98. Brasted Th Coll 69 Trin Coll Bris 71. **d** 73 **p** 74. C Clapham St Jas *S'wark* 73-74; C Ruskin Park St Sav and St Matt 74-77; C Hamworthy *Sarum* 77-80; V Bordesley St Andr *Birm* 80-83; V Bishop Sutton and Stanton Drew and Stowey *B & W* 83-09; rtd 09; Perm to Offic *Nor* and *St E* from 09. *129 St Martins Way, Thetford IP24 3QB* Tel (01842) 752655 E-mail rev.johnhiggins@btopenworld.com

HIGGINS, John Leslie. b 43. Open Univ BA79 Birm Univ MEd89 Univ of Cen England in Birm CQSW75. Lich Th Coll 64. **d** 66 **p** 67. C Sale St Anne *Ches* 66-69; C Bredbury St Mark 69-72; V Wharton 72-74; Hon C Annan and Lockerbie *Glas* 75-79; V Coseley Ch Ch *Lich* 79-89; R Arthuret *Carl* 89-96; Soc Resp Officer and Child Protection Co-ord 96-00; C Brampton and Farlam and Castle Carrock w Cumrew 96-00; Hon Can Carl Cathl 96-00; rtd 00; Hon C Annan *Glas* from 00; Perm to Offic *Carl* from 00. *Green Croft Cottage, The Haggs, Ecclefechan, Lockerbie DG11 3ED* Tel (01576) 300796 Fax 300790 Mobile 07867-505644 E-mail john_l_higgins@lineone.net

HIGGINS, Canon Kenneth. b 56. TCD BTh93. CITC 90. **d** 93 **p** 94. C Cregagh *D & D* 93-96; Bp's C Movilla 96-00; I 01-09; I Belfast St Donard from 09; Can Down Cathl from 06. *St Donard's Rectory, 421 Beersbridge Road, Belfast BT5 5DU* Tel (028) 9065 2321 Mobile 07986-866690 E-mail revkenhiggins@hotmail.com

HIGGINS, The Very Revd Michael John. b 35. OBE03. Birm Univ LLB57 G&C Coll Cam LLB59 PhD62. Ridley Hall Cam 63. **d** 65 **p** 65. C Ormskirk *Liv* 65-67; Selection Sec ACCM 67-74; Hon C St Marylebone St Mark w St Luke *Lon* 69-74; P-in-c Woodlands *B & W* 74-80; V Frome St Jo 74-80; TR Preston St Jo *Blackb* 80-91; Dean Ely 91-03; rtd 03; Perm to Offic *Ely* from 05. *Twin Cottage, North Street, Great Dunham, King's Lynn PE32 2LR* Tel (01328) 701058

HIGGINS, Richard Ellis. b 63. Univ of Wales BA84. St Mich Coll Llan 86. **d** 89 **p** 90. C Bargoed and Deri w Brithdir *Llan* 89-92; Zimbabwe 92-94; V Penmaen and Crumlin *Mon* 94-99; Chapl Glan Hafren NHS Trust 94-99; V Rhymney *Mon* 99-02; Chapl Pet Hosps NHS Trust from 03. *Chaplaincy Services, Peterborough Hospital NHS Trust, Thorpe Road, Peterborough PE3 6DA* Tel (01733) 874345 E-mail richard.higgins@pbh-tr.nhs.uk

HIGGINS, Rupert Anthony. b 59. Man Univ BA80. Wycliffe Hall Ox 82. **d** 85 **p** 86. C Plymouth St Andr w St Paul and St Geo *Ex* 85-90; C-in-c St Paul 88-90; Assoc V Clifton Ch Ch w Em *Bris* 90-95; V S Croydon Em *S'wark* 95-02; C Langham Place All So *Lon* 02-05; P-in-c Clifton Ch Ch w Em *Bris* 05-09; Asst Vacancy Development Adv Strategy Support 09-10; V Talbot Village *Sarum* from 10. *The Vicarage, 20 Alton Road, Bournemouth BH10 4AE* Tel (01202) 939799 E-mail rupert.higgins@gmail.com

HIGGINS, Mrs Sheila Margaret. b 46. STETS 09. **d** 10 **p** 11. NSM Aldingbourne, Barnham and Eastergate *Chich* from 10. *2 Orchard Terrace, The Street, Walberton, Arundel BN18 0PH* Tel (01243) 553901 Mobile 07884-495916 E-mail smhandaway@tiscali.co.uk

HIGGINS, Canon Timothy John. b 45. Bris Univ BEd70 Lanc Univ MA74. Cranmer Hall Dur. **d** 79 **p** 80. C Northampton All SS w St Kath *Pet* 79-82; V Whitton St Aug *Lon* 82-90; AD Hampton 86-90; TR Aylesbury w Bierton and Hulcott *Ox* 90-06; RD Aylesbury 94-04; Hon Can Ch 00-06; Can Res Bris Cathl from 06; P-in-c City of Bris 06-08; P-in-c Bris St Steph w St Jas and St Jo w St Mich etc from 08. *City Rectory, Apartment 8, 10 Unity Street, Bristol BS1 5HH* Tel 0117-929 4984 E-mail city.canon@bristol-cathedral.co.uk

HIGGINSON, Andrew John. b 62. Bradf Univ BTech85. Trin Coll Bris 02. **d** 04 **p** 05. C Quarrington w Old Sleaford *Linc* 04-08; C Silk Willoughby 04-08; P-in-c Freiston, Butterwick w Bennington, and Leverton from 08. *The Rectory, Butterwick Road, Freiston, Boston PE22 0LF* Tel (01205) 760480 E-mail andrewj.higginson@btopenworld.com

HIGGINSON, Richard Andrew. b 53. St Jo Coll Cam BA74 Man Univ PhD82. EAMTC 02. **d** 04 **p** 05. NSM Cambridge St Phil *Ely* from 04; Dir of Studies Ridley Hall Cam from 05. *15 Guest Road, Cambridge CB1 2AL* Tel (01223) 315667 *or* 741074 E-mail rah41@cam.ac.uk

HIGGINSON, Stanley. **d** 08. NSM Wigan St Mich *Liv* from 08. *12 Clifton Crescent, Wigan WN1 2LB* E-mail stanley.higginson33@yahoo.co.uk

HIGGON, David. Univ of Wales (Swansea) BA75 Birm Univ MBA96 Nottm Univ MA99. EMMTC 96. **d** 00 **p** 01. NSM Crich and S Wingfield *Derby* 00-04; Chapl HM Pris Dovegate 04-05; Perm to Offic *Derby* 05-07; Chapl HM Pris Ranby 07-11; NSM Crich and S Wingfield *Derby* from 11. *67 Main Road, Morton, Alfreton DE55 6HH* Tel (01773) 872332 E-mail dhiggon@btopenworld.com

HIGGOTT, Bryn Graham. b 54. Birm Poly BA76 Solicitor 79. NEOC 03. **d** 06 **p** 07. NSM Thirsk *York* 06-08. *19 Main Street, Mawsley, Kettering NN14 1GA* E-mail bghiggott@gmail.com

HIGGS, Andrew Richard Bowen. b 53. Man Univ BSc75. St Jo Coll Nottm 81. **d** 85 **p** 86. C Droylsden St Mary *Man* 85-88; C Harlow Town Cen w Lt Parndon *Chelmsf* 88-95; TV 95-02; Chapl Princess Alexandra Hosp NHS Trust 96-02; R Stifford

HIGGS

Chelmsf from 02. *The Rectory, High Road, North Stifford, Grays RM16 5UE* Tel (01375) 372733
E-mail andy@higgs4a.fsnet.co.uk

HIGGS, Michael John. b 53. Sarum & Wells Th Coll 76. **d** 80 **p** 81. C Cant St Martin and St Paul 80-84; C Maidstone St Martin 84-88; R Egerton w Pluckley 88-03; rtd 03. *8 Robinsons Mill, Mellis, Eye IP23 8DW* Tel (01379) 783926

HIGGS, Owen Christopher Goodwin. b 63. St Anne's Coll Ox BA84 MA88. St Steph Ho Ox 90. **d** 93 **p** 94. C Teddington St Mark and Hampton Wick *Lon* 93-96; C Lon Docks St Pet w Wapping St Jo 96-00; V Petts Wood *Roch* 00-09; V Bickley from 09. *The Vicarage, Bickley Park Road, Bromley BR1 2BE* Tel (020) 8467 3809 E-mail frhiggs@tiscali.co.uk

HIGHAM, Gerald Norman. b 40. St Aid Birkenhead 64. **d** 68 **p** 69. C Garston *Liv* 68-71; C Blundellsands St Nic 71-73; V Bolton All So w St Jas *Man* 73-78; V Tonge w Alkrington 78-84; P-in-c Edenfield 84-86; P-in-c Stubbins 84-86; V Edenfield and Stubbins 86-03; rtd 03; Perm to Offic *Blackb* from 03. *71 Cherry Tree Way, Rossendale BB4 4JZ* Tel (01706) 210143
E-mail revg.higham@rotary1280.org

HIGHAM, Canon Jack. b 33. Linc Coll Ox BA56 MA60 Union Th Sem (NY) STM61. Qu Coll Birm 58. **d** 60 **p** 61. C Handsworth *Sheff* 60-64; V Handsworth Woodhouse 64-70; USA 70-78; R Stoke Bruerne w Grafton Regis and Alderton *Pet* 78-83; RD Towcester 82-83; Can Res, Chan and Lib Pet Cathl 83-03; rtd 03; Perm to Offic *S'well* from 04. *44 Alma Hill, Kimberley, Nottingham NG16 2JF* Tel 0115-938 6063

HIGHAM, John Leonard. b 39. Wycliffe Hall Ox 62. **d** 65 **p** 66. C Prescot *Liv* 65-71; V Hollinfare 71-74; Adult and Youth Service Adv Knowsley 74-76; TV Padgate 76-84; V Farnworth 84-89; TR Sutton 89-02; rtd 02; Perm to Offic *Liv* from 03. *86 Ormskirk Road, Rainford, St Helens WA11 8DB*

HIGHAM (née ANNS), Canon Pauline Mary. b 49. Bris Univ BEd71. EMMTC 87. **d** 90 **p** 94. Par Dn Wirksworth w Alderwasley, Carsington etc *Derby* 90-92; Par Dn Lt Berkhamsted and Bayford, Essendon etc *St Alb* 92-94; C 94-96; P-in-c 96-05; R from 05; Jt RD Hertford and Ware from 05; Hon Can St Alb from 06. *1 Little Berkhamsted Lane, Little Berkhamsted, Hertford SG13 8LU* Tel (01707) 875940 Fax 875289

HIGHTON, Philip William. b 70. Liv Univ BSc91 Nottm Univ MSc92. Oak Hill Th Coll BA05. **d** 05 **p** 06. C Knutsford St Jo and Toft *Ches* 05-09; V Cheadle All Hallows from 09. *All Hallows' Vicarage, 222 Councillor Lane, Cheadle SK8 2JG* Tel 0161-428 9071 *or* 428 2804 E-mail phil highton@tiscali.co.uk

HIGHTON, William James. b 31. St Deiniol's Hawarden. **d** 82 **p** 83. NSM Thornton Hough *Ches* 82-84; C Cheadle 84-88; V Walton 88-99; rtd 99; Perm to Offic *Carl* from 01. *15 Mowbray Drive, Burton-in-Kendal, Carnforth LA6 1NF* Tel (01524) 782073

HIGMAN, John Charles. b 62. Plymouth Poly BSc84 MRSC01. SWMTC 03. **d** 06 **p** 07. NSM Peter Tavy, Mary Tavy, Lydford and Brent Tor *Ex* from 06. *Balwynd, Bal Lane, Mary Tavy, Tavistock PL19 9PE* Tel (01822) 810431

HIGTON, Anthony Raymond. b 42. Lon Sch of Th BD65. Oak Hill Th Coll 65. **d** 67 **p** 68. C Newark Ch Ch *S'well* 67-69; C Cheltenham St Mark *Glouc* 70-75; R Hawkwell *Chelmsf* 75-99; Gen Dir CMJ 99-05; R Jerusalem Ch Ch 03-05; R N w S Wootton *Nor* 06-09; rtd 09; Perm to Offic *Ely* and *Nor* from 09. *17 Church View, Marham, King's Lynn PE33 9HW* Tel (01760) 338342 Mobile 07815-891582 E-mail tony@higton.info

HILARY, Sister. *See* JORDINSON, Vera

HILBORN, David Henry Kyte. b 64. Nottm Univ BA85 PhD94 Mansf Coll Ox MA88. **d** 02 **p** 02. C Acton St Mary *Lon* 02-06; Dir Studies NTMTC 06-09; Dir 09-11; Asst Dean St Mellitus Coll *Lon* 09-11; Prin St Jo Coll Nottm from 11. *St John's College, Chilwell Lane, Bramcote, Nottingham NG9 3DS* Tel 0115-925 1114 Fax 943 6438

HILBORN, Mrs Mia Alison Kyte. b 63. City Univ BSc84 Mansf Coll Ox MA87. **d** 02 **p** 02. Chapl Team Ldr Guy's and St Thos' NHS Foundn Trust from 01; NSM N Lambeth *S'wark* from 02. *Guy's & St Thomas' NHS Foundn Trust, St Thomas Street, London SE1 9RT* Tel (020) 7188 5588 Mobile 07740-779585 E-mail mia.hilborn@gstt.sthames.nhs.uk

HILDITCH, Canon Janet. b 59. St Andr Univ MTheol81 PhD87. NOC 92. **d** 94 **p** 95. C Kirkholt *Man* 94-98; Chapl Rochdale Healthcare NHS Trust 97-98; Chapl N Man Health Care NHS Trust 98-00; Chapl Tameside and Glossop Acute Services NHS Trust from 00; Hon Can Man Cathl from 04. *Tameside General Hospital, Fountain Street, Ashton-under-Lyne OL6 9EW* Tel 0161-331 6000

HILDRED, David. b 61. Bath Univ BSc83 CertEd83. Wycliffe Hall Ox 86. **d** 89 **p** 90. C Westcliff St Mich *Chelmsf* 89-92; C Rayleigh 92-96; V Sidcup St Andr *Roch* 96-10; AD Sidcup 03-08; R Darfield *Sheff* from 10. *The Rectory, Church Street, Darfield, Barnsley S73 9JX* Tel (01226) 752236
E-mail david.hildred@talktalk.net

HILDRETH, Sarah Frances. b 72. St Mich Coll Llan BTh05. **d** 05 **p** 06. C Hawarden *St As* 05-08; V Bagillt from 08; P-in-c Mostyn

from 08. *The Vicarage, Bryntirion Road, Bagillt CH6 6BZ* Tel (01352) 732732 Mobile 07752-261931
E-mail revsarah3005@btinternet.com

HILDRETH, Steven Marcus. b 47. Leeds Univ LLB69 Solicitor 78. SNWTP 08. **d** 11. NSM Ches St Paul from 11. *3 Field Close, Tarvin, Chester CH3 8DL* Tel (01829) 749303
E-mail shildr1027@aol.com

HILES, Janet Rita. b 39. SAOMC 96. **d** 98 **p** 99. OLM Dorchester *Ox* 98-03; rtd 03; Perm to Offic *Portsm* from 04. *Malabar, The Broadway, Totland Bay PO39 0AN* Tel (01983) 752765
E-mail chrishiles@4thenet.co.uk

HILES, John Michael. b 32. Qu Coll Cam BA57 MA61. Sarum Th Coll 57. **d** 59 **p** 60. C Clifton St Jas *Sheff* 59-62; V Bramley St Fran 62-69; Hon C Holmfirth *Wakef* 69-89; Hon C Upper Holme Valley 89-91; Lic to Offic 91-97; Perm to Offic *Wakef* 97-03 and *Sarum* from 03. *22 Oldfield Road, Bishopdown, Salisbury SP1 3GQ* Tel (01722) 349951

HILL, Mrs Anne Doreen. b 40. **d** 88 **p** 94. Par Dn Bexleyheath St Pet *Roch* 88-90; Sub Chapl HM Pris Belmarsh 91-96; Dep Chapl 96-99; Hon C Lee St Mildred *S'wark* 93-04; rtd 04; Perm to Offic *Sarum* 05-08. *64 St Mary's Road, Poole BH15 2LL* Tel (01202) 666076 E-mail adhill40@hotmail.com

HILL, Barry Leon. b 79. Wycliffe Hall Ox BTh05. **d** 05 **p** 06. C Loughborough Em and St Mary in Charnwood *Leic* 05-09; Dioc Miss Enabler from 09. *1 Old Vicarage Mews, Sileby, Loughborough LE12 7FZ* E-mail barry@hill-home.co.uk

HILL, Canon Charles Bernard. b 50. Sheff Univ BA71 Qu Coll Ox DPhil76. Cant Sch of Min 91. **d** 94 **p** 95. NSM Sandgate St Paul w Folkestone St Geo *Cant* 94-98; NSM Folkestone H Trin w Ch 98-04; Eur Sec Coun for Chr Unity 99-08; Can Gib Cathl 03-08; P-in-c Benenden *Cant* 08-10; P-in-c Sandhurst w Newenden from 08; P-in-c Benenden and Sandhurst from 10. *The Vicarage, The Green, Benenden, Cranbrook TN17 4DL* Tel (01580) 240658 E-mail cbh.mail@ntlworld.com

HILL, Charles Merrick. b 52. Strathclyde Univ BA74. Qu Coll Birm. **d** 80 **p** 81. C Silksworth *Dur* 80-83; C Stockton St Pet 83-85; TV Southampton (City Cen) *Win* 85-87; V Portsea St Geo *Portsm* 87-94; P-in-c Bodenham w Hope-under-Dinmore, Felton etc *Heref* 94-04; P-in-c Hellingly and Upper Dicker *Chich* 04-05; V from 05. *The Vicarage, 14 Orchard Grange, Lower Dicker, Hailsham BN27 3PA* Tel (01323) 440246

HILL, Charles Winston. b 78. Lanc Univ BA99. St Steph Ho Ox 00. **d** 03 **p** 04. C Lt Marsden w Nelson St Mary *Blackb* 03-04; C Blackb St Thos w St Jude 04-07; C Blackb St Mich w St Jo and H Trin 04-07; Chapl HM Pris Preston 07-08; Chapl HM Pris Hindley 08-09; SSF 09-10; C from 10. *St Mark's Vicarage, 9 Rossendale Road, Burnley BB11 5DQ* Tel (01282) 428178
E-mail judopriest@orange.net

✠**HILL, The Rt Revd Christopher John.** b 45. K Coll Lon BD67 AKC67 MTh68. **d** 69 **p** 70 **c** 96. C Tividale *Lich* 69-73; C Codsall 73-74; Abp's Asst Chapl on Foreign Relns *Cant* 74-81; ARCIC from 74; Sec 74-90; Abp's Sec for Ecum Affairs *Cant* 82-89; Hon Can Cant Cathl 82-89; Chapl to The Queen 87-96; Can Res and Prec St Paul's Cathl 89-96; Select Preacher Ox Univ 90; Area Bp Stafford *Lich* 96-04; Bp Guildf from 04; Clerk of the Closet from 05. *Willow Grange, Woking Road, Guildford GU4 7QS* Tel (01483) 590500 Fax 590501
E-mail bishop.christopher@cofeguildford.org.uk

HILL, Christopher Murray. b 57. Lanchester Poly Cov BA78. Ox Min Course 05. **d** 07 **p** 08. NSM Warfield *Ox* from 07. *7 Shorland Oaks, Bracknell RG42 2JZ* Tel (01344) 867687 Mobile 07792-205124
E-mail chrismurrayhill@btopenworld.com

HILL, The Ven Colin. b 42. Leic Univ BSc64 Open Univ PhD88. Ripon Hall Ox 64. **d** 66 **p** 67. C Leic Martyrs 66-69; C Braunstone 69-71; Lect Ecum Inst Thornaby Teesside 71-72; V Worsbrough St Thos and St Jas *Sheff* 72-78; Telford Planning Officer *Lich* 78-96; RD Telford and Telford Severn Gorge *Heref* 80-96; Preb Heref Cathl 83-96; Can Res Carl Cathl 96-04; Dioc Sec 96-04; Adn W Cumberland 04-08; rtd 08. *1A Briery Bank, Arnside, Carnforth LA5 0HW* Tel (01524) 762629

HILL, Canon Colin Arnold Clifford. b 29. OBE96. Bris Univ 52 Univ of Wales (Ban) MPhil03. Ripon Hall Ox 55. **d** 57 **p** 58. C Rotherham *Sheff* 57-61; V Brightside St Thos 61-64; R Easthampstead *Ox* 64-73; Chapl RAF Coll Bracknell 68-73; V Croydon St Jo *Cant* 73-84; V Croydon St Jo *S'wark* 85-94; Chapl Abp Whitgift Foundn 73-94; Hon Can Cant Cathl 75-84; Hon Can *S'wark* Cathl 85-94; Chapl to The Queen 90-99; rtd 94. *Silver Birches, 70 Preston Crowmarsh, Wallingford OX10 6SL* Tel and fax (01491) 836102 E-mail colin.sb@btopenworld.com

HILL, David Rowland. b 34. Lon Univ BSc55. Qu Coll Birm. **d** 59 **p** 60. C Upper Tooting H Trin *S'wark* 59-61; C Cheam 61-63; C Richmond St Mary 63-68; V Sutton St Nicholas *Linc* 68-82; V Pinchbeck 82-99; rtd 99; Perm to Offic *Linc* 99-02 and from 05; Pet 04-11. *24 London Road, Spalding PE11 2TA* Tel (01775) 768912 E-mail revdandj.hill@virgin.net

HILL, David Royston. b 68. Westmr Coll Ox BTh96. ERMC 04. **d** 06 **p** 07. C Dereham and Distr *Nor* 06-09; R Quidenham Gp from 09; CF(V) from 09. *The Rectory, Church Hill, Banham, Norwich NR16 2HN* Tel (01953) 716014 Mobile 07827-815247 E-mail david.hill007@btinternet.com

HILL, Derek Stanley. b 28. AKC53. **d** 53 **p** 54. C Rushmere *St E* 53-55; S Africa 55-57; C Boreham Wood All SS *St Alb* 57-59; V Crowfield *St E* 59-67; P-in-c Stonham Aspal 59-61; R 61-67; V Bury St Edmunds St Geo 67-73; P-in-c Ampton w Lt Livermere and Ingham 68-73; V Gazeley w Dalham 73-75; P-in-c Lidgate w Ousden 73-74; P-in-c Gt Bradley 74-78; V Gazeley w Dalham and Moulton 75-78; V Gt Barton 78-86; V Bury St Edmunds All SS 86-93; rtd 93; Perm to Offic *St E* from 93. *Whinwillow, 38 Maltings Garth, Thurston, Bury St Edmunds IP31 3PP* Tel (01359) 230770

HILL, Elizabeth Jayne Louise. See DAVENPORT, Elizabeth Jayne Louise

HILL, Ernest. See HILL, George Ernest

HILL, Eugene Mark. b 48. Univ of Wales (Lamp) BA71. Sarum Th Coll 71. **d** 73 **p** 74. C Sutton St Nic *S'wark* 73-77; Hon C 77-80; Asst Chapl Em Sch Wandsworth 77-87; Chapl 87-04; Hon C St Helier *S'wark* 83-84; Hon C Caterham 84-98; Dir Chr Studies Course 85-04; Perm to Offic 98-07; Hon C Croydon St Jo 07-10. *22 Bramley Hill, South Croydon CR2 6LT* Tel (020) 8688 1387

HILL, Geoffrey Lionel. b 45. WEMTC 96. **d** 03 **p** 04. OLM Thornbury and Oldbury-on-Severn w Shepperdine *Glouc* 03-06; Perm to Offic Cyprus and the Gulf from 07. *4 Kalamionas Villas, Vasilikon Anavargos, 8025 Paphos, Cyprus* Tel (00357) (26) 910123 E-mail gl.hill@cytanet.com

HILL, George Ernest. b 25. St Jo Coll Nottm. **d** 85 **p** 87. OLM Selston *S'well* 85-93; Perm to Offic from 93. *103 Main Road, Jacksdale, Nottingham NG16 5HR* Tel (01773) 603446

HILL, Giles. See HILL, The Rt Revd Michael John Giles

HILL, Canon Gillian Beryl. b 53. Open Univ BA86 Portsm Univ PhD06. S Dios Minl Tr Scheme 87. **d** 90 **p** 94. NSM Southsea St Jude *Portsm* 90-95; C Southsea St Pet 95-01; V Catherington and Clanfield from 01; Hon Can Portsm Cathl from 03. *The Vicarage, 330 Catherington Lane, Catherington, Waterlooville PO8 0TD* Tel (023) 9259 3228 *or* 9259 3139 E-mail gillhill@inglisrd.freeserve.co.uk

HILL, Ian Maxwell. b 60. Loughb Univ BSc81 MCIT85. EMMTC 92. **d** 95 **p** 96. NSM Thurnby Lodge *Leic* 95-00; NSM Thurmaston 00-08; NSM Fosse from 08. *Shady Ash, 4 Sturrock Close, Thurnby, Leicester LE7 9QP* Tel 0116-243 1609

HILL, Ian Richard. b 69. Wycliffe Hall Ox 04. **d** 06 **p** 07. C Fareham St Jo *Portsm* 06-09; P-in-c Aspenden, Buntingford and Westmill *St Alb* from 09. *The Vicarage, Vicarage Road, Buntingford SG9 9BH* Tel (01763) 271552 E-mail ian@iansarahhill.co.uk

HILL, James. See HILL, Kenneth James

HILL, James Aidan Stuart. b 75. Ridley Hall Cam 06. **d** 09 **p** 10. C Cov H Trin from 09. *85 Stoney Road, Coventry CV3 6HH* Tel 07870-909439 (mobile) E-mail james.anglican@gmail.com

HILL, James Alexander Hart. b 82. K Coll Lon BA05. St Steph Ho Ox 05. **d** 07 **p** 08. C Tottenham St Paul *Lon* 07-11; C Tottenham St Benet Fink 10-11; P-in-c from 11. *St Benet Fink Vicarage, Walpole Road, London N17 6BH* Tel (020) 8888 4541 E-mail frjameshill@hotmail.co.uk

HILL, James Arthur. b 47. Ulster Univ BEd85. CITC 69. **d** 72 **p** 73. C Ballymena w Ballyclug *Conn* 72-74; C Arm St Mark w Aghavilly 74-78; C Derg w Termonamongan *D & R* 78-79; I Inver w Mountcharles, Killaghtee and Killybegs 79-87. *53 Dufferin Avenue, Bangor BT20 3AB* Tel (028) 9146 9090

HILL, Mrs Janice. Sheff Univ BEd79 Nottm Univ MA10. St Jo Coll Nottm 05. **d** 07 **p** 08. C Formby H Trin *Liv* 07-10; TV N Meols from 10. *The Rectory, 20 Moss Lane, Churchtown, Southport PR9 7QR* Tel (01704) 233547 E-mail janicehill.htc@talktalk.net

HILL, Mrs Jennifer Clare. b 50. City Univ BSc71 FBCO72. EMMTC 94. **d** 97 **p** 98. NSM Bottesford and Muston *Leic* 97-98; C Glen Parva and S Wigston 98-01; C Walsall Wood *Lich* 01-08; V Shelfield and High Heath 08-10; RD Walsall 05-10; TV Hemel Hempstead *St Alb* from 10; Dioc Adv for Women's Min from 11. *The Rectory, High Street, Hemel Hempstead HP1 3AE* Tel (01442) 265272 E-mail jennyhill@pawstime.co.uk

HILL, Mrs Jennifer Susan. b 50. Ex Univ BTh06 ALCM71 LLCM72 Gipsy Hill Coll of Educn CertEd75. SWMTC 03. **d** 06 **p** 07. C St Mewan w Mevagissey and St Ewe *Truro* 06-09; R W Buckrose *York* from 09. *The Rectory, 2 Sudnicton Croft, Westow, York YO60 7NB* Tel (01653) 618574 E-mail jenny@primrosemusic.btinternet.com

HILL, John Michael. b 34. FCA. Oak Hill NSM Course 81. **d** 85 **p** 86. NSM Rayleigh *Chelmsf* 85-96; Perm to Offic *Lon* 85-92; Chapl Rochford Gen Hosp 93-95; Chapl Southend Health Care NHS Trust 95-99; NSM Rochford *Chelmsf* 96-04; Perm to Offic from 04. *25D Belchamps Way, Hockley SS5 4NT* Tel (01702) 203287 E-mail michaelhill25@yahoo.co.uk

HILL, Mrs Judith Anne. b 47. RGN68. STETS 99. **d** 02 **p** 03. OLM Wool and E Stoke *Sarum* from 02. *9 High Street Close, Wool, Wareham BH20 6BW* Tel (01929) 462888 E-mail reverendjudy@tiscali.co.uk

HILL, Kenneth James. b 43. Leic Univ BA64 Lon Univ BD68. Oak Hill Th Coll 65. **d** 69 **p** 70. C Southall Green St Jo *Lon* 69-72; C Blackheath Park St Mich *S'wark* 72-75; C Bath Abbey w St Jas *B & W* 75-83; P-in-c Bath St Mich w St Paul 75-82; R 82-83; R Huntspill 83-91; Omega Order 91-98; Perm to Offic *B & W* and *Bris* 91-98; C Somerton w Compton Dundon, the Charltons etc *B & W* 98-07; rtd 07. *14 White Horse Road, Winsey, Bradford-on-Avon BA15 2JZ* Tel (01225) 864119 E-mail kjhill@tiscali.co.uk

HILL, Laurence Bruce. b 43. AKC67. **d** 69 **p** 70. C Feltham *Lon* 69-72; C-in-c Hampstead St Steph 72-77; V Finchley H Trin 77-10; rtd 10. *49 Abbots Gardens, London N2 0JG* Tel (020) 8444 0510 E-mail lorenzohill@yahoo.co.uk

HILL, Mrs Leonora Anne. b 59. Bath Univ BSc81 Westmr Coll Ox PGCE93. Ox Min Course 05. **d** 08 **p** 09. C Charlton Kings St Mary *Glouc* from 08. *20 Glynrosa Road, Charlton Kings, Cheltenham GL53 8QS* Tel (01242) 248858 Mobile 07773-137653 E-mail plcdhill@btinternet.com

HILL, Malcolm Crawford. b 43. Oak Hill Th Coll 68. **d** 71 **p** 72. C Maidstone St Luke *Cant* 71-74; C Longfleet *Sarum* 74-79; V Bexleyheath St Pet *Roch* 79-90; V Lee St Mildred *S'wark* 90-04; rtd 04; Perm to Offic *Sarum* from 05. *64 St Mary's Road, Poole BH15 2LL* Tel (01202) 666076 E-mail adhill40@hotmail.com

HILL, Mrs Marjorie Ann. b 38. MCSP60. St Jo Coll Nottm 92. **d** 94 **p** 95. C Hull St Martin w Transfiguration *York* 94-99; P-in-c Willerby w Ganton and Folkton 99-03; rtd 03; Perm to Offic *York* 03-06 and from 10; P-in-c Sigglesthorne w Nunkeeling and Bewholme 06-09; RD N Holderness 07-08. *40 Potterdale Drive, Little Weighton, Cottingham HU20 3UX* Tel (01482) 840544 E-mail marjoriehill28@googlemail.com

HILL, Mark. See HILL, Eugene Mark

HILL, Martyn William. b 43. Man Univ BSc64 Univ of Wales (Ban) PhD70 MInstP68 CPhys85. Westcott Ho Cam 90. **d** 92 **p** 93. C Horninglow *Lich* 92-95; TV Hawarden *St As* 95-00; V Bistre 00-05; rtd 05; Perm to Offic *St As* from 05. *Llys Penmaen, Penmaenpool, Dolgellau LL40 1YD* Tel (01391) 423305 Mobile 07835-238522 E-mail machillpenmaen@aol.com

HILL, Matthew Anthony Robert. b 71. Leeds Univ BA93 Univ of Wales (Cardiff) BD96. St Mich Coll Llan 94. **d** 97 **p** 98. C Cardiff St Jo *Llan* 97-00; Min Can Llan Cathl 00-04; P-in-c Dowlais and Penydarren 04-05; R 05-07; Chapl Univ of Wales (Trin St Dav) *St D* from 07. *The Chaplaincy, Forest Road, Lampeter SA48 8AN* Tel (01570) 424823 E-mail m.hill@trinitysaintdavid.ac.uk

HILL, Michael. See HILL, John Michael

✠**HILL, The Rt Revd Michael Arthur.** b 49. Ridley Hall Cam 74. **d** 77 **p** 78 **c** 98. C Addiscombe St Mary *Cant* 77-81; C Slough *Ox* 81-83; P-in-c Chesham Bois 83-90; R 90-92; RD Amersham 89-92; Adn Berks 92-98; Area Bp Buckm 98-03; Bp Bris from 03. *Bishop's Office, 58A High Street, Winterbourne, Bristol BS36 1JQ* Tel (01454) 777728 E-mail bishop@bristoldiocese.org

HILL, The Rt Revd Michael John Giles. b 43. S Dios Minl Tr Scheme 82. **d** 84 **p** 86. Community of Our Lady and St John from 67; Abbot from 90; Perm to Offic *Win* 84-92; Public Preacher from 92; Perm to Offic *Portsm* from 04. *Alton Abbey, Abbey Road, Beech, Alton GU34 4AP* Tel (01420) 562145 *or* 563575 Fax 561691

HILL, Miss Naomi Jean. b 75. Coll of Ripon & York St Jo BA96. Wycliffe Hall Ox BTh06. **d** 06 **p** 07. C Northampton St Giles *Pet* 06-10; C Nottingham St Nic *S'well* from 10; C Sneinton St Chris w St Phil from 10. *St Christopher's Vicarage, 180 Sneinton Boulevard, Nottingham NG2 4GL* Tel 07855-060410 (mobile) E-mail naomi.hill3@ntlworld.com

HILL, Nora. b 47. Univ of Wales BA95 PGCE97. St Mich Coll Llan 00. **d** 03 **p** 04. NSM Llandogo w Whitebrook Chpl and Tintern Parva *Mon* from 03. *3 Warwick Close, Chepstow NP16 5BU* Tel (01291) 626784

HILL, Patricia Frances. b 49. RGN90. SEITE 96. **d** 99 **p** 00. NSM Hythe *Cant* 99-01; Asst Chapl E Kent Hosps NHS Trust 99-00; Team Ldr Chapl from 01; NSM Saltwood *Cant* from 10; NSM Aldington w Bonnington and Bilsington etc from 10. *Springville, Sandling Road, Saltwood, Hythe CT21 4QJ* Tel (01303) 266649 *or* (01233) 633331 ext 88381 E-mail patricia.hill@ekht.nhs.uk

HILL, Peppie. See HILL, Stephanie Jane

HILL, Canon Peter. b 36. AKC60. St Boniface Warminster 60. **d** 61 **p** 62. C Gt Berkhamsted *St Alb* 61-67; R Bedford St Mary 67-69; P-in-c 69-70; V Goldington 69-79; V Biggleswade 79-90; RD Biggleswade 80-85; Hon Can St Alb 85-90; V Holbeach *Linc* 90-01; RD Elloe E 94-99; P-in-c The Suttons w Tydd 90-01; rtd 01; Perm to Offic *Nor* from 01 and *Ely* from 06. *Rayner Cottage, Low Street, Sloley, Norwich NR12 8HD* Tel (01692) 538744

HILL, The Ven Peter. b 50. Man Univ BSc71 Nottm Univ MTh90. Wycliffe Hall Ox 81. **d** 83 **p** 84. C Porchester *S'well* 83-86; V Huthwaite 86-95; P-in-c Calverton 95-04; RD S'well 97-01; Dioc Chief Exec 04-07; Adn Nottingham from 07; Hon Can S'well Minster 01-07. *4 Victoria Crescent, Sherwood, Nottingham NG5 4DA* Tel 0115-985 8641 E-mail archdeacon-nottm@southwell.anglican.org

HILL, Canon Richard Brian. b 47. Dur Univ BA68. Cranmer Hall Dur 68 Westcott Ho Cam 70. **d** 71 **p** 72. C Cockermouth All SS w Ch Ch *Carl* 71-74; C Barrow St Geo w St Luke 74-76; V Walney Is 76-83; Dir of Clergy Tr 83-90; P-in-c Westward, Rosley-w-Woodside and Welton 83-90; V Gosforth All SS *Newc* 90-05; rtd 05; Hon Can Newc Cathl from 05; Chapl St Mary Magd and H Jes Trust from 06; Asst Dioc Ecum Officer *Newc* from 08. *56 St Mary Magdalene Hospital, Claremont Road, Newcastle upon Tyne NE2 4NN* Tel 0191-261 2648 E-mail r.b.hill@lineone.net

HILL, Richard Hugh Oldham. b 52. CCC Ox BA74 BA77 MA78. Wycliffe Hall Ox 75. **d** 78 **p** 79. C Harold Wood *Chelmsf* 78-81; C Hampreston *Sarum* 81-86; TV N Ferriby *York* 86-97; V Swanland 97-08; R Church Stretton *Heref* from 08. *The Rectory, Ashbrook Meadow, Carding Mill Valley, Church Stretton SY6 6JF* Tel (01694) 722585

HILL, Robert Arthur. b 59. Trent Poly BSc83 Open Univ BA93. ACT 96. **d** 01 **p** 02. Sen Chapl Miss to Seafarers Australia 95-03; C Kettering SS Pet and Paul 03-08; Soc Resp Adv from 08. *19 Greenhill Road, Kettering NN15 7LW* Tel and fax (01536) 523603 E-mail robert.hill@peterborough-diocese.org.uk

HILL, Robert Joseph. b 45. Oak Hill Th Coll BA81. **d** 81 **p** 82. C W Derby St Luke *Liv* 81-84; P-in-c Devonport St Mich *Ex* 84-97; Chapl Morden Coll Blackheath 97-99; TV Manningham *Bradf* 99-04; P-in-c Davyhulme Ch Ch *Man* from 04. *Christ Church Vicarage, 14 Welbeck Avenue, Urmston, Manchester M41 0GJ* Tel 0161-748 2018 E-mail picdav.cc@virgin.net

HILL, Robin. b 35. Cranmer Hall Dur 59. **d** 62 **p** 63. C Aspley *S'well* 62-65; V Mansfield St Aug 65-71; R Hulland, Atlow and Bradley *Derby* 71-76; R Nollamara Australia 76-82; R Armadale 82-86; P-in-c Alkmonton, Cubley, Marston Montgomery etc *Derby* 86-93; P-in-c Ticknall, Smisby and Stanton-by-Bridge 93-99; P-in-c Barrow-on-Trent w Twyford and Swarkestone 94-99; rtd 99; Assoc P Fremantle Australia 99-05. *10/31 Pakenham Street, Freemantle WA 6160, Australia* Tel (0061) (8) 9336 4663

HILL, Rodney Maurice. b 44. Leeds Univ BA67 FCIPD. Ripon Coll Cuddesdon 04. **d** 05 **p** 06. NSM N Hinksey and Wytham *Ox* 05-10; NSM Osney from 10. *13 Hobson Road, Oxford OX2 7JX* Tel (01865) 426804 E-mail rodneymauricehill@hotmail.com

HILL, Canon Roger Anthony John. b 45. Liv Univ BA67 Linacre Coll Ox BA69 MA. Ripon Hall Ox 67. **d** 70 **p** 71. C St Helier *S'wark* 70-74; C Dawley Parva *Lich* 74-75; C Cen Telford 76-77; TV 77-81; TR 81-88; TR Newark *S'well* 88-02; RD Newark 90-95; Hon Can S'well Minster 98-02; R Man St Ann 02-07; AD Hulme 05-07; Bp's Missr 07-11; Hon Can Man Cathl 02-11; rtd 11; Perm to Offic *Man* from 11; Chapl to The Queen from 01. *4 Four Stalls End, Littleborough OL15 8SB* Tel (01706) 374719 E-mail hillraj@googlemail.com

HILL, Simon George. b 53. Reading Univ BSc75 MSc78 Lon Univ DMin10. S'wark Ord Course 80. **d** 83 **p** 84. NSM Croydon St Aug *Cant* 83-84; Swaziland 84-86; Fiji 86-88; NSM Croydon St Aug *S'wark* 88-90; Tanzania 90-94; Uganda 94-96; Swaziland 96-98; Perm to Offic *Chich* and *S'wark* 99-02; P-in-c Cockfield w Bradfield St Clare, Felsham etc *St E* 02-04; R Bradfield St Clare, Bradfield St George etc 04-11; RD Lavenham 09-11; V Copthorne *Chich* from 11. *The Vicarage, Church Road, Copthorne, Crawley RH10 3RD* Tel (01342) 712063 Mobile 07747-022903 E-mail mlima001@btinternet.com

HILL, Simon James. b 64. Sheff Univ BA85 Ex Univ PGCE88 Bris Univ MA09. Ripon Coll Cuddesdon BA84. **d** 95 **p** 96. C Manston *Ripon* 95-98; TV Dorchester *Ox* 98-03; Dir Berinsfield Progr Ripon Coll Cuddesdon 98-03; R Backwell w Chelvey and Brockley *B & W* 03-10; Dioc Dir of Clergy Development from 10. *87 Hawthorn Crescent, Yatton, Bristol BS49 4RG* Tel (01934) 832907 *or* (01749) 685107 E-mail simon.hill@bathwells.anglican.org

HILL, Stephanie Jane (Peppie). b 67. K Coll Lon LLB88. Wycliffe Hall Ox BTh05. **d** 05. C Loughborough Em and St Mary in Charnwood *Leic* 05-06. *1 Old Vicarage Mews, Sileby, Loughborough LE12 7FZ* E-mail pep@hill-home.co.uk

HILL, Stuart Graeme. b 64. Ripon Coll Cuddesdon BTh97. **d** 97 **p** 98. C Usworth *Dur* 97-99; C Monkwearmouth 99-01; TV 01-06; V Upper Derwent *York* from 06. *The Vicarage, 4 Cayley Lane, Brompton-by-Sawdon, Scarborough YO13 9DL* Tel (01723) 859694

HILL, Trevor Walton. b 30. Leeds Univ BA57. Coll of Resurr Mirfield. **d** 59 **p** 60. C Bollington St Jo *Ches* 59-62; C Woodchurch 62-64; V Addingham *Carl* 64-67; V Carl H Trin 67-71; R Wetheral w Warwick 71-80; P-in-c Doddington w Wychling *Cant* 80-82; P-in-c Newnham 80-82; rtd 95. *59 Medina Avenue, Newport PO30 1HG*

HILL, Walter Henry. b 06 **p** 07. Aux Min Cloyne Union *C, C & R* from 06. *Quetta, Glenatore, Conna, Co Cork, Republic of Ireland* Tel and fax (00353) (58) 56147 E-mail whill45@eircom.net

HILL, William. b 44. Man Univ BSc66 CEng73 MICE73. SEITE 95. **d** 98 **p** 99. NSM Farnham *Guildf* 98-01; P-in-c Smallburgh w Dilham w Honing and Crostwight *Nor* 01-05; rtd 05; Perm to

Offic *Nor* from 05; RD St Benet from 07. *Grange Farm House, Yarmouth Road, Worstead, North Walsham NR28 9LX* Tel (01692) 404917 E-mail revd.william.hill@btinternet.com

HILL-BROWN, Rachel Judith. b 65. Westmr Coll Ox BEd88. St Jo Coll Nottm MTh07. **d** 07. C Knowle *Birm* 07-10; C Tanworth 10-11; Hon C Dorridge from 11. *54 Glendon Way, Dorridge, Solihull B93 8SY* Tel (01564) 772472 E-mail rhillbrown@googlemail.com

HILL-BROWN, Timothy Duncan. b 65. Westmr Coll Ox BA87. Wycliffe Hall Ox 91. **d** 93 **p** 94. C Sparkhill w Greet and Sparkbrook *Birm* 93-97; C Sutton Coldfield H Trin 97-99; P-in-c Short Heath 99-00; V 00-06; V Dorridge from 06. *54 Glendon Way, Dorridge, Solihull B93 8SY* Tel (01564) 772472 E-mail duncan@ukonline.co.uk

HILLARY, Leslie Tyrone James. b 59. Cranmer Hall Dur 84. **d** 87 **p** 88. C Middlesbrough All SS *York* 87-89; C Stainton-in-Cleveland 89-91; C Filton *Bris* from 91. *clo MOD Chaplains (Army)* Tel (01264) 381140 Fax 381824

HILLAS, Ms Patricia Dorothy. b 66. E Lon Univ BA91 Middx Univ BA02. NTMTC 98. **d** 02 **p** 03. C Kensal Rise St Mark and St Martin *Lon* 02-05; V Northolt Park St Barn from 05. *The Vicarage, Raglan Way, Northolt UB5 4SX* Tel and fax (020) 8422 3775 E-mail mountainskies@btinternet.com

HILLEBRAND, Frank David. b 46. AKC68. St Boniface Warminster 68. **d** 69 **p** 70. C Wood Green St Mich *Lon* 69-72; C Evesham *Worc* 72-75; V Worc H Trin 75-80; V Kidderminster St Jo 80-90; TR Kidderminster St Jo and H Innocents 90-91; TV High Wycombe *Ox* 91-95; TR 95-00; Team Chapl Portsm Hosps NHS Trust 00-06; rtd 06. *40 Woodfield Park Road, Emsworth PO10 8BG* Tel (01243) 378846 E-mail frankandsue68@btinternet.com

HILLEL, Laurence Christopher Francis. b 54. Bris Univ BA76 Sheff Univ PGCE78 SOAS Lon MA84. Cuddesdon Coll 98. **d** 98 **p** 99. C Pinner *Lon* 98-00; NSM Eastcote St Lawr 01-04; Chapl Bp Ramsey Sch 01-04; NSM Brondesbury St Anne w Kilburn H Trin *Lon* from 04. *49 Keslake Road, London NW6 6DH* Tel (020) 8968 3898 E-mail revhillel@aol.com

HILLER, Ms Frances. b 53. Greenwich Univ BA93. NTMTC 07. **d** 09. Chapl to Suff Bp Eur from 09; Perm to Offic *S'wark* from 09. *14 Tufton Street, London SW1P 3QZ* Tel (020) 7898 1161 E-mail frances.hiller@churchofengland.org

HILLIAM, Mrs Cheryl. b 49. EMMTC. **d** 94 **p** 95. C Linc St Faith and St Martin w St Pet 94-98; P-in-c S Ormsby Gp from 98. *The Rectory, South Ormsby, Louth LN11 8QT* Tel (01507) 480236

HILLIARD, David. b 57. TCD BTh91. CITC 88. **d** 91 **p** 92. C Holywood *D & D* 91-94; C Seagoe 94-96; I Tartaraghan w Diamond *Arm* from 96. *The Rectory, 5 Tarthlogue Road, Portadown BT62 1RB* Tel and fax (028) 3885 1289 E-mail tartaraghan@armagh.anglican.org

HILLIARD, George Percival St John. b 45. TCD BA67. **d** 69 **p** 70. C Seapatrick *D & D* 69-73; C Carrickfergus *Conn* 73-76; I Fanlobbus Union *C, C & R* 76-85; Dean Cloyne 85-02; Prec Cork Cathl 85-02; I Cloyne Union 85-02; Chapl Univ Coll Cork 02-10; Can Cork and Cloyne Cathls 02-10; rtd 11; Perm to Offic *Nor* from 11. *Chestnut View, The Street, Rickinghall, Diss IP22 1EG* Tel (01379) 898096 E-mail gchilliard@hotmail.com

HILLIARD, Ms Lorelli Alison. b 60. St Mary's Coll Dur BSc82 Dur Univ MA07. Cranmer Hall Dur 04. **d** 06 **p** 07. C Drypool *York* 06-10; P-in-c Gt Marsden w Nelson St Phil *Blackb* from 10. *St Philip's Vicarage, 1 Victory Close, Nelson BB9 9ED* Tel (01282) 697011 E-mail lorelli.hilliard@googlemail.com

HILLIARD, Martin. b 45. TCD BA69 BTh08. CITC 05. **d** 08 **p** 09. C Larne and Inver and Glynn w Raloo *Conn* 08-11; I Kells Gp *C & O* from 11. *The Priory, Kells, Co Kilkenny, Republic of Ireland* Tel (00353) (56) 772 8367 Mobile 86-108 7432 E-mail revmartinhilliard@gmail.com

HILLIARD, Robert Godfrey. b 52. Portsm Univ BA(Ed)97 MA02. St Mich Coll Llan 72. **d** 75 **p** 76. C Whitchurch *Llan* 75-80; Chapl RNR 77-80; Chapl RN 80-06; Hon Chapl Portsm Cathl 03-06; Chapl Bradfield Coll Berks from 06. *Bradfield College, Bradfield, Reading RG7 6AU* Tel 0118-964 4763 E-mail ghilliard@bradfieldcollege.org.uk

HILLIARD, Russell Boston. b 57. Univ of N Carolina BA82 Zürich Univ Lic89 Vanderbilt Univ (USA) PhD95. St Jo Coll Nottm 01. **d** 03 **p** 04. C Zürich *Eur* 03-06; Perm to Offic 06-09; Asst Chapl Basle from 09. *Rebweg 12, 8309 Nürensdorf, Switzerland* Tel and fax (0041) (44) 836 9245 Mobile 79-501 4904 E-mail r.hilliard@anglicanbasel.ch

HILLIER, Andrew. b 68. RGN92. SWMTC 99. **d** 02 **p** 03. C Castle Cary w Ansford *B & W* 02-05; Chapl RN from 05. *Royal Naval Chaplaincy Service, Mail Point 1-2, Leach Building, Whale Island, Portsmouth PO2 8BY* Tel (023) 9262 5055 Fax 9262 5134 E-mail andrewhillier@bigfoot.com

HILLIER, Derek John. b 30. Sarum Th Coll 61. **d** 63 **p** 64. C Salisbury St Mark *Sarum* 63-65; C Weymouth H Trin 65-66; R Caundle Bishop w Caundle Marsh and Holwell 66-75; R The Caundles and Holwell 75-81; R The Caundles w Folke and Holwell 81-02; P-in-c Pulham 70-78; rtd 02; Perm to Offic *Sarum*

and *B & W* from 02. *Sarum House, Bishop's Caundle, Sherborne DT9 5ND* Tel and fax (01963) 23243
HILLIER, John Frederick. b 43. ARIBA67. **d** 01 **p** 02. OLM Merton St Mary *S'wark* 01-06; Perm to Offic *St Alb* 07; NSM Sandridge from 07. *21 Gonnerston, Mount Pleasant, St Albans AL3 4SY* Tel (01727) 812821 Mobile 07802-646374
HILLIER (née CHAPMAN), Mrs Linda Rosa. b 54. Middx Univ BA04. NTMTC 01. **d** 04 **p** 05. C W Drayton *Lon* 04-07; Faith and Work Development Officer Slough *Ox* from 07. *79 Torbay Road, Harrow HA2 9QG* Tel (020) 8864 5728 E-mail lindarosahillier@msn.com
HILLIER, Ms Marilyn Jean. b 51. Ches Coll of HE CertEd73. NTMTC BA08. **d** 08 **p** 09. NSM Gt Parndon *Chelmsf* from 08. *23 Chapel Hill, Stansted CM24 8AD* Tel (01279) 813833 E-mail lynhillier@btinternet.com
HILLIER, The Ven Michael Bruce. b 49. St Barn Coll Adelaide ThD73. **d** 74 **p** 75. C Plympton Australia 74-76; Assoc P Walkerville 76-80; C Tewkesbury w Walton Cardiff *Glouc* 81-86; P-in-c Whyalla Australia from 94; Adn Eyre Peninsula from 01. *37 Wood Terrace, PO Box 244, Whyalla SA 5600, Australia* Tel (0061) (8) 8644 0391 Fax 8644 0657 E-mail mjhillier@ozemail.com.au
HILLIER, Timothy John. b 55. Westmr Coll Ox CertEd77. Oak Hill Th Coll 94. **d** 96 **p** 97. C Chertsey *Guildf* 96-00; V 00-04; V Chertsey, Lyne and Longcross from 04; RD Runnymede from 07. *The Vicarage, London Street, Chertsey KT16 8AA* Tel and fax (01932) 563141 E-mail hillier@timp33.freeserve.co.uk
HILLMAN, Clive Ralph. b 71. York Univ BSc92. St Steph Ho Ox BA93. **d** 96 **p** 97. C Kingston upon Hull St Alb *York* 96-00; TV Ifield *Chich* 00-02, Chapl St Jo Coll Cam 02-06, V Betws-y-Coed and Capel Curig w Penmachno etc *Ban* from 06. *The Vicarage, Betws-y-Coed LL24 0AD* Tel (01690) 710313 E-mail crh41@cam.ac.uk
HILLMAN, John Anthony. b 32. St Chad's Coll Dur BA53. St Mich Coll Llan 54. **d** 55 **p** 56. C Llangollen *St As* 56-60; C Silvertown S Africa 60-64; P-in-c Matroosfontein 64-72; R Noorder Paarl 72-75; R Durbanville 75-80; R Somerset W 80-86; TV Wolstanton *Lich* 86-91; P-in-c E Goscote w Ratcliffe and Rearsby *Leic* 91-93; TV Syston 93-98; rtd 98. *7 Hafod Road West, Penrhyn Bay, Llandudno LL30 3PN* Tel (01492) 541374
HILLMAN, Jonathan. b 68. Man Univ BEng90. Ridley Hall Cam. **d** 00 **p** 01. C N Wingfield, Clay Cross and Pilsley *Derby* 00-03; TV Cove St Jo *Guildf* 03-10; R Windlesham from 10. *The Rectory, Kennel Lane, Windlesham GU20 6AA* Tel and fax (01276) 472363
HILLMAN, Peter. b 69. Spurgeon's Coll Lon BD. NTMTC. **d** 07 **p** 08. C Rayleigh *Chelmsf* 07-11. *Address temp unknown* E-mail pete@legacyweb.org
HILLMAN, Sarah Catherine. b 68. Selw Coll Cam BA90 MA94. St Jo Coll Nottm MA05. **d** 03 **p** 04. C Sandy *St Alb* 03-06; P-in-c Barkway, Reed and Buckland w Barley from 06. *The Rectory, 135 High Street, Barkway, Royston SG8 8ED* Tel (01763) 848077 E-mail sarah.c.hillman@tesco.net
HILLS, Alan Arthur. b 49. Sussex Univ BA73 Ches Coll of HE MEd94. **d** 09 **p** 10. OLM Ashton Ch Ch *Man* from 09. *41 Bollington Road, Stockport SK4 5ER* Tel 0161-432 2964 Fax 477 7459 Mobile 07752-162333 E-mail alan@cahills.co.uk
HILLS, Mrs Christine Ann. b 54. NTMTC BA05. **d** 05 **p** 06. C Romford Gd Shep *Chelmsf* 05-08; C Blackmore and Stondon Massey 08-10; P-in-c Mistley w Manningtree and Bradfield from 10. *The Rectory, 21 Malthouse Road, Manningtree CO11 1BY* Tel (01206) 392200 E-mail chris-hills@ntlworld.com
HILLS, Elaine. b 45. RN67. Mon Dioc Tr Scheme 02. **d** 04 **p** 08. NSM Caerleon w Llanhennock *Mon* 04-09; NSM Caerleon and Llanfrechfa from 09. *6 Anthony Drive, Caerleon, Newport NP18 3DS* Tel (01633) 421248 Mobile 07967-349096 E-mail rev.elaine@btinternet.com
HILLS, Jonathan Mark. b 84. Trin Coll Bris BA10. **d** 10 **p** 11. C Churchdown *Glouc* from 10. *11 Chapel Hay Lane, Churchdown, Gloucester GL3 2ET* Tel (01452) 856478 Mobile 07939-361180 E-mail jjhills@gmail.com
HILLS, Kenneth Hugh. b 30. Univ of NZ BCom54. Ripon Hall Ox 55. **d** 57 **p** 58. C Handsworth St Mary *Birm* 57-59; V Wanganui Paroch Distr New Zealand 59-61; V Porirua 61-67; Ind Chapl *Birm* 67-74; Chapl Aston Univ 74-82; rtd 91; Community Member Cluny Hill Coll 93-00. *2 O'Neills Place, Church Road, Holywood BT18 9BU* Tel (028) 9042 1545 E-mail ken.hills@findhorn.org *or* k_h@onetel.com
HILLS, Lee Anthony. b 74. St Jo Coll Nottm 04. **d** 06. Deanery Missr *Birm* 06-08. *23 Jubilee Gardens, Birmingham B23 5HS* Tel 0121-382 6887 Mobile 07796-137423 E-mail lee@djvicar.co.uk
HILLS, Michael Rae Buchanan. b 52. Univ of Wales (Lamp) BA81 Ex Univ BPhil83. St Steph Ho Ox 92. **d** 94 **p** 95. C Kingston upon Hull St Nic *York* 94-97; V Newington w Dairycoates 97-03; P-in-c 03-06; P-in-c Kingston upon Hull St Nic 05-06; N Humberside Ind Chapl 03-06; Sen Chapl from 07; Hon C Newington w Dairycoates 07-08; P-in-c Kingston upon Hull St Mary from 08. *St John's Vicarage, 203 St George's Road, Hull HU3 3SP* Tel (01482) 214551 E-mail vicar@kanga.karoo.co.uk

HILLS, Michael William John. b 54. Univ of Wales (Lamp) BA84. Westcott Ho Cam 85. **d** 87 **p** 88. C Reddish *Man* 87-91; V Bolton St Phil 91-00; V Northampton St Mich w St Edm *Pet* from 00; P-in-c Northampton H Sepulchre w St Andr and St Lawr 04-07; V from 07. *The Vicarage, 94 St Georges Avenue, Northampton NN2 6JF* Tel (01604) 230316 *or* 408111 Fax 635673 E-mail mickhills@btconnect.com
HILLS, Richard Leslie. b 36. Qu Coll Cam BA60 MA63 UMIST PhD68 FMA83. St Deiniol's Hawarden 85. **d** 87 **p** 88. C Urmston *Man* 87-89; C Gt Yarmouth *Nor* 89-90; NSM Mottram in Longdendale *Ches* 90-01; Perm to Offic from 01. *Stamford Cottage, 47 Old Road, Mottram, Hyde SK14 6LW* Tel (01457) 763104
HILLS, Roger Malcolm. b 42. Oak Hill Th Coll 83. **d** 86 **p** 87. NSM Mill Hill Jo Keble Ch *Lon* 86-98; NSM Mill Hill St Mich 86-98; Perm to Offic 98-00; V Queensbury All SS 00-07; rtd 07; Perm to Offic *Lon* from 08. *22 Sefton Avenue, London NW7 3QD* Tel (020) 8959 1931 E-mail roger.hills2@btinternet.com
HILLS, Sarah Ann St Leger. b 65. Sheff Univ MB, ChB89 Leeds Univ MA07. NOC 04. **d** 07 **p** 08. C Millhouses H Trin *Sheff* 07-10; Perm to Offic 10-11; Hon C Sheff St Pet and St Oswald from 11. *80 Crimicar Lane, Sheffield S10 4FB* Tel 0114-327 5114 E-mail sarahandrichard91@talktalk.net
HILLS, Stephen Alan. b 59. Sheff Univ BA81. Ridley Hall Cam 97. **d** 99 **p** 00. C Southborough St Pet w Ch Ch and St Matt etc *Roch* 99-02; TV from 02. *The Rectory, Rectory Drive, Bidborough, Tunbridge Wells TN3 0UL* Tel (01892) 528081 E-mail stephen.hills@diocese-rochester.org
HILLYER, Charles Norman. b 21. Lon Univ BD48 Lambeth STh67. ALCD48. **d** 48 **p** 49. C Finchley Ch Ch *Lon* 48-51; C New Malden and Coombe *S'wark* 51-54; V Hanley Road St Sav w St Paul *Lon* 54-59; Chapl City of Lon Maternity Hosp 54-59; V Ponsbourne *St Alb* 59-70; Chapl Tolmers Park Hosp 59-70; Lib Tyndale Ho Cam 70-73; Org Ed UCCF 73-79; Sec Tyndale Fellowship Bibl Research Cam 73-75; P-in-c Hatherleigh *Ex* 79-81; V 81-86; rtd 86; Perm to Offic *Sarum* 89-03 and *Leic* from 03. *c/o Mrs J V H White, Box House, 1 Clearbury Close, Odstock, Salisbury SP5 4NX* Tel (01722) 329610 E-mail norman.hillyer@btinternet.com
HILTON, Clive. b 30. K Coll Lon 54. **d** 58 **p** 59. C Wythenshawe Wm Temple Ch CD *Man* 58-61; C Newton Heath All SS 61-62; C-in-c Oldham St Chad Limeside CD 62-65; V Oldham St Chad Limeside 65-70; P-in-c Gravesend H Family *Roch* 70-71; R Killamarsh *Derby* 71-88; R Broughton w Loddington and Cransley etc *Pet* 88-91; rtd 92; Perm to Offic *Pet* and *Linc* from 98; *Ely* 05-08. *73A Tattershall Drive, Market Deeping, Peterborough PE6 8BZ* Tel (01778) 346217
HILTON, Ian Anthony. b 57. St Jo Coll Nottm 83. **d** 86 **p** 87. C Nottingham St Sav *S'well* 86-90; C Aspley 90-97; P-in-c Colchester, New Town and The Hythe *Chelmsf* 97-02; R from 02; RD Colchester from 06. *The Rectory, 24 New Town Road, Colchester CO1 2EF* Tel (01206) 530320 E-mail ian.hilton@ntlworld.com
HILTON, John. b 49. Ex Univ BA70. Cuddesdon Coll 71. **d** 73 **p** 74. C W Derby St Jo *Liv* 73-79; V Orford St Andr 79-96; V Leeds St Wilfrid *Ripon* from 96. *St Wilfrid's Vicarage, Chatsworth Road, Leeds LS8 3RS* Tel 0113-249 7724 E-mail john@the-oak-403.demon.co.uk
HILTON-TURVEY, Geoffrey Michael. b 34. Oak Hill Th Coll 80. **d** 81 **p** 82. C Bispham *Blackb* 81-85; V Inskip 85-99; rtd 99; Perm to Offic *Heref* from 00. *20 Cralves Mead, Tenbury Wells WR15 8EX* Tel (01584) 811153 E-mail gmh-t@gmh-t.freeserve.co.uk
HILTON-TURVEY, Keith Geoffrey Michael. b 59. Oak Hill Th Coll BA03. **d** 03 **p** 04. C S Mimms Ch Ch *Lon* 03-09; P-in-c Cricklewood St Pet from 09. *St Peter's Vicarage, 5 Farm Avenue, London NW2 2EG* Tel (020) 8438 8903 E-mail kht@fideste.freeserve.co.uk
HINA, Christine Magdeleine. b 66. SAOMC. **d** 01 **p** 02. C Stevenage St Hugh and St Jo *St Alb* 01-06; C Stevenage St Nic and Graveley from 06. *9 Providence Grove, Stevenage SG2 8PY* E-mail christine@anih.freeserve.co.uk
HINCHCLIFFE, Garry Anthony Frank. b 68. New Coll Edin BD94. Edin Th Coll 90. **d** 94 **p** 95. C Dumfries *Glas* 94-97; P-in-c Motherwell and Wishaw 97-00; V Hampsthwaite and Killinghall *Ripon* 00-04; V Hampsthwaite and Killinghall and Birstwith from 04. *The Vicarage, Church Lane, Hampsthwaite, Harrogate HG3 2HB* Tel (01423) 770337 E-mail garry.hinchcliffe@btinternet.com
HINCKLEY, Paul Frederick. b 61. Cranfield Inst of Tech MSc85. Ridley Hall Cam 92. **d** 94 **p** 95. C Ovenden *Wakef* 94-99; TV Billericay and Lt Burstead *Chelmsf* 99-06; R Yateley *Win* 06-10; TV Gt Marlow w Marlow Bottom, Lt Marlow and Bisham *Ox* from 10. *165 Marlow Bottom, Marlow SL7 3PL* Tel (01628) 298915
✠**HIND, The Rt Revd John William.** b 45. Leeds Univ BA66 Lambeth DD09. Cuddesdon Coll 70. **d** 72 **p** 73 **c** 91. C Catford (Southend) and Downham *S'wark* 72-76; V Forest Hill Ch Ch 76-82; P-in-c Forest Hill St Paul 81-82; Prin Chich Th Coll 82-91;

Wiccamical Preb Chich Cathl 82-91; Area Bp Horsham 91-93; Bp Eur 93-01; Asst Bp Chich 93-01; Bp Chich from 01. *The Palace, Chichester PO19 1PY* Tel (01243) 782161 Fax 531332 E-mail bishop.chichester@diochi.org.uk

HIND, Mrs Ruth Elizabeth. b 71. Cen Lancs Univ BA93. St Jo Coll Nottm MTh01. **d** 02 **p** 03. C Caldbeck, Castle Sowerby and Sebergham *Carl* 02-06; V Hutton Cranswick w Skerne, Watton and Beswick *York* 06-11; RD Harthill 10-11; P-in-c Kirklington w Burneston and Wath and Pickhill *Ripon* from 11. *The Rectory, Kirklington, Bedale DL8 2NJ* Tel (01845) 567429 E-mail ruth@hind8.orangehome.co.uk

HINDER, Doreen Patterson. b 38. Open Univ BA95. Selly Oak Coll 60 Bris Bapt Coll 68. **d** 97 **p** 98. NSM Stanwix *Carl* 97-99; P-in-c Glenurquhart *Mor* 99-03; rtd 03. *Hardies Byre, Kirkhill, Inverness IV5 7PP* Tel (01463) 831729

HINDER, Richard Alan. b 46. Birm Univ BSc67 CCC Cam PhD71 FRAS70 CEng82 FIEE80. S'wark Ord Course 04. **d** 07 **p** 08. NSM Croydon St Matt *S'wark* from 07. *18 Mapledale Avenue, Croydon CR0 5TB* Tel (020) 8123 5256 E-mail richard@richardhinder.com

HINDLE (*formerly* PARKER), Anne Margaret. b 57. Leeds Univ BSc78. EAMTC 96. **d** 99 **p** 00. C Greenstead w Colchester St Anne *Chelmsf* 99-04; TV 04-08; P-in-c Kingsley and Foxt-w-Whiston *Lich* 08-10; R Kingsley and Foxt-w-Whiston and Oakamoor etc from 10. *The Rectory, Holt Lane, Kingsley, Stoke-on-Trent ST10 2BA* Tel (01538) 754754 Mobile 07703-571879 E-mail anne.hindle@hotmail.co.uk

HINDLE, Miss Penelope Jane Bowyn. b 45. Trin Coll Bris 76. dss 84 **d** 87 **p** 94. Stoneycroft All SS *Liv* 84-89; Par Dn 87-89; Asst Chapl Broadgreen Hosp Liv 87-89; Asst Chapl R Free Hosp Lon 89-93; Chapl N Herts NHS Trust 93-02; rtd 02; Perm to Offic *B & W* from 07. *Cleeve House, Level Lane, Charlton Horethorne, Sherborne DT9 4NN* Tel (01963) 220055

HINDLEY, Canon Andrew David. b 59. Univ of Wales (Lamp) BA. Sarum & Wells Th Coll. **d** 82 **p** 83. C Huddersfield St Pet *Wakef* 82-84; C Huddersfield St Pet and All SS 84-86; P-in-c Holmfield 86-91; R Ribchester w Stidd *Blackb* 91-96; Bp's Adv for Leisure and Tourism 91-96; Chapl Ribchester Hosp from 91; Can Res Blackb Cathl from 96. *22 Billinge Avenue, Blackburn BB2 6SD* Tel (01254) 261152 *or* 51491 Fax 689666 E-mail andrew.hindley@blackburn.anglican.org

HINDLEY, Canon Anthony Talbot. b 41. Bernard Gilpin Soc Dur 61 Oak Hill Th Coll 62. **d** 66 **p** 67. C Stoke next Guildf St Jo 66-69; C Eldoret Kenya 70-72; V Menengai 72-78; C Redhill H Trin *S'wark* 78-79; P-in-c Eastbourne All So *Chich* 79-83; V 83-86; V S Malling 86-98; R Wainford *St E* 98-06; RD Beccles and S Elmham 00-03; Hon Can St E Cathl 05-06; rtd 06; Perm to Offic *St E* and *Nor* from 07. *Amani @ Mile End, Church Road, Earsham, Bungay NR35 2TL* Tel (01986) 894749 Mobile 07766-546601 E-mail anthony.hindley@ireverend.com

HINDLEY, John Philip Talbot. b 76. Ex Univ BA96 Oak Hill Th Coll BA01. **d** 01 **p** 02. C Astley Bridge *Man* 01-04; Assoc Miss Partner Crosslinks from 04. *40 Mill Road, Frettenham, Norwich NR12 7LQ* Tel (01603) 737974 Mobile 07790-007390 E-mail john@theplant.net

HINDLEY, Michael Alexander. b 72. Man Metrop Univ BA94. Wycliffe Hall Ox BTh05. **d** 05 **p** 06. C Clubmoor *Liv* 05-09; TV Fazakerley Em from 09. *Emmanuel Rectory, Higher Lane, Liverpool L9 9DJ* Tel 0151-525 5229 Mobile 07980-912768 E-mail revd.mike@btinternet.com

HINDLEY, Roger Dennis. b 48. Birm Univ BA70 Ox Univ BA77 MA83. Ripon Coll Cuddesdon 75 Qu Coll Birm 77. **d** 78 **p** 79. C Rubery *Birm* 78-81; C Henbury *Bris* 81-83; V Erdington St Chad *Birm* 83-89; V Hill 89-05; AD Sutton Coldfield 96-02; Hon Can Birm Cathl 00-05; TR Willington *Newc* from 05; rtd 11. *29 Thacker Drive, Lichfield WS13 6NS* E-mail rdhindley@yahoo.co.uk

HINDLEY, Thomas Richard. b 31. ARIBA54 Sheff Univ BA53 Lon Univ BD66. Clifton Th Coll 61. **d** 63 **p** 64. C Kenilworth St Jo *Cov* 63-67; C Cheadle *Ches* 67-70; R Harpurhey Ch Ch *Man* 70-95; R Harpurhey St Steph 72-95; rtd 96; Perm to Offic *Man* from 96. *15 Twyford Close, Didsbury, Manchester M20 2YR* Tel 0161-438 0387

HINDS, Francis. b 73. Bath Univ BSc96 Edge Hill Coll of HE PGCE98. Wycliffe Hall Ox 96. **d** 08. C Haydock St Mark *Liv* from 08; Dir Pioneer Min from 08. *1 Brookside Close, Haydock, St Helens WA11 0UQ* Tel 07736-176826 (mobile)

HINDS, Kenneth Arthur Lancelot. b 30. K Coll Lon BA00 Birkbeck Coll Lon MA04. Bps' Coll Cheshunt. **d** 64 **p** 65. C Sawbridgeworth *St Alb* 64-67; C Gt Berkhamsted 67-71; V Boreham Wood St Mich 71-75; Trinidad and Tobago 75-79; P-in-c Gt Ilford St Luke *Chelmsf* 79-81; V 81-95; rtd 95; Perm to Offic *Chelmsf* from 95. *214 Aldborough Road South, Ilford IG3 8HF* Tel (020) 8598 2963 E-mail frkalhinds@ntlworld.com

HINE, John Victor. b 36. Open Univ BA82. Carl Dioc Tr Course 85. **d** 88 **p** 89. NSM Dean *Carl* 88-92; NSM Clifton 88-92; C Millom 92-94; P-in-c Gt Broughton and Broughton Moor 94-02; P-in-c Brigham 99-02; rtd 02; Perm to Offic *Carl* from 02. *4 The Paddocks, Thursby, Carlisle CA5 6PB* Tel (01228) 712704 E-mail hine.hine@virgin.net

HINE, Keith Ernest. b 50. Bradf Univ BA Leeds Univ CertEd. NOC 89. **d** 89 **p** 90. C Wilmslow *Ches* 89-94; V Bowdon 94-08; R Tarporley from 08; C Acton and Worleston, Church Minshull etc from 10; RD Malpas from 10. *The Rectory, High Street, Tarporley CW6 0AG* Tel (01829) 732491 E-mail keith@hine24.freeserve.co.uk

HINE, Patrick Lewis. b 45. **d** 06 **p** 07. OLM Horfield H Trin *Bris* from 06. *16 Red House Lane, Bristol BS9 3RZ* Tel 0117-962 3861 E-mail patrick.hine@horfieldparishchurch.org.uk

HINES, Richard Arthur. b 49. Imp Coll Lon MSc73 PhD76 K Coll Lon MTh89. Oak Hill Th Coll 82. **d** 84 **p** 85. C Mile Cross *Nor* 84-87; Lect Oak Hill Th Coll 87-97; Vice-Prin NTMTC 94-97; R Happisburgh, Walcott, Hempstead w Eccles etc *Nor* 97-07; C Bacton w Edingthorpe w Witton and Ridlington 04-07; R Bacton, Happisburgh, Hempstead w Eccles etc 07; R Falkland Is from 07. *PO Box 160, The Deanery, 17 Ross Road, Stanley, Falkland Islands FIQQ 1ZZ* Tel (00500) 21100 E-mail christchurch@horizon.co.fk

HINEY, Thomas Bernard Felix. b 35. MC61. Open Univ BA07. Ridley Hall Cam 67. **d** 69 **p** 70. C Edgbaston St Aug *Birm* 69-71; CF 71-91; Chapl R Hosp Chelsea 91-01; Chapl Mercers' Coll Holborn 99-01; rtd 01. *7B Dagmar Road, Exmouth EX8 2AN* Tel (01395) 270688 E-mail thiney@onetel.net

HINEY, Thomas Robert Cornelius. b 70. Edin Univ MA92 St Jo Coll Dur MA11. Cranmer Hall Dur 09. **d** 11. C Dewsbury Wakef from 11. *Dewsbury Minster, Vicarage Road, Dewsbury WF12 8DD* Tel (01924) 457057 E-mail trchiney@gmail.com

HINGE, Canon David Gerald Francis. b 30. FRSA57. Wells Th Coll 64. **d** 66 **p** 67. C Brookfield St Anne, Highgate Rise *Lon* 66-69; C N Greenford All Hallows 69-71; V Winton *Man* 71-78; R Etherley *Dur* 78-96; Hon Can Dur Cathl 90-00; rtd 96. *9 Hillside, Ingleton, Darlington DL2 3JH* Tel (01325) 732002

HINGE, Derek Colin. b 36. Imp Coll Lon BSc58 CChem60 MRSC60. St Alb Minl Tr Scheme 84. **d** 88 **p** 89. NSM Bishop's Stortford St Mich *St Alb* from 88. *12 Avenue Road, Bishop's Stortford CM23 5NU* Tel (01279) 652173 E-mail derek.hinge@btinternet.com

HINGLEY, Christopher James Howard. b 48. Trin Coll Ox BA69 MA71. Wycliffe Hall Ox 81. **d** 80 **p** 81. C St Jo Cathl Bulawayo Zimbabwe 80-81; C Hillside Ascension 82-84; Tutor Wycliffe Hall Ox 84-88; Chapl Whitestone Sch Bulawayo 89-04; Headmaster Petra High Sch Bulawayo 04-06; R Petra Schs Bulawayo from 06. *Whitestone School, Private Bag 4, Bulawayo, Zimbabwe* E-mail hingley@yoafrica.com

HINGLEY (*née* EDWARDS), Mrs Helen. b 55. Natal Univ BSW75. St Steph Ho Ox 94. **d** 96 **p** 97. C Gravelly Hill *Birm* 96-01; TV Cen Wolverhampton *Lich* 01-05; P-in-c Hamstead St Bernard *Birm* from 05; AD Handsworth from 08. *The Vicarage, 147 Hamstead Road, Great Barr, Birmingham B43 5BB* Tel 0121-358 1286 E-mail h.hingley@btinternet.com

HINGLEY, Robert Charles. b 46. Ball Coll Ox BA69 MA74 Birm Univ CertEd73. Qu Coll Birm. **d** 73 **p** 74. C Charlton St Luke w H Trin *S'wark* 73-76; Asst Warden Iona Abbey 76-77; TV Langley Marish *Ox* 77-83; V Balsall Heath St Paul *Birm* 83-90; Perm to Offic 90-91; V Birm St Luke 91-96; Lic to Offic 96-05; Hon C Hamstead St Bernard from 05; Perm to Offic *Lich* from 01. *The Vicarage, 147 Hamstead Road, Great Barr, Birmingham B43 5BB* Tel 0121-357 4534

HINGLEY, Roderick Stanley Plant. b 51. St Chad's Coll Dur BA72. St Steph Ho Ox 74. **d** 75 **p** 76. C Lower Gornal *Lich* 75-79; C Tividale 79-82; C Broseley w Benthall *Heref* 82-84; C Wanstead St Mary *Chelmsf* 84-92; V Romford St Alb from 92. *St Alban's Vicarage, 3 Francombe Gardens, Romford RM1 2TH* Tel (01708) 473580

HINGSTON, Barry David. b 63. LSE BSc(Econ)84. NTMTC BA08. **d** 08 **p** 09. C Ealing St Paul *Lon* from 08. *20 Brookbank Avenue, London W7 3DW* Tel (020) 8578 2910 Mobile 07710-359483 E-mail barryhingston@btinternet.com

HINKLEY, Maureen. b 41. **d** 04. NSM Hollington St Jo *Chich* from 04. *8 Wadhurst Close, St Leonards-on-Sea TN37 7AZ* Tel (01424) 754872 E-mail hinkley872@btinternet.com

HINKS, David John. b 63. STETS 04. **d** 07 **p** 08. C Cowes H Trin and St Mary *Portsm* from 07. *St Faith's House, 2 St Faith's Road, Cowes PO31 7HH* Tel (01983) 280197 Mobile 07766-355196 E-mail julie@hinks42.freeserve.co.uk

HINKS, Margaret Anne. b 47. Birm Univ MB, ChB65. Qu Coll Birm 08. **d** 10 **p** 11. NSM Birm St Geo from 10. *29 Birchy Close, Shirley, Solihull B90 1QL* Tel (01564) 829088 E-mail annehinks@uwclub.net

HINKS (*née* CHAMBERS), Mrs Marion Patricia. b 48. Univ of Wales BDS72. SWMTC 97. **d** 97 **p** 98. NSM Plymstock and Hooe *Ex* from 97. *52 Southland Park Road, Wembury, Plymouth PL9 0HQ* Tel (01752) 862249 Mobile 07889-291228 E-mail marion@southlandpark.freeserve.co.uk

HINKSMAN, Adrian James Terence. b 43. Open Univ BA76. SAOMC 96. **d** 99 **p** 00. NSM Hemel Hempstead *St Alb* 99-02; Dioc CME Officer and NSM St Alb St Mary Marshalswick 02-07; rtd 07; NSM King's Walden and Offley w Lilley *St Alb*

from 07. *33 Sycamore Close, St Ippolyts, Hitchin SG4 7SN*   Tel (01462) 458260   E-mail adrian_hinksman@hotmail.com

HINKSMAN, Barrie Lawrence James. b 41. K Coll Lon BD64 AKC64 Birm Univ PhD02. St Boniface Warminster 64. **d** 65 **p** 66. C Crosby *Lic* 65-67; Ecum Development Officer Scunthorpe Coun of Chs 67-69; C Chelmsley Wood *Birm* 69-72; TV 72-75; P-in-c Offchurch *Cov* 75-79; Bp's Adv for Lay Tr 75-79; Perm to Offic 89-90; Hon Chapl Cov Cathl 90-01; Perm to Offic *Birm* from 01; Hon Sen Fell Warw Univ from 02. *c/o Crockford, Church House, Great Smith Street, London SW1P 3AZ*

HINSLEY, Robert Charles. b 77. Univ of Wales (Abth) BTh98 St Jo Coll Dur MATM06. Cranmer Hall Dur 03. **d** 05 **p** 06. C Carlton-in-Lindrick and Langold w Oldcotes *S'well* 05-08; P-in-c Felixstowe St Jo *St E* from 08; RD Colneys from 11. *The New Vicarage, 54 Princes Road, Felixstowe IP11 7PL*   Tel (01394) 286552   E-mail roberthinsley@tiscali.co.uk

HINTON, Mrs Frances Mary. b 43. EN(G)85. EMMTC 89. **d** 92 **p** 94. Par Dn Hornsey Rise Whitehall Park Team *Lon* 92-94; C 94-97; C Upper Holloway 97; TV Barking St Marg w St Patr *Chelmsf* 97-04; rtd 04. *5 Little Thorpe Lane, Thorpe-on-the-Hill, Lincoln LN6 9BL*   Tel (01522) 688886

HINTON, Geoffrey. b 34. Bede Coll Dur BA56 Em Coll Cam MA67 Sussex Univ PGCE72. Ridley Hall Cam 58. **d** 60 **p** 61. C Cheltenham St Mary *Glouc* 60-61; C Beverley Minster *York* 61-65; C Newark St Mary *S'well* 70-71; rtd 99. *1 Northmoor Place, Oxford OX2 6XB*   Tel (01865) 510267

HINTON, James William. b 63. Cov Poly BSc84 Leeds Univ PGCE86. St Jo Coll Nottm 00. **d** 02 **p** 03. C Thornbury *Bradf* 02-05; P-in-c Bowling St Steph from 05; C Lt Horton from 05; P-in-c Bankfoot from 09. *St Stephen's Vicarage, 48 Newton Street, Bradford BD5 7BH*   Tel (01274) 720784 *or* 391537   E-mail jimmy.hinton@bradford.anglican.org

HINTON, Michael Ernest. b 33. K Coll Lon 53 St Boniface Warminster 56. **d** 57 **p** 58. C Babbacombe *Ex* 57-60; S Africa 60-66; P-in-c Limehouse St Pet *Lon* 66-68; R Felmingham *Nor* 68-72; R Suffield 68-72; P-in-c Colby w Banningham and Tuttington 68-72; Bahamas 72-76; P-in-c Mylor w Flushing *Truro* 76-77; V 77-80; R The Deverills *Sarum* 82-87; Bermuda 87-89; Virgin Is 89-91; Chapl Sequoian Retreat and Conf Progr from 91; rtd 98; Perm to Offic *St E* 00-01; *Ex* from 02. *Le Petit Pain, St Ann's Chapel, Kingsbridge TQ7 4HQ*   Tel (01548) 810124   E-mail lacton.int@virgin.net

HINTON, Michael George. b 27. Mert Coll Ox BA48 MA51 Reading Univ PhD59. S Dios Minl Tr Scheme 81. **d** 83 **p** 84. NSM Weston-super-Mare St Paul *B&W* 83-85; NSM Sibertswold w Coldred *Cant* 85-87; NSM Eythorne and Elvington w Waldershare etc 87-95; Perm to Offic from 95. *212 The Gateway, Dover CT16 1LL*   Tel and fax (01304) 204198   E-mail michael@hintonm.demon.co.uk

HINTON, Nigel Keith. b 49. Univ Coll Lon BSc70 Worc Coll of Educn PGCE73 Lon Univ MA87. Oak Hill NSM Course 89. **d** 92 **p** 93. NSM Cudham and Downe *Roch* 92-07; Perm to Offic *Lon* from 03. *Address temp unknown*

HINTON, Paul Robin George. b 64. St Jo Coll Dur BA86. Qu Coll Birm BA05. **d** 05 **p** 06. C Rowley Regis *Birm* 05-09; V Warley Woods from 09. *St Hilda's Vicarage, Abbey Road, Smethwick, Warley B67 5NQ*   Tel 0121-429 1384   Fax 420 2386   Mobile 07777-603188   E-mail revpaulhinton@btinternet.com

HINTON, Robert Matthew. b 69. Lanc Univ BA91. Cranmer Hall Dur BA97. **d** 97 **p** 98. C Lache cum Saltney *Ches* 97-99; C Cheadle Hulme St Andr 99-02; V Hale Barns w Ringway 02-09; Ind Chapl *Ripon* from 09. *30 Huntington Crescent, Leeds LS16 5RT*   E-mail revrobhinton@hotmail.com

HIPKINS, Leslie Michael. b 35. Univ Coll Dur BA57 ACIS60. Oak Hill Th Coll 78 Westcott Ho Cam 89. **d** 81 **p** 82. NSM Halstead St Andr w H Trin and Greenstead Green *Chelmsf* 81-87; C Tolleshunt Knights w Tiptree and Gt Braxted 87-89; P-in-c Cratfield w Heveningham and Ubbeston etc *St E* 89-00; rtd 00; Perm to Offic *St E* 01-11. *72 Clarendon Road, Norwich NR2 2PW*   Tel (01603) 663100

HIPPISLEY-COX, Stephen David. b 63. Sheff Univ BSc85 PhD92 Peterho Cam BA98. Westcott Ho Cam 96. **d** 99 **p** 00. C Ollerton w Boughton *S'well* 99-02; NSM Wilford Hill 02-07; P-in-c Willoughby-on-the-Wolds w Wysall and Widmerpool from 07. *The Rectory, Keyworth Road, Wysall, Nottingham NG12 5QQ*   Tel (01509) 889706   E-mail s.d.hippisley.cox@gmail.com

HIRD, Matthew. b 83. Jes Coll Ox BA04. St Jo Coll Nottm MA09. **d** 09 **p** 10. C Penn *Lich* from 09. *Penhelig, Wynne Crescent, Wolverhampton WV4 4SW*   E-mail matthew.hird@hotmail.com

HIRONS, Malcolm Percy. b 36. Oriel Coll Ox BA59 MA62. Wycliffe Hall Ox 59. **d** 61 **p** 62. C Edgbaston St Aug *Birm* 61-64; Chapl Warw Sch 64-65; C Beverley Minster *York* 65-69; V Barnby upon Don *Sheff* 69-80; P-in-c Kirk Bramwith 75-80; P-in-c Fenwick 75-80; V Norton Woodseats St Paul 80-98; rtd 98; Perm to Offic *Nor* from 98. *Broome Lodge, 8 Lincoln Square, Hunstanton PE36 6DL*   Tel (01485) 532385

HIRST, Alan. b 44. CQSW74. Linc Th Coll 79. **d** 81 **p** 82. C Newton Heath All SS *Man* 81-84; Chapl to the Deaf 84-88; V Oldham St Chad Limeside 88-91; Dep Chapl HM Pris Liv 91-92; Chapl HM Pris Ranby 92-96 and 00-07; Chapl HM Pris Wakef 96-99; NSM Retford *S'well* from 07. *8 Maple Drive, Elkesley, Retford DN22 8AX*

HIRST, Anthony Melville (Anthony Mary). b 50. Cuddesdon Coll 74. **d** 77 **p** 78. C S Gillingham *Roch* 77-80; C Coity w Nolton *Llan* 80-83; OSB from 81; R Hallaton w Horninghold, Allexton, Tugby etc *Leic* 83-90; R Arthog w Fairbourne w Llangelynnin w Rhoslefain *Ban* 90-97; R Montgomery and Forden and Llandyssil *St As* 97-04; V Bedford Leigh *Man* 04-09; P-in-c S Ashford St Fran *Cant* from 09; P-in-c S Ashford Ch Ch from 09. *Christ Church Vicarage, 112 Beaver Road, Ashford TN23 7SR*   Tel (01233) 620600   E-mail ahirst@avnet.co.uk

HIRST, Mrs Carol Anne. b 46. Yorks Min Course 06. **d** 09 **p** 10. NSM Ripponden *Wakef* from 09; NSM Barkisland w W Scammonden from 09. *86 Crow Wood Park, Halifax HX2 7NR*   Tel (01422) 363095   Mobile 07977-210297   E-mail carolhirst1@btinternet.com

HIRST, David William. b 37. Man Univ BA78. Brasted Th Coll 59 St Aid Birkenhead 61. **d** 63 **p** 64. C Clayton *Man* 63-64; C Bury St Jo 64-66; C Wythenshawe Wm Temple Ch 67-70; V Oldham St Chad Limeside 70-79; V Friezland 79-91; R Ashton St Mich 91-95; Chapl HM Pris Buckley Hall 95-00; Chapl HM Pris Wolds 00-02; rtd 02; Perm to Offic *Blackb* from 09. *8 Priory Mews, Lytham St Annes FY8 4FT*   Tel 07833-353837 (mobile)

HIRST, Canon Godfrey Ian. b 41. Univ of Wales (Lamp) BA63 MBIM. Chich Th Coll 63. **d** 65 **p** 66. C Brierfield *Blackb* 65-68; Ind Chapl *Liv* 68-71; TV Kirkby 71-75; Ind Chapl *Blackb* 75-94; P-in-c Treales 75-87; Hon Can Blackb Cathl 83-87 and 94-06; Can Res 87-94; V Lytham St Cuth 94-06; AD Kirkham 98-06; rtd 06; Perm to Offic *Blackb* from 06. *11 Arundel Road, Lytham St Annes FY8 1AF*   Tel (01253) 732474   Mobile 07885-118331   E-mail ghirst1@compuserve.com

HIRST, John Adrian. b 49. St Jo Coll Nottm BTh78. **d** 78 **p** 79. C Cheltenham St Mark *Glouc* 78-84; TV 84-85; TV Swan *Ox* 85-89; R Denham from 89. *The Rectory, Ashmead Lane, Denham, Uxbridge UB9 5BB*   Tel (01895) 832771

HIRST, Mrs Judith. b 54. St Mary's Coll Dur BA76 LMH Ox PGCE77 Hull Univ MA86 St Jo Coll Dur BA94. Cranmer Hall Dur 91. **d** 94 **p** 95. Bp's Adv in Past Care and Counselling *Dur* 94-00; C Dur St Oswald 94-00; Dir Min Formation Cranmer Hall Dur 00-07; Local Min Development Officer *Dur* and *Newc* from 07. *Easdale, St Hild's Lane, Durham DH1 1QL*   Tel 0191-334 8540   E-mail judy.hirst@durham.ac.uk

HIRST, Malcolm. b 62. Ilkley Coll BA84. Moorlands Bible Coll 86 Trin Coll Bris BA00. **d** 00 **p** 01. C Bromley Common St Aug *Roch* 00-03; C Farnborough 03-08. *Address temp unknown*   E-mail malcolm@port-vale.freeserve.co.uk

HIRST, Mrs Rachel Ann. b 58. Portsm Poly BA79 Hull Univ PGCE81 ACII85. NEOC 99. **d** 02 **p** 03. NSM Clifton *York* 02-04; C 04-06; Par Development and Tr Officer (York Adnry) 06-11; V Norton juxta Malton from 11. *The Vicarage, 80 Langton Road, Norton, Malton YO17 9AE*   E-mail rachel.hirst40@googlemail.com

HISCOCK, Donald Henry. b 26. St Mich Th Coll Crafers 50 ACT ThL56. **d** 53 **p** 54. Australia 53 and from 65; SSM 54-82; C Averham w Kelham *S'well* 56-58; Lic to Offic 58-59; S Africa 59-60; Basutoland 60-61; rtd 92. *12 Charsley Street, Willagee WA 6156, Australia*   Tel (0061) (8) 9314 5192

HISCOCK, Gary Edward. b 43. Oak Hill Th Coll BA90. **d** 90 **p** 91. C Cheltenham St Luke and St Jo *Glouc* 90-94; V Hardwicke, Quedgeley and Elmore w Longney 95-96; rtd 96. *25 Bournside Road, Cheltenham GL51 3AL*   Tel (01242) 513002

HISCOCK, Peter George Harold. b 31. Wadh Coll Ox BA54 MA66. Ely Th Coll 54. **d** 58 **p** 59. C Edgehill St Dunstan *Liv* 58-61; C Kirkby 61-64; C Southport St Luke 64-66; Asst Dean of Residence TCD 66-68; Dean of Res TCD 68-73; Min Can St Patr Cathl Dublin 67-70; Chapl St Steph Coll Delhi 73-76; TV Jarrow *Dur* 77-82; Chapl Univ Coll Dur 82-87; P-in-c Dinnington *Newc* 87-88; TV Ch the King 88-94; RD Newc Cen 87-94; rtd 94; Perm to Offic *Lon* from 95. *8 Banbury Road, London E9 7DU*   Tel (020) 8986 2252

HISCOCK, Phillip George. b 47. Southn Univ CertEd68 MPhil90 MCIPD83. STETS 95. **d** 98 **p** 99. NSM Portchester and Chapl Portsm Docks 98-02; Chapl Dunkirk Miss to Seafarers *Eur* 02-08; C Alverstoke *Portsm* from 08. *36 Gomer Lane, Gosport PO12 2SA*   Tel and fax (023) 9234 6881   Mobile 07830-362149   E-mail phillip.hiscock@ntlworld.com

HISCOCKS, Nicholas Robin Thomas. b 75. Keble Coll Ox BA96 MA01 Anglia Poly Univ MA01. Ridley Hall Cam 99. **d** 01 **p** 02. C Bromley Ch Ch *Roch* from 01; Min Westbourne Ch Ch Chpl *Win* from 11. *134 Alumhurst Road, Bournemouth BH4 8HU*   Tel (01202) 762164 *or* 760952   E-mail nrth75@tiscali.co.uk

HISCOX, Miss Denise. b 47. Lon Univ TCert68 Lanchester Poly Cov BSc78. WMMTC 98. **d** 02 **p** 03. NSM Cov St Mary 01-05; NSM Leamington Priors All SS 05-07; NSM Leamington Spa H Trin and Old Milverton 05-07; Perm to Offic 07-08; NSM

Willenhall 08-10. *48 Wainbody Avenue North, Coventry CV3 6DB* Tel (024) 7641 1034 E-mail denise@dhiscox.co.uk

HISCOX, Jonathan Ronald James. b 64. Qu Coll Birm 87. **d** 89 **p** 90. C Wiveliscombe *B & W* 89-93; P-in-c Donyatt w Horton, Broadway and Ashill 93-94; TV Ilminster and Distr 94-02; R Rowde and Bromham *Sarum* 02-10. *58 Sadlers Mead, Chippenham SN15 3PL*

HISLOP, Martin Gregory. b 55. Jas Cook Univ Townsville BA78 Univ of S Aus MEd88. **d** 92 **p** 93. C N Mackay St Ambrose Australia 92-93; Dir Studies St Barn Coll of Min 93-94; Chapl Ballarat Univ 95-98; Asst Chapl St Mich Gr Sch and Assoc P E St Kilda 98; C Kingston St Luke *S'wark* 00-01; P-in-c 01-05; V from 05. *St Luke's Vicarage, 4 Burton Road, Kingston upon Thames KT2 5TE* Tel (020) 8546 4064 E-mail mhislop@btinternet.com

HISLOP, Mrs Patricia Elizabeth. b 42. Heythrop Coll Lon MA03. **d** 08 **p** 09. OLM Ewhurst Guildf from 08. *2 Napper Place, Cranleigh GU6 8DG* Tel (01483) 274359 E-mail patricia.hislop@dsl.pipex.com

HITCH, Canon Kim William. b 54. Leic Univ BSc75 K Coll Lon MA94 Birm Univ MPhil08. Trin Coll Bris 76. **d** 78 **p** 79. C Becontree St Mary *Chelmsf* 78-80; C Huyton Quarry *Liv* 80-83; V Hatcham St Jas *S'wark* 83-91; TR Kidbrooke 91-02; R Kidbrooke St Jas from 02; Lewisham Adnry Ecum Officer 03-06; Dir Ords (Woolwich Area) from 05; AD Charlton from 06; Hon Can S'wark Cathl from 08. *St James's Rectory, 62 Kidbrooke Park Road, London SE3 0DU* Tel (020) 8856 3438 E-mail kim.hitch@tiscali.co.uk

HITCHCOCK, David. b 37. MCIEH. S'wark Ord Course 70. **d** 73 **p** 74. NSM Milton next Gravesend Ch Ch *Roch* 73-94; NSM Chalk 96-98; CF (ACF) from 79; Perm to Offic Lon 93-02; NSM St Andr-by-the-Wardrobe w St Ann, Blackfriars 02-09; NSM St Jas Garlickhythe w St Mich Queenhithe etc 02-09. *148 Old Road East, Gravesend DA12 1PF* Tel (01474) 361091 E-mail hitch5@btinternet.com

HITCHEN, Miss Lisa Jan. b 73. Linc Univ NZ BPR&TM95 Graduate Sch of Educn Dip Teaching 01. Trin Coll Bris BA09. **d** 09 **p** 10. C Brinnington w Portwood *Ches* from 09. *10 Jura Close, Dukinfield SK16 4DE* Tel 0161-339 9850 Mobile 07769-800915 E-mail lisahitchen.angel@gmail.com

HITCHENS (née GREEN), Mrs Catherine Isabel. b 48. Cant Sch of Min 89. **d** 92 **p** 94. C Willesborough *Cant* 92-96; Sen Asst P E Dereham and Scarning *Nor* 96-97; Asst Chapl HM Pris Wayland 96-97; Chapl HM Pris Leic 97-00; Chapl HM YOI Castington 00-02; Chapl HM Pris Cant from 02. *The Chaplain's Office, HM Prison, 46 Longport, Canterbury CT1 1PJ* Tel (01227) 862984

HITCHINER, Mrs Elizabeth Ann. b 59. Birm Univ BSc80. WEMTC 03. **d** 06 **p** 07. NSM Cagebrook *Heref* from 06. *Dunan House, Clehonger, Hereford HR2 9SF* Tel (01432) 355980

HITCHINER, Sally Ann. b 80. Wycliffe Hall Ox. **d** 09 **p** 10. C W Ealing St Jo w St Jas *Lon* from 09. *41 Leighton Road, London W13 9EL* Tel (020) 8567 0241 Mobile 07761-661529 E-mail sallyhitchiner@hotmail.co.uk

HITCHING, His Honour Judge Alan Norman. b 41. Ch Ch Ox BA62 MA66 BCL63 Barrister-at-Law (Middle Temple) 64. **d** 01 **p** 02. NSM High Ongar w Norton Mandeville *Chelmsf* 01-06; Perm to Offic from 06. *9 Monkhams Drive, Woodford Green IG8 0LG* Tel (020) 8504 4260 E-mail anhitching@btinternet.com

HITCHINS, Graham Edward David. b 54. S Dios Minl Tr Scheme 91. **d** 94 **p** 95. C Bishop's Waltham *Portsm* 94-97; C Upham 94-97; C Honiton, Gittisham, Combe Raleigh, Monkton etc *Ex* 97-98; TV 98-03; Chapl RN 03-10; R Burnham Gp of Par *Nor* from 09. *The Rectory, The Pound, Burnham Market, King's Lynn PE31 8UL* E-mail revdgrahamhitchins@hotmail.com

HITCHMAN, Keith John. b 62. Middx Univ BSc90. Trin Coll Bris BA95. **d** 95 **p** 96. C Bestwood *S'well* 95-99; Chapl Glos Univ 99-04; C Cheltenham St Mary, St Matt, St Paul and H Trin *Glouc* 04-07; TV Cheltenham H Trin St Paul 07-10; Pioneer Min River in the City *Liv* from 10. *2 Rimsdale Close, Aigburth, Liverpool L17 6EX*

HITCHMOUGH, William. b 30. NOC. **d** 81 **p** 82. NSM Penketh *Liv* 81-83; Chapl Warrington Distr Gen Hosp 83-99; Perm to Offic *Liv* 83-03 and *Guildf* 00-09. *4 Rex Court, Haslemere GU27 1LJ* Tel (01428) 661504

HIZA, Douglas William. b 38. Richmond Univ Virginia BA60 MDiv63 Mankato State Univ MS70. Virginia Th Sem 60. **d** 63 **p** 64. C Calvary Cathl Sioux Falls USA 63-65; V Sioux Falls Gd Shep 65-66; V Vermillion St Paul 66-69; V New Ulm St Pet 71-80; Chapl Mankato State Univ 74-80; Chapl Hackney Hosp Gp Lon 80-95; Chapl Homerton Hosp Lon 80-95; Perm to Offic *Lon* 96-04; Hon C Smithfield St Bart Gt from 04; Perm to Offic *S'wark* from 06. *10 Meynal Crescent, London E9 7AS* Tel (020) 8985 7832 or 7253 3107 E-mail general@joanhudson.co.uk

HOAD, Anne Elizabeth. b 42. Bris Univ BA63. **dss** 69 **d** 94 **p** 95. Asst Chapl Imp Coll *Lon* 69-74; S'wark Lay Tr Scheme 74-77; Brixton St Matt *S'wark* 77-80; Charlton St Luke w H Trin 84-91; Project Worker Community of Women and Men 88-91; Voc Adv Lewisham from 91; Asst Chapl Lewisham Hosp 92-03; Hon C

Lee Gd Shep w St Pet 94-03; C 03-10; rtd 10; Perm to Offic *S'wark* from 11. *14 Silk Close, London SE12 8DL* Tel (020) 8297 8761 E-mail hoadanne@yahoo.co.uk

HOAD, Miss Rosemary Claire. b 60. Cranmer Hall Dur 92. **d** 94 **p** 95. C Epsom St Martin *Guildf* 94-97; TV Brentford *Lon* 97-05; V Spring Grove St Mary from 05. *St Mary's Vicarage, Osterley Road, Isleworth TW7 4PW* Tel (020) 8560 3555 E-mail rosemary.hoad@btinternet.com

HOAD, Mrs Shona Mary. b 66. Newc Univ BA88. STETS 07. **d** 10 **p** 11. C Dorking St Paul *Guildf* from 10. *3 South Terrace, Dorking RH4 2AB* Tel (01306) 877102 E-mail shona@stpaulsdorking.org.uk

HOARE, Carol. b 46. Lon Univ BA68 Birm Univ CertEd69. Qu Coll Birm 86 WMMTC 86. **d** 91 **p** 94. NSM Curdworth *Birm* 91-00; Perm to Offic from 00. *14 Elms Road, Sutton Coldfield B72 1JF* Tel 0121-354 1117 E-mail c.hoare@btinternet.com

HOARE, David Albert Sylvester. b 47. **d** 95. C Gibraltar Cathl 95-00. *3 Governor's Lane, Gibraltar*

HOARE, Canon David Marlyn. b 33. Bps' Coll Cheshunt 60. **d** 63 **p** 64. C Ampthill w Millbrook and Steppingley *St Alb* 63-67; C Bushey 67-70; V Harlington 70-76; V Oxhey All SS 76-81; V Hellesdon *Nor* 81-98; Hon Can Nor Cathl 95-98; rtd 98; Perm to Offic *Nor* from 98. *42 Starling Close, Aylsham, Norwich NR11 6XG* Tel (01263) 734565

HOARE, Diana Charlotte. Kent Univ BA78. WEMTC 02. **d** 05 **p** 06. C Bishop's Castle w Mainstone, Lydbury N etc *Heref* 05-09; P-in-c Bucknell w Chapel Lawn, Llanfair Waterdine etc from 09. *The Vicarage, Bucknell SY7 0AD* Tel (01547) 530340 Mobile 07989-432280 E-mail diana@stonescribe.com

HOARE (née CULLING), Elizabeth Ann. b 58. St Mary's Coll Dur BA76 St Jo Coll Dur PhD87 Rob Coll Cam BA88 PGCE80. Ridley Hall Cam 86. **d** 89 **p** 94. Par Dn S Cave and Ellerker w Broomfleet *York* 89-92; Tutor Cranmer Hall Dur 93-95; P-in-c Cherry Burton *York* 95-00; Abp's Sen Adv on Rural Affairs 95-98; Abp's Adv for Spiritual Direction 98-00; Chapl Bp Burton Coll *York* 95-00; Perm to Offic *York* 01-02; NSM Cowesby 02-07; NSM Felixkirk w Boltby 02-07; NSM Kirkby Knowle 02-07; NSM Leake w Over and Nether Silton and Kepwick 02-07; Tutor and Lect Cranmer Hall Dur 02-07; Tutor Wycliffe Hall Ox from 07. *Wycliffe Hall, 54 Banbury Road, Oxford OX2 6PW* Tel (01865) 274200 or 873412 E-mail liz.wildgoose@bigfoot.com

HOARE, Janet Francis Mary. See MILES, Ms Janet Francis Mary

HOARE, Patrick Gerard. See GERARD, Patrick Hoare

HOARE, Patrick Reginald Andrew Reid (Toddy). b 47. TD80 and Bar 88. Hull Univ MA90. Wycliffe Hall Ox 77. **d** 80 **p** 81. C Guisborough *York* 80-83; P-in-c Felixkirk w Boltby 83-07; P-in-c Kirkby Knowle 83-07; P-in-c Leake w Over and Nether Silton and Kepwick 83-07; P-in-c Cowesby 83-07; Chapl Yorks Agric Soc 92-09; CF (TA) 82-99; rtd 07; Perm to Offic *Ox* from 07. *Pond Farm House, Holton, Oxford OX33 1PY* Tel (01865) 873412 E-mail toddy100@btinternet.com

HOARE, Roger John. b 38. Tyndale Hall Bris 63. **d** 66 **p** 67. C Stoughton *Guildf* 66-70; C Chesham St Mary *Ox* 70-73; V Bath St Bart *B & W* 73-83; V Gt Faringdon w Lt Coxwell *Ox* 83-89; Deputation Appeals Org (NE Lon) Children's Soc 89-93; P-in-c Lambourne w Abridge and Stapleford Abbotts *Chelmsf* 93-03; Ind Chapl 93-03; rtd 03; Perm to Offic *Chelmsf* from 04. *44 Anchor Road, Tiptree, Colchester CO5 0AP* Tel (01621) 817236 E-mail rogerhoare@aol.com

✠**HOARE, The Rt Revd Rupert William Noel.** b 40. Trin Coll Ox BA61 MA66 Fitzw Ho Cam BA64 MA84 Birm Univ PhD73. Kirchliche Hochschule Berlin 61 Westcott Ho Cam 62. **d** 64 **p** 65 **c** 93. C Oldham St Mary w St Pet *Man* 64-67; Lect Qu Coll Birm 68-72; Can Th Cov Cathl 70-76; R Man Resurr 72-78; Can Res Birm Cathl 78-81; Prin Westcott Ho Cam 81-93; Area Bp Dudley and Hon Can Worc Cathl 93-00; Dean Liv 00-07; rtd 07; Hon Asst Bp Man from 08. *14 Shaw Hall Bank Road, Greenfield, Oldham OL3 7LD* Tel (01457) 820375

HOARE, Canon Simon Gerard. b 37. AKC61. **d** 62 **p** 63. C Headingley *Ripon* 62-65; C Adel 65-71; R Spofforth 68-71; R Spofforth w Kirk Deighton 71-77; V Rawdon *Bradf* 77-85; Hon Can Bradf Cathl 85-02; R Carleton and Lothersdale 85-02; Dioc Ecum Officer 85-94; rtd 02; Perm to Offic *Ripon* from 02. *Skell Villa, 20 Wellington Street, Ripon HG4 1PH* Tel (01765) 692187 E-mail sghoare@talktalk.net

HOARE, Toddy. See HOARE, Patrick Reginald Andrew Reid

HOARE, Mrs Valerie Mary. b 54. Ex Univ BTh07. SWMTC 04. **d** 07 **p** 08. NSM Chard St Mary *B & W* 07-10; C Chard St Mary w Combe St Nicholas, Wambrook etc from 10. *The Vicarage, Bracken House, Combe St Nicholas, Chard TA20 3LT* Tel (01460) 68799

HOBBINS, Mrs Susan. b 47. Birm Univ CertEd68. STETS 04. **d** 07 **p** 08. NSM Hatherden w Tangley, Weyhill and Penton Mewsey *Win* 07-09; NSM Pastrow from 09. *Whistlers Farm, Tangley, Andover SP11 0SB* Tel and fax (01264) 735533 E-mail suehobbins@yahoo.com

HOBBS (*formerly* **DUFFUS**)**, Mrs Barbara Rose.** b 51. EMMTC 95. **d** 98 **p** 99. C Linc St Faith and St Martin w St Pet 98-00; C Grantham 00-02; P-in-c Brothertoft Gp 02-04; Mental Health Chapl SE Lincs 02-04; P-in-c Hastings St Clem and All SS *Chich* 04-08; rtd 08. *Courtyard Cottage, Main Road, Westfield, Hastings TN35 4QE* Tel (01424) 756479 Mobile 07962-892156 E-mail barbara.r.hobbs@googlemail.com

HOBBS, Basil Ernest William. b 22. St Chad's Coll Dur BA49. **d** 51 **p** 52. C Mitcham St Mark *S'wark* 51-54; CF 54-68; Hon C Paddington H Trin w St Paul *Lon* 70-72; Asst Chapl St Mary's Hosp Praed Street Lon 69-72; Novice CR 72-74; Past Consultant Clinical Th Assn 74-84; Lic to Offic *S'well* 74-83; Chapl HM Pris Nottm 81-84; Hon C Nottingham St Andr *S'well* 83-84; C 84-86; TV Clifton 86-87; rtd 87; Perm to Offic *S'well* 87-00 and *Leic* from 99. *17 Stuart Court, High Street, Kibworth, Leicester LE8 0LR* Tel 0116-279 6367

HOBBS, Christopher Bedo. b 61. Jes Coll Cam BA83 BTh90. Ridley Hall Cam 88. **d** 91 **p** 92. C Langham Place All So *Lon* 91-95; C Hull St Jo Newland *York* 95-00; V Selly Park St Steph and St Wulstan *Birm* from 00. *18 Selly Wick Road, Selly Park, Birmingham B29 7JA* Tel 0121-472 0050 *or* 472 8253

HOBBS, Christopher John Pearson. b 60. Sydney Univ BA82 K Coll Lon BD89 AKC89. Wycliffe Hall Ox 89. **d** 91 **p** 92. C S Mimms Ch Ch *Lon* 91-94; C Jesmond Clayton Memorial *Newc* 94-97; V Oakwood St Thos *Lon* from 97. *St Thomas's Vicarage, 2 Sheringham Avenue, London N14 4UE* Tel (020) 8360 1749 *or* tel and fax 8245 9152 E-mail christopher.hobbs@blueyonder.co.uk

HOBBS, Edward Quincey. b 74. Bris Univ BSc95. Wycliffe Hall Ox BA99. **d** 00 **p** 01. C Stapenhill w Cauldwell *Derby* 00-03; C Newbury *Ox* 03-08; C Brompton H Trin w Onslow Square St Paul *Lon* 08-09; P-in-c Cullompton, Willand, Uffculme, Kentisbeare etc *Ex* from 09. *Windyridge, 10 Willand Road, Cullompton EX15 1AP* E-mail eqhobbs@gmail.com

HOBBS, Ian. *See* HOBBS, Kenneth Ian

HOBBS, James. b 42. K Alfred's Coll Win CertEd64 Open Univ BA89 Hull Univ MA94. Linc Th Coll 66. **d** 68 **p** 69. C Moseley St Mary *Birm* 68-73; V Kingstanding St Mark 73-77; R Rushbrooke *St E* 77-78; R Bradfield St Geo 77-80; P-in-c Bradfield St Clare 77-80; P-in-c Felsham w Gedding 77-80; R Bradfield St George w Bradfield St Clare etc 80-84; P-in-c Gt and Lt Whelnetham 84-85; R Gt and Lt Whelnetham w Bradfield St George 85-90; Ecum Chapl for F&HE Grimsby *Linc* 90-97; Chapl Humberside Univ (Grimsby Campus) 90-97; Gen Preacher 92-97; V Ingham w Cammeringham w Fillingham 97-01; R Aisthorpe w Scampton w Thorpe le Fallows etc 97-01; P-in-c N w S Carlton 97-01; P-in-c Burton by Linc 97-01; rtd 01; Perm to Offic *Linc* 01-04. *Courtyard Cottage, Main Road, Westfield, Hastings TN35 4QE* Tel (01424) 756479 Mobile 07726-302341 E-mail hobbs.jim1@googlemail.com

HOBBS, Jason Michael. b 74. Northumbria Univ BSc97 Sunderland Univ BA00. TISEC 07. **d** 10 **p** 11. C Aberdeen St Mary from 10. *21 Wallfield Place, Aberdeen AB25 2JR* Tel (01224) 641621 Mobile 07969-404380 E-mail jhobbs10@gmail.com

HOBBS, Mrs Joan Rosemary. b 39. Chelsea Coll Lon TDip61. WEMTC 97. **d** 00 **p** 01. NSM Cheltenham St Mary, St Matt, St Paul and H Trin *Glouc* 00-02; Perm to Offic 02-04; NSM Brimpsfield w Birdlip, Syde, Daglingworth etc 04-09; rtd 10; Perm to Offic *Glouc* from 10. *Manor Farmhouse, Woodmancote, Cirencester GL7 7EF* Tel and fax (01285) 831244 E-mail joan@hobbsjr.fsnet.co.uk

HOBBS, John Antony. b 36. S Dios Minl Tr Scheme. **d** 87 **p** 88. NSM Crowborough *Chich* from 87. *May Cottage, Alice Bright Lane, Crowborough TN6 3SQ* Tel (01892) 653909

HOBBS, Jonathan Noel Alan. b 70. Oak Hill Th Coll BA03. **d** 03 **p** 04. C Lindfield *Chich* 03-07; R Maresfield from 07; V Nutley from 07. *16 The Paddock, Maresfield, Uckfield TN22 2HQ* Tel (01825) 764536 E-mail jon@hobbs99.freeserve.co.uk

HOBBS, Kenneth Brian. b 47. Sussex Univ BA68 Lon Inst of Educn PGCE70. NTMTC 98. **d** 98 **p** 99. NSM Howell Hill *Guildf* 98-01; NSM Shere, Albury and Chilworth 01-11; rtd 11. *Yeoman's Acre, Farley Green, Albury, Guildford GU5 9DN* Tel (01483) 202165 E-mail hobbs@farleygreen.net

HOBBS, Kenneth Ian. b 50. Oak Hill Th Coll 74. **d** 77 **p** 78. C Southborough St Pet w Ch Ch and St Matt *Roch* 77-80; C Hoole *Ches* 80-84; V Barnston 84-95; P-in-c Bedworth *Cov* 95; TR 95-01; RD Nuneaton 00-01; TR Radipole and Melcombe Regis *Sarum* from 01; RD Weymouth and Portland from 08. *39 Icen Road, Weymouth DT3 5JL* Tel (01305) 785553 E-mail teamrector@radipoleparish.f2s.com

HOBBS, Leslie Robert. b 42. Sussex Univ BA64 Lon Bible Coll BD67. EAMTC 02. **d** 02 **p** 03. NSM Somerleyton, Ashby, Fritton, Herringfleet etc *Nor* 02-09; R from 09. *Nether End Cottage, Blacksmiths Loke, Lound, Lowestoft NR32 5LS* Tel (01502) 732536

HOBBS, Ms Maureen Patricia. b 54. Surrey Univ BSc76 Warwick Univ 92. Westcott Ho Cam 95. **d** 97 **p** 98. C Shrewsbury St Chad w St Mary *Lich* 97-01; R Baschurch and

Weston Lullingfield w Hordley 01-09; P-in-c Pattingham w Patshull from 09; RD Trysull from 09; Dioc Adv for Women in Min from 04. *The Vicarage, 20 Dartmouth Avenue, Pattingham, Wolverhampton WV6 7DP* Tel (01902) 700257 E-mail hobbsmaureen@yahoo.co.uk

HOBBS, Michael Bedo. b 30. Fitzw Ho Cam BA58 MA62. Clifton Th Coll 58. **d** 60 **p** 61. C Southsea St Jude *Portsm* 60-63; Paraguay 63-65; Argentina 65-67; V Potters Green *Cov* 68-75; Distr Sec BFBS 75-82; R Plaxtol *Roch* 82-96; Dioc Miss Audits Consultant 90-96; rtd 96; Perm to Offic *Sarum* from 96. *Falcons, Barkers Hill, Semley, Shaftesbury SP7 9BH* Tel (01747) 828920

HOBBS, Ms Sarah Kathleen. b 72. Liv Univ BA94 UMIST BSc98 PGCE95. Wycliffe Hall Ox BA05. **d** 05 **p** 06. C W Ealing St Jo w St Jas *Lon* 05-08; V Blockhouse Bay New Zealand from 08. *429A Blockhouse Bay Road, Blockhouse Bay, Auckland 0600, New Zealand* Tel (0064) (9) 627 8779 E-mail sarah@churchofthesaviour.org.nz

HOBBS, Sarah Louise. b 47. WEMTC 01. **d** 04 **p** 05. NSM Westbury-on-Severn w Flaxley, Blaisdon etc *Glouc* from 05. *Folly Cottage, Adsett Lane, Adsett, Westbury-on-Severn GL14 1PQ* Tel (01452) 760337 E-mail sarah@qhobbs.wanadoo.co.uk

HOBBS, Simon John. b 59. St Steph Ho Ox BA82 MA. **d** 83 **p** 84. C Middlesbrough Ascension *York* 83-85; C Stainton-in-Cleveland 85-88; C St Marylebone All SS *Lon* 88-90; P-in-c Paddington St Pet 90-94; C-in-c Grosvenor Chpl 94-08; C Hanover Square St Geo 94-08; Chapl Bonn w Cologne *Eur* 08-11. *Address temp unknown* E-mail bkchaplain@mac.com

HOBDAY, Hannah Elizabeth. b 80. Jes Coll Ox BA03 Cam Univ BA06. Ridley Hall Cam 04. **d** 07 **p** 08. C Margate H Trin *Cant* 07-09; C Cliftonville 07-09; Hon C Chesterton St Geo *Ely* from 09. *9 Hertford Street, Cambridge CB4 3AE* Tel (01223) 748872 Mobile 07792-923575 E-mail hannah.hobday@googlemail.com

HOBDAY, Peter Hugh Francis. b 34. IEng90. Oak Hill NSM Course 99. **d** 00 **p** 01. NSM Perivale *Lon* 00-05; Perm to Offic *Lon* 05-07 and *Pet* from 07. *48 Juniper Close, Towcester NN12 6XP* Tel (01327) 359045 Mobile 07778-007370 E-mail petehobday126@btinternet.com

HOBDAY, Philip Peter. b 81. Ex Coll Ox BA02 MA09 Fitzw Coll Cam BA05 MA09. Ridley Hall Cam 03. **d** 06 **p** 07. C St Peter-in-Thanet *Cant* 06-09; Chapl Cant Ch Ch Univ 06-09; Chapl and Fell Magd Coll Cam from 09. *Magdalene College, Cambridge CB3 0AG* Tel (01223) 332129 Mobile 07717-056951 E-mail pph21@cam.ac.uk

HOBDEN, Canon Brian Charles. b 38. Oak Hill Th Coll 63. **d** 66 **p** 67. C S Lambeth St Steph *S'wark* 66-70; C Cheadle *Ches* 70-76; R Brandon USA 76-87; R Portsm St Jo 87-98; R Mesilla Park St Jas from 98; rtd 03. *3160 Executive Hills Road, Las Cruces NM 88011-4724, USA* Tel (001) (505) 521 9435 Fax 526 4821 E-mail stjames@lascruces.com

HOBDEN, Christopher Martin. b 49. Lon Univ BSc71. Oak Hill Th Coll 80. **d** 87 **p** 88. NSM St Marylebone All So w SS Pet and Jo *Lon* 87-88; NSM Langham Place All So 88-95. *10 Kent Terrace, London NW1 4RP*

HOBDEN, David Nicholas. b 54. K Coll Lon BD76 AKC76 Cam Univ PGCE. Ripon Coll Cuddesdon 77. **d** 78 **p** 79. C Marlborough *Sarum* 78-80; C Salisbury St Thos and St Edm 81-85; V Shalford *Guildf* 85-99; Asst Chapl R Surrey Co Hosp NHS Trust 99-00; Sen Chapl from 00. *Department of Pastoral Care, Royal Surrey County Hospital, Egerton Road, Guildford GU2 5XX* Tel (01483) 406835 *or* 571122 E-mail cmhobden@aol.com *or* dhobden@royalsurrey.nhs.uk

HOBDEN, Geoffrey William. b 46. Trin Coll Bris 80. **d** 82 **p** 83. C Ex St Leon w H Trin 82-86; V Weston-super-Mare Ch Ch *B & W* 86-06; V Weston super Mare Ch Ch and Em 06-11; RD Locking 93-99; rtd 11. *21 Burrington Avenue, Weston-super-Mare BS24 9LP* Tel (01934) 813060 E-mail hobdenshouse@aol.com

HOBLEY, Ms Susan Elizabeth. b 51. Newc Univ BA74 Dur Univ PGCE75. NEOC 98. **d** 01 **p** 02. NSM Millfield St Mark and Pallion St Luke *Dur* 01-05; C Sheff St Mark Broomhill 05-09; V Wath-upon-Dearne from 09. *The Vicarage, Church Street, Wath-upon-Dearne, Rotherham S63 7RD* Tel (01709) 872299 E-mail sue.hobley@sheffield.anglican.org

HOBROUGH, Mrs Margaret Edith. b 40. OBE97. Man Univ BA63 Newc Univ MEd75 K Coll Lon MTh80 FRSA94. STETS 01. **d** 03 **p** 04. NSM Godalming *Guildf* 03-05; NSM Warkworth and Acklington *Newc* from 05. *3 St Lawrence Terrace, Warkworth, Morpeth NE65 0XE* Tel (01665) 711203 E-mail margarethobrough@v21.me.uk

HOBSON, Alexander. *See* HOBSON, John Alexander

HOBSON, Anthony Peter. b 53. St Jo Coll Cam BA74. St Jo Coll Nottm 75. **d** 77 **p** 78. C Brunswick *Man* 77-82; R Stretford St Bride 82-92; TR Hackney Marsh *Lon* 92-00; V Leic Martyrs 00-08; Dir St Martin's Ho from 09. *4 Church Road, Aylestone, Leicester LE2 8LB* Tel 0116-283 3251 E-mail petehobson@me.com

HOBSON, Barry Rodney. b 57. Open Univ BA98. Wilson Carlile Coll 82 EAMTC 97. **d** 98 **p** 99. CA from 85; C Warboys w

Broughton and Bury w Wistow *Ely* 98-01; P-in-c Roxwell *Chelmsf* 01-07; RD Chelmsf N 06-07; V Hornchurch St Andr from 07. *The Vicarage, 222 High Street, Hornchurch RM12 6QP* Tel (01708) 454594 *or* 441571 E-mail b.hobson@btinternet.com

HOBSON, Jeremy Graeme. b 71. Lon Univ BMedSci95 MB, BS96. Oak Hill Th Coll BA03. d 03 p 04. C Eastbourne H Trin *Chich* 03-07; C Clerkenwell St Jas and St Jo w St Pet *Lon* 07-08; Lic to AD Islington from 08. *47 Grange Grove, London N1 2NP* Tel (020) 7251 1190 E-mail thehobsons@onetel.com

HOBSON, John Alexander (Alex). b 70. LMH Ox BA91 MA02 York Univ MA94. Wycliffe Hall Ox BA01. d 02 p 03. C Aynho and Croughton w Evenley etc *Pet* 02-05; Chapl RAF from 05. *Chaplaincy Services, Valiant Block, HQ Air Command, RAF High Wycombe HP14 4UE* Tel (01494) 496800 Fax 496343

HOBSON, Canon Patrick John Bogan. b 33. MC53. Magd Coll Cam BA56 MA60 Ox Brookes Univ BA08. S'wark Ord Course 75 Qu Coll Birm 77. d 79 p 80. C St Jo in Bedwardine *Worc* 79-81; R Clifton-on-Teme, Lower Sapey and the Shelsleys 81-88; TR Waltham H Cross *Chelmsf* 88-98; Hon Can Chelmsf Cathl 95-98; rtd 98. *24 Cunliffe Close, Oxford OX2 7BL* Tel and fax (01865) 556206 E-mail patrick.hobson@btinternet.com

HOBSON, Peter. HOBSON, Anthony Peter

HOBSON, Mrs Yvonne Mary. b 45. Ex Univ BTh03. SWMTC 00. d 03 p 04. C St Illogan *Truro* 03-06; C Paul 06-10; rtd 10. *8 Donnington Road, Penzance TR18 4PQ* Tel (01736) 364354 E-mail yvonnehobson@btinternet.com

HOCKEN, Glen Rundle. b 59. Kent Univ BA80 Southlands Coll Lon PGCE90 ACA84. Wycliffe Hall Ox 90. d 92 p 93. C Cogges *Ox* 92-94; C Cogges and S Leigh 94-96; C Boldmere *Birm* 96-99; TV Southgate *Chich* 99-06; Chapl HM Pris Lewes from 06; Chapl St Pet and St Jas Hospice N Chailey from 05. *The Chaplain's Office, HM Prison, Brighton Road, Lewes BN7 1EA* Tel (01273) 785100 Fax 785101

HOCKEY, Ms Christine Helen. St Mich Coll Llan. d 09 p 10. NSM Maindee Newport *Mon* from 09. *134 Christchurch Road, Newport NP19 7SB* Tel (01633) 768900

HOCKEY (née LOOMES), Gaenor Mary. b 65. Hull Univ BA92 RGN86. St Jo Coll Nottm MPhil93. d 96 p 97. C Charles w Plymouth St Matthias *Ex* 96-00; C Devonport St Aubyn 00-05; Perm to Offic 05-06; P-in-c Seer Green and Jordans *Ox* from 06. *43 Long Grove, Seer Green, Beaconsfield HP9 2YN* Tel (01494) 675013

HOCKEY, Paul Henry. b 49. Oak Hill Th Coll BA86. d 86 p 87. C Dalton-in-Furness *Carl* 86-89; R Clifton, Brougham and Cliburn 89-94; V Fremington *Ex* 94-10; R Fremington, Instow and Westleigh from 10; Chapl Children's Hospice SW 97-07; RD Barnstaple from 07. *The Vicarage, Fremington, Barnstaple EX31 2NX* Tel (01271) 373879 E-mail paulhockey@talktalk.net

HOCKING, Canon Hugh Michael Warwick. b 12. VRD54. Ch Coll Cam BA34 MA38. Westcott Ho Cam 34. d 36 p 37. C Hackney St Jo *Lon* 36-37; C Stoke Damerel *Ex* 37-39; Chapl RNVR 39-46; V Madron w Morvah *Truro* 46-54; Chapl Poltair Hosp 50-54; V Bris St Ambrose Whitehall 54-62; R Guildf H Trin w St Mary 62-77; Chapl St Luke's Hosp Guildf 63-77; Hon Can Guildf Cathl 68-77; rtd 77; Chapl W Cornwall Hosp Penzance 78-97; Perm to Offic *Ex* from 97. *Ponsandane Care Home, Chyandour Terrace, Penzance TR18 3LT* Tel (01736) 330063

HOCKING, Paul Frederick. b 43. Chich Th Coll 84. d 86 p 87. C Whitton and Thurleston w Akenham *St E* 86-89; V Ipswich All Hallows 89-91; P-in-c Gt Cornard 91-98; V 98; P-in-c Woolpit w Drinkstone 98-03; R 03-05; rtd 05; Perm to Offic *St E* from 05. *22111 Town Walk Drive, Handen CT 06518-3759, USA* E-mail paulfhocking@gmail.com

HOCKLEY, Paul William. b 47. Chu Coll Cam BA68 MA72 Nottm Univ BA73. St Jo Coll Nottm 71. d 74 p 75. C Chatham St Phil and St Jas *Roch* 74-78; C Tunbridge Wells St Jo 78-81; V Penketh *Liv* from 81. *St Paul's Vicarage, 6 Poplar Avenue, Penketh, Warrington WA5 2EH* Tel (01925) 723492 Fax 486945 E-mail paul-hockley@lineone.net

HOCKLEY, Canon Raymond Alan. b 29. LRAM53 Em Coll Cam MA71. Westcott Ho Cam 56. d 58 p 59. C Endcliffe *Sheff* 58-61; P-in-c Wicker w Neepsend 61-63; Chapl Westcott Ho Cam 63-68; Chapl Em Coll Cam 68-76; Can Res and Prec York Minster 76-95; rtd 95; Perm to Offic *York* 95-05. *26 Buckingham Mews, Sutton Coldfield B73 5PR* Tel 0121-354 7083

HOCKNULL, Canon Mark Dennis. b 63. Surrey Univ BSc85 Univ Coll Lon PhD89 St Jo Coll Dur BA93. Cranmer Hall Dur 91. d 94 p 95. C Prenton *Ches* 94-96; C Runcorn All SS and Runcorn St Mich 96-99; V Gt Meols 99-05; CME Officer *Linc* 05-09; Lic Preacher 05-09; Can Res and Chan Linc Cathl from 09; Hd of Min Tr (Dioc Min Course) from 09. *The Chancery, 12 Eastgate, Lincoln LN2 1QG* Tel (01522) 561633 *or* 504025 E-mail mark.hocknull@lincoln.anglican.org

HOCKRIDGE, Joan. b 25. Girton Coll Cam BA47 MA50. St Steph Ho Ox 82. dss 83 d 87 p 94. Ealing Ascension Hanger Hill *Lon* 83-88; Hon C 87-88; Hon C Hanger Hill Ascension and W Twyford St Mary 88-92; Hon C Hillingdon St Jo 92-95; Perm

to Offic 95-00. *17 Mead Way, Ruislip HA4 7QW* Tel (01895) 622643

HODDER, Anthony Mark. b 56. d 11. C Heref S Wye from 11. *The Rectory, 91 Ross Road, Hereford HR2 7RJ* Tel (01432) 273004 E-mail tony.hodder@gmail.com

HODDER, Christopher John. b 75. Huddersfield Univ BA96. St Jo Coll Nottm BTh00. d 01 p 02. C Loughborough Em and St Mary in Charnwood *Leic* 01-05; Chapl Derby Univ and Derby Cathl 05-10; P-in-c Wilford Hill *S'well* from 10. *St Paul's Parsonage, Boundary Road, West Bridgford, Nottingham NG2 7DB* Tel 07833-592800 (mobile)

HODDER, John Kenneth. b 45. Edin Univ MA68. Cuddesdon Coll 71. d 73 p 74. C Kibworth Beauchamp *Leic* 73-76; C Whittlesey *Ely* 76-80; R Downham 80-87; P-in-c Coveney 80-81; R 81-87; R Nunney and Witham Friary, Marston Bigot etc *B & W* 87-10; rtd 10. *95 Nunney Road, Frome BA11 4LF* Tel (01373) 466063

HODDER, Trevor Valentine. b 31. Bps' Coll Cheshunt 65. d 67 p 68. C Oxhey All SS *St Alb* 67-70; C Digswell 70-73; V Colchester St Anne *Chelmsf* 74-96; rtd 96; Perm to Offic *Chelmsf* from 00. *30 Drury Road, Colchester CO2 7UX* Tel (01206) 766480

HODGE, Albert. b 40. NOC 84. d 87 p 88. C Huyton St Geo *Liv* 87-89; P-in-c Widnes St Paul 89-97; Chapl Halton Coll of FE 89-97; C Linton in Craven and Burnsall w Rylstone *Bradf* 97-05; rtd 05; Perm to Offic *Man* from 06. *Sunnyhurst, 50 Sandfield Road, Bacup OL13 9PD* Tel (01706) 873285 E-mail sergeant1832@aol.com

HODGE, Anthony Charles. b 43. AKC66. d 67 p 68. C Carrington *S'well* 67-69; C Bawtry w Austerfield 69-72; C Misson 69-72; Grenada 72-74; Trinidad and Tobago 74-76; V Tuckingmill *Truro* 76-78; V Worksop St Paul *S'well* 78-81; P-in-c Patrington w Hollym, Welwick and Winestead *York* 81-86; R 86-88; V York St Olave w St Giles 88-08; V York St Helen w St Martin 97-08; Chapl York Coll for Girls 88-96; rtd 08; P-in-c Duloe, Herodsfoot, Morval and St Pinnock *Truro* from 08. *The Rectory, Duloe, Liskeard PL14 4PW* Tel (01503) 264229 Mobile 07717-877430 E-mail anthonyhodge401@msn.com

HODGE, Colin. b 39. Sarum & Wells Th Coll. d 83 p 84. NSM Wareham *Sarum* 84-87; C Parkstone St Pet w Branksea and St Osmund 87-89; V Lilliput 89-00; rtd 00; Perm to Offic *Sarum* from 01. *35 Stowell Crescent, Wareham BH20 4PT* Tel (01929) 553222

HODGE, Canon Michael Robert. b 34. Pemb Coll Cam BA57 MA61. Ridley Hall Cam 57. d 59 p 60. C Harpurhey Ch Ch *Man* 59; C Blackpool St Mark *Blackb* 59-62; V Stalybridge Old St Geo *Man* 62-67; R Cobham w Luddesdowne and Dode *Roch* 67-81; Hon Can Roch Cathl 81-99; R Bidborough 81-99; rtd 99; Hon C Chale *Portsm* 99-06; Hon C Gatcombe 99-06; Hon C Shorwell w Kingston 99-06; Asst to RD W Wight 99-06; Perm to Offic from 06. *Braxton Cottage, Halletts Shute, Norton, Yarmouth PO41 0RH* Tel and fax (01983) 761121 Mobile 07941-232983 E-mail michael.hodge.1954@pem.cam.ac.uk

HODGE, Nigel John. b 61. BTh83 Open Univ BSc97 MIBiol98. St Mich Coll Llan 83. d 85 p 86. C Mynyddislwyn *Mon* 85-87; C Machen 87-89; TV Ebbw Vale 89-91; V Abercarn 91-98; Lic to Offic from 99. *6 Maple Terrace, Abercarn, Newport NP11 5JF* Tel (01495) 249014

HODGES, Mrs Christina Caroline. b 64. d 99 p 00. C Castle Church *Lich* 99-02; C Rugby *Cov* 02-03; TV 03-05; Perm to Offic *Sheff* 06-07; NSM Arbourthorne and Norfolk Park from 07. *St Paul and St Leonard's Vicarage, 458 East Bank Road, Sheffield S2 2AD* Tel 0114-265 3145 E-mail tina@thebeaconchurch.net

HODGES, Ian Morgan. Ridley Hall Cam. d 05 p 06. C Llantrisant 05-11; R Llanilid w Pencoed from 11. *The Rectory, 60 Coychurch Road, Pencoed, Bridgend CF35 5NA* Tel (01656) 860337 E-mail ian@hodgestowers.co.uk

HODGES, Mrs Jane Anne Christine. b 62. Leeds Univ BA84. SEITE 06. d 09 p 10. C Poplar *Lon* from 09. *164 St Leonard's Road, London E14 6PW* E-mail sussexjane@hotmail.com

HODGES, Jasper Tor. b 62. Leeds Univ BSc84 Sheff Univ MEng85 Lon Univ PGCE87. Trin Coll Bris BA94. d 94 p 95. C Holbeck *Ripon* 94-97; C Ealing St Steph Castle Hill *Lon* 97-04; V Arbourthorne and Norfolk Park *Sheff* from 04. *St Paul's and St Leonard's Vicarage, 458B East Bank Road, Sheffield S2 2AD* Tel 0114-265 3145 E-mail vicar@thebeaconchurch.net

HODGES, Keith Michael. b 53. Southn Univ BTh82 Heythrop Coll Lon MA04. Chich Th Coll 77. d 80 p 81. C Sydenham St Phil *S'wark* 80-84; Perm to Offic 85; C Leatherhead *Guildf* 86-89; V Aldershot St Aug from 89. *St Augustine's Vicarage, Holly Road, Aldershot GU12 4SE* Tel (01252) 320840 E-mail father.keith@ntlworld.com

HODGES, Mrs Laura. b 53. SAOMC 01. d 04 p 05. NSM Abingdon *Ox* from 04; Chapl SW Oxon Primary Care Trust from 07. *38 Baker Road, Abingdon OX14 5LW* Tel (01235) 527654 E-mail laura.hodges@btinternet.com

HODGES, Miss Stefanie Margaret. b 54. Trin Coll Bris 93. d 97 p 98. C Croydon Ch Ch *S'wark* 97-99; C Sutton St Nic 99-02; TV Mildenhall *St E* 02-08; TR Westborough *Guildf* from 08.

St Francis's Vicarage, Beckingham Road, Guildford GU2 8BU Tel (01483) 546412 E-mail stefanie@mhodges.co.uk

HODGES, Mrs Valerie Irene. b 44. **d** 06. NSM Newbridge *Mon* from 06. *Ty-Pwll House, The Pant, Newbridge, Newport NP11 5GF* Tel (01495) 244676
E-mail val.hodges@btinternet.com

HODGETT, Ms Tina Elizabeth. b 64. Leic Univ MBA05 Sheff Univ PGCE90 St Mary's Coll Dur BA88. Ridley Hall Cam 06. **d** 08 **p** 09. C Bestwood Em w St Mark *S'well* 08-11; TV Portishead *B & W* from 11. *110 Brampton Way, Portishead, Bristol BS20 6YT* Tel 07759-909106 (mobile)
E-mail tehodgett@ntlworld.com

HODGETTS, Alan Paul. b 54. Birm Poly BSc78 Heythrop Coll Lon MA96. St Steph Ho Ox 79. **d** 82 **p** 83. C Perry Barr *Birm* 82-85; C Broseley w Benthall *Heref* 85-87; V Effingham w Lt Bookham *Guildf* 87-96; R Merrow 96-06; Chapl HM Pris Woodhill from 06. *The Chaplaincy Department, HM Prison Woodhill, Tattenhoe Street, Milton Keynes MK4 4DA* Tel (01908) 722000 ext 2097 E-mail alan.hodgetts@hmps.gsi.gov.uk

HODGETTS, Colin William John. b 40. St D Coll Lamp BA61 Ripon Hall Ox 61. **d** 63 **p** 64. C Hackney St Jo *Lon* 63-68; Hon C St Martin-in-the-Fields 70-76; C Creeksea w Althorne *Chelmsf* 76-79; Perm to Offic *Ex* 84-03; C Parkham, Alwington, Buckland Brewer etc 03-06; Hon C from 06; rtd 06. *Quincott, Cheristowe, Hartland, Bideford EX39 6DA* Tel (01237) 441426
E-mail colin-julia@hartland.swinternet.co.uk

HODGETTS, Harry Samuel. b 30. Chich Th Coll 63. **d** 65 **p** 66. C Harton Colliery *Dur* 65-68; C Penzance St Mary *Truro* 68-70; V Penwerris 70-79; V Kettering St Mary *Pet* 79-94; rtd 95; Perm to Offic *Win* 03-09. *The Flat, Etal Manor, Etal, Cornhill-on-Tweed TD12 4TL* Tel (01890) 820378

HODGINS, Miss Kylie Anne. b 68. SEITE 98 Ridley Hall Cam 00. **d** 02 **p** 03. C Histon and Impington *Ely* 02-07; Chapl Sherborne Sch for Girls 07-08; P-in-c Cottenham *Ely* from 08; P-in-c Rampton from 09. *The Rectory, 6 High Street, Cottenham, Cambridge CB24 8SA* Tel (01954) 250454
E-mail kylie@gumnut.me.uk

HODGINS, Philip Arthur. b 57. Lanc Univ BA78 Bradf Univ MBA90 MCIPD94. Linc Th Coll 82. **d** 85 **p** 86. C Norton *Ches* 85-88; C Whitkirk *Ripon* 88-89; Perm to Offic *Bradf* 89-90 and *Chich* 91-02; Hon C Chiddingly w E Hoathly *Chich* 02-04; P-in-c 04-09; R from 09; RD Uckfield 06-11. *The Rectory, Rectory Close, East Hoathly, Lewes BN8 6EG* Tel (01825) 840270
E-mail philhodgins@btinternet.com

HODGKINSON, Canon John. b 27. Trin Hall Cam BA51 MA55. Linc Th Coll 51. **d** 53 **p** 54. C Penrith St Andr *Carl* 53-56; C Linc St Nic w St Jo Newport 56-58; C-in-c Lin St Jo Bapt CD 58-63; V Linc St Jo 63-66; R Old Brumby 66-71; V Kendal H Trin *Carl* 71-90; Hon Can Carl Cathl 84-90; rtd 90; Perm to Offic *Carl* from 90. *Boxtree Barn, Levens, Kendal LA8 8NZ* Tel (01539) 560806 E-mail boxtreebarn@hotmail.com

HODGKINSON, John David. b 57. Birm Univ BA78 Edin Univ BD89. Edin Th Coll 86. **d** 89 **p** 90. C Brier, Cliffe *Blackb* 89-92; C Darwen St Cuth w Tockholes St Steph 92-94; R Harrington *Carl* 94-00; V Walney Is from 00. *The Vicarage, Promenade, Walney, Barrow-in-Furness LA14 3QU* Tel (01229) 471268

HODGKINSON, Ms Amanda Jane. b 66. Westmr Coll Ox BA88 Heythrop Coll Lon MA99. Westcott Ho Cam 94. **d** 96 **p** 97. C Epping Distr *Chelmsf* 96-01; TV Wythenshawe *Man* 01-07; R Streatham St Leon *S'wark* from 07. *The Rectory, 1 Becmead Avenue, London SW16 1UH* Tel (020) 8769 4366
E-mail rectorstleonards@btinternet.com

HODGSON, Anthony Owen Langlois. b 35. Ripon Hall Ox 60. **d** 62 **p** 63. C Stiffkey w Morston and Blakeney w Lt Langham *Nor* 62-65; C Paddington Ch Ch *Lon* 66-70; Area Sec (Beds & Cambs) Chr Aid 70-74; (Herts & Hunts) 70-73; (Rutland & Northants) 73-74; V Gt w Lt Gidding and Steeple Gidding *Ely* 77-81; Warden Dovedale Ho 81-89; P-in-c Ilam w Blore Ray and Okeover *Lich* 81-89; Dir Chr Rural Cen 89-91; C Checkley and Stramshall 91-97; TV Uttoxeter Area 97-00; rtd 00. *9 Trent House, Station Road, Oundle, Peterborough PE8 4DE* Tel (01832) 275343 E-mail hodgson@phonecoop.coop

HODGSON, Antony Robert. b 66. Dundee Univ MA88 Jes Coll Cam BA92 MA96 Lanc Univ MA04 K Coll Lon MPhil10 AKC10. Westcott Ho Cam 90 Wm English Coll Rome 92. **d** 93 **p** 94. C Chorley St Geo *Blackb* 93-96; C Lytham St Cuth 96-99; V St Annes St Marg from 99. *St Margaret's Vicarage, 24 Chatsworth Road, Lytham St Annes FY8 2JN* Tel (01253) 722648

HODGSON, Barbara Elizabeth. b 46. N Riding Coll of Educn BEd85. NEOC 06. **d** 08 **p** 09. NSM Bridlington Em *York* 08-11; NSM Burton Fleming w Fordon, Grindale etc from 11. *The Vicarage, Back Street, Burton Fleming, Driffield YO25 3PD* Tel (01262) 470873 Mobile 07907-593234
E-mail vidara1972@talktalk.net

HODGSON, Christopher. b 24. Oriel Coll Ox BA49 MA54. Qu Coll Birm 50. **d** 52 **p** 53. C Cheltenham Ch Ch *Glouc* 52-55; C Liv Our Lady and St Nic 55-57; V Anfield St Columba 57-64; V Pembury *Roch* 64-82; Chapl Pembury Hosp Tunbridge Wells

66-82; R Aynho w Newbottle and Charlton *Pet* 82-85; Chapl Burrswood Chr Cen 85-94; C Castle Bromwich St Clem *Birm* 86-94; rtd 94. *Appledore, 29 Bramber Road, Seaford BN25 1AG* Tel (01323) 890735

HODGSON, Canon David George. b 54. Coll of Resurr Mirfield. **d** 82 **p** 83. C Stainton-in-Cleveland *York* 82-87; R Loftus 87; P-in-c Carlin How w Skinningrove 87; R Loftus and Carlin How w Skinningrove 87-93; V Middlesbrough Ascension from 93; P-in-c S Bank 03-07; RD Middlesbrough 98-05; Can and Preb York Minster from 01. *The Ascension Vicarage, Penrith Road, Middlesbrough TS3 7JR* Tel (01642) 244857

HODGSON, Canon David Peter. b 56. Fitzw Coll Cam BA77 MA81 Nottm Univ BA82 MTh85. St Jo Coll Nottm 80. **d** 83 **p** 84. C Guiseley w Esholt *Bradf* 83-86; Asst Chapl Loughb Univ 86-89; P-in-c Hatfield Broad Oak *Chelmsf* 89-90; P-in-c Bush End 89-90; P-in-c Hatfield Broad Oak and Bush End 90-97; Ind Chapl Harlow 89-97; R Wokingham All SS *Ox* from 97; AD Sonning from 04; Hon Can Ch Ch from 09. *The Rectory, 2A Norreys Avenue, Wokingham RG40 1TU* Tel 0118-979 2999
E-mail david@allsaints.prestel.co.uk

HODGSON, Gary Stuart. b 65. Ridley Hall Cam 95. **d** 98 **p** 99. C S Ossett *Wakef* 98-01; V Kirkburton 01-07; Chapl Huddersfield Univ and Hon C Fixby and Cowcliffe 07-09; P-in-c Cottingley *Bradf* from 09; RD Airedale from 10. *St Michael's Vicarage, 81 Littlelands, Bingley BD16 1AL* Tel (01274) 560761
E-mail gshodgson@sky.com

HODGSON, George. b 36. Qu Coll Birm 75. **d** 78 **p** 79. NSM Wordsley *Lich* 78-93; NSM Wordsley *Worc* from 93; Perm to Offic 84-93. *1 Newfield Drive, Kingswinford DY6 8HY* Tel (01384) 292543 Mobile 07811-733160
E-mail george@hodgson25.freeserve.co.uk

HODGSON, Mrs Helen Mary. b 66. NOC 01. **d** 04 **p** 05. C Emley and Flockton cum Denby Grange *Wakef* 04-05; NSM Kirkburton 05-07; Asst to RD Huddersfield 07-09; Lic to Offic *Bradf* 09-11; Hon C Thwaites Brow from 11. *St Michael's Vicarage, 81 Littlelands, Bingley BD16 1AL* Tel (01274) 560761
E-mail hmhodgson@sky.com

HODGSON, John. b 35. St Jo Coll Cam MA62 Lon Univ BD61. St Deiniol's Hawarden 80. **d** 81 **p** 82. Hon C Padiham *Blackb* 81-84; C W Burnley All SS 85-87; V 87-95; rtd 95; Perm to Offic *Worc* 95-02 and *Glouc* 98-02. *8 Rivergreen, Amble, Morpeth NE65 0GZ* Tel (01665) 713203

HODGSON, Kenneth Jonah. b 36. Open Univ BA79 CQSW89. Oak Hill Th Coll. **d** 69 **p** 70. C Rainford *Liv* 69-72; C Fazakerley Em 72-74; TV 74-78; Soc Worker 78-96; CF 79-82; rtd 00; C Wallasey St Hilary *Ches* 01-03; Perm to Offic from 03. *134 Rake Lane, Wallasey, Merseyside CH45 1JW* Tel and fax 0151-639 2980

HODGSON, Roger Vaughan. b 27. Magd Coll Cam BA49 MA54. Cuddesdon Coll 55. **d** 56 **p** 57. C Westmr St Matt *Lon* 56-59; C Pimlico St Pet w Westmr Ch Ch 59-65; R Lt Hadham *St Alb* 65-78; Chapl Oporto *Eur* 78-80; Chapl and Lect St Deiniol's Lib Hawarden 81-82; V Coldwaltham *Chich* 82-92; rtd 92; Asst Chapl Costa Blanca *Eur* 92-94; Perm to Offic *Chich* from 94. *2 Bakers Arms Hill, Arundel BN18 9DA* Tel (01903) 884708

HODGSON, The Ven Thomas Richard Burnham. b 26. FRMetS88. Lon Coll of Div BD52 ALCD52. **d** 52 **p** 53. C Crosthwaite Kendal *Carl* 52-55; C Stanwix 55-59; V Whitehaven St Nic 59-65; R Aikton 65-67; Bp's Dom Chapl and V Raughton Head w Gatesgill 67-73; Dir of Ords 70-74; Hon Can Carl Cathl 72-91; V Grange-over-Sands 73-79; RD Windermere 76-79; Adn W Cumberland 79-91; V Mosser 79-83; rtd 91; Perm to Offic *Carl* from 91. *58 Greenacres, Wetheral, Carlisle CA4 8LD* Tel (01228) 561159

HODGSON, Vernon Charles. b 34. MRPharmS58 Lon Univ BPharm58. Llan Dioc Tr Scheme 83. **d** 86 **p** 87. NSM Roath Llan 86-91; C Caerphilly 91-93; V Llanbister w Llanbadarn Fynydd w Llananno *S & B* 93-97; V Llanddewi Ystradenni 94-97; V Llanbister w Llanbadarn Fynydd w Llananno etc 97-01; rtd 01. *114 Carisbrooke Way, Cyncoed, Cardiff CF23 9HX* Tel (029) 2045 3403

HODKINSON, George Leslie. b 48. Qu Coll Birm 86. **d** 88 **p** 89. C Hall Green St Pet *Birm* 88-91; TV Solihull 91-96; P-in-c Billesley Common 96-00; V 00-05; AD Moseley 01-02; rtd 05; Chapl Countess of Chester Hosp NHS Foundn Trust from 05; Chapl Cheshire and Wirral Partnerships NHS Trust from 05. *2 Birch Close, Four Crosses, Llanymynech SY22 6NH* Tel (01691) 839946 or (01244) 364543

HODSON, Gordon George. b 35. St Chad's Coll Dur BA59. **d** 60 **p** 61. C Tettenhall Regis *Lich* 60-64; C Rugeley 64-68; V Shrewsbury St Mich 68-74; V Kinnerley w Melverley 74-87; P-in-c Knockin w Maesbrook 75-87; P-in-c Chebsey 87-91; P-in-c Seighford, Derrington and Cresswell 87-91; V Chebsey, Ellenhall and Seighford-with-Creswell 91-00; rtd 00; Perm to Offic *Lich* from 01. *27 Oak Drive, Oswestry SY11 2RU* Tel (01691) 662849

HODSON, Keith. b 53. Hatf Coll Dur BA74. Wycliffe Hall Ox 77. **d** 80 **p** 81. C Ashton-upon-Mersey St Mary Magd *Ches* 80-84; C

Polegate *Chich* 84-92; V Baddesley Ensor w Grendon *Birm* 92-08; R Beckbury, Badger, Kemberton, Ryton, Stockton etc *Lich* from 08; RD Edgmond and Shifnal from 10. *The Rectory, Beckbury, Shifnal TF11 9DG* Tel (01952) 750474 E-mail keithhodson@talk21.com

HODSON, Miss Margaret Christina. b 39. Linc Th Coll 88. **d** 90 **p** 94. Par Dn Old Trafford St Jo *Man* 90-94; C 94-95; P-in-c Calderbrook and Shore 95-01; rtd 01. *53 Lon Thelwal, Benllech, Tyn-y-Gongl LL74 8QH* Tel (01248) 852990

HODSON, Mrs Margot Rosemary. b 60. Bris Univ BSc82 PGCE83 Ox Brookes Univ BA06. All Nations Chr Coll 87 SAOMC 99. **d** 01 **p** 02. C Grove *Ox* 01-04; Chapl Jes Coll Ox 04-09; P-in-c Haddenham w Cuddington, Kingsey etc *Ox* from 09. *The Vicarage, 27A The Gables, Haddenham, Aylesbury HP17 8AD* Tel (01844) 291244 E-mail vicar@haddenhamstmarys.org

HODSON, Canon Raymond Leslie. b 42. St Chad's Coll Dur BSc64. **d** 66 **p** 67. C Adlington *Blackb* 66-68; C Cleveleys 68-72; V Ewood 72-77; V Nazeing *Chelmsf* 77-84; R Ampthill w Millbrook and Steppingley *St Alb* 84-95; Chapl Madrid *Eur* 95-04; Can Gib Cathl 02-04; rtd 04. *Mataro 1, 1 dcha, 28034 Madrid, Spain*

HODSON, Trevor. b 57. Sheff Univ BA78 Padgate Coll of Educn PGCE79 Leeds Univ MA06. NOC 04. **d** 06 **p** 07. NSM Broadheath *Ches* from 06. *40 Riversdale, Woolston, Warrington WA1 4PZ* Tel (01925) 811952 E-mail t.hodson@lathom.lancs.sch.uk

HODSON, William. b 42. Man Univ BA. Cranmer Hall Dur 81. **d** 82 **p** 83. C Ashton St Mich *Man* 82-86; V Tintwistle *Ches* 86-93; P-in-c Weston 93-99; rtd 99. *10 St Anne's Road, Horwich, Bolton BL6 7EJ* Tel (01204) 696172 E-mail bill.hodson@btopenworld.com

HOEY, David Paul. b 57. QUB BD79. CITC 79. **d** 81 **p** 82. C Belfast Whiterock *Conn* 81-83; C Portadown St Mark *Arm* 83-84; I Cleenish w Mullaghdun *Clogh* 84-90; I Magheracross 90-03; Dir of Ords 91-03; Can Clogh Cathl 95-03; Min Consultant for Ireland CPAS from 03. *44 Laragh, Ballycassidy, Enniskillen BT4 2JT* Tel (028) 6632 9655 Mobile 07712-873322 E-mail dphoey@btinternet.com *or* phoey@cpas.org.uk

HOEY, The Ven Raymond George. b 46. TCD BA70 MA. **d** 72 **p** 73. C Portadown St Mark *Arm* 72-78; I Camlough w Mullaglass from 78; Dom Chapl to Abp Arm from 86; Adn Arm from 92. *2 Maytown Road, Bessbrook, Newry BT35 7LY* Tel and fax (028) 3083 0301 E-mail archdeacon@armagh.anglican.org *or* rghoey@btinternet.com

HOEY, William Thomas. b 32. CITC 64. **d** 66 **p** 67. C Belfast St Mary *Conn* 66-68; C Lisburn Ch Ch 69-72; I Ballinderry 72-78; I Belfast St Simon w St Phil 78-02; rtd 02. *11 Carnshill Court, Belfast BT8 6TX* Tel (028) 9079 0595

HOFBAUER, Canon Andrea Martina. b 71. Johannes Gutenberg Univ Mainz Ox Univ MTh04. St Steph Ho Ox 00. **d** 02 **p** 03. C Teignmouth, Ideford w Luton, Ashcombe etc *Ex* 02-05; Chapl Ex Univ 05-09; Tutor SWMTC 05-09; PV Ex Cathl 06-09; Prec Wakef Cathl from 09. *4 Cathedral Close, Wakefield WF1 2DP* Tel (01924) 210008 *or* 373923 E-mail andi.hofbauer@wakefield-cathedral.org.uk

HOFFMANN, Jonathan Mark. b 60. Cranmer Hall Dur 95. **d** 97 **p** 99. C Eaton *Nor* 97-98; C Horsell *Guildf* 98-02; TV Aston cum Aughton w Swallownest and Ulley *Sheff* 02-06; P-in-c Freshford, Limpley Stoke and Hinton Charterhouse *B & W* from 06. *The Rectory, Crowe Lane, Freshford, Bath BA2 7WB* Tel (01225) 723135

HOFFMANN, Miss Rosalind Mary. b 49. **d** 10. OLM Loddon, Sisland, Chedgrave, Hardley and Langley *Nor* from 10. *Oakhurst, Briar Lane, Hales, Norwich NR14 6SY* Tel (01508) 548200 E-mail rhoffman12@aol.com

HOFREITER, Christian. b 75. **d** 10. NSM Ox St Aldate from 10. *40 Pembroke Street, Oxford OX1 1BP* Tel (01865) 254800 E-mail christian.hofreiter@staldates.org.uk

HOGAN, Edward James Martin. b 46. Trin Coll Bris. **d** 85 **p** 86. C St Austell *Truro* 85-88; V Gt Broughton and Broughton Moor *Carl* 88-94; V St Stythians w Perranarworthal and Gwennap *Truro* 94-10; RD Carnmarth N 03-08; rtd 10. *444 Buckfield Road, Leominster HR6 8SD* Tel (01568) 620064 E-mail martinhogan@mac.com

HOGAN, Miss Jennie. b 75. Goldsmiths' Coll Lon BA99 Fitzw Coll Cam BA03. Westcott Ho Cam 01. **d** 04 **p** 05. C Westmr St Steph w St Jo *Lon* 04-07; C All Hallows by the Tower etc 07-09; Chapl Chelsea Coll from 07; Chapl Lon Goodenough Trust from 09. *47 Mecklenburgh Square, London WC1N 2AJ* Tel 07515-486806 (mobile) E-mail jennie@goodenough.ac.uk

HOGAN, John James. b 24. St Edm Hall Ox BA51 MA56. Wells Th Coll 51. **d** 53 **p** 54. C Cannock *Lich* 53-55; C Drayton in Hales 55-58; V Woore 58-84; P-in-c Norton in Hales 82-84; V Woore and Norton in Hales 84-89; rtd 89; Perm to Offic *Lich* 89-00. *Wrekin Prospect, Audlem Road, Woore, Crewe CW3 9RJ* Tel (01630) 647677

HOGAN, William Riddell. b 22. Qu Coll Birm 48. **d** 51 **p** 52. C Brighouse *Wakef* 51-54; Singapore 55-58; V Greetland *Wakef*

59-73; V Greetland and W Vale 73-80; V Kellington w Whitley 80-87; rtd 87. *15 The Pastures, Carlton, Goole DN14 9QF* Tel (01405) 862233

HOGARTH, Alan Francis. b 58. Oak Hill Th Coll BA89. **d** 89 **p** 90. C Felixstowe SS Pet and Paul *St E* 89-93; R Beckington w Standerwick, Berkley, Rodden etc *B & W* 93-04; P-in-c Basildon w Aldworth and Ashampstead *Ox* 04-08; P-in-c Heapey and Withnell *Blackb* from 08. *34 Kittiwake Road, Heapey, Chorley PR6 9BA* Tel (01257) 231868 E-mail alan.hogarth@gmail.com

HOGARTH, Joseph. b 32. Edin Th Coll 65. **d** 67 **p** 67. C Walney Is *Carl* 67-71; V Whitehaven St Jas 71-76; V Millom H Trin w Thwaites 76-82; V Maryport 82-91; V Consett *Dur* 91-97; rtd 97; Perm to Offic *Roch* from 99. *56A Bexley Lane, Dartford DA1 4DD* Tel (01322) 526733

HOGARTH, Peter Robert. b 61. Bath Univ MSc97. Trin Coll Bris BA01. **d** 01 **p** 02. C Martock w Ash *B & W* 01-04; Asst Chapl Oslo w Bergen, Trondheim and Stavanger *Eur* from 04. *dragabergveien 11, 4085 Hundvåg, Stavanger, Norway* Tel (0047) 5155 5488 E-mail revpastorpete@yahoo.co.uk

HOGARTH MORGAN, Anthony. *See* MORGAN, Anthony Hogarth

HOGBEN, The Ven Peter Graham. b 25. Bps' Coll Cheshunt 60. **d** 61 **p** 62. C Hale *Guildf* 61-64; V Westborough 64-71; V Ewell 71-82; Hon Can Guildf Cathl 79-90; RD Epsom 80-82; Adn Dorking 82-90; rtd 90; Perm to Offic *Guildf* 90-08. *3 School Road, Rowledge, Farnham GU10 4EJ* Tel (01252) 793533

HOGG, Mrs Ann Grant. b 46. St Andr Univ MA68 Hughes Hall Cam PGCE70. NOC 99. **d** 02 **p** 03. NSM Bromborough *Ches* 02-04; Perm to Offic *St Alb* 04-05; NSM Watford Ch Ch 05-06; NSM Aldenham, Radlett and Shenley from 06. *The Vicarage, Church Fields, Christchurch Crescent, Radlett WD7 8EE* Tel (01923) 856606 E-mail wijoho@aol.com

HOGG, Anthony. b 42. Univ of Wales (Lamp) BA63. Linc Th Coll 64 Chich Th Coll 78. **d** 78 **p** 79. NSM Ridgeway *Ox* 78-86; NSM W w E Hanney 86-88; Hd Master New Coll Sch Ox 88-89; C Ridgeway *Ox* 90-91; P-in-c Hanney, Denchworth and E Challow 91-92; V 92-11; rtd 11. *11 Beckett House, Wallingford Street, Wantage OX12 8AZ* Tel (01235) 799240 E-mail victory@ukgateway.net

HOGG, Matthew. b 79. **d** 08 **p** 09. C Brompton H Trin w Onslow Square St Paul *Lon* 08-10; C Hammersmith St Paul from 10. *St Alban's Vicarage, 4 Margravine Road, London W6 8HJ*

HOGG, Neil Richard. b 46. BSc69. Ridley Hall Cam 82. **d** 84 **p** 85. C Bingham *S'well* 84-87; TV Bushbury *Lich* 87-00; V Worksop St Jo *S'well* 00-11; rtd 11. *4 Lowick, York YO24 2RF* Tel 07585-816697 (mobile) E-mail hogg350@btinternet.com

HOGG, William John. b 49. New Coll Ox MA71 Lon Univ CertEd72 Crewe & Alsager Coll MSc88. Edin Th Coll 86. **d** 88 **p** 89. C Oxton *Ches* 88-93; R Bromborough 93-04; P-in-c Radlett *St Alb* 04-05; TR Aldenham, Radlett and Shenley from 05. *The Vicarage, Church Fields, Christchurch Crescent, Radlett WD7 8EE* Tel (01923) 856606 E-mail wijoho@aol.lcom

HOGG, William Ritson. b 47. Leeds Univ BSc69. Qu Coll Birm. **d** 72 **p** 73. C Bordesley St Oswald *Birm* 72-76; TV Seacroft *Ripon* 76-82; V Hunslet St Mary 82-88; V Catterick 88-97; rtd 07. *c/o Crockford, Church House, Great Smith Street, London SW1P 3AZ* E-mail bill.denise@yahoo.co.uk

HOGGARD, Mrs Jean Margaret. b 36. NW Ord Course 76. **dss** 79 **d** 87 **p** 94. Northowram *Wakef* 79-94; Par Dn 87-94; C Ovenden 94-00; rtd 00; Perm to Offic *Wakef* from 01. *13 Joseph Avenue, Northowram, Halifax HX3 7HJ* Tel (01422) 201475

HOGGER, Clive Duncan. b 70. Sheff Univ BA92. Ridley Hall Cam 06. **d** 08 **p** 09. C Fletchamstead *Cov* from 08. *5 The Oaklands, Coventry CV4 9SY* Tel (024) 7646 2647 E-mail rev2b@tiscali.co.uk

HOGWOOD, Brian Roy. b 38. Bps' Coll Cheshunt. **d** 65 **p** 92. NSM Thetford *Nor* 91-93; Hon C 93-09; Chapl Aldenbrooke's NHS Trust 98-99. *31 Byron Walk, Thetford IP24 1JX* Tel (01842) 753915

HOLBEN, Bruce Frederick. b 45. STETS 99. **d** 02 **p** 03. NSM W Wittering and Birdham w Itchenor *Chich* from 02. *3 Elmstead Gardens, West Wittering, Chichester PO20 8NG* Tel (01243) 514129 Mobile 07940-759060

HOLBIRD, Thomas James. b 79. Leeds Univ BSc00. Ridley Hall Cam 08. **d** 11. C Gerrards Cross and Fulmer *Ox* from 11. *24 The Uplands, Gerrards Cross SL9 7JG* Tel (01753) 899318 Mobile 07870-682853 E-mail tomholbird@hotmail.co.uk

HOLBROOK, Ms Barbara Mary. b 58. Nottm Trent Univ BA94 Nottm Univ MA04. EMMTC 02. **d** 04 **p** 05. C Chesterfield H Trin and Ch Ch *Derby* 04-08; P-in-c Kimberley *S'well* from 08; P-in-c Nuthall from 08. *The Rectory, 1 Eastwood Road, Kimberley, Nottingham NG16 2HX* Tel 0115-938 3565 Mobile 07766-732514

HOLBROOK, Colin Eric Basford. *See* BASFORD HOLBROOK, Colin Eric

✠**HOLBROOK, The Rt Revd John Edward.** b 62. St Pet Coll Ox BA83 MA87. Ridley Hall Cam 82. **d** 86 **p** 87 **c** 11. C Barnes St Mary *S'wark* 86-89; C Bletchley *Ox* 89-93; C N Bletchley CD 89-93; V Adderbury w Milton 93-02; RD Deddington 00-02; R

Wimborne Minster *Sarum* 02-11; P-in-c Witchampton, Stanbridge and Long Crichel etc 02-11; P-in-c Horton, Chalbury, Hinton Martel and Holt St Jas 06-11; RD Wimborne 04-11; Chapl S and E Dorset Primary Care Trust 02-11; Can and Preb Sarum Cathl 06-11; Suff Bp Brixworth *Pet* from 11; Can Pet Cathl from 11. *Orchard Acre, 11 North Street, Mears Ashby, Northampton NN6 0DW* Tel 07534-716874 (mobile) E-mail jeholbrook@yahoo.co.uk

HOLCOMBE, Canon Graham William Arthur. b 50. Open Univ BA99. St Mich Coll Llan. **d** 80 **p** 81. C Neath w Llantwit 80-84; Asst Youth Chapl 81-84; PV Llan Cathl 84-86; V Pentyrch 86-00; V Pentyrch w Capel Llanillterne 00-02; Can Llan Cathl from 02. *1 White House, Cathedral Green, Llandaff, Cardiff CF5 2EB* Tel (029) 2056 9521

HOLDAWAY, Mark Daniel James. b 78. Selw Coll Cam MA02. Oak Hill Th Coll BA07. **d** 07 **p** 08. C Bury St Edmunds St Mary *St E* 07-11; R Kirby-le-Soken w Gt Holland *Chelmsf* from 11. *The Rectory, 10 Thorpe Road, Kirby Cross, Frinton-on-Sea CO13 0LT* Tel (01255) 675997 Mobile 07711-373427 E-mail markholdaway@btinternet.com

HOLDAWAY, Simon Douglas. b 47. Lanc Univ BA73 Sheff Univ PhD81. NOC 78. **d** 81 **p** 82. NSM Gleadless *Sheff* from 81; Sen Lect Sheff Univ from 81. *Address temp unknown*

HOLDAWAY, Canon Stephen Douglas. b 45. Hull Univ BA67. Ridley Hall Cam 67. **d** 70 **p** 71. C Southampton Thornhill St Chris *Win* 70-73; C Tardebigge *Worc* 73-78; Ind Chapl 73-78; Ind Chapl *Linc* 78-93; Co-ord City Cen Group Min 81-93; TR Louth from 93; RD Louthesk 95-11; Can and Preb Linc Cathl from 00. *The Rectory, 49 Westgate, Louth LN11 9YE* Tel (01507) 603213 *or* 610247 Fax 602991 E-mail stephen.holdaway@btinternet.com

HOLDEN, Canon Arthur Stuart James. b 23. ALCD51. **d** 51 **p** 52. C Barking St Marg *Chelmsf* 51-54; P-in-c Berechurch 54-55; V 55-61; V Earls Colne 61-82; P-in-c White Colne 66-67; V 68-82; V Earls Colne and White Colne 82-88; Hon Can Chelmsf Cathl 80-88; rtd 88; Perm to Offic *Chelmsf* from 88. *10 Wroxham Close, Colchester CO3 3RQ* Tel (01206) 560845

HOLDEN, Christopher Charles. b 54. Local Minl Tr Course. **d** 11. NSM Codnor *Derby* from 11; NSM Horsley and Denby from 11. *62 Waingroves Road, Waingroves, Ripley DE5 9TD* Tel (01773) 746411 E-mail cholden123@aol.com

HOLDEN, Christopher Graham. b 78. Lanc Univ BA06. Westcott Ho Cam 07. **d** 09 **p** 10. C Carnforth *Blackb* from 09. *10 Croasdale Close, Carnforth LA5 9UN* Tel (01524) 730760 Mobile 07790-202429 E-mail wilfriedgh@hotmail.com

HOLDEN, Geoffrey. b 26. FCII54. Oak Hill Th Coll 57. **d** 59 **p** 60. C Crookes St Thos *Sheff* 59-61; C Belper *Derby* 61-63; C Woking St Jo *Guildf* 63-66; R Bath St Mich w St Paul *B & W* 66-73; Chapl Bath Gp Hosps 73-91; rtd 91; Perm to Offic *B & W* from 91. *32 Crescent Gardens, Bath BA1 2NB* Tel (01225) 427933

HOLDEN, Jack Crawford (Simon). b 30. Leeds Univ BA59. Coll of Resurr Mirfield 59. **d** 61 **p** 61. C Middlesbrough All SS *York* 61-64; Lic to Offic *Wakef* 65-69 and from 98; CR from 67; Asst Chapl Univ Coll Lon 69-74; rtd 98. *House of the Resurrection, Stocks Bank Road, Mirfield WF14 0BN* Tel (01924) 494318

HOLDEN, Canon John. b 33. MBE76. Sheff Univ MA02 ACMA62. Ridley Hall Cam 65 Selly Oak Coll 71. **d** 67 **p** 68. C Flixton St Jo CD *Man* 67-71; Uganda 71-75; V Aston SS Pet and Paul *Birm* 75-87; RD Aston 86-87; Hon Can Birm Cathl 86-87; R Ulverston St Mary w H Trin *Carl* 87-98; RD Furness 90-94; Hon Can Carl Cathl 91-94; rtd 98; Perm to Offic *Carl* from 98 and *Heref* from 99. *3 Alison Road, Church Stretton SY6 7AT* Tel (01694) 724167

HOLDEN, John Norman. b 35. Heythrop Coll Lon MA97. Oak Hill Th Coll 91. **d** 95 **p** 96. NSM Codicote *St Alb* 95-96; Perm to Offic *St Alb* from 96 and *Ely* from 00. *4 Chapel Row, Shay Lane, Upper Dean, Huntingdon PE28 0LU* Tel (01234) 708928

HOLDEN, John Worrall. b 44. K Coll Lon AKC67. **d** 70 **p** 71. C Derby St Bart 70-72; Lic to Offic 72-74; Hon C St Helier *S'wark* 74-77; Hon C St Marylebone All SS *Lon* 80-83; Hon C St Botolph Aldgate w H Trin Minories 84-95. *4 Foster Lane, London EC2V 6HH*

HOLDEN, Mark Noel. b 61. Collingwood Coll Dur BA82 Edin Univ CQSW85 Warwick Univ TCert93 Birm Univ MA95. Qu Coll Birm 93. **d** 95 **p** 96. C Brumby *Linc* 95-99; P-in-c Wragby 99-00; R Wragby Gp from 00. *The Vicarage, Church Street, Wragby, Lincoln LN8 5RA* Tel (01673) 857825

HOLDEN, Norman. See HOLDEN, John Norman

HOLDEN, Paul Edward. b 53. BSc75 CEng79 MIM MIBF. Trin Coll Bris 82. **d** 86 **p** 87. C Harpurhey Ch Ch *Man* 86-88; C Harpurhey St Steph 88-93; Sen Min Harpurhey LEP 88-93. *2 Baywood Street, Harpurhey, Manchester M9 5XJ* Tel 0161-205 2938

HOLDEN, Richard Gary. **d** 04 **p** 05. C Louth *Linc* 04-07; P-in-c Clee from 07; P-in-c Cleethorpes St Aid from 07. *Old Clee Vicarage, 202 Clee Road, Grimsby DN32 8NG* Tel (01472) 581570 E-mail revrichard.holden@btinternet.com

HOLDEN, Mrs Rita. b 45. SAOMC 98. **d** 01 **p** 03. OLM Burghfield *Ox* 01-02; NSM Droitwich Spa *Worc* from 02.

40 Nightingale Close, Droitwich WR9 7HB Tel (01905) 772787 Mobile 07814-621389 E-mail rita@openv.clara.co.uk

HOLDEN, Simon. See HOLDEN, Jack Crawford

HOLDEN, Stuart. See HOLDEN, Canon Arthur Stuart James

HOLDER, Adèle Claire. See REES, Ms Adèle Claire

HOLDER, Canon John William. b 41. Chester Coll CertEd61 Open Univ BA73 Bath Univ MEd85. Trin Coll Bris MA94. **d** 87 **p** 88. C Brockworth *Glouc* 87-91; P-in-c Avening w Cherington 91-95; V Cinderford St Jo 95-05; P-in-c Lydbrook 99-03; P-in-c Coberley, Cowley, Colesbourne and Elkstone from 05; Hon Can Glouc Cathl from 03. *The Rectory, Cowley, Cheltenham GL53 9NJ* Tel (01242) 870183 E-mail canon.john@holder-net.co.uk

HOLDER, Kenneth William. b 29. Sarum Th Coll 60. **d** 61 **p** 62. C Crawley *Chich* 61-65; C-in-c Wick CD 65-73; V Hangleton 73-79; R Rotherfield 79-81; R Rotherfield w Mark Cross 81-83; Chapl Eastbourne Coll 83-84; C Farnborough *Roch* 85; TV Mildenhall *St E* 87-92; R Redgrave cum Botesdale w Rickinghall 92-99; rtd 99; Perm to Offic *Chich* from 01. *Flat 3, 13 Granville Road, Eastbourne BN20 7HE* Tel (01323) 410868

HOLDER, Rodney Dennis. b 50. Trin Coll Cam BA71 MA75 Ch Ch Ox MA75 DPhil78 FRAS75 CPhys91 MInstP91 CMath95 FIMA95. Wycliffe Hall Ox BA96. **d** 97 **p** 98. C Long Compton, Whichford and Barton-on-the-Heath *Cov* 97-01; C Wolford w Burmington 97-01; C Cherington w Stourton 97-01; C Barcheston 97-01; Perm to Offic 01-02; P-in-c The Claydons *Ox* 02-05; Course Dir Faraday Inst for Science and Relig from 06. *The Faraday Institute, St Edmund's College, Cambridge CB3 0BN* Tel (01223) 741284 *or* 364577 E-mail drandmrsr.holder@virginmedia.com

HOLDING, Kenneth George Frank. b 27. Sarum & Wells Th Coll 75. **d** 77 **p** 78. C Bexley St Mary *Roch* 77-80; Min Joydens Wood St Barn CD 80-85; R Mereworth w W Peckham 85-92; rtd 92; Perm to Offic *York* 92-04; P-in-c Willerby w Ganton and Folkton from 04. *Willerby Vicarage, Wains Lane, Staxton, Scarborough YO12 4SF* Tel (01944) 710364

HOLDRIDGE, The Ven Bernard Lee. b 35. Lich Th Coll 64. **d** 67 **p** 68. C Swinton *Sheff* 67-71; V Doncaster St Jude 71-81; R Rawmarsh w Parkgate 81-88; RD Rotherham 86-88; V Worksop Priory *S'well* 88-94; Adn Doncaster *Sheff* 94-01; rtd 01; Perm to Offic *Sheff* 01-06 and *Guildf* from 06. *35 Denehyrst Court, York Road, Guildford GU1 4EA* Tel (01483) 570791

HOLDSTOCK, Adrian Charles. b 51. Peterho Cam BA MA75 Nottm Univ MA03 CEng MIMechE MCMI. EMMTC 00. **d** 03 **p** 04. NSM Bosworth and Sheepy Gp *Leic* from 03; NSM Nailstone and Carlton w Shackerstone from 07. *34 Herald Way, Burbage, Hinckley LE10 2NX* Tel (01455) 251066 Mobile 07792-452669 E-mail adriancholdstock@yahoo.co.uk

HOLDSWORTH, Ian Scott. b 52. Sheff Poly BA75. Oak Hill Th Coll BA81. **d** 81 **p** 82. C Denham *Ox* 81-84; P-in-c S Leigh 84-89; P-in-c Cogges 84-88; V 88-89; Perm to Offic *Pet* 95; NSM Brackley St Pet w St Jas 96-99; P-in-c Northampton St Mary 99-04; V from 04. *St Mary's Vicarage, Towcester Road, Northampton NN4 9EZ* Tel (01604) 761104 Mobile 07912-639980 E-mail ianholdworth@aol.com

HOLDSWORTH, The Ven John Ivor. b 49. Univ of Wales (Abth) BA70 Univ of Wales (Cardiff) BD73 MTh75. St Mich Coll Llan 70. **d** 73 **p** 74. C Newport St Paul *Mon* 73-77; CF (TAVR) 75-90; V Abercraf and Callwen *S & B* 77-86; Bp's Chapl for Th Educn 80-97; V Gorseinon 86-97; Hon Lect Th Univ of Wales (Swansea) 88-96; Prin and Warden St Mich Coll Llan 97-03; Lect Th Univ of Wales (Cardiff) 97-03; Adn St D 4 Steynton *St D* 03-10; Adn Cyprus and Chapl Larnaca from 10. *15 Odyssea Androutsou, CY-7104 Aradippou, Cyprus* Tel (01646) 692867

HOLDSWORTH, The Very Revd Kelvin. b 66. Man Poly BSc89 St Andr Univ BD92 Edin Univ MTh96. TISEC 95. **d** 97 **p** 98. Prec St Ninian's Cathl Perth 97-00; R Bridge of Allan 00-06; Chapl Stirling Univ 00-06; Provost St Mary's Cathl from 06; R Glas St Mary from 06. *300 Great Western Road, Glasgow G4 9JB* Tel 0141-530 8643 E-mail kelvin@thurible.net *or* provost@thecathedral.org.uk

HOLDSWORTH, Michael Andrew. b 65. Univ Coll Dur BA88. Ripon Coll Cuddesdon BA92 MA96. **d** 93 **p** 94. C Cannock *Lich* 93-97; TV Shelf Manor 97-99; Tutor Ripon Coll Cuddesdon 97-99. *Address temp unknown*

HOLE, The Very Revd Derek Norman. b 33. De Montfort Univ Hon DLitt99 Leic Univ Hon LLD05. Linc Th Coll 57. **d** 60 **p** 61. C Knighton St Mary Magd *Leic* 60-62; S Africa 62-64; C Kenilworth St Nic *Cov* 64-67; R Burton Latimer *Pet* 67-73; V Leic St Jas 73-92; Hon Can Leic Cathl 83-92; RD Christianity S 83-92; Provost Leic 92-99; Chapl to The Queen 91-99; rtd 99; Perm to Offic *Leic* from 00. *25 Southernhay Close, Leicester LE2 3TW* Tel 0116-270 9988 E-mail dnhole@leicester.anglican.org

HOLE, Toby Kenton. b 72. Dur Univ BA94 MA95 Cam Univ BTh06. Ridley Hall Cam 03. **d** 06 **p** 07. C Islington St Mary *Lon*

HOLFORD, 06-10; V Woodseats St Chad *Sheff* from 10. *St Chad's Vicarage, 9 Linden Avenue, Sheffield S8 0GA* Tel 0114-274 9302 E-mail toby.hole@googlemail.com

HOLFORD, Andrew Peter. b 62. Nottm Univ BSc84. Cranmer Hall Dur 87. **d** 90 **p** 91. C Waltham Cross *St Alb* 90-93; C Northampton St Benedict *Pet* 93-95; V Pet Ch Carpenter 95-04; TR Baldock w Bygrave and Weston *St Alb* from 04. *The Rectory, 9 Pond Lane, Baldock SG7 5AS* Tel (01462) 896273 E-mail 2008luddite@googlemail.com

HOLFORD, Canon John Alexander. b 40. Chich Th Coll 65. **d** 67 **p** 68. C Cottingley *Bradf* 67-71; C Baildon 71-73; P-in-c Bingley H Trin 73-74; V 74-86; V Woodhall 86-93; C Shelf 93-94; TV Shelf w Buttershaw St Aid 94-99; rtd 99; P-in-c Embsay w Eastby *Bradf* 99-04; Hon Can Bradf Cathl 03-04; Perm to Offic from 04. *3 Wheelwrights Court, Hellifield, Skipton BD23 4LX* Tel (01729) 851740 E-mail john.holford@bradford.anglican.org

HOLFORD, Margaret Sophia. b 39. SAUMC 95. **d** 98 **p** 99. NSM Stevenage St Andr and St Geo *St Alb* 98-03; NSM Ickleford w Holwell 03-05; NSM Holwell, Ickleford and Pirton from 05. *Icknield House, Westmill Lane, Ickleford, Hitchin SG5 3RN* Tel (01462) 432794 Fax 436618

HOLGATE, David Andrew. b 54. Cape Town Univ BA77 Port Eliz Univ BA89 Rhodes Univ MTh90 PhD94. All Nations Chr Coll 80. **d** 82 **p** 84. S Africa 82-93; C Uitenhage St Kath 82-84; Asst P Port Elizabeth St Hugh 84-87; P-in-c Somerset E All SS 88-89; St Paul's Coll Grahamstown 90-93; CME Officer *Chelmsf* 93-96; P-in-c Felsted 93-96; V Felsted and Lt Dunmow 96-97; Dean of Studies STETS from 97; Vice-Prin 01-11; Prin from 11. *19 The Close, Salisbury SP1 2EE* Tel (01722) 424820 Fax 424811 E-mail daholgate@stets.ac.uk

✠**HOLLAND, The Rt Revd Alfred Charles.** b 27. St Chad's Coll Dur BA50. **d** 52 **p** 53 **c** 70. C W Hackney St Barn *Lon* 52-54; Australia 55-78 and from 94; R Scarborough 55-70; Asst Bp Perth 70-77; Bp Newcastle 78-92; rtd 92; Chapl St Geo Coll Jerusalem 93-94. *21 Sullivan Crescent, Wanniassa ACT 2903, Australia* Tel (0061) (2) 6231 8368 E-mail acjmholland@bigpond.com

✠**HOLLAND, The Rt Revd Edward.** b 36. AKC64. **d** 65 **p** 66 **c** 86. C Dartford H Trin *Roch* 65-69; C Mill Hill Jo Keble Ch *Lon* 69-72; Prec Gib Cathl 72-74; Chapl Naples Ch 74-79; Chapl Bromley Hosp 79-86; V Bromley St Mark *Roch* 79-86; Suff Bp Eur 86-95; Dean Brussels 86-95; Area Bp Colchester *Chelmsf* 95-01; rtd 01; Hon Asst Bp Lon from 02; Hon Asst Bp Eur from 02. *37 Parfrey Street, London W6 9EW* Tel (020) 8746 3636 E-mail ed.holland@btopenworld.com

HOLLAND, Geoffrey. *See* HOLLAND, William Geoffrey Bretton

HOLLAND, Mrs Gillaine. b 67. Kent Inst of Art & Design BA89. STETS 05. **d** 08 **p** 09. C Epsom St Martin *Guildf* 08-09; C Woking St Mary from 09. *11 Upper Edgeborough Road, Guildford GU1 2BJ* Tel 07969-067116 (mobile) E-mail gillaineholland@sky.com

HOLLAND, Glyn. b 59. Hull Univ BA Bris Univ CertEd. Coll of Resurr Mirfield 83. **d** 85 **p** 86. C Brighouse St Martin *Wakef* 85-89; V Ferrybridge 89-96; Chapl Pontefract Gen Infirmary 89-96; V Middlesbrough All SS *York* from 96. *All Saints' Vicarage, 14 The Crescent, Middlesbrough TS5 6SQ* Tel (01642) 820304

HOLLAND, Jesse Marvin Sean. b 66. Westmr Coll Ox MTh03. Oak Hill Th Coll BA97. **d** 98 **p** 99. C Thundersley *Chelmsf* 98-02; P-in-c Tedburn St Mary, Whitestone, Oldridge etc *Ex* 02-06; V Buller New Zealand 06-08; P-in-c Lyneham w Bradenstoke *Sarum* 08-10; Chapl RAF from 10. *Chaplaincy Services, Valiant Block, HQ Air Command, RAF High Wycombe HP14 4UE* Tel (01494) 496800 Fax 496343 E-mail revdjmsholland@aol.com

HOLLAND, John Stuart. b 52. Sarum & Wells Th Coll 77. **d** 80 **p** 81. C Wylde Green *Birm* 80-83; C Swanage and Studland *Sarum* 83-85; P-in-c Handley w Pentridge 85-88; TV Preston w Sutton Poyntz and Osmington w Poxwell 88-95; P-in-c Failsworth St Jo *Man* 95-01; V Ashton Ch Ch 01-07; P-in-c Carbis Bay w Lelant *Truro* 07-10; P-in-c Towednack and Zennor 08-10; P-in-c Oswaldtwistle Immanuel and All SS *Blackb* from 10; P-in-c Oswaldtwistle St Paul from 10. *The Vicarage, 29 Mayfield Avenue, Oswaldtwistle, Accrington BB5 3AA* Tel (01254) 231038 Mobile 07718-483817 E-mail vicar-cbl@fsmail.net

HOLLAND, Lesley Anne. *See* LEON, Mrs Lesley Anne

HOLLAND, Mrs Linda. b 48. Sarum & Wells Th Coll 91. **d** 93 **p** 94. Par Dn Queensbury All SS *Lon* 93-94; C 94-96; C Enfield St Jas 96-01; V Coney Hill *Glouc* 01-10; rtd 10. *3 Ryelands, Tuffley, Gloucester GL4 0QA* Tel (01452) 537493 E-mail revlynneholland@hotmail.com

HOLLAND, Matthew Francis. b 52. Lon Univ BA73. Qu Coll Birm. **d** 79 **p** 80. C Ecclesall *Sheff* 79-83; TV Gleadless Valley 83-86; TR 86-88; V Sheff Gillcar St Silas 88-92; V Sheff St Silas Broomhall 92-98; V Southsea St Simon *Portsm* from 98. *St Simon's Vicarage, 6 Festing Road, Southsea PO4 0NG* Tel (023) 9273 3068

HOLLAND, Paul William. b 55. Coll of Resurr Mirfield 78. **d** 80 **p** 81. C Parkstone St Pet w Branksea and St Osmund *Sarum* 80-83; CR 85-93; Asst Chapl Musgrove Park Hosp 93; Asst Chapl St Helier Hosp Carshalton 93-96; C Croydon St Jo *S'wark* 96-04; TV Barnes from 04. *39 Elm Bank Gardens, London SW13 0NX* Tel (020) 8876 5230 E-mail pauhold@mac.com

HOLLAND, Peter Christie. b 36. St Andr Univ BSc60. Cranmer Hall Dur 60. **d** 62 **p** 63. C Darlington St Jo *Dur* 62-64; C Bishopwearmouth Ch Ch 64-69; V Tudhoe 69-77; V New Seaham 77-89; V Totternhoe, Stanbridge and Tilsworth *St Alb* 89-01; rtd 02; Perm to Offic *Dur* from 02. *Bracken Ridge, Woodland, Bishop Auckland DL13 5RH* Tel (01388) 718881 E-mail hollandpeter90@supanet.com

HOLLAND, Simon Geoffrey. b 63. MHCIMA83. Trin Coll Bris BA. **d** 91 **p** 92. C Reigate St Mary *S'wark* 91-95; Chapl Lee Abbey 95-99; C Guildf St Sav 09-07; P-in-c Bath Walcot *B & W* from 07. *Swallowgate, Lansdown Road, Bath BA1 5TD* Tel (01225) 334748 E-mail simonholland150@hotmail.com

HOLLAND, Simon Paul. b 56. Westcott Ho Cam 79. **d** 81 **p** 82. C Uckfield *Chich* 81-84; TV Lewes All SS, St Anne, St Mich and St Thos 84-88; TR 88-91; R Glas St Matt 91-95; P-in-c Glas St Kentigern 95-96; R Aldingbourne, Barnham and Eastergate *Chich* from 96. *The Rectory, 97 Barnham Road, Barnham, Bognor Regis PO22 0EQ* Tel (01243) 554077 E-mail simonholland578@btinternet.com

HOLLAND, Mrs Tessa Christine. b 59. Hull Univ BA81. STETS 00. **d** 03 **p** 04. NSM Storrington *Chich* 03-05; NSM Pulborough 05-07; Lic to Offic from 07. *Wild Fortune, Sandgate Lane, Storrington, Pulborough RH20 3HJ* Tel (01903) 740487 E-mail wildfortune@btinternet.com

HOLLAND, William Geoffrey Bretton. b 36. Magd Coll Cam BA59 MA63. Westcott Ho Cam 61. **d** 63 **p** 64. C Cannock *Lich* 63-66; C Paddington Ch Ch *Lon* 66-69; Chapl Magd Coll Cam 69-73; V Twyford *Win* 74-78; V Twyford and Owslebury and Morestead 78-84; Chapl Twyford Sch Win 84-90; rtd 01. *68A Warwick Way, London SW1V 1RZ* Tel (020) 7630 8334

HOLLANDS, Derek Gordon. b 45. Brasted Th Coll Chich Th Coll 72. **d** 74 **p** 75. C Banstead *Guildf* 74-77; C Cranleigh 77-79; C Haywards Heath St Wilfrid *Chich* 79-80; TV 80-82; Chapl Hillingdon Area HA 82-86; Chapl W Suffolk Hosp Bury St Edm 86-95; Pres Coll Health Care Chapls 92-94; Sen Chapl R Cornwall Hosps Trust 95-98; rtd 99. *The Cedars, 59 Hardwick Lane, Bury St Edmunds IP33 2RB* Tel (01284) 386196 E-mail derek.hollands@tesco.net

HOLLANDS, Percival Edwin Macaulay. b 36. Edin Th Coll 57. **d** 60 **p** 61. C Greenock *Glas* 60-64; C Aberdeen St Mary 64-65; P-in-c Aberdeen St Clem 65-68; R Cruden Bay 68-70; CF 70-82; C Ribbleton *Blackb* 82-83; TV 83-88; C Penwortham St Mary 88-92; V Farington 92-98; rtd 98; Perm to Offic *Nor* from 00. *30 Teasel Road, Attleborough NR17 1XX* Tel (01953) 457372

HOLLANDS, Ray Leonard. b 42. MRICS02 MASI MRSH MCIOB. S'wark Ord Course 68. **d** 71 **p** 72. NSM Hanworth All SS *Lon* 71-77, 85-91, 95-98 and 02-03; NSM Hanworth St Geo 77-85; NSM Marshwood Vale *Sarum* 81-91; NSM Upper Sunbury St Sav *Lon* 98-01; rtd 03. *Yew Tree Cottage, Marshwood, Bridport DT6 5QF* Tel (01297) 678566 E-mail rlh.ltd@virgin.net

HOLLETT, Catherine Elaine. *See* DAKIN, Mrs Catherine Elaine

HOLLEY, Paul Robert. b 65. St Jo Coll Dur 91. **d** 94 **p** 95. C Tonge w Alkrington *Man* 94-98; P-in-c Salford St Phil w St Steph 98-00; P-in-c Salford Sacred Trin 99-00; R Salford Sacred Trin and St Phil 00-03; P-in-c La Côte *Eur* 03-10. *7 chemin du Couchant, 1260 Nyon, Switzerland* Tel (0041) (22) 364 0030 E-mail paul.holley@lineone.net

HOLLIDAY, Andrew. b 62. St Steph Ho Ox 89. **d** 92 **p** 93. C Marton *Blackb* 92-95; C Poulton-le-Fylde 95-97; V Leyland St Jas 97-04; AD Leyland 02-04; P-in-c Darwen St Pet w Hoddlesden 04-10; V Darwen St Pet from 10. *The Rectory, St Peter's Close, Darwen BB3 2EA* Tel (01254) 702411 E-mail andrew.holliday@tesco.net

HOLLIDAY, Peter Leslie. b 48. FCA79 Birm Univ BCom70 MA92. Qu Coll Birm 81. **d** 83 **p** 84. C Burton *Lich* 83-87; P-in-c Longdon 87-93; PV and Subchanter Lich Cath 87-93; R Stratford-on-Avon w Bishopton *Cov* 93-00; Dir St Giles Hospice Lich from 00; Chan's V Lich Cathl from 02. *St Giles Hospice, Fisherwick Road, Lichfield WS14 9LH* Tel (01543) 432031 E-mail plh@clara.net

HOLLIDAY, William. b 33. Qu Coll Cam BA56 MA60 McGill Univ Montreal BD58 LTh58. Montreal Dioc Th Coll 56 Linc Th Coll 58. **d** 58 **p** 59. C Stanningley St Thos *Ripon* 58-63; C Romaldkirk 63-64; India 64-77; V Thwaites Brow *Bradf* 77-86; RD S Craven 82-86; P-in-c Horton 86-98; P-in-c Bradf St Oswald Chapel Green 91-98; RD Bowling and Horton 95-98; rtd 98; Perm to Offic *Bradf* from 99. *61 Woodside Crescent, Bingley BD16 1RE* Tel (01274) 568413

HOLLIDAY, William John. b 49. Middleton St Geo Coll of Educn TCert72. CBDTI 05. **d** 07 **p** 08. NSM Kendal St Thos *Carl* from 07. *2 Michaelson Road, Kendal LA9 5JQ* Tel (01539) 730701 E-mail billholliday@googlemail.com

HOLLIMAN, The Ven John James. b 44. St D Coll Lamp BA66. **d** 67 **p** 68. C Tideswell *Derby* 67-71; CF 71-99; Dep Chapl Gen and Adn for the Army 96-99; QHC 94-99; V Funtington and Sennicotts *Chich* 99-09; R W Stoke 99-09; RD Westbourne 04-09; rtd 09. *3 Littledown, Shaftesbury SP7 9HD* Tel (01747) 853637

HOLLIN, Ian. b 40. Open Univ BA76 DCC91. Sarum Th Coll 67. **d** 70 **p** 71. C Lancaster Ch Ch *Blackb* 70-72; C S Shore H Trin 72-75; C Marton Moss 72-75; V Morecambe St Lawr 75-78; V Blackpool St Mary 78-83; PV and Succ Ex Cathl 83-87; Counsellor Coun for Chr Care and Tr 87-91; Admin Boniface Cen Ex 91-93; TV Maltby *Sheff* 93-96; R Handsworth 96-08; rtd 08; Perm to Offic *Blackb* from 08. *30 Sumpter Croft, Penwortham, Preston PR1 9UJ* Tel (01772) 749806

HOLLINGDALE, Derek Leslie. b 32. Ex & Truro NSM Scheme. **d** 83 **p** 84. NSM Tuckingmill *Truro* 83-85; NSM Illogan 85-92; NSM Treslothan 92-95; NSM Mithian w Mount Hawke 95-98; Perm to Offic from 05. *53 Tregrea, Beacon, Camborne TR14 7ST* Tel (01209) 612938

HOLLINGHURST, Mrs Anne Elizabeth. b 64. Trin Coll Bris BA96 Hughes Hall Cam MSt10. **d** 96 **p** 97. C Nottingham St Sav *S'well* 96-99; Chapl Derby Univ and Derby Cathl 99-05; Bp's Dom Chapl and Can Res Man Cathl 05-10; V St Alb St Pet *St Alb* from 10. *The Vicarage, 23 Hall Place Gardens, St Albans AL1 3SB* Tel (01727) 851464
E-mail annehollinghurst@hotmail.co.uk

HOLLINGHURST, Preb Stephen. b 59. St Jo Coll Nottm 81. **d** 83 **p** 84. C Hyde St Geo *Ches* 83-86; C Cropwell Bishop w Colston Bassett, Granby etc *S'well* 86-90; R Pembridge w Moor Court, Shobdon, Staunton etc *Heref* 90-02; R Presteigne w Discoed, Kinsham, Lingen and Knill from 02; RD Kington and Weobley 95-02 and from 07; Preb Heref Cathl from 08. *The Rectory, St David's Street, Presteigne LD8 2BP* Tel (01544) 267777 E-mail steve.hollinghurst@lineone.net

HOLLINGHURST, Stephen Patrick. b 63. Hull Univ BA84. Trin Coll Bris BA93 MA93. **d** 96 **p** 97. C Nottingham St Sav *S'well* 96-99; Chapl Nottm Trent Univ 99-03; Researcher CA from 03; Perm to Offic Derby 00-04; Chapl Derby Cathl 04-05. *The Vicarage, 23 Hall Place Gardens, St Albans AL1 3SB*

HOLLINGS, Ms Daphne. b 46. WMMTC 02. **d** 05 **p** 06. NSM Adbaston, High Offley, Knightley, Norbury etc *Lich* 05-09; NSM Edstaston, Fauls, Prees, Tilstock and Whixall from 09. *The Vicarage, Tilstock, Whitchurch SY13 3JL* Tel (01948) 880534 E-mail daphne.hollings@tiscali.co.uk

HOLLINGS, Miss Patricia Mary. b 39. CertEd59. S'wark Ord Course 84. **d** 87. Par Dn Wyke *Bradf* 87-94; C 94-96; rtd 96; Perm to Offic *Bradf* from 96 and *Wakef* from 10. *1 Greenacre Way, Wyke, Bradford BD12 9DJ* Tel (01274) 677439

HOLLINGS, Robert George. b 48. St Jo Coll Nottm. **d** 94 **p** 95. C Cotmanhay *Derby* 94-97; TV Godrevy *Truro* 97-02; V Newhall *Derby* from 02. *St John's Vicarage, Church Street, Newhall, Swadlincote DE11 0HY* Tel (01283) 214685
E-mail bobandjacqui@btinternet.com

HOLLINGSHURST, Christopher Paul. b 63. St Chad's Coll Dur BA85 Westmr Coll Ox PGCE86 Anglia Poly Univ MA04. Ridley Hall Cam 96. **d** 99 **p** 00. C Bourn and Kingston w Caxton and Longstowe *Ely* 99-00; C Papworth 00-03; V Hook *S'wark* from 03. *The Vicarage, 278 Hook Road, Chessington KT9 1PF* Tel (020) 8397 3521
E-mail chris.hollingshurst1@btopenworld.com

HOLLINGSWORTH, Geoffrey. b 53. MCIPD85. NOC 86. **d** 86 **p** 87. C Thorne *Sheff* 86-89; V Rawcliffe 89-96; V Airmyn, Hook and Rawcliffe 96-09; P-in-c Pocklington and Owsthorpe and Kilnwick Percy etc *York* 09-10; P-in-c Burnby 09-10; P-in-c Londesborough 09-10; P-in-c Nunburnholme and Warter and Huggate 09-10; P-in-c Shiptonthorpe and Hayton 09-10; R Pocklington Wold from 10; R Londesborough Wold from 10. *The Rectory, 29 The Balk, Pocklington, York YO42 2QQ* Tel (01759) 302133 or 306045
E-mail geoff.holly145@btinternet.com

HOLLINGSWORTH, James William. b 69. Southn Univ BA91 SS Coll Cam BA96. Aston Tr Scheme 92 Ridley Hall Cam 94. **d** 97 **p** 98. C Mildenhall *St E* 97-01; R Barcombe *Chich* from 01. *The Rectory, 1 The Grange, Barcombe, Lewes BN8 5AT* Tel (01273) 400260 E-mail james@barcombe.net

HOLLINGSWORTH, Miss Paula Marion. b 62. Van Mildert Coll Dur BSc83 Univ of Wales (Lamp) MA08. Trin Coll Bris BA91. **d** 91 **p** 94. C Keynsham *B & W* 91-95; C Balsall Heath St Paul *Birm* 95-98; Tutor Crowther Hall CMS Tr Coll Selly Oak 95-01; P-in-c Houghton-on-the-Hill, Keyham and Hungarton *Leic* 01-10; Bp's Adv for CME 01-04; P-in-c Westbury sub Mendip w Easton *B & W* from 10. *The Vicarage, Crow Lane, Westbury sub Mendip, Wells BA5 1HB* Tel (01749) 870293 Mobile 07909-631977
E-mail pmhollingsworth@btinternet.com

HOLLINGTON, David Mark. b 61. MCIEH83. Trin Coll Bris BA94. **d** 94. C Wednesbury St Paul Wood Green *Lich* 94-95; C Cannock 95-96. *Address temp unknown*

HOLLINS, Mrs Beverley Jayne. b 68. Univ of Wales (Abth) BLib90. SAOMC 00. **d** 03 **p** 04. C Milton Keynes *Ox* 03-06; Lic to Offic 06-07; Newport Deanery Development Facilitator from 07. *3 Castle Meadow Close, Newport Pagnell MK16 9EJ* Tel (01908) 614943 E-mail newportdd@talktalk.net

HOLLINS, John Edgar. b 35. St Jo Coll Cam BA58 MA62. Oak Hill Th Coll 58. **d** 60 **p** 61. C Whalley Range St Edm *Man* 60-63; C Highbury Ch Ch *Lon* 63-66; C St Alb St Paul *St Alb* 66-71; Hon C Halliwell St Paul *Man* 71-72; C Ravenhill St Jo 72-73; Perm to Offic *Birm* 79-81; V Millbrook *Ches* 81-89; rtd 89; Perm to Offic *Truro* from 89. *3 Victoria Close, Liskeard PL14 3HU* Tel (01579) 349963

HOLLINS (formerly SHIPP), Patricia Susan. b 54. Univ of Wales BA76. St Paul's Coll Grahamstown 77 Linc Th Coll 81. **d** 83 **p** 94. C Cyncoed *Mon* 83-87; Par Dn Lawrence Weston *Bris* 89-91; Par Dn Henbury 91-94; V Longwell Green 94-99; Hon Can Bris Cathl 97-99; Chapl Mt Vernon and Watford Hosps NHS Trust 99-00; Sen Co-ord Chapl W Herts Hosps NHS Trust 00-04; Lead Chapl (E) *Caring for the Spirit* NHS Project 04-09; P-in-c Boxley w Detling *Cant* from 09; AD N Downs from 09. *The Vicarage, The Street, Boxley, Maidstone ME14 3DX* Tel (01622) 600440 E-mail s.hollins540@btinternet.com

HOLLIS, Anthony Wolcott Linsley. b 40. McGill Univ Montreal BA61 Long Is Univ MA76. Gen Th Sem NY MDiv64. **d** 64 **p** 65. USA 64-92 and from 02; V Lonaconing St Pet 66-67; Chapl US Army 67-79; R Sherwood Ch Cockeysville 79-92; R St George St Pet Bermuda 92-02; rtd 02. *712 Murdock Road, Baltimore MD 21212, USA*

HOLLIS, The Ven Arnold Thaddeus. b 33. JP87. Stockton State Coll New Jersey BA74 NY Th Sem MDiv74 STM76 DMin78. Codrington Coll Barbados 56. **d** 59 **p** 60. C Wakef St Jo 60-62; Br Guiana 62-64; P-in-c Horbury Bridge *Wakef* 64-66; C Loughton St Jo *Chelmsf* 66-69; USA 69-77; Bermuda from 77; Hon Chapl RN from 77; Chapl HM Pris from 77; Chapl Miss to Seafarers from 90; Hon Can Bermuda Cathl from 87; Adn Bermuda 96-03; rtd 03. *3 Middle Road, Sandys SB 02, Bermuda* Tel (001441) 234 0834 or 234 2025 Fax 234 2723
E-mail athol@logic.bm

HOLLIS, Christopher Barnsley. b 28. Clare Coll Cam BA52 MA59. Wells Th Coll 60. **d** 62 **p** 63. C Baildon *Bradf* 62-64; V Esholt 64-66; V Heaton St Barn 66-85; RD Airedale 73-82; Hon Can Bradf Cathl 77-85; Chapl HM YOI Medomsley 85-90; V Medomsley *Dur* 85-90; P-in-c Denholme Gate *Bradf* 90-95; rtd 95; Perm to Offic *Bradf* from 95. *3 Oakwood Drive, Bingley BD16 4AH* Tel (01274) 823933

HOLLIS, Derek. b 60. Loughb Univ BA82. Cranmer Hall Dur 83. **d** 86 **p** 87. C Evington *Leic* 86-89; C Arnold *S'well* 89-93; V Beckingham w Walkeringham 93-03; P-in-c Gringley-on-the-Hill 95-03; V Beckingham w Walkeringham and Gringley 03-05; Hon Chapl Miss to Seafarers 03-04; Bp's Adv on Rural Affairs *S'well* from 04; P-in-c Elston w Elston Chapelry from 05; P-in-c E Stoke w Syerston from 05; P-in-c Shelton from 05; P-in-c Sibthorpe from 05; P-in-c Staunton w Flawborough from 05; P-in-c Kilvington from 05. *The Rectory, Top Street, Elston, Newark NG23 5NP* Tel (01636) 525383
E-mail rural.adviser@southwell.anglican.org

HOLLIS, Douglas John. b 32. S Dios Minl Tr Scheme. **d** 84 **p** 85. NSM Haywards Heath St Wilfrid *Chich* 84-98; Perm to Offic from 98. *Windrush, 1A High Point, Haywards Heath RH16 3RU* Tel (01444) 453688 E-mail douglas@cornerhouse.fslife.co.uk

HOLLIS, Mrs Lorna Mary. b 40. Cranmer Hall Dur 05. **d** 06 **p** 07. NSM Scarborough St Jas w H Trin *York* from 06; Asst Chapl Scarborough and NE Yorks Healthcare NHS Trust from 06. *30 Hartford Court, Filey Road, Scarborough YO11 2TP* Tel (01723) 351395 E-mail mary.hollis3@btinternet.com

HOLLIS, Rebecca Catherine. See MATHEW, Rebecca Catherine

HOLLIS, Timothy Knowles. b 28. RN Coll Dartmouth 45. St Steph Ho Ox 54. **d** 58 **p** 59. C Oatlands *Guildf* 58-60; C Crawley *Chich* 60-63; C Sotterley w Willingham *St E* 63-69; R Sotterley, Willingham, Shadingfield, Ellough etc 69-76; Gen Sec L'Arche UK 77-93; rtd 93; Perm to Offic *Chich* 93-02 and *Glouc* from 03. *9 Abbots Court Drive, Twyning, Tewkesbury GL20 6JJ* Tel (01684) 274903

HOLLIS, Mrs Valerie Elizabeth. b 40. Maria Grey Coll Lon CertEd61. St Alb Minl Tr Scheme 89. **d** 92 **p** 94. NSM Kempston Transfiguration *St Alb* 92-06; NSM Officer Bedford Adnry 06-10; Perm to Offic from 06. *33 Silverdale Street, Kempston, Bedford MK42 8BE* Tel (01234) 853397
E-mail nsmobeds@stalbans.anglican.org

HOLLOWAY, Canon David Dennis. b 43. Lich Th Coll 65. **d** 68 **p** 69. C Cricklade w Latton *Bris* 68-71; C Bris St Agnes and St Simon w St Werburgh 71-74; V Bitton 74-78; TV E Bris 78-80; P-in-c Tormarton w W Littleton 80-83; Dioc Ecum Officer 83-93; Hon C Bris St Mich 89-93; V Horfield St Greg 93-00; RD Horfield 97-99; Chapl St Monica Home Westbury-on-Trym 00-07; Hon Can Bris Cathl 92-07; rtd 07. *76 Marsworth Road, Pitstone, Leighton Buzzard LU7 9AS* Tel (01296) 662765 Mobile 07974-648556

HOLLOWAY, David Ronald James. b 39. Univ Coll Ox BA62 MA66. Ridley Hall Cam 65. **d** 67 **p** 68. C Leeds St Geo *Ripon* 67-71; Tutor Wycliffe Hall Ox 71-72; V Jesmond Clayton Memorial *Newc* from 73. *The Vicarage, 7 Otterburn Terrace, Jesmond, Newcastle upon Tyne NE2 3AP* Tel 0191-281 2001 *or* 281 2139

HOLLOWAY, Graham Edward. b 45. Chich Th Coll 69. **d** 72 **p** 73. C W Drayton *Lon* 72-75; P-in-c Hawton *S'well* 75-80; V Ladybrook 80-85; P-in-c Babworth 85-87; R Babworth w Sutton-cum-Lound 87-97; RD Retford 88-93; C Mansfield Woodhouse 97-04; P-in-c Mansfield St Aug from 04; P-in-c Pleasley Hill from 04. *St Augustine's Vicarage, 46 Abbott Road, Mansfield NG19 6DD* Tel (01623) 621247
E-mail padreg@btinternet.com

HOLLOWAY, Keith Graham. b 45. Linc Coll Ox BA67. Cranmer Hall Dur. **d** 73 **p** 74. C Gt Ilford St Andr *Chelmsf* 73-78; Hon C Squirrels Heath 78-80; Min Chelmer Village CD 80-87; V E Springfield 87-89; P-in-c Gt Dunmow 89-96; R Gt Dunmow and Barnston 96-02; R Upper Colne 02-10; rtd 10; Perm to Offic *Chelmsf* from 10. *5 Martens Meadow, Braintree CM7 3LB* Tel (01376) 334976 E-mail kanddway@aol.com

HOLLOWAY, Michael Sinclair. b 50. UEA BSc74 Southn Univ PGCE75. STETS 99. **d** 02 **p** 03. NSM Catherington and Clanfield *Portsm* 02-07; C Bishop's Cleeve *Glouc* 07-08; TV Bishop's Cleeve and Woolstone w Gotherington etc from 08. *The Rectory, 47 Malleson Road, Gotherington, Cheltenham GL52 9EX* Tel (01242) 675559
E-mail revmike.holloway@btinternet.com

✠**HOLLOWAY, The Rt Revd Prof Richard Frederick.** b 33. Lon Univ BD63 NY Th Sem STM68 Strathclyde Univ DUniv94 Aber Univ Hon DD95 Napier Univ Edin DLitt00 Glas Univ DD01 FRSE95. Edin Th Coll 58. **d** 59 **p** 60 **c** 86. C Glas St Ninian 59-63; P-in-c Glas St Marg 63-68; R Edin Old St Paul 68-80; R Boston The Advent MA USA 80-84; V Ox St Mary Magd 84-86; Bp Edin 86-00; Primus 92-00; rtd 00; Gresham Prof of Div 97-01. *6 Blantyre Terrace, Edinburgh EH10 5AE* Tel 0131-446 0696 Mobile 07710-254500
E-mail holloway.doc@googlemail.com

HOLLOWAY, Simon Anthony. b 50. Sussex Univ BSc72 Univ of Wales MA03. Trin Coll Bris 76. **d** 79 **p** 81. C Bushbury *Lich* 79-81; C Castle Church 81-84; P-in-c Sparkbrook Ch Ch *Birm* 84-91; V 91-02; AD Bordesley 92-99; TV Horley *S'wark* 02-11; Chapl SE Cyprus from 11. *PO Box 36101, 5386 Dherynia, Cyprus* Tel (00357) 97-769654 (mobile)
E-mail simonholloway55@yahoo.co.uk

HOLLOWOOD, Christopher George. b 54. K Alfred's Coll Win BEd76 Open Univ MA97. Ripon Coll Cuddesdon 83. **d** 86 **p** 87. C Tupsley *Heref* 86-89; R Much Birch w Lt Birch, Much Dewchurch etc 89-92; Hd RS Haywood High Sch Heref 92-97; Sen Teacher St Aug Upper Sch 97-00; Dep Hd N Bromsgrove High Sch 00-02; Headmaster Bp Llan Ch in Wales High Sch Cardiff from 02. *170 Kings Road, Cardiff CF11 9DG* Tel (029) 2056 2485 E-mail c.hollowood@ntlworld.com

HOLLOWOOD, Graham. b 56. Anglia Ruskin Univ MA07. St Steph Ho Ox 97. **d** 99 **p** 00. C Newport St Julian *Mon* 99-02; V Newport All SS 02-08; V Glodwick *Man* from 08. *St Mark's Vicarage, 1 Skipton Street, Oldham OL8 2JF* Tel and fax 0161-624 4964 Mobile 07748-106718
E-mail graham.hollowood@virgin.net

HOLLYWELL, Julian Francis. b 70. Liv Univ BSc91 Leeds Univ MA05. NOC 03. **d** 05 **p** 06. C W Didsbury and Withington St Chris *Man* 05-08; V Spondon *Derby* from 08; RD Derby N from 10. *St Werburgh's Vicarage, Gascoigne Drive, Spondon, Derby DE21 7GL* Tel (01332) 671503 Mobile 07963-420564

HOLMAN, Francis Noel. b 37. Sarum Th Coll 62. **d** 65 **p** 66. C Weston Favell *Pet* 65-68; C Eckington *Derby* 68-71; Asst Chapl St Thos Hosp Lon 72-77; Chapl Hope Hosp Salford 77-02; Chapl Salford R Hosp 77-93; Chapl Ladywell Hosp 77-99; Chapl Man and Salford Skin Hosp 88-94; rtd 02; Perm to Offic *Man* from 03. *90 Roxby Lane, Eccles, Manchester M30 9LY* Tel 0161-707 1180

HOLMAN, Geoffrey Gladstone. b 32. AKC56. **d** 57 **p** 58. C Eltham St Barn *S'wark* 57-60; CF 60-73; Dep Asst Chapl Gen 73-80; Asst Chapl Gen 80-84; QHC 82-84; V Wetwang and Garton-on-the-Wolds w Kirkburn *York* 84-92; RD Harthill 87-92; rtd 92; P-in-c Askham Bryan *York* 93-01; Perm to Offic from 01. *3 Westholme Drive, York YO30 5TH* Tel (01904) 624419 E-mail samegus@btopenworld.com

HOLMDEN, Miss Maria Irene. b 50. Trent Poly TCert72 BEd73. Oak Hill Th Coll 90. **d** 92 **p** 94. Par Dn Stratford St Jo and Ch Ch w Forest Gate St Jas *Chelmsf* 92-94; C St Jas Chelmsf All SS 96-01; V from 01. *All Saints' Vicarage, 47 Melbourne Road, London E10 7HF* Tel (020) 8558 8139
E-mail mholmden@tiscali.co.uk

HOLME, Thomas Edmund. b 49. Selw Coll Cam BA71 MA75. Coll of Resurr Mirfield 71. **d** 73 **p** 74. C Wyther *Ripon* 73-76; C Wimbledon *S'wark* 76-78; TV 78-79; V Bermondsey St Anne 79-81; V Stamford Baron *Pet* 83-89; P-in-c Tinwell 83-89; Hon Min Can Pet Cathl 84-89; Prec Worc Cathl 89-95; P-in-c

Penshurst and Fordcombe *Roch* 95-05; R from 05. *The Rectory, High Street, Penshurst, Tonbridge TN11 8BN* Tel (01892) 870316

HOLMES, Andrew Keith. b 69. Univ of Wales BEng93. St Mich Coll Llan BTh96. **d** 96 **p** 97. C Clydach *S & B* 96-98; C Swansea St Thos and Kilvey 98-00; P-in-c New Radnor and Llanfihangel Nantmelan etc 00-03; V Penrhiwceiber, Matthewstown and Ynysboeth *Llan* from 03. *The Vicarage, Penrhiwceiber, Mountain Ash CF45 3YF* Tel (01443) 473716
E-mail frandrew@penrhiwceiber.plus.com

HOLMES (née PLATT), Mrs Anne Cecilia. b 46. Birm Univ BA67 Ox Univ DipEd68 MInstGA96. SAOMC 99. **d** 02 **p** 03. NSM Marston w Elsfield *Ox* from 02; Chapl Headington Sch 02-04; Asst Chapl Oxon & Bucks Mental Health Partnership NHS Trust 04-09. *59 Oxford Road, Old Marston, Oxford OX3 0PH* Tel (01865) 794916 Mobile 07831-254727
E-mail anne@acholmes.demon.co.uk

HOLMES, Anthony David Robert. b 38. Oak Hill Th Coll 75. **d** 77 **p** 78. C Iver *Ox* 77-81 and 00-05; V Bucklebury w Marlston 81-00; rtd 05. *16 Lawrence Close, Aylesbury HP20 1DY* Tel (01296) 398945

HOLMES, Brian. b 41. NEOC 92. **d** 95 **p** 96. NSM Darlington St Matt and St Luke *Dur* 95-98; V 98-08; rtd 08. *2 Christchurch Close, Darlington DL1 2YL* Tel (01325) 482255
E-mail revbholmes@tiscali.co.uk

HOLMES (née KENYON), Caroline Elizabeth. b 40. SRN62. NOC 04. **d** 05 **p** 06. NSM Hale and Ashley *Ches* from 05. *1 Broomfield House, 134 Hale Road, Hale, Altrincham WA15 9HJ* Tel 0161-233 0761
E-mail caroline.holmes@btinternet.com

HOLMES, Clive Horace. b 31. Ox NSM Course. **d** 83 **p** 84. NSM Cumnor *Ox* 83-98; Perm to Offic from 98. *108 New Road, East Hagbourne, Didcot OX11 9JZ* Tel (01235) 811996

HOLMES, Craig Walter. b 72. Southn Univ BSc95 R Holloway & Bedf New Coll Lon PhD01 Fitzw Coll Cam BA03 MA07 CCC Cam MPhil04. Ridley Hall Cam 01. **d** 07 **p** 08. C Egham Guildf 07-10; V Hanworth St Rich *Lon* from 10. *St Richard's Vicarage, 35 Forge Lane, Feltham TW13 6UN* Tel (020) 8893 4935 E-mail craig@craigandbec.co.uk

HOLMES, Frank. b 22. NW Ord Course 75. **d** 78 **p** 79. NSM Hyde St Geo *Ches* 78-81; C Poynton 81-87; rtd 87; Perm to Offic *Ches* from 87. *277 Stockport Road, Marple, Stockport SK6 6ES* Tel 0161-449 9289

HOLMES, Geoffrey. See HOLMES, Robert John Geoffrey

HOLMES, Geoffrey Robert. b 67. Nottm Univ BSc89. Ridley Hall Cam BA92. **d** 93 **p** 94. C Clifton St Jas *Sheff* 93-98; V Worsbrough St Thos and St Jas 98-05. *16 Vernon Road, Worsbrough, Barnsley S70 5BD*
E-mail geoffrey.r.holmes@tesco.net

HOLMES, Grant Wenlock. b 54. St Steph Ho Ox BA78 MA83. **d** 79 **p** 80. C Benhilton *S'wark* 79-82; C-in-c S Kenton Annunciation CD *Lon* 82-86; Tutor Chich Th Coll 86-87; Bp's Dom Chapl *Chich* 86-88; V Mayfield 88-99; P-in-c Mark Cross 97-99; Asst Chapl Lewisham Hosp NHS Trust 99-01; Lead Chapl Kingston Hosp NHS Trust Surrey from 01; Hon C Barnes *S'wark* 01-06. *Kingston Hospitals NHS Trust, Galsworthy Road, Kingston upon Thames KT2 7QB* Tel (020) 8546 7711 ext 2292
E-mail grant.holmes@kingstonhospital.nhs.uk

HOLMES, Gregory Thomas. b 73. Open Univ MSc04 Cam Univ BTh11. Ridley Hall Cam 09. **d** 11. C Fareham St Jo *Portsm* from 11. *7A Upper St Michael's Grove, Fareham PO14 1DN* Tel 07773-477460 (mobile) E-mail gregjacqui@hotmail.com

HOLMES, Jane Margaret. b 57. Ridley Hall Cam 05. **d** 07 **p** 08. C Stamford Ch Ch *Linc* 07-11; P-in-c Gayton, Gayton Thorpe, E Walton, E Winch etc *Nor* from 11. *The Rectory, Grimston Road, Gayton, King's Lynn PE32 1QA* Tel (01553) 636227
E-mail jmh200@btinternet.com

HOLMES, Mrs Janet Ellen. b 61. Wolv Univ BSc95 RCN MSc99 RGN83. Qu Coll Birm MA09. **d** 09 **p** 10. C Hadley and Wellington Ch Ch *Lich* from 09. *Sutton Bank Farm, Sutton, Newport TF10 8DD* Tel (01952) 813658
E-mail janeteholmes@btinternet.com

HOLMES, Canon John Robin. b 42. Leeds Univ BA64. Linc Th Coll 64. **d** 66 **p** 67. C Wyther *Ripon* 66-69; C Adel 69-73; V Beeston Hill St Luke 73-76; V Holbeck 76-86; RD Armley 82-86; V Manston 86-93; Hon Can Ripon Cathl 89-98; Dioc Missr 93-98; Can Missr *Wakef* 98-07; rtd 07. *31 Detroit Avenue, Leeds LS15 8NU* Tel 0113-264 2667 Mobile 07712-044364
E-mail canon.john@sky.com

HOLMES, Jonathan Michael. b 49. Qu Coll Cam BA70 MA74 VetMB73 PhD78 MRCVS73. Ridley Hall Cam 87. **d** 88 **p** 89. Chapl Qu Coll Cam from 88; Dean of Chpl from 94. *Queens' College, Cambridge CB3 9ET* Tel (01223) 335545 Fax 335522 E-mail jmh38@cam.ac.uk

HOLMES, Nigel Peter. b 48. Nottm Univ BTh72 Lanc Univ CertEd72 Lon Univ BD76 Sheff Univ MEd84. Kelham Th Coll. **d** 72 **p** 73. C Barrow St Matt *Carl* 72-75; C Derby St Bart 75-78; P-in-c Gt Barlow 78-84; V Carl St Herbert w St Steph 84-91; V Keswick St Jo 91-94; V Mexborough *Sheff* 94-97; P-in-c Nether Hoyland St Pet 97-98; P-in-c Nether Hoyland St Andr 97-98; V

Hoyland 98-07; AD Tankersley 04-07; V Monk Bretton *Wakef* 07-09; rtd 09. *6 The Signals, Widdrington, Morpeth NE61 5QU* E-mail paxlives@btinternet.com

HOLMES, Mrs Patricia Ann. b 52. Bris Univ BA89 MA90. NOC 96. **d** 97 **p** 98. C Almondbury w Farnley Tyas *Wakef* 97-00; V Northowram from 00. *The Vicarage, Church Walk, Northowram, Halifax HX3 7HF* Tel (01422) 202551 E-mail patriciaholmes@sky.com

HOLMES, Peter Anthony. b 55. Univ of Wales (Ban) BA77 Brighton Poly CertEd78. Trin Coll Bris. **d** 88 **p** 89. C Croydon Ch Ch *S'wark* 88-93; V Norbiton from 93; RD Kingston 97-00. *The Vicarage, 21 Wolsey Close, Kingston upon Thames KT2 7ER* Tel (020) 8942 8330 *or* 8546 3212 E-mail revdrock@yahoo.co.uk

HOLMES, Prof Peter Geoffrey. b 32. Bris Univ BSc59 MSc69 Leic Univ PhD74 CEng FIEE. St Deiniol's Hawarden 74. **d** 76 **p** 77. NSM Glen Parva and S Wigston *Leic* 76-02; Prof Nottm Poly 85-92; Prof Nottm Trent Univ 92-96; rtd 02; Perm to Offic *Leic* from 02. *19 Windsor Avenue, Glen Parva, Leicester LE2 9TQ* Tel 0116-277 4534 E-mail peterholmes@iee.org

HOLMES, Peter John. b 41. Reading Univ TCert63 Open Univ BA76 K Coll Lon BA96 AKC96 MA97 Glas Univ PhD02. St Steph Ho Ox 03. **d** 04 **p** 05. NSM Beaconsfield *Ox* 04-08; Perm to Offic *Ox* 08-10 and *Pet* from 11. *14 Bayley Close, Uppingham, Oakham LE15 9TG* Tel (01572) 821834 E-mail peter.holmes@dial.pipex.com

HOLMES, Robert John Geoffrey. b 28. TCD BA53 MA57. Ely Th Coll 56. **d** 57 **p** 58. C Whitton St Aug CD *Lon* 57-59; C St Pancras w St Jas and Ch Ch 59-63; C Stepney St Dunstan and All SS 63-66; C Stepney St Aug w St Phil 66-68; Chapl The Lon Hosp (Whitechapel) 63-68, R Middelburg, Steynsburg and Colesburg S Africa 68-74; Perm to Offic *Ely* 74 and *Chich* 74-76; R Telscombe w Piddinghoe and Southease *Chich* 76-93; P-in-c Barlavington, Burton w Coates, Sutton and Bignor 93-96; rtd 95; Perm to Offic *Chich* 95-01. *7 Buckhurst Road, Telscombe Cliffs, Peacehaven BN10 7AH*

HOLMES, Roger Cockburn. b 46. Jes Coll Ox BA70 MA84 Edin Univ BD76. Edin Th Coll 73. **d** 84 **p** 85. Canada 84-88; R Ditchingham w Pirnough *Nor* 88-90; R Hedenham 88-90; R Broome 88-90; R Ditchingham, Hedenham and Broome 90-93; V Helmsley *York* 93-97; Perm to Offic *Wakef* 07. *16 Heslington Road, York YO10 5AT* Tel (01904) 629640 E-mail fatherholmes@hotmail.com

HOLMES, Roy Grant. b 37. Ox NSM Course 83. **d** 86 **p** 87. NSM Wokingham St Paul *Ox* from 86. *58 Copse Drive, Wokingham RG41 1LX* Tel 0118-978 4141

HOLMES, Stephen. b 54. St Andr Univ MTheol84. Chich Th Coll 84. **d** 86 **p** 87. C Croydon St Jo *S'wark* 86-89; C Tewkesbury w Walton Cardiff *Glouc* 89-92; P-in-c Bournemouth St Luke *Win* 92-94; V 94-10; P-in-c N Stoneham and Bassett from 10. *North Stoneham Rectory, 62 Glen Eyre Road, Southampton SO16 3NL* Tel (023) 8076 8123

HOLMES, Stephen John. b 50. CertEd72. Trin Coll Bris 81 Sarum & Wells Th Coll 88. **d** 89 **p** 90. C Skegness and Winthorpe *Linc* 89-93; P-in-c Mablethorpe w Trusthorpe 93-97; V Hadleigh St Barn *Chelmsf* 97-07; R Gt and Lt Leighs and Lt Waltham from 07. *141 Main Road, Great Leighs, Chelmsford CM3 1NP* Tel (01245) 361955 E-mail familyholmes@hotmail.co.uk

HOLMES, Susan. **d** 06 **p** 07. NSM Scotby and Cotehill w Cumwhinton *Carl* from 06. *Woodside, Great Corby, Carlisle CA4 8LL* Tel (01228) 560617 E-mail susan@gtcorby.plus.com

HOLMES, Theodore John. b 47. EMMTC 02. **d** 06 **p** 07. NSM Somercotes *Derby* from 06. *18 Leabrooks Road, Somercotes, Alfreton DE55 4HB* Tel (01773) 540186 Mobile 07837-574881 E-mail theodore.holmes@btopenworld.com

HOLMES, William John. b 49. **d** 97 **p** 98. Aux Min Billy w Derrykeighan *Conn* 97-02; Aux Min Ballymoney w Finvoy and Rasharkin from 02. *14 Glenlough Park, Coleraine BT52 1TY* Tel (028) 7035 5993

HOLMYARD, Deborah. *See* FRAZER, Deborah

HOLNESS, Edwin Geoffrey Nicholas. b 39. RGN. Sarum Th Coll 68. **d** 71 **p** 72. C Upper Beeding and Bramber w Botolphs *Chich* 71-74; C Munster Square St Mary Magd *Lon* 74-75; Perm to Offic *Chich* 75-76 and 77-99; C Brighton Annunciation 76-77; Chapl Brighton Hosp Gp 77-94; Chapl R Sussex Co Hosp Brighton 77-94; P-in-c Southwick St Pet *Chich* 99-02; rtd 02. *41 Wivelsfield Road, Saltdean, Brighton BN2 8FP* Tel (01273) 307025

HOLROYD, John Richard. b 54. Liv Univ BA75 PGCE77. Wycliffe Hall Ox 78. **d** 81 **p** 82. C Gt Stanmore *Lon* 81-84; Min Can, V Choral and Prec St E Cathl 84-89; TV Wolverton *Ox* 89-96; P-in-c Maidenhead St Luke 96-10; P-in-c Cotham St Sav w St Mary and Clifton St Paul *Bris* from 10. *12 Belgrave Road, Bristol BS8 2AB* Tel 0117-973 1564 E-mail richardholroyd@mac.com

HOLROYD, Stephen Charles. b 56. UEA BA79. St Jo Coll Nottm 84. **d** 87 **p** 88. C Barton Seagrave w Warkton *Pet* 87-91; V Eye 91-97; V Silsoe, Pulloxhill and Flitton *St Alb* from 97. *The Vicarage, Firtree Road, Silsoe, Bedford MK45 4EA* Tel (01525) 862380 E-mail silsoe.vicarage@tesco.net

HOLT, Mrs Claire Frances. b 66. Bris Univ BSc88 Kingston Poly PGCE89. STETS 02. **d** 05 **p** 06. C N Farnborough *Guildf* from 05. *27 Church Road East, Farnborough GU14 6QJ* Tel (01252) 655010 Mobile 07900-583403 E-mail clairefholt@hotmail.com

HOLT, Canon David. b 44. St Jo Coll Dur BSc67. **d** 70 **p** 71. C Blackley St Pet *Man* 70-73; C Radcliffe St Thos 73-74; C Radcliffe St Thos and St Jo 74-75; V Ashton St Pet 75-79; Dioc Youth Officer *Guildf* 80-85; V Bagshot 85-97; RD Surrey Heath 92-97; V Fleet 97-03; RD Aldershot 98-03; Hon Can Guildf Cathl 99-03; rtd 03; Perm to Offic *Guildf* from 03. *62 Lynwood Drive, Mytchett, Camberley GU16 6BY* Tel (01276) 507538 Mobile 07974-354411 E-mail david.holt@ntlworld.com

HOLT, Canon Douglas Robert. b 49. MA. Ridley Hall Cam. **d** 82 **p** 83. C Cambridge St Barn *Ely* 82-84; P-in-c 84-86; V 86-91; V Ealing St Mary *Lon* 91-98; Dir Par Development Team *Bris* 98-09; Can Res Bris Cathl 98-10; Hon Can and Dioc Dir Strategy Support from 10. *71 High Street, Malmesbury SN16 9AG* Tel (01666) 824885 *or* 0117-906 0100 E-mail douglas.holt@bristoldiocese.org

HOLT, Francis Thomas. b 38. Edin Th Coll 79. **d** 81 **p** 82. C Cullercoats St Geo *Newc* 81-83; C Ponteland 83-86; Chapl Worc Coll of HE 86-89; R Worc St Clem 86-93; V Finstall 93-96; Chapl Menorca *Eur* 96-97; Perm to Offic *Worc* from 97; rtd 98. *10 Ash Close, Malvern WR14 2WF* Tel (01684) 575507

HOLT, Jack Derek. b 38. Trin Coll Bris 71. **d** 73 **p** 74. C Daubhill *Man* 73-76; P-in-c Thornham w Gravel Hole 76-79; V 79-83; R Talke *Lich* 83-93; V Cornhamhay *Derby* 93-03; Chapl Derbyshire Mental Health Services NHS Trust 93-03; rtd 03; Perm to Offic *Lich* from 03. *31 Hatherton Close, Newcastle ST5 7SN* Tel (01782) 560845

HOLT, James Edward. b 49. St Martin's Coll Lanc BA94 PGCE95. NOC 99. **d** 02 **p** 04. NSM Holme-in-Cliviger w Worsthorne *Blackb* 02-03; NSM Whalley from 03. *5 Graham Street, Padiham, Burnley BB12 8RW* Tel (01282) 778319 E-mail jimeholt@btinternet.com

HOLT, Keith. b 37. CPFA62. S'wark Ord Course. **d** 82 **p** 83. NSM Selsdon St Jo w St Fran *Cant* 82-84; NSM Selsdon St Jo w St Fran *S'wark* 85-07; Perm to Offic from 07. *12 Ridge Langley, South Croydon CR2 0AR* Tel (020) 8651 1815

HOLT, Mrs Lucinda Jane. b 65. Open Univ BSc00. Wycliffe Hall Ox 01. **d** 03 **p** 04. C Newton Longville and Mursley w Swanbourne etc *Ox* 03-06; TV Riverside 06-08; V Eton w Eton Wick, Boveney and Dorney from 08. *The Vicarage, 69A Eton Wick Road, Eton Wick, Windsor SL4 6NE* Tel (01753) 852268 E-mail andrew-lucy@tinyworld.co.uk

HOLT, Michael. b 38. Univ of Wales (Lamp) BA61. St D Coll Lamp. **d** 63 **p** 64. C Stand *Man* 63-69; V Bacup St Jo 69-03; AD Rossendale 98-00; rtd 03; Perm to Offic *Man* from 03. *22 Windermere Road, Bacup OL13 9DN* Tel (01706) 877976

HOLT, Shirley Ann. b 98. **d** 98 **p** 99. OLM High Oak, Hingham and Scoulton w Wood Rising *Nor* from 98. *Westfield, 59 Church Lane, Wicklewood, Wymondham NR18 9QH* Tel (01953) 603668 E-mail saholt@talk21.com

HOLT, Stephen Richard. b 64. Leeds Univ BA11. Coll of Resurr Mirfield 09. **d** 11. C Gt Grimsby St Mary and St Jas *Linc* from 11. *3 Grosvenor Street, Grimsby DN32 0QH* Tel 07984-543892 (mobile)

HOLT, Stuart Henry. b 57. Bath Coll of HE BEd78. Ridley Hall Cam 84. **d** 87 **p** 88. C Locks Heath *Portsm* 87-90; Chapl RAF 90-91; C Worthing St Geo *Chich* 91-93; C Portchester *Portsm* 93-95; Perm to Offic 02-03; P-in-c Soberton w Newtown 03-09; R Meon Bridge from 09; AD Bishop's Waltham from 09. *The Rectory, Rectory Lane, Meonstoke, Southampton SO32 3NF* Tel (01489) 878222 E-mail stuart.holt2@btopenworld.com

HOLT, Susan Mary. b 45. Coll of Ripon & York St Jo MA98. NOC 97. **d** 97 **p** 98. NSM Longwood *Wakef* 97-00; NSM Liversedge w Hightown from 00. *229/231 Stainland Road, Holywell Green, Halifax HX4 9AJ* Tel (01422) 376481 E-mail susan@micromundi.net

✠**HOLTAM, The Rt Revd Nicholas Roderick.** b 54. Collingwood Coll Dur BA75 K Coll Lon BD78 AKC78 FKC05 Dur Univ MA89 Hon DCL05. Westcott Ho Cam 78. **d** 79 **p** 80 **c** 11. C Stepney St Dunstan and All SS *Lon* 79-83; Tutor Linc Th Coll 83-88; V Is of Dogs Ch Ch and St Jo w St Luke *Lon* 88-95; V St Martin-in-the-Fields 95-11; Bp Sarum from 11. *South Canonry, 71 The Close, Salisbury SP1 2ER* Tel (01722) 334031 Fax 413112 E-mail bishop.salisbury@salisbury.anglican.org

HOLTH, Oystein Johan. b 31. Open Univ BA75. AKC54. **d** 54 **p** 55. C Greenford H Cross *Lon* 54-56; Br N Borneo and Sarawak 56-63; E Malaysia 63-67; Chapl OHP 67-75; Chapl St Hilda's Sch Whitby 67-75; P-in-c Pimlico St Barn *Lon* 75-97; Ind Chapl 75-97; rtd 97; Perm to Offic *Lon* from 97. *13 Dollis Park, London N3 1HJ* Tel (020) 8346 8131

HOLY, Ravi. b 69. K Coll Lon MA09. Trin Coll Bris BA05. **d** 05 **p** 06. C Battersea St Luke *S'wark* 05-09; P-in-c Wye w Brook and Hastingleigh etc *Cant* from 10. *The Vicarage, Cherry Garden Crescent, Wye, Ashford TN25 5AS* Tel (01233) 813705 Mobile 07930-401963 E-mail raviholy@aol.com

HOLYER, Vincent Alfred Douglas. b 28. Ex Univ BA54. Oak Hill Th Coll 54. d 56 p 57. C Bethnal Green St Jas Less *Lon* 56-58; C Braintree *Chelmsf* 58-61; V Islington All SS *Lon* 61-65; R St Ruan w St Grade *Truro* 65-85; V Constantine 85-91; rtd 91; Perm to Offic *Truro* from 91. *32 Valley Gardens, Illogan, Redruth TR16 4EE* Tel (01209) 211509

HOLZAPFEL, Mrs Christine Anne. b 53. Ex Univ BA74 PGCE75. WMMTC 04. d 07 p 08. C Worc SE 07-10; P-in-c Finstall from 10; C Catshill and Dodford from 10. *The Vicarage, 15 Finstall Road, Bromsgrove B60 2EA* Tel 07749-898698 (mobile) E-mail cherrytree@tesco.net

HOLZAPFEL, Peter Rudolph. b 51. St Jo Coll Nottm 84. d 86 p 87. C St Jo in Bedwardine *Worc* 86-89; R Kempsey and Severn Stoke w Croome d'Abitot from 99. *The Rectory, 3 Oakfield Drive, Kempsey, Worcester WR5 3PP* Tel (01905) 820202

HOMDEN, Peter David. b 56. Moorlands Coll BA06. STETS 07. d 09 p 10. C Heatherlands St Jo *Sarum* from 09. *72 Alexandra Road, Poole BH14 9EW* Tel (01202) 770833 Mobile 07841-699094 E-mail homdenhome@btinternet.com

HOMER, Alan Fellows. b 30. Ridley Hall Cam 61. d 63 p 64. C Heref St Jas 63-66; V Brixton Hill St Sav *S'wark* 66-73; Dep Chapl HM Pris Brixton 66-70; CF (TA) 70-73; CF 73-76; V Heeley *Sheff* 75-87; R Cheveley *Ely* 87-95; R Ashley w Silverley 87-95; V Wood Ditton w Saxon Street 87-95; V Kirtling 87-95; RD Linton 94-95; rtd 95; Perm to Offic *Bris* from 95 and *Ox* 95-01. *62 The Willows, Highworth, Swindon SN6 7PH* Tel and fax (01793) 764023

HOMEWOOD, Michael John. b 33. Wells Th Coll 69. d 71 p 72. C Ilfracombe H Trin *Ex* 71-72; C Ilfracombe, Lee and W Down 72-75; P-in-c Woolacombe 76-78; TV Ilfracombe, Lee, W Down, Woolacombe and Bittadon 78-82; TR S Molton w Nymet St George, High Bray etc 82-97; RD S Molton 93-95; rtd 97; Perm to Offic *Sarum* from 97. *5 Avon Drive, Wareham BH20 4EL* Tel (01929) 556216

HOMEWOOD, Peter Laurence de Silvie. b 58. Oriel Coll Ox BA80 MA84. St Steph Ho Ox 90. d 92 p 93. C Ruislip St Martin *Lon* 92-96; R Hayes St Mary from 96; P-in-c Hayes St Anselm 03-07. *The Rectory, 170 Church Road, Hayes UB3 2LR* Tel (020) 8573 2470 E-mail peter@hayes-rectory.demon.co.uk

HOMFRAY, Kenyon Lee James. b 55. TCD BTh99 MA03 Univ of Wales (Cardiff) LLM02. CITC 96. d 99 p 00. C Convoy w Monellan and Donaghmore *D & R* 99-02; I 02-05; I Buncloody w Kildavin, Clonegal and Kilrush *C & O* from 05. *The Rectory, Bunclody, Enniscorthy, Co Wexford, Republic of Ireland* Tel (00353) (53) 937 7652

HONE, Canon Frank Leslie. b 11. Kelham Th Coll 32. d 38 p 39. C Sheff Arbourthorne 38-40; CF (EC) 40-45; C Sheff St Anne and St Phil 45-46; C Rotherham 46-49; V Brightside St Thos 49-53; R Attercliffe w Carbrook 53-60; P-in-c Sheff St Swithun 60-66; V Frodingham *Linc* 66-78; RD Manlake 69-76; Can and Preb Linc Cathl 72-78; rtd 78; Perm to Offic *Linc* from 78. *Cathedral Care Centre, 23 Nettleham Road, Lincoln LN2 1RQ* Tel (01522) 589828

HONES, Simon Anthony. b 54. Sussex Univ BSc75. Qu Coll Birm. d 79 p 80. C Win Ch Ch 79-82; C Basing 82-88; Min Chineham CD 88-90; V Surbiton St Matt *S'wark* 90-08; TR from 08. *St Matthew's Vicarage, 20 Kingsdowne Road, Surbiton KT6 6JZ* Tel (020) 8399 4853 E-mail simon.hones@blueyonder.co.uk

HONEY, Mrs Elizabeth Katherine. b 81. Keble Coll Ox MA07. Wycliffe Hall Ox 06. d 09 p 10. C Furze Platt *Ox* from 09. *33 Greenlands Court, Blenheim Road, Maidenhead SL6 5HF* Tel (01628) 674654 Mobile 07883-470158 E-mail beth.honey@hotmail.co.uk

HONEY, Canon Frederick Bernard. b 22. Selw Coll Cam BA48 MA72. Wells Th Coll 48. d 50 p 51. C S'wark St Geo 50-52; C Claines St Jo *Worc* 52-55; V Wollaston 55-87; RD Stourbridge 72-83; Hon Can Worc Cathl 75-87; rtd 87. *38 Park Farm, Bourton-on-the-Water, Cheltenham GL54 2HF* Tel (01451) 822218

HONEY, Canon Thomas David. b 56. Lon Univ BA78. Ripon Coll Cuddesdon 80. d 83 p 84. C Mill End and Heronsgate w W Hyde *St Alb* 83-86; C Stepney St Dunstan and All SS *Lon* 86-89; TV High Wycombe *Ox* 89-95; P-in-c Headington Quarry 95-07; Can Res and Treas Ex Cathl 07-10; V Ex St Dav from 10. *St David's Vicarage, 95 Howell Road, Exeter EX4 4LH* Tel (01392) 201100 E-mail vicar@stdavidschurchexeter.org.uk

HONEYMAN, Jennifer Mary. b 73. Leeds Univ BA08. NOC 05. d 08 p 09. C Crosland Moor and Linthwaite *Wakef* from 08. *The Vicarage, Church Lane, Linthwaite, Huddersfield HD7 5TA* Tel (01484) 843352 E-mail honeyman@ntlworld.com

HONG KONG ISLAND, Bishop of. See KWONG KONG KIT, The Most Revd Peter

HONG KONG SHENG KUNG HUI, Archbishop of. See KWONG KONG KIT, The Most Revd Peter

HONNOR, Jonathan Michael Bellamy. b 62. Leeds Univ BA84 Cant Ch Ch Univ Coll PGCE89. Stavanger Sch of Miss and Th 98. p 00. Norway 00-03; C Leigh Park and Warren Park *Portsm* 03-08; P-in-c Aylesham w Adisham *Cant* from 08. *The Rectory,* Dorman Avenue North, Aylesham, Canterbury CT3 3BL Tel (01304) 840266

HONNOR, Mrs Marjorie Rochefort. b 27. Birm Univ BA48. Cranmer Hall Dur 79. dss 81 d 87 p 94. Church Oakley and Wootton St Lawrence *Win* 81-87; Par Dn 87-89; rtd 89; Perm to Offic *Win* from 98. *15 Kernella Court, 51-53 Surrey Road, Bournemouth BH4 9HS* Tel (01202) 761021

HONOR MARGARET, Sister. See McILROY, Sister Honor Margaret

HONOUR, Colin Reginald. b 44. Lanc Univ CertEd69 Man Univ AdDipEd75 Newc Univ MEd80. NOC 88. d 91 p 92. NSM Walmsley *Man* 91; C Middleton 92-94; R Holcombe 94-01; P-in-c Hawkshaw Lane 99-01; P-in-c Aldingham, Dendron, Rampside and Urswick *Carl* 01-03; R 03-09; rtd 09. *1 Crow Wood, Heversham, Milnthorpe LA7 7ER* E-mail cnchonour@btinternet.com

HONOUR, Derek Gordon. b 59. Bath Univ BSc84. St Jo Coll Nottm. d 89 p 90. C High Wycombe *Ox* 89-91; C Brightside w Wincobank *Sheff* 91-94; P-in-c Dawley St Jerome *Lon* 94-01; C Derby St Alkmund and St Werburgh 01-05; V Stoke Hill *Guildf* 05-09; P-in-c Derby St Barn from 09. *St Barnabas' Vicarage, 122 Radbourne Street, Derby DE22 3BU* Tel (01332) 342553 E-mail derekhonour@compuserve.com

HONOUR, Mrs Joanna Clare. b 61. Westmr Coll Ox BEd83. St Jo Coll Nottm 86. d 89 p 94. Par Dn High Wycombe *Ox* 89-91; Par Dn Brightside w Wincobank *Sheff* 91-94; C 94; Dep Chapl HM Pris Wandsworth 95-97; Chapl HM Pris The Mount 97; NSM Dawley St Jerome *Lon* 96-01; Chapl HM Pris Foston Hall 01-05; Chapl HM Pris Coldingley 06-09; Chapl HM Pris Whatton from 09. *HM Prison Whatton, New Lane, Whatton, Nottingham NG13 9FQ* Tel (01949) 803200 Fax 803201 E-mail jo.honour@hmps.gsi.gov.uk

HONOUR, Jonathan Paul. b 68. Ox Brookes Univ BSc90 Greenwich Univ PGCE91. St Jo Coll Nottm MA98. d 99 p 00. C Tonbridge St Steph *Roch* 99-03; TV Woodley *Ox* 03-08; V Guernsey H Trin *Win* from 08. *Holy Trinity Vicarage, Brock Road, St Peter Port, Guernsey GY1 1RS* Tel (01481) 724382 Mobile 07752-241255 E-mail jonhonour@googlemail.com

HOOD, Mrs Doreen. b 38. Open Univ BA90 SRN59 RFN61. NEOC 90. d 93 p 94. NSM Cullercoats St Geo *Newc* 93-99; NSM Monkseaton St Pet 99-00; P-in-c Newc St Hilda 00-03; rtd 03. *24 Keswick Drive, North Shields NE30 3EW* Tel 0191-253 1762

HOOD, Mrs Elizabeth Mary. b 57. Ex Univ BA79. ERMC 05. d 08 p 09. C Boxmoor St Jo *St Alb* from 08. *136A Abbots Road, Abbots Langley WD5 0BL* Tel (01923) 269324 E-mail lizziehood@aol.com

HOOD, Miss Elizabeth Louise. St Mich Coll Llan. d 10 p 11. C Glanogwen and Llanllechid w St Ann's and Pentir *Ban* from 10. *The Rectory, Bryn Pistyll, Llanllechid, Bangor LL57 3SD* Tel (01248) 605017 E-mail jenniferhood.7@hotmail.co.uk

HOOD, Mrs Linda. b 47. Leeds Univ BA68. St Jo Coll Nottm 07. d 09 p 10. NSM Chase Terrace *Lich* from 09. *13 Mossbank Avenue, Burntwood WS7 4UN* Tel (01543) 301728 Mobile 07786-987114 E-mail linda.hood@stjohnscommunitychurch.org.uk

HOOD, Peter Michael. b 47. Sheff Univ BSc68. Wycliffe Hall Ox 70. d 73 p 74. C Soundwell *Bris* 73-76; P-in-c Walcot St Andr CD 76-77; TV Swindon St Jo and St Andr 77-80; V Esh and Hamsteels *Dur* 80-88; V Stockton St Paul 88-00; P-in-c Herrington 00-05; P-in-c Penshaw 00-05; P-in-c Shiney Row 00-05; R Herrington, Penshaw and Shiney Row 05-07; Lic to Adn Sunderland and Houghton Deanery from 07. *1 Victory Street East, Hetton le Hole, Houghton le Spring DH5 9DN* Tel 0191-526 9187 E-mail peter.hood@rohlfing-hood.freeserve.co.uk

HOOD, Canon Thomas Henry Havelock. b 24. Chich Th Coll 51. d 54 p 55. C Stella *Dur* 54-57; Australia from 57; Hon Can Brisbane from 88; rtd 93. *18 Moonyean Street, Bellbird Park Qld 4300, Australia* Tel (0061) (7) 3288 5106 E-mail havelock@gil.com.au

HOOGERWERF, John Constant. b 50. Bris Poly BA85 MCIH86. Oscott Coll (RC) 68. d 73 p 74. In RC Ch 73-84; NSM Davyhulme Ch Ch *Man* 84-93; Perm to Offic *Heref* 93-04; NSM Mold *St As* 04; Lic to Offic from 04. *2 Llys y Foel, Mold CH7 1EX* Tel (01352) 750701

HOOK, Canon Ian Kevin. b 57. Trin Coll Bris 93. d 95 p 96. C Dalton-in-Furness *Carl* 95-98; C Newbarns w Hawcoat 98-01; V Barrow St Mark from 01; RD Barrow from 06; Hon Can Carl Cathl from 10. *St Mark's Vicarage, Rawlinson Street, Barrow-in-Furness LA14 1BX* Tel (01229) 820405 E-mail ian@hooki.freeserve.co.uk

HOOK (née KAMINSKI), Mrs Julia Ann. b 55. WEMTC 07. d 10 p 11. NSM Winchcombe *Glouc* from 10. *18 Ratcliff Lawns, Southam, Cheltenham GL52 3PA* Tel (01242) 519346 Mobile 07715-953076 E-mail julia.hook@btinternet.com

HOOK, Neil. b 73. Univ of Wales (Swansea) BA94 Univ of Wales (Cardiff) BD96. St Mich Coll Llan 94. d 97 p 98. C Brecon St Mary and Battle w Llanddew *S & B* 97-99; Min Can Brecon

Cathl 97-99; P-in-c Llanllyr-yn-Rhos w Llanfihangel Helygen 99-00; V Upper Wye 00-05; P-in-c Trallwng w Bettws Penpont w Aberyskir etc 05-09; P-in-c Cynog Honddu 08-09; V Dan yr Eppynt from 10. *2 The Gardens, Cradoc, Brecon LD3 9LR* Tel (01874) 623183 E-mail frhooky@ukonline.co.uk

HOOKWAY, John Leonard Walter. b 73. St Jo Coll Dur BSc95. St Jo Coll Nottm MTh04. **d** 04 **p** 05. C St Alb St Paul *St Alb* 04-07; C Howell Hill w Burgh Heath *Guildf* 07-11; V Ware Ch Ch *St Alb* from 11. *The Vicarage, 15 Hanbury Close, Ware SG12 7BZ* Tel (01920) 463165
E-mail john@christchurchware.co.uk

HOOLE, Charles. b 33. St Aid Birkenhead 61. **d** 63 **p** 64. C Skerton St Luke *Blackb* 63-65; P-in-c Preston St Jas 65-69; V Lostock Hall 69-73; Chapl HM Pris Eastchurch 74-75; V St Annes St Marg *Blackb* 75-81; V S Shore St Pet 81-92; C Laneside 92-94; rtd 95; Perm to Offic *Blackb* from 95. *32 Hanover Crescent, Blackpool FY2 9DL* Tel (01253) 353564

HOOPER, Preb Derek Royston. b 33. St Edm Hall Ox BA57 MA65. Cuddesdon Coll 57. **d** 59 **p** 60. C Gt Walsingham *Nor* 59-62; C Townstall w Dartmouth *Ex* 62-65; V Lynton and Brendon 65-69; C Littleham w Exmouth 70-72; TV 72-79; R Wrington w Butcombe *B & W* 79-94; Preb Wells Cathl 93-94; rtd 94; Perm to Offic *Ex* 95; B & W 95-00. *23 Dagmar Road, Exmouth EX8 2AN* Tel (01395) 272831

HOOPER, Geoffrey Michael. b 39. MBE00. Univ of Wales (Ban) MA07. K Coll Lon 61. **d** 66 **p** 67. C Chesterfield St Mary and All SS *Derby* 66-69; Chapl RAF 69-74; P-in-c Hook Norton w Swerford and Wigginton *Ox* 74-80; P-in-c Gt Rollright 75-80; R Hook Norton w Gt Rollright, Swerford etc 80-82; Warden Manst Ho Univ Settlement Plaistow 82-00; Dir 86-00; rtd 03; Perm to Offic *Ban* from 09. *Ty'n Twll, Penbodlas, Llaniestyn, Pwllheli LL53 8SD* Tel (01758) 730526
E-mail geoffreyhooper@penbodlas.wanadoo.co.uk

HOOPER, Ian. b 44. St Jo Coll York CertEd67. Trin Coll Bris. **d** 88 **p** 89. C Martlesham w Brightwell *St E* 88-92; R Pakenham w Norton and Tostock 92-09; RD Ixworth 03-09; rtd 09; Perm to Offic *St E* from 09; Dioc Retirement Officer from 10. *26 Drake Close, Stowmarket IP14 1UP* Tel (01449) 770179
E-mail ianavrilhooper126@btinternet.com

✠**HOOPER, The Rt Revd Michael Wrenford.** b 41. Univ of Wales (Lamp) BA63. St Steph Ho Ox 63. **d** 65 **p** 66 **c** 02. C Bridgnorth St Mary *Heref* 65-70; P-in-c Habberley 70-78; R 78-81; V Minsterley 70-81; RD Pontesbury 75-80; Preb Heref Cathl 81-02; V Leominster 81-85; TR Leominster 85-97; P-in-c Eyton 81-85; RD Leominster 81-97; P-in-c Eye, Croft w Yarpole and Lucton 91-97; Adn Heref 97-02; Suff Bp Ludlow 02-09; Adn Ludlow 02-09; rtd 09. *6 Avon Drive, Eckington, Pershore WR10 3BU* Tel (01386) 751589
E-mail bishopmichael@btinternet.com

HOOPER, Canon Paul Denis Gregory. b 52. Man Univ BA75 Ox Univ BA80 MA87. Wycliffe Hall Ox 78. **d** 81 **p** 82. C Leeds St Geo *Ripon* 81-84; Dioc Youth Officer 84-87; Bp's Dom Chapl 87-95; Dioc Communications Officer 87-97; V Harrogate St Mark 95-09; AD Harrogate 05-09; Dir Clergy Development from 09; Hon Can Ripon Cathl from 08. *9 Fulwith Gate, Harrogate HG2 8HS* E-mail paulh@riponleeds-diocese.org.uk

HOOPER, Peter George. b 62. BSc PhD. EMMTC. **d** 06 **p** 07. C Melton Mowbray *Leic* 06-10; TR Bradgate Team from 10; Dioc Rural Officer from 11. *23 Ferndale Drive, Ratby, Leicester LE6 0LH* Tel 0116-239 4606

HOOPER, Sydney Paul. b 46. QUB BA68 Lanc Univ CertEd69. **d** 85 **p** 87. NSM Killaney w Carryduff *D & D* 85-91; Lic to Offic from 91; NSM Belfast St Chris 01-03; NSM Ballymacarrett from 03. *26 Manse Park, Carryduff, Belfast BT8 8RX* Tel (028) 9081 5607 *or* 9056 6289

HOOPER, William Gilbert. b 38. Ex Univ BA60. St Mich Coll Llan. **d** 82 **p** 83. C Hubberston w Herbrandston and Hasguard etc *St D* 82-85; R Llangwm and Freystrop 85-97; R Llangwm w Freystrop and Johnston 97-04; rtd 04. *5 Pen-y-Ffordd, St Clears, Carmarthen SA33 4DX* Tel (01994) 230069

HOOTON, David James. b 50. St Kath Coll Liv CertEd73. NOC 83. **d** 86 **p** 87. NSM Pemberton St Mark Newtown *Liv* 86-89; C Ashton-in-Makerfield St Thos 89-92; V Bryn 92. *The Vicarage, Log Bryn Road, Ashton-in-Makerfield, Wigan WN4 0AA* Tel (01942) 727114

HOPCRAFT, Jonathan Richard. b 34. Oriel Coll Ox BA55 DipEd66 MA66. Westcott Ho Cam 57. **d** 59 **p** 60. C Cannock *Lich* 59-63; N Rhodesia 63-64; S Rhodesia 64-65; Hon C Olton *Birm* 66-68; Antigua 68-72; C Gt Grimsby St Mary and St Jas *Linc* 72-74; P-in-c Stockwith 76-84; V Blyton w Pilham 76-84; P-in-c Laughton w Wildsworth 76-84; TV Bilston *Lich* 84-90; P-in-c Wolverhampton St Jo 90-98; C Wolverhampton 97-98; TV Cen Wolverhampton 98-00; rtd 00; Perm to Offic *Chelmsf* from 01. *13 Nabbott Road, Chelmsford CM1 2SW* Tel (01245) 263983 E-mail johnhopcraft@supanet.com

HOPE, Charles Henry. b 64. Regent's Park Coll Ox BA87 MA90. St Jo Coll Dur BA90. **d** 90 **p** 91. C Tynemouth St Jo *Newc* 90-94; V 94-03; P-in-c Prudhoe 03-07; V from 07. *The Vicarage, 5*

Kepwell Court, Prudhoe NE42 5PE Tel (01661) 836059 Mobile 07884-070619 E-mail charleshope@btopenworld.com

HOPE, Colin Frederick. b 49. St Mich Coll Llan 73. **d** 76 **p** 77. C Warrington St Elphin *Liv* 76-80; V Newton-le-Willows 80-84; CSWG from 84; Lic to Offic *Chich* from 88. *The Monastery, Crawley Down, Crawley RH10 4LH* Tel (01342) 712074

HOPE, Edith. b 43. Lanc Univ MA86 SRN64 SCM66. Wycliffe Hall Ox 89. **d** 91 **p** 94. Par Dn Droylsden St Mary *Man* 91-94; Par Dn Ecclesall *Sheff* 94; C 94-01; V Crosspool 01-08; rtd 08. *46 Gisborne Road, Sheffield S11 7HB* Tel 0114-263 1230
E-mail edithhope@btinternet.com

HOPE, Robert. b 36. Dur Univ BSc61. Clifton Th Coll 61. **d** 63 **p** 64. C Woking St Mary *Guildf* 63-66; C Surbiton Hill Ch Ch *S'wark* 66-68; Th Students' Sec IVF 68-71; Hon C Wallington *S'wark* 69-71; C Ox St Ebbe w St Pet 71-74; V Walshaw Ch Ch *Man* 74-87; TR Radipole and Melcombe Regis *Sarum* 87-93; rtd 93; Perm to Offic *St D* from 93. *1A Swiss Valley, Felinfael, Llanelli SA14 8BS* Tel (01554) 759199

HOPE, Susan. b 49. St Jo Coll Dur BA83 Sheff Univ MA04. Cranmer Hall Dur 80. **dss** 83 **d** 87 **p** 94. Boston Spa *York* 83-86; Brightside w Wincobank *Sheff* 86-97; Par Dn 87-89; Dn-in-c 89-94; V 94-97; V Chapeltown 97-02; Dioc Missr 02-07; RD Tankersley 00-02; Hon Can Sheff Cathl 00-09; Dir Tr Wilson Carlile Coll of Evang 07-08; P-in-c Shipley St Paul *Bradf* from 09; Dioc Adv in Evang from 09; Six Preacher Cant Cathl from 99. *31 South Edge, Shipley BD18 4RA* Tel (01274) 583652 Mobile 07736-774937

✠**HOPE OF THORNES, The Rt Revd and Rt Hon Lord (David Michael).** b 40. KCVO95 PC91. Nottm Univ BA62 Linacre Ho Ox DPhil65 Hon FGCM94. St Steph Ho Ox 62. **d** 65 **p** 66 **c** 85. C W Derby St Jo *Liv* 65-67 and 68-70; Chapl Bucharest *Eur* 67-68; V Orford St Andr *Liv* 70-74; Prin St Steph Ho Ox 74-82; V St Marylebone All SS *Lon* 82-85; Master of Guardians Shrine of Our Lady of Walsingham 82-93; Bp Wakef 85-91; Bp Lon 91-95; Dean of HM Chpls Royal and Prelate of OBE 91-95; Abp York 95-05; rtd 05; P-in-c Ilkley St Marg *Bradf* 05-06; Hon Asst Bp Bradf from 05; Hon Asst Bp Eur from 07; Hon Asst Bp Blackb from 08. *35 Hammerton Drive, Hellifield, Skipton BD23 4LZ*

HOPEWELL, Jeffery Stewart. b 52. Leic Univ BA75 ACA79. EMMTC 82. **d** 85 **p** 86. NSM Houghton on the Hill w Keyham *Leic* 85-88; NSM Houghton-on-the-Hill, Keyham and Hungarton 88-91; C Syston 91-93; TV Syston 93-97; Bp's Ecum Adv 91-97; P-in-c Wymeswold and Prestwold w Hoton 97-04; V Old Dalby, Nether Broughton, Saxelbye etc from 04; Dioc Ecum Officer from 03. *The Vicarage, Church Lane, Old Dalby, Melton Mowbray LE14 3LB* Tel (01664) 820064
E-mail jshopewell@btinternet.com

HOPKIN, David James. b 67. Birm Univ BTh92 CertEd91. Ripon Coll Cuddesdon 98. **d** 99 **p** 00. C Wickford and Runwell *Chelmsf* 99-02; TV Penistone and Thurlstone *Wakef* 02-06; TR from 06. *The Vicarage, Shrewsbury Road, Penistone, Sheffield S36 6DY* Tel (01226) 370954
E-mail david.hopkin@hotmail.com
or stjohns.pen@hotmail.com

HOPKINS, Mrs Angela Joan. b 42. Bp Otter Coll Chich CertEd64. S Dios Minl Tr Scheme 92. **d** 95 **p** 96. NSM Kingsbury H Innocents *Lon* from 95. *3 Regal Way, Harrow HA3 0RZ* Tel (020) 8907 1045 E-mail hopkinsangl@aol.com

HOPKINS, Miss Barbara Agnes. b 28. Lon Univ BSc60 Imp Coll Lon MPhil67. St Alb Minl Tr Scheme 82. **dss** 85 **d** 87. Bedford All SS *St Alb* 85-86; Chapl Asst Bedf Gen Hosp 86-88; Bedford St Mich *St Alb* 86-88; Hon Par Dn 87-88; Chapl Asst N Lincs Mental Health Unit 89-91; rtd 91; Perm to Offic *Linc* 93-95. *6 Olsen Court, Olsen Rise, Lincoln LN2 4UZ* Tel (01522) 513359

HOPKINS, Brenda Alison. b 63. St Martin's Coll Lanc BA95 Anglia Poly Univ MA97. Westcott Ho Cam 95. **d** 97 **p** 98. C Camberwell St Geo *S'wark* 97-00; Chapl Nor City Coll of F&HE 00-03. *Rose Tree Cottage, The Green, Stokesby, Great Yarmouth NR29 3EX* E-mail bhopkins@ccn.ac.uk

HOPKINS, Christopher Freeman. b 41. Dur Univ BA63. Wells Th Coll 63. **d** 65 **p** 66. C Spring Park *Cant* 65-69; C Mafeking S Africa 69-70; R Potchefstroom 70-78; Lic to Offic Botswana 78-81; R Beckley and Peasmarsh *Chich* from 81. *The Rectory, School Lane, Peasmarsh, Rye TN31 6UW* Tel and fax (01797) 230255 E-mail fr-christopher hopkins@bigfoot.com

HOPKINS, Gillian Frances. b 55. Bedf Coll Lon BA76 SS Mark & Jo Univ Coll Plymouth PGCE77 Cam Inst of Educn MA91. NTMTC BA07. **d** 07 **p** 08. C Wickford and Runwell *Chelmsf* 07-10; TV Waltham H Cross from 10. *15 Deer Park Way, Waltham Abbey EN9 3YN* E-mail gill hopkins@yahoo.co.uk

HOPKINS, Henry Charles. b 46. RD87. Edin Th Coll 65. **d** 71 **p** 72. C Dundee St Salvador *Bre* 71-74; C Dundee St Martin 71-74; Chapl RNVR 72-81; R Monifieth *Bre* 74-78; Chapl Miss to Seamen Kenya 78-85; Singapore 85-92; Offg Chapl NZ Defence Force 89-92; Chapl Miss to Seamen Teesside 92-94; V Middlesbrough St Thos *York* 94-97; V N Thornaby from 97.

HOPKINS *St Paul's Vicarage, 60 Lanehouse Road, Thornaby, Stockton-on-Tees TS17 8EA* Tel and fax (01642) 868086 E-mail harry.hopkins@ntlworld.com

HOPKINS, Hugh. b 33. TCD BA. **d** 62 **p** 63. C Ballymena *Conn* 62-64; C Belfast Ch Ch 64-67; I Ballintoy 67-72; I Belfast St Ninian 72-81; I Mossley 81-86; I Ballywillan 86-96; Can Belf Cathl 94-96; rtd 96. *2 Bush Gardens, Ballyness, Bushmills BT57 8AE* Tel (028) 2073 2981

HOPKINS, Ian Richard. b 70. Dur Univ BA92 Ox Univ BTh00. **d** 00 **p** 01. C Edin St Thos 00-04; R from 04. *16 Belgrave Road, Edinburgh EH12 6NF* Tel 0131-334 4434 *or* 316 4292 E-mail rector@saintthomas.org.uk

HOPKINS, John Dawson. b 39. Chich Th Coll 85. **d** 87 **p** 88. C Walker *Newc* 87-89; C Newc St Fran 89-92; V Horton 92-00; rtd 00; Perm to Offic *Newc* from 01. *Amen Cottage, 31 High Fair, Wooler NE71 6PA* Tel (07790) 915763

HOPKINS, Kenneth Victor John. b 45. Univ Coll Lon BA66 Lon Univ BD69 Hull Univ PhD84. Tyndale Hall Bris 66. **d** 69 **p** 70. C S Mimms Ch Ch *Lon* 69-72; C Branksome St Clem *Sarum* 72-75; P-in-c Trowbridge St Thos 75-76; V 76-81; R Wingfield w Rowley 76-81; Chapl and Lect NE Surrey Coll of Tech 81-84; Hd Student Services Essex Inst of HE 84-88; Kingston Poly 88-92; Kingston Univ 92-98; Dean of Students 98-03; Pro Vice-Chan 04-06; rtd 06. *Quarry Cottage, Duke Street, Withington, Hereford HR1 3QD* Tel (01432) 850933 E-mail ken_hopkins@dsl.pipex.com

HOPKINS, Lionel. b 48. Open Univ BA82. St D Coll Lamp. **d** 71 **p** 72. C Llandeilo Tal-y-bont *S & B* 71-74; C Morriston 74-78; P-in-c Waunarllwydd 78-80; V 80-86; Youth Chapl 84-86; V Llangyfelach 86-96; P-in-c Swansea Ch Ch 96-00, Chapl HM Pris Swansea from 96. *HM Prison, 200 Oystermouth Road, Swansea SA1 3SR* Tel (01792) 464030

HOPKINS, Miss Patricia Mary. b 46. Kingston Poly BEd78. Trin Coll Bris 83. **dss** 85 **d** 87 **p** 94. Gorleston St Andr *Nor* 85-88; C 87-88; C Woking St Jo *Guildf* 88-90; TD Barnham Broom *Nor* 90-94; TV 94-97; V Oxford *Roch* 97-07; rtd 07; Perm to Offic *Nor* from 08. *Hill Cottage, Broomhill, East Runton, Cromer NR27 9PF* Tel (01263) 512338

HOPKINS, Peter. b 54. Nottm Univ BSc75 Imp Coll Lon MSc79. Oak Hill Th Coll BA86. **d** 86 **p** 87. C Gee Cross *Ches* 86-90; R Gt Gonerby *Linc* 90-95; R Barrowby and Gt Gonerby from 95; RD Grantham 01-09. *The Rectory, 7 Long Street, Great Gonerby, Grantham NG31 8LN* Tel and fax (01476) 565737 E-mail peterhoppy@worldonline.co.uk

HOPKINS, Richard Clive John. b 74. Nottm Univ BA95 Ex Univ PGCE97. Wycliffe Hall Ox BTh02. **d** 02 **p** 03. C Duffield *Derby* 02-05; C Duffield and Lt Eaton 05-06; P-in-c Sileby, Cossington and Seagrave *Leic* 06-09; R from 09. *The Rectory, 11 Mountsorrel Lane, Sileby, Loughborough LE12 7NF* Tel (01509) 812493 E-mail hopkins@richardcj.fsnet.co.uk

HOPKINS, Robert James Gardner. b 42. Bris Univ BSc64 ACA76 FCA81. St Alb Minl Tr Scheme. **d** 79 **p** 80. NSM Chorleywood Ch Ch *St Alb* 79-83; NSM Parr Mt *Liv* 83-97; NSM Crookes St Thos *Sheff* 97-09; NSM Philadelphia St Thos from 09; Dir Angl Ch Planting Initiatives from 92. *70 St Thomas Road, Sheffield S10 1UX* Tel and fax 0114-267 8266 *or* 278 9378 E-mail admin@acpi.org.uk

HOPKINS, Victor John. b 44. UEA LLB82. CBDTI 06. **d** 07 **p** 08. NSM Sedbergh, Cautley and Garsdale *Bradf* from 07. *Brantrigg, Winfield Road, Sedbergh LA10 5AZ* Tel (015396) 21455 E-mail brantrigg@btinternet.com

HOPKINSON, The Ven Barnabas John. b 39. Trin Coll Cam BA63 MA67. Linc Th Coll 63. **d** 65 **p** 66. C Langley All SS and Martyrs *Man* 65-67; C Cambridge Gt St Mary w St Mich *Ely* 67-71; Asst Chapl Charterhouse Sch Godalming 71-75; P-in-c Preshute *Sarum* 75-76; TV Marlborough 76-81; RD Marlborough 77-81; TR Wimborne Minster and Holt 81-86; Can and Preb Sarum Cathl 83-04; RD Wimborne 85-86; Adn Sarum 86-98; P-in-c Stratford sub Castle 87-98; Adn Wilts 98-04; rtd 04. *Tanners Cottage, 22 Frog Street, Bampton, Tiverton EX16 9NT* Tel (01398) 331611

HOPKINSON, Benjamin Alaric. b 36. Trin Coll Ox BA59. Chich Th Coll 59. **d** 61 **p** 62. C Pallion *Dur* 61-66; Rhodesia 66-67; Botswana 67-74; Hon C Sherwood *S'well* 74-77; Hon C Carrington 74-77; V Lowdham 77-85; R Whitby *York* 85-95; Miss to Seafarers from 85; V Stainton w Hilton *York* 95-01; Chapl Cleveland Constabulary 95-01; rtd 01; Perm to Offic *Newc* from 01. *11 Watershaugh Road, Warkworth, Morpeth NE65 0TT* Tel and fax (01665) 714213 E-mail dumela@dial.pipex.com

HOPKINSON, Colin Edward. b 57. BA LLB. Ridley Hall Cam. **d** 84 **p** 85. C Chadwell *Chelmsf* 84-87; C Canvey Is 87-90; P-in-c E Springfield 90-98; RD Chelmsf N 95-99; R Langdon Hills from 98. *The Rectory, 105A Berry Lane, Basildon SS16 6AP* Tel (01268) 542156 E-mail cchopkinson@aol.com

HOPKINSON, David John. b 47. Ox NSM Course. **d** 79 **p** 80. NSM Wardington *Ox* 79-80; Hon C Didcot St Pet 80-83; C Headingley *Ripon* 83-87; P-in-c Leeds All So 87-91; R Middleton Tyas w Croft and Eryholme 91-95; V Leeds Belle Is St Jo and St Barn 95-98; rtd 98; Perm to Offic *Ripon* from 98 and *Wakef*

from 07. *11 Old Well Head, Halifax HX1 2BN* Tel (01422) 361226

HOPKINSON, William Humphrey. b 48. Lon Univ BSc69 Dur Univ MA78 Nottm Univ MPhil84 Man Poly MSc90 California State Univ MEd00 ARIC73. Cranmer Hall Dur. **d** 77 **p** 78. C Normanton *Derby* 77-80; C Sawley 80-82; V Birtles *Ches* 82-87; Dir Past Studies NOC 82-94; Dir Course Development 90-94; CME Officer *Ches* 87-94; P-in-c Tenterden St Mich *Cant* 94-96; Dir Min and Tr 94-02; Hon Can Cant Cathl 01-02; Perm to Offic 03-06; World Faith Manager Harmondsworth Immigration Removal Cen 04-05; Registrar Lon Academy of HE from 05. *London Academy of Higher Education, Boardman House, 64 Broadway, London E15 1NT* Tel (020) 8432 0388 Mobile 07734-202750 E-mail whhopkinson@f2s.com

HOPLEY, David. b 37. Wells Th Coll 62. **d** 65 **p** 66. C Frome St Jo *B & W* 65-68; R Staunton-on-Arrow w Byton and Kinsham *Heref* 68-81; P-in-c Lingen 68-81; P-in-c Aymestrey and Leinthall Earles 72-81; R Buckland Newton, Long Burton etc *Sarum* 81-02; rtd 02; Perm to Offic *B & W* from 07. *Sunnyside, Clatworthy, Taunton TA4 2EH* Tel (01984) 623842

HOPLEY, Gilbert. b 40. Univ of Wales (Ban) BA62. St D Coll Lamp LTh65. **d** 65 **p** 66. C St As and Tremeirchion *St As* 65-73; Warden Ch Hostel Ban 73-76; Chapl Univ of Wales (Ban) 73-76; V Meifod and Llangynyw *St As* 76-79; Chapl St Marg Sch Bushey 79-87; Hd Master St Paul's Cathl Choir Sch 87-97. *Plas Afon, Pentrefelin, Criccieth LL52 0PT* Tel (01766) 523588

HOPPER, Peter Edward. b 60. **d** 99 **p** 00. OLM Bermondsey St Mary w St Olave, St Jo etc *S'wark* 99-05. *56 Reverdy Road, London SE1 5QD* Tel (020) 7237 1543 *or* 7525 1831 E-mail phopper@phopper.screaming.net

HOPPER, Peter John. b 37. Univ Coll Dur BSc59 Lon Univ PGCE60. NOC 89. **d** 91 **p** 91. C Aston cum Aughton and Ulley *Sheff* 91-93; C Aston cum Aughton w Swallownest, Todwick etc 93-94; P-in-c Braithwell w Bramley 94-95; TV Bramley and Ravenfield w Hooton Roberts etc 95-00; rtd 00; Perm to Offic *Worc* from 00. *21 Hornsby Avenue, Worcester WR4 0PN* Tel (01905) 731618 E-mail peterjhopper@supanet.com

HOPPER, Canon Robert Keith. b 45. St Jo Coll Dur 74. **d** 77 **p** 78. C Oxclose *Dur* 77-80; C Hebburn St Jo 80-82; V Lobley Hill 82-04; P-in-c Marley Hill 02-04; V Hillside from 04; Hon Can Dur Cathl from 09. *All Saints' Vicarage, Rowanwood Gardens, Gateshead NE11 0DP* Tel and fax 0191-460 4409 Mobile 07960-754744 E-mail bob.hopper@durham.anglican.org

HOPPERTON, Thomas. b 33. Chich Th Coll 71. **d** 73 **p** 74. C Cheam *S'wark* 73-89; P-in-c St Alb Ch 76-89; P-in-c Rotherhithe St Kath w St Barn 89-92; P-in-c S Bermondsey St Bart 91-92; V Bermondsey St Kath w St Bart 92-01; rtd 01; Perm to Offic *York* 03-11. *8 Croft Heads, Sowerby, Thirsk YO7 1ND* Tel (01845) 524210 E-mail fathertom21@aol.com

HOPTHROW, Mrs Elizabeth Rosemary Gladys. b 45. **d** 01 **p** 02. NSM Aylesham w Adisham *Cant* 01-04; NSM Nonington w Wymynswold and Goodnestone etc 01-04; NSM Barham w Bishopsbourne and Kingston from 04; Chapl Pilgrims Hospice Cant 01-11. *146 The Street, Kingston, Canterbury CT4 6JQ* Tel (01227) 830070 *or* 812610 Mobile 07977-754920 E-mail lizziehopthrow@quista.net

HOPWOOD, Adrian Patrick. b 37. N Lon Poly BSc61 CBiol MIBiol MCIWEM. Ox Min Course 87. **d** 90 **p** 91. NSM Chesham Bois *Ox* 90-93; NSM Amersham 93-95; NSM Ridgeway 95-05; rtd 05; Perm to Offic *B & W* from 06. *15 Waverley, Somerton TA11 6SH* Tel (01458) 274527

HOPWOOD OWEN, Mrs Karen. b 58. Padgate Coll of Educn CertEd79 St Martin's Coll Lanc DASE90. **d** 95 **p** 96. OLM Peel *Man* 95-99; OLM Walkden and Lt Hulton from 99. *168 Manchester Road, Tyldesley, Manchester M29 8WY* Tel (01942) 894850

HORAN, Joan Anne. b 53. BA74 DipEd75. **d** 05 **p** 06. Australia 05-09; R Grimshoe *Ely* from 09. *The Rectory, 7 Oak Street, Feltwell, Thetford IP26 4DD* Tel (01842) 828034 E-mail joanhoran123@btinternet.com

HORAN, John Champain. b 52. WMMTC 95. **d** 98 **p** 99. NSM Leckhampton SS Phil and Jas w Cheltenham St Jas *Glouc* 98-08; Dioc Communications Officer 01-02. *38 Leckhampton Road, Cheltenham GL53 0BB* Tel (01242) 235370 E-mail horan.jc@btinternet.com

HORBURY, Prof William. b 42. Oriel Coll Ox BA64 MA67 Clare Coll Cam BA66 PhD71 DD00 FBA97. Westcott Ho Cam 64. **d** 69 **p** 70. Fell Clare Coll Cam 68-72; CCC Cam from 78; R Gt w Lt Gransden *Ely* 72-78; Lect Div Cam Univ 84-98; Prof Jewish and Early Chr Studies from 98; P-in-c Cambridge St Botolph *Ely* from 90. *5 Grange Road, Cambridge CB3 9AS* Tel (01223) 363529 Fax 462751 E-mail wh10000@cam.ac.uk

HORDER, Mrs Catharine Joy. b 51. Battersea Coll of Educn CertEd72 UWE BA98. S Dios Minl Tr Scheme 92. **d** 95 **p** 96. C Burrington and Churchill *B & W* 95-00; TV Yatton Moor 00-11; rtd 11. *The Sanctuary, Bridford, Exeter EX6 7HS* E-mail cathy.horder@btinternet.com

HORDER, Peter Alan Trahair. b 43. **d** 97 **p** 98. OLM Madron *Truro* 97-01; OLM Gulval 99-01; OLM Gulval and Madron from 01. *Kourion, 38 Boscathnoe Way, Heamoor, Penzance TR18 3JS* Tel (01736) 360813

HORDERN, Peter John Calveley. b 35. Jes Coll Cam BA59 MA64 McMaster Univ Ontario PhD72. Linc Th Coll 59. **d** 61 **p** 62. C Billingham St Aid *Dur* 61-65; Canada from 65; rtd 00. *346 Aberdeen Avenue, Brandon MB R7A 1N4, Canada* Tel (001) (204) 727 3324

HORE, Leslie Nicholas Peter. b 40. SWMTC 99. **d** 02 **p** 03. OLM Treverbyn *Truro* 02-10; rtd 10. *Tremore, Hallaze Road, Penwithick, St Austell PL26 8YW* Tel (01726) 851750 E-mail peterhore@hotmail.co.uk

HORE, Michael John. b 50. Man Univ BSc71. Linc Th Coll 75. **d** 78 **p** 79. C Maidstone St Martin *Cant* 78-81; C St Peter-in-Thanet 81-83; R Storrington *Chich* 83-93; RD Storrington 90-93; V Goring-by-Sea 93-02; R Cottenham *Ely* 02-07; R Upminster *Chelmsf* from 07. *The Rectory, 4 Gridiron Place, Upminster RM14 2BE* Tel (01708) 220174 E-mail mrthore@yahoo.co.uk

HORLESTON, Kenneth William. b 50. Oak Hill Th Coll BA86. **d** 86 **p** 87. C Wednesfield Heath *Lich* 86-89; V Blagreaves *Derby* 89-00; P-in-c Horsley 00-02; P-in-c Denby 00-02; V Horsley and Denby 02-10; C Morley w Smalley and Horsley Woodhouse 06-07; rtd 10. *11 Pegasus Way, Hilton, Derby DE65 5HW* Tel (01283) 735600 E-mail kenhorleston@tiscali.co.uk

HORLOCK, Andrew John. b 51. Bath Univ BSc74 Open Univ MPhil89 Nottm Univ PhD99. Ridley Hall Cam 03. **d** 05 **p** 06. C Crich and S Wingfield *Derby* 05-08; P-in-c Lugano *Eur* from 08. *St Edward the Confessor, via Maraini 6, 6900 Lugano, Switzerland* Tel (0041) (91) 968 1149 E-mail andrewhorlock@hotmail.com

HORLOCK, The Very Revd Brian William. b 31. OBE78. Univ of Wales (Lamp) BA55. Chich Th Coll 55. **d** 57 **p** 58. C Chiswick St Nic w St Mary *Lon* 57-61; C Witney *Ox* 61-62; V N Acton St Gabr *Lon* 62-68; Chapl Oslo w Bergen, Trondheim and Stavanger *Eur* 68-89; RD Scandinavia 75-79; Adn 80-89; Hon Can Brussels Cathl 80-89; Dean Gib 89-98; Chapl Gib 89-98; rtd 98; Perm to Offic *Eur* from 98; Hon C Wootton Bassett *Sarum* from 98. *1 Richard's Close, Wootton Bassett, Swindon SN4 7LE* Tel (01793) 848344 Fax 848378

HORLOCK, Louise Frances. **d** 10 **p** 11. NSM Hampreston *Sarum* from 10. *35 Award Road, Wimborne BH21 7NT*

HORLOCK, Peter Richard. b 76. UWE BA97. Oak Hill Th Coll BA04. **d** 04 **p** 05. C Rusholme H Trin *Man* from 04. *26 Croasdale Avenue, Manchester M14 6GU* Tel 0161-249 3957 Mobile 07890-860022 E-mail peter@plattchurch.org

HORLOCK, Timothy Edward. b 72. Anglia Poly Univ BSc94 Bath Univ PGCE96. Ridley Hall Cam 05. **d** 07 **p** 08. C Bedford Ch Ch *St Alb* 07-10; P-in-c Stevenage St Pet Broadwater from 10. *St Peter's House, 1 The Willows, Stevenage SG2 8AN* Tel (01483) 238236 Mobile 07787-968843 E-mail alextim_horlock@hotmail.com *or* vicar@stpeter-stevenage.co.uk

HORN, Colin Clive. b 39. CEng MIMechE. Cant Sch of Min. **d** 83 **p** 84. NSM Yalding w Collier Street *Roch* 83-91; V Kemsing w Woodlands 91-98; RD Shoreham 94-98; rtd 99; Perm to Offic *B & W* 00-07. *Saw Mill Cottage, Leigh Street, Leigh upon Mendip, Radstock BA3 5QQ* Tel and fax (01373) 812736 Mobile 07885-523190 E-mail colinhorn@hotmail.com

HORNBY (*née* CHRISTIAN), **Mrs Helen.** b 47. K Coll Lon BA68 AKC68 Lon Inst of Educn PGCE69. Cranmer Hall Dur 00. **d** 02 **p** 03. C Briercliffe *Blackb* 02-07; C Blackpool St Jo 07-11; C Blackpool St Mark from 11; C Blackpool St Mich from 11. *2 Arnside Avenue, Lytham St Annes FY8 3SA* Tel (01253) 711215 E-mail revhelenhornby@yahoo.co.uk

HORNE, Brian Edward. b 37. CEng68 MRAeS68 MIET68 EurIng92 Lon Univ BSc62 PhD78. WEMTC 92. **d** 95 **p** 96. OLM Cheltenham St Mark *Glouc* from 95. *87A Rowanfield Road, Cheltenham GL51 8AF* Tel (01242) 236786 E-mail lynbrihorne@btinternet.com

HORNE, Jack Kenneth. b 20. Linc Th Coll 68. **d** 70 **p** 71. C Danbury *Chelmsf* 70-75; V Frampton *Linc* 75-85; rtd 85; Perm to Offic *Linc* from 01. *33 Brick Kiln Place, Grantham NG31 7GJ*

HORNE, Mona Lyn Denison. b 38. Gipsy Hill Coll of Educn TCert58. WEMTC 98. **d** 99 **p** 00. OLM Cheltenham St Mark *Glouc* from 99. *87A Rowanfield Road, Cheltenham GL51 8AF* Tel (01242) 236786 Fax 691869 E-mail lynbrihorne@btinternet.com

HORNE, Simon Timothy. b 62. Ball Coll Ox BA86 MA90 Birm Univ PhD99 RN(MH)89. Qu Coll Birm BD94. **d** 95 **p** 96. C Basingstoke *Win* 95-99; C Fordingbridge 99-01; TV Fordingbridge and Breamore and Hale etc from 01. *29 Shaftesbury Street, Fordingbridge SP6 1JF* Tel 07502-146758 (mobile) E-mail simon.horne31@googlemail.com

HORNER, Eric. b 43. EMMTC 87. **d** 90 **p** 91. C Boultham *Linc* 90-93; P-in-c Frampton w Kirton in Holland 93-97; V Kirton in Holland 97-04; rtd 05. *24 Hurn Close, Ruskington, Sleaford NG34 9FE* Tel (01526) 834043 E-mail erichorner04@aol.com

HORNER, Graham. b 57. Grey Coll Dur BSc78 ACA81. St Jo Coll Nottm 93. **d** 93 **p** 94. C Longdon-upon-Tern, Rodington, Uppington etc *Lich* 93-95; C Wrockwardine Deanery 95-96; TV 96-02; TR 02-07; RD Wrockwardine 02-07; V Gt Wyrley from

07. *The Vicarage, 1 Cleves Crescent, Cheslyn Hay, Walsall WS6 7LR* Tel (01922) 414309 E-mail horner314@btinternet.com

HORNER, John Henry. b 40. Leeds Univ BA62 Middx Poly MA87. Oak Hill Th Coll 76. **d** 79 **p** 80. NSM Datchworth w Tewin *St Alb* 79-85; NSM Ware St Mary 85-91; C S Ashford Ch Ch *Cant* 91-94; C Bp's Hatfield *St Alb* 94-99; V Sandridge 99-02; rtd 02; P-in-c Broxbourne w Wormley *St Alb* 03-04. *41 St Leonard's Road, Hertford SG14 3JW* Tel (01992) 423725 E-mail john.horner1@ntlworld.com

HORNER, Richard Murray. b 61. Dur Univ BSc83. NTMTC 93. **d** 96 **p** 97. C Sherborne w Castleton and Lillington *Sarum* 96-99; Chapl Rugby Sch from 99. *11 Horton Crescent, Rugby CV22 5DJ* Tel (01788) 544939

HORNER, Sally. b 68. City Univ BSc94. Westcott Ho Cam 06. **d** 08 **p** 09. C Peckham St Jo w St Andr *S'wark* from 08. *10 Buller Close, London SE15 6UJ* Tel (020) 7639 0084 E-mail sally@sallyhorner.co.uk

HORNSBY, Edgar. b 23. AKC50. **d** 51 **p** 52. C Portsea St Mary *Portsm* 51-55; Chapl RAF 55-69; St Mary's Hall and Brighton Coll 69-74; Chapl St Swithun's Sch Win 74-88; rtd 88; Perm to Offic *B & W* 88-04 and *Sarum* 01-06. *4 Stirling Road, Chichester PO19 7DJ* Tel (01243) 536711

HORNSBY, William John. b 49. RIBA79. SEITE 98. **d** 01 **p** 02. C Faversham *Cant* 01-04; C Preston next Faversham, Goodnestone and Graveney 02-04; P-in-c Newington w Hartlip and Stockbury 04-07; P-in-c Iwade and Upchurch w Lower Halstow 05-07; Perm to Offic 07-08; V Goudhurst w Kilndown from 08; AD Weald from 10. *The Vicarage, Back Lane, Goudhurst, Cranbrook TN17 1AN* Tel (01580) 211352

HOROBIN, Timothy John. b 60. St Jo Coll Nottm 92. **d** 94 **p** 95. C Nelson St Phil *Blackb* 94-98; P-in-c Blackpool St Paul 98-00; Perm to Offic 05-06; Lic to Offic 06-10; P-in-c Lower Darwen St Jas from 10. *The Vicarage, Stopes Brow, Lower Darwen, Darwen BB3 0QP* Tel (01254) 53898 Mobile 07811-074063 E-mail tim.horobin@blackburn.anglican.org

HORREX, Mrs Gay Lesley. b 42. **d** 96 **p** 97. OLM Walton-on-Thames *Guildf* 96-07; rtd 07; Perm to Offic *Guildf* from 07 and *Portsm* from 08. *25 Pine Walk, Liss GU33 7AT* Tel (01730) 893827 E-mail glhorrex@homecall.co.uk

HORROCKS, Judith Anne. b 53. Univ of Calgary BSc76 Keele Univ MA99. St Jo Coll Nottm. **dss** 82 **d** 87 **p** 94. Denton Ch Ch *Man* 82-85; Whalley Range St Edm 85-97; Par Dn 87-97; C 94-97; Chapl Man R Infirmary 88-90; Chapl Christie Hosp NHS Trust Man 95-03; Chapl S Man Univ Hosps NHS Trust 98-03; Lic Preacher *Man* 97-03; Hon Can Man Cathl 02-03; Multifaith Chapl Co-ord Sheff Hallam Univ 03-05; Chapl St Ann's Hospice Manchester 05-09; Lect Bolton St Pet *Man* from 09. *Five Saints Rectory, 130A Highfield Road, Farnworth, Bolton BL4 0AJ* Tel (01204) 572334 Mobile 07725-957219 Fax 08709-138446 E-mail lecturer@boltonparishchurch.co.uk

HORROCKS, Oliver John. b 30. Clare Coll Cam BA53 MA57. Westcott Ho Cam 53. **d** 55 **p** 56. C Moss Side Ch Ch *Man* 55-58; C Arnold *S'well* 58-60; R Ancoats *Man* 60-67; R Barthomley *Ches* 67-96; rtd 96; Perm to Offic *Ches* from 98. *36 Station Road, Alsager, Stoke-on-Trent ST7 2PD* Tel (01270) 877284

HORROCKS, Robert James. b 56. Grey Coll Dur BSc78. St Jo Coll Nottm. **d** 82 **p** 83. C Denton Ch Ch *Man* 82-85; R Whalley Range St Edm 85-97; P-in-c Bolton St Paul w Em 97-06; P-in-c Daubhill 05-06; TR New Bury w Gt Lever from 06. *Five Saints Rectory, 130A Highfield Road, Farnworth, Bolton BL4 0AJ* Tel (01204) 572334 Fax 08709-138446 E-mail revbobhorrocks@yahoo.co.uk

HORSEMAN, Christopher Michael. b 54. Bris Sch of Min 84 Trin Coll Bris 87. **d** 88 **p** 89. C Weston-super-Mare Cen Par *B & W* 88-92; TV Yatton Moor 92-02; NSM 02-08. *6 Westaway Park, Yatton, Bristol BS49 4JU* Tel (01934) 834537 E-mail cfhors@globalnet.co.uk

HORSEMAN, Colin. b 46. Lon Coll of Div ALCD69 BD70 STh75. **d** 70 **p** 71. C Higher Openshaw *Man* 70-74; C Darfield *Sheff* 75-78; V Stainforth 78-88; V Heeley 88-95; P-in-c Ducklington *Ox* 95-99; P-in-c Gt Horkesley *Chelmsf* 99-02; P-in-c Wormingford 00-02; R W Bergholt and Gt Horkesley from 02; RD Dedham and Tey 03-08. *The Rectory, Ivy Lodge Road, Great Horkesley, Colchester CO6 4EN* Tel (01206) 271242 E-mail revcolin@tiscali.co.uk

HORSEY, Maurice Alfred. b 30. ACIB. S'wark Ord Course 61. **d** 64 **p** 65. C Oxhey All SS *St Alb* 64-67; C Coulsdon St Jo *S'wark* 67-71; P-in-c Champion Hill St Sav 71-76; Hon C Lewisham St Swithun 84-86; P-in-c Woolwich St Thos 86-90; R 90-94; rtd 94; Chapl Costa del Sol W *Eur* 94-98; Perm to Offic from 99. *6147 Marina de Casares, 29690 Casares (Malaga), Spain* Tel (0034) 952 892 166 E-mail dorothy@tiscali.es

HORSEY, Stanley Desmond. b 29. Ely Th Coll 46. **d** 49 **p** 50. C S Clevedon *B & W* 49-51; C Leigh-on-Sea St Marg *Chelmsf* 51-53; C Barbourne *Worc* 53-55; V Edgbaston St Jas *Birm* 55-60; V Brighton St Martin *Chich* 60-67; V Hove St Barn 67-77; V Hove St Barn and St Agnes 77-85; rtd 85; Perm to Offic *Chich* from 85. *27A Amesbury Crescent, Hove BN3 5RD* Tel (01273) 732081

HORSFALL, Andrew Stuart. b 64. Qu Coll Birm 93. **d** 06 **p** 06. Methodist Min 95-06; Chapl E Lancs Hosps NHS Trust 05-09; Chapl Co-ord from 09; NSM Feniscowles *Blackb* 06-07. *Royal Blackburn Hospital, Haslingden Road, Blackburn BB2 3HH* Tel (01254) 263555 *or* 736849 E-mail andrew.horsfall@elht.nhs.uk *or* revhors@aol.com

HORSFALL, David John. b 55. Bris Poly BA77. St Jo Coll Nottm 87. **d** 89 **p** 90. C Chaddesden St Mary *Derby* 89-92; V Swadlincote 92-11; RD Repton 99-09; R Chesterfield H Trin and Ch Ch from 11. *Holy Trinity Rectory, 31 Newbold Road, Chesterfield S41 7PG* Tel (01246) 220860 E-mail djhorsfall@hotmail.com

HORSFALL, Keith. b 39. Tyndale Hall Bris 62. **d** 65 **p** 66. C Walton Breck *Liv* 65-68; C Fazakerley Em 68-70; C Mile Cross *Nor* 70-73; V Gayton 73-80; TR Parr *Liv* 80-90; V Leyland St Andr *Blackb* 90-00; P-in-c Willand *Ex* 00-01; TV Cullompton, Willand, Uffculme, Kentisbeare etc 01-05, rtd 05. *8 Irwell Green, Taunton TA1 2TA* E-mail ritaandkeith@hotmail.com

HORSHAM, Archdeacon of. *See* COMBES, The Ven Roger Matthew

HORSHAM, Area Bishop of. *See* SOWERBY, The Rt Revd Mark Crispin Rake

HORSINGTON, Timothy Frederick. b 44. Dur Univ BA66. Wycliffe Hall Ox 67. **d** 69 **p** 70. C Halewood *Liv* 69-72; C Farnworth 72-75; C-in-c Widnes St Jo 72-75; P-in-c Llangarron w Llangrove *Heref* 75-82; P-in-c Whitchurch w Ganarew 77-82; R Llangarron w Llangrove, Whitchurch and Ganarew 83-84; R Highclere and Ashmansworth w Crux Easton *Win* 84-09; rtd 09. *27 Arlington Close, Yeovil BA21 3TB* Tel (01935) 410731

HORSLEY, Canon Alan Avery. b 36. St Chad's Coll Dur BA58 Pacific States Univ MA84 PhD85. Qu Coll Birm 58. **d** 60 **p** 61. C Daventry *Pet* 60-63; C Reading St Giles *Ox* 63-64; C Wokingham St Paul 64-66; V Yeadon St Andr *Bradf* 66-71; R Heyford w Stowe Nine Churches *Pet* 71-78; RD Daventry 76-78; V Oakham w Hambleton and Egleton 78-81; V Oakham, Hambleton, Egleton, Braunston and Brooke 81-86; Can Pet Cathl 79-86; V Lanteglos by Fowey *Truro* 86-88; Provost St Andr Cathl Inverness 88-91; R Inverness St Andr 88-91; P-in-c Culloden St Mary-in-the-Fields 88-91; P-in-c Strathnairn St Paul 88-91; V Mill End and Heronsgate w W Hyde *St Alb* 91-01; RD Rickmansworth 00-01; rtd 01; Perm to Offic Pet from 03. *3 Leicester Terrace, Northampton NN2 6AJ* Tel (01604) 628868 E-mail alanahorsley@hotmail.co.uk

HORSLEY, Amelia Mary Elizabeth. b 69. K Alfred's Coll Win BEd91. St Jo Coll Nottm MA97. **d** 98 **p** 99. C Southampton Maybush St Pet *Win* 98-01; Teacher Mansel Infant Sch Southampton 01; Teacher Highfields Primary Sch Leic from 01; Dep Hd from 05. *95 Aylestone Drive, Leicester LE2 8SB* Tel 0116-283 7710 E-mail amehorsley@aol.com

HORSLEY, Peter Alec. b 56. Leeds Metrop Univ CertEd98. Cranmer Hall Dur 99. **d** 01 **p** 02. C Acomb St Steph *York* 01-05; P-in-c Wheldrake w Thorganby 05-08; R Derwent Ings 08-11; V Acomb St Steph from 11. *The Vicarage, 32 Carr Lane, York YO26 5HX* Tel (01904) 781400 E-mail peterhorsley@tiscali.co.uk

HORSMAN, Andrew Alan. b 49. Otago Univ BA70 Man Univ MA72 PhD75. St Steph Ho Ox BA80 MA87. **d** 81 **p** 82. C Hillingdon All SS *Lon* 81-84; C Lt Stanmore St Lawr 84-87; TV Haxby w Wigginton *York* 87-98; V Acomb Moor from 98; P-in-c York All SS N Street from 03. *The Vicarage, 2 Sherringham Drive, York YO24 2SE* Tel (01904) 706047 E-mail andrew@horsmanz.plus.com

HORSWELL, Kevin George. b 48. Jes Coll Cam BA77 MA81 Nottm Univ BA81. St Jo Coll Nottm 79. **d** 82 **p** 83. C Bootle Ch Ch *Liv* 82-86; Chapl LMH Ox 86-91; C Ox St Giles and SS Phil and Jas w St Marg 86-91; R Dodleston *Ches* 91-00; R Llanaber w Caerdeon *Ban* from 00. *The Rectory, Mynach Road, Barmouth LL42 1RL* Tel (01341) 280516

HORTA, Nelson Pinto. b 40. Lisbon Univ Lic80 Catholic Univ of Portugal LicTh92. **d** 65 **p** 69. Portugal from 65; V Setbal H Spirit 69-71; V Lisbon St Paul 71-96; Asst Chapl Gtr Lisbon *Eur* 97-00. *Quinta da Cerieira, rua C, Lote 261, Vale de Figueira-Sobreda, 2800 Almada, Portugal* Tel (00351) (1) 295 7943

HORTON, Alan Michael. b 40. Univ of Wales BScTech71. Linc Th Coll 92. **d** 92 **p** 93. C Bexleyheath Ch Ch *Roch* 92-95; P-in-c Slade Green 95-99; V 99-03; P-in-c Southborough St Thos 03-08; rtd 08. *3 Bracken Row, Thurston, Bury St Edmunds IP31 3PT* Tel (01359) 231976 E-mail alan.horton28.plus.com

HORTON, Anne. *See* HORTON, Canon Roberta Anne

HORTON, Cathy Lynne Bosworth. b 62. BA JD. SEITE. **d** 99 **p** 00. NSM Warlingham w Chelsham and Farleigh *S'wark* 99-03; Assoc P Shaker Heights USA 03-07. *Address temp unknown*

HORTON, Canon Christopher Peter. b 26. Leeds Univ BA49. Coll of Resurr Mirfield 49. **d** 51 **p** 52. C Blyth St Mary *Newc* 51-55; C Delaval 55-59; V Grangetown *York* 59-91; Can and Preb York Minster 85-91; rtd 91; Perm to Offic *Newc* from 91. *51 Well Ridge Close, Seaton Grange, Whitley Bay NE25 9PN* Tel 0191-251 0742

HORTON, David Harold. b 49. St Jo Coll Dur BA72. NEOC 82. **d** 86 **p** 87. C Enfield St Jas *Lon* 86-90; Min Joydens Wood St Barn CD *Roch* 90-93; V Joydens Wood St Barn 93-99; P-in-c Rosherville 99-04; rtd 04. *5B Hawes Road, Bromley BR1 3JS* Tel (020) 8466 9211 E-mail davidhhorton@yahoo.com

HORTON, Canon Jeremy Nicholas Orkney. b 44. Cranmer Hall Dur 64. **d** 68 **p** 69. C Dalton-in-Furness *Carl* 68-70; C Penrith 70-73; V Hudswell w Downholme and Marske *Ripon* 73-75; R Middleton Tyas and Melsonby 75-81; P-in-c Croft 78-81; P-in-c Eryholme 78-81; V Wortley de Leeds 81-93; V Middleton St Mary 93-98; RD Armley 96-98; V Kirby-on-the-Moor, Cundall w Norton-le-Clay etc 98-09; Jt AD Ripon 01-04; Hon Can Ripon Cathl 01-09; rtd 09. *4 Downes Court, 70A South Street, Leominster HR6 8GB* Tel (01568) 610040 Mobile 07527-209028 E-mail nickhorton199@btinternet.com

HORTON, John. b 49. STETS 05. **d** 07 **p** 08. NSM Exhall *Cov* 07-11; NSM Stourdene Gp from 11. *The Vicarage, New Road, Alderminster, Stratford-upon-Avon CV37 8PE* E-mail john@horton6677.freeserve.co.uk

HORTON, John Ward. b 27. Leeds Univ BA50. Coll of Resurr Mirfield 50. **d** 52 **p** 53. C Balkwell CD *Newc* 52-55; C E Coatham *York* 55-58; C-in-c Acomb Moor CD 58-71; V Acomb Moor 71-93; rtd 93; Perm to Offic *Newc* from 93. *39 Billy Mill Lane, North Shields NE29 8BZ* Tel 0191-296 4082

HORTON, Mrs Joy. b 52. CertEd73 Kent Univ MA98. SEITE 94. **d** 97 **p** 98. C Dartford St Edm *Roch* 97-01; Chapl Bromley Hosps NHS Trust 01-02; C Erith St Jo *Roch* 02-03; Perm to Offic 03-04; Chapl Burrswood Chr Cen 04-08; Perm to Offic *St E* from 09. *3 Bracken Row, Thurston, Bury St Edmunds IP31 3PT* Tel (01359) 231976

HORTON, Melanie Jane. b 64. Birm Poly LLB85 Solicitor 86. Ripon Coll Cuddesdon BA95. **d** 96 **p** 97. C Lich St Chad 96-00; Chapl R Masonic Sch for Girls Rickmansworth 00-03; Chapl St Edm Sch Cant 03-08; R Colwall w Upper Colwall and Coddington *Heref* from 08. *The Rectory, Walwyn Road, Colwall, Malvern WR13 6EG* Tel (01684) 540330 Mobile 07748-842825 E-mail colwallrector@tiscali.co.uk

HORTON, Michael John. b 56. St Jo Coll Cam BA80 MA83 Univ of Wales (Swansea) PGCE83. Wycliffe Hall Ox BA88 MA92. **d** 89 **p** 90. C Northallerton w Kirby Sigston *York* 89-92; C Ulverston St Mary w H Trin *Carl* 92-94; V Lightwater *Guildf* 94-04; Chapl Wrekin Coll Telford from 04. *Five Gables, Prospect Road, Wellington, Telford TF1 3BE* Tel (01952) 415059 E-mail michael@hortonfamily.co.uk *or* mjhorton@wrekincollege.ac.uk

HORTON, Nicholas. *See* HORTON, Canon Jeremy Nicholas Orkney

HORTON, Ralph Edward. b 41. S'wark Ord Course 75. **d** 78 **p** 79. C Streatham St Leon *S'wark* 78-81; TV Catford (Southend) and Downham 81-88; V Ashford St Matt *Lon* from 88. *The Vicarage, 99 Church Road, Ashford TW15 2NY* Tel (01784) 252459

HORTON, Canon Roberta Anne. b 44. Leic Univ BSc66 CertEd67 Nottm Univ BCombStuds82. Linc Th Coll 79. **dss** 82 **d** 87 **p** 94. Cambridge St Jas *Ely* 82-86; Beaumont Leys *Leic* 86-91; Par Dn 87-91; Dioc Dir of Tr 91-00; P-in-c Swithland 94-99; R Woodhouse, Woodhouse Eaves and Swithland from 00; Hon Can Leic Cathl from 94. *The Rectory, 157 Main Street, Swithland, Loughborough LE12 8TQ* Tel and fax (01509) 891163 E-mail rahorton@leicester.anglican.org

HORTON, Mrs Wilma Alton. b 46. **d** 06 **p** 07. OLM Alford w Rigsby *Linc* from 06. *6 Wilyman Close, Sandilands, Mablethorpe LN12 2UG* Tel (01507) 443383 E-mail malc.horton@tiscali.co.uk

HORWELL, Elizabeth. b 54. Southn Univ BSc76 Essex Univ MA77 Birm Univ PhD84 Wolv Univ PGCE94. ERMC 04. **d** 07 **p** 08. C Wanstead St Mary w Ch Ch *Chelmsf* 07-11; R from 11. *The Rectory, 37 Wanstead Place, London E11 2SW* Tel (020) 8989 9101 Mobile 07835-450837 E-mail ehorwell@hotmail.com

HORWOOD, Graham Frederick. b 34. Univ of Wales (Cardiff) BA55. Coll of Resurr Mirfield 55. **d** 57 **p** 58. C Llantrisant 57-61; C Roath St Sav 61-62; C Roath 62-66; V Clydach Vale 66-77; V Canton St Luke 77-99; rtd 99. *26 Heol-yr-Onnen, Llanharry, Pontyclun CF72 9NJ* Tel (01443) 225777 E-mail ghorwood@freeuk.com

HORWOOD, Mrs Juliet Joy. b 51. Ex Univ BSc73. SWMTC 09. **d** 11. NSM Topsham *Ex* from 11; NSM Countess Wear from 11. *20 Higher Shapter Street, Topsham, Exeter EX3 0AW* Tel (01392) 875558 E-mail juliet horwood@yahoo.co.uk

HOSKIN, Brian. *See* HOSKIN, Henry Brian

HOSKIN, Canon David William. b 49. Hatf Coll Dur BSc71. Wycliffe Hall Ox 72. **d** 75 **p** 76. C Bridlington Priory *York* 75-78; C Rodbourne Cheney *Bris* 78-79; C Bebington *Ches* 79-82; R Lockington and Lund and Scorborough w Leconfield *York* 82-88; V Beverley St Mary 88-10; RD Beverley 97-07; Can and Preb York Minster 05-10; rtd 10. *24 Chestnut Avenue, Driffield YO25 6SH* E-mail david@hoskin.eu

HOSKIN, Canon Eric James. b 28. St Chad's Coll Dur BA50. **d** 52 **p** 53. C Coney Hill *Glouc* 52-54; C Stroud 54-57; R

Ruardean 57-63; P-in-c Lydbrook 61-63; V Cheltenham Em 63-70; R Dursley 70-86; RD Dursley 77-85; Hon Can Glouc Cathl 81-86; R Easington w Liverton *York* 86-96; rtd 96; Perm to Offic *York* from 96. *37A Algarth Rise, Pocklington, York YO42 2HX* Tel (01759) 305798

HOSKIN, Henry **Brian**. b 32. NW Ord Course 72. **d** 75 **p** 76. NSM Chesterfield St Aug *Derby* 75-79; NSM Bolsover 79-83; NSM Old Brampton and Loundsley Green 83-88; P-in-c Gt Barlow 88-94; rtd 97; Perm to Offic *Derby* from 97. *25 Barn Close, Chesterfield S41 8BD* Tel (01246) 201550

HOSKING, Canon Harold Ernest. b 19. Lich Th Coll 51. **d** 53 **p** 54. C Penwerris *Truro* 53-56; R Mawgan in Pyder 56-61; V Newlyn St Pet 61-69; V Newquay 69-74; TR Redruth 74-80; R Redruth w Lanner 80-84; Hon Can Truro Cathl 78-84; rtd 84; Perm to Offic *Ex* and *Truro* 84-03; *Ely* from 03. *Chestnut Cottage, Tunwells Lane, Great Shelford, Cambridge CB22 5LJ* Tel (01223) 840468

HOSKING, Suzanne Elizabeth. b 68. Wycliffe Hall Ox 07. **d** 10 **p** 11. C St Merryn and St Issey w St Petroc Minor *Truro* from 10. *7 Ivy Close, St Merryn, Padstow PL28 8FA* Tel (01841) 520643 Mobile 07533-310846 E-mail sehosking@hotmail.com

HOSKINS, Hugh George. b 46. S Dios Minl Tr Scheme. **d** 84 **p** 85. NSM Hilperton w Whaddon and Staverton etc *Sarum* 84-87; C Calne and Blackland 87-90; R W Lavington and the Cheverells 90-97; TR Upper Wylye Valley 97-04; RD Heytesbury 00-03; TR Pewsey and Swanborough 04-10; P-in-c Upavon w Rushall and Charlton 07-10; TR Vale of Pewsey from 10. *The Rectory, Church Street, Pewsey SN9 5DL* Tel (01672) 564357 Fax 563203 E-mail hahoskins@aol.com *or* hugh.hoskins@valcofpewsey.org.uk

HOSKINS, John Paul. b 79. Univ Coll Dur BA95 MA96 MLitt07 Trin Coll Cam BA99 MA04 Ox Univ MTh10. Westcott Ho Cam 97 Ripon Coll Cuddesdon 05. **d** 07 **p** 08. C Bakewell *Derby* 07-11; Bp's Chapl *Glouc* from 11. *2 College Green, Gloucester GL1 2LR* Tel (01452) 835513 Fax 308324 E-mail jphoskins@glosdioc.org.uk

HOSKINS, Preb Rosemary Anne. b 56. Surrey Univ BA03. Wesley Coll Bris 99 STETS 01. **d** 02 **p** 03. NSM Camelot Par *B & W* 02-06; NSM Cam Vale from 06; Warden of Readers Wells Adnry 05-09; RD Bruton and Cary from 10; Preb Wells Cathl from 09. *Springfields, Weston Bampfylde, Yeovil BA22 7HZ* Tel (01963) 440026 E-mail revrose@weston-bampfyle.freeserve.co.uk

HOTCHEN, Stephen Jeffrie. b 50. Bradf Coll of Educn. Linc Th Coll 85. **d** 87 **p** 88. C Morpeth *Newc* 87-90; TV High Wycombe *Ox* 90-91; R Dingwall and Strathpeffer *Mor* 91-94; V Rickerscote *Lich* 94-04; R Aylmerton, Runton, Beeston Regis and Gresham *Nor* 04-07; P-in-c Altofts *Wakef* from 07. *The Vicarage, 72A Church Road, Normanton WF6 2QG* Tel (01924) 892299 Mobile 07976-387199 E-mail stephenhotchen@btinternet.com

HOTCHIN, Mrs Hilary Moya. b 52. Birm Univ CertEd73. WMMTC 85. **d** 88 **p** 94. NSM Redditch St Steph *Worc* 88-91; Par Dn Handsworth *Sheff* 91-94; C 94-96; TV Maltby 96-98; NSM Marfleet *York* 06-08; NSM Sutton St Mich from 08. *8 Whisperwood Way, Bransholme, Hull HU7 4JT* Tel (01482) 828015 E-mail hotchin@hotchin.karoo.co.uk

HOUGH, Adrian Michael. b 59. Hertf Coll Ox BA80 MA84 DPhil84 MRSC CChem. Ripon Coll Cuddesdon BA91. **d** 92 **p** 93. C Martley and Wichenford, Knightwick etc *Worc* 92-96; Asst P Evesham Deanery 96-97; V Badsey w Aldington and Offenham and Bretforton 97-04; C Lerwick and Burravoe *Ab* 04-05; Perm to Offic *Worc* 05-06; Bp's Chapl and Asst *Ex* 06-11; Episc V and Chapl IME 4-7 from 08. *2 West Avenue, Exeter EX4 4SD* Tel (01392) 214867 *or* 272362 E-mail adrian.amhough@btinternet.com

HOUGH, Miss Carole Elizabeth. b 59. Lon Hosp SRN81. St Jo Coll Nottm 87. **d** 91 **p** 94. C Beoley *Worc* 91-95; Asst Chapl Addenbrooke's NHS Trust 95-98; Chapl Milton Keynes Hosp NHS Foundn Trust 98-09; Chapl Milton Keynes Primary Care Trust 98-09; Chapl St Jo Hospice Moggerhanger from 10. *St John's Hospice, St John's Road, Moggerhanger, Bedford MK44 3RJ* Tel (01767) 640622 Fax 641262

HOUGH, Michael Jeremy. b 61. Wilson Carlile Coll Oak Hill Th Coll 00. **d** 02 **p** 03. C Redhill H Trin *S'wark* 02-06; P-in-c Woodmansterne 06-11; R from 11. *The Rectory, Woodmansterne Street, Banstead SM7 3NL* Tel (01737) 352849 Mobile 07939-088867 E-mail mickhough@hotmail.com

HOUGH, Peter George. b 40. Dur Univ BA62. Wells Th Coll 62. **d** 64 **p** 65. C Stocking Farm CD *Leic* 64-68; V Leic St Aid 68-76; V Knutton *Lich* 76-05; P-in-c Silverdale and Alsagers Bank 93-94; V Alsagers Bank 01-05; rtd 05. *2 Station Road, Keele, Newcastle ST5 5AH* Tel (01782) 624282

HOUGH, Sharron Lesley. b 54. **d** 01 **p** 02. OLM Willenhall H Trin *Lich* 01-05; C Bentley 05-09; P-in-c 09-11; TV Bentley Em and Willenhall H Trin from 11. *10 Pineneedle Croft, Willenhall WV12 4BY* Tel (01902) 410458

HOUGH, Wendy Lorraine. b 63. Trin Coll Bris BA94 LLAM81. Cranmer Hall Dur 98. **d** 00 **p** 01. C The Hague *Eur* 00-03; Asst

Chapl Berne w Neuchâtel 05-07; C Bris St Mary Redcliffe w Temple etc from 07; Chapl St Mary Redcliffe and Temple Sch from 07. *2 Colston Parade, Bristol BS1 6RA* Tel 0117-930 0036 E-mail wendy@stmaryredcliffe.co.uk

HOUGHTON, Christopher Guy. b 64. W Surrey Coll of Art & Design BA86. Oak Hill Th Coll BA89. **d** 89 **p** 90. C Mossley Hill St Matt and St Jas *Liv* 89-92; C Ashton-in-Makerfield St Thos 92-95; C Southport St Phil and St Paul 95-96; Chapl Chorley and S Ribble NHS Trust 96-01; rtd 01; Perm to Offic *Blackb* from 03. *35 Deerfold, Chorley PR7 1UD*

HOUGHTON, David John. b 47. Edin Univ BSc(Econ)68. Cuddesdon Coll 69. **d** 71 **p** 72. C Prestbury *Glouc* 71-74; Prec Gib Cathl 74-76; Chapl Madrid 76-78; C Croydon St Jo *Cant* 78-80; Chapl Warw Sch 80-85; P-in-c Isleworth St Fran *Lon* 85-90; USA 90-91; TV Clapham Team *S'wark* 91-01; RD Clapham 93-01; V Clapham H Spirit 02; Chapl Paris St Geo *Eur* 02-07; P-in-c Surbiton St Andr and St Mark *S'wark* 07-10; V from 10; AD Kingston from 09. *The Vicarage, St Mark's Hill, Surbiton KT6 4LS* Tel (020) 8390 7749 E-mail davidhoughton@wanadoo.fr

HOUGHTON, Mrs Evelyn Mabel. b 44. Stockwell Coll of Educn TCert65. Oak Hill NSM Course 92. **d** 94 **p** 95. NSM Bedford St Jo and St Leon *St Alb* 94-98; C Reading St Agnes w St Paul *Ox* 98-10; rtd 10; Perm to Offic *St Alb* from 10. *1 Peashill Lane, Great Barford, Bedford MK44 3HG* Tel (01234) 871915 E-mail evehoughton@dsl.pipex.com

HOUGHTON, Ms Frances Mary. **d** 11. OLM Clifton H Trin, St Andr and St Pet *Bris* from 11. *3 Woodlands, Bridge Road, Leigh Woods, Bristol BS8 3PB* Tel 0117-973 9792 E-mail frances.houghton@virgin.net

HOUGHTON, Canon Geoffrey John. b 59. Ridley Hall Cam 87. **d** 90 **p** 91. C Sholing *Win* 90-94; P-in-c Jersey All SS 94-99; V 99-09; P-in-c Jersey St Simon 94-99; V 99-09; P-in-c Jersey H Trin 05-06; Vice-Dean Jersey from 99; Hon Chapl Jersey Hospice from 96; Hon Can Win Cathl from 11. *Holy Trinity Rectory, La Rue du Presbytere, Trinity, Jersey JE3 5JB* Tel and fax (01534) 861110 E-mail geoffhoughton@jerseymail.co.uk *or* gjh@super.net.uk

HOUGHTON, Graham. *See* HOUGHTON, Peter Graham

HOUGHTON, Hugh Alexander Gervase. b 76. St Jo Coll Cam BA97 MPhil98 MA01 Leeds Univ BA02 Birm Univ PhD06. Coll of Resurr Mirfield 00. **d** 03 **p** 04. NSM Weoley Castle *Birm* 03-06; NSM Headington Quarry *Ox* 06-09; Perm to Offic *Birm* from 09; Research Fell Birm Univ from 06. *68 Camp Lane, Handsworth, Birmingham B21 8JR* Tel 0121-682 1150 E-mail h.a.g.houghton@bham.ac.uk

HOUGHTON, Ian David. b 50. Lanc Univ BA71 Newc Univ CertEd74. Sarum & Wells Th Coll 80. **d** 82 **p** 83. C Newc St Geo 82-85; Chapl Newc Poly 85-92; Chapl Northumbria Univ 92-95; Master Newc St Thos Prop Chpl 90-95; Ind Chapl Black Country Urban Ind Miss *Lich* 95-04; Res Min Bilston 95-04; Chapl Pet City Cen 04-08; C Pet St Jo 04-08; P-in-c Osmotherley w Harlsey and Ingleby Arncliffe *York* 08-09; V from 09; P-in-c Leake w Over and Nether Silton and Kepwick 08-09; V from 09; P-in-c Felixkirk w Boltby 08-09; V from 09; P-in-c Kirkby Knowle 08-09; V from 09; P-in-c Cowesby 08-09; R from 09. *Leake Vicarage, Knayton, Thirsk YO7 4AZ* Tel (01845) 537277 E-mail ian.houghton@tiscali.co.uk

HOUGHTON, James Robert. b 44. AKC67 St Luke's Coll Ex CertEd73. St Boniface Warminster 67. **d** 68 **p** 69. C Herrington *Dur* 68-70; Asst Dioc Youth Chapl *Bris* 70-72; Perm to Offic *Ex* 73-74; C Heavitree 74-78; Perm to Offic *Lon* 78-80 and 83-88; Hon C W Drayton 80-83; Chapl Greycoat Hosp Sch 83-88; Chapl Stonar Sch Melksham 88-95; Chapl St Mary and St Anne's Sch Abbots Bromley 95-99; R Buxted and Hadlow Down *Chich* 99-02; V Eastbourne St Mich 02-08; rtd 09; Perm to Offic *Cant* from 09. *12A Audburnham Court, Earls Avenue, Folkestone CT20 2PN* Tel 07955-242324 (mobile) E-mail jamiehoughton@live.com

HOUGHTON, Josephine Elizabeth Mayer. b 80. Birm Univ BA01 PhD07. St Steph Ho Ox BA09. **d** 09 **p** 10. C Handsworth St Andr *Birm* from 09. *68 Camp Lane, Handsworth, Birmingham B21 8JR* Tel 0121-682 1150 E-mail josephine@houghtons.org.uk

HOUGHTON, Peter **Graham**. b 51. St Jo Coll Nottm 85. **d** 87 **p** 88. C Toxteth Park St Clem *Liv* 87-91; Chapl Winwick Hosp Warrington 91-94; Chapl Warrington Community Health Care NHS Trust 94-98; Chapl HM Pris Styal 98-01; Chapl St Helens and Knowsley Hosps NHS Trust 04-05. *40 Grange Drive, Penketh, Warrington WA5 2JN*

HOUGHTON, Prof Peter John. b 47. Chelsea Coll Lon BPharm68 PhD73 FRPharmS93 FRSC94. Dioc OLM tr scheme 05. **d** 08 **p** 09. NSM Balham Hill Ascension *S'wark* from 08. *7 Culverden Road, London SW12 9LR* Tel (020) 8673 7884 Mobile 07734-747688 E-mail peter.houghton@kcl.ac.uk

HOUGHTON, Mrs Rosemary Margaret Anne. b 46. **d** 00 **p** 01. OLM Earlham *Nor* from 00. *74 St Mildred's Road, West Earlham, Norwich NR5 8RS* Tel (01603) 502752 Mobile 07808-774811 E-mail rosemary.houghton@ntlworld.com

HOUGHTON, Mrs Susan Jeanette. b 39. Qu Mary Coll Lon BSc61 Nottm Univ PGCE62. WMMTC 98. **d** 99 **p** 00. OLM Dursley *Glouc* 99-02; rtd 02; NSM Offwell, Northleigh, Farway, Cotleigh etc *Ex* 02-09. *2 Combewater Cottages, Wilmington, Honiton EX14 9SQ* Tel (01404) 831887
E-mail sue.houghton2@btinternet.com

HOUGHTON, Thomas. b 17. NW Ord Course 71. **d** 74 **p** 75. NSM Newcastle w Butterton *Lich* 74-82; Perm to Offic from 82. *Madeley Manor Nursing Home, Heighley Castle Way, Madeley, Crewe CW3 9HF* Tel (01782) 750610

HOUGHTON, Timothy John. b 56. Kingston Poly BSc88. Oak Hill Th Coll BA93. **d** 97 **p** 98. C Normanton *Derby* 97-03. *Address temp unknown*

HOULDEN, Prof James Leslie. b 29. Qu Coll Ox BA52 MA56. Cuddesdon Coll 53. **d** 55 **p** 56. C Hunslet St Mary and Stourton *Ripon* 55-58; Tutor Chich Th Coll 58-59; Chapl 59-60; Chapl Trin Coll Ox 60-70; Prin Cuddesdon Coll 70-75; Prin Ripon Coll Cuddesdon 75-77; V Cuddesdon *Ox* 70-77; Hon Can Ch Ch 76-77; Sen Lect NT Studies K Coll Lon 77-87; Prof Th 87-94; rtd 94; Perm to Offic *S'wark* 94-99 and *Birm* from 99. *5 The Court, Fen End Road West, Knowle, Solihull B93 0AN* Tel (01564) 777138 E-mail leslie.houlden@btopenworld.com

HOULDING, Preb David Nigel Christopher. b 53. AKC76. **d** 77 **p** 78. C Hillingdon All SS *Lon* 77-81; C Holborn St Alb w Saffron Hill St Pet 81-85; V Hampstead St Steph w All Hallows from 85; AD N Camden 01-02; Preb St Paul's Cathl from 04. *All Hallows' House, 52 Courthope Road, London NW3 2LD* Tel (020) 7267 7833 *or* 7267 6317 Fax 7267 6317 Mobile 07710-403294 E-mail fr.houlding@lineone.net

HOULDSWORTH, Raymond Clifford. b 30. Bps' Coll Cheshunt 64. **d** 66 **p** 67. C Egham Hythe *Guildf* 66-70; C Cranbrook *Cant* 70-76; V Hernhill 76-82; V Minster w Monkton 82-95; rtd 95; Perm to Offic *Mon* from 95. *St Illtyd's, 11 Craig Road, Six Bells, Abertillery NP13 2LR* Tel (01495) 321934

HOULT, Roy Anthony. b 35. AKC58. **d** 59 **p** 60. C Walton St Mary *Liv* 59-63; Canada from 63; Hon Can Koot 75-79. *381 Huron Street, Toronto ON M5S 2G5, Canada*

HOULTON, David Andrew. b 58. Bradf Univ BEng80 MPhil86 CEng90 EurIng90 FIChemE98. Wycliffe Hall Ox BTh11. **d** 09 **p** 10. C Old Trafford St Bride *Man* from 09. *Flat 1, 78 Northumberland Road, Manchester M16 9PP* Tel 0161-872 4321 E-mail david.houlton@stbrides.org.uk

HOULTON, Neil James. b 54. STETS 04. **d** 07 **p** 08. NSM Pokesdown St Jas *Win* from 07; NSM Boscombe St Andr from 10. *27 Rebbeck Road, Bournemouth BH7 6LW* Tel (01202) 462476 E-mail neil.houlton@ntlworld.com

HOUNSELL, Mrs Susan Mary. b 49. STETS 04. **d** 07 **p** 08. NSM W Monkton *B & W* 07-11; NSM W Monkton w Kingston St Mary, Broomfield etc from 11. *33 Home Orchard, Hatch Beauchamp, Taunton TA3 6TG* Tel (01823) 480545 E-mail susanhounsell@tiscali.co.uk

HOUSE, Graham Ivor. b 44. Oak Hill Th Coll BA80. **d** 80 **p** 81. C Ipswich St Jo *St E* 80-84; V Ipswich St Andr 84-00; R Monks Eleigh w Chelsworth and Brent Eleigh etc 00-03; rtd 03; Perm to Offic *St E* from 03. *6 Through Duncans, Woodbridge IP12 4EA* Tel (01394) 386066 Mobile 07966-169372

HOUSE, Jack Francis. b 35. Bris Univ BEd70 Lon Univ MA80 Univ of Wales MTh94. Bris & Glouc Tr Course 79. **d** 80 **p** 81. NSM Bedminster *Bris* 80-92; Perm to Offic 92-94; NSM Knowle H Nativity 94-03; NSM Easton All Hallows 98-03; NSM Brislington St Anne 03-05; rtd 05; Perm to Offic *Bris* from 05. *48 Hendre Road, Bristol BS3 2LR* Tel 0117-966 1144 E-mail rhouse3766@talktalk.net

HOUSE, Mrs Janet. b 45. UEA BA67 Keswick Hall Coll PGCE68 Sussex Univ MA80. Ripon Coll Cuddesdon 93. **d** 95 **p** 96. C Swindon Ch Ch *Bris* 95-99; TV Worc SE 99-06; rtd 06; Perm to Offic *Nor* from 06. *11 Caernarvon Road, Norwich NR2 3HZ* Tel (01603) 762259 E-mail jhouse@waitrose.com

HOUSE, Miss Maureen Ruth (Mo). b 33. St Mich Ho Ox 56 LNSM course 95. **d** 98 **p** 99. NSM Charlton *S'wark* from 98. *88 Speedwell Street, London SE8 4AT* Tel (020) 8691 1637 *or* 8316 7695 E-mail plumbhouse@88speedwell.freeserve.co.uk

HOUSE, Simon Hutchinson. b 30. Peterho Cam BA65 MA67. Cuddesdon Coll 61. **d** 64 **p** 65. C Sutton St Jas *York* 64-67; C Acomb St Steph 67-69; V Allestree St Nic *Derby* 69-81; RD Duffield 74-81; V Bitterne Park *Win* 81-91; rtd 91; Perm to Offic *Win* from 91. *22 Stanley Street, Southsea PO5 2DS* Tel (023) 9283 8592

HOUSE, Vickery Willis. b 45. Kelham Th Coll. **d** 69 **p** 70. C Crediton *Ex* 69-76; TV Sampford Peverell, Uplowman, Holcombe Rogus etc 76-81; R Berwick w Selmeston and Alciston *Chich* 81-90; Chapl Ardingly Coll 90-94; V Brighton St Bart *Chich* 94-10; rtd 10. *1 Jessamine Cottages, Brighton Road, Handcross, Haywards Heath RH17 6BU* Tel (01444) 401496 E-mail vic4khouse@hotmail.com

HOUSEMAN, Patricia Adele. *See* CAMPION, Mrs Patricia Adele

HOUSLEY, Andrew Arthur. b 67. Wilson Carlile Coll 91 Ridley Hall Cam. **d** 02 **p** 03. C Ormskirk *Liv* 02-06; V Litherland

St Phil 06-09; R Aughton St Mich and Bickerstaffe from 09. *The Rectory, 10 Church Lane, Aughton, Ormskirk L39 6SB* Tel (01695) 423204 E-mail andrewjohousley@ukonline.co.uk

HOUSMAN, Arthur Martin Rowand. b 53. MA CertEd. Trin Coll Bris 81. **d** 83 **p** 84. C Croydon Ch Ch Broad Green *Cant* 83-84; C Croydon Ch Ch *S'wark* 85-87; TV Stratton St Margaret w S Marston etc *Bris* 87-93; Chapl Peterhouse Sch Zimbabwe 93-98; Chapl Nor Sch 98-07; Hon PV Nor Cathl 98-07; Hon C Raveningham Gp from 08. *Orchards, Beccles Road, Raveningham, Norwich NR14 6NW* Tel (01508) 548322 Mobile 07790-944860 E-mail orchardsone@uwclub.net

HOUSTON, Canon Arthur James. b 54. Trin Coll Bris BA87. **d** 87 **p** 88. C Chatham St Phil and St Jas *Roch* 87-91; I Carrigaline Union *C, C & R* 91-99; Can Cork Cathl 95-99; Can Ross Cathl 95-99; Dir of Ords 96-99; V Margate H Trin *Cant* 99-08; P-in-c Maidstone St Paul 08-10; AD Thanet 02-08; AD Maidstone 08-10; P-in-c Minster-in-Sheppey from 10; Hon Can Cant Cathl from 08. *4 Church Square, Lenham, Maidstone ME17 2PJ* Tel (01622) 858020
E-mail arthurjhouston@googlemail.com

HOUSTON, David William James. b 52. Th Ext Educn Coll. **d** 93 **p** 95. C Lyttelton S Africa 93-96; R Sabie w Lydenburg 96-00; P-in-c Elmsted w Hastingleigh *Cant* 00-06; P-in-c Petham and Waltham w Lower Hardres etc 00-06; V Stone Street Gp 06; R Southfleet *Roch* from 06. *The Rectory, Hook Green Road, Southfleet, Gravesend DA13 9NQ* Tel (01474) 833252
E-mail david@houstonclan.net

HOUSTON, Edward Davison. b 31. TCD BA56. **d** 57 **p** 58. C Conwall Union *D & R* 57-59; India 59-88; V Whittlebury w Paulerspury *Pet* 89-01; P-in-c Wicken 89-01; rtd 01; Perm to Offic *Pet* from 01. *38 Meadow Street, Market Harborough LE16 7JZ* Tel (01858) 433309

HOUSTON, Helen Sarah. b 70. Bris Univ BA91. St Jo Coll Nottm MA95. **d** 95 **p** 96. C Bourne *Guildf* 95-98; Perm to Offic *Bris* 98-99; Hon C Chippenham St Pet 99-00; C Ballyholme *D & D* 02-04; C Stretton and Appleton Thorn *Ches* 04-05; Asst to RD Gt Budworth 05; Chapl St Rocco's Hospice from 05; Hon C Stockton Heath *Ches* from 08. *St Rocco's Hospice, Lockton Lane, Bewsey, Warrington WA5 5BW* Tel (01925) 575780 *or* 211466 Fax 419777 E-mail helen@davehouston.fsnet.co.uk

HOUSTON, Kenneth. *See* HOUSTON, Prof Samuel Kenneth

HOUSTON, Maurice Iain. b 48. TISEC 99. **d** 02 **p** 03. C Edin Old St Paul 02-05; R Melrose from 05. *The Rectory, 20 High Cross Avenue, Melrose TD6 9SU* Tel (01896) 822626 Mobile 07866-074568 E-mail morrishouston@btinternet.com

HOUSTON, Michael Alexander. b 46. Lanc Univ MA92. Linc Th Coll 86. **d** 88 **p** 89. C Longton *Blackb* 88-91; C Woughton *Ox* 91-92; TV 92-98; TR 98-99; TR Gd Shep TM *Carl* 99-07; rtd 07. *East Wing, Eden Place, Kirkby Stephen CA17 4AP* Tel (01768) 371356 E-mail mike.greystoke@tiscali.co.uk

HOUSTON, Michael James. b 41. Dub Bible Coll St Jo Coll Nottm. **d** 95 **p** 97. Aux Min *D & D* 95-99; P-in-c Ballyphilip w Ardquin 99-07; Chapl Kyrenia St Andr Cyprus from 07. *PO Box 171, Girne, Mersin 10, Turkey* Tel (0090) (392) 815 4329 E-mail standrews@gawab.com

HOUSTON, Prof Samuel Kenneth. b 43. QUB BSc64 PhD67 FIMA73 MILT. CITC 81. **d** 85 **p** 86. NSM Belfast St Jas w St Silas *Conn* 85-91; NSM Belfast St Andr from 91; Prof Mathematical Studies Ulster Univ from 96. *29 North Circular Road, Belfast BT15 5HB* Tel (028) 9077 1830 *or* 9036 6953 Fax 9036 6859 Mobile 07929-725319
E-mail sk.houston@north-circular.demon.co.uk

HOUSTON, William Paul. b 54. QUB BSsc76 TCD BTh78. CITC 78. **d** 81 **p** 82. C Carrickfergus *Conn* 81-83; C Bangor St Comgall *D & D* 83-86; I Gilford 86-90; I Carnalea 90-99; I Clondalkin w Rathcoole *D & G* 99-09; I Castleknock and Mulhuddart w Clonsilla from 09; Min Can St Patr Cathl Dublin from 00. *The Rectory, 12 Hawthorn Lawn, Castleknock, Dublin 15, Republic of Ireland* Tel (00353) (1) 821 3083

HOVENDEN, Gerald Eric. b 53. York Univ BA75 Ox Univ MA85. Wycliffe Hall Ox 78. **d** 81 **p** 82. C Pitsmoor w Ellesmere *Sheff* 81-85; Chapl Lyon w Grenoble and St Etienne *Eur* 85-90; TV S Gillingham *Roch* 90-98; TR Southborough St Pet w Ch Ch and St Matt etc from 98. *The Vicarage, 86 Prospect Road, Southborough, Tunbridge Wells TN4 0EG* Tel (01892) 528534 *or* tel and fax 513680
E-mail gerald.hovenden@diocese-rochester.org

HOVEY, Richard Michael. b 58. City Univ Lon BScEng79 Cranfield Inst of Tech MBA84 CEng83 MIET83 EurIng73. Cranmer Hall Dur 93. **d** 95 **p** 96. C Cheddar *B & W* 95-99; TV Gtr Corsham *Bris* 99-01; TV Gtr Corsham and Lacock 01-05; S Team Ldr CMS from 05. *80 High Street, Corsham SN13 0HF* Tel (01249) 715407 E-mail crockford@richardhovey.co.uk

HOVIL, Jeremy Richard Guy. b 65. K Coll Lon BSc88 Spurgeon's Coll Lon MTh99 Stellenbosch Univ ThD05. Wycliffe Hall Ox BTh95. **d** 95 **p** 96. C Kensington St Barn *Lon* 95-99; Crosslinks Uganda 00-07; Field Dir Trust in Chr S Africa from 07. *11 Upper*

Towers Road, Muizenberg, Cape Town, 7945 South Africa Tel (0027) (21) 788 3313 Mobile 76-120 5888 E-mail jem@trustinchrist.org

HOVIL, Richard Guy. b 29. Ex Coll Ox BA51 MA57. Ridley Hall Cam. **d** 55 **p** 56. C Finchley Ch Ch *Lon* 55-58; Staff Worker Scripture Union 58-71; Chapl Monkton Combe Sch Bath 71-83; V Fremington *Ex* 83-94; rtd 94; Perm to Offic *Sarum* from 94. *22 The Downlands, Warminster BA12 9PN* Tel (01985) 214337 E-mail ricjanhovil@blueyonder.co.uk

HOW, Gillian Carol. See BUNCE, Gillian Carol

HOW, Canon John Maxloe. b 15. Magd Coll Cam BA37 MA49. Westcott Ho Cam 39. **d** 39 **p** 40. C Norton St Mary *Dur* 39-44; P-in-c W Pelton 44-45; P-in-c Stella 46-47; V Thornley 47-51; V Monkwearmouth St Andr 51-59; V Barton w Pooley Bridge *Carl* 59-73; RD Penrith 61-73; Hon Can Carl Cathl 72-81; V Kirkby Lonsdale w Mansergh 73-76; TR Kirkby Lonsdale 76-81; rtd 81; Perm to Offic *Carl* from 81. *The Laurels, 3 Belle Isle Terrace, Grange-over-Sands LA11 6EA* Tel (01539) 534117

HOWARD, Alan James. b 45. Bris Univ BA69. Clifton Th Coll. **d** 71 **p** 72. C Welling *Roch* 71-74; C Cromer *Nor* 74-78; V Sidcup St Andr *Roch* 78-86; V Leyton St Cath *Chelmsf* 86-93; V Leyton St Cath and St Paul 93-00; rtd 05. *4 Bower Close, Romford RM5 3SR* Tel (01708) 760905

HOWARD, Andrew. b 63. Man Univ BA95 Leeds Univ MA97. Coll of Resurr Mirfield 95. **d** 97 **p** 98. C Worksop Priory *S'well* 97-01; V Hemlington *York* 01-05; Chapl Teesside Univ from 05; C Middlesbrough St Jo the Ev from 05; C Middlesbrough St Columba w St Paul from 05. *St John's Vicarage, 45 Lothian Road, Middlesbrough TS4 2HS* Tel (01642) 242926 or 342708 E-mail a.howard@tees.ac.uk

HOWARD, Arthur Calvin. b 60. Leeds Univ LLB82 Barrister 83. Wycliffe Hall Ox 00. **d** 03 **p** 04. C Heswall *Ches* 03-04; C Weston 04-07; Chapl E Lancs Hospice 09-11; C Bispham *Blackb* from 11. *1 Prenton Gardens, Thornton-Cleveleys FY5 3RR* Tel (01253) 855283 E-mail calvin.howard@googlemail.com

HOWARD, Charles William Wykeham. b 52. Southn Univ BTh81. Sarum & Wells Th Coll 76. **d** 79 **p** 80. C St Mary-at-Latton *Chelmsf* 79-82; Chapl RN 82-06; Chapl Midi-Pyrénées and Aude *Eur* 06-09; V Funtington and Sennicotts *Chich* from 10. *The Vicarage, Church Lane, Funtington, Chichester PO18 9LH* Tel (01243) 575127 E-mail charlesww.howard@tiscali.co.uk

HOWARD, Clive Eric. b 65. Oak Hill Th Coll BA99. **d** 99 **p** 00. C Chipping Sodbury and Old Sodbury *Glouc* 99-03; V Tipton St Matt *Lich* from 03. *St Matthew's Vicarage, Dudley Road, Tipton DY4 8DJ* Tel 0121-557 1929 E-mail clive-howard@rev65.fsnet.co.uk

HOWARD, Daniel James. b 71. Nottm Univ BA94. Oak Hill Th Coll 04. **d** 06 **p** 07. C Deane *Man* 06-09; V Thornton Hough *Ches* from 09. *All Saints' Vicarage, Raby Road, Thornton Hough, Wirral CH63 1JP* Tel 0151-336 3429 *or* 336 1654

HOWARD, David John. b 47. Brasted Th Coll 68 Ripon Hall Ox 70. **d** 72 **p** 73. C Benchill *Man* 06-09; V Sedgley All SS *Lich* 75-77; C-in-c Lostock CD *Man* 77-85; V Lt Hulton 85-88; Perm to Offic 90-91; C E Leake *S'well* 91-92; C Costock 91-92; C Rempstone 91-92; C Stanford on Soar 91-92; C W Leake w Kingston-on-Soar and Ratcliffe-on-Soar 91-92; C E and W Leake, Stanford-on-Soar, Rempstone etc 92-94; P-in-c Bilborough w Strelley 94-98; Chapl HM YOI Werrington Ho 98-03; Chapl HM Pris Drake Hall from 03. *HM Prison and YOI Drake Hall, Eccleshall, Stafford ST21 6LQ* Tel (01785) 774144 E-mail david.howard3@hmps.gsi.gov.uk

HOWARD, David John. b 51. Lon Univ BSc73. Oak Hill Th Coll 74. **d** 77 **p** 78. C Radipole and Melcombe Regis *Sarum* 77-83; R Tredington and Darlingscott w Newbold on Stour *Cov* 83-90; P-in-c Binley 90-94; V 94-04; RD Cov E 95-99; V Potterne w Worton and Marston *Sarum* from 04. *The Vicarage, 4 Rookes Lane, Potterne, Devizes SN10 5NF* Tel (01380) 723189 E-mail howard@binleyvicarage.fsnet.co.uk

HOWARD, Mrs Erika Kathryn. b 49. SRN70 SCM72. S Dios Minl Tr Scheme 88. **d** 91 **p** 94. NSM New Shoreham and Old Shoreham *Chich* 91-94; C Kingston Buci 94-03; V Sompting from 03. *The Vicarage, West Street, Sompting, Lancing BN15 0AP* Tel (01903) 234511 E-mail rev.erikahoward@ntlworld.com

HOWARD, Canon Francis Curzon. b 27. St Aid Birkenhead 54. **d** 57 **p** 58. C Claughton cum Grange *Ches* 57-60; C Cheltenham St Paul *Glouc* 60-62; V Sheff St Barn 62-65; R Sandys Bermuda 65-71; Asst P Westfield Atonement USA 71-76; R Tariffville 76-98; rtd 98; Can Kaduna from 95. *PO Box 423, Simsbury CT 06070-0423, USA* Tel (001) (860) 658 1897

HOWARD, Frank Thomas. b 36. Lon Univ BSc57. Bps' Coll Cheshunt 59. **d** 61 **p** 62. C Macclesfield St Mich *Ches* 61-64; C Claughton cum Grange 64-66; V Lache cum Saltney 66-76; R Stanton *St E* 76-97; RD Ixworth 79-85; P-in-c Hempnall *Nor* 97-01; rtd 01; Perm to Offic *Nor* from 01. *55 Heywood Avenue, Diss IP22 4DN* Tel (01379) 640819

HOWARD, Geoffrey. b 30. Barrister-at-Law 83 Lon Univ LLB77. EMMTC. **d** 85 **p** 86. NSM Barton *Ely* 85-87; NSM Coton 85-87;

C W Walton 87-92; TV Daventry, Ashby St Ledgers, Braunston etc *Pet* 92-97; rtd 97; Perm to Offic *Ely* 97-00 and from 07. *11 Porson Court, Porson Road, Cambridge CB2 8ER* Tel (01223) 300738 E-mail geoffreyhoward@btinternet.com

HOWARD, Geoffrey. b 45. St Jo Coll Dur BA68. Cranmer Hall Dur 67. **d** 71 **p** 72. C Cheetham Hill *Man* 71-74; C Denton Ch Ch 74-77; V Pendleton St Ambrose 77-91; TR Pendleton St Thos w Charlestown 91-94; AD Salford 86-94; Perm to Offic from 04. *20 May Road, Swinton, Manchester M27 5FR* Tel 0161-950 7778 E-mail geoffrey.howard@ntlworld.com

HOWARD, Canon George Granville. b 47. Trin Coll Bris. **d** 88 **p** 89. C Downend *Bris* 88-92; V Clifton H Trin, St Andr and St Pet 92-99; Bp's Officer for Miss and Evang 92-99; V W Streatham St Jas *S'wark* from 99; P-in-c Streatham St Paul from 10; AD Tooting 02-07; Hon Can S'wark Cathl from 10. *St James's Vicarage, 236 Mitcham Lane, London SW16 6NT* Tel (020) 8664 6059 *or* 8677 3947 E-mail ghoward@ukonline.co.uk

HOWARD, George Victor Richard. b 69. Northn Univ MBA06. Ripon Coll Cuddesdon 07. **d** 09 **p** 10. C Iver *Ox* from 09. *6 Lawn Close, Datchet, Slough SL3 9JZ* Tel (01753) 591703 E-mail georgehoward01@btinternet.com

HOWARD, John. See HOWARD, Nicolas John

HOWARD, John Alexander. b 27. Wesley Coll Leeds 48 Coll of Resurr Mirfield 66. **d** 67 **p** 68. C Almondbury *Wakef* 67-71; V Skelmanthorpe 71-81; R Fontmoor *Mor* 81-94; R Cromarty 81-94; R Arpafeelie 81-94; rtd 94; Perm to Offic *Glouc* from 94. *2 Webbs Cottages, Stratford Road, Mickleton, Chipping Campden GL55 6SW*

HOWARD, Canon John Robert. b 60. NUI BA HDipEd. **d** 84 **p** 85. C Donaghcloney w Waringstown *D & D* 84-88; I Belfast St Ninian *Conn* 88-94; Bp's Dom Chapl 89-94; Chapl Ulster Univ 88-94; I Annahilt w Magherahamlet *D & D* from 94; Can Dromore Cathl from 06; Chapl HM Pris Maghaberry from 96. *Annahilt Rectory, 15 Ballykeel Road, Hillsborough BT26 6NW* Tel (028) 9263 8218 E-mail jrobert.howard@btinternet.com

HOWARD, Mrs Judith Marion. b 46. WEMTC 98. **d** 01 **p** 02. NSM Glouc St Jas and All SS 01-10; NSM Glouc St Jas and All SS and Ch Ch from 10. *Paulmead, Wells Road, Bisley, Stroud GL6 7AG* Tel (01452) 770776 E-mail judy.howard@homecall.co.uk

HOWARD, Keith. b 55. St Jo Coll Nottm 81. **d** 84 **p** 85. C Llanidloes w Llangurig *Ban* 84-87; R Llansantffraid Glan Conwy and Eglwysbach *St As* 87-00; V Heapey and Withnell *Blackb* 00-07; V Hooton *Ches* from 07. *Hooton Vicarage, Chester Road, Childer Thornton, Ellesmere Port CH66 1QF* Tel 0151-339 1655

HOWARD, Martin John Aidan. b 68. Lon Univ BA90 Open Univ MA96. St Jo Coll Nottm MA97. **d** 97 **p** 98. C Billericay and Lt Burstead *Chelmsf* 97-01; TV Kinson *Sarum* 01-06; TV Hampreston 06-08; TR from 08. *The Vicarage, 3 Dudsbury Road, West Parley, Ferndown BH22 8RA* Tel (01202) 876552 E-mail office@stmarys-ferndown.org.uk

HOWARD, Canon Michael Charles. b 35. Selw Coll Cam BA58 MA63 CQSW72. Wycliffe Hall Ox 58. **d** 60 **p** 61. C Stowmarket *St E* 60-64; CMS Nigeria 64-71; Hon Can Ondo 70-71; Hon C Southborough St Pet w Ch Ch and St Matt *Roch* 72-73; Perm to Offic *Ox* from 73; rtd 00. *17 Milton Road, Bloxham, Banbury OX15 4HD* Tel (01295) 720470

HOWARD, Michael John. b 51. Redland Coll of Educn CertEd74 Open Univ BA78. **d** 09 **p** 10. OLM Ness Gp *Linc* from 09. *East Dean House, East End, Langtoft, Peterborough PE6 9LP* Tel (01778) 349576 E-mail michaelj.howard@virgin.net

HOWARD, Natalie Delia. b 51. St Mich Coll Llan 99. **d** 02 **p** 03. NSM Magor *Mon* from 02. *8 The Meadows, Magor, Caldicot NP26 3LA* Tel (01633) 881714

HOWARD, Nicolas John. b 61. Nottm Univ BTh90. Aston Tr Scheme 85 Linc Th Coll 87. **d** 90 **p** 91. C Bracknell *Ox* 90-94; P-in-c Oldham St Chad Limeside *Man* 94-96; Perm to Offic *Birm* 96-99. *11 Chesterfield Court, Middleton Hall Road, Birmingham B30 1AF* Tel 0121-459 4975

HOWARD, Norman. b 26. AKC57. St Boniface Warminster 57. **d** 58 **p** 59. C Friern Barnet St Jas *Lon* 58-62; Jamaica 62-69; USA from 69; rtd 91. *766 Lake Forest Road, Clearwater FL 33765-2231, USA* Tel (001) (813) 799 3929

HOWARD, Paul David. b 47. Lanchester Poly Cov BA69. St Jo Coll Nottm 74. **d** 77 **p** 78. C Bedworth *Cov* 77-83; V Newchapel *Lich* 83-93; V Stretton w Claymills 93-04; P-in-c Talke 04-10; R from 10; Chapl Newcastle-under-Lyme Primary Care Trust from 07. *The Rectory, 26 Crown Bank, Talke, Stoke-on-Trent ST7 1PU* Tel (01782) 782348 E-mail paul.howard510.freeserve.co.uk

HOWARD, Canon Peter Leslie. b 48. Nottm Univ BTh77 Birm Univ MA80 Leeds Univ MEd91. St Jo Coll Nottm LTh77. **d** 77 **p** 78. C Gospel Lane St Mich *Birm* 77-81; P-in-c Nechells 81-85; V Stanley *Wakef* 85-92; P-in-c Nor Heartsease St Fran from 92; Dioc UPA/CUF Link Officer from 02; RD Nor E from 06; Hon Can Nor Cathl from 06. *St Francis's Vicarage, 100 Rider Haggard Road, Norwich NR7 9UQ* Tel (01603) 702799 E-mail plhoward@btinternet.com

HOWARD, Robert. See HOWARD, Canon John Robert

HOWARD, Canon Robert Weston (Robin). b 28. Pemb Coll Cam BA49 MA53. Westcott Ho Cam 51. **d** 53 **p** 54. C Bishopwearmouth St Mich *Dur* 53-56; C Cambridge Gt St Mary w St Mich *Ely* 56-60; Hong Kong 60-66; V Prenton *Ches* 66-75; RD Frodsham 74-82; P-in-c Dunham-on-the-Hill 75-77; V Helsby and Ince 75-77; V Helsby and Dunham-on-the-Hill 77-82; Hon Can Ches Cathl 78-82; V Moseley St Mary *Birm* 82-88; V Chalke Valley W *Sarum* 88-93; rtd 93; Perm to Offic *St D* and *Heref* 93-08; *Ox* from 08. *4 Hitchmans Drive, Chipping Norton OX7 5BG* Tel (01608) 641248

HOWARD, Ronald. b 40. AMIBF65 AMICME01. Cranmer Hall Dur 86. **d** 88 **p** 89. C Baildon *Bradf* 88-92; P-in-c Sutton 92-96; P-in-c St Tudy w St Mabyn and Michaelstow *Truro* 96-00; P-in-c Keyingham w Ottringham, Halsham and Sunk Is *York* 00-03; R 03-08; RD S Holderness 04-06; rtd 08; Perm to Offic *York* from 08. *Silver Gates, Withernsea Road, Hollym, Withernsea HU19 2QH* Tel (01964) 611270 E-mail fatherronald@btinternet.com

HOWARD, Simon Charles. b 60. Birm Univ BA81. Ridley Hall Cam 90. **d** 92 **p** 93. C Cambridge St Martin *Ely* 92-96; Chapl St Bede's Sch Cam 92-96; P-in-c Earley Trin *Ox* 96-05; P-in-c Ruscombe and Twyford from 05. *The Vicarage, Ruscombe, Reading RG10 9UD* Tel 0118-934 1092 *or* 934 1685 E-mail revsimon@lineone.net

HOWARD, Ms Susan. b 65. Lanc Univ BA86. Ripon Coll Cuddesdon 88. **d** 91 **p** 94. C Ditton St Mich *Liv* 91-94; C Kirkby 94-97; Adv for Youth and Young Adults *Man* 97-00; Governor HM Pris Styal from 01. *HM Prison, Styal, Wilmslow SK9 4HR* Tel (01625) 532141

HOWARD, Thomas Norman. b 40. St Aid Birkenhead 64. **d** 67 **p** 68. C Farnworth and Kearsley *Man* 67-70; C Prestwich St Marg 70-73; V Heyside 73-85; Warden Lamplugh Ho Angl Conf Cen 85-90; Hon C Langtoft w Foxholes, Butterwick, Cottam etc *York* 85-87; C 87-90; V Fence and Newchurch-in-Pendle *Blackb* 90-00; Dioc Ecum Officer 90-95; rtd 00; Hon C Stalybridge H Trin and Ch Ch *Ches* 01-03; Perm to Offic from 03. *36 Bridgeside, Carnforth LA5 9LF* Tel (01524) 736552

HOWARD, William Alfred. b 47. St Jo Coll Dur BA69. Wycliffe Hall Ox 74. **d** 77 **p** 79. C Norbiton *S'wark* 77-80; C Mile Cross *Nor* 80-84; R Grimston, Congham and Roydon from 84; Chapl Norfolk Constabulary from 00. *The Rectory, Watery Lane, Grimston, King's Lynn PE32 1BQ* Tel (01485) 600335 E-mail william.howard@dunelm.org.uk

HOWARD-COWLEY, Joseph Charles. b 27. Trin Coll Cam BA53 MA56. Wells Th Coll 53. **d** 55 **p** 56. C Newmarket All SS *St E* 55-58; Chapl Aycliffe Approved Sch Co Dur 58-61; V Aldringham *St E* 61-86; rtd 86; Perm to Offic *St E* 86-93 and *Truro* 93-03. *36 Bath Road, Wootton Bassett, Swindon SN4 7DF*

HOWARD JONES, Preb Raymond Vernon. b 31. AKC54. **d** 55 **p** 56. C Hutton *Chelmsf* 55-58; CF 58-62; V Walpole St Andrew *Ely* 62-64; Chapl St Crispin's Hosp Northampton 64-70; V Brockhampton w Fawley *Heref* 70-86; V Fownhope 70-86; RD Heref Rural 77-81; Preb Heref Cathl 81-97; Communications Adv and Bp's Staff Officer 86-97; rtd 97; Perm to Offic *Heref* from 97. *Kingfishers, Breinton, Hereford HR4 7PP* Tel (01432) 279371

HOWARTH, Christopher. b 47. Ch Ch Coll Cant CertEd69 Open Univ BA76. S Dios Minl Tr Scheme. **d** 83 **p** 84. NSM Uckfield *Chich* from 83; NSM Lt Horsted from 83; NSM Isfield from 83. *137 Rocks Park Road, Uckfield TN22 2BD* Tel (01825) 765352

HOWARTH, Delphine. See HOWARTH, Victoria Elizabeth Delphine

HOWARTH, Mrs Henriette. b 66. Utrecht Univ MTh94. Wycliffe Hall Ox 91. **d** 04 **p** 05. C Sparkbrook Ch Ch *Birm* 04-05; C Springfield 05-09; Perm to Offic from 09. *Address temp unknown* E-mail hentob@tiscali.co.uk

HOWARTH, Miles. b 58. **d** 08 **p** 09. OLM Failsworth St Jo *Man* from 08. *15 Grimshaw Street, Failsworth, Manchester M35 0DF* Tel 0161-688 7710 Mobile 07718-326321 E-mail miles@howarth8023.freeserve.co.uk

HOWARTH, Robert Francis Harvey. b 31. S'wark Ord Course 71. **d** 72 **p** 73. C St Marylebone All So w SS Pet and Jo *Lon* 72-73; C St Helen Bishopsgate w St Martin Outwich 73-78; V Harlow St Mary and St Hugh w St Jo the Bapt *Chelmsf* 78-88; P-in-c Victoria Docks Ascension 88-96; rtd 96. *14 Quinlan Court, 78 Mill Lane, Danbury, Chelmsford CM3 4HX*

HOWARTH, Canon Ronald. b 26. TCD BA51 MA54. Linc Th Coll 50. **d** 52 **p** 53. C Gannow *Blackb* 52-55; Nigeria 55-89; rtd 91. *4 Kingston Court, Walton Street, Oxford OX2 6ES* Tel (01865) 553046

HOWARTH, Toby Matthew. b 62. Yale Univ BA86 Birm Univ MA91 Free Univ of Amsterdam PhD01. Wycliffe Hall Ox 89. **d** 92 **p** 93. C Derby St Aug 92-95; Crosslinks India 95-00; The Netherlands 00-02; Vice Prin and Tutor Crowther Hall CMS Tr Coll Selly Oak 02-04; P-in-c Springfield *Birm* 04-11; Bp's Adv on Inter-Faith Relns 05-11; Abp's Sec for Internat and Inter-Relig Relns *Cant* from 11. *Lambeth Palace, London SE1 7JU* Tel (020) 7898 1247 E-mail toby.howarth@lambethpalace.org.uk *or* hentob@aya.yale.edu

HOWARTH, Victoria Elizabeth Delphine. d 11. OLM Penkridge *Lich* from 11. *Lower Farm House, Bednall, Stafford ST17 0SA* Tel (01785) 714527 E-mail delphine.howarth@ifdev.net

HOWAT, Jeremy Noel Thomas. b 35. Em Coll Cam BA59 MA62. Ridley Hall Cam 59. **d** 63 **p** 64. C Sutton *Liv* 63-65; C Kirk Ella *York* 65-66; C Bridlington Quay Ch Ch 66-69; R Wheldrake 69-78; Dioc Youth Officer 69-74; SAMS Argentina 78-81 and 90-97; P-in-c Newton upon Ouse *York* 81-82; V Shipton w Overton 81-82; P-in-c Skelton by York 81-82; R Skelton w Shipton and Newton on Ouse 82-89; C Elloughton and Brough w Brantingham 97-99; rtd 99; Perm to Offic *York* from 00. *18 Petersway, York YO30 6AR* Tel (01904) 628946 E-mail nowell@ntlworld.com

HOWDEN, Canon John Travis. b 40. RIBA62. Sarum Th Coll 66. **d** 69 **p** 70. C S Gillingham *Roch* 69-72; C Banbury *Ox* 72-73; Lic to Offic *York* 73-74; Hon C Hull St Jo Newland 74-81; Hon C Stock Harvard *Chelmsf* 82-86; R Doddinghurst and Mountnessing 86-91; P-in-c Pleshey and Warden Pleshey Retreat Ho 91-00; R Wickham Bishops w Lt Braxted 00-05; Hon Can Chelmsf Cathl 97-05; rtd 05; Perm to Offic *Chelmsf* from 05. *12A Back Road, Writtle, Chelmsford CM1 3PD* Tel (01245) 422023 E-mail johnhowden@realemail.co.uk

HOWDLE, Glyn. b 50. Bp Lonsdale Coll BEd72. St Alb Minl Tr Scheme 90. **d** 01 **p** 02. NSM Aspenden, Buntingford and Westmill *St Alb* from 01. *58 Ermine Street, Thundridge, Ware SG12 0SY* Tel and fax (01920) 469632 Mobile 07909-920437 E-mail glynjosealicia@howdle.fslife.co.uk

HOWE, Canon Alan Raymond. b 52. Nottm Univ BTh79. St Jo Coll Nottm 76. **d** 80 **p** 81. C Southsea St Simon *Portsm* 80-83; C Bexleyheath St Pet *Roch* 83-86; TV Camberley St Paul *Guildf* 86-93; P-in-c Mansfield St Jo *S'well* 93-96; P-in-c Wollaton Park 96-02; V 02-05; AD Nottingham W 99-05; V Chilwell from 05; P-in-c Lenton Abbey from 09; Hon Can S'well Minster from 11. *Christ Church Vicarage, 8 College Road, Beeston, Nottingham NG9 4AS* Tel 0115-925 7419 E-mail ar.howe1@ntlworld.com

HOWE, Anthony Graham. b 72. Qu Coll Ox BA93 MA99. St Steph Ho Ox BA00. **d** 01 **p** 02. C Newbury *Ox* 01-04; Dioc Communications Officer *Wakef* 04-05; C Athersley and Monk Bretton 05-06; V Staincliffe and Carlinghow from 06. *The Vicarage, Staincliffe Hall Road, Batley WF17 7QX* Tel (01924) 473343 Mobile 07795-095157 E-mail fatherhowe@tiscali.co.uk

HOWE, Brian Moore. b 48. **d** 10. NSM Ballymoney w Finvoy and Rasharkin *Conn* from 10. *10 Station Road, Portstewart BT55 7DA*

HOWE, Charles. b 30. Lon Univ BD65 Open Univ BA79. Tyndale Hall Bris 55. **d** 58 **p** 59. C Willowfield *D & D* 58-60; C Derryloran *Arm* 60-64; C Belfast St Bart *Conn* 64-65; I Tullyaughnish w Kilmacrennan and Killygarvan *D & R* 65-72; I Londonderry St Aug 73-95; Can Derry Cathl 85-95; Dioc Dir and Tutor for Aux Min 93-95; rtd 95. *43 Ashburn Avenue, Londonderry BT47 5QE* Tel (028) 7131 2305 E-mail charleshowe1@hotmail.com

HOWE, Canon David Randall. b 24. St Jo Coll Cam BA51 MA55. Wells Th Coll 51. **d** 53 **p** 54. C Basingstoke *Win* 53-59; V Rotherwick, Hook and Greywell 59-70; R Bossington w Broughton 70-81; R Broughton w Bossington and Mottisfont 81-86; R Broughton, Bossington, Houghton and Mottisfont 86-89; Hon Can Win Cathl 87-89; rtd 89; Perm to Offic *Sarum* and *Win* 89-05; *Ox* from 06. *Easter Cottage, 36 Britwell Road, Burnham, Slough SL1 8AG* Tel (01628) 603046

HOWE, Miss Frances Ruth. b 28. ACIB67. Cranmer Hall Dur IDC80. **dss** 80 **d** 87 **p** 94. Newc St Andr 80-82; Chapl Asst R Victoria Infirmary Newc 80-87; Chapl Wylam and Fleming Ch Hosp 82-87; Chapl St Oswald's Hospice Newc 86-92; C Newc Epiphany 87-90; rtd 92; Hon C Delaval Newc 92-98; Perm to Offic from 98. *18 Mason Avenue, Whitley Bay NE26 1AQ* Tel 0191-252 5163

HOWE, The Ven George Alexander. b 52. St Jo Coll Dur BA73. Westcott Ho Cam 73. **d** 75 **p** 76. C Peterlee *Dur* 75-79; C Norton St Mary 79-81; V Hart w Elwick Hall 81-85; R Sedgefield 85-91; RD Sedgefield 89-91; V Kendal H Trin *Carl* 91-00; RD Kendal 94-00; Hon Can Carl Cathl from 94; Adn Westmorland and Furness 00-11; Bp's Adv for Ecum Affairs 01-11; Bp's Chief of Staff and Dioc Dir of Ords from 11. *1 St John's Gate, Threlkeld, Keswick CA12 4TZ*

HOWE, Canon John. b 36. Ex Coll Ox BA58 MA63. St Steph Ho Ox 58. **d** 61 **p** 62. C Horninglow *Lich* 61-64; C Sedgley All SS 64-66; V Ocker Hill 66-73; V Gnosall 73-79; P-in-c Hoar Cross 79-82; Preb Lich Cathl 83-88; V Hoar Cross w Newchurch 83-88; Can Res Lich Cathl 88-96; Master St Jo Hosp Lich 96-00; rtd 00; Perm to Offic *Lich* from 01. *9 Cherry Street, The Leys, Tamworth B79 7ED* Tel (01827) 57817

HOWE, Canon Nicholas Simon. b 60. Man Univ BA81 K Coll Lon MTh85. Ridley Hall Cam 86. **d** 88 **p** 89. C Lich St Chad 88-92; TV Leeds City *Ripon* 92-01; Dioc Dir of Ords and Post-Ord Tr *Sheff* 01-06; Chapl Sheff Cathl 01-06; Can Res Sheff Cathl 03-06; Chapl Stockholm w Gävle and Västerås *Eur* from 06. *The English Church of Stockholm, Styrmansgatan 1, SE-114*

54, Stockholm, Sweden Tel (0046) (8) 663 8248 Fax 663 8911
E-mail anglican.church@chello.se

HOWE, Canon Rex Alan. b 29. Ch Coll Cam BA53 MA57. Coll of Resurr Mirfield 53. **d** 55 **p** 56. C Barnsley St Pet *Wakef* 55-57; C Helmsley *York* 57-60; V Middlesbrough St Martin 60-67; V Redcar 67-73; V Kirkleatham 67-73; RD Guisborough 67-73; Dean Hong Kong 73-76; Adn 75-76; TR Grantham *Linc* 77-85; RD Grantham 78-85; Can and Preb Linc Cathl 81-85; V Canford Cliffs and Sandbanks *Sarum* 85-94; RD Poole 92-94; rtd 94; Perm to Offic *Sarum* from 94. *18 St Nicholas Hospital, 5 St Nicholas Road, Salisbury SP1 2SW* Tel (01722) 326677

HOWE, Roy William. b 38. ALCD67. **d** 66 **p** 67. C Bradf Cathl 66-70; C Barnoldswick w Bracewell 70-72; V Yeadon St Jo 72-79; P-in-c Bainton *York* 79-86; P-in-c Middleton-on-the-Wolds 79-86; P-in-c N Dalton 79-86; RD Harthill 81-87; C Watton w Beswick and Kilnwick 82-86; R Bainton w N Dalton, Middleton-on-the-Wolds etc 86-87; TV Penrith w Newton Reigny and Plumpton Wall *Carl* 87-92; Dioc Chapl to Agric and Rural Life 87-92; V Cornhill w Carham *Newc* 92-98; V Branxton 92-98; P-in-c Coddenham w Gosbeck and Hemingstone w Henley *St E* 98-03; rtd 03; Perm to Offic *St E* from 04. *Ballaclague, 2 Halvasso Vean, Longdowns, Penryn TR10 9DN* Tel (01209) 860552

HOWE, Ruth. See HOWE, Miss Frances Ruth

HOWE, William Ernest. b 25. MRICS51. Westcott Ho Cam 68. **d** 70 **p** 71. C Anston *Sheff* 70-73; V 84-92; C Woodsetts 70-73; V Greasbrough 73-84; rtd 92; Perm to Offic *Sheff* from 92 and *S'well* from 97. *21 Broad Bridge Close, Kiveton Park, Sheffield S26 6SL* Tel (01909) 779779

HOWELL, Andrew John. b 44. Clifton Th Coll 68. **d** 71 **p** 72. C Halliwell St Pet *Man* 71-77; V Facit 77-95; P-in-c Wardle and Smallbridge from 95. *The Vicarage, 151 Wardle Road, Rochdale OL12 9JA* Tel (01706) 713529

HOWELL, Brian. b 43. MBE99. Newc Univ MA95. Cranmer Hall Dur 11. **d** 11. NSM Blaydon and Swalwell *Dur* from 11. *Hillcroft House, Sourmilk Hill Lane, Gateshead NE9 5RU* Tel 0191-482 3158 Mobile 07710-000654 E-mail howell2004@yahoo.co.uk

HOWELL, David. b 29. Clifton Th Coll 56. **d** 59 **p** 60. C Tipton St Martin *Lich* 59-62; V W Bromwich St Paul 62-71; V Deptford St Jo *S'wark* 71-81; Dir and Chapl Home of Divine Healing Crowhurst 81-89; rtd 90; Dir Ch Coun for Health and Healing 91-93; Hon Dioc Adv on Health and Healing *B & W* 93-00; Perm to Offic from 01. *60 Andrew Allan Road, Rockwell Green, Wellington TA21 9DY* Tel (01823) 664529
E-mail revshowell@waitrose.com

HOWELL (formerly WILLIAMS), David Paul. b 61. Coll of Resurr Mirfield 91. **d** 93 **p** 94. C Leic St Aid 93-97; P-in-c Edvin Loach w Tedstone Delamere etc *Heref* from 97. *The Rectory, Whitbourne, Worcester WR6 5RP* Tel (01886) 821285

HOWELL, Geoffrey Peter. b 52. Selw Coll Cam BA75 MA78 Leeds Univ MA01 K Alfred's Coll Win PGCE77 LTCL82. Cranmer Hall Dur 85. **d** 87 **p** 88. C Hartlepool St Luke *Dur* 87-90; TV Burford I, Nash and Boraston *Heref* 90-94; TV Whitton w Greete and Hope Bagot 90-94; TV Burford III w Lt Heref 90-94; TV Tenbury Wells 90-94; P-in-c Cradley w Mathon and Storridge 94-97; Succ Heref Cathl 97-99; Chapl Heref Cathl Jun Sch 97-99; Perm to Offic *Heref* from 99; Min Can St Woolos Cathl 02-10; TV Monkton *St D* from 10. *The Vicarage, 13 Reginald Close, Hundleton, Pembroke SA71 5RZ* Tel (01646) 687459 E-mail geoffrey.howell@tesco.net

HOWELL, Mrs Heather Ellen. b 40. Bp Otter Coll Chich TCert60 Sussex Univ BA83. Ripon Coll Cuddesdon 00. **d** 01 **p** 02. NSM Newhaven *Chich* 01-06; P-in-c Fletching 06-11; rtd 11. *1 Rookery Way, Seaford BN25 2SA* E-mail heather.howell@tiscali.co.uk

HOWELL, Martin John Hope. b 38. Bris Univ BA62. Tyndale Hall Bris 59. **d** 64 **p** 65. C Bolton St Paul *Man* 64-67; C Bishopsworth *Bris* 67-70; V Swindon St Aug 70-81; TR Stratton St Margaret w S Marston etc 81-93; RD Cricklade 88; RD Highworth 88-93; Chapl Lee Abbey 93-98; Chapl St Pet Viña del Mar Chile 99-03; rtd 03; Hon C Salcombe and Malborough w S Huish *Ex* 03-08. *7 Glen Walk, Exeter EX4 5EA* Tel (01548) 562402

HOWELL, Roger Brian. b 43. ALCD64. **d** 67 **p** 68. C Battersea Park St Sav *S'wark* 67-71; C Southgate *Chich* 71-76; V Pendeen and P-in-c Sancreed *Truro* 76-81; V Bedgrove *Ox* 81-91; R Purley 91-08; RD Bradfield 94-04; rtd 08; Perm to Offic *Ox* from 08. *246 Burwell Meadow, Witney OX28 5JJ* Tel (01993) 706893 E-mail rbh@bradean.fsnet.co.uk

HOWELL, Ronald William Fullerton. b 51. Man Univ BA72 CertEd Ox Univ BA78 MA. Ripon Coll Cuddesdon 76. **d** 79 **p** 80. C Newc St Fran 79-81; C Warmsworth *Sheff* 81-82; Dioc Educn Officer 82-85; V Millhouses H Trin 85-93; R Thornhill and Whitley Lower *Wakef* 93-96. *11 Hartington Road, Aldeburgh IP15 5HD* Tel (01728) 453000

HOWELL, Simon Gordon. b 63. Sheff Univ BMus84 Bath Coll of HE PGCE85 Anglia Ruskin Univ MA07 ACII90. Ridley Hall Cam 00. **d** 03 **p** 04. C Northwood Em *Lon* 03-06; TV Keynsham *B & W* from 06; Bp's Inter Faith Officer from 10. *9 Chelmer Grove, Keynsham, Bristol BS31 1QA* Tel 0117-377 9798 Mobile 07971-582332
E-mail revsimonhowell@blueyonder.co.uk

HOWELL, Preb Walter Ernest. b 17. St D Coll Lamp BA49. **d** 50 **p** 51. C Bromley St Mich *Lon* 50-56; V Somers Town 56-68; V Kentish Town St Benet and All SS 68-79; Preb St Paul's Cathl 78-84; V Alexandra Park St Sav 79-84; rtd 84; Perm to Offic *York* from 90. *6 Wattlers Close, Copmanthorpe, York YO23 3XR* Tel (01904) 702615

HOWELL-JONES, Canon Peter. b 62. Huddersfield Poly BMus84 Bretton Hall Coll PGCE85. St Jo Coll Nottm 90 MA96. **d** 93 **p** 94. C Walsall *Lich* 93-98; V Boldmere *Birm* 98-05; Can Res Birm Cathl from 05; Bp's Adv for Miss from 05; Asst Dean from 07. *Birmingham Cathedral, Colmore Row, Birmingham B3 2QB* Tel 0121-262 1840 Fax 262 1860 E-mail actingdean@birminghamcathedral.com

HOWELLS, Chan Arthur Glyn. b 32. Univ of Wales (Lamp) BA54. St Mich Coll Llan 54. **d** 56 **p** 57. C Oystermouth *S & B* 56-58; C Llangyfelach and Morriston 58-64; R Llandefalle and Llyswen w Boughrood etc 64-69; Youth Chapl 67-71; V Landore 70-80; Dioc Missr 80-89; Can Brecon Cathl 80-89; Can Treas 89-94; Dir St Mary's Coll Swansea 82-89; V Swansea St Jas *S & B* 89-98; Chan Brecon Cathl 94-98; RD Swansea 96-98; rtd 98. *2 Lilliput Lane, West Cross, Swansea SA3 5AQ* Tel (01792) 402133

HOWELLS, David. b 55. Grey Coll Dur BA78. Ripon Coll Cuddesdon 79. **d** 81 **p** 82. C Birtley *Dur* 81-84; Canada from 84. *5551 West Saanich Road, Victoria BC V9E 2G1, Canada* E-mail smaaac@telus.net

HOWELLS, David Morgan. b 24. Qu Coll Birm 72. **d** 75 **p** 76. NSM Radford *Cov* 75-87; rtd 87; Perm to Offic *Cov* 87-03 and *Roch* 98-03. *14 St Werburgh's Court, Pottery Road, Rochester ME3 9AP* Tel (01634) 251544

HOWELLS (formerly SMITHAM), Mrs Elizabeth Ann. b 62. St D Coll Lamp BA90 Univ of Wales (Lamp) MA04. St Mich Coll Llan. **d** 92 **p** 97. C Llangiwg *S & B* 92-94; C Morriston 94-98; P-in-c Llanfair-is-gaer and Llanddeiniolen *Ban* 98-00; V 00-03; V Llanddeiniolen w Llanfair-is-gaer etc 03-04; V Clydau w Egremont and Llanglydwen etc *St D* 04-06; P-in-c Llanpumsaint w Llanllawddog 06-08; V Llanilar w Rhostie and Llangwyryfon etc 09-10; V Llandybie from 10. *77 Kings Road, Llandybie, Ammanford SA18 2TL* Tel (01269) 850337

HOWELLS, Euryl. b 60. Univ of Wales (Cardiff) BD93. St Mich Coll Llan 90. **d** 93 **p** 94. C Deanery of Emlyn *St D* 93-97; V Llangeler w Pen-Boyr 97-03; P-in-c Tre-lech a'r Betws w Abernant and Llanwinio 03-06; Chapl Carmarthenshire NHS Trust 06-08; Chapl R Devon and Ex NHS Foundn Trust 08-09; V Grwp Bro Ystwyth a Mynach *St D* 09-10; Sen Chapl Hywel Dda Health Bd from 11. *Chaplaincy Office, Glangwili Hospital, Dolgwili Road, Carmarthen SA31 2AF* Tel (01267) 227563 E-mail euryl.howells@virgin.net

HOWELLS, Garfield Edwin. b 18. K Coll Lon 53 St Boniface Warminster 53. **d** 54 **p** 55. C Sanderstead All SS *S'wark* 54-57; CF 57-60; R Kingsdown *Roch* 60-64; Australia from 64; rtd 83. *301/17 Hefron Street, Rockingham WA 6168, Australia* Tel (0061) (8) 9592 8337

HOWELLS, Gordon. b 39. Univ of Wales (Cardiff) BSc61 DipEd62. Ripon Coll Cuddesdon 86. **d** 88 **p** 89. C Atherstone *Cov* 88-89; C Lillington 89-92; R Clymping and Yapton w Ford *Chich* 92-97; P-in-c Rackheath and Salhouse *Nor* 97-04; Chapl among Deaf People 97-04; rtd 04. *53 Abbey Road, Rhos on Sea, Colwyn Bay LL28 4NR* Tel (01492) 525899 E-mail g.howells.norwich@virgin.net

HOWELLS, Richard Grant. b 62. Univ of Wales (Lamp) BA83. Westcott Ho Cam 83 and 92. **d** 93 **p** 94. NSM Harston w Hauxton and Newton *Ely* from 93. *The Old School House, 8 High Street, Harston, Cambridge CB22 7PX* Tel (01223) 871902

HOWELLS, Mrs Sandra June. b 52. FBDO71. Mon Dioc Tr Scheme 90. **d** 93 **p** 97. NSM Caerwent w Dinham and Llanfair Discoed etc *Mon* 93-97; C Griffithstown 97-00; V Penallt and Trellech 00-07; V Trellech and Penallt from 07. *The Vicarage, Penallt, Monmouth NP25 4SE* Tel (01600) 716622

HOWES, Alan. b 49. Cinch Th Coll 76. **d** 79 **p** 80. C Bilborough St Jo *S'well* 79-82; TV Newark w Hawton, Cotham and Shelton 82-89; TV Newark 89-94; P-in-c Coseley St Chad *Worc* 94-96; V from 96. *St Chad's Vicarage, 3 Oak Street, Coseley, Bilston WV14 9TA* Tel (01902) 882285 Mobile 07941-284048 E-mail alan@heavensdoor.co.uk

HOWES, David. b 30. Open Univ BA75. Roch Th Coll 62. **d** 64 **p** 65. C Highweek *Ex* 64-67; C Clyst St George 67-71; P-in-c Woolfardisworthy w Kennerleigh 71-72; P-in-c Washford Pyne w Puddington 71-72; TR N Creedy 72-73; Perm to Offic 74-77; C Walworth *S'wark* 77-78; P-in-c Roundshaw LEP 78-83; R S'wark St Geo 83-90; P-in-c S'wark St Jude 84-90; P-in-c Risley *Derby* 90-93; Bp's Ind Adv 90-93; rtd 93; Perm to Offic *Derby* 93-00; *S'well* 95-00; *Win* from 01. *St Mary's House, Upper Swainswick, Bath BA1 8BX* Tel (01225) 851159

HOWES, Miss Judith Elizabeth. b 44. SRN RSCN. Ripon Coll Cuddesdon 83. d 89 p 94. Par Dn Ex St Sidwell and St Matt 89-92; Par Dn Brixham w Churston Ferrers and Kingswear 92-94; C 94-95; TV E Darlington *Dur* 95-97; TR 97-02; P-in-c Washington 02-04; P-in-c S Shields St Simon 04-08; C Hedworth 04-08; rtd 08. *25 Firtree Avenue, Harraton, Washington NE38 9BA*

HOWES, Mrs Kathleen Valerie. b 44. Surrey Univ BA05. STETS 03. d 05 p 06. NSM Droxford and Meonstoke w Corhampton cum Exton *Portsm* 05-08; NSM Cosham 08-09; NSM Bath St Sav w Swainswick and Woolley *B & W* from 09. *St Mary's House, Upper Swainswick, Bath BA1 8BX* Tel (01225) 851159 E-mail valerie.howes@btinternet.com

HOWES, Michael John Norton. b 43. Hull Univ BA66. Linc Th Coll 66. d 68 p 69. C Gt Berkhamsted *St Alb* 68-71; C Ampthill w Millbrook and Steppingley 71-72; Chapl RAF 72-88; V Thurlby w Carlby *Linc* 88-95; V Ness Gp 95-97; R Bassingham 97-00; V Aubourn w Haddington 97-00; V Carlton-le-Moorland w Stapleford 97-00; R Thurlby w Norton Disney 97-00; P-in-c Ashill w Saham Toney *Nor* 01-03; rtd 03. *182 Rookery Lane, Lincoln LN6 7PH* Tel (01522) 801514 E-mail mike.howes5@ntlworld.com

HOWES, Canon Norman Vincent. b 36. AKC61. d 62 p 63. C Radford *Cov* 62-66; V Napton on the Hill 66-72; V Exhall 72-83; R Walton d'Eiville and V Wellesbourne 83-03; RD Fosse 87-93; Hon Can Cov Cathl 89-03; rtd 03; Perm to Offic *Cov* from 03. *6 Brookside Avenue, Wellesbourne, Warwick CV35 9RZ* Tel (01789) 470902 E-mail norman@nhowes.freeserve.co.uk

HOWES, Valerie. See HOWES, Mrs Kathleen Valerie

HOWES, William John Lawrence. b 46. EAMTC. d 00 p 01. NSM Lexden *Chelmsf* 00-04; NSM Coggeshall w Markshall from 04. *26 Westfield Drive, Coggeshall, Colchester CO6 1PU* Tel and fax (01376) 561826 Mobile 07718-048574 E-mail frbill_105@fsmail.net

HOWETT, Miss Amanda Jane. b 68. Reading Univ BA91 Birm Univ MPhil08 Cam Univ BTh11. Ridley Hall Cam 09. d 11. C Boldmere *Birm* from 11. *19 Southam Drive, Sutton Coldfield B73 5PD* Tel 07891-250277 (mobile) E-mail amanda.howett@blueyonder.co.uk

HOWITT, Mrs Barbara Gillian. b 39. K Coll Lon BD60 PGCE61 MA95. EAMTC 99. d 00 p 01. NSM Longthorpe *Pet* 00-09; rtd 09; Perm to Offic *Pet* from 09. *8 Wakerley Drive, Orton Longueville, Peterborough PE2 7WF* Tel (01733) 391092 E-mail barbara@bhowitt.wanadoo.co.uk

HOWITT, Ivan Richard. b 56. Kent Univ BA81. Sarum & Wells Th Coll 83. d 85 p 86. C Herne Bay Ch Ch *Cant* 85-87; C St Laur in Thanet 87-90; R Owmby and Normanby w Glentham *Linc* 90-91; P-in-c Spridlington w Saxby and Firsby 90-91; R Owmby Gp 91-99; RD Lawres 96-99; Chapl Hull Miss to Seafarers 99-03; V Hedon w Paull *York* 03-09; P-in-c Sand Hutton from 09; P-in-c Whitwell w Crambe and Foston from 09. *The Vicarage, Sand Hutton, York YO41 1LB* Tel (01904) 468844 Mobile 07739-316019 E-mail ivan.howitt@btinternet.com

HOWITT, John Leslie. b 28. Lon Coll of Div 60. d 62 p 63. C Attenborough w Bramcote *S'well* 62-66; Chapl Rampton Hosp Retford 66-71; P-in-c Treswell and Cottam *S'well* 68-71; Chapl HM Pris Cardiff 71-75; Chapl HM Youth Cust Cen Dover 75-79; Chapl HM Pris Dartmoor 79-83; Chapl HM Pris Cant 83-87; Chapl HM Det Cen Aldington 83-87; Perm to Offic *Cant* 87-88; V Shobnall *Lich* 88-94; rtd 94; Perm to Offic *Chich* from 94. *7 Wish Court, Ingram Crescent West, Hove BN3 5NY* Tel (01273) 414535

HOWITZ (*formerly* **TEDD), Christopher Jonathan Richard.** b 74. Ch Ch Ox MEng96. Oak Hill Th Coll BA00. d 00 p 01. C Harpurhey Ch Ch *Man* 00-04; P-in-c Higher Openshaw from 05. *St Clement's Rectory, Ashton Old Road, Manchester M11 1HF* Tel 0161-370 1538 E-mail cjhowitz@hotmail.com

HOWLES, Kenneth. b 56. Oak Hill Th Coll 91. d 93 p 94. C Leyland St Andr *Blackb* 93-96; C Livesey 96-97; C Ewood 96-97; P-in-c 97-99; V 99-03; P-in-c Blackb Sav 01-03; V Chorley St Jas 03-10; rtd 10. *20 Waverley Drive, Tarleton, Preston PR4 6XX* Tel (01772) 815752 E-mail kenhowles@btinternet.com

HOWLETT, Mrs Elizabeth Mary. b 58. Southn Univ BA80. WMMTC 99. d 01 p 02. C Salter Street and Shirley *Birm* 01-04; Bp's Adv for Lay Adult Educn and Tr from 04. *6 Greenside, Shirley, Solihull B90 4HH* Tel (01564) 702233 E-mail liz@birmingham.anglican.org

HOWLETT, Richard Laurence. b 56. Kent Univ BA79. Trin Coll Bris. d 94 p 95. C Louth *Linc* 94-98; R Marston Morteyne w Lidlington *St Alb* 98-05; V Goldington from 05. *St Mary's Vicarage, Church Lane, Goldington, Bedford MK41 0AP* Tel (01234) 355024 E-mail richard@revhowlett.fslife.co.uk

HOWLETT, Victor John. b 43. S Dios Minl Tr Scheme 90. d 93 p 94. NSM Bris St Andr w St Bart 93-95; NSM Bishopston and Bris St Matt and St Nath 95-96; C Gtr Corsham 96-99; V Wick w Doynton and Dyrham 99-05; P-in-c Stratton St Margaret w S Marston etc 05-10; rtd 10. *11 Moor Park, Neston, Corsham SN13 9YJ* Tel (01225) 819954 E-mail victorhowlett@hotmail.co.uk

HOWMAN, Anne Louise. b 43. Ex Univ BA97. SWMTC 97. d 99 p 00. NSM Ex St Dav 99-02; C Salcombe and Malborough w S Huish 02-07; rtd 08. *28 Sentrys Orchard, Exminster, Exeter EX6 8UD* E-mail alhow@btinternet.com

HOWORTH, Sister Rosemary. b 44. Newnham Coll Cam MA. Westcott Ho Cam. d 98 p 99. NSM Derby St Andr w St Osmund 98-10; NSM Morley w Smalley and Horsley Woodhouse from 10; NSM Loscoe from 10. *The Convent of the Holy Name, Morley Road, Oakwood, Derby DE21 6HP* Tel (01332) 671716

HOWSE, Elizabeth Ann. See SMITH, Mrs Elizabeth Ann

HOWSE, Martin David. b 58. St Steph Ho Ox 97. d 99 p 00. C Colchester St Jas and St Paul w All SS etc *Chelmsf* 99-03; V Rush Green from 03. *St Augustine's Vicarage, 78 Birkbeck Road, Romford RM7 0QP* Tel (01708) 741460 Fax 732093 Mobile 07770-928167 E-mail martin.howse@virgin.net

HOWSON, Christopher Stewart. b 69. Bradf Univ BA94 St Jo Coll Dur BA02 CQSW94. Cranmer Hall Dur 99. d 02 p 03. C Tong *Bradf* 02-05; Miss P Bradf Adnry from 05. *Desmond Tutu House, 2 Ashgrove, Great Horton Road, Bradford BD7 1BN* Tel (01274) 727034 E-mail chris.howson@bradford.anglican.org

HOWSON, James Edward. b 62. Ridley Hall Cam 97 EAMTC 98. d 00 p 01. C Cogges and S Leigh *Ox* 00-05; Perm to Offic *Ox* and *Eur* 05-06; P-in-c Kiev *Eur* 06-08; R Alfriston w Lullington, Litlington and W Dean *Chich* from 09. *The Rectory, Sloe Lane, Alfriston, Polegate BN26 5UP* Tel (01323) 870376 E-mail jameshowson@rocketmail.com

HOY, Michael John. b 30. Reading Univ BSc52. Oak Hill Th Coll 57. d 59 p 60. C Worthing St Geo *Chich* 59-62; C Tulse Hill H Trin *S'wark* 62-66; R Danby Wiske w Yafforth and Hutton Bonville *Ripon* 66-76; V Camelsdale *Chich* 76-87; V Gt Marsden *Blackb* 87-96; rtd 96. *35 Hardwick Park, Banbury OX16 1YF* Tel (01295) 268744

HOY, Stephen Anthony. b 55. Leeds Poly BA76. Linc Th Coll 92. d 94 p 95. C Glen Parva and S Wigston *Leic* 94-98; V Linc St Jo from 98. *St John's Vicarage, 102 Sudbrooke Drive, Lincoln LN2 2EF* Tel (01522) 525621 E-mail fr-stephen@stjohnthebaptistparishchurch.org.uk

HOYAL, Richard Dunstan. b 47. Ch Ch Ox BA67 MA71 BA78. Ripon Coll Cuddesdon 76. d 79 p 80. C Stevenage St Geo *St Alb* 79-83; V Monk Bretton *Wakef* 83-89; V Ilkley St Marg *Bradf* 89-04; Dir of Ords 96-04; Hon Can Bradf Cathl 03-04; P-in-c Clifton All SS w St Jo *Bris* from 04; P-in-c Easton All Hallows from 04; P-in-c Ch Ch w St Ewen, All SS and St Geo from 09. *All Saints' Vicarage, 68 Pembroke Road, Bristol BS8 3ED* Tel 0117-974 1355 E-mail richard@rdhoyal.fsnet.co.uk

HOYLAND, John Gregory. b 50. Sussex Univ BEd73. Wycliffe Hall Ox 75. d 78 p 79. C Pudsey St Lawr *Bradf* 78-81; P-in-c Long Preston 81-84; V Long Preston w Tosside 84; CPAS Staff 85-87; Chapl York St Jo Coll 87-01; Lect York St Jo Univ from 01; Perm to Offic *York* from 01. *18 Caxton Avenue, York YO26 5SN* Tel (01904) 784140 or 876533

HOYLE, David Fredric. b 46. Lon Bible Coll. d 02 p 03. NSM Northwood Em *Lon* 02-05. *23 Cranleigh Gardens, Bournemouth BH6 5LE* Tel (01202) 386305 E-mail david.f.hoyle@lineone.net

HOYLE, The Very Revd David Michael. b 57. CCC Cam BA80 MA83 PhD91. Ripon Coll Cuddesdon 84. d 86 p 87. C Chesterton Gd Shep *Ely* 86-88; Chapl and Fell Magd Coll Cam 88-91; Dean and Fell 91-95; V Southgate Ch Ch *Lon* 95-02; Dir Post-Ord Tr Edmonton Area 00-02; Dioc Officer for Min *Glouc* 02-10; Dioc Can Res Glouc Cathl 02-10; Dean Bris from 10. *20 Charlotte Street, Bristol BS1 5PZ* Tel 0117-926 4879 E-mail dean@bristol-cathedral.co.uk

HOYLE, Pamela Margaret. See CLOCKSIN, Mrs Pamela Margaret

HOYLE, Stephen Jonathan. b 64. Leeds Univ BA87. Ripon Coll Cuddesdon 88. d 90 p 91. C Lt Stanmore St Lawr *Lon* 90-93; C Lon Docks St Pet w Wapping St Jo 93-96; Perm to Offic 01-02; TV Withycombe Raleigh *Ex* from 02. *St John's Vicarage, 3 Diane Close, Exmouth EX8 5QG* Tel (01395) 270094

HRYZIUK, Petro. b 57. Lanc Univ BEd80 Open Univ MA95. St Jo Coll Nottm 89. d 90 p 91. C Huyton St Geo *Liv* 90-93; C Goose Green 93-96; C Wavertree H Trin 96-98; TV Maghull 98-05; Chapl Shrewsbury and Telford NHS Trust from 05. *Chaplaincy Department, Royal Shrewsbury Hospital, Mytton Oak Road, Shrewsbury SY3 8XQ* Tel (01743) 261000 E-mail petroh@hotmail.com

HUARD, The Ven Geoffrey Robert. b 43. N Bapt Th Sem Illinois DMin95. Clifton Th Coll 65. d 70 p 71. C Barking St Marg *Chelmsf* 70-73; C Everton St Ambrose w St Tim *Liv* 73-74; C Everton St Pet 74-76; R Redfern and Waterloo Australia 76-78; R S Sydney St Sav 78-89; Adn Sydney and Cumberland 89-93; Adn Liverpool 93-08; C-in-c Cabramatta 97-99; R Chester Hill w Sefton 01-03; R Bankstown from 03. *34 Wigram Road, Austinmer NSW 2515, Australia* Tel (0061) (2) 4268 4243 Mobile 43-995 1571 E-mail gchuard@smartchat.net.au

HUBAND, Richard William. b 39. Trin Coll Cam BA62 MA66. Qu Coll Birm 76. d 78 p 79. C Norton *St Alb* 78-81; R Aspley Guise w Husborne Crawley and Ridgmont 81-91; V Elstow

91-03; rtd 03. *5 Shooters Paddock, Layton Lane, Shaftesbury SP7 8AB* Tel (01747) 854741

HUBBARD, David Harris. b 33. St Pet Hall Ox BA57 MA61 K Coll Lon MTh88. Ridley Hall Cam 59. **d** 60 **p** 61. C Dalston St Mark w St Bart *Lon* 60-63; C Stoke Newington St Olave 63-67; Hon C 67-68; Asst Master Dalston Sch 67-75; Hon C Hornsey Ch Ch 69-70; V 70-82; AD W Haringey 78-85; V Highgate All SS 82-02; rtd 02; Hon C W Hampstead St Cuth *Lon* 02-04; Perm to Offic from 04. *35 Sheppards College, London Road, Bromley BR1 1PF* Tel (020) 8695 7477

HUBBARD, Mrs Elisabeth Ann. b 41. EAMTC 82. **dss** 85 **d** 87 **p** 94. Cambridge H Trin w St Andr Gt *Ely* 85-86; Cherry Hinton St Jo 86-92; Par Dn 87-92; Par Dn Milton 92-94; C 94-95; R Willingham and Rampton 95-00; rtd 00; NSM Ely 01-06; Perm to Offic from 06. *3 Lodge Gardens, Haddenham, Ely CB6 3TR* Tel (01353) 741472 E-mail geolis@tiscali.co.uk

HUBBARD, Mrs Gillian. b 63. RGN84. WEMTC 05. **d** 08 **p** 09. NSM Glouc St Paul 08-09; NSM Glouc St Paul and St Steph from 09. *9 Pipers Grove, Highnam, Gloucester GL2 8NJ* Tel (01452) 413063 Mobile 07985-080680 E-mail gillyhubbard@hotmail.co.uk

HUBBARD, Haynes Quinton. b 68. Dalhousie Univ BA89. Wycliffe Coll Toronto MDiv95. **d** 96 **p** 96. C Elora Canada 96-99; R Dunville 99-07; Sen Chapl Algarve *Eur* from 07. *St Vincent, Casa do Jarim, Parque da Praia, Vila da Luz, 8600 Lagos, Portugal* Tel (00351) (282) 789660

HUBBARD, Ian Maxwell. b 43. FCollP83 ACP83 Surrey Univ BEd84 Goldsmiths' Coll Lon MA86. Sarum & Wells Th Coll 69. **d** 73 **p** 74. Hon C S'wark H Trin w St Matt 73-78; Hon C Camberwell St Mich w All So w Em 78 87; Hon C Dulwich St Barn 87-90; C Battersea St Mary 90-92; V Winscombe *B & W* 92-98; TR Yatton Moor from 98; RD Portishead 02-10. *The Rectory, 1 Well Lane, Yatton, Bristol BS49 4HT* Tel (01934) 835859 E-mail ian@hubbardi.freeserve.co.uk

HUBBARD, Ms Judith Frances. b 49. St Alb Minl Tr Scheme 79. **dss** 82 **d** 87 **p** 94. Hemel Hempstead *St Alb* 82-86; Longden and Annscroft w Pulverbatch *Heref* 86-87; Hon C 87-91; Vice Prin WEMTC 91-97; Acting Prin 94-95; Hon C Leominster *Heref* 94-97; Cathl Chapl and Visitors' Officer *Glouc* 97-02; I Kinneigh Union *C, C & R* 02-09; Warden of Readers 05-08; P-in-c Frampton on Severn, Arlingham, Saul etc *Glouc* 09-10; rtd 10. *Moorcott, Upper Ivington, Leominster HR6 0JN* Tel (01568) 720311 E-mail judithfrances@gmail.com

HUBBARD, Julian Richard Hawes. b 55. Em Coll Cam BA76 MA81. Wycliffe Hall Ox BA80 MA85. **d** 81 **p** 82. C Fulham St Dionis *Lon* 81-84; Chapl Jes Coll and Tutor Wycliffe Hall Ox 84-89; Selection Sec ACCM 89-91; Sen Selection Sec ABM 91-93; V Bourne *Guildf* 93-99; P-in-c Tilford 97-99; RD Farnham 96-99; Can Res Guildf Cathl and Dir Minl Tr 99-05; Adn Ox and Can Res Ch Ch 05-11; Dir Min Division Abps' Coun from 11. *Church House, Great Smith Street, London SW1P 3AZ* Tel (020) 7898 1390 Fax 7898 1421 E-mail julian.hubbard@churchofengland.org

HUBBARD, Laurence Arthur. b 36. Qu Coll Cam BA60 MA64. Wycliffe Hall Ox 60 CMS Tr Coll Chislehurst 65 CMS Tr Coll Selly Oak 93. **d** 62 **p** 63. C Widcombe *B & W* 62-65; CMS Kenya 66-73; V Pype Hayes *Birm* 73-79; P-in-c Norwich-over-the-Water Colegate St Geo 79-85; P-in-c Nor St Aug w St Mary 79-85; CMS 85-97; Area Sec *Cant* and *Roch* 85-93; Chapl Damascus, Syria 93-97; Miss to Seamen Aqaba, Jordan 97-00; rtd 00; Perm to Offic *Glouc* from 01. *31 Saddlers Road, Quedgeley, Gloucester GL2 4SY* Tel (01452) 728061

HUBBARD, Peter James. b 72. York Univ BA93 Nottm Univ PGCE97. Trin Coll Bris BA03. **d** 04 **p** 05. C Hinckley H Trin *Leic* 04-08; R Karrinyup Australia from 08. *53 Burroughs Road, Karrinyup, Perth WA 6018, Australia* Tel (0061) (8) 9341 5572 E-mail peterhubbardkac@bigpond.com

HUBBARD, Roy Oswald. b 32. Lich Th Coll 62. **d** 64 **p** 65. C Baswich *Lich* 64-68; P-in-c Ash 68-70; V Stevenage St Pet Broadwater *St Alb* 71-78; V Flitwick 78-90; RD Ampthill 87-90; R Sharnbrook and Knotting w Souldrop 90-96; rtd 96; Perm to Offic *St Alb* and *Pet* from 96. *11 Cowslip Close, Rushden NN10 0UD* Tel (01933) 419210

HUBBLE, Canon Raymond Carr. b 30. Wm Temple Coll Rugby 60. **d** 61 **p** 62. C Newbold w Dunston *Derby* 61-64; Chapl RAF 64-80; Asst Chapl-in-Chief RAF 80-85; QHC 84-85; P-in-c Odiham w S Warnborough and Long Sutton *Win* 85; P-in-c Odiham 85-86; V 86-95; RD Odiham 88-95; Hon Can Win Cathl 94-95; rtd 95; Perm to Offic *Win* from 95. *Dormers, Centre Lane, Everton, Lymington SO41 0JP*

HUBBLE, Canon Trevor Ernest. b 46. Bernard Gilpin Soc Dur 69 Chich Th Coll 70. **d** 76 **p** 77. C Eltham St Barn *S'wark* 76-79; C St Agnes Mission Teyateyaneng Lesotho 80-81; R Quthing H Trin 81-85; Adn S Lesotho 84-87; Warden Angl Tr Cen and Dir Chr Educn 85-87; Co-ord of Tr for Lay Min S Africa 87-89; R Matatiele St Steph 89-00; Adn Matatiele 91-00; V Gen Umzimvubu 95-00; Shared Min Tr Officer *Dur* 00-07; C Esh, Hamsteels, Langley Park and Waterhouses 00-07; Warden Lee Abbey Internat Students' Club Kensington from 07. *Lee Abbey*

International Students' Club, 57-67 Lexham Gardens, London W8 6JJ* Tel (020) 7244 2709 Fax 7244 8702 E-mail warden@leeabbeylondon.com

HUCKETT, Andrew William. b 50. AKC72. St Aug Coll Cant 72. **d** 73 **p** 74. C Chipping Sodbury and Old Sodbury *Glouc* 73-76; Miss to Seafarers from 76; Chapl Flushing 76-79; Chapl Teesside 79-82; Chapl Lagos Nigeria 82-85; Chapl Mombasa Kenya 85-86; Chapl Milford Haven 86-92; Chapl Medway Ports 92-03; Staff Chapl and Chapl Thames/Medway 03-05; Chapl Southampton from 05. *Southampton Seafarers' Centre, 12/14 Queens Terrace, Southampton SO14 3BP* Tel (023) 8033 3106 *or* 8071 4083 Mobile 07836-261324 E-mail southampton@mtsmail.org

HUCKLE, John Walford (Wally). b 39. EMMTC. **d** 89 **p** 90. C Nottingham St Pet and St Jas *S'well* 89-00; Commercial Chapl Nottingham City Cen 89-00; Dioc Adv on Ind Soc 96-97; rtd 00; Perm to Offic *S'well* from 00. *6 Lime Close, Radcliffe-on-Trent, Nottingham NG12 2DF* Tel 0115-933 2278 E-mail wally.huckle@ntlworld.com

HUCKLE, Peter. b 46. Ox Univ Inst of Educn CertEd69 Auckland Univ DipEd71. Educn for Min (NZ). **d** 90 **p** 91. New Zealand 90-91; Hon C N Walsham w Antingham *Nor* 91-92; C Gt Yarmouth 92-94; TV 94-96; Min Can and Chapl St Paul's Cathl 96-97; Asst Chapl Athens and Perm to Offic *Eur* 97; SSJE from 97; Superior from 02. *St Edward's House, 22 Great College Street, London SW1P 3QA* Tel (020) 7222 9234 Fax 7799 2641 E-mail superior@ssje.org.uk

HUCKLE, Stephen Leslie. b 48. Ch Ch Ox BA70 BA72 MA74. Coll of Resurr Mirfield 73. **d** 75 **p** 76. C Wednesbury St Paul Wood Green *Lich* 75-78, C Aylesbury *Ox* 78-83, C Farnham Royal w Hedgerley 85-88; V Fenny Stratford 88-98; V Stirchley Birm 98-05; P-in-c Kempston All SS *St Alb* from 05; P-in-c Biddenham from 05. *The Vicarage, Church End, Kempston, Bedford MK43 8RH* Tel (01234) 852241

HUCKLE, Walford. *See* HUCKLE, John Walford

HUDD, Philip Simon. b 68. Westmr Coll Ox BA90 Lanc Univ MA06. Westcott Ho Cam 91. **d** 93 **p** 94. C Kirkby *Liv* 93-97; TV 97-99; V Lancaster Ch Ch *Blackb* from 99; AD Lancaster 04-10. *Christ Church Vicarage, 1 East Road, Lancaster LA1 3EE* Tel (01524) 34430 E-mail p.hudd@uwclub.net

HUDDLESON, Robert Roulston. b 32. QUB BA55 TCD Div Test57. **d** 57 **p** 58. C Ballymena *Conn* 57-59; C Belfast St Jas 59-63; Ethiopia 65-69; Exec Asst WCC Geneva 69-75; Dep Sec Gen Syn Bd for Miss and Unity 75-81; Admin Sec *Dur* 81-86; Dioc Sec *Ex* 86-97; rtd 97; Perm to Offic *Ex* from 97. *6 Newton Court, Bampton, Tiverton EX16 9LG* Tel (01398) 331412

HUDDLESTON, Geoffrey Roger. b 36. TCD BA63 MA67. Ridley Hall Cam 63. **d** 65 **p** 66. C Tonbridge SS Pet and Paul *Roch* 65-69; Chapl RAF 69-85; V Lyonsdown H Trin *St Alb* 85-00; RD Barnet 94-99; rtd 00; Perm to Offic *Lich* from 01. *The Granary, Bellamour Lodge Farm, Colton Road, Colton, Rugeley WS15 3NZ* Tel (01889) 574052

HUDDLESTON, Mark Geoffrey. b 68. Bath Univ BSc90. Wycliffe Hall Ox 06. **d** 08 **p** 09. C Heigham H Trin *Nor* from 08. *14 Trinity Street, Norwich NR2 2BQ* Tel (01603) 443785 E-mail mhuddleston@onetel.com *or* curate@trinitynorwich.org

HUDGHTON, John Francis. b 56. BA. Cranmer Hall Dur 81. **d** 83 **p** 84. C Stockport St Geo *Ches* 83-85; C Witton 85-87; C Stockport St Alb Hall Street 87-90; V Thornton-le-Moors w Ince and Elton 90-95; Chapl RAF 95-01; P-in-c Burnby *York* 01-03; P-in-c Londesborough 01-03; P-in-c Nunburnholme and Warter and Huggate 01-03; P-in-c Shiptonthorpe and Hayton 01-03; TR Buxton w Burbage and King Sterndale *Derby* from 03. *The Rectory, 7 Lismore Park, Buxton SK17 9AU* Tel (01298) 22151 E-mail rectorofbuxton@hotmail.com

HUDSON, Andrew Julian. b 57. Cranmer Hall Dur 93. **d** 93 **p** 94. C Moldgreen *Wakef* 93-97; P-in-c Lundwood 97-01; V Dodworth 01-04; Ind Chapl *Chelmsf* from 04; C Aveley and Purfleet from 04. *St Stephen's Vicarage, London Road, Purfleet RM19 1QD* Tel (01708) 891242 Mobile 07989-988496 E-mail hudsona6@aol.com

HUDSON, Anthony George. b 39. NOC. **d** 84 **p** 85. C Harrogate St Mark *Ripon* 84-87; P-in-c Hampsthwaite 87-96; P-in-c Killinghall 87-94; V Hampsthwaite and Killinghall 96-99; rtd 99; Perm to Offic *Ripon* from 00. *26 Beckwith Crescent, Harrogate HG2 0BQ* Tel (01423) 858740

HUDSON, Brainerd Peter de Wirtz Goodwin. *See* GOODWIN HUDSON, Brainerd Peter de

HUDSON, Charles Edward Cameron. b 73. Univ Coll Ox BA94 MA08. Wycliffe Hall Ox BA07. **d** 08 **p** 09. C St Margaret's-on-Thames *Lon* from 08. *All Souls' Church, Northcote Road, Twickenham TW1 1PB* Tel (020) 8891 6820 E-mail charleshudson@allsoulschurch.org.uk

HUDSON, Christopher John. b 45. Bedf Coll Lon BSc68 MCIH73. Cranmer Hall Dur. **d** 77 **p** 78. C Bath Weston St Jo *B & W* 77-80; Youth Chapl 77-80; P-in-c Baltonsborough w Butleigh and W Bradley 80-84; V 84-87; P-in-c Shirwell w Loxhore *Ex* 87-89; P-in-c Kentisbury, Trentishoe, E Down and Arlington 88-89; TR Shirwell, Loxhore, Kentisbury, Arlington,

etc 90-91; P-in-c Trentishoe 90-91; RD Shirwell 88-91; R Huntspill *B & W* 91-94; rtd 01; Perm to Offic *B & W* from 98 and *Ex* from 06. *Achray, 5 Conigar Close, Hemyock, Cullompton EX15 3RE* Tel (01823) 680170
E-mail revchris@mhbruton.eclipse.co.uk

HUDSON, Clive. b 42. Nor City Coll CertEd66. **d** 03 **p** 04. OLM Redenhall, Harleston, Wortwell and Needham *Nor* from 03; Perm to Offic *St E* from 08. *9 Shotford Road, Harleston IP20 9JH* Tel (01379) 853284
E-mail clive.hudson@talktalk.net

HUDSON, John. *See* HUDSON, Reginald John

HUDSON, John. b 51. Oak Hill Th Coll 84. **d** 86 **p** 87. C Leyland St Andr *Blackb* 86-89; V Coppull from 89; P-in-c Coppull St Jo from 10. *The Vicarage, 209 Chapel Lane, Coppull, Chorley PR7 4NA* Tel (01257) 791218
E-mail saintjohns824@btinternet.com

HUDSON, Canon John Leonard. b 44. AKC66. St Boniface Warminster 66. **d** 67 **p** 68. C Dodworth *Wakef* 67-70; Prec Wakef Cathl 70-73; V Ravensthorpe 73-80; V Royston 80-09; P-in-c Carlton 90-09; RD Barnsley 93-04; Hon Can Wakef Cathl 97-09; rtd 09; Perm to Offic *Wakef* from 09 and *York* from 10. *Millbank Cottage, Thorpe Bassett, Malton YO17 8LU* Tel (01944) 718518
E-mail j.hudson93@btinternet.com

HUDSON, John Peter. b 42. AKC64. St Boniface Warminster 64. **d** 65 **p** 66. C S Shields St Hilda w St Thos *Dur* 65-68; Chapl RN 68-84; V Mellor *Blackb* 84-07; rtd 07; Perm to Offic *Blackb* from 07. *Hazel Mount, Bailrigg Lane, Bailrigg, Lancaster LA1 4XP* Tel (01524) 848693 E-mail jpeterhudson@btinternet.com

HUDSON, Prof John Richard Keith. b 35. St Pet Coll Ox BA60 MA64 State Univ NY PhD83. Linc Th Coll 60. **d** 62 **p** 63. C Tettenhall Wood *Lich* 62-65; Chapl and Lect Bp Grosseteste Coll Linc 65-71; Staff Officer Gen Syn Bd of Educn 72-73; Australia 73-79; Lect Riverina Coll of Advanced Educn Wagga 73-74; Lect Mt Gravatt Coll of Advanced Educn Brisbane 74-79; Master and Chapl Yardley Court Sch Tonbridge 79-82; Teaching Asst State Univ NY USA 82-83; Asst Prof Louisiana State Univ Alexandria 83-85; Asst R Alexandria St Jas 84-85; R Camden St Paul Delaware 85-05; Prof Wesley Coll Dover 85-92; Chapl Delaware Hospice 92-96; rtd 01. *1300 Morris Avenue, Villanova PA 19085-2131, USA* Tel (001) (610) 525 3131
E-mail jrkh65@msn.com

HUDSON, John Stephen Anthony. b 49. S Dios Minl Tr Scheme 85 Chich Th Coll 86. **d** 88 **p** 89. C Horsham *Chich* 88-91; TV Littlehampton and Wick from 91. *The Vicarage, 40 Beaconsfield Road, Wick, Littlehampton BN17 6LN* Tel (01903) 724990

HUDSON, Peter. *See* HUDSON, John Peter

HUDSON, Peter John. b 66. **d** 03 **p** 04. OLM Deptford St Paul *S'wark* 03-07; NSM Lewisham St Steph and St Mark from 07. *7A Blackheath Rise, London SE13 7PN* Tel (020) 8318 0483 Mobile 07908-640369 E-mail frpeter@sky.com

HUDSON, Philip Howard. b 50. St Steph Ho Ox 89. **d** 91 **p** 92. C Poulton-le-Fylde *Blackb* 91-95; V Blackpool St Wilfrid from 95. *St Wilfrid's Vicarage, 8 Langdale Road, Blackpool FY4 4RT* Tel (01253) 761532

HUDSON, Reginald John. b 47. FRSA CertSS. Linc Th Coll. **d** 83 **p** 84. C Merton St Mary *S'wark* 83-86; C Kirk Ella *York* 86-88; P-in-c Lenborough *Ox* 88-93; V Lenborough 93-03; P-in-c Tingewick w Water Stratford, Radclive etc 89-93; P-in-c Water Stratford 93-00; P-in-c Reading St Matt 03-10; rtd 11. *La Columbine, route d'Orbec, 61120 Canapville, France* Tel (0033) (2) 33 67 03 21 E-mail rjhfootsteps@virginmedia.com

HUDSON, Robert Antony. b 82. York Univ BA09. Wycliffe Hall Ox BA09. **d** 10. C Elburton *Ex* from 10. *Rosemorran, Wembury Road, Plymouth PL9 0DQ* Tel (01752) 863285 Mobile 07799-600147 E-mail roberthudson79@btinternet.com

HUDSON, Stephen. *See* HUDSON, John Stephen Anthony

HUDSON, Trevor. b 32. Dur Univ BA56. Cranmer Hall Dur. **d** 58 **p** 59. C Doncaster St Mary *Sheff* 58-62; C Attercliffe 62-64; V Stannington 64-79; V Abbeydale St Jo 79-88; V Worsbrough St Mary 88-95; rtd 95; Perm to Offic *Sheff* from 95. *Spring Villa Garden, 136A Langsett Road South, Oughtibridge, Sheffield S35 0HA* Tel 0114-286 3559

HUDSON, Walter Gerald. b 29. **d** 95 **p** 96. Hon C Eccleston Park *Liv* 95-99; Perm to Offic from 99. *31 Springfield Lane, Eccleston, St Helens WA10 5EW* Tel (01744) 24919

HUDSON, Wilfred. b 23. St Jo Coll Dur BA49. **d** 51 **p** 52. C Doncaster St Mary *Sheff* 51-56; V Brampton Bierlow 56-64; V Anston 64-74; V Woodsetts 64-74; V Sharrow St Andr 74-88; rtd 88; Perm to Offic *Sheff* from 88. *128 Totley Brook Road, Sheffield S17 3QU* Tel 0114-236 5558

HUDSON-WILKIN, Mrs Rose Josephine. b 61. WMMTC 89. **d** 91 **p** 94. Par Dn Wolverhampton St Matt *Lich* 91-94; C 94-95; C W Bromwich Gd Shep w St Jo 95-98; Black Anglican Concern 95-98; V Dalston H Trin w St Phil and Haggerston All SS *Lon* from 98; Chapl to The Queen from 08; Chapl to Speaker of Ho of Commons from 10; PV Westmr Abbey from 10. *The Vicarage, Livermere Road, London E8 4EZ* Tel (020) 7254 5062
E-mail revdrose@aol.com

HUDSPETH, Ralph. b 46. **d** 06 **p** 07. NSM Ripley w Burnt Yates *Ripon* from 06. *10 Winksley Grove, Harrogate HG3 2SZ* Tel (01423) 561918 Mobile 07867-772986
E-mail ralphhudspeth@hotmail.com

HUDSPITH, Colin John. b 46. Nottm Univ BA67. SWMTC 93. **d** 96 **p** 97. C Pilton w Ashford *Ex* 96-97; C Barnstaple 97-99; C Shirwell, Loxhore, Kentisbury, Arlington, etc 99-00; TV 00-11; rtd 11. *Brackendale, Heanton, Barnstaple EX31 4DG* Tel (01271) 812547

HUDSPITH, Mrs Susan Mary. b 49. St Alb Minl Tr Scheme 79. **dss** 82 **d** 87 **p** 94. Luton St Chris Round Green *St Alb* 82-92; Par Dn 87-88; NSM 88-92; Perm to Offic 92-94 and 00-05; NSM Luton St Mary 94-00; NSM Stevenage St Pet Broadwater 05-08; Perm to Offic from 08. *15 Waverley Close, Stevenage SG2 8RU* Tel (01438) 725030 E-mail geoff-sue.hudspith@virgin.net

HUGGETT, David John. b 34. Lon Univ BSc56 Southn Univ PhD59. Clifton Th Coll 64. **d** 67 **p** 68. C Heatherlands St Jo *Sarum* 67-70; C Cambridge St Sepulchre *Ely* 70-73; R Nottingham St Nic *S'well* 73-92; Cyprus 93-99; rtd 99. *101 Admirals Walk, West Cliff Road, Bournemouth BH2 5HF* Tel (01202) 558199

HUGGETT, John Victor James. b 39. Dur Univ BA64. Tyndale Hall Bris 64. **d** 66 **p** 67. C Hailsham *Chich* 66-69; C Worthing St Geo 69-71; C Woking St Pet *Guildf* 71-73; C Buckhurst Hill *Chelmsf* 73-76; V Meltham Mills *Wakef* 76-78; V Wilshaw 76-78; rtd 79; Jt Ldr Breath Fellowship from 79; Perm to Offic *Wakef* 79-84 and *Roch* from 84. *Breath Ministries Healing Centre, Weald House, 10A High Street, Tunbridge Wells TN1 1UX* Tel (01892) 512520 E-mail cjphuggett@yahoo.co.uk

HUGGETT, Kevin John. b 62. St Jo Coll Dur BA83. Trin Coll Bris 88. **d** 91 **p** 92. C Gt Ilford St Andr *Chelmsf* 91-94; Regional Manager for Uganda and Sudan CMS 94-01; Hon C Tonbridge SS Pet and Paul *Roch* 98-01; Chapl Lanc Univ from 01. *11 Alderman Road, Lancaster LA1 5FW* Tel (01524) 843091 *or* 594082/71 E-mail k.huggett@lancaster.ac.uk

HUGGETT, Michael George. b 38. Bris Univ BA60 Birm Univ CertEd61. EMMTC 85. **d** 88 **p** 89. C Sawley *Derby* 88-92; C Chaddesden St Phil 92-93; P-in-c Alkmonton, Cubley, Marston Montgomery etc 93-99; R 99-04; rtd 04. *12 Murray Road, Mickleover, Derby DE3 9LE*

HUGGINS, Stephen David. b 53. Sussex Univ BEd75 K Coll Lon MA80 Leic Univ DipEd79. STETS. **d** 01 **p** 02. NSM Bexhill St Aug *Chich* 01-02; NSM Sedlescombe w Whatlington 02-07; P-in-c Turners Hill 07-09; Angl Chapl Worth Sch 07-09; TV Bexhill St Pet *Chich* from 09. *20 Glassenbury Drive, Bexhill-on-Sea TN40 2NY* E-mail frshuggins@aol.com

HUGHES, Canon Adrian John. b 57. Newc Univ BA78 St Jo Coll Dur BA82. Cranmer Hall Dur 80. **d** 83 **p** 84. C Shard End *Birm* 83-86; TV Solihull 86-90; TV Glendale Gp *Newc* 90-94; P-in-c Belford 94-95; V Belford and Lucker 95-06; V Ellingham 95-02; AD Bamburgh and Glendale 97-06; Asst Dioc Dir of Ords 98-06; V Cullercoats St Geo from 06; AD Tynemouth from 09; Hon Can Newc Cathl from 05. *St George's Vicarage, 1 Beverley Gardens, North Shields NE30 4NS* Tel 0191-252 1817
E-mail revajh@btinternet.com

HUGHES, Canon Alan. b 46. TD. Edin Th Coll 71. **d** 74 **p** 75. C Edin St Cuth 74-76; P-in-c Edin St Luke 76-78; C Marske in Cleveland *York* 78-81; V New Marske 81-82; V Kirkbymoorside w Gillamoor, Farndale etc 84-94; CF 84-94; V Berwick H Trin and St Mary *Newc* from 94; Hon Can Newc Cathl from 08. *The Vicarage, Parade, Berwick-upon-Tweed TD15 1DF* Tel and fax (01289) 306136 Mobile 07941-757412
E-mail berwick.church@bigwig.net *or* skypilot@bigwig.net

HUGHES, Albert William. b 48. S Dios Minl Tr Scheme 90. **d** 92 **p** 93. Community of Our Lady and St John from 70; Prior from 90; Perm to Offic *Win* from 96. *Alton Abbey, Abbey Road, Beech, Alton GU34 4AP* Tel (01420) 562145 *or* 563575 Fax 561691

HUGHES, Alexander James. b 75. Greyfriars Ox BA97 MA03 St Edm Coll Cam MPhil99. Westcott Ho Cam 98. **d** 00 **p** 01. C Headington Quarry *Ox* 00-03; Bp's Dom Chapl *Portsm* 03-08; P-in-c Southsea St Pet from 08; P-in-c Portsea St Luke from 08. *St Peter's House, Playfair Road, Southsea PO5 1EQ* Tel (023) 9281 1999 E-mail alex.hughes@portsmouth.anglican.org

HUGHES, Allan Paul. b 45. Glam Coll of Educn CertEd69 Open Univ BA91. Abp's Sch of Min 01. **d** 02 **p** 03. Chapl St Olave's Sch York 02-05; NSM Skelton w Shipton and Newton on Ouse *York* 02-03; Asst to RD Easingwold 03-04; NSM York All SS Pavement w St Crux and St Mich from 04; NSM York St Denys from 04. *All Saints' Rectory, 52 St Andrewgate, York YO1 7BZ* Tel (01904) 643813 E-mail revd_al@hotmail.com

HUGHES, Andrew Karl William. b 58. St Steph Ho Ox 07 WEMTC 08. **d** 08 **p** 09. NSM N Cheltenham *Glouc* 08-09; C W Bromwich St Fran *Lich* from 09. *210 Friar Park Road, Wednesbury WS10 0GA* Tel 0121-505 4466
E-mail akwhughes@aol.com

HUGHES, Andrew Terrell. b 29. Bris Univ BA56 DipEd. Coll of Resurr Mirfield 65. **d** 66 **p** 67. C Weston-super-Mare St Sav *B & W* 66-70; C Yeovil St Jo w Preston Plucknett 70-73; TV

Yeovil 73-83; R Wincanton 83-88; rtd 89; Perm to Offic *Sarum* from 89. *2 Cove Street, Weymouth DT4 8TS* Tel (01305) 778639

HUGHES, Miss Angela Mary. b 52. Avery Hill Coll CertEd75. St Steph Ho Ox 90. **d** 92 **p** 94. Par Dn Kidderminster St Mary and All SS w Trimpley etc *Worc* 92-94; C 94-96; P-in-c Gilmorton w Peatling Parva and Kimcote etc *Leic* 96-01; RD Guthlaxton II 99-01; R Wyberton *Linc* 01-09; V Frampton 01-09; RD Holland W 04-09; R Carnoustie *Bre* from 09; R Monifieth from 09. *Holy Rood Rectory, 58 Maule Street, Carnoustie DD7 6AB* Tel (01241) 852202

HUGHES, Arthur John. b 41. MCIOB71 MRICS78. WEMTC 03. **d** 05 **p** 06. NSM Church Stretton *Heref* from 05. *Jacey, 2 Lawley Close, Church Stretton SY6 6EP* Tel (01694) 722582 E-mail jhnhughes6@aol.com

HUGHES, Arthur Lewis. b 36. St Deiniol's Hawarden 65. **d** 68 **p** 69. C Holywell *St As* 68-71; Lect Watford St Mary *St Alb* 71-75; V Thornton in Lonsdale w Burton in Lonsdale *Bradf* 75-84; V Daubhill *Man* 84-89; V Castle Town *Lich* 89-00; Chapl Staffs Univ 91-00; rtd 00; Perm to Offic *Ches* 00-04 and *Pet* from 05. *31 Hunt Close, Towcester NN12 7AD* Tel (01327) 358257

HUGHES, Benjamin John. b 65. Golds Coll Lon BEd91 Lon Metrop Univ MA08. Cranmer Hall Dur MTh97. **d** 99 **p** 00. NSM Fulham St Matt *Lon* 99-03; Chapl RN 03; Perm to Offic *Lon* from 04 and *S'wark* from 08. *101 Herne Hill Road, London SE24 0AD* E-mail benbassforty@yahoo.co.uk

HUGHES, Bernard Patrick. b 35. Oak Hill Th Coll. **d** 65 **p** 66. C Fulham St Matt *Lon* 65-69; Chapl St Steph Hosp Lon 69-89; Chapl St Mary Abbots Hosp Lon 69-97; Chapl Westmr Hosp Lon 89-94; Chapl Westmr Children's Hosp Lon 89-94; Sen Chapl Chelsea and Westmr Healthcare NHS Trust 94-97; rtd 97; Perm to Offic *Bris* and *Sarum* from 97. *Charis, 6 Priory Park, Bradford-on-Avon BA15 1QU* Tel (01225) 868679

HUGHES, Miss Carol Lindsay. b 51. Cam Inst of Educn CertEd72 Nottm Univ BEd86. Trin Coll Bris 91. **d** 93 **p** 94. C Ilkeston St Mary *Derby* 93-97; P-in-c Langley Mill 97-02; V 02-06; P-in-c Oakwood from 06; RD Heanor 99-06; rtd 11. *Address temp unknown* E-mail c.l.hughes@fsmail.net

HUGHES, Christopher Clarke. b 40. MRAC61. ALCD63. **d** 65 **p** 66. C Broadclyst *Ex* 65-68; C Chenies and Lt Chalfont *Ox* 68-70; TV Lydford w Bridestowe and Sourton *Ex* 70-72; TV Lydford, Brent Tor, Bridestowe and Sourton 72-74; V Buckland Monachorum 74-83; R Ashtead *Guildf* 83-98; R Aboyne and Ballater *Ab* 98-03; rtd 03. *Stone Farmhouse, Thorverton, Exeter EX5 5LL* Tel (01884) 855250

HUGHES, Clive. b 54. Univ of Wales BA77 MA82. St Mich Coll Llan BD95. **d** 95 **p** 96. C Carmarthen St Dav *St D* 95-97; TV Aberystwyth 97-04; P-in-c Hanmer, Bronington, Bettisfield, Tallarn Green *St As* 04-09; P-in-c Hanmer and Bronington and Bettisfield from 09. *The Vicarage, Hanmer, Whitchurch SY13 3DE* Tel (01948) 830448 E-mail clive@hughes2003.fsnet.co.uk

HUGHES, Cynthia May. b 45. **d** 10 **p** 11. NSM Middlewich w Byley *Ches* from 10. *90 Hartford Road, Davenham, Northwich CW9 8JF* Tel (01606) 350132

HUGHES, David Anthony. b 25. Trin Coll Cam BA48 MA55. Linc Th Coll 74. **d** 76 **p** 77. C Boston *Linc* 76-78; R Graffoe 78-90; rtd 90; Perm to Offic *Linc* from 91. *27 St Clement's Road, Ruskington, Sleaford NG34 9AF* Tel (01526) 832618

HUGHES, David Howard. b 55. Univ of Wales (Ban). St Mich Coll Llan. **d** 79 **p** 80. C Llanrhos *St As* 79-82; C Eckington w Handley and Ridgeway *Derby* 82-83; C Staveley and Barrow Hill 83-85; TV 85-89; V Whitworth St Bart *Man* 89-00. *2 Cromwell Road, Chesterfield S40 4TH* Tel (01246) 277361

HUGHES, Canon David Michael. b 41. Oak Hill Th Coll BD67. **d** 68 **p** 69. C Tunbridge Wells St Jo *Roch* 68-73; C Crookes St Thos *Sheff* 73-81; V Normanton *Wakef* 81-90; TR Didsbury St Jas and Em *Man* 90-09; AD Withington 00-04; Hon Can Man Cathl 06-09; rtd 09; Perm to Offic *Ches* and *Man* from 09. *41 Cross Lane, Marple, Stockport SK6 6DG* Tel 07929-114143 (mobile) E-mail davidmichaelhughes@btinternet.com

HUGHES, Debbie Ann. *See* PEATMAN, Mrs Debbie Ann

HUGHES, Mrs Elizabeth Jane. b 58. K Coll Lon BD81 AKC81. Ripon Coll Cuddesdon 81. **dss** 83 **d** 87 **p** 94. Chipping Barnet w Arkley *St Alb* 83-86; Dunstable 86-87; Hon Par Dn 87-93; NSM Boxmoor St Jo 93-03; Chapl Hospice of St Fran Berkhamsted from 99. *17 Lansdowne Road, Luton LU3 1EE* Tel (01582) 730722 E-mail liz.hughes@stfrancis.org.uk

HUGHES, The Ven Evan Arthur Bertram. b 25. St D Coll Lamp BA48 LTh50. **d** 50 **p** 51. C Abergwili w Llanfihangel-uwch-Gwili *St D* 50-53; C Llanelli 53-58; India 59-69; Adn Bhagalpur 65-66; C Llanstadwel *St D* 70-73; Pakistan 73-74; R Johnston w Steynton *St D* 74-80; Can St D Cathl 80-85; V Newcastle Emlyn 80-81; V Newcastle Emlyn w Llandyfriog and Troed-yr-aur 81-86; Adn Carmarthen 85-91; V Llanegwad w Llanfynydd 86-88; V Cynwil Elfed and Newchurch 88-91; rtd 91. *104 Bronwydd Road, Carmarthen SA31 2AW* Tel (01267) 237155

HUGHES, Canon Evelyn. b 31. Gilmore Ho 73. **dss** 79 **d** 87 **p** 94. Fetcham *Guildf* 79-82; Dioc Adv Lay Min 82-86; Farnborough

83-87; C 87-92; Bp's Adv for Women's Min 87-94; Dn-in-c Badshot Lea CD 92-94; C-in-c 94-96; Hon Can Guildf Cathl 94-96; rtd 96; Perm to Offic *Guildf* from 96. *4 Oaklands, Haslemere GU27 3RD* Tel (01428) 651576

HUGHES, Gareth Francis. b 73. St Jo Coll Dur MSc94 Wolfs Coll Ox MSt07 GInstP94. St Mich Coll Llan BD98. **d** 98 **p** 99. C Haughton le Skerne *Dur* 98-02; TV White Horse *Sarum* 02-06; Perm to Offic *Lon* from 09. *14 Erncroft Way, Twickenham TW1 1DA* Tel (020) 8892 4105 E-mail gareth.hughes@orinst.ox.ac.uk

HUGHES, The Very Revd Geraint Morgan Hugh. b 34. Keble Coll Ox BA58 MA63. St Mich Coll Llan 58. **d** 59 **p** 60. C Gorseinon *S & B* 59-63; C Oystermouth 63-68; R Llanbadarn Fawr, Llandegley and Llanfihangel etc 68-76; R Llandrindod w Cefnllys 76-87; R Llandrindod w Cefnllys and Disserth 87-98; Can Brecon Cathl 89-98; Prec Brecon Cathl 95-98; RD Maelienydd 95-98; Dean Brecon 98-00; V Brecon St Mary and Battle w Llanddew 98-00; rtd 00. *Hafod, Cefnllys Lane, Penybont, Llandrindod Wells LD1 5SW* Tel (01597) 851830

HUGHES, Canon Gerald Thomas. b 30. Lon Univ BD63 MTh. Qu Coll Birm 72. **d** 72 **p** 73. Lic to Offic *Cov* 72-80; P-in-c Birdingbury 80-81; P-in-c Leamington Hastings 80-81; V Leamington Hastings and Birdingbury 81-82; V Dunchurch 82-89; RD Rugby 85-89; Can Res Cov Cathl 89-94; rtd 94; Perm to Offic *Cov* and *Worc* from 94. *Loafers' Cottage, Lazy Lane, Fladbury, Pershore WR10 2QL* Tel (01386) 860650 E-mail gerald@loafers.plus.net

HUGHES, Canon Gwilym Berw. b 42. St Mich Coll Llan. **d** 68 **p** 69. C Conwy w Gyffin *Ban* 68-71; V Llandinorwig 71-75; TV Llandudno 75-80; V Dwygyfylchi 80-96; RD Arllechwedd 88-96; V Bodelwyddan *St As* 96-09; Can Cursal St As Cathl 08-09; rtd 09. *Glanfa, Glanyrafon Road, Dwygyfylchi, Penmaenmawr LL34 6UD* Tel (01492) 623365

HUGHES, Gwilym Lloyd. b 48. Univ of Wales (Cardiff) BD76 MA79 Univ of Wales (Ban) CertEd84. St Mich Coll Llan 71. **d** 99 **p** 00. NSM Caerwys and Bodfari *St As* from 99; Warden of Readers 99-02. *Adlonfa, Bodfari, Denbigh LL16 4DA* Tel (01745) 710385

HUGHES, Canon Gwyndaf Morris. b 36. Univ of Wales (Lamp) BA57 St Cath Soc Ox 57. St Steph Ho Ox 58 St Mich Coll Llan 59. **d** 59 **p** 60. C Glanogwen *Ban* 59-62; Chapl RN 62-78; R Llanfairpwll w Penmynydd *Ban* 78-90; R Beaumaris 90-03; RD Tindaethwy 88-02; AD 02-03; Can Ban Cathl 95-99; Prec 99-03; Preb 99-03; rtd 03. *Cae Pysgodlyn, Waterloo Port, Caernarfon LL55 1LW* Tel (01286) 677461

HUGHES, Harold John (Hadge). b 55. St Jo Coll Nottm 83. **d** 86 **p** 87. C Man Miles Platting 86-87; C Man Apostles w Miles Platting 87-89; V Roughtown 89-93; Chapl Chich Univ 04-09; TV Horsham *Chich* from 10. *St Leonard's Vicarage, Cambridge Road, Horsham RH13 5ED* Tel (01403) 265519

HUGHES, Canon Hazel. b 45. St Jo Coll Dur 75. **dss** 78 **d** 87 **p** 94. Lower Mitton *Worc* 78-81; Worc St Martin w St Pet, St Mark etc 82-87; Par Dn Worc SE 87-88; Dn-in-c Wribbenhall 88-94; V 94; P-in-c 94-10; Chapl to Mentally Handicapped 94-10; Hon Can Worc Cathl 95-10; rtd 11. *8 Hidcote Close, Worcester WR5 3SX* Tel (01905) 353817 E-mail hazel.hughes1@btopenworld.com

HUGHES, Heather Alice. b 48. Open Univ BA91 Kent Univ 97. **d** 99 **p** 00. NSM Pembury *Roch* from 99. *7 Henwoods Crescent, Pembury TN2 4LJ* Tel (01892) 822764 E-mail heather.hughes@diocese-rochester.org

HUGHES, Ian. b 67. Aston Tr Scheme Trin Coll Bris BA00. **d** 00 **p** 01. C Halton *Ches* 00-04; P-in-c Seacombe from 04; P-in-c Poulton from 06. *Seacombe Vicarage, 5 Brougham Road, Wallasey CH44 6PN* Tel 0151-638 9949 E-mail i_hughes@hotmail.com

HUGHES, Ian Peter. b 55. Fitzw Coll Cam BA76 MA93. Ridley Hall Cam 05. **d** 07 **p** 08. C Wadhurst *Chich* 07-11; C Howell Hill w Burgh Heath *Guildf* from 11. *19 Ballards Green, Burgh Heath, Tadworth KT20 6DA* Tel (01737) 373077 Mobile 07718-909695 E-mail ian@hughes.name

HUGHES, Preb Ivor Gordon. b 45. Culham Coll of Educn CertEd68 Westmr Coll Ox MTh94. Ripon Coll Cuddesdon 75. **d** 77 **p** 78. C Newport w Longford *Lich* 77-79; Children's Work Officer CMS 79-82; V Gt and Lt Bedwyn and Savernake Forest *Sarum* 82-86; P-in-c Urchfont w Stert 86-90; TR Redhorn 90-92; Nat Children's Officer Gen Syn Bd of Educn 92-95; R Yeovil w Kingston Pitney *B & W* 95-06; Preb Wells Cathl 02-06; RD Yeovil 04-06; Chapl St Marg Hospice Yeovil 04-06; P-in-c Klamath Falls and Bonanza USA 06-08; rtd 08. *6 Cole Mead, Bruton BA10 0DL* Tel (01749) 814873

HUGHES, Mrs Jackie Louise. b 50. ACP81 Birm Poly BEd86. WMMTC 89. **d** 92. NSM Edgbaston St Geo *Birm* 92-95; Tutor Qu Coll Birm 96-05; Lic to Offic *Birm* from 05. *267 Stoney Lane, Yardley, Birmingham B25 8YG* Tel 0121-628 4184 or 454 8597

HUGHES, James Thomas. b 74. St Anne's Coll Ox BA95 Liv Hope PGCE97. Oak Hill Th Coll BA02. **d** 03 **p** 04. C Virginia Water *Guildf* 03-07; C Hartford *Ches* from 07. *52 Stones Manor*

Lane, Hartford, Northwich CW8 1NU Tel (01606) 77740
E-mail james@christchurchgreenbank.org
HUGHES, John. *See* HUGHES, Arthur John
HUGHES, John David. b 58. Leeds Univ BA79 Man Univ
PGCE82. Ripon Coll Cuddesdon 97. **d** 99 **p** 00. C Wythenshawe
Man 99-06; P-in-c Old Trafford St Jo from 06; AD Stretford
from 10. *St John's Rectory, 1 Lindum Avenue, Manchester
M16 9NQ* Tel 0161-872 0500
E-mail john_dhughes@yahoo.co.uk
HUGHES, John Lloyd. b 48. **d** 08 **p** 09. NSM Abergavenny
St Mary w Llanwenarth Citra *Mon* 08-09; NSM Govilon w
Llanfoist w Llanelen from 09. *Emmanuel, 7 Orchard Close,
Gilwern, Abergavenny NP7 0EN* Tel (01873) 832368
E-mail john997hughes@btinternet.com
HUGHES, John Malcolm. b 47. Man Univ BSc68. Coll of Resurr
Mirfield 68. **d** 71 **p** 72. C Newton Nottage *Llan* 71-78; V
Llanwynno 78-92; R Cadoxton-juxta-Barry from 92; AD
Penarth and Barry from 08. *The Rectory, 21 Rectory Road,
Cadoxton, Barry CF63 3QB* Tel and fax (01446) 406690
E-mail johnmhughes@ntlworld.com
HUGHES, John Mark David. b 78. Jes Coll Cam BA00 MA04
Mert Coll Ox MSt02 Em Coll Cam PhD05. Westcott Ho Cam
01. **d** 05 **p** 06. C Ex St Dav 05-09; Chapl Jes Coll Cam from 09.
Jesus College, Jesus Lane, Cambridge CB5 8BL Tel (01223)
339339 Mobile 07967-744035 E-mail jmd3@cantab.net
HUGHES, Canon John Patrick. b 41. Oak Hill Th Coll. **d** 67 **p** 68.
C Chorleywood St Andr *St Alb* 67-71; C E Twickenham
St Steph *Lon* 71-76; TV High Wycombe *Ox* 77-92; Chapl
Wycombe Hosp 77-83; V Harborne Heath *Birm* 92-09; Hon Can
Birm Cathl 99-09; rtd 09; Perm to Offic *Ox* from 10. *59 Witney
Road, Ducklington, Witney OX29 7TS* Tel (01993) 358781
Mobile 07817-465996
E-mail johnandanniehughes@googlemail.com
HUGHES, John Tudor. b 59. Nottm Univ BSc81 Univ of Wales
(Cardiff) BD84. St Mich Coll Llan 81. **d** 84 **p** 85. C Mold *St As*
84-88; Asst Dioc Youth Chapl 86-90; Dioc Youth Chapl 90-97;
Min Can St As Cathl 88-90; Min St As and Tremeirchion 88-90;
V Holt 90-96; V Buckley 96-04; RD Mold 00-03; V Gresford
04-09; V Holt and Gresford from 09. *The Vicarage, Church
Green, Gresford, Wrexham LL12 8RG* Tel (01978) 852236
HUGHES, Leonard Mordecai. b 50. St Jo Coll Nottm 95. **d** 97
p 98. NSM N Evington *Leic* from 97. *68 Trevino Drive, Leicester
LE4 7PH* Tel 0116-266 9979
HUGHES, Lindsay. *See* HUGHES, Miss Carol Lindsay
HUGHES, Martin Conway. b 40. Ex Coll Ox BA61 MA67. Chich
Th Coll. **d** 63 **p** 64. C Roehampton H Trin *S'wark* 63-67; C
Addlestone *Guildf* 67-71; V Burpham 71-88; V Shamley Green
88-05; RD Cranleigh 90-95; rtd 05; Perm to Offic *Portsm* from
05. *22 Siskin Close, Bishops Waltham, Southampton SO32 1RQ*
Tel (01489) 890365 E-mail martin@mchughes.org.uk
HUGHES, Matthew James. b 66. K Coll Lon BD88. Westcott Ho
Cam 89. **d** 91 **p** 92. C Heston *Lon* 91-94; C Fulham All SS 94-96;
TV St Laur in Thanet *Cant* 96-01; R Farnborough *Roch* from
01. *The Rectory, Farnborough Hill, Orpington BR6 7EQ* Tel
(01689) 856931 E-mail jmath@btinternet.com
HUGHES, Michael John Minto. b 50. Liv Univ MB, ChB74
Westmr Coll Ox MTh94. Wycliffe Hall Ox 76. **d** 79 **p** 80. C
Stranton *Dur* 79-82; Chapl Intercon Ch Soc Peru 82-86; Perm to
Offic *Dur* 86-87 and *Carl* 87-89; TV Thetford *Nor* 89-97; P-in-c
Downham *Ely* 97-05; Hon C Ely from 05. *Georgian House, 6A
Station Road, Ely CB7 4BS* Tel (01353) 615682
E-mail mikeandsue.hughes@ntlworld.com
HUGHES, Neville Joseph. b 52. NUU BA79 MBIM93. CITC 97.
d 91 **p** 92. NSM Mullabrack w Markethill and Kilcluney *Arm*
91-98; I from 00; C Portadown St Mark 98-00. *The Rectory, 6
Mullurg Road, Markethill BT60 1QN* Tel (028) 3755 1092
HUGHES, The Ven Paul Vernon. b 53. Ripon Coll Cuddesdon 79.
d 82 **p** 83. C Chipping Barnet w Arkley *St Alb* 82-86; TV
Dunstable 86-93; P-in-c Boxmoor St Jo 93-98; V 98-03; RD
Hemel Hempstead 96-03; Adn Bedford from 03. *17 Landsowne
Road, Luton LU3 1EE* Tel (01582) 730722 Fax 877354
E-mail archdbedf@stalbans.anglican.org
HUGHES, Mrs Penelope Patricia. b 47. Sheff Univ LLB.
WMMTC 95. **d** 98 **p** 99. NSM Whitley *Cov* 98-01; NSM
Leamington Spa H Trin and Old Milverton 01-03; P-in-c
Berkswell 03-08; rtd 08. *8 Albany Terrace, Leamington Spa
CV32 5LP* Tel (01926) 330204 E-mail penhughes@aol.com
HUGHES, Peter. b 79. Nottm Univ BSc02. Westmr Th Cen 06.
d 08 **p** 09. C Bryanston Square St Mary w St Marylebone
St Mark *Lon* 08-09; Pioneer Min King's Cross from 10. *Flat B,
132 Hemingford Road, London N1 1DE*
E-mail pete@stmaryslondon.com
HUGHES, Peter John. b 43. Melbourne Univ BA67 Ch Ch Ox
BPhil77. Trin Coll Melbourne 64 ACT 69. **d** 70 **p** 70. C
Warrnambool Australia 70-72; C Croydon St Jo 72-74; Perm to
Offic *Ox* 75-77; Chapl Ripon Coll Cuddesdon 77-79; Chapl Lon
Univ 79-84; Australia from 84; rtd 08. *c/o P J Miller & Co, PO
Box 626, North Sydney NSW 2059, Australia*
E-mail pjmillerandco@ozemail.com.au

HUGHES, Peter John. b 59. Wolv Poly BA83 Lon Univ PGCE85.
Wycliffe Hall Ox 90. **d** 92 **p** 93. C Ecclesall *Sheff* 92-96; V
Kimberworth 96-05; R Wickersley from 05. *The Rectory, 5
Church Lane, Wickersley, Rotherham S66 1ES* Tel (01709)
543111 E-mail peter.j.hughes59@btinternet.com
HUGHES, Peter Knowles. b 61. Sarum & Wells Th Coll 87. **d** 90
p 91. C Whitchurch *Bris* 90-93; Perm to Offic *Worc* 93-97 and
from 02; Chapl Univ Coll Worc 97-02. *Woodside Farmhouse,
Blakes Lane, Guarlford, Malvern WR13 6NZ* Tel (01684) 311308
HUGHES, Canon Philip. b 47. St Jo Coll Nottm 79. **d** 81 **p** 82. C
Dolgellau w Llanfachreth and Brithdir etc *Ban* 81-83; Asst
Youth Chapl 82-83; R Llaneugrad w Llanallgo and
Penrhoslugwy etc 83-95; R Llanberis w Llanrug 95-03; Dioc
Youth Chapl 93-98; RD Arfon 00-02; R Llanfair-pwll and
Llanddaniel-fab etc from 03; AD Tindaethwy and Menai 07-10.
The Rectory, Ffordd Caergybi, Llanfairpwllgwyngyll LL61 5SX
Tel and fax (01248) 713746
E-mail revphiliphughes@yahoo.co.uk
HUGHES, Philip Geoffrey John. b 60. Nottm Univ
BCombStuds82. Qu Coll Birm 86. **d** 89 **p** 90. C Sedgley All SS
Worc 89-94; V Boscoppa *Truro* 94-96; Chapl Gatwick Airport
and Chapl Sussex Police 96-02; P-in-c Harmondsworth *Lon*
02-07; Chapl Heathrow Airport 02-07; Chapl Metrop Police
02-07; V Seghill *Newc* from 07; Chapl Northumbria Police from
07. *Seghill Vicarage, Mares Close, Seghill, Cramlington
NE23 7EA* Tel 0191-298 0925
E-mail p.hughes.1@btinternet.com
HUGHES, Philip John. b 70. Trin Coll Bris BA07. **d** 07 **p** 08. C
Ashby-de-la-Zouch and Breedon on the Hill *Leic* 07-10; V
Bishops Hull *B & W* from 10; Chapl Somerset Coll of Arts and
Tech from 10. *The Vicarage, Bishops Hull Hill, Bishops Hull,
Taunton TA1 5EB* E-mail phil2overflowing@tesco.net
HUGHES, Philip Stephen. b 34. Dur Univ BA59. Coll of Resurr
Mirfield 59. **d** 62 **p** 63. C Horfield St Greg *Bris* 62-66; C
Bedminster St Mich 66-69; P-in-c Chippenham St Pet 69-71; V
71-83; TR Bedminster 83-91; V Ashton Keynes, Leigh and
Minety 91-00; rtd 00; Perm to Offic *Worc* from 00. *19 Fairways,
Pershore WR10 1HA* Tel (01386) 552375
HUGHES, Poppy. *See* HUGHES, Veronica Jane
HUGHES, Richard Clifford. b 24. Pemb Coll Cam BA57 MA59.
Ely Th Coll 48. **d** 50 **p** 51. C Wandsworth St Anne *S'wark* 50-53;
S Rhodesia 53-65; S Africa 65-86; Adn Pinetown 75-80;
Australia from 86; rtd 89. *1/184 Springfield Road, Blackburn
North Vic 3130, Australia* Tel (0061) (3) 9894 4889
E-mail cherryh@smart.net.au
HUGHES, Richard Jeffrey. b 47. Trin Coll Carmarthen
CertEd68. St Mich Coll Llan 74. **d** 76 **p** 77. C Llanbeblig w
Caernarfon and Betws Garmon etc *Ban* 76-78; Dioc Youth
Chapl 78-82; TV Holyhead w Rhoscolyn w Llanfair-yn-Neubwll
78-83; R Llanfachraeth 83-92; R Llangefni w Tregaean and
Llangristiolus etc 92-95; TV Llanbeblig w Caernarfon and Betws
Garmon etc from 95. *Hafodty, 30 Bryn Rhos, Rhosbodrual,
Caernarfon LL55 2BT* Tel (01286) 674181
HUGHES, Richard Millree. b 33. Univ of Wales BA56 MA79.
St Mich Coll Llan 56. **d** 58 **p** 59. C Mold *St As* 58-61; V Choral
St As Cathl 61-64; V Towyn 64-67; Asst Master Marlborough
Sch Woodstock 77-79; R Whitchurch St Mary *Ox* 79-00; rtd 00.
Le Village, Saint-Antoine, 32340 Miradoux, France Tel (0033)
5 62 28 69 08 Mobile 07798-790369 E-mail rmillree@aol.com
HUGHES, Robert Elistan-Glodrydd. b 32. Trin Coll Ox BA54
MA58 Birm Univ MLitt85. Westcott Ho Cam 55. **d** 57 **p** 58. C
Stoke *Cov* 57-61; Ind Chapl *S'wark* 61-64; Birm Univ 64-69;
Chapl 64-69; Lodgings Warden and Student Welfare Adv 69-87;
Dir Housing Study Overseas Students Trust 88-91; Perm to Offic
Ban 88-94; V Harlech and Llanfair-juxta-Harlech etc 94-99; rtd
97. *Clogwyn Melyn, Ynys, Talsarnau LL47 6TP* Tel (01766)
780257 E-mail shebob.clog1@virgin.net
HUGHES, Robert John. b 46. Liv Univ MB, ChB69. St Jo Coll
Nottm 05. **d** 07 **p** 08. NSM Davenham *Ches* 07-11; V Sandiway
from 11. *The Vicarage, 50 Norley Road, Sandiway, Northwich
CW8 2JU* Tel (01606) 350132 Mobile 07966-470761
E-mail jh@doctors.org.uk
HUGHES, Robert Leslie. b 52. Qu Coll Birm 98. **d** 00 **p** 01. C The
Quinton *Birm* 00-05; P-in-c Appleby Gp *Leic* 05-08; TV
Woodfield 08-09; rtd 09. *42 Peto Avenue, Colchester CO4 5WJ*
E-mail roberthgs@mac.com
HUGHES, Rodney Thomas. b 39. Dur Univ BA60. Wycliffe Hall
Ox 60. **d** 62 **p** 63. C Edin St Thos 62-65; C Harlow New Town w
Lt Parndon *Chelmsf* 65-67; R Haworth *Bradf* 67-74; R W
Knighton w Broadmayne *Sarum* 74-77; R Broadmayne, W
Knighton, Owermoigne etc 77-82; V Crosthwaite Keswick *Carl*
82-02; rtd 02; Perm to Offic *Carl* from 02. *2 Bewcastle Close,
Carlisle CA3 0PU* Tel (01228) 401680
HUGHES, Roger. *See* HUGHES, Canon William Roger
HUGHES, Mrs Sally Lorraine. b 59. Open Univ BA98. EAMTC
99. **d** 02 **p** 03. NSM Gretton w Rockingham and Cottingham w
E Carlton *Pet* 02-05; Asst Chapl Kettering Gen Hosp NHS Trust
02-04; P-in-c Stoke Albany w Wilbarston and Ashley etc *Pet*
from 05; Rural Adv Oakham Adnry from 05. *28 Rushton Road,*

Wilbarston, Market Harborough LE16 8QL Tel and fax (01536) 770998 E-mail sally@hughes.uk.com
HUGHES, Mrs Sheila. b 52. NOC 92. **d** 95 **p** 96. NSM Birkenhead Priory *Ches* 95-97; C 97-99; P-in-c Northwich St Luke and H Trin 99-01; V 01-07; Bp's Adv for Women in Min 00-07; Chapl Mid Cheshire Hosps Trust 99-07; P-in-c Barrow St Jo *Carl* from 07. *St John's Vicarage, James Watt Terrace, Barrow-in-Furness LA14 2TS* Tel (01229) 821101 *or* 835909 E-mail revsheilahughes@hotmail.co.uk
HUGHES, Sheila Norah. b 40. **d** 06 **p** 07. NSM Ellesmere Port *Ches* 06-10; rtd 10. *13 Bridle Way, Great Sutton, Ellesmere Port CH66 2NJ* Tel 0151-339 9777 E-mail sheila.hughes67@ntlworld.com
HUGHES, Steven Philip. b 52. MBE01. St Jo Coll Dur BA80. Ridley Hall Cam 80. **d** 82 **p** 83. C Chilvers Coton w Astley *Cov* 82-86; TV Kings Norton *Birm* 86-91; Perm to Offic *Eur* 92-96; Asst Chapl Bucharest 96-98; P-in-c Bucharest w Sofia 98-01; P-in-c Belgrade 98-00; P-in-c Hoole *Blackb* 02-09; Inter-Faith Development Officer Chs Together from 09. *6 Park Avenue, Much Hoole, Preston PR4 4QL* Tel (01772) 611647 Mobile 07754-177689 E-mail steven.hughes24@btinternet.com
HUGHES, Trystan Owain. b 72. Univ of Wales (Ban) BD94 PhD98. Wycliffe Hall Ox MTh. **d** 05 **p** 07. C Llantwit Major 05-09; C Whitchurch 09; Chapl Cardiff Univ from 09. *The Chaplaincy, Cardiff University, 61 Park Place, Cardiff CF10 3AT* Tel (029) 2023 2550 E-mail hughest6@cardiff.ac.uk
HUGHES, Ms Valerie Elizabeth. b 53. Birm Univ BA75 CertEd76. Wycliffe Hall Ox 85. **d** 87 **p** 94. C Hallwood *Ches* 87-90; Par Dn Garston *Liv* 90-93; Asst Chapl Liv Univ 93; TD Gateacre 93-94, TV 94-00, C St Helens St Helen 00-09, TV Newton from 09. *Emmanuel Rectory, 333 Wargrave Road, Newton-le-Willows WA12 8RR* Tel (01925) 224920
HUGHES, Veronica Jane (Poppy). b 60. Ex Univ BA82 Birkbeck Coll Lon MSc04. SEITE 07. **d** 10 **p** 11. C Dulwich St Clem w St Pet *S'wark* from 10. *56 Sydenham Park Road, London SE26 4DL* E-mail poppy_hughes@hotmail.co.uk
HUGHES, William. *See* HUGHES, Albert William
HUGHES, William Piers Maximillian. b 76. Ex Univ BA99. Ripon Coll Cuddesdon 99. **d** 01 **p** 02. C Cley Hill Warminster *Sarum* 01-05; V Blackmoor and Whitehill *Portsm* 05-11; V Petersfield from 11; R Buriton from 11; AD Petersfield from 11. *The Vicarage, Shackleford House, 12 Dragon Street, Petersfield GU31 4AB* Tel (01730) 260464 E-mail will-hattie@lineone.net
HUGHES, Canon William Roger. b 47. ACCA MCIPD MBIM. Trin Coll Carmarthen. **d** 91 **p** 92. NSM Llan-non *St D* 91-93; Dio Officer for Soc Resp from 93; V Llangathen w Llanfihangel Cilfargen etc 93-10; V Catheiniog from 10; Hon Can St D Cathl 06-09; Can from 09; AD Llangadog and Llandeilo from 06. *The Vicarage, Llangathen, Carmarthen SA32 8QD* Tel (01558) 668455
HUGHMAN, June Alison. b 58. Kingston Poly BSc81 Southn Univ PhD84. Trin Coll Bris 86. **d** 89 **p** 94. Par Dn Penge St Jo *Roch* 89-93; C Woking Ch Ch *Guildf* 93-98; V Croydon Ch Ch *S'wark* 98-00; C Uxbridge *Lon* from 00; Town Cen Min from 00. *84 Harefield Road, Uxbridge UB8 1PN* Tel and fax (01895) 254121 *or* tel 258766 E-mail junehughman@tiscali.co.uk
HUGO, Canon Keith Alan. b 41. Nottm Univ BA62. Chich Th Coll 62. **d** 64 **p** 65. C Pontefract St Giles *Wakef* 64-68; C Chesterfield St Mary and All SS *Derby* 68-71; V Allenton and Shelton Lock 71-77; Dioc Communications Officer *Sarum* 77-89; V Potterne 77-84; V Worton 77-84; V Potterne w Worton and Marston 84-89; R Wyke Regis 89-06; Can and Preb Sarum Cathl 84-06; RD Weymouth 94-04; rtd 06. *15 Steepdene, Poole BH14 8TE* Tel (01202) 734971 E-mail keith.hugo@ntlworld.com
HUISH, Barnaby Thomas. b 71. St Chad's Coll Dur BA94 MA95. Ripon Coll Cuddesdon BA98. **d** 99 **p** 00. C Darlington H Trin *Dur* 99-02; Prec and Min Can St Alb Abbey 02-06; R Dur St Marg and Neville's Cross St Jo from 06. *St Margaret's Rectory, 10 Westhouse Avenue, Durham DH1 4FH*
HUITSON, Christopher Philip. b 45. Keble Coll Ox BA66 MA70. Cuddesdon Coll 67. **d** 69 **p** 70. C Croydon St Sav *Cant* 69-71; Soc Service Unit St Martin-in-the-Fields Lon 71-73; C St Alb St Pet *St Alb* 73-77; V Cople 77-78; P-in-c Willington 77-78; V Cople w Willington 78-89; V Leavesden 89-96; V Totteridge 96-11; RD Barnet 99-05; rtd 11. *Abbotsleigh, 1A Gainsborough Drive, Sherborne DT9 6DS* Tel (01935) 815187 E-mail c.huitson@btinternet.com
HULBERT, Hugh Forfar. b 22. Bris Univ BA49. Bible Churchmen's Coll Bris 46. **d** 50 **p** 51. C Summerstown *S'wark* 50-53; C Felixstowe SS Pet and Paul *St E* 53-55; Min Collier Row St Jas CD *Chelmsf* 55-59; SW Area Sec CPAS 59-63; V Portsea St Luke *Portsm* 63-75; V Worthing H Trin *Chich* 75-81; C-in-c Hove H Trin CD 81-85; C Hailsham 86-87; rtd 87; Perm to Offic *Chich* from 87. *8 Ramsay Hall, 11-13 Byron Road, Worthing BN11 3HN* Tel (01903) 209594
HULBERT, John Anthony Lovett. b 40. Trin Coll Cam BA63 MA67. Wells Th Coll 64. **d** 66 **p** 67. C Fareham H Trin *Portsm* 66-70; R Wickham 70-79; RD Bishop's Waltham 74-79; V

Bedford St Andr *St Alb* 79-92; RD Bedford 87-92; V Leighton Buzzard w Eggington, Hockliffe etc 92-03; Hon Can St Alb 91-03; C Stansted *Chich* 03-04; P-in-c Lynch w Iping Marsh and Milland 04-10; rtd 10; Perm to Offic *Chich* from 10 and *Portsm* from 11. *Cherry Trees, Buckshead Hill, Meonstoke, Southampton SO32 3NA* Tel (01489) 878289 E-mail anthonic@btinternet.com
HULBERT, Canon Martin Francis Harrington. b 37. Dur Univ BSc58 MA62. Ripon Hall Ox 58. **d** 60 **p** 61. C Buxton *Derby* 60-63; C Eglingham *Newc* 63-67; C-in-c Loundsley Green Ascension CD *Derby* 67-71; P-in-c Frecheville 71-73; R Frecheville and Hackenthorpe *Sheff* 73-77; P-in-c Hathersage *Derby* 77-83; V 83-90; RD Bakewell and Eyam 81-90; R Brailsford w Shirley and Osmaston w Edlaston 90-93; V Tideswell 93-02; RD Buxton 96-99; Hon Can Derby Cathl 89-02; rtd 02; Perm to Offic *Derby* from 02. *22 Yokecliffe Crescent, Wirksworth, Matlock DE4 4ER* Tel (01629) 825148 E-mail martin.hulbert1@btinternet.com
HULETT, Peter. b 31. CEng MIMechE62 Leeds Univ CertEd74. Wycliffe Hall Ox 75. **d** 77 **p** 78. C Eastwood *S'well* 77-80; C Granby w Elton 80-83; V Gilling and Kirkby Ravensworth *Ripon* 83-90; P-in-c Bishop Monkton and Burton Leonard 90-96; rtd 96; Perm to Offic *Bradf* from 96. *2 Cardan Drive, Ilkley LS29 8PH* Tel (01943) 604202
HULL, Mrs Bernadette Mary. b 46. E Lon Univ BA92 PGCE93. NTMTC 99. **d** 02 **p** 03. NSM Becontree S *Chelmsf* 02-04; NSM Marks Gate 04-09; P-in-c Romford Ascension Collier Row from 09. *Ascension Vicarage, 68 Collier Row Road, Romford RM5 2BA* Tel (01708) 741658 Mobile 07990-730293 E-mail bernadettchull@btinternet.com
HULL, David John. b 44. Linc Th Coll 88. **d** 90 **p** 91. C Mansfield Woodhouse *S'well* 90-93; P-in-c Mansfield St Lawr 93-00; V Mosbrough *Sheff* 00-03; V Elmton *Derby* 03-09; P-in-c Whitwell 05-09; rtd 10; Perm to Offic *Derby* and *S'well* from 10. *5 Beeley Close, Creswell, Worksop S80 4GA* Tel (01909) 724104 E-mail rev.dhull@tiscali.co.uk
HULL, John Hammond. b 36. Brasted Th Coll 58 Sarum Th Coll 60. **d** 61 **p** 62. C Gt Clacton *Chelmsf* 61-66; Area Chapl (E Anglia) Toc H 66-70; (Midl Region) 70-75; Lic to Offic *Chelmsf* 66-75; Chapl Toc H HQ 75-82; Lic to Offic *Ox* 75-01; rtd 01; Perm to Offic *Ox* from 01. *66 Grenville Avenue, Wendover, Aylesbury HP22 6AL* Tel (01296) 624487
HULL, The Very Revd Thomas Henry. b 55. QUB BD79. NTMTC 94. **d** 97 **p** 98. C Kidbrooke *S'wark* 97-99; TV 99-01; I Lecale Gp *D & D* from 01; Min Can Down Cathl 03-06; Dean Down from 06. *Lecale Rectory, 9 Quoile Road, Downpatrick BT30 6SE* Tel (028) 4461 3101 *or* 4461 4922 Fax 4461 4456 E-mail henryhull@downcathedral.org
HULL, Timothy David. b 60. Lon Bible Coll 87 K Coll Lon PhD97. St Jo Coll Nottm BTh90. **d** 90 **p** 91. C Leyton St Mary w St Edw *Chelmsf* 90-95; Chapl Havering Coll of F&HE 94-98; C Harold Hill St Geo *Chelmsf* 95-98; TV Becontree W 98-05; Co-ord NTMTC 98-01; Registrar 01-05; Tutor St Jo Coll Nottm from 05. *2 Peache Way, Chilwell Lane, Bramcote, Nottingham NG9 3DX* Tel 0115-943 6988 E-mail t.hull@stjohns-nottm.ac.uk
HULL, Suffragan Bishop of. *See* FRITH, The Rt Revd Richard Michael Cokayne
✠**HULLAH, The Rt Revd Peter Fearnley.** b 49. K Coll Lon BD71 AKC71 FRSA93. Cuddesdon Coll 73. **d** 74 **p** 75 **c** 99. Asst Chapl St Edw Sch Ox 74-77; C Summertown *Ox* 74-77; Chapl Sevenoaks Sch 77-82; Hon C Sevenoaks St Nic *Roch* 77-82; Hd Master Internat Cen Sevenoaks Sch 82-87; Hon C Kippington 82-87; Sen Chapl K Sch and Hon Min Can Cant Cathl 87-92; Hd Master Chetham's Sch of Music 92-99; Hon Can Man Cathl 96-99; Area Bp Ramsbury *Sarum* 99-05; Prin Northn Academy 05-11; NSM St Martin-in-the-Fields *Lon* from 11; Dir Ethos, United Learning Trust/Ch Schs Trust from 11. *62 St Margarets Road, Twickenham TW1 2LP*
HULLETT, Frederick Graham. St Jo Coll York CertEd53 Leeds Univ BA58. Coll of Resurr Mirfield 58. **d** 60 **p** 61. C Acton Green St Pet *Lon* 60-61; C W Hackney St Barn 61-64; C Paddington St Mary 64-67; Hon C 67-69; P-in-c Haggerston St Aug w St Steph 69-73; Lic to Offic 73-84; Perm to Offic *Linc* from 84; rtd 91. *16 James Street, Lincoln LN2 1QE* Tel (01522) 523516
HULLYER, Paul Charles. b 68. Anglia Poly Univ MA98 Lambeth MA04 FRSA04. Aston Tr Scheme 92 Westcott Ho Cam 94. **d** 97 **p** 98. C Stoke Newington St Mary *Lon* 97-00; C Addlestone *Guildf* 00-03; V Hillingdon All SS *Lon* 03-08; V Pinner from 08; Dir Post-Ord Tr from 10. *The Vicarage, 2 Church Lane, Pinner HA5 3AA* Tel (020) 8866 3869 E-mail paulhullyer.vicar@btinternet.com
HULME, Alan John. b 60. Birm Univ BSc81. Wycliffe Hall Ox BA90. **d** 91 **p** 92. C Chilwell *S'well* 91-96; TV Roxeth *Lon* 96-02; V S Harrow St Paul 02-08; TR Ely from 08. *St Mary's Vicarage, St Mary's Street, Ely CB7 4HF* Tel (01353) 662308 *or* 668787 E-mail alanjhulme@aol.com *or* alanhulme@elyparishchurch.org.uk

HULME (*née* **ASHLEY**), **Mrs Jane Isobel.** b 59. Birm Univ BSc81. **d** 05 **p** 06. NSM S Harrow St Paul *Lon* 05-08; NSM Ely from 08. *St Mary's Vicarage, St Mary's Street, Ely CB7 4ER* Tel (01353) 662308 *or* 668787 E-mail janehulme@aol.com *or* janehulme@elyparishchurch.org.uk

HULME, Ms Juliette Mary. b 57. Whitelands Coll Lon BEd81. Cranmer Hall Dur 94. **d** 94 **p** 95. C Crayford *Roch* 94-98; C Leatherhead *Guildf* 98-01; CF 02-05; Perm to Offic *Sarum* 05-08; Chapl Wells Cathl Sch from 06. *18 Vicars Close, Wells BA5 2UJ* Tel (01749) 834207 E-mail j.hulme@wells-cathedral-school.com

HULME, Norman. b 31. Kelham Th Coll 50. **d** 54 **p** 55. C Blackb St Pet 54-57; C Blakenall Heath *Lich* 57-59; V Gannow *Blackb* 59-64; V Anwick *Linc* 64-74; V S Kyme 64-74; V Moulton 74-83; V Earl Shilton w Elmesthorpe *Leic* 83-88; Chapl Harperbury Hosp Radlett 88-96; rtd 96. *Moorcroft, 9 Birch Grove, Spalding PE11 2HL* Tel (01775) 710127 E-mail norjoan@yahoo.co.uk

HULME, Susan. b 52. **d** 08 **p** 09. NSM Kinsley w Wragby *Wakef* from 08. *4 Balmoral Drive, Knottingley WF11 8RQ* Tel (01977) 676808 E-mail bedeuk@talk21.com

HULME, Suffragan Bishop of. Vacant

HULSE, William John. b 42. Dur Univ BA65. Linc Th Coll 65. **d** 67 **p** 68. C S Westoe *Dur* 67-70; Lic to Offic *Newc* 70-72; C Far Headingley St Chad *Ripon* 72-76; R Swillington 76-88; V Shadwell 88-95; V Oulton w Woodlesford 95-02; P-in-c Spennithorne w Finghall and Hauxwell from 02; Chapl MU from 03. *The Rectory, Spennithorne, Leyburn DL8 5PR* Tel (01969) 623010

HULT, Mrs Anna Eva Hildegard. b 73. Lund Univ Sweden MTh. Lund Inst Past Th 97. **p** 98. C Norrahammar Sweden 98-99; Asst V Ignaberga 99-00; Asst V Genard 00-03; Perm to Offic *Ely* 02-03; P-in-c Witchford w Wentworth 03-08; Spiritual Dir Växjö Sweden from 08. *Address temp unknown*

HUME, Miss Clephane Arrol. b 46. Open Univ BA87 Edin Univ MTh98 DipOT68. Edin Dioc NSM Course 88. **d** 92 **p** 94. NSM Edin St Jo from 92. *30 Findhorn Place, Edinburgh EH9 2JP* Tel 0131-667 2996 Fax 668 3568 E-mail cah@clephaneh.plus.com

HUME, Ernest. b 45. Linc Th Coll 77. **d** 79 **p** 80. C Ilkeston St Mary *Derby* 79-81; C Sheff Manor 81-82; TV 82-88; V Norton Woodseats St Chad 88-99; V Woodhouse St Jas 99-02; rtd 02. *Shadwell, 6 Canal Bridge, Killamarsh, Sheffield S21 1DJ* Tel 0114-248 1769 E-mail ehume@vicarage51.freeserve.co.uk

HUME, Martin. b 64. Coll of Resurr Mirfield 89. **d** 91 **p** 92. C Brentwood St Thos *Chelmsf* 91-94; P-in-c Corringham 94-04; V E Wickham *S'wark* 04-10; rtd 10; Perm to Offic *Chich* from 11. *45 Holland Mews, Hove BN3 1JG* Tel (01273) 206478 Mobile 07901-553522 E-mail martinhume@aol.com

HUME, Robert Roy. b 47. **d** 09 **p** 10. OLM Ashmanhaugh, Barton Turf etc *Nor* from 09. *Owls Dene, Ferry Cott Lane, Horning, Norwich NR12 8PP* Tel (01692) 630029 E-mail robhume1@btinternet.com

HUMMERSTONE, Jeremy David. Mert Coll Ox BA65 MA70. Wells Th Coll 70. **d** 72 **p** 73. C Helmsley and Pockley cum E Moors *York* 72-75; TV Swanborough *Sarum* 75-80; P-in-c Gt Torrington *Ex* 80-81; P-in-c Lt Torrington 80-81; P-in-c Frithelstock 80-81; V Gt and Lt Torrington and Frithelstock 81-10; rtd 10. *1 Undercliffe, Pickering YO18 7BB* E-mail jdhummerstone@tiscali.co.uk

HUMPHREY, Alan. b 48. Open Univ BA74. Qu Coll Birm 07. **d** 10 **p** 11. NSM Kirby Muxloe *Leic* from 10. *44 Somerfield Way, Leicester Forest East, Leicester LE3 3LX* Tel 0116-239 2404 Mobile 07768-374200 E-mail alan.humphrey@me.com

HUMPHREY, Mrs Betty. b 37. St Mich Ho Ox 59. **d** 90 **p** 94. C Hardwicke, Quedgeley and Elmore w Longney *Glouc* 90-93; Dn-in-c Swindon w Uckington and Elmstone Hardwicke 93-94; P-in-c 94-96; R 96-98; rtd 98; Perm to Offic *Glouc* from 00. *11 Lower Orchard, Tibberton, Gloucester GL19 3AX* Tel (01452) 790790

HUMPHREY, David Lane. b 57. Maine Univ BA79. St Jo Coll Nottm 84. **d** 88 **p** 89. C Springfield All SS *Chelmsf* 88-91; C Thundersley 91-96; V Standon *St Alb* 96-04; RD Bishop's Stortford 01-04; R Portland St Matt USA from 04. *11229 NE Prescott Street, Portland OR 97220-2457, USA* Tel (001) (503) 252 5720 E-mail humphrey@iinet.com

HUMPHREY, Derek Hollis. b 37. Chich Th Coll 69. **d** 72 **p** 73. C Havant *Portsm* 72-75; C Southsea H Spirit 75-78; V Finsbury Park St Thos *Lon* 78-88; V S Patcham *Chich* 88-03; rtd 03; C Clayton w Keymer *Chich* 03-05; C Bolney 05-07; C Lurgashall, Lodsworth and Selham 07-10; P-in-c Portslade Gd Shep from 10. *35 Stanley Avenue, Portslade, Brighton BN41 2WH* Tel (01273) 419518

HUMPHREY, Canon George William. b 38. Lon Bible Coll BD61 Lon Univ CertEd74. Oak Hill Th Coll 61. **d** 62 **p** 63. C Heigham H Trin *Nor* 62-64; P-in-c Buckenham w Hassingham and Strumpshaw 64-67; Chapl St Andr Hosp Norwich 64-67; Asst Master Mexborough Gr Sch 67-69; Hd RE Cheadle Gr Sch 69-76; Hon C Cheadle Hulme St Andr *Ches* 70-76; P-in-c Kellington w Whitley *Wakef* 76-80; Teacher Thurnscoe Comp Sch 76-80; RE Insp Glos Co Coun and Dio *Glouc* 80-93; Dioc

RE Adv 93-99; Hon Can Glouc Cathl 95-99; rtd 00; Perm to Offic *Glouc* from 00. *11 Lower Orchard, Tibberton, Gloucester GL19 3AX* Tel (01452) 790790

HUMPHREY, Heather Mary. b 46. CertEd68. WMMTC 87. **d** 90 **p** 94. NSM Overbury w Teddington, Alstone etc *Worc* 90-96; NSM Berrow w Pendock, Eldersfield, Hollybush etc 96-98; C Coseley Ch Ch 98-00; V from 00. *The Vicarage, Church Road, Coseley, Bilston WV14 8YB* Tel (01902) 353551

HUMPHREY, Timothy Martin. b 62. Ex Univ BA83. St Jo Coll Nottm 86. **d** 89 **p** 90. C Wallington *S'wark* 89-92; P-in-c 92-97; C Oakley w Wootton St Lawrence *Win* 97-02; Faith Development Field Officer 97-02; V Kensington St Barn *Lon* from 02. *St Barnabas's Vicarage, 23 Addison Road, London W14 8LH* Tel (020) 7471 7019 *or* 7471 7000 Fax 7471 7001 E-mail tim@stbk.org.uk

HUMPHREYS, Mrs Anne-Marie (Anna). b 44. SRN67 K Coll Lon BD92 AKC92 Man Univ MA96. NOC 92. **d** 95 **p** 96. NSM Manchester Gd Shep and St Barn 95-98; NSM Burnage St Nic 98-03; Chapl Cen Man Healthcare NHS Trust 96-01; Chapl Cen Man/Man Children's Univ Hosp NHS Trust 01-06; rtd 06. *Tyn-y-Coed, Henryd Road, Conwy LL32 8YF* Tel (01492) 573396

HUMPHREYS, Brian Leonard. b 29. MChS51 SRCh. Bp Attwell Tr Inst. **d** 87 **p** 88. NSM Maughold *S & M* 87-91; NSM S Ramsey St Paul 91-92; NSM Andreas 92-94; Perm to Offic from 94. *Thie Cassan Yack, Jack's Lane, Port E Vullen, Ramsey, Isle of Man IM7 1AW* Tel (01624) 813694

HUMPHREYS, Daniel Robert. b 74. K Coll Lon BA95 AKC95 Leeds Univ BA99. Coll of Resurr Mirfield 97. **d** 00 **p** 01. C Scarborough St Martin *York* 00-02; C Kilburn St Aug w St Jo *Lon* 02-08; V Willesden St Matt from 08. *St Matthew's Vicarage, 77 St Mary's Road, London NW10 4AU* Tel (020) 8965 3748 E-mail dhumphreys566@btinternet.com

HUMPHREYS, James Graham. b 36. Liv Univ BEng57 PhD60. Trin Coll Bris 61. **d** 63 **p** 64. C Denton Holme *Carl* 63-66; C St Helens St Mark *Liv* 66-68; V Houghton *Carl* 68-79; V Bramcote *S'well* 79-93; RD Beeston 85-90; rtd 93; Perm to Offic *S'well* 93-01; Perm to Offic *Carl* from 01. *383 London Road, Carlisle CA1 3HA* Tel (01228) 597108

HUMPHREYS, John Louis. b 51. Jes Coll Cam BA72 MA76 Nottm Univ BA75. St Jo Coll Nottm 73. **d** 76 **p** 77. C W Bromwich Gd Shep w St Jo *Lich* 76-79; C Woodford Wells *Chelmsf* 79-83; V Werrington *Lich* 83-08; Chapl HM YOI Werrington Ho 83-98; Perm to Offic *Lich* from 09. *18 Omega Way, Stoke-on-Trent ST4 8TF* Tel and fax (01782) 658575

HUMPHREYS, Canon Kenneth Glyn. b 28. Bps' Coll Cheshunt 64. **d** 66 **p** 67. C New Windsor St Jo *Ox* 66-67; C Whitley Ch Ch 67-70; V Compton 70-74; R Compton w E Ilsley 74-75; C Wokingham All SS 75-77; Chapl Lucas Hosp Wokingham (Almshouses) 77-81; V California *Ox* 81-94; RD Sonning 86-88; Hon Can Ch Ch 91-94; rtd 95; Perm to Offic *Ox* from 96. *3 Milton Court, Milton Road, Wokingham RG40 1DQ* Tel 0118-977 2096

HUMPHREYS, Mrs Lydia Ann. b 60. Sarum & Wells Th Coll 91. **d** 93 **p** 94. C Gaywood *Nor* 93-95 and 95-97; TV Cov E 97-10; P-in-c Kempston Transfiguration *St Alb* from 10. *The Vicarage, Cleveland Street, Kempston, Bedford MK42 8DW* Tel (01234) 854886 E-mail lydia@humphreys.clara.co.uk

HUMPHREYS, Canon Philip Noel. b 34. Bps' Coll Cheshunt 62. **d** 64 **p** 65. C Plymouth St Andr *Ex* 64-68; Chapl Lee Abbey 68-73; V Porchester *S'well* 73-82; RD W Bingham 82-87; P-in-c W Leake w Kingston-on-Soar and Ratcliffe-on-Soar 82-87; R W Bridgford 82-00; Hon Can S'well Minster 93-00; rtd 00; Perm to Offic *S'well* from 01. *2 Kirkfell Close, West Bridgford, Nottingham NG2 6QT*

HUMPHREYS, Canon Roger John. b 45. CertEd66 Open Univ BA76. Wycliffe Hall Ox 81. **d** 83 **p** 84. Chapl Dragon Sch Ox 83-87; C Ox St Andr 83-87; V Carterton 87-94; R Bladon w Woodstock 94-05; TR Blenheim 05-09; AD Woodstock 01-06; Chapl Cokethorpe Sch Witney from 09; Hon Can Ch Ch *Ox* from 05. *12 The Pieces, Bampton, Oxford OX18 2JZ* Tel (01993) 850199 Mobile 07788-717214 E-mail rev.rog@zen.co.uk *or* rjh@cokethorpe.org

HUMPHREYS, Stephen Robert Beresford. b 52. K Coll Lon BA98. K Coll Lon 74. **d** 76 **p** 77. C Northwood Hills St John *Lon* 76-79; C Manningham St Mary and Bradf St Mich 79-81; Chapl Bradf R Infirmary 82-86; C Leeds St Pet *Ripon* 87-90; Perm to Offic *B & W* 94-99; C Selworthy, Timberscombe, Wootton Courtenay etc 02-07; C Porlock and Porlock Weir w Stoke Pero etc from 07. *Stowey Farm, Timberscombe, Minehead TA24 7BW* Tel (01643) 841265 Mobile 07973-409536

HUMPHRIES, Anthony Roy. b 49. Lon Univ BSc73. Wycliffe Hall Ox. **d** 94 **p** 95. C Worksop St Jo *S'well* 94-96; C Retford St Sav 96-98; TV Grantham *Linc* 98-00; TV Bestwood *S'well* 00-03; V Branston w Tatenhill *Lich* 03-07. *57 Yeoman Street, Bonsall, Matlock DE4 2AA* Tel (01283) 568926 E-mail revtonyhumphries@hotmail.com

HUMPHRIES, Benjamin Paul. b 56. Man Univ BA77 FRGS85. Qu Coll Birm 82. **d** 85 **p** 86. C Hall Green Ascension *Birm* 85-88;

P-in-c Belmont *Man* 88-96; Fieldworker USPG *Blackb, Bradf, Carl* and *Wakef* 96-98; Area Co-ord Chr Aid (Cumbria, Lancs and Isle of Man) 98-07; C Shepherd's Bush St Steph w St Thos *Lon* from 07. *St Michael and St George Vicarage, 1 Commonwealth Avenue, London W12 7QR* Tel (020) 8743 7100 Mobile 07712-460860
E-mail ben.humphries@london.anglican.org
HUMPHRIES, Betty. *See* HUMPHRIES, Miss Marion Betty
HUMPHRIES, Catherine Elizabeth. *See* NICHOLLS, Mrs Catherine Elizabeth
HUMPHRIES, Canon Christopher William. b 52. St Jo Coll Cam BA73 MA77 Lon Inst of Educn CertEd74. St Jo Coll Nottm 71. **d** 79 **p** 80. C Eccleshill *Bradf* 79-82; Chapl Scargill Ho 82-86; TV Guiseley w Esholt *Bradf* 86-91; V Filey *York* 91-05; RD Scarborough 98-04; Can Res Ches Cathl from 05; Vice-Dean Ches from 11. *9 Abbey Street, Chester CH1 2JF* Tel (01244) 313812 E-mail canon.humphries@chestercathedral.com
HUMPHRIES, David. *See* HUMPHRIES, William David
HUMPHRIES, David Graham. b 48. St Mich Coll Llan 67. **d** 71 **p** 72. C Neath w Llantwit 71-72; C Bishop's Cleeve *Glouc* 81-83; C Cirencester 83-87; V Glouc St Steph 87-96; P-in-c Mickleton 96-03; Assoc P Up Hatherley 03-06; rtd 06; Chapl Glouc Charities Trust from 06. *19 Gurney Avenue, Tuffley, Gloucester GL4 0YJ* Tel (01452) 529582
HUMPHRIES, David John. b 51. BSc CertEd BD. Edin Th Coll. **d** 84 **p** 85. C Styvechale *Cov* 84-88; V Greetland and W Vale *Wakef* 88-96; V Shawbury *Lich* from 96; R Moreton Corbet from 96; V Stanton on Hine Heath from 96. *The Vicarage, Church Road, Shawbury, Shrewsbury SY1 1NH* Tel (01939) 250419
HUMPHRIES, Donald. b 43. Bris Univ BA66. Clifton Th Coll 66. **d** 68 **p** 69. C Selly Hill St Steph *Birm* 68-74; Chapl Warw Univ 74-79; V Bedford Ch Ch *St Alb* 79-85; V Cambridge H Trin w St Andr Gt *Ely* 85-92; V Cambridge H Trin 92-94; rtd 94; Perm to Offic *Ely* from 94. *25 Park Avenue, Beverley HU17 7AT* Tel (01482) 871471
HUMPHRIES, Miss Dorothy Maud. b 22. Bedf Coll Lon BA44 Lon Univ DipEd45. Gilmore Course 85. **dss** 79 **d** 87 **p** 94. Kidderminster Deanery *Worc* 79-97; NSM 87-97; Perm to Offic 98-09. *Address temp unknown*
HUMPHRIES, Grahame Leslie. b 44. Lon Coll of Div ALCD70 LTh. **d** 71 **p** 72. C Wandsworth St Mich *S'wark* 71-74; C Slough *Ox* 74-77; P-in-c Arley *Cov* 77-82; R 82-84; Norfolk Churches' Radio Officer 84-86; P-in-c Bawdeswell w Foxley 84-96; P-in-c Mayfield *Lich* 96-02; Local Min Adv (Stafford) 96-02; RD Uttoxeter 98-02; P-in-c Blockley w Aston Magna and Bourton on the Hill *Glouc* from 02; Local Min Officer from 02. *The Vicarage, The Square, Blockley, Moreton-in-Marsh GL56 9ES* Tel (01386) 700283
HUMPHRIES, Mrs Janet Susan. b 46. SAOMC 02. **d** 04 **p** 05. NSM Potton w Sutton and Cockayne Hatley *St Alb* 04-07; NSM Caldecote, Northill and Old Warden from 07. *7 Shakespeare Drive, Upper Caldecote, Biggleswade SG18 9DD* Tel (01767) 220365 E-mail janet.humphries1@ntlworld.com
HUMPHRIES, John. b 49. St Mich Coll Llan 73. **d** 76 **p** 77. C Pontnewynydd *Mon* 76-78; C Ebbw Vale 78-81; V Pet Ch Carpenter 81-86; P-in-c King's Cliffe 86-87; R King's Cliffe w Apethorpe 87-93; R King's Cliffe 93-97; V Finedon 97-09; Chapl Northants Fire and Rescue Service 03-09; TV Mynyddislwyn *Mon* from 09. *The Rectory, Vicarage Lane, Pontllanfraith, Blackwood NP12 2DP* Tel (01495) 224240 Mobile 07976-370434 E-mail frjohn13@aol.com
HUMPHRIES, Mrs Julie Ann. b 64. Birm Univ BA02. Qu Coll Birm 06. **d** 08 **p** 09. C Redditch H Trin *Worc* from 08. *4 Marshfield Close, Redditch B98 8RW* Tel (01527) 456635 E-mail julie1hum@tiscali.co.uk
HUMPHRIES, Miss Marion Betty. b 29. Open Univ BA84. Selly Oak Coll 51. **dss** 80 **d** 87 **p** 94. Newmarket St Mary w Exning St Agnes *St E* 80-82; Acomb St Steph *York* 83-86; Scarborough St Martin 86-93; Par Dn 87-93; C Cayton w Eastfield 94; rtd 94; Perm to Offic *Nor* from 95. *27 Wells Road, Walsingham NR22 6DL* Tel (01328) 820489
HUMPHRIES, Richard James Robert. b 44. FRAM95. EAMTC 99. **d** 01 **p** 02. NSM Heybridge w Langford *Chelmsf* 01-02; NSM Maldon All SS w St Pet 02-09; Asst Chapl Mid-Essex Hosp Services NHS Trust 01-04; Chapl Colchester Hosp Univ NHS Foundn Trust 04-09; rtd 09; Perm to Offic *Chelmsf* from 09. *116 Fronks Road, Harwich CO12 4EQ* Tel (01255) 502649 Mobile 07803-281036
E-mail richard.humphries1@btopenworld.com
HUMPHRIES, Robert William. b 36. Open Univ BA87. SWMTC 96. **d** 99 **p** 00. OLM Kenwyn w St Allen *Truro* from 99. *27 Penhalls Way, Playing Place, Truro TR3 6EX* Tel (01872) 862827 E-mail rev.bob@tiscali.co.uk
HUMPHRIES, Mrs Susan Joy. b 45. Open Univ BSc98. Cranmer Hall Dur 05. **d** 06 **p** 07. NSM Beverley Minster *York* 06-09; NSM N Cave w Cliffe from 09; NSM Hotham from 09. *The*

Vicarage, Church Lane, North Cave, Brough HU15 2LW Tel (01430) 470716
E-mail humphries22@humphries.22.karoo.co.uk
HUMPHRIES, William David. b 57. QUB BEd LTCL. CITC. **d** 86 **p** 87. C Ballyholme *D & D* 86-90; Min Can Belf Cathl from 89; V Choral 90-93; C Belfast St Anne *Conn* 90-93; I Stormont *D & D* from 93. *St Molua's Rectory, 3 Rosepark, Belfast BT5 7RG* Tel (028) 9048 2292 *or* 9041 9171
E-mail stormont@down.anglican.org
HUMPHRIS, Richard. b 44. Sarum & Wells Th Coll 69. **d** 72 **p** 73. C Cheltenham St Luke and St Jo *Glouc* 72-77; C Lydney w Aylburton 77-82; Chapl RAF 82-85; TV Kippax w Allerton Bywater *Ripon* 85-92; RSPCA 92-95; rtd 95; Perm to Offic *York* from 98. *4 Belle Vue Terrace, Bellerby, Leyburn DL8 5QL* Tel (01969) 622004
HUMPHRISS, Canon Reginald George. b 36. Kelham Th Coll 56. **d** 62 **p** 63. C Londonderry *Birm* 61-63; Asst Dir RE *Cant* 63-66; Dioc Youth Chapl 63-66; V Preston next Faversham 66-72; P-in-c Goodnestone St Bart and Graveney 71-72; V Spring Park 72-76; R Cant St Martin and St Paul 76-90; R Saltwood 90-01; RD Cant 82-88; Hon Can Cant Cathl 85-01; RD Elham 93-00; rtd 01; Perm to Offic *Cant* from 01. *Winsole, Faussett, Lower Hardres, Canterbury CT4 7AH* Tel (01227) 765264
HUMPHRY, Toby Peter. b 66. Man Univ BA88. Ripon Coll Cuddesdon BA90 MA96 Qu Coll Birm 92. **d** 93 **p** 94. C Westhoughton *Man* 93-96; C Westhoughton and Wingates 97; TV Atherton 97-99; TV Atherton and Hindsford 99-02; TV Atherton and Hindsford w Howe Bridge 02-03; Chapl K Sch Ely from 03; Min Can Ely Cathl from 03. *The King's School, Barton Road, Ely CB7 4DB* Tel (01353) 659653
E-mail chaplain@kings-ely.cambs.sch.uk
HUMPHRYES, Garry James. b 62. Coll of Resurr Mirfield 92. **d** 95 **p** 96. C Lt Marsden *Blackb* 95-98; C Darwen St Cuth w Tockholes St Steph 98-00; V Nelson St Bede 00-03; V Morecambe St Barn 03-08; Dioc Race and Community Relns Officer 98-03; CF from 08. *c/o MOD Chaplains (Army)* Tel (01264) 381140 Fax 381824
HUMPHRYS, Kevin Luke. b 73. Surrey Univ BA97. St Steph Ho Ox. **d** 99 **p** 00. C Moulsecoomb *Chich* 99-03. *2 Adur Court, 463 Brighton Road, Lancing BN15 8LF* Tel (01903) 609260 E-mail kevinhumphrys@hotmail.com
HUMPHRYS, Laura Frances. b 53. Goldsmiths' Coll Lon PGCE77. STETS 00. **d** 03 **p** 04. NSM Gatcombe, Chale and Shorwell w Kingston *Portsm* 03-07; Chapl HM Pris Is of Wight 07-09; Perm to Offic *Portsm* from 07. *Address temp unknown* E-mail laura.humphrys@virgin.net
HUNDLEBY, Alan. b 41. **d** 86 **p** 87. OLM Fotherby *Linc* 86-02; NSM Barnoldby le Beck from 02. *35 Cheapside, Waltham, Grimsby DN37 0HE* Tel (01472) 827159
HUNG, Frank Yu-Chi. b 45. Birm Univ BSc68 BA75 Liv Univ MSc71. Wycliffe Hall Ox 76. **d** 78 **p** 79. C Walton H Trin *Ox* 78-82; C Spring Grove St Mary *Lon* 82-85; TV Wexcombe *Sarum* 85-92; V Hatcham St Jas *S'wark* 92-98; Chapl Goldsmiths' Coll Lon 95-98; Chapl S Bank Univ 98-10; rtd 10; Hon C S'wark St Geo w St Alphege and St Jude from 10. *151 Graham Road, London SW19 3SL* Tel (020) 8542 1612
HUNGERFORD, Robin Nicholas. b 47. Redland Coll of Educn CertEd74. Trin Coll Bris 86. **d** 88 **p** 89. C Swindon Dorcan *Bris* 88-92; TV Melbury *Sarum* 92-01; P-in-c Winterbourne Stickland and Turnworth etc 01-05; V Winterborne Valley and Milton Abbas from 05. *The Rectory, North Street, Winterborne Stickland, Blandford Forum DT11 0NL* Tel and fax (01258) 880482 E-mail rjnk@rhungerford.freeserve.co.uk
HUNNISETT, John Bernard. b 47. AKC73. **d** 73 **p** 74. C Charlton Kings St Mary *Glouc* 73-77; C Portsea St Mary *Portsm* 77-80; V Badgeworth w Shurdington *Glouc* 80-87; R Dursley 87-99; TR Ross *Heref* 99-07; RD Ross and Archenfield 02-07; Chapl Huggens Coll Northfleet *Roch* from 07. *Chaplain's House, Huggens College, College Road, Northfleet DA11 9DL* Tel (01474) 352428 E-mail chaplain@huggenscollege.org
HUNNYBUN, Martin Wilfrid. b 44. Oak Hill Th Coll 67. **d** 70 **p** 71. C Ware Ch Ch *St Alb* 70-74; C Washfield, Stoodleigh, Withleigh etc *Ex* 74-75; TV 75-80; R Braunston *Pet* 80-85; Asst Chapl HM Pris Onley 80-85; R Berry and Kangaroo Valley Sydney Australia 85-94; Sen Chapl Angl Retirement Villages 94-98; TV Parkham, Alwington, Buckland Brewer etc *Ex* 98-00; Dioc Ecum Adv 98-00; R Glebe Australia 00-03. *Address temp unknown*
HUNT, Alan. b 31. GIMechE51 GIPE51. St Mich Coll Llan 65. **d** 67 **p** 68. C Standish *Blackb* 67-72; V Clitheroe St Paul Low Moor 72-76; Lic to Offic 76-85; rtd 85; Perm to Offic *Blackb* from 85. *68 Coniston Drive, Walton-le-Dale, Preston PR5 4RQ* Tel (01772) 339554
HUNT, Andrew Collins. b 54. Reading Univ BA77 Hull Univ PGCE79. St Alb Minl Tr Scheme 82 Sarum & Wells Th Coll 89 WEMTC 99. **d** 00 **p** 01. NSM Cainscross w Selsley *Glouc* 00-02;

NSM Wells St Thos w Horrington *B & W* from 07. *67 Wells Road, Glastonbury BA5 9BY* Tel (01458) 830914

HUNT, Ashley Stephen. b 50. St Jo Coll Nottm 81. **d** 83 **p** 84. C Southchurch H Trin *Chelmsf* 83-86; TV Droitwich *Worc* 86-87; USA 88-91; TV Melton St Framland *Leic* 92-93; TV Melton Mowbray 93-98; TV Grantham *Linc* 98-00; Chapl Mental Health 98-01; C Stamford All SS w St Jo 00-01; TV Mynyddislwyn *Mon* from 02. *The Vicarage, Commercial Road, Cwmfelinfach, Ynysddu, Newport NP11 7HW* Tel (01495) 200257 E-mail louhunt3@aol.com

HUNT, Beverley Cecilia. b 49. **d** 08 **p** 09. NSM E Molesey *Guildf* from 08. *422 Hurst Road, West Molesey KT8 1QS* Tel (020) 8979 8616

HUNT, Mrs Christina. b 24. Qu Mary Coll Lon BSc45. S Dios Minl Tr Scheme 78. **dss** 81 **d** 87 **p** 94. Alderbury and W Grimstead *Sarum* 81-87; Hon Par Dn 87-91; Hon Par Dn Alderbury Team 91-94; rtd 94; Perm to Offic *Sarum* 94-08. *The Heather, Southampton Road, Alderbury, Salisbury SP5 3AF* Tel (01722) 710601

HUNT, Christopher Paul Colin. b 38. Ch Coll Cam BA62 MA62. Clifton Th Coll 63. **d** 65 **p** 66. C Widnes St Paul *Liv* 65-68; Singapore 68-70; Malaysia 70-71; Hon C Foord St Jo *Cant* 72-73; Iran 74-80; Overseas Service Adv CMS 81-91; P-in-c Claverdon w Preston Bagot *Cov* 91-02; rtd 02; Perm to Offic *Worc* from 04. *Birchfield House, 18 Oaklands, Malvern WR14 4JE* Tel (01684) 578803

HUNT, David John. b 35. Kelham Th Coll 60. **d** 65 **p** 66. C Bethnal Green St Jo w St Simon *Lon* 65-69; C Mill Hill St Mich 69-73; R Staple Fitzpaine, Orchard Portman, Thurlbear etc *B & W* 73-79; P-in-c E Coker w Sutton Bingham 79-88; V E Coker w Sutton Bingham and Closworth 88-00; RD Merston 85-94; rtd 00; Perm to Offic *B & W* from 01. *Meadowside, Head Street, Tintinhull, Yeovil BA22 8QH* Tel (01935) 824554

HUNT, Derek Henry. b 38. ALCD61. **d** 62 **p** 63. C Roxeth Ch Ch *Lon* 62-66; C Radipole *Sarum* 66-70; P-in-c Shalbourne w Ham 70-72; V Burbage 72-73; V Burbage and Savernake Ch Ch 73-78; P-in-c Hulcote w Salford *St Alb* 78-88; R Cranfield 78-88; R Cranfield and Hulcote w Salford 88-95; rtd 95; Perm to Offic *St Alb* 95-98. *26 Jowitt Avenue, Kempston, Bedford MK42 8NW*

HUNT, Ernest Gary. b 36. Univ Coll Dur BA57. Carl Dioc Tr Inst 90. **d** 93 **p** 94. NSM Salesbury *Blackb* 93-95; NSM Blackb St Mich w St Jo and H Trin 95-98; NSM Balderstone 98-01; rtd 01; Perm to Offic *Blackb* from 01. *Dunelm, 10 Pleckgate Road, Blackburn BB1 8NN* Tel (01254) 52531 E-mail eg.andk.hunt@talktalk.net

HUNT, Miss Gabrielle Ann. b 59. STETS BA10. **d** 08 **p** 09. C Salisbury St Fran and Stratford sub Castle *Sarum* from 08; C Bourne Valley from 09. *20 Thistlebarrow Road, Salisbury SP1 3RT* Tel (01722) 415250 E-mail galehunt@btinternet.com

HUNT, Giles Butler. b 28. Trin Hall Cam BA51 MA55. Cuddesdon Coll 51. **d** 53 **p** 54. C N Evington *Leic* 53-56; C Northolt St Mary *Lon* 56-58; Bp's Dom Chapl *Portsm* 58-59; Bp's Chapl *Nor* 59-62; R Holt 62-67; R Kelling w Salthouse 63-67; C Pimlico St Pet w Westmr Ch Ch *Lon* 67-72; V Barkway w Reed and Buckland *St Alb* 72-79; V Preston next Faversham, Goodnestone and Graveney *Cant* 79-92; rtd 92; Perm to Offic *Nor* from 92. *The Cottage, The Fairstead, Cley-next-the-Sea, Holt NR25 7RJ* Tel (01263) 740471

HUNT, Canon Ian Carter. b 34. Chich Th Coll 61. **d** 64 **p** 65. C Plymouth St Pet *Ex* 64-67; C Daventry *Pet* 67-70; V Northampton St Paul 70-91; Can Pet Cathl 81-99; V Wellingborough All Hallows 91-99; rtd 99; Chapl Allnutt's Hosp Goring Heath 99-08. *Old School Cottage, Goring Heath, Reading RG8 7RR* Tel (01491) 680261

HUNT, James Allen. b 49. Linc Th Coll 92. **d** 92 **p** 93. C Huddersfield St Pet and All SS *Wakef* 92-95; V Longwood 95-10; rtd 10. *3 Moor Close, Huddersfield HD4 7BP* Tel (01484) 315498 E-mail jandchunt1@ntlworld.com

HUNT, James Castle. b 66. Univ of Ulster BSc90 MRICS92. Wycliffe Hall Ox 02. **d** 04 **p** 05. C N Farnborough *Guildf* 04-08; R Bishop's Waltham *Portsm* from 08; R Upham from 08. *The Rectory, Free Street, Bishops Waltham, Southampton SO32 1EE* Tel (01489) 892618

HUNT, Jeremy Mark Nicholas. b 46. Open Univ BA73 FRGS70. Ridley Hall Cam 83. **d** 85 **p** 86. C Leckhampton SS Phil and Jas w Cheltenham St Jas *Glouc* 85-87; Asst Chapl Vevey w Château d'Oex and Villars *Eur* 87-89; Chapl Berne w Neuchâtel 89-90; Dep Chapl HM Pris Pentonville 94-95; Chapl HM Pris Highpoint 95-05; TV Bury St Edmunds All SS w St Jo and St Geo *St E* 05-06; rtd 06; Perm to Offic *St E* from 06. *44 Queens Road, Bury St Edmunds IP33 3EP* Tel (01284) 723918

HUNT, John Barry. b 46. Lich Th Coll 70 Qu Coll Birm 72. **d** 73 **p** 74. C Auckland St Andr and St Anne *Dur* 73-77; C Consett 77-79; R Lyons 79-89; P-in-c Hebburn St Cuth 89-05; P-in-c Hebburn St Oswald 01-05; V Hebburn St Cuth and St Oswald 05-11; rtd 11. *11 Parklands, Gateshead NE10 8YP*

HUNT, John Edwin. b 38. ARCO Dur Univ BA60 DipEd. EMMTC 78. **d** 81 **p** 82. NSM Newbold w Dunston *Derby* 81-92;

NSM Chesterfield St Mary and All SS 92-02. *4 Ardsley Road, Ashgate, Chesterfield S40 4DG* Tel (01246) 275141 E-mail fredwin@cwcom.net

HUNT, John Stewart. b 37. Nor Ord Course 75. **d** 78 **p** 79. NSM Hunstanton St Edm *Nor* 78-81; NSM Hunstanton St Mary w Ringstead Parva, Holme etc 81-86; NSM Sedgeford w Southmere 84-86; C Lowestoft and Kirkley 86-89; R Blundeston w Flixton and Lound 89-93; P-in-c Kessingland w Gisleham 93-99; R Kessingland, Gisleham and Rushmere 99-00; rtd 00; Perm to Offic *Nor* from 00. *10 Peddars Drive, Hunstanton PE36 6HF* Tel (01485) 533424

HUNT, The Ven Judith Mary. b 57. Bris Univ BVSc80 Lon Univ PhD85 Fitzw Coll Cam BA90 MRCVS80. Ridley Hall Cam 88. **d** 91 **p** 94. Par Dn Heswall *Ches* 91-94; C 94-95; P-in-c Tilston and Shocklach 95-03; Bp's Adv for Women in Min 95-00; Can Res Ches Cathl and Dioc Dir of Min 03-09; Adn Suffolk *St E* from 09. *Glebe House, The Street, Ashfield, Stowmarket IP14 6LX* Tel (01728) 685497 E-mail archdeacon.judy@stedmundsbury.anglican.org

HUNT, Canon Kevin. b 59. St Jo Coll Dur BA80 Ox Univ BA84 MA88. St Steph Ho Ox 81. **d** 84 **p** 85. C Mansfield St Mark S'well 84-85; C Hendon and Sunderland *Dur* 85-88; V Sunderland St Mary and St Pet 88-95; TR Jarrow 95-02; V Walker *Newc* from 02; Asst Dioc Dir of Ords from 03; AD Newc E from 04; Hon Can Newc Cathl from 10. *Walker Vicarage, Middle Street, Newcastle upon Tyne NE6 4DB* Tel 0191-262 3666 E-mail kevin@hunt10.plus.com

HUNT, Mark. *See* HUNT, Jeremy Mark Nicholas

HUNT, Miss Nicola Mary. b 54. SRN77 RSCN77 RHV87. Ripon Coll Cuddesdon 93. **d** 95 **p** 96. C Broughton Astley and Croft w Stoney Stanton *Leic* 95-98; C Plymouth Em, St Paul Efford and St Aug *Ex* 98-01; V Ermington and Ugborough 01-10; TV Yelverton, Meavy, Sheepstor and Walkhampton from 10. *The Vicarage, 1 Manor Farm, Dousland, Yelverton PL20 6NR* Tel (01822) 855359

HUNT, Paul. *See* HUNT, Christopher Paul Colin

HUNT, Paul Edwin. b 47. Ripon Coll Cuddesdon 93. **d** 95 **p** 96. C Cleobury Mortimer w Hopton Wafers etc *Heref* 95-98; P-in-c Fritwell w Souldern and Ardley w Fewcott *Ox* 98-05; TR Cherwell Valley from 05; AD Bicester and Islip 05-08. *The Vicarage, 44 Forge Place, Fritwell, Bicester OX27 7QQ* Tel (01869) 346739 E-mail paul@cherwellvalleybenefice.co.uk

HUNT, Paul Michael. b 57. St Chad's Coll Dur BA79 K Coll Lon PGCE80 MA96 Univ of Wales (Lamp) MTh04. Chich Th Coll 91. **d** 92 **p** 93. Chapl Brighton Coll 92-93; NSM St Leonards SS Pet and Paul *Chich* 92-93; Chapl Mill Hill Sch Lon 93-98; Hon C Hendon St Paul Mill Hill *Lon* 95-98; P in O 96-98; V Southgate St Andr *Lon* 98-05; Warden of Readers Edmonton Area 01-05; Chapl Em Sch Wandsworth from 05. *Emanuel School, Battersea Rise, London SW11 1HS* Tel (020) 8870 4171 E-mail pmh@emanuel.org.uk

HUNT, Canon Peter John. b 35. AKC58. St Boniface Warminster. **d** 59 **p** 60. C Chesterfield St Mary and All SS *Derby* 59-61; C Matlock and Tansley 61-63; Chapl Matlock Hosp 61-63; Lect Matlock Teacher Tr Coll 61-63; V Tottington *Man* 63-69; CF (TA) 65-67 and from 75; V Bollington St Jo *Ches* 69-76; R Wilmslow 76-98; Hon Can Ches Cathl 94-02; P-in-c Brereton w Swettenham 98-02; rtd 02; Perm to Offic *Ches* from 02. *1 Varden Town Cottages, Birtles Lane, Over Alderley, Macclesfield SK10 4RZ* Tel (01265) 829593

HUNT, Philip Gerald. b 51. LCTP. **d** 11. NSM Rishton *Blackb* from 11. *11 Poplar Avenue, Great Harwood, Blackburn BB6 7RZ* Tel (01254) 889808 E-mail j.a.hunt@sky.com

HUNT, Canon Richard William. b 46. G&C Coll Cam BA67 MA71. Westcott Ho Cam 68. **d** 72 **p** 73. C Bris St Agnes and St Simon w St Werburgh 72-77; Chapl Selw Coll Cam 77-84; V Birchfield *Birm* 84-01; R Chich St Paul and Westhampnett from 01; RD Chich from 06; Can and Preb Chich Cathl from 10. *The Rectory, Tower Close, Chichester PO19 1QN* Tel (01243) 531624 E-mail richard@hunts.fsnet.co.uk

HUNT, Ms Rosalind Edna Mary. b 55. Man Univ BA76. St Steph Ho Ox 86. **d** 88 **p** 94. Chapl Jes Coll Cam 88-92; Hon Chapl to the Deaf *Ely* 92-04; C Cambridge St Jas 00; Perm to Offic *Man* from 05. *1 Thorne House, Wilmslow Road, Manchester M14 6DW* Tel 0161-257 0238 E-mail ros.hunt@virgin.net

HUNT, Canon Russell Barrett. b 35. NY Univ Virginia Univ Fitzw Ho Cam. Westcott Ho Cam 73. **d** 75 **p** 76. C Leic St Mary 75-78; V Leic St Gabr 78-82; Chapl Selw Coll Cam 77-84; V Birchfield *Birm* 84-01... Chapl Leic Gen Hosp 82-95; Hon Can Leic Cathl 88-95; rtd 95. *33 Braunstone Avenue, Leicester LE3 0JH* Tel 0116-254 9101

HUNT, Simon John. b 60. Pemb Coll Ox BA81 MA85. St Jo Coll Nottm 87. **d** 90 **p** 91. C Stalybridge St Paul *Ches* 90-93; C Heysham *Blackb* 93-99; V Higher Walton from 99. *The Vicarage, Blackburn Road, Higher Walton, Preston PR5 4EA* Tel (01772) 335406 E-mail simon.hunt15@btinternet.com

HUNT, Stephen. b 38. Man Univ BSc61 MSc62 PhD64 DSc80. Carl Dioc Tr Inst 88. **d** 91 **p** 92. C Broughton *Blackb* 91-95; Chapl Preston Acute Hosps NHS Trust 94-95; V Preston Em

Blackb 95-03; rtd 03; Perm to Offic *Blackb* from 05. *8 Wallace Lane, Forton, Preston PR3 0BA* Tel (01524) 792563

HUNT, Timothy Collinson. b 65. ASVA91 Univ of Wales (Cardiff) BD95 Ox Univ MTh98. Ripon Coll Cuddesdon 95. **d** 97 **p** 98. C Ex St Dav 97-01; Chapl Blundell's Sch Tiverton from 01. *1B Hillands, 39 Tidcombe Lane, Tiverton EX16 4EA* Tel (01884) 242343 E-mail tc@collhunt.fsnet.co.uk

HUNT, Vera Susan Henrietta. b 33. MBE06. S Dios Minl Tr Scheme 88. **d** 91 **p** 94. Hon Chapl RAD from 91; Perm to Offic *Lon* from 03. *54 Highway Avenue, Maidenhead SL6 5AQ* Tel (01628) 623909 E-mail vera@sh-hunt.fsnet.co.uk

HUNTE (*née* FRANKLIN), **Ms Roxanne Fay.** b 60. Gama Filho Univ Brazil BSc93 Huron Univ MBA94 Leeds Univ BA08. Coll of Resurr Mirfield 07. **d** 09 **p** 10. C Newington St Mary *S'wark* from 09. *89 Ambergate Street, London SE17 3RZ* Tel (020) 7735 1894 Mobile 07747-896779

HUNTER, Allan Davies. b 36. Univ of Wales (Lamp) BA57. Coll of Resurr Mirfield 57. **d** 59 **p** 60. C Cardiff St Jo *Llan* 59-68; V Llansawel 68-76; Youth Chapl 71-77; V Llansawel w Briton Ferry 76-79; V Canton St Cath 79-01; rtd 01. *9 Avonridge, Thornhill, Cardiff CF14 9AU* Tel (029) 2069 3054 E-mail allanhunter@talk21.com

HUNTER, David Hilliard Coman. b 48. Massey Univ (NZ) BA92. St Jo Coll Auckland LTh74. **d** 73 **p** 74. C Stoke New Zealand 73-75; C Christ Church Cathl 75-78; V Waimea 78-79; Chapl Tongariro Pris Farm 79-85; Chapl Waikune Pris 81-85; Chapl Rangipo Pris 81-85; Chapl Rimutuka Pris and Pris Staff Coll 86-92; P Asst Silverstream 86-92; Chapl NZ Army 88-92; P Asst Marton 92-97; P Asst Cambridge 97-01; Chapl Bruton Sch for Girls 02; P-in-c Stevington *St Alb* 03-06; Chapl Rockhampton Gr Sch Australia from 06. *Rockhampton Grammar School, Archer Street, Rockhampton Qld 4700, Australia* Tel (0061) (7) 4936 0600

HUNTER, Edwin Wallace. b 43. NUI BA83 FCIM. CITC 91. **d** 94 **p** 95. NSM Cork St Fin Barre's Union C, C & R from 94; Min Can Cork Cathl from 95; Bp's Dom Chapl from 03. *Cedar Lodge, Church Road, Carrigaline, Co Cork, Republic of Ireland* Tel (00353) (21) 437 2338 E-mail enjhunter@eircom.net

HUNTER, Canon Frank Geoffrey. b 34. Keble Coll Ox BA56 MA60 Fitzw Coll Cam BA58 MA62. Ridley Hall Cam 57. **d** 59 **p** 60. C Bircle *Man* 59-62; C Jarrow Grange *Dur* 62-65; V Kingston upon Hull St Martin *York* 65-72; V Linthorpe 72-76; V Heslington 76-99; RD Derwent 78-98; Can and Preb York Minster 85-99; rtd 99; Perm to Offic *Wakef* from 01. *2 Flexbury Avenue, Morley, Leeds LS27 0RG* Tel 0113-253 9213

HUNTER, Graham. b 78. K Coll Lon BA02. Ridley Hall Cam 05. **d** 07 **p** 08. C Holloway St Mary Magd *Lon* 07-10; C Hoxton St Jo w Ch Ch 10-11; V from 11. *St John's Vicarage, Crondall Street, London N1 6PT* Tel (020) 7739 9823 E-mail graham@stjohnshoxton.org.uk

HUNTER, Ian Paton. b 20. Em Coll Cam BA46 MA50. Tyndale Hall Bris 40. **d** 43 **p** 47. C Harrington *Pet* 43-47; C Portman Square St Paul *Lon* 47-50; V Furneux Pelham w Stocking Pelham *St Alb* 50-54; V Moulton *Pet* 54-60; V Danehill *Chich* 60-67; R Plumpton w E Chiltington 67-77; V Burwash Weald 77-83; P-in-c Stonegate 83-85; rtd 85; Perm to Offic *Chich* 86-08. *The College of St Barnabas, Blackberry Lane, Lingfield RH7 6NJ* Tel (01342) 872856

HUNTER, James. b 38. Union Th Coll Belf BD90. **d** 92 **p** 92. In Presbyterian Ch of Ireland 82-92; V Werneth *Man* 92-98; V Woking St Paul *Guildf* 98-05; Asst Chapl HM Pris Coldingley 01-05; rtd 06; Perm to Offic *Pet* from 06. *53 Rushton Road, Desborough, Kettering NN14 2RP* Tel (01536) 761290 E-mail jimo.hunter@virgin.net

HUNTER, John Crichton. b 38. Univ of Wales (Cardiff) BA59 DipEd60 LTCL. St Steph Ho Ox 98. **d** 99 **p** 00. NSM Walham Green St Jo w St Jas *Lon* 99-05; NSM S Kensington St Steph 05-08; Perm to Offic from 08. *57 Manor Court, 23 Bagleys Lane, London SW6 2BN* Tel (020) 7736 7544 E-mail frjohnhunter@hotmail.com

HUNTER, Canon John Gaunt. b 21. St Jo Coll Dur BA49 Leeds Univ MA94 Lanc Univ MPhil08. Ridley Hall Cam 49. **d** 51 **p** 52. C Bradf Cathl 51-54; C Compton Gifford *Ex* 54-56; V Bootle St Matt *Liv* 56-62; Prin Bp Tucker Coll Uganda 62-65; V Altcar *Liv* 65-78; Dioc Missr 65-71; Abp York's Adv in Miss 71-78; Hon Can Liv Cathl 71-78; R Buckhurst Hill *Chelmsf* 78-79; TR 79-89; Dioc Adv in Evang *Bradf* 89-92; rtd 92; Perm to Offic *Bradf* from 92. *Westhouse Lodge, Lower Westhouse, Ingleton, Carnforth LA6 3NZ* Tel (015242) 41305 E-mail canonjgh@gmail.com

HUNTER, Mrs Linda Margaret. b 47. STETS 95. **d** 98. NSM Wootton *Portsm* 98-02; NSM Chale, Gatcombe and Shorwell w Kingston 02-05; NSM Ruskington Gp *Linc* from 07. *12 Hillside Estate, Ruskington, Sleaford NG34 9TJ*

HUNTER, Lionel Lawledge Gleave. b 24. ALCD53. **d** 53 **p** 54. C Leic H Trin 53-56; C Northampton St Giles *Pet* 56-58; C Everton St Chrys *Liv* 58-59; P-in-c Liv St Mich 59-61; Chile 61-72; R Diddlebury w Bouldon and Munslow *Heref* 72-75;

P-in-c Abdon w Clee St Margaret 73-75; P-in-c Holdgate w Tugford 73-75; Canada 75-85; V N Elmham w Billingford *Nor* 85-89; R N Elmham w Billingford and Worthing 89-90; rtd 90; Perm to Offic *Heref* 93-07. *Flat 3, Manormead, Tilford Road, Hindhead GU26 6RA* Tel (01428) 602500

HUNTER, Malcolm Leggatt. b 61. Middx Univ BA97 MA97. SAOMC 03. **d** 05 **p** 07. NSM Old St Pancras *Lon* 05-06; C 06-09; Chapl HM Pris Bronzefield 09-10; Co-ord Chapl HM YOI Aylesbury from 10. *HM YOI Aylesbury, Bierton Road, Aylesbury HP20 1EH* Tel (01296) 444000

HUNTER, Michael John. b 45. CCC Cam BA67 MA71 PhD71 Ox Univ BA75. Wycliffe Hall Ox 73. **d** 76 **p** 77. C Partington and Carrington *Ches* 76-79; CMS 80-90; Uganda 80-89; C Penn Fields *Lich* 90-02; RD Trysull 97-02; V Dore *Sheff* from 02. *The Vicarage, 51 Vicarage Lane, Dore, Sheffield S17 3GY* Tel 0114-236 3335 E-mail dorevicar@aol.com

HUNTER, Canon Michael Oram. b 40. MBE10. K Coll Lon BD64 AKC64. **d** 65 **p** 66. C Tividale *Lich* 65-68; C Harrogate St Wilfrid *Ripon* 68-70; V Hawksworth Wood 70-78; V Whitkirk 78-86; TR Gt Grimsby St Mary and St Jas *Linc* 86-10; Can and Preb Linc Cathl 89-10; rtd 10. *12 Osborne Road, Harrogate HG1 2EA* Tel (01423) 313825 E-mail mo.hunter@talktalk.net

HUNTER, Paul. b 55. Huddersfield Poly BEd82 Cliff Coll MA05. Chich Th Coll 86. **d** 88 **p** 90. C Weymouth H Trin *Sarum* 88-92; P-in-c Hucknall Torkard *S'well* 92; TV 92-96; V Thurcroft *Sheff* 96-06; R Cleethorpes *Linc* from 06. *3 Taylors Avenue, Cleethorpes DN35 0LF* Tel (01472) 291156 E-mail paul@paulhunter03.wanadoo.co.uk

HUNTER, Paul Andrew. Trin Coll Bris 09. **d** 11. OLM Brislington St Chris from 11. *17 Friendship Road, Bristol BS4 2RW* Tel 0117-971 9390 E-mail paulzhunter@blueyonder.co.uk

HUNTER, Paul Graham. b 64. Sheff Univ LLB85 Solicitor 86. St Jo Coll Nottm MA96. **d** 04 **p** 05. Prin Morogoro Bible Coll Tanzania 04-06; Perm to Offic *Blackb* from 08. *1 Ferndale Close, Leyland PR25 3BS* Tel (01772) 624492 Mobile 07731-924289 E-mail pp.hunter@sky.com

HUNTER, Peter Wells. b 52. Bris Univ BSc73. Trin Coll Bris BA91. **d** 91 **p** 92. C New Borough and Leigh *Sarum* 91-97; P-in-c Warminster Ch Ch from 97. *The Vicarage, 13 Avon Road, Warminster BA12 9PR* Tel (01985) 212219 E-mail peter.wh@btopenworld.com

HUNTER, Robert. b 36. Man Univ BSc60. Clifton Th Coll. **d** 63 **p** 64. C Chadderton Ch Ch *Man* 63-65; C Balderstone 65-69; C Newburn *Newc* 69-73; TV Sutton St Jas and Wawne *York* 73-81; V Bilton St Pet 81-82; Hon C N Hull St Mich 82-91; TV Howden 91-97; P-in-c Ashton St Pet *Man* 97-99; TV Ashton 00-01; rtd 01; Perm to Offic *Bradf* 02-11. *2 Adel Park Gardens, Leeds LS16 8BN* Tel 0113-285 7088

HUNTER, Stephen Albert Paul. b 52. JP96. NOC 01. **d** 04 **p** 05. NSM Ecclesall *Sheff* from 04; Bp's Adv for SSM from 10. *Overhill, Townhead Road, Dore, Sheffield S17 3GE* Tel 0114-236 9978 Fax 275 9769 Mobile 07739-949473 E-mail stephen_hunter@btconnect.com

HUNTER DUNN, Jonathan. b 69. Sussex Univ BSc91 Uppsala Univ PhD98. Oak Hill Th Coll BA09. **d** 10 **p** 11. C Burford w Fulbrook, Taynton, Asthall etc *Ox* from 10. *20 Oxford Road, Burford OX18 4NR* Tel (01993) 823413 E-mail jonathanhunterdunn@btinternet.com

HUNTER SMART, Ian Douglas. b 60. St Jo Coll Dur BA83 MA99. Edin Th Coll 83. **d** 85 **p** 86. C Cockerton *Dur* 85-89; TV Jarrow 89-92; TV Sunderland 92-98; Chapl Sunderland Univ 92-98; Ecum Chapl Newcastle Coll of H&FE 96-98; Perm to Offic *Dur* from 98. *Gardeners Cottage, Carlton, Richmond DL11 7AG* Tel (01325) 710481 E-mail ihs@dunelm.org.uk

HUNTER SMART, William David. b 75. Bris Univ BSc97. Wycliffe Hall Ox BA01. **d** 02 **p** 03. C Watford *St Alb* 02-05; C Muswell Hill St Jas w St Matt *Lon* 05-11; TR Newbury *Ox* from 11. *The Rectory, 64 Northcroft Lane, Newbury RG14 1BN* Tel (01635) 47018 E-mail rector@st-nicolas-newbury.org

HUNTINGDON AND WISBECH, Archdeacon of. See McCURDY, The Ven Hugh Kyle

HUNTINGDON, Suffragan Bishop of. See THOMSON, The Rt Revd David

HUNTLEY, David Anthony. b 32. AMInstT56 MRTvS78 MILT98. Lon Bible Coll BA60 Fuller Sch of World Miss MTh81 Trin Coll Singapore 65. **d** 64 **p** 65. OMF Internat from 61; Singapore 61-71; Indonesia 72-73; Philippines 74-75; Hong Kong 77-81; Seychelles 82-87; Thailand 88-97; NSM S Croydon Em 76-77, 81-82, 87-88, 91-92 and 98-04. *42 Farnborough Avenue, South Croydon CR2 8HD* Tel (020) 8657 5673

HUNTLEY, David George. b 63. St Cuth Soc Dur BA02. Coll of Resurr Mirfield 05. **d** 07 **p** 08. C Owton Manor *Dur* 07-09; C Houghton le Spring from 09. *2 Waterworks Cottages, Stoneygate, Houghton le Spring DH4 4NN* Tel 0191-528 4077

HUNTLEY, Denis Anthony. b 56. Saltley Tr Coll Birm CertEd77. Qu Coll Birm 77. **d** 80 **p** 81. C Llanblethian w Cowbridge and Llandough etc 80-83; TV Glyncorrwg w Afan Vale and Cymmer

Afan 83-86; R 86-89; Chapl Asst Walsgrave Hosp Cov 89-92; Chapl Halifax Gen Hosp 92-94; Chapl Calderdale Healthcare NHS Trust 94-97; C Leeds City *Ripon* 97-02; Chapl to the Deaf 97-02; Chapl amongst Deaf People and Adv for Deaf Min 02-06; Chapl amongst Deaf and Deaf-blind People *Chelmsf* from 06. *17 Oakham Close, Langdon Hills, Basildon SS16 6NX* Tel (01268) 490471 *or* 546026
E-mail denis.huntley@btinternet.com

HUNTLEY, Heidi Anne. b 71. Ripon Coll Cuddesdon 07. **d** 09 **p** 10. C Sydenham St Bart *S'wark* from 09. *1 Ashleigh Court, 81 Lawrie Park Road, London SE26 6EX* Tel (020) 8659 9598
E-mail hahlive@yahoo.co.uk

HUNTLEY, Stuart Michael. b 73. BEng BA. Trin Coll Bris. **d** 08 **p** 09. C Jersey St Lawr *Win* from 08. *35 Nomond Avenue, La Pouquelaye, St Helier, Jersey JE2 3FW* Tel (01534) 758569 Mobile 07949-195026 E-mail stuart.huntley@jerseymail.co.uk

HUPFIELD, Mrs Hannah Elizabeth. b 84. New Hall Cam BA06 MA10. Westcott Ho Cam 08. **d** 11. C Woodbridge St Mary *St E* from 11. *40 Old Barrack Road, Woodbridge IP12 4ET* Tel (01394) 384594 E-mail hannahhupfield@cantab.net

HURCOMBE, Thomas William. b 45. BD74 AKC76. **d** 76 **p** 77. C Hampstead All So *Lon* 76-79; C Is of Dogs Ch Ch and St Jo w St Luke 79-83; C Bromley All Hallows 83-89; C E Greenwich Ch Ch w St Andr and St Mich *S'wark* 89-96; Ind Chapl 89-97; Dioc Urban Missr 90-96; Greenwich Waterfront Chapl 96-98; C Charlton St Luke w H Trin 97-98; P-in-c S Norwood St Mark from 98. *St Mark's Vicarage, 101 Albert Road, London SE25 4JE* Tel (020) 8656 6329 E-mail hurcomt@aol.com

HURD, Alun John. b 52. Trin Coll Bris BA86 New Coll Edin MTh97. **d** 86 **p** 87. C Chertsey *Guildf* 86-90; Chapl St Pet Hosp Chertsey 86-90; V W Ewell *Guildf* 90-04; Chapl NE Surrey Coll Ewell 01-05; CF (TA) 99-05; Distr P Lower Yorke Peninsular Australia 05-07; P-in-c Gt Wakering w Foulness *Chelmsf* from 08; P-in-c Barling w Lt Wakering from 08. *The Vicarage, 2 New Road, Great Wakering, Southend-on-Sea SS3 0AH* Tel (01702) 217493 Mobile 07941-417135
E-mail alunjhurd@googlemail.com

HURD, Canon Brenda Edith. b 44. Sittingbourne Coll DipEd75. Cant Sch of Min 87. **d** 92 **p** 94. NSM Birling, Addington, Ryarsh and Trottiscliffe *Roch* 92-02; P-in-c Wrotham from 02; RD Shoreham 06-11; Hon Can Roch Cathl from 09. *The Rectory, Borough Green Road, Wrotham, Sevenoaks TN15 7RA* Tel (01732) 882211 E-mail brenda.hurd@diocese-rochester.org *or* b.hurd@virgin.net

HURD, John Patrick. b 37. CertEd65 Open Univ BA73 Kent Univ MA92. S Dios Minl Tr Scheme 77. **d** 80 **p** 81. NSM Billingshurst *Chich* 80-82 and 89-94; NSM Itchingfield w Slinfold 82-89. *Groomsland Cottage, Parbrook, Billingshurst RH14 9EU* Tel (01403) 782167

HURFORD, Colin Osborne. b 33. Qu Coll Ox BA55 MA59. Wells Th Coll 55. **d** 57 **p** 58. C Barnoldswick w Bracewell *Bradf* 57-61; C Warrington St Elphin *Liv* 61-63; Malaysia 63-70; P-in-c Annscroft *Heref* 71-79; P-in-c Longden 71-79; P-in-c Pontesbury III 71-79; R Longden and Annscroft 79-85; P-in-c Church Pulverbatch 81-85; R Longden and Annscroft w Pulverbatch 85-86; Tanzania 86-87; TR Billingham St Aid *Dur* 87-96; rtd 96; Perm to Offic *Heref* from 96 and *Lich* 01-10. *14 Station Road, Pontesbury, Shrewsbury SY5 0QY* Tel (01743) 792605

✠**HURFORD, The Rt Revd Richard Warwick.** b 44. OAM99. Trin Coll Bris BA96 Univ of Wales MTh02 Hon FGCM96 MACE81. St Jo Coll Morpeth. **d** 69 **p** 70. cl. Prec Grafton Cathl Australia 69-70; P-in-c Tisbury *Sarum* 71-73; R 73-75; R Tisbury and Swallowcliffe w Ansty 75-76; TR Tisbury 76-78; P-in-c Chilmark 76-78; TR Coffs Harbour Australia 78-83; Dean Grafton 83-97; Adn The Clarence and Hastings 85-87; Adn Grafton 87-92; R Sydney St Jas 97-01; Bp Bathurst from 01. *Bishopscourt, 288 William Street, PO Box 23, Bathurst NSW 2795, Australia* Tel (0061) (2) 6331 3550 *or* 6331 1722 Fax 6331 3660 *or* 6332 2772 E-mail bxbishop@ix.net.au

HURLE, Canon Anthony Rowland. b 54. Lon Univ BSc Em Coll Cam PGCE. Wycliffe Hall Ox 80. **d** 83 **p** 84. C Ipswich St Mary at Stoke w St Pet *St E* 83-87; TV Barking St Marg w St Patr *Chelmsf* 87-92; V St Alb St Paul *St Alb* from 92; RD St Alb 95-05; Hon Can St Alb from 05. *St Paul's Vicarage, 7 Brampton Road, St Albans AL1 4PN* Tel and fax (01727) 836810 *or* tel 846281 E-mail tony@stpauls-stalbans.org *or* vicar@stpauls-stalbans.org

HURLE (née POWNALL), Mrs Lydia Margaret. b 53. SRN SCM. Wycliffe Hall Ox 78. **dss** 81 **d** 94 **p** 95. Ipswich St Mary at Stoke w St Pet etc *St E* 81-83; NSM St Alb St Paul *St Alb* from 93. *St Paul's Vicarage, 7 Brampton Road, St Albans AL1 4PN* Tel and fax (01727) 836810 E-mail tony.hurle@ntlworld.com

HURLEY, Daniel Timothy. b 37. St Mich Coll Llan 68. **d** 70 **p** 71. C Llanfabon 70-73; CF 73-79; R W Walton *Ely* 79-85; V Cwmdauddwr w St Harmon and Llanwrthwl *S & B* 86-02; rtd 02. *39 Ellesmere Orchard, Emsworth PO10 8TP* Tel (01243) 376923

HURLEY, Mark Tristan. b 57. Trin Coll Bris BA89. Sarum & Wells Th Coll 89. **d** 91 **p** 92. C Gainsborough All SS *Linc* 91-94; TV Grantham 94-00; V Donington and Bicker 00-02; Perm to Offic *Ox* 08-09; Hon C Wolverton from 09. *42 Fegans Court, Stony Stratford, Milton Keynes MK11 1LS* Tel (01908) 568809

HURLEY, Robert. b 64. Univ of Wales (Cardiff) BD86. Ridley Hall Cam 88. **d** 90 **p** 91. C Dagenham *Chelmsf* 90-93; C Egg Buckland *Ex* 93-96; C Devonport St Budeaux 96; P-in-c Camberwell All SS *S'wark* 96-99; V 99-02; R Oldbury *Sarum* 02-04. *Address temp unknown*
E-mail janeandbobhurley@aol.com

HURLOCK, Ronald James. b 31. BSc PhD. St Deiniol's Hawarden. **d** 83 **p** 84. C Oxton *Ches* 83-87; Chapl Asst Man R Infirmary 87-91; rtd 91. *78 Garwood Close, Westbrook, Warrington WA5 5TF* Tel (01925) 444583

HURLSTON, Mrs Jean Margaret. b 54. Crewe Coll of Educn CertEd75 Keele Univ BEd76. **d** 06 **p** 07. OLM High Crompton *Man* 06-10; OLM Oldham 10-11; OLM Oldham St Mary w St Pet from 11. *24 Taunton Lawns, Ashton-under-Lyne OL7 9EL* Tel and fax 0161-344 2854 Mobile 078885-406808
E-mail jeanhurlston@btinternet.com

HURN, Mrs June Barbara. b 32. Birm Univ CertEd53. Cant Sch of Min 87. **d** 90 **p** 94. NSM Chislehurst St Nic *Roch* from 90. *Hawkswing, Hawkwood Lane, Chislehurst BR7 5PW* Tel (020) 8467 2320

HURREN, Timothy John. b 46. York Univ BA74 ACIB70. NEOC 99. **d** 02 **p** 03. NSM High Harrogate St Pet *Ripon* 02-06; C from 06. *1 South Park Road, Harrogate HG1 5QU* Tel (01423) 541696 E-mail tim.hurren@ntlworld.com

HURRY, Lynn Susan. b 59. Middx Univ BA05. NTMTC 02. **d** 05 **p** 06. C Southchurch H Trin *Chelmsf* 05-08; V St Mary-at-Latton from 08. *St Mary-at-Latton Vicarage, The Gowers, Harlow CM20 2JP* Tel (01279) 424005
E-mail revlynn@btinternet.com

HURST, Alaric Desmond St John. b 24. New Coll Ox BA50 MA70. Wells Th Coll 48. **d** 51 **p** 53. C Huddersfield H Trin *Wakef* 51-52; C Leeds St Geo *Ripon* 52-54; Bp's Chapl for Rehabilitation *Roch* 55-56; C St Steph Walbrook and St Swithun etc *Lon* 57-59; V Pudsey St Paul *Bradf* 59-63; V Writtle *Chelmsf* 63-69; rtd 89. *9 Ganderton Court, Pershore WR10 1AW* Tel (01905) 840939

HURST, Canon Brian Charles. b 58. Nottm Univ BA Sheff Univ MA07. Ripon Coll Cuddesdon 82. **d** 84 **p** 85. C Cullercoats St Geo *Newc* 84-87; C Prudhoe 87-88; TV Willington 88-95; V Denton 95-03; RD Newc W 97-98; TV Glendale Gp 03-09; V Bamburgh from 09; V Ellingham from 09; AD Bamburgh and Glendale from 06; Hon Can Newc Cathl from 10. *The Vicarage, 7 The Wynding, Bamburgh NE69 7DB* Tel (01668) 214748
E-mail brian.hurst1@btopenworld.com

HURST, Colin. b 49. Linc Th Coll 88. **d** 90 **p** 91. C Wavertree H Trin *Liv* 90-93; C Croft and Stoney Stanton *Leic* 93-95; TV Broughton Astley and Croft w Stoney Stanton 95-97; V Wigan St Andr *Liv* from 97; AD Wigan W 03-05; AD Wigan 05-08; Hon Can Liv Cathl 03-08. *St Andrew's Vicarage, 3A Mort Street, Wigan WN6 7AU* Tel (01942) 243514
E-mail churst6000@aol.com

HURST, Colin. b 58. Westmr Coll Ox BA90. St Jo Coll Nottm MA95. **d** 95 **p** 96. C Warboys w Broughton and Bury w Wistow *Ely* 95-98; P-in-c Wisbech St Mary 98-04; P-in-c Guyhirn w Ring's End 98-04; V Wisbech St Mary and Guyhirn w Ring's End etc 05-07; P-in-c Eye *Pet* from 07; P-in-c Newborough from 07; P-in-c Thorney Abbey *Ely* from 07. *The Vicarage, Thorney Road, Eye, Peterborough PE6 7UN* Tel (01733) 222334
E-mail cehurst@globalnet.co.uk

HURST, Edward. b 57. SEITE 09. **d** 11. NSM S Gillingham *Roch* from 11. *83A Otterham Quay Lane, Rainham, Gillingham ME8 8NE* Tel (01634) 263580 Mobile 07791-994933
E-mail notfatherted@gmail.com

HURST, Canon Jeremy Richard. b 40. Trin Coll Cam BA61 MA MPhil FCP. Linc Th Coll 62. **d** 64 **p** 65. C Woolwich St Mary w H Trin *S'wark* 64-69; Perm to Offic *Ex* 69-76 and *Ox* 76-84; TV Langley Marish *Ox* 84-99; AD St 85-05; Hon Can Ch Ch 05; Chapl Thames Valley Univ 92-98; rtd 05. *Hortus Lodge, 22A Bolton Avenue, Windsor SL4 3JF* Tel (01753) 863693
E-mail jeremyhurst@lineone.net

HURST, John. b 31. NW Ord Course 76. **d** 79 **p** 80. C Flixton St Jo *Man* 79-82; P-in-c Hindsford 82-86; V 86-88; V Halliwell St Paul 88-93; rtd 93; Perm to Offic *Man* from 99. *26 Cornwall Avenue, Bolton BL5 1DZ* Tel (01204) 659233

HURT, Mrs Grenda Mary. b 36. LSE BSc(Econ)63. STETS 96. **d** 99 **p** 01. NSM Freshwater and Yarmouth *Portsm* 99-10; Asst Chapl Isle of Wight Healthcare NHS Trust 03-05; Chapl Earl Mountbatten Hospice 03-05; rtd 10; Perm to Offic *Portsm* from 10. *Benhams, Victoria Road, Freshwater PO40 9PP* Tel (01983) 759931 E-mail grenda.hurt@tiscali.co.uk

✠**HURTADO, The Rt Revd Jorge A Perera.** b 34. **d** 57 **p** 58 **c** 93. Bp Cuba from 94. *Calle 6 No 273, Vedado, Plaza de la Revolución,*

Havana 4, 10400, Cuba Tel (0053) (7) 35565, 38003, 321120 *or* 312436 Fax 333293 E-mail episcopal@ip.etecsa.cu

HUSS, David Ian. b 75. Jes Coll Ox MPhys97. Wycliffe Hall Ox BA07. **d** 07 **p** 08. C Banbury St Paul *Ox* 07-11; I Donegal w Killymard, Lough Eske and Laghey *D & R* from 11. *The Rectory, Ballyshannon Road, Donegal, Republic of Ireland* Tel (00353) (74) 972 1075 Mobile 07766-026041 E-mail david@huss.org.uk *or* donegal@raphoe.anglican.org

HUSSEY, Martin John. b 47. STETS 96. **d** 99 **p** 00. NSM Thames Ditton *Guildf* 99-11; NSM Oatlands from 11. *94 Wellington Close, Walton-on-Thames KT12 1BE* Tel (01932) 221914 E-mail martinhussey uk@yahoo.co.uk

HUTCHENS, Holly Blair. b 42. Univ of Michigan BA64 Univ of Chicago MA69. Seabury-Western Th Sem MDiv88. **d** 88 **p** 88. USA 88-05; P-in-c Glenurquhart *Mor* 05-11. *Address temp unknown* E-mail hollyhutchens@btinternet.com

HUTCHEON, Mrs Elsie. b 39. RGN63 CertEd UEA MEd98. EAMTC 89. **d** 92 **p** 94. NSM Heigham St Thos *Nor* 92-02; P-in-c Heigham St Barn w St Bart from 02; RD Nor S 06-09. *St Barnabas's Vicarage, 1 Russell Street, Norwich NR2 4QT* Tel (01603) 627859 E-mail elsie@rev.demon.co.uk

HUTCHIN, David William. b 37. Man Univ MusB58 CertEd59 DipEd59 LRAM ARCM LTCL. Glouc Sch of Min 85. **d** 88 **p** 89. NSM Northleach w Hampnett and Farmington *Glouc* 88-94; NSM Cold Aston w Notgrove and Turkdean 88-94; NSM Chedworth, Yanworth and Stowell, Coln Rogers etc 94-01; NSM Northleach 96-99; Perm to Offic *Leic* 01-06 and *Derby* 02-06; *Ripon* from 06. *Bank Side Garden, Glasshouses, Harrogate HG3 5QY* Tel (01423) 712733

HUTCHINGS, Colin Michael. b 36. Clifton Th Coll 66. **d** 68 **p** 69. C Worksop St Jo *S'well* 68-71; C Hampreston *Sarum* 71-76; TV Tisbury 76-82; R Waddesdon w Over Winchendon and Fleet Marston *Ox* 82-00; rtd 00; Perm to Offic *Pet* from 01. *Nimrod, 4 The Beeches, Pattishall, Towcester NN12 8LT* Tel (01327) 830563

HUTCHINGS, Ian James. b 49. Ches Coll of HE MA03. Clifton Th Coll 69 Trin Coll Bris 72. **d** 73 **p** 74. C Parr *Liv* 73-77; C Timperley *Ches* 77-81; V Partington and Carrington 81-96; V Huntington from 96; Chapl Bp's Blue Coat C of E High Sch from 96. *St Luke's Vicarage, 14 Celandine Close, Huntington, Chester CH3 6DT* Tel and fax (01244) 347345 or tel 344705 E-mail ihutchings@aol.com

HUTCHINGS, James Benjamin Balfour. b 62. Ex Univ BA84. STETS 03. **d** 06 **p** 07. C Ex St Jas 06-09; C Cen Ex from 09. *Glenn House, 96 Old Tiverton Road, Exeter EX4 6LD* Tel (01392) 202983 E-mail jhutchings@mail.com

HUTCHINGS, John Denis Arthur. b 29. Keble Coll Ox BA53 MA59 MSc59. Chich Th Coll 58. **d** 60 **p** 61. C St Pancras w St Jas and Ch Ch *Lon* 60-63; Asst Chapl Denstone Coll Uttoxeter 63-67 and 79-83; C Stepney St Dunstan and All SS *Lon* 67-78; V Devonport St Boniface *Ex* 83-86; TR Devonport St Boniface and St Phil 86-93; P-in-c Lydford and Brent Tor 93-95; rtd 96; Perm to Offic *Ex* from 96. *Maisonette, 40 Brook Street, Tavistock PL19 0HE* Tel (01822) 616946

HUTCHINS, Paul. b 79. Coll of Resurr Mirfield 99 NOC 04. **d** 05 **p** 06. C Royton St Paul *Man* 05-10; TV Swinton and Pendlebury from 10. *St Augustine's Vicarage, 23 Hospital Road, Pendlebury, Swinton, Manchester M27 4EY* Tel 0161-794 4298 Mobile 07818-022678 E-mail fr.hutchins@btinternet.com

HUTCHINSON, Alison Joyce. b 62. Leeds Univ BA84 RMN90. Aston Tr Scheme 92 Ripon Coll Cuddesdon 94. **d** 97 **p** 98. C Benfieldside *Dur* 97-00; C Bishopwearmouth St Nic 00-02; Perm to Offic *Carl* 02-07; C Penrith w Newton Reigny and Plumpton Wall 07-08; Perm to Offic 09; Hon C Crathorne *York* from 09; Hon C Kirklevington w Picton, and High and Low Worsall from 09; Hon C Rudby in Cleveland w Middleton from 09; Hon C Stokesley from 09. *The Rectory, Leven Close, Stokesley, Middlesbrough TS9 5AP* Tel (01642) 710405 E-mail alison.hutchinson@btinternet.com

HUTCHINSON, Canon Andrew Charles. b 63. Univ of Wales (Ban) BA84 MEd96. Aston Tr Scheme 85 Chich Th Coll 87. **d** 89 **p** 90. C Burnley St Cath w St Alb and St Paul *Blackb* 89-92; C Shrewsbury St Chad w St Mary *Lich* 92-94; Chapl Heref Cathl Sch 94-97; Succ Heref Cathl 94-97; Chapl Solihull Sch from 97; Can St Jo Pro-Cathl Katakwa from 00. *2 St Alphege Close, Church Hill Road, Solihull B91 3RQ* Tel 0121-704 3768

HUTCHINSON, Andrew George Pearce. b 78. Glos Univ BA01 PGCE02. Oak Hill Th Coll BA08. **d** 08 **p** 09. C Normanton *Derby* from 08. *18 Lawnlea Close, Sunnyhill, Derby DE23 1XQ* Tel (01332) 769503 Mobile 07877-831506 E-mail andy_hutchinson@hotmail.com

HUTCHINSON, Andrew Paul. b 65. Trin Hall Cam BA87 MA91 Solicitor 90. Aston Tr Scheme 92 Ripon Coll Cuddesdon BTh97. **d** 97 **p** 98. C Stanley *Dur* 97-99; C Sunderland 99-01; TV 01-02; Chapl Sunderland Univ 99-02; TV Penrith w Newton Reigny and Plumpton Wall *Carl* 02-09; Chapl Cumbria Campus Cen Lancs Univ 02-07; Chapl Cumbria Univ 07-09; R Stokesley w

Seamer *York* from 09. *The Rectory, Leven Close, Stokesley, Middlesbrough TS9 5AP* Tel (01642) 710405 E-mail paul.hutchinson5@btinternet.com

HUTCHINSON, Anthony Hugh. b 47. Open Univ BSc00 Liv Univ MA09. **d** 10 **p** 11. OLM Stafford *Lich* from 10. *Kilsall Hall, Kilsall, Shifnal TF11 8PL* Tel (01902) 373145 E-mail revdtony@softersolutions.co.uk

HUTCHINSON, Mrs Barbara Anne. b 55. **d** 05 **p** 06. OLM Holbeach Fen *Linc* from 05; Chapl United Lincs Hosps NHS Trust from 10. *3 Sholtsgate, Whaplode, Spalding PE12 6TZ* Tel (01406) 422354 E-mail revbarbara@uwclub.net

HUTCHINSON, Canon Cyril Peter. b 37. Dur Univ BA61. Wm Temple Coll Rugby 61. **d** 63 **p** 64. C Birm St Paul 63-67; Prin Community Relns Officer 66-69; Dir Bradf SHARE 69-76; Hon C Manningham *Bradf* 75-76; V Clayton 76-83; RD Bowling and Horton 80-83; TR Keighley St Andr 83-94; Hon Can Bradf Cathl 84-03; rtd 94; Hon C Keighley All SS *Bradf* 94-03. *Wellcroft, Laycock Lane, Laycock, Keighley BD22 0PN* Tel (01535) 606145

HUTCHINSON, David. See HUTCHINSON, Canon William David

HUTCHINSON, David Bamford. b 29. QUB BSc53 TCD Div Test55 QUB DipEd57. **d** 55 **p** 56. C Lisburn Ch Ch *Conn* 55-57; Uganda 57-65; I Kilkeel *D & D* 66-75; I Willowfield 75-82; V Longfleet *Sarum* 82-94; rtd 94; Perm to Offic *Sarum* 94-99. *Bethany, 3 Panorama Road, Poole BH13 7RA* Tel (01202) 664964

HUTCHINSON, Hugh Edward. b 27. CEng FICE. Bps' Coll Cheshunt. **d** 61 **p** 62. C Limehouse *St Anne Lon* 61 64; C Townstall w Dartmouth *Ex* 64-67; V Ex St Mark 67-75; P-in-c Foston on the Wolds *York* 75-77; P-in-c N Frodingham 75-77; R Beeford w Lissett 75-77; R Beeford w Frodingham and Foston 77-80; RD N Holderness 79-80; P-in-c Appleton Roebuck w Acaster Selby 80-84; P-in-c Etton w Dalton Holme 84-91; rtd 91; Perm to Offic *York* 91-11. *33 Limestone Grove, Burniston, Scarborough YO13 0DH* Tel (01723) 871116

HUTCHINSON, Jeremy Olpherts. b 32. Oriel Coll Ox BA55 MA60. St Jo Coll Dur. **d** 57 **p** 58. C Shoreditch St Leon *Lon* 57-60; V Hoxton St Jo w Ch Ch 60-78; Hon C Hackney 78-85; C Highbury Ch Ch w St Jo and St Sav 85-91; P-in-c Hanley Road St Sav w St Paul 91-92; TV Tollington 92-96; rtd 96; Perm to Offic *Lon* from 96. *8 Casimir Road, London E5 9NU* Tel (020) 8806 6492

HUTCHINSON, John Charles. b 44. K Coll Lon 64. **d** 69 **p** 70. C Portsea All SS *Portsm* 69-73; TV Fareham H Trin 73-78; P-in-c Pangbourne *Ox* 78-86; P-in-c Tidmarsh w Sulham 84-86; R Pangbourne w Tidmarsh and Sulham 86-96; Perm to Offic from 07. *90 Fir Tree Avenue, Wallingford OX10 0PL* Tel (01491) 832445 E-mail cavea@btinternet.com

HUTCHINSON, Jonathan Graham. b 62. Bris Univ BA01. Trin Coll Bris 98. **d** 01 **p** 02. C Church Stretton *Heref* 01-04; P-in-c Aspley *S'well* from 04. *St Margaret's Vicarage, 319 Aspley Lane, Nottingham NG8 5GA* Tel 0115-929 2920 *or* tel and fax 929 8899 E-mail jghutchinson@btinternet.com

HUTCHINSON, Jonathan Mark. b 45. Open Univ BA73 E Lon Univ MSc94. Cant Sch of Min 85. **d** 89 **p** 90. NSM Wickham Market w Pettistree and Easton *St E* 89-93; V Thorington w Wenhaston, Bramfield etc 94-97; TV Ipswich St Mary at Stoke w St Pet and St Fran 97-02; Perm to Offic *B & W* from 02. *27 Milton Lane, Wells BA5 2QS* Tel (01749) 676096 E-mail mark.hutchinson@which.net

HUTCHINSON, Canon Julie Lorraine. b 55. WMMTC 90. **d** 93 **p** 94. C Northampton St Mary *Pet* 93-95; P-in-c Morcott w Glaston and Bisbrooke 95-97; P-in-c Lyddington w Stoke Dry and Seaton etc 97-02; V 03; Dir of Ords and Voc 03-10; Bp's Chapl from 11; Can Pet Cathl from 09. *2 William Robinson House, 27 Minster Precincts, Peterborough PE1 1XZ* Tel (01733) 562492 Fax 890077 E-mail julie.hutchinson@peterborough-diocese.org.uk

HUTCHINSON, June. See HUTCHINSON, Mrs Margaret June

HUTCHINSON, Mrs Karen Elizabeth. b 64. LMH Ox BA85 MA89 Kent Univ MA06 Solicitor 89. Wycliffe Hall Ox. **d** 01 **p** 02. C Alton St Lawr *Win* 01-06; V Crondall and Ewshot *Guildf* from 06. *The Vicarage, Farm Lane, Crondall, Farnham GU10 5QE* Tel (01252) 850379

HUTCHINSON, Mrs Margaret June. b 45. ERMC 03. **d** 06 **p** 07. C Midi-Pyrénées and Aude *Eur* 06-10; Asst Chapl from 10. *Le Cru, 46150 Thedirac, France* Tel and fax (0033) 5 65 21 68 52 E-mail hutchinsonlecru@compuserve.com

HUTCHINSON, Mark. See HUTCHINSON, Jonathan Mark

HUTCHINSON, Moreen Anne. b 46. Ulster Univ BA84. CITC 98. **d** 01 **p** 02. NSM Larne and Inver *Conn* 01-04; P-in-c Ardclinis and Tickmacrevan w Layde and Cushendun 04-11; rtd 11; Bp's Dom Chapl *Conn* from 08. *St Mary's Rectory, 76 Largy Road, Carnlough, Ballymena BT44 0JJ* Tel and fax (028) 2888 5593 E-mail moreen.hutchinson@btinternet.com

HUTCHINSON, Paul. See HUTCHINSON, Andrew Paul

HUTCHINSON, Paul Edward. b 33. K Coll Lon. **d** 59 **p** 60. C Bromley St Mich *Lon* 59-63; C Mill Hill St Mich 63-66; C Sandridge *St Alb* 66-73; V St Alb St Mary Marshalswick 73-80; V Tunstall *Lich* 80-91; RD Stoke N 82-91; V Lower Gornal 91-93; V Lower Gornal *Worc* 93-98; rtd 98; Perm to Offic *Lich* from 99. *55 Mill Hayes Road, Burslem, Stoke-on-Trent ST6 4JB* Tel (01782) 813361

HUTCHINSON, Miss Pauline. b 49. St Jo Coll Nottm 88. **d** 90 **p** 94. Par Dn Sherwood *S'well* 90-94; C 94-95; TV Newark 95-09; Chapl Newark Hosp NHS Trust 95-04; rtd 09. *18 Cardinal Hinsley Close, Newark NG24 4NQ* Tel (01636) 681931

HUTCHINSON, Peter. See HUTCHINSON, Canon Cyril Peter

HUTCHINSON, Peter Francis. b 52. Sarum & Wells Th Coll 87. **d** 89 **p** 90. C Honiton, Gittisham, Combe Raleigh, Monkton etc *Ex* 89-93; V Valley Park *Win* from 93. *35 Raglan Close, Eastleigh SO53 4NH* Tel (023) 8025 5749 E-mail st.francis@ukgateway.net

HUTCHINSON, Raymond John. b 51. Liv Univ BSc73. Westcott Ho Cam 73. **d** 76 **p** 77. C Peckham St Jo *S'wark* 76-78; C Peckham St Jo w St Andr 78-79; C Prescot *Liv* 79-81; V Edgehill St Dunstan 81-87; P-in-c Litherland Ch Ch 87-89; P-in-c Waterloo Park 87-89; V Waterloo Ch Ch and St Mary 90-97; Chapl Wigan and Leigh Health Services NHS Trust 97-01; Chapl Wrightington Wigan and Leigh NHS Trust from 01; P-in-c Wigan All SS *Liv* 04-08; P-in-c Wigan St Geo 05-08; R Wigan All SS and St Geo from 08. *The Rectory, 6 Wrightington Street, Wigan WN1 2BX* Tel (01942) 244459 E-mail hutchinsons@glebehouse.fslife.co.uk

HUTCHINSON, Canon Stephen. b 38. St Chad's Coll Dur BA60. **d** 62 **p** 63. C Tividale *Lich* 62-68; V Walsall St Andr 68-73; R Headless Cross *Worc* 73-81; TR Redditch, The Ridge 81-91; RD Bromsgrove 85-91; V Stourbridge St Thos 91-03; Hon Can Worc Cathl 88-03; rtd 03; Perm to Offic *Worc* from 03. *251 Stourbridge Road, Kidderminster DY10 2XJ* Tel (01562) 631658

HUTCHINSON, Canon William David. b 27. Wycliffe Hall Ox 55. **d** 57 **p** 58. C Ipswich St Jo *St E* 57-60; R Combs 60-65; V Ipswich St Aug 65-76; R Ewhurst *Guildf* 76-81; V Aldeburgh w Hazlewood *St E* 81-92; RD Saxmundham 83-88; Hon Can St E Cathl 87-92; rtd 92. *Hazelwood, 1 Birch Close, Woodbridge IP12 4UA* Tel (01394) 383760

HUTCHINSON CERVANTES, Canon Ian Charles. b 62. Cant Univ (NZ) BSc84 Reading Univ MSc86 Jes Coll Cam BA89 MA92. Westcott Ho Cam 86. **d** 89 **p** 90. C Iffley *Ox* 89-92; USPG 92-04; Locum P Caracas Cathl Venezuela 93; P-in-c El Cayo St Andr Belize 93-97; USPG Staff 97-04; Chapl Madrid *Eur* from 04; Hon Can Madrid Cathl from 01; Hon Can Buenos Aires from 02; Can Gib Cathl from 10. *St George's Anglican Church, Núñez de Balboa 43, 28001 Madrid, Spain* Tel and fax (0034) 915 765 109 E-mail irhutch@ya.com

✠**HUTCHISON, The Most Revd Andrew Sandford.** b 38. Montreal Dioc Th Coll Hon DD93. Trin Coll Toronto. **d** 69 **p** 70 **c** 70. Canada from 69; Dean Montreal 84-90; Bp Montreal 90-04; Primate of Angl Ch of Canada from 04. *80 Hayden Street, Toronto ON M4Y 3G2, Canada* Tel (001) (416) 924 9119 Fax 924 0211 E-mail primate@national.anglican.ca

HUTCHISON, Geoffrey John. b 52. Trin Hall Cam MA76 Lon Univ CertEd76. Ridley Hall Cam 77. **d** 79 **p** 80. C Harold Wood *Chelmsf* 79-83; CF 83-89; Warden Viney Hill Chr Adventure Cen 89-96; P-in-c Viney Hill *Glouc* 89-96; V Wadsley *Sheff* from 96. *The Vicarage, 91 Airedale Road, Sheffield S6 4AW* Tel 0114-234 8481 E-mail rev.hutch@googlemail.com

HUTCHISON, Ross. b 61. Wadh Coll Ox BA83 MA86 DPhil88. SEITE 03. **d** 06 **p** 07. NSM Newington St Mary *S'wark* 06-10; NSM Kilburn St Mary w All So and W Hampstead St Jas *Lon* from 10. *12A Cumberland Mansions, West End Lane, London NW6 1LL* Tel (020) 7794 6087 E-mail ross.hutchison@kpmg.co.uk

HUTT, Canon David Handley. b 38. Lambeth MA05 AKC68. **d** 69 **p** 70. C Bedford Park *Lon* 69-70; C Westmr St Matt 70-73; PV and Succ S'wark Cathl 73-78; Chapl K Coll Taunton 78-82; V Bordesley SS Alb and Patr *Birm* 82-86; V St Marylebone All SS *Lon* 86-95; Can Steward Westmr Abbey 95-05; Sub-Dean and Adn Westmr 99-05; rtd 05; Perm to Offic *Lon* and *Eur* from 06. *3CC Morpeth Terrace, London SW1P 1EW*

HUTTON, Christopher. b 81. Sussex Univ BSc04. Wycliffe Hall Ox BTh10. **d** 10 **p** 11. C Southgate Chich from 10. *54 Dovedale Crescent, Crawley RH11 8SG* Tel (01293) 530850 Mobile 07971-336895 E-mail chrishutton@hotmail.com

HUTTON, Elizabeth. See HUTTON, Susan Elizabeth

HUTTON, Griffith Arthur Jeremy. b 31. Trin Hall Cam BA56 MA59. Linc Th Coll 56. **d** 58 **p** 59. C Hexham *Newc* 58-60; C Gosforth All SS 60-65; V Whitegate *Ches* 65-71; V Whitegate w Lt Budworth 71-78; R Dowdeswell and Andoversford w the Shiptons etc *Glouc* 78-91; V Newnham w Awre and Blakeney 91-96; rtd 96; Perm to Offic *Heref* from 99. *6 Farmington Rise, Northleach, Cheltenham GL54 3HU*

HUTTON, Joseph Charles. b 21. DFC41. Westcott Ho Cam 63. **d** 65 **p** 66. C St Marychurch *Ex* 65-67; V Warborough *Ox* 67-70;

V Earley St Pet 70-75; R Ludgvan *Truro* 75-79; rtd 79. *2 Baines Close, Bourton-on-the-Water, Cheltenham GL54 2PU*

HUTTON, Sarah Fielding. b 63. **d** 11. NSM Shere, Albury and Chilworth *Guildf* from 11. *Netley House, Shere Road, Gomshall, Guildford GU5 9QA*

HUTTON, Mrs Serena Quartermaine. b 35. Nottm Univ BA57 Lon Univ BA73 Stranmillis Coll PGCE68 FRSA87. SAOMC 95. **d** 98 **p** 99. OLM Chinnor, Sydenham, Aston Rowant and Crowell *Ox* from 98. *Elma Cottage, The Green, Kingston Blount, Chinnor OX9 4SE* Tel (01844) 354173

HUTTON, Susan Elizabeth. b 70. Univ of Wales (Cardiff) BD91. Ripon Coll Cuddesdon 93. **d** 95 **p** 96. C W Parley *Sarum* 95-99; C Trowbridge H Trin 99-05; P-in-c 05-09. *Address temp unknown* E-mail rev.beth@virgin.net

HUTTON-BURY, Canon David. b 44. BA. **d** 94 **p** 95. Aux Min Geashill w Killeigh and Ballycommon *M & K* 94-97; Aux Min Clane w Donadea and Coolcarrigan 97-00; Aux Min Mullingar, Portnashangan, Moylisear, Kilbixy etc 00-05; Aux Min Clane w Donadea and Coolcarrigan 05-10; P-in-c Geashill w Killeigh and Ballycommon from 10; Can Meath from 10. *Chorleyville Farm, Tullamore, Co Offaly, Republic of Ireland* Tel (00353) (57) 932 1813

HUXHAM, Hector Hubert. b 29. Bris Univ BA55. Tyndale Hall Bris 52. **d** 56 **p** 57. C Eccleston St Luke *Liv* 56-58; C Heworth H Trin *York* 59-60; V Burley *Ripon* 61-66; Chapl St Jas Univ Hosp Leeds 67-94; rtd 94; Perm to Offic *Bradf* 94-98 and *Ripon* from 94. *3 Oakwell Oval, Leeds LS8 4AL* Tel 0113-266 8851

HUXHAM, Canon Peter Richard. b 38. Worc Coll Ox BA61 MA74. St Steph Ho Ox 61. **d** 63 **p** 64. C Gillingham *Sarum* 63-67; C Osmondthorpe St Phil *Ripon* 67-70; V Parkstone St Osmund *Sarum* 70-75; TR Parkstone St Pet w Branksea and St Osmund 75-92; RD Poole 85-92; Can and Preb Sarum Cathl 85-92; Chapl Taunton and Somerset NHS Trust 92-03; rtd 03. *Salterns House, 34 Brownsea View Avenue, Poole BH14 8LQ* Tel (01202) 707431

HUXLEY, Edward Jonathan. b 74. Bris Univ BEng95. Trin Coll Bris BA04. **d** 05 **p** 06. C Sea Mills *Bris* 05-08. *Address temp unknown*

HUXLEY, Canon Stephen Scott. b 30. Linc Th Coll 53. **d** 56 **p** 57. C Cullercoats St Geo *Newc* 56-59; C Eglingham 59-60; C N Gosforth 60-63; V Nether Witton and Hartburn and Meldon 63-65; V Tynemouth Priory 65-74; V Warkworth and Acklington 74-78; P-in-c Tynemouth St Jo 78-81; V 81-87; Hon Can Newc Cathl 82-92; V Wylam 87-92; rtd 92; Perm to Offic *Newc* 92-10. *7 Langside Drive, Comrie, Crieff PH6 2HR* Tel (01764) 679877

HUXTABLE, Christopher Michael Barclay. b 61. Ex Univ BA83 Qu Coll Cam PGCE84. St Steph Ho Ox 93. **d** 95 **p** 96. C Chich 95-98; C Haywards Heath St Wilfrid 98-99; TV 99-01; Chapl Geelong Gr Sch (Timbertop) Australia 01-04; Chapl St Mary's Sch Wantage 04-05; C Blewbury, Hagbourne and Upton *Ox* 05-06; C S w N Moreton, Aston Tirrold and Aston Upthorpe 05-06; R Mansfield Australia 06-11; Chapl Westbourne Gr Sch from 11. *Westbourne Grammar School, PO Box 37, Werribee Vic 3030, Australia* Tel (0061) (3) 9731 9444

HUXTABLE, Peter Alexander. b 68. Southn Univ BEng90. St Jo Coll Nottm MTh01. **d** 01 **p** 02. C Kidderminster St Geo *Worc* 01-05; V Bestwood Em w St Mark *S'well* 05-10; P-in-c Stapleford from 10. *The Vicarage, 61 Church Street, Stapleford, Nottingham NG9 8GA* Tel 0115-875 0220

HUYSSE-SMITH, Georgina Leah. b 83. Nottm Univ BA05. Ripon Coll Cuddesdon 07. **d** 10 **p** 11. C Gt and Lt Coates w Bradley *Linc* from 10. *26 Meadowbank, Great Coates, Grimsby DN37 9PG* Tel (01472) 317114 E-mail georgehuyssesmith@hotmail.co.uk

HUYTON, Stuart. b 37. St D Coll Lamp BA62. **d** 63 **p** 64. C Kingswinford H Trin *Lich* 63-66; C Leek St Edw 66-69; V Wigginton 69-76; V Wombourne 76-89; RD Trysull 79-84; P-in-c Bobbington 85-89; TR Wombourne w Trysull and Bobbington 89-95; V Lt Aston 95-04; rtd 04. *14 Crosbie Close, Chichester PO19 8RZ* Tel (01243) 790119

HUYTON, Canon Susan Mary. b 57. Birm Univ BA79. Qu Coll Birm 83. **d** 86 **p** 97. C Connah's Quay *St As* 86-89; C Wrexham 89-90; Dn-in-c 90-91; TV 91-99; V Gwersyllt from 99; AD Gresford from 05; Can Cursal St As Cathl from 08. *The Vicarage, Old Mold Road, Gwersyllt, Wrexham LL11 4SB* Tel (01978) 756391 E-mail suehyton@aol.com

HUZZEY, Peter George. b 48. Trin Coll Bris 74. **d** 76 **p** 77. C Bishopsworth *Bris* 76-79; V 86-96; C Downend 79-80; TV Kings Norton *Birm* 80-86; TR Bishopsworth and Bedminster Down *Bris* 97-00; RD Bedminster 98-99; TR Kingswood from 00. *Holy Trinity Vicarage, High Street, Kingswood, Bristol BS15 4AD* Tel 0117-967 3627 E-mail peterhuzzey@tiscali.co.uk

HYATT, Robert Keith. b 34. Em Coll Cam BA59 MA63. Ridley Hall Cam 58. **d** 60 **p** 61. C Cheltenham St Mary *Glouc* 60-63; Asst Chapl K Edw Sch Witley 63-65; C Godalming *Guildf* 65-69; Hong Kong 69-78; V Claygate *Guildf* 78-91; TV Whitton *Sarum*

I

91-96 and 99-00; TR 96-99; rtd 00; Perm to Offic *B & W* 00-04 and *Bris* from 02; May Moore Chapl Malmesbury *Bris* 02-05; Chapl Kennet and N Wilts Primary Care Trust 02-05. *19 Dark Lane, Malmesbury SN16 0BB* Tel (01666) 829026 E-mail bobnhelen@dsl.pipex.com

HYDE, Ann. b 42. **d** 09 **p** 10. NSM Bramhall *Ches* from 09. *Mellor View, 25 St Martin's Road, Marple, Stockport SK6 7BY*

HYDE, Mrs Denise. b 54. WEMTC 05. **d** 08 **p** 09. OLM Fairford and Kempsford w Whelford *Glouc* 08; OLM Fairford Deanery from 09. *14 Park Street, Fairford GL7 4JJ* Tel (01285) 713285 Mobile 07816-500269 E-mail nisehyde@hotmail.co.uk

HYDE, Dennis Hugh. b 23. Leeds Univ BA56. Sarum Th Coll 60. **d** 60 **p** 61. C Farncombe *Guildf* 60-62; C Burgh Heath 62-65; V Shottermill 65-74; Past Consultant Clinical Th Assn 74-80; rtd 88. *c/o Miss M E M Hyde, 18 Lindsay Road, New Haw, Addlestone KT15 3BD* Tel (01932) 354682

HYDE, Edgar Bonsor. b 29. Clifton Th Coll 59. **d** 61 **p** 62. C Weston-super-Mare Ch Ch *B & W* 61-66; C Chipping Campden *Glouc* 66-70; R Longborough w Condicote and Sezincote 70-78; R Longborough, Sezincote, Condicote and the Swells 78-99; rtd 99; Perm to Offic *Glouc* from 99. *1 Turnpike Close, Primrose Court, Moreton-in-Marsh GL56 0JJ* Tel (01608) 652456

HYDE, Mrs Jacqueline. WEMTC. **d** 09 **p** 10. NSM Leckhampton SS Phil and Jas w Cheltenham St Jas *Glouc* 09; NSM S Cheltenham from 10. *2 Eldington Road, Cheltenham GL53 0AJ* Tel (01242) 234955 E-mail clanhyde@o2.co.uk

HYDE, Jeremy Richard Granville. b 52. Sch of Pharmacy Lon BPharm75 PhD80. SAOMC 01. **d** 04 **p** 05. NSM Furze Platt *Ox* from 04; AD Maidenhead and Windsor from 08. *2A Belmont Park Road, Maidenhead SL6 6HT* Tel (01628) 621651 E-mail jeremyrhyde@aol.com

HYDE-DUNN, Keith Frederick. b 43. Sarum Th Coll. **d** 69 **p** 70. C Selukwe St Athan Rhodesia 69-72; C Horsham *Chich* 73-77; P-in-c Fittleworth 77-86; P-in-c Graffham w Woolavington 86-00; Perm to Offic from 01; rtd 04. *The Hermitage, Church Place, Pulborough RH20 1AF* Tel (01798) 873892

HYDER-SMITH, Brian John. b 45. FInstAM MCMI MBIM. EAMTC 84. **d** 87 **p** 88. NSM Huntingdon *Ely* 87-90; P-in-c Abbots Ripton w Wood Walton 90-98; P-in-c Kings Ripton 90-98; C Whittlesey, Pondersbridge and Coates 98-99; TV 99-04; rtd 04; Hon C Ironstone *Ox* from 10. *The Vicarage, Lane Close, Horley, Banbury OX15 6BH* Tel (01295) 730951 E-mail revbh-s@hotmail.com

HYDON, Ms Veronica Weldon. b 52. N Lon Poly BA73 Maria Grey Coll Lon CertEd74. Aston Tr Scheme 87 Westcott Ho Cam 89. **d** 91 **p** 94. Par Dn Poplar *Lon* 91-94; C 94-95; P-in-c Roxwell *Chelmsf* 95-00; Lay Development Officer 95-00; V Forest Gate Em w Upton Cross 00-03; Assoc V Timperley *Ches* 03-07; V Bollington from 07. *The Vicarage, 35A Shrigley Road, Bollington, Macclesfield SK10 5RD* Tel (01625) 573162 E-mail vhydon@hotmail.com

HYETT, Dawn Barbara. b 53. Cyncoed Coll CertEd74 Open Univ BA79. WEMTC 99. **d** 02 **p** 03. NSM Bromyard *Heref* 02-08; NSM Bromyard and Stoke Lacy from 09. *Roberts Hill, Norton, Bromyard HR7 4PB* Tel (01885) 483747

HYETT, Derek Walter. b 79. Leeds Univ BA05. Coll of Resurr Mirfield 02. **d** 05 **p** 06. C Edmonton St Alphege *Lon* 05-08; C Ponders End St Matt 05-08. *Address temp unknown*

HYGATE, Paul. b 72. Bolton Inst of HE BA95. EMMTC 07. **d** 10 **p** 11. NSM Aston on Trent, Elvaston, Weston on Trent etc *Derby* from 10. *38 Oaklands Avenue, Littleover, Derby DE23 2QH* Tel (01332) 772779 E-mail paulhygate@fsmail.net

HYLAND, Cecil George. b 38. TCD BA62 MA78. CITC Div Test. **d** 63 **p** 64. C Belfast St Nic *Conn* 63-66; C Monkstown *D & G* 66-68; Ch of Ireland Youth Officer 68-73; Chapl TCD 73-79; I Tullow *D & G* 79-90; I Howth 90-05; Dir of Ords (Dub) 91-98; Can Ch Ch Cathl Dublin 91-05; Cen Dir of Ords 98-05; rtd 05. *34 The Vale, Skerries Road, Skerries, Co Dublin, Republic of Ireland* Tel (00353) (1) 810 6884 Mobile 86-838 5317 E-mail cecilhyland@hotmail.com

HYSLOP, Mrs Catherine Graham Young. b 53. Carl Dioc Tr Inst 90. **d** 92 **p** 94. NSM St Bees *Carl* 92-95; NSM Upperby St Jo 95-98; C 98-03; C S Carl from 03. *St John's Vicarage, Manor Road, Upperby, Carlisle CA2 4LH* Tel (01228) 523380 E-mail jim.hyslop@talk21.com

HYSLOP, Canon Thomas James (Jim). b 54. St Andr Univ BD76. Edin Th Coll 76. **d** 78 **p** 79. C Whitehaven *Carl* 78-81; C Walney Is 81-83; P-in-c Gt Broughton and Broughton Moor 83-85; V 85-88; V Kells 88-95; P-in-c Upperby St Jo 95-97; V 97-03; TR S Carl from 03; Dioc Chapl MU from 02; Hon Can Carl Cathl from 06. *St John's Vicarage, Manor Road, Upperby, Carlisle CA2 4LH* Tel (01228) 523380 E-mail jim.hyslop@talk21.com

HYSON, Peter Raymond. b 51. Open Univ BA80 Bris Univ MSc05. Oak Hill Th Coll BA86. **d** 87 **p** 88. C Billericay and Lt Burstead *Chelmsf* 87-92; TV Whitton *Sarum* 92-99; Perm to Offic *Lon* from 07. *23 Havana Road, London SW19 8EJ* Tel (020) 8715 0093 Mobile 07951-767113 E-mail peter@change-perspectives.com

I'ANSON, Frederick Mark. b 43. MRAC68. Carl Dioc Tr Inst 89. **d** 92 **p** 93. NSM Sedbergh, Cautley and Garsdale *Bradf* 92-98; P-in-c Kirkby-in-Malhamdale w Coniston Cold 98-08; rtd 08; Perm to Offic *Bradf* from 08. *The Bowers, Firbank, Sedbergh LA10 5EG* Tel (015396) 21757 Mobile 07815-552778 E-mail mark.ianson@bradford.anglican.org

IBADAN SOUTH, Bishop of. *See* AJETUNMOBI, The Rt Revd Jacob Ademola

IBALL, Charles Martin John. b 40. Lich Th Coll 67. **d** 69 **p** 70. C Dudley St Edm *Worc* 69-73; C W Bromwich St Jas *Lich* 73-76; V Oxley 76-80; Hon C Whittington w Weeford 86-10; Hon C Clifton Campville w Edingale and Harlaston 96-06; Hon C Hints 06-10; rtd 04. *21 Lion Court, Worcester WR1 1UT* Tel (01905) 724695

IBBETSON, Stephen Andrew. b 59. Portsm Poly BSc82. STETS 04. **d** 07 **p** 08. NSM Southbroom *Sarum* from 07. *12 Moonrakers, London Road, Devizes SN10 2DY* Tel (01380) 721953 E-mail s.ibbetson@btinternet.com

IBBOTSON, Miss Tracy Alexandra. b 63. Cranmer Hall Dur 01. **d** 03 **p** 04. NSM Knottingley *Wakef* 03-08; V Airedale w Fryston from 08. *Holy Cross Vicarage, The Mount, Castleford WF10 3JN* Tel (01977) 553157 E-mail ibbotson457@btinternet.com

IBE-ENWO, Ogbonnia. b 62. Univ of Nigeria BSc84 Univ of Northumbria at Newc MSc04 Ex Univ MSc11 MBCS05. Trin Coll Umuahia 00. **d** 00 **p** 02. C Unwana St Luke Nigeria 00-01; Chapl Akanu Ibiam Federal Poly Unwana 00-03 and 04-10; V Unwana Em 02-03; NSM Benwell *Newc* 03-04; V Unwana St Luke Nigeria 07-10; C Kenton, Mamhead, Powderham, Cofton and Starcross *Ex* from 11; C Exminster and Kenn from 11. *All Saints' House, Kenton, Exeter EX6 8NG* Tel (01626) 890034 Mobile 07760-927950 E-mail ibeenwo@yahoo.com

IBIAYO, David Akindayo Oluwarotimi. b 71. Lagos Univ BSc. Ridley Hall Cam. **d** 06 **p** 07. C Barking St Marg w St Patr *Chelmsf* 06-10; R Vange from 11; P-in-c Bowers Gifford w N Benfleet from 11. *Vange Rectory, 782 Clay Hill Road, Basildon SS16 4NG* Tel (01268) 581404 Mobile 07904-846028 E-mail david.ibiayo@hotmail.com

IDDON, Jonathan Richard. b 82. **d** 11. C Glascote and Stonydelph *Lich* from 11. *22 Melmerby, Wilnecote, Tamworth B77 4LP* Tel (01827) 895788 E-mail curate@stmartininthedelph.co.uk

IDDON, Roy Edward. b 40. TCert61 Lanc Univ MA88. NOC 83. **d** 83 **p** 84. Hd Teacher St Andr Primary Sch Blackb from 83; NSM Bolton St Matt w St Barn *Man* 83-88; Lic to AD Walmsley 88-93; NSM Walmsley 93-01; NSM Turton Moorland Min 01-04; NSM Bolton St Phil 04-10. *28 New Briggs Fold, Egerton, Bolton BL7 9UL* Tel (01204) 306589

IDLE, Christopher Martin. b 38. St Pet Coll Ox BA62. Clifton Th Coll 62. **d** 65 **p** 66. C Barrow St Mark *Carl* 65-68; C Camberwell Ch Ch *S'wark* 68-71; P-in-c Poplar St Matthias *Lon* 71-76; R Limehouse 76-89; R N Hartismere *St E* 89-95; Perm to Offic *S'wark* 95-03 and *St E* 01-03; rtd 03; Perm to Offic *Roch* from 04. *16 Cottage Avenue, Bromley BR2 8LQ* Tel and fax (020) 8462 1749

IEVINS, Mrs Catherine Ruth. b 54. LMH Ox BA77 MA80 Solicitor 81. EAMTC 98. **d** 01 **p** 02. C Pet Ch Carpenter 01-05; Perm to Offic 05-06; R Polebrook and Lutton w Hemington and Luddington 06-07; C Barnwell w Tichmarsh, Thurning and Clapton 06-07; R Barnwell, Hemington, Luddington in the Brook etc from 07. *The Rectory, Main Street, Polebrook, Peterborough PE8 5LN* Tel (01832) 270162 E-mail cievins@yahoo.co.uk

IEVINS, Peter Valdis. b 54. St Jo Coll Ox BA75 MA81 Solicitor 79. Westcott Ho Cam 86. **d** 88 **p** 89. C Sawston and Babraham *Ely* 88-91; NSM Pet Ch Carpenter 01-06; Lic to Offic from 06. *The Rectory, Main Street, Polebrook, Peterborough PE8 5LN* Tel (01832) 270162 E-mail peter.ievins@judiciary.gsi.gov.uk

IGENOZA, Andrew Olu. b 50. Ife Univ Nigeria BA75 Man Univ PhD82. Immanuel Coll Ibadan 87. **d** 88 **p** 89. Nigeria 88-99; C Gorton St Phil *Man* 00-01. *17 Northmoor Road, Longsight, Manchester M12 4NF* Tel 0161-248 8758

IJAZ, Luke Anthony. b 76. Univ Coll Lon MSci99 Lon Inst of Educn PGCE01. Wycliffe Hall Ox BA06. **d** 07 **p** 08. C Wallington *S'wark* 07-11; C Redhill H Trin from 11. *15 Earlsbrook Road, Redhill RH1 6DR* E-mail luke.ijaz@hotmail.com

IKIN, Gordon Mitchell. b 30. AKC57. **d** 58 **p** 59. C Leigh St Mary *Man* 58-61; V Westleigh St Paul 61-72; V Thornham St Jas 72-95; rtd 95; Perm to Offic *Man* 95-08. *3 Lygon Lodge, Newland, Malvern WR13 5AX*

ILECHUKWU, Gideon. b 70. Nnamdi Azikiwe Univ Nigeria MB, BS97. Trin Coll Umuahia 04. **d** 04 **p** 06. Chapl Univ of Nigeria Teaching Hosp 04-09; Dioc Dir of Ords and Miss and Adn Awgu/Aninri 07-09; NSM Dublin St Patr Cathl Gp 10;

Perm to Offic *Man* from 11. *12 Morrell Road, Manchester M22 4WH* Tel 0161-270 2656 Mobile 07411-239576 E-mail venerablegideon@yahoo.co.uk

ILES, Canon Paul Robert. b 37. FRCO65 Fitzw Coll Cam BA59 MA64 St Edm Hall Ox MA80. Sarum Th Coll 59. **d** 61 **p** 62. Chapl Bp Wordsworth Sch Salisbury 61-67; C Salisbury St Mich *Sarum* 61-64; Min Can Sarum Cathl 64-67; C Bournemouth St Pet *Win* 67-72; R Filton *Bris* 72-79; V Ox SS Phil and Jas w St Marg 79-83; Can Res and Prec Heref Cathl 83-03; rtd 03; Hon C Prestbury and All SS *Glouc* 03-08; Hon C N Cheltenham from 08. *24 Willowherb Close, Prestbury, Cheltenham GL52 5LP* Tel (01242) 579456

ILIFFE, Mrs Felicity Mary. b 57. Glam Univ BA79 Normal Coll Ban PGCE82. SEITE 06 WEMTC 07. **d** 09 **p** 10. C Ledbury *Heref* from 09. *21 Biddulph Way, Ledbury HR8 2HP* Tel (01531) 636840 *or* 631531 E-mail revfliss@googlemail.com

ILLING, Eric James. b 33. Kelham Th Coll 54 Chich Th Coll 55. **d** 57 **p** 58. C Leeds St Aid *Ripon* 57-60; C Leeds All SS 60-62; C E Grinstead St Swithun *Chich* 62-65; V Middleton St Mary *Ripon* 65-74; R Felpham w Middleton *Chich* 74-81; Chapl R Devon and Ex Hosp (Wonford) 81-91; TR Heavitree w Ex St Paul 81-91; R Bradninch and Clyst Hydon 91-94; rtd 94; Perm to Offic *B & W* from 94 and *Eur* from 98. *25 Pikes Crescent, Taunton TA1 4HS* Tel (01823) 289203

ILLINGWORTH, John Patrick Paul. b 34. New Coll Ox BA59 MA63. Chich Th Coll 61. **d** 63 **p** 64. C Brighouse *Wakef* 63-66; C Willesden St Andr *Lon* 66-70; Chapl Gothenburg w Halmstad and Jönköping *Eur* 70-74; Perm to Offic *Chich* 74; V Ryhill *Wakef* 74-82; R Weston Longville w Morton and the Witchinghams *Nor* 82-04; P-in-c Alderford w Attlebridge and Swannington 94-04; RD Sparham 95-00; rtd 04; Perm to Offic *Nor* from 04. *38 Eckling Road, Dereham NR20 3BB* Tel (01362) 690407

ILORI, Emmanuel. b 57. **d** 04 **p** 05. NSM New Addington *S'wark* from 04. *16 Birdhurst Avenue, South Croydon CR2 7DX* Tel (020) 7423 2822 Mobile 07734-929501 E-mail e.ilori@opmaritime.com

ILSLEY (née ROGERS), Mrs Anne Frances. b 50. Heythrop Coll Lon BA00 RGN72. Wycliffe Hall Ox 00. **d** 02 **p** 03. NSM Harefield *Lon* 02-06; NSM Dorchester *Ox* from 06. *The Vicarage, High Street, Long Wittenham, Abingdon OX14 4QQ* Tel (01865) 407605 Mobile 07956-374624 E-mail annefi36@aol.com

ILSON, John Robert. b 37. Leeds Univ BSc59 Lon Univ BD64 CertEd65. ALCD63. **d** 64 **p** 65. C Kennington St Mark *S'wark* 64-67; C Sydenham H Trin 67-70; Asst Dir RE *Sheff* 70-77; R Hooton Roberts 70-75; R Hooton Roberts w Ravenfield 75-77; P-in-c Kidderminster St Geo *Worc* 77-81; TR 81-85; P-in-c Powick 85-96; Chapl N Devon Healthcare NHS Trust 97-04; rtd 04. *14 Bromley College, London Road, Bromley BR1 1PE* Tel 020-8460 3927 E-mail jilson1@tiscali.co.uk

ILTON, Mrs Jennifer Jane. b 38. S Dios Minl Tr Scheme 92. **d** 95 **p** 96. NSM Jersey St Sav *Win* from 95. *38 Maison St Louis, St Saviour, Jersey JE2 7LX* Tel (01534) 722327

ILYAS, Marilyn. b 51. Oak Hill Th Coll 92. **d** 95 **p** 96. C Roch 95-98; TV S Chatham H Trin 98-01; TR from 01. *26 Mayford Road, Chatham ME5 8SZ* Tel (01634) 660922 E-mail marilyn.ilyas@diocese-rochester.org

IMAGE, Miss Isabella Christine. b 76. CCC Cam BA98 MPhil00 Southn Univ MSc06. Ripon Coll Cuddesdon BA09. **d** 10 **p** 11. C Luton All SS w St Pet *St Alb* from 10. *St Peter's House, 48 Harefield Road, Luton LU1 1TH* E-mail isabellaimage@gmail.com

IMPEY, Miss Joan Mary. b 35. Dalton Ho Bris 65. dss 74 **d** 87 **p** 94. Kennington St Mark *S'wark* 67-75; Barking St Marg w St Patr *Chelmsf* 75-81; Harwell w Chilton *Ox* 81-87; Par Dn 87-92; Par Dn Didcot All SS 92-94; C 94-97; rtd 98; Perm to Offic *Ox* from 99. *15 Loder Road, Harwell, Didcot OX11 0HR* Tel (01235) 820346

IMPEY, Canon Patricia Irene. b 45. Birm Univ BA67 Lanc Univ MPhil01. Carl Dioc Tr Course 88. **d** 90 **p** 94. Par Dn Blackpool St Paul *Blackb* 90-94; C 94-95; Chapl Asst Victoria Hosp Blackpool 94-95; Asst Chapl Norfolk and Nor Hosp 95-96; Hon C Sprowston w Beeston *Nor* 96; R King's Beck 96-02; V Ecclesfield *Sheff* 02-10; Bp's Adv for Women's Min 03-06; Dean of Women's Min 06-08; Hon Can Sheff Cathl 04-10; rtd 10; Perm to Offic *Blackb* from 11. *22 Hala Grove, Lancaster LA1 4PS* Tel (01524) 36617 E-mail patriciaimpey@btinternet.com

IMPEY, Richard. b 41. Em Coll Cam BA63 MA67 Harvard Univ ThM67. Ridley Hall Cam 67. **d** 68 **p** 69. C Birm St Martin 68-72; Dir of Tr *B & W* 72-79; Dir of Ords 76-79; V Blackpool St Jo *Blackb* 79-95; RD Blackpool 84-90; Hon Can Blackb Cathl 89-95; Dioc Dir of Tr *Nor* 95-00; P-in-c Heigham St Barn w St Bart 00-02; V Wentworth *Sheff* 02-06; Bp's Adv in Par Development 04-10; rtd 06; Perm to Offic *Blackb* from 10. *22 Hala Grove, Lancaster LA1 4PS* Tel (01524) 36617 E-mail richardimpey@btinternet.com

INALL, Mrs Elizabeth Freda. b 47. Univ of Wales (Lamp) MA06. St Alb Minl Tr Scheme 88. **d** 92 **p** 94. NSM Tring *St Alb* 92-01; C Harpenden St Nic 01-09; P-in-c Milton Ernest, Pavenham and Thurleigh from 09. *The Vicarage, Thurleigh Road, Milton Ernest, Bedford MK44 1RF* Tel (01234) 822885 E-mail elizabeth.inall@virgin.net

INCE, Peter Reginald. b 26. Bp's Coll Calcutta 48. **d** 51 **p** 52. C Calcutta St Jas India 51-52; V 52-53; Chapl Khargpur 53-54; Chapl Asansol 54-55; C Leek St Luke *Lich* 55-57; C Milton 57-59; C Lewisham St Jo Southend *S'wark* 59-62; R Loddington w Cransley *Pet* 62-75; V Snibston *Leic* 75-79; R Mickleham *Guildf* 79-92; rtd 92; Perm to Offic *Guildf* 92-03. *Bickerton, 8 Rockdale, Headley Road, Grayshott, Hindhead GU26 6TU* Tel (01428) 604694

IND, Dominic Mark. b 63. Lanc Univ BA87. Ridley Hall Cam 87. **d** 90 **p** 91. C Birch w Fallowfield *Man* 90-93; SSF 93-95; Perm to Offic *Glas* 95-96; C Byker St Martin *Newc* 96-98; C Walker 96-98; P-in-c Cambuslang and Uddingston *Glas* 98-07; R Bridge of Allan *St And* from 07; Chapl Stirling Univ from 07. *21 Fountain Road, Bridge of Allan FK9 4AT* Tel (01786) 832368 E-mail dom.ind@btinternet.com

IND, Philip William David. b 35. K Coll Lon BD82. Wycliffe Hall Ox 74 Cranmer Hall Dur 59. **d** 65 **p** 66. C Ipswich St Jo *St E* 65-67; C Charlton Kings St Mary *Glouc* 67-71; R Woolstone w Gotherington and Oxenton 71-74; Chapl Alleyn's Sch Dulwich 76-81; C Beckenham St Geo *Roch* 83-85; V Bromley St Jo 85-87; Perm to Offic *Ox* 88-91 and from 95; P-in-c Hurley 91-92; P-in-c Stubbings 91-92; rtd 92. *Stilegate, Tugwood Common, Cookham, Maidenhead SL6 9TT* Tel (01628) 477425 E-mail mtpipind@aol.com

✠**IND, The Rt Revd William.** b 42. Leeds Univ BA64. Coll of Resurr Mirfield 64. **d** 66 **p** 67 **c** 87. C Feltham *Lon* 66-71; C Northolt St Mary 71-73; TV Basingstoke *Win* 73-87; Vice-Prin Aston Tr Scheme 79-82; Dioc Dir of Ords *Win* 82-87; Hon Can Win Cathl 84-87; Suff Bp Grantham *Linc* 87-97; Dean Stamford 87-97; Can and Preb Linc Cathl 87-97; Bp Truro 97-08; rtd 08. *15 Dean Close, Melksham SN12 7EZ*

INDER, Patrick John. b 30. K Coll Lon BD54 AKC54 Huddersfield Univ MA98. St Boniface Warminster. **d** 55 **p** 56. C St Margaret's-on-Thames *Lon* 55-57; C Golders Green 57-61; V Hanwell St Mellitus 61-77; R Rawmarsh w Parkgate *Sheff* 77-80; rtd 80; Hon C Sheff St Matt 82-88; Perm to Offic *Wakef* from 98 and *Win* from 02. *Roucoulement, rue de la Brigade, St Andrews, Guernsey GY6 8RQ* Tel (01481) 234343 E-mail roucoulement@cwgsy.net

INESON, David Antony. b 36. ALCD62. **d** 62 **p** 63. C Sandal St Helen *Wakef* 62-65; C Birm St Geo 66-71; V Horton *Bradf* 71-80; RD Bowling and Horton 78-80; V Sedbergh, Cautley and Garsdale 80-86; C Firbank, Howgill and Killington 81-86; TV Langley and Parkfield *Man* 86-88; TR Banbury *Ox* 92-98; R 98-01; rtd 01; Perm to Offic *Ripon* from 01. *11 Church Close, Redmire, Leyburn DL8 4HF* Tel (01969) 624631 E-mail d.ineson@tiscali.co.uk

INESON, Emma Gwynneth. b 69. Birm Univ BA92 MPhil93 PhD98. Trin Coll Bris BA99. **d** 00 **p** 01. C Dore *Sheff* 00-03; Chapl Lee Abbey 03-06; Partnership P Inner Ring Partnership *Bris* from 06; NSM Bris St Matt and St Nath from 06; Tutor Trin Coll Bris from 07. *St Matthew's Vicarage, 11 Glentworth Road, Bristol BS6 7EG* Tel 0117-942 4186 E-mail emmaineson@blueyonder.co.uk

INESON, Mathew David. b 69. Birm Univ BEng91. Trin Coll Bris BA99 MA00. **d** 00 **p** 01. NSM Dore *Sheff* 00-03; Chapl Lee Abbey 03-06; P-in-c Bris St Matt and St Nath from 06; Min Inner Ring Partnership from 06; AD City from 10. *St Matthew's Vicarage, 11 Glentworth Road, Bristol BS6 7EG* Tel 0117-942 4186 Mobile 07896-997604 E-mail mat.ineson@bristol.anglican.org

INESON, Matthew. b 68. Leeds Univ BA00. Coll of Resurr Mirfield 97. **d** 00 **p** 01. C Owton Manor *Dur* 00-03; V Dalton *Sheff* from 03. *The Vicarage, 2 Vicarage Close, Dalton, Rotherham S65 3QL* Tel (01709) 850377 Mobile 07780-686310 E-mail frmatt_@excite.com

INGALL, David Lenox. b 81. Jes Coll Cam MA08. Wycliffe Hall Ox BA08. **d** 09 **p** 10. C Holborn St Geo w H Trin and St Bart *Lon* from 09. *Flat 3, 58 Lamb's Conduit Street, London WC1N 3LW* Tel 07968-119017 (mobile) E-mail davidingall@gmail.com

INGAMELLS, Ronald Sidney. b 32. FCIPD92. AKC56. **d** 57 **p** 58. C Leeds Gipton Epiphany *Ripon* 57-59; C Gt Yarmouth *Nor* 59-64; Dioc Youth Officer 64-79; Hon C Nor St Pet Mancroft 64-79; P-in-c Lemsford *St Alb* 79-02; Sec Tr Development and Chr Educn Nat Coun YMCAs 79-92; Consultant to Romania Euro Alliance YMCAs 93-97; rtd 02; Perm to Offic *Ely* from 03. *2 Aragon Close, Buckden, St Neots PE19 5TY* Tel (01480) 811608 E-mail rjingamells@btinternet.com

✠**INGE, The Rt Revd John Geoffrey.** b 55. St Chad's Coll Dur BSc77 MA94 PhD02 Keble Coll Ox PGCE79. Coll of Resurr Mirfield. **d** 84 **p** 85 **c** 03. Asst Chapl Lancing Coll 84-86; Jun

Chapl Harrow Sch 86-89; Sen Chapl 89-90; V Wallsend St Luke *Newc* 90-96; Can Res Ely Cathl 96-03; Vice-Dean 99-03; Suff Bp Huntingdon 03-07; Bp Worc from 07. *The Bishop's Office, The Old Palace, Deansway, Worcester WR1 2JE* Tel (01905) 731599 Fax 739382 E-mail bishop.worcester@cofe-worcester.org.uk

INGHAM, Anthony William. b 55. Ven English Coll Rome PhB75 STB78 NOC 98. **d** 78 **p** 79. In RC Ch 78-98; NSM Tottington *Man* 99-01; CF from 01. *clo MOD Chaplains (Army)* Tel (01264) 381140 Fax 381824

INGHAM, Miss Dawn. b 48. **d** 04 **p** 05. C Brownhill *Wakef* 04-07; P-in-c Wakef St Andr and St Mary from 07. *St Andrew's Vicarage, Johnston Street, Wakefield WF1 4DZ* Tel (01924) 384260 E-mail dawn_124@fsmail.net

INGHAM, John Edmund. b 34. Reading Univ BA56. Clifton Th Coll 58. **d** 60 **p** 61. C Rodbourne Cheney *Bris* 60-63; C Tunbridge Wells St Jo *Roch* 63-67; V Sevenoaks Weald 67-82; V Farrington Gurney *B & W* 82-92; V Paulton 82-92; RD Midsomer Norton 88-91; R Aspley Guise w Husborne Crawley and Ridgmont *St Alb* 92-99; rtd 99; Perm to Offic *B & W* from 00. *1 Garden Ground, Shepton Mallet BA4 4DJ* Tel (01749) 345403

INGHAM, Malcolm John. b 68. Wycliffe Hall Ox BTh99. **d** 99 **p** 00. C Moreton-in-Marsh w Batsford, Todenham etc *Glouc* 99-03; C Leckhampton SS Phil and Jas w Cheltenham St Jas 03-04; TV The Ortons, Alwalton and Chesterton *Ely* 04-10; P-in-c Elton w Stibbington and Water Newton 06-10; V Alwalton and Chesterton from 10. *St Andrew's Rectory, 4 Alwalton Hall, Alwalton, Peterborough PE7 3UN* Tel (01733) 239289 Mobile 07974-394984 E-mail malcolm.ingham@yahoo.com

INGHAM, Mrs Carol Helen. See PHARAOH, Carol Helen

INGHAM, Mrs Pamela. b 47. MBE96. NEOC 93. **d** 96 **p** 97. C Newc Epiphany 96-99; C Fawdon 99-00; P-in-c 00-06; Dioc Development Officer for Partners in Community Action 06-10; rtd 10. *15 St George's Road, Cullercoats NE30 3JZ* E-mail pimbe@o2.co.uk

INGLE-GILLIS, William Clarke. b 68. Baylor Univ (USA) BA90 MA95 K Coll Lon PhD04. Westcott Ho Cam 02. **d** 04 **p** 05. C Caldicot *Mon* 04-08; Dioc Soc Resp Officer 06-08; P-in-c Caerwent w Dinham and Llanfair Discoed etc from 08; Tutor St Mich Coll Llan from 07. *1 Vicarage Gardens, Caerwent, Caldicot NP26 5BH* Tel and fax (01291) 424984 E-mail w.c.ingle-gillis@cantab.net

INGLEBY, Canon Anthony Richard. b 48. Keele Univ BA72. Trin Coll Bris. **d** 83 **p** 84. C Plymouth St Jude *Ex* 83-88; R Lanreath *Truro* 88-97; V Pelynt 88-97; RD W Wivelshire 96-97; P-in-c Stoke Climsland 97-05; P-in-c Linkinhorne 03-05; P-in-c Liskeard and St Keyne from 05; Chapl Cornwall and Is of Scilly Primary Care Trust 05-09; Hon Can Truro Cathl from 04; RD W Wivelshire from 08; C Duloe, Herodsfoot, Morval and St Pinnock from 10. *The Rectory, Church Street, Liskeard PL14 3AQ* Tel (01579) 342178 E-mail revtonyingleby@gmail.com

INGLEDEW, Peter David Gordon. b 48. AKC77 Jo Dalton Coll Man CertEd73 Croydon Coll DASS92 CQSW92 Univ Coll Chich BA03. St Steph Ho Ox 77. **d** 78 **p** 79. C Whorlton *Newc* 78-81; C Poplar *Lon* 81-83; TV 83-85; V Tottenham H Trin 85-90; Perm to Offic *Chich* from 90. *11 St Luke's Terrace, Brighton BN2 2ZE* Tel (01273) 689765 Fax 389115 E-mail david.ingledew2@btinternet.com

INGLESBY, Preb Richard Eric. b 47. Birm Univ BSc69 Bris Univ CertEd74. Wycliffe Hall Ox 85. **d** 87 **p** 88. C Cheltenham Ch Ch *Glouc* 87-92; P-in-c Paulton *B & W* 92-94; V 94-01; P-in-c Farrington Gurney 92-94; V 94-01; P-in-c Moxley *Lich* 01-09; V from 09; C Darlaston All SS from 01; C Darlaston St Lawr from 01; Ecum Adv (Wolverhampton Area) 04-08; RD Wednesbury from 05; Preb Lich Cathl from 09. *The Vicarage, 5 Sutton Road, Moxley, Wednesbury WS10 8SG* Tel and fax (01902) 653084

INGLIS, Kelvin John. b 62. Ripon Coll Cuddesdon MTh00. **d** 00 **p** 01. C Southampton Maybush St Pet *Win* 00-04; V Whitchurch w Tufton and Litchfield from 04. *The Vicarage, Church Street, Whitchurch RG28 7AS* Tel (01256) 892535

INGLIS-JONES, Valentine Walter. b 72. UEA BA94 Univ of N Lon PGCE95 Cam Univ BTh07. Ridley Hall Cam 04. **d** 07 **p** 08. C Combe Down w Monkton Combe and S Stoke *B & W* 07-11; P-in-c Bramshott and Liphook *Portsm* from 11. *The Rectory, 22 Portsmouth Road, Liphook GU30 7DJ* Tel (01428) 723750 Mobile 07917-151108 E-mail vwi20@cam.ac.uk

INGRAM, Canon Bernard Richard. b 40. Lon Coll of Div 66. **d** 66 **p** 67. C Bromley Common St Aug *Roch* 66-70; C Gravesend St Geo 70-74; Chapl Joyce Green Hosp Dartford 75-83; V Dartford St Edm *Roch* 75-83; V Strood St Fran 83-04; RD Strood 91-97; Hon Can Roch Cathl 00-04; rtd 04; Perm to Offic *Heref* from 05. *1 Hillview Cottage, Upper Colwall, Malvern WR13 6DH* Tel and fax (01684) 540475

INGRAM, Clodagh Mary. b 65. **d** 10 **p** 11. C Tuffley *Glouc* from 10. *2 Coxmore Close, Hucclecote, Gloucester GL3 3SA* Tel (01452) 618255

INGRAM, Gary Simon. b 58. K Coll Lon BD AKC. Ripon Coll Cuddesdon. **d** 83 **p** 84. Chapl Nelson and Colne Coll 92-98; C Spalding *Linc* 83-87; C Heaton Ch Ch *Man* 87-89; V Colne H Trin *Blackb* 89-98; RD Pendle 96-98; R Poulton-le-Sands w Morecambe St Laur 98-09; AD Lancaster 98-04; P-in-c Ferring *Chich* from 09. *The Vicarage, 19 Grange Park, Ferring, Worthing BN12 5LS* Tel (01903) 241645 E-mail garyingram@care4free.net

INGRAM (née BURDEN), Mrs Joanna Mary. b 50. EMMTC 04. **d** 07 **p** 08. NSM Aston on Trent, Elvaston, Weston on Trent etc *Derby* from 07. *25 The Woodlands, Melbourne, Derby DE73 8DP* Tel (01332) 862548 E-mail joanna.ingram@rdplus.net

INGRAM, Canon Peter Anthony. b 53. NOC 83. **d** 86 **p** 87. C Maltby *Sheff* 86-89; TV Gt Snaith 89-92; R Adwick-le-Street w Skelbrooke 92-05; AD Adwick 01-05; V Millhouses H Trin from 05; AD Ecclesall from 07; Hon Can Sheff Cathl from 05. *The Vicarage, 80 Millhouses Lane, Sheffield S7 2HB* Tel 0114-236 2838 E-mail revingram@hotmail.co.uk

INGRAMS, Peter Douglas. b 56. Wheaton Coll Illinois BA77 Ox Univ BA80. Wycliffe Hall Ox 78. **d** 83 **p** 84. C Rowner *Portsm* 83-86; C Petersfield w Sheet 86-90; V Sheet 90-96; V Locks Heath 96-07; Local Min Officer *Cant* from 07. *12 Guildford Road, Canterbury CT1 3QD*

INKPIN, David Leonard. b 32. Liv Univ BSc54 CChem MRSC55. EMMTC 83. **d** 86 **p** 87. NSM Legsby, Linwood and Market Rasen *Linc* 86-04; Perm to Offic from 04. *Weelsby House, Legsby Road, Market Rasen LN8 3DY* Tel (01673) 843360 E-mail inkypens@yahoo.co.uk

INKPIN, Jonathan David Francis. b 60. Mert Coll Ox MA81 Dur Univ PhD96. Ripon Coll Cuddesdon BA85. **d** 86 **p** 87. C Hackney *Lon* 86-88; Tutor Ripon Coll Cuddesdon 88-90; C Cuddesdon *Ox* 88-90; TV Gateshead *Dur* 90-95; C Stanhope w Frosterley 95-01; C Eastgate w Rookhope 95-01; Dioc Rural Development Officer 95-01; Australia from 01. *78 Henry Parry Drive, PO Box 4255, Gosford East NSW 2250, Australia* Tel (0061) (2) 4324 2630

INMAN, Daniel David. b 84. Wycliffe Hall Ox BA05 Qu Coll Ox MSt06 DPhil09. Ripon Coll Cuddesdon 07. **d** 10 **p** 11. C Deddington w Barford, Clifton and Hempton *Ox* from 10. *7 Church Street, Barford St Michael, Banbury OX15 0UA* Tel (01869) 338582 Mobile 07747-016370 E-mail curatedan@gmail.com

INMAN, Malcolm Gordon. b 33. Edin Th Coll 58. **d** 60 **p** 61. C Lundwood *Wakef* 60-63; C Heckmondwike 63-70; V Wrenthorpe 70-75; Chapl Cardigan Hosp 70-73; Asst Chapl Pinderfields Gen Hosp Wakef 72-73; V Cleckheaton St Jo *Wakef* 75-98; rtd 98; Perm to Offic *Wakef* 00-07; Hon C Staincliffe and Carlinghow from 07. *14 Briestfield Road, Thornhill Edge, Dewsbury WF12 0PW* Tel (01924) 437171

INMAN, Mark Henry. b 31. Lon Univ BSc53. EAMTC 80. **d** 83 **p** 84. Hon C Orford w Sudbourne, Chillesford, Butley and Iken *St E* 83-85; Chapl HM YOI Hollesley Bay Colony 85-91; Hon C Alderton w Ramsholt and Bawdsey *St E* 85-92; P-in-c 92-00; P-in-c Shottisham w Sutton 92-00; TV Wilford Peninsula 00-01; rtd 01; Perm to Offic *Nor* from 01. *Mill Farm House, Newton Road, Sporle, King's Lynn PE32 2DB* Tel (01760) 722544

INMAN, Martin. b 50. K Coll Lon BD72 AKC73. St Aug Coll Cant 72. **d** 73 **p** 74. C Bridgnorth St Mary *Heref* 73-77; C Parkstone St Pet w Branksea and St Osmund *Sarum* 77-79; V Willenhall St Anne *Lich* 79-85; Chapl Yeovil Distr Gen Hosp 85-91; TV Yeovil *B & W* 85-88; R Barwick 88-91; Chapl Jersey Gen Hosp 91-99; Chapl Whittington Hosp NHS Trust 99-03; TV Smestow Vale *Lich* 03-09; RD Trysull 06-09; rtd 09; Perm to Offic *Lich* from 09. *28 Market Lane, Wolverhampton WV4 4UJ* Tel (01902) 345441 Mobile 07980-920462 E-mail martininman@hotmail.co.uk

INMAN, Canon Thomas Jeremy. b 45. Rhodes Univ BA67. St Steph Ho Ox 67. **d** 69 **p** 70. C Deptford St Paul *S'wark* 69-72; C Bellville S Africa 72-73; R Malmesbury 73-76; P-in-c Donnington *Chich* 76-80; V Hangleton 80-86; V Bosham 86-10; RD Westbourne 91-99; Can and Preb Chich Cathl 00-10; rtd 10; Perm to Offic *Bris* from 10. *35 Hunters Road, Bristol BS15 3EZ* Tel 0117-960 5045 Mobile 07941-834914 E-mail tjinman45@aol.com

INNES, Donald John. b 32. St Jo Coll Ox BA54 MA. Westcott Ho Cam 56. **d** 56 **p** 57. C St Marylebone St Mark Hamilton Terrace *Lon* 56-58; C Walton-on-Thames *Guildf* 58-67; Chapl Moor Park Coll Farnham 67-76; P-in-c Tilford *Guildf* 76-97; rtd 97; Perm to Offic *Guildf* from 97. *Watchetts, 67A Upper Hale Road, Farnham GU9 0PA* Tel (01252) 734597

INNES, Donald Keith. b 33. St Jo Coll Ox BA56 MA60 Lon Univ BD58 Bris Univ MPhil01. Clifton Th Coll 56. **d** 58 **p** 59. C Harold Hill St Paul *Chelmsf* 58-61; C Ealing Dean St Jo *Lon* 61-65; V Westacre and R Gayton Thorpe w E Walton *Nor* 65-70; V Woking St Paul *Guildf* 70-78; R Alfold and Loxwood 78-88; V Doddington w Wychling *Cant* 88-90; V Newnham 88-90; V Doddington, Newnham and Wychling 90-97; rtd 97; Perm to Offic *Chich* from 98. *6 Vicarage Close, Ringmer, Lewes BN8 5LF* Tel (01273) 814995

INNES, James Michael. b 32. Lon Univ BA56 BD59. Clifton Th Coll 59. **d** 59 **p** 60. C Blackpool St Thos *Blackb* 59-62; Tutor Clifton Th Coll 62-65; V Burton All SS *Lich* 65-73; V Ashton-upon-Mersey St Mary Magd *Ches* 73-90; P-in-c Brereton w Swettenham 90-91; R 91-97; Dioc Clergy Widows and Retirement Officer 93-97; rtd 97; Perm to Offic *Derby* from 97. *22 Sandown Avenue, Mickleover, Derby DE3 0QQ* Tel (01332) 516691 E-mail jminnes.9@tiscali.co.uk

INNES, Canon Robert Neil. b 59. K Coll Cam BA82 MA85 St Jo Coll Dur BA91 Dur Univ PhD95. Cranmer Hall Dur 89. **d** 95 **p** 96. C Dur St Cuth 95-97; C Shadforth and Sherburn w Pittington 97-99; Lect St Jo Coll Dur 95-99; P-in-c Belmont *Dur* 99-00; V 00-05; Sen Chapl and Chan Brussels Cathl from 05. *Avenue Princesse Paola 15, 1410 Waterloo, Belgium* Tel (0032) (2) 511 7183 E-mail chaplain@htbrussels.com

INNES, Ms Ruth. b 56. New Coll Edin BD00. TISEC 97. **d** 00 **p** 01. Prec St Ninian's Cathl Perth 00-02; P-in-c Linlithgow and Bathgate *Edin* 02-06; P-in-c Edin St Mark 06-10; R Falkirk from 10. *The Rectory, 55 Kerse Lane, Falkirk FK1 1RX* Tel (01324) 623709 E-mail ruth@ruthinnes.me.uk

INSLEY, Canon Michael George Pitron. b 47. Trin Coll Ox BA69 MA70 Nottm Univ MPhil85. Wycliffe Hall Ox 69. **d** 72 **p** 73. C Beckenham Ch Ch *Roch* 72-76; P-in-c Cowden 76-79; Lect St Jo Coll Nottm 79-85; V Tidebrook and Wadhurst *Chich* 85-98; P-in-c Stonegate 95-98; Can and Preb Chich Cathl 94-98; P-in-c Horsmonden and Dioc Rural Officer *Roch* 98-03; V Bromley Common St Luke from 03; Hon Can Th *Roch* Cathl from 06. *St Luke's Vicarage, 20 Bromley Common, Bromley BR2 9PD* Tel (020) 8464 2076 E-mail michael.insley@diocese-rochester.org

INSTON, Brian John. b 47. SAOMC 95. **d** 98 **p** 99. C Bentley *Sheff* 98-01; V Balby from 01; AD W Doncaster 07-11. *St John's Vicarage, 6 Greenfield Lane, Doncaster DN4 0PT* Tel and fax (01302) 853278 Mobile 07990-513120

INVERNESS, Provost of. *See* GORDON, The Very Revd Alexander Ronald

✠**INWOOD, The Rt Revd Richard Neil.** b 46. Univ Coll Ox BSc70 MA73 Nottm Univ BA73. St Jo Coll Nottm 71. **d** 74 **p** 75 **c** 03. C Fulwood *Sheff* 74-78; C St Marylebone All So w SS Pet and Jo *Lon* 78-81; V Bath St Luke *B & W* 81-89; R Yeovil w Kingston Pitney 89-95; Preb Wells Cathl 90-95; Adn Halifax *Wakef* 95-03; Suff Bp Bedford *St Alb* from 03; Cen Chapl MU from 05. *Bishop's Lodge, Bedford Road, Cardington, Bedford MK44 3SS* Tel (01234) 831432 Fax 831484 E-mail bishopbedford@stalbans.anglican.org

IPGRAVE, The Ven Michael Geoffrey. b 58. Oriel Coll Ox BA78 MA94 St Chad's Coll Dur PhD00 SOAS Lon MA04. Ripon Coll Cuddesdon BA81. **d** 82 **p** 83. C Oakham, Hambleton, Egleton, Braunston and Brooke *Pet* 82-85; Asst P Chiba Resurr Japan 85-87; TV Leic Ascension 87-90; TV Leic H Spirit 91-95; TR 95-99; P-in-c Leic St Mary 93-94; Bp's Adv on Relns w People of Other Faiths 91-99; Bp's Dom Chapl 92-99; Hon Can Leic Cathl 94-04; Adv Inter-Faith Relns Abp's Coun 99-04; Sec Ch's Commission Inter Faith Relns 99-04; Hon C Leic Presentation 02-04; Adn S'wark from 04; P-in-c S'wark St Geo w St Alphege and St Jude 06-07; P-in-c Peckham St Jo w St Andr 09-10; Can Missr from 10. *49 Colombo Street, London SE1 8DP* Tel (020) 7939 9409 *or* 7771 2858 Fax 7939 9467 E-mail michael.ipgrave@southwark.anglican.org

IPSWICH, Archdeacon of. *Vacant*

IQBAL, Canon Javaid. b 71. Birm Univ MA09. St Jo Coll Nottm BA97. **d** 97 **p** 99. C Lahore St Thos Pakistan 97-99; P-in-c Lahore Ch Ch 99-00; Dir Miss and Evang Raiwind 98-99; Perm to Offic *Leic* 00-05; C Evington 05-07; P-in-c Thurmaston 07-08; TV Troon from 08; Hon Can Leic Cathl from 11. *The Vicarage, 828 Melton Road, Thurmaston, Leicester LE4 8BE* Tel 0116-269 2555 Mobile 07782-169987 E-mail javaidiqbal7@aol.com *or* javaid.iqbal@leccofe.org

IREDALE, Simon Peter. b 56. Cam Univ BA78 MPhil80. Wycliffe Hall Ox 83. **d** 86 **p** 87. C Thirsk *York* 86-89; Asst Chapl Norfolk and Nor Hosp 89-90; P-in-c Kexby w Wilberfoss *York* 90-93; Sub-Chapl HM Pris Full Sutton 90-93; Chapl RAF 93-06. *5 Grange Road, Albrighton, Wolverhampton WV7 3LD*

IRELAND, David Arthur. b 45. Mert Coll Ox BA67 MA71 MICFM87. Cuddesdon Coll 67. **d** 69 **p** 70. C Chapel Allerton *Ripon* 69-72; C Harpenden St Nic *St Alb* 72-76; R Clifton 76-84; Perm to Offic *Guildf* 91-00; NSM Tattenham Corner and Burgh Heath 01-02; NSM Leatherhead and Mickleham from 02; Chapl Box Hill Sch from 05. *The Old London Road, Mickleham, Dorking RH5 6EB* Tel (01372) 378335 E-mail rev.ireland43@btinternet.com

IRELAND, Leslie Sydney. b 55. York Univ BA76. St Jo Coll Nottm 83. **d** 86 **p** 87. C Harwood *Man* 86-89; C Davyhulme St Mary 89-90; V Bardsley 90-99; R Levenshulme St Andr and St Pet 99-06; P-in-c Levenshulme St Mark 05-06; R Levenshulme from 06; AD Heaton from 04. *The Rectory, 27 Errwood Road, Levenshulme, Manchester M19 2PN* Tel 0161-224 5877 E-mail lesireland@compuserve.com

IRELAND, Mrs Lucy Annabel. b 53. Univ of Zimbabwe BSc74. St Jo Coll Nottm. **dss** 85 **d** 87 **p** 95. Mansfield St Jo *S'well* 85-87;

IRELAND, Mark Campbell. b 60. St Andr Univ MTheol81 Sheff Univ MA01. Wycliffe Hall Ox 82. **d** 84 **p** 85. C Blackb St Gabr 84-87; C Lancaster St Mary 87-89; Sub-Chapl HM Pris Lanc 87-89; V Baxenden *Blackb* 89-97; Dioc Missr *Lich* 98-07; TV Walsall 98-07; V Wellington All SS w Eyton from 07. *All Saints' Vicarage, 35 Crescent Road, Wellington, Telford TF1 3DW* Tel (01952) 641251 E-mail vicar@allsaints-wellington.org

IRELAND, Mrs Mary Janet. b 52. EMMTC 96. **d** 99 **p** 00. NSM Kibworth and Smeeton Westerby and Saddington *Leic* 99-02; C Lutterworth w Cotesbach and Bitteswell 02-05; P-in-c Glen Magna cum Stretton Magna etc from 05. *St Cuthbert's Vicarage, Church Road, Great Glen, Leicester LE8 9FE* Tel 0116-259 2238 E-mail mary_ireland@btinternet.com

IRELAND, Mrs Sharran. b 49. SEITE 95. **d** 98 **p** 99. C Appledore w Brookland, Fairfield, Brenzett etc *Cant* 98-01; TV St Laur in Thanet 01-03; TR from 03. *The Rectory, 2 Newington Road, Ramsgate CT11 0QT* Tel (01843) 592478

IRESON, David Christopher. b 45. Man Univ TCert67 Birm Univ BEd80. St Steph Ho Ox. **d** 93 **p** 94. C Minehead *B & W* 93-97; V St Decumans 97-08; rtd 08. *50 Camperdown Terrace, Exmouth EX8 1EQ* Tel (01395) 263307 E-mail decuman@hotmail.co.uk

IRESON, Ms Gillian Dorothy. b 39. Gilmore Ho 67. **dss** 72 **d** 87 **p** 94. Stepney St Dunstan and All SS *Lon* 72-99; Par Dn 87-94; C 94-99; rtd 99; Perm to Offic *Nor* from 00. *67 Glebe Road, Norwich NR2 3JH* Tel (01603) 451969

IRESON, Philip. b 52. Newc Univ BSc73. St Jo Coll Nottm. **d** 84 **p** 85. C Owlerton *Sheff* 84-87; V The Marshland 87-94; Perm to Offic *Linc* 90-93; Chapl HM YOI Hatfield 91-92; Bp's Rural Adv *Sheff* 91-00; R Firbeck w Letwell 94-01; V Woodsetts 94-01; Chapl HM Pris and YOI Doncaster 01-11; V Pitsmoor Ch Ch *Sheff* from 11. *The Vicarage, 257 Pitsmoor Road, Sheffield S3 9AQ* Tel 0114-272 7756 E-mail philip@iresonr.freeserve.co.uk

IRESON, Richard Henry. b 46. Linc Th Coll 69. **d** 71 **p** 72. C Spilsby w Hundleby *Linc* 71-74; TV Grantham w Manthorpe 74-76; R Claypole 76-79; P-in-c Westborough w Dry Doddington and Stubton 76-77; R 77-79; R Bratoft w Irby-in-the-Marsh 79-86; V Burgh le Marsh 79-86; V Orby 79-86; R Welton-le-Marsh w Gunby 79-86; R Wyberton 86-01; RD Holland W 95-97; V Frampton 97-01; V Alford w Rigsby 01-06; R Well 01-06; R Saleby w Beesby and Maltby 01-06; V Bilsby w Farlesthorpe 01-06; R Hannah cum Hagnaby w Markby 01-06; R N Beltisloe Gp 06-11; rtd 11. *36 St Michael's Road, Louth LN11 9DA* Tel (01507) 607170 E-mail r.ireson@uwclub.net

IRETON, Paul. b 65. Cranmer Hall Dur 99. **d** 01 **p** 02. C Southway *Ex* 01-06; P-in-c Torquay St Jo and Ellacombe from 06. *Silver Hill Lodge, Meadfoot Road, Torquay TQ1 2JP* Tel (01803) 392813 E-mail revpireton@eurobell.co.uk

IRETON, Robert John. b 56. Bris Univ BEd. Oak Hill Th Coll BA. **d** 84 **p** 85. C Bromley Ch Ch *Roch* 84-87; TV Greystoke, Matterdale, Mungrisdale etc *Carl* 87-90; V Falconwood *Roch* 90-97; V Stanwix *Carl* 97-04; P-in-c Erith St Jo *Roch* 04-10; Chapl Trin Sch Belvedere 04-10; P-in-c Brinklow *Cov* 10-11; P-in-c Harborough Magna 10-11; P-in-c Monks Kirby w Pailton and Stretton-under-Fosse 10-11; P-in-c Churchover w Willey 10-11; R Revel Gp from 11. *Kirby Moynes House, 1 Gate Farm Drive, Monks Kirby, Rugby CV23 0RY* Tel (01788) 833022 E-mail rireton@talktalk.net

IRONS, Nigel Richard. b 55. Aston Univ BSc77. St Jo Coll Nottm MA95. **d** 97 **p** 98. C Newchapel *Lich* 97-00; V Burton All SS w Ch Ch from 00. *All Saints' Vicarage, 242 Blackpool Street, Burton-on-Trent DE14 3AU* Tel (01283) 565134 E-mail mail@nigelirons.co.uk

IRONSIDE, John Edmund. b 31. Peterho Cam BA55 MA59. Qu Coll Birm 55. **d** 57 **p** 58. C Spring Park *Cant* 57-60; C Guernsey St Sampson *Win* 60-63; Thailand 63-66; V Guernsey St Jo *Win* 66-72; V Sholing 72-82; R Guernsey St Sampson 82-98; Miss to Seamen 82-98; rtd 98; Perm to Offic *Win* 98-07; P-in-c Guernsey St Andr 07-11; Perm to Offic *Chich* from 11. *1 Johnson Way, Ford, Arundel BN18 0TD* Tel (01903) 722884 E-mail sarniaford@hotmail.co.uk

IRVINE, Mrs Andrea Mary. b 49. Sussex Univ BA70 Ox Univ PGCE71. NTMTC 99. **d** 02. NSM Cov H Trin 02-05; Perm to Offic 05-06; NSM Cov Cathl from 06. *8 Priory Row, Coventry CV1 5EX* E-mail amirvine@lineone.net

IRVINE (formerly Ladbury), Ann Penrith. b 50. STETS 98. **d** 01 **p** 02. C Len Valley *Cant* 01-04; P-in-c Aylesham w Adisham 04-08; C Nonington w Wymynswold and Goodnestone etc 04-08; Perm to Offic 08-10. *Pilgrim Cottage, Le Kilmahougue Road, Moyarget, Ballycastle BT54 6JH* Tel (028) 2076 3748 E-mail revann@uwclub.net

IRVINE, Barry. *See* IRVINE, William Barry

IRVINE, Mrs Catherine Frances. b 70. K Coll Lon BA97. Ripon Coll Cuddesdon 99. **d** 01 **p** 02. C Romsey *Win* 01-05; TV

Richmond St Mary w St Matthias and St Jo *S'wark* 05-11; Chapl R Holloway and Bedf New Coll *Guildf* from 11. *The Chaplaincy Office, Royal Holloway College, Egham Hill, Egham TW20 0EX* Tel (01784) 443070 E-mail cate.irvine@rhul.ac.uk

IRVINE, Canon Christopher Paul. b 51. Nottm Univ BTh75 Lanc Univ MA76 St Martin's Coll Lanc PGCE77. Kelham Th Coll 73. **d** 76 **p** 76. Chapl Lanc Univ 76-77; C Stoke Newington St Mary *Lon* 77-80; Chapl Sheff Univ 80-85; Chapl St Edm Hall Ox 85-90; Tutor St Steph Ho Ox 85-90; Vice-Prin 91-94; V Cowley St Jo *Ox* 94-98; Prin Coll of Resurr Mirfield 98-07; Can Res and Lib Cant Cathl from 07. *19 The Precincts, Canterbury CT1 2EP* Tel (01227) 762862 E-mail irvinec@canterbury-cathedral.org

IRVINE, Clyde. *See* IRVINE, James Clyde

IRVINE, David John. b 50. Trin Coll Cam BA72 MA75. NOC 91. **d** 94 **p** 95. C Hexham *Newc* 94-99; P-in-c Blanchland w Hunstanworth and Edmundbyers etc from 99; P-in-c Slaley from 99; P-in-c Healey from 03; P-in-c Whittonstall from 03. *The Vicarage, Slaley, Hexham NE47 0AA* Tel (01434) 673609

IRVINE, Donald Andrew. b 45. Trin Coll Bris 94. **d** 96 **p** 97. C Allington and Maidstone St Pet *Cant* 96-99; P-in-c Harrietsham w Ulcombe 99-02; P-in-c Lenham w Boughton Malherbe 00-02; R Len Valley 02-07; TV Whitstable 07-10. *Pilgrim Cottage, 16 Kilmahamogue Road, Moyarget, Ballycastle BT54 6JH* Tel (028) 2076 3748 Mobile 07932-149495 E-mail don.irvine35@gmail.com

IRVINE, Gerard Philip. b 30. QUB BA52. Edin Th Coll 56. **d** 56 **p** 57. Chapl St Andr Cathl 56-58; Prec St Andr Cathl 58-59; C Belfast Malone St Jo *Conn* 61-66; Chapl Community of St Jo Ev Dublin 67-77; C Dublin Sandymount *D & G* 77-97; rtd 97. *12A Carraig na Greine House, Coliemore Road, Dalkey, Co Dublin, Republic of Ireland* Tel (00353) (1) 230 1430

IRVINE, James Clyde. b 35. QUB BA57 NUU BPhil(Ed)83. CITC 59. **d** 59 **p** 60. C Belfast St Luke *Conn* 59-62; C Lisburn Ch Ch Cathl 62-65; R Duneane w Ballyscullion 65-69; I Kilbride 69-74; Hd of RE Ballyclare High Sch 73-98; Bp's C Killead w Gartree 98-05; rtd 05. *1A Rathmena Avenue, Ballyclare BT39 9HX* Tel (028) 9332 2933 E-mail irvineclyde@live.co.uk

IRVINE, The Very Revd John Dudley. b 49. Sussex Univ BA70. Wycliffe Hall Ox BA80. **d** 81 **p** 82. C Brompton H Trin w Onslow Square St Paul *Lon* 81-85; P-in-c Kensington St Barn 85-94; V 94-01; Dean Cov from 01; P-in-c Cov St Fran N Radford from 06. *8 Priory Row, Coventry CV1 5EX* Tel (024) 7622 1992 E-mail john.irvine@coventrycathedral.org.uk

IRVINE, Simon Timothy. b 74. CITC 00. **d** 03 **p** 04. C Dublin Ch Ch Cathl Gp 03-06; Chapl Dublin Sandymount 06-11; Chapl Rathdown Sch 06-10. *Address temp unknown* Tel (00353) 87-944 4113 (mobile)

IRVINE, Stanley. b 35. TCD. **d** 83 **p** 84. C Arm St Mark w Aghavilly 83-85; I Kilmoremoy w Castleconnor, Easkey, Kilglass etc *T, K & A* 85-94; Dom Chapl to Bp Tuam 88-94; I Stranorlar w Meenglas and Kilteevogue *D & R* 94-05; Bp's Dom Chapl 01-05; Can Raphoe Cathl 02-05; rtd 05. *3 Inisfayle Crescent, Bangor BT19 1DT* Tel (028) 9146 2012

IRVINE, Mrs Suzanne. b 74. Huddersfield Univ BA96. St Jo Coll Nottm 99. **d** 03 **p** 04. C Wrose *Bradf* 03-06; Chapl Ripley St Thos C of E High Sch Lanc *Blackb* from 06. *Ripley St Thomas School, Ashton Road, Lancaster LA1 4RS* Tel (01524) 64496 Fax 847069 E-mail chocsxxx@hotmail.com

IRVINE, William Barry. b 48. QUB BD75. St Jo Coll Nottm 75. **d** 76 **p** 77. C Belfast St Mich *Conn* 76-80; C Mansfield SS Pet and Paul *S'well* 80-84; V Chapel-en-le-Frith *Derby* 84-90; Chapl Cheltenham Gen and Delancey Hosps 90-94; Chapl E Glos NHS Trust 94-02; Chapl Glos Hosps NHS Foundn Trust from 02. *Cheltenham General Hospital, Sandford Road, Cheltenham GL53 7AN* Tel (01242) 222222 ext 4286 or 274286

IRVINE-CAPEL, Luke Thomas. b 75. Greyfriars Ox BA97 MA01 Leeds Univ MA99. Coll of Resurr Mirfield 97. **d** 99 **p** 00. C Abertillery w Cwmtillery w Six Bells *Mon* 99-01; Chapl Gwent Tertiary Coll 99-01; Min Can St Woolos Cathl 01-03; Sub-Chapl HM Pris Cardiff 02-03; R Cranford *Lon* 03-08; V Pimlico St Gabr from 08. *St Gabriel's Vicarage, 30 Warwick Square, London SW1V 2AD* Tel (020) 7834 7520

IRVING, Canon Andrew. b 27. St Deiniol's Hawarden 62. **d** 65 **p** 66. C Benwell St Jas *Newc* 65-69; C Langley Marish *Ox* 69-73; V Moulsford 73-81; Canada from 81; rtd 92. *3615 Lever Court, Peachland BC V0H 1X5, Canada* Tel (001) (250) 767 9582

IRVING, Canon Michael John Derek. b 43. LVO07 DL09. BEd80. Qu Coll Birm 80. **d** 81 **p** 82. C Coleford w Staunton *Glouc* 81-84; V Dean Forest H Trin 84-91; RD Forest S 88-91; P-in-c Hempsted and Dir of Ords 91-96; R Minchinhampton 96-08; Hon Can Glouc Cathl 94-08; rtd 08. *9 Canton Acre, Painswick, Stroud GL6 6QX* Tel (01452) 814242 E-mail irvings@vale-view.co.uk

IRVING, Paul John. b 74. Univ of Wales (Ban) BA96 Bris Univ PGCE97. Trin Coll Bris BA10. **d** 10 **p** 11. C Galmington *B & W* from 10. *31 Essex Drive, Taunton TA1 4JX* Tel (01823) 336158 E-mail irvings@waitrose.com

IRWIN, Mrs Patricia Jane. b 49. CBDTI 02. **d** 05 **p** 06. NSM S Carl 05-10; rtd 10. *31 Blackwell Road, Carlisle CA2 4AB* Tel (01228) 526885

IRWIN, Patrick Alexander. b 55. BNC Ox BA77 MA81 Edin Univ BD81. Edin Th Coll 77 Liturgisches Inst Trier 79. **d** 81 **p** 82. Hon C Cambridge St Botolph *Ely* 81-84; Chapl BNC Ox 84-92; Lect Th 86-92; CF 92-99; Sen CF 99-10; Chapl Guards Chpl Lon 05-07; Dir of Ords 05-07; Chapl Udruga Hvrata Sv Dominik Gorazde 94-95; Perm to Offic *D & G* from 87; *Arm* from 96; *Eur* 08-10; Hon V Choral Arm Cathl 02-07; Chapl Bucharest w Sofia *Eur* from 10. *Chaplaincy, British Embassy - Bucharest, FCO, King Charles Street, London SW1A 2AH* Tel (0040) 740-243789 (mobile) E-mail patalexirwin@yahoo.co.uk *or* resurrectionbucharest@gmail.com

IRWIN, Stewart. b 53. Sarum & Wells Th Coll 80. **d** 83 **p** 84. C Brighouse *Wakef* 83-87; V Stockton St Jo *Dur* 87-95; V Howden-le-Wear and Hunwick from 95. *The Vicarage, Hunwick, Crook DL15 0JU* Tel (01388) 604456

IRWIN, Miss Susan Elizabeth. b 47. Cranmer Hall Dur 77. dss 79 **d** 87 **p** 94. Harborne St Faith and St Laur *Birm* 79-82; Caterham *S'wark* 82-88; Par Dn 87-88; Par Dn Kidlington w Hampton Poyle *Ox* 88-94; C 94-95; TV Gt Marlow w Marlow Bottom, Lt Marlow and Bisham 95-06; R Powick and Guarlford and Madresfield w Newland *Worc* from 06. *The Vicarage, 31 The Greenway, Powick, Worcester WR2 4RZ* Tel (01905) 830270 Mobile 07703-350301 E-mail vicarage@powickparish.org.uk

IRWIN, Canon William George. b 53. QUB BSc77. CITC 80. **d** 80 **p** 81. C Lisburn St Paul *Conn* 80-83; C Seagoe *D & D* 83-85; C Newtownards w Movilla Abbey 85-88; I Ballymacash *Conn* from 88; Preb Conn Cathl from 04. *St Mark's Rectory, 97 Antrim Road, Lisburn BT28 3EA* Tel (028) 9266 2393 E-mail wgirwin@btopenworld.com

IRWIN-CLARK, Peter Elliot. b 49. Univ Coll Lon LLB71 Barrister 72. Cranmer Hall Dur BA80. **d** 81 **p** 82. C Kirkheaton *Wakef* 81-86; V Shirley *Win* 86-96; Perm to Office *Chich* 96-97 and *S'wark* 97; V Prestonville St Luke *Chich* 97-03; Missr Warham Trust and Faith Development Officer (Basingstoke Adnry) *Win* 03-08; TR Broadwater *Chich* from 08. *The Rectory, 8 Sompting Avenue, Worthing BN14 8HN* Tel (01903) 823996 E-mail panddic@surfaid.org

ISAAC, Canon David Thomas. b 43. Univ of Wales BA65. Cuddesdon Coll 65. **d** 67 **p** 68. C Llandaff w Capel Llanilltern 67-71; P-in-c Swansea St Jas *S & B* 71-73; Chapl Ch in Wales Youth Coun 73-77; V Llangiwg *S & B* 77-79; Dioc Youth Officer *Ripon* 79-83; Nat Officer for Youth Work Gen Syn Bd of Educn 83-90; Can Res Portsm Cathl from 90; Dioc Dir of Educn 90-06; Hd Miss and Discipleship from 06; Warden of Readers from 11. *1 Pembroke Close, Portsmouth PO1 2NX* Tel (023) 9281 8107 *or* 9282 2053 Fax 9229 5081 Mobile 07768-997220 E-mail david.isaac@portsmouth.anglican.org

ISAAC, Edward Henry. b 20. Qu Coll Cam BA42 MA46. Ridley Hall Cam 45. **d** 47 **p** 48. C Wednesbury St Bart *Lich* 47-51; V Liv St Phil 51-56; V Knowsley 56-61; V Garston 61-66; V Millom St Geo *Carl* 66-85; rtd 85; Perm to Offic *Carl* from 86. *31 Lowther Road, Millom LA18 4PE* Tel (01229) 772332

ISAACS, John Kenneth. b 36. Cam Univ MA. EAMTC. **d** 82 **p** 83. NSM Ely 82-85; Chapl K Sch Ely 85-94; Lic to Offic *Ely* 85-94; P-in-c Denver 94-02; P-in-c Ryston w Roxham 94-02; P-in-c W Dereham 94-02; R Denver and Ryston w Roxham and W Dereham etc 02-03; rtd 03; Perm to Offic *Ely* from 03. *18 Barton Road, Ely CB7 4DE* Tel (01366) 666936 E-mail john.isaacs@ely.anglican.org

ISAACSON, Alan Timothy. b 55. York Univ BA77 Sheff Univ PGCE84 Leeds Univ MA97. NOC 94. **d** 96 **p** 97. C Kimberworth *Sheff* 96-99; TV Brinsworth w Catcliffe and Treeton 99-03; TV Rivers Team 03-07; R Bradfield from 07; Dioc Discipleship Development Officer from 07. *The Rectory, High Bradfield, Bradfield, Sheffield S6 6LG* Tel 0114-285 1225 E-mail alan.isaacson@sheffield.anglican.org

ISAACSON, Hilda Ruth. b 57. NOC 07. **d** 09 **p** 10. C Deepcar *Sheff* from 09. *The Rectory, High Bradfield, Bradfield, Sheffield S6 6LG* Tel 0114-285 1225 Mobile 07762-075687 E-mail hilda.isaacson@sheffield.anglican.org

ISABEL, Sister. *See* KEEGAN, Frances Ann

ISAM, Miss Margaret Myra Elizabeth (Wendy). b 35. Nottm Univ BEd73. EMMTC 78. dss 81 **d** 87 **p** 94. Humberston *Linc* 81-84; Gt Grimsby St Andr and St Luke 85-93; Dn-in-c 87-93; P-in-c Gt Grimsby St Andr w St Luke and All SS 94-97; V 97-00; rtd 00; Perm to Offic *Linc* from 00. *18 Grainsby Avenue, Cleethorpes DN35 9PA* Tel (01472) 699821 Mobile 07950-464542

ISBISTER, Charles. b 27. Chich Th Coll 58. **d** 60 **p** 61. C Tynemouth Ch Ch *Newc* 60-64; C Boyne Hill *Ox* 64-67; V Cookridge H Trin *Ripon* 67-93; rtd 93; Perm to Offic *Ripon* from 01. *2 Church Mount, Horsforth, Leeds LS18 5LE* Tel 0113-239 0813 Mobile 07714-356059

ISHERWOOD, Mrs Claire Virginia. b 54. Liv Univ BDS76 K Alfred's Coll Win PGCE92. **d** 10 **p** 11. OLM Camberley St Paul

Guildf from 10. *37 Watchetts Drive, Camberley GU15 2PQ* Tel (01276) 505015 Mobile 07854-549154 E-mail claire.isherwood@ntlworld.com
ISHERWOOD, Canon David Owen. b 46. BA68 Lon Univ MA95 MPhil87. Ridley Hall Cam 76. **d** 78 **p** 79. C Sanderstead All SS *S'wark* 78-82; C Horley 82-84; TV 84-88; P-in-c Streatham Immanuel and St Andr 88-89; V 89-95; TR Clapham Team 95-01; V Clapham H Trin and St Pet from 02; Hon Can S'wark Cathl from 06. *25 The Chase, London SW4 0NP* Tel (020) 7498 6879 *or* 7627 0941 Fax 7978 1327 *or* 7627 5065 E-mail rector@holytrinityclapham.org *or* david.htc@lineone.net
ISHERWOOD, Robin James. b 56. Hull Univ BA78 Uppsala Univ MDiv92. Ripon Coll Cuddesdon 92. **d** 94 **p** 95. C Bramhall *Ches* 94-98; V Alsager St Mary from 98; Hon Chapl ATC from 99. *St Mary's Vicarage, 37 Eaton Road, Alsager, Stoke-on-Trent ST7 2BQ* Tel (01270) 875748 E-mail vicar@pit6.fsnet.co.uk
ISHERWOOD, Samuel Peter. b 34. Lon Coll of Div ALCD62 LTh74. **d** 62 **p** 63. C Bacup St Sav *Man* 62-65; C Man Albert Memorial Ch 65-67; V Livesey *Blackb* 67-79; V Handforth *Ches* 79-99; RD Cheadle 92-99; rtd 99; Perm to Offic *York* from 00. *1 Andrew Drive, Huntington, York YO32 9YF* Tel (01904) 438116
ISIORHO, David John Phillip. b 58. Liv Poly BA80 Warwick Univ MA93 Bradf Univ PhD98. Westcott Ho Cam 87. **d** 90 **p** 91. C Nuneaton St Mary *Cov* 90-93; P-in-c Bradf St Oswald Chapel Green 93-96; P-in-c Brereton *Lich* 96-00; P-in-c Arthingworth, Harrington w Oxendon and E Farndon *Pet* 00-05; P-in-c Maidwell w Draughton, Lamport w Faxton 01-05; V Kempston Transfiguration *St Alb* 05-09; V Handsworth St Jas *Birm* from 09. *St James's Vicarage, 21 Austin Road, Birmingham B21 8NU* Tel 0121-554 4151 E-mail davidisiorho@catholic.org
ISIORHO (née NORTHALL), Mrs Linda Barbara. b 50. Birm Univ BA72 Worc Coll of Educn PGCE75. Qu Coll Birm 88. **d** 90 **p** 94. C Wood End *Cov* 90-91; Perm to Offic *Cov* 91-93 and *Bradf* 93-94; NSM Low Moor St Mark *Bradf* 94-96; Perm to Offic *Lich* 96-97; NSM Alrewas 97-00; Perm to Offic *Pet* 01-05 and *Birm* from 10. *St James's Vicarage, 21 Austin Road, Birmingham B21 8NU* Tel 0121-507 0370
ISITT, Norman. b 34. St Jo Coll Dur BA56. Cranmer Hall Dur. **d** 59 **p** 60. C Loughton St Mary *Chelmsf* 59-62; C Moulsham St Jo 62-64; Billericay Co Sch 64-90; Squirrels Heath Sch Romford 64-90; Althorpe and Keadby Co Sch 66-95; rtd 95. *21 Cambridge Avenue, Bottesford, Scunthorpe DN16 3LT* Tel (01724) 851489
ISKANDER, Mrs Susan Mary Mackay. Ox Univ BA85 MBA93. NTMTC 05. **d** 08 **p** 09. NSM Writtle w Highwood *Chelmsf* from 08. *44 Maltese Road, Chelmsford CM1 2PA* E-mail revsusaniskander@gmail.com
ISLE OF WIGHT, Archdeacon of. *See* BASTON, The Ven Caroline
ISON, Andrew Phillip. b 60. Imp Coll Lon BEng82 Penn Univ MSE83 Univ Coll Lon PhD87 Bris Univ BA01 CEng92 MIChemE92. Trin Coll Bris 99. **d** 01 **p** 02. C Cleethorpes *Linc* 01-05; V Bestwood Park w Rise Park *S'well* 05-07; Chapl Voorschoten *Eur* from 07. *Chopinlaan 17, 2253 BS Voorshoten, The Netherlands* Tel (0031) (71) 561 3020 E-mail minister@stjames.nl
ISON, The Very Revd Trevor John. b 54. Leic Univ BA76 Nottm Univ BA78 K Coll Lon PhD85. St Jo Coll Nottm 76. **d** 79 **p** 80. C Deptford St Nic and St Luke *S'wark* 79-85; Lect CA Tr Coll Blackheath 85-88; V Potters Green *Cov* 88-93; Jt Dir SWMTC *Ex* 93-95; Dioc Officer for CME 93-05; Bp's Officer for NSMs 97-05; Can Res Ex Cathl 95-05; Chan 97-05; Dean Bradf from 05. *The Deanery, 1 Cathedral Close, Bradford BD1 4EG* Tel (01274) 777722 Fax 777730 E-mail david.ison@bradfordcathedral.org
ISON, Mrs Hilary Margaret. b 55. Leic Univ BA76 E Lon Univ MA02. Gilmore Course 77. **d** 87 **p** 94. NSM Deptford St Nic and St Luke *S'wark* 87-88; NSM Potters Green *Cov* 88-90; C Rugby 90-93; Chapl Ex Hospiscare 93-00; C Ex St Mark, St Sidwell and St Matt 90-92; Bp's Adv for Women in Min 02-05; Area Tutor SWMTC 03-05; PV Ex Cathl 04-05; Tutor Coll of Resurr Mirfield 05-08; Selection Sec Min Division from 08; Hon C Calverley Deanery *Bradf* from 06. *The Deanery, 1 Cathedral Close, Bradford BD1 4EG* Tel (01274) 777727 E-mail hilary.ison@churchofengland.org
ISSBERNER, Norman Gunther Erich. b 34. Fitzw Ho Cam BA58 MA61. Clifton Th Coll 57. **d** 59 **p** 60. C Croydon Ch Ch Broad Green *Cant* 59-61; C Surbiton Hill Ch Ch *S'wark* 61-66; V Egham *Guildf* 66-75; V Wallington *S'wark* 75-86; UK Chmn Africa Inland Miss from 77; Adv on Miss and Evang *Chelmsf* 86-91; P-in-c Castle Hedingham 91-93; V Clacton St Paul 93-99; RD St Osyth 94-99; rtd 99; Perm to Offic *Chelmsf* from 99. *14 Darcy Close, Frinton-on-Sea CO13 0RR* Tel (01255) 673548
ITALY AND MALTA, Archdeacon of. *See* BOARDMAN, The Ven Jonathan
ITUMU, John Murithi. b 65. Lon Sch of Th BA04 Heythrop Coll Lon MA10. Lon Bible Coll 01. **d** 02 **p** 03. C Cricklewood

St Gabr and St Mich *Lon* 02-07; C Herne Hill *S'wark* 07-10; P-in-c Glouc St Cath from 10. *5 Kenilworth Avenue, Gloucester GL2 0QJ* Tel (01452) 502673 Mobile 07946-000364 E-mail vicar@stcatharine.org.uk
IVE, Jeremy George Augustus. b 57. Rhodes Univ BA81 Ch Coll Cam PhD86 K Coll Lon MPhil95. Wycliffe Hall Ox 89. **d** 91 **p** 92. NSM Ivybridge w Harford *Ex* 91-95; P-in-c Abbotskerswell 95-99; P-in-c Tudeley cum Capel w Five Oak Green *Roch* from 99; Dioc Lay Min Adv 99-01. *The Vicarage, Sychem Lane, Five Oak Green, Tonbridge TN12 6TL* Tel and fax (01892) 836653 Mobile 07720-841169 E-mail jeremy.ive@diocese-rochester.org *or* jeremy@tudeley.org
IVE (née KNOTT), Mrs Pamela Frances. b 58. Bedf Coll of Educn BEd79. Wycliffe Hall Ox 88. **d** 90. Par Dn Ivybridge w Harford *Ex* 90-95; Par Dn Abbotskerswell 95-99; Par Dn Tudeley cum Capel w Five Oak Green *Roch* from 99. *The Vicarage, Sychem Lane, Five Oak Green, Tonbridge TN12 6TL* Tel and fax (01892) 836653 *or* tel 835548 E-mail pamela.ive@diocese-rochester.org *or* pamela@tudeley.org
IVELL, Robert William. b 45. Lon Univ BSc71 Liv Univ CertEd. Ridley Hall Cam 83. **d** 85 **p** 86. C Wadsley *Sheff* 85-88; V Laughton w Throapham 88-96; V Wadworth w Loversall 96-06; rtd 06. *1 Wellbank, 20 Burrell Street, Crieff PH7 4DT* Tel (01764) 652057
IVES, Raymond Charles. b 27. St Mark & St Jo Coll Lon CertEd50. **d** 95 **p** 96. OLM Croydon St Pet *S'wark* 95-04; Perm to Offic from 04. *60 Windermere Road, West Wickham BR4 9AW* Tel (020) 8777 4956 E-mail revrayives@aol.com
IVES, Mrs Susan Ethel. b 48. EAMTC 98. **d** 01 **p** 02. NSM Moulsham St Luke *Chelmsf* 01-08; NSM Chelmsf St Andr from 08; Educn and Par Links Adv Chelmsf Deaneries from 07. *47 Long Brandocks, Writtle, Chelmsford CM1 3JL* Tel (01245) 420325 Mobile 07964-538485 E-mail sives@chelmsford.anglican.org
IVESON, Mrs Patricia Jill. b 35. Cam Univ CertEd55 K Coll Lon BD76 AKC76. **dss** 81 **d** 87 **p** 94. Wilmington *Roch* 81-87; Hon Par Dn 87-94; Hon C from 94; Chapl Dartford and Gravesham NHS Trust 87-04. *The Birches, 15 Wallis Close, Wilmington, Dartford DA2 7BE* Tel (01322) 279100 Mobile 07811-286219 E-mail pat.iveson@diocese-rochester.org
IVESON, Robert George. b 70. Oak Hill Th Coll BA01. **d** 01 **p** 02. C Cheadle All Hallows *Ches* 01-04; C-in-c Cheadle Hulme Em CD from 04. *198 Bruntwood Lane, Cheadle Hulme, Cheadle SK8 6BE* Tel 0161-485 1154 E-mail rob.iveson@btinternet.com
IVESON, Ronald Edward. b 68. Ches Coll of HE RMN92. Aston Tr Scheme 95 Oak Hill Th Coll BA00. **d** 00 **p** 01. C Lache cum Saltney *Ches* 00-03; V Bishton from 03. *The Vicarage, 6 Statham Road, Prenton CH43 7XS* Tel 0151-652 4852 *or* 653 4584 E-mail roniveson@hotmail.com
IVISON, Norman William. b 54. Hull Univ BA75 DipEd76. Trin Coll Bris. **d** 82 **p** 83. C Barrow St Mark *Carl* 82-85; Ecum Liaison Officer BBC Radio Furness 82-85; Chapl Barrow Sixth Form Coll 83-85; Dioc Broadcasting Officer *Lich* 85-91; Relig Progr Producer BBC Radio Stoke 85-91; Hon C Bucknall and Bagnall *Lich* 85-91; Asst Producer Relig Progr BBC TV Man 91-93; Producer Relig Progr BBC TV Man 93-05; Dir Tr and Events Fresh Expressions from 05; Dir Communications and Resources from 08; Perm to Offic *Blackb* from 98. *44 Peel Park Avenue, Clitheroe BB7 1JR* Tel and fax (01200) 442004 Mobile 07885-866317 E-mail norman.ivison@freshexpressions.org.uk
IVORSON, David. b 51. Mansf Coll Ox MA73 York Univ BPhil75 ACA80. SEITE 05. **d** 08 **p** 09. NSM E Grinstead St Swithun *Chich* from 08. *Woodhurst, Portland Road, East Grinstead RH19 4DZ* Tel (01342) 316451 Mobile 07787-155154 E-mail d@ivorson.com
IVORY, Canon Christopher James. b 54. Reading Univ BSc76. Qu Coll Birm. **d** 81 **p** 82. C Waltham Cross *St Alb* 81-84; C Is of Dogs Ch Ch and St Jo w St Luke *Lon* 84-88; V Streatham Ch Ch *S'wark* 88-03; Lambeth Adnry Ecum Officer 90-95; RD Streatham 00-03; R King's Lynn St Marg w St Nic *Nor* from 03; RD Lynn from 08; Hon Can Nor Cathl from 08. *St Margaret's Vicarage, St Margaret's Place, King's Lynn PE30 5DL* Tel (01553) 767090 E-mail vicar@stmargaretskingslynn.org.uk
IWANUSCHAK, Victor. b 51. Coll of Ripon & York St Jo MA00. NOC 97. **d** 00 **p** 01. C Pontefract All SS *Wakef* 00-03; P-in-c from 03. *All Saints' Vicarage, Grenton, South Baileygate, Pontefract WF8 2JL* Tel (01977) 695590 Mobile 07734-710254 E-mail iwanuschak@triom.net
IZOD, Mrs Wendy Janet. b 47. Sheff Univ BSc(Econ)68. SEITE 98. **d** 01 **p** 02. NSM Hever, Four Elms and Mark Beech *Roch* from 01; Chapl ATC from 01. *West Lodge, Stick Hill, Edenbridge TN8 5NJ* Tel (01342) 850738 Fax 850077 Mobile 07703-107496 E-mail izod.calligraphy@btinternet.com
IZZARD, David Antony. b 55. Trin Coll Bris 92. **d** 94 **p** 95. C E Bris 94-98; V Sea Mills from 98. *St Edyth's Vicarage, Avonleaze, Bristol BS9 2HU* Tel 0117-968 1912 *or* 968 6965 E-mail clan.izzard@ukgateway.net

IZZARD, Ms Susannah Amanda. b 59. Hatf Poly BA82 Birm Univ MEd93 Wolv Univ PGCE92. Trin Coll Bris BA86. **dss** 86 **d** 87 **p** 01. Birm St Martin w Bordesley St Andr 86-89; Par Dn 87-89; C Handsworth St Jas 89-91; Asst Chapl Qu Eliz Hosp Birm 90-91; Lect Birm Univ 93-02; NSM Selly Oak St Mary from 01; Bp's Adv for Pastoral Care from 07. *2 Hemyock Road, Birmingham B29 4DG* Tel and fax 0121-243 3745 E-mail susannah.izzard@blueyonder.co.uk

J

JABLONSKI, Andrew Philip. b 54. St Jo Coll Cam MA76 Nottm Univ MBA90 Anglia Ruskin Univ MA10 CEng90 FIMechE02. Ridley Hall Cam 07. **d** 09 **p** 10. NSM Grantham, Harrowby w Londonthorpe *Linc* from 09. *12 Lincoln Close, Grantham NG31 8RQ* Tel (01476) 403444 Mobile 07736-649401 E-mail andrewjab@virginmedia.com

JABLONSKI, Mrs Anne Judith. b 54. Girton Coll Cam BA76. Ridley Hall Cam 07. **d** 09 **p** 10. C Grantham *Linc* from 09. *12 Lincoln Close, Grantham NG31 8RQ* Tel 07739-661836 (mobile) E-mail annejab@ntlworld.com

JACK, Judith Ann. b 54. Wycliffe Hall Ox 03. **d** 05 **p** 06. C Tetbury, Beverston and Long Newnton and Shipton Moyne *Glouc* 05-10; P-in-c Baltonsborough w Butleigh, W Bradley etc *B & W* from 10. *The Vicarage, Old Hall House, Ham Street, Baltonsborough, Glastonbury BA6 8PX* Tel (01458) 851681 E-mail judithjack@talktalk.net

JACK, Paul. b 65. QUB BSc92 Univ Coll Galway MSc94 TCD BTh99. CITC 96. **d** 99 **p** 00. C Jordanstown *Conn* 99-01; C Seagoe *D & D* 01-07; I Belfast St Simon w St Phil *Conn* from 07; Bp's Dom Chapl from 09. *106 Upper Lisburn Road, Belfast BT10 0BB* Tel (028) 9061 7562 E-mail paul@jack11.wanadoo.co.uk

JACK, Philip Andrew. b 76. Nottm Univ BA98. Oak Hill Th Coll BA08. **d** 08 **p** 09. C Ox St Ebbe w H Trin and St Pet from 08. *81 Marlborough Road, Oxford OX1 4LX* Tel 07972-078148 (mobile) E-mail phil.a.jack@gmail.com

JACKLIN, John Frederick. b 30. Oak Hill Th Coll 72. **d** 72 **p** 72. Chile 72-75; C Roxeth Ch Ch *Lon* 75-78; V Selston *S'well* 78-95; rtd 95; Perm to Offic *Derby* from 97. *5 Rose Avenue, Borrowash, Derby DE7 3GA* Tel (01332) 669670

JACKS, David. b 59. Nottm Univ BTh87 Birm Univ MA95 PhD08. Linc Th Coll 84. **d** 87 **p** 88. C Oakham, Hambleton, Egleton, Braunston and Brooke *Pet* 87-90; V Weedon Bec w Everdon 90-98; P-in-c Dodford 96-98; V Weedon Bec w Everdon and Dodford 98-01; V Llandrillo-yn-Rhos *St As* from 01. *Llandrillo Vicarage, 36 Llandudno Road, Colwyn Bay LL28 4UD* Tel (01492) 548878 Mobile 07850-597891 E-mail david@llandrillo.fsbusiness.co.uk

JACKSON, Alan. b 44. Newc Univ BA67 DipEd68 MEd79. NEOC 79. **d** 81 **p** 82. NSM Jesmond H Trin Newc 81-82; Chapl Bp Wand Sch Sunbury-on-Thames 82-89; V Hanworth St Rich *Lon* 89-10; rtd 10. *7 Uxbridge Road, Feltham TW13 5EG* Tel (020) 8898 3093 E-mail alan1144@gmail.com

JACKSON, Barry. b 30. St Jo Coll Cam BA53 DipEd54 MA57. Westcott Ho Cam 63. **d** 65 **p** 66. C Stockport St Geo *Ches* 65-68; C Bridgwater St Mary, Chilton Trinity and Durleigh *B & W* 68-70; P-in-c Thurloxton 70-75; Chapl Wycliffe Coll Glos 75-88; V Heathfield *Chich* 88-97; rtd 97; Perm to Offic *Chich* from 98. *11 Glenleigh Walk, Robertsbridge TN32 5DQ* Tel (01580) 880067

JACKSON, Barry James. b 65. Sheff Univ BEng87. St Jo Coll Nottm 05. **d** 07 **p** 08. C Leamington Priors St Mary *Cov* 07-10; P-in-c Kineton from 10; P-in-c Combroke w Compton Verney from 10; P-in-c Warmington w Shotteswell and Radway w Ratley from 10. *Kalamunda, Warwick Road, Kineton, Warwick CV35 0HN* Tel (01926) 640248 E-mail barry.jackson@talktalk.net

JACKSON, The Very Revd Brandon Donald. b 34. Liv Univ LLB56 Bradf Univ Hon DLitt90. Wycliffe Hall Ox. **d** 58 **p** 59. C New Malden and Coombe *S'wark* 58-61; C Leeds St Geo *Ripon* 61-65; V Shipley St Pet *Bradf* 65-77; Relig Adv Yorkshire TV 69-79; Provost Bradf 77-89; Dean Linc 89-97; rtd 97; Perm to Offic *Ripon* from 98. *1 Kingston Way, Market Harborough LE16 7XB* Tel (01858) 462425 E-mail brandon.j@talktalk.net

JACKSON, Christopher John Wilson. b 45. St Pet Coll Ox BA67 MA87. Ridley Hall Cam 69. **d** 72 **p** 73. C Putney St Marg *S'wark* 72-76; C Battersea St Pet and St Paul 76-79; TV Preston St Jo *Blackb* 79-87; P-in-c Sandal St Cath *Wakef* 87-90; V Shenley

Green *Birm* 90-01; AD Kings Norton 95-99; P-in-c Chesterfield H Trin and Ch Ch *Derby* 01-10; R 10; rtd 10; Perm to Offic *Blackb* from 10. *5 Beech Grove, Ashton-on-Ribble, Preston PR2 1DX* Tel (01772) 721772 E-mail chrisaliz5@talktalk.net

JACKSON, Miss Cynthia. b 42. S'wark Ord Course 93. **d** 96 **p** 97. NSM Wimbledon *S'wark* from 96. *39 Panmuir Road, London SW20 0PZ* Tel (020) 8947 5940 *or* 7361 2396

JACKSON, Canon David. b 33. Leeds Univ BA60. Coll of Resurr Mirfield 60. **d** 62 **p** 63. C Lewisham St Steph *S'wark* 62-65; P-in-c New Charlton H Trin 65-69; C Charlton St Luke w St Paul 69-72; Sen Tutor Coll of the Resurr Mirfield 72-75; R Clapham H Trin 75-78; P-in-c Clapham St Pet 76-78; TR Clapham Old Town 78-84; Hon Can S'wark Cathl 80-96; V Battersea St Mary-le-Park 84-89; V Surbiton St Andr and St Mark 89-96; rtd 96; Chapl St Mich Convent Ham 96-03. *18 Tower Lane, Bearsted, Maidstone ME14 4JJ* Tel (01622) 730041

JACKSON, David. b 48. Open Univ BA85. St Deiniol's Hawarden 91. **d** 91 **p** 92. C Scotforth *Blackb* 91-95; C Banbury *Ox* 95-96; TV 96-98; V Banbury St Hugh 98-07; V Banbury St Fran from 07; Chapl Ox Radcliffe Hosps NHS Trust 95-00. *St Francis' House, Highlands, Banbury OX16 7FA* Tel (01295) 275449 E-mail vicardavyjax@tiscali.co.uk

JACKSON, David Hilton. b 62. Stanford Univ BA84 Princeton Th Sem MDiv90 Ox Univ MSt94. Wycliffe Hall Ox 94. **d** 95 **p** 96. C Ox St Andr 95-98; TV Thame 98-00; USA from 00; Assoc R and Chapl Upland St Mark 01-03; Sen Assoc for Par Life Pasadena All SS from 03. *614 Occidental Drive, Claremont CA 91711, USA* E-mail david.jackson@cgu.edu

JACKSON, David Reginald Estcourt. b 25. OBE. Qu Coll Cam BA43 MA49. St Jo Coll Dur 80. **d** 81 **p** 82. Hon C Douglas *Blackb* 81-82; C 82-87; rtd 90. *64 The Common, Parbold, Wigan WN8 7EA* Tel (01257) 462671

JACKSON, David Robert. b 51. Lon Univ BDS. Linc Th Coll 81. **d** 83 **p** 84. C Hatcham St Cath *S'wark* 83-87; V Sydenham St Bart 87-93; Perm to Offic *Lon* 03-05; Hon C St Martin-in-the-Fields from 05. *168 Manor Park, London SE13 5RH* Tel (020) 8297 9132 E-mail djsaab@aol.com

JACKSON, David William. b 53. Goldsmiths' Coll Lon BA75 PGCE76. Cranmer Hall Dur 90. **d** 92 **p** 93. C Desborough *Pet* 92-95; C Eastham *Ches* 95-98; P-in-c Taverham w Ringland *Nor* 98-05; R Taverham 05-06; R Redenhall, Harleston, Wortwell and Needham from 06. *The Rectory, 10 Swan Lane, Harleston IP20 9AN* Tel (01379) 852068 E-mail therec@talktalk.net

JACKSON, Canon Derek. b 26. Ex Coll Ox BA51 MA55. Westcott Ho Cam 51. **d** 53 **p** 54. C Radcliffe-on-Trent *S'well* 53-56; C Frome St Jo *B & W* 56-57; V Eaton Socon *St Alb* 57-63; V Boxmoor St Jo 63-74; V Bishop's Stortford St Mich 74-85; Hon Can St Alb 82-85; Bermuda 85-89; P-in-c Cerne Abbas w Godmanstone and Minterne Magna *Sarum* 89-95; rtd 95; Chapl Menorca *Eur* 95-96; Perm to Offic *St Alb* from 96 and *Chelmsf* from 97. *88 Stansted Road, Bishop's Stortford CM23 2DZ* Tel (01279) 652664

JACKSON, Canon Derek Reginald. b 49. K Coll Lon BD72 AKC72. **d** 73 **p** 74. C Westhoughton *Man* 73-75; C Kendal H Trin *Carl* 75-78; V Pennington w Lindal and Marton 78-83; Warden of Readers 82-92; V Kendal St Geo 83-94; Hon Can Carl Cathl 89-00; V Applethwaite 94-96; P-in-c Troutbeck 94-96; V Windermere St Mary and Troutbeck 96-00; RD Windermere 98-00; Can Res Bradf Cathl 00-03; P-in-c Bingley All SS 03-10; RD Airedale 05-10; rtd 10; Perm to Offic *Carl* from 11. *3 Ellas Orchard, Green Lane, Fockburgh, Grange-over-Sands LA11 7JT* Tel (015395) 58370 E-mail derekjackson2901@hotmail.com

JACKSON, Doreen May. b 35. SRN. S Dios Minl Tr Scheme. **d** 88 **p** 94. NSM Fareham H Trin *Portsm* 88-05; rtd 05. *134 Oak Road, Fareham PO15 5HR* Tel (01329) 841429

JACKSON, Mrs Elizabeth Barbara. b 67. EMMTC 07. **d** 10 **p** 11. C Linc St Pet-at-Gowts and St Andr from 10; C Linc St Botolph from 10; C Linc St Mary-le-Wigford w St Benedict etc from 10. *13 Earls Drive, Lincoln LN6 7TY* Tel (01476) 570207 Mobile 07799-724908 E-mail liz.jack@ntlworld.com

JACKSON, Mrs Elizabeth Mary. b 41. Man Univ BA67 Leeds Univ MA01. Ox Min Course 90. **d** 92 **p** 94. Chapl Asst Reading Hosps 86-95; NSM Reading St Mary w St Laur 92-94; Chapl R Berks and Battle Hosps NHS Trust 95-02; NSM Reading Deanery *Ox* 02-07. *The Hayloft, 2 Hall Court, Tallentire, Cockermouth CA13 0PU* Tel (01900) 825799 E-mail mjack2bl@aol.com

JACKSON, The Ven Frances Anne (Peggy). b 51. Somerville Coll Ox BA72 MA76 ACA76 FCA81. Ripon Coll Cuddesdon 85. **d** 87 **p** 94. C Ilkeston St Mary *Derby* 87-90; TM Hemel Hempstead *St Alb* 90-94; TV 94-98; TR Mortlake w E Sheen *S'wark* 98-09; RD Richmond and Barnes 00-05; Hon Can S'wark Cathl 03-09; Dean of Women's Min 04-09; Adn Llan from 09; P-in-c Penmark w Llancarfan w Llantrithyd from 09. *The Rectory, Llancarfan, Barry CF62 3AJ* Tel (01446) 750053 Fax 08701-323319 E-mail archdeacon.llandaff@churchinwales.org.uk

JACKSON, Miss Freda. b 41. Bp Otter Coll TCert61. **d** 92 **p** 94. OLM Middleton *Man* 92-94; OLM Middleton and Thornham from 94. *783 Manchester Old Road, Middleton, Manchester M24 4RE* Tel 0161-653 5876

JACKSON, Ms Gillian Rosemary. b 52. Newc Univ BA75 PGCE76 Aber Univ MLitt80 Nottm Univ MA04 AFBPsS. EMMTC 01. **d** 04 **p** 05. NSM Bosworth and Sheepy Gp *Leic* from 04. *Keeper's Cottage, Help out Mill, Shackerstone, Nuneaton CV13 0BT* Tel (01530) 264122 *or* 0116-248 7424
E-mail gill.jackson@leccofe.org

JACKSON, Harry Francis. b 30. K Coll Lon BD61 AKC61 Ex Univ BTh05 FBCO80. Sarum Th Coll 61. **d** 62 **p** 62. Bermuda 62-65; C Cobham *Guildf* 65-69; R Ash 69-96; Chapl RAF Farnborough 80-96; rtd 96; P-in-c Mawnan *Truro* 96-01; Perm to Offic from 02. *Rosnython, Treliever Road, Mabe Burnthouse, Penryn TR10 9EX* Tel (01326) 372532
E-mail harry.jackson4@btinternet.com

JACKSON, Hilary Walton. b 17. St Chad's Coll Dur BA40 MA48. **d** 46 **p** 47. C Selby Abbey *York* 46-49; C Middlesbrough All SS 49-51; V Thornley *Dur* 51-56; V Beamish 56-66; V Heighington 66-82; rtd 82. *54 Squires Court, Woodland Road, Darlington DL3 9XZ* Tel (01325) 389495
E-mail hilary.jackson@durham.anglican.org

JACKSON, Ian. b 53. Jes Coll Ox BA75. Linc Th Coll 76. **d** 78 **p** 79. C Holbeach *Linc* 78-82; V Newsome *Wakef* 82-85; V Newsome and Armitage Bridge 85-03; TR Em TM 03-04; P-in-c Corfe Castle, Church Knowle, Kimmeridge etc *Sarum* from 04. *The Rectory, East Street, Corfe Castle, Wareham BH20 5EE* Tel (01929) 480257

JACKSON, Mrs Isobel Margaret. b 69. Uganda Chr Univ BD04. **d** 04. CMS Uganda 04-05; C Lismore w Cappoquin, Kilwatermoy, Dungarvan etc *C & O* 05-10; I Templebreedy w Tracton and Nohoval *C, C & R* from 10. *Templebreedy Rectory, Church Road, Crosshaven, Co Cork, Republic of Ireland* Tel (00353) (21) 483 1236 Mobile 86-743 5424
E-mail isobel@nijackson.com *or* templebreedyrector@ccrd.ie

JACKSON, Mrs Janet Lesley. b 45. CQSW78. NEOC 93. **d** 96 **p** 97. NSM Whorlton *Newc* 96-98; Chapl St Oswald's Hospice Newc 98-07; Bereavement Services Co-ord Tynedale Hospice from 10. *1 St Andrews Road, Hexham NE46 2EY* Tel (01434) 602929

JACKSON, Mrs Joan. b 44. Bolton Coll of Educn CertEd71 Lanc Univ MA98. CBDTI 95. **d** 98 **p** 99. NSM Staveley, Ings and Kentmere *Carl* 98-00; Chapl Furness Hosps NHS Trust 98-00; Asst Chapl Bradf Hosps NHS Trust 00-04; NSM Bingley H Trin *Bradf* 03-07; Perm to Offic *Bradf* 07-10 and *Carl* from 11. *3 Ellas Orchard, Green Lane, Flookburgh, Grange-over-Sands LA11 7JT* Tel (015395) 58370
E-mail jjacksonddp@yahoo.co.uk

JACKSON, John Edward. b 29. K Coll Lon BD57 AKC57. St Boniface Warminster 57. **d** 58 **p** 59. C Crofton Park St Hilda w St Cypr *S'wark* 58-61; V Bremhill w Foxham *Sarum* 61-69; V Netheravon w Fittleton 69-73; V Netheravon w Fittleton and Enford 73-85; OCF 69-85; V Salisbury St Mark *Sarum* 85-92; P-in-c Bryngwyn and Newchurch and Llanbedr etc *S & B* 92-96; rtd 96. *Llwyndyrys Care Home, Llechryd, Cardigan SA43 2QP* Tel (01239) 682263

JACKSON, Miss Kathryn Dianne. b 64. Leeds Univ BA87 MA01. St Steph Ho Ox 87. **d** 90 **p** 94. Par Dn Headingley *Ripon* 90-94; C Hawksworth Wood 94-00; P-in-c Scarborough St Columba *York* from 00; Chapl St Cath Hospice Scarborough from 00. *160 Dean Road, Scarborough YO12 7JH* Tel (01723) 375070 E-mail kathryn.jackson@st-catherineshospice.org.uk

JACKSON, Kenneth William. b 30. MCSP53. Chich Th Coll 70. **d** 72 **p** 73. C Eastney *Portsm* 72-74; C Portchester 75-79; V Elson 79-95; rtd 95. *13 Jellicoe Avenue, Gosport PO12 2PA* Tel (023) 9258 7089

JACKSON, Lisa Helen. *See* BARNETT, Mrs Lisa Helen

JACKSON, Malcolm. b 58. NEOC 01. **d** 04 **p** 05. C Guisborough *York* 04-08; V Kirkleatham from 08. *The Vicarage, 130 Mersey Road, Redcar TS10 4DF* Tel (01642) 482073
E-mail mal_jacko@hotmail.com

JACKSON, Mrs Margaret Elizabeth. b 47. Lon Univ BSc68 MSc95 Univ of Wales (Lamp) MTh05 FCIPD91. S'wark Ord Course 80. **dss** 83 **d** 92 **p** 94. Surbiton Hill Ch *S'wark* 83-84; Saffron Walden w Wendens Ambo and Littlebury *Chelmsf* 84-85; Dulwich St Barn *S'wark* 86-97; Hon C *S'wark* 92-94; Personal Asst to Bp S'wark 92-94; Selection Sec Min Division 96-00 and from 03; NSM Churt *Guildf* 98-00; NSM The Bourne and Tilford 00-10; NSM Churt and Hindhead from 10; Convenor STETS 00-02; Dioc Dir of Ords *S'wark* 05-06; Dir of Ords Kingston Area from 10. *67 Parkhurst Fields, Churt, Farnham GU10 2PQ* Tel (01428) 714411 Fax 714426
E-mail revjackson@btinternet.com

JACKSON, Mrs Margaret Elizabeth. b 47. Mon Dioc Tr Scheme. **d** 87 **p** 94. C Chepstow *Mon* 87-90; C Exhall *Cov* 90-92; C Leamington Priors All SS 92-96; R Hulme Ascension *Man* 96-99; V Alstonfield, Butterton, Ilam etc *Lich* 99-08; RD Alstonfield 00-03; R Stonehaven *Bre* from 08; P-in-c Catterline from 08. *3 Ramsay Road, Stonehaven AB39 2HJ* Tel (01569) 764264 E-mail maggie.jackson@o2.co.uk

JACKSON, Margaret Jane. b 50. RGN72. S'wark Ord Course 89. **d** 92 **p** 94. Par Dn Hatcham St Cath *S'wark* 92-94; C 94-98; V Mottingham St Edw from 98. *St Edward's Vicarage, St Keverne Road, London SE9 4AQ* Tel (020) 8857 6278
E-mail margaretjjackson@compuserve.com

JACKSON, Ms Marie Ann. b 45. Nottm Univ BSc66. SAOMC 98. **d** 98 **p** 99. OLM High Wycombe *Ox* from 98. *19 New Road, Sands, High Wycombe HP12 4LH* Tel (01494) 530728

JACKSON, Mark Harding. b 51. Open Univ BA87. Sarum & Wells Th Coll 76. **d** 79 **p** 80. C Hobs Moat *Birm* 79-83; Chapl RN from 83. *Bush House, 12 Palmer Street, South Petherton TA13 5DB* Tel (01460) 242171
E-mail maundycottage@talktalk.net

JACKSON, Martin. b 56. Clare Coll Cam BA77 MA81 St Jo Coll Dur BA80 MA97. Cranmer Hall Dur. **d** 81 **p** 82. C Houghton le Spring *Dur* 81-84; C Bishopwearmouth St Mich w St Hilda 84-86; TV Winlaton 86; V High Spen and Rowlands Gill 86-94; P-in-c Benfieldside 94-97; V from 97; AD Lanchester 00-06. *St Cuthbert's Vicarage, Church Bank, Consett DH8 0NW* Tel (01207) 503019 E-mail martin.jackson@durham.anglican.org

JACKSON, Matthew Christopher. b 75. Univ of Wales (Abth) BD96 MTh98. Ripon Coll Cuddesdon. **d** 01 **p** 02. C King's Lynn St Marg w St Nic *Nor* 01-05; V Pembury *Roch* 05-10; R Attleborough w Besthorpe *Nor* from 10; RD Thetford and Rockland from 11. *The Rectory, Surrogate Street, Attleborough NR17 2AW* Tel (01953) 453185 E-mail therectory@me.com

JACKSON, Mrs Melanie Jane Susann. b 60. UWE BA83 Leic Univ MA94. SWMTC 97. **d** 00 **p** 01. C Ottery St Mary, Alfington, W Hill, Tipton etc *Ex* 00-04; Perm to Offic 04-08; NSM Linc St Jo from 08. *22 Kennington Close, Dunholme, Lincoln LN2 3QN* Tel (01673) 866129
E-mail melaniejackson.amia@btinternet.com

✠**JACKSON, The Most Revd Michael Geoffrey St Aubyn.** b 56. TCD BA79 MA82 St Jo Coll Cam BA81 MA85 PhD86 Ch Ch Ox MA89 DPhil89. CITC 86. **d** 86 **p** 87 **c** 02. C Dublin Zion Ch *D & G* 86-89; Chapl Ch Ch Ox 89-97; Student 93-97; Dean Cork *C, C & R* 97-02; I Cork St Fin Barre's Union 97-02; Chapl and Asst Lect Univ Coll Cork 98-02; Chapl Cork Inst of Tech 98-02; Bp Clogh 02-11; Abp Dublin *D & G* from 11. *The See House, 17 Temple Road, Dartry, Dublin 6, Republic of Ireland* Tel (00353) (1) 497 7849 Fax 497 6355
E-mail archbishop@dublin.anglican.org

JACKSON, Michael Ian. b 51. Southn Univ BA73. STETS 00. **d** 03 **p** 04. Dir St Jo Win Charity from 87; NSM Twyford and Owslebury and Morestead etc *Win* from 03. *Hill Farm Lodge, Morestead, Winchester SO21 1LZ* Tel (01962) 777277 *or* 854226
E-mail mijackson@ukgateway.net

JACKSON, Canon Michael James. b 44. Liv Univ BEng65 Newc Univ PhD84 CEng69 MICE69. NEOC 82. **d** 84 **p** 85. C Houghton le Spring *Dur* 84-87; V Millfield St Mark 87-95; V Ponteland *Newc* 95-07; AD Newc W 03-07; Hon Can Newc Cathl 06-07; rtd 07. *1 St Andrews Road, Hexham NE46 2EY* Tel (01434) 602929

JACKSON, Michael Richard. b 31. Selw Coll Cam BA54 MA58. Westcott Ho Cam 54. **d** 56 **p** 57. C Gosforth All SS *Newc* 56-62; R Dinnington *Sheff* 62-76; V Swinton 76-97; rtd 97; Perm to Offic *Sheff* from 97. *10 Elmhirst Drive, Rotherham S65 3ED* Tel (01709) 531065

JACKSON, Nicholas David. b 54. Wadh Coll Ox MA75 Bris Univ PGCE76. Wycliffe Hall Ox 06. **d** 08 **p** 09. C Branksome Park All SS *Sarum* from 08. *30 Canford Cliffs Road, Poole BH13 7AA* Tel (01202) 722967 Mobile 07969-831963
E-mail nick@thejacksons.freeserve.co.uk

JACKSON, Norman. b 20. CEng MIMechE53. S'wark Ord Course 74. **d** 77 **p** 78. NSM Erith Ch Ch *Roch* 77-82; NSM Bishopstoke *Win* 82-95; rtd 95; Perm to Offic *Win* 95-04. *7 Otter Close, Eastleigh SO50 8NF* Tel (023) 8069 5045

JACKSON, Paul Andrew. b 65. NEOC 05. **d** 08 **p** 09. NSM Haxby and Wigginton *York* from 08. *44 Windmill Way, Haxby, York YO32 3NJ* Tel (01904) 763921 E-mail pjacko99@aol.com

JACKSON, Peggy. *See* JACKSON, The Ven Frances Anne

JACKSON, Peter. *See* JACKSON, Thomas Peter

JACKSON, Peter Charles. b 71. Univ of Northumbria at Newc BA95. Oak Hill Th Coll BA01. **d** 02 **p** 03. C Lowestoft Ch Ch *Nor* 02-07; P-in-c Kendray *Sheff* 07-10; V from 10. *St Andrew's Vicarage, 84 Hunningley Lane, Barnsley S70 3DT* Tel (01226) 205826 E-mail jacko.pete@googlemail.com

JACKSON, Peter Jonathan Edward. b 53. St Pet Coll Ox BA74 MA78 PGCE78. St Steph Ho Ox 79. **d** 79 **p** 80. Lect Westmr Coll Ox 79-80; Hon C Ox St Mich w St Martin and All SS 79-80; C Malvern Link w Cowleigh *Worc* 79-82; Chapl Aldenham Sch Herts 82-89; Chapl and Hd RE Harrow Sch 89-01; Lect K Coll Lon 92-99; Dir Chr Educn and Assoc R Washington St Patr USA 01-03; V Southgate Ch Ch *Lon* from 03. *The Vicarage, 1 The Green, London N14 7EG* Tel (020) 8882 0917 *or* 8886 0384 E-mail peter.jackson@london.anglican.org

JACKSON, Peter Lewis. b 34. Bps' Coll Cheshunt 63. **d** 66 **p** 67. C Stockingford *Cov* 66-67; C Kenilworth St Nic 67-72; P-in-c Napton on the Hill 72-75; V 75-89; V Lower Shuckburgh 75-89;

R Napton-on-the-Hill, Lower Shuckburgh etc 89-99; rtd 99; Perm to Offic *Cov* from 99. *66 Arthur Street, Kenilworth CV8 2HE* Tel (01926) 864234

JACKSON, Philip Michael. b 74. Chelt & Glouc Coll of HE BA95 Brunel Univ PGCE97. Trin Coll Bris BA05. **d** 06 **p** 07. C W Kilburn St Luke w St Simon and St Jude *Lon* 06-09; C Reigate St Mary *S'wark* from 09. *63 Chart Lane, Reigate RH2 7EA* Tel 07545-054022 (mobile)
E-mail phil.jackson74@googlemail.com

JACKSON (née PRICE), Mrs Rachel Anne. b 57. **d** 03 **p** 04. OLM Barnham Broom and Upper Yare *Nor* from 03. *Red Hall, Red Hall Lane, Southburgh, Thetford IP25 7TG* Tel (01362) 821032 Fax 820145 E-mail revrachel@edwardjacksonltd.com

JACKSON, Richard Charles. b 61. Ch Ch Ox BA83 Cranfield Inst of Tech MSc85. Trin Coll Bris 92. **d** 94 **p** 95. C Lindfield *Chich* 94-98; V Rudgwick 98-09; RD Horsham 05-09; Dioc Adv for Miss and Renewal from 09. *The Vicarage, Cowfold Road, Bolney, Haywards Heath RH17 5QR* Tel (01444) 881301
E-mail rjac187233@aol.com

JACKSON, Richard Hugh. b 44. St Jo Coll York CertEd66 UEA MA84. **d** 98 **p** 99. OLM Stalham and E Ruston w Brunstead *Nor* 98-00; OLM Stalham, E Ruston, Brunstead, Sutton and Ingham from 00. *5 Rivermead, Stalham, Norwich NR12 9PH* Tel (01692) 581389 E-mail richard.jackson@intamail.com

JACKSON, Robert. b 69. Nottm Univ BA01. St Jo Coll Nottm 98. **d** 01 **p** 02. C Altham w Clayton le Moors *Blackb* 01-03; C Blackb St Gabr 03-05; TV Westhoughton and Wingates *Man* 05-10; TV Cartmel Peninsula *Carl* from 10; Lay Development Co-ord from 10. *The Vicarage, Boarbank Lane, Allithwaite, Grange-over-Sands LA11 7QR* Tel (015395) 32437 Mobile 07703-824849 E-mail jacksonsrt@aol.com

JACKSON, Robert Brandon. b 61. Lanchester Poly Cov BA86 Ox Univ BA88 MA95. Wycliffe Hall Ox 86. **d** 89 **p** 90. C Bromley Common St Aug *Roch* 89-92; P-in-c Stowe *Ox* 92-97; Asst Chapl Stowe Sch 92-97; Chapl Ld Wandsworth Coll Basingstoke 97-02; Chapl Stowe Sch from 02. *Stowe School, Buckingham MK18 5EH* Tel (01280) 818000 *or* 818144
E-mail rjackson@stowe.co.uk

JACKSON, Robert Fielden. b 35. St D Coll Lamp BA57. Sarum Th Coll 57. **d** 59 **p** 60. C Altham w Clayton le Moors *Blackb* 59-62; C Lytham St Cuth 62-64; V Skerton St Chad 64-69; V Preesall 69-90; RD Garstang 85-89; V Wray w Tatham and Tatham Fells 90-00; rtd 00; Perm to Offic *Blackb* from 01. *8 Squirrel's Chase, Lostock Hall, Preston PR5 5NE* Tel (01772) 338756

JACKSON, The Ven Robert William. b 49. K Coll Cam MA73 Man Univ MA. St Jo Coll Nottm 78. **d** 81 **p** 82. C Fulwood *Sheff* 81-84; V Grenoside and Chapl Grenoside Hosp 84-92; V Scarborough St Mary w Ch Ch and H Apostles *York* 92-01; Springboard Missr 01-04; Adn Walsall and Hon Can Lich Cathl 05-09; rtd 09. *4 Glebe Park, Eyam, Hope Valley S32 5RH* Tel (01433) 631212 E-mail archbob@gmail.com

JACKSON, Roger. b 57. Chich Th Coll 85. **d** 88 **p** 89. C Hale *Guildf* 88-92; V Barton w Peel Green *Man* 92-95; P-in-c Long Crendon w Chearsley and Nether Winchendon *Ox* 95-00; V 00-08; V Clevedon St Jo *B & W* from 08. *St John's Vicarage, 1 St John's Road, Clevedon BS21 7TG* Tel (01275) 341830

JACKSON, Canon Roger Brumby. b 31. Dur Univ BSc53 DipEd54. Ridley Hall Cam 57. **d** 59 **p** 60. C Rowner *Portsm* 59-61; C Drypool St Columba w St Andr and St Pet *York* 61-64; Asst Chapl HM Pris Hull 61-64; V Plumstead St Jas w St Jo *S'wark* 65-68; P-in-c Plumstead St Paul 65-68; V Plumstead St Jo w St Jas and St Paul 68-74; Sub-Dean Woolwich 71-74; Chapl Hulton Hosp Bolton 74-94; Chapl Bolton Hosp NHS Trust 94-01; V Deane *Man* 74-80; TR 80-01; AD Deane 80-85; Hon Can Man Cathl 90-01; rtd 01; Perm to Offic *Man* from 01. *17 Bentworth Close, Westhoughton, Bolton BL5 2GN* Tel (01942) 813209

JACKSON, Preb Roland Francis. b 20. Univ of Wales (Lamp) BA42. St Mich Coll Llan 42. **d** 44 **p** 45. C Risca *Mon* 44-49; C Chepstow St Arvan's w Penterry 49-54; R Haughton *Lich* 54-61; V Stafford St Paul Forebridge 61-72; RD Eccleshall 72-82; Chapl HM Pris Drake Hall 75-85; V Eccleshall *Lich* 72-85; Preb Lich Cathl 82-85; rtd 85; Perm to Offic *Lich* from 85. *Treginnis, 29 Meadow Drive, Haughton, Stafford ST18 9HQ* Tel (01785) 780571

JACKSON, Canon Ronald William. b 37. Lon Univ MA71 ALCD. **d** 69 **p** 70. C Crofton *Portsm* 69-74; V Wolverhampton St Matt *Lich* 74-85; V Bloxwich 85-89; C Tamworth 89-92; Bp's Officer for Par Miss and Development *Bradf* 92-98; Hon Can Bradf Cathl 94-98; rtd 98; Perm to Offic *Bradf* from 98. *94 Primrose Lane, Bingley BD16 4QP* Tel and fax (01274) 510642 E-mail rw.jackson@btinternet.com

JACKSON, Ruth Ellen. b 69. Dub City Univ BBS91. CITC BTh02. **d** 02 **p** 03. C Portadown St Mark *Arm* 02-05; C Carrigrohane Union *C, C & R* 05-10; I Mountmellick w Coolbanagher, Rosenallis etc *M & K* from 10. *The Rectory, Mountmellick, Co Laois, Republic of Ireland* Tel (00353) 87-052 3450 (mobile) E-mail ruthjnoble@gmail.com

JACKSON, Ruth Victoria. *See* HAKE, Mrs Ruth Victoria
JACKSON (née STAFF), Mrs Susan. b 59. Leeds Univ BA82. Ridley Hall Cam 88. **d** 90 **p** 94. Par Dn Mickleover All SS *Derby* 90-93; Par Dn Chatham St Wm *Roch* 93-94; C 94-97; TV Walton Milton Keynes *Ox* from 97. *The Rectory, London Road, Broughton, Milton Keynes MK10 9AA* Tel (01908) 667846

JACKSON, Thomas Peter. b 27. Univ of Wales (Lamp) BA50. St Mich Coll Llan 50. **d** 52 **p** 53. C Swansea St Mary and H Trin *S & B* 52-58; Area Sec (S Midl and S Wales) UMCA 58-60; V Glouc St Steph 60-73; R Upton St Leonards 73-92; RD Glouc N 82-91; rtd 92; Perm to Offic *Glouc* from 92. *44 Grebe Close, Gloucester GL4 9XL* Tel (01452) 533769

JACKSON, Mrs Wendy Pamela. b 45. Th Ext Educn Coll 99. **d** 00 **p** 02. Community P Woodlands S Africa 02-03; C Crediton, Shobrooke and Sandford etc *Ex* 03-05; P-in-c Southway from 05; C Tamerton Foliot from 06. *The Vicarage, 70 Inchkeith Road, Plymouth PL6 6EJ* Tel (01752) 782256
E-mail wendy@davwen.freeserve.co.uk

JACKSON, William Stafford. b 48. Sunderland Poly DCYW83 Sunderland Univ CertEd96. Linc Th Coll 86. **d** 89 **p** 90. C Heworth St Mary *Dur* 89-91; C Tudhoe Grange 91-92; Churches' Regional Commn in the NE 97-01; NSM Dipton and Leadgate 03-08; V Burnham *Ox* from 08. *The Rectory, The Precincts, Burnham, Slough SL1 7HU* Tel (01628) 559992 Mobile 07793-750652 E-mail jackson.bill39@yahoo.co.uk

JACKSON, Canon William Stanley Peter. b 39. St Mich Coll Llan 63. **d** 66 **p** 67. C Llandrindod w Cefnllys *S & B* 66-69; C Gowerton w Waunarlwydd 69-73; V Crickadarn w Gwenddwr and Alltmawr 73-79; R Llanfeugan w Llanthetty etc 79-04; Dioc GFS Chapl 84-92; Can Res Brecon Cathl 90-04; Prec 98-99; Treas 99-00; Chan 00-04; Dioc Communications Officer 92-94; RD Crickhowell 98-02; rtd 04. *9 St Peter's Avenue, Fforestfach, Swansea SA5 5BX* Tel (01792) 541229
E-mail canonjacko@aol.com

JACKSON NOBLE, Ruth Ellen. *See* JACKSON, Ruth Ellen
JACKSON-STEVENS, Preb Nigel. b 42. St Steph Ho Ox. **d** 68 **p** 69. C Babbacombe *Ex* 68-73; V Swimbridge 73-75; P-in-c W Buckland 73-75; V Swimbridge and W Buckland 75-84; P-in-c Mortehoe 84-85; V Ilfracombe, Lee, W Down, Woolacombe and Bittadon 84-85; TR Ilfracombe, Lee, Woolacombe, Bittadon etc 85-08; RD Barnstaple 93-97; Preb Ex Cathl 95-08; rtd 08. *Rose Cottage, Eastacombe, Barnstaple EX31 3NT* Tel (01271) 325283

JACOB, Mrs Amelia Stanley. b 52. Punjab Univ BA73. Oak Hill Th Coll. **d** 90 **p** 94. NSM Asian Chr Congregation All SS Tufnell Park *Lon* 90-92; NSM Alperton from 92. *62 Clifford Road, Wembley HA0 1AE* Tel (020) 8429 8633 *or* 8902 4592
E-mail stjames2000@breathemail.net

JACOB, John Lionel Andrew. b 26. Selw Coll Cam BA50 MA54. Westcott Ho Cam 50. **d** 52 **p** 53. C Brightside St Thos *Sheff* 52-55; C Maltby 55-58; V Doncaster Intake 58-67; V Sheff St Aid w St Luke 67-75; TR Sheff Manor 75-82; R Waddington *Linc* 82-91; rtd 91; Perm to Offic *Linc* 91-00. *Flat 21, Manormead, Tilford Road, Hindhead GU26 6RA* Tel (01428) 602559

JACOB, Canon Joseph. b 38. CITC 65. **d** 68 **p** 69. C Belfast St Aid *Conn* 68-70; Bp's Dom Chapl 70-71; I Kilscoran *C & O* 71-80; I Geashill *M & K* 80-83; Asst Warden Ch's Min of Healing 83-86; Gen Sec (Ireland) CMJ 87-91; I Ardamine, Kilnamanagh w Monamolin *C & O* 91-98; Preb Ferns Cathl 96-98; rtd 98. *Crannaulin, Clonmullen, Bunclody, Co Wexford, Republic of Ireland* Tel (00353) (53) 937 7532

JACOB, Neville Peter. b 60. Kent Univ BA82 Leeds Metrop Univ PGCE86. Ripon Coll Cuddesdon 94. **d** 96 **p** 97. C Market Harborough *Leic* 96-97; C Market Harborough Transfiguration 96-97; C Market Harborough and The Transfiguration etc 97-99; Chapl Miss to Seafarers 99-03; P-in-c Copythorne *Win* 03-11; Chapl Ibex 03-09; Perm to Offic from 11. *Address temp unknown*
E-mail raveknave@tinyworld.co.uk

JACOB, The Ven William Mungo. b 44. Hull Univ LLB66 Linacre Coll Ox BA69 MA73 Ex Univ PhD. St Steph Ho Ox 70. **d** 70 **p** 71. C Wymondham *Nor* 70-73; Asst Chapl Ex Univ 73-75; Dir Past Studies Sarum & Wells Th Coll 75-80; Vice-Prin 77-80; Selection Sec and Sec Cttee for Th Educn ACCM 80-86; Warden Linc Th Coll 85-96; Can and Preb Linc Cathl 86-96; Hon C Linc Minster Gp 88-96; Adn Charing Cross *Lon* from 96; Bp's Sen Chapl 96-00; R St Giles-in-the-Fields from 00. *15A Gower Street, London WC1E 6HW* Tel (020) 7636 4646 *or* 7323 1992 Fax 7937 2560 *or* 7323 4102
E-mail archdeacon.charingcross@london.anglican.org

JACOBS, Mrs Brenda Mary. b 61. Birm Univ BA85 Glos Univ PGCE04. WEMTC 06. **d** 09 **p** 10. C Holmer w Huntington *Heref* 09-11; C W Heref from 11. *6 Wetherby Drive, Hereford HR4 9TL* Tel (01432) 277392 E-mail ajacobs4.fsnet.co.uk

JACOBS, Prof Michael David. b 41. Ex Coll Ox BA63 MA67. Chich Th Coll 63. **d** 65 **p** 66. C Walthamstow St Pet *Chelmsf* 65-68; Chapl Sussex Univ 68-72; Student Cllr Leic Univ 72-84; Lect 84-97; Sen Lect 97-00; Dir Past Care *Derby, Linc* and *S'well*

84-94; Visiting Prof Bournemouth Univ from 03. *12 Atlantic Road, Swanage BH19 2EG* Tel and fax (01929) 423068

JACOBS, Neville Robertson Eynesford. b 32. Lon Coll of Div ALCD59. **d** 59 **p** 60. C Chesham St Mary *Ox* 59-62; CMS 62-67; C Keynsham *B & W* 67-71; R Croscombe and Dinder 72-80; R Pilton w Croscombe, N Wootton and Dinder 80-83; V Biddenham *St Alb* 83-89; W Chipping Sodbury and Old Sodbury *Glouc* 89-97; RD Hawkesbury 91-94; rtd 97; Perm to Offic S'wark from 98. *22 Comforts Farm Avenue, Hurst Green, Oxted RH8 9DH* Tel (01883) 714127

JACOBS, Peter John. b 33. JP. MICFM. SEITE 96. **d** 96 **p** 97. NSM Boughton under Blean w Dunkirk and Hernhill *Cant* 96-99; NSM Murston w Bapchild and Tonge 99-02; rtd 02; Perm to Offic *Cant* from 02. *13 Crown Gardens, Canterbury CT2 8LQ* Tel (01227) 455733 E-mail peter@pjacobs72.freeserve.co.uk

JACOBSON, Ian Andrew. b 61. FRGS94. STETS 02. **d** 05 **p** 06. NSM Ewell St Fran *Guildf* 05-08; NSM Headley w Box Hill from 08; CF (TA) from 07. *34 Woodlands Road, Epsom KT18 7HW* Tel (01372) 742281 E-mail andrew.jacobson@waitrose.com

JACQUES, Barry John. b 52. Open Univ BSc95. Wycliffe Hall Ox 00. **d** 02 **p** 03. NSM Attleborough *Cov* 02-03; C Weddington and Caldecote 03-07; Perm to Offic from 07. *6 Easedale Close, Nuneaton CV11 6EX* Tel (024) 7635 3400 E-mail barry@bjjacques.screaming.net

JACQUES, Mrs Margaret Irene. b 53. St Jo Coll Nottm BA03. **d** 03 **p** 04. C W Hallam and Mapperley w Stanley *Derby* 03-07; P-in-c Morton and Stonebroom w Shirland from 07. *The Rectory, Main Road, Shirland, Alfreton DE55 6BB* Tel (01773) 836003 E-mail margaret@ajacques.plus.com

JACQUES, Martin. b 62. Ch Ch Coll Cant BA05. Coll of Resurr Mirfield 00. **d** 02 **p** 03. C Margate St Jo *Cant* 02-06; P-in-c Bucharest w Sofia *Eur* 06-09; P-in-c Gainford *Dur* from 09; P-in-c Winston from 09. *The Vicarage, Low Green, Gainford, Darlington DL2 3DS* Tel (01325) 733268 Mobile 07706-875741 E-mail martinjacques@gmail.com

JACQUET, Linda. b 44. Hatf Poly BA84. ERMC 06. **d** 08 **p** 09. NSM Bungay H Trin w St Mary *St E* from 08. *The Old Red House, Barley Green, Stradbroke, Eye IP21 5LY* Tel (01379) 388846 Mobile 07890-216889 E-mail l.jacquet@tiscali.co.uk

JACQUET, Trevor Graham. b 56. Man Univ BSc77. Oak Hill Th Coll BA88. **d** 88 **p** 89. C Deptford St Nic and St Luke *S'wark* 88-92; Chapl HM Pris Brixton 92-95; Chapl HM Pris Elmley 95-08; Chapl HM Pris Belmarsh from 08. *HM Prison Belmarsh, Western Way, London SE28 0EB* Tel (020) 8331 4400 Fax 8331 4401 E-mail trevor@jacquet2.freeserve.co.uk

JACSON, Edward Shallcross Owen. b 38. St Steph Ho Ox 61. **d** 64 **p** 65. C Yate *Glouc* 64-67; C Churchdown 67-70; P-in-c Sandhurst 70-75; V Sherborne w Windrush and the Barringtons 75-76; V Sherborne, Windrush, the Barringtons etc 76-80; TV Shaston *Sarum* 80-87; Lic to Offic 87-03; Perm to Offic from 03. *Grove Farm House, Melbury Abbas, Shaftesbury SP7 0DE* Tel (01747) 853688

JAGE-BOWLER, Canon Christopher William. b 61. Nottm Univ BA83 Ch Ch Ox PGCE84 Down Coll Cam BA89 MA95. Ridley Hall Cam 87. **d** 90 **p** 91. C Downend *Bris* 90-94; Chapl Bris Univ 94-96; C Bris St Mich and St Paul 94-96; Asst Chapl Berlin *Eur* 96-97; Chapl from 97; Can Malta Cathl from 10. *Goethestrasse 31, 13158 Berlin, Germany* Tel and fax (0049) (30) 917 2248 E-mail office@stgeorges.de

JAGGER, The Ven Ian. b 55. K Coll Cam BA77 MA81 St Jo Coll Dur BA80 MA87. Cranmer Hall Dur 78. **d** 82 **p** 83. C Twickenham St Mary *Lon* 82-85; P-in-c Willen *Ox* 85-87; TV Stantonbury and Willen 87-94; TR Fareham H Trin *Portsm* 94-98; Dioc Ecum Officer 94-96; RD Fareham 96-98; Can Missr 98-01; Adn Auckland *Dur* 01-06; Dioc Rural Development Officer 01-06; Adn Dur and Can Res Dur Cathl from 06. *15 The College, Durham DH1 3EQ* Tel 0191-384 7534 or 386 6915 E-mail archdeacon.of.durham@durham.anglican.org

JAGGER (née GREEN), Mrs Ruth Valerie. b 56. Ex Univ CertEd77. Ox NSM Course 87. **d** 90 **p** 94. NSM Stantonbury and Willen *Ox* 90-94; NSM Fareham H Trin *Portsm* 94-98; NSM Portsm Deanery 98-01; Perm to Offic *Dur* from 02. *15 The College, Durham DH1 3EQ* Tel 0191-384 7534 or 386 6915

JAGO, Christine May. b 52. SRN73. **d** 94 **p** 95. OLM St Buryan, St Levan and Sennen *Truro* from 94. *Boscarne House, St Buryan, Penzance TR19 6HR* Tel (01736) 810374 Fax 810070 E-mail wandcmjago@btinternet.com

JAGO, David. b 48. Shoreditch Coll Lon CertEd69 Birm Univ BPhil77. St Steph Ho Ox 95. **d** 97 **p** 98. C S Bank *York* 97-00; V Middlesbrough St Martin w St Cuth 00-05; V Kingston upon Hull St Alb from 05. *St Alban's Vicarage, 62 Hall Road, Hull HU6 8SA* Tel (01482) 443566

JAKEMAN, Francis David. b 47. Leeds Univ BSc69. Cuddesdon Coll 71. **d** 74 **p** 75. C Gt Grimsby St Mary and St Jas *Linc* 74-77; Ind Chapl *Lon* 77-88; V Harrow Weald All SS 88-03; V Bexleyheath Ch Ch *Roch* from 03; AD Erith 04-09. *57 Townley Road, Bexleyheath DA6 7HY* Tel (020) 8301 5086 Mobile 07734-436879 E-mail francis.jakeman@diocese-rochester.org

JALLAND, Hilary Gervase Alexander. b 50. Ex Univ BA72. Coll of Resurr Mirfield 74. **d** 76 **p** 77. C Ex St Thos 76-80; C Portsea St Mary *Portsm* 80-86; V Hempton and Pudding Norton 86-90; TV Hawarden *St As* 90-93; R Llandysilio and Penrhos and Llandrinio etc 93-03; V Towyn and St George 03-06; rtd 06. *2 Church Cottages, Green Square, High Street, Llanfyllin SY22 5AB* Tel (01691) 649119 Mobile 07814-132259 E-mail hgaj@jalland1504.freeserve.co.uk

JAMES, Andrew Nicholas. b 54. BSc76. Trin Coll Bris 77. **d** 80 **p** 81. C Prescot *Liv* 80-83; C Upholland 83-85; V Hindley Green 85-91; V Dean Forest H Trin *Glouc* 91-06; RD Forest S 97-03; P-in-c Hardwicke and Elmore w Longney 06-09; V from 09. *Church House, Cornfield Drive, Hardwicke, Gloucester GL2 4QJ* Tel (01452) 720015 E-mail vicarage@inbox.com

JAMES, Andrew Peter. b 69. Glam Univ BSc96 Univ of Wales (Cardiff) BTh99. St Mich Coll Llan 96. **d** 99 **p** 00. C Roath *Llan* 99-01; C Radyr 01-06; TV Whitchurch from 06. *3 Lon Ganol, Cardiff CF14 6EB* Tel (029) 2065 4406 E-mail frjames@totalise.co.uk

JAMES, Anne Loraine. b 45. St Jo Coll Nottm. **d** 90 **p** 94. NSM Ellon and Cruden Bay *Ab* 90-99; NSM Alford 99-02; P-in-c from 02. *St Andrew's House, 53 Main Street, Alford AB33 8PX* Tel (01975) 564006 E-mail revanne.alford@virgin.net

JAMES, Barry Paul. b 49. BSc. Sarum & Wells Th Coll. **d** 82 **p** 83. C Bitterne Park *Win* 82-86; V Southampton St Mary Extra 86-00; R Fawley from 00. *The Rectory, 1 Sheringham Close, Southampton SO45 1SQ* Tel (023) 8089 3552 E-mail bpjames@gmail.com

JAMES, Brian. See JAMES, The Ven David Brian

JAMES, Brother. See PICKEN, James Hugh

JAMES, Brunel Hugh Grayburn. b 70. Selw Coll Cam BA93 MA97 Leeds Univ MA02. Wycliffe Hall Ox BA97. **d** 98 **p** 99. C Thornbury *Bradf* 98-02; R Barwick in Elmet *Ripon* 02-08; Abp's Dom Chapl *York* 08-10; P-in-c Cleckheaton St Luke and Whitechapel *Wakef* from 10; P-in-c Cleckheaton St Jo from 10. *The Vicarage, 33 Ashbourne Avenue, Cleckheaton BD19 5JH* Tel (01274) 873471 Mobile 07811-195280 E-mail bruneljames@orange.net

JAMES, Miss Carolyn Anne. b 65. Coll of Ripon & York St Jo BA87 Nottm Univ BTh91 Leeds Univ MA03. Linc Th Coll 88. **d** 91 **p** 94. Par Dn Middleton St Mary *Ripon* 91-94; C Wetherby 94-97; V Kirkstall 97-05; Chapl and Sen Warden Bp Grosseteste Coll Linc from 05. *Bishop Grosseteste College, Newport, Lincoln LN1 3DY* Tel (01522) 583607 E-mail carolyn.james@bgc.ac.uk

JAMES, Christyan Elliot. b 68. Westcott Ho Cam. **d** 09 **p** 10. C Maidstone St Martin *Cant* 09-11; rtd 11; Hon C Brighton Gd Shep Preston *Chich* from 11. *14 St Mary's Square, Brighton BN2 1FZ* Tel (01273) 241753 E-mail christyanj@yahoo.co.uk

JAMES, Colin Robert. b 39. Magd Coll Ox BA61 MA65 DipEd62. SAOMC 93. **d** 96 **p** 97. NSM Wokingham All SS *Ox* from 96. *7 Sewell Avenue, Wokingham RG41 1NT* Tel 0118-978 1515

JAMES, David. See JAMES, Richard David

JAMES, The Ven David Brian. b 30. FCA52 Univ of Wales (Swansea) BA63. St Mich Coll Llan 55. **d** 57 **p** 58. C Llandeilo Tal-y-bont *S & B* 57-59; C Swansea Ch Ch 59-63; V Bryngwyn and Newchurch and Llanbedr etc 63-70; R Llanfeugan w Llanthetty and Glyncollwng etc 70-79; V Ilston w Pennard 79-94; Hon Can Brecon Cathl 87-89; RD Gower 89-94; Can Brecon Cathl 89-94; Chan Brecon Cathl 93-94; Adn Brecon 94-99; P-in-c Llanllyr-yn-Rhos w Llanfihangel Helygen 94-99; Adn Gower 99-00; rtd 00. *1 Llys Ger-y-Llan, Pontarddulais, Swansea SA4 8HJ* Tel (01792) 883023

✠JAMES, The Rt Revd David Charles. b 45. Ex Univ BSc66 PhD71. St Jo Coll Nottm BA73. **d** 73 **p** 74 **c** 98. C Portswood Ch Ch *Win* 73-76; C Goring-by-Sea *Chich* 76-78; Chapl UEA *Nor* 78-82; V Ecclesfield *Sheff* 82-90; RD Ecclesfield 87-90; V Portswood Ch Ch *Win* 90-98; Hon Can Win Cathl 98; Suff Bp Pontefract *Wakef* 98-02; Bp Bradf 02-10; rtd 10. *7 Long Lane, Beverley HU17 0NH* E-mail davidcharlesjames@googlemail.com

JAMES, David Clive. b 40. Bris Univ BA61 K Coll Lon DipEd87. Lich Th Coll 62 St Steph Ho Ox 64. **d** 65 **p** 66. C Portslade St Nic *Chich* 65-68; C Haywards Heath St Wilfrid 68-71; Chapl Brighton Poly 71-75; Perm to Offic from 75. *22 Bradford Road, Lewes BN7 1RB* Tel (01273) 471851 E-mail davidcjames@talktalk.net

JAMES, David Henry. b 45. Univ of Wales MB, BCh68 Univ of Wales (Swansea) MA92 MRCPsych75. SWMTC 95. **d** 98. NSM Truro Cathl 98-00; rtd 00; Perm to Offic *Truro* 00-03 and *Sarum* 03-05; Lic to Offic *Arg* from 06. *Glencruitten House, Glencruitten, Oban PA34 4QB* Tel (01631) 562431 E-mail david.james.855@btinternet.com

JAMES, Preb David Howard. b 47. Ex Univ BA70 MA73 Pemb Coll Cam CertEd72. Linc Th Coll 81. **d** 83 **p** 84. C Tavistock and Gulworthy *Ex* 83-86; C E Teignmouth 86-88; C W Teignmouth 86-88; P-in-c Bishopsteignton 88-89; P-in-c Ideford, Luton and Ashcombe 88-89; TV Teignmouth, Ideford w Luton, Ashcombe etc 90-95; P-in-c Sidmouth, Woolbrook, Salcombe Regis,

Sidbury etc 95-97; TR from 97; Preb Ex Cathl from 99; RD Ottery from 03. *The Rectory, Glen Road, Sidmouth EX10 8RW* Tel (01395) 514223 E-mail rev.davidjames@btinternet.com

JAMES, David William. b 55. Birm Univ BA99. Coll of Resurr Mirfield 86. d 88 p 88. C New Rossington *Sheff* 88-90; V Yardley Wood *Birm* 90-95; P-in-c Allens Cross 95-96; V 96-06; P-in-c Rubery from 05. *160A New Road, Rubery, Rednal, Birmingham B45 9JA* Tel 0121-460 1278 Mobile 07511-918806 E-mail david.james5@btinternet.com

JAMES, Derek George. b 27. Sarum & Wells Th Coll 72. d 74 p 75. C Petersfield w Sheet *Portsm* 74-77; P-in-c Gosport Ch Ch 77-81; V 81-96; RD Gosport 90-96; rtd 96; Perm to Offic *Portsm* from 96. *2 Pyrford Close, Alverstoke, Gosport PO12 2RP* Tel (023) 9258 4753

JAMES, Elliot Paul. b 77. Univ of Wales (Lamp) BA08. Westcott Ho Cam 09. d 11. C Hertford *St Alb* from 11. *51 Port Vale, Hertford SG14 3AF* Tel (01992) 535068 Mobile 07824-553508 E-mail elliotpaul14@yahoo.com

JAMES, Canon Eric Arthur. b 25. K Coll Lon AKC50 BD51 FKC78 Trin Coll Cam MA55 Lambeth DD93 FRSA92. d 51 p 52. C Westmr St Steph w St Jo *Lon* 51-55; Chapl Trin Coll Cam 55-59; Warden Trin Coll Miss Camberwell 59-64; V Camberwell St Geo *S'wark* 59-64; Dir Par and People 64-69; Can Res and Prec S'wark Cathl 66-73; Dioc Missr *St Alb* 73-83; Can Res St Alb 73-83; Hon Can 83-90; Preacher Gray's Inn 78-97; Dir Chr Action 79-90; Hon Dir from 90; Chapl to The Queen 84-95; Extra Chapl to The Queen from 95; rtd 90; Perm to Offic *S'wark* 90-02. *Charterhouse Sutton's Hospital, The Charterhouse, Charterhouse Square, London EC1M 6AN*

JAMES, Gerwyn. *See* JAMES, Joshua John Gerwyn

JAMES, Gillian Mary. b 49. d 99. OLM Bassaleg *Mon* 99-05. *69 Hollybush Road, Cyncoed, Cardiff CF2 4SZ* Tel (029) 2073 2673

JAMES, Glyn. *See* JAMES, Henry Glyn

JAMES, Canon Godfrey Walter. b 36. Univ of Wales (Lamp) BA58 Univ of Wales (Cardiff) MA60 St Pet Coll Ox DipEd61 BA63 MA67. St Mich Coll Llan 63. d 64 p 65. C Canton St Jo *Llan* 64-71; V Williamstown 71-85; V Kenfig Hill 85-01; Hon Can Llan Cathl 96-01; rtd 01. *23 Crossfield Avenue, Porthcawl CF36 3LA*

✠**JAMES, The Rt Revd Graham Richard.** b 51. Lanc Univ BA72 Hon FGCM92. Cuddesdon Coll 72. d 75 p 76 c 93. C Pet Ch Carpenter 75-79; C Digswell *St Alb* 79-82; TV Digswell and Panshanger 82-83; Sen Selection Sec and Sec Cand Cttee ACCM 83-87; Abp's Chapl *Cant* 87-93; Hon Can Dallas from 89; Suff Bp St Germans *Truro* 93-99; Bp Nor from 99. *The Bishop's House, Norwich NR3 1SB* Tel (01603) 629001 Fax 761613 E-mail bishop@norwich.anglican.org

JAMES, Henley George. b 31. Sarum & Wells Th Coll 79. d 81 p 82. C Tottenham H Trin *Lon* 81-85; C Cricklewood St Pet 85-88; P-in-c 88-89; V Bearwood *Birm* 89-97; rtd 97. *33 Parkside Road, Birmingham B20 1EL*

JAMES, Henry Glyn. b 26. Keble Coll Ox BA50 MA58 Toronto Univ MEd74. Wycliffe Hall Ox 50. d 52 p 53. C Edgbaston St Aug *Birm* 52-54; C Surbiton St Matt *S'wark* 54-57; Housemaster Kingham Hill Sch Oxon 57-62; Chapl St Lawr Coll Ramsgate 62-68; Canada 68-73; Hon C Kidmore End *Ox* 74-77; K Jas Coll of Henley 74-87; Hon C Remenham *Ox* 77-88; Chapl The Henley Coll 87-88; Chapl Toulouse *Eur* 88-91; rtd 91; Perm to Offic *Win* from 93. *13 Harbour Road, Bournemouth BH6 4DD* Tel (01202) 427697 E-mail glyn.james50@aol.com

JAMES, Prof Ian Nigel. b 48. Leeds Univ BSc69 Man Univ PhD74. SAOMC 99. d 02 p 03. NSM Bracknell *Ox* 02-04; NSM Winkfield and Cranbourne 04-10; P-in-c Bootle, Corney, Whicham and Whitbeck *Carl* from 10. *The Rectory, Bootle, Millom LA19 5TH* Tel (01229) 718223 Mobile 07808-207422 E-mail dr.i.n.james@btinternet.com

JAMES, Jane Eva. b 55. Birm Univ BSc76 W Midl Coll of Educn PGCE77. St Mich Coll Llan 08. d 11. NSM Llanfair-ym-Mechain and Llanfechain *St As* from 11. *Pear Tree Farm, Llanfair Caereinion, Welshpool SY21 0BH* Tel (01938) 810031 Mobile 07748-697112 E-mail pilotjanej@aol.com

JAMES, Jeffrey Aneurin. b 53. Univ of Wales (Cardiff) BScEcon80 Bris Univ MSc85 MHSM83. WEMTC 98. d 01 p 02. NSM Minchinhampton *Glouc* 01-07; NSM Painswick, Sheepscombe, Cranham, The Edge etc from 07. *Jays Cottage, Keble Road, France Lynch, Stroud GL6 8LW* Tel (01453) 882481 E-mail jayscott@dsl.pipex.com

JAMES, Jeremy Richard. b 52. Jes Coll Cam BA73 MA77 York Univ CertEd77. Cranmer Hall Dur 86. d 88 p 89. C Broxbourne w Wormley *St Alb* 88-91; C Hailsham *Chich* 91-99; V Wadhurst from 99; V Tidebrook from 99; P-in-c Stonegate from 99; RD Rotherfield from 03. *The Vicarage, High Street, Wadhurst TN5 6AA* Tel (01892) 782083 E-mail jeremy@jrjames.freeserve.co.uk

JAMES, Mrs Joanna Elizabeth. b 72. SAOMC. d 06 p 07. C Northwood Em *Lon* 06-10; C S Mimms Ch Ch from 10. *8 Wentworth Road, Barnet EN5 4NT* Tel (020) 8441 0645

JAMES, John Charles. b 35. Keble Coll Ox BA59. Linc Th Coll 68. d 70 p 71. C S Shields St Hilda w St Thos *Dur* 70-77; P-in-c Jarrow Docks 77-78; Adn Seychelles 78-92; V Mylor w Flushing *Truro* 92-05; rtd 06. *172 Westoe Road, South Shields NE33 3PH*

JAMES, John David. b 23. CCC Cam MA. Wells Th Coll. d 50 p 51. C Romford St Edw *Chelmsf* 50-54; C Cannock *Lich* 54-56; R Wickham Bishops *Chelmsf* 56-61; V Stansted Mountfitchet 61-71; V Clacton St Jas 71-84; R Poulshot *Sarum* 84; V Rowde 84; R Rowde and Poulshot 84-88; rtd 88; Perm to Offic *Heref* from 92. *15 Beaconsfield Park, Ludlow SY8 4LY* Tel (01584) 873754

JAMES, John Hugh Alexander. b 56. St Jo Coll Dur BA78. St Mich Coll Llan. d 81 p 82. C Newton Nottage *Llan* 81-84; Prov Youth and Children's Officer Ch in Wales 84-92; V Llanfihangel-ar-arth *St D* 92-97; V Llanfihangel-ar-arth w Capel Dewi 97-04; RD Emlyn 01-04; V Cydweli and Llandyfaelog from 04; AD Cydweli 05-07. *The Vicarage, Vicarage Lane, Kidwelly SA17 4SY* Tel (01554) 890295 E-mail ficerdy@tiscali.co.uk

JAMES, John Morgan. b 21. Lon Univ BD43 MTh45. ALCD43. d 44 p 45. C Leyton St Mary w St Edw *Chelmsf* 44-47; C Southend St Sav Westcliff 47-50; Prec Chelmsf Cathl 50-53; V Kemp Town St Mark *Chich* 53-65; R Balcombe 65-67; V Sunbury *Lon* 67-77; RD Kemp Town *Chich* 55-65; Dir Coll of Preachers 77-85; Lic to Offic *Guildf* 77-86; rtd 85. *Fair Winds, 126 Pagham Road, Pagham, Bognor Regis PO21 4NN* Tel (01243) 264250

JAMES, John Paul. b 30. Sarum Th Coll 58. d 60 p 61. C Milton *Portsm* 60-65; C Stanmer w Falmer and Moulsecoomb *Chich* 65-69; PC Brighton H Trin 69-71; Canada from 71: R Saguenay St Jean 71; Dean Quebec 77-87; R Westmount St Matthias 87-96; rtd 96. *301-97 Huron Street, Stratford ON N5A 5S7, Canada* Fax (001) (519) 273 9226 E-mail helenandpaul@rogers.com

JAMES, Joshua John Gerwyn. b 31. St D Coll Lamp BA52. d 54 p 55. C Haverfordwest St Mary w St Thos *St D* 54-56; C Llanaber w Caerdeon *Ban* 56-57; CF 57-76; V Tidenham w Beachley and Lancaut *Glouc* 76-80; R Aberdovey *Ban* 80-82; V Quinton w Marston Sicca *Glouc* 82-90; RD Campden 88-90; P-in-c Upper Chelsea St Simon *Lon* 90-96; rtd 96; Perm to Offic *S'wark* from 97. *25 The Watergardens, Warren Road, Kingston upon Thames KT2 7LF* Tel (020) 8974 6889

JAMES, Mrs Julie Margaret. b 55. Shenstone Coll of Educn BEd77. Qu Coll Birm 01. d 04 p 05. NSM Salwarpe and Hindlip w Martin Hussingtree *Worc* 04-06; NSM St Jo in Bedwardine 06-09; NSM Abberton, The Flyfords, Naunton Beauchamp etc from 09. *Wyche Cottage, Plough Road, Tibberton, Droitwich WR9 7NQ* Tel (01905) 345688 Mobile 07751-465241 E-mail julie.m.james@btinternet.com.uk

JAMES, Keith Edward Arthur. b 38. Sarum & Wells Th Coll 85. d 87 p 88. C Hempnall *Nor* 87-91; R Roughton and Felbrigg, Metton, Sustead etc 91-98; V Ascension Is 98-01; rtd 02; Chapl Laslett's *Worc* 02-04; Perm to Offic *Nor* from 05. *30 Woodland Rise, Tasburgh, Norwich NR15 1NF* Tel (01508) 470032

JAMES, Keith Nicholas. b 69. Leeds Univ BA91. St Jo Coll Nottm MA93. d 93 p 94. C Crosby *Linc* 93-96; P-in-c Cherry Willingham w Greetwell 96-00; R S Lawres Gp 00-03; RD Lawres 01-03; R Ribbesford w Bewdley and Dowles *Worc* from 03; P-in-c Wribbenhall from 11; RD Kidderminster from 07. *The Rectory, 57 Park Lane, Bewdley DY12 2HA* Tel (01299) 402275 *or* 404773 E-mail kn.james@btinternet.com

JAMES, Malcolm. b 37. CEng MICE MIStructE. NOC 80. d 83 p 84. NSM Ripponden *Wakef* 83-10; Perm to Offic from 10. *Lower Stones, Bar Lane, Rishworth, Sowerby Bridge HX6 4EY* Tel (01274) 677439 E-mail malcolm@mjconsultancy.demon.co.uk

JAMES, Mark Nicholas. b 55. Jes Coll Ox BA77 MA80 PGCE79. Ridley Hall Cam 03. d 05 p 06. C Gt Dunmow and Barnston *Chelmsf* 05-09; R Bentley Common, Kelvedon Hatch and Navestock from 09. *The Rectory, 2 Church Road, Kelvedon Hatch, Brentwood CM14 5TJ* Tel (01277) 373486 Mobile 07884-185835 E-mail revmarkjames@btinternet.com

JAMES, Martin. b 40. ACII. d 94 p 95. OLM N Farnborough *Guildf* 94-08; OLM Camberley St Martin Old Dean 08-09; NSM 09-10; rtd 10; Perm to Offic *Guildf* from 10. *43 Ashley Road, Farnborough GU14 7HB* Tel (01252) 544698 Mobile 07786-013832 E-mail martinjean.james@ntlworld.com

JAMES, Michael Howard. b 55. Bris Univ LLB73 Solicitor 92. WEMTC 04. d 06 p 07. NSM Clifton H Trin, St Andr and St Pet *Bris* 06-08; NSM Westbury Park LEP from 08. *10 Hill Drive, Failand, Bristol BS8 3UX* Tel (01275) 393729 E-mail jamfam@jamfam4.wanadoo.co.uk *or* cranmer1662@hotmail.co.uk

JAMES, Michael John. b 29. ALA53 Heriot-Watt Univ CQSW81. Ho of Resurr Mirfield 57. d 59 p 60. C Applethwaite *Carl* 59-61; C Carl H Trin 61-63; C-in-c Carl St Luke Morton CD 63-67; R Lambley w Knaresdale *Newc* 67-72; Rossie Sch Montrose 75-83; Prin Redding Ho Falkirk 83-86; rtd 93. *28 Windsor Street, Edinburgh EH7 5JR* Tel 0131-556 4935

JAMES, Paul Maynard. b 31. Univ of Wales (Ban) BA52 Fitzw Ho Cam BA54 MA58. Ridley Hall Cam 56. **d** 57 **p** 58. C Newhaven *Chich* 57-60; Kenya 60-65; SW Area Sec CCCS 65-68; V Shrewsbury St Julian *Lich* 68-76; V Shrewsbury H Trin w St Julian 76-90; P-in-c Woore and Norton in Hales 90-98; Adn Salop's Adv on Evang 90-98; RD Hodnet 93-97; rtd 98; Perm to Offic *Heref* and *Lich* from 00. *Nettledene, Elms Lane, Little Stretton, Church Stretton SY6 6RD* Tel (01694) 722559
JAMES, Canon Peter David. b 42. Keble Coll Ox BA63 Lon Univ BD67. Tyndale Hall Bris 64. **d** 67 **p** 68. C Haydock St Mark *Liv* 67-69; C Ashton-in-Makerfield St Thos 69-74; V Whiston 74-80; V Harlech and Llanfair-juxta-Harlech etc *Ban* 80-94; R Botwnnog w Bryncroes 94-07; Hon Can Ban Cathl 02-07; rtd 07. *Tabor, Llithfaen, Pwllheli LL53 6NL* Tel (01758) 750202 E-mail peterjames@botwnnog.fsnet.co.uk
JAMES, Raymond John. b 36. Linc Th Coll 85. **d** 87 **p** 88. C Cov E 87-91; V Wolvey w Burton Hastings, Copston Magna etc 91-01; rtd 01. *46 Cornmore, Pershore WR10 1HX* Tel (01336) 556537
JAMES, Richard Andrew. b 44. Mert Coll Ox BA67 MA70. Tyndale Hall Bris. **d** 70 **p** 71. C Bebington *Ches* 70-73; C Histon Ely 73-77; Chapl Guildf Coll of Tech 77-80; C Guildf St Sav w Stoke-next-Guildford 77-80; Ecum Chapl Bedf Coll of HE *St Alb* 81-83; TV Ipsley *Worc* 84-89; R Mulbarton w Kenningham *Nor* 89-92; rtd 93. *5 Links Way, Harrogate HG2 7EW* Tel (01423) 889410
E-mail hilarygjames@hotmail.com
JAMES, Richard David. b 45. Cheltenham & Glouc Coll of HE MA97. Lon Coll of Div 66. **d** 70 **p** 71. C Boultham *Linc* 70-74; C New Waltham 74-77; TV Clecthorpes 77-87; TR E Bris 87-99; V E Bris St Ambrose and St Leon from 99. *St Ambrose Vicarage, 487 Whitehall Road, Bristol BS5 7DA* Tel 0117-951 2270 Mobile 07749-243407
JAMES, Richard David. b 65. Clare Coll Cam MA88 Lon Hosp MB, BChir90. Ridley Hall Cam 92. **d** 95 **p** 96. C Clifton Ch Ch w Em Bris 95-98; C Enfield Ch Ch Trent Park *Lon* 98-00; V from 00; AD Enfield from 09. *The Vicarage, 2A Chalk Lane, Cockfosters, Barnet EN4 9JQ* Tel (020) 8441 1230 *or* tel and fax 8449 0556 E-mail richard@ccc1.fsnet.co.uk
JAMES, Richard Lindsay. b 39. Kelham Th Coll 61. **d** 66 **p** 67. C Seacroft *Ripon* 66-74; rtd 04. *3 Cavendish Mews, Hove BN3 1AZ* Tel (01273) 324672
JAMES, Richard William. b 47. St D Coll Lamp. **d** 75 **p** 76. C Hubberston *St D* 75-78; R Pendine w Llanmiloe and Eglwys Gymyn w Marros 78-83; V Caerwent w Dinham and Llanfair Discoed etc *Mon* 83-84; Chapl Gothenburg w Halmstad, Jönköping etc *Eur* 84-89; P-in-c Shooters Hill Ch Ch *S'wark* 89-97; V Plumstead St Mark and St Marg 97-07; rtd 07. *Gärdesvägen 9H, 87162 Härnösand, Sweden* Tel (0046) (611) 435557 E-mail eva.jame@comhem.se
JAMES, Roger Michael. b 44. K Coll Lon BD66 AKC66. **d** 69 **p** 70. C Frindsbury w Upnor *Roch* 69-72; Lic to Offic *St Alb* 73-78; C Digswell 78-81; R Knebworth 81-92; P-in-c Upper Tean and Local Min Adv (Stafford) *Lich* 92-99; Dir Cottesloe Chr Tr Progr *Ox* 99-03; R Cusop w Blakemere, Bredwardine w Brobury etc *Heref* 03-09; RD Abbeydore 06-09; rtd 09. *Ty Siloh, Llandeilo'r Fan, Brecon LD3 8UD* Tel (01874) 636126 E-mail tysiloh@googlemail.com
JAMES, Sandra Kay. *See* GARDNER, Mrs Sandra Kay
JAMES, Sarah Alison Livingston. b 38. FCA73. **d** 06 **p** 06. NSM Churchdown *Glouc* 06-11; rtd 11. *Canton House, New Street, Painswick, Stroud GL6 6XH* Tel (01452) 812419
E-mail saljames@zetnet.co.uk
JAMES, Ms Sheridan Angharad. b 71. Univ of Wales (Abth) BA93 PGCE94 MPhil00. SEITE 04. **d** 07 **p** 08. C Catford (Southend) and Downham *S'wark* 07-11; V Hatcham St Cath from 11. *St Catherine's Vicarage, 102A Pepys Road, London SE14 5SG* Tel (020) 7639 1050 Mobile 07703-291594
E-mail revsheridanjames@gmail.com
JAMES, Stephen Lynn. b 53. Oak Hill Th Coll BA86. **d** 86 **p** 87. C Heigham H Trin *Nor* 86-89; C Vancouver St Jo Canada 89-93; R Bebington *Ches* 93-06; R Rusholme H Trin *Man* from 06. *Holy Trinity Rectory, Platt Lane, Manchester M14 5NF* Tel 0161-224 1123 Fax 224 1144 E-mail office@plattchurch.org
JAMES, Stephen Nicholas. b 51. Reading Univ MA87 Bris Univ EdD95 ARCM72 LTCL72 FTCL73 FRSA00. SAOMC 01. **d** 04 **p** 05. NSM Hanney, Denchworth and E Challow *Ox* 04-07; P-in-c Goetre w Llanover *Mon* from 07. *The Rectory, Nantyderry, Abergavenny NP7 9DW* Tel (01873) 880378 E-mail sueandstephen@btinternet.com
JAMES, Mrs Susan Margaret. b 58. SRN81 RSCN81 St Jo Coll Dur BA04. Cranmer Hall Dur 00. **d** 04 **p** 05. NSM Derby St Paul 04-07. *267 Victoria Avenue, Ockbrook, Derby DE72 3RL* Tel (01332) 673551 E-mail suzejames@hotmail.com
JAMES, Mrs Veronica Norma. b 59. STETS 99. **d** 02 **p** 03. NSM Ashton Keynes, Leigh and Minety *Bris* 02-05; R Merriott w Hinton, Dinnington and Lopen *B & W* 05-10; R The Guitings, Cutsdean, Farmcote etc *Glouc* from 10; AD N Cotswold from

10. *The Rectory, Copse Hill Road, Lower Slaughter, Cheltenham GL54 2HY* Tel (01451) 821777
E-mail rev.veronica@tiscali.co.uk
JAMES, William Glynne George. b 39. Trin Coll Carmarthen 82. **d** 85 **p** 86. NSM Gorseinon *S & B* 85-09; Perm to Offic from 09. *23 Cecil Road, Gowerton, Swansea SA4 3DF* Tel (01792) 872363
JAMESON, Miss Beverley Joyce. b 60. St Jo Coll Nottm 09. **d** 11. C Cen Telford *Lich* from 11. *32 Viscount Avenue, Telford TF4 3SW* Tel 07817-379583 (mobile)
E-mail bevjameson@live.co.uk
JAMESON, David Kingsbury. b 28. Mert Coll Ox BA50 MA55. Qu Coll Birm 50. **d** 53 **p** 54. C Leominster *Heref* 53-56; C Portsm Cathl 56-60; Dioc Youth Officer 58-61; V Gosport Ch Ch 60-65; V Portsea St Cuth 65-70; V Enfield Jes Chpl *Lon* 70-74; RD Nuneaton *Cov* 74-79; V Nuneaton St Nic 74-80; Org Sec (Leics and Northants) CECS 80-82; P-in-c Forty Hill Jes Ch *Lon* 82-87; V 87-91; rtd 91; Hon C Okehampton w Inwardleigh, Bratton Clovelly etc *Ex* 94-96; Hon C St Giles-in-the-Fields *Lon* 96-99; Perm to Offic *Chelmsf* 99-00 and *Cov* from 01. *20 Grasmere Crescent, Nuneaton CV11 6ED* Tel (024) 7674 6957
JAMESON, Canon Dermot Christopher Ledgard. b 27. TCD BA49 MA54. CITC 49. **d** 50 **p** 51. C Seagoe *D & D* 50-53; C Holywood 53-57; I Kilkeel 57-62; I Donaghcloney w Waringstown 62-79; Can Dromore Cathl 77-93; I Kilbroney 79-93; Treas Dromore Cathl 81-83; Prec Dromore Cathl 83-90; Chan Dromore Cathl 90-93; rtd 93. *Concord, 10B Kilbroney Road, Rostrevor, Newry BT34 3BH* Tel (028) 4173 9728
JAMESON, Geoffrey Vaughan. b 27. Culham Coll Ox CertEd51. Wycliffe Hall Ox 68. **d** 70 **p** 71. C Buckingham *Ox* 70-73; R Exton w Whitwell *Pet* 73-86; V Marystowe, Coryton, Stowford, Lewtrenchard etc *Ex* 86-90; rtd 90; Perm to Offic *Portsm* from 91 and *Win* from 03. *30 Green Haven Court, 84 London Road, Cowplain, Waterlooville PO8 8EW* Tel (023) 9223 2226
JAMESON, Howard Kingsley. b 63. Warwick Univ BSc84. Trin Coll Bris 99. **d** 02 **p** 03. C Wareham *Sarum* 02-05; P-in-c Monkton Farleigh, S Wraxall and Winsley 05-11; P-in-c Bradford-on-Avon Ch Ch 10-11; R N Bradford on Avon and Villages from 11. *The Rectory, 6 Millbourn Close, Winsley, Bradford-on-Avon BA15 2NN* Tel (01225) 722230
E-mail howard.jameson@virgin.net
JAMESON, Peter. b 31. Trin Coll Cam BA54 MA60. Linc Th Coll. **d** 62 **p** 63. C Earl's Court St Cuth w St Matthias *Lon* 62-68; C Notting Hill St Clem 68-72; C Notting Hill St Clem and St Mark 72-74; TV Notting Hill 74-77; V Stoke Newington St Olave 77-95; rtd 95; Perm to Offic *Chich* from 95. *Colemans, Warren Lane, Cross in Hand, Heathfield TN21 0TB* Tel (01435) 863414
JAMIESON, Douglas. *See* JAMIESON, William Douglas
JAMIESON, Guy Stuart. b 66. Leeds Univ BA98. Ripon Coll Cuddesdon. **d** 00 **p** 01. C Woodhall *Bradf* 00-03; V Southowram and Claremount *Wakef* from 03. *St Anne's Vicarage, Church Lane, Southowram, Halifax HX3 9TD* Tel (01422) 365229
E-mail guy.jamieson@virgin.net
JAMIESON, Kenneth Euan Oram. b 24. Roch Th Coll 60. **d** 62 **p** 63. C Bromley SS Pet and Paul *Roch* 62-66; R Colchester St Mary Magd *Chelmsf* 66-71; V Bexleyheath St Pet *Roch* 71-78; P-in-c Maidstone St Faith *Cant* 78-83; P-in-c Maidstone St Paul 78-83; Ind Chapl *St Alb* 83-89; rtd 89; Perm to Offic *B & W* from 89. *4 Ashley Road, Taunton TA1 5BP* Tel (01823) 289367
JAMIESON, Canon Marilyn. b 52. Cranmer Hall Dur IDC80. **d** 91 **p** 94. Par Dn Bensham *Dur* 91-93; Par Dn Ryton w Hedgefield 93-94; Chapl Metro Cen Gateshead 94-02 and from 06; Bp's Sen Chapl 02-05; Hon C Ryton 05-06; Hon Can Dur Cathl from 97. *Barmoor House, 64 Main Road, Ryton NE40 3AJ* Tel 0191-413 4592 *or* 493 0259
JAMIESON, Mrs Moira Elizabeth. b 50. **d** 08. C Lenzie *Glas* from 08. *5 Pinewood Place, Kirkintilloch, Glasgow G66 4JN* Tel 0141-775 1161 Mobile 07977-096446
E-mail moira.jamieson@ntlworld.com
JAMIESON, Peter Grant. b 64. Liv Univ BA87. Coll of Resurr Mirfield 93. **d** 93 **p** 94. C Charlton Kings St Mary *Glouc* 93-96. *3 Belmont Mews, Upper High Street, Thame OX9 3EJ* Tel (01844) 212895
JAMIESON, Miss Rosalind Heather. b 49. CertEd71. St Jo Coll Dur 79. **dss** 81 **d** 87 **p** 94. Queensbury All SS *Lon* 81-85; Richmond H Trin and Ch Ch *S'wark* 85-87; Par Dn 87-91; Par Dn Burnantofts St Steph and St Agnes *Ripon* 91-94; C 94-99; TV Seacroft from 99. *St Richard's Vicarage, Ramshead Hill, Leeds LS14 1BX* Tel 0113-273 2527
E-mail jamheat2002@tiscali.co.uk
JAMIESON, Mrs Susan Jennifer. b 49. Liv Univ SRN71. Dioc OLM tr scheme 97. **d** 00 **p** 01. OLM Clubmoor *Liv* from 00. *15 Winsford Road, Liverpool L13 0BJ* Tel 0151-475 7562 Mobile 07879-425277 E-mail susiejam@blueyonder.co.uk
JAMIESON, Thomas Lindsay. b 53. N Lon Poly BSc74. Cranmer Hall Dur. **d** 77 **p** 78. C Gateshead Fell *Dur* 77-80; C Gateshead 80-84; TV 84-90; P-in-c Gateshead St Cuth w St Paul 90-91; TV Bensham 91-93; P-in-c Ryton w Hedgefield 93-95; R 95-05; R

Ryton from 05; AD Gateshead W 94-98. *Barmoor House, 64 Main Road, Ryton NE40 3AJ* Tel 0191-413 4592 E-mail atl.jamieson@talk21.com
JAMIESON, William Douglas. b 38. Oak Hill Th Coll 63. **d** 66 **p** 67. C Shrewsbury St Julian *Lich* 66-68; C Bucknall and Bagnall 68-70; C Otley *Bradf* 70-74; TV Keighley 74-81; V Utley 81-00; rtd 00; Perm to Offic *Ches* from 00. *11 The Quay, Frodsham, Warrington WA6 7JG* Tel (01928) 731085 Mobile 07974-947838 E-mail douglasjamieson@lineone.net
JAMISON, William Mervyn Noel. b 66. CITC 03. **d** 07 **p** 08. NSM Ballybeen *D & D* 07-10; NSM Comber from 10. *Millview House, 1 Old Ballygowan Road, Comber, Newtownards BT23 5NP* Tel (028) 9187 1962 E-mail rev.merv@btinternet.com
JANES, Austin Steven. b 75. York Univ BA97. Ripon Coll Cuddesdon 06. **d** 08 **p** 09. C Crewe St Andr w St Jo *Ches* 08-11; Min Can St Alb Abbey from 11. *2 Dean Moore Close, St Albans AL1 1DW* Tel (01727) 890206 E-mail austinjanes@googlemail.com *or* mcy@stalbanscathedral.org.uk
JANES, David Edward. b 40. Lon Univ BSc67. Glouc Sch of Min 86. **d** 89 **p** 90. NSM Church Stretton *Heref* 89-00; rtd 00; Perm to Offic *Heref* from 00. *Bourton Westwood Farm, 3 Bourton Westwood, Much Wenlock TF13 6QB* Tel (01952) 727393
JANICKER, Laurence Norman. b 47. SS Mark & Jo Coll Chelsea DipEd69. St Jo Coll Nottm 83. **d** 85 **p** 86. C Beverley Minster *York* 85-89; R Lockington and Lund and Scorborough w Leconfield 89-94; V Cov St Geo 94-08; rtd 08; Perm to Offic *Nor* from 09. *136 Manor Road, Newton St Faith, Norwich NR10 3LG* Tel (01603) 898614 E-mail laurencejanicker@btinternet.com
JANSMA, Henry Peter. b 57. Ne Bible Coll (USA) BA79 Westmr Th Sem (USA) MA85 St Jo Coll Dur PhD91. Linc Th Coll 89. **d** 91 **p** 92. C Spalding *Linc* 91-96; P-in-c Cleethorpes St Aid 96-97; V 97-01; R Haddon Heights St Mary USA from 01. *501 Green Street, Haddon Heights NJ 08035-1903, USA* Tel (001) (856) 547 0565 *or* 547 3240 Fax 310 0565 E-mail stmaryshh@juno.com
JANSSON, Maria Patricia. b 55. Milltown Inst Dub MRelSc92. CITC 00. **d** 01 **p** 02. C Galway w Kilcummin *T, K & A* 01-02; C Wexford w Ardcolm and Killurin *C & O* 02-04; I 04-09; C Kilscoran w Killinick and Mulrankin 02-04; P-in-c 04-09; I Wexford and Kilscoran Union from 10. *The Rectory, Park, Wexford, Republic of Ireland* Tel (00353) (53) 914 0652 *or* 912 2377 Mobile 87-225 5793 E-mail miajansson@eircom.net
JANVIER, Philip Harold. b 57. Trin Coll Bris BA87. **d** 87 **p** 88. C Much Woolton *Liv* 87-90; TV Toxteth St Philemon w St Gabr and St Cleopas 90-97; TR Gateacre from 97. *St Stephen's Rectory, Belle Vale Road, Liverpool L25 2PQ* Tel and fax 0151-487 9338 E-mail philjanvier.home@virgin.net
JAONA, Ramahalefitra Hyacinthe Arsène. b 70. St Paul's Th Coll Ambatoharanana Madagascar 89. **d** 94 **p** 96. Madagascar 94-97 and from 98; C Caldicot *Mon* 97-98. *Mission Angelican, BP 126, 206 Antalaha, Antsiranana, Madagascar*
JAPAN, Primate of. *Vacant*
JAQUES, Geoffrey Sanderson. b 48. Man Univ BSc. NEOC 94. **d** 97 **p** 98. NSM Gt Ayton w Easby and Newton under Roseberry *York* from 97. *132 Roseberry Crescent, Great Ayton, Middlesbrough TS9 6EW* Tel (01642) 722979 E-mail jaques132@btinternet.com
JAQUISS, Mrs Gabrielle Clair. b 56. Clare Coll Cam BA79 MA83 LRAM76. NOC 06. **d** 08 **p** 09. NSM Bowdon *Ches* 08-11; NSM Hale Barns w Ringway from 11. *Ingersley, Belgrave Road, Bowdon, Altrincham WA14 2NZ* Tel 0161-928 0717 Mobile 07843-375494 E-mail clairjq@aol.com
JARAM, Peter Ellis. b 45. Lon Univ BSc70 CEng77 MIET77 MBIM88. Linc Th Coll 94. **d** 94 **p** 95. C Bridlington Priory *York* 94-96; C Rufforth w Moor Monkton and Hessay 96-97; C Healaugh w Wighill, Bilbrough and Askham Richard 96-97; P-in-c 97-01; Chapl Askham Bryan Coll 97-01; V Brompton by Sawdon w Hutton Buscel, Snainton etc *York* 01-05; rtd 05; Perm to Offic *York* from 05. *74 Eastgate, Pickering YO18 7DY* Tel (01751) 477831 E-mail pwj74@btinternet.com
JARDINE, Canon Anthony. b 38. Qu Coll Birm 64. **d** 67 **p** 68. C Baldock w Bygrave and Clothall *St Alb* 67-71; C N Stoneham *Win* 71-73; P-in-c Ecchinswell cum Sydmonton 73-79; P-in-c Burghclere w Newtown 78-79; R Burghclere w Newtown and Ecchinswell w Sydmonton 79-87; R Wonston and Stoke Charity w Hunton 87-97; P-in-c Chawton and Farringdon 97-04; Dioc Rural Officer 97-04; Hon Can Win Cathl 99-04; rtd 04; Hon C Knight's Enham and Smannell w Enham Alamein *Win* 04-08; Perm to Offic *Heref* from 09. *Longdendale, 4 Victoria Road, Kington HR5 3BX* E-mail rev_jardine@hotmail.com
JARDINE, David Eric Cranswick. b 30. CCC Ox BA53 MA57. Wycliffe Hall Ox 53. **d** 55 **p** 56. C Wavertree St Mary *Liv* 55-58; C Liv All So Springwood 58-62; C Horley *S'wark* 62-65; V Mitcham Ch Ch 65-72; V Iford *Win* 72-89; R Smannell w Enham Alamein 89-96; rtd 96; Perm to Offic *Sheff* from 96. *387 Redmires Road, Sheffield S10 4LE* Tel 0114-230 8721 E-mail d.jardine@uwclub.net

JARDINE, Canon David John (Brother David). b 42. QUB BA65. CITC 67. **d** 67 **p** 68. C Ballymacarrett St Patr *D & D* 67-70; Asst Chapl QUB 70-73; SSF from 73; Asst Chapl HM Pris Belfast 75-79; Chapl 79-85; USA 85-88; Sen Asst Warden Ch of Ireland Min of Healing 88-92; Dir Divine Healing Min 92-08; Can Belf Cathl from 07. *3 Richmond Park, Stranmillis, Belfast BT9 5EF* Tel (028) 9066 6200 *or* 9031 1532
JARDINE, Canon Norman. b 47. QUB BSc72. Trin Coll Bris 74. **d** 76 **p** 77. C Magheralin *D & D* 76-78; C Dundonald 78-80; Bp's C Ballybeen 80-88; I Willowfield 88-00; Dir Think Again 00-04; I Ballynafeigh St Jude from 04; Can Belf Cathl from 03. *10 Mornington, Belfast BT7 3JS* Tel (028) 9050 4976 E-mail norman.jardine2@ntlworld.com
JARDINE, Thomas Parker. b 44. Oak Hill Th Coll BA87. **d** 87 **p** 88. C Crowborough *Chich* 87-91; R Dersingham w Anmer and Shernborne *Nor* 91-00; P-in-c Southport SS Simon and Jude *Liv* 00-03; V Southport SS Simon and Jude w All So 03-09; C Southport All SS 03-09; rtd 09. *16 Donnelly Road, Bournemouth BH6 5NW*
JARMAN, Christopher (Kit). b 38. QUB BA63. Wells Th Coll 69. **d** 71 **p** 72. C Leckhampton SS Phil and Jas *Glouc* 71-73; Chapl RN 73-93; Chapl Rossall Sch Fleetwood 94; R Stirling *St And* 94-03; Chapl ATC 97-03; rtd 03; Warrant from 04. *Ground Floor Flat 2, 4 Branksome Park, Longsdale Road, Oban PA34 5JZ* Tel and fax (01631) 563535
JARMAN, John Geoffrey. b 31. IEng. S'wark Ord Course 75. **d** 78 **p** 79. NSM Chigwell *Chelmsf* 78-81; NSM Leytonstone St Marg w St Columba 81-87; C Walthamstow St Sav 87-89; V Gt Bentley and P-in-c Frating w Thorrington 89-92; C Wanstead St Mary w Ch Ch 92-95; rtd 95; Perm to Offic *Chelmsf* from 95. *18 Hillside Crescent, Holland-on-Sea, Clacton-on-Sea CO15 6PB* Tel (01255) 812746
JARMAN, Michael Robert. b 48. Trin Coll Bris 07. **d** 09 **p** 10. NSM Caerleon and Llanfrechfa *Mon* from 09. *Ahlan House, 4 Hafod Mews, Caerleon Road, Ponthir, Newport NP18 1PY* Tel (01633) 423619 E-mail michael@ahlan48.fsnet.co.uk
JARMAN, Robert Joseph. b 59. Van Mildert Coll Dur BA90. **d** 92 **p** 93. C Llanishen and Lisvane 92-93; C Whitchurch 93-94. *47 Penydre, Rhiwbina, Cardiff CF14 6EJ*
JARRATT, Canon Robert Michael. b 39. K Coll Lon BD62 AKC62 NY Th Sem DMin85. **d** 63 **p** 64. C Corby St Columba *Pet* 63-67; Lay Tr Officer *Sheff* 67-71; Ind Chapl *S'wark* 72-80; P-in-c Betchworth 76-80; V Ranmoor *Sheff* 80-01; P-in-c Worsbrough and Dir Post-Ord Tr 01-05; RD Hallam 87-94; Hon Can Sheff Cathl 95-05; rtd 05. *42 Storthwood Court, Storth Lane, Sheffield S10 3HP* Tel 0114-230 7036 E-mail michaeljarratt42@yahoo.co.uk
JARRATT, Stephen. b 51. Edin Univ BD76 St Kath Coll Liv CertEd77. **d** 78 **p** 79. C Horsforth *Ripon* 78-81; C Stanningley St Thos 81-84; P-in-c Fishponds St Jo *Bris* 84-85; V 85-92; V Chapel Allerton *Ripon* 92-04; AD Allerton 97-04; TR Clifton *S'well* 04-08; AD W Bingham 07-08; P-in-c Haxby and Wigginton *York* 08-09; R from 09. *The Rectory, 3 Westfield Close, Wigginton, York YO32 2JG* Tel (01904) 760455 E-mail jarratt312@btinternet.com
✠**JARRETT, The Rt Revd Martyn William.** b 44. K Coll Lon BD67 AKC67 Hull Univ MPhil91. **d** 68 **p** 69 **c** 94. C Bris St Geo 68-70; C Swindon New Town 70-74; C Northolt St Mary *Lon* 74-76; V Northolt St Jos 76-81; V Hillingdon St Andr 81-83; P-in-c Uxbridge Moor 82-83; V Uxbridge St Andr w St Jo 83-85; Selection Sec ACCM 85-88; Sen Selection Sec 89-91; V Chesterfield St Mary and All SS *Derby* 91-94; Suff Bp Burnley *Blackb* 94-00; Hon Can Blackb Cathl 94-00; Suff Bp Beverley (PEV) *York* from 00; Hon Asst Bp Dur, Ripon and Sheff from 00; Hon Asst Bp Man, S'well and Wakef from 01; Hon Asst Bp Bradf from 02; Hon Asst Bp Liv from 03; Hon Asst Bp Newc from 10; Hon Can Wakef Cathl 01-10. *3 North Lane, Roundhay, Leeds LS8 2QJ* Tel 0113-265 4280 Fax 265 4281 E-mail bishop-of-beverley@3-north-lane.fsnet.co.uk
JARRETT, René Isaac Taiwo. b 49. Milton Margai Teachers' Coll Sierra Leone TCert79 Lon Inst of Educn BEd94. Sierra Leone Th Hall 80. **d** 83 **p** 85. Dn Freetown St Luke Sierra Leone 83-85; C Freetown Bp Elwin Memorial Ch 85-89; Hon C St Pancras w St Jas and Ch Ch *Lon* 89-95; C Bloomsbury St Geo w Woburn Square Ch Ch 95-11; rtd 11; Perm to Offic *Lon* and *S'wark* from 11. *2 Woburn Mansions, Torrington Place, London WC1E 7HL* Tel (020) 7580 5165 Mobile 07853-348143 E-mail jarrorene@yahoo.co.uk
JARROW, Suffragan Bishop of. *See* BRYANT, The Rt Revd Mark Watts
JARVIS, Ian Frederick Rodger. b 38. Bris Univ BA60. Tyndale Hall Bris 61. **d** 63 **p** 64. C Penge Ch Ch w H Trin *Roch* 63-67; C Bilston St Leon *Lich* 67-71; V Lozells St Silas *Birm* 71-76; V Chaddesden St Mary *Derby* 76-95; V Newhall 95-02; rtd 02; Perm to Offic *Derby* from 02. *29 Springfield Road, Midway, Swadlincote DE11 0BZ* Tel (01283) 551589

JARVIS, Mrs Lynda Claire. b 46. Southn Univ CQSW87. STETS 95. d 98 p 99. C Chandler's Ford Win 98-01; rtd 01. Largo Santana 3, Tavira, 8800-701 Algarve, Portugal Tel (00351) (281) 323553 Mobile 961-166240

JARVIS, Miss Mary. b 35. Leeds Univ BA57 Lon Univ CertEd59. Cranmer Hall Dur 78. dss 80 d 87 p 94. Low Harrogate St Mary Ripon 80-84; Wortley de Leeds 84-87; C 87-88; C Upper Armley 88-94; C Holbeck 94-95; rtd 95; Perm to Offic Ripon from 01. 71 Burnsall Croft, Leeds LS12 3LH Tel 0113-279 7832 E-mail mjarvis@amserve.com

JARVIS, Nathan John. b 73. Ox Brookes Univ BA97 Leeds Univ MA04. St Steph Ho Ox BTh06. d 06 p 07. C Hartlepool H Trin Dur 06-09; V Kingstanding St Luke Birm from 09. The Vicarage, 49 Caversham Road, Birmingham B44 0LW Tel 0121-680 4919 E-mail fr.nathan@yahoo.com

JARVIS, Mrs Pamela Ann. b 51. Sussex Univ BEd74. SWMTC 97. d 00 p 01. C Braunton Ex 00-03; C Combe Martin, Berrynarbor, Lynton, Brendon etc 03-04; TV 04-10; rtd 10. Crocnamac, Tomouth Road, Appledore, Bideford EX39 1QD Tel (01237) 420454 Mobile 07773-900523 E-mail pajarvis@virgin.net

JARVIS, Peter Timothy. b 64. St Jo Coll Nottm 02. d 04 p 05. C Thatcham Ox 04-06; TV from 06. The Vicarage, 1 Cowslip Crescent, Thatcham RG18 4DE Tel (01635) 867336 Mobile 07713-113581 E-mail revdpj@btinternet.com

JARVIS, Rupert Charles Melbourne. b 69. St Andr Univ MA92 Univ of Wales (Swansea) MPhil96. Cuddesdon Coll 96. d 98 p 99. C Swansea St Mary w H Trin S & B 98-99; Min Can Brecon Cathl 99-01; CF 01-08; Asst Chapl Shiplake Coll Henley 08-09; Chapl Denstone Coll Uttoxeter from 09. Denstone College, Uttoxeter ST14 5HN Tel (01889) 590484

JARVIS, Stephen John. b 55. WEMTC 04. d 07 p 08. NSM Bisley, Chalford, France Lynch, and Oakridge Glouc from 07. 8 Ollney Road, Minchinhampton, Stroud GL6 9BX Tel (01453) 884566 Mobile 07921-548467 E-mail stephen@sjarvis.freeserve.co.uk

JARVIS, Steven. WEMTC. d 07 p 08. NSM Ludlow Heref from 07. 3 Townsend Close, Ludlow SY8 1UN Tel (01584) 874284

JARY, Ms Helen Lesley. b 69. Lanc Univ BA91. St Jo Coll Nottm 05. d 07 p 08. C Oulton Broad Nor 07-11; TV Thetford from 11. Cloverfield Vicarage, 24 Foxglove Road, Thetford IP24 2XF Tel (01842) 755769 Mobile 07990-501683 E-mail helenjary@btinternet.com

JASON, Mark Andrew. b 73. Madras Univ BA94 S Asia Inst for Advanced Chr Studies MA96. Gurukul Lutheran Th Coll & Research Inst BD00. p 01. India 01-03; Perm to Offic Ab from 03. 31 Gladstone Place, Aberdeen AB10 6UX Tel (01224) 321714 E-mail m.a.jason@abdn.ac.uk

JASPER, Prof David. b 51. Jes Coll Cam BA72 MA76 Keble Coll Ox BD80 Dur Univ PhD83 Ox Univ DD02 Uppsala Univ Hon ThD07 FRSE06. St Steph Ho Ox BA75 MA79. d 76 p 77. C Buckingham Ox 76-79; C Dur St Oswald 80; Chapl Hatf Coll Dur 81-88; Dir Cen Study of Lit and Th Dur 88-91; Prin St Chad's Coll Dur 88-91; Reader and Dir Cen Study of Lit and Th Glas Univ from 91; Vice-Dean of Div 95-98; Dean of Div 98-02; Lic to Offic Glas 91-08; NSM Hamilton from 08. Netherwood, 124 Old Manse Road, Wishaw ML2 0EP Tel and fax (01698) 373286 E-mail d.jasper@arts.gla.ac.uk

JASPER, David Julian McLean. b 44. Dur Univ BA66. Linc Th Coll 66. d 68 p 69. C Redruth Truro 68-72; TV 72-75; V St Just in Penwith 75-86; P-in-c Sancreed 82-86; C Reading St Matt Ox 96-00; P-in-c 00-02; R S Petherton w the Seavingtons B & W 02-11; rtd 11. East Barton, North Petherwin, Launceston PL15 8LR Tel (01566) 785996 Mobile 07767-814533 E-mail davidjasper5dy@btinternet.com

JASPER, James Roland. b 32. CA Tr Coll 56 NEOC 82. d 84 p 84. C Newburn Newc 84-86; V Ansley Cov 86-97; rtd 97; Perm to Offic Leic from 97 and Cov from 03. 69 Desford Road, Newbold Verdon, Leicester LE9 9LG Tel (01455) 822567

JASPER, Jonathan Ernest Farley. b 50. AKC72. St Aug Coll Cant 73. d 73 p 74. C Cheshunt St Alb 73-75; C Bedford St Paul 75-77; C Bedford St Pet w St Cuth 77-79; Chapl Southn Univ 77-80; Chapl Lon Univ Medical Students 80-86; PV Chich Cathl 86-89; P-in-c Earls Colne and White Colne Chelmsf 89-94; P-in-c Colne Engaine 89-94; R Earls Colne w White Colne and Colne Engaine 95-02; C Christchurch Win 03-08; Perm to Offic from 08. 18 Locksley Drive, Ferndown BH22 8JY Tel (01202) 894998 E-mail jefjasper@btinternet.com

JAUNDRILL, John Warwick. b 47. MCIM81. Qu Coll Birm 86. d 88 p 89. C Bistre St As 88-91; P-in-c Towyn and St George 91-92; V 92-02; C Llanrhos 06-09; C Rhos-Cystennin from 09. 5 Traeth Penrhyn, Penrhyn Bay, Llandudno LL30 3RN Tel (01492) 544845

JAY, Colin. b 62. Keble Coll Ox BA85 St Jo Coll Dur BA89. Cranmer Hall Dur 87. d 90 p 91. C Bishopwearmouth St Gabr Dur 90-94; C Newton Aycliffe 94; TV 94-96; TV Gt Aycliffe 96-03; AD Sedgefield 99-03; Chapl Co Dur & Darlington Priority Services NHS Trust from 03. Earls House Hospital, Lanchester Road, Durham DH1 5RD Tel 0191-333 6262 E-mail colsar@netscapeonline.co.uk

JAY, Ms Nicola Mary. b 37. SRN58. NEOC 88. d 91 p 94. Par Dn Whitburn Dur 91-94; C 94-95; P-in-c Sacriston and Kimblesworth 95-00; rtd 00. 29 Church Street, Sacriston, Durham DH7 6JL Tel 0191-371 0152

JAY, Richard Hylton Michael. b 31. Bris Univ BEd75. Sarum & Wells Th Coll 77. d 79 p 80. NSM Bath St Barn w Englishcombe B & W 79-81; NSM Saltford w Corston and Newton St Loe 81-88; R Hatch Beauchamp w Beercrocombe, Curry Mallet etc 89-97; rtd 97; Perm to Offic B & W from 97. Stableside, 5 Princess Road, Taunton TA1 4SY Tel (01823) 335531

JAYNE, Martin Philip. b 49. Man Univ BA71 MRTPI73. Carl Dioc Tr Course 87. d 90 p 91. NSM Natland Carl from 90; Dioc Officer for NSM 04-08. 12 Longmeadow Lane, Natland, Kendal LA9 7QZ Tel (01539) 560942 E-mail martjay@btinternet.com

JEANES, Gordon Paul. b 55. Ox Univ BA79 MA82 BD90 Univ of Wales (Lamp) PhD99. St Steph Ho Ox 80. d 82 p 83. C S Wimbledon H Trin and St Pet S'wark 82-85; C Surbiton St Andr and St Mark 85-90; Chapl St Chad's Coll Dur 90-93; Sub-Warden St Mich Coll Llan 94-98; Lect Th Univ of Wales (Cardiff) 94-98; V Wandsworth St Anne S'wark 98-08; P-in-c Wandsworth St Faith 05-08; V Wandsworth St Anne w St Faith from 08; Dioc Voc Adv from 99. St Anne's Vicarage, 182 St Ann's Hill, London SW18 2RS Tel (020) 8874 2809 E-mail gordon.jeanes@virgin.net

JEANS, The Ven Alan Paul. b 58. MIAAS84 MIBCO84 Southn Univ BTh89 Univ of Wales (Lamp) MA03. Sarum & Wells Th Coll 86. d 89 p 90. C Parkstone St Pet w Branksea and St Osmund Sarum 89-93; P-in-c Bishop's Cannings, All Cannings etc 93-98; Par Development Adv from 98; Can and Preb Sarum Cathl from 02; Adn Sarum from 03; RD Alderbury 05-07; Dioc Dir of Ords from 07. Herbert House, 118 Lower Road, Salisbury SP2 9NW Tel (01722) 336290 or (01380) 840373 Fax (01722) 411990 or (01380) 848247 E-mail adsarum@salisbury.anglican.org

JEANS, David Bockley. b 48. Mert Coll Ox BA71 MA80 PGCE73 Man Univ MPhil98. Trin Coll Bris 83. d 85 p 86. C Clevedon St Andr and Ch Ch B & W 85-88; V Wadsley Sheff 88-96; Dir Studies Wilson Carlile Coll of Evang 96; Prin 97-06; Dean Coll of S Cross New Zealand 06-08; P-in-c Deepcar Sheff from 08. St John's Vicarage, 27 Carr Road, Deepcar, Sheffield S36 2PQ Tel 0114-288 5138

JEANS, Miss Eleanor Ruth. b 75. Man Univ BMus97 GRNCM97. Ridley Hall Cam 09. d 11. C Thurnby w Stoughton Leic from 11. 59 Somerby Road, Thurnby, Leicester LE7 9PR Tel 07795-660144 (mobile) E-mail eleanor@thurnbychurch.org

JEAPES (née PORTER), Mrs Barbara Judith. b 47. Cam Inst of Educn TCert68. Carl Dioc Tr Inst 91. d 94 p 95. NSM Egremont and Haile Carl from 94. 15 Millfields, Beckermet CA21 2YY Tel (01946) 841489 E-mail barbara.jeapes@btinternet.com

JEAVONS, Mrs Margaret Anne. b 51. Liv Poly BA72 Bris Univ BA01 St Kath Coll Liv PGCE74. Trin Coll Bris 99. d 01 p 02. C Totnes w Bridgetown, Berry Pomeroy etc Ex 01-05; V Sutton St Mich York from 05. St Michael's Vicarage, 751 Marfleet Lane, Hull HU9 4TJ Tel (01482) 374509 E-mail jeavons2951@jeavons2951.karoo.co.uk

JEAVONS, Maurice. b 32. Ely Th Coll 60. d 62 p 63. C Longton St Jo Lich 62-68; V Wednesfield St Greg 68-81; V Lower Gornal 81-90; NSM Willenhall St Anne 92-93; C Tunstall 93-99; rtd 99; Hon C Wolverhampton St Steph Lich 99-09; Perm to Offic from 09. 17 Colaton Close, Wolverhampton WV10 9BB Tel (01902) 351118

JEE, Jonathan Noel. b 63. BNC Ox BA84 MA88. Wycliffe Hall Ox 85. d 88 p 89. C Brampton St Thos Derby 88-92; TV Hinckley H Trin Leic 92-00; V Leamington Priors St Paul Cov from 00. The Vicarage, 15 Lillington Road, Leamington Spa CV32 5YS Tel (01926) 772132 or 427149 E-mail jonathan.jee@ntlworld.com

JEFF, Canon Gordon Henry. b 32. St Edm Hall Ox BA56 MA60. Wells Th Coll 59. d 61 p 62. C Sydenham St Bart S'wark 61-64; C Kidbrooke St Jas 64-66; V Clapham St Paul 66-72; V Raynes Park St Sav 73-79; RD Merton 77-79; V Carshalton Beeches 79-86; P-in-c Petersham 86-90; Chapl St Mich Convent 90-96; Hon Can S'wark Cathl 93-96; rtd 96; Perm to Offic B & W from 07. 9 Barnetts Well, Draycott, Cheddar BS27 3TF Tel (01934) 744943

JEFFCOAT, Rupert Edward Elessing. b 70. St Cath Coll Cam BA92 MA96 FRCO91. WMMTC 02. d 05. NSM Brisbane Cathl Australia from 05. GPO Box 421, Brisbane Qld 4001, Australia Tel (0061) (7) 3835 2231 E-mail rjeffcoat@freenetname.co.uk

JEFFERIES, Michael Lewis. b 45. St Jo Coll Nottm. d 87 p 88. C Pudsey St Lawr and St Paul Bradf 87-93; V Beckenham St Jo Roch 93-00; TV Modbury, Bigbury, Ringmore w Kingston etc Ex 00-10; rtd 10. 6 Sherford Down Road, Sherford, Kingsbridge TQ7 2BQ Tel (01548) 531644 E-mail mandejefferies@fsmail.net

JEFFERIES, Preb Phillip John. b 42. St Chad's Coll Dur BA65 MA91. d 67 p 68. C Tunstall Ch Ch Lich 67-71; C

Wolverhampton St Pet 71-74; P-in-c Oakengates 74-80; V 80-82; P-in-c Ketley 78-82; V Horninglow 82-00; RD Tutbury 97-00; TR Stafford 00-07; Bp's Adv on Hosp Chapl 82-06; Preb Lich Cathl 99-07; rtd 07; Perm to Offic *Lich* from 07. *16 Morley's Hill, Burton-on-Trent DE13 0TA* Tel (01283) 544013

JEFFERS, Cliff Peter. b 69. CITC BTh98. **d** 98 **p** 99. C Limerick City *L & K* 98-01; I Clonenagh w Offerlane, Borris-in-Ossory etc *C & O* 01-04; I Athy w Kilberry, Fontstown and Kilkea *D & G* from 04. *The Rectory, Church Road, Athy, Co Kildare, Republic of Ireland* Tel (00353) (59) 863 1446 Fax 863 1490 E-mail athy@glendalough.anglican.org

JEFFERS, Neil Gareth Thompson. b 78. St Jo Coll Ox BA99 MA05. Oak Hill Th Coll MTh07. **d** 07 **p** 08. C Lowestoft Ch Ch *Nor* 07-11; Chapl Pangbourne Coll from 11. *Sunbeam, Bere Court Road, Pangbourne, Reading RG8 8JY* Tel 07769-586260 (mobile) E-mail neiljeffers2003@yahoo.co.uk

JEFFERSON, Charles Dudley. b 55. St Pet Coll Ox BA78 MA81. Ridley Hall Cam 79. **d** 81 **p** 82. C Chadkirk *Ches* 81-84; C Macclesfield St Pet 84-85; C Macclesfield Team 85-89; R Elworth and Warmingham 89-99; Chapl Framlingham Coll 99-01; Chapl Rendcomb Coll Cirencester and P-in-c Rendcomb *Glouc* 01-09; R Thrapston, Denford and Islip *Pet* from 09. *The Rectory, 48 Oundle Road, Thrapston, Kettering NN14 4PD* Tel (01832) 730814 E-mail revcjefferson@tiscali.co.uk

JEFFERSON, David Charles. b 33. Leeds Univ BA57. Coll of Resurr Mirfield 57. **d** 59 **p** 60. C Kennington Cross St Anselm *S'wark* 59-62; C Richmond St Mary 62-64; Chapl Wilson's Gr Sch Camberwell 64-93; Chapl Wilson's Sch Wallington 75-99; Public Preacher *S'wark* 64-74; Hon C Carshalton Beeches 74-04; rtd 93; Perm to Offic *S'wark* from 04. *15 Sandown Drive, Carshalton SM5 4LN* Tel (020) 8669 0640 *or* 8773 2931

JEFFERSON, Michael William. b 41. K Coll Lon AKC64. WMMTC 96. **d** 98 **p** 99. C Four Oaks *Birm* 98-02; P-in-c Longdon *Lich* 02-08; Local Min Adv (Wolverhampton) 02-08; rtd 08; Perm to Offic *Lich* and *Portsm* from 09; *Birm* from 10. *9 Soma House, 380 Springfield Road, Sutton Coldfield B75 7JH* Tel 0121-329 2214 E-mail rev michael.uk@yahoo.co.uk

✠**JEFFERTS SCHORI, The Most Revd Katharine.** b 54. Stanford Univ BS Oregon State Univ MS77 PhD83. Ch Div Sch of Pacific MDiv94 Hon DD01. **d** 94 **p** 94 **c** 01. C Corvallis Gd Samaritan USA 94-01; Chapl Benton Hospice Service 95-00; Instructor Oregon State Univ 96-99; Bp Nevada 01-06; Presiding Bp from 06. *Episcopal Church Center, 815 Second Avenue, New York NY 10017, USA* Tel (001) (212) 716 6271 Fax 490 3298 E-mail pboffice@episcopalchurch.org

JEFFERY, Graham. b 35. Qu Coll Cam BA58. Wells Th Coll 58. **d** 60 **p** 61. C Southampton Maybush St Pet *Win* 60-63; Australia 63-66; C E Grinstead St Swithun *Chich* 66-68; C-in-c The Hydneye CD 68-74; V Wick 74-76; V Hove 76-78; P-in-c Newtimber w Pyecombe 78-82; R Poynings w Edburton, Newtimber and Pyecombe 82-92; P-in-c Sullington and Thakeham w Warminghurst 92-95; rtd 96; NSM Poynings w Edburton, Newtimber and Pyecombe *Chich* 97-99; Perm to Offic from 00. *Eton Cottage, Compton, Chichester PO18 9HD* Tel (023) 9263 1220

JEFFERY (née CAW), Mrs Hannah Mary. b 69. Birm Univ BMus91. St Jo Coll Nottm MA95. **d** 95 **p** 96. C Northampton St Giles *Pet* 95-99; Hon C Hanger Hill Ascension and W Twyford St Mary *Lon* 99-04; TV Northampton Em *Pet* 04-11; Continuing Minl Development Officer from 11; Chapl Bp Stopford Sch from 11. *Bouverie Court, 6 The Lakes, Northampton NN4 7YD* E-mail hannahjeffery@classmail.co.uk

JEFFERY, Mrs Jennifer Ann. b 45. Philippa Fawcett Coll CertEd66. STETS. **d** 02 **p** 03. NSM Wilton *B & W* from 02; Chapl Bp Henderson Sch from 07. *4 Southwell, Trull, Taunton TA3 7HU* Tel (01823) 286589 E-mail jenny@jajeffery.freeserve.co.uk

JEFFERY, Jonathan George Piers. b 63. Man Univ LLB84. Ripon Coll Cuddesdon 95. **d** 97 **p** 98. C Lee-on-the-Solent *Portsm* 97-01; V Leigh Park from 01; V Warren Park from 01; AD Havant from 09. *The Vicarage, Riders Lane, Havant PO9 4QT* Tel (023) 9247 5276

JEFFERY, Kenneth Charles. b 40. Univ of Wales BA64 Linacre Coll Ox BA67 MA70. St Steph Ho Ox 64. **d** 67 **p** 68. C Swindon New Town *Bris* 67-68; C Summertown *Ox* 68-71; C Brighton St Pet *Chich* 71-77; V Ditchling 77-00; rtd 00. *62 Fruitlands, Malvern WR14 4XA* Tel (01684) 567042 E-mail kenneth@jeffery333.fslife.co.uk

JEFFERY, Michael Frank. b 48. Linc Th Coll 74. **d** 76 **p** 77. C Caterham Valley *S'wark* 76-79; C Tupsley *Heref* 79-82; P-in-c Stretton Sugwas 82-84; P-in-c Bishopstone 83-84; P-in-c Kenchester and Bridge Sollers 83-84; V Whiteshill *Glouc* 84-92; P-in-c Randwick 92; V Whiteshill and Randwick 93-02; TV Bedminster *Bris* 02-09; C from 09. *Bedminster Rectory, 287 North Street, Bedminster, Bristol BS3 1JP* Tel 0117-902 3866

JEFFERY, Peter James. b 41. Leeds Univ BSc63. Oak Hill Th Coll 64. **d** 66 **p** 67. C Streatham Park St Alb *S'wark* 66-70; C Northampton St Giles *Pet* 70-73; C Rushden St Pet 73-76; C Rushden w Newton Bromswold 77-78; V Siddal *Wakef* 78-85; V

Sowerby Bridge w Norland 85-98; P-in-c Cornholme 98-00; P-in-c Walsden 98-00; V Cornholme and Walsden 00-05; rtd 05; Perm to Offic *Wakef* from 07. *12 Highcroft Road, Todmorden OL14 5LZ* Tel (01706) 839781 E-mail jeffrey@cornden.freeserve.co.uk

JEFFERY, Peter Noel. b 37. Pemb Coll Ox BA60 MA64. Linc Th Coll 60. **d** 62 **p** 63. C W Smethwick *Birm* 62-64; P-in-c Bordesley St Andr 64-69; R Turvey *St Alb* 69-98; P-in-c Stevington 79-98; rtd 98. *Franconia Cottage, The Gardens, Adstock, Buckingham MK18 2JF* Tel (01296) 715770

JEFFERY, Richard William Christopher. b 43. Ex Univ BA65. Coll of Resurr Mirfield 66. **d** 68 **p** 69. C Widley w Wymering *Portsm* 68-71; C Salisbury St Mich *Sarum* 71-74; TV Ridgeway 74-80; V Stanford in the Vale w Goosey and Hatford *Ox* 80-89; V Topsham *Ex* 89-09; RD Aylesbeare 01-07; rtd 09; P-in-c Topsham *Ex* from 09; P-in-c Countess Wear from 09. *The Vicarage, Globefields, Topsham, Exeter EX3 0EZ* Tel (01392) 876120 E-mail richardwcj@blueyonder.co.uk

JEFFERY, The Very Revd Robert Martin Colquhoun. b 35. K Coll Lon BD58 AKC58 Birm Univ Hon DD99 FRSA91. **d** 59 **p** 60. C Grangetown *Dur* 59-61; C Barnes St Mary *S'wark* 61-63; Asst Sec Miss and Ecum Coun Ch Assembly 64-68; Sec Dept Miss and Unity BCC 68-71; V Headington *Ox* 71-78; RD Cowley 73-78; P-in-c Tong *Lich* 78-83; V 83-87; Dioc Missr 78-80; Adn Salop 80-87; Dean Worc 87-96; Can Res and Sub-Dean Ch Ch *Ox* 96-02; Select Preacher Ox Univ 91, 97, 98 and 02; rtd 02. *47 The Manor House, Bennett Crescent, Cowley, Oxford OX4 2UG* Tel (01865) 749706 E-mail rmci@btopenworld.com

JEFFERYES, June Ann. b 37. Dur Univ BA58. WMMTC 87. **d** 90 **p** 94. NSM Caverswall *Lich* 90-92; NSM Caverswall and Weston Coyney w Dilhorne 92-02; rtd 02; Perm to Offic *Lich* from 02. *24 Glen Drive, Alton, Stoke-on-Trent ST10 4DJ* Tel (01538) 702150 E-mail ann@jefferyes.co.uk

JEFFERYES, Preb Neil. b 37. St Andr Univ BSc60 Lon Univ BD62. Tyndale Hall Bris 60. **d** 63 **p** 64. C St Helens St Helen *Liv* 63-68; V Barrow St Mark *Carl* 68-77; RD Furness 74-77; P-in-c Tetsworth *Ox* 77-81; P-in-c Adwell w S Weston 77-81; P-in-c Stoke Talmage w Wheatfield 77-81; RD Aston 81-85; R Tetsworth, Adwell w S Weston, Lewknor etc 81-86; V Caverswall *Lich* 86-92; P-in-c Dilhorne 86-92; RD Cheadle 91-98; V Caverswall and Weston Coyney w Dilhorne 92-02; Preb Lich Cathl 97-02; rtd 02; Perm to Offic *Lich* from 02. *24 Glen Drive, Alton, Stoke-on-Trent ST10 4DJ* Tel (01538) 702150 E-mail neil@jefferyes.co.uk

JEFFORD, Mrs Margaret June. b 50. Univ of Wales RGN81. St Mich Coll Llan 94. **d** 96 **p** 97. C Risca *Mon* 96-98; C Pontypool 98-00; TV 00-02; V Newbridge w Crumlin 02-04; V Newbridge from 04. *St Paul's Vicarage, High Street, Newbridge, Newport NP11 4FW* Tel (01495) 243975

JEFFORD, Peter Ernest. b 29. AKC53. **d** 54 **p** 55. C Berkeley *Glouc* 54-57; C Petersfield w Sheet *Portsm* 57-61; Chapl Churcher's Coll 57-61; R Rollesby w Burgh w Billockby *Nor* 62-71; V Watton 71-81; V Watton w Carbrooke and Ovington 81-82; Offg Chapl RAF 71-82; P-in-c Brampford Speke *Ex* 82-83; P-in-c Cadbury 82-83; P-in-c Thorverton 82-83; P-in-c Upton Pyne 82-83; TR Thorverton, Cadbury, Upton Pyne etc 83-92; rtd 92; Perm to Offic *Ox* 92-96 and from 03; Hon C Ox St Mary V w St Cross and St Pet 96-99; P-in-c Whitchurch St Mary 00-03; Chapl Plater Coll 96-05. *22 Ashlong Road, Headington, Oxford OX3 0NH* Tel (01865) 760593

JEFFORD, Ronald. b 46. St Mich Coll Llan. **d** 91 **p** 92. C Ebbw Vale *Mon* 91-94; TV 94-95; R Bedwas and Rudry 95-98; V Abersychan and Garndiffaith 98-03; TV Mynyddislwyn 03-05; rtd 05; Perm to Offic *Mon* from 06. *1 Brecon Heights, Victoria, Ebbw Vale NP23 6WP* Tel (01495) 352909

JEFFREE, Robin. b 29. AKC54. **d** 55 **p** 56. C N Harrow St Alb *Lon* 55-59; C Hendon St Mary 59-62; V Manea *Ely* 62-67; V Hartford 67-83; R Denver 83-94; V Ryston w Roxham 83-94; V W Dereham 83-94; rtd 94; Perm to Offic *Nor* from 94. *3 Church Lane, Hindolveston, Dereham NR20 5BT* Tel (01263) 861857

JEFFREY, Katrina. *See* METZNER, Mrs Katrina

JEFFREYS, David John. b 45. S Dios Minl Tr Scheme 89. **d** 92 **p** 93. NSM Bexhill St Barn *Chich* 92-95; Chapl Hastings and Rother NHS Trust 95-02; Chapl E Sussex Hosps NHS Trust 02-05; Chapl Team Ldr 05-09; rtd 09; Perm to Offic *Chich* from 10. *4 Osbern Close, Bexhill-on-Sea TN39 4TJ* Tel (01424) 843672 E-mail frdavid@onetel.com

JEFFREYS (née DESHPANDE), Mrs Lakshmi Anant. b 64. Liv Univ BSc86 Ex Univ PGCE87. Wycliffe Hall Ox BTh94. **d** 94 **p** 95. C Long Eaton St Jo *Derby* 94-97; Chapl Nottm Trent Univ 98-03; Perm to Offic *Derby* 03-04; Dioc Miss Adv from 04. *43 White Street, Derby DE22 1HB* Tel (01332) 224432 E-mail lakshmi.jeffreys@derby.anglican.org

JEFFREYS, Timothy John. b 58. Man Univ BSc79. Cranmer Hall Dur 83. **d** 86 **p** 87. C Goodmayes All SS *Chelmsf* 86-88; Perm to Offic *S'wark* 92-93; Hon C S Lambeth St Anne and All SS 93-96; C Croydon St Jo 96-06; V Brixton Road Ch Ch from

06. *The Vicarage, 96 Brixton Road, London SW9 6BE* Tel (020) 7793 0621 E-mail tim.jeffreys@btopenworld.com
JEFFRIES, Miss Frances Alyx. b 59. Bris Poly BA82. Local Minl Tr Course 00. **d** 04 **p** 05. OLM Gainsborough and Morton *Linc* 04-11; C Skegness Gp from 11. *The Rectory, 2 Elmwood Drive, Ingoldmells, Skegness PE25 1QG* Tel (01754) 873439 E-mail francesjeffries789@btinternet.com
JEFFRIES, Keith. b 48. St Steph Ho Ox 91. **d** 93 **p** 94. C St Marychurch *Ex* 93-96; TV Wood Green St Mich w Bounds Green St Gabr etc *Lon* 96-98; V The Hydneye *Chich* 98-00; Chapl Univ of Greenwich *Roch* 00-02; Chapl Kent Inst of Art and Design 00-02; Chapl Tenerife Sur *Eur* 02-03; Perm to Offic *Roch* 03-04; Bp's Adv on Chr/Muslim Relns *Birm* 04-07; Chapl Oakington Immigration Reception Cen 07-09; rtd 09. *Edificio las Tejas, Bloque 3, Vivenda 12, Lugar Pasitos 38, Pueblo de Mogan, 35140 Las Palmas, Spain* E-mail fatherkeithjeffries@hotmail.com
JELF, Miss Pauline Margaret. b 55. Chich Th Coll 88. **d** 90 **p** 94. Par Dn Clayton *Lich* 90-94; C Knutton 94-98; P-in-c Silverdale and Alsagers Bank 94-98; Perm to Offic 98-02; C Clayton 02; C Betley and Madeley 02-04; C Trent Vale 03-06. *11 Stafford Avenue, Newcastle ST5 3BN* Tel (01785) 639545
JELLEY, Ian. b 54. Newc Univ MA94 Dur Univ MA03. NEOC 89. **d** 91 **p** 92. C Jarrow *Dur* 91-95; P-in-c Leam Lane 95-96; Chapl HM Pris Holme Ho 96-01; R Grindon, Stillington and Wolviston *Dur* 01-03; rtd 03; Perm to Offic *Dur* from 03. *1 Rievaulx Avenue, Billingham TS23 2BP*
JELLEY, James Dudley. b 46. Linc Th Coll 78. **d** 80 **p** 81. C Stockwell Green St Andr *S'wark* 80-85; V Camberwell St Phil and St Mark 85-93; Perm to Offic 93-96; V Camberwell St Luke from 96; RD Camberwell 00-06. *St Luke's Vicarage, 30 Commercial Way, London SE15 5JQ* Tel and fax (020) 7703 5587
JELLEY (née CAPITANCHIK), Mrs Sophie Rebecca. b 72. Leeds Univ BA93. Wycliffe Hall Ox MPhil97. **d** 97 **p** 98. C Shipley St Pet *Bradf* 97-00; CMS Uganda 00-03; C Churt and Hindhead *Guildf* 03-10; V Burgess Hill St Andr *Chich* from 10. *St Andrew's Vicarage, 2 Cants Lane, Burgess Hill RH15 0LG* Tel (01444) 232023 E-mail sophie@jelley.f9.co.uk
JENKIN, Canon the Hon Charles Alexander Graham. b 54. BScEng. Westcott Ho Cam 81. **d** 84 **p** 85. C Binley *Cov* 84-88; TV Canvey Is *Chelmsf* 88-94; TR Melton Mowbray *Leic* 94-08; RD Framland 98-02; Hon Can Leic Cathl 06-08; V Ipswich St Mary-le-Tower *St E* from 08; Bp's Interfaith Adv from 09. *The Vicarage, 18 Kingsfield Avenue, Ipswich IP1 3TA* Tel and fax (01473) 289001 E-mail charles@jenkin.uk.net
JENKIN, Christopher Cameron. b 36. BNC Ox BA61 MA64. Clifton Th Coll 61. **d** 63 **p** 64. C Walthamstow St Mary *Chelmsf* 63-68; C Surbiton Hill Ch Ch *S'wark* 68-78; V Newport St Jo *Portsm* 78-88; TR Newbarns w Hawcoat *Carl* 88-01; rtd 01; Perm to Offic *Carl* from 01. *Beckside, Orton, Penrith CA10 3RX* Tel (01539) 624410
JENKINS, Alan David. b 60. Bris Poly BA83 Spurgeon's Coll MTh02. Wycliffe Hall Ox 93. **d** 95 **p** 96. C Tunbridge Wells St Jas w St Phil *Roch* 95-01; TV S Gillingham 01-07; R Gt Bookham *Guildf* from 07. *The Rectory, 2A Fife Way, Bookham, Leatherhead KT23 3PH* Tel (01372) 452405 E-mail alan.jenkins@stnicolasbookham.org.uk
JENKINS, Allan Kenneth. b 40. Lon Univ BD63 AKC63 MTh69 PhD85. St Mich Coll Llan 63. **d** 64 **p** 65. C Llanblethian w Cowbridge 64-70; Lect Serampore Coll India 70-76; V Llanarth w Clytha, Llansantffraed and Bryngwyn *Mon* 76-78; Dir of Studies Chich Th Coll 78-83; P-in-c Fowlmere and Thriplow *Ely* 83-87; Sen Tutor EAMTC 84-87; Sen Chapl Cardiff Colls 87-95; Dioc Dir Post-Ord Tr *Llan* 88-95; P-in-c Sidlesham *Chich* 95-08; Tutor Chich Univ 95-09. *6 Clive Mews, Loftus Street, Cardiff CF5 1HY* Tel (029) 2035 9076 Mobile 07788-427159 E-mail allankjenkins@tiscali.co.uk
JENKINS, Miss Anne Christina. b 47. Birm Univ BA70 Hull Univ CertEd71 St Jo Coll Dur BA77. Cranmer Hall Dur 75. **dss** 78 **d** 87 **p** 94. E Coatham *York* 78-81; OHP 81-87; Perm to Offic *York* 81-87; Ghana 87-88; Par Dn Beeston *Ripon* 88-93; Par Dn Leeds Gipton Epiphany 93-94; V Leeds St Marg and All Hallows 94-99; rtd 99; Perm to Offic *York* from 00. *28 Hill Cottages, Rosedale East, Pickering YO18 8RG* Tel (01751) 417130
JENKINS, Audrey Joan. b 36. TCert61. St D Coll Lamp. **d** 01 **p** 06. Par Dn Marshfield and Peterstone Wentloog etc *Mon* 01-06; NSM Llanrumney from 06. *10 Cwrt Pencraig, 8 Caerau Crescent, Newport NP20 4HG* Tel (01633) 263470 E-mail glyn.jenkins@homecall.co.uk
JENKINS, Catherine. b 34. SWMTC 04. **d** 05 **p** 06. NSM Silverton, Butterleigh, Bickleigh and Cadeleigh *Ex* from 05. *Butterleigh House, Butterleigh, Cullompton EX15 1PH* Tel (01884) 855379
JENKINS, Clifford Thomas. b 38. Westmr Coll Ox MTh02 IEng MIEIecIE. Sarum & Wells Th Coll 74. **d** 77 **p** 78. Chapl Yeovil Coll 77-86; Hon C Yeovil w Kingston Pitney *B & W* 77-80; P-in-c 80-86; Chs FE Liaison Officer *B & W, Bris* and *Glouc* 87-90; Perm to Offic *B & W* from 87; FE Adv Gen Syn Bd of

Educn and Meth Ch 90-98; rtd 98. *Bethany, 10 Grove Avenue, Yeovil BA20 2BB* Tel (01935) 475043 E-mail clifford.jenkins@virgin.net
JENKINS, Clive Ronald. b 57. Chich Univ BA08. Ripon Coll Cuddesdon 81. **d** 84 **p** 85. C E Grinstead St Swithun *Chich* 84-87; C Horsham 87-88; TV 88-90; Dioc Youth Chapl 90-96; P-in-c Amberley w N Stoke and Parham, Wiggonholt etc 93-96; V Southbourne w W Thorney from 96; RD Westbourne from 11. *The Vicarage, 271 Main Road, Southbourne, Emsworth PO10 8JE* Tel (01243) 372436
JENKINS, David. See JENKINS, Canon William David
JENKINS, David. See JENKINS, Preb Richard David
✠**JENKINS, The Rt Revd David Edward.** b 25. Qu Coll Ox BA51 MA54 Dur Univ DD87. Linc Th Coll 52. **d** 53 **p** 54 **c** 84. C Birm Cathl 53-54; Lect Qu Coll Birm 53-54; Chapl Qu Coll Ox 54-69; Lect Th Ox Univ 55-69; Can Th Leic Cathl 66-82; Dir WCC Humanum Studies 69-73; Dir Wm Temple Foundn Man 73-78; Jt Dir 79-94; Prof Th and RS Leeds Univ 79-84; Bp Dur 84-94; rtd 94; Hon Asst Bp Ripon and Leeds from 94. *5 Chapel Court, Newgate, Barnard Castle DL12 8NG* Tel (01833) 631182
JENKINS, The Ven David Harold. b 61. SS Coll Cam BA84 MA87 Ox Univ BA88 MA94 Univ of Wales (Lamp) PhD08. Ripon Coll Cuddesdon 86. **d** 89 **p** 90. C Chesterton Gd Shep *Ely* 89-91; C Earley St Pet *Ox* 91-94; V Blackpool St Mich *Blackb* 94-99; V Broughton 99-04; AD Preston 04; Can Res Carl Cathl 04-10; Dir of Educn 04-10; Adn Sudbury *St E* from 10. *Sudbury Lodge, Stanningfield Road, Great Whelnetham, Bury St Edmunds IP30 0TL* Tel (01284) 386942 Mobile 07900-990073 E-mail archdeacon.david@stedmundsbury.anglican.org
JENKINS, David Noble. b 25. CCC Cam BA47 MA50. Cuddesdon Coll 48. **d** 50 **p** 51. C Northampton St Matt *Pet* 50-54; Chapl Hurstpierpoint Coll 54-59; USPG 60-65; Chapl Eastbourne Coll 66-74; V Jarvis Brook *Chich* 75-90; rtd 90; USA 90-92; Perm to Offic *Chich* from 92. *25 Ramsay Hall, 9-13 Byron Road, Worthing BN11 3HN* Tel (01903) 207524 E-mail dnjlittleb@waitrose.com
JENKINS, David Roland. b 32. Kelham Th Coll 55. **d** 59 **p** 60. C Middlesbrough St Jo the Ev *York* 59-60; C Kingston upon Hull St Alb 60-64; C Roehampton H Trin *S'wark* 64-68; V Dawley St Jerome *Lon* 68-73; R Harlington 73-98; rtd 98; Perm to Offic *Lon* 99-10. *19 Ramsay Hall, 9-13 Byron Road, Worthing BN11 3HN* Tel (01903) 369964
JENKINS, David Thomas. b 43. Ox Univ MA94 RIBA70. S'wark Ord Course 76. **d** 79 **p** 80. NSM Merthyr Tydfil and Cyfarthfa *Llan* 79-86; NSM Brecon St David w Llanspyddid and Llanilltyd *S & B* 86-91; P-in-c Llangiwg 91-92; V 92-01; Chapl Puerto de la Cruz Tenerife *Eur* 02-09; rtd 09. *15 Highmoor, Maritime Quarter, Swansea SA1 1YE* Tel 07974-748476 (mobile) E-mail djenkins@tinyonline.co.uk
JENKINS, The Ven David Thomas Ivor. b 29. K Coll Lon BD52 AKC52 Birm Univ MA63. **d** 53 **p** 54. C Bilton *Cov* 53-56; V Wolston 56-61; Asst Dir RE *Carl* 61-63; V Carl St Barn 63-72; V Carl St Cuth 72-76; P-in-c Carl St Mary w St Paul 72-76; V Carl St Cuth w St Mary 76-91; Dioc Sec 84-95; Hon Can Carl Cathl 76-91; Can Res 91-95; Adn Westmorland and Furness 95-99; rtd 99; Perm to Offic *Carl* from 00. *Irvings House, Sleagill, Penrith CA10 3HD* Tel (01931) 714400
JENKINS, Eric Robert. b 52. Poly Cen Lon BSc74. STETS 97. **d** 00 **p** 01. C Weybridge *Guildf* 00-04; R Cobham and Stoke D'Abernon from 04; RD Leatherhead from 08. *The Vicarage, St Andrew's Walk, Cobham KT11 3EQ* Tel (01932) 862109 Mobile 07747-844689 E-mail er.jenkins@btinternet.com
JENKINS, Mrs Fiona. b 59. Dur Univ BSc80 York St Jo Coll MA04. St Jo Coll Nottm 04. **d** 06 **p** 07. C Settle *Bradf* 06-08; C Linton in Craven from 08; C Kettlewell w Conistone, Hubberholme etc from 08; C Burnsall w Rylstone from 08. *The Rectory, Church Lane, Burnsall, Skipton BD23 6BP* Tel (01756) 720331 E-mail fiona.jenkins@bradford.anglican.org
JENKINS, The Very Revd Frank Graham. b 23. St D Coll Lamp BA47 Jes Coll Ox BA49 MA53. St Mich Coll Llan 49. **d** 50 **p** 51. C Llangeinor 50-53; Chapl Llan Cathl 53-60; CF (TA) 56-61; V Abertillery *Mon* 60-64; V Risca 64-75; Can St Woolos Cathl 67-76; V Caerleon 75-76; Dean Mon 76-90; rtd 90; Lic to Offic *Mon* 90-09. *Gravelly Close, Bottom Road, Radnage, High Wycombe HP14 4EQ*
JENKINS, Garry Frederick. b 48. Southn Univ BTh79. Chich Th Coll 75. **d** 79 **p** 80. C Kingsbury St Andr *Lon* 79-84; C Leigh St Clem *Chelmsf* 84-88; P-in-c Brentwood St Geo 88-94; V from 94; Chapl NE Lon Mental Health Tr from 02. *The Vicarage, 28 Robin Hood Road, Brentwood CM15 9EN* Tel (01277) 213618 E-mail g.f.jenkins@amserve.net
JENKINS, Canon Gary John. b 59. York Univ BA80 CertEd81. Oak Hill Th Coll BA89. **d** 89 **p** 90. C Norwood St Luke *S'wark* 89-94; P-in-c St Helier 94-95; V 95-01; V Redhill H Trin from 01; Hon Can S'wark Cathl from 06. *4 Carlton Road, Redhill RH1 2BX* Tel (01737) 779917 E-mail gary@htredhill.com
JENKINS, Canon Jeanette. b 42. St Jo Coll Nottm 83. **dss** 84 **d** 86 **p** 94. NSM Kilmarnock *Glas* 84-94; NSM Irvine St Andr LEP

84-94; NSM Ardrossan 84-94; Asst Chapl Crosshouse Hosp 86-94; Chapl Ayrshire Hospice 90-02; Can St Mary's Cathl from 99. *4 Gleneagles Avenue, Kilwinning KA13 6RD* Tel (01294) 553383 Mobile 07775-595901 E-mail revj.jenkins@btinternet.com

JENKINS, John Francis. b 46. Ripon Hall Ox 77 Ripon Coll Cuddesdon 75. **d** 77 **p** 78. C Filton *Bris* 77-79; C Bris St Andr Hartcliffe 79-84; P-in-c Bris H Cross Inns Court 84-85; V 85-95; R Odcombe, Brympton, Lufton and Montacute *B & W* from 95. *The Rectory, Street Lane, Higher Odcombe, Yeovil BA22 8UP* Tel (01935) 863184

JENKINS, John Howard David. b 51. Birm Univ BA72. St Steph Ho Ox 72. **d** 74 **p** 75. C Milford Haven *St D* 74-77; PV Llan Cathl 77-81; Chapl Lowther Coll and V Choral St As Cathl 81-84; C Neath w Llantwit 84-86; Chapl Colston's Sch Bris 86-91; Chapl Blue Coat Sch Birm 91-04; Chapl R Masonic Sch for Girls Rickmansworth 04-10; rtd 10. *Address temp unknown*

JENKINS, John Morgan. b 33. Open Univ BA96. Mon Dioc Tr Scheme 82. **d** 85 **p** 86. NSM Cwmbran *Mon* 85-02; rtd 02. *5 Ridgeway Avenue, Newport NP20 5AJ* Tel (01633) 662231

JENKINS, John Raymond. b 26. K Coll Lon 52. **d** 53 **p** 54. C Wrexham *St As* 53-56; Hon C 77-82; C Welshpool 56-57; V Mochdre 57-65; V Llandysul *St D* 67-70; V Llanfair Caereinion w Llanllugan *St As* 67-70; V Llanychaearn w Llanddeiniol *St D* 82-91; rtd 91; Chapl Lanzarote *Eur* 95-97. *24 Llys Hen Ysgol, North Road, Aberystwyth SY23 2ER* Tel (01970) 623994

JENKINS, John Richard. b 68. Dundee Univ LLB90 Leeds Univ MA98. St Steph Ho Ox BA94. **d** 94 **p** 95. C Brighouse and Clifton *Wakef* 94-97; C Barnsley St Mary 97-99; Dir Affirming Catholicism from 05. *St Matthew's House, 20 Great Peter Street, London SW1P 2BU* Tel (020) 7233 0235 E-mail director@affirmingcatholicism.org.uk

JENKINS, Julian James. b 56. St Mich Coll Llan 97. **d** 99 **p** 00. C Whitchurch *Llan* 99-01; TV Aberavon 01-05; TV Cowbridge 05-11; P-in-c Llandyfodwg and Cwm Ogwr from 11. *The Vicarage, Coronation Street, Ogmore Vale, Bridgend CF32 7HE* Tel (01656) 840248

JENKINS, Canon Lawrence Clifford. b 45. Open Univ BA77 AKC70. St Aug Coll Cant. **d** 71 **p** 72. C Osmondthorpe St Phil *Ripon* 71-74; C Monkseaton St Mary *Newc* 74-78; V Shiremoor 78-84; V Wheatley Hills *Sheff* 84-95; RD Doncaster 92-95; V Greenhill 95-10; Hon Can Sheff Cathl 08-10; rtd 10; Perm to Offic *Sheff* from 11. *10 Chiltern Crescent, Sprotbrough, Doncaster DN5 7RE* Tel (01302) 856587 E-mail lawriejenkins@virginmedia.com

JENKINS, Canon Paul Morgan. b 44. Sussex Univ BEd68 Fitzw Coll Cam BA73 MA76. Westcott Ho Cam 71. **d** 74 **p** 75. C Forest Gate St Edm *Chelmsf* 74-77; Chapl Bryanston Sch 77-85; P-in-c Stourpaine, Durweston and Bryanston *Sarum* 77-83; Asst Chapl and Housemaster Repton Sch Derby 84-89; Dean of Chpl 89-91; R Singleton *Chich* 91-97; V E Dean 91-97; V W Dean 91-97; Dir St Columba's Retreat and Conf Cen 97-07; Chapl Community of St Pet Woking 03-07; P-in-c Dunsfold and Hascombe *Guildf* from 07; Hon Can Guildf Cathl from 05. *The Rectory, Church Green, Dunsfold, Godalming GU8 4LT* Tel (01483) 200207 Mobile 07973-848941 E-mail pjenkins44@aol.com

JENKINS (née RICHARDSON), Pauline Kate. b 41. RGN62 Nottm Univ CertEd80 RNT83. St Jo Coll Nottm 91. **d** 94 **p** 98. Uganda 94-96; Perm to Offic *S'well* 96-98; NSM Selston 98-01; NSM Annesley w Newstead 01-03; rtd 03; Perm to Offic *S'well* from 03. *The Cottage, 5 Main Street, Stathern, Melton Mowbray LE14 4HW* Tel (01949) 869474

JENKINS, Richard. See JENKINS, John Richard

JENKINS, Preb Richard David. b 33. Magd Coll Cam BA58 MA. Westcott Ho Cam 59. **d** 61 **p** 62. C Staveley *Derby* 61-64; C Billingham St Aid *Dur* 64-68; V Walsall Pleck and Bescot *Lich* 68-73; R Whitchurch 73-97; RD Wem and Whitchurch 85-95; P-in-c Tilstock and Whixall 92-95; Preb Lich Cathl 93-97; rtd 97; Perm to Offic *Lich* from 99. *The Council House, Council House Court, Castle Street, Shrewsbury SY1 2AU* Tel (01743) 270051

JENKINS, Richard Morvan. b 44. St Mich Coll Llan 65. **d** 69 **p** 70. C Tenby *St D* 69-73; V Llanrhian w Llanhywel and Carnhedryn etc 73-80; R Johnston w Steynton 80-93; V St Ishmael's w Llan-saint and Ferryside 93-09; rtd 09. *Geirionydd, 7 Dwynant, Furnace Road, Burry Port SA16 0YQ* Tel (01554) 834761

JENKINS, Robert. See JENKINS, Eric Robert

JENKINS, Canon Robert Francis. b 33. BNC Ox BA57 MA59. Wycliffe Hall Ox 57. **d** 59 **p** 60. C Hall Green Ascension *Birm* 59-63; V Dosthill and Wood End 63-71; V Brandwood 71-85; V Sutton Coldfield St Columba 85-97; Hon Can S Malawi from 87; rtd 97; Perm to Offic *Birm* from 97 and *Lich* from 00. *4 The Pines, Lichfield WS14 9XA* Tel (01543) 252176

JENKINS, Timothy David. b 52. Pemb Coll Ox BA73 MLitt77 MA82 St Edm Ho Cam BA84 St Edm Ho Cam PhD01. Ridley Hall Cam 82. **d** 85 **p** 86. C Kingswood *Bris* 85-87; Sen Chapl Nottm Univ 88-92; Dean of Chpl Jes Coll Cam 92-10; Fell from

92; Can Th Leic Cathl 04-09. *50 Stanley Road, Cambridge CB5 8BL* Tel (01223) 363185 *or* 339303 E-mail tdj22@jesus.cam.ac.uk

JENKINS, Canon William David. b 42. Birm Univ BA63. St D Coll Lamp LTh65. **d** 65 **p** 66. C Gorseinon *S & B* 65-67; C Llanelli *St D* 67-72; V Clydach *S & B* 72-82; Chapl Gwynedd Hosp NHS Trust 82-97; V Llanrhos *St As* 82-97; RD Llanrwst 84-96; Can Cursal St As Cathl 93-97; TR Tenby *St D* 97-07; rtd 07. *Kildare, 96 Conway Road, Llandudno LL30 1PP* Tel 07791-738018 (mobile)

JENKINSON, Margaret. b 40. MCSP62. Carl Dioc Tr Inst 89. **d** 92 **p** 94. NSM Preesall *Blackb* 92-96; NSM Lanercost, Walton, Gilsland and Nether Denton *Carl* 96-04; P-in-c Lorton and Loweswater w Buttermere from 04. *The Vicarage, Loweswater, Cockermouth CA13 0RU* Tel (01900) 85237 E-mail m.jenkinson517@btinternet.com

JENKINSON, Rachel Elisabeth. b 66. Somerville Coll Ox BA87 Cranfield Univ MBA99. Ridley Hall Cam 05. **d** 07 **p** 08. C Chorleywood Ch Ch *St Alb* from 07. *4 Berry Way, Rickmansworth WD3 7EY* Tel (01923) 447185

JENKYNS, Preb Henry Derrik George. b 30. Sarum Th Coll 57. **d** 60 **p** 61. C Kettering SS Pet and Paul 60-64; V Shrewsbury St Geo *Lich* 64-71; V Wednesbury St Paul Wood Green 71-76; V Stokesay *Heref* 76-86; P-in-c Acton Scott 76-86; RD Condover 80-86; Preb Heref Cathl 83-96; R Kington w Huntington, Old Radnor, Kinnerton etc 86-96; rtd 96; Perm to Offic *Heref* from 96. *Llantroft, Newcastle, Craven Arms SY7 8PD* Tel (01588) 640314

JENKYNS, John Thomas William Basil. b 30. Univ of Wales (Lamp) BA34 St Cath Coll Ox BA37 MA62. Wycliffe Hall Ox 54. **d** 57 **p** 58. C Neasden cum Kingsbury St Cath *Lon* 57-60; C S Lyncombe *B & W* 60-64; V Gt Harwood St Bart *Blackb* 64-66; R Colne St Bart 66-69; V Chard St Mary *B & W* 69-87; Preb Wells Cathl 87; V Swaffham *Nor* 87-89; V Overbury w Teddington, Alstone etc *Worc* 89-95; rtd 95; Perm to Offic *St E* from 10. *9 Aldeburgh Road, Leiston IP16 4JY*

JENKYNS, Stephen. b 60. Univ of Wales (Cardiff) BTh02. St Mich Coll Llan 99. **d** 02 **p** 03. C Penarth w Lavernock *Llan* 02-04; C Penarth and Llandough 04-06; TV Cyncoed *Mon* 06-09; P-in-c Llandaff N from 09. *All Saints Vicarage, 59 Station Road, Llandaff North, Cardiff CF14 2FB* Tel (029) 2031 2510

JENNER, Miss Brenda Ann. b 54. Culham Coll Ox BEd80. St Jo Coll Nottm 86. **d** 88. Par Dn Leigh St Mary *Man* 88-92; Par Dn Leic Ch Sav 92-94. *18 Chatsworth Avenue, Wigston, Leicester LE18 4LF*

JENNER, Michael Albert. b 37. Oak Hill Th Coll 75. **d** 77 **p** 78. C Mile Cross *Nor* 77-80; P-in-c Easton *Ely* 80-86; P-in-c Ellington 80-86; P-in-c Grafham 80-86; P-in-c Spaldwick w Barham and Woolley 80-86; Perm to Offic *Roch* from 01; rtd 02. *Saffron Meadow, Manaccan, Helston TR12 6EN* Tel (01326) 231965 Mobile 07831-826954

JENNER, Peter John. b 56. Chu Coll Cam BA77 PhD80 MA81. St Jo Coll Nottm 82. **d** 85 **p** 86. C Upperby St Jo *Carl* 85-88; Chapl Reading Univ 88-96; P-in-c Mellor *Derby* 96-99; V 99-06; V Mellor *Ches* from 06; RD Chadkirk from 08. *The Vicarage, Church Road, Mellor, Stockport SK6 5LX* Tel 0161-427 1203 E-mail jennerfamily@btinternet.com

JENNER, William George. b 37. Nottm Univ BSc59 K Coll Lon PGCE60. **d** 97 **p** 98. OLM Gillingham w Geldeston, Stockton, Ellingham etc *Nor* 97-05; Perm to Offic from 05. *3 Woodland Drive, Kirby Cane, Bungay NR35 2PT* Tel (01508) 518229

JENNETT, The Ven Maurice Arthur. b 34. St Jo Coll Dur BA60. Cranmer Hall Dur 60. **d** 62 **p** 63. C Marple All SS *Ches* 62-67; V Withnell *Blackb* 67-75; V Stranton *Dur* 75-91; Crosslinks Zimbabwe 92-99; Asst P Nyanga St Mary Magd 92-93; R 93-99; Can and Adn Manicaland N 97; rtd 99; Perm to Offic *Ripon* from 01. *2 Southfield Avenue, Ripon HG4 2NR* Tel (01765) 607842 E-mail maurice@mjennett.fsnet.co.uk

JENNINGS, Anne. See SMITH, Mrs Anne

JENNINGS, Clive John. b 57. Trin Coll Bris. **d** 00 **p** 01. C Milton *B & W* 00-02; C Clevedon St Andr and Ch Ch from 02. *12 Princes Road, Clevedon BS21 7SZ* Tel (01275) 872134 E-mail clive.jennings@blueyonder.co.uk

✠**JENNINGS, The Rt Revd David Willfred Michael.** b 44. AKC66. **d** 67 **p** 68 **c** 00. C Walton St Mary *Liv* 67-69; C Christchurch *Win* 69-73; V Hythe 73-80; V Romford St Edw *Chelmsf* 80-92; RD Havering 85-92; Hon Can Chelmsf Cathl 87-92; Adn Southend 92-00; Suff Bp Warrington *Liv* 00-09; rtd 09; Perm to Offic *Ox* from 10; Hon Asst Bp Glouc from 10. *The Laurels, High Street, Northleach, Cheltenham GL54 3ET* Tel (01451) 860743

JENNINGS, Duncan William. b 54. UWE MA. STETS 05. **d** 08 **p** 09. C Southampton Thornhill St Chris *Win* from 08. *22 Lydgate Green, Southampton SO19 6LP* Tel (023) 8040 5313

JENNINGS, Canon Frederick David. b 48. K Coll Lon BD73 AKC73 Loughb Univ MPhil98. St Aug Coll Cant 73. **d** 74 **p** 75. C Halesowen *Worc* 74-77; Perm to Offic *Birm* 78-80; Perm to Offic *Leic* 78-80 and 85-87; P-in-c Snibston 80-85; Community Relns Officer 81-84; P-in-c Burbage w Aston Flamville 87-91; R

449

from 91; Hon Can Leic Cathl 03-10; Can Th from 10. *The Rectory, New Road, Burbage, Hinckley LE10 2AW* Tel (01455) 230512 Fax 250833 E-mail revdavidjennings@btinternet.com

JENNINGS, Ian. b 47. Leeds Univ MA98. NOC 95. **d** 97 **p** 97. NSM Hackenthorpe *Sheff* 97-01; Asst Chapl HM Pris Doncaster 97-98; Chapl HM Pris and YOI Doncaster 98-01; V Sheff St Cuth 01-06; TR Aston cum Aughton w Swallownest and Ulley from 06. *The Rectory, 91 Worksop Road, Aston, Sheffield S26 2EB* Tel 0114-287 2272

JENNINGS, Ian Richard. b 65. Liv Univ BA88 Wolv Poly PGCE91. Trin Coll Bris 07. **d** 09 **p** 10. C Pedmore *Worc* from 09. *25 Sandhurst Avenue, Pedmore, Stourbridge DY9 0XQ* Tel 07722-019096 (mobile) E-mail ianandsuejennings@googlemail.com

JENNINGS, Janet. b 38. SCM71 SRN74. Oak Hill Th Coll BA87. **d** 88 **p** 97. Par Dn Stevenage St Pet Broadwater *St Alb* 88-90; Perm to Offic *St As* from 92. *Pound House, Forden, Welshpool SY21 8NU* Tel (01938) 580400

JENNINGS, Jonathan Peter. b 61. K Coll Lon BD83. Westcott Ho Cam 84. **d** 86 **p** 87. C Peterlee *Dur* 86-89; C Darlington St Cuth 89-92; Dioc Communications Officer *Man* 92-95; Broadcasting Officer Gen Syn 95-01; Perm to Offic *S'wark* 95-98; Hon C Banstead *Guildf* 98-04; Abp Cant's Press Sec 01-08; Perm to Offic *Cant* and *Roch* 05-08; P-in-c Gillingham St Aug *Roch* from 08; RD Gillingham from 10. *St Augustine's Vicarage, Rock Avenue, Gillingham ME7 5PW* Tel (01634) 850288 E-mail revjpj@aol.com

JENNINGS, Margaret. b 50. **d** 11. OLM Marsh Green w Newtown *Liv* from 11. *26D Mill Lane, Upholland, Skelmersdale WN8 0HJ* Tel (01695) 627804

JENNINGS, Mervyn. b 39. Sarum & Wells Th Coll 83. **d** 85 **p** 86. C Knowle *Bris* 85-89; P-in-c Cressing and Rural Youth Development Officer *Chelmsf* 89-93; V Barkingside St Fran 93-08; rtd 08; Perm to Offic *Chelmsf* from 08. *36 Harris Close, Romford RM3 8PQ* Tel (01708) 341047 E-mail father.mervyn.jennings@o2.co.uk

JENNINGS, Mrs Pamela. b 49. SRN71. NEOC 05. **d** 08 **p** 09. NSM Scarborough St Mary w Ch Ch and H Apostles *York* from 08. *26 Ling Hill, Scarborough YO12 5HS* Tel (01723) 365528 E-mail kenandpamjennings@gmail.com

JENNINGS, Peter James. b 28. Univ of Wales (Lamp) BA56. St D Coll Lamp LTh57. **d** 57 **p** 58. C Dudley St Jo *Worc* 57-60; C Dudley St Thos 61-64; Chapl HM Borstal Portland 64-66; Chapl HM Pris Wakef 66-70; Chapl HM Pris Liv 70-76; RD Walton Liv 75-76; Chapl HM Pris Styal 76-77 and 88-92; N Regional Chapl 76-82; Asst Chapl Gen (N) 82-88; Perm to Offic *Man* 77-89 and 00-08; *Ches* from 79; rtd 93. *6 St Ann's Road South, Cheadle SK8 3DZ* Tel 0161-437 8828

JENNINGS, Robert Henry. b 46. St Jo Coll Dur BA69 MA79. Qu Coll Birm. **d** 72 **p** 73. C Dursley *Glouc* 72-74; C Coleford w Staunton 75-78; TV Bottesford w Ashby *Linc* 78-83; TV Witney *Ox* 83-89; V Lane End w Cadmore End from 89. *The Vicarage, 7 Lammas Way, Lane End, High Wycombe HP14 3EX* Tel (01494) 881913

JENNINGS, Thomas Robert. b 24. TCD BA47 MA51. **d** 48 **p** 49. C Drumragh *D & R* 48-51; CF 51-67; I Killeshandra *K, E & A* 67-70; I Newcastle w Newtownmountkennedy and Calary *D & G* 70-92; Can Ch Ch Cathl Dublin 88-92; rtd 92. *66 Seacourt, Newcastle, Greystones, Co Wicklow, Republic of Ireland* Tel (00353) (1) 281 0777 Mobile 87-763 3418 E-mail bojen66@yahoo.co.uk

JENNINGS, Walter James. b 37. Birm Univ BMus60 MA90. Qu Coll Birm 77. **d** 80 **p** 81. Hon C Hampton in Arden *Birm* 80-84; Chapl St Alb Aided Sch Highgate Birm 84-86; C Wotton-under-Edge w Ozleworth and N Nibley *Glouc* 86-89; V Pittville All SS 89-98; rtd 98; Chapl Beauchamp Community 98-00; Perm to Offic *Worc* from 98. *Flat 7, Leamington Court, Wells Road, Malvern WR14 4HF* Tel (01684) 561513 E-mail walter.linda@virgin.net

JENNO, Charles Henry. b 25. Wells Th Coll 65. **d** 66 **p** 67. C Shirehampton *Bris* 66-69; C Fishponds St Mary 69-73; V Thornes *Wakef* 73-78; V Carleton 78-82; V E Hardwick 78-82; rtd 82; Perm to Offic *Wakef* from 82. *32 Tower Avenue, Upton, Pontefract WF9 1EE* Tel (01977) 640925

JENSEN, Alexander Sönderup. b 68. Tübingen Univ 94 St Jo Coll Dur PhD97 Ox Univ MTh01. St Steph Ho Ox 97. **d** 99 **p** 00. C Norton St Mich *Dur* 99-02; Lect CITC 02-05; Lect Murdoch Univ Australia from 05. *School of Social Sciences and Humanities, Murdoch University, South Street, Murdoch, W Australia 6150* Tel (0061) (8) 9360 6625 Fax 9360 6480 E-mail a.jensen@murdoch.edu.au

JENSEN, Erik Henning. b 33. Copenhagen Univ BPhil51 Harvard Univ STM54 Worc Coll Ox BLitt58 DPhil69. Ripon Hall Ox. **d** 58 **p** 59. C Highwood *Chelmsf* 58-59; C Simanggang Sarawak 59-61; Borneo 61-62; Malaysia 63-03; rtd 02. *The Rook House, Maugersbury, Stow-on-the-Wold GL54 1HP* Tel (01451) 830171

✠**JENSEN, The Most Revd Peter Frederick.** b 43. Lon Univ BD70 Sydney Univ MA76 Ox Univ DPhil80. Moore Th Coll

Sydney. **d** 69 **p** 70 **c** 01. C Broadway Australia 69-76; Perm to Offic *Ox* 76-79; Lect Moore Th Coll 73-76 and 80-84; Prin 85-01; Can Sydney 89-01; Abp Sydney from 01. *PO Box Q190, QVB PO NSW 1230, Australia* Tel (0061) (2) 9265 1521 Fax 9265 1504

JENSON, Philip Peter. b 56. Ex Coll Ox BA78 MA82 Down Coll Cam BA80 MA86 PhD88. Ridley Hall Cam 80. **d** 87 **p** 88. C Gt Warley Ch Ch *Chelmsf* 87-89; Lect Trin Coll Bris 89-05; Lect Ridley Hall Cam from 05. *Ridley Hall, Cambridge CB3 9HG* Tel (01223) 746580 Fax 746581 E-mail ppj22@cam.ac.uk

JEPP, Malcolm Leonard. b 44. SWMTC 06. **d** 09 **p** 10. NSM Meneage *Truro* from 09. *Polpidnick Cottage, Porthallow, St Keverne, Helston TR12 6PL* Tel and fax (01326) 281031 Mobile 07797-505539 E-mail lenjepp@jeppassociates.co.uk

JEPP (*née* NUGENT), **Mrs Mary Patricia.** b 55. Mt St Vincent Univ Canada BA79 Univ of New Brunswick BEd80 Open Univ MA03. ERMC 05. **d** 08 **p** 09. C Godmanchester *Ely* 08-11; P-in-c Alconbury cum Weston from 11; P-in-c Winwick from 11; P-in-c Hamerton from 11; P-in-c Gt w Lt Gidding and Steeple Gidding from 11; P-in-c Upton and Copmanford from 11; P-in-c Buckworth from 11. *The Vicarage, Church Way, Alconbury, Huntingdon PE28 4DX* Tel (01480) 890284 E-mail m.jepp@btinternet.com

JEPPS, Philip Anthony. b 34. BNC Ox BA58 MA68. Wycliffe Hall Ox 58. **d** 60 **p** 73. C Elton All SS *Man* 60; Perm to Offic *Pet* 70-73; R Church w Chapel Brampton 74-80; P-in-c Harlestone 79-80; V Kettering St Andr 80-94; V Conisbrough *Sheff* 94-01; rtd 01; Perm to Offic *Heref* from 01. *2 Eagle Cottages, Church Lane, Orleton, Ludlow SY8 4HT* Tel (01568) 780517

JEPSON, Mrs Ann. **d** 11. NSM Hurst Green and Mitton *Bradf* from 11. *Ribblesdale View, Greenside, Ribchester, Preston PR3 3ZJ* Tel (01254) 878177

JEPSON, Joanna Elizabeth. b 76. Trin Coll Bris BA99 Cam Univ MA03. Ridley Hall Cam 01. **d** 03 **p** 04. C Plas Newton *Ches* 03-06; Chapl Lon Coll of Fashion 06-11; P-in-c Fulham St Pet 06-09. *Address temp unknown* E-mail joeyjep@yahoo.com

JERMAN, Edward David. b 40. Trin Coll Carmarthen CertEd61. **d** 87 **p** 88. NSM Llandrygarn w Bodwrog and Heneglwys etc *Ban* from 87. *Haulfre, Gwalchmai, Holyhead LL65 4SG* Tel (01407) 720856

JERMY, Jack. b 22. ACP65. Ripon Hall Ox 64. **d** 65 **p** 66. Hd Master SS Simon and Jude Primary Sch Bolton 62-80; C Bolton SS Simon and Jude *Man* 65-74; P-in-c Rivington 74-93; NSM Horwich and Rivington 93-95; rtd 95; Perm to Offic *Man* 95-08. *179 Preston Road, Whittle-le-Woods, Chorley PR6 7PR* Tel (01257) 480466

JERMY, Stuart John. b 66. Middx Univ BEd90. Wycliffe Hall Ox 01. **d** 03 **p** 04. C New Thundersley *Chelmsf* 03-07; V St Martins and Weston Rhyn *Lich* from 07. *The Vicarage, Church Lane, St Martins, Oswestry SY11 3AP* Tel (01691) 778468 Mobile 07801-071443 E-mail sjermy@toucansurf.com

JERSEY, Dean of. See KEY, The Very Revd Robert Frederick

JERVIS, Christopher. b 53. Loughb Univ BEd75. Wycliffe Hall Ox 80. **d** 82 **p** 83. C Woodford Wells *Chelmsf* 82-85; Chapl Felsted Sch 85-87; Chapl Canford Sch from 87. *Merryvale, Canford Magna, Wimborne BH21 3AF* Tel (01202) 887722 E-mail cj@canford.com

JERVIS, William Edward. b 47. MRICS74. Linc Th Coll 74. **d** 77 **p** 78. C W Bromwich All SS *Lich* 77-80; C Horsham Chich 80-86; R W Tarring from 86. *West Tarring Rectory, Glebe Road, Worthing BN14 7PF* Tel (01903) 235043 Fax 218877

JESSETT, David Charles. b 55. K Coll Lon BD77 AKC77 MTh. Westcott Ho Cam 78. **d** 79 **p** 80. C Aveley *Chelmsf* 79-82; C Walthamstow St Pet 82-85; P-in-c Hunningham *Cov* 85-91; P-in-c Wappenbury w Weston under Wetherley 85-91; Progr Dir Exploring Chr Min Scheme 85-91; Dir CME 87-90; Perm to Offic 90-97; P-in-c Barford w Wasperton and Sherbourne from 97; P-in-c Hampton Lucy w Charlecote and Loxley from 07. *The Rectory, Church Lane, Barford, Warwick CV35 8ES* Tel (01926) 624238 E-mail david@jessetts.freeserve.co.uk

JESSIMAN, Elaine Rae. b 59. Wall Hall Coll Aldenham BEd95. STETS 05. **d** 08 **p** 09. C Leigh Park *Portsm* 08-10; C Portsdown from 10. *The Vicarage, 61 Hart Plain Avenue, Waterlooville PO8 8RG* Tel (023) 9226 4551 E-mail elaine.jessiman@ntlworld.com

JESSIMAN, Timothy Edward. b 58. Portsm Univ MA06. Oak Hill Th Coll 88. **d** 91 **p** 92. C Baldock w Bygrave *St Alb* 91-95; C Bideford *Ex* 95-96; TV Bideford, Northam, Westward Ho!, Appledore etc 96-00; Chapl Grenville Coll Bideford 95-00; Chapl N Devon Healthcare NHS Trust 98-00; P-in-c Hartplain *Portsm* 00-06; V from 06. *The Vicarage, 61 Hart Plain Avenue, Waterlooville PO8 8RG* Tel (023) 9226 4551 E-mail tim.jessiman@ntlworld.com

JESSON, Alan Francis. b 47. TD89. Ealing Coll of Educn 70 Loughb Univ MLS77 Selw Coll Cam MA87 ALA70 FLA91 MBIM82. EAMTC 88. **d** 91 **p** 92. NSM Swavesey *Ely* 91-95; NSM Fen Drayton w Conington and Lolworth etc 95-00; CF (ACF) 92-96; Sen Chapl ACF from 96; R Outwell *Ely* from 00; R Upwell St Pet from 00; Perm to Offic *Nor* from 01. *The Rectory, 5*

New Road, Upwell, Wisbech PE14 9AB Tel (01945) 772213 Fax 07075-055234 E-mail alan.jesson@ely.anglican.org

JESSON, George Albert Oswald (Ossie). b 54. Trin Coll Bris 90. **d** 92 **p** 93. C Thorpe Acre w Dishley *Leic* 92-01; C Chilwell *S'well* 01-08. *The Rectory, Lincoln Road, East Markham, Newark NG22 0SH* Tel (01777) 870965 E-mail revo.jesson@ntlworld.com

JESSON, Julia Margaret. b 54. St Matthias Coll Bris CertEd75 Nottm Univ MA04. EMMTC 01. **d** 04 **p** 05. NSM Stapleford *S'well* 04-07; C Kimberley 07-08; P-in-c E Markham w Askham, Headon w Upton and Grove 08-11; P-in-c Dunham w Darlton, Ragnall, Fledborough etc 08-11; TV Retford Area from 11. *The Rectory, Lincoln Road, East Markham, Newark NG22 0SH* Tel (01777) 870965 E-mail julia.jesson@ntlworld.com

JESSOP, Canon Gillian Mary. b 48. Hatf Poly BSc71 Nottm Univ MEd85 Homerton Coll Cam PGCE80. EAMTC 91. **d** 94 **p** 95. C Gt Yarmouth *Nor* 94-97; R Gt w Lt Addington and Woodford *Pet* 97-02; R Passon from 02; Asst Dir Tr for Readers 00-02; Dir from 02; RD Pet from 10; Can Pet Cathl from 11. *The Rectory, 236 Fulbridge Road, Peterborough PE4 6SN* Tel (01733) 578228 E-mail rev.gill@tesco.net

JESSOP, John Edward. b 46. RMCS BSc71 CEng78 MIET78. S Dios Minl Tr Scheme 87 Ridley Coll Melbourne 89. **d** 90 **p** 90. Australia 90-02; C Mooroolbark 90-91; P-in-c S Yarra 92-93; I Blackburn St Jo 93-98; I Kew H Trin 98-02; P-in-c Brimpsfield w Birdlip, Syde, Daglingworth etc *Glouc* 02-04; R from 04; AD Cirencester from 08. *The Rectory, Church Road, Daglingworth, Cirencester GL7 7AG* Tel and Fax (01285) 640782

JESTY, Mrs Helen Margaret. b 51. York Univ BA72. Cranmer Hall Dur BA81. **dss** 82 **d** 87. S Lambeth St Steph *S'wark* 82-86; Norbiton 86-93; Par Dn 87-90; Hon Par Dn 91-93. *Fairfield, 1 Downside Road, Winchester SO22 5LT* Tel (01962) 849190

JESUDASON, Leslie Peter Prakash. b 58. Wycliffe Hall Ox 05. **d** 07 **p** 08. C Throop *Win* 07-11; TV Bracknell *Ox* from 11. *54 Vulcan Drive, Bracknell RG12 9GN* E-mail ljesudason@gmail.com

JEVONS, Alan Neil. b 56. Ex Univ BA77 Selw Coll Cam BA80 MA84. Ridley Hall Cam. **d** 81 **p** 82. C Halesowen *Worc* 81-84; C Heywood St Luke w All So *Man* 84-87; TV Heref St Martin w St Fran 87-93; P-in-c Much Birch w Lt Birch, Much Dewchurch etc 93-02; RD Ross and Archenfield 98-02; TR Tenbury Wells 02-07; Preb Heref Cathl 02-07; RD Ludlow 05-07; V Llyn Safaddan *S & B* from 07; Dioc Tourism Officer from 07; Asst Dioc Soc Resp Officer from 09. *The Vicarage, Llangorse, Brecon LD3 7UG* Tel (01874) 658298 E-mail alanjevons@mac.com

JEVONS, Harry Clifford. b 46. Bp Otter Coll 01. **d** 04 **p** 05. C Ifield *Chich* 04-07; C Milton *Win* from 07; rtd 11; C Ermington and Ugborough *Ex* from 11; C Diptford, N Huish, Harberton, Harbertonford etc from 11. *The Vicarage, Lutterburn Street, Ugborough, Ivybridge PL21 0NG* Tel 07881-527050 (mobile) E-mail harryjevons@supanet.com

JEWELL, Alan David John. b 59. St Cath Coll Ox MA86. Wycliffe Hall Ox 83. **d** 86 **p** 87. C Walton H Trin *Ox* 86-91; TV Sutton *Liv* 91-97; TV Halewood 97-01; TR from 01. *The Rectory, 3 Rectory Drive, Halewood, Liverpool L26 6LJ* Tel 0151-487 5610 E-mail alandjewell@btopenworld.com

JEWELL, Raymond Frederick. b 27. CA Tr Coll 56. **d** 05 **p** 05. NSM Tuffley *Glouc* from 05. *1 Bybrook Gardens, Tuffley, Gloucester GL4 0HQ*

JEWISS, Anthony Harrison. b 39. Virginia Th Sem MDiv92. **d** 92 **p** 93. Chapl to Bp Los Angeles USA 92-99; Can Prec Los Angeles 99; Dep Exec Officer Episc Ch Cen New York 99-07; rtd 07; Asst Chapl Midi-Pyrénées **and** Aude *Eur* from 09. *3 rue Mandrière, 11580 Alet-les-Bains, France* Tel (0033) 4 68 69 01 22 E-mail tonyjewiss@gmail.com

JEWITT, Martin Paul Noel. b 44. AKC69. St Aug Coll Cant. **d** 70 **p** 71. C Usworth *Dur* 70-74; TV 77-78; Tutor Newton Coll Papua New Guinea 74-77; V Balham Hill Ascension *S'wark* 78-93; R N Reddish *Man* 93-99; V Thornton Heath St Paul *S'wark* 99-10; rtd 10; Perm to Offic *Cant* from 10. *12 Abbott Road, Folkestone CT20 1NG* Tel (01303) 211491 Mobile 07981-754738 E-mail martin.jewitt@virginmedia.com

JEWSBURY, Jonathan Mark. b 64. St Jo Coll Dur BA86. NEOC 04. **d** 06 **p** 07. NSM E Rainton *Dur* from 06; NSM W Rainton from 06. *62 Grange Road, Durham DH1 1AL* E-mail j.jewsbury100@durhamlea.org.uk

JEYNES, Anthony James. b 44. AKC68. St Boniface Warminster 68. **d** 69 **p** 70. C Ellesmere Port *Ches* 69-73; C Birkenhead St Pet w St Matt 73-75; R Oughtrington 75-80; C Timperley 80-85; C Eastham 85-89; V New Brighton St Jas 89-96; P-in-c New Brighton Em 94-96; R Tarleton *Blackb* 96-04; P-in-c Kyrenia St Andr and Chapl N Cyprus 04-07; Chapl Paphos 07-09; rtd 09; Perm to Offic Cyprus and the Gulf from 09. *PO Box 54612, 3726 Limassol, Cyprus* Tel (00357) (25) 342908 Mobile 99-806109 E-mail tony_irene@cytanet.com.cy

JOACHIM, Margaret Jane. b 49. FGS91 St Hugh's Coll Ox BA70 MA74 W Midl Coll of Educn PGCE71 Birm Univ PhD77. S Dios Minl Tr Scheme 91. **d** 94 **p** 95. NSM Ealing St Barn *Lon* 94-97; NSM Ealing St Pet Mt Park from 97.

8 Newburgh Road, London W3 6DQ Tel (020) 8723 4514 *or* 8754 4547 E-mail margaret.joachim@london.anglican.org

JOB, Canon Evan Roger Gould. b 36. Magd Coll Ox BA60 MA64 ARCM55. Cuddesdon Coll 60. **d** 62 **p** 63. C Liv Our Lady and St Nic 62-65; V New Springs 65-70; Min Can and Prec Man Cathl 70-74; Prec and Sacr Westmr Abbey 74-79; Can Res, Prec and Sacr Win Cathl 79-94; Vice-Dean Win 91-94; Select Preacher Ox Univ 74 and 91; rtd 01; Perm to Offic *Win* from 94 and *Portsm* from 04. *Kitwood Farmhouse, Kitwood Lane, Ropley, Alresford SO24 0DB* Tel (01962) 772303

JOBBER, Barry William. b 38. N Staffs Poly BA84. Cuddesdon Coll 73. **d** 75 **p** 76. C Fenton *Lich* 76-79; V Goldenhill 79-80; Perm to Offic *Ches* 90-02; NSM Middlewich w Byley 02-08; NSM Witton from 08. *16 Angus Grove, Middlewich CW10 9GR* Tel (01606) 737386 Mobile 07974-380234 E-mail barry.jobber@uwclub.net

JOBLING, Jeremy Charles. b 72. Natal Univ BSc95. Wycliffe Hall Ox 03. **d** 05 **p** 06. C Watford *St Alb* 05-08; C Kenilworth S Africa from 08. *16 Summerley Road, Kenilworth, 7708 South Africa* Tel (0027) (21) 797 6332 E-mail jeremy.jobling@googlemail.com

JOBSON, Clifford Hedley. b 31. St Jo Coll Dur BA54 MA81. **d** 56 **p** 57. C Hall Green Ascension *Birm* 56-59; C Ambleside w Rydal *Carl* 59-60; R Arthuret 60-62; CF 62-73; Dep Asst Chapl Gen 73-78; Asst Chapl Gen 78-84; QHC from 80; V Fleet *Guildf* 84-96; rtd 96; Perm to Offic *B & W* 96-06. *Vine Cottage, 25 Silver Street, South Petherton TA13 5AL* Tel (01460) 241783

JOEL, Mrs Mary Tertia. b 35. **d** 99 **p** 00. OLM Blyth Valley *St E* 99-05; rtd 05; Perm to Offic *St E* from 05. *38 Saxmundham Road, Aldeburgh IP15 5JE* Tel (01728) 454886 Mobile 07790-910554 E-mail maryt@joel12.freeserve.co.uk

JOHN, Alexander Dominic. b 26. Madras Univ BA47. Episc Sem Austin Texas MDiv63. **d** 63 **p** 64. C Millhouses H Trin *Sheff* 63-65; Switzerland 65-68; India 68-78; Australia from 78; rtd 85. *12 Bentwood Avenue, Woodlands WA 6018, Australia* Tel (0061) (8) 9445 3530 E-mail remo@space.net.au

✠**JOHN, The Rt Revd Andrew Thomas Griffith.** b 64. Univ of Wales LLB. St Jo Coll Nottm BA. **d** 89 **p** 90 **c** 08. C Cardigan w Mwnt and Y Ferwig *St D* 89-91; C Aberystwyth 91-92; TV 92-99; V Henfynyw w Aberaeron and Llanddewi Aberarth etc 99-06; V Pencarreg and Llanycrwys 06-08; Adn Cardigan 06-08; Bp Ban from 08. *Ty'r Esgob, Upper Garth Road, Bangor LL57 2SS* Tel (01248) 362895 E-mail bishop.bangor@churchinwales.org.uk

JOHN, Canon Arun Andrew. b 54. **d** 77 **p** 78. India 77-96; S Africa 97-04; TV Manningham *Bradf* from 04. *St Paul's Rectory, 63 St Paul's Road, Manningham, Bradford BD8 7LS* Tel (01274) 490550 E-mail arun.john@bradford.anglican.org

JOHN, Barbara. b 34. Gilmore Ho. **dss** 67 **d** 80 **p** 97. Merthyr Tydfil *Llan* 67-71; Loughton St Jo *Chelmsf* 71-73; Newport St Woolos *Mon* 73-78; Asst Chapl Univ Hosp of Wales Cardiff 78-85; C Radyr *Llan* 85-00; rtd 00. *14 Pace Close, Cardiff CF5 2QZ* Tel (029) 2055 2989

JOHN, Canon Beverley Hayes. b 49. Qu Coll Birm 83. **d** 85 **p** 86. C Oystermouth *S & B* 85-87; C Morriston 87-88; V Cefn Coed w Vaynor from 88; AD Brecon from 99; Can Res Brecon Cathl from 04. *Ty Cefn Coed, 6 Lamb Road, Penderyn, Aberdare CF44 9JU* Tel (01685) 811810

JOHN, Brother. See HENNINGS, John Richard

JOHN, Caroline Victoria. b 64. Cam Univ BA86 MA90. St Jo Coll Nottm. **d** 90. NSM Cardigan w Mwnt and Y Ferwig *St D* 90-91; NSM Aberystwyth 91-96. *Ty'r Esgob, Upper Garth Road, Bangor LL57 2SS* Tel (01248) 362895

JOHN, Canon David Michael. b 36. Univ of Wales (Lamp) BA57. St Mich Coll Llan 57. **d** 59 **p** 60. C Pontypool *Mon* 59-61; C Roath *Llan* 61-66; Asst Chapl HM Pris Liv 66-67; Chapl HM Pris Ex 67-68; V Ystrad Rhondda *Llan* 68-76; V Pontyclun w Talygarn 76-84; R Newton Nottage 84-91; Can Llan Cathl 85-91; rtd 91; Perm to Offic *Llan* and *Mon* from 91. *1 Hornbeam Close, St Mellons, Cardiff CF3 0JA* Tel (029) 2079 7496

JOHN, David Wyndham. b 61. Lon Bible Coll. NTMTC. **d** 01 **p** 02. NSM Hampstead Em W End *Lon* 01-04; NSM W Hampstead St Cuth from 04; P-in-c from 06. *13 Kingscroft Road, London NW2 3QE* Tel (020) 8452 1913 Mobile 07719-333389

JOHN, The Ven Elwyn Crebey. b 36. Univ of Wales (Lamp) BA57. St Mich Coll Llan 57. **d** 59 **p** 60. C Llangiwg *S & B* 59-62; C Llandrindod w Cefnllys 62-66; V Beguildy and Heyope 66-79; Youth Chapl 72-79; Chapl Agric and Rural Soc 77-03; V Builth and Llanddewi'r Cwm w Llangynog etc 79-95; Can Brecon Cathl 88-95; Can Res Brecon Cathl 95-03; Prec 94-95; Treas 95-98; Chan 98-03; V Brecon St Mary w Llanddew 95-01; Adn Brecon 99-03; rtd 03. *17 Cae Castell, Builth Wells LD2 3BE* Tel (01982) 551553

JOHN, Canon James Richard. b 21. Ch Coll Cam BA47 MA49. Cuddesdon Coll 47. **d** 49 **p** 50. C Sidcup Ch Ch *Roch* 49-52; V Gillingham St Mary 52-66; RD Gillingham 60-66; V Bolton St Jas w St Chrys *Bradf* 66-78; R Guiseley 78-83; RD Otley 80-86; P-in-c Esholt 82-83; TR Guiseley w Esholt 83-87; Hon

Can Bradf Cathl 83-87; rtd 87; Perm to Offic *Bradf* from 87. *37 Croft House Drive, Otley LS21 2ER* Tel (01943) 461998

JOHN, The Very Revd Jeffrey Philip Hywel. b 53. Hertf Coll Ox BA75 Magd Coll Ox DPhil84. St Steph Ho Ox BA77 MA78. **d** 78 **p** 79. C Penarth w Lavernock *Llan* 78-80; Asst Chapl Magd Coll Ox 80-82; Fell and Dean of Div 84-91; Chapl and Lect BNC Ox 82-84; V Eltham H Trin *S'wark* 91-97; Chan and Can Th S'wark Cathl 97-04; Bp's Adv for Min 97-04; Dean St Alb from 04. *The Deanery, Sumpter Yard, St Albans AL1 1BY* Tel (01727) 890203 Fax 890227 E-mail dean@stalbanscathedral.org.uk

JOHN, Mrs Marie. b 48. **d** 04 **p** 05. OLM Camberwell St Geo *S'wark* from 04. *8 Caroline Gardens, Asylum Road, London SE15 2SQ* Tel (020) 7635 5534

JOHN, Mark Christopher. b 61. SS Mark & Jo Univ Coll Plymouth BA83. St Steph Ho Ox 84. **d** 87 **p** 88. C Treboeth *S & B* 87-90; V Swansea St Mark and St Jo 90-94; Chapl HM Pris Swansea 91-94; Chapl HM Pris Usk and Prescoed 94-97; Chapl HM Pris Cardiff from 97; Lic to Offic *Mon* from 99. *HM Prison Cardiff, Knox Road, Cardiff CF24 0UG* Tel (029) 2043 3100 ext 3233 Fax 2043 3318

JOHN, Meurig Hywel. b 46. St D Coll Lamp 67. **d** 71 **p** 72. C Llanelli Ch Ch *St D* 71-74; V Penrhyncoch and Elerch 74-79; V Llanfihangel Aberbythych 79-81; R Cilgerran w Bridell and Llantwyd 81-83; V Gwaun-cae-Gurwen 83-89; V Llanfihangel Genau'r-glyn and Llangorwen 89-95; V Newcastle Emlyn w Llandyfriog etc 95-01; Assoc V Lampeter and Llanddewibrefi Gp 01-03; rtd 03. *Arosfa, Llanybri, Carmarthen SA33 5HQ* Tel (01267) 241096

JOHN, Napoleon. b 55. Punjab Univ BA76. Lahetysteologisen Inst Ryttyla Finland 84 Oak Hill Th Coll BA93. **d** 93 **p** 94. C Leyton St Mary w St Edw *Chelmsf* 93-96; C Leyton St Mary w St Edw and St Luke 96-97; P-in-c Becontree St Elisabeth 97-04; V 04-07; TR Walton and Trimley *St E* from 07. *1 Parsonage Close, Felixstowe IP11 2QR* Tel (01394) 284803 E-mail napojohn@hotmail.com

JOHN, Nigel. b 59. Univ of Wales (Cardiff) BA87 Man Univ MPhil90. Westcott Ho Cam 88. **d** 91 **p** 92. C Carmarthen St Pet *St D* 91-94; Chapl Roehampton Inst *S'wark* 94-96; V Gors-las *St D* 96-98; V Llanelli Ch Ch 98-02; Chapl Univ of Wales (Swansea) *S & B* from 02. *23 Mayals Avenue, Blackpill, Swansea SA3 5DE* Tel (01792) 401703

JOHN, Richard. See JOHN, Canon James Richard

JOHN, Robert Michael. b 46. Edin Univ BSc67 Man Univ MSc68 PhD70 Otago Univ BD78. St Jo Coll Auckland 76. **d** 78 **p** 79. C Tauranga New Zealand 78-80; C Hastings 80-83; V Waipaoa 83-87; C Swansea St Jas *S & B* 87-88; V Otumoetai New Zealand 88-94; Chapl Auckland Hosps 94-09; Chapl Univ Hosps of Morecambe Bay NHS Trust 09-11; C N Barrow *Carl* from 11. *56 Flass Lane, Barrow-in-Furness LA13 0DF* Tel (01229) 821613 E-mail robertmichaeljohn@btinternet.com

JOHN, Stephen Michael. b 63. Univ of Wales (Lamp) BA85. Coll of Resurr Mirfield 87. **d** 89 **p** 90. C Coity w Nolton *Llan* 89-91; C Merthyr Dyfan 91-94; V Tredegar St Geo *Mon* 94-99; Chapl HM Pris Gartree 99-04; TV Tenby *St D* from 04. *9 Lamack Vale, Tenby SA70 8DN* Tel (01834) 844330

JOHN-FRANCIS, Brother. See FRIENDSHIP, Roger Geoffrey

JOHNES, Philip Sydney. b 45. St Mich Coll Llan 90. **d** 92 **p** 93. C Cardigan w Mwnt and Y Ferwig *St D* 92-95; V Llanegwad w Llanfynydd 95-10; rtd 10. *Keeper's Cottage, Ferryside SA17 5TY* Tel (01267) 267081 E-mail pjohnes@aol.com

JOHNS, Adam Aubrey. b 34. TCD BA57 MA76 NUU BA75. CITC Div Test 58. **d** 58 **p** 59. C Aghalee *D & D* 58-61; C Derriaghy *Conn* 61-63; I Billy 63-77; I Billy w Derrykeighan 77-03; Can Conn Cathl 98-03; rtd 03. *26 Chatham Road, Armoy, Ballymoney BT53 8TT* Tel (028) 2075 1978 E-mail chathambrae@btinternet.com

JOHNS, Canon Bernard Thomas. b 36. Birm Univ BSc58. St Mich Coll Llan 61. **d** 63 **p** 64. C Aberavon *Llan* 63-65; C St Andrews Major w Michaelston-le-Pit 65-70; V Cardiff St Andr and St Teilo 70-76; Asst Dioc Dir of Educn 72-91; V Roath 76-88; R Wenvoe and St Lythans 88-02; Dioc Dir Community Educn 91-02; Can Llan Cathl 96-02; rtd 02. *Bay Tree Cottage, 13 Badgers Meadow, Pwllmeyric, Chepstow NP16 6UE* Tel (01291) 623254

JOHNS, Mrs Patricia Holly. b 33. Girton Coll Cam BA56 MA60 Hughes Hall Cam PGCE57. Ox NSM Course 87. **d** 90 **p** 94. NSM Wantage *Ox* 90-94; NSM Marlborough *Sarum* 94-95; rtd 95; Perm to Offic *Sarum* 95-08. *1 Priory Lodge, 93 Brown Street, Salisbury SP1 2BX* Tel (01722) 328007

JOHNS, Canon Ronald Charles. b 37. TD. Dur Univ BA59. Wells Th Coll 59. **d** 61 **p** 62. C Wigan All SS *Liv* 61-66; TV Kirkby 66-75; Ho Master Ruffwood Sch Kirkby 70-75; TV Maghull 75-79; Dep Hd Master Maghull Old Hall High Sch 75-79; P-in-c Borrowdale *Carl* 79-84; V 84-89; RD Derwent 81-89; Hon Can Carl Cathl 87-89; Can Res 89-94; R Caldbeck, Castle Sowerby and Sebergham 94-00; rtd 01; Perm to Offic *Nor* from 01. *3 Kings Road, Coltishall, Norwich NR12 7DX*

JOHNS, Thomas Morton. b 43. Oak Hill Th Coll 67. **d** 70 **p** 71. C N Meols *Liv* 70-73; C Farnborough *Guildf* 73-76; P-in-c Badshot

Lea CD 76-83; Dep Chapl HM Pris Man 83; Chapl HM Youth Cust Cen Wellingborough 83-88; Chapl HM YOI Swinfen Hall 88-90; Chapl Tr Officer 88-95; Chapl HM Pris Service Coll 90-95; Asst Chapl Gen of Pris (HQ) 95-01; Acting Chapl Gen 00-01; P-in-c Colbury *Win* 02-08; Chapl Hants Constabulary 02-08; rtd 08; Perm to Offic *Portsm* from 02. *18 Southbrook Mews, Bishops Waltham, Southampton SO32 1RZ* Tel (01489) 891585 Mobile 07988-314928 E-mail tomjohns585@btinternet.com

JOHNS, Trevor Charles. b 33. St D Coll Lamp BA58. **d** 58 **p** 59. C Pembroke St Mary w St Mich *St D* 58-61; R Walwyn's Castle w Robeston W 61-67; CF 67-75; V Spittal and Treffgarne *St D* 75-79; C Tring *St Alb* 79-80; TV Tring 80-85; V Knighton and Norton *S & B* 85-86; V Merthyr Cynog and Dyffryn Honddu etc 86-98; rtd 98. *109 Hoel-y-Banc, Bancffosfelen, Llanelli SA15 5DF*

JOHNS, William Price. b 28. Keble Coll Ox BA51 MA56. St Mich Coll Llan 52. **d** 53 **p** 54. C Whitchurch *Llan* 53-56; C Pontypridd St Cath 56-59; Min Can Brecon Cathl 59-62; V Wellington *Heref* 62-78; R Wellington w Pipe-cum-Lyde and Moreton-on-Lugg 78-93; P-in-c Ford 63-69; rtd 93; Perm to Offic *Llan* from 93. *c/o Ms T Rabey, 8 Montgomery Street, Cardiff CF24 3LZ*

JOHNSEN, Edward Andrew. b 67. Birm Univ BTheol89. Qu Coll Birm 95. **d** 97 **p** 98. C Birm St Luke 97-01; C Handsworth St Mary 01-04; Perm to Offic 05-06; TV Eden, Gelt and Irthing *Carl* from 06. *The Vicarage, Hayton, Brampton CA8 9HR* Tel (01228) 670248 E-mail mail@johnsen3671.fsworld.co.uk

JOHNSON, Amanda Saffery. b 58. K Alfred's Coll Win BEd83. Wycliffe Hall Ox. **d** 97 **p** 98. C Oxhey All SS *St Alb* 97-00; C Bricket Wood 00-02; Teacher Bp Wand Sch Sunbury-on-Thames 02-04; C Dorking St Paul *Guildf* 05-09; C Bisley and W End 09-10; V Addiscombe St Mary Magd w St Martin *S'wark* from 10. *The Vicarage, 15 Canning Road, Addiscombe CR0 6QD* Tel (020) 8654 3459 or 8656 3457 Mobile 07905-893394 E-mail amanda@hut.co.uk

JOHNSON, Dom Andrew. b 59. **d** 08 **p** 09. OSB from 85. *Alton Abbey, Abbey Road, Beech, Alton GU34 4AP* Tel (01420) 562145 Fax 561691 E-mail altonabbey@supanet.com

JOHNSON, Andrew Paul. b 56. W Surrey Coll of Art & Design BA79 Kent Coll for Careers CertEd82 TCD BTh96. CITC 93. **d** 96 **p** 97. C Penarth w Lavernock *Llan* 96-99; R Walton W w Talbenny and Haroldston W *St D* from 99. *The Rectory, Walton West, Little Haven, Haverfordwest SA62 3UB* Tel (01437) 781279

JOHNSON, Andrew Peter. b 67. Westf Coll Lon BA89 St Jo Coll Nottm MA98 LTh99. Aston Tr Scheme 94. **d** 99 **p** 00. C Hitchin *St Alb* 99-03; V Batley All SS and Purlwell *Wakef* from 03. *The Vicarage, Churchfield Street, Batley WF17 5DL* Tel and fax (01924) 473049 E-mail johnsons@care4free.net

JOHNSON, Andrew Robert. b 68. Jes Coll Ox MA96 Univ of Wales (Abth) MLib93 PhD96. Cranmer Hall Dur 03. **d** 05 **p** 06. C Carmarthen St Pet *St D* 05-08; P-in-c Llanfihangel Ystrad and Cilcennin w Trefilan etc 08-11; P-in-c Gtr Corsham and Lacock *Bris* from 11. *The Rectory, Newlands Road, Corsham SN13 0BS* Tel (01249) 713232 E-mail teamrector@btinternet.com

JOHNSON, Mrs Angela Carolyn Louise. b 52. RGN76. STETS 00. **d** 03 **p** 04. NSM Catherington and Clanfield *Portsm* 03-07; NSM Denmead from 07. *90 Downhouse Road, Waterlooville PO8 0TY* Tel (023) 9264 4595 E-mail angela.johnson52@ntlworld.com

JOHNSON, Anthony. See JOHNSON, Edward Anthony

JOHNSON, Anthony Arthur Derry. b 15. Kelham Th Coll 31. **d** 39 **p** 40. C Pinner *Lon* 39-42; C Willesden St Andr 42-44; C Winchmore Hill H Trin 44-49; V Brookfield St Anne, Highgate Rise 49-60; V Mill Hill St Mich 60-73; R Chalfont St Giles *Ox* 73-80; rtd 80; Perm to Offic *Sarum* from 80. *Garden Close, Long Street, Sherborne DT9 3DD* Tel (01935) 813469

JOHNSON, Anthony Peter. b 45. K Coll Lon BD76 AKC76 MTh79. Wells Th Coll 67. **d** 70 **p** 71. C Goldington *St Alb* 70-73; C Hainault *Chelmsf* 73-76; TV Loughton St Mary 76-81; V Scunthorpe All SS *Linc* 81-85; V Alkborough 85-87; Chapl Man Univ and TV Man Whitworth 87-96; P-in-c Chorlton-cum-Hardy St Werburgh 96-00; R 00-05; P-in-c Yardley St Cypr Hay Mill *Birm* 05-08; V 08-10; rtd 10; Perm to Offic *Birm* from 10. *St Barnabas' Vicarage, 51 Over Green Drive, Kingshurst, Birmingham B37 6EY* Tel 0121-770 3972 E-mail ajohnson940@btinternet.com

JOHNSON, Anthony Warrington. b 40. Goldsmiths' Coll Lon CertEd60. St Jo Coll Nottm 86. **d** 88 **p** 89. C Lutterworth w Cotesbach *Leic* 88-92; V Countesthorpe w Foston 92-06; P-in-c Arnesby w Shearsby and Bruntingthorpe 94-01; rtd 06; Hon C Lutterworth w Cotesbach and Bitteswell *Leic* 06-09. *9 Forest Road, Loughborough LE11 3NW* Tel (01509) 210942

JOHNSON, Miss Barbara. b 45. St Jo Coll Nottm 04. **d** 07 **p** 08. NSM Royston *St Alb* 07-08; NSM Goldington 08-10; Chapl Beds and Luton Fire and Rescue Service from 07; Perm to Offic

Ely from 10 and *Ox* from 11. *4 Hicks Lane, Girton, Cambridge CB3 0JS* Tel (01223) 276282 Mobile 07768-560646 E-mail barbara.johnson@bedsfire.com

JOHNSON, Barry Charles Richard. b 48. EAMTC 96. **d** 99 **p** 00. NSM Billericay and Lt Burstead *Chelmsf* 99-01; C Gt Burstead 01-02; C Bowers Gifford w N Benfleet 02-04; P-in-c Woodham Mortimer w Hazeleigh 04-06; R Vange 06-10; P-in-c Bowers Gifford w N Benfleet 07-10; V Folkestone St Mary, St Eanswythe and St Sav *Cant* from 10. *The Vicarage, Priory Gardens, Folkestone CT20 1SW* Tel (01303) 252947 E-mail revbj@btinternet.com

JOHNSON, Beverley Charles. b 35. Bp Gray Coll Cape Town 59. **d** 61 **p** 62. S Africa 61-67 and from 91; C Woodstock St Mary 61-64; C Clanwilliam St Jo 64-65; C Plumstead St Mark 65-67; C Southsea St Pet *Portsm* 68-69; C Southwick St Cuth CD *Dur* 70-71; P-in-c Waterhouses 71-80; R Burnmoor 80-85; V Brandon 85-89; Australia 89-91; Asst P Sea Point St Jas 91-01; rtd 01. *43 Oxford Street, Goodwood, 7460 South Africa* Tel and fax (0027) (21) 592 1180 Mobile 82-202 5260

JOHNSON, Mrs Brenda Margaret. b 47. TISEC 93. **d** 00. NSM Edin St Salvador 00-03; NSM Wester Hailes St Luke 00-03; NSM Edin Gd Shep from 03. *58 Ratho Park Road, Ratho, Newbridge EH28 8PQ* Tel 0131-333 1742 Mobile 07713-154744 E-mail brenmj@btinternet.com

JOHNSON, Brian. b 42. S'wark Ord Course 84. **d** 87 **p** 88. NSM Dulwich St Barn *S'wark* 87-92; NSM Herne Hill 92-94; Perm to Offic 94-96; Chapl HM Pris Man 96-01; P-in-c Rotterdam *Eur* 01-02; Operations Manager ICS 03; Perm to Offic *Ches* from 04 and *Man* from 11. *11A Lynton Park Road, Cheadle Hulme, Cheadle SK8 6JA* Tel 0161-483 3787 E-mail revbfg@ntlworld.com

JOHNSON, Christopher Dudley. b 26. Worc Coll Ox BA44 MA51. Cuddesdon Coll 53. **d** 56 **p** 57. C Basingstoke *Win* 56-61; V Bethnal Green St Barn *Lon* 61-67; V Eton w Eton Wick and Boveney *Ox* 67-88; rtd 91; Perm to Offic *Sarum* from 96. *Lavinces Cottage, Netherbury, Bridport DT6 5LL*

JOHNSON, Christopher Frederick. b 43. MRICS67. Ripon Hall Ox 71. **d** 74 **p** 75. C Chatham St Steph *Roch* 74-78; V Slade Green 78-85; V Wilmington 85-95; R Chevening 95-09; rtd 09. *7 Kennedy Gardens, Sevenoaks TN13 3UG* Tel (01732) 456626 E-mail c.f.johnson@waitrose.com

JOHNSON, Christopher Paul. b 47. St Jo Coll Nottm BTh74. **d** 74 **p** 75. C Normanton *Wakef* 74-78; P-in-c Dewsbury St Mark 78-82; V Harden and Wilsden *Bradf* 82-88; P-in-c Holbeck *Ripon* 88-94; V 94-97; Asst Chapl Leeds Teaching Hosps NHS Trust 97-01; Chapl Bradf Hosps NHS Trust from 01. *Bradford Royal Infirmary, Duckworth Lane, Bradford BD9 6RJ* Tel (01274) 365819 E-mail chris.johnson@bradfordhospitals.nhs.uk

JOHNSON, Christopher Robert. b 43. Lon Coll of Div 66. **d** 70 **p** 71. C Everton St Geo *Liv* 70-71; C Childwall All SS 71-75; TV Gateacre 75-76; TV Bradninch *Lich* 76-87; R Burslem 87-10; rtd 10; Perm to Offic *Lich* from 11. *102 Chell Green Avenue, Stoke-on-Trent ST6 7LA* Tel (01782) 850169 E-mail rob.johnson60@talk21.com

JOHNSON, Claire Elisabeth. See PARR, Mrs Claire Elisabeth

JOHNSON, Canon Colin Gawman. b 32. Leeds Univ BA59. Coll of Resurr Mirfield 59. **d** 61 **p** 62. C Barrow St Matt *Carl* 61-67; V 90-96; V Addingham 67-71; V Carl H Trin 71-80; V Wigton 80-90; Hon Can Carl Cathl 85-96; rtd 96; Perm to Offic *Carl* from 97. *Hemp Garth, Ireby, Wigton CA7 1EA* Tel (01697) 371578

JOHNSON, Colin Leslie. b 41. Trin Coll Cam MA65. Cheshunt Coll Cam 62. **d** 93 **p** 94. Publications Dir Chr Educn Movement from 89; NSM Brailsford w Shirley and Osmaston w Edlaston *Derby* 93-04; Perm to Offic from 04. *33 The Plain, Brailsford, Ashbourne DE6 3BZ* Tel (01335) 360591 E-mail cj@acjohnson.plus.com

JOHNSON, Colin Stewart. b 46. SEITE 99. **d** 02 **p** 03. NSM Borden *Cant* 02-05; C Charlton-in-Dover 05-06; P-in-c from 06. *Holywell House, 3 Monastery Avenue, Dover CT16 1AB* Tel and fax (01304) 201143 Mobile 07740-775277 E-mail frcj@dsl.pipex.com

JOHNSON, Cyril Francis. b 22. St Cath Coll Cam BA49 MA54. Ely Th Coll 50. **d** 52 **p** 53. C Twickenham All Hallows *Lon* 52-56; C Kingsthorpe *Pet* 56-61; R Harpole 61-87; rtd 87; Perm to Offic *Chich* from 01. *16 Blake's Way, Eastbourne BN23 6EW* Tel (01323) 723491

JOHNSON, David. See JOHNSON, John David

JOHNSON, David Alan. b 43. Lon Univ BSc63 PhD67. Trin Coll Bris 78. **d** 80 **p** 81. C Watford *St Alb* 80-85; V Idle *Bradf* 85-08; P-in-c Greengates 08; rtd 08. *15 Blackburn Close, Bearpark, Durham DH7 7TQ* Tel 0191-373 7953 E-mail david@fss.me.uk

JOHNSON, David Bryan Alfred. b 36. Kelham Th Coll 56. **d** 61 **p** 62. C Streatham St Paul *S'wark* 61-63; Malaysia 63-71; V Worc St Mich 71-74; Warden Lee Abbey Internat Students' Club Kensington 74-77; V Plumstead St Mark and St Marg *S'wark* 77-86; Chapl W Park Hosp Epsom 86-96; Chapl Laslett's *Worc* 96-01; rtd 96. *3 St Birinus Cottages, Wessex Way, Bicester OX26 6DX* Tel (01869) 320839

JOHNSON, David Francis. b 32. Univ Coll Ox BA55 MA59. Westcott Ho Cam 55. **d** 57 **p** 58. C Earlsdon *Cov* 57-59; C Willenhall 59-61; C Attenborough w Bramcote *S'well* 61-62; V Ravenstone w Weston Underwood *Ov* 62-66; V Crewe Ch Ch *Ches* 66-70; P-in-c Crewe St Pet 67-70; V Thornton w Allerthorpe *York* 70-79; V N Hull St Mich 79-81; V Leyburn w Bellerby *Ripon* 81-88; V Coxwold and Husthwaite *York* 88-97; rtd 97; Perm to Offic *York* 98-03 and *Heref* from 05. *Nursery Cottage, The Park, Wormelow, Hereford HR2 8EQ* Tel (01981) 540967

JOHNSON, David John. b 49. Lanc Univ BA72. Linc Th Coll 78. **d** 81 **p** 82. C Stockport St Thos *Ches* 81-84; OGS from 83; C Stockton Heath *Ches* 84-88; V Tranmere St Paul w St Luke 88-99; P-in-c Antrobus 99-02; P-in-c Aston by Sutton 99-02; P-in-c Lt Leigh and Lower Whitley 99-02; V Antrobus, Aston by Sutton, Lt Leigh etc 02-07; C Coppenhall 07-10; rtd 11. *14 Manor Way, Crewe CW2 6JX* Tel (01270) 250256

JOHNSON, David Richard. b 67. Birm Univ BSc88. Ripon Coll Cuddesdon BA92 MA97. **d** 94 **p** 95. C Horfield H Trin *Bris* 94-97; V Two Mile Hill St Mich 97-01; Asst Chapl Haileybury Coll 01-02; Chapl Dauntsey's Sch Devizes from 02. *20 High Street, West Lavington, Devizes SN10 4HQ* Tel (01380) 814573 E-mail johnsoda@dauntseys.wilts.sch.uk

JOHNSON, David William. b 40. Oak Hill Th Coll BD64. **d** 65 **p** 66. C Tunbridge Wells St Jas *Roch* 65-68; C Kirby Muxloe *Leic* 68-72; V Burton Joyce w Bulcote *S'well* 72-83; V Mitford and Chapl Northgate Mental Handicap Unit Morpeth 83-87; Asst Chapl R Victoria Infirmary Newc 87-89; Chapl R Shrewsbury Hosps NHS Trust 89-04; rtd 04. *42 Hartlands, Bedlington NE22 6JG* Tel (01670) 828693

JOHNSON, David William. b 53. Selw Coll Cam BA76. Ripon Coll Cuddesdon 76. **d** 78 **p** 79. C Fulham St Etheldreda w St Clem *Lon* 78-82; Communications Sec Gen Syn Bd for Miss and Unity 82-87; PV Westmr Abbey 85-87; R Gilmorton w Peatling Parva and Kimcote etc *Leic* 87-91; R Cogenhoe *Pet* 91-95; R Whiston 93-95; rtd 95; Perm to Offic *Pet* from 00. *Seaview Cottage, 115 Hurst Street, Oxford OX4 1HE* Tel (01865) 793393

JOHNSON, Preb Derek John. b 36. St Aid Birkenhead 65. **d** 68 **p** 69. C Eccleshall *Lich* 68-73; C Stafford St Mary 73-75; Chapl New Cross Hosp Wolv 75-96; Preb Lich Cathl 83-96; rtd 96; Perm to Offic *St E* from 96. *6 St Paul's Close, Aldeburgh IP15 5BQ* Tel (01728) 452474

JOHNSON, Canon Diana Margaret. b 46. MCSP68 SRP68. Cranmer Hall Dur 92. **d** 94 **p** 95. C Birtley *Dur* 94-99; TV Gateshead 99-06; AD Gateshead 03-06; P-in-c Belmont 06-07; V Belmont and Pittington from 07; Hon Can Dur Cathl from 06. *Belmont Vicarage, Broomside Lane, Durham DH1 2QW* Tel 0191-386 1545

JOHNSON (née DEER), Mrs Diane Antonia. b 45. SEITE 97. **d** 00 **p** 01. C Hackington *Cant* 00-04; P-in-c Pitsea w Nevendon *Chelmsf* 04-06; R 06-09; RD Basildon 07-09; P-in-c Eastry and Northbourne w Tilmanstone etc *Cant* 09-10; AD Sandwich 09-10; rtd 10; Perm to Offic *Cant* from 11. *The Vicarage, Priory Gardens, Folkestone CT20 1SW* Tel (01303) 210205 Mobile 07957-758721 E-mail revdiane@btinternet.com

JOHNSON, Mrs Diane Pearl. b 47. Leeds Univ BA68 Cam Univ PGCE69. EAMTC 95. **d** 98 **p** 99. NSM Gt Bowden w Welham, Glooston and Cranoe *Leic* 98-01; C Evington and Leic St Phil 01-04; P-in-c Leic St Phil 04-07; rtd 07; Perm to Offic *Pet* from 10. *16 Oaklands Park, Market Harborough LE16 8EU* Tel (01858) 434118 E-mail gandi2007@btinternet.com

JOHNSON, Canon Donald Arnold. b 28. Linc Coll Ox BA51 MA59. Cuddesdon Coll 51. **d** 53 **p** 54. C Henfield *Chich* 53-55; C Horsham 55-59; V Oving w Merston 59-68; Bp's Dom Chapl 59-68; V Hellingly 68-78; V Upper Dicker 68-78; R W Stoke 78-98; V Funtington and Sennicotts 78-98; Can and Preb Chich Cathl 96-98; rtd 98; Perm to Offic *Chich* from 99. *Vectis, Commonside, Westbourne, Emsworth PO10 8TA* Tel (01243) 371433

JOHNSON, Mrs Dorothy. Leic Univ BSc89 Ox Univ MTh95 RGN FRSH91. Qu Coll Birm 77. **dss** 80 **d** 87 **p** 94. Coventry Caludon 80-81; Wolston and Church Lawford 81-86; NSM Stoneleigh w Ashow 87-08; Bp's Asst Officer for Soc Resp 87-96. *The Firs, Stoneleigh Road, Bubbenhall, Coventry CV8 3BS* Tel and fax (024) 7630 3712 E-mail firsjohn@supanet.com

JOHNSON, Douglas Leonard. b 45. St Paul's Coll Chelt CertEd67 Lon Bible Coll MA95. Tyndale Hall Bris 70. **d** 73 **p** 74. C New Malden and Coombe *S'wark* 73-76; P-in-c Upper Tulse Hill St Matthias 76-82; CPAS Staff 82-88; Lect and Tutor CA Coll 88-91; Dir Crossways Chr Educn Trust 92-08; Hon C Wimbledon Em Ridgway Prop Chpl *S'wark* 91-94; Lect Cornhill Tr Course 94-06; Crosslinks Kenya 08-10; rtd 11. *The Stables, Mudford, Yeovil BA21 5TD* Tel (01935) 432304 E-mail douglasjohnson@btinternet.com

JOHNSON, Edward Anthony (Tony). b 32. Univ of Wales (Swansea) BSc54. St Steph Ho Ox 79. **d** 81 **p** 82. C Wolvercote w Summertown *Ox* 81-84; P-in-c Ramsden 84-87; P-in-c Finstock and Fawler 84-87; P-in-c Wilcote 84-87; V Ramsden, Finstock and Fawler, Leafield etc 87-92; rtd 92; Hon C Kennington *Ox* 92-98; Perm to Offic from 98. *15 Cranbrook Drive, Kennington, Oxford OX1 5RR* Tel (01865) 739751

JOHNSON, Mrs Elizabeth Jane. b 47. St Hilda's Coll Ox MA69. Wycliffe Hall Ox 84. dss 86 d 87 p 94. NSM Ox St Aldate w St Matt 86-91; NSM Marston 91-94; NSM Ox St Clem 94-95; NSM Islip w Charlton on Otmoor, Oddington, Noke etc 95-99; OLM Officer (Dorchester) 99-00; Asst Chapl Oxon Mental Healthcare NHS Trust 00-04; NSM Bladon w Woodstock *Ox* 99-04; NSM Shill Valley and Broadshire 04-09 and from 11; Perm to Offic 09-11. *11 Oakey Close, Alvescot, Bampton OX18 2PX* Tel (01993) 846169
E-mail lizjohn@crecy.fsnet.co.uk

JOHNSON, Miss Emma Louise. b 82. St Mary's Coll Dur BA05 MA06. Ridley Hall Cam 07. d 09 p 10. C Cockfield *Dur* from 09; C Lynesack from 09. *The Vicarage, Brookside, Evenwood, Bishop Auckland DL14 9RA*
E-mail emmajohnson139@googlemail.com

JOHNSON, Eric. b 38. Nottm Univ BSc60 Man Univ CertEd65 Open Univ BA92 SS Paul & Mary Coll Cheltenham MA94 Birm Univ BA06. Qu Coll Birm 74. d 77 p 78. Sen Lect Cov Tech Coll 66-91; NSM Earlsdon *Cov* 77-81; NSM Wolston and Church Lawford 81-86; NSM Stoneleigh w Ashow and Baginton 90-98; FE Liaison Officer *B & W, Bris* and *Glouc* 91-93; Dioc Dir of Educn *Worc* 93-98; rtd 98. *The Firs, Stoneleigh Road, Bubbenhall, Coventry CV8 3BS* Tel and fax (024) 7630 3712 Mobile 07773-748967 E-mail e.djohnson@btinternet.com

JOHNSON, Frances Josephine. b 53. Leeds Univ CertEd74 Open Univ BA90. NOC 02. d 05 p 06. C Hall Green St Pet *Birm* 05-08; V Kingshurst from 08. *St Barnabas' Vicarage, 51 Overgreen Drive, Birmingham B37 6EY* Tel 0121-770 3972
E-mail j.johnson2@tiscali.co.uk

JOHNSON, Geoffrey Kemble. b 22. RD71. Roch Th Coll 62. d 64 p 65. C Hayes *Roch* 64-68; R Worlingham *St E* 68-84; rtd 84; Perm to Offic *Nor* 84-00 and *St E* from 84. *53 St Walstans Road, Taverham, Norwich NR8 6NG* Tel (01603) 860626

JOHNSON, Geoffrey Stuart. b 39. ALCD65 Wolv Poly DipEd Sussex Univ DPhil01. d 65 p 66. C Worksop St Jo *S'well* 65-68; Taiwan 68-71; C St Andr Cathl Singapore 71-76; Aber Univ 76-78; Perm to Offic *Heref* 78-82; P-in-c Hoarwithy, Hentland and Sellack 82-84; Chapl Horton Hosp Epsom 84-90; Distr Chapl Brighton HA 90-94; Managing Chapl Brighton Healthcare NHS Trust 94-99; Managing Chapl S Downs Health NHS Trust 94-99; rtd 99; Chapl S Downs Health NHS Trust 00-06; Chapl Sussex Partnership NHS Trust from 06; Perm to Offic *Chich* from 01. *5 Garden Mews, 15 Beachy Head Road, Eastbourne BN20 7QP* Tel (01323) 644083

JOHNSON, Gillian Margaret. b 55. Bretton Hall Coll CertEd76 Coll of Ripon & York St Jo MA03. NOC 00. d 03 p 04. C Thornhill and Whitley Lower *Wakef* 03-07; C Mirfield 07-10; Curriculum Development Officer Dioc Bd Educn from 10. *5 Wood Mount, Overton, Wakefield WF4 4SB* Tel (01924) 262181 Mobile 07880-901201
E-mail gilljohnson99@hotmail.com

JOHNSON, Gordon Edward. b 27. Oak Hill Th Coll 76. d 77 p 78. C Scarborough St Mary w Ch Ch and H Apostles *York* 77-82; V Hutton Cranswick w Skerne 82-86; P-in-c Watton w Beswick and Kilnwick 82-86; V Hutton Cranswick w Skerne, Watton and Beswick 86-88; V Bubwith w Skipwith 88-93; rtd 93; Perm to Offic *York* and *Ripon* from 93. *Greenacres, Lovesome Hill, Northallerton DL6 2PB* Tel (01609) 881512

JOHNSON, Graham. b 37. Westcott Ho Cam 66. d 68 p 69. C Stafford St Mary *Lich* 68-71; C Wombourne 71-74; Youth Chapl 74-77; P-in-c Tong 76-77; Res Min Wednesfield St Thos 77-78; TV 79-82; P-in-c Milwich and Weston upon Trent 82-88; P-in-c Gayton w Fradswell 84-88; V Fradswell, Gayton, Milwich and Weston 88-90; TV Wolstanton 90-96; V Oxley 96-02; rtd 03. *Ty Pab, 4 Church Street, Tremadog, Porthmadog LL49 9RA* Tel (01766) 513744 E-mail graham@typab.freeserve.co.uk

JOHNSON, Graham James. b 43. Leeds Univ BA67. Coll of Resurr Mirfield. d 70 p 71. C Heckmondwike *Wakef* 70-73; C Pet St Jude 73-76; V Gt w Lt Harrowden and Orlingbury 76-83; R Daventry 83-92; TR Daventry, Ashby St Ledgers, Braunston etc 92; RD Daventry 88-92; Chapl Danetre Hosp 83-93; P-in-c Loddington *Leic* 93-99; Warden Launde Abbey 93-99; RD Framland 94-96; Bp's Chapl and Interfaith Adv 00-02; P-in-c Humberstone 02-03; P-in-c Thurnby Lodge 02-03; TR Ascension TM 03-06; rtd 06. *16 Oaklands Park, Market Harborough LE16 8EU* Tel (01858) 434118
E-mail grahamanddiane@ntlworld.com

JOHNSON, Canon Hilary Ann. b 51. RGN72 RHV74. S'wark Ord Course 82. dss 85 d 87 p 94. Hon Par Dn Salfords *S'wark* 85-90; Chapl St Geo Hosp Lon 90-94; Chapl St Geo Healthcare NHS Trust Lon from 94; NSM Wimbledon *S'wark* 95-10; Hon Can S'wark Cathl from 07. *St George's Hospital, Blackshaw Road, London SW17 0QT* Tel (020) 8725 3070, 8725 3071 or 8397 0952 Fax 8725 1621
E-mail hilary.johnson@stgeorges.nhs.uk

JOHNSON, Ian Lawrence. b 44. Wells Th Coll 68. d 71 p 72. C Benhilton *S'wark* 71-73; C Weymouth H Trin *Sarum* 73-76; R Pewsey 76-81; R Maiden Newton and Valleys 81-83; Youth Officer (Sherborne Area) 81-83; Dioc Youth Officer 83-88; TR Langley and Parkfield *Man* 88-95; P-in-c Haughton St Anne 95-99; Dioc Adv on Evang 95-99; TR Southampton (City Cen) *Win* 99-08; rtd 08. *Farthing Cottage, 71 St Andrew Street, Tiverton EX16 6PL* Tel (01884) 251974

JOHNSON, Ian Leslie. b 51. Bede Coll Dur TCert73. Wycliffe Hall Ox 91. d 93 p 94. C Evington *Leic* 93-96; Sub Chapl HM Pris Gartree 96-97; C Foxton w Gumley and Laughton and Lubenham *Leic* 96-97; C Foxton w Gumley and Laughton 97-00; P-in-c from 00; Sub Chapl HM Pris Gartree from 97. *The Vicarage, Vicarage Drive, Foxton, Market Harborough LE16 7RJ* Tel (01858) 545245 E-mail ijoh270951@aol.com

JOHNSON (née SILINS), Ms Jacqueline. b 62. Coll of Ripon & York St Jo BA85. Ripon Coll Cuddesdon 01. d 03 p 04. C Torpoint *Truro* 03-08; P-in-c Harworth *S'well* from 08. *The Vicarage, Tickhill Road, Harworth, Doncaster DN11 8PD* Tel (01302) 744157 Mobile 07905-354723
E-mail jackie@benedict.f9.co.uk

✠JOHNSON, The Rt Revd James Nathaniel. b 32. Wells Th Coll 63. d 64 p 65 c 85. C Lawrence Weston *Bris* 64-66; P-in-c St Paul's Cathl St Helena 66-69; V 69-71; Hon Can from 75; Area Sec USPG *Ex* and *Truro* 72-74; R Combe Martin *Ex* 74-80; V Thorpe Bay *Chelmsf* 80-85; Bp St Helena 85-91; R Byfield w Boddington and Aston le Walls *Pet* 91-92; Asst Bp Pet 91-92; V Hockley *Chelmsf* 92-97; Asst Bp Chelmsf 92-97; Can Chelmsf Cathl 94-97; rtd 97; Hon Asst Bp Chelmsf 97-04; Hon Asst Bp Ox from 04; Perm to Offic *Cov* from 05. *St Helena, 28 Molyneux Drive, Bodicote, Banbury OX15 4AP* Tel (01295) 255357 E-mail bpjnj@onetel.com

JOHNSON, Canon John Anthony. b 18. Selw Coll Cam BA48 MA53 St Jo Coll Dur. d 51 p 52. C Battersea St Mary *S'wark* 51-54; C Merton St Mary 54-56; V Balderton *S'well* 56-60; V Mansfield Woodhouse 60-70; V Beeston 70-85; RD Beeston 81-85; Hon Can S'well Minster 82-85; rtd 86; Perm to Offic *Blackb* 90-02. *Driftwood, Ireleth Road, Askam-in-Furness LA16 7JD* Tel (01229) 462291

JOHNSON, John David. b 38. Handsworth Coll Birm 60 Claremont Sch of Th 65 St Deiniol's Hawarden 71. d 71 p 72. C Heref St Martin 71-73; P-in-c Ewyas Harold w Dulas 73-79; P-in-c Kilpeck 73-79; P-in-c St Devereux w Wormbridge 73-79; P-in-c Kenderchurch 73-79; P-in-c Bacton 78-79; TR Ewyas Harold w Dulas, Kenderchurch etc 79-81; R Kentchurch w Llangua, Rowlestone, Llancillo etc 79-81; Chapl Napsbury Hosp St Alb 81-96; Chapl Horizon NHS Trust Herts 96-00; Chapl Barnet Healthcare NHS Trust 96-00; Chapl Barnet and Chase Farm Hosps NHS Trust 00-05; Chapl Herts Partnerships NHS Trust 02-03; rtd 03. *25 Church Lane, Eaton Bray, Dunstable LU6 2DJ* Tel (01525) 222319

JOHNSON, Josephine. See JOHNSON, Frances Josephine

JOHNSON, Mrs Julie Margaret. b 47. d 98 p 99. OLM Welton and Dunholme w Scothern *Linc* 98-07; NSM Edgeley and Cheadle Heath *Ches* from 07. *10 Delaford Close, Stockport SK3 8XA* Tel 0161-456 6463 E-mail johnson-julie2@sky.com

JOHNSON, Kathryn Ann. d 03 p 04. C Wrexham *St As* 03-04; C Prestatyn 04-11; V Abergele and St George from 11. *The Vicarage, 109 High Street, Prestatyn LL19 9AR* Tel (01745) 853780

JOHNSON, Keith Henry. b 64. Keele Univ BA91 Leeds Univ BA97 CQSW91. Coll of Resurr Mirfield 95. d 97 p 98. C W Bromwich St Fran *Lich* 97-00; P-in-c Willenhall St Giles 00-05; V 05-06; Perm to Offic *Lich* from 06-08 and *Lich* 07-08; P-in-c Handsworth *Sheff* 08-10; R from 10. *St Mary's Rectory, Handsworth Road, Handsworth, Sheffield S13 9BZ* Tel 0114-269 2403 Mobile 07988-405572
E-mail keithhjohnson@hotmail.com

JOHNSON, Keith Martyn. b 68. St Jo Coll Nottm 04. d 06 p 07. C Ipsley *Worc* 06-10; V Chatham St Paul w All SS *Roch* from 10. *The Vicarage, 2A Waghorn Street, Chatham ME4 5LT* Tel 07772-642393 (mobile)
E-mail revkeithjohnson@btinternet.com

JOHNSON, The Very Revd Keith Winton Thomas William. b 37. K Coll Lon BD63 Open Univ MA06 AKC63. d 64 p 65. C Dartford H Trin *Roch* 64-69; Chapl Kuwait 69-73; V Erith St Jo *Roch* 73-80; V Bexley St Jo 80-91; V Royston *St Alb* 91-94; R Sandon, Wallington and Rushden w Clothall 94-97; Dean St Chris Cathl Bahrain 97-02; rtd 02; Hon C Balsham, Weston Colville, W Wickham etc *Ely* 04-10; RD Linton 07-09; Perm to Offic from 10. *17 The Rookery, Balsham, Cambridge CB21 4EU* Tel (01223) 890835 E-mail keith1412@hotmail.com

JOHNSON, Kenneth William George. b 53. Hull Univ BA76 PGCE77. EMMTC 92. d 95 p 96. NSM Ilkeston H Trin *Derby* 95-99; NSM Sandiacre from 99; Chapl Bluecoat Sch Nottm from 02. *18 Park Avenue, Awsworth, Nottingham NG16 2RA* Tel 0115-930 7830 E-mail kenjohnson@bluecoat.nottingham.sch.uk

JOHNSON, Miss Lesley Denise. b 47. WMMTC 95. d 98 p 99. NSM Stockingford *Cov* 98-01; TV Cov E 01-10; rtd 10.

212 Sedgemoor Road, Coventry CV3 4DZ Tel (024) 7630 1241
JOHNSON, Malcolm Arthur. b 36. Univ Coll Dur BA60 MA64
Lon Metrop Univ Hon MA02 Lambeth MA06 K Coll Lon
PhD10 FSA04. Cuddesdon Coll 60. **d** 62 **p** 63. C Portsea N End
St Mark *Portsm* 62-67; Chapl Qu Mary Coll *Lon* 67-74; V
St Botolph Aldgate w H Trin Minories 74-92; P-in-c
St Ethelburga Bishopgate 85-89; AD The City 85-90; Master R
Foundn of St Kath in Ratcliffe 93-97; Bp's Adv for Past Care and
Counselling *Lon* 97-01; rtd 02; Perm to Offic *Lon* from 07 and
Guildf from 09. *1 Foxgrove Drive, Woking GU21 4DZ* Tel
(01483) 720684 E-mail malcolm.johnson4@btinternet.com
JOHNSON, Canon Malcolm Stuart. b 35. AKC60. **d** 61 **p** 62. C
Catford St Laur *S'wark* 61-64; Hon C Hatcham St Cath 66-76;
P-in-c Kingstanding St Luke *Birm* 76-77; V 77-82; P-in-c
Peckham St Jo w St Andr *S'wark* 82-92; V 92-03; Hon Can
Sabongidda-Ora from 98; rtd 04. *34 Sheppard's College, London
Road, Bromley BR1 1PF* Tel (020) 8466 5276
JOHNSON, Canon Margaret Anne Hope. b 52. Fitzw Coll Cam
BA95. Ridley Hall Cam 93. **d** 95 **p** 96. C Northampton Em *Pet*
95-97; P-in-c 97-98; TR from 98; Adv in Women's Min 03-06;
Can Pet Cathl from 04. *13 Booth Lane North, Northampton
NN3 6JG* Tel (01604) 648974 or 402150
E-mail revmahj@aol.com
JOHNSON, Margaret Joan (Meg). b 41. S'wark Ord Course 92.
d 95 **p** 96. NSM Sanderstead St Mary *S'wark* 95-04. *Address
temp unknown*
JOHNSON, Mark. b 62. Leic Poly BSc84 Loughb Univ PhD88.
Ripon Coll Cuddesdon 88. **d** 94 **p** 95. C Bishop's Cleeve *Glouc*
94-98; TV Heref S Wye 98-09; R Wormelow Hundred from 09.
Becket House, Much Birch, Hereford HR2 8HT Tel (01981)
540390
JOHNSON, Michael. b 42. Birm Univ BSc63. S'wark Ord
Course 68. **d** 71 **p** 72. C Kidbrooke St Jas *S'wark* 71-74; NSM
Eynsford w Farningham and Lullingstone *Roch* 74-89; NSM
Selling w Throwley, Sheldwich w Badlesmere etc *Cant* from 89.
*1 Halke Cottages, North Street, Sheldwich, Faversham
ME13 0LR* Tel (01795) 536583 Mobile 07860-635728
E-mail onehalke@aol.com
JOHNSON, Canon Michael Anthony. b 51. Ex Univ BA76.
Ripon Coll Cuddesdon 76 Ch Div Sch of the Pacific (USA) 77.
d 78 **p** 79. C Primrose Hill St Mary w Avenue Road St Paul *Lon*
78-81; C Hampstead St Jo 81-85; TV Mortlake w E Sheen
S'wark 85-93; V Wroughton *Bris* from 93; RD Wroughton 97-99;
AD Swindon 99-06; Hon Can Bris Cathl from 99. *The Vicarage,
Church Hill, Wroughton, Swindon SN4 9JS* Tel (01793) 812301
Fax 814582 E-mail canonmike@hotmail.com
JOHNSON, Michael Colin. b 37. S'wark Ord Course 77. **d** 80
p 81. NSM New Eltham All SS *S'wark* 80-84; NSM
Woldingham 84-98; rtd 98; Perm to Offic *Chich* 99-07. *The
College of the Blessed St Barnabas, Blackberry Lane, Lingfield RH7 6NJ* Tel
(01342) 872832 E-mail tandem@collegeofstbarnabas.com
JOHNSON, Michael Gordon. b 45. Kelham Th Coll 64. **d** 68
p 69. C Holbrooks *Cov* 68-72; C Cannock *Lich* 72-75; V Coseley
Ch Ch 75-79; P-in-c Sneyd 79-82; R Longton 82-88; Chapl
Pilgrim Hosp Boston 88-96; TV Jarrow *Dur* 96-98; Chapl
Monkton and Primrose Hill Hosp 96-98; R Burghwallis and
Campsall *Sheff* 98-10; rtd 10; Perm to Offic *Sheff* from 10.
8 Harmby Close, Skellow, Doncaster DN6 8PA Tel (01302)
330700
JOHNSON, Michael Robert. b 68. Aston Business Sch BSc90.
Ridley Hall Cam 94. **d** 97 **p** 98. C E Greenwich *S'wark* 97-00; C
Perry Hill St Geo 00-03; Chapl W Lon YMCA 03-05; C
Wokingham All SS *Ox* from 05; Pioneer Min Sonning Deanery
from 11. *Vine House, 23 Broad Street, Wokingham RG40 1AU*
Tel 0118-979 0098 E-mail michael@stage-fright.org.uk
JOHNSON, Mrs Nancy May. b 46. TCert67 Sheff Poly MA86.
NOC 00. **d** 02 **p** 03. NSM Sheff Cathl 02-04; Asst Chapl Sheff
Teaching Hosps NHS Foundn Trust 04-10; rtd 10; Perm to Offic
Sheff from 10. *121 Rustlings Road, Sheffield S11 7AB* Tel
0114-266 6456 E-mail nancyjohnson@hotmail.co.uk
JOHNSON, Nigel Edwin. b 41. AKC64 St Boniface Warminster
64. **d** 65 **p** 66. C Poulton-le-Sands *Blackb* 65-68; Chapl RN
68-93; Perm to Offic *Cant* 93-00 and *Cant* from 00; rtd 99. *Mell
View, 9 Thirlmere Park, Penrith CA11 8QS* Tel (01768) 899865
JOHNSON, Canon Nigel Victor. b 48. ARCM68 LTCL75 Cam
Univ DipEd69. Linc Th Coll 80. **d** 82 **p** 83. C Lindley *Wakef*
82-85; P-in-c Upperthong 85-87; Perm to Offic *Derby* 88-89;
NSM Calow and Sutton cum Duckmanton 89-90; R 90-00; RD
Bolsover and Staveley 98-00; V Newbold w Dunston from 00;
RD Chesterfield from 02; Hon Can Derby Cathl from 05.
Newbold Rectory, St John's Road, Chesterfield S41 8QN Tel
(01246) 450374 E-mail nvjohnson@tiscali.co.uk
JOHNSON, Paul James. b 56. Teesside Coll of Educn BEd80
Dur Sch of Educn MA95. NEOC 06. **d** 09 **p** 10. NSM Whorlton
w Carlton and Faceby *York* from 09. *18 Priorwood Gardens,
Ingleby Barwick, Stockton-on-Tees TS17 0XH* Tel (01642)
761941 E-mail paul.johnson53@ntlworld.com
JOHNSON, Peter Colin. b 64. SS Mark & Jo Univ Coll Plymouth
BEd87 Univ of Wales (Lamp) PhD00. SWMTC 97. **d** 00 **p** 01.

NSM Godrevy *Truro* from 00. *Seascape, Trewelloe Road, Praa
Sands, Penzance TR20 9SU* Tel (01736) 763407
E-mail peterjohnson9@btconnect.com
JOHNSON, Canon Peter Frederick. b 41. Melbourne Univ BA63
Ch Ch Ox BA68 MA72. St Steph Ho Ox 68. **d** 69 **p** 70. C
Banbury *Ox* 69-71; Tutor St Steph Ho Ox 71-74; Chapl
St Chad's Coll Dur 74-80; Vice-Prin 78-80; Chapl K Sch Cant
80-90; Perm to Offic *Cant* 80-81; Hon Min Can Cant Cathl
81-90; Can Res Bris Cathl 90-08; rtd 08; Perm to Offic *Ox* from
08. *4 St John's Road, Windsor SL4 3QN* Tel (01753) 865914
E-mail pf.johnson@btinternet.com
JOHNSON, Prof Peter Stewart. b 44. Nottm Univ BA65 PhD70.
Cranmer Hall Dur 01. **d** 03 **p** 04. NSM Dur St Nic from 03.
126 Devonshire Road, Durham DH1 2BH Tel 0191-386 6334
Mobile 07949-680467
JOHNSON, Philip Anthony. b 69. All Nations Chr Coll BA97
MA98 FIBMS94. Ridley Hall Cam 00. **d** 02 **p** 03. C Witham
Chelmsf 02-06; P-in-c Holland-on-Sea from 06. *The Vicarage,
297 Frinton Road, Holland-on-Sea, Clacton-on-Sea CO15 5SP*
Tel (01255) 812424 E-mail revdphilip@aol.com
JOHNSON, Phillip Thomas. b 75. City Univ BA03 FRSA.
Ripon Coll Cuddesdon 06. **d** 08 **p** 09. C Cheam *S'wark* 08-11; V
Weston *Guildf* from 11. *All Saints' Vicarage, 1 Chestnut Avenue,
Esher KT10 8JL* Tel (020) 8398 9685 Mobile 07815-018846
E-mail vicar@allsaintschurchweston.org.uk
JOHNSON (née DAVIES), Rhiannon Mary Morgan. b 69.
St Anne's Coll Ox BA90 MA96 Univ of Wales (Cardiff) PhD94
BD96. St Mich Coll Llan 94. **d** 97 **p** 98. C Whitchurch *Llan*
97-99; NSM Walton W w Talbenny and Haroldston W *St D*
99-00; Chapl Trin Coll Carmarthen 00; NSM Walton W w
Talbenny and Haroldston W *St D* 00-08; P-in-c Walwyn's Castle
w Robeston W from 08; Dioc Course Dir for Exploring Faith
from 11. *The Rectory, Walton West, Little Haven, Haverfordwest
SA62 3UB* Tel (01437) 781279
JOHNSON, Richard Miles. b 59. Bris Univ BSc82. St Jo Coll
Nottm 87. **d** 90 **p** 91. C Bromley SS Pet and Paul *Roch* 90-94;
USPG/CMS Philippines 94-97; Ind Chapl *Roch* 97-06; C
Bexleyheath Ch Ch 97-06; Ind Chapl *Worc* from 06; TV
Redditch H Trin from 06. *120 Carthorse Lane, Redditch B97 6SZ*
Tel (01527) 61936 E-mail dickim@globalnet.co.uk
JOHNSON, Richard William. b 76. St Cath Coll Cam BA98 MA
Glos Univ PhD05. Westmr Th Cen. **d** 05 **p** 06. C Symonds Street
St Paul New Zealand 05-09; C Worc City from 09. *All Saints'
Church, Quay Turn, Quay Street, Worcester WR1 2JJ* Tel
(01905) 734625 E-mail rich@allsaintsworcester.org.uk
JOHNSON, Canon Robert Kenneth. b 48. NOC 83. **d** 86 **p** 87. C
Hattersley *Ches* 86-88; C Brinnington w Portwood 88-90; V
Gospel Lane St Mich *Birm* 90-97; P-in-c Birm St Geo 97-07; R
07; Hon Can Birm Cathl 05-07; rtd 07. *9 Briants Piece,
Hermitage, Thatcham RG18 9SX* Tel (01635) 203419
E-mail robkj@btopenworld.com
JOHNSON, Canon Robin Edward Hobbs. b 39. Fitzw Ho Cam
BA61 MA65. Ripon Hall Ox 61. **d** 63 **p** 64. C Tyldesley w
Shakerley *Man* 63-66; Lic to Offic *Leic* 66-71; V Castleton Moor
Man 71-77; Dir of Ords 76-81; V Prestwich St Gabr 77-81; V
Heaton Ch Ch 81-91; Hon Can Man Cathl 86-91; TR
Dorchester *Sarum* 91-00; RD Dorchester 99-00; rtd 00; Chapl
Torrevieja *Eur* 00-03. *11 Bampton Court, Gamston, Nottingham
NG2 6PA*
JOHNSON, Ronald George. b 33. Chich Th Coll 75. **d** 76 **p** 77.
NSM Shipley *Chich* 76-79; C Brighton St Matthias 79-82; R
Barlavington, Burton w Coates, Sutton and Bignor 82-93; rtd 93;
Perm to Offic *Chich* from 93. *1 Highdown Drive, Littlehampton
BN17 6HJ* Tel (01903) 732210
JOHNSON, The Very Revd Samuel Hugh Akinsope. b 30. K Coll
Lon BD61. Lich Th Coll 52. **d** 55 **p** 56. C Whitechapel St Paul w
St Mark *Lon* 55-58; C Sunbury 58-59; C Lisson Grove w
St Marylebone St Matt w Em 59-60; C St Martin-in-the-Fields
60-62; Nigeria from 63; Provost Lagos Cathl 70-95; rtd 95. *1 Oba
Nle Aro Crescent, Ilupeju, PO Box 10021, Marina, Lagos, Nigeria*
JOHNSON (née ROWE), Mrs Shiela. b 43. CITC 93. **d** 96 **p** 97.
Aux Min Urney w Denn and Derryheen *K, E & A* 96-97; Aux
Min Boyle and Elphin w Aghanagh, Kilbryan etc 97-01; Aux
Min Roscommon w Donamon, Rathcline, Kilkeevin etc 97-01;
P-in-c Clondevaddock w Portsalon and Leatbeg *D & R* 02-08;
rtd 08. *Rainbow's End, Carrickmacafferty, Derrybeg, Co Donegal,
Republic of Ireland* Tel (00353) (74) 953 2843
JOHNSON, Stanley. b 42. QUB BSc63 TCD BTh89. CITC 86.
d 89 **p** 90. C Kilmore w Ballintemple, Kildallan etc *K, E & A*
89-97; Adn Elphin and Ardagh 97-01; Can Elphin Cathl 97-01; I
Templemichael w Clongish, Clooncumber etc 97-01; I
Clondehorkey w Cashel *D & R* 01-09; Can Raphoe Cathl 08-09;
rtd 09. *Rainbow's End, Carrickmacafferty, Derrybeg, Co Donegal,
Republic of Ireland* Tel (00353) (74) 953 2843 Mobile 87-973
5775 E-mail sjohnsons@eircom.net
JOHNSON, Stephen. b 57. Cranmer Hall Dur. **d** 00 **p** 01. C
Longton *Blackb* 00-02; C Longridge 03-04; V Preston Em from
04; Chapl Cen Lancs Univ from 08. *Emmanuel Vicarage, 2*

Cornthwaite Road, Fulwood, Preston PR2 3DA Tel (01772) 717136 Mobile 07790-917504 E-mail stephen@johnsonstephen.orangehome.co.uk
JOHNSON, Stephen Ashley. b 79. York Univ BA01 MA02. Wycliffe Hall Ox BTh06. d 06 p 07. C Sunningdale Ox 06-09; V Sunninghill and S Ascot from 09. Sunninghill Vicarage, Church Lane, Ascot SL5 7DD Tel (01344) 873202 Mobile 07799-834250 E-mail steve79@tiscali.co.uk
JOHNSON, Stephen William. b 63. Trent Poly BEd86 Keele Univ MA94 Univ Coll Ches BA05 ALCM85. NOC 02. d 05 p 06. NSM Betley Lich 05-08; NSM Keele 05-08; NSM Madeley 05-08; NSM Silverdale 05-08; Perm to Offic from 10. 86 Dunnocksfold Road, Alsager, Stoke-on-Trent ST7 2TW Tel (01270) 874066 Mobile 07766-411090 E-mail sjohnsonone@talktalk.net
JOHNSON, Stuart. See JOHNSON, Geoffrey Stuart
JOHNSON, Mrs Susan Constance. b 46. EAMTC 01. d 03 p 04. NSM Heald Green St Cath Ches 03-07. 11A Lynton Park Road, Cheadle Hulme, Cheadle SK8 6JA Tel 0161-485 3787 E-mail revsusan@ntlworld.com
JOHNSON, Miss Susan Elaine. b 44. R Holloway Coll Lon BA66. EAMTC 99. d 03 p 03. C München Ascension and V Ingolstadt H Trin 03-06; NSM Cwmbran Mon 06-09; TV Papworth Ely 09-11; rtd 11. Address temp unknown Tel 07919-232211 (mobile) E-mail revsusan44@btinternet.com
JOHNSON, Terence John. b 44. Cov Poly BA89. ALCD70. d 69 p 70. C Woodside Ripon 69-72; C Leeds St Geo 72-76; C Heworth H Trin York 76-81; V Budbrooke Cov 81-97; Chapl Wroxall Abbey Sch 83-93; V Stone Ch Ch and Oulton Lich 97-02; P-in-c Collingtree w Courteenhall and Milton Malsor Pet 02-08; rtd 08; Perm to Offic Pet from 09. 18 Northgate, Towcester NN12 6HT Tel (01327) 351408 E-mail terencejohnson194@btinternet.com
JOHNSON, Thomas Bernard. b 44. BA CertEd. Oak Hill Th Coll. d 84 p 85. C Birkenhead St Jas w St Bede Ches 84-88; R Ashover and Brackenfield Derby 88-01; P-in-c Wessington 99-01; R Ashover and Brackenfield w Wessington 01-03; RD Chesterfield 97-02; V Swanwick and Pentrich 03-10; Hon Chapl Derbyshire St Jo Ambulance from 91; rtd 10. 11 The Spinney, Ripley DE5 3HW Tel (01773) 570375 E-mail t.b.johnson2000@gmail.com
JOHNSON, Victor Edward. b 45. Linc Th Coll 83. d 85 p 86. C Garforth Ripon 85-90; Dioc Video Officer 90-92; V Wyther 92-00; V Shelley and Shepley Wakef 00-01; rtd 01; Perm to Offic Bradf 02-04. Low Farm, Marsh Lane Gardens, Kellington, Goole DN14 0PG Tel (01977) 661629 E-mail vej@onetel.com
JOHNSON, Victoria Louise. b 75. Leic Univ BSc96 PhD00 SS Coll Cam BA06. Westcott Ho Cam 04 Yale Div Sch 06. d 07 p 08. C Baguley Man 07-10; P-in-c Flixton St Mich from 10. The Rectory, 348 Church Road, Urmston, Manchester M41 6HR Tel 0161-748 2884 Mobile 07761-030755 E-mail vickyjohnson@cantab.net
JOHNSTON, Alexander Irvine. b 47. Keele Univ BA70 LRAM. St Alb Minl Tr Scheme 77. d 80 p 81. NSM Hockerill St Alb 80-95; NSM High Wych and Gilston w Eastwick 95-96; TV Bottesford w Ashby Linc 96-01; P-in-c St Germans Truro from 01. The Vicarage, Quay Road, St Germans, Saltash PL12 5LY Tel (01503) 230690 E-mail alecjohnston@btinternet.com
JOHNSTON, Allen Niall. b 61. SAUB Univ BTh92 Kent Univ MA97 AMBIM87 MISM87 MInstD00. Sarum & Wells Th Coll 89. d 92 p 93. C Roehampton H Trin S'wark 92-95; Dir Past Services Richmond, Twickenham and Roehampton NHS Trust 95-98; Tutor SEITE 95-97; Perm to Offic Eur 01-02; Sierra Leone 02-03; Asst P St Jo Cathl Freetown 03; Perm to Offic Ely from 03 and D & R from 04. 50 Vestry Court, 5 Monck Street, London SW1P 2BW E-mail niall@nialljohnston.org
JOHNSTON, Austin. b 50. Huddersfield Poly CertEd76 BEd90. Chich Th Coll 92. d 94 p 95. C Peterlee Dur 94-97; C Stockton St Pet 97-00; TR Stanley and Tanfield 00-01; TR Ch the K from 01. The Rectory, Church Bank, Stanley DH9 0DU Tel (01207) 233936
JOHNSTON, Brian. See JOHNSTON, Wilfred Brian
JOHNSTON, Mrs Carole Ann. b 58. Worc Coll of Educn BA84. St Jo Coll Nottm 04. d 06 p 07. C Ilkley All SS Bradf 06-09; TV Turton Moorland Min Man 09-11. Address temp unknown E-mail carole.johnston@virgin.net
JOHNSTON, Charles Walter Barr. b 38. Lon Univ BSc61. Oak Hill Th Coll 62. d 64 p 65. C Holloway St Mark w Em Lon 64-68; Argentina from 68; SAMS 70-03; rtd 03. clo A Johnston Esq, 27 Cloister Crofts, Leamington Spa CV32 6QG Tel (01926) 336136
JOHNSTON, David George Scott. b 66. Avery Hill Coll BA88. SEITE 00. d 03 p 04. C Frindsbury w Upnor and Chattenden Roch 03-06; R Longfield from 06; C Chislehurst Ch Ch from 11. 56 Walden Road, Chislehurst BR7 5DL Tel (020) 8467 4610 E-mail rev.dj@btinternet.com
JOHNSTON, Canon Donald Walter. b 28. Trin Coll Melbourne BA51 Lon Univ PGCE52 Em Coll Cam BA63 MA67. Ridley Hall Cam 64. d 64 p 65. C Cottingham York 64-66; Australia from 66; Min Nunawading Melbourne 67-69; Chapl Brighton

Gr Sch Melbourne 70-73; Chapl Melbourne C of E Gr Sch 74-84; Angl Bd of Miss 85-90; Chapl H Name Sch Dogura 85; Hd Martyrs' Memorial Sch Popondetta 86-89; Hon Commissary from 91; Can Papua New Guinea from 90; rtd 91. 22 Albert Street, PO Box 114, Point Lonsdale Vic 3225, Australia Tel (0061) (3) 5258 2139 or 9690 0549 Fax 5258 3994 E-mail dncjohnston@al.com.au
JOHNSTON, Duncan Howard. b 63. Hull Univ BA85 Nottm Univ MA93. St Jo Coll Nottm 91. d 93 p 94. C Werrington Pet 93-96; V Gt Doddington and Wilby 96-01; Dioc Adv in Local Miss Dur 02-03; R Fremont St Jo USA from 03. 515 East Pine Street, Fremont MI 49412-1739, USA Tel (001) (231) 924 7120 E-mail djepisc@joimal.com
JOHNSTON, Edith Violet Nicholl. b 28. d 87. Par Dn Bentley Sheff 87-88; rtd 88; Perm to Offic Sheff 88-08. 30 Sharman Road, Belfast BT9 5FW Tel (028) 9066 6776
JOHNSTON, Elizabeth Margaret. b 37. QUB BA58 DipEd69 Serampore Univ BD87. Dalton Ho Bris. d 81 p 94. BCMS India 62-92; C Belfast St Chris D & D 93-94; Bp's C 94-03; Can Down Cathl 01-03; rtd 03. 103 Ballydorn Road, Killinchy, Newtownards BT23 6QB Tel (028) 9754 2518 Mobile 07762-821569 E-mail elizabeth_johnston@amserve.com
JOHNSTON, Frank. See JOHNSTON, William Francis
JOHNSTON, Geoffrey Stanley. b 44. Aston Univ MBA81 Birm Univ CertEd78. Kelham Th Coll 64. d 68 p 69. C Blakenall Heath Lich 68-72 and 73-75; C St Buryan, St Levan and Sennen Truro 72-73; P-in-c Willenhall St Steph Lich 75-76; C W Bromwich All SS 76-77; Lect W Bromwich Coll of Commerce and Tech 78-82; Ind Chapl Worc 82-94; TV Halesowen 82-94; NSM Dudley St Fran 94-99; P-in-c 99-08; P-in-c Dudley St Edm 04-08; rtd 08; P-in-c Nerja and Almuñécar Eur from 08. Church House, Calle Jilguero, Urbanizacion Almijara 2 Sur, Nerja, 29780 (Málaga), Spain Tel (0034) 952 521 339 E-mail anglicansnerja@yahoo.com
JOHNSTON, Mrs Helen Kay. b 48. SRN70. SAOMC 95. d 98 p 99. OLM Banbury St Paul Ox 98-01; P-in-c Flimby Carl 01-03; C Netherton 01-03; Perm to Offic Derby 04-11. Merryfields, Whitehorn Avenue, Barleston, Stoke-on-Trent ST12 9EF Tel (01782) 372618 E-mail kaybees@supanet.com
JOHNSTON, Miss Henrietta Elizabeth Ann. b 59. St Jo Coll Dur BA03. Cranmer Hall Dur 01. d 03 p 04. C Cov H Trin 03-07; C Dorridge Birm 07-11; V Lache cum Saltney Ches from 11. St Mark's Vicarage, 5 Cliveden Road, Chester CH4 8DR Tel (01244) 671702 Mobile 07796-948904 E-mail hennie.johnston@tiscali.co.uk
JOHNSTON, Kay. See JOHNSTON, Mrs Helen Kay
JOHNSTON, Malcolm. See JOHNSTON, William Malcolm
JOHNSTON, Michael David Haigh. b 44. S Dios Minl Tr Scheme 88. d 91 p 92. NSM Wootton Portsm 91-95; NSM Ryde H Trin 95-99; NSM Swanmore St Mich 95-99; P-in-c Cowes St Faith 99-03; Asst Chapl Isle of Wight NHS Primary Care Trust from 03; Chapl HM Pris Kingston (Portsm) 03-05. The Chaplaincy, St Mary's Hospital, Newport PO30 5TG Tel (01983) 524081 E-mail rvdmikej@fastmail.fm
JOHNSTON, Michael Edward. b 68. TCD BA97 MA04. CITC BTh00. d 00 p 01. Bp's V and Lib Kilkenny Cathl and C Kilkenny w Aghour and Kilmanagh C & O 00-03; V Waterford w Killea, Drumcannon and Dunhill 03-09; I Shinrone w Aghancon etc L & K from 09. St Mary's Rectory, Shinrone, Birr, Co Offaly, Republic of Ireland Tel (00353) (505) 47164 E-mail shinrone@killaloe.anglican.org
JOHNSTON, Niall. See JOHNSTON, Allen Niall
JOHNSTON, Patricia Anne. See FLEMING, Mrs Patricia Anne
JOHNSTON, Canon Robert John. b 31. Oak Hill Th Coll 64. d 64 p 65. C Bebington Ches 64-68; I Lack Clogh 68-99; Can Clogh Cathl 89-99; rtd 99. 2 Beechcroft, Semicock Road, Ballymoney BT53 6NF Tel (028) 2766 9317
JOHNSTON, Thomas Cosbey. b 15. Em Coll Cam BA40 MA44. Ridley Hall Cam 40. d 42 p 43. C Handsworth St Mary Birm 42-48; New Zealand from 48. 254 Main Road, Moncks Bay, Christchurch 8081, New Zealand Tel (0064) (3) 384 1224
JOHNSTON, Trevor Samuel. b 72. Ulster Univ BMus96 TCD BTh01. CITC 98. d 01 p 02. C Carrickfergus Conn 01-04; C Jordanstown and Chapl Jordanstown and Belf Campuses Ulster Univ 04-09; Crosslinks Ireland Team Ldr from 09. 18 Meadowview, Jordanstown, Newtownabbey BT37 0US Tel 07776-178248 (mobile) E-mail trev@tjohnston.net
JOHNSTON, Wilfred Brian. b 44. TCD BA67 MA70. Div Test 68. d 68 p 70. C Seagoe D & D 68-73; I Inniskeel D & R 73-82; I Castlerock w Dunboe and Fermoyle 82-02; Bp's C Gweedore, Carrickfin and Templecrone 02-08; Dioc Registrar 89-06; Can Derry Cathl 92-02; Preb 99-02; Can Raphoe Cathl 05-08; rtd 08. 2 The Apple Yard, Coleraine BT51 3PP Tel (028) 7032 6406 E-mail b.johnston@talk21.com
JOHNSTON, William Derek. b 40. CITC 68. d 68 p 69. V Choral Derry Cathl 68-70; I Swanlinbar w Templeport K, E & A 70-73; I Billis Union 73-84; Glebes Sec (Kilmore) 77-03; I Annagh w Drumaloor and Cloverhill 84-87; Preb Kilmore Cathl 85-89; I Annagh w Drumgoon, Ashfield etc 87-99; Adn Kilmore 89-03; I

Lurgan w Billis, Killinkere and Munterconnaught 99-03; rtd 03. *Ballaghanea, Mullagh Road, Virginia, Co Cavan, Republic of Ireland* Tel (00353) (49) 854 9960 Mobile 86-832 9911
JOHNSTON, William Francis (Frank). b 30. CB83. TCD BA55 MA69. **d** 55 **p** 56. C Orangefield *D & D* 55-59; CF 59-77; Asst Chapl Gen 77-80; Chapl Gen 80-87; P-in-c Winslow *Ox* 87-91; RD Claydon 89-94; R Winslow w Gt Horwood and Addington 91-95; rtd 95; Perm to Offic *Ex* from 95. *Lower Axehill, Chard Road, Axminster EX13 5ED* Tel (01297) 33259
JOHNSTON, Canon William John. b 35. Lon Univ BA85 MA90 PhD. CITC 67. **d** 70 **p** 71. C Belfast St Donard *D & D* 70-72; C Derg *D & R* 72-78; I Drumclamph w Lower and Upper Langfield 78-91; I Kilskeery w Trillick *Clogh* 91-10; Preb Clogh Cathl 04-10; Prec 09-10; rtd 10. *Ernedene, 61 Dublin Road, Enniskillen BT74 6HN* Tel (028) 6632 2268
JOHNSTON, William Malcolm. b 48. SAOMC 92. **d** 95 **p** 96. NSM Banbury *Ox* 95-01; P-in-c Netherton *Carl* 01-03; C Flimby 01-03; Perm to Offic *Derby* 04-11. *Merryfields, Whitehorn Avenue, Barleston, Stoke-on-Trent ST12 9EF* Tel (01782) 372618 E-mail kaybees@supanet.com
JOHNSTON, William McConnell. b 33. TCD BA57. **d** 58 **p** 59. C Ballymena w Ballyclug *Conn* 58-61; C Belfast St Thos 61-63; C Finaghy 63-66; R Kambula S Africa 66-74; Dean Eshowe 74-86; R Mtubatuba 86-99; rtd 00; Perm to Offic *Chich* from 04. *Honeysuckle Cottage, Redford, Midhurst GU29 0QG* Tel (01428) 741131
JOHNSTONE, William Henry Green. b 26. **d** 92 **p** 94. Belize 92-98; Hon C Tollard Royal w Farnham, Gussage St Michael etc *Sarum* 98-01; Hon C Chase from 01; OCF 94-98; OCM from 01. *Church Cottage, Chettle, Blandford Forum DT11 8DB* Tel (01258) 830396 E-mail padrewmchettle@aol.com
JOINT, Canon Michael John. b 39. Sarum & Wells Th Coll 79. **d** 79 **p** 79. CA from 61; Hon C Chandler's Ford *Win* 79-83; Youth Chapl 79-83; V Lymington 83-95; Co-ord Chapl R Bournemouth and Christchurch Hosps NHS Trust 96-03; Hon Can Win Cathl 00-03; rtd 03; Perm to Offic *Win* 03-04. *20 Wavendon Avenue, Barton on Sea, New Milton BH25 7LS* Tel (01425) 628952 E-mail michjoin@aol.com
JOLLEY, Andrew John. b 61. Nottm Univ BSc83 PhD06 Warwick Univ MBA88 CEng88 MIMechE88. St Jo Coll Nottm BTh97. **d** 98 **p** 99. C Sparkhill w Greet and Sparkbrook *Birm* 98-02; V Aston SS Pet and Paul 02-08; P-in-c Aston St Jas 05-08; P-in-c Nechells 05-08; V Aston and Nechells from 08; AD Aston from 05. *The Vicarage, Sycamore Road, Aston, Birmingham B6 5UH* Tel 0121-327 5856
E-mail andy@astonnechellscofe.org.uk
JOLLY, Leslie Alfred Walter. b 16. AKC40. **d** 40 **p** 41. C Bow w Bromley St Leon *Lon* 40-42; C Cheam Common St Phil *S'wark* 42-50; C Mottingham St Andr w St Alban 50-52; V Newington St Matt 52-57; R Chaldon 57-85; rtd 85; Perm to Offic *S'wark* 85-94 and *York* 85-04. *12 Roseneath Court, Greenwood Gardens, Caterham CR3 6RX* Tel (01883) 332463
JONAS, Alan Charles. b 56. Leeds Univ BA79 Univ of Wales (Abth) PGCE80. Wycliffe Hall Ox 92. **d** 94 **p** 95. C Hersham *Guildf* 94-98; P-in-c Westcott from 98; Chapl Priory Sch 01-07. *The Vicarage, Guildford Road, Westcott, Dorking RH4 3QB* Tel (01306) 885309 E-mail alchasjonas@aol.com
JONAS, Canon Ian Robert. b 54. St Jo Coll Nottm BTh80. **d** 80 **p** 81. C Portadown St Mark *Arm* 80-82; C Cregagh *D & D* 82-85; BCMS Sec *D & G* 85-90; V Langley Mill *Derby* 90-97; I Kilgariffe Union *C, C & R* 97-09; I Carrigrohane Union from 09; Can Cork Cathl from 11; Can Cloyne Cathl from 11. *The Rectory, Church Hill, Carrigrohane, Co Cork, Republic of Ireland* Tel (00353) (21) 487 1106 E-mail revianjonas@yahoo.co.uk
JONES, Alan David. b 32. ALCD58. **d** 58 **p** 59. C Ipswich All SS *St E* 58-60; C Southend St Jo *Chelmsf* 60-64; V Leyton St Cath 64-70; V Hatfield Broad Oak and P-in-c Bush End 70-77; V Theydon Bois 77-88; P-in-c Finchingfield and Cornish Hall End 88-93; rtd 94; Perm to Offic *Chelmsf* and *St E* from 94. *3 Grammar School Place, Sudbury CO10 2GE* Tel (01787) 370864
JONES, Preb Alan Brian. b 47. Nottm Univ BA71. Coll of Resurr Mirfield 71. **d** 73 **p** 74. C Sedgley St Mary *Lich* 73-76; C Cov St Jo 76-78; V W Bromwich St Fran *Lich* 78-94; V Ettingshall from 94; AD Wolverhampton from 03; Preb Lich Cathl from 11. *The Vicarage, Farrington Road, Wolverhampton WV4 6QH* Tel (01902) 884616
JONES, Alan Pierce. See PIERCE-JONES, Alan
JONES, Alison. See JONES, Ms Helen Alison
JONES, Alison. See WAGSTAFF, Ms Alison
JONES, Alun. b 52. Leeds Univ BA96. Cuddesdon Coll 94. **d** 96 **p** 97. C Newc St Geo 96-98; C Cowgate 98-99; C Fenham St Jas and St Basil 99-04; P-in-c Carl St Herbert w St Steph 04-07; V from 07. *St Herbert's Vicarage, Blackwell Road, Carlisle CA2 4RA* Tel (01228) 523375 E-mail alun52@btinternet.com
JONES, Alwyn Humphrey Griffith. b 30. Leeds Univ BSc51. Coll of Resurr Mirfield 53. **d** 55 **p** 56. C W Hackney St Barn *Lon* 55-58; C-in-c Dacca St Thos E Pakistan 58-64; Ox Miss to Calcutta India 65-68; Chapl R Bombay Seamen's Soc 68-73;

P-in-c Bedminster St Fran *Bris* 73-75; TR Bedminster 75-83; TV Langport Area *B & W* 83-85; Dep Chapl HM Pris Nor 85; Chapl HM Pris Preston 85-89; Chapl HM Pris Ashwell 89-91; C Acton Green *Lon* 91-93; rtd 93; NSM Langport Area *B & W* 93-98; Perm to Offic *B & W* and *Bris* from 98. *4 All Saints' House, 1 Upper York Street, Bristol BS2 8NT* Tel 0117-923 2331 E-mail alwyn j@btinternet.com
JONES, Alyson Elizabeth. See DAVIE, Mrs Alyson Elizabeth
JONES, Mrs Andrea Margaret. b 46. Qu Coll Birm 88. **d** 90 **p** 94. Par Dn Kidderminster St Geo *Worc* 90-94; TV 94-95; C Penn Fields *Lich* 95-00; C Gt Wyrley 00-06; rtd 06. *57 Woodward Road, Kidderminster DY11 6NY* Tel (01562) 823555 E-mail aam@jones46.fsbusiness.co.uk
JONES, Andrea Susan. b 55. **d** 10 **p** 11. OLM Davyhulme St Mary *Man* from 10. *80 Davyhulme Road, Urmston, Manchester M41 7DN* Tel 0161-202 9373 Fax 236 9321 E-mail andysjones@hotmail.co.uk
JONES, Andrew. See JONES, Ian Andrew
JONES, The Ven Andrew. b 61. Univ of Wales (Ban) BD82 PGCE82 TCD BTh85 MA91 Univ of Wales MPhil93. CITC 82 St Geo Coll Jerusalem 84. **d** 85 **p** 86. Min Can Ban Cathl 85-88; R Dolgellau 88-92; Warden of Readers 91-92; Dir Past Studies St Mich Coll Llan 92-96; Lect Th Univ of Wales (Cardiff) 92-96; Visiting Prof St Geo Coll Jerusalem from 94; Research Fell from 96; R Llanbedrog w Llannor w Llanfihangel etc *Ban* 96-01; R Llanbedrog w Llannor and Llangian from 01; Dioc CME and NSM Officer 96-00; AD Llyn and Eifionydd 99-10; Hon Can Ban Cathl 04-05; Can from 05; Dioc Dir of Ords from 06; Adn Meirionnydd from 10. *Ty'n Llan Rectory, Llanbedrog, Pwllheli LL53 7TU* Tel and fax (01758) 740919
E-mail archdeacon.meirionnydd@churchinwales.org.uk
JONES, Andrew. b 64. York Univ BA85. Westmr Th Sem (USA) MDiv91 St Jo Coll Nottm 92. **d** 94 **p** 95. C Win Ch Ch 94-98; C St Helen Bishopsgate w St Andr Undershaft etc *Lon* from 98. *89 Forest Road, London E8 3BL* Tel (020) 7254 5942 E-mail a.jones@st-helens.org.uk
JONES, Andrew Christopher. b 47. Southn Univ BA69 PhD75. Ridley Hall Cam 78. **d** 80 **p** 81. C Wareham *Sarum* 80-83; P-in-c Symondsbury 83; P-in-c Chideock 83; R Symondsbury and Chideock 84-91; V Shottermill *Guildf* 91-99; P-in-c Bishopsnympton, Rose Ash, Mariansleigh etc *Ex* from 99. *The Rectory, Bishops Nympton, South Molton EX36 4NY* Tel (01769) 550427 E-mail a.c.jones@bnrec.f9.co.uk
JONES, Andrew Collins. b 62. Univ Coll Dur BA83 MA84 MLitt92. St Steph Ho Ox 88. **d** 90 **p** 91. C Llangefni w Tregaean and Llangristiolus etc *Ban* 90-94; C Hartlepool St Aid *Dur* 94-98; Chapl Hartlepool Gen Hosp 94-98; R Hendon *Dur* from 98; CMP from 95. *St Ignatius' Rectory, Bramwell Road, Sunderland SR2 8BY* Tel 0191-567 5575
JONES, Anne. See FURNESS, Christine Anne
JONES, Anthony. b 43. WEMTC 99. **d** 01 **p** 02. OLM Lydney *Glouc* 01-07; NSM Woolaston w Alvington and Aylburton from 07. *The Rectory, Main Road, Alvington, Lydney GL15 5AT* Tel (01594) 529387 Mobile 07860-331755 E-mail jones_rev@yahoo.co.uk
JONES, Canon Anthony Spacie. b 34. AKC58. **d** 59 **p** 60. C Bedford St Martin *St Alb* 59-63; Br Guiana 63-66; Guyana 66-71; V Ipswich All Hallows *St E* 72-80; RD Ipswich 78-86; Bp's Dom Chapl 80-82; V Rushmere 82-91; Hon Can St E Cathl 83-99; R Brantham w Stutton 91-99; P-in-c Bentley w Tattingstone 95-99; rtd 99; Perm to Offic *St E* from 99. *6 Fritillary Close, Pinewood, Ipswich IP8 3QT* Tel (01473) 601848 E-mail tonyjones.pinewood@btinternet.com
JONES, Barbara Christine. b 48. St Hugh's Coll Ox BA71 MA74 Lady Spencer Chu Coll of Educn PGCE74. CBDTI 97. **d** 00 **p** 01. NSM Bolton-le-Sands *Blackb* 00-09; Bp's Adv on Healing from 09. *11 Sandown Road, Lancaster LA1 4LN* Tel (01524) 65598 E-mail bcjones@mypostoffice.co.uk
JONES, Barry Mervyn. b 46. St Chad's Coll Dur BA68. **d** 70 **p** 71. C Bloxwich *Lich* 70-72; C Norwood All SS *Cant* 72-76; C New Addington 76-78; Chapl Mayday Univ Hosp Thornton Heath 78-86; Chapl Qu and St Mary's Hosps Croydon 78-86; Chapl Bromsgrove and Redditch DHA 86-94; Chapl Alexandra Hosp Redditch 86-94; Chapl Alexandra Healthcare NHS Trust Redditch 94-00; Chapl Worcs Acute Hosps NHS Trust 00-05; Perm to Offic *Worc* from 05. *46 Barlich Way, Lodge Park, Redditch B98 7JP* Tel (01527) 520659
JONES, Canon Basil Henry. b 26. Bps' Coll Cheshunt 63. **d** 64 **p** 65. C Gt Berkhamsted *St Alb* 64-67; V Leagrave 68-74; RD Luton 71-74; P-in-c Bedford St Paul 74-75; V Wigginton 75-93; Hon Can St Alb 82-93; rtd 93; Perm to Offic *St Alb* from 00. *17 Lochnell Road, Northchurch, Berkhamsted HP4 3QD* Tel (01442) 864485 E-mail bazilhjones@aol.com
JONES, Benjamin Jenkin Hywel. b 39. Univ of Wales BA61. St Mich Coll Llan 61. **d** 64 **p** 65. C Carmarthen St Pet *St D* 64-70; V Cynwyl Gaeo w Llansawel and Talley 70-79; R Llanbadarn Fawr 79-82; V Llanbadarn Fawr w Capel Bangor and Goginan 82-92; V Llanychaearn w Llanddeiniol 92-05; Warden of Readers from 82; Can St D Cathl 86-90; RD

Llanbadarn Fawr 89-90; Adn Cardigan 90-06; rtd 06. *Dowerdd, Waun Fawr, Aberystwyth SY23 3QF* Tel (01970) 617100

JONES, Benjamin Tecwyn. b 17. Univ of Wales BA38. K Coll Lon 38. d 40 p 41. C Hawarden *St As* 40-45; C Pleasley *Derby* 45-46; C Ormskirk *Liv* 46-49; R Rufford *Blackb* 49-55; V S Shore St Pet 55-65; C Oldham St Mary w St Pet *Man* 65-69; Hd Master and Chapl St Mary's Sch Bexhill-on-Sea 69-71; V Blackb St Luke 71-72; P-in-c Griffin 71-72; V Blackb St Luke w St Phil 72-83; rtd 83; Perm to Offic *Blackb* from 83. *21 Fosbrooke House, 8 Clifton Drive, Lytham St Annes FY8 5RQ*

JONES, Bernard Lewis. b 48. Llan Dioc Tr Scheme 89. d 93 p 94. NSM Aberaman and Abercwmboi w Cwmaman *Llan* 93-99; V Hirwaun from 99; AD Cynon Valley from 08. *The New Vicarage, 6 Redhill Close, Hirwaun, Aberdare CF44 9NZ* Tel (01685) 811316

JONES, Brenda. See CAMPBELL, Mrs Brenda

JONES, Brenda. b 50. Cranmer Hall Dur 02. d 04 p 05. C Jarrow *Dur* 04-07; C-in-c Bishop Auckland Woodhouse Close CD from 07. *18 Watling Road, Bishop Auckland DL14 6RP* Tel (01388) 604807

JONES, Canon Brian Howell. b 35. Univ of Wales MPhil96. St Mich Coll Llan. d 61 p 62. C Llangiwg *S & B* 61-63; C Swansea St Mary and H Trin 63-70; R New Radnor w Llanfihangel Nantmelan etc 70-75; V Llansamlet 75-89; Dioc Dir of Stewardship 82-89; P-in-c Capel Coelbren 89-95; Dioc Missr 89-95; Can Res Brecon Cathl 89-00; Can Treas 98-00; Chan 99-00; RD Cwmtawe 89-93; V Killay 95-00; rtd 00. *12 Harlech Crescent, Sketty, Swansea SA2 9LP* Tel (01792) 421115

JONES, Canon Brian Michael. b 34. Trin Coll Bris 79 Oak Hill Th Coll BA82. d 84 p 84. CMS 82-93; Sierra Leone 84-93; Can Bo from 91; C Frimley *Guildf* 93-99; rtd 99; Perm to Offic *Newc* 00-01; Hon C N Tyne and Redesdale 01-08. *20 Campfield Road, Ulverston LA12 9PB* E-mail bmj.retired@btopenworld.com

JONES, Canon Brian Noel. b 32. Edin Th Coll 59. d 62 p 63. C Monkseaton St Mary *Newc* 62-65; C Saffron Walden *Chelmsf* 65-69; P-in-c Swaffham Bulbeck *Ely* 69-75; Dioc Youth Officer 69-75; RD St Ives 75-83 and 87-89; V Ramsey 75-89; V Upwood w Gt and Lt Raveley 75-89; P-in-c Ramsey St Mary's 82-89; Hon Can Ely Cathl 85-97; V Cherry Hinton St Jo 89-97; RD Cambridge 94-97; rtd 97; Perm to Offic *Nor* from 97. *11 Winns Close, Holt NR25 6NQ* Tel (01263) 713645

JONES, Brian Robert. b 53. Surrey Univ BSc76. SAOMC 02. d 05 p 06. NSM Greenham *Ox* from 05. *27 Three Acre Road, Newbury RG14 7AW* Tel (01635) 34875

JONES, Canon Bryan Maldwyn. b 32. St Mich Coll Llan. d 62 p 63. C Swansea St Barn *S & B* 62-69; V Trallwng and Betws Penpont 69-75; V Trallwng, Bettws Penpont w Aberyskir etc 75-00; RD Brecon II 80-91; RD Brecon 91-99; Hon Can Brecon Cathl 92-00; rtd 00. *Plas Mawydd, 8 Camden Crescent, Brecon LD3 7BY* Tel (01874) 625063

JONES, Bryan William. b 30. Selw Coll Cam BA53 MA57. Linc Th Coll 53. d 55 p 56. C Bedminster Down *Bris* 55-58; C Filton 58-62; P-in-c Bedminster St Mich 62-65; V 65-72; P-in-c Moorfields 72-75; TV E Bris 75-95; rtd 95; Perm to Offic *Bris* from 95. *89 Canterbury Close, Yate, Bristol BS37 5TU* Tel (01454) 316795

JONES, Bryn Parry. b 49. Univ of Wales BSc98 MCIH98 FCIH03. St As Minl Tr Course 04. d 06 p 10. NSM Connah's Quay *St As* from 06. *7 Fron Las, Pen y Maes, Holywell CH8 7HX* Tel (01352) 714781

JONES, Bryon. b 34. Open Univ BA84. St D Coll Lamp 61. d 64 p 65. C Port Talbot St Theodore *Llan* 64-67; C Aberdare 68-69; C Up Hatherley *Glouc* 69-71; C Oystermouth *S & B* 71-74; V Camrose *St D* 74-77; V Camrose and St Lawrence w Ford and Haycastle 77-04; rtd 04. *31 New Road, Haverfordwest SA61 1TU* Tel (01437) 760596

JONES, Mrs Carol. b 45. d 04 p 05. OLM Shirley St Geo *S'wark* from 04. *50 Belgrave Court, Sloane Walk, Croydon CR0 7NW* Tel (020) 8777 6247 E-mail caroljonesolm@yahoo.co.uk

JONES, Miss Celia Lynn. b 54. Univ of Wales (Lamp) MTh09. Trin Coll Bris. d 01 p 08. C Bris St Paul's 01-08; C Barton Hill St Luke w Ch Ch and Moorfields 08-09; TV Magor *Mon* from 09. *The Vicarage, Station Road, Llanwern, Newport NP18 2DW* Tel (01633) 413647 E-mail clynnjones@talktalk.net

JONES, Charles Derek. b 37. K Coll Lon BD60 AKC60. d 61 p 62. C Stockton St Chad *Dur* 61-64; C Becontree St Elisabeth *Chelmsf* 64-66; C S Beddington St Mich *S'wark* 66-73; Lic to Offic *Ex* 73-77; Perm to Offic *Liv* 77-99; rtd 02. *4 Bryn Glas, Graigfechan, Ruthin LL15 2EX* Tel (01824) 705015

JONES, Christopher Howell. b 50. BA FCCA. Oak Hill Th Coll 80. d 83 p 84. C Leyton St Mary w St Edw *Chelmsf* 83-86; C Becontree St Mary 86-90; P-in-c Bootle St Matt *Liv* 90-93; V 93-99; AD Bootle 97-99; V Ormskirk from 99; Chapl W Lancashire NHS Trust 99-11. *The Vicarage, Park Road, Ormskirk L39 3AJ* Tel (01695) 572143

JONES, Christopher Ian. b 63. Moorlands Coll BA98 Southn Univ PGCE03. Ripon Coll Cuddesdon 09. d 11. C Windermere *Carl* from 11. *Burnthwaite, Kendal Road, Bowness-on-*

Windermere, Windermere LA23 3EW* Tel 07745-410487 (mobile) E-mail agalliao@hotmail.co.uk

JONES, Christopher Mark. b 54. St Pet Coll Ox BA75 MA79 Selw Coll Cam MPhil80. Ridley Hall Cam 77. d 80 p 81. C Putney St Marg *S'wark* 80-83; C Ham St Andr 83-86; Chapl HM Rem Cen Latchmere Ho 83-86; Chapl St Jo Coll Dur 87-93; Tutor Cranmer Hall Dur 87-93; Chapl and Fell St Pet Coll Ox 93-04; Home Affairs Policy Adv Abps' Coun Bd for Soc Resp from 04. *Archbishops' Council, Church House, Great Smith Street, London SW1P 3AZ* Tel (020) 7898 1531 Fax 7898 1536 E-mail christopher.jones@churchofengland.org

JONES, Christopher Mark. b 56. St Jo Coll Cam BA78 MA82 Wycliffe Hall Ox BA81 MA85. d 82 p 83. C Walsall *Lich* 82-84; Chapl St Jo Coll Cam 84-89; Chapl Eton Coll from 89; Ho Master from 97. *The Hopgarden, Eton College, Windsor SL4 6EQ* Tel (01753) 671065 Fax 671067

JONES, Christopher Yeates. b 51. STETS 97. d 00 p 01. NSM Yeovil St Mich *B & W* from 00. *20 Bedford Road, Yeovil BA21 5UQ* Tel (01935) 420886 Mobile 07803-371617 E-mail cyjones@care4free.net

JONES, Clifford Albert. b 20. Edin Th Coll 54. d 56 p 57. C Dundee St Salvador *Bre* 56-58; C Linc St Swithin 58-59; C Grantham St Wulfram 59-60; R Dundee St Salvador *Bre* 60-69; V Bradford *B & W* 69-74; V Bridgwater St Jo 74-78; RD Bridgwater 76-80; R Bridgwater St Jo w Chedzoy 78-80; P-in-c Timsbury 80-85; R Timsbury and Priston 85; rtd 85; P-in-c Nor St Geo Tombland 85-90; Hon C St Marylebone All SS *Lon* 90-94; Perm to Offic *Nor* 94-99 and *Lon* from 97. *clo The Revd Canon M Sanders, The Rectory, Woodbridge Road, Grundisburgh, Woodbridge IP13 6UF* Tel (01473) 735182

JONES, Clive. b 51. BA82. Oak Hill Th Coll 79. d 82 p 83. C Brunswick *Man* 82-85; V Pendlebury St Jo 85-96; V Attleborough *Cov* from 96. *Attleborough Vicarage, 5 Fifield Close, Nuneaton CV11 4TS* Tel (024) 7635 4114 E-mail clivej@hta1.freeserve.co.uk

JONES, Clive Morlais Peter. b 40. Univ of Wales (Cardiff) BA63 CertEd64 LTCL71. Chich Th Coll 64. d 66 p 67. C Llanfabon 66-70; PV Llan Cathl 70-75; R Gelligaer 75-85; Prec and Can Llan Cathl 84-85; R Tilehurst St Mich *Ox* 85-94; Chapl Costa Blanca *Eur* 94-97; V Newton St Pet *S & B* 97-06; P-in-c Haarlem *Eur* 07-10; Perm to Offic *Ox* from 10. *31 Lowbury Gardens, Compton, Newbury RG20 6NN* Tel (01635) 579409 E-mail clive.jones857@btinternet.com

JONES, Clive Wesley. b 68. St Steph Ho Ox 95. d 98 p 99. C Swanley St Mary *Roch* 98-02; P-in-c Belvedere St Aug 02-07; V from 07; Chapl Trin Sch Belvedere 02-04. *The Vicarage, St Augustine's Road, Belvedere DA17 5HH* Tel (020) 8311 6307 E-mail clive.jones@diocese-rochester.org *or* frclive@tiscali.co.uk

JONES, Colin Stuart. b 56. Southn Univ LLB77. Coll of Resurr Mirfield 81. d 84 p 85. C Mountain Ash *Llan* 84-86; C Castle Bromwich SS Mary and Marg *Birm* 86-89; V Kingshurst 89-94; V Perry Barr 94-05; P-in-c Wordsley *Worc* 05-07; TR from 07. *The Rectory, 13 Dunsley Drive, 13 Dunsley Drive, Stourbridge DY8 5RA* Tel (01384) 400709

JONES, Collette Moyra Yvonne. b 50. Liv Univ BSc71 PhD75 ALCM91. SNWTP 08. d 11. NSM Gt Sutton *Ches* from 11. *17 Maplewood Grove, Saughall, Chester CH1 6AD* Tel (01244) 881585 Mobile 07790-334086 E-mail collettemyjones@jonesc94.freeserve.co.uk

JONES, Cyril Ernest. b 29. St D Coll Lamp BA54. d 56 p 57. C Llanedy *St D* 56-60; C Llanelli 60-63; V Mydroilyn w Dihewyd 63-66; V Llanybydder 66-73; V Llanybydder and Llanwenog w Llanwnnen 73-78; V Betws w Ammanford 78-81; V Cynwyl Gaeo w Llansawel and Talley 81-94; rtd 94. *21 Pontardulais Road, Tycroes, Ammanford SA18 3QD* Tel (01269) 596421

JONES, Daniel. b 78. St Andr Univ MTheol01 PGCE02. Qu Coll Birm 06. d 08 p 09. NSM Barbourne *Worc* 08-11; Chapl St Pet Sch York from 11. *St Peter's School, Clifton, York YO30 6AB* Tel (01904) 527412 E-mail daniel a jones@btopenworld.com

JONES, David. See JONES, Preb Wilfred David

JONES, David. See JONES, Canon William David

JONES, David. b 55. CA Tr Coll 74 St Steph Ho Ox 83. d 85 p 86. C Fleur-de-Lis *Mon* 85-87; V Ynysddu 87-93; V Blackwood 93-08; AD Bedwellty 06-08; V Landore w Treboeth *S & B* from 08. *St Alban's Vicarage, Heol Fach, Treboeth, Swansea SA5 9DE* Tel (01792) 310586

JONES, David Arthur. b 44. Liv Univ BA66 Sussex Univ MA68. St D Coll Lamp LTh74. d 74 p 75. C Tenby *St D* 74-76; C Chepstow *Mon* 76-78; P-in-c Teversal *S'well* 78-81; R 81-91; Chapl Sutton Cen 78-89; V Radford All So w Ch Ch and St Mich 91-04; Adv to Urban Priority Par 96-01; Officer for Urban Life and Miss 04-09; rtd 09. *37 Devonshire Road, Nottingham NG5 2EW* Tel 0115-962 2115 E-mail urbanrover@gmail.com

JONES, David Gornal. b 47. d 74 p 75. In RC Ch 75-80; Asst P Durban St Paul 87-88; R Durban St Aid 89-91; Justice and Reconciliation Officer Natal 92-94; Port Chapl Miss to Seafarers

Walvis Bay 95-00; Vlissingen (Flushing) *Eur* 00-02; R Ayr, Girvan and Maybole *Glas* 02-06; V Sunderland St Thos and St Oswald *Dur* from 06. *St Thomas's Vicarage, Parkhurst Road, Sunderland SR4 9DB* Tel 0191-534 2100
E-mail dgjones@clara.co.uk

JONES, David Hugh. b 34. St D Coll Lamp BA56. St Mich Coll Llan 58. **d** 58 **p** 59. C Swansea St Mary and H Trin *S & B* 58-61; Inter-Colleg Sec SCM (Liv) 61-63; Hon Chapl Liv Univ 61-63; C Swansea St Pet *S & B* 63-69; V Llanddewi Ystradenni and Abbey Cwmhir 69-75; R Port Eynon w Rhosili and Llanddewi and Knelston 75-83; V Swansea St Barn 83-92; rtd 92. *16 Lon Ger-y-Coed, Cockett, Swansea SA2 0YH*

✠**JONES, The Rt Revd David <u>Huw</u>.** b 34. Univ of Wales (Ban) BA55 Univ Coll Ox BA58 MA62. St Mich Coll Llan 58. **d** 59 **p** 60 **c** 93. C Aberdare *Llan* 59-61; C Neath w Llantwit 61-65; V Crynant 65-69; V Cwmavon 69-74; Lect Th Univ of Wales (Cardiff) 74-78; Sub-Warden St Mich Coll Llan 74-78; V Prestatyn *St As* 78-82; Dioc Ecum Officer 78-82; Dean Brecon *S & B* 82-93; V Brecon w Battle 82-83; V Brecon St Mary and Battle w Llanddew 83-93; Asst Bp St As 93-96; Bp St D 96-01; rtd 02. *31 The Cathedral Green, Llandaff, Cardiff CF5 2EB*

JONES, Prof David <u>Huw</u>. b 49. Univ of Wales MB, BCh72 MD79 Chelsea Coll Lon MSc78 FRCR83 FRCP96 Hon FFPM07. EAMTC 95. **d** 98 **p** 99. NSM Trumpington *Ely* 98-02; Perm to Offic 02; Dean's V G&C Coll Cam from 06; RD Cambridge S *Ely* from 11. *17 Barrow Road, Cambridge CB2 8AP* Tel (01223) 358458
E-mail drhuw@btopenworld.com

JONES, David Ian Stewart. b 34. Selw Coll Cam BA57 MA61. Westcott Ho Cam 57. **d** 59 **p** 60. C Oldham *Man* 59-63, V Elton All SS 63-66; Chapl Eton Coll 66-70; Sen Chapl 70-74; Hd Master Bryanston Sch 74-82; P-in-c Bris Ch Ch w St Ewen and All SS 82-84; P-in-c Bris St Steph w St Nic and St Leon 82-84; Soc Resp Adv 84-85; Dir Lambeth Endowed Charities 85-94; Hon PV S'wark Cathl 85-94; rtd 94; Perm to Offic *Ox* from 08. *3 Brackenwood, Naphill, High Wycombe HP14 4TD* Tel (01494) 564040

JONES, David James Hammond. b 45. Kelham Th Coll 65. **d** 70 **p** 70. C Cheadle *Lich* 70-73; Hon C W Bromwich All SS 78-83; Hon C Primrose Hill St Mary w Avenue Road St Paul *Lon* 91-03; Hon C Regent's Park St Mark 03-08; Perm to Offic *Lon* from 08 and *Lich* from 11. *26 Town Walls, Shrewsbury SY1 1TN* Tel (01743) 368284 Mobile 07850-206877
E-mail david@jones_gb.co.uk

JONES, David Mark. b 73. St Mich Coll Llan 03. **d** 06 **p** 07. C Llansamlet *S & B* 06-08; Min Can Brecon Cathl from 08. *The Clergy House, Cathedral Close, Brecon LD3 9DP* Tel (01874) 623886

JONES, David <u>Michael</u>. b 48. Chich Th Coll 75. **d** 78 **p** 79. C Yeovil *B & W* 78-84; C Barwick 81-84; V Cleeve w Chelvey and Brockley 84-92; V Heigham St Barn w St Bart *Nor* 92-00; V Writtle w Highwood *Chelmsf* from 00. *The Vicarage, 19 Lodge Road, Writtle, Chelmsford CM1 3HY* Tel (01245) 421282
E-mail revmjoneswrittle@aol.com

JONES, David <u>Ormond</u>. b 46. Llan Dioc Tr Scheme 90. **d** 94 **p** 95. NSM Resolven w Tonna *Llan* 94-01; C Skewen 01-07; C Neath from 07. *30 Henfaes Road, Tonna, Neath SA11 3EX* Tel (01639) 770930 E-mail ormond.jones@ntlworld.com

JONES, David <u>Raymond</u>. b 34. Univ of Wales (Lamp) BA54 St Cath Coll Ox BA57 MA61. Wycliffe Hall Ox 58. **d** 58 **p** 59. C Ex St Dav 58-60; C Bideford 60-63; Chapl Grenville Coll Bideford 63-66; Chapl RN 66-89; QHC 84-89; Dir and Warden Divine Healing Miss Crowhurst 89-97; rtd 97; Perm to Offic *Chich* from 97. *9 Perrots Lane, Steyning BN44 3NB* Tel (01903) 815236

JONES, David Robert Deverell. b 50. Sarum & Wells Th Coll 72. **d** 75 **p** 78. C Altrincham St Geo *Ches* 75-76; C Clayton *Lich* 77-80; Carriacou 80-81; P-in-c Baschurch *Lich* 81-83; R Baschurch and Weston Lullingfield w Hordley 83-96; RD Ellesmere 85-95; P-in-c Criftins 94-96; P-in-c Dudleston 94-96; P-in-c Jersey St Luke *Win* 96-99; V from 99; P-in-c Jersey St Jas 96-99; V from 99; R Jersey St Mary 02-07. *The Vicarage, Longueville Farm, Longueville Road, St Saviour, Jersey JE2 7WG* Tel (01534) 851445 Mobile 07797-757765

JONES, David Roy. b 47. Hull Univ BA74 CQSW76 Man Univ DipAdEd76 Bradf Univ MA85. NOC 77. **d** 80 **p** 81. C New Bury *Man* 80-83; NSM Ringley w Prestolee 92-97; NSM Belmont 97-01; TV Turton Moorland Min from 01. *The Vicarage, High Street, Bemont, Bolton BL7 8AP* Tel (01204) 811221

JONES, David <u>Sebastian</u>. b 43. St Cath Coll Cam BA67 MA73. Linc Th Coll 66. **d** 68 **p** 69. C Baguley *Man* 68-71; C Bray and Braywood *Ox* 71-73; V S Ascot 73-07; AD Bracknell 96-04; Chapl Heatherwood Hosp E Berks 81-94; Chapl Heatherwood and Wexham Park Hosp NHS Trust 94-07; rtd 07. *Fairhaven, 1 St Clement's Terrace, Mousehole, Penzance TR19 6SJ* Tel (01736) 732938 E-mail sebastianjones@talk21.com

JONES, David Victor. b 37. St Jo Coll Dur BA59. Cranmer Hall Dur Bossey Ecum Inst Geneva 61. **d** 62 **p** 63. C Farnworth *Liv*

62-65; CF 65-68; Asst Master Hutton Gr Sch Preston 68-97; rtd 02. *10 Houghton Close, Penwortham, Preston PR1 9HT* Tel (01772) 745306 E-mail d.v.jones@btinternet.com

JONES, David William. b 42. St Mark & St Jo Coll Lon CertEd64 Open Univ BA79. SEITE 97. **d** 00 **p** 01. NSM Coxheath, E Farleigh, Hunton, Linton etc *Roch* from 00; Perm to Offic *Cant* from 04. *13 Woodlands, Coxheath, Maidstone ME17 4EE* Tel (01622) 741474 E-mail david.jones@diocese-rochester.org

JONES, Denise Gloria. b 56. Cov Univ BA93 Leeds Univ MA06. WMMTC 95. **d** 98 **p** 99. C Hobs Moat *Birm* 98-02; C Olton and Chapl S Birm Mental Health NHS Trust 02-06; Chapl Manager Birm Women's Healthcare NHS Trust 06-08; TV Bridgnorth, Tasley, Astley Abbotts, etc *Heref* 08-10; rtd 10. *62 Balmoral Way, Birmingham B14 4NT* Tel 07747-385006 (mobile)
E-mail revddee@aol.com

JONES, Miss Diana. b 46. Qu Coll Birm 89. **d** 91 **p** 94. Par Dn Harnham *Sarum* 91-94; C 94-95; C Tidworth, Ludgershall and Faberstown 95-00; P-in-c Hazelbury Bryan and the Hillside Par 00-06; rtd 06. *47 Gloucester Road, Trowbridge BA14 0AB* Tel (01225) 755826

JONES, Canon Dick Heath Remi. b 32. Jes Coll Cam BA56. Linc Th Coll 56. **d** 58 **p** 59. C Ipswich St Thos *St E* 58-61; C Putney St Mary *S'wark* 61-65; P-in-c Dawley Parva *Lich* 65-75; P-in-c Lawley 65-75; RD Wrockwardine 70-72; P-in-c Malins Lee 72-75; RD Telford 72-80; P-in-c Stirchley 74-75; TR Cen Telford 75-80; Preb Lich Cathl 76-80; TR Bournemouth St Pet w St Swithun, H Trin etc *Win* 80-96; RD Bournemouth 90-95; Hon Can Win Cathl 91-96; rtd 96; Perm to Offic *Sarum* from 96. *Maltings, Church Street, Fontmell Magna, Shaftesbury SP7 0NY* Tel (01747) 812071 E-mail dick.jones@talk21.com

JONES, Dominic Jago Francis. St Jo Coll Nottm 09. **d** 11. C Ludgvan, Marazion, St Hilary and Perranuthnoe *Truro* from 11. *2 Bankfield, Trevenner Lane, Marazion TR17 0BL* Tel (01736) 711423 Mobile 07904-500882

JONES, Donald. b 50. BA BSc. St Jo Coll Nottm 79. **d** 82 **p** 83. C Hutton *Chelmsf* 82-86; C E Ham w Upton Park 86-88; TV 88-96; V Nuneaton St Nic *Cov* from 96; RD Nuneaton 01-06. *61 Ambleside Way, Nuneaton CV11 6AU* Tel (024) 7634 6900

JONES, Edward. b 36. Dur Univ BA60. Ely Th Coll 60. **d** 62 **p** 63. C S Shields St Hilda w St Thos *Dur* 62-65; C Cleadon Park 65-68; V Hebburn St Cuth 68-79; R Winlaton 79-00; rtd 00; Perm to Offic *Dur* from 00 and *Newc* from 01. *10 Melkridge Gardens, Benton, Newcastle upon Tyne NE7 7GQ* Tel 0191-266 4388

JONES, Elaine. b 62. SNWTP. **d** 10 **p** 11. C Wavertree St Mary *Liv* from 10. *2 Rutherford Road, Mossley Hill, Liverpool L18 0HJ* Tel 07787-550622 (mobile)

JONES, Miss Elaine Edith. b 58. St Jo Coll Nottm BA99. **d** 99 **p** 00. C Gainsborough and Morton *Linc* 99-02; C Netherton *Carl* 02-04; TV Maryport, Netherton and Flimby 04-05; Lay Tr Officer 02-05; V Binley *Cov* from 05. *The Vicarage, 68 Brandon Road, Binley, Coventry CV3 2JF* Tel (024) 7663 6334
E-mail elaine.jones@stbarts-binley.org.uk

JONES, Canon Elaine Joan. b 50. Oak Hill Th Coll. **d** 87 **p** 94. Par Dn Tottenham H Trin *Lon* 87-92; Par Dn Clay Hill St Jo and St Luke 92-94; C St Botolph Aldgate w H Trin Minories 94-96; V Hackney Wick St Mary of Eton w St Aug 96-04; AD Hackney 99-04; Can Res Derby Cathl from 04. *22 Kedleston Road, Derby DE22 1GU* Tel (01332) 208995
E-mail pastor@derbycathedral.org
or canon.pastor@ukonline.co.uk

JONES, Mrs Elizabeth Mary. b 48. QUB BA69. NOC 88. **d** 91 **p** 94. Par Dn Kippax w Allerton Bywater *Ripon* 91-94; C 94-95; R Swillington 95-00; TV Wordsley *Worc* 00-02; rtd 02. *33 Pill Way, Clevedon BS21 7UW* Tel (01275) 876297

JONES, Mrs Elizabeth Somerset. b 49. St Jo Coll Nottm. **d** 88 **p** 94. NSM Duns *Edin* 88-99; NSM Selkirk 89-90; Dioc Dir of Ords 95-05; NSM Dalkeith from 02; NSM Lasswade from 02. *255 Carnethie Street, Rosewell EH24 9DR* Tel 0131-653 6767 Fax 653 3646 E-mail esomersetjones@btinternet.com

JONES, Emile Conrad Modupe Kojo. b 50. Univ of Sierra Leone BA74 MA BD. Trin Coll Bris 74. **d** 77 **p** 78. C Kissy St Patr Sierra Leone 77-78; C Freetown H Trin 78-81; Asst Chapl and Lect OT Studies Fourah Bay Coll 81-85; Chapl Heidelberg *Eur* 86-97; Miss Partner CMS 97-03; C Holloway St Mary Magd *Lon* 97-04; Asst Chapl Whittington Hosp NHS Trust from 04; Hon C Walthamstow St Pet *Chelmsf* from 05; Hon C Tollington *Lon* from 05. *1 Beech Court, 28 Bisterne Avenue, London E17 3QX* Tel (020) 8521 1213 E-mail mynaekj@yahoo.co.uk

JONES, Ernest Edward <u>Stephen</u>. b 39. Lon Univ BD76. St D Coll Lamp. **d** 66 **p** 67. C N Meols *Liv* 66-69; C Kirkby 69-71; V Farnworth All SS *Man* 71-75; P-in-c Bempton *York* 75-78; R Rufford *Blackb* 78-84; V Cropredy w Gt Bourton and Wardington *Ox* 84-90; R York St Clem w St Mary Bishophill Senior 90-98; P-in-c York All SS N Street 90-98; V Northampton St Benedict *Pet* 98-05; rtd 05; P-in-c Wootton w Glympton and Kiddington *Ox* from 05; AD Woodstock from 06. *The Rectory, 22 Castle Road, Wootton, Woodstock OX20 1EG* Tel (01993) 812543 E-mail stephen@samarnic.wanadoo.co.uk

JONES, Evan Hopkins. b 38. St Mich Coll Llan 65. **d** 67 **p** 68. C Churston Ferrers w Goodrington *Ex* 67-70; C Tavistock and Gulworthy 70-73; R Ashprington and V Cornworthy 73-78; R S Hackney St Jo w Ch Ch *Lon* 78-92; AD Hackney 84-89; V Islington St Jas w St Pet 92-08; rtd 08; Perm to Offic *Lon* from 08. *5 St James's Close, Bishop Street, London N1 8PH* Tel (020) 7226 0104 E-mail fr.evan@virgin.net

JONES, Evan Trefor. b 32. Univ of Wales (Ban) BA54. Coll of Resurr Mirfield 54. **d** 56 **p** 57. C Ban St Mary 56-62; V Llandinorwig 62-71; TV Llanbeblig w Caernarfon and Betws Garmon etc 71-84; Ed dioc magazine *The Link* 79-89; R Llanfairfechan w Aber 84-97; Can Ban Cathl 95-97; rtd 97. *19 Marlborough Place, Vaughan Street, Llandudno LL30 1AE* Tel (01492) 878411

JONES, Frederick Morgan. b 19. Univ of Wales (Lamp) BA40 BD49. St Mich Coll Llan 42. **d** 42 **p** 43. C Llanelli St Paul *St D* 42-50; Org Sec (Wales) Ind Chr Fellowship 50-53; C-in-c Llwynhendy CD *St D* 52-56; C Llanelli 56-57; V Penrhyncoch and Elerch 57-61; R Llanbedrog and Penrhos *Ban* 61-74; R Llanbedrog w Llannor w Llanfihangel etc 74-84; C Llangefni w Tregaean and Llangristiolus etc 84-85; rtd 85; Perm to Offic *Ban* from 85. *15 Ponc-y-Fron, Llangefni LL77 7NY* Tel (01248) 722850

JONES, Gareth. b 35. St Aid Birkenhead 58. **d** 61 **p** 62. C Doncaster Ch Ch *Sheff* 61-65; Min Can Ripon Cathl 65-68; Chapl RAF 68-85; St Jo Cathl Hong Kong 85-89; R Spofforth w Kirk Deighton *Ripon* 89-00; rtd 00; Perm to Offic *Ripon* from 00 and *Dur* from 02. *36 Whitcliffe Lane, Ripon HG4 2JL* Tel (01765) 601745 E-mail garjones1549@yahoo.co.uk

JONES, Gareth Edward John Paul. b 79. Leeds Univ BA06. Coll of Resurr Mirfield 03. **d** 06 **p** 07. C Brighton St Mich *Chich* 06-10; P-in-c Gt Ilford St Mary *Chelmsf* from 10. *St Mary's Vicarage, 26 South Park Road, Ilford IG1 1SS* Tel (020) 8478 0546 E-mail fathergarethjones@gmail.com

JONES, Gareth Lewis. b 42. K Coll Lon BD64 AKC64. **d** 65 **p** 66. C Risca *Mon* 65-70; Perm to Offic *Win* 70-74; *Newc* 74-75; *Sarum* 75; C Pontesbury I and II *Heref* 75-77; P-in-c Presteigne w Discoed 77-79; TV Hemel Hempstead *St Alb* 79-86; R Longden and Annscroft w Pulverbatch *Heref* 86-93; TV Leominster 93-07; rtd 07; Perm to Offic *Heref* from 08. *33 Danesfield Drive, Leominster HR6 8HP* Tel (01568) 620453

JONES, Prof Gareth Lloyd. b 38. Univ of Wales BA61 Selw Coll Cam BA63 MA67 Yale Univ STM69 TCD BD70 Lon Univ PhD75. Episc Sem Austin Texas Hon DD90 Westcott Ho Cam 62. **d** 65 **p** 66. C Holyhead w Rhoscolyn *Ban* 65-68; USA 68-70; P-in-c Merton *Ox* 70-72; Tutor Ripon Hall Ox 72; Sen Tutor 73-75; Lect Ex Coll Ox 73-77; Tutor and Lib Ripon Coll Cuddesdon 75-77; Lect Th Univ of Wales (Ban) 77-89; Sen Lect 89-95; Reader and Hd of Sch from 95; Prof from 98; Sub-Dean Faculty of Th 80-89; Dean 89-92; Chan Ban Cathl 90-09; Select Preacher Ox Univ 89. *22 Bron-y-Felin, Llandegfan, Menai Bridge LL59 5UY* Tel (01248) 712786

JONES, Glyn Evan. b 44. Lon Coll of Div ALCD67 LTh. **d** 67 **p** 68. C Gt Horton *Bradf* 67-70; SAMS Argentina 71-78; V Idle *Bradf* 78-84; V Hyson Green *S'well* 84-87; V Nottingham St Steph 84-87; V Hyson Green St Paul w St Steph 87-89; V Hyson Green 89-91; V Basford w Hyson Green 91-92; V Worksop St Jo 92-99; RD Worksop 93-99; V Nottingham St Sav 99-08; rtd 08. *65 Conifer Crescent, Nottingham NG11 9PP* Tel 0115-846 9947 Mobile 07885-816697 E-mail chezjones@ntlworld.com

JONES, Canon Glyndwr. b 35. St Mich Coll Llan. **d** 62 **p** 63. C Clydach *S & B* 62-64; C Llangyfelach 64-67; C Sketty 67-70; V Bryngwyn and Newchurch and Llanbedr etc 70-72; Miss to Seafarers 72-00; Swansea 72-76; Port of Lon 76-81; Aux Min Sec 81-85; Asst Gen Sec 85-90; Sec Gen 90-00; V St Mich Paternoster Royal *Lon* 91-00; rtd 01; Hon Can Kobe Japan from 88; Chapl to The Queen 90-05; Perm to Offic *Chelmsf* from 91. *5 The Close, Grays RM16 2XU* Tel (01375) 375053 E-mail glynita.tomdavey@blueyonder.co.uk

JONES, Glynn. b 56. NEOC 91. **d** 94 **p** 95. NSM Glendale Gp *Newc* 94-97; Sen Chapl HM Pris Leeds 97-99; Chapl HM Pris Dur 99-00; Chapl HM YOI Wetherby 00-05; Chapl HM Pris Wymott 06-07; Co-ord Chapl HM Pris Haverigg from 07. *HM Prison, North Lane, Haverigg, Millom LA18 4NA* Tel (01229) 713152 *or* 713025 E-mail glynn.jones@hmps.gsi.gov.uk

JONES, Godfrey Caine. b 36. Dur Univ BA59 Lon Univ CertEd60 Birm Univ MEd71. St Deiniol's Hawarden 76. **d** 78 **p** 79. Hd Humanities Denbigh High Sch 75-81; NSM Ruthin w Llanrhydd *St As* 78-81; C 83-84; Sen Lect Matlock Coll 81-83; P-in-c Llanfwrog and Clocaenog and Gyffylliog 84-85; R 85-93; V Ruabon 93-02; RD Llangollen 93-02; rtd 02; Min Pradoe *Lich* 02-08; Perm to Offic from 08. *Idoma, Penylan, Ruabon, Wrexham LL14 6HP* Tel (01978) 812102 E-mail dorothy.e.jones@btopenworld.com

JONES, Canon Gordon Michael Campbell. b 33. St D Coll Lamp BA56. St Jo Coll Dur 56. **d** 58 **p** 59. C Maindee Newport *Mon* 58-60; C Penhow, St Brides Netherwent w Llandavenny etc 60-63; V Magor w Redwick 63-68; R Southern Cross Australia 68-71; R Kirkby Thore w Temple Sowerby *Carl* 72-73; R Kirkby

Thore w Temple Sowerby and Newbiggin 73-79; P-in-c Accrington St Jas *Blackb* 79-81; P-in-c Accrington St Andr 81-83; Chapl Ahmadi Kuwait 83-91; R Swardeston w E Carleton, Intwood, Keswick etc *Nor* 91-96; Chapl Limassol St Barn and Miss to Seafarers 96-03; Can Nicosia 01-03; rtd 03; Perm to Offic *Blackb* 03-08 and *Cov* from 08. *2 Margetts Close, Kenilworth CV8 1EN* Tel and fax (01926) 856759

JONES, Graham Frederick. b 37. Leeds Univ BA60 GradIPM63. ALCD66. **d** 66 **p** 67. C Chesterfield H Trin *Derby* 66-70; C Leeds St Geo *Ripon* 70-73; P-in-c Newcastle St Geo *Lich* 73-83; New Zealand 83-87; P-in-c Westcote w Icomb and Bledington *Glouc* 89-94; rtd 94. *7 Keynsham Bank, Cheltenham GL52 6ER* Tel (01242) 238680

JONES, Griffith Trevor. b 56. BSc MPS Univ of Wales BD. **d** 87 **p** 88. C Llandrygarn w Bodwrog and Heneglwys etc *Ban* 87-89; R Llangefni w Tregaean and Llangristiolus etc 89-91; TV Bangor 91-94; Chapl Ysbyty Gwynedd 91-94, Lic to Offic 94-00. *8 Carreg-y-Gad, Llanfairpwllgwyngyll LL61 5QF* Tel (01248) 713094

JONES, Canon Griffith William. b 31. St D Coll Lamp BA53 LTh55. **d** 55 **p** 56. C Llanycil w Bala and Frongoch *St As* 55-58; V Llandrillo 58-66; V Llandrillo and Llandderfel 66-96; RD Penllyn 83-96; Can Cursal St As Cathl from 87; rtd 96. *45 Yr Hafan, Bala LL23 7AU* Tel (01678) 520217

JONES, Gwynfryn Lloyd. b 35. Univ of Wales (Lamp) BA59. St Mich Coll Llan 59. **d** 61 **p** 62. C Rhyl w St Ann *St As* 61-64; C Prestatyn 64-67; V Whitford 67-75; V Llay 75-83; V Northop 83-98; rtd 98. *Tryfan, 41 Snowdon Avenue, Bryn-y-Baal, Mold CH7 6SZ* Tel (01352) 751036

JONES, Gwynn Rees. b 32. St D Coll Lamp BA55. **d** 57 **p** 58. C Llangystennin *St As* 57-59; C Llanrhos 59-64; R Cefn 64-68; R Llanfyllin 68-80; V Bistre 80-89; R Flint 89-97; rtd 97. *3 Lon Derw, Abergele LL22 7EA* Tel (01745) 825188

JONES, Canon Harold Desmond. b 22. Sarum Th Coll 52. **d** 55 **p** 56. C Bushey Heath *St Alb* 55-58; C Stevenage 58-64; V Milton Ernest and Thurleigh 64-80; RD Sharnbrook 70-81; Hon Can St Alb 78-90; V Sharnbrook 80-82; P-in-c Knotting w Souldrop 80-82; R Sharnbrook and Knotting w Souldrop 82-90; P-in-c Felmersham 82-87; RD Sharnbrook 86-90; rtd 90; Perm to Offic *St Alb* 00-04. *8 Capel Court, The Burgage, Prestbury, Cheltenham GL52 3EL* Tel (01242) 576510

JONES, Harold Philip. b 49. Leeds Univ BA72 St Jo Coll Dur BA84. Cranmer Hall Dur 82. **d** 85 **p** 86. C Scartho *Linc* 85-88; V Dodworth *Wakef* 88-91; C Penistone and Thurlstone 91-95; C Scunthorpe All SS *Linc* 95-96; TV Brumby 96-02; Chapl Derby Hosps NHS Foundn Trust from 02. *Derbyshire Royal Infirmary, London Road, Derby DE1 2QY* Tel (01332) 347141 Fax 290559 E-mail harold.jones@derbyhospitals.nhs.uk

JONES, Haydn Llewellyn. b 42. Edin Th Coll 63. **d** 65 **p** 66. C Towcester w Easton Neston *Pet* 65-68; C Northampton St Matt 68-72; CF 72-97; Perm to Offic *Roch* 97-98; *Ex* from 98; rtd 99. *11 Lady Park Road, Livermead, Torquay TQ2 6UA* Tel (01803) 690483

JONES (née JAMES), Ms Helen Alison. b 59. St Andr Univ BSc81. EMMTC 93. **d** 96 **p** 97. C Brocklesby Park *Linc* 96-98; Perm to Offic 06-08; C Bassingham Gp 08-10; R Dundee St Jo *Bre* from 10; R Dundee St Marg from 10; R Dundee St Martin from 10. *St Margaret's Rectory, 19 Ancrum Road, Dundee DD2 2JL* Tel (01382) 667227 Mobile 07814-789817 E-mail halisonjones@gmail.com

JONES, Hester. See JONES, Susannah Hester Everett

JONES, Hilary Christine. b 55. Ch Ch Coll Cant CertEd76 Lon Univ BEd77. SEITE. **d** 99 **p** 00. C Kennington *Cant* 99-02; R Cheriton St Martin from 02; P-in-c Cheriton All So w Newington from 06; Bp's Adv for Women's Min from 04; AD Elham 08-11. *St Martin's Rectory, Horn Street, Folkestone CT20 3JJ* Tel (01303) 238509 E-mail hilarycjones@lycos.co.uk

JONES, Howard. See JONES, John Howard

JONES, Hugh Vaughan. b 44. **d** 07 **p** 08. C Holyhead *Ban* 07-09; P-in-c Bodedern w Llanfaethlu 09-11; P-in-c Amlwch from 11. *The Rectory, Bull Bay Road, Amlwch LL68 9EA* Tel (01407) 830902 Mobile 07795-578932 E-mail hughvaughan.santelbod@btinternet.com

JONES, Hugh William Fawcett. b 68. Ripon Coll Cuddesdon. **d** 10 **p** 11. C Boston *Linc* from 10. *5 Irby Street, Boston PE21 8SA* Tel (01205) 352655 E-mail hugh.wf.jones@talk21.com

JONES, Hughie. See JONES, The Ven Thomas Hughie

JONES, Huw. See JONES, Prof David Huw

JONES, Ian. b 63. Trin Coll Carmarthen BEd88. St Mich Coll Llan 93. **d** 97 **p** 98. NSM Tycoch *S & B* 97-01; NSM Swansea St Nic 01-04; Chapl Wymondham Coll from 04. *Staff House 8, Wymondham College, Golf Links Road, Wymondham NR18 9SX* Tel (01953) 607120 E-mail ianjones99@yahoo.com

JONES, Ian Andrew. b 65. Lanc Univ BA87. St Mich Coll Llan. **d** 90 **p** 91. C Caerphilly *Llan* 90-96; Chapl RAF from 96. *Chaplaincy Services, Valiant Block, HQ Air Command, RAF High Wycombe HP14 4UE* Tel (01494) 496800 Fax 496343

JONES, Idris. b 31. **d** 88 **p** 94. NSM Llanfihangel Ysgeifiog and Llanffinan etc *Ban* 88-97; NSM Llangefni w Tregaean and Llangristiolus etc 98-01; NSM Llanfihangel Ysgeifiog w Llangristiolus etc 01-02. *8 Swn yr Engan, Gaerwen LL60 6LS* Tel (01248) 421797

✠**JONES, The Rt Revd Idris.** b 43. St D Coll Lamp BA64 NY Th Sem DMin86. Edin Th Coll 64. **d** 67 **p** 68 **c** 98. C Stafford St Mary *Lich* 67-70; Prec St Paul's Cathl Dundee 70-73; P-in-c Gosforth All SS *Newc* 73-80; R Montrose and Inverbervie *Bre* 80-89; Can St Paul's Cathl Dundee 84-92; Chapl Angl Students Dundee Univ 89-92; P-in-c Invergowrie 89-92; TR S Ayrshire TM 92-98; Bp Glas 98-09; Primus 06-09; rtd 09; Hon Fell Univ of Wales (Trin St Dav) from 07. *27 Donald Wynd, Largs KA30 8TH* E-mail idrisjones43@hotmail.co.uk

JONES, Ivor Wyn. b 56. Trin Coll Bris 92. **d** 94 **p** 95. C Gabalfa *Llan* 94-97; TV Daventry, Ashby St Ledgers, Braunston etc *Pet* 97-01; P-in-c Dawley St Jerome *Lon* 01-08; C-in-c Harlington Ch Ch CD 03-08; V W Hayes from 08. *St Jerome's Lodge, 42 Corwell Lane, Uxbridge UB8 3DE* Tel (020) 8561 7393 *or* 8573 1895 E-mail wynjones@blueyonder.co.uk

JONES, Jacqueline. **d** 09 **p** 10. NSM Chipping Norton *Ox* from 09. *Old Appleyard, 18 Kingham Road, Churchill, Chipping Norton OX7 6NE* Tel (01608) 658616 E-mail jackie.clark-jones@virgin.net

JONES, James Richard. b 65. SS Hild & Bede Coll Dur BA87 Open Univ MBA95. Wycliffe Hall Ox 02. **d** 04 **p** 05. C Ashtead *Guildf* 04-08; P-in-c Burscough Bridge *Liv* from 08. *St John's Vicarage, 253 Liverpool Road South, Ormskirk L40 7TD* E-mail jrj37@aol.com

✠**JONES, The Rt Revd James Stuart.** b 48. Ex Univ BA70 PGCE71 Hull Univ Hon DD99 Lincs & Humberside Univ Hon DLitt01. Wycliffe Hall Ox 81. **d** 82 **p** 83 **c** 94. C Clifton Ch Ch w Em *Bris* 82-90; V S Croydon Em *S'wark* 90-94; Suff Bp Hull *York* 94-98; Bp Liv from 98; Bp HM Pris from 07. *Bishop's Lodge, Woolton Park, Liverpool L25 6DT* Tel 0151-421 0831 Fax 428 3055 E-mail bishopslodge@liverpool.anglican.org

JONES, Canon Jaqueline Dorian. b 58. K Coll Lon BD80 AKC80 MTh81. Westcott Ho Cam 84. **dss** 86 **d** 87 **p** 94. Epsom St Martin *Guildf* 86-91; C 87-91; Chapl Chelmsf Cathl 91-97; V Bridgemary *Portsm* 97-03; Can Res S'well Minster from 03. *2 Vicars Court, Southwell NG25 0HP* Tel (01636) 813188 *or* 817282 E-mail jacquijones@southwellminster.org.uk

JONES, Jeffrey Lloyd. b 66. Univ of Wales (Abth) BD87 PGCE90. Wycliffe Hall Ox 95. **d** 97 **p** 98. C Lampeter Pont Steffan w Silian *St D* 97; C Carmarthen St Dav 97-00; TV Llantwit Major 00-08; V Llanddeiniolen w Llanfair-is-gaer etc *Ban* from 08; AD Arfon from 09. *The Vicarage, Y Felinheli LL56 4SQ* Tel (01248) 670212

JONES, Jennifer Margaret. b 49. Lon Univ CertEd. Cranmer Hall Dur 87. **d** 89 **p** 94. C Musselburgh *Edin* 89-93; Dn-in-c 93-94; P-in-c 94-95; R 95-02; C Prestonpans 89-93; Dn-in-c 93-94; P-in-c 94-95; R 95-02; Lic to Offic *Mor* from 02. *2 Stables, Balvatin Cottages, Perth Road, Newtonmore PH20 1BB* Tel (01540) 673042

JONES, Mrs Joanne. b 64. Warwick Univ BA88. St Mellitus Coll BA10. **d** 10 **p** 11. C Maldon All SS w St Pet *Chelmsf* from 10. *30 Minster Way, Maldon CM9 6YT* Tel (01621) 843075 E-mail revdjojones@gmail.com

JONES, John Bernard. b 49. Qu Coll Birm 86. **d** 88 **p** 89. C Mold *St As* 88-91; P-in-c Treuddyn and Nercwys and Eryrys 91-92; V Treuddyn w Nercwys from 92; RD Mold 95-00. *The Vicarage, Ffordd y Llan, Treuddyn, Mold CH7 4LN* Tel (01352) 770919 E-mail revjbj@hotmail.com

JONES, John Brian. St Mich Coll Llan. **d** 05 **p** 06. NSM Gors-las *St D* from 05. *Penpentre, 79 Carmarthen Road, Cross Hands, Lanelli SA14 6SU* Tel (01269) 842236

JONES, John David Emrys. b 36. Trin Coll Carmarthen. **d** 96 **p** 97. NSM Llanfihangel Ystrad and Cilcennin w Trefilan etc *St D* 96-97; P-in-c Llangeitho and Blaenpennal w Betws Leucu etc 97-06; Lic to Offic from 06. *Dolfor, Ciliau Aeron, Lampeter SA48 8DE* Tel (01570) 470569

JONES, John Hellyer. b 20. Birm Univ LDS43. Westcott Ho Cam 65. **d** 67 **p** 68. C Haddenham *Ely* 67-70; P-in-c Lolworth 70-79 and 81-85; P-in-c Conington 75-79 and 81-85; R Houghton w Wyton 79; rtd 85; Perm to Offic *Ely* 85-02. *13 High Street, Haddenham, Ely CB6 3XA* Tel (01353) 740530

JONES, John Howard. b 48. New Coll Ox BA69 MA73 K Coll Cam CertEd70. Sarum & Wells Th Coll 76. **d** 77 **p** 78. C Salisbury St Mark *Sarum* 77-78; C Morriston *St & B* 78-80; Dir of Ords 80-83; V Gowerton 80-83; V Swansea St Jas 85-89; Chapl Alleyn's Sch Dulwich 89-08; Hon C Dulwich St Barn *S'wark* 90-08; rtd 08. *Address temp unknown*

JONES, John Trevor. b 14. St D Coll Lamp BA42. **d** 43 **p** 44. C Rhosddu *St As* 43-52; C Timperley *Ches* 52-53; V Barnton 53-60; V Poulton 60-81; rtd 81; Perm to Offic *Ches* from 82. *21 Sandy Lane, Wallasey CH45 3JY* Tel 0151-639 4794

JONES, Canon Joyce Rosemary. b 54. Newnham Coll Cam BA76 MA82 Coll of Ripon & York St Jo MA97 Solicitor 79. NOC 94.

d 97 **p** 98. C Pontefract All SS *Wakef* 97-00; NSM Cumberworth, Denby and Denby Dale 00-01; Dioc Voc Adv 00-01; Asst Chapl Kirkwood Hospice Huddersfield 00-01; P-in-c Shelley and Shepley *Wakef* from 01; RD Kirkburton from 11; Hon Can Wakef Cathl from 10. *Oakfield, 206 Barnsley Road, Denby Dale, Huddersfield HD8 8TS* Tel and fax (01484) 862350 E-mail joycerjones@aol.com

JONES, Julie Ann. b 59. STETS. **d** 10 **p** 11. NSM W Meon and Warnford *Portsm* 10-11; NSM Portchester from 11. *Orchard View, Hill Pound, Swanmore, Southampton SO32 2UN* Tel (01489) 891402 Mobile 07800-553920 E-mail jones59ja@btinternet.com

JONES, Mrs Julie Denise. b 63. CBDTI 03. **d** 06 **p** 07. C Darwen St Pet w Hoddlesden *Blackb* 06-09; P-in-c Wesham and Treales from 09; V from 11. *The Vicarage, Mowbreck Lane, Wesham, Preston PR4 3HA* Tel (01772) 682206 Mobile 07814-500855 E-mail julie.jones.bpl@btinternet.com

JONES, Mrs Karen Elizabeth. b 64. Univ of Ulster BA87. Wycliffe Hall Ox 04. **d** 06 **p** 07. C Northolt Park St Barn *Lon* 06-07; NSM Longwell Green *Bris* 08-10; NSM Stoke Gifford from 10. *119 North Road, Stoke Gifford, Bristol BS34 8PE* Tel 0117-979 1656 Mobile 07876-752745 E-mail admin@karenjones.org.uk

JONES, Kathryn Mary. *See* BUCK, Kathryn Mary

JONES (née SANDELLS-REES), Ms Kathy Louise. b 68. Univ of Wales (Ban) BTh96. Qu Coll Birm 90. **d** 92 **p** 97. C Holyhead w Rhoscolyn w Llanfair-yn-Neubwll *Ban* 92-94; C Bangor 94-95; Chapl Gwynedd Hosp Ban 94-99; P-in-c Bangor 95-99; V Betws-y-Coed and Capel Curig w Penmachno etc 99-06; Chapl Newcastle upon Tyne Hosps NHS Foundn Trust from 06. *Freeman Hospital, Freeman Road, High Heaton, Newcastle upon Tyne NE7 7DN* Tel 0191-233 6161

JONES, Mrs Katie Ann. b 99. **p** 00. NSM Sutton Courtenay w Appleford *Ox* 99-04; Perm to Offic *Cant* 04-11. *Address temp unknown*

JONES, The Very Revd Keith Brynmor. b 44. Selw Coll Cam BA65 MA69. Cuddesdon Coll 67. **d** 69 **p** 70. C Limpsfield and Titsey *S'wark* 69-72; Dean's V St Alb Abbey 72-76; P-in-c Boreham Wood St Mich 76-79; TV Borehamwood 79-82; V Ipswich St Mary-le-Tower *St E* 82-96; RD Ipswich 92-96; Hon Can St E Cathl 93-96; Dean Ex 96-04; Dean York from 04. *The Deanery, York YO1 7JQ* Tel (01904) 557202 *or* 623618 Fax 557204 E-mail dean@yorkminster.org

JONES, Keith Bythell. b 35. BA CertEd ACP. Trin Coll Bris. **d** 83 **p** 84. C Bris St Mary Redcliffe w Temple etc 83-86; C Filton 86-88; TV Yate New Town 88-95; rtd 95; Perm to Offic *Mon* from 95. *3 Woodlands Close, St Arvans, Chepstow NP16 6EF* Tel (01291) 622377

JONES, Keith Ellison. b 47. Wycliffe Hall Ox 72. **d** 75 **p** 76. C Everton St Chrys *Liv* 75-79; C Buckhurst Hill *Chelmsf* 79-81; TV 81-88; TR Leek and Meerbrook *Lich* 88-99; V Formby H Trin *Liv* 99-11; AD Sefton 05-08; Hon Can Liv Cathl 05-08; rtd 11. *77 Woodhouse Lane, Biddulph ST8 7EN*

JONES, Kingsley Charles. b 45. Birm Univ BSc66 Open Univ BA75. Sarum Th Coll 66. **d** 69 **p** 70. C Penwortham St Mary *Blackb* 69-72; C Broughton 72-74; P-in-c Gt Wollaston *Heref* 74-77; Chapl RAF 77-83; V Colwich w Gt Haywood *Lich* 83-94; V Winshill *Derby* 94-01; P-in-c Glouc St Aldate 01-11; rtd 11. *Bella House, Sandhurst Road, Gloucester GL1 2SE* Tel (01452) 690406 E-mail arkj.kcj@care4free.net

JONES, Lesley Anne. b 46. Luton Coll of HE CertEd77. SAOMC 01. **d** 04 **p** 06. NSM Gravenhurst, Shillington and Stondon *St Alb* 04-06; NSM Leagrave from 06. *91 Manton Drive, Luton LU2 7DL* Tel (01582) 616888 E-mail lesleyjones31647@aol.com

JONES, Leslie Joseph. b 23. Linc Th Coll. **d** 57 **p** 58. C Penhill *Bris* 57-60; C-in-c Lockleaze St Mary CD 60-62; V Bris Lockleaze St Mary Magd w St Fran 62-69; V Bedminster St Aldhelm 69-75; TV Bedminster 75-80; V Abbots Leigh w Leigh Woods 80-88; rtd 88; Perm to Offic *Bris* from 88. *4 Summerleaze, Bristol BS16 4ER* Tel 0117-965 3597

JONES, Lloyd. *See* JONES, Jeffrey Lloyd

JONES, Lloyd. *See* JONES, Prof Gareth Lloyd

JONES, Miss Mair. b 41. Cartrefle Coll of Educn TCert61. St Mich Coll Llan 91. **d** 93 **p** 97. C Llangollen w Trevor and Llantysilio *St As* 93-97; V Llandrillo and Llandderfel 97-00; R Llanelian w Betws-yn-Rhos w Trofarth 00-03; R Llanelian 03-08; P-in-c Brynymaen 04-08; rtd 08. *5 Ffordd Bugail, Colwyn Bay LL29 8TN* Tel (01492) 517866 E-mail mair@jones6527.fsnet.co.uk

JONES, Malcolm. *See* JONES, Philip Malcolm

JONES, Malcolm Francis. b 44. Open Univ BA88 Hull Univ MA96 Univ of Wales (Cardiff) LLM05. Chich Th Coll 67. **d** 70 **p** 71. C Prestbury *Ches* 70-73; Chapl RAF 73-81; R Heaton Reddish *Man* 81-84; CF (ACF) 82-84 and from 98; CF (TA) 83-84; CF 84-93; CF (R of O) 93-99; TV Cleethorpes *Linc* 93-97; V Ryde H Trin *Portsm* 97-10; V Swanmore St Mich 97-10; rtd 10;

P-in-c Win H Trin from 10. *18 Lynford Way, Winchester SO22 6BW* Tel (01962) 869707 Mobile 07710-543155 E-mail frmalcolmjones@virginmedia.com

JONES, Malcolm Stuart. b 41. Sheff Univ BA62. Linc Th Coll 64. **d** 66 **p** 67. C Monkseaton St Mary *Newc* 66-69; C Ponteland 69-72; Chapl Lake Maracaibo Venezuela 73-75; C Hexham *Newc* 75-77; P-in-c Killingworth 77-92; V Delaval 92-01; TV Ch the King 01-07; rtd 07. *13 Valeside, Newcastle upon Tyne NE15 9LA*

JONES, Maldwyn Lloyd. b 17. St D Coll Lamp BA39. **d** 40 **p** 41. C Gorseinon *S & B* 40-43; Lic to Offic *Ox* 43-46; Chapl Nichteroy All SS Brazil 46-48; Hd Master St Paul's Sch Sao Paulo 48-50; Chapl Ch Ch Cathl Falkland Is 50-51; Chapl RN 52-68; Chapl Shattuck Sch Faribault USA 68-70; Chapl Lon Nautical Sch 71-72; Lic to Offic *Ban* 72-82; rtd 82; Perm to Offic *Ban* from 82. *12 Springfield Street, Dolgellau LL40 1LY* Tel (01341) 421715

JONES, Ms Margaret. b 28. TCD BA53 Man Univ PGCE54 Lon Univ BD66. **d** 87 **p** 94. NSM Stanstead Abbots *St Alb* 87-88; NSM Grappenhall *Ches* 89-98; rtd 98; Perm to Offic *Ches* from 98. *19 Hill Top Road, Grappenhall, Warrington WA4 2ED* Tel (01925) 261992

JONES, Mrs Margaret Angela. b 53. Wolv Univ CertEd91. Qu Coll Birm BA99. **d** 99 **p** 00. C Pershore w Pinvin, Wick and Birlingham *Worc* 99-03; TV Solihull *Birm* 03-11; P-in-c Pontesbury I and II *Heref* from 11. *The Deanery, Main Road, Pontesbury, Shrewsbury SY5 0PS* Tel (01743) 792221

JONES, Mrs Margaret Anne. b 47. Lon Univ TCert68 Ches Coll of HE BTh04. NOC 01. **d** 04 **p** 05. NSM Altrincham St Geo *Ches* 04-07; C from 07; C Altrincham St Jo from 07; Chapl Trin C of E High Sch Man 05-07; Perm to Offic *Man* from 06. *12 Moorland Avenue, Sale M33 3FH* Tel 0161-973 8020 Mobile 07748-645596 E-mail margaret.jones@talk21.com

JONES, Margaret Mary. b 47. Oak Hill Th Coll 92. **d** 95 **p** 96. C Sydenham H Trin *S'wark* 95-98; V Anerley St Paul *Roch* 98-09; TV Anerley 09-11; rtd 11. *10 Lower Road, Redhill RH1 6NN* Tel (01737) 247998

JONES, Mark. *See* JONES, Christopher Mark

JONES, Mark. b 70. Warwick Univ BSc92 Univ of Wales PGCE93. Ripon Coll Cuddesdon 06. **d** 08 **p** 09. C Old Basing and Lychpit *Win* from 08. *6 Copse View Close, Chineham, Basingstoke RG24 8EZ* Tel (01256) 323794 E-mail mark.kennington@btinternet.com

JONES, Mark Andrew. b 60. Southn Univ BSc82 Sussex Univ PGCE83. Oak Hill Th Coll BA91. **d** 91 **p** 92. C Wolverhampton St Luke *Lich* 91-96; I Inishmacsaint *Clogh* 96-01; V Padiham w Hapton and Padiham Green *Blackb* from 01; AD Burnley from 10. *The Vicarage, 1 Arbory Drive, Padiham, Burnley BB12 8JS* Tel (01282) 772442 E-mail jones.padiham@btinternet.com

JONES, Mark Vincent. b 60. St Mich Coll Llan 81. **d** 84 **p** 85. C Whitchurch *Llan* 84-89; V Pwllgwaun w Llanddewi Rhondda 89-90; CF from 90. *c/o MOD Chaplains (Army)* Tel (01264) 381140 Fax 381824

JONES, Martin. b 58. Leeds Univ BA07. NOC 04. **d** 07 **p** 08. NSM Winwick *Liv* from 07; Chapl St Helens and Knowsley Hosps NHS Trust from 09. *7 Longwood Close, Rainford, St Helens WA11 7QJ* Tel (01744) 889938 E-mail martinjones9558@aol.com

JONES, Martin Patrick. b 62. K Coll Lon BDS85. Dioc OLM tr scheme 02. **d** 05 **p** 06. NSM Kingsnorth and Shadoxhurst *Cant* 05-09; Perm to Offic 09-11; NSM Aldington w Bonnington and Bilsington etc from 11. *3 Hewitts Place, Willesborough, Ashford TN24 0AH* Tel (01233) 613271 E-mail martin.jones62@ntlworld.com

JONES, Mrs Mary Catherine Theresa Bridget. b 41. Westhill Coll Birm CertEd77 Birm Univ BA80. Qu Coll Birm 04. **d** 05 **p** 06. NSM Bromsgrove St Jo *Worc* from 05. *15 Greyfriars Drive, Bromsgrove B61 7LF* Tel (01527) 837018 E-mail theresa@supalife.com

JONES, Canon Mary Nerissa Anna. b 41. MBE02. Qu Mary Coll Lon BA86 FRSA91. Ripon Coll Cuddesdon 86. **d** 88 **p** 94. Par Dn St Botolph Aldgate w H Trin Minories *Lon* 88-93; P-in-c Wood End *Cov* 93-95; V 95-01; Hon Can Cov Cathl 01; rtd 01; P-in-c Askerswell, Loders and Powerstock *Sarum* 01-10; P-in-c Symondsbury 07-10. *Church Farm Cottage, West Milton, Bridport DT6 3SL* Tel (01308) 485304 E-mail nerissa@eurobell.co.uk

JONES, Canon Mary Valerie. b 37. Univ of Wales (Ban) BD84. St Deiniol's Hawarden 84. **d** 85 **p** 97. C Holyhead w Rhoscolyn w Llanfair-yn-Neubwll *Ban* 85-87; C Ynyscynhaearn w Penmorfa and Porthmadog 87-90; Dn-in-c Llansantffraid Glyn Ceirog and Llanarmon etc *St As* 90-97; V 97-98; R Overton and Erbistock and Penley 98-04; RD Bangor Isycoed 98-04; Can Cursal St As Cathl 01-04; rtd 04. *Cysgod y Coed, 12 Church View, Ruabon, Wrexham LL14 6TD* Tel (01978) 822206 E-mail valerie@hywyn.freeserve.co.uk

JONES, Matthew Brooks. b 58. St Fran Coll Brisbane BTh94. **d** 93 **p** 95. C Caloundra Australia 94-97; P-in-c Goondiwindi 97-01; R Ipswich St Paul 01-11; Adn Cunningham 05-11; Chapl

Hamburg *Eur* from 11. *St Thomas à Becket, Zeughausmarkt 22, 20459 Hamburg, Germany* Tel (0049) (40) 439 2334 E-mail st.thomas.becket@t-online.de

JONES, Matthew Christopher Howell. b 74. Leeds Univ BSc95 Cam Univ BTh01. Westcott Ho Cam 98. **d** 01 **p** 02. C Cheshunt *St Alb* 01-05; V Southgate St Andr *Lon* 05-10. *Address temp unknown* E-mail mchjones@lineone.net

JONES, Maurice Maxwell Hughes. b 32. Clifton Th Coll 56. **d** 60 **p** 61. C Islington St Andr w St Thos and St Matthias *Lon* 60-63; Argentina 63-71; C Whitchurch *Llan* 72-73; Area Sec (NW England) SAMS 73-77; V Haydock St Mark *Liv* 78-87; V Paddington Em Harrow Road *Lon* 87-97; rtd 98. *Glyn Orig, Cemmaes, Machynlleth SY20 9PR* Tel and fax (01650) 511632

JONES, Canon Melville Kenneth. b 40. Open Univ BA82. St D Coll Lamp. **d** 66 **p** 67. C Aberdare *Llan* 66-71; C Caerau w Ely 71-72; Chapl Pontypridd Hosps 72-89; V Graig *Llan* 72-89; P-in-c Cilfynydd 86-89; V Llantwit Fardre 89-07; Chapl E Glam Hosp 89-99; RD Pontypridd 99-05; Hon Can Llan Cathl 04-07; Chapl Pontypridd and Rhondda NHS Trust 99-01; rtd 07. *Nanteos, 7 Meadow Hill, Church Village, Pontypridd CF38 1RX* Tel (01443) 217213 E-mail melville k.jones@virgin.net

JONES, Michael. *See* JONES, David Michael

JONES, Michael. *See* JONES, Canon Gordon Michael Campbell

JONES, Michael. b 49. Leeds Univ BA71 Man Univ MA73 Padgate Coll of Educn PGCE73. Qu Coll Birm 83. **d** 85 **p** 86. C Leigh St Mary *Man* 85-88; C-in-c Holts CD 88-93; V Hamer 93-05; rtd 09; Perm to Offic *Man* from 06 and *St As* from 09. *Ty Coch Cottage, Llangynhafal, Ruthin LL15 1RT* Tel (01824) 703037 E-mail mike@ashborn.force9.co.uk

JONES, Michael Adrian. b 62. Reading Univ BSc83 PGCE84. Trin Coll Bris 87. **d** 09 **p** 10. C Bath Weston All SS w N Stoke and Langridge *B & W* from 09. *23 Lucklands Road, Bath BA1 4AX* Tel (01225) 471400 E-mail adrianjones.bath@tiscali.co.uk

JONES, Michael Barry. b 48. MCIEH88 MIOSH88. ERMC 04. **d** 07 **p** 08. NSM Whittlesey, Pondersbridge and Coates *Ely* from 07. *20 White Horse Gardens, March PE15 8AG* Tel (01354) 653456 E-mail michael.jones123@sky.com

JONES, Michael Christopher. b 67. Southn Univ BSc88. St Jo Coll Nottm MTh03 MA04. **d** 04 **p** 05. C Aldridge *Lich* 04-07; V Lilleshall and Muxton from 07. *The Vicarage, 25 Church Road, Lilleshall, Newport TF10 9HE* Tel (01952) 604281

JONES, Michael Denis Dyson. b 39. CCC Cam BA62 MA66 Lon Univ MSc73. Wycliffe Hall Ox. **d** 76 **p** 77. C Plymouth St Andr w St Paul and St Geo *Ex* 76-81; V Devonport St Budeaux 81-00; RD Plymouth Devonport 93-95; TV Barnstaple 00-07; RD Barnstaple 03-07; rtd 07. *The Spinney, 40 West Drive, Harrow HA3 6TS* Tel (020) 8954 1530 E-mail mddjamj@onetel.com

JONES, Michael Emlyn. b 47. Aber Univ MB, ChB72 MRCP75 FRCP95. **d** 79 **p** 79. Asst P Moshi St Marg Tanzania 79-82; NSM Duns *Edin* 83-99; NSM Dalkeith from 02; NSM Lasswade from 02. *255 Carnethie Street, Rosewell EH24 9DR* Tel 0131-440 2602 *or* 653 6767 Fax 653 3646 Mobile 07710-276208 E-mail michaelejones@doctors.org.uk

JONES, Michael Gerald. b 46. Ban Ord Course 05. **d** 07 **p** 08. NSM Ystumaner *Ban* 07-09; NSM Dolgellau w Llanfachreth and Brithdir etc from 09. *Bryn-Hyfryd, 1 St Mary's Terrace, Arthog LL39 1BQ* Tel (01341) 250406

JONES, Michael Kevin. b 57. Llan Ord Course 94. **d** 98 **p** 99. NSM Caerau w Ely *Llan* 98-00; NSM Cen Cardiff 01; P-in-c Tremorfa St Phil CD 02-05; Area Fundraising Manager Children's Soc *Llan* and *Mon* 98-00; Ch Strategy Manager Wales 01-02; Lic to Offic *Llan* 05-09; V Mountain Ash and Miskin from 09. *5 Lon-y-Felin, Cefn Pennar, Mountain Ash CF45 4ES* Tel (01443) 473700

JONES, Morgan. *See* JONES, Frederick Morgan

JONES, Canon Neil Crawford. b 42. Univ of Wales BA63 K Coll Lon BD66 AKC66. **d** 67 **p** 68. C Holywell *St As* 67-69; C Rhyl w St Ann 69-73; C Christchurch *Win* 73-77; V Stanmore 77-84; RD Win 82-84; V Romsey 84-07; RD Romsey 89-94; Hon Can Win Cathl 93-07; rtd 07. *1 The Brambles, Rosemary Lane, Leintwardine, Craven Arms SY7 0LR* Tel (01547) 540333

JONES, Nerissa. *See* JONES, Canon Mary Nerissa Anna

JONES, Canon Neville George. b 36. Univ of Wales (Ban) BA59. St Mich Coll Llan 59. **d** 61 **p** 62. C Broughton *St As* 61-65; C Newcastle *Llan* 65-68; V Laleston w Tythegston 68-84; V Llanishen and Lisvane 84-93; V Llanishen 93-02; Hon Can Llan Cathl 96-02; rtd 02. *21 Cwm Gwynlais, Tongwynlais, Cardiff CF15 7HU* Tel (029) 2081 1150

JONES, Nicholas Godwin. b 58. St Jo Coll Cam BA81 MA84 Hughes Hall Cam PGCE90. Ridley Hall Cam 91. **d** 93 **p** 94. C Cambridge H Trin *Ely* 93-97; Chapl St Bede's Sch Cam 97-00; C Fulbourn w Gt and Lt Wilbraham 97-00; V Harston w Hauxton and Newton 00-03; V Gt Horton *Bradf* 03-10; Chapl HM Pris Man from 10; Chapl HM Pris Hindley from 10. *Chaplaincy, HM Prison Hindley, Gibson Street, Bickershaw, Wigan WN2 5TH* Tel (01942) 663435

JONES, Nicholas Peter. b 55. St Mich Coll Llan. **d** 82 **p** 83. C St Andrews Major w Michaelston-le-Pit *Llan* 82-84; C Aberdare 84-88; Youth Chapl 85-89; V Abercynon 88-96; R Llanilid w

Pencoed 96-10; AD Bridgend 10. *22 Clos Brenin, Brynsadler, Pontyclun CF72 9GA* E-mail revnickjones@gmail.com

JONES, Nigel David. b 69. Qu Coll Cam MA95. Westcott Ho Cam 97. **d** 00 **p** 01. C Abbots Langley *St Alb* 00-03; TV Dunstable 03-08; V Caversham St Andr *Ox* from 08. *St Andrew's Vicarage, Harrogate Road, Reading RG4 7PW* Tel 0118-947 2788

JONES, Nigel Ivor. b 54. Sheff Univ MMin04. WMMTC 91. **d** 94 **p** 95. C Shirley *Birm* 94-99; TV Salter Street and Shirley 99-01; V Olton 01-08; Chapl HM Pris Rye Hill from 10. *HM Prison Rye Hill, Willoughby, Rugby CV23 8SZ* Tel (01788) 523300 E-mail revnigel@aol.com

JONES, Norman. b 50. Oak Hill Th Coll BA83. **d** 83 **p** 84. C Ulverston St Mary w H Trin *Carl* 83-87; Hong Kong 88-92; TR Eccles *Man* 92-01; AD Eccles 95-00; R Haslemere and Grayswood *Guildf* 01-10; RD Godalming 02-07; Chapl Wispers Sch Haslemere 01-10; rtd 11. *51 Freshwater Drive, Weston, Crewe CW2 5GR* Tel (01270) 829141 E-mail revnjones@aol.com

JONES, Norman Burnet. b 52. St Andr Univ BSc74 Man Univ PhD78 CChem81 CBiol78. SEITE 08. **d** 11. NSM Southgate Chich from 11. *1 Saxon Road, Crawley RH10 7SA* Tel (01293) 885209 Mobile 07766-367983 E-mail normanbjones1@virginmedia.com

JONES, Ormond. *See* JONES, David Ormond

JONES, Mrs Patricia Ann. b 43. **d** 97 **p** 98. OLM Bincombe w Broadwey, Upwey and Buckland Ripers *Sarum* 97-05; NSM 06-10; rtd 11; Perm to Offic *Sarum* from 11. *23 Camedown Close, Weymouth DT3 5RB* Tel (01305) 813056

JONES, Mrs Patricia Anne. b 55. CSS81. Oak Hill Th Coll 92. **d** 95. NSM Mill Hill Jo Keble Ch *Lon* 95-01; NSM Queensbury All SS 01-08; Perm to Offic from 08. *The Flat, St Paul's School, The Ridgeway, London NW7 1QU* Tel (020) 8201 1583

JONES, Canon Patrick Geoffrey Dickson. b 28. Ch Ch Ox BA51 MA55 Aber Univ MLitt98. St Deiniol's Hawarden 79. **d** 82 **p** 83. NSM Sandbach *Ches* 82-84; R Aboyne 84-96; R Ballater 84-96; P-in-c Braemar 84-96; rtd 96; Hon Can St Andr Cathl from 01. *Byebush of Fedderate, New Deer, Turriff AB53 6UL* Tel (01771) 644110 E-mail pg.dj@tiscali.co.uk

JONES, Patrick George. b 42. Cant Ch Ch Univ Coll MA99. Lich Th Coll 69. **d** 72 **p** 73. C Chesterton St Geo *Ely* 72-75; P-in-c Waterbeach 75-78; P-in-c Landbeach 76-78; R Charlton-in-Dover *Cant* 78-90; Chapl Cautley Ho Chr Cen 90-06; rtd 06. *149 London Road, Temple Ewell, Dover CT16 3DA* Tel (01304) 829377 E-mail patrickjones303@btinternet.com

JONES, Paul Anthony. b 72. Cov Univ BSc95. Ripon Coll Cuddesdon BTh99. **d** 99 **p** 00. C Dolgellau w Llanfachreth and Brithdir etc *Ban* 99-02; P-in-c Ffestiniog w Blaenau Ffestiniog 02-04; Perm to Offic *Ban* from 04-06 and *Newc* 06-07; Hon C Long Benton St Mary *Newc* 07-10; V Newc St Fran from 10. *St Francis's Vicarage, 66 Cleveland Gardens, Newcastle upon Tyne NE7 7QH* Tel 0191-266 1071 Mobile 07810-686072 E-mail paul.ajones@yahoo.co.uk

JONES, Paul Evan. b 62. York Univ BA84 CPFA89. SEITE 02. **d** 05 **p** 06. C Kingstanding St Luke *Birm* 05-09; P-in-c Babbacombe *Ex* from 09. *Babbacombe Vicarage, 4 Cary Park, Torquay TQ1 3NH* Tel (01803) 323002 E-mail liberty.hall@tiscali.co.uk

JONES, Paul Terence. b 35. Dur Univ BA60. Qu Coll Birm 60. **d** 62 **p** 63. C Rainford *Liv* 62-65; C Skelmersdale St Paul 65-68; V Huyton Quarry 68-78; V Widnes St Ambrose 78-00; rtd 00; Perm to Offic *Liv* from 00. *9 Hunter Court, Prescot L34 2UH* Tel 0151-430 6057

JONES, Pauline Edna. b 55. Liv Univ BA77. **d** 10 **p** 11. OLM Langley *Man* from 10. *9 Hopwood Avenue, Heywood OL10 2AX* Tel (01706) 368829 E-mail pej123@hotmail.co.uk

JONES, Penelope Howson. b 58. Girton Coll Cam BA80 MA83 LGSM79. Ripon Coll Cuddesdon BA85 MA88. dss 86 **d** 87 **p** 94. Hackney *Lon* 86-87; Par Dn 87-88; Tutor Ripon Coll Cuddesdon 88-90; Par Dn Cuddesdon *Ox* 88-90; Perm to Offic *Dur* 92-95; Dir Practical Th NEOC *Newc* 93-97; Hon C Eastgate w Rookhope *Dur* 93-97; Hon C Stanhope w Frosterley 93-97; Perm to Offic *York* 93-97; P-in-c Stanhope w Frosterley *Dur* 97-01; P-in-c Eastgate w Rookhope 97-01; Woman Adv in Min 97-01; Hon Can Dur Cathl 98-01; Sen Assoc P Gosford Australia from 01. *78 Henry Parry Drive, PO Box 4255, Gosford East NSW 2250, Australia* Tel (0061) (2) 4324 2630 E-mail redimp@bigpong.com

JONES, Canon Peter Anthony Watson. b 53. AKC75. Sarum & Wells Th Coll 76. **d** 77 **p** 78. C Hessle *York* 77-81; C Stainton-in-Cleveland 81-82; P-in-c Weston Mill *Ex* 82-84; Chapl Plymouth Poly 82-90; V Gt Ayton w Easby and Newton-in-Cleveland *York* 90-92; C Devonport St Aubyn *Ex* 92-98; P-in-c Yealmpton and Brixton 98-01; Team Chapl Portsm Hosps NHS Trust 01-05; Chapl Portsm Univ 05-09; Can Res Portsm Cathl 05-09; R Havant from 09; Dioc Interfaith Adv 06-11. *St Faith's Rectory, 5 Meadowlands, Havant PO9 2RP* Tel (023) 9248 3485 E-mail canon@stfaith.com

JONES, Peter Charles. b 57. Univ of Wales BA81 MA82 PGCE97. St Mich Coll Llan 80. **d** 83 **p** 84. C Pontnewynydd

Mon 83-85; C Bassaleg 85-87; TV Cwmbran 87-94; V Blaenavon w Capel Newydd 94-01; Chapl CME 00-01; Chapl and Fell Trin Coll Carmarthen 01-05; V Llangennech and Hendy *St D* from 05; AD Cydweli from 08. *The Vicarage, 2A Mwrwg Road, Llangennech, Llanelli SA14 8UA* Tel (01554) 820324 E-mail tadjones@btinternet.com

JONES, Peter David. b 48. S'wark Ord Course 89. **d** 92 **p** 93. NSM Coulsdon St Andr *S'wark* 92-04; Perm to Offic from 04. *79 Beverley Road, Whyteleafe CR3 0DU* Tel (020) 8668 6398

JONES, Peter Gordon Lewis. b 31. Llan Dioc Tr Scheme. **d** 82 **p** 83. NSM Llangynwyd w Maesteg 82-84; Deputation Appeals Org (S & M Glam) CECS 84-87; Appeals Manager (Wales and Glouc) Children's Soc 87-97; NSM Pyle w Kenfig *Llan* 89-97; rtd 97. *18 Fulmar Road, Porthcawl CF36 3UL* Tel (01656) 785455 Mobile 07785-755399

JONES, Peter Henry. b 50. Qu Coll Cam MA72 Ex Univ CertEd73 Bradf Univ MSc81 Nottm Univ MA05. EMMTC 02. **d** 05 **p** 06. NSM Annesley w Newstead *S'well* 05-11; NSM Hucknall Torkard from 11. *3 Roland Avenue, Nuthall, Nottingham NG16 1BB* Tel 0115-975 1868 E-mail maryandpeterjones@btinternet.com

JONES, Peter Owen. b 64. Hull Univ BSc86. Oak Hill Th Coll BA08. **d** 08 **p** 09. C Hubberston *St D* 08-11; P-in-c Llanfihangel Genau'r-glyn and Llangorwen from 11. *The Vicarage, Maes-y-Garn, Bow Street SY24 5DS* Tel (01970) 822267 E-mail peter@ojones.plus.com

JONES, Peter Robin. b 42. Open Univ BA75 Bp Otter Coll Chich CertEd68. EMMTC 79. **d** 82 **p** 83. NSM Doveridge *Derby* 82-97; NSM Doveridge, Scropton, Sudbury etc 98-10; NSM S Dales from 11; Bp's Inspector of Th Colls and Courses from 98; Perm to Offic *Lich* 93-10. *4 Cross Road, Uttoxeter ST14 7BN* Tel (01889) 565123 E-mail rev.jon@talktalk.net

JONES, Canon Peter Russell. b 48. St Jo Coll Cam BA71 MA75 Univ of Wales MTh86. Wycliffe Hall Ox. **d** 75 **p** 76. C Northampton All SS w St Kath *Pet* 75-79; C Ban Cathl 79-81; Min Can Ban Cathl 79-81; R Pentraeth and Llanddyfnan 81-85; V Conwy w Gyffin from 85; Lect Univ of Wales (Ban) 89-95; AD Arllechwedd *Ban* 96-09; Can and Treas Ban Cathl 99-09; Chan from 09. *The Vicarage, Rose Hill Street, Conwy LL32 8LD* Tel (01492) 593402

JONES, The Ven Philip Hugh. b 51. Solicitor. Chich Th Coll 92. **d** 94 **p** 95. C Horsham *Chich* 94-97; V Southwater 97-05; RD Horsham 02-04; Adn Lewes and Hastings from 05. *27 The Avenue, Lewes BN7 1QT* Tel (01273) 479530 E-mail archlandh@diochi.org.uk

JONES, Philip Malcolm. b 43. Qu Coll Birm. **d** 04 **p** 05. NSM Birm St Paul 04-08; P-in-c Heathfield St Rich *Chich* from 08. *St Richard's Vicarage, Hailsham Road, Heathfield TN21 8AF* Tel (01435) 862744 E-mail malcolm@peri.co.uk

JONES, Philip Smith. b 53. St Mich Coll Llan 75. **d** 79 **p** 80. C Milford Haven *St D* 79-82; Asst Chapl Miss to Seamen 82-84; C Orford St Andr *Liv* 84-85; C Walton St Luke 85-87; C Gt Crosby St Faith 87; C Blundellsands St Nic 87-88; Perm to Offic *St D* 05-07; Hon C Cwm Gwendraeth 07-08; P-in-c Llansteffan and Llan-y-bri etc from 08. *The Vicarage, Church Road, Llansteffan, Carmarthen SA33 5JT* Tel (01267) 241280 E-mail meryljones@lothlorien22.freeserve.co.uk

JONES, Philip Thomas Henry. b 34. Qu Coll Birm 58. **d** 60 **p** 61. C Castle Bromwich SS Mary and Marg *Birm* 60-67; C Reading St Mary V *Ox* 67-72; C-in-c Reading All SS CD 72-75; V Reading All SS 75-95; Perm to Offic *Portsm* from 97; Hon Chapl Portsm Cathl from 97. *13 Oyster Street, Portsmouth PO1 2HZ* Tel (023) 9275 6676

JONES, Canon Phillip Bryan. b 34. St Mich Coll Llan. **d** 61 **p** 62. C Hope *St As* 61-64; C Llanrhos 64-67; V Kerry 67-74; R Newtown w Llanllwchaiarn w Aberhafesp 74-97; RD Cedewain 76-97; Sec Ch in Wales Prov Evang Cttee 80-83; Hon Can St As Cathl 86-93; Can 93-97; rtd 97. *7 Dalton Drive, Shrewsbury SY3 8DA* Tel (01743) 351426

JONES, Phillip Edmund. b 56. Man Poly BA78 Fitzw Coll Cam BA84 MA88 GradCIPD79. Westcott Ho Cam 82. **d** 85 **p** 86. C Stafford St Jo and Tixall w Ingestre *Lich* 85-89; TV Redditch, The Ridge *Worc* 89-95; TV Worc SE 95-08; Ind Chapl 89-08; Team Ldr Worcs Ind Miss 01-08; Team Ldr and Chapl Faith at Work in Worcs from 08; C Worc St Barn w Ch Ch from 08. *7 Egremont Gardens, Worcester WR4 0QH* Tel (01905) 755037 E-mail phillipjones@faithatwork.co.uk

JONES, Phyllis Gwendoline Charlotte. b 44. **d** 05 **p** 06. OLM Talbot Village *Sarum* from 05. *Bluebell Cottage, 112 Wallisdown Road, Bournemouth BH10 4HY* Tel (01202) 528956 E-mail revphyllisjones@fsmail.net

JONES, Ray. *See* JONES, David Raymond

JONES, Raymond. b 43. NOC 99. **d** 02 **p** 03. NSM Ashton-in-Makerfield St Thos *Liv* 02-03; C Widnes St Mary w St Paul 03-05; V 05-08; rtd 08; Hon C Farnworth *Liv* from 10. *43 Hampton Drive, Widnes WA8 5DA*

JONES, Raymond Alban. b 34. RGN55 RMN63. Chich Th Coll 64. **d** 67 **p** 68. C Ocker Hill *Lich* 67-70; C Truro St Paul 70-71; Chapl Selly Oak Hosp *Birm* 71-76; USPG Bahamas 76-79;

Chapl Hospice of Our Lady and St Jo Willen 80-83; Chapl St Jas Hosp Balham 83-87; NSM Leamington Spa H Trin and Old Milverton *Cov* 87-92; TV Probus, Ladock and Grampound w Creed and St Erme *Truro* 92-94; rtd 94; Perm to Offic *Sarum* from 09. *2 St Catherine's Terrace, Rodden Row, Abbotsbury, Weymouth DT3 4JL* Tel (01305) 871836

JONES, Raymond Blake. b 29. K Coll Lon BD54 AKC54. **d** 55 **p** 56. C Fenny Stratford *Ox* 55-58; C Lt Brickhill 55-58; C Wooburn 58-60; C Southbourne St Kath *Win* 60-66; R Braiseworth *St E* 66-76; V Eye 66-76; P-in-c Yaxley 74-77; RD Hartismere 76-77; V Eye w Braiseworth and Yaxley 77; R Ufford 77-82; Chapl St Audry's Hosp Melton 77-82; V Southbourne St Kath *Win* 82-95; rtd 95; Perm to Offic *Win* from 95. *4 Russell Drive, Riverslea, Christchurch BH23 3PA* Tel (01202) 473205

JONES, Raymond Sydney. b 35. MSERT71. Glouc Th Course 85. **d** 87 **p** 88. NSM Madley *Heref* 87-89; NSM Preston-on-Wye w Blakemere 87-89; NSM Madley w Tyberton, Preston-on-Wye and Blakemere 89; Chapl St Mich Hospice Hereford 90-00; Perm to Offic *Heref* 00-06. *The Old Cedars, Much Birch, Hereford HR2 8HR* Tel (01981) 540851

JONES, Canon Raymond Trevor. b 35. Linc Th Coll. **d** 82 **p** 83. C Rushmere *St E* 82-85; Bp's Dom Chapl 85-86; CF 86-91; TV Ridgeway *Sarum* 91-97; Relig Programmes Producer BBC Wiltshire Sound 91-97; Chapl Fuengirola St Andr *Eur* 97-00; P-in-c Ypres 00-10; P-in-c Ostend 06-08; Can Gib Cathl 04-10; Perm to Offic *Portsm* from 10. *St Pierre, 3 Diana Close, Totland Bay PO39 0EE* E-mail raymondstg@hotmail.com

JONES, Miss Rhiannon Elizabeth. b 69. Univ of Wales (Cardiff) BA91 Ox Cen for Miss Studies MA04 Cam Univ BTh11. Ridley Hall Cam 09. **d** 11. C Man Cathl from 11. *9.6A Melia House, 19 Lord Street, Manchester M4 4AX* Tel 07765-241093 (mobile) E-mail rhinoharpy@yahoo.co.uk

JONES, Ms Rhiannon Elizabeth. b 72. Ex Univ BA93 Brunel Univ MA95 Anglia Poly Univ MA05. Ridley Hall Cam 98. **d** 00 **p** 01. C Huntingdon *Ely* 00-04; R Fulbourn 04-10; V Gt Wilbraham 04-10; R Lt Wilbraham 04-10; Transforming Ch Co-ord *Birm* from 10. *23 Hallewell Road, Birmingham B16 0LP* Tel 0121-454 5040 Mobile 07595-880584 E-mail rhiannonejones@me.com

JONES, Richard. *See* JONES, James Richard

JONES, Richard. b 23. BEM. St Deiniol's Hawarden 74. **d** 76 **p** 77. NSM Welshpool w Castle Caereinion *St As* 76-94; rtd 94. *Sherwood, Rhos Common, Llandrinio, Llanymynech SY22 6RN* Tel (01691) 830534

JONES, Canon Richard. b 28. St D Coll Lamp 54. **d** 56 **p** 57. C Llanaber w Caerdeon *Ban* 56-61; R Aberffraw w Llangwyfan 61-74; CF (TA) 61-71; V Llanfairisgaer *Ban* 74-79; Bp's Private Chapl 78-82; V Llanfair-is-gaer and Llanddeiniolen 79-89; RD Arfon 82-89; Can Ban Cathl from 86; V Llandegfan w Llandysilio 89-96; Chapl ATC from 90; rtd 96; Perm to Offic *Ban* from 96. *Bryniau, Rhostrehwfa, Llangefni LL77 7YS* Tel (01248) 724609

JONES, Richard Christopher Bentley. b 53. Pemb Coll Ox BA77 MA79. SEITE 03. **d** 06 **p** 07. NSM Clapham H Trin and St Pet *S'wark* from 06. *68 Mysore Road, London SW11 5SB* Tel (020) 7228 8965 E-mail rcb.jones@tiscali.co.uk

JONES, Richard Eifion. b 23. St D Dioc Tr Course 80 St Mich Coll Llan 84. **d** 82 **p** 83. NSM Llangennech and Hendy *St D* 82-84; C Llanbadarn Fawr w Capel Bangor and Goginan 84-86; V Llangadog and Gwynfe w Llanddeusant 86-91; rtd 91. *Gercoed, 186 St Teilo Street, Pontarddulais, Swansea SA4 8LH* Tel (01792) 882234

JONES, Richard Keith. b 40. Jes Coll Ox BA63. Wycliffe Hall Ox 61. **d** 63 **p** 64. C Blaenavon w Capel Newydd *Mon* 63-67; C Mynyddislwyn 67-71; C Pontypool 71; V Abercarn 71-81; V Penhow, St Brides Netherwent w Llandavenny etc 81-88. *32 Quantock Court, South Esplanade, Burnham-on-Sea TA8 1DL* Tel (01278) 458123

JONES, Robert. b 40. **d** 80 **p** 81. C St Laur in Thanet *Cant* 80-83. *Erbacher Strasse 72, 64287 Darmstadt, Germany* Tel (0049) (6151) 422913

JONES, Robert. b 45. Culham Coll Ox CertEd67. St Steph Ho Ox. **d** 85 **p** 86. C High Wycombe *Ox* 85-89; V Beckenham St Barn *Roch* 89-90; C Swanley St Mary 90-91; C Edenbridge from 91; C Crockham Hill H Trin from 91. *The Vicarage, Oakdale Lane, Crockham Hill, Edenbridge TN8 6RL* Tel (01732) 866515 Fax 864352 E-mail bob.jones@diocese-rochester.org

JONES, Robert Cecil. b 32. Univ of Wales (Abth) BA54 DipEd55. Qu Coll Birm 84. **d** 86 **p** 87. C Llanbadarn Fawr w Capel Bangor and Goginan *St D* 86-88; R Llanllwchaearn and Llanina 88-91; R Newport w Cilgwyn and Dinas w Llanllawer 91-98; rtd 98; Perm to Offic *Derby* from 05. *Old Craigstead Works, High Street, Stoney Middleton, Hope Valley S32 4TL* Tel (01433) 631857

JONES, Robert David. b 73. UCD BSc97 TCD BTh07. CITC 04. **d** 07 **p** 08. C Dublin St Patr Cathl Gp 07-10; V Dublin Rathmines w Harold's Cross from 10. *25 Knockwaree Avenue, Dublin 12, Republic of Ireland* Tel (00353) 86-285 4098 (mobile)

JONES, Canon Robert George. b 42. St Mich Coll Llan 93. **d** 95 **p** 96. NSM Treboeth *S & B* 95-02; P-in-c Treboeth 02-07; P-in-c Landore 03-07; Can Res Brecon Cathl 06-07; rtd 07. *Green Gables, 42 Heol Fach, Treboeth, Swansea SA5 9DE* Tel (01792) 424114

JONES, Canon Robert George. b 55. Hatf Coll Dur BA77 Ox Univ BA79 MA87. Ripon Coll Cuddesdon 77. **d** 80 **p** 81. C Foley Park *Worc* 80-84; V Dudley St Fran 84-92; TR Worc St Barn w Ch Ch 92-96; Dir Development from 06; RD Worc E 99-05; Hon Can Worc Cathl from 03. *4 Silverdale Avenue, Worcester WR5 1PY* Tel (01905) 769590 E-mail rjones@cofe-worcester.org.uk

JONES, Robert Ivan. b 33. Bede Coll Dur CertEd57. Westcott Ho Cam 85. **d** 85 **p** 86. NSM Wymondham *Nor* 85-86; C Epsom St Martin *Guildf* 87-89; V Hutton Cranswick w Skerne, Watton and Beswick *York* 89-94; RD Harthill 92-97; V Wetwang and Garton-on-the-Wolds w Kirkburn 94-98; V Waggoners 98-00; rtd 00; P-in-c Newbald *York* 00-04; Perm to Offic from 04. *North Wing, Saxby Hall, 72 Main Street, Saxby-All-Saints, Brigg DN20 0QB* Tel (01652) 618036 E-mail beemaj@onetel.com

JONES, The Very Revd Robert William. b 55. Open Univ BA85 MA88. Ian Ramsey Coll Brasted 75 Chich Th Coll 76 TCD Div Sch 77. **d** 79 **p** 80. C Seapatrick *D & D* 79; C Bangor Abbey 81-83; I Drumgath w Drumgooland and Clonduff 83-89; I Finaghy *Conn* 89-93; I Kilwaughter w Cairncastle and Craigy Hill 94-98; I Athlone w Benown, Kiltoom and Forgney *M & K* 98-02; Dean Clonmacnoise from 02; I Trim and Athboy Gp from 02. *St Patrick's Deanery, Loman Street, Trim, Co Meath, Republic of Ireland* Tel (00353) (46) 943 6698 Mobile 87-290 8344 E-mail trimdeanery@iolfree.ie

JONES, Robert William Aplin. b 32. Univ of Wales (Cardiff) BSc52 MSc65 FRSC71 CChem72. St Deiniol's Hawarden 72. **d** 73 **p** 74. C Bassaleg *Mon* 73-77; V Nantyglo 77-82; Perm to Offic 82-86; R Colwinston w Llandow and Llysworney 86-95; rtd 95; Perm to Offic *St D* from 99. *Golwg-y-Lan, Feidr Ganol, Newport SA42 0RR* Tel (01239) 820297 Mobile 07968-173759

JONES, Robin Dominic Edwin. b 78. St Chad's Coll Dur BA00 K Coll Lon MA01. St Steph Ho Ox MTh07. **d** 04 **p** 05. C Ealing Ch the Sav *Lon* 04-08; V Hammersmith St Luke from 08. *St Luke's Vicarage, 450 Uxbridge Road, London W12 0NS* Tel (020) 8749 7523 Mobile 07779-299924 E-mail fr.robin@stlukesw12.com

JONES, Roderick. b 48. Leeds Univ BA70 PGCE72. Westmr Th Sem (USA) 73 Oak Hill Th Coll 74. **d** 76 **p** 77. C Beckenham Ch Ch *Roch* 76-80; C Uphill *B & W* 80-84; R Springfield All SS *Chelmsf* 84-90; Selection Sec ABM 91-96; V Horsell *Guildf* from 96. *The Vicarage, Wilson Way, Horsell, Woking GU21 4QJ* Tel (01483) 772134 E-mail rjones2558@aol.com

JONES, Canon Roger. b 49. St Mich Coll Llan 84. **d** 86 **p** 87. C Llangynwyd w Maesteg 86-90; V Wiston w Walton E and Clarbeston *St D* 90-01; V Pembroke Gp 01-04; TV Monkton from 04; Can St D Cathl from 09. *The Vicarage, Lower Lamphey Road, Pembroke SA71 4AF* Tel and fax (01646) 682710 Mobile 07971-528933 E-mail roger@revjones.fsnet.co.uk

JONES, Russell Frederick. b 55. Man Univ BA77 Edin Univ BD84. Edin Th Coll 81. **d** 84 **p** 85. C Croxteth *Liv* 84-87; V Edgehill St Dunstan 87-98; R Glas St Bride 98-08; Hon Chapl Glas Univ 00-06; Chapl Marie Curie Hospice Glasgow from 08. *14B Hatfield Drive, Glasgow G12 0YA* Tel 0141-339 7989 or 531 1373 E-mail howisonandjones@btinternet.com

JONES, Mrs Sally. b 41. **d** 09 **p** 10. NSM Teme Valley N *Worc* from 09. *2 Old School House, Eastham, Tenbury Wells WR15 8PB* Tel (01584) 781526

JONES, Miss Sally Jennifer. St Mich Coll Llan. **d** 11. C Llanenddwyn w Llanddwywe, Llanbedr w Llandanwg *Ban* from 11. *Gwynfa, Dyffryn Ardudwy LL44 2EN* Tel (01341) 247857 E-mail sallyjjones@hotmail.com

JONES, Samuel. b 44. CITC. **d** 86 **p** 87. C Agherton *Conn* 86-88; I Connor w Antrim St Patr 88-97; I Whitehead and Islandmagee 97-01; Bp's C Kilbroney *D & D* 01-10; rtd 10. *2 The Brambles, Coleraine BT52 1PN* Tel (028) 7031 0076

JONES, Sarah Charlotte. b 57. SRN79. SAOMC 01. **d** 04 **p** 05. NSM Forest Edge *Ox* from 04. *4 Tower Hill, Witney OX28 5ER* Tel (01993) 200483 E-mail sarahtandem@hotmail.com

JONES, Ms Sarah Jane. b 61. St Hugh's Coll Ox BA95 MA03 Northumbria Univ MSc02. Westcott Ho Cam 02. **d** 04 **p** 05. C Ross *Heref* 04-07; P-in-c 07-08; R Ross w Walford from 08. *The Rectory, Church Street, Ross-on-Wye HR9 5HN* Tel (01989) 562175 E-mail sarah@revsarah.demon.co.uk

JONES, Sebastian. *See* JONES, David Sebastian

JONES, Sharon. b 74. Liv Univ MA00 PhD05. Westcott Ho Cam 05. **d** 07 **p** 08. C Warwick *Cov* 07-11; P-in-c New Springs and Whelley Liv from 11. *St Stephen's Vicarage, 141 Whelley, Wigan WN2 1BL* Tel (01942) 242579 E-mail rev.sharonjones@googlemail.com

JONES, Mrs Sharon Ann. b 60. St Kath Coll Liv BA82. Cranmer Hall Dur 83. **dss** 85 **d** 87 **p** 94. Chapl Birm 85-89; Par Dn 87-89; C-in-c Chelmsley Wood St Aug CD 89-92; Perm to Offic *Newc* 92-93; Chapl HM Pris Acklington 93-97; Chapl HM YOI

Castington 97-00; Chapl HM Pris Forest Bank 00-06; P-in-c Dearnley *Man* from 06; AD Salford 03-06; AD Rochdale 06-09. *St Andrew's Vicarage, Arm Road, Littleborough OL15 8NJ* Tel (01706) 378466 Mobile 07738-966271 E-mail vicar@dearnleyvicarage.plusnet.com

JONES, Mrs Shelagh Deirdre. b 46. St Mary's Coll Dur BA68. NEOC 01. **d** 04 **p** 05. NSM Burnby *York* 04-07; NSM Londesborough 04-07; NSM Nunburnholme and Warter and Huggate 04-07; NSM Shiptonthorpe and Hayton 04-07; Perm to Offic from 07; Chapl HM YOI Wetherby 04-10. *Red Gables, Fair View, Town Street, Shiptonthorpe, York YO43 3PE* Tel (01430) 872539 Fax 871612 E-mail revd-shelagh@amserve.com

JONES, Canon Sian Eira. b 63. Univ of Wales (Lamp) BA84 Southn Univ BTh88. Sarum & Wells Th Coll 85. **d** 88 **p** 97. C Llan-llwch w Llangain and Llangynog *St D* 88-93; Dn-in-c Llansteffan and Llan-y-bri etc 93-97; V 97-06; AD Carmarthen 00-06; TR Llanelli from 06; Can St D Cathl from 09. *The Vicarage, 1 Cysgod y Llan, Llanelli SA15 3HD* Tel (01554) 772072

JONES, Sian Hilary. See WIGHT, Mrs Sian Hilary

JONES, Simon. b 63. Trin Coll Bris BA89. **d** 89 **p** 90. C Hildenborough *Roch* 89-93; C Crofton *Portsm* 93-96; C Northwood *Em Lon* 96-01; Min in charge Ignite 01-07; TR Stoke Gifford *Bris* from 07; AD Kingswood and S Glos from 11. *119 North Road, Stoke Gifford, Bristol BS34 8PE* Tel 0117-979 1656 *or* 969 2486 Fax 959 9264 E-mail simon@st-michaels-church.org.uk

JONES, Simon Matthew. b 72. SS Hild & Bede Coll Dur BA93 MA94 Selw Coll Cam PhD00 Ox Univ MA02 DPhil03. Westcott Ho Cam 93. **d** 99 **p** 00. C Tewkesbury w Walton Cardiff and Twyning *Glouc* 99-02; Chapl and Fell Mert Coll Ox from 02. *Merton College, Oxford OX1 4JD* Tel (01865) 276365 *or* 281793 Fax 276361 E-mail simon.jones@merton.ox.ac.uk

JONES, Stella Frances. TCD BTh02. CITC. **d** 02 **p** 03. C Bandon Union *C, C & R* 02-05; I Clonenagh w Offerlane, Borris-in-Ossory etc *C & O* 05-10; I Kinneigh Union *C, C & R* from 10. *The Rectory, Ballineen, Co Cork, Republic of Ireland* Tel (00353) (23) 884 7047 E-mail sfjones@ccrd.ie

JONES, Stephen. See JONES, Ernest Edward Stephen

JONES, Stephen Frederick. b 53. Magd Coll Ox BA75 MA79 Lon Univ BD89 Leeds Univ MA96. Linc Th Coll BCombStuds84. **d** 84 **p** 85. C Kingswinford St Mary *Lich* 84-87; Min Can, Succ and Dean's V Windsor 87-94; C Howden *York* 94-96; Chapl St Elphin's Sch Matlock 96-01; C Worksop Priory *S'well* 01-03; R Longton *Lich* from 03. *The Rectory, Rutland Road, Stoke-on-Trent ST3 1EH* Tel (01782) 595098

JONES, Stephen Leslie. b 59. Hull Univ BA80 Lanc Univ MA06. Sarum & Wells Th Coll 82. **d** 85 **p** 86. C Perry Barr *Birm* 85-88; C Blackpool St Steph *Blackb* 88-90; V Greenlands 90-95; V Carnforth from 95. *The Vicarage, North Road, Carnforth LA5 9LJ* Tel (01524) 732948 E-mail stephenjones17@hotmail.com

JONES, Stephen Richard. b 49. Heythrop Coll Lon MA01. Oak Hill Th Coll 72. **d** 75 **p** 76. C Welling *Roch* 75-79; C Cheltenham St Mark *Glouc* 79-82; V Shiregreen St Jas and St Chris *Sheff* 82-86; P-in-c Harold Hill St Geo *Chelmsf* 86-88; V 88-97; P-in-c Harold Hill St Paul 94-95; V Kippington *Roch* 97-08; RD Sevenoaks 00-05; R Ightham from 08; RD Shoreham from 11. *The Rectory, Bates Hill, Ightham, Sevenoaks TN15 9BG* Tel (01732) 886827 *or* 884176 E-mail srjones49@hotmail.com *or* stephen.jones@diocese-rochester.org

JONES, Stephen William. b 46. K Coll Lon BD70 AKC70. **d** 71 **p** 72. C Streatham St Pet *S'wark* 71-76; C Leeds St Pet *Ripon* 76-79; C Leeds Richmond Hill 79-82; R Gourock *Glas* 85-88; V Porthleven w Sithney *Truro* 88-94; Miss to Seamen 88-94; P-in-c Portsea Ascension *Portsm* 96-00; V Grimsby St Aug *Linc* from 00. *St Augustine's Vicarage, 145 Legsby Avenue, Grimsby DN32 0LA* Tel (01472) 877109

JONES, Stewart William. b 57. Heriot-Watt Univ BA79 Bris Univ BA88. Trin Coll Bris 86. **d** 88 **p** 89. C Stoke Bishop *Bris* 88-92; P-in-c Brislington St Luke 92-97; Abp's Chapl and Dioc Missr *Cant* 97-03; P-in-c Cant All SS 01-05; AD Cant and Hon Prov Can Cant Cathl 02-05; R Birm St Martin w Bordesley St Andr from 05. *St Martin's Rectory, 37 Barlows Road, Birmingham B15 2PN* Tel 0121-604 0850 Mobile 07793-724949 E-mail stewart@bullring.org

JONES, Mrs Susan. b 55. Liv Hope BA03 St Jo Coll Dur MA05. Cranmer Hall Dur 03. **d** 05 **p** 06. C Skelmersdale St Paul *Liv* 05-09; TV Maghull and Melling from 09. *23 Green Link, Maghull L31 8DW* Tel 0151-526 6626 E-mail rev sue@talktalk.net

JONES, The Very Revd Susan Helen. b 60. Trin Coll Carmarthen BEd92 MPhil94 Univ of Wales (Ban) PhD. Ripon Coll Cuddesdon 93. **d** 95 **p** 97. Chapl Univ of Wales (Swansea) *S & B* 95-98; Hon C Sketty 95-98; Dir Past Studies St Mich Coll Llan 98-00; TV Bangor 00-09; AD Ogwen 07-09; Can Missr Ban Cathl 10-11; Dean Ban from 11. *The Deanery, Cathedral Close, Glanrafon, Bangor LL57 1LH* Tel (01248) 362840 E-mail suejone@netscapeonline.co.uk

JONES, Susan Jean. b 47. Bp Grosseteste Coll CertEd68 Heythrop Coll Lon MA01. SAOMC 93. **d** 96 **p** 97. C S Ascot *Ox* 96-07; NSM 01-07; rtd 07. *Fairhaven, 1 St Clement's Terrace, Mousehole, Penzance TR19 6SJ* Tel (01736) 732938 E-mail sebastian143@btinternet.com

JONES, Susannah Hester Everett. **d** 07 **p** 08. NSM Bris St Mary Redcliffe w Temple etc from 07. *18 Fairfield Road, Montpellier, Bristol BS6 5JP* E-mail hester.jones@stmaryredcliffe.co.uk

JONES, Tegid Owen. b 27. Univ of Wales (Abth) LLB47. St Deiniol's Hawarden. **d** 68 **p** 69. C Rhosddu *St As* 68-71; C Wrexham 71-75; R Marchwiel 75-83; R Marchwiel and Isycoed 83-92; RD Bangor Isycoed 86-92; rtd 92. *Teglys, 2 Bungalow, Pentre, Chirk, Wrexham LL14 5AW*

JONES, Theresa. See JONES, Mrs Mary Catherine Theresa Bridget

JONES, Thomas Glyndwr. b 41. Clifton Th Coll 65. **d** 65 **p** 66. C Islington St Mary *Lon* 65-69; USA from 69. *4425 Colchester Court, Columbus GA 31907-1682, USA* Tel (001) (706) 569 0314 E-mail welshwiz@knology.net

JONES, Canon Thomas Graham. b 33. St D Coll Lamp BA57. **d** 59 **p** 60. C Llanelli *St D* 59-64; V Ysbyty Cynfyn 64-69; V Ysbyty Cynfyn w Llantrisant 69-72; V Llanelli Ch Ch 72-94; RD Cydweli 89-93; V Carmarthen St Dav 94-00; Hon Can St D Cathl 93-99; Can from 99; RD Carmarthen 98-00; rtd 00. *32 Pen y Morfa, Llangunnor, Carmarthen SA31 2NP* Tel (01267) 231846

JONES, The Ven Thomas Hughie. b 27. Univ of Wales BA49 LLM94 Lon Univ BD53 Leic Univ MA72 FRSA. St Deiniol's Hawarden. **d** 66 **p** 67. Hon C Evington *Leic* 66-76; Hon C Kirby Muxloe 76-81; Dioc Adult Educn Officer 81-05; R Church Langton w Thorpe Langton and Tur Langton 81-85; Hon Can Leic Cathl 83-86; R Church Langton w Tur Langton, Thorpe Langton etc 85-86; Adn Loughborough 86-92; rtd 92; Perm to Offic *Leic* from 92. *Four Trees, 68 Main Street, Thorpe Satchville, Melton Mowbray LE14 2DQ* Tel (01664) 840262 E-mail thj@connectfree.co.uk

JONES, Thomas Percy Norman Devonshire. b 34. St Jo Coll Ox BA58 MA61 Lambeth MLitt02. Cuddesdon Coll 58. **d** 60 **p** 61. C Portsea St Cuth *Portsm* 60-61; C Portsea N End St Mark 61-67; Asst Chapl Portsm Tech Coll 67-70; Chapl Portsm Poly 70-73; Chapl Trin Coll Hartford USA 73-74; V Folkestone St Sav *Cant* 75-81; V Regent's Park St Mark *Lon* 81-00; rtd 00; Perm to Offic *Lon* from 00; Dir Art and Chr Enquiry Trust 94-06. *107 Crundale Avenue, London NW9 9PS* Tel and fax (020) 8204 7970 E-mail tomdevonshirejones@tiscali.co.uk

JONES, Canon Thomas Peter. b 20. Ex Coll Ox BA43 MA46. St Mich Coll Llan 43. **d** 45 **p** 46. C Wrexham *St As* 45-48; C Llandrillo-yn-Rhos 48-57; R Erbistock and Overton 57-83; Can St As Cathl 78-84; Preb and Prec St As Cathl 84-86; RD Bangor Isycoed 80-86; R Overton and Erbistock and Penley 83-86; rtd 86; Perm to Offic *Eve* 96-98; *St As* from 98. *18 All Hallows Close, Retford DN22 7UP* Tel (01777) 700481

JONES, Timothy Llewellyn. b 67. York Univ BA90. Ripon Coll Cuddesdon BA94. **d** 94 **p** 95. C Middlesbrough St Martin *York* 94-96; P-in-c Rounton w Welbury 96-02; Chapl HM YOI Northallerton 96-99; Adv for Young Adults and Voc (Cleveland) 99-02; R Corinth St Paul USA 02-07; P-in-c York St Hilda from 07; P-in-c York St Lawr w St Nic from 07. *St Hilda's Vicarage, 155 Tang Hall Lane, York YO10 3SD* Tel (01904) 412196 Mobile 07525-776406 E-mail tim.jones@yorklandh.org

JONES, Timothy Richard Nigel. b 54. Collingwood Coll Dur BSc75 Birm Univ MSc76 FGS. Trin Coll Bris 84. **d** 86 **p** 87. C Hailsham *Chich* 86-91; V Madley w Tyberton, Preston-on-Wye and Blakemere *Heref* 91-00; R Madley w Tyberton, Peterchurch, Vowchurch etc 00-06; V Taunton St Jas *B & W* from 06. *69 Richmond Road, Taunton TA1 1EN* Tel (01823) 333194 E-mail timjones@tesco.net

JONES, Trevor Blandon. b 43. Oak Hill Th Coll 77. **d** 80 **p** 81. NSM Homerton St Barn w St Paul *Lon* 80-83; NSM Harlow New Town w Lt Parndon *Chelmsf* 83-90; C 90-92; V Leyton Em 92-01; rtd 02; Perm to Offic *Chelmsf* from 03. *5 Wheatley Close, Sawbridgeworth CM21 0HS* Tel (01279) 600248 E-mail rev.trev@lineone.net

JONES, Trevor Edwin. b 49. Heythrop Coll Lon MA05. Ripon Coll Cuddesdon 74. **d** 76 **p** 77. C Cannock *Lich* 76-79; C Middlesbrough Ascension *York* 79-81; V Oldham St Steph and All Martyrs *Man* 81-84; V Perry Beeches *Birm* 84-90; P-in-c Saltley 90-93; P-in-c Shaw Hill 90-93; V Saltley and Shaw Hill 93-97; R Lon Docks St Pet w Wapping St Jo from 97. *St Peter's Clergy House, Wapping Lane, London E1W 2RW* Tel (020) 7481 2985 Fax 7265 1100 E-mail fatherjones@stpeterslondondocks.org.uk *or* frtejones@aol.com

JONES, The Ven Trevor Pryce. b 48. Southn Univ BEd76 BTh79 Univ of Wales (Cardiff) LLM04. Sarum & Wells Th Coll 73. **d** 76 **p** 77. C Glouc St Geo 76-79; Warden Bp Mascall Cen *Heref* 79-84; Dioc Communications Officer 81-86; TR Heref S Wye 84-97; Preb Heref Cathl 93-97; OCF 85-97; Adn Hertford and Hon Can St Alb from 97. *Glebe House, St Mary's Lane,*

Hertingfordbury, Hertford SG14 2LE Tel (01992) 581629 Fax 535349 E-mail archdhert@stalbans.anglican.org
JONES, Canon Tudor Howell. b 39. Univ of Wales (Cardiff) BD91. St Mich Coll Llan. **d** 68 **p** 69. C Clydach *S & B* 68-72; C Swansea St Pet 72-75; V Ystradfellte 75-79; V Llangiwg 79-91; V Manselton 91-05; RD Penderi 98-05; Can Res Brecon Cathl 00-05; rtd 05. *15 Glasfryn Close, Cockett, Swansea SA2 0FP*
JONES, Preb Wilfred David. b 22. Keble Coll Ox BA47 MA48. St Mich Coll Llan 47. **d** 48 **p** 49. C Aberaman *Llan* 48-50; C Cardiff St Jo 50-55; Chapl Kelly Coll Tavistock 55-62; V St Decumans *B & W* 62-76; V Ilminster w Whitelackington 76-92; RD Ilminster 78-87; Preb Wells Cathl from 81; rtd 92; Perm to Offic *B & W* 92-06. *Dragons, Lambrook Road, Shepton Beauchamp, Ilminster TA19 0NA* Tel (01460) 240967
JONES, Wilfred Lovell. b 39. Lon Univ BD71 Cam Univ CertEd. St D Coll Lamp. **d** 63 **p** 64. C Llanllyfni *Ban* 63-65; C Llanbeblig w Caernarfon 65-68; V Llanwnog w Penstrowed 68-73; V Llanwnnog and Caersws w Carno 73-75; Asst Chapl Dover Coll 77-90; Chapl Wrekin Coll Telford 91-94; V Llangollen w Trevor and Llantysilio *St As* 94-04; AD Llangollen 03-04; rtd 04. *7 Beech Hollows, Lavister, Rossett LL12 0DA* Tel (01244) 579225
JONES, Canon William. b 30. BTh92. St Mich Coll Llan 54. **d** 55 **p** 56. C Denio w Abererch *Ban* 55-60; V Aberdaron and Bodferin 60-66; R Llandwrog 66-71; R Llanstumdwy, Llangybi w Llanarmon 71-74; R Dolbenmaen w Llanystymdwy w Llangybi etc 74-99; RD Eifionydd 75-99; Can Ban Cathl 84-93; Can and Treas Ban Cathl 93-99; rtd 99; Perm to Offic *Ban* from 99. *Y Fachwen, Rhoshirwaun, Pwllheli LL53 8LB* Tel (01758) 760262
JONES, William David. **d** 10 **p** 11. NSM Bro Tefli Sarn Helen *St D* from 10. *Llwynteg, Felinfach, Lampeter SA48 8BQ* Tel (01570) 470691 E-mail dafydd.aeron1@btinternet.com
JONES, Canon William David. b 28. St D Coll Lamp BA48 Lon Univ BD57 Leeds Univ MA73. St Mich Coll Llan 48. **d** 51 **p** 52. C Risca *Mon* 51-54; C Chepstow St Arvan's w Penterry 54-55; C St Geo-in-the-East w Ch Ch w St Jo *Lon* 55-59; C Farnham Royal *Ox* 59-64; Lect Div Culham Coll 65-67; Hd RS Doncaster Coll of Educn 67-74; Vice-Prin St Bede Coll Dur 74; Vice-Prin SS Hild and Bede Coll Dur 75-89; Lect Th Dur Univ 75-89; Dir of Miss Ch in Wales 89-93; Metropolitical and Hon Can St D Cathl 90-93; rtd 93; Perm to Offic *Glouc* 93-08. *Triscombe Lodge, 55 Llantrisant Road, Cardiff CF5 2PU* Tel (029) 2019 3914 E-mail wdavidjones@ntlworld.com
JONES, William Douglas. b 28. St Fran Coll Brisbane ThL56. **d** 56 **p** 58. Australia 56-58; Papua New Guinea 58-72; C Manston *Ripon* 72-75; V Middleton St Mary 75-87; V Ireland Wood 87-94; rtd 94; Perm to Offic *Ripon* from 94. *6 Willow Court, Pool in Wharfedale, Otley LS21 1RX* Tel 0113-284 2028
JONES, William John. b 59. St Mich Coll Llan 91. **d** 93 **p** 94. C Pembroke Dock w Cosheston w Nash and Upton *St D* 93-96; C Tenby 96; TV 96-99; V Llanrhian w Llanhywel and Carnhedryn etc 99-00. *13 George Street, Milford Haven SA73 2AY* Tel (01646) 697094
JONES, William Lincoln. b 19. St D Coll Lamp BA41 St Mich Coll Llan 41. **d** 43 **p** 44. C Roath *Llan* 43-47; C Wooburn *Ox* 47-50; C Bridgwater w Chilton *B & W* 50-55; V Langford Budville w Runnington 55-60; V Winscombe 60-71; V Bishops Lydeard 71-73; V Bishops Lydeard w Cothelstone 73-80; P-in-c Bagborough 78-80; R Bishops Lydeard w Bagborough and Cothelstone 80-84; rtd 84; Perm to Offic *Ex* from 86. *Holme Lea, Well Mead, Kilmington, Axminster EX13 7SQ* Tel (01297) 32744
JONES, Mrs Wyn. **d** 01 **p** 02. OLM Linslade *Ox* 01-08; OLM Ouzel Valley *St Alb* from 08. *2 Woodside Way, Linslade, Leighton Buzzard LU7 7PN* Tel (01525) 373638
JONES, Wyn. *See* JONES, Ivor Wyn
JONES-BLACKETT, Enid Olive. b 40. Reading Univ BA61. **d** 97 **p** 98. OLM Hellesdon *Nor* 97-10; rtd 10; Perm to Offic *Nor* from 10. *8 Fastolf Close, Hellesdon, Norwich NR6 5RE* Tel (01603) 414895 E-mail enidjonesblackett@btinternet.com
JONES-CRABTREE, Stephen. b 56. Nottm Univ BTh80. Linc Th Coll 76. **d** 80 **p** 81. C Chorley St Pet *Blackb* 80-83; C Blackpool St Steph 83-84; C Penwortham St Mary 84-88; R Mareham-le-Fen and Revesby *Linc* 88-02; R Hameringham w Scrafield and Winceby 98-02; V Mareham on the Hill 98-02; R Washingborough w Heighington and Canwick from 02. *The Rectory, Church Hill, Washingborough, Lincoln LN4 1EJ* Tel (01522) 800240 E-mail stephen.jones-crabtree@ukonline.co.uk
JONGMAN, Kären Anngel Irene. b 43. EMMTC 97. **d** 01 **p** 02. NSM Northampton St Mary *Pet* 01-03; NSM Guilsborough w Hollowell and Cold Ashby 03-04; P-in-c Walgrave w Hannington and Wold and Scaldwell from 04; Chapl Northants Fire and Rescue Service from 03. *The Rectory, Lower Green, Walgrave, Northampton NN6 9QF* Tel and fax (01604) 781974 Mobile 07980-881252 E-mail jongman@ncountrus.co.uk
JORDAN, Anne. b 42. RGN66. **d** 02 **p** 03. OLM Crofton *Wakef* from 02. *55 Ashdene Avenue, Crofton, Wakefield WF4 1LY* Tel (01924) 865527 Mobile 07450-475184
JORDAN, Anthony John. b 50. Birm Univ BEd73. LNSM course. **d** 83 **p** 84. Asst Chapl Uppingham Sch 83-86; NSM Uppingham

w Ayston and Wardley w Belton *Pet* 83-86; Asst Chapl Sherborne Sch 86-87; NSM Bournemouth St Fran *Win* 88-03; Perm to Offic *Leic* 04-06; NSM Leic St Aid 06-08; V Eyres Monsell from 08. *St Hugh's Vicarage, 51 Pasley Road, Leicester LE2 9BU* Tel 0116-278 0940 Mobile 07798-860106 E-mail fathertonyjordan@ntlworld.com
JORDAN, Darryl Mark. b 62. Univ of Texas at Dallas BSc85 S Methodist Univ Dallas MDiv05. Perkins Sch of Th (USA) 01. **d** 04 **p** 04. C Dallas Ch Ch USA 04-05; C Bishop's Stortford St Mich *St Alb* 05-09; C Christchurch *Win* from 09. *6 Gleadowe Avenue, Christchurch BH23 1LR* Tel (01202) 470722
JORDAN, Mrs Elizabeth Ann. b 58. New Hall Cam MA82. St Jo Coll Nottm 82. **d** 87 **p** 94. Par Dn Blackpool St Jo *Blackb* 87-90; Par Dn Ewood 90-94; C 94-95; Asst Dir of Ords 90-95; Min Shelfield St Mark CD *Lich* 95-00; Local Min Adv (Wolverhampton) 95-05; OLM Course Ldr and Team Ldr Min Division 03-05; Dir Local Min Development 06-10; C Blakenall Heath 10-11; Lay Educn and Tr Adv *Chelmsf* from 11. *Diocesan Office, 53 New Street, Chelmsford CM1 1AT* Tel (01245) 294454 Fax 294477 E-mail ejordan@chelmsford.anglican.org
JORDAN, John Charles. b 37. CQSW81. NOC 84. **d** 87 **p** 88. C Southport Em *Liv* 87-90; V Abram and Bickershaw 90-95; V Bempton w Flamborough, Reighton w Speeton *York* 95-00; rtd 01; Perm to Offic *York* from 05. *35 Hollycroft, Barnston, Driffield YO25 8PP* Tel (01262) 468925 E-mail barmstonbonnie@yahoo.co.uk *or* bonnie.35@btinternet.com
JORDAN, Miss Pamela Mary. b 43. Univ of Wales (Cardiff) BSc64 Ox Univ DipEd65. WEMTC 02. **d** 05 **p** 06. NSM Coalbrookdale, Iron-Bridge and Lt Wenlock *Heref* from 05. *2 Madeley Wood View, Madeley, Telford TF7 5TF* Tel (01952) 583254
JORDAN, Patrick Glen. b 69. SEITE 01. **d** 04 **p** 05. C Charlton S'wark 04-07; C Catford (Southend) and Downham 07-08; TV from 08. *233 Bellingham Road, London SE6 1EH* Tel (020) 8697 3220 E-mail revpatrickjordan@yahoo.co.uk
JORDAN, Peter Harry. b 42. Leeds Univ BA64 Leeds Coll of Educn PGCE65. Cranmer Hall Dur 70. **d** 73 **p** 74. C Nottingham St Ann w Em *S'well* 73-77; C Edgware *Lon* 77-82; V Everton St Chrys *Liv* 82-94; Dioc Ev and V Bootle St Mary w St Paul 94-02; Chapl Barcelona *Eur* 02-08; rtd 08; Perm to Offic *Eur* from 08. *11 Stanford Avenue, Wallasey CH45 5AP* Tel 0151-639 7860 E-mail peterybarbara@gmail.com
JORDAN, Richard William. b 56. Lanchester Poly Cov BSc78 Sheff Univ MA07. St Jo Coll Nottm 84. **d** 87 **p** 88. C Blackpool St Jo *Blackb* 87-90; V Ewood 90-95; Perm to Offic *Lich* 95-97; Co-ord Walsall Town Cen Min 97-00; Ch Links Projects Officer 00-06; Dioc Ch and Soc Officer *Derby* 06-11; P-in-c Rawreth *Chelmsf* from 11. *The Rectory, Church Road, Rawreth, Wickford SS11 8SH* Tel (01268) 732078 E-mail rwjordan@gmx.com
JORDAN, Robert Brian. b 43. Qu Coll Birm 68. **d** 69 **p** 70. C Norton St Mich *Dur* 69-73; C Hastings St Clem and All SS *Chich* 73-74; C Carshalton *S'wark* 74-81; V Catford St Andr 81-08; rtd 08. *5 St Patrick's Road, Deal CT14 6AN* Tel (01304) 368607
JORDAN, Steven Paul. b 52. **d** 11. NSM Peopleton and White Ladies Aston w Churchill etc *Worc* from 11. *Chadbury House, Worcester Road, Chadbury, Evesham WR11 4TD*
JORDAN, Thomas. b 36. NW Ord Course 76. **d** 79 **p** 80. NSM Prenton *Ches* 79-84; NSM Egremont St Jo 84-91; C 91-96; Ind Chapl 91-96; TV Birkenhead Priory 96-01; rtd 01; Perm to Offic *Ches* from 02. *31 Willowbank Road, Birkenhead CH42 7JU* Tel 0151-652 4212 E-mail jordan@farndene.freeserve.co.uk
JORDAN, Trevor. b 44. Lon Hosp MB, BS67 LRCP68 MRCS68 Nottm Univ MA99. EMMTC 96. **d** 03 **p** 04. NSM Seamer *York* 03-07; Perm to Offic 07-11; NSM Long Buckby w Watford and W Haddon w Winwick *Pet* from 11. *The Vicarage, West End, West Haddon, Northampton NN6 7AY* Tel 07887-537244 (mobile) E-mail trevor@trevorsweb.net
JORDINSON, Vera (Sister Hilary). b 37. Liv Univ BA60 CertEd61. Westcott Ho Cam 88. **d** 89 **p** 94. CSF from 74; Prov Sec 90-01; Gen Sec 96-02; Sec for Miss SSF 96-99; Gift Aid Sec from 01; Lic to Offic *Heref* 89-92; Perm to Offic *Lich* 90-92; *Birm* 92-94 and 97-06; *B & W* 06-10; NSM Birchfield *Birm* 94-96. *St Francis House, 113 Gillott Road, Birmingham B16 0ET* E-mail hilarycsf@franciscans.org.uk
JORYSZ, Ian Herbert. b 62. Van Mildert Coll Dur BSc84 MA95 Liv Univ PhD87. Ripon Coll Cuddesdon BA89 MA95. **d** 90 **p** 91. C Houghton le Spring *Dur* 90-93; C Ferryhill 93-95; Research Officer to Bp of Bradwell from 95; P-in-c S Weald *Chelmsf* 95-00; V from 00; RD Brentwood from 08. *The Vicarage, Wigley Bush Lane, South Weald, Brentwood CM14 5QP* Tel (01277) 212054 Fax 262388 E-mail ian@jorysz.com
JOSEPH EMMANUEL, Brother. *See* DICKSON, Colin James
JOSS, Martin James Torquil. b 60. Univ of Wales (Lamp) BA99. EAMTC 03. **d** 03 **p** 04. C Harlow Town Cen w Lt Parndon *Chelmsf* 03-07; P-in-c Coalville and Bardon Hill *Leic* 07-09; C Ravenstone and Swannington 07-09; V Coalville w Bardon Hill

and Ravenstone from 09. *Christ Church Vicarage, 28 London Road, Coalville LE67 3JA* Tel (01530) 838287 Mobile 07875-494588 E-mail martin@thejosses.co.uk

JOUSTRA, The Very Revd Jan Tjeerd. b 57. Univ of Tasmania BA83 La Trobe Univ Vic MA97. Melbourne Coll of Div BTh91. **d** 89 **p** 91. Australia 89-97; C Melbourne E 90-91; C Wangaratta Cathl 91-93; R Rutherglen w Chiltern 93-97; P-in-c St Steph Chpl Hong Kong 97-03; Sen Chapl St Jo Cathl 00-03; Chapl Monte Carlo *Eur* 04-07; Dean Hamilton New Zealand from 07. *PO Box 338, Hamilton, New Zealand*

JOWETT, Ms Hilary Anne. b 54. Hull Univ BA75. Cranmer Hall Dur IDC80. **dss** 82 **d** 87 **p** 94. Sheff St Jo 80-83; Brampton Bierlow 83-87; Par Dn 87-89; Hon Par Dn Sharrow St Andr 89-95; Chapl Nether Edge Hosp Sheff 89-95; C Sheff St Mark Broomhill 95-97; C Mosbrough 97-00; TR Gleadless from 00. *The Rectory, 243 Hollinsend Road, Sheffield S12 2EE* Tel 0114-239 0757 E-mail hilary.jowett@izrmail.com

JOWETT, Canon Nicholas Peter Alfred. b 44. St Cath Coll Cam BA66 MA Bris Univ CertEd67. Qu Coll Birm 72. **d** 75 **p** 76. C Wales *Sheff* 75-78; TV Sheff Manor 78-83; V Brampton Bierlow 83-89; V Psalter Lane St Andr from 89; Dioc Ecum Adv 01-09; Hon Can Sheff Cathl from 06. *Shirley House, 31 Psalter Lane, Sheffield S11 8YL* Tel 0114 268 6550 E-mail njowett@sapl.ecclesallmethodist.org

JOWITT, Andrew Robert Benson. b 56. Down Coll Cam BA78 PGCE79 MA81. Wycliffe Hall Ox 88. **d** 90 **p** 91. C Northampton Em *Pet* 90-94; C Barking St Marg w St Patr *Chelmsf* 94-98; TV 98-00; TV Stantonbury and Willen *Ox* from 00; Bp'o Offiœr for Evang from 00. *Church House, 1A Atterbrook, Bradwell, Milton Keynes MK13 9EY* Tel (01908) 320850

JOWITT, David Arthur Benson. b 25. St Jo Coll Ox BA49 MA53. Sarum Th Coll 49. **d** 51 **p** 52. C Heckmondwike *Wakef* 51-56; C Harrogate St Wilfrid *Ripon* 56-59; V Kirkby Fleetham 60-69; R Langton on Swale 60-69; OGS from 65; Superior 75-81; P-in-c Edin St Ninian 69-77; Dioc Supernumerary 77-80; Chapl Edin R Infirmary 77-80; Syn Clerk *Edin* 77-90; Can St Mary's Cathl 77-90; Vice-Provost 81-86; P-in-c S Queenserry 86-90; rtd 90; Hon C Edin Old St Paul 91-99; Perm to Offic *S'wark* from 01. *16 The Quadrangle, Morden College, 19 St German's Place, London SE3 0PW* Tel (020) 8305 0811

JOWITT, John Frederick Benson. b 23. Oak Hill Th Coll 57. **d** 59 **p** 59. Uganda 59-63; CF 63-73; R Thrandeston, Stuston and Brome w Oakley *St E* 73-82; V Docking *Nor* 82-83; P-in-c Gt Bircham 82-83; R Docking w the Birchams 83-88; P-in-c Stanhoe w Barwick 85-88; R Docking w The Birchams and Stanhoe w Barwick 88; rtd 88; Perm to Offic *Nor* 88-06 and *St E* from 90. *White Lodge, The Street, North Cove, Beccles NR34 7PN* Tel (01502) 476404

JOY, Bernard David. b 50. Sarum & Wells Th Coll 90. **d** 92 **p** 93. C Shortlands *Roch* 92-94; C Henbury *Bris* 94-96; V Bristol St Aid w St Geo 96-03; P-in-c Bridgwater St Fran *B & W* 03-07; V from 07. *The Vicarage, Saxon Green, Bridgwater TA6 4HZ* Tel (01278) 422744 Mobile 07796-678478 E-mail rev.obejoyful@btopenworld.com

JOY, Canon Matthew Osmund Clifton. b 40. St Edm Hall Ox BA62 MA66. St Steph Ho Ox 62. **d** 64 **p** 65. C Brinksway *Ches* 64-66; C Southwick St Columba *Dur* 66-69; V Hartlepool H Trin 69-85; V Rotherham St Paul, St Mich and St Jo Ferham Park *Sheff* 85-88; V Masbrough 88-95; RD Rotherham 88-93; P-in-c Bordesley St Benedict *Birm* 95-01; V 01-05; Bp's Adv on Chr/Muslim Relns 95-05; rtd 05; Perm to Offic *Wakef* from 05 and *Sheff* from 06. *Lindisfarne, Eddyfield Road, Oxspring, Sheffield S36 8YH* Tel (01226) 762276

JOYCE, Canon Alison Jane. b 59. Univ of Wales (Swansea) BA81 Bris Univ MLitt87 Birm Univ PhD00 SS Coll Cam PGCE84. Ripon Coll Cuddesdon BA87 MA94. **d** 88 **p** 94. Par Dn Chalgrove w Berrick Salome *Ox* 88-90; Tutor WMMTC 90-95; Tutor Qu Coll Birm 95-96; NSM Moseley St Anne *Birm* 96-04; Dean NSMs 00-03; NSM Birm Cathl 04-05; P-in-c Edgbaston St Bart 05-11; V from 11; Chapl Birm Univ from 05; Chapl Elmhurst Sch for Dance from 05; Hon Can Birm Cathl from 06. *The Vicarage, 1B Arthur Road, Edgbaston, Birmingham B15 2UW* Tel 0121-454 0070 E-mail ajjoyce.oldedg@btinternet.com

JOYCE, Anthony Owen. b 35. Selw Coll Cam BA60 MA64. Wycliffe Hall Ox 60. **d** 62 **p** 63. C Birm St Martin 62-67; Rhodesia 67-70; V Birm St Luke 70-79; V Downend *Bris* 79-01; RD Stapleton 83-89; rtd 01; Perm to Offic *Bris* from 02. *116 Jellicoe Avenue, Stapleton, Bristol BS16 1WJ* Tel 0117-956 2510 E-mail tony@joycet.freeserve.co.uk

JOYCE, Gordon Franklin. b 51. Birm Univ BA72. St Jo Coll Nottm 86. **d** 88 **p** 89. C Didsbury St Jas and Em *Man* 88-92; V Tonge w Alkrington 92-96; C Bury St Mary from 06; Adv Rural from 00. *1A Pimhole Road, Bury BL9 7EY* Tel 0161-764 1157

JOYCE, Graham Leslie. b 49. Lon Univ CertEd71. Trin Coll Bris 87. **d** 89 **p** 90. C Heald Green St Cath *Ches* 89-93; R Church

Lawton from 93. *The Rectory, 1 Liverpool Road West, Church Lawton, Stoke-on-Trent ST7 3DE* Tel and fax (01270) 882103 E-mail grahamljoyce@btinternet.com

JOYCE, John Barnabas Altham. b 47. St Chad's Coll Dur BA69 Lon Univ DipEd86. St Steph Ho Ox 72. **d** 74 **p** 75. C Reading St Giles *Ox* 74-77; C Cowley St Jo 77-80; Dioc Youth and Community Officer 80-87; V Hangleton *Chich* 87-94; Dioc Adv for Schs and Dir Educn 94-99; R Hurstpierpoint from 99. *The Rectory, 21 Cuckfield Road, Hurstpierpoint, Hassocks BN6 9RP* Tel (01273) 832203 E-mail rector@hurstrectory.co.uk

JOYCE, Kingsley Reginald. b 49. MBE00 TD91. Man Univ BSc70. Cuddesdon Coll 70. **d** 73 **p** 74. C High Wycombe *Ox* 73-76; C Fingest 76-79; C Hambleden 76-79; C Medmenham 76-79; C Fawley (Bucks) 76-79; C Turville 76-79; P-in-c Hambleden Valley 79-80; R 80-87; R Friern Barnet St Jas *Lon* 87-91; CF 91-08; Chapl Naples w Sorrento, Capri and Bari *Eur* from 08. *Christ Church, Afsouth (Naples), BFPO 8, London* Tel (0039) (081) 411842 Fax 409789 E-mail vicar@christchurchnaples.org

JOYCE, Margaret. b 47. Oak Hill NSM Course 86. **d** 89 **p** 94. NSM Chadwell Heath *Chelmsf* 89-92; NSM Bath Odd Down w Combe Hay *B & W* from 92; Chapl Bath and West Community NHS Trust from 95. *69 Bloomfield Rise, Bath BA2 2BN* Tel (01225) 840864 E-mail margaretjoyce@stphilipstjames.org

JOYCE, Paul David. b 70. Qu Coll Birm 00. **d** 02 **p** 03. C Perry Beeches *Birm* 02-05; V Eastwood St Dav *Chelmsf* from 05. *St David's Vicarage, 400 Rayleigh Road, Leigh-on-Sea SS9 5PT* Tel (01702) 523126 E-mail joycefamily400@btinternet.com

JOYCE, Miss Penelope Anne. b 53. St Mary's Coll Chelt CertEd74. Wycliffe Hall Ox. **d** 00 **p** 01. C Ox St Clem 00-03; C Cogges and S Leigh 03-09; Hon C Bourne Valley *Sarum* from 11; Hon C Salisbury St Fran and Stratford sub Castle from 11. *Peacemere, Wavering Lane West, Gillingham SP8 4NR* Tel (01747) 822454 Mobile 07808-181885 E-mail pennyrie.joyce@btinternet.com

JOYCE, Philip Rupert. b 38. Selw Coll Cam BA68 MA72. Cranmer Hall Dur 68. **d** 70 **p** 71. C Newland St Jo *York* 70-73; C Woolwich St Mary w H Trin *S'wark* 73-77; Chapl Thames Poly 73-77; Chapl S Bank Poly 77-79; rtd 03. *37 Fulcher Avenue, Cromer NR27 9SG* Tel (01263) 519405 E-mail philipjoyce@ntlworld.com

JOYCE, Raymond. b 37. Keele Univ BA60 MA67 Linc Coll Ox BA62 MA68 Leic Univ MA97. St Steph Ho Ox 78. **d** 80 **p** 81. NSM Normanton *Derby* 80-83; NSM Derby St Alkmund and St Werburgh 83-87; Lic to Offic 87-97; NSM Mickleover All SS 97-00; Perm to Offic from 01. *23 Hindscarth Crescent, Mickleover, Derby DE3 9NN* Tel (01332) 519001

JOYCE, Canon Terence Alan. b 57. St Jo Coll Nottm BTh84. **d** 84 **p** 85. C Mansfield SS Pet and Paul *S'well* 84-88; V Greasley 88-00; Dioc Dir of Ords from 99; Dir Post-Ord Support and Tr from 01; Hon Can S'well Minster 02-11. *86 Main Road, Ravenshead, Nottingham NG15 9GW* Tel (01623) 489819 E-mail tjoyce@southwell.anglican.org

JOYNER, Mrs Susan Diane. b 58. Nene Coll Northn BA79 Open Univ MA99 Leic Univ PGCE84. NEOC 05. **d** 08 **p** 09. NSM Upper Coquetdale *Newc* from 08. *The Old Church, Harbottle, Morpeth NE65 7DQ* Tel (01669) 650385 E-mail suejoyner2@aol.com

JUBA, Bishop of. See MARONA, The Most Revd Joseph Biringi Hassan

JUCKES, Jonathan Sydney. b 61. St Andr Univ MA83. Ridley Hall Cam BA87. **d** 88 **p** 89. C Sevenoaks St Nic *Roch* 88-92; Proclamation Trust 92-95; C St Helen Bishopsgate w St Andr Undershaft etc *Lon* 95-98; TR Kirk Ella and Willerby *York* from 98. *The Rectory, 2 School Lane, Kirk Ella, Hull HU10 7NR* Tel (01482) 653040 E-mail juckes@juckes.karoo.co.uk

JUDD, Adrian Timothy. b 67. Lanc Univ BA88 St Jo Coll Dur BA92. Cranmer Hall Dur 90 Trin Coll Singapore 92. **d** 93 **p** 94. C Dudley St Aug Holly Hall *Worc* 93-97; V Stockbridge Village *Liv* 97-99; V Went Valley *Wakef* from 00. *The Vicarage, Marlpit Lane, Darrington, Pontefract WF8 3AB* Tel (01977) 704744 E-mail thevicar@darringtonchurch.com

JUDD, Colin Ivor. b 35. Dur Univ BA61. Ridley Hall Cam 61. **d** 63 **p** 64. C Stratford St Jo w Ch Ch *Chelmsf* 63-66; C Kimberworth *Sheff* 66-68; Area Sec CMS *Bradf* and *Wakef* 68-80; V Bradf St Columba w St Andr 80-00; rtd 00; Perm to Offic *Bradf* from 01. *57 Grosvenor Road, Shipley BD18 4RB* Tel (01274) 584775 E-mail thejudds@saltsvillage.co.uk

JUDD, Mrs Nicola Jane. b 51. Birm Coll of Educn CertEd72. S Dios Minl Tr Scheme 87. **d** 90 **p** 94. NSM Abbotts Ann and Upper and Goodworth Clatford *Win* 90-11; Adv for NSM 01-11; rtd 11. *13 Belmont Close, Andover SP10 2DE* Tel (01264) 363364 E-mail nicola.judd@ukonline.co.uk

JUDD, The Very Revd Peter Somerset Margesson. b 49. Trin Hall Cam BA71. Cuddesdon Coll 71. **d** 74 **p** 75. C Salford St Phil w St Steph *Man* 74-76; Chapl Clare Coll Cam 76-81; C Burnham *Ox* 81-82; TV Burnham w Dropmore, Hitcham and Taplow 82-88; V Iffley 88-97; RD Cowley 94-97; Provost Chelmsf 97-00;

Dean Chelmsf from 00. *The Deanery, 3 Harlings Grove, Chelmsford CM1 1YQ* Tel (01245) 354318 *or* 294480 E-mail dean@chelmsfordcathedral.org.uk

JUDD, Susan Elizabeth. b 48. Bris Univ BSc74 Univ of Wales MA04 ACA80. STETS 05. **d** 08 **p** 09. NSM Portsm Cathl from 08. *16 Bepton Down, Petersfield GU31 4PR* Tel (01730) 266819 E-mail susan.judd@ntlworld.com

JUDGE, Mrs Alison Gwendolyn. b 60. SEITE BA10. **d** 10. C W Wickham St Fran and St Mary *S'wark* from 10. *7 Woodland Way, West Wickham BR4 9LL* Tel (020) 8616 5794 Mobile 07939-495710 E-mail alison@judge-family.org.uk

JUDGE, Andrew Duncan. b 50. Cape Town Univ BCom72 Keble Coll Ox MA81. Pietermaritzburg Th Sem 82. **d** 83 **p** 84. S Africa 83-01; C Westville 84-87; R Prestbury 88-94; R Westville 94-01; TV Keynsham *B & W* from 01. *St Francis's Vicarage, Warwick Road, Keynsham, Bristol BS31 2PW* Tel 0117-373 7478 E-mail revjudge@blueyonder.co.uk

JUDGE, Mark Rollo. b 60. Chich Th Coll BTh92. **d** 92 **p** 93. C Forest Gate St Edm *Chelmsf* 92-96; V Gt Ilford St Luke 96-01; Asst Chapl Barking Havering and Redbridge Hosps NHS Trust 01-08. *Address temp unknown* E-mail markjudge_new.uk@excite.co.uk

JUDSON, Miss Christine Alison. b 64. Surrey Univ BSc86 Birm Univ PGCE88. Ripon Coll Cuddesdon 05. **d** 07 **p** 08. C Highbridge *B & W* 07-10; TV Portishead from 10. *77 Nightingale Rise, Portishead, Bristol BS20 8LX* Tel (01275) 397232 E-mail chris@cjudson.fslife.co.uk

JUDSON, Mrs Mary Ruth. b 47. Bretton Hall Coll DipEd68. NEOC 89. **d** 92 **p** 94. Par Dn Chester le Street *Dur* 92-94; C 94-96; V Millfield St Mark and Pallion St Luke 96-04; V Hartlepool St Luke from 04. *St Luke's Vicarage, 5 Tunstall Avenue, Hartlepool TS26 8NF* Tel (01429) 272893 E-mail mary.judson@durham.anglican.org

JUDSON, Paul Wesley. b 46. Leic Poly ATD71. Cranmer Hall Dur 87. **d** 89 **p** 90. C Lobley Hill *Dur* 89-92; C Chester le Street 92-96; Ed Dioc Publications and Sec Dioc Bd of Soc Resp 96-98; C Millfield St Mark and Pallion St Luke 96-04; C Hartlepool St Luke from 04; Dioc Publications Officer from 98; Dioc Dir of Communications from 02. *St Luke's Vicarage, 5 Tunstall Avenue, Hartlepool TS26 8NF* Tel (01429) 272893 E-mail director.of.communications@durham.anglican.org

JUDSON, Peter. b 39. Lon Univ BSc61 Plymouth Univ PGCE87. SWMTC 99. **d** 02 **p** 03. OLM Bude Haven and Marhamchurch *Truro* 02-09; rtd 09. *Meadowcroft, Bagbury Road, Bude EX23 8QJ* Tel and fax (01288) 356597 Mobile 07970-115538

JUKES, The Very Revd Keith Michael. b 54. Leeds Univ BA76. Linc Th Coll 77. **d** 78 **p** 79. C Wordsley *Lich* 78-81; C Wolverhampton 81-83; C-in-c Stoneydelph St Martin CD 83-90; TR Glascote and Stonydelph 90-91; RD Tamworth 90-91; TR Cannock and V Hatherton 91-97; Preb Lich Cathl 96-97; P-in-c Selby Abbey *York* 97-99; V 99-07; Dean Ripon from 07. *The Minster House, Bedern Bank, Ripon HG4 1PE* Tel (01765) 602609 *or* 603462 E-mail deankeith@riponcathedral.org.uk

JUKES (*née* **WEATHERHOGG), Mrs Susanne.** b 56. Leeds Univ BA77 Coll of Ripon & York St Jo PGCE78. NEOC 98. **d** 01 **p** 02. C Monk Fryston and S Milford *York* 01-05; P-in-c 05-07; Assoc Min Aldborough w Boroughbridge and Roecliffe *Ripon* 07-09; Asst Dir of Ords 07-09; Chapl HM Pris Full Sutton from 09. *The Chaplaincy, HM Prison Full Sutton, York YO41 1PS* Tel (01759) 475100 Fax 371206

JUMP, Elizabeth Anne. b 63. Liv Univ of Educn BA95. NOC 97. **d** 00 **p** 01. C Walkden and Lt Hulton *Man* 00-03; P-in-c Elton St Steph 03-05; C Ashton Ch Ch 05-06; Perm to Offic 06-07; TV Blackbourne *St E* from 07. *The Rectory, Church Road, Honington, Bury St Edmunds IP31 1RG* Tel (01359) 269265 E-mail revlizj@btinternet.com

JUMP, Paul Gordon. b 77. St Andr Univ BSc99. Oak Hill Th Coll 04. **d** 07 **p** 08. C Rusholme H Trin *Man* 07-10; NSM from 10. *2 The Grange, Manchester M14 5NY* Tel 0161-256 6547

JUNG, Mrs Jennifer Margaret. b 61. STETS 95. **d** 98 **p** 99. NSM Fareham H Trin *Portsm* 98-02. *42 Clifton Road, Winchester SO22 5BU*

JUPE, Canon Derek Robert. b 26. TCD BA53 Div Test54 MA67. **d** 54 **p** 55. C Lurgan Ch the Redeemer *D & D* 54-57; C Dublin Harold's Cross *D & G* 57-60; I Easkey w Kilglass *T, K & A* 60-65; Deputation Sec (Ireland) BCMS 65-72; R Man St Jerome w Ardwick St Silas 72-78; V Ardsley *Sheff* 78-83; I Tempo and Clabby *Clogh* 83-92; Can Clogh Cathl 89-92; rtd 92; Perm to Offic *Cov* 92-05 and *Edin* from 05. *4 Leithen Mills, Innerleithen EH44 6JJ* Tel (01896) 831701

✠**JUPP, The Rt Revd Roger Alan.** b 56. St Edm Hall Ox BA78 MA82 Surrey Univ PGCE96. Chich Th Coll 79. **d** 80 **p** 81 **c** 03. C Newbold w Dunston *Derby* 80-83; C Cowley St Jo *Ox* 83-85; C Islington St Jas w St Phil *Lon* 85-86; V Lower Beeding *Chich* 86-90; Dom Chapl to Bp Horsham 86-91; V Burgess Hill St Jo 90-93; TR Burgess Hill St Jo w St Edw 93-94; Perm to Offic 97-98; C Aldwick 98-00; Prin Newton Th Coll Papua New Guinea 00-03; Bp Popondota 03-05; Hon Asst Bp Chich from 05; P-in-c St Leonards Ch Ch and St Mary 05-06; R from 06.

Christ Church Rectory, 3 Silchester Road, St Leonards-on-Sea TN38 0JB Tel (01424) 444052 E-mail rajupp1@hotmail.com

JUPP, Vincent John. b 64. St Jo Coll Nottm BA(ThM)06. **d** 00 **p** 01. C Evington *Leic* 00-03; TV Ascension TM 03-07; TR 07-11; AD City of Leic 09-11; V Birstall and Wanlip from 11. *The Rectory, 251 Birstall Road, Birstall, Leicester LE4 4DJ* E-mail vince@nursery73.plus.com

JUSTICE, Keith Leonard. b 42. Wolv Univ BSc68 CEng83 MIMechE83. Wycliffe Hall Ox 91. **d** 93 **p** 94. C Penwortham St Mary *Blackb* 93-96; C Dovercourt and Parkeston w Harwich *Chelmsf* 96-98; V Wentworth *Sheff* 98-01; Chapl Rotherham Gen Hosps NHS Trust 98-01; Chapl Rotherham Priority Health Services NHS Trust 98-01; R Melrose *Edin* 01-04; P-in-c Royton St Anne *Man* 04-08; P-in-c Lawton Moor from 08. *The Vicarage, Orton Road, Manchester M23 0LH* Tel 0161-998 2461 E-mail keith.justice@ntlworld.com

JUSTICE, Simon Charles. b 66. Univ of Wales (Lamp) BD88 Edin Univ MTh90. Cranmer Hall Dur 90. **d** 92 **p** 93. C Tilehurst St Mich *Ox* 92-95; R Troy St Paul USA 95-01; R Tigard St Jas 01-04; Can All SS Cathl Albany 98-04; R Edin Ch Ch 04-06; R Corvallis Gd Samaritan USA from 06. *445 NW Elizabeth Drive, Corvallis OR 97330, USA* E-mail simon.justice@googlemail.com

JUTSUM, Linda Mary. *See* ELLIOTT, Mrs Linda Mary

K

KABOLEH, David Reardon. b 64. Westmr Coll Ox MTh00. Trin Coll Nairobi 88. **d** 90 **p** 91. C-in-c Nairobi St Phil 90-92; TV Nairobi St Luke and Immanuel 93-95; NSM Hoddesdon *St Alb* 95-97; NSM Ox St Matt 97-99; NSM Blackbird Leys 99-02; NSM Ox St Aldate 03-04; NSM Akeman 04-07; P-in-c Worminghall w Ickford, Oakley and Shabbington 07-10; R from 10. *The Rectory, 32A The Avenue, Worminghall, Aylesbury HP18 9LE* Tel (01844) 338839 E-mail kaboleh@aol.com

✠**KAFITY, The Rt Revd Samir.** b 33. Beirut Univ BA57. Near E Sch of Th 57. **d** 57 **p** 58 **c** 86. Israel 57-64 and 77-98; Lebanon 64-77; Adn Jerusalem 77-82; Bp Jerusalem 84-98; Pres Bp Episc Ch Jerusalem and Middle E 86-96; rtd 98. *11964 Callado Road, San Diego CA 92128, USA*

KAGGWA, Nelson Sonny. b 58. E Lon Univ BA91. Bp Tucker Coll Mukono 77. **d** 80 **p** 80. Kenya 80-83; USA 83; Hon C Ox SS Phil and Jas w St Marg 84-85; C W Ham *Chelmsf* 86-87; TV Walthamstow St Mary w St Steph 87-92; Perm to Offic *Sheff* 92-95; V Sheff St Paul 96-97; rtd 98. *Al-Salam, 36 Standish Gardens, Sheffield S5 8YD* Tel 0114-273 1428 Fax 273 1348 Mobile 07989-261278 E-mail kaggwanelsonibrahim@msn.com

KAJUMBA, The Ven Daniel Steven Kimbugwe. b 52. S'wark Ord Course. **d** 85 **p** 86. C Goldington *St Alb* 85-87; Uganda 87-99; TV Horley *S'wark* 99-01; Adn Reigate from 01. *84 Higher Drive, Purley CR8 2HJ* Tel (020) 8660 9276 *or* 8681 5496 Fax 8686 2074 Mobile 07949-594460 E-mail daniel.kajumba@southwark.anglican.org

KAKURU (*née* **ASHBRIDGE), Mrs Clare Patricia Esther.** b 80. QUB BTh03 MTh07. **d** 07 **p** 08. C Donaghcloney w Waringstown *D & D* from 07. *3 Banbridge Road, Waringstown, Craigavon BT66 7QA* Tel (028) 3882 0109

KALENIUK, Nicholas George. b 69. WEMTC. **d** 09 **p** 10. C Claines St Jo *Worc* from 09. *1 Tamarisk Close, Claines, Worcester WR3 7LE* Tel (01905) 458331

KALSI, Mrs Gina Louise. b 68. Leeds Univ BA09. NOC 06. **d** 09 **p** 10. C Netherthorpe St Steph *Sheff* from 09. *73 Burgoyne Road, Sheffield S6 3QB* Tel 0114-233 1455 Mobile 07787-578721 E-mail ginalkalsi@hotmail.co.uk

KALUS, Rupert. b 61. St Jo Coll Dur BA85 MA93 BA01 W Sussex Inst of HE PGCE87. Cranmer Hall Dur 99. **d** 02 **p** 03. C Dur N 02-06; P-in-c Shildon 06-07; V from 08. *St John's Vicarage, 1A Burnie Gardens, Shildon DL4 1ND* Tel (01388) 774494

KAMBLE-HANSELL, Anupama. b 76. Pune Univ India BSc97 Serampore Univ BD03 Birm Univ MA06. **d** 02 **p** 04. Perm to Offic *Nor* 03; C Birm St Martin w Bordesley St Andr 04-08; Chapl Aston Univ 05-08; TV Coventry Caludon 08-10; Perm to Offic *Nor* 10-11; C Brant Valley from 11. *The Vicarage, Back Lane, Buxton, Norwich NR10 5HD* Tel (01603) 279394 E-mail anupamakamble@hotmail.com

KAMEGERI, Stephen. *See* NSHIMYE, Stephen Kamegeri

KAMPALA, Bishop of. *See* OROMBI, The Most Revd Henry Luke

KAMUYU, Elpiety Wanjiku. b 53. St Jo Coll Nottm 06. d 93 p 09. Kenya 93-01; NSM Edgware Lon 01-03; NSM Bilborough w Strelley S'well 04-06; C Lenton 08-10; C Nottingham St Ann w Em from 10. 99 Allington Avenue, Lenton, Nottingham NG7 1JY Tel 0115-845 3922 Mobile 07985-424139 E-mail pietykamuyu@yahoo.co.uk

KANE, Peter David Colin. b 72. K Coll Lon BMus92 Fitzw Coll Cam BA05 MA09 ARCO91 ARCM94. Wycliffe Hall Ox BA08. d 09 p 10. C Chich St Paul and Westhampnett from 09. 37 Somerstown, Chichester PO19 6AL Tel (01243) 537121 E-mail p.kane.03@cantab.net

KANERIA, Rajni. b 57. Bath Univ BPharm82. Wycliffe Hall Ox 83. d 86 p 87. C Hyson Green S'well 86-87; C Hyson Green St Paul w St Steph 87-89; C Harold Hill St Geo Chelmsf 89-91; TV Oadby Leic 91-97. 32 Rendall Road, Leicester LE4 6LE Tel 0116-266 6613

KAOMA, John Kafwanka. b 66. Trin Coll Melbourne BTh97 Ridley Coll Melbourne MA00. St Jo Sem Lusaka 90. d 93 p 94. C Chingola St Barn Zambia 93-94; Perm to Offic Melbourne Australia 94-00; Lect St Jo Coll Lusaka Zambia 00-03; Prin 01-03; Regional Manager (S Africa) CMS 03-06; Research Officer Miss Dept Angl Communion Office 06-09; Dir for Miss from 09; Perm to Offic Lon from 06. 11 Silverhall Street, Isleworth TW7 6RF Tel (020) 7313 3940 Fax 7313 3999 Mobile 07901-987239 E-mail john.kafwanka@anglicancommunion.org

KARAMURA, Grace Patrick. b 62. Nat Teachers' Coll Uganda DipEd89 Rob Coll Cam MPhil95 Leeds Univ PhD98. Bp Tucker Coll Mukono BD92. d 92 p 93. C All SS Cathl Kampala Uganda 92-93; C Ebbw Vale Mon 98-01; TV 01-03; V Pontyclun w Talygarn Llan from 03. The Vicarage, Heol Miskin, Pontyclun CF72 9AJ Tel and fax (01443) 225477 E-mail gracekaramu@hotmail.com

KARRACH, Herbert Adolf. b 24. TCD BA46 MB, BCh48 BAO48. EAMTC 85. d 88 p 89. NSM Snettisham w Ingoldisthorpe and Fring Nor 88-95; Perm to Offic from 95. Narnia, 5 Docking Road, Fring, King's Lynn PE31 6SQ Tel (01485) 518346

KASHOURIS, Peter Zacharias. b 66. Peterho Cam BA89 MA93. St Steph Ho Ox 92. d 94 p 95. C Hampstead St Jo Lon 94-97; R Hartlepool St Hilda Dur 97-03; P-in-c Dur St Oswald 03-06; P-in-c Dur St Oswald and Shincliffe from 06; Dioc Ecum Officer 03-09. St Oswald's Vicarage, Church Street, Durham DH1 3DG Tel 0191-374 1681 E-mail p.j.kashouris@durham.anglican.org

KASIBANTE, Amos Sebadduka. b 54. Trin Coll Cam BA83 MA87 Yale Univ STM89. Bp Tucker Coll Mukono 76. d 79 p 80. C Lyantonde Uganda 79-80; Tutor Bp Tucker Coll Mukono 83-92; Tutor Coll of Ascension Selly Oak 92-95; Prin Simon of Cyrene Th Inst 95-97; Vice Prin St Mich Coll Llan 97-02; Chapl Leic Univ 02-09; P-in-c Burmantofts St Steph and St Agnes Ripon from 10; P-in-c Leeds St Cypr Harehills from 10. St Agnes' Vicarage, 21 Shakespeare Close, Leeds LS9 7UQ Tel 0113-248 2648 Mobile 07990-938122 E-mail amos.kasibante@virgin.net

KASOZI, Jackson Nsamba. b 50. Bp Tucker Coll Mukono BD91 Birm Univ MPhil94 All Nations Chr Coll MA00. d 83 p 84. Uganda 84-92 and 96-99; V St Andr Cathl Mityana 84-88; Adn 86-88; Chapl to Bp W Buganda 91-92; Perm to Offic Cov 93-94; Adn W Buganda 95-98; Acting Dean St Paul's Cathl 98-99; NSM Limehouse Lon 00-02; NSM Old Ford St Paul and St Mark 02-03; C Harold Hill St Geo Chelmsf 04-08; rtd 08. c/o Christian Vision Uganda, PO Box 37269, Kampala, Uganda E-mail christian.vision.uganda@live.com

KASSELL, Colin George Henry. b 42. Ripon Coll Cuddesdon 76. d 68 p 69. In RC Ch 69-75; Perm to Offic Ox 76-77; C Denham 77-80; V Brotherton Wakef 80-84; Chapl and Past Ldr St Cath Hospice Crawley 84-91; R Rogate w Terwick and Trotton w Chithurst Chich 91-94; C Heene 94-96; Chapl Worthing Hosp 94-07; rtd 07; P-in-c Worthing St Andr Chich from 06. Park House, 3 Madeira Avenue, Worthing BN11 2AT Tel (01903) 526571 Mobile 07802-259310 E-mail colin.kassell@ntlworld.com

KATE, Sister. See BURGESS, Kate Lamorna

KAUNHOVEN, Canon Anthony Peter. b 55. Leeds Univ BA78 Coll of Ripon & York St Jo PGCE79. Edin Th Coll 79. d 81 p 82. C Leeds St Aid Ripon 81-84; C Hawksworth Wood 84-89; V Upper Nidderdale 89-91; Hon C Rawdon Bradf 96-99; P-in-c Old Brampton Derby 99-07; P-in-c Gt Barlow 04-07; P-in-c Bakewell 07-11; C Ashford w Sheldon and Longstone 07-11; P-in-c Rowsley 07-11; V Bakewell, Ashford w Sheldon and Rowsley from 11; Dioc Ecum Officer from 01; Hon Can Derby Cathl from 11. The Vicarage, South Church Street, Bakewell DE45 1FD Tel (01629) 812256 E-mail jazzyrector@aol.com

KAVANAGH, John Paul. b 63. St Fran Coll Brisbane BTh94. d 94 p 96. C Indooroopilly Australia 94-95; C Centenary Suburbs 96-98; R Forest Lake 98; P-in-c Texas w Inglewood 99-00; Chapl Wolston Park Hosp and Asst Chapl R Brisbane Hosp 00-02; Chapl Matthew Flinders Angl Coll 02-08; I Kells Gp C & O 08-10; Chapl Dub Inst of Tech from 11. Dublin Institute of Technology, 143-149 Rathmines Road, Dublin 6, Republic of Ireland Tel (00353) (1) 402 3000 Mobile 85-840 2404 E-mail jpandmary@gmail.com or jp.kavanagh@dit.ie

KAVANAGH, Canon Michael Lowther. b 58. York Univ BA80 Newc Univ MSc82 Leeds Univ BA86 MBPsS90. Coll of Resurr Mirfield 84. d 87 p 88. C Boston Spa York 87-91; C Clifford 89-91; Chapl Martin House Hospice for Children Boston Spa 87-91; V Beverley St Nic York 91-97; RD Beverley 95-97; Abp's Dom Chapl and Dioc Dir of Ords 97-05; Chapl HM Pris Full Sutton 05-08; Angl Adv HM Pris Service from 08; Can Th Liv Cathl from 09. Chaplaincy HQ, Post Point 3.08, 3rd Floor Red Zone, Clive House, 70 Petty France, London SW1H 9HD Tel 03000-475182 Fax 03000-476822/3

KAY, Mrs Audrey Elizabeth. b 60. NOC 04. d 07 p 08. NSM Ramsbottom and Edenfield Man 07-10; V Cadishead from 10; Chapl Salford City Academy from 10. St Mary's Vicarage, Penry Avenue, Cadishead, Manchester M44 5ZE Tel 0161-775 2171 Mobile 07752-526140 E-mail kaynacg@aol.com

KAY, Dennis. b 57. St As Minl Tr Course 96. d 99 p 00. NSM Llangystennin St As 99-01; NSM Colwyn Bay w Brynymaen 01-03; NSM Petryal 03-07. 41 Ffordd Ffynnon, Rhuddlan, Rhyl LL18 2SP Tel 07748-312067 (mobile)

KAY, George Ronald. b 24. Sarum & Wells Th Coll 74. d 77 p 78. NSM Bemerton Sarum 77-87; rtd 87; Perm to Offic Sarum 89-00. The Lodge, 157 Wilton Road, Salisbury SP2 7JH Tel (01722) 338326

KAY, Ian Geoffrey. NOC. d 89 p 90. NSM Rochdale Man 89-91 and from 95; NSM Heywood St Luke w All So 91-95. 161 Norden Road, Rochdale OL11 5PT Tel (01706) 639497

KAY, Marjory Marianne Kate. b 61. d 97. NSM Godshill Portsm 97-05. 76A East Street, Bridport DT6 3LL Tel (01308) 422453

KAY, Peter Richard. b 72. St Cath Coll Cam BA93 MA00 PGCE95. Trin Coll Bris 09. d 11. C Letchworth St Paul w Willian St Alb from 11. 36 Howard Drive, Letchworth Garden City SG6 2BX Tel 07952-194565 (mobile) E-mail peterrkay08@googlemail.com

KAYE, Alistair Geoffrey. b 62. Reading Univ BSc85. St Jo Coll Nottm 87. d 90 p 91. C Gt Horton Bradf 90-94; C Rushden w Newton Bromswold Pet 94-98; V Upper Armley Ripon 98-08; Armley Deanery Missr from 08; AD Armley 05-08. 27 Hough End Lane, Leeds LS13 4EY Tel 0113-257 3702 Mobile 07881-804104 E-mail alistair@armley.freeserve.co.uk

KAYE, Bruce Norman. b 39. Lon Univ BD64 Sydney Univ BA66 Basel Univ DrTheol75. Moore Th Coll Sydney ThL64. d 64 p 65. Australia 64-66 and from 83; Perm to Offic Dur 67-68; Tutor St Jo Coll Dur 68-75; Sen Tutor 75-83; Vice Prin 79-83; rtd 04. 217 Hopetown Avenue, Watsons Bay NSW 2030, Australia Tel (0061) (2) 9337 6795

KAYE, Canon Gerald Trevor. b 32. Man Univ BSc54. Oak Hill Th Coll. d 56 p 57. C Widnes St Ambrose Liv 56-58; C St Helens St Mark 58-62; V Brixton Hill St Sav S'wark 62-65; Canada 65-85; Hon Can Keewatin 70-75; Adn Patricia 75-78; V Slough Ox 85-97; rtd 97; Lic to Offic Arg from 08. Craiguanach, Torlundy, Fort William PH33 6SW Tel (01397) 705395 E-mail eleanorado@aol.com

KAYE, Peter Alan. b 47. K Coll Lon BD71 AKC71 Leic Univ MA82 CQSW82. St Aug Coll Cant 71. d 72 p 73. C Fulham All SS Lon 72-74; Chapl Rubery Hill, Jo Conolly and Jos Sheldon Hosps Birm 74-80; Hon C Northfield Birm 80-83; Perm to Offic 99-06; P-in-c Stirchley from 06. Stirchley Vicarage, 18 Pineapple Grove, Birmingham B30 2TJ Tel 0121-443 1371 Mobile 07790-268754 E-mail peterakaye@googlemail.com

KAYE, Mrs Sharon Vernie. b 72. Bradf Coll of Educn BEd97. Trin Coll Bris 06. d 08 p 09. C Yeadon Bradf from 08. 37 Millbank, Yeadon, Leeds LS19 7AY Tel 0113-250 4522 Mobile 07871-768774 E-mail verniekaye@hotmail.com

KAYE, Stephen Michael. b 72. Trin Coll Bris 06. d 08 p 09. C Calverley Bradf from 08. 37 Millbank, Yeadon, Leeds LS19 7AY Tel 0113-250 4522 Mobile 07756-274011 E-mail revkaye@gmail.com

KAYE, Timothy Henry. b 52. Linc Th Coll 77. d 80 p 81. C Warsop S'well 80-83; C Far Headingley St Chad Ripon 83-86; P-in-c Birkby Wakef 86; TV N Huddersfield 86-91; R Stone St Mich w Aston St Sav Lich 91-95; V S Kirkby Wakef from 95. The Vicarage, Bull Lane, South Kirkby, Pontefract WF9 3QD Tel and fax (01977) 642795 E-mail mail@kaye5.fsworld.co.uk

KAYE-BESLEY, Mrs Lesley Kathleen. b 47. Cam Inst of Educn CertEd69 Kingston Univ MA94 FRSA85. d 04 p 05. OLM Walton-on-Thames Guildf 04-11; NSM Hinchley Wood from 11. Minggay, 1 Park Road, Esher KT10 8NP Tel (01372) 465185 E-mail lesley@waltonparish.org.uk

KAZIRO, Godfrey Sam. b 48. BDSc Lon Univ MSc FDSRCPSGlas FFDRCSI. d 02 p 03. OLM Waterloo St Jo w St Andr S'wark from 02. 19 Hampshire Road, Hornchurch RM11 3EU Tel (01708) 441609

KEAL, Barry Clifford. b 57. Leeds Univ BA06. NOC 03. d 06 p 07. NSM Halsall, Lydiate and Downholland Liv from 06. 46 Eastway, Liverpool L31 6BS Tel 0151-526 4508 E-mail barry@keal.me.uk

KEAN, Robert John. b 64. St Mellitus Coll BA11. **d** 11. C Black Notley *Chelmsf* from 11. *49 Brain Valley Avenue, Black Notley, Braintree CM77 8LS* Tel (01376) 331586 E-mail rob.kean@gmail.com

KEANE, Christian John. b 74. Rob Coll Cam BA95 MA99. Wycliffe Hall Ox BA06 MA06. **d** 06 **p** 07. C Eastrop *Win* 06-11; C Ex St Leon w H Trin from 11. *St Leonard's Church, Topsham Road, Exeter EX2 4NG* Tel (01392) 286995 E-mail chris@stlens.org.uk

KEANE, Damien. *See* O'CATHAIN, Damien

KEARLEY-HEYWOOD, Deiniol John Owen. b 73. K Coll Lon BA95 Peterho Cam MPhil03. Westcott Ho Cam 02. **d** 04 **p** 05. C Paddington St Jo w St Mich *Lon* 04-08; R Prestwood and Gt Hampden *Ox* from 08. *The Rectory, 140 Wycombe Road, Prestwood, Great Missenden HP16 0HJ* Tel (01494) 866530 E-mail rector@htprestwood.org.uk

KEARNEY, Mrs Sandra. b 55. Bolton Inst of HE BSc89 Univ Coll Ches BTh04. NOC 01. **d** 04 **p** 05. C Blackpool Ch Ch w All SS *Blackb* 04-08; P-in-c Ordsall and Salford Quays *Man* from 08. *The Rectory, Parsonage Close, Salford M5 3GS* Tel 0161-872 0800 E-mail rev.sandra@sky.com

KEARNS, Andrew Philip. b 76. Wycliffe Hall Ox. **d** 09 **p** 10. C Maidenhead St Andr and St Mary *Ox* from 09. *1 Hemsdale, Maidenhead SL6 6SL* Tel 07990-574431 (mobile) E-mail andrewpkearns@gmail.com

KEARNS, Mrs Mary Leah. b 38. **d** 87 **p** 94. Par Dn Morden *S'wark* 87-88; Asst Chapl HM Pris Holloway 88-98; rtd 99; Perm to Offic *Guildf* from 01. *48 The Orchard, North Holmwood, Dorking RH5 4JT* Tel (01306) 886858

KEARON, Canon Kenneth Arthur. b 53. TCD BA76 MA79 MPhil91. CITC 78. **d** 81 **p** 82. C Raheny w Coolock *D & G* 81-84; Lect TCD 82-90; Dean of Res TCD 84-90; I Tullow *D & G* 91-99; Can Ch Ch Cathl Dublin from 95; Dir Irish Sch Ecum 99-05; Sec Gen ACC from 05; Hon Prov Can Cant Cathl from 06. *Anglican Communion Office, 16 Tavistock Crescent, London W11 1AX* Tel (020) 7313 3900 Fax 7313 3999 E-mail kkearon@tcd.ie

KEARTON, Janet Elizabeth. b 54. Univ Coll Lon BSc78 Birkbeck Coll Lon MSc81. NEOC 01. **d** 04 **p** 05. C Richmond w Hudswell and Downholme and Marske *Ripon* 04-08; V Hipswell from 08. *The Vicarage, 7 Forest Drive, Colburn, Catterick Garrison DL9 4PN* Tel (01748) 833320 Mobile 07816-278267 E-mail revjan@btinternet.com

KEAST, William. b 43. Univ Coll Ox BA65 DipEd66. **d** 88 **p** 89. OLM Scotton w Northorpe *Linc* from 88. *4 Crapple Lane, Scotton, Gainsborough DN21 3QT* Tel (01724) 763190 E-mail wkeast@hotmail.com

KEATING, Mrs Ann Barbara. b 53. Open Univ BA85. STETS 06. **d** 09 **p** 10. NSM Fisherton Anger *Sarum* from 09. *1 The Old Orchard, High Street, Netheravon, Salisbury SP4 9QW* Tel (01980) 671010 Mobile 07510-588007 E-mail ann.keating@winchester.ac.uk

KEATING, Christopher Robin. b 39. K Coll Lon BD AKC84. Sarum Th Coll 62. **d** 65 **p** 66. C Baildon *Bradf* 65-67; CF 67-72; V Thornton Heath St Paul *Cant* 72-79; C Harold Hill St Geo *Chelmsf* 85-89; V Goodmayes All SS 89-07; rtd 07; Perm to Offic *York* from 09. *Ghyll View, Goathland, Whitby YO22 5AP* Tel (01947) 896406

KEATING, Geoffrey John. b 52. Open Univ BA94. St Steph Ho Ox 81. **d** 84 **p** 85. C Lancaster Ch Ch w St Jo and St Anne *Blackb* 84-85; C Rotherham *Sheff* 85-87; V Bentley 87-91; V Penponds *Truro* 91-96; V Pet St Jude from 96. *St Jude's Vicarage, 49 Atherstone Avenue, Peterborough PE3 9TZ* Tel and fax (01733) 264169 E-mail geoffkeatg@aol.com

KEAY, Alfred David. b 26. Aston Univ MSc72. Qu Coll Birm 76. **d** 79 **p** 80. Hon C Penkridge w Stretton *Lich* 79-82; C Rugeley 82-85; V Cheswardine 85-95; V Hales 85-95; rtd 95; Perm to Offic *Lich* from 98. *2 The Coppice, Farcroft Gardens, Market Drayton TF9 3UA* Tel (01630) 657924

KEAY, Charles Edward. b 70. Glos Univ BA94. St Steph Ho Ox 01. **d** 03 **p** 04. C Havant *Portsm* 03-07; P-in-c Alford w Rigsby *Linc* 07-11; TV Portsea N End St Mark *Portsm* from 11. *St Nicholas House, 90A Compton Road, Portsmouth PO2 0SR*

KEDDIE, Canon Tony. b 37. Qu Coll Birm 63. **d** 66 **p** 67. C Barnoldswick w Bracewell *Bradf* 66-69; C New Bentley *Sheff* 69-71; TV Seacroft *Ripon* 71-79; V Kippax 79-85; TR Kippax w Allerton Bywater 85-92; R Fountains Gp 92-02; Hon Can Ripon Cathl 94-02; rtd 02; Perm to Offic *Bradf* and *Ripon* from 02. *2 Westcroft, Station Road, Otley LS21 3HX* Tel (01943) 464146 E-mail tbmk@metronet.co.uk

KEEBLE, Leslie Bruce. b 32. Spurgeon's Coll Lon BD59. Bapt Th Sem Ruschlikon Zürich ThM63. **d** 08 **p** 08. NSM Harwell w Chilton *Ox* 08-11; Perm to Offic from 11. *13 Limetrees, Chilton, Didcot OX11 0HW* Tel (01235) 852203 E-mail bk@brucekeeble.org.uk

KEEBLE, Stephen Robert. b 56. K Coll Lon BD84 AKC84 MA98. Westcott Ho Cam 85. **d** 87 **p** 88. C Lt Stanmore St Lawr *Lon* 87-90; C Headstone St Geo 90-93; P-in-c 93-98; V from 98.

KEECH, April Irene. b 52. Penn State Univ BA76. Trin Coll Bris BA89. **d** 89 **p** 92. C Walthamstow St Luke *Chelmsf* 89-92; USA 92-95; V Deptford St Jo w H Trin *S'wark* 95-02; Asst Dioc Dir of Ords 96-00; Hon Can S'wark Cathl 99-02; V Hoxton St Jo w Ch Ch *Lon* 02-10; Chapl St Mary Magd Academy Lon from 10; Perm to Offic *Lon* from 10. *13 Regents Wharf, Wharf Place, London E2 9BD* Tel (020) 7739 7621 *or* 7697 0123 E-mail april.keech@smmacademy.org

KEEGAN, Frances Ann (Sister Isabel). b 44. SEN74. Franciscan Study Cen 87. **d** 99 **p** 00. NSM Sherborne w Castleton and Lillington *Sarum* 99-01; NSM Golden Cap Team 01-08; NSM Crosslacon Carl 08-11; NSM Brigham, Gt Broughton and Broughton Moor from 11. *The Vicarage, Arlecdon, Frizington CA26 3UB* Tel (01946) 861353 E-mail ifak@hotmail.co.uk

KEEGAN, Graham Brownell. b 40. Nottm Univ CertEd68. NOC 81. **d** 84 **p** 85. C Highfield *Liv* 84-87; V Ince St Mary 87-95; V Newton in Makerfield St Pet 95-05; rtd 05. *5 Scott Road, Lowton, Warrington WA3 2HD* Tel (01942) 713809

KEELER, Alan. b 58. City Univ BSc81. St Jo Coll Nottm MA01. **d** 90 **p** 91. C Paddock Wood *Roch* 90-94; V Blendon 94-06; V Plaistow St Mary from 06. *St Mary's Vicarage, 74 London Lane, Bromley BR1 4HE* Tel (020) 8460 1827 E-mail alan.keeler@diocese-rochester.org

KEELEY, John Robin. b 38. G&C Coll Cam BA62. Clifton Th Coll 62. **d** 64 **p** 65. C Onslow Square St Paul *Lon* 64-66; C Hove Bp Hannington Memorial Ch *Chich* 66-69; C Harborne Heath *Birm* 69-72; V Leic H Trin 72-74; V Leic H Trin w St Jo 74-80; Perm to Offic *St Alb* 81-86; NSM Carterton *Ox* 89-95; Tutor EAMTC *Ely* 95-99; TV Bishopsnympton, Rose Ash, Mariansleigh etc *Ex* 99-03; RD S Molton 01-03; rtd 03. *74 Pacific Parade, Mount Tamborine Qld 4272, Australia* Tel (0061) (7) 5545 0966 E-mail robandpaulkeeley@bigpond.com

KEELEY-PANNETT, Peter George. *See* PANNETT, Peter George

KEELING, Peter Frank. b 34. Kelham Th Coll. **d** 58 **p** 59. C S Elmsall *Wakef* 58-63; C Barnsley St Mary 63-67; V Ravensthorpe 67-73; V Cudworth 73-83; R Downham Market w Bexwell *Ely* 83-00; RD Fincham 83-94; V Crimplesham w Stradsett 85-00; rtd 00; P-in-c Hempton and Pudding Norton 00-04; Perm to Offic *Nor* from 04. *23 Cleaves Drive, Walsingham NR22 6EQ* Tel (01328) 820310

KEEN, David Mark. b 69. Oriel Coll Ox BA91. St Jo Coll Nottm BTh96 MPhil98. **d** 98 **p** 99. C Yeovil w Kingston Pitney *B & W* 98-02; C Haughton le Skerne *Dur* 02-06; C Preston Plucknett *B & W* from 06. *3 Poplar Drive, Yeovil BA21 3UL* Tel (01935) 422286 E-mail revdmkeen@btinternet.com

KEEN, Michael Spencer. b 41. St Pet Coll Ox BA68 MA72 GRSM62 ARCM Reading Univ CertEd. Westcott Ho Cam 68. **d** 73 **p** 74. NSM W Derby St Jo *Liv* 73-74; NSM Stanley 74-76; Chs Youth and Community Officer Telford *Lich* 77-82; Dioc Unemployment Officer *Sheff* 82-89; NSM Brixton Road Ch Ch *S'wark* 89-92; Employment Development Officer 89-92; Perm to Offic 92-99; NSM Camberwell St Giles w St Matt 99-01. *39 Bromley College, London Road, Bromley BR1 1PE* Tel (020) 8313 0490

KEEN, Miriam Frances. b 65. Ex Univ BSc87 Westmr Coll of Educn PGCE89. Wycliffe Hall Ox 03. **d** 05 **p** 06. C Cogges and S Leigh *Ox* from 05; C N Leigh from 08. *The Vicarage, New Yatt Road, North Leigh, Witney OX29 6TT* Tel (01933) 773844 E-mail miri@coggesparish.com

KEENAN, Leslie Herbert (Bertie). b 32. Cranmer Hall Dur. **d** 66 **p** 67. C Anston *Sheff* 66-70; C Woodsetts 66-70; Chapl HM Borstal Pollington 70-78; V Balne *Sheff* 70-78; V Poughill *Truro* 78-99; rtd 99; Perm to Offic *Chich* from 01. *Rosedene, Southdown Road, Seaford BN25 4JS* Tel (01323) 899507

KEENE, Canon David Peter. b 32. Trin Hall Cam BA56 MA60. Westcott Ho Cam. **d** 58 **p** 59. C Radcliffe-on-Trent *S'well* 58-61; C Mansfield SS Pet and Paul 61-64; V Nottingham St Cath 64-71; R Bingham 71-81; Dioc Dir of Ords 81-90; Can Res S'well Minster 81-97; rtd 97; Perm to Offic *S'well* from 02. *Averham Cottage, Church Lane, Averham, Newark NG23 5RB* Tel (01636) 708601 E-mail keene@averham.fsnet.co.uk

KEENE, Mrs Muriel Ada. b 35. dss 83 **d** 87 **p** 94. Dioc Lay Min Adv *S'well* 87-88; Asst Dir of Ords 88-90; Dn-in-c Oxton 90-93; Dn-in-c Epperstone 90-94; Dn-in-c Gonalston 90-94; NSM Lowdham w Caythorpe, and Gunthorpe 94-00; rtd 95; Perm to Offic *S'well* from 05. *Averham Cottage, Church Lane, Averham, Newark NG23 5RB* Tel (01636) 708601 E-mail keene@averham.fsnet.co.uk

KEEP, Andrew James. b 55. Collingwood Coll Dur BA77 Yale Univ STM84. Sarum & Wells Th Coll 78. **d** 80 **p** 81. C Banstead *Guildf* 80-83; Chapl Qu Eliz Hosp Banstead 80-83; USA 83-84; Chapl Cranleigh Sch Surrey 84-98; Chapl Wells Cathl Sch 98-06; PV Wells Cathl 01-06; Chapl Mall Hill Sch Lon 07-10; Perm to Offic *Lon* from 10. *118 Russell Court, Woburn Place, London WC1H 0LP* Tel (020) 7837 5327 Mobile 07740-647813 E-mail andrew.keep@lineone.net

KEETON, Barry. b 40. Dur Univ BA61 MA69 MLitt78 K Coll Lon BD63 AKC63. **d** 64 **p** 65. C S Bank *York* 64-67; C Middlesbrough St Cuth 67-69; C Kingston upon Hull St Alb 70-71; V Appleton-le-Street w Amotherby 71-74; Dioc Ecum Adv 74-81; R Ampleforth w Oswaldkirk 74-78; V Howden 78-79; P-in-c Barmby on the Marsh 78-79; P-in-c Laxton w Blacktoft 78-79; P-in-c Wressell 78-79; TR Howden 80-91; Can and Preb York Minster 85-91; RD Howden 86-91; TR Lewes All SS, St Anne, St Mich and St Thos *Chich* 91-96; R Cov St Jo 96-01; RD Cov N 97-01; rtd 01; Perm to Offic *Sheff* from 01 and *York* from 05. *19 Shardlow Gardens, Doncaster DN4 6UB* Tel (01302) 532045 E-mail barry.k3@ukonline.co.uk

KEFFORD, Canon Peter Charles. b 44. Nottm Univ BTh74. Linc Th Coll 70. **d** 74 **p** 75. C W Wimbledon Ch Ch *S'wark* 74-77; C All Hallows by the Tower etc *Lon* 77-81; C-in-c Pound Hill CD *Chich* 81; TV Worth 82-83; TR 83-92; R Henfield w Shermanbury and Woodmancote 92-01; Can Res and Treas Chich Cathl 01-09; Adv for Ord Min and Dioc Dir of Ords 01-06; Dioc Adv for Min 07-09; rtd 09. *17 North Close, Mickleover, Derby DE3 9JA* Tel (01332) 549534 E-mail peter.kefford@hotmail.com

KEGG, Mrs Georgina. b 47. Oak Hill Th Coll BA99. EAMTC 02. **d** 05 **p** 06. NSM Mattishall and the Tudd Valley *Nor* from 05. *The Vicarage, Back Lane, Mattishall, Dereham NR20 3PU* Tel (01362) 850243 E-mail gordonkegg@waitrose.com

KEGG, Gordon Rutherford. b 45. Reading Univ BSc66 Imp Coll Lon PhD71 Lon Univ CertEd74. Oak Hill Th Coll 88. **d** 90 **p** 91. C Luton Lewsey St Hugh *St Alb* 90-94; TV Hemel Hempstead 94-01; P-in-c Mattishall w Mattishall Burgh, Welborne etc *Nor* 01-08; P-in-c Hockering, Honingham, E and N Tuddenham 04-08; R Mattishall and the Tudd Valley from 08. *The Vicarage, Back Lane, Mattishall, Dereham NR20 3PU* Tel (01362) 850243 E-mail gordonkegg@waitrose.com

KEIGHLEY, Mrs Amanda Jane. b 56. Garnett Coll Lon CertEd85 Leeds Univ MA98. Cranmer Hall Dur 04. **d** 07 **p** 08. NSM Is of Dogs Ch Ch and St Jo w St Luke Lon from 07. *86 Saunders Ness Road, London E14 3EA* Tel (020) 7517 9628 Mobile 07889-486354 E-mail 42xfv@dsl.pipex.com

KEIGHLEY, Andrew Kenneth. b 62. Nottm Univ LLB84 Solicitor 85. Wycliffe Hall Ox 94. **d** 97 **p** 98. C Westminster St Jas the Less *Lon* 97-00; NSM 00-04; C Brompton H Trin w Onslow Square St Paul 04-06; P-in-c W Hampstead Trin 06-09; V from 09. *Holy Trinity Vicarage, 1A Akenside Road, London NW3 5BS* Tel (020) 7794 2975 Mobile 07747-611577

KEIGHLEY, David John. b 48. Open Univ BA88 CertEd. Sarum & Wells Th Coll 82. **d** 83 **p** 84. C Sawbridgeworth *St Alb* 83-86; TV Saltash *Truro* 86-89; V Lanlivery w Luxulyan 89-00; P-in-c The Candover Valley *Win* 00-08; P-in-c Wield 03-08; P-in-c Hurstbourne Tarrant, Faccombe, Vernham Dean etc from 08. *The Vicarage, The Dene, Hurstbourne Tarrant, Andover SP11 0AH* Tel (01264) 736222 Mobile 07736-799262 E-mail davidkeighley@hotmail.com

KEIGHLEY, Martin Philip. b 61. Edin Univ MA83. Westcott Ho Cam 86. **d** 88 **p** 89. C Lytham St Cuth *Blackb* 88-91; C Lancaster St Mary 91-93; R Halton w Aughton 93-00; V Poulton-le-Fylde 00-04; V Poulton Carleton and Singleton from 04; AD Poulton from 08. *The Vicarage, 7 Vicarage Road, Poulton-le-Fylde FY6 7BE* Tel (01253) 883086 E-mail martinkeighley@btconnect.com

KEIGHLEY, Thomas Christopher. b 51. Open Univ BA85. NEOC 00. **d** 03 **p** 04. NSM Upper Nidderdale *Ripon* 03-06; NSM Dacre w Hartwith and Darley w Thornthwaite 06-07; NSM Is of Dogs Ch Ch and St Jo w St Luke *Lon* from 07; Chapl St Joseph's Hospice Hackney 09-10. *86 Saunders Ness Road, London E14 3EA* Tel (020) 7517 9628 Mobile 07740-721032 E-mail nurprc@nursing.u-net.com

KEIGHTLEY, Canon Thomas. b 44. CITC 79. **d** 79 **p** 80. C Seagoe *D & D* 79-83; I Belvoir from 83; Can Down Cathl from 95; Treas 00-01; Prec from 01. *The Rectory, 86B Beechill Road, Belfast BT8 7QN* Tel (028) 9064 3777 Mobile 07919-366660 E-mail tmgktly@googlemail.com

KEIGHTLEY, Trevor Charles. b 54. St Jo Coll Nottm. **d** 03 **p** 04. C Wombwell *Sheff* 03-07; V Worsbrough Common w Worsbrough St Thos from 07. *St Thomas's Vicarage, 80 Kingwell Road, Worsbrough, Barnsley S70 4HG* Tel (01226) 286505 E-mail trevorkeightley@aol.com

KEILLER, Canon Jane Elizabeth. b 52. Westmr Coll Ox BEd74. Cranmer Hall Dur 76. dss 80 **d** 87 **p** 94. Cambridge H Trin w St Andr *St Ely* 80-86; NSM Cambridge St Barn 86-88 and 90-94; NSM Cambridge H Cross 95-02; Chapl and Tutor Ridley Hall Cam from 96; Hon Can Ely Cathl from 05. *68 Pierce Lane, Cambridge CB21 5DL* Tel (01223) 575776 *or* tel and fax 741061 E-mail jk271@cam.ac.uk

KEIR, Mrs Gillian Irene. b 44. Westf Coll Lon BA66 Somerville Coll Ox BLitt70 Lon Univ MA95. SAOMC 95. **d** 98 **p** 99. NSM St Alb St Steph *St Alb* from 98; NSM Officer St Alb Archd from 06. *17 Battlefield Road, St Albans AL1 4DA* Tel (01727) 839392

KEIRLE, Michael Robert. b 62. Trin Coll Bris BA89. **d** 89 **p** 90. C Orpington Ch Ch *Roch* 89-92; Zimbabwe 92-95; R Keston *Roch*

95-03; R Guernsey St Martin *Win* from 03. *St Martin's Rectory, La Grande Rue, St Martin, Guernsey GY4 6RR* Tel (01481) 238303 Fax 237710 E-mail mrkeirle@cwgsy.net

KEITH, Andrew James Buchanan. b 47. Qu Coll Cam BA69 MA73. Wycliffe Hall Ox 71. **d** 74 **p** 75. C Warrington St Elphin *Liv* 74-77; C Southgate *Chich* 77-80; C-in-c Broadfield CD 80-82; P-in-c Walberton w Binsted 82-85; P-in-c Aldingbourne 83-85; Chapl Oswestry Sch 85-95; Chapl HM Pris Liv 95-96; Chapl HM Pris Preston 96-01; Chapl HM Pris Garth 01-06; NSM Chipping Norton *Ox* from 07. *Juxon House, Little Compton, Moreton-in-Marsh GL56 0SE* Tel (01608) 674856 E-mail keith@janda.go-plus.net

KEITH, Gary Mark Wayne. b 71. Ripon Coll Cuddesdon 01. **d** 03 **p** 04. C Botley, Curdridge and Durley *Portsm* 03-06; Chapl RNR 05-06; Chapl RN 06-08; C N Hants Downs *Win* from 08. *The Vicarage, The Bury, Odiham, Hook RG29 1ND* Tel (01256) 704154 Mobile 07971-448049 E-mail thebishmeister@btinternet.com

KEITH, John. b 25. LRAM50 LGSM50 AGSM51. Cuddesdon Coll 60. **d** 62 **p** 63. C Lee-on-the-Solent *Portsm* 62-65; C Raynes Park St Sav *S'wark* 65-68; rtd 90. *7 Torr An Eas, Glenfinnan PH37 4LS* Tel (01397) 722314

KELHAM, Adèle. b 46. St Andr Univ BSc69. Cranmer Hall Dur. **d** 98 **p** 99. Asst Chapl Zürich *Eur* 98-01; P-in-c Bishop Middleham *Dur* 01-05; AD Sedgefield 03-05; P-in-c Lausanne *Eur* from 05; Dioc Adv for Women's Min from 05. *Avenue Floréal 3, 1006 Lausanne, Switzerland* Tel (0041) (21) 312 6563 E-mail info@christchurch-lausanne.ch

KELK, Michael Anthony. b 48. Sarum & Wells Th Coll. **d** 83 **p** 84. C Ross w Brampton Abbotts, Bridstow and Peterstow *Heref* 83-86; P-in-c Burghill 86-97; P-in-c Stretton Sugwas 86-97; P-in-c Walford and St John w Bishopswood, Goodrich etc 97-02; P-in-c Llangarron w Llangrove, Whitchurch and Ganarew 02-08. *Address temp unknown*

KELLAGHER, Christopher John Bannerman. b 55. Aber Univ MA79 UMIST MSc88. STETS MA09. **d** 09 **p** 10. NSM Aldershot H Trin *Guildf* from 09. *8 Elsenwood Crescent, Camberley GU15 2BA* Tel (01276) 508193 E-mail jkellagher@ntlworld.com

KELLEHER, Mrs Cheryl. b 56. Sheff Univ BA97. NOC 98. **d** 01 **p** 02. NSM Worsbrough St Mary *Sheff* 01-03; Perm to Offic from 04. *10 Fieldsend, Oxspring, Sheffield S36 8WH* Tel (01226) 763236 E-mail cheryl@kelnet.co.uk

KELLEN, David. b 52. St Mich Coll Llan 70. **d** 75 **p** 76. C Mynyddislwyn *Mon* 75-77; C Risca 77-78; C Malpas 78-81; V Newport All SS 81-88; V St Mellons from 88; R Michaelston-y-Fedw 89-96. *The Vicarage, Ty'r Winch Road, St Mellons, Cardiff CF3 5UP* Tel (029) 2079 6560

KELLETT, Garth. *See* KELLETT, Ronald Garth

KELLETT, Neil. b 41. Bps' Coll Cheshunt 64. **d** 66 **p** 67. C Ex St Thos 66-72; C Win H Trin 72-74; P-in-c Redditch St Geo *Worc* 74-77; Canada from 77. *39 Fox Avenue, St John's NL A1B 2H8, Canada* Tel (001) (709) 726 2883

KELLETT, Canon Richard. b 64. Leeds Univ BSc85 PhD89. St Jo Coll Nottm BTh95 MA96. **d** 96 **p** 97. C Nottingham St Jude *S'well* 96-00; P-in-c Skegby 00-02; P-in-c Teversal 00-02; R Skegby w Teversal from 02; AD Newstead from 06; Hon Can S'well Minster from 10. *The Vicarage, Mansfield Road, Skegby, Sutton-in-Ashfield NG17 3ED* Tel and fax (01623) 558800 E-mail richard@kellett.com

KELLETT, Ronald Garth. b 41. NOC 04. **d** 05 **p** 06. NSM Ilkley St Marg *Bradf* from 05. *8 Kingsway Drive, Ilkley LS29 9AG* Tel (01943) 601906 Fax 01943601906@talktalk.net

KELLEY, Neil George. b 64. ARCM85. Westcott Ho Cam 88. **d** 91 **p** 92. C Chiswick St Nic w St Mary 93-97; C Kirkby *Liv* 97-99; V Gt Crosby St Faith and Waterloo Park St Mary from 99; Dioc Adv on Worship and Liturgy from 06. *The Vicarage, Milton Road, Waterloo, Liverpool L22 4RE* Tel and fax 0151-928 3342 Mobile 07980-872203 E-mail frneilkelley@tiscali.co.uk

KELLY, Canon Albert Norman. b 21. TCD BA43 MA63. **d** 44 **p** 45. C Donaghcloney *D & D* 44-46; C Belfast Malone St Jo *Conn* 46-55; I Billy 55-63; C Dorking w Ranmore *Guildf* 63-66; C-in-c New Haw CD 66-72; V New Haw 72-78; RD Chertsey 73-75; RD Runnymede 75-78; V Egham Hythe 78-86; Hon Can Guildf Cathl 80-86; rtd 86; USPG Area Sec 88-93. *21 Rosetta Road, Belfast BT6 0LQ* Tel (028) 9069 3921

KELLY, Mrs Ann Clarke Thomson. b 60. WMMTC 04. **d** 07 **p** 08. C Stafford St Jo and Tixall w Ingestre *Lich* from 07. *31 The Oval, Stafford ST17 4LQ* Tel (01785) 251683 E-mail scottyann@blueyonder.co.uk

KELLY, Brian Eugene. b 56. Otago Univ BA77 Dunedin Coll PGCE79 Bris Univ PhD93. Trin Coll Bris BA89. **d** 90 **p** 91. NSM Redland *Bris* 90-93; C Scarborough St Mary w Ch Ch and H Apostles *York* 93-96; Dean Chpl Cant Ch Ch Univ Coll 96-03; Perm to Offic *Cant* from 06. *2 Riverside Close, Bridge, Canterbury CT4 5BN* Tel (01227) 831380 E-mail brian@kelly1915.fsnet.co.uk

KELLY, Canon Brian Horace. b 34. St Jo Coll Dur BA57 MA69. **d** 58 **p** 59. C Douglas St Geo and St Barn *S & M* 58-61; V Foxdale 61-64; V Bolton All So w St Jas *Man* 64-73; V Maughold *S & M* 73-77; Dir of Ords 76-93; V German 77-06; Can and Prec St German's Cathl 80-06; RD Castletown and Peel 97-04; rtd 06; Perm to Offic *S & M* from 09. *16 Slieau Whallian Park, St Johns, Isle of Man IM4 3JH* Tel (01624) 801479

KELLY, Canon Dennis Charles. b 31. Liv Univ BA52. Lich Th Coll 54. **d** 56 **p** 57. C Tranmere St Paul *Ches* 56-59; C-in-c Grange St Andr CD 59-63; P-in-c Grange St Andr 63-65; V 65-67; R Coppenhall 67-82; V W Kirby St Andr 82-01; Hon Can Ches Cathl 86-01; rtd 01; Perm to Offic *Ches* from 01. *26 Lyndhurst Road, Hoylake, Wirral CH47 7BP* Tel 0151-632 0335

KELLY, Desmond Norman. b 42. Oak Hill Th Coll 89. **d** 90 **p** 91. C Braintree *Chelmsf* 90-94; P-in-c Sible Hedingham w Castle Hedingham 94-95; R Sible Hedingham w Castle Hedingham 95-08; rtd 08; Perm to Offic *St E* from 11. *Wykhams, Mill Common, Westhall, Halesworth IP19 8RQ* Tel (01502) 575493 E-mail rev.des@btinternet.com

KELLY, Canon Edward William Moncrieff. b 28. AKC57. **d** 57 **p** 58. C Petersfield w Sheet *Portsm* 57-60; Papua New Guinea 60-65; Dioc Sec Samarai and Hon Chapl Miss to Seamen 61; V Gosport Ch Ch *Portsm* 65-69; Hon C Eltham St Jo *S'wark* 69-87; Org Sec New Guinea Miss 69-77; Org Sec Papua New Guinea Ch Partnership 77-87; Hon Can Papua New Guinea from 78; TR Trowbridge H Trin *Sarum* 87-94; Chapl St Jo Hosp Trowbridge 87-94; Acting RD Bradford 91-92; rtd 94; Perm to Offic *Portsm* from 94. *133 Borough Road, Petersfield GU32 3LP* Tel (01730) 260399

KELLY, John Adrian. b 49. Qu Coll Birm 70. **d** 73 **p** 74. C Formby St Pet *Liv* 73-77; Org Sec CECS *Liv, Blackb* and *S & M* 77-92; Deputation Appeals Org (Lancs and Is of Man) 88-92; Perm to Offic *Liv* 77-05; *Bradf* 77-00; *Man* 88-97. *39 Cornwall Way, Southport PR8 3SG*

KELLY, Canon John Dickinson. b 42. Nottm Univ BA63. Ripon Hall Ox 63. **d** 65 **p** 66. C Egremont *Carl* 65-67; C Upperby St Jo 67-70; V Arlecdon 70-73; V Barrow St Aid 73-79; V Milnthorpe 79-83; V Beetham and Milnthorpe 83-85; V Camerton St Pet 85-88; P-in-c Camerton H Trin W Seaton 86-88; V Camerton, Seaton and W Seaton 88-01; P-in-c Kells 01-05; Hon Can Carl Cathl from 00; Chapl N Cumbria Acute Hosps NHS Trust 03-05; rtd 05; P-in-c Kirkland, Lamplugh w Ennerdale *Carl* 05-07; Hon C Whitehaven from 07. *The Vicarage, Oakfield Court, Hillcrest, Whitehaven CA28 5TG* Tel (01946) 861310

KELLY, John Graham. b 60. Lanc Univ LLB82 Sheff Univ PhD95 Solicitor 84. St Jo. Coll Nottm BTh91. **d** 94 **p** 95. C Normanton *Derby* 94-97; P-in-c Ockbrook 97-01; Lect St Jo Coll Nottm 01-07; rtd 07. *15 Stanley Road, Whitstable CT5 4NJ* Tel (01227) 280209 E-mail jgkelly34@btinternet.com

KELLY, Malcolm Bernard. b 46. St Mich Coll Llan 72. **d** 74 **p** 75. C Tranmere St Paul w St Luke *Ches* 74-77; Chapl Bebington Hosp from 76; C Barnston *Ches* 77-80; R Thurstaston 80-92; R Grappenhall from 92. *The Rectory, 17 Hill Top Road, Stockton Heath, Warrington WA4 2ED* Tel (01925) 261546

KELLY, Martin Herbert. b 55. Selw Coll Cam MA90. Aston Tr Scheme 78 Ripon Coll Cuddesdon 80. **d** 83 **p** 84. C Clapham Old Town *S'wark* 83-87; Chapl and Fell Selw Coll Cam 87-92; Chapl Newnham Coll Cam 87-92; Chapl St Piers Hosp Sch Lingfield *S'wark* 95-01; C Limpsfield and Titsey 95-01; Chapl Basildon and Thurrock Gen Hosps NHS Trust 03-04; Chapl Dartford and Gravesham NHS Trust from 04. *Darent Valley Hospital, Darenth Wood Road, Dartford DA2 8DA* Tel (01322) 428100 ext 4640 E-mail martin.kelly@dvh.nhs.uk

KELLY, Neil Anthony. St Mich Coll Llan. **d** 10 **p** 11. C Llangollen w Trevor and Llantysilio *St As* from 10. *Rosslyn, Station Road, Trevor, Llangollen LL20 7TP* E-mail neilanthonykelly@gmail.com

KELLY, Nigel James (Ned). b 60. N Staffs Poly BSc83. Ripon Coll Cuddesdon 83. **d** 86 **p** 87. C Cen Telford *Lich* 86-90; TV 90-92; Chapl RN from 92. *Royal Naval Chaplaincy Service, Mail Point 1-2, Leach Building, Whale Island, Portsmouth PO2 8BY* Tel (023) 9262 5055 Fax 9262 5134

KELLY, Paul. b 60. Qu Coll Birm 02. **d** 04 **p** 05. C Ogley Hay *Lich* 04-07; V Stafford St Paul Forebridge from 07. *St Paul's Vicarage, 31 The Oval, Stafford ST17 4LQ* Tel (01785) 224634 Mobile 07815-452616

KELLY, Canon Peter Hugh. b 46. Sarum & Wells Th Coll 81. **d** 84 **p** 85. C Fareham H Trin *Portsm* 84-87; Chapl and Prec Portsm Cathl 87-90; V Eastney 90-97; P-in-c Swanmore St Barn 97-06; V 07-11; RD Bishop's Waltham 03-09; Hon Can Portsm Cathl 07-11; rtd 11. *16 Rosedale Close, Fareham PO14 4EL* Tel (01329) 849567

KELLY, Stephen Alexander. b 61. Man Univ BSc84. Ridley Hall Cam 03. **d** 05 **p** 06. C Meole Brace *Lich* 05-08; C Cen Telford from 08. *28 Bartholomew Road, Lawley Village, Telford TF4 2PW* Tel (01952) 501305 E-mail steve.kelly7@virgin.net

KELLY, Canon Stephen Paul. b 55. Keble Coll Ox BA77 MA07 Leeds Univ MA06. Linc Th Coll 77. **d** 79 **p** 80. C Illingworth *Wakef* 79-82; C Knottingley 82-84; V Alverthorpe 84-93; Dioc Ecum Officer 88-93; TR Bingley All SS *Bradf* 93-03; P-in-c Woolley *Wakef* from 03; Dioc CME Officer from 03; RD Wakef from 11; Hon Can Wakef Cathl from 08. *The Vicarage, Church Street, Woolley, Wakefield WF4 2JU* Tel (01226) 382550 E-mail stephen.kelly@wakefield.anglican.org

KELLY, Trevor Samuel. b 67. QUB BEd88 Open Univ CertEd09. CITC 06. **d** 10. NSM Craigs w Dunaghy and Killagan *Conn* from 10. *1 Galgorm Lodge, Ballymena BT42 1GL* Tel (028) 2565 4128 Mobile 07793-005275 E-mail tkhazelwood@yahoo.co.uk

KELLY, Canon William. b 35. Dur Univ BA58. Lambeth STh75 Wycliffe Hall Ox 58. **d** 60 **p** 61. C Walney Is *Carl* 60-66; R Distington 66-71; V Barrow St Matt 71-81; RD Furness 77-81; Hon Can Carl Cathl 79-00; Dir of Ords 81-97; V Dalston 81-92; RD Carl 83-88; P-in-c Raughton Head w Gatesgill 86-92; P-in-c Maryport 92-97; P-in-c Flimby 93-96; P-in-c Arthuret and Nicholforest and Kirkandrews on Esk 97-00; rtd 00; Perm to Offic *Carl* from 00. *73 Upperby Road, Carlisle CA2 4JE* Tel (01228) 514013

KELLY, William Norman. b 21. St Aid Birkenhead. **d** 64 **p** 65. Miss to Seamen 64-66; C Douglas St Geo and St Barn *S & M* 66-69; V Wingates *Man* 69-75; Perm to Offic 76-84; Chapl HM Pris Liv 77-78; Chapl HM Borstal Stoke Heath 78-84; V Castletown *S & M* 84-92; rtd 92; Perm to Offic *S & M* from 92. *9 Millhope Close, Hope Street, Castletown, Isle of Man IM9 1DJ* Tel (01624) 824768

KELSEY, George Robert. b 61. Imp Coll Lon BSc83 Newc Univ MSc84 PhD92. Cranmer Hall Dur 95. **d** 97 **p** 98. C Denton *Newc* 97-01; TV Glendale Gp 01-10; V Norham and Duddo from 10; P-in-c Cornhill w Carham from 10; P-in-c Branxton from 10; AD Norham from 10. *The Vicarage, Church Lane, Norham, Berwick-upon-Tweed TD15 2LF* Tel (01289) 382325 E-mail robert.josephkelsey@live.com

KELSEY, Michael Ray. b 22. FEPA57. Wycliffe Hall Ox 60. **d** 62 **p** 63. C Lower Broughton St Clem *Man* 62-64; V Ingleby Greenhow *York* 64-68; V Scarborough St Jas 68-71; Asst to the Gen Sec USCL 71-74; V Blackheath St Jo *S'wark* 74-87; rtd 87; Perm to Offic *St E* 88-05. *20 Sweet Briar, Marcham, Abingdon OX13 6PD* Tel (01865) 391835

✠**KELSHAW, The Rt Revd Terence.** b 36. Pittsburgh Th Sem DMin86. Oak Hill Th Coll. **d** 67 **p** 68 **c** 89. C Clifton Ch Ch w Em *Bris* 67-71; C Woking St Jo *Guildf* 71-73; V Bris H Trin 73-75; P-in-c Easton St Gabr w St Laur 73-75; V Easton H Trin w St Gabr and St Lawr 75-80; P-in-c Barton Hill St Luke w Ch 76-80; USA from 80; Bp Rio Grande 89-05; rtd 05. *12321 Key West Drive NE, Albuquerque NM 87111-2734, USA* Tel (001) (505) 299 0475 E-mail tkelshaw@aol.com

KELSO, Andrew John. b 47. Lon Univ BA70 LRAM73. St Jo Coll Nottm 83. **d** 85 **p** 86. C Gorleston St Mary *Nor* 85-87; C Hellesdon 87-90; TV Ipsley *Worc* 90-09; rtd 09. *2 The Close, Throckmorton, Pershore WR10 2JU* Tel (01386) 462087 Mobile 07795-431382 E-mail andykelso@blueyonder.co.uk

KEMM, William St John. b 39. Birm Univ BA62 MA65. Ridley Hall Cam 62. **d** 64 **p** 65. C Kingswinford H Trin *Lich* 64-68; C Redmarsh 68-71; V Hanbury 71-76; R Berrow and Breane *B & W* 76-92; V Hertford All SS *St Alb* 92-06; rtd 06. *Holtye, Nether Lane, Nutley, Uckfield TN22 3LE* Tel (01825) 713704 E-mail billkemm@waitrose.com

KEMP, Mrs Alice Mary Elizabeth. b 59. Kent Univ BA82 Thames Poly PGCE91. STETS 07. **d** 10 **p** 11. NSM Box w Hazlebury and Ditteridge *Bris* from 10. *Barn House, Barn Piece, Box, Corsham SN13 8LF* Tel (01225) 742128 E-mail amekemp@aol.com

KEMP, Canon Allan. b 43. Bps' Coll Cheshunt 65 Oak Hill Th Coll 67. **d** 68 **p** 69. C Tunbridge Wells St Jas *Roch* 68-76; V Becontree St Mary *Chelmsf* 76-90; RD Barking and Dagenham 81-86; V Gt w Lt Chesterford 90-07; Hon Can Chelmsf Cathl 99-07; rtd 07. *6 Freemans Orchard, Newent GL18 1TX* Tel (01531) 822041 E-mail canonkemp@waitrose.com

KEMP, Prof Anthony Eric. b 34. St Mark & St Jo Coll Lon CertEd57 LTCL63 FTCL63 Lon Inst of Educn DipEd70 Sussex Univ MA71 DPhil79 Hon FLCM83 CPsychol89 FBPsS97 Helsinki Univ Hon MusDoc03. SAOMC 96. **d** 98 **p** 99. NSM Wokingham All SS *Ox* 98-05; NSM Wokingham St Paul 05-09; Perm to Offic from 09. *18 Blagrove Lane, Wokingham RG41 4BA* Tel and fax 0118-978 2586 E-mail a.e.kemp@btinternet.com

KEMP, Ms Audrey. b 26. MSR49. Gilmore Ho 62. **dss** 69 **d** 87 **p** 94. Cranford *Lon* 67-70; S Ockendon Hosp 70-71; N Greenford All Hallows *Lon* 71-72; Feltham 72-80; Brentford St Faith 80-83; Hanworth All SS 83-85; Hanworth St Geo 85-87; Par Dn 87-88; rtd 88; Perm to Offic *B & W* 88-89 and 99-07; Hon Par Dn Ditcheat w E Pennard and Pylle 89-94; P-in-c 94-95; Perm to Offic *Win* 95-98. *Flat 5, Manormead, Tilford Road, Hindhead GU26 6RA* Tel (01428) 602500

KEMP, Christopher Michael. b 48. K Coll Lon BD71 AKC71. St Aug Coll Cant 75. **d** 76 **p** 77. C Weaverham *Ches* 76-79; C Latchford St Jas 79-82; P-in-c Sandbach Heath 82-88; V Macclesfield St Paul 88-89; C Cheadle Hulme All SS 89-93; C Oxton 93-98; P-in-c Seacombe 98-02; P-in-c Brereton w

Swettenham 02-05; P-in-c Brereton w Eaton and Hulme Walfield 05-10; rtd 10. *1 Orchard Rise, Droitwich WR9 8NU* Tel (01905) 774372

KEMP, Geoffrey Bernard. b 20. Lon Univ BD43. ALCD42. **d** 43 **p** 44. C Leyton All SS *Chelmsf* 43-46; C Woodford St Mary 46-49; V Barkingside St Laur 49-60; V Hadleigh St Barn 60-79; R Kelvedon Hatch 79-86; V Navestock 79-86; rtd 86; Perm to Offic *Chelmsf* and *St E* from 86. *24 Roman Way, Felixstowe IP11 9NJ* Tel (01394) 276691

KEMP, John Graham Edwin. b 29. Bris Univ BA51 PGCE52 Lon Univ BD65. Wells Th Coll 63. **d** 65 **p** 66. C Maidenhead St Luke *Ox* 65-70; R Rotherfield Greys 70-78; V Highmore 70-78; Dep Dir Tr Scheme for NSM 78-84; P-in-c Taplow 78-82; TV Burnham w Dropmore, Hitcham and Taplow 82-84; Prin EAMTC 84-92; rtd 92; Chapl Kyrenia Cyprus 92-95; Perm to Offic *St E* from 95. *Lea Cottage, The Street, Middleton, Saxmundham IP17 3NJ* Tel (01728) 648324
E-mail revdjgk@waitrose.com

KEMP, John Robert Deverall. b 42. City Univ BSc65 BD69. Oak Hill Th Coll 66. **d** 70 **p** 71. C Fulham Ch Ch *Lon* 70-73; C Widford *Chelmsf* 73-79; P-in-c New Thundersley 79-84; V 84-98; Chapl HM Pris Bullwood Hall 79-98; R S Shoebury *Chelmsf* 98-09; rtd 09; Perm to Offic *Chelmsf* from 09. *36 Macmurdo Road, Leigh-on-Sea SS9 5AQ*

KEMP, Mrs Pamela Ann. b 52. Coll of St Matthias Bris CertEd73 RMN98. Ripon Coll Cuddesdon BTh07. **d** 02 **p** 03. C Portland All SS w St Pet *Sarum* 02-04; C Verwood 04-06; R Highnam, Lassington, Rudford, Tibberton etc *Glouc* 06-11; P-in-c Stokenham, Slapton, Charleton w Buckland etc *Ex* from 11. *The Vicarage, Stokenham, Kingsbridge TQ7 2ST* Tel (01548) 580385 Mobile 07989-604543 E-mail pamelakemp@btinternet.com

KEMP, Ralph John. b 71. Wye Coll Lon BSc93 Trin Hall Cam BTh04. Ridley Hall Cam 01. **d** 04 **p** 05. C Astbury and Smallwood Ches 04-07; V Burton and Shotwick 07-08; NSM Plas Newton w Ches Ch Ch from 09. *38 Ethos Court, City Road, Chester CH1 3AT* Tel 07762-847211 (mobile)
E-mail ralphjkemp@googlemail.com

KEMP, Trevor George. b 62. Trin Coll Bris 98. **d** 00 **p** 01. C Old Catton *Nor* 00-03; V S Nutfield w Outwood *S'wark* from 03. *The Vicarage, 136 Mid Street, South Nutfield, Redhill RH1 5RP* Tel (01737) 822211 E-mail rev-trev@cc-nutfield.org.uk *or* sixkemps@tiscali.co.uk

KEMP, William. b 67. St Anne's Coll Ox BA91 Brunel Univ PGCE92 Wolfs Coll Cam BTh99. Ridley Hall Cam 96. **d** 99 **p** 00. C Kensington St Barn *Lon* 99-04; P-in-c Mid-Sussex Network Ch *Chich* from 04; C Hurstpierpoint from 04. *12 Western Road, Hurstpierpoint BN6 9TA* Tel (01273) 835829

KEMPSTER, Miss Helen Edith. b 49. **d** 00 **p** 01. OLM Weybridge *Guildf* 00-06; OLM Esher from 06. *28 Dorchester Road, Weybridge KT13 8PE* Tel (01932) 845861
E-mail helen.kempster@btinternet.com

KEMPSTER, Robert Alec. b 29. Selw Coll Cam MA53. Coll of Resurr Mirfield 53. **d** 55 **p** 56. C W Hackney St Barn *Lon* 55-57; C-in-c S'wark All Hallows CD 57-70; PV S'wark Cathl 57-60; Chapl Evelina Children's Hosp 57-70; Chapl Guy's Hosp Lon 70-81; Chapl Nat Hosp for Nervous Diseases Lon 81-89; Chapl Convent Companions Jes Gd Shep W Ogwell 89; rtd 90; Perm to Offic *Ex* from 90. *15A Seymour Road, Newton Abbot TQ12 2PT* Tel (01626) 361720

KEMPTHORNE, Renatus. b 39. Wadh Coll Ox BA60 MA64. Wycliffe Hall Ox 60. **d** 62 **p** 63. C Stoke *Cov* 62-65; Lect St Jo Coll Auckland New Zealand 65-68; R Wytham *Ox* 68-75; Chapl Bp Grosseteste Coll Linc 75-83; V Waimea New Zealand 83-90; Th Consultant 90-96; Researcher and Educator from 97; rtd 04. *140 Nile Street, Nelson 7010, New Zealand* Tel (0064) (3) 546 7447 E-mail kempthorne@xtra.co.nz

KENCHINGTON, Canon Jane Elizabeth Ballantyne. b 58. Hull Univ BSc79 Trin Coll Bris MA05 Hughes Hall Cam PGCE83. Westcott Ho Cam 88. **d** 90 **p** 94. C Winchcombe, Gretton, Sudeley Manor etc *Glouc* 90-96; Perm to Offic 96-99; NSM Dursley 99-02; Dir Reader Tr and Tutor WEMTC 01-06; Dean of Women Clergy 06-09; R Sodbury Vale from 09; Hon Can Glouc Cathl from 06. *The Vicarage, Horseshoe Lane, Chipping Sodbury, Bristol BS37 6ET* Tel (01454) 313159
E-mail jane@kenchington.plus.com

KENCHINGTON, Paul Henry. b 54. Worc Coll Ox MA76. St Jo Coll Nottm BA81. **d** 82 **p** 83. C Scarborough St Martin w Ch Ch and H Apostles *York* 82-85; C Caversham St Pet and Mapledurham etc *Ox* 85-89; V Hucclecote *Glouc* 89-00; V Kowloon St Andr Hong Kong 00-05; Chapl Versailles w Chevry *Eur* 05-11; P-in-c Combe Down w Monkton Combe and S Stoke *B & W* from 11. *Church Office, Avenue Place, Combe Down, Bath BA2 5EE* Tel (01225) 833152 *or* 835835

KENDAL, Henry David. b 59. ASVA83. Lon Bible Coll 90 Oak Hill NSM Course 92. **d** 94 **p** 95. C Roxeth Lon 94-99; C Woodside Park St Barn 99-06; V from 06. *78 Woodside Avenue, London N12 8TB* Tel (020) 8343 7776 *or* 8343 5775 Mobile 07977-521656 Fax (020) 8446 7492 *or* 8343 5771
E-mail henrykendal@compuserve.com
or henrykendal@stbarnabas.co.uk

KENDAL, Canon Stephen. b 35. Leeds Univ BA59. Coll of Resurr Mirfield 59. **d** 61 **p** 62. C Seaton Hirst *Newc* 61-63; C Newc St Geo 63-66; C Gosforth All SS 66-70; Ind Chapl *Llan* 70-78; Ind Chapl *Dur* 78-91; Hon C Houghton le Spring 78-90; Ind Chapl *Worc* 91-00; Hon Can Worc Cathl 98-00; rtd 00; Perm to Offic *Heref* from 00. *15 Coneybury View, Broseley TF12 5AX* Tel (01952) 882447 E-mail wimkiddy@aol.com

KENDALL, Edward Jonathan. b 76. Nottm Univ MA98 Ox Univ PGCE99. Oak Hill Th Coll BA10. **d** 10 **p** 11. C Fulham St Pet *Lon* from 10. *St Peter's Vicarage, St Peter's Terrace, London SW6 7JS* Tel (020) 3080 0904 Mobile 07813-610977
E-mail ed@stpetersfulham.co.uk

KENDALL, Edward Oliver Vaughan. b 33. Dur Univ BA59. Ridley Hall Cam 59. **d** 61 **p** 62. C Corsham *Bris* 61-64; C Portsea St Mary *Portsm* 64-67; Asst Chapl HM Pris Pentonville 67-68; Chapl HM Borstal Portland 68-71; Lic to Offic *Bradf* 71-94; rtd 94. *10 Halsteads Cottages, Settle BD24 9QJ* Tel and fax (01729) 822207

KENDALL, Frank. b 40. CCC Cam BA62 MA68 FRSA90. S'wark Ord Course 74. **d** 74 **p** 75. NSM Lingfield *S'wark* 74-75 and 78-82; NSM Sketty *S & B* 75-78; NSM Limpsfield and Titsey *S'wark* 82-84; Lic to Offic *Man* 84-89 and *Liv* 89-96; NSM Farington Moss and Lostock Hall *Blackb* 03-06; Perm to Offic from 06. *52 Kingsway, Penwortham, Preston PR1 0ED* Tel (01772) 748021

KENDALL, Giles. b 57. Lon Univ BA80 Univ Coll Lon BSc86 Lon Univ PhD90. STETS BTh98. **d** 98 **p** 99. C Wareham *Sarum* 98-01; V Sawston *Ely* 01-08; P-in-c Babraham 01-08; P-in-c Kingswinford St Mary *Worc* from 08. *The Rectory, 17 Penzer Street, Kingswinford DY6 7AA* Tel (01384) 273716
E-mail revg.kingswinford@btinternet.com

KENDALL, Gordon Sydney. b 41. **d** 72 **p** 74. NSM Old Ford St Paul w St Steph and St Mark *Lon* 72-82; NSM Homerton St Luke 86-92; Asst Chapl Hackney and Homerton Hosp Lon 87-92; Chapl S Devon Healthcare NHS Trust 92-06; rtd 06. *Shiloh, Beech Trees Lane, Ipplepen, Newton Abbot TQ12 5TW* Tel (01803) 814054

KENDRA, Neil Stuart. b 46. JP96. Leeds Univ BA67 Bradf Univ MSc80 PhD84. Linc Th Coll 67. **d** 69 **p** 70. C Allerton *Liv* 69-72; Ldr Leeds City Cen Detached Youth Work Project 73-75; Dioc Youth Officer *Ripon* 75-77; Lect Ilkley Coll 77-78; Sen Lect Bradf and Ilkley Community Coll 78-88; Hd Community and Youth Studies St Martin's Coll 88-94; Hd Applied Soc Sciences 94-06; Hd Sch Soc Sciences and Business Studies 01-06; P-in-c Settle *Bradf* 06-11; P-in-c Giggleswick and Rathmell w Wigglesworth 08-11; rtd 11. *Cravendale, Belle Hill, Giggleswick, Settle BD24 0BA* Tel (01729) 825307
E-mail neil.kendra@totalise.co.uk

KENDREW, Geoffrey David. b 42. K Coll Lon BD66 AKC66. **d** 67 **p** 68. C Bourne *Guildf* 67-70; C Haslemere 70-76; V Derby St Barn 76-95; R Deal St Leon w St Rich and Sholden etc *Cant* 95-07; Chapl E Kent NHS and Soc Care Partnership Trust 00-06; Chapl Kent & Medway NHS and Soc Care Partnership Trust 06-07; rtd 07. *2 Mill Lane, Butterwick, Boston PE22 0JE* Tel (01205) 760977 E-mail david-kendrew@supanet.com

KENDRICK, Dale Evans. b 62. Ch Ch Coll Cant BA86 Nottm Univ MA87 Leeds Univ MA95. Coll of Resurr Mirfield 94. **d** 95 **p** 96. C Tividale *Lich* 95-96; C Blakenall Heath 96-97; C Stafford 97-98; Dep Chapl HM Pris Birm 98-01; Chapl HM Pris Drake Hall 01-03; Chapl RAF 03-04; Chapl HM YOI Werrington Ho 04-08; Chapl HM Pris Lewes from 08. *HM Prison Lewes, 1 Brighton Road, Lewes BN7 1EA* Tel (01273) 785100

KENDRICK, Canon Desmond Max. b 22. Leeds Univ BA47. Wycliffe Hall Ox 50. **d** 52 **p** 53. C Glodwick St Mark *Man* 52-54; Chapl Leeds Road Hosp Bradf 54-77; V Bradf St Clem 54-77; RD Bradf 63-73; Hon Can Bradf Cathl 64-89; V Otley 77-89; Chapl Wharfedale Gen Hosp 77-90; rtd 89; Perm to Offic *Bradf* from 89. *26 Ashtofts Mount, Guiseley LS20 9DB* Tel (01943) 870430

KENDRICK, Mrs Helen Grace. b 66. Bris Univ BA88. SAOMC 96. **d** 99 **p** 00. C Icknield *Ox* 99-03; P-in-c Sutton Courtenay w Appleford from 03. *The Vicarage, 3 Tullis Close, Sutton Courtenay, Abingdon OX14 4BD* Tel (01235) 848297
E-mail helen@kendricks.fsnet.co.uk

KENNAR, Thomas Philip. b 66. Surrey Univ BA08. STETS 02. **d** 05 **p** 06. C Warblington w Emsworth *Portsm* 05-08; Chapl Portsm Coll 06-08; TR Portsea N End St Mark *Portsm* from 08. *The Rectory, 3A Wadham Road, Portsmouth PO2 9ED* Tel (023) 9234 2661 E-mail tomkennar@googlemail.com

KENNARD, Mark Philip Donald. b 60. Man Univ BSc82. Cranmer Hall Dur 85. **d** 88 **p** 89. C Newark w Hawton, Cotham and Shelton *S'well* 88-89; C Newark 89-91; C Cropwell Bishop w Colston Bassett, Granby etc 91-93; P-in-c Shireoaks 93-99; Chapl Bassetlaw Hosp and Community Services NHS Trust 93-96; Chapl RAF from 99. *Chaplaincy Services, Valiant Block, HQ Air Command, RAF High Wycombe HP14 4UE* Tel (01494) 496800 Fax 496343

KENNEDY, Alan. b 52. Liv Univ BSc95. NOC 01. **d** 03 **p** 04. C Westbrook St Phil *Liv* 03-07; TV Mossley Hill from 07. *The Vicarage, Rose Lane, Liverpool L18 8DB* Tel 0151-724 1915

KENNEDY, Ms Alison Mary. b 66. K Coll Lon BMus87 Heythrop Coll Lon MA95 LTCL90. NTMTC 96. **d** 99 **p** 00. C De Beauvoir Town St Pet *Lon* 99-02; TV Walthamstow *Chelmsf* 02-07; TV N Lambeth *S'wark* from 07. *10 Wincott Street, London SE11 4NT* Tel (020) 7820 9445
E-mail alison_m_kennedy@hotmail.com

KENNEDY, Anthony Reeves. b 32. Roch Th Coll 64. **d** 67 **p** 68. C Ross *Heref* 67-69; C Marfleet *York* 69-71; TV 72-76; V Lightwater *Guildf* 76-83; V W Ham *Chelmsf* 83-89; V Lutton w Gedney Drove End, Dawsmere *Linc* 89-94; Perm to Offic *Chich* from 94 and *Win* from 01; rtd 97. *40 Haydock Close, Alton GU34 2TL* Tel (01420) 549860
E-mail anthreev.kennedy@virgin.net

KENNEDY, Miss Carolyn Ruth. b 59. Univ of Wales (Ban) BA81 GradCertEd(FE)85. Ripon Coll Cuddesdon BA90. **d** 91 **p** 94. C Frodingham *Linc* 91-95; Chapl Cov Univ 95-00; R Uffington Gp *Linc* from 00. *The Rectory, 67 Main Road, Uffington, Stamford PE9 4SN* Tel (01780) 481786
E-mail rector@uffingtongroup.org.uk

KENNEDY, David George. b 46. Hull Univ BEd71 MA76. Linc Th Coll 77. **d** 79 **p** 80. C Linc St Faith and St Martin w St Pet 79-82; V Bilton St Pet *York* 82-90; V New Seaham *Dur* 90-92; Chapl Lincs and Humberside Univ 92-97; P-in-c Barrow St Matt *Carl* 97-99; TR 99-03; Chapl Furness Coll 97-03; P-in-c Blackb St Aid 03-04; V Blackb St Fran and St Aid 04-06; Chapl Nord Pas de Calais *Eur* 06-08; P-in-c Bierley *Bradf* from 08. *St John's Vicarage, Bierley Lane, Bradford BD4 6AA* Tel (01274) 681397
E-mail therevdavid@yahoo.com

KENNEDY, Canon David John. b 57. St Jo Coll Dur BA78 Nottm Univ MTh81 Birm Univ PhD96. St Jo Coll Nottm 79. **d** 81 **p** 82. C Tudhoe Grange *Dur* 81-87; C Merrington 84-87; Tutor Qu Coll Birm 88-96; R Haughton le Skerne *Dur* 96-01; Can Res Dur Cathl from 01; Chapl Grey Coll Dur 01-09. *7 The College, Durham DH1 3EQ* Tel 0191-375 0242 Fax 386 4267
E-mail canon.precentor@durhamcathedral.co.uk

KENNEDY, Gary. b 63. Qu Coll Birm BA02. **d** 03 **p** 04. C New Bury *Man* 03-06; C New Bury w St Lever 06; P-in-c Bolton SS Simon and Jude from 06. *The Vicarage, 15 Lowick Avenue, Bolton BL3 2DS* Tel (01204) 365063
E-mail therev@talktalk.net

KENNEDY, Ian Duncan. b 53. **d** 04 **p** 05. OLM Whitnash *Cov* 04-07; NSM Leek Wootton 07-08; P-in-c Fillongley and Corley from 08. *The Vicarage, Holbeche Crescent, Fillongley, Coventry CV7 8ES* Tel (01676) 540320 E-mail reviankennedy@aol.com

KENNEDY, James Edward. b 72. Magd Coll Cam MA97 Imp Coll Lon MB, BS97 Wolfs Coll Ox DPhil05. Wycliffe Hall Ox BA09. **d** 10 **p** 11. C High Wycombe *Ox* from 10. *Rye Cottage, 9 Bassetsbury Lane, High Wycombe HP11 1QU* Tel (01494) 529668 Mobile 07899-751931
E-mail james.kennedy@sac-hw.org.uk

KENNEDY, Mrs Jane Rowston. b 47. Dudley Coll of Educn CertEd70 Leic Univ DipEd93. EMMTC 04. **d** 07 **p** 08. NSM Gilmorton, Peatling Parva, Kimcote etc *Leic* from 07. *17 Cromwell Close, Walcote, Lutterworth LE17 4JJ* Tel (01455) 554065 E-mail jane@kennedyjane.wanadoo.co.uk

KENNEDY, Jason Grant. b 68. Oak Hill Th Coll BA95. **d** 98 **p** 99. C Beccles St Mich *St E* 98-01; R Hollington St Leon *Chich* 01-05; C Tonbridge St Steph *Roch* 05-10; V Ripley *Derby* from 10. *All Saints' Church Office, Moseley Street, Ripley DE5 3DA* Tel (01773) 570011
E-mail jason.kennedy@allsaintsripley.org.uk

KENNEDY, John Frederick. b 42. Birm Univ BSc64 PhD67 DSc73. Qu Coll Birm 05. **d** 06 **p** 07. NSM Edgbaston St Geo *Birm* 06-10. *Address temp unknown*

KENNEDY, Joseph. b 69. Edin Univ BSc91 BD94 Moray Ho Coll of Educn PGCE97 St Hugh's Coll Ox MSt00 Keble Coll Ox DPhil06. St Steph Ho Ox 98. **d** 02 **p** 03. C Stratfield Mortimer and Mortimer W End etc *Ox* 02-03; C Abingdon 03-05; Dean of Chpl, Chapl and Fell Selw Coll Cam 05-08; Chapl Newnham Coll Cam 05-08; Prin Coll of Resurr Mirfield 08-11; Hon Can Wakef Cathl 10-11; V Oxton *Ches* from 11. *Oxton Vicarage, 8 Wexford Road, Prenton CH43 9TB* Tel 0151-652 1194

KENNEDY, Canon Michael Charles. b 39. TCD BA63 MA79 BD79 Open Univ PhD87. TCD Div Sch 61. **d** 63 **p** 64. C Drumglass *Arm* 63-66; I Lisnadill w Kildarton from 66; Warden Dioc Guild of Lay Readers from 74; Hon V Choral Arm Cathl from 75; Tutor for Aux Min (Arm) from 82; Preb Yagoe St Patr Cathl Dublin from 92. *Lisnadill Rectory, 60 Newtownhamilton Road, Armagh BT60 2PW* Tel (028) 3752 3630
E-mail michaelkennedy2@btinternet.com

KENNEDY, Paul Alan. b 67. ACA92. St Steph Ho Ox BA95. **d** 95 **p** 96. C Romford St Andr *Chelmsf* 95-98; C Cheam *S'wark* 98-01; V Steep and Froxfield w Privett *Portsm* 01-08; R E Win from 08; Bp's Adv on Healing *Portsm* from 04. *The Rectory, 19 Petersfield Road, Winchester SO23 0JD* Tel (01962) 853777 Mobile 07877-211303
E-mail rectoreastwinchester@googlemail.com

KENNEDY, Paul Joseph Alan. b 57. Newc Univ MA93. Sarum & Wells Th Coll 81. **d** 84 **p** 85. C Shildon w Eldon *Dur* 84-86; C Shotton *St As* 86-88; V Waterhouses *Dur* 88-93; V Denton *Newc* 93-95; CF 95-98; P-in-c Leam Lane *Dur* 98-99; V 99-05; P-in-c S Westoe from 05. *St Michael's Vicarage, Westoe Road, South Shields NE33 3PD* Tel 0191-422 1299

KENNEDY, Miss Penelope Ann Cheney. b 49. STETS 08. **d** 11. NSM Buckland Newton, Cerne Abbas, Godmanstone etc *Sarum* from 11. *8 Abbots Walk, Cerne Abbas, Dorchester DT2 7JN* Tel (01300) 341390
E-mail penekennedy@tiscali.co.uk

KENNEDY, Brother Philip Bartholomew. b 47. STETS 95. **d** 98 **p** 99. SSF from 77; C Plaistow and N Canning Town *Chelmsf* from 08. *St Matthias' Vicarage, 45 Mafeking Road, London E16 4NS* Tel (020) 7511 7848
E-mail philipbartholomewssf@googlemail.com

KENNEDY, Ross Kenneth. b 40. Edin Th Coll 83. **d** 85 **p** 86. C Hexham *Newc* 85-89; TV Glendale Gp 89-93; TR Ch the King 93-05; rtd 05; Hon C Dunfermline *St And* from 05. *12 Calaisburn Place, Dunfermline KY11 4RD* Tel (01383) 625887 E-mail rk.kennedy@btinternet.com

KENNEDY, Samuel (Uell). b 51. Heriot-Watt Univ BSc72. CBDTI 06. **d** 07 **p** 08. NSM Baildon *Bradf* from 07; Development Officer Min and Miss from 02. *The Moorings, Hunsingore, Wetherby LS22 5HY* Tel (01535) 650531 Fax 650550 E-mail uell@kadugli.org.uk

KENNEDY, Wendy Patricia. b 58. STETS 00. **d** 03 **p** 04. NSM Warren Park and Leigh Park *Portsm* 03-07; Dioc Sec from 07; Perm to Offic from 07. *13 Ashcroft Lane, Waterlooville PO8 0AX* Tel (023) 9241 3190
E-mail wendy.kennedy@portsmouth.anglican.org

KENNERLEY, Katherine Virginia (Ginnie). Somerville Coll Ox BA58 MA65 TCD BA86 Princeton Th Sem DMin98. CITC 86. **d** 88 **p** 90. Lect Applied Th CITC 88-93; NSM Bray *D & G* 88-93; I Narraghmore and Timolin w Castledermot etc 93-05; Can Ch Ch Cathl Dublin 96-05; rtd 05. *4 Seafield Terrace, Dalkey, Co Dublin, Republic of Ireland* Tel (00353) (1) 275 0737 Mobile 87-647 5092 E-mail kennerley@eircom.net

KENNETT-ORPWOOD, Jason Robert. b 55. St Mich Coll Llan. **d** 78 **p** 79. Chapl St Woolos Cathl 78-82; Chapl St Woolos Hosp Newport 79-82; Dioc Youth Chapl *Mon* 82-85; V Cwmcarn 82-85; TV Wrexham *St As* 85-89; Dioc Ecum Officer 94-99; Chapl Wrexham Maelor Hosp 86-89; V Bistre 89-99. *94 Erddig Road, Wrexham LL13 7DR*

KENNEY, Canon Peter. b 50. Edin Univ BD75. Edin Th Coll 73. **d** 76 **p** 77. C Cullercoats St Geo *Newc* 76-81; TV Whorlton 81-88; TR Ch the King 88-93; P-in-c Newc St Jo 93-02; P-in-c Gosforth St Hugh 02-09; P-in-c Chapel House from 09; Dioc Adv in Past Care and Counselling from 02; Hon Can Newc Cathl from 04. *The Vicarage, 44 Queensbury Drive, North Walbottle, Newcastle upon Tyne NE15 9XF* Tel 0191-229 0136 E-mail kenney@globalnet.co.uk

KENNING, Canon Michael Stephen. b 47. St Chad's Coll Dur BA68. Westcott Ho Cam 69. **d** 71 **p** 72. C Hythe *Cant* 71-75; TV Bow w Bromley St Leon *Lon* 75-77; C-in-c W Leigh CD *Portsm* 77-81; V Lee-on-the-Solent 81-92; R N Waltham and Steventon, Ashe and Deane *Win* 92-10; RD Whitchurch 03-08; Hon Can Win Cathl 09-10; rtd 10. *20 Teal Crescent, Basingstoke RG25 5QX* E-mail michael.kenning@ukgateway.net

KENNINGTON, The Very Revd John Paul. b 61. Collingwood Coll Dur BA85. St Steph Ho Ox BA87 MA92. **d** 88 **p** 89. C Headington *Ox* 88-91; C Dulwich St Clem w St Pet *S'wark* 91-94; TV Mortlake w E Sheen 94-01; V Battersea St Mary 01-10; Dean Montreal Canada from 11. *1444 Union Avenue, Montreal QC H3A 2B8, Canada* E-mail pkennington@clara.net

KENNY, Charles John. b 39. QUB BA61 MEd78 LGSM74. CITC 69. **d** 69 **p** 70. C Belfast St Paul *Conn* 69-71; Hd of RE Grosvenor High Sch 71-94; V Choral Belf Cathl 94-00; Can Treas 95-00; rtd 00; Lic to Offic *Conn* from 84. *45 Deramore Drive, Belfast BT9 5JS* Tel (028) 9066 9632 or 9032 8332 Fax 9023 8855 E-mail c.kenny142@btinternet.com

KENNY, Frederick William Bouvier. b 28. TCD BA53 DipEd54 MA56. **d** 56 **p** 57. C Ballymacarrett St Patr *D & D* 56-58; C Blackpool St Jo *Blackb* 58-61; V Preston St Paul 61-66; Chapl Preston R Infirmary 61-66; Youth Adv CMS (Lon) 66-70; Youth Sec (Ireland) CMS 70-75; I Belfast St Clem *D & D* 75-80; V Preston St Cuth *Blackb* 80-86; TV Bushbury *Lich* 86-90; P-in-c Stambridge *Chelmsf* 90-97; Chapl Southend Community Care Services NHS Trust 90-97; rtd 97; Perm to Offic *Pet* 97-99 and *Chelmsf* from 99. *28 Cavendish Gardens, Westcliff-on-Sea SS0 9XP* Tel (01702) 344791 E-mail c-jkenny@dial.pipex.com

KENNY, Mark Anthony. b 74. Leeds Univ BA97 PGCE98. NTMTC 02. **d** 04 **p** 05. NSM Covent Garden St Paul *Lon* 04-08; NSM Aldersbrook *Chelmsf* 08-10; Perm to Offic from 10. *110 Perth Road, Ilford IG2 6AS* Tel (020) 8554 2492 Mobile 07974-572074 E-mail mark.kenny@btinternet.com

KENRICK, Kenneth David Norman. b 44. Liv Univ RMN. Ripon Hall Ox 70 NW Ord Course 77. d 77 p 78. C Stockport St Geo Ches 77-83; R Stockport St Thos 83-85; R Stockport St Thos w St Pet from 86; Chapl St Thos and Cheadle Royal Hospitals from 88. St Thomas's Rectory, 25 Heath Road, Stockport SK2 6JJ Tel 0161-483 2483 E-mail truefaith_@hotmail.com
KENSINGTON, Area Bishop of. See WILLIAMS, The Rt Revd Paul Gavin
KENT, Barry James. b 41. d 02 p 03. OLM Kinson Sarum 02-07; NSM Hordle Win from 07. Church Cottage, Sway Road, Tiptoe, Lymington SO41 6FR Tel (01425) 616670 E-mail kenthome@tiscali.co.uk
KENT, Christopher Alfred. b 48. Birm Univ BSc69 PhD72 CEng77 MIChemE77. St Jo Coll Nottm 82. d 84 p 85. C Bucknall and Bagnall Lich 84-86; Hon C Halesowen Worc 86-96; NSM Reddal Hill St Luke 96-01; NSM The Lye and Stambermill from 01. 40 County Park Avenue, Halesowen B62 8SP Tel 0121-550 3132 E-mail c.a.kent@bham.ac.uk
KENT, Miss Cindy. b 45. SEITE 05. d 07 p 08. NSM Whetstone St Jo Lon from 07; P-in-c from 10. St John the Apostle Vicarage, 1163 High Road, London N20 0PG Tel (020) 8445 3682 Mobile 07879-642100 E-mail cindykent58@hotmail.com
KENT, David. b 44. CEng MIMechE. NOC. d 83 p 84. NSM Huddersfield St Pet and All SS Wakef 83-98; NSM Newsome and Armitage Bridge 98-03; NSM Em TM from 03. 2 Hillside Crescent, Huddersfield HD4 6LY Tel (01484) 324049 Mobile 07949-762186 E-mail david.kent3@ntlworld.com
KENT, Frank. b 44. Open Univ BA82 ARCM76. Ridley Hall Cam. d 86 p 87. C Faversham Cant 86-89; R Lyminge w Paddlesworth, Stanford w Postling etc 89-99; P-in-c Sittingbourne St Mich 99-00; V Sittingbourne St Mary and St Mich 01-04; R Eastry and Northbourne w Tilmanstone etc 04-07; rtd 07. 3 Balfour Road, Walmer, Deal CT14 7HU Tel (01304) 375080 or 619366 E-mail revkent@francikent.freeserve.co.uk
KENT, Hugh. See KENT, Richard Hugh
KENT, Keith Meredith. b 32. St Aid Birkenhead 55. d 58 p 59. C Fulwood Ch Ch Blackb 58-60; C Everton St Chrys Liv 60-62; C Litherland St Phil 64-68; P-in-c Everton St Polycarp 68-74; V Liv All So Springwood 74-78; V Carr Mill 78-86; V Beddgelert Ban 86-91; rtd 91; Perm to Offic Blackb from 91. 14 Crow Hills Road, Penwortham, Preston PR1 0JE Tel (01772) 746831
KENT, Mrs Mary. b 51. Birm Univ BA72. St Steph Ho Ox 06. d 08 p 09. NSM Alveston Cov from 08. Elmhurst, Little Alne, Wootton Wawen, Henley-in-Arden B95 6HW Tel (01789) 488150
KENT, Canon Michael Patrick. b 27. St Edm Hall Ox BA50 MA52. Cuddesdon Coll 50. d 52 p 53. C W Hartlepool St Aid Dur 52-57; C-in-c Pennywell St Thos and Grindon St Oswald CD 57-70; V Cockerton 70-93; RD Darlington 79-84; Hon Can Dur Cathl 83-98; rtd 93; Chapl St Chad's Coll Dur 94-95. 21 Stitchell House, Greatham, Hartlepool TS25 2HS
KENT, Richard Hugh. b 38. Worc Coll Ox BA61 MA63. Chich Th Coll 61. d 63 p 64. C Emscote Cov 63-66; C Finham 66-70; V Parkend Glouc 70-75; V Glouc St Aldate 75-86; Chapl and Warden Harnhill Healing Cen 86-96; R N Buckingham Ox 96-04; AD Buckingham 00-04; rtd 04; Perm to Offic Pet from 05. 10 Booth Close, Pattishall, Towcester NN12 8JP Tel (01327) 836231 E-mail hugh.k@talk21.com
KENT, Ms Susan Elizabeth. b 52. St Aid Coll Dur BA74 St Mary's Coll Newc PGCE77. Ripon Coll Cuddesdon 98. d 00 p 01. C Westgate Common Wakef 00-03; P-in-c Oxclose Dur 03-08; R Upper Weardale from 08. The Rectory, 48 Front Street, Stanhope, Bishop Auckland DL13 2UE Tel (01388) 528722 Mobile 07884-024202 E-mail revsusan@arken.freeserve.co.uk
KENT-WINSLEY, Cindy. See KENT, Miss Cindy
KENTIGERN-FOX, Canon William Poyntere Kentigern. b 38. AKC63. d 64 p 65. C S Mimms St Mary and Potters Bar Lon 64-67; C S Tottenham 67-70; R Barrowden and Wakerley Pet 70-76; P-in-c Duddington w Tixover 70-76; P-in-c Morcott w S Luffenham 75-77; R Barrowden and Wakerley w S Luffenham 77-79; R Byfield w Boddington 79-86; V Northampton St Mich w St Edm 86-95; V Raunds 95-03; Can Pet Cathl 94-03; RD Higham 97-02; rtd 03. 41 Parkfield Road, Ruskington, Sleaford NG34 9HT Tel (01526) 830944
KENWARD, Roger Nelson. b 34. Selw Coll Cam BA58 MA62. Ripon Hall Ox 58. d 60 p 61. C Paddington St Jas Lon 60-63; Chapl RAF 64-82; Asst Chapl-in-Chief RAF 82-89; P-in-c Lyneham w Bradenstoke Sarum 72-76; QHC 85-89; R Laughton w Ripe and Chalvington Chich 90-95; Chapl Laughton Lodge Hosp 90-95; rtd 95; NSM Chiddingly w E Hoathly Chich 96; Perm to Offic from 96. The Coach House, School Hill, Old Heathfield, Heathfield TN21 9AE Tel (01435) 862618
KENWAY, Ian Michael. b 52. Leeds Univ BA74 Bris Univ PhD86. Coll of Resurr Mirfield 74. d 76 p 77. C Cov E 76-79; C Southmead Bris 79-81; P-in-c Shaw Hill Birm 82-88; Asst Sec Gen Syn Bd for Soc Resp 88-93; Chapl Essex Univ 93-99; Dir Studies Cen for Study of Th 93-99; Perm to Offic S & B from 01.

The Beast House, Cwmdu, Crickhowell NP8 1RT Tel (01874) 730143 Mobile 07748-223090 Fax 07092-315825 E-mail iank@cischr.org
KENWAY, Robert Andrew. b 56. Bris Univ BA78. Westcott Ho Cam 80. d 82 p 83. C Birchfield Birm 82-85; C Queensbury All SS Lon 87-89; R Birm St Geo 89-97; V Calne and Blackland Sarum 97-10; TR Marden Vale from 10. The Vicarage, Vicarage Close, Calne SN11 8DD Tel (01249) 812340 E-mail bobandsadie.kenway@btopenworld.com
KENYA, Archbishop of. See WABUKALA, The Most Revd Eliud
KENYON, Lee Stuart. b 78. Lanc Univ BA01 Leeds Univ BA04 MA05. Coll of Resurr Mirfield 02. d 05 p 06. C Darwen St Cuth w Tockholes St Steph Blackb 05-09; P-in-c Calgary St Jo Canada from 09. St John's Rectory, 1421 8th Avenue SE, Calgary AB T2G 0N1, Canada E-mail leekenyon@fsmail.net
KEOGH, Anthony. b 35. St Mich Coll Llan 63. d 66 p 67. C Aberaman and Abercwmboi Llan 66-70; Hon C Penarth All SS 70-76; R Jersey H Trin Win 76-05; rtd 05. 9 La Ville des Chenes, St John, Jersey JE3 4BG Tel (01534) 869655 E-mail jill.keogh@virgin.net
KEOGH, Henry James. b 39. TCD BA61 NUI BMus65. d 62 p 63. C Cork St Fin Barre's Cathl 62-65; C Belfast St Luke Conn 65-66; C Dromore Cathl 66-68; I Castlecomer C & O 68-85; I Kilscoran w Killinick and Mulrankin 85-02; Hon Chapl Miss to Seafarers 85-02; Preb Ferns Cathl 96-02; rtd 02. 5 Ard na Gréine, Dark Road, Midleton, Co Cork, Republic of Ireland Tel (00353) (21) 463 0841
KEOGH, Paul Anthony. b 37. Order of Friars Minor 55. d 62 p 63. In RC Ch 62-66; Hon C Eltham Park St Luke S'wark 00-07; Perm to Offic from 07. 78 Greenvale Road, London SE9 1PD Tel (020) 8850 9958 or 8303 4786
KEOGH, Robert Gordon. b 56. CITC. d 84 p 85. C Mossley Conn 84-87; I Taunagh w Kilmactranny, Ballysumaghan etc K, E & A 87-90; I Swanlinbar w Tomregan, Kinawley, Drumlane etc 90-02; Preb Kilmore Cathl 98-02; I Drumclamph w Lower and Upper Langfield D & R from 02. Drumclamph Rectory, 70 Greenville Road, Castlederg BT81 7NU Tel (028) 8167 1433 E-mail rkeogh@utvinternet.com
KEOWN, Paul. b 53. Univ of Wales (Swansea) BA95 PGCE97 LGSM76. Ripon Coll Cuddesdon 00 St Steph Ho Ox BTh06. d 02 p 03. C Llansamlet S & B 02-04; P-in-c Swansea St Nic 04-07; R Haddington Edin 07-08; V Salfords S'wark from 08. The Vicarage, Honeycrock Lane, Redhill RH1 5DF Tel (01737) 764712 E-mail frpaulkeown@mac.com
KER, Desmond Agar-Ellis. b 15. Wells Th Coll 58. d 58 p 60. C Wyken Cov 58-59; C Dawlish Ex 60-61; C Cockington 61-69; V Bovey Tracey St Jo 69-80; rtd 80; Perm to Offic S'wark 84-92; Perm to Offic Chich 92-97. Montcalm, 3 Clifton Crescent, Folkestone CT20 2EL
KER, Robert Andrew. b 65. d 05 p 06. Aux Min Larne and Inver Conn from 05. 24 Ravensdale, Newtownabbey BT36 6FA Tel (028) 9083 6901 E-mail a.ker@btinternet.com
KERLEY, Brian Edwin. b 36. St Jo Coll Cam BA57 MA61. Linc Th Coll 59. d 61 p 62. C Sheerness H Trin w St Paul Cant 61-64; C St Laur in Thanet 64-69; C Coulsdon St Andr S'wark 69-76; P-in-c Fulbourn Ely 76-77; R 77-03; P-in-c Gt and Lt Wilbraham 86-03; RD Quy 83-93 and 97-00; rtd 03; Perm to Offic Ely from 03. 11 Dalton Way, Ely CB6 1DS Tel (01353) 665641 E-mail brian.kerley@ely.anglican.org
KERLEY, Patrick Thomas Stewart. b 42. Linc Th Coll. d 85 p 86. Hon C Thorpe St Andr Nor 85-90; C Wymondham 90-94; C Gt Yarmouth 94-95; TV 95-00; TV Wilford Peninsula St E 00-07; rtd 07; Perm to Offic Nor from 08. 3 St Leonard's Close, Wymondham NR18 0JF Tel (01953) 606618 Mobile 07940-739769
KERNER, Vivienne Jane. b 49. Liv Univ CertEd71 BEd72. WEMTC 91. d 94 p 95. NSM Glouc St Jas and All SS 94-01; NSM Glouc St Mark and St Mary de Crypt w St Jo etc 01-02; Perm to Offic 02-04; NSM Hardwicke and Elmore w Longney 04-07; Hon Chapl Leckhampton Court Hospice 03-07; NSM Charfield and Kingswood Glouc 07-11; NSM Charfield and Kingswood w Wickwar etc from 11. The Rectory, 36 Wotton Road, Charfield, Wotton-under-Edge GL12 8TG Tel (01454) 261751 E-mail vivienne.kerner@btinternet.com
KERNEY, Barbara. See SHERLOCK, Mrs Barbara Lee Kerney
KERNOHAN, Jason William. b 79. TCD BTh10. CITC 07. d 10. C Drumachose D & R from 10. 45 Wood Road, Ballykelly, Limavady BT49 9PJ Tel (028) 7776 7889 E-mail jason.kernohan@btinternet.com
KERR, Mrs Alison. b 76. Ripon Coll Cuddesdon 06. d 09 p 10. C Lytchett Minster Sarum 09-10; C The Lytchetts and Upton from 10. Corfe View, Jenny's Lane, Lytchett Matravers, Poole BH16 6BP Tel 07833-450780 (mobile) E-mail rev.alison@hotmail.com
KERR, Andrew Harry Mayne. b 41. TCD BA63. Melbourne Coll of Div MMin98. d 65 p 66. C Belfast St Luke Conn 65-68; SCM Sec (Ireland) 68-72; C Clooney D & R 72-74; Australia from 74; C Swinburne 74-80; I Dallas 80-88; I Mont Albert 88-94; P-in-c W Geelong from 96. 101 Katrina Street, Blackburn North Vic

KERR

3130, Australia Tel (0061) (3) 5221 6694 *or* 9893 4946 Fax 9893 4946 E-mail ahmkerr@hotmail.com

KERR, Mrs Anita Dawn Christina. b 63. SRN81 SCM86 PGCE04. CITC 04. **d** 07 **p** 08. Aux Min Sligo w Knocknarea and Rosses Pt *K, E & A* 07-09; Lic to Offic *Clogh* 09-10; Chapl to Bp Clogh from 10; NSM Devenish w Boho from 10. *5 Oakhill Avenue, Killyhevlin, Enniskillen BT74 4EA* Tel (028) 6632 4626 E-mail st_kerr@btopenworld.com

KERR, Anthony. b 43. Sheff Univ BA64 Man Univ CertEd65. NOC. **d** 85 **p** 86. NSM Greenfield *Man* 85-87; NSM Leesfield 87-97; P-in-c Oldham St Steph and All Martyrs 97-02; NSM Lydgate w Friezland 02-03; NSM Saddleworth 03-09. *16 Netherlees, Lees, Oldham OL4 5BA* Tel 0161-620 6512

KERR, Arthur Henry. LRAM47 TCD BA48. **d** 49 **p** 50. C Templemore *D & R* 49-50; C Dublin Harold's Cross *D & G* 50-57; ICM 57-60; Chapl Rotunda Hosp 60-75; Lic to Offic *Conn* 58-94; P-in-c Clondevaddock w Portsalon and Leatbeg *D & R* 94-01; rtd 01. *Halothane, 172 Mountsandel Road, Coleraine BT52 1JE* Tel (028) 7034 4940

KERR, Bryan Thomas. b 70. QUB BD91 TCD MPhil96. CITC 94. **d** 96 **p** 97. C Enniskillen *Clogh* 96-99; I Garrison w Slavin and Belleek 99-05; I Lisbellaw from 05; Dioc Communications Officer from 00. *The Rectory, Faughard, Lisbellaw, Enniskillen BT94 5ES* Tel (028) 6638 7219 E-mail rector@lisbellaw.net *or* dco@clogher.anglican.org

KERR, Charles. *See* KERR, Ewan Charles

KERR, Charles Alexander Gray. b 33. Open Univ BA75 Birm Univ MA83 MA88. Edin Th Coll 63. **d** 67 **p** 68. C Hawick *Edin* 67-70; C Edgbaston St Geo *Birm* 70-72; Chapl Birm Skin Hosp 70-75; P-in-c Quinton Road W St Boniface *Birm* 72-79, V 79-84; R Musselburgh *Edin* 84-86; P-in-c Prestonpans 84-86; NSM Reighton w Speeton *York* 89-91; P-in-c Burton Pidsea and Humbleton w Elsternwick 91-95; V Anlaby Common St Mark 95; rtd 96; Perm to Offic *York* 96-02. *29 Kinsbourne Avenue, Bournemouth BH10 4HE*

KERR, David James. b 36. TCD BA58 MA61 BD61 HDipEd66. TCD Div Sch Div Test 59. **d** 60 **p** 61. C Belfast Trin Coll Miss *Conn* 60-63; Dean's V St Patr Cathl Dublin 63-66; Chapl Beechwood Park Sch St Alb 66-01; Hon C Flamstead *St Alb* 74-00; Perm to Offic from 00; rtd 01. *Trumpton Cottage, 12A Pickford Road, Markyate, St Albans AL3 8RU* Tel (01582) 841191 E-mail kerr_david@hotmail.com

KERR, Derek Preston. b 64. TCD BTh90. Oak Hill Th Coll 85. **d** 90 **p** 91. C Belfast St Donard *D & D* 90-93; C Carrickfergus *Conn* 93-96; I Devenish w Boho *Clogh* 96-07; I Drummaul w Duneane and Ballyscullion *Conn* from 07. *The Vicarage, 1A Glenkeen, Randalstown, Antrim BT41 3JX* Tel (028) 9447 2561

KERR, Miss Dora Elizabeth. b 41. QUB BA65 Southn Univ DipEd66. St Jo Coll Nottm 82. **dss** 84 **d** 87 **p** 94. Becontree St Mary *Chelmsf* 84-88; Par Dn 87-88; Par Dn Rushden w Newton Bromswold *Pet* 88-93; C Finham and Chapl Walsgrave Hosps NHS Trust 94-00; C Belper *Derby* 00-07; rtd 07. *23 Worcester Close, Allesley, Coventry CV5 9FZ* Tel (024) 7640 2413 E-mail elizabeth@ekerr.freeserve.co.uk

KERR, Ewan Charles. b 74. Fitzw Coll Cam BA96 MA00. Ripon Coll Cuddesdon MTh01. **d** 01 **p** 02. C Nor St Pet Mancroft w St Jo Maddermarket 01-04; Chapl Glenalmond Coll *St And* 04-07; Chapl St Edw Sch Ox from 07. *281 Woodstock Road, Oxford OX2 7NY* Tel (01865) 510210

KERR, Frank George. b 52. **d** 05 **p** 06. OLM Levenshulme *Man* from 05. *4 Limefield Terrace, Levenshulme, Manchester M19 2EP* Tel 0161-225 4200 E-mail frankkerr@btinternet.com

KERR, Canon Jean. b 46. Man Univ MA93 SS Hild & Bede Coll Dur CertEd69. NOC 84. **d** 87 **p** 94. NSM Peel *Man* 87-93; Par Dn Dixon Green 88-89; Par Dn New Bury 89-93; Par Dn Gillingham St Mark *Roch* 93-94; C 94-98; Chapl Medway Secure Tr Cen 98-01; Warden of Ev 98-05; NSM Roch St Justus 01-05; Hon Can Roch Cathl 03-05; Can Missr from 05; Tr Officer for Lay Minl Educn 03-05; Bp's Officer for Miss and Unity from 05. *Prebendal House, Kings Orchard, Rochester ME1 1TG* Tel and fax (01634) 844508 E-mail jean.kerr@rochester.anglican.org

KERR, John Maxwell. b 43. Toronto Univ BASc66 Leeds Univ MSc70 MSOSc88. Linc Th Coll 75. **d** 77 **p** 78. C New Windsor *Ox* 77-80; Asst Chapl Cheltenham Coll 80-81; Chapl 81-82; NSM Win St Lawr and St Maurice w St Swithun 82-94; Chapl Win Coll 82-92; Hd RS 86-97; Visiting Lect Dept of Continuing Educn Ox Univ 92-04; rtd 02; Perm to Offic *Portsm* 03-04; USA from 05. *111 Rolfe Road, Williamsburg VA 23185-3920, USA* E-mail jmk@kerr.newnet.co.uk

KERR, Canon Nicholas Ian. b 46. Em Coll Cam BA68 MA72. Westcott Ho Cam 74. **d** 77 **p** 78. C Merton St Mary *S'wark* 77-80; C Rainham *Roch* 80-84; Chapl Joyce Green Hosp Dartford 84-90; V Dartford St Edm *Roch* 84-90; V Lamorbey H Redeemer 90-11; RD Sidcup 98-03; Hon Can Roch Cathl 02-11; rtd 11. *11 Cobdown Grove, Rainham, Gillingham ME8 7PN* Tel (01634) 389960 Mobile 07885-619595 E-mail nicholasian@me.com

KERR, Paul Turner. b 47. Man Univ MA92. Cranmer Hall Dur 68. **d** 71 **p** 72. C Kingston upon Hull St Martin *York* 71-72; C Linthorpe 72-76; C Cherry Hinton St Jo *Ely* 76-78; Chapl Addenbrooke's Hosp Cam 76-78; TV Rochdale *Man* 78-84; Chapl Birch Hill Hosp Rochdale 78-84; V New Bury 84-87; TR 87-93; C Gillingham St Mark *Roch* 93-98; RD Gillingham 96-98; V Roch St Justus from 98; RD Roch from 02; Chapl Roch Cathl from 11. *Prebendal House, 1 Kings Orchard, Rochester ME1 1TG* Tel and fax (01634) 8444508 E-mail paul.kerr@diocese-rochester.org *or* ptkerr@hotmail.co.uk

KERR, Canon Stephen Peter. b 46. TCD BA68 Edin Univ BD71 MPhil80. **d** 71 **p** 72. C Belfast H Trin *Conn* 72-76; C Ballywillan 76-78; Lect Linc Th Coll 78-87; Dioc Officer for Adult Educn and Minl Tr *Worc* 87-99; P-in-c Ombersley w Doverdale from 87; P-in-c Hartlebury from 08; P-in-c Elmley Lovett w Hampton Lovett and Elmbridge etc from 10; Bp's Th Adv 99-07; RD Droitwich from 07; Hon Can Worc Cathl from 93. *The Rectory, Main Road, Ombersley, Droitwich WR9 0EW* Tel (01905) 620950 E-mail peter.kerr@cofe-worcester.org.uk

KERR, Terence Philip. b 54. QUB BD97. CITC 97. **d** 99 **p** 00. C Antrim All SS *Conn* 99-01; I Drummaul w Duneane and Ballyscullion 01-07; I Belfast St Aid from 07. *12 Royal Lodge Mews, Belfast BT8 7YT* Tel (028) 9079 0977 Mobile 07727-877830 E-mail terryrevkerr@talktalk.net

KERRIDGE, Donald George. b 32. Bede Coll Dur CertEd72 Hull Univ BA84. Wesley Coll Leeds 57 Bps' Coll Cheshunt 61. **d** 62 **p** 63. C Manston *Ripon* 62-66; C Hawksworth Wood 66-71; Asst Chapl Brentwood Sch Essex 72-74; Lic to Offic *Linc* 81-89; R Tetney, Marshchapel and N Coates 89-91; P-in-c Linc St Swithin 91-95; P-in-c Linc St Swithin w All SS 95-99; Asst Chapl Linc Co Hosp 91-94; rtd 99; Perm to Offic *S'wark* from 03. *28 Caverleigh Way, Worcester Park KT4 8DG* Tel (020) 8337 3886

KERRIN, Albert Eric. b 26. Aber Univ NA51. Edin Th Coll 51. **d** 53 **p** 54. C Dumfries *Glas* 53-55; P-in-c Cambuslang w Newton Cathl Miss 55-57; R Alford *Ab* 57-69; P-in-c Portpatrick *Glas* 69-98; P-in-c Stranraer 69-98; rtd 91; Perm to Offic *Glas* from 98. *15 London Road, Stranraer DG9 8AF* Tel (01776) 702822

KERRY, Martin John. b 55. Ox Univ MA78. St Jo Coll Nottm BA81 MTh83. **d** 82 **p** 83. C Everton St Geo *Liv* 82-85; Lic to Offic *S'well* 85-94; Chapl Asst Nottm City Hosp 85-89; Chapl 89-94; Hd Chapl Nottm City Hosp NHS Trust 94-04; Lead Chapl (NE) *Caring for the Spirit* NHS Project 04-07; Chapl Manager Sheff Teaching Hosps NHS Foundn Trust from 07. *Chaplaincy Services, Royal Hallamshire Hospital, Glossop Road, Sheffield S10 2JF* Tel 0114-271 2718 E-mail martin.kerry@sth.nhs.uk

KERSHAW, Diane Justine. b 11. NSM Philadelphia St Thos *Sheff* from 11. *St Thomas' Church, Philadelphia Campus, 6 Gilpin Street, Sheffield S6 3BL* Tel 0114-241 9560 E-mail diane.kershaw@missionorder.org

KERSHAW, John Harvey. b 51. Coll of Resurr Mirfield 84. **d** 86 **p** 87. C Hollinwood *Man* 86-89; V Audenshaw St Hilda from 89; Chapl Tameside Gen Hosp 90-94; Chapl Tameside and Glossop NHS Trust 94-95. *St Hilda's Vicarage, Denton Road, Audenshaw, Manchester M34 5BL* Tel 0161-336 2310

KERSHAW, Savile. b 37. Bernard Gilpin Soc Dur 60 Chich Th Coll 61. **d** 64 **p** 65. C Staincliffe *Wakef* 64-66; C Saltley *Birm* 66-68; C Birm St Aid Small Heath 68-72; Perm to Offic 88-02; rtd 02. *74 Longmore Road, Shirley, Solihull B90 3EE* Tel 0121-744 3470

KERSLAKE, Mrs Mary. b 39. Mary MacMillan Tr Coll Bradf QTS60. **d** 05 **p** 06. OLM Hethersett w Canteloff w Lt and Gt Melton *Nor* 05-09; rtd 09; Perm to Offic Nor from 10. *Melton Vista, Green Lane, Little Melton, Norwich NR9 3LE* Tel (01603) 811228 E-mail hjbk@btinternet.com

KERSLEY, Stuart Casburn. b 40. CEng MIET. Trin Coll Bris. **d** 82 **p** 83. C Lancing w Coombes *Chich* 82-87; TV Littlehampton and Wick 87-90; R Kingston Buci 90-98; V Kirdford 98-06; rtd 06; Hon C Appleshaw, Kimpton, Thruxton, Fyfield etc *Win* from 06. *St Peter's Vicarage, High Street, Shipton Bellinger, Tidworth SP9 7UF* Tel (01980) 842244

KERSWILL, Canon Anthony John. b 39. Lambeth STh85. Linc Th Coll 72. **d** 73 **p** 73. C Boultham *Linc* 73-76; P-in-c N Kelsey and Cadney 76-83; V Gainsborough St Geo 83-91; V Bracebridge 91-00; P-in-c Linc St Swithin 00-01; V Linc All SS 01-05; RD Christianity 96-02; Can and Preb Linc Cathl 02-05; rtd 05; Chapl Trin Hosp Retford from 05. *The Rectory Farm, Rectory Road, Retford DN22 7AY* Tel (01777) 862533 E-mail kerswill@btinternet.com

KERTON-JOHNSON, Peter. b 41. St Paul's Coll Grahamstown. **d** 81 **p** 82. S Africa 81-99; Perm to Offic *Sarum* 99-00; P-in-c Stoke sub Hamdon *B & W* 00-11; Chapl St Marg Hospice Yeovil 07-08; rtd 11. *1 Castle Street, Stoke-sub-Hamdon TA14 6RE* Tel (01935) 822529 E-mail peter.kertonjohnson@btinternet.com

KESLAKE, Peter Ralegh. b 33. Sarum & Wells Th Coll. **d** 64. C Glouc St Geo w Whaddon 83-86; P-in-c France Lynch 86-91; V Chalford and France Lynch 91-03; rtd 03; Perm to Offic *Glouc* from 04. *4 Farmcote Close, Eastcombe, Stroud GL6 7EG*

KESTER, Jonathan George Frederick. b 66. Ex Univ BA90. Coll of Resurr Mirfield 91. **d** 93 **p** 94. C Cheshunt *St Alb* 93-96; Chapl to Bp Edmonton *Lon* 96-00; Hon C Munster Square Ch Ch and St Mary Magd 96-00; V Gt Ilford St Mary *Chelmsf* 00-08; P-in-c Hampstead Em W End *Lon* from 08; Asst Dir of Ords from 09; CMP from 00. *Emmanuel Vicarage, Lyncroft Gardens, London NW6 1JU* Tel (020) 7435 1911 E-mail frjonathan@mac.com

KESTEVEN, Elizabeth Anne. b 79. Newc Univ LLB01. St Steph Ho Ox 05. **d** 08 **p** 09. C Bris St Steph w St Jas and St Jo w St Mich etc from 08. *78 Leighton Road, Southville, Bristol BS3 1NU* Tel 07973-917720 (mobile) E-mail simon@kesteven.orangehome.co.uk

KESTON, Marion. b 44. Glas Univ MB, ChB68 Edin Univ MTh95. St And Dioc Tr Course 87 Edin Th Coll 92. **d** 90 **p** 94. NSM W Fife Team Min *St And* 90-93; C Dunfermline 93-96; Priest Livingston LEP *Edin* 96-04; P-in-c Kinross *St And* 04-11; rtd 11. *Hattonburn Lodge, Milnathort, Kinross KY13 0SA* Tel (01577) 866834 E-mail marion.keston@btinternet.com

KETLEY, Christopher Glen. b 62. Aston Tr Scheme 91 Coll of Resurr Mirfield 93. **d** 95 **p** 96. C Gt Crosby St Faith *Liv* 95-98; C Swinton and Pendlebury *Man* 98-00; V Belfield 00-08. *8 Gordon Street, Elgin IV30 1JQ* E-mail cgketley@waitrose.com

KETLEY, Michael James. b 39. Oak Hill Th Coll 79. **d** 81 **p** 82. C Bedhampton *Portsm* 81-85; R St Ive w Quethiock *Truro* 85-86; NSM Basildon St Andr w H Cross *Chelmsf* 89-90; C Barkingside St Cedd 90-92; P-in-c 92-95; R Hadleigh St Jas 95-08; rtd 08; Perm to Offic *Chelmsf* from 08. *40 Commonhall Lane, Hadleigh, Benfleet SS7 2RN* Tel (01702) 556318 E-mail mikeketley@aol.com

KETTLE, Alan Marshall. b 51. Leeds Univ BA72. Wycliffe Hall Ox MA78. **d** 78 **p** 79. C Llantwit Fardre 78-81; Prov RE Adv Ch in Wales 81-84; Chapl Llandovery Coll 84-92; P-in-c Cil-y-Cwm and Ystrad-ffin w Rhandir-mwyn etc *St D* 85-92; Chapl W Buckland Sch Barnstaple from 92; Lic to Offic *Ex* from 92. *2 West Close, West Buckland, Barnstaple EX32 0ST* Tel (01598) 760542

KETTLE, Martin Drew. b 52. New Coll Ox BA74 Selw Coll Cam BA76 Cam Univ MA85. Ridley Hall Cam 74. **d** 77 **p** 78. C Enfield St Andr *Lon* 77-80; Chapl Ridley Hall Cam 80-84; V Hendon St Paul Mill Hill *Lon* 85-98; AD W Barnet 90-95; Perm to Offic *Ely* 03-04; Hon C Huntingdon 04-06; Hon C E Leightonstone 06-10; Hon C Hamerton, Winwick and Gt w Lt Gidding and Steeple Gidding 09-10. *Apple Tree House, 97 New Road, Bampton OX18 2NP* Tel (01993) 852454 E-mail mdkettle@msn.com

KETTLE, Mrs Patricia Mary Carole. b 41. Worc Coll of Educn CertEd61. Dalton Ho Bris 66. **d** 87 **p** 94. C Wonersh *Guildf* 87-98; C Wonersh w Blackheath 98-01; rtd 01; Perm to Offic *Guildf* from 02. *Wakehurst Cottage, Links Road, Bramley GU5 0AL* Tel (01483) 898856

KETTLE, Peter. b 51. K Coll Lon BD74 AKC74. St Aug Coll Cant 74. **d** 75 **p** 76. C Angell Town St Jo *S'wark* 75-78; C Putney St Mary 78-80; V Raynes Park St Sav 80-85; Perm to Offic *S'wark* from 85 and *Lon* from 03. *46 Allenswood, Albert Drive, London SW19 6JX* Tel (020) 8785 3797 E-mail peter@levelsix.plus.com

KEULEMANS, Andrew Francis Charles. b 68. Univ of Wales (Abth) BSc90. St Jo Coll Nottm BTh93. **d** 94 **p** 95. C Mold *St As* 94-97; TV Wrexham 97-02; Chapl Loretto Sch Musselburgh 02-10; R Musselburgh *Edin* from 10; R Prestonpans from 10. *12 Windsor Gardens, Musselburgh EH21 7LP* Tel 0131-653 4809

KEULEMANS, Michael Desmond. b 42. SS Mark & Jo Univ Coll Plymouth TCert65 Univ of Wales (Ban) MTh06 DMin10. St As Minl Tr Course 02. **d** 92 **p** 93. Perm to Offic *St As* from 03. *The Poplars, Llanyblodwel, Porth-y-Waen, Oswestry SY10 8LR* Tel (01691) 830010 E-mail roseandmike@tiscali.co.uk

KEVILL-DAVIES, Christopher Charles. b 44. AKC69. St Aug Coll Cant 70. **d** 70 **p** 71. C Folkestone St Sav *Cant* 70-75; V Yaxley *Ely* 75-78; R Chevington w Hargrave and Whepstead w Brockley *St E* 78-86; Perm to Offic *St Alb* 86-89; NSM Stansted Mountfitchet *Chelmsf* 87-89; R Barkway, Reed and Buckland w Barley *St Alb* 89-97; R Chelsea St Luke and Ch Ch *Lon* 97-05; rtd 06; Perm to Offic *S'wark* from 06; Hon Chapl S'wark Cathl from 06. *York House, 35 Clapham Common South Side, London SW4 9BS* Tel (020) 7622 9647 E-mail christopherkd@hotmail.com

KEVIN, Brother. *See* GOODMAN, Brother Kevin Charles

KEVIS, Lionel William Graham. b 55. York Univ BA. Wycliffe Hall Ox 83. **d** 86 **p** 87. C Plaistow St Mary *Roch* 86-90; R Ash and Ridley 90-00; P-in-c Bidborough 00-02; P-in-c Leigh 00-09; V from 09; RD Tonbridge 03-10. *The Vicarage, The Green, Leigh, Tonbridge TN11 8QJ* Tel (01732) 833022

KEW, William Richard. b 45. Lon Univ BD69. ALCD68. **d** 69 **p** 70. C Finchley St Paul Long Lane 69-72; C Stoke Bishop *Bris* 72-76; USA 76-07; C Hamilton and Wenham 76-79; R Rochester SS 79-85; Exec Dir SPCK 85-95; Co-ord Russian Min Network 95-00; Convenor US Angl Congregation 00-02; V Franklin Apostles 02-06; R Franklin Resurr 06-07; Development

KEY, Christopher Halstead. b 56. St Jo Coll Dur BA77 K Coll Lon MTh78. Ridley Hall Cam 79. **d** 81 **p** 82. C Balderstone *Man* 81-84; C Wandsworth All SS *S'wark* 84-88; C-in-c W Dulwich Em CD 88-93; V W Dulwich Em 93-95; R Ore St Helen and St Barn *Chich* from 95; RD Hastings from 03. *St Helen's Rectory, 266 Elphinstone Road, Hastings TN34 2AG* Tel (01424) 425172 E-mail chriskey5@talktalk.net

KEY, The Very Revd Robert Frederick. b 52. Bris Univ BA73. Oak Hill Th Coll 74. **d** 76 **p** 77. C Ox St Ebbe w St Pet 76-80; C Wallington *S'wark* 80-85; V Eynsham and Cassington *Ox* 85-91; V Ox St Andr 91-01; Gen Dir CPAS 01-05; Dean Jersey *Win* from 05; P-in-c Jersey St Helier from 05. *The Deanery, David Place, St Helier, Jersey JE2 4TE* Tel (01534) 720001 E-mail deanofjersey@gov.je *or* robert_f_key@yahoo.com

KEY, Roderick Charles Halstead. b 57. MTh. **d** 84 **p** 85. C Up Hatherley *Glouc* 84-87; V Glouc St Paul 87-04; TR Trunch *Nor* from 04. *The Rectory, Knapton Road, Trunch, North Walsham NR28 0QE* Tel (01263) 722725 *or* 834603

KEY, Roger Astley. b 49. Coll of Resurr Mirfield 72. **d** 74 **p** 75. Perm to Offic *Wakef* 74-75; P-in-c Khomasdal Grace Ch Namibia 75-77; R Luderitz 77-81; Adn The South 77-80; R Walvis Bay 81-85; Personal Asst to Bp Windhoek 85-86; Dean Windhoek 86-00; V Hopton w Corton *Nor* from 00. *The Vicarage, 51 The Street, Corton, Lowestoft NR32 5HT* Tel (01502) 730977 Mobile 07733-028048 E-mail thekeybunch@aol.com *or* rogerkey30@hotmail.com

KEYES, Graham George. b 44. St Cath Coll Cam BA65 MA68 Lanc Univ MA74 Nottm Univ MTh85 MPhil92. EMMTC 82. **d** 84 **p** 85. C Evington *Leic* 84-86; Vice-Prin NEOC 86-89; C Monkseaton St Mary *Newc* 86-89; P-in-c Newc St Hilda 89-94; TV Ch the King 94-99; rtd 99. *1 East Avenue, Newcastle upon Tyne NE12 9PH* Tel 0191-259 9024 E-mail simeon.and.anna@talk21.com

KEYMER, Philip John. b 72. Bris Univ BSc93. Oak Hill Th Coll 96. **d** 99 **p** 00. C Partington and Carrington *Ches* 99-02; C Cheadle 02-04; Perm to Offic *Man* from 05. *10 Central Avenue, Levenshulme, Manchester M19 2EN* Tel 0161-224 2384 E-mail phil.keymer@ntlworld.com

KEYS, Christopher David. b 56. Southn Univ BTh95. Trin Coll Bris. **d** 02 **p** 03. C Fressingfield, Mendham etc *St E* 02-04; C Ipswich St Helen, H Trin, and St Luke 04-05; P-in-c Swineshead and Brothertoft Gp *Linc* 05-07; P-in-c Weston Zoyland w Chedzoy *B & W* 07-10; V from 10. *The Vicarage, Church Lane, Weston Zoyland, Bridgwater TA7 0EP* Tel (01278) 691098 E-mail revchriskeys@btconnect.com

KEYT, Fitzroy John. b 34. Linc Th Coll. **d** 67 **p** 68. C Highters Heath *Birm* 67-70; Hon C Sheldon 70-73; Australia from 73; V Miles 73-76; R Rayton 76-86; R Coolangatta 86-98; P-in-c Clayfield 98-01. *58 Thompson Street, Zillmere Qld 4034, Australia* Tel (0061) (7) 3314 3011 E-mail dskeyt@optusnet.com.au

KHAKHRIA, Rohitkumar Prabhulal (Roy). b 60. Sheff Univ BSc82 PGCE83. Oak Hill Th Coll 94. **d** 96 **p** 97. C Muswell Hill St Jas w St Matt *Lon* 96-01; C Stoughton *Guildf* 01-04; V Boscombe St Jo *Win* from 04. *St John's Vicarage, 17 Browning Avenue, Bournemouth BH5 1NR* Tel (01202) 396667 *or* tel and fax 301916 E-mail roy.khakhria@lycosmax.co.uk

KHAMBATTA, Neville Holbery. b 48. St Chad's Coll Dur BA74. S'wark Ord Course 81. **d** 84 **p** 85. Asst Chapl Em Sch Wandsworth 84-87; Hon C Thornton Heath St Jude w St Aid *S'wark* 84-87; Asst Warden Horstead Cen 87-01; Hon C Coltishall w Gt Hautbois and Horstead *Nor* 87-01; V Ludham, Potter Heigham, Hickling and Catfield 01-11; rtd 11; Perm to Offic *Nor* from 11. *The Spinney, Butchers Common, Neatishead, Norwich NR12 8XH* Tel (01692) 630231 E-mail khambatta@lineone.net

KHAN, Rayman Anthony. b 63. Ripon Coll Cuddesdon 09. **d** 11. C Tamworth *Lich* from 11. *19 Perrycrofts Crescent, Tamworth B79 8UA* Tel 07952-170840 (mobile) E-mail captain.rayman@gmail.com

KHARITONOVA, Natalia. *See* CRITCHLOW, Mrs Natalia

KHOO, Boon-Hor. b 31. FBCO. Llan Dioc Tr Scheme. **d** 87 **p** 88. NSM Llandaff w Capel Llanilltern 87-96; Perm to Offic from 96. *38 The Cathedral Green, Llandaff, Cardiff CF5 2EB* Tel (029) 2056 1478

KHOVACS, Mrs Julie. b 67. Univ of California BA94 Leeds Univ MA04. Westcott Ho Cam 09. **d** 11. C Ashford *Cant* from 11. *24 Sweet Bay Crescent, Ashford TN23 3QA* Tel (01233) 620672 Mobile 07540-418623 E-mail khovacs@yahoo.com

KICHENSIDE, David Alexander. b 78. St Jo Coll Nottm BA10. **d** 10 **p** 11. C Lilleshall and Muxton *Lich* from 10. *3 Wild Thyme Drive, Muxton, Telford TF2 8RU* Tel (01952) 876204 E-mail david.kichenside@talktalk.net

KICHENSIDE, Mark George. b 53. Nottm Univ BTh83. St Jo Coll Nottm 80. **d** 83 **p** 84. C Orpington Ch Ch *Roch* 83-86; C Bexley St Jo 86-90; V Blendon 90-93; V Welling 93-00; R Flegg

KIDD, Coastal Benefice *Nor* 00-05; RD Gt Yarmouth 02-05; TV High Oak, Hingham and Scoulton w Wood Rising 05-10; TV Walton and Trimley *St E* from 10. *The Vicarage, 2 Blyford Way, Felixstowe IP11 2FW* Tel and fax (01394) 273581 E-mail markatk1che39@tiscali.co.uk

KIDD, Anthony John Eric. b 38. Solicitor. Oak Hill NSM Course. d 89 p 90. NSM Rawdon *Bradf* 89-91; C Ilkley All SS 91-93; Perm to Offic *Bradf* 93-95 and *York* 95-96; Hon C Gt and Lt Driffield *York* 96-98; Perm to Offic 98-04; P-in-c The Beacon 04-08; Perm to Offic *Chich* and *York* from 08. *135 Eighth Avenue, Bridlington YO15 2LY* Tel 07795-109090 (mobile)

KIDD, Canon Carol Ivy. b 47. Trent Park Coll of Educn CertEd69. Oak Hill Th Coll 92. d 95 p 96. C Bootle St Mary w St Paul *Liv* 95-99; TV Speke St Aid 99-05; TR from 05; Hon Can Liv Cathl from 03. *All Saints' Vicarage, Speke Church Road, Liverpool L24 3TA* Tel 0151-486 0292

KIDD, John Alan. b 32. Pemb Coll Cam BA58 MA61. Ridley Hall Cam 57. d 61 p 62. C Onslow Square St Paul *Lon* 61-65; R Bloemhof S Africa 65-67; Chapl Jinja Uganda 67-69; P-in-c Mayfair Ch Ch *Lon* 69-75; V 75-79; V Virginia Water *Guildf* 79-88; Lic to Offic 88-94; rtd 94. *c/o P J Kidd, 3 Ufford Street, London SE1 8QD*

KIDD, Kerry. d 08. NSM Alverthorpe *Wakef* from 08. *49 Wrenthorpe Lane, Wrenthorpe, Wakefield WF2 0PX* Tel (01924) 368811 E-mail kskrpe@hotmail.com

KIDD, Maurice Edward. b 26. d 55 p 56. C Wembley St Jo *Lon* 55-58; C Middleton *Man* 58-61; Chapl Pastures Hosp Derby 61-69; Chapl Guild of Health Lon 69-72; R Hanworth St Geo *Lon* 72-82; R Chartham *Cant* 82-91; rtd 91; Perm to Offic *Cant* from 91 and *Lon* 96-97. *4 Cornwallis Circle, Whitstable CT5 1DU* Tel (01227) 282658

KIDDLE, Canon John. b 58. Qu Coll Cam BA80 MA83 Heythrop Coll Lon MTh02. Ridley Hall Cam 79. d 82 p 83. C Ormskirk *Liv* 82-86; V Huyton Quarry 86-91; V Watford St Luke *St Alb* 91-08; RD Watford 99-04; Officer for Miss and Development from 08; Hon Can St Alb 05-10; Can Res from 10. *19 Stanbury Avenue, Watford WD17 3HW* Tel (01923) 460083 or (01727) 851748 E-mail john.kiddle@stalbans.anglican.org

KIDDLE, Mark Brydges. b 34. ACP61. Wycliffe Hall Ox. d 63 p 64. C Scarborough St Luke *York* 63-66; C Walthamstow St Sav *Chelmsf* 66-71; V Nelson St Bede *Blackb* 71-76; V Perry Common *Birm* 76-79; R Grayingham *Linc* 79-84; V Kirton in Lindsey 79-84; R Manton 79-84; Hon C St Botolph Aldgate w H Trin Minories *Lon* 85-91; Hon C St Clem Eastcheap w St Martin Orgar 91-08. *12 Tudor Rose Court, 35 Fann Street, London EC2Y 8DY* E-mail mk@fpsi.org

KIDDLE, Martin John. b 42. Open Univ BA80. St Jo Coll Nottm 74. d 76 p 77. C Gt Parndon *Chelmsf* 76-80; Asst Chapl HM Pris Wakef 80-81; Asst Chapl HM Youth Cust Cen Portland 81-88; Chapl HM Pris Cardiff 88-97; Chapl HM Pris Channings Wood 97-02; rtd 02; Perm to Offic *Ex* 02-09. *2 Cricketfield Close, Chudleigh, Newton Abbot TQ13 0GA* Tel (01626) 853980 E-mail mkiddle@talktalk.net

KIDDLE, Miss Susan Elizabeth. b 44. Birm Univ BSc66 Nottm Univ CertEd67. d 89 p 95. OLM Waddington *Linc* 89-97; OLM Bracebridge 98-06; Perm to Offic from 06. *Rose Cottage, 30 Finningley Road, Lincoln LN6 0UP*

KIGALI, Bishop of. *See* KOLINI, The Most Revd Emmanuel Musaba

KIGGELL, Mrs Anne. b 36. Liv Univ BA57. SAOMC 99. d 02 p 03. OLM Basildon w Aldworth and Ashampstead *Ox* from 02. *Straight Ash, Ashampstead Common, Reading RG8 8QT* Tel (01635) 201385 E-mail anne.kiggell@virgin.net

KIGHTLEY, Canon David John. b 39. AKC67. d 68 p 69. C Plymouth St Andr *Ex* 68-70; C Ex St Dav 70-73; Chapl Greenwich Distr Hosp & Brook Gen Hosp Lon 73-76; P-in-c Chippenham *Ely* 76-96; P-in-c Snailwell 76-96; P-in-c Isleham 76-96; RD Fordham 95-96; P-in-c Feltwell 96-98; P-in-c Methwold 96-98; R Feltwell and Methwold 98-05; RD Feltwell 96-04; RD Fincham 98-04; RD Fincham and Feltwell 04-05; Hon Can Ely Cathl 00-05; rtd 05; Perm to Offic *Nor* from 06 and *Ely* from 07. *53 Churchill Road, Thetford IP24 2JZ* Tel (01842) 753079 E-mail davidkightley@aol.com

KILBEY, Mrs Sarah. b 39. MBE98. Edin Univ MA75 Man Poly CETD82. Bp Otter Coll TDip59 Edin Dioc NSM Course 84. d 93 p 97. NSM Edin St Columba 93-96; NSM Edin St Martin from 96. *77 Morningside Park, Edinburgh EH10 5EZ* Tel 0131-447 2378

KILBOURN-MACKIE, Canon Mary Elizabeth. b 26. Toronto Univ MA48 Harvard Univ MA49. Trin Coll Toronto MDiv78 Hon DD02. d 77 p 78. Canada 77-00; C Norway St Jo and Chapl Toronto Gen Hosp 78-80; Dir Chapl Toronto 80-89; Hon Can Toronto from 95; Perm to Offic *Sarum* and *B & W* from 01. *17 Chatham Court, Station Road, Warminster BA12 9LS* Tel (01985) 216167 E-mail meskm1807@hotmail.co.uk

KILCOOLEY, Christine. *See* ROBINSON, Mrs Christine Margaret Anne

KILDARE, Archdeacon of. *See* STEVENSON, The Ven Leslie Thomas Clayton

KILDARE, Dean of. *See* MARSDEN, The Very Revd John Joseph

KILFORD, John Douglas. b 38. Oak Hill Th Coll 73. d 75 p 76. C Beckenham St Jo *Roch* 75-80; P-in-c Sinfin Moor *Derby* 80-83; V Penge St Jo *Roch* 83-92; Staff Member Ellel Min 92-03; rtd 03; Perm to Offic *Truro* 03-07 and *Ely* from 10. *33 London Road, Godmanchester, Huntingdon PE29 2HZ*

KILFORD, William Roy. b 38. Bris Univ BA60. Sarum & Wells Th Coll 82. d 84 p 85. C Herne *Cant* 84-87; Chapl Wm Harvey Hosp Ashford 87-93; R Mersham w Hinxhill *Cant* 87-93; P-in-c Sevington 87-93; V Reculver and Herne Bay St Bart 93-95; Chapl Paphos Cyprus 95-98; P-in-c Doddington, Newnham and Wychling *Cant* 98-02; P-in-c Lynsted w Kingsdown 98-02; P-in-c AD Ospringe 01-02; rtd 02; Chapl Nord Pas de Calais *Eur* 02-04; Hon C Burton Fleming w Fordon, Grindale etc *York* 04-08; Chapl St Jo Hosp Cant 08-09; P-in-c Burpham *Chich* from 09; P-in-c Poling from 09. *The Vicarage, Burpham, Arundel BN18 9RJ* Tel (01903) 882948

KILGOUR, The Very Revd Richard Eifl. b 57. Edin Univ BD85. Edin Th Coll 81. d 85 p 86. C Wrexham *St As* 85-88; V Whitford 88-97; Ind Chapl 89-97; R Newtown w Llanllwchaiarn w Aberhafesp 97-03; RD Cedewain 01-03; Provost St Andr Cathl from 03; R Aberdeen St Andr from 03; P-in-c Aberdeen St Ninian from 03. *St Andrew's Cathedral, King Street, Aberdeen AB24 5AX* Tel (01224) 640119 E-mail provost@aberdeen.anglican.org *or* newrect@hotmail.com

KILLALA AND ACHONRY, Archdeacon of. *Vacant*

KILLALA, Dean of. *Vacant*

KILLALOE, KILFENORA AND CLONFERT, Dean of. *See* WHITE, The Very Revd Stephen Ross

KILLALOE, KILFENORA, CLONFERT AND KILMACDUAGH, Archdeacon of. *See* CARNEY, The Ven Richard Wayne

KILLE, Vivian Edwy. b 30. Tyndale Hall Bris 60. d 62 p 63. C Dublin Miss Ch *D & G* 62-66; I Emlaghfad *T, K & A* 66-74; I Aghadrumsee w Clogh and Drumsnatt 74-05; Can Clogh Cathl 93-05; rtd 05. *16 Greer House, 115 Castlereagh Road, Belfast BT5 5FF* Tel (028) 9073 1135 E-mail vek@hallelujah.demon.co.uk

KILLOCK, Alfred Kenneth. b 26. Cranmer Hall Dur 72. d 74 p 75. C Moor Allerton *Ripon* 74-79; Hon C Bolton St Jas w St Chrys *Bradf* 79-83; P-in-c Oakenshaw cum Woodlands 84-90; P-in-c Allerton 90-91; rtd 91; Perm to Offic *Bradf* 91-10. *18 Thorpe View, Ossett, Wakefield WF5 9NS* Tel (01924) 272544

KILLWICK, Canon Simon David Andrew. b 56. K Coll Lon BD80 AKC80. St Steph Ho Ox 80. d 81 p 82. C Worsley *Man* 81-84; TV 84-97; P-in-c Moss Side Ch Ch 97-06; R from 06; Hon Can Man Cathl from 04; AD Hulme from 07. *Christ Church Rectory, Monton Street, Manchester M14 4LT* Tel and fax 0161-226 2476 E-mail frskillwick@tiscali.co.uk

KILMISTER, David John. b 46. Open Univ BA88. d 06 p 07. OLM Chippenham St Paul w Hardenhuish etc *Bris* from 06; OLM Kington St Michael from 06. *22 The Common, Langley Burrell, Chippenham SN15 4LQ* Tel and fax (01249) 650926 Mobile 07747-331971 E-mail dave@kilmister.eclipse.co.uk

KILMORE, Archdeacon of. *See* McCAULEY, The Ven Craig William Leslie

KILMORE, Dean of. *See* FERGUSON, The Very Revd Wallace Raymond

KILMORE, ELPHIN AND ARDAGH, Bishop of. *See* CLARKE, The Rt Revd Kenneth Herbert

KILNER, Canon Frederick James. b 43. Qu Coll Cam BA65 MA69. Ridley Hall Cam 67. d 70 p 71. C Harlow New Town w Lt Parndon *Chelmsf* 70-74; C Cambridge St Andr Less *Ely* 74-79; P-in-c Milton 79-88; R 88-94; P-in-c Ely 94-96; P-in-c Chettisham 94-96; P-in-c Prickwillow 94-96; P-in-c Stretham w Thetford 94-96; P-in-c Stuntney 95-96; TR Ely 96-08; Hon Can Ely Cathl 88-08; Hon C Somersham w Pidley and Oldhurst and Woodhurst from 08; RD St Ives from 10. *125 High Street, Somersham, Huntingdon PE28 3EN* Tel (01487) 842864 E-mail kilner@btinternet.com

KILNER, James Martin. b 51. Solicitor 77. St Jo Coll Nottm BA03. d 07 p 07. P-in-c Sheff St Bart 07-08; V Grenoside from 08. *St Mark's Vicarage, 19 Graven Close, Grenoside, Sheffield S35 8QT* Tel 0114-246 7513 Mobile 07931-582547 E-mail martin.kilner@sheffield.anglican.org

KILNER, Mrs Valerie June. b 42. Univ of Wales (Abth) BSc64 Hughes Hall Cam PGCE65 MICFM91. EAMTC 98. d 98 p 99. NSM Ely 98-08; Perm to Offic from 08. *125 High Street, Somersham, Huntingdon PE28 3EN* Tel (01487) 842864 E-mail vjkilner@btinternet.com

KILPATRICK, Alan William. b 64. Oak Hill Th Coll BA96. d 96 p 97. C Ealing St Paul *Lon* 96-01; Assoc R Mt Pleasant USA 01-04; P-in-c Prestonville St Luke *Chich* 04-09; S Africa from 09. *16 Waterloo Road, Wynberg Road, Cape Town, 7800 South Africa*

KILSBY, Miss Joyce (Jocelyn). b 40. Univ Coll Lon BSc62 Ox Univ DipEd63. NOC 98. d 01 p 02. NSM Stanley *Wakef* from

01. *18 Hazelwood Court, Outwood, Wakefield WF1 3HP* Tel (01924) 824396 E-mail hilkil.hazco@virgin.net
KIM, Crispin Ho-Kwan. b 68. Sung-Gong-Hoe Univ Korea BA98. Trin Coll Bris MA03. **d** 07 **p** 09. C Nam-Yang-Ju St Fran Korea 07-09; C Dae-Hak-Ro St Bede 09; C Hendon St Alphage *Lon* from 09; Chapl Angl Korean Community from 09. *18 Montrose Avenue, Edgware HA8 0DW* Tel (020) 8621 0174 Mobile 07834-831022 E-mail kimcrispin@hotmail.com
KIMARU, Benson Mbure. b 54. St Andr Coll Kabare 81. **d** 83 **p** 84. V Mitunguu Kenya 85; Dioc Radio Producer 86-88; Asst to Provost Nairobi 88; V Kangaru 89-90; V Kayole 91-94; V Nyari 95-98; V Maringo 99-02; V Githurai 03-05; Perm to Offic *Sheff* 06-07; NSM Brightside w Wincobank from 07. *The Vicarage, Manchester Road, Thurlstone, Sheffield S36 9QS* Tel (01226) 764225 Mobile 07919-988131
E-mail benititu@googlemail.com
KIMBALL, Melodie Irene. b 49. **d** 99 **p** 06. USA 99-01; Chapl Asst S Man Univ Hosps NHS Trust 01-02; Asst Chapl Qu Medical Cen Nottm Univ Hosp NHS Trust 02-03; Chapl Leeds Mental Health Teaching NHS Trust from 03; Hon C Far Headingley St Chad *Ripon* from 06. *The Becklin Centre, Alma Street, Leeds LS9 7BE* Tel 0113-305 6639
E-mail melodie.kimball@leedsmh.nhs.uk
KIMBER, Geoffrey Francis. b 46. Univ Coll Lon BA67 Birm Univ MPhil01. St Jo Coll Nottm 86. **d** 88 **p** 89. C Buckhurst Hill *Chelmsf* 88-92; R Arley *Cov* 92-02; P-in-c Ansley 97-02; CMS Romania 02-07; R Birm Bp Latimer w All SS from 07. *Winson Green Vicarage, 28 Handsworth New Road, Birmingham B18 4PT* Tel and fax 0121-598 9093
E-mail geoff.kimber@gmail.com
KIMBER, Mrs Gillian Margaret. b 48. Bedf Coll Lon BA70. Oak Hill Th Coll 89. **d** 91. NSM Buckhurst Hill *Chelmsf* 91-92; C Arley *Cov* 92-97; C Ansley 97-02; CMS Romania 02-07; Perm to Offic *Birm* from 08. *Winson Green Vicarage, 28 Handsworth New Road, Birmingham B18 4PT* Tel and fax 0121-598 9093
E-mail gillkimber@gmail.com
KIMBER, Mrs Hazel Olive. b 33. Lon Univ CertEd73. **d** 95 **p** 96. OLM W Dulwich Em *S'wark* from 95. *18 Michaelson House, Kingswood Estate, London SE21 8PX* Tel (020) 8670 5298
KIMBER, John Keith. b 45. Bris Univ BSc66. St Mich Coll Llan. **d** 69 **p** 70. C Caerphilly *Llan* 69-72; Chapl Birm Univ 72-75; TR Bris St Agnes and St Simon w St Werburgh 75-82; P-in-c Bris St Paul w St Barn 80-82; Hon C Westbury-on-Trym H Trin 82-83; Area Sec (Wales) USPG 83-89; TR Halesowen *Worc* 89-92; Chapl Geneva *Eur* 92-01; Chapl Monte Carlo 01-02; TR Cen Cardiff *Llan* 02-06; V Cardiff City Par 07-10; rtd 10. *13 Meadow Street, Cardiff CF11 9PY* Tel (029) 2023 5809
E-mail johnkeith.k@gmail.com
KIMBER, Jonathan Richard. b 69. K Coll Cam BA91 MA95 St Jo Coll Dur MA02. Cranmer Hall Dur 99. **d** 02 **p** 03. C Weston Favell *Pet* 02-05; P-in-c Northampton St Benedict 05-10; V from 10. *St Benedict's Vicarage, 16 Sentinel Road, Northampton NN4 9UF* Tel (01604) 768624
E-mail jrkimber@yahoo.co.uk
KIMBER, Stuart Francis. b 53. Qu Eliz Coll Lon BSc74 Fitzw Coll Cam BA79 MA83. Ridley Hall Cam 77. **d** 80 **p** 81. C Edgware *Lon* 80-83; C Cheltenham St Mark *Glouc* 83-84; TV 84-92; C Hawkwell *Chelmsf* 92-01; V Westcliff St Andr from 01. *St Andrew's Vicarage, 65 Electric Avenue, Westcliff-on-Sea SS0 9NN* Tel (01702) 302255
E-mail revskimber@blueyonder.co.uk
KIMBERLEY, Canon Carol Lylie Wodehouse, Countess of. b 51. St Hugh's Coll Ox BA73 MA77 CertEd74. Ripon Coll Cuddesdon 87. **d** 89 **p** 94. NSM Hambleden Valley *Ox* 89-02; P-in-c Hormead, Wyddial, Anstey, Brent Pelham etc *St Alb* from 02; P-in-c Sandon, Wallington and Rushden w Clothall from 10; RD Buntingford from 06; Hon Can St Alb from 10. *The Vicarage, Great Hormead, Buntingford SG9 0NT* Tel (01763) 289258 E-mail ck@womvic.demon.co.uk
KIMBERLEY, John Harry. b 49. Brasted Th Coll 72 St Steph Ho Ox 74. **d** 76 **p** 77. C W Tarring *Chich* 76-79; C Portslade St Nic 79-82; C-in-c Findon Valley CD 82-89; V Findon Valley 89-90; V E Preston w Kingston 90-95; Chapl Eastbourne Hosps NHS Trust 95-06. *Address temp unknown*
KIMBERLEY, The Ven Owen Charles Lawrence. b 27. Univ of NZ BCom53. Tyndale Hall Bris 57. **d** 59 **p** 60. C Higher Openshaw *Man* 59-62; New Zealand 62-94; C Nelson All SS 62-64; V Motupiko 64-69; V Kaikoura 69-76; V Tahunanui 76-85 76-85; Can Nelson Cathl 77-78; Adn Waimea 78-92; V Richmond 85-92; Egypt 94-98; Chapl Port Said 94-98; Adn Egypt 96-98. *11B Grigg Street, Richmond, Nelson 7020, New Zealand* Tel (0064) (3) 544 2115 E-mail okimberley@xtra.co.nz
KIME, Thomas Frederick. b 28. Linc Coll Ox BA50 MA53. Cuddesdon Coll 54. **d** 56 **p** 57. C Forest Gate St Edm *Chelmsf* 56-58; S Africa 58-74; R Ellisfield w Farleigh Wallop and Dummer *Win* 74-83; P-in-c Cliddesden 82-83; R Cliddesden and Ellisfield w Farleigh Wallop etc 83-94; rtd 94; Perm to Offic *Win* from 94. *6 Morley College, Market Street, Winchester SO23 9LF* Tel (01962) 870240

KIMMIS, Ms Sally Elizabeth. b 59. Westcott Ho Cam 08. **d** 10 **p** 11. C King's Lynn St Marg w St Nic *Nor* from 10. *10 Pilot Street, King's Lynn PE30 1QL* Tel 07548-741159 (mobile)
E-mail sally.kimmis@live.co.uk
KINAHAN, Canon Timothy Charles. b 53. Jes Coll Cam BA75. CITC 77. **d** 78 **p** 79. C Carrickfergus *Conn* 78-81; Papua New Guinea 81-84; I Belfast Whiterock *Conn* 84-90; I Gilnahirk *D & D* 90-96; I Helen's Bay from 06; Can Belf Cathl from 04. *The Rectory, 2 Woodland Avenue, Helen's Bay, Bangor BT19 1TX* Tel (028) 9185 3601
KINCH, Christopher David. b 81. K Alfred's Coll Win BTh02. St Steph Ho Ox 03. **d** 05 **p** 06. C Long Eaton St Laur *Derby* 05-09; TV Swindon New Town *Bris* 09-11; Partnership P Bris S from 11. *7 Petherton Road, Bristol BS14 9BP* Tel (01275) 834004
E-mail christopherkinch@btinternet.com
KINCHIN-SMITH, John Michael. b 52. Fitzw Coll Cam MA. Ridley Hall Cam 79. **d** 82 **p** 83. C Sanderstead All SS *S'wark* 82-87; TV Halesworth w Linstead, Chediston, Holton etc *St E* 87-92; R Mursley w Swanbourne and Lt Horwood *Ox* 92-02; R Newton Longville and Mursley w Swanbourne etc 03-06; R Chinnor, Sydenham, Aston Rowant and Crowell from 06. *The Rectory, High Street, Chinnor OX39 4DH* Tel (01844) 351309
E-mail johnks1881@aol.com
KINDER, David James. b 55. EAMTC 01. **d** 04 **p** 05. NSM Warboys w Broughton and Bury w Wistow *Ely* 04-08; Chapl HM Pris Littlehey from 08. *Chaplain, HM Prison Littlehey, Perry, Huntingdon PE28 0SR* Tel (01480) 335252
E-mail david.kinder@hmps.gsi.gov.uk
KINDER, Mark Russell. b 66. Univ of Wales (Swansea) BA(Econ)88. St Jo Coll Nottm 91. **d** 94 **p** 95. C Pleasley *Lich* 94-98; TV Tettenhall Regis 98-07; P-in-c Walsall St Paul 07-11; V from 11; C Walsall St Matt 07-11; V Walsall St Luke from 11; C Walsall Pleck and Bescot from 11. *St Paul's Vicarage, 57 Mellish Road, Walsall WS4 2DG* Tel (01922) 624963
KINDER, Mrs Sylvia Patricia. b 61. Ridley Hall Cam 03. **d** 05 **p** 06. C Warboys w Broughton and Bury w Wistow *Ely* 05-09; C Werrington *Pet* from 09. *6 Davids Close, Peterborough PE4 5AN* Tel 07876-204624 (mobile) E-mail sylvia@5kinders.com
KING, Mrs Angela Margaret. b 45. Bedf Coll Lon BA67 Lon Inst of Educn PGCE68. SEITE 00. **d** 03 **p** 04. NSM Bromley St Andr *Roch* from 03; P-in-c from 11. *4 Avondale Road, Bromley BR1 4EP* Tel and fax (020) 8402 0847
E-mail angelaking45@hotmail.com
KING, Anthony Richard. b 34. Trin Hall Cam BA58. Ely Th Coll 58 Linc Th Coll 61. **d** 62 **p** 63. C Benwell St Jas *Newc* 62-64; C Thirsk w S Kilvington *York* 64-67; V Halifax St Aug *Wakef* 67-74; R Upton on Severn *Worc* 74-99; RD Upton 86-92; rtd 99; Perm to Offic *Ex* from 99. *4 The Elms, Colyford, Colyton EX24 6QU* Tel (01297) 552666
KING, Benjamin John. b 74. Down Coll Cam BA96 MA00 Harvard Univ MTh03 Dur Univ PhD07. Westcott Ho Cam 97. **d** 00 **p** 00. C Boston the Advent USA 00-06; Chapl Harvard Univ 06-09; Asst Prof Univ of the South from 09. *University of the South, 335 Tennessee Avenue, Sewanee TN 37383, USA* Tel (001) (931) 598 1619 E-mail bjking@sewanee.edu
KING, Benjamin William. b 76. Dijon Univ BA97 Man Univ BA98 Univ Coll Lon MA Cam Univ BA05. Ridley Hall Cam 03. **d** 06 **p** 07. C Stanwix *Carl* 06-10; TV Chigwell and Chigwell Row *Chelmsf* from 10. *St Winifred's Vicarage, 115 Manor Road, Chigwell IG7 5PS* Tel (020) 8500 4608 Mobile 07752-708207
E-mail kingbw2001@yahoo.com
KING, Brian Henry. b 39. Chich Th Coll 63. **d** 65 **p** 66. C Castle Bromwich SS Mary and Marg *Birm* 65-67; C Southwick St Mich *Chich* 68-70; V Southwater 70-73; C Brighton St Alb Preston 73-74; TV Brighton Resurr 74-75; V Eastbourne St Elisabeth 75-96; rtd 96; Perm to Offic *Chich* 96-11. *17 Hartford House, Blount Road, Portsmouth PO1 2TN* Tel (023) 9281 7051
KING, Caroline Naomi. b 62. New Coll Edin BD94. Ripon Coll Cuddesdon 94. **d** 97 **p** 98. C Wheatley *Ox* from 97. *The Vicarage, Holton, Oxford OX33 1PR* Tel (01865) 873451
E-mail caroline.king1@ntlworld.com
KING, Christopher John. b 56. Chelsea Coll Lon BSc78 CertEd79. St Jo Coll Nottm LTh87. **d** 88 **p** 89. C Wandsworth All SS *S'wark* 88-92; Canada from 92; R Geraldton w Jellicoe, Longlac, Collins etc 92-97; R Toronto Lt Trin Ch from 97. *425 King Street East, Toronto ON M5A 1L3, Canada* Tel (001) (416) 367 0272 Fax 367 2074 E-mail chrisking@sympatico.ca
KING, Clare Maria. b 68. St Andr Univ BD91 K Coll Lon MPhil98. Westcott Ho Cam 91. **d** 94. Hon C Norbury St Phil *S'wark* 94-96; Chapl Croydon Coll 95-96; Asst Chapl Cen Sheff Univ Hosps NHS Trust 96-01; C Leic Presentation 02-08; C Leic St Chad from 08. *The Vicarage, 12 Saddington Road, Fleckney, Leicester LE8 8AW* Tel 0116-240 2215
KING, Mrs Daphne Eileen. b 37. EMMTC 78. **dss** 81 **d** 87 **p** 94. Theddlethorpe *Linc* 84-89; Dn-in-c 87-89; Saltfleetby 84-89; Dn-in-c 87-89; Dn-in-c Healing and Stallingborough 89-94; P-in-c 94-97; rtd 97; Perm to Offic *Linc* 99-02. *28 Charles Street, Louth LN11 0LE* Tel (01507) 606062
E-mail daphneking@lud28.freeserve.co.uk

KING, David Charles. b 52. K Coll Lon 73 Coll of Resurr Mirfield 77. **d** 78 **p** 79. C Saltburn-by-the-Sea *York* 78-81; Youth Officer 81-85; P-in-c Crathorne 81-85; Par Educn Adv *Wakef* 85-91; Min Coulby Newham LEP *York* 91-94; P-in-c Egton w Grosmont 94-00; P-in-c Goathland and Glaisdale 99-00; V Middle Esk Moor 00-07. *Address temp unknown*

KING, David Frederick. b 32. Sarum Th Coll 59. **d** 61 **p** 72. C Hanworth All SS *Lon* 61-62; Hon C Andover St Mich *Win* 71-83; P-in-c 83-88; V 88-90; Chapl R S Hants Hosp 90-92; Chapl Countess Mountbatten Hospice 90-92; Chapl Andover District Community Health Care NHS Trust from 92; Perm to Offic *Win* 92-97; rtd 97; P-in-c Smannell w Enham Alamein *Win* 97-04. *158 Weyhill Road, Andover SP10 3BG* Tel (01264) 365694

KING, David John. b 67. W Sussex Inst of HE BEd91. St Steph Ho Ox 98. **d** 00 **p** 01. C Bexhill St Pet *Chich* 00-03; TV 03-08; V Eastbourne St Andr from 08. *St Andrew's Vicarage, 425 Seaside, Eastbourne BN22 7RT* Tel (01323) 723739

KING, David Michael. b 73. St Jo Coll Dur BA95 PGCE96 Cam Univ BA02. Ridley Hall Cam 00. **d** 03 **p** 04. C Claygate *Guildf* 03-07; C Redhill H Trin *S'wark* 07-10; C Wallington from 10. *St Patrick's House, 47 Park Hill Road, Wallington SM6 0RU* Tel (020) 8647 1026 Mobile 07901-700958 E-mail davaid.king@stpats.org.uk

KING, Canon David Russell. b 42. Univ of Wales (Lamp) BA67. St D Coll Lamp. **d** 68 **p** 69. C Barrow St Geo w St Luke *Carl* 68-72; P-in-c Kirkland 72-74; V Edenhall w Langwathby 72-73; P-in-c Culgaith 72-73; V Edenhall w Langwathby and Culgaith 73-74; V Flookburgh 75-79; V Barrow St Jas 79-82; P-in-c Bolton w Ireby and Uldale 82-83; R 83-90; R Burgh-by-Sands and Kirkbampton w Kirkandrews etc 90-00; P-in-c Aikton and Orton St Giles 95-00; R Barony of Burgh 00-02; P-in-c Gt Broughton and Broughton Moor 02-05; V Brigham, Gt Broughton and Broughton Moor 05-07; Hon Can Carl Cathl 01-07; rtd 07; Hon C Aspatria w Hayton and Gilcrux *Carl* from 10. *27 King Street, Aspatria, Wigton CA7 3AF* Tel (01697) 323580 E-mail candrking@dsl.pipex.com

KING, David William Anthony. b 42. Ch Ch Ox BA63 MA68. Westcott Ho Cam 63. **d** 65 **p** 66. C Cayton w Eastfield *York* 65-68; C Southbroom *Sarum* 68-71; V Holt St Jas 71-72; R Hinton Parva 71-72; V Holt St Jas and Hinton Parva 72-75; P-in-c Horton and Chalbury 73-75; R Holt St Jas, Hinton Parva, Horton and Chalbury 75-79; TV Melton Mowbray w Thorpe Arnold *Leic* 79-83; V Foxton w Gumley and Laughton and Lubenham 83-90; P-in-c Boreham *Chelmsf* 90-00; R Tendring and Lt Bentley w Beaumont cum Moze 00-06; rtd 06; Perm to Offic *Ely* from 06. *14 The Hythe, Reach, Cambridge CB25 0JQ* Tel (01638) 742924

KING, Dennis. b 31. ACA53 FCA64. EMMTC 73. **d** 76 **p** 77. NSM Chesterfield St Mary and All SS *Derby* 76-00; Perm to Offic from 00. *Hillcrest, Stubben Edge, Ashover, Chesterfield S45 0EU* Tel (01246) 590279

KING, Dennis Keppel. b 33. Lich Th Coll 63. **d** 65 **p** 66. C Eccleston St Thos *Liv* 65-68; C W Derby St Mary 68-71; V Aintree St Giles 71-96; rtd 96; Perm to Offic *York* from 96 and *Liv* 00-05. *8 Whiteoak Avenue, Easingwold, York YO61 3GB* Tel (01347) 822625 E-mail dennis.k.king@btinternet.com

KING, Derek Edwin Noel. b 31. Qu Mary Coll Lon BSc54 Birkbeck Coll Lon PhD60. **d** 93 **p** 94. OLM Nacton and Levington w Bucklesham etc *St E* 93-09; Perm to Offic from 09. *Vindelis, 1 Eastcliff, Felixstowe IP11 9TA* Tel and fax (01394) 270815

KING, Canon Fergus John. b 62. St Andr Univ MA Edin Univ BD89. Edin Th Coll 86. **d** 89 **p** 90. Chapl St Jo Cathl Oban 89-92; C Oban St Jo 89-92; Tanzania 92-98; Hon Can and Can Th Tanga from 01; Perm to Offic *S'wark* 99-03; Hon C Thamesmead 03-05; R Kotara South Gd Shep Australia from 05. *The Rectory, 10 Melissa Avenue, Adamstown Heights NSW 2289, Australia* Tel (0061) (2) 4943 0103 E-mail revfking@bigpond.net.au

KING, George Henry. b 24. St Alb Minl Tr Scheme. **d** 79 **p** 80. Hon C Flamstead *St Alb* 79-98; Dioc Agric Chapl 90-98; Perm to Offic from 98. *Chad Lane Farm, Chad Lane, Flamstead, St Albans AL3 8HW* Tel (01582) 841648

KING, Mrs Gillian Daphne. b 38. EMMTC 79. **dss** 83 **d** 87 **p** 94. Knighton St Jo *Leic* 83-85; Clarendon Park St Jo w Knighton St Mich 86-89; Par Dn 87-89; Chapl Kingston and Esher Mental Health Services 89-93; Chapl Kingston and Esher Community Health Unit 93-97; Chapl Long Grove Hosp Epsom 90-92; Chapl Tolworth Hosp Surbiton 91-97; Chapl Kingston and Distr Community NHS Trust 94-97; TV Hale w Badshot Lea *Guildf* 99-05; V Egham Hythe 99-05; rtd 05; Perm to Offic *Guildf* from 06. *2 Fieldhurst Close, Addlestone KT15 1NN* Tel (01932) 846348 Mobile 07775-724090 E-mail g.king1nn@btinternet.com

KING, James Anthony. b 46. CBE76. K Coll Lon BA69 AKC69 Lon Inst of Educn DipEd77. SAOMC 99. **d** 01 **p** 02. NSM Gerrards Cross and Fulmer *Ox* 01-03; NSM S Tottenham St Ann *Lon* 03-08; NSM Chalfont St Peter *Ox* from 08.

7 Meadowcroft, Chalfont St Peter, Gerrards Cross SL9 9DH Tel (01753) 887386 E-mail jim@jimking.co.uk

KING, Canon Jeffrey Douglas Wallace. b 43. AKC67. **d** 68 **p** 69. C S Harrow St Paul *Lon* 68-71; C Garforth *Ripon* 71-74; V Potternewton 74-83; TR Moor Allerton 83-99; RD Allerton 85-89; P-in-c Thorner and Dioc Ecum Officer 99-08; Hon Can Ripon Cathl 90-08; rtd 08; Perm to Offic *Ripon* from 09. *17 Barleyfields Terrace, Wetherby LS22 6PW* Tel (01937) 520646

KING, Jennifer. b 48. **d** 08 **p** 09. OLM Chorlton-cum-Hardy St Clem *Man* from 08. *8 St Clements Road, Manchester M21 9HU* Tel 0161-861 0898 Mobile 07918-702572 E-mail jen.king@stclement-chorlton.org.uk

KING, Jennifer Mary. b 41. Lon Univ BDS65 MSc75 PhD. Ripon Coll Cuddesdon 86. **d** 88 **p** 94. NSM S Hackney St Mich w Haggerston St Paul *Lon* 88-99; Chapl St Bart's and RLSMD Qu Mary and Westf Coll from 98; NSM St John-at-Hackney from 99. *83 Victoria Park Road, London E9 7NA* Tel (020) 7377 7000 ext 3069 *or* 7377 7167 E-mail jenny.king@qmul.ac.uk

KING, Jeremy Norman. *See* CLARK-KING, Jeremy Norman

KING, John. **d** 05 **p** 06. NSM Buckingham *Ox* from 05. *Wood End Farm, 2 Wood End, Nash, Milton Keynes MK17 0EL* Tel (01908) 501860 E-mail john@kingsfold100.freeserve.co.uk

KING, John. b 38. S'wark Ord Course 77. **d** 80 **p** 81. C S Gillingham *Roch* 80-85; Min Joydens Wood St Barn CD 85-90; V Borstal 90-98; Chapl HM Pris Cookham Wood 90-98; Chapl The Foord Almshouses 90-98; rtd 98; Perm to Offic *Cant* from 99. *14 Lamberhurst Way, Cliftonville, Margate CT9 3HH* Tel (01843) 229405 Mobile 07889-277195

KING, John Andrew. b 50. Qu Coll Birm 72. **d** 75 **p** 76. C Halesowen *Worc* 75-77; C Belper Ch Ch and Milford *Derby* 78-81; Perm to Offic from 87. *11 Well Lane, Milford, Belper DE56 0QQ* Tel (01332) 841810

KING, John Charles. b 27. St Pet Hall Ox BA51 MA55. Oak Hill Th Coll 51. **d** 53 **p** 54. C Slough *Ox* 53-57; V Ware Ch Ch *St Alb* 57-60; Ed *C of E Newspaper* 60-68; Lic to Offic *St Alb* 60-70; Teacher St Fran Bacon Sch St Alb 68-71; Boston Gr Sch 71-88; Lic to Offic *Linc* 74-92; rtd 92. *6 Somersby Way, Boston PE21 9PQ* Tel (01205) 363061

KING, John Colin. b 39. Cuddesdon Coll 69. **d** 71 **p** 72. C Cookham *Ox* 71-75; Youth Chapl *B & W* 75-80; P-in-c Merriott 76-80; P-in-c Hinton w Dinnington 79-80; R Merriott w Hinton, Dinnington and Lopen 80-04; rtd 04. *Les Chênes, Les Arquies, St Henri, 46000 Cahors, France* Tel (0033) 5 65 31 14 46

KING, Joseph Stephen. b 39. St Chad's Coll Dur BA62 MPhil83. **d** 64 **p** 65. C Lewisham St Mary *S'wark* 64-69; Hon C Milton next Gravesend Ch Ch *Roch* 70-85; V 85-07; rtd 07. *40 Thistledown, Gravesend DA12 5EU* Tel (01474) 748121 E-mail patandjoe48@blueyonder.co.uk

KING, Mrs Katharine Mary. b 63. St Hugh's Coll Ox BA85 MA89 SS Coll Cam BA88. Ridley Hall Cam 86. **d** 89 **p** 94. C Ipswich St Aug *St E* 89-91; NSM Bures 92-02; NSM Bures w Assington and Lt Cornard from 02. *The Vicarage, Church Square, Bures CO8 5AA* Tel (01787) 227315 Mobile 07984-010485 E-mail kmking100@gmail.com

KING, Malcolm Charles. b 37. Chich Th Coll 67. **d** 70 **p** 71. C Mill End *St Alb* 70-72; Chapl RAF 72-76; R W Lynn *Nor* 76-81; V Croxley Green All SS *St Alb* 81-90; V Grimsby St Aug *Linc* 90-99; Asst Local Min Officer 90-95; V Bury w Houghton and Coldwaltham and Hardham *Chich* 99-02; rtd 02; OGS from 90; Perm to Offic *Chich* from 02; Warden Community of St Pet Woking 02-03. *25 Riverside Court, Station Road, Pulborough RH20 1RG* Tel (01798) 875213

KING, Malcolm Stewart. b 56. Sarum & Wells Th Coll 77. **d** 80 **p** 81. C Farnham *Guildf* 80-83; C Chertsey and Chapl St Pet Hosp Chertsey 83-86; V Egham Hythe *Guildf* 86-91; TR Cove St Jo 91-98; RD Aldershot 93-98; V Dorking w Ranmore 98-04; Hon Can Guildf Cathl 99-04; RD Dorking 01-04; P-in-c Portsea N End St Mark *Portsm* 04-06; TR 06-07; Warden Iona Community *Arg* from 07; Lic to Offic from 08. *The Abbey, Isle of Iona PA76 6SN* Tel (01681) 700404 Fax 700460 E-mail malcolmsking@gmail.com *or* warden@iona.org.uk

KING (née COWIE), Mrs Margaret Harriet. b 53. Glas Univ BSc76 AMA85 FMA97. TISEC 95. **d** 98 **p** 99. NSM Montrose and Inverbervie *Bre* 98-05; Dioc Dir of Ord 00-05; TV N Hinckford *Chelmsf* from 05. *The Vicarage, Great Henny, Sudbury CO10 7NW* Tel (01787) 269385 Mobile 07855-558056 E-mail mandgking39@hotmail.com

KING, Marie. b 40. CertEd78. **d** 03 **p** 04. OLM Addiscombe St Mildred *S'wark* 03-10; Perm to Offic from 10. *8 Annandale Road, Croydon CR0 7HP* Tel (020) 8654 2651 E-mail marieking@8annan.fsnet.co.uk

KING, Martin Harry. b 42. St Jo Coll Cam MA68 MBCS85. SAOMC 03. **d** 05 **p** 06. NSM Wheathampstead *St Alb* from 05; Dioc Environment Officer from 08. *29 Parkfields, Welwyn Garden City AL8 6EE* Tel (01707) 328905 E-mail martin@king-priestley.freeserve.co.uk

KING, Martin Peter James. b 73. Bris Univ BEng95. Oak Hill Th Coll BA05. **d** 05 **p** 06. C Leamington Priors St Paul *Cov* 05-09; V

Rudgwick *Chich* from 10. *The Vicarage, Cox Green, Rudgwick, Horsham RH12 3DD* Tel (01403) 822127
E-mail martinthevicar@googlemail.com

KING, Martin Quartermain. b 39. Reading Univ BA61. Cuddesdon Coll 62. **d** 64 **p** 65. C S Shields St Hilda w St Thos *Dur* 64-66; C Newton Aycliffe 66-71; V Chilton Moor 71-78; R Middleton St George 78-91; R Sedgefield 91-04; RD Sedgefield 91-96; Chapl Co Dur & Darlington Priority Services NHS Trust 91-04; rtd 04. *3 White House Drive, Sedgefield, Stockton on Tees TS21 3BX* Tel (01740) 620424
E-mail martin.king@durham.anglican.org

KING, Michael Charles. Worc Coll Ox BA56 MA60. Coll of Resurr Mirfield. **d** 62 **p** 63. Hon C Hampstead All So *Lon* 62-65; Ed Asst SCM Press 62-65; C Thorpe St Andr *Nor* 66-69; Ed Sec BRF 69-90; Hon C Queensbury All SS *Lon* 69-79; Hon C Lt Stanmore St Lawr 80-90; R Cawston w Haveringland, Booton and Brandiston *Nor* 91-96; P-in-c Heydon 94-96; R Cawston w Booton and Brandiston etc 96-01; rtd 01; Perm to Offic *Leic* from 01. *84 Beacon Road, Loughborough LE11 2BH* Tel (01509) 563103

KING, Nathan Richard. b 68. Whitelands Coll Lon BA89 Univ of Wales (Cardiff) BTh94 Man Univ MA00. St Mich Coll Llan 91. **d** 94 **p** 95. C Hawarden *St As* 94-99; P-in-c 99-00; P-in-c Coreley w Doddington *Heref* 00-02; P-in-c Knowbury w Clee Hill 00-02; TV Ellesmere Port *Ches* 02-07. *Thornycroft, Aston Hill, Ewloe CH5 3AL* E-mail nathanking@onetel.com

KING, Nicholas Bernard Paul. b 46. Wycliffe Hall Ox 72. **d** 75 **p** 76. C Pitsmoor w Wicker *Sheff* 75-78; C Erdington St Barn *Birm* 78-80; C Sutton Coldfield H Trin 80-84; V Lynesack *Dur* 84-92; rtd 93. *16 Chatsworth Avenue, Bishop Auckland DL14 6AX* Tel (01388) 605614

KING, Patrick Stewart. b 84. St Chad's Coll Dur BA06. Westcott Ho Cam 08. **d** 10 **p** 11. C Dorchester *Sarum* from 10. *10 Treves Road, Dorchester DT1 2HD* Tel (01305) 267641
E-mail patrick.s.king@gmail.com

KING, Peter Duncan. b 48. TD. K Coll Lon LLB70 AKC70 Fitzw Coll Cam BA72 MA77. Westcott Ho Cam 72. **d** 80 **p** 81. Hon C Notting Hill *Lon* 80-84; Hon C Mortlake w E Sheen *S'wark* from 84; Dean MSE from 99. *49 Leinster Avenue, London SW14 7JW* Tel (020) 8876 8997 Fax 8287 9329
E-mail kingpd@hotmail.com

KING, Peter John Ryland. b 49. Kent Univ BA72 Ex Univ BPhil76 Cam Univ PhD84. Qu Coll Birm 06. **d** 09. NSM Northampton Em *Pet* from 09. *7 Manor Road, Pitsford, Northampton NN6 9AR* Tel (01604) 880522
E-mail p.j.r.king@open.ac.uk

KING, Peter William Stephen. b 65. St Steph Ho Ox BTh01. **d** 01 **p** 02. C Abertillery w Cwmtillery w Six Bells *Mon* 01-06; C Abertillery w Cwmtillery 06; CF from 06. *c/o MOD Chaplains (Army)* Tel (01264) 381140 Fax 381824

KING, Miss Philipa Ann. b 65. Westcott Ho Cam 91. **d** 95 **p** 96. C Cambridge Ascension *Ely* 95-00; TV 00-02; TR from 02. *2 Stretten Avenue, Cambridge CB4 3EP* Tel (01223) 366665 *or* 315000 Mobile 07816-833363 E-mail pipking@btinternet.com *or* rectoratcastle@btinternet.com

KING, Richard Andrew. b 51. Linc Th Coll. **d** 84 **p** 85. C Bramhall *Ches* 84-87; V Heald Green St Cath 87-92; P-in-c Ashprington, Cornworthy and Dittisham *Ex* 92-99; RD Totnes 97-99; P-in-c Torquay St Jo and Ellacombe 99-02; P-in-c Stoneleigh and Dioc Spirituality Adv *Guildf* 02-07; P-in-c S Framland *Leic* from 08. *The Rectory, 7 Sycamore Lane, Wymondham, Melton Mowbray LE14 2AZ* Tel (01572) 787238 E-mail rking11@hotmail.com

KING, Richard David. b 63. Oak Hill Th Coll 87. **d** 90 **p** 91. C Foord St Jo *Cant* 90-94; P-in-c Orlestone w Snave and Ruckinge w Warehorne 94-02; Dioc Ecum Officer 97-02; CA Field Officer *Cant, Lon, Roch* and *S'wark* 02-06; Dioc Missr *Cant* 06-11; C Charing w Charing Heath and Lt Chart 06-11; P-in-c Kennington from 11. *The Vicarage, 212 Faversham Road, Kennington, Ashford TN24 9AF* Tel (01233) 622334
E-mail richarddking@hotmail.com

KING, Preb Robert Dan. b 57. Sarum & Wells Th Coll 92. **d** 94 **p** 95. C Heref H Trin 94-97; TV W Heref 97-00; V Weobley w Sarnesfield and Norton Canon from 00; P-in-c Letton w Staunton, Byford, Mansel Gamage etc 00-04; R from 04; Preb Heref Cathl from 10. *The Vicarage, Church Road, Weobley, Hereford HR4 8SD* Tel (01544) 318415
E-mail bobking@wbsnet.co.uk

KING, Canon Robin Lucas Colin. b 59. Dundee Univ MA81. Ridley Hall Cam 87. **d** 89 **p** 90. C Ipswich St Aug *St E* 89-92; V Bures 92-02; C Assington w Newton Green and Lt Cornard 00-02; V Bures w Assington and Lt Cornard from 02; RD Sudbury from 06; Hon Can St E Cathl from 08. *The Vicarage, Church Square, Bures CO8 5AA* Tel (01787) 227315 Mobile 07050-222719 E-mail robin@rolcking.orangehome.co.uk

KING, Stuart. b 77. **d** 10 **p** 11. NSM Bearwood *Ox* from 10; Chapl Bearwood Coll Wokingham from 10. *Bearwood College, Winnersh, Wokingham RG41 5BG* Tel 0118-974 8323
E-mail chaplain@bearwoodcollege.co.uk

KING, Tony Christopher. b 62. Lanc Univ BA83. Coll of Resurr Mirfield 83. **d** 86 **p** 87. C Stansted Mountfitchet *Chelmsf* 86-89; USPG 89-92; Botswana 90-92; C Chingford SS Pet and Paul *Chelmsf* 92-93. *252 Brettenham Road, London E17 5AY*

KING, Canon Walter Raleigh. b 45. New Coll Ox BA67 MA74. Cuddesdon Coll 71. **d** 74 **p** 75. C Wisbech SS Pet and Paul *Ely* 74-77; C Barrow St Geo w St Luke *Carl* 77-79; P-in-c Clifford *Heref* 79-83; P-in-c Cusop 79-83; P-in-c Hardwick 79-83; P-in-c Whitney w Winforton 81-84; R Cusop w Clifford, Hardwicke, Bredwardine etc 83-86; R Heref St Nic 86-92; Dir of Ords 86-92; Preb Heref Cathl 86-92; TR Huntingdon *Ely* 92-01; RD Huntingdon 94-99; Hon Can Ely Cathl 99-01; Vice Dean and Can Res Chelmsf Cathl 01-10; rtd 10. *20A Girdlers Road, London W14 0PU* Tel (020) 7603 2675
E-mail walterking@btinternet.com

KING, Zoë Elizabeth. St Mich Coll Llan. **d** 06 **p** 07. C Neath *Llan* 06-10; P-in-c Llansawel, Briton Ferry from 10. *14 Y Rhodfa, Tonna, Neath SA11 3JX* Tel (01639) 635738

KING-SMITH, Giles Anthony Beaumont. b 53. Univ Coll Ox BA75. Trin Coll Bris 86. **d** 88 **p** 89. C Gtr Corsham *Bris* 88-92; V Two Mile Hill St Mich 92-96; TV Ilfracombe, Lee, Woolacombe, Bittadon etc *Ex* from 96. *The Vicarage, Springfield Road, Woolacombe EX34 7BX* Tel (01271) 870467

KING-SMITH, Philip Hugh (Brother Robert Hugh). b 28. CCC Cam BA52 MA56. Cuddesdon Coll 52. **d** 54 **p** 55. C Stockton St Pet *Dur* 54-59; V Bishopwearmouth Gd Shep 59-64; SSF from 64; USA from 66; rtd 98. *San Damiano, 573 Dolores Street, San Francisco CA 94110-1564, USA* Tel (001) (415) 861 1372 Fax 861 7952

KINGCOME, John Purkon. b 18. CEng50 MIMechE50. 3a1 um Th Coll. 65. **d** 67 **p** 68. C Melksham *Sarum* 67-70; P-in-c Woodborough w Manningford Bohun etc 70-72; R Swanborough 72-75; TR Swanborough 75-79; RD Pewsey 75-84; Custos St Jo Hosp Heytesbury 79-84; rtd 84; Perm to Offic *B & W* from 85-95 and Bris from 92. *28 Pitch and Pay Park, Bristol BS9 1NL* Tel 0117-968 3719

KINGDOM, Paul Anthony. b 62. Ex Univ BA83 FCA86 ATII87. STETS 07. **d** 10 **p** 11. NSM Burnham *B & W* from 10. *1 Red House Road, East Brent, Highbridge TA9 4RX* Tel (01278) 760920 Mobile 07803-922605
E-mail paul@kingdom.fsnet.co.uk

KINGDON, Mrs Margaret Victoria. b 44. SAOMC95. **d** 98 **p** 99. OLM Wokingham St Sebastian *Ox* 98-03. *Address temp unknown*

KINGHAM, Derek Henry. b 29. Oak Hill Th Coll 56. **d** 58 **p** 59. C Deptford St Jo *S'wark* 58-60; C Normanton *Derby* 60-63; R Gaulby w Kings Norton and Stretton Parva *Leic* 63-73; V Bacup St Sav *Man* 73-95; rtd 95; Perm to Offic *Carl* from 95. *3 The Green, Blencogo, Wigton CA7 0DF* Tel (01697) 361435

KINGHAM, Mair Josephine. *See* TALBOT, Canon Mair Josephine

KINGMAN, Paul Henry Charles. b 64. Reading Univ BSc86. Wycliffe Hall Ox BTh95. **d** 95 **p** 96. C Whitton *Sarum* 95-99; C Harold Wood *Chelmsf* 99-03; V Stone Ch Ch and Oulton *Lich* from 03. *Christ Church Vicarage, Bromfield Court, Stone ST15 8ED* Tel (01785) 812669

KINGS, Mrs Frances Bridget (Biddi). b 48. City Univ BSc70 Birm Univ MSc77. WEMTC 00. **d** 03 **p** 04. NSM Eckington and Defford w Besford *Worc* 03-06; NSM Powick and Guarlford and Madresfield w Newland 06-08; Perm to Offic 08-09; NSM Bowbrook N from 09; NSM Bowbrook S from 09. *Merebrook Farm, Hanley Swan, Worcester WR8 0DX* Tel (01684) 310950
E-mail biddi@merebrook.clara.co.uk

✠**KINGS, The Rt Revd Graham Ralph.** b 53. Hertf Coll Ox BA77 MA80 Utrecht Univ PhD02. Ridley Hall Cam 78. **d** 80 **p** 81 **c** 09. C Harlesden St Mark *Lon* 80-84; CMS Kenya 85-91; Dir Studies St Andr Inst Kabare 85-88; Vice Prin 89-91; Lect Miss Studies Cam Th Federation 92-00; Overseas Adv Henry Martyn Trust 92-95; Dir Henry Martyn Cen Westmr Coll Cam 95-00; Hon C Cambridge H Trin *Ely* 92-96; Hon C Chesterton St Andr 96-00; V Islington St Mary *Lon* 00-09; Area Bp Sherborne *Sarum* from 09; Can and Preb Sarum Cathl from 09. *Sherborne House, Tower Hill, Iwerne Minster, Blandford Forum DT11 8NH* Tel (01258) 859110 Fax 859118 E-mail gsherborne@salisbury.anglican.org

KINGS, Mrs Jean Alison. *See* THORN, Mrs Jean Alison

KINGSBURY, Canon Richard John. b 41. Lon Univ BA63. Linc Th Coll 65. **d** 67 **p** 68. C Wallsend St Luke *Newc* 67-69; C Monkseaton St Mary 69-70; Chapl K Coll Lon 70-75; V Hungerford and Denford *Ox* 75-83; R Caversham St Pet and Mapledurham 83-07; Hon Can Ch Ch 92-07; rtd 07. *14 Emgate, Bedale DL8 1AL* Tel and fax (01677) 424530
E-mail rj.kingsbury@tinyworld.co.uk

KINGSLEY, Brian St Clair. b 26. St Steph Ho Ox 56. **d** 59 **p** 60. C Tilehurst St Mich *Ox* 59-63; CSWG from 63; Prior from 85. *The Monastery of the Holy Trinity, Cuttinglye Lane, Crawley Down, Crawley RH10 4LH* Tel (01342) 712074

KINGSLEY, Miss Mary Phyllis Lillian. b 48. ERMC. **d** 09 **p** 10. NSM Croxley Green All SS *St Alb* from 09. *19 The Cloisters, Rickmansworth WD3 1HL* Tel (01923) 771172

KINGSLEY-SMITH, John Sydney. b 45. ARCM. Ridley Hall Cam 78. **d** 80 **p** 81. C Nailsea H Trin *B & W* 80-84; TV Whitton *Sarum* 84-91; V Chorleywood Ch Ch *St Alb* 91-01; RD Rickmansworth 98-01; rtd 01; Perm to Offic *St Alb* from 01. *29 Lewes Way, Croxley Green, Rickmansworth WD3 3SW* Tel (01923) 249949

KINGSMILL-LUNN, Brooke. See LUNN, Preb Brooke Kingsmill

KINGSTON, Canon Albert William. b 47. Bernard Gilpin Soc Dur 68 Oak Hill Th Coll 69. **d** 72 **p** 73. C Walton Breck *Liv* 72-74; C Templemore *D & R* 74-76; I Kildallon w Newtowngore and Corrawallen *K, E & A* 76-82; Bp's C Ardagh w Tashinny, Shrule and Kilcommick from 82; Can and Preb Elphin Cathl from 95. *Oakhill Lodge, Ardrahan, Ballymahon, Co Longford, Republic of Ireland* Tel (00353) (90) 643 8945 Mobile 87-919 5473

KINGSTON, Mrs Avril Dawson. b 34. Local Minl Tr Course 91. **d** 94 **p** 95. Aux Min Douglas Union w Frankfield *C, C & R* 94-02; rtd 02. *Ballymartin House, Glencairn, Lismore, Co Waterford, Republic of Ireland* Tel (00353) (58) 56227 E-mail purdy@gaelic.ie

KINGSTON (*née* LUCAS), Mrs Barbara Margaret. b 44. Lon Univ CertEd70. **d** 06 **p** 07. NSM Lee Gd Shep w St Pet *S'wark* from 06. *375 Westmount Road, London SE9 1NS* Tel (020) 8856 6468 E-mail barbarakingston44@yahoo.co.uk

KINGSTON, Desmond. See KINGSTON, John Desmond George

KINGSTON, Canon Eric. b 24. **d** 69 **p** 70. C Ballymacarrett St Patr *D & D* 69-72; C Knock 72-76; I Annahilt w Magherahamlet 76-93; rtd 93; Can and Prec Dromore Cathl 93. *38 Kinedale Park, Ballynahinch BT24 8YS* Tel (028) 9756 5715

KINGSTON, George Mervyn. b 47. CITC 70. **d** 73 **p** 74. C Comber *D & D* 73-77; C Belfast St Donard 77-80; Min Can Down Cathl 80-84; Bp's C Lecale Gp 82-84; Bp's C Belfast St Andr *Conn* 84-90; I Ballymascanlan w Creggan and Rathcor *Arm* 90-03; V Choral Arm Cathl 03-07; rtd 07. *The Cloisters, 36 Seahill Road, Holywood BT18 0DJ* Tel and fax (028) 9042 5016 Mobile 07816-462107 E-mail creggan@iolfree.ie

KINGSTON, John Desmond George. b 40. TCD BA63 MA66. CITC 64. **d** 64 **p** 65. C Arm St Mark 64-70; Hon V Choral Arm Cathl 69-70; Chapl Portora R Sch Enniskillen 70-01; Lic to Offic *Clogh* 70-01; Can Clogh Cathl 96-01; rtd 01. *Ambleside, 45 Old Rossory Road, Enniskillen BT74 7LF* Tel (028) 6632 4493

KINGSTON, Canon Kenneth Robert. b 42. TCD BA65 MA69. **d** 66 **p** 67. C Enniscorthy *C & O* 66-72; C Ballymena *Conn* 70-72; C Drumragh w Mountfield *D & R* 72-78; I Badoney Lower w Greenan and Badoney Upper 78-84; I Desertmartin w Termoneeny from 84; Can Derry Cathl from 99. *25 Dromore Road, Desertmartin, Magherafelt BT45 5JZ* Tel (028) 7963 2455

KINGSTON, Malcolm Trevor. b 75. QUB BSc97 MSc98 TCD BTh04. CITC 01. **d** 04 **p** 05. C Portadown St Mark *Arm* 04-07; I Kilmore St Aid w St Sav from 07. *38 Vicarage Road, Portadown, Craigavon BT62 4HF* Tel (028) 3833 2664 E-mail malcolm.kingston@btinternet.com

KINGSTON, Michael Joseph. b 51. K Coll Lon BD73 AKC73. St Aug Coll Cant 73. **d** 74 **p** 75. C Reading H Trin *Ox* 74-77; C New Eltham All SS *S'wark* 77-83; V Plumstead Ascension 83-94; Sub-Dean Greenwich N 92-94; V Sydenham St Bart from 94; RD W Lewisham from 04. *St Bartholomew's Vicarage, 4 Westwood Hill, London SE26 6QR* Tel (020) 8778 5290 E-mail thekingstons@btopenworld.com

KINGSTON, Michael Marshall. b 54. St Jo Coll Nottm MA94. **d** 96 **p** 97. C Drayton w Felthorpe *Nor* 96-99; R Gt and Lt Plumstead w Thorpe End and Witton 99-09; RD Blofield 06-08; Chapl Norfolk Primary Care Trust 01-09; TR Hempnall *Nor* from 09. *The Rectory, The Street, Hempnall, Norwich NR15 2AD* Tel (01508) 498157

KINGSTON, Robert George. b 46. TCD BA68 Div Test69. **d** 69 **p** 72. C Belfast St Thos *Conn* 69-72; C Kilkenny St Canice Cathl 72-75; I Ballinasloe w Taughmaconnell *L & K* 77-79; I Maryborough w Dysart Enos and Ballyfin *C & O* 79-85; I Lurgan w Billis, Killinkere and Munterconnaught *K, E & A* 85-88; Registrar Kilmore 87-92; I Lurgan etc w Ballymachugh, Kildrumferton etc 88-92; I Tallaght *D & G* 92-98; Warden of Readers 93-98; I Mallow Union *C, C & R* 98-07; I Carrickmacross w Magheracloone *Clogh* from 07. *The Rectory, Drumconrath Road, Carrickmacross, Co Monaghan, Republic of Ireland* Tel (00353) (42) 966 1931 E-mail rgk@eircom.net

KINGSTON, Roy William Henry. b 31. Chich Th Coll 60. **d** 62 **p** 63. C Leeds St Aid *Ripon* 62-66; S Africa 66-73; V Bramley *Ripon* 74-81; TR Hemel Hempstead *St Alb* 81-85; TR Fareham H Trin *Portsm* 85-93; RD Alverstoke 89-90; RD Fareham 90-93; P-in-c Hambledon 93-97; rtd 97; Perm to Offic *Guildf, Portsm* and *Win* from 97. *8 Pengilly Road, Farnham GU9 7XQ* Tel (01252) 711371 Mobile 07855-457670 E-mail roy@roykingston.plus.com

KINGSTON-UPON-THAMES, Area Bishop of. See CHEETHAM, The Rt Revd Richard Ian

KINGTON, Canon David Bruce. b 45. Trin Coll Bris 72. **d** 72 **p** 73. C Wellington w Eyton *Lich* 72-77; C Boscombe St Jo *Win* 77-81; R Michelmersh, Timsbury, Farley Chamberlayne etc 81-98; R Michelmersh and Awbridge and Braishfield etc 86-10; RD Romsey 95-05; Hon Can Win Cathl 02-10; rtd 11; Perm to Offic *Win* from 11. *St Swithun's Cottage, Main Road, Littleton, Winchester SO22 6QS* Tel (01962) 882698 E-mail dbruce.kington245@btinternet.com

KINKEAD, John Alfred Harold. b 84. TCD BA06. CITC BTh10. **d** 10. C Cregagh *D & D* from 10. *54 Rochester Avenue, Belfast BT6 9JW* Tel (028) 9079 6193 E-mail kinkeadj@gmail.com

KINNA, Preb Michael Andrew. b 46. Chich Th Coll 84. **d** 86 **p** 87. C Leominster *Heref* 86-90; TV Wenlock 90-93; R Broseley w Benthall, Jackfield, Linley etc from 94; P-in-c Coalbrookdale, Iron-Bridge and Lt Wenlock 07-11; RD Telford Severn Gorge 03-10; Preb Heref Cathl from 07. *The Rectory, Church Street, Broseley TF12 5DA* Tel and fax (01952) 882647 E-mail mak@ridewise.fsnet.co.uk

KINNAIRD, Jennifer. b 41. Hull Univ BA62 Ex Univ PGCE63. NEOC 94. **d** 97 **p** 98. NSM Corbridge w Halton and Newton Hall *Newc* 97-11; rtd 11. *17 Glebelands, Corbridge NE45 5DS* Tel (01434) 632695 E-mail j.kinnaird@btopenworld.com

KINNAIRD, Keith. b 42. Chich Th Coll 72. **d** 75 **p** 76. C Didcot St Pet *Ox* 75-78; C Abingdon w Shippon 78-82; P-in-c Sunningwell 82-90; P-in-c Radley 88-90; R Radley and Sunningwell 90-95; Chapl Abingdon Hosp 79-92; V Old Shoreham *Chich* 95-00; V New Shoreham 95-00; V Caversham St Andr *Ox* 00-07; Voc Adv and Adv for Min of Healing 00-07; rtd 07; Perm to Offic *Ox* from 07. *2 Weaver Row, Garston Lane, Wantage OX12 7DZ* Tel and fax (01235) 760867 E-mail keithkinnaird@btinternet.com

KINSELLA, Joseph Thomas. b 78. St Jo Coll Nottm BA10. **d** 10. C Bromyard and Stoke Lacy *Heref* from 10. *12 Lower Thorn, Bromyard HR7 4AZ* Tel (01885) 489279

KINSELLA, Nigel Paul. b 66. Wolv Univ LLB95. Westcott Ho Cam 00. **d** 02 **p** 03. C Attleborough w Besthorpe *Nor* 02-03; C Quidenham Gp 03-05; R E w W Harling, Bridgham w Roudham, Larling etc 05-10; CF from 10. *c/o MOD Chaplains (Army)* Tel 01264 381140 Fax 381824 E-mail nigelkinsella@btinternet.com

KINSEY, Bruce Richard Lawrence. b 59. K Coll Lon BD81 AKC81 MTh86 MA94. Wycliffe Hall Ox. **d** 84 **p** 85. C Gt Stanmore *Lon* 84-88; C Shepherd's Bush St Steph w St Thos 88-91; Chapl and Fell Down Coll Cam 91-01; Hd Philosophy and RS Perse Sch Cam 01; Perm to Offic *Ely* from 07. *The Perse School, Hills Road, Cambridge CB2 8QF* Tel (01223) 3568266 E-mail brkinsey@perse.co.uk

KINSEY, Paul. b 56. Nottm Univ BTh89. Linc Th Coll 86. **d** 89 **p** 90. C Connah's Quay *St As* 89-91; Min Can St As Cathl 91-94; Asst Chapl Univ Coll Lon Hosps NHS Trust 94-00; R S Lynn *Nor* 00-11; Ind Chapl 00-11. *13 Bridewell Street, Little Walsingham, Fakenham NR22 6BJ* Tel (01328) 820925

KINSEY, Russell Frederick David. b 34. Sarum Th Coll 59. **d** 62 **p** 63. C Twerton *B & W* 62-66; C N Cadbury 66-76; C Yarlington 66-76; P-in-c Compton Pauncefoot w Blackford 66-76; P-in-c Maperton 66-76; P-in-c N Cheriton 66-76; TV Camelot Par 76-79; V Pill 79-82; P-in-c Easton-in-Gordano w Portbury and Clapton 80-82; V Pill w Easton in Gordano and Portbury 82-92; rtd 94. *25 Newbourne Road, Weston-super-Mare BS22 8NF*

KINSMEN, Barry William. b 40. Chan Sch Truro. **d** 74 **p** 75. NSM Padstow *Truro* 74-78; Dioc Adv in RE 79-95; P-in-c St Issey 80-81; P-in-c Lt Petherick 80-81; R St Issey w St Petroc Minor 81-95; rtd 95; Perm to Offic *Truro* from 95. *14 Old School Court, School Hill, Padstow PL28 8ED* Tel (01841) 532507

KIPLING, Miss Susan Jane. b 49. Girton Coll Cam BA70 MA73. Westcott Ho Cam 04. **d** 06 **p** 08. C Old Basing and Lychpit *Win* 06-07; C N Hants Downs 07-10; R Brington w Whilton and Norton etc *Pet* from 10. *The Rectory, Main Street, Great Brington, Northampton NN7 4JB* Tel (01604) 770402 E-mail suekipling@btinternet.com

KIPPAX, Canon Michael John. b 48. Open Univ BA82. SWMTC 89. **d** 92 **p** 93. C Camborne *Truro* 92-95; C Woughton *Ox* 95-96; TV 96-98; R St Illogan *Truro* from 98; Hon Can Truro Cathl from 08. *The Rectory, Robartes Terrace, Illogan, Redruth TR16 4RX* Tel (01209) 842233 E-mail mike@saint-illogan.org.uk

KIRBY, Antony Philip. b 60. Leeds Univ BA11. Yorks Min Course 08. **d** 11. C Richmond w Hudswell and Downholme and Marske *Ripon* from 11. *1 Wathcote Place, Richmond DL10 7SR* Tel (01748) 850349 Mobile 07594-615190 E-mail antonykirby01@btinternet.com

KIRBY, Barbara Anne June (Sister Barbara June). b 34. St Andr Univ MA55. SAOMC 95. **d** 96 **p** 97. NSM Cowley St Jo *Ox* 96-05; rtd 06; Perm to Offic *Ox* from 06. *Convent of the Incarnation, Fairacres, Oxford OX4 1TB* Tel (01865) 721301

KIRBY, Bernard William Alexander (Alex). b 39. Keble Coll Ox BA62. Coll of Resurr Mirfield 62. **d** 65 **p** 72. C Is of Dogs Ch Ch and St Jo w St Luke *Lon* 65-66; Hon C Battersea St Phil *S'wark* 72; Hon C Battersea St Phil w St Bart 73-76; Perm to Offic 76-78

and 83-95. *28 Prince Edward Road, Lewes BN7 1BE* Tel (01273) 474935 Fax 486685

KIRBY, David Anthony. b 42. Dur Univ BA64 PhD68 Huddersfield Univ Hon DLitt98. NOC 84. **d** 87 **p** 88. NSM Crosland Moor *Wakef* 87-00; Asst Chapl Algarve *Eur* 00-05; Perm to Offic *Ripon* from 05. *4 North Mead, Bramhope, Leeds LS16 9DT* Tel 0113-267 8695 E-mail revdakirby@hotmail.com

KIRBY, David Graham. b 58. Univ of Wales (Cardiff) BA80. Wycliffe Hall Ox BA85 MA92. **d** 86 **p** 87. C Northallerton w Kirby Sigston *York* 86-89; C Southport Ch Ch *Liv* 89-92; R Bishop Burton w Walkington *York* 92-07; R Weston Favell *Pet* from 07; Warden Lay Past Min from 10. *The Rectory, Church Way, Northampton NN3 3BX* Tel (01604) 413218

KIRBY, Mrs Elizabeth. b 56. City Univ BSc79. ERMC 06. **d** 10 **p** 11. NSM Bury St Edmunds All SS w St Jo and St Geo *St E* from 10. *56 Eastgate Street, Bury St Edmunds IP33 1YW* Tel (01284) 701788 E-mail liz.kirby@btinternet.com

KIRBY, Mrs Joan Florence. b 32. St Hugh's Coll Ox MA57 Lon Univ BA66. St Alb Minl Tr Scheme 79. **d** 87 **p** 94. NSM Hemel Hempstead *St Alb* 87-90; C Blisland w St Breward *Truro* 90-94; NSM Cardynham 94-96; rtd 96; Perm to Offic *Truro* 96-04. *Skyber Goth, Tresarrett, Bodmin PL30 4QF* Tel (01208) 850252

KIRBY, Miss Kathryn Margaret. b 59. Girton Coll Cam BA74 MA78 Hughes Hall Cam PGCE75 Leeds Univ MA08 MCLIP82. Coll of Resurr Mirfield 06. **d** 07 **p** 08. NSM Sale St Paul *Ches* 07-09; NSM Gatley 09-10; V Macclesfield St Paul from 10. *St Paul's Vicarage, Swallow Close, Macclesfield SK10 1QN* Tel (01625) 422910 Mobile 07745-434266 E-mail k.m.kirby@btinternet.com *or* kathy.kirby@mbs.ac.uk

KIRBY, Maurice William Herbert. b 31. K Coll Lon CertEd AKC. **d** 55 **p** 56. C Eltham Park St Luke *S'wark* 55-56; C Horley 56-59; C Westbury *Sarum* 59-62; R Poulshot w Worton 62-66; P-in-c Gt Cheverell 65; P-in-c Burcombe 66-68; V 68-70; V Salisbury St Mich 70-73; Chapl SS Helen and Kath Sch Abingdon 73-79; Chapl and Hd RS Wrekin Coll Telford 79-84; V Frensham *Guildf* 84-93; Dir of Reader Tr 84-93; rtd 93; Perm to Offic *Ex* 93-94; *Chich* 94-97; *York* 01-03 and 04-10. *28 Thirsk Close, Market Rasen LN8 3EB*

KIRBY, Meg. b 50. STETS 03. **d** 06 **p** 07. NSM Portsea St Cuth *Portsm* 06-09; NSM Calne and Blackland *Sarum* 09-10; TV Marden Vale from 09. *7 Richmond Road, Calne SN11 9UW* Tel (01249) 815964 Mobile 07757-646807 E-mail meg@kirby.myzen.co.uk *or* calnepcc@gotadsl.co.uk

KIRBY, Paul Michael. b 51. Wycliffe Hall Ox 74 Seabury-Western Th Sem DMin99. **d** 76 **p** 77. C Gateacre *Liv* 76-79; C Barton Seagrave w Warkton *Pet* 79-83; V Bidston *Ches* 83-93; V Ormskirk *Liv* 93-99; Team Ldr Chapl E Kent Hosps NHS Trust 99-00; Sen Team Ldr Chapl from 00; Chapl Manager E and Coastal Kent Primary Care Trust from 08; Bp's Adv for Hosp Chapl *Cant* from 02. *William Harvey Hospital, Kennington Road, Willesborough, Ashford TN24 0LZ* Tel (01233) 633331 Mobile 07811-134383 E-mail paul.kirby@ekht.nhs.uk

KIRBY, Richard Arthur. b 48. Lon Univ BSc69. **d** 05 **p** 06. OLM Wellington All SS w Eyton *Lich* 05-07; Perm to Offic from 07. *4 Donnerville Gardens, Admaston, Telford TF5 0DE* Tel (01952) 411358 E-mail richard.kirby@lichfield.anglican.org

KIRBY, Simon Thomas. b 67. Lon Bible Coll BA92. NTMTC 00. **d** 03 **p** 04. C Woodside Park St Barn *Lon* 03-06; Lic Preacher from 06; Chapl Wren Academy from 08. *48 Bawtry Road, London N20 0ST* Tel (020) 8361 1545 Mobile 07967-838272

KIRBY, Stennett Roger. b 54. St Pet Coll Ox BA75 MA79. Sarum & Wells Th Coll 75. **d** 77 **p** 78. C Belsize Park *Lon* 77-79; NSM Plumstead St Nic *S'wark* 88; C Leic Ch Sav 90-91; TV Hanley H Ev *Lich* 91-95; P-in-c Walsall St Pet 95-01; V 01-07; V W Ham *Chelmsf* from 07. *The Vicarage, 94 Devenay Road, London E15 4AZ* Tel (020) 8519 0955 E-mail skcse15@virgin.net

KIRK, Alastair James. b 71. St Jo Coll Dur BSc93 PhD98 Fitzw Coll Cam BA06. Ridley Hall Cam 04. **d** 07 **p** 08. C Tong *Bradf* 07-10; C Laisterdyke 08-10; Chapl Warw Univ from 10. *92 De Montfort Way, Coventry CV4 7DT* Tel 07725-991073 (mobile) E-mail alastair.kirk@yahoo.co.uk

KIRK, Andrew. See KIRK, John Andrew

KIRK, Clive John Charles. b 37. TD81. FIBMS66. Guildf Dioc Min Course 95. **d** 98 **p** 99. OLM E Molesey St Paul *Guildf* 98-04; NSM E Horsley and Ockham w Hatchford and Downside 04-10; rtd 10. *The Rectory, Ockham Lane, Ockham, Woking GU23 6NP* Tel (01483) 210167 E-mail candakirk@lineone.net

KIRK, Miss Erika Cottam. b 55. Nottm Univ LLB76 Solicitor 81. St Jo Coll Nottm MA98. **d** 98 **p** 99. NSM Epperstone, Gonalston, Oxton etc *S'well* 98-03; NSM Burton Joyce w Bulcote and Stoke Bardolph *S'well* 03-08; NSM Edingley w Halam 08-10; NSM Gedling from 11. *24 St Helen's Crescent, Burton Joyce, Nottingham NG14 5DW* Tel 0115-931 4125 E-mail erika.kirk@ntu.ac.uk

KIRK, Canon Gavin John. b 61. Southn Univ BTh Heythrop Coll Lon MA. Chich Th Coll 83. **d** 86 **p** 87. C Seaford w Sutton *Chich* 86-89; Chapl and Succ Roch Cath 89-91; Min Can 89-91; Hon PV 91-98; Asst Chapl K Sch Roch 91-98; Can Res Portsm Cathl

98-03; Can Res and Prec Linc Cathl from 03. *The Precentory, 16 Minster Yard, Lincoln LN2 1PX* Tel (01522) 561632 E-mail precentor@lincolncathedral.com

KIRK, Geoffrey. b 45. Keble Coll Ox BA67. Coll of Resurr Mirfield 71. **d** 72 **p** 73. C Leeds St Aid *Ripon* 72-74; C St Marylebone St Mark w St Luke *Lon* 74-76; C Kennington St Jo *S'wark* 77-79; C Kennington St Jo w St Jas 79-81; P-in-c Lewisham St Steph and St Mark 81-87; V from 87. *St Stephen's Vicarage, Cressingham Road, London SE13 5AG* Tel (020) 8318 1295 Fax 8318 1446

KIRK, Miss Geraldine Mercedes. b 49. Hull Univ MA89. **d** 87 **p** 94. Ind Chapl *Linc* 87-99; P-in-c Bridgwater St Jo *B & W* from 99; Chapl Somerset Primary Care Trust from 99. *St John's Vicarage, Blake Place, Bridgwater TA6 5AU* Tel (01278) 422540 E-mail geraldine@geraldinekirk.wanadoo.co.uk

KIRK, Henry Logan. b 52. Adelaide Univ BA74 New Coll Edin BD77 K Coll Lon MA96. **d** 80 **p** 81. Chapl Dioc Coll Cape Prov S Africa 80-85; Asst Master Haileybury Coll 86; Asst Chapl Rugby Sch 86-93; Dep Hd Dulwich Coll Prep Sch 93-94; NSM S Dulwich St Steph *S'wark* 93-94; C Linslade *Ox* 94-96; Chapl Birkenhead Sch Merseyside 96-03; Chapl Abingdon Sch from 04. *Abingdon School, Park Road, Abingdon OX14 1DA* Tel (01235) 849112 *or* 534674 E-mail henry.kirk@abingdon.org.uk

KIRK, John Andrew. b 37. Lon Univ BD61 AKC61 MPhil75 Fitzw Ho Cam BA63. Ridley Hall Cam 61. **d** 63 **p** 64. C Finchley Ch Ch *Lon* 63-66; Argentina 66-79; SAMS 79-81; CMS 82-90; Dean of Miss Selly Oak Coll Birm 90-99; Dept of Th Birm Univ 99-02; Perm to Offic *Glouc* from 99; rtd 02. *The Old Stable, Market Square, Lechlade GL7 3AB* Tel (01367) 253254

KIRK, Natalie Roberta. See GARRETT, Natalie Roberta

KIRK, Peter Fenwick. b 30. Leeds Univ 50. **d** 83 **p** 84. NSM Bathgate *Edin* 83-91; NSM Linlithgow 83-91; NSM Bathgate from 92. *18 Inch Crescent, Bathgate EH48 1EU* Tel (01506) 655369

KIRK, Canon Steven Paul. b 59. Ex Univ LLB80 Univ of Wales (Cardiff) BD87 LLM94. St Mich Coll Llan 84. **d** 87 **p** 88. C Ebbw Vale *Mon* 87-89; PV Llan Cathl 89-91; PV and Succ 91-94; V Port Talbot St Agnes w Oakwood 94-01; TR Aberavon 01-07; AD Margam 06-07; V Ystrad Mynach w Llanbradach from 07; Can Llan Cathl from 07. *The Vicarage, Cedar Way, Ystrad Mynach, Hengoed CF82 7DR* Tel (01443) 813246

KIRKBRIDE, Martin Lea. b 51. Oak Hill Th Coll BA94. **d** 97 **p** 98. C Lancaster St Thos *Blackb* 97-00; TV Hampreston *Sarum* 00-05; V Lenton *S'well* from 05. *The Vicarage, 35A Church Street, Nottingham NG7 2FF* Tel 0115-970 1059 E-mail martinkirkbride@aol.com

KIRKBY, Canon John Victor Michael. b 39. Lon Univ BScEng62 BD73. Ridley Hall Cam 65. **d** 67 **p** 68. C Muswell Hill St Jas *Lon* 67-70; Chapl Hatf Poly *St Alb* 71-75; V Wootton 75-86; RD Elstow 82-86; R Byfleet *Guildf* 86-92; P-in-c Potten End w Nettleden *St Alb* 92-97; V 97-05; TV Gt Berkhamsted, Gt and Lt Gaddesden etc 05-08; Chapl Ashridge Management Coll 92-08; rtd 08; Perm to Offic *St Alb* from 08; Can Masindi Uganda from 09. *3 Hillside Gardens, Berkhamsted HP4 2LE* Tel (01442) 872725 E-mail jvmkirkby@aol.com

KIRKE, Miss Annie Noreen. b 74. Univ of Wales (Cardiff) BA96 Reading Univ MA04. Westmr Th Cen 06. **d** 08 **p** 09. C Bryanston Square St Mary w St Marylebone St Mark *Lon* 08-09; Pioneer of Missional Communities from 09. *63 Oakmead Road, London SW12 9SH* Tel 07971 128498 (mobile) E-mail revkirke@gmail.com

KIRKE, Clive Henry. b 51. Ridley Hall Cam. **d** 83 **p** 84. C Ainsdale *Liv* 83-86; Gen Asst Bootle Deanery 86-89; P-in-c Litherland St Andr 89-98; V Ingrow w Hainworth *Bradf* from 98. *St John's Vicarage, Oakfield Road, Keighley BD21 1BT* Tel (01535) 604069 E-mail clive.kirke@bradford.anglican.org *or* thekirks@fsmail.net

KIRKER, Richard Ennis. b 51. Sarum & Wells Th Coll 72. **d** 77. C Hitchin *St Alb* 77-78; Chief Exec LGCM 79-08. *10 Coopers Close, London E1 4BB* Tel (020) 7791 1802 Mobile 07798-805428 E-mail richard@richardkirker.com

KIRKHAM, Alan. b 46. **d** 01 **p** 02. OLM Parr *Liv* from 01. *21 Avondale Road, Haydock, St Helens WA11 0HJ* Tel (01744) 28046

KIRKHAM, Clifford Gerald Frank. b 34. Open Univ BA91. Sarum & Wells Th Coll 72. **d** 74 **p** 75. C Worle *B & W* 74-76; C E Preston w Kingston *Chich* 76-78; C Goring-by-Sea 78-80; C-in-c Maybridge CD 80-82; V Maybridge 82-88; R N Chapel w Ebernoe 88-99; Chapl for Rural Affairs 89-99; rtd 99; Perm to Offic *Nor* from 99. *5 Meadow Way, Rollesby, Great Yarmouth NR29 5HA* Tel (01493) 749036

✠KIRKHAM, The Rt Revd John Dudley Galtrey. b 35. Trin Coll Cam BA59 MA63. Westcott Ho Cam 60. **d** 62 **p** 63 **c** 76. C Ipswich St Mary le Tower *St E* 62-65; Bp's Chapl for 65-69; P-in-c Rockland St Mary w Hellington 67-69; Papua New Guinea 69-70; C St Martin-in-the-Fields *Lon* 70-72; C Westmr St Marg 70-72; Abp's Dom Chapl *Cant* 72-76; Suff Bp Sherborne *Sarum* 76-81; Area Bp Sherborne 81-01; Can and Preb Sarum Cathl 77-01; Abp's Adv to the Headmasters' Conf from 90; Bp HM Forces 92-01; rtd 01; Hon Asst Bp Sarum from 01; Can and Preb Sarum Cathl from 02. *Flamstone House, Flamstone Street, Bishopstone, Salisbury SP5 4BZ* Tel (01722) 780221 E-mail jsherborne@salisbury.anglican.org

KIRKHAM, June Margaret. b 54. EMMTC 99. **d** 02 **p** 03. C Nottingham St Jude *S'well* 02-06; P-in-c Broxtowe from 06. *St Martha's Vicarage, 135 Frinton Road, Nottingham NG8 6GR* Tel 0115-927 8837 E-mail june@kirkham7260.fsnet.co.uk

KIRKHAM, Stephen Gawin. b 51. MC74. Ridley Hall Cam 96. **d** 98 **p** 99. C Histon and Impington *Ely* 98-02; P-in-c N Leigh *Ox* 02-07; rtd 07. *2 College Row, Crawley, Witney OX29 9TP* Tel (01993) 706405 E-mail sg.kirkham@btinternet.com

KIRKLAND, Richard John. b 53. Leic Univ BA75. St Jo Coll Dur 76. **d** 79 **p** 80. C Knutsford St Jo and Toft *Ches* 79-82; C Bebington 82-89; V Poulton Lancelyn H Trin 89-95; V Hoole from 95. *All Saints' Vicarage, 2 Vicarage Road, Chester CH2 3HZ* Tel (01244) 322056 E-mail j.kirkland@hender.org.uk

KIRKMAN, Richard Marsden. b 55. Cranmer Hall Dur. **d** 87 **p** 88. C Bridlington Priory *York* 87-90; TV Thirsk 90-96; R Escrick and Stillingfleet w Naburn from 96; RD Derwent 01-11; P-in-c Bubwith w Skipwith from 11. *The Rectory, York Road, Escrick, York YO19 6EY* Tel (01904) 728406 E-mail richard@kirkman.orangehome.co.uk

KIRKMAN, Trevor Harwood. b 51. Trin Hall Cam BA73 MA77. EMMTC 94. **d** 96 **p** 97. NSM Hickling w Kinoulton and Broughton Sulney *S'well* 96-01; NSM Keyworth and Stanton-on-the-Wolds and Bunny etc 01-10; P-in-c Plumtree from 10; Dioc Registrar and Bp's Legal Adv *Leic* from 02. *The Rectory, 1 Church Hill, Plumtree, Nottingham NG12 5ND* E-mail trevorkirkman@btinternet.com

KIRKPATRICK, The Very Revd Jonathan Richard. b 58. CA81 Goldsmiths' Coll Lon BA85 Otago Univ MBA02. Wilson Carlile Coll 78 S'wark Ord Course 83. **d** 85 **p** 85. C Lewisham St Mary *S'wark* 85-87; Chapl Lewisham Hosp 85-87; Selection Sec ACCM 88-91; Sec Aston Tr Scheme 89-91; Hon C Noel Park St Mark *Lon* 88-91; V Christchurch St Mich New Zealand 91-96; Dean Dunedin 96-01; V Gen 97-01; Lic to Offic Auckland from 02. *33 Haycock Avenue, Mount Roskill, Auckland 1041, New Zealand* Tel (0064) (9) 627 7225 E-mail jonrk@xtra.co.nz

KIRKPATRICK, Nigel David Joseph. b 68. CITC BTh96. **d** 96 **p** 97. C Portadown St Columba *Arm* 96-99; C Lecale Gp *D & D* 99-01; I Killinchy w Kilmood and Tullynakill 01-07; I Gilnahirk from 07. *The Rectory, 237 Lower Braniel Road, Belfast BT5 7NQ* Tel (028) 9079 1748 *or* 9070 4123 E-mail gilnahirk@down.anglican.org

KIRKPATRICK, Reginald. b 48. **d** 07 **p** 08. OLM Ditchingham, Hedenham, Broome, Earsham etc *Nor* from 07. *18 Clark Road, Ditchingham, Bungay NR35 2QQ* Tel (01986) 893645 E-mail regkpatrick@aol.com

KIRKPATRICK, Roger James (Brother Damian). b 41. FCA. **d** 86 **p** 87. SSF from 66; Guardian Belf Friary 80-88; Birm 89-93; Prov Min 91-02; NSM Belfast St Pet *Conn* 86-88; Chapl R Victoria Hosp Belf 86-88; Lic to Offic *Linc* 94-96; *Lon* 97-01; *Sarum* 01-03; V Holy Is *Newc* 03-10; rtd 10. *The Friary, Hilfield, Dorchester DT2 7BE* Tel (01300) 341345 E-mail damianssf@franciscans.org.uk

KIRKPATRICK, William John Ashley. b 27. SEN SRN RMN. Sarum Th Coll 63. **d** 68 **p** 70. NSM St Mary le Bow w St Pancras Soper Lane etc *Lon* 68-70; NSM Soho St Anne w St Thos and St Pet 70-75; SSF 76-79; NSM S Kensington St Aug *Lon* 79-80; NSM Earl's Court St Cuth w St Matthias 80-98; rtd 98; Perm to Offic *Lon* from 98. *c/o Ms V R F Tschudin, 26 Cathcart Road, London SW10 9NN*

KIRKUP, Nigel Norman. b 54. K Coll Lon BD79 AKC79. **d** 80 **p** 80. Hon C Catford (Southend) and Downham *S'wark* 80-83; Hon C Surbiton St Andr and St Mark 83-85; Hon C Shirley St Geo 85-93; Perm to Offic *Lon* 96-09. *10 Norfolk Buildings, Brighton BN1 2DZ* Tel 07817-458076 (mobile) E-mail nigelkirkup@hotmail.com

KIRKWOOD, Canon David Christopher. b 40. Pemb Coll Ox BA63. Clifton Th Coll 63. **d** 65 **p** 66. C Wilmington *Roch* 65-68; C Green Street Green 68-72; Youth and Area Sec BCMS 72-73; Educn and Youth Sec 73-80; Hon C Sidcup Ch Ch *Roch* 74-80; V Rothley *Leic* 80-92; RD Goscote II 84-88; RD Goscote 88-90; P-in-c Toxteth St Philemon w St Gabr and St Cleopas *Liv* 92-95; TR 95-01; TR Harlow Town Cen w Lt Parndon *Chelmsf* 01-07; AD Toxteth and Wavertree *Liv* 96-01; AD Harlow *Chelmsf* 04-07; Hon Can Chelmsf Cathl 07; rtd 07. *7 Dunoon Close, Sinfin, Derby DE24 9NF* E-mail davidk@minternet.org

KIRKWOOD, Jack. b 21. Worc Ord Coll 62. **d** 63 **p** 64. C Penwerris *Truro* 63-66; V Torpoint 66-73; V Turton *Man* 73-81; P-in-c Castleton All So 81-82; Hon C Heywood St Luke 82-84; rtd 86; Perm to Offic *Blackb* from 86 and *York* 89-94. *5 Duddle Lane, Walton-le-Dale, Preston PR5 4UP*

KIRLEW, John Richard Francis. b 52. STETS 92. **d** 05 **p** 06. NSM Castle Cary w Ansford *B & W* 05-08; P-in-c Colwyn *S & B* from

08; Dioc Rural Life Adv from 09. *The Rectory, Llanelwedd, Builth Wells LD2 3TY* Tel (01982) 551288 E-mail richard.kirlew@btinternet.com

KIRTLEY, Georgina. b 44. St Jo Coll Dur BA94. Cranmer Hall Dur. **d** 95 **p** 96. NSM Barnard Castle w Whorlton *Dur* 95-00; Chapl HM YOI Deerbolt from 00; Bp's Asst Adv Self-Supporting Min from 00. *Ryelands, Stainton, Barnard Castle DL12 8RB* Tel (01833) 630871

KIRTON, Canon Richard Arthur. b 43. Dur Univ BA67 MA73. Wycliffe Hall Ox 68. **d** 69 **p** 70. C Warsop *S'well* 69-72; C Newark St Mary 72-75; Lect Kolej Theoloji Malaysia 76-79; Dean of Studies Th Sem Kuala Lumpur 79-82; P-in-c Kuala Lumpur St Gabr 79-81; Hon Can Kuala Lumpur from 88; P-in-c Bleasby w Halloughton *S'well* 83-89; V Thurgarton w Hoveringham 83-89; V Thurgarton w Hoveringham and Bleasby etc 89-91; Bp's Adv on Overseas Relns 85-91; Tutor Wilson Carlile Coll of Evang 91-98; P-in-c Ollerton w Boughton *S'well* 98-08; rtd 08. *Hill Top, Mosscar Close, Warsop, Mansfield NG20 0BW* Tel (01623) 842915 Mobile 07803-627574 E-mail richardkirton1@btinternet.com

KISH, Paul Alexander. b 68. K Coll Lon BD92 AKC92 Leeds Univ MA96. St Steph Ho Ox 96. **d** 98 **p** 99. C Prestbury *Glouc* 98-01; Chapl Sutton Valence Sch Kent from 01. *1 Holdgate House, South Lane, Sutton Valence, Maidstone ME17 3BG* Tel (01622) 842814 *or* 842381 Fax 844208 Mobile 07760-355434 E-mail chaplain@svs.org.uk

KISSELL, Barrington John. b 38. Lon Coll of Div 64. **d** 67 **p** 68. C Camborne *Truro* 67-71; C Chorleywood St Andr *St Alb* 71-00; C Bryanston Square St Mary w St Marylebone St Mark *Lon* from 00; Dir Faith Sharing Min from 74. *Garden Flat, 19 Lena Gardens, London W6 7PY* Tel (020) 7258 5040 E-mail bkissell1@aol.com

KISSELL, Jonathan Mark Barrington. b 66. Trin Coll Bris 99. **d** 01 **p** 02. C Stevenage St Pet Broadwater *St Alb* 01-05; C Dublin St Patr Cathl Gp 05-11. *Address temp unknown*

KITCHEN, Ian Brian. b 60. Worc Coll Ox BA81 Southn Univ PGCE82. Wycliffe Hall Ox 98. **d** 00 **p** 01. C Brandesburton and Leven w Catwick *York* 00-03; P-in-c Coxwold and Husthwaite 03-11; V from 11; P-in-c Crayke w Brandsby and Yearsley 03-11; R from 11. *The Vicarage, Church Hill, Crayke, York YO61 4TA* Tel (01347) 821876 E-mail luddite2@tiscali.co.uk

KITCHEN, Martin. b 47. N Lon Poly BA71 K Coll Lon BD76 AKC77 Man Univ PhD88. S'wark Ord Course 77. **d** 79 **p** 80. Lect CA Tr Coll Blackheath 79-83; Hon C Kidbrooke St Jas *S'wark* 79-83; Chapl Man Poly 83-88; TV Man Whitworth 83-86; TR 86-88; Adv In-Service Tr *S'wark* 88-95; Dioc Co-ord of Tr 95-97; Can Res S'wark Cathl 88-97; Can Res Dur Cathl 97-05; Sub-Dean 99-05; Dean Derby 05-07; P-in-c S Rodings *Chelmsf* from 08. *The Rectory, Stortford Road, Leaden Roding, Dunmow CM6 1GY* Tel (01279) 876147 E-mail martinx.kitchen@btinternet.com

KITCHENER, Christopher William. b 46. Open Univ BA. Sarum & Wells Th Coll 82. **d** 84 **p** 85. C Bexleyheath Ch Ch *Roch* 84-88; V Gravesend St Mary 88-97; V Biggin Hill 97-07; V St Mary Cray and St Paul's Cray 07-11; rtd 11; Bp's Officer for retired Clergy Widows and Widowers *Roch* from 11. *St Lawrence Vicarage, Stone Street, Seal, Sevenoaks TN15 0LQ* Tel (01732) 761766 E-mail chris@chriskitchener.freeserve.co.uk

KITCHENER, Mrs Evarina Carol. b 51. Stockwell Coll of Educn CertEd70 Heythrop Coll Lon MA00. Cant Sch of Min 89. **d** 92 **p** 94. NSM Gravesend St Mary *Roch* 92-97; NSM Biggin Hill 97-07; Asst Chapl Bromley Hosps NHS Trust 98-99; Distr Evang Miss Enabler S Prov URC 99-01; Par Development Officer *Roch* 01-07; C Chislehurst St Nic 07-11; P-in-c Seal St Lawr from 11; P-in-c Underriver from 11. *St Lawrence Vicarage, Stone Street, Seal, Sevenoaks TN15 0LQ* Tel (01732) 761766 E-mail carol.kitchener@diocese-rochester.org

KITCHENER, Canon Michael Anthony. b 45. Trin Coll Cam BA67 MA70 PhD71. Cuddesdon Coll 70. **d** 71 **p** 72. C Aldwick *Chich* 71-74; C Caversham *Ox* 74-77; Tutor Coll of Resurr Mirfield 77-83; Prin NEOC *Dur* 83-90; Hon Can Newc Cathl 84-90; Can Res and Chan Blackb Cathl 90-95; P-in-c Rydal *Carl* 95-99; Warden Rydal Hall and Ldr Rydal Hall Community 95-99; Can Res Nor Cathl 99-05; Dioc Dir of Ords 99-04; Bp's Officer for Ord and Initial Tr 04-05; rtd 05; Perm to Offic *Edin* from 06. *Bullrock Cottage, Ford, Lochgilphead PA31 8RH* Tel (01546) 810062 E-mail kitcheners@yahoo.co.uk

KITCHIN, Kenneth. b 46. Trin Coll Bris. **d** 89 **p** 90. C Barrow St Mark *Carl* 89-93; C Dalton-in-Furness 93-95; P-in-c Dearham 95-01; P-in-c Clifton 01-07; P-in-c Dean 01-07; P-in-c Mosser 01-07; R Clifton, Dean and Mosser 07-10; rtd 10. *7 Allerdale, Cockermouth CA13 0BN* E-mail kenneth.kitchin@sky.com

KITCHING, Daphne. b 48. Yorks Min Course. **d** 09 **p** 10. NSM Swanland *York* from 09. *21 Old Pond Place, North Ferriby HU14 3JE* Tel (01482) 635159 E-mail daphnekitching@hotmail.com

KITCHING, David Monro. b 26. New Coll Ox BA49. Ridley Hall Cam 80. **d** 82 **p** 83. C Hornchurch St Andr *Chelmsf* 82-86; P-in-c

Graveley w Papworth St Agnes w Yelling etc *Ely* 86-90; rtd 91; Perm to Offic *Ely* from 91. *20 Victoria Park, Cambridge CB4 3EL* Tel (01223) 365687

KITCHING, Miss Elizabeth. b 49. Trent Park Coll of Educn CertEd74. St Jo Coll Nottm. **d** 01 **p** 02. C Northallerton w Kirby Sigston *York* 01-05; P-in-c Cloughton and Burniston w Ravenscar etc from 05. *The Vicarage, Mill Lane, Cloughton, Scarborough YO13 0AB* Tel (01723) 870270 Mobile 07889-425025 E-mail lizkitching@uwclub.net

KITELEY, Robert John. b 51. Hull Univ BSc73 Univ of Wales (Abth) MSc75 Lon Univ PhD82. Trin Coll Bris. **d** 83 **p** 84. C Bebington *Ches* 83-88; C Hoole 88-91; V Plas Newton 91-99; R Ashtead *Guildf* from 99. *The Rectory, Ashdene, Dene Road, Ashtead KT21 1EE* Tel and fax (01372) 805182 E-mail bobkiteley@ntlworld.com

KITLEY, Canon David Buchan. b 53. St Jo Coll Dur BA. Trin Coll Bris 78. **d** 81 **p** 82. C Tonbridge St Steph *Roch* 81-84; C-in-c Southall Em CD *Lon* 84-91; V Dartford Ch Ch *Roch* 91-09; RD Dartford 98-07; V Kippington from 09; Bp's Adv for Overseas Links from 09; Hon Can Roch Cathl from 05; Hon Can Mpwampwa from 05. *The Vicarage, 59 Kippington Road, Sevenoaks TN13 2LL* Tel (01732) 452112 E-mail kitley@clara.net

KITTS, Joseph. b 27. Tyndale Hall Bris 59. **d** 60 **p** 61. C Parr *Liv* 60-63; C Bootle St Leon 63-66; V Southport SS Simon and Jude 66-74; USA 74-94; rtd 92. *Windyridge, Cottage Lane, St Martin's, Oswestry SY11 3BL* Tel (01691) 777090

KIVETT, Michael Stephen. b 50. Bethany Coll W Virginia BA72. Chr Th Sem Indiana MDiv76 Sarum & Wells Th Coll 76. **d** 77 **p** 78. C Harnham *Sarum* 77-80; C E Dereham *Nor* 80-83; R S Walsham and V Upton 83-88; Chapl Lt Plumstead Hosp 84-88; V Chard St Mary *B & W* 88-99; TR Chard and Distr 99-04; RD Crewkerne and Ilminster 93-98; R Staplegrove w Norton Fitzwarren from 04. *The Rectory, Rectory Drive, Staplegrove, Taunton TA2 6AP* Tel (01823) 270211 E-mail kivett@btinternet.com

KLIMAS, Miss Lynda. b 58. Jes Coll Cam BA89 MA93. Cranmer Hall Dur 89. **d** 90 **p** 94. Par Dn Sandy *St Alb* 90-93; Par Dn Bishop's Stortford St Mich 93-94; C 94-98; P-in-c Weston and C Baldock w Bygrave 98-03; TV Baldock w Bygrave and Weston 03-04; V Cople, Moggerhanger and Willington from 04. *The Vicarage, 3 Grange Lane, Cople, Bedford MK44 3TT* Tel (01234) 838431

KNAPP, Antony Blair. b 48. Imp Coll Lon BSc68. NOC 86. **d** 89 **p** 90. C Bolton St Jas w St Chrys *Bradf* 89-92; V Kettlewell w Conistone, Hubberholme etc 92-00; TR Swindon Dorcan *Bris* from 00. *23 Sedgebrook, Swindon SN3 6EY* Tel (01793) 525130 E-mail tonybknapp@aol.com

KNAPP, Bryan Thomas. b 61. Trin Coll Bris BA91. **d** 91 **p** 92. C S Gillingham *Roch* 91-95; V Chatham St Paul w All SS 95-09; V Paddock Wood from 09. *The Vicarage, 169 Maidstone Road, Paddock Wood, Tonbridge TN12 6DZ* Tel (01892) 833917 E-mail bryan.knapp@diocese-rochester.org

KNAPP, Jeremy Michael. b 67. Westhill Coll Birm BEd91. Ripon Coll Cuddesdon BTh99. **d** 99 **p** 00. C Hill *Birm* 99-02; TV Salter Street and Shirley 02-09; V Olton from 09. *St Margaret's Vicarage, 5 Old Warwick Road, Solihull B92 7JU* Tel 0121-706 2318 E-mail revd.jeremy@btinternet.com

KNAPP (*née* STOCKER), **Mrs Rachael Ann.** b 64. Bris Univ BA86. Trin Coll Bris BA91. **d** 91 **p** 94. C Ditton *Roch* 91-95; C Chatham St Paul w All SS 95-08; Chapl Bennett Memorial Dioc Sch Tunbridge Wells from 08. *The Vicarage, 169 Maidstone Road, Paddock Wood, Tonbridge TN12 6DZ* Tel (01892) 833917 *or* 521595 E-mail knapp@bennett.kent.sch.uk

KNAPPER, Peter Charles. b 39. Lon Univ BA61. St Steph Ho Ox 61. **d** 63 **p** 64. C Carl H Trin 63-68; V Westfield St Mary 68-76; V Bridekirk 76-83; P-in-c Blackheath Ascension *S'wark* 83-96; P-in-c Holmwood *Guildf* 96-03; TV Surrey Weald 03-04; rtd 04; Perm to Offic *S'wark* from 09. *20 Boyne Road, London SE13 5AW* Tel (020) 8473 1501 E-mail peter/pat@pknapper.fsnet.co.uk

KNARESBOROUGH, Suffragan Bishop of. See BELL, The Rt Revd James Harold

KNEE, Geoffrey. b 31. Whitelands Coll Lon CertEd71 Anglia Poly Univ MA05. CA Tr Coll 56 Glouc Sch of Min 91. **d** 92 **p** 93. NSM Hampton *Worc* 92-97; Chapl St Richard's Hospice *Worc* 95-97; NSM Badsey w Aldington and Offenham and Bretforton *Worc* 97; rtd 97; Perm to Offic *Worc* from 98. *8 Mayfair, Fairfield, Evesham WR11 1JJ* Tel (01386) 443574 E-mail geoff@kneehome.freeserve.co.uk

KNEE, Jacob Samuel. b 66. LSE BSc(Econ)87 MSc(Econ)88. Ripon Coll Cuddesdon BA92. **d** 93 **p** 94. C Ashby-de-la-Zouch St Helen w Coleorton *Leic* 93-96; C Boston *Linc* 96-00; Chapl Boston Coll of FE 96-00; V Cam w Stinchcombe *Glouc* 00-07; V Billings St Steph USA from 07. *1241 Crawford Drive, Billings MT 59102, USA* Tel (001) (406) 259 5017 Fax 259 1150 E-mail jknee@global.net.uk

KNEE-ROBINSON, Keith Frederick. b 40. Thames Poly BSc75 MICE76. SAOMC 99. **d** 01 **p** 02. OLM Caversham St Pet and

Mapledurham *Ox* 01-10; OLM Caversham Thameside and Mapledurham from 10. *8 Hewett Close, Reading RG4 7ER* Tel 0118-947 7868 E-mail kkrmill@globalnet.co.uk

KNEEBONE, Mrs Patricia Jane. b 53. Man Univ BA74 Lon Univ BD94. SWMTC 08. **d** 10 **p** 11. NSM Newquay *Truro* from 10. *34 Henver Road, Newquay TR7 3BN* Tel 07966-703924 (mobile) E-mail janekneebone@gmail.com

KNEEN, Michael John. b 55. Univ Coll Lon BSc76 MSc77 St Jo Coll Dur BA85. Cranmer Hall Dur 83. **d** 86 **p** 87. C Bishop's Castle w Mainstone *Heref* 86-90; TV Bridgnorth, Tasley, Astley Abbotts, etc 90-08; TV Leominster 08-10; TR from 10. *The Rectory, Church Street, Leominster HR6 8NH* Tel (01568) 615709 E-mail michael@kneenmichael.orangehome.co.uk

KNELL, John George. b 35. Cant Sch of Min 79. **d** 82 **p** 83. Hd Master St Geo C of E Middle Sch Sheerness 80-87; NSM Sheerness H Trin w St Paul *Cant* 82-87; NSM Minster-in-Sheppey 87-06; rtd 06; Perm to Offic *Cant* 06-08. *The Annex, Old Mill House, Old Mill Drive, Pulham St Mary, Diss IP21 4NB*

KNELL, Canon Raymond John. b 27. Qu Coll Cam BA48 MA52. Ridley Hall Cam 50. **d** 52 **p** 53. C Bishopwearmouth St Gabr *Dur* 52-57; C S Shields St Hilda 57-58; P-in-c Hebburn St Oswald 58-67; V Castleside 67-76; V Heworth St Mary 76-93; RD Gateshead 83-87; Hon Can Dur Cathl 87-93; rtd 93. *40 St Andrew's Drive, Low Fell, Gateshead NE9 6JU* Tel 0191-442 1069

KNIBBS, Peter John. b 55. Birm Univ BDS78 DDS93. SWMTC 04. **d** 07 **p** 08. NSM St Illogan *Truro* 07-11; P-in-c Chacewater w St Day and Carharrack from 11; P-in-c St Stythians w Perranarworthal and Gwennap from 11; P-in-c Devoran from 11; P-in-c Feock from 11. *Hillywych, Sunnyvale Road, Portreath, Redruth TR16 4NE* Tel (01209) 842005 E-mail peter.knibbs@lineone.net

KNIFTON, Gladys Elizabeth. b 52. Kingston Univ BSc95 SRN73 SCM75 TCert84. NTMTC 95. **d** 98 **p** 99. NSM Churt *Guildf* 98-01; Asst Chapl Surrey Hants Borders NHS Trust 01-05; Chapl Acorn Chr Foundn from 05; Hon C Grayshott *Guildf* from 07. *Bryanston, Boundary Road, Grayshott, Hindhead GU26 6TX* Tel and fax (01428) 604977 E-mail elizabeth@knifton.com *or* eknifton@acornchristian.org

KNIGHT, The Very Revd Alexander Francis (Alec). b 39. OBE06. St Cath Coll Cam BA61 MA65. Wells Th Coll. **d** 63 **p** 64. C Hemel Hempstead *St Alb* 63-68; Chapl Taunton Sch 68-75; Dir Bloxham Project 75-81; Dir of Studies Aston Tr Scheme 81-83; P-in-c Easton and Martyr Worthy *Win* 83-91; Adn Basingstoke 90-98; Can Res Win Cathl 91-98; Dean Linc 98-06; rtd 06. *Shalom, Clay Street, Whiteparish, Salisbury SP5 2ST* Tel (01794) 884402 E-mail sheelagh_knight@hotmail.com

KNIGHT, Andrew. b 67. **d** 06 **p** 07. C Wolstanton *Lich* 06-09; TR from 09. *St Barnabas' Vicarage, Oldcastle Avenue, Newcastle ST5 8QG* Tel (01782) 636161 E-mail andykn@aol.com

KNIGHT, Canon Andrew James. b 50. Grey Coll Dur BA72 Ox Univ BA74 MA81. Wycliffe Hall Ox 72. **d** 75 **p** 76. Min Can Brecon Cathl 75-78; C Brecon w Battle 75-78; C Morriston 78-82; V Llanwrtyd w Llanddulas in Tir Abad etc 82-89; RD Cwmtawe 97-00; V Sketty from 00; Can Res Brecon Cathl 98-04; Treas from 04. *The Vicarage, De La Beche Road, Sketty, Swansea SA2 9AR* Tel (01792) 202767 E-mail andrewknight@phonecoop.coop

KNIGHT, Mrs Ann. b 54. Lanc Univ CertEd75. Trin Coll Bris. **dss** 84 **d** 87 **p** 94. Wigan St Jas w St Thos *Liv* 84-87; Par Dn 87-90; C Costessey *Nor* 90-96; R Gt and Lt Ellingham, Rockland and Shropham etc 96-03; Chapl Norwich Primary Care Trust 96-02; P-in-c Worthen *Heref* 03-07; P-in-c Hope w Shelve 03-07; TV Ross 07-08; V Brampton from 08. *The Rectory, Brampton Abbotts, Ross-on-Wye HR9 7JD* Tel (01989) 562010

KNIGHT, Arthur Clifford Edwin. b 42. Univ of Wales BSc64. Wells Th Coll 64. **d** 66 **p** 67. C Llangyfelach and Morriston *S & B* 66-68; C Oystermouth 68-73; Chapl RAF 73-95; Perm to Offic *Heref* 95-97; P-in-c Brant Broughton and Beckingham *Linc* 97-99; P-in-c Credenhill w Brinsop and Wormsley etc *Heref* 99-10; RD Heref Rural 05-07; rtd 10. *26 Meadow Drive, Credenhill, Hereford HR4 7EE* Tel (01432) 760530 E-mail cknight@aol.com

KNIGHT, Mrs Barbara. b 46. St Alb Minl Tr Scheme 86. **d** 90 **p** 94. NSM Weston and Ardeley *St Alb* 90-95; C Norton 95-97; R Barkway, Reed and Buckland w Barley 97-05; rtd 05. *16 Keynshambury Road, Cheltenham GL52 6HB* Tel (01242) 238805

KNIGHT, Mrs Barbara Mary. b 43. SRN64 SCM70. EMMTC 94. **d** 97 **p** 98. NSM Market Harborough and The Transfiguration etc *Leic* 97-99; C Church Langton cum Tur Langton etc 99-02; P-in-c Billesdon and Skeffington 02; R Church Langton cum Tur Langton etc 02-07; rtd 07; Perm to Offic *Blackb* from 07. *1 Whittlewood Drive, Accrington BB5 5DJ* Tel (01254) 395549 E-mail revbarbarak@btopenworld.com

KNIGHT, Brenda Evelyn. b 27. SAOMC 96. **d** 98 **p** 99. OLM Wheatley *Ox* 98-09; Perm to Offic from 09. *22 Middle Road, Stanton St John, Oxford OX33 1HD* Tel (01865) 351227

KNIGHT, Christopher. b 61. Wycliffe Hall Ox 94. **d** 96 **p** 97. C Banbury Ox 96-98; C Banbury St Paul 98-01; Chapl HM Pris Lowdham Grange from 01. *HM Prison Lowdham Grange, Nottingham NG14 7DQ* Tel 0115-966 9308
E-mail 2cv@clara.net

KNIGHT, Christopher Colson. b 52. Ex Univ BSc73 Man Univ PhD77 SS Coll Cam MA90. Sarum & Wells Th Coll BTh83. **d** 81 **p** 82. Chapl St Mary's Cathl Edin 81-84; V Chesterton Cov 84-87; R Lighthorne 84-87; V Newbold Pacey w Moreton Morrell 84-87; Chapl and Fell SS Coll Cam 87-92; Sen Research Assoc St Edm Coll Cam from 92. *Hope Cottage, Hindringham Road, Walsingham NR22 6DR* Tel (01328) 820108

KNIGHT, Clifford. See KNIGHT, Arthur Clifford Edwin

KNIGHT, David Alan. b 59. Lanc Univ BA81. Ripon Coll Cuddesdon 82. **d** 85 **p** 86. C Stretford All SS Man 85-88; C Charlestown 88-89; TV Pendleton St Thos w Charlestown 89-94; V Tysoe w Oxhill and Whatcote Cov 94-05; RD Shipston 04-05; Chapl Marie Curie Cen Solihull 06-08; Chapl St Richard's Hospice Worc from 06. *St Richard's Hospice, Wild Wood Drive, Worcester WR5 2QT* Tel (01905) 763963
E-mail chaplain@strichards.org.uk

KNIGHT, David Charles. b 32. Clare Coll Cam BA55 MA59. Tyndale Hall Bris 55. **d** 57 **p** 58. C Cambridge St Paul Ely 57-58; C St Alb Ch Ch St Alb 58-61; C-in-c Wimbledon Em Ridgway Prop Chpl S'wark 61-67; Publications Sec BCMS 67-68; Ed Asst The Christian 68-69; V Lannarth Truro 69-75; RD Carnmarth N 72-75; V Fremington Ex 75-83; C Edmonton All SS w St Mich Lon 83; Chapl N Middx Hosp 83; rtd 94; Perm to Offic Chelmsf from 94. *Tudor Court, High Street, Hatfield Broad Oak, Bishop's Stortford CM22 7HF* Tel (01279) 718650
E-mail david-knight@amserve.com

KNIGHT, Canon David Charles. b 45. Lon Univ BA66 St Edm Hall Ox BA68 MA73 ATCL63. St Steph Ho Ox 68. **d** 70 **p** 71. C Northwood H Trin Lon 70-73; C Stevenage All SS Pin Green St Alb 73-77; C Cippenham CD Ox 77-78; TV W Slough 78-83; Dep Min Can Windsor 81-08; R Lt Stanmore St Lawr Lon 83-91; Ecum Officer to Bp Willesden 83-91; Prec and Can Res Chelmsf Cathl 91-01; V Ranmoor Sheff 01-08; rtd 08; Perm to Offic Ox from 09. *12 Bankside, Headington, Oxford OX3 8LT* Tel (01865) 761476 E-mail david.knight@bethere.co.uk

KNIGHT, Canon David Lansley. b 33. Em Coll Cam BA58 MA61 PGCE76. Ridley Hall Cam 57. **d** 59 **p** 60. C Chatham St Steph Roch 59-63; C Plymouth St Andr Ex 63-65; V Gravesend St Aid Roch 65-71; V Bexley St Mary 71-98; RD Sidcup 93-97; Hon Can Roch Cathl 97; rtd 98; Perm to Offic Chich from 98. *1 Newlands Avenue, Bexhill-on-Sea TN39 4HA* Tel (01424) 212120

KNIGHT (née SMITH), Frances Mary. b 48. St Jo Coll York CertEd69. EMMTC 98. **d** 03 **p** 04. NSM Braunstone Leic 03-07; NSM The Abbey Leic from 07. *32 Aster Way, Burbage, Hinckley LE10 2UQ* Tel (01455) 618218
E-mail frances@knight-t.freeserve.co.uk

KNIGHT, Gavin Rees. b 65. St Andr Univ MTheol94. Ripon Coll Cuddesdon MTh96. **d** 98 **p** 99. C Solihull Birm 98-02; P-in-c Fulham St Andr Lon 02-05; P-in-c Fulham St Alb w St Aug 04-05; Chapl Mon Sch from 05. *Monmouth School, Almshouse Street, Monmouth NP25 3XP* Tel (01600) 713143 Fax 772701
E-mail chaplain@monmouthschool.org

KNIGHT, Henry Christian. b 34. Fitzw Ho Cam BA62 MA66. Ridley Hall Cam 62. **d** 63 **p** 64. Succ Bradf Cathl 63-64; Chapl 64-66; Chapl Tel Aviv Israel 67-79; CMJ 79-86; V Allithwaite Carl 86-93; rtd 93; Perm to Offic Leic from 93. *20 Saxon Way, Ashby-de-la-Zouch LE65 2JR* Tel (01530) 460709

KNIGHT, Canon John Bernard. b 34. Fuller Th Sem California DMin91 ACIS60. Oak Hill Th Coll 61. **d** 65 **p** 66. C Morden S'wark 65-69; USA 69-71; V Summerfield Birm 71-07; Hon Can Birm Cathl 01-07; rtd 07. *102 High Haden Road, Cradley Heath B64 7PN* Tel 0121-559 0108

KNIGHT, Canon John Francis Alan Macdonald. b 36. Coll of Resurr Mirfield 59. **d** 61 **p** 62. C Gwelo S Rhodesia 61-66; R Melfort 66-68; C Highlands and P-in-c Chikwata 68-70; Lic to Offic Mashonaland 70-75; R Umtali 76-81; Dean Mutare 81-87; TR Northampton Em Pet 87-97; RD Northn 88-92; P-in-c Greens Norton w Bradden and Lichborough 97-05; Bp's Adv for Min of Healing 99-05; Can Pet Cathl 01-05; rtd 05; Perm to Offic Pet from 06. *16 Glebe Drive, Brackley NN13 7BX* Tel (01280) 706258 E-mail theknights16@tiscali.co.uk

KNIGHT, Jonathan Morshead. b 59. Fitzw Coll Cam BA81 MA85 Jes Coll Cam PhD91 Jes Coll Ox MA87 Worc Coll Ox DPhil02 W Lon Inst of HE PGCE82 Sheff Univ PGCE00. Wycliffe Hall Ox 86. **d** 88 **p** 89. C Hillingdon St Jo Lon 88-91; NSM Baslow Derby 91-92; NSM Curbar and Stoney Middleton 91-92; Lect Bibl Studies Sheff Univ 91-92; Research Fell 92-94; NSM Sheff St Paul 92-94; Bp's Research Asst Ely 94-98; NSM Whittlesford LEP 95-96; Bp's Dom Chapl 96; Sec Doctrine Commn 96-98; P-in-c Holywell w Needingworth Ely 98-01; Tutor Westcott Ho Cam 98-99; OCM from 99; CF (TAVR) 00-03; Hon Lect Th Kent Univ 00-03; Chapl Worc Coll Ox 02-03; Visiting Fell York St Jo Univ from 07; Tutor Grey Coll Dur from 10. *36 Ninth Street, Peterlee SR8 4LZ* Tel 07549-170031 (mobile) E-mail jonathanknight5@hotmail.com

KNIGHT, Mrs June. b 28. Glouc Sch of Min 85. **d** 87 **p** 94. NSM Leckhampton SS Phil and Jas w Cheltenham St Jas Glouc 87-96; rtd 96; Perm to Offic Glouc from 96. *31 St Michael's Road, Woodlands, Cheltenham GL51 5RP* Tel (01242) 517911

KNIGHT, Mrs June Elizabeth. b 42. St Alb Minl Tr Scheme 90. **d** 93 **p** 94. NSM Stanstead Abbots St Alb 93-96; NSM Gt Amwell w St Margaret's and Stanstead Abbots 96-97; NSM Lt Hadham w Albury 97-98; NSM Bishop's Stortford St Mich from 98. *The White Cottage, Albury Hall Park, Albury, Ware SG11 2HX* Tel (01279) 771756
E-mail june.e.knight@btopenworld.com

KNIGHT, Keith Kenneth. b 36. Southn Univ BSc58. Wycliffe Hall Ox 59. **d** 62 **p** 63. C Lower Darwen St Jas Blackb 62-64; C Leyland St Andr 64-68; P-in-c Blackb All SS 68-71; Dioc Youth Chapl 71-88; Hon C Burnley St Pet 71-74; Warden Scargill Ho 88-01; rtd 01; Perm to Offic Bradf from 01. *4 The Hawthorns, Sutton-in-Craven, Keighley BD20 8BP* Tel (01535) 632920

KNIGHT, Mrs Margaret Owen. b 34. Oak Hill Th Coll 78. **dss** 80 **d** 87 **p** 94. Chorleywood St Andr St Alb 80-04; Par Dn 87-94; C 94-04; rtd 94; Perm to Offic St Alb from 04. *15A Blacketts Wood Drive, Chorleywood, Rickmansworth WD3 5PY* Tel (01923) 283832 E-mail moknight@waitrose.com

KNIGHT, Canon Michael Richard. b 47. St Jo Coll Dur BA69 MA79 Fitzw Coll Cam BA73 MA78 St Cross Coll Ox MA92. Westcott Ho Cam 71. **d** 74 **p** 75. C Bishop's Stortford St Mich St Alb 74-75; C Bedford St Andr 75-79; Chapl Angl Students Glas 79-86; V Riddings and Ironville Derby 86-91; Lib Pusey Ho 91-94; Fell St Cross Coll Ox 92-94; V Chesterfield St Mary and All SS Derby from 94; P-in-c Chesterfield St Aug 05-09; Hon Can Derby Cathl from 06. *28 Cromwell Road, Chesterfield S40 4TH* Tel (01246) 232937 or 206506
E-mail vicar.chesterfield@virgin.net

KNIGHT, Paul James Joseph. b 50. Oak Hill Th Coll. **d** 84 **p** 85. C Broadwater St Mary Chich 84-87; R Itchingfield w Slinfold 87-92; Chapl Highgate Sch Lon from 92. *15A Bishopswood Road, London N6 4PB* Tel (020) 8348 9211 or 8340 1524
E-mail paul.knight@highgateschool.org.uk

KNIGHT, Paul Jeremy. b 53. **d** 94 **p** 95. CA 77-04; C Moreton Say Lich 94-97; V Birstall Wakef from 97. *St Peter's Vicarage, King's Drive, Birstall, Batley WF17 9JJ* Tel and fax (01924) 473715
E-mail vicar@stpetersbirstall.co.uk

KNIGHT, Peter John. b 51. AKC73 Ch Ch Coll Cant CertEd77. Sarum & Wells Th Coll 79. **d** 80 **p** 81. C Greenford H Cross Lon 80-83; C Langley Marish Ox 83; NSM W Acton St Martin Lon 88-90; C E Acton St Dunstan w St Thos 90-92; V Malden St Jo S'wark 92-02; Co-ord Chapl HM Pris Long Lartin 02-05; TR Malvern Link w Cowleigh Worc 05-10; V from 10. *St Matthias' Rectory, 12 Lambourne Avenue, Malvern WR14 1NL* Tel (01684) 566054 E-mail revpeterknight@hotmail.com

KNIGHT, Peter Malcolm. b 55. Cam Univ BA76 Lon Hosp MB, BS76 MRCGP85. Trin Coll Bris BA94. **d** 94 **p** 95. C Quidenham Nor 94-97; R Thurton from 97; RD Loddon 99-05. *The Rectory, 29 Ashby Road, Thurton, Norwich NR14 6AX* Tel (01508) 480738

KNIGHT, Peter Michael. b 47. St Luke's Coll Ex BEd71. Trin Coll Bris 90. **d** 92 **p** 93. C Bris Ch the Servant Stockwood 92-95; Chapl St Brendan's Sixth Form Coll 92-94; C W Swindon and the Lydiards Bris 95-96; TV 96-07; P-in-c The Claydons Ox 07-09; TV The Claydons and Swan from 09. *The Rectory, Queen Catherine Road, Steeple Claydon, Buckingham MK18 2PY* Tel (01296) 738055 E-mail peterknight15@tiscali.co.uk

KNIGHT, Philip Stephen. b 46. Ian Ramsey Coll Brasted 74 Oak Hill Th Coll 75. **d** 77 **p** 78. C Pennycross Ex 77-80; C Epsom St Martin Guildf 80-83; V Clay Hill St Jo Lon 83-86; TV Washfield, Stoodleigh, Withleigh etc Ex 86-90; Chapl ATC from 86; Chapl S Warks Hosps 90-94; Chapl S Warks Health Care NHS Trust 94-05; Perm to Offic Cov from 05 and Ex from 10; rtd 11. *Coombeside, 122 Alexandria Road, Sidmouth EX10 9HG* Tel (01395) 514166 E-mail psk54@hotmail.co.uk

KNIGHT, Canon Roger George. b 41. Culham Coll Ox CertEd63. Linc Th Coll 65. **d** 67 **p** 68. C Bris St Andr Hartcliffe 67-69; Hd Master Twywell Sch Kettering 69-74; V Naseby Pet 74-79; P-in-c Haselbeech 74-79; R Clipston w Naseby and Haselbech 79-82; P-in-c Kelmarsh 79-82; TR Corby SS Pet and Andr w Gt and Lt Oakley 82-88; R Irthlingborough 88-99; RD Higham 89-94; R Burton Latimer 99-03; Can Pet Cathl 92-03; rtd 03; Perm to Offic Pet from 03. *9 Hollow Wood Road, Burton Latimer, Kettering NN15 5RB* Tel (01536) 721726
E-mail rogerknight01@yahoo.co.uk

KNIGHT, Roger Ivan. b 54. K Coll Lon BD79 AKC79. Ripon Coll Cuddesdon 79. **d** 80 **p** 81. C Orpington All SS Roch 80-84; C St Laur in Thanet Cant 84-87; R Cuxton and Halling Roch from 87. *The Rectory, 6 Rochester Road, Cuxton, Rochester ME2 1AF* Tel (01634) 717134 E-mail roger.knight@diocese-rochester.org or rogerknight@aol.com

KNIGHT, Stephen. See KNIGHT, Philip Stephen

KNIGHT, Ms Sue Elizabeth. b 47. Southlands Coll Lon CertEd68. SEITE 01. **d** 03 **p** 04. NSM Lee St Mildred *S'wark* 03-09. *101 Lyme Farm Road, London SE12 8JH* Tel (020) 8852 1781

KNIGHT, Mrs Susan Jane. b 57. Open Univ BSc99. NTMTC BA09. **d** 09 **p** 10. C Harlow Town Cen w Lt Parndon *Chelmsf* from 09. *92 Ram Gorse, Harlow CM20 1PZ* Tel 07801-701084 (mobile) E-mail sue@kerryknight.co.uk

KNIGHT, Mrs Susan Margaret. **d** 02 **p** 03. C Clydach *S & B* 02-03; C Cen Swansea 04-05; TV from 05. *The Vicarage, 27 Bowen Street, Swansea SA1 2NA* Tel (01792) 473047

KNIGHT, Suzanne. b 55. **d** 00 **p** 01. NSM Reading St Jo *Ox* from 00. *9 Victoria Way, Reading RG1 3HD* Tel 0118-967 5645 E-mail suz-knight@yahoo.co.uk

KNIGHT, William Lawrence. b 39. Univ Coll Lon BSc61 PhD65. Coll of Resurr Mirfield 75. **d** 77 **p** 78. C Bp's Hatfield *St Alb* 77-81; Asst Chapl Brussels Cathl 81-84; V Pet H Spirit Bretton 84-89; P-in-c Marholm 84-89; TR Riverside *Ox* 89-04; rtd 04. *90 Norfolk Gardens, Littlehampton BN17 5PF* Tel (01903) 716750 E-mail knightsmvd@dial.pipex.com

KNIGHTS, Christopher Hammond. b 61. St Jo Coll Dur BA83 PhD88. Linc Th Coll 87. **d** 89 **p** 90. C Stockton St Pet *Dur* 89-92; C Chich St Paul and St Pet 92-94; Tutor Chich Th Coll 92-94; V Ashington *Newc* 94-00; V Monkseaton St Mary 00-04; Dioc Moderator Reader Tr 03-10; P-in-c Scotswood 04-11; R Kelso *Edin* from 11; P-in-c Coldstream from 11. *The Rectory, 6 Forestfield, Kelso TD5 7BX* Tel (01573) 224163 E-mail revchrisknights@gmail.com

KNIGHTS, James William. b 34. AKC66. **d** 67 **p** 68. C Kettering St Andr *Pet* 67-71; V Braunston w Brooke 71-81; V Dudley St Jo *Worc* 81-97; rtd 97; Perm to Offic *Worc* from 98. *192 Brook Farm Road, Malvern WR14 3SL* Tel (01684) 561358

KNIGHTS JOHNSON, Nigel Anthony. b 52. Ealing Tech Coll BA74 Westmr Coll Ox MTh99. Wycliffe Hall Ox 78. **d** 80 **p** 81. C Beckenham Ch Ch *Roch* 80-84; CF 84-07; P-in-c Ockley, Okewood and Forest Green *Guildf* from 07. *The Rectory, Stane Street, Ockley, Dorking RH5 5SY* Tel (01306) 711550 E-mail nknightsj@hotmail.com

KNILL-JONES, Jonathan Waring (Jack). b 58. Univ Coll Lon BSc79. St Jo Coll Nottm 88. **d** 90 **p** 91. C Northolt St Jos *Lon* 90-94; C Hayes St Nic CD 94-99; V Airedale w Fryston *Wakef* 99-07; V Teddington SS Pet and Paul and Fulwell *Lon* from 07; Chapl Richmond and Twickenham Primary Care Trust from 08. *The Vicarage, 1 Bychurch End, Teddington TW11 8PS* Tel (020) 8977 0054 E-mail jackknill@aol.com

KNOPP, Alexander Edward Robert. b 09. St Jo Coll Cam BA33 MA37. Ridley Hall Cam 32. **d** 34 **p** 35. C Loughton St Mary *Chelmsf* 34-38; C Prittlewell St Mary 38-40; R Nevendon 40; R N Benfleet w Nevendon 41-48; V Walthamstow St Jo 48-50; V Pampisford *Ely* 50-59; V Babraham 50-59; R Quendon w Rickling *Chelmsf* 59-68; R Gt Yeldham 68-73; R Gt w Lt Snoring *Nor* 73-76; rtd 76; Perm to Offic *Ely* 77-00. *c/o Ms S Chapman, The Pump House, 28 High Street, Meldreth, Royston SG8 6JU* Tel (01763) 261944

KNOTT, Graham Keith. b 53. Oak Hill Th Coll BA80. **d** 80 **p** 81. C Normanton *Derby* 80-83; C Ripley 83-87; TV Newark w Hawton, Cotham and Shelton *S'well* 87-89; TV Newark 89-97; P-in-c Mansfield St Jo 97-06; AD Mansfield 03-06; P-in-c Croajingolong Australia 06-09; P-in-c Watford *St Alb* from 09. *St Mary's Vicarage, 14 Cassiobury Drive, Watford WD17 3AB* Tel (01923) 254005 E-mail graham.knott@stmaryswatford.org

KNOTT, Preb Janet Patricia. b 50. Avery Hill Coll CertEd71. S Dios Minl Tr Scheme MTS91. **d** 92 **p** 94. NSM Clutton w Cameley *B & W* 92-99; Chapl R Sch Bath 94-98; Chapl R High Sch Bath 98-99; R Farmborough, Marksbury and Stanton Prior *B & W* from 99; Chapl Bath Spa Univ from 99; RD Chew Magna *B & W* from 04; Preb Wells Cathl from 07. *The Rectory, Church Lane, Farmborough, Bath BA3 1AN* Tel (01761) 479311 E-mail rayjanknott@btinternet.com

KNOTT, Pamela Frances. See IVE, Mrs Pamela Frances

KNOTT, Miss Wendy Gillian. b 47. Adelaide Univ BA78. Melbourne Coll of Div BD95. **d** 94 **p** 96. NSM Sandy Bay Australia 94-98; NSM New Town St Jas 98-01; NSM Franklin w Esperance 01-05; Hon Chapl Ch Coll Tasmania 97-06; R Wick *Mor* from 06; P-in-c Thurso from 06. *5 Naver Place, Thurso KW14 7PZ* Tel (01847) 893393 E-mail rev.wendy@btinternet.com

KNOWD, George Alexander. b 31. St Deiniol's Hawarden. **d** 88 **p** 89. NSM Aghalurcher w Tattykeeran, Cooneen etc *Clogh* 88-91; Dioc Communications Officer 89-90 and 92-97; NSM Ballybay w Mucknoe and Clontibret 91-92; C *C & O* 96-97; I Clonmel w Innislounagh, Tullaghmelan etc *C & O* 97-06; Can Ossory Cathl 05-06; rtd 06. *Sunhaven, Knockelly Road, Fethard, Co Tipperary, Republic of Ireland* Tel and fax (00353) (52) 613 0821 Mobile 87-284 2350 E-mail gknowd@eircom.net

KNOWERS, Stephen John. b 49. K Coll Lon BD72 AKC72. **d** 73 **p** 74. C Bp's Hatfield *St Alb* 73-77; C Cheshunt 77-81; P-in-c Barnet Vale St Mark 81-83; V 83-85; Chapl S Bank Poly *S'wark* 85-92; Chapl S Bank Univ 92-94; V Croydon St Pet 94-06; P-in-c

---

Croydon St Aug 04-06; V S Croydon St Pet and St Aug 06-07; V Shirley St Jo from 07. *The Vicarage, 49 Shirley Church Road, Croydon CR0 5EF* Tel (020) 8654 1013 E-mail frstiiv@hotmail.com

KNOWLES, Andrew John. b 66. Wimbledon Sch of Art BA88. St Jo Coll Nottm 05. **d** 07 **p** 08. C Long Buckby w Watford and W Haddon w Winwick and Ravensthorpe *Pet* 07-11; V Camberley St Mary *Guildf* from 11. *St Mary's Vicarage, 37 Park Road, Camberley GU15 2SP* Tel and fax (01276) 22085 or 685167 E-mail vicar@stmaryscamberley.org.uk

KNOWLES, Canon Andrew William Allen. b 46. St Cath Coll Cam BA68 MA72. St Jo Coll Nottm 69. **d** 71 **p** 72. C Leic H Trin 71-74; C Cambridge H Trin *Ely* 74-77; C Woking St Jo *Guildf* 77-81; V Goldsworth Park 81-93; V Wyke 93-98; Dioc Officer Educn and Development of Lay People 93-98; Can Res Chelmsf Cathl from 98. *2 Harlings Grove, Chelmsford CM1 1YQ* Tel (01245) 355041 or 294484 E-mail andrew.knowles@btinternet.com

KNOWLES, Charles Howard. b 43. Sheff Univ BSc65 Fitzw Coll Cam BA69 MA73. Westcott Ho Cam 67. **d** 69 **p** 70. C Bilborough St Jo *S'well* 69-72; V Choral S'well Minster 72-82; V Cinderhill 82-94; AD Nottingham W 91-94; V Cov St Mary 94-06; AD Cov S 96-02; C Burnsall w Rylstone *Bradf* 06-08; C Linton in Craven 06-08; C Kettlewell w Conistone, Hubberholme etc 06-08; rtd 08; Perm to Offic *Bradf* from 08. *Ivy Cottage, Linton, Skipton BD23 5HH* E-mail charles.knowles@sky.com

KNOWLES, Clay. See KNOWLES, Melvin Clay

KNOWLES, Clifford. b 35. Open Univ BA82. NW Ord Course 74. **d** 77 **p** 78. C Urmston *Man* 77-80, V Chadderton St Luke 80-87; V Heywood St Luke w All So 87-95; AD Heywood and Middleton 92-95; Perm to Offic *Linc* 95-98; rtd 00; Perm to Offic *Linc* from 02. *12B Far Lane, Coleby, Lincoln LN5 0AH* Tel (01522) 810720

KNOWLES, Canon Eric Gordon. b 44. WMMTC 79. **d** 82 **p** 83. NSM Gt Malvern St Mary *Worc* 82-83; NSM Malvern H Trin and St Jas 83-90; NSM Lt Malvern, Malvern Wells and Wyche 90-99; NSM Lt Malvern 99-00; P-in-c from 00; Hon Can Worc Cathl from 05. *45 Wykewane, Malvern WR14 2XD* Tel (01684) 567439

KNOWLES, George. b 37. **d** 95 **p** 96. NSM Hucknall Torkard *S'well* 95-02; rtd 02; Perm to Offic *S'well* from 02. *8 North Hill Avenue, Hucknall, Nottingham NG15 7FE* Tel 0115-955 9822 E-mail g.knowles3@ntlworld.com

✠**KNOWLES, The Rt Revd Graeme Paul.** b 51. AKC73. St Aug Coll Cant 73. **d** 74 **p** 75 **c** 03. C St Peter-in-Thanet *Cant* 74-79; C Leeds St Pet *Ripon* 79-81; Chapl and Prec Portsm Cathl 81-87; Chapter Clerk 85-87; V Leigh Park 87-93; RD Havant 90-93; Adn Portsm 93-99; Dean Carl 99-03; Bp S & M 03-07; Dean St Paul's *Lon* from 07. *The Deanery, 9 Amen Court, London EC4M 7BU* Tel (020) 7236 2827 Fax 7332 0298 E-mail thedean@stpaulscathedral.org.uk

KNOWLES, Irene. See KNOWLES, Margaret Irene

KNOWLES, Mrs Jane Frances. b 44. GGSM66 Lon Inst of Educn TCert67. Ox Min Course 90. **d** 93 **p** 94. NSM Sandhurst *Ox* 93-97; C Wargrave 97-99; P-in-c Ramsden, Finstock and Fawler, Leafield etc 99-01; V Forest Edge 01-09; rtd 09. *41 Martin's Road, Keevil, Trowbridge BA14 6NA* Tel (01380) 870325 E-mail janeknowles@tiscali.co.uk

KNOWLES, John Geoffrey. b 48. Man Univ BSc69 Ox Univ PGCE70 Lon Univ MSc75 FRSA. WMMTC 95. **d** 98 **p** 99. NSM The Lickey *Birm* 99-04; R Hutcheson's Gr Sch 99-04; P-in-c Woodford *Ches* from 05; Dioc Warden of Readers from 05. *The Vicarage, 531 Chester Road, Woodford, Stockport SK7 1PR* Tel 0161-439 2286 E-mail john.knowles2@virgin.net

KNOWLES, Margaret Irene. b 48. EAMTC 96. **d** 99 **p** 00. C Gt Yarmouth *Nor* 99-03; TV 03-11; RD Gt Yarmouth 05-10; Chapl Norfolk & Waveney Mental Health NHS Foundn Trust 00-11; R Bunwell, Carleton Rode, Tibenham, Gt Moulton etc *Nor* from 11. *The Rectory, Chapel Road, Carleton Rode, Norwich NR16 1RN* Tel (01953) 788161 Mobile 07713-30382 E-mail revmik@hotmail.co.uk

KNOWLES, Melvin Clay. b 43. Stetson Univ (USA) BA66 Ex Univ MA73. Ripon Coll Cuddesdon 75. **d** 77 **p** 78. C Minchinhampton *Glouc* 77-80; St Helena 80-82; TV Haywards Heath St Wilfrid *Chich* 82-88; Adult Educn Adv 88-94; TR Burgess Hill St Jo w St Edw 94-06; V Burgess Hill St Jo 00-09; rtd 09. *32 Livingstone Road, Burgess Hill RH15 8QP* Tel (01444) 254429 E-mail cknowles@waitrose.com

KNOWLES, Philip Andrew. b 63. Leeds Univ BA87. NOC 04. **d** 07 **p** 08. C Blackb St Mich w St Jo and H Trin 07-10; C Blackb St Thos w St Jude 07-10; P-in-c Lt Marsden w Nelson St Mary and Nelson St Bede 10-11; V from 11. *St Paul's Vicarage, Bentley Street, Nelson BB9 0BS* Tel (01254) 615888 E-mail philip.knowles1@btinternet.com

KNOWLES, The Very Revd Philip John. b 48. MA PhD BTh LTCL ALCM LLAM. CITC 76. **d** 76 **p** 77. C Lisburn St Paul *Conn* 76-79; I Cloonclare w Killasnett and Lurganboy *K, E & A* 79-87; I Gorey w Kilnahue *C & O* 87-89; I Gorey w Kilnahue,

Leskinfere and Ballycanew 89-95; Preb Ferns Cathl 91-95; Dean Cashel from 95; I Cashel w Magorban, Tipperary, Clonbeg etc from 95; Chan Waterford Cathl from 95; Chan Lismore Cathl from 95; Can Ossory and Leighlin Cathls from 96; Can St Patr Cathl Dublin from 08. *The Deanery, Cashel, Co Tipperary, Republic of Ireland* Tel (00353) (62) 61232 *or* 61944 E-mail knowlesph@iolfree.ie

KNOWLES, Richard John. b 47. EAMTC 00. d 01 p 02. C Burlingham St Edmund w Lingwood, Strumpshaw etc *Nor* 01-04; TV Gt Yarmouth 04-10; rtd 11; Perm to Offic *Nor* from 11. *The Rectory, Chapel Road, Carleton Rode, Norwich NR16 1RN* Tel (01953) 788161 Mobile 07855-165008 E-mail revrjk@hotmail.co.uk

KNOWLES-BROWN, Canon John Henry. b 30. AKC53. d 54 p 55. C Hertford St Andr *St Alb* 54-58; C Bushey 58-61; Chapl RAF 61-65; C-in-c Farley Hill St Jo CD *St Alb* 65-69; V Farley Hill St Jo 69-72; V Totteridge 72-95; RD Barnet 79-89; Hon Can St Alb 85-95; rtd 95; Perm to Offic *Ex* from 97. *1 Ascerton Close, Sidmouth EX10 9BS* Tel (01395) 579286

KNOWLING, Richard Charles. b 46. K Coll Lon BSc67 St Edm Hall Ox BA70 MA89. St Steph Ho Ox 69. d 71 p 72. C Hobs Moat *Birm* 71-75; C Shrewsbury St Mary w All SS and St Mich *Lich* 75-77; V Rough Hills 77-83; Dir Past Th Coll of Resurr Mirfield 83-90; V Palmers Green St Jo *Lon* 90-05; AD Enfield 96-01; V Edmonton St Alphege from 05; P-in-c Ponders End St Matt from 05. *St Alphege's Vicarage, Rossdale Drive, London N9 7LG* Tel (020) 8245 3588 E-mail richard.knowling@london.anglican.org

KNOX, Canon Geoffrey Martin. b 44. Dur Univ BA66 Sheff City Coll of Educn DipEd73. St Chad's Coll Dur 63. d 67 p 68. C Newark St Mary *S'well* 67-72; Perm to Offic *Derby* 72-74; V Woodville 74-81; RD Repton 79-81; V Long Eaton St Laur 81-00; V Somercotes 00-09; RD Alfreton 04-09; Hon Can Derby Cathl 08-09; rtd 09. *9 Treveryn Parc, Budock Water, Falmouth TR11 5EH* Tel (01326) 373142

KNOX, Iain John Edward. b 46. TCD BA70 MA74 Hull Univ BPhil76. CITC 71. d 71 p 72. C Belfast Malone St Jo *Conn* 71-74; Bp's Dom Chapl 72-74; Perm to Offic *D & R* 74-76; I Gweedore Union 76-80; I Clonmel w Innislounagh, Tullaghmelan etc *C & O* 80-96; Bp's Dom Chapl 82-97; Press and Radio Officer (Cashel) 90-95; Dioc Info Officer (Cashel and Waterford) 92-95; Lic to Offic from 96; V Choral Cashel Cathl from 03. *Rossnowlagh, Heywood Road, Clonmel, Co Tipperary, Republic of Ireland* Tel (00353) (52) 27107 Mobile 87-236 8186

KNOX, Canon Ian Stephen. b 44. Leeds Univ LLB64 Solicitor 66 Brunel Univ MPhil03. d 05 p 05. Perm to Offic *Cov* 05-06 and *Newc* from 06; Exec Dir 40:3 Trust from 05. *16 East Moor, Loughoughton, Alnwick NE66 3JB* Tel (01665) 572939 E-mail office@fortythreetrust.com

KNOX, Janet. b 57. d 11. NSM Quinton Road W St Boniface *Birm* from 11. *405 Simons Drive, Birmingham B32 2UH* Tel 0121-426 3575

KNOX, Matthew Stephen. b 75. Man Univ BSc98 Newc Univ PGCE02 St Jo Coll Dur BA07. Cranmer Hall Dur 04. d 07 p 08. C Newburn *Newc* 07-11; P-in-c Tweedmouth from 11; P-in-c Spittal from 11; P-in-c Scremerston from 11. *The Vicarage, 124 Main Street, Tweedmouth, Berwick-upon-Tweed TD15 2AW* Tel (01289) 305296 E-mail knoxmatthew@yahoo.com

KNUCKEY, William Thomas. b 47. Qu Coll Birm 02. d 05 p 06. NSM Amington *Birm* 05-10; P-in-c Deloraine Australia from 10. *14 Marlendy Drive, Deloraine TA 7304, Australia* E-mail bill.knuckey@sky.com

KOCH, John Dunbar. Washington & Lee Univ BA00. d 07 p 08. C Wiesbaden Austria 07-09; C Vienna *Eur* from 09. *Christ Church, 17-19 Jaurèsgasse, A-1030 Vienna, Austria* Tel and fax (0043) (1) 714 8900

KOHNER, Canon Jeno George. b 31. K Coll Lon BD56 AKC56 Concordia Univ Montreal MA82. Westcott Ho Cam 56. d 57 p 58. C Eccleston St Thos *Liv* 57-60; Canada from 60; Hon Can Montreal from 75. *H3-850 Lakeshore Drive, Dorval QC H9S 5T9, Canada* Tel (001) (514) 631 0066

KOLAWOLE, Canon Peter Adeleke. b 36. Immanuel Coll Ibadan 91. d 85 p 86. C Lagos Abp Vining Memorial Ch Nigeria 85-87; P Isolo St Paul 88-96; P Lagos Cathl 97-99; Can Res 99-03; Perm to Offic *Chelmsf* from 04. *58 Shaftesbury Point, High Street, London E13 0AB* Tel (020) 8471 5144

✠KOLINI, The Most Revd Emmanuel Musaba. b 44. Balya Bible Coll Uganda 67 Can Werner Coll Burundi 68 Bp Tucker Coll Mukono 75. d 69 c 80. Uganda 69-79; Kyangwali 69-74; Bulinda 77-79; Zaïre 80-97; Adn Bukavu 80; Asst Bp Bukavu 81-85; Bp Shaba 86-97; Bp Kigali from 97; Abp Rwanda from 98. *PO Box 61, Kigali, Rwanda* Tel (00250) 576340 Fax 573213 *or* 576504 E-mail eak@rwanda1.com

KOLOGARAS, Mrs Linda Audrey. b 48. Humberside Univ BA97. EMMTC 89. d 95 p 96. NSM Gt and Lt Coates w Bradley *Linc* 95-98; C Immingham 98-02; R Rosewood Australia 03-07. *Address temp unknown*

KOMOR, Michael. b 60. Univ of Wales BSc83. Chich Th Coll 83. d 86 p 87. C Mountain Ash *Llan* 86-89; C Llantwit Major 89-91;

TV 91-00; V Ewenny w St Brides Major 00-05; R Coity, Nolton and Brackla from 05; AD Bridgend 04-10. *Nolton Rectory, Merthyr Mawr Road North, Bridgend CF31 3NH* Tel (01656) 652247 E-mail mkomor@talk21.com

KONIG, Peter Montgomery. b 44. Univ of Wales (Lamp) MA10. Westcott Ho Cam 80. d 82 p 83. C Oundle *Pet* 82-86; Chapl Westwood Ho Sch Pet 86-92; Chapl Pet High Sch 92-95; Chapl Worksop Coll Notts 95-99; Chapl Glenalmond Coll *St And* 99-04; rtd 04; Perm to Offic *Pet* from 04. *Crossways, Main Street, Yarwell, Peterborough PE8 6PR* Tel (01780) 782873 E-mail pandakonig@talktalk.net

KOPSCH, Hartmut. b 41. Sheff Univ BA63 Univ of BC MA66 Lon Univ PhD70. Trin Coll Bris 78. d 80 p 81. C Cranham Park *Chelmsf* 80-85; V Springfield *Birm* 85-92; V Dover St Martin *Cant* 92-96; R Bath Walcot *B & W* 96-06; rtd 06; Perm to Offic *Glouc* 07-09. *10 St Edyths Road, Bristol BS9 2ES* Tel 0117-968 8683 E-mail harmutandjane@gmail.com

KOREA, Presiding Bishop of. *Vacant*

KORNAHRENS, Wallace Douglas. b 43. The Citadel Charleston BA66 Gen Th Sem (NY) STB69. d 69 p 70. USA 69-72; C Potters Green *Cov* 72-75; Chapl Community of Celebration Wargrave Oxon 75-76; P-in-c Cumbrae (or Millport) *Arg* 76-78; R Grantown-on-Spey *Mor* 78-83; R Rothiemurchus 78-83; R Edin H Cross from 83. *Holy Cross Rectory, 18 Barnton Gardens, Edinburgh EH4 6AF* Tel 0131-336 2311

KOSLA, Mrs Ann Louise. b 56. Middx Univ BA04. NTMTC 01. d 04 p 05. NSM Thorley *St Alb* 04-07; NSM Chelmsf S Deanery 08-10; NSM Boreham *Chelmsf* from 10. *7 Yonge Close, Boreham, Chelmsford CM3 3GY* Tel (01245) 465773 E-mail ann.kosla@sky.com

KOSLA, Charles Antoni. b 58. Ridley Hall Cam 97. d 99 p 00. C Widford *Chelmsf* 99-03; C Thorley *St Alb* 03-07; Dioc Adv for Miss and Par Development *Chelmsf* from 07; Hon C E Springfield from 08. *7 Yonge Close, Boreham, Chelmsford CM3 3GY* Tel (01245) 294419 *or* 465773 E-mail ckosla@chelmsford.anglican.org

KOTHARE, Jayant Sunderrao. b 41. Bombay Univ BA Heidelberg Univ MDiv. d 86 p 87. C Handsworth St Mich *Birm* 86-89; C Southall St Geo *Lon* 89-92; TV Thamesmead *S'wark* 92-97; Dioc Community Relns Officer *Man* 97-00; P-in-c Moston St Chad 97-02; rtd 02; Perm to Offic *Man* from 09. *27 Charlesworth Court, 18 Bingley Close, Manchester M11 3RF* E-mail jaysohum@yahoo.co.uk

KOUBLE (*née* MACKIE)**, Fiona Mary.** b 66. Anglia Ruskin Univ BA94 MSc95 St Jo Coll Dur BA09 RGN88. Cranmer Hall Dur 07. d 11. C Hillsborough and Wadsley Bridge *Sheff* from 11. *486 Loxley Road, Loxley, Sheffield S6 6RS* Tel 0114-232 3506 Mobile 07817-167386 E-mail fionakouble@yahoo.co.uk

KOUSSEFF, Mrs Karen Patricia. b 60. Ex Univ BA83. STETS 06. d 09 p 10. NSM Lower Dever *Win* from 09. *15 Long Barrow Close, South Wonston, Winchester SO21 3ED* Tel (01962) 885114 E-mail kkousseff@tiscali.co.uk

KOVOOR, Canon George Iype. b 57. Delhi Univ BA77 Serampore Univ BD80. Union Bibl Sem Yavatmal 78. d 80 p 80. Chapl Leprosy Miss Hosp Kothara India 80-81; Assoc Presbyter Shanti Nivas Ch Faridabad 82; Presbyter Santokh Majra 83; Dean St Paul's Cathl Ambala 84-88; Chapl St Steph Hosp Delhi 88-90; C Derby St Aug 90-94; Min Derby Asian Chr Min Project 90-94; Tutor Crowther Hall CMS Tr Coll Selly Oak 94-97; Prin 97-05; Hon Can Worc Cathl 01-05; Prin Trin Coll Bris from 05; Chapl to The Queen from 03; Can Th Niger Delta N from 10; Can Missiologist Sabah from 10. *Trinity College, Stoke Hill, Bristol BS9 1JP* Tel 0117-968 2803 *or* 968 2646 Fax 968 7470 E-mail principal@trinity-bris.ac.uk

KRAFT (*née* STEVENS)**, Mrs Jane.** b 45. SRN66 SCM68. NTMTC 01. d 03 p 04. NSM Finchley St Mary *Lon* 03-07; TV Chipping Barnet *St Alb* from 07. *St Stephen's Vicarage, 1 Spring Close, Barnet EN5 2UR* Tel (020) 8275 0858 Mobile 07803-868482 E-mail revd.janekraft@btinternet.com

KRAMER, Beaman Kristopher (Kris). b 67. Mars Hill Coll (USA) BS88 Duke Univ (USA) MTS95. Wycliffe Hall Ox MTh98. d 98 p 99. C Hersham *Guildf* 98-99; C Paddington St Jo w St Mich *Lon* 99-00; R Radford Grace USA 00-10; Perm to Offic *Ox* from 10. *69 Bishops Drive, Wokingham RG40 1WA* Tel 0118-979 9956 E-mail frkris@gmail.com

KRAMER, Mrs Caroline Anne. b 70. Wycliffe Hall Ox BTh98. d 98. C Oatlands *Guildf* 98-99; USA 00-10; C Wokingham All SS *Ox* from 10. *69 Bishops Drive, Wokingham RG40 1WA* Tel 0118-979 9956 Mobile 07772-605107 E-mail revcarolinekramer@googlemail.com

KROLL, Una Margaret Patricia. b 25. Girton Coll Cam MB51 BChir51. S'wark Ord Course 68. d 88 p 97. NSM Monmouth 88-97; Lic to Offic *Mon* from 04. *6 Hamilton House, 57 Hanson Street, Bury BL9 6LR* Tel 0161-797 7877

KRONBERGS, Paul Mark. b 55. NEOC 02. d 05 p 06. NSM Middlesbrough St Columba w St Paul *York* from 05. *39 Northumberland Grove, Stockton-on-Tees TS20 1PB* Tel (01642) 365160 E-mail fr-paul.kronbergs@hotmail.com

KRONENBERG, John Simon. b 59. Greenwich Univ BSc85 Open Univ BA00 MRICS87 MBEng94. Ripon Coll Cuddesdon 02. **d** 02 **p** 03. C Chandler's Ford *Win* 02-06; V Hinchley Wood *Guildf* from 06. *The Vicarage, 98 Manor Road North, Esher KT10 0AD* Tel (020) 8786 6391 Mobile 07956-517065 E-mail j.kronenberg@btinternet.com

KRONENBERG, Selwyn Thomas Denzil. b 32. Univ of Wales (Swansea) BA54 St Cath Soc Ox BA57 MA60 Leic Univ MA72 California Univ MA82. Wycliffe Hall Ox 54. **d** 57 **p** 58. C Surbiton St Matt *S'wark* 57-59; C Luton St Mary *St Alb* 59-61; P-in-c Loscoe *Derby* 61-65; Lect RE Bulmershe Coll 65-67; Whitelands Coll 67-97; rtd 97; Perm to Offic *Guildf* 77-07. *58 Woodfield Lane, Ashtead KT21 2BS* Tel (01372) 272505

KROUKAMP, Nigel John Charles. b 53. Cen Lancs Univ BSc93 Bolton Inst of HE CertEd86 RNMH75 RGN78. LCTP 05. **d** 08 **p** 09. NSM Colne and Villages *Blackb* from 08. *56 Kelswick Drive, Nelson BB9 0SZ* Tel (01282) 698261 Mobile 07725-858433 E-mail nigelkroukamp@googlemail.com

KRZEMINSKI, Stefan. b 51. Nottm Univ BTh77. Linc Th Coll 74. **d** 77 **p** 78. C Sawley *Derby* 77-79; Asst Chapl Bluecoat Sch Nottm 79-86; Hon C W Hallam and Mapperley *Derby* 84-96; Hd of RE Nottm High Sch from 86; Perm to Offic *Derby* from 96. *12 Newbridge Close, West Hallam, Ilkeston DE7 6LY* Tel 0115-930 5052

KUHRT, The Ven Gordon Wilfred. b 41. Lon Univ BD63 Middx Univ DProf01. Oak Hill Th Coll 65. **d** 67 **p** 68. C Illogan *Truro* 67-70; C Wallington *S'wark* 70-73; V Shenstone *Lich* 73-79; P-in-c S Croydon Em *Cant* 79-81; V S Croydon Em *S'wark* 81-89; RD Croydon Cen *Cant* 81-86; Hon Can S'wark Cathl 87-89, Adn Lewisham 89-96, Chief Sec ADM 96-02, Dir Min Division Abps' Coun 99-06; rtd 06; Hon C Tredington and Darlingscott *Cov* from 06; Hon C Ilmington w Stretton-on-Fosse etc from 06. *The Rectory, Tredington, Shipston-on-Stour CV36 4NG* Tel (01608) 661264 E-mail omkuhrt@tiscali.co.uk

KUHRT, Martin Gordon. b 66. Nottm Univ LLB88. Trin Coll Bris 93. **d** 96 **p** 97. C Morden *S'wark* 96-00; Chapl Lee Abbey 00-02; TV Melksham *Sarum* 02-08; C Atworth w Shaw and Whitley 07-08; P-in-c Bedgrove *Ox* 08-09; V from 09. *The Vicarage, 252 Wendover Road, Aylesbury HP21 9PD* Tel (01296) 435546 E-mail mgkuhrt555@btinternet.com

KUHRT, Stephen John. b 69. Man Univ BA91 Lon Inst of Educn PGCE93. Wycliffe Hall Ox BA03. **d** 03 **p** 04. C New Malden and Coombe *S'wark* from 03; P-in-c from 07. *12 Roseberry Avenue, New Malden KT3 4JS* Tel (020) 8942 2523

KUIN LAWTON, Theresa. b 69. St Aid Coll Dur BA91 TCD MPhil96. Ox Min Course 05. **d** 07 **p** 08. NSM Bampton w Clanfield *Ox* 07-10; Chapl Magd Coll Sch Ox from 09. *Manor Croft, Church Close, Bampton OX18 2LW* Tel (01993) 850468 E-mail tessa.lawton@onetel.com

KUMAR, Suresh. b 59. Madras Univ MSc81 Leic Univ MA91 Alagappa Univ MA05. Serampore Th Coll BD85. **d** 85 **p** 88. India 85-08; C Braunstone Park *Leic* 08-09; TV Emmaus Par Team from 09. *10 Park Hill Drive, Leicester LE2 8HR* Tel 0116-283 4031 Mobile 07824-813202 E-mail suresh@skumar.plus.com

KURK, Pamela Ann. b 56. Univ of Wales (Ban) BTh06. **d** 04 **p** 05. NSM Wandsworth St Mich w St Steph *S'wark* 04-11; Chapl St Cecilia's Wandsworth C of E Sch from 07. *64 Pulborough Road, London SW18 5UJ* Tel (020) 8265 8985 Mobile 07774-437471 E-mail thekurks@aol.com *or* akurk@saintcecilias.wandsworth.sch.uk

KURRLE, Canon Stanley Wynton. b 22. OBE82. Melbourne Univ BA47 St Cath Soc Ox BA50 MA54. Wycliffe Hall Ox 49. **d** 52 **p** 53. C Sutton *Liv* 52-54; Australia from 54; Fell St Paul's Coll Univ of Sydney from 69; Can Sydney 81-95; Can Emer 95. *25 Marieba Road, PO Box 53, Kenthurst NSW 2156, Australia* Tel (0061) (2) 9654 1334 Mobile 427-277919 Fax 9654 1368 E-mail mathourastation@bigpond.com

KURTI, Peter Walter. b 60. Qu Mary Coll Lon LLB82 K Coll Lon MTh89. Ch Div Sch of Pacific 82 Ripon Coll Cuddesdon 83. **d** 86 **p** 87. C Prittlewell *Chelmsf* 86-90; Chapl Derby Coll of HE 90-92; Chapl Derby Univ 92-94; Dep Hd Relig Resource and Research Cen 90-94; Australia from 94; Prec St Geo Cathl Perth 94-97; R Scarborough 97-01; R Sydney St Jas from 01. *Level 1, 169-171 Phillip Street, Sydney NSW 2000, Australia* Tel (0061) (2) 9363 3335 *or* 9232 3022 Mobile 412-049271 Fax 9232 4182 E-mail peter.kurti@bigpond.com

KUSTNER, Ms Jane Lesley. b 54. Lanchester Poly Cov BA76 FCA79. St Steph Ho Ox 03. **d** 05 **p** 06. C Waterloo St Jo w St Andr *S'wark* 05-08; P-in-c Lewisham St Swithun from 08. *St Swithun's Vicarage, 191 Hither Green Lane, London SE13 6QE* Tel 00734-113741 (mobile) E-mail jane.kustner@btinternet.com

✠**KWONG KONG KIT, The Most Revd Peter.** b 36. Kenyon Coll Ohio BSc65 DD86 Hong Kong Univ DD00. Bexley Hall Div Sch Ohio MTh71 DD98. **d** 65 **p** 66 **c** 81. P-in-c Hong Kong Crown of Thorns 65-66; C Hong Kong St Paul 71-72; Bp Hong Kong and Macao 81-98; Bp Hong Kong Is from 98; Abp Hong Kong

Sheng Kung Hui from 98. *Bishop's House, 1 Lower Albert Road, Hong Kong, China* Tel (00852) 2526 5355 Fax 2525 2537 E-mail office1@hkskh.org

KYEI-BAFFOUR, Jacob Owusu. b 62. Kwame Nkrumah Univ Ghana BA02 Univ of the Arts Lon MA05. St Nic Th Coll Ghana 90. **d** 93 **p** 94. C Jameso-Nkwatah Ghana 93-94; Perm to Offic *S'wark* 94-95; P-in-c Cape Coast St Monica Ghana 95-98; Asst Chapl Kwame Nkrumah Univ 98-02; Asst P Ch Ch Cathl Cape Coast 02-03; Perm to Offic *Lon* 03-06; Hon C Willesden Green St Andr and St Fran 06-09. *Address temp unknown* Tel 07906-718708 (mobile) E-mail kyei baffourcl@fsmail.net

KYLE, Miss Sharon Patricia Culvinor. b 55. Open Univ BA90 Edin Univ BD94 MTh96. Coates Hall Edin 91. **d** 94 **p** 95. C Edin SS Phil and Jas 94-96; C Neston *Ches* 96-99; TV Kirkby *Liv* 99-01. *22 Oak Tree Close, Kingsbury, Tamworth B78 2JF* Tel (01827) 874445

KYRIACOU, Brian George. b 42. Lon Univ LLB64. Oak Hill Th Coll 79. **d** 81 **p** 82. C Becontree St Mary *Chelmsf* 81-83; C Becontree St Cedd 83-85; C Becontree W 85; TV 85-87; V Shiregreen St Jas and St Chris *Sheff* 87-92; TV Schorne *Ox* 92-98; V Edmonton All SS w St Mich *Lon* 98-07; rtd 07; Perm to Offic *Chelmsf* from 07. *28 Morant Road, Colchester CO1 2JA* Tel (01206) 520699 Mobile 07970-719094 E-mail brian.kyriacou@ntlworld.com

KYRIAKIDES-YELDHAM, Anthony Paul Richard. b 48. Birkbeck Coll Lon BSc82 Warwick Univ MSc90 CQSW83 CPsychol91. K Coll Lon BD73 AKC73. **d** 74 **p** 75. C Dalston H Trin w St Phil *Lon* 74-78; NSM Lon Docks St Pet w Wapping St Jo 79-81; NSM Hackney Wick St Mary of Eton w St Aug 81-05; NSM Wandsworth Common St Mary *S'wark* 85 87; Chapl Wandsworth HA Mental Health Unit 87-93; Chapl Springfield Univ Hosp Lon 87-93; Perm to Offic *Ex* 94-98; Lic to Offic 98-08; Sen Chapl Plymouth Hosps NHS Trust 98-08; P-in-c Kingsbridge and Dodbrooke *Ex* 08-11; Preb Ex Cathl 07-11; Chapl Imp Coll Healthcare NHS Trust from 11. *14 Neville House, 19 Page Street, London SW1P 4JX* Tel 07929-775228 (mobile) E-mail tony.yeldham@talk21.com

KYTE, Eric Anthony. b 62. Leeds Univ BSc84 PGCE85. Trin Coll Bris BA98. **d** 98 **p** 99. C Pudsey St Lawr and St Paul *Bradf* 98-01; P-in-c Gisburn and Hellifield 01-11; New Zealand from 11. *353 Highgate, Roslyn, Dunedin, New Zealand* E-mail thereverick@aol.com

KYUMU MOTUKO, Norbert. *See* CHUMU MUTUKU, Norbert

L

LABDON, David William. b 64. St Jo Coll Nottm 07. **d** 09 **p** 10. C Bebington *Ches* from 09. *125 West Vale, Neston CH64 0TJ* Tel 0151-336 7865 E-mail davidlabdon@btinternet.com

LABDON, John. b 32. Oak Hill Th Coll. **d** 84 **p** 85. C Formby H Trin *Liv* 84-87; P-in-c St Helens St Mark 87-97; rtd 97; Perm to Offic *Ches* from 97. *28 Burton Road, Little Neston, Neston CH64 9RA* Tel 0151-336 7039

LABOUREL, Elaine Odette. b 58. St Jo Coll Nottm 03. **d** 05 **p** 06. C Paris St Mich *Eur* 05-08; P-in-c Rouen All SS 06-08; Asst Chapl Versailles w Chevry from 08. *4 avenue de Savigny, 91700 Ste Geneviève des Bois, France* Tel (0033) 1 69 04 09 91 Mobile 6 60 59 65 98 E-mail elaine.labourel@wanadoo.fr

LABRAN, Stuart. b 79. Leeds Univ BA00 PGCE02 Clare Coll Cam MPhil09. Westcott Ho Cam 07. **d** 09 **p** 10. C Stratford-upon-Avon, Luddington etc *Cov* from 09. *2 St John's Close, Stratford-upon-Avon CV37 9AB* Tel (01789) 268836 E-mail stuartlabran@hotmail.com

LACEY, Allan John. b 48. Sheff Univ MA02. Wycliffe Hall Ox. **d** 82 **p** 83. C Greasbrough *Sheff* 82-85; R Treeton 85-92; V Thorpe Hesley 92-00; R Rossington 00-07; CMS Uganda from 07. *Church Mission Society, Watlington Road, Oxford OX4 6BZ* Tel 08456-201799 E-mail allanandanne@btinternet.com

LACEY, Brian. d 10. C Ballymena w Ballyclug *Conn* from 10. *The Gate Lodge, St Patrick's Church, 50 Castle Street, Ballymena BT43 7BT* Tel (028) 2564 7040 E-mail brianlacey@hotmail.co.uk

LACEY, Mrs Carol Ann. b 62. Qu Coll Birm 07. **d** 09 **p** 10. NSM Leic St Anne, St Paul and St Aug from 09. *Willow Cottage, 22A Chapel Street, Blaby, Leicester LE8 4GB* Tel 0116-278 8817 Mobile 07971-519705 E-mail carolannlacey@googlemail.com

LACEY, Eric. b 33. Cranmer Hall Dur 69. **d** 71 **p** 72. C Blackpool St Jo *Blackb* 71-75; V Whittle-le-Woods 75-88; R Heysham 88-98; rtd 98; Perm to Offic *Blackb* from 98. *143 Bredon Avenue, Chorley PR7 6NS* Tel (01257) 273040

LACEY, Nigel Jeremy. b 59. St Jo Coll Nottm BTh94. **d** 94 **p** 95. C Mildenhall *St E* 94-97; C Selly Park St Steph and St Wulstan *Birm* 97-01; P-in-c W Wycombe w Bledlow Ridge, Bradenham and Radnage *Ox* 01-09; R from 09. *The Rectory, Church Lane, West Wycombe, High Wycombe HP14 3AH* Tel (01494) 529988 E-mail nigel.lacey@whsmithnet.co.uk

LACK, Miss Catherine Mary. b 59. Clare Coll Cam BA81 Ox Univ MTh00 ARCM78. Qu Coll Birm 90. **d** 92 **p** 94. C Leiston *St E* 92-95; TV Ipswich St Mary at Stoke w St Pet and St Fran 95-98; Chapl Keele Univ 98-07; Cultural and Relig Affairs Manager Yarl's Wood Immigration Removal Cen 07-08; Warden Ferrar House Lt Gidding Community 08-09; Chapl Newc Univ from 09; Master Newc St Thos Prop Chpl from 09. *9 Chester Crescent, Newcastle upon Tyne NE2 1DH* Tel 0191-231 2750 Mobile 07913-721989 E-mail catherine.lack50@gmail.com

LACK, Martin Paul. b 57. St Jo Coll Ox MA79 MSc80. Linc Th Coll 83. **d** 86 **p** 87. C E Bowbrook and W Bowbrook *Worc* 86-89; C Bowbrook S and Bowbrook N 89-90; R Teme Valley S 90-01; rtd 01. *Colbridge Cottage, Bottom Lane, Whitbourne, Worcester WR6 5RT* Tel (01886) 821978

LACKEY, Michael Geoffrey Herbert. b 42. Oak Hill Th Coll 73. **d** 75 **p** 76. C Hatcham St Jas *S'wark* 75-81; V New Barnet St Jas *St Alb* 81-91; V Hollington St Jo *Chich* 91-02; Dir Crowhurst Chr Healing Cen 02-05; rtd 05; Hon C Gt Amwell w St Margaret's and Stanstead Abbots *St Alb* 05-09. *5 Vicarage Close, St Albans AL1 2PU* E-mail glackey@toucansurf.com

LACKEY, William Terence Charles. b 32. St Mich Coll Llan 80. **d** 82 **p** 83. C Wrexham *St As* 82-85; V Gwersyllt 85-93; R Trefnant 93-98; rtd 98. *24 Old Farm Road, Rhostyllen, Wrexham LL14 4DX* Tel (01978) 311969

LACY, Melanie June. b 75. TCD BA98 All Hallows Coll Dublin MA00. CITC 98. **d** 00. C Bangor St Comgall *D & D* 00-02; N Ireland Regional Co-ord Crosslinks 02-06; C Knutsford St Jo and Toft *Ches* 06-09; Dir Youth and Children's Min Oak Hill Th Coll from 10. *Oak Hill College, Chase Side, London N14 4PS* Tel (020) 8449 0467 Fax 8441 5996 E-mail mel@oakhill.ac.uk

LACY, Sarah Frances. b 49. Sarum Th Coll 93. **d** 96 **p** 97. C Weston Zoyland w Chedzoy *B & W* 96-00; C Middlezoy and Othery and Moorlinch 00-01; R Berrow and Breane from 01. *The Rectory, 1 Manor Way, Berrow, Burnham-on-Sea TA8 2RG* Tel (01278) 751057 E-mail sally@lacys.freeserve.co.uk

LACY-SMITH, Mrs Joanna. b 56. STETS 05. **d** 08 **p** 09. OLM Dorchester *Sarum* from 08. *2 Ackerman Road, Dorchester DT1 1NZ* Tel (01305) 266721 E-mail jolacysmith@copperstream.co.uk

LADD, Mrs Anne de Chair. b 56. Nottm Univ BA78 CQSW80. St Jo Coll Nottm. dss 86 **d** 87 **p** 94. Bucknall and Bagnall *Lich* 86-91; Par Dn 87-91; NSM Bricket Wood *St Alb* 91-01; Chapl Garden Ho Hospice Letchworth 98-06; Befriending Co-ord Mencap from 07; Perm to Offic *Ely* 01-09. *5 Peache Way, Chilwell Lane, Bramcote, Nottingham NG9 3DX* Tel 0115-967 7019

LADD, John George Morgan. b 36. Univ of Wales (Ban) BA58 MA65. St Mich Coll Llan. **d** 90 **p** 91. NSM Nevern and Y Beifil w Eglwyswrw and Meline etc *St D* 90-92; NSM Llandysilio w Egremont and Llanglydwen etc 92-93; V Gwaun-cae-Gurwen 93-04; rtd 04. *Penybanc, Rhiw Road, Swansea SA9 2RE*

LADD, Nicholas Mark. b 57. Ex Univ BA78 Selw Coll Cam BA81 Anglia Ruskin Univ MA03. Ridley Hall Cam 79. **d** 82 **p** 83. C Aston SS Pet and Paul *Birm* 82-86; TV Bucknall and Bagnall *Lich* 86-91; V Bricket Wood *St Alb* 91-01; V Cambridge St Barn *Ely* 01-09; Dean and Lect St Jo Coll Nottm from 09. *St John's College, Chilwell Lane, Bramcote, Nottingham NG9 3DS* Tel 0115-925 1114 Fax 943 6438 E-mail n.ladd@stjohns-nottm.ac.uk

✠**LADDS, The Rt Revd Robert Sidney.** b 41. Lon Univ BEd71 LRSC72. Cant Sch of Min 79. **d** 80 **p** 81 **c** 99. C Hythe *Cant* 80-83; R Bretherton *Blackb* 83-91; Chapl Bp Rawstorne Sch Preston 83-87; Bp's Chapl for Min and Adv Coun for Min *Blackb* 86-91; P-in-c Preston St Jo 91-96; R Preston St Jo and St Geo 96-97; Hon Can Blackb Cathl 93-97; Adn Lancaster 97-99; Suff Bp Whitby *York* 99-08; rtd 08; Hon C Hendon St Mary and Ch Ch *Lon* from 09. *Christ Church House, 76 Brent Street, London NW4 2ES* Tel (020) 8202 8123

LADIPO, Canon Adeyemi Olalekan. b 37. Trin Coll Bris 63. **d** 66 **p** 76. C Bilston St Leon *Lich* 66-68; Nigeria 68-84; V Canonbury St Steph *Lon* 85-87; Sec for Internat Miss BCMS 87-90; Hon C Bromley SS Pet and Paul *Roch* 89-90; V Herne Hill *S'wark* 90-99; Hon Can Jos from 95; V S Malling *Chich* 99-02; rtd 02; Perm to Offic *Chich* from 03 and *S'wark* from 07. *63 Elm Grove, London SE15 5DB* Tel (020) 7639 8150

LAFFORD, Sylvia June. b 46. Middx Univ BA04. NTMTC 01. **d** 04 **p** 05. NSM Hayes St Edm *Lon* from 04; Asst Chapl Hillingdon Hosp NHS Trust from 10. *17 Audley Court, Pinner HA5 3TQ* Tel (020) 8868 2574 E-mail sylvialafford@aol.com

LAIDLAW, Juliet. *See* MONTAGUE, Mrs Juliet

LAIN-PRIESTLEY, Ms Rosemary Jane. b 67. Kent Univ BA89 K Coll Lon MA02. Carl Dioc Tr Course 92. **d** 96 **p** 97. C Scotforth *Blackb* 96-98; SC St Martin-in-the-Fields *Lon* 98-06;

LAING, Canon Alexander Burns. b 34. RD90. Edin Th Coll 57. **d** 60 **p** 61. C Falkirk *Edin* 60-62; C Edin Ch Ch 62-70; Chapl RNR 64-91; P-in-c Edin St Fillan 70-74; Chapl Edin R Infirmary 74-77; Dioc Supernumerary *Edin* from 77; R Helensburgh *Glas* 77-03; Can St Mary's Cathl 87-03; rtd 03; Lic to Offic *Glas* from 06. *13 Drumadoon Drive, Helensburgh G84 9SF* Tel (01436) 675705

LAING, William Sydney. b 32. TCD BA54 MA62. **d** 55 **p** 56. C Dublin Crumlin *D & G* 55-59; C Dublin St Ann 59-65; I Carbury *M & K* 65-68; I Dublin Finglas *D & G* 68-80; I Tallaght 80-91; Can Ch Ch Cathl Dublin 90-94; Preb 94-97; I Dublin Crumlin w Chapelizod 91-97; rtd 97. *42 Hazelwood Crescent, Clondalkin, Dublin 22, Republic of Ireland* Tel (00353) (1) 459 3893 Mobile 87-760 1210

LAIRD, Alisdair Mark. b 60. Auckland Univ BA84. Trin Coll Bris BA92. **d** 92 **p** 93. C Linthorpe *York* 92-98; V Hull St Cuth 98-06; P-in-c Alne and Brafferton w Pilmoor, Myton-on-Swale etc 06-07; Lic to Offic 07-08; Perm to Offic from 08; Chapl Hull and E Yorks Hosps NHS Trust from 09. *Hull Royal Infirmary, Anlaby Road, Hull HU3 2JZ* Tel (01482) 875875 E-mail aml12375@lairds.org.uk

LAIRD, Canon John Charles. b 32. Sheff Univ BA53 MA54 St Cath Coll Ox BA58 MA62 Lon Univ DipEd70. Ripon Hall Ox 56. **d** 58 **p** 59. C Cheshunt *St Alb* 58-62; Chapl Bps' Coll Cheshunt 62-64; Vice-Prin 64-67; Prin 67-69; V Keysoe w Bolnhurst and Lt Staughton *St Alb* 69-01; Hon Can St Alb 87-02; Lic to Offic from 01. *The Chaplaincy, Fore Street Lodge, Hatfield Park, Hatfield AL9 5NQ* Tel (01707) 274941

LAIRD, Robert George (Robin). b 40. TCD Div Sch 58 Edin Th Coll 63. **d** 65 **p** 66. C Drumragh *D & R* 65-68; CF 68-93; QHC 91-93; Sen Chapl Sedbergh Sch 93-98; Lic to Offic *Bradf* 93-98; rtd 98; Perm to Offic *Ex* and *Sarum* from 98. *Barrule, Hillside Road, Sidmouth EX10 8JD* Tel (01395) 513948

LAIRD, Stephen Charles Edward. b 66. Oriel Coll Ox BA88 MA92 MSt93 K Coll Lon MTh91 Kent Univ PhD06 FRSA00. Wycliffe Hall Ox MPhil96. **d** 94 **p** 95. C Ilfracombe, Lee, Woolacombe, Bittadon etc *Ex* 94-98; Chapl Kent Univ 98-03; Dean of Chapl from 03; Hon Lect from 98; Hon C Hackington *Cant* from 09. *24 Tyler Hill Road, Blean, Canterbury CT2 9HT* Tel (01227) 763373 or 787476 Mobile 07970-438840 E-mail s.c.e.laird@kent.ac.uk

LAKE, David Michael. b 57. St Mary's Sem Oscott 76. St Jo Coll Nottm BA01. **d** 01 **p** 02. C Lilleshall, Muxton and Sheriffhales *Lich* 01-05; P-in-c Crick and Yelvertoft w Clay Coton and Lilbourne *Pet* 05-09; R from 09. *The Rectory, Main Road, Crick, Northampton NN6 7TU* Tel (01788) 822147 E-mail davidlake@mailserver97.freeserve.co.uk

LAKE, Eileen Veronica. *See* CREMIN, Mrs Eileen Veronica

LAKE, Kevin William. b 57. St Mich Coll Llan 97. **d** 99 **p** 00. C Penarth w Lavernock *Llan* 99-02; Chapl Marie Curie Cen Holme Tower 02-04; P-in-c Cwm Ogwr *Llan* 04-06; P-in-c Llandyfodwg and Cwm Ogwr 06-08; V Aberdare St Fagan from 08. *5 Redwood Court, Aberdare CF44 8RX* Tel (01685) 881435 E-mail kevin.lake1@btinternet.com

LAKE, The Very Revd Stephen David. b 63. Southn Univ BTh. Chich Th Coll 85. **d** 88 **p** 89. C Sherborne w Castleton and Lillington *Sarum* 88-92; P-in-c Branksome St Aldhelm 92-96; V 96-01; RD Poole 00-01; Can Res and Sub-Dean St Alb 01-11; Dean Glouc from 11. *The Deanery, 1 Miller's Green, Gloucester GL1 2BP* Tel (01452) 524167 E-mail dean@gloucestercathedral.org.uk

LAKE, Thomas Wesley Cellan. b 77. Univ Coll Lon MEng01. Oak Hill Th Coll BTh08. **d** 08 **p** 09. C Enfield Ch Ch Trent Park *Lon* from 08. *2 Chalk Lane, Barnet EN4 9JQ* E-mail curate@cockfosters.org.uk

LAKE, Vivienne Elizabeth. b 38. Westcott Ho Cam 84. dss 86 **d** 87 **p** 94. Chesterton Gd Shep *Ely* 86-90; C 87-90; Ecum Min K Hedges Ch Cen 87-90; NSM Bourn Deanery 90-01; NSM Papworth Everard 94-96; Perm to Offic from 01. *15 Storey's House, Mount Pleasant, Cambridge CB3 0BZ* Tel (01223) 369523

LAKE, Wynne Vaughan. b 34. St D Coll Lamp BA55. St Mich Coll Llan 55. **d** 57 **p** 58. C Cadoxton-juxta-Barry *Llan* 57-61; C Roath St Sav 61-64; V Oakwood 64-67; V Oakwood w Bryn 67-72; R Shirenewton and Newchurch *Mon* 72-77; rtd 99. *32 Belvedere Close, Kittle, Swansea SA3 3LA*

LAKER, Clive Sheridan. b 59. Greenwich Univ BSc92 RGN82. Aston Tr Scheme 93 SEITE 95. **d** 98 **p** 99. C Bridlington Quay Ch Ch *York* 98-00; C Bridlington Em 00-01; TV Bucknall *Lich* 01-04; C Surbiton St Matt *S'wark* 04-08; TV from 08. *127 Hamilton Avenue, Surbiton KT6 7QA* E-mail lakerfamily@ntlworld.com

LAKER, Grace. *See* SWIFT, Mrs Grace

LAKEY, Elizabeth Flora. b 46. DipOT69 Open Univ BA81. SAOMC 98. **d** 01 **p** 02. OLM Nettlebed w Bix, Highmoor, Pishill

etc *Ox* from 01. *Bank Farm, Pishill, Henley-on-Thames RG9 6HJ* Tel and fax (01491) 638601 Mobile 07799-752933 E-mail bankfarm@btinternet.com
LALL, Mrs Julia Carole. b 56. Ch Ch Coll Cant CertEd78 BEd79. ERMC 07. **d** 10 **p** 11. C Bacton w Wyverstone, Cotton and Old Newton etc *St E* from 10. *7 Silver Street, Old Newton, Stowmarket IP14 4HF* Tel (01449) 774646 Mobile 07837-785607 E-mail julia.lall@hotmail.co.uk
LAMB, Mrs Alison. b 60. Ches Coll of HE BTh04. NOC 01. **d** 04 **p** 05. C Rossington *Sheff* 04-08; V Worsbrough w Elsecar from 08. *The Vicarage, Wath Road, Elsecar, Barnsley S74 8HJ* Tel (01226) 351806 E-mail alison.lamb@sheffield.anglican.org
LAMB, Miss Alyson Margaret. b 55. LMH Ox BA77 MA80. Ridley Hall Cam 03. **d** 05 **p** 06. C York St Mich-le-Belfrey 05-09; V Eastbourne St Jo *Chich* from 09. *St John's Vicarage, 9 Buxton Road, Eastbourne BN20 7LL* Tel (01323) 721105
LAMB, Bruce. b 47. Keble Coll Ox BA69 MA73. Coll of Resurr Mirfield 70. **d** 73 **p** 74. C Romford St Edw *Chelmsf* 73-76; C Canning Town St Cedd 76-79; V New Brompton St Luke *Roch* 79-83; Chapl RN 83-87; C Rugeley *Lich* 87-88; V Trent Vale 88-92; Bereavement Cllr Cruse 94-99; Hon C Chorlton-cum-Hardy St Clem *Man* 98-99; Asst Chapl N Man Health Care NHS Trust 99-02; P-in-c Barton w Peel Green *Man* from 02. *St Michael's Vicarage, 684 Liverpool Road, Eccles, Manchester M30 7LP* Tel 0161-789 3751
LAMB, Bryan John Harry. b 35. Leeds Univ BA60. Coll of Resurr Mirfield 60. **d** 62 **p** 63. C Solihull *Birm* 62-65 and 88-89; Asst Master Malvern Hall Sch Solihull 65-74; Alderbrook Sch and Hd of Light Hall Adult Educn Cen 74-88; V Wragby *Linc* 89; Dioc Dir of Readers 89; Perm to Offic *Birm* from 89; rtd 93. *27 Ladbrook Road, Solihull B91 3RN* Tel 0121-705 2489
LAMB, Canon Christopher Avon. b 39. Qu Coll Ox BA61 MA65 Birm Univ MA78 PhD87. Wycliffe Hall Ox BA63. **d** 63 **p** 64. C Enfield St Andr *Lon* 63-69; Pakistan 69-75; Tutor Crowther Hall CMS Tr Coll Selly Oak 75-78; Co-ord BCMS/CMS Other Faiths Th Project 78-87; Dioc Community Relns Officer *Cov* 87-92; Can Th Cov Cathl from 92; Sec Inter Faith Relns Bd of Miss 92-99; R Warmington w Shotteswell and Radway w Ratley *Cov* 99-06; rtd 06; Perm to Offic *Cov* from 06. *8 Brookside Avenue, Wellesbourne, Warwick CV35 9RZ* Tel (01789) 842060 E-mail christophertinalamb@tiscali.co.uk
LAMB, David Andrew. b 60. Liv Inst of HE BA94 Man Univ MA01. NOC 90. **d** 94 **p** 95. C Formby H Trin *Liv* 94-97; C St Helens St Matt Thatto Heath 97-98; C Halewood 98-01; Lect Liv Hope 99-00; V Birkenhead St Jas w St Bede *Ches* 01-08; NSM Wallasey St Nic w All SS from 08. *66 Chapelhill Road, Wirral CH46 9QN*
LAMB, Graeme William. b 68. Open Univ BA. Trin Coll Bris 99. **d** 01 **p** 02. C Heald Green St Cath *Ches* 01-06; P-in-c Whaley Bridge 06-09. *Address temp unknown*
LAMB, Mrs Jean Evelyn. b 57. Reading Univ BA79 Nottm Univ MA88. St Steph Ho Ox 81. **dss** 84 **d** 88 **p** 01. Leic H Spirit 84-87; Asst Chapl Leic Poly 84-87; Par Dn Beeston *S'well* 88-91; Hon C and Artist in Res Nottingham St Mary and St Cath 92-95; Hon Par Dn Sneinton St Steph w St Alb 97-01; NSM Rolleston w Fiskerton, Morton and Upton 01-02; Perm to Offic 02-04; C Bilborough St Jo 04-11; C Bilborough w Strelley 04-11; C Colwick from 11. *St Alban's House, 4 Dale Street, Nottingham NG2 4JX* Tel 0115-958 5892 Mobile 07851-792552
LAMB, Mary. b 52. **d** 10 **p** 11. OLM Framlingham w Saxtead *St E* from 10. *2 The Coach House, The Square, Dennington, Woodbridge IP13 8AB* Tel (01728) 638897 E-mail marylamb1952@googlemail.com
LAMB, Nicholas Henry. b 52. St Jo Coll Dur BA74. St Jo Coll Nottm 76. **d** 79 **p** 80. C Luton Lewsey St Hugh *St Alb* 79-84; Bethany Fellowship 84-86; In Bapt Min 86-94; Perm to Offic *Chich* 97-99; C E Grinstead St Swithun 99-04; V Forest Row from 04. *The Vicarage, Ashdown Road, Forest Row RH18 5BW* Tel (01342) 822595 E-mail revnicklamb@hotmail.com
LAMB, Philip Richard James. b 42. Sarum & Wells Th Coll. **d** 83 **p** 84. C Wotton-under-Edge w Ozleworth and N Nibley *Glouc* 83-86; TV Worc SE 86-91; R Billingsley w Sidbury, Middleton Scriven etc *Heref* 91-96; R St Dominic, Landulph and St Mellion w Pillaton *Truro* from 96. *The Rectory, St Mellion, Saltash PL12 6RN* Tel (01579) 350061 E-mail frlamb@stmellion141.freeserve.co.uk
LAMB, Phillip. b 68. NEOC 00. **d** 03 **p** 04. C Bridlington Priory *York* 03-06; V Hornsea w Atwick from 06. *The Vicarage, 59 Newbegin, Hornsea HU18 1AB* Tel (01964) 532531 Mobile 07803-239611 E-mail phil_lamb2002@yahoo.co.uk
LAMB, Scott Innes. b 54. Edin Univ BSc86 Fitzw Coll Cam BA92. Ridley Hall Cam 90. **d** 93 **p** 94. C E Ham w Upton Park *Chelmsf* 93-97; V W Holloway St Luke *Lon* 97-00; P-in-c Hammersmith H Innocents 00-03; Chapl RN 03-09; V Bexley St Jo *Roch* from 09. *St John's Vicarage, 29 Parkhill Road, Bexley DA5 1HX* Tel (01322) 521786 E-mail lambscott@sky.com
LAMB, William Robert Stuart. b 70. Balliol Coll Ox BA91 MA95 Peterho Cam MPhil94 Sheff Univ PhD10. Westcott Ho Cam 92. **d** 95 **p** 96. C Halifax *Wakef* 95-98; TV Penistone and Thurlstone

98-01; Chapl Sheff Univ 01-10; Can Res Sheff Cathl 05-10; Vice-Prin Westcott Ho Cam from 10. *Westcott House, Jesus Lane, Cambridge CB5 8BP* Tel (01223) 741013
LAMBERT, Antony. *See* LAMBERT, John Clement Antony
LAMBERT, David Francis. b 40. Oak Hill Th Coll 72. **d** 74 **p** 75. C Paignton St Paul Preston *Ex* 74-77; C Woking Ch Ch *Guildf* 77-84; P-in-c Willesden Green St Gabr *Lon* 84-91; P-in-c Cricklewood St Mich 85-91; V Cricklewood St Gabr and St Mich 92-93; R Chenies and Lt Chalfont, Latimer and Flaunden *Ox* 93-01; Chapl Izmir (Smyrna) w Bornova *Eur* 01-03; TV Brixham w Churston Ferrers and Kingswear *Ex* 03-05; rtd 05. *54 Brunel Road, Broadsands, Paignton TQ4 6HW* Tel (01803) 842076
LAMBERT, David Hardy. b 44. AKC66. **d** 67 **p** 68. C Marske in Cleveland *York* 67-72; V 85-09; V N Ormesby 73-85; RD Guisborough 86-91; rtd 09; Perm to Offic *York* from 10. *13 Fell Briggs Drive, Marske-by-the-Sea, Redcar TS11 6BU* Tel (01642) 490235 E-mail david@lambert9139.freeserve.co.uk
LAMBERT, David Joseph. b 66. Coll of Resurr Mirfield 99. **d** 01 **p** 02. C Camberwell St Geo *S'wark* 01-04; C Walworth St Jo 04-06; V Stoke Newington St Faith, St Matthias and All SS *Lon* from 06. *St Matthias Vicarage, Wordsworth Road, London N16 8DD* Tel (020) 7254 5063 E-mail frdavidlambert@aol.com
LAMBERT, David Nathaniel. b 34. Headingley Meth Coll 58 Linc Th Coll 66. **d** 66 **p** 67. In Methodist Ch 58-66; C Canwick *Linc* 66-68; C-in-c Bracebridge Heath CD 68-69; R Saltfleetby All SS w St Pet 69-73; R Saltfleetby St Clem 70-73; V Skidbrooke 70-73; V Saltfleetby 73-80; R Theddlethorpe 74-80; RD Louthesk 76-82; R N Ormsby w Wyham 80; R Fotherby 81-94; rtd 94; Perm to Offic *Linc* 94-03; *York* and *Ripon* 03-03; *Dur* from 06. *Sandcroft, Market Place, Houghton-le-Spring DH5 8AJ* Tel 0191-584 1387
LAMBERT, Ian Anderson. b 43. Lon Univ BA72 Nottm Univ MTh87. Ridley Hall Cam 66. **d** 67 **p** 68. C Bermondsey St Mary w St Olave, St Jo etc *S'wark* 67-70; R Lluidas Vale Jamaica 71-75; Chapl RAF 75-98; rtd 98; P-in-c N and S Muskham *S'well* 01-03; P-in-c Averham w Kelham 01-03; Bp's Adv for Past Care and Counselling from 04. *34 Hayside Avenue, Balderton, Newark NG24 3GB* Tel (01636) 659101 Mobile 07788-171958 E-mail revianlambert@mac.com
LAMBERT, John Clement Antony. b 28. St Cath Coll Cam BA48 MA52. Cuddesdon Coll 50. **d** 52 **p** 53. C Hornsea and Goxhill *York* 52-55; C Leeds St Pet *Ripon* 55-59; R Carlton in Lindrick *S'well* 59-93; rtd 93; Perm to Offic *Derby* from 93 and *S'well* 93-00. *4 Old Tatham, Holme-on-Spalding-Moor, York YO43 4BN* Tel (01430) 860531
LAMBERT, John Connolly. b 61. Univ of Wales (Ban) BTh04. EAMTC 01. **d** 04 **p** 05. C Paris St Mich *Eur* 04-08; C Preston-on-Tees and Longnewton *Dur* 08-10; P-in-c from 10. *The Vicarage, Quarry Road, Eaglescliffe, Stockton-on-Tees TS16 9BD* Tel (01642) 789814 E-mail johnlambert@allsaints-church.co.uk
LAMBERT, Malcolm Eric. b 58. Leic Univ BSc80 Fitzw Coll Cam BA89 Nottm Univ MPhil02 RMN84. Ridley Hall Cam 87. **d** 90 **p** 91. C Humberstone *Leic* 90-94; R S Croxton Gp 94-99; V Birstall and Wanlip 99-05; TR Leic Resurr 05-07; RD Christianity N 05-07; Warden of Readers 97-05; Dir Angl Th Inst Belize 08-09; TR Chigwell and Chigwell Row *Chelmsf* from 09. *The Rectory, 66 High Road, Chigwell IG7 6QB* Tel (020) 8500 0914 E-mail malcolm.lambert@gmail.com
LAMBERT, Michael Roy. b 25. Univ Coll Dur BSc49. Cuddesdon Coll 52. **d** 52 **p** 53. C Middlesbrough St Oswald *York* 52-56; C Romsey *Win* 56-59; C Cottingham *York* 59-64; Chapl Hull Univ 59-64; V Saltburn-by-the-Sea 64-72; P-in-c Shaftesbury H Trin *Sarum* 72-73; R Shaston 74-78; R Corfe Mullen 78-91; rtd 91; Perm to Offic *Glouc* from 91. *16 Pheasant Way, Cirencester GL7 1BL* Tel (01285) 654657
LAMBERT, Neil James. b 58. Goldsmiths' Coll Lon BA81. Ridley Hall Cam 02. **d** 04 **p** 05. C Wisley w Pyrford *Guildf* 04-08; V Ash Vale from 08. *The Vicarage, 203 Vale Road, Ash Vale, Aldershot GU12 5JE* Tel (01252) 325295 Mobile 07812-385392
LAMBERT, Miss Olivia Jane. b 48. Matlock Coll of Educn BEd70. Trin Coll Bris 84. **dss** 86 **d** 87 **p** 94. York St Luke 86-90; Par Dn 87-90; Chapl York Distr Hosp 86-90; Par Dn Huntington *York* 90-94; C 94-95; TV 95-00; TV Marfleet 00-07; C Harrogate St Mark *Ripon* 07-08; rtd 08. *58 Almsford Drive, Harrogate HG2 8EE* Tel (01423) 810357 E-mail oliviajlambert@aol.com
LAMBERT, Peter George. b 29. Coll of Resurr Mirfield 86. **d** 87 **p** 88. NSM Rothwell w Orton, Rushton w Glendon and Pipewell *Pet* 87-93; P-in-c Corby Epiphany w St Jo 93-96; rtd 96; Perm to Offic *Pet* from 96. *4 Cogan Crescent, Rothwell, Kettering NN14 6AS* Tel (01536) 710692 E-mail pglambert@tiscali.co.uk
LAMBERT, Canon Philip Charles. b 54. St Jo Coll Dur BA75 Fitzw Coll Cam BA77 MA81. Ridley Hall Cam 75. **d** 78 **p** 79. C Upper Tooting H Trin *S'wark* 78-81; C Whorlton *Newc* 81-84; P-in-c Alston cum Garrigill w Nenthead and Kirkhaugh 84-87; TV Alston Team 87-89; R Curry Rivel w Fivehead and Swell *B & W* 89-01; RD Crewkerne and Ilminster 98-01; TR Dorchester *Sarum* 01-06; RD Dorchester 02-06; Can Res Truro

Cathl from 06. *Foxhayes, 3 Knights Hill, Truro TR1 3UY* Tel (01872) 272866 E-mail philiplambert@dsl.pipex.com

LAMBERT (*née* JOHNSON), Mrs Ruth Alice Edna. b 59. Leic Univ BA80 PGCE93 Nottm Univ MA01 RGN85. EMMTC 98. d 01 p 02. C Mountsorrel Ch Ch and St Pet *Leic* 01-04; Chapl Univ Hosps Leic NHS Trust 04-07; P-in-c Belmopan St Ann Belize 08-09; Chapl Barking Havering and Redbridge Hosps NHS Trust from 09. *The Rectory, 66 High Road, Chigwell IG7 6QB* Tel (020) 8500 0914 E-mail ruth.lambert@gmail.com

LAMBETH, Archdeacon of. See SKILTON, The Ven Christopher John

LAMBOURN, David Malcolm. b 37. Lanc Univ BEd76 Man Univ MEd78 Warwick Univ PhD01. Linc Th Coll 63. d 65 p 66. C Camberwell St Geo *S'wark* 65-67; C Mottingham St Andr w St Alban 67-70; rtd 03. *28 Frederick Road, Birmingham B15 1JN* Tel 0121-242 3953 E-mail david.lambourn@blueyonder.co.uk

LAMBOURNE, John Brian. b 36. Chich Th Coll 62. d 65 p 66. C Cant St Greg 65-67; C St Mary in the Marsh 67-68; C E Grinstead St Swithun *Chich* 68-70; C Storrington and Sullington 70-76; V Salehurst 76-06; CF (TA) 87-96; Agric Chapl and Bp's Adv on Rural Affairs *Chich* 89-06; rtd 06; Chapl Vinehall Sch Robertsbridge from 06. *2 Walden Terrace, Lower Lake, Battle TN33 0AU* Tel (01580) 880408

LAMDIN, Canon Keith Hamilton. b 47. Bris Univ BA69. Ripon Coll Cuddesdon 86. d 86 p 87. Adult Educn Officer *Ox* 83-98; Team Ldr Par Resources Dept from 88; Dioc Dir Tr 94-08; Prin Sarum Coll from 08; NSM Cowley St Jo *Ox* 98-06; P-in-c Upper Kennet *Sarum* 08-10; Hon Can Ch Ch *Ox* from 97; Hon Can Kimberley S Africa from 08; Can and Preb Sarum Cathl from 09. *2 Forge Close, West Overton, Marlborough SN8 4PG* Tel (01672) 861550 E-mail klamdin@sarum.ac.uk

LAMEY, Richard John. b 76. Keble Coll Ox BA98 MA02 Em Coll Cam BA01 MA05. Westcott Ho Cam 99. d 02 p 03. C Stockport SW *Ches* 02-05; P-in-c Newton in Mottram 05-11; P-in-c Newton in Mottram w Flowery Field from 11; RD Mottram from 08. *St Mary's Vicarage, 39 Bradley Green Road, Hyde SK14 4NA* Tel 0161-368 1489 E-mail richardlamey@btinternet.com

LAMMAS, Miss Diane Beverley. b 47. Trin Coll Bris 76. dss 79 d 87 p 94. Lenton Abbey *S'well* 79-84; Wollaton Park 79-84; E Regional Co-ord and Sec for Voc and Min CPAS 84-89; Hon C Cambridge St Paul *Ely* 87-90; Voc and Min Adv CPAS 89-92; Sen Voc and Min Adv CPAS 92-95; R Hethersett w Canteloff w Lt and Gt Melton *Nor* from 95; RD Humbleyard 98-03. *The Rectory, 27 Norwich Road, Hethersett, Norwich NR9 3AR* Tel (01603) 810273 E-mail di.lammas@freeuk.com

LAMMENS, Erwin Bernard Eddy. b 62. Catholic Univ Leuven BA86 Gregorian Univ Rome MDiv90. Grootseminarie Gent 84. d 87 p 88. In RC Ch 87-96; Asst Chapl Antwerp St Boniface *Eur* 98-05; TV Harwich Peninsula *Chelmsf* 05-10; R Wivenhoe from 10. *The Rectory, 44 Belle Vue Road, Wivenhoe, Colchester CO7 9LD* Tel (01206) 822511 E-mail erwinlammens@btinternet.com

LAMMING, Sarah Rebecca. b 77. Middx Univ BA02. Westcott Ho Cam 03 Yale Div Sch 05. d 06 p 07. C Handsworth St Jas *Birm* 06-09; USA from 09. *30 South 22nd Street Apt 4, Philadelphia PA 19103, USA* E-mail sarah@sarahlamming.com

LAMOND, Stephen Paul. b 64. Trin Coll Bris BA99. d 99 p 00. C Weston-super-Mare Ch Ch *B & W* 99-02; C Congresbury w Puxton and Hewish St Ann 02-03; Chapl RAF from 03. *Chaplaincy Services, Valiant Block, HQ Air Command, RAF High Wycombe HP14 4UE* Tel (01494) 496800 Fax 496343

LAMONT, Canon Euphemia Margaret (Fay). b 53. N Coll of Educn BA98. TISEC 00. d 00 p 00. C Monifieth and Carnoustie *Bre* 00-07; P-in-c Dundee St Ninian from 07; Can St Paul's Cathl Dundee from 08. *St Ninian's Church House, Kingsway East, Dundee DD4 7RW* Tel (01382) 453818 Mobile 07931-222092 E-mail fay.lamont@sky.com

LAMONT, Roger. b 37. Jes Coll Ox BA60 MA62 MBACP00. St Steph Ho Ox 59. d 61 p 62. C Northampton St Alb *Pet* 61-66; V Mitcham St Olave *S'wark* 66-73; V N Sheen St Phil and All SS 73-85; P-in-c Richmond St Luke 82-85; Chapl St Lawr Hosp Caterham 85-94; Chapl Lifecare NHS Trust 92-99; Chapl Surrey Oaklands NHS Trust 99-01; rtd 01; Perm to Offic *S'wark* from 01. *8 Montague Drive, Caterham CR3 5BY* Tel (01883) 340803

LAMONT, Ms Veronica Jane (Ronni). b 56. Bp Grosseteste Coll CertEd77 Anglia Poly Univ MA06. St Jo Coll Nottm 90. d 92 p 94. Par Dn St Alb St Pet *St Alb* 92-94; C 94-96; TV Hemel Hempstead 96-01; V Bexley St Jo *Roch* 01-08; Perm to Offic *Cant* and *Roch* from 08. *86 Ufton Lane, Sittingbourne ME10 1EX* Tel (01795) 553603 Mobile 07802-793910 E-mail ronni@lamonts.org.uk

LAMPARD, Ms Ruth Margaret. b 65. St Jo Coll Dur BA87 Jes Coll Cam BA99 MA04 Heythrop Coll Lon MA04. Westcott Ho Cam 97 Berkeley Div Sch 99. d 00 p 01. C Ealing St Pet Mt Park *Lon* 00-01; C Eastcote St Lawr 01-04; Hon C Norton *St Alb* 05-06; Perm to Offic *S'wark* from 06; Chapl to Bp Kensington *Lon* 07-08; C W Brompton St Mary w St Peter and St Jude from

08. *St Barnabas' Vicarage, 146A Lavenham Road, London SW18 5EP* Tel (020) 7835 1440 E-mail ruthlampard3@gmail.com

LANCASTER, Mrs Jennifer. b 48. NEOC 00. d 03 p 04. C Walker Newc 03-07; TV Jarrow *Dur* from 07. *St Andrew's House, Borough Road, Jarrow NE32 5BL* Tel 0191-423 4109 *or* 489 1925 E-mail jenny.lancaster@gmail.com

LANCASTER, John Rawson. b 47. BSc. NOC. d 82 p 83. C Bolton St Jas w St Chrys *Bradf* 82-86; V Barnoldswick w Bracewell from 86. *The Vicarage, 131 Gisburn Road, Barnoldswick BB18 5JU* Tel (01282) 812028 Fax 850346 E-mail john.lancaster@bradford.anglican.org

LANCASTER, Ronald. b 31. MBE93. St Jo Coll Dur BA53 MA56 Hon MSc09 FRSC83 CChem83. Cuddesdon Coll 55. d 57 p 58. C Morley St Pet w Churwell *Wakef* 57-60; C High Harrogate St Pet *Ripon* 60-63; Lic to Offic *Ely* 63-88; Chapl Kimbolton Sch 63-88; Asst Chapl 88-91; Perm to Offic *Ely* from 88; rtd 96. *7 High Street, Kimbolton, Huntingdon PE28 0HB* Tel (01480) 860498 Fax 861277

LANCASTER, Mrs Susan Louise. b 47. Leic Univ BA79. EMMTC 88. d 93 p 94. NSM Clarendon Park St Jo w Knighton St Mich *Leic* 93-97; Perm to Offic 97-01; NSM Roundhay St Edm *Ripon* 01-09. *38 Talbot Avenue, Leeds LS17 6SB* Tel 0113-228 0145

LANCASTER, Archdeacon of. See EVERITT, The Ven Michael John

LANCASTER, Suffragan Bishop of. See PEARSON, The Rt Revd Geoffrey Seagrave

LANCHANTIN, Mrs Eveline. b 51. Sorbonne Univ Paris BA79 MA80 MPhil83. Protestant Inst of Th Paris BDiv95 MDiv99. d 07 p 08. C Ashford *Cant* 07-10. *Address temp unknown* Tel 07806-483434 (mobile) E-mail santiago31@free.fr

LAND, Michael Robert John. b 43. Ripon Hall Ox BA72 MA. d 72 p 73. C Newbury St Nic *Ox* 72-75; TV Chigwell *Chelmsf* 75-80; V Walthamstow St Andr 80-08; rtd 08; Perm to Offic *Heref* from 08. *20 St Mary's Lane, Burghill, Hereford HR4 7QL* Tel (01432) 760452 E-mail land117@btinternet.com

LANDALL, Capt Allan Roy. b 55. Qu Coll Birm BA98. d 98 p 99. C Thurnby w Stoughton *Leic* 98-02; R Walsoken *Ely* from 02. *The Rectory, Church Road, Wisbech PE13 3RA* Tel (01945) 583740 E-mail arlandall@btinternet.com

LANDALL, Richard. b 57. St Jo Coll Dur 85. d 88 p 89. C Nailsea H Trin *B & W* 88-92; CF 92-99; TV Westborough *Guildf* 99-01; R Armthorpe *Sheff* from 01. *The Rectory, Church Street, Armthorpe, Doncaster DN3 3AD* Tel and fax (01302) 831231 E-mail richard.landall@virgin.net

LANDEN, Edgar Sydney. b 23. ARCM46 FRCO46 St Jo Coll Dur BA54 BMus55. d 55 p 56. Succ Leeds *Ripon* 55-58; Prec Chelmsf Cathl 58-60; V Bathampton *B & W* 60-65; Perm to Offic *Glouc* 65-69; C Cirencester 69-76; Min Can Ch Ch *Ox* 76-88; R Wytham 76-88; rtd 88; Perm to Offic *B & W* 88-98. *The Old Vicarage, Bakers Hill, Tiverton EX16 5NE* Tel (01884) 256815

LANDER, Mrs Eileen. b 47. d 09 p 10. NSM Maidstone St Paul *Cant* from 09. *47 Bargrove Road, Maidstone ME14 5RT* Tel (01622) 685975 E-mail eileenlander@yahoo.co.uk

LANDER, Mrs Elizabeth Anne. b 69. St Andr Univ BSc93 Ox Univ PGCE94. Wycliffe Hall Ox 00. d 02 p 03. C Glascote and Stonydelph *Lich* 02-07; C Beckenham St Jo *Roch* from 08. *91 The Grove, West Wickham BR4 9LA* Tel (020) 3417 6285 Mobile 07790-212302 E-mail landerliz@yahoo.co.uk

LANDER, John Stanley. b 55. d 04 p 05. OLM Uttoxeter Area *Lich* from 04. *9 Overcroft, Bramshall, Uttoxeter ST14 5NQ* Tel (01889) 565228 E-mail john_lander@lineone.net

LANDMAN, Denis Cooper. b 21. MBE60 OM(Ger)80. Lon Univ BA41 DipEd52. St Deiniol's Hawarden 79. d 82 p 83. Hon C Tranmere St Paul w St Luke *Ches* 82-86; Australia from 86; C Southport St Pet 86-88; P-in-c Biggera Waters 88-92; rtd 92. *1/24 Stretton Drive, Helensvale Qld 4212, Australia* Tel (0061) (7) 5573 4660 Mobile 407-758376

LANDMANN, Ulrike Helene Kathryn. b 57. d 06 p 07. NSM Balsall Heath and Edgbaston SS Mary and Ambrose *Birm* from 06. *57 Lea House Road, Birmingham B30 2DB*

LANE, Alexander John. b 71. Leeds Univ BA02. Coll of Resurr Mirfield 99. d 02 p 03. C Eastbourne St Andr *Chich* 02-06; C Littlehampton and Wick 06-08; V Hunslet w Cross Green *Ripon* from 08; CMP from 08. *The Vicarage, Church Street, Hunslet, Leeds LS10 2QY* Tel 0113-271 9661 E-mail fr.alex.lane@googlemail.com

LANE, Andrew Harry John. b 49. MBE92. Lanc Univ BA71. Cuddesdon Coll 71. d 73 p 74. C Abingdon w Shippon *Ox* 73-78; Chapl Abingdon Sch 75-78; Chapl RAF 78-94; rtd 94; Perm to Offic *Nor* 94-01; Public Preacher 01; RD Repps 02-05. *Society of St Luke, 32B Beeston Common, Sheringham NR26 8ES* Tel (01263) 825623 Fax 820334 E-mail superior@ssluke.org.uk

LANE, Anthony James. b 29. Leeds Univ BA53. Coll of Resurr Mirfield 53. d 55 p 56. C Tilehurst St Mich *Ox* 55-60; Min Can Win Cathl 60-63; R Handley w Pentridge *Sarum* 64-80; V

Thurmaston *Leic* 80-85; TV Bournemouth St Pet w St Swithun, H Trin etc *Win* 85-93; rtd 93. *5 Richards Way, Salisbury SP2 8NT* Tel (01722) 332163

LANE, Anthony Richard. b 42. St Jo Coll Nottm 07. **d** 09 **p** 10. C Gtr Athens *Eur* from 09. *Kefalas, Chania 73008, Crete, Greece* Tel (0030) (282) 502 2345 Mobile 6944-131257 E-mail kritilanes@yahoo.co.uk

LANE, Canon Antony Kenneth. b 58. Ripon Coll Cuddesdon 84. **d** 87 **p** 88. C Crediton and Shobrooke *Ex* 87-90; C Amblecote *Worc* 90-94; C Sedgley All SS 94-95; TV 95-00; R Crayford *Roch* from 00; AD Erith from 09; Hon Can Roch Cathl from 09. *The Rectory, Claremont Crescent, Crayford, Dartford DA1 4RJ* Tel (01322) 522078 Mobile 07931-603470 E-mail antony.lane@diocese-rochester.org

LANE, Bernard Charles. b 59. Cam Coll of Art & Tech BA81 Anglia Poly Univ MA01. Trin Coll Bris BA91 Ridley Hall Cam 99. **d** 02 **p** 03. C Sittingbourne St Mary and St Mich *Cant* 01-05. *Address temp unknown* E-mail lane@train66.fsnet.co.uk

LANE, Christopher George. b 48. Sarum & Wells Th Coll 84. **d** 86 **p** 87. C Petersfield *Portsm* 86-90; P-in-c Barton 90-95; Perm to Offic from 95. *Carisbrooke Priory, 39 Whitcombe Road, Carisbrooke, Newport PO30 1YS* Tel (01983) 523354

LANE, Denis John Victor. b 29. Lon Univ LLB49 BD55. Oak Hill Th Coll 50. **d** 53 **p** 54. C Deptford St Jo *S'wark* 53-56; C Cambridge St Steph CD *Ely* 56-59; OMF S Perak Malaysia 60-66; Promotion Sec OMF Singapore 66-70; Overseas Dir 70-82; Dir Home Min 82-88; Internat Min 88-94; Lic to Offic *Chich* 91-94; rtd 94; Perm to Offic *Chich* from 94. *2 Parry Drive, Rustington, Littlehampton BN16 2QY* Tel and fax (01903) 785430

LANE, Ms Elizabeth Jane Holden. b 66. St Pet Coll Ox BA89 MA93. Cranmer Hall Dur 91. **d** 93 **p** 94. C Blackb St Jas 93-96; Perm to Offic *York* 96-99; Family Life Educn Officer *Ches* 00-02; TV Stockport SW 02-07; Asst Dir of Ords 05-07; V Hale and Ashley from 07; Dean of Women in Min from 10. *St Peter's Vicarage, 1 Harrop Road, Hale, Altrincham WA15 9BU* Tel 0161-928 4182 E-mail libby.lane@btinternet.com

LANE, Gareth Ernest. b 71. Westmr Univ BSc94 Univ of Wales MA08. Wycliffe Hall Ox 08. **d** 10 **p** 11. C Bedgrove *Ox* from 10. *263 Tring Road, Aylesbury HP20 1PH* Tel 07919-332859 (mobile) E-mail garethlane@hotmail.com

LANE, George David Christopher. b 68. St Pet Coll Ox BA89 MA93. Cranmer Hall Dur 91. **d** 93 **p** 94. C Blackb St Jas 93-96; C Beverley Minster *York* 96-99; V Heald Green St Cath *Ches* 99-07; Perm to Offic *Ches* from 07 and *Man* from 08. *St Peter's Vicarage, 1 Harrop Road, Hale, Altrincham WA15 9BU* Tel 0161-928 4182 E-mail george dcl@yahoo.co.uk

LANE, Canon Gerald. b 29. Bede Coll Dur BA52 MA96. Sarum Th Coll 52. **d** 54 **p** 55. C Camberwell St Giles *S'wark* 54-58; C Gillingham St Aug *Roch* 58-59; V Camberwell St Phil and St Mark *S'wark* 59-67; V Plumstead St Nic 67-73; V Gillingham St Aug *Roch* 73-78; V Hadlow 78-94; Hon Can Roch Cathl 87-94; rtd 94; Perm to Offic *Roch* 94-97; Perm to Offic *St Alb* 97-03. *6 Windsor Drive, Norristhorpe, Liversedge WF15 7RA* Tel (01924) 235254

LANE, Iain Robert. b 61. CCC Ox BA83. Ripon Coll Cuddesdon BA86 MA88. **d** 87 **p** 88. C Rotherhithe St Mary w All SS *S'wark* 87-91; V Bierley *Bradf* 91-00; Can Res St Alb 00-08; Admin St Alb Cen for Chr Studies from 08; Perm to Offic from 08. *Hill House, Wild Hill, Hatfield AL9 6EB* Tel (01707) 660485 E-mail iain.lane@christianstudies.org.uk

LANE, John Ernest. b 39. OBE94. MBIM76 Cranfield Info Tech Inst MSc80. Handsworth Coll Birm 58. **d** 80 **p** 80. In Methodist Ch 62-80; Hon C Peckham St Jo w St Andr *S'wark* 80-95; Hon C Greenwich St Alfege 98-99; Dir St Mungo Housing Assn 80-94; Dir Corporate Affairs from 94; Perm to Offic 95-98; Perm to Offic from 02. *2 Tregony Rise, Lichfield WS14 9SN* Tel (01543) 415078

LANE, Mrs Lilian June. b 37. Stockwell Coll Lon TCert59. **d** 02 **p** 03. OLM E Knoyle, Semley and Sedgehill *Sarum* 02-08; OLM St Bartholomew 08-09; Chapl St Mary's Sch Shaftesbury from 09. *Ashmede, Watery Lane, Donhead St Mary, Shaftesbury SP7 9DP* Tel (01747) 828427

LANE, Mrs Linda Mary. b 41. Lon Univ BD87 ACIB66. Gilmore Ho. **dss** 82 **d** 87 **p** 94. Hadlow *Roch* 82-94; Hon Par Dn 87-94; Perm to Offic 94-96; C Dartford H Trin 96-97; V Kensworth, Studham and Whipsnade *St Alb* 97-03; rtd 03; Perm to Offic *Wakef* from 05. *6 Windsor Drive, Norristhorpe, Liversedge WF15 7RA* Tel (01924) 235254

LANE, Malcolm Clifford George. b 48. JP. ACIB. St D Coll Lamp. **d** 02 **p** 05. Par Dn Abergavenny St Mary w Llanwenarth Citra *Mon* 02-08; P-in-c Michaelston-y-Fedw from 08; Asst Chapl Gwent Healthcare NHS Trust from 02. *The Rectory, Michaelston-y-Fedw, Cardiff CF3 6XS* Tel (01633) 681566 E-mail st8711@msn.com

LANE, Martin Guy. b 70. Oak Hill Th Coll BA08. **d** 08 **p** 09. C Herne Bay Ch Ch *Cant* from 08. *26 Linden Avenue, Herne Bay CT6 8TZ* Tel (01227) 371457 Mobile 07765-861939 E-mail martlane@hotmail.com

LANE, Martin John. b 69. Open Univ BSc03 Cardiff Univ LLM08. Coll of Resurr Mirfield 92. **d** 95 **p** 96. C Liss *Portsm* 95-98; C Warren Park and Leigh Park 98-00; TV Littlehampton and Wick *Chich* 00-04; P-in-c Harting w Elsted and Treyford cum Didling 04-10; RD Midhurst 06-10; V Bosham from 10. *The Vicarage, Bosham Lane, Bosham, Chichester PO18 8HX* Tel (01243) 573228 E-mail martinjlane@btinternet.com

LANE, Mrs Pamela. b 44. **d** 00 **p** 01. OLM Betley *Lich* from 00. *Brandon, Main Road, Betley, Crewe CW3 9BH* Tel (01270) 820258

LANE, Richard Peter. b 60. Linc Th Coll 85. **d** 88 **p** 89. C Towcester w Easton Neston *Pet* 88-91; Asst Chapl Oslo w Bergen, Trondheim, Stavanger etc *Eur* 91-93; V Writtle w Highwood *Chelmsf* 93-99; Chapl Whitelands Coll Roehampton Inst *S'wark* 99-03; P-in-c W Wimbledon Ch Ch 03-04; V from 04. *The Vicarage, 16 Copse Hill, London SW20 0HG* Tel (020) 8946 4491

LANE, Robert David. b 66. St Steph Ho Ox 05. **d** 07 **p** 08. C Corringham *Chelmsf* 07-10; V Petts Wood *Roch* from 10. *St Francis's Vicarage, 60 Willett Way, Orpington BR5 1QE* Tel (01689) 829971 Mobile 07807-224748 E-mail robert.lane2@virgin.net

LANE, Ms Rosalind Anne. b 69. Trevelyan Coll Dur BA91 Heythrop Coll Lon MTh93 Man Univ MA01. Westcott Ho Cam. **d** 95 **p** 96. C Huddersfield St Pet and All SS *Wakef* 95-99; Sub Chapl HM Pris and YOI New Hall 97-99; Asst Chapl HM Pris and YOI Doncaster 99-01; Chapl 01; Chapl HM Pris Wymott 01-05; Chapl HM Pris Kirkham 05-08; Chapl HM Pris Whitemoor 08-11; Chapl HM Pris Ashwell 11; Chapl N Essex Partnership NHS Foundn Trust from 11. *The Derwent Centre, Princess Alexandra Hospital, Hamstel Road, Harlow CM20 1QX* Tel (01279) 827268

LANE, Roy Albert. b 42. Bris Sch of Min 82. **d** 85 **p** 86. NSM Bedminster *Bris* 85-97; Perm to Offic 97-02; NSM Bishopsworth and Bedminster Down from 02. *20 Ashton Drive, Bristol BS3 2PW* Tel 0117-983 0747 Mobile 07747-808972 E-mail roypeg@blueyonder.co.uk

LANE, Simon. See DOUGLAS LANE, Charles Simon Pellew

LANE, Stuart Alexander Rhys. See LANE, Alexander John

LANE, Terry. b 50. STETS 94. **d** 97 **p** 98. NSM Freemantle *Win* 97-99; Chapl HM Pris Kingston (Portsm) 99-01; Chapl HM Pris Parkhurst 01-06; Co-ord Chapl HM Pris Win from 06. *HM Prison Winchester, Romsey Road, Winchester SO22 5DF* Tel (01962) 723000

LANE, William Henry Howard. b 63. Bris Poly BA85. Trin Coll Bris 00. **d** 02 **p** 03. C Frome H Trin *B & W* 02-06; P-in-c Woolavington w Cossington and Bawdrip 06-08; V from 09; RD Sedgemoor 09-11; V Bridgwater H Trin and Durleigh from 11. *The New Vicarage, Hamp Avenue, Bridgwater TA6 6AN* E-mail reverend.lane@googlemail.com

LANG, Geoffrey Wilfrid Francis. b 33. St Jo Coll Ox BA56 MA61. Cuddesdon Coll 56. **d** 58 **p** 59. C Spalding *Linc* 58-61; Asst Chapl Leeds Univ 61-62; C Chesterton St Luke *Ely* 62-63; C-in-c Chesterton Gd Shep CD 63-69; V Chesterton Gd Shep 69-72; V Willian *St Alb* 72-76; Dioc Dir of Educn 72-76; R N Lynn w St Marg and St Nic *Nor* 77-86; V Hammersmith St Pet Lon 86-00; rtd 00. *53A Ridgmount Gardens, London WC1E 7AU* Tel (020) 7580 4692

LANG, The Very Revd John Harley. b 27. LRAM Em Coll Cam MA60 K Coll Lon AKC49 BD60 Keele Univ Hon DLitt88. St Boniface Warminster 49. **d** 52 **p** 53. C Portsea St Mary *Portsm* 52-57; PV and Sacr S'wark Cathl 57-60; Chapl Em Coll Cam 60-64; Asst Hd Relig Broadcasting BBC 64-67; Hd Relig Progr BBC Radio 67-71; Hd Relig Broadcasting BBC 71-80; C Sacombe *St Alb* 73-80; Chapl to The Queen 77-80; Dean Lich 80-93; rtd 93; Perm to Offic *Glouc* 93-96. *1 Abbotsdene, 6 Cudnall Street, Charlton Kings, Cheltenham GL53 8HT* Tel and fax (01242) 577742 E-mail jhlang@email.com

LANG, Nicholas. b 45. SEITE 94. **d** 97 **p** 98. NSM Beckenham St Jo *Roch* 97-98; NSM Penge Lane H Trin 98-01; Chapl St Chris Hospice Lon 00; V Beckenham St Jo *Roch* from 01. *St John's Vicarage, 249 Eden Park Avenue, Beckenham BR3 3JN* Tel and fax (020) 8650 6110 Mobile 07968-985051 E-mail niklang@ntlworld.com *or* nick.lang@diocese-rochester.org

LANG, William David. b 51. K Coll Lon BD74 MA94 AKC74. St Aug Coll Cant 74. **d** 75 **p** 76. C Fleet *Guildf* 75-79; C Ewell St Fran 79-82; C W Ewell 79-82; V Holmwood 82-92; R Elstead 92-10; V Thursley 92-10; P-in-c Redhorn *Sarum* from 10; P-in-c Bishop's Cannings, All Cannings etc from 11. *The Rectory, High Street, Urchfont, Devizes SN10 4QP* Tel (01380) 840672 E-mail william@lang.net

LANGAN, Mrs Eleanor Susan. b 56. Homerton Coll Cam BEd78. Ripon Coll Cuddesdon 84. **d** 87 **p** 94. Hon Par Dn Grays Thurrock *Chelmsf* 87-89; Lic to Offic 89-94; NSM Creeksea w Althorne, Latchingdon and N Fambridge 94-95; NSM S Woodham Ferrers 95-99; NSM Overstrand, Northrepps, Sidestrand etc 99-03; Chapl Norfolk and Nor Univ Hosp NHS Trust 00-10; Lead Chapl from 10. *Norfolk and Norwich*

University Hospital, Colney Lane, Cromer NR4 7UY Tel (01603) 287470 E-mail eleanor.langan@nnuh.nhs.uk

LANGAN, Michael Leslie. b 54. Cam Univ BA PGCE. Cranmer Hall Dur. **d** 84 **p** 85. C Grays Thurrock *Chelmsf* 84-89; R Creeksea w Althorne, Latchingdon and N Fambridge 89-95; RD Maldon and Dengie 92-95; P-in-c S Woodham Ferrers 95-99; R Overstrand, Northrepps, Sidestrand etc 99-11; RD Repps 05-10; rtd 11. *The Rectory, 22A Harbord Road, Overstrand, Cromer NR27 0PN* Tel (01263) 579350 E-mail ml@netcom.co.uk

LANGDON, John Bonsall. b 21. Linc Coll Ox BA51 MA55. Ripon Hall Ox 52. **d** 54 **p** 55. C Erith St Jo *Roch* 54-57; C Christchurch *Win* 57-60; Min Can Ripon Cathl 60-63; R Swillington 63-75; P-in-c Wrangthorn 75-76; V Leeds All Hallows w St Simon 75-76; V Leeds All Hallows w Wrangthorn 76-87; P-in-c Woodhouse St Mark 85-87; V Woodhouse and Wrangthorn 87-92; rtd 92; Perm to Offic *Ripon* from 92; Hon Min Can Ripon Cathl from 02. *32 Magdalen's Road, Ripon HG4 1HT* Tel (01765) 606814

LANGDON, Ms Susan Mary. b 48. RN69. Ripon Coll Cuddesdon 01. **d** 03 **p** 04. C Amesbury *Sarum* 03-06; Jt Ldr Pilgrimage Community of St Wite from 06. *St Wite House, Whitchurch Canonicorum, Bridport DT6 6RQ* Tel (01297) 489401 E-mail stwitehouse@btinternet.com

LANGDON-DAVIES, Mrs Stella Mary. b 44. Bris Univ BSc85 Nottm Univ MBA97. St Jo Coll Nottm MTh01. **d** 01 **p** 02. C Stamford All SS w St Jo *Linc* 01-04; V Herne *Cant* 04-06; P-in-c Saxonwell *Linc* 06-08; rtd 08. *5 Manor Paddock, Allington, Grantham NG32 2DL* Tel (01400) 281395 Mobile 07976-380659 E-mail stellalangdondavies@btinternet.com

LANGDOWN, Jennifer May. b 48. STETS 95. **d** 98 **p** 99. C S Petherton w the Seavingtons *B & W* 98-02; R Curry Rivel w Fivehead and Swell from 02. *The Rectory, Curry Rivel, Langport TA10 0HQ* Tel (01458) 251375

LANGE-SMITH, Michael Leslie. b 56. Bris Univ BSc83 Lon Bible Coll MA90. Trin Coll Bris 87. **d** 90 **p** 91. C Greendale Zimbabwe 91-92; R Melfort 93-98; Dir Th Educn by Ext Coll of Zimbabwe 99-02; R Chinnor, Sydenham, Aston Rowant and Crowell *Ox* 03-05; P-in-c Jersey Grouville *Win* 05-06; R from 06. *The Rectory, La Rue à Don, Grouville, Jersey JE3 9GB* Tel (01534) 853073

LANGERHUIZEN, Sandra Marilyn. b 45. **d** 11. NSM Birkenhead St Jas w St Bede *Ches* from 11. *43 Shamrock Road, Birkenhead CH41 0EG*

LANGFORD, Mrs Carol Mary. b 60. Southn Univ BTh93 MTh97 SS Mark & Jo Univ Coll Plymouth PGCE06. STETS 03. **d** 06 **p** 07. C Parkstone St Pet and St Osmund w Branksea *Sarum* 06-09; C Lilliput 09-10; P-in-c from 10; Chapl Talbot Heath Sch Bournemouth from 09. *The Vicarage, 55 Lilliput Road, Poole BH14 8JX* Tel (01202) 708567 E-mail carol.langford@tinyworld.co.uk

LANGFORD, David Laurence. b 51. **d** 88 **p** 89. OLM Scotton w Northorpe *Linc* from 88. *1 Westgate, Scotton, Gainsborough DN21 3QX* Tel (01724) 763139

LANGFORD, Prof Michael John. b 31. New Coll Ox BA54 MA58 Cam Univ MA59 Lon Univ PhD66. Westcott Ho Cam 55. **d** 56 **p** 57. C Bris St Nath w St Kath 56-59; Chapl Qu Coll Cam 59-63; C Hampstead St Jo *Lon* 63-67; Philosophy Dept Memorial Univ Newfoundland 67-96; Prof Philosophy 82-96; Prof Medical Ethics 87-96; rtd 96; Perm to Offic *Ely* from 96. *19 High Street, Dry Drayton, Cambridge CB23 8BS* Tel (01954) 789593 E-mail mjm29@hermes.cam.ac.uk

LANGFORD, Peter Francis. b 54. Sarum & Wells Th Coll 76. **d** 79 **p** 80. C N Ormesby *York* 79-82; Ind Chapl 83-91; V Middlesbrough St Chad 91-96; R Easington w Liverton 96-07; rtd 07. *17 The Cranbrooks, Wheldrake, York YO19 6AZ* Tel (01904) 448944 E-mail peterlan2@aol.com

LANGFORD, Peter Julian. b 53. Selw Coll Cam BA58. Westcott Ho Cam 59. **d** 60 **p** 61. C E Ham St Mary *Chelmsf* 60-67; Hon C 67-71; Hon C Beccles St Mich *St E* 71-76; Warden Ringsfield Hall Suffolk 71-87; P-in-c Ringsfield w Redisham *St E* 76-80; TV Seacroft *Ripon* 87-98; rtd 98; Perm to Offic *St E* from 99. *22 Alexander Road, Beccles NR34 9UD* Tel (01502) 710034

LANGHAM, Paul Jonathan. b 60. Ex Univ BA81 Fitzw Coll Cam BA86 MA91. Ridley Hall Cam 84. **d** 87 **p** 88. C Bath Weston All SS w N Stoke *B & W* 87-91; Chapl and Fell St Cath Coll Cam 91-96; V Combe Down w Monkton Combe and S Stoke *B & W* 96-10; P-in-c Clifton Ch Ch w Em *Bris* from 10. *Christ Church Clifton Church Office, Linden Gate, Clifton Down Road, Bristol BS8 4AH* Tel 0117-973 6524 Fax 904 7065 E-mail paul@christchurchclifton.org.uk

LANGILLE, Canon Melvin Owen. b 58. St Mary's Univ Halifax NS BA79. Atlantic Sch of Th MDiv82. **d** 82 **p** 83. Dn-in-c Falkland Canada 82; R Lockeport and Barrington 83-86; R French Village 87-90; R Cole Harbour St Andr 90-96; R Yarmouth H Trin 97-03; P-in-c Brora *Mor* 03-09; P-in-c Dornoch 03-09; R Arpafeelie from 09; R Cromarty from 09; R Fortrose from 09; Syn Clerk and Can St Andr Cathl Inverness from 07. *The Rectory, 1 Deans Road, Fortrose IV10 8TJ* Tel 07780-512990 (mobile) E-mail mel@langille.freeserve.co.uk

LANGLEY, Ms Emma Louise. b 70. Bris Univ BA93 MA98. STETS 01. **d** 03 **p** 04. C Horfield H Trin *Bris* 03-07; P-in-c Westbury-on-Trym St Alb from 07; Min Westbury Park LEP from 07. *St Alban's Vicarage, 21 Canowie Road, Bristol BS6 7HR* Tel 0117-951 9771 Mobile 07974-658619 E-mail emmalang@aol.com

LANGLEY, Canon Myrtle Sarah. b 39. TCD BA61 HDipEd62 MA67 Bris Univ PhD76 Lon Univ BD66 FRAI. Dalton Ho Bris 64. **d** 88 **p** 94. Dir Chr Development for Miss *Liv* 87-89; Dir Dioc Tr Inst *Carl* 90-98; Dioc Dir of Tr 90-98; Hon Can Carl Cathl 91-98; P-in-c Long Marton w Dufton and w Milburn 98-06; rtd 06. *Grania, 9 St John's Close, Cotehill, Carlisle CA4 0ED* Tel (01228) 562679 E-mail canonmlangley@hotmail.com

LANGLEY, The Ven Robert. b 37. St Cath Soc Ox BA61. St Steph Ho Ox. **d** 63 **p** 64. C Aston cum Aughton *Sheff* 63-68; Midl Area Sec Chr Educn Movement 68-71; HQ Sec Chr Educn Movement 71-74; Prin Ian Ramsey Coll Brasted 74-77; Can Res St Alb and Dir St Alb Minl Tr Scheme 77-85; Can Res Newc Cathl 85-01; Dioc Missr 85-98; Dioc Dir of Min and Tr 98-01; Adn Lindisfarne 01-07; Local Min Development Officer 01-07; rtd 08; Perm to Offic *York* from 09. *Brook House, Middlewood Lane, Fylingthorpe, Whitby YO22 4TT* Tel (01947) 880355 E-mail kca83@dial.pipex.com

LANGMAN, Barry Edward. b 46. Master Mariner 73. Cant Sch of Min 87. **d** 90 **p** 91. NSM St Margarets-at-Cliffe w Westcliffe etc *Cant* 90-92; C Sandgate St Paul w Folkestone St Geo 92-95; P-in-c Headcorn 95-01; V 01-08; rtd 08; Perm to Offic *Cant* from 08. *19 Hazel Heights, Lodge Wood Drive, Ashford TN25 4GF* Tel (01233) 664199

LANGRELL, Gordon John. b 35. Cant Univ (NZ) BA58. Ridley Hall Cam 65. **d** 67 **p** 68. C Tonbridge SS Pet and Paul *Roch* 67-71; New Zealand from 71; rtd 05. *11A Henry Wigram Drive, Hornby, Christchurch 8042, New Zealand* Tel (0064) (3) 348 9554 E-mail gorlang@paradise.net.nz

✠**LANGRISH, The Rt Revd Michael Laurence.** b 46. Birm Univ BSocSc67 Fitzw Coll Cam BA73 MA77. Ridley Hall Cam 71. **d** 73 **p** 74 **c** 93. C Stratford-on-Avon w Bishopton *Cov* 73-76; Chapl Rugby Sch 76-81; P-in-c Offchurch *Cov* 81-87; Dioc Dir of Ords 81-87; P-in-c Rugby 87-91; Hon Can Cov Cathl 90-93; TR Rugby 91-93; Suff Bp Birkenhead *Ches* 93-00; Bp Ex from 00. *The Palace, Exeter EX1 1HY* Tel (01392) 272362 Fax 430923 E-mail bishop.of.exeter@exeter.anglican.org

✠**LANGSTAFF, The Rt Revd James Henry.** b 56. St Cath Coll Ox BA77 MA81 Nottm Univ BA80. St Jo Coll Nottm 78. **d** 81 **p** 82 **c** 04. C Farnborough *Guildf* 81-84 and 85-86; P-in-c 84-85; P-in-c Duddeston w Nechells *Birm* 86; V 87-96; RD Birm City 95-96; Bp's Dom Chapl 96-00; P-in-c Short Heath 98-00; R Sutton Coldfield H Trin 00-04; AD Sutton Coldfield 02-04; Suff Bp Lynn *Nor* 04-10; Bp Roch from 10. *Bishopscourt, 24 St Margaret's Street, Rochester ME1 1TS* Tel (01634) 842721 Fax 831136 E-mail bishops.secretary@rochester.anglican.org

LANGSTON, Clinton Matthew. b 62. Derby Coll of Educn BCombStuds86. Qu Coll Birm 87. **d** 90 **p** 91. C Shirley *Birm* 90-94; CF from 94. *c/o MOD Chaplains (Army)* Tel (01264) 381140 Fax 381824

LANGTON, Robert. b 45. SAOMC 97. **d** 00 **p** 01. C Boyne Hill *Ox* 00-03; Chapl St Mich Hospice 03-08; TV Cwmbran *Mon* from 08. *The Vicarage, 87 Bryn Eglwys, Croesyceiliog, Cwmbran NP44 2LF* Tel (01633) 483945

LANHAM, Geoffrey Peter. b 62. Cam Univ MA84 Ox Univ MPhil86. Wycliffe Hall Ox 86. **d** 89 **p** 90. C Southborough St Pet w Ch Ch and St Matt *Roch* 89-92; C Harborne Heath *Birm* 92-00; C Birm St Paul 00-07; Deanery Missr 00-09; C Birm Cathl 07-09; V Selly Park Ch Ch from 09. *16 Over Mill Drive, Selly Park, Birmingham B29 7JL* Tel 0121-472 7074 E-mail geoff@b1church.net

LANHAM, Richard Paul White. b 42. Dur Univ BA64. Wycliffe Hall Ox 65. **d** 67 **p** 68. C Gerrards Cross *Ox* 67-69; C Horwich H Trin *Man* 69-72; C Worsley 72-74; V Accrington St Andr *Blackb* 74-80; V Shillington *St Alb* 80-85; V Upper w Lower Gravenhurst 80-85; rtd 85; Perm to Offic *St Alb* from 85. *10 Alexander Close, Clifton, Shefford SG17 5RB* Tel (01462) 813520

LANKESTER, Mrs Jane Elizabeth. b 53. Qu Mary Coll Lon BScEcon74 SS Mark & Jo Univ Coll Plymouth MA04. SWMTC 05. **d** 08. NSM Totnes w Bridgetown, Berry Pomeroy etc *Ex* from 08. *Beeches, 4 Greenfield Drive, South Brent TQ10 9QF* Tel (01364) 72948 Mobile 07812-945622 E-mail jane@lankester.entadsl.com

LANKSHEAR, Jane Frances. *See* MAINWARING, Jane Frances

LANSDALE, Canon Charles Roderick. b 38. Leeds Univ BA59. Coll of Resurr Mirfield 59. **d** 61 **p** 62. C Nunhead St Antony S'wark 61-65; Swaziland 65-71; V Benhilton S'wark 72-78; TR Catford (Southend) and Downham 78-87; TR Moulsecoomb *Chich* 87-97; V Eastbourne St Mary 97-08; Can and Preb Chich Cathl 98-08; rtd 08; Perm to Offic *Chich* from 08. *102 Channel View Road, Eastbourne BN22 7LJ* Tel (01323) 646655

LANYON-HOGG, Mrs Anne Chester. b 49. St Anne's Coll Ox BA71 MA75 Worc Coll of Educn PGCE92. WEMTC 01. **d** 04 **p** 05. NSM Colwall w Upper Colwall and Coddington *Heref* from 04; NSM Malvern H Trin and St Jas *Worc* from 07. *7 Lockyear Close, Colwall, Malvern WR13 6NR* Tel (01684) 541979 Mobile 07890-995297 E-mail annelh@tiscali.co.uk

LANYON JONES, Keith. b 49. Southn Univ BTh79. Sarum & Wells Th Coll 74. **d** 77 **p** 78. C Charlton Kings St Mary *Glouc* 77-81; Sen Chapl Rugby Sch 81-99; Lic to Offic *Truro* 83-00; P-in-c St Cleer from 00; C St Ive and Pensilva w Quethiock from 02; Chapl Kelly Coll Tavistock from 08. *The Vicarage, St Cleer, Liskeard PL14 5DN* Tel (01579) 343240 E-mail lanyon67@hotmail.com

LAPAGE, Michael Clement. b 23. Selw Coll Cam BA47 MA73. Clifton Th Coll 60. **d** 61 **p** 62. C Weithaga Kenya 61-65; V Nanyuki 65-72; Chapl Bedford Sch 73-75; Chapl Lyon w Grenoble *Eur* 76-79; V Walford w Bishopswood *Heref* 79-88; P-in-c Goodrich w Welsh Bicknor and Marstow 83-88; rtd 88; Perm to Offic *Ex* from 88. *Moorlands, 20 Watts Road, Tavistock PL19 8LG* Tel (01822) 615901

LAPHAM, Canon Fred. b 31. Univ of Wales (Lamp) BA53 PhD00. Vancouver Sch of Th LTh55 BD58. **d** 55 **p** 55. Canada 55-59; C Wallasey St Hilary *Ches* 59-62; V Over St Jo 62-70; V Upton Ascension 70-82; R Grappenhall 82-91; RD Gt Budworth 85-91; Hon Can Ches Cathl 88-91; rtd 91. *1 Coppice Gate, Lyth Hill, Shrewsbury SY3 0BT* Tel (01743) 872284

LAPWOOD, Robin Rowland John. b 57. Selw Coll Cam MA. Ridley Hall Cam 80. **d** 82 **p** 83. C Bury St Edmunds St Mary *St E* 82-86; P-in-c Bentley w Tattingstone 86-93; P-in-c Copdock w Washbrook and Belstead 86-93; TV High Wycombe *Ox* 93-96; P-in-c Marcham w Garford 96-02; Asst Master Summer Fields Sch Ox from 02. *Summer Fields School, Mayfield Road, Oxford OX2 7EN* Tel (01865) 454433 E-mail robin.lapwood@bigfoot.com

LARCOMBE, Paul Richard. b 57. Portsm Poly BSc79 CEng MIET. Trin Coll Bris 94. **d** 96 **p** 97. C Werrington *Pet* 96-98; C Longthorpe 98-00; V Pet St Paul 00-07; TR Worle *B & W* from 07. *The Vicarage, 93 Church Road, Worle, Weston-super-Mare BS22 9EA* Tel (01934) 510694

LARGE, William Roy. b 40. Dur Univ BA DipEd. Edin Th Coll 82. **d** 84 **p** 85. C Leamington Priors All SS *Cov* 84-88; V Bishop's Tachbrook 88-99; Warden of Readers and Sen Tutor 88-99; TV N Tyne and Redesdale *Newc* 99-01; TR 01-05; rtd 05. *4 Osborne Court, Osborne Avenue, Newcastle upon Tyne NE2 1LE* Tel 0191-281 1894

LARK, William Donald Starling. b 35. Keble Coll Ox BA59 MA63. Wells Th Coll 59. **d** 61 **p** 62. C Wyken *Cov* 61-64; C Christchurch *Win* 64-66; V Yeovil St Mich *B & W* 66-75; V Earley St Pet *Ox* 75-85; V Prittlewell *Chelmsf* 85-88; V Dawlish *Ex* 88-00; rtd 00; P-in-c Lanzarote *Eur* 00-05. *Las Alondras, 6 Cummings Court, Cummings Cross, Liverton, Newton Abbot TQ12 6HJ* Tel (01626) 824966 E-mail lanzalarks2000@yahoo.co.uk

LARKEY, Mrs Deborah Frances. b 63. Univ of Wales (Abth) BA85 Liv Inst of Educn PGCE90. **d** 98 **p** 99. OLM Toxteth St Cypr w Ch Ch *Liv* 98-01; OLM Edge Hill St Cypr w St Mary 01-04; C Netherton 04-07; TV Vale of Pewsey *Sarum* from 07. *The Vicarage, Church Road, Woodborough, Pewsey SN9 5PH* Tel (01672) 851746 E-mail deborah.larkey@valeofpewsey.org.uk

LARKIN, Andrew Brian. b 70. Warwick Univ BEng92 PhD95. Trin Coll Bris BA06. **d** 06 **p** 07. C Littleover *Derby* 06-08; C Brailsford w Shirley, Osmaston w Edlaston etc 08-10; R Fenny Bentley, Thorpe, Tissington, Parwich etc from 10. *The Vicarage, Parwich, Ashbourne DE6 1QD* Tel (01335) 390226 Mobile 07758-704452 E-mail andy@larkin.me.uk

LARKIN, Mrs Karen Maria. b 74. Qu Coll Birm BA08. **d** 08 **p** 09. C Coleshill *Birm* from 08; C Maxstoke from 08. *52 Oakthorpe Drive, Birmingham B37 6HY* Tel 0121-694 4442 Mobile 07956-923653 E-mail karen_larkin@hotmail.co.uk

LARKIN, Canon Peter John. b 39. ALCD62. **d** 62 **p** 63. C Liskeard St Keyne *Truro* 62-65; C Rugby St Andr *Cov* 65-67; Sec Bp Cov Call to Miss 67-68; V Kea *Truro* 68-78; P-in-c Bromsgrove St Jo *Worc* 78-81; R Torquay St Matthias, St Mark and H Trin *Ex* 81-97; Can Sokoto Nigeria 91-98; Can Kaduna from 98; TR Plymouth Em, St Paul Efford and St Aug *Ex* 97-00; rtd 00; Perm to Offic *Ex* from 00. *Picklecombe, 57 Babbacombe Downs Road, Torquay TQ1 3LP* Tel (01803) 326888 E-mail larkin@petermolly.freeserve.co.uk

LARKIN, Simon George David. b 69. Birm Univ BSocSc90 PGCE92 Reading Univ MA96. Trin Coll Bris BTh09. **d** 09 **p** 10. C Kensington St Barn *Lon* from 09. *17 Devonport Road, London W12 8NZ* Tel 07954-600258 (mobile) E-mail me@sarahsi.com

LARLEE, David Alexander. b 78. Univ of W Ontario MA01. Wycliffe Hall Ox BTh04. **d** 04 **p** 05. NSM Battersea Rise St Mark *S'wark* from 04. *24 Parma Crescent, London SW11 1LT* Tel (020) 7326 9426 *or* 7223 6188 E-mail david_larlee@yahoo.com

LARNER, Gordon Edward Stanley. b 30. Brasted Th Coll 54 Oak Hill Th Coll 55. **d** 59 **p** 60. C Peckham St Mary Magd *S'wark* 59-62; C Luton w E Hyde *St Alb* 62-68; V Lower Sydenham St Mich *S'wark* 68-73; Ind Chapl 73-84; Chapl HM Pris Ranby 84-92; rtd 92. *Glen Rosa, Meshaw, South Molton EX36 4NE*

LARSEN, Clive Erik. b 55. St Jo Coll Nottm 88. **d** 90 **p** 91. C Weaverham *Ches* 90-92; C Alvanley and Helsby and Dunham-on-the-Hill 92-95; P-in-c Cheadle Heath 95-02; P-in-c N Reddish *Man* from 05. *The Rectory, 551 Gorton Road, Stockport SK5 6NX* Tel 0161-223 0692 Mobile 07789-915263 E-mail clive.larsen@ntlworld.com

LASKEY, Cyril Edward. b 44. RMN71 RGN74. Llan Dioc Tr Scheme 85. **d** 88 **p** 89. NSM Troedrhiwgarth *Llan* 88-93; NSM Caerau St Cynfelin 94-01; P-in-c Glyncorrwg and Upper Afan Valley 01-10; rtd 10. *207 Bridgend Road, Maesteg CF34 0NL* Tel (01656) 734639

LASKEY, Stephen Allan. b 56. Manitoba Univ BA85. St Jo Coll Winnipeg MDiv88. **d** 89 **p** 89. C Labrador W Canada 89; C Battle Harbour 89-91; R 91-96; R Goulds St Paul 96-99; Assoc P Foxtrap All SS 00-01; C Paddington St Jo w St Mich *Lon* 01-02; P-in-c Sydenham H Trin *S'wark* 02-07; P-in-c Forest Hill St Aug 03-07; V Sydenham H Trin and St Aug 07-09; R Dartmouth Ch Ch Canada from 09. *172 Green Village Lane, Dartmouth NS B2Y 4V4, Canada* E-mail stephenlaskey@onetel.com

LASLETT, Christopher John. b 42. Leeds Univ BA64 Lon Univ PGCE73. Lich Th Coll 64. **d** 66 **p** 67. C Bradf St Clem 66-69; C Upper Armley *Ripon* 69-70; Perm to Offic *Dur* 71-72; Hon C Stranton 79-81; Perm to Offic *Ripon* 87-88; rtd 07. *1 Locksley Grange, 74 St Marychurch Road, Torquay TQ1 3HX* Tel (01803) 310613 E-mail mfl@ntlworld.com

LAST, Eric Cyril. b 30. Oak Hill Th Coll 77. **d** 79 **p** 80. C Wandsworth All SS *S'wark* 79-83; V Earlsfield St Andr 83-88; V S Merstham 88-96; Asst RD Reigate 92-96; rtd 96; Hon C Upper Tean *Lich* 96-10; Perm to Offic from 10. *29 Vicarage Road, Tean, Stoke-on-Trent ST10 4LE* Tel and fax (01538) 723551 E-mail eric.last1@btopenworld.com

LAST, Michael Leonard Eric. b 60. St Jo Coll Nottm 92. **d** 94 **p** 95. C Tettenhall Wood *Lich* 94-98; V Pelsall 98-02; V Alton w Bradley-le-Moors and Oakamoor w Cotton 02-09; P-in-c Mayfield and Denstone w Ellastone and Stanton 06-09; I Saskatchewan Gateway Canada 09-11; R Adderley, Ash, Calverhall, Ightfield etc *Lich* from 11. *The Rectory, Moreton Say, Market Drayton TF9 3RS* Tel (01630) 638054 Mobile 07510-179425 E-mail rev.last@btinternet.com

LAST, Norman Percy George. b 31. BA CertEd. Sarum & Wells Th Coll 77 Wycliffe Hall Ox 80. **d** 81 **p** 82. C Walton-on-Thames *Guildf* 81-83; C Farnham 83-87; R Monks Eleigh w Chelsworth and Brent Eleigh etc *St E* 87-90; P-in-c Bradworthy *Ex* 91-97; rtd 97; Perm to Offic *Ex* from 98; C Stansted *Chich* 00-02. *9 Wensley Gardens, Emsworth PO10 7RA* Tel (01243) 374174

LATHAM, Christine Elizabeth. b 46. S'wark Ord Course 87. **d** 90 **p** 94. Par Dn Battersea St Pet and St Paul *S'wark* 90-94; Par Dn S'wark Ch Ch 94; C 94-97; C Merstham and Gatton 97-05; Chapl E Surrey Learning Disability NHS Trust 97-05; Chapl R Marsden NHS Foundn Trust 05-10; rtd 10. *46 Myrtle Road, Sutton SM1 4BX* Tel (020) 8395 4701

LATHAM, Henry Nicholas Lomax. b 64. Reading Univ BA86. Wycliffe Hall Ox BTh93. **d** 93 **p** 94. C Aberystwyth *St D* 93-99; P-in-c Stoke Poges *Ox* 99-08; V from 08. *The Vicarage, Park Road, Stoke Poges, Slough SL2 4PE* Tel (01753) 642261 E-mail harryandmary@isaiah61.freeserve.co.uk

LATHAM, John Montgomery. b 37. Univ of NZ BA Cam Univ MA Cant Univ (NZ) MEd. Westcott Ho Cam 60. **d** 62 **p** 63. C Camberwell St Geo *S'wark* 62-65; Chapl Trin Coll Cam 65-70; Chapl Wanganui Colleg Sch New Zealand 71-79; Min Enabler N New Brighton 96-01; V Christchurch St Luke 98-02; rtd 02. *43 Rugby Street, Christchurch 8014, New Zealand* Tel (0064) (3) 355 6654 Fax 355 6658 E-mail latham@xtra.co.nz

LATHAM, John Westwood. b 31. Ely Th Coll 57. **d** 60 **p** 61. C Cleckheaton St Jo *Wakef* 60-63; C Hemel Hempstead *St Alb* 63-65; C Wakef Cathl 65-67; V Outwood 67-72; TV Daventry w Norton *Pet* 72-79; V Flore w Dodford and Brockhall 79-96; rtd 96; Perm to Offic *Leic* from 97. *53 Lubenham Hill, Market Harborough LE16 9DG* Tel (01858) 469023

LATHAM, Robert Norman. b 53. Qu Coll Birm 82. **d** 85 **p** 86. C Tamworth *Lich* 85-89; TV Wordsley 89-96; P-in-c Hallow *Worc* 96-97; R Hallow and Grimley w Holt from 97. *Hallow Vicarage, 26 Baveney Road, Worcester WR2 6DS* Tel (01905) 748711 E-mail robert@hallowvicarage.freeserve.co.uk

LATHAM, Roger Allonby. b 69. Leic Univ BA90 Warwick Univ MA92 Leeds Univ PGCE93 Nottm Univ PhD07. St Jo Coll Nottm BTh98. **d** 99 **p** 00. C Paston *Pet* 99-02; TV Cartmel Peninsula *Carl* 02-09; Officer for IME 4-7 from 08; Vice-Prin LCTP and C Beacon from 09. *The Vicarage, Greyrigg, Kendal LA8 9BU* E-mail rogerlatham54@aol.com

LATHAM, (née WEBSTER), Mrs Rosamond Mary. b 54. Coll of Ripon & York St Jo BEd90 MA00. Westcott Ho Cam 00. **d** 02 **p** 03. C Frodingham *Linc* 02-05; TV Dur N 05-07; TV Dorchester *Ox* from 07. *The Vicarage, Cherwell Road,*

Berinsfield, Wallingford OX10 7PB Tel (01865) 340460 Mobile 07779-784320 E-mail bbdparishoffice@googlemail.com
LATHAM, Trevor Martin. b 56. BD84. Ripon Coll Cuddesdon 84. **d** 86 **p** 87. C Cantril Farm *Liv* 86-89; TV Croxteth Park 89-98; V 98-99; TR Walton-on-the-Hill from 99. *The Rectory, Walton Village, Liverpool L4 6TJ* Tel and fax 0151-525 3130 E-mail trevor.latham@talktalk.net
LATHE, Canon Anthony Charles Hudson. b 36. Jes Coll Ox BA59 MA64. Lich Th Coll 59. **d** 61 **p** 62. C Selby Abbey *York* 61-63; V Hempnall *Nor* 63-72; R Woodton w Bedingham 63-72; R Fritton w Morningthorpe w Shelton and Hardwick 63-72; R Topcroft 63-72; R Banham 72-76; TR Quidenham 76-83; P-in-c New Buckenham 78-79; V Heigham St Thos 83-94; Hon Can Nor Cathl 87-99; RD Nor S 90-94; P-in-c Sheringham 94-99; rtd 99; Perm to Offic *Nor* 99-06. *15A Kingsdale Road, Berkhamsted HP4 3BS* Tel (01442) 863115
LATIFA, Andrew Murdoch. b 73. Univ of Wales (Abth) BTh96 Univ of Wales (Cardiff) MTh00. St Mich Coll Llan 99. **d** 01 **p** 02. C Betws w Ammanford *St D* 01-03; C Llangynwyd w Maesteg 03-05; CF from 05. *c/o MOD Chaplains (Army)* Tel (01264) 381140 Fax 381824
LATIMER, Andrew John. b 78. Qu Coll Cam MA04 Lon Univ MB, BS05. Oak Hill Th Coll BTh10. **d** 10 **p** 11. C Limehouse *Lon* from 10. *84 Saunders Ness Road, London E14 3EA* Tel (020) 7538 1576 Mobile 07740-287545 E-mail andrew@thelatimers.com
LATIMER, Clifford James. b 45. City Univ BSc68. **d** 99 **p** 00. OLM Burntwood *Lich* 99-10; rtd 10; Perm to Offic *Lich* from 11. *24 Dove Close, Burntwood WS7 9JL* Tel (01543) 671471 E-mail cliff.latimer@btinternet.com
LATTEY, Susan. *See* CUMMING-LATTEY, Mrs Susan Mary Ruth
LATTIMORE, Anthony Leigh. b 35. Dur Univ BA57. Lich Th Coll 60. **d** 62 **p** 63. C Aylestone *Leic* 62-66; C-in-c Eyres Monsell CD 66-69; V Eyres Monsell 69-73; V Somerby, Burrough on the Hill and Pickwell 73-86; RD Goscote I 80-86; R Glenfield 86-95; rtd 95; Perm to Offic *Leic* and *Pet* from 95. *28 Elizabeth Way, Uppingham, Oakham LE15 9PQ* Tel (01572) 823193
LATTY, Howard James. b 54. SRCh71. WEMTC 98. **d** 01 **p** 02. NSM Bath St Mich w St Paul *B & W* 01-08; NSM Chewton Mendip w Ston Easton, Litton etc from 08. *The Rectory, Lower Street, Chewton Mendip, Radstock BA3 4GP* Tel (01761) 241189 E-mail howard.latty@yahoo.co.uk
LAU, Paul Chow Sing. b 49. Nat Chengchi Univ BA74 Chinese Univ of Hong Kong MDiv80. **d** 80 **p** 81. Hong Kong 80-82 and 83-94; C Hong Kong H Trin 80-82; Macao 82-83; V Macao St Mark 82-83; P-in-c Hong Kong Ch of Our Sav 83-94; New Zealand 94-01; V Ang Chinese Miss Ch *Wellington* 94-01; Chapl Chinese Congregation *Lon* from 01. *3 Strutton Court, 54 Great Peter Street, London SW1P 2HH* Tel (020) 7233 4027 *or* 7766 1106 E-mail paul.lau@smitf.org
LAUCKNER, Averil Ann. b 55. Lanc Univ BSc76. Ripon Coll Cuddesdon 03. **d** 04 **p** 05. C Royston *St Alb* 04-07; C Lich Ch Ch and Lich St Mich w St Mary and Wall 07-09; P-in-c Lich Ch Ch 09-11; P-in-c Hatfield Hyde *St Alb* from 11. *St Mary Magdalene Vicarage, Hollybush Lane, Welwyn Garden City AL7 4JS* Tel (01707) 322313 E-mail averil.lauckner@btinternet.com
LAUGHTON, Derek Basil. b 24. Worc Coll Ox BA49 MA52. Westcott Ho Cam 49. **d** 51 **p** 52. C Wareham w Arne *Sarum* 51-53; CF 53-56; C Hemel Hempstead St Mary *St Alb* 56-59; V Stretton cum Wetmoor *Lich* 59-64; Chapl Wellington Sch Somerset 64-73; Chapl Ardingly Coll 73-77; R Plumpton w E Chiltington *Chich* 77-88; Perm to Offic *B & W* from 88; rtd 89. *13 Pyles Thorne Road, Wellington TA21 8DX* Tel (01823) 667386
LAURENCE, Brother. *See* EYERS, Frederick Thomas Laurence
LAURENCE, The Ven John Harvard Christopher. b 29. Trin Hall Cam BA53 MA57. Westcott Ho Cam 53. **d** 55 **p** 56. C Linc St Nic w St Jo Newport 55-59; V Crosby 59-74; Can and Preb Linc Cathl 74-79 and 85-94; Dioc Missr 74-79; Bp's Dir of Clergy Tr *Lon* 80-85; Adn Lindsey *Linc* 85-94; rtd 94; Perm to Offic *Linc* 94-97. *5 Haffenden Road, Lincoln LN2 1RP* Tel (01522) 531444
LAURENCE, John-Daniel. b 79. Mansf Coll Ox MPhys02. Trin Coll Bris BA09 MA10. **d** 10 **p** 11. C Aberystwyth *St D* from 10. *Fenton, Queen's Square, Aberystwyth SY23 2HL* Tel (01970) 624537 E-mail jd@stmikes.net
LAURENCE, Julian Bernard Vere. b 60. Kent Univ BA82. St Steph Ho Ox 86. **d** 88 **p** 89. C Yeovil St Mich *B & W* 88-91; Chapl Yeovil Coll 90-91; Chapl Yeovil Distr Gen Hosp 91; P-in-c Barwick *B & W* 91-94; V Taunton H Trin from 94. *Holy Trinity Vicarage, 18 Holway Avenue, Taunton TA1 3AR* Tel (01823) 337890 E-mail jlaurence@htvicarage.fsnet.co.uk
LAURIE, Canon Donovan Hugh. b 40. Man Univ MSc. Oak Hill NSM Course. **d** 82 **p** 83. NSM Cudham and Downe *Roch* 82-84; C Tunbridge Wells St Jas 84-88; P-in-c Ventnor St Cath *Portsm* 88-99; V 99-04; P-in-c Ventnor H Trin 88-99; V 99-04; P-in-c Bonchurch 00-03; R 03-04; Hon Chapl St Cath Sch Ventnor

88-04; Hon Can Portsm Cathl 01-04; rtd 04. *39 Cleveland, Tunbridge Wells TN2 3NH* Tel (01892) 539951 E-mail don@dlaurie.fsbusiness.co.uk
LAUT, Graham Peter. b 37. Chich Th Coll 63. **d** 67 **p** 68. C Corringham *Chelmsf* 67-68; C Leytonstone St Marg w St Columba 68-71; P-in-c Leytonstone St Andr 71-75; V 75-80; V Romford Ascension Collier Row 80-06; rtd 06; Perm to Offic *Chelmsf* from 07. *11 Archers Close, Billericay CM12 9YF* Tel (01277) 630395 E-mail glaut10497@aol.com
LAUTENBACH, Edward Wayne. b 59. Univ Coll Ches BTh04. St Paul's Coll Grahamstown 85. **d** 88 **p** 88. C Weltevredenpark St Mich S Africa 88-89; Asst P Florida St Gabr 89-91; Sen Asst P Bryanston St Mich 91-94; R Brakpan St Pet 94-99; P-in-c Grange St Andr *Ches* 99-04; P-in-c Runcorn H Trin 99-04; V Prenton from 04. *The Vicarage, 1 Vicarage Close, Birkenhead CH42 8QX* Tel 0151-608 1808 E-mail waynelautenbach@sky.com
LAUTENBACH, Mrs Glynnis Valerie. b 59. Leeds Univ BA08. NOC 05. **d** 08 **p** 09. C Oxton *Ches* from 08. *The Vicarage, 1 Vicarage Close, Birkenhead CH42 8QX* E-mail glynn.laut@sky.com
LAVENDER, Christopher Piers. b 61. Ridley Hall Cam 08. **d** 10 **p** 11. C Headcorn and The Suttons *Cant* from 10. *The Vicarage, Chart Road, Sutton Valence, Maidstone ME17 3AW* Tel (01622) 844340 Mobile 07910-442247 E-mail chris.piers@yahoo.com
LAVERTY, Canon Walter Joseph Robert. b 49. CITC 70 Glouc Th Course 73. **d** 73 **p** 74. C Belfast St Donard *D & D* 73-77; C Ballymacarrett St Patr 77-82; I Kilwarlin Upper w Kilwarlin Lower 82-86; I Orangefield w Moneyreagh from 86; Warden of Readers from 96; Can Down Cathl 97-00; Preb 97-00; Treas from 01. *The Rectory, 397 Castlereagh Road, Belfast BT5 6AB* Tel and fax (028) 9070 4493
LAVERY, Edward Robinson. Lon Univ BA. St Aid Birkenhead 65. **d** 67 **p** 68. C Belfast Trin Coll Miss *Conn* 67-69; C Belfast St Mary Magd 69-71; CF (TA) 70-95; OCM from 75; I Belfast St Phil *Conn* 71-74; I Craigs w Dunaghy and Killagan 74-83; I Ballymoney w Finvoy and Rasharkin 83-05; Dioc Info Officer 83-05; Can Conn Cathl 96-05; Treas 98-01; Chan 01-05; rtd 05; P-in-c Ballysculion *D & R* from 09. *11 Drummanallaght Park, Ballymoney BT53 7QZ* Tel (028) 2766 9147
LAW, Andrew Philip. b 61. BNC Ox BA83 MA93 G&C Coll Cam PGCE86 Leic Univ MBA04. WEMTC 90. **d** 93 **p** 94. C Tupsley w Hampton Bishop *Heref* 93-95; Chapl Heref Sixth Form Coll 94-95; Chapl City of Lon Freemen's Sch 95-97; Lic to Offic *Guildf* 95-97; Chapl and Hd RS Heref Cathl Sch 97-02; Chapl Malvern Coll from 02; Ho Master 05-07; Perm to Offic *Heref* from 02. *The Chaplain's House, College Road, Malvern WR14 3DD* Tel (01684) 581540 Fax 581617 E-mail apl@malcol.org
LAW, David Richard. b 61. Keble Coll Ox BA82 Wolfs Coll Ox MA89 DPhil89. NOC 98 Predigerseminar Preetz Germany 99. **d** 01 **p** 02. NSM Ashton-upon-Mersey St Martin *Ches* 01-09; NSM Timperley from 09. *2 Winston Close, Sale M33 6UG* Tel 0161-962 0297 E-mail david.law@manchester.ac.uk
LAW, Mrs Elizabeth Ann. b 49. Doncaster Coll of Educn CertEd70 Loughb Univ MA01. EAMTC 99. **d** 01 **p** 02. C Wickham Bishops w Lt Braxted *Chelmsf* 01-05; P-in-c Rattlesden w Thorpe Morieux, Brettenham etc *St E* 05-08; R from 08; Asst Dioc Dir of Ords from 08. *The Rectory, High Street, Rattlesden, Bury St Edmunds IP30 0RA* Tel (01449) 737993 E-mail rev.liz@btinternet.com
LAW, Jeremy Stuart Alan. b 67. RMN93 Man Metrop Univ BSc96. Westcott Ho Cam. **d** 00 **p** 01. C Newton Heath *Man* 00-01; C Wythenshawe 01-04; P-in-c Lawton Moor 04-07; Chapl Cen Man/Man Children's Univ Hosp NHS Trust from 07. *Manchester Royal Infirmary, Cobbett House, Oxford Road, Manchester M13 9WL* Tel 0161-276 1234 E-mail jeremylaw@ntlworld.com
LAW, Jeremy Thomson. b 61. Univ of Wales (Abth) BSc82 Southn Univ BTh89 Ox Univ DPhil00. Sarum & Wells Th Coll 84. **d** 87 **p** 88. C Wimborne Minster and Holt *Sarum* 87-90; C Highfield Ox 90-94; Chapl and Lect Ex Univ 94-03; Dean of Chpl Cant Ch Ch Univ from 03. *Canterbury Christ Church University, North Holmes Road, Canterbury CT1 1QU* Tel (01227) 782747 E-mail jeremy.law@canterbury.ac.uk
LAW, John Francis. b 35. Bps' Coll Cheshunt 65. **d** 67 **p** 68. C Styvechale *Cov* 67-71; P-in-c Cov St Anne and All SS 71-73; TV Cov E 73-77; P-in-c Fillongley 77-82; P-in-c Corley 77-82; V Fillongley and Corley 82-00; RD Nuneaton 90-95; rtd 00; Perm to Offic *Cov* from 00. *10 Brodick Way, Nuneaton CV10 7LH* Tel (024) 7632 5582
LAW, Canon John Michael. b 43. Open Univ BA79. Westcott Ho Cam 65. **d** 68 **p** 69. C Chapel Allerton *Ripon* 68-72; C Ryhope *Dur* 72-73; Mental Health Chapl Fulbourn Hosp Cam 74-04; Chapl Ida Darwin Hosp Cam 74-96; Hon Can Ely Cathl 04-05; rtd 04; PV Ely Cathl 06-08; Perm to Offic from 08. *2 Suffolk Close, Ely CB6 3EW* Tel (01353) 659084
LAW, Nicholas Charles. b 58. Trin Coll Bris BA89. **d** 89 **p** 90. C Goldington *St Alb* 89-92; C Teignmouth, Ideford w Luton,

Ashcombe etc *Ex* 92-97; R Bere Ferrers from 97. *The Rectory, Bere Alston, Yelverton PL20 7HH* Tel (01822) 840229 E-mail nicklaw@breathemail.net

LAW, Peter James. b 46. Ridley Hall Cam 85. **d** 87 **p** 88. C Bournemouth St Jo w St Mich *Win* 87-91; V Chineham 91-96; V Luton Lewsey St Hugh *St Alb* 96-11; rtd 11. *7 Anmore Drive, Waterlooville PO7 6DY* Tel (023) 9226 8336 E-mail revpjl@btinternet.com

LAW, Richard Antcliffe Kelway. b 57. UWIST BEng79. St Jo Coll Nottm MA(TS)01 99. **d** 01 **p** 02. C Brundall w Braydeston and Postwick *Nor* 01-04; V Hollingworth w Tintwistle *Ches* from 04. *The Vicarage, 10 Church Street, Tintwistle, Glossop SK13 1JR* Tel (01457) 852575 E-mail richardaklaw@tiscali.co.uk

LAW, Richard Lindsey. b 34. Univ Coll Ox BA58 MA63 St Pet Coll Birm DipEd70. Cuddesdon Coll 58. **d** 60 **p** 61. C Leighton Buzzard *St Alb* 60-63; Trinidad and Tobago 63-67; V Stotteseden *Heref* 67-72; P-in-c Farlow 67-72; Chapl Framlingham Coll 72-83; V Leigh-on-Sea St Marg *Chelmsf* 83-91; Warden Framlingham Ho of Prayer and Retreat 91-94; rtd 96. *19 Durns Road, Wotton-under-Edge GL12 7JD*

LAW, Canon Robert Frederick. b 43. St Aid Birkenhead 67. **d** 69 **p** 70. C Bengeo *St Alb* 69-72; C Sandy 72-76; P-in-c St Ippolyts 76-81; Chapl Jersey Gp of Hosps 81-84; V Crowan w Godolphin Truro 84-92; RD Kerrier 90-91; R St Columb Major w St Wenn 92-02; RD Pydar 95-02; P-in-c St Minver 02-05; Hon Can Truro Cathl 98-05; rtd 05; Perm to Offic *Truro* from 07. *24 Parkfield, Stillington, York YO61 1JW* Tel (01347) 810754 Mobile 07842-111525 E-mail robertlaw@freeuk.com

LAW, Robert James. b 31. Lon Univ MB, BS55. Ridley Hall Cam 62. **d** 64 **p** 65. C Barnehurst *Roch* 64-66; C Edgware *Lon* 66-72; V Halwell w Moreleigh *Ex* 72-94; P-in-c Woodleigh and Loddiswell 76-79; R 79-94; rtd 96. *38 Wheatlands Road, Paignton TQ4 5HU* Tel (01803) 559450

LAW, Simon Anthony. b 55. Middx Univ BA93 K Coll Lon MA10. NTMTC 94. **d** 96 **p** 97. NSM Forest Gate St Mark *Chelmsf* 96-98; C Becontree W 98-99; TV 99-02; TR 02-07; V Becontree St Cedd 07-10; R Pitsea w Nevendon from 10. *The Rectory, Rectory Road, Pitsea, Basildon SS13 2AA* Tel (01268) 556874 E-mail simon@revlaw.co.uk

LAW-JONES, Peter Deniston. b 55. Newc Univ BA77 Man Univ PGCE81 Nottm Univ BTh87 Lanc Univ MA03. Linc Th Coll 84. **d** 87 **p** 88. C Chorley St Laur *Blackb* 87-91; V Feniscliffe 91-96; V St Annes St Thos from 96; AD Kirkham from 09; Chapl Blackpool, Wyre and Fylde Community NHS Trust 97-04. *The Vicarage, St Thomas Road, Lytham St Annes FY8 1JL* Tel (01253) 723750 E-mail peter.lawjones@tesco.net

LAWAL, Miss Basirat Adebanke Amope (Ade). b 67. Lon Bible Coll BTh02. SAOMC 03. **d** 05 **p** 06. C Blurton *Lich* 05-09; V Wyther Ripon from 09; Racial Justice Officer from 10. *Wyther Vicarage, Houghley Lane, Leeds LS13 4AU* Tel 0113-279 8014 E-mail rev.chick@hotmail.co.uk

LAWES, David Alan. b 33. Lon Bible Coll BD57 PGCE58 Lon Inst of Educn MA70. Cranmer Hall Dur 90. **d** 91 **p** 92. NSM Shaston *Sarum* 91-94; Hon C Diptford, N Huish, Harberton and Harbertonford *Ex* 94-98; rtd 98; Perm to Offic *Sarum* 98-07. *47 Grosvenor Road, Shaftesbury SP7 8DP* Tel (01747) 855621

LAWES, Geoffrey Hyland. b 37. St Jo Coll Dur BA58 Hertf Coll Ox BA60 MA64 Newc Univ PGCE76 MEd79. Cranmer Hall Dur 61. **d** 63 **p** 64. C Millfield St Mark *Dur* 63-66; C Jarrow Grange 66-69; Hon C 69-86; Lic to Offic 86-90; V Collierley w Annfield Plain 90-05; rtd 05; Hon C Satley, Stanley and Tow Law *Dur* from 05. *Netherwood, St Mary's Avenue, Crook DL15 9HY* Tel (01388) 766585

LAWES, Stephen George. b 40. Nottm Univ PGCE75. St Jo Coll Nottm BTh74. **d** 82 **p** 83. NSM Hillmorton *Cov* 82-86; NSM Daventry Deanery Pet 87-03. *Irrisfree, Barleyfield, Kilbrittain, Co Cork, Republic of Ireland*

LAWES, Timothy Stanley. b 57. Nottm Univ BTh88. Linc Th Coll 85. **d** 88 **p** 89. C Wymondham *Nor* 88-92; R Felmingham, Skeyton, Colby, Banningham etc 92-96; Sweden from 96; Asst V Byske Sweden 98-09; TR Skelleftea Landsforsamling from 11. *Asgatan 33A, 931 40 Skelleftea, Sweden (46646) (910) 787901* E-mail timothylawes@hotmail.com

LAWLESS, Mrs Patricia Angela. b 36. Bris Univ BA58 PGCE59. S Dios Minl Tr Scheme 91. **d** 93 **p** 94. NSM Frome Ch Ch *B & W* 93-95; NSM Mells w Buckland Dinham, Elm, Whatley etc 96; NSM Frome St Jo and St Mary 96-00; Chapl Victoria Hosp Frome 96-98; rtd 00; Perm to Offic *B & W* from 00. *22 Braithwaite Way, Frome BA11 2XG* Tel (01373) 466106

LAWLEY, Peter Gerald Fitch. b 52. Chich Th Coll 77. **d** 80 **p** 81. C Pet St Jo 80-83; C Daventry 83-87; P-in-c Syresham w Whitfield 87-90; TV Cen Telford *Lich* 90-98; V Priors Lee and St Georges from 98. *The Vicarage, Ashley Road, Telford TF2 9LF* Tel and fax (01952) 612923 E-mail peterlawley@talktalk.net

LAWLEY, Rosemary Ann. b 47. WMMTC 00. **d** 03 **p** 04. NSM Kinver and Enville *Lich* 03-07; TV Kidderminster St Mary and All SS w Trimpley etc *Worc* from 07; Ind Chapl from 07.

186 Birmingham Road, Kidderminster, Worcester DY10 2SJ Tel (01562) 748274 E-mail rosemarylawley@tiscali.co.uk

LAWLOR, Colin Robert. b 63. Lanc Univ BA89 MPhil97 St Martin's Coll Lanc PGCE90. Chich Th Coll 90. **d** 93 **p** 94. C Moulsecoomb *Chich* 93-97; TV 97-99; Chapl Brighton Univ from 99. *204 Bevendean Crescent, Brighton BN2 4RD* Tel 07733-225263 (mobile) E-mail c.r.lawlor@bton.ac.uk

LAWLOR, Paul. b 60. Nottm Univ BSc82. St Jo Coll Nottm 06. **d** 08 **p** 09. C Warsop *S'well* from 08. *19 Wood Street, Warsop NG20 0AX* Tel (01623) 844517 Mobile 07807-611090 E-mail paul@pjlawlor.me.uk

LAWRANCE, Hugh Norcliffe. b 49. N Riding Coll of Educn BEd79. Linc Th Coll 83. **d** 85 **p** 86. C Lindley *Wakef* 85-87; C Barkisland w W Scammonden and Ripponden 87-92; V Knottingley 92-98; C Thorp Arch w Walton, Boston Spa and Clifford *York* 98-00; P-in-c Bramham and Clifford 00-08; C Whitby w Ruswarp from 08. *23 Abbeville Avenue, Whitby YO21 1JD* E-mail frhugh@norcliffe.com

LAWRANCE, Canon Robert William. b 63. Jes Coll Ox BA85 MA89 Man Univ MA93. Ripon Coll Cuddesdon BA87. **d** 88 **p** 89. C Astley *Man* 88-91; Lect Bolton St Pet 91-94; V Bury St Jo w St Mark 94-00; Chapl Bury Healthcare NHS Trust 95-00; Dir of Ords *Dur* 00-08; Chapl Hatf Coll Dur 00-05; Chapl Collingwood Coll Dur 05-08; TR Dur N from 08; AD Dur from 10; Hon Can Dur Cathl from 10; Hon Chapl Dur and Darlington Fire and Rescue Brigade from 09. *St Cuthbert's Vicarage, 1 Aykley Court, Durham DH1 4NW* Tel 0191-386 0146

LAWRENCE, Charles Anthony Edwin. b 53. AKC75. St Aug Coll Cant 75. **d** 76 **p** 77. C Mitcham St Mark *S'wark* 76-80; C Haslemere *Guildf* 80-82; P-in-c Ashton H Trin *Man* 82-84; V Effingham w Lt Bookham *Guildf* 97-05; Chapl Manor Ho Sch 97-05; R Shere, Albury and Chilworth *Guildf* 05-09; R Northfield *Birm* from 09. *The Rectory, Rectory Road, Birmingham B31 2NA* Tel 0121-477 3111 E-mail fathercharles@hotmail.co.uk

LAWRENCE, Christopher David. b 55. Wycliffe Hall Ox 01. **d** 03 **p** 04. C Wadhurst *Chich* 03-07; C Tidebrook 03-07; C Stonegate 03-07; P-in-c Framfield 07-11; V from 11. *The Vicarage, Brookhouse Road, Framfield, Uckfield TN22 5NH* Tel (01825) 890365 Mobile 07941-557537 E-mail cdsjlawrence@tiscali.co.uk

LAWRENCE, Christopher David. b 73. Liv Jo Moores Univ BEd98. Ridley Hall Cam 03. **d** 05 **p** 06. C Letchworth St Paul w Willian *St Alb* 05-08; Chapl RAF from 08. *Chaplaincy Services, Valiant Block, HQ Air Command, RAF High Wycombe HP14 4UE* Tel (01494) 496800 Fax 496343 E-mail revchrislawrence@yahoo.co.uk

LAWRENCE, Canon David Ian. b 48. Univ Coll Lon BSc74 AIMLS71 MIBiol76. Glouc Sch of Min 84 Sarum & Wells Th Coll 87. **d** 88 **p** 89. C Wotton St Mary *Glouc* 88-91; P-in-c Cheltenham St Mich 91-93; V 93-06; V Coleford, Staunton, Newland, Redbrook etc from 06; Hon Can Glouc Cathl from 06. *The Vicarage, 40 Boxbush Road, Coleford GL16 8DN* Tel (01594) 833379 E-mail dandhlawrence@tiscali.co.uk

LAWRENCE, Miss Helen. b 30. St Mich Ho Ox 62. dss 74 **d** 87 **p** 94. Braintree *Chelmsf* 74-87; Par Dn 87-90; rtd 90. Perm to Offic *Chelmsf* 90-08 and *Ely* from 09. *28 Storeys House, Mount Pleasant, Cambridge CB3 0BZ* Tel (01223) 360017

LAWRENCE, Isaac Sartaj. b 72. Peshawar Univ BSc95 Philippine Chr Univ MBA97. **d** 08 **p** 09. C Ripon H Trin from 08. *14 Filey Avenue, Ripon HG4 2DH* Tel (01765) 603146 Mobile 07837-395770 E-mail isaaclawrence28@yahoo.co.uk

LAWRENCE, James Conrad. b 62. St Jo Coll Dur BA85. Ridley Hall Cam 85. **d** 87 **p** 88. Min Bar Hill LEP *Ely* 87-93; Deanery Adv in Evang 90-93; CPAS Evang 93-98; Perm to Offic *Cov* from 93; Springboard Missr from 97; CPAS Dir Evang Projects from 99. *Cotton Mill Spinney, Cubbington, Leamington Spa CV32 7XH* Tel (01926) 426761 or 334242 Fax 337613 E-mail jlawrence@cpas.org.uk

LAWRENCE, Mrs Janet Maureen. b 43. Hockerill Teacher Tr Coll TCert64. Ox Min Course 89. **d** 92 **p** 94. Hon Par Dn Bletchley *Ox* 92-94; NSM N Bletchley CD 94-05; rtd 05; Perm to Offic *Ox* 05-08; Hon C Gayhurst w Ravenstone, Stoke Goldington etc from 08. *The Rectory, Mount Pleasant, Stoke Goldington, Newport Pagnell MK16 8LL* Tel (01908) 551221 E-mail jmlawrence@talktalk.net

LAWRENCE, John Graham Clive. b 47. ACIB. Trin Coll Bris. **d** 78 **p** 79. C Chatham St Phil and St Jas *Roch* 78-83; V Roch St Justus 83-97; Asst Chapl HM Pris Roch 83-97; UK Dir CMJ 97-00; Internat Co-ord Light to the Nations UK 00-10; Chapl Maidstone and Tunbridge Wells NHS Trust 03-04; Chapl W Kent NHS and Soc Care Trust 05-06; Chapl Kent & Medway NHS and Soc Care Partnership Trust 06-08; Chapl Team Ldr Bucks Hosps NHS Trust 08-10; rtd 10. *55 Staines Square, Dunstable LU6 3JG* Tel (01582) 603408 Mobile 07984-951534 E-mail jgcl1@sky.com

LAWRENCE, Mrs Judith Patricia. b 53. WEMTC 01. **d** 04 **p** 05. C Glastonbury w Meare *B & W* 04-09. *Address temp unknown* Tel 07969-381488 (mobile) E-mail lawrence@wedmore100.fsnet.co.uk

LAWRENCE, Canon Leonard Roy. b 31. Keble Coll Ox BA56 MA59. Westcott Ho Cam 56. **d** 58 **p** 59. C Stockport St Geo *Ches* 58-62; V Thelwall 62-68; V Hyde St Geo 68-75; V Prenton 75-96; Hon Can Ches Cathl 86-96; rtd 96; Perm to Offic *Ches* from 96; Acorn Chr Foundn from 97. *39 Mockbeggar Drive, Wallasey CH45 3NN* Tel 0151-346 9438

LAWRENCE, Leslie. b 44. S'wark Ord Course 86. **d** 88 **p** 89. NSM Stanwell *Lon* 88-92; C Hounslow H Trin w St Paul 92-97; P-in-c Norwood St Mary 97-06; R 06-09; rtd 09. *22 Chestnut Road, Ashford TW15 1DG* Tel (01784) 241773 Mobile 07765-551637 E-mail leslie.lawrence@tesco.net

LAWRENCE, Lorraine Margaret. b 58. **d** 11. NSM Gravesend St Geo *Roch* from 11. *39 Darnley Street, Gravesend DA11 0PH* Tel (01474) 326268 E-mail lorraine lawrence@btinternet.com

LAWRENCE, Martin Kenneth. b 59. Univ Coll Dur BA82. St Steph Ho Ox 94. **d** 96 **p** 97. C Wanstead St Mary w Ch Ch *Chelmsf* 96-00; PV Westmr Abbey 99-00; Chapl Malta and Gozo *Eur* 00-01; C Becontree S *Chelmsf* 02; C Romford St Edw 02-05; P-in-c Cranham 05-08; rtd 08. *13A Guildford Road, Brighton BN1 3LU* Tel (01273) 245812 Mobile 07905-290849 E-mail martinlawrence@dunelm.org.uk

LAWRENCE, Norman. b 45. Lon Univ BEd75. S'wark Ord Course 77. **d** 80 **p** 81. NSM Hounslow H Trin *Lon* 80-88; NSM Hounslow H Trin w St Paul from 88. *89 Bulstrode Avenue, Hounslow TW3 3AE* Tel (020) 8572 6292 E-mail nlawrence@lampton.hounslow.sch.uk

LAWRENCE, Canon Patrick Henry Andrew. b 51. TCD Div Test 79 BA81. **d** 81 **p** 82. C Templemore *D & R* 81-84; C Kilkenny St Canice Cathl 84-85; I Templebreedy w Tracton and Nohoval *C, C & R* 85-92; I Geashill w Killeigh and Ballycommon *M & K* 92-98; Can Kildare Cathl 92-09; Adn Kildare 93-09; Adn Meath 97-09; Warden of Readers 97-09; I Julianstown and Colpe w Drogheda and Duleek 98-09; I Monkstown *D & G* from 09; Preb Monmohenock St Patr Cathl Dublin from 00. *62 Monkstown Road, Monkstown, Co Dublin, Republic of Ireland* Tel (00353) (1) 280 6596 E-mail patricklawrence@eircom.net

LAWRENCE, Canon Peter Anthony. b 36. Lich Th Coll 67. **d** 69 **p** 70. C Oadby *Leic* 69-74; P-in-c Northmarston and Granborough *Ox* 74-81; P-in-c Hardwick St Mary 74-81; P-in-c Quainton 76-81; P-in-c Oving w Pitchcott 76-81; TR Schorne 81-91; RD Claydon 84-88; V Ivinghoe w Pitstone and Slapton 91-97; Hon Can Ch Ch 97; rtd 97; Perm to Offic *Ox* 99-07 and *Worc* from 01. *Hill House, Back Lane, Malvern WR14 2HJ* Tel (01684) 564075

LAWRENCE, Ralph Guy. b 55. Trin Coll Bris 87. **d** 89 **p** 90. C Cotmanhay *Derby* 89-93; P-in-c Tansley, Dethick, Lea and Holloway 93-04; R Ashover and Brackenfield w Wessington from 04; C N Wingfield, Clay Cross and Pilsley from 06. *The Rectory, Narrowleys Lane, Ashover, Chesterfield S45 0AU* Tel (01246) 590246 E-mail ralphlawrence@tiscali.co.uk

LAWRENCE, Roy. See LAWRENCE, Canon Leonard Roy

LAWRENCE (*née* MASON), **Sarah Catherine.** b 79. K Coll Lon BA02 PGCE03 Chu Coll Cam MPhil06. Ridley Hall Cam 05. **d** 08 **p** 10. NSM Carr Dyke Gp *Linc* 08-10; C Shifnal and Sheriffhales *Lich* from 10. *7 Oakfield Road, Shifnal TF11 8HT* Tel (01952) 463944 Mobile 07766-348170 E-mail revsarahlawrence@yahoo.co.uk

LAWRENCE, Simon Peter. b 60. TD. Nottm Univ BTh88 MA97 Indiana State Univ DMin01. St Jo Coll Nottm 85. **d** 88 **p** 89. C Holbeach *Linc* 88-90; C Alford w Rigsby 90-91; R Rattlesden w Thorpe Morieux and Brettenham *St E* 91-93; V Churchdown *Glouc* 93; V Maenclochog w Henry's Moat and Mynachlogddu etc *St D* 93-94; R Overstrand, Northrepps, Sidestrand etc 95-98; CF (TA) 89-05; CF (ACF) 90-05; Perm to Offic *Nor* 02-06; Public Preacher 06-07; R Stalham, E Ruston, Brunstead, Sutton and Ingham from 07; Dioc Chapl MU from 11. *The Rectory, Camping Field Lane, Stalham, Norwich NR12 9DT* Tel (01692) 580250 E-mail simon.stalham@btinternet.com

LAWRENCE, Timothy Hervey. b 25. Ripon Hall Ox 58. **d** 60 **p** 61. C Newmarket All SS *St E* 60-62; V Kentford w Higham Green 62-84; P-in-c Herringswell 78-84; rtd 84. *The Dairy, Parsonage Farm, Parsonage Downs, Dunmow CM6 2AT* Tel (01371) 874818

LAWRENCE (*née* FOREMAN), **Mrs Vanessa Jane.** b 73. Ch Ch Coll Cant BA95. Westcott Ho Cam. **d** 00 **p** 01. C N Stoneham *Win* 00-04; NSM Swaythling 04-07; NSM Chilworth w N Baddesley 07-10; NSM Ampfield 08-10; NSM Ampfield, Chilworth and N Baddesley from 10; Chapl Hants Partnership NHS Trust from 09. *Address temp unknown* E-mail vanessalawrence@waitrose.com

LAWRENCE, Victor John. b 43. ACII. Oak Hill Th Coll. **d** 83 **p** 84. C Paddock Wood *Roch* 83-87; R Milton next Gravesend w Denton 87-09; RD Gravesend 05-09; rtd 09. *7 Sarnia House, 17 Darley Road, Eastbourne BN20 7PE* E-mail victorjlaw@googlemail.com

LAWRENCE-MARCH, David Lawrence. b 61. Univ of Wales (Lamp) BA83. Coll of Resurr Mirfield 83. **d** 85 **p** 86. C Pet St Jude 85-89; Chapl St Aug Sch Kilburn 89-92; C Kilburn St Aug w St Jo *Lon* 89-90; C Paddington St Mary 90-92; Chapl Bearwood Coll Wokingham 92-96; R Holt w High Kelling *Nor* 96-98; Sen Chapl Bedford Sch 98-09; Chapl Ardingly Coll from 09. *Ardingly College, Haywards Heath RH17 6SQ* Tel (01444) 892656 E-mail father.david@ardingly.com

LAWRENSON, Michael. b 35. Leeds Univ BA60 Liv Univ CertSS65 Newc Univ DASS69. Coll of Resurr Mirfield 60. **d** 74 **p** 74. NSM Glenrothes *St And* 74-90; Dioc Supernumerary 90-95; Chapl HM Pris Perth 91-95; NSM Glenrothes *St And* 95-00; NSM Leven 95-00; NSM Lochgelly 95-00; NSM St Andrews St Andr 95-00; rtd 00. *Hollyburn, West Port, Falkland, Cupar KY15 7BW* Tel (01337) 857311 E-mail lawrenson@hollyburn.plus.com

LAWRENSON, Ronald David. b 41. CITC 68. **d** 71 **p** 72. C Seapatrick *D & D* 71-78; Min Can Down Cathl 78-79; V Choral Belf Cathl 79-86; Bp's C Tynan w Middletown *Arm* 86-93; Hon V Choral Arm Cathl 87-02; Bp's C Tynan w Middletown 92-93; I Donaghmore w Upper Donaghmore 93-98; rtd 02. *Riverbrook Apartments, 5 Brookland Drive, Whitehead, Carrickfergus BT38 9SL* Tel (028) 9337 3625

LAWRIE (*née* VENTON), **Ms Kathryn Magdelana.** b 56. Reading Univ BA78. NEOC 03. **d** 06 **p** 07. C Skelton w Upleatham *York* 06-10; P-in-c Hedon w Paull from 10. *The Vicarage, 44 New Road, Hedon, Hull HU12 8BS* Tel (01482) 897693

LAWRIE, Paul Edward. b 12. Freiburg Univ LLD35 St Cath Soc Ox BA48 MA53. Wycliffe Hall Ox 46. **d** 48 **p** 49. C Walkley *Sheff* 48-51; C Thrybergh 51-54; V Drax 54-64; R Todwick 64-78; rtd 78; Chapl Rotherham Distr Gen Hosp 78-85; Hon C Handsworth Woodhouse *Sheff* 85-88; Hon C Aston cum Aughton w Swallownest, Todwick etc 88-92; Perm to Offic from 92. *15 Haddon Way, Aston, Sheffield S26 2EH* Tel 0114-287 4864

LAWRIE, Peter Sinclair. b 39. Clifton Th Coll 62. **d** 65 **p** 66. C Derby St Chad 65-68; C Toxteth Park St Philemon w St Silas *Liv* 68-71; V Ramsey St Mary's w Ponds Bridge *Ely* 71-81; V Whitwick St Jo the Bapt *Leic* 81-96; P-in-c Felixstowe SS Pet and Paul *St E* 96-03; rtd 03. *71 Lincroft, Oakley, Bedford MK43 7SS* Tel (01234) 824055 E-mail p.lawrie@talk21.com

LAWRINSON, Leslie Norman. b 35. IEng MCIPD90 MCMI84. **d** 99 **p** 00. OLM Onchan *S & M* 99-05; NSM Scarisbrick *Liv* 05-08; rtd 08; Perm to Offic *S & M* from 09. *8 Hillary Wharf Apartments, South Quay, Douglas, Isle of Man IM1 5BL* Tel (01624) 627664 Mobile 07749-687469 E-mail leslawrinson05@aol.com

LAWRY, Mrs Fianach Alice Moir. b 35. St And Dioc Tr Course 85. **d** 88 **p** 94. NSM Dollar *St And* from 88; Chapl HM Pris Glenochil 91-07. *Sunnybank, Muckhart, Dollar FK14 7JN* Tel (01259) 781426 E-mail f.lawry@virgin.net

LAWRY, Richard Henry. b 57. Bris Univ BA79 Wolfs Coll Cam PGCE81. St Jo Coll Nottm MA01. **d** 99 **p** 00. C Macclesfield Team *Ches* 99-02; P-in-c Stalybridge St Paul 02-06; V 06-09; V Norbury from 09. *Norbury Vicarage, 75 Chester Road, Hazel Grove, Stockport SK7 5PE* Tel 0161-483 8640 E-mail richardlawry@talk21.com

LAWS, Clive Loudon. b 54. UEA BEd76 Leeds Univ CertEd75. Wycliffe Hall Ox 79. **d** 82 **p** 83. C Newcastle w Butterton *Lich* 82-85; C Gabalfa *Llan* 85-88; R Pendine w Llanmiloe and Eglwys Gymyn w Marros *St D* 89-94; CF 89-94; Perm to Offic *B & W* 95-96; C Portishead 96-02; TV 02-08; P-in-c High Laver w Magdalen Laver and Lt Laver etc *Chelmsf* 08-10; Chapl St Clare Hospice 08-10; rtd 10. *36 Alexandra Close, Illogan, Redruth TR16 4RS* Tel (01209) 843117 E-mail clive anne@yahoo.co.uk

LAWSON, Anne. See LAWSON, Miss Sarah Anne

LAWSON, Canon Alma Felicity. b 51. St Hugh's Coll Ox BA73 MA78. St Jo Coll Nottm. **d** 98 **p** 99. Dean of Min and Dir of Ords *Wakef* 93-00; Hon C Wakef Cathl 98-00; V Gildersome from 00; Hon Can Wakef Cathl from 01; RD Birstall from 10. *St Peter's House, 2A Church Street, Gildersome, Morley, Leeds LS27 7AF* Tel and fax 0113-253 3339 E-mail felicity.lawson@tiscali.co.uk

LAWSON, Anne. See LAWSON, Miss Sarah Anne

LAWSON, David McKenzie. b 47. Glas Univ MA69 Edin Univ BD76. Edin Th Coll 73. **d** 76 **p** 77. C Glas St Mary 76-82; V Keighley All SS *Bradf* 82-85; Chapl Asst Univ Coll Hosp Lon 85-91; Hon C St Pancras w St Jas and Ch Ch *Lon* 86-91; R Smithfield St Bart Gt 91-93; Hon C Paddington St Jas 94-00; TV Chambersbury *St Alb* 00-03; TR 03-09; TR Langelei from 09; RD Hemel Hempstead from 08. *The Rectory, The Glebe, Kings Langley WD4 9HY* Tel (01923) 262939 Mobile 07939-473717 E-mail davidmlawson@btinternet.com

LAWSON, David William. b 50. ACA. Linc Th Coll. **d** 82 **p** 83. C Stafford *Lich* 82-85; TV Redruth w Lanner *Truro* 85-87; P-in-c Whitley *Cov* 87-93; Chapl Whitley Hosp Cov 87-94; Chapl Gulson Road Hosp Cov 87-94; Chapl Cov and Warks Hosp 87-94; V S Leamington St Jo *Cov* from 93. *St John's Vicarage,*

Tachbrook Street, Leamington Spa CV31 3BN Tel (01926) 422208

LAWSON, Felicity. *See* LAWSON, Canon Alma Felicity

LAWSON, The Very Revd Frederick Quinney (Rick). b 45. Leic Univ BA. St Steph Ho Ox. **d** 83 **p** 84. Hon C Loughborough Em *Leic* 83-86; NSM Somerby, Burrough on the Hill and Pickwell 86-87; USA from 87; Hon Can Salt Lake City 87-02; Dean from 02. *4294 Adonis Drive, Salt Lake City UT 84124, USA* Tel (001) (801) 595 5380 *or* 322-3400 Fax 278 5903 E-mail rlawson@stmarkscathedral-ut.org

LAWSON, Gary Austin. b 53. Man Univ BA80. Ripon Coll Cuddesdon 80. **d** 82 **p** 83. C Nunhead St Antony *S'wark* 82-86; Hon C Reddish *Man* 86-87; Hon C Longsight St Jo w St Cypr 87-88; V Wythenshawe St Rich 88-98; Chapl Bolton Inst of F&HE 98-03; C Bolton St Pet 98-03; TR Westhoughton and Wingates from 03; C Daisy Hill from 11. *The Rectory, Market Street, Westhoughton, Bolton BL5 3AZ* Tel (01942) 859251

LAWSON, James Barry. b 68. Edin Univ MA91 New Coll Ox DPhil96. Coll of Resurr Mirfield 98. **d** 99 **p** 00. C Poplar *Lon* 99-02; Chapl CCC Cam 02-07; Bp's Sen Chapl *Sarum* 07-08; V Stoke Newington Common St Mich *Lon* from 09. *St Michael's Vicarage, 55 Fountayne Road, London N16 7ED* Tel (020) 8806 4225

LAWSON, Canon John Alexander. b 62. Sheff Univ BA84 Nottm Univ MA97 PhD06. St Jo Coll Nottm 85. **d** 87 **p** 88. C Wellington All SS w Eyton *Lich* 87-92; TV Dewsbury *Wakef* 92-98; P-in-c Birchencliffe 98-05; Dioc Vocations Adv and Asst Dir of Ords 02-05; Can Res Wakef Cathl from 05; Dioc Dir Tr from 05; Warden Wakef Mln Scheme from 06. *7 Belgravia Road, Wakefield WF1 3JP* Tel (01924) 380182 *or* 371802 E-mail john.lawson@wakefield.anglican.org

LAWSON, Jonathan Halford. b 68. St Chad's Coll Dur BA90 Heythrop Coll Lon MA04. Westcott Ho Cam 91. **d** 93 **p** 94. C Sedgefield *Dur* 93-96; C Usworth 96-97; TV 97-00; TV Epping Distr *Chelmsf* 00-04; Chapl St Hild and St Bede Coll *Dur* from 04. *The College of St Hild and St Bede, St Hild's Lane, Durham DH1 1SZ* Tel 0191-334 8522 Fax 334 8301 E-mail j.h.lawson@durham.ac.uk

LAWSON, June Margaret. b 62. Birm Univ BA83 Didsbury Coll of Educn PGCE84 St Jo Coll York MA02. NOC 00. **d** 02 **p** 03. C Huddersfield H Trin *Wakef* 02-05; Dir Adult Chr Educn Mirfield Cen 05-08; Dir Mirfield Cen from 08; Hon C Wakef Cathl from 05; Dean of Women's Min from 09. *The Mirfield Centre, Stocks Bank Road, Mirfield WF14 0BW* Tel (01924) 481911 E-mail jlawson@mirfield.org.uk

LAWSON, Matthew Charles Outram. b 71. Trin Coll Bris. **d** 11. C Bury St Edmunds St Mary *St E* from 11. *18 Vinery Road, Bury St Edmunds IP33 2JR* Tel 07834-507086 (mobile) E-mail mattisfound@gmail.com

LAWSON, Matthew James. b 67. St Andr Univ MTheol91 FRSA02. Ripon Coll Cuddesdon MTh94. **d** 94 **p** 95. C Bedford St Andr *St Alb* 94-97; Chapl and Hd RS St Jo Sch Leatherhead 97-07; Tutor Dioc Min Course *Guildf* 98; Chapl Tsurippoint Coll 07-10. *54 Hipwell Court, Olney MK46 5QB* Tel 07768-515950 (mobile) E-mail frlawson@aol.com

LAWSON, The Ven Michael Charles. b 52. Sussex Univ BA75. Trin Coll Bris. **d** 78 **p** 79. C Horsham *Chich* 78-81; C St Marylebone All So w SS Pet and Jo *Lon* 81-87; V Bromley Ch Ch *Roch* 87-99; Adn Hampstead *Lon* 99-10; R Guildf St Sav from 10. *St Saviour's Rectory, Wharf Road, Guildford GU1 4RP* Tel (01483) 577811 E-mail m.c.lawson@btinternet.com

LAWSON, Rick. *See* LAWSON, The Very Revd Frederick Quinney

LAWSON, Robert William. b 60. MIBiol89. CITC 05. **d** 08 **p** 09. NSM Celbridge w Straffan and Newcastle-Lyons *D & G* from 08. *6 Roselawn Close, Castleknock, Dublin 15, Republic of Ireland* Tel (00353) (1) 820 5129 Mobile 86-394 3151 E-mail lawson.rw@gmail.com

LAWSON, Russell Thomas. b 70. Leeds Univ BA92 Ox Univ BTh98. St Steph Ho Ox 98. **d** 98 **p** 99. C Cheshunt *St Alb* 98-02; C Cheam *S'wark* 02-06; TV 06-07; P-in-c S Norwood St Alb from 07. *The Vicarage, 6 Dagmar Road, London SE25 6HZ* Tel 07703-176001 (mobile) E-mail rtl70@btopenworld.com

LAWSON, Miss Sarah Anne. b 66. Ches Coll of HE BA87. Ridley Hall Cam. **d** 00 **p** 01. C Hollingworth w Tintwistle *Ches* 00-05; V Haslington w Crewe Green from 05. *The Vicarage, 163 Crewe Road, Haslington, Crewe CW1 5RL* Tel (01270) 582388 E-mail revanne@uwclub.net

LAWSON-JONES, Christopher Mark. b 68. Open Univ BA98. St Mich Coll Llan 98. **d** 00 **p** 01. C Risca *Mon* 00-03; Chapl Cross Keys Campus Coleg Gwent 00-03; TV Cyncoed 03-06; Dioc Soc Resp Officer 04-06; P-in-c Magor 06-09; TR Magor from 09. *The Rectory, Redwick Road, Magor, Caldicot NP26 3GU* Tel (01633) 880266 E-mail church.office@ymail.com

LAWTON, David Andrew. b 62. Man Univ BA83. Cranmer Hall Dur. **d** 00 **p** 01. C Deptford St Jo w H Trin *S'wark* 00-04; TV

Walton H Trin *Ox* 04-09; V Southcourt from 09. *60 Grenville Road, Aylesbury HP21 8EY* Tel (01296) 424175 E-mail revdave15@aol.com

LAXON, Canon Colin John. b 44. FRSA. Cant Sch of Min 86. **d** 89 **p** 90. C Folkestone St Mary and St Eanswythe *Cant* 89-94; P-in-c Barrow St Jas *Carl* 94-01; Soc Resp Officer 01-09; C Brampton and Farlam and Castle Carrock w Cumrew 01-02; TV Eden, Gelt and Irthing 02-06; C Carl St Cuth w St Mary 06-09; Hon Can Carl Cathl 06-09; rtd 09. *15 Knowefield Avenue, Carlisle CA3 9BQ* Tel (01228) 544215 E-mail c.laxon@btinternet.com

LAY, Mrs Alison Margaret. b 57. **d** 07 **p** 09. OLM Needham Market w Badley *St E* 07-08; OLM Combs and Lt Finborough from 08. *The Hideaway, Park Road, Needham Market, Ipswich IP6 8BH* Tel (01449) 721115 E-mail ali@divineone.f9.co.uk

LAY, Brian Robert. b 37. Bernard Gilpin Soc Dur 59 Chich Th Coll 60. **d** 63 **p** 64. C Battyeford *Wakef* 63-66; C Belhus Park *Chelmsf* 66-73; P-in-c Sutton on Plym *Ex* 73-80; V 80-07; rtd 07; Perm to Offic *Ex* from 09. *18 Dunstone Drive, Plymouth PL9 8SQ* Tel (01752) 407348

LAY, Geoffrey Arthur. b 54. Leic Poly BA77 Man Univ MA83 Lon Univ BD88. Ridley Hall Cam 90. **d** 92 **p** 93. C St Neots *Ely* 92-95; P-in-c Long Stanton w St Mich 95-01; P-in-c Dry Drayton 95-97; R Chailey *Chich* 01-06; Chapl Chailey Heritage Hosp Lewes 01-06; rtd 06. *77 Firle Road, Peacehaven BN10 7QH* Tel (01273) 588048 E-mail geofflay@btinternet.com

LAYBOURNE, Michael Frederick. b 37. Qu Coll Birm 81. **d** 83 **p** 84. C High Elswick St Phil *Newc* 83-85; C High Elswick St Phil and Newc St Aug 86; C Cramlington 86-87; TV 87-95; C Killingworth 95-02; rtd 02; Perm to Offic *Newc* from 02. *16 Rockcliffe Gardens, Whitley Bay NE26 2NL* Tel 0191-251 0115 E-mail mikelaybourne@waitrose.com

LAYCOCK, Charles. b 37. Open Univ BA88. NOC 80. **d** 83 **p** 84. C Astley Bridge *Man* 83-86; R Crumpsall 86-94; V Ashton Ch Ch 94-00; rtd 00; Perm to Offic *Man* from 00 and *Ches* from 03. *23 The Mere, Ashton-under-Lyne OL6 9NH* Tel 0161-330 2824

LAYCOCK, Lawrence. b 42. St Deiniol's Hawarden 86. **d** 89 **p** 90. C Blackpool St Mich *Blackb* 89-94; P-in-c Worsthorne 94-99; P-in-c Holme 96-99; V Holme-in-Cliviger w Worsthorne 99-08; rtd 08; Hon C Burnley St Steph *Blackb* 08-11; Hon C Burnley St Pet and St Steph from 11; AD Burnley 04-10. *St Stephen's Vicarage, 154 Todmorden Road, Burnley BB11 3ER* Tel (01282) 424733 E-mail revrover@btinternet.com

LAYNESMITH, Mark David. b 74. York Univ BA97 MA99. Ripon Coll Cuddesdon BA01. **d** 02 **p** 03. C Tadcaster w Newton Kyme *York* 02-05; Chapl Reading Univ from 05. *30 Shinfield Road, Reading RG2 7BW* Tel 0118-987 1495

LAYTON, Miss Norene. b 39. Trin Coll Bris 84. dss 86 **d** 87 **p** 94. Lindfield *Chich* 86-92; Par Dn 87-92; Par Dn Loughborough Em *Leic* 92-94; C Loughborough Em and St Mary in Charnwood 94-96; V Hengrove *Bris* 96-04; rtd 04. *104 Outwoods Drive, Loughborough LE11 3LU* Tel (01509) 218127

LAYZELL, Martyn Paul. b 75. Wycliffe Hall Ox 08. **d** 10 **p** 11. C Onslow Square and S Kensington St Aug *Lon* from 10. *56 Drakefield Road, London SW17 8RP* Tel (020) 8767 7369 Mobile 07891-015221 *or* 07702-968022 E-mail martyn.layzell@htb.org.uk

LAZENBY, Donna Jannine. b 83. Qu Coll Cam BA04 MPhil05 PhD09. Westcott Ho Cam 09. **d** 11. C Wallington Springfield Ch *S'wark* from 11. *The Vicarage, 3 Valley Road, Kenley CR8 5DJ* Tel (020) 8660 6981 *or* (020) 8660 1914 Mobile 07732-175107 E-mail donna.lazenby@btinternet.com

LE BAS, Mrs Jennifer Anne. b 60. Hull Univ BSc81 Univ of Wales (Lamp) MA06. S Dios Minl Tr Scheme 90. **d** 93 **p** 94. C Alverstoke *Portsm* 93-96; C Elson 97-01; P-in-c Gosport Ch Ch and Dioc FE Officer 01-04; Perm to Offic *Roch* 05-06; P-in-c Seal SS Pet and Paul from 06. *The Vicarage, Church Street, Seal, Sevenoaks TN15 0AR* Tel (01732) 762955 E-mail annelebas@dsl.pipex.com

LE BILLON, Mrs Janet. b 42. STETS 99. **d** 02 **p** 03. NSM Guernsey St Jo *Win* 02-06; NSM Guernsey Ste Marie du Castel from 06; NSM Guernsey St Matt from 06; Chapl States of Guernsey Bd of Health from 02. *Tranquillité, Clos des Quatre Vents, St Martin, Guernsey GY4 6SU* Tel (01481) 234283

LE COUTEUR, Miss Tracy. STETS. **d** 09 **p** 10. NSM Jersey St Clem *Win* from 09. *2 La Cachette, La Cache du Bourg, St Clement, Jersey JE2 6FX* Tel (01534) 857693 E-mail tracylecouteur@hotmail.com

LE DIEU, Miss Heather Muriel. b 41. Birm Univ BA62 MA67. St Jo Coll Dur 77. dss 79 **d** 87. Birchfield *Birm* 79-82; Kings Heath 82-84; Walsall Pleck and Bescot *Lich* 84-88; Par Dn 87-88; rtd 88. *159 Swarthmore Road, Selly Oak, Birmingham B29 4NW* Tel 0121-475 1236

LE GRICE, Elizabeth Margaret. b 53. Man Univ BA75 MA(Theol)78. N Bapt Coll 75 Westcott Ho Cam 87. **d** 88 **p** 97. In Bapt Ch 78-82; C Whitchurch *Llan* 88-95; Chapl among the Deaf SE Wales *Mon* from 95; Lic to Offic from 95. *9 Hawarden Road, Newport NP19 8JP*

LE GRYS, Alan Arthur. b 51. K Coll Lon BD73 AKC73 MTh90. St Aug Coll Cant 73. **d** 74 **p** 75. C Harpenden St Jo *St Alb* 74-77;

C Hampstead St Jo *Lon* 77-81; Chapl Westf Coll and Bedf Coll 81-84; V Stoneleigh *Guildf* 84-91; Lect Ripon Coll Cuddesdon 91-96; Prin SEITE 96-05; Hon PV Roch Cathl from 96. *265 Dale Street, Chatham ME4 6QR* Tel (01634) 402678 *or* 832299 Fax 819347 Mobile 07958-547053
E-mail alan@alegrys.freeserve.co.uk
LE ROSSIGNOL, Richard Lewis. b 52. Aston Univ BSc75. Oak Hill Th Coll BA79. **d** 79 **p** 80. C E Ham St Paul *Chelmsf* 79-81; C Willesborough w Hinxhill *Cant* 81-85; Perm to Offic 85-94; NSM Brabourne w Smeeth 94-01; NSM Mersham w Hinxhill and Sellindge 01-06; NSM Smeeth w Monks Horton and Stowting and Brabourne 06-07; P-in-c from 07; P-in-c Mersham w Hinxhill and Sellindge from 07. *The Rectory, Church Road, Smeeth, Ashford TN25 6SA* Tel (01303) 812697
E-mail rlerossi@ntlworld.com
LE SÈVE, Mrs Jane Hilary. b 63. SS Hild & Bede Coll Dur BA86. EAMTC 01. **d** 04 **p** 05. NSM Brightlingsea *Chelmsf* 04-08; TV Greenstead w Colchester St Anne from 08. *The Vicarage, 1 Blackwater Avenue, Colchester CO4 3UY* Tel 05602-299409 E-mail revhilary@btinternet.com
LE SUEUR, Paul John. b 38. Lon Univ BSc59. Wycliffe Hall Ox 60. **d** 62 **p** 63. C Mortlake w E Sheen *S'wark* 62-65; C Witney *Ox* 65-69; R Sarsden w Churchill 69-74; P-in-c Clifton Hampden 74-77; P-in-c Rotherfield Greys H Trin 77-82; V 82-90; V Blacklands Hastings Ch Ch and St Andr *Chich* 90-97; V Ticehurst and Flimwell 97-00; rtd 00; Perm to Offic *Chich* from 01. *80 Barnhorn Road, Bexhill-on-Sea TN39 4QA* Tel (01424) 844747 E-mail halomanpaul@talk21.com
LE VASSEUR, Mrs Linda Susan. b 48. Shenstone Coll of Educn CertEd70. S Dios Minl Tr Scheme 92. **d** 95 **p** 96. NSM Guernsey Ste Marie du Castel *Win* 95-01; NSM Guernsey St Matt 95-01; NSM Guernsey St Sav from 01; NSM Guernsey St Marguerite de la Foret from 01. *Coin des Arquets, Les Arquets, St Pierre du Bois, Guernsey GY7 9HE* Tel (01481) 264047
LE VAY, Clare Forbes Agard Bramhall Joanna. b 41. St Anne's Coll Ox BA64 MA66 Univ of Wales (Abth) MSc72 PhD86. Westcott Ho Cam 86. **d** 88 **p** 94. C Stamford Hill St Thos *Lon* 88-89; C Hackney 89-92; Asst Chapl Brook Gen Hosp *Lon* 92-95; Asst Chapl Greenwich Distr Hosp *Lon* 92-95; Chapl Greenwich Healthcare NHS Trust 95-01; Perm to Offic *S'wark* 02-06; *Lon* 04-06; *Glouc* from 09. *Winton, Beards Lane, Stroud GL5 4HD* Tel (01453) 767020 Mobile 07816-468112
E-mail clarelevay@yahoo.com
LE-WORTHY, Michael Raymond. b 50. **d** 98 **p** 99. OLM Glascote and Stonydelph *Lich* from 98. *15 Abbey Road, Glascote, Tamworth B77 2QE* Tel (01827) 55762
E-mail michael.leworthy1@btinternet.com
LEA, Carolyn Jane. See COOKE, Mrs Carolyn Jane
LEA, Canon Montague Brian. b 34. OBE00. St Jo Coll Cam BA55 Lon Univ BD71. St Jo Coll Nottm 68. **d** 71 **p** 72. C Northwood Em *Lon* 71-74; Chapl Barcelona *Eur* 74-79; V Hove Bp Hannington Memorial Ch *Chich* 79-86; Adn N France *Eur* 86-94; Chapl Paris St Mich 86-94; Hon Can Gib Cathl from 95; R Chiddingly w E Hoathly *Chich* 94-96; Chapl The Hague *Eur* 96-00; rtd 01; Perm to Offic *Chich* from 01. *35 Summerdown Lane, East Dean, Eastbourne BN20 0LE* Tel (01323) 423226
E-mail brian.lea@freedom255.co.uk
LEA, Norman. b 42. JP89. Univ of Wales (Lamp) BA67. Coll of Resurr Mirfield 66. **d** 68 **p** 69. C Newton St Pet *S & B* 68-71; C Oystermouth 71-73; C Brecon w Battle 73-74; TV Cwmbran *Mon* 74-77; V Talgarth and Llanelieu *S & B* 77-84; V Port Talbot St Theodore *Llan* 84-95; Hon Chapl Miss to Seafarers 84-08; V Cadoxton-juxta-Neath *Llan* 95-08; P-in-c Tonna 04-08; rtd 08. *67 Leonard Street, Neath SA11 3HW*
LEA, Canon Richard John Rutland. b 40. Trin Hall Cam BA63 MA67. Westcott Ho Cam 63. **d** 65 **p** 66. C Edenbridge *Roch* 65-68; C Hayes 68-71; V Larkfield 71-86; P-in-c Leybourne 76-86; RD Malling 79-84; V Chatham St Steph 86-88; Can Res and Prec Roch Cathl 88-98; V Iffley *Ox* 98-06; rtd 06. *The Gate House, Malling Abbey, Swan Street, West Malling ME19 6LP* Tel (01732) 522887 E-mail richard.lea@lineone.net
LEA-WILSON, Nicholas Hugh. b 61. Man Poly BA83 Univ Coll Ches BA08 MLI90. NOC 05. **d** 08. C Gateacre *Liv* from 08. *12 Dudlow Gardens, Liverpool L18 2HA* Tel 0151-488 0990 Fax 487 8480 Mobile 07968-290553
E-mail hugh.leawilson@virgin.net
LEACH, Alan Charles Graham. b 46. Univ Coll Ches BTh04 Master Mariner 73. NOC 04. **d** 05 **p** 06. NSM Neston *Ches* 05-08; NSM Heswall from 08. *8 Hill Top Lane, Ness, Neston CH64 4EL* Tel 0151-336 5046 Mobile 07802-622143
E-mail alan.leach5@btinternet.com
LEACH, Alan William Brickett. b 28. MSc CEng FIStructE FASI FICE. S'wark Ord Course. **d** 89 **p** 90. NSM Forest Row *Chich* 89-98; Perm to Offic from 98. *High Beeches, Priory Road, Forest Row RH18 5HP* Tel (01342) 823778
E-mail alanleach@mail.adsl4less.com
LEACH, Andrew John Philip. b 54. Univ of Wales (Lamp) BA77 Univ of Wales (Abth) PGCE78. WEMTC 07. **d** 10 **p** 11. NSM Painswick, Sheepscombe, Cranham, The Edge etc *Glouc* from

10. *Melrose Cottage, Cheltenham Road, Painswick GL6 6SJ* Tel (01452) 813609 Mobile 07564-448692
E-mail ajpleach@googlemail.com
LEACH, Miss Bethia Morag. b 62. Sheff Univ BA84 Liv Inst of Educn PGCE85. Ripon Coll Cuddesdon 95. **d** 97 **p** 98. C Stafford *Lich* 97-00; TV Bilston 00-07; V Pensnett *Worc* 07-10; rtd 10. *66 Lichfield Road, Walsall WS4 2DJ* Tel (01922) 446956
E-mail bethialeach@virginmedia.com
LEACH, Clive. See LEACH, James Clive
LEACH, Gerald. b 27. Sarum & Wells Th Coll 85. **d** 73 **p** 74. NSM Cyncoed *Mon* 73-86; C 86-87; V Dingestow and Llangovan w Penyclawdd etc 87-94; rtd 94; Perm to Offic *Heref* from 95; Lic to Offic *Mon* from 98. *19 Grange Park, Whitchurch, Ross-on-Wye HR9 6EA* Tel (01600) 890397
LEACH, James Clive. b 65. Homerton Coll Cam BEd88 Open Univ MA98. SWMTC 04. **d** 09 **p** 10. NSM Calbourne w Newtown *Portsm* from 09; NSM Shalfleet from 09. *1 Brinton Close, East Cowes PO32 6GH* Tel 07535-670089 (mobile)
E-mail rev.clive@gmail.com
LEACH, James Roger. b 66. Ball Coll Ox BA89 MA99. Wycliffe Hall Ox BA98. **d** 99 **p** 00. C Knowle *Birm* 99-06; C Gerrards Cross and Fulmer *Ox* from 06. *3 The Uplands, Gerrards Cross SL9 7JQ* Tel (01753) 886480
E-mail james@jrleach.freeserve.co.uk
LEACH, Jeffrey Alan. b 64. Bournemouth Univ MSc00. Qu Coll Birm BA11. **d** 11. NSM Wednesfield St Greg *Lich* from 11; Chapl Sandwell Coll from 11. *36 Clewley Drive, Wolverhampton WV9 5LB* Tel 07805-273277 (mobile)
E-mail fr.jcffrcylcach@btinternet.com
LEACH, John. b 52. K Coll Lon BD79 AKC79 St Jo Coll Dur MA83 Lambeth STh02. **d** 81 **p** 82. C N Walsham w Antingham *Nor* 81-85; C Crookes St Thos *Sheff* 85-89; V Styvechale *Cov* 89-97; Dir Angl Renewal Min 97-02; R Jersey St Lawr *Win* 02-04; Par Development Adv *Mon* 04-09; V Foord St Jo *Cant* from 09. *St John's Vicarage, 4 Cornwallis Avenue, Folkestone CT19 5JA* Tel (01303) 250805
E-mail revjohn.leach@tiscali.co.uk
LEACH, Mrs Rebecca Mary. b 65. St Aid Coll Dur BA87 Bris Univ PGCE90. ERMC 05. **d** 08 **p** 09. C E Barnet *St Alb* 08-11; C Harpenden St Nic from 11. *122 Hazelwood Drive, St Albans AL4 0UZ* Tel (01727) 840182 E-mail p.r.leach@ntlworld.com
LEACH, Robert Neville. b 54. Trin Coll Bris 91. **d** 93 **p** 94. C Towcester w Easton Neston *Pet* 93-96; P-in-c Cowley *Lon* 96-01; P-in-c Brandon and Santon Downham w Elveden *St E* 01-04; P-in-c Lakenheath 02-04; R Brandon and Santon Downham w Elveden etc 04-10; P-in-c Chirbury *Heref* from 10; P-in-c Marton from 10; P-in-c Trelystan from 10; P-in-c Middleton from 10. *The Vicarage, Chirbury, Montgomery SY15 6BN* Tel (01938) 561822
E-mail revtrebor@hotmail.com
LEACH, Samuel Mark. b 76. Westmr Coll Ox BEd99. Ridley Hall Cam 05. **d** 08 **p** 09. C Walsall St Paul *Lich* from 08. *11 The Cloisters, Walsall WS4 2AJ* Tel 07915-668714 (mobile)
E-mail samuelmw@hotmail.co.uk
LEACH, Stephen Lance. b 42. St Steph Ho Ox 66. **d** 69 **p** 70. C Higham Ferrers w Chelveston *Pet* 69-72; TV Ilfracombe H Trin *Ex* 72-74; V Barnstaple St Mary 74-77; R Goodleigh 74-77; P-in-c Barnstaple St Pet w H Trin 76-77; P-in-c Landkey 77-79; TR Barnstaple and Goodleigh 77-79; TR Barnstaple, Goodleigh and Landkey 79-82; V Paignton St Jo 82-95; Chapl Paignton and Kings Ash Hosps 82-95; Gen Sec ACS 95-08; Public Preacher *Birm* from 95; rtd 07; Perm to Offic *Ex* from 07. *16 Kings Avenue, Paignton TQ3 2AR* Tel (01803) 552335
LEACH, Stephen Windsor. b 47. St Chad's Coll Dur BSc70 Linacre Coll Ox BA72 MA76. Ripon Hall Ox 70. **d** 73 **p** 74. C Swinton St Pet *Man* 73-77; C Oldham St Chad Limeside 77-79; V Shaw 79-87; V St Just in Penwith *Truro* from 87; V Sancreed from 87. *The Vicarage, St Just, Penzance TR19 7UB* Tel (01736) 788672
LEACH, Timothy Edmund. b 41. Dur Univ BA63. Ridley Hall Cam 63. **d** 65 **p** 66. C Ecclesfield *Sheff* 65-68; C Stocksbridge 68-71; C-in-c W Bessacarr CD 71-80; V Goole and Hon Chapl Miss to Seamen 80-95; V Wath-upon-Dearne *Sheff* 95-08; rtd 08; Perm to Offic *Sheff* from 09. *6 Sawn Moor Avenue, Thurcroft, Rotherham S66 9DQ* Tel (01709) 701263
E-mail komedy@btopenworld.com
LEADBEATER, Canon Nicolas James. b 20. Univ of Wales BA43 LLM95. St Steph Ho Ox 43. **d** 45 **p** 46. C Abergavenny H Trin *Mon* 45-47; C Coleford w Staunton *Glouc* 47-55; PC Moreton Valence and V Whitminster 55-67; V Westcote 67-72; P-in-c Icomb 67-72; V Westcote w Icomb 72-79; V Westcote w Icomb and Bledington 79-88; Hon Can Glouc Cathl 83-88; rtd 88; Perm to Offic *Glouc* 88-06. *19 The Cotswold Home, Woodside Drive, Bradwell Grove, Burford OX18 4XA* Tel (01993) 823182
LEADBEATER, Richard Paul. b 77. Birm Univ BA04. Wycliffe Hall Ox 08. **d** 10 **p** 11. C Selly Park St Steph and St Wulstan *Birm* from 10. *103 Bournbrook Road, Selly Park, Birmingham B29 7BY* Tel 0121-472 8881
E-mail richardleadbeater@hotmail.com

LEADER, Miss Janette Patricia. b 46. EAMTC 94. **d** 97 **p** 98. C Desborough, Brampton Ash, Dingley and Braybrooke *Pet* 97-01; V Wellingborough St Barn from 01. *St Barnabas' Vicarage, St Barnabas Street, Wellingborough NN8 3HB* Tel and fax (01933) 226337 E-mail revjanleader@talktalk.net

LEADER, Stephen. b 64. Ripon Coll Cuddesdon 99. **d** 01 **p** 02. C Battersea St Luke *S'wark* 01-04; V Enfield St Jas *Lon* from 04. *St James's Vicarage, 144 Hertford Road, Enfield EN3 5AY* Tel (020) 7640 9932 E-mail therevstelea@waitrose.com

LEAF, Edward David Hugh. b 65. Oak Hill Th Coll BA97. **d** 98 **p** 99. C Bath St Bart *B & W* 98-01; C Minehead 01-05; V Chadderton Em *Man* from 05. *Emmanuel Vicarage, 15 Chestnut Street, Chadderton, Oldham OL9 8HB* Tel 0161-688 8655 *or* 681 1310 E-mail david.leaf@btopenworld.com

LEAF, William Peter Geard. b 67. Edin Univ BEng90. Ridley Hall Cam 08. **d** 10 **p** 11. C Fulham St Dionis *Lon* from 10. *16 Parsons Green, London SW6 4TS* Tel (020) 7731 1900 E-mail will@stdionis.org.uk

LEAH, William Albert. b 34. K Coll Lon BA56 AKC57 K Coll Cam MA63. Ripon Hall Ox 60. **d** 62 **p** 63. C Falmouth K Chas *Truro* 62-63; Chapl K Coll Cam 63-67; Min Can Westmr Abbey 67-74; V Hawkhurst *Cant* 74-83; Hon Min Can Cant Cathl 78-83; V St Ives *Truro* 83-94; rtd 98. *Trerice Cottage, Sancreed Newbridge, Penzance TR20 8QR* Tel (01736) 810987

LEAHY, David Adrian. b 56. Open Univ BA90. Qu Coll Birm. **d** 85 **p** 86. C Tile Cross *Birm* 85-88; C Warley Woods 88-91; V Hobs Moat 91-07; AD Solihull 97-04; V Four Oaks from 07. *The Vicarage, 26 All Saints Drive, Sutton Coldfield B74 4AG* Tel 0121-308 5315 E-mail adrian.leahy@btinternet.com

LEAK, Adrian Scudamore. b 38. Ch Ch Ox BA60 MA65 BD89. Cuddesdon Coll 64. **d** 66 **p** 67. C Cov St Mark 66-69; C Dorchester *Ox* 69-73; V Badsey *Worc* 73-80; V Wickhamford 73-80; P-in-c Monkwearmouth St Pet *Dur* 80-81; V Choral and Archivist York Minster 81-86; Can Res and Prec Guildf Cathl 86-90; Hon C Guildf H Trin w St Mary 96-00; Hon C Worplesdon 00-06; P-in-c Withyham St Mich *Chich* from 06. *The Rectory, Withyham, Hartfield TN7 4BA* Tel (01892) 770241 E-mail adrian.leak@btinternet.com

LEAK, Harry Duncan. b 30. St Cath Coll Cam BA53 MA57. Ely Th Coll 53. **d** 54 **p** 55. S Africa 54-57; Portuguese E Africa 57-61; C Eccleshall *Lich* 62-64; V Normacot 64-66; C Stoke upon Trent 66-68; V Hanley All SS 68-71; R Swynnerton 71-80; Perm to Offic 80-03; rtd 92. *15 Sutherland Road, Tittensor, Stoke-on-Trent ST12 9JQ* Tel (01782) 374341

LEAK, John Michael. b 42. St Jo Coll Nottm. **d** 84 **p** 85. NSM Beeston *Ripon* 84-87; C Far Headingley St Chad 87-88; Hon C 88-90; C Headingley 90-95; TV Bramley 95-98; rtd 98. *23 Arthington Close, Tingley, Wakefield WF3 1BT* Tel 0113-253 3061

✠LEAKE, The Rt Revd Martin. b 35. CBE03. ALCD59. **d** 59 **p** 60 **c** 69. C Watford *St Alb* 59-61; Lect 61-63; SAMS Argentina 63-69; Asst Bp Paraguay 69-73; Asst Bp N Argentina 69-80; Bp 80-90; Bp Argentina 90-02; rtd 02; Hon Asst Bp Nor from 03; Perm to Offic from 03. *The Anchorage, Lower Common, East Runton, Cromer NR27 9PG* Tel (01263) 513536 E-mail david@leake8.wanadoo.co.uk

LEAKE, Duncan Burton. b 49. Leeds Univ BA71 Leeds and Carnegie Coll PGCE72 Keele Univ MA85. Oak Hill Th Coll 90. **d** 92 **p** 93. C Stanwix *Carl* 92-97; C Chasetown *Lich* 97-00; V Chase Terrace from 00. *The Vicarage, 3 Chapel Street, Burntwood WS7 1NL* Tel (01543) 306649 *or* 304611 Fax 304642 E-mail duncan.leake@ntlworld.com

LEAKEY, Ian Raymond Arundell. b 24. K Coll Cam BA47 MA49. Ridley Hall Cam 48. **d** 50 **p** 51. C Litherland St Jo and St Jas *Liv* 50-53; Rwanda Miss 53-73; Can Burundi 66; V Cudham *Roch* 73-76; P-in-c Downe; V Cudham and Downe 76-89; rtd 89; Perm to Offic *Sarum* from 89. *10 Francis Court, Spire View, Salisbury SP2 7GE* Tel (01722) 329243 E-mail iandf.leakey@btinternet.com

LEAKEY, Peter Wippell. b 39. Lon Univ BSc60. Trin Coll Bris 73. **d** 75 **p** 76. C Colne St Bart *Blackb* 75-79; V Copp 79-85; V Pennington *Man* 85-05; AD Leigh 93-05; Hon Can Man Cathl 02-05; rtd 05; Perm to Offic *Man* from 05. *28 Gilda Road, Worsley, Manchester M28 1BP* Tel 0161-703 8076

LEAL, Malcolm Colin. b 33. Chich Th Coll 72. **d** 75 **p** 76. NSM Shoreham St Giles CD *Chich* 75-87; Chapl NE Surrey Coll Ewell 87-95; NSM Arundel w Tortington and S Stoke *Chich* 88-95; Perm to Offic 95-06. *8 West Park Lane, Goring-by-Sea, Worthing BN12 4EK* Tel (01903) 244160

LEALMAN, Helen. b 46. NOC 03. **d** 05 **p** 06. NSM Ben Rhydding *Bradf* 05-06; NSM Bolton St Jas w St Chrys 06-10; NSM Shipley St Paul from 10. *8 Parkfield Road, Shipley BD18 4EA* Tel (01274) 584569 E-mail helen.lealman@bradford.anglican.org

LEAMY, Stuart Nigel. b 46. Pemb Coll Ox BA68 MA73 ACA76 FCA81. Sarum Th Coll 68. **d** 70 **p** 71. C Upholland *Liv* 70-78; Lic to Offic *Lon* 78-83 and 94-97; NSM Pimlico St Mary Bourne Street from 97. *92 Gloucester Road, Hampton TW12 2UJ* Tel (020) 8979 9068 E-mail leamy@blueyonder.co.uk

LEAN, The Very Revd David Jonathan Rees. b 52. Coll of Resurr Mirfield 74. **d** 75 **p** 76. C Tenby *St D* 75-81; V Llanrhian w Llanhywel and Carnhedryn etc 81-88; V Haverfordwest St Martin w Lambston 88-00; RD Roose 99-00; Can St D Cathl from 00; TV Dewisland 01-09; TR from 09; Dean St D from 09. *The Deanery, St Davids, Haverfordwest SA62 6RD* Tel (01437) 720202

LEANING, The Very Revd David. b 36. Lambeth MA01 Nottm Trent Univ Hon MA03. Lich Th Coll 58. **d** 60 **p** 61. C Gainsborough All SS *Linc* 60-65; R Warsop *S'well* 65-76; RD Kington and Weobley *Heref* 76-80; R Kington w Huntington 76-80; Adn Newark *S'well* 80-91; Provost *S'well* 91-00; Dean 00-06; P-in-c Rolleston w Fiskerton, Morton and Upton 91-93; P-in-c Edingley w Halam 02-06; rtd 06; Perm to Offic *S'well* from 06. *52 Greetwell Road, Lincoln LN2 4AX* Tel (01522) 531361 Fax 521903 E-mail davidleaning@btinternet.com

LEAR, Peter Malcolm. b 45. FCMA. SEITE 95. **d** 98 **p** 99. NSM Ham St Andr *S'wark* 98-03; NSM Wandsworth St Anne 03-04; NSM Upper Coquetdale *Newc* 04-11; rtd 11; Perm to Offic *York* from 11. *39 Farmanby Close, Thornton Dale, Pickering YO18 7TD* E-mail peter@learpm.com

LEARMONT, Oliver James. b 62. UEA BA83 Wolv Univ LLM96 SS Coll Cam BTh07. Westcott Ho Cam 05. **d** 07 **p** 08. C Hitchin *St Alb* from 07. *67 Whitehill Road, Hitchin SG4 9HP* Tel 07966-459315 (mobile) E-mail oliver@learmont.com

LEARMOUTH, Michael Walter. b 50. FCA. Oak Hill Th Coll 84. **d** 84 **p** 85. C Harlow St Mary and St Hugh w St Jo the Bapt *Chelmsf* 84-89; V Hainault 89-97; TR Harlow Town Cen w Lt Parndon 97-00; TR Barnsbury *Lon* from 00; AD Islington from 08. *The Rectory, 10 Thornhill Square, London N1 1BQ* Tel (020) 7607 9039 *or* 7607 4552 E-mail michael@learmonth.fsworld.co.uk

LEARY, Thomas Glasbrook. b 42. AKC66. **d** 67 **p** 68. C W Bromwich All SS *Lich* 67-70; TV Croydon St Jo *Cant* 70-75; C Limpsfield and Titsey *S'wark* 75-83; V Sutton New Town St Barn 83-92; V Merton St Mary 92-07; RD Merton 98-01; rtd 07. *South Barn, Knighton LD7 1NE* Tel (01547) 529194 E-mail glassbrook@msn.com

LEATHARD, Preb Brian. b 56. Sussex Univ BA Cam Univ MA Loughb Univ PhD91. Westcott Ho Cam 79. **d** 82 **p** 83. C Seaford w Sutton *Chich* 82-85; Chapl Loughb Univ 85-89; V Hampton Hill *Lon* 89-06; R Chelsea St Luke and Ch Ch from 06; Dir of Ords from 99; Preb St Paul's Cathl from 05. *The Rectory, 64A Flood Street, London SW3 5TE* Tel (020) 7352 6331 *or* 7351 7365 E-mail brianleathard@chelseaparish.org

LEATHERBARROW, Ronald. b 35. Chester Coll TCert59. NW Ord Course 71. **d** 75 **p** 76. C Eccleston Ch Ch *Liv* 75-80; C Eccleston St Thos 80-83; R Kirklinton w Hethersgill and Scaleby *Carl* 83-86; R Blackley St Mark White Moss *Man* 86-99; rtd 99. *1 Chapel Street, St Helens WA10 2BG* Tel (01744) 614426

LEATHERS, Brian Stanley Peter. b 61. Nottm Univ BSc83. Oak Hill Th Coll BA89. **d** 89 **p** 90. C Watford *St Alb* 89-92; C Welwyn w Ayot St Peter 92-96; V Heacham *Nor* 96-99; P-in-c Stapenhill Immanuel *Derby* 99-00; V 00-09; V Alton w Bradley-le-Moors and Oakamoor w Cotton *Lich* 09-10; P-in-c Denstone w Ellastone and Stanton 09-10; P-in-c Mayfield 09-10; V Alton w Bradley-le-Moors and Denstone etc from 10; RD Uttoxeter from 11. *The New Vicarage, Limekiln Lane, Alton, Stoke-on-Trent ST10 4AR* Tel (01538) 702469 E-mail briantopsey@googlemail.com

LEATHES, David Burlton de Mussenden. b 49. St Jo Coll Nottm 90. **d** 92 **p** 93. C Kirkby Stephen w Mallerstang etc *Carl* 92-00; C Brough w Stainmore, Musgrave and Warcop 94-00. *Low Beck House, Rookby, Kirkby Stephen CA17 4HX* Tel (01768) 371713

LEATHLEY, Susan Mary. b 57. Bath Univ BPharm78 Trin Coll Bris MA98 MRPharmS. Oak Hill Th Coll 92. **d** 94 **p** 98. C Weston-super-Mare Ch Ch *B & W* 94-95; C Toxteth St Philemon w St Gabr and St Cleopas *Liv* 97-01; TV Maghull 01-08; TV Mildenhall *St E* from 08. *The Rectory, 8 Church Walk, Mildenhall, Bury St Edmunds IP28 7ED* Tel (01638) 711930 E-mail sueleathley@aol.com

LEATHLEY, Terence Michael. b 63. Coll of Resurr Mirfield 99. **d** 01 **p** 02. C Whitby w Aislaby and Ruswarp *York* 01-04; TV 04-07; V S Bank from 07; V Middlesbrough St Thos from 07. *The Vicarage, 259 Normanby Road, Middlesbrough TS6 6TB* Tel (01642) 453679 Mobile 07678-986916 E-mail terence.leathley@ntlworld.com

LEATON, Martin John. b 46. Clifton Th Coll 68. **d** 71 **p** 72. C Kenilworth St Jo *Cov* 71-74; C Stratford-on-Avon w Bishopton 74-77; P-in-c Meriden 77-81; R Meriden and Packington 82-84; R Heanton Punchardon w Marwood *Ex* 84-87; Perm to Offic 95-97; P-in-c Rampton w Laneham, Treswell, Cottam and Stokeham *S'well* 97-06; P-in-c N and S Leverton 03-06; rtd 06; Hon C Tysoe w Oxhill and Whatcote *Cov* from 06. *The Vicarage, Peacock Lane, Tysoe, Warwick CV35 0SG* Tel (01295) 680201 E-mail martinleaton@yahoo.co.uk

LEAVER, David Noel. b 63. Hatf Coll Dur BA85. Wycliffe Hall Ox 89. **d** 91 **p** 92. C Blackheath Park St Mich *S'wark* 91-95; C

Upton (Overchurch) *Ches* 95-98; C Wilmslow 98-99; Perm to Offic from 99. *42 Hill Top Avenue, Cheadle Hulme, Cheadle SK8 7HY* Tel 0161-485 4302 E-mail davidleaver@btconnect.com

LEAVER, Mrs Janice Patricia. b 56. EAMTC 03. **d** 06 **p** 07. C Desborough, Brampton Ash, Dingley and Braybrooke *Pet* 06-09; TV Wilford Peninsula *St E* from 09. *The Vicarage, 11 Walnut Tree Avenue, Rendlesham, Woodbridge IP12 2GG* Tel (01394) 460547 Mobile 07913-977218 E-mail revdjleaver@googlemail.com

LEAVER (*née* SMYTH), **Mrs Lucinda Elizabeth Jane (Liz).** b 67. New Hall Cam BA88 MA92. Wycliffe Hall Ox BTh93. **d** 93 **p** 94. C Cambridge St Barn *Ely* 93-97; Chapl St Kath Hall Liv Inst of HE 97-98; TV Stockport SW *Ches* 99-01; Chapl Stockport Gr Sch from 99. *42 Hill Top Avenue, Cheadle Hulme, Cheadle SK8 7HY* Tel 0161-485 4302 E-mail liz.leaver@boltblue.net

LEAVER, Prof Robin Alan. b 39. Groningen Univ DTh87. Clifton Th Coll 62. **d** 64 **p** 65. C Gipsy Hill Ch Ch *S'wark* 64-67; C Gt Baddow *Chelmsf* 67-71; P-in-c Reading St Mary Castle Street Prop Chpl *Ox* 71-77; P-in-c Coggeshall 74-78; Chapl Luckley-Oakfield Sch Wokingham 73-75; Lect Wycliffe Hall Ox 84-85; Prof Ch Music Westmr Choir Coll USA 84-08; Visiting Prof Liturgy Drew Univ 88-00; Visiting Prof Juilliard Sch from 04; Visiting Prof Yale Univ from 08; Visiting Prof QUB from 08. *10 Finch Lane, Dover NH 03820-4707, USA* Tel (001) (603) 343 4251 E-mail leaver@rider.edu

LEAVES (*née* CRAIG), **Julie Elizabeth.** b 63. Southn Univ BTh87. Sarum & Wells Th Coll 82. **dss** 86 **d** 87 **p** 92. Thatcham *Ox* 86-87; Par Dn 87-88; Hong Kong 88-92; Assoc P Fremantle Australia 92-95; Chapl St Mary's Angl Girls' Sch Karrinyup from 96. *Wollaston College, Wollaston Road, Mount Claremont WA 6010, Australia* Tel (0061) (8) 9383 2774 *or* 9341 9102 Fax 9341 9222 E-mail jleaves@stmarys.wa.edu.au

LEAVES, Nigel. b 58. Keble Coll Ox BA80 MA83 K Coll Lon PGCE81 MA86. Sarum & Wells Th Coll 84. **d** 86 **p** 87. C Boyne Hill *Ox* 86-88; Chapl Hong Kong Cathl 88-92; Australia from 92; Abp's Chapl and R W Perth *Perth* 92-98; Tutor and Research Fell Murdoch Univ 98-00; Warden Wollaston Coll & Dir Cen for Belief, Spirituality and Aus Culture from 00. *Wollaston College, Wollaston Road, Mount Claremont WA 6010, Australia* Tel (0061) (8) 9384 5511 *or* tel and fax 9383 2774 Fax 9385 3364 E-mail leaves@iinet.net.au

LEAWORTHY, John Owen. b 40. Univ of Wales (Swansea) BSc62. Oak Hill Th Coll 80. **d** 82 **p** 83. C Compton Gifford *Ex* 82-85; C Plymouth Em w Efford 85-86; P-in-c Marks Tey w Aldham and Lt Tey *Chelmsf* 86-88; R 88-89; Chapl HM Pris Full Sutton 89-91; NSM Portree *Arg* 96-04; rtd 05; Perm to Offic *Chelmsf* from 05. *46 Wilkin Drive, Tiptree, Colchester CO5 0QP* Tel (01621) 810905 E-mail jleaworthy@btinternet.com

LECK, Stuart David. b 62. ACIB84. SEITE 03. **d** 06 **p** 07. NSM Brockley Hill St Sav *S'wark* 06-10; NSM Nunhead St Antony w St Silas from 10. *55 Algiers Road, London SE13 7JD* Tel (020) 8314 5848 E-mail stuart.leck@btinternet.com

LECKEY, Paul Robert. b 61. QUB. Ripon Coll Cuddesdon Aston Tr Scheme. **d** 96 **p** 97. C Eastleigh *Win* 96-01; P-in-c Upton St Leonards *Glouc* from 01. *The Rectory, Bond Road End, Upton St Leonards, Gloucester GL4 8AG* Tel (01452) 617443 E-mail paul@pleckey.abel.co.uk

LECLÉZIO, Ms Marie Katryn. b 62. Natal Univ BA83 All Nations Chr Coll MA00. WEMTC 05. **d** 08 **p** 09. C Halas *Worc* from 08. *36 Albrighton Road, Halesowen B63 4JY* Tel and fax 0121-501 1913 E-mail katryn.leclezio@virgin.net

LEDBETTER, Shannon Carroll. b 64. Louisville Univ (USA) BA85 Liv Univ PhD00. Virginia Th Sem MTS96. **d** 03 **p** 04. NSM Knowsley *Liv* 03-08; NSM W Derby St Mary and St Jas from 08. *7 Cathedral Close, Liverpool L1 7BR* Tel 07720-072787 (mobile) E-mail scledbetter2008@yahoo.co.uk

LEDGARD, Canon Frank William Armitage. b 24. Wells Th Coll 49. **d** 52 **p** 53. C Ipswich St Mary le Tower *St E* 52-55; V Tottington *Man* 55-62; V Kirkby Malzeard w Dallow Gill *Ripon* 62-66; R Bedale 66-87; RD Wensley 79-85; Hon Can Ripon Cathl 80-89; Bp's Adv on Chr Healing 87-89; rtd 89; Perm to Offic *Ripon* from 89. *c/o Wrigleys Solicitors, 19 Cookridge Street, Leeds LS2 3AG* Tel 0113-244 6100 Fax 244 6101

LEDGER, James Henry. b 23. Oak Hill Th Coll 68. **d** 70 **p** 71. C Spitalfields Ch Ch w All SS *Lon* 70-75; V Chitts Hill St Cuth 75-91; rtd 91; Perm to Offic *Lon* 93-96; *St Alb* from 93. *6 Acorn Street, Hunsdon, Ware SG12 8PB* Tel (01279) 842878

LEDGER, Mrs Margaret Phyllis. b 47. **d** 04 **p** 05. OLM Newburn *Newc* from 04. *14 Woodside Avenue, Throckley, Newcastle upon Tyne NE15 9BE* Tel 0191-267 2953 E-mail margaret.p.ledger@btinternet.com

LEDWARD, John Archibald. b 30. Lon Univ BD58 Man Univ MA81 FRSA85. ALCD57. **d** 58 **p** 59. C St Helens St Helen *Liv* 58-62; V Dearham *Carl* 62-66; V Mirehouse 66-71; V Daubhill *Man* 71-77; R Newcastle w Butterton *Lich* 77-88; R Rockland St Mary w Hellington, Bramerton etc *Nor* 88-94; P-in-c Kirby Bedon w Bixley and Whitlingham 92-94; R Rockland St Mary w Hellington, Bramerton etc 94-95; RD Loddon 92-95; rtd 95;

Perm to Offic *Nor* from 95. *41 Lackford Close, Brundall, Norwich NR13 5NL* Tel (01603) 714745

LEE, Agnes Elizabeth. b 31. Open Univ BA87 Whitelands Coll Lon TCert51 ACP76. NOC 97. **d** 98 **p** 99. NSM Dewsbury *Wakef* 98-02; rtd 02; Perm to Offic *Wakef* from 02. *1 Moor Park Court, Dewsbury WF12 7AU* Tel (01924) 467319

LEE, Mrs Anne Louise. b 65. St Jo Coll Nottm BTh90. Wycliffe Hall Ox 94. **d** 95 **p** 96. C Wembley St Jo *Lon* 95-98; NSM S Gillingham *Roch* 98-07; Jt P-in-c Locking *B & W* 07-09; Jt P-in-c Hutton and Locking from 09. *The Vicarage, The Green, Locking, Weston-super-Mare BS24 8DA* Tel (01934) 823556 E-mail revdannelee@yahoo.co.uk

LEE, Anthony Maurice. b 35. Bps' Coll Cheshunt 62. **d** 65 **p** 66. C Pinner *Lon* 65-71; Asst Youth Chapl *Glouc* 71-72; V Childswyckham 72-73; R Aston Somerville 72-73; V Childswyckham w Aston Somerville 73-91; P-in-c Buckland 88-91; P-in-c Stanton w Snowshill 88-91; R Childswyckham w Aston Somerville, Buckland etc 91-94; RD Winchcombe 86-94; rtd 94. *11 Holly Close, Broadclyst, Exeter EX5 3JB*

LEE, Canon Brian. b 37. Linc Th Coll 78. **d** 80 **p** 81. C Duston *Pet* 80-84; P-in-c Spratton 84-89; V 89-06; Jt P-in-c Maidwell w Draughton, Lamport w Faxton 89-01; Jt P-in-c Cottesbrooke w Gt Creaton and Thornby 89-06; RD Brixworth 94-01; Can Pet Cathl 98-06; rtd 06; Perm to Offic *Pet* from 06. *8 Clive Close, Kettering NN15 5BQ* Tel (01536) 484407 E-mail brian.lee18@btopenworld.com

LEE, Canon Brian Ernest. b 32. ACA59 FCA70. Linc Th Coll 60. **d** 62 **p** 63. C Birch St Jas *Man* 62-65; C Withington St Paul 65-66; R Abbey Hey 66-70; Hon C Gatley *Ches* 86-88; V Egremont St Jo 88-97; RD Wallasey 91-96; OGS from 92; Hon Can Ches Cathl 96-97; rtd 97; Perm to Offic *Nor* from 97. *St Fursey House, Convent of All Hallows, Ditchingham, Bungay NR35 2DZ* Tel (01986) 892308 Fax 894215

LEE, Brian John. b 51. K Coll Lon BD78 AKC78. Coll of Resurr Mirfield 78. **d** 79 **p** 80. C Ham St Rich *S'wark* 79-82; C Surbiton St Andr and St Mark 82-85; V Shirley St Geo 85-93; V St Botolph Aldgate w H Trin Minories *Lon* 93-08; rtd 08. *10 Norfolk Buildings, Brighton BN1 2PZ*

LEE, Christopher John Bodell. b 82. Kingston Univ BA01 Cam Univ BTh11. Ridley Hall Cam 08. **d** 07 **p** 11. C Onslow Square and S Kensington St Aug *Lon* from 11. *26 Chancellors Wharf, Crisp Road, London W6 9RT* Tel 07824-365905 (mobile) E-mail revchris7@gmail.com

LEE, Clifford Samuel (Sam). b 53. **d** 95 **p** 96. OLM S Elmham and Ilketshall *St E* 95-10; NSM Worlingham w Barnby and N Cove from 10. *Packway Lodge, Park Road, Flixton, Bungay NR35 1NR* Tel (01986) 782300

LEE, Clive Warwick. b 34. St Pet Coll Ox BA58 MA62 Ox Univ PGCE73. Coll of Resurr Mirfield 58. **d** 60 **p** 61. C W End *Win* 60-64; C Upper Norwood St Jo *Cant* 65-69; Chapl Vinehall Sch Robertsbridge 69-94; rtd 94; Perm to Offic *Cant* from 04. *28 St Radigund's Street, Canterbury CT1 2AA* Tel (01227) 780624

LEE, Colin John Willmot. b 21. Wycliffe Hall Ox 57. **d** 59 **p** 59. C Gravesend St Jas *Roch* 59-62; V Dartford St Edm 62-67; Bp's Ind Adv *Derby* 67-91; C-in-c Ilkeston St Bart CD 67-69; P-in-c Stanton by Dale 69-76; V Ilkeston St Jo 76-91; rtd 91; Perm to Offic *Derby* and *S'well* from 91. *3 Buttermead Close, Trowell, Nottingham NG9 3QT* Tel 0115-949 7608

LEE, The Ven David John. b 46. Bris Univ BSc67 Fitzw Coll Cam BA76 MA79 Birm Univ PhD96. Ridley Hall Cam 74. **d** 77 **p** 78. C Putney St Marg *S'wark* 77-80; Tutor Bp Tucker Th Coll Uganda 80-86; Tutor Crowther Hall CMS Tr Coll Selly Oak 86-91; P-in-c Wishaw and Middleton *Birm* 91-96; Can Res Birm Cathl 96-04; Dir Dioc Bd for Miss 96-04; Adn Bradf from 04. *47 Kirkgate, Shipley BD18 3EH* Tel (01274) 200698 *or* tel and fax 730196 Mobile 07711-671351 E-mail david.lee@bradford.anglican.org

LEE, The Ven David Stanley. b 30. Univ of Wales (Cardiff) BSc51 St Mich Coll Llan 56. **d** 57 **p** 58. C Canvau w Ely *Llan* 57-60; C Port Talbot St Agnes 60-70; Ind Chapl 60-70; R Merthyr Tydfil 70-72; Chapl Merthyr Tydfil Hosp 70-91; R Merthyr Tydfil and Cyfarthfa *Llan* 72-91; RD Merthyr Tydfil 82-91; Can Llan Cath 84-97; Adn Llan 91-97; R Llanfabon 91-97; rtd 97; Perm to Offic *Llan* from 97; *Mon* from 98. *2 Old Vicarage Close, Llanishen, Cardiff CF14 5UZ* Tel (029) 2075 2431

LEE, David Wight Dunsmore. b 39. Wells Th Coll 61. **d** 63 **p** 64. C Middlesbrough St Oswald *York* 63-67; C Northallerton w Kirby Sigston 67-69; R Limbe w Thyolo and Mulanje Malawi 69-71; R S Highlands 71-75; V Newington Transfiguration 76-81; P-in-c Sheriff Hutton 81-85; P-in-c Sheriff Hutton and Farlington 85-97; V Sheriff Hutton, Farlington, Stillington etc 97-04; rtd 04; Perm to Offic *York* from 04. *Kirkstone Cottage, Main Street, Oswaldkirk, York YO62 5XT* Tel (01439) 788283 E-mail dawdle@dwdlee.plus.net *or* dwdlee@talk21.com

LEE, Derek Alfred. **d** 00. Hon Par Dn Llantilio Pertholey w Bettws Chpl etc *Mon* 00-05; Hon Par Dn Llanfihangel Crucorney w Oldcastle etc from 05. *94 Croesonen Parc, Abergavenny NP7 6PF* Tel (01873) 855042

LEE, Edmund Hugh. b 53. Trin Coll Ox BA75 MA79 Goldsmiths' Coll Lon BMus83 K Coll Lon MA98. Ripon Coll Cuddesdon 93. d 95 p 96. C Malden St Jas S'wark 95-99; TV Mortlake w E Sheen 99-08. *67 North Worple Way, London SW14 8PP* Tel (020) 8876 5270 E-mail edknife@aol.com

LEE, Elizabeth. See LEE, Agnes Elizabeth

LEE, Gilbert (Sai Kuen). b 51. Hong Kong Univ BD80 Kent Univ MA98. Chung Chi Coll Hong Kong 77. d 80 p 81. C Angl Ch Hong Kong 80-81; V 81-88; NSM St Martin-in-the-Fields *Lon* 88-00; Chapl to Chinese in London 88-00; I St Jo Chinese Ch Toronto 00-07; I Markham All SS from 07. *142 Dunbar Crescent, Markham ON L3R 6V8, Canada* Tel (001) (905) 946 1637 Fax 946 9782 E-mail allsts@arex.com

LEE, Hugh. See LEE, John Charles Hugh Mellanby

LEE, Canon Hugh Gordon Cassels. b 41. St Andr Univ BSc64. Edin Th Coll 64. d 67 p 68. C Dumfries *Glas* 67-70; C Totteridge *St Alb* 70-73; R Glas St Jas 73-80; R Bishopbriggs 80-86; R St Fillans *St And* 86-89; R Crieff and Comrie 86-01; P-in-c Muthill 86-01; P-in-c Lochearnhead 89-01; R Dunoon *Arg* 01-06; Dioc Dir of Ord from 06; Can St Jo Cathl Oban from 04; Can Cumbrae from 04. *Chapel Hall, Toward, Dunoon PA23 7UA* Tel (01369) 870237 E-mail fish4hill@yahoo.co.uk

LEE, Miss Iris Audrey Olive. b 26. Gilmore Ho. dss 76 d 87. N Weald Bassett *Chelmsf* 76-87; rtd 87; NSM Clacton St Jas *Chelmsf* 87-00; Chapl Clacton Hosp 90-95; Perm to Offic 00-04. *30 Marine Court, Marine Parade West, Clacton-on-Sea CO15 1ND* Tel (01255) 423719

LEE, Mrs Jayne Christine. b 53. Dundee Univ MA75. d 06 p 07. OLM Robertown w Hartshead *Wakef* from 06; OLM Heckmondwike from 06; OLM Liversedge w Hightown from 06. *58 Prospect View, Liversedge WF15 8BD* Tel (01924) 401264 E-mail jaynelee@hotmail.com

LEE, Mrs Jennifer. b 42. Westf Coll Lon BA64 CQSW78. NOC 01. d 03 p 04. NSM Millhouses H Trin *Sheff* 03-06; NSM Compton w Shackleford and Peper Harow *Guildf* from 07. *The Old Cottage Barn, Peper Harow Park, Peper Harow, Godalming GU8 6BQ* Tel (01483) 424468 E-mail revjenny@btinternet.com

LEE, John. b 47. Univ of Wales (Swansea) BSc70 MSc73 MInstGA87. Ripon Hall Ox 73. d 75 p 76. C Swansea St Pet *S & B* 75-78; C St Botolph Aldgate w H Trin Minories *Lon* 79-84; P-in-c Chiddingstone w Chiddingstone Causeway *Roch* 84-89; R 89-98; Clergy Appts Adv from 98; Chapl to The Queen from 10. *The Wash House, Lambeth Palace, London SE1 7JU* Tel (020) 7898 1898 Fax 7898 1899 E-mail admin.caa@churchofengland.org

LEE, John Charles Hugh Mellanby. b 44. Trin Hall Cam BA66 MA69 Brunel Univ MTech71. Ox NSM Course 78. d 81 p 82. NSM Amersham on the Hill *Ox* 81-88; NSM Ox St Aldate w St Matt 88-93; NSM Wheatley 93-95; Dioc Development Officer Miss in Work and Economic Life 95-02; P-in-c Ox St Mich w St Martin and All SS 02-09; Lic to Offic from 09. *12 Walton Street, Oxford OX1 2HG* Tel and fax (01865) 316245 E-mail hugh.lee@btinternet.com

LEE, John Michael Andrew. b 62. Leeds Univ BA84. Trin Coll Bris 88. d 90 p 91. C Norbiton *S'wark* 90-92; C Leic H Trin w St Jo 94-02; R York St Paul from 02. *St Paul's Rectory, 100 Acomb Road, York YO24 4ER* Tel (01904) 792304 E-mail johnmalee@btinternet.com

LEE, John Samuel. b 47. Chich Th Coll 74. d 77 p 78. C Bramley *Ripon* 77-80; C Bideford *Ex* 81-84; TV Littleham w Exmouth 84-90; P-in-c Sidbury 90-91; TV Sidmouth, Woolbrook, Salcombe Regis, Sidbury etc 91-04; rtd 04. *Westward Ho!, Torpark Road, Torquay TQ2 5BQ* Tel (01803) 293086 E-mail johnslee@glensidf.freeserve.co.uk

LEE, Joseph Patrick. b 53. St Jos Coll Upholland 72 Ushaw Coll Dur 75. d 78 p 79. In RC Ch 78-99; Hon C Charlton *S'wark* 99-09; Hon C E Greenwich from 09. *45 Chestnut Rise, London SE18 1RJ* Tel (020) 8316 4674 Mobile 07956-294429 Fax 8317 7304 E-mail joe_lee@lineone.net

LEE, Mrs Judith Mary. b 44. Doncaster Coll of Educn TCert65. d 06 p 07. OLM Frenchay and Winterbourne Down *Bris* from 06. *8 Beaufort Road, Frampton Cotterell, Bristol BS36 2AD* Tel (01454) 772381 E-mail jrplee@btinternet.com

LEE, Canon Kenneth Peter. b 45. Em Coll Cam BA67 MA71. Cuddesdon Coll 67. d 69 p 70. C Stoke Poges *Ox* 69-72; C Witton *Ches* 72-74; V Frankby w Greasby 74-92; R Christleton 92-10; Hon Can Ches Cathl 05-10; rtd 10. *16 Rookery Drive, Tattenhall, Chester CH3 9QS* Tel (01829) 770292 E-mail kpeter.lee@btinternet.com

LEE, Luke Gun-Hong. b 37. Univ of Yon Sei BTh62. St Jo Coll Morpeth 64. d 67 p 68. Lic to Offic Taejon Korea 67-79; C Bloxwich *Lich* 79-83; TV Dunstable *St Alb* 83-90; V Croxley Green All SS 90-07; rtd 07. *101 Larkvale, Aylesbury HP19 0YP* Tel (01296) 423133 E-mail luke.gh.lee@gmail.com

LEE, Miss Lynley Hoe. b 52. St Jo Coll Nottm BTh89 K Coll Lon MA93. d 90 p 94. Par Dn Pitsea *Chelmsf* 90-95; Singapore 95-98; C Gt Ilford St Andr *Chelmsf* 99-02; TV Grays Thurrock 02-07;

Chapl Salford R Hosps NHS Foundn Trust from 07. *Hope Hospital, Stott Lane, Salford M6 8HD* Tel 0161-789 7373 E-mail lynleyhoe@aol.com

LEE, Mrs Margaret. b 48. Coll of Ripon & York St Jo BEd71. NEOC 03. d 06 p 07. NSM Houghton le Spring *Dur* from 06. *2 Rectory View, Shadforth, Durham DH6 1LF* Tel 0191-372 0595 E-mail margaretlee595@hotmail.com

LEE, Martin Paul. b 66. Aston Tr Scheme 91 Linc Th Coll 93 St Steph Ho Ox 94. d 96 p 97. C Wells St Thos w Horrington *B & W* 96-00; P-in-c Brent Knoll, E Brent and Lympsham 00-01; R 01-08; RD Axbridge 03-08; V Long Benton *Newc* from 08. *The Vicarage, 3 Station Road, Benton, Newcastle upon Tyne NE12 8AN* Tel 0191-266 1921 E-mail frmlee@aol.com

LEE, Michael. b 45. d 07 p 08. OLM Chickerell w Fleet *Sarum* from 07. *45 Lower Way, Chickerell, Weymouth DT3 4AR* Tel (01305) 777031 E-mail michaellynda@googlemail.com

LEE, Nicholas Knyvett. b 54. Trin Coll Cam BA76 MA77. Cranmer Hall Dur 82. d 85 p 86. C Brompton H Trin w Onslow Square St Paul *Lon* 85-11; C Onslow Square and S Kensington St Aug from 11; Chapl R Brompton and Harefield NHS Trust 86-90 and from 94. *St Paul's Church House, Onslow Square, London SW7 3NX* Tel 08456-447533 E-mail nicky.lee@htb.org.uk

LEE, Peter. See LEE, Canon Kenneth Peter

LEE, Peter Alexander. b 44. Hull Univ BSc(Econ)65. Ex & Truro NSM Scheme 80. d 83 p 84. NSM Ex St Sidwell and St Matt 83-89; NSM Ex St Dav 90-98; C Paignton St Jo 98-01; Perm to Offic 01-03; Hon C Ex St Dav from 03. *Windyridge, Beech Avenue, Exeter EX4 6HF* Tel (01392) 254118

LEE, The Rt Revd Peter John. b 47. St Jo Coll Cam BA69 MA73 CertEd70 Lambeth BD06. Ridley Hall Cam 70 St Jo Coll Nottm 72. d 73 p 74 c 90. C Onslow Square St Paul *Lon* 73-76; S Africa from 76; V-Gen and Bp Ch the K from 90. *PO Box 1653, Rosettenville, 2130 South Africa* Tel (0027) (11) 435 0097 or 942 1179 Fax 435 2868 E-mail dckpeter@netactive.co.za

LEE, Peter Kenneth. b 44. Selw Coll Cam BA66 MA69. Cuddesdon Coll 67. d 69 p 70. C Manston *Ripon* 69-72; C Bingley All SS *Bradf* 72-77; Chapl Bingley Coll of Educn 72-77; V Cross Roads cum Lees *Bradf* 77-90; V Auckland St Pet *Dur* 90-09; Tutor NEOC 91-09; rtd 09; Tutor NEITE from 03; Perm to Offic *York* from 10. *2 Winston Court, Northallerton DL6 1PY* Tel (01609) 777539

LEE, Canon Raymond John. b 30. St Edm Hall Ox BA53 MA57. Tyndale Hall Bris 54. d 56 p 57. C Tooting Graveney St Nic *S'wark* 56-59; C Muswell Hill St Jas *Lon* 59-62; V Woking St Mary *Guildf* 62-70; V Gt Crosby St Luke *Liv* 70-82; Dioc Adv NSM 79-95; V Allerton 82-94; P-in-c Altcar 94-98; Hon Can Liv Cathl 89-95; rtd 95; Perm to Offic *Liv* from 96. *15 Barkfield Lane, Liverpool L37 1LY* Tel (01704) 872670 E-mail rjlee@btinternet.com

LEE, Richard. See LEE, Thomas Richard

LEE, Richard Alexander. b 63. St Jo Coll Nottm BTh91. d 91 p 92. C Gt Stanmore *Lon* 91-95; C Edgware 95-98; TV S Gillingham *Roch* 98-07; Jt P-in-c Locking *B & W* 07-09; Jt P-in-c Hutton and Locking from 09. *The Vicarage, The Green, Locking, Weston-super-Mare BS24 8DA* Tel (01934) 823556 E-mail revdannelee@yahoo.co.uk

LEE, Robert David. b 53. QUB BD75. CITC 77. d 77 p 78. C Comber *D & D* 77-83; I Mt Merrion 83-87; CMS 89-92; Egypt 89-97; R Peebles *Edin* 97-11; P-in-c Innerleithen 97-11; rtd 11. *Address temp unknown* E-mail rdlee@dsl.pipex.com

LEE, Robert William. b 31. Keele Univ BA54 St Cath Soc Ox BA58 MA63. Ripon Hall Ox 56. d 59 p 60. C Dawley St Jerome *Lon* 59-62; C Bromley H Trin *Roch* 62-65; R Clayton *Man* 65-70; P-in-c Man St Paul 65-70; TV Hemel Hempstead *St Alb* 70-72; TV Corby SS Pet and Andr w Gt and Lt Oakley 72-80; V Weedon Lois w Plumpton and Moreton Pinkney etc 80-88; R Thornhams Magna and Parva, Gislingham and Mellis *St E* 88-96; rtd 96; Perm to Offic *Bradf* and *Carl* from 96. *2 Guldrey Fold, Sedbergh LA10 5DY* Tel (01539) 621907

LEE, Roderick James. b 50. Linc Th Coll 88. d 90 p 91. C Rushden w Newton Bromswold *Pet* 90-93; C Kingsthorpe w Northampton St Dav 93-94; TV 94-99; R Mears Ashby and Hardwick and Sywell etc 99-04; P-in-c Corby St Columba from 04; RD Corby from 07; Chapl Northants Fire and Rescue Service from 08. *St Columba's Vicarage, 157 Studfall Avenue, Corby NN17 1LG* Tel (01536) 204158 *or* 261436 E-mail rlee103400@aol.com

LEE, Sai Kuen. See LEE, Gilbert

LEE, Sam. See LEE, Clifford Samuel

LEE, Steven Michael. b 56. Van Mildert Coll Dur BA78. Trin Coll Bris 80. d 83 p 84. C Beckenham St Jo *Roch* 83-86; C Leic Martyrs 86-90; V Coalville and Bardon Hill 90-95; P-in-c Kibworth and Smeeton Westerby and Saddington 95-00; P-in-c Foxton w Gumley and Laughton 96-00; R Kibworth and Smeeton Westerby and Saddington 00-06; Chapl St Lawr Coll Ramsgate 06-08; R Newcastle w Butterton *Lich* from 08. *The Rectory, Seabridge Road, Newcastle ST5 2HS* Tel (01782) 616397 E-mail revslee@btinternet.com

LEE, Stuart Graham. b 73. Roehampton Inst BA94. St Steph Ho Ox BTh00. **d** 00 **p** 01. C Eltham H Trin *S'wark* 00-03; TV Wimbledon 03-10; TV Mortlake w E Sheen from 10. *86 East Sheen Avenue, London SW14 8AU* E-mail stuartlee73@blueyonder.co.uk

LEE, Stuart Michael. b 67. SEITE 06. **d** 09 **p** 10. NSM St Jo on Bethnal Green *Lon* from 09. *29 Brierly Gardens, London E2 0TE* Tel (020) 8980 1699 Mobile 07855-703766 E-mail stuartm.lee@virgin.net

LEE, Thomas Richard. b 52. AKC73 FRSA03. St Aug Coll Cant 74. **d** 75 **p** 76. C Leam Lane CD *Dur* 75-80; Chapl RAF 80-09; Prin Armed Forces Chapl Cen Amport Ho 03-06; Hon C St Mary le Strand w St Clem Danes *Lon* 06-09; QHC 06-09; TR Egremont and Haile *Carl* from 09. *The Rectory, Grove Road, Egremont CA22 2LU* Tel and fax (01946) 820268 E-mail lee535877@aol.com

LEE, Veronica. b 47. Redland Coll of Educn TCert68 Open Univ BA84 Bris Poly MEd89. STETS 02. **d** 05 **p** 06. NSM Bishopston and St Andrews *Bris* from 05. *48 Chesterfield Road, Bristol BS6 5DL* Tel 0117-949 8325 E-mail vronlee@hotmail.com

LEE-PHILPOT, Derreck. d 11. NSM Cholsey and Moulsford *Ox* from 11. *49 Elmhurst Road, Thatcham RG18 3DQ*

LEECE, Roderick Neil Stephen. b 59. Wadh Coll Ox BA81 MA85 Leeds Univ BA84 ARCM85. Coll of Resurr Mirfield 82. **d** 85 **p** 86. C Portsea St Mary *Portsm* 85-91; V Stamford Hill St Bart *Lon* 91-05; R Hanover Square St Geo from 05. *21A Down Street, London W1J 7AW* Tel (020) 7629 0874 E-mail rleece@lineone.net

LEECH, Kenneth. b 39. Lon Univ BA61 AKC61 Trin Coll Ox BA63 MA71 Lambeth DD98. St Steph Ho Ox 62. **d** 64 **p** 65. C Hoxton H Trin w St Mary *Lon* 64-67; C Soho St Anne w St Thos and St Pet 67-71; Tutor St Aug Coll Cant 71-74; R Bethnal Green St Matt *Lon* 74-79; Field Officer Community & Race Relns Unit BCC 80; Race Relns Officer Gen Syn Bd for Soc Resp 81-87; Hon C Notting Hill St Clem and St Mark *Lon* 82-85; Hon C Notting Dale St Clem w St Mark and St Jas 85-88; Dir Runnymede Trust 87-90; Hon C St Botolph Aldgate w H Trin Minories *Lon* 91-04; rtd 04; Perm to Offic *Man* from 05 and *Ches* from 06. *89 Manchester Road, Mossley, Ashton-under-Lyne OL5 9LZ* Tel (01457) 835119 E-mail kenleech@aol.com

LEECH, Pieter-Jan Bosdin. b 73. K Alfred's Coll Win BA(QTS)96. St Jo Coll Nottm 08. **d** 10 **p** 11. C Stalham, E Ruston, Brunstead, Sutton and Ingham *Nor* from 10. *1 Bullemer Close, Stalham, Norwich NR12 9AY* Tel 07504-171311 (mobile) E-mail peter.leech@live.co.uk

LEEDS, Archdeacon of. See BURROWS, The Ven Peter

LEEFIELD, Michael John. b 37. Liv Univ BA60 K Coll Lon BD65 AKC65. St Boniface Warminster 62. **d** 66 **p** 67. C Gt Yarmouth *Nor* 66-70; V Trowse 70-75; V Arminghall 70-75; R Caistor w Markshall 70-75; Chapl Norfolk and Nor Hosp 70-75; V Lydney w Aylburton *Glouc* 75-84; RD Forest S 82-84; Lic to Offic from 85; rtd 01. *Brays Court, Awre, Newnham GL14 1EP* Tel (01594) 510483

LEEKE, Charles Browne. b 39. Stranmillis Coll CertEd62. CITC 80. **d** 83 **p** 84. C Ballymoney w Finvoy and Rasharkin *Conn* 83-86; I Faughanvale *D & R* 86-97; Chapl Port Londonderry Miss to Seamen 92-97; Bp's Dom Chapl *D & R* 92-96; Can Derry Cathl 96-00; I Drumragh w Mountfield 97-00; Reconciliation Development Officer *D & D* 00-06; Can Dromore Cathl 05-06; rtd 06; I Dromara w Garvaghy *D & D* from 08. *The Rectory, 58 Banbridge Road, Dromara, Dromore BT25 1NE* Tel (028) 9753 3063 E-mail charlie@reconcile-think.fsnet.co.uk

LEEKE, Canon Stephen Owen. b 50. EAMTC 82 Ridley Hall Cam 83. **d** 84 **p** 85. C Cherry Hinton St Andr *Ely* 84-87; P-in-c Warboys 87-91; P-in-c Bury 87-91; P-in-c Wistow 87-91; R Warboys w Broughton and Bury w Wistow 91-01; RD St Ives 92-01; V Cambridge St Martin from 01; Hon Can Ely Cathl from 05. *St Martin's Vicarage, 127 Suez Road, Cambridge CB1 3QD* Tel (01223) 214203 or 519291 E-mail stephen.leeke@ely.anglican.org

LEEMAN, John Graham. b 41. NOC 78. **d** 80 **p** 81. NSM Hull St Mary Sculcoates *York* 80-96; Perm to Offic 96-99; Hon C Hull St Mary Sculcoates 99-04; P-in-c from 04; Hon C Hull St Steph Sculcoates 99-04; Hon C Sculcoates St Paul w Ch Ch and St Silas 99-04. *1 Snuff Mill Lane, Cottingham HU16 4RY* Tel (01482) 840355

LEEMING, Jack. b 34. Kelham Th Coll 56. **d** 61 **p** 62. C Sydenham St Phil *S'wark* 61-64; Chapl RAF 64-84; Chapl Salisbury Gen Infirmary 84-89; R Barford St Martin, Dinton, Baverstock etc *Sarum* 89-99; rtd 99; Perm to Offic *Sarum* from 01. *8 Bower Gardens, Salisbury SP1 2RL* Tel (01722) 416800

LEEMING, Mrs Janice Doreen. b 45. EMMTC 97. **d** 00 **p** 01. NSM Lenton *S'well* 00-06; NSM Radford All So and St Pet from 06. *5 Hollinwell Avenue, Wollaton, Nottingham NG8 1JY* Tel 0115-928 2145

LEEMING, John Maurice. b 24. CEng MIMechE MIProdE FIED. NW Ord Course 72. **d** 75 **p** 76. NSM Endcliffe *Sheff* 75-78; C Norton 78-80; V Bolsterstone 80-89; Jt Min Stocksbridge Chr Cen LEP 80-89; Ind Chapl 81-89; rtd 89; Perm

to Offic *S'well* from 89; *Sheff* from 93; *Derby* from 98. *Beck House, Toftdyke Lane, Clayworth, Retford DN22 9AH* Tel (01777) 817795 E-mail maurice@leeming02.freeserve.co.uk

LEES, Allan Garside. b 39. **d** 99 **p** 00. OLM Hurst *Man* 99-09; rtd 09; Perm to Offic *Man* from 10. *1 Exeter Drive, Ashton-under-Lyne OL6 8BZ* Tel 0161-339 3105

LEES, Brian James. b 52. Lon Univ BA74 Leeds Univ BA08 Univ of Wales (Abth) PGCE75. NOC 05. **d** 08 **p** 09. NSM Hutton Cranswick w Skerne, Watton and Beswick *York* from 08. *The Old Post House, Beswick, Driffield YO25 9AS* Tel (01377) 270806 E-mail brianjlees@tiscali.co.uk

LEES, Charles Alan. b 38. RGN TCert. WMMTC 78. **d** 81 **p** 82. NSM Yardley St Cypr Hay Mill *Birm* 81-84 and 86-87; Hon C Dorridge 84-86; Chapl E Birm Hosp 85-87; Hon C Leamington Spa H Trin and Old Milverton *Cov* 89-90; Perm to Offic *Birm* 95-01. *8 Fairlawn Close, Leamington Spa CV32 6EN*

LEES, Christopher John. b 58. Fitzw Coll Cam BA80 Birkbeck Coll Lon MA86 FCIPD. NOC 01. **d** 04 **p** 05. NSM Wilmslow *Ches* from 04; Asst Dir of Ords from 07. *110 Grove Park, Knutsford WA16 8QB* Tel (01565) 631625 E-mail johnlees@dsl.pipex.com

LEES, John Raymond. b 57. Selw Coll Cam BA78 MA82. St Steph Ho Ox 89. **d** 91 **p** 92. C Eastbourne St Mary *Chich* 91-93; Min Can and Succ St Paul's Cathl 93-98; TR Swindon New Town *Bris* 98-01; Asst to AD Swindon and C Highworth w Sevenhampton and Inglesham etc 01-02; Perm to Offic *Lon* 02-05; *Pet* and *Ely* 04-06; Can Res and Prec Wakef Cathl 06-09; rtd 09; Perm to Offic *Lich* from 09. *71 Merridale Road, Wolverhampton WV3 9SE* Tel (01902) 714744 E-mail frjrl@btinternet.com

LEES, Mrs Kathleen Marion. b 30. Birkbeck Coll Lon BA60. S'wark Ord Course 77. **dss** 80 **d** 87 **p** 94. Epping St Jo *Chelmsf* 80-86; Hon C Hunstanton St Mary w Ringstead Parva, Holme etc *Nor* 87-88; Perm to Offic 88-94; Chapl King's Lynn and Wisbech Hosps NHS Trust 94-00; NSM Gaywood *Nor* 94-00; rtd 00; Perm to Offic *Nor* from 00. *20 North Hirne Court, St Anns Street, King's Lynn PE31 1LT* Tel (01553) 661294

LEES, Peter John. b 39. St Jo Coll Nottm 91. **d** 95 **p** 96. NSM Buckie and Turriff *Ab* 95-00; P-in-c Fraserburgh 00-01; R 01-06; rtd 06; Hon C Turriff *Ab* from 06. *7 Whitefield Court, Buckie AB56 1EY* Tel (01542) 835011 Mobile 07929-668027

LEES, Peter John William. b 37. **d** 02. NSM Walsall St Paul *Lich* from 02. *66 Cresswell Crescent, Bloxwich, Walsall WS3 2UH* Tel (01922) 497869

LEES, Stephen. b 55. St Jo Coll York CertEd77 BEd78 Nottm Univ MA96. St Jo Coll Nottm 88. **d** 90 **p** 91. C Mansfield St Jo *S'well* 90-93; TV Bestwood 93-98; V Baxenden *Blackb* 98-08; P-in-c Halifax All SS *Wakef* from 08. *All Saints' Vicarage, Greenroyd Avenue, Halifax HX3 0LP* Tel (01422) 251016 E-mail theleeslot@blueyonder.co.uk

LEES, Stephen David. b 63. Sheff City Poly BA84 Bradf Coll of Educn PGCE92 St Jo Coll Dur BA09. Cranmer Hall Dur 07. **d** 09 **p** 10. C Frizinghall St Marg *Bradf* from 09. *2B Nab Lane, Shipley BD18 4HB* Tel (01274) 583487 E-mail stelees2004@yahoo.co.uk

LEES, Stuart Charles Roderick. b 62. Trin Coll Bris BA. **d** 89 **p** 90. C Woodford Wells *Chelmsf* 89-93; C Brompton H Trin w Onslow Square St Paul *Lon* 93-97; Chapl Stewards Trust 93-97; P-in-c Fulham Ch Ch 97-03; V from 03. *Christ Church Vicarage, 40 Clancarty Road, London SW6 3AA* Tel (020) 7736 4261 E-mail stuart@ccfulham.com

LEES-SMITH, Anthony James. b 77. Selw Coll Cam BA99 MA02 St Jo Coll Dur BA08 Westmr Inst of Educn PGCE02. Cranmer Hall Dur 06. **d** 09 **p** 10. C Chesterton Gd Shep *Ely* from 09. *258 Milton Road, Cambridge CB4 1LQ* Tel (01223) 425338 Mobile 07967-353857 E-mail singers99@talktalk.net

LEESE, Arthur Selwyn Mountford. b 09. K Coll Lon BD31 AKC31 St Cath Soc Ox BA33 MA44. Ripon Hall Ox 31. **d** 33 **p** 34. C Bexleyheath Ch Ch *Roch* 33-37; C Cockington *Ex* 37-39; C Langley Mill *Derby* 39-51; V Hawkhurst *Cant* 51-74; rtd 74; Perm to Offic *Cant* from 74 and *Chich* 75-08. *84 Wickham Avenue, Bexhill-on-Sea TN39 3ER* Tel (01424) 213137

LEESE, Mrs Jane Elizabeth. b 50. Man Univ BA(Econ)72 Avery Hill Coll PGCE73. Sarum Th Coll 93. **d** 96 **p** 97. NSM Kempshott *Win* 96-01; NSM Herriard w Winslade and Long Sutton etc 01-08; NSM N Hants Downs from 08. *The Rectory, Greywell Road, Up Nately, Hook RG27 9PL* Tel (01256) 765547 E-mail reverendjane@hotmail.co.uk

LEESON, Bernard Alan. b 47. Bris Univ CertEd68 Open Univ BA75 Southn Univ MA78 Sheff Univ PhD97 FCollP92 FRSA92. EMMTC 84. **d** 87 **p** 88. Dep Hd Master Ripley Mill Hill Sch 80-91; NSM Breadsall *Derby* 87-91; Hd St Aid C of E Tech Coll Lancs 91-06; NSM Officer *Blackb* 92-96; Clergy Support and Development Officer 06-09; Perm to Offic 91-92; Lic to Offic from 92. *The Lodge, Daggers Lane, Preesall, Poulton-le-Fylde FY6 0QN* Tel (01253) 811020 E-mail bernard.leeson@mail.org

LEESON, David Harry Stanley. b 45. Glouc Th Course 82. **d** 85 **p** 86. NSM Stratton w Baunton *Glouc* 85-94; NSM N Cerney w Bagendon 91-94; NSM Stratton, N Cerney, Baunton and

Bagendon from 95. *83 Cheltenham Road, Stratton, Cirencester GL7 2JB* Tel (01285) 651186

LEESON, Mrs Sally Elizabeth. b 57. Sussex Univ BA79. Westcott Ho Cam 83. **dss** 85 **d** 87 **p** 94. Battersea St Pet and St Paul *S'wark* 85-90; Par Dn 87-90; Par Dn Limpsfield and Titsey 90-94; Perm to Offic from 94; Chapl Bp Wand Sch Sunbury-on-Thames from 05. *32 Albany Road, New Malden KT3 3NY* Tel (020) 8942 5198

LEFFLER, Christopher. b 33. Em Coll Cam BA57 MA61. Linc Th Coll. **d** 59 **p** 60. C Bermondsey St Mary w St Olave and St Jo *S'wark* 59-60; C Herne Hill St Paul 60-63; C-in-c Canley CD *Cov* 63-67; R Gt and Lt Glemham *St E* 67-72; R Badwell Ash w Gt Ashfield, Stowlangtoft etc 72-82; R Trimley 82-99; rtd 99; Perm to Offic *St E* from 99. *308 High Street, Felixstowe IP11 9QJ* Tel (01394) 672279 E-mail chrisleffler@quista.net

LEFFLER, Jeremy Paul (Jem). b 62. Westmr Coll Ox BEd88. Wycliffe Hall Ox BTh94. **d** 94 **p** 95. C Ormskirk *Liv* 94-97; C Much Woolton 97-00; P-in-c Widnes St Ambrose 00-03; V from 03. *St Ambrose Vicarage, 45 Hargreaves Court, Widnes WA8 0QA* Tel and fax 0151-420 8044 E-mail info@stambrose.fsnet.co.uk

LEFROY, John Perceval. b 40. Trin Coll Cam BA62. Cuddesdon Coll 64. **d** 66 **p** 67. C Maidstone St Martin *Cant* 66-69; C St Peter-in-Thanet 69-74; V Barming Heath 74-82; V Upchurch w Lower Halstow 82-05; P-in-c Iwade 95-05; rtd 05. *23 Heather Avenue, Melksham SN12 6FX* Tel (01225) 704012 E-mail jclefroy@tiscali.co.uk

LEFROY (*née* CLARK), Kathleen Christine. *See* ENGLAND, Mrs Kathleen Christine

LEFROY, Matthew William. b 62. Trin Coll Cam BA84 Keele Univ PGCE91. St Jo Coll Nottm MTh02. **d** 02 **p** 03. C Portswood Ch Ch *Win* 02-06; TV Madeley *Heref* from 06; RD Telford Severn Gorge from 11. *The Vicarage, Park Lane, Madeley, Telford TF7 5HN* Tel (01952) 588958 E-mail matthew@mjlefroy.freeserve.co.uk

LEFROY-OWEN, Neal. b 62. Bradf Univ BA99. NOC 00. **d** 03 **p** 04. C Sandal St Cath *Wakef* 03-06; Asst Chapl HM Pris Hull 06-08; Chapl HM Pris Lindholme from 08. *HM Prison Lindholme, Bawtry Road, Hatfield Woodhouse, Doncaster DN7 6EE* Tel (01302) 848829 E-mail neal@owen21.fslife.co.uk

LEGG, Adrian James. b 52. St Jo Coll Nottm BTh82. **d** 82 **p** 83. C Haughton le Skerne *Dur* 82-85; C Llanishen and Lisvane 85-89; V Llanwddyn and Llanfihangel-yng-Nghwynfa etc *St As* 89-93; V Llansadwrn w Llanwrda and Manordeilo *St D* 93-10; Chapl Wadham Sch Crewkerne from 11. *The Rectory, Cucklington, Wincanton BA9 9PY* Tel (01747) 840230 E-mail adrianlegg@btinternet.com

LEGG, Joanna Susan Penberthy. *See* PENBERTHY, Joanna Susan

LEGG, Margaret. b 50. SEITE. **d** 07 **p** 08. NSM Paddington St Jo w St Mich *Lon* from 07. *9 Wilton Street, London SW1X 7AF* Tel (020) 7235 4944

LEGG, Peter Ellis. b 51. STETS 02. **d** 05 **p** 06. NSM Radipole and Melcombe Regis *Sarum* from 05. *449 Dorchester Road, Weymouth DT3 5BW* Tel (01305) 815342 Mobile 07779-334520 E-mail pleggwey@aol.com

LEGG, Richard. b 37. Selw Coll Cam BA62 MA66 Brunel Univ MPhil77 NY Th Sem DMin85. Coll of Resurr Mirfield 63. **d** 65 **p** 66. C Ealing St Pet Mt Park *Lon* 65-68; Chapl Brunel Univ 68-78; Wychcroft Ho (Dioc Retreat Cen) *S'wark* 78-81; C Chipping Barnet w Arkley *St Alb* 81-83; TV 83-85; R St Buryan, St Levan and Sennen *Truro* 85-93; Subwarden St Deiniol's Lib Hawarden 93; Perm to Offic *Truro* from 00; TV Beaminster Area *Sarum* 93-97; P-in-c Veryan w Ruan Lanihorne *Truro* 97-00; rtd 01; Perm to Offic *Truro* 08-09 and *B & W* from 10. *27A Bath Road, Wells BA5 3HR* Tel (01749) 670468 E-mail richardlegg@blue-earth.co.uk

LEGG, Roger Keith. b 35. Lich Th Coll 61. **d** 63 **p** 64. C Petersfield w Sheet *Portsm* 63-66; C Portsea St Mary 66-70; Rhodesia 70-75; V Clayton *Lich* 75-00; rtd 01; Perm to Offic *Lich* from 01. *High Crest, Chapel Lane, Hookgate, Market Drayton TF9 4QP* Tel (01630) 672766 E-mail rogjud@aol.com

LEGG, Miss Ruth Helen Margaret. b 52. Hull Univ BA74 Homerton Coll Cam CertEd75. Trin Coll Bris 86. **d** 88 **p** 94. C Clevedon St Andr and Ch Ch *B & W* 88-92; C Nailsea Ch Ch 92-96; C Nailsea Ch Ch w Tickenham 96-97; V Pill, Portbury and Easton-in-Gordano from 97. *The Rectory, 17 Church Road, Easton-in-Gordano, Bristol BS20 0PQ* Tel (01275) 372804

LEGGATE, Colin Archibald Gunson. b 44. Bris Sch of Min 86. **d** 88 **p** 89. NSM Brislington St Luke 88-97; Asst Chapl Frenchay Healthcare NHS Trust Bris 97-99; Asst Chapl N Bris NHS Trust from 99. *Frenchay Hospital, Frenchay Park Road, Bristol BS16 1LE* Tel 0117-970 1212 or 965 1434

LEGGE, Mrs Anne Christine. b 53. Ex Univ BA73 BPhil76 PGCE94. Trin Coll Bris BA10. **d** 10. C Newton Ferrers w Revelstoke *Ex* from 10. *Church Hill House, Church Hill, Holbeton, Plymouth PL8 1LN* Tel (01752) 830641 Mobile 07929-153132 E-mail annelegge@live.com

LEGGE, Robert James. b 63. BSc92. Ox Min Course. **d** 09 **p** 10. C Walton H Trin *Ox* from 09. *55 Highbridge Road, Aylesbury HP21 7EX* Tel 07809-227660 (mobile) E-mail rjlegge@live.co.uk

LEGGE, Trevor Raymond. b 42. Liv Univ BEng63. **d** 11. NSM Oughtrington and Warburton *Ches* from 11. *17 Wychwood Avenue, Lymm WA13 0NE* Tel (01925) 756872 E-mail trlegge@talktalk.net

LEGGETT, James Henry Aufrere. b 61. Oak Hill Th Coll 91. **d** 93 **p** 94. C Hensingham *Carl* 93-97; C-in-c Ryde St Jas Prop Chpl *Portsm* from 97. *84 Pellhurst Road, Ryde PO33 3BS* Tel (01983) 565621 or 566381 E-mail jleggett@onetel.com

LEGGETT, Nicholas William Michael. b 62. St Steph Ho Ox 00. **d** 02 **p** 04. C Clevedon St Jo *B & W* 02-06; P-in-c Bridgwater H Trin and Durleigh 06-07; V Tile Hill *Cov* from 10; Hon Chapl ATC from 04. *St Oswald's Vicarage, 228 Jardine Crescent, Coventry CV4 9PL* Tel 07762-156380 (mobile) E-mail leggett1uwe@yahoo.co.uk

LEGGETT, Vanessa Gisela. *See* CATO, Ms Vanessa Gisela

LEGH, Mrs Jane Mary. b 52. Southn Univ BSc73. Qu Coll Birm 08. **d** 09 **p** 10. NSM S Dales *Derby* from 09; NSM Boylestone, Church Broughton, Dalbury, etc from 09. *Cubley Lodge, Cubley, Ashbourne DE6 2FB* Tel (01335) 330297 E-mail jane.legh@cubleylodge.com

LEGOOD, Giles Leslie. b 67. K Coll Lon BD88 AKC88 Heythrop Coll Lon MTh98 Derby Univ DMin04. Ripon Coll Cuddesdon 90. **d** 92 **p** 93. C N Mymms *St Alb* 92-95; Chapl R Veterinary Coll *Lon* 95-07; Chapl R Free and Univ Coll Medical Sch 95-07; Chapl RAuxAF 04-07; Chapl RAF from 08. *Chaplaincy Services, Valiant Block, HQ Air Command, RAF High Wycombe HP14 4UE* Tel (01494) 496800 Fax 496343

LEGRAND, Nigel Stuart. b 51. STETS 96. **d** 99 **p** 00. NSM Boscombe St Jo *Win* 99-03; NSM Pokesdown All SS 03-07; NSM Holdenhurst and Iford from 07; NSM Southbourne St Chris from 03. *50 Meon Road, Bournemouth BH7 6PP* Tel (01202) 428603 Fax 300400 E-mail nlegrandfamily@aol.com

LEHANEY, Frank George. b 44. MCIT75 MILT99 MIAM78. **d** 99 **p** 00. OLM Brockham Green *S'wark* 99-07; NSM from 07; OLM Leigh 99-07; NSM from 07; Chapl Surrey and Sussex Healthcare NHS Trust from 99. *Twelve Trees, Small's Hill Road, Leigh, Reigate RH2 8PE* Tel (01306) 611201

LEICESTER, Archdeacon of. *See* ATKINSON, The Ven Richard William Bryant

LEICESTER, Bishop of. *See* STEVENS, The Rt Revd Timothy John

LEICESTER, Dean of. *See* FAULL, The Very Revd Vivienne Frances

LEIGH, Mrs Alison Margaret. b 40. CertEd63 Goldsmiths' Coll Lon BEd75. Sarum & Wells Th Coll 85. **d** 87 **p** 94. C Chessington *Guildf* 87-90; C Green Street Green *Roch* 90-92; Dn-in-c E Peckham and Nettlestead 92-94; P-in-c 94-95; R 95-01; rtd 01; Perm to Offic *Heref* from 02. *17 Orchard Green, Marden, Hereford HR1 3ED* Tel (01432) 882032 E-mail alison.leigh@which.net

LEIGH, Arnold Robert. b 36. AKC60. **d** 61 **p** 62. C Lewisham St Mary *S'wark* 61-66; C Stockwell Green St Andr 66-69; V 69-72; TV Withycombe Raleigh *Ex* 72-74; TR 74-80; V Devonport St Bart 80-93; P-in-c Moretonhampstead, N Bovey and Manaton 93-96; R Moretonhampstead, Manaton, N Bovey and Lustleigh 96-00; rtd 00; Perm to Offic *Win* from 03. *1 Southwick Road, Bournemouth BH6 5PR* Tel (01202) 420135

LEIGH, Dennis Herbert. b 34. Lon Univ BSc56. Chich Th Coll 58. **d** 60 **p** 61. C Roehampton H Trin *S'wark* 60-62; C E Wickham 62-67; C Plumstead St Mark and St Marg 67-73; C Corby Epiphany w St Jo *Pet* 73-74; C Paston 84-86; C Aylestone St Andr w St Jas *Leic* 86-95; rtd 95; Perm to Offic *Pet* 95-10 and *Leic* from 00. *14 Willowbrook Road, Corby NN17 2EB* Tel (01536) 263405

LEIGH, Mary Elizabeth. b 42. K Coll Lon BA64 Univ of Wales (Lamp) MMin06. Westcott Ho Cam 89. **d** 91 **p** 94. NSM Chesterfield St Mary and All SS *Derby* 91-92; C Hall Green Ascension *Birm* 92-94; Asst P Yardley St Edburgha 94-97; Chapl and Tutor NOC 97-08; rtd 08; Perm to Offic *Lich* from 99. *Downing Cottage, Jaggers Lane, Hathersage, Hope Valley S32 1AZ* Tel 07796-980636 (mobile) E-mail maryelizabethleigh@gmail.com

LEIGH, Michael John. b 69. Leeds Univ BA02 LWCMD93. Coll of Resurr Mirfield 00. **d** 02 **p** 03. C N Hull St Mich *York* 02-06; P-in-c Newby from 06. *St Mark's Vicarage, 77 Green Lane, Scarborough YO12 6HT* Tel (01723) 363205 E-mail mike@singingvicar.co.uk

LEIGH, Raymond. b 37. Lon Univ BEd81. Clifton Th Coll 65. **d** 68 **p** 69. C Chadwell *Chelmsf* 68-71; Chapl RAF 71-77; Asst Teacher Swakeleys Sch Hillingdon 81-82; Hd RE 83-88; NSM Hillingdon *Lon* from 87-88; C Rowley Regis *Birm* 88-90; V Londonderry 90-95; R Westbury w Turweston, Shalstone and Biddlesden *Ox* 95-99; CF (ACF) 95-02; rtd 99; Perm to Offic

Chich 99-07 and *Guildf* from 07. *10 Nursery Close, Epsom KT17 1NH* Tel (020) 8394 2477 Mobile 07745-493014 E-mail rayleigh37@talktalk.net

LEIGH, Richenda Mary Celia. b 71. St Mary's Coll Strawberry Hill BA93. Ripon Coll Cuddesdon BTh98. **d** 99 **p** 00. C Dalston H Trin w St Phil and Haggerston All SS *Lon* 99-02; Asst Chapl R Free Hampstead NHS Trust 02-05; Chapl Lon Metrop Univ 05-10; Chapl Derby Cathl from 10; Chapl Derby Univ from 10. *1 Peet Street, Derby DE22 1RE* Tel (01332) 591878 Mobile 07971-659534

LEIGH, Roy Stephen. b 28. Imp Coll Lon BSc49. S'wark Ord Course 87. **d** 90 **p** 92. NSM Green Street Green *Roch* 90-92; NSM E Peckham and Nettlestead 92-00; Perm to Offic *Roch* 01 and *Heref* from 02. *17 Orchard Green, Marden, Hereford HR1 3ED* Tel (01432) 882032 E-mail roy@leighmarden.plus.com

LEIGH-HUNT, Edward Christopher. b 22. Univ Coll Dur BA47. Ely Th Coll 48. **d** 50 **p** 51. C Wandsworth St Anne *S'wark* 50-54; C Bethnal Green St Matt *Lon* 54-56; C Lewisham St Jo Southend *S'wark* 56-57; C Ealing St Barn *Lon* 57-66; C St Bart Less 66-73; Chapl Asst St Barts Hosp Lon 66-73; Chapl Middx Hosp 73-86; rtd 87; Perm to Offic *Lon* 95-02. *The College of St Barnabas, Blackberry Lane, Lingfield RH7 6NJ* Tel (01342) 872823

LEIGH-HUNT, Nicolas Adrian. b 46. MIEx70. Qu Coll Birm 85. **d** 87 **p** 88. C Tilehurst St Geo *Ox* 87-91; TV Wexcombe *Sarum* 91-99; TR 99-02; TR Savernake 02-11; RD Pewsey 97-10; rtd 11. *Rose Cottage, Hawkchurch, Axminster EX13 5XD* Tel (01297) 678408 E-mail leighhunt@aol.com

LEIGHLIN, Dean of. *See* GORDON, The Very Revd Thomas William

LEIGHTON, Adrian Barry. b 44. LTh. Lon Coll of Div 65. **d** 69 **p** 70. C Erith St Paul *Roch* 69-72; C Ipswich St Marg *St E* 72-75; P-in-c Ipswich St Helen 75-82; R 82-88; P-in-c Holbrook w Freston and Woolverstone 88-97; P-in-c Wherstead 94-97; R Holbrook, Freston, Woolverstone and Wherstead 97-98; RD Samford 90-93; P-in-c Woore and Norton in Hales *Lich* 98-09; Local Min Adv (Shrewsbury) 99-09; rtd 09. *2 Tollgate Drive, Audlem, Crewe CW3 0EA* Tel (01270) 812209

LEIGHTON, Alan Granville Clyde. b 37. MInstM AMIDHE. S'wark Ord Course 73. **d** 76 **p** 77. C Silverhill St Matt *Chich* 76-79; C Eston *York* 79-82; V 82-84; TR Eston w Normanby 84-02; rtd 02; Perm to Offic *York* from 02. *Priory Lodge, 86B Church Lane, Eston, Middlesbrough TS6 9QR* Tel (01642) 504798 Fax 283016 E-mail aleighton@argonet.co.uk

LEIGHTON, Anthony Robert. b 56. Trin Coll Bris BA88. **d** 88 **p** 89. C Harrow Trin St Mich *Lon* 88-92; TV Ratby cum Groby *Leic* 92-94; TR Bradgate Team 94-00; P-in-c Newtown Linford 95-98; V Thorpe Acre w Dishley 00-08; NSM S Croxton Gp from 08. *The Rectory, 19 Main Street, South Croxton, Leicester LE7 3RJ* Tel (01664) 840245 E-mail tony0leighton@btinternet.com

LEIGHTON, Mrs Susan. b 58. Bretton Hall Coll BEd80. Trin Coll Bris BA89. **d** 89 **p** 94. Par Dn Harrow Weald All SS *Lon* 89-92; NSM Ratby cum Groby *Leic* 92-96; C Bradgate Team 96-00; Asst Warden of Readers 96-00; NSM Thorpe Acre w Dishley 00-08; TV S Croxton Gp 08-10; P-in-c from 10; P-in-c Burrough Hill Pars from 10. *The Rectory, 19 Main Street, South Croxton, Leicester LE7 3RJ* Tel (01664) 840245 E-mail susan.leighton2@btinternet.com

LEIPER, Nicholas Keith. b 34. SS Coll Cam BA55 MB58 BChir58 MA65. St Jo Coll Nottm LTh82. **d** 84 **p** 85. C Bidston *Ches* 84-87; TV Gateacre *Liv* 87-92; P-in-c Bickerstaffe 92-94; P-in-c Melling 92-94; V Bickerstaffe and Melling 94-00; rtd 00; Perm to Offic *Liv* from 00. *31 Weldale House, Chase Close, Southport PR8 2DX* Tel (01704) 566393

LEITCH, Peter William. b 36. FCA58 ATII59. Coll of Resurr Mirfield 83. **d** 85 **p** 86. C Newsome and Armitage Bridge *Wakef* 85-88; P-in-c Upper Hopton 88-91; P-in-c Mirfield Eastthorpe St Paul 88-91; Chapl Rouen Miss to Seamen *Eur* 92-94; Sen Chapl Rotterdam Miss to Seamen 94-97; Chapl Felixstowe Miss to Seafarers *St E* 97-01; rtd 01; Perm to Offic *St E* from 01. *104 St Andrew's Road, Felixstowe IP11 7ED* Tel (01394) 285320

LEITHEAD, Mrs Lynette. b 54. SEITE. **d** 08 **p** 09. NSM Kippington *Roch* from 08. *45 Chipstead Park, Sevenoaks TN13 2SL* Tel (01732) 742272 Mobile 07958-145959 E-mail lynetteleithead@hotmail.co.uk

LEMMEY, William Henry Michael. b 59. Jes Coll Cam BA81 Jes Coll Ox PGCE82. Westcott Ho Cam 03. **d** 05 **p** 06. C Milton *Win* 05-09; R Porlock and Porlock Weir w Stoke Pero etc *B & W* from 09. *The Rectory, Parsons Street, Porlock, Minehead TA24 8QL* Tel (01643) 863135 E-mail billlemmey@yahoo.co.uk

LENDRUM, William Henry. b 24. TCD BA50 MA62. CITC 50. **d** 50 **p** 51. C Belfast St Mich *Conn* 50-53; C Lisburn Ch Ch Cathl 53-61; P-in-c Belfast Whiterock 61-69; I Belfast St Mary Magd 69-91; Can Conn Cathl 87-91; rtd 91. *38 Lancefield Road, Belfast BT9 6LL* Tel (028) 9028 0635 Mobile 07929-117924

LENG, Bruce Edgar. b 38. St Aid Birkenhead 68. **d** 69 **p** 70. C Sheff St Swithun 69-74; TV Speke St Aid *Liv* 74-78; TV Yate New Town *Bris* 78-82; R Handsworth *Sheff* 82-95; R Thrybergh 95-05; Warden for Past Workers 96-05; rtd 05. *41 Hall Close Avenue, Whiston, Rotherham S60 4AH* Tel (01709) 533819 E-mail bruce@faith.f9.co.uk

LENNARD, Mrs Elizabeth Jemima Mary Patricia (Mary Pat). b 21. Edin Dioc NSM Course 78. **dss** 82 **d** 86 **p** 94. Falkirk *Edin* 82-86; Hon C 86-91; Asst Dioc Supernumerary 91-96; rtd 92; Hon C Grangemouth *Edin* 96-04; Hon C Bo'ness 96-04. *36 Heugh Street, Falkirk FK1 5QR* Tel (01324) 623240

LENNOX, Joan Baxter. *See* LYON, Joan Baxter

LENNOX, Mark. CITC. **d** 09 **p** 10. NSM Maghera w Killelagh *D & R* from 09. *Address temp unknown*

LENOX-CONYNGHAM, Andrew George. b 44. Magd Coll Ox BA65 MA73 CCC Cam PhD73. Westcott Ho Cam 72. **d** 74 **p** 75. C Poplar *Lon* 74-77; TV 77-80; Chapl Heidelberg *Eur* 80-82 and 91-96; Chapl Ch Coll Cam 82-86; Chapl and Fell St Cath Coll Cam 86-91; V Birm St Luke from 96; AD Birm City Cen from 04. *St Luke's Vicarage, 29 Bradshaw Close, Birmingham B15 2DD* Tel 0121-666 6089 *or* 622 2435 Fax 622 4532 E-mail lenox@birm.eclipse.co.uk

LENS VAN RIJN, Robert Adriaan. b 47. St Jo Coll Nottm 78. **d** 80 **p** 81. C Gt Baddow *Chelmsf* 80-83; C Edgware *Lon* 83-86; C Derby St Pet and Ch w H Trin 86-90; Chapl Eindhoven *Eur* 91-00; Chapl Burrswood Chr Cen 04-08; rtd 08; Perm to Offic *York* from 09; Chapl Dove Ho Hospice Hull from 09. *15 Spinnaker Close, Hull HU9 1UL* Tel (01482) 212082 E-mail rlvr@iae.nl

LENTHALL, Mrs Nicola Yvonne. b 73. Southn Univ BA95. Westcott Ho Cam. **d** 99 **p** 00. C Leighton Buzzard w Eggington, Hockliffe etc *St Alb* 99-03; V Kensworth, Studham and Whipsnade from 03. *The Vicarage, Clay Hall Road, Kensworth, Dunstable LU6 3RF* Tel (01582) 872223

LENTON, Colin William. b 23. CertEd. Cuddesdon Coll 80. **d** 81 **p** 81. NSM Cowley St Jo *Ox* 81-82; NSM Oakley 82-85; V Langtoft w Foxholes, Butterwick, Cottam etc *York* 85-89; rtd 89; Perm to Offic *Ripon* from 89. *Flat 3, 24 South Drive, Harrogate HG2 8AU* Tel (01423) 564751

LENTON, John Robert. b 46. Ex Coll Ox BA69 Harvard Univ MBA74. Oak Hill Th Coll. **d** 00. NSM Muswell Hill St Jas w St Matt *Lon* 00-09; NSM Hampstead St Jo Downshire Hill Prop Chpl 09-10; NSM Bramley *Win* from 10. *Address temp unknown* Tel 07714-237235 (mobile) E-mail johnlenton@iname.com

LENTON, Patricia Margarita. *See* DICKIN, Mrs Patricia Margarita

LEON (née HOLLAND), Mrs Lesley Anne. b 52. Univ Coll Chich BA04. STETS 04. **d** 07 **p** 08. NSM Northanger *Win* from 07; Perm to Offic *Portsm* from 11. *11A Tilmore Gardens, Petersfield GU32 2JQ* E-mail lesley.leon@ntlworld.com

LEONARD, Ms Ann Cressey. b 50. Open Univ BA90. S Dios Minl Tr Scheme 90. **d** 94 **p** 95. C Portsea St Cuth *Portsm* 94-96; C Farlington 96-00; Asst to RD Petersfield 00-03; Deanery Co-ord for Educn and Tr 00-03; V Hayling Is St Andr from 03; V N Hayling St Pet from 03; Dioc Ecum Officer from 02. *29 Selsmore Road, Hayling Island PO11 9JZ* E-mail ann.leonard@ukgateway.net

LEONARD, John Francis. b 48. Lich Th Coll 69. **d** 72 **p** 73. C Chorley St Geo *Blackb* 72-75; C S Shore H Trin 75-80; V Marton Moss 81-89; V Kingskerswell w Coffinswell *Ex* from 89; P-in-c Abbotskerswell from 06. *The Vicarage, Pound Lane, Kingskerswell, Newton Abbot TQ12 5DW* Tel (01803) 407217 *or* 873006 E-mail kingskerswell.parish.church@tinyworld.co.uk

LEONARD, Canon John James. b 41. Southn Univ BSc62. Sarum Th Coll 63. **d** 65 **p** 66. C Loughborough Em *Leic* 65-70; V New Humberstone 70-78; C-in-c Rushey Mead CD 78-85; V Leic St Theodore 85-05; Hon Can Leic Cathl 96-05; RD Christianity N 97-05; rtd 05. *1339 Melton Road, Syston, Leicester LE7 2EP* Tel 0116-269 2691

LEONARD, Canon Peter Michael. b 47. Portsm Poly BSc MRTPI. Sarum & Wells Th Coll 82. **d** 84 **p** 85. C Llantwit Major 84-88; V Cymmer and Porth 88-96; R Colwinston, Llandow and Llysworney from 96; AD Vale of Glam 02-08 and from 11; Can Llan Cathl from 11. *The Rectory, Llandow, Cowbridge CF71 7NT* Tel and fax (01656) 890205 E-mail peter@theleonards.org.uk

LEONARD, Peter Philip. b 70. Trin Coll Bris BA94. **d** 97 **p** 98. C Haslemere *Guildf* 97-00; C Haslemere and Grayswood 00-01; C Woodham 01-06; Perm to Offic 07-10. *Address withheld by request* Tel 07817-722219 (mobile) E-mail peter.revleonard@ntlworld.com

LEONARD, Vaughan Thomas. b 51. Coll of Resurr Mirfield 94. **d** 96 **p** 97. C Broadstone *Sarum* 96-99; C Worth *Chich* 99-00; TV 00-06; V Leesfield *Man* 06-09; P-in-c Rhodes 09-10. *5 Wentworth Road, Middleton, Manchester M24 4DB* E-mail frvaughan@btinternet.com

LEONARD-JOHNSON, Canon Philip Anthony. b 35. Selw Coll Cam BA58 MA60. Linc Th Coll 63. **d** 65 **p** 66. C Wymondham *Nor* 65-68; Zimbabwe 69-82; V Drayton in Hales *Lich* 82-92; R

Adderley 82-92; P-in-c Moreton Say 88-92; S Africa 92-98; rtd 97; Hon Can Grahamstown from 97; Perm to Offic *Lich* from 99. *Hillside, Mount Lane, Market Drayton TF9 1AG* Tel (01630) 655480

LEONARDI, Jeffrey. b 49. Warwick Univ BA71. Carl Dioc Tr Course 85. **d** 88 **p** 89. C Netherton *Carl* 88-91; V Cross Canonby 91-97; V Allonby 91-97; Bp's Adv for Past Care and Counselling *Lich* from 97; C Colton, Colwich and Gt Haywood 97-10; C Abbots Bromley, Blithfield, Colton, Colwich etc from 11. *The New Rectory, Bellamour Way, Colton, Rugeley WS15 3JW* Tel and fax (01889) 570897 E-mail jeff.leonardi@btinternet.com

LEPINE, Canon Jeremy John. b 56. BA. St Jo Coll Nottm 82. **d** 84 **p** 85. C Harrow Trin St Mich *Lon* 84-88; TV Horley *S'wark* 88-95; Evang Adv Croydon Area Miss Team 95-02; Dioc Evang Adv and Hon Chapl S'wark Cathl 97-02; R Wollaton *S'well* from 02; AD Nottingham N from 08; Hon Can S'well Minster from 09. *St Leonard's Rectory, 143 Russell Drive, Nottingham NG8 2BD* Tel 0115-928 1798 E-mail jerry.lepine@btopenworld.com

LEPPINGTON, Dian Marjorie. b 46. Leeds Univ BA85. Cranmer Hall Dur 81. **dss** 83 **d** 87 **p** 94. Potternewton *Ripon* 83-85; Ind Chapl 85-97; Chapl Teesside Univ 97-04; Can and Preb York Minster 03-04; Par Resources Adv *Man* from 05. *3 Booth Clibborn Court, Salford M7 4PJ* Tel 0161-792 8820 E-mail dianleppington@hotmail.com

LERRY, Keith Doyle. b 49. St Mich Coll Llan 69. **d** 72 **p** 73. C Caerau w Ely *Llan* 72-75; C Roath St Martin 75-84; V Glyntaff 84-11; rtd 11. *8 Wenvoe Terrace, Barry CF62 7AS*

LERVY, Hugh Martin. b 68. Univ of Wales (Lamp) BA89. Qu Coll Birm 89. **d** 91 **p** 92. C Brecon St Mary and Battle w Llanddew *S & B* 91-93; C Oystermouth 93-95; V Glantawe 95-00; V Morriston from 00. *The Vicarage, Vicarage Road, Morriston, Swansea SA6 6DR* Tel (01792) 771329 Mobile 07976-725644 E-mail hugh@lervy.net

LESITER, The Ven Malcolm Leslie. b 37. Selw Coll Cam BA61 MA65. Cuddesdon Coll 61. **d** 63 **p** 64. C Eastney *Portsm* 63-66; C Hemel Hempstead *St Alb* 66-71; TV 71-73; V Leavesden 73-88; RD Watford 81-88; V Radlett 88-93; Hon Can St Alb Abbey 90-93; Adn Bedford 93-03; rtd 03; Perm to Offic *Ely* from 03 and *Chelmsf* from 04. *349 Ipswich Road, Colchester CO4 0HN* Tel (01206) 841479

LESLIE, Christopher James. b 42. Open Univ BA75. Wycliffe Hall Ox 03. **d** 05 **p** 06. NSM Loddon Reach *Ox* from 05. *Church Farm House, Church Lane, Shinfield, Reading RG2 9BY* Tel 0118-988 8642 E-mail cj.leslie@btinternet.com

LESLIE, David Rodney. b 43. Liv Univ MEd94 Birm Univ PhD01 AKC67. **d** 68 **p** 69. C Belmont *Lon* 68-71; C St Giles Cripplegate w St Bart Moor Lane etc 71-75; TV Kirkby *Liv* 76-84; TR Ditton St Mich 84-98; V Ditton St Mich w St Thos 98-03; V Croxteth Park 03-08; rtd 08. *10 Eversley Close, Frodsham WA6 6AZ* Tel (01928) 723463 E-mail david_leslie@lineone.net

LESLIE, Richard Charles Alan. b 46. ACIB71. St Alb Minl Tr Scheme 76. **d** 79 **p** 91. NSM Redbourn *St Alb* 79-88; NSM Newport Pagnell w Lathbury and Moulsoe *Ox* 88-94; Stewardship Adv St Alb Adnry *St Alb* 94-97; TV Borehamwood 97-05; TV Elstree and Borehamwood from 05. *St Michael's Vicarage, 142 Brook Road, Borehamwood WD6 5EQ* Tel (020) 8953 2362 *or* 8905 1365 E-mail rcaleslie@idreamtime.com

LESTER, David Charles. b 46. BSc. **d** 99 **p** 00. NSM Trowell *S'well* 99-02; NSM Trowell, Awsworth and Cossall 02-06; rtd 06. *25 Ruby Street, Saltburn-by-the-Sea TS12 1EF* E-mail d.lester@ntlworld.com

LESTER, Trevor Rashleigh. b 50. CITC 83. **d** 89 **p** 90. NSM Douglas Union w Frankfield *C, C & R* 89-93; Bp's V and Lib Kilkenny Cathl and C Kilkenny w Aghour and Kilmanagh *C & O* 93-95; I Abbeystrewry Union *C, C & R* 95-03; Dean Waterford *C & O* 03-11; I Waterford w Killea, Drumcannon and Dunhill 03-11; I Kilmoe Union *C, C & R* from 11. *Altar Rectory, Toormore, Skibbereen, Co Cork, Republic of Ireland* Tel (00353) (28) 28249

L'ESTRANGE, Timothy John Nicholas. b 67. Surrey Univ BA90. St Steph Ho Ox BA92 MA96. **d** 93 **p** 94. C Halesworth w Linstead, Chediston, Holton etc *St E* 93-96; Dom Chapl to Bp Horsham *Chich* 96-98; R Beeding and Bramber w Botolphs 98-08; R Monken Hadley *Lon* 08-11; V N Acton St Gabr from 11. *The Rectory, Hadley Common, Barnet EN5 5QD* Tel (020) 8449 2414 Mobile 07845-211617 E-mail sacerdotal@gmail.com

LETALL, Ronald Richard. b 29. ACII76. Linc Th Coll 82. **d** 84 **p** 85. C Scarborough St Martin *York* 84-86; C Middlesbrough St Thos 86-88; R Kirby Misperton w Normanby, Edston and Salton 88-92; TV Louth *Linc* 90-94; rtd 94; Perm to Offic *Sheff* from 95; *Wakef* 95-97; *Chich* 97-99 and from 01. *20 Greenwood Drive, Angmering, Littlehampton BN16 4ND* Tel (01903) 859469 E-mail ronald@letall.f.snet.co.uk

LETCHER, Canon David John. b 34. K Coll Lon 54. Chich Th Coll 56. **d** 58 **p** 59. C St Austell *Truro* 58-62; C Southbroom *Sarum* 62-64; R Odstock w Nunton and Bodenham 64-72; RD Alderbury 68-73 and 77-82; V Downton 72-85; Can and Preb

Sarum Cathl 79-99; TV Dorchester 85-97; RD Dorchester 89-95; rtd 97; Perm to Offic *Sarum* from 97; CF (ACF) 97-00. *6 Longmoor Street, Poundbury, Dorchester DT1 3GN* Tel (01305) 257764 E-mail letcher@uwclub.net

LETHBRIDGE, Christopher David. b 43. NOC 90. **d** 93 **p** 94. NSM S Elmsall *Wakef* 93-95; C Knottingley 95-97; R Badsworth 97-01; P-in-c Bilham *Sheff* from 01; Chapl HM YOI Hatfield 01-03; Chapl HM Pris Moorland from 03. *Bilham Vicarage, Churchfield Road, Clayton, Doncaster DN5 7DH* Tel (01977) 643756

LETHEREN, William Neils. b 37. St Aid Birkenhead 61. **d** 64 **p** 65. C Liv St Mich 64-67; V 71-75; C Kirkdale St Athanasius 67-69; C Walsall Wood *Lich* 69-71; V W Derby St Jas *Liv* 75-84; R Newton in Makerfield Em 84-88; V Garston 88-04; rtd 04. *24 Pitville Avenue, Liverpool L18 7JG* Tel 0151-724 5543

LETSCHKA, Mrs Alison. b 58. Sussex Univ BA79 Anglia Ruskin Univ BA08. Westcott Ho Cam 06. **d** 08 **p** 09. C Haywards Heath St Wilfrid *Chich* from 08. *The Presentation Vicarage, 1 Marylands, New England Road, Haywards Heath RH16 3JZ* Tel (01444) 454179 Mobile 07950-152229 E-mail acletschka@yahoo.co.uk

LETSOM-CURD, Clifford John. *See* CURD, Clifford John Letsom

LETSON, Barry. b 55. Univ of Wales (Lamp) BA77. St Deiniol's Hawarden 82. **d** 83 **p** 84. C Flint *St As* 83-86; V Llansantffraid Glyn Ceirog and Llanarmon etc 86-89; R Montgomery and Forden and Llandyssil 89-96; RD Pool 92-96; V Mountain Ash *Llan* 96-97; V Mountain Ash and Miskin 97-02; V Crickhowell w Cwmdu and Tretower *S & B* from 02. *The Rectory, Rectory Road, Crickhowell NP8 1DW* Tel (01873) 810017

LETTS, The Ven Kenneth John. b 42. Melbourne Univ BA65 DipEd67. Coll of Resurr Mirfield 68. **d** 71 **p** 72. C Mt Waverley St Steph Australia 71-74; Chapl Melbourne C of E Gr Sch 74-81; P-in-c Albert Park 81-94; Sen Chapl St Mich Sch 82-94; Chapl Nice w Vence *Eur* from 94; Can Gib Cathl from 04; Adn France from 07. *11 rue de la Buffa, 06000 Nice, France* Tel (0033) 4 93 87 19 83 Fax 4 93 82 25 09 E-mail anglican@free.fr

LEUNG, Peter. b 36. Trin Coll Singapore BTh60 St Andr Univ PhD73. SE Asia Sch of Th MTh69. **d** 60 **p** 61. Singapore 60-62 and 65-76; Br N Borneo 62-63; Malaysia 63-65; Lect Congr Coll Man 76-77; USPG 77-83; Perm to Offic *Roch* 83-89; BCC 83-90; CTBI from 90; Perm to Offic *S'wark* 88-94; Hon C Shortlands *Roch* 90-01; Regional Sec (S and E Asia) CMS 91-99; rtd 99. *35 Tufton Gardens, West Molesey KT8 1TD* Tel (020) 8650 4157

LEVASIER, James Arjen. b 67. Heriot-Watt Univ BSc95. Wycliffe Hall Ox 07. **d** 09 **p** 10. C Ashtead *Guildf* from 09. *17 Loraine Gardens, Ashtead KT21 1PD* Tel (01372) 813366 E-mail levasier@googlemail.com

LEVASIER, Joanna Mary. b 68. Jes Coll Cam BA89 MA90. Wycliffe Hall Ox 07. **d** 09 **p** 10. C Ashtead *Guildf* from 09. *17 Loraine Gardens, Ashtead KT21 1PD* E-mail j.levasier@ntlworld.com

LEVELL, Peter John. b 40. Bris Univ BA62 CertEd63. STETS 99. **d** 02 **p** 03. NSM Guildf St Sav 02-10; rtd 10. *23 Mountside, Guildford GU2 4JD* Tel (01483) 871656 E-mail plevell@ntlworld.com

LEVER, Julian Lawrence Gerrard. b 36. Fitzw Coll Cam BA60 MA64. Sarum Th Coll 60. **d** 62 **p** 63. C Amesbury *Sarum* 62-66; R Corfe Mullen 66-78; RD Wimborne 73-75; P-in-c Wilton w Netherhampton and Fugglestone 78-82; R 82-86; R Salisbury St Martin 86-94; Perm to Offic *Win* from 96; rtd 98. *6 St John's Close, Wimborne BH21 1LY* Tel (01202) 848249

LEVERTON, James. *See* LEVERTON, Peter James Austin

LEVERTON, Mrs Judith. b 55. Eaton Hall Coll of Educn CertEd76. St Jo Coll Nottm 02. **d** 04 **p** 05. C Doncaster St Jas *Sheff* 04-07; TV Rivers Team from 07; Chapl to Deaf People from 09. *The Rectory, Church Lane, Treeton, Rotherham S60 5PZ* Tel 0114-269 6542 Mobile 07960-573529 E-mail judy.leverton@yahoo.co.uk

LEVERTON, Michael John. b 52. K Coll Lon BD76 AKC76 MTh77. Cant Sch of Min 84. **d** 87 **p** 88. NSM Elham w Denton and Wootton *Cant* 87-92; C Yelverton, Meavy, Sheepstor and Walkhampton *Ex* 92-93; TV 93-98; C Tavistock and Gulworthy 98-00; P-in-c Stevenage All SS Pin Green *St Alb* 00-10; P-in-c Ardeley from 10; P-in-c Cottered w Broadfield and Throcking from 10; P-in-c Benington w Walkern from 10. *The Rectory, Cottered, Buntingford SG9 9QA* Tel (01763) 281218 E-mail michael.leverton@btinternet.com

LEVERTON, Peter James Austin. b 33. Nottm Univ BA55. Ripon Coll Cuddesdon 79. **d** 81 **p** 82. C St Jo in Bedwardine *Worc* 81-84; V Worc St Mich 84-88; TR Worc St Barn w Ch Ch 88-92; V Riddings and Ironville *Derby* 92-00; rtd 00; Perm to Offic *Derby* from 00. *2 George Street, Langley Mill, Nottingham NG16 4DJ* Tel (01773) 710243 E-mail jim@rev-levs.freeserve.co.uk

LEVERTON, Peter Robert. b 25. Lich Th Coll 59. **d** 60 **p** 61. C Shepshed *Leic* 60-64; Australia 64-69; V Marshchapel *Linc* 70-73; V Grainthorpe w Conisholme 70-73; R N Coates 70-73; Miss to Seamen 73-77; P-in-c Brislington St Luke 77-84; V

Avonmouth St Andr 84-87; Ind Chapl 84-87; P-in-c Ugborough *Ex* 87-91; P-in-c Ermington 88-91; rtd 91; Perm to Offic *Ex* from 91. *4 Drakes Avenue, Sidford, Sidmouth EX10 9QY* Tel (01395) 579835

LEVETT, The Ven Howard. b 44. AKC67. **d** 68 **p** 69. C Rotherhithe St Mary w All SS *S'wark* 68-72; P-in-c Walworth St Jo 72-77; V Walworth St Jo 77-80; P-in-c Walworth Lady Marg w St Mary 78; RD S'wark and Newington 78-80; Adn Egypt 80-94; Miss to Seafarers 80-10; JMECA 80-10; V Holborn St Alb w Saffron Hill St Pet *Lon* 94-10; rtd 10; P-in-c Venice w Trieste *Eur* from 10. *Chaplain's House, 253 Dorsoduro, 30123 Venice, Italy* Tel (0039) (041) 520 0571 E-mail stgeorgesvenice@virgilio.it

LEVETT, Julie. d 10 **p** 11. OLM Knaphill w Brookwood *Guildf* from 10. *7 Larks Way, Knaphill, Woking GU21 2LE* Tel (01483) 850623 E-mail julie-levett@ntlworld.com

LEVICK, Brian William. b 30. Solicitor 51. Westcott Ho Cam 63. **d** 64 **p** 65. C Bourne *Linc* 64-69; C Deeping St James 69-70; C Hemel Hempstead *St Alb* 70-71; TV 71-77; Hon C Sedbergh, Cautley and Garsdale *Bradf* 77-83; V Firbank, Howgill and Killington 77-83; V Cononley w Bradley 83-90; Methodist Min 83-90; rtd 90; C Kettlewell w Conistone, Hubberholme etc *Bradf* 90-93; Hon C New Sleaford *Linc* 93-97; Dioc Ecum Officer 93-97; Ecum Officer Chs Together Lincs and S Humberside 93-97; Perm to Offic *Bradf* 99-10 and *Blackb* from 10. *11 Fosbrooke House, Clifton Drive, Lytham St Annes FY8 5RG* Tel (01253) 667026

LEVISEUR, Nicholas Templer. b 56. Magd Coll Ox MA82 Barrister 79. STETS 97 Ven English Coll Rome 00. **d** 00 **p** 01. NSM Hartfield w Coleman's Hatch *Chich* from 00. *Tye House East, Edenbridge Road, Hartfield TN7 4JR* Tel (01892) 770451

LEVY, Christopher Charles. b 51. Southn Univ BTh82. Sarum & Wells Th Coll 79. **d** 82 **p** 83. C Rubery *Birm* 82-85; C Stratford-on-Avon w Bishopton *Cov* 85-87; TV Clifton *S'well* 87-95; V Egmanton from 95; R Kirton from 95; V Walesby from 95; P-in-c Kneesall w Laxton and Wellow from 07; Chapl Center Parcs Holiday Village from 01. *St Edmund's Vicarage, Walesby, Newark NG22 9PA* Tel (01623) 860522 E-mail chris@walesbyvic.fsnet.co.uk

LEW, Henry. b 39. **d** 96 **p** 97. Manager Brabazon Trust Sheltered Housing 96-00; NSM Dublin Whitechurch *D & G* 96-99; Lic to Offic from 99; NSM Powerscourt w Kilbride from 00. *Lotts Cottage, Drummin West, The Downs, Delgany, Co Wicklow, Republic of Ireland* Tel (00353) (1) 287 2957 Mobile 87-628 8049 E-mail healew@iol.ie

LEWER ALLEN, Mrs Patricia (Paddy). b 47. UNISA BA79 HDipEd85 Cape Town Univ BA86 SRN70. Th Ext Educn Coll 94. **d** 97 **p** 98. P-in-c Dunbar *Edin* 98-08; R Comrie *St And* from 08; R Crieff from 08; R Lochearnhead from 08. *3B Gavelmore Street, Crieff PH7 4DN* E-mail paddyallen@aol.com

LEWERS, The Very Revd Benjamin Hugh. b 32. Selw Coll Cam BA60 MA64. Linc Th Coll. **d** 62 **p** 63. C Northampton St Mary *Pet* 62-65; C Hounslow Heath St Paul *Lon* 65-68; C-in-c Hounslow Gd Shep Beavers Lane CD 65-68; Chapl Heathrow Airport 68-75; V Newark St Mary *S'well* 75-80; TR Newark w Hawton, Cotham and Shelton 80-81; P-in-c Averham w Kelham 79-81; Provost Derby 81-97; rtd 98; Perm to Offic *Sarum* from 98 and *B & W* from 00. *Thimble Cottage, Marshwood, Bridport DT6 5QF* Tel (01297) 678515

LEWES AND HASTINGS, Archdeacon of. See JONES, The Ven Philip Hugh

LEWES, Area Bishop of. See BENN, The Rt Revd Wallace Parke

LEWIS, Prof Andrew Dominic Edwards. b 49. St Jo Coll Cam LLB71 MA74. SWMTC 04. **d** 07 **p** 08. NSM St Endellion w Port Isaac and St Kew *Truro* from 07; NSM St Minver from 07. *Drakes, 15 Rose Hill, Port Isaac PL29 3RL* Tel (01208) 880947 E-mail a.d.e.lewis@ucl.ac.uk

LEWIS, Ann Theodora Rachel. b 33. Univ of Wales (Ban) BA55. Qu Coll Birm 78. **d** 80 **p** 97. C Swansea St Mary w H Trin *S & B* 80-96; Chapl St Mary's Coll 90-96; rtd 96; Public Preacher *St D* from 96. *Fisherywish, Maes yr Eglwys, Llansaint, Kidwelly SA17 5JE* Tel (01267) 267386

LEWIS, Arthur Jenkin Llewellyn. b 42. Univ of Wales (Cardiff) MPS67 BPharm. Coll of Resurr Mirfield 71. **d** 73 **p** 74. C Cardiff St Jo *Llan* 73-78; C Christchurch *Win* 78-82; R Lightbowne *Man* 82-04; rtd 07. *25 Dene Street Gardens, Dorking RH4 2DN* Tel (01306) 879743

LEWIS, Brian James. b 52. Cant Univ (NZ) BA75. St Jo Coll Auckland 76. **d** 78 **p** 79. C Ashburton New Zealand 78-80; C Shrub End *Chelmsf* 80-82; P-in-c Colchester St Barn 82-84; V 84-88; P-in-c Romford St Andr 88-90; R 90-99; RD Havering 93-97; R Lt Ilford St Mich from 99. *The Rectory, 124 Church Road, London E12 6HA* Tel (020) 8478 2182 E-mail brian@littleilford.fsnet.co.uk

LEWIS, Mrs Cheryl Irene. b 11. NSM Blaina and Nantyglo *Mon* from 11. *13 Newchurch Road, Ebbw Vale NP23 5NL* Tel (01495) 303388

LEWIS, The Very Revd Christopher Andrew. b 44. Bris Univ BA69 CCC Cam PhD74. Westcott Ho Cam 71. **d** 73 **p** 74. C

Barnard Castle *Dur* 73-76; Dir Ox Inst for Ch and Soc 76-79; Tutor Ripon Coll Cuddesdon 76-79; Sen Tutor 79-81; Vice-Prin 81-82; P-in-c Aston Rowant w Crowell *Ox* 78-81; V Spalding *Linc* 82-87; Can Res Cant Cathl 87-94; Dir of Minl Tr 89-94; Dean St Alb 94-03; Dean Ch Ch *Ox* from 03. *The Deanery, Christ Church, Oxford OX1 1DP* Tel (01865) 276161 Fax 276238 E-mail rachel.perham@chch.ox.ac.uk

LEWIS, Canon Christopher Gouldson. b 42. K Coll Cam BA64 MA68. Cuddesdon Coll 65. **d** 67 **p** 68. C Gosforth All SS *Newc* 67-71; Sarawak 71-74; V Luton St Chris Round Green *St Alb* 74-80; RD Reculver Cant 80-86 and 92-93; V Whitstable All SS w St Pet 80-84; TR Whitstable 84-93; Dir Post-Ord Tr 88-93; Hon Can Cant Cathl 91-93; Can Res Bradf Cathl 93-01; Bp's Officer for Min and Tr 93-01; P-in-c Riding Mill *Newc* 01-07; Chapl Shepherd's Dene Retreat Ho 01-07; Adv for Spirituality and Spiritual Direction 02-07; Hon Can Newc Cathl from 07; rtd 07. *The Old School, Bingfield, Hexham NE46 4HR* Tel (01434) 672729

LEWIS, David Antony. b 48. Dur Univ BA69 Nottm Univ MTh84. St Jo Coll Nottm 81. **d** 83 **p** 84. C Gateacre *Liv* 83-86; V Toxteth St Cypr w Ch Ch 86-01; V Edge Hill St Cypr w St Mary 01-07; AD Liv N 94-03; Urban Development Adv 07-08; rtd 08. *48 Coulsdon Road, Sidmouth EX10 9JP* Tel (01395) 516762 E-mail davenwend@gmail.com

LEWIS, David Hugh. b 45. Oak Hill Th Coll 88. **d** 90 **p** 91. C Oakham, Hambleton, Egleton, Braunston and Brooke *Pet* 90-94; R Ewhurst *Guildf* 94-99; V Southway *Ex* 99-03; RD Plymouth Moorside 01-03; P-in-c Anglesey Gp *Ely* 03-04; V from 04; rtd 11. *The Vicarage, 86 High Street, Bottisham, Cambridge CB25 9BA* Tel (01223) 812367 E-mail revdavidhlewis@msn.com

LEWIS, David Tudor. b 61. Jes Coll Cam BA83. Trin Coll Bris BA88. **d** 88 **p** 89. C Tile Cross *Birm* 88-91; C Woking St Jo *Guildf* 91-95; TV Carl H Trin and St Barn 95-97; Chapl Carl Hosps NHS Trust 95-97; Asst Chapl Oslo w Bergen, Trondheim and Stavanger *Eur* 97-04; TV E Richmond *Ripon* from 04. *The Rectory, Great Smeaton, Northallerton DL6 2EP* Tel (01609) 881205 E-mail dtlewis@freenet.co.uk

LEWIS, David Tudor Bowes. b 63. Keele Univ BA85 Univ of Wales (Cardiff) BTh90. St Mich Coll Llan 87. **d** 90 **p** 91. C Llangollen w Trevor and Llantysilio *St As* 90-93; C Bistre 93-97; V Berse and Southsea 97-02; V Bwlchgwyn w Berse w Southsea 02-04; R Overton and Erbistock and Penley from 04; AD Bangor Isycoed from 09. *The Rectory, 4 Sundorne, Overton, Wrexham LL13 0EB* Tel (01978) 710229

LEWIS, Canon David Vaughan. b 36. Trin Coll Cam BA60 MA64. Ridley Hall Cam 60. **d** 62 **p** 63. C Rugby St Matt *Cov* 62-65; Asst Chapl K Edw Sch Witley 65-71; Hon C Rainham *Chelmsf* 71-76; V Stoke Hill *Guildf* 76-87; V Wallington *S'wark* 87-03; Hon Can S'wark Cathl 95-03; RD Sutton 97-00; rtd 03; Perm to Offic *Ely* from 03. *11 The Meadows, Haslingfield, Cambridge CB23 1JD* Tel (01223) 874029 E-mail david@hmlewis.freeserve.co.uk

LEWIS, Canon David Watkin. b 40. Univ of Wales (Lamp) BA61. Wycliffe Hall Ox 61. **d** 63 **p** 64. C Skewen *Llan* 63-66; Field Tr Officer Prov Youth Coun Ch in Wales 66-68; C Gabalfa 68-71; P-in-c Marcross w Monknash and Wick 71-73; R 73-83; RD Llantwit Major and Cowbridge 81-83; V Baglan 83-10; Can Llan Cathl 00-10; Treas Llan Cathl 04-10; rtd 10. *23 St Illtyd's Close, Baglan, Port Talbot SA12 8BA* Tel (01639) 821778

LEWIS, Edward John. b 58. JP93. Univ of Wales BEd80 BA82 Surrey Univ MA07 FRSA97 MInstD01. Chich Th Coll 82. **d** 83 **p** 84. C Llangiwg *S & B* 83-85; C Morriston 85-87; Asst Chapl Morriston Hosp 85-87; V Tregaron w Ystrad Meurig and Strata Florida *St D* 87-89; Chapl Tregaron Hosp 87-89; Chapl Manor Hosp Walsall 89-92; Distr Co-ord Chapl Walsall Hosps 90-92; Sen Chapl Walsall Hosps NHS Trust 92-00; Chapl Walsall Community Health Trust 92-00; Chief Exec and Dir Tr Gen Syn Hosp Chapl Coun 00-10; Perm to Offic *Lich* from 00 and *St Alb* 02-10; P-in-c Watford St Jo *St Alb* 10-11; V Kenton *Lon* from 11; Visiting Lect St Mary's Univ Coll Twickenham from 04; PV Westmr Abbey from 07; Chapl to The Queen from 08. *St Mary's Vicarage, 3 St Leonard's Avenue, Harrow HA3 8EJ* Tel (020) 8907 2914 Mobile 07500-557953 E-mail fr.edward@ntlworld.com

LEWIS, Ella Pauline. b 41. SWMTC 94. **d** 98. NSM Paignton Ch Ch and Preston St Paul *Ex* 98-07; NSM Torquay St Luke from 07. *Roselands, 5 Great Headland Road, Paignton TQ3 2DY* Tel (01803) 555171 E-mail paulinelewis@eclipse.co.uk

LEWIS, Elsie Leonora. b 26. Cranmer Hall Dur 72. **dss** 78 **d** 87 **p** 94. S Westoe *Dur* 78-80; Ryton 80-86; rtd 86. *53 Cushy Cow Lane, Ryton NE40 3NL* Tel 0191-413 5845

LEWIS, Eric. b 47. NEOC 04. **d** 07 **p** 08. NSM Monkseaton St Mary *Newc* 07-11; P-in-c Ovingham from 11. *The Vicarage, 2 Burnside Close, Ovingham, Prudhoe NE42 6BS* Tel (01661) 836072 E-mail e.lewis129@gmail.com

LEWIS, Frederick Norman. b 23. Leeds Univ BA47. Coll of Resurr Mirfield 47. **d** 49 **p** 50. C Haydock St Jas *Liv* 49-51; C Dresden *Lich* 51-55; C Stafford St Mary 55-56; V Wednesfield

St Thos 56-65; V Shrewsbury St Chad 65-69; V Kingswinford St Mary 69-88; rtd 88; Perm to Offic *Lich* from 88. *27 Bramblewood Drive, Wolverhampton WV3 9DB* Tel (01902) 334934

LEWIS, Gary. b 61. Lanc Univ BA85. Ripon Coll Cuddesdon 86. **d** 89 **p** 90. C Blackb St Mich w St Jo and H Trin 89-92; C Altham w Clayton le Moors 92-95; V Lea 95-01; V Skerton St Luke from 01. *St Luke's Vicarage, Slyne Road, Lancaster LA1 2HU* Tel (01524) 63249

LEWIS, Graham Rhys. b 54. Loughb Univ BTech76 Cranfield Inst of Tech MBA89. SEITE 95. **d** 98 **p** 99. NSM S Gillingham *Roch* from 98. *53 Oastview, Gillingham ME8 8JG* Tel (01634) 373036 *or* tel and fax 389224 Mobile 07740-915826 E-mail graham.lewis@diocese-rochester.org

LEWIS, Gwynne. See LEWIS, Hywel Gwynne

LEWIS, Ms Hannah Margaret. b 71. CCC Cam BA93 MA96 Birm Univ PhD03. Qu Coll Birm 95. **d** 97 **p** 98. C Cannock *Lich* 97-00; NSM Cen Telford 00-06; Team Ldr Past Services for Deaf Community *Liv* from 06. *9 Hougoumont Avenue, Liverpool L22 0LL* Tel 0151-705 2130 E-mail hannah.lewis@liverpool.anglican.org

LEWIS, Hubert Godfrey. b 33. Univ of Wales (Lamp) BA59. **d** 60 **p** 61. C Merthyr Tydfil *Llan* 60-64; C Caerphilly 64-66; Perm to Offic *S'wark* 66-76 and *Cant* 76-82; Hon C Shirley St Jo *S'wark* 82-93; Hon C Whitchurch *Llan* from 94. *2 Heol Wernlas, Cardiff CF14 1RY* Tel (029) 2061 3079

LEWIS, Hywel Gwynne. b 37. FCA75. St D Dioc Tr Course 94. **d** 97 **p** 98. NSM Henfynyw w Aberaeron and Llanddewi Aberarth etc *St D* 97-07; rtd 07; Perm to Offic *St D* from 07. *Dunycoed, Lampeter Road, Aberaeron SA46 0ED* Tel (01545) 570577

LEWIS, Ian. b 33. Lon Univ MB, BS57. Oak Hill Th Coll 61. **d** 63 **p** 64. C Heatherlands St Jo *Sarum* 63-66; Hd CMJ Ethiopia 66-73; Hon C Bath Walcot *B & W* 75-77; Lic to Offic 78-98; Hon C Bath St Bart 80-04; rtd 98; Perm to Offic *B & W* from 04. *22C Ashley Road, Bathford, Bath BA1 7TT* Tel (01225) 859818 E-mail ian@iclewis.co.uk

LEWIS, Preb Ian Richard. b 54. Sheff Univ BA76 Ox Univ BA83 MA87. Wycliffe Hall Ox 81. **d** 84 **p** 85. C Rusholme H Trin *Man* 84-88; C Sandal St Helen *Wakef* 88-91; V Bath St Bart *B & W* from 91; Preb Wells Cathl from 11. *St Bartholomew's Vicarage, 5 Oldfield Road, Bath BA2 3ND* Tel and fax (01225) 422070 E-mail ian.ir.lewis@btinternet.com *or* ianlewis@stbartsbath.org

LEWIS, James Edward. b 22. St D Coll Lamp BA50. **d** 51 **p** 52. C Gorseinon *S & B* 51-52; C Defynnog 52-56; R Llangynllo w Troed-yr-aur *St D* 56-61; V Brynamman 61-72; R Llangathen w Llanfihangel Cilfargen 72-82; V Llangathen w Llanfihangel Cilfargen etc 82-90; RD Llangadog and Llandeilo 85-89; rtd 90. *4 Ger y Llan, The Parade, Carmarthen SA31 1TN* Tel (01267) 221660

LEWIS, James Michael. b 51. Trin Coll Carmarthen CertEd73 Open Univ BA86 MA91. St Mich Coll Llan 98. **d** 02 **p** 03. NSM Laleston w Tythegston and Merthyr Mawr *Llan* 02-09; NSM Laleston and Merthyr Mawr from 09. *19 Austin Avenue, Laleston, Bridgend CF32 0LG* Tel (01656) 660648 Mobile 07951-300206 E-mail mike.lewis11@virgin.net

LEWIS, Jean Anwyl. b 34. Surrey Univ BA03. K Coll Lon MA05. **d** 05 **p** 06. OLM Windlesham *Guildf* from 05. *2 Hillside Cottages, Broadway Road, Windlesham GU20 6BY* Tel (01276) 472681 E-mail jean.lewis1@btopenworld.com

LEWIS, Jocelyn Vivien. b 49. Trevelyan Coll Dur BSc70 Sheff Univ PhD75. EMMTC 91. **d** 94 **p** 95. NSM Brimington *Derby* 94-99; P-in-c Whittington 99-09; Dioc Dir Reader Tr 99-09; P-in-c New Whittington 00-09; rtd 09. *13 Gower Crescent, Chesterfield S40 4LX* Tel (01246) 229539

LEWIS, The Ven John Arthur. b 34. Jes Coll Ox BA56 MA60. Cuddesdon Coll 58. **d** 60 **p** 61. C Prestbury *Glouc* 60-63; C Wimborne Minster *Sarum* 63-66; R Eastington and Frocester *Glouc* 66-70; V Nailsworth 70-78; Chapl Memorial and Querns Hosp Cirencester 78-88; V Cirencester *Glouc* 78-88; RD Cirencester 84-88; Hon Can Glouc Cathl 85-98; Adn Cheltenham 88-98; rtd 98; Perm to Offic *Glouc* from 98. *5 Vilverie Mead, Bishop's Cleeve, Cheltenham GL52 7YY* Tel (01242) 678425

LEWIS, John Edward. b 31. SS Mark & Jo Coll Chelsea CertEd53. Qu Coll Birm 83. **d** 85 **p** 86. C Leominster *Heref* 85-87; TV 87-95; rtd 95; Perm to Offic *Heref* from 97. *The Holms, 253 Godiva Road, Leominster HR6 8TB* Tel (01568) 612287

LEWIS, John Goddard. b 52. Houston Bapt Univ (USA) BA74 JD77 Ox Univ 98. Virginia Th Sem MDiv97. **d** 97. USA 97-98 and from 01; Hon C Bladon w Woodstock *Ox* 98-01; Min Cen for Faith in the Workplace San Antonio from 01. *2015 NE Loop 410, San Antonio TX 78217, USA* Tel (001) (210) 599 4224

LEWIS, John Herbert. b 42. Selw Coll Cam BA64 MA68. Westcott Ho Cam 64. **d** 66 **p** 67. C Wyken *Cov* 66-70; C Bedford St Andr *St Alb* 70-73; Lib Pusey Ho and Bp's Chapl for Graduates *Ox* 73-77; TV Woughton 78-82; TV Gt Chesham 82-88; P-in-c Newport Pagnell w Lathbury and Moulsoe 88-91;

R 91-07; rtd 07; Perm to Offic *Ox* from 08. *54 Sparrows Way, Oxford OX4 7GE*

LEWIS, John Horatio George. b 47. Southn Univ BEd72 MA85. Ox NSM Course 86. **d** 89 **p** 90. NSM Newbury *Ox* 89-04; Perm to Offic *Win* 94-04; P-in-c Borden *Cant* 05-08; V from 08; AD Sittingbourne from 09. *The Vicarage, School Lane, Borden, Sittingbourne ME9 8JS* Tel (01795) 472986 Mobile 07973-406622 E-mail fr.johnlewis@tiscali.co.uk

✠**LEWIS, The Rt Revd John Hubert Richard.** b 43. AKC66. **d** 67 **p** 68 **c** 92. C Hexham *Newc* 67-70; Ind Chapl 70-77; Communications Officer *Dur* 77-82; Chapl for Agric *Heref* 82-87; Adn Ludlow 87-92; V Ludlow and Bp *B & W* 92-97; Bp St E 97-07; rtd 07. *Kenwater House, 14A Green Lane, Leominster HR6 8QJ* Tel (01568) 613982 E-mail lewis310@btinternet.com

LEWIS, John Malcolm. b 41. Reading Univ BEd. Trin Coll Bris. **d** 82 **p** 83. C Kingswood *Bris* 82-85; TV Weston-super-Mare Cen Par *B & W* 85-91; Dioc Children's Adv *Nor* 91-97; TV Bishopsworth and Bedminster Down *Bris* 97-06; Hon Min Can Bris Cathl 04-06; rtd 06. *35 Lodge Way, Weymouth DT4 9UU* Tel (01305) 776560 E-mail monandjohn@btinternet.com

LEWIS, John Pryce. b 65. Trin Coll Carmarthen BA87. Wycliffe Hall Ox 92. **d** 94 **p** 95. C Carmarthen St Pet *St D* 94-97; V Nevern and Y Beifil w Eglwyswrw and Meline etc 97-07; V Henfynyw w Aberaeron and Llanddewi Aberarth etc from 07. *The Vicarage, Panteg Road, Aberaeron SA46 0EP* Tel (01545) 570433 E-mail vicar@aberaeronparish.org.uk

LEWIS, The Very Revd John Thomas. b 47. Jes Coll Ox BA69 MA73 St Jo Coll Cam BA72 MA92. Westcott Ho Cam 71. **d** 73 **p** 74. C Whitchurch *Llan* 73-77, C Llanishen and Lisvane 77-80; Asst Chapl Univ of Wales (Cardiff) 80-85; Warden of Ords 81-85; V Brecon St David w Llanspyddid and Llanilltyd *S & B* 85-91; Sec Prov Selection Panel and Bd Ch in Wales 87-94; V Bassaleg *Mon* 91-96; TR 96-00; Bp's Chapl for CME 98-00; Dean Llan from 00; V Llandaff from 00. *The Deanery, The Cathedral Green, Llandaff, Cardiff CF5 2YF* Tel (029) 2056 1545

LEWIS, Joycelyn. See LEWIS-GREGORY, Mrs Joycelyn

LEWIS, Kevin James. b 76. Nottm Univ BA98. St Jo Coll Nottm MTh04 MA(MM)05. **d** 05 **p** 06. C Southgate *Chich* 05-09; C St Helier *S'wark* from 09. *59 Wigmore Road, Carshalton SM5 1RG* Tel (020) 8644 9203 Mobile 07739-139389 E-mail kevinjlewis@btinternet.com

LEWIS, Leslie. b 28. LRAM56. St Aid Birkenhead 61. **d** 63 **p** 64. C Eastham *Ches* 63-66; C W Kirby St Bridget 66-72; V Rainow w Saltersford 72-73; V Rainow w Saltersford and Forest 73-02; Dioc Clergy Widows and Retirement Officer 88-93; rtd 02; Perm to Offic *Ches* from 02. *25 Appleby Close, Macclesfield SK11 8XB* Tel (01625) 616395

LEWIS, Mrs Mary Carola Melton. b 51. LRAM72 S Glam Inst HE CertEd76 Lon Univ BD93. St Mich Coll Llan 97. **d** 98 **p** 99. NSM Aberedw w Llandeilo Graban and Llanbadarn etc *S & B* 98-03. *Brynglocsen, Dolanog, Welshpool SY21 0LJ* Tel (01938) 811202 E-mail marylewis@btinternet.com

LEWIS, Maureen. b 50. Ches Coll of HE BA92. St Jo Coll Nottm 92. **d** 94 **p** 95. C Ellesmere Port *Ches* 94-98; C Prenton 98-00; C New Brighton St Jas w Em 00-05; rtd 05; Perm to Offic *Ches* from 06. *27 Wimborne Avenue, Wirral CH61 7UL* Tel 0151-648 0605

LEWIS, Melville. See LEWIS, William George Melville

LEWIS, Michael. See LEWIS, James Michael

✠**LEWIS, The Rt Revd Michael Augustine Owen.** b 53. Mert Coll Ox BA75 MA79. Cuddesdon Coll 78. **d** 78 **p** 79. C Salfords *S'wark* 78-80; Chapl Thames Poly 80-84; V Welling 84-91; TR Worc SE 91-99; RD Worc E 93-99; Hon Can Worc Cathl 98-99; Suff Bp Middleton *Man* 99-07; Bp Cyprus and the Gulf from 07. *PO Box 22075, CY 1517-Nicosia, Cyprus* Tel (00357) (22) 671220 Fax 674553 E-mail bishop@spidernet.com.cy *or* maolewis 2000@yahoo.com

LEWIS, Canon Michael David Bennett. b 41. Portsm Univ MA01. St Mich Coll Llan 65. **d** 68 **p** 69. C Penarth w Lavernock *Llan* 68-72; Chapl RAF 72-74; C Llanishen and Lisvane 74-77; V Penyfai w Tondu 77-82; Chapl Ardingly Coll 82-90; R Merrow *Guildf* 90-95; RD Guildf 94-95; V Southsea H Spirit *Portsm* 95-11; RD Portsm 06-11; Hon Can Portsm Cathl 06-11; rtd 11; Perm to Offic *St D* from 11. *Stepping Stones, Reynalton, Kilgetty SA68 0PG* Tel (01834) 891529 Mobile 07808-609912 E-mail fr.lewis@btinternet.com

LEWIS, Michael John. b 37. LLAM86. St Aid Birkenhead 64. **d** 66 **p** 67. C Whitnash *Cov* 66-69; C Nuneaton St Nic 69-73; TV Basildon St Martin w H Cross and Laindon *Chelmsf* 73-79; V W Bromwich St Jas *Lich* 79-85; TV Buxton w Burbage and King Sterndale *Derby* 85-95; P-in-c Brampton St Mark 95-02; rtd 02; Perm to Offic *Cov* from 03. *15 Langley Street, Basford, Stoke-on-Trent ST4 6DX* Tel (01782) 622762

LEWIS, Norman. See LEWIS, Frederick Norman

LEWIS, Norman Eric. b 34. SRN55 Open Univ BA77. Roch Th Coll 59 Lich Th Coll 60. **d** 63 **p** 64. C Hope St Jas *Man* 63-67; V Hindsford 67-77; V Bolton SS Simon and Jude 77-90; rtd 90;

Perm to Offic *York* from 90. *Millbank Cottage, Kirby Misperton, Malton YO17 6XZ* Tel (01653) 668526
E-mail normanl@btinternet.com

LEWIS, Patrick Mansel. *See* MANSEL LEWIS, Patrick Charles Archibald

LEWIS, Peter. *See* LEWIS, Thomas Peter

LEWIS, Peter Andrew. b 67. Pemb Coll Ox MA PhD Univ of Wales (Abth) Bris Univ BA. Trin Coll Bris. **d** 96 **p** 97. C Cardigan w Mwnt and Y Ferwig *St D* 96-98; C Gabalfa *Llan* 98-01; V Aberpergwm and Blaengwrach 01-04; V Vale of Neath from 04; AD Neath from 10. *99A Neath Road, Resolven, Neath SA11 4AN* Tel (01639) 711262
E-mail rev.peterlewis@virgin.net

LEWIS, Peter Richard. b 40. Dur Univ BA62. Qu Coll Birm 62. **d** 64 **p** 65. C Moseley St Mary *Birm* 64-67; C Sherborne w Castleton and Lillington *Sarum* 67-71; P-in-c Bishopstone w Stratford Tony 72-80; V Amesbury 80-02; rtd 02; Perm to Offic *Sarum* from 02 and *B & W* from 05. *Rose Cottage, Silton Road, Bourton, Gillingham SP8 5DE*

LEWIS, Miss Rachel Veronica Clare. b 59. St Jo Coll Dur BA80 Man Univ PGCE81 Univ of Wales (Cardiff) MSc. Sarum & Wells Th Coll 86. **d** 86 **p** 94. C Caereithin *S & B* 86-88; Par Dn Bolton St Pet *Man* 88-91; Chapl Bolton Colls of H&FE 88-91; Chapl Trin Coll Carmarthen 91-94; C Yatton Keynell *Bris* 94-97; P-in-c 97-99; C Biddestone w Slaughterford 94-97; P-in-c 97-99; C Castle Combe 94-97; P-in-c 97-99; C W Kington 94-97; P-in-c 97-99; C Nettleton w Littleton Drew 94-97; P-in-c 97-99; P-in-c Grittleton and Leigh Delamere 94-99; TR By Brook 99-02; I Adare and Kilmallock w Kilpeacon, Croom etc *L & K* 02-07; P-in-c Peterston-super-Ely w St Brides-super-Ely *Llan* from 07; P-in-c St Nicholas w Bonvilston and St George-super-Ely from 07; P-in-c Pendoylan w Welsh St Donats from 07. *The Rectory, Peterston-super-Ely, Cardiff CF5 6LH* Tel (01446) 760687
E-mail revlewis@btinternet.com

LEWIS, Ray Arthur. b 63. Oak Hill Th Coll 87. **d** 90 **p** 91. C Holloway St Mary Magd *Lon* 90-93; TV Forest Gate St Sav w W Ham St Matt *Chelmsf* 93-97; St Vincent 97-98; Grenada 98-99. *45 Avenue Road, London E7 0LA*

LEWIS, Raymond James. b 34. Univ of Wales (Cardiff) BA Open Univ BSc. St Mich Coll Llan. **d** 91 **p** 92. C Llanelli *St D* 91-94; rtd 99. *36 Yorath Road, Whitchurch, Cardiff CF14 1QD* Tel (029) 2061 6267

LEWIS, Richard. *See* LEWIS, The Rt Revd John Hubert Richard

LEWIS, The Very Revd Richard. b 35. Fitzw Ho Cam BA78 MA63. Ripon Hall Ox 58. **d** 60 **p** 61. C Hinckley St Mary *Leic* 60-63; C Sanderstead All SS *S'wark* 63-66; V S Merstham 67-72; V S Wimbledon H Trin 72-74; P-in-c S Wimbledon St Pet 72-74; V S Wimbledon H Trin and St Pet 74-79; V Dulwich St Barn 79-90; Chapl Alleyn's Foundn Dulwich 79-90; RD Dulwich *S'wark* 83-90; Hon Can S'wark Cathl 87-90; Dean Wells *B & W* 90-03; Warden of Readers 91-03; rtd 03; Perm to Offic *Worc* 03-08. *1 Monmouth Court, Union Street, Wells BA5 2PX*
E-mail dean.richard@btopenworld.com

LEWIS, Canon Richard Charles. b 44. Univ of Wales (Lamp) MA94 Sheff Univ MEd96. ALCD69. **d** 69 **p** 70. C Kendal H Trin *Carl* 69-72; C Chipping Barnet *St Alb* 72-76; V Watford Ch Ch from 76; Chapl Abbots Hill Sch Hemel Hempstead 81-96; Hon Can St Alb Abbey from 90. *Christ Church Vicarage, Leggatts Way, Watford WD24 5NQ* Tel (01923) 672240 Fax 279919 E-mail vicar@ccwatford.u-net.com
or rts@ccwatford.u-net.com

LEWIS, Robert. b 38. St Pet Coll Ox BA62 MA66. Cuddesdon Coll 62. **d** 64 **p** 65. C Kirkby *Liv* 64-67 and 70-71; TV 71-75; Chapl St Boniface Coll Warminster 68-69; Tutor St Aug Coll Cant 69-70; Abp's Dom Chapl and Dir of Ords *York* 76-79; TR Thirsk 79-92; Chapl Oslo w Bergen, Trondheim, Stavanger etc *Eur* 93-96; P-in-c Danby *York* 96-98; V 98-04; RD Whitby 98-04; rtd 04; Perm to Offic *York* from 04. *19 Long Street, Thirsk YO7 1AW* Tel (01845) 523256

LEWIS, Canon Robert George. b 53. Lanc Univ BEd76. Ripon Coll Cuddesdon. **d** 78 **p** 79. C Liv Our Lady and St Nic w St Anne 78-81; Asst Dir of Educn 81-88; P-in-c Newchurch 88-89; P-in-c Glazebury 88-89; R Newchurch and Glazebury 89-94; R Winwick 94-09; R Glazebury w Hollinfare 04-09; AD Winwick 01-09; Hon Can Liv Cathl from 01; Chapl Liv Univ from 09; Chapl Liv Jo Moores Univ from 09; Bp's Adv Sector Min from 11. *10 Ladychapel Close, Liverpool L1 7BZ* Tel 0151-707 2988 E-mail thelewises@hotmail.com

LEWIS, Roger Gilbert. b 49. St Jo Coll Dur BA70. Ripon Hall Ox 70. **d** 72 **p** 73. C Boldmere *Birm* 72-76; C Birm St Pet 76-77; TV Tettenhall Regis *Lich* 77-81; V Ward End *Birm* 81-91; rtd 91; Perm to Offic *Birm* from 91. *8 Tudor Terrace, Ravenhurst Road, Birmingham B17 9SB* Tel 0121-427 4915

LEWIS, Simon William. b 66. Westmr Coll Ox BTh94 Roehampton Inst PGCE95. STETS 03. **d** 06 **p** 07. C Ventnor St Cath, Ventnor H Trin and Bonchurch *Portsm* 06-09; P-in-c Brent Knoll, E Brent and Lympsham *B & W* from 09. *The Rectory, 3 Ash Trees, East Brent, Highbridge TA9 4DQ* Tel (01278) 760496 E-mail rev.simonlewis@gmail.com

LEWIS, Stuart William. b 54. Newc Univ BA79 Newc Poly PGCE80. Edin Th Coll 84. **d** 86 **p** 87. C Ledbury w Eastnor *Heref* 86-89; Chapl Malvern Coll 89-96; Chapl and Prec Portsm Cathl 96-97; TV Ross *Heref* 97-01; P-in-c Lower Wharfedale *Ripon* 01-03; R from 03; Chapl St Aid Sch Harrogate 01-05. *Hayfield House, Strait Lane, Huby, Leeds LS17 0EA*
E-mail stuartlewis@wyenet.co.uk

LEWIS, Thomas Peter. b 45. Selw Coll Cam BA67 MA. Ripon Hall Ox 68. **d** 70 **p** 71. C Bp's Hatfield *St Alb* 70-74; C Boreham Wood All SS 74-78; Chapl Haileybury Coll 78-85; Chapl Abingdon Sch 86-03; R Narberth w Mounton w Robeston Wathen etc *St D* from 03. *The Rectory, Adams Drive, Narberth SA67 7AE* Tel (01834) 860370
E-mail revtplewis@btinternet.com

LEWIS, Timothy Mark Philip. b 82. Worc Coll Ox BA05. Wycliffe Hall Ox MA11. **d** 11. C Yeovil w Kingston Pitney *B & W* from 11. *9 Park Gardens, Yeovil BA20 1DW* Tel (01935) 509102 Mobile 07739-026939
E-mail timothymplewis@hotmail.co.uk

LEWIS, Timothy Paul. b 84. Nottm Univ BA07. Trin Coll Bris MA11. **d** 11. C Cottingley *Bradf* from 11. *6 Canon Pinnington Mews, Bingley BD16 1AQ* Tel 07951-132418 (mobile)
E-mail tim.paul.lewis@gmail.com

LEWIS, Trevor Arnold. b 55. NEOC 06. **d** 09 **p** 10. NSM Middlesbrough St Martin w St Cuth *York* 09-10; NSM Osmotherley w Harlsey and Ingleby Arncliffe from 10; NSM Leake w Over and Nether Silton and Kepwick from 10; NSM Felixkirk w Boltby from 10; NSM Kirkby Knowle from 10; NSM Cowesby from 10. *Orchard House, Ingleby Arncliffe, Northallerton DL6 3LN* Tel (01609) 882937
E-mail revtrevor02@sky.com

LEWIS, Vera Elizabeth. b 45. Lon Univ BA66 Univ of Wales (Abth) DipEd67. St As Minl Tr Course 82. **d** 85 **p** 97. NSM Garthbeibio and Llanerfyl and Llangadfan *St As* 85-86; C 87-88; NSM Llanfair Caereinion w Llanllugan 85-86; C 87-88; Dn-in-c Llanrhaeadr-ym-Mochnant etc 88-96; Dn-in-c Llanddulas and Llysfaen 96-97; R 97-03; rtd 03. *Heulwen, Bronwylfa Square, St Asaph LL17 0BU*

LEWIS, Canon Walter Arnold. b 45. NUI BA68 TCD MPhil91. TCD Div Sch 71. **d** 71 **p** 72. C Belfast Whiterock *Conn* 71-73; C Belfast St Mark 73-80; Bp's C Belfast St Andr 80-84; I Belfast St Thos from 84; Can Belf Cathl from 97. *St Thomas's Rectory, 1A Eglantine Avenue, Belfast BT9 6DW* Tel and fax (028) 9066 3332 E-mail walter.lewis@ntlworld.com

LEWIS, William George Melville. b 31. Open Univ BA. S'wark Ord Course. **d** 69 **p** 70. C Coulsdon St Jo *S'wark* 69-71; C Perry Hill St Geo 71-74; V Eltham St Barn 74-80; V Reigate St Mark 80-89; V Ham St Rich 89-97; rtd 97; Hon C Kew *S'wark* 97-00; Perm to Offic from 03. *20 Avenue Court, The Avenue, Tadworth KT20 5BG* Tel (01737) 819748

LEWIS, William George Rees. b 35. Hertf Coll Ox BA59 MA63. Tyndale Hall Bris 61. **d** 63 **p** 64. C Tenby w Gumfreston *St D* 63-66; C Llanelli St Paul 66-69; R Letterston 69-84; R Jordanston w Llanstinan 73-78; R Punchestown and Lt Newc 78-84; R Hubberston w Herbrandston and Hasguard etc 84-90; Prov Officer for Evang and Adult Educn 90-94; V Gabalfa *Llan* 94-00; rtd 00. *5 Westaway Drive, Hakin, Milford Haven SA73 3EG* Tel (01646) 692280

LEWIS, William Rhys. b 20. St Mich Coll Llan 53. **d** 55 **p** 56. C Ystrad Mynach *Llan* 55-58; C Bassaleg *Mon* 58-59; V Cwmtillery 59-62; V Newport St Andr 62-64; TR Ebbw Vale 64-73; R Llangattock and Llangynidr *S & B* 73-78; V Swansea St Luke 78-85; rtd 85; Perm to Offic *Llan* from 85. *6 Beech Avenue, Llantwit Major CF61 1RT* Tel (01446) 796741

LEWIS-ANTHONY, Justin Griffith. b 64. LSE BA86. Ripon Coll Cuddesdon BA91 MA97. **d** 92 **p** 93. C Cirencester *Glouc* 92-98; Prec Ch Ch *Ox* 98-03; R Hackington *Cant* from 03. *The Rectory, St Stephen's Green, Canterbury CT2 7JU* Tel (01227) 765391 E-mail rector@ststephenscanterbury.net

LEWIS-GREGORY, Mrs Joycelyn. b 60. Qu Coll Birm. **d** 08 **p** 09. C Hall Green St Pet *Birm* from 08. *4 Etwall Road, Birmingham B28 0LE* Tel 0121-777 8547

LEWIS-JENKINS, Christopher Robin. b 50. St Mich Coll Llan 94. **d** 96 **p** 97. C Barry All SS *Llan* 96-01; V Dinas and Penygraig w Williamstown from 01; AD Rhondda from 06. *The Vicarage, 1 Llanfair Road, Penygraig, Tonypandy CF40 1TA* Tel (01443) 423364

LEWIS LLOYD, Canon Timothy David. b 37. Clare Coll Cam BA58 MA62. Cuddesdon Coll 58. **d** 60 **p** 61. C Stepney St Dunstan and All SS *Lon* 60-64; C St Alb Abbey 64-67; Prec St Alb Abbey 67-69; V St Paul's Walden 69-78; V Braughing w Furneux Pelham and Stocking Pelham 78-79; P-in-c Lt Hadham 78-79; V Braughing, Lt Hadham, Albury, Furneux Pelham etc 79-82; V Cheshunt 82-95; RD Cheshunt 89-94; Hon Can St Alb 94-01; V Sawbridgeworth 95-01; rtd 01. *c/o M Lewis Lloyd Esq, 219C Goldhawk Road, London W12 8ER* Tel (020) 8576 6122

LEWISHAM AND GREENWICH, Archdeacon of. *See* HARDMAN, The Ven Christine Elizabeth

LEWORTHY, Graham Llewelyn. b 47. Reading Univ BA69. S Dios Minl Tr Scheme 91. **d 94 p** 95. C Sark *Win* 94-11; rtd 11. *Carrefour, Route De Cobo, Castel, Guernsey GY5 7UH* Tel (01481) 256081

LEYDEN, Michael John. b 85. St Pet Coll Ox MA07 MSt08. St Jo Coll Nottm 08. **d** 11. C Rainhill *Liv* from 11. *26 Calder Drive, Rainhill, Prescot L35 0NW* Tel 07771-923672 (mobile) E-mail michael.leyden@spc.oxon.org

LEYLAND, Derek James. b 34. Lon Univ BSc55. Qu Coll Birm 58. **d 60 p** 61. C Ashton-on-Ribble St Andr *Blackb* 60-63; V 80-87; C Salesbury 63-65; V Preston St Oswald 65-67; V Pendleton 67-74; Dioc Youth Chapl 67-69; Ind Youth Chapl 70-74; R Brindle 74-80; V Garstang St Helen Churchtown 87-94; Sec SOSc 90-94; rtd 94; Perm to Offic *Blackb* from 94. *Greystocks, Goosnargh Lane, Goosnargh, Preston PR3 2BP* Tel (01772) 865682

LEYLAND, Stephen Robert. b 63. Portsm Poly BSc84. St Seiriol Cen 07. **d** 11. C Llandegfan w Llandysilio *Ban* from 11. *18 Coed-y-Castell, Bangor LL57 1PH* Tel (01248) 521156 E-mail curate.steve@gmail.com

LEYLAND, Tyrone John. b 49. Aston Univ BSc68. St Jo Coll Nottm 89. **d 91 p** 92. C Lich St Mary w St Mich 91-94; TV Willenhall H Trin 94-99; P-in-c The Ridwares and Kings Bromley 99-08; R from 08. *The Rectory, Alrewas Road, Kings Bromley, Burton-on-Trent DE13 7HP* Tel and fax (01543) 472932 E-mail t.leyland@btinternet.com

LEYSHON, Philip Alan. b 76. Glam Univ BA. Ripon Coll Cuddesdon BTh03. **d 03 p** 04. C Newton Nottage *Llan* 03-07; C Caerphilly 07-09; V Tonypandy w Clydach Vale from 09. *The Vicarage, Richards Terrace, Tonypandy CF40 2LD* Tel (01443) 423037

LEYSHON, Simon. b 63. Trin Coll Carmarthen BA86 Southn Univ BTh89. Sarum & Wells Th Coll. **d 89 p** 90. C Tenby *St D* 89-92; TV 92-96; Chapl and Hd RS Llandovery Coll 96-02; Chapl Ld Wandsworth Coll Basingstoke from 02. *Kimbers, Lord Wandsworth College, Long Sutton, Hook, Basingstoke RG29 1TB* Tel (01256) 862206 E-mail simonleyshon@hotmail.com

LIBBY, Canon John Ralph. b 55. Trin Coll Cam BA83. Ridley Hall Cam 89. **d 91 p** 92. C Enfield St Andr *Lon* 91-93; C Northwood Em 93-96; V Denton Holme *Carl* from 96; RD Carl 04-10; Hon Can Carl Cathl from 08. *St James's Vicarage, Goschen Road, Carlisle CA2 5PF* Tel (01228) 515639 *or* 810616 Fax 524569 E-mail john.libby@btinternet.com

LICHFIELD, Archdeacon of. *See* LILEY, The Ven Christopher Frank

LICHFIELD, Bishop of. *See* GLEDHILL, The Rt Revd Jonathan Michael

LICHFIELD, Dean of. *See* DORBER, The Very Revd Adrian John

LICHTENBERGER, Miss Ruth Eileen. b 34. NY Th Sem 64 NOC 95. **d 96 p** 97. NSM Warrington H Trin *Liv* 96-05; rtd 05. *8 Towers Court, Warrington WA5 0AH* Tel (01925) 656763

LICKESS, Canon David Frederick. b 37. St Chad's Coll Dur BA63. **d 65 p** 66. C Howden *York* 65-70; V Rudby in Cleveland w Middleton 70-07; Can and Preb York Minster 90-07; RD Stokesley 93-00; rtd 07; Perm to Offic *York* from 07. *Bridge House, Snape, Bedale DL8 2SZ* Tel (01677) 470077 E-mail davidlickess@gmail.com

LIDDELL, Mark. b 55. Birm Univ BA00. Coll of Resurr Mirfield 96. **d 98 p** 99. C Wednesbury St Jas and St Jo *Lich* 98-00; C Walsall St Andr 00-01; P-in-c 01-05; V 06-08; V Nuneaton St Mary *Cov* from 08. *St Mary's Abbey Vicarage, 99 Bottrill Street, Nuneaton CV11 5JB* Tel (024) 7638 2936

LIDDELL, Canon Peter Gregory. b 40. St Andr Univ MA63 Linacre Ho Ox BA65 MA70 Andover Newton Th Sch DMin75. Ripon Hall Ox 63. **d 65 p** 66. C Bp's Hatfield *St Alb* 65-71; USA 71-76; P-in-c Kimpton w Ayot St Lawrence *St Alb* 77-83; Dir of Past Counselling 80-05; Hon Can St Alb 99-05; rtd 05. *12 Old Hall Court, Horn Hill, Whitwell, Hitchin SG4 8AS* Tel (01438) 832266 E-mail petermary.liddell@btinternet.com

LIDDELOW, Peter William. b 33. Oak Hill NSM Course. **d** 82 **p** 83. NSM Finchley Ch Ch *Lon* 82-84; NSM S Mimms Ch Ch from 84; Perm to Offic *St Alb* from 09; Chapl Magic Circle from 02. *23 King's Road, Barnet EN5 4EF* Tel (020) 8441 2968 E-mail chaplain@themagiccircle.co.uk

LIDDLE, George. b 48. NEOC 88. **d 90 p** 91. C Auckland St Andr and St Anne *Dur* 90-92; C Crook 92-94; C Stanley 92-94; P-in-c Evenwood 94-96; V 96-03; R Blackhall, Castle Eden and Monkhesleden from 03. *The Rectory, The Crescent, Blackhall Colliery, Hartlepool TS27 4LE* Tel 0191-586 4202

LIDDLE, Harry. b 36. Wadh Coll Ox BA57 MA61. Wycliffe Hall Ox 62. **d 64 p** 65. C Withington St Paul *Man* 64-68; R Broughton St Jo 68-73; V Balby *Sheff* 73-82; R Firbeck w Letwell 82-94; V Woodsetts 82-94; TV Aston cum Aughton w Swallownest, Todwick etc 94-01; rtd 01; Perm to Offic *Sheff* from 01. *30 Meadow Grove Road, Totley, Sheffield S17 4FF* Tel 0114-236 4941

LIDDLE, Stephen John. b 60. St Jo Coll Ox BA81 PGCE82. Linc Th Coll 88. **d 91 p** 92. C Morpeth *Newc* 91-95; P-in-c Byker St Mich w St Lawr 95-98; R Bothal and Pegswood w Longhirst 98-05; P-in-c Billingham St Aid *Dur* 05-10. *Address temp unknown*

LIDSTONE, Vernon Henry. b 43. SWMTC 89. **d 92 p** 93. NSM Bovey Tracey SS Pet, Paul and Thos w Hennock *Ex* 92-94; Sub-Chapl HM Pris Channings Wood 92-96; Asst Dioc Chr Stewardship Adv 92-93; Dioc Chr Stewardship Adv 93-96; Dioc Officer for Par Development *Glouc* 96-97; Chapl HM Pris Leyhill 97-03; rtd 03. *The Pike House, Saul, Gloucester GL2 7JD* Tel (01452) 741410 E-mail vernon@lidstone.net

LIDWILL, Canon Mark Robert. b 57. CITC. **d 87 p** 88. C Annagh w Drumgoon, Ashfield etc *K, E & A* 87-90; I Urney w Denn and Derryheen from 90; Dioc Youth Adv from 92; Preb Kilmore Cathl from 98. *The Rectory, Keadue Lane, Cavan, Co Cavan, Republic of Ireland* Tel (00353) (49) 436 1016

LIEVESLEY, Mrs Joy Margaret. b 48. Lady Mabel Coll CertEd69. Guildf Dioc Min Course 98. **d 00 p** 01. NSM Farnham *Guildf* from 00. *3 Kingfisher Close, Church Crookham, Fleet GU52 6JP* Tel (01252) 690223 E-mail joy.lievesley@ntlworld.com

LIGHT, Mrs Madeline Margaret. b 54. Girton Coll Cam BA77 MA80 Lon Inst of Educn PGCE78. EAMTC 96. **d 99 p** 00. C Eaton *Nor* 99-02; P-in-c Nor St Helen 02-09; Chapl Gt Hosp Nor 02-09; P-in-c Nor St Stephen from 09. *86 Grove Walk, Norwich NR1 2QH* Tel (01603) 219927 E-mail madelinelight@gmail.com

LIGHT, Mrs Penelope Ann. b 46. Madeley Coll of Educn TCert71 N Lon Poly BEd81. WEMTC 06. **d 09 p** 10. NSM Cirencester *Glouc* from 09. *Toad Cottage, 22 Bingham Close, Cirencester GL7 1HJ* Tel (01285) 640125 E-mail jonpen22@tiscali.co.uk

LIGHTFOOT, The Very Revd Vernon Keith. b 34. St Jo Coll Dur BA58. Ripon Hall Ox 58. **d 60 p** 61. C Rainhill *Liv* 60-62; C Liv Our Lady and St Nic 62-65; V Stanley 65-75; Chapl St Edm Coll Liv 66-68; Chapl Rathbone Hosp Liv 70-75; V Mt Albert St Luke New Zealand 75-85; Dean Waikato 85-97; rtd 98. *16C Acacia Crescent, Hamilton 3206, New Zealand* Tel and fax (0064) (7) 843 1381 E-mail keith.jennie@xtra.co.nz

LIGHTOWLER, Joseph Trevor. b 33. **d 79 p** 80. Hon C Leverstock Green *St Alb* 79-80; Hon C Chambersbury 80-84; C Woodmansterne *S'wark* 84-88; R Odell and Pavenham *St Alb* 88-97; rtd 97; Perm to Offic *St Alb* from 97. *18 The Dell, Sandpit Lane, St Albans AL1 4HE* Tel (01727) 833422

LILBURN, Robert Irvine Terence. b 47. CITC 07. **d** 10. NSM Kilternan *D & G* from 10. *13 Churchfields, Dundrum Road, Milltown, Dublin 14, Republic of Ireland* Tel (00353) (1) 260 0003 Mobile 86-886 5361 E-mail terrylilburn@gmail.com

LILES, Malcolm David. b 48. Nottm Univ BA69. St Steph Ho Ox 69. **d** 71 **p** 72. C Corby Epiphany w St Jo *Pet* 71-74; C New Cleethorpes *Linc* 74-76; TV Lt Coates 76-77; TV Gt and Lt Coates w Bradley 78-82; Soc Resp Sec 82-93; Hon C Gt Grimsby St Mary and St Jas 82-93; P-in-c Grimsby All SS 88-93; TV Dronfield w Holmesfield *Derby* 93-98; TR Crawley *Chich* from 98. *The Rectory, 1 Southgate Road, Crawley RH10 6BL* Tel (01293) 535856 *or* 520421 E-mail rectorcrawley@btinternet.com

LILEY, The Ven Christopher Frank. b 47. Nottm Univ BEd70. Linc Th Coll 72. **d 74 p** 75. C Kingswinford H Trin *Lich* 74-79; TV Stafford 79-84; V Norton *St Alb* 84-96; RD Hitchin 89-94; P-in-c Shrewsbury St Chad w St Mary *Lich* 96-01; P-in-c Shrewsbury St Alkmund 96-01; Adn Lich from 01; Can Res and Treas Lich Cathl from 01. *24 The Close, Lichfield WS13 7LD* Tel (01543) 306145 Fax 306147 E-mail archdeacon.lichfield@lichfield.anglican.org

LILEY, Peter James. b 60. Liv Univ BA82 Westmr Coll Ox PGCE83. Oak Hill Th Coll 91. **d 93 p** 94. C Exning St Martin w Landwade *St E* 93-96; V Acton w Gt Waldingfield 96-00; TV Bottesford w Ashby *Linc* 00-05; TR from 05. *The Vicarage, 10 Old School Lane, Bottesford, Scunthorpe DN16 3RD* Tel (01724) 867256 *or* 842732 E-mail peter.liley@ntlworld.com

LILEY, Stephen John. b 65. Liv Univ BA87 MMus88 ARCM93. Wycliffe Hall Ox 97. **d 99 p** 00. C Throop *Win* 99-03; V Clapham *St Alb* from 03; RD Elstow from 08. *The Vicarage, Green Lane, Clapham, Bedford MK41 6ER* Tel (01234) 352814 E-mail the.lileys@talkgateway.net

LILLEY, Canon Christopher Howard. b 51. FCA75 FTII83. LNSM course 83 St Jo Coll Nottm 91. **d 85 p** 86. OLM Skegness and Winthorpe *Linc* 85-93; C Limber Magna w Brocklesby 93-96; Perm to Offic *S'well* 93-96; P-in-c Middle Rasen Gp *Linc* 96-97; R 97-02; V Scawby, Redbourne and Hibaldstow 02-10; P-in-c Bishop Norton, Wadingham and Snitterby 06-10; P-in-c Kirton in Lindsey w Manton 06-10; RD Yarborough 02-09; Hon C Mablethorpe w Trusthorpe from 10; Hon C Sutton, Huttoft and Anderby from 10; Can and Preb Linc Cathl from 05. *The Chrysalis, 12 Hillside Avenue, Sutton-on-Sea, Mablethorpe LN12 2JH* Tel (01507) 440039 E-mail c.lilley@btinternet.com

LILLEY, Ivan Ray. b 32. Bps' Coll Cheshunt 58. **d** 61 **p** 62. C Kettering SS Pet and Paul 61-64; C Gt Yarmouth *Nor* 64-75; P-in-c Tottenhill w Wormegay *Ely* 76-83; P-in-c Watlington 76-83; P-in-c Holme Runcton w S Runcton and Wallington 76-83; V Tysoe w Oxhill and Whatcote *Cov* 83-86; C Langold *S'well* 87-91; P-in-c 91-98; rtd 98; Perm to Offic *Nor* from 98. *Linden Lea, 41 Cedar Drive, Attleborough NR17 2EY* Tel and fax (01953) 452710

LILLEY, Thomas Robert. b 84. UEA BA05 PGCE06 Fitzw Coll Cam BTh11. Westcott Ho Cam 08. **d** 11. C Attleborough w Besthorpe *Nor* from 11. *39 Cedar Drive, Attleborough NR17 2EX* Tel 07984-181919 (mobile) E-mail tom.lilley@gmail.com

LILLIAN, Mother. *See* MORRIS, Lillian Rosina

LILLICRAP, Peter Andrew. b 65. Hatf Poly BEng87 CEng93 MIMechE93. Trin Coll Bris 00. **d** 02 **p** 03. C Kineton *Cov* 02-04; C Napton-on-the-Hill, Lower Shuckburgh etc 04-07; V Acton and Worleston, Church Minshull etc *Ches* from 07. *St Mary's Vicarage, Chester Road, Acton, Nantwich CW5 8LG* Tel (01270) 628864 E-mail revlills@homecall.co.uk

LILLICRAP, Stephen Hunter. b 58. Newc Univ MB, BS81 MRCGP85. SEITE 00. **d** 03 **p** 04. C Wye w Brook and Hastingleigh etc *Cant* 03-08; C Stone Street Gp 06-08; C Mersham w Hinxhill and Sellindge 08; P-in-c Teynham w Lynsted and Kingsdown from 08; P-in-c Norton from 08. *The Vicarage, 76 Station Road, Teynham, Sittingbourne ME9 9SN* Tel (01795) 522510 Mobile 07971-224094 E-mail steve.lillicrap@btopenworld.com

LILLIE, Judith Virginia. *See* THOMPSON, Mrs Judith Virginia

LILLIE, Mrs Shona Lorimer. b 49. St Jo Coll Nottm BA03. **d** 03 **p** 04. C Bishopbriggs *Glas* 03-06; Dioc Supernumerary 06-07; Assoc P Glas St Mary 07-09; R Cambuslang from 09; R Uddingston from 09. *5 Brownside Road, Cambuslang G72 8NL* E-mail shonalillie@hotmail.com

LILLINGTON (née POLLIT), Mrs Ruth Mary. b 65. SS Paul & Mary Coll Cheltenham BA88. St Jo Coll Nottm 88. **d** 90 **p** 94. Par Dn Caverswall *Lich* 90-92; Par Dn Caverswall and Weston Coyney w Dilhorne 92-93; Par Dn Luton St Mary *St Alb* 93-94; C 94-97; Chapl Luton Univ 93-97. *20 Harcourt Road, Bracknell RG12 7JD* Tel (01344) 423025

LILLISTONE, Canon Brian David. b 38. SS Coll Cam BA61 MA65. St Steph Ho Ox 61. **d** 63 **p** 64. C Ipswich All Hallows *St E* 63-66; C Stokesay *Heref* 66-71; P-in-c Lyonshall w Titley 71-76; R Martlesham w Brightwell *St E* 76-03; Hon Can St E Cathl 98-03; rtd 03; Perm to Offic *St E* from 03. *23 Woodland Close, Risby, Bury St Edmunds IP28 6QN* Tel (01284) 811330 E-mail canon.b.lillistone@onetel.net

LIMBERT, Kenneth Edward. b 25. CEng69 MIMechE. S'wark Ord Course 72. **d** 75 **p** 76. NSM Northwood Hills St Edm *Lon* 75-90; Perm to Offic from 90. *55 York Road, Northwood HA6 1JJ* Tel (01923) 825791

LIMBRICK, Gordon. b 36. Open Univ BA88. St Jo Coll Nottm. **d** 87 **p** 91. Hon C Troon *Glas* 87-90; Hon C Yaxley *Ely* 90-97; Hon C Yaxley and Holme w Conington 97-04; rtd 04; Perm to Offic *Pet* from 98 and *Ely* from 04. *271 Broadway, Yaxley, Peterborough PE7 3NR* Tel (01733) 243170 E-mail moandgol@ntlworld.com

LIMERICK AND ARDFERT, Dean of. *Vacant*

LIMERICK, ARDFERT AND AGHADOE, Archdeacon of. *See* WARREN, The Ven Robert

LIMERICK, ARDFERT, AGHADOE, KILLALOE, KILFENORA, CLONFERT, KILMACDUAGH AND EMLY, Bishop of. *See* WILLIAMS, The Rt Revd Trevo

LINAKER, David Julian John Ramage. b 65. Ripon Coll Cuddesdon BTh95. **d** 95 **p** 96. C Colehill *Sarum* 95-99; V Mere w W Knoyle and Maiden Bradley 99-06; P-in-c Salisbury St Thos and St Edm from 06; RD Salisbury from 07. *Little Bower, Campbell Road, Salisbury SP1 3BG* Tel (01722) 504462 *or* 322537 E-mail david.linaker@ntlworld.com

LINCOLN, Archdeacon of. *See* BARKER, The Ven Timothy Reed

LINCOLN, Bishop of. *See* LOWSON, The Rt Revd Christopher

LINCOLN, Dean of. *See* BUCKLER, The Very Revd Philip John Warr

LIND-JACKSON, Peter Wilfrid. b 35. Leeds Univ BA67. Linc Th Coll 67. **d** 68 **p** 69. C Heref St Martin 68-71; P-in-c Burghill 71-78; V 78-82; V Barnard Castle *Dur* 82-83; P-in-c Whorlton 82-83; V Barnard Castle w Whorlton 83-00; rtd 00; Perm to Offic *Ripon* from 03. *5 Gill Lane, Barnard Castle DL12 9AS* Tel (01833) 630027 E-mail lindjacksons@googlemail.com

LINDARS, Frank. b 23. Wycliffe Hall Ox 54. **d** 56 **p** 57. C Beeston Hill St Luke *Ripon* 56-59; C Harrogate St Wilfrid 59-61; V Shadwell 61-80; RD Allerton 73-78; V Masham and Healey 80-88; rtd 88; Perm to Offic *Ripon* from 88. *Hope Cottage, Reeth, Richmond DL11 6SF* Tel (01748) 884685

LINDECK, Peter Stephen. b 31. Oak Hill Th Coll 57. **d** 59 **p** 60. C Homerton St Luke *Lon* 59-62; C Salterhebble All SS *Wakef* 62-63; C Islington St Andr w St Thos and St Matthias *Lon* 64-67; Perm to Offic *Derby* and *St Alb* 67-68; V Toxteth Park

St Bede *Liv* 68-74; V Kano St Geo Nigeria 74-76; C Netherton *Liv* 76-77; C Ollerton and Boughton *S'well* 77-80; V Whitgift w Adlingfleet and Eastoft *Sheff* 80-86; P-in-c Swinefleet 81-86; V Kilnhurst 86-94; Chapl Montagu Hosp Mexborough 86-94; rtd 94; Perm to Offic *Sheff* 94-06. *1 Stuart Court, High Street, Kibworth, Leicester LE8 0LR* Tel 0116-279 6347 E-mail peter@lindeck.freeserve.co.uk

LINDISFARNE, Archdeacon of. *See* ROBINSON, The Ven Peter John Alan

LINDLEY (née FLYNN), Mrs Anna Therese. b 42. Leeds Univ BSc63 Surrey Univ MPhil72 Westmr Coll Ox DipEd64. Yorks Min Course 08. **d** 09 **p** 11. NSM York St Mich-le-Belfrey from 09. *35 Manor Garth, Wigginton, York YO32 2WZ*

LINDLEY, Graham William. b 47. CIPFA77. **d** 97 **p** 98. OLM E Crompton *Man* 97-02; NSM Newhey 02-08; P-in-c from 08; P-in-c Belfield from 09. *37 Jordan Avenue, Shaw, Oldham OL2 8DQ* Tel (01706) 845677 E-mail g.lindley7@ntlworld.com

LINDLEY, Harold Thomas. b 28. St Jo Coll Ox BA51 MA73. Wells Th Coll 51. **d** 53 **p** 54. C Normanton *Wakef* 53-57; C-in-c Rawthorpe CD 57-63; P-in-c Longstone *Derby* 63-67; V 68-74; P-in-c Barrow w Twyford 74-84; V Barrow-on-Trent w Twyford and Swarkestone 84-93; rtd 93. *Gorwel, 35 Nant Bychan, Moelfre LL72 8HE* Tel (01248) 410484

LINDLEY, Canon Richard Adrian. b 44. Hull Univ BA65 Man Univ MA79. Cuddesdon Coll 66. **d** 68 **p** 69. C Ingrow w Hainworth *Bradf* 68-70; Perm to Offic *Birm* 70-74; TV Ellesmere Port *Ches* 74-79; V Westborough *Guildf* 79-80; TR 80-84; Dir of Educn *Birm* 84-96; Hon Can Birm Cathl 96; Dir of Educn *Win* 96-04; Hon Can Win Cathl 03-04; Perm to Offic from 04. *28 Denham Close, Winchester SO23 7BL* Tel (01962) 621851 Mobile 07743-758639 E-mail lindleyrs@ntlworld.com

LINDOP, Andrew John. b 57. Cam Univ MA. Cranmer Hall Dur 80. **d** 82 **p** 83. C Brinsworth w Catcliffe *Sheff* 82-85; C S Shoebury *Chelmsf* 85-89; V Mosley Common *Man* 89-99; V Astley Bridge 99-11; AD Walmsley 02-10; TR Ramsbottom and Edenfield from 11. *St Andrew's Vicarage, 2 Henwick Hall Avenue, Ramsbottom, Bury BL0 9YH* Tel and fax (01706) 826482 E-mail andylindop95@tiscali.co.uk

LINDOP, Canon Kenneth. b 45. Linc Th Coll 71. **d** 74 **p** 75. C Leic St Phil 74-77; C Cov H Trin 77-80; P-in-c Cubbington 80-82; V 82-07; RD Warwick and Leamington 91-96; Jt P-in-c Leamington Spa H Trin and Old Milverton 03-07; Hon Can Cov Cathl 04-07; rtd 07. *2 Grove House, Blue Anchor, Minehead TA24 6JU* Tel (01643) 821940 E-mail rev.lindop@btinternet.com

LINDSAY, Alan. *See* LINDSAY, Canon Richard John Alan

LINDSAY, Alexandra Jane (Sandra). b 43. CITC 90. **d** 93 **p** 94. Lic to Offic *K, E & A* 93-94; Aux Min Bailieborough w Knockbride, Shercock and Mullagh 94-05; Aux Min Roscommon w Donamon, Rathcline, Kilkeevin etc from 05. *Clementstown House, Cootehill, Co Cavan, Republic of Ireland* Tel and fax (00353) (49) 555 2207

LINDSAY, Anne. *See* LINDSAY, Mrs Mary Jane Anne

LINDSAY, Anthony. b 38. Trin Coll Bris 92. **d** 89 **p** 90. CMS 76-92; Dioc Admin Bo Sierra Leone 89-92; C Rainham w Wennington *Chelmsf* 93-96; R Quendon w Rickling and Wicken Bonhunt etc 96-03; rtd 03; Perm to Offic *York* 03-07 and from 10; P-in-c Langtoft w Foxholes, Butterwick, Cottam etc 07-10. *17 Hall Garth, Pickering YO18 7AW* Tel (01751) 476849 E-mail tonyandpamlindsay@yahoo.co.uk

LINDSAY, Ashley. *See* LINDSAY, Robert Ashley Charles

LINDSAY, Calum Oran. b 73. Edin Univ BEng97. Ridley Hall Cam 09. **d** 11. C St Margaret's-on-Thames *Lon* from 11. *25 Brantwood Avenue, Isleworth TW7 9EX* Tel (020) 8891 6820 Mobile 07773-392542 E-mail revcalumlindsay@gmail.com

LINDSAY, David Macintyre. b 46. Trin Hall Cam BA68 MA72. Cuddesdon Coll 68. **d** 71 **p** 72. C Gosforth All SS *Newc* 71-74; C Keele *Lich* 74-78; Perm to Offic *St E* 79-80; Chapl Haberdashers' Aske's Sch Elstree 80-06; rtd 06; Perm to Offic *St Alb* 06-07 and *Portsm* from 07; Co-ord Reader Tr *Portsm* from 10. *Kentmere, Ashling Close, Waterlooville PO7 6NQ* Tel (023) 9225 7662 Mobile 07769-814165 E-mail lindsay d46@hotmail.com

LINDSAY, Eric Graham. b 30. Witwatersrand Univ BA51 Lon Univ MA80 DipAdEd78. Coll of Resurr Mirfield 55. **d** 57 **p** 59. C Stella *Dur* 57-58; C W Hartlepool St Aid 58-60; C St Geo Grenada 60-61; Perm to Offic *Win* 61-65; *Roch* 65-72; and *Chelmsf* 72-84; C Stepney St Dunstan and All SS *Lon* 84-85; P-in-c Stepney St Dunstan LEP 84-85; R Bridge of Weir *Glas* 85-98; R Kilmacolm 85-98. *1 Woodrow Court, 26-32 Port Glasgow Road, Kilmacolm PA13 4QA* Tel (01505) 874668

LINDSAY, Canon John Carruthers. b 50. Edin Univ MA72 BD82. Edin Th Coll 79. **d** 82 **p** 83. C Broughty Ferry *Bre* 82-84; C Edin St Hilda 84-85; TP 85-88; C Edin St Fillan 84-85; TP 85-88; R N Berwick from 88; R Gullane from 88; Can St Mary's Cathl from 00. *The Rectory, 2 May Terrace, North Berwick EH39 4BA* Tel (01620) 892154 Mobile 07977-520277 E-mail johnlindsay@bigfoot.com

LINDSAY (née CLEALL), Mrs Mary Jane Anne. b 54. Keele Univ BA77 Herts Univ PGCE92. SAOMC 00. **d** 03 **p** 04. C

Chipping Barnet *St Alb* 03-07; Chapl Portsm Hosps NHS Trust from 07. *Kentmere, Ashling Close, Waterlooville PO7 6NQ* Tel (023) 9225 7662 *or* 9228 6000 Mobile 07769-814166 E-mail anne.lindsay@porthosp.nhs.uk

LINDSAY, Richard John. b 46. Sarum & Wells Th Coll 74. **d** 78 **p** 79. C Aldwick *Chich* 78-81; C Almondbury w Farnley Tyas *Wakef* 81-84; V Mossley *Man* from 84. *The Vicarage, Stamford Street, Mossley, Ashton-under-Lyne OL5 0LP* Tel (01457) 832219

LINDSAY, Canon Richard John **Alan.** b 24. TCD BA46 BD52. **d** 49 **p** 50. C Denton Holme *Carl* 49-52; CMS Burundi 52-64; Chapl and Tutor CMS Tr Coll Chislehurst 65-68; R Chich St Pancras and St Jo 68-74; Chapl Maisons-Laffitte *Eur* 74-82; Can Brussels Cathl 81-88; Chapl The Hague w Leiden and Voorschoten 82-89; rtd 89; Perm to Offic *Heref* 88-01; *Portsm* from 01; *Guildf* from 03. *Flat 24, Moormead, Tilford Road, Hindhead GU26 6RA* Tel (01428) 601524

LINDSAY, Canon Robert. b 16. St Jo Coll Dur BA37 MA40. **d** 39 **p** 40. C Gateshead St Mary *Dur* 39-43; P-in-c Sacriston 43-45; P-in-c Benfieldside 45-46; V Lanercost w Kirkcambeck *Carl* 46-55; V Hawkshead and Low Wray 55-70; R Dean 70-74; RD Derwent 70-81; Hon Can Carl Cathl 72-81; V Loweswater w Buttermere 74-81; rtd 81; Perm to Offic *Ex* from 81. *58 Primley Road, Sidmouth EX10 9LF* Tel (01395) 577882

LINDSAY, Robert Andrew Duquemin. b 58. St Mich Coll Llan. **d** 09 **p** 10. C Blaenavon w Capel Newydd *Mon* from 09. *The Vicarage, Vicarage Lane, Abersychan, Pontypool NP4 8PX* Tel (01495) 772213

LINDSAY, Robert **Ashley** **Charles.** b 43. Leeds Univ BA66 Ex Univ BPhil81. Coll of Resurr Mirfield 66. **d** 68 **p** 69. C Mill Hill Jo Keble *Ch Lon* 68-72; C Sherborne w Castleton and Lillington *Sarum* 73-78; Chapl Coldharbour Hosp Dorset 73-78; Perm to Offic *Leic* 87-92; rtd 08. *Breezedown Cottage, East Melbury, Shaftesbury SP7 0DS* Tel (01747) 850145

LINDSAY, Sandra. See LINDSAY, Alexandra Jane

LINDSAY-PARKINSON, Michael. b 28. Edin Th Coll 66. **d** 67 **p** 68. C Edin Ch Ch 67-70; C Helensburgh *Glas* 70-72; R Lockerbie 72-83; R Annan 72-83; S Africa 83-88; V Alsager St Mary *Ches* 88-93; rtd 93; Perm to Offic *Ches* 93-98. *10 Cherry Tree Avenue, Church Lawton, Stoke-on-Trent ST7 3EL* Tel (01270) 875574

LINDSAY-SMITH, Kevin Roy. b 55. **d** 05 **p** 06. OLM Glascote and Stonydelph *Lich* from 05. *34 Castlehall, Tamworth B77 2EJ* Tel (01827) 251557 E-mail lindsay-smith1@sky.com

LINDSEY, Anna Elizabeth. b 65. Cuddesdon Coll 95. **d** 97 **p** 98. C Limpsfield and Titsey *S'wark* 97-00; C Warlingham w Chelsham and Farleigh 00-03; TV 03-06; rtd 06. *23 Omana, Milford, Auckland 0620, New Zealand* E-mail anna@heffs.demon.co.uk

LINDSEY, Archdeacon of. See SINCLAIR, The Ven Jane Elizabeth Margaret

LINES, Canon Andrew John. b 60. Univ Coll Dur BA82. All Nations Chr Coll 88. **d** 97 **p** 98. Paraguay 91-99; Dir Caleb Bible Cen 91-99; SAMS 97-00; Miss Dir/Chief Exec Officer Crosslinks from 00; Hon Can Paraguay from 00. *59 Woodside Road, New Malden KT3 3AW* Tel (020) 8942 2179 *or* 8691 6111 Fax 8694 8023 E-mail alines@crosslinks.org

LINES, Graham Martin. b 55. St Jo Coll Nottm 97. **d** 99 **p** 00. C Crosby *Linc* 99-02; C Bottesford w Ashby 02-03; TV from 03. *The Rectory, St Paul's Road, Ashby, Scunthorpe DN16 3DL* Tel (01724) 842083 E-mail graham@ml47.sflife.co.uk

LINES, Nicholas David John. b 64. St Jo Coll Nottm 94. **d** 96 **p** 97. C Burton All SS w Ch Ch *Lich* 96-01; P-in-c Rodbourne Cheney *Bris* 01-02; R from 02. *St Mary's Rectory, 298 Cheney Manor Road, Swindon SN2 2PF* Tel (01793) 522379 E-mail nick.lines1@gmail.com

LINFORD, Preb John Kenneth. b 31. Liv Univ BA52. Chich Th Coll 54. **d** 56 **p** 57. C Stoke upon Trent *Lich* 56-61; V Tunstall Ch Ch 61-70; V Sedgley All SS 70-78; Chapl Chase Hosp Cannock 78-91; TR Cannock *Lich* 78-91; V Hatherton 80-91; Preb Lich Cathl 88-98; rtd 91; Perm to Offic *Lich* 91-00. *16 School Lane, Hill Ridware, Rugeley WS15 3QN* Tel (01543) 492831

LING, Adrian Roger. b 66. Goldsmiths' Coll Lon BA89 Leeds Univ BA02. Coll of Resurr Mirfield 00. **d** 02 **p** 03. C Mill End and Heronsgate w W Hyde *St Alb* 02-06; P-in-c Flegg Coastal Benefice *Nor* 06-08; R from 08. *The Rectory, Somerton Road, Winterton-on-Sea, Great Yarmouth NR29 4AW* Tel (01493) 393227 E-mail adrianrling@btinternet.com

LING, Andrew Joyner. b 35. ACP69 St Luke's Coll Ex TCert63 Open Univ BA80. SWMTC 83. **d** 86 **p** 87. NSM St Dominic, Landulph and St Mellion w Pillaton *Truro* 86-90; C Saltash 90-94; TV 94-97; Chapl Montreux w Gstaad *Eur* 98-03; rtd 03. *Martinets, chemin des Martinets 7, 1872 Troistorrents, Switzerland* Tel (0041) (24) 477 2408

LING, Rebecca (Jordan). b 75. Leic Univ BSc00. St Jo Coll Nottm 04. **d** 08 **p** 09. C Leic St Chris from 08. *20 The Fairway, Leicester LE2 6LN* E-mail jordanling@ntlworld.com

LING, Timothy Charles. b 61. Ex Univ BA85 Selw Coll Cam BA91. Ridley Hall Cam 89. **d** 92 **p** 93. C Gerrards Cross and

Fulmer *Ox* 92-96; C Woking St Pet *Guildf* 96-00; V Bathford *B & W* 00-09. *Address temp unknown* E-mail tim.ling@whsmithnet.co.uk

LINGARD, Colin. b 36. Kelham Th Coll 58. **d** 63 **p** 64. C Middlesbrough St Martin *York* 63-66; C Stainton-in-Cleveland 66-71; V Eskdaleside w Ugglebarnby 71-77; P-in-c Redcar w Kirkleatham 77; V Kirkleatham 78-86; RD Guisborough 83-86; V Linc St Botolph 86-89; Dioc Dir of Readers 86-89; R Washington *Dur* 89-93; P-in-c Middleton St George 93-97; R 97-01; Chapl Teesside Airport from 97; rtd 01. *29 Belgrave Terrace, Hurworth Place, Darlington DL2 2DW* Tel 07752-179418 (mobile)

LINGARD, Jennifer Mary. See ALIDINA, Jennifer Mary

LINGARD, Keith **Patrick.** b 30. AKC53. **d** 54 **p** 55. C Bedford Park *Lon* 54-56; C Ruislip St Martin 56-58; C Kempston All SS *St Alb* 58-63; Metrop Area Sec UMCA 63-65; V S Farnborough *Guildf* 65-75; R Glaston w Bisbrooke *Pet* 75-76; R Morcott w Glaston and Bisbrooke 77-95; rtd 95. *13 Woodside East, Thurlby, Bourne PE10 0HT* Tel (01778) 425572

LINGS, Canon George William. b 49. Nottm Univ BTh74 Ox Univ PGCE75 Lambeth MLitt93 Man Univ PhD09. St Jo Coll Nottm 70. **d** 75 **p** 76. C Harold Wood *Chelmsf* 75-78; C Reigate St Mary *S'wark* 78-85; V Deal St Geo *Cant* 85-97; First Dir CA Sheff Cen for Ch Planting and Evang from 97; NSM Norfolk Park St Leonard CD *Sheff* 97-05; Hon Can Sheff Cathl from 11. *The Sheffield Centre, 50 Cavendish Street, Sheffield S3 7RZ* Tel 0114-272 7451 E-mail g.lings@churcharmy.org.uk

LINGWOOD, Preb David Peter. b 51. Lon Univ BEd73 Southn Univ BTh80. Sarum & Wells Th Coll 75. **d** 78 **p** 79. C Ashford St Hilda *Lon* 78-01; TV Redditch, The Ridge *Worc* 81-86; TR Blakenall Heath *Lich* 86-96; V Rushall 96-04; RD Walsall 98-03; TR Stoke-upon-Trent from 04; RD Stoke from 07; Preb Lich Cathl from 02. *Stoke Rectory, 172 Smithpool Road, Stoke-on-Trent ST4 4PP* Tel (01782) 747737 E-mail dp.lingwood@btinternet.com

LINKENS, Timothy Martin. b 67. Strathclyde Univ MEng90. Wycliffe Hall Ox BTh99. **d** 99 **p** 00. C Blackheath St Jo *S'wark* 99-03; V Kidbrooke St Nic from 03. *66A Whetstone Road, London SE3 8PZ* Tel (020) 8856 6317

LINN, Frederick Hugh. b 37. Em Coll Cam BA61 MA65. Ripon Hall Ox 61. **d** 63 **p** 64. C Bramhall *Ches* 63-68; V Liscard St Mary 68-71; V Liscard St Mary w St Columba 71-74; V Wybunbury 74-82; R Eccleston and Pulford 82-98; rtd 98; Perm to Offic *Ches* from 98. *4 Stonewalls, Rossett, Wrexham LL12 0LG* Tel (01244) 571942 *or* (01407) 810372

LINNEGAR, George Leonard. b 33. CGA. Kelham Th Coll 63. **d** 62 **p** 63. C Wellingborough St Mary *Pet* 62-65; Lic to Offic *Lich* 65-69; *B & W* 69-80; Hon C Lewes All SS, St Anne, St Mich and St Thos *Chich* 80-86; C 87-99; rtd 99; Perm to Offic *Chich* from 99. *20 Morris Road, Lewes BN7 2AT* Tel (01273) 478145

LINNEY, Barry James. b 64. Spurgeon's Coll BD97 Anglia Poly Univ MA02. Westcott Ho Cam 99. **d** 01 **p** 02. C Chingford SS Pet and Paul *Chelmsf* 01-04; V Cherry Hinton St Andr *Ely* from 04. *The Vicarage, 2 Fulbourn Old Drift, Cherry Hinton, Cambridge CB1 9NE* Tel (01223) 247740 E-mail standrews.cherryhinton@btinternet.com

LINNEY, Gordon Charles Scott. b 39. CITC 66. **d** 69 **p** 70. C Agherton *Conn* 69-72; Min Can Down Cathl 72-75; V Dublin St Cath w St Jas *D & G* 75-80; Preb Tipperkevin St Patr Cathl Dublin 77-80; I Glenageary *D & G* 80-04; Adn Dublin 88-04; Lect CITC 89-93; rtd 04. *208 Upper Glenageary Road, Glenageary, Co Dublin, Republic of Ireland* Tel (00353) (1) 284 8503 Mobile 87-254 1775 E-mail glinney@eircom.net

LINTERN, John. b 61. Linc Th Coll BTh93. **d** 93 **p** 94. C Preston on Tees *Dur* 93-96; Asst Dioc Youth Adv 96-99; P-in-c W Pelton 96-07; P-in-c Pelton 99-07; V Pelton and W Pelton from 07. *The Vicarage, West Pelton, Stanley DH9 6RT* Tel 0191-370 2146 Fax 07971-114359 E-mail john.lintern@durham.anglican.org

LINTERN, Robert George. **d** 10 **p** 11. OLM Codsall *Lich* from 10. *43 Castle Street, Oswestry SY11 1JZ* Tel (07971) 403157 E-mail lintern@gmail.com

LINTHICUM, James Douglas. b 58. Towson State Univ (USA) BSc81 Leeds Univ MA00. Wesley Th Sem Washington MDiv86. **d** 01 **p** 02. Chapl Barnet and Chase Farm Hosps NHS Trust 01-06; NSM Monken Hadley *Lon* 01-06; Sen Chapl Gt Ormond Street Hosp for Children NHS Trust from 06. *Great Ormond Street Hospital, Great Ormond Street, London WC1N 3JH* Tel (020) 7813 8232 Mobile 07921-140825 E-mail jlinth5481@aol.com

LINTON, Alan Ross. b 28. St Aid Birkenhead 57. **d** 60 **p** 61. C Blundellsands St Nic *Liv* 60-62; C Southport St Phil 62-63; C Aigburth 63-66; V Glazebury 66-67; C Formby St Pet 67-69; C Douglas *Blackb* 69-71; P-in-c Appley Bridge All SS CD 71-76; P-in-c Scorton and Calder Vale w Admarsh 76-85; R Hoole 85-93; rtd 93; Perm to Offic *Blackb* from 93. *12 Clive Road, Penwortham, Preston PR1 0AT* Tel (01772) 747513

LINTON, Mrs Angela Margaret. b 45. SAOMC 97. **d** 00 **p** 01. NSM Langtree *Ox* from 00. *10 Yew Tree Court, Goring, Reading RG8 9HF* Tel and fax (01491) 874236 Mobile 07884-346552

LINTON, Barry Ian. b 76. Glas Univ BSc98 TCD BTh04 MCIBS01. CITC 01. **d** 04 **p** 05. C Enniskillen *Clogh* 04-08; I Drumcliffe w Lissadell and Munninane *K, E & A* from 08. *The Rectory, Drumcliffe, Co Sligo, Republic of Ireland* Tel (00353) (71) 916 3125 E-mail drumcliffe@elphin.anglican.org

LINTON, Joseph Edmund. b 19. St Andr Univ MA46. Sarum Th Coll 46. **d** 48 **p** 49. C Monkseaton St Mary *Newc* 48-53; CF (TA) 50-54; C-in-c Lynemouth St Aid CD *Newc* 53-59; V Beltingham w Henshaw 59-93; rtd 93; Perm to Offic *Newc* from 93. *4 Dipton Close, Eastwood Grange, Hexham NE46 1UG* Tel (01434) 601457

LINTOTT, William Ince. b 36. St Cath Coll Cam BA58. Ely Th Coll 58. **d** 60 **p** 61. C Brighton St Wilfrid *Chich* 60-62; C Chingford SS Pet and Paul *Chelmsf* 62-66; Chapl Fulbourn Hosp Cam 66-73; Lic to Offic *Ely* 66-97; rtd 01. *7 Haverhill Road, Stapleford, Cambridge CB22 5BX* Tel (01223) 842008

LINZEY, Prof Andrew. b 52. K Coll Lon BD73 PhD86 AKC73 Lambeth DD01. St Aug Coll Cant 75. **d** 75 **p** 76. C Charlton-by-Dover SS Pet and Paul *Cant* 75-77; Chapl and Lect Th NE Surrey Coll of Tech 77-81; Chapl Essex Univ 81-92; Dir of Studies Cen for Study of Th 87-92; Sen Research Fell Mansf Coll Ox 92-00; Tutor Chr Ethics 93-00; Special Prof Th Nottm Univ 92-96; Special Prof St Xavier Univ Chicago from 96; Hon Prof Birm Univ 97-07; Sen Research Fell Blackfriars Hall Ox 00-06; Dir Ox Cen for Animal Ethics from 06; Hon Prof Win Univ from 07; Hon Res Fell St Steph Ho Ox from 08. *91 Iffley Road, Oxford OX4 1EG* Tel (01865) 201565 E-mail andrewlinzey@aol.com *or* director@oxfordanimalethics.com

LIONEL, Brother. See PEIRIS, Lionel James Harold

LIPP-NATHANIEL, Julie Christiane. b 41. Melbourne Univ BA63 MA72. **d** 95 **p** 95. Tutor United Coll of Ascension Selly Oak 96-99; Lic to Offic *Birm* 96-99; Regional Desk Officer S Asia & Middle East USPG 99-05; Perm to Offic *S'wark* 00-05; rtd 05. *Frankentobel Strasse 4, 73079 Suessen, Germany* Tel (0049) (71) 625846 E-mail julinath@aol.com

LIPPIATT, Michael Charles. b 39. Oak Hill Th Coll BD71. **d** 71 **p** 72. C Ardsley *Sheff* 71-74; C Lenton *S'well* 74-78; V Jesmond H Trin *Newc* 78-87; rtd 96. *69 Lansdowne Crescent, Stanwix, Carlisle CA3 9ES* Tel (01228) 537080

LIPPIETT, Canon Peter Vernon. b 47. Lon Univ MB, BS73 MRCGP80 Univ of Wales (Lamp) MA08. Ripon Coll Cuddesdon 86. **d** 88 **p** 89. C Pinner *Lon* 88-91; V Twyford and Owslebury and Morestead *Win* 91-99; P-in-c Rydal *Carl* 99-03; Warden Rydal Hall and Ldr Rydal Hall Community 99-03; Dioc Spirituality Adv *Portsm* 03-10; Hon Can Portsm Cathl 10; rtd 11. *Pax Lodge, Coxs Hill, Twyford, Winchester SO21 1PQ*

LIPSCOMB, Ian Craig. b 30. Wells Th Coll 61. **d** 63 **p** 64. C Feltham *Lon* 63-65; Australia from 65; rtd 94. *South Hill, Garroorigang Road, PO Box 118, Goulburn NSW 2580, Australia* Tel and fax (0061) (2) 4821 9591

LIPSCOMB, Canon Timothy William. b 52. Chich Th Coll 82. **d** 85 **p** 86. C Sevenoaks St Jo *Roch* 85-89; C Stanningley St Thos *Ripon* 89-92; V Armley w New Wortley 92-05; AD Armley 98-05; R Preston St Jo and St Geo *Blackb* from 05; AD Preston from 08; Hon Can Blackb Cathl from 10. *The Rectory, 13 Ribblesdale Place, Preston PR1 3NA* Tel (01772) 252528 Mobile 07855-396452 E-mail lavish@ermine2.fsnet.co.uk

LIPSCOMBE, Brian. b 37. Bris Univ BA62. Tyndale Hall Bris 62. **d** 64 **p** 65. C Eccleston Ch Ch *Liv* 64-66; C Halliwell St Pet *Man* 66-69; C Frogmore St Alb 69-72; V Richmond Ch Ch *S'wark* 72-75; TV Mortlake w E Sheen 76-80; P-in-c Streatham Vale H Redeemer 80-85; V 85-91; R Norris Bank *Man* 91-96; V Droylsden St Martin 96-02; rtd 02; Perm to Offic *Ripon* from 02. *15 St Anne's Drive, Leeds LS4 2SA* Tel 0113-275 1893 Mobile 07743-168641 E-mail yvonne@ylipscombe.freeserve.co.uk

LISK, Stewart. b 62. Regent's Park Coll Ox BA84 MA88. St Mich Coll Llan 86. **d** 88 **p** 89. C Glan Ely *Llan* 88-92; Chapl Cardiff Inst of HE 92-96; Chapl Welsh Coll of Music and Drama 92-96; Asst Chapl Univ of Wales (Cardiff) 92-96; V Glan Ely 96-06; AD Llan 04-06; V Roath from 06. *Roath Vicarage, Waterloo Road, Cardiff CF23 5AD* Tel (029) 2048 4808

LISMORE, Dean of. See DRAPER, The Very Revd Paul Richard

LISTER, Mrs Jennifer Grace. b 44. Totley Hall Coll CertEd65. NOC 87. **d** 92 **p** 94. C Cowgate *Newc* 92-95; C Wall and Lich St Mary w St Mich 95-96; P-in-c Yoxall and Asst P The Ridwares and Kings Bromley 96-07; rtd 07. *81 Kingsley Road, Bishops Tachbrook, Leamington Spa CV33 9RZ* Tel (01926) 427922 E-mail jenny.lister@waitrose.com

LISTER (née AISBITT), Mrs Joanne. b 69. St Jo Coll Dur BA91. St Steph Ho Ox 91. **d** 93. NSM Mill End and Heronsgate w W Hyde *St Alb* 93-96. *Address temp unknown* E-mail listerwilliam@hotmail.com

LISTER, Joseph Hugh. b 38. Tyndale Hall Bris 61. **d** 64 **p** 65. C Pemberton St Mark Newtown *Liv* 64-68; Hon C Braintree *Chelmsf* 68-71; C Darfield *Sheff* 71-73; P-in-c Sheff St Swithun 73-76; TV Sheff Manor 76-80; TR Winfarthing w Shelfanger *Nor* 80-81; P-in-c Burston 80-81; P-in-c Gissing 80-81; P-in-c Tivetshall 80-81; R Winfarthing w Shelfanger w Burston w

Gissing etc 81-88; P-in-c Sandon, Wallington and Rushden w Clothall *St Alb* 88-89; R 89-93; R Nether and Over Seale *Derby* 93-96; V Lullington 93-96; R Seale and Lullington 96-98; RD Repton 96-98; Dean Ndola Zambia 99-02; rtd 02; Hon C Hartington, Biggin and Earl Sterndale *Derby* 02-04; C Stoke Canon, Poltimore w Huxham and Rewe etc *Ex* 05-06. *The Bungalow, Queens Park, Millom LA18 5DY* E-mail joe@ndolarola.co.uk

LISTER, Miss Mary Phyllis. b 28. St Andr Ho Portsm 52. **dss** 80 **d** 87. Inkberrow w Cookhill and Kington w Dormston *Worc* 80-82; Ancaster *Linc* 82-87; C 87-88; rtd 88; Perm to Offic *Worc* 88-00 and *Leic* from 00. *6 Stuart Court, High Street, Kibworth, Leicester LE8 0LR* Tel 0116-279 3763

LISTER, Peter. b 42. Leeds Univ BA64 Newc Univ PGCE75. Coll of Resurr Mirfield 63. **d** 65 **p** 66. C Monkseaton St Pet *Newc* 65-68; C Cramlington 68-70; Hon C 71-78; C Morpeth 79-83; V Shilbottle 83-88; Asst Dioc Dir of Educn 83-88; Dir of Educn 88-95; Hon Can Newc Cathl 88-95; Dioc Dir of Educn *Lich* 95-06; rtd 07; Perm to Offic *Lich* 07-09. *81 Kingsley Road, Bishops Tachbrook, Leamington Spa CV33 9RZ* Tel (01926) 427922 E-mail peter-lister@supanet.com

LISTER, Peter William Ryley. b 56. **d** 10 **p** 11. OLM Bourne *Linc* from 10. *4 Linden Rise, Bourne PE10 9TD* Tel (01778) 423730 E-mail pwr.lister@btinternet.com

LISTER, William Bernard. b 67. Keble Coll Ox BA88 MA92. St Steph Ho Ox BA91. **d** 92 **p** 93. C Mill End and Heronsgate w W Hyde *St Alb* 92-96; CF 96-06; Sen CF from 06. *c/o MOD Chaplains (Army)* Tel (01980) 615804 Fax 615800 E-mail listerwilliam@hotmail.com

LITHERLAND, Norman Richard. b 30. Lon Univ BA51 BA52 Man Univ MEd72. NOC 78. **d** 81 **p** 82. NSM Flixton St Mich *Man* 81-94; rtd 94; Perm to Offic *Man* from 94. *1 Overdale Crescent, Urmston, Manchester M41 5GR* Tel 0161-748 4243

LITHERLAND, Terence. b 46. **d** 93 **p** 94. OLM Horwich and Rivington *Man* from 93; OLM Blackrod from 11. *61 Tomlinson Street, Horwich, Bolton BL6 5QR* Tel (01204) 692201

LITJENS, Shan Elizabeth. b 55. **d** 95. C Fareham SS Pet and Paul *Portsm* 95-96; C Fareham H Trin 96-99; NSM Hedge End St Jo *Win* from 00. *11 Abraham Close, Botley, Southampton SO30 2RQ* Tel (01489) 796321 E-mail shanlitjens@aol.com

LITTLE, Andrew. b 27. Open Univ BA83 UEA BA03. AKC51. **d** 52 **p** 53. C Fulham All SS *Lon* 52-54; C Epsom St Barn *Guildf* 54-61; V Northwood *Lich* 61-72; P-in-c Hixon 72-86; V Stowe 72-86; V Hixon w Stowe-by-Chartley 86-89; rtd 89; Perm to Offic *Nor* 89-09; Hon PV Nor Cathl 93-09. *4 Capel Court, The Burgage, Prestbury, Cheltenham GL52 3EL* Tel (01242) 285800

LITTLE, Ms Christine. b 60. Lanc Univ BA83. St Jo Coll Nottm 88. **d** 91 **p** 94. Par Dn Meltham *Wakef* 91-94; C Hatcham St Jas *S'wark* 94-99; P-in-c 99-04; C Nottingham St Pet and All SS *S'well* 04-07; C Nottingham All SS, St Mary and St Pet from 07. *15 Hamilton Drive, Nottingham NG7 1DF* Tel 0115-924 3354

LITTLE, David John. b 65. Oak Hill Th Coll BA94. **d** 94 **p** 95. C Chislehurst Ch Ch *Roch* 94-98; TV Bath Twerton-on-Avon *B & W* 98; Dep Chapl HM Pris Bris 98-99; Chapl HM Pris Reading from 99. *The Chaplain's Office, HM Prison, Forbury Road, Reading RG1 3HY* Tel 0118-908 5000

LITTLE, Derek Peter. b 50. St Jo Coll Dur BA72. Trin Coll Bris. **d** 75 **p** 76. C Bradley *Wakef* 75-78; C Kidderminster St Geo *Worc* 78-82; V Lepton *Wakef* 82-85; E Regional Sec CPAS 85-88; V Canonbury St Steph 88-96; R Bedhampton *Portsm* 96-99; rtd 09. *13 Queensland Avenue, London SW19 3AD* Tel (020) 8542 2604 E-mail deepy@blueyonder.co.uk

LITTLE, George Nelson. b 39. CITC 70. **d** 72 **p** 73. C Portadown St Mark *Arm* 72-76; I Newtownhamilton w Ballymoyer and Belleek 76-80; I Aghaderg w Donaghmore *D & D* 80-82; I Aghaderg w Donaghmore and Scarva 82-05; Can Dromore Cathl 93-05; Treas 93-05; Chan 03-05; rtd 05. *22 Willow Dean, Markethill, Armagh BT60 1QG* Tel (028) 3755 2848

LITTLE, Herbert Edwin Samuel. b 21. Lon Univ BA54 BD68. NEOC 79. **d** 80 **p** 81. NSM Dur St Cuth 80-88; rtd 88. *Orchard Close, Bourne Lane, Twyford, Winchester SO21 1NX*

LITTLE, Ian Dawtry Torrance. b 49. Keele Univ BEd72. SWMTC 81. **d** 85 **p** 86. NSM St Stythians w Perranarworthal and Gwennap *Truro* 85-97; NSM Chacewater w St Day and Carharrack 97-06; Perm to Offic from 06. *Kernyk, Crellow Fields, Stithians, Truro TR3 7RE*

LITTLE, James Harry. b 57. York Univ BA79. Qu Coll Birm 84. **d** 87 **p** 88. C Wollaton *S'well* 87-90; C N Wheatley, W Burton, Bole, Saundby, Sturton etc 90-93; R E Markham w Askham, Headon w Upton and Grove 93-06; P-in-c Dunham w Darlton, Ragnall, Fledborough etc 04-06; TR Howden *York* from 06; RD Howden from 10. *The Minster Rectory, Market Place, Howden, Goole DN14 7BL* Tel (01430) 432056 E-mail revjlittle@aol.com

LITTLE, Nigel James. b 73. Middx Univ BA93. Oak Hill Th Coll 98. **d** 01 **p** 02. C Highgate St Mich *Lon* 01-07; TV Kirk Ella and Willerby *York* from 07. *St Luke's Vicarage, 2A Chestnut Avenue, Hull HU10 6PA* Tel (01482) 658974 E-mail nigel_little@yahoo.com

LITTLE, Rebekah Mary. b 70. Oak Hill Th Coll. **d** 97 **p** 03. NSM Chislehurst Ch Ch *Roch* 97-98; NSM Bath Twerton-on-Avon *B & W* 98; Perm to Offic *Ox* 00-04; NSM Reading St Mary w St Laur 04-05. *Address withheld by request*

LITTLE, Canon Stephen Clifford. b 47. Man Univ MEd81. AKC72. **d** 72 **p** 73. C Grange St Andr *Ches* 72-73; C E Runcorn w Halton 73-75; P-in-c Newbold *Man* 75-77; P-in-c Broughton and Milton Keynes *Ox* 77-82; Sector Min Milton Keynes Chr Coun 77-84; TR Warwick *Cov* 84-93; R Harvington and Norton and Lenchwick *Worc* 93-96; R Harvington 96-98; Exec Officer Dioc Bd for Ch and Soc *Man* 98-05; Exec Officer Dioc Bd for Min and Soc 01-05; Hon Can Man Cathl 00-05; Perm to Offic from 05. *12 Redwood, Westhoughton, Bolton BL5 2RU* Tel 0161-832 5253

LITTLEFAIR, David. b 38. ACCA71 FCCA85 Lon Univ BD79. Trin Coll Bris 76. **d** 79 **p** 80. C Bursledon *Win* 79-82; V Charles w Plymouth St Matthias *Ex* 82-89; Warden Lee Abbey Internat Students' Club Kensington 89-94; V Malmesbury w Westport and Brokenborough *Bris* 94-03; rtd 03. *6 Matford Mews, Matford, Exeter EX2 8XP* Tel (01392) 218784

LITTLEFORD, Peter John. b 40. St Mark & St Jo Coll Lon CertEd63 ACP65 Birkbeck Coll Lon BSc70 Lon Inst of Educn DipEd73 MA76. SAOMC 96. **d** 99 **p** 00. NSM Bedf St Mark *St Alb* 99-10; Chapl De Montfort Univ 99-01; rtd 10; Perm to Offic *St Alb* from 10. *1 Bindon Abbey, Bedford MK41 0AZ* Tel (01234) 356645 E-mail plittlef@dmu.ac.uk

LITTLEJOHN, Keith Douglas. b 59. Ripon Coll Cuddesdon BTh03. **d** 03 **p** 04. C Horsham *Chich* 03-07; P-in-c Bolney from 07; P-in-c Cowfold from 07. *The Vicarage, Horsham Road, Cowfold, Horsham RH13 8AH* Tel (01403) 865945 Mobile 07905-544366 E-mail keithdlj@aol.com

LITTLER, Eric Raymond. b 36. AMIC93. Roch Th Coll 65. **d** 68 **p** 69. C Hatfield Hyde *St Alb* 68-73; Chapl Welwyn Garden City Hosp 70-73; TV Pemberton St Jo *Liv* 73-78; Chapl Billinge Hosp Wigan 76-81; V Pemberton St Fran Kitt Green *Liv* 78-81; V White Notley, Faulkbourne and Cressing *Chelmsf* 81-88; V Westcliff St Andr 88-96; Chapl Westcliff Hosp 88-96; Chapl Southend HA 89-96; R E and W Tilbury and Linford *Chelmsf* 96-98; Chapl Orsett Hosp 96-98; RD Thurrock *Chelmsf* 96-98; R Gt Oakley w Wix and Wrabness 98-02; Chapl Essex Rivers Healthcare NHS Trust 98-02; rtd 02; Perm to Offic *Sarum* from 98; *Chelmsf* and *B & W* from 02; Chapl St Jo Hosp Heytesbury 03-08. *Minster Hall, 1 Pound Row, Warminster BA12 8NQ* Tel (01985) 218818 E-mail ericandsuzette@uwclub.net

LITTLER, Keith Trevor. b 35. Lon Univ BSc(Soc)63 TCert64 York Univ MA82 Hull Univ PhD89 Westmr Coll Ox MTh98 Univ of Wales (Ban) DMin06. St D Dioc Tr Course 89 St Mich Coll Llan 94. **d** 92 **p** 93. NSM Betws w Ammanford *St D* 92-94; C 94; R Pendine w Llanmiloe and Eglwys Gymyn w Marros 94-03; RD St Clears 98-03; rtd 03; Hon Research Fell Ban Univ from 06. *Myrtle Hill Cottage, Broadway, Laugharne, Carmarthen SA33 4NS* Tel (01994) 427779

LITTLER, Malcolm Kenneth. b 34. Univ of Wales (Lamp) BA55. **d** 57 **p** 58. C Llanelli *St D* 57-60; C Llandeilo Fawr 60-61; R Puncheston, Lt Newcastle and Castle Bythe 61-64; R Lampeter Velfrey 64-68; V Llanwnda w Goodwick and Manorowen 68-74; V Llanfynydd 74-78; V The Suttons w Tydd *Linc* 87-90; R Graffoe 90-94; rtd 94; Perm to Offic *Linc* 94-97. *Summerdown, Beaumont Fee, Lincoln LN1 1EZ* Tel (01522) 531075

LITTLEWOOD, Alan James. b 51. Man Poly BEd77. **d** 95 **p** 96. OLM Gosberton *Linc* 95-97; OLM Gosberton, Gosberton Clough and Quadring 97-01; C Bourne 01-03; P-in-c Leasingham and Cranwell 03-08; P-in-c Ancaster Wilsford Gp from 08. *The Rectory, 117 Ermine Street, Ancaster, Grantham NG32 3QL* Tel (01400) 231145 E-mail alan@littlewood35.freeserve.co.uk

LITTLEWOOD, Alistair David. b 68. St Cath Coll Ox BA89. Qu Coll Birm 93. **d** 96 **p** 97. C Keyworth and Stanton-on-the-Wolds *S'well* 96-00; Chapl Birm Univ 00-05; P-in-c Edwinstowe *S'well* 05-10; P-in-c Perlethorpe 05-10; Hon C Mansfield Deanery from 10. *St Lawrence Vicarage, 3 Shaw Street, Mansfield NG18 2NP*

LITTLEWOOD, Miss Jacqueline Patricia. b 52. Linc Th Coll 77. **dss** 80 **d** 87 **p** 94. Crayford Roch 80-84; Gravesend H Family w Ifield 84-87; Par Dn 87-93; rtd 93; NSM Gravesend St Aid *Roch* from 93. *25 Beltana Drive, Gravesend DA12 4BT* Tel (01474) 560106

LITTLEWOOD, Mrs Penelope Anne. b 47. WEMTC 05. **d** 08 **p** 09. NSM Burghill *Heref* from 08; NSM Pipe-cum-Lyde and Moreton-on-Lugg from 08; NSM Stretton Sugwas from 08. *Cobwebs, Burghill, Hereford HR4 7RL* Tel (01432) 760835 Mobile 07734-347327 E-mail penny.cobwebs@virgin.net

LITTON, Alan. b 42. Ridley Hall Cam 66. **d** 69 **p** 70. C Bolton St Bede *Man* 69-71; C Ashton St Mich 71-73; V Haslingden St Jo Stonefold *Blackb* 73-77; Ind Chapl *York* 77-81; V Crewe All SS and St Paul *Ches* 81-84; Ind Chapl *Liv* 84-89; V Spotland *Man* 89-94; R Newchurch *Liv* 94-02; P-in-c Croft w Southworth 94-02; R Newchurch w Croft 02; rtd 02; Perm to Offic *Liv* 03-08; Hon C Burtonwood from 08. *3 Rosemary Close, Great Sankey, Warrington WA5 1TL* Tel (01925) 222944

LIVERPOOL, Archdeacon of. *See* PANTER, The Ven Richard James Graham

LIVERPOOL, Bishop of. *See* JONES, The Rt Revd James Stuart

LIVERPOOL, Dean of. *Vacant*

LIVERSIDGE, Mrs Linda Sheila. b 48. Oak Hill Th Coll BA98. **d** 98 **p** 99. C Kensal Rise St Mark and St Martin *Lon* 98-01; TV N Wingfield, Clay Cross and Pilsley *Derby* 01-11; P-in-c Willingham *Ely* from 11. *The Rectory, 23 Rampton End, Willingham, Cambridge CB24 5JB* Tel (01954) 263187 Mobile 07941-667616 E-mail revlin@me.com

LIVERSUCH, Ian Martin. b 56. St Jo Coll Dur BA79. Wycliffe Hall Ox 79. **d** 83 **p** 84. C Newport St Mark *Mon* 83-85; C Risca 85-88; P-in-c Newport All SS 88-91; Canada from 91; R Hemmingford w Clarenceville 92-98; R La Salle St Lawr from 98. *350 120 John, La Salle QC H8P 3P7, Canada* Tel (001) (514) 364 5718 E-mail islwyn@total.net

LIVESEY, Miss Rachel Elizabeth. b 67. Univ of Wales (Cardiff) BSc89 MBA96 Homerton Coll Cam BTh04 Ridgefield Univ PGCE99. Ridley Hall Cam 07. **d** 09 **p** 10. C Streetly *Lich* from 09. *36 Foley Road East, Streetly, Sutton Coldfield B74 3JL* Tel 07977-310049 (mobile) E-mail rachel.livesey@googlemail.com

LIVESLEY, John. b 80. Magd Coll Ox BA02 MSt03 MA07 Leeds Univ MA07. Coll of Resurr Mirfield 04. **d** 07 **p** 08. C Swinton and Pendlebury *Man* 07-10; P-in-c Tudhoe Grange *Dur* from 10; P-in-c Cassop cum Quarrington from 10. *St Andrew's Vicarage, St Andrew's Road, Spennymoor DL16 6NE* Tel (01388) 814817 Mobile 07796-117568 E-mail johnlivesley1980@yahoo.co.uk

LIVINGSTON, Andrew Stuart. b 56. Sheff Univ BSc79 Man Univ PGCE85. ENWTP 07. **d** 10 **p** 11. NSM Poynton *Ches* from 10. *5 Eveside Close, Cheadle Hulme, Cheadle SK8 5RW* Tel 0161-291 0650 Mobile 07925-589841 E-mail revandylivo@gmail.com

LIVINGSTON, Bertram. TCD BA56. **d** 57 **p** 58. C Enniscorthy *C & O* 57-59; I Carrickmacross *Clogh* 59-61; I Carrickmacross w Magheracloone 61-63; C-in-c Derryvolgie *Conn* 63-78; I 78-79; I Monaghan *Clogh* 79-86; I Desertlyn w Ballyeglish *Arm* 86-94; rtd 94. *6 The Green, Portadown, Craigavon BT63 5LH* Tel (028) 3835 1859

LIVINGSTON, Richard. b 46. Qu Coll Birm. **d** 83 **p** 84. C Hobs Moat *Birm* 83-87; V Droylsden St Martin *Man* 87-95; P-in-c Wolverton w Norton Lindsey and Langley *Cov* from 95; Chapl to the Deaf 95-03; P-in-c Snitterfield w Bearley from 03; P-in-c Aston Cantlow and Wilmcote w Billesley from 08. *The Rectory, Wolverton, Stratford-upon-Avon CV37 0HF* Tel (01789) 731278 E-mail richard@livingston.freeserve.co.uk

LIVINGSTONE, Canon Francis Kenneth. b 26. TCD BA48 MA64. TCD Div Sch Div Test49. **d** 49 **p** 50. C Dublin Santry Union w Coolock *D & G* 49-52; C Dublin St Geo 52-57; I Castledermot Union 57-62; C Arm St Mark 62-66; Hon V Choral Arm Cathl 63-92; I Portadown St Sav 66-78; I Kilmore St Aid w St Sav 78-83; I Donaghmore w Upper Donaghmore 83-92; Preb Yagoe St Patr Cathl Dublin 85-92; rtd 92. *9 Castle Parade, Richhill, Armagh BT61 9QQ* Tel (028) 3887 1574

LIVINGSTONE, Canon John Morris. b 28. Peterho Cam BA53 MA56. Cuddesdon Coll 53. **d** 55 **p** 56. C Hunslet St Mary and Stourton *Ripon* 55-60; Chapl Liddon Ho Lon 60-63; V Notting Hill St Jo *Lon* 63-74; P-in-c Notting Hill St Mark 66-73; P-in-c Notting Hill All SS w St Columb 67-74; P-in-c Notting Hill St Clem 68-74; TR Notting Hill 74-75; Chapl Paris St Geo *Eur* 75-84; Adn N France 79-84; Adn Riviera 84-93; Chapl Nice w Vence 84-93; Chapl Biarritz 93-05; rtd 93. *47 Côte des Basques, 64200 Biarritz, France* Tel and fax (0033) 5 59 24 71 18 E-mail biarritz.cofe@infonie.fr

LIVINGSTONE, John Philip. b 51. Univ of Wales (Abth) BA PGCE. St D Dioc Tr Course. **d** 96 **p** 97. NSM Maenclochog w New Moat etc *St D* 96-02; V Elerch w Penrhyncoch w Capel Bangor and Goginan from 02; AD Llanbadarn Fawr from 10. *The Vicarage, 78 Ger y Llan, Penrhyncoch, Aberystwyth SY23 3HQ* Tel (01970) 820988

LIVINGSTONE, Kenneth. *See* LIVINGSTONE, Canon Francis Kenneth

LIYANAGE, Sylvester. b 78. Kingston Univ BEng01 Surrey Univ MSc03 Cam Univ BTh08. Ridley Hall Cam 05. **d** 08 **p** 09. C Kingston Hill St Paul *S'wark* from 08. *78 Kelvedon Close, Kingston upon Thames KT2 5LF* Tel (020) 8541 0577 E-mail sylvester.liyanage@stpaulskingston.org.uk

LLANDAFF, Archdeacon of. *See* JACKSON, The Ven Frances Anne

LLANDAFF, Bishop of. *See* MORGAN, The Most Revd Barry Cennydd

LLANDAFF, Dean of. *See* LEWIS, The Very Revd John Thomas

⊞**LLEWELLIN, The Rt Revd John Richard Allan.** b 38. Fitzw Ho Cam BA64 MA78. Westcott Ho Cam 61. **d** 64 **p** 65 **c** 85. C Radlett *St Alb* 64-68; C Johannesburg Cathl S Africa 68-71; V Waltham Cross *St Alb* 71-79; R Harpenden St Nic 79-85; Hon Can Truro Cathl 85-92; Suff Bp St Germans 85-92; Suff Bp Dover *Cant* 92-99; Bp at Lambeth (Hd of Staff) 99-03; rtd 03;

Perm to Offic *Truro* 04-07; Hon Asst Bp Cant from 08. *193 Ashford Road, Canterbury CT1 3XS* Tel (01227) 789515 E-mail rllewellin@clara.co.uk

LLEWELLYN, Brian Michael. b 47. Univ of Wales (Cardiff) LLM99 MRICS73. Sarum & Wells Th Coll 78. **d** 80 **p** 81. C Farncombe *Guildf* 80-83; Chapl RAF 83-87; R Hethersett w Canteloff w Lt and Gt Melton *Nor* 87-95; RD Humbleyard 94-95; P-in-c Smallburgh w Dilham w Honing and Crostwight 95-98; R 98-00; P-in-c Folkestone St Sav *Cant* 00-07; rtd 07; P-in-c Ypres *Eur* from 10. *Haiglaan 12, 8900 Ieper, Belgium* Tel (0032) (57) 215685 Fax 215927 E-mail bllewy@gmail.com

LLEWELLYN, Canon Christine Ann. b 46. Univ of Wales (Ban) BA69 DipEd70. **d** 89 **p** 97. NSM Arthog w Fairbourne w Llangelynnin w Rhoslefain *Ban* 90-93; NSM Holyhead w Rhoscolyn w Llanfair-yn-Neubwll 93-94; C 94-95; C Holyhead 95-97; TV 97-04; R from 04; Hon Can Ban Cathl 03-07; Can Cursal from 07. *The Old School, Rhoscolyn, Holyhead LL65 2RQ* Tel (01407) 763001

LLEWELLYN, Neil Alexander. b 55. LWCMD78. Westcott Ho Cam 79 Sarum & Wells Th Coll 83. **d** 84 **p** 85. C Heref St Martin 84-86; Chapl Rotterdam Miss to Seamen *Eur* 86-89; R Docking w The Birchams and Stanhoe w Barwick *Nor* 89-92; Chapl Ypres *Eur* 92-95; Toc H 92-95; CF 95-06; P-in-c Newport w Cilgwyn and Dinas w Llanllawer *St D* 06-07; V Newport w Cilgwyn and Nevern and Y Beifil etc from 07. *The Rectory, Long Street, Newport SA42 0TJ* Tel (01239) 820380

LLEWELLYN, Richard Morgan. b 37. CB91 OBE79 MBE76. FCMI81. Sarum & Wells Th Coll 91. **d** 93 **p** 94. C Brecon St Mary and Battle w Llanddew *S & B* 93-95; Min Can Brecon Cathl 93-95; Chapl Ch Coll Brecon from 95. *Llangattock Court, Llangattock, Crickhowell NP8 1PH* Tel (01873) 810116

LLEWELLYN-MACDUFF, Ms Lindsay. b 75. Kent Univ BA97. St Mich Coll Llan 97. **d** 99 **p** 00. C Milton next Sittingbourne *Cant* 99-01; C Barham w Bishopsbourne and Kingston 01-03; C Margate All SS and Westgate St Sav 03-05; P-in-c Gt Finborough w Onehouse, Harleston, Buxhall etc *St E* 05-09; Chapl HM Pris Littlehey from 10. *Chaplaincy, HM Prison Littlehey, Perry, Huntingdon PE28 0SR* Tel (01480) 335252 E-mail lindsay.llewellyn-macduff@hmp.gsi.gov.uk

LLEWELYN, Miss Gabrielle Jane. b 48. Trin Coll Bris 08. **d** 09 **p** 10. NSM Fair Oak *Win* from 09. *Clover Cottage, 1 Victena Road, Fair Oak, Eastleigh SO50 7FY* Tel (023) 8069 6793 Mobile 07817-731036 E-mail gabbyllewelyn@googlemail.com

LLEWELYN, Canon Robert John. b 32. Keble Coll Ox BA54 MA58 Cheltenham & Glouc Coll of HE PhD01. Cuddesdon Coll 65. **d** 66 **p** 67. C Bedford St Andr *St Alb* 66-69; C Cheltenham St Luke and St Jo *Glouc* 69-75; V S Cerney w Cerney Wick 75-80; V Glouc St Cath 80-99; P-in-c Glouc St Mark 87-89; Hon Can Glouc Cathl 94-99; rtd 99; Perm to Offic *Glouc* from 99. *2 The Limes, South Cerney, Cirencester GL7 5RF* Tel (01285) 861529 E-mail robert@llewe4.freeserve.co.uk

LLEWELLYN-EVANS, Catherine Ruth. b 55. St Mary's Coll Dur BA76 Southlands Coll Lon PGCE78. STETS 99. **d** 02 **p** 03. NSM Yatton Moor *B & W* from 02. *The Court House, The Triangle, Wrington, Bristol BS40 5LB* Tel (01934) 863269 E-mail cthlle@btinternet.com

LLOYD, Canon Bernard James. b 29. AKC56. **d** 57 **p** 58. C Laindon w Basildon *Chelmsf* 57-65; V E Ham St Geo 65-82; RD Newham 76-82; Hon Can Chelmsf Cathl 82-94; R Danbury 82-94; P-in-c Woodham Ferrers 87-90; rtd 94; Perm to Offic *Chelmsf* from 94. *Chanterelle, 47 Seaview Avenue, West Mersea, Colchester CO5 8HE* Tel (01206) 383892

LLOYD, Bertram John. b 26. St Mich Coll Llan 81. **d** 83 **p** 84. C Malpas *Mon* 83-85; V Blaenavon w Capel Newydd 85-93; rtd 93; Lic to Offic *Mon* 93-96; St Vincent 96-02. *91 Hillside Avenue, Blaenavon, Pontypool NP4 9JL* Tel (01495) 792616 E-mail llwydunion@caribsurf.com

LLOYD, The Ven Bertram Trevor. b 38. Hertf Coll Ox BA60 MA64. Clifton Th Coll 62. **d** 64 **p** 65. C S Mimms Ch Ch *Lon* 64-70; V Wealdstone H Trin 70-84; RD Harrow 77-82; P-in-c Harrow Weald St Mich 80-84; V Harrow Trin St Mich 84-89; Adn Barnstaple *Ex* 89-02; Preb Ex Cathl 91-02; rtd 02. *8 Pebbleridge Road, Westward Ho!, Bideford EX39 1HN* Tel (01237) 424701 E-mail trevor@stagex.fsnet.co.uk

LLOYD, Mrs Carole Barbara. b 53. Sheff Univ BA74 Coll of Ripon & York St Jo MA03 Leeds Metrop Univ PGCE93. NOC 00. **d** 03 **p** 04. C Bolton St Jas w St Chrys *Bradf* 03-06; C Gt Aycliffe and Chilton *Dur* 06-07; TV Gt Aycliffe 07-09; P-in-c Chilton 09-11; P-in-c Kelloe and Coxhoe 08-11; P-in-c Swanwick and Pentrich *Derby* from 11. *The Vicarage, 4 Broom Avenue, Swanwick, Alfreton DE55 1DQ* Tel (01773) 607947 E-mail carole.lloyd@amnos.co.uk

LLOYD, David Edgar Charles. b 59. St Mich Coll Llan 97. **d** 99 **p** 00. C Newton Nottage *Llan* 99-03; V Newcastle from 03. *The Vicarage, 1 Walters Road, Bridgend CF31 4HE* Tel (01656) 655999 E-mail revd.lloyd@virgin.net

LLOYD, David Hanbury. b 28. Univ of Wales (Abth) BSc49 Reading Univ PhD70. LNSM course 97. **d** 97 **p** 98. NSM

Swanage and Studland *Sarum* 97-98; Perm to Offic 98-06. *Scar Bank House, Russell Avenue, Swanage BH19 2ED* Tel (01929) 426015

LLOYD, David John. b 52. Lon Univ BD82. Burgess Hall Lamp 73. **d** 76 **p** 77. C Pembroke St Mary w St Mich *St D* 76-77; C Llanelli 77-80; V Cil-y-Cwm and Ystrad-ffin w Rhandir-mwyn etc 80-82; Oman 82-84; R Llanllwchaearn and Llanina *St D* 84-88; V Llangennech and Hendy 88-90; Perm to Offic *St Alb* 91-95; V Bampton w Clanfield *Ox* from 96; AD Witney 02-03. *5 Deanery Court, Broad Street, Bampton OX18 2LY* Tel (01993) 851222 E-mail revdjlloyd@aol.com

LLOYD, David John Silk. b 37. Univ of Wales (Lamp) BA62. St Steph Ho Ox 71. **d** 73 **p** 74. C Brentwood St Thos *Chelmsf* 73-77; C Hockley 77-80; C Wickford 80-81; C Wickford and Runwell 81-83; TV 83-88; Chapl Runwell Hosp Wickford 81-88; S Africa from 88; Perm to Offic *Chelmsf* from 88; rtd 97. *D4 Argyll House, Seaforth Road, Westcliff-on-Sea SS0 7SJ*

LLOYD, David Matthew. b 76. SS Hild & Bede Coll Dur BA98. Oak Hill Th Coll 06. **d** 09 **p** 10. C St Helen Bishopsgate w St Andr Undershaft etc *Lon* from 09. *2 Disbrowe Road, London W6 2QF* Tel 07721-745165 (mobile) E-mail dmattlloyd@yahoo.co.uk

LLOYD, David Peter. b 58. Kingston Poly BA81 DipArch84. Sarum & Wells Th Coll 88. **d** 90 **p** 91. C N Dulwich St Faith *S'wark* 90-94; TV Bedminster *Bris* 94-00; V Henbury from 00; Tutor STETS from 11. *Henbury Vicarage, Station Road, Bristol BS10 7QQ* Tel and fax 0117-950 0536 Mobile 07939-264261 E-mail dlloyd@stets.ac.uk

LLOYD, David Zachary. b 80. Wycliffe Hall Ox BA01 Solicitor 05. Ridley Hall Cam 08. **d** 10 **p** 11. C Hampton St Mary *Lon* from 10. *24 Upper Sunbury Road, Hampton TW12 2DL* Tel 07916-295154 (mobile) E-mail davidzlloyd@hotmail.co.uk

LLOYD, Dennis John. b 46. BSc70 MSc74 PhD81. S Dios Minl Tr Scheme. **d** 90 **p** 91. C Hamworthy *Sarum* 90-92; Chapl UEA *Nor* 92-97; P-in-c Malvern St Andr *Worc* 97-99; V 99-01; Chapl Defence Evaluation Research Agency 97-01; RD Malvern 98-01; P-in-c Rowlands Castle *Portsm* 01-11; Warden of Readers 01-11; rtd 11; Perm to Offic *Portsm* from 11. *24 Forest Hills, Newport PO30 5NQ* E-mail revdrdjlloyd@aol.com

LLOYD, Derek James. b 78. Birm Univ BA00 Leeds Univ BA03. Coll of Resurr Mirfield 02. **d** 04 **p** 05. C Burnley St Andr w St Marg and St Jas *Blackb* 04-07; C W Burnley All SS 07-09; V Cross Heath *Lich* from 09; V Newcastle St Paul from 09; CMP from 05. *St Michael's Presbytery, Linden Grove, Newcastle ST5 9LJ* Tel (01782) 662839

LLOYD, Dyfrig Cennydd. b 80. K Coll Lon BA01. Ripon Coll Cuddesdon 01. **d** 04 **p** 05. C Llandysul w Bangor Teifi w Henllan etc *St D* 04-06; C Bro Teifi Sarn Helen 06-07; TV 07-11; V Cardiff Dewi Sant *Llan* from 11. *6 Rachel Close, Cardiff CF5 2SH* Tel (029) 2056 6001 E-mail dyfriglloyd@hotmail.com

LLOYD, Edward Gareth. b 60. K Coll Cam BA81 MA85 Dur Univ PhD98. Ridley Hall Cam 85. **d** 88 **p** 89. C Jarrow *Dur* 88-91; C Monkwearmouth St Pet 91-92; P-in-c 92-96; TV Monkwearmouth 97-99; V Birtley from 99. *6 Ruskin Road, Birtley, Chester le Street DH3 1AD* Tel 0191-410 2115 E-mail gareth@dunelm.org.uk

LLOYD, Eileen. See TAVERNOR, Mrs Eileen

LLOYD, Canon Elizabeth Jane. b 52. GRIC74 CChem MRIC77. Linc Th Coll 77. **dss** 80 **d** 87 **p** 94. Linc St Nic w St Jo Newport 80-81; Lic to Offic *Sarum* 81-87; Hon Par Dn Lytchett Matravers 87-92; Chapl Poole Gen Hosp 85-94; Chapl Poole Hosp NHS Trust from 94; Can and Preb Sarum Cathl from 03; Pres Coll of Health Care Chapl 02-04. *The Rectory, 19 Springfield Road, Poole BH14 0LG* Tel (01202) 748860 or 442167 E-mail jane.lloyd@poole.nhs.uk or jane@jalloyd.fsnet.co.uk

LLOYD, Gareth. See LLOYD, Edward Gareth

LLOYD, Geoffrey. See LLOYD, William Geoffrey

LLOYD, Graham. b 36. Brasted Th Coll 62 St Aid Birkenhead 64 Glouc Sch of Min 86. **d** 89 **p** 90. NSM Churchstoke w Hyssington and Sarn *Heref* 89-97; NSM Lydbury N w Hopesay and Edgton 97-01; rtd 01; Perm to Offic *Heref* from 01. *The Pullets Cottage, Church Stoke, Montgomery SY15 6TL* Tel (01588) 620285

LLOYD, Gwilym Wyn. b 50. Leic Univ BA72 Birm Univ MSc73 Lon Univ LLB78. Trin Coll Bris 83. **d** 87 **p** 88. C Bexleyheath Ch Ch *Roch* 87-91; R Darlaston St Lawr *Lich* 91-98. *24 Grosvenor Avenue, Streetly, Sutton Coldfield B74 3PB*

LLOYD, Hamilton William John Marteine. b 19. Jes Coll Ox BA41 MA45. Ripon Hall Ox. **d** 43 **p** 44. C Falmouth K Chas *Truro* 43-47; R Gerrans w St Anthony in Roseland 47-51; Min Bournemouth H Epiphany CD 51-53; V Bournemouth H Epiphany *Win* 53-60; V Whitchurch w Tufton 60-68; V Whitchurch w Tufton and Litchfield 68-71; V Lyndhurst 71-73; V Lyndhurst and Emery Down 73-84; rtd 84; Perm to Offic *Win* from 86. *Post Office House, Litchfield, Whitchurch RG28 7PT* Tel (01256) 893507

LLOYD, Harry James. b 22. Univ of Wales (Lamp) BA50. **d** 51 **p** 52. C Hay *S & B* 51-55; C Llanigon 51-55; C Hillingdon St Jo *Lon* 55-56; C Marlborough *Sarum* 56-60; V Kingston and Worth

Matravers 60-83; C Milton Abbas, Hilton w Cheselbourne etc 83-87; rtd 87; Perm to Offic *Sarum* 87-00. *Riverside Cottage, 35 Rockbridge Park, Presteigne LD8 2NF* Tel (01547) 560115
LLOYD, Jane. *See* LLOYD, Canon Elizabeth Jane
LLOYD, John Francis. b 21. d 01 p 02. OLM Tettenhall Regis *Lich* from 01. *The Barn, West Trescott Farm, Bridgnorth Road, Trescott, Wolverhampton WV6 7EU* Tel (01902) 765612
LLOYD, The Ven Jonathan Wilford. b 56. Surrey Univ & City of Lon Poly BSc80 N Lon Poly MA86 CQSW82 DASS82. S'wark Ord Course 87. d 90 p 91. NSM Sydenham St Bart *S'wark* 90-93; P-in-c 93-94; Dir of Soc Resp 91-95; Bp's Officer for Ch in Soc 95-97; Hon PV S'wark Cathl 91-97; Chapl Team Ldr Bath Univ 97-04; P-in-c Charlcombe w Bath St Steph 04-09; Copenhagen w Aarhus *Eur* from 09; Adn Germany and N Eur from 10; Can Brussels Cathl from 10. *Tuborgvej 82, 2900 Hellerup, Copenhagen, Denmark* Tel (0045) (39) 627736
E-mail adjonathan@live.com
LLOYD, Marc Andrew. b 78. LMH Ox BA99 Middx Univ MA02. Oak Hill Th Coll 04. d 07 p 08. C Eastbourne H Trin *Chich* 07-11; P-in-c Warbleton and Bodle Street Green from 11. *Warbleton Rectory, Rookery Lane, Rushlake Green, Heathfield TN21 9QJ* Tel (01435) 830421 Mobile 07812-054820
E-mail marc lloyd@hotmail.com
LLOYD, Matthew. *See* LLOYD, David Matthew
LLOYD, Michael Francis. b 57. Down Coll Cam BA79 MA82 St Jo Coll Dur BA83 Worc Coll Ox DPhil97. Cranmer Hall Dur 81. d 84 p 85. C Locks Heath *Portsm* 84-87; Asst Chapl Worc Coll Ox 89-90; Chapl Ch Coll Cam 90-94; Chapl Fitzw Coll Cam 95-96; Hon C Westminster St Jas the Less *Lon* 96-03; Tutor St Steph Ho Ox 03-06; Tutor St Paul's Th Cen *Lon* from 06; C St Andr Holborn 06-10; Chapl Qu Coll Ox from 10. *37 Buckingham Street, Oxford OX1 4LH* Tel (01865) 726223 Mobile 07852-907604
LLOYD, Canon Nigel James Clifford. b 51. Nottm Univ BTh81 Lambeth STh90. Linc Th Coll 77. d 81 p 82. C Sherborne w Castleton and Lillington *Sarum* 81-84; R Lytchett Matravers 84-92; TR Parkstone St Pet w Branksea and St Osmund 92-02; R Parkstone St Pet and St Osmund w Branksea from 02; Ecum Officer (Sherborne Area) from 92; Dioc Ecum Officer 00-01; RD Poole 01-09; Can and Preb Sarum Cathl from 02. *The Rectory, 19 Springfield Road, Poole BH14 0LG* Tel (01202) 748860 *or* 749085 Fax 08700-558534 E-mail nigel@branksea.co.uk
LLOYD, Mrs Pamela Valpy. b 25. Gilmore Ho 48 St Aug Coll Cant 76. dss 76 d 87 p 94. Chartham *Cant* 76-78; Cant All SS 78-85; rtd 85; Chapl Asst Kent and Cant Hosp 87; Chapl Chaucer Hosp Cant 87-90; NSM Elham w Denton and Wootton *Cant* 87-93; Sub-Chapl HM Pris Cant 88-96; Hon C Cant St Martin and St Paul 93-95; Perm to Offic from 96. *Cavendish House, 9 North Holmes Road, Canterbury CT1 1QJ* Tel (01227) 457782
LLOYD (née WALMSLEY), Patricia Jane. b 62. Bris Univ BSc83 PhD87 Trin Coll Cam BTh01. Ridley Hall Cam 99. d 01 p 02. C Bowdon *Ches* 01-05; V Over Peover w Lower Peover from 05. *The Vicarage, The Cobbles, Lower Peover, Knutsford WA16 9PZ* Tel (01565) 722304
E-mail janelloyd6.wanadoo.co.uk
LLOYD, Canon Peter John. b 32. TD78. Wells Th Coll 59. d 61 p 62. C Walmer *Cant* 61-63; CF (TA) 62-73 and 77-87; C Maidstone All SS w St Phil *Cant* 63-66; V Milton next Sittingbourne 66-69; R Brinkley, Burrough Green and Carlton *Ely* 69-73; CF 73-77; V Chessington *Guildf* 77-85; RD Epsom 82-87; V Epsom St Martin 85-92; rtd 92; Perm to Offic *B & W* from 92. *74 Southover, Wells BA5 1UH* Tel (01749) 672213
LLOYD, Peter Vernon James. b 36. Sx Coll *Cam* BA61 MA. Ridley Hall Cam 60. d 62 p 63. C Keynsham w Queen Charlton *B & W* 62-65; Perm to Offic *Sarum* from 65; NSM Bournemouth St Jo w St Mich *Win* 87-90; NSM Bournemouth St Pet w St Swithun, H Trin etc 90-93; Perm to Offic *Win* 93-95; rtd 01. *18 Cornelia Crescent, Branksome, Poole BH12 1LU* Tel and fax (01202) 741422
LLOYD, Richard Gary. b 75. Ex Coll Ox BA98 St Jo Coll Dur MA00. Cranmer Hall Dur 98. d 00 p 01. C Dibden *Win* 00-03; Asst Chapl Charterhouse Sch Godalming 04-11; C Claygate *Guildf* from 11. *27 Cavendish Drive, Claygate, Esher KT10 0QE* Tel 07753-835784 (mobile)
LLOYD, Robert Graham. b 42. St Jo Coll Nottm 82. d 84 p 85. C Tonyrefail *Llan* 84-87; V Martletwy w Lawrenny and Minwear and Yerbeston *St D* 87-91; V Monkton 91-96; V Cymmer and Porth *Llan* 96-07; AD Rhondda 04-06; rtd 07. *7 Greenhill Park Drive, Haverfordwest SA61 1LS* Tel (01437) 783682
LLOYD, Robert James Clifford. b 18. Selw Coll Cam BA41 MA49. Linc Th Coll 46. d 47 p 48. C Clapham H Trin *S'wark* 47-50; C High Wycombe All SS *Ox* 50-53; CF (TA) 50-53; C Hampstead St Jo *Lon* 53-55; V Wellington w W Buckland *B & W* 55-66; P-in-c Nynehead 56-57; V 57-66; RD Wellington 59-66; R Chartham *Cant* 66-81; RD W Bridge 75-81; Hon C Elham w Denton and Wootton 81-92; rtd 92; Perm to Offic *Cant* from 83. *Cavendish House, 9 North Holmes Road, Canterbury CT1 1QJ* Tel (01227) 457782

LLOYD, Roger Bernard. b 58. K Coll Lon BA. Cranmer Hall Dur. d 84 p 85. C Hornchurch St Andr *Chelmsf* 84-87; C Gt Parndon 87-94; V Elm Park St Nic Hornchurch 94-99. *494 Heathway, Dagenham RM10 7SH* Tel (020) 8984 9887 Mobile 07703-383176
LLOYD, Ronald. b 37. St Mich Coll Llan. d 83 p 84. C Penarth All SS *Llan* 83-85; V Cwmbach 85-91; Perm to Offic from 91. *23 Teilo Street, Cardiff CF11 9JN*
LLOYD, Canon Ronald Henry. b 32. Univ of Wales (Lamp) BA52 LTh54. d 54 p 56. C Manselton *S & B* 54-56; C Sketty 56-59; C Swansea St Mary 59-63; CF (TA) 59-65; V Elmley Castle w Netherton and Bricklehampton *Worc* 63-69; Chapl Dragon Sch Ox 69-82; Chapl St Hugh's Coll Ox 75-80; P-in-c Ox St Marg 75-76; Chapl Magd Coll Ox 75-82; Prec and Chapl Ch Ch *Ox* 82-87; R Alvescot w Black Bourton, Shilton, Holwell etc 87-95; P-in-c Broughton Poggs w Filkins, Broadwell etc 94-95; R Shill Valley and Broadshire 95-01; rtd 01; Perm to Offic *Glouc* and *Ox* from 02. *2 The Farriers, Southrop, Lechlade GL7 3RL* Tel (01367) 850071
LLOYD, Mrs Sandra Edith. b 48. Sarum & Wells Th Coll 83. dss 86 d 87 p 94. Freshwater *Portsm* 86-87; C 87-89; C Whitwell 89-95; V from 95; C Niton 89-95; P-in-c 95-96; R from 96; R St Lawrence 96-04. *The Rectory, Pan Lane, Niton, Ventnor PO38 2BT* Tel and fax (01983) 730595
E-mail rhadegunde@aol.com
LLOYD, Simon David. b 58. Portsm Poly BA79 RGN91 RSCN95. Wycliffe Hall Ox 80. d 83 p 84. C Cotmanhay *Derby* 83-85; Chapl Asst Nottm City Hosp 85-87; Chapl Basford Hosp Nottm 85-87; Perm to Offic *Birm* 91-97; TV Solihull 97-04; V Minehead *B & W* 04-10. *1 Cyril Street, Taunton TA2 6HW* Tel (01823) 618028 E-mail fathersi@dsl.pipex.com
LLOYD, Stephen Russell. b 47. Worc Coll Ox BA69 MA77 CertEd. Oak Hill Th Coll 76. d 77 p 78. C Canonbury St Steph *Lon* 77-80; C Braintree *Chelmsf* 80-92; V Braintree St Paul 92-01; V Ipswich St Andr *St E* from 01. *The Vicarage, 286 Britannia Road, Ipswich IP4 5HF* Tel (01473) 714341
E-mail rev.lloyd@tiscali.co.uk
LLOYD, Canon Stuart George Errington. b 49. TCD BA72. d 75 p 76. C Cloughfern *Conn* 75-79; C Cregagh *D & D* 79-82; I Eglantine *Conn* 82-89; I Ballymena w Ballyclug from 89; Can Conn Cathl from 97; Preb 97-01; Prec from 01. *St Patrick's Rectory, 102 Galgorm Road, Ballymena BT42 1AE* Tel and fax (028) 2565 2253 *or* tel 2563 0741
E-mail ballymena@connor.anglican.org
LLOYD, Timothy David Lewis. *See* LEWIS LLOYD, Canon Timothy David
LLOYD, Trevor. *See* LLOYD, The Ven Bertram Trevor
LLOYD, William Geoffrey. b 48. Man Univ BA70. Oak Hill Th Coll 92. d 95 p 96. C Plaistow St Mary *Roch* 95-99; TV Ottery St Mary, Alfington, W Hill, Tipton etc *Ex* 99-04; P-in-c Sampford Spiney w Horrabridge 04-11; RD Tavistock 07-11; rtd 11. *24 Mills Bakery, 4 Royal William Yard, Plymouth PL1 3GD* Tel (01752) 227680 E-mail geofflloyd@ukgateway.net
LLOYD-DAVIES, Arthur (Lloyd). b 31. Univ of Wales BA55. Cuddesdon Coll 55. d 57 p 58. C Tonypandy w Clydach Vale *Llan* 57-59; C Merthyr Dyfan 59-62; C Amersham *Ox* 62-65; V Tilehurst St Geo 65-73; R Wokingham St Paul 73-84; R Nuthurst *Chich* 84-90; I Fiddown w Clonegam, Guilcagh and Kilmeaden *C & O* 90-96; rtd 96; Hon C Bratton, Edington and Imber, Erlestoke etc *Sarum* 96-99. *Garthwaite, 135 Horsham Road, Cranleigh GU6 8DZ*
LLOYD HUGHES, Gwilym. *See* HUGHES, Gwilym Lloyd
LLOYD-JAMES, Duncan Geraint. b 66. St Steph Ho Ox BTh94. d 94 p 96. C St Leonards Ch Ch and St Mary *Chich* 94-96; C Rottingdean 96-99; R Brede w Udimore 99-07; rtd 07; Perm to Offic *Guildf* 08-10. *62 Richmond Street, Brighton BN2 9PE* Tel (01273) 606550 Mobile 07511-772256
E-mail duncanlj@btinternet.com
LLOYD JONES, Ieuan. b 31. St Cath Coll Cam BA51 MA54 FBIM. Sarum & Wells Th Coll 80. d 83 p 84. NSM Claygate *Guildf* 83-89; Perm to Offic *Ox* 89-06 and *Guildf* from 07. *20 Aldersey Road, Guildford GU1 2ES* Tel (01483) 449605 E-mail lloyd.jones4@ntlworld.com
LLOYD MORGAN, Richard Edward. b 48. Trin Coll Cam MA70 Ox Univ DipEd71. SEITE 95. d 98 p 99. NSM Clapham St Paul *S'wark* 98-03; Chapl K Coll Cam from 03. *King's College, Cambridge CB2 1ST* Tel (01223) 331100
E-mail chaplain@kings.cam.ac.uk
LLOYD-RICHARDS, David Robert. b 48. Open Univ BA84 Hull Univ MA87. St D Coll Lamp. d 71 p 72. C Skewen *Llan* 71-73; C Neath w Llantwit 73-76; Miss to Seamen 76-77; V Pontlottyn w Fochriw *Llan* 77-84; R Merthyr Dyfan 84-90; Chapl Barry Neale-Kent Hosp 84-90; Tutor Open Univ 85-10; Sen Chapl Univ Hosp of Wales Cardiff 90-95; Sen Chapl Univ Hosp of Wales and Llandough NHS Trust 95-00; Sen Chapl Manager Cardiff and Vale NHS Trust 00-08; rtd 08. *Jeantique, La Butte, La Trinité des Laitiers, Gace, 61230 Orne, France* Tel (0033) (2) 33 36 11 15 E-mail robertlloydrichards@googlemail.com

LLOYD ROBERTS, Mrs Kathleen Ada May. b 49. Bordesley Coll of Educn CertEd71. Qu Coll Birm 03. **d** 06 **p** 07. NSM Temple Balsall *Birm* 06-09; V from 09. *The Master's House, Temple Balsall, Knowle, Solihull B93 0AL* Tel 0121-684 3844 E-mail klloydr@citycol.ac.uk

LLOYD WILLIAMS, Martin Clifford. b 65. Westmr Coll Lon BEd87. Trin Coll Bris BA93. **d** 93 **p** 94. C Bath Walcot *B & W* 93-97; R Bath St Mich w St Paul from 97; RD Bath from 10. *71 Priory Close, Combe Down, Bath BA2 5AP* Tel (01225) 835490 E-mail martin.lloydwilliams@stmichaelsbath.org.uk

LO, Peter Kwan Ho. b 54. Chinese Univ of Hong Kong BD84 Stirling Univ MBA92 K Coll Lon LLB99 QTS02. **d** 84 **p** 85. Hong Kong 84-91; Perm to Offic *Chich* 02-03; C Uckfield 03-06; R Monterey Park USA from 07. *133 East Graves Avenue, Monterey Park CA 91755-3915, USA* Tel (001) (626) 571 2714 E-mail peterkwanholo@hotmail.com

lo POLITO, Nicola. b 59. Catholic Th Union Chicago MDiv85 MA(Theol)87. Comboni Miss. **d** 85 **p** 86. In RC Ch 85-94; Egypt 86-88; Sudan 88-91; Italy 91-94; Asst Chapl Malta and Gozo *Eur* 94-98; C Castle Bromwich SS Mary and Marg *Birm* 98-01; TV Salter Street and Shirley 01-05; Chapl Birm Univ from 05. *258 Mary Vale Road, Birmingham B30 1PJ* Tel 0121-458 7432 *or* 414 7001 Fax 414 7002 E-mail nlopolito@hotmail.com

LOAT, Canon Andrew Graham. b 61. Aber Univ BD83 Univ of Wales (Ban) MTh00. St Jo Coll Nottm. **d** 87 **p** 88. C Llangynwyd w Maesteg 87-90; C Llansamlet *S & B* 90-91; R Whitton and Pilleth and Cascob etc 91-98; R Llandrindod w Cefnllys and Disserth 98-09; R Lower Ithon Valley from 09; V Upper Ithon Valley from 09; Warden of Readers 02-08; Can Res Brecon Cathl from 03; AD Maelienydd from 06. *The Rectory, Crossgates, Llandrindod Wells LD1 6RU* Tel (01597) 851204 E-mail andrew.loat@googlemail.com

LOBB, Edward Eric. b 51. Magd Coll Ox BA74 MA76. Wycliffe Hall Ox 73. **d** 76 **p** 77. C Haughton St Mary *Man* 76-80; C Rusholme H Trin 80-84; P-in-c Whitfield *Derby* 84-90; V 90-92; V Stapenhill w Cauldwell 92-03; rtd 03; Perm to Offic *Derby* 03-05. *Middleton House, Beith KA15 1HX* Tel (01505) 500232

LOBB, Miss Josephine Mary. b 57. SRN83. **d** 96 **p** 97. OLM St Germans *Truro* from 96. *19 Lowertown Close, Landrake, Saltash PL12 5DG* Tel (01752) 851488

LOCK, Mrs Beverley. b 59. Loughb Univ BA81 Bris Univ PGCE82. CBDTI 01. **d** 04 **p** 05. C Kendal St Geo *Carl* 04-07; C Beacon 07-08; P-in-c Orton and Tebay w Ravenstonedale etc from 08; P-in-c Shap w Swindale and Bampton w Mardale from 08. *The Vicarage, Orton, Penrith CA10 3RQ* Tel (015396) 24045 E-mail rev.bev@btinternet.com

LOCK, Graham Robert. b 39. Hertf Coll Ox BA63 MA67. Ridley Hall Cam 62. **d** 64 **p** 65. C Bexleyheath St Pet *Roch* 64-66; C Roch St Justus 66-71; C St Mary Cray and St Paul's Cray 71-75; V Chatham St Paul w All SS 75-83; R Lambourne w Abridge and Stapleford Abbotts *Chelmsf* 83-92; V Barkingside St Laur 92-03; rtd 04. *107 Spencer Road, Benfleet SS7 3HS* Tel (01268) 750882

LOCK, Mrs Jacqueline. b 43. **d** 08 **p** 09. OLM High Wycombe *Ox* from 08. *15 Kingsley Crescent, High Wycombe HP11 2UN* Tel (01494) 532216 E-mail jackie@thelocks.org.uk

LOCK, Paul Alan. b 65. St Chad's Coll Dur BA86. Coll of Resurr Mirfield 87. **d** 89 **p** 90. C Upholland *Liv* 89-92; C Teddington SS Pet and Paul and Fulwell *Lon* 92-95; V 95-99; V Wigan St Anne *Liv* 99-05. *151 Mossy Lea Road, Wrightington, Wigan WN6 9RE* Tel (01257) 424817 E-mail paul.a lock@virgin.net

LOCK, The Ven Peter Harcourt D'Arcy. b 44. AKC67. **d** 68 **p** 69. C Meopham *Roch* 68-72; C Wigmore w Hempstead 72; C S Gillingham 72-77; R Hartley 77-83; R Fawkham and Hartley 83-84; V Dartford H Trin 84-93; Hon Can Roch Cathl 90-01; V Bromley SS Pet and Paul 93-01; RD Bromley 96-01; Adn Roch and Can Res Roch Cathl 01-09; rtd 09; Perm to Offic *Cant* from 11. *53 Preston Park, Faversham ME13 8LH* Tel (01795) 529161 E-mail peter.lock123@btinternet.com

LOCK, Thomas. **d** 05 **p** 06. OLM N Poole Ecum Team *Sarum* from 05. *103 Copeland Drive, Poole BH14 8NP* E-mail thomas@thomaslock.orangehome.co.uk

LOCKE, Mrs Jennifer Margaret. b 52. Edin Univ BEd74. Ox Min Course 06. **d** 08 **p** 09. NSM Wexham *Ox* from 08. *Hazeldene House, 20 Seer Mead, Seer Green, Beaconsfield HP9 2QL* Tel (01494) 759734 E-mail jmlocke1@gmail.com

LOCKE, Nigel Richard. See HESFORD-LOCKE, Richard Nigel

LOCKE, Robert Andrew. b 52. St Steph Ho Ox 89. **d** 92 **p** 93. C Colchester St Jas, All SS, St Nic and St Runwald *Chelmsf* 92-95; CF 95-00; V Burnham *Chelmsf* 00-04. *331 Broomfield Road, Chelmsford CM1 4DU* Tel (01245) 440745 Mobile 07949-862867 E-mail robert@robertlocke.wanadoo.co.uk

LOCKE, Stephen John. b 60. St Chad's Coll Dur BA82. Sarum & Wells Th Coll 84. **d** 86 **p** 87. C Blackb St Mich w St Jo and H Trin 86-89; C Oswaldtwistle Immanuel and All SS 89-92; V Blackb St Mich w St Jo and H Trin 92-98; Chapl to the Deaf 98-04; V Owton Manor *Dur* from 04. *The Vicarage, 18 Rossmere Way, Hartlepool TS25 5EF* Tel (01429) 290278

LOCKETT, Preb Paul. b 48. Sarum & Wells Th Coll 73. **d** 76 **p** 77. C Horninglow *Lich* 76-78; C Tewkesbury w Walton Cardiff *Glouc* 78-81; P-in-c W Bromwich St Pet *Lich* 81-90; R Norton Canes 90-95; V Longton St Mary and St Chad from 95; Dean's V Lich Cathl from 91; Preb Lich Cathl from 04. *St Mary and St Chad's Presbytery, 269 Anchor Road, Stoke-on-Trent ST3 5DH* Tel (01782) 313142

LOCKETT, Simon David. b 66. Stirling Univ BA96. Wycliffe Hall Ox 00. **d** 02 **p** 03. C Ray Valley *Ox* 02-06; R Madley w Tyberton, Peterchurch, Vowchurch etc *Heref* from 06. *The Vicarage, Madley, Hereford HR2 9LP* Tel (01981) 250245 E-mail simonlizlockett@hotmail.com

LOCKEY, Malcolm. b 45. Sunderland Poly BA67 Newc Univ DipEd68 FRSA75. NEOC 87. **d** 90 **p** 91. NSM Yarm *York* 90-97; C 97-98; TV Whitby w Aislaby and Ruswarp 98-03; Hon Chapl Miss to Seafarers 98-03; Chapl RNLI 00-03; P-in-c Coldstream *Edin* 04-09; R Kelso 05-09; Offg Chapl RAF and Chapl ATC 02-03; rtd 09. *12 St Helen's Terrace, Spittal, Berwick-upon-Tweed TD15 1RJ* Tel (01289) 306911 Mobile 07710-467785 E-mail macbrac@hotmail.com

LOCKHART, Clare Patricia Anne (Sister Clare). b 44. Bris Univ BA74 Newc Univ MLitt96. Cranmer Hall Dur 84. **d** 87 **p** 94. Sisters of Charity from 63; Chapl Asst Sunderland Distr Gen Hosp 84-89; Chapl 89-95; NSM N Hylton St Marg Castletown *Dur* 87-95; P-in-c 95-99; NSM Eorropaidh *Arg* from 99; Perm to Offic *Dur* from 02. *The Sisters of Charity, Carmel, 7A Gress, Isle of Lewis HS2 0NB* Tel (01851) 820484 E-mail srlockhart@btinternet.com

LOCKHART, David. b 68. QUB BSc90 TCD BTh93. CITC 90. **d** 93 **p** 94. C Belfast St Mary w H Redeemer *Conn* 93-96; I Belfast St Steph w St Luke 96-03; I Cloughfern from 03. *Cloughfern Rectory, 126 Doagh Road, Newtownabbey BT37 9QR* Tel (028) 9086 2437 E-mail dandblockhart@btinternet.com

LOCKHART, Eileen Ann. b 52. Open Univ BA93 ACII74. EAMTC 95. **d** 98 **p** 99. NSM Shenfield *Chelmsf* from 98. *6 Granary Meadow, Wyatts Green, Brentwood CM15 0QD* Tel and fax (01277) 822537 E-mail eileenlockhart@gmail.com

LOCKHART, Patricia May. b 50. Open Univ BA90 Lon Inst of Educn CertEd73. **d** 06 **p** 07. Hd Teacher Kingussie Primary Sch from 86; NSM Rothiemurchus *Mor* from 07. *Craigentor, Middle Terrace, Kingussie PH21 1EY* Tel (01540) 661873 Mobile 07979-540999 E-mail patricialockhart79@hotmail.com

LOCKHART, Raymond William. b 37. Qu Coll Cam BA58 MA61 LLB60. St Jo Coll Nottm 72. **d** 74 **p** 75. C Aspley *S'well* 74-76; V 81-88; R Knebworth *St Alb* 76-81; Warden Stella Carmel Haifa (CMJ) 88-91; R Jerusalem Ch Ch 91-99; Dir CMJ Israel 99-02; rtd 02; Perm to Offic *B & W* from 03. *2 Paddock Woods, Combe Down, Bath BA2 7AD* Tel (01225) 840432 Mobile 07817-330831 E-mail lockhart@xalt.co.uk

LOCKLEY, Miss Pauline Margaret. b 41. **d** 02. OLM Stoke-upon-Trent *Lich* from 02. *Highfields, 89 Tolkien Way, Stoke-on-Trent ST4 7SJ* Tel (01782) 849806 E-mail plock@cix.co.uk

LOCKWOOD, Richard John. b 46. **d** 01 **p** 02. OLM Glascote and Stonydelph *Lich* from 01. *26 Mossdale, Wilnecote, Tamworth B77 4PJ* Tel (01827) 738105 *or* 330306

LOCKWOOD, Mrs Thelma. b 42. WEMTC 01. **d** 03 **p** 04. OLM Bourton-on-the-Water w Clapton etc *Glouc* 03-07; NSM Wimborne Minster *Sarum* from 07. *82 Merley Ways, Wimborne BH21 1QR* Tel (01202) 882488

LOCKYER, David Ralph George. b 41. Wells Th Coll 65. **d** 67 **p** 68. C Bottesford *Linc* 67-69; C Eling *Win* 69-73; TV Eling, Testwood and Marchwood 73-77; TR Speke St Aid *Liv* 77-84; V Halifax St Jude *Wakef* 84-96; Chapl Halifax R Infirmary 84-96; V Banwell *B & W* 96-06; rtd 06. *The Old Quarry, Stour Provost, Gillingham SP8 5SB* Tel (01747) 839970 E-mail david.r.g.lockyer@btinternet.com

LOCKYER, Peter Weston. b 60. Linc Coll Ox BA80 MA83 PGCE98. St Jo Coll Nottm 84. **d** 87 **p** 88. C Rowner *Portsm* 87-90; C Beaconsfield *Ox* 90-91; TV 91-95; Dep Chapl HM YOI Glen Parva 95; Chapl Wellingborough Sch 96-00; R Ewhurst *Guildf* 00-03; Hd Schs & Youth Chr Aid from 03. *3 King George Avenue, Petersfield GU32 3EU* Tel (01730) 269661 E-mail peterlockyer@btinternet.com

LOCOCK (née MILES), Mrs Jillian Maud. b 33. Lon Univ BSc55. NOC 81. **dss** 84 **d** 87 **p** 95. Didsbury Ch Ch *Man* 84-86; Chapl Asst Man R Infirmary 85-87; Chapl Asst Withington Hosp 86-88; Chapl Asst RN 88-93; NSM Dumbarton *Glas* 93-96; Perm to Offic *Ex* from 02. *Glebe Cottage, Dousland, Yelverton PL20 6LU* Tel (01822) 854098 E-mail rjbirtles@aol.com

LODER, Sister Helen. b 43. S'wark Ord Course 91. **d** 94 **p** 95. Soc of St Marg from 70; Hon C S Hackney St Mich w Haggerston St Paul *Lon* 94-01; Hon C Bethnal Green St Matt w St Jas the Gt 02-10. *St Saviour's Priory, 18 Queensbridge Road, London E2 8NS* Tel (020) 7613 1464 E-mail helenloder@aol.com

LODGE, Michael John. b 53. Wycliffe Hall Ox 87. **d** 89 **p** 90. C Highworth w Sevenhampton and Inglesham etc *Bris* 89-93; P-in-c Cheltenham St Luke and St Jo *Glouc* 93-05; TR Rayleigh

Chelmsf from 05; RD Rochford from 08. *The Rectory, 3 Hockley Road, Rayleigh SS6 8BA* Tel (01268) 742151
E-mail mike.lodge@btinternet.com
LODGE, Mrs Patricia Evelyn. b 46. City of Birm Coll CertEd68. **d** 08 **p** 09. OLM Ashton *Man* from 08. *250 Yew Tree Lane, Dukinfield SK16 5DE* Tel 0161-338 5303
E-mail patterry@lodge250.freeserve.co.uk
LODGE, Robin Paul. b 60. Bris Univ BA82 Ch Ch Coll Cant PGCE83. Chich Th Coll 88. **d** 90 **p** 91. C Calne and Blackland *Sarum* 90-94; Asst Chapl St Mary's Sch Calne 90-94; TV Wellington and Distr *B & W* 94-03; V Highbridge 03-09; V Taunton St Andr from 09. *The Vicarage, 118 Kingston Road, Taunton TA2 7SR* Tel (01823) 365730 Mob 07707-439808
E-mail robin.lodge1@btinternet.com
LODGE, Roy Frederick. b 38. MBE97. BTh DPhil93. Tyndale Hall Bris 63. **d** 66 **p** 67. C Tardebigge *Worc* 66-67; Chapl and Warden Probation Hostel Redditch 67-69; Chapl RAF 69-75; C Kinson *Sarum* 76; Lic to Offic *Pet* 76-77; Asst Chapl HM Pris Stafford 77-78; Chapl HM Pris Ranby 78-84; Chapl HM Pris Long Lartin 84-93; Chapl HM Pris Service Coll 87-93; Chapl HM Pris Hewell Grange 93-98; Chapl HM Pris Brockhill 93-98; rtd 98; Perm to Offic *Cov* from 98 and *Glouc* from 99. *44 Eton Road, Stratford-upon-Avon CV37 7ER*
LODGE, Mrs Sally Nicole. b 61. Keele Univ BA83 St Jo Coll Dur BA09. Cranmer Hall Dur 07. **d** 09 **p** 10. C Halstead Area *Chelmsf* from 09. *47 Tidings Hill, Halstead CO9 1BL* Tel (01787) 475528 Mobile 07747-612817
E-mail sally.lodge@btinternet.com
LODWICK, Canon Brian Martin. b 40. Leeds Univ BA61 MPhil76 Linacre Coll Ox BA63 MA67 Univ of Wales PhD87. St Steph Ho Ox 61. **d** 64 **p** 65. C Aberaman *Llan* 64-66; C Newton Nottage 66-73; R Llansannor and Llanfrynach w Penllyn etc 73-94; R Llandough w Leckwith 94-04; RD Llantwit Major and Cowbridge 83-94; Warden of Readers 92-03; Chan Llan Cathl 92-02; Treas 02-04; Chapl Llandough Hosp 94-99; Chapl Univ Hosp of Wales and Llandough NHS Trust 99-01; rtd 04. *26 New Road, Neath Abbey, Neath SA10 7NH*
LODWICK, Stephen Huw. b 64. Plymouth Poly BSc85. St Mich Coll Llan. **d** 94 **p** 95. C Clydach *S & B* 94-95; Chapl St Woolos Cathl 95-98; R Grosmont and Skenfrith and Llangattock etc 98-01; CF from 01. *c/o MOD Chaplains (Army)* Tel (01264) 381140 Fax 381824
LOEWE, Jost Andreas. b 73. St Pet Coll Ox BA95 MA99 MPhil97 Selw Coll Cam PhD01. Westcott Ho Cam 97. **d** 01 **p** 02. C Upton cum Chalvey *Ox* 01-04; C Cambridge Gt St Mary w St Mich *Ely* 04-09; Chapl Trin Coll Melbourne Australia from 09; Lect Th Trin Coll Th Sch from 10. *Trinity College, University of Melbourne, Royal Parade, Parkville Vic 3052, Australia* Tel (0061) (3) 9348 7192 Fax 9348 7610
E-mail aloewe@trinity.unimelb.edu.au
LOEWENDAHL, David Jacob (Jake). b 50. SS Coll Cam BA74 MA77. Ripon Coll Cuddesdon 75. **d** 77 **p** 78. C Walworth *S'wark* 77-80; Chapl St Alb Abbey 80-83; Chapl St Alb Sch 80-83; Team Ldr Community Service Volunteers 84-90; Perm to Offic *Lon* 83-90; R E and W Tilbury and Linford *Chelmsf* 90-95; V Menheniot *Truro* 95-98; RD W Wivelshire 97-98; rtd 98; Perm to Offic *Truro* from 98. *Ashpark House, Ash Park Terrace, Liskeard PL14 4DN* Tel (01579) 348205
LOFT, Edmund Martin Boswell. b 25. St Jo Coll Cam BA49 MA55. Ely Th Coll 49. **d** 51 **p** 52. C Carl H Trin 51-54; C Barrow St Geo 54-56; V Allonby w W Newton 56-62; V Fillongley *Cov* 62-77; V Earlsdon 77-90; rtd 90; Perm to Offic *Sheff* from 90. *10 Quarry Road, Sheffield S17 4DA* Tel 0114-236 0759
LOFTHOUSE, Canon Alexander Francis Joseph. b 30. Keble Coll Ox BA54 MA58. St Steph Ho Ox 54. **d** 56 **p** 57. C Barrow St Jas *Carl* 56-59; C Castleford All SS *Wakef* 59-60; V Airedale w Fryston 60-70; V Maryport *Carl* 70-78; V Helsington 78-95; V Underbarrow 78-95; V Levens 78-95; Hon Can Carl Cathl 85-95; rtd 95; Perm to Offic *Blackb* and *Carl* from 95. *Hazel Grove House, Yealand Redmayne, Carnforth LA5 9RW* Tel (01524) 782405
LOFTHOUSE, Canon Brenda. b 33. RGN60 RM62 RNT69. NOC 84. **d** 87 **p** 94. Hon Par Dn Greengates *Bradf* 87-89; Par Dn Farsley 89-94; V Bolton St Jas w St Chrys 94-00; Hon Can Bradf Cathl 98-00; rtd 00; Perm to Offic *Bradf* from 00. *33 Myrtle Court, Bingley BD16 2LP* Tel (01274) 771476
E-mail brenloft@blueyonder.co.uk
LOFTHOUSE, Mrs Diane Lesley. b 66. Yorks Min Course 08. **d** 11. NSM Moor Allerton and Shadwell *Ripon* from 11. *33 Jackson Avenue, Leeds LS8 1NT* Tel 0113-266 6495
E-mail dianelofthouse@virginmedia.com
LOFTUS, Francis. b 52. Newc Univ BA73 St Andr Univ BPhil76 York St Jo Coll PGCE76 FRSA94. NEOC 93. **d** 96 **p** 97. Hd Master Barlby High Sch 90-10; rtd 10; NSM Barlby w Riccall *York* 96-10; P-in-c from 10; NSM Hemingbrough 06-10; P-in-c from 10. *29 Green Lane, North Duffield, Selby YO8 5RR* Tel (01757) 288030 *or* 706161 Mobile 07850-839419
E-mail francisloftus@btinternet.com

LOFTUS, John Michael. b 52. Sheff Univ BSc74 Solicitor 77. **d** 00 **p** 01. OLM Hundred River *St E* from 00. *Keld House, Hulver Street, Henstead, Beccles NR34 7UE* Tel (01502) 476257 Fax 533001 E-mail jloftus@nortonpeskett.co.uk
LOGAN, Ms Alexandra Jane. b 73. Trin Coll Carmarthen BA94. Ridley Hall Cam 99. **d** 02 **p** 03. C Penwortham St Mary *Blackb* 02-07; V Bethnal Green St Jas Less *Lon* from 07. *St James the Less Vicarage, St James's Avenue, London E2 9JD* Tel and fax (020) 8980 1612 E-mail alexandra.logan@btopenworld.com
LOGAN, Elisabeth Jane. b 59. **d** 10 **p** 11. NSM Copthorne *Chich* from 10. *Fermandy House, Fermandy Lane, Crawley Down, Crawley RH10 4UB* Tel (01342) 713338
LOGAN, Ms Joanne. b 64. Ch Coll Cam BA87 St Jo Coll Dur BA04 MA05. Cranmer Hall Dur 02. **d** 05 **p** 06. C Harrogate St Mark *Ripon* 05-09; Perm to Offic *Lich* from 11. *65 Riches Street, Wolverhampton WV6 0EA*
E-mail jo_logan@btopenworld.com
LOGAN, Kevin. b 43. Oak Hill Th Coll 73. **d** 75 **p** 76. C Blackb Sav 75-78; C Leyland St Andr 78-82; V Gt Harwood St Jo 82-91; V Accrington Ch Ch 91-08; rtd 08; Perm to Offic *Blackb* from 08. *119 Kingsway, Church, Accrington BB5 5EL* Tel (01254) 396139 Mobile 07776-007694 E-mail kevin-logan@sky.com
LOGAN, Samuel Desmond. b 39. TEng. CITC. **d** 78 **p** 79. NSM Belvoir *D & D* 78-85; NSM Knock 85-87; NSM Belfast St Brendan 87-91; Lic to Offic 91-95; C Bangor Abbey 95-97; I Belfast St Clem from 97. *8 Casaeldona Crescent, Belfast BT6 9RE* Tel (028) 9079 5473
LOGUE, Mrs Rosemary Christine. TCD BTh93. CITC 90. **d** 93 **p** 94. C Clooney w Strathfoyle *D & R* 93-96; I Londonderry St Aug 96-03; I Tullyaughnish w Kilmacrennan and Killygarvan 03-05; I Sixmilecross w Termonmaguirke *Arm* 05-08; P-in-c Cambuslang and Uddingston *Glas* 08; I Kilskeery w Trillick *Clogh* from 11. *The Rectory, 130 Kilskeery Road, Trillick, Omagh BT78 3RJ* Tel (028) 8956 1228 E-mail r.logue@btinternet.com
LOH, Tom. b 79. UEA BSc01. Wycliffe Hall Ox BTh11. **d** 11. C Billericay and Lt Burstead *Chelmsf* from 11. *9 Arundel Close, Billericay CM12 0FN* Tel 07905-743419 (mobile)
E-mail tomloh79@yahoo.co.uk
LOMAS, Anthony David. b 59. Cranfield Inst of Tech BSc81. WEMTC 04. **d** 07 **p** 08. C Sevenhampton w Charlton Abbots, Hawling etc *Glouc* 07-11; R Redmarley D'Abitot, Bromesberrow, Pauntley etc from 11. *The Rectory, Redmarley, Gloucester GL19 3HS* Tel (01531) 650715 Mobile 07793-564877 E-mail adlomas@aol.com
LOMAS, Mrs Catherine Mary. b 72. St Jo Coll Cam MA93. STETS 07. **d** 10 **p** 11. C Wellingborough All SS *Pet* from 10; C Wellingborough All Hallows from 11. *12 Bush Close, Wellingborough NN8 3GL* Tel (01933) 385430
E-mail revdcatherine@virginmedia.com
LOMAS, David Xavier. b 39. St Jo Coll Dur BA78. Cranmer Hall Dur 75. **d** 78 **p** 79. C Chester le Street *Dur* 78-81; C-in-c Newton Hall LEP 81-85; Chapl Scunthorpe Distr HA 85-93; Sen Chapl Linc and Louth NHS Trust 93-01; Sen Chapl Chapl Manager United Lincs Hosps NHS Trust 01-04; rtd 04. *9 Hazel Grove, Welton, Lincoln LN2 3JZ* Tel (01673) 861409
E-mail xavlomas@aol.com
LOMAS, Canon John Derrick Percy. b 58. St Mich Coll Llan 94. **d** 94 **p** 95. C Rhyl w St Ann *St As* 94-00; Chapl RN 00-01; V Holywell *St As* from 01; AD Holywell from 08; Can Cursal St As Cathl from 08. *The Vicarage, 1 Llys Bychan, Holywell CH8 7SX* Tel (01352) 710010
LOMAX, Canon Barry Walter John. b 39. Lambeth STh Lon Coll of Div 63. **d** 66 **p** 67. C Sevenoaks St Nic *Roch* 66-71; C Southport Ch Ch *Liv* 71-73; V Bootle St Matt 73-78; P-in-c Litherland St Andr 76-78; V New Borough and Leigh *Sarum* 78-94; Can and Preb Sarum Cathl 91-02; R Blandford Forum and Langton Long 94-02; rtd 02; Perm to Offic *Sarum* from 03. *Shiloh, 2 Colborne Avenue, Wimborne BH21 2PZ* Tel (01202) 856104 E-mail barry.lomax@virgin.net
LOMAX, Eric John. b 64. St Jo Coll Dur BA96 Leeds Univ PGCE04. Cranmer Hall Dur 93. **d** 96 **p** 97. C Goodshaw and Crawshawbooth *Man* 96-00; V Copmanthorpe *York* 00-01; P-in-c Colsterworth Gp *Linc* from 10. *The Rectory, 13A Back Lane, Colsterworth, Grantham NG33 5NJ* Tel (01476) 861959 E-mail ericjohnlomax64@aol.com
LOMAX, Mrs Kate Jane. b 73. RGN96. St Jo Coll Nottm BA02. **d** 02 **p** 03. C Luton St Mary *St Alb* 02-04; Asst Chapl Cam Univ Hosps NHS Foundn Trust 04-05; Chapl 05-07; NSM Penn Fields *Lich* 08-10; NSM Bayston Hill from 10. *The Vicarage, 42 Eric Lock Road West, Bayston Hill, Shrewsbury SY3 0QA* Tel (01743) 872472 E-mail kate.lomax@btinternet.com
LOMAX, Timothy Michael. b 73. Derby Univ BEd95 Nottm Univ MA11. Ridley Hall Cam 05. **d** 07 **p** 08. C Penn Fields *Lich* 07-10; V Bayston Hill from 10. *The Vicarage, 42 Eric Lock Road West, Bayston Hill, Shrewsbury SY3 0QA* Tel (01743) 872472 E-mail tim.lomax@btinternet.com
LONDON (St Paul's), Dean of. See KNOWLES, The Rt Revd Graeme Paul

LONDON, Archdeacon of. *See* MEARA, The Ven David Gwynne

LONDON, Bishop of. *See* CHARTRES, The Rt Revd and Rt Hon Richard John Carew

LONEY, Mark William James. b 72. Cen Lancs Univ BSc94 MA97 TCD BTh03. CITC 00. **d** 03 **p** 04. C Larne and Inver *Conn* 03-06; I Ahoghill w Portglenone from 06. *The Rectory, 42 Church Street, Ahoghill, Ballymena BT42 2PA* Tel (028) 2587 1240 E-mail rev.loney@btopenworld.com

LONG, Canon Anne Christine. b 33. Leic Univ BA56 Ox Univ DipEd57 Lon Univ BD65 ALBC. **dss** 80 **d** 87 **p** 94. Lect St Jo Coll Nottm 73-84; Acorn Chr Healing Trust 85-98; Stanstead Abbots *St Alb* 85-92; Hon Par Dn 87-92; Hon Par Dn Camberley St Paul *Guildf* 92-94; Hon C 94-03; Hon Can Guildf Cathl 96-03. *3 Chiselbury Grove, Salisbury SP2 8EP* Tel (01722) 341488

LONG, Anthony Auguste. b 45. Linc Th Coll 79. **d** 81 **p** 82. C Kingswinford St Mary *Lich* 81-84; TV Ellesmere Port *Ches* 84-87; V Witton 87-97; P-in-c Wybunbury w Doddington 97-02; V 02-10; rtd 10. *23 Osborne Grove, Shavington, Crewe CW2 5BY* Tel (01270) 561113 E-mail tojolong@tiscali.co.uk

LONG, Anthony Robert. b 48. SS Mark & Jo Coll Chelsea CertEd70 Southn Univ BTh93 UEA MA96 Lambeth MA04. Chich Th Coll 74. **d** 77 **p** 78. C Chiswick St Nic w St Mary *Lon* 77-80; C Earley St Pet *Ox* 80-85; P-in-c Worstead w Westwick and Sloley *Nor* 85-92; R Worstead, Westwick, Sloley, Swanton Abbot etc from 92; P-in-c Tunstead w Sco' Ruston from 85; Chapl Nor Cathl from 85. *The Vicarage, Withergate Road, Worstead, North Walsham NR28 9SE* Tel (01692) 536800

LONG, Bill. *See* LONG, Edward Percy Eades

LONG, Bradley. b 65. St Jo Coll Dur BA08 Lon Inst of Educn PGCE94. Cranmer Hall Dur 06. **d** 08. C The Hague *Eur* from 08. *Ary van der Spuyweg 1, 2585 HA The Hague, The Netherlands* Tel (0031) (70) 887 6108 Mobile 68-236 6789 E-mail bradley_long4@hotmail.com

LONG, The Ven Christopher William. b 47. MBE94. Nottm Univ BTh78 Open Univ BA80. Linc Th Coll 75. **d** 78 **p** 79. C Shiregreen St Jas and St Chris *Sheff* 78-81; V 81-82; Chapl RAF 82-05; I Enniscorthy w Clone, Clonmore, Monart etc *C & O* from 05; Adn Ferns from 08. *The Rectory, St John's, Enniscorthy, Co Wexford, Republic of Ireland* Tel (00353) (53) 923 9009 E-mail chriswlong1@eircom.net

LONG, David William. b 47. St Aug Coll Cant 70. **d** 72 **p** 73. C Stanley *Liv* 72-73; C W Derby St Luke 73-76; C Cantril Farm 76-79; V Warrington St Barn 79-81; V Westbrook St Jas 82-96; V Ince St Mary from 96; AD Wigan E and Hon Can Liv Cathl 03-05. *St Mary's Vicarage, 240A Warrington Road, Ince, Wigan WN3 4NH* Tel (01942) 864383 E-mail david@scars.org.uk

LONG, Edward Percy Eades (Bill). b 14. Liv Univ BA36 MA38. Linc Th Coll 73. **d** 73 **p** 74. C Sedbergh, Cautley and Garsdale *Bradf* 73-84; rtd 85; Perm to Offic *Bradf* from 85. *4 Derry Cottages, Sedbergh LA10 5SN* Tel (015396) 20577

LONG, Mrs Frances Mary. b 58. SEITE 98. **d** 01 **p** 02. NSM Caterham *S'wark* 01-05; Chapl Surrey and Sussex Healthcare NHS Trust 01-03; C Riddlesdown *S'wark* 05-08; P-in-c Purley St Mark from 08; P-in-c Purley St Swithun from 08. *2 Church Road, Purley CR8 3QQ* E-mail franyb8@hotmail.com

LONG, Frederick Hugh. b 43. EMMTC 90. **d** 90 **p** 91. NSM Grantham *Linc* 90-00; C 00-01; TV 01-02; V Grantham St Anne New Somerby and Spitalgate 02-08; rtd 08; Hon C Drybrook, Lydbrook and Ruardean *Glouc* from 08. *The Rectory, High Street, Ruardean GL17 9US* Tel (01594) 541070

LONG, Geoffrey Lawrence. b 47. La Sainte Union Coll BTh93 PGCE94. Portsm Dioc Tr Course 88. **d** 89 **p** 98. NSM Whippingham w E Cowes *Portsm* 89-01; Chapl HM Pris Maidstone from 01. *HM Prison, County Road, Maidstone ME14 1UZ* Tel (01622) 755611

LONG, Hermione Jane. b 66. Univ of Wales (Swansea) BSc97 RGN88. St Mich Coll Llan 05. **d** 07 **p** 08. C Bassaleg *Mon* from 07. *St Anne's Church House, 2 High Cross Drive, Rogerstone, Newport NP10 9AB* Tel (01633) 895441

LONG, John. b 48. ACIB72. Yorks Min Course 09. **d** 10 **p** 11. NSM Utley *Bradf* from 10. *Rosslyn House, Cold Street, Haworth BD22 8AY* Tel (01535) 646592 E-mail haworthlongs@tiscali.co.uk

LONG, Canon John Sydney. b 25. Lon Univ BSc49. Wycliffe Hall Ox 50. **d** 51 **p** 52. C Plaistow St Andr *Chelmsf* 51-54; C Keighley *Bradf* 54-57; C-in-c Horton Bank Top CD 57-59; V Buttershaw St Aid 59-64; V Barnoldswick w Bracewell 64-85; Hon Can Bradf Cathl 77-91; RD Skipton 83-90; R Broughton, Marton and Thornton 85-91; rtd 91; Perm to Offic *Bradf* from 91. *1 Church Villa, Carleton, Skipton BD23 3DQ* Tel (01756) 799095

LONG, Kingsley Edward. b 41. CITC 90. **d** 93 **p** 94. NSM Swords w Donabate and Kilsallaghan *D & G* 93-94 and 96-99; NSM Howth 94-96; NSM Holmpatrick w Balbriggan and Kenure 99-01; NSM Dublin Clontarf 02-03; NSM Swords w Donabate and Kilsallaghan from 03. *Crimond, 125 Seapark, Malahide, Co Dublin, Republic of Ireland* Tel (00353) (1) 845 3179

LONG, Canon Michael David Barnby. b 32. AKC55. **d** 56 **p** 57. C Whitby *York* 56-59; C Cottingham 59-61; V Elloughton 61-66; P-in-c Brantingham 61-66; V Sheff St Cecilia Parson Cross 66-68; V Flamborough *York* 68-73; R Litcham w Kempston w E and W Lexham *Nor* 73-75; P-in-c York St Luke 75-77; V 77-80; V Hatton w Haseley and Rowington w Lowsonford *Cov* 80-82; V Derringham Bank *York* 82-85; R Castleacre w Newton, Rougham and Southacre *Nor* 85-86; TV Grantham *Linc* 86-89; V Cayton w Eastfield *York* 89-98; RD Scarborough 94-98; Can and Preb York Minster 97-03; rtd 98; P-in-c York St Clem w St Mary Bishophill Senior 98-03; P-in-c Trowse *Nor* from 03. *19 Ipswich Grove, Norwich NR2 2LU* Tel (01603) 613224 E-mail michael-long@amserve.com

LONG, Peter Ronald. b 48. Cuddesdon Coll 71. **d** 73 **p** 74. Chapl RAFVR 74-99; C Bodmin *Truro* 73-75; C Newquay 75-76; Asst Youth Chapl 75-76; Dioc Youth Chapl 76-79; Perm to Offic *Eur* 76, 78-85 and 87-98; Public Preacher *Truro* 77; P-in-c Mawgan w St Martin-in-Meneage 79-82; Chapl Helston-Meneage Community and Geriatric Hosp 80-95; Miss to Seamen 80-98; P-in-c Cury w Gunwalloe *Truro* 80-82; R Cury and Gunwalloe w Mawgan 83-98; Perm to Offic *Ex* 82-93; Ecum Th in UK Rail Ind from 97; rtd 08. *26 Jubilee Street, Newquay TR7 1LA* Tel 07780-976113 (mobile) Fax (01637) 877060 E-mail ipsn2009@yahoo.co.uk

LONG, Richard John William. b 59. Hull Univ BA80 PGCE81. Cranmer Hall Dur 03. **d** 05 **p** 06. C Beverley St Nic *York* 05-09; TV Marfleet from 09. *St Philip's House, 107 Amethyst Road, Hull HU9 4JG* Tel (01482) 376208 E-mail richlong@fsmail.net

LONG, Roger Eric. b 36. Univ Coll Dur BSc59 PhD62. NEOC 90. **d** 93 **p** 94. C Street *York* 93-97; P-in-c Coxwold and Husthwaite 97-02; rtd 02. *Ivy House, Coxwold, York YO61 4AD* Tel (01347) 868301

LONG, Samuel Allen. b 48. EAMTC 03. **d** 05 **p** 06. NSM Barrow *St E* 05-08; NSM Pakenham w Norton and Tostock 08-10; P-in-c Badwell and Walsham from 10. *The Rectory, The Causeway, Walsham-le-Willows, Bury St Edmunds IP31 3AB* Tel (01359) 259310 Mobile 07732-971925 E-mail valerielong16@aol.com

LONG, Canon Samuel Ernest. b 18. JP68. ALCD50 LTh MTh ThD. **d** 49 **p** 50. C Belfast St Clem *D & D* 49-52; C Willowfield 52-56; I Dromara w Garvaghy 56-85; Can Dromore Cathl 81-85; Treas 82-85; rtd 85. *9 Cairnshill Court, Saintfield Road, Belfast BT8 4TX* Tel (028) 9079 3401

LONG, Simon Richard. b 40. Bernard Gilpin Soc Dur 61 Ely Th Coll 62 Coll of Resurr Mirfield 64. **d** 65 **p** 66. C Bournemouth St Fran *Win* 65-68; C Brussels *Eur* 68; V Portales and Fort Sumner USA 69-79; V Lincoln St Mark 79-81; V Martin St Kath 81-83; R Lousville Em 83-86; V Elizabethtown Ch Ch 86-88; P-in-c Medbourne cum Holt w Stockerston and Blaston *Leic* 88-89; P-in-c Bringhurst w Gt Easton 88-89; R Six Saints circa Holt 90-99; RD Gartree I 93-97; rtd 99. *17C Craft Village, Balnakeil, Durness, Lairg IV27 4PT* Tel (01971) 511757

LONG, William Thomas. b 53. Dur Univ MA88 QUB PhD99. **d** 81 **p** 82. C Orangefield *D & D* 81-84; C Portadown St Mark *Arm* 84-86; I Dromara w Garvaghy *D & D* 86-91; I Aghalurcher w Tattykeeran, Cooneen etc *Clogh* 91-96; I Annalong *D & D* 96-03; I Belfast St Simon w St Phil *Conn* 03-06; I Carnteel and Crilly *Arm* from 06. *St James's Rectory, 22 Carnteel Road, Aughnacloy BT69 6DU* Tel (028) 8555 7682 Mobile 07748-857312 E-mail wlhudhud@bushinternet.com

LONGBOTTOM, Canon Frank. b 41. Ripon Hall Ox 65. **d** 68 **p** 69. C Epsom St Martin *Guildf* 68-72; Asst Chapl St Ebbas Hosp Epsom 68-72; Asst Chapl Qu Mary's Hosp Carshalton 68-72; Asst Chapl Henderson Hosp Sutton 68-72; Chapl Highcroft Hosp Birm 72-94; Chapl Northcroft Hosp Birm 74-94; Dioc Adv for Past Care of Clergy & Families 89-94; Bp's Adv 94-06; Bp's Adv on Health and Soc Care *Birm* 01-06; P-in-c Middleton 99-00; Hon Can Birm Cathl 91-06; rtd 07. *46 Sunnybank Road, Sutton Coldfield B73 5RE* Tel and fax 0121-350 5823

LONGBOTTOM, Canon Paul Edward. b 44. Kent Univ MA02 AKC67. **d** 68 **p** 69. C Rainham *Roch* 68-71; C Riverhead 71-75; C Dunton Green 71-75; V Penge Lane H Trin 75-84; V Chatham St Wm 84-94; V Shorne and Dioc Dir of Ords 94-09; Hon Can Roch Cathl 96-09; rtd 09; Perm to Offic *Roch* from 09 and *Cant* from 10. *Advent House, Primrose Lane, Bredgar, Sittingbourne ME9 8EH* Tel (01622) 884593 E-mail paul.longbottom@ymail.com

LONGDEN, Lee Paul. b 70. Peterho Cam BA91 MA95 Ches Coll of HE MTh03 FRCO91 LLCM93 ARCM93 LRSM96. Qu Coll Birm 03. **d** 05 **p** 06. C Langley and Parkfield *Man* 05-08; V Ashton Ch Ch from 08; Hon Assoc Dir of Ords from 09. *Christ Church Vicarage, Vicarage Road, Ashton-under-Lyne OL7 9QY* Tel 0161-330 1601 E-mail vicar@christchurch-ashton.org.uk

LONGDON, Anthony Robert James. b 44. STETS 00. **d** 03 **p** 04. OLM N Bradley, Southwick and Heywood *Sarum* 03-08; OLM N Bradley, Southwick, Heywood and Steeple Ashton from 08. *1A Holbrook Lane, Trowbridge BA14 0PP* Tel and fax (01225) 754771 E-mail tony.longdon@homecall.co.uk

LONGE, David John Hastings. b 75. New Coll Edin BD99. Ripon Coll Cuddesdon 07. **d** 09 **p** 10. C N Lambeth *S'wark* from 09. *12 Moat Place, London SW9 0BS* Tel (020) 7735 3403
LONGE, James Robert. b 46. EAMTC 02. **d** 04 **p** 05. NSM Pakenham w Norton and Tostock *St E* 04-07; NSM St Edm Way from 07. *Bush House, Bradfield St Clare, Bury St Edmunds IP30 0EQ*
LONGFELLOW, Erica Denise. b 74. Duke Univ (USA) BA97 Linc Coll Ox MSt98 DPhil01. SEITE 02. **d** 05 **p** 06. NSM Kew St Phil and All SS w St Luke *S'wark* 05-09; NSM Surbiton St Andr and St Mark from 09. *The Coach House, 1 Church Hill Road, Surbiton KT6 4UG* Tel (020) 8390 9129 E-mail e.longfellow@kingston.ac.uk
LONGFOOT, Canon Richard. b 46. Oak Hill Th Coll 76. **d** 78 **p** 79. C Chaddesden St Mary *Derby* 78-81; C Cambridge St Martin *Ely* 81-83; R Folksworth w Morborne 83-89; R Stilton w Denton and Caldecote 83-89; R Stilton w Denton and Caldecote etc from 90; RD Yaxley 02-07; Hon Can Ely Cathl from 04. *The Rectory, Stilton, Peterborough PE7 3RF* Tel (01733) 240282 E-mail richard.lfoot@lineone.net
LONGMAN, Edward. b 37. Hatf Coll Dur BSc62 Fitzw Coll Cam BA66 MA70. Clifton Th Coll 62. **d** 66 **p** 67. C Lower Homerton St Paul *Lon* 66-72; C Parr *Liv* 72-73; TV 74-85; Perm to Offic *Liv* 87-02 and *Ches* from 96. *21 Canadian Avenue, Hoole, Chester CH2 3HG* Tel (01244) 317544 Fax 400450 Mobile 07779-650791 E-mail elongman@onetel.com
LONGMAN, Edward George. b 35. St Pet Hall Ox BA58 MA62. Westcott Ho Cam 59. **d** 61 **p** 62. C Sheff St Mark Broomhall 61-65; V Brightside St Thos 65-74; V Yardley St Edburgha *Birm* 74-84, RD Yardley 77-84, Hon Can Birm Cathl 81-96, R Sutton Coldfield H Trin 84-96; RD Sutton Coldfield 94-96; Chapl Gd Hope Distr Gen Hosp Sutton Coldfield 84-90; P-in-c Cerne Abbas w Godmanstone and Minterne Magna *Sarum* 96-02; RD Dorchester 00-02; rtd 02; Perm to Offic *B & W* from 04. *5 Old Wells Road, Shepton Mallet BA4 5XN* Tel (01749) 343699 E-mail ed@roseted.co.uk
LONGUET-HIGGINS, John. b 62. Leeds Univ BA85. St Jo Coll Nottm 88. **d** 91 **p** 92. C Kidlington w Hampton Poyle *Ox* 91-95; TV N Huddersfield *Wakef* 95-01; V Painswick, Sheepscombe, Cranham, The Edge etc *Glouc* from 02. *The Vicarage, Orchard Mead, Painswick, Stroud GL6 6YD* Tel (01452) 812334
LONSDALE, Mrs Gillian. b 36. Qu Mary Coll Lon BA57 MA59 Ex Univ MPhil81 AIMSW91. SWMTC 96. **d** 99 **p** 00. NSM Duloe, Herodsfoot, Morval and St Pinnock *Truro* 99-06; NSM Lansallos and Talland 01-03; RD W Wivelshire 03-06; rtd 06. *Woodhill Manor, Liskeard PL14 6RD* Tel (01579) 340697 Mobile 07801-301031 E-mail gill@glonsdale.freeserve.co.uk
LONSDALE, Ms Linda. b 49. SWMTC 08. **d** 10 **p** 11. NSM Alderley Edge *Ches* from 10. *27 Willow Lane, Goostrey, Crewe CW4 8PP* Tel (01477) 549303 E-mail linda.goostrey@talktalk.net
LOOKER, Clare Margaret. *See* FLEMING, Miss Clare Margaret
LOOMES, Gaenor Mary. *See* HOCKEY, Gaenor Mary
LORAINE, Kenneth. b 34. Cranmer Hall Dur 63. **d** 66 **p** 67. C Hartlepool All SS Stranton *Dur* 66-69; C Darlington St Cuth 69-72; V Preston on Tees 72-79; V Staindrop 79-87; P-in-c Haynes *St Alb* 87-96; Dioc Stewardship Adv 87-96; rtd 96; Perm to Offic *York* from 96. *116 Turker Lane, Northallerton DL6 1QD* Tel (01609) 771277
LORD, Alexander. b 13. ALCD43. **d** 43 **p** 44. C Wakef St Mary 43-45; P-in-c Thornham St Jas *Man* 45-47; R Clitheroe St Jas *Blackb* 47-55; V Madeley *Heref* 55-69; R Illogan *Truro* 70-81; rtd 81; C Letton w Staunton, Byford, Mansel Gamage etc *Heref* 81-84. *44 Church Street, Davenham, Northwich CW9 8NF*
LORD, Andrew Michael. b 66. Warwick Univ BSc87 Birm Univ MA99 PhD10 Fitzw Coll Cam BA02. Ridley Hall Cam 00. **d** 03 **p** 04. C Long Buckby w Watford *Pet* 03-06; C W Haddon w Winwick and Ravensthorpe 03-06; R Trowell, Awsworth and Cossall *S'well* from 06. *The Rectory, 47 Nottingham Road, Trowell, Nottingham NG9 3PF* Tel 0115-849 5195 E-mail revandylord@gmail.com
LORD, Clive Gavin. b 69. St Martin's Coll Lanc BA. St Steph Ho Ox BTh. **d** 96 **p** 97. C Penwortham St Leon *Blackb* 96-98; C Blackpool St Mary 98-01; P-in-c 01-04; V 04-06; Chapl Blackpool, Fylde and Wyre Hosps NHS Trust from 06. *Chaplaincy Office, Victoria Hospital, Whinney Heys Road, Blackpool FY3 8NR* Tel (01253) 306875 E-mail livecg@aol.com *or* clive.lord@bfwhospitals.nhs.uk
LORD, Stuart James. b 59. K Coll Lon BD81 AKC81. Sarum & Wells Th Coll 83. **d** 85 **p** 86. C Darwen St Pet w Hoddlesden *Blackb* 85-88; C Otley *Bradf* 88-93; P-in-c Low Moor St Mark 93-02; TV Brighouse and Clifton *Wakef* 02-09; R Norton in the Moors *Lich* from 10. *The New Rectory, Norton Lane, Stoke-on-Trent ST6 8BY* Tel (01484) 534622
LORD, Mrs Tanya Marie. b 66. Trin Coll Bris. **d** 09 **p** 10. C Bris St Matt and St Nath from 09. *157 Bishop Road, Bristol BS7 8NA* Tel 0117-908 2797 Mobile 07852-928881 E-mail tanyalord@aol.com

LORD-LEAR, Mark. b 40. Ex Univ DipEd70 Sussex Univ MA74. SWMTC 10. **d** 11. *Orchard Lodge, 109B Ilsham Road, Torquay TQ1 2HY* Tel (01803) 290404 E-mail markll@talktalk.net
LORDING, Miss Claire Ann. b 75. Roehampton Inst BA96. Ripon Coll Cuddesdon BTh96. **d** 99 **p** 00. C Ledbury *Heref* 99-02; TV Tenbury Wells 02-08; TR 08-10; P-in-c Clee Hill 09-10; TR Tenbury from 10; RD Ludlow from 10. *The Vicarage, Church Street, Tenbury Wells WR15 8BP* Tel (01584) 810811 E-mail claire.lording@virgin.net
LORIMER, Eileen Jean. b 35. CertEd56. Dalton Ho Bris 62. dss 84 **d** 89 **p** 94. Chiddingstone w Chiddingstone Causeway *Roch* 84-04; NSM 89-04; Perm to Offic from 04. *3 Causeway Cottages, Chiddingstone Causeway, Tonbridge TN11 8JR* Tel (01892) 871393
LORT-PHILLIPS, Mrs Elizabeth Priscilla. b 47. STETS 02. **d** 05 **p** 06. NSM Redhorn *Sarum* from 05. *The Cottage on the Green, 1 Manor Farm Lane, Patney, Devizes SN10 3RB* Tel (01380) 84071 E-mail e.lortphillips@btinternet.com
LOSACK, Marcus Charles. b 53. Ch Coll Cam BA76 MA78 MPhil. Sarum & Wells Th Coll 78. **d** 80 **p** 81. C Hattersley *Ches* 80-82; C Dublin Zion Ch *D & G* 83-86; Libya 86-89; CMS Jerusalem 89-92; I Newcastle w Newtownmountkennedy and Calary *D & G* 93-95; Exec Dir Céile Dé from 95. *Céile Dé, Castlekevin, Annamoe, Bray, Co Wicklow, Republic of Ireland* Tel and fax (00353) (404) 45595
LOTHIAN, Iain Nigel Cunningham. b 59. Aber Univ MA84 Bath Univ PGCE86 Leeds Univ MA05. NOC 02. **d** 05 **p** 06. C Sheff St Pet Abbeydale 05-09; C Sheff St Pet and St Oswald 09; Perm to Offic from 09. *33 Gatefield Road, Sheffield S7 1RD* Tel 0114-250 9736 E-mail i.lothian@btopenworld.com
LOTT, Eric John. b 34. Lon Univ BA65 Lanc Univ MLitt70 PhD77. Richmond Th Coll BD59. **d** 60 **p** 61. India 60-88; Prof United Th Coll Bangalore 77-88; Wesley Hall Ch and Community Project Leics 88-94; rtd 94; Perm to Offic *Leic* from 94. *16 Main Road, Old Dalby, Melton Mowbray LE14 3LR* Tel (01664) 822405 E-mail eric.lott@breathemail.net
LOUDEN, Canon Terence Edmund. b 48. Ch Coll Cam BA70 MA74. Sarum & Wells Th Coll 72. **d** 75 **p** 76. C Portsea N End St Mark *Portsm* 75-78; C-in-c Leigh Park St Clare CD 78-81; R Chale 81-88; R Niton 81-88; P-in-c Whitwell 82-84; V Cosham 88-96; Hon Can Portsm Cathl from 92; V E Meon from 96; V Langrish from 96; CME Officer 96-03. *The Vicarage, Church Street, East Meon, Petersfield GU32 1NH* Tel (01730) 823221 Mobile 07711-319752 E-mail telouden@cwcom.net
LOUDON (*née* KING), Mrs Ellen Francis. b 67. Liv Poly BA90 Liv Univ MA96. Trin Coll Bris 06. **d** 08. C Everton St Pet w St Chrys *Liv* from 08. *The Vicarage, St John Chrysostom, Queens Road, Liverpool L6 2NF* Tel 0151-260 8289 Mobile 07718-806831 E-mail ellen@ellenloudon.com
LOUGHBOROUGH, Archdeacon of. *See* NEWMAN, The Ven David Maurice Frederick
LOUGHEED, Brian Frederick Britain. b 38. TCD BA60. CITC 61. **d** 61 **p** 62. C Dublin St Pet w St Audoen *D & G* 61-63; C Glenageary 63-66; I Rathmolyon Union *M & K* 66-79; I Killarney w Aghadoe and Muckross *L & K* 79-04; Can Limerick and Killaloe Cathls 87-95; Preb Taney St Patr Cathl Dublin 89-04; Dioc Info Officer (Limerick) *L & K* 90-91; Radio Officer 91-04; rtd 04. *2 Arlington Heights, Park Road, Killarney, Co Kerry, Republic of Ireland* Tel (00353) (64) 21642 E-mail brianlougheed1@eircom.net
LOUGHLIN, Canon Alfred. b 10. Clifton Th Coll 37. **d** 39 **p** 40. C Preston St Mark *Blackb* 39-44; Chapl RAFVR 41-43; Org Sec (SE Area) CPAS 44-48; V Sneinton St Chris *S'well* 48-54; R Kinson *Sarum* 54-81; Can and Preb Sarum Cathl 75-81; rtd 81. *2 Friars Close, Wilmslow SK9 5PP* Tel (01625) 530403
LOUGHLIN, George Alfred Graham. b 43. Clifton Th Coll 65. **d** 69 **p** 70. C Plumstead All SS *S'wark* 69-73; C Bromley Ch Ch *Roch* 73-76; P-in-c Bothenhampton w Walditch *Sarum* 76-79; TV Bridport 79-83; V Heatherlands St Jo 83-08; rtd 08. *239 rue de Florièye, 83460 Taradeau, France* E-mail vicar@gagl.co.uk
LOUGHTON, Michael. b 34. K Coll Lon BD58 AKC58. **d** 59 **p** 60. C Chingford SS Pet and Paul *Chelmsf* 59-62; C Eastbourne St Elisabeth *Chich* 62-65; R Lewes St Jo sub Castro 65-74; Perm to Offic from 87 rtd 99. *Green Woodpecker, 1 Kammond Avenue, Seaford BN25 3JL* Tel (01323) 893506
LOUIS, Ms Emma Christine. b 69. Coll of Ripon & York St Jo BA92 St Jo Coll Dur BA96. Cranmer Hall Dur 94. **d** 97 **p** 98. C Birm St Martin w Bordesley St Andr 97-00; Arts Development Officer 97-00; Asst Chapl Harrogate Health Care NHS Trust 00-02; Chapl Co-ord St Mich Hospice Harrogate 01-02; Asst Chapl Birm Heartlands and Solihull NHS Trust 02-04; Lead Chapl Sandwell Mental Health NHS and Social Care Trust from 04. *Sandwell Mental Health Trust, Delta House, Greets Green Road, West Bromwich B70 9PL* Tel 0121-612 8067 Mobile 07813-015325 E-mail emma.louis@smhsct.nhs.uk
LOUIS, Canon Peter Anthony. b 41. St Cath Coll Ox BA63 MA77 Man Univ MPhil85 Jes Coll Cam CertEd64. Wells Th Coll 66. **d** 68 **p** 70. C E Grinstead St Mary *Chich* 68-75; C Radcliffe-on-

Trent S'well 75-80; Hd Master Blue Coat Comp Sch Cov 80-85; V Welwyn Garden City St Alb 85-08; Chapl Oaklands Coll 93-95; Hon Can St Alb 04-08; rtd 08. 27 Aylesbury Road, Wendover, Aylesbury HP22 6JG Tel (01296) 582683 E-mail plouis@ntlworld.com

LOVATT, Bernard James. b 31. Lich Th Coll 64. **d** 65 **p** 66. C Burford III w Lt Heref 65-67; C Cleobury Mortimer w Hopton Wafers 67-68; C Bradford-on-Avon H Trin Sarum 68-69; C Wootton Bassett 69-72; C Broad Town 69-72; R Bishopstrow and Boreham 72-79; P-in-c Brighton St Geo Chich 79-83; V Brighton St Anne 79-83; V Brighton St Geo and St Anne 83-86; P-in-c Kemp Town St Mark and St Matt 85-86; V Brighton St Geo w St Anne and St Mark 86-95; rtd 95; Perm to Offic Ex from 95. 7 Cambridge Terrace, Salcombe Road, Sidmouth EX10 8PL Tel (01395) 514154

LOVATT, James Arthur Roy. b 36. **d** 08 **p** 09. OLM Horton, Lonsdon and Rushton Spencer Lich from 08. 25 Kent Drive, Endon, Stoke-on-Trent ST9 9EH Tel (01782) 504723 E-mail jarl25kd@tiscali.co.uk

LOVATT, Mrs Pamela. b 50. **d** 98 **p** 99. OLM Warrington St Ann Liv from 98; Chapl Warrington Community Health Care NHS Trust from 99. 59 Amelia Street, Warrington WA2 7QD Tel (01925) 650049 or 655221 E-mail pam.lovatt@ntlworld.com

LOVATT, William Robert. b 54. SS Coll Cam MA75 K Coll Lon PGCE77 MA78. Oak Hill Th Coll 85. **d** 87 **p** 88. C Warrington St Budeaux Ex 87-90; Asst Chapl Paris St Mich Eur 90-94; P-in-c Lenton S'well 94-00; V 00-04; V Eastbourne All SS Chich from 04; RD Eastbourne 06-09. All Saints' Vicarage, 1A Jevington Gardens, Eastbourne BN21 4HR Tel (01323) 410033 Mobile 07815-138202 E-mail robertlovatt@tiscali.co.uk

LOVE, Mrs Alison Jane. b 63. Lanc Univ BA84 Westmr Coll Ox PGCE85 Win Univ BA11. STETS 08. **d** 11. NSM Chippenham St Pet Bris from 11. 5 Stainers Way, Chippenham SN14 6YE Tel (01249) 653004 E-mail palove@tiscali.co.uk

LOVE, Ms Anette. b 53. Matlock Coll of Educn CertEd74 Nottm Univ BEd75. St Jo Coll Dur 88. **d** 90 **p** 94. Par Dn Gresley Derby 90-92; C Heanor 92-94; C Loscoe 94-02; V Horsley from 02. The Vicarage, Main Road, Heath, Chesterfield S44 5RX Tel (01246) 850339

LOVE, Joel. b 77. Birm Univ BA99 MPhil04 PhD08 Cam Univ BA11. Westcott Ho Cam 09. **d** 11. C Lancaster St Mary w St John and St Anne Blackb from 11. Chauntry Cottage, 1 Priory Close, Lancaster LA1 1YZ Tel (01524) 381936 Mobile 07745-902735 E-mail joel.loves.trees@gmail.com

LOVE, Richard Angus. b 45. AKC67. **d** 68 **p** 69. C Balham Hill Ascension S'wark 68-71; C Amersham Ox 71-73; R Scotter w E Ferry Linc 73-79; P-in-c Petham w Waltham and Lower Hardres w Nackington Cant 79-85; R Petham and Waltham w Lower Hardres etc 85-90; V Sittingbourne H Trin w Bobbing 90-02; P-in-c Aldington w Bonnington and Bilsington etc 02-10; rtd 10; Perm to Offic Cant from 10. 45 Greystones Road, Bearsted, Maidstone ME15 8PD E-mail revralove@msn.com

LOVE, Robert. b 45. Bradf Univ BSc68 PhD74 NE Lon Poly PGCE89. Trin Coll Bris. **d** 75 **p** 76. C Bowling St Jo Bradf 75-79; TV Forest Gate St Sav w W Ham St Matt Chelmsf 79-85; P-in-c Becontree St Elisabeth 85-96; V S Hornchurch St Jo and St Matt 96-10; AD Havering 08-10; rtd 10. 7 Chelmer Drive, South Ockendon RM15 6EE Tel (01708) 530915 E-mail revboblove@tiscali.co.uk

LOVEDAY, Mrs Jean Susan. b 47. Ex Univ BTh10. SWMTC 09. **d** 11. NSM Braunton Ex from 11. Cowley, Parracombe, Barnstaple EX31 4PQ Tel (01598) 763373 E-mail jean@castlemaker.com

LOVEDAY, Joseph Michael. b 54. AKC75. St Aug Coll Cant 75. **d** 78 **p** 79. C Kettering SS Pet and Paul 78-81; C Upper Teddington SS Pet and Paul Lon 81-84; CF from 84. c/o MOD Chaplains (Army) Tel (01264) 381140 Fax 381824

LOVEDAY, Susan Mary. b 49. Sussex Univ BA70 Surrey Univ MSc81. STETS 94. **d** 97 **p** 98. NSM New Haw Guildf 97-03; NSM Egham Hythe from 03; Ecum Co-ord Churches Together in Surrey from 00. 10 Abbey Gardens, Chertsey KT16 8RQ Tel (01932) 566920 E-mail sue.loveday.ctsurrey@lineone.net

LOVEGROVE, Anne Maureen. b 44. Oak Hill Th Coll 88. **d** 90 **p** 94. Par Dn Thorley St Alb 90-94; C 94-95; V Croxley Green St Oswald 95-02; V Letchworth St Paul w Willian 02-09; rtd 09. 24 Chenies Avenue, Amersham HP6 6PP Tel (01494) 763151 E-mail anne.lovegrove1@btinternet.com

LOVEGROVE, Michael John Bennett. b 42. FCII FCIPD ACIArb. SEITE. **d** 00 **p** 01. NSM Saffron Walden w Wendens Ambo, Littlebury etc Chelmsf 00-08; TV 05-08; rtd 08; Perm to Offic Chelmsf from 09. Craigside, 8 Beck Road, Saffron Walden CB11 4EH Tel (01799) 528232 Mobile 07980-103541 E-mail lovegrove8 @btinternet.com

LOVELESS, Christopher Hugh. b 61. Trin Coll Ox BA84 MA91. Linc Th Coll 89. **d** 91 **p** 92. C Walkington Chich 91-95; C Goring-by-Sea 95-99; V Warnham from 99. The Vicarage, Church Street, Warnham, Horsham RH12 3QW Tel (01403) 265041 E-mail nloveless@hotmail.com

LOVELESS, Martin Frank. b 46. N Bucks Coll of Educn CertEd68. Wycliffe Hall Ox 72. **d** 75 **p** 76. C Caversham Ox 75-81; V Carterton 81-86; Chapl RAF 86-02; Chapl K Coll Taunton 02-04; Perm to Offic Heref 04-05 and from 07; P-in-c Glossop Derby 05-07. Ridge Cottage, Staunton-on-Wye, Hereford HR4 7LP Tel (01981) 500311 Mobile 07810-002079 E-mail martinloveless@hotmail.com

LOVELESS, Mrs Natalie. b 78. Southn Univ BA01. SEITE 08. **d** 11. NSM Horsham Chich from 11. The Vicarage, Church Street, Warnham, Horsham RH12 3QW Tel (01403) 243254 E-mail revnloveless@gmail.com

LOVELESS, Robert Alfred. b 43. Birm Univ BA66. Westcott Ho Cam 66. **d** 68 **p** 69. C Kenilworth St Nic Cov 68-72; C Costessey Nor 73-75; R Colney 75-80; R Lt w Gt Melton, Marlingford and Bawburgh 75-80; V Lt and Gt Melton w Bawburgh 80-82; P-in-c Westwood Sarum 82-83; P-in-c Wingfield w Rowley 82-83; R Westwood and Wingfield 83-87; Chapl Stonar Sch Melksham 82-87; R Paston Pet 87-93; V Nassington w Yarwell and Woodnewton 93-07; rtd 07. 93 The Pollards, Bourne PE10 0FR Tel (01778) 393561

LOVELESS, Canon William Harry. b 21. Lon Univ BSc60. Ridley Hall Cam 61. **d** 63 **p** 64. C Danbury Chelmsf 63-65; C Cambridge St Mary w St Mark Ely 65-67; V Cambridge St Mark 67-87; RD Cambridge 81-84; Hon Can Ely Cathl 81-87; rtd 87; Perm to Offic Ely 87-03. Langdon House, 20 Union Lane, Cambridge CB4 1QB Tel (01223) 303279

LOVELL, Charles Nelson. b 34. Oriel Coll Ox BA57 MA61. Wycliffe Hall Ox. **d** 59 **p** 60. C Walsall St Matt Lich 59-63; C St Giles-in-the-Fields Lon 63; Argentina 64-67; C Cambridge H Trin Ely 64; V Esh Dur 67-75; V Hamsteels 67-75; Chapl Winterton Hosp Sedgefield 75-83; R Stanhope Dur 83-86; Chapl Horn Hall Hosp Weardale 83-97; R Stanhope w Frosterley Dur 86-97; V Eastgate w Rookhope 86-97; RD Stanhope 87-97; rtd 97. 10 Riverside, Wolsingham, Bishop Auckland DL13 3BP Tel (01388) 527038 E-mail charles@thefreeinternet.co.uk

LOVELL, David John. b 38. JP89. Univ of Tasmania BEcon86. Qu Coll Birm 60. **d** 62 **p** 63. C Glouc St Steph 60-64; C Lower Tuffley St Geo CD 64-67; V Lydbrook 67-73; R Oatlands Australia 73-75; Perm to Offic Tas 76-81; rtd 98. 26 Lynden Road, Bonnet Hill Tas 7053, Australia Tel (0061) (3) 6229 2838

LOVELL, Mrs Gillian Jayne. b 58. Univ of Wales (Ban) BA79 PGCE80. Qu Coll Birm MA04. **d** 04 **p** 05. C Burnham Ox 04-08; P-in-c Burghfield 08-10; R from 10; R Sulhamstead Abbots and Bannister w Ufton Nervet from 10. The Rectory, Hollybush Lane, Burghfield Common, Reading RG7 3JL Tel 0118-983 4433 E-mail gill.lovell@stmarysburghfield.org

LOVELL, Helen Sarah. See HOUSTON, Helen Sarah

LOVELL, Keith Michael Beard. b 43. K Coll Lon 67. **d** 68 **p** 69. C Romford St Edw Chelmsf 68-73; P-in-c Elmstead 73-79; V Tollesbury w Salcot Virley 79-09; rtd 09; Perm to Offic Chelmsf from 09. 14 Brierley Avenue, West Mersea, Colchester CO5 8HG Tel (01206) 386626 E-mail keith@mary.freewire.co.uk

LOVELL, Laurence John. b 31. St D Coll Lamp BA54 Tyndale Hall Bris 54. **d** 56 **p** 57. C Penge Ch Ch w H Trin Roch 56-61; C Illogan Truro 61-63; V St Keverne 63-68; C-in-c Oatley Australia 68-72; R 72-95; rtd 95. Donald Robinson Village, 105/81 Flora Street, Kirrawee NSW 2223 Australia E-mail ljl01@bigpond.com

LOVELUCK, Canon Allan (Illtyd). b 30. Univ of Qld BSW74 MSocWork79. St D Coll Lamp BA52 St Mich Coll Llan 52. **d** 55 **p** 56. C Dowlais Llan 55-58; SSF 58-79; Lic to Offic Chelmsf 62-64; Australia from 64; Hon Can Brisbane 92-00; rtd 95. 5/48 Dunmore Terrace, Auchenflower Qld 4066, Australia Tel (0061) (7) 3719 5342 or 3870 2566 Mobile 414-500837

LOVELUCK, Canon Graham David. b 34. Univ of Wales (Abth) BSc55 PhD58 CChem FRSC. St Deiniol's Hawarden 77. **d** 78 **p** 79. NSM Llanfair Mathafarn Eithaf w Llanbedrgoch Ban 78-87; NSM Llaneugrad w Llanallgo and Penrhosllugwy etc 87-96; P-in-c 96-03; R 03-04; Dioc Dir of Educn 92-03; Can Cursal Ban Cathl 00-04; rtd 04. Gwenallt, Marianglas LL73 8PE Tel (01248) 853741

LOVEMAN, Mrs Ruth. b 45. STETS 01. **d** 04 **p** 05. NSM Portsea N End St Mark Portsm 04-09; NSM Cowplain from 09. 3 Cotwell Avenue, Waterlooville PO8 9AP Tel (023) 9259 1933 E-mail ruthlvm@googlemail.com

LOVERIDGE, Douglas Henry. b 52. Sarum & Wells Th Coll. **d** 84 **p** 85. C Earley St Pet Ox 84-88; V Hurst 88-03; Asst Chapl R Berks NHS Foundn Trust 03-07; Chapl Mid-Essex Hosp Services NHS Trust 07-09; Chapl W Herts Hosps NHS Trust from 09. All Saints' Vicarage, Churchfields, Hertford SG13 8AE Tel (01992) 584899 or (01923) 217994 E-mail dhloveridge@hotmail.com or douglas.loveridge@whht.nhs.uk

LOVERIDGE, Emma Warren. b 65. St Jo Coll Cam BA87 MA90 PhD01. **d** 99 **p** 00. NSM Highbury Ch Ch w St Jo and St Sav Lon 99-02; NSM Islington St Mary 03-05; Prin Adv to Abp York 06-07. 6 Prior Bolton Street, London N1 2NX Tel 07000-777977 (mobile) E-mail eloveridge@windsandstars.co.uk

LOVERIDGE (née RODEN), Ms Joan Margaretha Holland (Jo). b 57. K Coll Lon BD78 AKC78 Regent's Park Coll Ox MTh98. SAOMC 95. **d** 97 **p** 98. NSM Caversham St Jo *Ox* 97-98; C Earley St Pet 98-03; P-in-c Burghfield 03-07; AD Bradfield 04-07; P-in-c Hertford All SS *St Alb* 07-08; TR Hertford from 08. *All Saints' Vicarage, Churchfields, Hertford SG13 8AE* Tel (01992) 584899
E-mail jonloveridge@hotmail.com
LOVERING, Mrs Jennifer Mary. b 39. Eastbourne Tr Coll CertEd59. Wycliffe Hall Ox 81. **dss** 84 **d** 87 **p** 94. Abingdon w Shippon *Ox* 84-87; Par Dn Abingdon 87-94; C 94-97; rtd 98. *5 Monksmead, Brightwell-cum-Sotwell, Wallingford OX10 0RL* Tel (01491) 825329
LOVERING, Martin. b 35. Imp Coll Lon BScEng57. Wycliffe Hall Ox 82. **d** 84 **p** 85. NSM Abingdon w Shippon *Ox* 84-88; C Abingdon 88-89; TV 89-00; rtd 01. *5 Monks Mead, Brightwell-cum-Sotwell, Wallingford OX10 0RL* Tel (01491) 825329
LOVERN, Mrs Sandra Elaine. b 48. Trin Coll Bris BA07. **d** 07 **p** 08. NSM Chew Magna w Dundry, Norton Malreward etc *B & W* from 07. *Willow Lodge, Breach Hill Lane, Chew Stoke, Bristol BS40 8YA* Tel (01275) 332657
E-mail sandra.lovern@yahoo.com
LOVESEY, Katharine Patience Beresford. b 62. Trin Coll Bris 01. **d** 03 **p** 04. C Nor Lakenham St Jo and All SS and Tuckswood 03-08; C Stoke H Cross w Dunston, Arminghall etc 08-10. *3 Alexander Court, Norwich NR4 6RL*
E-mail katelovesey@aol.com
LOVETT, Frances Mary Anderson. b 46. Plymouth Univ BA92. NOC 00. **d** 03 **p** 04. Ind Chapl *Liv* 03-10; NSM Newton in Makerfield St Pet 03-05; Hon Chapl Liv Cathl 05-10; rtd 10; Perm to Offic *Liv* from 10. *28 New Street, Torrington EX38 8BN* Tel (01805) 938219 Mobile 07989-099483
E-mail fran.lovett@googlemail.com
LOVETT, Francis Roland. b 25. Glouc Th Course. **d** 85 **p** 86. NSM Ludlow *Heref* 85-91; rtd 92; Perm to Offic *Heref* 96-05. *7 Poyner Road, Ludlow SY8 1QT* Tel (01584) 872470
LOVETT, Ian Arthur. b 43. NE Lon Poly BSc74. Linc Th Coll 85. **d** 87 **p** 88. C Uppingham w Ayston and Wardley w Belton *Pet* 87-91; R Polebrook and Lutton w Hemington and Luddington 91-04; Asst to RD Corby 05-08; rtd 08; Perm to Offic *Pet* from 09. *38 Northbrook, Corby NN18 9AX* Tel (01536) 747644
E-mail ian.lovett@tiscali.co.uk
LOVETT, Canon Ian James. b 49. JP99. CertEd72 BTh89 MA92. S'wark Ord Course 73. **d** 76 **p** 77. NSM Gravesend St Geo *Roch* 76-77; NSM Wellesborough w Hinxhill *Cant* 77-83; NSM Landcross, Littleham, Monkleigh etc *Ex* 83-85; C Compton Gifford 85-86; TV Plymouth Em w Efford 86-92; TV Plymouth Em, St Paul Efford and St Aug 93-97; Chapl Aintree Hosps NHS Trust Liv 97-10; Bp's Adv for Hosp Chapl *Liv* 03-10; Hon Can Liv Cathl 08-10; TV Bideford, Northam, Westward Ho!, Appledore etc *Ex* from 11. *The Rectory, Fore Street, Northam, Bideford EX39 1AW* Tel (01237) 470183
LOVITT, Gerald Elliott. b 25. St Mich Coll Llan 59. **d** 61 **p** 62. C Aberdare *Llan* 61-66; C Whitchurch 66-71; V Grangetown 71-76; V Rockfield and Llangattock w St Maughan's *Mon* 76-83; V Rockfield and St Maughen's w Llangattock 83-93; rtd 93; Perm to Offic *Llan* from 93; Lic to Offic *Mon* from 93. *104B Albany Road, Cardiff CF24 3RT* Tel (029) 2041 1697
LOW, Andrew Andrew. b 56. UEA BSc77 Hull Univ MSc78 Nottm Univ MA10 CertEd82 FBCS FIMA CEng CITP. EMMTC 08. **d** 10 **p** 11. NSM Alrewas *Lich* from 10; NSM Wychnor from 10. *Griffin Lodge, Bellamour Way, Colton, Rugeley WS15 3LL* Tel (01889) 577888 Mobile 07766-520365
E-mail a.a.low@staffs.ac.uk
LOW, Alastair Graham. b 43. Brunel Univ BSc68 Reading Univ PhD74. Ripon Coll Cuddesdon 90. **d** 92 **p** 93. C Brighton Gd Shep Preston *Chich* 92-96; TV Ifield 96-99; TV Horsham 99-08; Chapl Surrey and Sussex Healthcare NHS Trust 02-08; rtd 08; Perm to Offic *Ox* from 08. *3 Sheepway Court, Iffley, Oxford OX4 4JL* Tel (01865) 777257
E-mail graham@glowpigs.freeserve.co.uk
LOW, Mrs Christine Mabel. b 48. Southlands Coll Lon CertEd69 SS Mark & Jo Univ Coll Plymouth BEd87. SWMTC. **d** 99 **p** 00. NSM Bideford, Northam, Westward Ho!, Appledore etc *Ex* 99-03; P-in-c Thornton in Lonsdale w Burton in Lonsdale *Bradf* 03-08; NSM Bingley All SS from 08; NSM Bingley H Trin from 08. *Winston Grange, Otley Road, Eldwick, Bingley BD16 3DE* Tel (01274) 564694 Mobile 07870-766634
E-mail chris.low@talktalk.net
or chris.low@bradford.anglican.org
LOW, Canon David Anthony. b 42. AKC66. **d** 67 **p** 68. C Gillingham St Barn *Roch* 67-70; V 82-88; C Wallingford *Ox* 70-73; V Spencer's Wood 73-82; P-in-c Grazeley and Beech Hill 77-82; Chapl Medway Hosp Gillingham 86-88; V Hoo St Werburgh *Roch* 88-02; RD Strood 97-02; Hon Can Roch Cathl 01-02; rtd 02. *12 Stonecrop Close, St Mary's Island, Chatham ME4 3HA*
LOW, Canon David Michael. b 39. Cape Town Univ BA60. Cuddesdon Coll 61. **d** 63 **p** 64. C Portsea St Cuth *Portsm* 63-65; S

Africa 65-69; C Havant *Portsm* 69-72; V St Helens 72-88; V Sea View 81-88; V Sandown Ch Ch 88-95; V Lower Sandown St Jo 88-95; R Brading w Yaverland 95-01; Hon Can Portsm Cathl 00-01; rtd 01. *Copeland, Lane End Close, Bembridge PO35 5UF* Tel (01983) 874306
LOW, Mrs Jennifer Anne. b 49. St Anne's Coll Ox MA70 Nottm Univ PGCE71. Trin Coll Bris 01. **d** 03 **p** 04. C Bris St Andr Hartcliffe 03-07; P-in-c Lawrence Weston and Avonmouth from 07; Deanery Growth Officer Bris W from 07. *The Vicarage, 335 Long Cross, Bristol BS11 0NN* Tel 0117-982 5863
E-mail jennilow@yahoo.com
LOW, Peter James. b 52. Nottm Univ BTh89. Linc Th Coll 86. **d** 89 **p** 90. C Dartford H Trin *Roch* 89-92; C Plympton St Mary *Ex* 92-94; TR Devonport St Boniface and St Phil 94-08; V Heybridge w Langford *Chelmsf* from 08. *The Vicarage, 1A Crescent Road, Heybridge, Maldon CM9 4SJ* Tel (01621) 841274 E-mail peter@lowuk.wanadoo.co.uk
LOW, Robbie. See LOW, William Roberson
LOW, Stafford. b 42. N Lon Poly BSc65. Trin Coll Bris 82. **d** 85 **p** 86. C Yeovil *B & W* 85-88; C Glastonbury w Meare, W Pennard and Godney 88-92; R Berrow and Breane 92-00; R Wincanton 00-07; R Pen Selwood 00-07; Chapl Voc and Min 97-07; RD Bruton and Cary 03-06; rtd 07. *Les Acacias, route d'Uzès Prolongée, Le Moulinet, 30500 Saint-Ambroix, France* E-mail lowandco@aol.com
LOW, Terence John Gordon. b 37. Oak Hill Th Coll 75. **d** 77 **p** 78. C Kensal Rise St Martin *Lon* 77-79; C Longfleet *Sarum* 79-83; P-in-c Maiden Newton and Valleys 83-84; TV Melbury 84-88; TV Buckhurst Hill *Chelmsf* 88-92; R Gt Hallingbury and Lt Hallingbury 92-01; rtd 01; Perm to Offic *Sarum* from 02. *37 Vicarage Lane, Charminster, Dorchester DT2 9QF* Tel (01305) 260180
LOW, William Roberson (Robbie). b 50. Pemb Coll Cam BA73 MA77. Westcott Ho Cam 76. **d** 79 **p** 80. C Poplar *Lon* 79-83; Chapl St Alb Abbey 83-88; V Bushey Heath 88-03; rtd 10. *3 Trewince Lane, Bodmin Hill, Lostwithiel PL22 0AJ* Tel (01208) 871517 E-mail robbielow2@hotmail.com
LOWATER, Canon Jennifer Blanche. b 34. Eastbourne Tr Coll TCert54. Sarum & Wells Th Coll 82. **dss** 85 **d** 87 **p** 94. Locks Heath *Portsm* 85-88; Hon C 87-88; NSM Southsea St Pet 88-94; NSM Hook w Warsash 94-01; Asst Dir of Ords 91-99; Hon Can Portsm Cathl 95-97; rtd 97. *Lower Gubbles, Hook Lane, Warsash, Southampton SO31 9HH* Tel (01489) 572156 Fax 572252
E-mail jenny.lowater@care4free.net
LOWDON, Christopher Ian. b 63. Plymouth Univ LLB93 Barrister 94. Aston Tr Scheme 86 St Mich Coll Llan 04. **d** 06 **p** 07. C Chaddesden St Phil *Derby* 06-09; TV Buxton w Burbage and King Sterndale from 09. *St Mary's Vicarage, 2A New Market Street, Buxton SK17 6LP* Tel (01298) 213212 Mobile 07871-087294 E-mail chris.lowe@bradford.anglican.org
E-mail frchris@buxtonparish.org.uk
LOWE, Anthony Richard. b 45. York Univ BA66. Qu Coll Birm 66. **d** 69 **p** 70. C Greasbrough *Sheff* 69-71; C Thrybergh 71-75; P-in-c Sheff St Mary w St Simon w St Matthias 75-78; V Shiregreen St Hilda 78-85; V Hoxne w Denham St Jo and Syleham *St E* 85-89; P-in-c Wingfield 86-89; R Hoxne w Denham, Syleham and Wingfield 90-05; rtd 06. *9 Alfred Road, Dover CT16 2AB* Tel (01304) 214047
LOWE, Mrs Brenda June. b 53. Cranmer Hall Dur 75. **d** 88 **p** 94. Chapl to Families Trin Coll and Mortimer Ho Bris 86-91; NSM Clifton Ch Ch w Em *Bris* 88-91; Asst Chapl Southmead Health Services NHS Trust 86-91; NSM Marple All SS *Ches* from 91; Perm to Offic *Man* 91-97; Asst Chapl Wythenshawe Hosp Man 94-96; Chapl Stockport Acute Services NHS Trust 96-98; Sen Chapl Stockport NHS Trust from 98. *4 Greenway Road, Heald Green, Cheadle SK8 3NR* Tel 0161-282 3850 or 419 5889
E-mail malowe@mail.com
LOWE, Christopher Alan. b 75. Imp Coll Lon MEng97. Oak Hill Th Coll MTh08. **d** 08 **p** 09. C Cambridge St Andr Less *Ely* from 08. *4 Parsonage Street, Cambridge CB5 8DN* Tel (01223) 354207 Mobile 07962-060786
E-mail chris.lowe@christchurchcambridge.org.uk
LOWE, Canon David Charles. b 43. Kelham Th Coll 62. **d** 67 **p** 68. C Wingerworth *Derby* 67-70; C Greenhill St Pet 70-73; TV Eckington 73-74; TV Eckington w Handley and Ridgeway 74-78; V Bury St Edmunds St Geo *St E* 78-86; V Leiston 86-98; RD Saxmundham 88-96; P-in-c Felixstowe St Jo 86-98; Hon Can St E Cathl 98-08; rtd 08; Perm to Offic *St E* from 08. *21 Firebrass Lane, Sutton Heath, Woodbridge IP12 3TS* Tel (01394) 421722 E-mail david_lowechurch@lineone.net
LOWE, David Reginald. b 42. K Coll Lon BD65 AKC65. St Boniface Warminster 65. **d** 67 **p** 68. C Tupsley *Heref* 66-69; C Lewes St Anne *Chich* 69-73; C Heref H Trin 73-77; P-in-c Lyonshall w Titley 77-88; V Lyonshall w Titley, Almeley and Kinnersley 88-96; Perm to Offic 97-00; rtd 00. *26 Chapel Street, Penzance TR18 4AP* Tel (01736) 331068
LOWE, Donald. b 33. Lich Th Coll 57. **d** 60 **p** 61. C Horwich H Trin *Man* 60; C Wythenshawe W Martin CD 60-62; C Bury St Paul 62-65; V Gannow *Blackb* 70-73; R Virginia St Alb S Africa 73-81; V Colne H Trin 81-89; TV

Melbury *Sarum* 89-94; RD Beaminster 93-94; rtd 94; Perm to Offic *Bradf* from 94. *28 High Bank, Threshfield, Skipton BD23 5BU* Tel (01756) 752344

LOWE, Mrs Elaine Mary. b 55. **d** 98 **p** 99. OLM Bardsley *Man* from 98. *5 Danisher Lane, Bardsley, Oldham OL8 3HU* Tel 0161-633 4535

LOWE, The Ven Frank McLean Rhodes. b 26. ACT 59. **d** 61 **p** 63. Australia 61-86 and from 87; Hon Can Gippsland 73-81; Adn Latrobe Valley 81-86; Adn Gippsland 81-86; P-in-c Kirkby in Ashfield St Thos *S'well* 86-87; C Mansfield Woodhouse 87; rtd 91. *Unit 2, 3 Berg Street, Morwell Vic 3840, Australia* Tel (0061) (3) 5134 1338

LOWE, Mrs Janet Eleanor. b 56. Univ Coll Lon BSc77. NTMTC 98. **d** 01 **p** 02. C Hendon St Paul Mill Hill *Lon* from 01. *12 Frobisher Road, London N8 0QS* Tel (020) 8340 8764 E-mail janlowe@btinternet.com

LOWE, Canon John Bethel. b 30. TCD BA52 BD65. Ridley Hall Cam 55. **d** 55 **p** 56. C Belfast St Mary Magd *Conn* 55-57; Sudan 59-64; Uganda 64-74; Warden CMS Fellowship Ho Foxbury 74-76; V Kippington *Roch* 76-96; Dioc Dir of Ords 82-96; Hon Can Roch Cathl 85-96; rtd 96; Perm to Offic *Ely* from 96. *228 Cambridge Road, Great Shelford, Cambridge CB22 5JU* Tel (01223) 840019

LOWE, John Forrester. b 39. Nottm Univ BA61. Lich Th Coll 61. **d** 64 **p** 65. C N Woolwich *Chelmsf* 64-70; V Marks Gate 70-74; V Moulsham St Jo 74-79; V N Woolwich w Silvertown 79-82; V Birm St Pet 82-86; Gen Sec SOMA UK 86-91; V Heckmondwike *Wakef* 92-98; rtd 98; Perm to Offic *Heref* from 99. *37 Jubilee Close, Ledbury HR8 2XA* Tel (01531) 631890

LOWE, Jonathan David. b 66. ACII04. Trin Coll Bris 08. **d** 10 **p** 11. C Icknield Way Villages *Chelmsf* from 10. *8 Colts Croft, Great Chishill, Royston SG8 8SF* Tel (01763) 836962 Mobile 07771-850705 E-mail jonathan@worship.org.uk

LOWE, Keith Gregory. b 50. Sarum & Wells Th Coll 91. **d** 93 **p** 94. C Wallasey St Hilary *Ches* 93-94; C W Kirby St Bridget 94-98; V Sandbach Heath w Wheelock 98-01; V High Lane 01-04; Chapl Stockport NHS Trust 01-04; Asst Chapl Sheff Teaching Hosps NHS Trust 04-06; Chapl Sheff Teaching Hosps NHS Foundn Trust from 06. *169 Mortomley Lane, High Green, Sheffield S35 3HT* Tel 0114-284 4076 E-mail keithglowe@aol.com

LOWE, Canon Michael Arthur. b 46. Lon Univ BD67 Hull Univ MA85. Cranmer Hall Dur. **d** 76 **p** 77. C Thorpe Edge *Bradf* 76-79; C N Ferriby *York* 79-84; TV 84-86; Dir Past Studies Trin Coll Bris 86-91; V Marple All SS *Ches* 91-00; RD Chadkirk 95-00; Dir of Miss and Unity 00-05; C Delamere 00-02; C Wilmslow 05-08; Hon Can Ches Cathl 00-08; rtd 08; Dioc Ecum Officer *Ches* from 09; Hon C Cheadle from 10. *4 Greenway Road, Heald Green, Cheadle SK8 3NR* Tel 0161-282 3850 E-mail malowe@mail.com

LOWE, Samuel. b 35. St D Coll Lamp. **d** 65 **p** 66. C Tenby w Gumfreston *St D* 65-67; C Lower Mitton *Worc* 67-69; C Halesowen 69-72; R Droitwich St Nic w St Pet 72-73; TV Droitwich 73-77; P-in-c Claines St Geo 77-78; P-in-c Worc St Mary the Tything 77-78; P-in-c Worc St Geo w St Mary Magd 78-84; V 84-00; rtd 00. *57 Camp Hill Road, Worcester WR5 2HG* Tel (01905) 357807

LOWE, Preb Stephen Arthur. b 49. Nottm Univ BSc71. Cuddesdon Coll 71. **d** 74 **p** 75. C Mansfield St Mark *S'well* 74-77; Chapl Martyrs' Sch Papua New Guinea 77-78; P-in-c Nambaiyufa 79; V Kirkby Woodhouse 80-86; V Beeston 86-99; TR Wenlock *Heref* from 99; RD Condover from 06; Preb Heref Cathl from 10. *The Rectory, New Road, Much Wenlock TF13 6EQ* Tel (01952) 727396 E-mail rector@wenlockchurches.co.uk

✠**LOWE, The Rt Revd Stephen Richard.** b 44. Lon Univ BSc66. Ripon Hall Ox 68. **d** 68 **p** 69 **c** 99. C Gospel Lane St Mich *Birm* 68-72; C-in-c Woodgate Valley CD 72-75; V E Ham w Upton Park *Chelmsf* 75-76; TR 76-88; Hon Can Chelmsf Cathl 85-88; Adn Sheff 88-99; Can Res Sheff Cathl 88-99; Suff Bp Hulme *Man* 99-09; rtd 09. *2 Pen y Glyn, Bryn-y-Maen, Colwyn Bay LL28 5EW* Tel (01492) 533510 Mobile 07801-505277 E-mail lowehulme@btinternet.com

LOWE, Mrs Valerie Anne. CBDTI. **d** 07 **p** 08. NSM Skipton Ch Ch w Carleton *Bradf* from 07. *126A Keighley Road, Skipton BD23 2QT* Tel (01756) 790132

LOWELL, Ian Russell. b 53. AKC75. St Aug Coll Cant 75. **d** 76 **p** 77. C Llwynderw *S & B* 76-79; C Swansea St Mary w H Trin and St Mark 79-81; Chapl Ox Hosps 81-83; TV Gt and Lt Coates w Bradley *Linc* 83-88; V Wellingborough St Mark *Pet* 88-02; V Northampton St Alb from 02; Chapl Northants Ambulance Service 92-03; Officer for Major Emergencies from 03. *St Alban's Vicarage, Broadmead Avenue, Northampton NN3 2RA* Tel (01604) 407074 E-mail ianlowell@btinternet.com

LOWEN, Mrs Anne Lois. b 60. DipCOT82. ERMC 03. **d** 06 **p** 07. NSM Basle *Eur* from 06; Asst Chapl from 11. *Im Wygaertli 15, 4114 Hofstetten, Switzerland* Tel (0041) (61) 731 1485 E-mail anne.lowen@bluewin.ch

LOWEN, David John. b 42. Sussex Univ BSc74 Univ of Wales (Lamp) MA84. Llan Dioc Tr Scheme 86. **d** 88 **p** 89. C Carmarthen St Pet *St D* 88-90; P-in-c Walwyn's Castle w Robeston W 90-92; R 92-08; rtd 08. *The Vicarage, Rock Lane, Llawhaden, Narberth SA67 8HL*

LOWEN, John Michael. b 47. Nottm Univ BTh77. Linc Th Coll 73. **d** 77 **p** 78. C Beeston *S'well* 77-80; C Stratford-on-Avon w Bishopton *Cov* 80-82; V Monkseaton St Mary *Newc* 82-90; V Ponteland 90-95; Chapl HM Pris Leeds 95; P-in-c Sutton St Mary *Linc* 95-00; R Dunvegan Canada 00-05; rtd 07. *9 Alden Hubley Drive, RR1, Annapolis Royal NS B0S 1A0, Canada* Tel (001) (902) 532 1981

LOWER, David John. b 77. Huddersfield Univ BA99. Wycliffe Hall Ox 08. **d** 10 **p** 11. C Sileby, Cossington and Seagrave *Leic* from 10. *52 Main Street, Cossington, Leicester LE7 4UU* Tel 07709-451681 (mobile) E-mail davidandnaomi@o2.co.uk

LOWLES, Martin John. b 48. Thames Poly BSc72. Cranmer Hall Dur. **d** 78 **p** 79. C Leyton St Mary w St Edw *Chelmsf* 78-81; C Waltham Abbey 81-85; V E Ham St Paul 85-95; TR N Huddersfield *Wakef* 95-06; V Birkenshaw w Hunsworth from 06. *The Vicarage, 6 Vicarage Gardens, Birkenshaw, Bradford BD11 2EF* Tel (01274) 683776 E-mail martin.lowles@btinternet.com

LOWMAN, The Ven David Walter. b 48. K Coll Lon BD73 AKC73. St Aug Coll Cant 73. **d** 75 **p** 76. C Notting Hill *Lon* 75-78; C Kilburn St Aug w St Jo 78-81; Selection Sec and Voc Adv ACCM 81-86; TR Wickford and Runwell *Chelmsf* 86-93; Dioc Dir of Ords 93-01; C Chelmsf All SS 93-01; C Chelmsf Ascension 93-01; Hon Can Chelmsf Cathl 93-01; Adn Southend from 01. *The Archdeacon's Lodge, 136 Broomfield Road, Chelmsford CM1 1RN* Tel (01245) 258257 Fax 250845 E-mail a.southend@chelmsford.anglican.org

LOWNDES, Charles. b 22. MISW57 CQSW72. **d** 87 **p** 88. NSM Hanley H Ev *Lich* 87-97; rtd 97. *7 Beacon Rise, Stone ST15 0AL* Tel (01785) 812698

LOWNDES, Harold John (Nobby). b 31. SAOMC 96. **d** 99 **p** 00. OLM Lamp *Ox* from 99. *98 Wolverton Road, Haversham, Milton Keynes MK19 7AB* Tel (01908) 319939 E-mail hlowndes@vivao.net

LOWNDES, Canon Richard Owen Lewis. b 63. Univ of Wales (Ban) BD86. Coll of Resurr Mirfield 87. **d** 89 **p** 90. C Milford Haven *St D* 89-91; C Roath St German *Llan* 91-94; Chapl Cardiff Royal Infirmary 91-94; V Tylorstown w Ynyshir *Llan* 94-96; Asst Chapl St Helier NHS Trust 96-98; Chapl Team Ldr W Middx Univ Hosp NHS Trust 98-03; Chapl Team Ldr Ealing Hosp NHS Trust 01-03; Chapl Team Ldr Southn Univ Hosps NHS Trust from 03; Hon Can Win Cathl from 11. *Trust Management Offices, Southampton General Hospital, Tremona Road, Southampton SO16 6TD* Tel (023) 8077 7222 Fax 8079 4153

LOWRIE, Ronald Malcolm. b 48. Bath Spa Univ MA07. Ripon Hall Ox 70. **d** 72 **p** 73. C Knowle *Birm* 72-75; C Bourton-on-the-Water w Clapton *Glouc* 75-79; R Broadwell, Evenlode, Oddington and Adlestrop 79-81; TV Trowbridge H Trin *Sarum* 81-88; P-in-c Westwood and Wingfield 88-90; R from 90; P-in-c Bradford-on-Avon Ch Ch 03-10; Chapl Wilts and Swindon Healthcare NHS Trust 88-05. *The Rectory, Westwood, Bradford-on-Avon BA15 2AF* Tel (01225) 863109 or 867040 E-mail rmlowrie@btinternet.com

LOWRY, The Very Revd Stephen Harold. b 58. QUB BSc79 CertEd80. CITC 82. **d** 85 **p** 86. C Coleraine *Conn* 85-88; I Greenisland 88-98; I Dromore Cathl from 98; Dean Dromore from 02. *Dromore Cathedral Rectory, 28 Church Street, Dromore BT25 1AA* Tel (028) 9269 2275 or 9269 3968 Mobile 07834-584932 E-mail cathedral@dromore.anglican.org

✠**LOWSON, The Rt Revd Christopher.** b 53. AKC75 Heythrop Coll Lon MTh96 Univ of Wales (Cardiff) LLM03. St Aug Coll Cant 76 Pacific Sch of Relig Berkeley STM78. **d** 77 **p** 78 **c** 11. C Richmond St Mary *S'wark* 77-79; C Richmond St Mary w St Matthias and St Jo 79-82; P-in-c Eltham H Trin 82-83; V 83-91; R Buriton *Portsm* 91-99; V Petersfield 91-99; RD Petersfield 95-99; Adn Portsdown 99-06; Bp's Liaison Officer for Pris 00-03; Bp's Adv to Hosp Chapl 03-06; Dir Min Division Abps' Coun 06-11; PV Westmr Abbey 06-11; Bp Linc from 11. *The Old Palace, Lincoln LN2 1PU* Tel (01522) 504050 E-mail bishop.lincoln@lincoln.anglican.org

LOWSON, Geoffrey Addison. b 47. Bede Coll Dur BEd70 PGCE70. NEOC 95. **d** 98 **p** 99. NSM Sherburn in Elmet w Saxton *York* 98-04; Fieldworker (NE England) USPG 98-06; P-in-c Tynemouth Priory *Newc* from 06. *Holy Saviour Vicarage, 1 Crossway, North Shields NE30 2LB* Tel 0191-257 1636 E-mail geoffl@freenet.co.uk

LOWTHER, Ms Kareen Anne. b 59. Loughb Univ BSc81. WMMTC 98. **d** 01 **p** 02. C Lich St Mich w St Mary and Wall 01-04; TV Bloxwich from 04. *9 Sanstone Road, Walsall WS3 3SJ* Tel (01922) 711225 Mobile 07940-936033

LOWTHER, Peter Mark. b 56. GTCL77. NTMTC BA08. **d** 08 **p** 09. NSM Pimlico St Pet w Westmr Ch Ch *Lon* from 08. *19 Marlborough Yard, London N19 4ND* Tel (020) 7561 0173 Mobile 07801-258503 E-mail mark.lowther@virgin.net

LOWTON, Nicholas Gerard. b 53. St Jo Coll Ox BA76 FRSA94. Glouc Sch of Min 86. **d** 89 **p** 90. NSM Prestbury *Glouc* 89-94; V Clodock and Longtown w Craswall, Llanveynoe etc *Heref* from 10. *Forest Mill, Craswall, Hereford HR2 0PW* Tel (01981) 510675

LOXHAM, Edward. b 49. BEd. **d** 04 **p** 05. OLM Birkdale St Pet *Liv* from 04. *34 Alma Road, Southport PR8 4AN* Tel (01704) 568141

LOXHAM, Geoffrey Richard. b 40. Hull Univ BA62. Cranmer Hall Dur. **d** 65 **p** 66. C Darwen St Barn *Blackb* 65-68; C Leyland St Andr 68-72; V Preston St Mark 72-79; V Edgeside *Man* 79-91; P-in-c Heapey and Withnell *Blackb* 91-92; V 92-99; V Grimsargh 99-10; rtd 10; Perm to Offic *Blackb* from 10. *63 Preston Road, Preston PR3 3AY* Tel (01772) 780511

LOXLEY, Mrs Deirdre. b 41. **d** 96 **p** 97. OLM Heacham *Nor* 96-05; NSM Knaresborough *Ripon* 05-08; rtd 08; Perm to Offic *Nor* from 08. *6 Holkham Avenue, Swaffham PE37 7RX* Tel (01760) 723235 E-mail banddloxley@btinternet.com

LOXLEY, Harold. b 43. NOC 79. **d** 82 **p** 83. NSM Sheff St Cecilia Parson Cross 82-87; C Gleadless 87-90; V Sheff St Cath Richmond Road from 90. *St Catherine's House, 300 Hastilar Road South, Sheffield S13 8EJ* Tel 0114-239 9598 E-mail father.loxley@sky.com

LOXLEY, Ronald Alan Keith. b 26. St Jo Coll Ox BA51 MA55. Wm Temple Coll Rugby 66 Cuddesdon Coll 67. **d** 68 **p** 69. C Swindon Ch Ch *Bris* 68-71; Ind Chapl *Lon* 71-83; Ind Chapl and P-in-c Theydon Garnon *Chelmsf* 83-92; rtd 92; Perm to Offic *Linc* 92-09. *30 Chancellor House, Mount Ephraim, Tunbridge Wells TN4 8RT* Tel (01892) 513330

LOXTON, John Sherwood. b 29. Bris Univ BSc50 Birm Univ BA53. Handsworth Coll Birm 50 Chich Th Coll 80. **d** 80 **p** 81. In Meth Ch 50-80; C Haywards Heath St Wilfrid *Chich* 80-82; TV 82-89; V Turners Hill 89-96; rtd 96; Perm to Offic *Chich* 96-10. *4 Caerleon Drive, Andover SP10 4DE*

LOXTON, Mrs Susan Ann. b 57. EAMTC 02. **d** 05 **p** 06. NSM Colchester, New Town and The Hythe *Chelmsf* 05-08; P-in-c Fressingfield, Mendham etc *St E* from 08; C Hoxne w Denham, Syleham and Wingfield from 08. *The Vicarage, 2 Tansy Meadow, Fressingfield, Eye IP21 5RQ* Tel (01379) 586040 E-mail susan.loxton@mypostoffice.co.uk

LOZADA-UZURIAGA, Ernesto. b 61. Wycliffe Hall Ox. **d** 02 **p** 03. C Henley w Remenham *Ox* 02-06; P-in-c Milton Keynes from 06. *1 Cottage Common, Loughton, Milton Keynes MK5 8AE* Tel (01908) 231260 E-mail leon-judah@hotmail.com

LUBBOCK, David John. b 34. S'wark Ord Course. **d** 87 **p** 88. NSM Tulse Hill H Trin and St Matthias *S'wark* 87-04; rtd 04; Perm to Offic *S'wark* from 04. *The Old Vicarage, 107 Upper Tulse Hill, London SW2 2RD* Tel (020) 8674 6146 E-mail lubodj@dircon.co.uk

LUBKOWSKI, Richard Jan. b 51. Westmr Coll Ox BEd75 Warw Univ MA79. St Jo Coll Dur 86. **d** 88 **p** 89. C Duston *Pet* 88-90; C Hellesdon *Nor* 90-91; Perm to Offic *Sheff* 91-94; In RC Ch 94-00; Chapl HM Pris Ashwell 10-; P-in-c Cottesmore and Barrow w Ashwell and Burley *Pet* 10; V Cottesmore and Burley, Clipsham, Exton etc from 11. *The Rectory, 38 Main Street, Cottesmore, Oakham LE15 7DJ* Tel (01572) 813120 Mobile 07449-122406 E-mail richardman812@btinternet.com

LUCAS, Anthony Stanley. b 41. Man Univ BA62 K Coll Lon MA99. Qu Coll Birm 63. **d** 65 **p** 66. C Hammersmith St Kath *Lon* 65-69; C W Wimbledon Ch Ch *S'wark* 69-74; C Caterham 74-78; P-in-c Stockwell St Mich 78-86; V 86-91; R S'wark St Geo the Martyr w St Jude 91-94; P-in-c S'wark St Alphege 92-94; R S'wark St Geo w St Alphege and St Jude 95-06; rtd 06; Perm to Offic *S'wark* from 10. *23 Clements Road, London SE16 4DW* Tel (020) 7064 9088 E-mail tonyslucas@btinternet.com

LUCAS, Arthur Edgar. b 24. Clifton Th Coll 60. **d** 62 **p** 63. C Hyson Green *S'well* 62-66; V Willoughby-on-the-Wolds w Wysall 66-74; P-in-c Widmerpool 71-74; R Collyhurst *Man* 75-80; V Heapey *Blackb* 80-91; rtd 91; Perm to Offic *Blackb* from 91 and *Liv* 91-00. *18 Parkway, Standish, Wigan WN6 0SJ*

LUCAS, The Ven Brian Humphrey. b 40. CB93. FRSA93 Univ of Wales (Lamp) BA62. St Steph Ho Ox 62. **d** 64 **p** 65. C Llandaff w Capel Llanilltern 64-67; C Neath w Llantwit 67-70; Chapl RAF 70-87; Asst Chapl-in-Chief RAF 87-91; Chapl-in-Chief RAF 91-95; QHC from 88; Perm to Offic *Llan* from 88; Can and Preb Linc Cathl 91-95; P-in-c Caythorpe 96-00; R 00-03. *Pen-y-Coed, 6 Arnhem Drive, Caythorpe, Grantham NG32 3DQ* Tel (01400) 272085 E-mail brian.lucas@savageclub.com

LUCAS, Mrs Carolyn. b 61. Surrey Univ MSc06. SEITE 06. **d** 09 **p** 10. NSM New Malden and Coombe *S'wark* from 09. *10 Presburg Road, New Malden KT3 5AH* E-mail clucas@blueyonder.co.uk

LUCAS, Glyn Andrew. b 63. Oak Hill Th Coll. **d** 09 **p** 10. C Cheadle *Ches* from 09. *39 Oakfield Avenue, Cheadle SK8 1EF*

LUCAS, Mrs Jane Eleanor. b 49. SWMTC 00. **d** 03 **p** 04. NSM N Creedy *Ex* 03-07; NSM Burrington, Chawleigh, Cheldon, Chulmleigh etc 07-08; P-in-c Ashwater, Halwill, Beaworthy, Clawton etc from 08. *The Rectory, Ashwater, Beaworthy EX21 5EZ* Tel and fax (01409) 211205 E-mail jane.e.lucas@btinternet.com

LUCAS, John Kenneth. b 32. LNSM course 92. **d** 95 **p** 96. NSM Deptford St Nic and St Luke *S'wark* 95-97; Perm to Offic 97-00 and from 03. *4 The Colonnade, Grove Street, London SE8 3AY* Tel (020) 8691 3161

LUCAS, John Maxwell. b 34. TD85. Cranmer Hall Dur 59. **d** 62 **p** 63. C Lancaster St Mary *Blackb* 62-65; C Lytham St Cuth 65-68; V Blackb St Aid 68-72; V Sparkhill St Jo *Birm* 72-78; CF (TAVR) from 73; V Edgbaston St Aug *Birm* 78-85; V Slyne w Hest *Blackb* 85-89; Chapl HM YOI Stoke Heath 89-93; rtd 93. *2 Glendon Close, Market Drayton TF9 1NX* Tel (01630) 652977

LUCAS, Lorna Yvonne. b 48. Bp Lonsdale Coll TCert69. EMMTC 95. **d** 98 **p** 99. NSM Haxey and Owston *Linc* 98-00; NSM Scawby, Redbourne and Hibaldstow 00-04; NSM Lea Gp from 05. *4 Willingham Road, Lea, Gainsborough DN21 5EH* Tel (01427) 811463 E-mail lorna.lucas@virgin.net

LUCAS, Mark Wesley. b 62. Man Univ BSc83. Oak Hill Th Coll BA94. **d** 94 **p** 95. C Harold Wood *Chelmsf* 94-98; Dir Oast Ho Retreat Cen *Chich* 98-00; Co-ord for Adult Educn (E Sussex Area) 98-00; V Polegate 00-10; R Barton Seagrave w Warkton *Pet* from 10. *The Rectory, St Botolph's Road, Kettering NN15 6SR* Tel (01536) 513629 *or* 414052 Mobile 07788-100757 E-mail vicar@polegate.org.uk

LUCAS, Maxwell. *See* LUCAS, John Maxwell

LUCAS, Ms Pamela Turnbull. b 68. Westmr Coll Ox BA91 Glas Univ MSW98 Edin Univ MTh99 UNISA MTh05. TISEC 98. **d** 00 **p** 01. C Easington, Easington Colliery and S Hetton *Dur* 00-04; CSC 04-06; Asst Chapl Basingstoke and N Hants NHS Foundation Trust 06-09; Chapl St Mich Hosp Toronto Canada from 09; Hon C Toronto St Monica 09-10; Hon C Toronto St Pet from 11. *St Michael's Hospital, Spiritual Care, Room 3-018a, 30 Bond Street, Toronto ON M5B 1W8, Canada* Tel (001) (647) 238 1499 E-mail revd ptlucas@yahoo.co.uk

LUCAS, Paul de Neufville. b 33. Ch Ch Ox BA59 MA59 Cam Univ MA63. Cuddesdon Coll 57. **d** 59 **p** 60. C Westmr St Steph w St Jo *Lon* 59-63; Chapl Trin Hall Cam 63-69; V Greenside *Dur* 69-73; Chapl Shrewsbury Sch 73-77; V Batheaston w St Cath B & W 78-88; Preb Wells Cathl 87-88; Can Res and Prec 88-99; rtd 99; Perm to Offic *Sarum* from 01. *11 Fisherton Island, Salisbury SP2 7TG* Tel and fax (01722) 325266

LUCAS, Peter Stanley. b 21. Sarum Th Coll 48. **d** 50 **p** 51. C Gillingham *Sarum* 50-53; Min Heald Green St Cath CD *Ches* 53-58; V Heald Green St Cath 58-62; V Egremont St Jo 62-65; Canada from 66. *404-1241 Fairfield Road, Victoria BC V8V 3B3, Canada* E-mail pmlucas@smartt.com

LUCAS, Preb Richard Charles. b 25. Trin Coll Cam BA49 MA57. Ridley Hall Cam. **d** 51 **p** 52. C Sevenoaks St Nic *Roch* 51-55; Cand Sec CPAS 55-61; Asst Sec 61-67; R St Helen Bishopsgate w St Martin Outwich *Lon* 61-80; P-in-c St Andr Undershaft w St Mary Axe 77-80; R St Helen Bishopsgate w St Andr Undershaft etc 80-98; Preb St Paul's Cathl 85-98; rtd 98. *16 Merrick Square, London SE1 4JB* Tel (020) 7407 4164

LUCAS, Ronald James. b 38. St Aid Birkenhead 64. **d** 67 **p** 68. C Swindon Ch Ch *Bris* 67-71; C Knowle St Martin 71-74; V Swindon St Jo 74-77; TR Swindon St Jo and St Andr 77-81; V Wroughton 81-83; TV Liskeard w St Keyne, St Pinnock and Morval *Truro* 83-87; R St Ive w Quethiock 87-91; R St Ive and Pensilva w Quethiock 91-01; rtd 01; Perm to Offic *Truro* from 01. *Ough's Folly, Castle Lane, Liskeard PL14 3AH* Tel (01579) 345611 E-mail ronjulialucas@hotmail.com

LUCAS, Ms Susan Catherine. b 59. City of Lon Poly BSc90. STETS 97. **d** 00 **p** 01. C Streetly *Lich* 00-02; C Pheasey 02-04; Chapl HM Pris Albany 04-09; Chapl HM Pris Wandsworth from 09. *HM Prison Wandsworth, PO Box 757, Heathfield Road, London SW18 3HS* Tel (020) 8588 4000

LUCAS, Susan Joyce. b 61. Bedf Coll Lon BA83 Univ of Wales (Swansea) PGCE90 Birkbeck Coll Lon MPhil95 PhD07 Leeds Univ MA08. **d** 08 **p** 09. NSM St Marg *Liv* from 08. *39 Westbury Close, Liverpool L17 5BD* Tel 0151-727 3251 Mobile 07976-901389 E-mail sue.lucas@dsl.pipex.com

LUCAS, Mrs Vivienne Kathleen. b 44. Sarum & Wells Th Coll 84. **d** 87 **p** 94. Chapl Asst W Middx Univ Hosp Isleworth 87-92; Par Dn Whitton St Aug *Lon* 87-94; C Isleworth St Jo 94-97; P-in-c Isleworth St Mary 97-01; Perm to Offic *Guildf* 01-06; rtd 06; Perm to Offic *York* from 07. *36 Harthill Avenue, Leconfield, Beverley HU17 7LN* Tel and fax (01964) 551519 E-mail vivienne.lucas@sky.com

LUCAS, William Wallace. b 29. Sarum Th Coll 56. **d** 59 **p** 60. C Stockton St Jo *Dur* 59-63; V Norton St Mich 63-81; R Broseley w Benthall *Heref* 81-93; P-in-c Jackfield and Linley w Willey and Barrow 81-93; rtd 93; Perm to Offic *Dur* 93-02. *1 Beckwith Mews, Seaham Street, Sunderland SR3 1HN*

LUCK, Benjamin Paul. b 53. BD. St Mich Coll Llan 80. **d** 83 **p** 84. C Blakenall Heath *Lich* 83-87; C Torpoint *Truro* 87-89; V Tuckingmill 89-96; C Knowle St Barn and H Cross Inns Court *Bris* 96-02; V Inns Court H Cross 02-05; C Washfield, Stoodleigh, Withleigh etc *Ex* 05-07; Chapl N Devon Hospice from 07. *The Rectory, Withleigh, Tiverton EX16 8JQ* Tel (01884) 250509

LUCKCUCK, Anthony Michael. b 47. Lon Univ BA70. Wycliffe Hall Ox 70. **d** 77 **p** 78. C Mansfield Woodhouse *S'well* 77-79; C Beeston 79-82; V Harworth 82-85; V Carlton from 85. *The Vicarage, 261 Oakdale Road, Carlton, Nottingham NG4 1BP* Tel 0115-987 2216 Mobile 07734-032900 E-mail amlclerc@btinternet.com

LUCKETT, Nicholas Frank. b 43. Ch Ch Ox BA65 DipEd66 MA69. OLM course 95. **d** 98 **p** 99. Hd Master St Edw C of E Middle Sch Leek 94-00; OLM Ipstones w Berkhamsytch and Onecote w Bradnop *Lich* 98-02; NSM Siddington w Preston *Glouc* 02-07; NSM S Cerney w Cerney Wick, Siddington and Preston 07-08; rtd 08; Perm to Offic *Nor* from 09. *Shillingstone, Church Road, Beetley, Dereham NR20 4AB* Tel (01362) 860738 E-mail nandeluckett@hotmail.com

LUCKETT, Virginia. b 67. **d** 11. NSM Isleworth All SS *Lon* from 11. *156 Windmill Road, Brentford TW8 9NQ*

LUCKING, Mrs Linda Pauline. b 61. St Jo Coll Nottm BA10. **d** 10 **p** 11. NSM Caverswall and Weston Coyney w Dilhorne *Lich* from 10. *5 Welsh Close, Lightwood Grange, Stoke-on-Trent ST3 4TQ* Tel (01782) 321246 Mobile 07778-896584 E-mail linda.lucking.me@googlemail.com

LUCKMAN, David Thomas William. b 71. Oak Hill Th Coll BA95 K Coll Lon PGCE96. CITC 98. **d** 00 **p** 01. C Portadown St Mark *Arm* 00-02; C Enniskillen *Clogh* 02-03; I Galloon w Drummully and Sallaghy 03-04; N Ireland Field Worker ICM 05-08; C Ardmore w Craigavon *D & D* 10-11. *53 Taughrane Lodge, Dollingstown, Craigavon BT66 7UH* Tel (028) 9167 7376 E-mail daveluckman@hotmail.com

LUCKRAFT, Christopher John. b 50. K Coll Lon BD80 AKC80. Ripon Coll Cuddesdon 80. **d** 81 **p** 82. C Sherborne w Castleton and Lillington *Sarum* 81-84; Bermuda 84-87; Chapl RN 87-07; R Merrow *Guildf* from 07. *St John's Rectory, 232 Epsom Road, Guildford GU4 7AA* Tel (01483) 452390 E-mail chrisluckraft@sky.com

LUCKRAFT, Ian Charles. b 47. Qu Coll Ox BA70 BSc81. Ripon Hall Ox 70. **d** 73 **p** 74. C Totteridge *St Alb* 73-77; C Broxbourne w Wormley 77-78; Lect Harrow Tech Coll 78-81; Perm to Offic *Ox* from 06. *4 Willes Close, Faringdon SN7 7DU* Tel (01367) 240135

LUCY CLARE, Sister. *See* WALKER, Margaret

LUDKIN, Miss Linda Elaine. b 50. NEOC 02. **d** 05 **p** 06. NSM Dunnington *York* 05-10; NSM Ireland Wood *Ripon* from 10. *St Paul's Vicarage, Raynel Drive, Leeds LS16 6BS* Tel 0113-230 1564 E-mail l.e.ludkin@btinternet.com

LUDLOW, Brian Peter. b 55. Lon Univ MB, BS78 Birm Univ MMedSc90 LRCP90 MRCS90 MRAeS87 AFOM90 MFOM92 FFOM01. WEMTC 01. **d** 04 **p** 05. NSM Winchcombe *Glouc* 04-06; NSM Cainscross w Selsley 06-09; NSM Rodborough from 09. *The Rectory, Walkley Hill, Stroud GL5 3TX* Tel (01453) 752659 Mobile 07836-667530 E-mail revbrian@btopenworld.com

LUDLOW, Mrs Lesley Elizabeth. b 43. SEITE 97 OLM course 04. **d** 06 **p** 07. NSM Allington and Maidstone St Pet *Cant* 06-10; NSM Bearsted w Thurnham from 11. *37 Tudor Avenue, Maidstone ME14 5HJ* Tel (01622) 673536 Mobile 07778-027031 E-mail lesley.ludlow@blueyonder.co.uk

LUDLOW, Lady Margaret Maude. b 56. WEMTC 98. **d** 01 **p** 02. C Winchcombe *Glouc* 01-05; P-in-c Rodborough from 05. *The Rectory, Walkley Hill, Stroud GL5 3TX* Tel (01453) 751344 E-mail revpeggy@btopenworld.com

LUDLOW, Archdeacon of. *See* MAGOWAN, The Rt Revd Alistair James

LUDLOW, Suffragan Bishop of. *See* MAGOWAN, The Rt Revd Alistair James

LUFF, Canon Alan Harold Frank. b 28. Univ Coll Ox MA54 ARCM77 Hon FGCM93. Westcott Ho Cam 54. **d** 56 **p** 57. C Stretford St Matt *Man* 56-59; C Swinton St Pet 59-61; Prec Man Cathl 61-68; V Dwygyfylchi *Ban* 68-79; Prec and Sacr Westmr Abbey 79-86; Prec 86-92; Can Res Birm Cathl 92-96; rtd 96; Perm to Offic *Llan* from 96. *12 Heol Ty'n-y-Cae, Cardiff CF14 6DJ* Tel and fax (029) 2061 6023

LUFF, Mrs Caroline Margaret Synia. b 44. St Hild Coll Dur BA65 Bris Univ CertEd66. SWMTC 87. **d** 90 **p** 94. NSM Teignmouth, Ideford w Luton, Ashcombe etc *Ex* 90-07; Chapl Trin Sch Teignmouth 97-11; C Diptford, N Huish, Harberton, Harbertonford etc *Ex* from 07; C Ermington and Ugborough from 11. *The Vicarage, Harberton, Totnes TQ9 7SA* Tel (01803) 868445 E-mail pgandcmsl@btinternet.com

LUFF, John Edward Deweer. b 46. STETS 04. **d** 07 **p** 08. NSM Guernsey St Peter Port *Win* from 07; Chapl States of Guernsey Bd of Health from 07. *La Neuve Maison Cottage, Rue de la Neuve Maison, St Saviour, Guernsey GY7 9TG* Tel (01481) 264772 E-mail johnluff@cwgsy.net

LUFF, Matthew John. b 70. Brighton Univ BA(QTS)95. Wycliffe Hall Ox 07. **d** 09 **p** 10. C Broadwater *Chich* from 09. *20 Grove Road, Worthing BN14 9DG* Tel (01903) 525619 Mobile 07875-190203 E-mail luff925@hotmail.com

LUFF, Preb Philip Garth. b 42. St Chad's Coll Dur BA63. **d** 65 **p** 66. C Sidmouth St Nic *Ex* 65-69; C Plymstock 69-71; Asst Chapl Worksop Coll Notts 71-74; V Gainsborough St Jo *Linc* 74-80; V E Teignmouth *Ex* 80-89; P-in-c W Teignmouth 85-89; TR Teignmouth, Ideford w Luton, Ashcombe etc 90-07; RD Kenn 01-05; Preb Ex Cathl 02-07; Chapl S Devon Healthcare NHS Trust 85-07; Chapl Trin Sch Teignmouth 88-97; rtd 07; Perm to Offic *Ex* from 07. *The Vicarage, Harberton, Totnes TQ9 7SA* Tel (01803) 868445 E-mail pgandcmsl@btinternet.com

LUGG, Donald Arthur. b 31. St Aid Birkenhead 56. **d** 59 **p** 60. C Folkestone H Trin w Ch Ch *Cant* 59-62; V Seasalter 62-66; Iran 67-73; V Cliftonville *Cant* 74-94; rtd 94; Perm to Offic *Cant* from 94. *Redcroft, Vulcan Close, Whitstable CT9 1DF* Tel (01227) 770434

LUGG, Stuart John. b 26. Glouc Th Course 74. **d** 76 **p** 77. NSM Fairford *Glouc* 76-79; P-in-c Kempsford w Welford 80-88; Perm to Offic 88-05. *Content, Station Road, South Cerney, Cirencester GL7 5UB* Tel (01285) 860498

LUKE, Anthony. b 58. Down Coll Cam BA81 MA85. Ridley Hall Cam 82. **d** 84 **p** 85. C Allestree *Derby* 84-87; C Oakham, Hambleton, Egleton, Braunston and Brooke *Pet* 87-88; V Allenton and Shelton Lock *Derby* 88-02; Dir Reader Tr 95-97; Warden of Readers 97-00; R Aston on Trent, Elvaston, Weston on Trent etc from 02; RD Melbourne from 07. *The Rectory, Rectory Gardens, Aston-on-Trent, Derby DE72 2AZ* Tel (01332) 792658 E-mail tonyluketenor@aol.com

LUKE, Denise Elaine. b 60. Wolv Univ BEd92 Leeds Univ BA08. NOC 05. **d** 08 **p** 09. NSM Leesfield *Man* 08-09; NSM Rhodes and Parkfield 09-10; NSM Chadderton St Matt w St Luke from 10. *11 The Grove, Dobcross, Oldham OL3 5RR* Tel (01457) 875830 Mobile 07894-046606 E-mail deniseluke@btinternet.com

LUMB, David Leslie. b 28. Jes Coll Cam BA52 MA56. Oak Hill Th Coll 52. **d** 54 **p** 55. C Walcot *B & W* 54-58; C Lenton *S'well* 58-60; V Handforth *Ches* 60-71; V Plymouth St Jude *Ex* 71-87; V Southminster *Chelmsf* 87-93; rtd 93; Perm to Offic *Worc* from 93. *13 Glebe Close, Redditch B98 0AW* Tel (01527) 528623

LUMBY, Jonathan Bertram. b 39. Em Coll Cam BA62 MA66 Lon Univ PGCE66. Ripon Hall Ox 62. **d** 64 **p** 65. C Moseley St Mary *Birm* 64-65; Asst Master Enfield Gr Sch 66-67; C Hall Green Ascension 67-70; V Melling *Liv* 70-81; P-in-c Milverton w Halse and Fitzhead *B & W* 81-82; R 82-86; P-in-c Gisburn and Dioc Rural Adv *Bradf* 90-93; P-in-c Easton w Colton and Marlingford *Nor* 95-98; Dioc Missr 95-98; R Eccleston and Pulford *Ches* 98-05; rtd 05; Hon C Redmarley D'Abitot, Bromesberrow, Pauntley etc *Glouc* 05-08. *Valentines Cottage, Hollybush, Ledbury HR8 1ET* Tel (01531) 650641

LUMBY, Simon. b 70. Coll of Resurr Mirfield 99. **d** 02 **p** 03. C Worksop Priory *S'well* 02-06; P-in-c Leic St Aid 06-09; V from 09. *St Aidan's Vicarage, St Oswald's Road, Leicester LE3 6RJ* Tel 0116-287 2342 Mobile 07983-609290 E-mail fathersimonlumby@btinternet.com

LUMBY, Simon John. b 56. Hull Univ BSc80 Open Univ MTh01. St Jo Coll Nottm 99. **d** 01 **p** 04. C Wirksworth *Derby* 01-06; R Clifton Campville w Edingale and Harlaston *Lich* 06-10; P-in-c Thorpe Constantine 06-10; P-in-c Elford 06-10; Perm to Offic from 10; Chapl OHP from 10. *St Hilda's Priory, Sneaton Castle, Whitby YO21 3QN* Tel (01947) 602079 Fax 820854 E-mail ohppriorywhitby@btinternet.com

LUMGAIR, Michael Hugh Crawford. b 43. Lon Univ BD71. Oak Hill Th Coll 66. **d** 71 **p** 72. C Chorleywood Ch Ch *St Alb* 71-74; C Prestonville St Luke *Chich* 74-75; C Attenborough *S'well* 75-80; R Tollerton 80-91; V Bexleyheath St Pet *Roch* 91-06; rtd 06. *11 Bromley College, London Road, Bromley BR1 1PE* Tel (020) 8290 2011 E-mail michael@lumgair.plus.com

LUMLEY (née HATFIELD), Rebecca Alison. b 76. St Andr Univ MTheol99. Cranmer Hall Dur 02. **d** 04 **p** 05. C Haughton le Skerne *Dur* 04-09; V Windy Nook St Alb from 09. *The Vicarage, Coldwell Park Drive, Gateshead NE10 9BY* Tel 0191-438 1720 Mobile 07930-631936

LUMMIS, Elizabeth Howieson. *See* McNAB, Mrs Elizabeth Howieson

LUMSDON, Keith. b 45. Linc Th Coll 68. **d** 71 **p** 72. C S Westoe *Dur* 71-74; C Jarrow St Paul 74-77; TV Jarrow 77-88; V Ferryhill 88-07; P-in-c Cornforth 03-07; V Cornforth and Ferryhill from 07; AD Sedgefield from 05. *St Luke's Vicarage, Church Lane, Ferryhill DL17 8LT* Tel (01740) 651438

LUND, David Peter. b 46. NOC 88. **d** 91 **p** 92. C Maghull *Liv* 91-94; V Hindley All SS 94-01; V Teddington St Mark and Hampton Wick *Lon* from 01. *The Vicarage, 23 St Mark's Road, Teddington TW11 9DE* Tel (020) 8977 4067 Mobile 07813-493761 E-mail saintsteddington@btinternet.com

LUND, John Edward. b 48. St Jo Coll Dur 78. **d** 80 **p** 81. C Peterlee *Dur* 80-83; C Bishopton w Gt Stainton 83-85; C Redmarshall 83-85; C Grindon and Stillington 83-85; V Hart w Elwick Hall 85-09; Hon Chapl Miss to Seamen 85-99; Chapl Hartlepool and E Durham NHS Trust 94-99; Chapl N Tees and Hartlepool

NHS Trust 99-04; rtd 09. *16 Chelker Close, Hartlepool TS26 0QW* E-mail lund@telco4u.net

✠LUNGA, The Rt Revd Cleophus. b 66. UNISA BTh00. Bp Gaul Th Coll Harare 91. d 93 p 94 c 09. Zimbabwe 94-03 and from 09; TV Coventry Caludon 03-09; Bp Matabeleland from 09. *PO Box 2422, Bulawayo, Zimbabwe* Tel (00263) (9) 61370 Fax 68353

LUNN, Preb Brooke Kingsmill. b 32. TCD BA62 MA66. Chich Th Coll 62. d 64 p 65. C Northolt Park St Barn *Lon* 64-66; C N St Pancras All Hallows 66-68; P-in-c Hornsey St Luke 68-79; V Stroud Green H Trin 79-02; AD W Haringey 90-95; Preb St Paul's Cathl 96-02; rtd 02; Perm to Offic *Lon* from 02. *The Charterhouse, Charterhouse Square, London EC1M 6AN* Tel (020) 7251 5143

LUNN, Christopher James Edward. b 34. AKC58. d 59 p 60. C Clapham H Trin *S'wark* 59-62; C Cranleigh *Guildf* 63-64; C Ham St Andr *S'wark* 64-66; V Ham St Rich 66-75; V Coulsdon St Andr 75-96; rtd 96. *24 Penally Heights, Penally, Tenby SA70 7QP* Tel (01834) 845277

LUNN, David. b 47. Bris Univ BSc69. St Jo Coll Dur BA73. d 74 p 75. C Aigburth *Liv* 74-77; C Slough *Ox* 77-81; P-in-c Haversham w Lt Linford 81-84; R Haversham w Lt Linford, Tyringham w Filgrave 84-93; RD Newport 86-92; TR Walton Milton Keynes from 93; Dioc Ecum Officer 00-10. *The Rectory, Walton Road, Wavendon, Milton Keynes MK17 8LW* Tel (01908) 582839

✠LUNN, The Rt Revd David Ramsay. b 30. K Coll Cam BA53 MA57. Cuddesdon Coll 53. d 55 p 56 c 80. C Sugley *Newc* 55-59; C N Gosforth 59-63; Chapl Linc Th Coll 63-66; Sub-Warden 66-70; V Cullercoats St Geo *Newc* 71-72; TR 72-80; RD Tynemouth 75-80; Bp Shelt 80-97; rtd 97; Perm to Offic *York* 97-99; Hon Asst Bp York from 99. *Rivendell, 28 Southfield Road, Wetwang, Driffield YO25 9XX* Tel (01377) 236657

LUNN, Graham Edward. b 86. Wycliffe Hall Ox BA08. St Steph Ho Ox 09. d 11. C Reading All SS *Ox* from 11; C Reading St Mark from 11. *32 Baker Street, Reading RG1 7XY* Tel 0118-958 4842 E-mail graham.lunn@gmail.com

LUNN, Leonard Arthur. b 42. Culham Coll of Educn CertEd64. Trin Coll Bris 69. d 72 p 73. C Walthamstow St Mary w St Steph *Chelmsf* 72-75; V Collier Row St Jas 75-85; V Collier Row St Jas and Havering-atte-Bower 86-87; Sen Chapl St Chris Hospice Sydenham *S'wark* 87-04; Hon C Redlynch and Morgan's Vale *Sarum* 04-06; Hon C Forest and Avon 06-09. *Summerhayes, Whiteshoot, Redlynch, Salisbury SP5 2PR* Tel (01725) 510322 E-mail len.lunn@btopenworld.com

LUNN, Maureen Susan. b 48. Middx Univ BSc00. NTMTC BA07. d 07. NSM Enfield St Jas *Lon* 07-10; NSM Enfield Chase St Mary from 10. *62 First Avenue, Enfield EN1 1BN* Tel (020) 8366 0592

LUNN, Mrs Rosemary Christine. b 51. Bris Univ BA72. Trin Coll Bris 98. d 00 p 01. NSM Stoke Bishop *Bris* 00-01; C Chippenham St Pet 01-04; Hon Min Can Bris Cathl 02-04; P-in-c Wraxall *B & W* 04-09; R from 09. *41 Vowles Close, Wraxall BS48 1PP* Tel (01275) 857086 Mobile 07786-118762 E-mail rosemarylunn@btinternet.com

LUNN, Sarah Anne. b 63. Lanc Univ BMus84 Man Metrop Univ MA93. Cranmer Hall Dur 00. d 02 p 03. C Kirkby Lonsdale *Carl* 02-07; P-in-c Long Marton w Dufton and w Milburn 07-08; TV Heart of Eden 08-10; TR from 10; P-in-c Kirkby Thore w Temple Sowerby and Newbiggin from 11. *The Rectory, Long Marton, Appleby-in-Westmorland CA16 6BN* Tel (01768) 361269 E-mail sarahlunn@care4free.net

LUNNON, Canon Robert Reginald. b 31. K Coll Lon BD55 AKC55 Kent Univ MA99. St Boniface Warminster 55. d 56 p 57. C Maidstone St Mich *Cant* 56-58; C Deal St Leon 58-62; V Sturry 63-68; V Norbury St Steph 68-77; V Orpington All SS *Roch* 77-96; RD Orpington 79-95; Hon Can Roch Cathl 96; rtd 96; Perm to Offic *Cant* from 96. *10 King Edward Road, Deal CT14 6QL* Tel (01304) 364898

LUNT, Colin Peter. b 54. York Univ BA75 Bris Univ MA02. Trin Coll Bris 95. d 97 p 98. C Westbury-on-Trym H Trin *Bris* 97-00; V Coalpit Heath from 00. *The Vicarage, Beesmoor Road, Coalpit Heath, Bristol BS36 2RP* Tel and fax (01454) 775129 E-mail colin@lunt.co.uk

LUNT, Margaret Joan. b 44. Leeds Univ MB, ChB68. Cranmer Hall Dur 91. d 94 p 95. C Stanford-le-Hope w Mucking *Chelmsf* 94-97; C Rayleigh 97-00; TV 00-03; TV Rivers Team *Sheff* 03-10; rtd 10; Hon C Todwick *Sheff* 10-11. *1 Rodwell Close, Treeton, Rotherham S60 5UF* Tel 0114-269 4479 E-mail margaretlunt@yahoo.co.uk

LURIE, Miss Gillian Ruth. b 42. LRAM62 GNSM63. Gilmore Ho 68. dss 74 d 87 p 94. Camberwell St Phil and St Mark *S'wark* 74-76; Haddenham *Ely* 76-79; Dioc Lay Min Adv 79-81; Longthorpe *Pet* 79-81; Pet H Spirit Bretton 81-86; Bramley *Ripon* 86-93; C 87-88; TD 88-93; P-in-c Methley w Mickletown 93-98; R 98-01; rtd 02; Perm to Offic *Cant* from 02. *42A Cuthbert Road, Westgate-on-Sea CT8 8NR* Tel and fax (01843) 831698 E-mail gillandjean@hotmail.com

LURY, Anthony Patrick. b 49. K Coll Lon BD71 AKC71. St Aug Coll Cant 71. d 72 p 73. C Richmond St Mary *S'wark* 72-76;

P-in-c Streatham Hill St Marg 76-81; V Salfords 81-90; V Emscote *Cov* 90-01; P-in-c Ascot Heath *Ox* 01-06; NSM The Churn 06-10; Perm to Offic *St E* from 11. *8 St Anthonys Crescent, Ipswich IP4 4SY* Tel (01473) 273395 E-mail anthonyplury@btinternet.com

LUSBY, Dennis John. b 27. Brentwood Coll of Educn CertEd70. d 93 p 94. NSM Grayshott *Guildf* 93-99; Perm to Offic from 99. *Squirrels Drey, Waggoners Way, Grayshott, Hindhead GU26 6DX* Tel (01428) 604419 E-mail dennis.j.lusby@btinternet.com

LUSCOMBE, John Nickels. b 45. Birm Univ BA99. AKC68. d 69 p 70. C Stoke Newington St Faith, St Matthias and All SS *Lon* 69-74; V Tottenham St Phil 74-81; Zimbabwe 82-86; V Queensbury All SS *Lon* 86-99; V Estover *Ex* 99-01; Dioc Ecum Officer 99-01; V Norton *St Alb* 01-10; RD Hitchin 02-07; rtd 10. *8 Manor Way, Totnes TQ9 5HP* Tel (01803) 864514 E-mail jnluscombe@btinternet.com

✠LUSCOMBE, The Rt Revd Lawrence Edward (Ted). b 24. Dundee Univ LLD87 MPhil91 PhD93 ACA52 FSA80 FRSA87. K Coll Lon 63. d 63 p 64 c 75. C Glas St Marg 63-66; R Paisley St Barn 66-71; Provost St Paul's Cathl Dundee 71-75; R Dundee St Paul 71-75; Bp Bre 75-90; Primus 85-90; rtd 90; Perm to Offic *Bre* from 90. *Woodville, Kirkton of Tealing, Dundee DD4 0RD* Tel (01382) 380331

LUSITANIAN CHURCH, Bishop of the. See SOARES, The Rt Revd Fernando da Luz

LUSTED, Jack Andrew. b 58. Sussex Univ BSc79 PGCE81. St Steph Ho Ox 88. d 90 p 91. C Moulsecoomb *Chich* 90-93; C Southwick St Mich 93-97; R Lurgashall, Lodsworth and Selham 97-07; V Salehurst from 07. *Salehurst Vicarage, Fair Lane, Robertsbridge TN32 5AR* Tel (01580) 880408 E-mail jack.lusted@btinternet.com

LUSTY, Tom Peter. b 71. Glas Univ BD94 Leeds Univ MA06. Coll of Resurr Mirfield 97. d 99 p 00. C Billingshurst *Chich* 99-02; Asst Chapl Leeds Teaching Hosps NHS Trust 02-06; Chapl Wheatfields Hospice 06-11; P-in-c Far Headingley St Chad *Ripon* from 11. *St Chad's Vicarage, Otley Road, Leeds LS16 5JT* Tel 0113-275 2224

LUTHER, Canon Richard Grenville Litton. b 42. Lon Univ BD64. Tyndale Hall Bris 66. d 68 p 69. C Preston St Mary *Blackb* 68-70; C Bishopsworth *Bris* 70-71; C Radipole *Sarum* 72-76; TV Radipole and Melcombe Regis 77-90; TR Hampreston 90-07; Can and Preb Sarum Cathl 00-07; rtd 07. *49 North Street, Charminster, Dorchester DT2 9RN* Tel (01305) 251547

✠LUXMOORE, The Rt Revd Christopher Charles. b 26. Trin Coll Cam BA50 MA54. Chich Th Coll 50. d 52 p 53 c 84. C Newc St Jo 52-55; C-in-c Newsham St Bede CD 55-57; V Newsham 57-58; Trinidad and Tobago 58-66; V Headingley Ripon 67-81; Hon Can Ripon Cathl 80-81; Can Res and Prec Chich Cathl 81-84; Bp Bermuda 84-89; Adn Lewes and Hastings *Chich* 89-91; rtd 91; Provost Woodard Corp (S Division) 89-96; Hon Asst Bp Chich from 91. *42 Willowbed Drive, Chichester PO19 8JB* Tel (01243) 784680

LYALL, Canon Graham. b 37. Univ of Wales (Lamp) BA61. Qu Coll Birm 61. d 63 p 64. C Middlesbrough Ascension *York* 63-67; C Kidderminster St Mary *Worc* 67-72; V Dudley St Aug Holly Hall 72-79; P-in-c Barbourne 79-81; V 81-93; RD Worc E 83-89; TR Malvern Link w Cowleigh 93-04; Hon Can Worc Cathl 85-04; rtd 04; Perm to Offic *Worc* from 04. *44 Victoria Street, Worcester WR3 7BD* Tel (01905) 20511

LYALL, Richard Keith. b 70. Glas Univ BSc92 MSc95 Strathclyde Univ MSc97. Trin Coll Bris BA02. d 02 p 03. C Gateacre *Liv* 02-06; C Haydock St Mark 06-08; Canada 08-09. *Address temp unknown* E-mail rklyall@yahoo.com

LYDDON, David Andrew. b 47. Lon Univ BDS70 LDS70. SWMTC 90. d 93 p 94. NSM Tiverton St Pet *Ex* 93-95; NSM Tiverton St Pet w Chevithorne 95-96; NSM W Exe 96-01; NSM Tiverton St Geo and St Paul from 01. *Hightrees, 19 Patches Road, Tiverton EX16 5AH* Tel (01884) 257250 E-mail dlyddon597@aol.uk

LYDON, Mrs Barbara. b 34. Gilmore Ho 64. dss 72 d 87 p 94. Rastrick St Matt *Wakef* 72-85; Upper Hopton 85-87; Par Dn 87; Dn-in-c Kellington w Whitley 87-94; P-in-c 94-95; rtd 95; Perm to Offic *Wakef* from 95. *17 Garlick Street, Brighouse HD6 3PW* Tel (01484) 722704

LYES-WILSON, Canon Patricia Mary. b 45. Open Univ BA87 ALA65. Glouc Sch of Min 84 Qu Coll Birm 86. d 87 p 94. C Thornbury *Glouc* 87-94; P-in-c Cromhall w Tortworth and Tytherington 94-03; Asst Dioc Dir of Ords 90-98; Dioc Voc Officer 94-01; RD Hawkesbury 98-04; R Cromhall, Tortworth, Tytherington, Falfield etc 02-09; Dioc Adv for Women's Min 01-09; Hon Can Glouc Cathl 02-09; rtd 09. *24 Maple Avenue, Thornbury, Bristol BS35 2JW* E-mail revd.pat@virgin.net

LYMBERY, Peter. b 32. JP73. SAOMC 95. d 98 p 99. OLM Stewkley w Soulbury and Drayton Parslow *Ox* 98-05; Hon C 05-09; Hon C Stewkley w Soulbury from 09; Dep Chapl Guild of Servants of the Sanctuary from 00; P Assoc Shrine of Our Lady of Walsingham from 00. *19 White House Court, Hockliffe Street, Leighton Buzzard LU7 1FD* Tel (01525) 371235

LYNAS, Canon Norman Noel. b 55. St Andr Univ MTheol78. CITC 78. **d** 79 **p** 80. C Knockbreda *D & D* 79-81; C Holywood 81-85; I Portadown St Columba *Arm* 85-91; Dioc Communications Officer 86-89; Tutor for Aux Min (Arm) 88-91; Radio Officer (Arm) 90-91; I Kilkenny w Aghour and Kilmanagh *C & O* 91-09; Dean Ossory 91-09; Can Leighlin Cathl 91-09; Dioc Dir of Ords 05-09; Can Res Bermuda from 09. *Address temp unknown*

LYNAS, Preb Stephen Brian. b 52. MBE00. St Jo Coll Nottm BTh77. **d** 78 **p** 79. C Penn *Lich* 78-81; Relig Progr Org BBC Radio Stoke-on-Trent 81-84; C Hanley H Ev 81-82; C Edensor 82-84; Relig Progr Producer BBC Bris 85-88; Relig Progr Sen Producer BBC S & W England 88-91; Hd Relig Progr TV South 91-92; Community (and Relig) Affairs Ed Westcountry TV 92-96; Abps' Officer for Millennium 96-01; Dioc Resources Adv *B & W* 01-07; Sen Chapl and Adv to Bps B & W and Taunton from 07; Preb Wells Cathl from 07. *Old Honeygar Cottage, Honeygar Lane, Westhay, Glastonbury BA6 9TS* Tel (01749) 672341 E-mail chaplain@bathwells.anglican.org

LYNCH, Canon Eithne Elizabeth Mary. b 43. TCD BTh. CITC 94. **d** 97 **p** 98. C Douglas Union w Frankfield *C, C & R* 97-01; I Kilmoe Union 01-10; I Mallow Union from 10; Min Can Cork Cathl 98-07; Bp's Dom Chapl from 99; Can Cork and Ross Cathls from 09. *The Rectory, Lower Bearforest, Mallow, Co Cork, Republic of Ireland* Tel (00353) (22) 21473 Mobile 86-253 5002 E-mail eithnel@eircom.net or mallowunion@eircom.net

LYNCH, James. b 44. EAMTC 93. **d** 96 **p** 97. NSM High Oak *Nor* 96-97; NSM High Oak, Hingham and Scoulton w Wood Rising 97-99; Asst Chapl Norfolk Mental Health Care NHS Trust 99-03; P-in-c Nor St Steph 99-03; NSM Blanchland w Hunstanworth and Edmundbyers etc *Newc* from 03; NSM Slaley from 03; NSM Healey from 03; NSM Whittonstall from 03. *The Vicarage, Blanchland, Consett DH8 9ST* Tel (01434) 675141

LYNCH, Ms Sally Margaret. b 60. St Jo Coll Dur BA81 UEA MA94 FRSA96. Westcott Ho Cam 04. **d** 08 **p** 09. C Romford St Edw *Chelmsf* 08-11; V Maidenhead St Luke *Ox* from 11. *St Luke's Vicarage, 26 Norfolk Road, Maidenhead SL6 7AX* Tel (01628) 783033 E-mail sally514@btinternet.com

LYNCH, Sheila. b 56. **d** 09 **p** 10. OLM Rossendale Middle Valley *Man* from 09. *70 Fairfield Avenue, Rossendale BB4 9TH* Tel (01706) 217438 Mobile 07711-992004 E-mail sheila.lynch@btinternet.com

LYNCH, Mrs Victoria. **d** 09 **p** 10. Lic to Offic *L & K* from 09. *Address temp unknown*

LYNCH-WATSON, Graham Leslie. b 30. AKC55. **d** 56 **p** 57. C New Eltham All SS *S'wark* 56-60; C W Brompton St Mary *Lon* 60-62; V Camberwell St Bart *S'wark* 62-66; V Purley St Barn 67-77; C Caversham *Ox* 77-81; C Caversham St Pet and Mapledurham etc 81-85; P-in-c Warwick St Paul *Cov* 85-86; V 86-92; rtd 92; Perm to Offic *Ox* 96-00. *11 Crouch Street, Banbury OX16 9PP* Tel (01295) 263172

LYNE, Peter. b 27. Sheff Univ BA51. Qu Coll Birm 51. **d** 53 **p** 54. C Newland St Aug *York* 53-55; C Harworth *S'well* 55-56; C Burbage *Derby* 56-58; V Horsley Woodhouse 58-62; V Rawcliffe *Sheff* 62-69; V Elvaston and Shardlow *Derby* 69-74; P-in-c Ashbourne St Jo 74-80; P-in-c Kniveton w Hognaston 75-80; P-in-c Fenny Bentley, Thorpe and Tissington 77-78; P-in-c Osmaston w Edlaston 78-80; P-in-c Lt Eaton 80-84; P-in-c Holbrooke 80-84; V Holbrook and Lt Eaton 84-91; rtd 91; Perm to Offic *Derby* from 91. *3 Vicarage Close, High Street, Belper DE56 1TB* Tel (01773) 829188

LYNESS, Nicholas Jonathan. b 55. Oak Hill Th Coll BA97. **d** 97. C Reading Greyfriars *Ox* 97-98. *3 Roe Green Cottages, Roe Green, Sandon, Buntingford SG9 0QE* Tel (01763) 288172 Mobile 07802-730485

LYNETT, Anthony Martin. b 54. K Coll Lon BD75 AKC75 Darw Coll Cam PGCE76. Sarum & Wells Th Coll 77. **d** 78 **p** 79. C Swindon Ch Ch *Bris* 78-81; C Leckhampton SS Phil and Jas w Cheltenham St Jas *Glouc* 81-83; Asst Chapl HM Pris Glouc 83-88; Chapl 91-98; V Coney Hill *Glouc* 83-88; Chapl HM YOI Deerbolt 88-91; P-in-c Glouc St Mark 91-99; P-in-c Glouc St Mary de Crypt w St Jo, Ch Ch etc 98-99; Chapl HM Pris Wellingborough 99-01; V Wellingborough All SS *Pet* from 01; P-in-c Wellingborough All Hallows from 10; RD Wellingborough from 07. *The Vicarage, 154 Midland Road, Wellingborough NN8 1NF* Tel (01933) 227101 E-mail tartleknock@btinternet.com

LYNN, Anthony Hilton. b 44. Golds Coll Lon TCert66 Open Univ BA80. SAOMC 95. **d** 98 **p** 99. NSM Stanford in the Vale w Goosey and Hatford *Ox* 98-00; NSM Cherbury w Gainfield 00-03; TV Hermitage from 03. *The Rectory, Yattendon, Thatcham RG18 0UR* Tel (01635) 201213 E-mail revtonylynn@btinternet.com

LYNN, Mrs Antonia Jane. b 59. Girton Coll Cam BA80 MA84. St Steph Ho Ox 82. dss 84 **d** 87. Portsm Cathl 84-87; Dn-in-c Camberwell St Mich w All So w Em *S'wark* 87-91; Par Dn Newington St Mary 87-91; Perm to Offic 91-94; Chapl Horton

Hosp Epsom 91-94; Gen Sec Guild of Health from 94; Hon Par Dn Ewell *Guildf* 94-99. *7 Kingsmead Close, West Ewell, Epsom KT19 9RD* Tel (020) 8786 8983

LYNN, Frank Trevor. b 36. Keble Coll Ox BA61 MA63. St Steph Ho Ox 61. **d** 63 **p** 64. C W Derby St Mary *Liv* 63-65; C Chorley *Ches* 65-68; V Altrincham St Jo 68-72; Chapl RN 72-88; Hon C Walworth St Jo *S'wark* 88-90; C Cheam 90-96; rtd 99. *7 Kingsmead Close, West Ewell, Epsom KT19 9RD* Tel (020) 8786 8983

LYNN, Jeffrey. b 39. Moore Th Coll Sydney 67 EMMTC 76. **d** 79 **p** 80. C Littleover *Derby* 79-80; Hon C Allestree 80-85; Chapl HM Pris Man 85-86; Kirkham 86-93; Wakef 93-95; Sudbury and Foston Hall 95-96; rtd 96; Perm to Offic *Blackb* from 98. *48 South Park, Lytham St Annes FY8 4QQ* Tel (01253) 730490

LYNN, Peter Anthony. b 38. Keele Univ BA62 St Jo Coll Cam BA64 MA68 PhD72. Westcott Ho Cam 67. **d** 68 **p** 69. C Soham *Ely* 68-72; Min Can St Paul's Cathl 72-78; Perm to Offic *St Alb* 78-86; Min Can and Sacr St Paul's Cathl 86-88; C Westmr St Matt 89-91; V Glynde, W Firle and Beddingham *Chich* 91-03; rtd 03. *119 Stanford Avenue, Brighton BN1 6FA* Tel (01273) 553361

LYNN, Trevor. See LYNN, Frank Trevor

LYNN, Archdeacon of. See ASHE, The Ven Francis John

LYNN, Suffragan Bishop of. See MEYRICK, The Rt Revd Cyril Jonathan

LYON, Adrian David. b 55. Coll of Resurr Mirfield 84. **d** 87 **p** 88. C Crewe St Andr *Ches* 87-90; C Altrincham St Geo 90-91; TV Accrington *Blackb* 91-00; TR Accrington Ch the King 00-10; P-in-c St Annes St Anne from 10; V from 11. *St Anne's Vicarage, 4 Oxford Road, Lytham St Annes FY8 2EA* Tel (01253) 722725 E-mail david.lyon1955@googlemail.com

LYON, Christopher David. b 55. Strathclyde Univ LLB75 Edin Univ BD81. Edin Th Coll 78. **d** 81 **p** 82. C Dumfries *Glas* 81-84; P-in-c Alexandria 84-88; R Greenock 88-00; R Ayr, Girvan and Maybole 00-02; Chapl Luxembourg *Eur* from 02. *89 rue de Mühlenbach, L-2168 Luxembourg* Tel and fax (00352) 439593 E-mail chris.lyon@escc.lu

LYON, Dennis. b 36. Wycliffe Hall Ox 64. **d** 67 **p** 68. C Woodthorpe *S'well* 67-70; Warden Walton Cen 70-72; V W Derby Gd Shep *Liv* 72-81; V Billinge 81-00; AD Wigan W 89-00; rtd 00; Perm to Offic *Liv* from 01. *10 Arniam Road, Rainford, St Helens WA11 8BU* Tel (01744) 885623

LYON, Miss Jane Madeline. b 50. Derby Univ MA05. Ripon Coll Cuddesdon 07. **d** 09 **p** 10. NSM Derby St Andr w St Osmund from 09. *21 Cedar Close, Ashbourne DE6 1FJ* Tel (01335) 345408 Mobile 07974-806636 E-mail janelyon0910@tiscali.co.uk

LYON, Joan Baxter. b 50. Strathclyde Univ BA70. TISEC 94. **d** 96 **p** 00. NSM Glas E End 96-00; Asst Chapl Luxembourg *Eur* 05-11; TV Sole Bay *St E* from 11. *Address temp unknown* E-mail joanblyon@hotmail.com

LYON, John Forrester. b 39. Edin Th Coll CertEd95. **d** 95 **p** 96. C Greenock *Glas* 95-98; C Gourock 95-98; Chapl Ardgowan Hospice 95-98; P-in-c Glas Gd Shep and Ascension 98-07; rtd 07. *28 Demondale Road, Arbroath DD11 1TR* E-mail revjohnlyon@btinternet.com

LYON, John Harry. b 51. S Dios Minl Tr Scheme 86. **d** 89 **p** 90. NSM S Patcham *Chich* 89-91; C Chich St Paul and St Pet 91-94; R Earnley and E Wittering 94-04; V E Preston w Kingston from 04. *The Vicarage, 33 Vicarage Lane, East Preston, Littlehampton BN16 2SP* Tel (01903) 783318 E-mail revdjohnlyon@dsl.pipex.com

LYON, Mark John. b 82. St Steph Ho Ox 08. **d** 11. C Brighton St Mich *Chich* from 11. *59 Avalon, West Street, Brighton BN1 2RP* Tel (01273) 590889 E-mail frmarklyon@gmail.com

LYONS, Bruce Twyford. b 37. K Alfred's Coll Win CertEd61. Tyndale Hall Bris. **d** 70 **p** 71. C Virginia Water *Guildf* 70-73; Chapl Ostend w Knokke and Bruges *Eur* 73-78; V E Ham St Paul *Chelmsf* 78-85; V St Alb Ch Ch *St Alb* 85-91; Chapl Wellingborough Sch 92-95; P-in-c Stogumber w Nettlecombe and Monksilver *B & W* 96-98; P-in-c Ostend w Knokke and Bruges *Eur* 98-00; NSM Newbury Deanery *Ox* 01; Chapl Milton Abbey Sch Dorset 01-02; rtd 02; Perm to Offic *Sarum* 01-11. *Berkeley House, 18 Moore Road, Bourton-on-the-Water, Cheltenham GL54 2AZ* Tel (01451) 810388 E-mail bruce.lyons1@virgin.net

LYONS, Canon Edward Charles. b 44. Nottm Univ BTh75 LTh. St Jo Coll Nottm 71. **d** 75 **p** 76. C Cambridge St Martin *Ely* 75-78; P-in-c Bestwood Park *S'well* 78-85; R W Hallam and Mapperley *Derby* 85-98; P-in-c Brownsover CD *Cov* 98-02; V Brownsover 02-06; V Clifton w Newton and Brownsover 07-09; RD Rugby 99-06; Dioc Ecum Officer 03-06; Hon Can Cov Cathl 07-09; rtd 09. *68 Juliet Drive, Rugby CV22 6LY* E-mail ted.lyons@btinternet.com

LYONS, Graham Selby. b 29. MBE84. Open Univ BA79. **d** 97 **p** 98. OLM New Eltham All SS *S'wark* 97-04. *56 Cadwallon Road, London SE9 3PY* Tel (020) 8850 6576 E-mail holyons2@aol.com

LYONS, Margaret Rose Marie. b 47. **d** 89. OLM Gainsborough All SS *Linc* 89-91; Hon C Low Moor *Bradf* 04-05; Hon C Oakenshaw, Wyke and Low Moor from 06. *1C Common Road, Low Moor, Bradford BD12 0PN* Tel 07940-558062 (mobile)

LYONS, Paul. b 67. Ulster Univ BA91. TCD Div Sch BTh98. **d** 98 **p** 99. C Seapatrick *D & D* 98-03; I Greenisland *Conn* from 03. *4 Tinamara, Upper Station Road, Greenisland, Carrickfergus BT38 8FE* Tel (028) 9086 3421 *or* 9085 9676 Mobile 07791-472225 E-mail greenisland@connor.anglican.org

LYONS, Paul Benson. b 44. Qu Coll Birm 68. **d** 69 **p** 70. C Rugby St Andr *Cov* 69-70; C Moston St Jo *Man* 70-72; PV Llan Cathl 73-74; C Brookfield St Anne, Highgate Rise *Lon* 74-75; Perm to Offic 76-82; C Westmr St Sav and St Jas Less 82-86; V Gt Cambridge Road St Jo and St Jas from 86. *St John's Vicarage, 113 Creighton Road, London N17 8JS* Tel (020) 8808 4077 E-mail stjohnstjames@hotmail.com

LYONS, William. b 22. LNSM course 78. **d** 80 **p** 81. NSM Glenrothes *St And* 80-81; NSM Kirkcaldy 81-91; NSM Kinghorn 81-91; rtd 91. *24 Auchmithie Place, Glenrothes KY7 4TY* Tel (01592) 630757

LYSSEJKO, Mrs Janet Lesley. b 64. **d** 10 **p** 11. OLM Walmersley Road, Bury *Man* from 10. *31 Burrs Lea Close, Bury BL9 5HT* Tel 0161-764 6882 E-mail janetlyssejko@sky.com

LYTHALL, Andrew Simon. b 86. Keele Univ BSc07 St Jo Coll Dur BA09. Cranmer Hall Dur 07. **d** 10 **p** 11. C Stockport St Geo *Ches* from 10. *40 Beechfield Road, Stockport SK3 8SF* Tel 0161-425 7992 Mobile 07706-036425 E-mail alythall@btinternet.com

LYTHALL, Jennifer Elizabeth. *See* MAYO-LYTHALL, Ms Jennifer Elizabeth

LYTTLE, Norma Irene. b 47. CITC. **d** 01 **p** 02. Aux Min Drumachose *D & R* 01-04; Aux Min Dungiven w Bovevagh 04-07; Bp's C Leckpatrick w Dunnalong 07-09; I from 09. *The Rectory, 1 Lowertown Road, Ballymagorry, Strabane BT82 0LE* Tel and fax (028) 7188 3545 Mobile 07742-836688 E-mail leckpatrick@derry.anglican.org

M

MABBS, Miss Margaret Joyce. b 24. St Hilda's Coll Ox BA45 MA47 DipEd46. S'wark Ord Course 79. **dss** 82 **d** 87 **p** 94. Eltham Park St Luke *S'wark* 82-05; NSM 87-05; Perm to Offic from 05. *70 Westmount Road, London SE9 1JE* Tel (020) 8850 4621

McADAM, Gordon Paul. b 66. QUB BSc88 TCD BTh93. CITC 90. **d** 93 **p** 94. C Drumglass w Moygashel *Arm* 93-96; I Dungiven w Bovevagh *D & R* 96-02; I Loughgall w Grange *Arm* from 02. *The Rectory, 2 Main Street, Loughgall, Armagh BT61 8HZ* Tel (028) 3889 1587 E-mail loughgall@armagh.anglican.org

McADAM, Canon Michael Anthony. b 30. K Coll Cam BA52 MA56. Westcott Ho Cam 54. **d** 56 **p** 57. C Towcester w Easton Neston 56-59; Chapl Hurstpierpoint Coll 60-68; Bp's Chapl *Lon* 69-73; R Much Hadham *St Alb* 73-95; Hon Can St Alb 89-95; rtd 95; RD Oundle Pet 96-97; Perm to Offic *Pet* from 98 and *St Alb* from 03. *Parkers Patch, 55 Barnwell, Peterborough PE8 5PG* Tel (01832) 273451

McALISTER, Canon David. b 39. St Jo Coll Nottm 83. **d** 87 **p** 88. NSM Arpafeelie *Mor* 87-93; NSM Cromarty 87-93; NSM Fortrose 87-93; C Broughty Ferry *Bre* 93-95; P-in-c Nairn *Mor* 95-09; P-in-c Kishorn 08-09; P-in-c Lochalsh 08-09; P-in-c Poolewe 08-09; Chapl Inverness Airport 98-09; Can St Andr Cathl Inverness 01-09; Hon Can from 09; OCM from 03; rtd 09. *36 Feddon Hill, Fortrose IV10 8SP* Tel (01381) 622530 E-mail david.mcalister@tesco.net

McALISTER, Kenneth Bloomer. b 25. TCD BA51. **d** 51 **p** 53. C Cregagh *D & D* 51-54; C Monaghan *Clogh* 54-57; C Portadown St Mark *Arm* 57-62; R Ripley *Ripon* 62-91; rtd 91; Perm to Offic *Ripon* from 91. *31 Wetherby Road, Knaresborough HG5 8LH* Tel (01423) 860705

McALISTER, Margaret Elizabeth Anne (Sister Margaret Anne). b 55. St Mary's Coll Dur BA78 Ex Univ PGCE79. Wycliffe Hall Ox 83 SAOMC 99. **d** 01 **p** 02. ASSP from 91; NSM Cowley St Jas *Ox* 01-04; NSM Cowley St Jo 04-09; NSM Ox St Mary Magd 09-11; Perm to Offic from 11. *All Saints Convent, St Mary's Road, Oxford OX4 1RU* Tel (01865) 200479 Fax 726547 E-mail margaretanne@socallss.co.uk

McALLEN, James. b 38. Lon Univ BD71. Oak Hill Th Coll 63. **d** 66 **p** 67. C Blackheath St Jo *S'wark* 66-69; C Edin St Thos 69-73; V Selby St Jas *York* 73-80; V Wistow 75-80; V Houghton

Carl 80-91; Gen Sec Lon City Miss 92-03; Hon C Blackheath St Jo *S'wark* 94-04; rtd 04; Perm to Offic *Carl* from 04. *205 Brampton Road, Carlisle CA3 9AX* Tel (01228) 540505

McALLEN, Robert Roy. b 41. Bps' Coll Cheshunt 62. **d** 65 **p** 66. C Seagoe *D & D* 65-67; C Knockbreda 67-70; CF 70-96; Chapl R Memorial Chpl Sandhurst 87-92; Chapl Guards Chpl Lon 92-96; Perm to Offic *Guildf* 96-98; R Ockley, Okewood and Forest Green 98-06; rtd 06. *Maranatha, Church Street, Rudgwick, Horsham RH12 3EG* Tel (01403) 823172 E-mail roy-gill@mcallenr.freeserve.co.uk

MACAN, Peter John Erdley. b 36. Bp Gray Coll Cape Town 58. **d** 60 **p** 61. C Matroosfontein S Africa 60-64; C Maitland Gd Shep 64-67; C S Lambeth St Ann *S'wark* 68-71; V Nunhead St Silas 72-81; P-in-c Clapham H Spirit 81-87; TV Clapham Team 87-90; V Dulwich St Clem w St Pet 90-02; rtd 02; Perm to Offic *S'wark* from 04; Retirement Officer Croydon Area from 08. *19 The Windings, South Croydon CR2 0HW* Tel (020) 8657 1398 E-mail peter.macan@virgin.net

McARTHUR, Claudette. **d** 08 **p** 09. NSM Norbury St Oswald *S'wark* from 08. *2 Quince House, Hemlock Close, London SW16 5PN* Tel (020) 8715 1341 E-mail claudettemac1@aol.com

McARTHUR, Duncan Walker. b 50. Strathclyde Univ BSc73 Moore Th Coll Sydney ThL80 Melbourne Univ BD82 Newc Univ MA94. **d** 82 **p** 82. C Hornsby Australia 82-85; Asst Min 88-89; Asst Chapl Barker Coll Hornsby 86-88; P-in-c Harraby *Carl* 90-93; R Hurstville Australia 93-95; Hon Asst P Wauchope St Matt from 99; Chapl St Columba Sch Port Macquarie from 02. *43 Narran River Road, Wauchope NSW 2446, Australia* Tel (0061) (2) 6505 1147 *or* 6583 6999 Mobile 412 828341 Fax (2) 6583 6982 E-mail dmcarthe@bigpond.net.au

MACARTHUR, Helen Anne. b 45. Ulster Univ BEd90 QUB MSc96. CITC 05. **d** 08 **p** 09. NSM Derriaghy w Colin *Conn* from 08. *16 Halftown Road, Lisburn BT27 5RD* Tel (028) 9262 1703 Mobile 07818-027040 E-mail helenmacar@btinternet.com

McARTHUR-EDWARDS, Mrs Judith Sarah. b 71. Westmr Coll Ox BTh94. Cranmer Hall Dur 97. **d** 99 **p** 00. C Cradley *Worc* 99-02; C Quarry Bank 02-03; Asst Chapl Frimley Park Hosp NHS Trust 04-05; Asst Chapl R Surrey Co Hosp NHS Trust from 05. *The Vicarage, 37 Sturt Road, Frimley Green, Camberley GU16 6HY* Tel (01252) 835179 E-mail scott-edwards@btopenworld.com

MACARTNEY, Gerald Willam. b 52. TCD BTh03. CITC. **d** 03 **p** 04. C Drumglass w Moygashel *Arm* 03-05; I Milltown from 05; Dioc Communications Officer 09-10 and from 11. *10 Derrylileagh Road, Portadown, Craigavon BT62 1TQ* Tel (028) 3885 2626 Mobile 07850-040027 E-mail milltown@armagh.anglican.org

McATEER (née ROBINSON), Katharine Mary. b 51. NUU BA73. CITC 03. **d** 06 **p** 07. NSM Conwal Union w Gartan *D & R* 06-08; NSM Londonderry Ch Ch, Culmore, Muff and Belmont from 08. *27 Northland Road, Londonderry BT48 7NF* Tel (028) 7137 4544 Fax 7127 1991 Mobile 07813-885145 E-mail kmcateer51@gmail.com

MACAULAY (née BRAYBROOKS), Mrs Bridget Ann. b 63. Trin Coll Bris BA92 DipCOT84. TISEC 96. **d** 98 **p** 99. C Edin Old St Paul 98-01; C Edin St Pet 01-06; Dir Coracle Trust from 01. *Address temp unknown* E-mail kbmac@gmx.net

MACAULAY, John Roland. b 39. Man Univ BSc61 Liv Inst of Educn PGCE80. Wells Th Coll 61. **d** 63 **p** 64. C Padgate Ch Ch *Liv* 63-66; C Upholland 66-73; TV 73-75; V Hindley St Pet 75-81; Chapl Liv Coll 81-96; Sub-Chapl HM Pris Risley 85-96; R Lowton St Luke *Liv* 96-05; rtd 05. *58 Rectory Road, Ashton-in-Makerfield, Wigan WN4 0QD* Tel (01942) 711336

MACAULAY, Kenneth Lionel. b 55. Edin Univ BD78. Edin Th Coll 74. **d** 78 **p** 79. C Glas St Ninian 78-80; Dioc Youth Chapl 80-87; P-in-c Glas St Matt 80-87; R Glenrothes *St And* 87-89; Chapl St Mary's Cathl 89-92; Min Glas St Mary 89-92; Min Glas St Serf 92-94; Perm to Offic 94-96; NSM Glas St Oswald 96-98; P-in-c 98-01; Chapl HM Pris Glas (Barlinnie) 99-00; P-in-c Dumbarton *Glas* 01-06; R from 06. *The Rectory, 54 Helenslee Crescent, Dumbarton G82 4HS* Tel (01389) 602261 *or* 734514 Mobile 07734-187250 E-mail frkenny@btinternet.com

MACAULAY, Kenneth Russell. b 63. Strathclyde Univ BSc85. TISEC 95. **d** 98 **p** 99. C Edin Old St Paul 98-01; C Edin St Pet 01-06; Dir Coracle Trust from 01. *Address temp unknown* E-mail kbmac@gmx.net

McAULAY, Mark John Simon. b 71. Lanc Univ LLB92 Leeds Univ BA04 Barrister-at-Law (Inner Temple) 93. Coll of Resurr Mirfield 02. **d** 04 **p** 05. C Ruislip St Martin *Lon* 04-07; V New Southgate St Paul from 07. *The Vicarage, 11 Woodland Road, London N11 1PN* Tel (020) 8361 1946 E-mail frmarkmcaulay@hotmail.com

McAUSLAND, Canon William James. b 36. Edin Th Coll 56. **d** 59 **p** 60. C Dundee St Mary Magd *Bre* 59-64; R 71-79; R Glas H Cross 64-71; Chapl St Marg Old People's Home 79-85; R Dundee St Marg *Bre* 79-01; Chapl St Mary's Sisterhood 82-87; Chapl Ninewells Hosp 85-01; Can St Paul's Cathl Dundee 93-01; Hon Can St Paul's Cathl Dundee from 01; rtd 01. *18 Broadford*

Terrace, Broughty Ferry, Dundee DD5 3EF Tel (01382) 737721 E-mail billmcausland@talktalk.net

McAVOY, George Brian. b 41. MBE78. TCD BA61 MA72. Div Test 63. d 63 p 65. C Cork St Luke w St Ann *C, C & R* 63-66; I Timoleague w Abbeymahon 66-68; Chapl RAF 68-88; Asst Chapl-in-Chief RAF 88-95; QHC 91-95; Chapl Fosse Health NHS Trust 95-98; Chapl Oakham Sch 98-03; rtd 03; Perm to Offic *Pet* 03-11 and *Leic* from 05; Past Care and Counselling Adv *Pet* 04-10. *1 The Leas, Cottesmore, Oakham LE15 7DG* Tel (01572) 812404 Mobile 07967-967803 E-mail laurel.cottage@tiscali.co.uk

McAVOY, Philip George. b 63. Imp Coll Lon BSc85 SS Coll Cam BA90. Westcott Ho Cam 88. d 91 p 92. C W End *Win* 91-95; TV Swanage and Studland *Sarum* 95-00; P-in-c Littleton *Lon* 00-06; V Weston *Guildf* 06-10; Perm to Offic from 10. *Four Acorns, Molesey Road, Walton-on-Thames KT12 3PP* E-mail pandk.mac@btinternet.com

MACBAIN, Patrick. b 77. G&C Coll Cam BA99. Oak Hill Th Coll BTh06. d 09 p 10. C Worksop St Anne *S'well* from 09. *27 Sunnyside, Worksop S81 7LN* Tel (01909) 470433 E-mail pmacbain@yahoo.co.uk

McBETH, David Ronald. d 06 p 07. C Glendermott *D & R* 06-09; Australia 09-11; I Dungiven w Bovevagh *D & R* from 11. *The Rectory, 14 Main Street, Dungiven, Londonderry BT47 4LB* Tel (028) 7774 1226

McBRIDE, Ms Catherine Sarah. b 64. Trent Poly BSc87. Ridley Hall Cam 06. d 08 p 09. C Meole Brace *Lich* from 08. *7 Dargate Close, Shrewsbury SY3 9QE* Tel (01743) 369322 E-mail cathmcb@yahoo.co.uk

McBRIDE, Murray. b 61. Trin Coll Bris BA00. d 00 p 01. C S Lawres Gp *Linc* 00-04; V Aspatria w Hayton and Gilcrux *Carl* 04-06; CF 06-09; V Shrewsbury St Geo w Greenfields *Lich* from 09. *The Vicarage, St George's Street, Shrewsbury SY3 8QA* Tel (01743) 235461

McBRIDE, Peter William Frederick. b 66. Trin Coll Ox BA88 MA03 Solicitor 91. SEITE 03. d 06 p 07. C Guildf H Trin w St Mary 06-09; TV Poplar *Lon* 09-11. *G10 The School House, Pages Walk, London SE1 4HG* Tel (020) 7252 2328 Mobile 07887-551077

McBRIDE, The Ven Stephen Richard. b 61. QUB BSc84 TCD BTh89 MA92 QUB PhD96. CITC 84. d 87 p 88. C Antrim All SS *Conn* 87-90; I Belfast St Pet 90-95; Bp's Dom Chapl 94-02; I Antrim All SS from 95; Adn Conn from 02; Prec Belfast St Anne from 02. *The Vicarage, 10 Vicarage Gardens, Antrim BT41 4JP* Tel and fax (028) 9446 2186 Mobile 07718-588191 E-mail archdeacon@connor.anglican.org

McCABE, Alan. b 37. Lon Univ BScEng61. Ridley Hall Cam 61. d 63 p 64. C Bromley SS Pet and Paul *Roch* 63-67; PV Roch Cathl 67-70; V Bromley H Trin 70-77; V Westerham 77-88; V Eastbourne St Jo *Chich* 88-99; rtd 00; Perm to Offic *Chich* from 00. *94 Baldwin Avenue, Eastbourne BN21 1UP* Tel and fax (01323) 643731 E-mail mccabe@talktalk.net

McCABE, Carol. b 49. d 03 p 04. OLM Blackrod *Man* from 03; OLM Horwich and Rivington from 11. *27 Lymbridge Drive, Blackrod, Bolton BL6 5TH* Tel (01204) 669775

McCABE, John Hamilton. b 59. St Edm Hall Ox MA82 PGCE84. Trin Coll Bris MA01. d 01 p 02. C Burpham *Guildf* 01-05; Lic to Offic 05-06; R Byfleet from 06. *The Rectory, 81 Rectory Lane, Byfleet, West Byfleet KT14 7LX* Tel (01932) 342374 Mobile 07710-094357 E-mail john.h.mccabe@btinternet.com

McCABE, The Ven John Trevor. b 33. RD78. Nottm Univ BA55. Wycliffe Hall Ox 57. d 59 p 60. C Compton Gifford *Ex* 59-63; P-in-c Ex St Martin, St Steph, St Laur etc 63-66; Chapl RNR 63-03; Chapl Ex Sch 64-66; V Capel *Guildf* 66-71; V Scilly Is *Truro* 71-74; TR Is of Scilly 74-81; Can Res Bris Cathl 81-83; V Manaccan w St Anthony-in-Meneage and St Martin *Truro* 83-96; RD Kerrier 87-90 and 94-96; Chmn Cornwall NHS Trust for Mental Handicap 91-00; Hon Can Truro Cathl from 93; Adn Cornwall 96-99; rtd 00; Non Exec Dir Cornwall Healthcare NHS Trust from 99; Perm to Offic *Truro* from 99. *1 Sunhill, School Lane, Budock Water, Falmouth TR11 5DG* Tel (01326) 378095

McCABE, Terence John. b 46. Sarum Th Coll 71. d 74 p 75. C Radford *Cov* 74-77; P-in-c Bris St Paul w St Barn 77-80; TV E Bris 80-84; USA 84-90; R Eynesbury *Ely* from 90. *The Rectory, 7 Howitt's Lane, Eynesbury, St Neots PE19 2JA* Tel (01480) 403884 *or* 385364 E-mail terry.mccabe@ntlworld.com

McCABE, William Alexander Beck. b 27. QUB BA50 PhD65. d 74 p 74. Sec Sheff Coun of Chs 74-80; Hon C Millhouses H Trin *Sheff* 74-80; TV Sheff Manor 80-83; C Mosbrough 83; C Portsea St Cuth *Portsm* 83-86; C S w N Hayling 86-87; V Mickleover St Jo *Derby* 87-91; rtd 91; Perm to Offic *Derby* from 91. *4 Rowan House, Flookersbrook, Chester CH2 3AA* Tel (01244) 321623

McCAFFERTY, Andrew. See McCAFFERTY, William Andrew

McCAFFERTY, Canon Christine Ann. b 43. FCA76. Gilmore Course 76. dss 79 d 87 p 94. Writtle w Highwood *Chelmsf* 79-94; C 87-94; Chapl to Bp Bradwell 87-92; Dioc NSM Officer 87-94; TR Wickford and Runwell 94-00; Hon C Lt Baddow 00-09; Hon Can Chelmsf Cathl 91-09; rtd 09; Perm to Offic *Chelmsf* from 09.

3 Hanlee Brook, Great Baddow, Chelmsford CM2 8GB Tel (01245) 476371 E-mail mccafferty@jcmcc.freeserve.co.uk

McCAFFERTY, (née BACK), Mrs Esther Elaine. b 52. Saffron Walden Coll CertEd74. Trin Coll Bris 79 Oak Hill Th Coll BA81. dss 81 d 87 p 94. Collyhurst *Man* 81-84; Upton (Overchurch) *Ches* 84-88; Par Dn 87-88; Par Dn Upper Holloway St Pet w St Jo *Lon* 88-90; Min in charge 90-97; P-in-c Pitsea w Nevendon *Chelmsf* 97-02; R Basildon St Martin from 02; RD Basildon 99-04. *The Rectory, St Martin's Square, Basildon SS14 1DX* Tel and fax (01268) 522455 E-mail emccafferty@talk21.com

McCAFFERTY, Keith Alexander. See DUCKETT, Keith Alexander

McCAFFERTY, William Andrew. b 49. Open Univ BA93. SWMTC 94. d 97 p 98. NSM Lapford, Nymet Rowland and Coldridge *Ex* 97-00; CF 00-04; TR Crosslacon *Carl* 04-08; R Forfar *St And* from 08; R Lunan Head from 08. *St John's Rectory, 24 St James Road, Forfar DD8 1LG* Tel (01307) 463440 Mobile 07891-119684 E-mail normandy08@btinternet.com

McCAGHREY, Mark Allan. b 66. Warwick Univ BSc87. St Jo Coll Nottm BTh93. d 94 p 95. C Byfleet *Guildf* 94-97; V Lowestoft St Andr *Nor* from 97. *The Vicarage, 51 Beresford Road, Lowestoft NR32 2NQ* Tel (01502) 511521 Fax 08701-377567 E-mail mark@romanhill.org.uk

McCALL, Adrienne. b 49. d 08 p 09. OLM Hawkhurst *Cant* 08-11; NSM St Nicholas at Wade w Sarre and Chislet w Hoath from 11. *Invicta House, Queens Road, Hawkhurst, Cranbrook TN18 4HH* Tel (01580) 754334 E-mail adie.mac@tiscali.co.uk

McCALLA, Robert Ian. b 31. AKC55. St Boniface Warminster 56. d 56 p 57. C Barrow St Jo *Carl* 56-58; C Penrith St Andr 58-61; R Greenheys St Clem *Man* 61-64; V Glodwick 64-71; R Distington *Carl* 71-73; V Howe Bridge *Man* 73-87; Chapl Atherleigh Hosp 75-98; R Heaton Mersey *Man* 87-92; V Tyldesley w Shakerley 92-98; rtd 98; Perm to Offic *Carl* from 98. *17 Brunswick Square, Penrith CA11 7LW* Tel (01768) 895212

McCALLIG, Darren. d 05 p 06. C Monkstown *D & G* 05-07; Dean of Res and Chapl TCD from 07. *House 27, Trinity College, College Green, Dublin 2, Republic of Ireland* Tel (00353) (1) 896 1402 Mobile 87-286 6637 E-mail darrenmccallig@hotmail.com

MacCALLUM, The Very Revd Norman Donald. b 47. Edin Univ LTh70. Edin Th Coll 67. d 71 p 72. TV Livingston LEP *Edin* 71-82; P-in-c Bo'ness and R Grangemouth 82-00; Syn Clerk 96-00; Can St Mary's Cathl 96-00; Provost St Jo Cathl Oban from 00; R Oban St Jo from 00; R Ardchattan from 00; R Ardbrecknish from 00; Dean Arg from 05. *The Rectory, Ardconnel Terrace, Oban PA34 5DJ* Tel and fax (01631) 562323 E-mail provostoban@argyll.anglican.org

McCAMLEY, Gregor Alexander. b 42. TCD BA64 MA67. CITC 65. d 65 p 66. C Holywood *D & D* 65-68; C Bangor St Comgall 68-72; I Carnalea 72-80; I Knock 80-07; Stewardship Adv 89-07; Can Down Cathl 90-07; Dioc Registrar 90-95; Adn Down and Chan Belf Cathl 95-07; rtd 07. *1 Rocky Lane, Seaforde, Downpatrick BT30 8PW* Tel (028) 4481 1111

McCAMMON, John Taylor. b 42. QUB BSc65 Lon Univ BD70. Clifton Th Coll 67. d 71 p 72. C Lurgan Ch the Redeemer *D & D* 71-75; I Kilkeel 75-82; I Lisburn Ch Ch Cathl 82-98; Treas 94-96; Prec 96; Chan 96-98; Can Conn Cathl 85-95; CMS Kenya 99-05; CMS Ireland 05-09; rtd 09. *9 Beechfield Park, Coleraine BT52 2HZ* Tel (028) 7032 6046 E-mail jmmccammon@hotmail.com

McCANDLESS, John Hamilton Moore. b 24. QUB BA Ulster Poly BEd. d 63 p 64. C Belfast St Matt *Conn* 63-66; I Termonmaguirke *Arm* 66-69; C Jordanstown *Conn* 69-70; I Ballinderry, Tamlaght and Arboe *Arm* 70-74; I Killyman w Rossnowlagh and Drumholm *D & R* 84-87; rtd 87. *4 Greenhill Drive, Ballymoney BT53 6DE* Tel (028) 2766 2078 E-mail jack@theloughan.fsnet.co.uk

McCANN, Alan. See McCANN, Thomas Alan George

McCANN, Hilda. b 36. NOC. d 03. OLM Parr *Liv* from 03. *25 Newton Road, St Helens WA9 2HZ* Tel (01744) 758759

McCANN, Michael Joseph. b 61. Man Univ BSc82 TCD BTh91 FCA. d 91 p 92. C Derryloran *Arm* 91-94; I Dunmurry *Conn* 94-99; I Kilroot and Templecorran from 99. *Kilroot Rectory, 29 Downshire Gardens, Carrickfergus BT38 7LW* Tel (028) 9336 2387

McCANN, Roland Neil. b 39. Serampore Coll BD73. Bp's Coll Calcutta. d 70 p 73. C Calcutta St Jas 70-73; V Calcutta St Thos 73-74; C Earley St Bart *Ox* 74-77; C-in-c Harlington Ch Ch CD *Lon* 77-99; rtd 99; Perm to Offic *Lon* from 02. *195 Park Road, Uxbridge UB8 1NP* Tel (01895) 259265

McCANN, Stephen Thomas. b 60. Benedictine Coll Kansas BA83 Boston Coll (USA) MA89 Creighton Univ Nebraska MA94. Pontifical Gregorian Univ 96. d 97 p 98. In RC Ch 97-01; Rydal Hall *Carl* 02-05; C Kendal H Trin 05-10; I Ballydehob w Aghadown *C, C & R* from 10. *The Rectory, Church Road, Ballydehob, Co Cork, Republic of Ireland* Tel (00353) (28) 37117 E-mail stmccann@live.com

McCANN, Thomas Alan George. b 66. Ulster Univ BA90 TCD BTh93 QUB MPhil99. CITC 90. d 93 p 94. C Carrickfergus

Conn 93-00; I Woodburn H Trin from 00. *20 Meadow Hill Close, Carrickfergus BT38 9RQ* Tel (028) 9336 2126 E-mail alan@thehobbit.fsnet.co.uk

McCARTAN, Mrs Audrey Doris. b 50. Keele Univ CertEd71 BEd72 Lanc Univ MA75 Northumbria Univ MSc99. NEOC 01. **d** 04 **p** 05. NSM Gosforth St Hugh *Newc* 04-07; P-in-c Heddon-on-the-Wall from 07. *St Andrew's Vicarage, The Towne Gate, Heddon-on-the-Wall, Newcastle upon Tyne NE15 0DT* Tel (01661) 853142

McCARTER, Mrs Suzanne. b 63. Hull Univ BA85 PGCE86. CBDTI 04. **d** 07 **p** 08. C Standish *Blackb* 07-10; C Cullingworth *Bradf* from 10; Area Missr S Craven Deanery from 10. *The Vicarage, Halifax Road, Cullingworth, Bradford BD13 5DE* Tel (01535) 270687 E-mail suzanne_mccarter@msn.com

McCARTHY, Christopher James. b 61. NEOC 04. **d** 06 **p** 07. C Bessingby *York* 06-08; C Bridlington Quay Ch Ch 06-08; V Bridlington Em from 08; P-in-c Skipsea w Ulrome and Barmston w Fraisthorpe 08-09; P-in-c Skipsea and Barmston w Fraisthorpe from 09. *Emmanuel Vicarage, 72 Cardigan Road, Bridlington YO15 3JT* Tel (01262) 671952 E-mail chrismbrid@aol.com

McCARTHY, Daniel Michael. b 76. Wolv Univ LLB98. Trin Coll Bris 08. **d** 10 **p** 11. C Long Benton *Newc* from 10. *5 Balroy Court, Newcastle upon Tyne NE12 9AW* Tel 0191-266 8490 Mobile 07855-941184 E-mail danielmccarthy7x77@yahoo.com

McCARTHY, David William. b 63. Edin Th Coll BD88. **d** 88 **p** 89. C Edin St Paul and St Geo 88-91; P-in-c S Queensferry 91-95; R Glas St Silas from 95. *77 Southbrae Drive, Glasgow G13 1PU* Tel 0141-954 9368 E-mail david@stsilas.org.uk

MacCARTHY, Denis Francis Anthony. b 60. St Patr Coll Maynooth BD85 CITC 05. **d** 85 **p** 86. In RC Ch 85-05; C Bandon Union *C, C & R* 06-08; I from 10; I Mallow Union 08-10. *The Rectory, Castle Road, Bandon, Co Cork, Republic of Ireland* Tel (00353) (23) 884 1259 E-mail noden1@eircom.net

McCARTHY, Lorraine Valmay. *See* REED, Mrs Lorraine Valmay

McCARTHY, Peter James. b 25. OBE. Cranmer Hall Dur. **d** 85 **p** 86. Hon C Farnham w Scotton, Staveley, Copgrove etc *Ripon* 85-87; V Startforth w Bowes 87-92; rtd 92; C Dufftown *Ab* 92-95; Perm to Offic *Ripon* from 95 and *Newc* from 99. *Manderley, Farnham Lane, Ferrensby, Knaresborough HG5 9JG* Tel (01423) 340503

MacCARTHY, The Very Revd Robert Brian. b 40. TCD BA63 MA66 PhD83 NUI MA65 Ox Univ MA82. Cuddesdon Coll 77. **d** 79 **p** 80. C Carlow w Urglin and Staplestown *C & O* 79-81; Lic to Offic Cashel, Waterford and Lismore 81-86; Lib Pusey Ho and Fell St Cross Coll Ox 81-82; C Bracknell *Ox* 82-83; TV 83-86; Bp's V and Lib Kilkenny Cathl and C Kilkenny w Aghour and Kilmanagh *C & O* 86-88; Chapl Kilkenny Coll 86-88; Bp's Dom Chapl 86-89; I Castlecomer w Colliery Ch, Mothel and Bilboa 88-95; Dioc Info Officer (Ossory and Leighlin) 88-90; Glebes Sec (Ossory and Leighlin) 92-94; Preb Monmohenock St Patr Cathl Dublin 94-99; Provost Tuam *T, K & A* 95-99; I Galway w Kilcummin 95-99; Chapl Univ Coll Galway 95-99; Dean St Patr Cathl Dublin from 99. *The Deanery, Upper Kevin Street, Dublin 8, Republic of Ireland* Tel (00353) (1) 475 5449 or 453 9472

McCARTHY, Sandra Ellen. *See* MANLEY, Mrs Sandra Ellen

MacCARTHY, Stephen Samuel. b 49. ACII81 Univ Coll Chich BA02. **d** 01. NSM Burgess Hill St Edw *Chich* from 01. *St Edward's House, 9 Coopers Close, Burgess Hill RH15 8AN* Tel (01444) 248520 Mobile 07802-734903 E-mail ssmaccarthy@aol.com

McCARTNEY, Terence Arthur. b 46. Open Univ BA90. Kelham Th Coll 66. **d** 70 **p** 71. C Gt Burstead *Chelmsf* 70-74; C Wickford 74-76; TV E Runcorn w Halton *Ches* 76-80; V Runcorn H Trin 80-84; Chapl HM Pris Liv 84; Chapl HM Pris Acklington 84-92; Chapl HM Pris Holme Ho from 92. *The Chaplaincy, HM Prison Holme House, Stockton-on-Tees TS18 2QU* Tel (01642) 744115

McCARTNEY, Adrian Alexander. b 57. Stranmillis Coll BEd79 TCD BTh88. CITC 86. **d** 88 **p** 89. C Jordanstown w Monkstown *Conn* 88-91; Bp's C Monkstown 91-94; I 94-96; C Belvoir *D & D* from 02. *94 Comber Road, Dundonald, Belfast BT16 2AG* Tel (028) 9067 3379 Mobile 07970-626384 E-mail adrian@boringwells.org

McCARTNEY, Darren James. **d** 03. P-in-c Pangnirtung Canada 03-06; C Carrickfergus *Conn* 06-09; I Knocknamuckley *D & D* from 09. *The Rectory, 30 Moss Bank Road, Ballynagarrick, Portadown BT63 5SL*

McCARTNEY, Ellis. b 47. Univ Coll Lon BSc73 Lon Inst of Educn MA82. NTMTC 94. **d** 97 **p** 98. NSM Tollington *Lon* 97-05. *6 Elfort Road, London N5 1AZ* Tel (020) 7226 1533 E-mail macfour@btinternet.com

McCARTNEY, Robert Charles. CITC. **d** 85 **p** 85. C Portadown St Mark *Arm* 85-88; I Errigle Keerogue w Ballygawley and Killeshil 88-89; CF 89-94; I Belfast St Donard *D & D* 04-08; I Aghalee from 08. *The Rectory, 39 Soldierstown Road, Aghalee, Craigavon BT67 0ES* Tel (028) 9265 0407 Mobile 07846-610977 E-mail dunroamin.mccartney@btopenworld.com

McCARTY, Colin Terence. b 46. Loughb Univ BTech68 PhD71 Lon Univ PGCE73 FRSA89. EAMTC 91. **d** 94 **p** 95. NSM Exning St Martin w Landwade *St E* from 94; Bp's Officer for Self-Supporting Min from 09. *1 Seymour Close, Newmarket CB8 8EL* Tel (01638) 669400 *or* (01223) 552716 Mobile 07970-563166 Fax (01223) 553537 E-mail mccarty.c@ucles.org.uk *or* test_and_eval@btinternet.com

MacCARTY, Paul Andrew. b 34. Sarum & Wells Th Coll 73. **d** 75 **p** 76. Ind Chapl *Win* 75-80; C Bournemouth St Andr 75-84; Hon C Christchurch 80-91; C 91-99; rtd 99; Perm to Offic *Win* from 01. *3 Douglas Avenue, Christchurch BH23 1JT* Tel (01202) 483807 E-mail paulmaccarty@aol.com

McCASKILL, James Calvin. b 73. Wheaton Coll Illinois BA95 Leeds Univ MA02. Coll of Resurr Mirfield 00. **d** 02 **p** 03. C Mt Lebanon St Paul USA 02-04; P-in-c Lundwood *Wakef* 04-09; R Bailey's Crossroads USA from 09. *The Rectory, 5850 Glen Forest Drive, Falls Church VA 22041-2527, USA* Tel (001) (828) 335 1382 E-mail james@mccaskill.info

McCATHIE, Neil. b 62. N Staffs Poly BA84 De Montfort Univ MA00 Huddersfield Univ PGCE93 MAAT96. St Jo Coll Nottm 03. **d** 05 **p** 06. C Shipley St Pet *Bradf* 05-09; TV Parr *Liv* from 09. *St Peter's Vicarage, Broad Oak Road, St Helens WA9 2DZ*

McCAULAY, Stephen Thomas John. b 61. Coll of Resurr Mirfield BA98. **d** 98 **p** 99. C Chaddesden St Phil *Derby* 98-02; V Mackworth St Fran 02-04; CF from 04. *c/o MOD Chaplains (Army)* Tel (01264) 381140 Fax 381824 E-mail mccaulay@ntlworld.com

McCAULEY, The Ven Craig William Leslie. b 72. Glam Univ BA95 TCD BTh99 CITC 96. **d** 99 **p** 00. C Knaresbrit *D & D* 99-02; C Kill *D & G* 02-04; I Lurgan w Billis, Killinkere and Munterconnaught *K, E & A* from 04; Adn Kilmore from 10. *The Rectory, Virginia, Co. Cavan, Republic of Ireland* Tel (00353) (49) 854 8465 E-mail virginia@kilmore.anglican.org

McCAUSLAND, Norman. b 58. TCD BTh89. CITC 89. **d** 89 **p** 90. C Portadown St Columba *Arm* 89-91; P-in-c Clonmel Union *C, C & R* 91-94; Miss to Seamen 91-94; CMS 94-95; Bp's V and Lib Ossory Cathl 96; Chapl and Tutor CITC 96-00; PV Ch Ch Cathl Dublin 96-00; CMS 00-01; Lic to Offic *D & G* from 01. *102 Killiney Hill Road, Killiney, Co Dublin, Republic of Ireland* Tel (00353) (1) 275 1661 E-mail mccausln@tcd.ie

M'CAW, Stephen Aragorn. b 61. Magd Coll Cam BA83 Lon Univ MB, BS86 FRCS90 MRCGP92. Cranmer Hall Dur 97. **d** 99 **p** 00. C Thetford *Nor* 99-02; R Steeple Aston w N Aston and Tackley *Ox* 02-10; AD Woodstock 06-09; TR Keynsham *B & W* from 10. *68 Park Road, Keynsham, Bristol BS31 1DE* Tel 0117-986 4437 E-mail samcaw@talk21.com

McCLAY, Canon David Alexander. b 59. TCD MA87. **d** 87 **p** 88. C Magheralin w Dollingstown *D & D* 87-90; I Kilkeel 90-01; I Willowfield from 01; P-in-c Mt Merrion from 07; Can Belf Cathl from 05. *Willowfield Rectory, 149 My Lady's Road, Belfast BT6 8FE* Tel and fax (028) 9046 0105 *or* 9045 7654 E-mail mcclayd@googlemail.com

McCLEAN, Derek Alistair. b 69. Poly of Wales BA92 QUB PGCE94. Ridley Hall Cam 08. **d** 10 **p** 11. C Drayton *Nor* from 10. *6 Cricket Close, Drayton, Norwich NR8 6YA* Tel 07889-28491 (mobile) E-mail revdmac@googlemail.com

McCLEAN, Lydia Margaret Sheelagh. *See* COOK, Mrs Lydia Margaret Sheelagh

McCLEAN, Robert Mervyn. b 38. Greenwich Univ BTh91. Edgehill Th Coll Belf 57. **d** 85 **p** 88. NSM Seapatrick *D & D* 85-99. *2 Kiloanin Crescent, Banbridge BT32 4NU* Tel (028) 4062 7419 E-mail r.m.mcclean@btinternet.com

McCLELLAN, Andrew David. b 71. St Jo Coll Cam BA93 MA96. Oak Hill Th Coll BA05. **d** 05. C Sevenoaks St Nic *Roch* 05-09; P-in-c Bromley St Jo from 09; Chapl St Olave's Gr Sch Orpington from 09. *St John's Vicarage, 9 Orchard Road, Bromley BR1 2PR* Tel (020) 8460 1844 Mobile 07931-731062 E-mail aj_mcc@btinternet.com

McCLENAGHAN, John Mark. b 61. TCD BTh05. CITC 02. **d** 05 **p** 06. C Portadown St Columba *Arm* 05-08; I Keady w Armaghbreague and Derrynoose from 08; Hon V Choral Arm Cathl from 07. *The Rectory, 31 Crossmore Road, Armagh BT60 3JY* Tel (028) 3753 1230 E-mail jm.mcclenaghan@btinternet.com *or* keady@armagh.anglican.org

MACCLESFIELD, Archdeacon of. *See* BISHOP, The Ven Ian Gregory

McCLINTOCK, Darren John. b 77. Hull Univ BA98 Open Univ MA(TS)00. St Jo Coll Nottm 98. **d** 01 **p** 02. C Drypool *York* 01-04; C Bilton *Ripon* 04-06; TV from 06; Dioc Ecum Adv 08-09. *8 Pecketts Way, Harrogate HG1 3EW* Tel (01423) 560863 E-mail darren@djmcclintock.freeserve.co.uk

McCLOSKEY, Robert Johnson. b 42. Stetson Univ (USA) AB63. Gen Th Sem NY STB67. **d** 67 **p** 68. C Gt Medford USA 67-69; R Somerville W St Jas and Chapl Tufts Univ 69-72; Dioc Adv for Liturgy and Music Massachusetts 71-76; R Westford St Mark 72-76; R Blowing Rock St Mary 76-82; Liturg and Musical Adv and Ecum Officer Dio W N Carolina 76-81; Dio SE Florida 90-93; Ecum Officer Dio Long Is 81-89; R Bay Shore St Pet and

St Pet Sch 82-89; R Miami St Steph and St Steph Sch 89-01; Staff Officer Lambeth Conf 98; rtd 01. *Address temp unknown*

McCLURE, Mrs Catherine Abigail. b 63. Birm Univ BA84 SS Hild & Bede Coll Dur PGCE85. Ripon Coll Cuddesdon BTh07. **d** 03 **p** 04. C Cirencester *Glouc* 03-07; Chapl Glos Hosps NHS Foundn Trust from 07. *Cheltenham General Hospital, Sandford Road, Cheltenham GL53 7AN* Tel 08454-224286 ext 4286 *or* (01242) 681139 Fax 08454-221214 Mobile 07824-476505 E-mail katie.mcclure@glos.nhs.uk

McCLURE, John. d 07 **p** 08. NSM Skerry w Rathcavan and Newtowncrommelin *Conn* 07-09; C Belfast St Mich from 09; Bp's Dom Chapl from 11. *69 Parkgate Road, Kells, Ballymena BT42 3PF* Tel (028) 2589 2324 *or* 9024 1640 E-mail mcclurejohn@hotmail.com *or* belfast@icm-online.ie

McCLURE, Robert (Roy). b 30. Open Univ BA92. TCD Div Sch 68. **d** 70 **p** 71. C Monaghan *Clogh* 70-72; C Belfast St Matt *Conn* 72-76; Chapl HM Pris Liv 76-77; Chapl HM Pris Preston 77-82; V Foulridge *Blackb* 82-88; rtd 88; Perm to Offic *Liv* from 89. *4 Mill Lane Crescent, Southport PR9 7PF* Tel (01704) 227476

McCLURE, The Ven Timothy Elston. b 46. St Jo Coll Dur BA68. Ridley Hall Cam 68. **d** 70 **p** 71. C Kirkheaton *Wakef* 70-73; C Chorlton upon Medlock *Man* 74-79; Chapl Man Poly 74-82; TR Man Whitworth 79-82; Gen Sec SCM 82-92; Bp's Soc and Ind Adv and Dir Chs' Coun for Ind and Soc Resp LEP *Bris* 92-99; Hon Can Bris Cathl from 92; Hon C Cotham St Sav w St Mary 96; Chapl Lord Mayor's Chpl 96-99; Adn Bris from 99. *10 Great Brockeridge, Bristol BS9 3TY* Tel 0117-962 1433 Fax 962 9438 E-mail tim.mcclure@bristoldiocese.org

McCLUSKEY, Coralie Christine. b 52. Univ of Wales (Cardiff) BEd74. SAOMC 98. **d** 01 **p** 02. C Welwyn w Ayot St Peter *St Alb* 01-04; P-in-c Datchworth 04-05; TV Welwyn 05-11; P-in-c Eaton Bray w Edlesborough from 11; Agric Chapl for Herts from 09. *The Vicarage, High Street, Eaton Bray, Dunstable LU6 2DN* Tel (01525) 220261 E-mail coralie mccluskey@yahoo.co.uk

McCLUSKEY, James Terence. b 65. Coll of Resurr Mirfield 01. **d** 03 **p** 04. C Swanley St Mary *Roch* 03-06; V Prittlewell St Luke *Chelmsf* from 06. *The Vicarage, St Luke's Road, Southend-on-Sea SS2 4AB* Tel and fax (01702) 467620 Mobile 07761-632734 E-mail mccluskey@katy-james.freeserve.co.uk

McCLUSKEY, Miss Lesley. b 45. Hull Univ LLB72 Bolton Coll of Educn PGCE77. NOC 89. **d** 92 **p** 94. C Bootle St Mary w St Paul *Liv* 92-94; C Wigan St Anne 94-98; P-in-c Newton in Makerfield Em 98-07; TV Newton 08; Chapl St Helens and Knowsley Hosps NHS Trust 98-08; rtd 09. *9 Mulberry Court, Stockton Heath, Warrington WA4 2DB* Tel (01925) 602286 E-mail lesley-mccluskey@yahoo.co.uk

McCOACH, Jennifer Sara. *See* CROFT, Jennifer Sara

McCOLLUM, Alastair Colston. b 69. Whitelands Coll Lon BA91. Westcott Ho Cam 95. **d** 96 **p** 97. C Hampton All SS *Lon* 96-98; C S Kensington St Aug 98-00; Chapl Imp Coll 98-00; TV Papworth *Ely* 00-08; V Kilmington, Stockland, Dalwood, Yarcombe etc *Ex* from 08. *The Vicarage, Whitford Road, Kilmington, Axminster EX13 7RF* Tel (01297) 32160 E-mail alastair.mccollum@btinternet.com

McCOLLUM, Charles James. b 41. TCD BTh89. CITC 85. **d** 89 **p** 90. C Larne and Inver *Conn* 89-91; Bp's C Belfast Whiterock 91-96; I Belfast St Pet and St Jas 96-08; I Dunleckney w Nurney, Lorum and Kiltennel *C & O* from 08. *St Mary's Rectory, Dunleckney, Muine Bheag, Co Carlow, Republic of Ireland* Tel and fax (00353) (59) 972 0934 Mobile 87-288 5019 E-mail charlesjmccollum@gmail.com

McCOMB, Samuel. b 33. CITC 70. **d** 71 **p** 72. C Belfast St Mich *Conn* 71-74; C Lisburn Ch Ch *Conn* 75-79; I Ballinderry *Arm* 79-83; I Lisburn Ch Ch *Conn* 83-04; Can Conn Cathl 98-04; Treas 01-04; rtd 04. *209 Hillsborough Old Road, Lisburn BT27 5QE* Tel (028) 9260 5812

McCONACHIE, Robert Noel. b 40. Goldsmiths' Coll Lon BA86. Oak Hill Th Coll 86. **d** 88 **p** 89. C Larkfield *Roch* 88-93; R Mereworth w W Peckham 93-10; rtd 11. *25 Sturmer Court, Kings Hill, West Malling ME19 4ST* Tel (01732) 874195 E-mail r.mcconachie105@btinternet.com

McCONKEY, Brian Robert. b 53. Kansas Wesleyan Univ (USA) BA75 Yale Univ MusM77. Yale Div Sch MDiv79. **d** 83 **p** 84. Dn Ch Cathl Salina USA 83-84; C S Lake Anchorage 84-85; P-in-c Louisville St Luke 85-86; R Warrensburgh H Cross 86-94; Can Capitular All SS Cath Albany 88-93; R Belvedere St Eliz Zimbabwe 94-03; P-in-c Norton St Fran and St Jas 94-99; Lect Bp Gaul Coll 94-01; TR Swindon New Town *Bris* from 03. *18 Park Lane, Swindon SN1 5EL* Tel (01793) 619403 E-mail frdbmcconkey@bigpond.com *or* swindonnewtown@btinternet.com

McCONKEY, David Benton. b 53. Kansas Wesleyan Univ (USA) BA75 Yale Univ MusM77. Yale Div Sch MDiv79. **d** 83 **p** 84. Dn Ch Cathl Salina USA 83-84; C S Lake Anchorage 84-85; P-in-c Louisville St Luke 85-86; R Warrensburgh H Cross 86-94; Can Capitular All SS Cath Albany 88-93; R Belvedere St Eliz Zimbabwe 94-03; P-in-c Norton St Fran and St Jas 94-99; Lect Bp Gaul Coll 94-01; TR Swindon New Town *Bris* from 03. *18 Park Lane, Swindon SN1 5EL* Tel (01793) 619403 E-mail frdbmcconkey@bigpond.com *or* swindonnewtown@btinternet.com

McCONNAUGHIE, Adrian William. b 66. Jes Coll Ox BA89 MA06 Lon Univ PhD93 Cam Univ PGCE96. Trin Coll Bris

BA08. **d** 08 **p** 09. C Bath Abbey w St Jas *B & W* from 08. *20A Bellotts Road, Bath BA2 3RT* Tel (01225) 314029 E-mail adrian@bathabbey.org

McCONNELL, Canon Brian Roy. b 46. St Paul's Coll Grahamstown. **d** 71 **p** 72. C Plumstead S Africa 71-74; C St Geo Cathl Cape Town 74-77; C Prestwich St Marg *Man* 77-79; R Sea Point S Africa 79-85; V Liscard St Mary w St Columba *Ches* 85-90; V Altrincham St Geo 90-06; RD Bowdon 95-03; Hon Can Ches Cathl 97-06; Can Res Carl Cathl from 06. *3 The Abbey, Carlisle CA3 8TZ* Tel (01228) 521834

McCONNELL, Peter Stuart. b 54. Linc Th Coll 89. **d** 91 **p** 92. C N Shields *Newc* 91-95; V Balkwell 95-03; C Killingworth 03-07; P-in-c Longhorsley and Hebron 08-10; P-in-c Longhorsley from 11; Sen Chapl Northumbria Police from 98. *The Vicarage, Longhorsley, Morpeth NE65 8UU* Tel (01670) 788218 E-mail mcconnell@balkwell.freeserve.co.uk

McCONNELL, Robert Mark. b 60. Oak Hill Th Coll BA88. **d** 89 **p** 90. C Bedford Ch Ch *St Alb* 89-92; C Bangor St Comgall *D & D* 92-94; I Killyleagh 94-99; I Ballynure and Ballyeaston *Conn* from 99. *The Rectory, 11 Church Road, Ballyclare BT39 9UF* Tel (028) 9332 2350 E-mail s+j-cc@yahoo.co.uk

McCORMACK, Alan William. b 68. Jes Coll Ox BA90 MA94 DPhil94. CITC 93. **d** 96 **p** 97. C Knock *D & D* 96-98; Dean of Res and Chapl TCD 98-07; P-in-c St Botolph without Bishopgate *Lon* from 07; P-in-c St Vedast w St Mich-le-Querne etc from 07. *St Vedast's Rectory, 4 Foster Lane, London EC2V 6HH* Tel (020) 7588 3388 E-mail rector@botolph.org.uk

McCORMACK, Colin. b 47. QUB Sch TD DipEd71. St Jo Coll Nottm BA75. **d** 78 **p** 79. C Carl St Jo 78-81; C Ballynafeigh St Jude *D & D* 81-84; V Harraby *Carl* 84-89; NSM Carl H Trin and St Barn 95-99; Asst Chapl Costa Blanca *Eur* 00-04; Chapl Torrevieja 04-08. *3C The Pines, Hillsborough BT26 6NT* Tel (028) 9268 9262 E-mail colinmccormack6@btinternet.com

McCORMACK, Canon David Eugene. b 34. Wells Th Coll 66. **d** 68 **p** 69. C Lillington *Cov* 68-71; C The Lickey *Birm* 71-75; V Highters Heath 75-82; V Four Oaks 82-00; Hon Can Birm Cathl 95-00; rtd 00; Perm to Offic *Linc* and *Pet* from 00; *Birm* from 05. *27 Rockingham Close, Market Deeping, Peterborough PE6 8BY* Tel (01778) 347569

McCORMACK, George Brash. b 32. ACIS65 FCIS75. S'wark Ord Course 82. **d** 85 **p** 86. Hon C Crofton St Paul *Roch* 85-89; C Crayford 89-91; R Fawkham and Hartley 91-97; rtd 97; Perm to Offic *Roch* from 98. *11 Turnpike Drive, Pratts Bottom, Orpington BR6 7SJ*

McCORMACK, Ian Douglas. b 80. St Anne's Coll Ox BA02 MA06 MSt03 Leeds Univ MA10. Coll of Resurr Mirfield 07. **d** 10 **p** 11. C Horbury w Horbury Bridge *Wakef* from 10. *1C Westfield Drive, Ossett WF5 8HJ* Tel (01924) 609701 E-mail fatherianmccormack@hotmail.co.uk

McCORMACK, John Heddon. b 58. Chich Th Coll 85. **d** 88 **p** 89. C Cleobury Mortimer w Hopton Wafers *Heref* 88-90; C Lymington *Win* 90-92; C Portsea N End St Mark *Portsm* 92-95; Chapl St Barn Hospice Worthing 95-06. *10 Columbia Walk, Worthing BN13 2ST* Tel (01903) 263700 Mobile 07974-603518 E-mail humanrites1@sky.com

McCORMACK, Canon Kevan Sean. b 50. Chich Th Coll 77. **d** 80 **p** 81. C Ross *Heref* 80-81; C Ross w Brampton Abbotts, Bridstow and Peterstow 81-83; C Leominster 83; TV 84-87; Chapl R Hosp Sch Holbrook 87-00; R Woodbridge St Mary *St E* from 00; Hon Can St E Cathl from 09. *St Mary's Rectory, Church Street, Woodbridge IP12 1DS* Tel and fax (01394) 610424 E-mail rector@stmaryswoodbridge.org

McCORMACK, Canon Lesley Sharman. b 50. EAMTC. **d** 93 **p** 94. Hon Par Dn Chevington w Hargrave and Whepstead w Brockley *St E* 88-95; Asst Chapl W Suffolk Hosp Bury St Edm 88-95; Chapl Kettering Gen Hosp NHS Trust 95-09; Chapl Cransley Hospice from 09; NSM Kettering SS Pet and Paul from 09; Bp's Hosp Chapl Adv from 00; Can Pet Cathl from 03. *Barnbrook, Water Lane, Chelveston, Wellingborough NN9 6AP* Tel (01933) 626636 E-mail lesleybarnbrook@hotmail.co.uk

MacCORMACK, Michael Ian. b 54. Kent Univ BA77 Ch Ch Coll Cant MA87 Bris Univ PGCE78. STETS 02. **d** 05 **p** 06. NSM Martock w Ash *B & W* from 05. *12A Middle Street, Montacute TA15 6UZ* Tel (01935) 827823 Mobile 07717-878736 E-mail michael.maccormack@nationaltrust.org.uk

McCORMACK, Mrs Susan. b 60. NEOC 00. **d** 03 **p** 04. C Newburn *Newc* 03-07; P-in-c Fawdon from 07. *St Mary's Vicarage, 7 Fawdon Lane, Newcastle upon Tyne NE3 2RR* Tel 0191-285 5403 E-mail suemc@mccormacks4.fsnet.co.uk

McCORMICK, Mrs Anne Irene. b 67. Sheff Univ BA89 Hull Univ PGCE90. Ripon Coll Cuddesdon 90. **d** 92 **p** 94. C Spalding *Linc* 92-96; C Gt Grimsby St Mary and St Jas 96-01; C Gt and Lt Coates w Bradley from 98; Chapl Rotherham, Doncaster and S Humber NHS Trust from 07. *The Glebe House, 11 Church Lane, Limber, Grimsby DN37 8JN* Tel (01469) 561082 E-mail anneoflimber@btinternet.com

McCORMICK, David Mark. b 68. Univ of Wales (Ban) BD89. Ripon Coll Cuddesdon 90. **d** 92 **p** 93. C Holbeach *Linc* 92-96;

TV Gt Grimsby St Mary and St Jas 96-01; Prin Linc Min Tr Course 01-09; CME Officer from 09. *Diocesan Office, Church House, The Old Palace, Minster Yard, Lincoln LN2 1PU* Tel (01522) 504030 E-mail david.mccormick@lincoln.anglican.org
McCOSH, Canon Duncan Ian. b 50. Edin Dioc NSM Course 82. **d** 91 **p** 92. C Dalkeith *Edin* 91-96; C Lasswade 91-96; P-in-c Falkirk 96-97; R 97-03; R Galashiels from 03; Hon Can Cape Coast from 06. *The Rectory, 6 Parsonage Road, Galashiels TD1 3HS* Tel (01896) 753118 E-mail stpeters.gala@btopenworld.com
McCOUBREY, William Arthur. b 36. CEng MIMechE. Sarum & Wells Th Coll 86. **d** 89 **p** 90. C Bedhampton *Portsm* 89-92; V Stokenham w Sherford *Ex* 92-96; R Stokenham w Sherford and Beesands, and Slapton 96-02; rtd 02; Perm to Offic *Chich* and *Portsm* from 02. *19 Warblington Road, Emsworth PO10 7HE* Tel (01243) 374011
McCOULOUGH, David. b 61. Man Univ BA84 St Jo Coll Dur BA88. Cranmer Hall Dur 86. **d** 89 **p** 90. C Man Apostles w Miles Platting 89-92; C Elton All SS 92-94; V Halliwell St Marg 94-98; Min Can Ripon Cathl 98-01; Chapl Univ Coll of Ripon and York St Jo 98-01; Ind Chapl *S'well* 01-07; Chapl Boots PLC 01-07; C Nottingham St Pet and St Jas 01-02; C Nottingham St Pet and All SS 02-07; Assoc Dir Partnerships from 07. *15 Adams Row, Southwell NG25 0FF* Tel (01636) 812029
McCOULOUGH, Thomas Alexander. b 32. AKC59. **d** 60 **p** 61. C Norton St Mich *Dur* 60-63; USPG India 63-67; P-in-c Derby St Jas 67-72; Ind Chapl *York* 72-82; P-in-c Sutton on the Forest 82-96; Dioc Sec for Local Min 83-89; Lay Tr Officer 89-96; rtd 96; Perm to Offic *Newc* from 96. *1 Horsley Gardens, Holywell, Whitley Bay NE25 0TU* Tel 0191-298 0332
McCRACKEN, William. d 08 **p** 09. C Camlough w Mullaglass *Arm* from 08. *1 Aughlish Road, Tandragee, Craigavon BT62 2EE* Tel (028) 3884 0655
McCREA, Basil Wolfe. b 21. QUB BA49. Wycliffe Hall Ox 51. **d** 53 **p** 54. C Kingston upon Hull H Trin *York* 53-56; C Dundela St Mark *D & D* 56-59; C Cork H Trin w St Paul, St Pet and St Mary *C, C & R* 59-61; I Tullyaughnish *D & R* 61-65; I Rathkeale *L & K* 65-68; I Cork H Trin *C, C & R* 68-72; I Carrigaline Union 72-90; rtd 90. *30 Somerville, Carrigaline, Co Cork, Republic of Ireland* Tel (00353) (21) 437 1538
McCREA, Christina Elizabeth. b 53. **d** 08 **p** 09. NSM Glanogwen and Llanllechid w St Ann and Pentir *Ban* from 08. *2 Bron-y-Waun, Rhiwlas, Bangor LL57 4EX* Tel (01248) 372249 E-mail christinaemcc@aol.com
McCREA, Francis. b 53. BTh. **d** 91 **p** 92. C Dundonald *D & D* 91-94; I Belfast St Brendan from 94. *St Brendan's Rectory, 36 Circular Road, Belfast BT4 2GA* Tel (028) 9076 3458
McCREADIE, Mrs Lesley Anne. b 51. Bp Otter Coll CertEd73 Open Univ BA93. STETS BA10. **d** 10 **p** 11. NSM Sherborne w Castleton, Lillington and Longburton *Sarum* from 10. *5 Kings Close, Longburton, Sherborne DT9 5PW* Tel (01963) 210548 E-mail revdlesley@aol.com
McCREADY, Kennedy Lemar. b 26. Birkbeck Coll Lon BSc59 Sussex Univ MA94 Garnett Coll Lon TCert54 CEng56 FIEE56. Chich Th Coll 91. **d** 92 **p** 99. NSM Mayfield *Chich* 92-97; Perm to Offic 97-00; NSM New Groombridge 99-01; Perm to Offic from 01. *Quarry House, Groombridge Road, Groombridge, Tunbridge Wells TN3 9PS* Tel (01892) 864297
McCRORY, Canon Peter. b 34. Chich Th Coll 63. **d** 67 **p** 68. C St Marychurch *Ex* 67-72; R Kenn w Mamhead 72-76; R Kenn 76-78; Bp's Dom Chapl *S'wark* 78-81; V Kew 81-90; RD Richmond and Barnes 84-89; Hon Can S'wark Cathl 90-00; rtd 00; Perm to Offic *Nor* from 00. *Dane House, The Street, Kettlestone, Fakenham NR21 0AU* Tel (01328) 878455
McCROSKERY, Andrew. b 74. Glas Univ BD97 TCD MPhil99. CITC 98. **d** 99 **p** 00. C Newtownards *D & D* 99-02; Dean's V Cork Cathl 02-04; I Youghal Union 04-08; Chapl Univ Coll Cork 04-08; Bp's Dom Chapl 03-08; Min Can Cork Cathl 04-08; I Dublin St Bart w Leeson Park *D & G* from 08. *The Rectory, 12 Merlyn Road, Ballsbridge, Dublin 4, Republic of Ireland* Tel (00353) (1) 269 4813 E-mail wolfram100@hotmail.com
McCRUM, Michael Scott. b 35. Glas Univ BSc57 UNISA BTh85. **d** 85 **p** 85. S Africa 85-89; Asst F Lynnwood 86-87; P-in-c Mameloli 87; P-in-c Villieria 87-88; Kerygma Internat Chr Min 89-92; Perm to Offic *Nor* 93-94; NSM Chesham Bois *Ox* 94-95; Perm to Offic *St Alb* 95-98 and from 05; Hon C Chorleywood St Andr 98-05. *Cranbrook, 31 South Road, Chorleywood, Rickmansworth WD3 5AS* Tel and fax (01923) 336897 Mobile 07792-621587 E-mail michael.s.mccrum@gmail.com
McCULLAGH, Elspeth Jane Alexandra. *See* SAVILLE, Mrs Elspeth Jane Alexandra
McCULLAGH, Canon John Eric. b 46. TCD BA68 BTh88 QUB DipEd70. **d** 88 **p** 89. C Stillorgan w Blackrock *D & G* 88-91; Chapl and Hd of RE Newpark Sch Dub 90-99; I Clondalkin w Rathcoole 91-99; Sec Gen Syn Bd of Educn 99-08; I Rathdrum w Glenealy, Derralossary and Laragh *D & G* from 08; Can Ch Ch Cathl Dublin from 99; Treas from 09. *The Rectory,*

Rathdrum, Co Wicklow, Republic of Ireland Tel (00353) (404) 43814 E-mail rathdrum@glendalough.anglican.org
McCULLAGH, Canon Mervyn Alexander. b 44. TCD BA BAI68. CITC 79. **d** 79 **p** 80. C Larne and Inver *Conn* 79-83; C Ballymacash 83-85; C Dublin St Ann w St Mark and St Steph *D & G* 85-88; I Baltinglass w Ballynure etc *C & O* from 88; Warden of Readers 90-05; Can Ossory and Leighlin Cathls 92-96; Treas from 96; P-in-c Kiltegan w Hacketstown, Clonmore and Moyne 00-03. *The Rectory, Baltinglass, Co Wicklow, Republic of Ireland* Tel (00353) (59) 648 1321
McCULLOCH, Alistair John. b 59. Univ of Wales (Lamp) BA81 Leeds Univ BA86 Lon Univ MA07. Coll of Resurr Mirfield 84. **d** 87 **p** 88. C Portsm Cathl 87-90; C Portsea St Mary 90-94; V Reading St Matt *Ox* 94-95; Perm to Offic *S'wark* 99; Chapl King's Coll Hosp NHS Trust 00-04; Chapl R Marsden NHS Foundn Trust from 04. *The Royal Marsden Hospital, Fulham Road, London SW3 6JJ* Tel (020) 7808 2818 E-mail alistair.mcculloch@rmh.nhs.uk
McCULLOCH, Mrs Celia Hume. b 53. Leeds Univ BA08. NOC 05. **d** 08 **p** 09. C Cheetham *Man* 08-10; rtd 10; Perm to Offic *Man* from 11. *Bishopscourt, Bury New Road, Salford, Manchester M7 4LE* Tel 07943-366331 (mobile) E-mail celiamcculloch@yahoo.co.uk
MacCULLOCH, Prof Diarmaid Ninian John. b 51. Chu Coll Cam BA72 MA76 PhD77 FSA78 FRHistS81. Ripon Coll Cuddesdon 86. **d** 87. NSM Clifton All SS w St Jo *Bris* 87-88. *St Cross College, St Giles, Oxford OX1 3LZ* Tel (01865) 270794 Fax 270795 E-mail diarmaid.macculloch@theology.ox.ac.uk
✠**McCULLOCH, The Rt Revd Nigel Simeon.** b 42. Selw Coll Cam BA64 MA69. Cuddesdon Coll 64. **d** 66 **p** 67 **c** 86. C Ellesmere Port Chos 66-70; Dir Th Studies Ch Coll Cam 70-75; Chapl 70-73; Dioc Missr *Nor* 73-78; P-in-c Salisbury St Thos and St Edm *Sarum* 78-81; R 81-86; Adn Sarum 79-86; Can and Preb Sarum Cathl 79-86; Suff Bp Taunton *B & W* 86-92; Preb Wells Cathl 86-92; Bp Wakef 92-02; Bp Man from 02; High Almoner from 97. *Bishopscourt, Bury New Road, Salford, Manchester M7 4LE* Tel 0161-792 2096 Fax 792 6826 E-mail bishop@bishopscourt.manchester.anglican.org
McCULLOCK, Mrs Patricia Ann. b 46. CertEd72. EMMTC 87. **d** 90 **p** 94. C Bottesford w Ashby *Linc* 90-95; P-in-c Wragby 95-98; Chapl N Lincs Coll of FE 95-98; Ind Chapl 98-01; rtd 01; Perm to Offic *Linc* 01-11. *1 Jackson Street, North Shields NE30 2JA* E-mail patricia.mcculock@virgin.net
McCULLOUGH, Mrs Aphrodite Maria. b 47. Derby Univ MSc95. EMMTC 97. **d** 00 **p** 01. NSM Kirby Muxloe *Leic* 00-04; TV 04-08; rtd 08. *33 Alton Road, Leicester LE2 8QB* Tel 0116-283 7887 E-mail aphro.mccullough@btinternet.com
McCULLOUGH, Canon Roy. b 46. Brasted Th Coll 69 Linc Th Coll 70. **d** 73 **p** 74. Chapl Highfield Priory Sch Lancs 73-77; C Ashton-on-Ribble St Andr *Blackb* 73-77; V Rishton 77-86; V Burnley St Matt w H Trin 86-97; RD Burnley 91-97; Chapl Victoria Hosp Burnley 86-88; V Walton-le-Dale St Leon w Samlesbury St Leon 97-11; Hon Can Blackb Cathl 97-11; rtd 11; Perm to Offic *Blackb* from 11. *West Coe, Kirkby Thore, Penrith CA10 1XE* Tel (01768) 361656
McCURDY, The Ven Hugh Kyle. b 58. Portsm Poly BA Univ of Wales (Cardiff) PGCE. Trin Coll Bris. **d** 85 **p** 86. C Egham *Guildf* 85-88; C Woking St Jo 88-91; V Histon *Ely* 91-05; P-in-c Impington 98-05; RD N Stowe 94-05; Hon Can Ely Cathl 04-05; Adn Huntingdon and Wisbech from 05. *Whitgift House, The College, Ely CB7 4DL* Tel (01353) 658404 *or* 652709 Fax 652745 E-mail archdeacon.handw@ely.anglican.org
McDERMID, The Ven Norman George Lloyd Roberts. b 27. St Edm Hall Ox BA49 MA52. Wells Th Coll 49. **d** 51 **p** 52. C Leeds St Pet *Ripon* 51-56; V Bramley 56-64; Dioc Stewardship Adv 64-76; R Kirkby Overblow 64-80; Hon Can Ripon Cathl 72-93; Dioc Stewardship Adv *Wakef* 73-76; Dioc Stewardship Adv *Bradf* 73-76; RD Harrogate *Ripon* 77-83; V Knaresborough 80-83; Adn Richmond 83-93; rtd 93; Perm to Offic *Ripon* from 93. *Greystones, 10 North End, Bedale DL8 1AB* Tel (01677) 422210 Mobile 07704-977035 E-mail norman@gmcdermid.fsbusiness.co.uk
McDERMOTT, Christopher Francis Patrick. b 54. Southeastern Coll USA BA84 Wheaton Coll Illinois MA87. EAMTC. **d** 95 **p** 96. C Gt Ilford St Clem and St Marg *Chelmsf* 95-99. *17 Benton Road, Ilford IG1 4AT*
McDERMOTT, Fraser Graeme. b 65. NTMTC 97. **d** 98 **p** 00. NSM Oak Tree Angl Fellowship *Lon* 98-02; V N Wembley St Cuth from 02. *St Cuthbert's Vicarage, 214 Carlton Avenue West, Wembley HA0 3QY* Tel (020) 8904 7657 *or* 8904 8599 E-mail fraser@stcuths.org
MACDONALD, Preb Alan Hendry. b 49. St Steph Ho Ox 86. **d** 88 **p** 89. C Heavitree w Ex St Paul 88-91; C Withycombe Raleigh 91-92; TV 92-95; R Silverton, Butterleigh, Bickleigh and Cadeleigh from 95; RD Tiverton 00-02; Preb Ex Cathl from 10. *The Rectory, 21A King Street, Silverton, Exeter EX5 4JG* Tel (01392) 860350 E-mail almac1@talktalk.net
MacDONALD, Alastair Douglas. b 48. Cranmer Hall Dur 71. **d** 74 **p** 75. C Mottingham St Andr w St Alban *S'wark* 74-78; C

Woolwich St Mary w St Mich 78-81; V S Wimbledon St Andr 81-89; V Brighton St Matthias *Chich* 89-94; Chapl Southn Community Services NHS Trust 94-01; Mental Health Chapl Hants Partnerships NHS Trust 01-04. *Episkopi, Fontwell Avenue, Eastergate, Chichester PO20 3RU* Tel (01243) 542771

MacDONALD, Alastair Robert. b 72. Edin Univ MA94 MTh03. TISEC. **d** 02 **p** 03. C Edin St Thos 02-06; Asst Chapl Amsterdam w Den Helder and Heiloo *Eur* from 06. *Christ Church, Groenburgwal 42, 1011 HW Amsterdam, The Netherlands* Tel (0031) (20) 624 8877 E-mail alastair@christchurch.nl

MACDONALD, Cameron. b 51. Open Univ BA89. Wilson Carlile Coll 76 NEOC 89. **d** 90 **p** 91. CA from 76; C Nairn *Mor* 90-92; P-in-c 92-95; CF 95-05; Chapl HM YOI Thorn Cross 05-07; Port Chapl Aqaba Jordan from 07. *Church of St Peter and St Paul, PO Box 568, Aqaba 77110, Jordan* Tel (00962) (3) 201 8630 E-mail mtsaqaba@go.com.jo

McDONALD, Carollyn Elisabeth. b 54. Edin Univ BSc76. EMMTC 07. **d** 09 **p** 10. C Sawley *Derby* from 09. *10 Brecon Close, Long Eaton, Nottingham NG10 4JW* Tel 0115-972 4762 E-mail sawleycurate@fsmail.net

MACDONALD, Christopher Kenneth. b 57. Ex Univ BA79 PGCE80. Trin Coll Bris 91. **d** 93 **p** 94. C Eastbourne All SS *Chich* 93-96; C Polegate 96-99; Chapl Eastbourne Coll from 99. *14A Grange Road, Eastbourne BN21 4HJ* Tel (01323) 452317 E-mail ckm@eastbourne-college.co.uk

MACDONALD, Colin. b 47. St Jo Coll Nottm 87. **d** 89 **p** 90. C Limber Magna w Brocklesby *Linc* 89-92; P-in-c Barrow and Goxhill 92-97; V 97-99; R Hemingby, V Fulletby and R Belchford *Linc* 99-02; TV Wilford Peninsula *St E* 02-09; rtd 09; P-in-c Siddal *Wakef* from 09. *The Vicarage, 15 Whitegate Road, Halifax HX3 9AD* Tel (01422) 364423 E-mail cmacdonald@aol.com

MACDONALD, Canon Donald Courtenay. b 45. Nottm Univ BTh74 St Martin's Coll Lanc CertEd75. Kelham Th Coll 70. **d** 75 **p** 76. C Clifton All SS w Tyndalls Park *Bris* 75-78; C Clifton All SS w St Jo 78-79; Chapl Derby Lonsdale Coll 79-84; V Derby St Andr w St Osmund 84-10; RD Derby S 89-99; Dioc Communications Officer 89-93; Hon Can Derby Cathl 95-10; rtd 10. *13 Langford Road, Mickleover, Derby DE3 0PD* E-mail donald.c.macdonald@btinternet.com

MACDONALD, Helen Maria. See BARTON, Helen Maria

McDONALD, Ian Henry. b 40. TD. St Aid Birkenhead 65. **d** 68 **p** 69. C Kingston upon Hull H Trin *York* 68-70; C Drumglass *Arm* 70-73; I Eglish w Killylea 73-80; I Maghera w Killelagh *D & R* 80-91; I Killowen 91-98; I Errigal w Garvagh 98-05; Can Derry Cathl 94-00; Preb 00-05; CF (TAVR) 91-05; rtd 05. *4 Ballylagan Lane, Aghadowey, Coleraine BT51 4DD* Tel (028) 7086 9150 Mobile 07740-708402 E-mail ihmcd@hotmail.co.uk

McDONALD, James Damian (Jack). b 66. Pemb Coll Cam BA87 MA91 K Coll Lon MA96 SS Hild & Bede Coll Dur PGCE88 Strasbourg Univ Dr Théol07. Qu Coll Birm 90. **d** 92 **p** 93. C Camberwell St Geo *S'wark* 92-95; Chapl G&C Coll Cam 95-99; Fell and Dean 99-06; Sen Proctor Cam Univ 02-03; Headmaster Sancton Wood Sch 06-09; Perm to Offic *Eur* from 09. *11 rue Ausone, 57000 Metz, France* Tel (0033) 6 84 87 69 76 E-mail pasteurjackmcdonald@yahoo.fr

McDONALD, Lawrence Ronald. b 32. St Alb Minl Tr Scheme 84. **d** 87 **p** 88. NSM Sharnbrook and Knotting w Souldrop *St Alb* 87-90; C Bromham w Oakley and Stagsden 90-93; P-in-c Renhold 93-98; rtd 99; P-in-c Stevington *St Alb* 99-02; Perm to Offic from 02. *16 Townsend Road, Sharnbrook, Bedford MK44 1HY* Tel (01234) 782849 E-mail fathermac@ukgateway.net

MACDONALD, Malcolm Crawford. b 75. St Andr Univ MA97 MLitt98. Wycliffe Hall Ox BTh05. **d** 05 **p** 06. C Kensington St Barn *Lon* 05-09; V Loughton St Mary *Chelmsf* from 09. *The Vicarage, 4 St Mary's Close, Loughton IG10 1HA* Tel (020) 8508 7892 Mobile 07821-011435 E-mail malcolmandcaroline@talktalk.net

MACDONALD, Martin Stanley Harrison. b 51. Dur Univ BSc72 ACA75 FCA82. SAOMC 98. **d** 01 **p** 02. NSM Tring *St Alb* 01-08; Perm to Offic *Wakef* from 09. *Broad Head End, Cragg Vale, Hebden Bridge HX7 5RT* Tel (01422) 881543 Mobile 07883-091787 E-mail mshmacdonald@gmail.com

MACDONALD, Canon Murray Somerled. b 23. Pemb Coll Cam BA46 MA49. Ely Th Coll 47. **d** 48 **p** 49. C Hendon St Mary *Lon* 48-51; C Hanover Square St Geo 51-53; P-in-c Upton and Copmanford *Ely* 53-54; R Sawtry 53-54; R Sawtry, Upton and Copmanford 54-57; V Upwood w Gt and Lt Raveley 57-62; R Wood Walton 57-62; V Fenstanton 62-70; V Hilton 62-70; RD Huntingdon 69-76; R Huntingdon All SS w St Jo 70-82; R Huntingdon St Mary w St Benedict 71-82; Hon Can Ely Cathl 72-82; Can Res 82-88; rtd 89; Perm to Offic *Linc* 89-01 and *Ely* 89-97. *4 Hacconby Lane, Morton, Bourne PE10 0NT* Tel (01778) 570711

McDONALD, Robert William. b 72. Otago Univ BA94 MA96 Cam Univ BA06 MPhil07 LTCL95. Ridley Hall Cam 04. **d** 10 **p** 11. C Shrewsbury St Geo w Greenfields *Lich* from 10. *5 Bayford Drive, Shrewsbury SY1 3XQ* Tel (01743) 350906

MACDONALD (formerly WIFFIN), Susan Elizabeth. b 51. Edin Th Coll 93. **d** 96 **p** 97. NSM Jedburgh *Edin* 96-98; C Galashiels 98-01; P-in-c Fochabers and Dioc Miss Co-ord *Mor* 01-05; Can St Andr Cathl Inverness 03-05; Miss and Min Officer *Ab* 05-07; R Edin Ch Ch from 07. *4 Morningside Road, Edinburgh EH10 4DD* Tel 0131-229 0090 Mobile 07753-684923 E-mail susan@6a.org.uk

MACDONALD, Warren. Monash Univ Aus BEng Leeds Univ MPhil Gothenburg Univ PhD00 CEng CPEng MIEAust. Trin Coll Bris 93. **d** 95 **p** 96. NSM Iford *Win* 95-98; Perm to Offic from 98. *5 St James's Square, Bournemouth BH5 2BX* Tel (01202) 422131 Fax 422101 Mobile 07774-497872 E-mail warren@warrenmacdonald.com

MACDONALD-MILNE, Canon Brian James. b 35. CCC Cam BA58 MA62 St Pet Coll Ox MA81. Cuddesdon Coll 58. **d** 60 **p** 61. C Fleetwood St Pet *Blackb* 60-63; Solomon Is 64-78; Vanuatu 78-80; Acting Chapl Trin Coll Ox 81; Acting Chapl St Pet Coll Ox 81-82; Relief Chapl HM Pris Grendon and Spring Hill 81-82; Research Fell Qu Coll Birm 82-83; Hon Asst P Bordesley SS Alb and Patr *Birm* 82-83; R Landbeach *Ely* 83-88; V Waterbeach 83-88; OCF 83-88; R Radwinter w Hempstead *Chelmsf* 88-97; RD Saffron Walden 91-97; P-in-c The Sampfords 95-97; rtd 97; Perm to Offic *Ely* from 97 and *Chelmsf* from 02; Dioc Rep Melanesian Miss and Papua New Guinea Ch Partnership from 99; Chapl Ely Chapter Guild of Servants of the Sanctuary from 00; Adv Melanesian Brotherhood 05-11; Perm to Offic Melanesia from 07; Can Honiara from 07. *39 Way Lane, Waterbeach, Cambridge CB25 9NQ* Tel (01223) 861631 E-mail bj.macdonaldmilne@homecall.co.uk

McDONNELL, David. b 80. TCD BEd02 BTh09 MA09. CITC. **d** 09 **p** 10. C Dublin Ch Ch Cathl Gp from 09. *32 Shandon Drive, Phibsboro, Dublin 7, Republic of Ireland* Tel (00353) (1) 838 0469 E-mail christchurchcurate@gmail.com

McDONNELL, Mrs Mavis Marian. b 42. **d** 98 **p** 99. OLM Warrington St Ann *Liv* from 98. *32 Shaws Avenue, Warrington WA2 8AX* Tel (01925) 634408 E-mail mmavis@aol.com

McDONOUGH, David Sean. b 55. **d** 89 **p** 90. C Moseley St Mary *Birm* 89-92; TV Glascote and Stonydelph *Lich* 92-11; R Anstey and Thurcaston w Cropston *Leic* from 11. *The Rectory, 1 Hurd's Close, Anstey, Leicester LE7 7GH* Tel 0116-236 2176 E-mail david@dmcdonough.freeserve.co.uk

McDONOUGH, Terence. b 57. St Jo Coll Nottm LTh86. **d** 89 **p** 90. C Linthorpe *York* 89-94; TV Heworth H Trin 94-98; V Heworth Ch Ch from 98; P-in-c York St Thos w St Maurice 06-09. *Christ Church Vicarage, 13 Lawnway, York YO31 1JD* Tel (01904) 425678

McDOUGAL, John Anthony Phelps Standen. See STANDEN

McDOUGAL, Canon John Anthony Phelps

McDOUGALL, David Robin. b 61. Avery Hill Coll CertEd BEd84. Ridley Hall Cam 85. **d** 87 **p** 88. C Bletchley *Ox* 87-91; C High Wycombe 91-93; C E Twickenham St Steph *Lon* 93-02; P-in-c Upper Sunbury St Sav from 02; AD Spelthorne from 10. *St Saviour's Vicarage, 205 Vicarage Road, Sunbury-on-Thames TW16 7TP* Tel (01932) 782800 E-mail david@st-saviours-sunbury.org.uk

McDOUGALL, Mrs Denise Alma. b 48. Ban Coll TCert69. NOC 00. **d** 03. NSM Waterloo Ch Ch and St Jo *Liv* 03-09; Chapl St Fran of Assisi City Academy Liv 05-09; NSM Gt Crosby St Faith and Waterloo Park St Mary *Liv* from 09. *27 Mayfair Avenue, Crosby, Liverpool L23 2TL* Tel 0151-924 8870 E-mail denisemcdougall@yahoo.co.uk

MacDOUGALL, Canon Iain William. b 20. TCD BA43 MA59. CITC 43. **d** 43 **p** 44. C Belfast St Steph *Conn* 43-45; C Enniskillen and Trory *Clogh* 45-48; I Drumlane *K, E & A* 48-50; I Ballinaclash *D & G* 51-54; I Moate *M & K* 54-58; I Ballyloughloe 54-58; I Ferbane 54-58; I Mullingar, Portnashangan, Moyliscar, Kilbixy etc 58-85; Can Meath 81-85; rtd 85. *18 Denville Court, Killiney, Co Dublin, Republic of Ireland* Tel (00353) (1) 285 4751

McDOUGALL, Sally-Anne. b 64. Glas Univ BMus86 Edin Univ BD04. TISEC 01. **d** 04 **p** 11. C Glas St Marg 04-06; C Studley *Sarum* from 10. *26 Holbrook Lane, Trowbridge BA14 0PP* Tel (01225) 755145 E-mail sal@mcdougall.gg

McDOUGALL, Stuart Ronald. b 28. Leeds Univ DipAdEd MEd84. Roch Th Coll 64. **d** 66 **p** 67. C Gravesend St Aid *Roch* 66-69; C Wells St Thos w Horrington *B & W* 69-70; TV Tong *Bradf* 70-73; V Cononley w Bradley 73-82; C Thornthwaite w Thruscross and Darley *Ripon* 82-83; P-in-c Dacre w Hartwith 83-86; rtd 86; Perm to Offic *Sarum* 90-08. *13 Bromley College, London Road, Bromley BR1 1PE* Tel (020) 8313 1342

MacDOUGALL, William Duncan. b 47. Nottm Univ BTh74 LTh74. St Jo Coll Nottm 69. **d** 74 **p** 75. C Highbury New Park St Aug *Lon* 74-77; SAMS 77-82; Argentina 78-82; V Rashcliffe and Lockwood *Wakef* 83-87; V Tonbridge St Steph *Roch* 87-03; RD Tonbridge 01-03; Dir Past and Evang Studies Trin Coll Bris from 03. *15 Cranleigh Gardens, Bristol BS9 1HD* Tel 0117-968 2028 E-mail bill.macdougall@btinternet.com

McDOWALL, Julian Thomas. b 39. CCC Cam BA62 MA67 Barrister 61. Linc Th Coll 62. **d** 64 **p** 65. C Rugby St Andr *Cov*

64-70; C-in-c Stoke Hill CD *Guildf* 70-72; V Stoke Hill 72-76; R Elstead 76-91; V Thursley 82-91; TV Wellington and Distr *B & W* 91-93; C Lymington *Win* 93-04; rtd 04; Perm to Offic *Win* from 04. *Juniper Cottage, 20 Solent Avenue, Lymington SO41 3SD* Tel (01590) 676750

McDOWALL, Robert Angus (Robin). b 39. AKC66. d 67 p 68. C Bishopwearmouth St Mich w St Hilda *Dur* 67-69; CF 69-05; Sen CF 80-91; Asst Chapl Gen 91-94; QHC 93-05; rtd 04; Perm to Offic *York* from 05. *clo Crockford, Church House, Great Smith Street, London SW1P 3AZ* Tel (01482) 862504

McDOWALL, Roger Ian. b 40. AKC64. d 65 p 66. C Peterlee *Dur* 65-68; C Weaste *Man* 68-70; C Tonge Moor 70-73; V Whitworth St Bart 73-80; TV Torre *Ex* 80-88; V Torre All SS 88-00; Chapl S Devon Tech Coll Torbay 80-00; rtd 04. *1 Dunanellerich, Dunvegan, Isle of Skye IV55 8ZH* Tel (01470) 521271 E-mail mcdowall@lineone.net

✠**McDOWELL, The Rt Revd Francis John.** b 56. QUB BA78. CITC BTh93. d 96 p 97 c 11. C Antrim *Conn* 96-99; I Ballyrashane w Kildollagh 99-02; I Dundela St Mark *D & D* 02-11; Bp Clogh from 11. *The See House, Ballagh Road, Fivemiletown BT75 0QP* Tel and fax (028) 8952 2475 E-mail bishop@clogher.anglican.org

McDOWELL, Ian. b 67. Ch Coll Cam MA88 BA92. Westcott Ho Cam 90. d 93 p 94. C Hackney *Lon* 93-96; Asst Chapl Homerton Hosp NHS Trust Lon 96-98; Chapl Newham Healthcare NHS Trust Lon 98-03. *37 Hemsworth Street, London N1 5LF* Tel (020) 7363 8053 E-mail mcdow@dircon.co.uk

McDOWELL, Ian James. b 37. St Jo Coll Morpeth ACT ThL60 St Aug Coll Cant. d 61 p 62. C Naracoorte Australia 61-63; P-in-c Elliston Miss 63-66; C S Harrow St Paul *Lon* 66; C Southgate Ch 67; V Ganton *York* 67-71; P-in-c Foxholes and Butterwick 67-68; R 68-71; R Angaston Australia 71-76; R Colonel Light Gardens 76-94; R Gawler 94-98; R Merriwa 98-02; rtd 02. *1516 New England Highway, Harpers Hill NSW 2321, Australia* Tel (0061) (2) 4930 9051

McDOWELL, John. *See* McDOWELL, The Rt Revd Francis John

McDOWELL, Peter Kerr. b 69. QUB BA91. CITC BTh94. d 94 p 95. C Lisburn St Paul *Conn* 94-98; C Arm St Mark 98-99; I Belfast Upper Malone (Drumbeg) *Conn* 99-05; I Ballywillan from 05. *The Rectory, 10 Coleraine Road, Portrush BT56 8EA* Tel (028) 7082 4298 Mobile 07724-072944 E-mail revpetermcdowell@hotmail.co.uk

McDOWELL, Sheilah Rosamond Girgis. b 72. d 05. NSM Hammersmith H Innocents and St Jo *Lon* from 05. *36 Avenue Gardens, Teddington TW11 0BH* Tel (020) 8943 9259 E-mail rosamond.mcdowell@collyerbristow.com

MACE, Alan Herbert. b 28. Lon Univ BA49 Ex Inst of Educn TCert50. Wycliffe Hall Ox 59. d 60 p 61. C Disley *Ches* 60-63; C Folkestone H Trin w Ch Ch *Cant* 63-67; Lic to Offic *Win* 67-93; rtd 93; Public Preacher *Win* from 93. *15 Bassett Heath Avenue, Southampton SO16 7GP* Tel (023) 8076 8161

MACE, David Sinclair. b 37. Cam Univ BA61. d 95 p 96. OLM Godalming *Guildf* 95-07; rtd 07; Perm to Offic *Guildf* from 07. *Torridon, Grosvenor Road, Godalming GU7 1NZ* Tel (01483) 414646 E-mail dsmace@btinternet.com

MACE, Robert Alfred Beasley. b 24. Leeds Univ BA49. Coll of Resurr Mirfield 48. d 50 p 51. C Callander *St And* 50-53; C Newc St Mary 53-54; C Penton Street St Silas w All SS *Lon* 54-56; C Aylesbury *Ox* 56-59; P-in-c Glas St Gabr 59-61; R Campbeltown *Arg* 61-65; V Barnsley St Pet *Wakef* 65-72; V Barnsley St Pet and St Jo 72-84; rtd 85; Perm to Offic *Wakef* from 85. *18 Chestnut Court, Barnsley S70 4HW* Tel (01226) 280729

McELHINNEY, Canon Mary Elizabeth Ellen. b 45. TCD BSSc67 BA67. CITC BTha94. d 97 p 98. C Magheralin w Dollingstown *D & D* 97-01; I Calry *K, E & A* 01-07; Preb Elphin Cathl 04-07; rtd 07. *10 Taughrane Heights, Dollingstown, Craigavon BT66 7RS* Tel (028) 3831 0113 E-mail lizmcelhinney@hotmail.com

McELHINNEY, Robert Stephen. b 70. Aston Univ BSc91. CITC BTh05. d 05 p 06. C Kill *D & G* 05-08; C Drumglass w Moygashel *Arm* 08-11; I Derryvolgie *Conn* from 11. *The Rectory, 35 Kirkwoods Park, Lisburn BT28 3RR* E-mail scrap5@eircom.net

McELWEE, Rachel. d 10. NSM Clapham St Paul *S'wark* from 10. *Flat 4, 84 Northcote Road, Clapham SW11 6QN*

McENDOO, Canon Neil Gilbert. b 50. TCD BA72. CITC 75. d 75 p 76. C Cregagh *D & D* 75-79; C Dublin St Ann *D & G* 79-82; I Dublin Rathmines w Harold's Cross from 82; Can Ch Ch Cathl Dublin 92-02; Preb from 02; Chan from 05. *The Rectory, Purser Gardens, Church Avenue, Rathmines, Dublin 6, Republic of Ireland* Tel (00353) (1) 497 1797 E-mail neil.mcendoo@oceanfree.net

McEUNE, Patrick John. b 55. d 04 p 05. NSM White Horse *Sarum* from 04; TV from 07; Liturg Chapl Bp Ramsbury from 09; Perm to Offic *Nor* from 08. *82 Danvers Way, Westbury BA13 3UF* Tel 07544-588121 (mobile) E-mail mceune@googlemail.com

McEVITT, Canon Peter Benedict. b 58. Coll of Resurr Mirfield 91. d 93 p 94. C Swinton and Pendlebury *Man* 93-96; TV 96-97; V Darwen St Cuth w Tockholes St Steph *Blackb* 97-02; P-in-c Failsworth H Family *Man* 02-04; R 04-08; AD Oldham 02-08; Dioc Stewardship Officer 08-11; V Royton St Paul and Shaw from 11; Hon Can Man Cathl from 07. *The Vicarage, 13 Church Road, Shaw, Oldham OL2 7AT* Tel (01706) 844395 E-mail petermcevitt@hotmail.com

MACEY, Preb Anthony Keith Frank. b 46. St Steph Ho Ox 69. d 71 p 72. C Ex St Thos 71-76; V Wembury 76-88; RD Ivybridge 83-91; V Cockington from 88; RD Torbay 98-03; Preb Ex Cathl from 05. *The Vicarage, 22 Monterey Close, Torquay TQ2 6QW* Tel (01803) 607957 Fax 690338 E-mail smacey@lineone.net *or* cockington@lineone.net

MACEY, Michael David. b 81. Ex Univ BA03 Dur Univ MATM08. Cranmer Hall Dur 03. d 05 p 06. C Dartmouth and Dittisham *Ex* 05-08; Min Can Westmr Abbey from 08. *7 Little Cloister, Dean's Yard, London SW1P 3PL* Tel (020) 7654 4813 *or* 7654 4855 Fax 7654 4859 E-mail frmacey@hotmail.com *or* michael.macey@westminster-abbey.org

McFADDEN, Canon Ronald Bayle. b 30. TCD BA53 MA55. d 54 p 55. C Drumglass *Arm* 54-58; S Africa 58-62; Bp's Dom Chapl *D & D* 62-64; C Dundela St Mark 62-64; V Pateley Bridge and Greenhow Hill *Ripon* 64-73; V Knaresborough St Jo 73-79; P-in-c Knaresborough H Trin 78-79; Can Res Ripon Cathl 79-90; rtd 90; Chapl Qu Mary's Sch Baldersby Park 90-00; Perm to Offic *Ripon* from 90 and *York* from 97. *12 Ure Bank Terrace, Ripon HG4 1JG* Tel (01765) 604043

McFADDEN, Terrance. b 61. NTMTC 05. d 08 p 09. C Greenstead w Colchester St Anne *Chelmsf* from 08. *10 Goldcrest Close, Colchester CO4 3FN*

McFADYEN, Donald Colin Ross. b 63. Wolfs Coll Cam BTh00 Peterho Cam MPhil02. Ridley Hall Cam 97. d 01 p 02. NSM Haslingfield w Harlton and Gt and Lt Eversden *Ely* 01-05; P-in-c Bassingbourn from 05; P-in-c Whaddon from 05; Course Dir Ridley Hall Cam from 05. *The Vicarage, 21 North End, Bassingbourn, Royston SG8 5NZ* Tel (01763) 244836 Fax 243119 Mobile 07763-401567 E-mail donald.mcfadyen@me.com

McFADYEN, Canon Phillip. b 44. K Coll Lon BD69 AKC69 MTh70 ATD. St Aug Coll Cant 69. d 71 p 72. C Sheff St Mark Broomhall 71-74; Chapl Keswick Hall Coll of Educn 74-79; V Swardeston *Nor* 79-81; P-in-c E Carleton 79-81; P-in-c Intwood w Keswick 79-81; R Swardeston w E Carleton, Intwood, Keswick etc 81-90; R Ranworth w Panxworth, Woodbastwick etc 90-05; Dioc Clergy Tr Officer 90-98; P-in-c Nor St Geo Colegate from 05; Hon Can Nor Cathl from 97; Bp's Officer for Visual Arts from 01; Relig Adv Anglia TV from 01. *12 The Crescent, Chapel Field Road, Norwich NR2 1SA* Tel (01603) 621570 E-mail phillipmcfadyen@aol.com

McFARLAND, Alan Malcolm. b 24. Lon Univ BA53. Bris Sch of Min 82. d 85 p 86. NSM Westbury-on-Trym H Trin *Bris* 85-88; Asst Lect Bris Sch of Min 85-88; Perm to Offic *Glouc* 88-89; NSM Lechlade 89-93; Perm to Offic *Sarum* 93-08. *11 The Seahorse, Higher Sea Lane, Charmouth, Bridport DT6 6BB* Tel (01297) 560414

McFARLAND, Darren William. b 71. QUB BA93. CITC BTh96. d 96 p 97. C Greystones *D & G* 96-98; PV Ch Ch Cathl Dublin 97-99; P-in-c Clydebank *Glas* 99-02; Asst Dioc Miss 21 Co-ord 99-02; R Paisley St Barn and Paisley H Trin 02-11; V Headington *Ox* from 11. *The Vicarage, 33 St Andrew's Road, Oxford OX3 9DL* Tel (01865) 761094 Mobile 07773-772610 E-mail vicar.headington@gmail.com

MACFARLANE, Miss Elizabeth Clare. b 71. St Hugh's Coll Ox BA92. Ripon Coll Cuddesdon BA02. d 03 p 04. C Watford St Mich *St Alb* 03-06; TV Gt Marlow w Marlow Bottom, Lt Marlow and Bisham *Ox* 06-11; Chapl and Fell St Jo Coll Ox from 11. *St John's College, Oxford OX1 3JP* Tel (01865) 277435

MACFARLANE, Iain Philip. b 64. Essex Univ BSc85 W Sussex Inst of HE PGCE88. Trin Coll Bris BA99. d 99 p 00. C Fishponds St Jo *Bris* 99-03; TV Yate New Town from 03. *The Vicarage, 57 Brockworth, Bristol BS37 8SJ* Tel (01454) 322921 E-mail imacfarlane@ukonline.co.uk

MACFARLANE, Iain Scott. b 70. St Jo Coll Nottm 02. d 04 p 05. C Malvern St Andr and Malvern Wells and Wyche *Worc* 04-07; V Taunton Lyngford *B & W* from 07. *62 Eastwick Road, Taunton TA2 7HD* Tel (01823) 275085 Mobile 07834-191507 E-mail revmcfarlane@gmail.com

McFARLANE, The Ven Janet Elizabeth. b 64. Sheff Univ BMedSci87 St Jo Coll Dur BA92. Cranmer Hall Dur 93. d 93 p 94. Par Dn Stafford *Lich* 93-94; C 94-96; Chapl and Min Can Ely Cathl 96-99; Dioc Communications Officer *Nor* from 99; Hon PV Nor Cathl 00-09; Bp's Chapl 01-09; Adn Nor from 09. *31 Bracondale, Norwich NR1 2AT* Tel (01603) 620007 E-mail archdeacon@norwich.anglican.org

MACFARLANE, Katy Antonia. b 69. STETS. d 09. NSM Crofton *Portsm* from 09. *20 Shannon Road, Fareham PO14 3RS* Tel (01329) 668920

MACFARLANE, William Angus. b 17. Worc Coll Ox BA39 MA43. Wycliffe Hall Ox 39. **d** 40 **p** 41. C Charles w Plymouth St Luke *Ex* 40-45; C Reading St Jo *Ox* 45-47; CMS Tr Coll Blackheath 47-48; C Brompton H Trin *Lon* 48-49; R Bighton *Win* 49-52; V Bishop's Sutton 49-52; V Southwold *St E* 52-59; V Plaistow St Mary *Roch* 59-71; V Bexleyheath Ch Ch 71-79; Perm to Offic *B & W* 79-95 and 04-07; Chapl Sandhill Park Hosp Taunton 80-87; rtd 82. *Moorlands, Blue Anchor, Minehead TA24 6JZ* Tel (01643) 821564

McGAFFIN, Judi. CITC. **d** 09 **p** 10. NSM Donagheady *D & R* from 09. *Address temp unknown*

McGANITY, Canon Steven. b 61. Nottm Univ BTh93. St Jo Coll Nottm 90. **d** 93 **p** 94. C Gateacre *Liv* 93-97; V Clubmoor from 97; AD W Derby from 08; Hon Can Liv Cathl from 08. *St Andrew's Vicarage, 176 Queen's Drive, West Derby, Liverpool L13 0AL* Tel 0151-226 1977 E-mail smcganity@bigfoot.com

McGARAHAN, Kevin Francis. b 51. Oak Hill Th Coll BA84 MA90. **d** 84 **p** 85. C Balderstone *Man* 84-87; C Stoughton *Guildf* 87-89; Par Lect Ashton St Mich *Man* 89-92; TV Madeley *Heref* 92-96; CF 96-99; TV Woughton *Ox* 99-06; rtd 07; Hon C Hanger Hill Ascension and W Twyford St Mary *Lon* 07-10. *7 Wesley Terrace, Pensilva, Liskeard PL14 5PD* Tel (01579) 363336 E-mail revkev_mcgarahan@hotmail.co.uk

McGEARY, Peter. b 59. K Coll Lon BD AKC. Chich Th Coll 84. **d** 86 **p** 87. C Brighton St Pet and St Nic w Chpl Royal *Chich* 86-90; C St Marylebone All SS *Lon* 90-95; P-in-c Hayes St Anselm 95-97; V 97-98; V St Geo-in-the-East St Mary from 98; PV Westmr Abbey from 00. *The Clergy House, All Saints Court, 68 Johnson Street, London E1 0BQ* Tel and fax (020) 7790 0973 E-mail mcgcary@mcg.pvedg.demon.co.uk

McGEE, The Very Revd Stuart Irwin. b 30. TCD BA53 MA68. **d** 53 **p** 54. C Belfast St Simon *Conn* 53-55; Chapl Miss to Seamen Singapore 55-58; I Drumholm and Rossnowlagh *D & R* 58-65; CF 65-77; Dep Asst Chapl Gen 77-88; Can Achonry Cathl 89-92; I Achonry w Tubbercurry and Killoran 89-92; Dean Elphin and Ardagh and I Sligo w Knocknarea and Rosses Pt *K, E & A* 92-99; rtd 99. *Teach na Mara, Strandhill, Sligo, Republic of Ireland* Tel (00353) (71) 916 8910 Mobile 86-050 9272

MacGEOCH, David John Lamont. b 64. Bath Univ BSc90 CQSW90. Westcott Ho Cam 97. **d** 99 **p** 00. C Midsomer Norton w Clandown *B & W* 99-03; V Puriton and Pawlett 03-08; P-in-c Glastonbury w Meare from 08. *24 Wells Road, Glastonbury BA6 9DJ* E-mail all@macgeoch.fsnet.co.uk

McGHIE, Clinton Adolphus. b 41. Univ of W Indies. **d** 78 **p** 79. Jamaica 78-96; Perm to Offic *Chelmsf* 96-97; P-in-c Highams Park All SS 97-02; V from 02; rtd 11. *10 Sussex Way, Billericay CM12 0FA* Tel (01277) 634389

McGILL, Francis Leonard. b 31. **d** 93 **p** 94. NSM Howell Hill *Guildf* 93-01; Perm to Offic from 02. *27 Hampton Grove, Ewell, Epsom KT17 1LA* Tel (020) 8393 2226

MacGILLIVRAY, Canon Alexander Buchan. b 33. Edin Univ MA55 Aber Univ DipEd67. Edin Th Coll 55. **d** 57 **p** 58. Chapl St Ninian's Cathl Perth 57-59; Chapl Aberlour Orphanage 59-62; C Aberluar *Mor* 59-62; R Oldmeldrum and Whiterashes *Ab* 62-07; R Fyvie and Insch 74-81; Can St Andr Cathl 78-07; rtd 07. *Address temp unknown*

MacGILLIVRAY, Jonathan Martin. b 53. Aber Univ MA75. Coll of Resurr Mirfield. **d** 80 **p** 81. C Hulme Ascension *Man* 80-84; P-in-c Birch St Agnes 84-85; R 85-91; V Hurst 91-96; Chapl Tameside Gen Hosp 92-96; Dir of Ords and OLM Officer *Man* 96-02; V Carrington *S'well* from 02. *Carrington Vicarage, 6 Watcombe Circus, Nottingham NG5 2DT* Tel 0115-962 1291 E-mail j.macg@virgin.net

McGINLEY, Canon Jack Francis. b 36. ALCD65. **d** 65 **p** 66. C Erith St Paul *Roch* 65-70; C Morden *S'wark* 70-74; V New Catton Ch Ch *Nor* 74-94; RD Nor N 84-89; Hon Can Nor Cathl 90-94; R Carlton-in-the-Willows *S'well* 94-02; R Colwick 96-02; rtd 02; Perm to Offic *Nor* from 03. *14 Clovelly Drive, Norwich NR6 5EY* Tel (01603) 788848 E-mail jack.mcginley@talk21.com

McGINLEY, John Charles. b 69. Birm Univ BSocSc90. Trin Coll Bris BA96. **d** 96 **p** 97. C Hounslow H Trin w St Paul *Lon* 96-00; TV Hinckley H Trin *Leic* 00-04; TR 04-09; V Leic H Trin w St Jo from 09. *5 Ratcliffe Road, Leicester LE2 3JE* E-mail john.mcginley1@ntlworld.com

McGINTY, Ms Nicola Jane. b 61. Bath Univ BSc83 Warwick Univ MBA06. Qu Coll Birm 06. **d** 09 **p** 10. NSM Barrow upon Soar w Walton le Wolds *Leic* from 09; NSM Wymeswold and Prestwold w Hoton from 09. *5 Station Road, Rearsby, Leicester LE7 4YX* Tel (01664) 424869 E-mail nicky@njmcginty.co.uk

McGIRR, Canon William Eric. b 43. CITC 68. **d** 71 **p** 72. C Carrickfergus *Conn* 71-74; C Mt Merrion *D & D* 74-77; I Donacavey w Barr *Clogh* 77-88; I Ballybeen *D & D* 88-94; I Magheraculmoney *Clogh* 94-10; Can Clogh Cathl 95-10; Chan 06-10; rtd 10. *Address temp unknown*

McGIVERN, Mrs Ann Margaret. b 49. Newc Poly BSc79 MPhil92 Newc Univ PGCE80. Lindisfarne Regional Tr Partnership 10. **d** 11. NSM Long Benton *Newc* from 11.

9 Albany Avenue, Newcastle upon Tyne NE12 8AS Tel 0191-2665442 Mobile 07940-211004 E-mail annpope@hotmail.com

McGLADDERY, David John. b 62. Homerton Coll Cam BEd85 Univ of Wales (Cardiff) MA93. St Mich Coll Llan 02. **d** 05 **p** 06. NSM Monmouth w Overmonnow etc 05-09; V from 09; Asst Chapl Mon Sch from 05. *The Vicarage, The Parade, Monmouth NP25 3PA* Tel (01600) 715941 E-mail mcgladdery5@btinternet.com

McGLASHAN, Alastair Robin. b 33. Ch Ch Ox BA57 MA58 St Jo Coll Cam BA59 MA63 SaPH 84. Ridley Hall Cam 58. **d** 60 **p** 61. C St Helens St Helen *Liv* 60; C Ormskirk 60-62; CMS India 63-74; USA 74-75; C Lamorbey H Redeemer *Roch* 75-77; Chapl W Park Hosp Epsom 77-85; Chapl Maudsley Hosp Lon 85-87; Perm to Offic *S'wark* 86-06; rtd 98. *102 Westway, London SW20 9LS* Tel (020) 8542 2125

McGLINCHEY, Patrick Gerard. b 59. NUU BA82 Nottm Univ BTh95 MA06. St Jo Coll Nottm 93. **d** 95 **p** 96. C Kettering Ch the King *Pet* 95-97; C Gorleston St Andr *Nor* 97-02; Assoc Min Cliff Park Community Ch 99-02; Chapl and Dean of Res QUB 03-09; Lect Ch of Ireland Th Inst from 09. *74 Locksley Park, Belfast BT10 0AS* Tel (028) 9062 6887 Mobile 07799-061718

McGONIGLE, Martin Leo Thomas. b 64. Univ of Greenwich BA94 Anglia Poly Univ MA99. EAMTC 96. **d** 98 **p** 99. C Forest Gate All SS and St Edm *Chelmsf* 98-01; Perm to Offic *Lon* 01-02; Chapl Asst Cen Man/Man Children's Univ Hosp NHS Trust 02-03; Lead Chapl 03-07; Spiritual Care Co-ord 07-11; Chapl Springhill Hospice 06-11; V Southgate St Andr *Lon* from 11. *St Andrew's Vicarage, 184 Chase Side, London N14 5HN* Tel (020) 8886 9503

McGONIGLE, Thomas. b 22. TCD BA45 MA65. TCD Div Sch 43. **d** 46 **p** 47. C Drumglass *Arm* 46-50; I Clogherny 50-53; I Magherafelt 53-61 and 74-88; I Portadown St Mark 61-74; Can Arm Cathl 72-88; Treas 79-83; Chan 83-88; Prec 88; rtd 88; Lic to Offic *Arm* from 88. *91 Kernan Gardens, Portadown, Craigavon BT63 5RA* Tel (028) 3833 0892

McGOWAN, Anthony Charles. b 57. Jes Coll Cam BA79 MA83. Coll of Resurr Mirfield 80. **d** 82 **p** 83. C Milford Haven *St D* 82-85; C Penistone and Thurlstone *Wakef* 85-88; Asst Chapl Radcliffe Infirmary Ox 91-94; Chapl Radcliffe Infirmary NHS Trust 94-99; Chapl Ox Radcliffe Hosps NHS Trust 99-04; V Northampton H Trin and St Paul *Pet* from 05. *The Vicarage, 24 Edinburgh Road, Northampton NN2 6PH* Tel (01604) 711468 E-mail anthony.mcgowan@tiscali.co.uk

McGOWAN, Daniel Richard Hugh. b 71. Oak Hill Th Coll. **d** 03 **p** 04. C Peterlee *Dur* 03-07; TV Morden *S'wark* from 07. *49 Camborne Road, Morden SM4 4JL* Tel (020) 8542 2966

McGOWAN, James. b 83. York St Jo Coll BA04 St Hild Coll Dur PGCE05 St Jo Coll Dur BA11. Cranmer Hall Dur 08. **d** 11. C St Germain's Cathl from 11. *Thie Manninagh, Peveril Road, Peel, Isle of Man IM5 1PQ* Tel (01624) 843373 E-mail revdjamesmcgowan@hotmail.co.uk

McGRANAGHAN, Patrick Joseph Colum. b 46. Glas Univ BSc68 Lanc Univ MA72. St Alb Minl Tr Scheme 82. **d** 85 **p** 86. NSM Markyate Street *St Alb* 85-91; NSM Johnstone *Glas* 91-99; NSM Renfrew 97-99; P-in-c Kilmacolm from 99; P-in-c Bridge of Weir from 99. *The Rectory, 4 Balmore Court, Kilmacolm PA13 4LX* Tel (01505) 872733 *or* tel and fax 872961 Mobile 07932-643893 E-mail colum.mcgranaghan@talk21.com

McGRATH, Prof Alister Edgar. b 53. Wadh Coll Ox BA75 Mert Coll Ox MA78 DPhil78 BD83 DD01 FRSA05. Westcott Ho Cam 78. **d** 80 **p** 81. C Wollaton *S'well* 80-83; Chapl St Hilda's Coll Ox 83-87; Tutor Wycliffe Hall Ox from 83; Prin 95-04; Prof Systematic Th Regent Coll Vancouver 93-97; Research Lect in Th Ox Univ 93-99; Prof Hist Th 99-08; Dir Ox Cen for Evang and Apologetics 04-08; Hd Cen for Th, Relig and Culture K Coll Lon from 08. *King's College London, Franklin-Wilkins Building, Waterloo Road, London SE1 9NH* Tel (020) 7848 3778

McGRATH, Ian Denver. b 47. Leeds Univ CertEd72. **d** 87 **p** 88. OLM Ancaster Wilsford Gp *Linc* 87-92; C Spilsby w Hundleby 92-95; P-in-c Asterby Gp 95-99; R 99-09; rtd 09. *14 Park Crescent, Metheringham, Lincoln LN4 3HH* Tel (01526) 321918 E-mail ian@idmcgrath.fsnet.co.uk

McGRATH, Joanna Ruth. See COLLICUTT McGRATH, Joanna Ruth

McGRATH, John. b 49. Salford Univ BSc78 Univ of Wales (Lamp) MA10 Man Poly CertEd79. NOC 82. **d** 85 **p** 86. C Horwich *Man* 85-88; P-in-c Hillock 88-89; V 89-94; V York St Luke 94-97; V Hollinwood *Man* 97-02; P-in-c Oldham St Chad Limeside 97-02; V Hollinwood and Limeside 02-03; TV Turton Moorland Min 03-07; P-in-c Littleborough from 07; P-in-c Calderbrook from 07; P-in-c Shore from 07. *The Vicarage, 4 Stansfield Hall, Littleborough OL15 9RH* Tel (01706) 378055 E-mail johnbede@live.co.uk

McGRATH, Kenneth David. b 59. Surrey Univ BSc82 QUB PGCE83 TCD BTh03. CITC 00. **d** 03 **p** 04. C Lisburn Ch Ch Cathl 03-05; V 05-09; I Kilkeel *D & D* from 09. *The Rectory, 44 Manse Road, Kilkeel, Newry BT34 4BN* Tel (028) 4176 2300 *or* 4176 5994 E-mail revken.mcgrath@btopenworld.com

McGRATH, Patrick Desmond. b 64. Liv Univ LLB86. Wycliffe Hall Ox 92. **d** 96 **p** 97. C Netherton *Liv* 96-98; C Ravenhead 98-02; P-in-c Ightham *Roch* 02-07; Perm to Offic *Cant* from 08. *c/o Crockford, Church House, Great Smith Street, London SW1P 3AZ*

MacGREGOR, Alan John. b 31. Jes Coll Ox MA57. S Tr Scheme 94. **d** 97 **p** 98. NSM Worting *Win* 97-00; Perm to Offic *Lon* 01 and *Sarum* 03-08. *7 Sterte Avenue, Poole BH15 2AJ* Tel (01202) 667267

McGREGOR, Alexander Scott. b 72. Ch Ch Ox BA95 MA00 Barrister 96. SAOMC 03. **d** 06 **p** 07. NSM Harrow St Mary *Lon* 06-09; NSM Pimlico St Barn from 09; NSM Pimlico St Mary Bourne Street from 09; Legal Adv Legal Office Nat Ch Inst 06-08; Dep Legal Adv Gen Syn and Abps' Coun from 09; Dep Chan *Ox* from 07. *30 Bourne Street, London SW1W 8JJ* Tel (020) 7730 2423 E-mail asmcg@hotmail.com

McGREGOR, Manuel Alistair Darrant. b 45. ALCD69. **d** 69 **p** 70. C Streatham Immanuel w St Anselm *S'wark* 69-73; C Somerset St Jas Bermuda 73-76; Warden St Mich Cen New Cross 76-80; C Hatcham St Jas *S'wark* 76-80; V Nor Heartsease St Fran 80-87; TR Thetford 87-96; P-in-c Kilverstone 87-90; P-in-c Croxton 87-90; RD Thetford and Rockland 90-96; TR Gt Baddow *Chelmsf* 96-08; rtd 08. *10 Portland Road, West Bridgford, Nottingham NG2 6DL* Tel 0115-981 0689 E-mail asmcgregor@plusnet.co.uk

MacGREGOR, Colin Highmoor. b 19. Lon Univ BSc45 Magd Coll Cam BA47 MA50. Wells Th Coll 54. **d** 56 **p** 57. C Camberwell St Giles *S'wark* 56-60; V Clapham St Pet 60-73; V Riddlesdown 73-87; rtd 87; Perm to Offic *S'wark* from 03. *5 Longacre Court, 21 Mayfield Road, South Croydon CR2 0BG* Tel (020) 8651 2615

MacGREGOR, Donald Alexander Thomson. b 52. Loughb Univ BSc75 Nottm Univ MA97 Leic Univ CertEd78. St Jo Coll Nottm 91. **d** 93 **p** 94. C Walmley *Birm* 93-96; C Braunstone *Leic* 96-97; TV 97-99; Chapl Loughb Univ 99-04; V Fishguard w Llanychar and Pontfaen w Morfil etc *St D* from 04. *The Vicarage, High Street, Fishguard SA65 9AU* Tel (01348) 872895 E-mail don@macgregors.wanadoo.co.uk

McGregor, Mrs Eileen. b 50. Ex Univ BA71. STETS 07. **d** 10 **p** 11. NSM Fulham All SS *Lon* from 10. *44 Abinger Road, London W4 1EX* Tel (020) 8994 2088 Mobile 07899-928785 E-mail mcgeileen@aol.com

McGREGOR, Mrs Lorraine Louise. b 59. Sarum Th Coll 02. **d** 05 **p** 06. OLM Colehill *Sarum* from 05. *Tapiola, Marianne Road, Wimborne BH21 2SQ* Tel (01202) 886519 E-mail lorraine@hayeswood.dorset.sch.uk

McGREGOR, Mrs Lynn. b 61. Ches Coll of HE BTh00. NOC 97. **d** 00 **p** 01. C Colne and Villages *Blackb* 00-03; C Gt Harwood 03-06; P-in-c Wigan St Mich *Liv* 06-07; V 07-10; P-in-c Platt Bridge from 10. *The Vicarage, Ridyard Street, Platt Bridge, Wigan WN2 3TD* Tel (01942) 865553 E-mail ian.mcgregor@homecall.co.uk

MacGREGOR, Preb Neil. b 35. Keble Coll Ox BA60 MA80. Wells Th Coll. **d** 65 **p** 66. C Bath Bathwick St Mary w Woolley *B & W* 65-70; R Oare w Culbone 70-74; C Lynton, Brendon, Countisbury and Lynmouth *Ex* 70-74; P-in-c Kenn w Kingston Seymour *B & W* 74-76; R 76-80; R Wem and V Lee Brockhurst *Lich* 80-01; P-in-c Loppington w Newtown 95-01; RD Wem and Whitchurch 95-01; Preb Lich Cathl 97-01; rtd 01; Perm to Offic *Heref* from 01. *19 Castle View Terrace, Ludlow SY8 2NG* Tel (01584) 872671 E-mail hatchment@talktalk.net

McGREGOR, Nigel Selwyn. b 47. FCA69. Sarum & Wells Th Coll 87. **d** 89 **p** 90. C Charlton Kings St Mary *Glouc* 89-92; P-in-c Seale *Guildf* 92-95; P-in-c Puttenham and Wanborough 92-95; R Seale, Puttenham and Wanborough 95-04; R Barming *Roch* from 04. *The Rectory, Church Lane, Barming, Maidstone ME16 9HA* Tel (01622) 726263 E-mail nigel.mcgregor@diocese-rochester.org *or* mcgregorn@aol.com

McGREGOR, Stephen Paul. b 55. **d** 03 **p** 04. OLM Tonge Fold *Man* 03-10; OLM Leverhulme from 10. *32 Rawcliffe Avenue, Bolton BL2 6JX* Tel (01204) 391205 E-mail steve.mcgregor2@ntlworld.com

McGUFFIE, Duncan Stuart. b 45. Man Univ MA70 Regent's Park Coll Ox DPhil80. S Dios Minl Tr Scheme 84. **d** 85 **p** 85. C Sholing *Win* 85-89; V Clavering and Langley w Arkesden etc *Chelmsf* 89-10; rtd 10; Perm to Offic *Sheff* from 11. *April Cottage, 15 High Street, Snaith, Goole DN14 9HF*

McGUINNESS, Gordon Baxter. b 57. St Andr Univ BSc79 BNC Ox MSc80. Oak Hill NSM Course 86. **d** 89 **p** 90. NSM Loudwater *Ox* 89-92; C Chilwell *S'wark* 92-01; TR Ellesmere Port *Ches* 01-09; R from 09. *The Rectory, Vale Road, Whitby, Ellesmere Port CH65 9AY* Tel 0151-356 8351 *or* 355 2516 E-mail revgordon@supanet.com

McGUIRE, Alec John. b 51. K Coll Cam BA73 MA76 MRSH86 FRSH90. Westcott Ho Cam 74. **d** 78 **p** 79. C Hungerford and Denford *Ox* 78-81; Prec Leeds St Pet *Ripon* 81-86; Perm to Offic from 86; rtd 01. *34 Gledhow Wood Road, Leeds LS8 4BZ* Tel 0113-240 0336

McGUIRE, John. b 31. Oak Hill Th Coll 59. **d** 62 **p** 65. C Tooting Graveney St Nic *S'wark* 62-64; C Normanton *Derby* 64-67; N Area Sec ICM 67-71; Chapl RNR 67-81; R Biddulph Moor *Lich* 71-00; rtd 00; Perm to Offic *Blackb* from 00. *25 Victoria Road, Fulwood, Preston PR2 8NE* Tel (01772) 719549 E-mail jmcguire@argonet.co.uk

McGURK, Michael Joseph Patrick. b 68. St Jo Coll Nottm 05. **d** 07 **p** 08. C Haughton St Mary *Man* 07-09; C Harpurhey 09-10; R from 10. *The Rectory, 95 Church Lane, Manchester M9 5BG* Tel and fax 0161-205 4020 Mobile 07811-360432 E-mail rev.mikemcgurk@hotmail.com

MACHA, David. b 65. Keele Univ BA88 CertEd88 St Jo Coll Dur BA97 Nottm Univ MA03. Cranmer Hall Dur 94. **d** 97 **p** 98. C Loughborough Em and St Mary in Charnwood *Leic* 97-01; CMS Tanzania 02-09; R Linton in Craven *Bradf* from 09; P-in-c Burnsall w Rylstone from 09. *The Rectory, Hebden Road, Grassington, Skipton BD23 5LA* Tel (01756) 752575 E-mail mchdmacha@gmail.com

McHAFFIE, Alistair. b 57. Oak Hill Th Coll 92. **d** 94 **p** 95. C Braintree *Chelmsf* 94-98; R Falkland Is 98-03; V Leyland St Jo *Blackb* from 03. *St John's Vicarage, Leyland Lane, Leyland PR25 1XB* Tel (01772) 621646 E-mail alistair@mchaffie.com

McHALE, John Michael. b 61. Ch Ch Coll Cant BA84 Kingston Univ PGCE89 Univ of Wales (Cardiff) BTh08. St Mich Coll Llan 03. **d** 08 **p** 09. NSM Llandingat w Myddfai and Chapl Llandovery Coll 08-10; Chapl Lich Cathl Sch from 10; Prec's V Lich Cathl from 10. *1 The Close, Lichfield WS13 7LD* Tel (01543) 898132 Mobile 07912-143374 E-mail john.mchale8@btinternet.com

MACHAM, Miss Anna. b 77. Trin Coll Ox BA98 Cam Univ BA02 MPhil04. Ridley Hall Cam 00. **d** 04 **p** 05. C Cheshunt *St Alb* 04-07; Succ S'wark Cathl from 07; Chapl K Coll Lon from 07. *St Paul's Vicarage, 54 Kipling Street, London SE1 3RU* Tel (020) 7407 8290 Mobile 07796-590024 E-mail anna.macham@southwark.anglican.org *or* anna.macham@kcl.ac.uk

McHARDIE, Douglas John Low. b 64. Dundee Univ MA85. St Jo Coll Nottm 08. **d** 10 **p** 11. C Horley *S'wark* from 10. *84 Balcombe Road, Horley RH6 9AY* Tel (01293) 782218 Mobile 07958-675530 E-mail revdougmch@btinternet.com

McHARDY, David William. b 61. Edin Univ BD88 BD90 PhD97 Aber Coll of Educn DCE82. Edin Th Coll 85. **d** 88 **p** 03. C Dumfries *Glas* 88-89; Lect in World Religions Open Univ 97-08; Hon C Oldmeldrum *Ab* 99-08; P-in-c 08; Chapl Blue Coat Sch Reading 08-10; V Meir Heath and Normacot *Lich* from 10. *St Francis's Vicarage, Sandon Road, Stoke-on-Trent ST3 7LH* Tel (01782) 398585 Mobile 07855-581714 E-mail david.mchardy@hotmail.co.uk

MACHELL, Leigh Douglas. b 64. Leic Poly BSc85. St Jo Coll Nottm MTh03. **d** 03 **p** 04. C Beoley *Worc* 03-07; P-in-c Churchill and Langford *B & W* 07-10. *Address temp unknown* E-mail rev.leigh@ntlworld.com

McHENRY, Brian Edward. b 50. CBE08. New Coll Ox BA73 MA77 Barrister 76. SEITE 05. **d** 08 **p** 09. NSM Deptford St Paul *S'wark* 08-11; V Orpington All SS *Roch* from 11. *The Vicarage, 1A Keswick Road, Orpington BR6 0EU* Tel (01689) 824624 Mobile 07887-802641 E-mail brian@mchenry.co.uk

MACHIN, Mrs Jacqueline June. b 62. STETS. **d** 10 **p** 11. C Romsey *Win* from 10. *c/o Crockford, Church House, Great Smith Street, London SW1P 3AZ* E-mail jax.machin@btinternet.com

MACHIN, Roy Anthony. b 38. BA79. Oak Hill Th Coll 76. **d** 79 **p** 80. C Halliwell St Pet *Man* 79-83; V Eccleston St Luke *Liv* 83-91; V Kendal St Thos and Crook *Carl* 91-99; V Wigan St Barn Marsh Green *Liv* 99-03; rtd 03; Perm to Offic *Man* from 03. *56 Ferndown Road, Harwood, Bolton BL2 3NN* Tel and fax (01204) 362220 E-mail roy.machin@btinternet.com

MACHIRIDZA, Douglas Tafara. b 71. Univ of Zimbabwe BSW99 Birm Univ BPhil07 St Edm Coll Cam BTh10. Westcott Ho Cam 08. **d** 10 **p** 11. C Perry Barr *Birm* from 10; C Perry Beeches from 10. *45 Epwell Road, Birmingham B44 8DH* Tel 0121-356 5300 Mobile 07887-741029 E-mail dtmachiridza@yahoo.co.uk

McHUGH, Brian Robert. b 50. York Univ BA72 Keele Univ CertEd73 IEng92 MIMA98 CMath98. S Dios Minl Tr Scheme 79. **d** 82 **p** 83. NSM Sarisbury *Portsm* 82-86; NSM Shedfield 86-06; NSM Shedfield and Wickham from 07. *28 Siskin Close, Bishops Waltham, Southampton SO32 1RQ* Tel (01489) 896658 E-mail brian.mchugh@bcs.org.uk *or* mchughb@tauntons.ac.uk

McHUGH, Michael. b 57. **d** 87 **p** 88. In RC Ch 87-05; NSM Cley Hill Warminster *Sarum* 05-07; C Salisbury St Thos and St Edm 07-10; TV Vale of Pewsey from 10. *The Vicarage, Wilcot, Pewsey SN9 5NS* Tel (01672) 563676 E-mail mtmch@hotmail.com

McILROY, Sister Honor Margaret. b 44. LRAM44 GRSM45. **d** 98 **p** 99. CSMV from 55. *St Mary's Convent, Challow Road, Wantage OX12 9DJ* Tel (01235) 763141 E-mail sisterscsmv@btinternet.com

McINDOE, Darren Lee. b 76. Univ of Wales (Lamp) BA97. Trin Coll Bris BA05. **d** 06 **p** 07. C Stratford St Jo w Ch Ch and St Jas

Chelmsf 06-09; C Forest Gate Em w Upton Cross 09-10; R Burslem *Lich* from 10. *The Rectory, 16 Heyburn Crescent, Burslem, Stoke-on-Trent ST6 4DL* Tel (01782) 838932 Mobile 07886 502307 E-mail rev.darren.mcindoe@gmail.com

MACINNES, Canon David Rennie. b 32. Jes Coll Cam BA55 MA59. Ridley Hall Cam 55. **d** 57 **p** 58. C Gillingham St Mark *Roch* 57-61; C St Helen Bishopsgate w St Martin Outwich *Lon* 61-67; Prec Birm Cathl 67-78; Angl Adv ATV 67-82; Angl Adv Cen TV 82-93; Dioc Missr *Birm* 79-87; Hon Can Birm Cathl 81-87; R Ox St Aldate w St Matt 87-94; R Ox St Aldate 95-02; Hon Can Ch Ch 98-02; rtd 02. *Pear Tree Cottage, Milcombe, Banbury OX15 4RS* Tel (01295) 721119

MacINNES, Harry Campbell. b 67. Nottm Poly BA89. Wycliffe Hall Ox BTh94. **d** 97 **p** 98. C E Twickenham St Steph *Lon* 97-00; P-in-c St Margaret's-on-Thames 00-04; R Shill Valley and Broadshire Ox from 04. *The Rectory, Church Lane, Shilton, Burford OX18 4AE* Tel (01993) 845954

MACINTOSH, Andrew Alexander. b 36. St Jo Coll Cam BA59 MA63 BD80 DD97. Ridley Hall Cam 60. **d** 62 **p** 63. C S Ormsby Gp *Linc* 62-64; Lect St D Coll Lamp 64-67; Lic to Offic *Ely* from 67; Chapl St Jo Coll Cam 67-69; Asst Dean 69-79; Dean 79-02; Lect Th from 70; Pres 95-99. *St John's College, Cambridge CB2 1TP* Tel (01223) 338709 E-mail aam1003@cus.cam.ac.uk

MacINTOSH, Canon George Grant. b 41. St Jo Coll Dur BA75. Cranmer Hall Dur. **d** 76 **p** 77. C Ecclesall *Sheff* 76-79; Hon C Sheff St Oswald 79-81; Research Fell Sheff Univ 79-81; Dioc Adult Educn Officer 81-88; V Crookes St Tim 81-88; V Abbeydale St Jo 88-97; RD Ecclesall 89-94; P-in-c Cuminestown and Turriff *Ab* 97-06; Dioc Dir Ords 01-03; Can St Andr Cathl 01-06; rtd 06. *9 Millar Street, Carnoustie, Angus DD7 7AS* Tel (01241) 854678 E-mail gmacintosh@onetel.com

McINTOSH, Ian MacDonald. b 64. Jes Coll Cam BA86. Trin Coll Bris BA90. **d** 90 **p** 91. C Belmont *Lon* 90-92; C Frenze 92-95; Chapl Leic Univ 96-02; TV Leic H Spirit 96-02; Co-ord Reader Tr 00-02; Dir Cen for Ecum Studies Westcott Ho Cam 02-04; C Milton Ernest, Pavenham and Thurleigh *St Alb* 02-06; Hon C 06-08; RD Sharnbrook 04-06; Lect and Dir Studies ERMC *Ely* 06-07; Prin from 07. *31 Paddock Close, Clapham, Bedford MK41 6BD* Tel (01234) 302362 *or* (01223) 741740 E-mail mcintosh@ermc.cam.ac.uk

McINTOSH, Mrs Nicola Ann. b 60. Trin Coll Bris 87. **d** 90 **p** 94. Par Dn Queensbury All SS *Lon* 90-93; Par Dn Ruislip Manor St Paul 93-94; C 94-95; NSM Clarendon Park St Jo w Knighton St Mich *Leic* 96-02; Asst Dioc Dir of Ords 00-02; V Milton Ernest, Pavenham and Thurleigh *St Alb* 02-08; Perm to Offic from 08. *31 Paddock Close, Clapham, Bedford MK41 6BD* Tel (01234) 302362

McINTYRE, Ms Iris Evelyn. b 60. Worc Coll Ox BA82 MA90. St Steph Ho Ox 82. **dss** 84 **d** 87 **p** 97. Southbroom *Sarum* 84-86; Oakdale 86-88; Par Dn 87-88; Par Dn Ireland Wood *Ripon* 88-89; Area Co-ord (NW) Chr Aid 92-94; Hon C W Derby St Mary *Liv* 94-98; R Bangor Monachorum and Worthenbury *St As* 98-03; Chapl HM Pris Brockhill 03-06; V Stourport and Wilden *Worc* from 06. *The Vicarage, 20 Church Avenue, Stourport-on-Severn DY13 9DD* Tel (01299) 822041 E-mail evacymru@btinternet.com

McINTYRE, Robert Mark. b 69. Nottm Univ BA91. Coll of Resurr Mirfield 92. **d** 94 **p** 95. C Wednesbury St Jas and St Jo *Lich* 94-97; TV Wolstanton 97-05; P-in-c Rickerscote 05-10; V 10-11; C Stafford 05-11; V Walsall St Gabr Fulbrook from 11; CMP from 97. *St Gabriel's Vicarage, Walstead Road, Walsall WS5 4LZ* Tel (01922) 622583 E-mail frmark.mcintyre@ntlworld.com

MACIVER, Donald. b 46. Heriot-Watt Univ BSc69 Nazarene Th Coll Man ThB82 Lon Univ BD82. **d** 08 **p** 09. OLM Heatons *Man* from 08. *20 Withnell Road, Manchester M19 1GH* Tel 0161-431 5814 E-mail dmaciver@eclipse.co.uk

McIVER, Lyn Cavell. b 56. SNWTP. **d** 10 **p** 11. C Toxteth Park Ch Ch and St Mich w St Andr *Liv* from 10. *29 Moel Famau View, Liverpool L17 7ET* Tel 0151-547 2988 Mobile 07791-650911

MACK, Mrs Gillian Frances. b 50. SCM72. Cant Sch of Min 84. **d** 87 **p** 94. NSM Deal St Geo *Cant* 87-88; NSM Deal St Leon and St Rich and Sholden 88-92; Par Dn 93-94; C 94-97; rtd 97; Perm to Offic *Cant* 97-06; Hon Chapl Cautley Ho Chr Cen 98-06; Hon C Hurst Green and Mitton *Bradf* 06-07; P-in-c from 07; Hon C Waddington from 06; Pioneer Min Craven Adnry 08-11. *The Vicarage, Shire Lane, Hurst Green, Clitheroe BB7 9QR* Tel (01254) 826686 E-mail gillmack@tiscali.co.uk

McKAE, William John. b 42. Liv Univ BSc63 St Mark & St Jo Coll Lon PGCE64. Wells Th Coll 68. **d** 71 **p** 72. C Tranmere St Paul w St Luke *Ches* 71-74; C Midsomer Norton *B & W* 74-75; TV Birkenhead Priory *Ches* 75-80; R Oughtrington 80-91; Chapl Asst Hope, Salford R and Ladywell Hosps Man 91-92; Lic Preacher *Man* 91-92; R Heaton Reddish 92-06; rtd 06; Perm to Offic *Ches* from 06. *3 Grantham Close, Wirral CH61 8SU* Tel 0151-648 0858 E-mail john.g4ila@tiscali.co.uk

MACKARILL, Ian David. b 54. York St Jo Univ BA09. NEOC 01. **d** 04 **p** 05. NSM Waggoners *York* from 04. *The Old*

Farmhouse, Fridaythorpe, Driffield YO25 9RT Tel (01377) 288369 Fax 288459 Mobile 07730-314093 E-mail rev@mackarill.co.uk

McKAVANAGH, Dermot James. b 51. TCD BA75 MA78 K Coll Lon BD78 AKC78. **d** 78 **p** 79. C Croydon H Sav *Cant* 78-82; Asst Chapl Wellington Coll Berks 82-87; Chapl RAF 87-00; rtd 02. *42 Freshfields, Lea, Preston PR2 1TJ*

McKAY, Brian Andrew. b 39. Sarum Th Coll 69. **d** 71 **p** 72. C Walker *Newc* 71-74; C Wooler Gp 74-77; TV 77-81; V Long Benton St Mary 81-89; TV Bellingham/Otterburn Gp 89-91; TV N Tyne and Redesdale 91-02; rtd 02. *26 Punchards Down, Totnes TQ9 5FB* Tel (01803) 840675

MACKAY, Canon Douglas Brysson. b 27. Edin Th Coll 56. **d** 58 **p** 59. Prec St Andr Cathl Inverness 58-61; P-in-c Fochabers 61-70; R 70-72; Chapl Aberlour Orphanage 64-67; P-in-c Aberlour 64-72; Syn Clerk 65-72; Can St Andr Cathl Inverness 65-72; Hon Can 72; R Carnoustie *Bre* 72-98; Can St Paul's Cathl Dundee 81-97; Hon Can from 98; Syn Clerk 81-97; Tutor Dundee Univ from 97; Chapl St Paul's Cathl Dundee from 99. *24 Philip Street, Carnoustie DD7 6ED* Tel (01241) 852362 E-mail db.mackay@btinternet.com

MACKAY, Hedley Neill. b 27. St Aid Birkenhead 53. **d** 56 **p** 57. C Beverley St Mary *York* 56-59; C Scarborough St Mary 59-60; Nigeria 61-70; C Wawne *York* 70-71; TV Sutton St Jas and Wawne 72-76; V Huntington 76-82; TR 82-93; rtd 93; Perm to Offic *York* from 93; Rtd Clergy and Widows Officer (York Adnry) 94-98. *2 Elmfield Terrace, Heworth, York YO31 1EH* Tel (01904) 412971

MACKAY, James Hugh. b 57. Ridley Hall Cam. **d** 09 **p** 10. C Walesby *Linc* from 09. *The Rectory, Beelsby Road, Swallow, Market Rasen LN7 6DG* Tel 07946-054218 (mobile) E-mail jandl.mackay@virgin.net

McKAY, Margaret McLeish. *See* HALE, Mrs Margaret McLeish

MACKAY, Neill. *See* MACKAY, Hedley Neill

MACKAY, Paul Douglas. b 60. Trin Coll Bris. **d** 00 **p** 01. C Becontree St Mary *Chelmsf* 00-03; V Mile Cross *Nor* from 03; RD Nor N from 10. *St Catherine's Vicarage, Aylsham Road, Norwich NR3 2RJ* Tel (01603) 426767 E-mail vicar@stcatherinesmilecross.org.uk

MACKAY, Phyllis Marion. *See* BAINBRIDGE, Mrs Phyllis Marion

MACKAY, Rupert. b 61. Oak Hill Th Coll BA00. **d** 00 **p** 01. C Knutsford St Jo and Toft *Ches* 00-04; Min Hadley Wood St Paul Prop Chpl *Lon* from 04. *28 Beech Hill, Barnet EN4 0JP* Tel and fax (020) 8449 2572 E-mail rupmac@mac.com

McKEACHIE, The Very Revd William Noble. b 43. Univ of the South (USA) BA66. Trin Coll Toronto STB70. **d** 70 **p** 70. Asst Chapl St Jo Coll Ox 70-72; Dioc Th Toronto Canada 73-78; USA from 78; Dir Ch Relns and Tutor Univ of the South 78-80; R Baltimore St Paul 81-95; Dean S Carolina and R Charleston Cathl from 95. *126 Coming Street, Charleston SC 29403-6151, USA* Tel (001) (843) 722 7345 Fax 722 2105 E-mail cathchlp@dycon.com

McKEARNEY, Andrew Richard. b 57. Selw Coll Cam MA. Edin Th Coll 81. **d** 82 **p** 83. Prec St Ninian's Cathl Perth 82-84; Chapl St Mary's Cathl 84-88; R Hardwick and Toft w Caldecote and Childerley *Ely* 88-94; RD Bourn 92-94; V Chesterton Gd Shep 94-06; V Iffley *Ox* from 06. *The Rectory, Mill Lane, Iffley, Oxford OX4 4EJ* Tel (01865) 773516 E-mail theophan@surfaid.org

McKEE, Douglas John Duncan. b 34. Univ of W Aus BA65. St Mich Th Coll Crafers 54. **d** 57 **p** 58. Australia 57-72 and from 85; SSM from 58; Lic to Offic *S'well* 73-85. *12 Kensington Mews, 69 Maesbury Street, Kensington, SA 5068 Australia* Tel (0061) (8) 8331 3853 *or* 8416 8445 Fax 8416 8450 E-mail dunstan.mckee@flinders.edu.au

McKEE, Nicholas John. b 71. Nottm Univ MEng02. Ridley Hall Cam 05. **d** 08 **p** 09. C Didsbury St Jas and Em *Man* 08-11; V Astley Bridge from 11. *St Paul's Vicarage, Sweetloves Lane, Bolton BL1 7ET* Tel (01204) 304119 E-mail rev.nick@live.co.uk

McKEE, Patrick Joseph. b 49. Ripon Coll Cuddesdon 92. **d** 94 **p** 95. C Oakham, Hambleton, Egleton, Braunston and Brooke *Pet* 94-97; V Ryhall w Essendine and Carlby from 97. *The Vicarage, Church Street, Ryhall, Stamford PE9 4HR* Tel (01780) 762398 E-mail revpaddymckee@aol.com

McKEEMAN, David Christopher. b 36. AKC58 DipEd76. **d** 60 **p** 61. C Catford St Andr *S'wark* 60-64; P-in-c W Dulwich Em 64-69; Lic to Offic *Win* 70-82; R Silchester 82-01; rtd 01; Perm to Offic *Heref* from 01. *The Maltings, Woodend Lane, Stoke Lacy, Bromyard HR7 4HQ* Tel (01885) 490705 E-mail david.mckeeman@ntlworld.com

McKEGNEY, Canon John Wade. b 47. TCD BA70 MA81. CITC 70. **d** 72 **p** 73. C Ballynafeigh St Jude *D & D* 72-75; C Bangor St Comgall 75-80; I Drumgath w Drumgooland and Clonduff 80-83; I Gilnahirk 83-90; I Arm St Mark from 90; Can Arm Cathl from 01. *St Mark's Rectory, 14 Portadown Road, Armagh BT61 9EE* Tel and fax (028) 3752 2970 *or* 3752 3197 Mobile 07801-866555 E-mail john.mckegney@virgin.net *or* armagh@armagh.anglican.org

MacKEITH (née GODFREY), Mrs Ann Veronica. b 35. Bris Univ BSc57 CertEd. Gilmore Course 78. **dss** 79 **d** 87 **p** 94. Bishopwearmouth Ch Ch *Dur* 79-83; Bishopwearmouth St Gabr 83-86; Ryhope 86-88; Par Dn 87-88; Par Dn Darlington H Trin 88-94; C 94-95; Family Life Officer 95-97; rtd 98. *26 Withdean Court, London Road, Brighton BN1 6RN* Tel (01273) 552376 E-mail annmackeith@webportal.co.uk

McKELLAR, John Lorne. b 19. Sarum Th Coll 70. **d** 72 **p** 73. C Warminster St Denys *Sarum* 72-75; USA 75-79 and 81-84; P-in-c Colchester St Barn *Chelmsf* 79-81; rtd 84; Perm to Offic *Sarum* from 84. *Corrie, 105A Clay Street, Crockerton, Warminster BA12 8AG* Tel (01985) 213161

McKELLEN, Pamela Joyce. b 47. Homerton Coll Cam TCert69 BEd70. Cranmer Hall Dur 01. **d** 02 **p** 03. C Ox St Matt 02-04; P-in-c Radley and Sunningwell from 04; P-in-c Kennington from 09; AD Abingdon from 07. *The Vicarage, Kennington Road, Radley, Abingdon OX14 2JN* Tel (01235) 554739 E-mail pjmck@compuserve.com

McKELVEY, Mrs Jane Lilian. b 48. Liv Inst of Educn BA94. N Bapt Coll 94. **d** 97 **p** 98. C Aughton St Mich *Liv* 97-01; TV Gateacre from 01. *St Mark's Vicarage, Cranwell Road, Liverpool L25 1NZ* Tel 0151-487 9634

McKELVEY, The Very Revd Robert Samuel James Houston. b 42. OBE10 QVRM00 TD. QUB BA65 MA(Ed)88 Garrett-Evang Th Sem DMin93. CITC 67. **d** 67 **p** 68. C Dunmurry *Conn* 67-70; CF (TAVR) 70-99; P-in-c Kilmakee *Conn* 70-77; I 77-81; Sec Gen Syn Bd of Educn (N Ireland) 81-01; Preb Newcastle St Patr Cathl Dublin 89-01; Dean Belf 01-11; rtd 11. *9 College Park, Coleraine BT51 3HE* Tel (028) 7035 3621 Mobile 07802-207825 E-mail houston.mckelvey@btinternet.com

McKEMEY, Mrs Norma Edith. b 47. St Mary's Coll Chelt CertEd71. STETS BA10. **d** 10 **p** 11. NSM Swindon Ch Ch *Bris* from 10. *Bethany, Greens Lane, Wroughton, Swindon SN4 0RJ* Tel (01793) 845917 Mobile 07760-457739 E-mail mckemeyn@talktalk.net

McKENDREY, Susan Margaret. b 55. **d** 02 **p** 03. NSM Allonby, Cross Canonby and Dearham *Carl* 02-08; TV Maryport, Netherton and Flimby from 08. *The Vicarage, Church Street, Maryport CA15 6HE* Tel (01900) 813077 E-mail s.mckendrey@btinternet.com

MACKENNA, Christopher. *See* MACKENNA, Robert Christopher Douglass

McKENNA, Dermot William. b 41. TCD BA63 MA66. CITC 64. **d** 64 **p** 65. C Enniscorthy *C & O* 64-66; I Killeshin 66-84; rtd 84. *20 Sherwood, Pollerton, Carlow, Republic of Ireland* Tel (00353) (59) 913 0915 E-mail dermotmckennasherwood@gmail.com

McKENNA, Edward Patrick. b 48. Liv Univ BTh02. NOC 05. **d** 06 **p** 07. NSM Stretton and Appleton Thorn *Ches* 06-09; Asst Chapl HM Pris Risley 08-09; P-in-c Low Marple *Ches* from 09. *15 Brabyns Brow, Marple Bridge, Stockport SK6 5DT* Tel 0161-427 2736 Mobile 07979-624271 E-mail ed1mckenna@aol.com

McKENNA, Lindsay Taylor. b 62. Glas Univ MA83 Aber Univ BD86. Edin Th Coll 87. **d** 87 **p** 88. C Broughty Ferry *Bre* 87-90; C Wantage *Ox* 90-93; V Illingworth *Wakef* 93-99; Dir CARA Dundee 08-09; R Dundee St Paul 08-09; Perm to Offic *Win* 09-10; P-in-c Catford St Andr *S'wark* from 10. *St Andrew's Parsonage, 119 Torridon Road, London SE6 1RG* Tel (020) 8697 2600 E-mail lindsay.m@virgin.net

MACKENNA, Richard William. b 49. Pemb Coll Cam BA71 MA75. Ripon Coll Cuddesdon BA77 MA81. **d** 78 **p** 79. C Fulham St Dionis *Lon* 78-81; C Paddington St Jas 81-85; Tutor Westcott Ho Cam 85-89; V Kingston All SS w St Jo *S'wark* 90-91; Perm to Offic *S'wark* 94-01 and *Nor* 99-04. *Flat 5, 11 Grassington Road, Eastbourne BN20 7BJ* Tel (01323) 730477

MACKENNA, Robert Christopher Douglass. b 44. Oriel Coll Ox BA72 MA75 MBAP85. Cuddesdon Coll 71. **d** 73 **p** 74. C Farncombe *Guildf* 73-77; C Tattenham Corner and Burgh Heath 77-80; P-in-c Hascombe 80-90; R 90-00; RD Godalming 91-96; Hon Can Guildf Cathl 99-00; Dir St Marylebone Healing and Counselling Cen from 00; NSM St Marylebone w H Trin *Lon* from 00; rtd 09. *37 Clifden Road, Worminghall, Aylesbury HP18 9JR* Tel (01844) 338213 *or* (020) 7935 5066 E-mail chrismackenna@aol.com *or* cmackenna@stmarylebone.org

MACKENZIE, Andrew John Kett. b 46. Southn Univ BA68. Guildf Dioc Min Course 98. **d** 91 **p** 92. Fullbrook Sch New Haw 76-99; OLM Woodham *Guildf* 91-99; C Aldershot St Mich 99-05; V Effingham w Lt Bookham from 05. *The Rectory, 4 Leewood Way, Effingham, Leatherhead KT24 5JN* Tel (01372) 458314 Mobile 07944-996475 E-mail rectorandy@aol.com

MACKENZIE, Miss Ann. b 54. CertEd76. Trin Coll Bris 82. **dss** 85 **d** 87 **p** 94. Normanton *Wakef* 85-90; Par Dn 87-90; Par Dn Bletchley *Ox* 90-94; C 94-98; TV W Swindon and the Lydiards *Bris* 98-04; P-in-c E Springfield *Chelmsf* from 04. *The Vicarage, Ashton Place, Chelmsford CM2 6ST* Tel (01245) 462387 E-mail annmackenzie@tregoze.fsnet.co.uk

McKENZIE, Mrs Ann Elizabeth. b 45. Leic Univ BA67 PGCE68. STETS 95. **d** 98 **p** 99. NSM Appleshaw, Kimpton, Thruxton, Fyfield etc *Win* from 98. *The Post House, Thruxton, Andover SP11 8LZ* Tel (01264) 772788 E-mail ann.mckenzie@tinyonline.co.uk

McKENZIE, Cilla. *See* McKENZIE, Mrs Priscilla Ann

MACKENZIE, David Stuart. b 45. Open Univ BA95 FRSA00. Linc Th Coll 66. **d** 69 **p** 70. C Bishopwearmouth St Mary V w St Pet CD *Dur* 69-72; C Pontefract St Giles *Wakef* 72-74; Chapl RAF 74-02; Chapl OHP 02-08; RD Whitby *York* 04-08; QHC from 00; Perm to Offic *Ely* from 09. *57 London Road, Godmanchester, Huntingdon PE29 2HZ* Tel (01480) 413120 E-mail ds@mack60.wanadoo.co.uk

MACKENZIE, Duncan. *See* MACKENZIE, Preb Lawrence Duncan

McKENZIE, Ian Colin. b 31. CA56. EMMTC 89. **d** 93. NSM Edin St Mark and Edin St Andr and St Aid 93-94; Perm to Offic *S'well* from 01. *21 Crafts Way, Southwell NG25 0BL* Tel (01636) 815755

MACKENZIE, Ian William. b 46. Trin Coll Bris 93. **d** 95 **p** 96. C Bideford *Ex* 95-96; C Bideford, Northam, Westward Ho!, Appledore etc 96-99; TV Littleham w Exmouth 99-11; rtd 11. *1 Brynview Close, Reynoldston, Swansea SA3 1AG* E-mail billandmaggiemackenzie@gmail.com

McKENZIE, Jack Llewellyn. b 29. FRSH AMIEHO MAMIT. S'wark Ord Course. **d** 79 **p** 80. Hon C Stonebridge St Mich *Lon* 79-88; Hon C Willesden St Mary 88-91; Perm to Offic *St Alb* 00-08. *2 Beckets Square, Berkhamsted HP4 1BZ* Tel (01442) 874265

MACKENZIE, Miss Janet. b 62. Westmr Coll Ox BEd86 Anglia Ruskin Univ BA08. Westcott Ho Cam 04. **d** 06 **p** 07. C Sandy *St Alb* 06-10; P-in-c Luton St Aug Limbury from 10. *The Vicarage, 215 Icknield Way, Luton LU3 2JR* Tel (01582) 572415 E-mail revjanetmackenzie@tiscali.co.uk

McKENZIE (née DOORES), Mrs Jennifer Mary. b 78. Hull Univ BA99 St Jo Coll Dur BA03. Cranmer Hall Dur 01. **d** 04 **p** 05. C Old Swinford Stourbridge *Worc* 04-08; V Cam w Stinchcombe *Glouc* from 08. *The Vicarage, Church Road, Cam, Dursley GL11 5PQ* Tel (01453) 542084 E-mail mckenzie.jennifer@btinternet.com

MacKENZIE, John Christopher Newman. b 67. Trin Coll Bris 02. **d** 04 **p** 05. C Staplehurst *Cant* 04-07; P-in-c Willesborough from 07; P-in-c Sevington from 07. *The Rectory, 66 Church Road, Willesborough, Ashford TN24 0JG* Tel (01233) 624064 E-mail john@jjsmack.me.uk

MACKENZIE, Preb Lawrence Duncan. b 30. St Aid Birkenhead 52. **d** 55 **p** 56. C Blackb St Gabr 55-58; C Burnley St Pet 58-60; C St Giles-in-the-Fields *Lon* 60-63; V Queensbury All SS 63-85; V Hillingdon St Jo 85-96; Preb St Paul's Cathl 89-96; rtd 96; NSM Gt Stanmore *Lon* 96-99; Perm to Offic *Lon* from 99 and *Ely* 99-11. *Room 48, Manormead, Tilford Road, Hindhead GU26 6RA* E-mail duncanmackenzie123@tiscali.co.uk

MACKENZIE, Peter Sterling. b 65. Univ Coll Lon BSc88. Oak Hill Th Coll BA95. **d** 95 **p** 96. C Roxeth *Lon* 95-99; Assoc V 99-00; TV 00-08; V W Ealing St Jo w St Jas from 08. *23 Culmington Road, London W13 9NJ* Tel (020) 8566 3462 E-mail petersmackenzie@btinternet.com

MACKENZIE, Canon Peter Thomas. b 44. Lon Univ LLB67 Westmr Coll Ox MTh97 Univ of E Lon MA01. Cuddesdon Coll 68. **d** 70 **p** 71. C Leigh Park *Portsm* 70-75; P-in-c Sittingbourne St Mary *Cant* 75-82; V Folkestone St Sav 82-90; RD Elham 89-90; C Sant St Martin and St Paul 90-99; RD Cant 95-99; V Goudhurst w Kilndown 99-07; Hon Can Cant Cathl 97-07; AD Cranbrook 01-06; rtd 07; Perm to Offic *Cant* from 09; P-in-c Turvey *St Alb* from 11; P-in-c Stevington from 11. *The Rectory, Bamford Lane, Turvey, Bedford MK43 8DS* E-mail canonmack@talk21.com

McKENZIE, Mrs Priscilla Ann. b 47. St Jo Coll Nottm 87. **d** 93 **p** 94. NSM Ellon *Ab* 93-96; NSM Cruden Bay 93-96; Perm to Offic *Roch* 96-99 and from 04; Chapl Medway NHS Trust 99-04. *Iona, Linton Hill, Linton, Maidstone ME17 4AW* Tel (01622) 741318 E-mail johncilla.mckenzie@onetel.net

MACKENZIE, Richard Graham. b 49. St Aug Coll Cant 72. **d** 73 **p** 74. C Deal St Leon Cant 73-75; C Deal St Leon w Sholden 75-78; C Herne 78-81; Canada from 81; I Pakenham 81-88; I Richmond 88-90; I Petawawa from 90. *1179 Victoria Street, Petawawa ON K8H 2E6, Canada* Tel (001) (613) 687 2218

McKENZIE, Robin Peter. b 61. Sheff Univ BEng82 Birm Univ MSc(Eng)87 Dur Univ BA02 Warwick Univ EngD02 CEng MIET. Cranmer Hall Dur 00. **d** 03 **p** 04. C Shrewsbury St Chad w St Mary *Lich* 03-07; P-in-c Hilton *Ely* 07-11; P-in-c Fenstanton from 07. *The Vicarage, 16 Church Street, Fenstanton, Huntingdon PE28 9JL* Tel (01480) 466162 E-mail mckenzie_robin@hotmail.com

MACKENZIE, Simon Peter Munro. b 52. Univ Coll Ox BA74. Coll of Resurr Mirfield 82. **d** 85 **p** 86. C Tipton St Jo *Lich* 85-91; V Perry Beeches *Birm* from 91. *St Matthew's Vicarage, 313 Beeches Road, Birmingham B42 2QR* Tel 0121-360 2100

McKENZIE, Stephen George. b 58. Leeds Univ BSc80 Imp Coll Lon PhD85. Oak Hill Th Coll 03. **d** 05 **p** 06. C Barton Seagrave w Warkton *Pet* 05-08; P-in-c Swynnerton and Tittensor *Lich* 08-09; C Broughton w Croxton and Cotes Heath w Standon 08-09; R Cotes Heath and Standon and Swynnerton etc from 09. *3 Rectory Gardens, Swynnerton, Stone ST15 0RT* Tel (01782) 796564 Mobile 07986-558861 E-mail stegliverpool@aol.com

McKENZIE, William. *See* MACKENZIE, Ian William

MACKENZIE MILLS, David Graham. b 75. Bris Univ BA96 St Jo Coll Dur BA01. Cranmer Hall Dur. **d** 01 **p** 02. C Glas St Marg 01-04; Chapl Trin Coll Cam 04-09; Min Can and Prec Cant Cathl from 09. *Cathedral House, 11 The Precincts, Canterbury CT1 2EH* Tel (01227) 762862 E-mail precentor@canterbury-cathedral.org

McKEON, Linda. **d** 09 **p** 10. OLM Gentleshaw *Lich* from 09. *17 Bradwell Lane, Rugeley WS15 4RW* Tel (01543) 670739

McKEOWN, Trevor James. b 53. CITC 01. **d** 04 **p** 05. Aux Min Dromore Cathl from 04. *39 Cedar Park, Portadown, Craigavon BT63 5LL* Tel (028) 3832 1217

McKERAN, James Orville. b 71. Kent Univ BA94 K Coll Lon MA06 Leeds Univ MA08 Solicitor 98 ACIArb08 FRGS11. Coll of Resurr Mirfield 06. **d** 08 **p** 09. C Altrincham St Geo and Altrincham St Jo *Ches* 08-11; Chapl Trafford Coll 08-11; SSM from 11; Perm to Offic Lesotho from 11. *SSM Maseru Priory, PO Box 1579, Maseru 100, Lesotho* E-mail james.mckeran@yahoo.com

MACKEY, John. b 34. Lich Th Coll. **d** 64 **p** 65. C Kells *Carl* 64-67; C Barrow St Matt 67-70; R Clayton *Man* 70-75; V Low Marple *Ches* 75-83; R Coppenhall 83-00; rtd 00; Perm to Offic *Ches* from 00. *361 Hungerford Road, Crewe CW1 5EZ* Tel (01270) 254951

McKIBBIN, Gordon. b 29. St Aid Birkenhead 55. **d** 58 **p** 59. C Dundela St Mark *D & D* 58-60; C Knotty Ash St Jo *Liv* 61-64; V Gt Sankey 64-97; rtd 97; Perm to Offic *Liv* from 97. *6 Penmark Close, Warrington WA5 5TG* Tel (01925) 445125

MacKICHAN, Gillian Margaret. b 34. Cam Univ CertEd56 CQSW80. S Dios Minl Tr Scheme 90. **d** 93 **p** 94. NSM Upper Kennet *Sarum* 93-04; TV 95-04; RD Marlborough 02-04; rtd 04; Perm to Offic *Sarum* from 08. *West Bailey, Lockeridge, Marlborough SN8 4ED* Tel (01672) 861629 E-mail lalmack@globalnet.co.uk

MACKIE, Andrew. b 53. Glas Univ BSc74 CEng MIET. SAOMC 00. **d** 00 **p** 01. OLM Purley *Ox* from 00. *12 Church Mews, Purley-on-Thames, Pangbourne, Reading RG8 8AG* Tel 0118-941 7170 E-mail mackie.family@btinternet.com

MACKIE, Ian William. b 31. Lon Univ BSc53 Ex Univ PGCE54. Linc Th Coll 81. **d** 83 **p** 84. C Market Rasen *Linc* 83-87; V Bracebridge Heath 87-96; RD Christianity 92-96; rtd 96; Perm to Offic *Sheff* 96-02. *57 Bridle Crescent, Chapeltown, Sheffield S35 2QX* Tel 0114-284 4073

MACKIE, Kenneth Johnston. b 20. Univ of NZ BA45 MA46 La Trobe Univ Vic BEd77. St Jo Coll Auckland 46. **d** 47 **p** 48. New Zealand 46-66; C Whangarei 47-51; P-in-c S Hokianga 51-53; V Opotiki 53-56; V Napier St Aug 56-61; Gen Sec NZ Coun for Chr Educn 62-66; Australia 66-72 and 74-94; Chapl Traralgon and Macleod High Schs 66-70; Chapl Univ of Papua New Guinea 72-75; Perm to Offic Melbourne and Gippsland 75-89; Hon P-in-c Nerang 91-94; Perm to Offic *Roch* 97-08. *Address temp unknown*

McKIE, The Very Revd Kenyon Vincent. b 60. Aus Nat Univ BA83 ACT BTh88 K Coll Lon MTh92 Canberra Coll DipEd84. **d** 86 **p** 87. Australia 86-89 and from 91; Dn Queanbeyan 86; C 87; Lucas-Tooth Scholar K Coll Lon 89-91; Hon C Coulsdon St Andr *S'wark* 89-91; R Monaro S 91-94; R Bega 94-99; Adn S Coast and Monaro 96-99; Dean Goulburn from 99. *PO Box 205, Goulburn NSW 2580, Australia* Tel (0061) (2) 4821 9192 *or* 4821 2206 Fax 4822 2639 E-mail mesacgbn@tpgi.com.au *or* deanery@tpgi.com.au

McKILLOP, Mrs Caroline Annis. b 47. Glas Univ MB, ChB72 PhD77. TISEC 95. **d** 98 **p** 99. NSM Glas St Matt 98-01; Chapl Stobhill NHS Trust 99-00; NSM Glas St Mary from 02. *Flat 1, 6 Kirklee Gate, Glasgow G12 0SZ* Tel 0141-339 7000 E-mail caroline.mckillop@yahoo.co.uk

McKILLOP, Iain Malcolm. b 54. Man Univ BA75 Man Poly PGCE76 Kingston Univ MA95. Guildf Dioc Min Course 07. **d** 10 **p** 11. NSM Effingham w St Lawrence H Broadham *Guildf* from 10. *10 Hopfield Avenue, Byfleet, West Byfleet KT14 7PE* Tel (01932) 341687 E-mail imckillopi@aol.com

McKINLEY, Canon Arthur Horace Nelson. b 46. TCD BA69 MA79. CITC 70. **d** 70 **p** 71. C Taney Ch Ch *D & G* 71-76; I Dublin Whitechurch from 76; Preb Dunlavin St Patr Cathl Dublin from 91. *The Vicarage, Whitechurch Road, Rathfarnham, Dublin 16, Republic of Ireland* Tel (00353) (1) 493 3953 *or* 493 4972 E-mail whitechurchparish@ireland.com

McKINLEY, George Henry. b 23. TCD BA44 MA51. **d** 46 **p** 47. C Waterford Ch Ch *C & O* 46-49; I Fiddown 49-51; I Fiddown w Kilmacow 51-54; C S Harrow St Paul *Lon* 54-58; V Stonebridge St Mich 58-65; R Hackney St Jo 65-72; TR Hackney 72-77; V Painswick w Sheepscombe *Glouc* 77-83; Bp's Chapl 83-87; C Sandhurst 83-85; C Twigworth, Down Hatherley, Norton, The

Leigh etc 85-87; rtd 88; Perm to Offic *Heref* and *Worc* from 96. *Middlemarch, 2 Old Barn Court, Bircher, Leominster HR6 0AU* Tel (01568) 780795

McKINNEL, Preb Nicholas Howard Paul. b 54. Qu Coll Cam BA75 MA79. Wycliffe Hall Ox BA79 MA86. **d** 80 **p** 81. C Fulham St Mary N End *Lon* 80-83; Chapl Liv Univ 83-87; P-in-c Hatherleigh *Ex* 87-88; R Hatherleigh, Meeth, Exbourne and Jacobstowe 88-94; P-in-c Plymouth St Andr w St Paul and St Geo 94-95; TR Plymouth St Andr and Stonehouse from 95; RD Plymouth Sutton from 01; Preb Ex Cathl from 02. *St Andrew's Vicarage, 13 Bainbridge Avenue, Plymouth PL3 5QZ* Tel (01752) 772139 *or* 661414 E-mail nick@standrewschurch.org.uk

McKINNEY, James Alexander. b 52. Ex Univ BA74 Hull Univ MA87. Ripon Coll Cuddesdon 75. **d** 78 **p** 79. C Wath-upon-Dearne w Adwick-upon-Dearne *Sheff* 78-82; V Doncaster Intake 82-87; Ind Chapl 84-87; Chapl Bramshill Police Coll *Win* 87-92; V Cleator Moor w Cleator *Carl* 92-96; Chapl Cumbria Constabulary 93-96; P-in-c Frizington and Arlecdon 94-96; V Roehampton H Trin *S'wark* from 96. *The Vicarage, 7 Ponsonby Road, London SW15 4LA* Tel (020) 8788 9460 E-mail mckinneyja@hotmail.com

McKINNEY, Canon Mervyn Roy. b 48. St Jo Coll Nottm. **d** 81 **p** 82. C Tile Cross *Birm* 81-84; C Bickenhill w Elmdon 84-89; V Addiscombe St Mary *S'wark* 89-93; V Addiscombe St Mary Magd w St Martin 93-99; P-in-c W Wickham St Fran 99-02; V W Wickham St Fran and St Mary from 02; AD Croydon Addington from 04; Hon Can S'wark Cathl from 05. *The Vicarage, The Avenue, West Wickham BR4 0DX* Tel (020) 8777 5034 E-mail mervmckinney@btinternet.com

MacKINNON, Mrs Karen Audrey. b 64. Ex Univ BA85. Linc Th Coll 92. **d** 92 **p** 94. Par Dn Filton *Bris* 92-93; Par Dn Bris Lockleaze St Mary Magd w St Fran 93-94; C 94-96; P-in-c 96-98; V 98-00; Asst Chapl Southn Univ Hosps NHS Trust 00-03; Chapl 03-04; Dep Team Ldr from 04. *Chaplaincy Department, Southampton General Hospital, Tremona Road, Southampton SO16 6YD* Tel (023) 8079 8517

McKINNON, Neil Alexander. b 46. Wycliffe Hall Ox 71. **d** 74 **p** 75. C Deptford St Nic w Ch Ch *S'wark* 74-76; C St Helier 76-79; Min W Dulwich All SS and Em 79-81; TV Thamesmead 87-95; R S'wark H Trin w St Matt from 95. *The Rectory, Meadow Row, London SE1 6RG* Tel (020) 7407 1707 *or* tel and fax 7357 8532 E-mail neilatelephany@yahoo.com

MACKINTOSH, Canon Robin Geoffrey James. b 46. Rhodes Univ BCom71 Cranfield Inst of Tech MBA78. Ripon Coll Cuddesdon BA85 MA91. **d** 86 **p** 87. C Cuddesdon *Ox* 86; C Cannock *Lich* 86-89; R Girton *Ely* 89-01; Exec Dir The Leadership Inst 01-06; Dir Min and Tr *Cant* from 06; Hon Can Cant Cathl from 09. *4 Loop Court Mews, Sandwich CT13 9HF* Tel (01227) 459401 E-mail rmackintosh@diocant.org

McKINTY, Norman Alexander (Fionn). b 46. Westcott Ho Cam 97. **d** 99 **p** 00. C Yeovil St Mich *B & W* 99-03; C Gillingham and Milton-on-Stour *Sarum* 03-05; P-in-c Portland All SS w St Andr 05-09; TV Portland from 10. *The Vicarage, Straits, Portland DT5 1HG* Tel (01305) 861285 E-mail fionn@mckinty.fsworld.co.uk

McKITTRICK, The Ven Douglas Henry. b 53. St Steph Ho Ox 74. **d** 77 **p** 78. C Deptford St Paul *S'wark* 77-80; C W Derby St Jo *Liv* 80-81; TV St Luke in the City 81-89; V Toxteth Park St Agnes and St Pancras 89-97; V Brighton St Pet w Chpl Royal *Chich* 97-02; RD Brighton 98-02; Can and Preb Chich Cathl 98-02; Adn Chich from 02. *2 Yorklands, Dyke Road Avenue, Hove BN3 6RW* Tel (01273) 505330 *or* 421021 E-mail archchichester@diochi.org.uk

McKITTRICK, Noel Thomas Llewellyn. b 28. TCD BA50 MA57 BD71. **d** 51 **p** 53. C Londonderry Ch Ch *D & R* 51-52; C Belfast St Aid *Conn* 52-54; C Knockbreda *D & D* 54-58; C Keynsham w Queen Charlton *B & W* 58-59; V Glastonbury St Benedict 59-82; V Weston-super-Mare St Paul 82-92; rtd 93; Perm to Offic *Ex* 94-09. *Priory Lodge, 87A Latimer Road, Exeter EX4 7JP* Tel (01392) 496744

MACKLEY, Robert Michael. b 78. Ch Coll Cam BA99 MA03. Westcott Ho Cam 00. **d** 03 **p** 04. C Clerkenwell H Redeemer and St Mark *Lon* 03-06; C Liv Our Lady and St Nic 06-09; Asst Chapl Em Coll Cam from 09. *Emmanuel College, Cambridge CB2 3AP* Tel 07866-445877 (mobile) E-mail rob_mackley@hotmail.com

MACKLIN, Reginald John. b 29. Bris Univ BA52. Ely Th Coll 54. **d** 55 **p** 56. C W Hackney St Barn *Lon* 55-58; C E Ham St Mary *Chelmsf* 58-61; C Northolt St Mary *Lon* 61-64; Jordan 64-68; Palma de Mallorca and Balearic Is *Eur* 68-69; P-in-c Hammersmith St Matt *Lon* 69-70; V Stanwell 70-82; V Kimbolton *Ely* 82-88; V Stow Longa 82-88; RD Leightonstone 82-88; P-in-c Keyston and Bythorn 85-88; P-in-c Catworth Magna 85-88; P-in-c Tilbrook 85-88; P-in-c Covington 85-88; R Coveney 88-96; R Downham 88-96; RD Ely 89-96; rtd 96; Perm to Offic *Ely* from 96. *11 Castlehythe, Ely CB7 4BU* Tel and fax (01353) 662205 E-mail macklinrj@aol.com

MACKNESS, Paul Robert. b 73. Univ of Wales (Lamp) BA96 Univ of Wales (Cardiff) BA01. St Mich Coll Llan 98. **d** 01 **p** 02. C Llanelli *St D* 01-04; P-in-c Maenordeifi and Capel Colman w Llanfihangel etc 04-05; R 05-07; R Maenordeifi Gp 07-10; AD Cemais and Sub-Aeron 08-10; V Haverfordwest from 10. *St Martin's Vicarage, Barn street, Haverfordwest SA61 1TD* Tel (01437) 762303 E-mail paulr@pmackness.fsnet.co.uk

MACKNEY, John Pearson. b 17. Univ of Wales BA39 Lon Univ MA81 PGCE73. St D Coll Lamp 39. **d** 41 **p** 42. C Gelligaer *Llan* 41-44; CF 44-47; C Llangeinor 47-49; P-in-c Cardiff All SS 49-58; Chapl HM Pris Cardiff 49-58; V Mountain Ash *Llan* 58-69; Hon C Streatley w Moulsford *Ox* 81-04; Hon C Cholsey and Moulsford 04-07; Perm to Offic 07-08. *Merlebank, Moulsford, Wallingford OX10 9JG* Tel (01491) 651347

McKNIGHT, Thomas Raymond. b 48. QUB BEd71. CITC 74. **d** 77 **p** 78. C Lisburn Ch Ch Cathl 77-80; C Carrickfergus 80-82; I Kilcronaghan w Draperstown and Sixtowns *D & R* 82-86; I Magheragall *Conn* 86-91; CF 91-07; I Urney w Sion Mills *D & R* 07-11; rtd 11. *5 Pembury Mews, Brompton on Swale, Richmond DL10 7SG*

MACKRELL, Ms Catherine Anita. b 64. St Mary's Coll Dur BSc85 MSc88. Ox Min Course 06. **d** 10 **p** 11. NSM Earley Trin *Ox* from 10. *7 Woodmere Close, Earley, Reading RG6 5QU* Tel and fax 0118-975 3463 Mobile 07885-593103 E-mail cath@hineni.plus.com

MACKRIELL, Peter John. b 64. Mansf Coll Ox BA85 MA93 Man Univ PGCE87. St Jo Coll Nottm BTh93 MA94. **d** 94 **p** 95. C Hale and Ashley *Ches* 94-96; C Marple All SS 96-98; V Brandwood *Birm* 98-01; V Pontblyddyn *St As* 01-05; Chapl to Deaf People 01-11; Dioc Communications Officer 06-11; V Kelsall *Ches* from 11. *St Philip's Vicarage, Chester Road, Kelsall, Tarporley CW6 0SA* Tel (01829) 752639 E-mail vicar@kelsallparishchurch.org.uka

MACKRILL, Mrs Deirdre Anne. b 49. ACIS95. SAOMC 01. **d** 05 **p** 06. NSM Hemel Hempstead *St Alb* 05-09. *Address temp unknown* E-mail deirdre@brewhouse4.freeserve.co.uk

MACKRILL, Robert John. b 51. Univ Coll Lon BSc73 RIBA79. EMMTC 92. **d** 93 **p** 94. NSM Stamford All SS w St Jo *Linc* 93-97; P-in-c Stamford Ch Ch 97-10; RD Aveland and Ness w Stamford 09-10; C Oakham, Hambleton, Egleton, Braunston and Brooke *Pet* 10; TV Oakham, Ashwell, Braunston, Brooke, Egleton etc from 11. *The Rectory, 3 Paddock Close, Whissendine, Oakham LE15 7HW* Tel (01664) 474283 E-mail bobmackrill@btinternet.com

MacLACHLAN (née GRIFFITHS), Mrs Margaret. b 44. Birm Poly CertEd81 Open Univ BA82 SRN67. WMMTC 92. **d** 95 **p** 96. NSM Tile Cross *Birm* 95-08; NSM Garretts Green 07-08; NSM Garretts Green and Tile Cross from 08; Chapl Heart of England NHS Foundn Trust from 08. *Wayside, 17 Chester Road, Birmingham B36 9DA* Tel 0121-747 2340

MacLACHLAN, Michael Ronald Frederic. b 39. Wycliffe Hall Ox 75. **d** 75 **p** 76. C Mansfield SS Pet and Paul *S'well* 75-78; P-in-c Newark Ch Ch 78-80; TV Newark w Hawton, Cotham and Shelton 80-86; P-in-c Sparkhill St Jo *Birm* 86-90; P-in-c Sparkbrook Em 86-90; V Sparkhill w Greet and Sparkbrook 90-92; RD Bordesley 90-92; P-in-c Kugluktuk Canada 92-97; R Stoke-next-Guildf 97-05; rtd 05; Hon C Drayton Bassett *Lich* from 05; Hon C Canwell from 09. *35 Moat Drive, Drayton Bassett, Tamworth B78 3UG* Tel (01827) 259730 E-mail michaelmaclachlan@btinternet.com

McLACHLAN, Canon Sheila Elizabeth. b 52. SRN73 Kent Univ MA89. Wycliffe Hall Ox 80. **dss** 83 **d** 87 **p** 94. Chapl Kent Univ 83-94; Dep Master Rutherford Coll 87-94; Dn-in-c Kingsnorth w Shadoxhurst 94; P-in-c Kingsnorth and Shadoxhurst from 94; AD Ashford 03-09; Hon Can Cant Cathl from 08. *The Rectory, Church Hill, Kingsnorth, Ashford TN23 3EG* Tel (01233) 620433 Mobile 07771-691164 E-mail sheila.mclachlan@tesco.uk

MacLAREN, Ms Clare. b 67. Edin Univ LLB88. Linc Th Coll BTh95. **d** 95 **p** 96. C Benchill *Man* 95-98; C Bilton *Ripon* 98-03; TV Seacroft 03-10; P-in-c Heaton St Martin *Bradf* from 10; P-in-c Heaton St Barn from 10. *The Vicarage, 130 Haworth Road, Bradford BD9 6LL* Tel (01274) 543004 E-mail claremaclaren@googlemail.com

MacLAREN, Duncan Arthur Spencer. b 69. Oriel Coll Ox BA90 MA96 K Coll Lon MA97 PhD03. Oak Hill Th Coll 92. **d** 94 **p** 95. C Ox St Clem 94-97; Chapl St Edm Hall Ox 97-04; Assoc R Edin St Paul and St Geo 04-09; R Edin St Jas from 09. *43/9 Rattray Drive, Edinburgh EH10 5TH* Tel 0131-447 4424 E-mail rector@stjamesleith.org *or* duncan@maclarens.org

MacLAREN (née ALEXANDER), Mrs Jane Louise. b 69. LMH Ox BA90 MA96. Oak Hill Th Coll BA03. **d** 95 **p** 96. C Ox St Clem 95-98; Chapl St Aug Sch 98-02; Chapl Ox Brookes Univ 02-04; Assoc R Edin St Paul and St Geo 04-09; NSM Edin St Jas from 09. *43/9 Rattray Drive, Edinburgh EH10 5TH* Tel 0131-447 4424

McLAREN, Mrs Jeanette Moira. b 59. **d** 95 **p** 96. C Dulwich St Clem w St Pet *S'wark* 95-99; P-in-c Brixton St Paul 99-05; P-in-c Brixton St Paul w St Sav 05-08; V Biggin Hill *Roch* from

08. *St Mark's Vicarage, 10 Church Road, Biggin Hill, Westerham TN16 3LB* Tel (01959) 540482 E-mail jmmclaren@tiscali.co.uk

McLAREN, Richard Francis. b 46. S'wark Ord Course 72. **d** 75 **p** 76. C Charlton St Luke w H Trin *S'wark* 75-78; C Kensington St Mary Abbots w St Geo *Lon* 78-81; Hon C St Marylebone w H Trin 82-96; P-in-c 96-97; Development Officer CUF 97; Chmn Art and Christianity Enquiry Trust from 97; Hon C Regent's Park St Mark from 97. *8 Gray's Court, 51-53 Gray's Inn Road, London WC1X 8PP* Tel and fax (020) 7404 5642 E-mail richard@mclaren7.fsnet.co.uk

McLAREN, Robert Ian. b 62. Bris Univ BSc84 St Jo Coll Dur BA87. Cranmer Hall Dur 85. **d** 88 **p** 89. C Birkenhead Ch Ch *Ches* 88-90; C Bebington 90-95; V Cheadle All Hallows 95-05; V Poynton from 05; RD Cheadle from 09. *The Vicarage, 41 London Road North, Poynton, Stockport SK12 1AF* Tel (01625) 850524 *or* 879277 E-mail vicar@orange.net

McLAREN-COOK, Paul Raymond. b 43. **d** 66 **p** 67. C Mt Lawley Australia 66-67; C Perth Cathl 67-69; R Carnarvon 69-72; V Seremban Malaysia 72-75; Warden Coll of Th 75-76; R Kensington 76-79; R Narrogin 79-84; P-in-c Berridge Australia 84-85; R Eugowra 85-86; P-in-c Berrigan 86-87; P-in-c Hay 87-88; P-in-c Yass 88; R Moruya 88-90; R Heywood 90-92; R Warracknabeal 92-95; Chapl Ballarat Base and St Jo of God Hosps 95-00; R Kansas City St Mary USA 00-03; R Stanway *Chelmsf* from 03. *The Rectory, Church Lane, Stanway, Colchester CO3 5LR* Tel (01206) 210407 E-mail mclarencook@btinternet.com

McLARNON, Mrs Sylvia Caroline Millicent. b 45. S Dios Minl Tr Scheme 92. **d** 95 **p** 96. NSM Burgess Hill St Andr *Chich* 95-99; C 99-09; rtd 09; Asst Chapl St Pet and St Jas Hospice N Chailey from 05. *23 The Warren, Burgess Hill RH15 0DU* Tel (01444) 233902

McLAUGHLIN, Adrian. **d** 07 **p** 08. C Bangor Abbey *D & D* from 07. *9 Pinehill Crescent, Bangor BT19 6FS* Tel (028) 9147 7182 E-mail revadrian@nireland.com

McLAUGHLIN, Hubert James Kenneth. b 45. CITC 85. **d** 88 **p** 89. NSM Donaghedy *D & R* 88-89; NSM Glendermott 89-98; P-in-c Inver w Mountcharles, Killaghtee and Killybegs 98-02; I 02-10; rtd 10. *9 Cadogan Park, Londonderry BT47 5QW* E-mail revadrian@nireland.com

McLAUGHLIN, Capt Michael Anthony. b 48. **d** 97 **p** 98. C Gt Chart *Cant* 97-01; C-in-c Parkwood CD from 01; rtd 11. *12 Medway Road, Gillingham ME7 1NH* Tel 07977-051649 (mobile) E-mail macl@blueyonder.co.uk

MACLAURIN, Ms Anne Fiona. b 62. St Andr Univ MA84. Ridley Hall Cam. **d** 99 **p** 00. C Crookes St Thos *Sheff* 99-04; TV 04-05; Miss P Philadelphia St Thos 05-10; V Cambridge St Barn *Ely* from 10. *The Vicarage, 57 St Barnabas Road, Cambridge CB1 2BX*

MACLAY, Christopher Willis. b 64. Stirling Univ BA88 Reading Univ MA92. Trin Coll Bris BA99. **d** 01 **p** 02. C Bedhampton *Portsm* 01-05; P-in-c Ashington, Washington and Wiston w Buncton *Chich* 05-11; R from 11. *The Rectory, Mill Lane, Ashington, Pulborough RH20 3BX* Tel (01903) 893878

McLAY, Robert James. b 49. Cant Univ (NZ) BA71. St Jo Coll Auckland. **d** 73 **p** 74. C Fendalton New Zealand 73-75; Hon C Yardley St Edburgha *Birm* 75-77; V Banks Peninsular New Zealand 77-80; V Marchwiel 80-83; V Huntly 83-89; Lect St Jo Coll 86-88; V Stokes Valley 89-93; V Pauatahanui 93-04; V Brooklyn from 04; Can Wellington Cathl 96-00. *13 Garfield Street, Brooklyn, Wellington 6021, New Zealand* Tel (0064) (4) 389 8003 *or* 389 3470 E-mail stmattes@actrix.gen.nz

MACLEAN, Canon Allan Murray. b 50. Edin Univ MA72. Cuddesdon Coll 72. **d** 76 **p** 77. Chapl St Mary's Cathl 76-81; Tutor Edin Univ 77-80; R Dunoon *Arg* 81-86; R Tighnabruaich 84-86; Provost St Jo Cathl Oban 86-99; R Oban St Jo 86-99; R Ardbrecknish 86-99; R Ardchattan 89-99; Hon Can St Jo Cathl Oban from 99; Perm to Offic *Mor* from 00. *5 North Charlotte Street, Edinburgh EH2 4HR* Tel 0131-225 8609

McLEAN, Bradley Halstead. b 57. McMaster Univ Ontario BSc Toronto Univ MDiv MTh PhD. **d** 83 **p** 84. C Dur St Giles 83-84; Canada from 84. *38 Tweedsmuir Road, Winnipeg MB R3P 1Z2, Canada*

McLEAN, The Ven Donald Stewart. b 48. TCD BA70. CITC 70. **d** 72 **p** 73. C Glendermott *D & R* 72-75; I Castledawson 75-87 and from 03; Dioc Dir of Ords 79-96; I Londonderry Ch Ch 87-03; Can Derry Cathl from 91; Adn Derry from 96. *12 Station Road, Castledawson, Magherafelt BT45 8AZ* Tel (028) 7946 8235 E-mail archdeacon@derry.anglican.org *or* dsmclean@iol.ie

McLEAN, Mrs Eileen Mary. b 44. City Univ BSc67. NOC 85. **d** 88 **p** 94. Par Dn Burley in Wharfedale *Bradf* 88-92; Par Dn Nottingham St Pet and St Jas *S'well* 92-94; C 94-02; AD Nottingham Cen 98-02; V Bamburgh *Newc* 02-08; V Ellingham 02-08; rtd 08. *3 The Green, Bewerley, Harrogate HG3 5HU* Tel (01423) 712467

MACLEAN, Kenneth John Forbes. b 31. St Deiniol's Hawarden 80. **d** 81 **p** 82. C Sedgley All SS *Lich* 81-85; V Shareshill 85-90; R Bicton, Montford w Shrawardine and Fitz 90-96; rtd 96; Perm to

Offic *Lich* from 99. *7 The Armoury, Wenlock Road, Shrewsbury SY2 6PA* Tel (01743) 243308

MacLEAN, Lawrence Alexander Charles. b 61. K Coll Lon BD84 AKC84. Chich Th Coll 86. **d** 88 **p** 89. C Cirencester *Glouc* 88-91; C Prestbury 91-96; Perm to Offic 01-02; Chapl Florence w Siena *Eur* 02-11; P-in-c Gt and Lt Torrington and Frithelstock *Ex* from 11. *The Vicarage, Calf Street, Torrington EX38 8EA* Tel (01805) 622166 E-mail lawrence.maclean@virgilio.it

McLEAN, Ms Margaret Anne. b 62. Birm Univ BA91 Heythrop Coll Lon MA99. Qu Coll Birm 88. **d** 91 **p** 94. Par Dn Bedford All SS *St Alb* 91-94; C 94; Chapl St Alb High Sch for Girls 94-98; Asst Soc Resp Officer *Derby* 98-99; Chapl Huddersfield Univ 99-02; P-in-c Scholes 02-09; P-in-c Cleckheaton St Luke and Whitechapel 02-09; P-in-c Battyeford from 09; Dioc Tr Officer (Reader Formation) from 09. *Battyeford Vicarage, 107A Stocksbank Road, Mirfield WF14 9QT* Tel (01924) 493277 Mobile 07777-673172 E-mail m.a.mclean@btinternet.com

McLEAN, Canon Michael Stuart. b 32. Dur Univ BA57. Cuddesdon Coll 57. **d** 59 **p** 60. C Camberwell St Giles *S'wark* 59-61; Lic to Offic *Nor* 61-68; R Marsham 68-74; R Burgh 68-74; RD Ingworth 70-74; P-in-c Nor St Pet Parmentergate w St Jo 74-75; TV 75-78; TR 78-86; Hon Can Nor Cathl 82-86; Can Res Nor Cathl 86-94; P-in-c Nor St Mary in the Marsh 87-94; Perm to Offic from 94; rtd 97. *8 Blickling Court, Recorder Road, Norwich NR1 1NW* Tel (01603) 630394

McLEAN, Peter. b 50. **d** 94 **p** 95. NSM Mold *St As* 94-02; Perm to Offic 02-03; P-in-c Bodedern w Llanfaethlu *Ban* 03-05; R Llangefni w Tregaean from 05; AD Malltraeth from 06. *Llety'r Llan, 50 Bro Ednyfed, Llangefni LL77 7WB* Tel (01248) 722667

McLEAN, Canon Robert Hedley. b 47. St Jo Coll Dur BA69. Ripon Hall Ox 69. **d** 71 **p** 72. C Redhill St Jo *S'wark* 71-74; C S Beddington St Mich 74-77; C-in-c Raynes Park H Cross CD 77; P-in-c Motspur Park 77-80; V 80-84; Hon C Tadworth 84-00; Asst RD Reigate 92-93; RD Reigate 93-00; R Morpeth *Newc* from 00; AD Morpeth 04-08; Chapl Northd Mental Health NHS Trust 00-09; Chapl Northumbria Healthcare NHS Trust 00-09; Hon Can Newc Cathl from 11. *The Rectory, Cottingwood Lane, Morpeth NE61 1ED* Tel (01670) 513517 E-mail robert@morpeth-rectory.fsnet.co.uk

McLEAN-REID, Robert. b 43. Oak Hill Th Coll 81. **d** 83 **p** 84. C Rainham *Chelmsf* 83-86; R Challoch w Newton Stewart *Glas* 86-87; R Aberdeen St Pet 87-90; P-in-c Aberdeen St Clem 89-90; V Easington Colliery *Dur* 90-95; rtd 95; Hon C Hampsthwaite and Killinghall and Birstwith *Ripon* 08-11. *14 Manor Orchards, Knaresborough HG5 0BW* E-mail mcleanreid2nj@btinternet.com

MacLEAY, Angus Murdo. b 59. Univ Coll Ox BA81 MA86 Man Univ MPhil92 Solicitor 83. Wycliffe Hall Ox 85. **d** 88 **p** 89. C Rusholme H Trin *Man* 88-92; V Houghton *Carl* 92-01; R Sevenoaks St Nic *Roch* from 01. *The Rectory, Rectory Lane, Sevenoaks TN13 1JA* Tel (01732) 740340 Fax 742810 E-mail angus.macleay@diocese-rochester.org

MacLEOD, Alan Roderick Hugh (Roddie). b 33. St Edm Hall Ox BA56 MA61 Ox Univ DipEd62. Wycliffe Hall Ox 56. **d** 58 **p** 59. C Bognor St Jo *Chich* 58-61; Chapl Wadh Coll Ox 62; Hd of RE Picardy Boys' Sch Erith 62-68; C Erith St Jo *Roch* 63-69; Dean Lonsdale Coll Lanc Univ 70-72; Hd of RE K Edw VI Sch Totnes 72-73; Dir of Resources St Helier Boys' Sch Jersey 73-84; V Shipton Bellinger *Win* 84-02; rtd 02; Perm to Offic *Win* from 02. *Pippins Toft, Lashmar's Corner, East Preston, Littlehampton BN16 1EZ* Tel (01903) 783523

McLEOD, David Leo Roderick. b 71. Westmr Coll Ox BA92 DipCOT96. **d** 05 **p** 06. OLM Coddenham w Gosbeck and Hemingstone w Henley *St E* 05-10; OLM Crowfield w Stonham Aspal and Mickfield 05-10; Chapl Team Co-ord Univ Campus Suffolk 07-10; Chapl Team Co-ord Suffolk New Coll 07-10; C Wokingham St Sebastian *Ox* from 10. *St Sebastian's Lodge, Nine Mile Ride, Wokingham RG40 3AT* Tel 07906-880820 (mobile) E-mail davidmcleod01@btinternet.com

McLEOD, Everton William. b 57. Oak Hill Th Coll 89. **d** 91 **p** 92. C New Ferry *Ches* 91-93; C Moreton 93-98; Chapl R Liv Univ Hosp NHS Trust 98-01; R Weston-super-Mare St Nic w St Barn *B & W* 01-11; V Trentham *Lich* from 11; V Hanford from 11. *The Vicarage, Trentham Park, Stoke-on-Trent ST4 8AE* Tel (01782) 658194 E-mail mcleod@xalt.co.uk

MACLEOD, John Bain Maclennan. b 50. Aber Univ LLB86 Solicitor 89. TISEC 06. **d** 06. NSM Hamilton *Glas* from 06. *Greenrig Barn, Greenrig Road, Lesmahagow, Lanark ML11 9QB* Tel (01555) 664866 E-mail macleod.greenrig@btinternet.com

MacLEOD, John Malcolm (Jay). b 61. Harvard Univ AB84 Pemb Coll Ox BA87 MA91. Linc Th Coll MDiv93. **d** 93 **p** 94. C Chesterfield St Aug *Derby* 93-96; C Stalybridge St Paul *Ches* 96-98; P-in-c Micklehurst 98-03; P-in-c Bedford All SS *St Alb* from 03; Dioc Interfaith Adv from 03. *All Saints' Vicarage, 1 Cutcliffe Place, Bedford MK40 4DF* Tel (01234) 266945 E-mail macasher@dial.pipex.com

McLEOD, Neil Raymond. b 61. Trin Coll Bris 06. **d** 08 **p** 09. C N w S Wootton *Nor* from 08. *Ambleside, 34 Castle Rising Road, South Wootton, King's Lynn PE30 3JB* Tel (01553) 684064

McLEOD, Paul Douglas. b 66. Cuddesdon Coll BTh95. **d** 98 **p** 99. C Morpeth *Newc* 98-02; V Newbiggin Hall 02-10; R Silverstone and Abthorpe w Slapton etc *Pet* from 10; RD Towcester from 11. *The Vicarage, 24A High Street, Silverstone, Towcester NN12 8US* Tel (01327) 858101 Mobile 07780-834099 E-mail revpaulmcleod@btinternet.com

MacLEOD, Roderick. *See* MacLEOD, Alan Roderick Hugh

McLEOD, Canon Ronald. b 17. Lon Univ BA39 BA50 BD71 Ex Univ BA56 Man Univ MA59 Ex Univ MPhil01. Bps' Coll Cheshunt 39. **d** 41 **p** 42. C Plymouth St Pet *Ex* 41-44; Chapl RAF 44-69; Prin RAF Chapl Sch and Asst Chapl-in-Chief RAF 69-73; QHC 72-73; R Itchen Abbas cum Avington *Win* 73-91; Hon Can Win Cathl 84-91; rtd 91; Perm to Offic *Ex* 92-09. *Melfort, High Wall, Sticklepath, Barnstaple EX31 2DP* Tel (01271) 343636

McLEOD, Ms Susan Margaret. b 48. SEN69 Sheff Poly CQSW89. NOC 92. **d** 95 **p** 96. NSM Charlesworth and Dinting Vale *Derby* 95-02; Chapl Asst S Man Univ Hosps NHS Trust 97-02. *Address temp unknown*

MacLEOD, Talisker Isobel. b 81. St Andr Univ MA03. Ripon Coll Cuddesdon BTh11. **d** 11. C Hove All SS *Chich* from 11. *The Parsonage, Blatchington Road, Hove BN3 3TA* Tel (01273) 778938 E-mail revd@alathea.org.uk

MacLEOD-MILLER, The Ven Peter Norman. b 66. **d** 91 **p** 91. C Cardiff Australia 91-92; C Hillston 92-94; C Fitzroy 95-97; Perm to Offic Melbourne 97-01; P-in-c Risby w Gt and Lt Saxham *St E* 02-04; V Barrow 05-10; Min Can St E Cathl 05-10; R Albury and Adn Hume Australia from 10. *St Matthew's Rectory, PO Box 682, Albury NSW 2640, Australia* Tel (0061) (2) 6021 3022 *or* 6041 1916

McLOUGHLIN, Ian Livingstone. b 38. CEng MICE64. Carl Dioc Tr Course 78. **d** 83 **p** 84. NSM Stanwix *Carl* 83-88; C Barrow St Geo w St Luke 88-90; R Kirkby Thore w Temple Sowerby and Newbiggin 90-01; rtd 01; Perm to Offic *Bradf* and *Carl* from 01. *29 Wordsworth Drive, Kendal LA9 7JW*

McLOUGHLIN, John Robert. b 70. QUB BEng92 Open Univ MSc02. CITC BTh09. **d** 09 **p** 10. C Arm St Mark from 09. *6 Ashley Avenue, Armagh BT60 1HD* Tel (028) 3752 6180 *or* 3752 3197 Mobile 07515-353023 E-mail johnnymcloughlin@gmail.com

McLUCKIE, John Mark. b 67. St Andr Univ BD89. Edin Th Coll MTh91. **d** 91 **p** 92. C Perth St Ninian *St And* 91-94; Chapl K Coll Cam 94-96; TV Glas E End 96-00; Assoc R Edin St Jo 00-03; Perm to Offic 08-10; Chapl Asst R Marsden NHS Foundn Trust from 10. *Royal Marsden NHS Foundation Trust, Fulham Road, London SW3 6JJ* Tel (020) 7352 8171 E-mail john.mcluckie@hotmail.co.uk

MACLUSKIE, Mrs Linda. b 55. Lanc Univ MA99. CBDTI 95. **d** 98 **p** 99. NSM Halton w Aughton *Blackb* 98-02; NSM Bolton-le-Sands 02-10; P-in-c Sandylands 10-11; V from 11. *St John's Vicarage, 2 St John's Avenue, Morecambe LA3 1EU* Tel (01524) 411039 Mobile 07827-923222 E-mail linda.macluskie@virgin.net

McMAHON, George Ian Robertson. b 23. Monmouth Coll Illinois BA64 Univ of N Carolina BA44 MA49 Ox Univ MLitt61 Birm Univ PhD73. Gen Th Sem NY STB52. **d** 52 **p** 53. P-in-c Roxboro, Yanceyville and Milton USA 52-57; Perm to Offic *Ox* 57-64; Prin Lect Homerton Coll Cam 65-88; P-in-c Cambridge St Clem *Ely* 89-04; Perm to Offic from 04. *44 Grantchester Road, Cambridge CB3 9ED* Tel (01223) 350988

McMAHON, Stephen. b 66. Newc Univ BSc87 MSc89 Leeds Univ BA03 CEng97 MBES97. Coll of Resurr Mirfield 01. **d** 04 **p** 04. C Lancaster St Mary w St John and St Anne *Blackb* 03-07; P-in-c Lowther and Askham and Clifton and Brougham *Carl* 07-10; P-in-c Kirkby Thore w Temple Sowerby and Newbiggin 07-10; Chapl Rossall Sch Fleetwood 10; NSM Lancaster St Mary w St John and St Anne *Blackb* from 10. *St David's Vicarage, 211 Broadway, Fleetwood FY7 8AZ* Tel (01253) 770405 E-mail steve1345.mcmahon@virgin.net

McMANN, Duncan. b 34. Jes Coll Ox BA55 MA60. Clifton Th Coll 55. **d** 58 **p** 59. C Newburn *Newc* 58-60; C Bishopwearmouth St Gabr *Dur* 60-62; N Area Sec BCMS 62-66; Midl and E Anglia Area Sec 66-92; Support Co-ord 84-92; Lic to Offic *Man* 62-66 and *Cov* 66-92; P-in-c Awsworth w Cossall *S'well* 92-99; Chapl Notts Constabulary 93-99; rtd 99; Perm to Offic *Nor* from 00. *7 Evans Drive, Lowestoft NR32 2RX* Tel (01502) 531337

McMANN, Canon Judith. b 46. Hull Univ BTh96. EMMTC MA98. **d** 98 **p** 99. NSM Gt Grimsby St Mary and St Jas *Linc* 98-08; NSM Caistor Gp from 08; Can and Preb Linc Cathl from 05. *23 Grasby Crescent, Grimsby DN37 9HE* Tel (01472) 887523 E-mail jmcmann@btopenworld.com

McMANNERS, John Roland. b 46. Liv Univ LLB68. Cranmer Hall Dur 99. **d** 01 **p** 02. C Monkwearmouth *Dur* 01-05; P-in-c Bishopwearmouth St Gabr from 05. *The Vicarage, St Gabriel's Avenue, Sunderland SR4 7TF* Tel 0191-567 5200

McMANUS, James Robert. b 33. Wycliffe Hall Ox 56. **d** 58 **p** 59. C Leic H Trin 58-60; C Aylestone 60-63; India 66-79; V Oldham St Barn *Man* 79-83; Asst Regional Sec CMS 83-85; V Wolverhampton St Matt *Lich* 85-93; V Lapley w Wheaton Aston

93-99; P-in-c Blymhill w Weston-under-Lizard 93-99; rtd 99; Perm to Offic *Lich* from 99. *Delamere, McBean Road, Wolverhampton WV6 0JQ* Tel (01902) 833436 Fax 834170 E-mail jimvicar@aol.com
McMANUS-THOMPSON, Elizabeth Gray. See THOMPSON, Elizabeth Gray McManus
McMASTER, James Alexander. b 43. **d** 69 **p** 70. C Dundonald *D & D* 69-73; C Antrim All SS *Conn* 73-78; I Tempo and Clabby *Clogh* 78-83; I Knocknamuckley *D & D* 83-95; I Carrickfergus *Conn* 95-08; rtd 08. *78 Murray Wood, Waringstown, Craigavon BT66 7SX* Tel (028) 3882 0741
MacMASTER, Mrs Norma. QUB BA DipEd McGill Univ Montreal MEd. **d** 04 **p** 05. NSM Dublin St Geo and St Thos *D & G* 04-07; rtd 07. *1 The Orchard, Tennis Court Lane, Skerries, Co Dublin, Republic of Ireland* Tel (00353) (1) 849 1387 E-mail nmacmaster@eircom.net
McMASTER, Richard Ian. b 32. Edin Th Coll 57. **d** 60 **p** 61. C Carl H Trin 60-63; Chapl St Andr Tr Coll Korogwe Tanzania 63-66; V Broughton Moor 66-69; V Burnley St Steph *Blackb* 69-77; V New Longton 77-89; P-in-c Woodhall Spa and Kirkstead *Linc* 89-91; P-in-c Langton w Woodhall 89-91; P-in-c Bucknall w Tupholme 89-91; P-in-c Horsington w Stixwould 89-91; R Woodhall Spa Gp 92-97; rtd 97; Perm to Offic *Birm* from 97. *18 Marsden Close, Solihull B92 7JR* Tel 0121-707 6208 E-mail bettyandianmc@aol.com
McMASTER, William Keith. b 45. TCD. **d** 82 **p** 84. C Portadown St Columba *Arm* 82-84; C Erdington St Barn *Birm* 84-87; TV Shirley 87-00; TV Salter Street and Shirley 00-02; rtd 02. *1 Hockley Terrace, Scava Road, Banbridge BT32 3QB* Tel (028) 4062 2582
MACMATH, Terence Handley. See HANDLEY MACMATH, Terence
McMICHAEL, Andrew Hamilton. b 48. Univ of Wales (Ban) BA77. Chich Th Coll 87. **d** 89 **p** 90. C Chorley St Geo *Blackb* 89-92; C Burnley St Andr w St Marg 92-94; Chapl Burnley Health Care NHS Trust 92-94; R Eccleston *Blackb* 94-99; V Lt Marsden w Nelson St Mary 99-04; P-in-c Tain, Lochinver and Invergordon St Ninian *Mor* 04-07; P-in-c Harrington *Carl* 07-09; R Port Glas from 09. *St Mary's Rectory, Bardrainney Avenue, Port Glasgow PA14 6HB* E-mail andrew.mcmichael@tesco.net
MacMILLAN, Douglas Michael. b 41. St Thos Hosp Lon MB, BS66 FRCS70 FTCL82 AMusLCM80 FLCM83. Guildf Dioc Min Course 96. **d** 00. NSM Guildf Cathl 00-02; Perm to Offic 02-04; NSM E and W Clandon from 04. *Rivendell, 50 Speedwell Close, Guildford GU4 7HE* Tel (01483) 533019
✠**McMULLAN, The Rt Revd Gordon.** b 34. ACIS57 QUB BSc61 PhD71 TCD MPhil90 Univ of the South (USA) DMin95. Ridley Hall Cam 61. **d** 62 **p** 63 **c** 80. C Ballymacarrett St Patr *D & D* 62-67; Cen Adv on Chr Stewardship to Ch of Ireland 67-70; C Knock 70-71; I 76-80; I Belfast St Brendan 71-76; Offg Chapl RAF 71-78; Bp's Dom Chapl *D & D* 73-78; Adn Down 79-80; Bp Clogh 80-86; Bp D & D 86-97; rtd 97. *26 Wellington Park, Bangor BT20 4PJ* Tel (028) 9146 0821
McMULLEN, Philip Kenneth. b 55. RMN80. St Mich Coll Llan 93. **d** 95 **p** 96. C Coity w Nolton *Llan* 95-98; V Fleur-de-Lis *Mon* 98-04. *29 Clos Coed Bach, Blackwood NP12 1GT* Tel (01495) 220210
McMULLEN, Ronald Norman. b 36. TCD BA61 MA66 California Inst of Integral Studies MA92. Ridley Hall Cam 61. **d** 63 **p** 64. C Fulham St Mary N End *Lon* 63-67; C Cambridge St Sepulchre *Ely* 67-70; C Everton St Ambrose w St Tim *Liv* 70-73; Community Work Course & Research Asst York Univ 73-75; P-in-c Heanor *Derby* 75-79; V 79-88; RD Heanor 76-83; USA 88-93; rtd 98. *Apple Tree Cottage, 38A Main Street, Lowick, Berwick-upon-Tweed TD15 2UA* Tel and fax (01289) 388301
McMULLON, Andrew Brian. b 56. Sheff Univ BSc. St Jo Coll Nottm. **d** 83 **p** 84. C Stainforth *Sheff* 83-86; V Blackb Redeemer 86-90; Chapl RAF from 90. *Chaplaincy Services, Valiant Block, HQ Air Command, RAF High Wycombe HP14 4UE* Tel (01494) 496800 Fax 496343
McMUNN, Lee James. b 78. LSE BSc99. Wycliffe Hall Ox BA04. **d** 05 **p** 06. C Hull St Jo Newland *York* from 05. *32 Riversdale Road, Hull HU6 7HA* Tel (01482) 802611 Mobile 07957-898884 E-mail lee@stjohnnewland.org.uk
McMURRAY, Gary. b 81. QUB BA02. CITC BTh08. **d** 08 **p** 09. C Dundonald *D & D* 08-11; I Aghavea *Clogh* from 11. *The Rectory, Lurgan, Brookeborough, Enniskillen BT94 4EE* Tel (028) 8953 1210 E-mail garymcmurray@gmail.com
McMURRAY, Matthew Paul. b 79. Westcott Ho Cam 08. **d** 11. C Hawes Side and Marton Moss *Blackb* from 11. *St Nicholas' House, 189 Common Edge Road, Blackpool FY4 5DJ* Tel (01253) 694208 E-mail frmatthew@cantab.net
McNAB (née LUMMIS), Mrs Elizabeth Howieson. b 44. Lon Univ BDS68 LDS68. St Jo Coll Nottm 85. **d** 88 **p** 95. NSM Lerwick *Ab* from 88; NSM Burravoe from 88. *Waters Edge, Bridge of Walls, Shetland ZE2 9NP* Tel (01595) 809441

MCNAIR SCOTT, Benjamin Guthrie. b 76. K Coll Lon BA98 MA05. Ridley Hall Cam 05. **d** 07 **p** 08. NSM Guildf Ch Ch w St Martha-on-the-Hill from 07. *3 Newlands Crescent, Guildford GU1 3JS* Tel (01483) 455645 Mobile 07968-617084 E-mail jbenjaming@lycos.co.uk
McNAMARA, Barbara. See SMITH, Mrs Barbara Mary
McNAMARA, Michael Ian. b 59. Van Mildert Coll Dur BA81. Ridley Hall Cam 83. **d** 85 **p** 86. C Bedford Ch Ch *St Alb* 85-89; BCMS Tanzania 89-92; TV Bolton St Paul w Em *Man* 93-97; C Galleywood Common *Chelmsf* 97-03; R Elmswell *St E* from 03; RD Lavenham from 11. *The Rectory, Church Road, Elmswell, Bury St Edmunds IP30 9DY* Tel (01359) 240512 E-mail mwanza@lineone.net
McNAUGHTAN-OWEN, James Thomas (Tom). b 48. Liv Univ MA00. Linc Th Coll 77. **d** 80 **p** 81. C Palmers Green St Jo *Lon* 80-84; C Timperley *Ches* 84-87; C Bramhall 87-92; V Latchford St Jas from 92; RD Gt Budworth 96-03. *St James's Vicarage, Manx Road, Warrington WA4 6AJ* Tel (01925) 631893
MACNAUGHTON, Mrs Diana. b 54. St Hugh's Coll Ox BA76 MA90 Dur Univ PGCE78. NEOC 95. **d** 98 **p** 99. NSM Gosforth All SS *Newc* 98-01; C Willington 01-04; Chapl Team Ldr Northumbria Healthcare NHS Trust from 04. *The Rectory, North Terrace, Wallsend NE28 6PY* Tel 0191-234 0371 Mobile 07950-627799 E-mail dmacnaughton@btinternet.com
MACNAUGHTON, James Alastair. b 54. St Jo Coll Ox BA78 MA82 Fitzw Coll Cam BA80. Ridley Hall Cam 78. **d** 81 **p** 82. C Rounds Green *Birm* 81-85; TV Bestwood Park *S'well* 85-86; TV Bestwood 86-90; V Amble *Newc* 90-97; TR Cramlington 97-07; Jt Newc/Dur Development Officer for Educn for Discipleship from 07. *The Rectory, North Terrace, Wallsend NE28 6PY* Tel 0191-234 0371 E-mail macnaughton@btinternet.com
McNAUGHTON, John. b 29. St Chad's Coll Dur. **d** 54 **p** 55. C Thorney Close CD *Dur* 54-58; C-in-c E Herrington St Chad CD 58-62; PC E Herrington 62-66; CF 66-94; V Hutton Cranswick w Skerne, Watton and Beswick *York* 94-99; rtd 99; Perm to Offic *York* from 99. *47 Southgate, Cranswick, Driffield YO25 9QX* Tel (01377) 270869
MACNAUGHTON, Mrs Pamela Jean. Ox Min Course. **d** 08 **p** 09. NSM Acaster Malbis *York* from 08; NSM Appleton Roebuck w Acaster Selby from 08; NSM Bishopthorpe from 08. *64 Copmanthorpe Lane, Bishopthorpe, York YO23 2RS* Tel (01904) 700141 E-mail workspacepjm@aol.com
MACNAUGHTON, William Malcolm. b 57. Qu Coll Cam BA80. Ridley Hall Cam 79. **d** 81 **p** 82. C Haughton le Skerne *Dur* 81-85; P-in-c Newton Hall 85-90; TV Shoreditch St Leon and Hoxton St Jo *Lon* 90-00; AD Hackney 94-99; V Hoxton St Jo w Ch Ch 00-02; R Hambleden Valley *Ox* 02-07; AD Wycombe 05-07; Chief of Staff to Abp York from 07. *The Palace, Bishopthorpe, York YO23 2GE* Tel (01904) 707021 Fax 709204 E-mail malcolm.macnaughton@archbishopofyork.org
McNEE, Canon William Creighton. Ulster Univ MA NUU MA FCIPD. **d** 82 **p** 83. C Larne and Inver *Conn* 82-84; I Donagheady *D & R* 84-91; I Kilwaughter w Cairncastle and Craigy Hill *Conn* 91-93; I Ardstraw w Baronscourt, Badoney Lower etc *D & R* 93-04; P-in-c Londonderry Ch Ch 04-05; I 05-09; I Londonderry Ch Ch, Culmore, Muff and Belmont 08-09; Bp's Dom Chapl 96-07; Can Derry Cathl 00-09; rtd 09. *72 Brookview Glen, Eglinton, Londonderry BT47 3GW* E-mail billmcnee@usa.net
MACNEICE, Alan Donor. b 34. TCD Div Sch 62. **d** 64 **p** 65. C Ballymoney w Finvoy and Rasharkin *Conn* 64-67; R Christiana Jamaica 67-70; C Winchmore Hill H Trin *Lon* 71-76; C Harringay St Paul 76-77; C Kensington St Barn 77-78; P-in-c 78-79; USA 83-06; rtd 99. *29Eo, Street 178, Commond Choychom, nas Distrib Daun Penh, Phnom Penh, Cambodia* Tel (00855) (23) 986064 E-mail donor@online.com.kh
McNEICE, Kathleen Mary. SEITE. **d** 07 **p** 08. NSM Folkestone Trin *Cant* from 07. *19 Beachborough Road, Folkestone CT19 4AA* Tel (01303) 278791
McNEIL, Mrs Ann. b 41. **d** 89 **p** 94. NSM Henfield w Shermanbury and Woodmancote *Chich* 89-99; Perm to Offic from 00. *6 The Daisy Croft, Henfield BN5 9LH* Tel (01273) 492606 E-mail annmcneil@onetel.com
McNEILE, Donald Hugh. b 30. Trin Coll Cam BA53. Coll of Resurr Mirfield 53. **d** 55 **p** 56. C Wigan All SS *Liv* 55-57; C W Derby Gd Shep 57-61; rtd 95. *Monks Barn, North Hinksey Village, Oxford OX2 0NA* Tel (01865) 245473
MACNEILL, Nicholas Terence. b 62. St Steph Ho Ox BTh93. **d** 93 **p** 94. C Ex St Thos and Em 93-97; TV 97-98; V Cople, Moggerhanger and Willington *St Alb* 98-03; R Toddington and Chalgrave 03-06; rtd 07. *20 Black Path, Polegate BN26 5AP* Tel (01323) 485399 E-mail nick.macneill@ntlworld.com
McNELLY, Mrs Nicola. b 62. Cranmer Hall Dur 07. **d** 09. C Edin St Mary from 09. *32 Manor Place, Edinburgh EH3 7EB* Tel 0131-220 2375 Mobile 07825-440580 E-mail nicki.mcnelly@googlemail.com
McNICOL, Andrew Norman. b 69. Westmr Coll of Educn CertEd69 Open Univ BA79 Westmr Coll Ox MA90. Westcott Ho Cam 92. **d** 92 **p** 93. C Whitstable *Cant* 92-95; V Ferring *Chich* 95-00; P-in-c Willesborough *Cant* 00-06; P-in-c Tunstall w

McNIVEN

Rodmersham 06-11; R Tunstall and Bredgar from 11. *The Rectory, Tunstall, Sittingbourne ME9 8DU* Tel (01795) 423907 E-mail akmcnicol@tesco.net

McNIVEN, Mrs Betty. b 47. Lanc Univ BA68. NOC 83. **dss** 86 **d** 87 **p** 94. Baguley *Man* 86-87; Hon Par Dn 87-88; Par Dn Newton Heath All SS 88-91; Par Dn E Farnworth and Kearsley 91-94; TV 94-95; P-in-c Spotland 95-02; Hon Can Man Cathl 00-02; TV Cwm Gwendraeth *St D* 02-06; rtd 07; P-in-c Llansteffan and Llan-y-bri etc *St D* 07-08. *105 Homegower House, St Helens Road, Swansea SA1 4DN* Tel (01792) 469995 E-mail betty.mcniven@talk21.com

MACONACHIE, Charles Leslie. b 27. TCD BA71 MA74 MDiv85 PhD90. Em Coll Saskatoon 47. **d** 50 **p** 51. C Clooney *D & R* 50-54; P-in-c Lower Tamlaght O'Crilly 54-61; Chapl Newsham Gen Hosp Liv 61-63; Chapl RAF 63-67; C Londonderry Ch Ch *D & R* 69-75; I Belmont 75-78; Warden for Min of Healing 75-96; I Culmore w Muff and Belmont 78-96; Warden Irish Internat Order of St Luke Physician 82-96; Can Derry Cathl 85-96; rtd 96; Chmn Ch's Min of Healing from 96. *3 Broomhill Court, Waterside, Londonderry BT47 6WP* Tel (028) 7134 8942

MACOURT, William Albany. b 19. TCD BA40 MA46. CITC 41. **d** 42 **p** 43. C Ballymena *Conn* 42-46; C Belf Cathl 46-48; I Duneane w Ballyscullion *Conn* 48-51; I Belfast St Mark 51-64; I Ballymacarrett St Patr *D & D* 64-69; Preb Swords St Patr Cathl Dublin 75-89; Adn Down *D & D* 80-89; Chan Belf Cathl 85-89; rtd 89; Dioc Info Officer *D & D* 89-97. *19 Abbey Court, Abbey Gardens, Belfast BT5 7JE* Tel (028) 9048 2041

McPHATE, The Very Revd Gordon Ferguson. b 50. Aber Univ MB, ChB74 Fitzw Coll Cam BA77 MA81 MD88 Surrey Univ MSc86 Edin Univ MTh94 FRCPEd98. Westcott Ho Cam 75. **d** 78 **p** 79. NSM Sanderstead All SS *S'wark* 78-81; Hon PV S'wark Cathl 81-86; Lect Lon Univ 81-86; Chapl St Andr Univ 86-02; Lect 86-93; Sen Lect 93-02; Dean Ches from 02. *The Deanery, 7 Abbey Street, Chester CH1 2JF* Tel (01244) 500956 or 500971 Fax 341110 E-mail dean@chestercathedral.com

MacPHEE, Canon Roger Hunter. b 43. Leeds Univ BSc65. EAMTC. **d** 86 **p** 87. NSM Trunch *Nor* from 86; Dioc NSM Officer from 97; Hon Can Nor Cathl from 03. *8 Lawn Close, Knapton, North Walsham NR28 0SD* Tel (01263) 720045 E-mail rmacphee4@aol.com

McPHERSON, Andrew Lindsay. b 58. St Jo Coll Dur BA79 MCIPD84. **d** 88 **p** 89. C Bitterne *Win* 88-92; V Weston 92-99; V Holdenhurst and Iford from 99; P-in-c Southbourne St Chris from 07; AD Bournemouth from 08. *The Vicarage, 53A Holdenhurst Avenue, Bournemouth BH7 6RB* Tel (01202) 425978 E-mail parish.office@stsaviours.f2s.com

MACPHERSON, Canon Anthony Stuart. b 56. Qu Coll Birm 77. **d** 80 **p** 81. C Morley St Pet w Churwell *Wakef* 80-84; C Penistone 84-85; P-in-c Thurlstone 85-86; TV Penistone and Thurlstone 86-88; V Grimethorpe 88-95; P-in-c Westgate Common 95-96; V 96-07; P-in-c Horbury Junction 02-07; RD Wakef 99-07; Hon Can Wakef Cathl 06-07; Can Missr from 07. *14 Belgravia Road, Wakefield WF1 3JP* Tel (01924) 275274 Mobile 07780-990354 Fax 275311 E-mail tony.macpherson@wakefield.anglican.org

MACPHERSON, Archibald McQuarrie. b 27. Edin Th Coll 50. **d** 52 **p** 53. Asst Chapl St Andr Cathl 52-55; Prec 55-56; P-in-c Airdrie *Glas* 56-63; R Dumbarton 63-92; rtd 92. *29 Bramblehedge Path, Alexandria G83 8PH* Tel (01389) 753981

MACPHERSON, Miss Catherine Annunciata. b 86. Univ of Wales (Lamp) BA07 Em Coll Cam MPhil10. Westcott Ho Cam 08. **d** 10 **p** 11. C Mirfield *Wakef* from 10. *4 Hopton Hall Lane, Mirfield WF14 8EL* Tel (01924) 503877 Mobile 07961-699486 E-mail catherine.a.macpherson@gmail.com

MacPHERSON, David Alan John. b 42. Lon Univ BD75 Open Univ BA83 Hatf Poly MSc89. Clifton Th Coll 69 Trin Coll Bris 72. **d** 72 **p** 73. C Drypool St Columba w St Andr and St Pet *York* 72-76; Asst Chapl HM Pris Hull 72-76; P-in-c Bessingby and Carnaby *York* 76-78; Chapl RAF 78-83; P-in-c Chedgrave w Hardley and Langley *Nor* 83-87; R 87-97; Chapl Langley Sch Nor 83-97; P-in-c Brington w Whilton and Norton *Pet* 97-98; R Brington w Whilton and Norton etc 98-02; rtd 02; Perm to Offic *Pet* from 02; Chapl to Retired Clergy and Clergy Widows' Officer from 10. *24 Coldstream Close, Daventry NN11 9HL* Tel (01327) 704500 E-mail dmacp@compuserve.com

MACPHERSON, Ewan Alexander. b 43. Toronto Univ BA74. Wycliffe Coll Toronto MDiv78. **d** 78 **p** 79. C Toronto St Cuth 78-81; C Toronto Apostles 81-86; V Priddy and Westbury sub Mendip w Easton *B & W* 86-06; rtd 06. *20 Tuddington Gardens, Wells BA5 2EJ* Tel (01749) 675876

MACPHERSON, John. b 28. Lon Univ BSc50 Ex Univ DipEd51 Univ of W Indies HDipEd65. St Alb Minl Tr Scheme 82. **d** 89 **p** 90. NSM Gt Berkhamsted *St Alb* 89-95; Perm to Offic from 00. *Little Tanglewood, Luton Road, Markyate, St Albans AL3 8PZ* Tel (01582) 841219

MACPHERSON, Peter Sinclair. b 44. Lich Th Coll 68. **d** 71 **p** 72. C Honiton, Gittisham and Combe Raleigh *Ex* 71-72; C Bideford 72-74; C Devonport St Mark Ford 74-75; V Thorncombe *Sarum*

75-79; TV Dorchester 79-85; Chapl Jersey Gp of Hosps 85-90; Chapl Derriford Hosp Plymouth 90-98; rtd 98; Perm to Offic *Ex* 04-09. *Pump Cottage, 1 Rosemary Lane, Musbury, Axminster EX13 6AT* Tel (01297) 552524

McQUILLEN, Brian Anthony. b 45. Ripon Hall Ox 73. **d** 75 **p** 76. C Northfield *Birm* 75-78; C Sutton Coldfield H Trin 78-80; V Bearwood 80-89; V Glouc St Geo w Whaddon 89-96; R St Martin w Looe *Truro* 96-11; RD W Wivelshire 98-03 and 06-08; rtd 11. *7 Bonython Drive, Grampound, Truro TR2 4RL* Tel (01726) 883184 E-mail revmcq.looe@btinternet.com

McQUILLEN-WRIGHT, Christopher Charles. b 71. Kent Univ BA92. Westcott Ho Cam 92. **d** 95 **p** 96. C Hayle, St Erth and Phillack w Gwithian and Gwinear *Truro* 95-96; C Godrevy 96-99; TV Bodmin w Lanhydrock and Lanivet 99-02; P-in-c St Columb Minor and St Colan from 02. *The Vicarage, Parkenbutts, Newquay TR7 3HE* Tel (01637) 873496 *or* 877165

MACRAE, Charles. b 27. RD71. Edin Univ BDS62. S Dios Minl Tr Scheme 88. **d** 91 **p** 92. NSM Heene *Chich* 91-94; NSM Portsea St Alb *Portsm* 94-96; OGS from 96; Perm to Offic *Chich* from 96. *64 Stone Lane, Worthing BN13 2BQ* Tel (01903) 691660

McRAE, Keith Alban. b 44. S'wark Ord Course 68. **d** 73 **p** 74. NSM Crawley *Chich* 73-78; NSM Ifield 78-90. *52 Downsview, Small Dole, Henfield BN5 9YB*

MacRAE, Mrs Rosalind Phyllis. b 41. Sarum & Wells Th Coll 81. **dss** 84 **d** 87 **p** 94. Feltham *Lon* 84-87; Asst Chapl R Cornwall Hosps Trust 87-88; Chapl Mt Edgcumbe Hospice 88-92; Chapl St Austell Hosp 88-92; Chapl Penrice Hosp St Austell 88-92; NSM St Austell *Truro* 88-92; Chapl R Cornwall Hosps Trust 92-95; rtd 95. *16 Rosparc, Probus, Truro TR2 4TJ*

McREYNOLDS, Canon Kenneth Anthony. b 48. **d** 83 **p** 84. C Ballymena w Ballyclug *Conn* 83-86; I Rathcoole 86-90; I Lambeg from 90; Can Conn Cathl from 08. *Lambeg Rectory, 58 Belfast Road, Lisburn BT27 4AT* Tel and fax (028) 9266 3872 E-mail kenmcreynolds@btinternet.com

MacROBERT, Iain. b 49. Wolv Univ BA80 PGCE81 Birm Univ MA85 PhD89. **d** 00 **p** 00. NSM S Queensferry *Edin* from 00. *21 Long Crook, South Queensferry EH30 9XR* Tel and fax 0131-319 1558 *or* tel 244 0651 E-mail iain0macrobert@aol.com

McROBERTS, Ms Tracey. b 68. QUB BTh99 PGCE00 Dub City Univ MA09. CITC 08. **d** 09 **p** 10. C Belfast St Thos *Conn* from 09; Bp's Dom Chapl from 11. *23 Lower Courtyard, Belfast BT7 3LH* Tel (028) 9064 8990 Mobile 07718-490040 E-mail tracey.mcroberts@btinternet.com

McROSTIE, Ms Lyn. b 50. Canberra Univ BA77 Portsm Univ MA03 MIInfSc81. STETS 95. **d** 98 **p** 99. C Portsea St Cuth *Portsm* 98-02; P-in-c Shadwell St Paul w Ratcliffe St Jas *Lon* 02-04; Course Ldr NTMTC 04-06; P-in-c Northwood *Portsm* 06-07; R from 07; P-in-c Gurnard 06-07; V from 07; P-in-c Cowes St Faith 06-07; V from 07. *The Rectory, Chawton Lane, Cowes PO31 8PR* Tel (01983) 298370 Mobile 07718-300732 E-mail lyn.mcrostie@mcrostie.info

MACROW-WOOD, Antony Charles. b 60. York Univ BA82 Jes Coll Cam BA91 ACA86. Westcott Ho Cam 89. **d** 92 **p** 93. C Swindon St Jo and St Andr *Bris* 92-96; TV Preston w Sutton Poyntz and Osmington w Poxwell *Sarum* 96-04; P-in-c N Poole Ecum Team 04-06; TR from 06. *The Rectory, 99 Darby's Lane, Poole BH15 3EU* Tel (01202) 660612 Mobile 07775-574971 E-mail amacrowwood@mac.com

MacSWAIN, Robert Carroll. b 69. Liberty Univ USA BA92 Princeton Th Sem MDiv95 Edin Univ MTh96 St Andr Univ PhD10. Virginia Th Sem 99. **d** 01 **p** 02. C Kinston St Mary USA 01-04; Chapl and Fell St Chad's Coll Dur 05-08; Instructor Univ of the South USA 09-10; Asst Prof from 10. *The School of Theology, University of the South, Sewanee TN 37383-0001, USA* E-mail robert.macswain@sewanee.edu

McTEER, Canon Robert Ian. b 56. Chich Th Coll 90. **d** 92 **p** 93. C S Shields All SS *Dur* 92-95; P-in-c Auckland St Helen 95-97; V from 97; Chapl Bishop Auckland Hospitals NHS Trust 95-98; Chapl S Durham Healthcare NHS Trust 98-02; Hon Can Koforidua from 07. *The Vicarage, 8 Manor Road, St Helen Auckland, Bishop Auckland DL14 9EN* Tel (01388) 604152 E-mail fr.r.mcteer@btinternet.com

McTIGHE, Ann-Margaret. b 67. Brunel Univ BSc97 PGCE98. Trin Coll Bris BA10. **d** 10 **p** 11. C Woodford St Mary w St Phil and St Jas *Chelmsf* from 10. *33 Elmhurst Drive, London E18 1BP* Tel (020) 8530 7217 Mobile 07940-892391 E-mail anniemct@btinternet.com

MacVANE, Ms Sara Ann Andrew. b 44. Wellesley Coll (USA) BA66 Univ of Wales (Ban) BA05. EAMTC 03. **d** 05 **p** 06. C Rome *Eur* 05-09; Asst Dir Angl Cen Rome 05-09; P-in-c Nord Pas de Calais *Eur* from 09. *Appt EA2, Domaine de la Barre, 23 Place de l'Esplanade, 62500 St Omer, France* Tel (0033) 3 21 39 63 35 E-mail macvanesara@gmail.com

McVEAGH, Paul Stuart. b 56. Southn Univ BA78. Oak Hill Th Coll BA88. **d** 88 **p** 89. C Bebington *Ches* 88-92; Crosslinks Portugal 92-95; R High Halstow w All Hallows and Hoo St Mary *Roch* 95-02; V Westerham from 02. *The Vicarage, Borde*

Hill, *Vicarage Hill, Westerham TN16 1TL* Tel and fax (01959) 563127 E-mail paul.mcveagh@diocese-rochester.org *or* pmcveagh@aol.com

McVEETY, Ian. b 46. NOC 82. **d** 85 **p** 86. C Langley and Parkfield *Man* 85-89; V Castleton Moor 89-99; AD Heywood and Middleton 95-99; V Baguley from 99; AD Withington from 06. *St John's Vicarage, 186 Brooklands Road, Sale M33 3PB* Tel 0161-973 5947

McVEIGH, Miss Dorothy Sarah. b 67. QUB BA89 TCD BTh93. CITC 90. **d** 93 **p** 94. C Belfast St Matt *Conn* 93-96; C Carrickfergus 96-99; C Lurgan Ch the Redeemer *D & D* 99-04; I Annaghmore *Arm* from 04. *54 Moss Road, Portadown, Craigavon BT62 1NB* Tel (028) 3885 2751 Mobile 07786-454346

McVEIGH, Canon Samuel. b 49. CITC 77. **d** 79 **p** 80. C Drumragh w Mountfield *D & R* 79-82; I Dromore *Clogh* 82-90; I Drumachose *D & R* from 90; Can Derry Cathl from 01. *49 Killane Road, Limavady BT49 0DJ* Tel (028) 7776 2680

MACVICAR, Miss Mary. b 23. Edin Univ MA44 Ox Univ DipEd45. Ripon Coll Cuddesdon 85. **dss** 86 **d** 87 **p** 94. Bishop's Waltham *Portsm* 86-89; Hon C 87-89; Perm to Offic 89-94; Hon C Portsm Cathl 94-95; Hon Chapl from 94; rtd 95; Perm to Offic *Portsm* 95-09. *8/17 Victoria Grove, Southsea PO5 1NF* Tel (023) 9275 1207

McWATT, Glenn Ellsworth. b 48. S'wark Ord Course 89. **d** 92 **p** 93. NSM Tulse Hill H Trin and St Matthias *S'wark* 92-99; C New Malden and Coombe 99-03; C Reigate St Mary 03-08; C Gillingham St Mark *Roch* from 08. *The Garden House, Vicarage Road, Gillingham ME7 5JA* Tel (01634) 575280 E-mail glennmcwatt@btinternet.com

McWHIRTER, James Angus. b 58. Portsm Poly BA91 Trin Coll Carmarthen PGCE93 Warwick Univ PGCE07. St Steph Ho Ox 00. **d** 02 **p** 03. C Shifnal *Lich* 02-06; CF from 07. *c/o MOD Chaplains (Army)* Tel (01264) 381140 Fax 381824 E-mail revdjames.mcwh@btopenworld.com

McWHIRTER (née BELL), Jennifer Kathryn. b 77. Harper Adams Univ Coll BSc99. CITC BTh04. **d** 04 **p** 05. Asst Chapl R Group of Hosps Health and Soc Services Trust 04-06; Asst Chapl Belfast City Hosp Health and Soc Services Trust 04-06; Chapl Belfast Health and Soc Care Trust from 06; C Belfast St Anne *Conn* 04-06; C Belfast St Nic 06-08; I Templepatrick w Donegore from 08; Bp's Dom Chapl from 08. *The Vicarage, 926 Antrim Road, Templepatrick, Ballyclare BT39 0AT* Tel (028) 9443 2330 E-mail revjkmcwhirter@yahoo.co.uk

MacWILLIAM, The Very Revd Alexander Gordon. b 23. Univ of Wales BA43 Lon Univ BD47 PhD52. St Mich Coll Llan 43. **d** 45 **p** 46. C Llanllyfni *Ban* 46-49; Min Can Ban Cathl 49-55; C Ban St Mary 50-53; C Ban St Jas 53-55; R Llanfaethlu w Llanfwrog 55-56; R Llanfaethlu w Llanfwrog and Llanrhuddlad etc 56-58; Hd of RE Dept Lic to Offic *St D* 60-78; Trin Coll Carmarthen 60-70; Hd Sch of Soc Studies 70-84; Visiting Prof Th Cen Univ Iowa USA 83-84; Can St D Cathl 78-84; Prec, V, and Dean 84-90; rtd 90. *Pen Parc, Smyrna Road, Llangain, Carmarthen SA33 5AD* Tel (01267) 241333

McWILLIAMS, Amelia. CITC. **d** 09 **p** 10. NSM Brackaville w Donaghendry and Ballyclog *Arm* from 09. *Address temp unknown*

McWILLIAMS, Mrs Laura Jane. b 67. Cranmer Hall Dur 01. **d** 03 **p** 04. C Kingston upon Hull St Aid Southcoates *York* 03-07; V Seamer w East Ayton from 07. *The Vicarage, 3 Stockshill, Seamer, Scarborough YO12 4QG* Tel (01723) 863102 Mobile 07984-003660 E-mail revlaurajane@yahoo.co.uk

MACY, Jonathan Edward Gordon. b 68. Oak Hill Th Coll BA96 Heythrop Coll Lon MTh98 K Coll Lon PhD04. Wycliffe Hall Ox MTh09. **d** 10 **p** 11. C Plumstead St Jo w St Jas and St Paul *S'wark* from 10. *34 Earl Rise, Plumstead SE18 7NH* Tel (020) 8855 1827 Mobile 07707-755108 E-mail jegmacy@googlemail.com

MADDEN, Kenneth John. b 48. St Jo Coll Dur BA70 Lon Inst of Educn PGCE73. WEMTC 06. **d** 09 **p** 10. NSM Newent and Gorsley w Cliffords Mesne *Glouc* from 09. *Plantation Cottage, Ganders Green, May Hill, Longhope GL17 0NJ* Tel (01452) 831401 Mobile 07894-208501 E-mail kenlibby@talktalk.net

MADDERN, James Thomas. b 76. New Coll Edin BD99. Wycliffe Hall Ox MTh03. **d** 02 **p** 03. C Stratford St Jo w Ch Ch and St Jas *Chelmsf* 02-06; Perm to Offic *Ox* 07-09; TV Brize Norton and Carterton from 09. *The Vicarage, 8 Trefoil Way, Carterton OX18 1JQ* Tel (01993) 844175 E-mail vicbrizecarterton@btinternet.com

MADDOCK (née FARLEY), Mrs Claire Louise. b 69. Man Univ BA91 Heythrop Coll Lon MTh99. Westcott Ho Cam 96. **d** 99 **p** 00. C Sherborne w Castleton and Lillington *Sarum* 99-00; C Weymouth H Trin 00-02; Chapl Barts and The Lon NHS Trust 02-03; Chapl Ealing Hosp NHS Trust 03-06; Chapl W Middx Univ Hosp NHS Trust from 08; C Pimlico St Pet w Westmr Ch Ch *Lon* from 08. *18 Ekarro House, 49A Guildford Road, London SW8 2DT* Tel (020) 7720 6239 E-mail claire@themaddocks.co.uk

MADDOCK, David John Newcomb. b 36. Qu Coll Cam BA60 MA64. Oak Hill Th Coll 60. **d** 62 **p** 63. C Bispham *Blackb* 62-65; R 82-93; RD Blackpool 90-93; Miss Payne Bay Canada 65-69; R Frobisher Bay 70; R Walsoken *Ely* 70-77; V Ore Ch Ch *Chich* 77-82; V Fowey *Truro* 93-02; Chapl Cornwall Healthcare NHS Trust 94-02; rtd 02; Perm to Offic *Truro* from 02. *3 The Moorings, 25 St John's Road, Eastbourne BN20 7NL* Tel (01323) 749172

MADDOCK, Nicholas Rokeby. b 47. ABSM72 Birm Coll of Educn CertEd73. Linc Th Coll 82. **d** 82 **p** 83. C Romford St Edw *Chelmsf* 82-87; V Sway *Win* 87-94; V Taunton St Mary *B & W* 94-04; R Wrington w Butcombe and Burrington from 04. *The Rectory, 3 Alburys, Wrington, Bristol BS40 5NZ* Tel (01934) 862201 E-mail n.maddock@rectory.org.uk

MADDOCK, Philip Arthur Louis. b 47. Open Univ BA82 Lanc Univ MPhil02. Oak Hill Th Coll 75. **d** 78 **p** 79. C New Ferry *Ches* 78-81; C Barnston 81-82; V Over St Jo 82-85; V Norley and Chapl to the Deaf 85-88; P-in-c Treales and Chapl to the Deaf *Blackb* 88-96; Chapl to the Deaf *Lich* 96-02; C Yoxall and The Ridwares and Kings Bromley 98-02; Adv for Deaf and Disabled People Min Div from 03; NSM Alrewas *Lich* from 03; NSM Wychnor from 03. *23 Jackman Road, Fradley, Lichfield WS13 6PF* Tel (01543) 415088 *or* 306085 Mobile 07984-911488 E-mail philip.maddock@churchofengland.org

MADDOCK, Canon Philip Lawrence. b 20. Bris Univ BA42. Cuddesdon Coll 42. **d** 43 **p** 44. C Kilburn St Aug *Lon* 43-48; C Weston-super-Mare All SS *B & W* 48-57; Chapl Community of the Epiphany Truro 57-60; Sub-Warden 60-63; Chapl HM Pris Wandsworth 63-64; HM Pris Birm 64-67; Ex 67-69; Chapl St Lawr Hosp Bodmin 69-76; Can Res and Treas Truro Cathl 76-88; rtd 88; Perm to Offic *Truro* from 88. *32A Coinagehall Street, Helston TR13 8EQ*

MADDOCKS, Alison Julie. b 63. Birm Univ BSc84 Loughb Univ MBA92. St Jo Coll Nottm MTh03. **d** 03 **p** 04. C Wollaton *S'well* 03-06; Retail Chapl Birm City Cen 06-08; Ind Chapl *S'well* 08-11; C Nottingham All SS, St Mary and St Pet 08-11; P-in-c Breadsall *Derby* from 11. *The Rectory, 57 Rectory Lane, Breadsall, Derby DE21 5LL* Tel (01332) 835465 E-mail revmaddocks@aol.com *or* alison.maddocks@derby.anglican.org

MADDOX, David John. b 34. AIMLS58. Sarum & Wells Th Coll 92. **d** 81 **p** 93. In RC Ch 81-91; NSM Wimborne Minster and Holt *Sarum* 93-95; NSM Broadstone 95-01; Perm to Offic *Sarum* 00-08 and *Win* from 00. *298 Wimborne Road, Poole BH15 3EG* Tel (01202) 672597

MADDOX, Derek Adrian James. b 64. Kingston Poly BA88. Trin Coll Bris 02. **d** 04 **p** 05. C Mitcham St Mark *S'wark* 04-07; P-in-c S Yardley St Mich *Birm* 07-08; V from 08. *St Michael's Vicarage, 60 Yew Tree Lane, Yardley, Birmingham B26 1AP* Tel 0121-706 7811 E-mail maddoxmob@blueyonder.co.uk

MADDOX, Hugh Inglis Monteath. b 37. CCC Cam BA60. Westcott Ho Cam 61. **d** 63 **p** 64. C Attercliffe *Sheff* 63-66; C Maidstone All SS w St Phil *Cant* 66-67; C Folkestone St Mary and St Eanswythe 67-69; C St Martin-in-the-Fields *Lon* 69-73; R Sandwich *Cant* 73-81; V St Peter-in-Thanet 81-84; V Red Post *Sarum* 84-03; rtd 03; Perm to Offic *Sarum* from 03. *36 Corfe Road, Stoborough, Wareham BH20 5AD* Tel (01929) 550872

MADDY, Kevin. b 58. Selw Coll Cam BA83 GRNCM79 FRSA96. Westcott Ho Cam 81. **d** 85 **p** 86. C St Peter-in-Thanet *Cant* 85-88; Perm to Offic *Nor* 88-91; Chapl RAF 88-02; CF 02-07; Regional Chapl Hong Kong Miss to Seafarers 07-11; V Monk Bretton *Wakef* from 11; P-in-c Lundwood from 11. *St Paul's Vicarage, Burton Road, Barnsley S71 2HQ* Tel (01226) 203159 E-mail kevinmaddy@hotmail.com

MADELEY, Mark Keith. b 68. AVCM96. Oak Hill Th Coll BA93. **d** 93 **p** 94. C Mickleover All SS *Derby* 93-96; C Charlesworth and Dinting Vale 96-99; Chapl Chr Tours (UK) Ltd 99-00; NSM Moldgreen and Rawthorpe *Wakef* 99-00; V Coley from 00. *Coley Vicarage, 41 Ing Head Terrace, Shelf, Halifax HX3 7LB* Tel and fax (01422) 202292 Mobile 07050-021860 E-mail mark@mibtravel.co.uk

MADGE, Francis Sidney. b 35. AKC58. **d** 59 **p** 60. C York St Mary Bishophill Senior 59-62; C Sutton St Mich 62-64; C Ex St Jas 64-69; R Sutton by Dover w Waldershare *Cant* 69-78; P-in-c W Wickham St Mary 78-81; V 81-02; rtd 02; Perm to Offic *Chich* from 03. *1 Callums Walk, Bexhill-on-Sea TN40 2JF* Tel (01424) 222756

MADGWICK, Mrs Philippa Jane. b 60. Magd Coll Ox BA83 DPhil86. SAOMC 04 ERMC 05. **d** 07 **p** 08. NSM St Alb St Steph *St Alb* from 07. *22 Blenheim Road, St Albans AL1 4NR* Tel (01727) 842449 E-mail pippa.madgwick1@btinternet.com

MADZIMURE, Dominic Makusha. b 52. Middx Univ MA03. **d** 77 **p** 78. Zimbabwe 77-99; Perm to Offic *Cant* 01-03; P-in-c Woodchurch 03-06; P-in-c Byker St Ant *Newc* from 06. *St Anthony's Vicarage, Enslin Gardens, Newcastle upon Tyne NE6 3ST* Tel 0191-265 1683 E-mail dominic@madzimure.fsnet.co.uk

MAGEE, Frederick Hugh. b 33. Yale Univ BA56. Westcott Ho Cam 58. **d** 59 **p** 60. C Bury St Mark *Man* 59-62; USA 63-64 and

87-05; Chapl St Paul's Cathl Dundee 74-79; P-in-c Invergowrie 76-79; R St Andrews St Andr *St And* 79-83; R Forfar 83-87; rtd 05. *17 North Street, St Andrews KY16 9PW* Tel (01334) 470446 E-mail hugh@twomagees.plus.com

MAGEE, Keith Robert. b 60. Bris Univ BA95 PGCE96. Trin Coll Bris 92 Westcott Ho Cam 99. **d** 01 **p** 02. C S Woodham Ferrers *Chelmsf* 01-05; V Moulsham St Jo from 05. *St John's Vicarage, Vicarage Road, Chelmsford CM2 9PH* Tel (01245) 352344 E-mail keith.magee@btinternet.com

MAGILL, Robert James Henderson. b 59. Paisley Coll of Tech BSc81. Sarum & Wells Th Coll 92. **d** 94 **p** 95. C W Moors *Sarum* 94-98; P-in-c Hilperton w Whaddon and Staverton etc 98-05; Community Affairs Chapl 02-05. *The Vicarage, 1A The Weir, Edington, Westbury BA13 4PX*

MAGNESS, Anthony William John. b 37. New Coll Ox BA62 MA65. Coll of Resurr Mirfield 78. **d** 80 **p** 81. C Gt Crosby St Faith *Liv* 80-83; C Newc St Jo 83-85; P-in-c Newc St Luke 85-88; P-in-c Newc St Andr 88; V Newc St Andr and St Luke 89-99; Chapl Hunter's Moor Hosp 89-95; P-in-c Cambois *Newc* 99-00; P-in-c Sleekburn 99-00; V Cambois and Sleekburn 00-03; rtd 03; Perm to Offic *Newc* from 03. *59 Firtree Crescent, Newcastle upon Tyne NE12 7JU* Tel and fax 0191-268 4596

MAGNUSSON, Lisbet Maria. b 50. Mid-Sweden Univ BSc85 Uppsala Univ MDiv93 ML98. Past Inst Uppsala 93. **p** 94. In Ch of Sweden 94-98; C Crosby *Linc* 98-99; TV Gainsborough and Morton 99-04; P-in-c Swallow and Chapl Doncaster and S Humber Healthcare NHS Trust 04-06; Sweden from 06. *Haggkullevagen 26, 184 37 Akersberga, Stockholm, Sweden* Tel (0046) (8) 1205 9082 *or* (278) 41023 Mobile 72-231 5990 E-mail dalhemrectory@hotmail.com

MAGOR, Robert Jolyon. b 47. Sarum & Wells Th Coll 91. **d** 93 **p** 94. C Plaistow *Chelmsf* 93-96; TV Plaistow and N Canning Town 96-99; V Leigh-on-Sea St Aid 99-01; C Thorpe Bay 01-06; R E and W Tilbury and Linford 06-09; rtd 09. *31 Selwyn Road, Southend-on-Sea SS2 4DR* E-mail robert.magor@googlemail.com

MAGORRIAN, Brian Geoffrey. b 64. St Aid Coll Dur BSc85 York Univ DPhil89. St Jo Coll Nottm. **d** 01 **p** 02. C Bishopwearmouth St Gabr *Dur* 01-04; P-in-c Brough w Stainmore, Musgrave and Warcop *Carl* 04-10; C Whitfield *Derby* from 10. *Church House, Fauvel Road, Glossop SK13 7AR* Tel (01457) 899105 E-mail brianmagorrian@tiscali.co.uk *or* brian@glossop.org

✠**MAGOWAN, The Rt Revd Alistair James.** b 55. Leeds Univ BSc77 Ox Univ MTh02. Trin Coll Bris 78. **d** 81 **p** 82 **c** 09. C Owlerton *Sheff* 81-84; C Dur St Nic 84-89; Chapl St Aid Coll 85-89; V Egham *Guildf* 89-00; RD Runnymede 93-98; Adn Dorset *Sarum* 00-09; Can and Preb Sarum Cathl 00-09; Suff Bp Ludlow *Heref* from 09; Adn Ludlow from 09. *Bishop's House, Corvedale Road, Halford, Craven Arms SY7 9BT* Tel (01588) 673571 Fax 673585 E-mail bishopofludlow@btinternet.com

MAGOWAN, Harold Victor. b 34. QUB BA55 BSc(Econ)66 DipEd69 ACII69 FCII73. TCD Div Sch Div Test57. **d** 57 **p** 58. C Antrim All SS w Muckamore *Conn* 57-59. *6 Fold Mews, 22 Ballyholme Road, Bangor BT20 5JS* Tel (028) 9146 5091

MAGOWAN, Ian Walter. b 51. St Paul's Coll Chelt CertEd73 Ulster Poly BEd82 TCD BTh07. CITC 04. **d** 07 **p** 08. C Killowen *D & R* 07-10; I Connor w Antrim St Patr from 10. *Connor Rectory, 50 Church Road, Kells, Ballymena BT42 3JU* Tel (028) 2589 1254 Mobile 07810-636167 E-mail iwmagowan@hotmail.co.uk

MAGUIRE, Alan. b 45. CBDTI 03. **d** 06 **p** 07. NSM Croglin *Carl* from 06; NSM Holme Eden and Wetheral w Warwick from 06. *21 Hill Head, Scotby, Carlisle CA4 8BH* Tel (01228) 513638 E-mail alan.maguire@virgin.net

MAGUIRE, Canon Brian William. b 33. Hull Univ BTh84 MA88. Coll of Resurr Mirfield 70. **d** 72 **p** 73. C Guisborough *York* 72-76; TV Haxby w Wigginton 76-77; TR 78-89; V Huddersfield St Pet and All SS *Wakef* 89-00; Hon Can Wakef Cathl 94-00; rtd 00; Perm to Offic *Wakef* from 00; Bp's Dom Chapl 03-04. *33 Chapel Lane, Lichfield WS14 9BA* Tel (01543) 305936

MAGUIRE, Michael Timothy Gale (Tim). b 34. Ox Univ Inst of Educn DipEd61. Wycliffe Hall Ox 58. **d** 61 **p** 62. C Southampton St Mary Extra *Win* 61-63; Bp's Youth Chapl 63-66; Perm to Offic *Win* from 97 and *Truro* from 02; rtd 99. *23 Wharf Hill, Winchester SO23 9NQ* Tel (01962) 841375

MAGUIRE (formerly GRATTON), Canon Patricia Margaret. b 46. Leeds Univ BTh94 MA96 SRN67 TCert84 CertEd88. EMMTC 89 NOC 96. **d** 97 **p** 98. NSM Shipley St Pet *Bradf* 97-99; C Brighouse and Clifton *Wakef* 99-00; Chapl Wakef Cathl Sch 00-05; P-in-c Lupset *Wakef* 05-11; P-in-c Thornes 00-11; RD Wakef 08-11; Hon Can Wakef Cathl 07-11; rtd 11. *33 Chapel Lane, Lichfield WS14 9BA* Tel (01543) 305936 E-mail revmaguire@virginmedia.com

MAGUMBA, Canere Patrick John. b 53. Bp Tucker Coll Mukono BD85 Makerere Univ Kampala PGDE88 Birm Univ MA92 Leeds Univ PhD03. **d** 79 **p** 80. Uganda 79-90 and 93-04; C Kamuli 79-81; V Kaliro 86-90; Sub-Dean Busoga 90; Hon C

Harborne Heath *Birm* 91-93; Sen Lect Uganda Chr Univ Mukono 93-04; TV S Rochdale *Man* 04-11; V Deeplish and Newbold from 11; Hon Can Th Orlu from 05. *St Luke's Vicarage, 9 Deeplish Road, Rochdale OL11 1NY* Tel (01706) 354628 Mobile 07901-782329 E-mail jmagumba@hotmail.com

MAHER, David James. b 70. St Jo Coll Dur BA01. Cranmer Hall Dur 98. **d** 01 **p** 02. C Hounslow H Trin w St Paul *Lon* 01-04; C Staines 04-07; Chapl to Bp Kensington 04-07; V Chesterton Gd Shep *Ely* from 07. *The Good Shepherd Vicarage, 51 Highworth Avenue, Cambridge CB4 2BQ* Tel (01223) 351844 *or* 312933 E-mail vicar@churchofthegoodshepherd.co.uk

MAHILUM, Bello. **d** 10 **p** 11. NSM Notting Hill St Jo *Lon* from 10. *5 Faith Court, Cooper's Road, London SE1 5HD* E-mail belkiewtz@aol.com

MAHONEY, William Denis. b 35. 77. **d** 79 **p** 95. In RC Ch USA 79-87; NSM Egremont and Haile *Carl* 92-93; NSM Kells 93-96; R Cohoes USA 96-98; P-in-c Beckermet St Jo and St Bridget w Ponsonby *Carl* 98-05; rtd 05. *2 Bowden Drive, Huntington Station NY 11746-4218, USA* E-mail vlwd17@aol.com

MAHONY, Conal Martin. b 38. Pontificio Ateneo Antoniano Rome Lic in Sacred Th 64 Lateran Univ Rome ThD66. Franciscan Ho of Studies 57. **d** 62 **p** 63. In RC Ch 62-89; Dir Folkestone Family Care Cen 86-92; Lic to Offic *Cant* 89-92; C Hempnall *Nor* 92-94; TV 94-97; TR 97-08; rtd 08; Perm to Offic *Nor* from 08. *6 Rigby Close, Framingham Earl, Norwich NR14 7TL* Tel (01508) 491646

MAIDEN, Charles Alistair Kingsley. b 60. Trent Poly BSc84. St Jo Coll Nottm LTh88. **d** 89 **p** 90. C Porchester *S'well* 89-93; C Selston 93-96; P-in-c Huthwaite from 96. *The Vicarage, Blackwell Road, Huthwaite, Sutton-in-Ashfield NG17 2QT* Tel (01623) 555053 E-mail charliemaiden@hotmail.com

MAIDMENT, Thomas John Louis. b 43. Lon Univ BSc65. St Steph Ho Ox. **d** 67 **p** 68. C Westmr St Steph w St Jo *Lon* 67-73; P-in-c Twickenham Common H Trin 73-77; V 77-80; V Heston 80-98; V Bolton-le-Sands *Blackb* 98-08; P-in-c Tunstall w Melling and Leck 02-03; AD Tunstall 99-05; rtd 08; Perm to Offic *Blackb* from 08. *69 Aintree Road, Thornton-Cleveleys FY5 5HW* Tel (01253) 829399 E-mail t.j.l.m@btinternet.com

MAIDSTONE, Archdeacon of. See TAYLOR, The Ven Stephen Ronald

MAIDSTONE, Suffragan Bishop. *Vacant*

MAIN, Mrs Brigid Mary Harvey. b 49. EAMTC 96. **d** 99 **p** 00. NSM Tillingham *Chelmsf* 99-03; NSM Pleshey from 03. *Parsonage Cottage, The Street, Pleshey, Chelmsford CM3 1HA* Tel (01245) 237012 E-mail bmain@chelmsford.anglican.org

MAIN, Clive Timothy. b 53. St Andr Univ MA75 Cam Univ PGCE76. Oak Hill Th Coll BA94. **d** 96 **p** 97. C Alperton *Lon* 96-00; V Highbury New Park St Aug from 00. *St Augustine's Vicarage, 108 Highbury New Park, London N5 2DR* Tel (020) 7226 6870 E-mail clivemain@blueyonder.co.uk

MAIN, Canon David Murray. b 28. Univ Coll Ox BA52 MA56. St Deiniol's Hawarden 73. **d** 73 **p** 74. C Glas St Marg 73-75; R Challoch w Newton Stewart 75-79; R Kilmarnock 79-93; Can St Mary's Cathl 85-93; rtd 93; Hon Can St Mary's Cathl from 93. *Sunnybrae, 50 Abercromby Road, Castle Douglas DG7 1BA* Tel (01556) 504669

MAINA, Simon Mwangi. b 52. Nairobi Univ 85. **d** 80 **p** 81. Kenya 80-95; C Acton St Mary *Lon* 95-97; Worthing Churches Homeless Project from 98; rtd 08. *49 Cambourne Court, Shelley Road, Worthing BN11 4BQ* Tel (01903) 205042

MAINE, Michael John. b 57. FGMS95. Coll of Resurr Mirfield 09. **d** 11. C Willingdon *Chich* from 11. *37 Church Street, Willingdon, Eastbourne BN20 9HT* Tel 07895-415143 (mobile) E-mail michaelmaine@houlgate.eclipse.co.uk

MAINES, Canon Trevor. b 40. Leeds Univ BSc63. Ripon Hall Ox 63. **d** 65 **p** 66. C Speke All SS *Liv* 65-70; C Stevenage St Geo *St Alb* 70-73; V Dorridge *Birm* 73-78; Org Sec CECS 79-80; Hon C Tiverton St Pet *Ex* 79-80; Org Sec (Wales) CECS 80-87; Hon C Newton Nottage *Llan* 81-83; Perm to Offic *Mon* 83-87; V Arlesey w Astwick *St Alb* 87-95; RD Shefford 91-95; V Goldington 95-05; RD Bedford 98-05; Hon Can St Alb 04-05; rtd 05; Hon C Beedon and Peasemore w W Ilsley and Farnborough *Ox* 05-07; Hon C Brightwalton w Catmore, Leckhampstead etc 05-07. *1 Adlam Villas, Greenham Road, Newbury RG14 7HX* Tel (01635) 551352 E-mail trevor.maines@tesco.net

MAINEY, Ian George. b 51. CertEd73. Oak Hill Th Coll BA87. **d** 87 **p** 88. C Denton Holme *Carl* 87-91; V Hensingham 91-02; RD Calder 01-02; TR Deane *Man* 02-09; P-in-c Birkdale St Jas *Liv* from 09; P-in-c Birkdale St Pet from 09. *The Vicarage, 26 Lulworth Road, Southport PR8 2BQ* Tel (01704) 566255 E-mail ian.mainey@lineone.net

MAINWARING, Islwyn Paul. b 52. Univ of Wales (Swansea) BD75. St Mich Coll Llan 77. **d** 79 **p** 80. C Llanilid w Pencoed 79-82; C Llanishen and Lisvane 82-85; V Cwmbran *Mon* 85-88; V Troedyrhiw w Merthyr Vale *Llan* 88-91. *Pennant, 109 Penygroes Road, Blaenau, Ammanford SA18 3BZ* Tel (01269) 850350

MAINWARING (née LANKSHEAR), Jane Frances. b 70. Leeds Univ BA92 Trin Coll Carmarthen MPhil97 PhD99. EAMTC 98. **d** 00 **p** 01. C Sudbury and Chilton *St E* 00-03; TV Hitchin *St Alb* from 03. *St Mark's Vicarage, St Mark's Close, Hitchin SG5 1UR* Tel (01462) 422862 *or* 434686 E-mail jane@stmarks-hitchin.org.uk

MAIRS, Canon Adrian Samuel. b 43. Oak Hill Th Coll 76. **d** 78 **p** 79. C Rugby St Matt *Cov* 78-82; P-in-c Mancetter 82-84; V 84-08; P-in-c Hartshill 97-01; Hon Can Cov Cathl 03-08; rtd 08. *21 Cleverley Drive, Nuneaton CV10 0JZ* Tel (024) 7639 2852

MAIS, Jeremy Hugh. b 47. **d** 00 **p** 01. NSM Bibury w Winson and Barnsley *Glouc* 00-02; P-in-c 04-08; NSM Stratton, N Cerney, Baunton and Bagendon 02-04; NSM Fairford Deanery 09; NSM Hambleden Valley *Ox* from 09. *The Vicarage, Turville, Henley-on-Thames RG9 6QU* Tel (01491) 638539 E-mail jeremy.mais@tiscali.co.uk

MAITIN, Ito. b 36. Open Univ BA. Kelham Th Coll 63. **d** 68 **p** 69. C Longton St Jo *Lich* 68-69; C Leek St Edw 69-71; C Lich St Chad 71-74; C Tamworth 74-81; V Penkhull 81-06; rtd 06; Perm to Offic *Lich* 06-08; C Hanley H Ev 08-09; C Stoke-upon-Trent from 10. *18 Crescent Grove, Stoke-on-Trent ST4 6EN* Tel (01782) 878788

MAITLAND, The Hon Sydney Milivoje Patrick. b 51. Edin Univ BSc MRTPI. St Jo Coll Nottm. **d** 86 **p** 87. Hon C Glas St Geo 86-01; Hon C Glas St Bride from 03. *14 Kersland Street, Glasgow G12 8BL* Tel 0141-339 4573 E-mail sydney@maitland50.freeserve.co.uk

MAJOR, Richard James Edward. b 54. Trin Coll Bris 78. **d** 81 **p** 82. C Parr *Liv* 81-84; V Burton Fleming w Fordon *York* 84-85; V Grindale and Ergham 84-85; P-in-c Wold Newton 84-85; V Burton Fleming w Fordon, Grindale etc 85-91; V Bilton St Pet from 91. *The Vicarage, 14 Cherry Tree Close, Bilton, Hull HU11 4EZ* Tel (01482) 811441 E-mail richard@revmajor.karoo.co.uk

MAJOR, Richard John Charles. b 63. Massey Univ (NZ) BA85 Ex Coll Ox BA91 MA93 Magd Coll Ox DPhil91. St Steph Ho Ox 92. **d** 94 **p** 95. C Truro Cathl 94-97; C Putney St Mary *S'wark* 97-98; Chapl Florence w Siena *Eur* 98-01; USA from 01. *Nansough Manor, Ladock, Truro TR2 4PB* Tel (01726) 883315 *or* (001) (718) 442 1589 Fax (001) (718) 442 4555 E-mail richard@richardmajor.com

MAKAMBWE, Canon Francis James. b 40. St Jo Sem Lusaka. **d** 65 **p** 67. Zambia 65-91; Miss Partner CMS 91-10; C Waterloo St Jo w St Andr *S'wark* 91-96; V Hatcham St Cath 96-10; AD Deptford 05-07; Hon Can S'wark Cathl 03-10; rtd 10; Perm to Offic *S'wark* from 11. *St Michael's Vicarage, Champion Crescent, London SE26 4HJ* Tel (020) 8778 7196 E-mail fmakam@aol.com

MAKEL, Arthur. b 39. AKC63. **d** 64 **p** 65. C Beamish *Dur* 64-68; Ind Chapl *York* 68-72; Ind Chapl and P-in-c Scotton w Northorpe *Linc* 72-81; R Epworth 81-89; P-in-c Wroot 81-89; R Epworth and Wroot 89-92; R Sigglesthorne and Rise w Nunkeeling and Bewholme *York* 92-04; P-in-c Aldbrough, Mappleton w Goxhill and Withernwick 98-04; rtd 04; Perm to Offic *York* 04-11. *43 Lowfield Road, Beverley HU17 9RF* Tel (01482) 865798

MAKEPEACE, David Norman Harry. b 51. Magd Coll Ox BA74. Trin Coll Bris 83. **d** 85 **p** 86. C Romford Gd Shep *Chelmsf* 85-88; Tanzania 88-89; C York St Paul 89-91; TV Radipole and Melcombe Regis *Sarum* 91-98; V Sandgate St Paul w Folkestone St Geo *Cant* 98-00; Perm to Offic from 01. *10 Limes Road, Folkestone CT19 4AU* Tel (01303) 274011 E-mail dnhm@talk21.com

MAKEPEACE, Preb James Dugard. b 40. Keble Coll Ox BA63 MA67. Cuddesdon Coll 63. **d** 65 **p** 66. C Cullercoats St Geo *Newc* 65-68; Lib Pusey Ho and Chapl Wadh Coll Ox 68-72; V Romford St Edw *Chelmsf* 72-79; V Tettenhall Regis *Lich* 79-80; TR 80-99; RD Trysull 87-97; Preb Lich Cathl 96-99; rtd 00; Perm to Offic *Lich* from 00. *3 Shaw Lane, Albrighton WV7 3DS* Tel (01902) 375472

✠**MAKHULU, The Most Revd Walter Paul Khotso.** b 35. CMG00. Kent Univ Hon DD88 Gen Th Sem NY Hon DD99. St Pet Rosettenville Selly Oak Coll. **d** 57 **p** 58 **c** 79. S Africa 57-61; Bechuanaland 61-63; C Poplar All SS w St Frideswide *Lon* 64-66; C Pentonville St Silas w Barnsbury St Clem 66-68; V Battersea St Phil *S'wark* 68-73; V Battersea St Phil w St Bart 73-75; Bp Botswana 79-00; Abp Cen Africa 80-00; rtd 00. *16 Downside, 8-10 St John's Avenue, London SW15 2AE* E-mail makhulu@btinternet.com

MAKIN, Miss Pauline. b 45. Cranmer Hall Dur 75. **dss** 78 **d** 87 **p** 94. Ashton-in-Makerfield St Thos *Liv* 78-89; Par Dn 87-89; Par Dn Rainford 89-94; C 94-95; C Farnworth 95-10; Asst Dioc Chapl to the Deaf 89-10; rtd 10. *50 Farm Meadow Road, Orrell, Wigan WN5 8TE* Tel (01695) 624995 E-mail paulinemakin@aol.com

MAKIN, Valerie Diana. S'wark Ord Course 86. **d** 88 **p** 94. Hon Par Dn Bryanston Square St Mary w St Marylebone St Mark *Lon* 88-95; Chapl St Marylebone Healing and Counselling Cen 88-94; NSM Godalming *Guildf* 94-95; Perm to Offic *Lon* 95-97 and *Guildf* 95-05. *Address temp unknown*

MÄKIPÄÄ, Tuomas. b 78. Helsinki Univ MTh06. **d** 05 **p** 10. C Helsinki *Eur* from 05. *Rastilantie 5 B 16, Helsinki FI-00980, Finland* Tel (00358) (50) 309 9132 E-mail assistant-curate@anglican.fi

MAKOWER, Canon Malory. b 38. TCD BA61 MA68 St Jo Coll Ox MA64 DPhil64. Ridley Hall Cam 64. **d** 66 **p** 67. C Onslow Square St Paul *Lon* 66-69; Tutor Ridley Hall Cam 69-71; Sen Tutor 71-76; P-in-c Lode and Longmeadow *Ely* 76-84; Warden EAMTC 77-79; Prin 79-84; Dir of Post-Ord Tr for NSM *Nor* 84-90; C Gt Yarmouth 84-89; TV 89-95; Dioc NSM Officer 88-95; Hon Can Nor Cathl 94-97; Prin LNSM Tr Scheme 94-97; rtd 97; Perm to Offic *Nor* from 98. *114 Yarmouth Road, Lowestoft NR32 4AQ* Tel (01502) 574769

MALAN, Victor Christian de Roubaix. b 39. Cape Town Univ BA60 Linacre Coll Ox BA63 MA68. Wycliffe Hall Ox 61. **d** 63 **p** 64. C Springfield *Birm* 63-66; P-in-c 66-67; C New Windsor *Ox* 67-69; Chapl St Jo Coll Cam 69-74; V Northampton All SS w St Kath *Pet* 74-86; V Stockport St Geo *Ches* 86-89; R N Mundham w Hunston and Merston *Chich* 89-06; rtd 06; Perm to Offic *Cant* from 07. *40 St Lawrence Forstal, Canterbury CT1 3PA* Tel (01227) 785752

✠**MALANGO, The Rt Revd Bernard Amos.** b 43. TCD MPhil84. St Jo Sem Lusaka. **d** 71 **p** 72 **c** 88. Malawi 71-88 and from 02; Bp N Zambia 88-02; Bp Upper Shire 02-07; Abp Cen Africa 00-07; rtd 07. *Address temp unknown* E-mail bernardmalango@hotmail.com

MALBON, Canon John Allin. b 36. Oak Hill Th Coll 62. **d** 65 **p** 66. C Wolverhampton St Jude *Lich* 65-68; C Hoole *Ches* 68-71; P-in-c Crewe Ch Ch 71-75; V 75-79; V Plemstall w Guilden Sutton 79-01; Hon Can Ches Cathl 96-01; rtd 01; Perm to Offic *Ches* from 02. *22 Hawksey Drive, Nantwich CW5 7GF* Tel (01270) 611584

MALCOLM, Andrew Alexander. b 55. Open Univ BA99 Leic Univ MSc Leeds Univ BA08. NOC. **d** 08 **p** 09. NSM Salesbury *Blackb* from 08. *Townhead Old Barn, 49A Downham Road, Chatburn, Clitheroe BB7 4AU* Tel (01200) 441220 E-mail andrewmalcolm@dsl.pipex.com

MALCOLM, Brother. See FOUNTAIN, David Roy

MALCOLM, Miss Mercia Alana. b 54. St Andr Univ MA77. S'wark Ord Course 84. **d** 87 **p** 94. C Dartford Ch Ch *Roch* 87-91; Par Dn Stockport St Geo *Ches* 91-94; C Jordanstown *Conn* 95-99; Chapl Ulster Univ 95-03; I Carnmoney *Conn* from 03. *Coole Glebe, 20 Glebe Road, Newtownabbey BT36 6UW* Tel (028) 9083 6337 E-mail carnmoney@connor.anglican.org

MALE, David Edward. b 62. Southn Univ BA83 St Jo Coll Dur BA90. Cranmer Hall Dur 88. **d** 91 **p** 92. C Leic St Chris 91-94; C Kirkheaton *Wakef* 94-98; P Missr Huddersfield 99-06; Dioc Fresh Expressions Adv *Ely* from 06; Tutor Ridley Hall Cam from 06. *130 Hulatt Road, Cambridge CB1 8TH* Tel (01223) 410581 *or* 741102 E-mail dm432@cam.ac.uk

✠**MALECDAN, The Most Revd Edward Pacyaya.** Episc Th Sem of the SW MA93 Hon DD. St Andr Th Sem Manila BTh77 MDiv85. **d** 79 **p** 80 **c** 97. Philippines from 79; Dean St Andr Th Sem 94-97; Bp N Philippines 97-09; Prime Bp from 09. *Provincial Office, PO Box 10321, Broadway Centrum, 1112 Quezon City, Philippines* Tel (0063) (2) 722 8478 *or* 722 8481 Fax 721 1923 E-mail ednpvic@hotmail.com

MALEK, Mark Mayool. b 44. Khartoum Univ BSc69 Salford Univ BSc76 Bradf Coll of Educn PGCE93. **d** 03 **p** 04. NSM Horton *Bradf* 03-04; NSM Bradf St Oswald Chapel Green 03-04; NSM Lt Horton from 04. *26 Martlett Drive, Bradford BD5 8QG* Tel (01274) 732712

MALES, Jeanne Margaret. b 49. Reading Univ BA71 Lon Univ MPhil73 Surrey Univ PhD86 AFBPsS75 CPsychol88. S'wark Ord Course 93. **d** 96 **p** 97. NSM Caterham *S'wark* 96-00; C Addington 00-03; V from 03. *Addington Vicarage, Spout Hill, Croydon CR0 5AN* Tel (01689) 841838 *or* 842167 E-mail rev.jeanne@tiscali.co.uk

MALINS, Mrs Judith. b 47. Birm Univ BA69. STETS 97. **d** 00 **p** 01. NSM Wilton w Netherhampton and Fugglestone *Sarum* 00-04; P-in-c Kingston, Langton Matravers and Worth Matravers 04-10; P-in-c Wrington w Butcombe and Burrington *B & W* from 10. *4 Ashford Road, Redhill, Bristol BS40 5TH* Tel (01275) 474106 *or* 475151 E-mail judith.malins@tesco.net

MALKIN, Thomas Ross. b 64. Hertf Coll Ox BA86. Trin Coll Bris BA98 MPhil00. **d** 99 **p** 00. C Old Trafford St Bride *Man* 99-03; P-in-c Firswood and Gorse Hill 03-10; R from 10. *The Rectory, 24 Canute Road, Stretford, Manchester M32 0RJ* Tel 0161-865 1802 Mobile 07973-240023 E-mail rev.trm@ntlworld.com

MALKINSON, Canon Christopher Mark. b 47. Chich Th Coll 84. **d** 86 **p** 87. C Stroud and Uplands w Slad *Glouc* 86-89; V Cam w Stinchcombe 89-00; P-in-c Tywardreath w Tregaminion *Truro* 00-02; P-in-c St Sampson 00-02; V Padstow from 02; RD Pydar from 03; Hon Can Truro Cathl from 07; Chapl Miss to Seafarers from 00. *The Vicarage, 46 Treverbyn Road, Padstow PL28 8DN* Tel (01841) 533776 E-mail chrismalk@hotmail.com

MALKINSON, Michael Stephen. b 43. St Steph Ho Ox 65. **d** 68 **p** 69. C New Addington *Cant* 68-71; C Blackpool St Steph *Blackb* 71-74; V Wainfleet St Mary *Linc* 74-81; R Wainfleet All

SS w St Thos 74-81; P-in-c Croft 80-81; V Lund *Blackb* 81-93; V Heyhouses on Sea 93-00; R Balcombe *Chich* 00-09; P-in-c Staplefield Common 00-03; rtd 09. *8 Haines Avenue, Wyre Piddle, Pershore WR10 2RQ* Tel (01386) 556102 E-mail malkinson@msn.com

MALLAS, Mrs Wendy Norris. b 42. Cov Coll of Educn CertEd63 Reading Univ MA91. STETS 00. **d** 03 **p** 04. NSM Liss *Portsm* 03-07; NSM Blackmoor and Whitehill from 07; NSM Bordon *Guildf* from 07. *Mayfield, 45 Hogmoor Road, Whitehill, Bordon GU35 9ET* Tel (01420) 478883 E-mail wendy.mallas@mayfieldjays.co.uk

MALLESON, Michael Lawson. b 42. Univ of Wales (Swansea) BA64 Nottm Univ MA92. Linc Th Coll 67. **d** 70 **p** 71. C Wakef St Jo 70-73; C-in-c Holmfield St Andr CD 73-75; V Holmfield 75-80; V Heworth St Alb *Dur* 80-93; V Killingworth *Newc* 93-06; rtd 06. *8 Slingsby Gardens, Newcastle upon Tyne NE7 7RX* Tel 0191-209 2880 E-mail michaelmalleson@aol.com

MALLETT, John Christopher. b 44. EAMTC. **d** 82 **p** 83. NSM Hethersett w Canteloff *Nor* 82-85; NSM Hethersett w Canteloff w Lt and Gt Melton 85-90; Chapl Wayland Hosp Norfolk 88-94; Chapl Norwich Community Health Partnership NHS Trust 94-00; Perm to Offic *Nor* 00-03; NSM Hethersett w Canteloff w Lt and Gt Melton 03-10; rtd 10. *2 Bailey Close, Hethersett, Norwich NR9 3EU* Tel (01603) 811010 E-mail christophersheila@tiscali.co.uk

MALLETT, Marlene Rosemarie. b 59. Sussex Univ BA81 Warwick Univ PhD94. SEITE 01. **d** 04 **p** 05. C Brixton Road Ch Ch *S'wark* 04-07; P-in-c Angell Town St Jo from 07. *St John's Vicarage, 49 Wiltshire Road, London SW9 7NE* Tel (020) 7733 0585 E-mail rosemarie.mallett@btinternet.com

MALLINSON, Peter Albert. b 57. St Jo Coll Nottm 06. **d** 08 **p** 09. NSM Allestree St Edm and Darley Abbey *Derby* from 08. *68 High Lane West, West Hallam, Ilkeston DE7 6HQ* Tel 0115-944 3134 E-mail petermallinson@smartemail.co.uk

MALLINSON, Canon Ralph Edward. b 40. Oriel Coll Ox BA63 MA66. St Steph Ho Ox 63. **d** 66 **p** 67. C Bolton St Pet *Man* 66-68; C Elton All SS 68-72; V Bury St Thos 72-76; V Bury Ch King 76-81; P-in-c Goodshaw 81-82; V 82-84; V Goodshaw and Crawshawbooth 84-93; AD Rossendale 83-93; V Unsworth 93-06; Hon Can Man Cathl 92-06; Vice Prin Dioc OLM Scheme 98-06; rtd 06; Perm to Offic *Man* from 06. *18 Woodgate Avenue, Bury BL9 7RU* Tel 0161-797 2006 E-mail ralphandhelen@rmallinson.fsnet.co.uk

MALLON, Allister. b 61. Sheff Univ BA83 TCD BTh89 MA. CITC. **d** 87 **p** 88. C Ballymoney w Finvoy and Rasharkin *Conn* 87-90; C Belfast St Mary w H Redeemer 90-92; Bp's C Belfast St Mary Magd 92-00; Bp's C Stoneyford 00-11; Chapl R Group of Hosps Health and Soc Services Trust from 00. *9 The Rose Garden, Dunmurry, Belfast BT17 9GZ* Tel (028) 9030 1272 E-mail bigal@talk21.com

MALLORY, George Henry. b 14. JP. Lon Univ BSc63. St Deiniol's Hawarden. **d** 80 **p** 81. NSM Oaks in Charnwood and Copt Oak *Leic* 80-88; rtd 88; Perm to Offic *Leic* 88-91; Perm to Offic *Worc* from 91. *Claudina, Bewdley Road North, Stourport-on-Severn DY13 8PX* Tel (01299) 827969

MALMESBURY, Archdeacon of. See FROUDE, The Ven Christine Ann

MALONE, Richard Patrick. b 66. Wycliffe Hall Ox BTh03. **d** 03 **p** 04. C Fulham Ch Ch *Lon* 03-06; C Battersea St Pet and St Paul *S'wark* from 06. *29 Winstanley Road, London SW11 2EZ* Tel (020) 7585 3303 Mobile 07973-104941 E-mail patrick.malone@stmarks-battersea.org.uk

MALONEY, Ms Fiona Elizabeth. b 60. Bradf Univ BSc82 St Jo Coll Dur BA91. NOC 91. **d** 92 **p** 94. Par Dn Castleton Moor *Man* 92-94; C 94-96; C Pendlebury St Jo 96-99; C Fatfield *Dur* 99-03; NSM Harrow Trin St Mich *Lon* 03-05; NSM Wealdstone H Trin from 05. *The Vicarage, 39 Rusland Park Road, Harrow HA1 1UN* Tel (020) 8863 5844 or 8863 6131 E-mail fiona@cofe.org.uk

MALONEY, Terence Mark. b 63. York Univ BSc84. Cranmer Hall Dur 88. **d** 91 **p** 92. C Blackley St Andr *Man* 91-96; P-in-c Pendlebury St Jo 96-99; P-in-c Fatfield *Dur* 99-03; P-in-c Harrow Trin St Mich *Lon* 03-05; V Wealdstone H Trin from 05. *The Vicarage, 39 Rusland Park Road, Harrow HA1 1UN* Tel (020) 8863 5844 or 8863 6131 E-mail mark@cofe.org.uk

MALTBY, Canon Geoffrey. b 38. Leeds Univ BA62. Wells Th Coll 68. **d** 70 **p** 71. C Mansfield St Mark *S'well* 70-73; V Skegby 73-78; V Carrington 78-87; C Rainworth 87-90; Chapl for People w Learning Disability (Mental Handicap) 90-03; Hon Can *S'well* Minster 99-03; rtd 03; Perm to Offic *S'well* from 03. *18 Beverley Close, Rainworth, Mansfield NG21 0LW* Tel (01623) 474452

MALTBY, Canon Judith Diane. b 57. Illinois Univ BA79 Newnham Coll Cam PhD92 FRHistS99. S Dios Minl Tr Scheme 89. **d** 92 **p** 94. Tutor Sarum & Wells Th Coll 87-93; Hon Par Dn Wilton w Netherhampton and Fugglestone *Sarum* 92-93; Chapl and Fell CCC Ox from 93; Reader Ch Hist Ox Univ from 04; Can Th Leic Cathl from 04; Hon Can Ch Ch *Ox* from 06; Can Th Win Cathl from 11. *Corpus Christi College, Oxford OX1 4JF* Tel (01865) 276722 E-mail judith.maltby@ccc.ox.ac.uk

MALTIN, Basil St Clair Aston. b 24. Qu Coll Cam BA49 MA54. Westcott Ho Cam 50. **d** 51 **p** 52. C Dursley *Glouc* 51-53; C Bathwick w Woolley *B & W* 53-57; V Frome Ch Ch 57-63; P-in-c Marston Bigot 57-59; V Bishops Lydeard 63-71; R Pulborough *Chich* 71-90; RD Storrington 84-89; rtd 90; Perm to Offic *Chich* from 90. *13 Somerstown, Chichester PO19 6AG* Tel (01243) 786740

MALTON, William Peter Antony. b 33. K Coll Lon AKC56. **d** 57 **p** 58. C N Hammersmith St Kath *Lon* 57-60; C-in-c Blackbird Leys CD *Ox* 60-65; R Pitsford *Pet* 65-66; Canada from 66; rtd 93. *5589 Highway 221, Woodville NS B0P 1V0, Canada*

MAN, Archdeacon of the Isle of. See SMITH, The Ven Brian

MANCHESTER, Canon John Charles. b 45. Lon Univ BD69. ALCD68. **d** 69 **p** 70. C Scarborough St Martin *York* 69-73; C Selby Abbey 73-76; P-in-c Old Malton 76-79; V 79-10; RD Bulmer and Malton 85-91; Can and Preb York Minster 05-10; rtd 10; Perm to Offic *York* from 10. *18 Castle Howard Road, Malton YO17 7AY* Tel (01653) 690671

MANCHESTER, Archdeacon of. See ASHCROFT, The Ven Mark David

MANCHESTER, Bishop of. See McCULLOCH, The Rt Revd Nigel Simeon

MANCHESTER, Dean of. See GOVENDER, The Very Revd Rogers Morgan

MANCO, Gwenda Diane. b 54. NOC 97. **d** 99 **p** 00. NSM Rochdale *Man* 99-02; NSM Dearnley 02-04 and from 06; NSM Spotland 04-06; Asst Chapl HM Pris Buckley Hall 99-03; Chapl HM Pris Styal 03. *5 Stansfield Hall, Littleborough OL15 9RH* Tel (01706) 370264 Mobile 07966-217252 E-mail gwenda.manco@tesco.net

MANCOR, Neil McKay. Univ of BC MA Reading Univ PhD. Wycliffe Hall Ox. **d** 99 **p** 00. C Llandeilo Fawr and Taliaris *St D* 99-02; Canada from 02. *1490 Nanton Avenue, Vancouver BC V6H 2E2, Canada* E-mail neilmancor@hotmail.com

MANDER, Peter John. b 52. Liv Univ BA85. Sarum & Wells Th Coll 85. **d** 87 **p** 88. C Hale and Ashley *Ches* 87-90; TV Grantham *Linc* 90-00; P-in-c Quarrington w Old Sleaford 00-08; P-in-c Silk Willoughby 00-08; RD Lafford 03-07; Can and Preb Linc Cathl 05-08; R Cruden Bay *Ab* from 08; R Ellon from 08. *The Rectory, Craighall, South Road, Ellon AB41 9NF* E-mail peter.mander@gmail.com

MANDER, Canon Thomas Leonard Frederick. b 33. Roch Th Coll 59 Ely Th Coll 60. **d** 62 **p** 63. C Cov St Mary 62-66; V Bishop's Tachbrook 66-70; V Earlsdon 70-76; V Chesterton 76-83; R Lighthorne 76-83; V Newbold Pacey w Moreton Morrell 76-83; Hon Can Cov Cathl 80-92; P-in-c S Leamington St Jo 83-84; V 84-92; rtd 92; Perm to Offic *Cov* from 92. *59 Murcott Road East, Whitnash, Leamington Spa CV31 2JJ* Tel (01926) 339950

MANDERSON, Robert Dunlop (Leslie). b 35. LDS59 FDS65. Ox Min Course 92. **d** 94 **p** 95. NSM Maidenhead St Andr and St Mary *Ox* 94-00; Perm to Offic 00-02; NSM Chipping Norton 02-03; rtd 03; Perm to Offic *Ox* 03-04 and *Ely* from 04. *67 Park Street, Dry Drayton, Cambridge CB23 8DA* Tel (01954) 782388 E-mail lesmanderson@tiscali.co.uk

MANGA, Amos Morris Yorobama. **d** 06 **p** 07. C Helsinki *Eur* from 06. *The Anglican Church in Finland, Bulevardi 54B, 00120 Helsinki, Finland* Tel (00358) (9) 680 1515 Fax 698 6302

MANHOOD, Phyllis. See DELVES, Canon Phyllis

✠**MANKTELOW, The Rt Revd Michael Richard John.** b 27. Ch Coll Cam BA48 MA52. Chich Th Coll 51. **d** 53 **p** 54 **c** 77. C Boston *Linc* 53-56; Chapl Ch Coll Cam 57-61; Chapl Linc Th Coll 61-63; Sub-Warden 64-66; V Knaresborough St Jo *Ripon* 66-73; RD Harrogate 72-77; V Harrogate St Wilfrid 73-77; P-in-c Harrogate St Luke 75-77; Hon Can Ripon Cathl 75-77; Suff Bp Basingstoke *Win* 77-93; Can Res Win Cathl 77-91; Hon Can 91-93; Vice-Dean 87-93; rtd 93; Hon Asst Bp Chich from 94; Hon Asst Bp Eur from 94; Wiccamical Preb Chich Cathl 97-02. *14 Little London, Chichester PO19 1NZ* Tel (01243) 531096

MANLEY, Mrs Gillian. b 59. St Martin's Coll Lanc BEd80. St Jo Coll Nottm MA00. **d** 00 **p** 01. C Eckington and Ridgeway *Derby* 00-04; TV Wirksworth 04-09; V Blackwell w Tibshelf from 09. *The Vicarage, 67 High Street, Tibshelf, Alfreton DE55 5NU* Tel (01773) 873305 E-mail gill-manley@sky.com

MANLEY, Canon Gordon Russell Delpratt. b 33. Ch Coll Cam BA56 MA60. Linc Th Coll 57. **d** 59 **p** 60. C Westbury-on-Trym St Alb *Bris* 59-61; Chapl Ch Coll Cam 61-66; V Radlett *St Alb* 66-75; V Faversham *Cant* 75-99; RD Ospringe 84-90; Hon Can Cant Cathl 90-99; rtd 99; Perm to Offic *Cant* from 99; Retirement Officer (Cant Adnry) 01-10. *170 Old Dover Road, Canterbury CT1 3EX* Tel (01227) 784016

MANLEY, Mrs Jane Elizabeth. b 58. Ox Min Course 05. **d** 08 **p** 09. C Bracknell *Ox* from 08. *4 Windlesham Way, Forest Park, Bracknell RG12 0XX* Tel (01344) 420167 Mobile 07711-613057 E-mail johnandjane2@btinternet.com

MANLEY, Canon Michael Alan. b 60. SS Hild & Bede Coll Dur BA82. Trin Coll Bris. **d** 86 **p** 87. C Accrington St Jo w Huncoat *Blackb* 86-90; V Preston St Luke and St Oswald 90-96; V

Blackpool St Jo 96-07; Can Res Carl Cathl from 07; RD Carl from 10. *1 The Abbey, Carlisle CA3 8TZ* Tel (01228) 542790 E-mail canonmissioner@carlislecathedral.org.uk

MANLEY (*née* **McCARTHY**), **Mrs Sandra Ellen.** b 56. Man Univ MusB77 Goldsmiths' Coll Lon PGCE79 ARCM75 FRCO77 GRNCM78. S'wark Ord Course 92. **d** 95 **p** 96. C Beckenham St Geo *Roch* 95-99; V Heybridge w Langford *Chelmsf* 99-06; R Creeksea w Althorne, Latchingdon and N Fambridge 06-09; P-in-c Purleigh, Cold Norton and Stow Maries 08-09; V Althorne and Latchingdon w N Fambridge from 09; V Cold Norton w Stow Maries from 09; RD Maldon and Dengie from 11. *The Vicarage, Fambridge Road, Althorne, Chelmsford CM3 6BZ* Tel (01621) 742947 Mobile 07722-425942 E-mail sandra.manley@btinternet.com

MANLEY-COOPER, Simon James. b 46. S Dios Minl Tr Scheme 91. **d** 94 **p** 95. NSM Soho St Anne w St Thos and St Pet *Lon* 94-96; Ind Chapl 94-96; P-in-c Bedford St Mich *St Alb* 96-01; Ind Chapl 96-01; R Bramfield, Stapleford, Waterford etc 01-02; Chapl E and N Herts NHS Trust 03-11; rtd 11. *19 Barnfield Road, Harpenden AL5 5TH* Tel (01582) 460797 E-mail manley-c@hotmail.co.uk

MANN, Alexandrina Elizabeth. b 67. Westmr Coll Ox BA92 PGCE93 Birm Univ MA95. Trin Coll Bris 01. **d** 03 **p** 04. C Austrey and Warton *Birm* 03-06; V Hanbury, Newborough, Rangemore and Tutbury *Lich* from 06. *The Vicarage, 62 Redhill Lane, Tutbury, Burton-on-Trent DE13 9JW* Tel (01283) 810099 Mobile 07761-263849 E-mail alexandrina.shalom@virgin.net

MANN, Ms Angela. b 58. Bath Univ BA80 Bris Univ PGCE83. Trin Coll Bris 92. **d** 94 **p** 95. C Marlborough *Sarum* 94-97; Perm to Offic *Sarum* 97-98 and *Ox* 98-09; NSM The Claydons and Swan *Ox* from 09. *The Rectory, Grendon Underwood, Aylesbury HP18 0SY* Tel (01296) 770240 Mobile 07982-770161 E-mail angela.mann@o2.co.uk

MANN, Lt Comdr Anthony James. b 34. Open Univ BA76. St Jo Coll Nottm 85. **d** 88 **p** 89. NSM Helensburgh *Glas* 88-01; rtd 01. *Address temp unknown* E-mail didnpud@supanet.com

MANN, Canon Charmion Anne Montgomery. b 36. Liv Univ BA57 CertEd62 AdDipEd79 Univ of Wales (Lamp) MA06. Trin Coll Bris 80. **dss** 82 **d** 87 **p** 94. Bris St Nath w St Kath 82-84; Bris St Matt and St Nath 84-85; Asst Chapl City Cen Hosps Bris 85-88; Chapl Bris Maternity Hosp 88-94; Chapl Bris R Hosp for Sick Children 88-94; Chapl Bris R Infirmary 88-94; Hon Can Bris Cathl 93-00; P-in-c Lacock w Bowden Hill 94-00; C Gtr Corsham 97-00; rtd 00; Perm to Offic *Bris* 00-06; *Sarum* 01-06; *Ex* from 07. *21 Oak Gardens, Ivybridge PL21 0NB* Tel (01752) 896636 E-mail charmion.mann@danmat.co.uk

MANN, Christopher John. b 57. Glas Univ BSc79. Westcott Ho Cam 83. **d** 86 **p** 87. C Worc SE 86-89; Min Can and Sacr St Paul's Cathl 89-96; R Upminster *Chelmsf* 96-06; Chapl to Bp Bradwell 06-10; C Corringham 07-10; P-in-c Christchurch *Win* from 10. *8 Warren Edge Road, Bournemouth BH6 4AU* E-mail christopher@crispysalad.com

MANN, David. b 57. St Jo Coll Dur BA78. Ridley Hall Cam. **d** 82 **p** 83. C Monkwearmouth St Andr *Dur* 82-86; Chapl Sheff Cathl 86-87; C Leeds St Geo *Ripon* 87-94; V Ripon H Trin 94-06; Asst Dir of Ords 02-06; Nat Adv for Pre-Th Educn and Selection Sec Min Division 06-09; Dioc Voc Adv *York* from 09. *3 Glebe Close, Bolton Percy, York YO23 7HB* Tel (01904) 744619 E-mail david.mann@yorkdiocese.org

MANN, Donald Leonard. b 22. Westcott Ho Cam. **d** 47 **p** 48. C S'well Minster 47-49; C Edwinstowe 49-51; C St Alb St Paul *St Alb* 51-54; C Baldock w Bygrave and Clothall 54-56; V Guilden Morden *Ely* 56-59; V Rocester *Lich* 59-63; V Gnosall w Knightley 63-69; V Sheen 69-76; P-in-c Calton 72-76; P-in-c Ellastone 76; rtd 76; Perm to Offic *Ches* from 93. *Bungalow 24, Lyme Green Settlement, Macclesfield SK11 0LD* Tel (01260) 252209

MANN (*née* **WELLS**), **Ms Gillian Mary.** b 46. Bedf Coll Lon BA67 Goldsmiths' Coll Lon TCert68 MCIPD89. EMMTC 99. **d** 01 **p** 02. NSM Wirksworth *Derby* 01-05; P-in-c The Sampfords and Radwinter w Hempstead *Chelmsf* from 05. *The Rectory, Walden Road, Radwinter, Saffron Walden CB10 2SW* Tel (01799) 599332 Mobile 07719-470363 E-mail gillianmann@eidosnet.co.uk

MANN, Ivan John. b 52. Brunel Univ BTech74 Southn Univ BTh80. Sarum & Wells Th Coll 75. **d** 78 **p** 79. C Hadleigh w Layham and Shelley *St E* 78-81; C Whitton and Thurleston w Akenham 81-83; V Leiston 83-86; Perm to Offic 86-89; R Aldringham w Thorpe, Knodishall w Buxlow etc 89-93; V Ipswich St Jo 93-96; Chapl St Mary's Convent Wantage 96-00; Asst Chapl R Berks and Battle Hosps NHS Trust 00; TV Gt Yarmouth *Nor* 00-03; Team Member Loyola Hall Jesuit Spirituality Cen Prescot 03-04; Prec and Hon Can Cumbrae *Arg* 04-06; Can St Jo Cathl Oban 04-06; rtd 06. *140 Somerleyton Gardens, Norwich NR2 2BS* Tel (01603) 929591 E-mail ivan@ivanmann.f2s.com

MANN, Mrs Joan. **d** 98. NSM Eastbourne St Mary *Chich* 98-02; NSM The Hydneye 02-10; NSM Hampden Park and The

Hydnye from 10. *39 Cherry Garden Road, Eastbourne BN20 8HF* Tel (01323) 728259

MANN, John. b 35. ISO91. Oak Hill NSM Course 89. **d** 92 **p** 93. NSM Springfield All SS *Chelmsf* 92-05; RD Chelmsf N 99-04; rtd 05; Perm to Offic *Chelmsf* from 05. *18 Humber Road, Chelmsford CM1 7PE* Tel (01245) 259596

MANN, The Very Revd John Owen. b 55. QUB BD77 MTh86 MPhil98. CITC 79. **d** 79 **p** 81. C Cloughfern *Conn* 79-82; C Knock *D & D* 82-85; I Ballyrashane w Kildollagh *Conn* 85-89; R Bentworth and Shalden and Lasham *Win* 89-93; RD Alton 92-93; I Cloughfern *Conn* 93-02; I Belfast Malone St Jo 02-11; I Belfast St Anne from 11; Dean Belf from 11; Preb Clonmethan St Patr Cathl Dublin from 99. *The Deanery, 5 Deramore Drive, Belfast BT9 5JQ* Tel (028) 9066 0980 *or* 9032 8332 E-mail secstjohns@malo98.freeserve.co.uk

MANN, Julia Corinne. b 52. Open Univ BA92 Anglia Poly Univ BA03 RGN91. **d** 08 **p** 09. OLM Bury St Edmunds All SS w St Jo and St Geo *St E* from 08. *23 Westgate Street, Bury St Edmunds IP33 1QG* Tel (01284) 753984 E-mail jc.mann@btinternet.com

MANN, Julian Farrer Edgar. b 64. Peterho Cam MA90. Oak Hill Th Coll BA93. **d** 96 **p** 97. C Hoole *Ches* 96-00; V Oughtibridge *Sheff* from 00. *The Vicarage, Church Street, Oughtibridge, Sheffield S35 0FU* Tel 0114-286 2317 E-mail julianlisa@oughtimann.freeserve.co.uk

✠**MANN, The Rt Revd Michael Ashley.** b 24. KCVO89. CBIM. Wells Th Coll 55. **d** 57 **p** 58 **c** 74. C Wolborough w Newton Abbot *Ex* 57-59; V Sparkwell 59-62; V Port Harcourt Ch Ch Nigeria 62-67; Home See Miss to Seamen 67-69; Can Res Nor Cathl 69-74; Vice-Dean 73-74; Dioc Ind Adv 69-74; Suff Bp Dudley *Worc* 74-76; Dean Windsor and Dom Chapl to The Queen 76-89; rtd 89; Hon Asst Bp Glouc 89-11. *c/o Ms Caroline Pepys, 53 Hayfield Road, Oxford OX2 6TX*

MANN, Mrs Patricia Ann. b 62. STETS 08. **d** 11. C Havant *Portsm* from 11. *Christchurch Bungalow, 39 Snowberry Crescent, Havant PO9 2FE* Tel 07890-304670 (mobile) E-mail patmann12@yahoo.co.uk

MANN, Paul William. b 63. Leeds Univ BSc84 CEng MIET. EAMTC 01. **d** 04 **p** 05. NSM Lawford *Chelmsf* from 04. *8 Cherrywoods, Great Bentley, Colchester CO7 8QF* Tel (01206) 252420 E-mail lima3papa-lawford@yahoo.co.uk

MANN, Peter Eric. b 51. St Jo Coll Dur BA73. Westcott Ho Cam 73. **d** 75 **p** 76. C Barrow St Jo *Carl* 75-78; C Egremont 78-80; V Carl St Luke Morton 80-86; TR Egremont and Haile 86-93; P-in-c Barrow St Geo w St Luke 93-99; TR S Barrow 99-06; P-in-c Barrow St Jo 95-96; RD Furness 94-01; RD Barrow 01-06; Hon Can Carl Cathl 95-06; TR Harwich Peninsula *Chelmsf* from 06; RD Harwich from 09. *The Rectory, 51 Highfield Avenue, Harwich CO12 4DR* Tel (01255) 502033 E-mail cookbird@gmail.com

MANN, Philip David. b 78. **d** 08 **p** 09. NSM Guildf St Sav 08-10; C Gerrards Cross and Fulmer *Ox* from 10. *Willowbrook, 54 The Uplands, Gerrards Cross SL9 7JG* Tel (01753) 887118 E-mail philip.mann@saintjames.org.uk

MANN, Ms Rachel. b 70. Lanc Univ BA91 MA93. Qu Coll Birm 03. **d** 05 **p** 06. C Stretford St Matt *Man* 05-08; P-in-c Burnage St Nic from 08. *The Rectory, 408 Kingsway, Burnage, Manchester M19 1PL* Tel 0161-432 7009 Mobile 07834-403195 E-mail rachel.mann@ntlworld.com

MANN, Ralph Norman. b 27. BNC Ox BA51 MA55 DipEd52. Ox NSM Course 79. **d** 82 **p** 83. NSM Kingham w Churchill, Daylesford and Sarsden *Ox* 82-85; S Area See BCMS 82-89; P-in-c Broadwell, Evenlode, Oddington and Adlestrop *Glouc* 89-97; rtd 97; P-in-c Upton St Leonards *Glouc* 97-00. *2 Whittons Close, Hook Norton, Banbury OX15 5QG* Tel (01608) 730327

MANN, Robin. b 45. Fitzw Coll Cam BA76 MA80 MRTPI73. Ridley Hall Cam 73. **d** 77 **p** 78. C Wetherby *Ripon* 77-80; V Hipswell 80-86; V Mamble w Bayton, Rock w Heightington etc *Worc* 86-96; V Avon Valley *Sarum* 96-02; R Selworthy, Timberscombe, Wootton Courtenay etc *B & W* 02-07; rtd 07. *Hoarthorns Cottage, Malvern Way, Edge End, Coleford GL16 7DZ* Tel (01594) 833576 E-mail hoarthorns@tiscali.co.uk

MANN, Stephen Paul. b 52. Staffs Univ BA76 Keele Univ PGCE78. Cranmer Hall Dur 96. **d** 98 **p** 99. C Spennymoor, Whitworth and Merrington *Dur* 98-03; Chapl Dur Constabulary 99-03; Chapl Butterwick Hospice Bishop Auckland 00-03; TV Madeley *Heref* 03-04; rtd 05. *42 The Crescent, Montford Bridge, Shrewsbury SY4 1EA* E-mail steve.mann99@telco4u.net

MANN, Terence John. b 47. GGSM68 LRSM79 FTCL79 Miami Univ MA80 Lon Univ PGCE69. Ox Min Course 91. **d** 94 **p** 95. NSM Kingham w Churchill, Daylesford and Sarsden *Ox* 94-00; Chapl HM Pris Camp Hill from 00. *HM Prison, Camp Hill, Newport PO30 5PB* Tel (01983) 527661 Fax 520505

MANN, Mrs Tessa. STETS. **d** 08 **p** 09. NSM Bourne Valley *Sarum* from 08; NSM Salisbury St Fran and Stratford sub Castle from 09. *Barton Mead, Tanners Lane, Winterbourne Earls, Salisbury SP4 6HD*

MANNALL, Michael John Frederick. b 37. St Mich Coll Llan 61. **d** 63 **p** 64. C Clapham H Spirit *S'wark* 63-66; C Brighton St Bart

Chich 66-68; C Willesden St Matt *Lon* 68-69; C-in-c Cricklewood St Pet CD 69-73; R Broughton *Pet* 73-75; Hon C Kingston St Luke *S'wark* 76-94; rtd 84; Perm to Offic *Nor* from 95. *The Blessings, 55 Sculthorpe Road, Fakenham NR21 9ET* Tel (01328) 863496 E-mail michael.mannall@btinternet.com

MANNERS, Jennifer Helen Edith. b 50. K Coll Lon MB, BS73 AKC73. d 06 p 07. OLM Bearsted w Thurnham *Cant* from 06. *9 Tilefields, Hollingbourne, Maidstone ME17 1TZ* Tel (01622) 880363 E-mail jhemanners@hotmail.com

MANNERS, Kenneth. b 29. NOC. d 84 p 85. NSM Brayton *York* 84-00; rtd 00; Perm to Offic *York* 00-11. *16 Wistow Road, Selby YO8 3LY* Tel (01757) 702129

MANNING, Adrian Peter. b 63. St Cath Coll Cam MA88 K Coll Lon PGCE88 St Cath Coll Cam BA84. Ridley Hall Cam 92. d 95 p 96. C Oxhey All SS *St Alb* 95-97; Asst Chapl Bedford Sch 97-02; Chapl St Geo Sch Harpenden from 02. *12 Crecy Gardens, Redbourn, St Albans AL3 7JP* Tel (01582) 716231

MANNING, Mrs Ann. b 42. Liv Univ CertEd75. St Jo Coll Nottm 93 NOC 94. d 95 p 96. NSM Grasmere *Carl* 95-96; NSM Delamere *Ches* 96-99; C Middlewich w Byley 99-02; Chapl Mid Cheshire Hosps Trust 99-02; P-in-c Dunton w Wrestlingworth and Eyeworth *St Alb* 02-05; R 05-08; rtd 08. *27 Barley Croft, Great Boughton, Chester CH3 5SP* Tel (01244) 316781 E-mail revmanning@hotmail.co.uk

MANNING, David Godfrey. b 47. Trin Coll Bris 73. d 76 p 77. C Richmond H Trin and Ch Ch *S'wark* 76-79; C Anston *Sheff* 79-83; V Blackpool St Mark *Blackb* 83-91; V Creech St Michael *B & W* 91-08; Perm to Offic from 10. *The Priest Hole, 11 Bittern Avenue, Portishead BS20 7NT* Tel (01275) 848016

MANNING, Mrs Jean Margaret. b 46. Oak Hill NSM Course 07. d 08 p 09. NSM Herstmonceux and Wartling *Chich* from 08. *Little Bathurst Farm, Cowbeech Road, Rushlake Green, Heathfield TN21 9QA* Tel and fax (01435) 831105 Mobile 07711-052131 E-mail jmm60@btinternet.com

MANNING, Neville Alexander. b 41. Lon Univ BD68. ALCD68. d 68 p 69. C Belvedere All SS *Roch* 68-71; C Hollington St Leon *Chich* 71-73; C Hersham *Guildf* 73-77; V Dawley St Jerome *Lon* 77-94; R Denton w S Heighton and Tarring Neville *Chich* 94-06; rtd 06. *7 Salvador Close, Eastbourne BN23 5TB* Tel (01323) 479359

MANNING, Virginia Ann. b 47. Univ of Wales (Ban) BTh07. d 07 p 08. OLM N Hartismere *St E* from 07. *Fernleigh, Mill Road, Winfarthing, Diss IP22 2DZ* Tel (01379) 644229 E-mail colgin.manning@tesco.net

MANNINGS, Andrew James. b 52. Trent Park Coll of Educn CertEd73. St Jo Coll Nottm 90. d 92 p 94. C Over St Chad *Ches* 92-93; C Sale St Anne 93-96; C Timperley 96-98; P-in-c Egremont St Jo 98-04; P-in-c Liscard St Mary w St Columba 03-04; V Liscard Resurr from 04; RD Wallasey 02-07. *The Vicarage, 107 Manor Road, Wallasey CH45 7LU* Tel 0151-638 4360 Fax 513 0172 Mobile 07814-878175 E-mail frandrew2004@yahoo.co.uk

MANNS, Edwin Ernest. b 30. Portsm Dioc Tr Course 84. d 85. C Paulsgrove *Portsm* 85-95; Chapl St Mary's Hosp Portsm 90-91; Team Chapl Portsm Hosp 91-95; rtd 95. *17 Kelvin Grove, Portchester, Fareham PO16 8LQ* Tel (023) 9232 4818

MANSBRIDGE, The Ven Michael Winstanley. b 32. Southn Univ BA54. Ridley Hall Cam 56. d 58 p 59. C Ware St Mary *St Alb* 58-60; C Claverdon w Preston Bagot *Cov* 60-62; Kenya 62-65; Asst P Nairobi Cathl and Chapl Nairobi Univ 62-65; V Chilvers Coton w Astley *Cov* 65-75; RD Nuneaton 66-73; V Leamington Priors H Trin 75-83; Chapl Abu Dhabi St Andr UAE 83-97; Adn the Gulf 83-91; Adn Cyprus and the Gulf 91-99; Can Nicosia 86-99; Provost 97-99; Can Bahrain 87-99; rtd 97; Hon Can Nicosia and Bahrain from 99. *Blue Skies, 7 Norman Way, Wootton Bridge, Ryde PO33 4NJ* Tel (01983) 882394 E-mail fiona mansbridge@compuserve.com

MANSEL LEWIS, Patrick Charles Archibald. b 53. Solicitor 79. St Mich Coll Llan 01. d 04 p 05. NSM Llandeilo Fawr and Taliaris *St D* from 04. *Stradey Castle, Pwll, Llanelli SA15 4PL* Tel (01554) 774626 E-mail patmanlew@btconnect.com

MANSELL, Carol. b 52. Lon Bible Coll BA75 Nottm Univ MA86 CQSW86 Leic Univ MBA05. ERMC 08. d 10 p 11. NSM Rattlesden w Thorpe Morieux, Brettenham etc *St E* from 10. *Dawning, Rags Lane, Woolpit, Bury St Edmunds IP30 9SG* Tel (01359) 242776 Mobile 07788-157147 E-mail carol.mansell@btinternet.com

MANSELL, The Ven Clive Neville Ross. b 53. Leic Univ LLB74 Solicitor 77. d 82 p 83. C Gt Malvern St Mary *Worc* 82-85; Min Can Ripon Cathl 85-89; R Kirklington w Burneston and Wath and Pickhill 89-02; AD Wensley 98-02; Adn Tunbridge *Roch* from 02. *3 The Ridings, Blackhurst Lane, Tunbridge Wells TN2 4RU* Tel and fax (01892) 520660 E-mail archdeacon.tonbridge@rochester.anglican.org

MANSELL, Paul John. b 67. Staffs Univ MSc05. Ripon Coll Cuddesdon 05. d 07 p 08. C Schorne *Ox* 07-10; V Forest Edge from 10. *The Vicarage, Mount Skippett, Ramsden, Chipping Norton OX7 3AP* Tel (01993) 868687 Mobile 07983-707560 E-mail paul@deepblueocean.co.uk

MANSFIELD, Alastair John Fraser. b 60. Ex Univ BA82 Ch Coll Cam PGCE84 City Univ MSc92. SEITE. d 99 p 00. C Palmers Green St Jo *Lon* 99-02; P-in-c Enfield St Mich 02-07; Chapl RN from 08. *Royal Naval Chaplaincy Service, Mail Point 1-2, Leach Building, Whale Island, Portsmouth PO2 8BY* Tel (023) 9262 5055 Fax 9262 5134

MANSFIELD, Glen Robert. b 76. St Jo Coll Ox BA97. Oak Hill Th Coll BA11. d 11. C Aldershot H Trin *Guildf* from 11. *13 Vixen Drive, Aldershot GU12 4FN*

MANSFIELD, Gordon Reginald. b 35. Lon Univ BA CertEd. Clifton Th Coll 58. d 63 p 64. C Carl St Jo 63-65; C Westcombe Park St Geo *S'wark* 65-68; C Rashcliffe *Wakef* 68-70; V Woodlands *Sheff* 70-80; V Steeple Bumpstead and Helions Bumpstead *Chelmsf* 80-02; Perm to Offic *Ely* 03-04; *Heref* and *S & B* from 04. *18 Caefelyn, Norton, Presteigne LD8 2UB* Tel (01544) 260380

MANSFIELD, Julian Nicolas (Nick). b 59. K Coll Lon BD AKC. Edin Th Coll 83. d 85 p 86. C Kirkby *Liv* 85-89; TV Ditton St Mich 89-96; P-in-c Preston St Oswald *Blackb* 96-01; V Penwortham St Leon from 01. *St Leonard's Vicarage, Marshall's Brow, Penwortham, Preston PR1 9HY* Tel (01772) 742367 E-mail nickthevic1@googlemail.com

MANSFIELD, Robert William. b 45. d 88 p 89. OLM Louth *Linc* from 88. *The Old Railway House, Stewton, Louth LN11 8SD* Tel (01507) 327533 E-mail mansfieldstewton@hotmail.com

MANSFIELD, Simon David. b 55. Brunel Univ BSc81 Lon Univ MA94 Univ of Wales (Ban) MPhil06. Ripon Coll Cuddesdon 88. d 90 p 91. C N Harrow St Alb *Lon* 91-93; C Birchington w Acol and Minnis Bay *Cant* 93-97; TV Accrington *Blackb* 97-00; TV Accrington Ch the King 00-05; P-in-c Wednesfield St Greg *Lich* from 05. *St Gregory's Vicarage, 112 Long Knowle Lane, Wolverhampton WV11 1JQ* Tel (01902) 731677 E-mail smansfield@toucansurf.com

MANSFIELD, Stephen McLaren. b 59. FGA. Cranmer Hall Dur 86. d 89 p 90. C Poynton *Ches* 89-92; C Bromborough 92-94; V Bidston 94-02; C Heswall 02-09; V Birkenhead St Jas w St Bede from 09. *St James's Vicarage, 56 Tollemache Road, Prenton CH43 8SZ* Tel 0151-652 1016 E-mail steve.mansfield@mac.com

MANSHIP, Charmian Margaret. b 45. RCM BMus68 ARCM65 GRSM67 FRCO68. SAOMC 95. d 98 p 99. NSM Abingdon *Ox* 98-04; Succ and Min Can Worc Cathl from 04. *22 Stanmore Road, Worcester WR2 4PW* Tel (01905) 421147

MANSHIP, Canon David. b 27. ARCO Keble Coll Ox BA52 MA58. Qu Coll Birm 52. d 54 p 55. C Hackney St Jo *Lon* 54-58; C Preston Ascension 58-61; C St Andr Holborn 61-65; Members' Tr Officer C of E Youth Coun 65-68; Clergy Tr Officer 68-70; Dir of Educn *Win* 70-79; Hon Can Win Cathl 74-79; R Old Alresford 76-79; V Abingdon w Shippon *Ox* 79-89; TR Abingdon 89-93; V Shippon 89; RD Abingdon 87-90; rtd 93; Perm to Offic *Ox* 93-03 and *Worc* from 04. *22 Stanmore Road, Worcester WR2 4PW* Tel (01905) 421147

MANSLEY, Colin Edward. b 56. Edin Univ MA80 BA85. Ripon Coll Cuddesdon 83. d 86 p 87. C Worle *B & W* 86-89; C Baguley *Man* 89-91; C Radcliffe St Mary 91; TV Radcliffe 91-96; V Bartley Green *Birm* 96-08; R Cefn w Trefnant w Tremeirchion *St As* from 08. *The Rectory, Trefnant, Denbigh LL16 5UG* Tel (01745) 730584 E-mail colin@archangel.clara.co.uk

MANSON-BRAILSFORD, Andrew Henry. b 64. NUU BA86 Liv Univ MPhil98 Sussex Univ DPhil06. Ripon Coll Cuddesdon 87. d 90 p 91. C Warrington St Elphin *Liv* 90-93; C Torrisholme *Blackb* 93-96; V Brighton St Geo w St Anne and St Mark *Chich* from 96; RD Brighton from 10; Chapl St Mary's Hall Brighton from 97. *St George's House, 6 Sussex Mews, Brighton BN2 1GZ* Tel (01273) 625538 E-mail revmanson-brailsford@hotmail.co.uk

MANTON, Paul Arthur. b 45. Oak Hill Th Coll BD77. d 77 p 78. C Wolverhampton *Lich* 77-80; Ind Chapl *Lon* 80-87; Hon C St Marylebone All So w SS Pet and Jo 80-87; Perm to Offic from 03. *75 Homefield Gardens, London N2 0XL* Tel (020) 3224 3001 Mobile 07847-425946

MANUEL, Paul. b 55. Univ of Wales (Ban) BA76 Lon Sch of Th MA09 ACIS79 FCIS88. SAOMC 97. d 00 p 01. NSM Luton St Paul *St Alb* 00-03; C Chorleywood Ch Ch 03-07; P-in-c New Milverton *Cov* 07-10; V from 10; AD Warwick and Leamington from 10. *St Mark's Vicarage, 2 St Mark's Road, Leamington Spa CV32 6DL* Tel (01926) 421004 E-mail paul.manuel4@ntlworld.com

MAPES, David. Brunel Univ BSc71 CEng75 MIET74 MIMechE78 EurIng89 FInstD77 MBACP99. NTMTC BA07. d 07 p 08. NSM Feltham *Lon* 07-10; P-in-c Southampton St Mark *Win* from 10. *St Mark's Vicarage, 54 Archers Road, Southampton SO15 2LU* Tel (023) 8063 6425 Mobile 07885-635378 E-mail davemapes@aol.com

MAPLE, David Charles. b 34. Sarum Th Coll 64. d 66 p 66. C Buckland in Dover *Cant* 66-67; C St Laur in Thanet 67-71; Chapl RAF 71-75; P-in-c Ivychurch 75-76; P-in-c Newchurch *Cant* 75-78; P-in-c Burmarsh 75-78; P-in-c St Mary in the Marsh 75-76; R Dymchurch 76-78; R Dymchurch w Burmarsh and

Newchurch 78-81; Hon Min Can Cant Cathl from 79; Abp's Dioc Chapl 81-91; Chapl St Jo Hosp Cant 91-95; rtd 95; Perm to Offic *Cant* from 98. *1 Mount Pleasant, Blean, Canterbury CT2 9EU* Tel (01227) 459044

MAPLE, John Philip. b 50. Chich Th Coll 71. d 74 p 79. C Notting Hill St Mich and Ch *Lon* 74-75; Lic to Offic 78-79; C Barnsbury St Dav w St Clem 79-80; C Cotham St Sav w St Mary *Bris* 80-83; TV St Marylebone Ch Ch *Lon* 83-91; R St Marylebone St Paul 91-99; P-in-c Fulham St Alb w St Aug 99-04; P-in-c Fulham St Pet 99-02; Community Min Adv from 04. *London Diocesan House, 36 Causton Street, London SW1P 4AU* Tel (020) 7932 1122 E-mail jack.maple@london.anglican.org

MAPLEY, Mrs Barbara Jean. b 46. Guy's Hosp Medical Sch MCSP69. Oak Hill NSM Course 86. d 89 p 94. NSM Kelvedon *Chelmsf* 89-93; C Witham 93-94; TV 94-01; R Belbroughton w Fairfield and Clent *Worc* from 01. *The Rectory, Bradford Lane, Belbroughton, Stourbridge DY9 9TF* Tel (01562) 730531 E-mail barbaramapley@waitrose.com

MAPPLEBECKPALMER, Richard Warwick. b 32. CCC Cam BA56 MA60. Cuddesdon Coll 56. d 58 p 59. C Redcar *York* 58-60; C Drypool St Jo 61-63; V Pendleton St Ambrose *Man* 63-77; P-in-c Piddington *Ox* 77; P-in-c Ambrosden w Arncot and Blackthorn 77; P-in-c Merton 77; V Ambrosden w Merton and Piddington 77-88; USA from 88; rtd 97. *472 Dale Road, Martinez CA 94553-4829, USA* Tel (001) (510) 228 5252

MAPSON, Preb John Victor. b 31. Lon Univ BA60. Oak Hill Th Coll 55. d 60 p 61. C Littleover *Derby* 60-62; C Wandsworth St Mich *S'wark* 62-65; R Willand *Ex* 65-71; P-in-c Axmouth 71-72, V 72-75, V Axmouth w Musbury 75-77, RD Honiton 76-77; V Cullompton 77-89; R Kentisbeare w Blackborough 77-89; RD Cullompton 81-89; P-in-c Sidmouth All SS 89-96; Preb Ex Cathl 91-01; RD Ottery 94-96; rtd 96; Ed *Exeter Diocesan Directory* 00-10. *47 Head Weir Road, Cullompton EX15 1NN* Tel (01884) 38037 E-mail jmapson@care4free.net

MAPSTONE, Trevor Anthony. b 63. Lanc Univ BSc84 MA96. St Jo Coll Nottm 86. d 89 p 90. C Hoole *Ches* 89-92; C Lancaster St Thos *Blackb* 92-96; V Harrow Trin St Mich *Lon* 96-03; Dir of Ords Willesden Area 98-03; V S Croydon Em *S'wark* from 03; AD Croydon Cen from 09. *33 Hurst Way, South Croydon CR2 7AP* Tel (020) 8688 6676 E-mail tmapstone@emmanuelcroydon.org.uk

MARAIS, Rudolph James. b 41. St Bede's Coll Umtata BTh. d 81 p 82. S Africa 81-85 and from 87; C Belmont *S'wark* 85-87. *PO Box 101, Jefferys Bay, 6300 South Africa* Tel (0027) (42) 291 1659 Mobile 82-578 7522

MARBUS, Alida Janny. See WHITTOCK, Alida Janny

MARCER, Graham John. b 52. Ripon Coll Cuddesdon 75. d 78 p 79. C Sherborne w Castleton and Lillington *Sarum* 78-81; C Christchurch *Win* 81-84; V Southampton St Jude 84-90; P-in-c Moordown 90-91; C Sheff St Cecilia Parson Cross 91-93; V Balby 93-00; RD W Doncaster 97-00; V Radford *Cov* 00-11; AD Cov N 01-04; rtd 11. *1 Bosworth Close, Ashby de la Zouch LE65 1LB* Tel (01530) 563767 E-mail graham.marcer@btinternet.com

MARCETTI, Alvin Julian. b 41. San Jose State Univ BA66 Santa Clara Univ MA76. Cranmer Hall Dur 85. d 87 p 88. C Stepney St Dunstan and All SS *Lon* 87-91; Chapl City of Lon Poly 91-92; Chapl Lon Guildhall Univ 92-96; Chapl Homerton Univ Hosp NHS Trust Lon 96-03; Chapl City and Hackney Community Services NHS Trust 96-03; rtd 03. *1145 East Whitton Avenue, Unit 1003, Phoenix AZ 85014-5088, USA* E-mail almarcetti@yahoo.co.uk

MARCH, Alan Mervyn. b 48. Open Univ BA91 CPFA73. EAMTC 00. d 03 p 04. NSM Northampton St Alb *Pet* 03-06; NSM Northampton Ch Ch from 06; NSM Northampton H Sepulchre w St Andr and St Lawr from 06; NSM Northampton St Mich w St Edm from 06; NSM Northampton H Trin and St Paul from 06. *236 Beech Avenue, Northampton NN3 2LE* Tel (01604) 405722 E-mail alan@march100.freeserve.co.uk

MARCH, Andrew. b 81. UEA BA03. St Jo Coll Nottm MA09. d 09 p 10. C Werrington and Wetley Rocks *Lich* from 09. *360 Ash Bank Road, Werrington, Stoke-on-Trent ST9 0JS* Tel 07816-998642 (mobile) E-mail revandymarch@googlemail.com

MARCH, Anthony. See MARCH, Charles Anthony Maclea

MARCH, Charles Anthony Maclea (Tony). b 32. CCC Cam BA55 MA70. Oak Hill Th Coll 55. d 57 p 58. C S Croydon Em *Cant* 57-60; C Eastbourne H Trin *Chich* 60-63; V Whitehall Park St Andr Hornsey Lane *Lon* 63-67; V Tunbridge Wells H Trin w Ch Ch *Roch* 67-82; V Prestonville St Luke *Chich* 82-97; rtd 97; Perm to Offic *Roch* from 99. *The Barn, 2 Town Farm Dairy, Brenchley Road, Brenchley, Tonbridge TN12 7PA* Tel (01892) 722802

MARCH, Gerald. b 44. Nottm Univ BA75. Oak Hill Th Coll 92. d 95 p 96. C Sandgate St Paul w Folkestone St Geo *Cant* 95-99; P-in-c Southampton St Mark *Win* 99-03; V 03-09; Perm to Offic *Ox* from 10. *Dovetrees, 2B Curbridge Road, Witney OX28 5JR* Tel (01993) 700479 E-mail rev.gerald@gmail.com

MARCH, Jonathan. b 79. Wycliffe Hall Ox. d 05 p 06. C

Brompton H Trin w Onslow Square St Paul *Lon* 05-11; V Oseney Crescent St Luke from 11. *22 Castle Road, London NW1 8PP* Tel (020) 7052 0301

MARCHAND, Canon Rex Anthony Victor (Toby). b 47. K Coll Lon BD69 AKC69. St Aug Coll Cant 69. d 70 p 71. C Leigh Park *Portsm* 70-73; C Bp's Hatfield *St Alb* 73-80; R Deal St Leon and St Rich and Sholden *Cant* 80-95; RD Sandwich 91-94; Hon Can Cant Cathl 94-95; V Bishop's Stortford St Mich *St Alb* from 95; RD Bishop's Stortford 03-06; Hon Can St Alb from 08. *St Michael's Vicarage, 8 Larkspur Road, Bishop's Stortford CM23 4LL* Tel (01279) 651415 E-mail tandmmarchand@ntlworld.com

MARCHANT, Canon Iain William. b 26. Wells Th Coll 59. d 60 p 61. C Dalston *Carl* 60-63; V Hawkesbury *Glouc* 63-76; R Newent 76-85; Hon Can Glouc Cathl 84-92; R Newent and Gorsley w Cliffords Mesne 85-92; rtd 92; Perm to Offic *Glouc* from 92. *34 Parklands, Wotton-under-Edge GL12 7LT* Tel (01453) 844779

MARCHANT, John Bennet. b 46. St Jo Coll Nottm. d 06 p 07. Aux Min Powerscourt w Kilbride *D & G* from 06; Chapl Dublin City Univ from 07. *276 Harolds Grange Road, Dublin 16, Republic of Ireland* Tel (00353) (1) 494 2408 Mobile 87-239 3682 E-mail revjmarchant@yahoo.ie *or* john.marchant@dcu.ie

MARCHANT, Canon Ronald Albert. b 26. Em Coll Cam BA50 MA52 PhD57 BD64. Ridley Hall Cam 50. d 54 p 55. C Acomb St Steph *York* 54-57; C Willian *St Alb* 57-59; V Laxfield *St E* 59-92; RD Hoxne 73-78; Hon Can St E Cathl 75-92; P-in-c Wilby w Brundish 86-92; rtd 92; Perm to Offic *York* 93-11. *34 The Paddock, Boroughbridge Road, York YO26 6AW* Tel (01904) 798446

MARCHMENT, Mrs Ethel Diane. b 53. Ridley Hall Cam. d 11. NSM Douglas St Ninian *S & M* from 11. *Thie Peddyr, Glen Vine Road, Glen Vine, Isle of Man IM4 4HG* Tel (01624) 851754 E-mail dianemarchment@hotmail.com

MARCUS, Mrs Candice Ann. b 52. FInstLEx80. Trin Coll Bris 05. d 07 p 08. C Timsbury and Priston *B & W* 07-11; TV Whitton *Sarum* from 11. *The Vicarage, Back Lane, Aldbourne, Marlborough SN8 2BP* Tel (01672) 540311 Mobile 07788-437063 E-mail revcandicemarcus@gmail.com

MARCUS, Sarah Caroline. See ROWLAND JONES, Sarah Caroline

MARCUSSEN, Mrs Yolande Roberta. b 47. SEITE 98. d 01 p 02. NSM Bromley Common St Aug *Roch* 01-03; NSM Orpington All SS 03; Asst Chapl HM Pris Roch 01-03; Chapl 03-06; rtd 06. *24 Lucerne Road, Orpington BR6 0EP* Tel (01689) 833599 E-mail revyolandemarcussen@gmail.com

MARGAM, Archdeacon of. See MORRIS, The Ven Philip Gregory

MARGARET ANNE, Sister. See McALISTER, Margaret Elizabeth Anne

MARGARET JOY, Sister. See HARRIS, Margaret Claire

MARINER, Aris. b 43. Alexandria Univ BSc65. St Alb Minl Tr Scheme 84. d 87. NSM Stevenage H Trin *St Alb* from 87. *13 Church Lane, Stevenage SG1 3QS* Tel (01438) 365596

MARION EVA, Sister. See RECORD, Sister Marion Eva

MARK, Timothy John. b 34. Bris Univ BA57 PGCE58 MLitt68 MEd71 Leeds Univ PhD79. Didsbury Methodist Coll 54. d 59 p 61. India 59-69; Perm to Offic *Sheff* 73-08. *Spindrift, 61 Craig-yr-Eos Road, Ogmore-by-Sea, Bridgend CF32 0PH* Tel (01665) 880908 E-mail tjm@timothymark.plus.com

MARKBY, Archibald Campbell. b 15. Em Coll Cam BA37 MA41. Ridley Hall Cam 37. d 39 p 39. C Bradf St Clem 39-42; C Ox St Aldate 42-46; V Kilburn St Mary *Lon* 46-53; V Hornsey Ch Ch 53-64; R Ickenham 64-68; V Crowfield w Stonham Aspal *St E* 68-71; V Damerham *Sarum* 71-80; V Martin 71-80; rtd 80; Perm to Offic *Sarum* 80-00. *c/o A G C Markby Esq, 17 Sandell Court, The Parkway, Southampton SO16 3PH*

MARKBY, Ms Jane Elizabeth. b 67. Em Coll Cam BA88 Homerton Coll Cam PGCE89. Ridley Hall Cam 00. d 02 p 03. NSM Edmonton All SS w St Mich *Lon* 02-06; Chapl Haberdashers' Aske's Sch Elstree 06-10; Chapl Berkhamsted Sch Herts from 10. *Adelbert House, Mill Street, Berkamsted HP4 2AN* Tel (01442) 358095 E-mail jmarkby@berkhamstedschool.org

MARKBY, Peter John Jenner. b 38. Em Coll Cam BA60. Clifton Th Coll 62. d 64 p 65. C Tufnell Park St Geo *Lon* 64-68; C Crowborough *Chich* 68-73; C Polegate 73-77; R Southover 77-02; rtd 02; Perm to Offic *Chich* from 02. *66 Leylands Road, Burgess Hill RH15 8AJ* Tel (01444) 870831 E-mail petermarkby@onetel.com

MARKER, Janet. b 63. WEMTC 02. d 06 p 07. NSM Bris Lockleaze St Mary Magd w St Fran from 06. *165 Landseer Avenue, Bristol BS7 9YT* Tel 0117-969 3248 E-mail janet.marker@getreal.co.uk

MARKEY, Andrew John. b 73. Univ of Wales (Swansea) BSc96. Westcott Ho Cam BTh02. d 02 p 03. C Wotton-under-Edge w Ozleworth, N Nibley etc *Glouc* 02-06; Chapl Ox Brookes Univ from 09. *The Chaplaincy, Oxford Brookes University, Headington, Oxford OX3 0BP* Tel (01865) 484690 E-mail chaplaincy@brookes.ac.uk

MARKHAM, Deryck O'Leary. b 28. Oak Hill Th Coll 66. **d** 68 **p** 69. C Purley Ch Ch *S'wark* 68-72; V E Budleigh and Bicton *Ex* 72-93; RD Aylesbeare 89-93; rtd 93; Perm to Offic *Ex* 93-03 and *Win* from 03. *8 Milford House, Milford on Sea, Lymington SO41 0QJ* Tel (01590) 643515 E-mail dolm@onetel.com

MARKS, Allan Willi. b 56. Cranmer Hall Dur 92. **d** 94 **p** 95. C Barnoldswick w Bracewell *Bradf* 94-96; C Willington *Newc* 96-98; TV 98-02; V Newc H Cross 02-09; P-in-c Newc Ch Ch w St Ann from 09. *St Ann's Vicarage, 11 Gibson Street, Newcastle upon Tyne NE1 6PY* Tel 0191-232 0516 E-mail fatherallan@blueyonder.co.uk

MARKS, Anthony Alfred. b 28. AKC53. **d** 54 **p** 55. C Fleetwood St Pet *Blackb* 54-58; V Burnley St Cuth 58-63; Chapl RN 63-83; P-in-c Bradninch *Ex* 83-88; R Bradninch and Clyst Hydon 88-90; rtd 90; Perm to Offic *B & W* from 90; QHC from 81. *45 Mondyes Court, Milton Lane, Wells BA5 2QX*

MARKS, Anthony Wendt. b 43. G&C Coll Cam BA63 MA67 PhD70 BNC Ox DPhil72. St Steph Ho Ox 70. **d** 72 **p** 73. C Withington St Crispin *Man* 72-75; Chapl Lon Univ Medical Students 75-80; Warden Liddon Ho Lon 80-92; C-in-c Grosvenor Chpl *Lon* 80-92; V Shrewsbury All SS w St Mich *Lich* 92-99; V Fareham SS Pet and Paul *Portsm* 99-09; rtd 09; Perm to Offic *York* from 10. *9A Throxenby Lane, Scarborough YO12 5HN* Tel (01723) 377504

MARKS, Dennis Ray. b 37. Lon Univ BSc58 PhD67 PGCE59 Univ of Wales (Ban) BTh04 CChem85 MRSC85. **d** 06 **p** 07. OLM Woking St Mary *Guildf* from 06. *Green Tiles, Shaftesbury Road, Woking GU22 7DU* Tel (01483) 762030 E-mail ray@raymarks.fsnet.co.uk

MARKS, Mrs June Margaret. b 49. LCTP. **d** 08. NSM Oakworth *Bradf* 08-09. *49 Larkfield Terrace, Oakworth, Keighley BD22 7HJ* Tel (01535) 648328 E-mail emrysandjune@talktalk.net

MARKS, Robert Wesley. b 58. Guelph Univ (Canada) BSc81. Cranmer Hall Dur 03. **d** 05 **p** 06. C Baxenden *Blackb* 05-06; C Anchorsholme 06-09; P-in-c Ribby cum Wrea and Weeton 09-11; V from 11. *The Vicarage, 1 Vicarage Close, Wrea Green, Preston PR4 2PQ* Tel (01772) 687644 Mobile 07906-175379 E-mail wesmarks@supanet.com

MARKS, Timothy John. b 45. Man Univ BA76 Anglia Poly Univ MA96. **d** 88 **p** 89. NSM Burton and Sopley *Win* 88-91; R Croxton and Eltisley *Ely* 91-96; R Graveley w Papworth St Agnes w Yelling etc 91-96; Dir Network Counselling and Tr 96-05; Nat Adv for Personal/Spiritual Development YMCA 05-07. *58 Meadow Road, Malvern WR14 2SD* Tel (01684) 564925 Mobile 07817-465213 E-mail tim@timmarksconsulting.com

MARL, David John. b 42. ARCA67. **d** 01 **p** 02. OLM Okeford Sarum from 01. *Bow Cottage, Shute Lane, Iwerne Minster, Blandford Forum DT11 8LZ* Tel (01747) 812048 E-mail burgoyne.marl@tiscali.co.uk

MARLEY, The Very Revd Alan Gordon. b 59. Birm Univ BA89. Qu Coll Birm 87. **d** 89 **p** 90. C Blandford Forum and Langton Long *Sarum* 89-93; Chapl HM YOI Aylesbury 93-97; I Fermoy Union *C, C & R* 97-03; Bp's Dom Chapl 99-03; Dean Cloyne from 03; I Cloyne Union from 03; Dioc Dir of Ords from 05. *The Deanery, Deanery Road, Midleton, Co Cork, Republic of Ireland* Tel (00353) (21) 463 1449 E-mail dean@cloyne.anglican.org

MARLOW, Jonathan James. b 76. SS Hild & Bede Coll Dur MEng99. Wycliffe Hall Ox BTh06. **d** 06 **p** 07. C Elburton *Ex* 06-10; P-in-c Pennycross from 10. *St Pancras' Vicarage, 66 Glentor Road, Plymouth PL3 5TR* Tel (01752) 395300 E-mail jon.marlow@stps.co.uk

MARLOW (née SIBBALD), Mrs Olwyn Eileen. b 57. Aston Tr Scheme 85 Linc Th Coll 87. **d** 89 **p** 94. Par Dn Wythenshawe St Martin *Man* 89-93; Par Dn Baguley 93-94; C 94-95; Asst Chapl Cen Man Healthcare NHS Trust 95-00; NSM Newall Green St Fran *Man* 97-98; rtd 01; NSM Wythenshawe *Man* 01-05; Perm to Offic *Ches* and *Man* from 05. *28 Arcadia Avenue, Sale M33 3SA* Tel 0161-962 9292

MARNHAM, Preb Charles Christopher. b 51. Jes Coll Cam BA73 MA77. Cranmer Hall Dur. **d** 77 **p** 78. C Brompton H Trin *Lon* 77-78; C Brompton H Trin w Onslow Square St Paul 78-80; C Linthorpe *York* 80-84; R Haughton le Skerne *Dur* 84-95; V Ches Square St Mich w St Phil *Lon* from 95; Preb St Paul's Cathl from 10. *St Michael's Vicarage, 4 Chester Square, London SW1W 9HH* Tel (020) 7730 8889 Fax 7730 0043 E-mail charles@stmichaelschurch.org.uk

MARNS, Nigel Geoffrey. b 63. Univ of Wales (Abth) BSc(Econ)85 Birm Univ BD92. Qu Coll Birm 90. **d** 93 **p** 94. C Addington *S'wark* 96; P-in-c W Bromwich Gd Shep w St Jo *Lich* 96-01; V Bromsgrove St Jo *Worc* 01-09; R Ludgvan, Marazion, St Hilary and Perranuthnoe *Truro* from 09. *The Rectory, Ludgvan, Penzance TR20 8EZ* Tel (01736) 740784

✠**MARONA, The Most Revd Joseph Biringi Hassan.** b 41. Bp Gwynne Th Coll 78. **d** 81 **p** 82 **c** 84. Chapl Rumbek State Secondary Sch Sudan 81-82; Chapl Maridi Teachers' Tr Coll 82-83; Area Bp Maridi 85-89; Bp Maridi 89-00; Dean of Prov from 98; Abp Sudan and Bp Juba from 00. *ECS Liaison Office,*

PO Box 604, Khartoum, Sudan Tel (00249) (811) 20040 *or* (11) 485720 Fax (811) 20065 *or* (11) 485717 E-mail ecsprovince@hotmail.com

MARQUEZ, Edilberto. b 57. Bible Sem Alliance Peru BA80 Westmr Coll Ox MTh93. St Steph Ho Ox 92. **d** 94 **p** 95. C Reading St Jo *Ox* 94-98; C New Malden and Coombe *S'wark* 98-01; P-in-c Bucklebury w Marlston *Ox* 01-08; P-in-c Bradfield and Stanford Dingley 04-08; P-in-c Woodley 08-09; V Woodley from 09. *6 Denmark Avenue, Woodley, Reading RG5 4RS* Tel 0118-969 6540 E-mail emarquez@tiscali.co.uk

MARQUIS-FAULKES, Edmund. b 62. Hatf Coll Dur BA85. Ridley Hall Cam 87 Coates Hall Edin 90. **d** 91 **p** 92. C Broughty Ferry *Bre* 91-93; P-in-c Dundee St Ninian 93-02; R Bieldside *Ab* 02-07. *Address temp unknown* E-mail marquisfaulkes@yahoo.com

MARR (née PARKER), Mrs Anne Elizabeth. b 46. Hull Univ BSc67 CertEd68. NEOC 91. **d** 96. NSM Whorlton *Newc* 96-97; NSM Chapel House from 97; Chapl Newc City Health NHS Trust 96-01; Chapl Newc Mental Health Unit from 01. *26 The Chesters, Newcastle upon Tyne NE5 1AF* Tel 0191-267 4808

MARR, Derek Paul. b 33. Dur Univ TCert69. **d** 00 **p** 01. OLM Chapel House *Newc* from 00. *26 The Chesters, West Denton, Newcastle upon Tyne NE5 1AF* Tel 0191-267 4808

MARR, Canon Donald Radley. b 37. K Coll Lon 57. St Aid Birkenhead 61. **d** 64 **p** 65. C Macclesfield St Mich *Ches* 64-66; C Sale St Anne 66-67; V Marthall 67-72; C W Kirby St Bridget 72-76; R Waverton 76-83; R Nantwich 83-87; RD Nantwich 86-87; RD Malpas 87-91; V Bunbury 87-91; rtd 91; Dioc Rural Officer *Ches* 91-07; Hon Can Ches Cathl 91-92; Perm to Offic *Truro* from 94 and *Ches* from 07. *St Boniface, 5 Hockenhull Crescent, Tarvin, Chester CH3 8LJ,* or *The Parsonage, Tresco TR24 0QQ* Tel (01829) 741302 *or* (01720) 423176

MARR, Mrs Margaret Rose. b 36. JP81. St Mary's Coll Ban TCert56 Open Univ BA00. Ripon Coll Cuddesdon 02. **d** 02 **p** 03. NSM Tarvin *Ches* from 02; Perm to Offic *Truro* from 02. *St Boniface, 5 Hockenhull Crescent, Tarvin, Chester CH3 8LJ,* or *The Parsonage, Tresco TR24 0QQ* Tel (01829) 741302 *or* (01720) 423176 E-mail donald@donaldmarr.wanadoo.co.uk

MARR, Peter. b 36. Reading Univ PhD78. Ox NSM Course 84. **d** 87 **p** 88. NSM Reading St Giles *Ox* 87-89; C Beverley Minster *York* 90-92; P-in-c Beckenham St Barn *Roch* 92-96; V 96-03; rtd 03; Perm to Offic *Ex* from 04. *31 Kingsley Road, Plymouth PL4 6QP* Tel (01752) 228426 E-mail pbmarr@dircon.co.uk

MARRIAGE, Sophia Briony. b 71. Rob Coll Cam BA93 Edin Univ PhD98 Glas Univ MTh05. TISEC 03. **d** 05 **p** 06. C Edin St Martin from 05. *St Martin's Church, 232 Dalry Road, Edinburgh EH11 2GJ* Tel 0131-337 5493

MARRIOTT (née REID), Mrs Amanda Joy. b 63. Nottm Univ BTh92. Linc Th Coll 89. **d** 92 **p** 96. Par Dn Rothwell *Ripon* 92-94; C 94-95; C Manston 95-97; C Wetherby 97-01; P-in-c Water Eaton *Ox* 01-06; AD Milton Keynes 05-06; P-in-c Sherington w Chicheley, N Crawley, Astwood etc 06-09; R from 09. *The Rectory, 21 School Lane, Sherington, Newport Pagnell MK16 9NF* Tel (01908) 610521 E-mail ajmarriott@tiscali.co.uk

MARRIOTT, Frank Lewis. b 29. Lich Th Coll 57. **d** 60 **p** 61. C Earlsdon *Cov* 60-64; R Tysoe w Compton Winyates and Oxhill 64-70; P-in-c Cov St Marg 70-77; R Ufton 77-83; V Long Itchington 77-83; RD Southam 82-89; V Long Itchington and Marton 83-95; rtd 95; Perm to Offic *Heref* from 95. *12 Traherne Close, Ledbury HR8 2JF* Tel (01531) 634576

MARRIOTT, Stanley Richard. b 36. AKC60 Warwick Univ MA92. **d** 61 **p** 62. C Coleshill *Birm* 61-64; C Maxstoke 61-64; V Ansley *Cov* 64-78; Org Sec (E Midl) CECS 79-83; P-in-c Baxterley w Hurley and Wood End and Merevale etc *Birm* 83-84; R 84-87; R Newton Regis w Seckington and Shuttington 87-97; rtd 97; Perm to Offic *B & W* from 97. *Dunkery Pleck, Wootton Courtenay, Minehead TA24 8RH* Tel (01643) 841058

MARRISON, Geoffrey Edward. b 23. Lon Univ BA48 PhD67. Bps' Coll Cheshunt 49 Kirchliche Hochschule Berlin 50. **d** 51 **p** 52. C Wormley *St Alb* 51-52; SPG Miss Selangor Malaya 52-55; C St Andr Cathl Singapore 55-56; C Radlett *St Alb* 56-57; C St Botolph Aldgate w H Trin Minories *Lon* 57-58; V Crookes St Tim *Sheff* 58-61; SPG India 62-64; Perm to Offic *Cant* 64-69; Lic to Offic 69-82; Perm to Offic *Carl* 83-07; Tutor Carl Dioc Tr Course 83-07. *1 Ainsworth Street, Ulverston LA12 7EU* Tel (01229) 586874

MARROW, David Edward Armfield. b 42. Nottm Univ BA65 MA. Tyndale Hall Bris 65. **d** 67 **p** 68. C Clifton Ch Ch w Em *Bris* 67-70; BCMS Ethiopia 70-75; N Area Sec BCMS 75-77; C-in-c Ryde St Jas Prop Chpl *Portsm* 77-84; V Worthing St Geo *Chich* 84-07; rtd 07. *West View, 65 St Michael's Road, St Helens, Ryde PO33 1YJ* Tel (01983) 872729

MARSBURG, John Edward. b 53. Oak Hill Th Coll BA96. Coll of Resurr Mirfield 98. **d** 99 **p** 00. NSM Selby Abbey *York* 99-02; R Lenzie *Glas* 02-06; I Donacavey w Barr *Clogh* from 06. *The Rectory, 247 Tattyreagh Road, Fintona, Omagh BT78 2DA* Tel (028) 8284 1644 E-mail fintona@clogher.anglican.org

MARSDEN, Andrew Philip. b 63. Keble Coll Ox BA85 MA90 Birm Univ MA86. Wycliffe Hall Ox BA90. d 91 p 92. C Newport St Jo *Portsm* 91-94; C Cowplain 94-97; V Wokingham St Sebastian *Ox* from 97. *St Sebastian's Vicarage, Nine Mile Ride, Wokingham RG40 3AT* Tel (01344) 761050

MARSDEN, Andrew Robert. b 49. AKC71. St Aug Coll Cant 68. d 72 p 73. C New Addington *Cant* 72-75; C Prudhoe *Newc* 75-77; Asst Chapl HM Pris Wakef 77; Chapl HM Borstal Portland 77-82; Chapl HM YOI Onley 82-89; V Ulceby Gp *Linc* 89-98; Chapl Calderdale Healthcare NHS Trust 98-01; Chapl St Andr Hospice Grimsby 01-05; Community Chapl *Linc* 01-05; Chapl Hull and E Yorks Hosps NHS Trust from 05. *The Chaplaincy Office, Hull Royal Infirmary, Anlaby Road, Hull HU3 2JZ* Tel (01482) 674427 E-mail andrew.marsden@hey.nhs.uk

MARSDEN, Mrs Carole. b 44. Avery Hill Coll TCert65 Sheff Poly DipEd87. NOC 88. d 91 p 94. NSM Saddleworth *Man* 91-92; Par Dn 92-94; C 94-95; P-in-c Oldham St Paul 95-02; C Werneth 98-02; P-in-c Shap w Swindale and Bampton w Mardale *Carl* 02-08; P-in-c Orton and Tebay w Ravenstonedale etc 07-08. *Fairfield, Faraday Road, Kirby Stephen CA17 4QL* Tel (017683) 71279 Mobile 07866-006849 E-mail revmothershap@hotmail.com

MARSDEN, Mrs Diana Marion (Dodie). b 53. Deakin Univ Australia BEd88. STETS 00. d 03 p 04. NSM Hurstbourne Priors, Longparish etc *Win* from 03. *Little Brook House, Church Street, St Mary Bourne, Andover SP11 6BG* Tel (01264) 738211 E-mail dodie.marsden@ukgateway.net

MARSDEN, The Very Revd John Joseph. b 53. York Univ BA74 Nottm Univ MTh81 Kent Univ PhD88. St Jo Coll Nottm 77. d 80 p 81. C *Leigh* St Mary *Man* 80-83; Hon C Chatham St Steph *Roch* 83-91; Ind Chapl 83-91; Lect Systematic Th CITC and TCD from 91; I Newbridge w Carnalway and Kilcullen M & K from 97; I Kildare w Kilmeague and Curragh from 06; Dean Kildare from 06. *The Rectory, Morristown, Newbridge, Co Kildare, Republic of Ireland* Tel (00353) (45) 438185 E-mail johnmarsen@eircom.net

MARSDEN, John Robert. b 22. Linc Coll Ox BA48 MA49. Ripon Hall Ox 57. d 58 p 59. C Dur St Cuth 58-61; Chapl Dur Sch 61-85; rtd 85. *Prebends, High Kilburn, York YO61 4AJ* Tel (01347) 868597

MARSDEN, Canon Joyce. b 47. Eliz Gaskell Coll Man TCert68. Trin Coll Bris 78. dss 83 d 87 p 94. Wavertree H Trin *Liv* 83-85; Much Woolton 85-97; Par Dn 87-94; C 94-97; TV Parr 97-05; C 05-07; Hon Can Liv Cathl 03-07; rtd 07. *4 Mackets Close, Liverpool L25 9NU* Tel 0151-428 2798 E-mail joyceamarsden@hotmail.co.uk

MARSDEN, Michael John. b 59. St Mich Coll Llan 78. d 82 p 83. C Neath w Llantwit 82-85; Asst Chapl Univ Hosp of Wales Cardiff 85-89; V Graig *Llan* 89-93; P-in-c Cilfynydd 89-93; R Merthyr Tydfil St Dav 93-01; Chapl Gwent Healthcare NHS Trust from 01. *Nevill Hall Hospital, Brecon Road, Abergavenny NP7 7EG* Tel (01873) 732112 E-mail michael.marsden@gwent.wales.nhs.uk

MARSDEN, Robert. b 59. Ch Ch Ox BA81 PGCE82. Oak Hill Th Coll BA92. d 92 p 93. C Sevenoaks St Nic *Roch* 92-95; Chapl Fettes Coll Edin 95-99; C-in-c Buxton Trin Prop Chpl *Derby* from 99. *37 Temple Road, Buxton SK17 9BA* Tel (01298) 73656 E-mail robert@marsden8833.freeserve.co.uk

MARSDEN, Robert James. b 56. Ch Ch Coll Cant BEd79. Oak Hill Th Coll 90. d 94 p 95. C Margate H Trin *Cant* 94-98; P-in-c Brinton, Briningham, Hunworth, Stody etc *Nor* 98-08; P-in-c Gressenhall w Longham w Wendling etc from 08. *The Rectory, Bittering Street, Gressenhall, Dereham NR20 4EB* Tel (01362) 860211 E-mail robert@camelhome.co.uk

MARSDEN, Robert William. b 24. TCD BA49 MA52. CITC 50. d 50 p 51. C Dublin St Jas *D & G* 50-54; Asst Chapl Miss to Seamen 54-58; I Currin w Drum *Clogh* 58-66; I Clones w Killeevan 66-94; Prec Clogh Cathl 86-94; rtd 94. *30 Claremont Park, Sandymount, Dublin 4, Republic of Ireland* Tel (00353) (1) 668 0210

MARSDEN, Samuel Edward. b 44. Keble Coll Ox BA66 MA85. Linc Th Coll 66. d 68 p 69. C Liskeard w St Keyne *Truro* 68-72; R Gerrans w St Anthony in Roseland 72-77; V Kowloon Ch Ch Hong Kong 77-81; P-in-c Ingrave *Chelmsf* 81-82; P-in-c Gt Warley w Childerditch 81-82; R Gt Warley w Childerditch and Ingrave 82-89; R Gilgandra Australia 89-93; R Kelso 94-00; Adn Wylde 00-01; R Parkes 01-07; Adn Bathurst 05-07; R Coffs Harbour 07-10; rtd 10; Perm to Offic *Ely* from 10. *27 Archers Avenue, Feltwell, Thetford IP26 4BY* Tel (01842) 829772 E-mail samuelmarsden@hotmail.com

MARSDEN-JONES, Watkin David. b 22. St D Coll Lamp BA48. d 49 p 50. C Flint *St As* 49-54; C Forest Row *Chich* 54-56; V Copthorne 56-70; RD E Grinstead 66-70; V Bosham 70-86; rtd 86. *10 Fairfield Road, Bosham, Chichester PO18 8JH* Tel (01243) 575053

MARSH, Anderson Jason. b 74. STETS 06. d 09. NSM Sheet *Portsm* from 09. *12 Rother Close, Petersfield GU31 4DN* Tel (01730) 268156 E-mail amarsh@rotherbank.co.uk

MARSH, Anthony David. b 29. Roch Th Coll 64. d 66 p 67. C Liskeard w St Keyne *Truro* 66-69; R Wrentham w Benacre and Covehithe *St E* 69-75; R Wrentham w Benacre, Covehithe, Frostenden etc 75-80; P-in-c Beyton and Hessett 80-86; C Felixstowe St Jo 86-88; rtd 88; Perm to Offic *St E* 88-03 and from 07; *B & W* 01-03. *24 Winston Close, Felixstowe IP11 2FA*

MARSH, Carol Ann. *See* HATHORNE, Mrs Carol Ann

MARSH, Colin Arthur. b 54. Edin Univ PhD02. St Jo Coll Nottm 79. d 82 p 83. C Kirkby *Liv* 82-86; TV St Luke in the City 86-91; P-in-c Chingola St Barn Zambia 91-95; Perm to Offic *Edin* 95-03; Tutor United Coll of Ascension Selly Oak from 03. *19 St Denis Road, Birmingham B29 4LN* E-mail c.marsh@bham.ac.uk

MARSH, David. b 32. St Jo Coll Dur BA54. Cranmer Hall Dur. d 57 p 58. C Bilston St Leon *Lich* 57-62; Lic to Offic Dio Maseno Kenya 63-66; Chapl Scargill Ho 67-69; Adn S Maseno 70-72; V Meole Brace *Lich* 72-77; V Westlands St Andr 77-86; V Trentham 86-96; P-in-c Alstonfield, Butterton, Warslow w Elkstone etc 96-99; rtd 99; Perm to Offic *Ches* from 99; Chapl Mid Cheshire Hosps Trust from 02. *31 Spring Gardens, Nantwich CW5 5SH* Tel (01270) 610079 E-mail dlmarsh@btinternet.com

MARSH, Donald. b 32. WMMTC. d 90 p 91. NSM Wednesbury St Bart *Lich* 90-03; NSM Wednesbury Deanery from 03. *Holly Rise, 19 Trouse Lane, Wednesbury WS10 7HR* Tel and fax 0121-556 0095

MARSH, Mrs Elaine Daphne. b 42. d 07 p 08. OLM Askerswell, Loders, Powerstock and Symondsbury *Sarum* from 07. *Powerstock Mill Farm, West Milton, Bridport DT6 3SL* Tel (01308) 485213 Fax 485160

MARSH, Francis John. b 47. York Univ BA69 DPhil76 ATCL65 ARCM66 ARCO71. Oak Hill Th Coll 72 Selw Coll Cam 73. d 75 p 76. C Cambridge St Matt *Ely* 75-78; C Pitsmoor w Wicker Sheff 79; C Pitsmoor w Ellesmere 79-81; C Crookes St Thos 81-85; V S Ossett Wakef 85-96; RD Dewsbury 93-96; Adn Blackb 96-01; Bp's Adv on Hosp Chapls 96-01; P-in-c Emley Wakef from 11; P-in-c Flockton cum Denby Grange from 11. *14 Grange Drive, Emley, Huddersfield HD8 9SF* Tel (01924) 849161 E-mail john.marsh747@sky.com

MARSH, Gordon Bloxham. b 25. Cant Sch of Min 82. d 85 p 86. NSM Loose *Cant* 85-86; NSM New Romney w Old Romney and Midley 86-90; NSM Asst to RD S Lympne 90-94; rtd 94; Perm to Offic *Cant* from 94. *1 Yew Tree House, Ashford Road, Tenterden TN30 7AD*

MARSH, John. d 10 p 11. OLM Ockley, Okewood and Forest Green *Guildf* from 10. *2 Chatsworth Row, Caburn Heights, Crawley RH11 8RT* Tel (01293) 401639 E-mail home@john-marsh.co.uk

MARSH, Lawrence Allan. b 36. Sarum Th Coll 66. d 67 p 68. C Waterlooville *Portsm* 67-70; V Shedfield 70-76; R Fen Ditton *Ely* 76-01; P-in-c Horningsea 83-01; rtd 01; Perm to Offic *Ely* from 01. *The Old Bakery, 22 High Street, Bottisham, Cambridge CB25 9DA* Tel (01223) 811314 E-mail landjmarsh@aol.com

MARSH, Leonard Stuart Alexander. b 55. Hull Univ BA77 SOAS Lon MA00. Linc Th Coll 77. d 79 p 80. C Eltham St Barn *S'wark* 79-81; C Camberwell St Giles 81-83; Hon C Clifton St Paul *Bris* 83-86; Asst Chapl Bris Univ 83-86; Area Sec (Dio S'wark) USPG 86-91; Chapl Guildhall Sch of Music and Drama *Lon* 91-97; Chapl City Univ 91-98; NSM Clerkenwell H Redeemer and St Mark 94-95; P-in-c Finsbury St Clem w St Barn and St Matt 95-01; P-in-c Upper Norwood All SS *S'wark* from 01. *The Vicarage, 49 Chevening Road, London SE19 3TD* Tel (020) 8653 2820

MARSH, Mrs Margaret Ann. b 37. Nottm Univ BSc59 Ox Univ DipEd60 Lambeth STh87 Newc Univ MA93 Man Univ MPhil95. Carl Dioc Tr Course 86. d 87. Asst Chapl Garlands Hosp 87-92; Dn Carl Cathl 87-93; NSM Carl St Luke Morton 93-94; Hon Chapl Carl Hosps NHS Trust 94-00; rtd 00; Perm to Offic *Carl* 00-02 and *St Alb* 02-10. *1 The Maltings, Leighton Buzzard LU7 4BS* Tel (01525) 384655

MARSH, Canon Margaret Evaline. b 47. STETS 96. d 99 p 00. NSM Tattenham Corner and Burgh Heath *Guildf* 99-03; NSM Epsom St Martin 03-04; P-in-c Walton-on-the-Hill from 04; Hon Can Guildf Cathl from 10. *The Rectory, Breech Lane, Tadworth KT20 7SD* Tel (01737) 812105 Fax 814333 E-mail margaret.marsh@talk21.com

MARSH, Miss Maxine Dorothy. b 49. Bretton Hall Coll TCert72. Westcott Ho Cam 90. d 92 p 94. C Kings Norton *Birm* 92-95; P-in-c Kingsbury 95-96; V 96-02; P-in-c Middleton 99; AD Polesworth 99-02; P-in-c Glastonbury w Meare *B & W* 02-07; rtd 07. *7 Millar House, Merchants Road, Clifton, Bristol BS8 4HA* Tel 0117-973 2229 E-mail maxatglastonbury@yahoo.co.uk

MARSH, Michael John. b 47. Reading Univ BA69 DipEd70 York Univ MA91 Leeds Univ BA07. Coll of Resurr Mirfield 05. d 07 p 08. NSM Castleford *Wakef* 07-11; NSM Knottingley and Kellington w Whitley from 11. *The Vicarage, 1 Manor Farm Close, Kellington, Goole DN14 0PF* Tel 07802-734900 (mobile) E-mail mikej.marsh@talktalk.net

MARSH, Peter Charles Ernest. b 57. Southn Univ CertEd03 IEng87. WEMTC 04. d 06 p 07. NSM Wotton-under-Edge w

Ozleworth, N Nibley etc *Glouc* from 06. *1 Pitt Court Villas, Pitt Court, North Nibley, Dursley GL11 6EB* Tel (01453) 547521 E-mail pete.marsh@cityofbristol.ac.uk

MARSH, Phillip Edward. b 73. Univ of Wales (Abth) BSc94 Ch Ch Coll Cant PGCE96. Wycliffe Hall Ox BTh02. **d** 02 **p** 03. C Hubberston *St D* 02-05; C Werrington *Pet* 05-09; P-in-c Wilford *S'well* from 09. *St Wilfrid's New Rectory, Main Road, Wilford, Nottingham NG11 7AJ* Tel 0115-981 7328 Mobile 07766-314957 E-mail revdphilmarsh@aol.com

MARSH, Ralph. b 42. Ches Coll of HE CertEd63 Birm Univ BPhil77 Liv Univ MA00 ACP65. St Deiniol's Hawarden 86. **d** 88 **p** 89. NSM Tranmere St Paul w St Luke *Ches* 88-90; C Guiseley w Esholt *Bradf* 90-92; V Broughton *St As* 92-94; Hon C W Derby St Jo *Liv* 94; C Ribbleton *Blackb* 94-97; NSM Man Victoria Park 98-00; NSM Croxteth *Liv* 00-07; rtd 07. *47 Rolleston Drive, Wallasey CH45 6XE*

MARSH, Richard John Jeremy. b 60. Keble Coll Ox BA82 MA86 Dur Univ PhD91. Coll of Resurr Mirfield 83. **d** 85 **p** 86. C Grange St Andr *Ches* 85-87; Solway Fell and Chapl Univ Coll Dur 87-92; Abp's Asst Sec for Ecum Affairs *Cant* 92-95; Abp's Sec for Ecum Affairs 95-01; Hon C Westmr St Steph w St Jo *Lon* 94-96; Assoc P Westmr St Matt 96-01; Can Gib Cathl 95-01; Hon Prov Can Cant Cathl 98-01; Can Res Cant Cathl 01-06; Dir of Educn 01-05. *6 Barrack Square, Winchelsea TN36 4EG*

MARSH, Robert Christopher. b 53. Ex Univ BEd76. St Steph Ho Ox 86. **d** 88 **p** 89. C St Leonards Ch Ch and St Mary *Chich* 88-91; TV Crawley 91-00; V Maybridge 00-02. *67 Hythe Crescent, Seaford BN25 3TZ* E-mail rmarsh6204@aol.com

MARSH, Roger Philip. b 44. K Coll Lon BD72 AKC72 Sussex Univ MA95. St Aug Coll Cant 73. **d** 73 **p** 74. C Leagrave *St Alb* 73-76; Asst Youth Officer 76-77; Resources Officer 77-80; Chapl Marlborough Coll 80-86; Master Ardingly Coll Jun Sch Haywards Heath 86-95; Hd Master St Geo Sch Windsor 95-99; Chapl Lancing Coll 99-09; rtd 09; Perm to Offic *Cant* from 09. *107 College Road, Deal CT14 6BU* Tel (01304) 362851 E-mail frrogermarsh@hotmail.com

MARSH, Mrs Shelley Ann. b 54. SRN75 SCM76. St Jo Coll Nottm 84. **d** 89 **p** 94. Hon C Glas Gd Shep and Ascension 89-96; P-in-c Johnstone and Renfrew 96-06; R Bishopbriggs from 06; Chapl Paisley Univ 98-00. *St James's Rectory, 5 Meadowburn, Bishopbriggs, Glasgow G64 3HA* Tel 0141-563 5154 E-mail revshelleymarsh@ntlworld.com

MARSH, Simon Robert. b 59. Sarum & Wells Th Coll 79. **d** 82 **p** 83. C Mottram in Longdendale w Woodhead *Ches* 82-85; Bp's Dom Chapl *Bradf* 85-87; V Ashton Hayes *Ches* 87-90; V Macclesfield St Paul 90-96; V Ringway 96-01; V Bollington St Jo 01-06; V Bramhall from 06. *The Vicarage, 66 St Michael's Avenue, Bramhall, Stockport SK7 2PG* Tel 0161-439 6532 E-mail frsimon@btinternet.com

MARSH, Susan Edith. b 42. Southn Univ BA63 CertEd64. SAOMC 01. **d** 01 **p** 02. NSM Bp's Hatfield *St Alb* 01-05; NSM Bp's Hatfield, Lemsford and N Mymms from 05. *141 Handside Lane, Welwyn Garden City AL8 6TA* Tel (01707) 329744 E-mail susanianmarsh@ntlworld.com

MARSHALL, Alexander John. Leeds Univ BSc. **d** 95 **p** 96. OLM Holbrook, Stutton, Freston, Woolverstone etc *St E* 95-05; Perm to Offic 05-06 and from 09. *Well Cottage, 1 The Street, Freston, Ipswich IP9 1AF* Tel (01473) 780738

MARSHALL, Alexander Robert. b 43. Glouc Sch of Min 84. **d** 87 **p** 88. NSM Newtown w Llanllwchaiarn w Aberhafesp *St As* 87-00; P-in-c Mochdre 00-06. *31 Bromley College, London Road, Bromley BR1 1PE* Tel (020) 8464 9727 E-mail marshall@rhayapow.kc3ltd.co.uk

MARSHALL, Mrs Alison Mary. b 54. Middx Hosp MB, BS79 MRCGP84. SAOMC 98. **d** 01 **p** 02. NSM Reading St Jo *Ox* from 01. *36 Bulmershe Road, Reading RG1 5RJ* Tel 0118-966 8794 Mobile 07740-944102 E-mail ali.marshall@ntlworld.com

MARSHALL, Ms Alison Rose Marie. b 60. Leic Univ BA83 Birkbeck Coll Lon MA86 UEA PGCE87. Ridley Hall Cam. **d** 95 **p** 96. C Whittlesey, Pondersbridge and Coates *Ely* 95-98; Dep Chapl HM Pris Nor 98-99; Chapl HM Pris Northallerton 99-03; TV Sunderland and Chapl Sunderland Univ 03-04; rtd 04. *9 Glamis Avenue, Sunderland SR4 8PB* Tel 0191-520 2580 Mobile 07905-173171

MARSHALL, Andrew Stephen. b 74. UNISA BTh00. Coll of Resurr Mirfield 02. **d** 99 **p** 00. C Port Elizabeth St Hugh S Africa 00-02; C Port Elizabeth St Jo 02; C Easthampstead *Ox* 03-06; Sen Chapl Southn Solent Univ 06-09; Chapl Portsm Univ from 09; Dioc Interfaith Adv from 11. *15 Grays Court, Portsmouth PO1 2PN* Tel (023) 9284 3030 E-mail andyroo74@btinternet.com

MARSHALL, Mrs Angela. b 48. Trin Coll Bris 74. **d** 88 **p** 96. Hon Par Dn Newcastle St Geo *Lich* 88-92; Lic to Offic *Eur* 92-94; Dn Versailles 94-96; Asst Chapl 96-04; Perm to Offic *St E* 04-07; Hon C Collier Row St Jas and Havering-atte-Bower *Chelmsf* from 07. *St James's Vicarage, 24 Lower Bedfords Road, Romford RM1 4DG* Tel (01708) 746614 E-mail revdave@dsl.pipex.com

MARSHALL, Basil Eustace Edwin. b 21. OBE69. Westcott Ho Cam 71. **d** 73 **p** 74. C Edenbridge *Roch* 73-78; P-in-c Matfield

78-85; P-in-c Lamberhurst 78-85; C Farnborough 85-86; rtd 86; Perm to Offic *Roch* from 86 and Chich from 01. *7 Boyne Park, Tunbridge Wells TN4 8EL* Tel (01892) 521664

MARSHALL, Canon Bryan John. b 40. Chich Th Coll 63. **d** 65 **p** 66. C Poulton-le-Fylde *Blackb* 65-68; C S Shore H Trin 68-70; V Wesham 70-74; PV Chich Cathl 74-82; V Boxgrove 82-91; P-in-c Tangmere 82-84; R 84-91; R Westbourne 91-95; V E Preston w Kingston 95-03; Can and Preb Chich Cathl 94-10; rtd 03. *11 Priory Close, Boxgrove, Chichester PO18 0EA* Tel (01243) 536337

MARSHALL, Christine. *See* MARSHALL, Melinda Christine

MARSHALL, Mrs Christine Anne. b 40. Leeds Univ BSc64. **d** 95 **p** 96. OLM Holbrook, Stutton, Freston, Woolverstone etc *St E* 95-05; Perm to Offic 05-06 and from 09. *Well Cottage, 1 The Street, Freston, Ipswich IP9 1AF* Tel (01473) 780738 E-mail marshall@freston40.freeserve.co.uk

MARSHALL, Christopher John. b 56. BEd79. St Alb Minl Tr Scheme 83. **d** 86 **p** 87. C Biggleswade *St Alb* 86-89; Chapl Asst S Beds Area HA 89-91; Chapl St Helier Hosp Carshalton 91-93; Sen Chapl St Helier NHS Trust 93-98; Gen Office and Bereavement Manager Newham Healthcare NHS Trust from 98; Gen Services Manager from 99. *Newham General Hospital, Glen Road, London E13 8SL* Tel (020) 7363 8462

MARSHALL, Preb Christopher John Bickford. b 32. TD78. AKC56. **d** 57 **p** 58. C Leatherhead *Guildf* 57-60; C Crewkerne *B & W* 60-63; V Long Sutton 63-72; V Long Sutton w Long Load 72-76; V Wiveliscombe 76-93; RD Tone 78-87; Preb Wells Cathl 88-96; P-in-c Chipstable w Huish Champflower and Clatworthy 93; R Wiveliscombe w Chipstable, Huish Champflower etc 93-96; rtd 96; Perm to Offic *B & W* from 96. *Tap Cottage, High Street, Milverton, Taunton TA4 1LL* Tel (01823) 400419

MARSHALL, Craig Laurence. b 64. Southn Univ BEd87 Open Univ MA93. St Jo Coll Nottm MTh01. **d** 01 **p** 02. C Staplegrove w Norton Fitzwarren *B & W* 01-04; Chapl K Coll Taunton 04-06; R Aisholt, Enmore, Goathurst, Nether Stowey etc *B & W* from 06. *The Rectory, 25 St Mary Street, Nether Stowey, Bridgwater TA5 1LJ* Tel (01278) 734777 E-mail craig785@btinternet.com

MARSHALL, David. b 66. Liv Univ BA88. Ripon Coll Cuddesdon 89. **d** 92 **p** 93. C Dovecot *Liv* 92-96; P-in-c Westbrook St Jas 96-98; Dioc Communications Officer *Liv* 95-98; *Ches* 98-03; *Man* from 06; Lic to Offic *Ches* 98-06. *Diocesan Church House, 90 Deansgate, Manchester M3 2GJ* Tel 0161-828 1421 E-mail dmarshall@manchester.anglican.org

MARSHALL, David Charles. b 52. St Chad's Coll Dur BA73. Trin Coll Bris 74. **d** 76 **p** 77. C Meole Brace *Lich* 76-78; C W Teignmouth *Ex* 78-80; C Broadwater St Mary *Chich* 80-84; V Newcastle St Geo *Lich* 84-92; Chapl Versailles w Chevry *Eur* 92-04; Min Southgate LEP *St E* 04-07; P-in-c Collier Row St Jas and Havering-atte-Bower *Chelmsf* from 07; AD Havering from 10. *St James's Vicarage, 24 Lower Bedfords Road, Romford RM1 4DG* Tel (01708) 746614 E-mail revdave@dsl.pipex.com

MARSHALL, Canon David Evelyn. b 63. New Coll Ox BA85 Birm Univ MA88 PhD96. Ridley Hall Cam 88. **d** 90 **p** 91. C Roundhay St Edm *Ripon* 90-92; Chapl Ex Coll Ox 95-98; Lect St Paul's United Th Coll Limuru Kenya 98-99; P-in-c Buckden and Hail Weston *Ely* 99-00; Abp's Dom Chapl *Cant* 00-05; Hon Can All SS Cathl Cairo from 02; Perm to Offic *S'wark* 05-09 and Carl from 09. *2A Eskin Street, Keswick CA12 4DH* Tel (01768) 772467 E-mail revdem63@yahoo.co.uk

MARSHALL, The Very Revd Geoffrey Osborne. b 48. St Jo Coll Dur BA71. Coll of Resurr Mirfield 71. **d** 73 **p** 74. C Waltham Cross *St Alb* 73-76; C Digswell 76-78; P-in-c Belper Ch Ch and Milford *Derby* 78-86; V Spondon 86-93; Chapl Derby High Sch 87-01; RD Derby N 90-95; Can Res Derby Cathl 93-02; Dioc Dir of Ords 95-00; TR Wrexham *St As* 02-08; AD Wrexham 02-08; Dean Brecon *S & B* from 08; V Brecon St Mary w Llanddew from 08; Warden of Readers from 08. *The Deanery, Cathedral Close, Brecon LD3 9DP* Tel (01874) 623344 Fax 623716 E-mail admin@breconcathedral.org.uk

MARSHALL, Mrs Gillian Kathryn. b 54. Glouc Sch of Min 84. **d** 87 **p** 91. NSM Newtown w Llanllwchaiarn w Aberhafesp *St As* 87-98; P-in-c Betws Cedewain and Tregynon and Llanwyddelan 98-02; V 02-06. *31 Bromley College, London Road, Bromley BR1 1PE* Tel (020) 8464 9727

MARSHALL, Graham George. b 38. Dur Univ BA60 St Chad's Coll Dur. **d** 65 **p** 66. C Ashton-on-Ribble St Mich *Blackb* 65-67; C Lancaster St Mary 67-71; R Church Eaton *Lich* 71-75; Prec Man Cathl 75-78; R Reddish 78-85; V Chadderton St Luke 87-02; rtd 02; Perm to Offic *Man* from 02. *7 The Woods, Rochdale OL11 3NT* Tel (01706) 642139 E-mail ggm@manutd.com

MARSHALL (née CHADWICK), Mrs Helen Jane. b 63. UEA BA84. St Jo Coll Nottm MTh91. **d** 91 **p** 94. Par Dn Easton H Trin w St Gabr and St Lawr and St Jude *Bris* 91-94; C 94-95; Perm to Offic *Ox* 95-98; Lect St Paul's Th Coll Limuru Kenya 98-99; Perm to Offic *Ely* 99-00; Chapl K Coll Lon 01-05; P-in-c Addiscombe St Mildred *S'wark* 05-06; V 06-09; Perm to Offic

Carl from 09. *2A Eskin Street, Keswick CA12 4DH* Tel (01768) 772467 E-mail helenmarshall2592@yahoo.co.uk

MARSHALL, Canon Hugh Phillips. b 34. SS Coll Cam BA57 MA61. Linc Th Coll 57. **d** 59 **p** 60. C Westmr St Steph w St Jo *Lon* 59-65; V Tupsley *Heref* 65-74; V Wimbledon *S'wark* 74-78; TR 78-87; RD Merton 79-86; V Mitcham SS Pet and Paul 87-90; Hon Can S'wark Cathl 89-90; Perm to Offic 90-96; Chief Sec ABM 90-96; V Wendover *Ox* 96-01; P-in-c Halton 96-01; rtd 01; Hon Can Bulawayo from 96; Perm to Offic *Ox* from 01. *7 The Daedings, Deddington, Banbury OX15 0RT* Tel (01869) 337761 E-mail hughm34@btinternet.com

MARSHALL, James Hudson. b 48. Sheff Univ CertEd70 Open Univ BA74 Cumbria Univ BA08. LCTP 05. **d** 08 **p** 09. NSM Lamplugh w Ennerdale *Carl* from 08. *Iona, Sandwith, Whitehaven, CA28 9UG* E-mail j.h.marshall@talk21.com

MARSHALL, Mrs Jean. b 36. SWMTC 84. **d** 87 **p** 94. NSM Stratton *Truro* 87-89; NSM Bodmin w Lanhydrock and Lanivet 89-94; P-in-c Lawhitton and S Petherwin w Trewen 94-98; rtd 98; Hon C Bodmin w Lanhydrock and Lanivet *Truro* 00-06; Perm to Offic from 06. *10 Springwell View, Love Lane, Bodmin PL31 2QP* Tel (01208) 79891

MARSHALL, John. b 37. Kelham Th Coll 53. **d** 62 **p** 63. C Winshill *Derby* 62-64; C Chaddesden St Phil 64-65; Chapl HM Borstal Morton Hall 65-75; V Swinderby *Linc* 66-77; R Church Aston *Lich* 77-84; V Auckland St Andr and St Anne *Dur* 84-02; P-in-c Hunwick 88-90; Chapl Bishop Auckland Gen Hosp 84-94; Chapl Bishop Auckland Hospitals NHS Trust 94-98; Chapl S Durham Healthcare NHS Trust 98-00; rtd 02; Perm to Offic *Derby* 02-06; Hon C S Darley, Elton and Winster from 06. *Croft House, West Bank, Winster, Matlock DE4 2DQ* Tel (01629) 650310

MARSHALL, John. b 50. St Luke's Coll Ex CertEd74 W Lon Inst of HE DEHC79. S'wark Ord Course 88. **d** 91 **p** 92. Hon C Brixton Hill St Sav *S'wark* 91-95; Hon C Clapham St Jas from 95. *57A Kingscourt Road, London SW16 1JA* Tel (020) 8769 3665

MARSHALL, John Douglas. b 23. Univ of Wales (Cardiff) BA43. St Alb Minl Tr Scheme 76. **d** 79 **p** 80. Hon C Radlett *St Alb* 79-86; Lic to Offic *Llan* from 86. *Meiros, 3 River Walk, Cowbridge CF71 7DW* Tel (01446) 773930

MARSHALL, John Linton. b 42. Worc Coll Ox BA64 MA68 Bris Univ MLitt75. Wells Th Coll 66. **d** 68 **p** 69. C Bris St Mary Redcliffe w Temple etc 68-71; Tutor Sarum & Wells Th Coll 71-73; Perm to Offic *Pet* 74-77; Lic to Offic *S'well* 77-81; V Choral S'well Minster 79-81; R Ordsall 81-88; P-in-c Grove 84-88; RD Retford 84-88; V Northowram *Wakef* 88-99; P-in-c Glouc St Mark and St Mary de Crypt w St Jo etc 99-00; R Glouc St Mary de Lode and St Mary de Crypt etc 00-09; rtd 09. *166 Calton Road, Gloucester GL1 5ER* E-mail cyprianus@btopenworld.com

MARSHALL, Mrs Julie. b 62. **d** 08 **p** 09. OLM Bucknall *Lich* from 08. *27 Meadow Avenue, Wetley Rocks, Stoke-on-Trent ST9 0BD* Tel (01782) 550993 E-mail julie.marshall@stokecoll.ac.uk

MARSHALL, Ms Karen Lesley. b 59. Coll of Ripon & York St Jo BA82 Leeds Metrop Univ BSc96 Huddersfield Univ MA05. NEOC 04. **d** 07 **p** 08. C Horsforth *Ripon* 07-11; P-in-c Leeds All SS w Osmondthorpe from 11. *St Philip's Vicarage, 68 Osmondthorpe Lane, Leeds LS9 9EF* E-mail karenlmarshall@btinternet.com

MARSHALL, Kirstin Heather. *See* FREEMAN, Kirstin Heather

MARSHALL, Canon Lionel Alan. b 41. TEng. St Deiniol's Hawarden 84 Qu Coll Birm 86. **d** 87 **p** 88. C Llandudno *Ban* 87-90; V Rhayader and Nantmel *S & B* 90-01; P-in-c Llanbister w Llanbadarn Fynydd w Llananno etc 01-06; AD Maelienydd 98-06; Hon Can Brecon Cathl 00-04; Can Res 04-06; rtd 06. *46 Gordon Road, Blackwood NP12 1DW* Tel (01495) 223371

MARSHALL, Mrs Margaret Elizabeth. b 60. New Hall Cam BA81 MA84. EAMTC 01. **d** 04 **p** 05. C St Neots *Ely* 04-09; P-in-c Riversmeet *St Alb* from 09. *The Vicarage, 57 High Street, Great Barford, Bedford MK44 3JJ* Tel (01234) 870363 E-mail riversmeetvicar@ntlworld.com

MARSHALL, Canon Maurice Peter. b 23. Oak Hill Th Coll 59. **d** 61 **p** 62. C Haydock St Mark *Liv* 61-64; V New Ferry *Ches* 64-79; V Hartford 79-89; Hon Can Ches Cathl 87-89; rtd 89; Perm to Offic *Ches* from 89. *27 East Lane, Sandiway, Northwich CW8 2QQ* Tel (01606) 888591

MARSHALL, Melinda Christine. b 54. Cov Coll of Educn CertEd76. Ridley Hall Cam. **d** 01 **p** 02. C Exning St Martin w Landwade *St E* 01-05; TV Heatons *Man* 05-10. *52 Osborne Road, Tweedmouth TD15 2HS*

MARSHALL, Michael David. b 51. BSc. Trin Coll Bris. **d** 84 **p** 85. C Kennington St Mark *S'wark* 84-88; V Streatham Park St Alb 88-96; RD Tooting 90-96; V Blackheath St Jo 96-06; RD Charlton 01-06; Chapl Bishop's Stortford Coll 06-11; V St Austell *Truro* from 11. *12 North Hill Park, St Austell PL25 4BJ* Tel (01726) 64990 *or* 61930 E-mail mikemarshall51@hotmail.com

✠**MARSHALL, The Rt Revd Michael Eric.** b 36. Ch Coll Cam BA58 MA60. Cuddesdon Coll 58. **d** 60 **p** 61 **c** 75. C Birm St Pet 60-62; Tutor Ely Th Coll 62-64; Min Can Ely Cathl 62-64; Chapl Lon Univ 64-69; V St Marylebone All SS 69-75; Suff Bp Woolwich *S'wark* 75-84; Episc Dir Angl Inst Missouri 84-92; Abps' Adv Springboard for Decade of Evang 92-97; Hon Asst Bp Lon 84-07; Hon Asst Bp Chich from 92; Can and Preb Chich Cathl 90-99; Bp in Res Upper Chelsea H Trin *Lon* 97-02; R 02-07; rtd 07. *53 Oakley Gardens, London SW3 5QQ* Tel (020) 7351 0928 Mobile 07710-215131

MARSHALL, Mrs Michèle Jane. b 60. SEN82. NTMTC 05. **d** 08 **p** 09. C Orsett and Bulphan and Horndon on the Hill *Chelmsf* 08-11; C Pitsea w Nevendon from 11. *The Glebe House, High Road, Fobbing, Stanford-le-Hope SS17 9JH* Tel (01375) 672285 E-mail mjmarshall@fastmail.co.uk

MARSHALL, Pauline Nikola. b 49. WMMTC 84. **d** 87 **p** 94. C Walsgrave on Sowe *Cov* 87-91; TD Grantham *Linc* 91-94; TV 94-96; Ind Chapl 91-96; Perm to Offic 01-02; C Boston 02-05; TV 05-06; Mental Health Chapl Lincs Partnership NHS Trust 05-06; Lead Chapl Mental Health Beds and Luton Mental Health and Soc Care NHS Trust 06-11. *39 Moat Lane, Luton LU3 1UU* Tel (01582) 517824 Mobile 07792-981768 E-mail nikola.marshall@ntlworld.com

MARSHALL, Canon Peter Arthur. b 31. AKC58. **d** 59 **p** 60. C Hutton *Chelmsf* 59-61; C Rickmansworth *St Alb* 61-66; Chapl Orchard View and Kingsmead Court Hosps 66-94; R Lexden *Chelmsf* 66-94; RD Colchester 88-93; Hon Can Chelmsf Cathl 90-94; rtd 94; Perm to Offic *Win* from 94. *21 Manor Close, Wickham, Fareham PO17 5BZ* Tel (01329) 832988

MARSHALL, Peter James. b 48. Qu Coll Birm 78. **d** 80 **p** 81. C Ormskirk *Liv* 80-83; V Dallam from 83. *St Mark's Vicarage, Longshaw Street, Warrington WA5 0DY* Tel (01925) 631193 E-mail pjorm.marshall@btinternet.com

MARSHALL, The Very Revd Peter Jerome. b 40. Westcott Ho Cam 61. **d** 63 **p** 64. C E Ham St Mary *Chelmsf* 63-66; C Woodford St Mary 66-71; C-in-c S Woodford 66-71; V Walthamstow St Pet 71-81; Can Res Chelmsf Cathl 81-85; Dep Dir of Tr 81-84; Can Res Ripon Cathl and Dioc Dir of Tr *Ripon* 85-97; Dean Worc 97-06; rtd 06. *433 Gordon Avenue, Peterborough ON K9J 6G6, Canada* Tel (001) (705) 876 3381 E-mail petermarshall@bell.net

MARSHALL, Peter John Charles. b 35. Bris Univ BA60. Ridley Hall Cam 60. **d** 62 **p** 63. C Lindfield *Chich* 62-65; Travelling Sec Scripture Union 65-83; Hon C Nottingham St Nic *S'well* 65-67; Hon C Cheadle Hulme St Andr *Ches* 67-83; V Ilkley All SS *Bradf* 83-98; RD Otley 92-97; rtd 98; Perm to Offic *Ches* 00-03 and *St As* from 03. *Creuddyn Barn, Glanwydden, Llandudno Junction LL31 9JL* Tel (01492) 547352 E-mail revmarsh35@yahoo.co.uk

MARSHALL, Richard Albert. b 38. Open Univ BA73 Westmr Coll Ox MTh97 ACIS82. **d** 06 **p** 06. OLM Ray Valley *Ox* 06-09; NSM Perm to Offic from 09. *21 Ancil Avenue, Launton, Bicester OX26 5DL* Tel (01869) 243546 E-mail marshra@aol.com

MARSHALL, Richard Arthur Howard. b 66. Regent's Park Coll Ox BA88 MA92 SS Coll Cam PGCE89. Wycliffe Hall Ox BTh99. **d** 98 **p** 99. C Broughton *Man* 98-02; Asst Chapl Sedbergh Sch 02-03; Sub Chapl HM Pris Man 02-04; V Blackb Redeemer from 04. *2 Kendall Close, Blackburn BB2 4FB* Tel (01254) 51206 E-mail vicar@the-redeemer.org.uk

MARSHALL, Robert David. b 52. TCD BA75 MA00 Solicitor 77. CITC 99. **d** 02 **p** 03. NSM Stillorgan w Blackrock *D & G* from 02. *The Tontine, 84 The Rise, Mount Merrion, Co Dublin, Republic of Ireland* Tel (00353) (1) 288 6170 *or* 649 2137 Fax 649 2649 E-mail curate@stillorgan.dublin.anglican.org

MARSHALL, Robert Paul. b 60. Sheff Univ BA81 St Jo Coll Dur MA85. Cranmer Hall Dur 81. **d** 83 **p** 84. C Kirkstall *Ripon* 83-85; C Otley *Bradf* 85-87; Dioc Communications Officer 87-91; P-in-c Embsay w Eastby 87-91; Dioc Communications Officer *Lon* 91-95; P-in-c S Kensington St Aug 95-00; Media Adv to Abp *York* 95-05; Communications Adv *Sheff* from 04; Public Relns Adv Fresh Expressions from 05; Hd of Marketing St Mary's Univ Coll Twickenham 05-07; Hon C Kensington St Mary Abbots w Ch Ch and St Phil from 07. *4 Kensington Church Court, London W8 4SP* Tel 07917-272833 (mobile) E-mail robmarshalluk@gmail.com

MARSHALL, Canon Rodney Henry. b 46. Bernard Gilpin Soc Dur 71 St Steph Ho Ox 72. **d** 75 **p** 76. C Gorton Our Lady and St Thos *Man* 75-78; C Bedford Leigh 78-82; V Goldthorpe w Hickleton *Sheff* 82-90; Dioc Dir of In-Service Tr 88-90; NSM Hemsworth *Wakef* 96-97; P-in-c Athersley 97-98; V from 98; P-in-c Monk Bretton 07-10; P-in-c Carlton from 10; Hon Can Wakef Cathl from 07. *St Helen's Vicarage, 27 Laithes Lane, Barnsley S71 3AF* Tel (01226) 245361

MARSHALL, Simon. b 54. Kingston Poly BSc77 Leeds Univ PGCE78 MA(Ed)79. Qu Coll Birm 91. **d** 93 **p** 94. C Gt Clacton *Chelmsf* 93-97; TV Chigwell and Chigwell Row 97-02; C Woodford Wells from 02. *107 Monkhams Avenue, Woodford Green IG8 0ER* Tel (020) 8220 5143 E-mail simon.marshall17@ntlworld.com

MARSHALL, Simon Hardy. b 69. Bp Grosseteste Coll BA92. St Jo Coll Nottm 00. **d** 02 **p** 03. C Bartley Green *Birm* 02-05; TV Solihull from 05. *Oak Cottage, Bryanston Road, Solihull B91 1BS* Tel 0121-704 4730

MARSHALL, Mrs Sonia Margaret Cecilia. b 49. Westf Coll Lon BA71 Nottm Univ MA03. EMMTC 01. **d** 03 **p** 04. NSM Deeping St James *Linc* from 03. *135C Eastgate, Deeping St James, Peterborough PE6 8RB* Tel (01778) 346420 E-mail curate@dsj.org.uk

MARSHALL, Sonya Tolley. b 62. Hull Univ BA84 Lon Inst of Educn PGCE85. NOC 04. **d** 06 **p** 07. NSM Southport Ch Ch *Liv* from 06. *112 Linaker Street, Southport PR8 5DG* Tel 07834-170070 (mobile)

MARSHALL, Susan. *See* PANTER MARSHALL, Canon Susan Lesley

MARSHALL, Trevor. b 60. SEITE. **d** 11. NSM Bognor *Chich* from 11. *48 Southview Road, Southwick, Brighton BN42 4TT* Tel (01273) 592160

MARSHALL, William John. b 35. TCD BA57 BD61 PhD75. TCD Div Sch 59. **d** 59 **p** 60. C Ballyholme *D & D* 59-61; India 62-72; Asst Dean of Residence TCD 73-76; I Rathmichael *D & G* 76-92; Can Ch Cath Dublin 90-02; Chan 91-02; Vice-Prin CITC 92-02; rtd 02. *115 The Elms, Abberley, Killiney, Co Dublin, Republic of Ireland* Tel (00353) (1) 239 0832

MARSHALL, William Michael. b 30. Pemb Coll Ox BA53 MA57 DipEd65 Bris Univ MLitt72 PhD79. Wells Th Coll 63 Sarum & Wells Th Coll 79. **d** 80 **p** 81. Asst Chapl Millfield Sch Somerset 80-96; Hon C Glastonbury St Jo w Godney *B & W* 80-84; Hon C Glastonbury w Meare, W Pennard and Godney 84-96; rtd 96; Perm to Offic *Portsm* and *Win* 96-01 and *Ely* 01-08. *7 The Paddock, Ely CB6 1TP* Tel and fax (01353) 612287 E-mail william.m247@gmail.com

MARSHMAN, Mrs Elizabeth Maryan. b 53. York St Jo Coll CertEd74 Leeds Univ BEd75. NEOC 03. **d** 06 **p** 07. C Clifton *York* 06-10; P-in-c Lockington and Lund and Scorborough w Leconfield from 10. *Rectory House, Church Lane, Lockington, Driffield YO25 9SU* Tel (01430) 810604 E-mail emmarshman@yahoo.co.uk

MARSTON, David Howarth. b 48. St Jo Coll Dur BA69. Edin Th Coll 69. **d** 71 **p** 72. C Kendal H Trin *Carl* 71-75; Perm to Offic *Glas* 75-78; NSM Barrow St Matt *Carl* 79-86; Perm to Offic *York* 86-91; *Liv* 91-93 and 99-00; NSM Southport All SS and All So *Liv* 93-99; NSM Southport St Luke 00-09; Perm to Offic from 11. *33 Sandringham Road, Ainsdale, Southport PR8 2NY* Tel (01704) 578303

MARSTON, Neville Charles. b 37. Univ of Wales (Cardiff) BA65 Waterloo Univ (Canada) MA67. Ox Cen for Miss Studies 95. **d** 97 **p** 99. Dioc Dir Tr Seychelles 92-00; C Coven *Lich* 00-02; rtd 02; Perm to Offic *York* 05-11. *8 Appleton Gardens, South Cave, Brough HU15 2EN* Tel (01430) 471093 Mobile 07866-935844 E-mail nevillemarston@aol.com

MARSTON, William Thornton. b 59. Worc Coll Ox BA81 MA85 Cam Univ CertEd83. St Steph Ho Ox BA87. **d** 88 **p** 89. C Beckenham St Geo *Roch* 88-92; TV Ifield *Chich* 92-97; C-in-c Middleton-on-Sea CD 97-99; V Middleton from 99. *The Vicarage, 106 Elmer Road, Middleton-on-Sea, Bognor Regis PO22 6LJ* Tel (01243) 586348 E-mail w.marston@btinternet.com

MARSZALEK, Mrs Rachel Emma. b 74. St Jo Coll Nottm 08. **d** 11. C Belper *Derby* from 11. *7 Ashdene Gardens, Belper DE56 1TG* Tel 07906-632972 (mobile) E-mail rachel@ansteadsolutions.co.uk

MART, Terence Eugene. b 47. CertEd76 BA82. St Jo Coll Nottm LTh87. **d** 87 **p** 88. C Prestatyn *St As* 87-91; Chapl Theatr Clwyd Mold 87-91; R Llangystennin 91-01; RD Llanrwst 96-00; V Llanfair DC, Derwen, Llanelidan and Efenechtyd 01-07. *Woodville, Uppergate Street, Conwy LL32 8RF*

MARTIN, Mrs Adele Joan. b 51. BSc74. Cranmer Hall Dur 05. **d** 07 **p** 08. C Seacroft *Ripon* 07-11; P-in-c Dinsdale w Sockburn *Dur* from 11; P-in-c Hurworth from 11; Chapl HM YOI Deerbolt from 11. *HM YOI Deerbolt, Bowes Road, Barnard Castle DL12 9BG* Tel (01833) 633325

MARTIN, Alexander Lewendon. b 26. Em Coll Cam BA47 MA51. Ridley Hall Cam 56. **d** 57 **p** 58. C Ashtead *Guildf* 57-59; Asst Chapl Tonbridge Sch 59-64; Chapl Felsted Sch 64-74; Chapl Sedbergh Sch 74-84; R Askerswell, Loders and Powerstock *Sarum* 84-89; RD Lyme Bay 86-89; rtd 89; Perm to Offic *Ex* from 89. *Thirtover, 7 Alexandra Way, Crediton EX17 2EA* Tel (01363) 776206 E-mail alexmartin777@hotmail.com

MARTIN, Angela Frances. b 66. SEITE 05. **d** 08 **p** 09. C Henfield w Shermanbury and Woodmancote *Chich* from 08. *Glebe House, 41 Furner Mead, Henfield BN5 9JA* Tel (01273) 494509 E-mail ange.martin@virgin.net

MARTIN, Angela Lee. EMMTC 00. **d** 03 **p** 04. NSM Derby St Barn 03-08; P-in-c Hatton from 08. *The Joiners' Arms, 60 Church Road, Quarndon, Derby DE22 5JA* Tel (01332) 552876 Mobile 07967-180531 E-mail hattonlee1968@yahoo.co.uk

MARTIN, Brother. *See* COOMBE, John Morrell

MARTIN, Bryan Robert. b 71. TCD BTh01. CITC 98. **d** 01 **p** 02. C Magheralin w Dollingstown *D & D* 01-04; C Knockbreda 04-07; I Dromore *Clogh* 07-10; I Donaghcloney w Waringstown *D & D* from 10. *The Rectory, 54 Banbridge Road, Waringstown, Craigavon BT66 7QD* Tel (028) 3888 1218 E-mail brymrtn@aol.com *or* bryan.martin@btinternet.com

MARTIN, Canon Cameron Anthony Brian. b 56. Cape Town Univ BA93 Cant Univ (NZ) MBA02 MA05. St Bede's Coll Umtata 82. **d** 84 **p** 85. C Nigel Ch the K S Africa 84-86; R Ennerdale St Nic 87-89; R Eldorado Park Transfiguration 89-90; P-in-c Kenwyn 90-95; R Woodlands 95-02; Adn Mitchell's Plain 98-02; Dioc Admin Kimberley and Kuruman 02-05; Can Kimberley and Kuruman from 03; P-in-c Brumby *Linc* 05-07; TR from 07. *St Hugh's Rectory, 114 Ashby Road, Scunthorpe DN16 2AG* Tel (01724) 343652 E-mail cameron.martin@ntlworld.com

MARTIN, Christopher Edward. b 70. Bris Poly BA92 ACA97. Trin Coll Bris 07. **d** 09 **p** 10. C Newton Flotman, Swainsthorpe, Tasburgh, etc *Nor* from 09. *The New Rectory, Church Hill, Tasburgh, Norwich NR15 1NB* Tel (01508) 470768 E-mail chris.martin2@blueyonder.co.uk

MARTIN, Christopher John. b 45. Ball Coll Ox BA67 MA87. Wycliffe Hall Ox 86. **d** 88 **p** 89. C Edin St Thos 88-90; R Duns 90-00; Chapl Lyon *Eur* from 00. *38 chemin de Taffignon, 69110 Ste-Foy-lès-Lyon, France* Tel (0033) 4 78 59 67 06 E-mail lyonchurch@aol.com

MARTIN, Prof David Alfred. b 29. LSE BSc PhD. Westcott Ho Cam. **d** 83 **p** 84. Hon C Guildf Cathl 83-99; Perm to Offic from 99. *174 St John's Road, Woking GU21 7PQ* Tel (01483) 762134

MARTIN, David Howard. b 47. Worc Coll Ox BEd79. AKC70 St Aug Coll Cant 70. **d** 71 **p** 72. C Sedgley All SS *Lich* 71-75; Dioc Youth Chapl *Worc* 75-81; P-in-c Worc St Andr and All SS w St Helen 75-81; R Newland, Guarlford and Madresfield 81-91; R Alvechurch from 91. *The Rectory, Alvechurch, Birmingham B48 7SB* Tel 0121-445 1087 E-mail davidmartin@lynkserve.net

MARTIN, Donald Philip (Ralph). b 30. Trin Coll Toronto MA55 STB55. **d** 54 **p** 55. Canada 54-57; C Toronto St Simon 55-57; Tutor Kelham Th Coll 57-73; SSM from 60; P-in-c Willen *Ox* 73-81; Japan 81-82; Ghana 83-89; Dir Cleveland Lay Tr Course 89-91; C Middlesbrough All SS *York* 89-91; Kuwait 92-93; Italy 93-94; Canada 94-95; Tutor SAOMC *Ox* 95-96; Chapl OHP 96; Lesotho 97-00; rtd 98. *All Saints Convent, St Mary's Road, Oxford OX4 1RU* Tel (01865) 727276 E-mail ralphssm@yahoo.co.uk

MARTIN, Edward Eldred William. b 37. Cranfield Inst of Tech MSc84 Herts Univ MA88. S'wark Ord Course 65. **d** 68 **p** 69. C Greenwich St Alfege w St Pet S'wark 68-71; C Kidbrooke St Jas 71-75; V Peckham St Jo 75-78; P-in-c Peckham St Andr w All SS 76-78; V Peckham St Jo w St Andr 78-81; Hon Chapl S'wark Cathl 81-02; Chapl Guy's Hosp Lon 81-88; rtd 02; Perm to Offic S'wark 02-03 and from 07; Hon C Lee St Marg 03-07. *17 Honor Oak Rise, London SE23 3QY* Tel (020) 8699 2303 Mobile 07956-204869 E-mail emartin1722@yahoo.co.uk

MARTIN, Edward James Russell. b 76. Hull Univ BA98 Leeds Univ BA02 MA06. Coll of Resurr Mirfield 00. **d** 03 **p** 04. C Carrington S'well 03-06; P-in-c Chapel St Leonards w Hogsthorpe *Linc* 06-09; R Searby from 09. *St Giles's Rectory, 44 Waltham Road, Grimsby DN33 2LX* Tel (01472) 239758 Mobile 07736-711360 E-mail fatheredward@ntlworld.com

MARTIN, Mrs Eileen. b 43. City of Portsm Coll of Educn TCert65. **d** 03. OLM Queen Thorne *Sarum* 03-08. *School House, Trent, Sherborne DT9 4SW* Tel (01935) 851078 E-mail rev_eileenm@yahoo.co.uk

MARTIN, Miss Eileen Susan Kirkland. b 45. LCST66. Cranmer Hall Dur 77. **dss** 83 **d** 86. Kilmarnock *Glas* 84-86; Par Dn Heanor *Derby* 87-92; Perm to Offic 92-95. *1 Malin Court, Hardings Close, Hemel Hempstead HP3 9AQ* Tel (01442) 216768

MARTIN, Mrs Elizabeth Anne. b 60. Sheff Univ BMedSci82. ERMC 05. **d** 09 **p** 10. C Gaywood *Nor* from 09. *28 Jermyn Road, King's Lynn PE30 4AE* Tel (01553) 772896

MARTIN, George Cobain. b 34. TCD BA57 MA65. **d** 57 **p** 58. C Bangor St Comgall *D & D* 57-64; I Kircubbin 64-74; R Ashby by Partney *Linc* 75-78; R Partney w Dalby 75-78; V Skendleby 75-78; P-in-c Candlesby w Scremby 77-78; R Partney 78-95; rtd 95; Perm to Offic *Linc* 95-98. *Hapstead Cottage, 26 Mill Leat, Baltonsborough, Glastonbury BA6 8HX* Tel (01458) 850590

MARTIN, Glenn. b 52. Qu Coll Birm 84. **d** 86 **p** 87. C Chatham St Wm *Roch* 86-89; Chapl Pastures Hosp Derby 89-94; Chapl Kingsway Hosp Derby 89-94; Sen Chapl S Derbys Mental Health NHS Trust 94-97; Sen Chapl Community Health Sheff NHS Trust 97-01; Professional Development Officer for Chapl and Spiritual Healthcare 01-07; NSM Gilmorton, Peatling Parva, Kimcote etc *Leic* 04-07; NSM Guilsborough w Hollowell and Cold Ashby *Pet* 07-08; NSM Cottesbrooke w Gt Creaton and Thornby 07-08; NSM Spratton 07-08; NSM Naseworthy 07-08; R Sutton Bonington w Normanton-on-Soar S'well 08-11; P-in-c Derby St Andr w St Osmund from 11; P-in-c Allenton

and Shelton Lock from 11. *St Edmund's Vicarage, Sinfin Avenue, Derby DE24 9JA* E-mail glenn.martinrev@btinternet.com
MARTIN, Graham Rowland. b 39. Liv Univ CertEd58 Lon Univ BD70 Bris Univ BEd73 FRSA LCP. Wells Th Coll 71. **d** 71 **p** 72. Hon C Glouc St Cath 71-76; P-in-c Brookthorpe w Whaddon 76-78; Perm to Offic 78-80; Hon C Hucclecote 80-82; Hon C Tuffley 82-88; NSM Hardwicke, Quedgeley and Elmore w Longney 88-89; V Kemble, Poole Keynes, Somerford Keynes etc 89-96; P-in-c Bibury w Winson and Barnsley 96-04; Dioc Ecum Officer 96-04; rtd 04; Perm to Offic *Glouc* from 04. *Wharf Cottage, Wharf Lane, Lechlade GL7 3AU* Tel (01367) 252825
MARTIN, Henry Rowland Felix. b 67. Leeds Univ BA89 SS Coll Cam BA95. Ridley Hall Cam 93. **d** 96 **p** 97. C Becontree St Mary *Chelmsf* 96-00; C Broughton *Man* 00-02; TR 02-10; Chapl HM Pris Man from 10. *HM Prison Manchester, 1 Southall Street, Manchester M60 9AH* Tel 0161-817 5600
E-mail h3nrymartin@googlemail.com
MARTIN, James Alwyn. b 47. St Paul's Coll Grahamstown 76. **d** 78 **p** 79. Zimbabwe 78-04; C Highlands St Mary 78-80; P-in-c Lowveld 80-84; R Masvingo St Mich 84-87; Adn Victoria 82-87; R Borrowdale Ch Ch 87-98; Adn Harare S 96-98; Dean Bulawayo 98-04; V Aldershot St Mich *Guildf* from 05. *St Michael's Vicarage, 120 Church Lane East, Aldershot GU11 3SS* Tel (01252) 320108 Mobile 07749-770035
E-mail jamesmartin858@btinternet.com
MARTIN, James Smiley. b 32. MBE98. TCD 65. **d** 67 **p** 68. C Glenavy *Conn* 67-70; C Belfast St Mary 70-73; I Carnmoney 73-74; I Malusk 74-94; rtd 94. *21 Dundesert Road, Nutts Corner, Crumlin BT29 4SL* Tel (028) 9082 5636
MARTIN, Mrs Jane Juliet. b 36. Warwick Univ BA77 Solicitor 81. ERMC 03. **d** 06 **p** 07. NSM Huntingdon w the Stukeleys *Ely* from 06. *The Old School House, Barham Road, Buckworth, Huntingdon PE28 5AN* Tel (01480) 891543
E-mail jjmandsm@aol.com
MARTIN, Jessica Heloise. b 63. Trin Hall Cam BA86 PhD93. EAMTC 00. **d** 03 **p** 04. NSM Trin Coll Cam 03-09; NSM Fen Ditton, Horningsea and Teversham 08-09; P-in-c Duxford *Ely* from 10; P-in-c Hinxton from 10; P-in-c Ickleton from 10. *The Rectory, 13 St John's Street, Duxford, Cambridge CB2 4RA* Tel (01223) 832137 Mobile 07780-704006
E-mail jessicamartin@virginmedia.com
MARTIN, John Eric Terence. b 75. SS Coll Cam MA99 MEng99. Wycliffe Hall Ox BTh10. **d** 10 **p** 11. C Wolverhampton St Luke *Lich* from 10. *20 Waterside Close, Wolverhampton WV2 1HN* Tel (01902) 457672 Mobile 07941-978856
E-mail johnmartin@yahoo.co.uk
MARTIN, John Henry. b 42. St Jo Coll Cam BA63 MA67. St Jo Coll Nottm BA73. **d** 73 **p** 74. C Ecclesall *Sheff* 73-77; C Hednesford *Lich* 77-82; V Walsall Pleck and Bescot 82-92; V Whittington w Weeford 92-08; V Hints 05-08; rtd 08. *2 Churn Close, South Cerney, Cirencester GL7 6HX* Tel (01285) 869585
MARTIN, John Hunter. b 42. AKC64. **d** 65 **p** 66. C Mortlake w E Sheen *S'wark* 65-69; C-in-c Bermondsey St Hugh CD 69-72; V Bermondsey St Anne 72-78; P-in-c Lt Ouse *Ely* 78; V Littleport 78-89; V Attercliffe *Sheff* 89-90; P-in-c Darnall 89-90; TR Darnall-cum-Attercliffe 90-96; TR Attercliffe, Darnall and Tinsley 96; R Kirk Sandall and Edenthorpe 96-07; rtd 07. *Salara Haven, Sandgreen, Gatehouse of Fleet, Castle Douglas DG7 2DU* Tel (01557) 815068
MARTIN, Canon John Pringle. b 24. Bris Univ BA50. Clifton Th Coll 50. **d** 52 **p** 53. C Braintree *Chelmsf* 52-56; C St Alb St Paul *St Alb* 56-59; V Congleton St Pet *Ches* 59-81; R Brereton w Swettenham 81-90; RD Congleton 74-85; Hon Can *Ches* Cathl 80-90; rtd 90; Perm to Offic *B & W* from 90. *49 Parkhouse Road, Minehead TA24 8AD* Tel (01643) 706769
MARTIN, Canon Jonathan Patrick McLeod. b 55. Leic Univ BA81. Sarum & Wells Th Coll 84. **d** 86 **p** 87. C Southampton Thornhill St Chris *Win* 86-89; Perm to Offic 89-92; C Heatherlands St Jo *Sarum* 92-97; Dioc Link Officer for ACUPA 95-97; Chief Exec Dame Agnes Weston's R Sailors' Rests from 97; Perm to Offic 98-01; NSM Parkstone St Pet and St Osmund w Branksea 01-09; Can and Preb Sarum Cathl from 06. *32 Gladstone Road, Poole BH12 2LY* Tel (01202) 733580
E-mail jonathan.martin@poole.gov.uk
MARTIN, Joseph Edward. b 35. Bps' Coll Cheshunt 58. **d** 60 **p** 61. C Short Heath *Birm* 60-62; C Caterham Valley *S'wark* 63-66; R W Hallam and Mapperley *Derby* 66-70; P-in-c Mapperley 66-67; V Wykeham and Hutton Buscel *York* 71-78; Chapl HM Pris Askham Grange 78-82; V Askham Bryan w Askham Richard *York* 78-82; R Amotherby w Appleton and Barton-le-Street 82-84; C Banbury *Ox* 85-88; C Warsop *S'well* 88-90; V Tuxford w Weston and Markham Clinton 90-00; rtd 00; Perm to Offic *Carl* from 03. *Windsmead, Allithwaite Road, Cartmel, Grange-over-Sands LA11 7SB* Tel (01539) 532693
MARTIN, Kenneth. b 20. Univ of Wales (Lamp) BA47. Bp Burgess Hall Lamp. **d** 48 **p** 49. C Rumney *Mon* 48-49; C Griffithstown 49-51; CF (TA) from 52; Perm to Offic *Llan* from 51. *21 Earls Court Road, Penylan, Cardiff CF23 9DE* Tel (029) 2049 3796

MARTIN, Lee. *See* MARTIN, Angela Lee
MARTIN (née BULLEN), Mrs Marilyn Patricia. b 46. Liv Hope Univ Coll BA(Theol)00 MA05. NOC 06. **d** 06 **p** 07. NSM Stretton and Appleton Thorn *Ches* 06-09; Asst Chapl HM YOI Thorn Cross from 06. *Thorn Cross, Arley Road, Appleton Thorn, Warrington WA4 4RL* Tel (01925) 805100
E-mail malmartin@btinternet.com
MARTIN, Miss Marion. b 47. Oak Hill Th Coll 83. **dss** 86 **d** 87. Ditton *Roch* 86-88; C 87-88; Perm to Offic *Glouc* 89-01; rtd 07. *16 Garborough Close, Crosby, Maryport CA15 6RZ* Tel (01900) 810776
MARTIN, Nicholas Roger. b 53. St Jo Coll Dur BA74. Ripon Coll Cuddesdon 75. **d** 77 **p** 78. C Wolvercote w Summertown *Ox* 77-80; C Kidlington 80-82; TV 82-84; V Happisburgh w Walcot *Nor* 84-85; P-in-c Hempstead w Lessingham and Eccles 84-85; R Happisburgh w Walcot, Hempstead, Lessingham etc 85-89; R Blakeney w Cley, Wiveton, Glandford etc 89-97; TR Totnes w Bridgetown, Berry Pomeroy etc *Ex* 97-05; RD Totnes 99-03; Co-ord Chapl HM Pris Channings Wood from 05. *HM Prison, Channings Wood, Denbury, Newton Abbot TQ12 6DW* Tel (01803) 814647 E-mail nick.martin@hmps.gsi.gov.uk
MARTIN, Paul Dexter. b 50. Wabash Coll (USA) BA72 Univ of the South (USA) MDiv75. **d** 75 **p** 76. Educn Tutor Cov Cathl 75-76; C Norbury St Phil *Cant* 76-80; USA from 80. *275 Southfield Road, Shreveport LA 71105, USA* Tel (001) (318) 865 8469 E-mail pdmartin@iamerica.net
MARTIN, Canon Penelope Elizabeth. b 44. Cranmer Hall Dur 83. **dss** 86 **d** 87 **p** 94. Seaham w Seaham Harbour *Dur* 86-89; Par Dn 87-89; Par Dn Cassop cum Quarrington 89-93; Par Dn Sherburn w Pittington 93-94, C 94-95, V 95-02, R Shadforth 95-02, R Pittington, Shadforth and Sherburn 02-03; Hon Can Dur Cathl 01-03; rtd 03. *34A Rosemount, Durham DH1 5GA* Tel 0191-386 1742 E-mail penny.martin@charis.co.uk
MARTIN, Preb Peter. b 50. MCIH75. Linc Th Coll 82. **d** 84 **p** 85. C Taunton H Trin *B & W* 84-86; C Bath Bathwick 86-88; R Cannington, Otterhampton, Combwich and Stockland from 88; RD Sedgemoor 00-06; Warden of Readers Taunton Adnry from 06; Chapl Cannington Coll from 89; Preb Wells Cathl from 09. *The Rectory, 27 Brook Street, Cannington, Bridgwater TA5 2HP* Tel (01278) 652953 E-mail revd.petermartin@tiscali.co.uk
MARTIN, Peter. b 66. Univ of Wales (Ban) BD89. Qu Coll Birm 90. **d** 92 **p** 93. C Kingswinford St Mary *Lich* 92-93; C Kingswinford St Mary *Worc* 93-95; Sen Chapl Redbridge Health Care NHS Trust 95-01; Sen Chapl Barking Havering and Redbridge Hosps NHS Trust 01-06; Hd Past Services Lancs Teaching Hosps NHS Trust 06-08. *Address temp unknown*
MARTIN, Philip James. b 58. Cam Univ BA. Coll of Resurr Mirfield. **d** 84 **p** 85. C Pontefract St Giles *Wakef* 84-88; C Wantage *Ox* 88-90; C Didcot All SS 90; V Alderholt *Sarum* from 90. *The Vicarage, Daggons Road, Alderholt, Fordingbridge SP6 3DN* Tel (01425) 653179
E-mail vicar@stjamesalderholt.org.uk
MARTIN, Ralph. *See* MARTIN, Donald Philip
MARTIN, Raymond William. b 32. Lon Univ BSc66 MBIM. Glouc Th Course 73. **d** 76 **p** 76. NSM Glouc St Mary de Lode and St Nic 76-77; NSM Redmarley D'Abitot, Bromesberrow w Pauntley etc 77-84; R 84-91; P-in-c Falfield w Rockhampton 91-98; P-in-c Oldbury-on-Severn 91-98; Chapl HM YOI Eastwood Park 91-92; rtd 98; Perm to Offic *Glouc* 98-00; Clergy Widows' Officer (Glouc Adnry) from 99; P-in-c Shipton Moyne w Westonbirt and Lasborough 00-02; Perm to Offic *Glouc, Heref* and *Worc* from 03. *Tree Tops, 35 Thirlstane Road, Malvern WR14 3PL* Tel (01684) 562714
MARTIN, Rhys Jonathan. b 68. Heythrop Coll Lon BD98. EAMTC 98. **d** 00 **p** 01. C Stansted Mountfitchet w Birchanger and Farnham *Chelmsf* 00-02; C Dovercourt and Parkeston w Harwich 02-04; R Fingringhoe w E Donyland and Abberton etc from 04. *St Lawrence House, Rectory Road, Rowhedge, Colchester CO5 7HR* Tel (01206) 728640
E-mail rhys.martin@zetnet.co.uk
MARTIN, Richard. b 34. Rhodes Univ BA54 Em Coll Cam BA57 MA58. Wells Th Coll 57. **d** 59 **p** 60. C Portsea St Mary *Portsm* 59-60; S Africa 60-87; C Bloemfontein Cathl 60-62; R Wepener 62-64; R Odendaalsrus 64-67; R Newton Park St Hugh 67-76; Chapl St Bede's Coll Umtata 77-79; R Hillcrest 79-87; C Aldershot St Mich *Guildf* 87-94; R Wick *Mor* 94-99; P-in-c Thurso 94-99; rtd 99; Hon C Diptford, N Huish, Harberton, Harbertonford etc *Ex* 99-01; Perm to Offic 01-03; Lic to Offic *Mor* from 03. *10 Royal Oak Drive, Invergordon IV18 0RP* Tel (01349) 853787 E-mail martin@chilledthames.com
MARTIN, Richard Arthur. b 59. Leeds Univ BA91 MA97 Cant Ch Ch Univ Coll PGCE03. SEITE 07. **d** 09 **p** 10. C Gravesend St Aid *Roch* from 09. *81 Laburnum Road, Rochester ME2 2LB* Tel (01634) 721868 Mobile 07789-238627
E-mail ramartin@talktalk.net
MARTIN, Richard Charles de Villeval. b 41. St Jo Coll Ox BA63 MA67. Ox Ord Course. **d** 84 **p** 85. NSM Ox St Thos w St Frideswide and Binsey 84-04; Asst Chapl Highgate Sch Lon 86-92; Asst Master Magd Coll Sch Ox 92-02; Chapl 94-02; rtd

04; Lic to Offic *Ox* from 05. *11 Benson Place, Oxford OX2 6QH* Tel (01865) 510694 E-mail richardcmartin@tiscali.co.uk
MARTIN, Richard Hugh. b 55. Van Mildert Coll Dur BA78 St Jo Coll Nottm BA81 Leeds Univ MA01. Cranmer Hall Dur 79. **d** 82 **p** 83. C Gateshead *Dur* 82-85; C Redmarshall 85-88; V Scarborough St Jas w H Trin *York* 88-96; Chapl R Wolv Hosps NHS Trust 96-02; V Bris St Andr Hartcliffe from 02. *St Andrew's Vicarage, Peterson Square, Bristol BS13 0EE* Tel 0117-964 3554 Mobile 07709-429631 E-mail richardtherev@blueyonder.co.uk
✠**MARTIN, The Rt Revd Robert David Markland.** b 49. Trin Coll Cam BA71 MA74 FCA80. Trin Coll Bris BA91. **d** 91 **p** 92 **c** 08. C Kingswood *Bris* 91-95; V Frome H Trin *B & W* 95-08; RD Frome 03-08; Suff Bp Marsabit Kenya from 08. *ACK Marsabit Mission Area, clo MAF Kenya, PO Box 21123/00505, Nairobi, Kenya*
MARTIN, Robert Paul Peter. b 58. Chich Th Coll. **d** 83 **p** 84. C Anfield St Columba *Liv* 83-86; C Orford St Marg 86-87; R Blackley H Trin *Man* 87-90; C Oseney Crescent St Luke *Lon* 90-93; C Kentish Town 93-96; V Harringay St Paul 96-09; P-in-c W Green Ch Ch w St Pet 04-08; Chapl St Paul's Coll Hong Kong from 09; CMP from 01. *St Paul's College, 69 Bonham Road, Hong Kong, China* Tel (00852) 2546 2241 E-mail fr.robert@btinternet.com
MARTIN, Robin. See MARTIN, Thomas Robin
MARTIN, Robin Hugh. b 35. Rhodes Univ BA56. **d** 58 **p** 59. C Darnall *Sheff* 58-62; C-in-c Kimberworth Park 62-65; Lic to Offic *Sheff* 65-66 and *Newc* 67-71; Perm to Offic *Man* 79-93; *Lich* 97-99; *Heref* from 97; P-in-c Maesbury *Lich* 99-11. *Offa House, Treflach, Oswestry SY10 9HQ* Tel (01691) 657090
MARTIN, Roger Allen. b 38. Westmr Coll Lon CertEd59 Birkbeck Coll Lon BA64 FRMetS79. SAOMC 97. **d** 99 **p** 00. NSM Bramfield, Stapleford, Waterford etc *St Alb* 99-06; NSM Broxbourne w Wormley 06-10; rtd 10; Perm to Offic *St Alb* from 10. *41 The Avenue, Bengeo, Hertford SG14 3DS* Tel (01992) 422441 E-mail roger.martin@ntlworld.com
MARTIN, Canon Roger Ivor. b 42. MCMI. Cant Sch of Min. **d** 85 **p** 86. NSM Saltwood *Cant* 85-90; P-in-c Crundale w Godmersham 90-01; Dioc Exec Officer for Adult Educn and Lay Tr 90-96; CME Officer 94-96; Chapl to Bp Maidstone 96-01; R Saltwood 01-09; Hon Can Cant Cathl 09; rtd 09; Perm to Offic *Cant* 09-11; Hon C Aldington w Bonnington and Bilsington etc from 11. *Kwetu, 23 Tanners Hill Gardens, Hythe CT21 5HY* Tel (01303) 237204 E-mail rogmartin@btinternet.com
MARTIN, Mrs Rosanna Stuart. b 60. Bris Univ BA81. Wycliffe Hall Ox 89. **d** 92 **p** 94. Par Dn Stanford in the Vale w Goosey and Hatford *Ox* 92-94; C 94-96; C Abingdon 96-00; Perm to Offic 00-04; P-in-c Uffington, Shellingford, Woolstone and Baulking from 04. *St Mary's Vicarage, Broad Street, Uffington, Faringdon SN7 7RA* Tel (01367) 820633
MARTIN, Rupert Gresley. b 57. Worc Coll Ox BA78 Ox Univ MA95. Trin Coll Bris 89. **d** 91 **p** 92. C Yateley *Win* 91-95; V Sandal St Helen *Wakef* from 95. *The Vicarage, 333 Barnsley Road, Wakefield WF2 6EJ* Tel (01924) 255441 E-mail office@sandalmagna.fsnet.co.uk
MARTIN, Russell Derek. b 47. St Jo Coll Dur 71. **d** 74 **p** 75. C Hartlepool H Trin *Dur* 74-78; C Swindon St Jo and St Andr *Bris* 78-79; V Penhill 79-91; V Haselbury Plucknett, Misterton and N Perrott *B & W* 91-99. *59 North Street, Martock TA12 6EH* Tel (01935) 829266 Mobile 07770-783843
MARTIN, Scott. b 73. Herts Univ BA99 Leeds Univ BA04 MA05. Coll of Resurr Mirfield 02. **d** 05 **p** 06. C Leagrave *St Alb* 05-09; P-in-c Bishop's Stortford from 09. *Holy Trinity Vicarage, 69 Havers Lane, Bishop's Stortford CM23 3PA* Tel (01279) 656546 Mobile 07706-295678 E-mail scottmar73@hotmail.com
MARTIN, Sean Cal Hugh. b 69. Wycliffe Coll Toronto MDiv04. **d** 04 **p** 05. C Rio Grande St Andr USA 05-06; Asst P ICM 06-08; Canada from 08. *587 Laurel Crescent, Campbell River BC V9W 6K8, Canada*
MARTIN, Steven. b 50. Qu Coll Birm BA08. **d** 08 **p** 09. C Malvern St Andr and Malvern Wells and Wyche *Worc* from 08. *96 Fruitlands, Malvern WR14 4XB* Tel (01684) 893146 E-mail smartin1006@sky.com
MARTIN, Miss Susan. b 56. Nottm Univ BA77. Edin Th Coll 86. **d** 88 **p** 94. C Leigh Park *Portsm* 88-91; C Sandown Ch Ch 91-94; C Portsea St Cuth 94-95; rtd 95; Perm to Offic *Portsm* 95-01 and from 04; NSM Portsea St Geo 01-04. *7 Farthingdale Terrace, Peacock Lane, Portsmouth PO1 2TL* Tel (023) 9229 7994
MARTIN, Mrs Susan Jane. b 69. SEITE BA10. **d** 10 **p** 11. C Minster-in-Sheppey *Cant* from 10. *The Vicarage, North Road, Queenborough ME11 5HA* Tel (01795) 663791 E-mail revsuemartin@btinternet.com
MARTIN, Mrs Susan Mary. b 49. UEA BEd94. ERMC 04. **d** 09 **p** 10. NSM Gayton, Gayton Thorpe, E Walton, E Winch etc *Nor* from 09. *The Limes, Lynn Road, Gayton, King's Lynn PE32 1QJ* Tel and fax (01553) 636570 Mobile 07801-701677
MARTIN, Sylvia. b 24. **dss** 75 **d** 87 **p** 94. NSM Selsdon St Jo w St Fran *S'wark* 87-99; Perm to Offic 99-07. *17 Frobisher Court, Sydenham Rise, London SE23 3XH* Tel (020) 8699 6247

MARTIN, Sylvia. b 43. Sarum Th Coll 94. **d** 97 **p** 98. NSM Locks Heath *Portsm* 97-02; Perm to Offic 02-04; NSM Fareham H Trin and Chapl Fareham Coll 04-07; rtd 07; Perm to Offic *Portsm* from 07. *9 Harvester Drive, Fareham PO15 5NR* Tel (01329) 312269 E-mail sylvia.martin43@yahoo.com
MARTIN, Thomas Robin. b 40. Bps' Coll Cheshunt 64. **d** 67 **p** 68. C Ripley *Derby* 67-70; C Ilkeston St Mary 70-74; V Chinley w Buxworth 74-83; V Knighton St Mich *Leic* 83-85; V Thurmaston 85-05; rtd 05; C Braunstone Park *Leic* 08-09; C Birstall and Wanlip 10-11. *22 Sycamore Road, Birstall, Leicester LE4 4LT* Tel 0116-267 1651 E-mail tr.martin@btinternet.com
MARTIN, Warrick David. b 71. Stirling Univ BA94. Oak Hill Th Coll BA09. **d** 09 **p** 10. C Lt Heath *St Alb* from 09. *128 Holwell Road, Welwyn Garden City AL7 3RW* Tel 07738-127587 (mobile)
MARTIN, William Harrison. b 38. Sarum & Wells Th Coll 91. **d** 87 **p** 88. NSM Rushen *S & M* 87-92; C German 92-97; V Lonan and Laxey 97-08; rtd 08; Perm to Offic *S & M* from 09. *Crossag Villa, Crossag Road, Ballasalla, Isle of Man IM9 3EF* Tel (01624) 825982 E-mail billmartin@manx.net
MARTIN, William Matthew. b 28. Ch Coll Cam BA52 MA56 TCert81. Ridley Hall Cam 52. **d** 54 **p** 55. C Weaste *Man* 54-56; V 56-61; CF (TA) 58-61; CF 61-82; Dep Asst Chapl Gen 73-82; Asst Master St Jo Southworth RC High Sch Preston 82-88; Lic to Offic *Blackb* 82-93; rtd 93; Perm to Offic *Blackb* from 93. *31 Fosbrooke House, 8 Clifton Drive, Lytham St Annes FY8 5RQ* Tel (01253) 667052
MARTIN-DOYLE, Mrs Audrey Brenda. b 35. Cranmer Hall Dur 80. **dss** 82 **d** 87 **p** 95. The Lye and Stambermill *Worc* 82-86; Chapl Lee Abbey 86-88; Ldr Aston Cottage Community 88-93; C Cheltenham St Mary, St Matt, St Paul and H Trin *Glouc* 94-97; rtd 97; Perm to Offic *Glouc* from 97. *39 Moorend Street, Cheltenham GL53 0EH* Tel (01242) 510352 E-mail audrey@martin-doyle.freeserve.co.uk
MARTIN-SMITH, Paul. b 38. TCD BA64 Lon Univ MSc67 FIPEM88. WMMTC 94. **d** 97 **p** 98. NSM Tile Hill *Cov* 97-99; Perm to Offic *Ex* 00-09. *12 Emmasfield, Exmouth EX8 2LS* Tel (01395) 269505
MARTINDALE, Mrs Patricia Ann. b 24. Qu Coll Birm. **dss** 84 **d** 87 **p** 94. Rugby *Cov* 84-94; NSM 87-94; Perm to Offic from 95. *54 Hillmorton Road, Rugby CV22 5AD* Tel (01788) 543038
MARTINEAU, Canon Christopher Lee. b 16. Trin Hall Cam BA38 MA70. Linc Th Coll 39. **d** 41 **p** 42. C Hinckley St Mary *Leic* 41-43; Chapl RNVR 43-46; C St Alb Abbey 46-48; V Balsall Heath St Paul *Birm* 48-54; P-in-c Shard End 54-58; V 58-65; R Skipton H Trin *Bradf* 65-83; Hon Can Bradf Cathl 72-83; rtd 83; Perm to Offic *Bradf* 83-02 and *Heref* from 03. *70 New Street, Ledbury HR8 2EE* Tel (01531) 635479
MARTINEAU, Canon David Richards Durani. b 36. AKC59. **d** 60 **p** 61. C Ches St Jo 60-64; S Africa 64-69; C St Mark's Cathl George 64; C Riversdale 64-66; R Beaufort W and Victoria W 66-69; C Jarrow St Paul *Dur* 69-72; TV 72-75; TR Jarrow 76-85; V Gildersome *Wakef* 85-00; Hon Can Wakef Cathl 94-00; rtd 00; Perm to Offic *Linc* from 00; Hon Asst Chapl Voorschoten *Eur* 02-03. *Harlough, St Chad, Barrow-upon-Humber DN19 7AU* Tel (01469) 531475 E-mail david-martineau@harlough.freeserve.co.uk
MARTINEAU, Canon Jeremy Fletcher. b 40. OBE03. K Coll Lon BD65 AKC65. **d** 66 **p** 67. C Jarrow St Paul *Dur* 66-73; Bp's Ind Adv 69-73; P-in-c Raughton Head w Gatesgill *Carl* 73-80; Chapl to Agric 73-80; Ind Chapl *Bris* 80-90; Sec Abps' Commission on Rural Affairs 88-90; Nat Rural Officer Gen Syn Bd of Miss 90-03; Hon Can Cov Cathl 01-03; rtd 04; Lic to Offic *St D* from 05. *11 New Hill Villas, Goodwick SA64 0DT* Tel (01348) 874886 E-mail jeremy.m@talktalk.net
MARTINSON, Matthew. b 74. Mattersey Hall BA03. St Jo Coll Nottm. **d** 09 **p** 10. C Beverley St Nic *York* from 09. *7 St Nicholas' Drive, Beverley HU17 0QY* Tel (01482) 862770 E-mail matt@martinson.org.uk
MARTLEW, Andrew Charles. b 50. Nottm Univ BTh76 Lanc Univ MA80. Linc Th Coll 72. **d** 76 **p** 77. C Poulton-le-Fylde *Blackb* 76-79; Hon C Lancaster Ch Ch 79-80; Malaysia 81-83; V Golcar *Wakef* 83-89; Dioc Schs Officer 89-95; V Warmfield 89-95; Dioc Dir of Educn *York* 95-02; CF 02-10; Chapl HM Pris Ranby 10-11; rtd 11; Perm to Offic *Wakef* from 10 and *York* from 11. *Balne Moor Farm, Balne Moor Road, Balne, Goole DN14 0EN* Tel (01405) 862484
MARVELL, John. b 32. Lon Univ BD63 Leic Univ MEd73 PhD85. Oak Hill Th Coll 79. **d** 80 **p** 81. NSM Colchester Ch Ch w St Mary V *Chelmsf* 80-85; Perm to Offic 85-87; P-in-c Stisted w Bradwell and Pattiswick 87-98; rtd 98. *3 impasse de Genets, 35800 Dinard, France* Tel (0033) 2 99 16 56 74 E-mail jmarvell@nordnet.fr
MARVIN, David Arthur. b 51. St Jo Coll Nottm 96. **d** 97 **p** 98. C Mansfield St Jo *S'well* 97-01; P-in-c Greasley from 01. *The Vicarage, 36 Moorgreen, Newthorpe, Nottingham NG16 2FB* Tel (01773) 712509 E-mail dave.marvin1@ntlworld.com
MARWOOD, Canon Timothy John Edmonds. b 51. Whitelands Coll Lon CertEd72 Open Univ BA89 Lon Inst of Educn MA91.

S'wark Ord Course 92. **d** 95 **p** 96. NSM Putney St Mary *S'wark* 95-00; Perm to Offic *Ex* 00-07; P-in-c Petersham *S'wark* 07-11; V from 11; Chapl K Coll Sch Wimbledon 08-10; AD Richmond and Barnes *S'wark* from 10; Hon Can S'wark Cathl from 08. *The Vicarage, Bute Avenue, Richmond TW10 7AX* Tel (020) 8940 8435 Mobile 07973-518742 E-mail timmarwood@yahoo.co.uk

MARY CLARE, Sister. *See* FOGG, Cynthia Mary

MARY STEPHEN, Sister. *See* BRITT, Sister Mary Stephen

MASCALL, Mrs Margaret Ann. b 43. LRAM64 Bris Univ CertEd65 St Jo Coll Dur BA71 MA79. Cranmer Hall Dur 69. **dss** 76 **d** 87 **p** 94. Hertford St Andr *St Alb* 75-79; Herne Bay Ch Ch *Cant* 79-82; Seasalter 82-84; Whitstable 84-90; Par Dn 87-90; Perm to Offic 91-94; Hon C Hackington 94-95; V Newington w Hartlip and Stockbury 95-03; rtd 03; Perm to Offic *Cant* from 03. *48 Holmside Avenue, Minster on Sea, Sheerness ME12 3EY* Tel (01795) 663095
E-mail margaret.mascall@btopenworld.com

MASCARENHAS, Felix Pedro Antonio. b 55. Bombay Univ BA80 Pontifical Univ Rome JCD88. Pilar Major Th Sem Goa BTh81. **d** 82 **p** 82. In RC Ch 82-02; C Chich St Paul and Westhampnett 02-06; P-in-c Brighton Gd Shep Preston from 06. *The Vicarage, 272 Dyke Road, Brighton BN1 5AE* Tel (01273) 882987 Mobile 07814-739312 E-mail felixmas@hotmail.com

MASDING, John William. b 39. Magd Coll Ox BA61 DipEd63 MA65 Univ of Wales (Cardiff) LLM94 FRSA96. Ridley Hall Cam 63. **d** 65 **p** 66. C Boldmere *Birm* 65-71; V Hamstead St Paul 71-97; rtd 97; Perm to Offic *B & W* from 97 and *Bris* from 00. *The Old School House, Norton Hawkfield, Pensford, Bristol BS39 4HB* Tel and fax (01275) 830017
E-mail john.masding@magd.oxon.org

MASH, William Edward John. b 44. Imp Coll Lon BSc75 Open Univ MA00 ARCS. St Jo Coll Nottm 87. **d** 89 **p** 90. C Beverley Minster *York* 89-93; V Elloughton and Brough w Brantingham 93-01; P-in-c Newcastle St Geo *Lich* 01-08; V 08-10; P-in-c Knutton 06-08; V 08-10; Chapl Town Cen and Newcastle Coll of H&FE 01-10; Team Ldr Black Country Urban Ind Miss *Lich* from 10; Dioc Officer for Miss in the Economy from 10. *20 Mahogany Drive, Stafford ST16 2TS*
E-mail bcuim@btconnect.com

MASHEDER, Peter Timothy Charles. b 49. AKC71. St Aug Coll Cant 71. **d** 72 **p** 73. C Barkingside St Fran *Chelmsf* 72-75; C Chingford SS Pet and Paul 75-91; P-in-c High Laver w Magdalen Laver and Lt Laver etc 91-98; R 98-07; RD Ongar 02-04; R Ray Valley *Ox* from 07; AD Bicester and Islip from 08. *St Mary's Rectory, Church Walk, Ambrosden, Bicester OX25 2UJ* Tel (01869) 247813 E-mail chasmash@ic24.net

MASHITER, Mrs Marion. b 48. CBDTI 01. **d** 04 **p** 05. NSM Burneside *Carl* 04-07; NSM Beacon from 07. *The Maples, 5 Esthwaite Avenue, Kendal LA9 7NN* Tel (01539) 731957 Mobile 07748-771836 E-mail marionmashiter@lineone.net

MASIH, Wilson. d 11. NSM Hanwell St Mellitus w St Mark *Lon* from 11. *37 West Avenue, Southall UB1 2AP*

MASKELL, John Michael. b 45. Sarum & Wells Th Coll 86. **d** 88 **p** 89. C Swanborough *Sarum* 88-91; Chapl RAF 91-95; P-in-c Ollerton w Boughton *S'well* 95-97; P-in-c Capel *Guildf* 97-02; TV Walton H Trin *Ox* 02-03; Healing Co-ord Acorn Chr Foundn 03-04; rtd 04; Perm to Offic *Chich* 04-10; P-in-c Chailey from 10. *The Rectory, Chailey Green, Lewes BN8 4DA* Tel 07929-134962 (mobile) E-mail johnm1@madasafish.com

MASKELL, Miss Rosemary Helen. b 58. Ripon Coll Cuddesdon. **d** 00 **p** 01. C Goodrington *Ex* 00-04; V Littleport *Ely* from 04. *St George's Vicarage, 30 Church Lane, Littleport, Ely CB6 1PS* Tel (01353) 860207 Mobile 07803-499755
E-mail revrose@goodevon.fsnet.co.uk

MASKREY, Mrs Susan Elizabeth. b 43. Cranmer Hall Dur IDC70. **dss** 76 **d** 92 **p** 94. Littleover *Derby* 76-77; Sec to Publicity Manager CMS Lon 77-78; Stantonbury and Willen *Ox* 78-88; Billingham St Aid *Dur* 88-95; C 92-95; Asst Chapl HM Pris Holme Ho 94-95; Asst Chapl HM Pris Preston 95-01; Chapl HM Pris Kirkham 01-05; rtd 05; Perm to Offic *Blackb* from 05. *c/o the Bishop of Blackburn, Bishop's House, Ribchester Road, Blackburn BB1 9EF*

MASLEN (*formerly* **CHILD**), **Mrs Margaret Mary.** b 44. ALA76 Open Univ BA79. S Dios Minl Tr Scheme 89. **d** 92 **p** 94. C Portishead *B & W* 92-93; C Ilminster w Whitelackington 93-94; C Ilminster and Distr 94-96; C Tatworth 96-00; TV Chard and Distr 00-05; Chapl Taunton and Somerset NHS Trust 97-05; rtd 05; Hon C Sherston Magna, Easton Grey, Luckington etc *Bris* from 06; Hon C Hullavington, Norton and Stanton St Quintin from 06. *2 Woods Close, Sherston, Malmesbury SN16 0LF* Tel (01666) 840387 E-mail maslens@tiscali.co.uk

MASLEN, Richard Ernest. b 34. S Dios Minl Tr Scheme 89. **d** 92 **p** 93. NSM Sherston Magna, Easton Grey, Luckington etc *Bris* 92-93; NSM Ilminster w Whitelackington *B & W* 93-94; NSM Ilminster and Distr 94-96; P-in-c Tatworth 96-99; TV Chard and Distr 99-00; rtd 00; Perm to Offic *B & W* 00-05. *2 Woods Close, Sherston, Malmesbury SN16 0LF* Tel (01666) 840387

MASLEN, Canon Stephen Henry. b 37. CCC Ox BA62 MA65. Ridley Hall Cam 62. **d** 64 **p** 65. C Keynsham w Queen Charlton

MASON, Adrian Stanley. b 54. Hatf Poly BSc77 QTS01. Ripon Coll Cuddesdon 77. **d** 80 **p** 81. C Mill End and Heronsgate w W Hyde *St Alb* 80-83; TV Axminster, Chardstock, Combe Pyne and Rousdon *Ex* 83-87; TV Halesworth w Linstead, Chediston, Holton etc *St E* 87-88; R Brandon and Santon Downham 88-91; R Glemsford, Hartest w Boxted, Somerton etc 91-95; Min Can St E Cathl 95-97; R S Hartismere 06-11; P-in-c Stoke by Nayland w Leavenheath and Polstead from 11. *The Vicarage, Bear Street, Nayland, Colchester CO6 4LA* Tel and fax (01206) 262316
E-mail fr.adrian.mason@gmail.com

MASON, Alan Hambleton. b 27. Lon Univ BD59. Wycliffe Hall Ox 56. **d** 59 **p** 60. C Norbiton *S'wark* 59-63; V 73-84; V Thornton St Jas *Bradf* 63-73; V Wavertree St Thos *Liv* 84-92; rtd 92; Perm to Offic *Liv* from 92. *c/o Ms F E Mason, 44 St Margarets Road, Lowestoft NR32 4HT*

MASON, Ambrose. *See* MASON, Canon Thomas Henry Ambrose

MASON, Andrew. b 73. **d** 10 **p** 11. NSM Chelsea St Jo w St Andr *Lon* from 10. *Flat 2, 465 Kings Road, London SW10 0LU* Tel (020) 7351 1447 E-mail andymason73@yahoo.com

MASON, Andrew John. b 77. St Jo Coll Nottm BA06. **d** 06 **p** 07. C Bemerton *Sarum* 06-09; TV Kingswood *Bris* from 09. *60 Lavers Close, Bristol BS15 9ZG* Tel 0117-960 3195
E-mail revandymason06@hotmail.co.uk

MASON, Miss Beverley Anne. Trin Coll Bris BA00. **d** 01 **p** 03. C Rusthall *Roch* 01-02; C Rainham 02-05; V Upper Norwood St Jo *S'wark* from 05; AD Croydon N from 10. *St John's Vicarage, 2 Sylvan Road, London SE19 2RX* Tel (020) 8653 0378
E-mail revdbev@tiscali.co.uk

MASON, Miss Chantal Marie. b 73. Ex Univ BA96 St Luke's Coll Ex PGCE98. Trin Coll Bris MA08. **d** 08. C Alphington, Shillingford St George and Ide *Ex* from 08. *13 Sydney Road, Exeter EX2 9AJ* Tel (01392) 427568
E-mail revchantalmason@yahoo.co.uk

MASON, Charles Oliver. b 51. Jes Coll Cam BA73 MA99 St Jo Coll Dur BA79. **d** 80 **p** 81. C Cheltenham St Mary, St Matt, St Paul and H Trin *Glouc* 80-84; C Enfield Ch Ch Trent Park *Lon* 84-88; P-in-c W Hampstead St Cuth 88-93; V 93-01; AD N Camden 98-01; V Braintree *Chelmsf* from 01. *St Michael's Vicarage, 10A Marshalls Road, Braintree CM7 2LL* Tel (01376) 322840 E-mail revdcom@btinternet.com

MASON, Christina Mary. b 42. Univ of Wales Ban63 MA67 BSc(Econ)70 Dundee Univ PhD84 Middx Univ MSc02. St Jo Coll Nottm 81. **d** 83 **p** 10. Lic to Offic *Bre* 83-92; Perm to Offic *Nor* from 99. *44 Long Street, Great Ellingham, Attleborough NR17 1LN* Tel (01953) 451354 E-mail cmason@patsltd.co.uk

MASON, Mrs Christine Mary. b 43. Sarum & Wells Th Coll 91. **d** 93 **p** 94. Par Dn Blakenall Heath *Lich* 93-94; C 94-97; TV Rugeley 97-06; TV Brereton and Rugeley 06-08; rtd 08; Perm to Offic *Lich* from 09. *The Old School, Sutton Maddock, Shifnal TF11 9NQ* Tel (01952) 730442

MASON, Christopher David. b 51. Lanc Univ BA72 Leic Univ MEd82. EAMTC 91. **d** 94 **p** 95. NSM Pet St Mary Boongate 94-00 and 03-05; P-in-c Newborough 00-02; Chapl Pet High Sch 05-10; rtd 10. *74 Derby Drive, Peterborough PE1 4NQ* Tel (01733) 700000 E-mail mason.cd@virgin.net

MASON, Clive Ray. b 34. St Chad's Coll Dur BA57. Qu Coll Birm 57. **d** 59 **p** 60. C Gateshead St Mary *Dur* 59-62; C Bishopwearmouth Ch Ch 62-64; V Darlington St Jo 64-74; P-in-c Southwick H Trin 75-84; R 84-89; V Bearpark 89-95; rtd 95; Perm to Offic *Dur* from 95. *41 Harbour View, Littlehaven, South Shields NE33 1LS* Tel 0191-454 0234

MASON, David Gray. b 37. Birm Univ LDS61 K Coll Lon MPhil94. St Alb Minl Tr Scheme 83. **d** 95 **p** 95. NSM Biddenham *St Alb* 95-98; P-in-c Felmersham 98-05; NSM Sharnbrook, Felmersham and Knotting w Souldrop from 05; RD Sharnbrook from 06. *2A Devon Road, Bedford MK40 3DF* Tel and fax (01234) 309737
E-mail david.mason93@ntlworld.com

MASON, Dawn Lavinia. b 53. Ripon Coll Cuddesdon 95. **d** 97 **p** 98. C Wisbech St Aug *Ely* 97-00; V Emneth and Marshland St James 00-09; P-in-c Elm and Friday Bridge w Coldham 04-09; V Fen Orchards from 09. *The Vicarage, 72 Church Road, Emneth, Wisbech PE14 8AF* Tel (01945) 583089
E-mail dmason889@btinternet.com

MASON, Dennis Wardell. b 28. Ox NSM Course 83. **d** 86 **p** 87. NSM Ox St Barn and St Paul 86-08. *26 John Lopes Road, Eynsham, Witney OX29 4JR* Tel (01865) 880440

MASON, Edward. *See* MASON, Preb Thomas Edward

MASON, Mrs Elizabeth Ann. b 42. Homerton Coll Cam TCert64 Open Univ BA90. Ox Min Course 91. **d** 94 **p** 95. NSM Worminghall w Ickford, Oakley and Shabbington *Ox* 94-95;

NSM Swan 95-98; TV 98-05; rtd 05. *35 Common Road, North Leigh, Witney OX29 6RD* Tel (01993) 883966

MASON, Francis Robert Anthony. b 56. Trin Coll Bris BA90. **d** 90 **p** 91. C Denham *Ox* 90-94; P-in-c Jersey Grouville *Win* 94-98; R 98-04; R Tendring and Lt Bentley w Beaumont cum Moze *Chelmsf* from 07. *The Rectory, The Street, Tendring, Clacton-on-Sea CO16 0BW* Tel (01255) 830586
E-mail francismason@jerseymail.co.uk

MASON, Canon Geoffrey Charles. b 48. K Coll Lon BD74 AKC74. St Aug Coll Cant 74. **d** 75 **p** 76. C Hatcham Park All SS *S'wark* 75-78; V Bellingham St Dunstan 78-87; RD E Lewisham 82-87; C Catford (Southend) and Downham 87-88; Bp's Adv for Min Development 88-00; Dioc Dir of Ords 00-10; P-in-c Nunhead St Antony w St Silas from 10; Dir Ords (Woolwich Area) from 10; Hon Can S'wark Cathl from 07. *13 Halons Road, London SE9 5BS* Tel (020) 8859 7614
E-mail geoff.mason@southwark.anglican.org

✠**MASON, The Rt Revd James Philip.** b 54. Solomon Is Coll of HE TCert73 St Jo Coll Auckland STh86. Bp Patteson Th Coll (Solomon Is) 78. **d** 81 **p** 82 **c** 91. C St Barn Cathl Honiara Solomon Is 81-82; Sec to Abp Melanesia 83-86; Lect Bp Patteson Th Coll 87; Dean Honiara 88-91; Bp Hanuato'o 91-04; P-in-c Plympton St Maurice *Ex* from 05; Hon Asst Bp Ex from 07. *St Maurice's Rectory, 31 Wain Park, Plymouth PL7 2HX* Tel (01752) 346114 Mobile 07875-160159
E-mail jamesphilipmason@stmaurice.eclipse.co.uk

MASON, John Evans. b 32. RD. Linc Th Coll 57. **d** 59 **p** 60. C Putney St Mary *S'wark* 59-62; C Berry Pomeroy *Ex* 62-64; Chapl RN 64-68; V Hopton *Nor* 68-72; Chapl RNR 69-82; P-in-c Roydon St Remigius *Nor* 72-76; R Diss 72-80; Dir YMCA Cam 80-85; Prin YMCA Dunford Coll 85-88; Perm to Offic *Glouc* 88-97 and *Ox* 89-99; rtd 96; Perm to Offic *Nor* 98-02; *Sarum* 02-04; *B & W* from 05. *Barretts House Farm, Yeovil Road, Halstock, Yeovil BA22 9RP* Tel (01935) 891400

MASON, John Martin. b 41. UMIST BSc63. Glouc Sch of Min 80 Qu Coll Birm 82. **d** 84 **p** 85. C Tuffley *Glouc* 84-87; P-in-c Willersey, Saintbury, Weston-sub-Edge etc 87-92; R Yeovil, Selling w Throwley, Sheldwich w Badlesmere etc *Cant* 96-06; Dioc Rural Officer 96-06; rtd 06; Perm to Offic *Cant* from 06. *4 Old Garden Court, Chartham, Canterbury CT4 7GA* Tel (01227) 733486 Mobile 07951-024355
E-mail ruraljoe@btinternet.com

MASON, Canon Jonathan Patrick. b 55. Edin Th Coll 90. **d** 92 **p** 93. C Edin Ch Ch 92-94; C Edin Old St Paul 94-96; R St Andrews All SS *St And* from 96; Chapl St Andr Univ from 97; Can St Ninian's Cathl Perth from 07. *All Saints' Rectory, North Street, St Andrews KY16 9AQ* Tel and fax (01334) 473193
E-mail jpm2@st-and.ac.uk

MASON, Ms Josephine Margaret. b 41. Edin Univ BMus64. WMMTC 88. **d** 93 **p** 94. Chapl Asst S Birm Mental Health NHS Trust 91-06; C Birm St Jo Ladywood 93-01; C Ladywood St Jo and St Pet 01-06; rtd 06; Perm to Offic *Birm* from 06. *340 Selly Oak Road, Birmingham B30 1HP* Tel 0121-451 1412
E-mail jo.mason@freeuk.com

MASON, Julia Ann. b 43. St Jo Coll Nottm 89. **d** 91 **p** 95. NSM Troon *Glas* 91-93; NSM Ayr, Maybole and Girvan 93-05; Lic to Offic *Edin* from 08; Perm to Offic *Glas* from 08. *13/2 Rocheid Park, Edinburgh EH4 1RU* Tel 0131-343 1165
E-mail revdjuliamason@btinternet.com

MASON, Canon Kenneth Staveley. b 31. ARCS53 Lon Univ BSc53 BD64. Wells Th Coll 56. **d** 58 **p** 59. C Kingston upon Hull St Martin *York* 58-61; C Pocklington w Yapham-cum-Meltonby, Owsthorpe etc 61-63; C Millington w St Givendale 61-63; V Thornton w Allerthorpe 63-69; Sub-Warden St Aug Coll Cant 69-76; Abp's Adv in Past Min 76-77; Dir Cant Sch of Min 77-81; Prin 81-89; Sec to Dioc Bd of Min 77-87; Six Preacher Cant Cathl 79-84; Hon Can Cant Cathl 84-89; Prin Edin Th Coll 89-95; Can St Mary's Cathl 89-96; rtd 95; Perm to Offic *Ripon* from 96. *2 Williamson Close, Ripon HG4 1AZ* Tel (01765) 607041

MASON, Lesley Jane. b 55. Newnham Coll Cam BA76 FInstLD. St Jo Coll Nottm 04. **d** 07 **p** 08. NSM Busbridge and Hambledon *Guildf* 07-10; Chapl HM Pris Send from 10. *HM Prison Send, Ripley Road, Woking GU23 7LJ* Tel (01483) 471000
E-mail ljmason@btinternet.com

MASON, Nigel Frederick. b 60. Wycliffe Hall Ox 93. **d** 95 **p** 96. C Highbury Ch Ch w St Jo and St Sav *Lon* 95-98; C Seaford w Sutton *Chich* 98-01; R Rotherfield w Mark Cross from 01. *The Rectory, Mayfield Road, Rotherfield, Crowborough TN6 3LU* Tel (01892) 852536

MASON, Nigel James. b 56. Culham Coll of Educn BEd78. St Steph Ho Ox 95. **d** 97 **p** 98. C Hove *Chich* 97-00; V Kemp Town St Mary 00-07; Chapl St Mary's Hall Brighton 03-07; V Smethwick *Birm* from 07; P-in-c Smethwick St Matt w St Chad from 10. *Old Church Vicarage, 93A Church Road, Smethwick B67 6EE* Tel 0121-558 1763 E-mail n.mason@talktalk.net

MASON, Paul. b 51. Cranmer Hall Dur 93. **d** 93 **p** 94. C Handforth *Ches* 93-97; V Partington and Carrington 97-04; V

Church Hulme from 04. *The Vicarage, 74 London Road, Holmes Chapel, Crewe CW4 7BD* Tel and fax (01477) 533124

MASON, Mrs Pauline. b 49. LCTP. **d** 08 **p** 09. NSM Chorley St Geo *Blackb* from 08. *33 Park Road, Chorley PR7 1QS* Tel (01257) 264300 E-mail pollymason@qualitas.f9.co.uk

MASON, Peter Charles. b 45. K Coll Lon BD72 AKC72 Birm Univ PGCE89. St Aug Coll Cant 72. **d** 73 **p** 74. C Ilkeston St Mary *Derby* 73-76; C Bridgnorth St Mary *Heref* 76-78; TV Bridgnorth, Tasley, Astley Abbotts, etc 78-88; RE Teacher from 89; rtd 10; Perm to Offic *Heref* 89-04 and *St D* from 04. *63 Nun Street, St Davids, Haverfordwest SA62 6NU* Tel (01437) 721715

MASON, Canon Peter Joseph. b 34. Lon Univ BA58. Coll of Resurr Mirfield 58. **d** 60 **p** 61. C Belhus Park CD *Chelmsf* 60-63; Lic to Offic *Eur* 63-64; Asst Chapl Lon Univ 64-70; Chapl City Univ 66-70; R Stoke Newington St Mary 70-78; V Writtle *Chelmsf* 78-81; P-in-c Highwood 78-81; V Writtle w Highwood 81-86; R Shenfield 86-93; Hon Can Chelmsf Cathl 89-00; P-in-c Maldon All SS w St Pet 93-95; V 95-00; RD Maldon and Dengie 95-00; rtd 00; Perm to Offic *Chelmsf* from 00. *32 Providence, Burnham-on-Crouch CM0 8JU* Tel (01621) 785921
E-mail peter@franknox.demon.co.uk

MASON, Robert Herbert George. b 48. ACII. Oak Hill Th Coll 82. **d** 84 **p** 85. C Ware Ch Ch *St Alb* 84-88; V Eastbourne All So *Chich* 88-98; P-in-c Poole *Sarum* 98-01; R from 01; Chapl Miss to Seafarers from 98. *The Rectory, 10 Poplar Close, Poole BH15 1LP* Tel (01202) 672694 Fax 677117
E-mail revbobmelmason@hotmail.com

MASON, Canon Roger Arthur. b 41. Lon Univ BSc65 K Coll Lon BD68 AKC68. **d** 69 **p** 70. C Enfield St Andr *Lon* 69-72; P-in-c Westbury and Yockleton *Heref* 72-78; P-in-c Gt Wollaston 77-78; V Willesden St Mary *Lon* 78-88; V Prittlewell *Chelmsf* 88-06; P-in-c Prittlewell St Steph 92-04; Hon Can Chelmsf Cathl 01-06; rtd 06; Perm to Offic *Leic* and *Eur* from 07; Hon C Empingham, Edith Weston, Lyndon, Manton etc Pet from 08. *4 Westhorpe Close, Wing, Oakham LE15 8RJ* Tel (01572) 737014 E-mail randjmason@sky.com

MASON, Mrs Sally Lynne. b 52. EMMTC 05. **d** 08 **p** 09. NSM Alfreton *Derby* from 08. *27 Stretton Road, Morton, Alfreton DE55 6GW* Tel (01773) 873508 E-mail sallymason@live.co.uk

MASON, Mrs Sally-Anne. b 55. Open Univ BA86 C F Mott Coll of Educn CertEd77. SNWTP 07. **d** 10 **p** 11. NSM Childwall St Dav *Liv* from 10; NSM Stoneycroft All SS from 10. *2 Reedale Road, Liverpool L18 5HL* Tel 0151-724 1142 Mobile 07889-584885 E-mail sallyanne.mason@o2.co.uk

MASON *(formerly FOALE)*, **Sheila Rosemary.** b 40. Saffron Walden Coll CertEd61 ARCM62. SWMTC 98. **d** 01 **p** 02. NSM Shebbear, Buckland Filleigh, Sheepwash etc *Ex* 01-04; C Cobham and Stoke D'Abernon *Guildf* 04-08; rtd 08. *1 Heron Place, Broughty Ferry, Dundee DD5 3PR* Tel (01382) 350568 Mobile 07712-086540 E-mail rosemary@foale16.fsworld.co.uk

MASON, Simon Ion Vincent. b 60. Birm Univ BA82. Trin Coll Bris BA00. **d** 00 **p** 01. C Nottingham St Nic *S'well* 00-05; P-in-c Newent and Gorsley w Cliffords Mesne *Glouc* from 05. *The Rectory, 43 Court Road, Newent GL18 1SY* Tel (01531) 820248 E-mail mason.simon@ntlworld.com
or stmarys.church@talk21.com

MASON, Stephen David. b 65. Univ of Wales (Lamp) BA87. Ripon Coll Cuddesdon 89. **d** 92 **p** 93. C Gt Grimsby St Mary and St Jas *Linc* 92-97; V Southborough St Thos *Roch* 97-02; V Paddington St Jo w St Mich *Lon* from 02. *18 Somers Crescent, London W2 2PN* Tel (020) 7262 1732 Fax 7706 4475
E-mail parishadmin@stjohns-hydepark.com

MASON, Terry Mathew. b 56. Trin Coll Bris 94. **d** 96 **p** 97. C Bexleyheath Ch Ch *Roch* 96-99; P-in-c Stone 99-03; V Broadway w Wickhamford *Worc* 03-11; RD Evesham 05-10; P-in-c Wootton Wawen *Cov* from 11; P-in-c Claverdon w Preston Bagot from 11. *The Vicarage, Stratford Road, Wootton Wawen, Henley-in-Arden B95 6BD*

MASON, Preb Thomas Edward. b 52. Bris Univ MEd80. Trin Coll Bris BA91. **d** 91 **p** 92. C Glouc St Jas and All SS 91-94; V Churchdown 94-04; RD Glouc N 99-04; R Bath Abbey w St Jas *B & W* from 04; Preb Wells Cathl from 05. *The Rectory, 12 Cleveland Walk, Bath BA2 6JX* Tel (01225) 318267 or 422462
E-mail rector@bathabbey.org

MASON, Canon Thomas Henry Ambrose. b 51. Solicitor 75. Oak Hill Th Coll BA86. **d** 86 **p** 87. C W Drayton *Lon* 86-89; Field Officer Oak Hill Ext Coll 89-94; Eur Sec ICS 94-95; Dir of Tr *Eur* 95-03; Dir Min and Dir of Ords 01-03; Can Brussels Cathl 00-03; Hon Can 03-07; R Grosmont and Skenfrith and Llangattock etc *Mon* 03-08; Dioc Dir Min from 06. *The Rectory, Gwernesney, Usk NP15 1HP* Tel (01291) 672152
E-mail ambrose@rectorygwernesney.com

MASON, William Frederick. b 48. Linc Th Coll 75. **d** 78 **p** 79. C Ipswich St Aug *St E* 78-81; TV Dronfield *Derby* 81-88; V Ellesmere St Pet *Sheff* 88-91; V Bedgrove *Ox* 91-00; C Hazlemere 00-07; V Penn Street from 07. *The Vicarage, Penn Street, Amersham HP7 0PX* Tel (01494) 715195
E-mail willfmason@aol.com

MASSEY, Mrs Elizabeth Ann. b 53. N Staffs Poly BSc75. STETS 04. **d** 07 **p** 08. C Whitton *Sarum* 07-10; TV Marden Vale from 10. *The Vicarage, Church Road, Derry Hill, Calne SN11 9NN* Tel 07777-800084 (mobile) E-mail ea.massey@btinternet.com

MASSEY, George Douglas. b 44. St Jo Coll Nottm 91. **d** 93 **p** 94. C Higher Bebington *Ches* 93-98; V Messingham *Linc* from 98. *The Vicarage, 12 Holme Lane, Messingham, Scunthorpe DN17 3SG* Tel (01724) 762823 E-mail george.massey@ntlworld.com

MASSEY, Mrs Kate Ishbel. b 77. Aber Univ MB, ChB99. Qu Coll Birm 08. **d** 11. C Kenilworth St Nic *Cov* from 11. *St Barnabas House, 145 Albion Street, Kenilworth CV8 2FY* Tel (01926) 402859 E-mail katemassey@virginmedia.com

MASSEY, Keith John. b 46. Oak Hill Th Coll 69. **d** 72 **p** 73. C Bermondsey St Jas w Ch Ch *S'wark* 72-76; C Benchill *Man* 76-82; V Clifton Green 82-97; V Flixton St Jo from 97. *St John's Vicarage, Irlam Road, Urmston, Manchester M41 6AP* Tel 0161-748 6754

MASSEY, Margaret. **d** 10 **p** 11. OLM Frimley *Guildf* from 10. *69 Old Pasture Road, Frimley, Camberley GU16 8RT* Tel (01276) 684907

MASSEY, Michelle Elaine (Shellie). Plymouth Univ BA00. Trin Coll Bris BA04. **d** 04 **p** 05. C Barrowby and Gt Gonerby *Linc* 04-09; P-in-c Saxonwell from 09. *15 Manor Drive, Long Bennington, Newark NG23 5GZ* Tel (01400) 282696 Mobile 07876-645786 E-mail revdmichellem@aol.com

MASSEY, Nigel John. b 60. Birm Univ BA81 MA82. Wycliffe Hall Ox. **d** 87 **p** 88. C Bearwood *Birm* 87-90; C Warley Woods 90; C Tottenham St Paul *Lon* 91-94; USA from 94. *French Church du St Spirit, 111 East 60th Street #4, New York NY 10022, USA* Tel (001) (212) 838 5680 E-mail stesprit@msn.com

MASSEY, Paul Daniel Shaw. b 70. Nottm Univ BA93. Westcott Ho Cam 94. **d** 96 **p** 97. C Ashby-de-la-Zouch St Helen w Coleorton *Leic* 96-01; R Cotgrave *S'well* from 01; P-in-c Owthorpe from 01. *The Rectory, 2 Thurman Drive, Cotgrave, Nottingham NG12 3LG* Tel and fax 0115-989 2223 E-mail pdsmassey@tiscali.co.uk

MASSEY, Peter William. b 45. St Mark & St Jo Coll Lon TCert66 Open Univ BA75. WMMTC 96. **d** 99 **p** 00. Lay Tr Officer *Heref* 97-09; NSM Holmer w Huntington 99-03; NSM Heref St Pet w St Owen and St Jas from 03. *15 Thoresby Drive, Hereford HR2 7RF* Tel and fax (01432) 270248 Mobile 07803-826728 E-mail p.massey@hereford.anglican.org

MASSEY, Shellie. *See* MASSEY, Michelle Elaine

MASSEY, Stephen William. b 56. Hatf Poly BSc79 PhD86 MIMA04. ERMC 06. **d** 09 **p** 10. NSM Watford St Luke *St Alb* from 09. *19 South Riding, Bricket Wood, St Albans AL2 3NG* Tel (01923) 662368 E-mail swmportraits@xalt.co.uk

MASSEY, Wayne Philip. b 74. Brunel Univ BSc97. Wycliffe Hall Ox BA05. **d** 06 **p** 07. C Clifton Ch Ch w Em *Bris* from 06. *The Vicarage, 6 Goldney Avenue, Clifton, Bristol BS8 4RA* Tel 0117-973 5220 E-mail wayne@christchurchclifton.org.uk

MASSEY, Preb William Cyril. b 32. Lich Th Coll 58. **d** 61 **p** 62. C Heref St Martin 61-66; V Kimbolton w Middleton-on-the-Hill 66-75; V Alveley 75-83; P-in-c Quatt 81-83; R Alveley and Quatt 84-85; R Llangarron w Llangrove, Whitchurch and Ganarew 85-97; Preb Heref Cathl 92-97; rtd 97; Perm to Offic *Heref* from 97. *Hollybush Cottage, Pencombe, Bromyard HR7 4RW* Tel (01885) 400713

MASSEY, William Peter. b 50. CITC 96. **d** 99 **p** 00. C Fermoy Union C, C & R 99-00; C Carrigrohane Union and Kinsale Union 00-03; Perm to Offic *Eur* from 04. *1801 chemin des Pailles, 83510 Lorgues, France* Tel (0033) 4 94 73 93 37 or 4 94 99 40 74 E-mail peter@themasseys.fr

MASSHEDAR, Richard Eric. b 57. Nottm Univ BTh86. Linc Th Coll 83. **d** 86 **p** 87. C Cassop cum Quarrington *Dur* 86-89; C Ferryhill 89-91; V Leam Lane 91-94; P-in-c Hartlepool St Paul 94-96; V from 96. *St Paul's Vicarage, 6 Hutton Avenue, Hartlepool TS26 9PN* Tel (01429) 272934 E-mail r.masshedar@ntlworld.com

MASSINGBERD-MUNDY, Roger William Burrell. b 36. TD. Univ of Wales (Lamp) BA59. Ridley Hall Cam 59. **d** 61 **p** 62. C Benwell St Jas *Newc* 61-64; C Whorlton 64-72; TV 73; P-in-c Healey 73-85; Dioc Stewardship Adv 73-85; Hon Can Newc Cathl 82-85; CF (TA) 63-68; CF (TAVR) 71-83; R S Ormsby w Ketsby, Calceby and Driby *Linc* 85-86; P-in-c Harrington w Brinkhill 85-86; P-in-c Haugh 85-86; P-in-c Oxcombe 85-86; P-in-c Ruckland w Farforth and Maidenwell 85-86; P-in-c Somersby w Bag Enderby 85-86; P-in-c Tetford and Salmonby 85-86; R S Ormsby Gp 86-96; RD Bolingbroke 88-96; rtd 96; Chapl Taverham Hall Sch from 03. *The Old Post Office, West Raynham, Fakenham NR21 7AD* Tel (01328) 838611 Fax 838698 E-mail rogermundy@markeaton.co.uk

MASSON, Canon Philip Roy. b 52. Hertf Coll Ox BA75 Leeds Univ BA77. Coll of Resurr Mirfield 75. **d** 78 **p** 79. C Port Talbot St Theodore *Llan* 78-82; V Penyfai w Tondu 82-92; Dioc Dir Post-Ord Tr 85-88; Warden of Ords 88-01; R Newton Nottage from 92; AD Margam 01-06; Can Llan Cathl from 02. *The*

Rectory, 64 Victoria Avenue, Porthcawl CF36 3HE Tel and fax (01656) 782042 *or* 786899 E-mail porthcawl.church@tiscali.co.uk *or* philipmasson@hotmail.com

MASTERMAN, Malcolm. b 49. City Univ MSc00. K Coll Lon 73 Chich Th Coll 76. **d** 77 **p** 78. C Peterlee *Dur* 77-80; Chapl Basingstoke Distr Hosp 80-85; Chapl Freeman Hosp Newc 85-95; Tr and Development Officer Hosp Chapl Coun 96-00; Sen Chapl N Dur Healthcare NHS Trust 00-02; Sen Chapl Co Durham and Darlington Acute Hosps NHS Trust 02-06; Lead Chapl S Tees Hosps NHS Trust from 06; Bp's Adv on Hosp Chapl (Whitby Area) *York* from 06. *James Cook University Hospital, Marton Road, Middlesbrough TS4 3BW* Tel (01642) 854802 *or* 850850 E-mail malcolm.masterman@stees.nhs.uk

MASTERMAN, Miss Patricia Hope. b 28. St Mich Ho Ox 59. dss 79 **d** 87. Asst CF 79-90; rtd 90; Perm to Offic *Chich* from 90. *33 Sea Lane Gardens, Ferring, Worthing BN12 5EQ* Tel (01903) 245231

MASTERS, Kenneth Leslie. b 44. Leeds Univ BA68. Cuddesdon Coll 68. **d** 70 **p** 71. C Wednesbury St Paul Wood Green *Lich* 70-71; C Tettenhall Regis 71-75; TV Chelmsley Wood *Birm* 75-79; R Harting *Chich* 79-87; V Rustington 87-00; TR Beaminster Area *Sarum* 00-09; rtd 09. *9 Carrington Way, Wincanton BA9 9NX* Tel (01963) 824209 E-mail k2masters4@btinternet.com

MASTERS, Rupert Paul Falla. b 52. Hull Univ BA74 Ex Univ PGCE75 Lon Inst of Educn MA88. **d** 10 **p** 11. OLM Stoughton *Guildf* from 10. *32 Sheepfold Road, Guildford GU2 9TT* Tel (01483) 573785 E-mail rupert.masters@talk21.com

MASTERS, Stephen Michael. b 52. **d** 87 **p** 88. C Primrose Hill St Mary w Avenue Road St Paul *Lon* 87-90; C Hornsey St Mary w St Geo 90-91; Bp's Dom Chapl *Chich* 91-96; V Brighton St Mich 96-99; C Eastbourne St Andr 00-01; Chapl to Bp Lewes 00-01; Asst to Adn Lewes and Hastings 00-01; P-in-c Alderney Win 01-03; V from 03. *The New Vicarage, La Vallee, Alderney, Guernsey GY9 3XA* Tel (01481) 824866

MASTIN, Brian Arthur. b 38. Peterho Cam BA60 MA63 BD80 Mert Coll Ox MA63. Ripon Hall Ox 62. **d** 63 **p** 64. Asst Lect Hebrew Univ Coll of N Wales (Ban) 63-65; Lect Hebrew 65-82; Sen Lect 82-98; Chapl Ban Cathl 63-65; Lic to Offic 65-98; rtd 98; Perm to Offic *Ely* from 98. *2A Gurney Way, Cambridge CB4 2ED* Tel (01223) 355078

MATABELELAND, Bishop of. *See* LUNGA, The Rt Revd Cleophus

MATANA, Bishop of. *See* NTAHOTURI, The Most Revd Bernard

MATCHETT, Christopher Jonathan. b 65. QUB BSSc TCD BTh98. **d** 98 **p** 99. C Ballynafeigh St Jude *D & D* 98-01; C Holywood 01-04; I Magheracross *Clogh* from 04. *The Rectory, 27 Craghan Road, Ballinamallard, Enniskillen BT94 2BT* Tel and fax (028) 6638 8238 E-mail magheracross@clogher.anglican.org

MATCHETT, Miss Diane Margaret. b 71. Open Univ BA98. TCD Div Sch BTh05. **d** 05 **p** 06. C Lisburn Ch Ch *Conn* 05-08; I Castlerock w Dunboe and Fermoyle *D & R* from 08. *The Rectory, 52 Main Street, Castlerock, Coleraine BT51 4RA* Tel (028) 7084 8127 Mobile 07853-186509 E-mail revdiane@hotmail.co.uk

MATHER, Cuthbert. b 15. Tyndale Hall Bris 36. **d** 40 **p** 41. C Bebington *Ches* 40-42; C Stapenhill w Cauldwell *Derby* 43-51; C Cambridge St Andr Less *Ely* 51-52; C Dagenham *Chelmsf* 53-57; V Needham w Rushall *Nor* 57-80; rtd 80; Perm to Offic *Nor* from 80. *9 Gorselands, 25 Sandringham Road, Hunstanton PE36 5DP* Tel (01485) 533084

MATHER, David Jonathan. b 65. New Coll Ox BA88 MA95. St Steph Ho Ox BTh95. **d** 95 **p** 96. C Pickering w Lockton and Levisham *York* 95-98; P-in-c Bridlington H Trin and Sewerby w Marton 98-99; V from 99. *Sewerby Vicarage, Cloverley Road, Bridlington YO16 5TX* Tel (01262) 675725

MATHER, Mrs Elizabeth Ann. b 45. CertEd66. Dalton Ho Bris IDC70 St Jo Coll Nottm 92. **d** 94 **p** 95. NSM Littleover *Derby* 94-02; Lic to Offic *St Alb* 02-05; rtd 05; Perm to Offic *Nor* 05-10. *Angel Court, 2 Rose Street, Fortrose IV10 8TN* Tel (01381) 621745 E-mail revlib@libbymather.freeserve.co.uk

MATHER, James William. b 63. Sheff Univ BA86. St Steph Ho Ox 88. **d** 91 **p** 92. C Doncaster St Leon and St Jude *Sheff* 91-94; C Cantley 94-95; V Lakenheath *St E* 95-01; P-in-c Downham Market w Bexwell *Ely* 01-02; P-in-c Crimplesham w Stradsett 01-02; R Downham Market and Crimplesham w Stradsett from 02; RD Fincham and Feltwell 06-09. *The Rectory, King's Walk, Downham Market PE38 9LF* Tel (01366) 382187 E-mail james.mather@ely.anglican.org

MATHER, Stephen Albert. b 54. Qu Coll Birm 85. **d** 87 **p** 88. C Sutton *Liv* 87-90; TV 90-96; V Abram 96-99; V Bickershaw 96-99; V Hindley St Pet from 99. *St Peter's Vicarage, 122 Wigan Road, Hindley, Wigan WN2 3XF* Tel (01942) 55505

MATHER, William Bernard George. b 45. St Jo Coll Nottm 77. **d** 79 **p** 80. C St Leonards St Leon *Chich* 79-82; TR Netherthorpe *Sheff* 82-90; V Littleover *Derby* 90-02; Assoc Dir SOMA UK

02-05; TR Drypool *York* 05-10; rtd 10. *Angel Court, 2 Rose Street, Fortrose IV10 8TN* Tel (01381) 621745 E-mail williammather@gmail.com

MATHERS, Alan Edward. b 36. Lon Univ BA FPhS. Oak Hill Th Coll 61. **d** 64 **p** 65. C Ox St Matt 64-66; C Bootle St Leon *Liv* 66-68; C Hampreston *Sarum* 68-70; P-in-c Damerham 70-71; V Queniborough *Leic* 71-76; USA 76-77; V Tipton St Matt *Lich* 77-86; P-in-c Tipton St Paul 77-84; V 85-86; V Sutton Ch Ch *S'wark* 86-95; Chapl Cannes *Eur* 95-98; rtd 98; Perm to Offic *S'wark* and *Chich* from 98. *52 The Meadow, Copthorne, Crawley RH10 3RQ* Tel (01342) 713325 E-mail alanandmuriel@talktalk.net

MATHERS, David Michael Brownlow. b 43. Em Coll Cam BA65 MA69. Clifton Th Coll 65. **d** 67 **p** 68. C Branksome St Clem *Sarum* 67-70; C Bromley Ch Ch *Roch* 70-73; V Bures *St E* 73-80; Brazil 80-82; P-in-c Old Newton w Stowupland *St E* 82-86; V 87-90; V Thurston from 90; RD Ixworth 94-03. *The Rectory, Church Lane, Laughton, Lewes BN8 6AH* Tel (01323) 811624 *or* 811177

MATHERS, Derek. b 48. NOC 82. **d** 85 **p** 86. C Huddersfield St Jo *Wakef* 85-86; C N Huddersfield 86-88; TV Almondbury w Farnley Tyas 88-92; V Marsden 92-02; R Badsworth from 02. *The Rectory, Main Street, Badsworth, Pontefract WF9 1AF* Tel (01977) 643642 E-mail father.derek@badsworth.com

MATHERS, Kenneth Ernest William. b 56. Trin Coll Bris 93. **d** 95 **p** 96. C Bournemouth St Jo w St Mich *Win* 95-99; NSM Darenth *Roch* 99-04; Chapl Dartford and Gravesham NHS Trust 01-04; Chapl N Devon Healthcare NHS Trust from 05. *The Rectory, Newton Tracey, Barnstaple EX31 3PL* Tel (01271) 858292 E-mail revkmathers@btinternet.com

MATHERS, Mrs Kim Deborah. b 61. Southn Univ LLB82. Trin Coll Bris 86. **d** 89 **p** 94. Par Dn Bitterne *Win* 89-93; NSM Stoke Bishop *Bris* 93-95; NSM Bournemouth St Jo w St Mich *Win* 95-99; P-in-c Darenth *Roch* 99-04; TR Newton Tracey, Horwood, Alverdiscott etc *Ex* from 04; RD Torrington from 09. *The Rectory, Newton Tracey, Barnstaple EX31 3PL* Tel (01271) 858292 E-mail revkimmathers@btinternet.com

MATHESON, Alexander John. b 59. Lon Bible Coll BA84 S Tr Scheme 94. **d** 97 **p** 98. NSM Cowplain *Portsm* 97-01; C Portchester 01-04; V Sarisbury from 04. *The Vicarage, 149 Bridge Road, Sarisbury Green, Southampton SO31 7EN* Tel (01489) 572207 E-mail sandy@mathesonuk.com

MATHEW, Laurence Allen Stanfield. b 47. Sarum Th Coll 99. **d** 02 **p** 03. OLM Warminster Ch Ch *Sarum* from 02. *Chalvedune, 25 King Street, Warminster BA12 8DG* Tel (01985) 217282 Mobile 07768-006245 E-mail laurence01@blueyonder.co.uk

MATHEW (*née* HOLLIS), **Rebecca Catherine.** b 78. St Martin's Coll Lanc BA99. Ripon Coll Cuddesdon BTh03. **d** 03 **p** 04. C Broughton *Blackb* 03-07; C Mirihana Ch Ch Sri Lanka 07-08; Chapl St Thos Coll Mt Lavinia 08-11; TV Bicester w Bucknell, Caversfield and Launton *Ox* from 11. *The Vicarage, The Spinney, Launton, Bicester OX25 6EP* E-mail revdrebh@hotmail.com

MATHEWS, Richard Twitchell. b 27. Bps' Coll Cheshunt 57. **d** 59 **p** 60. C Leic St Phil 59-62; Chapl Beirut 62-63; Qatar 63-67; V Riddlesden *Bradf* 67-74; Australia 74-78; P-in-c Medbourne cum Holt w Stockerston and Blaston *Leic* 78-82; Chapl Alassio *Eur* 82-83; Chapl San Remo 82-83; Chapl Palma and Balearic Is w Ibiza etc 83-87; P-in-c Witchford w Wentworth *Ely* 87-91; rtd 91; Perm to Offic *Cant* 96-09. *Rosecroft, Church Lane, Ringwould, Deal CT14 8HR* Tel (01304) 367554

MATHEWS, Trevor John. b 50. Goldsmiths' Coll Lon MSc98. St Steph Ho Ox 87. **d** 89 **p** 90. C Cheltenham St Steph *Glouc* 89-91; C Up Hatherley 89-91; Perm to Offic *Chelmsf* from 08; CF from 09. *c/o MOD Chaplains (Army)* Tel (01264) 381140 Fax 381824 E-mail mathews@conflict.co.uk

MATHIAS, John Maelgwyn. b 15. St D Coll Lamp BA38 St Mich Coll Llan 40. **d** 40 **p** 41. C Ban St Mary 40-44; C Swansea St Pet *S & B* 44-49; V Mydroilyn w Dihewyd *St D* 49-54; R Cellan w Llanfair Clydogau 54-83; Lect St Jo Ch Coll Ystrad Meurig 67-77; rtd 83. *Bronallt, Capel Seion Road, Drefach, Llanelli SA14 7BN* Tel (01269) 844350

MATHIAS, Ms Lesley. b 49. Portsm Poly BA72 Nottm Univ MTh90. EMMTC 93. **d** 96 **p** 97. C Oadby *Leic* 96-98; Asst Chapl United Bris Healthcare NHS Trust 98-99; C Pet St Mary Boongate 99-01; V Kings Heath 01-06; Bp's Interfaith Adv 01-05; Perm to Offic *Pet* from 06 and *Ely* from 08. *4 Manor Walk, Hanging Houghton, Northampton NN6 9EP* Tel (01604) 880968 E-mail lesley@mathias.me.uk

MATHIAS-JONES, Edward Lloyd. b 71. Univ of Wales (Lamp) BA93. St Mich Coll Llan BD96. **d** 97 **p** 98. C Llanelli *St D* 97-00; C Milford Haven 00-04; V Newport St Steph and H Trin *Mon* from 04. *St Stephen's Vicarage, Adeline Street, Newport NP20 2HA* Tel (01633) 265192 E-mail frmathias-jones@aol.com

MATHIE, Patricia Jean (**Sister Donella**). b 22. Worc Coll of Educn CertEd49. **dss** 79 **d** 87. CSA from 74; Asst Superior 82-94; Mother Superior 94-00; Notting Hill St Jo 79-80; Abbey Ho Malmesbury 81-82; Notting Hill St Clem and St Mark 82-84; Kensal Town St Thos w St Andr and St Phil

---

85-87; Hon C 87-96; Perm to Offic 00-09. *40 Homecross House, 21 Fishers Lane, London W4 1YA* Tel (020) 8747 0001

MATHOLE, Paul Mark. b 76. St Anne's Coll Ox BA98 R Holloway Coll Lon MA00 PhD04. Oak Hill Th Coll 07. **d** 10 **p** 11. C Rusholme H Trin *Man* from 10. *3A Eileen Grove West, Manchester M14 5NW* Tel 07733-185670 (mobile) E-mail paulmathole@yahoo.co.uk

MATLOOB, Nazir Ahmad Barnabas. b 48. Punjab Univ BA79. Gujranwala Th Sem BTh77 BD81 MDiv85. **d** 78 **p** 78. Pakistan 78-93; Perm to Offic *Chelmsf* 94-97; C Forest Gate All SS and St Edm 98-06; C Lt Ilford St Barn 06; Inter-Faith Worker Newham Deanery from 07. *64 Henderson Road, London E7 8EF* Tel (020) 8552 4280

MATON, Oswald. b 24. St Aug Coll Cant 75. **d** 77 **p** 78. NSM Chatham St Steph *Roch* 77-94; Perm to Offic 94-04. *304 Maidstone Road, Chatham ME4 6JJ* Tel (01634) 843568

MATSON de LAURIER, Mrs Sarah Kennerley. b 46. EMMTC 00. **d** 02 **p** 03. NSM Hilton w Marston-on-Dove *Derby* from 02. *1 Park Way, Etwall, Derby DE65 6HU* Tel (01283) 732859 E-mail pskmdl@aol.com

MATTACKS, Mrs Lesley Anne. b 58. Birm Univ BA79 K Coll Lon MA86 Leeds Univ BA07 W Lon Inst of HE PGCE80. NOC 04. **d** 07 **p** 08. C Birkenshaw w Hunsworth *Wakef* 07-10; P-in-c Middlestown from 10. *The Vicarage, 6 Coxley Dell, Horbury, Wakefield WF4 5LF* Tel (01924) 283533 Mobile 07952-375176 E-mail revles.mattacks@hotmail.co.uk

MATTAPALLY, Sebastian Thomas. b 57. N Bengal Univ BA77 Pontifical Salesian Univ BTh84 Pontifical Gregorian Univ LTh98 DTh05. **d** 83 **p** 83. In RC Ch 83-00; Perm to Offic *Eur* 01-04; C Patcham *Chich* 05-07; P-in-c Kirdford 07-10; V Eastbourne St Mich from 10. *St Michael's Vicarage, 15 Long Acre Close, Eastbourne BN21 1UF* Tel (01323) 646569 E-mail smattapally@btinternet.com

MATTEN, Derek Norman William. b 30. Man Univ BA51. Wycliffe Hall Ox 54. **d** 56 **p** 57. C Farnworth *Liv* 56-59; C Walton H Trin *Ox* 59-62; Chapl Kampala and Entebbe Uganda 62-69; Lic to Offic *Eur* 69-93; W Germany 69-90; Germany 90-93; rtd 93; Hon C Modbury, Bigbury, Ringmore w Kingston etc *Ex* 95-00; Perm to Offic from 01. *1 Bramley Meadow, Landkey, Barnstaple EX32 0PB* Tel (01271) 830952 E-mail dnwm@supanet.com

MATTHEWS, Adrian James. b 51. Edge Hill Coll of HE CertEd73. NOC. **d** 87 **p** 88. C Blackley St Andr *Man* 87-90; NSM Tonge w Alkrington 96-01; R Failsworth St Jo from 01. *St John's Rectory, Pole Lane, Manchester M35 9PB* Tel and fax 0161-681 2734

MATTHEWS, The Rt Revd Alan Montague (**Dom Basil**). b 37. Ex Univ BA86. **d** 02 **p** 02. OSB from 65; Abbot Elmore Abbey from 88. *Elmore Abbey, Church Lane, Speen, Newbury RG14 1SA* Tel (01635) 33080 Fax 580729

MATTHEWS, Anita Kathryn. b 70. Dur Univ BTh91. Ripon Coll Cuddesdon 93. **d** 97 **p** 98. C E Barnet *St Alb* 97-01; Chapl Derby High Sch 01-05; Nat Adv for Children's Work CMS from 05. *5 Bamford Avenue, Derby DE23 8DT* Tel (01332) 270917

MATTHEWS, Mrs Anna Ruth. b 78. Rob Coll Cam BA99 MA03 MPhil03. Westcott Ho Cam 01. **d** 03 **p** 04. C Abbots Langley *St Alb* 03-06; Min Can St Alb Abbey from 06. *1 The Deanery, Sumpter Yard, Holywell Hill, St Albans AL1 1BY* Tel (01727) 890207 Mobile 07974-647226 E-mail mcl@stalbanscathedral.org.uk

MATTHEWS, Barry Alan. b 46. AKC68. St Boniface Warminster 68 St Paul's Coll Grahamstown 69. **d** 69 **p** 70. S Africa 69-74, 77-83 and 01-04; C De Aar 69-72; C Kimberley St Aug 72-74; P-in-c Kimberley St Matt 74-75; C Leeds St Aid *Ripon* 75-77; R Vryburg St Steph 77-81; Dioc Missr 81-82; R Kimberley St Aug 82-83; C Shotton *St As* 83-84; R Hwange St Jas Zimbabwe 84-89; R Bulawayo N St Marg 89-95; R Nkulumane H Family 95-97; Adn N Matabeleland 89-97; Sen P St Mary's Cathl Harare 97-00; rtd 01. *23 Clovelly Drive, Newburgh, Wigan WN8 7LY*

MATTHEWS, Basil. *See* MATTHEWS, The Rt Revd Alan Montague

MATTHEWS, Canon Campbell Thurlow. b 33. Lon Univ BA56 Dur Univ DipEd57. St Jo Coll Nottm 70. **d** 71 **p** 72. C Ryton *Dur* 71-74; Chapl R Victoria Infirmary Newc 74-82; V Greenside *Dur* 74-82; R Wetheral w Warwick *Carl* 82-93; RD Brampton 83-91; P-in-c Farlam and Nether Denton 87-93; P-in-c Gilsland 87-93; Hon Can Carl Cathl 87-00; P-in-c Thornthwaite cum Braithwaite and Newlands 93-00; P-in-c Borrowdale 97-00; rtd 00; Perm to Offic *Carl* from 00 and *Newc* from 01. *The Hayes, Newcastle Road, Corbridge NE45 5LP* Tel (01434) 632010

MATTHEWS, Celia Inger. b 30. St Chris Coll Blackheath 50. **d** 86 **p** 94. Dioc Missr *St And* from 86; rtd 95. *24 Barossa Place, Perth PH1 5HH* Tel (01738) 623578 E-mail cmatthews@tiscali.co.uk

MATTHEWS, Cilla. *See* MATTHEWS, Mrs Francilla Lacey

MATTHEWS, Canon Colin John. b 44. Jes Coll Ox BA67 MA71 Fitzw Coll Cam BA70 MA74. Ridley Hall Cam 68. **d** 71 **p** 72. C

Onslow Square St Paul *Lon* 71-74; C Leic H Apostles 74-78; Bible Use Sec Scripture Union 78-89; Dir Ch Cen Guildf St Sav 89-95; V Burpham from 95; RD Guildf 01-06; Hon Can Guildf Cathl from 02. *272 London Road, Burpham, Guildford GU4 7LF* Tel 07787-575923 (mobile) E-mail vicarage@ntlworld.com

MATTHEWS, David Charles. b 61. TCD BA84 HDipEd86 MA87 BTh95 Lille Univ LèsL85. CITC 95. **d** 95 **p** 96. C Arm St Mark 95-97; Hon V Choral Arm Cathl 96-97; Min Can and Chapl St Woolos Cathl 97-01; V Marshfield and Peterstone Wentloog etc from 01. *The Vicarage, Church Lane, Marshfield, Cardiff CF3 2UF* Tel (01633) 680257 E-mail david@hebron97.freeserve.co.uk

MATTHEWS, David William. b 49. St Paul's Coll Grahamstown 88. **d** 90 **p** 91. S Africa 90-03; C Port Eliz St Sav 90-91; C Port Eliz St Paul 91-94; R Zwartkops River Valley Par 94-00; Chapl Miss to Seafarers 00-03; R Boxford, Edwardstone, Groton etc *St E* 03-09; P-in-c Southampton St Anne Bermuda from 09. *St Anne's Rectory, 74 Middle Road, Southampton SB 04, Bermuda* Tel (001) (441) 238 0370 E-mail stannesrectory@logic.bm

MATTHEWS, David William Grover. b 73. Acadia Univ (NS) BA93 Toronto Univ MDiv98. Trin Coll Toronto 95. **d** 98 **p** 99. C Newport St Teilo *Mon* 98-00; NSM Cobbold Road St Sav w St Mary *Lon* 00-03; P-in-c Hammersmith H Innocents 03-05; P-in-c Hammersmith H Innocents and St Jo from 05. *35 Paddenswick Road, London W6 0UA* Tel (020) 8741 6480 E-mail holyinnocentsw6@yahoo.com

MATTHEWS, Mrs Deborah Lynne. b 57. Southn Univ BTh98 MCIPD92. Ripon Coll Cuddesdon MTh01. **d** 00 **p** 01. C Southampton (City Cen) *Win* 00-04; V Clapham St Paul S *wark* from 04. *St Paul's Vicarage, Rectory Grove, London SW4 0DX* Tel (020) 7622 2128 E-mail revdebmatthews@waitrose.com

MATTHEWS, Mrs Diana Elizabeth Charlotte. b 43. MCSP65. **d** 93 **p** 96. OLM Merrow *Guildf* from 93. *Avila, 13 Wells Road, Guildford GU4 7XQ* Tel (01483) 839738 E-mail diana.matthews@ntlworld.com

MATTHEWS, Mrs Francilla Lacey. b 37. S'wark Ord Course 83. **dss** 86 **d** 87 **p** 94. Bromley St Mark *Roch* 86-90; Hon Par Dn 87-90; Par Dn Hayes 90-94; C 94-02; rtd 02; Perm to Offic *Roch* from 02. *71 Hayes Road, Bromley BR2 9AE* Tel (020) 8464 4083

MATTHEWS, Frederick Peter. b 45. Grey Coll Dur BA66 MA68 K Coll Lon PGCE68 Lon Univ BSc(Econ)75. Sarum & Wells Th Coll 70. **d** 72 **p** 73. C W Wickham St Jo *Cant* 72-74; C Sholing *Win* 74-77; Lic to Offic 78-79; V Woolston 79-03; P-in-c Over Wallop w Nether Wallop 03-07; Dioc Ecum Officer 03-07; rtd 07; Perm to Offic *Sarum* and *Win* from 07. *19 Berkshire Road, Salisbury SP2 8NY* Tel (01722) 340508 E-mail fpetermatthews@gmail.com

MATTHEWS, George Charles Wallace. b 27. Sarum Th Coll 58. **d** 60 **p** 61. C Coppenhall St Paul *Ches* 60-63; C Lewes St Anne *Chich* 63-67; V Wheelock *Ches* 67-76; V Mossley 76-93; rtd 93; Perm to Offic *Ches* from 93. *145 Primrose Avenue, Haslington, Crewe CW1 5QB* Tel (01270) 587463

MATTHEWS, Gerald Lancelot. b 31. Bris Univ LLB50. Ripon Hall Ox 55. **d** 57 **p** 58. C The Quinton *Birm* 57-60; C Olton 60-63; V Brent Tor *Ex* 63-72; P-in-c Lydford w Bridestowe and Sourton 70-72; TR Lydford, Brent Tor, Bridestowe and Sourton 72-78; P-in-c Black Torrington, Bradford w Cookbury etc 78-90; Perm to Offic from 94. *The Larches, Black Torrington, Beaworthy EX21 5PU* Tel (01409) 231228

MATTHEWS, Harold James. b 46. Leeds Univ BSc68 Fitzw Coll Cam BA70 MA74 Goldsmiths' Coll Lon PGCE71. Westcott Ho Cam 68. **d** 71 **p** 72. C Mossley Hill St Matt and St Jas *Liv* 71-74; C Stanley 77-70; TV Hackney Lon 76-78; Chapl Forest Sch Snaresbrook 78-83; Hd Master Vernon Holme Sch Cant 83-88; Hd Master Heath Mt Sch Hertf 88-06; Chapl Roedean Sch Brighton 06-08; Chapl Kent Coll Pembury from 10. *18 Oak Hall Road, London E11 2JT* Tel (020) 8257 2925 Mobile 07515-857110 E-mail hjmatth46@hotmail.co.uk

MATTHEWS, Hayley Deborah Yeshua. b 68. Ridley Hall Cam 05. **d** 07 **p** 08. C Lancaster St Mary w St John and St Anne *Blackb* 07-10; Chapl MediaCityUK *Man* from 10. *Holy Angels Vicarage, 90 Radford Road, Salford M6 7QD* Tel 0161-737 1835 E-mail chaplain@anchormediacity.org

MATTHEWS, Mrs Heather Ann. b 49. Bris Univ BA71 Lon Univ CertEd72. Trin Coll Bris 87. **d** 89 **p** 94. C Blagdon w Compton Martin and Ubley *B & W* 89-93; Dn-in-c 93-94; R 94-01; R Hodnet w Weston under Redcastle *Lich* 01-03; C Skipton Ch Ch *Bradf* 03-04; rtd 04. *The Sett, Yate Lane, Oxenhope, Keighley BD22 9HL* Tel (01535) 649095

MATTHEWS, Canon Joan Muriel. b 53. NOC 89. **d** 92 **p** 94. C Aughton St Mich *Liv* 92-97; R Wavertree St Mary 97-06; AD Toxteth and Wavertree 04-06; Hon Can Liv Cathl 04-06 and from 07; P-in-c Newton in Makerfield St Pet 06-07; P-in-c Earlestown 06-07; TR Newton from 08; AD Winwick from 09. *8 Parchments, Newton-le-Willows WA12 9SR* Tel (01925) 220795 E-mail revjoan@hotmail.com

MATTHEWS, John Goodman. b 77. Univ of Wales BTh99. St Mich Coll Llan 99. **d** 02 **p** 03. C Lampeter and Llanddewibrefi

Gp *St D* 02-05; P-in-c Aberporth w Tremain w Blaenporth and Betws Ifan 05-07; V 07-09; P-in-c Tregarth and Llandygai and Maes y Groes *Ban* from 09. *Pentir Vicarage, Pentir, Bangor LL57 4YB* Tel (01248) 364991

MATTHEWS, Lewis William (Bill). b 29. St Jo Coll Dur BA53 MSc76. **d** 55 **p** 56. C Eston *York* 55-57; Ind Chapl *Sheff* 57-61; V Copt Oak *Leic* 61-64; R Braunstone 64-70; V Thornaby on Tees St Paul *York* 70-72; TR Thornaby on Tees 72-78; Dir Dioc Bd for Soc Resp *Lon* 79-84; Perm to Offic 84-94; Warden Durning Hall Chr Community Cen Forest Gate 84-94; rtd 94; Hon C Jersey Gouray St Martin *Win* 94-06. *2 Malvern, La Ruelle es Ruaux, St Brelade, Jersey JE3 8BB* Tel (01534) 498368 Mobile 07797-731143 E-mail billmatthews@jerseymail.co.uk

MATTHEWS, Liam. See MATTHEWS, William Temple Atkinson

MATTHEWS, Canon Melvyn William. b 40. St Edm Hall Ox BA63 MA68. K Coll Lon BD66 AKC67. **d** 67 **p** 68. C Enfield St Andr *Lon* 67-70; Asst Chapl Southn Univ 70-72; Lect Univ of Nairobi Kenya 72-76; V Highgate All SS *Lon* 76-79; P-in-c Clifton St Paul *Bris* 79-87; Sen Chapl Bris Univ 79-87; Dir Ammerdown Cen for Study and Renewal 87-93; V Chew Magna w Dundry *B & W* 93-97; Can and Chan Wells Cathl 97-05; rtd 05; Perm to Offic *B & W* from 05. *Yew Tree House, 22 Beaufort Avenue, Midsomer Norton, Radstock BA3 2TG* Tel (01761) 413630 E-mail mwmatthews@onetel.com

MATTHEWS, Michael Raymond. b 55. JP96. Huddersfield Univ MBA96 Leeds Univ BA04 CQSW82. Coll of Resurr Mirfield 02. **d** 04 **p** 05. C Featherstone and Purston cum S Featherstone *Wakef* 04-07; P-in-c Haslingfield w Harlton and Gt and Lt Eversden *Ely* 07 10; TV Lordsbridge from 10; RD Bourn from 10. *The Vicarage, Broad Lane, Haslingfield, Cambridge CB3 7JF* Tel (01223) 870285 E-mail frmichaelmatthews@yahoo.co.uk

MATTHEWS, Paul. b 47. Brunel Univ BTech70. S Dios Minl Tr Scheme 89. **d** 92 **p** 93. NSM Goring-by-Sea *Chich* from 92. *7 Denton Close, Goring-by-Sea, Worthing BN12 4TZ* Tel (01903) 505859

MATTHEWS, Peter. See MATTHEWS, Frederick Peter

MATTHEWS, Peter Henry. b 22. Sarum Th Coll 62. **d** 64 **p** 65. C Wareham w Arne *Sarum* 64-67; P-in-c Houghton 67; C Sholing Staverton 71-72; V 72-78; P-in-c Milborne St Andrew w Dewlish 78-87; rtd 87; Perm to Offic *B & W* from 87. *Holmlands, Lambrook Road, Shepton Beauchamp, Ilminster TA19 0LZ* Tel (01460) 40938

MATTHEWS, Peter John. b 69. Leic Poly BEng92. Wycliffe Hall Ox 07. **d** 09 **p** 10. C Catterick *Ripon* from 09; Chapl St Fran Xavier Sch Richmond from 09. *24 Low Green, Catterick, Richmond DL10 7LP* Tel 07590-698333 (mobile) E-mail peterthelong@gmail.com

MATTHEWS, Canon Rodney Charles. b 36. Sarum Th Coll 62. **d** 64 **p** 65. C Gt Clacton *Chelmsf* 64-68; C Loughton St Mary 68-74; TV 74-76; V Goodmayes All SS 76-87; V Woodford Bridge 87-02; Hon Chapl Sail Tr Assn from 89; P-in-c Barkingside St Cedd 90-92; Hon Can Chelmsf Cathl 99-02; rtd 02; Perm to Offic *Chelmsf* from 03. *93 King's Head Hill, London E4 7JG* Tel (020) 8529 4372

MATTHEWS, Canon Roger Charles. b 54. Man Univ BSc75 Nottm Univ MA02 MBCS82 CEng90. Trin Coll Bris 87. **d** 89 **p** 90. C Gt Baddow *Chelmsf* 89-93; P-in-c Chigwell Row 93-94; TV Chigwell and Chigwell Row 94-96; Dioc Miss Officer 96-00; Millenium Ecum Officer 98-00; Bp's Adv for Miss and Min from 01; Hon C Gt Baddow from 01; Hon Can Chelmsf Cathl from 00. *62 Longmead Avenue, Great Baddow, Chelmsford CM2 7EY* Tel (01245) 478959 or 294455 Fax 294477 E-mail rmatthews@chelmsford.anglican.org

MATTHEWS, Canon Roy Ian John. b 27. TD71. St Cath Soc Ox BA52 MA56. St Steph Ho Ox 52. **d** 54 **p** 55. C Barnsley St Mary *Wakef* 54-58; V Staincliffe 58-65; CF (TA) 58-92; V Penistone w Midhope *Wakef* 65-72; V Brighouse 72-84; Hon Can Wakef Cathl 76-92; V Darrington 84-92; Dioc Schs Officer 84-89; Dep Dir of Educn 85-89; rtd 92; Perm to Offic *Wakef* and *York* from 92; P-in-c Selby Abbey *York* 96-97. *14 Spring Walk, Brayton, Selby YO8 9DS* Tel (01757) 707259

MATTHEWS, Canon Royston Peter. b 39. Univ of Wales (Lamp) BA61. St Mich Coll Llan 61. **d** 64 **p** 65. C Fairwater CD *Llan* 64-67; C Cadoxton-juxta-Barry 67-71; V Bettws *Mon* 71-84; V Abergavenny H Trin 84-05; Hon Can St Woolos Cathl 05; rtd 05. *1 Hoburne Gardens, Christchurch BH23 4PP*

MATTHEWS, Canon Stuart James. b 37. St Jo Coll Dur BA60. Bps' Coll Cheshunt 60. **d** 62 **p** 63. C Horsham *Chich* 62-65; C Rednal *Birm* 65-67; Min Brandwood St Bede CD 67-68; C Northfield 68-73; V Thurcroft *Sheff* 73-82; RD Laughton 79-82; R Sprotbrough 82-00; RD Adwick 84-89; Hon Can Sheff Cathl 92-00; rtd 00; Perm to Offic *Sheff* from 00. *43 Dinnington Road, Woodsetts, Worksop S81 8RL* Tel (01909) 560160

MATTHEWS, Terence Leslie. b 35. Handsworth Coll Birm 55. **d** 61 **p** 62. C W Acklam *York* 61-64; V Horden *Dur* 64-72; R Witton Gilbert 72-77; P-in-c Grangetown 77-85; V Cleadon 85-86; V Hebburn St Cuth 86-88; rtd 88; Perm to Offic *Lich* from 08. *22 Bankfield Grove, Scot Hay, Newcastle ST5 6AR*

MATTHEWS, Thomas Bartholomew Hall. *See* HALL, Thomas Bartholomew Berners

MATTHEWS, Timothy John. b 73. Univ of Wales (Cardiff) BScEcon97 PhD00 ACA03. Wycliffe Hall Ox 06. **d** 08 **p** 09. C Brompton H Trin w Onslow Square St Paul *Lon* 08-11; C Onslow Square and S Kensington St Aug from 11. *90 Abercrombie Street, London SW11 2JD* Tel (020) 7228 8774

MATTHEWS, William. *See* MATTHEWS, Lewis William

MATTHEWS, Canon William Andrew. b 44. Reading Univ BA65 MA94. St Steph Ho Ox 65. **d** 67 **p** 68. C Westbury-on-Trym St Alb *Bris* 67-70; C Marlborough *Sarum* 70-73; P-in-c Winsley 73-75; V 75-81; V Bradford-on-Avon H Trin 81-09; RD Bradford 84-94; Can and Preb Sarum Cathl 88-09; rtd 09; Chapl to The Queen from 01. *21 Williams Lane, Fernwood, Newark-on-Trent NG24 3FN* Tel (01636) 646927 E-mail wajematthews@gmail.com

MATTHEWS, William John Joseph. b 48. **d** 08 **p** 08. NSM Lee-on-the-Solent *Portsm* 08-10; TV St Helens Town Cen *Liv* from 11. *St Thomas's Vicarage, 21 St Georges Road, St Helens WA10 4LH* Tel (01744) 22295 E-mail wjjmatthews@hotmail.com

MATTHEWS, William Temple Atkinson (Liam). b 47. EMMTC 86. **d** 83 **p** 83. SSF 83-86; C Brinsley w Underwood *S'well* 86-89; TV Hitchin *St Alb* 89-97; R Toddington and Chalgrave 97-03; R N Albury Australia from 03; RD Murray Valley from 05. *St Mark's Rectory, 328 Gulpha Street, North Albury NSW 2640, Australia* Tel (0061) (2) 5794 2443 E-mail liammatthews@bigpond.com

MATTHEWS-LOYDALL, Mrs Elaine. b 63. Bp Otter Coll BA85. St Jo Coll Nottm 87. **d** 90 **p** 94. Par Dn Nottingham All SS *S'well* 90-94; C 94-95; Asst Chapl to the Deaf 91-93; Chapl to the Deaf 93-99; Chapl for Deaf People *Leic* 99-10; TV Leic H Spirit 99-10. *Pumpkin Cottage, 54 Wilne Road, Long Eaton, Nottingham NG10 3AN* Tel 0115-972 8943

MATTHIAE, Canon David. b 40. Fitzw Ho Cam BA63 MA69. Linc Th Coll 63. **d** 65 **p** 66. C New Addington *Cant* 65-70; C Charlton-by-Dover St Pet and Paul 70-75; V Cant All SS 75-84; P-in-c Tunstall 84-87; R Tunstall w Rodmersham 87-05; RD Sittingbourne 88-94; Hon Can Cant Cathl 99-05; rtd 05; Perm to Offic *Ely* from 06. *7 Bustlers Rise, Duxford, Cambridge CB22 4QU* Tel (01223) 835471 Mobile 07719-716240 E-mail david@matthiae.demon.co.uk

MATTHIAS, George Ronald. b 30. CertEd51. St Deiniol's Hawarden 76. **d** 78 **p** 79. NSM Broughton *St As* 78-83; NSM Wrexham 83-85; C 85-87; V Brymbo 87-95; rtd 95. *Bryn Adref, Pisgah Hill, Pentre Hill, Wrexham LL11 5DB* Tel (01978) 750757

MATTHIAS, John Rex. b 61. St Mich Coll Llan. **d** 94 **p** 95. C Llandrillo-yn-Rhos *St As* 94-98; R Llanfair Talhaearn and Llansannan etc 98-03; V Petryal 03-10; P-in-c Betws-yn-Rhos 03-10; Warden of Readers 09-10; P-in-c Newport St Julian *Mon* from 10. *The Vicarage, 41 St Julian's Avenue, Newport NP19 7JT* Tel (01633) 258046 E-mail ssjuliusandaaron@ntlworld.com

MATTHIAS, Paul. b 47. Philippa Fawcett Coll CertEd75 Kent Univ DipEd84. Cant Sch of Min 92. **d** 94 **p** 95. Head RE Hever Sch Maidstone 80-94; Chapl Ch Ch High Sch Ashford 94-07; NSM Gillingham St Aug *Roch* 94-10; P-in-c New Brompton St Luke from 10. *33 Malvern Road, Gillingham ME7 4BA* Tel (01634) 576197 E-mail paul.matthias@diocese-rochester.org

MATTOCK, Colin Graham. b 38. Chich Th Coll. **d** 84 **p** 85. C Hove All SS *Chich* 84-87; C Bexhill St Pet 87-90; V Henlow *St Alb* 90-96; V Linslade *Ox* 96-00; P-in-c Pebworth w Dorsington and Honeybourne *Glouc* 00-02; R Pebworth, Dorsington, Honeybourne etc 02-10; AD Campden 06-10; rtd 10. *14 Mullings Court, Cirencester GL7 2AW* Tel (01285) 653828 E-mail colin.mattock@btinternet.com

MATTOCKS, Mrs Margaret. b 61. **d** 06 **p** 07. C Tettenhall Regis *Lich* 06-09; V Burntwood from 09. *The Vicarage, Church Road, Burntwood, Walsall WS7 9EA* Tel (01543) 675014

MATTY, Horace Anthony (Tony). b 36. Ely Th Coll 61. **d** 63 **p** 64. C Minchinhampton *Glouc* 63-66; C Hunslet St Mary and Stourton *Ripon* 66-69; TV Wendy w Shingay *Ely* 69-71; V Parson Drove 71-74; V Southea cum Murrow 71-74; V Coven *Lich* 74-82; TV Hednesford 82-85; TV Basildon St Martin w Nevendon *Chelmsf* 85-92; P-in-c Basildon St Andr w H Cross 85-92; P-in-c Sandon 92-98; P-in-c E Hanningfield 92-98; rtd 98; Perm to Offic *Truro* 00-01 and 03-04. *7 Calvin Close, Fordhouses, Wolverhampton WV10 6LN* Tel (01902) 781789

MAUCHAN, Andrew. b 44. Hertf Coll Ox BA65 MA69 Man Univ CertEd66. Oak Hill Th Coll 88. **d** 90 **p** 91. C Bridlington Priory *York* 90-94; V Alverthorpe *Wakef* 94-01; R Wombwell *Sheff* 01-07; rtd 07. *Hollins Barn, Top o' the Hill, Slaithwaite, Huddersfield HD7 5UA* Tel (01484) 846371 E-mail andrew.mauchan@yahoo.co.uk

MAUDE, Canon Alan. b 41. Lon Univ BD69 Newc Univ MSc90 Lambeth STh74. Oak Hill Th Coll 66. **d** 69 **p** 70. C Balderstone *Man* 69-73; C Crumpsall St Matt 73-75; Asst Chapl Crumpsall and Springfield Hosps 73-75; Chapl R Victoria Infirmary Newc 75-94; Chapl R Victoria Infirmary and Assoc Hosps NHS Trust 94-98; Chapl Newcastle upon Tyne Hosps NHS Trust 98-06; Hon Can Newc Cathl 88-06; P-in-c Costa del Sol W *Eur* from 06. *Calle Juan de Fuca 27, Urb Beverly Hill, 29680 Estepona, Málaga, Spain* Tel (0034) 952 808 605 E-mail alanmarj@hotmail.com

MAUDE, Alexander. b 53. Bingley Coll of Educn TCert74. NOC. **d** 02 **p** 03. NSM Erringden *Wakef* from 02; Chapl Ravenscliffe High Sch from 02. *47 Vicar Park Drive, Norton Tower, Halifax HX2 0NN* Tel (01422) 355856 Mobile 07816-597074 E-mail sandiemaude@hotmail.com

MAUDE, Gillian Hamer. b 53. St Anne's Coll Ox BA75 MA79 Edin Univ MSc77. St Steph Ho Ox 99. **d** 01 **p** 02. C Hackney Wick St Mary of Eton w St Aug *Lon* 01-05; P-in-c Goodrington *Ex* 05-06; V from 06; RD Torbay from 09. *The Vicarage, 17 Seafields, Paignton TQ4 6NY* Tel (01803) 846335 Mobile 07932-056071 E-mail gillian.maude@btinternet.com

MAUDLIN, David. b 39. EAMTC 92. **d** 95 **p** 96. NSM Bury St Edmunds St Jo *St E* 95-97; NSM Haverhill w Withersfield 97-98; P-in-c The Sampfords and Radwinter w Hempstead *Chelmsf* 98-04; RD Saffron Walden 00-04; rtd 04; Perm to Offic *Leic, Pet* and *Eur* from 04. *3 Goldfinch Road, Uppingham LE15 9UJ* Tel (01572) 820181

MAUDSLEY, Canon George Lambert. b 27. St Jo Coll Nottm 74. **d** 75 **p** 76. C Binley *Cov* 75-77; Chapl Barn Fellowship Winterborne Whitechurch 77-83; V Salford Priors *Cov* 83-94; RD Alcester 87-92; Hon Can Cov Cathl 91-94; rtd 94; Perm to Offic *Cov* and *Worc* from 94. *75 Rawnsley Drive, Kenilworth CV8 2NX* Tel (01926) 512206 E-mail maudsley@tiscali.co.uk

MAUDSLEY, Keith. b 51. York Univ BA72. Ripon Hall Ox 72. **d** 75 **p** 76. C Rugby St Andr *Cov* 75-79; C Cambridge Gt St Mary w St Mich *Ely* 79-82; Chapl Girton Coll 79-82; P-in-c Binley *Cov* 82-89; RD Cov E 87-89; P-in-c Leek Wootton 89-91; Dioc Policy Development Adv 89-91; Dioc Adv on UPA *Liv* 91-97; Soc Resp Officer 91-97; R Lymm *Ches* from 97. *The Rectory, 46 Rectory Lane, Lymm WA13 0AL* Tel (01925) 752164 E-mail keith@maudsley5234.wanadoo.co.uk

MAUDSLEY, Canon Michael Peter. b 38. St Andr Univ BSc61. Oak Hill Th Coll 65. **d** 67 **p** 68. C Blackpool St Mark *Blackb* 67-70; C Hartford *Ches* 70-72; R Balerno *Edin* 72-82; V Stapenhill w Cauldwell *Derby* 82-91; Assoc R Edin St Paul and St Geo 91-95 and 00-03; R 95-00; rtd 03. *44 Buckstone Loan, Edinburgh EH10 6UG*

MAUDSLEY, Richard Leonard. b 55. Trent Park Coll of Educn BEd76. NTMTC 04. **d** 07 **p** 08. NSM Clay Hill St Jo and St Luke *Lon* 07-09; NSM Silverton, Butterleigh, Bickleigh and Cadeleigh *Ex* from 09. *The Old Coach House, 5B Fore Street, Silverton, Exeter EX5 4HP* Tel (01392) 860883 E-mail richard.maudsley@exeter.anglican.org

MAUGHAN, Angela. b 54. Newc Univ BA93. NEOC 94. **d** 97 **p** 98. C Willington *Newc* 97-01; V Weetslade from 01. *Weetslade Vicarage, 59 Kirklands, Burradon, Cramlington NE23 7LE* Tel 0191-268 9366

MAUGHAN, Geoffrey Nigel. b 48. CCC Cam BA69 MA73 Wycliffe Hall Ox MA98. Oak Hill Th Coll 75. **d** 77 **p** 78. C New Malden and Coombe *S'wark* 77-81; C Abingdon w Shippon *Ox* 81-89; TV Abingdon 89-98; Dir of Min and Chapl Wycliffe Hall Ox 98-07; V Cumnor *Ox* from 07. *The Vicarage, 1 Abingdon Road, Cumnor, Oxford OX2 9QN* Tel (01865) 865402

MAUGHAN, John. b 28. Keble Coll Ox BA51 MA55. Linc Th Coll 51. **d** 53 **p** 54. C Heworth St Mary *Dur* 53-56; C Winlaton 56-59; R Penshaw 59-72; V Cleadon Park 72-93; rtd 93. *South Chowdene Care Home, Chowdene Bank, Gateshead NE9 6JE* Tel 0191-491 0861

MAUND, Mrs Margaret Jennifer. b 42. RGN64 RM65. Llan Dioc Tr Scheme 89. **d** 94 **p** 97. NSM Cymmer and Porth *Llan* 94-97; NSM Pwllgwaun w Llanddewi Rhondda 97-04. *27 Mile Street, Tonyrefail, Porth CF39 8AB* Tel (01443) 670085

MAUNDER, Alan John. b 52. UWIST BSc74. Oak Hill Th Coll 88. **d** 90 **p** 91. C Birkenhead Ch Ch *Ches* 90-95; P-in-c Poulton 95-05; V Cwmaman *St D* from 05. *The Vicarage, 118 Heol Cae Gurwen, Gwaun-cae-Gurwen, Ammanford SA18 1PD* Tel (01269) 822426 E-mail ajmaunder@lineone.net

MAUNDER, Miss Vicky Alexandra. b 73. Leeds Univ BA95. Ripon Coll Cuddesdon BA01. **d** 02 **p** 03. C Swaythling *Win* 02-05; C Pimlico St Pet w Westmr Ch Ch *Lon* 05-07; TV Kingston All SS w St Jo *S'wark* from 07. *30 Bloomfield Road, Kingston upon Thames KT1 2SE* Tel (020) 8546 9882

MAURICE, David Pierce. b 50. Pemb Coll Cam BA72 MA76 BChir76. Dioc OLM tr scheme. **d** 01 **p** 02. OLM Marlborough *Sarum* from 01. *Isbury House, Kingsbury Street, Marlborough SN8 1JA* Tel (01672) 514119 E-mail david.maurice2000@yahoo.com

✠**MAURICE, The Rt Revd Peter David.** b 51. St Chad's Coll Dur BA72. Coll of Resurr Mirfield. **d** 75 **p** 76 **c** 06. C Wandsworth St Paul *S'wark* 75-79; TV Mortlake w E Sheen 79-85; V Rotherhithe H Trin 85-96; RD Bermondsey 91-96; V Tooting All SS 96-03; Adn Wells, Can Res and Preb Wells Cathl 03-06; Suff Bp Taunton from 06. *The Palace, Wells BA5 2PD* Tel (01749) 672341 Fax 679355 E-mail bishop.taunton@bathwells.anglican.org

MAW, Mrs Jacqueline. b 59. Wycliffe Hall Ox 04. **d** 06 **p** 07. C Iwerne Valley *Sarum* 06-10; TV Wareham from 10. *St Martin's Vicarage, 9 Keysworth Road, Wareham BH20 7BD* Tel (01929) 556796 Mobile 07747-561375 E-mail jackiemaw@yahoo.co.uk

MAWBEY, Diane. *See* COUTURE, Mrs Diane

MAWDITT, Stephen Donald Harvey. b 56. **d** 96 **p** 97. OLM Ashill w Saham Toney *Nor* 96-05; OLM Watton w Carbrooke and Ovington 00-05; Min Fountain of Life from 05. *43 Cressingham Road, Ashill, Thetford IP25 7DG* Tel (01760) 440363 E-mail themawditts@tiscali.co.uk

MAWER, Canon David Ronald. b 32. Keble Coll Ox BA55 MA58 Dur Univ BA57 McGill Univ Montreal PhD77. Wells Th Coll 58. **d** 59 **p** 60. C Cullercoats St Geo *Newc* 59-61; Canada 61-92; Co-ord Angl Studies St Paul Univ Ottawa 81-92; Can Ottawa from 85; rtd 92; Perm to Offic *Newc* from 93. *Moorside, Church Lane, Thropton, Morpeth NE65 7JA* Tel (01669) 620597

MAWSON, Canon Arthur Cyril. b 35. St Pet Coll Ox BA56 MA61. Wycliffe Hall Ox 61. **d** 62 **p** 63. C Walsall *Lich* 62-66; V Millhouses H Trin *Sheff* 66-73; Selection Sec ACCM 73-79; Can Res and Treas Ex Cathl 79-98; Dioc Dir of Ords 81-87; rtd 99. *4 Woodlands Close, Headington, Oxford OX3 7RY* Tel (01865) 764099

MAXFIELD, Roberta. WMMTC. **d** 09 **p** 10. NSM Oxley *Lich* from 09. *53 Swan Bank, Wolverhampton WV4 5PZ* Tel (01902) 834023

MAXIM, Claire Margaret Astrid. b 68. Birm Univ BEng90 Reading Univ MBA03 MIET95. Qu Coll Birm 07. **d** 10 **p** 11. C Ampfield, Chilworth and N Baddesley *Win* from 10. *188 Rownhams Lane, North Baddesley, Southampton SO52 9LQ* Tel (023) 8073 9145 E-mail claire@themaxims.co.uk

MAXTED, Neil Andrew. b 58. Aston Tr Scheme 88 Sarum & Wells Th Coll 90. **d** 92 **p** 93. C Folkestone St Sav *Cant* 92-96; CF 96-05; P-in-c Frome Ch *B & W* from 05; V Frome St Mary from 11. *The Vicarage, 73 Weymouth Road, Frome BA11 1HJ* Tel (01373) 473249 E-mail vicarchchfrome@aol.com

MAXWELL, Alan. b 75. Strathclyde Univ BSc96 Aber Univ MSc97 Selw Coll Cam BTh08. Ridley Hall Cam 05. **d** 08 **p** 09. C Gosforth All SS *Newc* from 08. *1 Northfield Road, Newcastle upon Tyne NE3 3UL* Tel 07790-913581 (mobile) E-mail alan.maxwell@hotmail.co.uk

MAXWELL, Christopher John Moore (Bill). b 31. Qu Coll Cam MA75 MRCS59 LRCP59. Trin Coll Bris 74. **d** 75 **p** 76. SAMS Chile 75-81; Hon C Homerton St Luke *Lon* 81-94; Chapl Ibiza *Eur* 94-99; rtd 99; Perm to Offic *Chich* 99-08 and *Win* from 08. *Willowbank, Sycamore Close, Milford on Sea, Lymington SO41 0RY* Tel (01590) 643110 E-mail abmaxwell@metronet.co.uk

MAXWELL, Marcus Howard. b 54. Liv Univ BSc76 Man Univ MPhil89. St Jo Coll Nottm BA79. **d** 80 **p** 81. C Chadderton St Matt *Man* 80-84; V Bircle 84-93; P-in-c Heaton Mersey 93-02; TR Heatons from 02; AD Heaton 98-04. *St John's Rectory, 15 Priestnall Road, Stockport SK4 3HR* Tel 0161-442 1932 E-mail marcus.maxwell@ntlworld.com

MAY, Charles Henry. b 29. ALCD58. **d** 58 **p** 59. C Bethnal Green St Jas Less *Lon* 58-61; C Woking St Pet *Guildf* 61-64; Area Sec (W Midl) CPAS 64-67; V Homerton St Luke *Lon* 67-80; Home Sec SAMS 80-84; V Fulham Ch Ch *Lon* 84-94; rtd 94; Perm to Offic *Ely* and *Pet* from 94; *Linc* from 95. *16 Kilverstone, Werrington, Peterborough PE4 5DX* Tel (01733) 328108 E-mail cclergyman@aol.com

MAY, Mrs Deborah Kim. b 60. Trin Coll Bris. **d** 01 **p** 02. C Haughley w Wetherden and Stowupland *St E* 01-04; R Ashwater, Halwill, Beaworthy, Clawton etc *Ex* 04-08; R Melville Australia from 08. *6 Donovan Road, Murdoch, Perth WA 6150, Australia* Tel (0061) (8) 9310 7767 Mobile 41-817 8688 E-mail revd.debbie@gmail.com

MAY, Donald Charles Leonard. b 25. Chich Th Coll 72. **d** 73 **p** 74. C Barkingside H Trin *Chelmsf* 73-77; V Aldersbrook 77-91; rtd 92; Perm to Offic *Chelmsf* from 92. *236 Prospect Road, Woodford Green IG8 7NQ* Tel (020) 8504 6119

MAY, George Louis. b 27. Selw Coll Cam BA52 MA55 Cam Univ PGCE67 AdDipEd78. Ridley Hall Cam 52. **d** 54 **p** 55. C St Mary Cray and St Paul's Cray *Roch* 54-56; C St Paul's Cray St Barn CD 56-57; C-in-c Elburton CD *Ex* 57-66; Asst Master Guthlaxton Sch Wigston 67-70; Ixworth Sch 70-72; Thurston Upper Sch 73-74; Perias Sch New Alresford 75-85; Hon C Ropley w W Tisted *Win* 78-79; Perm to Offic 79-96; rtd 92; Perm to Offic *Derby* from 97. *Oven House, Water Lane, Eyam, Hope Valley S32 5RG* Tel (01433) 630599

MAY, Janet Isabel. b 51. Lon Univ CertEd72. **d** 00 **p** 01. OLM Gt and Lt Ellingham, Rockland and Shropham etc *Nor* 00-05; Perm to Offic from 05. *The Mill House, Church Street, Great Ellingham, Attleborough NR17 1LE* Tel (01953) 452198 E-mail rev.may@btopenworld.com

MAY, Preb John Alexander Cyril. b 52. K Coll Lon BD77 PhD98 Ch Ch Ox PGCE78. Linc Th Coll 79. **d** 80 **p** 81. C Tynemouth Ch Ch *Newc* 80-82; C Tynemouth Ch Ch w H Trin 82-85; C Tynemouth St Aug 82-85; TV Glendale Gp 85-90; V Wotton-under-Edge w Ozleworth, N Nibley etc *Glouc* 90-07; P-in-c

St Endellion w Port Isaac and St Kew *Truro* from 07; P-in-c St Minver from 07; Preb St Endellion from 07. *The Rectory, St Endellion, Port Isaac PL29 3TP* Tel (01208) 881041 E-mail may187@hotmail.com

MAY, Peter Richard. b 43. St Jo Coll Cam BA64 MA68 MICE70. Trin Coll Bris 77. **d** 79 **p** 80. C Lancaster St Thos *Blackb* 79-85; V Darwen St Barn 85-91; Chapl Lyon w Grenoble *Eur* 91-92; Chapl Lyon 92-94; Perm to Offic *S'wark* 94-95; TR Horley 95-02; rtd 03; Perm to Offic *Chich* 04-11. *North Lodge, Exminster, Exeter EX6 8AT* Tel (01392) 823047 E-mail openhearts.2@btinternet.com

MAY, Roger Austin. b 45. SWMTC 07. **d** 10 **p** 11. NSM Bodmin w Lanhydrock and Lanivet *Truro* from 10. *12 Hanson Road, Liskeard PL14 3NT* Tel (01579) 342924 Mobile 07779-349257 E-mail rogermay@clara.co.uk

MAY, Preb Simon George. b 47. Ex Univ BA69 Univ of Wales (Ban) CertEd72 FCA77. Sarum & Wells Th Coll 86. **d** 88 **p** 89. C Tamworth *Lich* 88-92; V Whitchurch *Ex* 92-07; Warden of Readers (Plymouth Adnry) 00-07; RD Tavistock 02-07; TV Barnstaple from 07; Preb Ex Cathl from 09. *Holy Trinity Vicarage, Victoria Road, Barnstaple EX32 9HP* Tel (01271) 344321 E-mail vicar@trinitybarnstaple.eclipse.co.uk

MAY, Stephen Charles Arthur. b 52. Mert Coll Ox BA73 Edin Univ BD78 Aber Univ PhD86. Ridley Hall Cam 84. **d** 86 **p** 87. C Sawley *Derby* 86-88; Lect St Jo Coll Auckland New Zealand 88-01; V Norden w Ashworth *Man* 01-11; rtd 11. *St Paul's Vicarage, Heap Road, Rochdale OL12 7SN* Tel (01706) 641001 E-mail smaysfiction@hotmail.com

MAY, Toby Sebastian. b 67. Bris Univ BEng89. St Jo Coll Nottm MTh02. **d** 02 **p** 03. C Kendal St Thos *Carl* 02-06; V Alsager Ch Ch *Ches* from 06. *Christ Church Vicarage, 43 Church Road, Alsager, Stoke-on-Trent ST7 2HS* Tel (01270) 873727 E-mail toby@mays-in-grace.co.uk

MAYBEE, Christine. *See* DALE, Ms Christine

MAYBURY, David Kaines. b 32. G&C Coll Cam BA55 MA59. Ridley Hall Cam 55. **d** 57 **p** 58. C Sydenham H Trin *S'wark* 57-60; C Rainham *Chelmsf* 60-63; R Edin St Jas 63-75; R Jedburgh 75-84; NSM Duns 84-91; Warden Whitchester Conf Cen 84-91; NSM Hawick *Edin* 91-97; Warden Whitchester Chr Guest Ho and Retreat Cen 91-97; Admin from 97; rtd 97. *DaDo Heights, Borthaugh, Hawick TD9 7LN* Tel and fax (01450) 370809 or tel 377477 Mobile 07941-448402 E-mail dado@maybud.fsnet.co.uk

MAYBURY, Doreen Lorna. b 33. RGN54 SCM56. Edin Th Coll 76. **dss** 81 **d** 95 **p** 95. Jedburgh *Edin* 81-84; Warden Whitchester Conf Cen 84-91; Duns 84-91; Hawick 91-97; NSM 95-97; rtd 97; Chapl Borders Gen Hosp NHS Trust 98-04. *DaDo Heights, Borthaugh, Hawick TD9 7LN* Tel and fax (01450) 370809 Mobile 07801-354134 E-mail dado@maybud.fsnet.co.uk

MAYBURY, Canon John Montague. b 30. G&C Coll Cam BA53 MA57. Ridley Hall Cam 53. **d** 55 **p** 56. C Allerton *Liv* 55-59; C Rowner *Portsm* 59-62; V Wroxall 62-67; V Southsea St Simon 67-78; V Crofton 78-91; Hon Can Portsm Cathl 81-95; C Locks Heath 91-95; rtd 95; Perm to Offic *Portsm* from 95. *19 Netley Road, Titchfield Common, Fareham PO14 4PE* Tel (01489) 584168

MAYBURY, Paul. b 31. St Deiniol's Hawarden 87. **d** 88 **p** 90. NSM Sutton St Geo *Ches* 88-94; Perm to Offic 94-98 and 01-08; P-in-c Towednack *Truro* 98-00. *Address temp unknown*

MAYBURY, Paul Dorian. b 58. Trin Coll Bris 93. **d** 95 **p** 96. C Spondon *Derby* 95-99; V Gawthorpe and Chickenley Heath *Wakef* 99-02; P-in-c Ossett cum Gawthorpe 01-02; V Ossett and Gawthorpe from 02; RD Dewsbury from 08. *The Vicarage, 12 Fearnley Avenue, Ossett WF5 9ET* Tel (01924) 217379 or 263497 Fax 08701-375994 E-mail paul@trinityossett.org.uk

MAYCOCK, Ms Jane Ellen. b 66. Somerville Coll Ox BA90 MA95 Glas Univ MPhil98. Cranmer Hall Dur 90. **d** 92 **p** 94. Par Dn Harrow Trin St Mich *Lon* 92-94; C 94-95; C Kendal H Trin *Carl* 95-99; Dir of Ords 01-07. *The Rectory, Longlands Road, Bowness-on-Windermere, Windermere LA23 3AS* Tel (01539) 443063 E-mail jemaycock@lineone.net

MAYELL, Howard John. b 50. Bris Sch of Min 81. **d** 84 **p** 88. NSM Patchway *Bris* 84-86; NSM Weston-super-Mare Cen Par *B & W* 87-88; C N Stoneham *Win* 88-91; P-in-c Black Torrington, Bradford w Cookbury etc *Ex* 91-97; C Ledbury w Eastnor *Heref* 97-98; TV Ledbury from 98. *27 Hazle Close, Ledbury HR8 2XX* Tel (01531) 631530

MAYER, Alan John. b 46. AKC70. St Aug Coll Cant 70. **d** 71 **p** 72. C Stanningley St Thos *Ripon* 71-74; C St Helier *S'wark* 74-79; TV Wimbledon 79-85; V Reigate St Luke S Park 85-00; R Oxted and Tandridge 00-11; rtd 11; Perm to Offic *S'wark* from 11. *17 Saxon Crescent, Horsham RH12 2HX* E-mail aandkmayer@gmail.com

MAYER, Graham Keith. b 46. St Cath Coll Ox BA68 Nottm Univ PGCE69 Ex Univ MA93. Linc Th Coll 78. **d** 80 **p** 81. C Paignton St Jo *Ex* 80-93; Perm to Offic 93-96; P-in-c Christow, Ashton and Bridford 96-10; P-in-c Dunchideock 97-10; V Christow, Ashton, Bridford, Dunchideock etc from 10; RD Kenn from 05. *The Rectory, Dry Lane, Christow, Exeter EX6 7PE* Tel (01647) 252845 E-mail rivertide@btinternet.com

MAYER, Mrs Paula Denise. b 45. St Hilda's Coll Ox BA68 Nottm Univ CertEd69. SWMTC 84. **d** 88 **p** 07. Hon Par Dn Paignton St Jo *Ex* 88-90; Par Dn 90-93; Perm to Offic from 93. *The Haven, 1 Parkside Road, Paignton TQ4 6AE* Tel (01803) 558727 E-mail paula.haven@aniserve.com

MAYER-JONES, Miss Fiona Ruth. b 70. Westcott Ho Cam 08. **d** 10 **p** 11. C Beverley Minster *York* from 10. *23 Outer Trinities, Beverley HU17 0HN* Tel (01482) 888249 E-mail fionaruth@gmail.com

MAYES, Miss Alexier Olwen. St Mich Coll Llan 08. **d** 11. C Bistre *St As* from 11. *11 Bron yr Eglwys, Mynydd Isa, Mold CH7 6YQ* Tel (01352) 744872 E-mail rev.alex@btinternet.com

MAYES, Canon Andrew Dennis. b 56. K Coll Lon BD79 AKC79 Man Univ MA97. Armenian Orthodox Sem Jerusalem 79 St Steph Ho Ox 80. **d** 81 **p** 82. C Hendon St Alphage *Lon* 81-84; C Hockley *Chelmsf* 84-87; V Kingstanding St Mark *Birm* 87-92; V Saltdean *Chich* 92-01; P-in-c Ovingdean 01-09; CME Officer 01-09; Course Dir St Geo Coll and C St Geo Cathl Jerusalem from 09; Hon Can Niger Delta from 96. *St George's College Jerusalem, PO Box 1248, Jerusalem 91000, Israel* Tel (00972) (2) 626 4704

MAYES, Aonghus William Alun. **d** 05 **p** 06. C Cregagh *D & D* 05-10; I Moy w Charlemont *Arm* from 10; Dioc Communications Officer 10-11. *The Rectory, 37 The Square, Moy, Dungannon BT71 7SG* Tel (028) 8778 4312 E-mail aonghusmayes@yahoo.ie

MAYES, John Charles Dougan. b 44. Bps' Coll Cheshunt 63. **d** 67 **p** 68. C Portadown St Mark *Arm* 67-74; I Aghadowey w Kilrea *D & R* 74-86; USPG Area Sec 77-94; I Clooney w Strathfoyle 86-07; Can Derry Cathl 92-96; Preb 96-07; rtd 07. *10 Ebrington Park, Londonderry BT47 6JE* Tel (028) 7131 2973

✠**MAYES, The Rt Revd Michael Hugh Gunton.** b 41. TCD BA62 Lon Univ BD85. TCD Div Sch Div Test64. **d** 64 **p** 65 **c** 93. C Portadown St Columba *Arm* 64-68; USPG Kobe Japan 68-69; Tokyo 69-70; Yokkaichi 70-74; Area Sec USPG *C & O, C, C & R, L & K* and *T, K & A* 75-93; I Cork St Mich Union *C, C & R* 75-86; Adn Cork, Cloyne and Ross 86-93; I Moviddy Union 86-88; I Rathcooney Union 88-93; Bp K, E & A 93-00; Can Elphin Cathl 93-00; Bp L & K 00-08; rtd 08. *4 Langford Place, Langford Row, Cork, Republic of Ireland* Tel (00353) (21) 496 7688

MAYES, Canon Stephen Thomas. b 47. St Jo Coll Nottm 67. **d** 71 **p** 72. C Cullompton *Ex* 71-75; C Cheltenham St Mark *Glouc* 76-84; P-in-c Water Orton *Birm* 84-91; V from 91; AD Coleshill 99-05; Hon Can Birm Cathl from 05. *The Vicarage, Vicarage Lane, Water Orton, Birmingham B46 1RX* Tel 0121-747 2751 Fax 749 7294 E-mail stmayes@yahoo.co.uk

MAYES, Suzanne Janette. b 55. NTMTC 95. **d** 98 **p** 99. NSM E Ham w Upton Park *Chelmsf* 98-02; Chapl HM Pris Wellingborough 02-04; Sessional Chapl HM Pris Chelmsf 05-07; HM Pris Wormwood Scrubs 07-08; HM Pris Hollesley Bay 07-10; HM Pris and YOI Warren Hill 07-10; Chapl HM Pris Bullwood Hall from 11; Perm to Offic *Chelmsf* 04-11; Hon C Romford St Andr from 11. *HM Prison Bullwood Hall, Bullwood Hall Lane, Hockley SS5 4TE* Tel (01702) 562800 E-mail suzannemayes@btinternet.com

✠**MAYFIELD, The Rt Revd Christopher John.** b 35. G&C Coll Cam BA57 MA61 Cranfield Inst of Tech MSc83. Wycliffe Hall Ox 61. **d** 63 **p** 64 **c** 85. C Birm St Martin 63-67; Lect 67-71; V Luton St Mary *St Alb* 71-80; RD Luton 74-80; Adn Bedford 80-85; Suff Bp Wolverhampton *Lich* 85-92; Area Bp Wolverhampton 92-93; Bp Man 93-02; rtd 02; Hon Asst Bp Worc from 02. *Harewood House, 54 Primrose Crescent, Worcester WR5 3HT* Tel (01905) 764822

MAYFIELD, Timothy James Edward. b 60. LMH Ox BA82. Trin Coll Bris BA88. **d** 88 **p** 89. C Ovenden *Wakef* 88-92; V Mount Pellon 92-03; V Cheltenham Ch Ch *Glouc* from 03. *Christ Church Vicarage, Malvern Road, Cheltenham GL50 2NU* Tel (01242) 515983

MAYFIELD, Timothy John Joseph. b 59. BA MA. **d** 99 **p** 00. C Battersea Rise St Mark *S'wark* 99-10; C Fairfax Truro Ch USA from 10. *10520 Main Street, Fairfax VA 22030-3380, USA* Tel (001) (703) 273 1300

MAYHEW, David Francis. b 51. Ch Ch Ox BA72 MA76 Wycliffe Hall Ox BA75. NEOC 89. **d** 91 **p** 92. NSM High Elswick St Paul *Newc* 91-94; Toc H 91-94; V Mitford *Newc* 94-09; C Longhorsley and Hebron 07-09; Chapl Northgate and Prudhoe NHS Trust 94-09; V Cov H Trin from 09. *Holy Trinity Vicarage, 4 Bishop's Walk, Coventry CV5 6PY* Tel (024) 7671 2114 E-mail dfmayhew@aol.com

MAYHEW (née GURNEY), Jean Elizabeth. b 39. OBE97. New Hall Cam MA85 K Coll Lon BD84 AKC84 PGCE85 Ulster Univ Hon DUniv98 FKC00. SEITE 02. **d** 05 **p** 06. NSM Maidstone St Paul *Cant* 05-10; Perm to Offic from 11. *Twysden, Riseden Lane, Kilndown, Cranbrook TN17 2SG* Tel (01580) 211820 Fax 212232 Mobile 07773-404554 E-mail jean@jmayhew.free-online.co.uk

MAYLAND, Mrs Jean Mary. b 36. JP77. LMH Ox BA58 MA61 TCert60. St Deiniol's Hawarden 91. **d** 91 **p** 94. NSM York

Minster 91-93; Lect and Tutor NOC 91-93; Lect NEOC 93-96 Dioc Ecum Officer *Dur* 93-96; Local Unity Officer Dur Ecum Relns Gp 93-96; Assoc Sec CCBI 96-99; Co-ord Sec for Ch Life CTBI 99-03; Asst Gen Sec 99-03; rtd 03; Perm to Offic *York* 03-09 and *Newc* from 04. *5 Hackwood Glade, Hexham NE46 1AL* Tel (01434) 600339 E-mail jeanmayland@btinternet.com

MAYLAND, Canon Ralph. b 27. VRD63. Ripon Hall Ox 57. **d** 59 **p** 60. C Lambeth St Andr w St Thos *S'wark* 59-62; Chapl RNR 61-94; C-in-c Worksop St Paul CD *S'well* 62-68; V Brightside St Marg *Sheff* 68-72; Ind Chapl 68-81; V Ecclesfield 72-81; Can Res and Treas York Minster 82-94; rtd 94; Hon C Brancepeth *Dur* 94-96; Perm to Offic *York* from 96 and *Chelmsf* 01-03 *5 Hackwood Glade, Hexham NE46 1AL* Tel (01434) 600339

MAYLOR, David Charles. b 59. Lanc Univ BSc80 Edge Hill Coll of HE PGCE81. St Jo Coll Nottm 89. **d** 91 **p** 92. C Hindley All SS *Liv* 91-94; P-in-c Spalding St Paul *Linc* 94-07; Chapl United Lincs Hosps NHS Trust 99-07; Lic Gen Preacher *Linc* from 07; Music Dir Stamford St Geo w St Paul from 07. *St Martin's Rectory, Pinfold Lane, Stamford PE9 2LS* Tel (01780) 767993

MAYLOR, Miles Edward. b 55. St Andr Univ BD85 Glam Univ PhD00 PGCE02. St Mich Coll Llan 03. **d** 05 **p** 06. NSM Mountain Ash and Miskin *Llan* 05; NSM Wheatley Ox 06-09 NSM Ox St Barn and St Paul from 09. *30 Skene Close, Headington, Oxford OX3 7XQ* Tel (01865) 769554 Mobile 07967-584670 E-mail miles.maylor@virgin.net

MAYNARD, John William. b 37. Lon Univ BSc58. Ripon Hall Ox 60. **d** 62 **p** 63. C St Laur in Thanet *Cant* 62-67; C S Ashford Ch Ch 67-70; V Pagham *Chich* 70-00; rtd 00. *Two Hedges, Lower Budleigh, East Budleigh, Budleigh Salterton EX9 7DL* Tel (01395) 443869

MAYNARD, Jonathan Mark (Josh). b 80. Ex Univ BA02. Trin Coll Bris BA09. **d** 10 **p** 11. C Woodchester and Brimscombe *Glouc* from 10. *Red House Cottage, Westrip Lane, Stroud GL5 4PL* Tel (01453) 765175 Mobile 07825-795257 E-mail jmaynard1044@googlemail.com

MAYNARD, Canon Richard Edward Buller. b 42. AKC66. **d** 67 **p** 68. C St Ives *Truro* 67-71; C Falmouth K Chas 71-74; V St Germans 74-85; RD E Wivelshire 81-85; TR Saltash 85-08; Hon Can Truro Cathl 82-08; Chapl St Barn Hosp Saltash 90-93; Chapl Cornwall Healthcare NHS Trust 93-02; Chapl N and E Cornwall Primary Care Trust 02-06; Chapl Cornwall and Is of Scilly Primary Care Trust 06-08; rtd 08; C Altarnon w Bolventor Laneast and St Clether *Truro* from 11. *Harewood, Dunheved Road, Launceston PL15 9JJ* Tel (01752) 843142 E-mail canonrichardmaynard@btinternet.com

MAYNE, Canon Brian John. b 52. Univ of Wales (Cardiff) BA73 LTCL75 MRICS81. NEOC 82 Coll of Resurr Mirfield 84. **d** 85 **p** 86. C Stainton-in-Cleveland *York* 85-89; P-in-c Rounton w Welbury 89-96; Chapl HM YOI Northallerton 89-96; Chapl HM YOI Lanc Farms 96-10; Chapl HM Pris Kirkham from 10; Hon Can Blackb Cathl from 09. *HM Prison Kirkham, Freckleton Road, Kirkham, Preston PR4 2RN* Tel (01772) 675625 E-mail brianmayne@tiscali.co.uk

MAYNE, John Andrew Brian. b 34. QUB BA55 Lon Univ BD62 TCD Div Sch Div Test 57. **d** 57 **p** 58. C Ballymoney *Conn* 57-60 C Knock *D & D* 60-62; P-in-c Knocknagoney 62-68; P-in-c Belvoir 68-71; I 71-80; Dean Waterford *C & O* 80-84; I Lecale Gp *D & D* 84-01; Can Down Cathl 87-01; Prec 91-00; Chan 00-01; Sec Gen Syn Liturg Cttee 89-99; rtd 01. *114 Ballydugan Road, Downpatrick BT30 8HF* Tel (028) 4461 2521 Mobile 07092-207229 E-mail jab@brianmayne.co.uk *or* editor.bcp@ireland.anglican.org

MAYO, Christopher Paul. b 68. Heythrop Coll Lon BD91 Birm Univ PGCE96. Qu Coll Birm 91. **d** 93 **p** 94. C Wednesfield *Lich* 93-94; C Bilston 94-95; Dioc Miss P *Mor* from 10. *9 Academy Street, Brora KW9 6QP* Tel (01408) 621539

MAYO, Deborah Ann. See MURPHY, Mrs Deborah Ann

MAYO, Inglis John. b 46. FCA. Ripon Hall Ox 74. **d** 77 **p** 78. C Bitterne Park *Win* 77-81; C Christchurch 81-86; P-in-c Sturminster Marshall *Sarum* 86-89; P-in-c Kingston Lacy and Shapwick 86-89; V Sturminster Marshall, Kingston Lacy and Shapwick 89-00; P-in-c Lilliput 00-06; V 06-08; rtd 08; Perm to Offic *Sarum* and *Win* from 08. *49B St Catherine's Road, Bournemouth BH6 4AQ* Tel (01202) 424971 E-mail inglis.mayo@btinternet.com

MAYO, Robert William. b 61. Keble Coll Ox BA83 Trin Coll Carmarthen PhD00. Cranmer Hall Dur 85. **d** 87 **p** 88. C Luton Lewsey St Hugh *St Alb* 87-90; Hd Cam Univ Miss and NSM Bermondsey St Jas w Ch Ch *S'wark* 90-95; Chapl S Bank Univ 95-98; Dir Youth Work Tr Ridley Hall Cam 98-05; V Shepherd's Bush St Steph w St Thos *Lon* from 05. *St Stephen's Vicarage, 1 Coverdale Road, London W12 8JJ* Tel (020) 8743 3166 Mobile 07977-003227 E-mail bobmayo43@gmail.com

MAYO, Mrs Susan. b 53. Didsbury Coll Man BEd78. St Jo Coll Nottm 08. **d** 10 **p** 11. NSM Edgeley and Cheadle Heath *Ches* from 10; Chapl Stockport Academy from 11. *38 Brookhead Drive, Cheadle SK8 2JA* Tel 0161-428 5375 E-mail mayos32@waitrose.com *or* sue@edgeleyandcheadleheath.org.uk

MAYO-LYTHALL, Ms Jennifer Elizabeth. b 83. St Jo Coll Dur BA10. Cranmer Hall Dur 07. **d** 10 **p** 11. C Norbury *Ches* from 10. *40 Beechfield Road, Stockport SK3 8SF* Tel 0161-425 7992 Mobile 07749-949830 E-mail jmayo-lythall@hotmail.com

MAYO-SMITH, Peter. b 49. Open Univ BA80. Ridley Hall Cam 05. **d** 06 **p** 07. C Greengates *Bradf* 06-09; C Idle 06-09; C Cottingley 08-09; P-in-c Haworth from 09; P-in-c Cross Roads cum Lees from 09; P-in-c Oxenhope from 10. *78 Prince Street, Haworth, Keighley BD22 8JD* Tel (01535) 648464 Mobile 07880-866222 E-mail peter@mayo-smith.net

MAYOR, Henry William. b 39. Oriel Coll Ox BA62. Westcott Ho Cam 62. **d** 64 **p** 65. C The Quinton *Birm* 64-66; C Dudley St Thos *Worc* 67-71; R Birch St Agnes *Man* 71-83; Community Chapl Aylesbury *Ox* 83-89; Community Chapl Aylesbury w Bierton and Hulcott 89; R Cheetham St Luke and Lower Crumpsall St Thos *Man* 89-96; R Cheetham and Lower Crumpsall 97-01; rtd 01; Perm to Offic *Man* from 01. *57 Hill Street, Manchester M20 3FY* Tel 0161-434 2955 Mobile 07960-767155 E-mail henrywmayor@hotmail.com

MAYOR, Janet Hilary. See TAYLOR, Mrs Janet Hilary

MAYOSS, Anthony (Aidan). b 31. Leeds Univ BA55. Coll of Resurr Mirfield 55. **d** 57 **p** 58. C Meir *Lich* 57-62; Lic to Offic *Wakef* 62-72 and from 78; CR from 64; S Africa 73-75; Asst Chapl Lon Univ 76-78; Bursar CR 84-90; rtd 98; Perm to Offic *Lon* 98-07. *House of the Resurrection, Stocks Bank Road, Mirfield WF14 0BN* Tel (01924) 483330 E-mail amayoss@mirfield.org.uk

MAYOSS-HURD, Canon Susan Patricia. b 59. Lanc Univ BA81. Cranmer Hall Dur 82. **dss** 84 **d** 87 **p** 94. Ribbesford w Bewdley and Dowles *Worc* 84-88; Par Dn 87-88; Chapl W Heath Hosp 88-96; C W Heath *Birm* 88-96; V 96-03; V Peachland St Marg Canada from 03. *6146 Turner Avenue, Peachland BC V0H 1X4, Canada* Tel (001) (250) 767 9682 E-mail revsuemh@shaw.ca

MAZUR, Mrs Ann Carol. b 47. St Mich Coll Sarum CertEd69. TISEC 01. **d** 04 **p** 05. NSM St Ninian's Cathl Perth 04-07; Prec from 07; Chapl Craigclowan Sch Perth 04-07. *8 Netherlea, Scone, Perth PH2 6QA* Tel (01738) 551351 E-mail ann@mazur.org.uk

MBALI, Escourt Zolile. b 40. Fort Hare Univ BA68 Ox Univ BA71. St Bede's Coll Umtata 62. **d** 71 **p** 72. S Africa 71-74 and from 93; Botswana 74-81; V Preston on Tees *Dur* 81-83; C Knighton St Mary Magd *Leic* 84-88; P-in-c Church Langton w Tur Langton, Thorpe Langton etc 88-92; Community Relns Officer 88-93; Hon Can Leic Cathl 92-93; rtd 02. *1 Halford Road, Berea, Durban, 4001 South Africa* Tel (0027) (31) 201 6195

MDUMULLA, Jonas Habel. b 50. Nairobi Univ Hull Univ BTh87 MA89. St Phil Coll Kongwa. **d** 74 **p** 75. Tanzania 74-82; C Sutton St Jas and Wawne *York* 82-96; P-in-c Carlton and Drax from 96; Ind Chapl from 96. *The Vicarage, 2 Church Dike Lane, Drax, Selby YO8 8NZ* Tel (01757) 618313

MEACHAM, John David. b 24. AKC51 QTS60 Lambeth STh77 Open Univ MPhil90. **d** 52 **p** 53. C Maidenhead St Luke *Ox* 52-55; Asst Master Linton Ho Maidenhead 52-55; C Croydon St Jo *Cant* 55-58; V Sittingbourne St Mich 58-74; Teacher St Jo Boys' High Sch 64-74; V Brenchley *Roch* 74-83; Teacher Tunbridge Wells Girls' Gr Sch 78-83; P-in-c St Wishford and S Newton *Sarum* 83-85; Bp's Chapl and Research Asst 83-86; Sec C of E Doctrine Commn 84-89; rtd 88; Perm to Offic *Sarum* 88-98. *Trewinnard, Grams Road, Walmer, Deal CT14 7NT* Tel (01304) 239613

MEAD, Arthur Hugh. b 39. K Coll Cam BA60 MA64 New Coll Ox BLitt66. St Steph Ho Ox 61. **d** 80 **p** 80. NSM Hammersmith St Jo *Lon* 80-05; NSM Hammersmith H Innocents and St Jo from 05; Chapl St Paul's Sch Barnes 82-97; rtd 97; Dep P in O 85-90 and from 95; P in O 90-95; Reader of The Temple from 95. *11 Dungarvan Avenue, London SW15 5QU* Tel (020) 8876 5833

MEAD, Colin Harvey. b 26. FCA. S Dios Minl Tr Scheme 81. **d** 84 **p** 85. NSM Talbot Village *Sarum* 84-96; rtd 96; Perm to Offic *Sarum* 96-07. *22 Melton Court, 37 Lindsay Road, Poole BH13 6BH* Tel (01202) 763647

MEAD, Canon John Harold. b 37. Wells Th Coll 69. **d** 71 **p** 72. C Charlton Kings St Mary *Glouc* 71-75; R Stratton w Baunton 75-82; R Bishop's Cleeve 82-00; RD Tewkesbury 88-97; Hon Can Glouc Cathl 90-00; rtd 00; Perm to Offic *Glouc* from 00. *13 Cleevemount Close, Cheltenham GL52 3HW* Tel (01242) 241050

MEAD, Mrs Lynda Roberta. b 44. Open Univ BA91. STETS. **d** 99 **p** 00. NSM Hythe *Win* 99-04. *22 Furzedale Park, Hythe, Southampton SO45 3HW* Tel (023) 8084 8901

MEAD, Nicholas Charles. b 50. Newc Univ BEd73 Reading Univ MA76. Ridley Hall Cam 83. **d** 85 **p** 86. C Bilton *Cov* 85-88; C Whittlesey *Ely* 88-89; Hd of Relig Studies Neale-Wade Community Coll March 89-97; Fell Farmington Inst for Chr Studies Ox from 96; Sen Lect RE Westmr Coll Ox 97-00; Sen Lect RE Ox Brookes Univ from 00. *Westminster Institute of Education, Oxford Brookes University, Harcourt Hill, Oxford OX2 9AT* Tel (01865) 488294 E-mail nmead@brookes.ac.uk

MEAD, Peter Tony. b 63. St Jo Coll Dur BA08. Cranmer Hall Dur 06. **d** 08 **p** 09. C Yeovil H Trin w Barwick *B & W* from 08. *19 Foxglove Way, Yeovil BA22 8PU* Tel (01935) 476692 Mobile 07726-959659 E-mail pete.mead@talktalk.net

MEADEN, Philip George William. b 40. Open Univ BA75. Lich Th Coll 63. **d** 66 **p** 67. C Aston SS Pet and Paul *Birm* 66-70; V Lozells St Paul 70-76; Asst Chapl HM Pris Brixton 76-77; Chapl HM Pris Lewes 77-84; Chapl HM Pris Aylesbury 84-88; Chapl HM Pris Wandsworth 88-01; rtd 01; Perm to Offic *St E* 01-05. *2 Waterloo Lane, Fairford GL7 4BP* Tel (01285) 713917

MEADER, Jennifer Lindsay. b 68. UEA BA89. Westcott Ho Cam. **d** 01 **p** 02. C Teversham and Cherry Hinton St Andr *Ely* 01-05; C Westmr St Jas *Lon* from 05. *St James's Church, 197 Piccadilly, London W1J 9LL* Tel (020) 7734 4511 E-mail revlindsaym@gmail.com

MEADER, Philip John. b 44. Oak Hill Th Coll 73. **d** 75 **p** 76. C E Ham St Paul *Chelmsf* 75-77; CMJ 77-90; TV Lowestoft and Kirkley *Nor* 90-94; V Lowestoft St Andr 94-96; R Panfield and Rayne *Chelmsf* 96-09; RD Braintree 06-09; rtd 09. *39 Langdale Avenue, Chichester PO19 8JQ* Tel (01243) 528783 E-mail philip@revmeader.fsnet.co.uk

MEADOWS, Mrs Freda Angela. b 46. CertEd68. Oak Hill Th Coll 93. **d** 96 **p** 97. NSM N Wembley St Cuth *Lon* 96-01; NSM Roxeth 01-07; rtd 07; Perm to Offic *Lon* from 07. *48 Torrington Drive, Harrow HA2 8NF* Tel (020) 8248 3523 E-mail fam@revfredmead.freeserve.co.uk

MEADOWS, Philip Michael. b 71. Univ of Wales (Lamp) BA95. St Steph Ho Ox BTh01. **d** 01 **p** 03. C W Bromwich St Fran *Lich* 01; C Leeds Belle Is St Jo and St Barn *Ripon* 02-06; Perm to Offic *Ches* from 06; CMP from 04. *13 Naburn Close, Stockport SK5 8JQ* Tel 0161-494 8073 Mobile 07971-035513 E-mail frmeadows@hotmail.co.uk

MEADS, William Ivan. b 35. Qu Mary Coll Lon BA56 ACIS67 ACMA75. Linc Th Coll 75. **d** 77 **p** 78. C Cheltenham St Luke and St Jo *Glouc* 77-81; Chapl HM Pris Pentonville 81-82; Preston 82-85; Wakef 85-88; P-in-c Wroxton w Balscote and Shenington w Alkerton *Ox* 88-90; R Broughton w N Newington and Shutford etc 90-95; P-in-c Week St Mary w Poundstock and Whitstone *Truro* 95-97; rtd 97; Perm to Offic *B & W* 97-00 and *St E* from 08. *The Meads, Briswell Green, Thorndon, Eye IP23 7JF* Tel (01379) 678670 E-mail nanmeads@whsmithnet.co.uk

MEADWAY, Prof Jeanette Valerie. b 47. Edin Univ MB, ChB69 FRCP87 FRCPEd87. Oak Hill NSM Course 89. **d** 93 **p** 94. NSM Stratford St Jo w Ch Ch and St Jas *Chelmsf* from 93; Perm to Offic *Lon* 99-03; Hon Prof Gulu Univ Uganda from 09; Lon Mbale Cathl from 09. *4 Glebe Avenue, Woodford Green IG8 9HB* Tel (020) 8504 1958 E-mail drjeanettemeadway@btinternet.com

MEAKIN, Canon Anthony John. b 28. TD76. Down Coll Cam BA52 MA56. Westcott Ho Cam 52. **d** 54 **p** 55. C Gosforth All SS *Newc* 54-60; V Alnwick St Paul 60-71; V Edlingham 62-71; CF (TA) 63-81; R Whickham *Dur* 71-88; RD Gateshead W 78-88; Hon Can Dur Cathl 83-93; Bp's Sen Chapl and Exec Officer for Dioc Affairs 88-93; rtd 93. *73 Oakfields, Burnopfield, Newcastle upon Tyne NE16 6PQ* Tel (01207) 270429

MEAKIN, Catherine Mary. b 77. LMH Ox BA99 Selw Coll Cam BA02. Ridley Hall Cam 02. **d** 04 **p** 05. NSM Cambridge H Trin *Ely* from 04. *Holy Trinity Church, Market Street, Cambridge CB2 3NZ* Tel (01223) 355397 E-mail cat.meakin@htcambridge.org.uk

MEAKIN, David John. b 61. Hull Univ BA82 Dur Univ MA96 Hughes Hall Cam PGCE83 Lambeth STh88. Westcott Ho Cam 86. **d** 88 **p** 89. C Upminster *Chelmsf* 88-92; Prec and Sacr Dur Cathl 92-97; V Ryhope 97-04; P-in-c Schorne *Ox* from 04. *The Rectory, 1 Green Acres Close, Whitchurch, Aylesbury HP22 4JP* Tel (01296) 641606 E-mail d.meakin@btinternet.com

MEANEY, Ashley John. b 67. Ridley Hall Cam 04. **d** 06 **p** 07. C Hammersmith St Paul *Lon* from 06. *39 Rosaville Road, London SW6 7BN* E-mail ash.meaney@sph.org

MEARA, The Ven David Gwynne. b 47. Oriel Coll Ox BA70 MA73. Lambeth STh76 Cuddesdon Coll 71. **d** 73 **p** 74. C Whitley Ch Ch *Ox* 73-77; Chapl Reading Univ 77-82; V Basildon 82-87; P-in-c Aldworth and Ashampstead 85-87; V Basildon w Aldworth and Ashampstead 87-94; RD Bradfield 90-94; V Buckingham w Radclive cum Chackmore 94-97; P-in-c Nash w Thornton, Beachampton and Thornborough 96-97; R Buckingham 97-00; RD Buckingham 95-00; Hon Can Ch Ch 98-00; R St Bride Fleet Street w Bridewell etc *Lon* from 00; Adn Lon from 09; P-in-c St Mary Aldermary from 10. *St Bride's Rectory, Fleet Street, London EC4Y 8AU* Tel (020) 7353 7999 *or* 7427 0133 Fax 7583 4867 E-mail info@stbrides.com *or* archdeacon.london@london.anglican.org

MEARDON, Canon Brian Henry. b 44. Reading Univ BSc66 PhD71. Oak Hill Th Coll MPhil84. **d** 79 **p** 80. C Reading St Jo *Ox* 79-82; V Warfield 82-09; Hon Can Ch Ch 03-09; rtd 09; Hon C Bemerton *Sarum* from 10. *382 Devizes Road, Salisbury SP2 9LY* E-mail brianmeardon@googlemail.com

MEARDON, Mark James. b 73. Southn Univ BSc94. Trin Th Coll Singapore MTS07 St Jo Coll Nottm MA09. **d** 09 **p** 10. C Hazlemere *Ox* from 09. *Church House, 70 Georges Hill, Widmer End, High Wycombe HP15 6BH* Tel 07905-887125 (mobile) E-mail mark.meardon@gmail.com

MEARNS, Christopher Lee. b 30. Worc Coll Ox BA54 MA58. Ripon Hall Ox BTh56. **d** 57 **p** 58. C Greenhill St Jo *Lon* 57-60; Vice-Prin Qu Coll St John's Canada 60-62; Lect Ripon Coll of Educn 63-75; Sen Lect Coll of Ripon and York St Jo 75-85; Lect New Clairvaux Abbey USA 87 and 89; Tutor Ridley Hall Cam 88; Chapl St Phil Th Coll Seychelles 88-90; Perm to Offic *Ripon* 90-06. *The College of St Barnabas, Blackberry Lane, Lingfield RH7 6NJ* Tel (01342) 872820

MEARS, Mrs Hannah Marie. b 80. St Cuth Soc Dur BA02 St Mary's Ho Dur MA03. Trin Coll Bris 06. **d** 08 **p** 09. NSM Henbury *Bris* 08-09; C St Austell *Truro* from 09. *St Luke's House, 5 Penhaligon Way, St Austell PL25 3AR* Tel (01726) 69857

✠**MEARS, The Rt Revd John Cledan.** b 22. Univ of Wales (Abth) BA43 Univ of Wales MA48. Wycliffe Hall Ox 43. **d** 47 **p** 48 **c** 82. C Mostyn *St As* 47-49; C Rhosllannerchrugog 49-56; V Cwm 56-59; Lic to Offic *Llan* 59-73; Chapl St Mich Coll Llan 59-67; Lect Th Univ of Wales (Cardiff) 59-73; Sub-Warden St Mich Coll Llan 67-73; V Gabalfa *Llan* 73-82; Hon Can Llan Cathl 81-82; Bp Ban 82-92; rtd 92; Perm to Offic *Llan* from 92. *Isfryn, 23 Avonridge, Cardiff CF14 9AU* Tel (029) 2061 5505

MEARS, Oliver Harry John. b 80. Ball Coll Ox BA02. Trin Coll Bris BA08. **d** 09 **p** 10. C St Austell *Truro* from 09. *St Luke's House, 5 Penhaligon Way, St Austell PL25 3AR* Tel (01726) 69857 E-mail ollymears@yahoo.co.uk

MEARS, Phillip David. b 40. Dur Univ BA62. **d** 65 **p** 66. C Sandylands *Blackb* 65-68; C Chorley St Geo 68-71; V Leyland St Ambrose 71-81; Chapl Warrington Distr Gen Hosp 81-00; Perm to Offic 81-06; Hon C Schorne *Ox* from 06. *The Rectory, Church Street, Quainton, Aylesbury HP22 4AP* Tel (01296) 655237

MEATH AND KILDARE, Bishop of. *See* CLARKE, The Most Revd Richard Lionel

MEATH, Archdeacon of. *See* STEVENSON, The Ven Leslie Thomas Clayton

MEATHREL, Timothy James. b 78. **d** 08 **p** 09. C Harborne Heath *Birm* from 08. *33 Margaret Road, Birmingham B17 0EU* Tel 0121-426 2585 Mobile 07818-401372 E-mail timmeathrel@stjohns-church.com

MEATS, Canon Alan John. b 41. Univ of Wales (Cardiff) BA62 DipEd63 Lon Univ BD70. St Mich Coll Llan 68. **d** 70 **p** 71. C Pontypridd St Cath *Llan* 70-73; TV Ystradyfodwg 73-75; Dioc Insp of Schs 73-75 and 83-89; V Llandeilo Tal-y-bont *S & B* 75-83; RD Llwchwr 81-83; V Aberdare St Fagan *Llan* 83-89; V Felin-foel *St D* 89-01; Asst Dioc Dir of Educn 89-92; Dioc Dir of Educn 92-97; V Pen-bre 01-07; Can St D Cathl 94-07; rtd 07; Perm to Offic *St D* from 07. *77 Parc Tyisha, Burry Port SA16 0RR*

MEATYARD, Mrs Christina. b 51. SRN74. STETS 96. **d** 99 **p** 01. NSM S Hayling *Portsm* 99-05; NSM N Hayling St Pet and Hayling Is St Andr 05-06. *38 Staunton Avenue, Hayling Island PO11 0EW* Tel (023) 9234 8886 *or* 9263 7649 Mobile 07979-096779

MECHANIC, Mrs Bridget Elisheva. b 54. Cape Town Univ TDip74 Nazarene Th Coll Man BA08 Anglia Ruskin Univ MA10. Ridley Hall Cam 08. **d** 10 **p** 11. C Ipswich St Jo *St E* from 10. *34 Holland Road, Ipswich IP4 4EF* Tel (01473) 720564 Mobile 07738-115691 E-mail elishevamechanic@virgin.net

MECHANIC, Rodney Ian (Roni). b 48. Man Univ MA(Theol)00. **d** 78 **p** 78. S Africa 78-98; P-in-c Shebbear, Buckland Filleigh, Sheepwash etc *Ex* 98-01; Australia 01-02; TV Heatons *Man* 02-08; TV Mildenhall *St E* from 08. *The Vicarage, 1 The Street, Barton Mills, Bury St Edmunds IP28 6AP* Tel (01638) 715112 Mobile 07753-177280 E-mail ronimechanic@googlemail.com

MEDCALF, James Gordon. b 31. CB. Solicitor 63. S'wark Ord Course 87. **d** 90 **p** 91. NSM Shortlands *Roch* 90-00. *15 Losecoat Close, Stamford PE9 1DU* Tel (01780) 482583

MEDCALF, John Edward. b 19. Oak Hill Th Coll 47. **d** 50 **p** 51. C Rugby St Matt *Cov* 50-53; TR Chell *Lich* 53-61; V Wednesfield Heath 61-85; rtd 85; Perm to Offic *Heref* from 86. *9 Richmond Care Village, St Joseph's Way, Nantwich CW5 6TD* Tel (01270) 623244

MEDCALF, William Henry. b 15. TCD BA45 MA49. CITC 46. **d** 46 **p** 47. C Belfast St Mich *Conn* 46-48; C Bedford St Pet *St Alb* 48-50; SE Sec CMJ 50-63; Dir Exhibitions CMJ 63-80; rtd 80; Perm to Offic Lon 80-08. *c/o Mrs O H Thompson, Swans View, 26 Wilhelmina Close, Leamington Spa CV32 5JT* Tel (01926) 337577

MEDFORTH, Allan Hargreaves. b 27. Qu Coll Cam BA48 MA52. Westcott Ho Cam 50. **d** 51 **p** 52. C Hexham *Newc* 51-55; PV S'well Minster 55-59; V Farnsfield 59-72; RD S'well 66-72; V St Alb St Pet *St Alb* 72-95; RD St Alb 74-84; rtd 95; Perm to Offic *St Alb* from 95. *62 Cuckmans Drive, St Albans AL2 3AF* Tel (01727) 836437

MEDHURST, Mrs June. b 44. St Hild Coll Dur TCert66. NOC 99. **d** 02 **p** 03. C Silsden *Bradf* 02-06; P-in-c Oxenhope 06-10. *100 Langley Lane, Baildon, Shipley BD17 6TD* Tel (01274) 599177 E-mail medjune@tiscali.co.uk

MEDHURST, Prof Kenneth Noel. b 38. Edin Univ MA61 Man Univ PhD69. **d** 91 **p** 93. NSM Baildon *Bradf* 91-06; NSM Oxenhope 06-09; Perm to Offic from 10; Can Th Bradf Cathl from 00. *100 Langley Lane, Baildon, Shipley BD17 6TD* Tel (01274) 599177 E-mail kenmed@btinternet.com

MEDHURST, Leslie John. b 56. TCD BTh90 MA93 Open Univ BA91. **d** 85 **p** 86. C Seapatrick *D & D* 85-90; I Belfast St Mark *Conn* 90-97; I Helen's Bay *D & D* 97-05. *55 Abbey Park, Bangor BT20 4BZ*

MEDLEY, Philip James Anthony. b 81. St Jo Coll Dur BA03 PGCE04. Trin Coll Bris 08. **d** 10 **p** 11. C Walker *Newc* from 10. *27 Scrogg Road, Newcastle upon Tyne NE6 4EX* Tel 0191-265 5373 Mobile 07735-990077 E-mail phil.medley@hotmail.com

MEDLEY, Canon Philip Roger. b 46. Birm Univ CertEd73 Sheff Univ MA00 FCollP96. SWMTC. **d** 85 **p** 86. NSM Ottery St Mary, Alfington and W Hill *Ex* 85-86; C S Hill w Callington *Truro* 86-89; C Linkinhorne 86-89; V 89-03; Dioc Officer for Evang 93-99; Warden Cornwall Preachers' Coll 93-99; Hon Can Truro Cathl 01-03; Dioc Missr *B & W* from 03. *The Old Deanery, Wells BA5 2UG* Tel (01749) 670777 E-mail roger.medley@bathwells.anglican.org

MEDWAY, Mrs Christine Jean. b 57. Qu Coll Birm 93. **d** 95 **p** 98. C Milton *Win* 95-97; C Southampton St Mary Extra 97-01; P-in-c Haselbury Plucknett, Misterton and N Perrott *B & W* 01-03; rtd 03. *40 Lime Avenue, Southampton SO19 8NZ* Tel (023) 8044 5105

MEDWAY, Daron. b 72. Univ of N Lon BA98. Wycliffe Hall Ox BTh04. **d** 04 **p** 05. C Crofton *Portsm* 04-08; V Penge St Jo *Roch* from 08. *The Vicarage, St Johns Road, London SE20 7EQ* Tel (020) 8778 6176 Mobile 07900-574691 E-mail d.medway@mac.com

MEE, Colin Henry. b 36. Reading Univ BSc58. Bris Sch of Min 83. **d** 85 **p** 86. NSM Stanton St Quintin, Hullavington, Grittleton etc *Bris* 85-87; C Swindon Ch Ch 88-90; TV Washfield, Stoodleigh, Withleigh etc *Ex* 90-95; TR 95-99; Chapl Marie Curie Foundn (Tidcombe Hall) 95-99; rtd 99; Perm to Offic *B & W* 99-02. *Rickstones, Burgundy Road, Minehead TA24 5QJ* Tel (01643) 706048

MEEHAN, Cyril Frederick. b 52. St Jo Coll Nottm BTh80. **d** 80 **p** 81. C Keresley and Coundon *Cov* 80-83; P-in-c Linton and Castle Gresley *Derby* 83-90; P-in-c Alvaston 90-00; V 00; Chapl Asst Freeman Gp of Hosps NHS Trust 00-03; Chapl Northumbria Healthcare NHS Trust 03-04. *Address temp unknown*

MEEK, Anthony William. b 45. ACIB. Ox NSM Course 80. **d** 83 **p** 84. NSM Gt Chesham *Ox* 83-01; Perm to Offic *Ex* from 01; Clergy Widow(er)s Officer from 02. *The Willows, Orley Road, Ipplepen, Newton Abbot TQ12 5SA* Tel (01803) 814370 E-mail frtonymeek@aol.com

MEERE, Mrs Alison Elizabeth. b 44. SRN65. Ripon Coll Cuddesdon 85. **d** 87 **p** 94. Par Dn Hengrove *Bris* 87-88; Par Dn Winterbourne 88-91; Par Dn Southmead 91-93; Par Dn Hackney *Lon* 93-94; TV 94-95; Asst Chapl R Berks Hosp Reading 95-96; Asst Chapl Battle Hosp Reading 95-96; Indonesia 02-03; rtd 03. *19 St Elmos Road, London SE16 1SA* Tel (020) 7231 2601 Mobile 07754-808579

MEERING, Laurence Piers Ralph. b 48. Man Univ BSc70. Trin Coll Bris 79. **d** 81 **p** 82. C Downend *Bris* 81-84; C Crofton *Portsm* 84-87; V Witheridge, Thelbridge, Creacombe, Meshaw etc *Ex* 87-94; TV Southgate *Chich* 94-02; TV Walton H Trin *Ox* 02-07; P-in-c Bedgrove 02-07; P-in-c Newton Longville and Mursley w Swanbourne etc 07-08; R 08-09; V Newton Longville, Mursley, Swanbourne etc from 09; AD Mursley from 11. *1 St Mary's Close, Mursley, Milton Keynes MK17 0HP* Tel (01296) 728055 E-mail laurencemeering@yahoo.co.uk

MEESE, Dudley Noel. b 63. Leic Univ BA86 Nottm Univ PGCE87. Ridley Hall Cam 99. **d** 01 **p** 02. C Sheff St Jo 01-05; Chapl Lee Abbey from 05. *Lee Abbey Fellowship, Lee Abbey, Lynton EX35 6JJ* Tel (01598) 752621

MEGAHEY, Alan John. b 44. Selw Coll Cam BA65 MA69 QUB PhD69. Westcott Ho Cam 69. **d** 70 **p** 71. Asst Chapl Wrekin Coll Telford 70-73; Ho Master Cranleigh Sch Surrey 73-83; Zimbabwe 84-93; Chapl Uppingham Sch 93-01; R Brant Broughton and Beckingham *Linc* from 01; R Leadenham from 01; R Welbourn from 01; RD Loveden from 03. *The Rectory, Church End, Leadenham, Lincoln LN5 0PX* Tel (01400) 273987 E-mail rector.leadenham@btopenworld.com

MEGARRELL, Miss Joanne Myrtle. b 70. QUB BA93 PGCE94 CITC BTh03. **d** 03 **p** 04. C Moira *D & D* from 03. *27 Danesfoot, Moira, Craigavon BT67 0SG* Tel (028) 9261 7346 E-mail jmegarrell@talk21.com *or* joanne@moiraparish.org.uk

✠**MEHAFFEY, The Rt Revd James.** b 31. TCD BA52 MA56 BD56 QUB PhD75 Ulster Univ Hon DLitt99. **d** 54 **p** 55 **c** 80. C Ballymacarrett St Patr *D & D* 54-56; C Deptford St Jo *S'wark* 56-58; C Down Cathl 58-60; C-in-c Ballymacarrett St Chris 60-62; I Kilkeel 62-66; I Cregagh 66-80; Bp's Private Chapl 72-76 Preb Down Cathl 76-80; Dioc Missr 76-80; Bp D & R 80-02; rtd 02. *10 Clearwater, Londonderry BT47 6BE* Tel (028) 7134 2624 E-mail james.mehaffey@btinternet.com

MEHEN, Donald Wilfrid. b 44. Birkbeck Coll Lon BSc72 CertEd66. **d** 00 **p** 01. OLM Sproughton w Burstall, Copdock w Washbrook etc *St E* from 00. *19 The Link, Bentley, Ipswich IP9 2DJ* Tel (01473) 310383 E-mail don@mehen.freeserve.co.uk

MEIER, Paul. b 64. St Jo Coll Nottm BA98. **d** 98 **p** 99. C Highley w Billingsley, Glazeley etc *Heref* 98-01; C Hildenborough *Roch* 01-07; Storrington Deanery Youth Missr *Chich* 07-10; P-in-c Horsmonden *Roch* from 10. *The Rectory, Goudhurst Road, Horsmonden, Tonbridge TN12 8JU* Tel (01892) 722521 E-mail paul.meier@diocese-rochester.org *or* paulmeier@bleev.co.uk

MEIKLE, Canon David Skene. b 39. St Cath Coll Cam BA60 MA89. Westcott Ho Cam. **d** 63 **p** 64. C Hawick *Edin* 63-67; C Edin SS Phil and Jas 67-72; C Banbury *Ox* 72-73; TV 74-78; R Ipswich St Matt *St E* 78-91; Hon Can St E Cathl 90-01; TR Mildenhall 91-01; rtd 01; Perm to Offic *St E* from 01. *172 Nacton Road, Ipswich IP3 9JN* Tel (01473) 439113 E-mail dandrmeikle@ntlworld.com

MEIN, The Very Revd James Adlington. b 38. Nottm Univ BA60. Westcott Ho Cam 61. **d** 63 **p** 64. C Edin St Columba 63-67; Bp's Dom Chapl 65-67; Malawi 67-72; R Grangemouth *Edin* 72-82; P-in-c Bo'ness 76-82; TV Livingston LEP 82-90; R Edin Ch Ch 90-04; Can St Mary's Cathl 90-01; Syn Clerk 00-01; Dean Edin 01-04; rtd 04. *Cardhu, Bridgend, Linlithgow EH49 6NH* Tel (01506) 834317 E-mail jim@meins.plus.com

MEIN, Canon Peter Simon. b 27. Nottm Univ BA55 MA59. Kelham Th Coll 48. **d** 55 **p** 56. SSM 54-70; Chapl Kelham Th Coll 55-61; Warden 62-70; Prior 64-70; Chapl St Andr Sch Delaware USA 71-92; Hon Can Delaware 89; rtd 92. *PO Box 13, Odessa DE 19730-0013, USA* Tel (001) (302) 378 9160 E-mail simmein@verizon.net

MEIRION-JONES, Dafydd Padrig ap Geraint. b 70. Magd Coll Cam BA91 PGCE92. Oak Hill Th Coll BA01. **d** 01 **p** 02. C Ex St Leon w H Trin 01-05; V Preston All SS *Blackb* from 05. *All Saints' Vicarage, 94 Watling Street Road, Fulwood, Preston PR2 8BP* Tel (01772) 700672 Mobile 07989-390028 E-mail dafandboo@hotmail.com *or* daf@allsaintspreston.org.uk

MEIRION-JONES, Canon Huw Geraint (Gary). b 39. K Coll Lon AKC69 BD71 MA84 MRAC61. St Aug Coll Cant 69. **d** 70 **p** 71. C Harlescott *Lich* 70-73; C Worplesdon *Guildf* 73-77; V Ash Vale 77-85; TR Westborough 85-96; Dioc Press Officer 85-94; P-in-c Shere 96-98; P-in-c Albury 97-98; R Shere, Albury and Chilworth 98-04; Hon Can Guildf Cathl 99-04; Dioc Rural Adv 99-03; RD Cranleigh 00-04; rtd 04; Perm to Offic *Guildf* from 04 and *Ban* 04-06; Lic to Offic *Ban* from 06. *Parc Newydd, Rhosgadfan, Caernarfon LL54 7LF* Tel (01286) 831195 Fax 830141 Mobile 07880-707414

MEIRIONNYDD, Archdeacon of. *See* JONES, The Ven Andrew

MELANESIA, Archbishop of. *See* VUNAGI, The Most Revd David

MELANIPHY, Miss Angela Ellen. b 55. SRN79. Cranmer Hall Dur 87. **d** 90 **p** 94. Par Dn Leytonstone St Jo *Chelmsf* 90-94; C 94-95; TV Harlow Town Cen w Lt Parndon 95-06; TV Hackney Marsh *Lon* from 06. *105 Mayola Road, London E5 0RG* Tel (020) 8533 4034 E-mail angels25@ntlworld.com

MELBOURNE, Brian Kenneth. b 45. Trin Coll Toronto 79. **d** 82 **p** 82. R Fogo Is Canada 82-84; R Welland 84-87; C Pembroke Bermuda 88-94; P-in-c Biddenden and Smarden *Cant* 94-97; Hon C Isfield *Chich* 01-06; R Ponoka Canada 06-10. *Calle San Antonio 6, 29754 Competa (Málaga), Spain* Tel (0034) 951 088 478 E-mail melbournesinspain@yahoo.es

MELDRUM, Andrew John Bruce. b 66. Univ of Wales (Abth) LLB89 Lon Univ MA98. Westcott Ho Cam 91. **d** 94 **p** 95. C Paddington St Jas *Lon* 94-99; P-in-c Brookfield St Anne, Highgate Rise 99-02; V from 02; Communications Adv to Bp Edmonton from 00; AD S Camden from 08. *St Anne's Vicarage, 106 Highgate West Hill, London N6 6AP* Tel and fax (020) 8340 5190 E-mail javintner@aol.com

MELDRUM, David Peter John. b 73. St Andr Univ MA95. Oak Hill Th Coll BA01. **d** 01 **p** 02. C Leyton St Mary w St Edw and St Luke *Chelmsf* 01-03; C Cranham Park 03-05; C Wandsworth St Steph *S'wark* 05-06; C Wandsworth St Mich w St Steph 06-10; S Africa from 10. *Address temp unknown* E-mail davidpjmeldrum@gmail.com

MELINSKY, Canon Michael Arthur Hugh. b 24. Ch Coll Cam BA47 MA49. Ripon Hall Ox 57. **d** 57 **p** 59. C Wimborne Minster *Sarum* 57-59; C Wareham w Arne 59-61; V Nor St Steph 61-68; Chapl Norfolk and Nor Hosp 61-68; Hon Can Nor Cathl and Can Missr 68-73; Chief Sec ACCM 73-78; Prin NOC 78-88; rtd 88; Perm to Offic *Nor* from 88. *15 Parson's Mead, Norwich NR4 6PG* Tel (01603) 455042

MELLERUP, Miss Eiler Mary. b 37. Saffron Walden Coll CertEd58. **d** 96 **p** 97. OLM Happisburgh, Walcott, Hempstead w Eccles etc *Nor* 96-08; Perm to Offic from 08. *Channings, The Crescent, Walcott, Norwich NR12 0NH* Tel (01692) 651393

MELLING, Canon Leonard Richard. b 13. St Aid Birkenhead 38. **d** 41 **p** 42. C W Acklam *York* 41-45; C Scarborough St Mary

45-48; V Newby 48-54; Borneo 54-59; Area Sec USPG *Ox* and *Cov* 59-64; *York* 64-67; V Osbaldwick w Murton *York* 67-78; RD Bulmer 72-78; Malaysia 78-81; Dean Kuching 78-81; rtd 81; Perm to Offic *York* 81-11. *82 Tranby Avenue, Osbaldwick, York YO10 3NN* Tel (01904) 413796

MELLISH, John. b 26. Cranmer Hall Dur 67. **d** 69 **p** 70. C Ulverston St Mary w H Trin *Carl* 69-72; V Bromfield 72-73; V Bromfield w Waverton 73-79; P-in-c Allonby w W Newton 77-79; V Shap w Swindale 79-86; RD Appleby 82-86; V Bassenthwaite, Isel and Setmurthy 86-90; rtd 90; Perm to Offic *Carl* from 90. *Wyndham, 3 Old Road, Longtown, Carlisle CA6 5TH* Tel (01228) 791441

MELLOR, The Very Revd Kenneth Paul. b 49. Southn Univ BA71 Leeds Univ MA72. Cuddesdon Coll 72. **d** 73 **p** 74. C Cottingham *York* 73-76; C Ascot Heath *Ox* 76-80; V Tilehurst St Mary 80-85; V Menheniot *Truro* 85-94; Hon Can Truro Cathl 90-94 and from 03; Can Res and Treas 94-03; RD W Wivelshire 88-96; R Guernsey St Peter Port *Win* from 03; P-in-c Sark from 03; Dean Guernsey from 03; Hon Can Win Cathl from 03. *The Deanery, Cornet Street, St Peter Port, Guernsey GY1 1BZ* Tel (01481) 720036 Fax 722948 E-mail paul@townchurch.org.gg

MELLOR, Roy. b 52. Lanc Univ BA92. Cuddesdon Coll 94. **d** 96 **p** 97. C Oakdale *Sarum* 96-00; TV Kingsthorpe w Northampton St Dav *Pet* 00-03; R Blisworth and Stoke Bruerne w Grafton Regis etc 03-10; P-in-c Malton Malsor 09-10; rtd 10; Perm to Offic *Dur* from 11. *1 Surtees Drive, Crossgate Moor, Durham DH1 4AR* Tel 0191-383 2698 Mobile 07914-767191 E-mail roy_mellor2002@yahoo.co.uk

MELLOR, Sarah Victoria. b 80. St Hilda's Coll Ox BA02 Liv Hope Univ Coll PGCE03 Man Univ MA05. Wycliffe Hall Ox 07. **d** 09 **p** 10. C Dur St Nic from 09. *95 Rochester Road, Durham DH1 5PN* Tel 0191-383 1148 E-mail victoriamellor26@yahoo.co.uk

MELLORS, Derek George. b 38. Bris Univ CertEd60 Lon Univ BSc71 Nottm Univ DipEd74 Liv Univ MEd83. NOC 81. **d** 84 **p** 85. NSM Eccleston Ch Ch *Liv* 84-92; C Lowton St Mary 92-93; V Ashton-in-Makerfield St Thos 93-99; rtd 99; Perm to Offic *Liv* from 00. *20 Millbrook Lane, Eccleston, St Helens WA10 4QU* Tel (01744) 28424

MELLORS, James. b 32. Kelham Th Coll 52. **d** 56 **p** 57. C Horbury *Wakef* 56-61; V Scholes 61-72; V Mirfield 72-88; Hon Can Wakef Cathl 83-88; V Leyburn w Bellerby *Ripon* 88-93; rtd 93; Perm to Offic *Ripon* from 93. *Broomhill, 22 The Shawl, Leyburn DL8 5DG* Tel (01969) 622452 E-mail jj.ww@virgin.net

MELLOWS, Canon Alan Frank. b 23. Qu Coll Cam BA45 MA49. Tyndale Hall Bris 47. **d** 49 **p** 50. C Morden *S'wark* 49-54; V Brimscombe *Glouc* 54-62; R Mileham *Nor* 62-74; P-in-c Beeston next Mileham 62-66; R 66-74; P-in-c Stanfield 62-74; P-in-c Gt w Lt Dunham 70-73; R Ashill 74-79; P-in-c Saham Toney 78-79; R Ashill w Saham Toney 79-88; Hon Can Nor Cathl 82-88; rtd 88; Perm to Offic *Nor* from 88. *8 Smugglers Close, Hunstanton PE36 6JU* Tel (01485) 534271

MELLOWSHIP, Robert John. b 52. St Mich Coll Llan BD92. **d** 92 **p** 93. C Brecon St Mary and Battle w Llanddew *S & B* 92-94; Min Can Brecon Cathl 92-94; C Pontypool *Mon* 94-95; TV 95-97; P-in-c Bressingham w N Lopham and Fersfield *Nor* 97-07; P-in-c Roydon St Remigius 04-07; R Upper Waveney from 07. *The Rectory, High Road, Bressingham, Diss IP22 2AT* Tel and fax (01379) 688267 E-mail robmellowship@msn.com

MELLUISH, Mark Peter. b 59. Oak Hill Th Coll. **d** 89 **p** 90. C Ashtead *Guildf* 89-93; V Ealing St Paul *Lon* from 93. *St Paul's Vicarage, 102 Elers Road, London W13 9QE* Tel and fax (020) 8567 4628 *or* tel 8799 3779 E-mail mark.melluish@stpauls-ealing.org

MELLUISH, Stephen. b 60. Trin Coll Bris 91. **d** 93 **p** 94. C Gipsy Hill Ch Ch *S'wark* 93-96; V Wandsworth St Steph 96-06; P-in-c Wandsworth St Mich 01-06; V Wandsworth St Mich w St Steph from 06. *St Michael's Vicarage, 73 Wimbledon Park Road, London SW18 5TT* Tel (020) 8874 5610 *or* 8877 3003 E-mail smelluish@aol.com

MELLY, Aleck Emerson. b 24. Oak Hill Th Coll 50. **d** 53 **p** 54. C Chadderton Ch Ch *Man* 53-56; C Cheltenham St Mark *Glouc* 56-59; V Tipton St Paul *Lich* 59-68; R Kemberton w Sutton Maddock 68-80; P-in-c Stockton 74-80; R Kemberton, Sutton Maddock and Stockton 81-89; rtd 89; Perm to Offic *Lich* 89-03 and *Heref* from 90. *Bethany, 47 Greenfields Road, Bridgnorth WV16 4JG* Tel (01746) 762711

MELTON, Mrs Anne. b 54. N Riding Coll of Educn CertEd65. St Jo Coll Dur 80. **dss** 83 **d** 87 **p** 94. Newton Aycliffe *Dur* 83-88; Par Dn 87-88; Par Dn Shildon w Eldon 88-94; Asst Dir of Ords 88-94; P-in-c Suxworth 94-96; TR 96-06; rtd 06. *4 Lindisfarne, High Shincliffe, Durham DH1 2PH* Tel 0191-416 3533

MELVILLE, Dominic. b 63. Sussex Univ BA84 Southn Univ BTh90. Sarum & Wells Th Coll 87. **d** 90 **p** 91. C Willenhall H Trin *Lich* 90-94; V Wednesfield St Greg 94-99; V Worc St Wulstan 99-11; TV Halas from 11. *506 Bromsgrove Road, Hunnington, Halesowen B62 0JJ*

MELVIN, Gordon Thomas. b 55. BA86. Sarum & Wells Th Coll 86. **d** 88 **p** 89. C Linc St Faith and St Martin w St Pet 88-91; TV

Horsham *Chich* 91-94; Chapl Horsham Gen Hosp 91-94; Chapl Ipswich Hosp NHS Trust 94-00; Sen Chapl from 00; Chapl Local Health Partnerships NHS Trust 94-00; Sen Chapl from 00; Perm to Offic *St E* from 04. *The Ipswich Hospital NHS Trust, Heath Road, Ipswich IP4 5PD* Tel (01473) 704100 *or* 712233

MENDEL, Canon Thomas Oliver. b 57. Down Coll Cam BA79 MA82. Cranmer Hall Dur 79. **d** 81 **p** 82. Chapl Down Coll Cam 81-86; Fell 84-86; Hon C Cambridge St Mary Less *Ely* 81-86; V Minsterley *Heref* 86-92; R Habberley 86-92; Chapl Shrewsbury Sch 93-95; Chapl Milan w Genoa and Varese *Eur* 95-96; Chapl Copenhagen w Aarhus 96-04; Sen Chapl Malta and Gozo 04-08; Can and Chan Malta Cathl 04-08; V Eastbourne St Mary *Chich* from 08. *St Mary's Vicarage, 2 Glebe Close, Eastbourne BN20 8AW* Tel (01323) 720420

✠**MENIN, The Rt Revd Malcolm James.** b 32. Univ Coll Ox BA55 MA59. Cuddesdon Coll 55. **d** 57 **p** 58 **c** 86. C Southsea H Spirit *Portsm* 57-59; C Fareham SS Pet and Paul 59-62; V Nor St Jas w Pockthorpe 62-72; P-in-c Nor St Martin 62-74; P-in-c Nor St Mary Magd 68-72; V Nor St Mary Magd w St Jas 72-86; RD Nor E 81-86; Hon Can Nor Cathl 82-86; Suff Bp Knaresborough *Ripon* 86-97; rtd 97; Perm to Offic *Nor* 97-04; Hon Asst Bp Nor from 00. *32C Bracondale, Norwich NR1 2AN* Tel (01603) 627987

MENNISS, Canon Andrew Philip. b 49. Univ of Wales (Swansea) BSc73. Sarum & Wells Th Coll 83. **d** 85 **p** 86. C Horsell *Guildf* 85-89; V Bembridge *Portsm* from 89; RD E Wight 95-00; Hon Can Portsm Cathl from 09. *The Vicarage, Church Road, Bembridge PO35 5NA* Tel (01983) 872175 Fax 875255 E-mail apmenniss@aol.com

MENON, Nicholas Anthony Thotekat. b 39. Mert Coll Ox BA61 MA65. St Steph Ho Ox 61. **d** 63 **p** 64. C Paddington Ch Ch *Lon* 63-66; Hon C 66-70; V Thorpe *Guildf* 70-76; V Ox SS Phil and Jas w St Marg 76-79; Chapl Surrey Univ 79-82; Chapl and Ho Master Cranleigh Sch Surrey 82-00; Asst Chapl Malvern Coll 00-06; rtd 04-06; Perm to Offic *Worc* from 05 and *Heref* from 06. *Pilgrim Cottage, 187 West Malvern Road, Malvern WR14 4BB* Tel (01684) 577189 E-mail nicholasmenon159@btinternet.com

MENON, Suresh. b 64. Man Poly BA88. Oak Hill Th Coll 96. **d** 98 **p** 99. C Braintree *Chelmsf* 98-02; C Leic H Trin w St Jo 02-05; C Ox St Ebbe w H Trin and St Pet from 10. *St Ebbe's Church, 2 Roger Bacon Lane, Oxford OX1 1QE* E-mail smenon@stebbes.org.uk

MENSINGH, Gregg Richard. b 69. Portsm Univ BSc94. Westcott Ho Cam 95. **d** 97 **p** 98. C Birchfield *Birm* 97-01; V Gravelly Hill from 01. *All Saints' Vicarage, Broomfield Road, Birmingham B23 7QA* Tel 0121-373 0730 E-mail greggm@onetel.com

MENTZEL, Kevin David. b 60. Reading Univ BSc82 Down Coll Cam BA87 MA91 QUB MTh04 Heythrop Coll Lon MA09. Ridley Hall Cam 85. **d** 88 **p** 89. C Ditton *Roch* 88-91; Asst Chapl Eton Coll 91-93; Asst Chapl R Hosp Sch Holbrook 93-94; Sen C Fulham St Dionis *Lon* 94-97; CF from 97. *c/o MOD Chaplains (Army)* Tel (01264) 381140 Fax 381824 E-mail kdmentzel@gmail.com

MENZIES, James Kingsley. b 86. St Jo Coll Dur BA08. Cranmer Hall Dur 08. **d** 10 **p** 11. C Hetton-Lyons w Eppleton *Dur* from 10. *Lyons Rectory, High Street, Easington Lane, Houghton le Spring DH5 0JN* Tel 0191-526 2300

MENZIES, Stanley Hay. b 33. Edin Univ MA55 BD58. New Coll Edin 55. **d** 02 **p** 03. NSM Boston Spa *York* 02-10; rtd 10; Perm to Offic *York* from 10. *Cairn Croft, 2 Crag Gardens, Bramham, Wetherby LS23 6RP* Tel and fax (01937) 541047

MEON, Archdeacon of the. *See* COLLINS, The Ven Gavin Andrew

MEPHAM, Alistair. b 75. Trin Coll Bris BA07. **d** 07 **p** 08. C Warminster Ch Ch *Sarum* 07-10; TV The Lytchetts and Upton from 10. *The Rectory, Jenny's Lane, Lytchett Matravers, Poole BH16 6BP* Tel (01929) 459200 Mobile 07540-745210 E-mail ali@smlm.co.uk

MEPHAM, Stephen Richard. b 64. K Coll Lon BD85 AKC85. Linc Th Coll 87. **d** 89 **p** 90. C Newark *S'well* 89-92; C Cheshunt *St Alb* 92-95; C-in-c Turnford St Clem CD 95-98; V Rickmansworth 98-06. *46 Thellusson Way, Rickmansworth WD3 8RQ* E-mail sr.mepham@ntlworld.com

MERCER, James John. b 56. Bp Otter Coll Chich BEd79 Lon Inst of Educn MA85. Ridley Hall Cam 00. **d** 02 **p** 03. C Heref St Pet w St Owen and St Jas 02-07; V Harrow Weald All SS *Lon* from 07; Lic Lay Min Tr Officer Willesden Area from 08. *All Saints' Vicarage, 175 Uxbridge Road, Harrow HA3 6TP* Tel (020) 8954 0247 Mobile 07940-506188 E-mail james_ashw@mac.com

MERCER, Canon John James Glendinning. b 20. TCD BA49 MA55. **d** 50 **p** 51. C Newtownards *D & D* 50-51; C Bangor St Comgall 53-55; I Ballyholme 55-90; Can Belf Cathl 76-88; Preb Wicklow St Patr Cathl Dublin 88-90; rtd 90. *6 Hillfoot, Groomsport, Bangor BT19 6JJ* Tel (028) 9147 2979

MERCER, Lt Col Nicholas Justin. b 62. St Andr Univ BD85 Cardiff Univ LLM99 Solicitor 91. Ripon Coll Cuddesdon 08. **d** 11. C Gillingham and Milton-on-Stour *Sarum* from 11. *The Vicarage, 49 Fern Brook Lane, Gillingham SP8 4FL* Tel 07912-619533 (mobile) E-mail mercer-family@hotmail.com

MERCER, Preb Nicholas Stanley. b 49. Selw Coll Cam BA72 MA76 PGCE73 Spurgeon's Coll BA78 Lon Bible Coll MPhil86. Cranmer Hall Dur 95. **d** 95 **p** 95. C Northwood Hills St Edm *Lon* 95-98; C Pimlico St Mary Bourne Street 98-03; Dir of Min 03-07; V Gen Lon Coll of Bps from 07; Hon C Wilton Place St Paul from 04; Preb St Paul's Cathl from 08. *The Old Deanery, Dean's Court, London EC4V 5AA* Tel (020) 7489 4274 Mobile 07782-250377 E-mail nick.mercer@london.anglican.org

MERCER, Canon Timothy James. b 54. Fitzw Coll Cam BA76 MA80. Westcott Ho Cam 78. **d** 81 **p** 82. C Bromley SS Pet and Paul *Roch* 81-85; R Swanscombe 85-96; Chapl Bromley Hosps NHS Trust 96-09; Chapl S Lon Healthcare NHS Trust from 09; Hon Can Roch Cathl from 10. *Princess Royal University Hospital, Farnborough Common, Orpington BR6 8ND* Tel (01689) 863912 *or* 821171 E-mail tim.mercer@diocese-rochester.org

MERCERON, Daniel John. b 58. Lon Univ BA81. Westcott Ho Cam 88. **d** 90 **p** 91. C Clevedon St Jo *B & W* 90-94; CF from 94. *c/o MOD Chaplains (Army)* Tel (01264) 381140 Fax 381824

MERCHANT, Robert Ian. b 73. Keele Univ BA98. Wycliffe Hall Ox BA00. **d** 01 **p** 02. C Harborne Heath *Birm* 01-04; C Cheltenham St Mark *Glouc* 05-06; C Cheltenham St Mich and Cheltenham St Luke and St Jo 06-10; R Ashleworth, Corse, Hartpury, Hasfield etc from 10. *The Rectory, Over Old Road, Hartpury, Gloucester GL19 3BJ* E-mail rob@robmerchant.com

MERCHANT, Mrs Tamsin Laetitia Rachel. b 70. Wycliffe Hall Ox BTh01. **d** 01 **p** 02. C Harborne Heath *Birm* 01-04; Chapl Glos Univ from 04. *The Rectory, Over Old Road, Hartpury, Gloucester GL19 3BJ* Tel (01242) 532735 Mobile 07715-041525 E-mail tmerchant@glos.ac.uk

MERCURIO, Frank James Charles. b 46. Webster Univ (USA) BA73 MA75. St Alb Minl Tr Scheme 87. **d** 89 **p** 90. C Cheshunt *St Alb* 89-93; TV Hitchin 93-00; RD Hitchin 94-00; TR Tring 00-07; P-in-c Alfreton *Derby* from 07; P-in-c Riddings and Ironville from 08. *The Vicarage, 13 Church Street, Alfreton DE55 7AH* Tel (01773) 833280 E-mail frankmercurio@dialstart.net

MEREDITH, Andrew James MacPherson. b 59. St Jo Coll Nottm 91. **d** 93 **p** 94. C Killay *S & B* 93-97; V Waunarllwydd 97-00; V Swansea St Thos and Kilvey from 00. *The Vicarage, Lewis Street, St Thomas, Swansea SA1 8BP* Tel (01792) 652891

MEREDITH, Ian. b 53. Univ of Wales BA85 Lon Univ MTh89 Edin Univ MTh96 Dur Univ PhD07. K Coll Lon 86. **d** 02 **p** 03. Assoc Min Dumfries *Glas* 02-07; R Ayr from 07; R Girvan from 07; R Maybole from 07. *The Rectory, 12 Barns Terrace, Ayr KA7 2DB* Tel (01292) 261145 E-mail rectorayr@yahoo.co.uk

MEREDITH, Canon Roland Evan. b 32. Trin Coll Cam BA55 MA59. Cuddesdon Coll 55. **d** 57 **p** 58. C Bishopwearmouth St Mich *Dur* 57-59; Dioc Chapl *Birm* 59-60; C Kirkby *Liv* 60-63; V Hitchin St Mary *St Alb* 63-72; V Preston St Jo *Blackb* 72-76; TR 76-79; RD Preston 72-79; Hon Can Blackb Cathl 77-79; TR Witney *Ox* 79-94; P-in-c Hailey w Crawley 79-82; RD Witney 89-97; Hon Can Ch Ch 92-97; rtd 94; Perm to Offic *Ox* from 97; *Eur* from 98; *Glouc* from 03. *37 Otters Court, Priory Mill Lane, Witney OX28 1GJ* Tel (01993) 703698 Mobile 07971-370647 E-mail roland@canonmeredith.free-online.co.uk

MERIVALE, Charles Christian Robert. b 44. Cranmer Hall Dur 76. **d** 78 **p** 79. C Highbury Ch Ch w St Jo *Lon* 78-81; P-in-c Hawes *Ripon* 81-82; P-in-c Hardrow and St Jo w Lunds 81-82; V Hawes and Hardraw 82-84; Chapl R Cornwall Hosps Trust 85-92; Perm to Offic *B & W* 92-00 and *Ex* 00-02; TV Shebbear, Buckland Filleigh, Sheepwash etc *Ex* 02-08; rtd 08. *The Cider House, Coxs Close, North Cadbury, Yeovil BA22 7DY* E-mail cjmerivale@milestonenet.co.uk

MERRICK, Harry. **d** 10. NSM Pontefract All SS *Wakef* from 10. *18 Eastbourne Terrace, Pontefract WF8 2HF* Tel (01977) 780831 E-mail harry.merrick1a@btinternet.com

MERRICK, Canon John. b 51. New Univ of Ulster BA72 DipAdEd75 TCD HDipEd73. CITC 89. **d** 92 **p** 93. Hd Master Sligo Gr Sch from 86; Lic to Offic *K, E & A* from 92; Preb Elphin Cathl from 01. *Pier Lodge, Dunfanaghy PO, Letterkenny, Co Donegal, Republic of Ireland* Tel and fax (00353) (74) 913 6971 Mobile 87-227 4978

MERRICK, Richard Christopher. b 57. Qu Coll Birm 08. **d** 11. C Bushbury *Lich* from 11. *11 Eldridge Close, Wolverhampton WV9 5PX* Tel (01902) 784185 E-mail revrichstmarys@gmail.com

MERRIMAN, Stephen Richard. b 74. Leeds Univ BA02. Coll of Resurr Mirfield 99. **d** 02 **p** 03. C Littlehampton and Wick *Chich* 02-06; TV from 06; C Brighton St Matthias 06-08. *St James's Vicarage, 12 Cornwall Road, Littlehampton BN17 6EE* Tel (01903) 724311

MERRINGTON, Bill. b 55. Sheff Hallam Univ BSc78 Birm Univ MPhil95 Warwick Univ PhD03. Cranmer Hall Dur 80. **d** 83 **p** 84. C Harborne Heath *Birm* 83-88; V Leamington Priors St Paul *Cov* 88-99; RD Warwick and Leamington 97-99; R Ilmington w Stretton-on-Fosse etc 99-07; R Tredington and Darlingscott 05-07; RD Shipston 99-03; Hon Can Cov Cathl 01-07; Sen Chapl Bournemouth Univ from 07. *Chaplaincy,*

Bournemouth University, Fern Barrow, Poole BH12 5BB   Tel (01202) 965383 E-mail billmerri@aol.com

MERRY, David Thomas (Tom). b 48. St Chad's Coll Dur BA70. AKC73. **d** 74 **p** 75. C Cirencester *Glouc* 74-78; TV Bridgnorth, Tasley, Astley Abbotts and Oldbury *Heref* 78-83; P-in-c Quatford 81-83; P-in-c Stroud H Trin *Glouc* 83-87; V 87-01; Chapl Stroud Gen Hosp 83-93; Chapl Severn NHS Trust 93-01; Chapl Cheltenham Ladies' Coll from 01; Hon Min Can Glouc Cathl from 04. *The Cheltenham Ladies' College, Bayshill Road, Cheltenham GL50 3EP*   Tel (01242) 520691

MERRY, Ivor John. b 28. WMMTC 84. **d** 87 **p** 88. NSM Redditch, The Ridge *Worc* 87-94; NSM Astwood Bank 94-98; Perm to Offic from 98. *186 Moorcroft Gardens, Redditch B97 5WQ*

MERRY, Rex Edwin. b 38. AKC67. **d** 68 **p** 69. C Spalding St Jo *Linc* 68-73; C Boxmoor St Jo *St Alb* 73-83; TV Hemel Hempstead 83-95; V Farley Hill St Jo 95-06; rtd 06; Perm to Offic *St Alb* from 06. *4 Wellcroft, Hemel Hempstead HP1 3EG*   Tel (01442) 401122

MERRY, Thomas. See MERRY, David Thomas

MERRYWEATHER, Mrs Rosalynd. b 50. Hull Coll of Educn CertEd72. NEOC. **d** 00 **p** 01. NSM Beverley St Nic *York* from 00. *10 West Close, Beverley HU17 7JJ*   Tel (01482) 867958

MESLEY, Mark Terence. b 59. Plymouth Poly BSc88. St Steph Ho Ox 98. **d** 00 **p** 01. C Bickleigh and Shaugh Prior *Ex* 00-03; P-in-c Llanhilleth *Mon* 03-06; P-in-c Llanhilleth w Six Bells 06-08; P-in-c Penwerris *Truro* from 08; Chapl Miss to Seafarers from 08. *The Vicarage, Pellew Road, Falmouth TR11 2NS*   Tel (01326) 218947 E-mail revmarkmesley@btinternet.com

MESLEY-SPONG, Terence John. b 32. Roch Th Coll 63. **d** 66 **p** 67. C Forton *Portsm* 66-68; Rhodesia 68-80; Zimbabwe 80-84; R Christow, Ashton, Trusham and Bridford *Ex* 84-86; Chapl Puerto de la Cruz Tenerife *Eur* 86-93; Miss to Seamen 86-93; rtd 93; Perm to Offic *Win* from 93; Chapl R Bournemouth and Christchurch Hosps NHS Trust 97-98. *14B Stuart Road, Highcliffe, Christchurch BH23 5JS*   Tel (01425) 277833

MESSAM, Paul James. b 65. Lon Coll of Printing BA87. Cranmer Hall Dur 01. **d** 03 **p** 04. C Market Harborough and The Transfiguration etc *Leic* 03-07; P-in-c Bulkington *Cov* from 07; Lead Chapl Cov Blue Coat C of E Sch from 07. *St James's Vicarage, School Road, Bulkington, Nuneaton CV12 9JB*   Tel (024) 7631 8241 Mobile 07711-098209 E-mail paul.messam@virgin.net

MESSENGER, Paul. b 38. Univ of Wales (Lamp) BA63. Coll of Resurr Mirfield 63. **d** 65 **p** 66. C Battersea St Luke *S'wark* 65-69; C Ainsdale *Liv* 69-71; V Wigan St Steph 71-74; Asst Chapl St Marg Convent E Grinstead 74-76; Chapl Kingsley St Mich Sch W Sussex 74-76; P-in-c Southwater *Chich* 76-81; V 81-97; R Sullington and Thakeham w Warminghurst 97-07; rtd 07. *122 Ninfield Road, Bexhill-on-Sea TN39 5BB*   Tel (01424) 220044

MESSER, David Harry. b 61. MCIH93. EAMTC 01. **d** 04 **p** 05. C Stanton, Hopton, Market Weston, Barningham etc *St E* 04-07; R from 07. *The Rectory, Old Rectory Gardens, Stanton, Bury St Edmunds IP31 2JH*   Tel (01359) 250239 E-mail david@dmesser.freeserve.co.uk

MESSERVY, Mrs Cassandra. b 75. Ox Brookes Univ BA99 PGCE02. Ripon Coll Cuddesdon BTh11. **d** 11. C Beaconsfield *Ox* from 11. *26 Candlemas Mead, Beaconsfield HP9 1AP*   Tel 07886-331714 (mobile) E-mail cassamesservy@gmail.com

MESSHAM, Canon Barbara Lynn. b 52. Bretton Hall Coll CertEd75. STETS 96. **d** 99 **p** 00. C The Bourne and Tilford *Guildf* 99-03; V Guildf All SS from 03; RD Guildf 06-11; Hon Can Guildf Cathl from 10. *All Saints' Vicarage, 18 Vicarage Gate, Guildford GU2 7QJ*   Tel (01483) 572006   Mobile 07932-615132 E-mail barbara@messhams.co.uk

METCALF, Preb Michael Ralph. b 37. Clare Coll Cam BA61 MA65 Birm Univ MA80. Ridley Hall Cam 63. **d** 64 **p** 65. C Downend *Bris* 64-67; Perm to Offic *Birm* 68-78 and *Lich* 72-81; Lect W Midl Coll of Educn 72-77; Sen Lect 77-81; Dioc Dir of Educn *Lich* 83-94; V Stafford St Paul Forebridge 94-05; Preb Lich Cathl 91-05; RD Stafford 00-05; rtd 05; Perm to Offic *Heref* from 87 and *Lich* from 05. *196 Stone Road, Stafford ST16 1NT*   Tel and fax (01785) 600260 E-mail prebmetcalf@hotmail.com *or* berylm@ntlworld.com

METCALF, The Ven Robert Laurence. b 35. Dur Univ BA60. Cranmer Hall Dur. **d** 62 **p** 63. C Bootle Ch Ch *Liv* 62-65; C Farnworth 65-67; V Wigan St Cath 67-75; R Wavertree H Trin 75-94; Chapl Blue Coat Sch Liv 75-94; Dir of Ords *Liv* 82-94; Hon Can Liv Cathl 87-02; Adn Liv 94-02; rtd 02; P-in-c Garston *Liv* from 04. *32 Storrsdale Road, Liverpool L18 7JY*   Tel 0151-724 3956 Fax 729 0587 E-mail bobmetcalf@ukgateway.net

METCALFE, Alan. b 22. St Aid Birkenhead 49. **d** 52 **p** 53. C Cleckheaton St Jo *Wakef* 52-55; C Todmorden 55-56; C Thornhill Lees 56-58; V Middlestown 58-60; V S Crosland 60-64; V Upwood w Gt and Lt Raveley *Ely* 64-69; Chapl RAF 64-68; V Wakef St Matt and St Jo *Wakef* 69-71; Warden Bridgehead Hostel Cardiff 71-73; Field View Hostel Stoke Prior 73-75; McIntyre Ho Nuneaton 75-79; C Southam w Stockton *Cov*

79-84; P-in-c Kinwarton w Gt Alne and Haselor 84-87; rtd 87; Hon C Yarcombe w Membury and Upottery *Ex* 89-92; Perm to Offic *St E* from 92. *3 Mays Court, Garrison Road, Felixstowe IP11 7ST*   Tel (01394) 271665

METCALFE, Bernard. See METCALFE, Canon William Bernard

METCALFE, Reginald Herbert. b 38. **d** 79. Hon C Aspley Guise *St Alb* 79; Hon C Aspley Guise w Husborne Crawley and Ridgmont 80-84; Hon C Bovingdon 84-03. *30 Manorville Road, Hemel Hempstead HP3 0AP*   Tel (01442) 242952   Fax 213137

METCALFE, Canon Ronald. BA. Edin Th Coll 67. **d** 69 **p** 70. C Saltburn-by-the-Sea *York* 69-72; P-in-c Crathorne 73-77; Youth Officer 73-77; Dioc Adult Tr Officer 78-88; Can Res York Minster 88-00; Sec for Miss and Min 88-00; V Kendal H Trin *Carl* 00-07; rtd 07. *50 Carlton Moor Crescent, Darlington DL1 4RF*   Tel (01325) 367219

METCALFE, Canon William Bernard. b 47. St Jo Coll Cam BA69 MA73 Ball Coll Ox BA71. Ripon Hall Ox 70. **d** 72 **p** 73. C Caversham *Ox* 72-75; C Aylesbury 75-79; Ind Chapl 75-79; TV Thamesmead *S'wark* 79-84; TR Totton *Win* 84-94; R Gt Bentley and Frating w Thorrington *Chelmsf* 94-10; V Gt Bentley from 10; RD St Osyth 99-07; Hon Can Chelmsf Cathl from 06. *The Rectory, Moors Close, Great Bentley, Colchester CO7 8QL*   Tel (01206) 250476 E-mail bernard.metcalfe@btinternet.com

METHUEN, Canon Charlotte Mary. b 64. Girton Coll Cam BA85 MA89 New Coll Edin BD91 PhD95. Edin Th Coll 87. **d** 98 **p** 99. C E Netherlands *Eur* 98-01; C Bonn w Cologne 01-03; Hon Asst Chapl 03-05; Dioc Dir of Tr 03-05; Hon C Offenbach (Old Catholic Ch) 05-07; Hon C Bottrop (Old Catholic Ch) from 08; Lect Ecclesiastical Hist Ox Univ 05-11; Dioc Can Th Glouc from 07; Lect Ripon Coll Cuddesdon 09-11; Lect Ch History Glas Univ from 11. *Theology and Religious Studies, 4 The Square, University of Glasgow, University Avenue, Glasgow G12 8QQ*   Tel 0141-330 2501 E-mail charlotte.methuen@glasgow.ac.uk

METHVEN, Alexander George. b 26. Lon Univ BD52 Em Coll Cam BA54 MA58. ACT ThL47 Lon Coll of Div 50. **d** 52 **p** 53. C Cambridge St Andr Less *Ely* 52-54; Chapl RAF 55-60; V Lower Sydenham St Mich *S'wark* 60-67; Australia from 68; rtd 91. *PO Box 494, Belgrave Vic 3160, Australia*   Tel (0061) (3) 9754 8056 E-mail agmethven@hotmail.com

METIVIER, Canon Robert John. b 31. Lon Univ BA68. Lambeth STh61 Ch Div Sch of the Pacific (USA) BD66 MDiv69 Codrington Coll Barbados 56. **d** 60 **p** 61. Trinidad and Tobago 61-64 and 68-78; USPG 66-67; C Gt Berkhamsted *St Alb* 78-82; V Goff's Oak St Jas 82-90; V Tokyngton St Mich *Lon* 90-01; Hon Can Trinidad from 98; rtd 01; Perm to Offic *Lon* from 02. *17 Willowcourt Avenue, Kenton, Harrow HA3 8ET*   Tel (020) 8909 1371

METRY, Sameh Farid. b 63. **d** 09 **p** 10. C W Ealing St Jo w St Jas *Lon* from 09. *9 Fermoy Road, Greenford UB6 9HX*   Tel and fax (020) 8575 0568   Mobile 07971-257287 E-mail smetry@msn.com

METTERS, Anthony John Francis. b 43. AKC65. **d** 68 **p** 69. C Heavitree *Ex* 68-74; V Plymouth Crownhill Ascension 74-79; RD Plymouth 77-79; Chapl RN 79-99; rtd 99. *Knightshayes, 1 De Port Heights, Corhampton, Southampton SO32 3DA*

METTERS, Mrs Henrietta Louise. b 83. Dur Univ BA05. NTMTC 08. **d** 10 **p** 11. C Onslow Square and S Kensington St Aug *Lon* from 10. *7 Broughton Road, London SW6 2LE*   Tel 07862-258706 (mobile) E-mail henriettametters@yahoo.co.uk

METZNER (née JEFFREY), Mrs Katrina. b 73. St Jo Coll Ox BA96 MA01. St Steph Ho Ox 97. **d** 99 **p** 00. C Glouc St Geo w Whaddon 99-00; C Parkstone St Pet and St Osmund w Branksea *Sarum* 00-04; Perm to Offic *S'wark* from 05. *All Saints' Vicarage, 84 Franciscan Road, London SW17 8DQ*   Tel (020) 8672 3706

METZNER, Simon David. b 64. Magd Coll Ox BA85 K Coll Lon MA95 St Luke's Coll Ex PGCE93. St Steph Ho Ox 88. **d** 90 **p** 01. C Branksome St Aldhelm *Sarum* 00-04; V Tooting All SS *S'wark* from 04. *All Saints' Vicarage, 84 Franciscan Road, London SW17 8DQ* E-mail simon.metzner@ntlworld.com

MEWIS, Canon David William. b 47. Leeds Inst of Educn CertEd68 Leeds Poly BA83. NOC 87. **d** 90 **p** 91. C Skipton Ch Ch *Bradf* 90-92; R Bolton by Bowland w Grindleton from 92; C Hurst Green and Mitton from 05; C Waddington from 05; RD Bowland 99-08; Hon Can Bradf Cathl from 00. *The Rectory, Sawley Road, Grindleton, Clitheroe BB7 4QS*   Tel (01200) 441154 E-mail david.mewis@bradford.anglican.org

MEWS, Stuart Paul. b 44. Leeds Univ BA64 MA67 Trin Hall Cam PhD74 FRHistS75. Westcott Ho Cam 86. **d** 87 **p** 88. Lect Lanc Univ 68-92; NSM Caton w Littledale *Blackb* 87-90; Hon C Lancaster St Mary 88-92; Reader RS Cheltenham and Glouc Coll of HE 92-00; Acting P-in-c Croxton and Eltisley *Ely* 97-98; P-in-c Tilbrook 00-07; P-in-c Keyston and Bythorn 00-07; P-in-c Catworth Magna 00-07; P-in-c Covington 00-07; P-in-c Grantchester from 07. *The Vicarage, 44 High Street, Grantchester, Cambridge CB3 9NF*   Tel (01223) 845664

MEYER, Jonathan Peter. b 55. Keble Coll Ox BA76 MA. SAOMC 03. **d** 05 **p** 06. NSM Kintbury w Avington *Ox* 05-08; NSM W Woodhay w Enborne, Hampstead Marshall etc 05-09; P-in-c Ewelme, Brightwell Baldwin, Cuxham w Easington from 09. *The Rectory, Ewelme, Wallingford OX10 6HP* Tel (01491) 837823 E-mail revdjonathan@btinternet.com

MEYER, William John. b 46. ACIB. Cranmer Hall Dur 83. **d** 85 **p** 86. C Merrow *Guildf* 85-89; V Grayshott 89-98; R Binfield *Ox* 98-11; rtd 11. *27A Oxford Drive, Bognor Regis PO21 5QU* E-mail bill.meyer@hotmail.com

MEYNELL, Canon Andrew Francis. b 43. Westcott Ho Cam 70. **d** 73 **p** 74. C Cowley St Jas *Ox* 73-79; TV 79-81; P-in-c Halton 81-95; V Wendover 81-95; P-in-c Monks Risborough 95-98; TV Risborough 98-08; Dir Ords Bucks Adnry 95-08; Hon Can Ch Ch 01-08; rtd 08; Perm to Offic *Ox* from 09. *Pettits House, The Green, Great Milton, Oxford OX44 7NT* Tel (01844) 277912 E-mail andrew.meynell@oxford.anglican.org

MEYNELL, Mrs Honor Mary. b 37. EMMTC 84. **d** 87 **p** 94. NSM Kirk Langley *Derby* 87-03; NSM Mackworth All SS 87-03; NSM Mugginton and Kedleston 87-03; rtd 04; Perm to Offic *Derby* from 04. *The Coachman's Cottage, Meynell Langley, Kirk Langley, Ashbourne DE6 4NT* Tel (01332) 824207

MEYNELL, Mark John Henrik. b 70. New Coll Ox MA93. Ridley Hall Cam MA97. **d** 97 **p** 98. C Fulwood *Sheff* 97-01; Dean Kampala Evang Sch of Th Uganda 01-05; C Langham Place All So *Lon* from 05. *2 St Paul's Court, 56 Manchester Street, London W1U 3AF* Tel (020) 7486 0006 Fax 7436 3019 E-mail mark.meynell@allsouls.org

✠**MEYRICK, The Rt Revd Cyril Jonathan.** b 52. St Jo Coll Ox BA73 MA77. Sarum & Wells Th Coll 74. **d** 76 **p** 77 **c** 11. C Bicester *Ox* 76-78; Bp's Dom Chapl 78-81; Tutor Codrington Coll Barbados 81-84; TV Burnham w Dropmore, Hitcham and Taplow *Ox* 84-90; TR Tisbury *Sarum* 90-98; Link Officer Black Angl Concerns 90-98; RD Chalke 97-98; Can Res Roch Cathl 98-05; Dean Ex 05-11; P-in-c Cen Ex 06-11; Suff Bp Lynn *Nor* from 11. *The Old Vicarage, Priory Road, Castle Acre, King's Lynn PE32 2AA* Tel (01760) 755553 Fax 755085 E-mail bishoplynn@norwich.anglican.org

MEYRICK, Thomas Henry George. b 67. Magd Coll Ox BA88 MA92 Leeds Univ PhD05. St Steph Ho Ox BA94. **d** 95 **p** 96. C Bierley *Bradf* 95-99; Chapl Oriel Coll Ox 99-04; P-in-c Ox St Thos w St Frideswide and Binsey 04-05; P-in-c Newbold de Verdun and Kirkby Mallory *Leic* 05-10; P-in-c Barlestone 09-10; R Newbold de Verdun, Barlestone and Kirkby Mallory from 10; AD Sparkenhoe W from 08. *The Rectory, 6 The Paddock, Newbold Verdon, Leicester LE9 9NW* Tel (01455) 824986 E-mail tom_meyrick@ekit.com

MIALL, Peter Brian. b 30. Scawsby Coll of Educn TCert69. **d** 89 **p** 89. Hon C Bolsterstone *Sheff* 89-98; Perm to Offic from 98. *Waldershaigh Cottage, Heads Lane, Bolsterstone, Sheffield S36 3ZH* Tel 0114-288 5558

MICHAEL, Canon Ian MacRae. b 40. Aber Univ MA62 Hertf Coll Ox DPhil66. Westcott Ho Cam 77. **d** 79 **p** 80. C Kings Heath *Birm* 79-82; Vice-Provost St Paul's Cathl Dundee 82-88; V Harborne St Faith and St Laur *Birm* 88-03; RD Edgbaston 91-98; Hon Can Birm Cathl 00-03; rtd 03; Perm to Offic *Birm* from 03 and *St And* from 04. *46 Argyle Court, St Andrews KY16 9BW* Tel (01334) 473901

MICHAEL, Stephen David. b 71. Ripon Coll Cuddesdon 01. **d** 03 **p** 04. C St Blazey *Truro* 03-07; C Tywardreath w Tregaminion 03-07; C Lanlivery w Luxulyan 03-07; P-in-c Treverbyn from 07; P-in-c Boscoppa from 07. *The Vicarage, Treverbyn Road, Stenalees, St Austell PL26 8TL* Tel (01726) 851923 E-mail sdm.554@gmail.com

MICHAELS, David Albert Emmanuel. b 49. Bede Coll Dur BA72 Barrister-at-Law (Inner Temple) 73. Westcott Ho Cam 86. **d** 88 **p** 89. C Hampstead St Jo *Lon* 88-91; TV Wolvercote w Summertown *Ox* 91-04; P-in-c Launceston *Truro* from 04. *The Rectory, Dunheved Road, Launceston PL15 9JE* Tel (01566) 772101 E-mail david.michaels@dunelm.org.uk

MICHELL, Canon Francis Richard Noel. b 42. St Cath Coll Cam BA64 MA68. Tyndale Hall Bris 64. **d** 66 **p** 67. C Northampton St Giles *Pet* 66-69; C Gateacre *Liv* 69-72; V Litherland St Paul Hatton Hill 72-79; V Rainhill 79-88; V Rainford 88-07; Hon Can Liv Cathl 06-07; rtd 07; Hon C Ludgvan, Marazion, St Hilary and Perranuthnoe *Truro* from 07. *The Rectory, St Hilary, Penzance TR20 9DQ* Tel (01736) 710229 E-mail noelmichell@uk7.net

MICHELL, Philip Leonard. b 69. Trin Coll Bris 08. **d** 10 **p** 11. C Brailsford w Shirley, Osmaston w Edlaston etc *Derby* from 10. *7 Sundial Close, Brailsford, Ashbourne DE6 3DP* Tel (01335) 360339 Mobile 07815-940409 E-mail phil.michell@live.co.uk

MICKLEFIELD, Andrew Mark. b 71. K Alfred's Coll Win BEd93. Ridley Hall Cam 04. **d** 06 **p** 07. C Alton *Win* 06-10; P-in-c Itchen Valley from 10. *Itchen Valley Rectory, Chillandham Lane, Itchen Abbas, Winchester SO21 1AS* Tel (01962) 779832 Mobile 07766-732735 E-mail itchenvalleyrectory@gmail.com

MICKLETHWAITE, Andrew Quentin. b 67. Univ Coll Dur BA89. Trin Coll Bris BA94. **d** 94 **p** 95. C Abington *Pet* 94-97; TV Duston 97-04; V Castle Donington and Lockington cum Hemington *Leic* from 04. *The Vicarage, 6 Delven Lane, Castle Donington, Derby DE74 2LJ* Tel (01332) 810364 E-mail revandrew@talk21.com

MICKLETHWAITE, Mrs Dorothy Eileen. b 41. SAOMC 98. **d** 01 **p** 02. NSM Astwell Gp *Pet* from 01; Asst Chapl O Radcliffe Hosps NHS Trust 02-09; Perm to Offic *Ox* 02-04 *54 Stuart Road, Brackley NN13 6HZ* Tel (01280) 703697 E-mail dorothy.mick@talktalk.net

MICKLETHWAITE, Jane Catherine. b 56. Lanc Univ BSc78 Trin Coll Bris 92. **d** 95 **p** 96. C Kings Heath *Pet* 95-98; Chap Nene Coll of HE Northn 97-98; Perm to Offic *Pet* 98-01; NSM Kings Heath 01-04; Perm to Offic *Leic* from 04. *The Vicarage, 6 Delven Lane, Castle Donington, Derby DE74 2LJ* Tel (01332) 810364 E-mail j.micklethwaite@talk21.com

MICKLETHWAITE, Peter William. b 62. Peterho Cam BA84 MA88. St Jo Coll Nottm 87. **d** 90 **p** 91. C Leatherhead *Guildf* 90-93; C Wisley w Pyrford 93-97; R Windlesham 97-09; Perm to Offic *Portsm* from 09. *Cloncaird, Durford Wood, Petersfield GU31 5AS*

MIDDLEBROOK, David John. b 61. Newc Univ BSc83 Cranfield Inst of Tech MSc85. Trin Coll Bris BA98. **d** 98 **p** 99. C Chorleywood Ch Ch *St Alb* 98-02; TV Hemel Hempstead 02-08; P-in-c Watford St Luke from 08; RD Watford from 09. *St Luke's Vicarage, Devereux Drive, Watford WD17 3DD* Tel (01923) 231205 E-mail dmiddlebrook@btinternet.com

MIDDLEDITCH, Terry Gordon. b 30. Univ of Wales (Lamp) BA62 St Martin's Coll Lanc PGCE68. St D Coll Lamp 59. **d** 62 **p** 64. C Poulton-le-Fylde *Blackb* 63-65; C-in-c Heysham 65-67 Sch Master 68-88; Hon C Cheltenham St Pet *Glouc* 75-87; Hor C Badgeworth w Shurdington 75-87; Hon C Up Hatherley 75-87; C Poulton-le-Sands w Morecambe St Laur *Blackb* 88-91 V Stalmine 91-00; rtd 00; Perm to Offic *Blackb* from 00 *93 Thornton Road, Morecambe LA4 5PG* Tel (01524) 413378 Mobile 07879-426173

MIDDLEMISS, Fritha Leonora. b 47. Man Univ BA68 CertEd69. Glouc Sch of Min 86. **d** 89 **p** 94. NSM Bengeworth *Worc* 89-94; NSM Stoulton w Drake's Broughton and Pirton etc 94-96; Chapl Malvern Girls' Coll 96-03; Asst Chapl HM Pris Long Lartin 13-08. *1 Ravensdowne, Berwick-upon-Tweed TD15 1HX* Tel (01289) 308553

MIDDLEMISS, Mrs Justine. b 68. Aston Univ BSc90. Ripor Coll Cuddesdon 00. **d** 02 **p** 03. C Lee St Marg *S'wark* 02-06 P-in-c Beddington 06; R from 06. *The Rectory, 18 Bloxworth Close, Wallington SM6 7NL* Tel (020) 8647 1973

MIDDLESEX, Archdeacon of. See WELCH, The Ven Stephan John

MIDDLETON, Alan Derek. b 46. St Jo Coll Dur BA68 MA85 Bris Univ PGCE70 Sheff Univ MMin00. Qu Coll Birm. **d** 72 **p** 73. C Cannock *Lich* 72-76; Warden St Helen's Youth & Community Cen Bp Auckd 76-79; V Darlington St Jo *Dur* 79-89; TR E Darlington 89-90; V Upper Norwood All SS *S'wark* 90-99; TR Warlingham w Chelsham and Farleigh from 99; Bp's Ecum Adv 96-11; AD Caterham 05-11; rtd 11. *Address temp unknown* E-mail alan.middleton@southwark.anglican.org

MIDDLETON, Arthur. See MIDDLETON, Canon Thomas Arthur

MIDDLETON, Barry Glen. b 41. Lich Th Coll 68. **d** 70 **p** 71. C Westhoughton *Man* 70-73; C Prestwich St Marg 73-74; TV Buxton w Burbage and King Sterndale *Derby* 74-77; Chapl Wore R Infirmary 77-83; Chapl Fairfield Hosp Hitchin 83-85; P-in-c Erpingham w Calthorpe *Nor* 85-86; R Erpingham w Calthorpe Ingworth, Aldborough etc 86-92; R Badingham w Bruisyard Cransford and Dennington *St E* 92-96; V Sidcup St Jo *Roch* 96-98; V Gt and Lt Bardfield w Gt and Lt Saling *Chelmsf* 98-00 rtd 00; Perm to Offic *St E* from 00. *20 Lynwood Avenue Felixstowe IP11 9HS* Tel (01394) 286506

MIDDLETON, David Jeremy. b 68. Ex Univ BSc90. Wycliff Hall Ox 01. **d** 03 **p** 04. C Ipswich St Jo *St E* 03-06; Hon C Wimbledon Park St Luke *S'wark* 06-09; C Fulwood *Shef* 09-11; C Heeley and Gleadless Valley from 11. *The Vicarage 5 Blackstock Close, Sheffield S14 1AE* Tel 0114-239 3808 E-mail djm.middleton@googlemail.com

MIDDLETON, Hugh Charles. b 50. Nottm Univ BTh77. Linc Tl Coll 73. **d** 77 **p** 78. C New Sleaford *Linc* 77-81; C Grantham 81 TV 81-83; R Caythorpe 83-95; P-in-c Bracebridge Heath 97-00 V from 00; P-in-c Bracebridge from 07. *The Vicarage, 1 Salisbury Drive, Bracebridge Heath, Lincoln LN4 2SW* Te (01522) 540460

MIDDLETON, Miss Jennifer Ann. b 82. St Jo Coll Dur BA03 St Jo Coll Nottm 06. **d** 08 **p** 09. C Fatfield *Dur* from 08. *80 Rowan Avenue, Washington NE38 9AF* Tel 0191-416 7405

MIDDLETON, Canon Michael John. b 40. Dur Univ BSc62 Fitzw Ho Cam BA66 MA70. Westcott Ho Cam 63. **d** 66 **p** 67. C Newc St Geo 66-69; V 77-85; Chapl St Geo Gr Sch Cape Town 69-72; Chapl K Sch Tynemouth 72-77; R Hexham *Newc* 85-92 Hon Can Newc Cathl 90-92; Adn Swindon *Bris* 92-97; Can and Treas Westmr Abbey 97-04; rtd 04. *37 High Fellside, Kendal LA9 4JG* Tel (01539) 729320

MIDDLETON, Rodney. b 54. St Andr Univ BD80. St Steph Ho Ox 80. **d** 82 **p** 83. C Walton St Mary *Liv* 82-87; C-in-c Kew St Fran CD 87-94; V Kew 94-95; Chapl Southport and Formby Distr Gen Hosp 87-95; V Haydock St Jas from 95. *The Vicarage, 169 Church Road, Haydock, St Helens WA11 0NJ* Tel (01942) 727956 E-mail rodmid169@yahoo.co.uk

MIDDLETON, Canon Thomas Arthur. b 36. Dur Univ MLitt95 FRHistS04. K Coll Lon AKC61 St Boniface Warminster 61. **d** 62 **p** 63. C Sunderland *Dur* 62-63; C Auckland St Helen 63-67; C Winlaton 67-70; C-in-c Pennywell St Thos and Grindon St Oswald CD 70-79; Chapl Grindon Hall Hosp 73-79; R Boldon 79-03; Adv in Stewardship Dur Adnry 87-92; Acting Prin St Chad's Coll Dur 97; Hon Fell from 07; Hon Can Dur Cathl 98-03; rtd 03. *1 St Mary's Drive, Sherburn Village, Durham DH6 1RL* Tel 0191-372 3436 E-mail thomas@thomas.middleton.wanadoo.co.uk

MIDDLETON, Suffragan Bishop of. See DAVIES, The Rt Revd Mark

MIDDLETON-DANSKY, Serge Wladimir. b 45. Cuddesdon Coll 74. **d** 77 **p** 78. C Wisbech SS Pet and Paul *Ely* 77-79; Lic to Offic Adnry Riviera *Eur* from 80; C Ox St Giles and SS Phil and Jas w St Marg 83-86; Perm to Offic *Ox* 86-88 and *Truro* 88-90; P-in-c Zennor and Towednack *Truro* 90-96; Perm to Offic 97-99; Lic to Offic from 99. *The Old Vicarage, Zennor, St Ives TR26 3BY* Tel (01736) 796955

MIDDLEWICK, Robert James. b 44. Lon Univ BD76 K Alfred's Coll Win CertEd67. Ripon Coll Cuddesdon 75. **d** 77 **p** 78. C Bromley SS Pet and Paul *Roch* 77-81; C Belvedere All SS 81-84; P-in-c Lamberhurst 85-88; P-in-c Matfield 85-88; V Lamberhurst and Matfield 88-99; rtd 09. *12 Mill Stream Place, Tonbridge TN9 1QJ* Tel (01732) 352480 E-mail middlewick@btinternet.com

MIDGLEY, George William. b 38. NOC. **d** 83 **p** 84. C Penistone and Thurlstone *Wakef* 88-89; TV 89-94; TR 94-04; rtd 04; Perm to Offic *Wakef* from 06. *20 Smithies Moor Lane, Batley WF17 9AR* Tel (01924) 472289

MIDGLEY, Stephen Nicholas. b 60. Jes Coll Cam BA83 MA86 Lon Hosp MB, BS86. Wycliffe Hall Ox. **d** 97 **p** 98. C Hove Bp Hannington Memorial Ch *Chich* 97-01; C Cambridge H Sepulchre *Ely* 01-04; P-in-c Cambridge St Andr Less 04-09; V from 09. *St Andrew the Less Vicarage, 21 Parsonage Street, Cambridge CB5 8DN* Tel (01223) 353794 *or* 362574 E-mail steve.midgley@stag.org

MIDLANE, Colin John. b 50. Qu Mary Coll Lon BA72. Westcott Ho Cam 73 Sarum & Wells Th Coll 77. **d** 78 **p** 79. C Bethnal Green St Pet w St Thos *Lon* 78-82; P-in-c Haggerston All SS 82-88; Chapl Hengrave Hall Ecum Cen 88-89; P Cllr St Botolph Aldgate *Lon* 89-94; C St Botolph Aldgate w H Trin Minories 93-94; TV Haywards Heath St Wilfrid *Chich* 94-97; C Brighton St Geo w St Anne and St Mark 97-01; Chapl Brighton and Sussex Univ Hosps NHS Trust 01-03; rtd 03; Perm to Offic *Lon* from 04. *30 Damien Court, Damien Street, London E1 2HL* Tel (020) 7791 0001

MIDWINTER, Sister Josie Isabel. b 46. Open Univ BA84 Univ of Wales (Lamp) MA98. CA Tr Coll IDC71. **d** 87 **p** 99. CA from 71; CMS 84-93; Uganda 85-91; Kenya 92-96; C Didcot All SS Ox 98-05; P-in-c Drayton St Pet (Berks) 05-10; rtd 06; Perm to Offic *Ox* from 10. *32 Barnes Close, Didcot OX11 8JN* Tel (01235) 759398 E-mail josie.midwinter@lineone.net

MIDWOOD, Canon Peter Stanley. b 47. CertEd69. Linc Th Coll 80. **d** 82 **p** 83. C Garforth *Ripon* 82-85; C-in-c Grinton w Arkengarthdale, Downholme and Marske 85-86; C-in-c Melbecks and Muker 85-86; V Swaledale 86-97; R Romaldkirk w Laithkirk 97-08; AD Richmond 97-08; R Walkingham Hill from 08; Hon Can Ripon Cathl from 05. *The Rectory, Main Street, Staveley, Knaresborough HG5 9LD* Tel (01423) 340275 E-mail ps.midwood@virgin.net

MIELL, David Keith. b 57. BSc PhD BA. Westcott Ho Cam 83. **d** 86 **p** 87. C Blackbird Leys CD *Ox* 86-89; C Walton Milton Keynes 89-90; TV 90-96; RD Milton Keynes 93-95; TR Upton cum Chalvey 96-05; AD Burnham and Slough 02-05; Perm to Offic 05-08; Perm to Offic *Sarum* 10-11; P-in-c Ringwood *Win* from 11. *The Vicarage, 65 Southampton Road, Ringwood BH24 1HE* Tel (01425) 473219 E-mail dkmiell@googlemail.com

MIER, Ms Catherine Elizabeth. b 60. Bris Univ BSc81 Chelsea Coll Lon MSc84 Dur Univ BA95. Cranmer Hall Dur 93. **d** 96 **p** 97. C Royston *St Alb* 96-00; C Bilton *Cov* 00-04; P-in-c Wellesbourne from 04; P-in-c Walton d'Eiville from 04; AD Fosse from 11. *The Vicarage, Church Street, Wellesbourne, Warwick CV35 9LS* Tel (01789) 840262 E-mail kate.mier@virgin.net

MIGHALL, Robert. b 33. St Pet Coll Ox BA57 MA61. Wycliffe Hall Ox 57. **d** 58 **p** 59. C Stoke Cov 58-62; C Rugby St Andr 62-64; V Newbold on Avon 64-76; V Combroke w Compton Verney 76-96; V Kineton 76-96; rtd 96; Perm to Offic *Glouc* from 97. *The Dairy House, Quarleston Farm, Clenston Road, Winterborne Stickland, Blandford Forum DT11 0NP* Tel (01258) 881467 E-mail randm@qvalley.tesco.net

MIHILL, Dennis George. b 31. St Alb Minl Tr Scheme 78. **d** 81 **p** 82. NSM Harpenden St Nic *St Alb* 81-86; C Sawbridgeworth 86-89; V Motspur Park *S'wark* 89-96; rtd 96; Perm to Offic *St Alb* 96-98 and 01-08; Hon C Biddenham 98-01; Perm to Offic *Roch* from 06. *7 Bourchier Close, Sevenoaks TN13 1PD* Tel (01732) 459760

MIKHAIL, Stella Frances. See JONES, Stella Frances

MILBANK, (née LEGG), Alison Grant. b 54. Girton Coll Cam BA78 MA81 PGCE79 Lanc Univ PhD88. EMMTC 05. **d** 06 **p** 07. NSM Lambley *S'well* 06-09; PV S'well Minster from 09. *Burgage Hill Cottage, Burgage, Southwell NG25 0EP* Tel (01636) 819224 E-mail alison.milbank@nottingham.ac.uk

MILBURN, John Frederick. b 56. Westmr Coll Ox BA84. Sarum & Wells Th Coll 84. **d** 86 **p** 87. C Leavesden *St Alb* 86-89; C Broxbourne w Wormley 89-93; CF (TA) 90-93; R Inglewood w Texas Australia 93-98; P-in-c Holland Park 98-04; R Bulimba from 04. *171 Oxford Street, PO Box 271, Bulimba Qld 4171, Australia* Tel (0061) (7) 3397 1508 Fax 3397 3253 Mobile 415-838239 E-mail johnmilburn@hotmail.com *or* anglicanbulimba@ozemail.com.au

MILES, Mrs Beverley Anne. b 54. **d** 09. NSM Findon Valley *Chich* from 09. *2 Maxwell Cottages, Findon Road, Findon, Worthing BN14 0RA* Tel (01903) 877191

MILES, Damian Stewart. b 76. Fitzw Coll Cam BTh02. Westcott Ho Cam 99. **d** 02 **p** 03. C Willingdon *Chich* 02-06; P-in-c Nork Guildf 06-11; P-in-c Thorpe from 11. *The Vicarage, Church Approach, Egham TW20 8TQ* Tel (01932) 565986 Mobile 07815-848735 E-mail damomiles@btinternet.com

MILES, Gerald Christopher Morgan. b 36. Peterho Cam BA57 MA72 Cranfield Inst of Tech MSc72 CEng MIET. Wycliffe Hall Ox 74. **d** 76 **p** 77. C Tunbridge Wells St Jas *Roch* 76-80; V Leigh 80-90; R Addington w Trottiscliffe 90-91; P-in-c Ryarsh w Birling 90-91; R Birling, Addington, Ryarsh and Trottiscliffe 91-00; Hon Chapl London and SE Region ATC from 96; rtd 00; Perm to Offic *Roch* from 00. *2 Spa Close, Hadlow, Tonbridge TN11 0JX* Tel and fax (01732) 852323 E-mail cmiles@supanet.com

MILES, (née HOARE), Ms Janet Francis Mary. b 48. St Aid Coll Dur BA70 Bris Univ MEd84. Sarum & Wells Th Coll 91. **d** 93 **p** 94. C Bruton and Distr *B & W* 93-98; P-in-c Llangarron w Llangrove, Whitchurch and Ganarew *Heref* 98-02; Dixton and Whitchurch w Ganarew 02-04; P-in-c Chewton Mendip w Ston Easton, Litton etc *B & W* 04-08; Dir Studies WEMTC 04-07; rtd 08. *1 Millier Road, Cleeve, Bristol BS49 4NL* Tel (01934) 830276 E-mail jfm2@btinternet.com

MILES, Malcolm Robert. b 36. AKC60. **d** 61 **p** 62. C Northampton St Mary *Pet* 61-63; C E Haddon 63-67; R Broughton 67-73; Asst Chapl Nottm Univ 73-74; V Northampton H Trin *Pet* 75-84; V Painswick w Sheepscombe *Glouc* 84-97; V Painswick w Sheepscombe and Cranham 97-01; RD Bisley 90-94; rtd 01; P-in-c Wensley and W Witton *Ripon* 01-05; Perm to Offic *York* from 06. *32 Turker Lane, Northallerton DL6 1PZ* Tel (01609) 773133 E-mail rachel@milesr.freeserve.co.uk

MILES, Marion Clare. b 41. S Dios Minl Tr Scheme 86. **d** 88 **p** 94. Hon Par Dn Blandford Forum and Langton Long *Sarum* 88-94; Hon C 94-01; Chapl Blandford Community Hosp from 88; NSM Winterborne Valley and Milton Abbas from 01. *153 Salisbury Road, Blandford Forum DT11 7SW* Tel (01258) 452010 E-mail marionclare07@yahoo.co.uk

MILES, Ms Patricia Ellen. b 56. RGN79. STETS 00. **d** 03 **p** 04. NSM Verwood *Sarum* from 03. *4 Firs Glen Road, Verwood BH31 6JB* Tel (01202) 824211 E-mail pe.miles@btinternet.com

MILES, Robert. See MILES, Malcolm Robert

MILES, Robert Anthony. b 71. Nottm Univ BSc92 PGCE94 All Nations Chr Coll BA01. Wycliffe Hall Ox MTh08. **d** 08 **p** 09. C Moulton *Pet* from 08. *8 Cubleigh Close, Moulton, Northampton NN3 7BG* Tel (01604) 491062 E-mail robmiles100@btinternet.com

MILES, Canon Robert William. b 27. Magd Coll Cam BA50 MA55. Westcott Ho Cam 50. **d** 52 **p** 53. C Bury St Mary *Man* 52-55; Bp's Dom Chapl *Chich* 55-58; Kenya 58-63; Provost Mombasa 58-63; R Dalmahoy *Edin* 65-70; R Batsford w Moreton-in-Marsh *Glouc* 70-77; rtd 77; Perm to Offic *Glouc* from 79. *Boilingwell, Winchcombe, Cheltenham GL54 5JB* Tel (01242) 603337

MILES, Miss Sharon Elizabeth Ann. b 66. Westcott Ho Cam 00. **d** 02 **p** 03. C Shrub End *Chelmsf* 02-05; P-in-c Rivenhall 05-10; P-in-c St Osyth from 10; Adv for Ordained Women's Min (Colchester Area) from 07. *The Vicarage, The Bury, St Osyth, Clacton-on-Sea CO16 8NX* Tel (01255) 822055 E-mail revdsmiles@hotmail.com

MILES, Stephen John. b 44. Monash Univ Aus BA66 Worc Coll Ox DipEd68 Univ Coll Lon MA75 California Univ PhD80. Melbourne Coll of Div BTheol86. **d** 87 **p** 88. Australia 87-97 and from 03; C E Malvern St Jo 87; C Clifton Hill St Andr 87-89; Chapl Co-ord and Angl Chapl Monash Medical Cen 89-97; Asst Chapl Bonn w Cologne *Eur* 97-00; Chapl 00-03; rtd 03. *24 Dorothea Crescent, Dromana Vic 3936, Australia*

MILFORD, Canon Catherine Helena. b 39. LMH Ox BA61 MA65 FRSA92. Gilmore Course 81. **dss** 82 **d** 87 **p** 94. Heaton St Barn *Bradf* 82-88; Par Dn 87-88; Adult Educn Adv *Win* 88-96; TR Barnham Broom *Nor* 96-00; P-in-c Reymerston w Cranworth, Letton, Southburgh etc 96-00; TR Barnham Broom and Upper Yare 00-04; Hon Can Nor Cathl 00-04; rtd 04; Perm to Offic *Bradf* from 05. *6 Leylands Grove, Bradford BD9 5QP*

MILFORD, Graham Alan. b 57. Trin Coll Bris 00. **d** 02 **p** 03. C Wolborough and Ogwell *Ex* 02-08; P-in-c Newburgh w Westhead *Liv* 08-10; V from 10. *The Vicarage, Back Lane, Newburgh, Wigan WN8 7XB* Tel (01257) 463267 E-mail grahammilford@btinternet.com

MILFORD, Mrs Nicola Claire. b 75. Univ Coll Ches BTh03. Trin Coll Bris 00 NOC 02. **d** 04 **p** 05. C Alphington, Shillingford St George and Ide *Ex* 04-08; Dioc Adv NSM *Liv* from 11. *The Vicarage, Back Lane, Newburgh, Wigan WN8 7XB* Tel (01257) 463267 E-mail milford.nicola@virgin.net

MILLER, Alan William. b 46. Toronto Univ MDiv. **d** 00 **p** 01. C Drumglass w Moygashel *Arm* 00-02; I Dromara w Garvaghy *D & D* 02-06; I Rathcoole *Conn* 06-11; rtd 11. *Address temp unknown* E-mail alan.millar3@btinternet.com

MILLAR, Alexander. *See* MILLAR, The Rt Revd John Alexander Kirkpatrick

MILLAR, Andrew Charles. b 48. Hull Univ BSc69. Cuddesdon Coll 71. **d** 73 **p** 74. C Rushmere *St E* 73-76; C Ipswich All Hallows 76-79; Dioc Youth Chapl *Sheff* 79-83; Youth Chapl *Win* 83-92; V Colden 92-08; V Twyford and Owslebury and Morestead etc 08-10; rtd 10. *22 Fford Bryn Estyn, Mold CH7 1TJ* E-mail acmillar@btinternet.com

MILLAR, Christine. *See* WHEELER, Mrs Christine

MILLAR, David Glassell. b 43. Dur Univ BSc64 St Cath Coll Cam BA66 MA71 Birkbeck Coll Lon BSc78 Leeds Univ MSc80. Cuddesdon Coll 86. **d** 68 **p** 69. C Pershore w Wick *Worc* 68-72; C Malden St Jas *S'wark* 72-73; V W Dean *Chich* 73-75; rtd 08. *5 Beacon Hill, London N7 9LY* Tel and fax (020) 7607 3809

MILLAR, Gary. b 67. St Mich Coll Llan 88. **d** 91 **p** 92. C Tonyrefail w Gilfach Goch *Llan* 91-93; C Barry All SS 93-95; TV Cowbridge 95-97; I Dromara w Garvaghy *D & D* 97-01; I Kilkeel 01-08; I Belfast St Paul w St Barn *Conn* from 08. *The Rectory, 50 Sunningdale Park, Belfast BT14 6RW* Tel (028) 9071 5413 Mobile 07817-968357 E-mail stpaulandbarnabas@btinternet.com

✠**MILLAR, The Rt Revd John Alexander Kirkpatrick (Sandy).** b 39. Trin Coll Cam BA62 MA66. St Jo Coll Dur 74. **d** 76 **p** 77 **c** 05. C Brompton H Trin w Onslow Square St Paul *Lon* 76-85; V 85-05; Hon C 05-11; Hon C Onslow Square and S Kensington St Aug from 11; P-in-c Tollington 03-10; AD Chelsea 89-94; Preb St Paul's Cathl from 97; Asst Bp Uganda from 05. *Fairlawn, 37 Alde Lane, Aldeburgh IP15 3DZ* Tel (01728) 452926

MILLAR, Mrs Julie Ann. b 65. Bris Poly BA87 Ex Univ BTh08 FCA09. SWMTC 02. **d** 05 **p** 06. NSM Penzance St Mary w St Paul and St Jo *Truro* 05-08; Asst Chapl R Cornwall Hosps Trust from 08; NSM St Agnes and Mount Hawke w Mithian *Truro* from 10. *6 Brunel Court, Truro TR1 3AE* Tel (01872) 274351 ext 214 E-mail julie.millar@truro.anglican.org

MILLAR, Sandra Doreen. b 57. Univ of Wales (Cardiff) BA79 Warwick Univ MA94 PhD99. Ripon Coll Cuddesdon 98. **d** 00 **p** 01. C Chipping Barnet w Arkley *St Alb* 00-03; TV Dorchester *Ox* 03-07; Dioc Children's Officer *Glouc* from 07. *18 Overbury Road, Gloucester GL1 4EA* Tel (01452) 382998 Mobile 07787-842674 E-mail revdocsand@aol.com

MILLARD, Canon Jane Mary. b 43. Open Univ BA80. Edin Dioc NSM Course 81. **d** 90 **p** 94. Chapl HIV/AIDS 90-94; NSM Edin St Mary 90-94; C 94-98; Can St Mary's Cathl 95-09; Vice Provost 98-09; rtd 09. *14 Grosvenor Crescent, Edinburgh EH12 5EL* Tel 0131-346 2469 Mobile 07712-898805 E-mail jmmillard@btinternet.com

MILLARD, Jonathan Neil. b 62. Aston Univ BSc83 Barrister-at-Law (Gray's Inn) 84. Wycliffe Hall Ox 89. **d** 92 **p** 93. C Haddenham w Cuddington, Kingsey etc *Ox* 92-94; R Washington Trin USA 94-00; R Church Stretton *Heref* 00-03; R Pittsburgh Ascension USA from 04. *4729 Ellsworth Avenue, Pittsburgh PA 15213-2888, USA* Tel (001) (412) 621 5378 Fax 621 5746 E-mail jonathan.millard@comcast.net

MILLARD, Malcolm Edoric. b 38. Lon Univ BA60 AKC60 Lon Inst of Educn PGCE61. St Jo Coll Nottm 80. **d** 77 **p** 81. Dn Banjul Cathl The Gambia 77-79; Dn Lamin St Andr 79-81; P-in-c 81-82; P-in-c Fajara St Paul 82-88; V Gen 86-88; P-in-c Farafenni Ch of African Martyrs 89-95; C S Shoebury *Chelmsf* 95-97; C Rainham w Wennington 97-02; P-in-c N Ockendon 02-08; Perm to Offic *Sarum* from 08. *29 Moorcombe Drive, Preston, Weymouth DT3 6NP* Tel (01305) 834060 E-mail weeksmary@gmail.com

MILLARD, Richard Stuart Marsh. b 33. St Pet Coll Ox BA57 MA. Oak Hill NSM Course 90. **d** 93 **p** 94. NSM Laleham *Lon* 93-94; NSM Neatishead, Barton Turf and Irstead *Nor* 94-95; NSM Ashmanhaugh, Barton Turf etc 95-99; rtd 99; Perm to Offic *Nor* from 99. *Semaphore Lodge, 30 Weybourne Road, Sheringham NR25 8HF*

MILLER, Adrian David. b 74. Open Univ BSc02. St Jo Coll Nottm MTh06. **d** 06 **p** 07. C Newton Flotman, Swainsthorpe, Tasburgh, etc *Nor* 06-09; TV from 09. *The Rectory, The Street Saxlingham Nethergate, Norwich NR15 1AJ* Tel (01508) 49831 Mobile 07871-085013 E-mail aidymiller@i12.com

MILLER, Andrew. *See* MILLER, Ronald Andrew Brian

MILLER, Andrew Philip. b 72. Liv Univ BSc94 PhD98. Cranmer Hall Dur 09. **d** 11. C Barnard Castle w Whorlton *Dur* from 11. *17 Mayfield, Barnard Castle DL12 8EA* Tel (01833) 63088 Mobile 07747-191989 E-mail a235miller@btinternet.com

MILLER, Anthony. *See* MILLER, Ronald Anthony

MILLER, Anthony Talbot. b 37. Univ of Wales (Lamp) BA59 Coll of Resurr Mirfield. **d** 61 **p** 62. C Panteg w Llanddewi Fach and Llandegfeth *Mon* 61-63; C Monmouth 63-65; V Holm Cultram St Mary *Carl* 65-76; Lic to Offic *Lich* 76-78; P-in-c Wrockwardine Wood 78-80; R 80-94; OCF 92-94; rtd 94. *Smallhythe, 26 Rosemary Lane, Whitchurch SY13 1EG* Tel (01948) 662120

MILLER, Barry. b 42. Bede Coll Dur TCert63 Open Univ BA7? Leic Univ MEd86. Linc Th Coll 63. **d** 65 **p** 66. C Greenside *Dur* 65-68; C Auckland St Andr and St Anne 68-71; Adv in Educn *Leic* 71-77; C Leic St Nic 77-80; Asst Chapl Leic Univ 77-8C Lect RS Leic Poly 77-80; Children's Officer Gen Syn Bd o Educn 80-84; Hd RS W Midl Coll of HE 84-89; Hd Initi Teacher Educn Wolv Poly 89-92; Wolv Univ 92-93; Hd Teache Educn Bradf Coll from 94; Perm to Offic *Bradf* from 07. *32 Na Lane, Shipley BD18 4HH* Tel (01274) 590630 E-mail b.miller@bradfordcollege.ac.uk

MILLER, Charles. *See* MILLER, Ernest Charles

MILLER, Charles Irvine. b 35. Nottm Univ BEd76. Bps' Co. Cheshunt 61. **d** 63 **p** 64. C Anlaby Common St Mark *York* 63-66 C Whitby 66-68; R Ingoldmells w Addlethorpe *Linc* 68-72 P-in-c Bishop Norton 72-76; V Scunthorpe St Jo 76-83; Chap Manor Hosp Walsall 83-89; rtd 89; Perm to Offic *Ely* 89-98 an from 99; P-in-c Isleham 98-99. *The Old Studio, 6 Chapel Street Duxford, Cambridge CB22 4RJ*

MILLER, Darren Noel. b 67. Birm Univ BSocSc89. Chich T Coll BTh95 Coll of Resurr Mirfield 94. **d** 95 **p** 96. C Weole Castle *Birm* 95-98; C Shard End 98-00; V Castle Vale St Cut 00-06; AD Sutton Coldfield 04-06; TR Cheam *S'wark* from 06 *The Rectory, 33 Mickleham Gardens, Cheam, Sutton SM3 8Q.* Tel (020) 8641 4664 Mobile 07747-858697 E-mail dnmiller@dandsmiller.me.uk

MILLER, Canon David George. b 54. Oriel Coll Ox BA76 MA8C Ripon Coll Cuddesdon 78. **d** 81 **p** 82. C Henfield v Shermanbury and Woodmancote *Chich* 81-84; C Monk Bretto *Wakef* 84-87; V Rastrick St Jo 87-93; TR Helston and Wendro *Truro* from 93; Chapl R Cornwall Hosps Trust 95-01; Chapl W of Cornwall Primary Care Trust 01-06; Hon Can Truro Cath from 06. *St Michael's Rectory, Church Lane, Helston TR13 8P* Tel (01326) 572516 E-mail millerourrectory@googlemail.com

MILLER, David James Tringham. b 45. AKC70. Sarum & Well Th Coll 76. **d** 77 **p** 78. C Abington *Pet* 77-80; TV Corby SS P and Andr w Gt and Lt Oakley 80-83; V Kettering All SS 83-94 RD Kettering 87-94; V Pet All SS 94-09; rtd 09; C Penrith v Newton Reigny and Plumpton Wall *Carl* 10-11. *27 Drover Terrace, Penrith CA11 9EN* Tel (01768) 840406 E-mail djtmiller@o2.co.uk

MILLER, David John. b 37. Louvain Univ Belgium Lic e Sciences Catéchétiques 68. Chich Th Coll 60. **d** 62 **p** 63. C Southsea H Spirit *Portsm* 62-65; C Roehampton H Trin *S'war* 67-68; Chapl Luxembourg *Eur* 68-72; Chapl Lausanne 72-9 Asst Chapl 91-93; P-in-c Gstaad 82-88; Chapl Le Rosey Sc. Switzerland 72-02; rtd 02; Perm to Offic *Eur* from 94. *63 avent de Savoie, 74500 Publier, France* Tel (0033) 4 50 26 89 41

MILLER, David Robert. b 47. Middx Univ BA98. ERMC 9 **d** 08 **p** 09. C Eaton Socon *St Alb* from 08. *32 Cornwall Cour Eaton Socon, St Neots PE19 8PR* Tel (01480) 471132 E-mail davidmiller@care4free.net

MILLER, Ernest Charles. b 56. Franklin & Marshall Coll (USA BA78 Univ of Michigan MA79 Keble Coll Ox DPhil90 Nashotah Ho MDiv82. **d** 82 **p** 83. C Dallas St Andr USA 82-84 Warden Ho of SS Greg and Macrina 84-90; Asst Chapl Kebl Coll Ox 84-88; P-in-c New Marston *Ox* 91-96; Ramsey Prof T Nashotah Ho Wisconsin USA 96-00; R New Yor Transfiguration 00-04; Adjunct Prof Ch Hist Gen Th Sem 02-0 TR Abingdon *Ox* from 06. *The Rectory, St Helen's Cour Abingdon OX14 5BS* Tel (01235) 532722 Mobile 07726-74392 E-mail echarlesmiller@yahoo.com

MILLER, Francis Rogers. b 54. Ex Univ BA86. St Steph Ho O 86. **d** 88 **p** 89. C Wednesfield *Lich* 88-93; P-in-c Caldmore 93-9 V 99-02; C Walsall St Mary and All SS Pleck etc 97-99; P-in 97-02; V Caldmore w Palfrey from 02; rtd 11. *12 Brooke Roa Braunston, Oakham LE15 8QR* E-mail rogermiller@live.co.uk

MILLER, Gareth. *See* MILLER, John Gareth

MILLER, Gary Russell. b 58. **d** 07 **p** 08. OLM Wythenshawe *Ma* from 07. *77 Mayfair Road, Manchester M22 9ZE* Tel 0161-43 8151 E-mail gary-miller@hotmail.co.uk

MILLER, The Ven Geoffrey Vincent. b 56. Dur Univ BEd78 Newc Univ MA94. St Jo Coll Nottm 81. **d** 83 **p** 84. C Jarrow *Dur* 83-86; TV Billingham St Aid 86-92; Dioc Urban Development Officer 91-97; Community Chapl Stockton-on-Tees 92-94; P-in-c Darlington St Cuth 94-96; V 96-99; Soc Resp Officer 97-99; Can Res Newc Cathl 99-05; Dioc Urban Officer 99-05; Adn Northd and Can Res Newc Cathl from 05. *80 Moorside North, Newcastle upon Tyne NE4 9DU* Tel 0191-273 8245 Fax 226 0286 E-mail g.miller@newcastle.anglican.org

MILLER, The Ven George Charles Alexander. b 20. TCD BA45. CITC Div Test 46. **d** 46 **p** 47. C Wexford w Rathaspeck *C & O* 46-49; Asst Chapl Miss to Seamen Belf 49; Chapl Miss to Seamen Immingham 49-51; Chapl Pernis Miss to Seamen *Eur* 51-55; I Billis w Ballyjamesduff *K, E & A* 55-57; I Knockbride w Shercock 57-65; I Urney w Denn and Derryheen 65-89; Preb Kilmore Cathl 77-87; Adn Kilmore 87-89; rtd 89. *Wavecrest, Blenacup, Cavan, Republic of Ireland* Tel (00353) (49) 436 1270

MILLER, Graham William. b 71. St Andr Univ BD94 Dur Univ MA98. Westcott Ho Cam 99. **d** 01 **p** 02. C Ex St Dav 01-03; C Sunderland St Mary and St Pet *Dur* 03-07; C Sunderland Pennywell St Thos 03-07; C Paddington St Jas *Lon* from 07. *61 Pembroke House, Hallfield Estate, London W2 6HQ* Tel (020) 7706 1248 E-mail grahamwmiller@aol.com

MILLER, The Rt Revd Harold Creeth. b 50. TCD BA73 MA78. St Jo Coll Nottm BA75. **d** 76 **p** 77 **c** 97. C Carrickfergus *Conn* 76-79; Dir Ext Studies St Jo Coll Nottm 79-84; Chapl QUB 84-89; I Carrigrohane Union *C, C & R* 89-97; Bp's Dom Chapl 91-97; Can Cork and Cloyne Cathls 94-96; Treas Cork Cathl 96-97; Can Cork Cathl 96-97; Preb Tymothan St Patr Cathl Dublin 96-97, Bp D & D from 97. *The See House, 32 Knockdene Park South, Belfast BT5 7AB* Tel (028) 9047 1973 *or* 9023 7602 Fax 9023 1902 E-mail bishop@down.anglican.org

MILLER (née BLUNDEN), Mrs Jacqueline Ann. b 63. Leic Univ BA86 SS Coll Cam BA90. Ridley Hall Cam 88. **d** 91. Par Dn Bedford St Paul *St Alb* 91-94; C 94-95; Perm to Offic *Lon* from 05. *39 Bounds Green Road, London N22 8HE* Tel (020) 8829 0450

MILLER, Canon John David. b 50. Nottm Univ BTh73 Lanc Univ CertEd74 Newc Univ MA93. Kelham Th Coll 68. **d** 74 **p** 75. C Horden *Dur* 74-79; C Billingham St Aid 79-80; TV 80-84; TR S Shields All SS 84-10; Hon Can Dur Cathl 04-10; rtd 10. *6 Tynedale Road, South Shields NE34 6EX* Tel 0191-455 6911

MILLER, John David. b 76. Ch Ch Ox BA98 MA07. Oak Hill Th Coll BA10. **d** 10 **p** 11. C Bath St Bart *B & W* from 10. *59 Longfellow Avenue, Bath BA2 4SH* Tel (01225) 444247 Mobile 07821-180901 E-mail johnmiller.jdm@gmail.com

MILLER, John Douglas. b 24. FCA60. NOC 74. **d** 77 **p** 78. C Prestbury *Ches* 77-80; V Ashton Hayes 80-87; rtd 87; Perm to Offic *Ex* 87-09. *35 Branscombe Close, Colyford, Colyton EX24 6RF* Tel (01297) 553581

MILLER, John Gareth. b 57. St Jo Coll Dur BA78. Ridley Hall Cam 79 Ven English Coll Rome 80. **d** 81 **p** 82. C Addiscombe St Mary *Cant* 81-84; TV Melbury *Sarum* 84-88; TR 88-91; V Leamington Priors All SS *Cov* 91-94. *Chelwood, Market Street, Charlbury, Chipping Norton OX7 3PL* Tel (01608) 811410 E-mail garethmiller@tiscali.co.uk

MILLER, John Selborne. b 32. RMN70. S'wark Ord Course 64. **d** 71 **p** 72. C Kenton *Lon* 71-74; C Fulham St Etheldreda w St Clem 74-78; Asst at Convent of the Epiphany Truro 79-80; Hon C Pimlico St Sav 80-84; C Shirley *Birm* 84-86; rtd 86; Perm to Offic *Nor* 86-01 and from 08. *28 Knight Street, Walsingham NR22 6DA* Tel (01328) 820824

MILLER (née BAILEY), Judith Elizabeth Anne. b 61. RGN RSCN84. Trin Coll Carmarthen 96. **d** 99 **p** 00. OLM Blyth Valley *St E* 99-07; OLM Bungay H Trin w St Mary from 11; OLM Wainford from 11. *Moonrakers, Back Road, Wenhaston, Halesworth IP19 9DY* Tel (01502) 478882 E-mail judym61@btinternet.com

MILLER, Kenneth Leslie. b 50. Lanc Univ BEd74 Liv Univ BPhil94 FRSA. NOC 78. **d** 80 **p** 81. NSM Formby St Pet *Liv* 80-87; NSM Anfield St Columba from 87; Chapl St Marg C of E High Sch Aigburth Liv from 86. *9 Hampton Road, Liverpool L37 6EJ* Tel (01704) 831256 E-mail jenke 82@hotmail.co.uk

MILLER, Kim Hurst. b 49. Ex Univ PhD89. Canberra Coll of Min BTh82. **d** 82 **p** 83. Australia 82-85 and from 89; C Goulburn Cathl 83-84; P-in-c Koorawatha 84-85; Perm to Offic *Ex* 85-89; R Wagga Wagga St Alb 89-98; Chapl Bathurst Gaol from 98. *3 Oates Place, Eglinton NSW 2795, Australia* Tel (0061) (2) 6337 1841 *or* 6338 3282 E-mail kkmiller@globalfreeway.com.au

MILLER, The Ven Luke Jonathan. b 66. SS Coll Cam BA87 MA91. St Steph Ho Ox BA90. **d** 91 **p** 92. C Oxhey St Matt *St Alb* 91-94; C Tottenham St Mary *Lon* 94-95; V 95-10; AD E Haringey 05-10; Adn Hampstead from 10; P-in-c Winchmore Hill H Trin from 11. *39 Bounds Green Road, London N22 8HE* Tel (020) 8829 0450 E-mail archdeacon.hampstead@london.anglican.org

MILLER, Martin Michael. b 55. St Jo Coll Dur BSc78. Trin Coll Bris 94. **d** 96 **p** 97. C Leamington Priors St Paul *Cov* 96-99; C Bermondsey St Anne and St Aug *S'wark* 99-05; R Newhaven

Chich from 05. *The Rectory, 36 Second Avenue, Newhaven BN9 9HN* Tel (01273) 515251 E-mail martinmrev@aol.com

MILLER, Michael Andrew. b 58. Ripon Coll Cuddesdon 03. **d** 05 **p** 06. C Hockerill *St Alb* 05-08; P-in-c Kensal Town St Thos w St Andr and St Phil *Lon* from 08. *St Thomas's Vicarage, 231 Kensal Road, London W10 5DB* Tel (020) 8960 3703 Mobile 07778-617482 E-mail mmiller363@tiscali.com

MILLER, Michael Daukes. b 46. Qu Coll Cam MA71 Lon Univ BCh70 MB71 MRCGP74. Glouc Th Course 82. **d** 85 **p** 94. NSM Lydney w Aylburton *Glouc* 85-95; NSM Lydney 95-06; Asst Chapl HM Pris Ex from 07; Perm to Offic *Ex* from 07. *HM Prison, 30 New North Road, Exeter EX4 4EX* Tel (01392) 415650 E-mail mmiller@btinternet.com

MILLER, Patrick Figgis. b 33. Ch Coll Cam BA56 MA60 Surrey Univ PhD95. Cuddesdon Coll 56. **d** 58 **p** 59. C Portsea St Cuth *Portsm* 58-61; C Cambridge Gt St Mary w St Mich *Ely* 61-63; Chapl SCM 61-63; Hd RS Man Gr Sch 63-69; Can Res and Lib S'wark Cathl 69-72; Dir of Soc Studies Qu Mary's Coll Basingstoke 72-79; Prin Sunbury Coll 79-80; Prin Esher Coll 81-98; Project Dir Learning for Living 00-05; Chapl London Flotilla from 00; Perm to Offic *Guildf* from 01. *9 Fairfax Avenue, Epsom KT17 2QN* Tel (020) 8394 0970 Mobile 07740-909414 E-mail patrickmiller@ntlworld.com

MILLER, Canon Paul. b 49. Oak Hill Th Coll 71. **d** 74 **p** 75. C Upton *Ex* 74-77; C Farnborough *Guildf* 77-78; P-in-c Torquay St Luke *Ex* 78-81; V 81-86; V Green Street Green *Roch* 86-94; V Green Street Green and Pratts Bottom 94-01; RD Orpington 96-01; V Shortlands from 01; Hon Can Roch Cathl from 00; AD Beckenham from 09; Chapl to The Queen from 05. *The Vicarage, 37 Kingswood Road, Bromley BR2 0HG* Tel (020) 8460 4989 *or* 8460 5682 Fax 8289 7577 Mobile 07940-582040 E-mail canonpmiller@aol.com

MILLER, Paul Richard. b 37. K Coll Lon BSc60 AKC60. Linc Th Coll 60. **d** 62 **p** 63. C Sheff St Geo 62-65; C Bottesford *Linc* 65-67; Bp's Youth Chapl 67-69; C Corringham 67-69; Dioc Youth Officer *Ripon* 69-74; Sec Nat Coun for Voluntary Youth Services 74-79; Hd Youth Nat Coun of Soc Services 74-79; P-in-c Battlesden and Pottesgrove *St Alb* 79-80; P-in-c Eversholt w Milton Bryan 79-80; P-in-c Woburn 79-80; V Woburn w Eversholt, Milton Bryan, Battlesden etc 80-98; rtd 98; Perm to Offic *Heref* from 98 and *Lich* from 03. *6 Elms Paddock, Little Stretton, Church Stretton SY6 6RD* Tel (01694) 724596 E-mail paulmiller@macunlimited.net

MILLER, Canon Philip Harry. b 58. Leeds Univ BA79. Chich Th Coll 80. **d** 82 **p** 83. C Reddish *Man* 82-86; R Lower Broughton Ascension 86-94; P-in-c Cheetwood St Alb 91-94; P-in-c Langley and Parkfield 95-00; TR 00-10; V Langley from 10; AD Heywood and Middleton from 10; Hon Can Man Cathl from 07. *The Rectory, Wood Street, Middleton, Manchester M24 5GL* Tel 0161-643 5013

MILLER, Philip Howard. b 40. Tyndale Hall Bris 67. **d** 72 **p** 73. Argentina 72-73; C Rusholme H Trin *Man* 73-74; SAMS Paraguay 74-77; C Toxteth St Cypr w Ch Ch *Liv* 78-80; V Burscough Bridge 80-85; V Woodbridge St Jo *St E* 85-91; P-in-c Combs 91-92 and 93-96; Chapl Burrswood Chr Cen 92-93; V Yoxford and Peasenhall w Sibton *St E* 96-01; rtd 01; Perm to Offic *St E* from 01. *Salta, 54 Orchard Close, Melton, Woodbridge IP12 1LD* Tel (01394) 388615 E-mail phm914@lineone.net

MILLER, Richard Bracebridge. b 45. Wycliffe Hall Ox 68. **d** 70 **p** 71. C Lee Gd Shep w St Pet *S'wark* 70-74; C Roehampton H Trin 74-77; C Earley St Pet *Ox* 77-80; V Aldermaston w Wasing and Brimpton 80-96; C Newbury 96-01; Perm to Offic from 03. *14 Burcot Park, Burcot, Abingdon OX14 3DH* Tel (01865) 407521 E-mail rbmoxford@breathe.com

MILLER, Robert Stephen. b 71. QUB BSc92. CITC BTh95. **d** 95 **p** 96. C Lurgan Ch the Redeemer *D & D* 95-99; I Tullylish 99-03; I Maghera w Killelagh *D & R* 03-10; I Londonderry Ch Ch, Culmore, Muff and Belmont from 10. *The Rectory, 1B Heathfield, Londonderry BT48 8JD* Tel (028) 7135 2396 *or* 7127 1803 Mobile 07711-748406 E-mail robsmiller@btinternet.com

MILLER, Ronald Andrew John. b 46. **d** 96 **p** 97. OLM Heywood *Man* 96-09. *16 Bryn Morfa, Bodelwyddan, Rhyl LL18 5TP* Tel (01745) 530055 E-mail andrew.miller1@virgin.net

MILLER, Ronald Anthony. b 41. CEng CPA MRAeS City Univ BSc63. S'wark Ord Course 69. **d** 72 **p** 80. NSM Crookham *Guildf* 72-73 and 80-85; NSM New Haw 85-95; NSM Effingham w Lt Bookham 95-04; Perm to Offic 05-09; NSM Nork 09-11; rtd 11. *Glen Anton, Horsley Road, Downside, Cobham KT11 3JZ* Tel and fax (01932) 863394 Mobile 07710-294786

MILLER, Rosamund Joy. See SEAL, Mrs Rosamund Joy

MILLER, Mrs Rosslyn Leslie. b 43. St Andr Univ MA65 Ox Univ DipEd66. **dss** 72 **d** 87. Dir of Studies Inst of Chr Studies 72; St Marylebone All SS *Lon* 72; Adult Educn Officer 73-78; Alford w Rigsby *Linc* 86-87; C 87-90; Dioc Dir of Readers 90-03; rtd 03. *59 Malham Drive, Lincoln LN6 0XD* Tel (01522) 831294 E-mail rosslyn.miller@ntlworld.com

MILLER, Roy. b 29. **d** 88 **p** 93. NSM Leic Cathl 88-91; NSM Leic H Apostles 91-97; Perm to Offic 97-99. *5 Bratmyr, Fleckney, Leicester LE8 8BJ* Tel 0116-240 2004

MILLER, Miss Sarah Lydia. b 65. St Andr Univ BD90 Hughes Hall Cam PGCE91. EAMTC 98. d 01 p 02. NSM Nor St Pet Mancroft w St Jo Maddermarket 01-03; C Wythenshawe *Man* 03-07; C Tewkesbury w Walton Cardiff and Twyning *Glouc* from 07; V Newbiggin Hall *Newc* from 11. *St Wilfrid's House, Trevelyan Drive, Newcastle upon Tyne NE5 4DA* Tel 0191-271 4005 E-mail revsarah1@tiscali.co.uk

MILLER, Stephen Michael. b 63. NE Lon Poly BSc86 Nottm Univ BTh91. Linc Th Coll 88. d 91 p 92. C Dudley St Fran *Worc* 91-94; V Sedgley St Mary 94-99; Miss to Seafarers from 99; Chapl Rotterdam w Schiedam Miss to Seafarers *Eur* 99-02; Chapl Dubai and UAE 02-11; Sen Chapl Hong Kong from 11. *The Mission to Seafarers, 11 Middle Road, Kowloon, Hong Kong, China* Tel (00852) 2368 8261 Fax 2366 0928 E-mail seamenhk@biznetvigator.com

MILLER, Stuart William. b 71. Univ of Wales (Cardiff) BA92. Trin Coll Bris BA97. d 97 p 98. C Fordingbridge *Win* 97-98; C Bursledon 98-02; V W Moors *Sarum* 02-05; Chapl Bournemouth and Poole Coll of FE *Win* 05-10; C Bournemouth Town Cen 05-10; V Moordown from 10. *St Birinus House, 31 Lonsdale Road, Bournemouth BH3 7LY* Tel (01202) 520920 E-mail millersw@bpc.ac.uk

MILLER, William David. b 45. Man Univ BA66. Linc Th Coll 69. d 71 p 72. C Newc St Geo 71-74; C Corbridge w Halton 74-77; C N Gosforth 77-81; TV Whorlton 81-90; Chapl K Sch Tynemouth 90-09; rtd 09. *7 Strawberry Terrace, Hazlerigg, Newcastle upon Tyne NE13 7AR* Tel 0191-236 5024

MILLETT, Maxwell Roy. b 45. Clare Coll Cam BA67. S Dios Minl Tr Scheme 92. d 95 p 96. NSM Southsea St Pet *Portsm* 95-03; Perm to Offic from 03. *70 Waverley Road, Southsea PO5 2PR* Tel (023) 9281 7216 E-mail max.millett@ntlworld.com

MILLGATE, Victor Frederick. b 44. St Mich Coll Llan 81. d 83 p 84. C Pembroke St Mary w St Mich *St D* 83-85; V Manorbier and St Florence w Redberth 85-04; TR Carew 04-09; AD Castlemartin 03-09; rtd 09. *3 George Drive, Pembroke SA71 5QB* Tel (01646) 621683 E-mail esmillgate@yahoo.co.uk

MILLICHAMP, Mrs Penelope Mary. b 39. CertEd60. WMMTC 82. dss 85 d 87 p 94. Wednesfield *Lich* 85-94; Par Dn 87-90; TD 90-94; Perm to Offic 94-95; NSM Wrockwardine Deanery 95-99; rtd 99; Perm to Offic *Lich* 99-00 and from 06. *18 Nursery Walk, Tettenhall, Wolverhampton WV6 8QY* Tel (01902) 741996 Mobile 07971-421562 E-mail penny@millichamp.com

MILLIER, Gordon. b 28. St Aid Birkenhead 63. d 65 p 66. C Congresbury *B & W* 65-69; P-in-c Badgworth w Biddisham 69-76; R Weare w Badgworth and Biddisham 76-84; R Pilton w Croscombe, N Wootton and Dinder 84-93; rtd 93; Perm to Offic *Ex* from 93. *28 Withy Close, Canal Hill, Tiverton EX16 4HZ* Tel (01884) 253128

MILLIGAN, Peter John. b 52. d 01 p 02. NSM Putney St Marg *S'wark* 01-06; NSM Angell Town St Jo from 06. *39 Stapleton Road, London SW17 8BA* Tel (020) 8767 3497

MILLIGAN, Canon William John (Barney). b 28. OBE95. Em Coll Cam BA49. Cuddesdon Coll 53. d 55 p 56. C Portsea N End St Mark *Portsm* 55-62; V New Eltham All SS *S'wark* 62-71; V Roehampton H Trin 71-79; Can Res St Alb 79-86; Chapl Strasbourg *Eur* 86-95; Angl Rep Eur Insts 90-95; rtd 95; Perm to Offic *S'wark* 95-00 and *Sarum* from 00. *3 East Street, Beaminster DT8 3DS* Tel (01308) 862806

MILLING, David Horace. b 29. Oriel Coll Ox BA51 MA54 Cam Univ PhD73. Cuddesdon Coll 54. d 56 p 57. C Bris St Mary Redcliffe w Temple 56-59; C Fishponds St Jo 59-62; India 62-69; Lect St D Coll Lamp 73-75; C Caversham *Ox* 77-81; C Mapledurham 77-81; C Caversham St Andr 81-86; TV Upper Kennet *Sarum* 86-88; rtd 88; Perm to Offic *Glouc* 90-99 and *Ex* 00-09. *16 Loram Way, Exeter EX2 8GG* Tel (01392) 436261

MILLINGTON, Stuart. b 45. Lich Th Coll 67. d 70 p 71. C Boulton *Derby* 70-73; C Moseley St Mary *Birm* 73-76; TV Staveley and Barrow Hill *Derby* 76-82; R Wingerworth 82-99; RD Chesterfield 91-97; P-in-c Elton All SS *Man* 99-09; P-in-c Woolfold 07-09; V Kirklees Valley 09-10; AD Bury 05-10; rtd 10; Perm to Offic *Man* from 10. *33 Westways, Wrenthorpe, Wakefield WF2 0TE* Tel (01924) 375996 E-mail stuart@revmillington.wanadoo.co.uk

MILLS, Alan Francis. b 29. Ch Coll Cam BA52 MA91. Linc Th Coll 52. d 54 p 55. C Hucknall Torkard *S'well* 54-58; C Bath Bathwick St Jo *B & W* 58-70; V Drayton 70-76; V Muchelney 70-76; V Alcombe 76-99; rtd 99; Perm to Offic *B & W* from 00. *194 Locking Road, Weston-super-Mare BS23 3LU* Tel (01934) 622679

MILLS, Alexandra. b 56. Univ of Wales (Abth) BMus78 CertEd79. Ripon Coll Cuddesdon 88. d 90 p 94. Par Dn Earlsfield St Andr *S'wark* 90-94; C Kingston All SS w St Jo 94-99; C Brixton Road Ch Ch 99-00; Perm to Offic from 05. *121A Transmere Road, London SW18 3QP* Tel (020) 8944 1641 Mobile 07900-543068

MILLS, Anne. *See* MILLS, Mrs Leslie Anne

MILLS, Anthony James. b 55. Nottm Univ BA. Linc Th Coll. d 84 p 85. C Mexborough *Sheff* 84-86; C Howden *York* 86-89; V

Fylingdales and Hawsker cum Stainsacre 89-95; V Scarborough St Sav w All SS 95-09; P-in-c Scarborough St Martin 02-05; V 05-09; R Failsworth H Family *Man* from 09. *The Rectory, 190 Lord Lane, Failsworth, Manchester M35 0QS* Tel and fax 0161-681 3644 E-mail tony.mills@talktalk.net

MILLS, David Francis. b 51. Oak Hill Th Coll 76. d 79 p 80. C Rodbourne Cheney *Bris* 79-82; C Wolverhampton St Matt *Lich* 82-85; CF 85-88; TV Braunstone *Leic* 88-95; Past Asst to Adn Leic 95-97; C Barkestone w Plungar, Redmile and Stathern 97-99; C Bottesford and Muston 97-99; C Harby, Long Clawson and Hose 97-99; C Vale of Belvoir 00-02; R Winfarthing w Shelfanger w Burston w Gissing etc *Nor* from 02. *The Rectory, Church Lane, Winfarthing, Diss IP22 2EA* Tel (01379) 643646 E-mail revdfmills1812@gmail.com

MILLS, David Graham Mackenzie. *See* MACKENZIE MILLS, David Graham

MILLS (née SHAW), Mrs Elaine Rosemary. b 42. SRN63. d 07 p 08. OLM Bris Lockleaze St Mary Magd w St Fran from 07. *15 Blake Road, Bristol BS7 9UJ* E-mail elaine.mills@lycos.co.uk

MILLS, Canon Geoffrey Charles Malcolm. b 33. Wycliffe Hall Ox 59. d 61 p 62. C Buckhurst Hill *Chelmsf* 61-65; C Ecclesall *Sheff* 65-69; V Endcliffe 69-78; R Whiston 79-99; Hon Can Sheff Cathl 96-99; rtd 99; Perm to Offic *Sheff* from 99. *8 Hall Road, Rotherham S60 2BP* Tel (01709) 373863

MILLS, Miss Glenys Christine. b 38. Open Univ BA81. Dalton Ho Bris 64. d 87 p 94. Par Dn Clifton Ch Ch w Em *Bris* 87-94; C 94-95; P-in-c Gt w Lt Abington *Ely* 95-00; Chapl Arthur Rank Hospice Cam 95-00; Perm to Offic *Bris* from 00. *14 St Bartholomew's Road, Bristol BS7 9BJ* Tel 0117-909 8859

MILLS, Gordon Derek. b 35. Lich Th Coll 60. d 63 p 64. C W Derby St Mary *Liv* 63-65; C Clifton w Glapton *S'well* 65-67; V N Wilford St Faith 67-72; V Farnsfield 72-82; P-in-c Kirklington w Hockerton 77-82; P-in-c Brindle and Asst Dir of Educn *Blackb* 82-86; V Gt Budworth *Ches* 86-88; P-in-c Antrobus 87-88; V Gt Budworth and Antrobus 88-92; V Gt Budworth 92-00; rtd 00 Perm to Offic *Blackb* 01-04; *York* and *Bradf* from 04; *Dur* from 06. *Holmelands House, Raby Lane, East Cowton, Northallerton DL7 0BW* Tel (01325) 378798

MILLS, Canon Hubert Cecil. b 44. TCD BA66 MA71 HDipEd73. CITC 67. d 67 p 68. C Dublin Rathfarnham *D & G* 67-72; C Dublin St Steph and St Ann 72-77; I Holmpatrick w Balbriggan and Kenure 77-86; I Killiney H Trin 86-11; Min Can St Patr Cathl Dublin 69-92; Succ 77-92; Preb Rathmichael St Patr Cathl Dublin 92-01; Treas from 01; rtd 11. *Address temp unknown*

MILLS, Ian Anderson. b 35. Coll of Resurr Mirfield 60 K Coll Lon AKC65. d 65 p 70. C S'wark St Alphege 65-67; C Hartlepool St Paul *Dur* 69-72; NSM Hartlepool St Hilda 90-95; Perm to Offic from 95. *7 Claypool Farm Close, Hutton Henry, Hartlepool TS27 4QZ* Tel (01429) 836204

MILLS, Jack Herbert. b 14. Selw Coll Cam BA38 MA42 Cuddesdon Coll 39. d 40 p 41. C Camberwell St Geo *S'wark* 40-42; C Southfields St Barn 42-46; USPG 46-47; Chapl Hurstpierpoint Coll 47-52; Chapl K Coll Auckland New Zealand 52-56; Asst Chapl St Pet Colleg Sch Adelaide 57-59 Chapl St Paul's Colleg Sch Hamilton New Zealand 59-61; Chapl Guildford Gr Sch Perth Australia 62-66; Hd Master Carpentaria Coll Darwin 66-73; Hd Master St Wilfrid's Sch Ex 74-79; Chapl Community of St Wilfrid 74-79; Hon C Ewhurst *Chich* 79-81 Hon C Bodiam 79-81; Perm to Offic *Ex* 81-85 and *Chich* 85-87 rtd 87; New Zealand from 87. *14/28 Maranui Avenue, Point Chevalier 1002, Auckland, New Zealand* Tel (0064) (9) 849 2243

MILLS, Jennifer Clare. *See* TOMLINSON, Mrs Jennifer Clare

MILLS, John Kettlewell. b 53. BA. Cranmer Hall Dur. d 84 p 85 C Ashton-upon-Mersey St Mary Magd *Ches* 84-87; TV Didsbury St Jas and Em *Man* 87-98; V Styvechale *Cov* from 98 *Styvechale Vicarage, 16 Armorial Road, Coventry CV3 6GJ* Tel (024) 7641 6074 or 7669 2299 E-mail jkm@stivichall.freeserve.co.uk

MILLS, Mrs Leslie Anne. b 44. K Alfred's Coll Win CertEd65 SWMTC 99. d 02 p 03. NSM Kilmington, Stockland, Dalwood Yarcombe etc *Ex* from 02. *Gorse Bungalow, Cotleigh, Honiton EX14 9JB* Tel (01404) 861430 E-mail revannemills@googlemail.com

MILLS, Michael Henry. b 51. AKC73. St Aug Coll Cant. d 74 p 75. C Newton Aycliffe *Dur* 74-78; C Padgate *Liv* 78-79; TV 79-95; V Frodsham *Ches* from 95. *The Vicarage, Vicarage Lane Frodsham, Warrington WA6 7DU* Tel (01928) 733378 E-mail mikehmills@mac.com

MILLS, Michael John. b 52. St Andr Univ BSc75 Cam Univ PGCE76. Cranmer Hall Dur 97. d 99 p 00. C Brockmoor *Worc* 99-03; P-in-c St Leonards St Ethelburga *Chich* 04-09; P-in-c St Leonards St Leon 04-09; R St Leonards St Ethelburga and St Leon from 09. *The Rectory, 81A Filsham Road, St Leonards on-Sea TN38 0PE* Tel (01424) 422199 Mobile 07789-913013 E-mail michael_mills@talktalk.net

MILLS, Pamela Ann. b 44. Southn Univ DAES82. S Tr Scheme 94. d 97 p 98. NSM Hurstbourne Tarrant, Faccombe, Vernham

Dean etc *Win* 97-11; rtd 11. *Sunnyside, The Dene, Hurstbourne Tarrant, Andover SP11 0AS* Tel (01264) 736286

MILLS, Peter James. b 32. Univ Coll Lon LLB58. **d** 99 **p** 00. NSM Woodchurch *Ches* 99-03; rtd 03; Perm to Offic *Ches* from 03. *6 West Heath Court, Gerard Road, West Kirby, Wirral CH48 4ES* Tel 0151-625 4459 Mobile 07989-374499 E-mail pjmills@uwclub.net

MILLS, Peter John. b 52. Sarum & Wells Th Coll 87. **d** 89 **p** 90. C Chatham St Wm *Roch* 89-92; V Perry Street 92-95; V E Malling 95-00; CF from 00. *c/o MOD Chaplains (Army)* Tel (01264) 381140 Fax 381824

MILLS, Philippa Jane. b 63. STETS. **d** 09 **p** 10. NSM Hook w Warsash *Portsm* from 09. *Lower Lapstone, Botley Road, Fair Oak, Eastleigh SO50 7AN*

MILLS, Roger Conrad. b 58. Selw Coll Cam BA79 MA83. St Jo Coll Nottm 83. **d** 85 **p** 86. C Jesmond H Trin *Newc* 85-88; C Alnwick 88-91; Chapl Newc Univ 91-00; P-in-c Newc St Barn and St Jude 95-97; V Kingston Park from 00. *12 Shannon Court, Newcastle upon Tyne NE3 2XF* Tel and fax 0191-286 4050 E-mail rogermills123@yahoo.co.uk

MILLS, Timothy John. b 57. Wye Coll Lon BSc79. Trin Coll Bris 01. **d** 03 **p** 04. C Chislehurst Ch Ch *Roch* 03-07; V Ticehurst and Flimwell *Chich* from 07. *The Vicarage, Church Street, Ticehurst, Wadhurst TN5 7AB* Tel (01580) 200316 Mobile 07786-540819 E-mail tim.mills60@tinternet.com

MILLS-POWELL, Mark Oliver McLay. b 55. Edinburg Th Sem Virginia. **d** 83 **p** 84. C Huyton St Mich *Liv* 83-86; USA 86-95; P-in-c Basildon w Aldworth and Ashampstead *Ox* 95-02; TR Linton *Ely* 02-08; Warden Guild of St Jo and St Mary Magd from 08. *102 Warren Close, Cambridge CB2 1LE* Tel (01223) 314294

MILLSON, Brian Douglas. b 53. Univ of W Ontario BA76 Huron Coll MDiv84. Westcott Ho Cam 82. **d** 83 **p** 84. C Walton-on-Thames *Guildf* 83-86; Canada 86-98; R Par of the Six Nations 86-89; Canadian Forces Chapl 89-98; CF from 98. *c/o MOD Chaplains (Army)* Tel (01264) 381140 Fax 381824 E-mail brian.millson@btinternet.com

MILLSON, Mrs Margaret Lily. b 41. CertEd61. EMMTC 83. **dss** 86 **d** 87 **p** 94. NSM Bottesford w Ashby *Linc* 86-87; P-in-c St Tudy w St Mabyn and Michaelstow *Truro* 01-10; rtd 10. *Winterbourne, 2 Gwelmeneth Park, St Cleer, Liskeard PL14 5HU* Tel (01579) 346338 E-mail mlmillson@aol.com

MILLWOOD, Stephen Grant. b 44. Sheff City Coll of Educn CertEd77 Open Univ BA92. St Jo Coll Nottm 92. **d** 94 **p** 95. C Anston *Sheff* 94-98; V Kimberworth Park 98-09; Bp's Urban Adv 05-09; rtd 09. *6 Quarryfield Drive, Sheffield S9 5AG* Tel 0114-243 4948 E-mail steveandjanetm@mac.com

✠**MILNE, The Rt Revd Douglas.** b 21. CBE83. St Pet Hall Ox BA46 MA46. Clifton Th Coll 47. **d** 47 **p** 48 **c** 73. C Ilfracombe SS Phil and Jas *Ex* 47-50; C Slough *Ox* 50-53; Chile 54-69; Adn N Chile, Bolivia and Peru 63-69; Hon Can Chile from 69; Area Sec SAMS 69-72; Bp Paraguay 73-85; rtd 86. *1C Clive Court, 24 Grand Parade, Eastbourne BN21 3DD* Tel (01323) 734159

MILMINE, Canon Neil Edward Douglas. b 46. Kent Univ BSc70. Wycliffe Hall Ox 80. **d** 82 **p** 83. C Hailsham *Chich* 82-86; C Horsham 86; TV 86-93; V Patcham 93-11; Can and Preb Chich Cathl 00-11; RD Brighton 02-09; rtd 11. *8 The Willows, Barcombe, Lewes BN8 5FJ* Tel and fax (01273) 401521 E-mail n.milmine@yahoo.co.uk

MILNE, Alan. b 54. RMN SRN TCert. Cranmer Hall Dur 89. **d** 91 **p** 92. C Hartlepool St Luke *Dur* 91-94; P-in-c Dalton le Dale 94-00; V 00-05; P-in-c Hawthorn 94-00; R 00-05; R Hawthorn and Murton from 05; AD Easington from 03. *The Vicarage, Church Lane, Murton, Seaham SR7 9RD* Tel 0191-526 2410

MILNE, Miss Christine Helen. b 48. LTCL71. S'wark Ord Course 83. **dss** 86 **d** 87 **p** 90. S Lambeth St Steph *S'wark* 86-91; Par Dn 87-89; New Zealand from 89. *NGA Tawa School, Private Bag 1101, Marton 4741, New Zealand* Tel (0064) (6) 355 4566 Fax 327 7954 E-mail hmilne@xtra.co.nz

MILNE, James Harley. b 73. Univ of Wales (Lamp) BD94 New Coll Edin MTh96. TISEC 95. **d** 98 **p** 99. C Dundee St Mary Magd *Bre* 98-01; Chapl St Marg Res Home Dundee 98-01; R Dundee St Marg 01-09; Chapl Ninewells Hosp Dundee 01-09; R Glas St Bride from 09. *St Bride's Rectory, Flat 1/1, 25 Queensborough Gardens, Glasgow G12 9QP*

MILNE, Norma Campbell. b 45. TISEC 01. **d** 02 **p** 06. OLM Huntly *Mor* 02-03; NSM Aberlour from 05; NSM Dufftown from 05; NSM Elgin w Lossiemouth from 05. *26 Green Road, Huntly AB54 8BE* Tel and fax (01466) 793841 E-mail normamilne@fsmail.net

MILNER, Catherine Mary. b 56. **d** 99 **p** 00. OLM Uttoxeter Area *Lich* 99-03; Sub Chapl HM Pris Foston Hall and Werrington YOI 99-03; Chapl Blue Coat Comp Sch Walsall 03-05; Hon Chapl Lich Cathl 99-03; rtd 05. *29 Crown Meadow, Alvechurch, Birmingham B48 7NZ* Tel 0121-445 0477 Mobile 07754-444770

MILNER, Darryl Vickers. b 43. Natal Univ BA63. St Chad's Coll Dur 64. **d** 66 **p** 67. C Oswestry H Trin *Lich* 66-69; S Africa 69-76;

New Zealand from 76. *The Vicarage, 47 Church Street, Northcote, North Shore 0627, New Zealand* Tel (0064) (9) 480 7568 Fax 419 7459 E-mail dvmilner@clear.net.nz

MILNER, David. *See* MILNER, William David

MILNER, David. b 38. St Aid Birkenhead 63. **d** 66 **p** 67. C Ulverston H Trin *Carl* 66-68; C Mickleover All SS *Derby* 68-71; C Mickleover St Jo 68-71; V 71-82; P-in-c Sandiacre 82-86; P-in-c Doveridge 86-97; P-in-c Sudbury and Somersal Herbert 92-97; R Doveridge, Scropton, Sudbury etc 98-03; RD Longford 86-96 and 01-03; rtd 03; Perm to Offic *Lich* from 04. *21 Greenwood Park, Hednesford WS12 4DQ* Tel (01543) 428972

✠**MILNER, The Rt Revd Ronald James.** b 27. Pemb Coll Cam BA49 MA52. Wycliffe Hall Ox 51. **d** 53 **p** 54 **c** 88. Succ Sheff Cathl 53-58; V Westwood *Cov* 58-64; V Fletchamstead 64-70; R Southampton St Mary w H Trin *Win* 70-72; P-in-c Southampton St Matt 70-72; Lic to Offic 72-73; TR Southampton (City Cen) 73-83; Hon Can Win Cathl 75-83; Adn Linc 83-88; Can and Preb Linc Cathl 83-88; Suff Bp Burnley *Blackb* 88-93; rtd 93; Hon Asst Bp S'well and Nottm from 94. *7 Crafts Way, Southwell NG25 0BL* Tel (01636) 816256

MILNER, William David. b 52. St Jo Coll Nottm. **d** 93 **p** 94. C Wollaton *S'well* 93-97; P-in-c Daybrook 97; C W Bridgford 98-99; TV Clifton 99-04; P-in-c Collingham w S Scarle and Besthorpe and Girton 04-10; P-in-c E Trent 10-11; P-in-c Farndon w Thorpe, Hawton and Cotham from 11. *The Rectory, 3 Marsh Lane, Farndon, Newark NG24 3SS*

MILNES, David Ian. b 45. Chich Th Coll 74. **d** 76 **p** 77. C Walthamstow St Sav *Chelmsf* 76-80; C Chingford SS Pet and Paul 80-83; P-in-c Gt Ilford St Alb 83-87; V 87-09; rtd 09. *Walsingham House, Main Road, Hadlow Down, Uckfield TN22 4ES* Tel (01825) 830076 E-mail frmilnes@aol.com

MILNES, James Clark. b 79. St Chad's Coll Dur BA00 MA01. Westcott Ho Cam 03. **d** 05 **p** 06. C Newbold w Dunston *Derby* 05-08; R Alderley w Birtles *Ches* from 08. *St Mary's Rectory, Congleton Road, Nether Alderley, Macclesfield SK10 4TW* Tel (01625) 585444 E-mail jamesclarkmilnes@yahoo.co.uk

MILSON, Julian James. b 70. De Montfort Univ BEd96. Oak Hill Th Coll BA04. **d** 04 **p** 05. C Bramcote *S'well* 04-07; C Hove Bp Hannington Memorial Ch *Chich* from 07. *43 Hogarth Road, Hove BN3 5RH* Tel (01273) 777020 E-mail jmilson@bigfoot.com

MILTON, Andrew John. b 54. BD. St Steph Ho Ox. **d** 83 **p** 84. C Highfield *Ox* 83-87; TV Banbury 87-95; P-in-c Thorney Abbey *Ely* 95-02; TR Huntingdon 02-07; P-in-c Gt w Lt Stukeley 04-07; TR Huntingdon w the Stukeleys from 07. *The Rectory, 1 The Walks East, Huntingdon PE29 3AP* Tel (01480) 412674 E-mail miltons@walkseast.fsnet.co.uk

MILTON, Miss Angela Daphne. b 50. FInstLEx79. Oak Hill Th Coll 84. **d** 87 **p** 94. NSM Watford *St Alb* 87-95; NSM St Alb St Mary Marshalswick 95-97; C Stevenage St Mary Shephall w Aston 97-02; P-in-c E Molesey St Paul *Guildf* 02-05; V E Molesey 05-10; rtd 10. *34 Woodhurst Avenue, Watford WD25 9RQ* Tel (01923) 682047 E-mail angelamilton@msn.com

MILTON, Claudius James Barton. b 29. K Coll Lon BD52 AKC53. **d** 53 **p** 54. C Sudbury St Andr *Lon* 53-56; Asst Chapl Bedford Sch 57-65; Asst Master 57-65; Chapl Cranbrook Sch Kent 65-74; Asst Master and Housemaster 65-74; Chapl & Asst Master Claysemore Sch Blandford 74-89; Claysemore Prep Sch 74-89; rtd 89. *28 Oakwood Drive, Iwerne Minster, Blandford Forum DT11 8QT* Tel (01747) 811792

MILTON, Robert. **d** 07 **p** 08. NSM Southport Ch Ch *Liv* from 11. *28 Dover Road, Southport PR8 4TB* Tel 07721-414724 (mobile) E-mail robert.uk.milton@openwork.uk.com

MILTON-THOMPSON, Jonathan Patrick. b 51. Nottm Univ BA76. Oak Hill Th Coll 86. **d** 88 **p** 89. C Bispham *Blackb* 88-92; C Darfield *Sheff* 92; C-in-c Gt Houghton CD 92-03; P-in-c Livesey *Blackb* from 05; P-in-c Blackb St Barn from 10. *St Andrew's Vicarage, 112 Full View, Blackburn BB2 4QB* Tel (01254) 59422 E-mail jarpmt51hotmail.co.uk

MILVERTON, The Revd and Rt Hon Lord (Fraser Arthur Richard Richards). b 30. Bps' Coll Cheshunt. **d** 57 **p** 58. C Beckenham St Geo *Roch* 57-59; C Sevenoaks St Jo 59-60; C Gt Bookham *Guildf* 60-63; V Okewood 63-67; R Christian Malford w Sutton Benger etc *Bris* 67-93; Public Preacher 93-95; rtd 95; Perm to Offic *Sarum* from 96. *7 Betjeman Road, Marlborough SN8 1TL* Tel (01672) 514068

MILVERTON, Mrs Ruth Erica. b 32. Open Univ BA78 Southn Univ MA82. Sarum Th Coll 83. **dss** 86 **d** 87 **p** 95. Weymouth H Trin *Sarum* 86-87; Hon Par Dn 87-95; NSM 95-02; Dioc NSM Officer 89-97; rtd 02; Perm to Offic *Sarum* 02-07. *4 Compass South, Rodwell Road, Weymouth DT4 8QT* Tel (01305) 788930 E-mail rev.milv.compass@care4free.net

MILWARD, Terence George. b 23. Ripon Hall Ox 66. **d** 68 **p** 69. C Selly Oak St Mary *Birm* 68-70; C Edgbaston St Bart 70-75; TV Bournemouth St Pet w St Swithun, H Trin etc *Win* 75-81; R Smannell w Enham Alamein 81-88; rtd 88; Perm to Offic *Guildf* 88-10. *Church House Flat, Church Lane, Witley, Godalming GU8 5PN* Tel (01428) 685308

MINALL, Peter. b 26. Lon Univ BSc47. Bps' Coll Cheshunt 51. **d** 53 **p** 54. C Bishop's Stortford St Mich *St Alb* 53-57; C Luton w E Hyde 57-63; C Tuffley *Glouc* 63-65; Asst Youth Chapl 65-69; V Stroud 69-84; RD Bisley 78-84; P-in-c Barnwood 84-91; rtd 91; Chapl Coney Hill Hosp Glouc 86-95; Chapl Severn NHS Trust 95-06; Perm to Offic *Glouc* from 06. *Amberwood, Knapp Lane, Painswick, Stroud GL6 6YE* Tel (01452) 813730
E-mail peter.minall@btinternet.com

MINAY, Francis Arthur Rodney. b 44. Westcott Ho Cam 66. **d** 68 **p** 69. C Edenbridge *Roch* 68-73; C Bromley St Mark 73-75; V Tudeley w Capel 75-79; TV Littleham w Exmouth 79-82; P-in-c Bolton Percy and Asst Chapl to Arts and Recreation in the NE *York* 82-06; rtd 06; Lic to Offic *Mor* from 07; Hon C Kishorn 07-08. *Rosedyke, Achintee, Strathcarron IV54 8YX* Tel (01520) 722144

MINCHER, John Derek Bernard. b 31. **d** 60 **p** 61. OSB 54-80; Lic to Offic *Ox* 60-80; Perm to Offic *St E* 81-87; C Halesworth w Linstead, Chediston, Holton etc 87-90; P-in-c Worlingworth, Southolt, Tannington, Bedfield etc 90-91; R 91-96; rtd 96; Perm to Offic *St E* 96-09 and Guildf from 09. *Flat 7, Manormead, Tilford Road, Hindhead GU26 6RA*

MINCHEW, Donald Patrick. b 48. Univ of Wales (Cardiff) BD76. St Mich Coll Llan 72. **d** 76 **p** 77. C Glouc St Aldate 76-80; P-in-c Sharpness CD 80-81; V Sharpness w Purton and Brookend 81-95; Miss to Seafarers from 81; V Croydon St Mich w St Jas *S'wark* from 95. *St Michael's Vicarage, 39 Oakfield Road, Croydon CR0 2UX* Tel (020) 8680 8413

MINCHIN, Anthony John. b 35. St Cath Coll Cam BA59 MA. Wells Th Coll 59. **d** 61 **p** 62. C Cheltenham St Pet *Glouc* 61-64; C Bushey *St Alb* 64-67; V Cheltenham St Mich *Glouc* 67-74; V Lower Cam 74-82; V Tuffley 82-92; R Huntley and Longhope 92-00; rtd 00; Perm to Offic *Glouc* from 00. *2 Melbourne Drive, Stonehouse GL10 2PJ* Tel (01453) 828899

MINCHIN, Charles Scott. b 51. Trin Coll Cam BA72 MA75. Linc Th Coll 73. **d** 75 **p** 76. C Gt Wyrley *Lich* 75-78; TV Wilnecote 78-82; C Tamworth 82-84; C-in-c Glascote CD 84-88; R Brierley Hill 88-93; R Brierley Hill *Worc* 93-03; P-in-c Stonehouse *Glouc* from 03. *The Vicarage, Elms Road, Stonehouse GL10 2NP* Tel (01453) 822332 E-mail cminchin@lineone.net

MINION, Arthur. b 65. TCD BTh92. CITC 89. **d** 92 **p** 93. C Bandon Union *C, C & R* 92-95; I Taunagh w Kilmactranny, Ballysumaghan etc *K, E & A* 95-99; I Shinrone w Aghancon etc *L & K* 99-08; I Crosspatrick Gp *C & O* from 08. *The Rectory, Churchlands, Tinahely, Co Wicklow, Republic of Ireland* Tel (00353) (402) 28922 Mobile 86-825 1065
E-mail arthurminion@gmail.com

MINION, Hazel Elizabeth Alice. b 47. TCD BA68 HDipEd69. CITC 00. **d** 03 **p** 04. Aux Min Templebreedy w Tracton and Nohoval *C, C & R* 03-04; Aux Min Carrigaline Union from 04; Chapl Ashton Sch Cork 03-07. *22 Inchvale Drive, Shamrock Lawn, Douglas, Cork, Republic of Ireland* Tel (00353) (21) 436 1924 E-mail hminion22@hotmail.com

MINKKINEN, Mrs Janet Mary. b 63. **d** 10 **p** 11. *12 Oakfield Avenue, Slough SL1 5AE* Tel (01753) 552354 Mobile 07856-047960 E-mail janetminkkinen@hotmail.co.uk

MINNS, David Andrew. b 59. St Jo Coll Nottm 95. **d** 97 **p** 98. C Burpham *Guildf* 97-00; C Knaphill w Brookwood 00-04; R Ewhurst from 04. *The Rectory, The Street, Ewhurst, Cranleigh GU6 7PX* Tel (01483) 277584
E-mail dlkminns@btinternet.com

MINNS, John Alfred. b 38. Oak Hill Th Coll 63. **d** 68 **p** 69. C Cheadle Hulme St Andr *Ches* 68-72; C Hartford 72-74; V Wharton 74-85; V Halliwell St Paul *Man* 85-87; C Halliwell St Pet 87-91; rtd 91; Perm to Offic *Glouc* 91-97. *39 Hambidge Lane, Lechlade GL7 3BJ* Tel (01367) 253549

MINNS, Canon John Charles. b 42. EAMTC. **d** 85 **p** 86. NSM Heigham St Barn w St Bart *Nor* 85-91; P-in-c Nor St Geo Tombland from 91; Asst Chapl Norfolk and Nor Hosp 92-95; Chapl Nor Sch of Art and Design 99-03; Hon Can Nor Cathl from 05. *18 Thunder Lane, Norwich NR7 0PX* Tel (01603) 437000 Mobile 07951-434485 E-mail john.minns@virgin.net

MINORS, Canon Graham Glyndwr Cavil. b 44. Glouc Sch of Min. **d** 79 **p** 79. Hon C Lower Cam *Glouc* 79-83; C Leckhampton SS Phil and Jas w Cheltenham St Jas 83-89; V Cainscross w Selsley 89-99; RD Stonehouse 97-99; TR Bodmin w Lanhydrock and Lanivet *Truro* from 99; Chapl N and E Cornwall Primary Care Trust 02-06; Hon Can Truro Cathl from 07. *The Rectory, Priory Road, Bodmin PL31 2AB* Tel (01208) 73867 E-mail revgrminors@hotmail.com

MINSON, Roger Graham. b 41. Leeds Univ BA64. Coll of Resurr Mirfield 64. **d** 66 **p** 67. C Horfield St Greg *Bris* 66-70; C Southmead 70-73; V Lawrence Weston 74-81; TV Knowle 81-93; V Knowle St Martin 93-95; V Fishponds St Mary 95-06; rtd 06. *2 Box Tree Cottage, Turners Tump, Ruardean GL17 9XG* Tel (01594) 546821

MINTON, Bernard John. b 68. St Chad's Coll Dur BA89 MRICS00. Coll of Resurr Mirfield 00. **d** 04 **p** 05. C Lancing w Coombes *Chich* 04-08; TV Ouzel Valley *St Alb* from 08. *St Barnabas' Vicarage, Vicarage Road, Leighton Buzzard LU7 2LP* E-mail bernardminton@aol.com

MINTY, Kenneth Desmond. b 25. Ch Ch Ox BA48 MA51. Lich Th Coll 71 Qu Coll Birm 72. **d** 73 **p** 74. Asst Chapl Wrekin Coll Telford 73-84; Chapl 84-86; Hon C Lawley *Lich* 74-75; Hon C Cen Telford 75-81; Hon C Longdon-upon-Tern, Rodington, Uppington etc 81-89; V Ercall Magna 89-95; V Rowton 89-95; rtd 95; Perm to Offic *Lich* from 95. *8 Glebelands, High Ercall, Telford TF6 6BB* Tel (01952) 770487

MINTY, Selwyn Francis. b 34. St D Coll Lamp 58. **d** 61 **p** 62. C Tonyrefail *Llan* 61-66; C Pontypridd St Cath 66-69; V Cilfynydd 69-84; V Crynant 84-00; rtd 00. *24 Derwen Fawr, Cilfrew, Neath SA10 8NX*

MIRZANIA, Ms Bassirat Bibi (Bassi). b 43. Tehran Univ MS74 Thames Valley Coll of HE BSc83. **d** 04 **p** 05. Chapl Persian Community from 04; NSM Guildf Ch Ch w St Martha-on-the-Hill from 04. *Shiraz, 11 Nelson Gardens, Guildford GU1 2NZ* Tel (01483) 569316 E-mail bassi.mirzania@btinternet.com

MISTLIN, Mrs Donna Jane. b 68. RGN89. STETS 03. **d** 08 **p** 09. NSM Crookham *Guildf* from 08. *18 Prospect Road, Ash Vale, Aldershot GU12 5ED* Tel (01252) 692720
E-mail djmistl@aol.com

MITCHAM, Andrew Mark. b 66. Kent Univ BA87 Leeds Univ BA90. Coll of Resurr Mirfield 88. **d** 91 **p** 92. C Downham Market w Bexwell *Ely* 91-94; P Shrine of Our Lady of Walsingham 94-96; V W Worthing St Jo *Chich* 96-04; R Eye *St E* from 04; RD Hartismere from 10. *The Vicarage, 41 Castle Street, Eye IP23 7AW* Tel (01379) 870277
E-mail andrew@redmail.co.uk

MITCHELL, Albert George. b 25. TCD MA. **d** 88 **p** 89. Bp's C Skreen w Kilmacshalgan and Dromard *T, K & A* 88-00; Can Killala Cathl 96-00; rtd 00. *The Glebe, Kilglass, Enniscrone, Co Sligo, Republic of Ireland* Tel (00353) (96) 36258

MITCHELL, Alec Silas. b 52. Man Univ BA75 MPhil95. N Bapt Coll 77 Coll of Resurr Mirfield 98. **d** 99 **p** 99. C Ashton *Man* 99-05; TV 05-07; P-in-c Haughton St Anne from 07; Dioc Officer for Racial Justice from 02; Borough Dean Tameside from 10. *St Anne's Rectory, St Anne's Drive, Denton, Manchester M34 3EB* Tel 0161-336 2374 *or* 828 1400 Mobile 07746-873164
E-mail fathermit@hotmail.com

MITCHELL, Allan. b 52. Kelham Th Coll 74 Linc Th Coll 78. **d** 78 **p** 79. C Kells *Carl* 78-81; C Upperby St Jo 81-83; V Pennington w Lindal and Marton 83-88; V Westfield St Mary 88-98; P-in-c Dalton-in-Furness 98-02; V Dalton-in-Furness and Ireleth-with-Askam from 02. *The Vicarage, Market Place, Dalton-in-Furness LA15 8AZ* Tel (01229) 462526

MITCHELL, Andrew Patrick (Paddy). b 37. English Coll Valladolid 59 Ripon Coll Cuddesdon 84. **d** 64 **p** 65. In RC Ch 64-85; C Woolwich St Mary w St Mich *S'wark* 85-87; V Wickham 87-94; P-in-c Walsall St Andr *Lich* 94-00; TV Sedgley All SS *Worc* 00-03; rtd 03; Perm to Offic *Birm* 03-04 and from 05. *714 Pershore Road, Selly Oak, Birmingham B29 7NR* Tel 0121-415 5828

MITCHELL, Anthony. b 54. St Jo Coll Nottm 05. **d** 07 **p** 08. C Plas Newton w Ches Ch 07-10; P-in-c Halton from 10. *27 Halton Brow, Halton, Runcorn WA7 2EH*
E-mail tony@tlmitchell.co.uk

MITCHELL, Mrs Brenda Margaret. b 53. Leeds Univ BA06. NOC 03. **d** 06 **p** 07. C Golcar *Wakef* 06-10; P-in-c Oldham Moorside *Man* from 10. *The Vicarage, 1 Glebe Lane, Oldham OL1 4SJ* Tel 0161-652 6452 Mobile 07976-305011
E-mail brenda_m_mitchell@hotmail.com

MITCHELL, Christopher Allan. b 51. Newc Univ BA72. Oak Hill Th Coll 82. **d** 84 **p** 85. C Guisborough *York* 84-87; C Thornaby on Tees 87-88; TV 88-92; V Dent w Cowgill *Bradf* 92-98; R Barney, Fulmodeston w Croxton, Hindringham etc *Nor* 98-03; R Hulland, Atlow, Kniveton, Bradley and Hognaston *Derby* from 03; RD Ashbourne from 09. *The Rectory, 16 Eaton Close, Hulland Ward, Ashbourne DE6 3EX* Tel (01335) 372138 E-mail pennychris@tiscali.co.uk

MITCHELL, Christopher Ashley. b 69. Leeds Univ BA(Econ)91. Ridley Hall Cam 92. **d** 95 **p** 96. Min Can St As Cathl 95-98; CF 98-02; Chapl RAF from 02. *Chaplaincy Services, Valiant Block, HQ Air Command, RAF High Wycombe HP14 4UE* Tel (01494) 496800 Fax 496343

MITCHELL, Christopher Derek. b 61. Univ of Wales (Lamp) BA85 Leic Univ MA86 Qu Coll Cam BA88 MA92 Auckland Univ of Tech MHSc04. Westcott Ho Cam 87. **d** 89 **p** 90. C Streetly *Lich* 89-92; C Brookfield St Mary *Lon* 92-96; Hon C Hornsey St Mary w St Geo 99-02; Lic to Offic Dio Auckland New Zealand 03-07; C Hendon St Mary and Ch Ch 07-08; V Edmonton St Pet w St Martin from 08. *St Peter's Vicarage, St Peter's Road, London N9 8JP* Tel (020) 8807 7431
E-mail fatherchris@btinternet.com

MITCHELL, Clare. *See* GRIFFITHS, Mrs Clare Elizabeth

MITCHELL, Canon David George. b 35. QUB BA56. Sarum Th Coll 59. **d** 61 **p** 62. C Westbury-on-Trym H Trin *Bris* 61-64; C Cricklade w Latton 64-68; V Fishponds St Jo 68-77; RD Stapleton 76-77; TR E Bris 77-87; R Syston 87-94; V Warmley 87-94; P-in-c Bitton 87-94; R Warmley, Syston and Bitton 94-01; RD Bitton 87-93; Hon Can Bris Cathl 87-01; rtd 01; P-in-c

Chedworth, Yanworth and Stowell, Coln Rogers etc *Glouc* 01-09; AD Northleach 04-09; Perm to Offic *Bris* from 01. *32 Flower Way, Longlevens, Gloucester GL2 9JD* Tel (01452) 500119 E-mail canongeorgemitchell@btinternet.com

MITCHELL, Preb David Norman. b 35. Tyndale Hall Bris 64. **d** 67 **p** 68. C Marple All SS *Ches* 67-70; C St Helens St Helen *Liv* 70-72; V S Lambeth St Steph *S'wark* 72-78; P-in-c Brixton Road Ch 73-75; SE Area Sec CPAS 78-81; R Uphill *B & W* 81-92; TR 92-01; Chapl Weston Area Health Trust 86-01; Preb Wells Cathl from 90; rtd 01; Perm to Offic *B & W* from 02. *3 Pizey Close, Clevedon BS21 7TP* Tel (01275) 349176

MITCHELL, Canon Edwin. b 44. St Jo Coll Nottm BTh74. **d** 74 **p** 75. C Worksop St Jo *S'well* 74-77; C Waltham Abbey *Chelmsf* 77-80; V Whiston *Liv* 80-91; R Wombwell *Sheff* 91-99; V Mortomley St Sav High Green from 99; P-in-c Stocksbridge 06-07; AD Ecclesfield 01-07; Hon Can Sheff Cathl 07-11; rtd 11. *3 North View, Lothersdale, Keighley BD20 8EX* Tel (01535) 631837 E-mail edwin.mitchell1@btopenworld.com

MITCHELL, Eric Sidney. b 24. S Dios Minl Tr Scheme 77. **d** 80 **p** 81. NSM Portland All SS w St Pet *Sarum* 80-83; C 88-92; Bermuda 83-88; Chapl HM Pris The Verne 91-92; rtd 92; Perm to Offic *Sarum* from 92. *10 Underhedge Gardens, Portland DT5 2DX* Tel (01305) 821059

MITCHELL, Geoffrey. b 36. SS Coll Cam BA60 MA64 Nottm Univ PhD74 CEng66 FIMechE76 FCIT92. EMMTC 88. **d** 91 **p** 92. NSM Oaks in Charnwood and Copt Oak *Leic* 91-94; NSM Loughborough All SS w H Trin 94-00; P-in-c Oaks in Charnwood and Copt Oak 00-03; NSM Shepshed and Oaks in Charnwood 03-04; Dioc NSM Officer 98-02; rtd 04; Perm to Offic *Leic* from 04. *56 Brick Kiln Lane, Shepshed, Loughborough LE12 9EL* Tel (01509) 502280 E-mail mitchell.household@talk21.com

MITCHELL, Geoffrey Peter. b 30. Liv Univ BEng57 Man Univ MSc68. Wells Th Coll 57. **d** 59 **p** 60. C Bradford cum Beswick *Man* 59-61; R Man St Pet Oldham Road w St Jas 61-64; Lic to Offic 64-68; Hon C Unsworth 68-86; V Woolfold 86-95; rtd 95; Perm to Offic *Man* from 95. *14 Redfearn Wood, Rochdale OL12 7GA* Tel (01706) 638180

MITCHELL, George. See MITCHELL, Canon David George

MITCHELL, George Alfred. b 23. TCD BA45 MA56. **d** 46 **p** 47. C Belfast St Matt *Conn* 46-48; C Ballymoney 48-51; C Belf Cathl Miss 51-52; I Broomhedge 52-58; I Carrickfergus 59-70; I Bangor St Comgall *D & D* 70-88; Can Belf Cathl 78-88; rtd 88. *2 Glendun Park, Bangor BT20 4UX* Tel (028) 9146 0882

MITCHELL, Geraint Owain. b 71. Univ Coll Ches & Humberside Univ BA96 Leeds Univ BA. Coll of Resurr Mirfield 99. **d** 02 **p** 03. C Bridlington Em *York* 02-05; V Brigg, Wrawby and Cadney cum Howsham *Linc* from 05; V Bonby from 10; V Worlaby from 10. *The Vicarage, 10 Glanford Road, Brigg DN20 8DJ* Tel (01652) 653989 E-mail owain.mitchell@btopenworld.com

MITCHELL, Gordon Frank Henry. b 26. FIFireE. Sarum & Wells Th Coll 74. **d** 77 **p** 78. NSM Alderbury and W Grimstead *Sarum* 77-91; NSM Alderbury Team 91-96; Perm to Offic 96-07. *Seefeld, Southampton Road, Whaddon, Salisbury SP5 3EB* Tel (01722) 710516

MITCHELL, Graham Bell. b 40. Otago Univ BA64 MA65 Worc Coll Ox BA73 MA76. St Chad's Coll Dur 66. **d** 68 **p** 69. C Bris St Agnes w St Simon 68-71; C Bedminster St Mich 73-76; V Auckland St Pet *Dur* 76-78; Vice-Prin Chich Th Coll 78-83; C Brighton St Pet w Chpl Royal and St Jo *Chich* 83-86; P-in-c Scaynes Hill 86-96; V 96-04; rtd 04. *18B Ballin Street, Ellersie, Auckland 1051, New Zealand* Tel (0064) (9) 579 6988

MITCHELL, Mrs Helen Miranda. b 55. **d** 10 **p** 11. NSM Sudbury and Chilton *St E* from 10. *The Vicarage, Church Street, Stoke by Nayland, Colchester CO6 4QL* Tel (01206) 262612 E-mail helenoldvic@hotmail.com

MITCHELL, Ian. See MITCHELL, Stuart Ian

MITCHELL, Jolyon Peter. b 64. Selw Coll Cam BA88 MA90 Edin Univ PhD97. St Jo Coll Dur MA93. **d** 93 **p** 94. NSM St Mary's Cath 93-97; NSM Edin Ch Ch 97-01; NSM Edin St Jas from 01; Lect Edin Univ 93-01; Sen Lect from 01; Visiting Fell Clare Hall Cam 02. *11 Eildon Street, Edinburgh EH3 5JU* Tel 0131-226 1092 *or* 650 8900 E-mail jolyon.mitchell@ed.ac.uk

MITCHELL, Karen Irene. b 68. Westcott Ho Cam 07. **d** 09 **p** 10. C Cheshunt St Alb from 09. *156 Churchgate, Cheshunt, Waltham Cross EN8 9DX* Tel (01992) 620659 Mobile 07834-322943 E-mail curate.cheshunt@virginmedia.com

MITCHELL, Kevin. b 49. Newc Univ BSc71 Ox Univ BA83. Ripon Coll Cuddesdon 81. **d** 83 **p** 84. C Cantril Farm *Liv* 83-86; Chapl N Middx Hosp 86-90; C Gt Cambridge Road St Jo and St Jas *Lon* 86-90; P-in-c Cricklewood St Pet 90-96; V Whetstone St Jo 96-10; rtd 10. *32 Guildford Street, Brighton BN1 3LS* Tel (01273) 203429 E-mail kevin.mitchell.49@googlemail.com

MITCHELL, Owain. See MITCHELL, Geraint Owain

MITCHELL, Paddy. See MITCHELL, Andrew Patrick

MITCHELL, The Very Revd Patrick Reynolds. b 30. FSA81 Mert Coll Ox BA52 MA56. Wells Th Coll 52. **d** 54 **p** 55. C Mansfield St Mark *S'well* 54-57; Chapl Wells Th Coll and PV Wells Cathl 57-61; V Milton *Portsm* 61-67; V Frome St Jo and P-in-c

Woodlands *B & W* 67-73; Dir of Ords 70-74; Dean Wells 73-89; Dean Windsor and Dom Chapl to The Queen 89-98; rtd 98; Perm to Offic *Ex* from 98 and *Sarum* from 00. *Wolford Lodge, Dunkeswell, Honiton EX14 4SQ* Tel (01404) 841244

MITCHELL, Canon Richard John Anthony. b 64. St Martin's Coll Lanc BA85 PGCE86. Sarum & Wells Th Coll 88. **d** 91 **p** 92. C Kendal H Trin *Carl* 91-95; TV Kirkby Lonsdale 95-04; P-in-c Badgeworth, Shurdington and Witcombe w Bentham *Glouc* 04-09; R from 09; AD Glouc N 04-09; AD Severn Vale from 09; Hon Can Glouc Cathl from 10. *The Vicarage, School Lane, Shurdington, Cheltenham GL51 4TF* Tel (01242) 702911 E-mail richard.mitchell@talk21.com

MITCHELL, Robert Hugh. b 53. Ripon Coll Cuddesdon. **d** 82 **p** 83. C E Dulwich St Jo *S'wark* 82-86; C Cambridge Gt St Mary w St Mich *Ely* 86-90; Chapl Girton Coll Cam 86-90; Asst Chapl Win Coll 90-91; Assoc Chapl Addenbrooke's Hosp Cam 91-93; Chapl Portsm Hosps NHS Trust 93-95; Chapl St Mary's Hosp Portsm 93-95; Chapl R Free Hampstead NHS Trust from 95. *The Chaplains' Office, The Royal Free Hospital, Pond Street, London NW3 2QG* Tel (020) 7794 0500 ext 3096 *or* 7830 2742 E-mail robert.mitchell@royalfree.nhs.uk

MITCHELL, Robert McFarlane. b 50. Man Univ BA72 Lambeth STh92. Wycliffe Hall Ox 73. **d** 75 **p** 76. C Tonbridge SS Pet and Paul *Roch* 75-80; CF 80-08; P-in-c Tillington *Chich* from 08. *The Rectory, Tillington, Petworth GU28 9AH* Tel (01798) 342827 Mobile 07530-852896 E-mail robert@revbobm.plus.com

MITCHELL, Roger Sulway. b 36. Chich Th Coll 70. **d** 71 **p** 71. C Sidcup St Jo *Roch* 71-74; C Pembury 74-76; Chapl St Lawr Hosp Bodmin 76-96; Chapl Cornwall and Is of Scilly Mental Health Unit 88-96; Chapl Cornwall Healthcare NHS Trust 96-00; TV Bodmin w Lanhydrock and Lanivet *Truro* 97-00; rtd 00. *12 Beacon Road, Bodmin PL31 1AS* Tel (01208) 76357 Mobile 07771-881258

MITCHELL, Miss Sandra Helen. b 47. ERMC 03. **d** 06 **p** 07. NSM Wroxham w Hoveton and Belaugh *Nor* 06-07; NSM Martham and Repps with Bastwick, Thurne etc from 07. *White House Farm, Tower Road, Repps with Bastwick, Great Yarmouth NR29 5JW* Tel (01692) 670439 E-mail shmitch@tiscali.co.uk

MITCHELL, Sarah Rachel. See TAN, Mrs Sarah Rachel

MITCHELL, Sheila Rosemary. b 53. Univ Coll Ches CertEd74 AdDipEd80. NOC 93. **d** 96 **p** 97. NSM Plemstall w Guilden Sutton *Ches* 96-98; C New Brighton St Jas w Em 98-00; C New Brighton All SS 98-00; P-in-c Weston 00-02; V 02-07; Perm to Offic from 07. *Casa Robila 21, Calle Jilguero, Mondron, 29710 Periana (Málaga), Spain* E-mail revsmitchel@aol.com

MITCHELL, Stephen Andrew John. b 56. Ch Ch Coll Cant CertEd78 K Coll Lon AKC77 BD80 MA02 Lambeth STh90 Heythrop Coll Lon MTh05 PhD10. Coll of Resurr Mirfield 80. **d** 82 **p** 83. C Chatham St Steph *Roch* 82-87; C Edenbridge 87-91; V from 91; P-in-c Crockham Hill H Trin from 91; Chapl Invicta Community Care NHS Trust from 91. *The Vicarage, Mill Hill, Edenbridge TN8 5DA* Tel (01732) 862258 Fax 864335 E-mail ssppvicarage@hotmail.com

MITCHELL, Canon Stephen John. b 51. Ex Univ BA73 Fitzw Coll Cam BA78 MA. Ridley Hall Cam 76. **d** 79 **p** 80. C Gt Malvern St Mary *Worc* 79-81; Prec Leic Cathl 82-85; R Barrow upon Soar w Walton le Wolds 85-02; P-in-c Gazeley w Dalham, Moulton and Kentford *St E* 02-04; V Dalham, Gazeley, Higham, Kentford and Moulton from 05; Min Can St E Cathl from 05; RD Mildenhall from 08; Hon Can St E Cathl from 10. *All Saints' Vicarage, The Street, Gazeley, Newmarket CB8 8RB* Tel (01638) 552630 E-mail smitch4517@aol.com

MITCHELL, Steven. b 58. St Jo Coll Nottm BTh83. **d** 83 **p** 84. C Ovenden *Wakef* 83-87; V Gawthorpe and Chickenley Heath 87-98; V Birkenshaw w Hunsworth 98-05; R Newport w Longford, Chetwynd and Forton *Lich* 05-11; V Newport w Longford, Chetwynd and Forton from 11. *10 Forton Glade, Newport TF10 8BP* Tel (01952) 810099

MITCHELL, Stuart. b 53. Cranmer Hall Dur 01. **d** 03 **p** 04. C Pocklington and Owsthorpe and Kilnwick Percy etc *York* 03-06; P-in-c Edith Weston w N Luffenham and Lyndon w Manton *Pet* 06-10; P-in-c Preston and Ridlington w Wing and Pilton 06-10; C Empingham and Exton w Horn w Whitwell 06-10; R Empingham, Edith Weston, Lyndon, Manton etc 11; R Stour Valley *St E* from 11. *The Vicarage, 14 High Street, Clare, Sudbury CO10 8NY*

MITCHELL, Stuart Ian. b 50. Wadh Coll Ox BA71 DPhil74. S'wark Ord Course 81. **d** 85 **p** 87. NSM Charlton St Luke w H Trin *S'wark* 85-86; NSM Kidbrooke St Jas 86-88; NSM Newbold w Dunston *Derby* 88-94; C 94-96; C Newbold and Gt Barlow 96-97; P-in-c Matlock Bank 97-03; RD Wirksworth 98-03; P-in-c Mackworth All SS 03-10; P-in-c Mugginton and Kedleston 03-10; P-in-c Kirk Langley 03-10; rtd 10. *22 Old Hall Close, Pilsley, Chesterfield S45 8JD* E-mail ianandmarym@tiscali.co.uk

MITCHELL, Tim. b 63. Trin Coll Bris 95. **d** 97 **p** 98. C Cromer *Nor* 97-01; P-in-c Selston *S'well* 01-05; P-in-c Sutton in Ashfield St Mich from 05. *The Vicarage, 11A Deepdale Gardens, Sutton-in-Ashfield NG17 4ER* Tel (01623) 441743 E-mail timmitchell.t@googlemail.com

MITCHELL, Wendy Mary. b 47. Glas Univ MA70 Callendar Park Coll of Educn Falkirk PGCE71. Trin Coll Bris 99. **d** 01 **p** 02. C Yatton Moor *B & W* 01-07; TV Parkham, Alwington, Buckland Brewer etc *Ex* from 07. *The Rectory, Old Market Drive, Woolsery, Bideford EX39 5QF* Tel (01237) 431160 E-mail revwendym@aol.com

MITCHELL-INNES, Charles William. b 47. Pemb Coll Cam BA69 MA73. Sarum Th Coll 83. **d** 86 **p** 87. Asst Chapl Sherborne Sch 86-89; Chapl Milton Abbey Sch Dorset 90-96; Conduct Eton Coll 96-07; rtd 07; V of Close Sarum Cathl from 07. *32 The Close, Salisbury SP1 2EJ* Tel (01722) 328361 *or* 555192 E-mail voc@salcath.co.uk

MITCHELL-INNES, James Alexander. b 39. Ch Ch Ox BA64 MA66. Lon Coll of Div 65. **d** 67 **p** 68. C Cullompton *Ex* 67-71; Nigeria 71-75; P-in-c Puddletown w Athelhampton and Burleston *Sarum* 75-78; R Puddletown and Tolpuddle 78-82; V Win Ch Ch 82-92; V Titchfield *Portsm* 92-98; rtd 98; Perm to Offic *Win* from 99. *115 Battery Hill, Winchester SO22 4BH* Tel (01962) 859039 E-mail jamesminnes@o2.co.uk

MITCHINSON, Frank. b 37. AKC60. **d** 61 **p** 62. C Cross Heath *Lich* 61-64; C Forrabury w Minster and Trevalga *Truro* 64-68; C Harpenden St Nic *St Alb* 68-70; R Southwick St Mich *Chich* 70-83; V Billingshurst 83-88; V Preston 88-02; rtd 02; P-in-c Bolney *Chich* 02-05. *7 St Cyr, 26 Douglas Avenue, Exmouth EX8 2HA* Tel (01395) 268438

MITCHINSON, Canon Ronald. b 35. Westmr Coll Ox MA91. Linc Th Coll 66. **d** 68 **p** 69. C Heworth St Mary *Dur* 68-72; C Banbury *Ox* 72-73; TV 73-76; New Zealand 76-82; TR Banbury *Ox* 82-86; RD Deddington 84-86; Ind Chapl 86-92; Hon Can Ch Ch 90-92; TV Brayton York 92-96; Sen Chapl Selby Coalfield Ind Chapl 92-96; rtd 96; Perm to Offic *York* 04-11. *6 St John's Crescent, York YO31 7QP* Tel (01904) 642382 E-mail rmitchinson@freire.org

MITFORD, Bertram William Jeremy (Bill). b 27. Wells Th Coll 62. **d** 64 **p** 65. C Hollinwood *Man* 64-67; C Atherton 67-68; C Frome St Jo *B & W* 68-71; V Cleeve 72-74; V Cleeve w Chelvey and Brockley 74-79; Chapl HM Pris Shepton Mallet 79-92; C Shepton Mallet *B & W* 79-84; C Shepton Mallet w Doulting 84-92; rtd 92. *21 Monkton Road, Honiton EX14 1PZ* Tel (01404) 42632

MITRA, Avijit (Munna). b 53. Keble Coll Ox BA76. Ox NSM Course 84. **d** 88 **p** 89. NSM Abingdon *Ox* 88-96; Asst Chapl Abingdon Sch 88-96; Sen Chapl Ch Hosp Horsham 96-09; Hd Classics K Sch Roch from 09. *The Old Archdeaconry Flat, The Precinct, Rochester ME1 1SX* Tel (01634) 400576 Mobile 07713-727708 E-mail avijit@mitra1953.plus.com *or* amm@ksr.org.uk

MITRA, Mrs Nicola Jane. b 54. St Hugh's Coll Ox BA76 MA81 PGCE77. Ox Min Course 92. **d** 94 **p** 95. NSM Abingdon *Ox* 94-96; Asst Chapl Ch Hosp Horsham 96-08; Asst Chapl Maidstone and Tunbridge Wells NHS Trust from 08. *The Old Archdeaconry Flat, The Precinct, Rochester ME1 1SX* Tel (01634) 400576 *or* (01622) 224569 Mobile 07976-966105 E-mail nicola@mitra1953.plus.com *or* nicolamitra@nhs.net

MITSON, Mrs Carol Mae. b 46. SRN SCM. Oak Hill NSM Course 89. **d** 93 **p** 94. NSM Lawford *Chelmsf* 93-96; NSM Elmstead 96-98; NSM Harwich 96-98; NSM Dedham 98-00; Perm to Offic from 01. *Drift Cottage, The Drift, Dedham, Colchester CO7 6AH* Tel and fax (01206) 323116 E-mail mitson@onetel.net.uk

MITSON, John Dane. b 29. Solicitor 56 SS Coll Cam MA53 LLM54. Oak Hill Th Coll 91 EAMTC 93. **d** 94 **p** 95. Dioc Registrar and Legal Sec to Bp St E 75-97; NSM Greenstead *Chelmsf* 94-96; NSM Elmstead 96-98; NSM Dedham 98-00; Perm to Offic from 00. *Drift Cottage, The Drift, Dedham, Colchester CO7 6AH* Tel and fax (01206) 323116 E-mail mitson@onetel.net.uk

MITSON, Miss Joyce. b 37. Man Univ CertEd64. Trin Coll Bris 77. **dss** 79 **d** 87 **p** 94. Wellington w Eyton *Lich* 79-85; Farnworth *Liv* 85-91; Par Dn 87-91; TD Bilston *Lich* 91-94; TV 94; Lich Local Min Adv 91-94; C W Bromwich St Jas 94-97; C W Bromwich St Jas w St Paul 97-98; rtd 98; Perm to Offic *Man* from 00. *13 Birkenhills Drive, Bolton BL3 4TX* Tel (01204) 655081

MITTON, Michael Simon. b 53. Ex Univ BA75. St Jo Coll Nottm 76. **d** 78 **p** 79. C High Wycombe *Ox* 78-82; TV Kidderminster St Geo *Worc* 82-89; Dir Angl Renewal Min 89-97; Dep Dir Acorn Chr Foundn 97-03; Renewing Min Project Officer *Derby* 03-06; Miss and Min Development Adv 06-09; Dioc Fresh Expressions Adv and P-in-c Derby St Paul from 09. *20 Statham Street, Derby DE22 1HQ* Tel (01332) 552448 E-mail michaelmitton@btinternet.com

MLEMETA, Kedmon Hezron. b 60. CertEd78. CA Tr Coll Nairobi 86. **d** 89 **p** 90. Tanzania 89-96 and from 99; P-in-c Loughb Gd Shep *Leic* 96-99. *The Diocese of Mount Kilimanjaro, PO Box 1057, Arusha, Tanzania*

MOAT, Terry. b 61. Nottm Univ BTh92. Aston Tr Scheme 86 Linc Th Coll 88. **d** 92 **p** 93. C Caterham *S'wark* 92-96; Hon C Tynemouth Priory *Newc* 04-06; C Morpeth 06-09; V Choppington from 09. *The Vicarage, Scotland Gate, Choppington NE62 5SX* Tel (01670) 822216

MOATE, Gerard Grigglestone. b 54. BA FRSA01. Oak Hill Th Coll 79. **d** 82 **p** 83. C Mildmay Grove St Jude and St Paul *Lon* 82-85; C Hampstead St Jo 85-88; P-in-c Pinxton *Derby* 88; V Charlesworth and Dinting Vale 88-95; V Dedham *Chelmsf* from 95; RD Dedham and Tey 98-03. *The Vicarage, High Street, Dedham, Colchester CO7 6DE* Tel (01206) 322136 E-mail gerard@moate.org *or* vicar@dedham-parishchurch.org.uk

MOATE, Phillip. b 47. RGN70 RNT75. NOC 87. **d** 90 **p** 91. NSM Upper Holme Valley *Wakef* 90-92; NSM Almondbury Deanery 92-94; NSM Honley 94-95; P-in-c Roos and Garton w Tunstall, Grimston and Hilston *York* 95-02; R Lockington and Lund and Scorborough w Leconfield 02-09; rtd 09; Perm to Offic *York* from 09. *58 Pilmar Lane, Roos, Hull HU12 0HN* Tel (01964) 671321 E-mail phillipmoate@btinternet.com

MOATT, Canon Richard Albert. b 54. K Coll Lon BD76 AKC76. Linc Th Coll 80. **d** 81 **p** 82. C Egremont and Haile *Carl* 81-85; V Addingham, Edenhall, Langwathby and Culgaith 85-04; P-in-c Skirwith, Ousby and Melmerby w Kirkland 98-04; V Cross Fell Gp from 04; RD Penrith from 09; Hon Can Carl Cathl from 10. *1 Low Farm, Langwathby, Penrith CA10 1NH* Tel (01768) 881212 E-mail moatt@btinternet.com

MOBBERLEY, Keith John. b 56. BA. Westcott Ho Cam. **d** 84 **p** 85. C Coventry Caludon 84-87; C Kenilworth St Nic 87-92; V Keresley and Coundon 92-98; P-in-c Hatton w Haseley, Rowington w Lowsonford etc 98-00; R from 00. *North Ferncumbe Rectory, Hatton Green, Hatton, Warwick CV35 7LA* Tel (01926) 484332

MOBBERLEY, Mrs Susan. b 57. Kent Univ BA79. Westcott Ho Cam 81. **dss** 84 **d** 90 **p** 94. Coventry Caludon 84-87; Lic to Offic 87-92; NSM Keresley and Coundon 92-98; NSM Hatton w Haseley, Rowington w Lowsonford etc from 98. *North Ferncumbe Rectory, Hatton Green, Hatton, Warwick CV35 7LA* Tel (01926) 484332

MOBBS, Bernard Frederick. b 26. Open Univ BA. S'wark Ord Course 71. **d** 72 **p** 73. C Purley St Barn *S'wark* 72-74; Vice-Prin S'wark Ord Course 74-80; P-in-c Sydenham St Bart *S'wark* 80-87; V Dormansland 87-92; rtd 92; Perm to Offic *Chich* from 92. *19 Ramsay Hall, 11-13 Byron Road, Worthing BN11 3HN* Tel (01903) 237663

MOBERLY (née McCLURE), Mrs Jennifer Lynne. b 62. Ball State Univ (USA) BSc84. Cranmer Hall Dur 98. **d** 01 **p** 02. C Belmont *Dur* 01-08; Chapl St Mary's Coll Dur from 09. *St Mary's College, Elvet Hill Road, Durham DH1 3LR* E-mail j.l.moberly@durham.ac.uk

MOBERLY, Richard Hamilton. b 30. Trin Hall Cam BA53 MA57. Cuddesdon Coll 53. **d** 55 **p** 56. C Walton St Mary *Liv* 55-59; C Kensington St Mary Abbots w St Geo *Lon* 59-63; R Chingola Zambia 63-66; V Kennington Cross St Anselm *S'wark* 67-73; TV N Lambeth 74-80; Ind Chapl 80-95; Perm to Offic *S'wark* from 95. Flat 2, *1 Chester Way, London SE11 4UT* Tel (020) 7735 2233 E-mail richard@richardmoberly.org.uk

MOBERLY, Robert Walter Lambert. b 52. New Coll Ox MA77 Selw Coll Cam MA80 Trin Coll Cam PhD81. Ridley Hall Cam 74. **d** 81 **p** 82. C Knowle *Birm* 81-85; Lect Dur Univ from 85; Perm to Offic *Dur* from 85. *Department of Theology, Abbey House, Palace Green, Durham DH1 3RS* Tel 0191-334 3953 E-mail r.w.l.moberly@durham.ac.uk

MOBEY, Jonathan. Wycliffe Hall Ox 05. **d** 08 **p** 09. NSM Ox St Andr from 08. *St Andrew's Church, Linton Road, Oxford OX2 6UG* Tel (01865) 468044 E-mail jonathan.mobey@standrewsoxford.org

MOBSBY, Ian Jonathan. b 68. Leeds Univ BHSc93 SROT93 Anglia Ruskin Univ MA06. EAMTC 00. **d** 04 **p** 05. C Westmr St Matt *Lon* 04-11; C St Mary Aldermary from 11. *Moot Community, St Mary Aldermary, Watling Street, London EC4M 9BW* Tel (020) 7248 4906 E-mail ian.mobsby@moot.uk.net

MOCK, David Lawrence. b 64. Whitman Coll Washington BA86 Heythrop Coll Lon MTh01. Trin Coll Bris BA98. **d** 98 **p** 99. C Tadworth *S'wark* 98-01; P-in-c Sutton St Geo *Ches* 01-02; C Macclesfield Team 01-02; TV N Lambeth 74-80. *St George's Vicarage, 88 Byrons Lane, Macclesfield SK11 7JS* Tel (01625) 432919 E-mail revdavem@googlemail.com

MOCKFORD (née WATKINS), Mrs Betty Anne. b 45. Leeds Univ BA66 Nottm Univ CertEd67. EAMTC 94. **d** 97 **p** 98. C Ipswich St Aug *St E* 97-00; P-in-c Charsfield w Debach, Monewden, Hoo etc 01-06; rtd 06; Perm to Offic *St E* from 06. *Mirembe, 10 Castle Brooks, Framlingham, Woodbridge IP13 9SF* Tel (01728) 724193 Mobile 07890-110741

MOCKFORD, Canon John Frederick. b 28. Em Coll Cam BA52 MA56. Ridley Hall Cam 52. **d** 54 **p** 55. C Ardwick St Silas *Man* 54; C Harpurhey Ch Ch 54-57; V Bootle St Leon *Liv* 57-64; CMS 65-73; Can Missr Kampala 72-73; V Bushbury *Lich* 73-77; TR 77-84; Preb Lich Cathl 81-84; Dir Miss and Past Studies Ridley Hall Cam 84-88; V Ipswich St Marg *St E* 88-93; rtd 93; Perm to Offic *St E* from 93. *Mirembe, 10 Castle Brooks, Framlingham, Woodbridge IP13 9SF* Tel (01728) 724193

MOCKFORD, Peter John. b 57. Nottm Univ BSc79 St Jo Coll Dur BA88. Cranmer Hall Dur 86. **d** 89 **p** 90. C Tamworth *Lich* 89-94; V Blurton from 94; P-in-c Dresden from 04; P-in-c Longton Hall from 08. *The Vicarage, School Lane, Stoke-on-Trent ST3 3DU* Tel (01782) 312163
E-mail p.mockford@ukgateway.net

MODY, Rohintan Keki. b 63. New Coll Ox BA85 MA88 Fitzw Coll Cam MPhil05 Aber Univ PhD08. Oak Hill Th Coll BA00. **d** 00 **p** 01. C Wolverhampton St Luke *Lich* 00-03; C Virginia Water *Guildf* 08-11; P-in-c Throop *Win* from 11. *St Paul's Vicarage, 1 Chesildene Avenue, Bournemouth BH8 0AZ* Tel (01202) 531064 E-mail romody@hotmail.com

MOESEL, Joseph Sams. b 65. Villanova Univ USA BA90 Harris Man Coll Ox BTh93 Regent's Park Coll Ox MTh03. Ripon Coll Cuddesdon 93. **d** 95 **p** 96. C Twigworth, Down Hatherley, Norton, The Leigh etc *Glouc* 95-98; CF 98-06; Sen CF from 06. *clo MOD Chaplains (Army)* Tel (01980) 615804 Fax 615800

MOFFAT, Canon George. b 46. Edin Univ BD77 Open Univ BA87 Bradf Univ MA04. Edin Th Coll 67. **d** 72 **p** 73. C Falkirk *Edin* 73-76; C Edin St Pet 76-81; Chapl Edin Univ 77-81; C Heston *Lon* 81-84; V S Elmsall *Wakef* 84-93; TR Manningham *Bradf* 93-07; R Bolton Abbey from 07; Chapl to The Queen from 00; Hon Can Bradf Cathl from 02. *The Rectory, Bolton Abbey, Skipton BD23 6AL* Tel (01756) 710326 *or* 710238
E-mail rectorboltonpriory@btinternet.com

MOFFATT, Joseph Barnaby. b 72. Fitzw Coll Cam BA96 MA99. Ripon Coll Cuddesdon MTh99. **d** 99 **p** 00. C Cen Wolverhampton *Lich* 99-03; C Chelsea St Luke and Ch Ch *Lon* 03-09; V Teddington St Mary w St Alb from 09. *The Vicarage, 11 Twickenham Road, Teddington TW11 8AQ* Tel (020) 8977 2767

MOFFATT, Canon Neil Thomas. b 46. Fitzw Coll Cam BA68 MA72. Qu Coll Birm 69. **d** 71 **p** 72. C Charlton St Luke w St Paul *S'wark* 71-74; C Walworth St Pet 74-75; C Walworth 75-77; V Dormansland 77-86; TR Padgate *Liv* 86-96; V Padgate 96-98; TR Thatcham *Ox* 98-10; AD Newbury 02-10; S Africa 10-11; Hon Can Ch Ch *Ox* 10-11; rtd 11. *7 Jeffs Close, Upper Tysoe, Warwick CV35 0TQ* Tel (01295) 688030
E-mail rev.tom.moffatt@googlemail.com

MOFFETT, Mrs Marie-Louise. b 25. St Andr Univ MA46. **d** 87 **p** 94. St Andr Univ Angl Chapl Team 87-91; C St Andrews All SS *St And* from 91. *10 Queen's Gardens, St Andrews KY16 9TA* Tel (01334) 473678

MOFFETT-LEVY, Joanna. b 11. NSM Ox St Mich w St Martin and All SS from 11. *15 Third Acre Rise, Oxford OX2 9DA* Tel (01865) 862715

MOFFITT, Mrs Vivien Louisa. b 37. LSE BSc59. Sarum & Wells Th Coll 90. **d** 91 **p** 94. NSM Chandler's Ford *Win* 91-99; NSM Twyford and Owslebury and Morestead 99-01; rtd 01. *13 Velmore Road, Eastleigh SO53 3HD* Tel (023) 8026 5327

MOGER, Canon Peter John. b 64. Mert Coll Ox BA85 BMus86 MA89 St Jo Coll Dur BA93 ARSCM08 Hon FGCM10. Cranmer Hall Dur 89. **d** 93 **p** 94. C Whitby *York* 93-95; Prec, Sacr and Min Can Ely Cathl 95-01; V Godmanchester 01-05; Nat Worship Development Officer Abps' Coun 05-10; Perm to Offic *Ely* 05-10; Sec Liturg Commn 09-10; Can Res and Prec York Minster from 10. *2 Minster Court, York YO1 7JJ* Tel (01904) 557205 *or* 557265 Mobile 07970-694021
E-mail precentor@yorkminster.org

MOGFORD, Canon Stanley Howard. b 13. St Pet Hall Ox BA35 MA39. Westcott Ho Cam 36. **d** 37 **p** 38. C Aberdare *Llan* 37-41; C Llan Cathl 41-48; V Cyfarthfa 48-54; V Pontypridd St Cath 54-63; V Llanblethian w Cowbridge 63-66; V Llanblethian w Cowbridge and Llandough etc 66-80; RD Llantwit Major and Cowbridge 69-80; Can Llan Cathl 71-80; rtd 80; Perm to Offic *Llan* from 80. *Fortis Green, 19 Plas Treoda, Cardiff CF14 1PT* Tel (029) 2061 8839

MOGHAL, Dominic Jacob. See MUGHAL, Dominic Jacob

MOGRIDGE, Christopher James. b 31. Culham Coll of Educn CertEd62 LCP70 FCollP86. St Steph Ho Ox 93. **d** 94 **p** 95. NSM Wellingborough St Andr *Pet* 94-98; NSM Ecton 98-02; rtd 02; Perm to Offic *Pet* from 02. *April Cottage, Little Harrowden, Wellingborough NN9 5BB* Tel (01933) 678412

MOIR, Canon David William. b 38. St Aid Birkenhead 64. **d** 67 **p** 68. C Danbury *Chelmsf* 67-70; C Bollington St Jo *Ches* 70-72; V Sutton St Jas 72-81; V Prestbury 81-95; RD Macclesfield 88-89; P-in-c Bosley and N Rode w Wincle and Wildboarclough 95-98; V 98-03; Hon Can Ches Cathl 96-03; Chapl E Cheshire NHS Trust 96-03; rtd 04; Perm to Offic *Heref* from 04. *Dove Top, Bentlawnt, Minsterley, Shrewsbury SY5 0HE* Tel (01743) 891209 E-mail moirdl@compuserve.com

MOIR, Nicholas Ian. b 61. G&C Coll Cam BA82 MA86 Ox Univ BA86 MA91 Lon Univ MTh92. Wycliffe Hall Ox 84. **d** 87 **p** 88. C Enfield St Andr *Lon* 87-91; Bp's Dom Chapl *St Alb* 91-94; Chapl St Jo Coll Cam 94-98; V Waterbeach and R Landbeach *Ely* 98-07; RD N Stowe 05-07; V Chesterton St Andr from 07; RD Cambridge N from 11. *The Vicarage, 10 Lynfield Lane, Cambridge CB4 1DR* Tel (01223) 303469
E-mail nicholas.moir@ntlworld.com
or vicar@standrews-chesterton.org

MOLD, Peter John. b 33. **d** 63 **p** 64. C Boston *Linc* 63-66; C Scarborough St Mary w Ch Ch, St Paul and St Thos *York* 67-68; Australia from 68; rtd 91. *Stone Grange, 29 Newcastle Street, PO Box 355, York WA 6302, Australia* Tel (0061) (8) 9641 1965

MOLE, David Eric Harton. b 33. Em Coll Cam BA54 MA58 PhD62. Ridley Hall Cam 55. **d** 59 **p** 59. C Selly Hill St Steph *Birm* 59-62; Tutor St Aid Birkenhead 62-63; Chapl Peterho Cam 63-69; Ghana 69-72; Lect Qu Coll Birm 72-76; Tutor USPG Coll of the Ascension Selly Oak 76-87; C Burton *Lich* 87-93; Chapl Burton Gen Hosp 90-93; Chapl Ostend w Knokke and Bruges *Eur* 93-98; rtd 98; Perm to Offic *Birm* from 99. *48 Green Meadow Road, Selly Oak, Birmingham B29 4DE* Tel 0121-475 1589
E-mail susananddavidmole@yahoo.co.uk

MOLE, Canon Jennifer Vera. b 49. CertEd70. Qu Coll Birm 82. **d** 84 **p** 97. C Pontypool *Mon* 84-87; C Cyncoed 87-88; TV 88-96; C Caerleon 96-99; V Maesglas and Duffryn 99-07; R Panteg w Llanfihangel Pontymoile from 07; AD Pontypool from 08; Can St Woolos Cathl from 07. *Panteg Rectory, The Highway, New Inn, Pontypool NP4 0PH* Tel (01495) 763724

MOLESWORTH, Canon Anthony Edward Nassau. b 23. Pemb Coll Cam BA45 MA48. Coll of Resurr Mirfield 45. **d** 46 **p** 47. C Blyth St Mary *Newc* 46-51; C High Elswick St Phil 51-52; Swaziland 52-68; Can 68-71; Can Zululand 63-68; R Huish Episcopi w Pitney *B & W* 71-78; P-in-c High Ham 76-78; TR Langport Area 78-84; R Charlton Musgrove, Cucklington and Stoke Trister 84-90; RD Bruton 86-90; rtd 90; Perm to Offic *B & W* and *Sarum* from 90. *3 Barrow Hill, Stourton Caundle, Sturminster Newton DT10 2LD* Tel (01963) 362337

MOLL, Christopher David Edward. b 67. St Cath Coll Cam BA89 MA93. Ridley Hall Cam 94. **d** 98 **p** 99. C Byker St Mark and Walkergate St Oswald *Newc* 98-02; C Eastrop *Win* 02-06; V Wembdon *B & W* from 07. *The Vicarage, 12 Greenacre, Wembdon, Bridgwater TA6 7RD* Tel (01278) 423647
E-mail ed@sgw.org.uk

MOLL, Nicola. b 47. Bedf Coll Lon BA69. TISEC 99. **d** 03 **p** 04. C Edin Gd Shep from 03; C Edin St Salvador from 03. *9/3 Forth Street, Edinburgh EH1 3JX* Tel 0131-558 3729 *or* 557 0718
E-mail mollnicola@hotmail.com

MOLL, Randell Tabrum. b 41. Lon Univ BD65. Wycliffe Hall Ox 62. **d** 66 **p** 67. C Drypool St Columba w St Andr and St Pet *York* 66-70; Asst Chapl HM Pris Hull 66-70; Asst Master Hull Gr Sch 66-70; C Netherton *Liv* 70-74; C Sefton 70-72; Ind Chapl 70-74 and 92-99; Belgium 75-76; P-in-c Brockmoor *Lich* 76-81; Team Ldr Black Country Urban Ind Miss 76-81; Dir Chilworth Home Services 81-84; Asst Master Bp Reindorp Sch Guildf 84-90; France and Iraq 91; Chapl Sedbergh Sch 92; Sen Chapl Miss in the Economy (Merseyside) 92-99; Hon Can Liv Cathl 97-99; Chapl Campsfield Ho Immigration and Detention Cen 00-02; Sen Chapl Immigration Detention Services 01-02; Team Ldr Workplace Min *St Alb* 03-07; rtd 08. *Penn Cottage, Green End, Granborough, Buckingham MK18 3NT* Tel and fax (01296) 670970 E-mail randellmoll@yahoo.co.uk

MOLLAN, Patricia Ann Fairbanks. b 44. QUB BSc67 PhD70 BD97. **d** 97 **p** 98. Aux Min *D & D* from 97; Aux Min Lecale Gp 02-04; Dep Dir Ch's Min of Healing from 04. *Echo Sound, 69 Killyleagh Road, Downpatrick BT30 9BN* Tel (028) 4482 1620 Fax 9073 8665 E-mail pat@mollan.net *or* cmhbel@btconnect.com

MOLLAN, Prof Raymond Alexander Boyce. b 43. QUB MB, BCh69 BAO69 MD84 FRCS. CITC 97. **d** 97 **p** 98. Aux Min *D & D* from 97; NSM Comber 02-10; NSM Orangefield w Moneyreagh from 10. *Echo Sound, 69 Killyleagh Road, Downpatrick BT30 9BN* Tel (028) 4482 1620
E-mail rab@mollan.net

MOLLER, George Brian. b 35. TCD BA60 MA64 Div Test 61 Lon Univ BD84. **d** 61 **p** 62. C Belfast St Pet *Conn* 61-64; C Larne and Inver 64-68; P-in-c Rathcoole 68-69; I 69-86; Dioc Dir Ords 82-92; I Belfast St Bart 86-01; Chapl Stranmillis Univ Coll Belf 88-01; Preb Conn Cathl 90-96; Treas 96; Prec 96-98; Dean 98-01; rtd 01. *Deneholme, 7 Sunningdale Park, Bangor BT20 4UU* Tel (028) 9145 5903 E-mail gb@moller2.plus.com

MOLLOY, Mrs Heather. b 54. Bradf Univ BTech76. **d** 95 **p** 96. OLM Harwood *Man* from 95. *7 Fellside, Bolton BL2 4HB* Tel (01204) 520395

MOLONEY, Charles Michael Stephen. b 81. Leeds Univ BA03 Cant Ch Ch Univ CDTS05. Ridley Hall Cam 07. **d** 09 **p** 10. C Retford Area *S'well* from 09. *East Retford Vicarage, 1 Chapelgate, Retford DN22 6PL*

MOLONY, Canon Nicholas John. b 43. St Jo Coll Dur BA67 Birm Univ MA78 Fuller Th Sem California DMin06. Qu Coll Birm 67. **d** 70 **p** 71. C Beaconsfield *Ox* 70-75; P-in-c Chesham Ch Ch 75-80; TV Gt Chesham 80-81; P-in-c Weston Turville 81-90; P-in-c Stoke Mandeville 87-89; P-in-c Gt Marlow 90-93; P-in-c Bisham 90-93; TR Gt Marlow w Marlow Bottom, Lt Marlow and Bisham 93-10; rtd 10; Hon Can Kimberley and Kuruman from 08; Perm to Offic *Ox* from 11. *9 Culverton Hill, Princes Risborough HP27 0DZ* Tel (01844) 273895
E-mail nick.molony@btopenworld.com

MOLYNEUX, Ms Tina Mercedes. b 68. Ox Min Course 07. **d** 10 **p** 11. NSM Burchetts Green *Ox* from 10. *1 Littlewick Place, Coronation Road, Littlewick Green, Maidenhead SL6 3RA* Tel (01628) 822813 E-mail tina.molyneux@btconnect.com

MONAGHAN, Mrs Hilary Alice. b 78. Edin Univ MA01 Cam Univ BA04. Ridley Hall Cam 02. **d** 06 **p** 07. C Gerrards Cross and Fulmer *Ox* 06-10. *14 Wellington Drive, Bristol BS9 4SR*

MONBERG, Canon Ulla Stade. b 52. Copenhagen Univ BA79. Westcott Ho Cam 88. **d** 90 **p** 94. C Westmr St Jas *Lon* 90-94; Dean Women's Min and Area Dir of Ords Cen Lon 94-99; Dean Women's Min Kensington 94-99; C Paddington St Jo w St Mich 96-98; P-in-c S Kensington H Trin w All SS 98-02; Dir of Ords Two Cities Area 99-02; Denmark from 02; Dioc Adv for Women's Min *Eur* 04-05; Dioc Dir of Tr from 05; Can Brussels Cathl from 10. *Borgmester Jensens Alle 9, 2th, DK-2100 Copenhagen 0, Denmark* Tel (0045) 3526 0660 E-mail ullamonberg@msn.com

✠**MONDAL, The Rt Revd Barnabas Dwijen.** b 37. Dhaka Univ BA61 Serampore Univ BD64. Bp's Coll Calcutta 61. **d** 64 **p** 65 **c** 75. Barisal Bangladesh 64-67; Khulna 67-69; Rhode Is USA 69-70; Bollorepur 70-71; Thakurpukur 71-72; Prin Coll of Chr Th 72-74; Dhaka St Thos 74-75; Asst Bp Dhaka 75; Bp Dhaka and Moderator Ch of Bangladesh 75-03; rtd 03. *Merlin Apartment, 59/A-1 Barobagh, Dhaka 1216, Bangladesh* Tel (00880) (2) 805 1656 Mobile 172-031350

MONDON, Simon Charles. b 57. WEMTC. **d** 02 **p** 03. OLM Worfield *Heref* 02-09; V Goodrich, Marstow, Welsh Bicknor, Llangarron etc from 09. *The Vicarage, Llangrove, Ross-on-Wye HR9 6EZ* Tel (01989) 770341 E-mail revsimon@btinternet.com

MONDS, Anthony John Beatty. b 53. Solicitor 77. **d** 97 **p** 00. OLM Queen Thorne *Sarum* 97-04; C Sherborne w Castleton, Lillington and Longburton 04-06; V Piddle Valley, Hilton, Cheselbourne etc from 06. *The Vicarage, Church Lane, Piddletrenthide, Dorchester DT2 7QY* Tel (01300) 348211 E-mail tony.monds@btinternet.com

MONEY, John Charles. b 69. Wycliffe Hall Ox 01. **d** 03 **p** 04. C Porchester *S'well* 03-06; TV Plymouth St Andr and Stonehouse *Ex* from 06. *88 Durnford Street, Stonehouse, Plymouth PL13 3QW* Tel (01752) 223774 Mobile 07711-285217 E-mail john.stjames@ntlworld.com

MONEY, Mrs Lynn Astrid. b 59. St Martin's Coll Lanc BEd80. WEMTC 03. **d** 06 **p** 07. C Letton w Staunton, Byford, Mansel Gamage etc *Heref* 06-09; R Bredenbury from 09. *The Rectory, Bredenbury, Bromyard HR7 4TF* Tel (01885) 482236 Mobile 07836-295627

MONGER, John Dennis. b 26. **d** 99 **p** 99. NSM Ewyas Harold w Dulas, Kenderchurch etc *Heref* 99-04; RD Abbeydore 00-02; rtd 04; Perm to Offic *Heref* from 04. *Chapel Cottage, Longtown, Hereford HR2 0LE* Tel (01873) 860306

MONGER, Paul James. b 54. Reading Univ BEd77 Greenwich Univ MSc99. NTMTC 07. **d** 10 **p** 11. NSM Chingford St Edm *Chelmsf* from 10. *25 Stanmore Road, London E11 3BU* Tel 07739-905363 (mobile) E-mail james.monger@yahoo.com

MONK, Carol Lorna. b 57. STETS 08. **d** 11. NSM Ash *Guildf* from 11. *The Hawthorns, 2 Rowhill Avenue, Aldershot GU11 3LU* Tel (01252) 313239 E-mail clmonk@virginmedia.com

MONK, Mrs Mary. b 38. CertEd58. S'wark Ord Course 85. **d** 88 **p** 94. NSM Lee Gd Shep w St Pet *S'wark* 88-99; NSM Harpenden St Jo *St Alb* 99-07; Perm to Offic from 07. *3 Hawthorn Close, Harpenden AL5 1HN* Tel (01582) 462567

MONK, Nicholas John. b 32. Westcott Ho Cam 61. **d** 63 **p** 64. C Bris H Cross Inns Court 63-67; C Stoke Bishop 67-69; V Swindon All SS 69-75; V Ashton Keynes w Leigh 75-87; P-in-c Minety w Oaksey 82-87; RD Malmesbury 85-88; V Ashton Keynes, Leigh and Minety 87-91; TR Swindon St Jo and St Andr 91-97; rtd 97; Perm to Offic *Heref* from 97. *The Riddings Cottage, Newcastle on Clun, Craven Arms SY7 8QT* Tel (01686) 670929

MONK, Paul Malcolm Spenser. b 65. Ex Univ BSc86 PhD90 Leeds Univ MA07 CChem MRSC. NOC 05. **d** 07 **p** 08. C Oldham *Man* 07-09; TV Medlock Head from 09. *St Barnabas Vicarage, 1 Arundel Street, Oldham OL4 1NL* Tel 0161-624 7708 Mobile 07854-776410 E-mail paul and jo monk@yahoo.co.uk

MONK, Stephen David. b 74. Leuven Univ Belgium STB03. Qu Coll Birm 05. **d** 00 **p** 01. C Knighton St Mary Magd *Leic* 06-08; C Wigston Magna from 08. *8 Harrogate Way, Wigston LE18 3YB* Tel 0116-288 8806 Mobile 07967-825277 E-mail rev.stephenmonk@btinternet.com

MONKHOUSE, Henry Alistair. b 34. **d** 99 **p** 00. OLM Quidenham Gp *Nor* 99-05; Perm to Offic from 05. *Wildwood, Mill Road, Old Buckenham, Attleborough NR17 1SG* Tel (01953) 860845 E-mail henrym45@btinternet.com

MONKHOUSE, William Stanley. b 50. Qu Coll Cam BA72 MA76 MB, BChir75 Nottm Univ PhD85 MA06. EMMTC 04. **d** 06 **p** 07. C Wirksworth *Derby* 06-08; P-in-c Old Brampton 08-09; P-in-c Gt Barlow 08-09; P-in-c Old Brampton and Great Barlow 09-11; R 11; P-in-c Loundsley Green 09-11; Asst Dir of Ords 09-11; I Maryborough w Dysart Enos and Ballyfin

C & O from 11. *The Rectory, Coote Street, Portlaoise, Co Laois, Republic of Ireland* Tel (00353) (57) 862 1154 E-mail stanleymonkhouse@gmail.com

MONKS, Ian Kay. b 36. K Coll Lon BA60 Lon Inst of Educn PGCE61. Oak Hill NSM Course 90. **d** 93 **p** 94. NSM Woodford Bridge *Chelmsf* 93-06; Perm to Offic from 06. *46 Summit Drive, Woodford Green IG8 8QP* Tel (020) 8550 2390

MONMOUTH, Archdeacon of. See PAIN, The Ven Richard Edward

MONMOUTH, Bishop of. See WALKER, The Rt Revd Edward William Murray

MONMOUTH, Dean of. Vacant

MONTAGUE (née LAIDLAW), Mrs Juliet. b 52. Nottm Univ BTh82. Linc Th Coll 78. **dss** 82 **d** 87 **p** 94. Gainsborough All SS *Linc* 82-86; Chapl Linc Cathl and Linc Colls of FE 86-92; Dn-in-c Gedney Hill and Whaplode Drove 92-94; P-in-c 94-99; P-in-c Crawley and Littleton and Sparsholt w Lainston *Win* 99-03; R 03-08; R Downs Benefice from 08. *The Rectory, Church Lane, Littleton, Winchester SO22 6QY* Tel (01962) 881898 E-mail revdjuliet@montague.me.uk

MONTAGUE-YOUENS, Canon Hubert Edward. b 30. Ripon Hall Ox 55. **d** 58 **p** 59. C Redditch St Steph *Worc* 58-59; C Halesowen 59-62; V Kempsey 62-69; V Kidderminster St Geo 69-72; R Ribbesford w Bewdley and Dowles 72-81; RD Kidderminster 74-81; Hon Can Worc Cathl 78-81; TR Bridport *Sarum* 81-86; RD Lyme Bay 82-86; V Easebourne *Chich* 86-89; Chapl K Edw VII Hosp Midhurst 86-89; rtd 89; Perm to Offic *Worc* from 89; *Glouc* 89-95 and from 98; P-in-c Twyning *Glouc* 96-98. *6 Harbour View, Bredon Road, Tewkesbury GL20 5AZ* Tel (01684) 292363

MONTEITH, Canon David Robert Malvern. b 68. St Jo Coll Dur BSc89 Nottm Univ BTh92 MA93. St Jo Coll Nottm 90. **d** 93 **p** 94. C Kings Heath *Birm* 93-97; C St Martin-in-the-Fields *Lon* 97-02; P-in-c S Wimbledon H Trin and St Pet *S'wark* 02-09; TR Merton Priory 09; AD Merton 04-09; Can Res and Chan Leic Cathl from 09. *39 Meadowcourt Road, Leicester LE2 2PD* Tel 0116-248 7400 Mobile 07952-238291 E-mail david.monteith@leccofe.org

MONTGOMERIE, Alexander (Sandy). b 47. St Jo Coll Nottm 89. **d** 94 **p** 96. NSM Irvine St Andr LEP *Glas* from 94; NSM Ardrossan from 94. *105 Sharphill Road, Saltcoats KA21 5QU* Tel and fax (01294) 465193 E-mail sandy.montgomerie@btinternet.com

MONTGOMERIE, Andrew Simon. b 60. Keble Coll Ox BA82. Ridley Hall Cam 83. **d** 85 **p** 86. C Childwall All SS *Liv* 85-87; C Yardley St Edburgha *Birm* 87-90; TV Solihull 90-96; V Balsall Common 96-05; P-in-c Eyam *Derby* 05-11; C Baslow w Curbar and Stoney Middleton 06-11; R Baslow and Eyam from 11; RD Bakewell and Eyam from 07. *The Rectory, Church Street, Eyam, Hope Valley S32 5QH* Tel (01433) 630821 E-mail asmontgomerie@hotmail.co.uk

MONTGOMERY, Canon Anthony Alan. b 33. Trin Hall Cam BA56. Edin Th Coll 56. **d** 58 **p** 59. C Dumfries *Glas* 58-63; P-in-c Airdrie 63-66; R 66-68; Asst Chapl Gordonstoun Sch 68-93; Can St Andr Cathl Inverness from 81; rtd 93. *Easter Hillside, Mosstowie, Elgin IV30 8XE* Tel and fax (01343) 850282

MONTGOMERY, Canon Ian David. b 44. St Andr Univ LLB66 Univ of the South (USA) DMin02 FCA69. Wycliffe Hall Ox 71. **d** 75 **p** 76. C Fulham St Dionis *Lon* 75-78; Chapl Amherst Coll USA 78-83; R New Orleans St Phil 83-92; R Nashville St Bart 92-97; R Menasha St Thos 97-99; rtd 09; SAMS Peru from 09; Can Peru from 10. *Iglesia Anglicana del Perú, Calle Doa Maria 141, Surco, Lima 13, Peru* Tel (001) (802) 428 4762 *or* 463 2175 E-mail frianm@aol.com

MONTGOMERY (née YOUATT), Canon Jennifer Alison. b 49. St Aid Coll Dur BSc70 Homerton Coll Cam PGCE71. NOC 89. **d** 92 **p** 94. NSM Ripon H Trin from 92; Warden of Readers from 99; Dioc Adv on Women's Min from 10; Hon Can Ripon Cathl from 10. *Washington House, Littlethorpe, Ripon HG4 3LJ* Tel (01765) 605276 *or* tel and fax 609930 E-mail montgomery@littlethorpe97.freeserve.co.uk

MONTGOMERY, Jennifer Susan. b 54. QUB MB, BCh77 Leeds Univ MA05. NOC 02. **d** 05 **p** 06. NSM Ackworth *Wakef* 05-10; P-in-c Goodshaw and Crawshawbooth *Man* from 10. *Goodshaw Vicarage, Goodshawfold Road, Rossendale BB4 8QN* Tel (01706) 601262 Mobile 07780-764233 E-mail jsm1954@hotmail.com

MONTGOMERY, Laura Alice. b 77. Lon Bible Coll BTh99. St Jo Coll Nottm MTh09. **d** 09. C Newton Liv from 09. *St John's Vicarage, 63 Market Street, Newton-le-Willows WA12 9BS* Tel (01925) 223727 Mobile 07511-030948 E-mail la.monty@yahoo.co.uk

MONTGOMERY, Mark. b 77. **d** 10 **p** 11. NSM Upton (Overchurch) *Ches* from 10. *18 Kingfisher Way, Wirral CH49 4PR*

MONTGOMERY, Pembroke John Charles. b 24. Codrington Coll Barbados. **d** 53 **p** 55. C St Geo Cathl St Vincent 55-73; R Biabou 56-65; R Calliaqua 65-73; Can Kingstown Cathl 63-73; P-in-c Derby St Jas 73-74; V 74-90; rtd 90. *39 Church Street, Tutbury, Burton-on-Trent DE13 9JE* Tel (01283) 814887

MONTGOMERY, Rachel. *See* TREWEEK, The Ven Rachel

MONTGOMERY, Stanley. b 18. Lich Th Coll. **d** 52 **p** 53. P-in-c Hitcham w Lt Finborough, Kettlebaston etc 93-95; Perm to Offic *St E* 95-05. *34 Drovers Rise, Stanton, Bury St Edmunds IP31 2BW* Tel (01359) 250359 E-mail freddie@fmontgomery.fslife.co.uk

MONTGOMERY, Canon Thomas Charles Osborne. b 59. Edin Univ BD81. Edin Th Coll 77. **d** 82 **p** 83. C Glas St Mary 82-85; C Dumfries 85-88; R Hamilton 88-96; R Glas St Marg 96-10; R Troon from 10; Can St Mary's Cathl from 94. *70 Bentinck Drive, Troon KA10 6HZ* Tel (01292) 313731

MONTGOMERY, Canon Timothy Robert. b 59. Hull Univ BA82 Cam Univ PGCE83. EAMTC 90. **d** 93 **p** 94. Dir Romsey Mill Community Cen 93-94; NSM Cambridge St Phil 93-96; Warden Kepplewray Cen Broughton-in-Furness 96-00; NSM Kendal St Thos *Carl* 96-00; V from 00; Hon Can Carl Cathl from 06. *St Thomas's Vicarage, South View Lane, Kendal LA9 4QN* Tel (01539) 729617 *or* 730683 Fax 729010 E-mail vicar@saintthomaskendal.net

MONTGOMERY, Archdeacon of. *See* THELWELL, The Ven John Berry

MONTROSE, Michelle Ann. b 57. NOC 05. **d** 08. NSM W Derby St Mary *Liv* 08-09; NSM W Derby St Mary and St Jas from 09. *1 Highfield View, Liverpool L13 3BP* Tel 0151-220 1746 Mobile 07528-331316 E-mail michelleamontrose@yahoo.co.uk

MOODY, Christopher John Everard. b 51. New Coll Ox BA72 Lon Univ MSc90. Cuddesdon Coll BA74. **d** 75 **p** 76. C Fulham All SS *Lon* 75-79; C Surbiton St Andr and St Mark *S'wark* 79-82; Chapl K Coll Lon 82-87; V S Lambeth St Anne and All 33 *S'wark* 87-95; RD Lambeth 90-95; P-in-c Market Harborough *Leic* 95-97; P-in-c Market Harborough Transfiguration 95-97; V Market Harborough and The Transfiguration etc 97-05; Hon Can Leic Cathl 04-05; V Greenwich St Alfege *S'wark* from 05. *The Vicarage, Park Vista, London SE10 9LZ* Tel (020) 8858 6828 E-mail chrisjemoody@btinternet.com

MOODY, Colin John. b 36. Chich Th Coll 61. **d** 63 **p** 64. C Hove All SS *Chich* 63-69; C Dulwich St Barn *S'wark* 69-70; Perm to Offic *Bris* 70-71; *Chich* 72-78 and from 90; Lic to Offic *Ely* 78-89; rtd 01. *11 Hewitts, Henfield BN5 9DT* Tel and fax (01273) 495062

MOODY, Ms Elizabeth Jane. b 61. Hull Univ BA82 Westmr Coll Ox PGCE84. Ridley Hall Cam 00. **d** 02 **p** 03. C Uxbridge *Lon* 02-05; C Hanwell St Mary w St Chris from 05. *26 Tentelow Lane, Southall UB2 4LE* Tel 07796-988302 (mobile) E-mail lizmoody@blueyonder.co.uk

MOODY, Preb George Henry. b 27. ACIS56 ARCA68. Cranmer Hall Dur 69. **d** 71 **p** 72. C Marske in Cleveland *York* 71-74; Chapl to the Deaf *Lich* 74-89; Preb Lich Cathl 83-89; rtd 89; Perm to Offic *York* from 90. *21 Priestcrofts, Marske-by-the-Sea, Redcar TS11 7HW* Tel (01642) 489660

MOODY, Canon Ivor Robert. b 57. K Coll Lon BD80 AKC Anglia Ruskin Univ MA03. Coll of Resurr Mirfield. **d** 82 **p** 83. C Leytonstone St Marg w St Columba *Chelmsf* 82-85; C Leigh-on-Sea St Marg 85-88; V Tilbury Docks 88-96; Chapl Anglia Ruskin Univ 96-10; Hon Can Chelmsf Cathl 09-10; Vice-Dean and Can Res Chelmsf Cathl from 10. *83 Ridgewell Avenue, Chelmsf CM1 2GF* Tel (01245) 267773 *or* 294493 E-mail vicedean@chelmsfordcathedral.org.uk

MOODY, John Kelvin. b 30. St Fran Coll Brisbane ThL55. **d** 56 **p** 57. C Warwick Australia 56-57; C Southport 57-58; C Dalby 58-61; C Earl's Court St Cuth w St Matthias *Lon* 61-64; Chapl Ankara *Eur* 64-69; Chapl Istanbul 64-66; Chapl Palma 69-75; Chapl Tangier 75-79; Can Ldn Cathl 74-79; Hon Can from 79; Australia from 79; rtd 01. *1 Short Street, Watsons Bay NSW 2030, Australia* Tel (0061) (2) 9337 2871 E-mail jm986672@bigpond.net.au

MOOKERJI, Michael Manoje. b 45. Baring Union Coll Punjab BSc69. Ridley Hall Cam 83. **d** 85 **p** 86. C Heanor *Derby* 85-92; V Codnor and Loscoe 92-93; V Codnor 93-02; V Winshill from 02. *The Vicarage, 54 Mill Hill Lane, Burton-on-Trent DE15 0BB* Tel (01283) 545143

MOON, Arthur Thomas. b 22. ACP53 LCP56. Sarum Th Coll 65. **d** 66 **p** 67. C Fulwood Ch Ch *Blackb* 66-71; Hon C Bispham 71-80; C 80-87; rtd 87; Perm to Offic *Blackb* from 87. *15 Kirkstone Drive, Thornton-Cleveleys FY5 1QQ* Tel (01253) 853521

MOON, Sister Catherine Joy. b 48. LRAM68 ARCM69. Gen Th Sem NY 84. **d** 84 **p** 85. USA 84-02; CSF from 87; Chapl Ashworth Hosp Maghull from 04. *42 Boxtree Close, Liverpool L12 0PN* Tel 07906-365962 (mobile)

MOON, John Charles. b 23. Sarum Th Coll 49. **d** 51 **p** 52. C Bottesford *Linc* 51-54; C Habrough 54-55; V Immingham 55-61; V Weaste *Man* 61-67; V Spalding St Jo *Linc* 67-82; V Spalding St Jo w Deeping St Nicholas 82-86; rtd 86; Perm to Offic *Linc* 87-02. *14 Harrox Road, Moulton, Spalding PE12 6PR* Tel (01406) 370111

MOON, Philip. b 59. CCC Ox BA80 Warwick Univ PhD92. Wycliffe Hall Ox BTh01. **d** 01 **p** 02. C Otley *Bradf* 01-05; V Lt Aston *Lich* from 05. *The Vicarage, 3 Walsall Road, Little Aston, Sutton Coldfield B74 3BD* Tel 0121-353 0798 E-mail familyofmoon@aol.com

MOON, Philip Russell. b 56. Em Coll Cam BA78 MA81 Reading Univ PGCE79. Wycliffe Hall Ox BA82. **d** 85 **p** 86. C Crowborough *Chich* 85-87; Hd of CYFA (CPAS) 87-94; V Lowestoft Ch Ch *Nor* 94-04; P-in-c Hove Bp Hannington Memorial Ch *Chich* 04-06; V from 06; RD Hove 05-08. *82 Holmes Avenue, Hove BN3 7LD* Tel (01273) 732821

MOON, Thomas Arnold. b 24. Lon Univ BA51. Oak Hill Th Coll 49. **d** 52 **p** 53. C Fazakerley Em *Liv* 52-56; V Everton St Benedict 56-70; V Formby St Luke 70-95; rtd 95; Perm to Offic *Liv* from 95. *8 Harington Road, Formby, Liverpool L37 1NU* Tel (01704) 872249

MOONEY, The Very Revd Paul Gerard. b 58. St Patr Coll Maynooth BD84 Asian Cen for Th Studies and Miss Seoul ThM92 Protestant Th Faculty Brussels DrTheol02. **d** 84 **p** 85. In RC Ch 84-90; Chapl Miss to Seamen Korea 90-94; Hon Can Pusan from 94; Chapl Antwerp Miss to Seamen 94-97; Asst Chapl Antwerp St Boniface *Eur* 94-97; C Galway w Kilcummin *T, K & A* 97-98; I New w Old Ross, Whitechurch, Fethard etc *C & O* 98-07; Hon Chapl New Ross and Waterford Miss to Seamen 98-07; Prec Ferns Cathl 01-07; Adn Ferns 02-07; Chapl Seoul Cathl Korea 07-11; Dean Ferns *C & O* from 11; I Ferns w Kilbride, Toombe, Kilcormack etc from 11. *The Deanery, Ferns, Enniscorthy, Co Wexford, Republic of Ireland* Tel (00353) (53) 936 6124 E-mail pgmoon@hotmail.com

MOOR, Simon Alan. b 65. Nottm Univ BTh93. Linc Th Coll 90. **d** 93 **p** 94. C Skegness and Winthorpe *Linc* 93-96; C Airedale w Fryston *Wakef* 96-98, V Hoylandswaine and Silkstone w Stainborough 98-11; V Huddersfield St Pet from 11; Bp's Adv for Ecum Affairs from 08. *59 Lightridge Road, Fixby, Huddersfield HD2 2HF* Tel (01484) 544558 E-mail samoor@talktalk.net

MOORCROFT, Steven James. b 73. Wye Coll Lon BSc95. Cranmer Hall Dur 05. **d** 07 **p** 08. C Kendal St Thos *Carl* 07-09. *Little Pendene, Fore Street, Grampound, Truro TR2 4RS* Tel (01726) 882242 E-mail s.j.moorcroft@btinternet.com

MOORE, Albert William (Bill). b 47. WMMTC 91. **d** 94 **p** 95. C Hobs Moat *Birm* 94-98; V Dosthill 98-06; V Hill from 06. *61 Mere Green Road, Sutton Coldfield B75 5BW* Tel 0121-308 0074

MOORE, Andrew Jonathan. b 57. York Univ BA82 Wycliffe Hall Ox BA84 MA89 Worc Coll Ox DPhil99. **d** 86 **p** 86. C Camberwell St Jo Australia 86-87; Assoc P S Yarra Ch Ch 87-90; Asst/Acting Chapl Worc Coll Ox 91-94; Chapl Jes Coll Ox 94-99; Voc Adv *Ox* 98-04; Dir of Ords from 04; Hon Chapl Cen for Mediaeval and Renaissance Studies Ox 99-04; Research Fell Regent's Park Coll Ox 01-04; Chapl St Pet Coll Ox 04-07. Theology Faculty, *41 St Giles, Oxford OX1 3LW* Tel (01865) 270731 E-mail andrew.moore@spc.ox.ac.uk

MOORE, Anthony Harry. b 34. Westcott Ho Cam 88. **d** 90 **p** 91. C Eyke w Bromeswell, Rendlesham, Tunstall etc *St E* 90-93; V Aldeburgh w Hazlewood 93-02; rtd 02; Perm to Offic *St E* and *Chelmsf* from 02. *5 Kings Meadow, Great Cornard, Sudbury CO10 0HP* Tel (01787) 377967

MOORE, Anthony Michael. b 71. Ex Univ BA94 Leeds Univ BA98 MA99 PhD10 Cam Univ MA10. Coll of Resurr Mirfield 96. **d** 99 **p** 00. C Carnforth *Blackb* 99-03; Fell and Past Tutor Coll of Resurr Mirfield 03-04; C Wilton Place St Paul *Lon* 04-07; Chapl R Academy of Music 04-07; Chapl and Fell St Cath Coll Cam from 07. *St Catharine's College, Trumpington Street, Cambridge CB2 1RL* Tel (01223) 338346 E-mail amm21@cam.ac.uk *or* chaplain@caths.cam.ac.uk

MOORE, Anthony Richmond. b 36. Clare Coll Cam BA59 MA63. Linc Th Coll 59. **d** 61 **p** 62. C Roehampton H Trin *S'wark* 61-66; C New Eltham All SS 66-70; P Missr Blackbird Leys CD *Ox* 70-81; Dioc Ecum Officer 80-98; TV Dorchester 81-93; R Enstone and Heythrop 93-01; rtd 01; Perm to Offic *Ox* from 01. *13 Cobden Crescent, Oxford OX1 4LJ* Tel (01865) 244673 E-mail moore.t@which.net

MOORE, Arlene. b 64. Dundee Univ BSc87 N Coll of Educn PGCE90 TCD BTh95. CITC 92. **d** 95 **p** 96. C Portadown St Mark *Arm* 95-99; Perm to Offic *Sheff* 99-02 and 03-09; C Crookes St Thos 02-03; Chapl Belfast Health and Soc Care Trust 09-10; P-in-c Monkstown *Conn* from 09. *Monkstown Rectory, 27 Twinburn Gardens, Newtownabbey BT37 0EW* Tel (028) 9086 4902 Mobile 07921-864024 E-mail sendmyemails2me@yahoo.com

MOORE, Arthur Lewis. b 33. Dur Univ BA58 PhD64. Cranmer Hall Dur. **d** 62 **p** 63. C Stone *Roch* 62-66; C Clevedon St Andr *B & W* 66-68; Chapl Wycliffe Hall Ox 68-70; Vice-Prin 70-83; P-in-c Ampfield *Win* 83-84; V Hursley and Ampfield 84-92; TV Ewyas Harold w Dulas, Kenderchurch etc *Heref* 92-94; P-in-c 94-98; rtd 98. *2 Tollstone Way, Grosmont, Abergavenny NP7 8ER* Tel (01981) 240415

MOORE, Canon Bernard Geoffrey. b 27. New Coll Ox BA47 MA52. Ely Th Coll 49. **d** 51 **p** 52. C Chorley St Pet *Blackb* 51-54; Bp's Dom Chapl 54-55; C-in-c Blackpool St Mich CD 55-67;

Chapl Victoria Hosp Blackpool 58-67; V Morecambe St Barn *Blackb* 67-81; R Standish 81-88; Hon Can Blackb Cathl 86-92; RD Chorley 86-92; V Charnock Richard 88-92; rtd 92; Perm to Offic *Ex* from 92; *Carl* from 01; *Win* from 00. *29 Wiltshire Close, Exeter EX4 1LU* Tel (01392) 258686

MOORE, Bernard George. b 32. Qu Coll Birm 57. **d** 60 **p** 62. C Middlesbrough St Columba *York* 60-62; C Kimberley Cathl S Africa 62-64; R Kimberley St Matt 64-69; Chapl RN 70-74; C Milton *Portsm* 74-76; V Glenfield New Zealand 76-80; V Kaitaia 80-84; V Gisborne 84-86; rtd 97. *45 Feasegate Street, Manurewa 2102, New Zealand* Tel (0064) (9) 267 6924
E-mail freesaxon2000@yahoo.com

✠**MOORE, The Rt Revd Bruce Macgregor.** b 31. Univ of NZ BA55. Coll of Resurr Mirfield. **d** 57 **p** 58 **c** 92. C Blackpool St Steph *Blackb* 57-61; New Zealand from 61; Hon Can Auckland 78-96; Adn Manukau 81-90; Asst Bp Auckland 92-97. *5 Pokaka Crescent, Taupo 3330, New Zealand* Tel (0064) (7) 378 4849 E-mail brucemoore@xtra.co.nz

MOORE, Caroline Judith. *See* FALKINGHAM, Mrs Caroline Judith

MOORE, Miss Catherine Joy. b 63. Bretton Hall Coll BEd85 Anglia Poly Univ MEd94. St Mellitus Coll BA10. **d** 10 **p** 11. NSM Springfield All SS *Chelmsf* from 10. *33 Church Street, Witham CM8 2JP* Tel (01376) 501128 Mobile 07860-459465 E-mail katejmoore@aol.com

MOORE, Charles David. b 59. Dundee Univ BSc82 BArch85 Open Univ MA96 RIBA86. St Jo Coll Nottm 91. **d** 93 **p** 94. C Deane *Man* 93-97; Crosslinks 98-02; R and Sub Dean Mutare Zimbabwe 98-02; R Bermondsey St Mary w St Olave, St Jo etc *S'wark* from 02. *The Rectory, 193 Bermondsey Street, London SE1 3UW* Tel (020) 7357 0984

MOORE, Christopher Kevin William. b 69. Ox Brookes Univ BSc92 Bris Univ BA01 Trin Coll Bris PhD10 MRICS95. Bris Bapt Coll 98. **d** 09 **p** 10. C Tenbury *Heref* from 09. *Deepcroft Cottage, Worcester Road, Newnham Bridge, Tenbury Wells WR15 8JA* Tel (01584) 781157 E-mail chris@cm5j.com

MOORE, Preb Clive Granville. b 31. St Pet Hall Ox BA54 MA58. Wycliffe Hall Ox 54. **d** 55 **p** 56. C Newbarns w Hawcoat *Carl* 55-57; CF 57-61; Chapl Joyce Green Hosp Dartford 61-69; R Stone *Roch* 61-69; R Radstock *B & W* 69-71; P-in-c Writhlington 69-71; R Radstock w Writhlington 71-83; RD Midsomer Norton 81-83; R S Petherton w the Seavingtons 83-95; RD Crewkerne 83-92; R S Crewkerne and Ilminster 93; Preb Wells Cathl 90-95; rtd 95; Perm to Offic *B & W* from 95. *Mowries Stable, West Street, Somerton TA11 6NA* Tel (01458) 274649

MOORE, Canon Colin Frederick. b 49. CITC 69. **d** 72 **p** 73. C Drumglass w Moygashel *Arm* 72-80; I Newtownhamilton w Ballymoyer and Belleek from 80; Hon V Choral Arm Cathl 85-96; Can and Preb from 97; Asst Dioc and Prov Registrar 96-09; Dioc and Prov Registrar from 09. *71 Ballymoyer Road, Whitecross, Armagh BT60 2LA* Tel (028) 3750 7256

MOORE, Darren Lee. b 73. Kingston Univ BEng95. Oak Hill Th Coll BA01. **d** 01 **p** 02. C Camberwell All SS *S'wark* 01-04; P-in-c Tranmere St Cath *Ches* 04-07; V from 07. *St Catherine's Vicarage, 39 Westbank Road, Birkenhead CH42 7JP* Tel 0151-652 7379 E-mail darren@stcatherinestranmere.co.uk

MOORE, Darren Richard. b 70. Univ of Wales (Abth) BD91 Hull Univ PGCE97 St Jo Coll York MA(Ed)03 Leeds Univ MA04. Coll of Resurr Mirfield 02. **d** 04 **p** 05. C Scarborough St Martin *York* 04-07; R Brayton 07-09; Chapl Ranby Ho Sch Retford 09-11; P-in-c Leeds Halton St Wilfrid *Ripon* from 11. *St Wilfrid's Vicarage, Selby Road, Leeds LS15 7NP* Tel 0113-264 7000 Mobile 07745-296406 E-mail frdmoore@gotadsl.co.uk

MOORE, David James Paton. b 60. Sheff Univ BEng82. Cranmer Hall Dur 88. **d** 91 **p** 92. C Pemberton St Mark Newtown *Liv* 91-94; C St Helens St Helen 94-97; V Canonbury St Steph *Lon* 97-07; NSM Easton H Trin w St Gabr and St Lawr and St Jude *Bris* from 08. *St Michael's Vicarage, St Michael's Court, Kingswood, Bristol BS15 1BE* Tel 0117-967 9446

MOORE, David Leonard. b 51. **d** 80 **p** 82. Hon C Brixton St Matt *S'wark* 80-82; C 82-84; TV Bris St Agnes and St Simon w St Werburgh 84-86; Perm to Offic *Bris* 86-88 and *Blackb* from 88. *154 Victoria Road, Fulwood, Preston PR2 8NQ*

MOORE, David Metcalfe. b 41. Hull Univ BA64 PhD69. Trin Coll Bris 76. **d** 78 **p** 79. C Marple All SS *Ches* 78-82; V Loudwater *Ox* 82-90; V Chilwell *S'well* 90-93; rtd 93; Perm to Offic *Ely* from 05. *12 Rhugarve Gardens, Linton, Cambridge CB21 4LX* Tel (01223) 894315
E-mail davidmmoore@mypostoffice.co.uk

MOORE, David Roy. b 39. Clare Coll Cam BA61. Ripon Hall Ox 61. **d** 63 **p** 64. C Melton Mowbray w Thorpe Arnold *Leic* 63-66; C St Steph Walbrook and St Swithun etc *Lon* 66-72; Dep Dir The Samaritans 66-72; Public Preacher *S'well* 72-77; C Daybrook 77-80; V 80-87; V Ham St Andr *S'wark* 87-99; P-in-c Rothbury *Newc* 99-04; rtd 04; P-in-c Kneesall w Laxton and Wellow *S'well* 04-07. *Lily Cottage, Far Back Lane, Farnsfield, Newark NG22 8JX*

MOORE, Donald John. b 31. Chich Th Coll 86. **d** 87 **p** 88. C Uckfield *Chich* 87-88; C Southwick St Mich 88-90; Bermuda from 90; Asst P St Geo 90-97; P-in-c St Dav 90-97; Chapl St Brendan's Psychiatric Hosp 92-97; rtd 97. *PO Box HM122, Hamilton HM AX, Bermuda* Tel (001) (441) 296 8962

MOORE, Douglas Gregory. b 49. Bris Univ BA71 CertEd72. Coll of Resurr Mirfield 87. **d** 89 **p** 90. C Hessle *York* 89-93; P-in-c Micklefield w Aberford 93-95; V Aberford w Micklefield 95-04; P-in-c Darwen St Cuth w Tockholes St Steph *Blackb* from 04. *21 The Meadows, Darwen BB3 0PF* Tel (01254) 771196
E-mail douglasgmoore@yahoo.co.uk

MOORE, Edward James. b 32. TD85. TCD BA56 MA59. **d** 56 **p** 57. C Belfast St Luke *Conn* 56-59; CF 59-62; C Dunmurry *Conn* 62-64; P-in-c Kilmakee 64-70; I Belfast H Trin 70-80; I Jordanstown w Monkstown 80-91; I Jordanstown 91-97; Chapl Ulster Poly 80-84; Chapl Ulster Univ 84-88; CF (ACF) 66-70 and 88-97; CF (TAVR) 70-88; Can Belf Cathl 89-97; rtd 97. *16 Langford Close, Carrickfergus BT38 8HG* Tel (028) 9336 7209 E-mail ejm@ejmoore.plus.com

MOORE, Geoffrey David. b 51. Poly Cen Lon BA73. ERMC 04. **d** 07 **p** 08. NSM Brackley St Pet w St Jas 07-11; NSM Aston-le-Walls, Byfield, Boddington, Eydon etc from 11. *The New Vicarage, Parsons Street, Woodford Halse, Daventry NN11 3RE* Tel (01327) 261477 E-mail geoff@ccvp.co.uk

MOORE, Geoffrey Robert. b 46. WEMTC 03. **d** 06 **p** 07. NSM Upton-on-Severn, Ripple, Earls Croome etc *Worc* from 06. *12 Hill View Gardens, Upton-upon-Severn WR8 0QJ* Tel (01684) 594531 Mobile 07876-162402

MOORE, Mrs Gillian Mary. NTMTC. **d** 09 **p** 10. NSM Harwich Peninsula *Chelmsf* from 09. *15 Lushington Road, Manningtree CO11 1EE* Tel (01206) 397493

MOORE, Henry James William. b 33. TCD BA55 MA70. **d** 56 **p** 57. C Mullabrack *Arm* 56-61; C Drumglass 61-63; I Clogherny 63-81; I Ballinderry, Tamlaght and Arboe 81-08; Can Arm Cathl 90-08; Chan 98-01; Prec 01-08; rtd 08. *20 Laragh Road, Beragh, Omagh BT79 0TH* Tel (028) 8075 7384

✠**MOORE, The Rt Revd Henry Wylie.** b 23. Liv Univ BCom50 Leeds Univ MA72. Wycliffe Hall Ox 50. **d** 52 **p** 53 **c** 83. C Farnworth *Liv* 52-54; C Middleton *Man* 54-56; CMS 56-60; Iran 57-60; R Burnage St Marg *Man* 60-63; R Middleton 60-74; Home Sec CMS 74-80; Exec Sec CMS 80-83; Bp Cyprus and the Gulf 83-86; Gen Sec CMS 86-90; rtd 90; Asst Bp Dur 90-94; Perm to Offic *Heref* from 94. *Fern Hill Cottage, Hopesay, Craven Arms SY7 8HD* Tel (01588) 660248

MOORE, Preb Hugh Desmond. b 37. St Cath Soc Ox BA58 MA64. St Steph Ho Ox 58. **d** 61 **p** 62. C Kingston St Luke *S'wark* 61-68; Asst Chapl Lon Univ 68-70; Chapl Edgware Community Hosp 70-92; Chapl Wellhouse NHS Trust 92-99; V Hendon St Alphage *Lon* from 70; AD W Barnet 85-90; Preb St Paul's Cathl from 95. *The Vicarage, Montrose Avenue, Edgware HA8 0DN* Tel (020) 8952 4611
E-mail hugh.moore@tesco.net

MOORE, Ivan. b 46. MA BTh. **d** 90 **p** 91. C Knock *D & D* 90-93; I Taney *D & G* 97-99; Chapl Bancroft's Sch Woodford Green from 99. *41 Wynndale Road, London E18 1DY* Tel (020) 8559 2791 *or* 8505 4821 Fax 8559 0032

MOORE, James. *See* MOORE, Edward James

MOORE, Canon James Kenneth. b 37. AKC62. St Boniface Warminster 62. **d** 63 **p** 64. C W Hartlepool St Oswald *Dur* 63-66; C-in-c Manor Park CD *Sheff* 66-76; TV Sheff Manor 76-78; R Frecheville and Hackenthorpe 78-87; V Bilham 87-91; V Sheff St Oswald 91-02; Hon Can Sheff Cathl 93-02; rtd 02; Perm to Offic *Sheff* from 02. *115 Greenhill Main Road, Sheffield S8 7RG* Tel 0114-283 9634

MOORE (formerly BEVAN), Ms Janet Mary. b 46. Bris Poly CertEd86. WMMTC. **d** 98 **p** 99. C Bishop's Cleeve *Glouc* 98-02; V Overbury w Teddington, Alstone etc *Worc* 02-08; Faith Co-ord Surrey Police *Guildf* 08-11; rtd 11. *8 St John's Close, Cirencester GL7 2JA* Tel (01285) 640077
E-mail therevjan@btinternet.com

MOORE, Janis. **d** 05 **p** 06. OLM Bridport *Sarum* from 05. *61 North Allington, Bridport DT6 5DZ* Tel (01305) 425644

MOORE, John. b 22. St Aid Birkenhead 54. **d** 57 **p** 58. C Glenavy w Tunny and Crumlin *Conn* 57-59; I Kingscourt w Syddan *M & K* 60-63; C Carnmoney *Conn* 63-65; P-in-c Templepatrick w Donegore 65-68; I Templepatrick 68-85; rtd 85. *13 Brookhill House, 2 Newmills Road Lower, Coleraine BT52 2JR* Tel (028) 7032 6753 E-mail jack@cuthona.fsnet.co.uk

MOORE, John. b 26. Univ of Wales (Lamp) BA51. Oak Hill Th Coll 51. **d** 53 **p** 54. C Illogan *Truro* 53-57; C Margate H Trin *Cant* 57-58; C Abingdon w Shippon *Ox* 58-67; V Retford St Sav *S'well* 67-73; R Aspenden and Layston w Buntingford *St Alb* 73-86; V Stanstead Abbots 86-91; rtd 91; Perm to Offic *Ox* from 95. *20 Radley Road, Abingdon OX14 3PQ* Tel (01235) 532518

MOORE, John. b 53. Haverford Coll (USA) BA75 Columbia Univ MBA78. ERMC. **d** 08 **p** 09. C Paris St Mich *Eur* from 08. *32 avenue Bugeaud, 75116 Paris, France* Tel (0033) 1 44 05 93 43 Mobile 6 17 01 53 06
E-mail johnmoore@saintmichaelsparis.org

MOORE, John Arthur. b 33. Cuddesdon Coll 70. **d** 71 **p** 72. Hon C Gt Burstead *Chelmsf* 71-74; Chapl Barnard Castle Sch 74-97; rtd 97; Perm to Offic *Dur* from 97 and *Ripon* from 02. *39 Woodside, Barnard Castle DL12 8DY* Tel (01833) 690947

MOORE, John Cecil. b 37. TCD BA61 MA67 BD69. CITC 62. **d** 62 **p** 63. C Belfast St Matt *Conn* 62-65; C Holywood *D & D* 65-70; I Ballyphilip w Ardquin 70-77; I Mt Merrion 77-79; I Donaghcloney w Waringstown 79-02; Treas Dromore Cathl 90-93; Chan 93-02; rtd 02. *22 Kensington Court, Dollingstown, Craigavon BT66 7HU* Tel (028) 3832 1606 E-mail johncmoore@talktalk.net

MOORE, John David. b 30. St Chad's Coll Dur BA54 DipEd56. **d** 56 **p** 57. C Wallsend St Pet *Newc* 56-60; C Leamington Priors All SS *Cov* 60-62; V Longford 62-75; P-in-c Nuneaton St Mary 75-77; V 77-83; V St Ives *Ely* 83-00; rtd 00; Perm to Offic *Chelmsf* from 01. *25 Felmongers, Harlow CM20 3DH* Tel (01279) 436496 Mobile 07890-976056 E-mail frjdavid@aol.com

MOORE, John Henry. b 35. Nottm Univ BMus56 CertEd57 MA61. EMMTC 87. **d** 90 **p** 91. NSM Gotham *S'well* 90-95; NSM Kingston and Ratcliffe-on-Soar 90-95; NSM Bunny w Bradmore 95-00; P-in-c 97-00; rtd 00. *19 Hall Drive, Gotham, Nottingham NG11 0JT* Tel 0115-983 0670 E-mail john@moorerev.freeserve.co.uk

MOORE, John Keith. b 26. Sarum & Wells Th Coll 78. **d** 81 **p** 82. NSM Guildf All SS 81-86; NSM Guildf H Trin w St Mary 86-94; Dean of Chapter 90-94; Perm to Offic *Chich* 94-06 and *Guildf* from 94. *4 Grover's Manor, Wood Road, Hindhead GU26 6JP* Tel (01428) 605871

MOORE, John Michael. b 48. Em Coll Cam BA70 MA73. Cuddesdon Coll 72. **d** 74 **p** 75. C Almondbury *Wakef* 74-78; TV Basingstoke *Win* 78-88; P-in-c Southampton St Alb 88-91; V Swaythling 91-99; rtd 99; Chapl St Jo Win Charity from 99. *13 Priors Way, Winchester SO22 4HQ* Tel (01962) 862341 *or* 854226 Fax 840602 E-mail office@stjohnswinchester.co.uk

MOORE, Canon John Richard. b 35. Lambeth MA01. St Jo Coll Nottm 56. **d** 59 **p** 60. C Northwood Em *Lon* 59-63; V Burton Dassett *Cov* 63-66; Dioc Youth Chapl 63-71; Dir Lindley Lodge Educn Trust Nuneaton 71-82; TR Kinson *Sarum* 82-88; Gen Dir CPAS 83-96; Hon Can Cov Cathl 95-01; Internat Dir ICS 96-01; rtd 01; Perm to Offic *Cov* from 01. *26 Jourdain Park, Heathcote, Warwick CV34 6FJ* Tel (01926) 429299

MOORE, Canon John Richard. b 45. Linc Th Coll 80. **d** 82 **p** 83. C Gt Grimsby St Mary and St Jas *Linc* 82-86; V Skirbeck Quarter 86-95; P-in-c Coningsby w Tattershall 95-99; R 99-06; R Bain Valley Gp 06-10; Can and Preb Linc Cathl 09-10; rtd 11. *23 Church Lane, Hutton, Alford LN13 9RD* Tel (01507) 490246

MOORE, Mrs Joyce. b 48. TCD BA70 HDipEd71 ARIAM68. CITC 98. **d** 01 **p** 02. NSM Camlough w Mullaglass *Arm* 01-07; NSM Drogheda w Ardee, Collon and Termonfeckin from 07; Hon V Choral Arm Cathl from 07. *Dundalk Road, Dunleer, Co Louth, Republic of Ireland* Tel (00353) (41) 685 1327 E-mail am.drogheda@armagh.anglican.org

MOORE, Leonard Richard. b 22. Leeds Univ BA47. Coll of Resurr Mirfield 47. **d** 49 **p** 50. C Hendon St Mary *Lon* 49-54; C Stevenage *St Alb* 54-60; V Bedford All SS 60-68; Lic to Offic 68-70; P-in-c Bedford H Trin 70-74; rtd 87; Hon C Cardington *St Alb* 87-91; Perm to Offic from 92. *22 Dart Road, Bedford MK41 7BT* Tel (01234) 357536 E-mail leonard@moore9926.fsnet.co.uk

MOORE, Margaret Louise. b 62. DipOT85. SAOMC 04. **d** 06 **p** 07. C Bp's Hatfield, Lemsford and N Mymms *St Alb* 06-10; C Letchworth St Paul w Willian from 10; Chapl Garden Ho Hospice Letchworth from 09. *St Paul's Vicarage, 177 Pixmore Way, Letchworth SG6 1QT* Tel (01462) 483934 Mobile 07729-385830 E-mail louisemoore85@btinternet.com

MOORE, Matthew Edward George. b 38. Oak Hill Th Coll 77. **d** 77 **p** 78. C Larne and Inver *Conn* 77-80; I Desertmartin w Termoneeny *D & R* 80-84; I Milltown *Arm* 84-96; I Culmore w Muff and Belmont *D & R* 96-06; Dioc Warden for Min of Healing 97-06; Can Derry Cathl 04-06; rtd 06. *9 Glen House Mews, Main Street, Eglinton, Londonderry BT47 3AA* Tel (028) 7181 1208 Mobile 07720-036211 E-mail mmoore9@toucansurf.com

MOORE, Canon Michael Mervlyn Hamond. b 35. LVO99. Pemb Coll Ox BA60 MA63. Wells Th Coll 62. **d** 62 **p** 63. C Bethnal Green St Matt *Lon* 62-66; Chapl Bucharest w Sofia and Belgrade *Eur* 66-67; Asst Gen Sec C of E Coun on Foreign Relns 67-70; Gen Sec 70-72; Abp's Chapl on Foreign Relns *Cant* 72-82; Hon C Walworth St Pet *S'wark* 67-80; Hon Can Cant Cathl 74-90; Chapl Chpl Royal Hampton Court Palace 82-99; Dep P in O 92-99; rtd 99. *The College of St Barnabas, Blackberry Lane, Lingfield RH7 6NJ* Tel (01342) 872859

MOORE, Michael Peter John. b 60. Qu Coll Birm 05. **d** 08 **p** 09. C Pet St Mary Boongate 08-11; V from 11. *St Mary's Vicarage, 214 Eastfield Road, Peterborough PE1 4BD* Tel (01733) 343418 E-mail revmichael@tiscali.co.uk

MOORE, Paul Henry. b 59. Ball Coll Ox BA82 DPhil86. Wycliffe Hall Ox 87. **d** 89 **p** 90. C Ox St Andr 89-93; V Kildwick *Bradf* 93-01; V Cowplain *Portsm* from 01; RD Havant 04-09. *The*

Vicarage, Padnell Road, Cowplain, Waterlooville PO8 8DZ Tel (023) 9226 2295 E-mail p.h.moore@btinternet.com

MOORE, Philip. b 49. York Univ MA71 Leeds Univ MA05 PGCE72. NOC 02. **d** 05 **p** 06. NSM Heworth Ch Ch *York* 05-09; P-in-c York St Thos w St Maurice from 09. *14 Whitby Avenue, York YO31 1ET* Tel (01904) 425250 E-mail phil.moore@stthomaswithstmaurice.org.uk

MOORE, Raymond. b 47. QUB BSc70. **d** 87 **p** 88. Aux Min Belfast All SS *Conn* 87-95; NSM 95-96; Aux Min Kilmakee 96-04; P-in-c Drung w Castleterra, Larah and Lavey etc *K, E & A* 04-09; NSM Albert Park Australia from 09. *Address temp unknown* E-mail rmoore@rmoore.uklinux.net

MOORE, Richard William Robert. b 39. UCD BA70 TCD HDipEd71. CITC 98. **d** 01 **p** 02. Aux Min Drogheda w Ardee, Collon and Termonfeckin *Arm* 01-05; Aux Min Dundalk w Heynestown from 05; Aux Min Ballymascanlan w Creggan and Rathcor from 05. *Dundalk Road, Dunleer, Co Louth, Republic of Ireland* Tel (00353) (41) 685 1327 E-mail richwmoore@yahoo.ie

MOORE, Richard Noel. b 34. TCD BA56 MA60. **d** 57 **p** 58. C Derry Cathl 57-60; I Clondehorkey 60-66; I Stranorlar w Meenglas and Kilteevogue 66-76; I Glendermott 76-00; Can Derry Cathl 89-00; rtd 00. *Evergreen House, 37 Mullanahoe Road, Dungannon BT71 5AT* Tel (028) 8673 7112

MOORE, Richard Norman Theobald. b 39. St Andr Univ BSc62 Lon Univ BD66. Clifton Th Coll. **d** 66 **p** 67. C Stowmarket *St E* 66-69; C New Humberstone *Leic* 69-72; P-in-c Leic Martyrs 73; V 73-84; Chapl Manor Hosp Epsom 84-94; Chapl Surrey Oaklands NHS Trust 94-00; rtd 00; Perm to Offic *Guildf* 02-07 and *St E* from 07. *9 Cranmer Cliff Gardens, Felixstowe IP11 7NH* Tel (01394) 273889

MOORE, Robert Allen. b 32. Univ of the Pacific BA54 Boston Univ STB58 STM59. **d** 63 **p** 63. USA 63-80; V Farington *Blackb* 80-83; TV Preston St Jo 83-85; P-in-c Fleetwood St Pet 85-87; V Leyland St Jas 87-97; rtd 97; Perm to Offic *Blackb* from 97. *19 Lea Road, Whittle-le-Woods, Chorley PR6 7PF* Tel (01257) 265701 E-mail rmoore1980@aol.com

MOORE, Mrs Roberta. b 46. CITC 03. **d** 06 **p** 07. Aux Min Drung w Castleterra, Larah and Lavey etc *K, E & A* 06-09; NSM Albert Park Australia from 09. *Address temp unknown* E-mail bobbie@rmoore.uklinux.net

MOORE, Robin Hugh. b 52. CertEd BEd QUB BD. **d** 84 **p** 85. C Derryloran *Arm* 84-86; C Knock *D & D* 86-89; Bp's C Belfast St Steph w St Luke *Conn* 89-94; I 94-96; I Whitehouse 96-03; Bp's C Belfast St Mary Magd 03-07; I Belfast St Mark from 07. *9 Sycamore Park, Newtownabbey BT37 0NR* Tel (028) 9086 9569

MOORE, Shaun Christopher. b 52. Open Univ BA92 NE Lon Poly CertEd75 K Coll Lon MA10. NTMTC BA08. **d** 08 **p** 09. NSM Leyton St Mary w St Edw and St Luke *Chelmsf* 08-11; TV Walthamstow from 11. *17 Rayfield, Epping CM16 5AD* Tel (01992) 570684 E-mail shaunmoore@freeola.com

MOORE, Simon Quentin. b 61. Sheff Univ BA83 PGCE84. St Jo Coll Nottm MA99. **d** 00 **p** 01. C St Alb St Paul *St Alb* 00-03; TV Digswell and Panshanger 03-10; P-in-c Letchworth St Paul w Willian from 10. *St Paul's Vicarage, 177 Pixmore Way, Letchworth SG6 1QT* Tel (01462) 483934 E-mail sqmoore@btinternet.com

MOORE, Thomas Sydney. b 50. St Paul's Coll Grahamstown 77. **d** 79 **p** 80. C Rondebosch St Thos S Africa 79-82 and 83-84; C Bredasdorp 82-83; R Green Pt 84-88; C Bushey *St Alb* 97-08; C Aldershot St Mich *Guildf* from 08. *Ascension House, Ayling Hill, Aldershot GU11 3LL* Tel (01252) 330224 E-mail ts.moore@virgin.net

MOORE, Mrs Wendy. b 44. Westcott Ho Cam 92. **d** 94 **p** 95. C Rotherham *Sheff* 94-97; V Laughton w Throapham 97-01; V Bromsgrove All SS *Worc* 01-09; rtd 09; TV Saffron Walden w Wendens Ambo, Littlebury etc *Chelmsf* from 09. *Ashdown Vicarage, Radwinter Road, Ashdown, Saffron Walden CB10 2ET* Tel (01799) 584171 E-mail wendywmoor@aol.com

MOORE, William. *See* MOORE, Albert William

MOORE, William Henry. b 14. K Coll Lon 34. **d** 38 **p** 39. C Mill End *St Alb* 38-41; C Tring 41-44; C Gt Yarmouth *Nor* 44-46; New Zealand 46-52; R Houghton Conquest *St Alb* 52-56; Canada 56-59; R Filby w Thrigby *Nor* 60-62; P-in-c Mautby 60-62; Perm to Offic 62-71; Asst Master Mildenhall Sec Sch 68-73; Heartsease Sch Nor 73-75; C Mildenhall *St E* 71-73; rtd 79; Perm to Offic *Nor* from 88. *21 Green Court, Avenue Green, Norwich NR7 0DN* Tel (01603) 432758

MOORE, William Morris. b 33. QUB BSc55 TCD. **d** 61 **p** 62. C Belfast St Mich *Conn* 61-64; I 70-80; C Belfast All SS 64-70; I Ballynafeigh St Jude *D & D* 80-03; Can Belf Cathl 95-03; rtd 03. *10 Hollygate Park, Carryduff, Belfast BT8 8DZ* Tel (028) 9081 4896

MOORE-BICK, Miss Elizabeth Mary. b 77. Qu Coll Cam BA99 MA03 Anglia Poly Univ BA04. Westcott Ho Cam 02. **d** 05 **p** 06. C Hillingdon St Jo *Lon* 05-09; TV Clarendon *Sarum* from 09. *The Rectory, 5 The Copse, Alderbury, Salisbury SP5 3BL* Tel (01722) 711144 Mobile 07803-044217 E-mail lizmoore_bick@yahoo.co.uk *or* emm25@cam.ac.uk

MOORE BROOKS, Dorothy Anne. b 66. York Univ BA87 Hughes Hall Cam PGCE88. Ridley Hall Cam 96. d 98 p 99. C S Kensington St Jude *Lon* 98-01; Perm to Offic 02-08; Chapl Gt Ormond Street Hosp for Children NHS Trust 02-08; NSM Hoddesdon *St Alb* 01-10; Chapl Isabel Hospice 08-10; NSM Amersham *Ox* from 11. *The Rectory, Wycombe End, Beaconsfield HP9 1NB* Tel (01494) 673949
E-mail moorebrooks@ntlworld.com

MOORHEAD, Michael David. b 52. BSc BA. St Steph Ho Ox. d 83 p 84. C Kilburn St Aug w St Jo *Lon* 83-87; C Kenton 87-89; Chapl Cen Middx Hosp NHS Trust from 89; V Harlesden All So *Lon* from 89; P-in-c Willesden St Matt 92-02. *All Souls' Vicarage, 3 Station Road, London NW10 4UJ* Tel and fax (020) 8965 4988
E-mail michael@allsoulschurch.fsnet.co.uk

MOORHOUSE, Christine Susan. b 49. K Coll Lon BD71 AKC71. WMMTC. dss 86 d 87 p 94. NSM Stourbridge St Thos *Worc* 86-99; Perm to Offic 02-07. *Address temp unknown*

MOORHOUSE, Humphrey John. b 18. Oak Hill Th Coll 37. d 41 p 42. C Dalston St Mark w St Bart *Lon* 41-42; C Chadwell Heath *Chelmsf* 42-45; R Vange 45-83; rtd 83; Perm to Offic *Chelmsf* from 83. *12 Waverley Road, Benfleet SS7 4AZ* Tel (01268) 754952

MOORHOUSE, Peter. b 42. Liv Univ BSc64 Hull Univ CertEd. Linc Th Coll 79. d 81 p 82. C Horsforth *Ripon* 81-85; R Ackworth *Wakef* 85-96; Dep Chapl HM Pris Leeds 96-97; Chapl HM Pris Stocken 97-98; Chapl HM Pris Everthorpe 98-07; rtd 07; Perm to Offic *York* from 07. *65 Eastfield Lane, Dunnington, York YO19 5ND* Tel (01904) 481055

MOORSE, Michael William. b 36. Culham Coll of Educn TCert63. Guildf Dioc Min Course 96. d 98 p 99. OLM Woking St Pet *Guildf* 98-06; Perm to Offic from 06. *4 Bonners Close, Woking GU22 9RA* Tel (01483) 767460

MOORSOM, Christopher Arthur Robert. b 55. Ox Univ MA. Sarum & Wells Th Coll 79. d 82 p 83. C Bradford-on-Avon H Trin *Sarum* 82-85; R Broad Town, Clyffe Pypard and Tockenham 85-89; V Banwell *B & W* 89-96; R Upper Stour *Sarum* from 96. *The Rectory, Portnells Lane, Zeals, Warminster BA12 6PG* Tel (01747) 840221
E-mail chrisliz.moorsom@btopenworld.com

MORAN, Adrian Peter. CITC. d 09 p 10. NSM Cork St Ann's Union *C, C & R* 09-10; NSM Fermoy Union from 10. *22 Rosehill East, Ballinacurra, Midleton, Co Cork, Republic of Ireland* Tel (00353) (21) 463 1611 Mobile 87-228 2931
E-mail adrianpmoran@yahoo.ie

MORAY, ROSS AND CAITHNESS, Bishop of. See STRANGE, The Rt Revd Mark Jeremy

MORAY, ROSS AND CAITHNESS, Dean of. See PIPER, The Very Revd Clifford John

MORBY, Canon Helen Mary. b 62. Wolv Univ BA99. Ripon Coll Cuddesdon 99. d 01 p 02. C Lich St Chad 01-04; V Farnworth *Liv* from 04; AD Widnes 05-07; Hon Can Liv Cathl from 05. *The Vicarage, Coroners Lane, Widnes WA8 9HY* Tel 0151-424 2735
E-mail helen@morby.freeserve.co.uk

MORDECAI, Mrs Betty. b 27. Birm Univ BA48 Cam Univ CertEd49. Wycliffe Hall Ox 85. dss 86 d 87 p 94. Leamington Priors All SS *Cov* 86-89; Hon Par Dn 87-89; C Worc City St Paul and Old St Martin etc 89-94; rtd 94; Perm to Offic *Cov* from 00. *8 Swain Crofts, Leamington Spa CV31 1YW* Tel (01926) 882001
E-mail bettyhoward@btinternet.com

MORDECAI, Thomas **Huw.** b 59. Bris Univ BA81 St Jo Coll Dur BA85 MA92. Cranmer Hall Dur 83. d 87 p 88. C Gillingham St Mary *Roch* 87-90; Chapl Warw Sch 90-96; Chapl Giggleswick Sch 96-98; Chapl Westmr Sch and PV Westmr Abbey 98-01; Chapl Geelong Gr Sch Australia 02-04; Chapl Malvern Coll 05-07; Chapl K Wm's Coll Is of Man from 07. *King William's College, Castletown, Isle of Man IM9 1TP* Tel (01624) 820400

MORE, Canon Richard David Antrobus. b 48. St Jo Coll Dur BA70. Cranmer Hall Dur 70. d 72 p 73. C Macclesfield St Mich *Ches* 72-77; Chapl Lee Abbey 77-82; V Porchester *S'well* 82-96; RD Gedling 90-96; Bp's Dom Chapl *Chelmsf* 96-01; Dioc Dir of Ords from 01; Dioc NSM Officer from 01; Hon Can Chelmsf Cathl from 06. *25 Roxwell Road, Chelmsford CM1 2LY* Tel (01245) 264187 Fax 348789
E-mail ddo@chelmsford.anglican.org

MORELAND, Andrew John. b 64. St Jo Coll Nottm 09. d 11. C Bridlington Priory *York* from 11. *20 The Lawns, Bridlington YO16 6FL* Tel (01262) 675919
E-mail andrew.moreland@talktalk.net

MORETON, Ann Louise. b 32. d 02 p 03. OLM Whitstable *Cant* 02-10; Perm to Offic from 11. *Church House, 24 Freemans Close, Seasalter, Whitstable CT5 4BB* Tel (01227) 277140
E-mail annmoreton@hotmail.com

MORETON, Harley. See MORETON, Philip Norman Harley

MORETON, Preb Mark. b 39. Jes Coll Cam BA64 MA68. Westcott Ho Cam 63. d 65 p 66. C Portsea All SS *Portsm* 65-70; C St Martin-in-the-Fields *Lon* 70-72; Chapl Jes Coll Cam 72-77; R Stafford St Mary and St Chad *Lich* 77-79; P-in-c Stafford Ch Ch 77-79; TR Stafford 79-91; P-in-c Marston w Whitgreave 77-79; V W Bromwich All SS 91-04; Preb Lich Cathl 99-04; rtd

04. *Rosemont, Dry Mill Lane, Bewdley DY12 2BL* Tel (01299) 401965

MORETON, Michael Bernard. b 44. St Jo Coll Cam BA66 MA70 Ch Ch Ox BA66 MA69 DPhil69. St Steph Ho Ox 66. d 68 p 69. C Banstead *Guildf* 68-74; R Alburgh *Nor* 74-75; R Denton 74-75; R Middleton Cheney w Chacombe *Pet* 75-87; Perm to Offic *Cant* from 00. *Waterloo House, 56-58 High Street, Rolvenden, Cranbrook TN17 4LN* Tel (01580) 241287

MORETON, Preb Michael Joseph. b 17. Univ Coll Lon BA40 Ch Ch Ox BA47 MA53. Wells Th Coll 47. d 48 p 49. C Rowbarton *B & W* 48-52; C Ilfracombe H Trin *Ex* 52-59; Lect Th Ex Univ 57-86; R Ex St Mary Steps 59-86; P-in-c 86-92; RD Christianity 83-89; Preb Ex Cathl 85-86; rtd 86; Perm to Offic *Ex* from 86. *3 Glenthorne Road, Duryard, Exeter EX4 4QU* Tel (01392) 438083

MORETON, Philip Norman **Harley.** b 28. Linc Th Coll. d 57 p 58. C Howden *York* 57-60; C Bottesford *Linc* 60-65; V Linc St Giles 65-70; V Bracebridge Heath 71-77; V Seasalter *Cant* 77-84; TV Whitstable 84-88; rtd 88; Perm to Offic *York* 96-06. *112 Grantham Road, Bracebridge Heath, Lincoln LN4 2QF* Tel (01522) 534672 Mobile 07851-717891

MORETON, Rupert Robert James. b 66. TCD BA89. CITC BTh92. d 92 p 93. C Dublin Ch Ch Cathl Gp 92-96; Asst Chapl Costa Blanca *Eur* 96-98; Chapl Helsinki from 98. *Kuutamokatu 4A22, 02210 Espoo, Finland* Tel 08458-674751 Mobile (00358) 405-728372 E-mail rupert.moreton@icon.fi
or chaplain@anglican.fi

MORFILL, Mrs Mary Joanna. b 46. Seaford Coll of Educn TCert67. STETS 01. d 04 p 08. NSM Swanmore St Barn *Portsm* from 04. *Whistlers, New Road, Swanmore, Southampton SO32 2PF* Tel (01489) 878227 Mobile 07906-755145
E-mail mary@swanmore.net

✠MORGAN, The Rt Revd Alan Wyndham. b 40. OBE05. Univ of Wales (Lamp) BA62. St Mich Coll Llan 62. d 64 p 65 c 89. C Llangyfelach and Morriston *S & B* 64-69; C Swansea St Pet 69-72; C Cov E 72-73; TV 73-83; Bp's Officer for Soc Resp 78-83; Adn Cov 83-89; Suff Bp Sherwood *S'well* 89-04; rtd 04. *10 Station Road, Alcester B49 5ET* Tel (01789) 762486

MORGAN, Alison Jean. b 59. Girton Coll Cam BA82 MA85 Darw Coll Cam PhD86. EMMTC 93. d 96 p 97. NSM Oadby *Leic* 96; NSM Leic H Trin w St Jo 98-08; Thinker and writer ReSource from 04. *10 Dairy Close, Wells BA5 2ND* Tel (01749) 600341 E-mail alisonmorgan@resource-arm.net

MORGAN, Anthony Hogarth. b 42. St Josef Missiehuis Holland 60 St Jos RC Coll Lon 62. d 65 p 66. In RC Ch 66-93; NSM Handsworth Woodhouse *Sheff* 93-94; C Sheff St Leon Norwood 94-97; P-in-c Shiregreen St Hilda 97-05; C Shiregreen St Jas and St Chris 05-07; rtd 07; Perm to Offic *York* from 09. *3 Belvedere Mansions, Lonsdale Road, Scarborough YO11 2QU* Tel (01723) 37372

MORGAN, Anthony Paul George. b 57. Sarum & Wells Th Coll 89. d 91 p 92. C Plymstock *Ex* 91-95; P-in-c Wolborough w Newton Abbot 95-00; V York St Hilda 01-06; rtd 06; Perm to Offic *Derby* 07-10. *54 Macaulay Road, Luton LU4 0LP* E-mail tony@thefms.fsnet.co.uk

✠MORGAN, The Most Revd Barry Cennydd. b 47. Lon Univ BA69 Selw Coll Cam BA72 MA74 Univ of Wales PhD86. Westcott Ho Cam 70. d 72 p 73 c 93. Chapl Bryn-y-Don Community Sch 72-75; C St Andrews Major w Michaelston-le-Pit *Llan* 72-75; Ed *Welsh Churchman* 75-82; Lect Th Univ of Wales (Cardiff) 75-77; Chapl and Lect St Mich Coll Llan 75-77; Warden Ch Hostel Ban 77-84; Chapl and Lect Th Univ of Wales (Ban) 77-84; In-Service Tr Adv *Ban* 78-84; Dir of Ords 82-84; Can Ban Cathl 83-84; TR Wrexham *St As* 84-86; Adn Meirionnydd *Ban* 86-93; R Criccieth w Treflys 86-93; Bp Ban 93-99; Bp Llan from 99; Abp Wales from 03. *Llys Esgob, The Cathedral Green, Llandaff, Cardiff CF5 2YE* Tel (029) 2056 2400 Fax 2057 7129
E-mail archbishop@churchinwales.org.uk

MORGAN, Miss Beryl. b 30. dss 63 d 87 p 94. Rickerscote *Lich* 63-69; Hd Dss 70-87; Dioc Lay Min Adv 70-93; Willenhall H Trin 80-93; Par Dn 87-93; rtd 93; Hon C Penn *Lich* 94-01; Perm to Offic *Lich* 01-04 and *Leic* from 05. *12 Stuart Court, High Street, Kibworth, Leicester LE8 0LR* Tel 0116-279 6345

MORGAN, Charles Nicholas Brendan. b 55. Milw91. Open Univ BSc94 Leeds Univ BA08. NOC 05. d 08 p 09. C Derwent Ings *York* from 08. *The Rectory, Church Lane, Elvington, York YO41 4AD* Tel (01904) 607121 Mobile 07902-033174
E-mail dadintheditch@hotmail.com

✠MORGAN, The Rt Revd Christopher Heudebourck. b 47. Lanc Univ BA73 Heythrop Coll Lon MTh91. Kelham Th Coll 66. d 73 p 74 c 01. C Birstall *Leic* 73-76; Asst Chapl Brussels *Eur* 76-80; P-in-c Redditch St Geo *Worc* 80-81; TV Redditch, The Ridge 81-85; V Sonning *Ox* 85-96; Prin Berks Chr Tr Scheme 85-89; Dir Past Studies Ox Min Course 92-96; Dioc Can Res Glouc Cathl and Bp's Officer for Min 96-01; Area Bp Colchester *Chelmsf* from 01. *1 Fitzwalter Road, Colchester CO3 3SS* Tel (01206) 576648 Fax 763868
E-mail b.colchester@chelmsford.anglican.org

MORGAN, Christopher John. b 46. Brasted Th Coll 68 Linc Th Coll 70. **d** 72 **p** 73. C Earley St Pet *Ox* 72-76; C Epsom St Martin *Guildf* 76-79; V Stoneleigh 79-83; Ind Chapl *York* 83-92; NACRO 87-91; V York St Hilda 92-96; TV E Greenwich *S'wark* 96-03; P-in-c Norbury St Oswald 03-05; V from 05. *The Vicarage, 2B St Oswald's Road, London SW16 3SB* Tel (020) 8764 2853

MORGAN, Clive. b 41. **d** 02. Par Dn Blaina and Nantyglo *Mon* from 02. *26 Victoria Street, Blaina, Abertillery NP13 3BG* Tel (01495) 291637

MORGAN, David Farnon Charles. b 43. Leeds Univ BA68. Coll of Resurr Mirfield 68. **d** 70 **p** 71. C Swinton St Pet *Man* 70-73; C Langley All SS and Martyrs 73-75; R Salford St Clem w St Cypr Ordsall 75-76; R Salford Ordsall St Clem 76-86; V Adlington *Blackb* 86-11; AD Chorley 98-04. *Address temp unknown* E-mail morgyvic@talktalk.net

MORGAN, David Joseph (Joe). b 47. Bp Burgess Hall Lamp 66 St Deiniol's Hawarden 74. **d** 74 **p** 75. C Pembroke Dock *St D* 74-77; C Burry Port and Pwll 77-80; Miss to Seafarers from 80; Sen Chapl and Sec Welsh Coun from 85. *25 Glanmor Park Road, Sketty, Swansea SA2 0QG* Tel (01792) 206637

MORGAN, Deiniol Tudur. **d** 02 **p** 03. Min Can Ban Cathl 02-04; P-in-c Llandinorwig, Llanrug and Llandinorwig 04-05; Min Can and Prec Westmr Abbey 05-08; CF from 08. *c/o MOD Chaplains (Army)* Tel (01264) 381140 Fax 381824

MORGAN, Sister Enid May. b 37. St Luke's Coll Ex CertEd69 Ex Univ DipEd76 Univ of Wales (Lamp) BA04. **d** 07 **p** 07. NSM Llanfrechfa and Llanddewi Fach w Llandegfeth *Mon* 07-08. *Llety'r Pererin, Whitchurch, Solva, Haverfordwest SA62 6UD* E-mail enidmorgan@onetel.com

MORGAN, Canon Enid Morris Roberts. b 40. St Anne's Coll Ox BA61 Univ of Wales (Ban) MA73. United Th Coll Abth BD81. **d** 84 **p** 97. C Llanfihangel w Llanafan and Llanwnnws etc *St D* 84-86; Dn-in-c 86-93; Dir Bd of Miss Ch in Wales 93-00; V Llangynwyd w Maesteg 00-05; Hon Can Llan Cathl 02-05; rtd 05. *Rhiwlas, Cliff Terrace, Aberystwyth SY23 2DN* Tel (01970) 624648

MORGAN, Gareth Morison Kilby. b 33. Bris Univ BA56. Cuddesdon Coll 57 Bangalore Th Coll. **d** 61 **p** 62. C St Helier *S'wark* 61-65; Chapl Scargill Ho 65-70; Dir RE *Linc* 71-74; Dioc Dir of Educn *St E* 74-81; TR Hanley H Ev *Lich* 81-89; TR Cen Telford 89-92; Warden Glenfall Ho *Glouc* 92-98; rtd 98; Perm to Offic *Win* from 00; Chapl Hants Partnership NHS Trust from 08. *St Neots, Kanes Hill, Southampton SO19 6AH* Tel (023) 8046 6509 E-mail geejaymo@aol.com

MORGAN, Gary. b 61. Westmr Inst of Educn BA03. St Steph Ho Ox 04. **d** 06 **p** 07. C Spilsby Gp *Linc* 06-10; P-in-c Kirton in Holland from 10; P-in-c Algarkirk and Fosdyke from 10. *The Vicarage, Penny Gardens, Kirton, Boston PE20 1HN* Tel (01205) 722380 Mobile 07879-068196 E-mail fathergaz@yahoo.co.uk

MORGAN, Geoffrey. See MORGAN, James Geoffrey Selwyn

MORGAN, Gerwyn. See MORGAN, William Charles Gerwyn

MORGAN, Glyn. b 21. Oak Hill Th Coll 73. **d** 76 **p** 77. NSM Barton Seagrave w Warkton *Pet* 76-00; Perm to Offic from 00. *St Edmund's House, Warkton, Kettering NN15 5AB* Tel (01536) 520610

MORGAN, Glyn. b 33. Univ of Wales (Ban) BA55 MA69. Coll of Resurr Mirfield 55. **d** 57 **p** 58. C Dolgellau *Ban* 57-60; C Conway 60-63; V Corris 63-68; Hd of RE Friars' Sch Ban 69-70; Lic to Offic 70-71; Hd of RE Oswestry Boys' Modern Sch 70-74; Hd of RE Oswestry High Sch for Girls 74-79; Hon C Oswestry H Trin *Lich* 71-79; Hd of RE Fitzalan Sch Oswestry 79-88; V Meifod and Llangynyw *St As* 88-01; RD Caereinion 89-01; rtd 01. *Crib y Gwynt Annexe, Trefnanney, Meifod SY22 6XX* Tel (01938) 500066

MORGAN, Graham. b 47. Kt00. S'wark Ord Course. **d** 83 **p** 84. NSM S Kensington St Steph *Lon* 83-90; NSM Hammersmith H Innocents 90-02; NSM Bedford Park from 02. *24 Charleville Court, Charleville Road, London W14 9JG* Tel (020) 7381 3211 E-mail graham.morgan@nwlh.nhs.uk

MORGAN, Mrs Hilary. WEMTC. **d** 09 **p** 10. NSM Tenbury *Heref* from 09. *The Steps, Bleathwood, Ludlow SY8 4LR* Tel (01584) 819971 E-mail hilsandbern@btinternet.com

MORGAN, Canon Ian David John. b 57. Hull Univ BA78 LTCL75. Ripon Coll Cuddesdon 80. **d** 83 **p** 84. C Heref H Trin 83-86; C New Shoreham *Chich* 86-88; Researcher, Producer & Presenter BBC Local Radio 88-92; V Ipswich All Hallows *St E* 92-95; TR Ipswich St Mary at Stoke w St Pet 95-97; TR Ipswich St Mary at Stoke w St Pet and St Fran from 97; CUF Link Officer from 06; RD Ipswich from 08; Hon Can St E Cathl from 09. *1 Salmet Close, Ipswich IP2 9BA* Tel (01473) 601895 Fax 683303 E-mail ianmorgan@aol.com

MORGAN, Ian Stephen. b 50. Open Univ BA88. Sarum & Wells Th Coll 86. **d** 88 **p** 89. C Baldock w Bygrave *St Alb* 88-91; C S Elmham and Ilketshall *St E* 91-95; V Bungay H Trin w St Mary 95-05; R Lt Barningham, Blickling, Edgefield etc *Nor* 05-10; rtd 10. *Plessey Cottage, Oulton, Norwich NR11 6NX* Tel (01263) 587535 Mobile 07808-451350 E-mail smorganciho@yahoo.co.uk

MORGAN, James Geoffrey Selwyn. b 59. Ex Univ BA81 PGCE82 Open Univ MPhil97. Cranmer Hall Dur 88. **d** 91 **p** 92. C Reading St Agnes w St Paul *Ox* 91-93; C Bromham w Oakley and Stagsden *St Alb* 94-95; Perm to Offic *Pet* 96-98; C Epsom St Martin *Guildf* 98-01; Ox Cen for Miss Studies 01-05; Perm to Offic *Guildf* and *Ox* from 01; Chapl Imp Coll Healthcare NHS Trust from 11. *26 Cheam Road, Epsom KT17 1SY* Tel (020) 8393 4635 E-mail jgs_morgan@talktalk.net

MORGAN, Joe. See MORGAN, David Joseph

MORGAN, John. See MORGAN, William John

MORGAN, John Geoffrey Basil. b 21. Wells Th Coll 59. **d** 60 **p** 61. C Oakdale St Geo *Sarum* 60-64; C Talbot Village 64-67; C-in-c Ensbury St Thos CD 67-69; V Ensbury 69-82; C W Parley 82-86; rtd 86; Perm to Offic *Sarum* 01-05. *Widgery, 32 Church Road, Ferndown BH22 9EU* Tel (01202) 861207

MORGAN, John Laurence. b 41. Melbourne Univ BA62 Oriel Coll Ox BA69 MA73 DPhil76. **d** 68 **p** 69. Acting Chapl Oriel Coll Ox 69 and 70-76; USA 77-78; Australia from 78. *St John's College, College Road, St Lucia Qld 4067, Australia* Tel (0062) (7) 3371 3741 *or* 3842 6600 Fax 3870 5124 E-mail john.morgan@mailbox.uq.edu.au

MORGAN, John Roland. b 31. Birm Univ BA54. Bps' Coll Cheshunt 54. **d** 55 **p** 56. C Selly Oak St Mary *Birm* 55-57; C Yardley Wood 57-58; C Hamstead St Paul 58-61; V Smethwick St Chad 61-68; V Balsall Common 68-82; V N Leigh *Ox* 82-95; RD Woodstock 87-92; rtd 95; Perm to Offic *Ely* from 95. *Dyn Caryn, 2 Hayling Close, Godmanchester, Huntingdon PE29 2XB* Tel (01480) 459522

MORGAN, John William Miller. b 34. Lon Univ BSc56. Wycliffe Hall Ox 61. **d** 63 **p** 64. C St Alb Ch *St Alb* 63-68; V Luton St Matt High Town 68-79; V Mangotsfield *Bris* 79-90; P-in-c Stanton St Quintin, Hullavington, Grittleton etc 90-95; R Hullavington, Norton and Stanton St Quintin 95-99; rtd 99; Perm to Offic *Bris* from 00. *3 Bouverie Park, Stanton St Quintin, Chippenham SN14 6EE* Tel (01666) 837670 E-mail johnwmmorgan@compuserve.com

MORGAN, Mrs Judith. b 62. CBDTI 96. **d** 99 **p** 00. C Brigham and Gt Broughton and Broughton Moor *Carl* 99-04; P-in-c Doxford St Wilfrid *Dur* from 04. *2 Whitebark, Sunderland SR3 2NX* Tel 0191-522 7639 E-mail morgjud@aol.com

MORGAN, Katharine. b 41. **d** 91 **p** 97. NSM Loughor S & B from 91. *68 Borough Road, Lougher, Swansea SA4 6RT* Tel (01792) 524901

MORGAN, Kathleen Irene. b 52. St Martin's Coll Lanc CertEd74. WEMTC 93. **d** 96 **p** 97. NSM Barnwood *Glouc* 96-99; C Coney Hill 99-02; V Churchdown St Jo and Innsworth from 02. *The Vicarage, St John's Avenue, Churchdown, Gloucester GL3 2DA* Tel (01452) 713421 E-mail revkaty@aol.com

MORGAN, Linda Marianne. b 48. Bris Univ BSc69 Surrey Univ MSc72 Lon Univ PhD77 FRCPath01. STETS 99. **d** 02 **p** 03. NSM Claygate *Guildf* from 02. *8 Melbury Close, Claygate KT10 0EX* Tel (01372) 462911 E-mail lindamorgan@holytrinityclaygate.org.uk

MORGAN, Mrs Marian Kathleen Eleanor. b 38. Birm Univ MA94 FCMI82. WEMTC. **d** 00 **p** 01. NSM Cusop w Blakemere, Bredwardine w Brobury etc *Heref* 00-03; P-in-c New Radnor and Llanfihangel Nantmelan etc *S & B* 03-07; rtd 08; Hon C Aberedw w Llandeilo Graban and Llanbadarn etc *S & B* from 10; Hon C Bryngwyn and Newchurch and Llanbedr etc from 10. *Trefechan, Aberedw, Builth Wells LD2 3UH* Tel (01982) 560702 Mobile 07977-477212 E-mail mkemorgan@btinternet.com

MORGAN, Mark Anthony. b 58. LLB. Chich Th Coll. **d** 84 **p** 85. C Thorpe St Andr *Nor* 84-87; C Eaton 87-90; V Southtown 90-92; Perm to Offic from 92. *Nethergate End, The Street, Saxlingham, Nethergate, Norwich NR15 1AJ* Tel (01603) 762850

MORGAN, Mark Steven Glyn. b 60. Essex Univ BSc83 RGN86. Ridley Hall Cam 95. **d** 97 **p** 99. C Herne Bay Ch Ch *Cant* 97-02; TV Ipswich St Mary at Stoke w St Pet and St Fran *St E* from 02. *St Peter's Church House, Stoke Park Drive, Ipswich IP2 9TH* Tel (01473) 601438 E-mail hama.morgan-@tinyworld.co.uk

MORGAN, Martin Paul. b 46. St Steph Ho Ox 71. **d** 73 **p** 74. C Kettering St Mary *Pet* 73-76; C Fareham SS Pet and Paul *Portsm* 76-80; V Portsea Ascension 80-94; V Rottingdean *Chich* from 94. *The Vicarage, Steyning Road, Rottingdean, Brighton BN2 7GA* Tel (01273) 309216 E-mail martin.morgan43@ntlworld.com

MORGAN, Mrs Melanie Jane. b 54. RMN. Qu Coll Birm 98. **d** 02 **p** 03. NSM Derby St Andr w St Osmund 02-05. *16 Brading Close, Alvaston, Derby DE24 0UW* Tel (01332) 754419 E-mail clifden@btinternet.com

MORGAN, Michael. b 32. Lon Univ BSc57 MSc67 PhD63. **d** 74 **p** 75. NSM Portsdown *Portsm* 74-98; Perm to Offic from 98.

12 East Cosham Road, Cosham, Portsmouth PO6 2JS Tel (023) 9237 7442

MORGAN, Michael John. b 45. Nottm Univ BA66 MEd71. Linc Th Coll 80. **d** 82 **p** 83. C Bulkington *Cov* 82-83; C Bulkington w Shilton and Ansty 83-85; V Longford 85-89; R Norton *Sheff* 89-99; R Lapworth *Birm* 99-09; R Baddesley Clinton 99-09; rtd 09; Perm to Offic *Birm* from 09. *77 Tiverton Drive, Nuneaton CV11 6XJ*

MORGAN, Morley Roland. b 47. Univ of Wales (Lamp) BA76. St Steph Ho Ox 76. **d** 77 **p** 78. C Merthyr Dyfan *Llan* 77-78; C Llantrisant 78-80; TV Coventry Caludon 80-86; Chapl N Man Gen Hosp 86-93; Chapl N Man Health Care NHS Trust 93-02; Chapl Pennine Acute Hosps NHS Trust 02-07; Hon C Bury St Jo w St Mark *Man* 05-07; rtd 07; Perm to Offic *Man* from 08. *14 Rectory Road, Manchester M8 5EA* Tel 0161-740 9925

MORGAN, Canon Nicholas John. b 50. K Coll Lon BD71 AKC71 CertEd. St Aug Coll Cant 72. **d** 73 **p** 74. C Wythenshawe Wm Temple Ch *Man* 73-76; C Southam w Stockton *Cov* 76-79; V Brailes from 79; R Sutton under Brailes from 79; P-in-c Tysoe w Oxhill and Whatcote from 06; RD Shipston 90-98; Hon Can Cov Cathl from 03. *The Vicarage, Brailes, Banbury OX15 5HT* Tel (01608) 685230

MORGAN, Nicola. b 64. Nottm Univ BA86. Linc Th Coll BTh95. **d** 95 **p** 96. C Lillington *Cov* 95-98; C Gospel Lane St Mich *Birm* 98-01; P-in-c Gt Paxton *Ely* 01-05; P-in-c Lt Paxton 01-05; P-in-c Diddington 01-05; V The Paxtons w Diddington 05; Perm to Offic *Pet* 06-08; P-in-c Hallaton and Allexton, w Horninghold, Tugby etc *Leic* from 08. *The Rectory, 19 Churchgate, Hallaton, Market Harborough LE16 8TY* Tel (01858) 555363

MORGAN, Peter Neville. b 36. Univ of Wales (Cardiff) BSc60 BD63 Sussex Univ PGCE82. S Wales Bapt Coll 60. **d** 98 **p** 99. NSM Ardingly *Chich* 98-06; P-in-c 04-06; P-in-c Poynings w Edburton, Newtimber and Pyecombe 06-09; rtd 09. *Address temp unknown* E-mail revpnm98@aol.com

MORGAN, Philip. b 51. Lon Univ BSc75 Univ of Wales (Cardiff) BD78. St Mich Coll Llan 75. **d** 78 **p** 79. C Swansea St Nic *S & B* 78-81; C Morriston 81-83; C Swansea St Mary w H Trin 83-84; USA from 84. *17476 Hawthorne Avenue, Culpeper VA 22701-8003, USA* E-mail padre4u@hotmail.com

MORGAN, Canon Philip Brendan. b 35. G&C Coll Cam BA59 MA63. Wells Th Coll 59. **d** 61 **p** 62. C Paddington Ch Ch *Lon* 61-66; C Trunch w Swafield *Nor* 66-68; P-in-c Nor St Steph 68-72; Sacr Nor Cathl 72-74; Can Res and Sub-Dean St Alb 74-81; Hon Can St Alb 81-94; R Bushey 81-94; RD Aldenham 91-94; Can Res and Treas Win Cathl 94-01; rtd 01; Perm to Offic *Win* from 01. *9 Clifton Hill, Winchester SO22 5BL* Tel (01962) 867549

MORGAN, Canon Philip Reginald Strange. b 27. St D Coll Lamp BA51 Keble Coll Ox BA53 MA57. Wells Th Coll 57. **d** 57 **p** 58. C Fleur-de-Lis *Mon* 57-59; C Bassaleg 59-62; CF (TA) 62-74; V Dingestow and Wanastow *Mon* 62-65; V Dingestow and Penrhos 65-66; R Machen and Rudry 66-75; R Machen 75-76; V Caerleon 76-95; Can St Woolos Cathl 84-95; rtd 95; Lic to Offic *Mon* from 95. *4 Anthony Drive, Caerleon, Newport NP18 3DS* Tel (01633) 422238

MORGAN, Philip Richard Llewelyn. b 27. Wadh Coll Ox BA50 MA52. St Steph Ho Ox 53. **d** 55 **p** 56. C Warlingham w Chelsham and Farleigh *S'wark* 55-58; Chapl Haileybury Coll 58-73; Hd Master Haileybury Jun Sch Berks 73-87; R The Deverills *Sarum* 87-94; rtd 94; Perm to Offic *Guildf* and *Win* from 95. *6 Phillips Close, Headley, Bordon GU35 8LY* Tel and fax (01428) 712194 E-mail philipmorgan@msn.com

MORGAN, Canon Reginald Graham. b 25. St D Coll Lamp BA46 LTh48. **d** 48 **p** 49. C Chirk *St As* 48-50; C Llangollen and Trevor 50-55; R Llanwyddelan w Manafon 55-66; V Rhuddlan 66-94; RD St As 78-94; Hon Can St As Cathl 83-89; Can from 89; rtd 94. *Manafon, 49 Ffordd Ffynnon, Rhuddlan, Rhyl LL18 2SP* Tel (01745) 591036

MORGAN, The Ven Reginald Graham Tharle. b 46. St Jo Coll Nottm LTh75. **d** 75 **p** 76. C Oadby *Leic* 75-78; S Africa from 79; R Greytown St Jas from 88; Adn Estcourt from 95. *PO Box 112, Greytown, Natal, 3250 South Africa* Tel and fax (0027) (334) 71240 or tel 71241 E-mail beehive@cybertrade.co.za

MORGAN, Rhys Bryn. b 65. E Lon Univ BA94. St Mich Coll Llan 00. **d** 02 **p** 03. C Carmarthen St Pet *St D* 02-05; P-in-c Cil-y-Cwm and Ystrad-ffin w Rhandir-mwyn etc 05-09. *Rhiwlas, Cliff Terrace, Aberystwyth SY23 2DN* Tel (01970) 624648 Mobile 07973-254062 E-mail rhys.morgan1@btinternet.com

MORGAN, Richard Mervyn. b 50. Wadh Coll Ox BA73 MA75 K Alfred's Coll Win PGCE74. **d** 92 **p** 93. CMS 85-94; Kenya 88-94; Perm to Offic *S'wark* 95-96; R Therfield w Kelshall *St Alb* from 96; Tutor ERMC *Ely* from 99. *The Rectory, Church Lane, Therfield, Royston SG8 9QD* Tel (01763) 287364 E-mail rm@therfieldrectory.freeserve.co.uk

MORGAN, Richard Thomas. b 70. Peterho Cam BA91 MA95. Wycliffe Hall Ox 94. **d** 96 **p** 97. C Bath Twerton-on-Avon *B & W* 96-99; Chapl Lee Abbey 99-01; R Marks Tey and Aldham

Chelmsf 01-08; C Fisherton Anger *Sarum* from 08. *14 Wyndham Park, Salisbury SP1 3BA* Tel (01722) 333808 E-mail richardtmorgan@ic24.net

MORGAN, Robert Chowen. b 40. St Cath Coll Cam BA63 MA67. St Chad's Coll Dur 64. **d** 66 **p** 67. C Lancaster St Mary *Blackb* 66-76; Lect Th Lanc Univ 67-76; Fell Linacre Coll Ox from 76; Lect Th Ox Univ 76-97; Reader from 97; P-in-c Sandford-on-Thames *Ox* from 87. *Lower Farm, Sandford-on-Thames, Oxford OX4 4YR* Tel (01865) 748848 E-mail robert.morgan@theology.oxford.ac.uk

MORGAN, Canon Robert Harman. b 28. OBE94. Univ of Wales (Cardiff) BA55. Coll of Resurr Mirfield 55. **d** 57 **p** 58. C Penarth w Lavernock *Llan* 57-61; C Caerau w Ely 61-67; V Glan Ely 67-95; Hon Can Llan Cathl 94-95; rtd 95; Perm to Offic *St D* and *Llan* from 95. *Y Felin Wynt, St Davids, Haverfordwest SA62 6QS* Tel (01437) 720130

MORGAN, Canon Roger William. b 40. Mert Coll Ox BA62 Cam Univ MA67. Ridley Hall Cam 80. **d** 81 **p** 82. NSM Claregate St Paul *Ely* 81-84; V Corby St Columba *Pet* 84-90; V Leic H Trin w St Jo 90-08; C-in-c Leic St Leon CD 01-08; Hon Can Leic Cathl 06-08. *10 Dairy Close, Wells BA5 2ND* Tel (01749) 679865 Mobile 07799-403346 E-mail rogermorgan@resource-arm.net

MORGAN, Simon John. b 58. Univ of Wales (Swansea) BA81 Univ of Wales (Cardiff) BD86 MA94 Sussex Univ PGCE03 FRGS03 FRSA07. St Mich Coll Llan 83. **d** 86 **p** 87. C Penarth All SS *Llan* 86-87; C Port Talbot St Theodore 87-89; C Gelligaer 89-91; R Dowlais 91-96; Asst P Peacehaven and Telscombe w Piddinghoe and Southease *Chich* 96; P-in-c E Dean w Friston and Jevington 96-99; NSM Hellingly and Upper Dicker 99-05; NSM Fairwarp 05-08; Chapl St Bede's Sch Upper Dicker 99-08; Asst Master Abbey Sch Reading 08-10; SS Helen and Kath Sch Abingdon from 10. *19 Lister Close, Exeter EX2 4SD*

MORGAN, Stephen. See MORGAN, Ian Stephen

MORGAN, Stephen John. b 67. UEA BA89 SS Coll Cam BA02. Westcott Ho Cam 99. **d** 02 **p** 03. C Pitlochry and Kilmaveonaig *St And* 02-04; P-in-c E Knoyle, Semley and Sedgehill *Sarum* 05-08; P-in-c St Bartholomew 08-09; R from 09. *The Rectory, Semley, Shaftesbury SP7 9AU* Tel (01747) 830174 E-mail revstevemorgan@tiscali.co.uk

MORGAN, Canon Steve Shelley. b 48. St Mich Coll Llan 67. **d** 71 **p** 72. C Llanharan w Peterston-super-Montem 71; C Llandaff w Capel Llanilltern 71-74; C Neath w Llantwit 74-77; TV Merthyr Tydfil and Cyfarthfa 77-91; V Merthyr Tydfil Ch Ch from 91; RD Merthyr Tydfil 93-04; Can Llan Cathl from 98. *Mandian House, Brondeg, Heolgerrig, Merthyr Tydfil CF48 1TW* Tel (01685) 268088 E-mail smorgan842@yahoo.com

MORGAN, Mrs Susan Dianne. b 53. Univ of Wales (Lamp) BA74 Westmr Coll Ox PGCE75. NOC 03. **d** 05 **p** 06. C Droylsden St Martin *Man* 05-07; P-in-c Kirkholt from 08. *St Thomas's Vicarage, Cavendish Road, Rochdale OL11 2QX* Tel (01706) 649373 Mobile 07837-706037 E-mail sue_morgan14@hotmail.com

MORGAN, Teresa Jean. b 68. Clare Coll Cam BA90 MA94 PhD95 Oriel Coll Ox MA98 BA01 LRAM91. SAOMC 00. **d** 02 **p** 03. NSM Littlemore *Ox* from 02. *Oriel College, Oxford OX1 4EW* Tel (01865) 276579 E-mail teresa.morgan@classics.ox.ac.uk

MORGAN, Trevor. b 45. **d** 01 **p** 05. C Fleur-de-Lis *Mon* 01-06; P-in-c from 06; AD Bedwellty from 08. *The Tidings, Woodfieldside, Blackwood NP12 0PJ* Tel and fax (01495) 222198 E-mail tmo1036014@aol.com

MORGAN, Verna Ireta. b 42. NEOC. **d** 89 **p** 94. NSM Potternewton *Ripon* 89-92; Par Dn Longsight St Luke *Man* 92-94; C 94-95; P-in-c Gorton St Phil 95-02; rtd 02. *Butler's Village, St James's Parish, Nevis, St Kitts and Nevis*

MORGAN, William Charles Gerwyn. b 30. Univ of Wales (Lamp) BA52. St Mich Coll Llan 52. **d** 56 **p** 57. C Hubberston *St D* 56-62; V Ambleston w St Dogwells 62-68; Miss to Seamen 68-93; V Fishguard w Llanychar *St D* 68-85; V Fishguard w Llanychar and Pontfaen w Morfil etc 85-93; Can St D Cathl 85-93; Chan 91-93; rtd 93. *Wrth y Llan, Pontycleifion, Cardigan SA43 1DW* Tel (01239) 613943

MORGAN, William John. b 38. Selw Coll Cam BA62 MA66. Cuddesdon Coll 62. **d** 65 **p** 66. C Cardiff St Jo *Llan* 65-68; Asst Chapl Univ of Wales (Cardiff) 68-70; Perm to Offic *Lon* 70-73; C Albany Street Ch Ch 73-78; P-in-c E Acton St Dunstan 78-80; V E Acton St Dunstan w St Thos 80-95; V Isleworth All SS 95-04; P-in-c St Margaret's-on-Thames 95-00; rtd 04. *Marvol, 24310 Bourdeilles, France* Tel (0033) 5 53 54 18 90 E-mail marvol24@orange.fr

MORGAN, William Stanley Timothy. b 41. Univ of Wales (Lamp) BA63. Wycliffe Hall Ox 63. **d** 66 **p** 67. C Aberystwyth St Mich *St D* 66-69; V Ambleston w St Dogwells 69-70; V Ambleston, St Dogwells, Walton E and Llysyfran 70-74; V Llan-non 74-80; V Lampeter 80-87; V Lampeter Pont Steffan w Silian 87-01; V Llanbadarn Fawr 01-08; rtd 08. *16 Eddystone Close, Cardiff CF11 8EB* Tel (029) 2115 6388

MORGAN-CROMAR, Christopher. *See* MORGAN, Christopher

MORGAN-GUY, John Richard. b 44. St D Coll Lamp BA65 Univ of Wales PhD85 ARHistS80 FRHistS05 FRSM81. St Steph Ho Ox 65. **d** 67 **p** 68. C Canton St Cath *Llan* 67-68; C Roath St Sav 68-70; Chapl Llandough Hosp 70-71; C Machen and Rudry *Mon* 71-74; R Wolvesnewton w Kilgwrrwg and Devauden 74-80; Perm to Offic *B & W* 80-93; V Betws Cedewain and Tregynon and Llanwyddelan *St As* 93-97; RD Cedewain 97; Lect Univ of Wales (Lamp) 98-03; Research Fell Lect Univ of Wales (Trin St Dav) from 04; Research Fell Cen for Adv Welsh & Celtic Studies 99-04; Tutor Welsh Nat Cen for Ecum Studies Carmarthen from 00. *Tyngors, Silian, Lampeter SA48 8AS* Tel (01570) 422710

MORGAN-JONES, Canon Christopher John. b 43. Bris Univ BA66 Chicago Univ MBA68 McMaster Univ Ontario MA69. Cuddesdon Coll 70. **d** 73 **p** 74. C Folkestone St Sav *Cant* 73-76; P-in-c Swalecliffe 76-82; V Addington 82-84; V Addington *S'wark* 85-92; RD Croydon Addington 85-90; V Maidstone All SS and St Phil w Tovil *Cant* from 92; Hon Can Cant Cathl from 99. *The Vicarage, Priory Road, Maidstone ME15 6NL* Tel (01622) 756002 Fax 692320
E-mail maidstoneallsaints.wanadoo.co.uk

MORGANNWG, Archdeacon of. *See* SMITH, The Ven Christopher Blake Walters

MORGANS, Paul Hywel. b 61. LWCMD83. Chich Th Coll 86. **d** 90 **p** 91. C Johnston w Steynton *St D* 90-92; C Caerau w Ely *Llan* 92-95; V Pentre 95-99; Hon C Roath St German 99-00. *5 Docks Chapel, Embankment Road, Llanelli SA15 2BT*

MORIARTY, Mrs Susan Margaret. b 43. Cartrefle Coll of Educn TCert65. St As Minl Tr Course. **d** 02 **p** 09. Par Dn Gorsedd w Brynford, Ysgeifiog and Whitford *St As* from 02. *7 St Michael's Drive, Caerwys, Mold CH7 5BS* Tel (01352) 720874

MORING, Sally Margaret. b 61. St Martin's Coll Lanc BEd84 Middx Univ BA06. NTMTC 03. **d** 06 **p** 07. NSM Northolt St Mary *Lon* 06-09; V Hayes St Edm from 09. *St Edmund's Vicarage, 1 Edmund's Close, Hayes UB4 0HA* Tel (020) 8573 9965 E-mail vicar@stedmundschurch.com

MORISON, John Donald. b 34. ALCD60. **d** 61 **p** 62. C Rayleigh *Chelmsf* 61-64; C St Austell *Truro* 64-67; V Meltham Mills *Wakef* 67-71; Youth Chapl *Cov* 71-76; S Africa 76-82; Can Port Elizabeth 80-82; Bardsley Missr 82-86; Lic to Offic *S'wark* 82-86; Dioc Missr *Derby* 86-99; V Quarndon 86-99; rtd 99; Perm to Offic *Sarum* from 01. *Flat 1, Canford Place, 59 Cliff Drive, Canford Cliffs, Poole BH13 7JX* Tel (01202) 709377
E-mail kayandjohn@waitrose.com

MORLEY, Athelstan John. b 29. Linc Coll Ox BA52 MA56. Ridley Hall Cam. **d** 54 **p** 55. C Surbiton St Matt *S'wark* 54-57; Succ Chelmsf Cathl 57-60; R Mistley w Manningtree 60-69; R Hadleigh St Jas 69-94; rtd 94; Hon C Prittlewell *Chelmsf* 94-97; Perm to Offic from 94; P-in-c St Martin Ludgate *Lon* 01-04. *38 Bridgwater Drive, Westcliff-on-Sea SS0 0DH* Tel (01702) 339335

MORLEY, Georgina Laura (George). b 63. Dur Univ BA84 Nottm Univ MTh95 PhD99. Cranmer Hall Dur. **d** 03 **p** 03. Dir Studies NEOC 99-04; NSM Osmotherley w Harlsey and Ingleby Arncliffe *York* 03-08; Lect Cranmer Hall Dur 07-10. *Beacon Hill, High Street, Low Pittington, Durham DH6 1BE* Tel 0191-372 0385

MORLEY, Miss Gillian Dorothy. b 21. Greyladies Coll 49. **dss** 70 **d** 87. Lewisham St Swithun *S'wark* 70-82; Sturry w Fordwich and Westbere w Hersden *Cant* 82-87; Perm to Offic 87-10. *28 Glen Iris Avenue, Canterbury CT2 8HP* Tel (01227) 459992

MORLEY, John. *See* MORLEY, Athelstan John

MORLEY, John. b 43. AKC67. St Deiniol's Hawarden 67. **d** 68 **p** 69. C Newbold on Avon *Cov* 69-73; C Solihull *Birm* 73-77; C-in-c Elmdon Heath CD 76-77; Chapl RAF 77-93; TR Wallingford *Ox* 93-99; RD Wallingford 95-99; Dean St Paul's Cathl and Chapl Nicosia 99-02; V Henlow and Langford *St Alb* 02-08; RD Shefford 06-08; rtd 08; Perm to Offic *Leic* 08-11; *Pet* from 08; *Lich* from 09; P-in-c Gaulby from 11. *31 Walcot Road, Market Harborough LE16 9DL* Tel (01858) 419714 Mobile 07900-892566 E-mail revjmorley@talktalk.net

MORLEY, Keith. b 44. St Chad's Coll Dur BA66 Open Univ BSc93. **d** 67 **p** 68. C S Yardley St Mich *Birm* 67-70; C Solihull 70-73; V Shaw Hill 73-77; P-in-c Burton Coggles *Linc* 77-79; P-in-c Boothby Pagnell 77-79; V Lenton w Ingoldsby 77-79; P-in-c Bassingthorpe w Bitchfield 77-79; R Ingoldsby 79-87; RD Beltisloe 84-87; P-in-c Old Dalby and Nether Broughton *Leic* 87-94; RD Framland 88-90; Perm to Offic *Linc* from 03; rtd 04. *11 Swallow Close, Quarrington, Sleaford NG34 7UU*

MORLEY, Canon Leslie James. b 45. K Coll Lon BD67 AKC67 MTh68. St Boniface Warminster 68. **d** 69 **p** 70. C Birm St Pet 69-72; C W Bromley St Mary *Lon* 72; C W Bromley St Mary w St Pet 73-74; Chapl Nottm Univ 74-80; Dir Post-Ord Tr 80-85; Can Res and Vice-Provost S'well Minster 80-85; Hon Can 85-99; Chapl Bluecoat Sch Nottm 85-90; R Nottingham St Pet and St Jas *S'well* 85-99; AD Nottingham Cen 90-93; Dioc Rural

Officer *Ripon* 99-10; Hon Chapl Yorks Agric Soc 09-10; rtd 10. *Beacon Hill, High Street, Low Pittington, Durham DH6 1BE* Tel 0191-372 0385 Mobile 07879-470752
E-mail leslie.morley@virgin.net

MORLEY, Peter. b 36. St Jo Coll Nottm 81. **d** 83 **p** 84. C Sheff St Jo 83-87; Chapl The Shrewsbury Hosp Sheff 85-87; V Worsbrough Common *Sheff* 87-93; Chapl Mt Vernon Hosp Barnsley 87-93; R Harthill and Thorpe Salvin *Sheff* 93-99; rtd 99. *39 Hallcroft Road, Retford DN22 7LE* Tel (01777) 719081

MORLEY, Stephen Raymond. b 55. Birm Univ LLB76. STETS 07. **d** 10 **p** 11. C Aisholt, Enmore, Goathurst, Nether Stowey etc *B & W* from 10. *2 Cole Close, Nether Stowey, Bridgwater TA5 1JU* Tel (01278) 733669 Mobile 07723-786688
E-mail steve.morley@btinternet.com

MORLEY, Terence Martin Simon. b 49. SS Hild & Bede Coll Dur CertEd78. St Steph Ho Ox 71. **d** 74 **p** 75. C Kingston upon Hull St Alb *York* 74-76; C Middlesbrough All SS 76-77; Perm to Offic *Dur* 77-78; Hon C Worthing St Andr *Chich* 78-80; C Brighton Ch Ch 80-82; C Hove St Patr 80-82; C Ayr *Glas* 83-86; C Maybole 83-84; P-in-c Coatbridge 86-88; R 88-92; P-in-c 92; V Plymouth St Jas Ham *Ex* 93-09; Chapl Plymouth Community Services NHS Trust 96-98; rtd 09. *37 Great College Street, Brighton BN2 1HJ*

MORLEY, Trevor. b 39. Man Univ BSc62 MPS62 MRSH84. Ripon Hall Ox 65. **d** 67 **p** 68. C Compton Gifford *Ex* 67-70; Chapl Hammersmith Hosp Lon 70-83; Hon C N Hammersmith St Kath *Lon* 70-83; Chapl Univ Coll Hosp Lon 83-94; Chapl Univ Coll Lon Hosps NHS Trust 94-99; Hon Chapl St Luke's Hosp for the Clergy 89-99; V Linthwaite *Wakef* 99-06; rtd 06; Perm to Offic *Sheff* from 06. *19 Queenswood Road, Sheffield S6 1RR* Tel 0114-232 5232 E-mail tmqwr@tiscali.co.uk

MORLEY-BUNKER, John Arthur. b 27. Wells Th Coll 67. **d** 68 **p** 69. C Horfield H Trin *Bris* 68-71; P-in-c Easton All Hallows 71-75; V 75-82; RD Bris City 74-79; V Horfield St Greg 82-93; rtd 93; Perm to Offic *Bris* from 93. *1 Knoll Court, Knoll Hill, Bristol BS9 1QX* Tel 0117-968 5837

MORLEY-JONES, Anthony Roger. St Mich Coll Llan. **d** 04 **p** 05. NSM Cydweli and Llandyfaelog *St D* from 04. *11 Westhill Crescent, Cydweli SA17 4US* Tel (01554) 890458

MORLING, David Arthur. b 45. Saltley Tr Coll Birm CertEd66 Open Univ BA78. S Dios Minl Tr Scheme 83 Linc Th Coll. **d** 85 **p** 86. NSM Chich 85-97; P-in-c Doncaster Intake *Sheff* 97-02; P-in-c Doncaster H Trin 97-02; rtd 02; Perm to Offic *Bradf* from 02. *Lorindell, 61 Layton Lane, Rawdon, Leeds LS19 6RA* Tel 0113-250 3488 E-mail david.morling@bradford.anglican.org *or* david@morling.co.uk

MORONEY, Kevin John. b 61. Valley Forge Chr Coll Pennsylvania BS86. Gen Th Sem NY MDiv92. **d** 92 **p** 93. Asst Pastor Metuchen St Luke USA 92-94; R Metuchen All SS 94-98; Chapl St James Sch St James Maryland 98-00; Chapl and Tutor CITC 00-05; P-in-c Dublin Sandymount *D & G* 01-05; Dir Educn Radnor St Dav USA from 05. *St James School, 17641 College Road, St James MD 21781, USA* Tel (001) (301) 733 9330 E-mail kjmcoi@yahoo.com

MORPHY, George David. b 49. Birm Univ BEd71 Lon Univ BA75 Warwick Univ MA90. WMMTC. **d** 89 **p** 90. NSM Ribbesford w Bewdley and Dowles *Worc* 89-06; NSM Barbourne from 06; Dioc Dir of Educn 99-11. *41 Hallow Road, Worcester WR2 6BX* Tel (01905) 422007 Mobile 07867-525779 E-mail dmorphy@cofe-worcester.org

MORPHY, Canon Michael John. b 43. Newc Univ BSc65 Dur Univ MSc66 QUB PhD73. Ripon Coll Cuddesdon 82. **d** 84 **p** 85. C Halifax *Wakef* 84-86; V Luddenden w Luddenden Foot 86-97; V Corbridge w Halton and Newton Hall *Newc* 97-08; Hon Can Newc Cathl 07-08; rtd 08. *7 Mallard Drive, Montrose DD10 9NB* Tel (01674) 675277 E-mail mj.morphy@tiscali.co.uk

MORRELL, Mrs Jennifer Mary. b 49. NOC 84. **d** 87 **p** 94. Par Dn Crewe All SS and St Paul *Ches* 87-90; Par Dn Padgate *Liv* 90-94; C 94-95; TV Kirkby 95-00; V Croxteth Park 00-02. *24 Oak Tree Close, Kingsbury, Tamworth B78 2JF* Tel (01827) 874445

MORRELL, Canon Nigel Paul. b 38. S'wark Ord Course 73. **d** 76 **p** 77. C Letchworth St Paul w Willian *St Alb* 76-85; V Farley Hill St Jo 85-95; RD Luton 90-94; V Cardington 95-03; Hon Can St Alb 01-03; RD Elstow 03-08; rtd 03. *22 Sunderland Place, Shortstown, Bedford MK42 0FD* Tel and fax (01234) 743202
E-mail nigel.morrell@btopenworld.com

MORRELL, Paul Rodney. b 49. SRN70. SWMTC 91. **d** 93 **p** 94. C Heavitree w Ex St Paul 93-02; C Heavitree and St Mary Steps 02-05; TV from 05. *1A St Loyes Road, Exeter EX2 5HA* Tel (01392) 273430

MORRELL, His Honour Peter Richard. b 44. Univ Coll Ox MA71 Solicitor 70 Barrister-at-Law (Gray's Inn) 74. ERMC 06. **d** 08 **p** 09. NSM Uppingham w Ayston and Wardley w Belton *Pet* 10-11; NSM Nassington w Yarwell and Woodnewton w Apethorpe from 10. *New Sulehay Lodge, Nassington, Peterborough PE8 6QT* Tel and fax (01780) 782281 Mobile 07860-573597 E-mail pmorrell@btinternet.com

MORRELL, Mrs Susan Marjorie. b 46. Open Univ BA94. SEITE 93. d 96 p 97. NSM E Peckham and Nettlestead *Roch* from 96; Chapl Kent Coll Pembury 99-00. *7 Pippin Road, East Peckham, Tonbridge TN12 5BT* Tel (01622) 871150

MORRIS, Alan Ralph Oakden. b 29. Roch Th Coll 59. d 61 p 62. C Riverhead *Roch* 61-62; C Roch St Pet w St Marg 62-66; C Wrotham 66-74; V Biggin Hill 74-82; R Kingsdown 82-88; V Seal SS Pet and Paul 88-92; rtd 92; P-in-c Renhold *St Alb* 92-93; Perm to Offic *Roch* from 93. *268 Woolwich Road, London SE2 0DW* Tel (020) 8310 7860

MORRIS, Miss Alison Mary. b 58. W Midl Coll of Educn BEd81 Wolv Univ PGCE00 MA02. Qu Coll Birm 06. d 09 p 10. NSM Pelsall *Lich* from 09. *32 Chestnut Road, Leamore, Walsall WS3 1BD* Tel (01922) 477734 Mobile 07837-649756 E-mail a.morris125@btinternet.com

MORRIS, Andy. *See* MORRIS, Edward Andrew

MORRIS, Mrs Ann. b 52. N Co Coll Newc CertEd73. WEMTC 00. d 03 p 04. C Churchdown St Jo and Innsworth *Glouc* 03-07; P-in-c Barnwood from 07. *The Vicarage, 27A Barnwood Avenue, Gloucester GL4 3AB* Tel (01452) 619531

MORRIS, Mrs Ann Veronica Marsham. b 46. Open Univ BA83. WEMTC 99. d 01 p 02. NSM Amberley *Glouc* 01-09; NSM Minchinhampton w Box and Amberley from 09. *The Rectory, Amberley, Stroud GL5 5JG* Tel (01453) 878515 E-mail ann.morris@amberley.org

MORRIS, Anne. *See* MORRIS, Ms Margaret Anne

MORRIS (*née* ALLEN), Mrs Anne. b 47. LMH Ox BA69 MA72 Lon Univ BD82. NOC 01. d 03 p 04. NSM Leamington Priors All SS *Cov* from 03; NSM Leamington Spa H Trin from 03. *20 Hayle Avenue, Warwick CV34 5TW* Tel (01926) 403512

MORRIS, Anthony David. b 61. Aston Univ BSc83. Qu Coll Birm 06. d 09. NSM Droitwich Spa *Worc* from 09. *15 Elgar Crescent, Droitwich WR9 7SP* Tel (01905) 771040 E-mail david.morris@droitwich777.freeserve.co.uk

MORRIS, Bernard Lyn. b 28. St Aid Birkenhead 55. d 58 p 59. C-in-c Hartcliffe St Andr CD *Bris* 58-61; C Bishopston 61-63; R Ardwick St Thos *Man* 63-69; R Aylton w Pixley, Munsley and Putley *Heref* 69-79; P-in-c Tarrington w Stoke Edith 72-77; R 77-79; P-in-c Queen Camel, Marston Magna, W Camel, Rimpton etc *B & W* 79-80; R 80-87; R Queen Camel w W Camel, Corton Denham etc 87-95; rtd 95; Perm to Offic *B & W* from 95 and *Ex* from 01. *Canterbury Bells, Ansford Hill, Castle Cary BA7 7JL* Tel (01963) 351154 E-mail revblmorris@supanet.com

MORRIS, Beti Elin. b 36. CertEd57. Sarum & Wells Th Coll 87. d 89 p 97. C Llangeitho and Blaenpennal w Betws Leucu etc *St D* 89-92; C-in-c Pencarreg and Llanycrwys 92-97; V 97-05; rtd 05. *Bro Mihangel, Maes y Tren, Felinfach, Lampeter SA48 8AH* Tel (01570) 470845

MORRIS, Brian. *See* MORRIS, Reginald Brian

MORRIS, Brian Michael Charles. b 32. S Dios Minl Tr Scheme 82. d 85 p 86. NSM Denmead *Portsm* 85-89; C S w N Hayling 89-96; P-in-c Shalfleet 96-97; rtd 97; Perm to Offic *Portsm* from 97. *Ashleigh, 5 Ashwood Close, Hayling Island PO11 9AX* Tel (023) 9246 7292 E-mail bmc_morris@btinternet.com

MORRIS, Ms Catharine Mary. b 75. Regent's Park Coll Ox BA96 MA00. Ridley Hall Cam 99. d 01 p 02. C Malpas *Mon* 01-06; C Reading Greyfriars *Ox* from 06. *93 York Road, Reading RG1 8DU* Tel 0118-957 1585 E-mail catharine.morris@greyfriars.org.uk

MORRIS, Canon Christopher John. b 45. K Coll Lon AKC67 BD68. d 68 p 69. C W Bromwich All SS *Lich* 68-72; C Porthill 72-74; Min Can Carl Cathl 74-77; Ecum Liaison Officer BBC Radio Carl 74-77; Dioc Communications Officer *Carl* 77-83; V Thursby 77-83; Angl Adv Border TV from 82; V Upperby St Jo *Carl* 83-91; P-in-c Lanercost w Kirkcambeck and Walton 91-99; P-in-c Gilsland w Nether Denton 96-99; R Lanercost, Walton, Gilsland and Nether Denton 99-10; RD Brampton 98-05; Hon Can Carl Cathl 98-10; rtd 10. *15 Nook Lane Close, Dalston, Carlisle CA5 7JA* Tel (01228) 711872

MORRIS, Prof Colin. b 28. Qu Coll Ox BA48 BA51 MA53 FRHistS71. Linc Th Coll 51. d 53 p 54. Fell and Chapl Pemb Coll Ox 53-69; Prof Medieval Hist Southn Univ 69-92; rtd 92; Public Preacher *Win* from 69. *12 Bassett Crescent East, Southampton SO16 7PB* Tel (023) 8076 8176

MORRIS, Preb David Meeson. b 35. Trin Coll Ox BA56 MA60. Chich Th Coll 57. d 60 p 61. C Westmr St Steph w St Jo *Lon* 60-65; Lib Pusey Ho 65-68; Chapl Wadh Coll Ox 67-68; C Sheff St Leon Norwood 68-69; Ind Chapl 68-72; C Brightside St Marg 69-72; R Adderley *Lich* 72-82; V Drayton in Hales 72-82; RD Tutbury 82-95; Chapl Burton Gen Hosp 82-90; P-in-c Burton St Modwen *Lich* 82; V Burton 82-99; Preb Lich Cathl 93-99; P-in-c Shobnall 94-99; rtd 99; Perm to Offic *Heref* and *Lich* from 99. *Watling House, All Stretton, Church Stretton SY6 6HH* Tel (01694) 722243

MORRIS, David Michael. b 59. Ox Univ MA84 Cam Univ PGCE91. Sarum & Wells Th Coll 82. d 84 p 85. C Angell Town St Jo *S'wark* 84-87; C Mitcham SS Pet and Paul 87-90; V Llandygwydd and Cenarth w Cilrhedyn etc *St D* 90-98; Lect Th St D Coll Lamp from 90; Hd RE Lampeter Comp Sch from 98. *Bronant, Rhydargaeau, Carmarthen SA32 7DR*

MORRIS, Canon David Pryce. b 39. St Mich Coll Llan 62. d 63 p 64. C Colwyn Bay *St As* 63-70; R St George 70-76; Dioc Children's Adv 75-87; V Bodelwyddan and St George 76-79; V Connah's Quay 79-95; St As Dioc Adult Lay Tr Team 88-06; Ed *St Asaph Diocesan News* from 89; Dioc Communications Officer 90-06; V Shotton 95-06; Hon Can St As Cathl 96-00; Can Cursal St As Cathl 00-06; rtd 07. *7 Rhuddlan Road, Buckley CH7 3QA* Tel (01244) 540779 Mobile 07711-519752 E-mail david@dandpmorris.net

MORRIS, David Thomas. St Mich Coll Llan. d 09 p 10. C Merthyr Tydfil St Dav *Llan* 09-10; C Merthyr Tydfil St Dav and Abercanaid from 10. *4 Lancaster Terrace, Merthyr Tydfil CF47 8SL* Tel (01685) 386072 E-mail fr.davidmorris@hotmail.co.uk

MORRIS, Dennis Gordon. b 41. ALCM58. St D Coll Lamp. d 67 p 68. C Neath w Llantwit 67-92; V Troedrhiwgarth 92-10; rtd 10. *12 Cwrt yr Hen Ysgol, Tondu, Bridgend CF32 9GE*

MORRIS, Edward Andrew (Andy). b 57. St Jo Coll Nottm BTh93. d 96 p 97. C Conisbrough *Sheff* 96-01; Perm to Offic *S'well* 01-04; V Bestwood St Matt w St Phil from 04. *St Matthew's Vicarage, Padstow Road, Nottingham NG5 5GH* Tel 0115-927 7229 Mobile 07775-925297 E-mail andy-morris@ntlworld.com

MORRIS, Mrs Elizabeth Anne. b 59. BA05. d 00 p 01. OLM Darsham and Westleton w Dunwich *St E* 00-04; C Hadleigh, Layham and Shelley 04-06; C Yoxmere 08-09; C Aquitaine *Eur* from 10. *Maison Neuve, Plaisance, 24650 Issigeac, France* Tel (0033) 5 53 58 71 90 E-mail cookingcurate@tiscali.co.uk

MORRIS, Geoffrey. *See* MORRIS, Canon Martin Geoffrey Roger

MORRIS, Geoffrey David. b 43. Fitzw Coll Cam BA65 MA69 Westmr Coll Ox DipEd67. NOC. d 82 p 83. C Man Clayton St Cross w St Paul 82-85; V Lower Kersal 85-03; P-in-c Priors Hardwick, Priors Marston and Wormleighton *Cov* 03-08; Asst Chapl HM Pris Rye Hill 03-07; rtd 08. *20 Hayle Avenue, Warwick CV34 5TW* Tel (01926) 403512

MORRIS, Graham Edwin. b 60. Sarum & Wells Th Coll 83. d 86 p 87. C Coalbrookdale, Iron-Bridge and Lt Wenlock *Heref* 86-90; TV Bilston *Lich* 90-99; R Northwood *Portsm* 99-05; V Gurnard 99-05; P-in-c Ventnor H Trin 05-06; V from 06; P-in-c Ventnor St Cath 05-06; V from 06; P-in-c Bonchurch 05-06; R from 06; RD E Wight from 05. *The Vicarage, Maples Drive, Ventnor PO38 1NR* Tel (01983) 853729 E-mail graham.morris@btinternet.com

MORRIS, Preb Henry James. b 47. Lon Univ BSc69. Wycliffe Hall Ox MA. d 79 p 80. C Woodford Wells *Chelmsf* 79-82; C Gt Baddow 82-87; R Siddington w Preston *Glouc* 87-01; RD Cirencester 97-01; TR Madeley *Heref* from 01; Preb Heref Cathl from 09. *St Michael's Vicarage, Church Street, Madeley, Telford TF7 5BN* Tel and fax (01952) 586645 *or* tel 585718 E-mail henrym@dircon.co.uk

MORRIS, Ian Henry. b 42. Sarum & Wells Th Coll 73. d 75 p 76. C Lawrence Weston *Bris* 75-78; C St Buryan, St Levan and Sennen *Truro* 78-81; P-in-c Lanteglos by Fowey 81-84; V 84-85; R Lanteglos by Camelford w Advent 85-95; RD Trigg Minor and Bodmin 93-95; TR Probus, Ladock and Grampound w Creed and St Erme 95-07; RD Powder 01-04; rtd 07. *43 Abbots Way, West Kirby, Wirral CH48 6EN* Tel 0151-625 8474

MORRIS, Miss Jane Elizabeth. b 50. York Univ BA71 CertEd72 MSc80. NEOC 92. d 92 p 94. NSM York St Mich-le-Belfrey 92-95; C Leeds St Geo *Ripon* 95-05; V Cricklewood St Gabr and St Mich *Lon* from 05. *St Gabriel's Vicarage, 156 Anson Road, London NW2 6BH* Tel (020) 8452 6305 E-mail janemorris@ntlworld.com

MORRIS, Jeremy Nigel. b 60. Ball Coll Ox MA81 DPhil86 Clare Coll Cam BA92. Westcott Ho Cam 90. d 93 p 94. C Battersea St Mary *S'wark* 93-96; Dir Studies Westcott Ho Cam 96-01; Vice-Prin 97-01; Dean and Chapl Trin Hall Cam 01-10; Dean K Coll Cam from 10. *King's College, Cambridge CB2 1ST* Tel (01223) 331100 E-mail jnm20@cam.ac.uk

MORRIS, Mrs Joanna Elizabeth. b 60. N Riding Coll of Educn CertEd81. Qu Coll Birm 07. d 09 p 10. C Riddings and Ironville *Derby* from 09. *The Vicarage, Vicarage Lane, Ironville, Nottingham NG16 5PT* Tel (01773) 528136 E-mail jomorris17@googlemail.com

MORRIS, Canon John. b 25. Westcott Ho Cam. d 65 p 66. C St Alb St Mich *St Alb* 65-68; V Leverstock Green 68-80; TR Chambersbury 80-82; V Mymms 82-90; RD Hatfield 83-88; Hon Can St Alb 89-90; rtd 90; Perm to Offic *St Alb* 90-02; *Nor* 92-94 and 95-10; *Pet* from 11; P-in-c Barney, Fulmodeston w Croxton, Hindringham etc *Nor* 94-95. *Highfield, 20 Teigh Road, Market Overton, Oakham LE15 7PW* Tel (01572) 767212

MORRIS, John Douglas. b 37. Cam Univ BA58 Lon Inst of Educn PGCE60 Univ of E Africa MEd67 Ex Univ PhD87. S Dios Minl Tr Scheme 94. d 95 p 96. NSM Twyford and Owslebury and Morestead *Win* 95-01; Perm to Offic from 01; Chapl Twyford Sch *Win* from 96. *Gifford House, St Giles Hill, Winchester SO23 0JH* Tel (01962) 869720 E-mail johnmarymorris@btopenworld.com

MORRIS, John Dudley. b 33. Ball Coll Ox BA57 MA61. Wycliffe Hall Ox 58. **d** 60 **p** 61. C Tonbridge SS Pet and Paul *Roch* 60-65; C Enfield Ch Ch Trent Park *Lon* 65-69; Chapl Elstree Sch Woolhampton 70-74; Hd Master Handcross Park Sch W Sussex 74-89; V Rudgwick *Chich* 89-98; RD Horsham 93-98; rtd 98; Perm to Offic *Chich* from 98. *13 Hoadlands, Handcross, Haywards Heath RH17 6HB* Tel (01444) 400184

MORRIS, John Edgar. b 20. Keble Coll Ox BA42 MA50. Wycliffe Hall Ox 42. **d** 44 **p** 45. C Eccleston St Thos *Liv* 44-48; C Warrington H Trin 48-50; V Newton-le-Willows 50-57; R Wavertree H Trin 57-66; V Ainsdale 66-82; R Broadwell, Evenlode, Oddington and Adlestrop *Glouc* 82-88; rtd 89; Perm to Offic *Glouc* 89-97 and 01-07. *Pen y Dref, Rhosneigr, Anglesey LL64 5JH* Tel (01407) 810202

MORRIS, John Owen. b 56. Nottm Univ BCom82. Linc Th Coll 79. **d** 82 **p** 83. C Morriston *S & B* 82-84; C Kingstone w Clehonger and Eaton Bishop *Heref* 84-87; P-in-c Lugwardine w Bartestree and Weston Beggard 87-92; Chapl RN from 92. *Royal Naval Chaplaincy Service, Mail Point 1-2, Leach Building, Whale Island, Portsmouth PO2 8BY* Tel (023) 9262 5055 Fax 9262 5134

MORRIS, Jonathan Richard. b 57. Lanc Univ BA78 Trin Coll Ox MSc84. WEMTC 99. **d** 02 **p** 03. C Taunton St Andr *B & W* 02-06; C Wulfric Benefice from 06. *The Rectory, New Street, North Perrott, Crewkerne TA18 7ST* Tel (01460) 72356 E-mail jonbea@supanet.com

MORRIS, Kevin John. b 63. Univ of Wales (Ban) BMus84. Westcott Ho Cam 85. **d** 88 **p** 89. C Roath *Llan* 88-91; C Holborn St Alb w Saffron Hill St Pet *Lon* 91-96; V Bedford Park from 96; Dir Post-Ord Tr from 99. *The Vicarage, Priory Gardens, London W4 1TT* Tel (020) 8994 0139 *or* 8994 1380 E-mail kevin.john.morris@ukgateway.net

MORRIS, Kirsteen Helen Grace. b 44. STETS 99. **d** 02 **p** 03. NSM Cowes H Trin and St Mary *Portsm* from 02. *Meda, Medham Farm Lane, Cowes PO31 8PH* Tel (01983) 289585 Fax 292919 E-mail morris.scawfell@onwight.net

MORRIS, Lillian Rosina (Mother Lillian). b 29. dss 70 **d** 87. CSA 68-97; Mother Superior 82-94 and from 00; Sherston Magna w Easton Grey *Bris* 71-73; Notting Hill All SS w St Columb *Lon* 74-82. *40 Homecross House, 21 Fishers Lane, London W4 1YA* Tel (020) 8747 0001

MORRIS, Lyn. See MORRIS, Bernard Lyn

MORRIS, Mrs Lynne. b 48. STETS 07. **d** 10 **p** 11. NSM Horton, Chalbury, Hinton Martell and Holt St Jas *Sarum* from 10; NSM Witchampton, Stanbridge and Long Crichel etc from 11. *The Vicarage, Witchampton, Wimborne BH21 5AP* Tel (01258) 840445 E-mail lynnemorrislp@btinternet.com

MORRIS, Mrs Lynne Margaret. b 53. SEN. WMMTC 95. **d** 98 **p** 99. NSM Wrockwardine Wood *Lich* 98-01; Chapl Birm Specialist Community Health NHS Trust from 01. *5 Kingston Road, Trench, Telford TF2 7HT* Tel (01952) 618158 *or* 0121-442 4321 E-mail lynne.morris@southbirminghampct.nhs.uk

MORRIS, Ms Margaret Anne. b 61. Man Univ BA82 MA91. NOC 94. **d** 96 **p** 97. C Bury St Pet *Man* 96-98; C Accrington St Jo w Huncoat *Blackb* 98-01; V Knuzden from 01. *St Oswald's Vicarage, 68 Bank Lane, Blackburn BB1 2AP* Tel (01254) 698321 E-mail rev_anne_morris@gn.apc.org

MORRIS, Canon Margaret Jane. Ox Univ MTh96 Leic Univ Hon LLM96. EMMTC 86. **d** 89 **p** 94. NSM Quorndon *Leic* 89-96; Chapl for People affected by HIV 94-05; NSM Loughborough All SS w H Trin 96-98; Chapl Asst Leic R Infirmary NHS Trust 98-00; Chapl Asst Univ Hosps Leic NHS Trust 00-10; Hon Can Leic Cathl 97-10; rtd 10. *10 Toller Road, Quorn, Loughborough LE12 8AH* Tel and fax (01509) 412092 E-mail morris@rog15.freeserve.co.uk

MORRIS, Canon Martin Geoffrey Roger. b 41. Trin Coll Cam BA63 MA67. St D Coll Lamp 63. **d** 66 **p** 67. C Newport St Paul *Mon* 66-72; R Lampeter Velfrey *St D* 72-74; R Lampeter Velfrey and Llanddewi Velfrey 74-98; RD St Clears 83-98; Can St D Cathl 92-08; Chan 03-08; rtd 08. *Greenfield Cottage, Gilfach Hill, Lampeter Velfrey, Narberth SA67 8UL*

MORRIS, Ms Mary. b 27. Birm Univ BA49 CertEd50 MA56. dss 68 **d** 87 **p** 94. Kinver *Lich* 83-87; Hon Par Dn Kinver and Enville 87-94; Hon C from 94. *12 Pavilion End, Prestwood, Stourbridge DY7 5PF* Tel (01384) 877245 E-mail marymorris12@tiscali.co.uk

MORRIS, Michael Alan. b 46. Jes Coll Cam BA70 MA74. Coll of Resurr Mirfield 79. **d** 81 **p** 82. C Leamington Priors All SS *Cov* 81-83; C Milton *Portsm* 83-88; R Petworth *Chich* 88-90; R Egdean 88-90; Chapl St Pet Hosp Chertsey 90-95; Hon C Thorpe *Guildf* 90-95; P-in-c Harbledown Cant 95-97; R from 97; Chapl St Nic Hosp Cant from 95. *The Rectory, Summer Hill, Harbledown, Canterbury CT2 8NW* Tel (01227) 464117 Fax 760530 E-mail michael@summer-hill.freeserve.co.uk

MORRIS, Michael James. b 70. Univ of Wales (Abth) BScEcon92. Qu Coll Birm BA. **d** 00 **p** 01. C Tupsley w Hampton Bishop *Heref* 00-04; TV Watling Valley *Ox* from 04. *21 Edzell Crescent, Westcroft, Milton Keynes MK4 4EU* Tel (01908) 507123 E-mail mike.morris@wvep.org

MORRIS (née ROBERTS), Nia Wyn. b 64. Univ of Wales (Ban) BA86 PGCE87 CQSW90 Anglia Poly Univ MA00. Westcott Ho Cam 98. **d** 00 **p** 01. C Rhyl w St Ann *St As* 00-03; R Bala from 03. *Y Rheithordy, 13 Heol-y-Castell, Bala LL23 7YA* Tel (01678) 521047 Mobile 07833-302312

MORRIS, Norman Foster Maxwell. b 46. Ex Univ BA68 MA71 Leic Univ PGCE69 K Coll Lon MTh85 Univ of Wales (Cardiff) MA91 Cheltenham & Glouc Coll of HE MA98. S'wark Ord Course 75. **d** 78 **p** 79. C Hackbridge and N Beddington *S'wark* 78-81; Chapl Tonbridge Sch 81-85; Chapl Mon Sch 85-00; Asst Warden Jones Almshouses Mon 89-00; R Wentnor w Ratlinghope, Myndtown, Norbury etc *Heref* from 00; P-in-c Churchstoke w Hyssington from 04; CF (ACF) from 02. *The Rectory, Wentnor, Bishops Castle SY9 5EE* Tel (01588) 650244 Mobile 07974-771069 E-mail revnorm@btinternet.com

MORRIS, Paul David. b 56. St Jo Coll Nottm BTh79. **d** 80 **p** 81. C Billericay and Lt Burstead *Chelmsf* 80-84; C Luton Lewsey St Hugh *St Alb* 84-89; Dioc Adv on Evang *S'well* 89-00; Dioc Millennium Officer 97-01; Min Tommy's (ch for the unchurched) 96-01; C Barton in Fabis 01-02; C Gotham 01-02; C Thrumpton 01-02; C Kingston and Ratcliffe-on-Soar 01-02; C Sutton Bonington w Normanton-on-Soar 01-02; Dir Evang Chr Associates Internat 02-04; Assoc Eur Dir 04-06; Eur Dir 06-08; Brussels Team 08-09; P-in-c Derby St Pet and Ch Ch w H Trin from 09. *St Peter's Vicarage, 16 Farley Road, Derby DE23 6BX* Tel (01332) 204686 E-mail paul@stpetersderby.org.uk

MORRIS, Peter. b 45. Leeds Univ CertEd66. Tyndale Hall Bris 68. **d** 71 **p** 72. C Southport SS Simon and Jude *Liv* 71-74; Min-in-c Ch Ch Netherley LEP 74-76; V Bryn 76-91; R Redenhall, Harleston, Wortwell and Needham *Nor* 91-05; rtd 05. *9 Bromley College, London Road, Bromley BR1 1PE* Tel (020) 8460 3455 E-mail petermorris203@btinternet.com

MORRIS, The Ven Philip Gregory. b 50. Leeds Univ BA71 MPhil74. Coll of Resurr Mirfield 71. **d** 73 **p** 74. C Aberdare *Llan* 74-77; C Neath w Llantwit 77-80; V Cymmer and Porth 80-88; TV Llantwit Major 88-01; Dioc Missr 88-99; Can Res Llan Cathl 00-01; Adn Margam from 02; TV Aberavon 02; P-in-c Kenfig Hill 02-05; P-in-c Ewenny w St Brides Major from 05. *The Vicarage, Southerndown Road, St Brides Major, Bridgend CF32 0SD* Tel (01656) 880108 E-mail pmorri@globalnet.co.uk

MORRIS, Philip John. b 50. FCIPD96. St Mich Coll Llan 97. **d** 99 **p** 00. NSM Builth and Llanddewi'r Cwm w Llangynog etc *S & B* 99-04; NSM Aberedw w Llandeilo Graban and Llanbadarn etc from 04. *Lochaber, 22 North Road, Builth Wells LD2 3BU* Tel (01982) 552390

MORRIS, Canon Raymond. b 48. Open Univ BA88. NOC 80. **d** 83 **p** 84. C Tonge w Alkrington *Man* 83-86; R Blackley St Paul 86-91; V Heyside from 91; AD Tandle 02-09; Hon Can Man Cathl from 07. *St Mark's Vicarage, Perth Street, Royton, Oldham OL2 6LY* Tel (01706) 847177

MORRIS, Raymond Arthur. b 42. Trin Coll Ox BA64 MA66 Lon Univ LLB71 CQSW72. Clifton Th Coll 66. **d** 67 **p** 91. C Greenstead *Chelmsf* 67-68; Perm to Offic *York* 69-91; NSM Linthorpe from 91. *3 Medina Gardens, Middlesbrough TS5 8BN* Tel (01642) 593726 E-mail morris101@btinternet.com

MORRIS, Reginald Brian. b 31. St Mich Coll Llan 56. **d** 59 **p** 60. C St Jo in Bedwardine *Worc* 59-61; P-in-c Tolladine 61-62; CF 62-78; V Cheswardine *Lich* 78-84; V Hales 78-84; Perm to Offic 84-86; C Cen Telford 86-89; rtd 89; Perm to Offic *Heref* 90-07 and *Lich* from 07. *Woodside Cottage, School Lane, Prees, Whitchurch SY13 2BU* Tel (01948) 840090

MORRIS, Canon Robert John. b 46. Leeds Univ BA67. Coll of Resurr Mirfield 74. **d** 76 **p** 77. C Beeston Hill St Luke *Ripon* 76; C Holbeck 76-78; C Moseley St Mary *Birm* 78-83; P-in-c Handsworth St Jas 83-88; V 88-99; P-in-c Handsworth St Mich 86-87; AD Handsworth 92-99; TR Kings Norton from 99; Hon Can Birm Cathl from 97. *The Rectory, 273 Pershore Road South, Kings Norton, Birmingham B30 3EX* Tel 0121-459 0560 Fax 486 2825 Mobile 07973-389427 E-mail morrisrob4@aol.com

MORRIS, Robert Lee. b 47. W Virginia Univ BA69. Gen Th Sem (NY) MDiv73. **d** 73 **p** 74. USA 73-74 and from 84; Community of Celebration 74-94; P-in-c Cumbrae (or Millport) *Arg* 75-76 and 79-84. *St Dunstan's Episcopal Church, 14301 Stuebner Airline Road, Houston TX 77069 USA* Tel (001) (281) 440 1600

MORRIS, Canon Robin Edward. b 32. St Jo Coll Ox BA55 MA60. Westcott Ho Cam 55. **d** 57 **p** 58. C Halliwell St Thos *Man* 57-61; V Castleton Moor 61-71; V Stalybridge 71-80; R Heswall *Ches* 80-97; Hon Can Ches Cathl 91-97; RD Wirral N 93-97; rtd 97; Perm to Offic *Man* from 97. *122 Kiln Lane, Milnrow, Rochdale OL16 3HA* Tel (01706) 642846

MORRIS, The Ven Roger Anthony Brett. b 68. Imp Coll Lon BSc89 Trin Coll Cam BA92 MA08 ARCS89. Ridley Hall Cam 90. **d** 93 **p** 94. C Northleach w Hampnett and Farmington etc *Glouc* 93-96; P-in-c Sevenhampton w Charlton Abbotts and Hawling etc 96-00; P-in-c Dowdeswell and Andoversford w the Shiptons etc 96-00; R Sevenhampton w Charlton Abbots, Hawling etc 00-03; Dioc Dir Par Development and Evang *Cov* 03-08; Adn Worc from 08. *The Archdeacon's House, Walkers*

Lane, Whittington, Worcester WR5 2RE Tel 07590-696212 (mobile) E-mail roger.morris@me.com

MORRIS, Mrs Sally Jane. b 69. Imp Coll Lon BSc91. Qu Coll Birm 07. **d** 10 **p** 11. NSM Bowbrook S *Worc* from 10. *The Archdeacon's House, Walkers Lane, Whittington, Worcester WR5 2RE* E-mail sjmorris@mypostoffice.co.uk

MORRIS (née GILES), Ms Sarah Jayne. b 76. Aston Univ BSc98. St Jo Coll Nottm MTh06. **d** 06 **p** 07. C Ten Telford *Lich* 06-10; Perm to Offic from 10; Chapl HM YOI Stoke Heath from 11. *HM Young Offender Institution, Stoke Heath, Market Drayton TF9 2JL* Tel (01630) 636000 E-mail morris.sarah33@btinternet.com

MORRIS, Shaun Anthony. b 64. Keele Univ BSocSc85. Oak Hill Th Coll 04. **d** 06 **p** 07. C Westlands St Andr *Lich* 06-10; C Hanford from 10; C Trentham from 10. *Hanford Vicarage, 76 Church Lane, Stoke-on-Trent ST4 4QD* E-mail morris.shaun@btinternet.com

MORRIS, Simon John. b 83. St Jo Coll Dur BA05. St Steph Ho Ox BA07. **d** 08 **p** 09. C Tottenham St Mary *Lon* from 08. *The Mission House, Mitchley Road, London N17 9HG* Tel (020) 8808 5027

MORRIS, Stanley James. b 35. Keble Coll Ox BA58 MA63. Chich Th Coll 59. **d** 61 **p** 62. C Tunstall Ch Ch *Lich* 61-64; C W Bromwich All SS 64-67; V Wilnecote 67-88; V Alrewas and Wychnor 88-00; rtd 01; Perm to Offic *Derby* from 01. *44 Pinfold Close, Repton, Derby DE65 6FR* Tel (01283) 703453

MORRIS, Stephen Bryan. b 54. Linc Th Coll 88. **d** 90 **p** 91. C Glouc St Geo w Whaddon 90-94; Chapl for the Deaf from 94; C Glouc St Mary de Crypt w St Jo, Ch Ch etc 94-99; C Glouc St Mark and St Mary de Crypt w St Jo etc 00-02; C Barnwood 02-03. *The Vicarage, 27A Barnwood Avenue, Gloucester GL4 3AB* Tel (01452) 610450

MORRIS, Stephen Francis. b 52. St Jo Coll Nottm BTh79. **d** 79 **p** 80. C N Hinksey *Ox* 79-82; C Leic H Apostles 82-85; TV Shenley and Loughton *Ox* 85-88; TV Watling Valley 88-95; V Chatham St Wm *Roch* 95-98; TR S Chatham H Trin 98-00; Lect Nottingham St Mary and St Cath *S'well* 00-07; Lect Nottingham All SS, St Mary and St Pet from 07; AD Nottingham Cen 02-08; Dioc Ecum Officer from 10. *21 Private Road, Sherwood, Nottingham NG5 4DD* Tel 0115-960 4477 or 947 2476 E-mail parishoffice@stmarysnottingham.org

MORRIS, Steven Ralph. b 62. UEA BA84 MA85. Wycliffe Hall Ox 08. **d** 10 **p** 11. C Ealing St Steph Castle Hill *Lon* from 10. *26 Kings Avenue, London W5 2SH* Tel (020) 8998 7884 E-mail steve wycliffe@hotmail.co.uk

MORRIS, Canon Stuart Collard. b 43. AKC66. St Boniface Warminster 66. **d** 67 **p** 68. C Hanham *Bris* 67-71; C Whitchurch 71-74; P-in-c Westerleigh and Wapley w Codrington and Dodington 74-77; P-in-c Holdgate w Tugford *Heref* 77-82; P-in-c Abdon w Clee St Margaret 77-82; R Diddlebury w Bouldon and Munslow 77-82; P-in-c Sotterley, Willingham, Shadingfield, Ellough etc *St E* 82-87; RD Beccles and S Elmham 83-94; P-in-c Westhall w Brampton and Stoven 86-88; P-in-c Flixton w Homersfield and S Elmham 86-92; Hon Can St E Cathl 87-99; V Bungay H Trin w St Mary 87-94; P-in-c Hadleigh w Layham and Shelley 94-96; R Hadleigh 96-99; Dean Bocking 94-99; RD Hadleigh 94-98; rtd 99; Perm to Offic *Ely* from 07. *Blackbank Farm, Black Bank, Southery, Downham Market PE38 0NL* Tel (01366) 377567 E-mail stuart@bartimaeuscommunity.org.uk

MORRIS, Canon Timothy David. b 48. Lon Univ BSc69. Trin Coll Bris. **d** 75 **p** 76. C Edin St Thos 75-77; R Edin St Jas 77-83; R Troon *Glas* 83-85; R Galashiels *Edin* 85-02; R Edin Gd Shep 02-08; Dean Edin 92-01; Hon Can St Mary's Cathl from 01; rtd 08. *2 The Firs, Foulden Newton, Berwick-upon-Tweed TD15 1UL* Tel (01289) 386615 E-mail timdmorris@blueyonder.co.uk

MORRIS, Mrs Valerie Ruth. b 46. St Hugh's Coll Ox BA68 MA72. Gilmore Course 76. dss 78 **d** 87 **p** 05. Drayton in Hales *Lich* 78-82; Burton 82-90; Par Dn 87-91; Perm to Offic *Heref* 04-05; Hon C Church Stretton from 05. *Watling House, All Stretton, Church Stretton SY6 6HH* Tel (01694) 722243 E-mail valerieanddavid@caradoc-as.fsnet.co.uk

MORRIS, William Hazlitt. b 62. Trin Coll Cam BA84 MA88 Virginia Univ LLM89 Solicitor 88. NTMTC BA09. **d** 09 **p** 10. NSM St Martin-in-the-Fields *Lon* from 09. *St Martin-in-the-Fields, 6 St Martin's Place, London WC2N 4JH* Tel (020) 7766 1100 E-mail william.morris@smitf.org

MORRIS, William Humphrey Francis. b 29. Univ of Wales BA54 MA72 Trin Coll Cam BA62 MA66 PhD75 Par Wales MEd76 PhD80 Ox Univ DPhil85 DD88 FRAS84 FInstP92. Qu Coll Birm 56. **d** 58 **p** 59. C Prestbury *Ches* 58-60; C Neston 60-65; V Sandbach Heath 65-68; Lic to Offic 69-93; rtd 84; Lic to Offic *Lich* from 93; Perm to Offic *Ches* from 93. *Stonyflats Farm, Smallwood, Sandbach CW11 2XH* Tel (01477) 500354

MORRIS, William James. b 23. St Deiniol's Hawarden 72. **d** 73 **p** 74. NSM Brecon Adnry 73-78; NSM Crickhowell w Cwmdu and Tretower *S & B* 78-98; rtd 98. *The School House, Cwmdu, Crickhowell NP8 1RU* Tel (01874) 730355

MORRIS, William Richard Price. b 23. FCollP82. Glouc Sch of Min 86. **d** 88 **p** 89. Hon C Bussage *Glouc* 88-90; Perm to Offic

90-91; Hon C France Lynch 91; Hon C Chalford and France Lynch 91-93; rtd 93; Perm to Offic *Glouc* from 93. *Langendun House, Manor Close, Michinhampton, Stroud GL6 9DG* Tel (01453) 886382

MORRISON, Barbara Anne. b 29. St Andr Univ BSc50. **d** 95 **p** 96. NSM Eorropaidh *Arg* from 95; P-in-c 00-04; rtd 04. *46 Upper Coll, Back, Isle of Lewis HS2 0LT* Tel and fax (01851) 820559 E-mail barbara.stmoluag@care4free.net

MORRISON, Barry John. b 44. Pemb Coll Cam BA66 MA70. ALCD69. **d** 69 **p** 70. C Stoke Bishop *Bris* 69-72; C Edgware *Lon* 72-76; Chapl Poly Cen Lon 76-83; Hon C Langham Place All So 76-83; P-in-c W Hampstead St Luke 83-88; V 88-98; Chapl Westf Coll 84-92; R Rushden St Mary w Newton Bromswold *Pet* 98-08; rtd 08; Perm to Offic *Pet* from 09. *11 Lytham Park, Oundle, Peterborough PE8 4FB* Tel (01832) 274242 E-mail gandbmorrison@btinternet.com

MORRISON, Bryony Clare. b 47. Lon Univ CertEd77 Brentwood Coll of Educn BEd86. NTMTC 96. **d** 99 **p** 00. C Epping Distr *Chelmsf* 99-05; TV from 05; Chapl Epping Forest Primary Care Trust 02-05. *Theydon Garnon Vicarage, Fiddlers Hamlet, Epping CM16 7PQ* Tel (01992) 573672 Mobile 07850-876304 E-mail revbry@dibleyhouse.com

MORRISON, Mrs Caroline Frances. b 63. SEITE. **d** 09 **p** 10. C Bexleyheath Ch Ch *Roch* from 09. *50 Martin Dene, Bexleyheath DA6 8NA* Tel 07765-244724 (mobile) E-mail carol.morrison@ntlworld.com

MORRISON, Diana Mary (Sister Diana). b 43. St Kath Coll Liv CertEd64. EAMTC 02. **d** 05 **p** 06. NSM Breadsall *Derby* from 05. *The Convent of the Holy Name, Morley Road, Chaddesden, Derby DE21 4QZ* Tel (01332) 671716 Fax 669712 E-mail dianachn@tiscali.co.uk

MORRISON, Iain Edward. b 36. St Steph Ho Ox 76. **d** 78 **p** 79. C Brighton St Aug and St Sav *Chich* 78-81; C Felpham w Middleton 81-83; P-in-c Barnham and Eastergate 83-85; R Aldingbourne, Barnham and Eastergate 85-91; V Jarvis Brook 91-98; R Hastings St Clem and All SS 98-03; rtd 03; P-in-c Arlington, Folkington and Wilmington *Chich* 03-10. *2 Priory Close, Hastings TN34 1UJ* Tel (01424) 420499 E-mail revmorrison@btinternet.com

MORRISON, Preb James Wilson Rennie. b 42. Aber Univ MA65. Linc Th Coll 76. **d** 78 **p** 79. C Whitley Ch Ch *Ox* 78-81; R Burghfield 81-87; CF 87-97; P-in-c Burghill *Heref* 97-03; V 03-11; P-in-c Stretton Sugwas 97-03; R 03-11; P-in-c Pipe-cum-Lyde 97-03; P-in-c Pipe-cum-Lyde and Moreton-on-Lugg 03-11; Preb Heref Cathl 08-11; rtd 11. *Brambles, 8 Dernside Close, Wellington, Hereford HR4 8BP*

MORRISON, The Ven John Anthony. b 38. Jes Coll Cam BA60 MA64 Linc Coll Ox MA68. Chich Th Coll 61. **d** 64 **p** 65. C Birm St Pet 64-68; C Ox St Mich 68-71; Chapl Linc Coll Ox 68-74; C Ox St Mich w St Martin and All SS 71-74; V Basildon 74-82; RD Bradfield 78-82; V Aylesbury 82-89; RD Aylesbury 85-89; TR Aylesbury w Bierton and Hulcott 89-90; Adn Buckingham 90-98; P-in-c Princes Risborough w Ilmer 96-97; Adn Ox and Can Res Ch Ch 98-05; rtd 05; Perm to Offic *Ox* from 05. *39 Crown Road, Wheatley, Oxford OX33 1UJ* Tel (01865) 876625 E-mail morrison039@btinternet.com

MORRISON, Keith Charles. b 63. Wycliffe Hall Ox. **d** 01 **p** 02. C Ipswich St Aug *St E* 01-04; Asst Chapl Cam Univ Hosps NHS Foundn Trust from 04. *Addenbrooke's Hospital, Hills Road, Cambridge CB2 0QQ* Tel (01223) 217769 Mobile 07798-965651 E-mail keith.morrison@addenbrookes.nhs.uk

MORRISON, Raymond. See MORRISON, Walter John Raymond

MORRISON, Richard James. b 55. Sarum & Wells Th Coll 87. **d** 89 **p** 90. C Boston *Linc* 89-93; P-in-c Digby 93-99; V Whaplode Drove from 99; V Gedney Hill from 99; P-in-c Whaplode from 10; P-in-c Holbeach Fen from 10. *The Vicarage, 1 Broadgate, Whaplode Drove, Spalding PE12 0TN* Tel (01406) 330392

MORRISON, Canon Robin Victor Adair. b 45. Nottm Univ BA67. Bucharest Th Inst 67 Ripon Hall Ox 68. **d** 70 **p** 71. C Hackney St Jo *Lon* 70-73; Chapl Newc Univ 73-76; P-in-c Teversal *S'well* 76-78; Chapl Sutton Cen 76-78; Asst Hd Deans Community Sch Livingston *Edin* 78-80; R Edin St Columba 80-81; Chapl Birm Univ 81-88; Prin Soc Resp Officer *Derby* 88-96; TV Southampton (City Cen) *Win* 96-01; Ind Chapl 96-01; Non Exec Dir Southampton and SW Hants HA 00-01; Officer for Ch and Soc Ch in Wales Prov Coun from 01; Hon Can Llan Cathl from 09. *1 Dannog y Coed, Barry CF63 1HF* Tel (01446) 741900 E-mail robinmore@tiscali.co.uk

MORRISON, Walter John Raymond (Ray). b 30. Jes Coll Cam BA55 MA58. Westcott Ho Cam 55. **d** 57 **p** 58. C Dalston St Mark w St Bart *Lon* 57-60; C Totteridge *St Alb* 60-63; V Letchworth St Paul 63-71; RD Hitchin 70-71; R Ludlow *Heref* 72-83; RD Ludlow 78-83; Preb Heref Cathl 78-83; P-in-c Ludlow, Ludford, Ashford Carbonell etc 80-83; Chapl St Thos Hosp Lon 83-86; Chapl Eastbourne Distr Gen Hosp 86-95; rtd 95; Perm to Offic *Worc* 95-10. *24 West Grange Court, Lovedays Mead, Stroud GL5 1XB* E-mail ray_morrison@tiscali.co.uk

MORROW, Daniel Ross. b 77. Oklahoma Bapt Univ BA01. Claremont Sch of Th MDiv06. **d** 07 **p** 08. C San Clemente USA 07-08; Asst Chapl Zürich *Eur* 08-11; P-in-c Oregon City St Paul USA from 11. *Address temp unknown* Tel (001) (503) 656 9842 E-mail revdanmorrow@gmail.com

MORROW, David. b 63. NUU BSc86 TCD BTh89. CITC 86. **d** 89 **p** 90. C Portadown St Mark *Arm* 89-91; C Ballymena w Ballyclug *Conn* 91-94; I Tempo and Emo *Clogh* 94-01; I Kilcronaghan w Draperstown and Sixtowns *D & R* 01-11; Bp's Dom Chapl 07-11. *Address temp unknown* Tel 07784-738217 (mobile) E-mail davidmorrow763@btinternet.com

MORROW, Canon Henry Hugh. b 26. TCD BA49 MA67 Flinders Univ Aus BSocAdmin76. TCD Div Sch Div Test49. **d** 49 **p** 50. C Dublin St Thos *D & G* 49-53; I Rathmolyon *M & K* 53-58; I Killoughter *K, E & A* 58-63; C Portadown St Columba *Arm* 63-65; I Ballinderry w Tamlaght 65-70; Australia from 70; Hon Can Adelaide from 84. *5 Allendale Grove, Stonyfell SA 5066, Australia* Tel (0061) (8) 8332 5890

MORROW, Canon Joseph John. b 54. JP87. Edin Univ BD79 Dundee Univ LLB92 NY Th Sem DMin87. Edin Th Coll 76. **d** 79 **p** 80. Chapl St Paul's Cathl Dundee 79-82; P-in-c Dundee St Martin 82-85; R 85-90; P-in-c Dundee St Jo 85-08; P-in-c Dundee St Ninian 02-07; Can St Paul's Cathl Dundee 00-08; Dioc Chan from 08. *Milton Haugh, Tealing, Dundee DD4 0QZ* Tel (01382) 380501 E-mail j.jmorrow@btinternet.com

MORROW, Nigel Patrick. b 68. Dur Univ BA94 TCD MPhil02 Anglia Ruskin Univ MA05. Westcott Ho Cam 03. **d** 05 **p** 06. C Linc St Botolph and Linc St Pet-at-Gowts and St Andr 05-08; C Camberwell St Giles w St Matt *S'wark* 08-10; Chapl K Coll Lon 08 10; Chapl and Inter Faith Adv Brunel Univ from 11. *26 Church Road, Uxbridge UB8 3NA* Tel (01895) 273656 *or* 266460 Mobile 07515-770440 E-mail patrickmorrow@live.co.uk

MORSE, Mrs Elisabeth Ann. b 51. New Hall Cam MA73 Qu Eliz Coll Lon MSc74 Heythrop Coll Lon MA97. S'wark Ord Course 91. **d** 94 **p** 95. C Wimbledon *S'wark* 94-99; C Fulham All SS Lon 99-08; V Battersea St Luke *S'wark* from 08. *52 Thurleigh Road, London SW12 8UD* Tel (020) 8673 6506 E-mail morseelisabeth@yahoo.co.uk

MORSHEAD, Ivo Francis Trelawny. b 27. ACA52 FCA63. Cuddesdon Coll 61. **d** 63 **p** 64. C Bris St Mary Redcliffe w Temple etc 63-68; C Wimbledon *S'wark* 68-73; V Elham *Cant* 73-78; V Whitchurch *Ex* 78-91; rtd 91; Perm to Offic *Lon* from 91. *28 Edge Street, London W8 7PN* Tel (020) 7727 5975

MORSON, Mrs Dorothy Mary. b 29. Linc Th Coll 71. **d** 87. Par Dn Cen Telford *Lich* 87-89; rtd 89; Perm to Offic *Lich* 89-00. *Ashleigh, Hunter Street, Shrewsbury SY3 8QN* Tel (01743) 369225

MORSON, Mrs Eleanor. b 42. CA Tr Coll 63 TISEC 95. **d** 96 **p** 96. NSM Kirkwall *Ab* 96-01; R Edin St Mark 01-05. *17 Pickering Drive, Blaydon-on-Tyne NE21 5GA*

MORSON, John. b 41. CA Tr Coll 62. **d** 88 **p** 92. NSM Duns *Edin* 88-89; CF 89-92; R Kirkwall *Ab* 92-01; R Stromness 92-01; NSM Edin St Mark 01-05; rtd 06. *17 Pickering Drive, Blaydon-on-Tyne NE21 5GA*

MORT, Alister. b 52. BSc BA. Oak Hill Th Coll. **d** 82 **p** 83. C Cheadle Hulme St Andr *Ches* 82-85; C Rodbourne Cheney *Bris* 86-87; TV 87-90; V New Milverton *Cov* 90-05; Perm to Offic 05-09; TR Bilton *Ripon* from 09. *Bilton Vicarage, Bilton Lane, Harrogate HG1 3DT* Tel (01423) 525349 E-mail alistermort@mac.com

MORT, Ivan Laurence (Laurie). b 61. Nottm Univ BTh87. Linc Th Coll 84. **d** 87 **p** 88. C Aston cum Aughton and Ulley *Sheff* 87-90; C Greenstead *Chelmsf* 90-94; Chapl Toulouse *Eur* 94-05. *19 rue Bel Soulhel, 31700 Cornebarrieu, France* E-mail laurie.mort@tiscali.fr

MORT, Canon Margaret Marion. b 37. Edin Univ MA. S Tr Scheme 94. **d** 97 **p** 98. NSM Swanmore St Barn *Portsm* 97-07; Hon Can Portsm Cathl 01-07; rtd 07; Perm to Offic *Portsm* from 07. *Rivendell, High Street, Shirrell Heath, Southampton SO32 2JN* Tel and fax (01329) 832178 Mobile 07761-225222 E-mail marian@colinholy.f2s.com

MORTER, Canon Ian Charles. b 54. AKC77. Coll of Resurr Mirfield 77. **d** 78 **p** 79. C Colchester St Jas, All SS, St Nic and St Runwald *Chelmsf* 78-82; C Brixham w Churston Ferrers *Ex* 82-83; TV 84-86; TV Sidmouth, Woolbrook, Salcombe Regis, Sidbury etc 86-95; P-in-c Exminster and Kenn 95-00; TR Littleham w Exmouth 00-10; RD Aylesbeare 07-10; Preb Ex Cathl 08-10; Can Res Ex Cathl from 10. *9 Cathedral Close, Exeter EX1 1EZ* Tel (01392) 285983 E-mail pastor@exeter-cathedral.org.uk

MORTIBOYS, John William. b 45. K Coll Lon BD69 AKC69. Sarum Th Coll 71. **d** 71 **p** 72. C Reading All SS *Ox* 71-95; Perm to Offic *Portsm* from 97. *13 Oyster Street, Portsmouth PO1 2HZ* Tel (023) 9275 6676 Fax 9266 2626

MORTIMER, Aileen Jane. b 46. Edin Univ MA67 CQSW69. ERMC 05. **d** 08 **p** 09. NSM E Bergholt and Brantham *St E* from 08. *20 Leggatt Drive, Bramford, Ipswich IP8 4ET* Tel (01473) 747419 E-mail ajmortimer@hotmail.co.uk

MORTIMER, Anthony John. b 42. Sarum & Wells Th Coll 68. **d** 71 **p** 72. C Heref St Martin 71-79; V Kingstone 79-85; P-in-c Clehonger and Eaton Bishop 80-85; TR Pinhoe and Broadclyst *Ex* 85-05; rtd 05. *97 Egremont Road, Exmouth EX8 1SA* Tel (01395) 271390 E-mail themortimers@totalise.co.uk

MORTIMER, Mrs Elizabeth Anne. b 69. RGN92. Ripon Coll Cuddesdon 05. **d** 07 **p** 08. C Minehead *B & W* 07-10; P-in-c Castle Cary w Ansford from 10. *The Vicarage, Church Street, Castle Cary BA7 7EJ* Tel (01963) 351615 E-mail fr.liz@talktalk.net

MORTIMER, Jonathan Michael. b 60. Bris Univ BA83. Oak Hill Th Coll BA92. **d** 92 **p** 93. C Rugby St Matt *Cov* 92-96; C Southgate *Chich* 96-98; TR 98-07; Through Faith Miss Ev 07-11; V Camberwell All SS *S'wark* from 11. *78 Talford Road, London SE15 5NZ* Tel (020) 7252 7549 E-mail mortimerj@btinternet.com

MORTIMER, Canon Lawrence George. b 45. St Edm Hall Ox BA67 MA71. St Chad's Coll Dur. **d** 70 **p** 71. C Rugby St Andr *Cov* 70-75; V Styvechale 75-89; Dioc Broadcasting Officer 80-89; Dioc Communications Officer 89-03; P-in-c Wootton Wawen 95-10; C Claverdon w Preston Bagot 03-10; Hon Can Cov Cathl 98-10. *3 Top Street, Whittington, Oswestry SY11 4DR* Tel (01691) 657986 E-mail l.mortimer@btinternet.com

MORTIMER, Peter Aled. **d** 10 **p** 11. NSM Whitchurch *Llan* from 10. *2 Forsythia Drive, Cardiff CF23 7HP* Tel (029) 2031 2326

MORTIMER, Canon Peter Jackson. b 41. MBE95 TD73. St Jo Coll York CertEd63 Essex Univ MA71 FRSA97. EAMTC 97. **d** 98 **p** 99. NSM Needham Market w Badley *St E* 98-02; NSM Ringshall w Battisford, Barking w Darmsden etc 98-02; Bp's Ecum Adv from 02; Chapl to Suffolk Fire Service from 03; Hon Can St E Cathl from 06. *20 Leggatt Drive, Bramford, Ipswich IP8 4ET* Tel (01473) 747419

MORTIMER, Richard James. b 63. Ex Univ BSc85 Lon Bible Coll BA97. Oak Hill Th Coll. **d** 01 **p** 02. C Ore St Helen and St Barn *Chich* 01-05; Chapl Hastings Univ and C Hastings H Trin 05-10; V Dartford Ch Ch *Roch* from 10. *The Vicarage, 67 Shepherds Lane, Dartford DA1 2NS* Tel (01322) 220036 E-mail richardrmortimer123@btinternet.com

MORTIMER, William Raymond. b 31. MIET66. St Deiniol's Hawarden 68. **d** 69 **p** 70. C Flint *St As* 69-71; Lic to Offic 72-73; V Llanwddyn and Llanfihangel-yng-Nghwynfa etc 73-85; RD Llanfyllin 83-84; R Llanrwst and Llanddoget and Capel Garmon 85-96; rtd 96. *1 Coed Masarn, Woodlands Estate, Abergele LL22 7EE* Tel (01745) 822306

MORTIMORE, David Jack. b 42. Master Mariner 69. St Mich Coll Llan 90. **d** 91 **p** 92. C Pembroke St Mary w St Mich *St D* 91-92; C Bargoed and Deri w Brithdir *Llan* 92-97; Perm to Offic 98-02; P-in-c Llangeinor 02-04; P-in-c Llangeinor and the Garw Valley from 04. *The Vicarage, St Davids Street, Pontycymer, Bridgend CF32 8LT* Tel (01656) 870280 E-mail davidmortimore139@btinternet.com

MORTIMORE, Robert Edward. b 39. Kelham Th Coll 61 Wells Th Coll 66. **d** 69 **p** 70. C Byfleet *Guildf* 69-72; C Fitzroy New Zealand 72-75; C Remuera 76-78; Min Bell Block 77-79; V Te Kuiti 79-85; Offic Min Auckland 86-89; Sen Asst P Whangarei 89-92; V Avondale 92-98; V Milford 98-04; Offic Min from 04. *69 Crawford Crescent, Kamo, Whangarei 0112, New Zealand* Tel and fax (0064) (9) 435 1285 E-mail b.jmortimore@xtra.co.nz

MORTIMORE, Robin Malcolm. b 46. **d** 11. NSM Yardley St Edburgha *Birm* from 11. *33 Stonebow Avenue, Solihull B91 3UP* Tel 0121-705 9116 Mobile 07812-728526

MORTIS, Lorna Anne. b 54. Moray Ho Coll of Educn DipEd76 Open Univ BA88. TISEC 95. **d** 98 **p** 99. NSM Gullane and N Berwick *Edin* 98-02; P-in-c Edin St Marg 02-08; Hon C Musselburgh from 08; Hon C Prestonpans from 08. *Rosebank, 2 Main Street, Athelstaneford, North Berwick EH39 5BE* Tel (01620) 880505 Mobile 07779-553807 E-mail anrola@aol.com

MORTON, Adrian Ian. b 65. Brighton Poly BSc87 Brunel Univ MSc93. Ridley Hall Cam 98. **d** 00 **p** 01. C Kettering Ch the King *Pet* 00-04; P-in-c Bozeat w Easton Maudit 04-06; P-in-c Wollaston and Strixton 04-06; V Wollaston w Strixton and Bozeat etc from 06. *The Vicarage, 31 Irchester Road, Wollaston, Wellingborough NN29 7RW* Tel (01933) 664256 E-mail adrian-morton@supanet.com

MORTON, Albert George. b 34. Saskatchewan Univ BA61 McGill Univ Montreal MA73. Em Coll Saskatoon 56. **d** 61 **p** 61. Canada 61-65; C Stanford-le-Hope *Chelmsf* 66-69; V Linc St Geo Swallowbeck 69-82; R Lt Munden w Sacombe *St Alb* 82-89; R The Mundens w Sacombe 89-96; rtd 96; Perm to Offic *Sarum* from 00. *10 Church Green, Bishop's Caundle, Sherborne DT9 5NN* Tel (01963) 23383

MORTON, Andrew Edward. b 51. Lon Univ BA72 BD74 AKC74 Univ of Wales (Cardiff) MPhil93. St Aug Coll Cant 75. **d** 76 **p** 77. C Feltham *Lon* 76-79; C Pontlottyn w Fochriw *Llan* 79-81; V Ferndale w Maerdy 81-88; V Tylorstown w Ynyshir 88-93; Dir of Studies Llan Ord Course 91-93; R Llangybi and Coedypaen w Llanbadoc *Mon* from 93; Chapl Coleg Gwent from 93; Dioc FE Officer from 93; Prov HE Officer from 01; Dioc Dir NSM

Studies from 00. *The Rectory, Parc Road, Llangybi, Usk NP15 1NL* Tel (01633) 450214 E-mail mortonae@hotmail.com

MORTON, Mrs Christine Mary. b 39. Linc Th Coll 78. **dss** 80 **d** 87 **p** 94. Ore St Helen and St Barn *Chich* 80-84; Southwick St Mich 84-85; Winchmore Hill St Paul *Lon* 85-87; Par Dn 87-94; C 94-99; Hon C 00-02; rtd 00; Perm to Offic *Lon* from 02. *122 Bourne Hill, London N13 4BD* Tel (020) 8886 3157

MORTON, Clive Frederick. b 47. Lon Univ BA70 Birm Univ MA98. Cranmer Hall Dur 78. **d** 80 **p** 81. C Countesthorpe w Foston *Leic* 80-83; C Glen Parva and S Wigston 83-86; Asst Chapl HM Youth Cust Cen Glen Parva 83-86; V Birm St Pet 86-98; Miss Partner CMS 99-02; Chapl St Petersburg *Eur* 99-02; Lect St Petersburg Th Academy and Sem 99-02; V Kingsbury H Innocents *Lon* from 02. *Kingsbury Vicarage, 54 Roe Green, London NW9 0PJ* Tel (020) 8204 7531 Mobile 07947-883559 E-mail holyinnocents.kingsbury@virgin.net

MORTON, Howard Knyvett. b 30. St Jo Coll Cam BA51 MA67. Linc Th Coll 55. **d** 57 **p** 58. C Hatfield Hyde *St Alb* 57-60; Hd RE Heaton Gr Sch Newc 60-66 and 72-75; CMS 66-72; Heworth Grange Sch Dur 75-83; Regional Org Oxfam 88-91; Grainger Gr Sch Newc 91-94; Lic to Offic *Newc* 73-93; Dioc World Development Officer 94-95; rtd 95; Perm to Offic *Dur* 95-98 and *Newc* from 96. *Daisy Cottage, Hawthorn Lane, Rothbury, Morpeth NE65 7TL* Tel (01665) 577958

MORTON, Mrs Jacqueline Mavis. b 46. UEA BSc67 York Univ BSc82. EMMTC 97. **d** 00 **p** 01. NSM Sibsey w Frithville *Linc* from 00. *8 Lucan Close, Sibsey, Boston PE22 0SH* Tel (01205) 751378 E-mail jacqui.morton@care4free.net

MORTON, Jennifer. b 50. Bedf Coll Lon BA72 Leic Univ PGCE73. EMMTC 87. **d** 90 **p** 94. C New Mills *Derby* 90-94; Chapl Asst Nottm City Hosp NHS Trust 94-98; Chapl Basford Hosp Nottm 94-98; Chapl S Derbyshire Acute Hosps NHS Trust 98-02; Vice Prin EMMTC *S'well* 02-10; rtd 10. *56 Marshall Drive, Beeston, Nottingham NG9 3LD* Tel 0115-939 5784 E-mail home@jennifer3.plus.com

MORTON, Mrs Judith. b 58. St Jo Coll Nottm 04. **d** 06 **p** 07. C Shaftesbury *Sarum* 06-10; V St Leonards and St Ives *Win* from 10. *The Vicarage, 30 Pine Drive, St Ives, Ringwood BH24 2LN* Tel (01425) 483283 Mobile 07932-630232 E-mail revjude@tiscali.co.uk

MORTON, Mark Paul. b 58. Univ of Wales (Swansea) BA79 Univ of Wales (Lamp) MA99 Cardiff Univ MTh08. Ridley Hall Cam 90. **d** 92 **p** 93. C Daventry, Ashby St Ledgers, Braunston etc *Pet* 92-95; Chapl Danetre Hosp 93-94; CF (TA) 93-95; CF 95-03; Sen CF from 03. *c/o MOD Chaplains (Army)* Tel (01980) 615804 Fax 615800 E-mail revmpmorton@hotmail.com

MORTON, Michelle. b 67. Ripon Coll Cuddesdon 00. **d** 02 **p** 03. C Buckingham *Ox* 02-05; P-in-c Stewkley w Soulbury and Drayton Parslow 05-09. *Address temp unknown* E-mail squarenalo@hotmail.com

MORTON, Rex Gerald. b 61. St Jo Coll Nottm 96. **d** 98 **p** 99. C Bury St Edmunds All SS *St E* 98-01; C Woodside Park St Barn *Lon* 01-07; V Golders Green from 07. *The Vicarage, 3 St Alban's Close, London NW11 7RA* Tel (020) 8455 4525 Mobile 07968-088714 E-mail sj@morton4.swinternet.co.uk

MORTON, Sister Rita. b 34. Wilson Carlile Coll. **dss** 85 **d** 87 **p** 94. CA from 76; Par Dn Harlow New Town w Lt Parndon *Chelmsf* 87-89; C Harold Hill St Geo 89-94; rtd 94; NSM Elm Park St Nic Hornchurch *Chelmsf* from 94. *16 Cheviot Road, Hornchurch RM11 1LP* Tel (01708) 709842

MORTON, Robert Hart. b 28. Moray Ord Course 91. **d** 94. Hon C St Andr Cathl Inverness from 94. *75 Fairfield Road, Inverness IV3 5LJ* Tel (01463) 223525

MORTON, Miss Rosemary Grania. b 65. Qu Coll Birm BA05. **d** 05 **p** 06. C Kings Heath *Birm* 05-07; C Handsworth St Mary 07-09; Asst Chapl Northn Gen Hosp NHS Trust from 09. *5 Radleigh Close, Northampton NN4 8RE* Tel 07771-530232 (mobile) E-mail rosie morton@yahoo.co.uk *or* rosie.morton@ngh.nhs.uk

MORTON, Ms Rosemary Jane. b 79. LRAM02 Lon Univ BMus03. Westcott Ho Cam 07. **d** 10 **p** 11. C Coggeshall w Markshall *Chelmsf* from 10. *55 Church Street, Coggeshall, Colchester CO6 1TY* Tel (01376) 562864 E-mail rjmorton@cantab.net

MORTON, Mrs Sheila. b 44. Leeds Univ. Sarum & Wells Th Coll 79. **dss** 84 **d** 87 **p** 94. HM Forces Düsseldorf 84-86; Cov St Mary 86-89; Par Dn 87-89; Par Dn Boston Spa *York* 89-92; C Flitwick *St Alb* 93-00; R Wilden w Colmworth and Ravensden from 00. *The New Rectory, High Street, Wilden, Bedford MK44 2PB* Tel (01234) 772895 E-mail revsheila@vicarage727freeserve.co.uk

MORTON, The Very Revd William Wright. b 56. ALAM TCD BTh88 MA95 QUB PhD96. CITC. **d** 88 **p** 89. C Drumachose *D & R* 88-91; I Conwal Union w Gartan 91-97; Bp's Dom Chapl 92-97; Can Raphoe Cathl 94-97; Dean Derry from 97; I Templemore from 97. *The Deanery, 30 Bishop Street, Londonderry BT48 6PP* Tel (028) 7126 2746 E-mail dean@derry.anglican.org

MOSEDALE, Jonathan Ralph. b 69. Imp Coll Lon BSc90 York Univ MSc91 Trin Coll Ox DPhil95. Protestant Th Inst

Montpellier Lic99 Ripon Coll Cuddesdon 07. **d** 09 **p** 10. C St Endellion w Port Isaac and St Kew *Truro* from 09; C St Minver from 09. *The Vicarage, Churchtown, St Minver, Wadebridge PL27 6QH* Tel (01208) 862398 Mobile 07760-275087 E-mail mosedale@metanoa.com

MOSELEY, David John Reading. b 30. Univ Coll Ox BA54 MA58. Wells Th Coll 54. **d** 56 **p** 57. C Farnworth and Kearsley *Man* 56-59; Trinidad and Tobago 59-63; V Bedminster St Paul *Bris* 63-75; TV Bedminster 75-78; V Kilmington w Shute *Ex* 78-95; P-in-c Stockland w Dalwood 90; rtd 95; Perm to Offic *Ex* 95-09. *3 Nevada Court, Havenview Road, Seaton EX12 2PF* Tel (01297) 24174

MOSELEY, Canon Hugh Martin. b 47. St Jo Coll Dur BA70. Westcott Ho Cam 71. **d** 73 **p** 74. C Hythe *Cant* 73-77; P-in-c Eythorne w Waldershare 77-83; V Ringmer *Chich* 83-99; RD Lewes and Seaford 93-97; P-in-c E Dean w Friston and Jevington 99-00; R 00-03; TR Rye 03-09; RD Rye 03-09; Can and Preb Chich Cathl 07-09; rtd 09; Perm to Offic *Cant* from 11. *5 Sandhurst Close, Bodiam Road, Sandhurst, Cranbrook TN18 5LJ* Tel (01580) 850151 E-mail hugh@rabbitwarren13.freeserve.co.uk

MOSELEY, Michael. b 45. Oak Hill Th Coll 02. **d** 04 **p** 05. NSM Forty Hill Jes Ch *Lon* 04-07; P-in-c Murston w Bapchild and Tonge *Cant* from 07. *Bapchild Rectory, School Lane, Sittingbourne ME9 9NL* Tel (01795) 474557 E-mail michaelmoseley07@googlemail.com

MOSELEY, Roger Henry. b 38. Edin Th Coll 60. **d** 63 **p** 64. C Friern Barnet All SS *Lon* 63-66; C Grantham St Wulfram *Linc* 66-69; P-in-c Swaton w Spanby 69-73; P-in-c Horbling 69-73; V Soberton w Newtown *Portsm* 73-80; V Sarisbury 80-03; rtd 03; Perm to Offic *Portsm* from 03. *53 B St Michael's Road, St Helens, Ryde PO33 1YJ* Tel (01983) 875203 E-mail roger.moseley@tesco.net

MOSELING, Peter. b 48. WMMTC 92. **d** 95 **p** 96. C Daventry, Ashby St Ledgers, Braunston etc *Pet* 95-97; P-in-c Northampton H Trin 97-99; P-in-c Northampton St Paul 98-99; V Northampton H Trin and St Paul 99-05; Chapl Univ Coll Northn 99-05; P-in-c Bletchingley *S'wark* 05-06; R Bletchingley and Nutfield from 06. *The Rectory, Outwood Lane, Bletchingley, Redhill RH1 4LR* Tel (01883) 743252 E-mail p.moseling@tiscali.co.uk

MOSES, The Very Revd John Henry. b 38. KCVO06. Nottm Univ BA59 PhD65. Linc Th Coll 62. **d** 64 **p** 65. C Bedford St Andr *St Alb* 64-70; P-in-c Cov St Pet 70-73; P-in-c Cov St Mark 71-73; TR Cov E 73-77; RD Cov E 73-77; Adn Southend *Chelmsf* 77-82; Provost Chelmsf 82-96; Chmn Coun of Cen for Th Study Essex Univ 87-96; Dean St Paul's *Lon* 96-06; rtd 06. *Chestnut House, Burgage, Southwell NG25 0EP* Tel (01636) 814880

MOSES, Preb Leslie Alan. b 49. Hull Univ BA71 Edin Univ BD76. Edin Th Coll 73. **d** 76 **p** 77. C Edin Old St Paul 76-79; R Leven *St And* 79-85; R Edin Old St Paul 85-95; P-in-c Edin St Marg 86-92; V St Marylebone All SS *Lon* from 95; AD Westmr St Marylebone from 01; Preb St Paul's Cathl from 10. *All Saints' Vicarage, 7 Margaret Street, London W1W 8JG* Tel (020) 7636 1788 *or* 7636 9961 Fax 7436 4470 E-mail alan@moses.org.uk

MOSFORD, Canon Denzil Huw Erasmus. b 56. Florida State Univ MTh04 AKC78. Sarum & Wells Th Coll 77. **d** 79 **p** 80. C Clydach *S & B* 79-82; V 87-97; Jamaica 82-85; V Ystalyfera *S & B* 85-87; Dioc World Miss Officer 91-10; RD Cwmtawe 93-97; V Gorseinon 97-10; AD Llwchwr 00-10; Hon Can Brecon Cathl 01-04; Can Res 04-10; Dir of Min Miss to Seafarers from 10. *The Mission to Seafarers, St Michael Paternoster Royal, College Hill, London EC4R 2RL* Tel (020) 7248 5202 E-mail chaplaincy@missiontoseafarers.org

MOSLEY, Edward Peter. b 38. Clifton Th Coll 62. **d** 67 **p** 68. C Mirehouse *Carl* 67-69; C Newbarns w Hawcoat 69-72; R Aikton and Orton St Giles 72-77; V Silloth 77-78; CF 78-94; Hon C Rothiemurchus and Grantown-on-Spey *Mor* 94-95; rtd 98; P-in-c Strathnairn St Paul *Mor* 03-09. *52 Castle Heather Crescent, Inverness IV2 4BF* Tel (01463) 232552 E-mail epmos@onetel.com

MOSLEY, Robin Howarth. b 46. Birm Univ LLB67 Leeds Univ BA09 Solicitor 71. NOC 06. **d** 09 **p** 10. NSM Ches St Mary from 09. *Brookside, Sandy Lane, Higher Kinnerton, Chester CH4 9BJ* Tel (01244) 661097 E-mail robinm243@btinternet.com

MOSS, Barbara Penelope. b 46. St Anne's Coll Ox BA66 MA70 Lon Univ BD97 Middx Univ MA00. EAMTC 95. **d** 97 **p** 98. NSM Leytonstone H Trin and St Aug Harrow Green *Chelmsf* 97-00; C Cambridge Gt St Mary w St Mich *Ely* 00-05; P-in-c Gothenburg w Halmstad, Jönköping etc *Eur* from 05; Chapl Gothenburg Univ and Chalmers Univ of Tech from 05. *St Andrew's Church Flat, Norra Liden 15, S411-18 Gothenburg, Sweden* Tel and Fax (0046) (31) 711 1915 E-mail bar@barmoss.demon.co.uk *or* st.andrews.got@telia.com

MOSS, Catherine. b 53. ERMC. **d** 09 **p** 10. NSM Guilsborough and Hollowell and Cold Ashby etc Pet from 09. *Saxon Spires Practice, West Haddon Road, Guilsborough, Northampton NN6 8QE* Tel (01604) 740210 Fax 740869 Mobile 07779-000897 E-mail cattimoss@aol.com

MOSS (née **BELL**), **Mrs Catherine Ann.** b 63. Trin Coll Bris BA88. **d** 89 **p** 94. Par Dn Southsea St Jude *Portsm* 89-94; C 94-97; C Luton St Mary *St Alb* from 97; Chapl Luton Univ 97-02. *2 Saxtead Close, Luton LU2 9SQ* Tel (01582) 391125

MOSS, Christopher Ashley. b 52. Ex Univ BA73 Southn Univ DASS78 CQSW78. Wycliffe Hall Ox 89. **d** 91 **p** 92. C Malvern H Trin and St Jas *Worc* 91-96; V Longdon, Castlemorton, Bushley, Queenhill etc from 96. *The Vicarage, Longdon, Tewkesbury GL20 6AT* Tel and fax (01684) 833256
E-mail cmoss@holyplace.feeserve.co.uk

MOSS, David Glyn. b 62. St Anne's Coll Ox BA83 Em Coll Cam BA89. Westcott Ho Cam 87. **d** 90 **p** 91. C Halesowen *Worc* 90-93; Tutor St Steph Ho Ox 93-03; Vice-Prin 00-03; Dioc Tr Officer *Ex* 03-04; Prin SWMTC from 04; Preb Ex Cathl from 10. *SWMTC Office, Amory Building, University of Exeter, Rennes Drive, Exeter EX4 4RJ* Tel (01392) 264403
E-mail principal@swmtc.org.uk

MOSS, David Sefton. b 59. Sunderland Poly BSc80 Anglia Poly Univ MA05 MRPharmS81. Ridley Hall Cam 91. **d** 93 **p** 94. C Highworth w Sevenhampton and Inglesham etc *Bris* 93-97; V Bedminster St Mich from 97. *St Michael's Vicarage, 153 St John's Lane, Bedminster, Bristol BS3 5AE* Tel 0117-977 6132 Mobile 07890-262334 E-mail vicar@stmichaelandallangels.info

MOSS, Canon Denis. b 32. St Jo Coll Auckland LTh83. **d** 74 **p** 75. New Zealand 74-92; Chapl Budapest *Eur* 92-10; Hon Can Malta Cathl 01-10. *Address temp unknown*

MOSS, James Wilfred. b 15. Oak Hill Th Coll 75. **d** 76 **p** 77. Hon C Frogmore *St Alb* 76-78 and 81-93; Hon C Watford St Luke 78-81; Perm to Offic 93-08. *8A The Rise, Park Street, St Albans AL2 2NT* Tel (01727) 812467

MOSS, Preb Kenneth Charles. b 37. Imp Coll Lon BSc59 PhD62 ARCS59. **d** 66 **p** 67. Canada 66-73; Chapl Ex Univ 73-83; V St Marychurch 83-02; RD Ipplepen 87-93; Preb Ex Cathl from 92; rtd 02. *3 Mondeville Way, Northam, Bideford EX39 1DQ* Tel (01237) 422251

MOSS, The Ven Leonard Godfrey. b 32. K Coll Lon BD59 AKC59. **d** 60 **p** 61. C Putney St Marg *S'wark* 60-63; C Cheam 63-67; R Much Dewchurch w Llanwarne and Llandinabo *Heref* 67-72; Dioc Ecum Officer 69-83; V Marden w Amberley 72-80; V Marden w Amberley and Wisteston 80-84; P-in-c 92-94; Preb Heref Cathl 79-97; Can Heref Cathl 84-91; Dioc Soc Resp Officer 84-91; Adn Heref 91-97; rtd 97; Perm to Offic *Heref* from 97. *10 Saxon Way, Ledbury HR8 2QY* Tel (01531) 631195

MOSS, Leslie. b 52. **d** 02 **p** 03. OLM Ditton St Mich w St Thos *Liv* from 02. *105 Heath Road, Widnes WA8 7NU* Tel 0151-423 1100

MOSS, Miss Lindsey. b 70. St Jo Coll Nottm 07. **d** 09 **p** 10. C Standon and The Mundens w Sacombe *St Alb* from 09. *Parish Office, Standon Vicarage, Kents Lane, Standon, Ware SG11 1PJ* Tel 07974-823727 (mobile)
E-mail lindseymoss822@yahoo.co.uk

MOSS, Mrs Nelva Elizabeth. b 44. Bp Grosseteste Coll TCert66 Sussex Univ BEd73. S Dios Minl Tr Scheme 90. **d** 93 **p** 94. NSM Bincombe w Broadwey, Upwey and Buckland Ripers *Sarum* 93-96; NSM Langtree *Ox* 96-98; TV 98-09; rtd 09. *5 Wynnes Rise, Sherborne DT9 6DH* Tel (01935) 814329
E-mail nelvamoss@hotmail.com

MOSS, Peter Hextall. b 34. Clare Coll Cam BA59 MA62. Linc Th Coll 59. **d** 61 **p** 62. C Easington Colliery *Dur* 61-63; C Whickham 63-65; C-in-c Town End Farm CD 65-72; TV Mattishall *Nor* 72-75; P-in-c Welborne 75-84; P-in-c Mattishall w Mattishall Burgh 75-84; P-in-c Yaxham 80-84; TR Hempnall 84-89. *High House Cottage, Gunn Street, Foulsham, Dereham NR20 5RN* Tel (01362) 683823

MOSS, Peter John. b 41. K Coll Cam BA64 MA67. Westcott Ho Cam 63. **d** 84 **p** 85. NSM Leighton Buzzard w Eggington, Hockliffe etc *St Alb* 84-93; NSM Luton St Sav 93-98; NSM Houghton Regis 03-05; P-in-c Devizes St Pet *Sarum* from 05. *St Peter's Vicarage, Bath Road, Devizes SN10 2AP* Tel (01380) 722621 E-mail peter.moss87@ntlworld.com

MOSSE, Mrs Barbara Ann. b 51. CertEd73 Open Univ BA77 Univ of Wales (Lamp) MA99 Lambeth STh83. CA Tr Coll IDC81. **d** 90 **p** 95. CA 81-91; NSM Southbourne w W Thorney *Chich* 90-93; Community Mental Health Chapl Fareham/Gosport 94-97; NSM Purbrook *Portsm* 95-03; Team Chapl Portsm Hosps NHS Trust 01-09; Asst Dioc Spirituality Adv *Portsm* 05-09. *Drogo, 1 Grenfield Court, Emsworth PO10 7SA* Tel (01243) 376155
E-mail barbaramosse@btinternet.com

MOSSLEY, Iain Stephen. b 72. Univ of Wales (Ban) BTh94. St Steph Ho Ox 95. **d** 98 **p** 99. C Ribbleton *Blackb* 98-01; C Marton Moss 01-03; V Burnley St Matt w H Trin 03-08; P-in-c Leyland St Jas from 08. *St James's Vicarage, 201 Slater Lane, Leyland PR26 7SH* Tel (01772) 421034
E-mail fatheriain@blueyonder.co.uk

MOSSMAN, Mrs Margaret. b 46. NOC 97. **d** 00 **p** 01. NSM Beighton *Sheff* 00-02; C 02-04; V Owston from 04. *The Vicarage, 11 Crabgate Lane, Skellow, Doncaster DN6 8LE* Tel (01302) 337101

MOSSOP, Patrick John. b 48. Solicitor St Jo Coll Cam MA LLB. Linc Th Coll BTh93. **d** 93 **p** 94. C Halstead St Andr w H Trin and Greenstead Green *Chelmsf* 93-97; Assoc Chapl Essex Univ 97-99; Chapl 99-04; V Forest Gate Em w Upton Cross 04-09; TR Plaistow and N Canning Town from 09. *The Rectory, 19 Abbey Street, London E13 8DT* Tel (020) 7511 4657 *or* 7511 6110
E-mail pat.mos@btinternet.com

MOSTON, William Howard. b 47. **d** 10 **p** 11. OLM E Crompton *Man* from 10. *36 Clough Road, Shaw, Oldham OL2 8QD* Tel (01706) 847940 Mobile 07824-507354
E-mail whmoston@hotmail.com

MOTE, Gregory Justin. b 60. Oak Hill Th Coll BA83. **d** 86 **p** 87. C W Ealing St Jo w St Jas *Lon* 86-90; C St Helen Bishopsgate w St Andr Undershaft etc 90-95; V Poulton Lancelyn H Trin *Ches* 96-04; Perm to Offic *Blackb* from 04. *22 Evergreen Avenue, Leyland PR25 3AW* E-mail gjmote@aol.com

MOTH, Miss Susan. b 44. Leic Univ BA65 K Coll Lon CertEd66. Linc Th Coll 83. **dss** 85 **d** 87 **p** 94. Churchdown St Jo *Glouc* 85-93; C 87-93; Dn-in-c The Rissingtons 93-94; P-in-c 94-05; rtd 05. *19 Cunliffe Close, Oxford OX2 7BJ*

MOTHERSDALE, Paul John. b 52. NOC 94. **d** 97 **p** 98. C Kirkleatham *York* 97-00; V Middlesbrough St Agnes 00-05; R Thornton Dale w Allerston, Ebberston etc from 05; RD Pickering 06-09; RD N Ryedale from 09. *The Rectory, High Street, Thornton Dale, Pickering YO18 7QW* Tel (01751) 474244
E-mail p.mothersdale@live.co.uk

MOTHERSOLE, Hugh Robert. b 43. Essex Univ BA70 MSc73. **d** 11. OLM Halstead Area *Chelmsf* from 11. *10 Park Lane, Earls Colne, Colchester CO6 2RJ* Tel (01787) 222211 Mobile 07803-699268 E-mail hrmsteam@btinternet.com

MOTHERSOLE, John Robert. b 25. Lon Univ MA99. Chich Th Coll. **d** 84 **p** 85. NSM Hayes St Anselm *Lon* 84-93; NSM Hayes St Edm 93-98; P-in-c St Mary Aldermary 98-10; rtd 10. *116 Nestles Avenue, Hayes UB3 4QD* Tel (020) 8848 0626
E-mail jm041t1045@blueyonder.co.uk

MOTT, Julian Ward. b 52. Loughb Univ BSc77. Ripon Coll Cuddesdon 78. **d** 81 **p** 82. C Aylestone *Leic* 81-84; C Gt Ilford St Mary *Chelmsf* 84-88; R Chevington w Hargrave and Whepstead w Brockley *St E* 88-99; V Lower Gornal *Worc* from 99. *The Vicarage, Church Street, Lower Gornal, Dudley DY3 2PF* Tel (01902) 882023

MOTT, Peter John. b 49. Ch Coll Cam BA70 MA75 Dundee Univ PhD73. St Jo Coll Nottm BA79. **d** 80 **p** 81. C Hull St Jo Newland *York* 80-83; C Selly Park St Steph and St Wulstan *Birm* 83-87; C Mosbrough *Sheff* 87-92; R Colne St Bart *Blackb* 92-98; TV Colne and Villages 98-01; P-in-c Keighley St Andr *Bradf* from 01; Dioc Ecum Officer from 04. *The Rectory, 3 Westview Grove, Keighley BD20 6JJ* Tel (01535) 601499
E-mail peter.mott@bradford.anglican.org

✠**MOTTAHEDEH, The Rt Revd Iraj Kalimi.** b 32. United Th Coll Bangalore 56. **d** 59 **p** 60 **c** 86. C Isfahan St Luke Iran 59-62; V Shiraz St Simon 62-66; V Tehran St Paul 67-75; V Isfahan St Luke 75-83; Adn Iran 83-86; Asst Bp Iran 86-90; Bp Iran 90-02; Pres Bp Episc Ch Jerusalem and Middle E 00-02; rtd 02; Interim Bp Iran 02-04; Hon Asst Bp Birm and Lich from 05. *2 Highland Road, Newport TF10 7QE* Tel (01952) 813615
E-mail bishraj@btinternet.com

MOTTERSHEAD, Derek. b 39. Open Univ BA74 BEd. Chich Th Coll 65. **d** 69 **p** 70. C Walthamstow St Barn and St Jas Gt *Chelmsf* 69-72; C Chelmsf All SS 72-77; P-in-c Cold Norton w Stow Maries 77-80; V Leytonstone St Andr 80-92; V Eastbourne St Sav and St Pet *Chich* 92-04; Miss to Seafarers 92-04; Perm to Offic *Cant* 05-06 and from 11; Hon C Preston next Faversham, Goodnestone and Graveney 06-10. *Sherwood, 25B The Paddock, Spring Lane, Canterbury CT1 1SX* Tel (01227) 453118 E-mail dmottershead11@btinternet.com

MOTTRAM, Andrew Peter. b 53. AKC77. Ripon Coll Cuddesdon 77. **d** 78 **p** 79. C E Bedfont *Lon* 78-81; C Bp's Hatfield *St Alb* 81-84; V Milton Ernest 84-91; V Thurleigh 84-91; P-in-c Heref All SS 91-06; RD Heref City 02-03; Perm to Offic from 06. *Ecclesiastical Property Solutions, Mulberry Dock, Pencombe, Bromyard HR7 4SH* Tel (01885) 400311 Mobile 07960-726717 E-mail andrew@abetterview.co.uk

MOTYER, John Alexander. b 24. TCD BA46 MA51 BD51 Lambeth DD97. Wycliffe Hall Ox 47. **d** 47 **p** 48. C Penn Fields *Lich* 47-50; C Bris H Trin and Tutor Clifton Th Coll 51-54; Vice-Prin 54-65; Tutor Tyndale Hall Bris 52-54; V W Hampstead St Luke *Lon* 65-70; Dep Prin Tyndale Hall Bris 70-71; Prin and Dean Trin Coll Bris 71-81; Min Westbourne Ch Ch Prop Chpl *Win* 81-89; rtd 89; Perm to Offic *Ex* from 90. *27 Georges Road West, Poynton, Stockport SK12 1JY*

MOTYER, Stephen. b 50. Pemb Coll Cam BA73 MA77 Bris Univ MLitt79 K Coll Lon PhD93. Trin Coll Bris 73. **d** 76 **p** 77. Lect Oak Hill Th Coll 76-83; C Braughing, Lt Hadham, Albury, Furneux Pelham etc *St Alb* 83-87; Lect Lon Sch of Th from 87; Perm to Offic *Lon* and *St Alb* from 87. *7 Hangar Ruding, Watford WD19 5BH* Tel (020) 8386 6829 *or* (01923) 826061
E-mail s.motyer@londonbiblecollege.ac.uk

MOUGHTIN, Ross. b 48. St Cath Coll Cam BA70 St Jo Coll Dur BA75. **d** 76 **p** 77. C Litherland St Paul Hatton Hill *Liv* 76-79; C Heswall *Ches* 79-84; Chapl Edw Unit Rochdale Infirmary 83-92; V Thornham w Gravel Hole *Man* 84-92; V Aughton Ch Ch *Liv* from 92; Chapl W Lancashire NHS Trust 94-11. *Christ Church Vicarage, 22 Long Lane, Aughton, Ormskirk L39 5AT* Tel (01695) 422175 E-mail ross.moughtin@lineone.net

MOUGHTIN-MUMBY, Andrew Denis Paul. b 78. Birm Univ BA00 SS Coll Cam BA05 MA09. Westcott Ho Cam 03. **d** 06 **p** 07. C Walworth St Chris *S'wark* 06-10; R Walworth St Pet from 10. *St Peter's Rectory, 12 Villa Street, London SE17 2EJ* Tel (020) 7703 3139 E-mail rector@stpeterswalworth.org

MOUGHTIN-MUMBY, Sharon. b 76. St Jo Coll Dur BA97 MA98 Worc Coll Ox DPhil04. Westcott Ho Cam 05. **d** 06 **p** 07. C Walworth St Pet *S'wark* 06-10; Dioc Miss Th 10-11; Hon C S'wark St Geo w St Alphege and St Jude from 10. *St Peter's Rectory, 12 Villa Street, London SE17 2EJ* Tel 07980-611347 (mobile) E-mail sharon.mm@btinternet.com

MOUL, Russell Derek. b 56. Reading Univ BA83. Oak Hill Th Coll 97. **d** 99 **p** 00. C Harold Wood *Chelmsf* 99-02; C Harold Hill St Paul 02-03; V from 03. *St Paul's Vicarage, Redcar Road, Romford RM3 9PT* Tel (01708) 341225 E-mail russell@themouls.fslife.co.uk

MOULAND, Norman Francis. b 38. OLM course 98. **d** 99 **p** 00. OLM Verwood *Sarum* from 99. *13 Park Drive, Verwood BH31 7PE* Tel (01202) 825320

MOULD, Mrs Jacqueline. b 66. QUB BD88. CITC BTh91. **d** 91 **p** 92. C Belfast St Aid *Conn* 91-94; C Drumragh w Mountfield *D & R* 94-96; NSM Kinson *Sarum* 97-00; C Belvoir *D & D* from 03. *10A Ballyclough Road, Lisburn BT28 3UY* Tel (028) 9264 7912 *or* 9049 1436 E-mail jjmould@hotmail.com

MOULD, James Michael. b 46. SEITE 95. **d** 98 **p** 99. NSM Wallington *S'wark* 98-03; NSM W Wittering and Birdham w Itchenor *Chich* from 03. *Quinneys, Itchenor Road, Itchenor, Chichester PO20 7DD* Tel (01243) 513600 E-mail revd.jim@btinternet.com

MOULD, Jeremy James. b 63. Nottm Univ BA85 TCD BTh91. CITC 88. **d** 91 **p** 92. C Mossley *Conn* 91-94; C Drumragh w Mountfield *D & R* 94-96; C Kinson *Sarum* 97-00. *10A Ballyclough Road, Lisburn BT28 3UY* Tel (028) 9264 7912

MOULDEN, David Ivor. b 52. Cant Ch Ch Univ BA02. SEITE 05. **d** 08 **p** 09. C Madeley *Heref* from 08. *7 Mellor Close, Madeley, Telford TF7 5SS* Tel (01952) 275287 E-mail davidmoulden@hotmail.com

MOULDER, John William Michael Cornock. b 39. City of Lon Poly ACIB67. Glouc Sch of Min 82. **d** 86 **p** 86. C Broken Hill Australia 86-88; P-in-e Berrigan 88-94; P-in-c Edenhope 94-98; C Tividale *Lich* 98-01; P-in-c W Bromwich St Pet 01-04; rtd 04; Hon Asst P Cobram Australia from 04. *Goldwick, 130 Jerilderie Street, Berrigan NSW 2712, Australia* Tel and fax (0061) (3) 5885 2913 E-mail fatherm@dragnet.com.au

MOULDER, Kenneth. b 53. Lon Univ BEd75. Ridley Hall Cam 78. **d** 81 **p** 82. C Harold Wood *Chelmsf* 81-84; C Darfield *Sheff* 84-88; V Walkergate *Newc* 88-92; P-in-c Byker St Mark 90-92; V Byker St Mark and Walkergate St Oswald from 92. *St Oswald's Parsonage, Woodhead Road, Newcastle upon Tyne NE6 4RX* Tel 0191-263 6249

MOULT, Jane Elizabeth Kate. b 61. Trin Coll Bris 91. **d** 94 **p** 95. C St Jo in Bedwardine *Worc* 94-97; NSM Bilton *Cov* 97-99; Chapl Staunton Harold Hosp 00-01; Sen Chapl Leics Partnership NHS Trust 01-07; Perm to Offic *Leic* from 07. *17 The Leascroft, Ravenstone, Coalville LE67 2BL* Tel (01530) 833160 E-mail jane.moult@btinternet.com

MOULT, Simon Paul. b 66. Trin Coll Bris BA94. **d** 94 **p** 95. C St Jo in Bedwardine *Worc* 94-97; C Bilton *Cov* 97-99; P-in-c Thringstone St Andr *Leic* 99-05; RD Akeley S 03-05; Chapl N Warks NHS Trust from 05; Chapl Geo Eliot Hosp NHS Trust Nuneaton from 05. *The Chaplaincy, George Eliot Hospital, College Street, Nuneaton CV10 7DJ* Tel (024) 7686 5046 *or* 7635 1351

MOULTON, Canon Paul Oliver. b 43. NOC 77. **d** 80 **p** 81. C Wilmslow *Ches* 80-85; V Knutsford St Cross 85-92; Chapl Mary Dendy Hosp Knutsford 86-92; V Gatley *Ches* 92-01; Chapl Cen Man Healthcare NHS Trust 92-01; P-in-c Capesthorne w Siddington and Marton *Ches* 01-11; Hon Can Ches Cathl 07-11; rtd 11. *52 Longdown Road, Congleton CW12 4QP* Tel (01260) 272627 E-mail paulo.moulton@btinternet.com

MOUNCER, David Peter. b 65. Univ of Wales (Abth) BA86. Oak Hill Th Coll BA94. **d** 94 **p** 95. C Foord St Jo *Cant* 94-98; Min Grove Green LEP 98-03; R Brampton St Thos *Derby* 03-07; C Walton St Jo from 07. *5 Foxbrook Drive, Chesterfield S40 3JR*

MOUNSEY, William Lawrence Fraser. b 51. St Andr Univ BD75. Edin Th Coll 76. **d** 78 **p** 79. C Edin St Mark 78-81; Chapl RAF 81-90 and 96-06; R Dalmahoy and Chapl Heriot-Watt Univ 90-96; Perm to Offic *Eur* from 06; C Roslin (Rosslyn Chpl) *Edin* from 06. *9 Upper Coltbridge Terrace, Edinburgh EH12 6AD* Tel 07967-322651 (mobile) E-mail wlfm@hotmail.co.uk

MOUNSTEPHEN, Philip Ian. b 59. Southn Univ BA80 Magd Coll Ox MA87 PGCE. Wycliffe Hall Ox 85. **d** 88 **p** 89. C

Gerrards Cross and Fulmer *Ox* 88-92; V W Streatham St Jas *S'wark* 92-98; Hd Pathfinders CPAS 98-02; Dir CY Network 01-02; Hd Min 02-07; Dep Gen Dir 04-07; Chapl Paris St Mich *Eur* from 07. *St Michael's Church, 5 rue d'Aguesseau, 75008 Paris, France* Tel (0033) 1 47 42 70 88 Fax 1 47 42 74 75 E-mail office@saintmichaelsparis.org

MOUNT, Canon Judith Mary. b 35. Bedf Coll Lon BA56 Lon Univ CertEd57. Ripon Coll Cuddesdon 81. **dss** 83 **d** 87 **p** 94. Carterton *Ox* 83-85; Charlton on Otmoor and Oddington 85-87; Dioc Lay Min Adv and Asst Dir of Ords 86-89; Par Dn Islip w Charlton on Otmoor, Oddington, Noke etc 87-94; V Charlton on Otmoor, Oddington, Noke etc 87-94; Assoc Dioc Dir Ords and Adv for Women in Ord Min 89-95; Hon Can Ch Ch 92-95; rtd 95; Perm to Offic *Ox* 95-10 and *Glouc* from 99. *The Owl House, Bell Lane, Poulton, Cirencester GL7 5JF* Tel (01285) 850242 E-mail can.mj@tiscali.co.uk

MOUNTFORD, Canon Brian Wakling. b 45. Newc Univ BA66 Cam Univ MA73 Ox Univ MA90. Westcott Ho Cam 66. **d** 68 **p** 69. C Westmr St Steph w St Jo *Lon* 68-69; C Paddington Ch Ch 69-73; Chapl SS Coll Cam 73-78; V Southgate Ch Ch *Lon* 78-86; V Ox St Mary V w St Cross and St Pet from 86; Chapl St Hilda's Coll Ox from 89; Hon Can Ch Ch *Ox* from 98. *9A Norham Gardens, Oxford OX2 6PS* Tel (01865) 515778 *or* 279111 E-mail brian.mountford@oriel.ox.ac.uk

MOUNTFORD, Ian David. b 65. St Jo Coll Nottm BTh93. **d** 96 **p** 97. C Chilwell *S'well* 96-00; TV Thame *Ox* from 00. *22 Stuart Way, Thame OX9 3WP* Tel (01844) 216508

MOUNTNEY, Frederick Hugh. b 14. St Chad's Coll Dur BA36 MA39. Lich Th Coll 36. **d** 37 **p** 38. C Beighton *Derby* 37-39; C Spondon 39-40; C Byker St Laur *Newc* 40-44; C Backworth St Jo 44-48; V N Gosforth 48-51; R Lillingstone Lovell *Ox* 51-56; V Heref All SS 56-75; Chapl Victoria Eye Hosp Heref 56-75; Dioc Ecum Officer 63-69; Chapl Bonn w Cologne *Eur* 75-79; rtd 79; Perm to Offic *Heref* 79-90; *Nor* 82-00; *St E* 82-02; *Eur* 90-02. *The Grange, 3 Church Road, Rennington, Alnwick NE66 3RR* Tel (01665) 577344

MOURANT, Julia Caroline. b 58. Sheff Univ BA79. St Jo Coll Nottm 82. **dss** 84 **d** 92 **p** 94. Cropwell Bishop w Colston Bassett, Granby etc *S'well* 84-86; Marple All SS *Ches* 86-89; Harlow St Mary and St Hugh w St Jo the Bapt *Chelmsf* 89-92; NSM 92-04; Asst Dir of Min 98-04; CME Officer 00-02; Perm to Offic *Win* from 04; Lay Tr Officer 05-07; Voc, Recruitment and Selection Officer from 07. *The Vicarage, Knapp Lane, Ampfield, Romsey SO51 9BT* Tel (01794) 367195

MOURANT, Sidney Eric. b 39. Lon Univ BD73. Oak Hill Th Coll. **d** 89 **p** 90. C Oxton *Ches* 89-92; V Douglas All SS and St Thos *S & M* 92-96; I Rathkeale w Askeaton, Kilcornan and Kilnaughtin *L & K* 96-00; I Nenagh 00-04; rtd 04. *12 Breezemount, Hamiltonsbawn, Armagh BT61 9SB* Tel (00353) (48) 3887 2203 Mobile 87-239 9785 E-mail hmt3bwn@sky.com

MOURANT, Stephen Philip Edward. b 54. St Jo Coll Nottm BTh83. **d** 83 **p** 84. C Cropwell Bishop w Colston Bassett, Granby etc *S'well* 83-86; C Marple All SS *Ches* 86-89; P-in-c Harlow St Mary and St Hugh w St Jo the Bapt *Chelmsf* 89-90; V 90-04; P-in-c Bitterne *Win* 04-08; C Fair Oak from 08. *The Vicarage, Knapp Lane, Ampfield, Romsey SO51 9BT* Tel (01794) 367195 E-mail stephen.mourant@btinternet.com

MOUSIR-HARRISON, Stuart Nicholas. b 68. SW Poly Plymouth BSc89 Nottm Univ MSc92 St Martin's Coll Lanc PhD99 St Jo Coll Dur BA99. Cranmer Hall Dur. **d** 00 **p** 01. C Oadby *Leic* 00-03; C W Malling w Offham *Roch* 03-07; C Mereworth w W Peckham 03-07; P-in-c Dallington *Pet* from 07; Chapl Northn Univ from 07. *The Vicarage, The Bartons Close, Northampton NN5 7HQ* Tel (01604) 751478 E-mail rev.moose@mousir.org

MOVERLEY, Ruth Elaine. b 55. K Alfred's Coll Win CertEd76. St Mich Coll Llan. **d** 90 **p** 97. C Llangynwyd w Maesteg 90-95; C Glan Ely 95-97; V Llanharan w Peterston-super-Montem 97-05; V Tonyrefail w Gilfach Goch from 05. *The Vicarage, High Street, Tonyrefail, Porth CF39 8PL* Tel (01443) 670330

MOWBRAY, David. b 38. Fitzw Ho Cam BA60 MA64 Lon Univ BD62. Clifton Th Coll. **d** 63 **p** 64. C Northampton St Giles *Pet* 63-66; Lect Watford St Mary *St Alb* 66-70; V Broxbourne 70-77; R Broxbourne w Wormley 77-84; V Hertford All SS 84-91; V Darley Abbey *Derby* 91-03; Asst Chapl Derby R Infirmary 91-94; Chapl Derbyshire Mental Health Services NHS Trust 99-03; rtd 03. *Blackbird Cottage, 169 Newport, Lincoln LN1 3DZ* Tel (01522) 546753

MOWBRAY, James Edward. b 78. Univ of Wales (Abth) BTh00 Leeds Univ BA03. Coll of Resurr Mirfield 01. **d** 03 **p** 04. C Perry Street *Roch* 03-07; V Swanley St Mary from 07. *St Mary's Vicarage, London Road, Swanley BR8 7AQ* Tel (01322) 662201 E-mail vicarofswanley@sky.com

MOWBRAY, Ms Jill Valerie. b 54. Sussex Univ BEd76 Lon Inst of Educn MA86 Anglia Poly Univ MA01. Ridley Hall Cam 99. **d** 01 **p** 02. C Tufnell Park St Geo and All SS *Lon* 01-04; V Whitton SS Phil and Jas 04-09; CME Adv *Chelmsf* from 09; C Walthamstow from 10. *39 Kings Road, London E11 1AU* E-mail revjillmowbray@googlemail.com

MOWER, Miss Marguerite Mary. b 36. Bris Univ BA57. Cant Sch of Min 90. **d** 93 **p** 94. NSM Eythorne and Elvington w Waldershare etc *Cant* 93-03; NSM Denholme and Harden and Wilsden *Bradf* 04-07; Perm to Offic *Cant* from 07. *Meadow Bank, Eythorne Road, Shepherswell, Dover CT15 7PN*

MOWLL, John William Rutley. b 42. Sarum Th Coll 63. **d** 66 **p** 67. C Oughtibridge *Sheff* 66-69; C Hill *Birm* 69-73; Ind Chapl and V Upper Arley *Worc* 73-78; P-in-c Upton Snodsbury and Broughton Hackett etc 78-81; R 81-83; V Boughton under Blean w Dunkirk *Cant* 83-89; V Boughton under Blean w Dunkirk and Hernhill 89-07; RD Ospringe 95-01; Hon Min Can Cant Cathl 96-07; rtd 07; Chapl to The Queen from 00; Perm to Offic *Cant* from 07. *Holly Cottage, Water Lane, Ospringe, Faversham ME13 8TS* Tel (01795) 597597

MOXLEY, Mrs Elizabeth Jane. b 52. St Jo Coll Nottm. **d** 05 **p** 06. C Aston Clinton w Buckland and Drayton Beauchamp *Ox* 05-08; R from 08. *The Rectory, 23 New Road, Aston Clinton, Aylesbury HP22 5JD* Tel (01296) 632488 E-mail elizabethmoxley@hotmail.com

MOXON, John. **d** 02 **p** 03. NSM Birm St Luke 02-04. *41 Mariner Avenue, Birmingham B16 9DF* Tel 0121-456 1628 *or* 472 0726 Mobile 07887-573122 E-mail john.moxon@birminghamchristiancollege.ac.uk

MOXON, Michael Anthony. b 42. LVO98. Lon Univ BD78 Heythrop Coll Lon MA96. Sarum Th Coll 67. **d** 70 **p** 71. C Kirkley *Nor* 70-74; Min Can St Paul's Cathl 74-81; Sacr 77-81; Warden Coll of Min Canons 79-81; V Tewkesbury w Walton Cardiff *Glouc* 81-90; Chapl to The Queen 86-98; Can Windsor and Chapl in Windsor Gt Park 90-98; Dean Truro and R Truro St Mary 98-04; Chapl Cornwall Fire Brigade HQ 98-04, rtd 05. *St Neots, 79 Moresk Avenue, Truro TR1 1BT* Tel (01872) 274666

MOY, Miss Elizabeth. b 55. Leeds and Carnegie Coll CertEd76. LCTP 07. **d** 10. NSM Harden and Wilsden *Bradf* from 10; NSM Cullingworth from 10; NSM Denholme from 10. *3 Parkside Court, Cross Roads, Keighley BD22 9DS* Tel (01535) 645991 E-mail li2@kadugli.org.uk

MOY, Mrs Joy Patricia. b 35. Cant Sch of Min 87. **d** 90 **p** 94. NSM Cranbrook *Cant* 90-96; Perm to Offic *Win* 96-02. *Address temp unknown*

MOY (née PLUMB), Mrs Nicola Louise. b 80. Birm Univ BA01 Bris Univ MA03 PGCE04. St Jo Coll Nottm 06. **d** 08 **p** 09. C Wolverhampton St Jude *Lich* from 08. *21 St Jude's Road, Wolverhampton WV6 0EB* Tel (01902) 653942 E-mail nicolamoy@hotmail.com

MOY, Richard John. b 78. St Cath Coll Cam BA99. Trin Coll Bris MA03. **d** 04 **p** 05. C Wolverhampton St Jude *Lich* 04-07; Pioneer Min Wolv City Cen 07-10; Fresh Expressions Adv from 10. *21 St Jude's Road, Wolverhampton WV6 0EB* Tel (01902) 653942 E-mail notintheratrace@yahoo.co.uk

MOYES (née WATSON), Mrs Stephanie Abigail. b 61. Heriot-Watt Univ BA84. Cranmer Hall Dur 86. **d** 90 **p** 94. C Bishop's Castle w Mainstone *Heref* 90-93; Dep Chapl HM Pris Dur 93-95; Chapl HM Rem Cen Low Newton 95-98; V Chilton and Cornforth *Dur* 98-02; Chapl Wrekin Coll Telford 02-04; Perm to Offic *Worc* from 04. *7 Birchanger Green, Worcester WR4 0DW* Tel (01905) 619181

MOYNAGH, David Kenneth. b 46. LRCP70 MRCS70 MRCGP76 Lon Univ MB, BS70. S Dios Minl Tr Scheme 88. **d** 91 **p** 92. NSM Ore St Helen and St Barn *Chich* 91-99; Perm to Offic *Win* from 01. *White Cottage, Jordan's Lane, Sway, Lymington SO41 6AR* Tel (01590) 682475

MOYNAGH, Michael Digby. b 50. Southn Univ BA73 Lon Univ MA74 Aus Nat Univ PhD78 Bris Univ MA85. Trin Coll Bris. **d** 85 **p** 86. C Northwood Em 85-89; P-in-c Wilton *B & W* 89-90; TR 90-96; Dir Cen for Futures Studies St Jo Coll Nottm 96-04; Co-Dir Tomorrow Project from 04. *Address temp unknown*

MOYNAN, Canon David George. b 53. **d** 86 **p** 87. C Seagoe *D & D* 86-88; C Taney *D & G* 88-89; I Arklow w Inch and Kilbride 89-94; Dioc Stewardship Adv from 92; Dioc Ch of Ireland Bps' Appeal Rep from 92; I Kilternan from 94; Dioc Dir for Decade of Evang from 96; Can Ch Ch Cathl Dublin from 97. *Kilternan Rectory, Kilternan, Dublin 18, Republic of Ireland* Tel and fax (00353) (1) 295 5603 *or* tel 295 2643 E-mail moynandg@gmail.com

MOYO, Edmore Illingworth. b 71. Bedfordshire Univ MSc08. Bp Gaul Th Coll Harare 99. **d** 02. NSM Luton St Mary *St Alb* 06-08. *Address temp unknown* Tel 07909-671876 (mobile) E-mail edmorei@yahoo.co.uk

MOYSE, Mrs Pauline Patricia. b 42. Ex Univ CertEd62. S Dios Minl Tr Scheme 88. **d** 91 **p** 94. NSM Fleet *Guildf* 91-92; C 93-97; Chapl Farnborough Coll of Tech 96-97; P-in-c Stoneleigh *Guildf* 97-02; Warden of Readers 97-07; Dioc Adv Lay Min 01-07; Tr Officer for Past Assts 07-09; rtd 07. *Beechend, 2 Hillcrest, Fleet GU51 4PZ* Tel (01252) 671382

✠**MPALANYI-NKOYOYO, The Rt Revd Livingstone.** b 37. **d** 69 **p** 70 **c** 80. Kasubi Uganda 69-75; Nsangi 75-77; Adn Namirembe 77-79; Suff Bp 80-81; Suff Bp Mukono 81-94; Abp Uganda and

Bp Kampala 94-03; rtd 03. *PO Box 14123, Kampala, Uganda* E-mail couab@uol.co.ug

MPUNZI, Nduna Ananias. b 46. Federal Th Coll S Africa 69. **d** 71 **p** 72. C Galeshewe St Jas S Africa 71-74; C Taung 74-75; C Vaal Hartz 75-77; R Vryburg St Phil 77-78; Lic to Offic *Glas* 82-84; C Bilston *Lich* 84-86; TV 86-90; P-in-c Walsall St Mary and All SS Palfrey 90-97; P-in-c Caldmore 90-93; P-in-c Shobnall 02-04; TV Worc St Barn w Ch Ch 04-08. *Address temp unknown*

✠**MTETEMELA, The Rt Revd Donald Leo.** b 47. St Phil Th Coll Kongwa Wycliffe Hall Ox 75. **p** 71 **e** 82. Asst Bp Cen Tanganyika 82-90; Bp Ruaha from 90; Abp Tanzania 98-08. *Box 1028, Iringa, Tanzania* Tel (00255) (262) 270 1211 Fax 270 2479 E-mail ruaha@anglican.or.tz

MUDD, Mrs Linda Anne. b 59. WMMTC 00. **d** 03 **p** 04. C Exhall *Cov* 03-07; Chapl Geo Eliot Hosp NHS Trust Nuneaton 07-11; TV Coventry Caludon from 11. *The Vicarage, 56 Wyken Croft, Coventry CV2 3AD* Tel (024) 7661 8329 E-mail muddie@mudda.freeserve.co.uk

MUDDIMAN, John Bernard. b 47. Keble Coll Ox BA67 MA72 DPhil76 Selw Coll Cam BA71 MA75. Westcott Ho Cam 69. **d** 72 **p** 73. Hon C Ox St Giles 72-83; Chapl New Coll Ox 72-76; Tutor St Steph Ho Ox 76-83; Vice-Prin 80-83; Lect Th Nottm Univ 83-90; Fell Mansf Coll Ox from 90; Chapl from 97; Lic to Offic *Ox* 90-02; NSM Littlemore from 97. *Mansfield College, Oxford OX1 3TF* Tel (01865) 270999 E-mail john.muddiman@mansfield.ox.ac.uk

MUDGE, Frederick Alfred George. b 31. Leeds Univ BSc58 Univ of Wales BD67. St Mich Coll Llan 58. **d** 61 **p** 62. C Cwmavon *Llan* 61-64; PV Llan Cathl 64-70; R Llandough w Leckwith 70-88, V Penarth All SS 88-96; rtd 96. *Pathways, 6 Fairwater Road, Llandaff, Cardiff CF5 2LD*

MUDIE, Martin Bruce. b 54. Goldsmiths' Coll Lon BA76. Sarum & Wells Th Coll 92. **d** 92 **p** 93. C Bromley St Mark *Roch* 92-95; rtd 95; Perm to Offic *B & W* 02-03; Hon C Glastonbury w Meare 03-10. *20 Oriel Road, Street BA16 0JL* Tel (01458) 448034

MUFFETT, Mrs Sarah Susan. b 53. STETS 02. **d** 05 **p** 06. NSM Okeford *Sarum* from 05. *Prides Cottage, High Street, Child Okeford, Blandford Forum DT11 8EH* Tel (01258) 860010 E-mail sarahmuffett@btopenworld.com

MUGAN, Miriam Ruth. b 56. RNMH77. Oak Hill Th Coll 93. **d** 96 **p** 97. NSM St Alb St Sav *St Alb* 96-07; P-in-c Croxley Green All SS from 07. *All Saints' Vicarage, The Green, Croxley Green, Rickmansworth WD3 3HJ* Tel (01923) 772109 E-mail miriam.mugan@btopenworld.com

MUGGLETON, James. b 55. Bris Univ BA80. Chich Th Coll 81 EAMTC 99. **d** 01 **p** 02. NSM E Leightonstone *Ely* 01-03; C 03-04; C Buckworth and Alconbury cum Weston 04; R Barney, Fulmodeston w Croxton, Hindringham etc *Nor* from 04. *The Rectory, The Street, Hindringham, Fakenham NR21 0AA* Tel (01328) 878159 E-mail jamiemuggs@aol.com

MUGGLETON, Major George. b 25. Chich Th Coll 55. **d** 57 **p** 58. C Oldham St Mary *Man* 57-59; C Ashton St Mich 59-61; V Croydon H Trin *Cant* 61-68; R Stisted *Chelmsf* 68-69; P-in-c Pattiswick 68-69; P-in-c Bradwell 68-69; R Stisted w Bradwell and Pattiswick 69-87; rtd 87. *Curvalion House, Creech St Michael, Taunton TA3 5QF* Tel (01823) 443842

MUGHAL, Dominic Jacob. b 59. Asian Soc Inst Manila MSc88 Edin Univ MTh93 Leeds Univ MPhil05. St Jo Coll Nottm 05. **d** 07 **p** 08. C Fairweather Green *Bradf* 07-09; Community Outreach P from 09; C Thornbury from 09; C Woodhall from 09; C Bradf St Aug Undercliffe from 09; C Bradf St Clem from 09. *11 Daleside Road, Pudsey LS28 8EX* Tel (01274) 656245 Mobile 07821-246891 E-mail dominic moghal@hotmail.com

MUGRIDGE, Mrs Gloria Janet. b 45. R Holloway Coll Lon BA66. S Dios Minl Tr Scheme 92. **d** 95 **p** 96. NSM Dorchester *Sarum* 95-97; Asst Chapl Weymouth Coll 95-97; Chapl 97-04; NSM Melbury *Sarum* 97-02; NSM Stour Vale 04-06. *3 Hedgehog Path, Gillingham SP8 4GD* Tel (01747) 821562 E-mail janetmug@aol.com

MUIR, David Murray. b 49. Glas Univ MA70. St Jo Coll Nottm BA72. **d** 76 **p** 77. C Fulham St Mary N End *Lon* 76-80; C Aspley *S'well* 80; India 81-85; Dir Ext Studies St Jo Coll Nottm 85-02; C Upton (Overchurch) *Ches* 02-04; Adult Educn and Par Development Adv *Ex* 04-08; Pioneer Min Okehampton Deanery from 08. *The Rectory, South Tawton, Okehampton EX20 2LQ* Tel (01837) 840867 Mobile 07854-845067 E-mail david.muir@exeter.anglican.org

MUIR, David Trevor. b 49. TCD MA MLitt93. CITC 75. **d** 78 **p** 79. C Dublin Clontarf *D & G* 78-80; C Monkstown St Mary 80-83; I Kilternan 83-94; I Delgany 94-97; Can Ch Ch Cathl Dublin 95-97; Chapl to Ch of Ireland Assn of Deaf People from 97. *Luogh North, Doolin, Co Clare, Republic of Ireland* Tel (00353) (65) 707 4778 Fax 707 4871 E-mail muirdt@gmail.com

MUIR, John William. b 38. Dur Univ BA59 Mansf Coll Ox MA65. Chich Th Coll 78. **d** 78 **p** 79. In Congr Ch 62-70; United Ch of Zambia 70-78; C Brighouse *Wakef* 78-80; V Northowram 80-87; V Sowerby 87-01; rtd 01; Perm to Offic *Wakef* from 02. *8 Whitley Drive, Holmfield, Halifax HX2 9SJ* Tel (01422) 244163 Mobile 07733-152089 E-mail jmuir@msn.com

MUIR, Peter Robert James. b 49. Ex Univ BSc71. **d** 09 **p** 10. OLM Thursley *Guildf* from 09; OLM Elstead from 09. *Yew Cottage, Thursley, Godalming GU8 6QA* Tel (01252) 702360 *or* 703857 Mobile 07747-793253 E-mail peter@cellarworld.co.uk *or* peter.muir@thursleychurch.org.uk

MUKHERJEE (or MUKHOPADHYAY), Supriyo. b 42. Calcutta Univ BA70 Serampore Th Coll BD76 Derby Univ MA97. Bp's Coll Calcutta 70. **d** 75 **p** 76. India 75-91; C Crook *Dur* 91-92; V Nelson in Lt Marsden *Blackb* 92-95; Dioc Community Relns Officer *Cov* 95-02; TV Cov E 95-02; rtd 02; Perm to Offic *Cov* from 02. *30 Ulverscroft Road, Coventry CV3 5EZ* Tel (024) 7650 1559 E-mail samukh@lineone.net

MUKHOLI, Eshuchi Patrick. b 60. Nairobi Univ BSc86. Nairobi Evang Graduate Sch of Th MDiv98. **d** 98 **p** 99. Dioc Youth Adv Mombasa Kenya 98-02; Dioc Miss and Communications Officer 99-02; Chapl St Aug Prep Sch 99-02; NSM Blackbird Leys *Ox* 02-08. *Address temp unknown* Tel 07781-489070 (mobile) E-mail pmukholi@yahoo.com

MUKUNGA, James. b 74. Univ of Zimbabwe BA00. Bp Gaul Th Coll Harare 95. **d** 97 **p** 99. Zimbabwe 97-04; R Kadoma All SS 01-02; R Mabelreign St Pet and Lect Bp Gaul Coll 02-04; Perm to Offic *Ox* 04-06; C High Wycombe 06-07; C Peckham St Sav *S'wark* 07-10; Perm to Offic from 11. *173 Choumert Road, London SE15 4AW* Tel 07886-235698 (mobile) E-mail jamesmukunga@yahoo.com

MULCAHY, Richard Patrick. b 67. SW Poly Plymouth BSc90. St Mich Coll Llan 02. **d** 05 **p** 06. NSM Bassaleg *Mon* from 05. *9 High Cross Drive, Rogerstone, Newport NP10 9AB* Tel (01633) 894641 E-mail richard-mulcahy@ntlworld.com

MULFORD, Robert. b 57. Middx Poly CertEd79 Open Univ BA87 MA93. Oak Hill Th Coll BA03 ERMC 05. **d** 07 **p** 08. C Billing *Pet* from 07. *80 Worcester Close, Northampton NN3 9GD* Tel (01604) 788728 Mobile 07768-960896 E-mail robert@mulford.me.uk

MULHALL, James Gerard. b 60. NUI DipSW92 CQSW92. Carlow Coll BA95. **d** 86 **p** 87. C Clonmel w Innislounagh, Tullaghmelan etc *C & O* 09-10; C Lismore w Cappoquin, Kilwatermoy, Dungarvan etc from 10. *St James's Rectory, Church Lane, Stradbally, Co Waterford, Republic of Ireland* Tel (00353) (51) 293129 Mobile 87-240 1913 E-mail jamesgmulhall@gmail.com

MULHOLLAND, Canon Nicholas Christopher John. b 44. Chich Th Coll 77. **d** 79 **p** 80. C Thornbury *Glouc* 79-83; R Boxwell, Leighterton, Didmarton, Oldbury etc from 83; RD Tetbury 00-03; Hon Can Glouc Cathl 06-11; rtd 11. *The Vicarage, Badminton GL9 1ET* Tel (01454) 218427

MULKERN, Richard Neville. b 39. S'wark Ord Course 88. **d** 91 **p** 92. NSM Leytonstone St Andr *Chelmsf* 91-93; Min Sec and Welfare Officer Miss to Seamen 91-93; Welfare Sec 93-94; Dir N Region 94-00; Perm to Offic *Wakef* 93-06; NSM Oulton w Woodlesford *Ripon* 96-99; rtd 00. *120 Norwood Road, Birkby, Huddersfield HD2 2XX* Tel (01484) 480864

MULLALLY, Dame Sarah Elisabeth. b 62. DBE05. S Bank Univ BSc84 MSc92 Bournemouth Univ Hon DSc01 Wolv Univ Hon DSc04 Herts Univ Hon DSc05 RGN84. SEITE 98. **d** 01 **p** 02. C Battersea Fields *S'wark* 01-06; TR Sutton from 06. *The Rectory, 34 Robin Hood Lane, Sutton SM1 2RG* Tel (020) 8642 3499 Mobile 07909-595752 E-mail sarah.mullally@btinternet.com

MULLANEY, Mrs Jane Megan. b 48. Kingston Poly BA72. **d** 04 **p** 05. OLM Kenilworth St Jo *Cov* from 04. *5 Knightlow Close, Kenilworth CV8 2PX* Tel (01926) 850723 E-mail jane_m.mullaney@tiscali.co.uk

MULLEN, Canon Charles William. b 64. CITC BTh92. **d** 92 **p** 93. C Lecale Gp *D & D* 92-95; I Gorey w Kilnahue, Leskinfere and Ballycanew *C & O* 95-00; Dean's V St Patr Cathl Dublin from 00; Preb Rathmichael St Patr Cathl Dublin from 08. *35A Kevin Street Upper, Dublin 8, Republic of Ireland* Tel (00353) (1) 453 9472 Mobile 87-261 8878 E-mail deans.vicar@stpatrickscathedral.ie

MULLEN, Lee Ross. b 73. Cranmer Hall Dur 05. **d** 07 **p** 08. C Chelmsf St Andr 07-11; V Southend St Sav Westcliff from 11. *St Saviour's Vicarage, 33 King's Road, Westcliff-on-Sea SS0 8LL* Tel 07976-311906 (mobile) E-mail tdyp@msn.com

MULLEN, Peter John. b 42. Liv Univ BA70 Middx Univ PhD00. St Aid Birkenhead 66. **d** 70 **p** 71. C Manston *Ripon* 70-72; C Stretford All SS *Man* 72-73; C Oldham St Mary w St Pet 73-74; Lic to Offic 74-77; V Tockwith and Bilton w Bickerton *York* 77-89; Perm to Offic 97-98; P-in-c St Mich Cornhill w St Pet le Poer etc *Lon* 94-03; R from 03; P-in-c St Sepulchre w Ch Ch Greyfriars etc from 98; Chapl City Inst Stock Exchange from 98. *The Watch House, Giltspur Street, London EC1A 9DE* Tel and fax (020) 7248 3826 E-mail citychurches@pmullen.freeserve.co.uk

MULLENGER, William. b 44. Linc Th Coll 68. **d** 69 **p** 70. C Clapham St Jo *S'wark* 69-73; C Hook 73-81; P-in-c Camberwell St Phil and St Mark 81-85; V Hackbridge and N Beddington 85-93; rtd 93; Perm to Offic *Roch* from 93. *30 Constance Crescent, Bromley BR2 7QJ*

MULLER, Vernon. b 40. Natal Univ BA62 Birm Univ MPhil93. St Chad's Coll Dur 62. **d** 64 **p** 65. S Africa 64-76; C Durban N St Martin 64-68; R Queensburgh 68-76; C Hendon St Mary *Lon* 76-77; Chapl Friern Hosp Lon 77-91; Chapl R Berks Hosp and Battle Hosp Reading 91-95; Dep Dir Bodey Ho Counselling Cen 95-05; rtd 05; Perm to Offic *Chelmsf* from 95. *8 Ruskin Road, Chelmsford CM2 6HN* Tel (01245) 345865 E-mail vernonmuller@aol.com

MULLETT, John St Hilary. b 25. St Cath Coll Cam BA47 MA49. Linc Th Coll. **d** 50 **p** 51. C Tottenham All Hallows *Lon* 50-52; R Que Que S Rhodesia 52-61; V Bollington St Jo *Ches* 61-69; V Oxton 69-77; R Ashwell *St Alb* 77-90; RD Buntingford 82-88; rtd 90; Fell St Cath Coll Cam from 90; Perm to Offic *Ely* from 90. *Queen's Head Cottage, 20 Main Street, Wardy Hill, Ely CB6 2DF* Tel (01353) 778171

MULLEY, Mrs Margery Ann Oclanis. b 38. **d** 07 **p** 08. OLM Iwerne Valley *Sarum* from 07. *Hellum Farmhouse, Iwerne Courtney, Blandford Forum DT11 8QF*

MULLIGAN, Colin Arthur. b 42. Llan Ord Course 96. **d** 96 **p** 97. NSM Neath w Llantwit 96-01; NSM Neath 01-07; rtd 07. *12 Chestnut Road, Cimla, Neath SA11 3PB* Tel (01639) 630409

MULLIGAN, Ronald Leslie. b 53. LCTP. **d** 08 **p** 09. NSM Haslingden w Grane and Stonefold *Blackb* from 08. *3 Chatburn Close, Rossendale BB4 8UT* Tel (01706) 220749 E-mail ronmulligan@talktalk.net

MULLIN, Horace Boies (Dan). b 44. **d** 00 **p** 01. OLM Mildenhall *St E* from 00. *47 Oak Drive, Beck Row, Bury St Edmunds IP28 8UA* Tel (01638) 718200 E-mail dan-martha@mullin47.freeserve.co.uk

MULLINER, Denis Ratliffe. b 40. BNC Ox BA62 MA66. Linc Th Coll 70. **d** 72 **p** 73. C Sandhurst *Ox* 72-76; Chapl Bradfield Coll Berks 76-99; Chapl Chpl Royal Hampton Court Palace from 00; Dep P in O from 00. *Chapel Royal, Hampton Court Palace, East Molesey KT8 9AU* Tel (020) 3166 6515

MULLINGS, Paulette Patricia Yvonne. b 53. **d** 07 **p** 08. NSM Cobbold Road St Sav w St Mary *Lon* from 07. *53A Melina Road, London W12 9HY* Tel (020) 7386 1262 Mobile 07751-374857 E-mail pmullings@aol.com

MULLINS, Caroline Anne. b 56. Ex Univ BA78 St Anne's Coll Ox CertEd79. SEITE 04. **d** 07 **p** 08. NSM Wandsworth St Paul *S'wark* 07-11; NSM Hinchley Wood *Guildf* from 11. *1 Chesterfield Drive, Esher KT10 0AH* E-mail rev.caroline@blueyonder.co.uk

MULLINS, Joe. b 20. MC45. Trin Coll Ox BA49 MA59. Ridley Hall Cam 48. **d** 50 **p** 51. C Portman Square St Paul *Lon* 50-52; India 52-74; Australia from 74; rtd 86. *33/31 Cockcroft Avenue, Monash ACT 2904, Australia* Tel (0061) (2) 6291 0345 E-mail emullins@autarmetro.com.au

MULLINS, Malcolm David. b 42. St Edm Hall Ox BA63. St Steph Ho Ox 63. **d** 65 **p** 66. C Kirkby *Liv* 65-69; C Lamorbey H Redeemer *Roch* 69-75; C Solihull *Birm* 75-77; Perm to Offic *Lon* from 06. *843 Field End Road, Ruislip HA4 0QN* Tel (020) 8864 8733 Mobile 07710-313922

MULLINS, Mrs Margaret. b 49. Southn Univ CertEd70. Sarum & Wells Th Coll 94. **d** 94 **p** 95. C Bishopstoke *Win* 94-98; TV Bicester w Bucknell, Caversfield and Launton *Ox* 98-10; rtd 10. *5 Hardings Lane, Fair Oak, Eastleigh SO50 8GL* E-mail mgt.mullins@tiscali.co.uk

MULLINS, Canon Peter Matthew. b 60. Ch Ch Ox BA82 MA86 Irish Sch of Ecum MPhil90. Qu Coll Birm 82. **d** 84 **p** 85. C Caversham St Pet and Mapledurham etc *Ox* 84-88; Perm to Offic *D & G* 88-89; TV Old Brumby *Linc* 89-94; Clergy Tr Adv 94-99; TR Gt and Lt Coates w Bradley from 99; Can and Preb Linc Cathl from 02; RD Grimsby and Cleethorpes 05-10. *The Rectory, 23 Littlecoates Road, Grimsby DN34 4NG* Tel (01472) 346986 E-mail p.m.mullins@virgin.net

MULLINS, Timothy Dougal. b 59. Wycliffe Hall Ox 83. **d** 85 **p** 86. C Reading Greyfriars *Ox* 85-89; C Haughton le Skerne *Dur* 89-95; Chapl Eton Coll 95-05; Chapl Radley Coll from 05. *Radley College, Radley, Abingdon OX14 2HR* Tel (01235) 543190 E-mail tdm@radley.org.uk

MULLIS, Robert Owen. b 49. Bris Univ BA71 CertEd71. St Mich Coll Llan 93. **d** 93 **p** 94. NSM Llangenni and Llanbedr Ystrad Yw w Patricio *S & B* 93-04. *2 Ivy Place, Lyonshall, Kington HR5 3JN*

MULRAINE, Miss Margaret Haskell. b 24. Birm Univ BA45 DipEd46. Sarum Th Coll 83. **dss** 86 **d** 87 **p** 94. Wareham *Sarum* 86-93; Hon Par Dn 87-93; Perm to Offic 93-08. *9 Turnworth Close, Broadstone BH18 8LS* Tel (01202) 640292

MULRYNE, Thomas Mark. b 70. St Cath Coll Cam BA91 MA95 Lon Inst of Educn PGCE93. Oak Hill Th Coll BA02. **d** 02 **p** 03. C W Streatham St Jas *S'wark* 02-06; C Gt Clacton *Chelmsf* from 06. *112 Woodlands Close, Clacton-on-Sea CO15 4RU* Tel (01255) 425159 E-mail mark_and_caroline_mulryne@hotmail.com

MUMBY, Andrew. *See* MOUGHTIN-MUMBY, Andrew Denis Paul

MUMFORD, Clare. *See* VAN DEN BOS, Mrs Clare

MUMFORD, David. *See* MUMFORD, Michael David

MUMFORD, David Bardwell. b 49. MRCPsych86 St Cath Coll Cam BA71 MA75 Bris Univ MB, ChB81 MD92 Edin Univ MPhil89. Bp's Coll Calcutta 71 Cuddesdon Coll 73. **d** 75. C Bris St Mary Redcliffe w Temple etc 75-76; NSM 76-82; NSM Edin St Columba 82-86; NSM Calverley *Bradf* 86-92; Perm to Offic *B & W* 92-06. *14 Clifton Vale, Clifton, Bristol BS8 4PT* Tel 0117-927 2221 E-mail david.mumford@bristol.ac.uk

MUMFORD, The Very Revd David Christopher. b 47. Mert Coll Ox BA68 MA74 York Univ MSW CQSW81. Linc Th Coll 84. **d** 86 **p** 87. C Shiremoor *Newc* 86-89; C N Shields 89-91; V Byker St Ant 91-97; RD Newc E 96-97; V Cowgate 97-02; Internat Co-ord Internat Fellowship of Reconciliation 02-07; R Brechin from 07; R Tarfside from 07; Dean Bre from 08. *St Andrew's Rectory, 9 Castle Street, Brechin DD9 6JW* Tel (01356) 622708 E-mail dmumford3@btinternet.com

MUMFORD, Geoffrey Robert. b 70. York Univ BSc92 St Jo Coll Nottm MA00. **d** 00 **p** 01. C Rowley Regis *Birm* 00-03; TV Darwen St Pet w Hoddlesden *Blackb* 03-08; P-in-c Copmanthorpe *York* from 08; P-in-c Askham Bryan from 08; P-in-c Bolton Percy from 08. *The Vicarage, 17 Sutor Close, Copmanthorpe, York YO23 3TX* Tel (01904) 707716 E-mail gmumford@talktalk.net

MUMFORD, Grenville Alan. b 34. Richmond Th Coll. **d** 78 **p** 78. C Witham *Chelmsf* 78-81; C-in-c Gt Ilford St Marg CD 81-85; V Gt Ilford St Marg 85-87; P-in-c Everton and Mattersey w Clayworth *S'well* 87-89; R 89-96; RD Bawtry 93-96; rtd 96; Perm to Offic *Ches* from 96. *146 Audlem Road, Nantwich CW5 7EB* Tel (01270) 610221

MUMFORD, Canon Hugh Raymond. b 24. Oak Hill Th Coll 50. **d** 53 **p** 54. C Bethnal Green St Jas Less *Lon* 53-57; C Watford St Mary *St Alb* 57-69; R Thetford St Pet w St Nic *Nor* 59-69; RD Thetford 68-69; V Nether Cerne *Sarum* 69-71; R Godmanstone 69-71; R Cerne Abbas w Upcerne 69-71; R Minterne Magna 69-71; V Cerne Abbas w Godmanstone and Minterne Magna 71-89; RD Dorchester 75-79; Can and Preb Sarum Cathl 77-89; rtd 89; Perm to Offic *Sarum* from 89. *10 South Walks Road, Dorchester DT1 1ED* Tel (01305) 264971

MUMFORD, Joyce Mary. b 42. St Hilda's Coll Ox BA64 Ox Univ Inst of Educn DipEd64. TISEC 07. **d** 11. C Arbroath *Bre* from 11; C Auchmithie from 11. *St Andrew's Rectory, 9 Castle Street, Brechin DD9 6JW* Tel (01356) 622708 E-mail jmmumford@btinternet.com

MUMFORD, Michael David. b 29. **d** 79 **p** 80. Chapl Lister Hosp Stevenage 79-83; C Royston *St Alb* 83-87; P-in-c Kelshall and Therfield 83-88; C Barkway, Reed and Buckland w Barley 87-88; V Bodiam and R Ewhurst *Chich* 88-94; RD Rye 90-91; rtd 94; Perm to Offic *Chich* 94-09. *9 Colonel Stevens Court, 10A Granville Road, Eastbourne BN20 7HD* Tel (01323) 730323 Mobile 07803-004492

MUNBY, Canon David Philip James. b 52. Pemb Coll Ox BA75 MA80. St Jo Coll Nottm 76. **d** 78 **p** 79. C Gipsy Hill Ch Ch *S'wark* 78-82; C-in-c W Dulwich Em CD 82-88; V Barnsley St Geo *Wakef* from 88; Asst Dioc Ecum Officer 99-01; Can Bungoma from 04. *St George's Vicarage, 100 Dodworth Road, Barnsley S70 6HL* Tel (01226) 203870 E-mail david.munby@bigfoot.com

MUNCEY, William. b 49. Oak Hill Th Coll BA80. **d** 80 **p** 81. C Wandsworth St Mich *S'wark* 80-84; C Morden 84-88; TV 88-01; RD Merton 00-01; P-in-c Croydon Ch Ch 01-04; V from 04. *Christ Church Vicarage, 34 Longley Road, Croydon CR0 3LH* Tel (020) 8665 9664

MUNCH, Philip Douglas. b 55. Witwatersrand Univ BMus. Cranmer Hall Dur. **d** 88 **p** 89. C Walvis Bay Namibia 88-89; P-in-c 89-92; Warden Ho of Prayer Luderitz 92-99; Prec Port Elizabeth S Africa 99-02; Warden Emmaus Ho of Prayer Northampton from 02; NSM Northampton St Mich w St Edm *Pet* from 02. *Emmaus House of Prayer, St Michael's Church, Perry Street, Northampton NN1 4HL* Tel (01604) 627669 Fax 230316 E-mail emmaushouse@btconnect.com

MUNCHIN, David Leighfield. b 67. Imp Coll Lon BSc88 K Coll Lon MA00 Heythrop Coll Lon PhD09. Ripon Coll Cuddesdon 89. **d** 92 **p** 93. C Golders Green *Lon* 92-96; Prec and Min Can St Alb Abbey 96-02; P-in-c Hatfield Hyde 02-10; TR Welwyn from 10. *The Rectory, 2 Ottway Walk, Welwyn AL6 9AS* Tel (01483) 714150 Mobile 07787-567747 E-mail davidmunchin@talktalk.net *or* rector@welwyn.org.uk

MUNCHIN, Ysmena Rachael. *See* PENTELOW, Mrs Ysmena Rachael

MUNDAY, Elaine Jeanette. b 56. SWMTC. **d** 10 **p** 11. NSM Bodmin w Lanhydrock and Lanivet *Truro* from 10. *70 St Mary's Crescent, Bodmin PL31 1NP* Tel (01208) 77945 E-mail themunday.family@virgin.net

MUNDAY, Nicholas John. b 54. Jes Coll Cam BA76 PGCE77 MA97. Ripon Coll Cuddesdon 09. **d** 11. C Monmouth w Overmonnow etc from 11. *St Thomas' Vicarage, St Thomas' Square, Monmouth NP25 5ES* Tel (01600) 711756 E-mail n.j.munday@btinternet.com

MUNDAY, Mrs Sandra Anne. b 61. St Jo Sem Wonersh BTh89 Ripon Coll Cuddesdon 97. **d** 99 **p** 00. C Esher *Guildf* 99-02; Team Chapl R United Hosp Bath NHS Trust 02-03; Perm to Offic *B & W* from 03. *18 Chestnut Walk, Saltford, Bristol BS31 3BG* Tel (01225) 342740 E-mail sandy.munday@fastblue.net

MUNDELL, Mrs Christine Elizabeth. b 49. WEMTC 01. **d** 04 **p** 05. C Ledbury *Heref* 04-08; TV Leominster from 08. *118 Buckfields Road, Leominster HR6 8SQ* Tel (01568) 615514

MUNDEN, Alan Frederick. b 43. Nottm Univ BTh74 Birm Univ MLitt80 Dur Univ PhD87. St Jo Coll Nottm. **d** 74 **p** 75. C Cheltenham St Mary *Glouc* 74-76; C Cheltenham St Mary, St Matt, St Paul and H Trin 76; Hon C Jesmond Clayton Memorial *Newc* 76-80; C 80-83; V Cheylesmore *Cov* 83-01; R Weddington and Caldecote 01-03; rtd 03; Hon C Jesmond Clayton Memorial *Newc* from 03. *11 The Crescent, Benton, Newcastle upon Tyne NE7 7ST* Tel 0191-266 1227

MUNGAVIN, David Stewart. b 60. Stirling Univ BA80. Edin Th Coll 87. **d** 90 **p** 91. C Glas St Marg 90-92; P-in-c Airdrie, Coatbridge and Gartcosh 92-96; R 96-99; R Troon 99-09; I Greystones *D & G* from 09. *The Rectory, Church Road, Greystones, Co Wicklow, Republic of Ireland* Tel (00353) (1) 287 4077 E-mail davidmungavin@gmail.com

MUNGAVIN, Canon Gerald Clarence. b 27. Edin Th Coll 51. **d** 54 **p** 55. C Dunfermline *St And* 54-55; C Glas Gd Shep 55-57; CF 57-60; C Stanwix *Carl* 60-62; Chapl RAF 62-75; R Turriff *Ab* 75-81; R Cuminestown 75-81; R Banff 75-81; R Banchory 81-92; R Kincardine O'Neil 81-92; Can St Andr Cathl 89-92; Hon Can from 92; rtd 92. *5 Lade Court, Lochwinnoch PA12 4BT* Tel (01505) 043972

MUNN, Canon Carole Christine. b 45. EMMTC 83. **d** 90 **p** 94. NSM Long Bennington w Foston *Linc* 90-95; NSM Saxonwell 95-98; NSM Claypole 98-08; Asst Chapl HM Pris Linc 94-01; Chapl HM Pris Morton Hall from 01; Gen Preacher *Linc* from 01; Can and Preb Linc Cathl from 05. *HM Prison, Morton Hall, Swinderby, Lincoln LN6 9PT* Tel (01522) 666739

MUNN, George. b 44. Master Mariner 72. Linc Th Coll 85. **d** 87 **p** 88. C Boston *Linc* 87-90; R Claypole 90-08; rtd 08. *15 The Meadow, Caistor, Market Rasen LN7 6XD* Tel (01472) 852203 E-mail g.munn@tiscali.co.uk

MUNN, Richard Probyn. b 45. Selw Coll Cam BA67 MA69. Cuddesdon Coll 67. **d** 69 **p** 70. C Cirencester *Glouc* 69-71; USPG Zambia 71-79; Chapl St Mark's Sch Mapanze 72-74; R Livingstone 75-79; adn S Zambia 79; P-in-c Kings Stanley *Glouc* 80-83; R Lezant w Lawhitton and S Petherwin w Trewen *Truro* 84-92; Lesotho from 93; rtd 01. *Reavenall, PO Box 249, Leribe 300, Lesotho* Tel (00266) 877 8553

MUNNS, John Millington. b 76. Univ Coll Dur BA99 MA00 Bris Univ MPhil07 Em Coll Cam PhD10 FRSA04. Westcott Ho Cam 01. **d** 03 **p** 04. C Bridgwater St Mary and Chilton Trinity *B & W* 03-06; Asst Chapl Em Coll Cam 06-10; Lect Bris Univ from 10. *Department of Historical Studies, 11 Woodland Road, Bristol BS8 1TB* E-mail jmm8@cantab.net

MUNNS, Stuart Millington. b 36. OBE77. St Cath Coll Cam BA58 MA62 MCIPD91. Cuddesdon Coll 58. **d** 60 **p** 61. C Allenton and Shelton Lock *Derby* 60-63; C Brampton St Thos 63-65; C-in-c Loundsley Green Ascension CD 65-66; Bp's Youth Chapl 66-72; Nat Dir of Community Industry 72-77; Hon C Hornsey Ch Ch *Lon* 72-77; Dioc Missr *Liv* 77-82; V Knowsley 77-82; P-in-c Stramshall *Lich* 82-88; V Uttoxeter w Bramshall 82-88; RD Uttoxeter 82-87; P-in-c Kingstone w Gratwich 84-88; P-in-c Marchington w Marchington Woodlands 84-88; P-in-c Checkley 86-88; Perm to Offic *B & W* 88-90; NSM Wells St Thos w Horrington 90-94; P-in-c Fosse Trinity 94-02; rtd 02; Dioc Pre-Th Educn Co-ord *B & W* 02-03; Perm to Offic from 03. *Applewood House, Ham Street, Baltonsborough, Glastonbury BA6 8PX* Tel (01458) 851443 E-mail munns@ukonline.co.uk

MUNOZ-TRIVINO, Daniel. b 75. Hatf Coll Dur BA99. Wycliffe Hall Ox MTh01. **d** 01 **p** 02. C Hazlemere *Ox* 01-04; TV Gt Marlow w Marlow Bottom, Lt Marlow and Bisham 04-09. *Hacienda los Olivos, Haza Llana, Sierra de Mondujar, 18656 Lecrin, Spain* Tel (01865) 600698 E-mail daniel.munoz@haciendalosolivos.org

MUNRO, Basil Henry. b 40. Ripon Hall Ox 73. **d** 75 **p** 76. C N Mymms *St Alb* 75-78; C St Alb St Steph 78-80; V 80-87; R Aston-on-Trent and Weston-on-Trent *Derby* 87-99; P-in-c Elvaston and Shardlow 98-99; R Aston on Trent, Elvaston, Weston on Trent etc 99-01; Chapl Aston Hall Hosp Derby 87-93; Chapl S Derbyshire Community Health Services NHS Trust 93-01; rtd 01; Perm to Offic *Derby* from 01. *40 Brisbane Road, Mickleover, Derby DE3 9JZ*

MUNRO, Duncan John Studd. b 50. Magd Coll Ox BA72 MA76 Warwick Univ MBA96 CDir05. Wycliffe Hall Ox 73. **d** 76 **p** 77. C Ecclesall *Sheff* 76-77; C Sheff St Barn and St Mary 78-80; Lic to Offic 80-86; Perm to Offic 97-05; Lic to Offic *Edin* 06-08; NSM Musselburgh from 08; NSM Prestonpans from 08. *Little Acre, Westerdunes Park, North Berwick EH39 5HJ* Tel (01620) 890513

MUNRO, Ingrid Phyllis. b 51. Herts Univ BEd80. St Jo Coll Nottm MA96 St Alb Minl Tr Scheme 83. **d** 98 **p** 99. NSM

Walbrook Epiphany *Derby* 98-01 and 05-09; NSM Alvaston from 09. *40 Brisbane Road, Mickleover, Derby DE3 9JZ*

MUNRO, Robert. b 40. Leeds Univ BA62 Bris Univ PGCE63. SWMTC 95. **d** 98 **p** 99. NSM Saltash *Truro* 98-03; NSM Calstock 03-11. *15 Valley Road, Saltash PL12 4BT* Tel (01752) 844731 E-mail bobmu@valley151.fsnet.co.uk

MUNRO, Robert Speight. b 63. Bris Univ BSc84 Man Univ PGCE87. Oak Hill Th Coll BA93. **d** 93 **p** 94. C Hartford *Ches* 93-97; R Davenham 97-03; R Cheadle from 03. *The Rectory, 1 Depleach Road, Cheadle SK8 1DZ* Tel 0161-428 3440 *or* 428 8050 E-mail rob@munro.org.uk

MUNRO, Canon Terence George. b 34. Jes Coll Cam BA56 MA60. Linc Th Coll 59. **d** 61 **p** 62. C Far Headingley St Chad *Ripon* 61-64; Jamaica 64-70; R Methley w Mickletown *Ripon* 70-79; V Hunslet Moor St Pet and St Cuth 79-85; R Barwick in Elmet 85-93; V Woodhouse and Wrangthorn 93-99; Dioc Ecum Officer 93-99; Hon Can Ripon Cathl 94-99; rtd 99; Perm to Offic *York* from 00. *45 Laburnum Drive, Beverley HU17 9UQ* Tel (01482) 861237

MUNRO, Teresa Frances. b 51. Leeds Poly CertEd73 Leeds Univ BEd74. SEITE 03. **d** 06 **p** 07. NSM Coulsdon St Andr *S'wark* from 06. *Burach, 23 Purley Knoll, Purley CR8 3AF* Tel (020) 8763 2927

MUNRO-SMITH, Alison Jean. *See* WATERS, Alison Jean

MUNT, Cyril. b 27. AKC52. **d** 53 **p** 54. C Ashford *Cant* 53-56; C Dorking w Ranmore *Guildf* 56-60; R Cheriton w Newington *Cant* 60-68; R Harbledown 68-83; R Porlock w Stoke Pero *B & W* 83-92; rtd 92; Perm to Offic *B & W* from 92. *Applegarth, 26 Hood Close, Glastonbury BA6 8ES* Tel (01458) 831842

MUNT, Mrs Linda Christine. b 55. NEOC 92. **d** 95 **p** 96. C Beverley St Nic *York* 95-98; Chapl E Yorkshire Hosps NHS Trust 97-99; V Bridlington Em *York* 99-03; P-in-c Skipsea w Ulrome and Barmston w Fraisthorpe 02-03; Chapl Martin House Hospice for Children Boston Spa 03-05; Hon C Boston Spa, Thorp Arch w Walton etc 03-05; V Market Weighton *York* 05-10; V Sancton 05-10; R Goodmanham 05-10; rtd 10; Perm to Offic *York* from 10. *53 Eastgate, Hornsea HU18 1NB* Tel 07862-289705 (mobile) E-mail l.munt@btinternet.com

MUNYANGAJU, Canon Jerome Cassian. b 53. Serampore Univ BD85 Open Univ MA97. St Phil Coll Kongwa 73. **d** 75 **p** 76. Tanzania 75-80 and 85-95; India 80-85; Hon Can Kagera from 91; Overseas Resource Person *D & D* 95-97; C Bangor Abbey *D & D* 98-00; I Killyleagh from 00. *The Rectory, 34 Inishbeg, Killyleagh, Downpatrick BT80 9TR* Tel and fax (028) 4482 8231 E-mail jmunyangaju@yahoo.co.uk

MURCH, Canon Robin Norman. b 37. Wells Th Coll. **d** 67 **p** 68. C Wisbech St Aug *Ely* 67-70; C Basingstoke *Win* 70-73; C Whitstable All SS *Cant* 73-76; V Queenborough 76-99; Hon Can Cant Cathl 96-99; rtd 99; Perm to Offic *Ex* from 00. *Flat 3, Narenta, 2 Barton Crescent, Dawlish EX7 9QL* Tel (01626) 863532 Mobile 07836-514528

MURDOCH, Alexander Edward Duncan. b 37. Oak Hill Th Coll 68. **d** 71 **p** 72. C Kensington St Helen w H Trin *Lon* 71-72; C Kensington St Barn 73-74; CF 74-78; C W Kirby St Bridget *Ches* 78-84; V N Shoebury *Chelmsf* 84-87; V W Poldens *B & W* 87-96; R Gayhurst w Ravenstone, Stoke Goldington etc *Ox* 96-07; rtd 07. *Hopp House, Back Lane, Old Bolingbroke, Spilsby PE23 4EU* Tel (01790) 763603

MURDOCH, David John. b 58. Birm Univ BSocSc81 Leeds Univ MA03. Ripon Coll Cuddesdon 81. **d** 84 **p** 85. C Penwortham St Leon *Blackb* 84-87; C Wirksworth w Alderwasley, Carsington etc *Derby* 87-89; R Shirland 89-97; Dioc World Development Officer 96-00; P-in-c New Mills 97-01; V 01-05; RD Glossop 04-05; TR Wilford Peninsula *St E* from 05. *The Rectory, 109A Front Street, Orford, Woodbridge IP12 2LN* Tel (01394) 450336 E-mail murdochs@btopenworld.com

MURDOCH, Canon Lucy Eleanor. b 41. STETS BTh99. **d** 99 **p** 00. NSM Warbleton and Bodle Street Green *Chich* 99-02; NSM Rye 02-11; TV 03-11; RD Rye 10-11; Can and Preb Chich Cathl 10-11; rtd 11. *Vert House, Whitesmith, Lewes BN8 6JQ* Tel (01825) 872451 E-mail dog.home@virgin.net

MURFET, Edward David. b 36. Qu Coll Cam BA59 MA63. Chich Th Coll 59. **d** 61 **p** 62. C Croydon St Mich *Cant* 61-64; C Hunslet St Mary and Stourton *Ripon* 64-65; C Hackney Wick St Mary of Eton w St Aug *Lon* 65-69; Chapl Berne *Eur* 69-71; Chapl Naples 71-74; Chapl Rome 74-77; Lic to Offic *Bris* 78-81; Gen Sec CEMS 81-86; C Leeds St Pet *Ripon* 87-89; P-in-c 89-90; C Leeds City 91-93; Min Can Ripon Cathl 93-03; rtd 03; Perm to Offic *Ripon* from 03. *3 Old Deanery Close, St Marygate, Ripon HG4 1LZ* Tel (01765) 608422

MURFET, Gwyn. b 44. Linc Th Coll 71. **d** 74 **p** 75. C Scalby w Ravenscar and Staintondale *York* 74-77; P-in-c S Milford 77-83; R 83-84; V Kirkby Ireleth *Carl* 84-05; rtd 05. *75 Portsmouth Street, Walney, Barrow-in-Furness LA14 3AJ* Tel(01229) 471157

MURFITT, Mrs Ruth Margaret. b 48. **d** 09 **p** 10. NSM St Goran w Caerhays *Truro* from 09. *Haven Cottage, Gorran, St Austell PL26 6HN* Tel (01726) 844891 E-mail ruthmurfitt@hotmail.com

MURPHIE, Andrew Graham. b 65. Reading Univ BA86. St Jo Coll Nottm BTh91 MA92. **d** 92 **p** 93. C Boulton *Derby* 92-96; C Marston on Dove w Scropton 96-97; V Hilton w Marston-on-Dove from 98; RD Longford from 04. *The Vicarage, 28 Back Lane, Hilton, Derby DE65 5GJ* Tel (01283) 733433 E-mail andymurphie@btinternet.com

MURPHY, Alexander Charles. b 28. St Edm Coll Ware 50. **d** 55 **p** 56. NSM Edin St Jas 88-90; TV Edin St Mark 90-93; TV Edin St Andr and St Aid 90-93; TV Edin St Marg 93-96; rtd 96. *Ardleven, 48 Victoria Street, Dumbarton G82 1HP* Tel (01389) 733755 E-mail almagda328@hotmail.com

MURPHY, Mrs Deborah Ann. b 67. Newc Univ BA89. Qu Coll Birm BD92. **d** 93 **p** 94. C Bloxwich *Lich* 93-97; TV Gt Grimsby St Mary and St Jas *Linc* 97-00; Chapl N Lincs and Goole Hosps NHS Trust 99-00; Perm to Offic *St Alb* 01-05; Asst Chapl Walsall Hosps NHS Trust 05-08; TV Blakenall Heath *Lich* 08-10; Chapl Gd Hope Hosp NHS Trust Sutton Coldfield from 10. *Chaplains' Office, Good Hope Hospital, Rectory Road, Sutton Coldfield B75 7RR* Tel 0121-424 7676 E-mail deborahamurphy@tiscali.co.uk

MURPHY, Gerry. *See* MURPHY, Canon John Gervase Maurice Walker

MURPHY, Ms Hilary Elizabeth. b 57. St Martin's Coll Lanc BSc00. St Jo Coll Nottm MTh05. **d** 05 **p** 06. C S Shore H Trin *Blackb* 05-08; C Bloemfontein Cathl S Africa from 08. *St Andrew's Cathedral, PO Box 1523, Bloemfontein, 9300 South Africa* Tel (0027) (51) 448 3010

MURPHY, Jack. b 27. NOC 83. **d** 86 **p** 87. C Armley w New Wortley *Ripon* 86-90; C Hawksworth Wood 90-94; rtd 94; Perm to Offic *York* from 96. *70 Avocet Way, Bridlington YO15 3NT* Tel (01262) 609477

MURPHY, James Royse. b 54. Bris Univ MB, ChB77 MRCGP81. Glouc Sch of Min 89. **d** 92 **p** 94. NSM Glouc St Cath 92-98; NSM Glouc St Paul 98-09; NSM Glouc St Paul and St Steph from 09. *52 Lansdown Road, Gloucester GL1 3JD* Tel (01452) 505080 E-mail jrmurphy@supanet.com

MURPHY, Canon John Gervase Maurice Walker (Gerry). b 26. LVO87. TCD BA52 MA55. **d** 52 **p** 53. C Lurgan Ch the Redeemer *D & D* 52-55; CF 55-73; Asst Chapl Gen 73-77; V Ranworth w Panxworth *Nor* 77-79; RD Blofield 79; Dom Chapl to The Queen 79-87; Chapl to The Queen 87-96; R Sandringham w W Newton *Nor* 79-87; RD Heacham and Rising 85-87; Hon Can Nor Cathl 86-87; Chapl ICS 87-91; R Ch Ch Cathl Falkland Is 87-91; Miss to Seamen 87-91; rtd 91; Chapl St Pet-ad-Vincula at HM Tower of Lon 91-96; Dep P in O 92-96; Extra Chapl to The Queen from 96; Perm to Offic *Nor* from 98. *Saffron Close, 17 Ringstead Road, Heacham, King's Lynn PE31 7JA* Tel (01485) 572351

MURPHY, Ms Julia Mary. b 58. Essex Univ BA81 Lon Bible Coll BTh00. Wycliffe Hall Ox MTh07. **d** 07 **p** 08. C Thetford *Nor* 07-11; TV Forest Gate St Sav w W Ham St Matt *Chelmsf* from 11. *St Matthew's Vicarage, 38 Dyson Road, London E15 4JX* Tel (020) 8519 2524 Mobile 07779-266034 E-mail juliamurphy22@btinternet.com

MURPHY, Owen. b 52. Open Univ BA85 Liv Univ MA04. Chich Th Coll 92. **d** 94 **p** 95. C Oxhey St Matt *St Alb* 94-96; C Watford St Mich 96-98; P-in-c Shinfield *Ox* 98-05; V Barnehurst *Roch* 05-07; Dir St Columba's Retreat and Conf Cen from 07. *70 Sandy Lane, Woking GU22 8BH* Tel (01483) 750739 *or* 766498 Fax 776208 E-mail omurphy@globalnet.co.uk *or* director@stcolumbashouse.org.uk

MURPHY, Peter Frederick. b 40. AKC65. **d** 67 **p** 68. C Paddington St Jo w St Mich *Lon* 67-72; P-in-c Basingstoke *Win* 72-76; TV 76-81; V Hythe 81-92; V Lyndhurst and Emery Down 92-99; P-in-c Minstead 95-99; V Lyndhurst and Emery Down and Minstead 99-05; rtd 05; Hon C Fordingbridge and Breamore and Hale etc *Win* from 05. *Smuggler's Cottage, 20 Shaftesbury Street, Fordingbridge SP6 1JF* Tel (01425) 650209 Mobile 07815-050096 E-mail petermurf@gmail.com

MURPHY, Philip John Warwick. b 65. Kent Univ BA87 Southn Univ BTh93. Chich Th Coll 88. **d** 91 **p** 92. C Broadstone *Sarum* 91-94; C Teddington SS Pet and Paul and Fulwell *Lon* 94-96; V Leytonstone St Marg w St Columba *Chelmsf* 96-01; P-in-c Leytonstone St Andr 96-97; R Benalla Australia 04-10; V Fitzroy 04-10; Exec Officer Catchment Youth Services from 10. *PO Box 207, Fitzroy Vic 3065, Australia* E-mail pjwm65@hotmail.com

MURPHY, Ronald Frederick. b 38. **d** 84 **p** 85. NSM Swindon Dorcan *Bris* 84-87; P-in-c N Cerney w Bagendon *Glouc* 87-90. *Anemone Cottage, The Village, Ashreigney, Chulmleigh EX18 7LU*

MURPHY, Rosalyn Frances Thomas. b 55. Marquette Univ (USA) BA85 Ustinov Coll Dur MTh00 Union Th Sem Virginia MDiv99 St Jo Coll Dur PhD05. Cranmer Hall Dur 04. **d** 05 **p** 06. C Dur St Nic 05-08; P-in-c Blackpool St Thos *Blackb* from 08. *St Thomas's Vicarage, 80 Devonshire Road, Blackpool FY3 8AE* Tel (01253) 392544 E-mail stthomasvicar@btinternet.com

MURPHY, Royse. *See* MURPHY, James Royse

MURPHY, Canon William Albert. b 43. MBE98. Lon Univ BD73 QUB MTh78. **d** 73 **p** 74. C Lisburn Ch Ch *Conn* 73-79; Supt & Chapl Ulster Inst for the Deaf 79-98; Chapl HM Pris Maze from 82; Dioc Dir Ords *Conn* from 92; Chapl Ch of Ireland Min to Deaf people from 98; Can Belf Cathl from 04. *2 Maghaberry Manor, Moira, Craigavon BT67 0JZ* Tel (028) 9261 9140 E-mail murphy43@btinternet.com

MURPHY, Mrs Yvonne Letita. b 52. Brunel Univ BA90 PGCE91. SEITE 95. **d** 98 **p** 99. NSM Hampton St Mary *Lon* 98-01; NSM Staines St Mary and St Pet 01-04; Chapl Bp Wand Sch 98-04; P-in-c Kennington *Cant* 04-09; TV High Wycombe *Ox* from 09. *175 Dashwood Avenue, High Wycombe HP12 3DB* Tel (01494) 474996 E-mail ylm.bwm@virgin.net

MURRAY, Alan. b 61. St Jo Coll Nottm BTh92. **d** 92 **p** 93. C Wombwell *Sheff* 92-95; C Mortomley St Sav High Green 95-99; P-in-c Doncaster St Jas 99-01; V from 01. *The Vicarage, 54 Littlemoor Lane, Doncaster DN4 0LB* Tel (01302) 365544

MURRAY, Mrs Anne. b 53. MCSP75. NOC 03. **d** 06 **p** 07. NSM Fairfield *Liv* 06-10; NSM Liv All SS from 11. *75 Priorsfield Road, Liverpool L25 8TL* Tel 0151-428 2254 E-mail annel25@yahoo.co.uk

MURRAY, Christine Jean. *See* MEDWAY, Mrs Christine Jean

MURRAY, Christopher James. b 49. Open Univ BA78. St Jo Coll Nottm 79. **d** 81 **p** 82. C Heatherlands St Jo *Sarum* 81-84; C Hamworthy 84-90; R Passenham *Pet* from 90. *The Rectory, Wicken Road, Deanshanger, Milton Keynes MK19 6JP* Tel (01908) 262371 E-mail chris@murrayfamily.org.uk

MURRAY, David McIlveen. b 36. ALCD61. **d** 61 **p** 62. C Mortlake w E Sheen *S'wark* 61-64; C Lyncombe *B & W* 64-67; C Horsham *Chich* 67-73; V Devonport St Bart *Ex* 73-79; R Chalfont St Peter *Ox* 79-95; RD Amersham 86-89; R Lower Windrush 95-03; rtd 03; Perm to Offic *Glouc* from 03. *Collum End Farm, 88 Church Road, Leckhampton, Cheltenham GL53 0PD* Tel (01242) 528008

MURRAY, Elaine Mary Edel. b 58. TCD BTh05 MICS97. CITC 02. **d** 05 **p** 06. Bp's V and Lib Kilkenny Cathl from 05; C Kilkenny w Aghour and Kilmanagh 05-08; V from 08. *St Canice's Library, Cathedral Close, Kilkenny, Republic of Ireland* Tel (00353) (56) 777 1998 Mobile 87-236 3100 E-mail emit@eircom.net

MURRAY, Elizabeth. b 57. **d** 10 **p** 11. NSM Eastwood *S'well* from 10; NSM Brinsley w Underwood from 10. *The Vicarage, 102A Church Lane, Brinsley, Nottingham NG16 5AB* Tel (01773) 713978

MURRAY, Elizabeth Ruth. **d** 03 **p** 04. C Antrim All SS *Conn* 03-06; I Woodschapel w Gracefield *Arm* from 06. *The Rectory, 140 Ballyronan Road, Magherafelt BT45 6HU* Tel (028) 7941 8311 E-mail ruth@mdroll.fsnet.co.uk

MURRAY, Gordon John. b 33. St Cath Coll Cam BA57 MA61. Clifton Th Coll 57. **d** 59 **p** 60. C Heref St Jas 59-61; C Uphill *B & W* 62-65; C-in-c Reading St Mary Castle Street Prop Chpl *Ox* 65-68; Ed *English Churchman* 65-71; Prin Kensit Coll Finchley 68-75; Hd of RE Sandown High Sch 76-78; rtd 98. *18 Longcroft, Felixstowe IP11 9QH* Tel (01394) 273372

MURRAY, Gordon Stewart. b 33. Birkbeck Coll Lon BSc72. Ripon Coll Cuddesdon 76. **d** 78 **p** 79. C Kenilworth St Nic *Cov* 78-81; V Potterspury w Furtho and Yardley Gobion *Pet* 81-83; V Potterspury, Furtho, Yardley Gobion and Cosgrove 84; TV Wolvercote w Summertown *Ox* 84-90; P-in-c Walworth *S'wark* 90-95; R Walworth St Pet 95-98; rtd 98; P-in-c Tillington, Duncton and Up Waltham *Chich* 98-01; Perm to Offic *York* from 05. *26 Burton Stone Lane, York YO30 6BU* Tel (01904) 330401 E-mail gordon.murray11@ntlworld.com

MURRAY, Heather. b 62. BSc NEOC 04. **d** 07 **p** 08. NSM Burnopfield *Dur* from 07. *33 Church Street, Castleside, Consett DH8 9QW* Tel (01207) 581156 E-mail heather.murray0@btinternet.com

MURRAY, Preb Ian Hargraves. b 48. Man Univ BSc71. St Jo Coll Nottm 79. **d** 81 **p** 82. C Erith St Paul *Roch* 81-84; C Willenhall H Trin *Lich* 84-87; TV 87-92; P-in-c Moxley 92-00; C Darlaston St Lawr 99-00; TR Glascote and Stonydelph from 00; RD Tamworth 04-09; Preb Lich Cathl from 11. *20 Melmerby, Wilnecote, Tamworth B77 4LP* Tel (01827) 737326 *or* 330306 E-mail rockin.rev@ntlworld.com

MURRAY, Ian William. b 32. Lon Univ BA53 PGCE54. Oak Hill NSM Course 80. **d** 83 **p** 84. NSM Pinner *Lon* 83-03; Perm to Offic from 03. *4 Mansard Close, Pinner HA5 3FQ* Tel (020) 8866 2984 E-mail bimurray@talk21.com

MURRAY, James Beattie. b 67. Goldsmiths' Coll Lon BMus87 Southlands Coll Lon PGCE89. Oak Hill Th Coll 01. **d** 03 **p** 04. C Upper Holloway *Lon* 03-07; C Chesham Bois *Ox* from 07. *The Vicarage, 22 Green Lane, Chesham Bois, Amersham HP6 5LQ* E-mail jamiebmurray@yahoo.co.uk

MURRAY, The Ven John Grainger. b 45. CITC 67. **d** 70 **p** 71. C Carlow *C & O* 70-72; C Limerick St Mary *L & K* 72-77; I Rathdowney w Castlefleming, Donaghmore etc *C & O* from 77; Can Leighlin Cathl 83-88; Treas 88-89; Chan 89-90; Prec 90-92; Preb Ossory Cathl 83-88; Treas 88-89; Chan 89-90; Prec 90-92; Adn Ossory and Leighlin from 92; Adn Cashel, Waterford and Lismore from 94. *The Rectory, Rathdowney, Portlaoise, Co Laois, Republic of Ireland* Tel (00353) (505) 46311 Fax 46540 E-mail venjgm@iol.ie *or* archdeacon@cashel.anglican.org

MURRAY, John Louis. b 47. Keble Coll Ox BA67 MA69. **d** 82 **p** 83. Asst Chapl Strasbourg *Eur* 82-05; P-in-c 05-09. *Aumônerie Anglicane, 2 Quai Mathiss, 67000 Strasbourg, France* Tel and fax (0033) 3 88 36 93 90 E-mail john.murray@coe.int

MURRAY, Mrs Kim Margaret. b 58. **d** 07 **p** 09. OLM Camberley St Mich Yorktown *Guildf* from 07. *190 Upper College Ride, Camberley GU15 4HD* Tel (01276) 28213 E-mail k.murray208@btinternet.com

MURRAY, Mrs Margaret Janice. b 46. Carl Dioc Tr Course. dss 86 **d** 87 **p** 94. Walney Is *Carl* 86-87; Hon Par Dn 87-89; Par Dn Carl H Trin and St Barn 89-94; Chapl Cumberland Infirmary 90-94; C Harraby *Carl* 94-97; P-in-c 97-00; V 00-02; Chapl to the Deaf and Hard of Hearing 94-02; rtd 02; Perm to Offic *Carl* from 02. *6 Follyskye Cottages, Tindale Fell, Brampton CA8 2QB* Tel (01697) 746400

MURRAY, Paul Ridsdale. b 55. BEd. Hull Bp Ox 80. **d** 83 **p** 84. C Hartlepool St Oswald *Dur* 83-86; C S Shields All SS 86-88; V Sacriston and Kimblesworth 88-94; P-in-c Waterhouses 94-98; P-in-c Chopwell from 98; Perm to Offic *Newc* from 99. *St John's Vicarage, Derwent View, Chopwell, Newcastle upon Tyne NE17 7AN* Tel (01207) 561248 Fax 563850 Mobile 07803-906727 E-mail p.r.murray@durham.anglican.org

MURRAY, Roy John. b 47. Open Univ BA92 Wolv Poly CertEd89 RGN75 RMN77. WMMTC 01. **d** 04 **p** 05. NSM Solihull *Birm* 04-08; C Torquay St Jo and Ellacombe *Ex* from 08. *3 Redgate Close, Torquay TQ1 3UG* Tel (01803) 313042 Mobile 07768-436363 E-mail roy.j.murray@btinternet.com

MURRAY, Ruth. *See* MURRAY, Elizabeth Ruth

MURRAY, Mrs Ruth Elizabeth. b 55. Dur Univ BA77 Man Coll of Educn CertEd78. BA. **d** 94 **p** 95. NSM Alloa *St And* 94-98; Chapl Stirling Univ 94-99. *2 Wallace Street, Alloa FK10 3RZ* Tel (01259) 217432 E-mail ruthemurray@lineone.net

MURRAY, Mrs Sheila Elizabeth. b 53. Ripon Coll Cuddesdon 10. **d** 11. NSM Taunton St Mary *B & W* from 11. *Courtlands, Staplehay, Trull, Taunton TA3 7HT* Tel (01823) 326876 E-mail revsmurray@aol.com

MURRAY (née GOULD), Mrs Susan Judith. b 61. Poly of Wales BSc83 Open Univ MA95. St Jo Coll Nottm 90. **d** 91 **p** 94. Par Dn Stokesley *York* 91-94; CMS 94-95; Argentina 95-03; P-in-c Haddlesey w Hambleton and Birkin *York* 03-09; TV Crawley *Chich* from 09. *St Richard's Vicarage, 1 Crossways, Crawley RH10 1QF* Tel (01293) 533727

MURRAY, Canon William Robert Craufurd. b 44. St Chad's Coll Dur BA66. **d** 68 **p** 69. C Workington St Mich *Carl* 68-71; C Harrogate St Wilfrid *Ripon* 71-74; P-in-c Sawley 74; V Winksley cum Grantley and Aldfield w Studley 74; R Fountains 75-81; V Hutt New Zealand 81-87; V Fendalton and Chapl Medbury Sch 87-00; V Merivale 00-09; Can Christchurch Cathl 91-09; rtd 09. *Oriel Cottage, 28 High Street, Waddington 7500, New Zealand* Tel (0064) (3) 318 3068 E-mail craufurd@xtra.co.nz

MURRAY-LESLIE, Adrian John Gervase. b 46. Lich Th Coll 67. **d** 69 **p** 70. C Sheff St Cuth 69-73; C Mosbrough 73-75; C-in-c Mosborough CD 75-80; P-in-c Edale and Warden The Peak Cen 80-11; rtd 11. *Woodside House, New Road, Barlborough, Chesterfield S43 4HY* Tel (01246) 819021

MURRAY-PETERS, Mrs Nancy Susan. b 48. WEMTC 09. **d** 11. NSM Worc St Barn w Ch Ch from 11. *Wee Wee Cottage, Worcester Road, Wyre Piddle, Pershore WR10 2HR* Tel (01386) 553286 E-mail nmp.murraypeters@btinternet.com

MURRAY, THE, Bishop of. *See* DAVIES, The Rt Revd Ross Owen

MURRELL, Canon John Edmund. b 28. Westcott Ho Cam. **d** 66 **p** 67. C Ivychurch w Old Romney and Midley *Cant* 66-70; R Bardwell *St E* 70-75; Perm to Offic *Ely* 75-77; V Wenhaston w Thorington and Bramfield w Walpole *St E* 77-86; V Thorington w Wenhaston and Bramfield 86-92; P-in-c Walberswick w Blythburgh 86-92; V Thorington w Wenhaston, Bramfield etc 92-93; RD Halesworth 85-90; Hon Can St E Cathl 89-93; rtd 93; Perm to Offic *St E* from 93. *Strickland Cottage, 12 Lorne Road, Southwold IP18 6EP* Tel (01502) 722074

MURRIE, Clive Robert. b 44. Ripon Coll Cuddesdon 77. **d** 79 **p** 80. C Kenton Ascension *Newc* 79-80; C Prudhoe 80-83; V Burnopfield *Dur* 83-87; R Stella 87-91; V Coalpit Heath *Bris* 91-95; P-in-c Sittingbourne St Mich *Cant* 95-98; Chapl HM Pris Stocken 98-03; Chapl HM YOI Castington 03-04; rtd 04; Perm to Offic *Pet* 04-08; P-in-c Publow w Pensford, Compton Dando and Chelwood *B & W* 08-09. *1 Kingsway Cottages, Corston, Malmesbury SN16 0HW* Tel (01666) 838887 E-mail c.murrie@btinternet.com

MURRIN, Robert Staddon. b 42. Reading Univ BA68 Open Univ MA96. WMMTC 90. **d** 93 **p** 95. NSM Peterchurch w Vowchurch, Turnastone and Dorstone *Heref* 93-95; NSM Tupsley w Hampton Bishop 95-97; Chapl Kemp Hospice Kidderminster 97-05; Perm to Offic *Heref* from 06. *Albion Cottage, Peterchurch, Hereford HR2 0RP* Tel (01981) 550656 *or* 550467 Fax 550432

✠**MURSELL, The Rt Revd Alfred Gordon.** b 49. BNC Ox BA70 MA73 BD87 Birm Univ Hon DD05 ARCM74. Cuddesdon Coll 71. **d** 73 **p** 74 **c** 05. C Walton St Mary *Liv* 73-77; V E Dulwich St Jo *S'wark* 77-86; Tutor Sarum Th Coll 87-91; TR Stafford *Lich* 91-99; Provost Birm 99-02; Dean Birm 02-05; Area Bp Stafford *Lich* 05-10; rtd 10; Can Th Leic Cathl from 10. *Blackbrigg, Borgue, Kirkcudbright DG6 4ST* Tel (01557) 870307 E-mail muirmursell@btinternet.com

MUSGRAVE, James Robert Lord. b 20. MBE97. TCD BA43 MA51. **d** 44 **p** 45. C Belfast St Andr *Conn* 44-46; C Derriaghy 46-51; R Duneane w Ballyscullion 51-54; I Belfast St Steph 54-64; I Magheragall 64-85; Can Conn Cathl 82-85; Bp's C Killead w Gartree 87-95; rtd 95. *14 Earlsfort, Moira, Craigavon BT67 0LY* Tel (028) 9261 2047

MUSHEN, Canon Francis John. b 34. Birm Univ BA60. Ripon Hall Ox 60. **d** 62 **p** 63. C Foleshill St Laur *Cov* 62-65; C Halesowen *Worc* 65-69; V Stourbridge St Mich Norton 69-81; Hon Can Worc Cathl 81-99; P-in-c Bromsgrove St Jo 81-87; V 87-92; R Kempsey and Severn Stoke w Croome d'Abitot 92-99; rtd 99; Perm to Offic *Worc* from 99. *16 Longheadland, Ombersley, Droitwich WR9 0JB* Tel (01905) 621461

MUSINDI, Mrs Beatrice Nambuya Balibali. b 64. Birm Univ MA94. Bp Tucker Coll Mukono BD90. **d** 03 **p** 04. C Caerleon w Llanhennock *Mon* 03-07; C Malpas 07-08; Perm to Offic *Cant* from 09. *St Andrew's House, 29 Reading Street, Broadstairs CT10 3AZ* Tel (01843) 579945 Mobile 07889-469938

MUSINDI, Philip. b 63. Bp Tucker Coll Mukono BD91 Univ of Wales (Cardiff) MA94. **d** 87 **p** 90. C and Sch Chapl Naigana Uganda 87-89; C Builth and Llanddewi'r Cwm w Llangynog etc *S & B* 92-94; C Newport St Teilo *Mon* 94-97; P-in-c Newport St Matt 97-04; V Newport St Andr 04-09; Min Thanet St Andr CD *Cant* from 09. *St Andrew's House, 29 Reading Street, Broadstairs CT10 3AZ* Tel (01843) 579945

✠**MUSK, The Rt Revd Bill Andrew.** b 49. Ox Univ BA70 MA75 Fuller Th Sem California ThM80 UNISA D Litt et Phil84. Trin Coll Bris. **d** 81 **p** 82. C 08. Egypt 81-86; CMS 88-89; TV Maghull *Liv* 89-97; V Tulse Hill H Trin and St Matthias *S'wark* 97-08; Hon Can S'wark Cathl 07-08; Area Bp N Africa and R Tunis St Geo from 08. *5 rue Ahmed Beylem, 1006 Tunis Bab Souika, Tunisia* Tel (00216) 7133 5493 E-mail billmusk@gmail.com

MUSODZA, Archford. b 72. Univ of Zimbabwe BA00 MPhil03 UNISA PhD08. Bp Gaul Th Coll Harare 96. **d** 98 **p** 99. C Avondale St Mary Zimbabwe 99-00; R Marlborough St Paul 00-01; R Greendale St Luke 01-02; Prin Bp Gaul Coll 02-03; Lect Coll of Transfiguration S Africa 04-06; Adn The North and R Francistown Botswana 06-08; Regional Desk Officer (Africa) USPG 09-10; Regional Manager (Cen and S Africa) from 10; Hon C E Dulwich St Jo *S'wark* from 11. *36B Keston Road, London SE15 4JB* Tel (020) 7378 5672 Fax 7378 5650 Mobile 07565-244860 E-mail archfordm@uspg.org.uk

MUSSER, Ms Christine. b 55. Ex Univ 96. **d** 00 **p** 01. C Torpoint *Truro* 00-03; P-in-c Boscastle w Davidstow 03-07; P-in-c Pirbright *Guildf* from 07. *The Vicarage, The Green, Pirbright, Woking GU24 0JE* Tel (01483) 473332 E-mail revdchrismusser@aol.com

MUSSON, David John. b 46. Open Univ BA86 Univ of Wales (Lamp) MPhil96 Univ of Wales (Ban) PhD00. Linc Th Coll 70. **d** 73 **p** 74. C New Sleaford *Linc* 73-76; C Morton 76-80; P-in-c Thurlby 80-86; R Quarrington w Old Sleaford 86-99; P-in-c Silk Willoughby 86-87; R 87-99; Perm to Offic *Chich* from 01. *Flat 9, Regency Court 4-5, South Cliff, Eastbourne BN20 7AE* Tel (01323) 723345 E-mail davidmusson@tiscali.co.uk

MUSSON, Mrs Joanne Chatterley. b 60. Qu Coll Birm 07. **d** 09 **p** 10. C Redditch Ch the K *Worc* from 09. *2 Compton Close, Redditch B98 7NL* Tel (01527) 551996 Mobile 07590-514115

MUSSON, John Keith. b 39. Nottm Univ BSc61 PhD66 CEng MIMechE. St As Minl Tr Course 85. **d** 88 **p** 89. Assoc Prin NE Wales Inst of HE 80-93; NSM Holywell *St As* 88-93; C 93-95; R Caerwys and Bodfari 95-02; rtd 02; Perm to Offic *Lich* from 02. *4 Hayes View, Oswestry SY11 1TP* Tel (01691) 656212

MUSSON, William John. b 58. UMIST BSc80 Open Univ MA02. St Jo Coll Nottm 88. **d** 91 **p** 92. C Nantwich *Ches* 91-94; C Finchley Ch Ch *Lon* 94-97; V Lynchmere and Camelsdale *Chich* 97-10; V Cudham and Downe *Roch* from 10. *The Boundary, Hangrove Hill, Downe, Orpington BR6 7LQ* Tel (01959) 540012 E-mail stpandp@googlemail.com

MUST, Albert Henry. b 27. Clifton Th Coll 61. **d** 63 **p** 64. C Becontree St Mary *Chelmsf* 63-68; V Highbury Vale St Jo *Lon* 68-78; V Highbury New Park St Aug 78-84; V Walthamstow St Jo *Chelmsf* 84-93; rtd 93; Perm to Offic *Cant* from 93. *24 Nightingale Avenue, Whitstable CT5 4TR* Tel and fax (01227) 772160

MUST, Mrs Shirley Ann. b 35. St Mich Ho Ox 61. **dss** 82 **d** 87 **p** 94. Highbury New Park St Aug *Lon* 82-84; Walthamstow St Jo *Chelmsf* 84-93; Hon Par Dn 87-93; Perm to Offic *Cant* 93-94; Hon C Herne Bay Ch Ch 94-05; Perm to Offic from 05. *24 Nightingale Avenue, Whitstable CT5 4TR* Tel and fax (01227) 772160

MUSTARD, James Edmond Alexander. b 74. Ex Univ BA95 Clare Coll Cam BA04 MA08. Westcott Ho Cam 02 Berkeley Div Sch 04. **d** 05 **p** 06. C Nor St Pet Mancroft w St Jo Maddermarket 05-08; C Pimlico St Pet w Westmr Ch Ch *Lon* from 08. *3 St Peter's House, 119 Eaton Square, London SW1W 9AL* Tel (020) 7235 4480 E-mail curate@stpetereatonsquare.co.uk

MUSTOE, Alan Andrew. b 52. Man Univ BA74. Qu Coll Birm. **d** 78 **p** 79. C Chatham St Wm *Roch* 78-82; R Burham and Wouldham 82-88; Dioc Info Officer 83-88; V Strood St Nic w St Mary 88-99; V Orpington All SS 99-10; AD Orpington 05-10; R Chislehurst St Nic from 10. *The Rectory, 2 Cardinal Close, Chislehurst BR7 6SA* Tel (020) 8467 4405 Mobile 07949-817540 E-mail alan.mustoe@akmustoe.co.uk

MUSTON, David Alan. b 33. Nottm Univ BA60. Ridley Hall Cam 62. **d** 64 **p** 65. C Tankersley *Sheff* 64-67; C Goole 67-70; Sec Ind Cttee of Gen Syn Bd for Soc Resp 70-76; Asst Gen Sec Bd for Soc Resp 74-76; Ind Chapl *Win* 77-79; V Leigh St Mary *Man* 79-83; R Otham w Langley *Cant* 83-97; rtd 97; Perm to Offic *Ox* 01-10. *7 The Homestead, Bladon, Woodstock OX20 1XA* Tel (01993) 812650 E-mail musto33@tiscali.co.uk

MUSTON, James Arthur. b 48. Open Univ BA92 Derby Univ MA. EMMTC 89. **d** 91 **p** 92. NSM Chaddesden St Mary *Derby* 91-95; Community Min E Marsh Grimsby *Linc* 95-99; V Gresley *Derby* 99-04; rtd 04; Perm to Offic *Derby* from 04. *20 Whitmore Road, Chaddesden, Derby DE21 6HR* Tel (01332) 678073 Mobile 07946-575563

MUTCH, Canon Sylvia Edna. b 36. St Mich Ho Ox 57. **dss** 79 **d** 87 **p** 94. Clifton *York* 79-95; Par Dn 87-94; C 94-95; Chapl Clifton Hosp York 81-94; R Flvington w Sutton on Derwent and E Cottingwith *York* 95-01; Can and Preb York Minster 98-01; rtd 01; Perm to Offic *York* from 01. *18 Waite Close, Pocklington, York YO42 2YU* Tel (01759) 307894

MUTETE, Lameck. b 61. Bp Gaul Th Coll Harare 94. **d** 96 **p** 97. C Harare St Luke Zimbabwe 96-97; Asst P Harare Cathl 97-01; P-in-c 01; Adn Harare E 01; Can Harare 01-04; Perm to Offic *Bradf* 04; P-in-c Tattenhall and Handley *Ches* 04-10; R 10-11; R Tattenhall w Burwardsley and Handley from 11. *The Rectory, 4 Rean Meadow, Tattenhall, Chester CH3 9PU* Tel (01829) 770245 Mobile 07940-512748 E-mail lameckmutete@yahoo.co.uk

MUTHALALY, Varghese Malayil Lukose (Saju). b 79. S Asia Bible Coll Bangalore BTh01. Wycliffe Hall Ox BTh08. **d** 08 **p** 09. C Lancaster St Thos *Blackb* from 08. *6 Jackson Close, Lancaster LA1 5EY* Tel (01524) 590417 E-mail sajudoq@yahoo.com *or* saju@st.tees.org.uk

MUXLOW, Judy Ann. b 47. Univ of Wales (Cardiff) BSc69 St Luke's Coll Ex CertEd73. SEITE. **d** 00 **p** 01. Chapl Ch Ch High Sch Ashford 00-03; Bp's Officer for NSM *Cant* 03-07; NSM Biddenden and Smarden 00-06; NSM Appledore w Brookland, Fairfield, Brenzett etc 06-08; NSM Wittersham w Stone and Ebony 06-08; NSM Woodchurch 06-08; Perm to Offic *Roch* from 00 and *Cant* from 09. *29 The Meadows, Biddenden, Ashford TN27 8AW* Tel (01580) 291016 E-mail judy@mucat.eclipse.co.uk

MWANGI, Capt Joel Waweru. b 59. CA Tr Coll Nairobi 81. **d** 93 **p** 94. Kenya 93-96 and from 00; C Sheff St Mary Bramall Lane 96-99. *PO Box 57227, Nairobi, Kenya*

MWAURA, Nicholas Chege. b 65. **d** 90 **p** 91. Nairobi 91-95; NSM Limehouse *Lon* 99-00. *75 Harold Road, London E11 4QX*

MYANMAR, Archbishop of. *See* SAN SI HTAY, The Most Revd Samuel

MYATT, Edwin Henry. b 54. MA. Ripon Coll Cuddesdon. **d** 84 **p** 85. C W Bromwich St Fran *Lich* 84-88; C Sedgley All SS 88-93; V Trent Vale 93-94. *The Conifers, 5 Prestwick Road, Kingswinford ST4 6JY*

MYATT, Francis Eric. b 60. St Jo Coll Nottm 89. **d** 92 **p** 93. C W Derby St Luke *Liv* 92-95; TV Sutton 95-98; V Liv St Chris Norris Green 98-01; CF from 01. *c/o MOD Chaplains (Army)* Tel (01264) 381140 Fax 381624

MYATT, Philip Bryan. b 29. Wycliffe Hall Ox 54. **d** 57 **p** 58. C Fareham St Jo *Portsm* 57-61; C Westgate St Jas *Cant* 61-64; R Woodchester *Glouc* 64-70; R Bath Walcot *B & W* 70-91; R The Edge, Pitchcombe, Harescombe and Brookthorpe *Glouc* 91-94; rtd 94; Perm to Offic *Glouc* from 94. *West Cottage, Littleworth, Amberley, Stroud GL5 5AL*

MYCOCK, Geoffrey John Arthur. b 22. Open Univ BA76. St Deiniol's Hawarden 76. **d** 77 **p** 78. Hon C Ches H Trin 77-79; Bp's Dom Chapl 79-80; P-in-c Hargrave 79-80; V Sandbach Heath 80-82; Chapl and Lect St Deiniol's Lib Hawarden 82-85; V Holt *St As* 85-90; rtd 90; Perm to Offic *St A* from 90 and *Ches* from 91. *20 Eaton Close, Broughton, Chester CH4 0RF* Tel (01244) 531214

MYERS, Mrs Alison Margaret. b 66. Bris Univ BSc88. SEITE 04. **d** 07 **p** 08. NSM Cambourne *Ely* 07-10; TV Lordsbridge from 10. *The Rectory, 50 Main Street, Hardwick, Cambridge CB23 7QS* Tel (01954) 212815 Mobile 07884-370933 E-mail alisonmyers@lordsbridge.org

MYERS, Andrew Thomas Christopher. b 57. Leeds Univ BA81 Ches Coll of HE MTh05. NOC 02. **d** 04 **p** 05. C Leeds St Aid *Ripon* 04-08; P-in-c Middleton St Cross from 08; P-in-c Middleton St Mary from 08. *St Cross Vicarage, Middleton Park Avenue, Leeds LS10 4HT* Tel 0113-271 6398 Mobile 07876-431183 E-mail andymyers@elmet4.freeserve.co.uk

MYERS, Duncan Frank. b 57. Warwick Univ BSc. St Jo Coll Nottm 81. **d** 84 **p** 85. C Upton cum Chalvey *Ox* 84-86; C Farnborough *Guildf* 86-90; Chapl Nottm Poly *S'well* 90-92; Chapl Nottm Trent Univ 92-95; Sen Past Adv 95-02; Hon Min Can Dur Cathl 04-08; Chapl Hatf Coll Dur 06-08; Chapl Salford Univ from 08. *2 Booth Clibborn Court, Salford M7 4PJ* Tel 0161-792 0979 E-mail duncanmyers@ymail.com

MYERS, Canon Gillian Mary. b 57. Warwick Univ BSc78 Nottm Univ MA96. St Jo Coll Nottm 83. **d** 95 **p** 97. C Nottingham St Jude *S'well* 95-97; NSM Gedling 97-00; P-in-c Nottingham All SS 00-02; Succ, Sacr and Min Can Dur Cathl 02-08; Can Res Man Cathl from 08. *2 Booth Clibborn Court, Salford M7 4PJ* Tel 0161-792 0979 E-mail gilly@myers.uk.net

MYERS, John Bulmer. b 19. Worc Ord Coll 64. **d** 66 **p** 67. C Linthorpe *York* 66-68; NSM Huddersfield St Jo *Wakef* 74-76; C 76-79; V Cornholme 79-88; rtd 88; Perm to Offic *Wakef* 88-04. *2 Pine Close, Redcar TS10 3BL*

MYERS, Paul Henry. b 49. ALA72. Qu Coll Birm 74. **d** 77 **p** 78. C Baildon *Bradf* 77-80; C W Bromwich All SS *Lich* 80-83; Chapl RAF 83-86; V Milton *Lich* 87-92; C Baswick 96-99; C Hixon w Stowe-by-Chartley 99-02; TV Mid Trent 02-05; TR Blakenall Heath from 05. *Christ Church Rectory, Blakenall Heath, Walsall WS3 1HT* Tel (01922) 479593 E-mail rev.paulmyers@btinternet.com

MYERS, Peter John. b 60. St Jo Coll Dur BA81. Linc Th Coll 84. **d** 84 **p** 85. C Bulwell St Mary *S'well* 84-88; C Shrewsbury H Cross *Lich* 88-92; rtd 92. *21-22 Eastcliff, Dover CT16 1LU* Tel (01304) 332179

MYERS, Robert William John. b 57. Aus Nat Univ BSc80 Newc Univ Aus DipEd82. Trin Coll Bris 93. **d** 95 **p** 96. C Addiscombe St Mary Magd w St Martin *S'wark* 95-98; C Surbiton St Matt 98-03; P-in-c Blayney Australia from 04. *88 Adelaide Street, PO Box 125, Blayney NSW 2799, Australia* Tel (0061) (2) 6368 2065 Fax 6368 4185 E-mail rwjmyers@netscape.net

MYERS, Sally Ann. b 65. Leic Univ BA86 Nottm Univ MA06. EMMTC 02. **d** 06 **p** 07. C Grantham *Linc* 06-08; Vice-Prin Dioc Min Tr Course 08-09; Dir of Studies Dioc Min Tr Course from 09. *15 Wain Well Mews, Lincoln LN2 4BF* Tel (01522) 567804 or 504050 E-mail sally.myers@lincoln.anglican.org

MYERSCOUGH, Robin Nigel. b 44. K Coll Lon BD69 Nottm Univ PGCE70. Coll of Resurr Mirfield 66. **d** 81 **p** 82. Hon C Diss *Nor* 81-84; Chapl Nor Sch 81-84; Hd RS Sedbergh Sch 84-85; Chapl and Hd RS Dur Sch 85-92; Chapl Gresham's Sch Holt 92-01; Asst Chapl 01-04; rtd 04; Perm to Offic *Nor* from 04. *Hamer, The Street, Bodham, Holt NR25 6NW* Tel (01263) 588859 E-mail robin@myerscough3.freeserve.co.uk

MYLNE, Mrs Christine. b 44. Open Univ BA76 Univ of Wales (Lamp) MA03. St Alb Minl Tr Scheme 89 NEOC 04. **d** 04 **p** 05. NSM Norham and Duddo *Newc* 04-06; NSM Cornhill w Carham 04-06; NSM Branxton 04-06; P-in-c Challoch *Glas* from 06. *All Saints' Rectory, Challoch, Newton Stewart DG8 6RB* Tel (01671) 402101

MYLNE, Denis Colin. b 31. Kelham Th Coll 69. **d** 71. Perm to Offic *Glas* 74-84 and *Ab* 84-88; C Bedford All SS *St Alb* 88-91; C Harpenden St Jo 91-96; rtd 96; Perm to Offic *Newc* 96-06; Hon C Kelso *Edin* 99-03. *All Saints' Rectory, Challoch, Newton Stewart DG8 6RB* Tel (01671) 402101

MYNORS, James Baskerville. b 49. Peterho Cam BA70 MA74. Ridley Hall Cam 70 St Jo Coll Nottm 77. **d** 78 **p** 80. Hon C Leic H Apostles 78-79; C Virginia Water *Guildf* 79-83; C Patcham *Chich* 83-88; P-in-c Fowlmere and Thriplow *Ely* 88-01; Sen Tutor EAMTC 88-90; Vice-Prin 90-97; P-in-c Gt w Lt Abington 01-07; P-in-c Hildersham 01-07; Dioc Rural Miss Officer 01-07; R Aldwincle, Clopton, Pilton, Stoke Doyle etc *Pet* from 07. *The Rectory, Main Street, Aldwincle, Kettering NN14 3EP* Tel (01832) 720613 E-mail jim@mynors.me.uk

N

NADARAJAH (née GOODDEN), Mrs Stephanie Anne. b 81. Fitzw Coll Cam MA04. Ripon Coll Cuddesdon MTh10. **d** 10. C Caterham *S'wark* from 10. *70 Spencer Road, Caterham CR3 5LB* Tel (01883) 330961 E-mail stephnadarajah@gmail.com

NADEN, Anthony Joshua. b 38. Jes Coll Ox BA62 MA64 SOAS Lon PhD73. Wycliffe Hall Ox 60. **d** 62 **p** 63. C Rowner *Portsm* 62-66; C Fisherton Anger *Sarum* 69-72; Ghana 72-10; Perm to Offic *Ox* from 10. *Lost Marbles, 31 Reading Road, Pangbourne, Reading RG8 7HY* Tel 0118-984 2368 E-mail tanddbusiness@yahoo.com

NADIN, Dennis Lloyd. b 37. St D Coll Lamp BA60 Man Univ MEd81. Ridley Hall Cam 60. **d** 64 **p** 65. C Childwall All SS *Liv* 64-67; P-in-c Seacroft *Ripon* 67-69; Project Officer Grubb Inst 69-70; Lect CA Tr Coll Blackheath 70-72; Community Educn Essex Co Coun 73-80; Public Preacher *Chelmsf* from 73; Perm to Offic *St Alb* 01-03. *The Hermitage, 201 Willowfield, Harlow CM18 6RZ* Tel (01279) 325904

NAGEL, Canon Lawson Chase Joseph. b 49. Univ of Michigan BA71 K Coll Lon PhD82 ARHistS75. Sarum & Wells Th Coll 81. **d** 83 **p** 84. C Chiswick St Nic w St Mary *Lon* 83-86; C Horsham *Chich* 86; TV 86-91; V Aldwick from 91; Sec Gen Confraternity of the Blessed Sacrament 85-10; Hon Can Popondota from 05. *The Vicarage, 25 Gossamer Lane, Aldwick, Bognor Regis PO21 3AT* Tel (01243) 262049 E-mail lawson@nagel.me.uk

NAHABEDIAN, Canon Harold Joseph. b 39. Toronto Univ BA63 MA66. Trin Coll Toronto STB70 Armenian Orthodox Sem Jerusalem 70. **d** 73 **p** 74. C Vancouver St Jas Canada 73-76; Chapl Trin Coll Toronto 76-81; V Toronto St Thos 81-83; P-in-c Toronto St Mary Magd 83-88; R 88-09; Hon Can Toronto from 93; rtd 09; P-in-c Strasbourg *Eur* from 10. *Aumônerie Anglicane, 2 Quai Mathiss, 67000 Strasbourg, France* Tel and fax (0033) 3 88 36 93 90 E-mail hj.nahabedian@gmail.com

NAIDU, Michael Sriram. b 28. Univ of the South (USA) 81. Ridley Hall Cam 86. **d** 80 **p** 85. Acting Chapl Stuttgart *Eur* 85-91; Chapl 91-00; rtd 00. *Kloster Kirchberg, 72172 Sulz am Neckar, Stuttgart, Germany* Tel (0049) (7454) 883136 or 87418 Fax 883250

NAIRN, Frederick William. b 43. TCD 64. Luther NW Th Sem DMin88. **d** 67 **p** 68. C Larne and Inver *Conn* 67-70; Chapl RAF 70-74; P-in-c Harmston *Linc* 75-77; V 77-84; V Coleby 78-84; USA from 84; rtd 04. *5895 Stoneybrook Drive, Minnetonka MN 55345-6434, USA*

NAIRN, Canon Stuart Robert. b 51. K Coll Lon BD75 AKC75 Univ of Wales (Lamp) MTh04 FRSA01. St Aug Coll Cant 75. **d** 76 **p** 77. C E Dereham *Nor* 76-80; TV Hempnall 80-88; V Narborough w Narford 88-99; R Pentney St Mary Magd w W Bilney 88-99; R Narborough w Narford and Pentney 99-10; P-in-c Castleacre, Newton, Westacre and Southacre 97-10; R Nar Valley from 11; RD Lynn 91-99; RD Breckland from 06; Hon Can Nor Cathl from 03. *The Rectory, Main Road, Narborough, King's Lynn PE32 1TE* Tel (01760) 338552 or 338562 E-mail nairn.nvgoffice@btinternet.com

NAIRN-BRIGGS, The Very Revd George Peter. b 45. AKC69. St Aug Coll Cant 69. **d** 70 **p** 71. C Catford St Laur *S'wark* 70-73; C Raynes Park St Sav 73-75; V Salfords 75-81; V St Helier 81-87; Dioc Soc Resp Adv *Wakef* 87-97; Can Res Wakef Cathl 92-97; Provost Wakef 97-00; Dean Wakef 00-07; rtd 07; Perm to Offic *Wakef* from 09. *Abbey House, 2 St James Court, Park Avenue, Wakefield WF2 8DN* Tel (01924) 291029 Mobile 07770-636840 E-mail nairnbriggs@btinternet.com

NAISH, Miss Annie Claire. b 65. St Jo Coll Dur BA04 MA08. Cranmer Hall Dur. **d** 05 **p** 06. C Gorleston St Andr *Nor* 05-09; Dioc Ecum Miss Enabler *B & W* from 09. *Diocesan Office, The Old Deanery, Wells BA5 2UG* Tel (01749) 670777 E-mail annie.naish@bathwells.anglican.org

NAISH, Mrs Hilary Marilyn. b 43. Edin Univ MA04. TISEC 04. **d** 05 **p** 07. NSM Edin Gd Shep and Edin St Salvador 05-09. *51 Lauderdale Street, Edinburgh EH9 1DE* Tel 0131-447 2068 E-mail hmnaish@talk21.com

NAISH, Mrs Joanna Mary. b 60. Bris Univ BA81 Southn Univ MA92 Sheff Univ PGCE82. STETS 06. **d** 09 **p** 10. NSM Woodford Valley w Archers Gate *Sarum* from 09. *44 Balmoral Road, Salisbury SP1 3PX* Tel (01722) 504934 Mobile 07810-810231 E-mail joanna.naish@ntlworld.com

NAISH, Timothy James Neville. b 57. St Jo Coll Ox BA80 MA88 Bris Univ PhD05. WMMTC 86. **d** 87 **p** 88. CMS 81-00; C Cov H Trin 87; Dir Th Formation (Shaba) Zaïre 88-91; Research Fell, Tutor, and Lect Qu Coll Birm 92-93; Tutor and Lect Bp Tucker Th Coll Uganda 93-00; R Hanborough and Freeland *Ox* 00-06; Dir Studies Ox Min Course from 06. *307 London Road, Headington, Oxford OX3 9EJ* Tel (01865) 766627

NAISMITH, Mrs Carol. b 37. St Andr Univ MA59 Edin Univ MTh98. Edin Dioc NSM Course 85. **d** 90 **p** 94. NSM Edin Gd St Paul from 90; Hon C Edin St Salvador 00-03. *38 Castle Avenue, Edinburgh EH12 7LB* Tel 0131-334 4486 E-mail carol.naismith@tiscali.co.uk

✠**NALEDI, The Rt Revd Theophilus Tswere.** b 36. UNISA BTh82 K Coll Lon MTh84. St Bede's Coll Umtata LTh59. **d** 59 **p** 60 **c** 87. S Africa 59-70; R Kimberley St Jas 67-70; Botswana 71-83 and 85-87; R Gaborone 71-73; Adn and R Lobatse 74-83; C Wimbledon *S'wark* 83-85; Prov Sec Ch of the Prov of Cen Africa

86-87; Bp Matabeleland Zimbabwe 87-01; Bp Botswana 01-04; rtd 04. *PO Box 237, Gaborone, Botswana*

NALL, Sheila Ann. b 48. Univ of Wales (Ban) BA69. WMMTC 00. **d** 03 **p** 04. NSM Worc St Wulstan 03-07; Chapl HM Pris Hewell 07-09. *108 Ombersley Road, Worcester WR3 7EZ* Tel (01905) 26284 E-mail nall.mail@tiscali.co.uk

NANCARROW, Mrs Rachel Mary. b 38. Cam Inst of Educn TCert59. EAMTC 87. **d** 90 **p** 94. NSM Girton *Ely* 90-95; P-in-c Foxton 95-01; P-in-c Shepreth 98-01; C Fulbourn and Gt and Lt Wilbraham 01-03; rtd 03; Perm to Offic *Pet* from 04. *Thimble Cottage, 11 Geeston, Ketton, Stamford PE9 3RH* Tel (01780) 729382 E-mail r.m.nancarrow@skogen.co.uk

NANKIVELL, Christopher Robert Trevelyan. b 33. Jes Coll Ox BA55 MA63 Birm Univ MSocSc79. Linc Th Coll 56. **d** 58 **p** 59. C Bloxwich *Lich* 58-60; C Stafford St Mary 60-64; P-in-c Malins Lee 64-72; Soc Welfare Sector Min to Milton Keynes Chr Coun 73-76; Tutor Qu Coll Birm 76-81; rtd 96. *77 Pereira Road, Birmingham B17 9JA* Tel 0121-427 1197

NAPIER, Graeme Stewart Patrick Columbanus. b 66. Magd Coll Ox BA MA MPhil LRSM. St Steph Ho Ox. **d** 95 **p** 96. C Inverness St Andr *Mor* 95-98; Asst P St Laurence Ch Ch Australia 98-02; Min Can and Succ Westmr Abbey from 02. *4B Little Cloister, Westminster Abbey, London SW1P 3PL* Tel (020) 7654 4850 E-mail graeme.napier@westminster-abbey.org

NAPIER, Lady (Jennifer Beryl). See BLACK, Jennifer Beryl

NARUSAWA, Masaki Alec. b 53. K Coll Lon BD77 AKC77. Linc Th Coll 77. **d** 78 **p** 79. C Hendon St Alphage *Lon* 78-81; C Eastcote St Lawr 81-84; V Glodwick *Man* 84-99; P-in-c Withington St Crispin 99-03; Perm to Offic *Blackb* from 03. *21 Regency Gardens, Blackpool FY2 0WX* Tel (01253) 593336 Fax 594606 E-mail masaki.narusawa@sky.com

NASCIMENTO COOK, Mrs Anesia. b 62. Mogidas Cruces Univ BA86. Porto Allegre Th Sem BTh91. **d** 91 **p** 93. Brazil 91-94; Lic to Offic *St Alb* 96-97; C Dinnington *Sheff* 97-99; P-in-c Shiregreen St Jas and St Chris 99-07; P-in-c Shiregreen St Hilda 05-07; V Shiregreen 07-08; C Rotherham from 08. *7 Oxley Court, Rotherham S60 2RE* Tel (01709) 365145

NASH, Alan Frederick. b 46. Sarum & Wells Th Coll 72. **d** 75 **p** 76. C Foley Park *Worc* 75-79; P-in-c Mildenhall *Sarum* 79-82; Wilts Adnry Youth Officer 79-82; TV N Wingfield, Pilsley and Tupton *Derby* 82-85. *17 Chapel Road, Astwood Bank, Redditch B96 6AL* Tel (01527) 894294 E-mail alan.nash@bigfoot.com

NASH, David. b 25. K Coll Lon BD51 AKC51. **d** 52 **p** 53. C Buckhurst Hill *Chelmsf* 52-58; Min St Cedd CD Westcliff 58-66; R Rownhams 66-83; P-in-c Boscastle w Davidstow *Truro* 83-85; TR 85-90; rtd 90; Perm to Offic *Truro* from 90. *9 Boscundle Avenue, Falmouth TR11 5BU*

NASH, Preb David John. b 41. Pemb Coll Ox BA64 MA70. Wells Th Coll 65. **d** 67 **p** 68. C Preston Ascension *Lon* 67-70; TV Hackney 70-75; TV Clifton *S'well* 76-82; V Winchmore Hill St Paul *Lon* 82-98; AD Enfield 87-91; R Monken Hadley 98-08; AD Cen Barnet 00-04; Preb St Paul's Cathl 96-08; rtd 08; Perm to Offic *Lon* from 08. *36 Birkbeck Road, Enfield EN2 0DX* Tel (020) 8367 6873 E-mail prebdjnash@yahoo.co.uk

NASH, Mrs Ingrid. b 36. SRN57 RNT80 BEd78. S'wark Ord Course 91. **d** 94 **p** 95. NSM Eltham Park St Luke *S'wark* 94-06; Perm to Offic *Roch* from 97 and *S'wark* from 06. *13 Crookston Road, London SE1 1YH* Tel (020) 8850 0750 E-mail ingrid.nash@btopenworld.com

NASH, James Alexander. b 56. St Jo Coll Nottm BA94. **d** 97 **p** 98. C Trunch *Nor* 97-01; R Stratton St Mary w Stratton St Michael etc 01-10; R N w S Wootton from 10. *The Rectory, 47 Castle Rising Road, South Wootton, King's Lynn PE30 3JA* E-mail james.nash8@btopenworld.com

NASH, James David Gifford. b 76. New Coll Ox MEng98. Wycliffe Hall Ox BTh03. **d** 03 **p** 04. C Plymouth St Andr and Stonehouse *Ex* 03-07; Hon C Preston All SS *Blackb* 07-11; C W Preston from 11. *The Vicarage, 240 Tulketh Road, Ashton-on-Ribble, Preston PR2 1ES* Tel (01772) 726848 Mobile 07889-424907 E-mail jdgnash@gmail.com

NASH, Mrs Jane. b 58. ERMC 05. **d** 08 **p** 09. C Kempston All SS *St Alb* from 08; C Biddenham from 08. *The Vicarage, 57 Church End, Biddenham, Bedford MK40 4AS* Tel (01234) 351265 E-mail janenash@hotmail.co.uk

NASH, Paul. See NASH, William Paul

NASH, Paul. b 59. WMMTC 94. **d** 97 **p** 98. C Aston SS Pet and Paul *Birm* 97-02; Asst Chapl Birm Children's Hosp NHS Trust from 02; Tutor St Jo Coll Nottm from 02. *13 Jaffray Road, Birmingham B24 8AZ* Tel 0121-384 6034 or 333 8526 Fax 333 8527 E-mail paulandsal@msn.com or p.nash@bch.nhs.uk

NASH, Paul Alexander. b 20. Glouc Th Course 73. **d** 76 **p** 76. NSM Coleford w Staunton *Glouc* 76-88; Perm to Offic from 88. *16 Orchard Road, Coleford GL16 8AU* Tel (01594) 832758

NASH, Penelope Jane. b 71. Trin Coll Bris 04. **d** 06 **p** 07. C Downend *Bris* 06-09; TV Gt Berkhamsted, Gt and Lt Gaddesden etc *St Alb* from 09. *The Vicarage, Church Road, Potton End, Berkhamsted HP4 2QY* Tel (01442) 865217 E-mail penny@jeznash.co.uk

NASH, Robin Louis. b 51. Open Univ BA87. Aston Tr Scheme 80 Chich Th Coll 82. **d** 84 **p** 85. C Lymington *Win* 84-86; C Andover w Foxcott 86-90; R Kegworth *Leic* 90-01; P-in-c Bournemouth St Alb *Win* 01-10; V from 10; V Bournemouth St Luke from 10. *17 Linwood Road, Bournemouth BH9 1DW* Tel (01202) 534193 E-mail my quarters@yahoo.co.uk

NASH, Thomas James. b 82. SS Hild & Bede Coll Dur BA03 MA04. Wycliffe Hall Ox 07. **d** 09 **p** 10. C St Helen Bishopsgate w St Andr Undershaft etc *Lon* from 09. *64 Arbery Road, London E3 5DD* Tel (020) 7283 2231

NASH, The Ven Trevor Gifford. b 30. Clare Coll Cam BA53 MA57. Cuddesdon Coll 53. **d** 55 **p** 56. C Cheshunt *St Alb* 55-57; CF (TA) 56-61; C Kingston All SS *S'wark* 57-61; C Stevenage *St Alb* 61-63; V Leagrave 63-67; Dir Luton Samaritans 66-67; Chapl St Geo Hosp Lon 67-73; R Win St Lawr and St Maurice w St Swithun 73-82; Bp's Adv Min of Healing 73-98; P-in-c Win H Trin 77-82; RD Win 75-82; Hon Can Win Cathl 80-90; Adn Basingstoke 82-90; Exec Co-ord Acorn Chr Healing Trust 90-97; Pres Guild of Health 92-97; Warden Guild of St Raphael 95-98; Perm to Offic *Win* from 95; rtd 97; Hon Chapl Win Cathl from 98. *The Corner Stone, 50B Hyde Street, Winchester SO23 7DY* Tel (01962) 861759

NASH, William Henry. b 31. Oak Hill Th Coll 58. **d** 61 **p** 62. C New Milverton *Cov* 61-64; C Toxteth Park St Philemon w St Silas *Liv* 64-67; V Bryn 67-76; NW Area Sec CPAS 76-82; V Penn Fields *Lich* 82-99; rtd 99; Perm to Offic *Lich* from 01. *29 Peterdale Drive, Penn, Wolverhampton WV4 5NY* Tel (01902) 344745

NASH, William Paul. b 48. St Mich Coll Llan 86. **d** 87 **p** 88. C Pembroke Dock *St D* 87-89; P-in-c Llawhaden w Bletherston and Llanycefn 89-90; V Wiston *St D* 90-92; P-in-c E Brixton St Jude *S'wark* 92-96; V 96-99; V Cwmaman *St D* 99-04; R Pendine w Llanmiloe and Eglwys Gymyn w Marros from 04. *The Rectory, Pendine, Carmarthen SA33 4PD* Tel (01994) 453405

NASH-WILLIAMS, Mrs Barbara Ruth. b 66. St Martin's Coll Lanc BA88 Anglia Poly Univ MA03. EAMTC 96. **d** 99 **p** 00. C Tettenhall Wood and Perton *Lich* 99-02; NSM Cheswardine, Childs Ercall, Hales, Hinstock etc 04-06; Dioc Development Officer for Youth Work *Newc* from 06. *The Vicarage, Stamfordham, Newcastle upon Tyne NE18 0QQ* Tel (01661) 886853 E-mail bar@nash-williams.name

NASH-WILLIAMS, Mark Christian Victor. b 64. Trin Hall Cam BA86 MA90 PGCE87. Qu Coll Birm BD01. **d** 02 **p** 03. C Edgmond w Kynnersley and Preston Wealdmoors *Lich* 02-06; P-in-c Stamfordham w Matfen *Newc* from 06. *The Vicarage, Stamfordham, Newcastle upon Tyne NE18 0QQ* Tel (01661) 886853 E-mail mark@nash-williams.name

NASH-WILLIAMS, Canon Piers le Sor Victor. b 35. Trin Hall Cam BA57 MA61. Cuddesdon Coll 59. **d** 61 **p** 62. C Milton *Win* 61-64; Asst Chapl Eton Coll 64-66; Perm to Offic *Chich* 66-68; C Furze Platt *Ox* 69-72; V Newbury St Geo Wash Common 72-73; TV Newbury 73-91; R Ascot Heath 91-01; Hon Can Ch Ch 01; rtd 01; Perm to Offic *Ox* from 02. *18 Chiltern Close, Newbury RG14 6SZ* Tel (01635) 31762 E-mail pnashwilliams@tesco.net

NASHASHIBI, Pauline. b 48. **d** 11. NSM Finsbury Park St Thos *Lon* from 11. *36A Woodstock Road, London N4 3EX*

NASON, Canon Thomas David. b 44. Open Univ BA92 ACA68 FCA78. Ripon Coll Cuddesdon 84. **d** 86 **p** 87. C Banstead *Guildf* 86-89; Chapl Prebendal Sch Chich from 89; PV Chich Cathl from 89; Can and Preb Chich Cathl from 06. *1 St Richard's Walk, Canon Lane, Chichester PO19 1QA* Tel (01243) 775615 Mobile 07732-114279 E-mail d.nason@tesco.net

NASSAR, Nadim. b 64. Near E Sch of Th BTh88. **d** 03 **p** 04. Prin Trin Foundn for Christianity and Culture 03-05; Dir from 05; Hon C Upper Chelsea H Trin *Lon* from 03. *Holy Trinity Church, Sloane Street, London SW1X 9DF* Tel (020) 7730 8830 Mobile 07961-968193 E-mail director@tfccinternational.com

NATHANAEL, Brother. See THOMPSON, Kenneth

NATHANAEL, Martin Moses. b 43. Lon Univ BEd73 K Coll Lon MTh77. Ripon Coll Cuddesdon 77. **d** 79 **p** 80. C Hampton All SS *Lon* 79-82; P-in-c Kensal Town St Thos w St Andr and St Phil 82-83; Hd Div Bp Stopford Sch Lon 83-91; TV Tring *St Alb* 91-00; rtd 00. *5 Carvers Croft, Woolmer Green, Knebworth SG3 6LX* Tel (01438) 815853 E-mail martinascend@aol.com

NATHANIEL, Garth Edwin Peter. b 61. Brunel Univ BTh99. Lon Bible Coll 96. **d** 98 **p** 99. NSM Hanwell St Mary w St Chris *Lon* 98-99; C Lt Stanmore St Lawr 99-01; P-in-c Brockmoor *Worc* 02-07; TV Brierley Hill 07-10; TR Ipsley from 10. *The Rectory, Icknield Street, Ipsley, Redditch B98 0AN* Tel (01527) 522847 Mobile 07949-490265 E-mail gn004d6359@blueyonder.co.uk

NATHANIEL, Ivan Wasim. Punjab Univ MA65. Bp's Coll Calcutta 59. **d** 62 **p** 64. India 63-68; C Newland St Aug *York* 68-70; Hon C Crawley *Chich* 70-98; Chapl H Trin Sch Crawley 76-97; Hd RS 76-97; Perm to Offic *Chich* from 97. *13 Haywards, Crawley RH10 3TR* Tel (01293) 882932 E-mail i.nathaniel@btopenworld.com

NATHANIEL, Leslie Satianathan. b 54. Bangalore Univ BA74 Jawaharlal Nehru Univ Delhi BA79 Birm Univ PhD08. **d** 01 **p** 02. Interchange Adv CMS 99-04; Germany from 04; Abp's

Dep Sec Ecum Affairs and Eur Sec Coun for Chr Unity from 09. *Frankentobelstrasse 4, 73079 Suessen, Germany* Tel (020) 7898 1474 E-mail leslie.nathaniel@churchofengland.org

NATTRASS, Elizabeth Jane. b 59. CBDTI 97. **d** 00 **p** 01. C Dalston w Cumdivock, Raughton Head and Wreay *Carl* 00-03; TV S Barrow 03-08; P-in-c 08; TR 08-10; P-in-c York St Olave w St Giles from 10; P-in-c York St Helen w St Martin from 10; P-in-c York All SS Pavement w St Crux and St Mich from 10; P-in-c York St Denys from 10. *St Olave's Vicarage, 52 Bootham, York YO30 7BZ* Tel (01904) 623559 E-mail nattrassjane@aol.com

NATTRASS, Michael Stuart. b 41. CBE98. Man Univ BA62. Cuddesdon Coll 62. **d** 64 **p** 65. C Easington Colliery *Dur* 64-65; C Silksworth 65-68; Perm to Offic *S'well* 68-72; Lic to Offic *Dur* 72-76; Perm to Offic *Lon* 76-78 and from 05; Hon C Pinner 78-05; rtd 05. *36 Waxwell Lane, Pinner HA5 3EN* Tel (020) 8866 0217 Fax 8930 0622 E-mail msnattrass@btinternet.com

NAUDÉ, John Donald. b 62. Ridley Hall Cam 95. **d** 97 **p** 98. C Kettering Ch the King *Pet* 97-00; C Wellingborough All Hallows 00-06; Dioc Disability Adv 05-06; V Crookhorn *Portsm* from 06. *The Vicarage, 87 Perseus Place, Waterlooville PO7 8AW* Tel (023) 9226 7647 E-mail john@naudeuk.com

NAUMANN, Canon David Sydney. b 26. Ripon Hall Ox 54. **d** 55 **p** 56. C Herne Bay Ch Ch *Cant* 55-58; Asst Chapl United Sheff Hosps 58-60; V Reculver *Cant* 60-64; Dioc Youth Chapl 63-70; R Eastwell w Boughton Aluph 65-67; V Westwell 65-67; Warden St Gabr Retreat Ho Westgate 68-70; V Littlebourne 70-82; RD E Bridge 78-82; Hon Can Cant Cathl 81-00; R Sandwich 82-91; RD Sandwich 85-90; rtd 91; Perm to Offic *Cant* from 91. *2 The Forrens, The Precincts, Canterbury CT1 2ER* Tel (01227) 458939

NAUNTON, Hugh Raymond. b 38. Whitelands Coll Lon CertEd69 Open Univ BA75. Bernard Gilpin Soc Dur 59 Chich Th Coll 60. **d** 63 **p** 64. C Stanground *Ely* 63-66; NSM Woolwich St Mary w H Trin *S'wark* 66-67; NSM Wandsworth St Anne 67-69 and 71-73; NSM Paddington St Sav *Lon* 69-71; NSM Cuddington *Guildf* 73-78; Hd RE Raynes Park High Sch 69-76; Hd RE Paddington Sch 76-78; Sen Teacher and Hd RE Ch Sch Richmond 79-93; Hon C Cheam Common St Phil *S'wark* 79-95; C Cheam 95-02; Perm to Offic *Guildf* 97-02 and from 04; TV Selsdon St Jo w St Fran *S'wark* 02-03; rtd 03; Perm to Offic *S'wark* from 04. *35 Farm Way, Worcester Park KT4 8RZ* Tel (020) 8395 1748 E-mail hugh.naunton@blueyonder.co.uk

NAY, Ms Imogen Joyce. b 79. York Univ BA00 Warwick Univ MA02 Cam Univ BA08. Westcott Ho Cam 06. **d** 09 **p** 10. C Surbiton St Andr and St Mark *S'wark* from 09. *1 The Mall, Surbiton KT6 4EH* Tel (020) 8399 6806 Mobile 07828-064710 E-mail imogen.nay1@btinternet.com

NAYLOR, Alison Louise. See CHESWORTH, Mrs Alison Louise
NAYLOR, Barry. See NAYLOR, Canon James Barry
NAYLOR, Fiona. b 68. CQSW93. St Jo Coll Nottm 02. **d** 05 **p** 08. C Len Valley *Cant* 05-06; Hon C Lower Darwen St Jas *Blackb* 07-10; P-in-c Lea from 10. *45 Abingdon Drive, Ashton-on-Ribble, Preston PR2 1EY* Tel (01772) 729197 E-mail revfionanaylor@btinternet.com

NAYLOR, Canon Frank. b 36. Lon Univ BA58 Liv Univ MA63. NW Ord Course 75. **d** 75 **p** 76. NSM Eccleston Ch Ch *Liv* 75-92; Asst Dioc Chapl to the Deaf 92-94; Sen Chapl from 94; Hon Can Liv Cathl from 01. *27 Daresbury Road, Eccleston, St Helens WA10 5DR* Tel (01744) 757034

NAYLOR, Grant Lambert. b 87. Univ of Wales (Lamp) BA09. St Steph Ho Ox 09. **d** 11. C Auckland St Helen *Dur* from 11. *22 Challener Way, St Helen Auckland, Bishop Auckland DL14 9EH* Tel (01388) 662570 E-mail father.naylor@gmail.com

NAYLOR, Ian Frederick. b 47. AKC70 Open Univ BA92 Heythrop Coll Lon MA00. St Aug Coll Cant 70. **d** 71 **p** 72. C Camberwell St Giles *S'wark* 71-74; OSB 74-86; Chapl RN 86-04; rtd 04; P-in-c Pau *Eur* from 08. *Appt 23, 3 bis rue Pasteur, 64000 Pau, France* Tel (0033) 5 59 30 91 84 Mobile 6 81 20 80 03 E-mail if.naylor@orange.fr

NAYLOR, Ian Stuart. b 63. Wycliffe Hall Ox. **d** 01 **p** 02. C Ipswich St Marg *St E* 01-04; P-in-c Martlesham w Brightwell 04-11; P-in-c Coalbrookdale, Iron-Bridge and Lt Wenlock *Heref* from 11. *The Rector's House, Paradise, Coalbrookdale, Telford TF8 7NR* Tel (01952) 433248 Mobile 07712-309848 E-mail iandjnaylor@hotmail.co.uk

NAYLOR, Canon James Barry. b 50. Lon Univ BSc71 St Benet's Hall Ox BA75. Wycliffe Hall Ox 72. **d** 76 **p** 76. C Catford (Southend) and Downham *S'wark* 76-79; TV 79-82; P-in-c Lewisham St Swithun 82-87; V E Dulwich St Jo 87-97; RD Dulwich 90-97; P-in-c Blythburgh w Reydon *St E* 97-99; P-in-c Frostenden, Henstead, Covehithe etc 97-99; P-in-c Southwold 97-99; P-in-c Uggeshall w Sotherton, Wangford and Henham 97-99; TR Sole Bay 99-02; Chapl Supervisor St Felix Sch Southwold 99-02; Can Res Leic Cathl from 02; C The Abbey Leic 02-08; P-in-c from 08; C Leic H Spirit 02-08; P-in-c from 08. *St Andrew's House, 53B Jarrom Street, Leicester LE2 7DH* Tel 0116-255 0031 *or* 248 7471 E-mail barry.naylor@leccofe.org

NAYLOR, Miss Jean. b 29. Linc Th Coll 77. **dss** 79 **d** 87. Charlton St Luke w H Trin *S'wark* 79-84; Crofton Park St Hilda w St Cypr 84-89; Par Dn 87-89; rtd 89; Perm to Offic *Wakef* from 89. *12 Winter Terrace, Barnsley S75 2ES* Tel (01226) 204767

NAYLOR, Martin. b 72. Leeds Univ BA10 Darw Coll Cam PhD98 Hertf Coll Ox BA94 ALCM90. Coll of Resurr Mirfield 08. **d** 10 **p** 11. C Bedford All SS *St Alb* from 10. *16 Wingfield Close, Queen's Park, Bedford MK40 4PB* Tel (01234) 304167 E-mail martin.mna@gmail.com

NAYLOR, Canon Peter Aubrey. b 33. Kelham Th Coll 54 Ely Th Coll 57. **d** 58 **p** 59. C Shepherd's Bush St Steph *Lon* 58-62; C Portsea N End St Mark *Portsm* 62-66; Chapl HM Borstal Portsm 64-66; V Foley Park *Worc* 66-74; V Maidstone All SS w St Phil and H Trin *Cant* 74-81; P-in-c Tovil 79-81; V Maidstone All SS and St Phil w Tovil 81-91; Hon Can Cant Cathl 79-93; RD Sutton 80-86; R Biddenden and Smarden 91-93; P-in-c Leic St Marg and All SS 93-96; P-in-c Leic St Aug 93-96; TR The Abbey Leic 96; rtd 98; Perm to Offic *Chich* 98-02; P-in-c Crowborough St Jo 02-09. *11 Park View, Buxted, Uckfield TN22 4LS* Tel (01825) 731840

NAYLOR, Peter Edward. b 30. Linc Th Coll 58. **d** 61 **p** 62. C S Beddington St Mich *S'wark* 61-64; V S Lambeth St Ann 64-77; V Nork *Guildf* 77-90; R Ecton *Pet* 90-97; Warden Ecton Ho 90-97; rtd 97; Perm to Offic *Ely* 97-01 and *Eur* from 03. *51 avenue du Bezet, 64000 Pau, France* Tel (0033) 5 59 62 41 68 E-mail peternaylor30@hotmail.com

NAYLOR, Peter Henry. b 41. MIMechE. Chich Th Coll 64. **d** 67 **p** 68. C Filton *Bris* 67-70; C Brixham *Ex* 70-72; C Leckhampton St Pet *Glouc* 72-76; V Brockworth 76-94; P-in-c St Witcombe 91-94; RD Glouc N 91-94; P-in-c The Ampneys w Driffield and Poulton 94-95; R 95-99; P-in-c Cheltenham Em w St Steph 99-07; rtd 07. *11 The Yarnolds, Shurdington, Cheltenham GL51 4SJ* Tel (01242) 861329

NAYLOR, Robert James. b 42. CQSW66. NOC 74. **d** 77 **p** 78. C Aigburth *Liv* 77-80; Soc Resp Officer *Glouc* 80-85; Leonard Cheshire Foundn (Lon) 85-91; Dir The Stable Family Home Trust (Hants) 91-07; NSM The Lulworths, Winfrith Newburgh and Chaldon *Sarum* 98-00; P-in-c 00-07; RD Purbeck 02-07; R Jersey St Mary *Win* from 07. *The Rectory, La route de Ste Marie, St Mary, Jersey JE3 3DB* Tel (01534) 484678 E-mail rjn-rectory@tiscali.co.uk

NAYLOR, Russell Stephen. b 45. Leeds Univ BA70. St Chad's Coll Dur 70. **d** 72 **p** 73. C Chapel Allerton *Ripon* 72-75; Ind Chapl *Liv* 75-81; P-in-c Burtonwood 81-83; V 83-05; rtd 05; Perm to Offic *Ches* from 05. *6 Hillside Avenue, Runcorn WA7 4BW* Tel (01928) 835139 E-mail russnaylor@ntlworld.com

NAYLOR, Mrs Shelagh. b 47. I M Marsh Coll of Physical Educn Liv CertEd68 MBACP. Ban Ord Course 06. **d** 07 **p** 08. NSM Ardudwy *Ban* from 07. *Tanyffridd, Heol y Bryn, Harlech LL46 2TU* Tel (01766) 780922 Mobile 07855-057037

NAYLOR, Vivien Frances Damaris. See BRADLEY, Ms Vivien Frances Damaris

✠**NAZIR-ALI, The Rt Revd Michael James.** b 49. Karachi Univ BA70 St Edm Hall Ox BLitt74 MLitt81 Fitzw Coll Cam MLitt77 ACT ThD85 Bath Univ Hon DLitt03 Greenwich Univ Hon DLitt03 Kent Univ Hon DD04 Westmr Coll Penn (USA) DHumLit04 Lambeth DD05. Ridley Hall Cam 70. **d** 74 **p** 76 **c** 84. C Cambridge H Sepulchre w All SS *Ely* 74-76; Tutorial Supervisor Th Cam Univ 74-76; Sen Tutor Karachi Th Coll Pakistan 76-81; Provost Lahore 81-84; Bp Raiwind 84-86; Asst to Abp Cant 86-89; Co-ord of Studies and Ed Lambeth Conf 86-89; Hon C Ox St Giles and SS Phil and Jas w St Marg 86-89; Gen Sec OMS 89-94; Asst Bp S'wark 89-94; Hon C Limpsfield and Titsey 89-94; Can Th Leic Cathl 92-94; Bp Roch 94-09; Visiting Prof Th and RS Univ of Greenwich from 96; Hon Fell St Edm Hall Ox from 99. *PO Box 54, Orpington BR5 9RT* E-mail oxtrad@gmail.com

✠**NDUNGANE, The Most Revd Winston Hugh Njongonkulu.** b 41. K Coll Lon BD78 AKC78 MTh. St Pet Coll Alice 71. **d** 73 **p** 74 **c** 91. C Atholone S Africa 73-75; C Mitcham St Mark *S'wark* 75-76; C Hammersmith St Pet *Lon* 76-77; C Primrose Hill St Mary w Avenue Road St Paul 77-79; Asst Chapl Paris St Geo *Eur* 79; R Elsies River S Africa 80-81; Prov Liaison Officer 81-84; Prin St Bede's Th Coll Umtata 85-86; Prov Exec Officer 87-91; Bp Kimberley and Kuruman 91-96; Abp Cape Town 96-07. *Address temp unknown*

NEAL, Alan. b 27. Linc Coll Bris 82. **d** 84 **p** 85. Hon C Broughty Ferry *Bre* 84-85; P-in-c Dundee St Ninian 85-86; R Lockerbie and Annan *Glas* 86-94; rtd 94. *clo Mr and Mrs Graham Rew, 3 Vallance Drive, Lockerbie DG11 2DU*

NEAL, Canon Anthony Terrence. b 42. Open Univ BA84 Leeds Univ CertEd73. Chich Th Coll 65. **d** 68 **p** 69. C Cross Green St Saw and St Hilda *Ripon* 68-73; NSM Hawksworth Wood 73-78; Asst Chapl and Hd RE Abbey Grange High Sch Leeds 73-81; NSM Farnley *Ripon* 78-81; Dioc Adv in RE *Ripon* 81-85; Children's Officer 85-87; Stewardship Adv 87-88; P-in-c St Erth 81-84; V 84-96; P-in-c Phillack w Gwithian and Gwinear 94-96; P-in-c Hayle 94-96; TR Godrevy 96-06; Hon Can Truro Cathl

94-06; C Feock from 10; C Devoran from 10; C St Stythians w Perranarworthal and Gwennap from 10; C Chacewater w St Day and Carharrack from 10. *11 Adelaide Street, Camborne TR14 8HH* Tel (01209) 712733
E-mail steamerneal@talktalk.net

NEAL, Canon Christopher Charles. b 47. St Pet Coll Ox BA69. Ridley Hall Cam 69. **d** 72 **p** 73. C Addiscombe St Mary *Cant* 72-76; C Camberley St Paul *Guildf* 76-83; TV 83-86; V Thame w Towersey *Ox* 86-98; TR Thame 98-03; Hon Can Ch Ch 98-03; Dir Miss and Community CMS from 03. *Church Mission Society, Watlington Road, Cowley, Oxford OX4 6BZ* Tel 08456-201799 Fax (01865) 776375
E-mail chris.neal@cms-uk.org

NEAL, Miss Frances Mary. b 37. BEd76. S'wark Ord Course 94. **d** 96 **p** 97. NSM Catford (Southend) and Downham *S'wark* 96-07; Perm to Offic 07-08. *29 Ballamore Road, Downham, Bromley BR1 5LN* Tel (020) 8698 6616

NEAL, Gary Roy. b 57. St Jo Coll Nottm 03. **d** 05 **p** 06. C Kinson *Sarum* 05-09; TV Broadwater *Chich* from 09. *St Stephen's Vicarage, 37 Angola Road, Worthing BN14 8DU* Tel (01903) 235054 E-mail gary@cofekinson.org.uk

NEAL, Canon Geoffrey Martin. b 40. AKC63. **d** 64 **p** 65. C Wandsworth St Paul *S'wark* 64-66; USA 66-68; C Reigate St Mark *S'wark* 68-70; P-in-c Wandsworth St Faith 70-72; V 72-75; V Houghton Regis *St Alb* 75-95; Hon Can St Alb 93-95; rtd 00; Perm to Offic *St Alb* from 00 and *Pet* from 10. *63 The Moor, Carlton, Bedford MK43 7JS* Tel (01234) 720938

NEAL, John Edward. b 44. Nottm Univ BTh74 Heythrop Coll Lon MA04. Linc Th Coll 70. **d** 74 **p** 75. C Lee St Marg *S'wark* 74-77; C Clapham St Jo 77; C Clapham Ch Ch and St Jo 77-81; P-in-c Eltham St Barn 81-83; V 83-98; Sub-Dean Eltham 89-91; Sub-Dean Greenwich S 91-97; RD Greenwich S 97-01; V Eltham St Jo 98-09; rtd 09; Perm to Offic *Eur* from 10. *4 Square Mantegna, 37000 Tours, France* Tel (0033) 2 47 64 07 92
E-mail johnlesneal@orange.fr

NEAL, Mrs Maxine Elner. b 56. Univ of Wales (Abth) BA78 Wolv Univ PGCE94. WEMTC 09. **d** 11. OLM Ford *Heref* from 11; OLM Alberbury w Cardeston from 11; OLM Gt Wollaston from 11. *Bank House, Coedway, Shrewsbury SY5 9AR* Tel (01743) 884095 E-mail nealmaxine@hotmail.com

NEAL, Stephen Charles. b 44. K Coll Lon BSc66 MCMI76. NOC 90. **d** 93 **p** 94. C Walmsley *Man* 93-96; P-in-c Bolton St Matt w St Barn 96-98; TV Halliwell 98-02; Chapl Bolton Hospice 02-05; Perm to Offic *Man* 05-08; *Derby* and *Eur* from 08; rtd 09; Asst Chapl Derby Hosps NHS Foundn Trust from 09. *21 Utah Close, Hilton, Derby DE65 5JA* Tel (01283) 480450 Mobile 07775-794890
E-mail stephencneal@yahoo.co.uk

NEALE, Alan James Robert. b 52. LSE BSc(Econ)73. Wycliffe Hall Ox BA76 MA81. **d** 77 **p** 78. C Plymouth St Andr w St Paul and St Geo *Ex* 77-80; C Portswood Ch Ch *Win* 80-82; V Stanstead Abbots *St Alb* 82-85; Asst Master Chelmsf Hall Sch Eastbourne 85-88; R Brookings St Paul USA 88-90; R Middletown St Columba 91-04; R Philadelphia H Trin from 04. *316 S 16th Street, Philadelphia PA 19102, USA* Tel (001) (215) 567 1267 Fax 567 3766

NEALE, Andrew Jackson. b 58. Oak Hill Th Coll 97. **d** 99 **p** 00. C Harold Hill St Geo *Chelmsf* 99-02; C Bentley Common, Kelvedon Hatch and Navestock 02-03; TV Chigwell and Chigwell Row 03-10; Perm to Offic from 10. *Pilgrims' Hall, Ongar Road, Brentwood CM15 9SA* Tel (01277) 372206
E-mail andy.neale2pray@btopenworld.com

NEALE, David. b 50. Lanchester Poly Cov BSc72. St Mich Coll Llan BD83. **d** 83 **p** 84. Min Can St Woolos Cathl 83-87; Chapl St Woolos Hosp Newport 85-87; R Blaina and Nantyglo *Mon* 87-91; Video and Tech Officer Bd of Miss 91-01; TV Cyncoed 99-01; Creative Resources Officer 01-03; V Maindee Newport from 03; AD Newport from 09. *St John's Vicarage, 25 St John's Road, Newport NP19 8GR* Tel (01633) 674155
E-mail dneale@ntlworld.com

NEALE, Edward. See NEALE, Canon James Edward McKenzie

NEALE, Geoffrey Arthur. b 41. Brasted Th Coll 61 St Aid Birkenhead 63. **d** 65 **p** 66. C Stoke Cov 65-68; C Fareham H Trin *Portsm* 68-71; TV 71-72; R Binstead 72-77; TR Bottesford w Ashby *Linc* 77-80; V Horncastle w Low Toynton 80-90; V Brigg 90-95; V Blockley w Aston Magna and Bourton on the Hill *Glouc* 95-01; Local Min Officer 95-01; V Heath and Reach *St Alb* 01-05; TV Billington, Egginton, Hockliffe etc 06; RD Dunstable 02-04; rtd 06; Perm to Offic *Cant* from 06. *46 Cavendish Road, Herne Bay CT6 5BB* Tel (01227) 360717 Mobile 07703-174761
E-mail revd.geoffn@gmail.com

NEALE, Hannah. b 40. SEITE. **d** 99 **p** 00. NSM Mitcham St Mark *S'wark* 99-00; NSM Merton St Jo 00-09; NSM Merton Priory 09; Perm to Offic from 09. *42 Palestine Grove, London SW19 2QN* Tel (020) 8648 5405

NEALE, Canon James Edward McKenzie (Eddie). b 38. MBE04. Selw Coll Cam BA61 Nottm Trent Univ Hon DLitt00 Nottm Univ Hon DD03. Clifton Th Coll 61. **d** 63 **p** 64. C Everton St Ambrose w St Tim *Liv* 63-72; Relig Adv BBC Radio

Merseyside 72-76; V Bestwood St Matt *S'well* 76-86; Dioc Urban Officer 86-91; V Nottingham St Mary and St Cath 91-03; Hon Can S'well Minster 91-03; rtd 03; Perm to Offic *S'well* from 03. *Church Cottage, Church Lane, Maplebeck, Nottingham NG22 0BS* Tel (01636) 636559
E-mail eddie@neale007.freeserve.co.uk

NEALE, Mrs Jan Celia. b 42. EMMTC 92. **d** 92 **p** 94. C Gt and Lt Coates w Bradley *Linc* 92-96; TV 96-01; TV Chambersbury *St Alb* 01-07; rtd 07. *1 Dickens Close, St Albans AL3 5PP* Tel (01727) 853936

✠**NEALE, The Rt Revd John Robert Geoffrey.** b 26. AKC54 St Boniface Warminster 54. **d** 55 **p** 56 **c** 74. C St Helier *S'wark* 55-58; Chapl Ardingly Coll 58-62; Recruitment Sec CACTM 63-66; ACCM 66-68; R Hascombe *Guildf* 68-74; Can Missr and Dir Post-Ord Tr 68-74; Hon Can Guildf Cathl 68-74; Adn Wilts *Sarum* 74-80; Suff Bp Ramsbury 74-81; Area Bp Ramsbury 81-88; Can and Preb Sarum Cathl 74-88; Sec Partnership for World Miss 89-91; Hon Asst Bp Lon and S'wark 89-91; rtd 91; Hon Asst Bp B & W 91-08; Bris from 92; Glouc from 94. *26 Prospect, Corsham SN13 9AF* Tel (01249) 712557

NEALE, Martyn William. b 57. G&C Coll Cam BA78 MA82. Ripon Coll Cuddesdon 78. **d** 81 **p** 82. C Perry Hill St Geo *S'wark* 81-83; C Purley St Mark 83-85; V Abbey Wood 85-97; V Hawley H Trin *Guildf* from 97; V Minley from 97. *The Vicarage, Hawley, Blackwater, Camberley GU17 9BN* Tel (01276) 35287
E-mail frmartyn@aol.com

NEALE, Paul Edward. b 46. Portsm Coll of Tech BSc68. **d** 07 **p** 08. OLM Cromer *Nor* from 07. *30 Fulcher Avenue, Cromer NR27 9SG* Tel (01263) 513563
E-mail paulneale127@btinternet.com

NEARY (née TAYLOR), Mrs Joanna Beatrice. b 74. Warwick Univ BA96 Homerton Coll Cam PGCE97. St Jo Coll Nottm 04. **d** 06 **p** 07. C Northolt St Jos *Lon* 06-09. *7 Cedar Road, Charlton Down, Dorchester DT2 9UL* Tel (01305) 267708 Mobile 07939-062409 E-mail jo@joneary.com

NEAUM, David Andrew. b 79. Trin Coll Melbourne BA01 SS Coll Cam BA06 Em Coll Cam MPhil08. Westcott Ho Cam 04 Yale Div Sch 06. **d** 07 **p** 08. NSM Cambridge St Mary Less *Ely* 07-08; C Marnhull *Sarum* 08-11; C Ox St Mary V w St Cross and St Pet from 11. *22 Stratford Street, Oxford OX4 1SW*
E-mail david.neaum@gmail.com

NEAVE, Garry Reginald. b 51. Leic Univ BA72 MA73 PGCE74 MCMI. S'wark Ord Course. **d** 82 **p** 83. NSM Harlow St Mary Magd *Chelmsf* 82-87 and from 92; NSM St Mary-at-Latton 87-92; Chapl and Asst Prin Harlow Tertiary Coll 84-99; Dir Student Services and Admin W Herts Coll 99-04; Educn Dir Girls' Day Sch Trust from 04. *35 Perry Spring, Harlow CM17 9DQ* Tel (01279) 411775

NEED, The Very Revd Philip Alan. b 54. AKC75. Chich Th Coll 76. **d** 77 **p** 78. C Clapham Ch Ch and St Jo *S'wark* 77-79; C Luton All SS w St Pet *St Alb* 80-83; V Harlow St Mary Magd *Chelmsf* 83-89; P-in-c Chaddesden St Phil *Derby* 89-91; Bp's Dom Chapl *Chelmsf* 91-96; R Bocking St Mary from 96; Dean Bocking from 96; RD Braintree 00-06 and from 09; Hon Can Chelmsf Cathl from 07. *The Deanery, Deanery Hill, Braintree CM7 5SR* Tel (01376) 324887 *or* 553092
E-mail thedeanofbocking@tiscali.co.uk

NEED, Stephen William. b 57. K Coll Lon BD79 MTh83 PhD93 AKC79 FRSA95. **d** 08 **p** 08. Dean St Geo Coll Jerusalem 05-11; C St Geo Cathl 08-11; P-in-c Stock Harvard *Chelmsf* from 11; P-in-c W Hanningfield from 11. *The Rectory, 61 High Street, Stock, Ingatestone CM4 9BN* Tel (01277) 840442

NEEDHAM, Mrs Marian Ruth. b 52. Birm Univ BMus74 City Univ MA96. NOC 06. **d** 08 **p** 09. NSM Ches H Trin from 08. *14 Roselands Court, Chester Road, Rossett, Wrexham LL12 0DD* Tel (01244) 610339 Fax 571857
E-mail marianrnmailbox-rev@yahoo.co.uk

NEEDHAM, Brother Peter Douglas. b 56. Chich Th Coll 86. **d** 88 **p** 88. SSF from 80; C S Moor *Dur* 88-90; Chapl RN 91-93; Lic to Offic *Newc* 91-96 and *Lon* 97-99; C Ealing Ch the Sav *Lon* 99-02; P-in-c Grimethorpe *Wakef* 02-05; V Grimethorpe w Brierley from 05. *St Luke's Vicarage, High Street, Grimethorpe, Barnsley S72 7JA* Tel (01226) 717561 E-mail needham278@oal.com

NEEDLE, Mrs Jill Mary. b 56. Matlock Coll of Educn TCert77 BEd78. St Jo Coll Nottm 03. **d** 05 **p** 06. NSM Allestree St Nic *Derby* from 05; NSM Quarndon from 05. *117 Hazelwood Road, Duffield, Belper DE56 4AA* Tel (01332) 840746
E-mail jill.needle@btinternet.com

NEEDLE, Paul Robert. b 45. Oak Hill Th Coll 67. **d** 70 **p** 71. C Gt Horton *Bradf* 70-74; C Pudsey St Lawr 74-77; Hon C Horton and Chapl St Luke's Hosp Bradf 78-80; NSM Irthlingborough *Pet* 87-90; NSM Gt w Lt Addington 90-98; Bp's Media Adv 94-02; NSM Higham Ferrers w Chelveston 02-06; Bp's Communications Officer *Eur* from 05; P-in-c Costa Azahar from 07; Perm to Offic *Pet* from 07. *Apdo Correos 136, 12579 Alcossebre, Spain, or Countess Gardens, Bell Street, Henley-on-Thames RG9 2BN* Tel (0034) 964 413 166 Mobile 07833-372439 E-mail paulneedle@aol.com

NEEDLE, Richard John. b 57. Bath Univ BPharm78 PhD83 MRPharmS79. ERMC 04. **d** 07 **p** 08. NSM Sproughton w Burstall, Copdock w Washbrook etc *St E* 07-11; NSM E Bergholt and Brantham from 11. *Meadowside, Gandish Road, East Bergholt, Colchester CO7 6UR* Tel (01206) 298859 E-mail richard.needle@btinternet.com

NEEDS, Michael John. b 42. Open Univ BA82 Univ of Wales (Swansea) MSc84 PhD87. Wycliffe Hall Ox 91. **d** 93 **p** 94. C Aberystwyth *St D* 93-96; R Llanllwchaearn and Llanina 96-06; rtd 07; P-in-c Martletwy w Lawrenny and Minwear etc *St D* 07-09. *5 Pentwyn Road, Nelson, Treharris CF46 6HE* Tel (01443) 453137 E-mail michaeljohnneeds@aol.com

NEIL, Prof Peter Sydney. b 62. Edin Univ MA83 MEd86 QUB PhD95 MDiv03. **d** 08 **p** 09. NSM Elerch w Penrhyncoch w Capel Bangor and Goginan *St D* 08-09; NSM Ayr *Glas* from 09. *7 Genoch Mews, Ayr KA7 4GX*

NEILAND, Paul Andrew. b 62. CITC 00. **d** 01 **p** 02. Aux Min Enniscorthy w Clone, Clonmore, Monart etc *C & O* 01-05; Aux Min Wexford w Ardcolm and Killurin 05-09; Aux Min Wexford and Kilscoran Union from 10. *Butlerstown, Killinick, Co Wexford, Republic of Ireland* Tel (00353) (53) 913 5701 Mobile 87-242 2842

NEILL, Barbara June. b 39. St Jo Coll Nottm. **d** 00 **p** 01. NSM Bestwood Park w Rise Park *S'well* 00-09; rtd 09. *17 Harvest Close, Nottingham NG5 9BW* Tel 0115-975 3378 E-mail barbjn@btopenworld.com

✠**NEILL, The Rt Revd John Robert Winder.** b 45. TCD BA66 MA69 Jes Coll Cam BA68 MA72 NUI Hon LLD03. Ridley Hall Cam 67. **d** 69 **p** 70 **c** 86. C Glenageary *D & G* 69-71; Lect CITC 70-71 and 82-84; Dioc Registrar (Ossory, Ferns and Leighlin) *C & O* 71-74; Bp's V, Lib and Chapter Registrar Kilkenny Cathl 71-74; I Abbeystrewry *C, C & R* 74-78; I Dublin St Bart w Leeson Park *D & G* 78-84; Chapl Community of St Jo the Ev 78-84; Dean Waterford *C & O* 84-86; Prec Lismore Cathl 84-86; Adn Waterford 84-86; I Waterford w Killea, Drumcannon and Dunhill 84-86; Bp T, K & A 86-97; Bp C & O 97-02; Abp Dublin *D & G* 02-11; Preb Cualaun St Patr Cathl Dublin 02-11; rtd 11. *Knockglass, Annamult Road, Bennettsbridge, Co Kilkenny, Republic of Ireland* Tel (00353) (56) 772 7707 E-mail jrwneill@eircom.net

NEILL, Richard Walter. b 67. Wadh Coll Ox BA89 Em Coll Cam BA92. Westcott Ho Cam 90. **d** 93 **p** 94. C Abbots Langley *St Alb* 93-97; C Wisley w Pyrford *Guildf* 97-00; V Winkfield and Cranbourne *Ox* 00-08; V Wedmore w Theale and Blackford *B & W* from 08. *The Vicarage, Manor Lane, Wedmore BS28 4EL* Tel (01934) 713566 E-mail neill.hall@care4free.net

NEILL, Canon Robert Chapman. b 51. Lon Univ BD82. CITC 77. **d** 77 **p** 78. C Lurgan Ch the Redeemer *D & D* 77-82; I Tullylish 82-88; I Mt Merrion 88-98; I Drumbo from 98; Can Down Cathl from 07. *Drumbo Rectory, 5 Pinehill Road, Ballylesson, Belfast BT8 8LA* Tel (028) 9082 6225 E-mail rc.neill@talktalk.net

NEILL, Canon Stephen Mahon. b 69. TCD BA91. CITC 91. **d** 93 **p** 94. C Monkstown *D & G* 93-95; Dom Chapl to Bp of Killaloe and Clonfert *L & K* from 95; C Limerick City 95-98; I Cloughjordan w Borrisokane etc from 98; Can Limerick Cathl from 04. *Modreeny Rectory, Cloughjordan, Co Tipperary, Republic of Ireland* Tel and fax (00353) (505) 42183 Mobile 87-232 8172 E-mail paddyanglican@eircom.net

NEILL, The Ven William Barnet. b 30. TCD BA61. **d** 63 **p** 64. C Belfast St Clem *D & D* 63-66; C Dundonald 66-72; I Drumgath 72-80; I Drumgooland 78-80; I Mt Merrion 80-83; I Dromore Cathl 83-97; Adn Dromore 85-97; rtd 97. *10 Cairnshill Court, Saintfield Road, Belfast BT8 4TX* Tel (028) 9079 2969

NEILL, Canon William Benjamin Alan. b 46. Open Univ BA76. CITC 68. **d** 71 **p** 72. C Dunmurry *Conn* 71-74; C Coleraine 75-77; C Dublin St Ann w St Steph *D & G* 77-78; I Convoy w Monellan and Donaghmore *D & R* 78-81; I Faughanvale 81-86; I Waterford w Killea, Drumcannon and Dunhill *C & O* 86-97; Dean Waterford 86-97; Prec Lismore Cathl 86-97; Prec Cashel Cathl 87-97; Can Ossory and Leighlin Cathls 96-97; I Dalkey St Patr *D & G* from 97; Can Ch Ch Cathl Dublin from 04. *The Rectory, Barnacoille Park, Church Road, Dalkey, Co Dublin, Republic of Ireland* Tel (00353) (1) 280 3369

NELLIST, Canon Valerie Ann. b 48. SRN69 SCM71. St And Dioc Tr Course 87. **d** 90 **p** 94. NSM W Fife Team Min *St And* 90-99; Hon Can St Ninian's Cathl Perth from 97; R Aberdour from 99; R Burntisland from 99; R Inverkeithing from 99. *28 Glamis Gardens, Dalgety Bay, Dunfermline KY11 9TD* Tel (01383) 824066 Fax 824668 E-mail atgn02@dsl.pipex.com

NELMES, Mrs Christine. b 41. St Mary's Coll Chelt Dip Teaching63 UWE BA97. S Dios Minl Tr Scheme 92. **d** 95 **p** 96. NSM Winscombe *B & W* 95-99; Perm to Offic 00-03; P-in-c Mark w Allerton 03-08. *Yarrow Farm, Yarrow Road, Mark, Highbridge TA9 4LW* Tel (01278) 641650 E-mail revcnelmes@btinternet.com

NELSON, Christopher James. b 57. Lanc Univ MA91. Aston Tr Scheme 83 St Jo Coll Nottm BTh88. **d** 88 **p** 89. C Blackpool St Thos *Blackb* 88-90; C Altham w Clayton le Moors 90-92; V

Knuzden 92-01; V Penwortham St Mary from 01; AD Leyland from 04. *St Mary's Vicarage, 14 Cop Lane, Penwortham, Preston PR1 0SR* Tel (01772) 743143 Mobile 07858-772421 E-mail kitnel@btinternet.com

NELSON, Gibson. *See* NELSON, Robert Gibson

NELSON, Graham William. b 61. St Jo Coll Nottm BA91. **d** 91 **p** 92. C Pype Hayes *Birm* 91-93; C Lancaster St Mary *Blackb* 94-97; Chapl HM Pris Lanc Castle 94-97; P-in-c Preston St Jude w St Paul *Blackb* 97-06; P-in-c Preston St Oswald 01-06; P-in-c Preston St Oswald w St Jude from 06. *Deepdale Vicarage, 97 Garstang Road, Preston PR1 1LD* Tel (01772) 252987 E-mail gw.nelson@btinternet.com

NELSON, Hugh Edmund. b 72. Worc Coll Ox BA94. Ripon Coll Cuddesdon 07. **d** 09 **p** 10. C Upchurch w Lower Halstow *Cant* from 09; C Iwade from 09; C Newington w Hartlip and Stockbury from 09. *The Vicarage, Church Lane, Newington, Sittingbourne ME9 7JU* Tel (01795) 844345 E-mail revhughnelson@googlemail.co.uk

NELSON, Jane. b 42. **d** 94 **p** 99. Par Dn Muchalls *Bre* 94-99; C 99-04; Asst Chapl Grampian Healthcare NHS Trust 93-97; NSM Brechin from 04; NSM Tarfside from 05. *4 St Michael's Road, Newtonhill, Stonehaven AB39 3RW* Tel (01569) 730967 E-mail nelson.jane1@btinternet.com

NELSON, Mrs Julie. b 52. St Aid Coll Dur BA73 Ex Univ MA95. SWMTC 92. **d** 95 **p** 96. NSM Tavistock and Gulworthy *Ex* 95-01; Germany 01-04; P-in-c Kirklington w Burneston and Wath and Pickhill *Ripon* 04-10; AD Wensley 08-10; Dioc Adv on Women's Min 08-10; R Panfield and Rayne *Chelmsf* from 10; Dioc Rural Officer from 10. *The Rectory, Shalford Road, Rayne, Braintree CM77 6DT* Tel (01376) 341357 E-mail revjulie@tiscali.co.uk

NELSON, Michael. b 44. Newc Univ Aus BSc68 BA72 St Jo Coll Cam BA74 Cam Univ MA78. Westcott Ho Cam 74. **d** 75 **p** 76. Perm to Offic *Newc* 75; Australia from 77. *185 Burbong Street, Chapel Hill Qld 4069, Australia* Tel (0061) (7) 3720 1283 Fax 3720 1620 E-mail mnelson@hradvantage.com.au

NELSON, Canon Michael. b 44. Lon Univ BD66. Coll of Resurr Mirfield 66. **d** 68 **p** 69. C Newbold w Dunston *Derby* 68-72; C N Gosforth *Newc* 72-77; V Seaton Hirst 77-83; V Blyth St Mary 83-93; P-in-c Horton 86-87; RD Bedlington 88-93; R Hexham 93-03; Hon Can Newc Cathl 94-09; P-in-c Ovingham 03-09; RD Corbridge 03-09; rtd 09; Perm to Offic *Newc* from 09. *25 The Chase, Bedlington NE22 6BY* Tel (01670) 820784 E-mail canon.michael.nelson@care4free.net

NELSON, Sister Norma Margaret. b 34. Liv Univ DASS77 CQSW77. CA Tr Coll IDC60. **d** 93 **p** 94. TD Kirkby *Liv* 93-94; TV 94-95; rtd 95; Perm to Offic *Liv* from 95. *15 Pateley Close, Kirkby, Liverpool L32 4UT* Tel 0151-292 0255

NELSON, Canon Paul John. b 52. Nottm Univ BCombStuds84. Linc Th Coll 81. **d** 84 **p** 85. C Waltham Cross *St Alb* 84-87; C Sandridge 87-90; V 90-98; R Hundred River *St E* from 98; C Wainford from 06; RD Beccles and S Elmham 03-11; Hon Can St E Cathl from 08. *The Rectory, Moll's Lane, Brampton, Beccles NR34 8DB* Tel (01502) 575859

NELSON, Peter Joseph. b 46. Nottm Poly BSc73. N Bapt Coll 82 NEOC 99. **d** 99 **p** 99. In Bapt Min 85-99; Chapl R Hull Hosps NHS Trust 94-99; Chapl Hull and E Yorks Hosps NHS Trust 99-02; Sen Chapl from 02; NSM Sutton St Mich *York* 99-06. *Cobblestones, 1 Low Street, Sancton, York YO43 4QZ* Tel (01430) 828779 *or* (01482) 674427

NELSON, Ralph Archbold. b 27. St Cuth Soc Dur BA50. Bps' Coll Cheshunt 50. **d** 52 **p** 53. C Penwortham St Mary *Blackb* 52-57; C Eglingham *Newc* 57-58; V Featherstone *Wakef* 58-80; V Kirkham *Blackb* 80-92; RD Kirkham 88-91; rtd 92; Perm to Offic *Blackb* from 92. *6 Blundell Lane, Penwortham, Preston PR1 0EA* Tel (01772) 742573

NELSON, Robert Gibson. b 34. ALCD61. **d** 61 **p** 62. C Isleworth St Mary *Lon* 61-64; C-in-c Reading St Barn CD *Ox* 64-69; R Margaret River Australia 69-72; V Guernsey St Jo *Win* 72-78; R Guernsey Ste Marie du Castel 78-86; V Guernsey St Matt 84-86; rtd 86; Perm to Offic *Win* from 86. *Le Petit Feugre, Clos des Mielles, Castel, Guernsey GY5 7XB* Tel (01481) 52726

NELSON, Robert Towers. b 43. MSOSc Liv Coll of Tech BSc65. NW Ord Course 76. **d** 79 **p** 80. NSM Liv Our Lady and St Nic w St Anne 79-83; NSM Liscard St Thos *Ches* 83-87; P-in-c from 87; Ind Missr from 87; Asst Sec SOSc from 89; Perm to Offic *Liv* 89-98; Chapl Wirral and W Cheshire Community NHS Trust 98-03. *5 Sedbergh Road, Wallasey CH44 2BR* Tel 0151-630 2830

NELSON, Roger Charles. b 44. ATII74 Newc Univ LLB66 Solicitor 69. Cant Sch of Min 88. **d** 91 **p** 92. NSM Deal St Leon and St Rich and Sholden *Cant* 91-96; NSM Northbourne and Gt Mongeham w Ripple and Sutton by Dover 96-97; Perm to Offic *Cant* 97-00 and *Wakef* from 01. *26 Meal Hill Road, Holme, Holmfirth HD9 2QQ* Tel (01484) 680309 E-mail nelsontrap@aol.com

NELSON, Warren David. b 38. TCD BA67. **d** 68 **p** 69. C Belfast St Mich *Conn* 68-70; I Kilcooley w Littleton, Crohane, Killenaule etc *C & O* 70-76; Chapl Coalbrook Fellowship Hosp Ho Thurles 76-94; Perm to Offic (Cashel, Waterford and

Lismore) 93-94; I Lurgan w Billis, Killinkere and Munterconnaught *K, E & A* 94-98; rtd 98. *6 Mucklagh, Tullamore, Co Offaly, Republic of Ireland* Tel (00353) (57) 932 4218 E-mail wnelson@eircom.net

NELSON, William. b 38. Oak Hill Th Coll 74. **d** 76 **p** 77. C Hensingham *Carl* 76-81; V Widnes St Paul *Liv* 81-89; R Higher Openshaw *Man* 89-03; AD Ardwick 96-00; rtd 03; Perm to Offic *S'well* from 03. *215 Stapleford Road, Trowell, Nottingham NG9 3QE* Tel 0115-932 2910

NENER, Canon Thomas Paul Edgar. b 42. Liv Univ MB, ChB FRCSEd71 FRCS71. Coll of Resurr Mirfield 78. **d** 80 **p** 81. C Warrington St Elphin *Liv* 80-83; V Haydock St Jas 83-95; V W Derby St Jo 95-10; Hon Can Liv Cathl 95-10; rtd 10. *16 Princes Park Mansions, Croxteth Road, Liverpool L8 3SA* Tel 0151-726 7003

NENO, David Edward. b 62. SS Mark & Jo Univ Coll Plymouth BA85. Ripon Coll Cuddesdon 85. **d** 88 **p** 89. C Chapel Allerton *Ripon* 88-91; C Acton St Mary *Lon* 91-94; V Kingsbury H Innocents 94-02; R Brondesbury Ch Ch and St Laur from 02. *The Rectory, Chevening Road, London NW6 6DU* Tel (020) 8969 5961 Mobile 07976-905294 E-mail d.s.neno@dial.pipex.com

NESBITT, Heather Hastings. b 48. S'wark Ord Course 88. **d** 90 **p** 94. Par Dn Camberwell St Luke *S'wark* 90-94; C Addiscombe St Mary Magd w St Martin 94-01; TV Sutton St Jas and Wawne *York* 01-10; rtd 10. *36 Peterborough Way, Sleaford NG34 8TW* Tel (01529) 419298 E-mail h.nesbitt@yahoo.co.uk

NESBITT, Patrick Joseph. b 72. St Martin's Coll Lanc BA96. St Jo Coll Nottm 00. **d** 03 **p** 04. C Blackpool St Thos *Blackb* 03-07; TV Kinson and W Howe *Sarum* from 07. *St Andrew's Rectory, 51 Milhams Road, Bournemouth BH10 7LJ* Tel (01202) 571996 Mobile 07879-660100 E-mail patricknesbitt72@hotmail.com

NESBITT, Canon Ronald. b 58. Sheff Univ LLB. CITC 82. **d** 85 **p** 86. C Ballymena w Ballyclug *Conn* 85-88; C Holywood *D & D* 88-90; I Helen's Bay 90-96; I Bangor Abbey from 96; Can Belf Cathl from 04. *The Abbey Rectory, 5 Downshire Road, Bangor BT20 3TW* Tel (028) 9146 0173 E-mail ronnienesbitt@aol.com *or* bangorabbeyparish@gmail.com

NESBITT, Miss Wilhelmina. b 65. Qu Coll Birm 98. **d** 00 **p** 01. C Bridgnorth, Tasley, Astley Abbotts, etc *Heref* 00-04; TV Saddleworth *Man* 04-08; I Fanlobbus Union *C, C & R* from 08. *The Rectory, Sackville Street, Dunmanway, Co Cork, Republic of Ireland* Tel and fax (00353) (23) 884 5151 E-mail willinesbitt@eircom.net

NETHERWAY, Diana Margaret. b 47. Bp Otter Coll 94. **d** 96. NSM Northwood *Portsm* from 96; NSM Gurnard from 96; Asst Chapl Isle of Wight NHS Primary Care Trust from 09. *138 Bellevue Road, Cowes PO31 7LD* Tel (01983) 298505 E-mail revdiana@onwight.net

NETHERWAY, Robert Sydney. b 37. Bp Otter Coll 94. **d** 96. NSM Cowes St Faith *Portsm* 96-07; Perm to Offic from 07. *138 Bellevue Road, Cowes PO31 7LD* Tel (01983) 298505 E-mail revbob@onwight.net

NETHERWOOD, Mrs Anne Christine. b 43. Liv Univ BArch66 Lon Univ BD92 ARIBA68. St Deiniol's Hawarden 88. **d** 91 **p** 94. NSM Ellesmere and Welsh Frankton 91-94; C Dudleston 94-97; C Criftins 94-97; C Criftins w Dudleston and Welsh Frankton 97; P-in-c Criftins w Dudleston and Welsh Frankton 97-10; rtd 10; Perm to Offic *Lich* from 10. *11 Cottage Fields, St Martins, Oswestry SY11 3EJ* Tel (01691) 778495 E-mail anne_netherwood@talk21.com

NEUDEGG, Mrs Joan Mary. b 36. Cant Sch of Min 81. dss 84 **d** 87 **p** 94. Chalk *Roch* 84-86; Hon C Dean Forest H Trin *Glouc* 87-90; Hon C Woolaston w Alvington 90-95; Hon C Woolaston w Alvington and Aylburton 95-96; rtd 96; Perm to Offic *Ex* from 96. *48 Marker Way, Honiton EX14 2EN* Tel (01404) 43957

NEUPERT, Douglas Alan. b 46. Chris Newport Univ (USA) BA78. Dioc OLM tr scheme 97. **d** 99 **p** 00. OLM Blackbourne *St E* from 99. *Hall Farm, Troston, Bury St Edmunds IP31 1EZ* Tel (01359) 269614 Mobile 07944-214417 E-mail doug_neupert@eu.odedodea.edu

NEVILL, James Michael. b 50. Cranmer Hall Dur 84. **d** 86 **p** 87. C Sowerby Bridge w Norland *Wakef* 86-91; CF 91-94; TV Broadwater *Chich* 94-99; Chapl St Mich Hospice Hereford 99-05; Spiritual Care Co-ord St Cath Hospice from 05. *St Catherine's Hospice, Malthouse Road, Crawley RH10 6BH* Tel (01293) 447333 Fax 611977

NEVILL, Mavis Hetty. b 45. Bradf Univ BEd95. NOC 92. **d** 95 **p** 96. NSM Mount Pellon *Wakef* 95-99; P-in-c Mixenden 99-04; Hon C Harden and Wilsden *Bradf* 06-07; P-in-c Steeton 07-11; rtd 11. *1 Willow Bank Close, Allerton, Bradford BD15 7YL* E-mail mh.nevill@btinternet.com

NEVILLE, Alfred John. b 21. K Coll Lon BA40. Sarum & Wells Th Coll 80. **d** 83 **p** 84. NSM Weston-super-Mare St Paul *B & W* 83-93; Perm to Offic from 93. *10 Clarence House, 17 Clarence Road North, Weston-super-Mare BS23 4AS* Tel (01934) 631116

NEVILLE, David Bruce. b 61. Ravensbourne Coll of Art & Design BA83. St Jo Coll Nottm 87. **d** 91 **p** 92. C Broxtowe *S'well* 91-94; C Attenborough 94-95; Perm to Offic 95-97; C Carrington

97-99; C Bulwell St Mary 99-02; Perm to Offic from 02. *3 Inham Road, Beeston, Nottingham NG9 4FL* Tel 0115-854 5648 E-mail rev.dnev@virgin.net

NEVILLE, Michael Robert John. b 56. Hatf Coll Dur BA80 Hughes Hall Cam PGCE81. Wycliffe Hall Ox 82. **d** 85 **p** 86. C E Twickenham St Steph *Lon* 85-88; Asst Dir Proclamation Trust 88-93; R Fordham *Chelmsf* 93-11; P-in-c Upper Chelsea St Sav and St Simon *Lon* from 11. *St Simon Zelotes Vicarage, 34 Milner Street, London SW3 2QF* Tel (020) 7589 8999 E-mail mike.neville@btinternet.com

NEVILLE, Paul Stewart David. b 61. Wycliffe Hall Ox 98. **d** 00 **p** 01. C Chester le Street *Dur* 00-03; R Middleton St George from 03; R Sadberge from 03. *17 Hunters Green, Middleton St George, Darlington DL2 1DZ* Tel (01325) 332017

NEVIN, Alan Joseph. b 51. Univ Coll Galway BA72 MCIPD80. CITC 87. **d** 92 **p** 93. Aux Min Youghal Union *C, C & R* 92-94; Aux Min Waterford w Killea, Drumcannon and Dunhill *C & O* 94-95; C 95-98; I Bunclody w Kildavin, Clonegal and Kilrush 98-04; I Clonfert Gp *L & K* from 04. *The Rectory, Banagher, Birr, Co Offaly, Republic of Ireland* Tel and fax (00353) (57) 915 1269 Mobile 87-285 8251 E-mail clonfert@clonfert.anglican.org

NEVIN, Graham Harold. b 45. QUB BSc68 MSc72 Ulster Poly CertEd74 FGS75. St Jo Coll Nottm 06. **d** 09 **p** 10. NSM Billy w Derrykeighan *Conn* from 09. *11 Carthall Crescent, Coleraine BT51 3LT* Tel (028) 7035 3713 E-mail graham@carthall.fsnet.co.uk

NEW, David John. b 37. Lon Univ BScEng58. Chich Th Coll 65. **d** 67 **p** 68. C Folkestone St Mary and St Eanswythe *Cant* 67-72; C Kings Heath *Birm* 72-74; V S Yardley St Mich 74-83; V Moseley St Agnes 83-00; rtd 00; Perm to Offic *Worc* from 00. *6 Falmouth, Worcester WR4 0TE* Tel (01905) 458084 E-mail david@revnew.freeserve.co.uk

NEW, Derek. b 30. **d** 86 **p** 87. NSM Brondesbury St Anne w Kilburn H Trin *Lon* 86-98; NSM Willesden St Matt 99-02; Perm to Offic from 02. *20 Lynton Road, London NW6 6BL* Tel (020) 7912 0640

NEW, Canon Thomas Stephen. b 30. K Coll Cam BA52 MA56. Cuddesdon Coll 52. **d** 54 **p** 55. C Greenford H Cross *Lon* 54-55; C Old St Pancras w Bedford New Town St Matt 55-58; C Woodham *Guildf* 58-64; V Guildf All SS 64-72; V Banstead 72-93; RD Epsom 76-80; Hon Can Guildf Cathl 79-93; Sub-Chapl HM Pris Downview 88-93; rtd 93; Perm to Offic *Ex* from 94. *St Katharine's, North Street, Denbury, Newton Abbot TQ12 6DJ* Tel (01803) 813775

NEW ZEALAND, Archbishop of. *See* TUREI, The Most Revd William Brown

NEWALL, Arthur William. b 24. Univ of Wales (Lamp) BA49. Chich Th Coll 49. **d** 51 **p** 52. C Hulme St Phil *Man* 51-53; C Fallowfield 53-55; V Oldham St Barn 55-60; V Aspull *Liv* 60-68; R Foots Cray *Roch* 68-78; V Henlow St Alb 78-89; rtd 89; Perm to Offic *Liv* from 89. *38 Fairhaven Road, Southport PR9 9UH* Tel (01704) 26045

NEWALL, Richard Lucas. b 43. K Coll Lon AKC66. **d** 66 **p** 67. C Roby *Liv* 66-69; C Douglas St Geo and St Barn *S & M* 69-71; Lic to Offic *Man* 72-75; C Ban St Mary 75-77; R Newborough w Llangeinwen w Llangaffo etc 77-97; R Newborough w Llanidan and Llangeinwen etc 98-07; AD Tindaethwy and Menai 03-07; V Llanilar w Rhostie and Llangwyryfon etc *St D* 07-09; rtd 09. *Himmelbjerg, 18 Maesydderwen, Cardigan SA43 1PE* Tel (01239) 623816

NEWARK, Archdeacon of. Vacant.

NEWBOLD, Mrs Caroline Sarah. b 62. K Alfred's Coll Win BA83 Homerton Coll Cam PGCE85. St Mellitus Coll BA10. **d** 10 **p** 11. C Yiewsley *Lon* from 10. *St Stephen's Vicarage, Sherborne Gardens, London W13 8AQ* Tel 07958-073583 (mobile) E-mail caroline.newbold@tiscali.co.uk

NEWBOLD, Stephen Mark. b 60. Trin Coll Bris 01. **d** 03 **p** 04. C Roxeth *Lon* 03-09; V Ealing St Steph Castle Hill from 09. *St Stephen's Vicarage, Sherborne Gardens, London W13 8AQ* Tel (020) 8864 4929

NEWBON, Kenneth. b 29. Wells Th Coll 67. **d** 69 **p** 70. C Church Stretton *Heref* 69-72; P-in-c Cressage w Sheinton 72-75; R Braunstone *Leic* 75-81; TR 81-84; P-in-c Eardisley w Bollingham and Willersley *Heref* 84-88; P-in-c Brilley w Michaelchurch on Arrow 84-88; P-in-c Whitney w Winforton 84-88; RD Kington and Weobley 87-95; R Eardisley w Bollingham, Willersley, Brilley etc 88-96; rtd 96; Perm to Offic *Heref* from 96. *Grace Dieu House, Staunton-on-Wye, Hereford HR4 7LT* Tel (01981) 500188

NEWBON, Michael Charles. b 59. Oak Hill Th Coll 92. **d** 94 **p** 95. C Bedford St Jo and St Leon *St Alb* 94-99; V Luton St Fran 99-11; P-in-c Georgeham *Ex* from 11. *The Rectory, Newberry Road, Georgeham, Braunton EX33 1JS* Tel (01271) 890616 E-mail mikenewbon@aol.com

NEWBORN, Carol Margaret. b 45. **d** 05 **p** 06. OLM Styvechale *Cov* from 05. *76 The Park Paling, Coventry CV3 5LL* Tel (024) 7650 3707 E-mail rev.carol@newborn.org.uk

NEWBY, Mrs Ailsa Ballantyne. b 56. Collingwood Coll Dur BA78. St Steph Ho Ox 98. **d** 98 **p** 99. C Streatham Ch Ch *S'wark*

98-01; V S Lambeth St Anne and All SS 01-10; TR Putney St Mary from 10; Dir IME Kingston Area from 10. *21 Landford Road, London SW15 1AQ* Tel (020) 8785 6019
E-mail ailsanewby@f2s.com

NEWBY, Peter Gordon. b 23. d 64 p 65. C Leic St Phil 64-69; R Lt Bowden St Nic 69-72; V Jersey Gouray St Martin *Win* 72-77; Chapl Jersey Gp of Hosps 78-80; R Much Birch w Lt Birch, Much Dewchurch etc *Heref* 80-88; rtd 89; Perm to Offic *Ex* from 90. *The Shippen, Lower Hampton Farm, Shute, Axminster EX13 7PA*

NEWBY, Mrs Susan. b 48. Lady Spencer Chu Coll of Educn CertEd70 BEd71. d 04 p 05. OLM Adderbury w Milton *Ox* 04-10; NSM Banbury from 10. *2 Meadow View, Adderbury, Banbury OX17 3LZ* Tel 07766-716659 (mobile)
E-mail susan@newby4448.freeserve.co.uk

NEWCASTLE (AUSTRALIA), Dean of. See RIGNEY, The Very Revd James Thomas

NEWCASTLE, Bishop of. See WHARTON, The Rt Revd John Martin

NEWCASTLE, Dean of. See DALLISTON, The Very Revd Christopher Charles

NEWCOMBE, Andrew Charles. b 70. Melbourne Univ BA92 BMus93 Monash Univ Aus DipEd96 LTCL93. St Steph Ho Ox 03. d 05 p 06. C Tottenham St Mary *Lon* 05-08; C Edmonton St Alphege from 08; C Ponders End St Matt from 08. *St Matthew's Vicarage, 1 Church Road, Enfield EN3 4NT* Tel (020) 8443 2255 Mobile 07931-700675
E-mail andrewnewcombe@yahoo.co.uk

NEWCOMBE, John Adrian. b 61. Univ of Wales (Lamp) BA83 SS Paul & Mary Coll Cheltenham PGCE85, Ripon Coll Cuddesdon 90. d 92 p 93. C Stroud and Uplands w Slad *Glouc* 92-96; C Nailsworth 96-01; P-in-c Childswyckham w Aston Somerville, Buckland etc 01-05; TV Winchcombe from 05. *New Vicarage, Buckland Road, Childswickham, Broadway WR12 7HH* Tel (01386) 853824

NEWCOMBE, John Charlie. BSc. Ridley Hall Cam. d 07 p 08. NSM Wimbledon Em Ridgway Prop Chpl *S'wark* 07-10; Asst Chapl Tervuren *Eur* from 10. *St Paul's Church Centre, Hoornzeelstraat24, 3080 Tervuren, Belgium* Tel (0032) (2) 767 3435 Fax 688 0989 E-mail charlienewc@clara.co.uk

NEWCOMBE, Canon Timothy James Grahame. b 47. AKC75. St Aug Coll Cant 75. d 76 p 77. C Heref St Martin 76-79; C Hitchin *St Alb* 79-85; R Croft and Stoney Stanton *Leic* 85-91; P-in-c Launceston *Truro* 91-92; V Launceston 92-97; TR Launceston 97-03; Hon Can Truro Cathl 01-03; Chapl Cornwall Healthcare NHS Trust 96-03; V Wotton St Mary *Glouc* from 03. *Holy Trinity Vicarage, Church Road, Longlevens, Gloucester GL2 0AJ* Tel (01452) 524129 E-mail tnewco@tiscali.co.uk

✠**NEWCOME, The Rt Revd James William Scobie.** b 53. Trin Coll Ox BA74 MA78 Selw Coll Cam BA77 MA81. Ridley Hall Cam 75. d 78 p 79 c 02. C Leavesden *St Alb* 78-82; P-in-c Bar Hill LEP *Ely* 82-92; V Bar Hill 92-94; Tutor Ridley Hall Cam 83-88; P-in-c Dry Drayton *Ely* 89-94; RD N Stowe 93-94; Can Res Ches Cathl and Dioc Dir of Ords 94-02; Dir of Educn and Tr 96-02; Suff Bp Penrith *Carl* 02-09; Bp Carl from 09. *Bishop's House, Ambleside Road, Keswick CA12 4DD* Tel (01768) 773430
E-mail bishop.carlisle@carlislediocese.org.uk

NEWELL, Aubrey Francis Thomas. b 20. St D Coll Lamp BA43. d 45 p 46. C Rhosddu *St As* 45-49; C Llanwnog *Ban* 49-50; C Gabalfa *Llan* 50-51; C Gt Marlow *Ox* 53-57; R Lavendon w Cold Brayfield 57-62; V Gawcott and Hillesden 62-77; P-in-c Radclive 69-72; RD Buckingham 70-76 and 82-84; P-in-c Padbury w Adstock 72-77; V Lenborough 77-87; rtd 87; Perm to Offic *Ox* 89-00 and *St D* from 07. *Station House, Glandyfi, Machynlleth SY20 8SS* Tel (01654) 781307

NEWELL, Christopher David. b 53. Ex Univ MA03. S'wark Ord Course 84. d 87 p 88. C Stockwell St Mich *S'wark* 87-90; Asst Chapl R Lon Hosp (Whitechapel) 90-92; Asst Chapl R Lon Hosp (Mile End) 90-92; R Birch St Agnes *Man* 92-96; P-in-c Longsight St Jo w St Cypr 94-96; R Birch St Agnes w Longsight St Jo w St Cypr 97; R Lansallos and V Talland *Truro* 97-98; Asst P Liskeard and Keyne 00-02; C Duloe, Herodsfoot, Morval and St Pinnock 02-03; P-in-c 03-05; C Lansallos and Talland 02-03; Chapl Cornwall Partnership NHS Trust from 02. *4 Russell Street, Liskeard PL14 4BP* Tel (01579) 349617
E-mail christopher.newell@cpt.cornwall.nhs.uk

NEWELL, David Walter. b 37. Nottm Univ BSc57. WEMTC 01. d 03 p 04. OLM Painswick, Sheepscombe, Cranham, The Edge etc *Glouc* from 03. *Woodside, Kingsmill Lane, Painswick, Stroud GL6 6SA* Tel (01452) 812083
E-mail d.newell083@btinternet.com

NEWELL, Canon Edmund John. b 61. Univ Coll Lon BSc83 Nuff Coll Ox DPhil88 MA89 FRHistS98 FRSA08. Ox Min Course 89 Ripon Coll Cuddesdon 92. d 94 p 95. C Deddington w Barford, Clifton and Hempton *Ox* 94-98; Bp's Dom Chapl 98-01; Chapl Headington Sch 98-01; Can Res St Paul's Cathl 01-08; Chan 03-08; Can Res and Sub-Dean Ch Ch *Ox* from 08. *Christ Church, Oxford OX1 1DP* Tel (01865) 276278
E-mail edmund.newell@chch.ox.ac.uk

NEWELL, Jack Ernest. b 26. CEng FIChemE ARCS BSc. Glouc Th Course 80. d 83 p 84. NSM Hempsted *Glouc* 83-96; Perm to Offic from 96. *Hempsted House, Rectory Lane, Hempsted, Gloucester GL2 5LW* Tel (01452) 523320

NEWELL, Kenneth Ernest. b 22. S Dios Minl Tr Scheme 77. d 79 p 80. NSM Lynton, Brendon, Countisbury, Lynmouth etc *Ex* 79-85; TR 85-89; RD Shirwell 84-89; rtd 89; Perm to Offic *Ex* 89-09. *Mole End, Lydiate Lane, Lynton EX35 6HE*

NEWELL, Samuel James. b 28. TCD BA53 MA63. TCD Div Sch Div Test54. d 54 p 55. C Belfast St Mary *Conn* 54-57; C Derriaghy 57-60; C Reading St Mary V *Ox* 60-63; V Chesham Ch Ch 63-74; P-in-c Wraysbury 74-78; TV Riverside 78-94; rtd 94; Perm to Offic *Ox* 97-10. *41 Redford Road, Windsor SL4 5ST* Tel (01753) 862300

NEWELL OF STAFFA, Gerald Frederick Watson. b 34. Sarum Th Coll 56. d 59 p 61. C Southampton SS Pet and Paul w All SS *Win* 59-61; C Overton w Laverstoke and Freefolk 61-63; CF (TA) 61-63; CF 63-66; R Spennithorne *Ripon* 66-68; R Finghall 66-68; R Hauxwell 66-68; Hon C Steyning *Chich* 74-78; Perm to Offic *Ex* 93-95 and 99-00; P-in-c Breamore *Win* 95-98; rtd 99; P-in-c Palermo w Taormina *Eur* 99-00; R Glencarse *Bre* 00-03; Perm to Offic *Ox* 04-06 and from 10. *Church Cottage, Compton Beauchamp, Swindon SN6 8NN* Tel (01738) 710334

NEWELL PRICE, John Charles. b 29. SS Coll Cam BA50 MA MB, BChir MRCGP. d 91 p 94. OLM Frensham *Guildf* 91-99; rtd 99; Perm to Offic *Guildf* 99-05. *The Linney, Clamoak, Bere Alston, Yelverton PL20 7BU* Tel (01822) 841126

NEWEY, Edmund James. b 71. Linc Coll Ox BA95 MA97 Em Coll Cam BA99 Man Univ PhD08. Westcott Ho Cam 97. d 00 p 01. C Birch w Fallowfield *Man* 00-03; R Newmarket St Mary w Exning St Agnes *St E* 03-07; V Handsworth St Andr *Birm* from 07. *St Andrew's Vicarage, 55 Laurel Road, Handsworth, Birmingham B21 9PB* Tel 0121-551 2097 Mobile 07986-530511
E-mail ejnewey@waitrose.com

NEWHAM, Simon Frank Eric. b 65. Sheff Univ BSc87 MSc89. Trin Coll Bris BA00. d 00 p 01. C Horsham *Chich* 00-04; P-in-c Wisborough Green 04-09; V 09-10; RD Petworth 06-09; TR Ifield from 10. *Capella, Rusper Road, Ifield, Crawley RH11 0LR* Tel (01293) 543126
E-mail simon_newham@revd.fsbusiness.co.uk

✠**NEWING, The Rt Revd Dom Kenneth Albert.** b 23. Selw Coll Cam BA53 MA57. Coll of Resurr Mirfield 53. d 55 p 56 c 82. C Plymstock *Ex* 55-63; R Plympton St Maurice 63-82; RD Plympton 71-76; Preb Ex Cathl 75-82; Adn Plymouth 78-82; Suff Bp Plymouth 82-88; Lic to Offic *Ox* 88-93; OSB from 89; rtd 93. *St Benedict's Priory, 19A The Close, Salisbury SP1 2EB*

NEWING, Peter. b 33. Birm Univ CertEd55 Dur Univ BA63 Bris Univ BEd76 State Univ NY BSc85 EdD88 FRSA60 FSAScot59 ACP67 MCollP86 FCollP95 APhS63 FVCM01. Cranmer Hall Dur 63. d 65 p 66. C Blockley w Aston Magna *Glouc* 65-69; P-in-c Taynton 69-75; P-in-c Tibberton 69-75; R Brimpsfield w Elkstone and Syde 75-83; R Brimpsfield, Cranham, Elkstone and Syde 83-97; P-in-c Daglingworth w the Duntisbournes and Winstone 95-97; R Brimpsfield w Birdlip, Syde, Daglingworth etc 97-01; C Redmarley D'Abitot, Bromesberrow, Pauntley etc 01-02; NSM 02-10; rtd 02; Perm to Offic *Heref* from 02; *Worc* from 04; *Glouc* from 10. *1 Hambutts Mead, Painswick, Stroud GL6 6RP* Tel (01452) 814360

NEWITT, Mark Julian. b 76. Bradf Univ BSc97 St Jo Coll Dur BA02. Cranmer Hall Dur 00. d 03 p 04. C Billing *Pet* 03-06; Asst Chapl Sheff Teaching Hosps NHS Foundn Trust from 06. *Chaplaincy Services, Royal Hallamshire Hospital, Glossop Road, Sheffield S10 2JF* Tel 0114-271 1900

NEWLAND, Mrs Patricia Frances. b 35. Edin Univ MA56. EAMTC 96. d 97 p 98. NSM Duxford *Ely* 97-02; NSM Hinxton 97-02; NSM Ickleton 97-02; rtd 02; Perm to Offic *Ely* from 02. *Ickleton Lodge, 14 Frogge Street, Ickleton, Saffron Walden CB10 1SH* Tel (01799) 530268 Fax 531146
E-mail patricia.newland@googlemail.com

NEWLANDS, Christopher William. b 57. Bris Univ BA79. Westcott Ho Cam 81. d 84 p 85. C Bishop's Waltham *Portsm* 84-87; Hon C Upham 85-87; Prec, Sacr and Min Can Dur Cathl 87-92; Chapl Bucharest w Sofia *Eur* 92-95; V Shrub End *Chelmsf* 96-04; Bp's Chapl 04-10; P-in-c Lancaster St Mary w St John and St Anne *Blackb* 10-11; V from 11. *The Vicarage, Priory Close, Lancaster LA1 1YZ* Tel (01524) 63200
E-mail cnewlands@gmail.com

NEWLANDS, Prof George McLeod. b 41. Edin Univ MA63 DLitt05 Heidelberg Univ BD66 PhD70 Ch Coll Cam MA73 FRSE08. d 82 p 82. Lect Cam Univ 73-86; Fell and Dean Trin Hall Cam 82-86; Prof Div Glas Univ 86-08; Perm to Offic *Glas* from 86. *12 Jamaica Street Lane, Edinburgh EH3 6HQ*, or *49 Highsett, Cambridge CB2 1NZ* Tel 0131-225 2545 or (01223) 569984 Mobile 07979-691966
E-mail newlands71@hotmail.com

NEWLYN, Canon Edwin. b 39. AKC64. d 65 p 66. C Belgrave St Mich *Leic* 65-68; Miss to Seamen 68-81; Chapl Santos Brazil 68-69; Asst Chapl Glas and C Glas St Gabr 69-73; Chapl E Lon S Africa 73-76; R W Bank St Pet 75-76; V Fylingdales *York* 81;

P-in-c Hawsker 81; V Fylingdales and Hawsker cum Stainsacre 81-88; RD Whitby 85-92; Sec Dioc Adv Cttee for Care of Chs 87-01; P-in-c Goathland 88-99; Can and Preb York Minster 90-08; rtd 01; Perm to Offic *York* from 01. *The Garden Flat, 12 Royal Crescent, Whitby YO21 3EJ* Tel (01947) 604533 E-mail edwin.newlyn@talktalk.net

✠NEWMAN, The Rt Revd Adrian. b 58. Bris Univ BSc80 MPhil89. Trin Coll Bris 82. d 85 p 86 c 11. C Forest Gate St Mark *Chelmsf* 85-89; V Hillsborough and Wadsley Bridge *Sheff* 89-96; RD Hallam 94-96; R Birm St Martin w Bordesley St Andr 96-05; Hon Can Birm Cathl 01-05; Dean Roch 05-11; Area Bp Stepney *Lon* from 11. *63 Coborn Road, London E3 2DB* Tel (020) 8981 2323 Fax 8981 8015 E-mail bishop.stepney@london.anglican.org

NEWMAN, Mrs Alison Myra. b 55. K Coll Lon BD77. SEITE 99. d 02 p 03. C Bromley SS Pet and Paul *Roch* 02-06; C Shortlands 06-08; C Farnborough from 08. *Church House, Leamington Avenue, Orpington BR6 9QB* Tel (01689) 854451 E-mail alison@st-nicks.org.uk

NEWMAN, Christopher David. b 81. Bath Univ BSc02 Anglia Ruskin Univ BA10. Ridley Hall Cam 07. d 11. C Canonbury St Steph *Lon* from 11. *16A Cleveland Road, London N1 3ET* Tel 07788-413611 (mobile) E-mail chris@stsc.org.uk

NEWMAN, David. *See* NEWMAN, Richard David

NEWMAN, David Malcolm. b 58. FSAScot81 Aber Univ BTh. St Steph Ho Ox 89. d 91 p 92. C St Mary-at-Latton *Chelmsf* 91-94; R Weeley and Lt Clacton from 94. *The Vicarage, 2 Holland Road, Little Clacton, Clacton-on-Sea CO16 9RS* Tel (01255) 860241

NEWMAN, The Ven David Maurice Frederick. b 54. Hertf Coll Ox BA75 MA79. St Jo Coll Nottm. d 79 p 80. C Orpington Ch Ch *Roch* 79-83; C Bushbury *Lich* 83-86; V Ockbrook *Derby* 86-97; TR Loughborough Em and St Mary in Charnwood *Leic* 97-09; RD Akeley E 99-06; Hon Can Leic Cathl 06-09; Adn Loughborough from 09. *The Archdeaconry, 21 Church Road, Glenfield, Leicester LE3 8DP* Tel 0116-231 1632

NEWMAN, Mrs Diana Joan. b 43. Sarum Th Coll 81. dss 84 d 87 p 94. Parkstone St Pet and St Osmund w Branksea *Sarum* from 84; NSM from 87; TV 96-02. *62 Vale Road, Poole BH14 9AU* Tel and fax (01202) 745136 E-mail diana.n@ntlworld.com

NEWMAN, Ms Elizabeth Ann. b 57. K Coll Lon BD79 Hull Univ CQSW81. d 05 p 06. OLM Charlton *S'wark* from 05; Chapl Blackheath Bluecoat C of E Sch from 11. *66 Annandale Road, London SE10 0DB* Tel (020) 8305 0642 E-mail newman66@btopenworld.com

NEWMAN, Mrs Helen Margaret. b 58. York Univ BA80 Nottm Univ MA02. EMMTC 99. d 02 p 03. NSM Thorpe Acre w Dishley *Leic* 02-05; NSM Loughborough Em and St Mary in Charnwood 05-09; Chapl LOROS Hospice from 09. *The Archdeaconry, 21 Church Road, Glenfield, Leicester LE3 8DP* Tel 0116-231 1632 E-mail helen@astad.org

NEWMAN, James Edwin Michael. b 59. Nottm Univ BA80 Ox Univ BA90. Wycliffe Hall Ox 88. d 91 p 92. C Bidston *Ches* 91-95; C Cheadle from 95. *4 Cuthbert Road, Cheadle SK8 2DT* Tel 0161-428 3983 E-mail mike@stcuthberts.org

NEWMAN, John Humphrey. b 17. ALCD49. d 49 p 50. C Hove Bp Hannington Memorial Ch *Chich* 49-52; V Welling *Roch* 52-64; V Penge St Jo 64-74; R Knockholt 74-82; rtd 82; Perm to Offic *Chich* from 82. *Lauriston Christian Care Home, 40 The Green, St Leonards-on-Sea TN38 0SY*

NEWMAN, Kevin Richard. b 74. Warwick Univ BSc95 PGCE96. Oak Hill Th Coll BA06. d 06 p 07. C Crowborough *Chich* 06-10. *Address temp unknown* E-mail kev@kevandfran.co.uk

NEWMAN, Mrs Lynda Elizabeth. b 61. Univ of Wales (Swansea) DipEd81 BEd83 MEd93. St Mich Coll Llan 07. d 10 p 11. NSM Neath *Llan* from 10. *22 Falcon Drive, Cimla, Neath SA11 3SG* Tel (01639) 633354 E-mail l newman50@hotmail.com

NEWMAN, Michael Alan. b 40. Chich Th Coll 67. d 70 p 71. C Kilburn St Aug *Lon* 70-73; C St Geo-in-the-East St Mary 75-78; rtd 78. *April Cottage, Georges Lane, Storrington, Pulborough RH20 3JH* Tel (01903) 744354 E-mail tcepriest@tiscali.co.uk

NEWMAN, Preb Michael John. b 50. Leic Univ BA72 MA75. Cuddesdon Coll 73. d 75 p 76. C Tettenhall Regis *Lich* 75-79; C Uttoxeter w Bramshall 79-82; R Norton Canes 82-89; TR Rugeley 89-06; TR Brereton and Rugeley from 06; RD Rugeley from 07; Preb Lich Cathl from 02. *The Rectory, 20 Church Street, Rugeley WS15 2AB* Tel (01889) 582149

NEWMAN, Canon Michael Robert. b 30. K Coll Lon BD61. St Jo Coll Auckland LTh53. d 54 p 55. New Zealand 54-58; C Hampstead St Jo *Lon* 58-61; New Zealand from 61; Can Auckland 81-93. *2/26 Alfriston Road, Manurewa East, Manukau 2102, New Zealand* Tel (0064) (9) 267 4357 E-mail bobnewman@xtra.co.nz

NEWMAN, Paul. b 65. St Martin's Coll Lanc BA90. Oak Hill Th Coll. d 00 p 01. C Poynton *Ches* 00-04; V Barnton from 04. *The Vicarage, Church Road, Barnton, Northwich CW8 4JH* Tel (01606) 74358 E-mail scallyvic@yahoo.com

NEWMAN, Paul Anthony. b 48. Lon Univ BSc70. Coll of Resurr Mirfield 73. d 76 p 77. C Catford St Laur *S'wark* 76-81; TV

Grays All SS *Chelmsf* 81-83; TV Lt Thurrock St Mary 81-83; Youth Chapl W Ham Adnry 83-87; P-in-c Forest Gate All SS 83-89; V 89-91; Dep Chapl HM Pris Wormwood Scrubs 91-92; Chapl HM Pris Downview 92-02; Chapl HM Pris Win 02-07; Chapl HM Pris Kingston (Portsm) from 07. *HM Prison Kingston, 122 Milton Road, Portsmouth PO3 6AS* Tel (023) 9295 3229 E-mail paul.anthony.newman@hmps.gsi.gov.uk

NEWMAN, Richard David. b 38. BNC Ox BA60 MA63. Lich Th Coll 60. d 62 p 63. C E Grinstead St Swithun *Chich* 62-66; C Gt Grimsby St Jas *Linc* 66-69; C Gt Grimsby St Mary and St Jas 69-73; TV 73-74; V St Nicholas at Wade w Sarre *Cant* 74-75; P-in-c Chislet w Hoath 74-75; V St Nicholas at Wade w Sarre and Chislet w Hoath 75-81; V S Norwood H Innocents 81-84; V S Norwood H Innocents *S'wark* 85-04; rtd 04; Perm to Offic *B & W* from 04. *10 Hardy Court, Lang Road, Crewkerne TA18 8JE* Tel (01460) 271496 E-mail david.newman123@btinternet.com

NEWMAN, William Nigel Edward. b 61. St Jo Coll Dur BA83 Bris Univ PGCE86. Westcott Ho Cam 99. d 01 p 02. C Halstead Area *Chelmsf* 01-04; Chapl St Jo Cathl Hong Kong from 04; P-in-c Stanley St Steph from 04. *Bungalow 5, St Stephen's College, 22 Tung Tau Wan Road, Stanley, Hong Kong, China* E-mail willanddot@netvigator.org

NEWNHAM, Eric Robert. b 43. FCA. Sarum & Wells Th Coll 70. d 75 p 76. NSM Blackheath Ascension *S'wark* 75-06; NSM Deptford St Jo w H Trin and Ascension from 06. *27 Morden Hill, London SE13 7NN* Tel (020) 8692 6507 or 8691 6559

NEWPORT, Derek James. b 39. Acadia Univ (NS) BA82 MEd84. Sarum & Wells Th Coll 74. d 76 p 77. C Tavistock and Gulworthy *Ex* 76-78; Canada 78-86; V Malborough w S Huish, W Alvington and Churchstow *Ex* 86-95; TR Widecombe-in-the-Moor, Leusdon, Princetown etc 95-04; rtd 04. *Woodland Cottage, Southdown Woods, Yarnscombe, Barnstaple EX31 3LZ* Tel (01271) 858685 E-mail dereknewport@dnewport.fsnet.co.uk

NEWPORT, Prof Kenneth George Charles. b 57. Columbia Union Coll (USA) BA83 Andrews Univ (USA) MA84 Linacre Coll Ox MSt85 St Hugh's Coll Ox DPhil88. NOC 98. d 00 p 01. Reader Chr Thought Liv Hope 99-01; Prof Th and RS Liv Hope Univ from 01; Asst Vice Chan from 05; Hon Research Fell Man Univ from 98; NSM Bolton St Pet from 00; Perm to Offic *Liv* from 00. *Theology and Religious Studies, Liverpool Hope, Hope Park, Taggart Avenue, Liverpool L16 9JD* Tel 0151-291 3510 Fax 291 3772 E-mail knewport@hope.ac.uk

NEWPORT, Archdeacon of. *See* HACKETT, The Ven Ronald Glyndwr

NEWSOME, David Ellis. b 55. St Jo Coll Dur BA77. Westcott Ho Cam 80. d 82 p 83. C Finchley St Mary *Lon* 82-85; C Fulham All SS 85-87; Bp's Dom Chapl *Birm* 87-91; V Gravelly Hill 91-00; P-in-c Stockland Green 93-96; AD Aston 95-00; TR Tettenhall Regis *Lich* 00-08; Dioc Dir of Ords from 08. *10 The Brambles, Lichfield WS14 9SE* Tel (01543) 306220

NEWSOME, Canon John Keith. b 49. Mert Coll Ox BA73 MA76. Ripon Coll Cuddesdon 73. d 76 p 77. C Bywell *Newc* 76-78; C Berwick H Trin 78-82; Chapl Bonn w Cologne *Eur* 86-93; Chapl Hamburg 93-00; Chapl Zürich from 00; Can Brussels Cathl from 98. *Promenadengasse 9, 8001 Zürich, Switzerland* Tel (0041) (44) 252 6024 or 261 2241 Fax 252 6042 E-mail jknewsome@anglican.ch

NEWSOME, Monica Jane. b 55. WMMTC 96. d 99 p 00. NSM Kingshurst *Birm* 99-00; Asst Chapl HM YOI Stoke Heath 00-10; Chapl HM Pris Swinfen Hall from 10. *HM Young Offender Institution, Swinfen Hall, Swinfen, Lichfield WS14 9QS* Tel (01543) 484000

NEWSON, Julie. b 60. Southn Univ BA97. Bp Otter Coll 00. d 03. NSM Brighton St Pet w Chpl Royal *Chich* 03-09; NSM Brighton Chpl Royal 09-10; C Brighton St Luke Queen's Park from 10. *St Luke's Vicarage, Queen's Park Terrace, Brighton BN2 9YA* Tel (01273) 570978 Mobile 07803-750147 E-mail julie.newson@btinternet.com

NEWSTEAD, Dominic Gerald Bruno. b 65. Wycliffe Hall Ox BTh95. d 95 p 96. C Windlesham *Guildf* 95-00; Asst Chapl Fontainebleau *Eur* 00-05; V Southwater *Chich* 05-09; C Bebington *Ches* from 09. *22 Woodhey Road, Wirral CH63 9PD*

NEWSUM, Alfred Turner Paul. b 28. Coll of Resurr Mirfield 52. d 53 p 54. C Roath St German *Llan* 53-59; C Westmr St Matt *Lon* 59-60; C Washwood Heath *Birm* 60-68; P-in-c Small Heath St Greg 68-78; V Birm St Aid Small Heath 72-80; V Stockland Green 80-93; rtd 93; Perm to Offic *Llan* and *Mon* from 93. *Ty'r Offeiriad, 18 Almond Drive, Cardiff CF23 8HD*

NEWTH, Barry Wilfred. b 33. Bris Univ BA56. ALCD58. d 58 p 59. C Upton (Overchurch) *Ches* 58-62; C Kimberworth *Sheff* 62-63; V Clifton *Man* 63-72; V Radcliffe St Thos 72-74; V Radcliffe St Thos and St Jo 74-81; R Heaton Mersey 81-86; V Kirkby Malham *Bradf* 86-87; P-in-c Coniston Cold 86-87; V Kirkby-in-Malhamdale w Coniston Cold 87-97; rtd 97; Perm to Offic *Man* 00-08. *1 Higher Ridings, Bromley Cross, Bolton BL7 9HP* Tel (01204) 451927

NEWTON, Angela Margaret. b 48. RGN70. Ripon Coll Cuddesdon 06. d 07 p 08. NSM Luton St Aug Limbury *St Alb* from 07. *The Rectory, 2 Manor Farm Close, Barton-le-Clay, Bedford MK45 4TB* Tel (01582) 881873 Mobile 07940-824206 E-mail angela.m.newton@talktalk.net

NEWTON, Miss Ann. b 46. Trin Coll Bris 75. d 87 p 94. Par Dn Rothley *Leic* 87-91; Par Dn Becontree St Mary *Chelmsf* 91-94; C 94-01; V Canley *Cov* 01-08; rtd 08. *35 Mossford Street, London E3 4TH* Tel (020) 8981 5764 E-mail revanew@aol.com

NEWTON, Barrie Arthur. b 38. Dur Univ BA61. Wells Th Coll 61. d 63 p 64. C Walton St Mary *Liv* 63-67; C N Lynn w St Marg and St Nic *Nor* 67-69; Chapl Asst The Lon Hosp (Whitechapel) 69-71; Chapl K Coll Hosp Lon 72-77; P-in-c Bishops Sutton w Stowey *B & W* 77-81; P-in-c Compton Martin w Ubley 79-81; P-in-c Bridgwater St Jo w Chedzoy 81-83; Chapl St Mary's Hosp Praed Street Lon 83-94; Chapl St Mary's NHS Trust Paddington 94-99; rtd 00; Perm to Offic *Lon* from 04. *10 Brondesbury Park Mansions, 132 Salusbury Road, London NW6 6PD* Tel and fax (020) 7328 0397

NEWTON, Brian Karl. b 30. Keble Coll Ox BA55 MA59. Wells Th Coll 56. d 58 p 59. C Barrow St Geo *Carl* 58-61; Trinidad and Tobago 61-69 and 71-77; Gen Ed USPG 69-71; P-in-c Gt Coates *Linc* 77; TV Gt and Lt Coates w Bradley 78-88; V Burgh le Marsh 88-94; R Bratoft w Irby-in-the-Marsh 88-94; V Orby 88-94; R Welton-le-Marsh w Gunby 88-94; rtd 94; Perm to Offic *Linc* 94-97. *27 Somersby Way, Boston PE21 9PQ* Tel (01205) 362433

NEWTON, Canon Christopher Wynne. b 25. Trin Hall Cam BA46, Westcott Ho Cam 48. d 50 p 51. C Gateshead Ch Ch *Dur* 50-52; Canada 52-55; C Harrow Weald All SS *Lon* 55-58; V Radlett *St Alb* 58-66; RD St Alb 63-66; TR Hemel Hempstead 66-72; RD Milton Keynes *Ox* 72-77; TV Swan 78-84; RD Claydon 78-84; Dioc Ecum Officer 79-84; Hon Can Ch Ch 80-83; P-in-c Lt Gaddesden *St Alb* 84-86; rtd 86; Perm to Offic *St Alb* from 86. *24 Slade Court, Watling Street, Radlett WD7 7BT* Tel (01923) 859131

NEWTON, David Ernest. b 42. Sarum & Wells Th Coll 72. d 74 p 75. C Wigan All SS *Liv* 74-80; V Choral York Minster 80-85; R Ampleforth w Oswaldkirk 85-86; P-in-c E Gilling 85-86; R Ampleforth w Oswaldkirk and Gilling E 86-97; V Ampleforth w Oswaldkirk, Gilling E etc 98-01; RD Helmsley 94-99; P-in-c Overton *Blackb* 01-10. *4 Lunesdale Court, Derwent Road, Lancaster LA1 3ET* Tel (01524) 599101 E-mail davidnoot@aol.com

NEWTON, Derek. b 50. NEOC 89. d 92 p 93. NSM Houghton le Spring *Dur* 92-96; C 06-09; NSM Deanery of Houghton 97-06; P-in-c Chilton Moor from 09. *Pine Lodge, Warwick Drive, Houghton le Spring DH5 8JR*

NEWTON, Canon Fiona Olive. b 46. GTCL67. WMMTC 96. d 99 p 00. C Southam and Ufton *Cov* 99-03; P-in-c Laxfield, Cratfield, Wilby and Brundish *St E* 03-04; R from 04; C Hoxne w Denham, Syleham and Wingfield from 06; RD Hoxne from 07; RD Hartismere 08-10; Hon Can St E Cathl from 11. *The Vicarage, 15 Noyes Avenue, Laxfield, Woodbridge IP13 8EB* Tel (01986) 798998 E-mail fionanewton@rmplc.co.uk

NEWTON, George Peter Howgill. b 62. Pemb Coll Cam BA84 MA88. Oak Hill Th Coll BA93. d 93 p 94. C Blackpool St Thos *Blackb* 93-99; P-in-c Aldershot H Trin *Guildf* 99-03; V from 03; Chapl Farnborough Coll of Tech from 00. *2 Cranmore Lane, Aldershot GU11 3AS* Tel (01252) 320618 E-mail g@gjsk.prestel.co.uk

NEWTON, Gerald Blamire. b 30. Lich Th Coll. d 69 p 70. C Leeds Halton St Wilfrid *Ripon* 69-73; C Gt Yarmouth *Nor* 73-74; P-in-c Cattistock w Chilfrome and Rampisham w Wraxall *Sarum* 74-77; V Coney Hill *Glouc* 77-79; V Bryneglwys and Llandegla *St As* 79-80; R Llandegla and Bryneglwys and Llanarmon-yn-Ial 80-86; P-in-c Burythorpe, Acklam and Leavening w Westow *York* 86-95; rtd 95; Perm to Offic *York* 95-09. *9 Ropery Walk, Malton YO17 7JS* Tel (01653) 698980

NEWTON, Gordon. b 81. Cant Ch Ch Univ Coll BA03. Coll of Resurr Mirfield 07. d 09 p 10. C Armley w New Wortley *Ripon* from 09. *7 Stephenson Drive, Leeds LS12 5TN* Tel 0113-219 4646 *or* 289 0824 E-mail gnewton@mirfield.org.uk

NEWTON, Canon Graham Hayden. b 47. AKC69. St Aug Coll Cant 70. d 70 p 71. C St Mary-at-Lambeth *S'wark* 70-73; TV Catford (Southend) and Downham 73-78; P-in-c Porthill *Lich* 78-79; TV Wolstanton 79-86; V Stevenage H Trin *St Alb* 86-96; TR Dunstable 96-04; RD Dunstable 96-02; R Barton-le-Cley w Higham Gobion and Hexton from 04; Hon Can St Alb from 04. *The Rectory, 2 Manor Farm Close, Barton-le-Cley, Bedford MK45 4TB* Tel (01582) 881873 E-mail rector@stnicholas-barton.org.uk

NEWTON, Ian. b 66. Westmr Coll Ox BEd89 Leeds Univ BA03. Coll of Resurr Mirfield 01. d 03 p 04. C Horninglow *Lich* 03-06; V W Bromwich St Pet 06-10; Chapl Quainton Hall Sch Harrow 10-11; V Paulsgrove *Portsm* from 11. *St Michael's Vicarage, Hempsted Road, Portsmouth PO6 4AS* Tel (023) 9237 8808 E-mail fatheriannewton@yahoo.co.uk

NEWTON, John. b 39. AKC65. d 66 p 67. C Whipton *Ex* 66-68; C Plympton St Mary 68-74; V Broadwoodwidger 74-81; R Kelly w Bradstone 74-81; R Lifton 74-81; Chapl All Hallows Sch Rousdon 81-94; Lic to Offic *Ex* 81-94; rtd 99. *Flat 2, 5 Eyewell Green, Seaton EX12 2BN* Tel (01297) 625887

NEWTON, Miles Julius Albert. b 69. K Alfred's Coll Win BA91. Qu Coll Birm BTh96. d 97 p 98. C Sholing *Win* 97-01; C Bitterne Park 01-03; V Woolston from 03; P-in-c Southampton St Mary Extra from 11. *St Mark's Vicarage, 117 Swift Road, Southampton SO19 9ER* Tel (023) 8044 1124 *or* 8032 6908

NEWTON, Canon Nigel Ernest Hartley. b 53. Jo Coll Nottm 87. d 89 p 90. C Largs *Glas* 89-92; Angl Chapl Ashbourne Home Largs 89-92; P-in-c Eyemouth *Edin* 92-95; Chapl Miss to Seamen 92-95; P-in-c Challoch *Glas* 95-04; R 04-06; Can St Mary's Cathl 04-06; Hon Can from 06; rtd 06. *Glenairlie, 7 Wigtown Road, Newton Stewart DG8 6JZ* Tel (01671) 401228 Mobile 07885-436892 E-mail glenairlie@btinternet.com

NEWTON, Miss Pauline Dorothy. b 48. Southn Univ BA70 PGCE71 MPhil79. Sarum Th Coll 79. dss 82 d 87 p 94. Bemerton *Sarum* 82-06; Hon C 87-06; Dep Hd Malvern Girls' Coll 86-06; rtd 06; Perm to Offic *Heref* from 07. *16 Weston Park, Weston under Penyard, Ross-on-Wye HR9 7FR* Tel (01989) 564414 E-mail pnewton48@hotmail.com

NEWTON, Peter. b 39. St Jo Coll Nottm 73. d 75 p 76. C Porchester *S'well* 75-79; R Wilford 79-99; rtd 99; Perm to Offic *S'well* and *Leic* from 00; Warden Advent Ho Healing Min Birmingham USA from 99. *Advent House, 2317 Arlington Avenue, Birmingham AL 35205, USA, or 20 Main Street, Eaton, Grantham NG32 1SE* Tel (001) (205) 918 0120 *or* (01476) 870024

NEWTON, Richard. b 47. Trin Coll Bris 72. d 73 p 74. C Fareham St Jo *Portsm* 73-76; C Cheltenham St Mark *Glouc* 76-83; P-in-c Malvern St Andr *Worc* 83-95; TR Kingswood *Bris* 95-99; Master St Jo Hosp Bath 00-07; rtd 07. *61 Columbia Drive, Worcester WR2 4DB* Tel (01905) 426702 E-mail 2antiques41@talktalk.net

NEWTON, Richard John Christopher. b 60. Bris Univ BSc81. Qu Coll Birm 85. d 88 p 89. C Bris Ch the Servant Stockwood 88-92; C Dorking w Ranmore *Guildf* 92-96; P-in-c Hagley *Worc* 96-00; R from 00. *The Rectory, 6 Middlefield Lane, Hagley, Stourbridge DY9 0PX* Tel (01562) 882442 *or* 886363 Fax 887833 E-mail richard.kathy@yescomputers.co.uk *or* hagley.pcc@freeuk.com

NEWTON, Ruth Katherine. d 10 p 11. NSM Rowley w Skidby *York* from 10. *6 Manor Barns, Little Weighton, Cottingham HU20 3UA* Tel (01482) 841875 E-mail newtonrk@network.karoo.co.uk

NGOY, Lusa. See NSENGA-NGOY, Lusambo

NGURURI, Miss Naomi. b 73. St Jo Coll Nottm 07. d 09 p 10. C Hackney Marsh *Lon* from 09. *Basement Flat, 306A Amhurst Road, London N16 7UE* Tel (020) 7249 9746 Mobile 07896-970367 E-mail naomingururi02@yahoo.com

NIASSA, Bishop of. See VAN KOEVERING, The Rt Revd Mark Allan

NIBLOCK, Mark. b 78. Fitzw Coll Cam MA03 Milltown Inst Dub MA08. CITC 06. d 08 p 09. C Agherton *Conn* from 08. *23 Cappaghmore Manor, Portstewart BT55 7RD* Tel and fax (028) 7083 4606 E-mail curate.agherton@connor.anglican.org

NICE, Canon John Edmund. b 51. Univ of Wales (Ban) BA73. Coll of Resurr Mirfield 74. d 76 p 77. C Oxton *Ches* 76-79; C Liscard St Mary w St Columba 79-82; V Latchford St Jas 82-92; R Holyhead w Rhoscolyn w Llanfair-yn-Neubwll *Ban* 92-95; R Holyhead 95-04; RD Llifon and Talybolion 97-01; AD 01-04; R Llandudno from 04; Can Cursal Ban Cathl 02-04; Can and Preb Ban Cathl from 04; AD Arllechwedd from 10. *The Rectory, Church Walks, Llandudno LL30 2HL* Tel (01492) 876624 E-mail john.nice2@btopenworld.com

NICHOL, William David. b 58. Hull Univ BA84. Ridley Hall Cam 84. d 87 p 88. C Hull St Jo Newland *York* 87-90; C Kirk Ella 90-92; TV 92-98; P-in-c Powick *Worc* 98-99; R Powick and Guarlford and Madresfield w Newland 99-05; V Malvern H Trin and St Jas from 05; RD Malvern from 07. *Holy Trinity Vicarage, 2 North Malvern Road, Malvern WR14 4LR* Tel (01684) 561126 E-mail david@trinityandthewest.wanadoo.co.uk

NICHOLAS, Ernest Milton. b 25. ACP50 Newc Univ DipAdEd69 Lanc Univ MA78. NEOC 85. d 86 p 87. NSM Hexham Newc 86-96; Perm to Offic from 96. *Hillside, Eilansgate, Hexham NE46 3EW* Tel (01434) 603609

NICHOLAS, Jonathan. b 78. Cranmer Hall Dur 08. d 10 p 11. C Lt Horton *Bradf* from 10. *St Matthew's Vicarage, Carr Bottom Road, Bradford BD5 9AA*

NICHOLAS, Malcolm Keith. b 46. Open Univ BA79 FIBMS71. S Dios Minl Tr Scheme 81. d 84 p 85. NSM Gatcombe *Portsm* 84-92; NSM Shorwell w Kingston 88-92; C Hartley Wintney, Elvetham, Winchfield etc 92-96; TV Grantham *Linc* 96-02; V Grantham, Harrowby w Londonthorpe 02-03; V Carr Dyke Gp 03-11; rtd 11. *20 Marrams Avenue, Cromer NR27 9BB* E-mail revmalc14@yahoo.co.uk

NICHOLAS, Maurice Lloyd. b 30. Kelham Th Coll 54. d 58 p 59. C Stepney St Dunstan and All SS *Lon* 58-60; C Sevenoaks St Jo

Roch 60-65; Chapl RADD 65-75; C Northolt St Mary *Lon* 75-85; rtd 85; Hon C Upper Teddington SS Pet and Paul *Lon* 85-90; Perm to Offic from 91. *clo N C Ward Esq, 23 Thames Haven, Portsmouth Road, Surbiton KT6 4JA* Tel (020) 8399 5003

NICHOLAS, Milton. See NICHOLAS, Ernest Milton

NICHOLAS, Patrick. b 37. Selw Coll Cam BA60 MA65. Wells Th Coll 60. **d** 62 **p** 63. C Camberwell St Giles *S'wark* 62-63; C Warlingham w Chelsham and Farleigh 63-65; C Oxted 65-68; Hong Kong 68-74; C Portsea St Mary *Portsm* 75; Hd of Ho St Chris Fellowship Chiswick 76-79; Dept of Soc Services Glos Co Coun 79-92; Probation Officer Glouc Probation Service 92-97; rtd 97; Chapl St Jo Coll Hong Kong 97-00; Perm to Offic *Glouc* from 02. *35 Norwich Drive, Cheltenham GL51 3HD* Tel (01242) 510007 E-mail patnic@btinternet.com

NICHOLAS, Paul James. b 51. Univ of Wales (Lamp) BA. Coll of Resurr Mirfield 73. **d** 74 **p** 75. C Llanelli *St D* 74-78; C Roath *Llan* 78-84; P-in-c Leic St Pet 84-87; V Shard End *Birm* 87-96; rtd 96; Perm to Offic *Birm* from 96. *50 Delrene Road, Shirley, Solihull B90 2HJ* Tel 0121-745 7339 E-mail frpaul@oikos.screaming.net

NICHOLAS ALAN, Brother. See WORSSAM, Brother Nicholas Alan

NICHOLL, Mrs Karen. b 65. Bradf Univ BA99 Leeds Univ BA07. Coll of Resurr Mirfield 05. **d** 07 **p** 08. C Lindley *Wakef* 07-10; P-in-c Gomersal from 10. *St Mary's Vicarage, 404 Spen Lane, Gomersal, Cleckheaton BD19 4LS* E-mail nicholl.karen@googlemail.com

NICHOLLS, Brian Albert. b 39. LBIPP LMPA. WMMTC 90. **d** 93 **p** 94. NSM Oakham, Hambleton, Egleton, Braunston and Brooke *Pet* 93-96; R Edith Weston w N Luffenham and Lyndon w Manton 96-05; P-in-c Empingham w Whitwell 02-05; rtd 05; Perm to Offic *Pet* and *Leic* from 05. *28 Heron Road, Oakham LE15 6BN* Tel (01572) 759657 E-mail lizbriannicholls@tiscali.co.uk

NICHOLLS (née HUMPHRIES), Mrs Catherine Elizabeth. b 53. Anglia Poly Univ MA97. Trin Coll Bris BA87. **d** 87 **p** 94. C Bath Twerton-on-Avon *B & W* 87-90; Personnel Manager and Tr Officer TEAR Fund 90-95; Hon C Norbiton *S'wark* 91-95; Perm to Offic *Ely* 95-97; Dir Past Studies EAMTC 97-03; Vice Prin 01-03; Hon Min Can Pet Cathl 97-03; Perm to Offic *Nor* 03-05; Dioc Dir CME 05-10. *North Cottage, King John's Thorn, Hethel, Norwich NR14 8HE* Tel (01508) 570557

NICHOLLS, Christopher Alan. Leic Univ BSc81 Reading Univ MSc82 FGS91. ERMC 07. **d** 10 **p** 11. C Utrecht w Zwolle *Eur* from 10. *Baronielaan 37, 2242 RB Wassenaar, The Netherlands* Tel (0031) (70) 517 5291 Mobile 610-973 164 E-mail cajwnicholls@hetnet.nl

NICHOLLS (née TOVAR), Mrs Gillian Elaine. b 48. Sussex Univ CertEd69. Trin Coll Bris BA86. dss 86 **d** 87 **p** 94. Tonbridge SS Pet and Paul *Roch* 86-00; Par Dn 87-94; C 94-00; V Gillingham H Trin 00-10; rtd 10. *29 The Gables, Haddenham, Aylesbury HP17 8AD* Tel (01844) 291993 E-mail gilltovar2008@gmail.com

NICHOLLS, Irene. **d** 09 **p** 10. OLM Penkridge *Lich* from 09. *79 Croydon Drive, Penkridge, Stafford ST19 5DW* Tel (01785) 714686

✠**NICHOLLS, The Rt Revd John.** b 43. AKC66. **d** 67 **p** 68 **c** 90. C Salford St Clem Ordsall *Man* 67-69; C Langley All SS and Martyrs 69-72; V 72-78; Dir Past Th Coll of Resurr Mirfield 78-83; Can Res Man Cathl 83-90; Suff Bp Lancaster *Blackb* 90-97; Bp Sheff 97-08; rtd 08; Hon Asst Bp Derby from 09. *77 Rowton Grange Road, Chapel-en-le-Frith, High Peak SK23 0LD*

NICHOLLS, Keith Barclay. b 57. Nottm Univ BA78. Wycliffe Hall Ox 03. **d** 05 **p** 06. C Bisley and W End *Guildf* 05-09; V Burchetts Green *Ox* from 09. *The Vicarage, Burchetts Green Road, Burchetts Green, Maidenhead SL6 6QS* Tel (01628) 828822 E-mail kbnicholls@hotmail.com

NICHOLLS, Mark Richard. b 60. LSE BSc(Econ)82 Leeds Univ BA88. Coll of Resurr Mirfield 86. **d** 89 **p** 90. C Warrington St Elphin *Liv* 89-92; V Wigan St Andr 92-96; R North End St Marg Zimbabwe 96-00; Shrine P Shrine of Our Lady of Walsingham 00-02; V Mill End and Heronsgate w W Hyde *St Alb* 02-07; P-in-c Rotherhithe St Mary w All SS *S'wark* 07-10; R from 10. *St Mary's Rectory, 72A St Marychurch Street, London SE16 2JE* Tel 07909-546659 (mobile) E-mail mmarini2001@aol.com

NICHOLLS, Mark Simon. b 57. Down Coll Cam MA79. Ripon Coll Cuddesdon 92. **d** 94 **p** 95. C Farnham *Guildf* 94-98; P-in-c Crookham 98-03; V from 03. *The Vicarage, 14 Gally Hill Road, Church Crookham, Fleet GU52 6LH* Tel (01252) 617130 E-mail office@christchurch.crookham.org.uk

NICHOLLS, Michael Stanley. b 34. AKC59. St Boniface Warminster 59. **d** 60 **p** 61. C Torquay St Martin Barton CD *Ex* 60-63; C E Grinstead St Mary *Chich* 63-66; C-in-c Salfords CD *S'wark* 66-68; V Salfords 68-75; V Tunbridge Wells St Barn *Roch* 75-97; rtd 97; Perm to Offic *Cant* 98-99 and *Chich* from 99. *30 St Itha Road, Selsey, Chichester PO20 0AA* Tel (01243) 603837

NICHOLLS, Neil David Raymond. b 65. Univ Coll Lon BA86. Wycliffe Hall Ox BA90. **d** 91 **p** 92. C Westmr St Steph w St Jo *Lon* 91-94; C Islington St Mary 94-96; Chapl LSE 96-00; C St Bride Fleet Street w Bridewell etc 99-00; V Ealing St Barn 00-05; V Hatcham St Jas *S'wark* from 05; AD Deptford from 07. *St James's Vicarage, St James's, London SE14 6AD* Tel (020) 8691 2167 E-mail rev.neil@tiscali.co.uk

NICHOLLS, Rachel. b 62. BA MPhil. **d** 00 **p** 01. NSM Chesterton St Geo *Ely* 00-04; Perm to Offic 04-07; NSM Cambridge St Benedict from 07. *5 Eachard Road, Cambridge CB3 0HZ* Tel (01223) 359167 E-mail rachel.nicholls2@btinternet.com

NICHOLLS, Robert Graham. b 56. Sheff Univ BEng77 CEng MIET07. STETS 05. **d** 08 **p** 09. NSM Fair Oak *Win* from 08. *20 The Spinney, Eastleigh SO50 8PF* Tel (023) 8069 3716 Mobile 07837-804366 E-mail bob.nicholls@dsl.pipex.com

NICHOLLS, Roger. b 43. Ox Univ MA Cam Univ DipEd. **d** 01 **p** 02. OLM Kenwyn w St Allen *Truro* 01-04; NSM Truro St Paul and St Clem 04-08; NSM Truro St Geo and St Jo 04-08; P-in-c Mylor w Flushing from 08. *17 Olivey Place, Mylor Bridge, Falmouth TR11 5RX* Tel (01326) 374408 E-mail rognicholls@tesco.net

NICHOLLS, Simon James. b 53. Anglia Ruskin Univ MA08 Trent Park Coll of Educn CertEd76. Ridley Hall Cam. **d** 00 **p** 01. C Nuneaton St Nic *Cov* 00-04; R Markfield, Thornton, Bagworth and Stanton etc *Leic* from 04. *The Rectory, 3A The Nook, Markfield LE67 9WE* Tel (01530) 242844 E-mail markfield.rector@virgin.net

NICHOLS, Barry Edward. b 40. ACA63 FCA73. S'wark Ord Course 66. **d** 69 **p** 70. NSM Surbiton St Andr and St Mark *S'wark* 69-92; Dean for MSE Kingston 90-92; Hon Can S'wark Cathl 90-92; Perm to Offic 99-01; NSM Upper Tooting H Trin 01-04; NSM Upper Tooting H Trin w St Aug from 04. *19 Arterberry Road, London SW20 8AF* Tel and fax (020) 8879 0154 E-mail barrynichols@btinternet.com

NICHOLS, Dennis Harry. b 25. Kelham Th Coll 47. **d** 52 **p** 53. C Oakham *Pet* 52-55; C Kettering St Mary 55-57; P-in-c Spalding St Paul *Linc* 57-61; V Bury H Trin *Man* 61-81; V St Gluvias *Truro* 81-90; RD Carnmarth S 85-90; rtd 90; Perm to Offic *Truro* 90-08. *15 Ramsay Hall, 9-13 Byron Road, Worthing BN11 3HN*

NICHOLS, Mrs Elizabeth Margaret. b 45. WEMTC 00. **d** 02 **p** 03. NSM Ledbury *Heref* 02-05; NSM Boxwell, Leighterton, Didmarton, Oldbury etc *Glouc* from 05. *The Rectory, The Meads, Leighterton, Tetbury GL8 8UW* Tel (01666) 890635 E-mail reverend.elizabeth@cotswoldwireless.co.uk

NICHOLS, Frank Bernard. b 43. Kelham Th Coll 64. **d** 68 **p** 69. C Luton St Andr *St Alb* 68-72; C Cheshunt 72-76; C-in-c Marsh Farm CD 76-81; Australia 05-10; Perm to Offic Brisbane 08-10; Perm to Offic *Nor* from 10. *8 Carterford Drive, Norwich NR3 4DW* Tel (01603) 446311 Mobile 07503-932804 E-mail frank.nichols@virginmedia.com

NICHOLS, Howard Keith. b 41. CCC Ox BA64 MA68 CEng86 FIEE92 EurIng94. WEMTC 98. **d** 01 **p** 02. NSM Ledbury *Heref* 01-04; NSM Boxwell, Leighterton, Didmarton, Oldbury etc *Glouc* from 04. *The Rectory, The Meads, Leighterton, Tetbury GL8 8UW* Tel (01666) 890635 E-mail reverend.howard@cotswoldwireless.co.uk

NICHOLS, Mark Steven. b 68. Lon Bible Coll BA94 Ridley Hall Cam 95. **d** 97. C Balham Hill Ascension *S'wark* 97-99. *Address temp unknown* E-mail markn1968uk@yahoo.co.uk

NICHOLS, Canon Raymond Maurice. b 22. ALCD53. **d** 53 **p** 54. C Childwall All SS *Liv* 53-56; Kenya 56-64; Home Sec SPCK 64-71; Overseas Sec 67-73; Publisher 73-74; P-in-c Dorchester *Ox* 74-78; P-in-c Newington 77-78; TR Dorchester 78-87; V Warborough 78-87; Hon Can Ch Ch 84-87; rtd 87; Perm to Offic *Sarum* 91-08 and *Ox* from 09. *14 Augustine Way, Oxford OX4 4DG* Tel (01865) 747772

NICHOLS, Robert Warren. b 54. Biola Univ (USA) BA77 Fuller Th Sem California MA81. SAOMC 93. **d** 96 **p** 97. C Headington Quarry *Ox* 96-00; Sen Asst P Wymondham *Nor* 00-05; Lect 01-05; R Caston, Griston, Merton, Thompson etc from 05. *The Rectory, 4 Hunters Ride, Caston, Attleborough NR17 1DE* Tel (01953) 483222 E-mail revbobnichols@gmail.com

NICHOLS, Stephen Robert Chamberlain. b 73. Ch Coll Cam BA96 MA00 SOAS Lon MA98 Bris Univ PhD11. Wycliffe Hall Ox BA06. **d** 09 **p** 10. C Plymouth St Andr and Stonehouse *Ex* from 09. *18 Glenhurst Road, Plymouth PL3 5LT* Tel (01752) 267025 E-mail stephen.nichols@virgin.net

NICHOLSON, Andrew John. b 69. Leeds Univ BA93 MA00. St Jo Coll Nottm MTh04. **d** 05 **p** 06. C E Richmond *Ripon* 05-09; P-in-c Barwick in Elmet from 09; P-in-c Thorner from 09. *The Vicarage, Church View, Thorner, Leeds LS14 3ED* Tel 0113-289 2437 Mobile 07723-345917 E-mail andydebbie80@hotmail.com

NICHOLSON, Mrs Barbara Ruth. b 39. Nor City Coll TCert59. Dioc OLM tr scheme 99. **d** 02 **p** 03. OLM Reculver and Herne Bay St Bart *Cant* from 02. *34 Cliff Avenue, Herne Bay CT6 6LZ* Tel (01227) 364606 Fax 365384

NICHOLSON, Brian Warburton. b 44. ALCD73 LTh74. St Jo Coll Nottm 70. **d** 73 **p** 74. C Canford Magna *Sarum* 73-77; C E Twickenham St Steph *Lon* 77-80; V Colchester St Jo *Chelmsf* 80-96; R Oakley w Wootton St Lawrence *Win* 96-09; rtd 09; Perm to Offic *Win* from 09. *Nuthatches, 16 St Vigor Way, Colden Common, Winchester SO21 1UU* Tel (01962) 713433 E-mail brian.nic@talktalk.net

NICHOLSON, Christina. d 08. OLM Mossley Hill *Liv* from 08. *9 Mossville Road, Liverpool L18 7JN* E-mail christnanic099@aol.com

NICHOLSON, Miss Clare. b 46. RMN80 Keele Univ BA70 CertEd70. St Jo Coll Nottm 83. **dss** 85 **d** 87 **p** 94. Bletchley *Ox* 85-89; Par Dn 87-89; Par Dn Milton Keynes 89-90; Par Dn Prestwood and Gt Hampden 90-94; C 94-99; P-in-c E Springfield *Chelmsf* 99-03; V Aldborough Hatch from 03. *The Vicarage, 89 St Peter's Close, Ilford IG2 7QN* Tel (020) 8599 0524 E-mail revdclare@stpetersah.org.uk *or* revclare46@aol.com

NICHOLSON, David. b 57. Sarum & Wells Th Coll 80. **d** 83 **p** 84. C Trevethin *Mon* 83-85; C Ebbw Vale 85-87; V Newport St Steph and H Trin 87-95; V Abertillery w Cwmtillery w Six Bells 95-97; Hon Chapl Miss to Seamen 87-97; P-in-c Cudworth *Wakef* 97-98; V from 98; P-in-c Lundwood 01-04; Dioc Urban Officer from 08. *The Vicarage, St John's Road, Cudworth, Barnsley S72 8DE* Tel (01226) 710279 E-mail frnicholson@aol.com

NICHOLSON, Mrs Diane Maureen. b 45. Birm Coll of Educn CertEd68. **d** 97 **p** 98. OLM Ludham, Potter Heigham, Hickling and Catfield *Nor* from 97. *25 Latchmoor Park, Ludham, Great Yarmouth NR29 5RA* Tel (01692) 678683

NICHOLSON, Dorothy Ann. b 40. Surrey Univ Roehampton MSc04. S'wark Ord Course 81. **dss** 84 **d** 87 **p** 94. Carshalton Beeches *S'wark* 84-88; Par Dn 87-88; Par Dn Brixton Road Ch Ch 88-89; C Malden St Jo 89-95; V Balham St Mary and St Jo 95-05; rtd 05. *13 Tebbs Close, Countesthorpe, Leicester LE8 5XG* Tel 0116-277 5737 E-mail nicholsonda@btopenworld.com

NICHOLSON, Eric. b 33. **d** 01 **p** 02. OLM W Wycombe w Bledlow Ridge, Bradenham and Radnage *Ox* 01-07; Lic to Offic *Mor* from 07. *Gordon Chapel Rectory, 40 Castle Street, Fochabers IV32 7DW* Tel (01343) 820337 E-mail eric@torrington67.freeserve.co.uk

NICHOLSON, Prof Ernest Wilson. b 38. Comdr OM (Italy)90. TCD BA60 MA64 Glas Univ PhD64 Cam Univ MA67 BD71 DD78 Ox Univ DD79 FBA87. Westcott Ho Cam 69. **d** 69 **p** 70. Lect Div Cam Univ 67-79; Fell, Chapl and Dir of Th Studies Pemb Coll Cam 69-79; Dean 73-79; Prof of Interpr of H Scripture Oriel Coll Ox 79-90; Provost 90-03; Pro-Vice-Chan Ox Univ 93-03; rtd 03; Lic to Offic *Ox* 84-10; Perm to Offic from 10. *39A Blenheim Drive, Oxford OX2 8DJ* E-mail ernest.nicholson@oriel.ox.ac.uk

NICHOLSON, Gary. b 62. Open Univ BA89. Cranmer Hall Dur 91 NEOC 92. **d** 95 **p** 96. NSM Whitworth w Spennymoor *Dur* 95-97; NSM Spennymoor, Whitworth and Merrington 97-00; C Coundon and Eldon 00-02; P-in-c from 02. *St James's Vicarage, 2A Collingwood Street, Coundon, Bishop Auckland DL14 8LG* Tel (01388) 603312 E-mail frgary@hotmail.com

NICHOLSON, Harold Sydney Leonard. b 35. Garnett Coll Lon PGCE67 Open Univ BA77. Oak Hill NSM Course 92. **d** 94 **p** 95. NSM Stanwell *Lon* 94-00; NSM Sunbury 98-00; NSM Shepperton 00-05; Perm to Offic from 05. *7 Academy Court, Fordbridge Road, Sunbury-on-Thames TW16 6AN* Tel (01932) 787690 E-mail hslnicholson@onetel.com

NICHOLSON, James Benjamin. NEOC. **d** 08 **p** 09. NSM Helmsley *York* from 08; NSM Upper Ryedale from 08. *5 Bells Court, Helmsley, York YO62 5BA* Tel (01439) 772150 E-mail bnicuk@aol.com

NICHOLSON, John Paul. b 57. Sarum Th Coll. **d** 82 **p** 83. C Kirkby *Liv* 82-85; TV Speke St Aid 85-95; Ind Chapl *Ox* 95-04; Chapl Cambs and Pet NHS Founda Trust from 04. *Chaplaincy Office, Kent House, Fulbourn Hospital, Cambridge CB21 5EF* Tel (01223) 218598 E-mail john.nicholson@cpft.nhs.uk

NICHOLSON, Kevin Smith. b 47. CQSW76. Edin Th Coll 89. **d** 91 **p** 92. C W Fife Team Min *St And* 91-94; P-in-c 94-95; R Kinross 95-03; rtd 03. *Oldshoremore, 3A West Huntingtower, Perth PH1 3NU* Tel (01738) 583555 E-mail keith.nicholson@virgin.net *or* keithsnicholson@yahoo.co.uk

NICHOLSON, Canon Nigel Patrick. b 46. DL07. Sarum & Wells Th Coll 72. **d** 75 **p** 76. C Farnham *Guildf* 75-78; C Worplesdon 78-81; CF (ACF) from 80; P-in-c Compton *Guildf* 81-85; R Compton w Shackleford and Peper Harow 85-89; R Cranleigh from 89; RD Cranleigh 95-00; Hon Can Guildf Cathl from 01. *The Rectory, High Street, Cranleigh GU6 8AS* Tel (01483) 273620 E-mail stnicoloff@aol.com

NICHOLSON, Miss Pamela Elizabeth. b 47. Ripon Coll Cuddesdon. **d** 92 **p** 94. C Balsall Heath St Paul *Birm* 92-95; V Smethwick St Matt w St Chad 95-09; Perm to Offic from 09. *1 Acresfield, Colne BB8 0PT* Tel (01282) 862717 E-mail pamela.nicholson1@btinternet.com

NICHOLSON, Paul Shannon. b 52. York Univ BA74 Middx Univ BA02 ARCO74 ARCM75. NTMTC 99. **d** 02 **p** 03. C

Primrose Hill St Mary w Avenue Road St Paul *Lon* 02-06; P-in-c S Hampstead St Sav from 06; P-in-c Belsize Park from 06. *St Saviour's Vicarage, 30 Eton Villas, London NW3 4SQ* Tel (020) 7586 6522 Mobile 07971-223764 E-mail nicholsongarrison@hotmail.com

NICHOLSON, Canon Peter Charles. b 25. OBE92. Lambeth MA89 Chich Th Coll 57. **d** 59 **p** 60. C Sawbridgeworth *St Alb* 59-62; Min Can, Prec and Sacr Pet Cathl 62-67; V Wroxham w Hoveton *Nor* 67-74; V Lyme Regis *Sarum* 74-80; Gen Sec St Luke's Hosp for the Clergy 80-93; NSM Harlington *Lon* 80-87; Hon Chapl S'wark Cathl from 87; Can and Preb Chich Cathl 89-93; rtd 93. *St Luke's Cottage, 13 Brearley Close, Uxbridge UB8 1JJ* Tel (01895) 233522

NICHOLSON, Peter Charles. b 44. Oak Hill Th Coll 74. **d** 76 **p** 77. C Croydon Ch Ch Broad Green *Cant* 76-80; C Gt Baddow *Chelmsf* 80-88; TV 88-96; V Westcliff St Mich from 96. *St Michael's Vicarage, 5 Mount Avenue, Westcliff-on-Sea SS0 8PS* Tel (01702) 478462 E-mail pedinic@tiscali.co.uk

NICHOLSON, Canon Rodney. b 45. Mert Coll Ox BA68 MA71. Ridley Hall Cam 69. **d** 72 **p** 73. C Colne St Bart *Blackb* 72-75; C Blackpool St Jo 75-78; V Ewood 78-90; V Clitheroe St Paul Low Moor from 90; P-in-c Chatburn and Downham from 03; Hon Can Blackb Cathl from 06. *The Vicarage, St Paul's Street, Clitheroe BB7 2LS* Tel and fax (01200) 458019 E-mail rodnic@btopenworld.com

NICHOLSON, Roland. b 40. Sarum & Wells Th Coll 72. **d** 74 **p** 75. C Morecambe St Barn *Blackb* 74-78; V Feniscliffe 78-90; V Sabden and Pendleton 90-02; C Poulton-le-Fylde 02-04; C Poulton Carleton and Singleton 04-07; rtd 08. *13 Laurel Bank Terrace, Feniscowles, Blackburn BB2 5JA*

NICHOLSON, Mrs Samantha. b 69. St Jo Coll York BA92. St Jo Coll Nottm MA95 LTH93. **d** 96 **p** 97. C Toxteth St Cypr w Ch Ch *Liv* 96-01; P-in-c W Derby St Luke 01-08; P-in-c Ince Ch Ch 08-09; P-in-c Wigan St Cath 08-09; V Ince Ch Ch w Wigan St Cath from 09. *The Vicarage, 70 Belle Green Lane, Ince, Wigan WN2 2EP* Tel (01942) 495831

NICHOLSON, Stephen Lee. b 65. St Jo Coll Cam BA87 MA91 PhD94 Ox Univ MTh01. St Steph Ho Ox 98. **d** 00 **p** 01. C Middlesbrough All SS *York* 00-05; Asst Chapl HM Pris Holme Ho 00-05; Chapl York Univ 05-08; NSM Howden-le-Wear and Hunwick *Dur* from 09. *44 Briardene, Lanchester, Durham DH7 0QD* Tel 07875-909792 (mobile)

NICHOLSON, Trevor Parry. b 35. St Edm Hall Ox BA58 MA. Wycliffe Hall Ox 58. **d** 60 **p** 61. C Eastbourne Ch Ch *Chich* 60-63; C Ifield 63-67; Asst Youth Chapl *Win* 67-73; Chapl Shoreham Gr Sch 73-78; P-in-c Capel *Guildf* 78-85; V 85-90; Chapl Qu Anne's Sch Caversham 90-00; rtd 00; P-in-c N Chapel w Ebernoe *Chich* 00-05. *Lexham, Dodsley Lane, Easebourne, Midhurst GU29 9BB* Tel (01730) 810452

NICHOLSON, Miss Velda Christine. b 44. Charlotte Mason Coll of Educn TCert65. Cranmer Hall Dur 81. **dss** 82 **d** 87 **p** 94. Gt and Lt Driffield *York* 82-86; Newby 86-88; Par Dn 87-88; TD Cramlington *Newc* 88-94; TV 94-96; Perm to Offic from 96; rtd 04. *24 Glendale, Amble, Morpeth NE65 0RG* Tel (01665) 713796

NICHOLSON, Veronica Mary. See WILSON, Mrs Veronica Mary

NICKLAS-CARTER, Derath May. See DURKIN, Mrs Derath May

NICKLESS, Christopher John. b 58. Univ of Wales BA79. Coll of Resurr Mirfield 79. **d** 81 **p** 82. C Bassaleg *Mon* 81-85; TV Ebbw Vale 85-93; V Newport St Teilo 93-99. *c/o Bishopstow Stow Hill, Newport NP9 4EA* Tel (01633) 263510

NICKLIN, Ivor. b 41. FRSA68 BEd MTh73 PhD76 MA84. Wycliffe Hall Ox. **d** 84 **p** 85. NSM Weaverham *Ches* 84-89; P-in-c Kings Walden *St Alb* 89-91; P-in-c Offley w Lilley 89-91; V King's Walden and Offley w Lilley 91-93; V Basford *Lich* 93-98; rtd 98; Perm to Offic *Ches* from 99 and *Lich* 00-11. *232 Manor Way, Crewe CW2 6PH* Tel (01270) 669080

NICKOLS, James Alexander. b 75. Regent's Park Coll Ox BA96. Ridley Hall Cam 98. **d** 00 **p** 01. C Plymouth St Jude *Ex* 00-04; C Camberwell All SS *S'wark* 04-08; Hon C Camberwell Ch Ch from 09. *Christ Church, 676-680 Old Kent Road, London SE15 1JF* Tel 07968-062339 (mobile) E-mail jamesnkls@aol.com

NICKOLS-RAWLE, Peter John. b 44. St Luke's Coll Ex CertEd73. Sarum & Wells Th Coll 76. **d** 78 **p** 79. C Ex St Thos 78-80; Old and New Shoreham *Chich* 80-86; P-in-c Donnington 86-90; Chapl RAF 90-92; TV Ottery St Mary, Alfington, W Hill, Tipton etc *Ex* 92-97; V Breage w Germoe and Godolphin *Truro* 98-01; rtd 01; Perm to Offic *Truro* 01-05. *14 The Copse, Exmouth EX8 4EY* Tel (01395) 270068

NICKSON, Canon Ann Louise. b 58. New Hall Cam BA80 Fitzw Coll Cam BA95 Solicitor 81. Ridley Hall Cam PhD98. **d** 98 **p** 99. C Sanderstead All SS *S'wark* 98-01; P-in-c Norbury St Steph and Thornton Heath 01-05; V 05-10; AD Croydon N 06-10; TR Mortlake w E Sheen from 10; Hon Can S'wark Cathl from 10. *The Rectory, 170 Sheen Lane, London SW14 8LZ* Tel (020) 8876 4816 E-mail annnickson@aol.com

NICOL, David Christopher. b 56. Westmr Coll Ox BEd84 Ox Univ Inst of Educn 91. SAOMC 95. **d** 98 **p** 99. NSM Deddington w Barford, Clifton and Hempton *Ox* 98-01; V Longnor, Quarnford and Sheen *Lich* 01-08; P-in-c Woore and Norton in Hales from 09; Local Par Development Adv Shrewsbury Area from 10. *The Vicarage, Nantwich Road, Woore, Crewe CW3 9SA* Tel (01630) 642801
E-mail fr.david@tinyworld.co.uk
NICOL, Harvie Thomas. b 61. Aston Tr Scheme 95 St Jo Coll Nottm 97. **d** 99 **p** 00. C Balderstone *Man* 99; C S Rochdale 00-03; TV Ashton 03-08; P-in-c Ashton St Pet 03-08; V Formby St Luke *Liv* from 08. *St Luke's Vicarage, St Luke's Church Road, Liverpool L37 2DF* Tel (01704) 877655
NICOL, Stephen Trevor. b 52. Oak Hill Th Coll BA82. **d** 82 **p** 83. C Harold Hill St Geo *Chelmsf* 82-85; C Greenstead 85-88. *24 rue du Pré des Dames, 87330 Nouic, France* Tel 07811-138957 (mobile) E-mail stephen.nicol@nvoy.co.uk
NICOLE, Bruce. b 54. K Coll Lon MA96 ACIB. Wycliffe Hall Ox 89. **d** 91 **p** 92. C Headley All SS *Guildf* 91-95; V Camberley St Mich Yorktown from 95; RD Surrey Heath 02-06. *The Vicarage, 286 London Road, Camberley GU15 3JP* Tel (01276) 23602 E-mail revbrucenicole@aol.com
NICOLL, Alexander Charles Fiennes Jack. b 34. Lon Coll of Div 66. **d** 68 **p** 69. C Trentham *Lich* 68-71; C Hednesford 72-74; P-in-c Quarnford 74-84; V Longnor 74-84; P-in-c Sheen 80-84; V Longnor, Quarnford and Sheen 85-00; RD Alstonfield 96-00; rtd 00; Perm to Offic *Lich* from 00. *110 Stone Road, Uttoxeter ST14 7QW* Tel (01889) 569361
NICOLL, Miss Angela Olive Woods. b 50. Linc Th Coll 77. **dss** 79 **d** 87 **p** 94. Catford St Laur *S'wark* 79-83; Peckham St Jo w St Andr 83-88; Par Dn 87-88; Par Dn New Addington 88-94; C 94-02; S Africa 02-06; Perm to Offic *Ely* from 06. *15 Manor Park, Watton, Thetford IP25 6HH*
NICOLLS, Andrew John. b 67. Regents Th Coll BA03. Trin Coll Bris MA05. **d** 05 **p** 06. C Higher Bebington *Ches* 05-08; P-in-c Bulwell St Mary *S'well* from 08. *The Rectory, Station Road, Bulwell, Nottingham NG6 9AA* Tel 0115-927 8468
NICOLLS, Mrs Louise Victoria. b 71. Ch Ch Coll Cant BA93. St Jo Coll Nottm 07. **d** 10 **p** 11. C Arnold *S'well* from 10. *The Rectory, Station Road, Bulwell, Nottingham NG6 9AA* Tel 07969-572731 (mobile) E-mail louisestmarys@aol.com
NICOLSON, Paul Roderick. b 32. Cuddesdon Coll 65. **d** 67 **p** 68. C Farnham Royal *Ox* 67-68; Lic to Offic *St Alb* 69-82; C Hambleden Valley *Ox* 82-99; rtd 99. *93 Campbell Road, London N17 0AX* Tel (020) 8376 5455 Fax 8376 5319 Mobile 07961-177889 E-mail paul@nicolson.com
NIEMIEC, Paul Kevin. b 56. EAMTC 03. **d** 05 **p** 06. Youth Officer *Pet* 97-08; NSM Thrapston, Denford and Islip 05-08; TV Barnstaple *Ex* from 08. *The Vicarage, 40 Chichester Road, Newport, Barnstaple EX32 9EH* Tel (01271) 376285
E-mail pkniemiec@gmail.com
NIGER, Bishop on the. *See* OKEKE, The Rt Revd Ken Sandy Edozie
NIGERIA, Archbishop of. *See* AKINOLA, The Most Revd Peter Jasper
NIGHTINGALE, Catherine. b 72. **d** 01 **p** 02. C Birchencliffe *Wakef* 01-04; C to Dioc Chapl among Deaf People 01-04; TV E Farnworth and Kearsley *Man* 04-08; P-in-c Roughtown from 08; Chapl among Deaf People from 04. *The Vicarage, Carrhill Road, Mossley, Ashton-under-Lyne OL5 0BL* Tel (01457) 832250 E-mail cathy.nightingale@clearclergy.org.uk
NIGHTINGALE, Mrs Jennifer. b 66. Wolv Univ BA99. Qu Coll Birm. **d** 04 **p** 05. C Walsall St Paul *Lich* 04-07; C Holdenhurst and Iford *Win* from 07; Chapl Bp Win Comp Sch from 07. *13 Brackendale Road, Bournemouth BH8 9HY* Tel (01202) 533356 Mobile 07703-558668
NIGHTINGALE, Canon John Brodie. b 42. Pemb Coll Ox BA64 Qu Coll Cam BA67. Westcott Ho Cam 65. **d** 67 **p** 68. C Wythenshawe St Martin *Man* 67-70; Nigeria 70-76; P-in-c Amberley w N Stoke *Chich* 76-79; Adult Educn Adv 76-79; Asst Home Sec Gen Syn Bd for Miss and Unity 80-84; Miss Sec 84-87; P-in-c Wolverton w Norton Lindsey and Langley *Cov* 87-95; Dioc Miss Adv 87-95; V Rowley Regis *Birm* 95-07; Hon Can Birm Cathl 01-07; Warden of Readers 03-07; rtd 07; Perm to Offic *Birm* from 07. *19 Berberry Close, Birmingham B30 1TB* Tel 07811-128831 (mobile)
E-mail john.nightingale@btinternet.com
NIGHTINGALE, Susan Kay. b 44. Keele Univ BA66 Seabury-Western Th Sem DMin99. S'wark Ord Course 90. **d** 93 **p** 94. NSM St Giles Cripplegate w St Bart Moor Lane etc *Lon* 93-99; Perm to Offic *York* 93-99; Asst Chapl H Trin Geneva *Eur* 99-02; P-in-c Sutton on the Forest *York* 03-06. *Westfield Farm, Sheriff Hutton, York YO60 6QQ* Tel (01347) 878423
E-mail suenightingale@barbicannet.demon.co.uk
NIMMO, The Very Revd Alexander Emsley. b 53. Aber Univ BD76 PhD97 Edin Univ MPhil83 FSAScot93. Edin Th Coll 76. **d** 78 **p** 79. Prec St Andr Cathl Inverness 78-81; P-in-c Stornoway *Arg* 81-83; R 84; R Edin St Mich and All SS 84-90; Chapl HM Pris Saughton 87-90; R Aberdeen St Marg from 90; Can St Andr

Cathl from 96; Syn Clerk 01-08; Dean Ab from 08. *St Margaret's Clergy House, Gallowgate, Aberdeen AB25 1EA* Tel (01224) 644969 Fax 630767 E-mail alexander306@btinternet.com
NIND, Robert William Hampden. b 31. Ball Coll Ox BA54 MA60. Cuddesdon Coll 54. **d** 56 **p** 57. C Spalding *Linc* 56-60; Jamaica 60-67; P-in-c Battersea St Bart *S'wark* 67-70; V Brixton St Matt 70-82; Lic to Offic 82-84; Ind Chapl 84-89; Ind Chapl *Ox* 89-95; rtd 95. *19 Binswood Avenue, Headington, Oxford OX3 8NY* Tel (01865) 66604
E-mail bawalker@rwhnind.freeserve.co.uk
NINEHAM, Prof Dennis Eric. b 21. Qu Coll Ox BA43 MA46 Cam Univ BD64 Birm Univ Hon DD72. Linc Th Coll 44. **d** 44 **p** 45. Asst Chapl Qu Coll Ox 44-46; Chapl 46-54; Prof Bibl and Hist Th K Coll Lon 54-58; Prof Div Lon Univ 58-64; Regius Prof Div Cam Univ 64-69; Warden Keble Coll Ox 69-79; Hon Can Bris Cathl 80-86; Prof Th Bris Univ 80-86; rtd 86; Perm to Offic *Ox* from 87. *9 Fitzherbert Close, Iffley, Oxford OX4 4EN* Tel (01865) 715941
NINIS, The Ven Richard Betts. b 31. Linc Coll Ox BA53 MA62 Derby Univ Hon DUniv99. Linc Th Coll 53. **d** 55 **p** 56. C Poplar All SS w St Frideswide *Lon* 55-62; V Heref St Martin 62-71; V Upper and Lower Bullinghope w Grafton 68-71; R Dewsall w Callow 68-71; Dioc Missr 69-74; Preb Heref Cathl 70-74; Telford Planning Officer *Lich* 70-74; Can Res and Treas Lich Cathl 74-98; Adn Stafford 74-80; Adn Lich 80-98; rtd 98; Perm to Offic *B & W* from 00. *Hill View, 32 Robert Street, Williton, Taunton TA4 4QL* Tel and fax (01984) 634987
NISBECK, Peter. b 51. SOAS Lon BA73 Aston Univ MSc94. NOC 03. **d** 06 **p** 07. NSM Newcastle w Butterton *Lich* from 06. *210 Seabridge Lane, Newcastle ST5 3LS* Tel (01782) 662379
NISBET, Gillian Ruth. b 65. NOC 00. **d** 03 **p** 04. NSM Childwall St Dav *Liv* 03-06; NSM Abu Dhabi St Andr UAE from 06. *PO Box 60534, Al Bateen PO, Abu Dhabi, UAE* Tel (00971) 508-173234 E-mail gilliannisbet@hotmail.co.uk
NISBETT, Canon Thomas Norman. b 25. OBE91. Codrington Coll Barbados. **d** 62 **p** 63. Barbados 62-64; Bermuda from 65; Hon Can Bermuda Cathl from 81; rtd 97. *2 Shelton Road, Pembroke HM 20, Bermuda* Tel and fax (001441) 236 0537
NIXON, David John. b 59. St Chad's Coll Dur BA81 Ex Univ PhD02. St Steph Ho Ox 88. **d** 91 **p** 92. C Plymouth St Pet *Ex* 91-94; Chapl Ex Univ 94-03; P-in-c Stoke Damerel 03-09; P-in-c Devonport St Aubyn 03-09; R Stoke Damerel and Devonport St Aubyn from 09. *The Rectory, 6 Underhill Road, Plymouth PL3 4BP* Tel (01752) 562348 E-mail rev.dave@virgin.net
NIXON, Frances (Isobel). b 34. TCD BA62. **d** 94 **p** 95. NSM Rossorry *Clogh* from 94. *59 Granshagh Road, Enniskillen BT92 2BL* Tel (028) 6634 8723 Mobile 07710-307263
E-mail agfin@btinternet.com
NIXON, John David. b 38. Leeds Univ BSc60 CEng70 MICE. Linc Th Coll 76. **d** 78 **p** 79. C Rugby *Cov* 78-83; TV Bicester w Bucknell, Caversfield and Launton *Ox* 86-98; USA from 98; rtd 03. *1209 W 21st Street, Lawrence KS 66046-2833, USA* E-mail frjdn@hotmail.com *or* allsaintskcrector@juno.com
NIXON, Ms Naomi Jane. b 75. Keele Univ BA97. St Jo Coll Nottm MA00. **d** 01 **p** 02. C Ludlow, Ludford, Ashford Carbonell etc *Heref* 01-04; Chapl N Warks and Hinckley Coll of FE from 04; NSM Lillington and Old Milverton *Cov* from 10. *North Warks and Hinckley College, Hinckley Road, Nuneaton CV11 6BH* Tel (024) 7624 3355
E-mail naomi.nixon@nwhc.ac.uk
NIXON, Pauline Margaret. b 49. **d** 05 **p** 06. NSM Perranzabuloe *Truro* 05-10; NSM Crantock w Cubert 09-10; NSM Perranzabuloe and Crantock w Cubert from 10. *3 Dorrington House, Granny's Lane, Perranporth TR6 0HB* Tel (01872) 571697 *or* 552340 E-mail paulinenixon@btinternet.com
NIXON, Canon Phillip Edward. b 48. Ch Ch Ox MA73 DPhil73 Trin Coll Cam BA80 K Coll Lon MA00. Westcott Ho Cam 78. **d** 81 **p** 82. C Leeds Halton St Wilfrid *Ripon* 81-84; V Goring *Ox* 84; V Goring w S Stoke 84-03; RD Henley 94-02; Hon Can Ch Ch 00-03; P-in-c Northampton St Jas *Pet* from 03; Warden of Readers from 05. *St James's Vicarage, Vicarage Road, Northampton NN5 7AX* Tel (01604) 751164
E-mail phillipn@btinternet.com
NIXON, Miss Rosemary Ann. b 45. Bp Grosseteste Coll CertEd66 Dur Univ MA83 Edin Univ MTh95. Dalton Ho Bris BD73. **d** 87 **p** 94. Tutor St Jo Coll w Cranmer Hall Dur 75-89; Dir St Jo Coll Ext Progr 82-89; NSM Chester le Street *Dur* 87-89; TD Gateshead 89-92; Dir Cranmer Hall Urban Studies Unit 89-92; Staff Member Edin Th Coll 92-95; Prin TISEC 95-99; Can St Mary's Cathl 96-99; V Cleadon *Dur* 99-07; rtd 07. *6 Wearside Drive, Durham DH1 1LE* Tel 0191-384 6558
NIXON, Mrs Tonya. b 69. Plymouth Univ BSc93 St Mark & St Jo Coll Lon PGCE94. Qu Coll Birm 06. **d** 09 **p** 10. C Farmborough, Marksbury and Stanton Prior *B & W* from 09. *The Gables, Stanton Prior, Bath BA2 9HT*
E-mail tonya39n@btinternet.com
NIXON, William Samuel. Reading Univ BSc94 TCD BTh00. **d** 00 **p** 01. C Lisburn St Paul *Conn* 00-02; C Hillsborough *D & D*

02-06; P-in-c Edin Clermiston Em 06-08; I Killaney w Carryduff *D & D* from 08; Warden of Readers from 11. *The Rectory, 700 Saintfield Road, Carryduff, Belfast BT8 8BU* Tel (028) 9081 2342 Mobile 07764-277771 E-mail cazza-willie@hotmail.com

NIXSON, Peter. b 27. Ball Coll Ox BA51 MA59 Ex Univ PGCE67 DipEd72. Coll of Resurr Mirfield 51. **d** 53 **p** 54. C Babbacombe *Ex* 53-56; C Swindon New Town *Bris* 56-57; C Boyne Hill *Ox* 57-60; C-in-c Bayswater St Mary CD 60-66; Perm to Offic *Ex* 66-67 and 70-85; Perm to Offic *Lich* 67-69; Hd RE Oswestry Boys' High Sch 67-69; Hon C Oswestry H Trin 69-70; Sch Coun Tiverton 70-75; Newton Abbot 75-85; V Winkleigh *Ex* 85-92; R Ashreigney 85-92; V Broadwoodkelly 85-92; V Brushford 85-92; RD Chulmleigh 87-93; rtd 93; Perm to Offic *Ex* from 93. *40 Lidford Tor Avenue, Paignton TQ4 7ED* Tel (01803) 522698

NIXSON, Rosemary Clare. See WARD, Mrs Rosemary Clare

NJENGA, Kennedy Samuel. b 60. Oak Hill Th Coll Qu Coll Birm. **d** 01 **p** 02. C Old Trafford St Jo *Man* 01-04; P-in-c Pheasey *Lich* 04-10; V W Bromwich Gd Shep w St Jo from 10; Chapl Sandwell Coll from 10. *The Vicarage, 4 Bromford Lane, West Bromwich B70 7HP* Tel 0121-525 5530 E-mail njambinjenga@aol.com

NJENGA, Lukas. b 68. Natal Univ BTh97 MTh98. Trin Coll Nairobi. **d** 92 **p** 93. V Kitengela Kenya 92-96; R Sobantu S Africa 96-01; Lect Carlile Coll Nairobi 01-02; R Glas St Geo 02-05; Chapl Glas Caledonian Univ 05-11; Chapl York St Jo Univ from 11. *The Vicarage, York Road, Barlby, Selby YO8 5JP* Tel (01904) 876606 Mobile 07534-719450 E-mail l.njenga@yorksj.ac.uk

✠**NJOJO, The Rt Revd Patrice Byankya.** b 38. BA76. Montreal Dioc Th Coll 77. **d** 70 **p** 00. C Dp Doga from 00; Abp Congo 92-02. *PO Box 25586, Kampala, Uganda* Tel (00256) 77-647495 E-mail eac-mags@infocom.co.uk

NJOKA, Stanley. b 80. St Andr Coll Kabare 01 Lon Sch of Th 06. **d** 04 **p** 05. Kenya 04-06; Perm to Offic *Lon* 06-07 and *S'wark* 08-10; NSM Peckham St Jo w St Andr *S'wark* 10-11; NSM Camberwell St Giles w St Matt from 11; Chapl King's Coll Hosp NHS Trust from 10. *The Chaplaincy, King's College Hospital, Denmark Hill, London SE5 9RS* Tel (020) 3299 3522 Mobile 07846-759133 E-mail sknjoka@yahoo.co.uk

NJOKU, Chinenye Ngozi. b 63. Trin Coll Bris. **d** 09 **p** 10. C Goldington *St Alb* from 09. *1 Atholl Walk, Bedford MK41 0BG* Tel (01234) 343326 Mobile 07515-171579 E-mail gozy78@hotmail.com

NJOROGE, John Kibe Mwangi. b 47. **d** 79 **p** 79. C Llantwit Major 07-10; Chapl HM Pris Elmley from 11. *HM Prison Elmley, Church Road, Eastchurch, Sheerness ME12 4DZ* Tel (01795) 882130 E-mail john.njoroge@hmps.gsi.gov.uk *or* john.njoroge@btinternet.com

NJUGUNA, Daniel Cahira. b 73. St Jo Coll Nottm BA04. **d** 00 **p** 01. Kenya 00-03; C Balderton and Barnby-in-the-Willows *S'well* 04-06; TV Hucknall Torkard 06-11; V Wednesbury St Paul Wood Green *Lich* from 11. *St Paul's Vicarage, 68 Wood Green Road, Wednesbury WS10 9QT* Tel 07817-577436 (mobile) E-mail dcahira@yahoo.co.uk

NJUGUNA, Timothy. b 49. St Paul's Coll Limuru BD84 Presbyterian Th Coll Seoul ThM89 San Francisco Th Sem DMin03. **d** 83 **p** 84. V Nairobi St Mary Kenya 84-86; V Karura 86-87; V Kirangari 89-90; Dioc Sec Mt Kenya S 91-93; P-in-c San Bruno USA 99-03; Perm to Offic *S'wark* 05-07; Hon C Falkirk *Edin* from 07. *55 Kerse Lane, Falkirk FK1 1RX* Tel (01324) 877405 Mobile 07805-690363 E-mail tegssa@yahoo.com

NOAH, Michael John. b 44. WEMTC 00. **d** 02 **p** 03. NSM Hucclecote *Glouc* 02-05; NSM Malmesbury w Westport and Brokenborough *Bris* 05-11; NSM Frampton on Severn, Arlingham, Saul etc *Glouc* from 11. *1 Athelstan Court, Malmesbury SN16 0FD* Tel (01666) 826564 E-mail mikenoah@supanet.com

NOAKES, Mrs Dorothy. b 35. Derby Coll of Educn CertEd55 Ex Univ BEd85 BPhil(Ed)92. **d** 96 **p** 97. OLM Helston and Wendron *Truro* from 96. *6 Tenderah Road, Helston TR13 8NT* Tel (01326) 573239 E-mail dorothy@dorothy1.wanadoo.co.uk

NOBBS, Charles Henry ffrench. b 67. Hatf Coll Dur BSc89 St Jo Coll Dur BA99 CEng96. Cranmer Hall Dur 97. **d** 99 **p** 00. C Northampton St Giles *Pet* 99-02; C Collingtree w Courteenhall and Milton Malsor 02-11; Min Grange Park LEP from 11; Police Chapl Co-ord from 03. *10 Foxglove Close, Grange Park, Northampton NN4 5DD* Tel (01604) 875188 Mobile 07742-590789 E-mail charlie@dunelm.org.uk

NOBBS, John Ernest. b 35. Tyndale Hall Bris 60. **d** 63 **p** 64. C Walthamstow St Mary *Chelmsf* 63-66; C Braintree 66-69; C Wakef St Andr and St Mary 69-71; C Tooting Graveney St Nic *S'wark* 71-74; C Woking St Pet *Guildf* 74-78; C Worthing St Geo *Chich* 78-88; C Rayleigh *Chelmsf* 88-94; rtd 94; Perm to Offic *Chelmsf* from 00. *89 Panfield Lane, Braintree CM7 5RP* Tel (01376) 322901

NOBEL, Johannes. b 81. Evang Th Faculty Leuven BA03 Utrecht Univ MA05 St Jo Coll Dur MA08. Cranmer Hall Dur 06. **d** 08 **p** 09. C Norton St Mary *Dur* from 08; C Stockton St Chad from

08. *St Chad's Vicarage, Ragpath Lane, Stockton-on-Tees TS19 9JN* Tel (01642) 672502 E-mail johannes.nobel@gmail.com

NOBLE, Alexander Frederick Innes (Sandy). b 30. Selw Coll Cam BA53 MA58. Lon Coll of Div ALCD55. **d** 55 **p** 56. C Stratton St Margaret *Bris* 55-57; C Brislington St Luke 57-59; Chapl Pierrepont Sch Frensham 59-61; Asst Chapl Repton Sch Derby 61-63; Chapl 63-66; Chapl Blundell's Sch Tiverton 66-72; St Jo C of E Sch Cowley 73-77; Chapl Cranbrook Sch Kent 77-81; Chapl St Geo Sch Harpenden 81-90; Hon C Herriard w Winslade and Long Sutton etc 90-94; rtd 95; P-in-c Oare w Culbone *B & W* 95-99; Perm to Offic from 00. *Upway, Church Street, Minehead TA24 5JU* Tel (01643) 708976

NOBLE, Anne Valerie. b 60. Univ Coll Ox BA82 Toronto Univ MSc84 PhD91. St Jo Coll Nottm 04. **d** 07 **p** 08. C Wollaton *S'well* 07-11; TV Clifton from 11. *St Mary's House, 58 Village Road, Clifton, Nottingham NG11 8NE* Tel 0115-921 1188 E-mail nobles1@btinternet.com

NOBLE, Christopher John Lancelot. b 58. Oak Hill Th Coll 88. **d** 90 **p** 91. C Tonbridge SS Pet and Paul *Roch* 90-95; P-in-c Stansted w Fairseat and Vigo 95-98; R from 98. *The Rectory, 9 The Coach Drive, Meopham, Gravesend DA13 0SZ* Tel (01732) 822494

NOBLE, David. b 37. S Dios Minl Tr Scheme 84. **d** 87 **p** 88. C Alverstoke *Portsm* 87-89; R Jerramungup Australia 90-93; R Bridgetown 93-97; R Willetton 97-02; rtd 02. *Quill Studio, 9 Chaparral Crescent, Willetton WA 6155, Australia* Tel and fax (0033) (8) 9259 0323 Mobile 41-717 2542 E-mail thenobles@surak.com.au

NOBLE, Mrs Eileen Joan. b 45. NEOC 90. **d** 93 **p** 94. C Gosforth All SS *Newc* 93-96; C Cramlington 96-97; TV 97-01; V Ashington 01-06; rtd 06; Hon C Monkseaton St Mary *Newc* from 07. *34 Gorsedene Road, Whitley Bay NE26 4AH* E-mail revnoble2000@yahoo.com

NOBLE, Canon Graham Edward. b 49. Open Univ BA74 SS Paul & Mary Coll Cheltenham CertEd71. EAMTC 85. **d** 88 **p** 89. C Kesgrave *St E* 88-90; P-in-c Gt and Lt Blakenham w Baylham and Nettlestead 90-95; P-in-c Debenham w Aspall and Kenton 95-04; P-in-c Helmingham w Framsden and Pettaugh w Winston 99-04; R Debenham and Helmingham 04-05; RD Loes 99-05; Hon Can St E Cathl 03-05; rtd 05; Perm to Offic *St E* from 05. *36 Gracechurch Street, Debenham, Stowmarket IP14 6RE* Tel (01728) 861008 E-mail graham@noblefamily.fsnet.co.uk

NOBLE, Paul Vincent. b 54. Leeds Univ BA75 PGCE76 Ox Univ BA81 MA85. St Steph Ho Ox 79. **d** 82 **p** 83. C Prestbury *Glouc* 82-85; P-in-c Avening w Cherington 85-90; V The Suttons w Tydd *Linc* 90-98; R Skirbeck St Nic from 98. *The Rectory, Fishtoft Road, Skirbeck, Boston PE21 0DJ* Tel (01205) 362734 E-mail frpnoble@skirbeckrectory.freeserve.co.uk

NOBLE, Canon Philip David. b 46. Glas Univ BSc67 Edin Univ BD70. Edin Th Coll 67. **d** 70 **p** 71. C Edin Ca Th 70-72; C Port Moresby Papua New Guinea 72-73; P-in-c Sakarina 73-75; R Cambuslang *Glas* 76-83; R Uddingston 76-83; Ev Prestwick 83-85; R Prestwick 85-11; Can St Mary's Cathl 99-11; rtd 11. *28 Duncraig Street, Inverness IV3 5DJ* Tel (01463) 233612

NOBLE, Robert. b 43. TCD BA66 BD73. **d** 68 **p** 69. C Holywood *D & D* 68-71; Chapl RAF 71-98; Chapl Holmewood Ho Sch Tunbridge Wells 98-04; Perm to Offic *Chich* 01-08 and *Heref* from 08. *Temperance Cottage, Weston under Penyard, Ross-on-Wye HR9 7NX* Tel (01989) 566748 E-mail rjnobles@tiscali.co.uk

NOBLES, Mrs Mary Joy. b 37. WEMTC 04. **d** 05 **p** 06. NSM Malvern Link w Cowleigh *Worc* from 05. *4 Hamilton Close, Powick, Worcester WR2 4NH* Tel (01905) 831925 E-mail m.nobles@btopenworld.com

NOBLET, David. b 62. Cranmer Hall Dur 97. **d** 99 **p** 00. C Standish *Blackb* 00-03; P-in-c Langho Billington 03-11; Lic to Offic from 11; Chapl HM Pris Kirkham from 08. *HM Prison Kirkham, Freckleton Road, Kirkham, Preston PR4 2RN* Tel (01772) 675625 E-mail davidnoblet@aol.com

NOBLETT, The Ven William Alexander. b 53. Southn Univ BTh78 Westmr Coll Ox MTh99. Sarum & Wells Th Coll 74. **d** 78 **p** 79. C Sholing *Win* 78-80; I Ardamine w Kiltennel, Glascarrig etc *C & O* 80-82; Chapl RAF 82-84; V Middlesbrough St Thos *York* 84-87; Asst Chapl HM Pris Wakef 87-89; Chapl 89-92; Chapl HM Pris Nor 92-97; Chapl HM Pris Full Sutton 97-01; Chapl Gen of Pris and Adn to HM Pris from 01; Can and Preb York Minster from 01; Lic to Offic from 01; Chapl to The Queen from 05; Hon Can Liv Cathl from 09. *Chaplaincy HQ, Post Point 3.08, 3rd Floor Red Zone, Clive House, 70 Petty France, London SW1H 9HD* Tel 03000-475184 Fax 03000-476822/3

NOCK, Peter Arthur. b 15. Keble Coll Ox BA36 MA42. Bps' Coll Cheshunt 37. **d** 39 **p** 40. C Gt Harwood St Bart *Blackb* 39-40; C Lancaster Priory Ch 40-45; V Over Wyresdale 45-50; V Darwen St Cuth 50-64; V Sparkhill St Jo *Birm* 64-71; RD Bordesley 67-71; V Maney 71-81; rtd 81; Perm to Offic *Carl* from 81. *Westlands, Linden Fold, Grange-over-Sands LA11 7AY* Tel (01539) 535139

NOCK, Roland George William. b 62. St Andr Univ BSc84 BD89. Edin Th Coll 91. **d** 91 **p** 92. C Dunfermline *St And* 91-93; C W Fife Team Min 91-93; R Cupar 93-96; CF 96-99. *46 Heol Y Parc, Cefneithin, Llanelli SA14 7DL* Tel (01269) 845847 E-mail roland@nock.screaming.net

NOCKELS, John Martin. b 46. Lich Th Coll Qu Coll Birm 73. **d** 73 **p** 74. C Eccleshill *Bradf* 73-76; C Fawley *Win* 76-78; V Southampton St Jude 78-84; R Tadley St Pet 84-98; P-in-c Gt and Lt Massingham and Harpley *Nor* 98-99; P-in-c S Raynham, E w W Raynham, Helhoughton, etc 98-99; R Gt w Lt Massingham, Harpley, Rougham etc 99-06; rtd 06. *96 Church Lane, Beeston Regis, Sheringham NR26 8EY* Tel (01263) 825404

NODDER, Marcus Charles Colmore. b 67. Pemb Coll Cam BA89 PGCE90. Oak Hill Th Coll BA01. **d** 01 **p** 02. C Denton Holme *Carl* 01-04; C Limehouse *Lon* from 04. *13 Storers Quay, London E14 3BZ* Tel (020) 7515 7947 E-mail mnodder@hotmail.com *or* marcus@nodder.fsbusiness.co.uk

NODDER, Thomas Arthur (Brother Arnold). b 20. K Coll Lon 58. **d** 60 **p** 61. Brotherhood of the H Cross from 49; C Rotherhithe St Mary w All SS *S'wark* 60-63; SSF from 63; Lic to Offic *Chelmsf* 63-66; C Plaistow St Andr 66-68; Lic to Offic *Newc* 69-70 and *Birm* 70-83; Perm to Offic *Birm* 90-98; Lic to Offic *Sarum* 83-89; rtd 90; Perm to Offic *Chelmsf* from 98. *Society of St Francis, 42 Balaam Street, London E13 8AQ* Tel (020) 7476 5189

NODDINGS, John Henry. b 39. Chich Th Coll 80. **d** 81 **p** 82. C Southborough St Pet w Ch Ch and St Matt *Roch* 81-83; C Prittlewell *Chelmsf* 83-86; V Clay Hill St Jo *Lon* 86-88; V Clay Hill St Jo and St Luke 88-02; Chapl Chase Farm Hosp Enfield 88-94; Chapl Chase Farm Hosps NHS Trust 94-95; P-in-c Gt Coxwell w Buscot, Coleshill etc *Ox* 03-10; rtd 03; Perm to Offic *Sarum* from 10. *9 Fisherton Island, Salisbury SP2 7TG* Tel (01722) 320177 E-mail johnnoddings@btinternet.com

NOKE, Christopher. b 48. Ex Coll Ox BA69 MA79 LSE MSc78 ACA72 FCA79. SEITE 03. **d** 06 **p** 07. NSM Raynes Park St Sav and S Wimbledon All SS *S'wark* from 06. *Cedar Lodge, Church Road, Ham, Richmond TW10 5HG* Tel (020) 8948 7986

NOKES, Michael David Patrick. b 44. York St Jo Coll MA05. **d** 02 **p** 03. Ca from 88; NSM Heworth Ch Ch *York* 02-08; Perm to Offic *Bradf* from 02; *Ripon* from 03; *York* from 08; rtd 10. *5 Fox Covert, York YO31 9EN* Tel (01904) 674879 Mobile 07776-252440 E-mail michaelanddi@talktalk.net

NOKES, Canon Peter Warwick. b 48. Leic Univ BA71. Westcott Ho Cam 79. **d** 81 **p** 82. C Northfield *Birm* 81-84; C Ludlow *Heref* 84-87; P-in-c Writtle w Highwood *Chelmsf* 87-91; V 91-92; P-in-c Epping St Jo 92-95; P-in-c Coopersale 93-95; TR Epping Distr 95-99; R Nor St Pet Mancroft w St Jo Maddermarket from 99; Hon Can Nor Cathl from 10. *37 Unthank Road, Norwich NR2 2PB* Tel (01603) 627816 *or* 610443 Fax 766652 Mobile 07711-384009 E-mail pwnokes@o2.co.uk

NOKES, Robert Harvey. b 39. Keble Coll Ox BA61 MA65. Qu Coll Birm 61. **d** 63 **p** 64. C Totteridge *St Alb* 63-67; C Dunstable 67-73; V Langford 73-90; R Braughing w Furneux Pelham and Stocking Pelham 90-04; Perm to Offic *Ox* from 04. *92 Western Drive, Hanslope, Milton Keynes MK19 7LE* Tel (01908) 337939 E-mail nokes@easykey.com

NOLAN, James Charles William. b 44. Chich Th Coll 75. **d** 77 **p** 78. C Crewe St Andr *Ches* 77-79; C Sale St Anne 79-83; R Holme Runcton w S Runcton and Wallington *Ely* from 83; V Tottenhill w Wormegay from 83; R Watlington from 83. *The Rectory, Downham Road, Watlington, King's Lynn PE33 0HS* Tel (01553) 810305

NOLAN, Marcus. b 54. Bris Univ BEd. Ridley Hall Cam. **d** 83 **p** 84. C Dagenham *Chelmsf* 83-86; C Finchley St Paul and St Luke *Lon* 86-90; V W Hampstead Trin 90-98; rtd 99; Perm to Offic *Derby* 00-06. *55 Blanch Croft, Melbourne, Derby DE73 8GG*

NOLES, Mrs Gillian. BEd86. St Paul's Th Cen Lon. **d** 10 **p** 11. NSM Colchester St Jo *Chelmsf* from 10. *6 Baronia Croft, Colchester CO4 9EE*

NOLES, Jeremy Andrew. b 67. St Jo Coll Nottm 02. **d** 04 **p** 05. C Southchurch Ch Ch *Chelmsf* 04-07; C Colchester St Jo from 07. *6 Baronia Croft, Colchester CO4 9EE* Tel 07719-652333 (mobile)

NOLLAND, John Leslie. b 47. New England Univ (NSW) BSc67 Clare Coll Cam PhD78. Moore Th Coll Sydney ThL70 BD71. **d** 71 **p** 72. Australia 71-78; Canada 78-86; Asst Prof NT Studies Regent Coll Vancouver 78-86; Tutor Trin Coll Bris from 86; Vice Prin 91-97. *Trinity College, Stoke Hill, Bristol BS9 1JP* Tel 0117-968 2083 *or* 968 4053 Fax 968 7470 E-mail john.nolland@trinity-bris.ac.uk

NOLLER, Hilda Elizabeth Mary (Sister Elizabeth Mary). b 26. MSR47 FSR53. **d** 95 **p** 96. Lic to Offic *Chelmsf* 96-02; Sister Superior CSD from 00. *Retired Nurses Home, Riverside Avenue, Bournemouth BH7 7EE* Tel (01202) 397014

NOON, Canon Edward George. b 16. Selw Coll Cam BA38 MA42. Bps' Coll Cheshunt 38. **d** 40 **p** 41. C Kingston St Jo *S'wark* 40-43; C Dulwich St Barn 43-48; P-in-c S Wimbledon St Pet 48-50; V 50-55; V Mitcham St Mark 55-65; V Horley 65-77; RD

Reigate 72-76; Hon Can S'wark Cathl 72-83; P-in-c Purley St Barn 77-83; rtd 83; Hon C Overbury w Teddington, Alstone etc *Worc* 83-86; Perm to Offic *Glouc* 86-95. *40 Shepherds Leaze, Wotton-under-Edge GL12 7LQ* Tel (01453) 844978

NOORDANUS, Francis Peter. b 61. Cant Univ (NZ) BA82 ACT BTh90. **d** 92 **p** 93. New Zealand 92-02; C Ashburton 92-94; V Masterton St Matt 94-02; Chapl Eindhoven *Eur* from 02. *Paradijslaan 76, 5611 KR Eindhoven, The Netherlands* Tel (0031) (40) 245 0601 E-mail f.p.noordanus@planet.nl

NORBURN, Christopher Richard. b 62. Cov Poly BSc85. Aston Tr Scheme 92 Ridley Hall Cam 94. **d** 96 **p** 97. C Exning St Martin w Landwade *St E* 96-99; P-in-c Redgrave cum Botesdale w Rickinghall 99-01; R from 01. *The Rectory, Bury Road, Rickinghall, Diss IP22 1HA* Tel (01379) 898685

NORBURN, The Very Revd Richard Evelyn Walter. b 21. Witwatersrand Univ BA44 TDip44. St Paul's Coll Grahamstown 49. **d** 51 **p** 53. Vice-Prin Dioc Tr Coll Pretoria S Africa 51-56; Dioc Dir RE and R Potgietersrus 56-62; C Croydon St Sav *Cant* 63-64; V Norbury St Phil 65-75; V Addington 75-81; Hon Can Cant Cathl 79-81; RD Croydon Addington 81; Dean Botswana 81-88; rtd 89; Perm to Offic *Cant* 98-05. *The College of St Barnabas, Blackberry Lane, Lingfield RH7 6NJ* Tel (01342) 872839

NORBURN, Canon Richard Henry. b 32. MBE97. St Edm Hall Ox BA57. Wycliffe Hall Ox 57. **d** 59 **p** 59. C Sudbury St Greg and St Pet *St E* 59-65; Dioc Youth Officer 65-74; P-in-c Gt Livermere 74-81; R Ampton w Lt Livermere and Ingham 74-81; RD Thingoe 78-88; Hon Can St E Cathl 81-97; R Ingham w Ampton and Gt and Lt Livermere 81-92; TV Blackbourne 92-97; rtd 97; Perm to Offic *St E* from 97. *69 Churchgate Street, Bury St Edmunds IP33 1RL* Tel (01284) 702644 E-mail richardhnorburn@btopenworld.com

NORBURY, Robert John. b 60. Southn Univ BA83 Univ of Wales (Ban) BTh07. S'wark Ord Course 01. **d** 04 **p** 05. OLM Eltham Park St Luke *S'wark* 04-07; Perm to Offic *Chich* 07-08; NSM Crowborough St Jo from 08; P-in-c from 09; Chapl Wandsworth Primary Care Trust 09-10; Dir of Ords Croydon Area *S'wark* from 10. *St John's Vicarage, St John's Road, Crowborough TN6 1RZ* Tel (01892) 668188 Mobile 07715-595828 E-mail frrobnorbury@aol.com

NORBY, Dean Luverne. **d** 11. C Edin St Paul and St Geo from 11. *53 Balgreen Road, Edinburgh EH12 5TY* Tel 07821-712500 (mobile)

NORFIELD, David Jonathan. b 67. Humberside Univ BA89. Linc Th Coll MA94 Westcott Ho Cam 95. **d** 97 **p** 98. C Halstead St Andr w H Trin and Greenstead Green *Chelmsf* 97-01; V Moulsham St Jo 01-04; Chapl RAF from 04. *Chaplaincy Services, Valiant Block, HQ Air Command, RAF High Wycombe HP14 4UE* Tel (01494) 496800 Fax 496343 E-mail davidnorfield@hotmail.com

NORFOLK, The Ven Edward Matheson. b 21. Leeds Univ BA44. Coll of Resurr Mirfield 41. **d** 46 **p** 47. C Greenford H Cross *Lon* 46-47; C S Mymms K Chas 47-50; C Bushey *St Alb* 50-53; PC Waltham Cross 53-59; V Welwyn Garden City 59-69; R Gt Berkhamsted 69-81; Hon Can St Alb 72-82; V Kings Langley 81-82; Adn St Alb 82-87; rtd 87; Perm to Offic *Ex* 87-09. *5 Fairlawn Court, Sidmouth EX10 8UR* Tel (01395) 514222

NORFOLK, Archdeacon of. *See* HAYDEN, The Ven David Frank

NORGATE, Norman George. b 32. Qu Coll Cam BA55 MA58. Ridley Hall Cam. **d** 57 **p** 58. C Erith St Paul *Roch* 57-60; C E Twickenham St Steph *Lon* 60-63; V Bexleyheath St Pet *Roch* 63-71; V Woking St Mary *Guildf* 71-83; V Tunbridge Wells St Jas *Roch* 83-92; TR Tunbridge Wells St Jas w St Phil 92-97; rtd 97; Perm to Offic *St E* from 97. *Crathie, 58 Sexton Meadows, Bury St Edmunds IP33 2SB* Tel (01284) 767363

NORKETT, Alan. b 45. Sarum & Wells Th Coll 85. **d** 87 **p** 88. C Shrewsbury St Giles w Sutton and Atcham *Lich* 87-90; V Mow Cop 90-94; NSM Astbury and Smallwood *Ches* 96-97; NSM Sandbach Heath w Wheelock 97-98; C Castleford All SS and Whitwood *Wakef* 98-01; C Glass Houghton 98-01; R Shrawley, Witley, Astley and Abberley *Worc* 01-10; rtd 10. *15 New Road, Far Forest, Kidderminster DY14 9TQ* E-mail vicaralan@aol.com

NORMAN, Canon Andrew Herbert. b 54. K Coll Lon BD77 AKC77 Lon Univ PhD88. St Steph Ho Ox 77. **d** 78 **p** 79. C Deal St Leon w Sholden *Cant* 78-81; C Maidstone All SS and St Phil w Tovil 81-84; V Tenterden St Mich 84-93; Chapl Benenden Hosp 86-91; Dir Post-Ord Tr *Cant* 91-93; R Guildf St Nic from 93; Hon Can Guildf Cathl from 05. *The Rectory, 3 Flower Walk, Guildford GU2 4EP* Tel (01483) 504895 E-mail fr-andrew@st-nicholas.freeserve.co.uk

NORMAN, Canon Andrew Robert. b 63. Univ Coll Ox BA84 MA99 Selw Coll Cam BA94 MA99 Birm Univ MPhil08 AIL89. Ridley Hall Cam 92. **d** 95 **p** 96. C Chapl Paris St Mich *Eur* 95-00; C Clifton Ch Ch w Em *Bris* 00-02; Abp's Asst Sec for Ecum and Angl Affairs *Cant* 02-05; Abp's Prin Sec for Internat, Ecum and Angl Communion Affairs 05-08; Prin Ridley Hall

Cam from 09; Hon Prov Can Cant Cathl from 06. *Ridley Hall, Cambridge CB3 9HG* Tel (01223) 746580 Fax 746581 E-mail arn1000@cam.ac.uk

NORMAN, Ann. *See* NORMAN, Margaret Ann

NORMAN, Catherine. b 51. Nottm Univ BSc73 N Counties Coll Newc CertEd74. Linc Th Coll 95. **d** 95 **p** 96. C Scartho *Linc* 95-99; V Ulceby Gp 99-02; TV Guiseley w Esholt *Bradf* 02-08; P-in-c Rawdon from 08; RD Otley from 09. *The Vicarage, Layton Avenue, Rawdon, Leeds LS19 6QQ* Tel 0113-250 3263 E-mail caytenorman@aol.com *or* office@stpetersrawdon.co.uk

NORMAN, Canon Edward Robert. b 38. Selw Coll Cam BA61 PhD64 MA65 BD67 DD78 FRHistS72 FRSA88. Linc Th Coll 65. **d** 65 **p** 71. Fell Jes Coll Cam 64-71; Lect Cam Univ 65-88; Dean Peterho Cam 71-88; Dean of Chpl Ch Ch Coll of HE Cant 88-95; Six Preacher Cant Cathl 84-90; Can Res York Minster 95-04; Treas 95-99; Chan 99-04; Hon Prof York Univ from 96; Hon C St Andr-by-the-Wardrobe w St Ann, Blackfriars *Lon* from 05; Hon C St Jas Garlickhythe w St Mich Queenhithe etc from 05. *Peterhouse, Cambridge CB2 1RD*

NORMAN, Mrs Elizabeth Ann. b 43. SAOMC 95. **d** 98 **p** 99. OLM Amersham *Ox* 98-04; Perm to Offic *Ex* from 11. *Lamorna, Main Road, Bickington, Barnstaple EX31 2NA* Tel (01271) 859314

NORMAN, The Ven Garth. b 38. St Chad's Coll Dur BA62 MA68 UEA MEd84 Cam Inst of Educn PGCE68. **d** 63 **p** 64. C Wandsworth St Anne *S'wark* 63-66; C Trunch w Swafield *Nor* 66-71; R Gimingham 71-77; TR Trunch 77-83; RD Repps 75-83; Prin Chiltern Chr Tr Course *Ox* 83-87; C W Wycombe w Bledlow Ridge, Bradenham and Radnage 83-87; Dir of Tr *Roch* 88-94; Adn Bromley and Bexley 94-03; Hon Can Roch Cathl 91-03; rtd 03; Perm to Offic *S'well* from 03; Chapl to Retired Clergy 04-09; Perm to Offic *Ely* from 10. *32 Scotsdowne Road, Trumpington, Cambridge CB2 9HU* Tel (01223) 844303 E-mail garthnorman@btinternet.com

NORMAN, Gary. b 64. Newc Univ BA87. Ripon Coll Cuddesdon 02. **d** 04 **p** 05. C Spennymoor and Whitworth *Dur* 04-09; P-in-c Croxdale and Tudhoe from 08; P-in-c Merrington from 09. *The Vicarage, 21 York Villas, Spennymoor DL16 6LP* Tel (01388) 811108

NORMAN, Jillianne Elizabeth. b 59. Ridley Hall Cam 85. **d** 88 **p** 94. Par Dn Fishponds St Jo *Bris* 88-92; Perm to Offic 92-94; Hon C Warmley, Syston and Bitton from 94; Chapl Univ Hosps Bris NHS Foundn Trust from 02. *74 Blackhorse Road, Mangotsfield, Bristol BS16 9AY* Tel 0117-956 1551 Fax 904 6894 E-mail jilliannenorman@blueyonder.co.uk

NORMAN, Linda Mary. b 48. Man Univ BSc69 CertEd70 St Jo Coll Dur BA82. dss 83 **d** 87. York St Mich-le-Belfrey 83-88; Par Dn 87-88; rtd 88. *23 Ainsty Avenue, Dringhouses, York YO24 1HH* Tel (01904) 706152

NORMAN, Lynette Dianne. b 52. Sussex Univ CertEd73 Univ of Wales (Ban) BEd89. Ripon Coll Cuddesdon 00. **d** 02 **p** 03. C Welshpool w Castle Caereinion *St As* 02-04; R LLanrwst 04-11; C Llanrhaeadr ym Mochnant etc from 11. *The Vicarage, Llanrhaeadr-ym-Mochnant, Oswestry SY10 0JZ* Tel (01691) 860408 Mobile 07889-184517

NORMAN, Margaret Ann. b 48. N Lon Poly CertEd76 ALA73. SEITE 09. **d** 11. NSM Erith St Paul *Roch* from 11. *27 Kempton Close, Erith DA8 3SR* Tel (01322) 430902 E-mail ann.norman@hotmail.com

NORMAN, Michael John. b 59. Southn Univ LLB82. Wycliffe Hall Ox 82. **d** 85 **p** 86. C Woodley St Jo the Ev *Ox* 85-89; C Uphill *B & W* 89-92; TV 92-98; R Bath St Sav w Swainswick and Woolley from 98. *St Saviour's Rectory, Claremont Road, Bath BA1 6LX* Tel (01225) 311637 E-mail michael@stsaviours.org.uk

NORMAN, Michael John. b 61. St Jo Coll Ox BSc83 Univ Coll Lon MSc84. Aston Tr Scheme 89 St Jo Coll Nottm 91. **d** 93 **p** 94. C Haughton le Skerne *Dur* 93-97; R Sapcote and Sharnford w Wigston Parva *Leic* from 97; RD Sparkenhoe W 02-07. *The Rectory, 4 Sharnford Road, Sapcote, Leicester LE9 4JN* Tel (01455) 272215 E-mail micknorman@msn.com

NORMAN, Peter John. b 42. Culham Coll of Educn TCert66 Lon Inst of Educn DipEd83 MA86. STETS 95. **d** 98 **p** 99. NSM Bath Weston All SS w N Stoke and Langridge *B & W* from 98. *5 Rockliffe Avenue, Bathwick, Bath BA2 6QP* Tel (01225) 463348

NORMAN, Peter John. b 59. Chich Th Coll 84. **d** 87 **p** 88. C Farncombe *Guildf* 87-91; C Cockington *Ex* 91-94; V Winkleigh from 94; R Ashreigney from 94; R Broadwoodkelly from 94; V Brushford from 94. *The Vicarage, Torrington Road, Winkleigh EX19 8HR* Tel (01837) 83719

NORMAN, Canon Richard Hudson. b 58. Louisiana State Univ BS84 MA88. Gen Th Sem NY MDiv93 STM93. **d** 92 **p** 93. C Southgate St Andr *Lon* 92 and 97-98; USA 92-97 and from 02; Assoc New York City St Matt and St Tim 92-93; R Abbeville St Paul 93-95; Assoc R Chevy Chase All SS 95-97; V Mill Hill St Mich *Lon* 98-02; R Greenville Redeemer 02-05; Sen Can St Mark's Cathl Minneapolis from 05. *3734 Pleasant Avenue, Minneapolis MN 55409, USA* Tel (001) (612) 870 7800 Fax 870 7802 E-mail richardn@ourcathedral.org

NORMAN, Richard Jonathan. b 88. Ch Ch Ox BA10 Leeds Univ MA11. Coll of Resurr Mirfield 09. **d** 11. C Rotherhithe St Mary w All SS *S'wark* from 11. *26 Elizabeth Square, London SE16 5XN* Tel (020) 7740 1877 Mobile 07752-732324 E-mail rjnorman@hotmail.co.uk

NORMAN, Timothy. b 68. Jes Coll Cam BA91 Univ Coll Lon PhD95. Spurgeon's Coll 95 Wycliffe Hall Ox BA00. **d** 01 **p** 02. C Chipping Norton *Ox* 01-04; Asst Chapl Paris St Mich *Eur* 04-06; Perm to Offic 06-08; C Rugby W *Cov* from 09. *58 Park Road, Rugby CV21 2QH* E-mail tim.norman@bigfoot.com

NORMAN, Canon William Beadon. b 26. Trin Coll Cam BA49 MA55. Ridley Hall Cam 52. **d** 52 **p** 53. C Beckenham St Jo *Roch* 52-54; CMS Miss and Tutor Buwalasi Th Coll Uganda 55-65; Hon Can Mbale 63-65; V Alne *York* 65-74; RD Warley *Birm* 74-79; V Blackheath 74-79; Hon Can Birm Cathl 78-91; TR Kings Norton 79-91; RD Kings Norton 82-87; Warden Dioc Readers Bd 84-91; rtd 91; Perm to Offic *S'wark* from 91; Preacher Lincoln's Inn 94-06. *37 Cloudesdale Road, London SW17 8ET* Tel (020) 8673 9134 Fax 8675 6890 E-mail bbnorman@hotmail.com

NORMAN-WALKER, Canon Anna Elizabeth. b 67. RGN89. St Jo Coll Nottm BA03. **d** 03 **p** 04. C Cullompton, Willand, Uffculme, Kentisbeare etc *Ex* 03-06; TV 06-10; Can Res Ex Cathl from 10; Dioc Missr from 10. *3 Spicer Road, Exeter EX1 1SX* Tel 07986-450330 (mobile) E-mail anna.norman-walker@exeter.anglican.org

NORMAND, Stephen Joseph William. b 48. N Texas State Univ BSEd80. Sarum & Wells Th Coll 90. **d** 92 **p** 93. C Norton *St Alb* 92-94; C St Alb St Pet 95-97; Chapl Oaklands Coll 95-97; TV Horsham *Chich* 97-01; R Wimbotsham w Stow Bardolph and Stow Bridge etc *Ely* 01-04; rtd 04; Perm to Offic *Ely* 05-09. *97 Mitre Road, London SE1 8PT* Tel (020) 7633 0012 E-mail normasteph@aol.com

NORRINGTON, Paul Richard. b 57. Brighton Poly BSc80. Trin Coll Bris 96. **d** 98 **p** 99. C Prittlewell St Pet w Westcliff St Cedd *Chelmsf* 98-02; R Colchester Ch Ch w St Mary V from 02. *The Rectory, 21 Cambridge Road, Colchester CO3 3NS* Tel (01206) 563478 E-mail pnozzer@tesco.net

NORRIS, Mrs Alison. b 55. St Andr Univ MTheol77 Dur Univ PGCE78. Cant Sch of Min 80. dss 82 **d** 87 **p** 94. Warlingham w Chelsham and Farleigh *S'wark* 82-85; Willingham *Ely* 85-90; Hon Par Dn 87-90; Hon Par Dn Worle *B & W* 90-94; NSM Milverton w Halse and Fitzhead 94-02; P-in-c Deane Vale 02-10; R from 10. *6 Cole Close, Cotford St Luke, Taunton TA4 1NZ* Tel (01823) 431567 E-mail revalison@revsnorris.co.uk

NORRIS, Allan Edward. b 43. St Jo Coll Dur BA72. Cranmer Hall Dur 69. **d** 73 **p** 74. C Plumstead St Jo w St Jas and St Paul *S'wark* 73-78; C Battersea Park St Sav 78-82; C Battersea St Geo w St Andr 78-82; V Grain w Stoke *Roch* 82-92; V Sissinghurst w Frittenden Cant from 92. *The Rectory, Oakleaves, Frittenden, Cranbrook TN17 2DD* Tel (01580) 852275 E-mail revco@amserve.com

NORRIS, Andrew David. b 54. St Andr Univ BSc78 Lon Univ MPhil80 CPsychol. EAMTC 87. **d** 90 **p** 91. C Worle *B & W* 90-94; R Milverton w Halse and Fitzhead 94-08; RD Tone 01-07; Nat Chapl Adv Methodist Homes for the Aged from 08. *6 Cole Close, Cotford St Luke, Taunton TA4 1NZ* Tel (01823) 431567 E-mail revandrew@revsnorris.co.uk

NORRIS, Andrew Peter. b 62. Aston Univ BSc83. St Jo Coll Nottm BA86. **d** 87 **p** 88. C Mountsorrel Ch Ch and St Pet *Leic* 87-90; C Harborne Heath *Birm* 90-91; P-in-c Edgbaston St Germain 91-92; V 92-99; P-in-c Hook w Warsash *Portsm* 99-00; V from 00. *The Vicarage, 113 Church Road, Warsash, Southampton SO31 9GF* Tel and fax (01489) 572324

NORRIS, Barry John. b 46. Nottm Univ MTh86 Open Univ BA80 K Coll Lon PhD95 CQSW75. St Jo Sem Wonersh. **d** 70 **p** 71. In RC Ch 70-72; C Wisbech SS Pet and Paul *Ely* 76-78; TV E Ham w Upton Park *Chelmsf* 78-81; Chapl RAF 81-87; V N Tadley St Mary *Win* from 87; rtd 11. *Address temp unknown* E-mail baz.norris@btinternet.com

NORRIS, Canon Clifford Joseph. b 29. Codrington Coll Barbados. **d** 61 **p** 68. Antigua 61-62; C Penton Street St Silas w All SS *Lon* 68-70; C Stepney St Dunstan and All SS 70-73; P-in-c Bethnal Green St Jas the Gt w St Jude 73-82; V Aveley and Purfleet *Chelmsf* 82-98; Hon Can NE Caribbean from 95; rtd 98; Perm to Offic *Chelmsf* from 98. *20 Hayhouse Road, Earls Colne, Colchester CO6 2PD* Tel (01787) 222015

NORRIS, Eric Richard. b 43. Bernard Gilpin Soc Dur 65 Ripon Hall Ox 66. **d** 69 **p** 70. C Huyton St Mich *Liv* 69-72; C Mexborough *Sheff* 72-74; V Dalton 74-78; Org Sec CECS *Carl* 78-89; Area Appeals Manager N Co 89-93; TR Thirsk *York* 93-02; RD Mowbray 00-02; V Boosbeck w Moorsholm 02-06; Abp's Adn in Tourism 02-06; rtd 06; Perm to Offic from 06. *39 Upleatham Street, Saltburn-by-the-Sea TS12 1JX* Tel (01287) 280940 E-mail dtoyork@gmail.com

NORRIS, Mrs Helen. b 53. Univ of Wales (Abth) LLB74 Univ Coll Lon LLM76 Solicitor 78. **d** 04 **p** 05. OLM Coddenham w Gosbeck and Hemingstone w Henley *St E* from 04; OLM Crowfield w Stonham Aspal and Mickfield from 04. *The Villa,*

The Street, Stonham Aspal, Stowmarket IP14 6AQ Tel (01449) 711395 E-mail helen.norris@btinternet.com

NORRIS, Julie Mary. b 63. Westmr Coll Ox BA84 Fitzw Coll Cam MPhil88 Birm Univ PhD03. Wesley Ho Cam 86. **d** 06 **p** 06. C Orwell Gp *Ely* 06-09; P-in-c Gt w Lt Abington from 09; P-in-c Hildersham from 09; TV Linton from 09; P-in-c Balsham, Weston Colville, W Wickham etc from 10. *The Vicarage, 35 Church Lane, Little Abington, Cambridge CB21 6BQ* Tel (01223) 891350 E-mail julienorris1323@aol.com

NORRIS, Keith David. b 47. E Lon Univ BA89 MIAM76 MBIM80. NTMTC 95. **d** 98 **p** 02. NSM Cranham Park *Chelmsf* 98-99; NSM S Hornchurch St Jo and St Matt 01-06; NSM Rainham w Wennington from 06. *Still Waters, 8 Hesselyn Drive, Rainham RM13 7EJ* Tel (01708) 780767 E-mail keithdnorris@hotmail.co.uk

NORRIS, Mark. b 68. Brunel Univ BEng90. Oak Hill Th Coll BA93. **d** 93 **p** 94. C Roby *Liv* 93-97; C St Helens St Helen 97-00; TV Gateacre 00-09; Asst Dioc Dir of Ords 05-09; Leadership Development Adv (Voc) CPAS from 09. *CPAS, Athena Drive, Tachbrook Park, Warwick CV34 6NG* Tel (01926) 458461 E-mail mnorris@cpas.org.uk

NORRIS, Michael Charles Latham. b 69. Reading Univ LLB. Wycliffe Hall Ox 99. **d** 01 **p** 02. C Bryanston Square St Mary w St Marylebone St Mark *Lon* 01-03; V Symonds Street St Paul New Zealand from 04. *PO Box 6049, Wellesley Street, Auckland 1141, New Zealand* Tel (0064) (9) 373 3268 E-mail mikenorris1@hotmail.com

NORRIS, Paul. b 48. **d** 10 **p** 11. OLM Woughton *Ox* from 10. *20 Thirsk Gardens, Bletchley, Milton Keynes MK3 5LH* Tel (01908) 371824 Mobile 07840-296676 E-mail paul88547@aol.com

NORTH, Barry Albert. b 46. **d** 82 **p** 83. C Brampton St Thos *Derby* 82-84; C Chesterfield St Aug 84-88; P-in-c Derby St Mark 88-91; R Coalbrookdale, Iron-Bridge and Lt Wenlock *Heref* 91-97; Ch and Community Worker (Manlake Deanery) *Linc* 97-00; Adv for Ch in Soc *Chich* from 00; C Brighton St Nich from 00. *2 Windlesham Road, Brighton BN1 3AG* Tel (01273) 269274 *or* 725806 E-mail barry.north@diochi.org.uk

NORTH, Christopher David. b 69. Trin Coll Bris BA01. **d** 01 **p** 02. C Bathampton w Claverton *B & W* 01-05; P-in-c Chilcompton w Downside and Stratton on the Fosse from 05. *The Rectory, The Street, Chilcompton, Radstock BA3 4HN* Tel (01761) 232219 E-mail chris.north1@tesco.net

NORTH, Preb David Roland. b 45. Lich Th Coll 70 Qu Coll Birm 72. **d** 73 **p** 74. C Salesbury *Blackb* 73-76; C Marton 76-79; V Penwortham St Leon 79-87; R Whittington St Jo *Lich* 87-10; P-in-c W Felton 96-10; RD Oswestry 02-09; Chapl Robert Jones/Agnes Hunt Orthopaedic NHS Trust 00-01; Preb Lich Cathl 07-10; rtd 11; Perm to Offic *Lich* from 11. *Honeycroft, Daisy Lane, Whittington, Oswestry SY11 4EA* Tel (01691) 676130

NORTH, Lyndon Percival. b 55. Lon Bible Coll BA77. NTMTC. **d** 00 **p** 01. NSM Sudbury St Andr *Lon* 00-04 and from 05; C Roxbourne St Andr 04-05. *143 Abbotts Drive, Wembley HA0 3SH* Tel (020) 8904 2408 Mobile 07774-685906 E-mail lyndonnorth@hotmail.com

NORTH, Mark Richard. b 71. St Steph Ho Ox 03. **d** 05 **p** 06. C Sevenoaks St Jo *Roch* 05-09; V Burnham *Chelmsf* from 09. *The Vicarage, 2A Church Road, Burnham-on-Crouch CM0 8DA* Tel (01621) 782071 Mobile 07776-231681 E-mail frmarknorth@btinternet.com

NORTH, Philip John. b 66. York Univ BA88. St Steph Ho Ox BA91 MA01. **d** 92 **p** 93. C Sunderland St Mary and St Pet *Dur* 92-96; V Hartlepool H Trin 96-02; AD Hartlepool 00-02; P Admin Shrine of Our Lady of Walsingham 02-08; P-in-c Hempton and Pudding Norton 04-07; TR Old St Pancras *Lon* from 08; CMP from 97. *The Rectory, 191 St Pancras Way, London NW1 9NH* Tel (020) 7485 5791 *or* 7485 0724 Mobile 07919-180788 E-mail fr.philip@posp.co.uk

NORTH, Preb Robert. b 54. Lon Univ BSc77. Ripon Coll Cuddesdon 78. **d** 81 **p** 82. C Leominster *Heref* 81-86; TV Heref St Martin w St Fran, Dewsall etc 86-92; P-in-c Heref St Nic 92-97; TR W Heref from 97; Dir of Ords 92-00; Preb Heref Cathl from 94; Dioc Chapl MU from 05. *St Nicholas's Rectory, 76 Breinton Road, Hereford HR4 0JY* Tel (01432) 273810 Pager 07623-476523

NORTH, Canon Vernon Leslie. b 26. Bps' Coll Cheshunt 61. **d** 63 **p** 64. C N Holmwood *Guildf* 63-65; C Dunstable *St Alb* 65-68; V Stotfold 68-91; V Stotfold and Radwell 91-92; RD Shefford 79-91; Hon Can St Alb 89-92; rtd 92; Perm to Offic *Ely* from 96 and *St Alb* from 00. *Hunters Moon, 10 High Street, Little Paxton, St Neots PE19 6HA* Tel (01480) 471146

NORTH, William Walter. b 77. Ox Brookes Univ BA03. St Jo Coll Nottm 07. **d** 09 **p** 10. C N Farnborough *Guildf* from 09. *14 Wilton Court, Farnborough GU14 7EL* Tel 07766-560793 (mobile) E-mail wilnorth@hotmail.com

NORTH INDIA, Moderator of the Church of. *Vacant*

NORTH SYDNEY, Bishop of. *See* DAVIES, The Rt Revd Glenn Naunton

NORTH WEST EUROPE, Archdeacon of. *See* DE WIT, The Ven John

NORTHALL, Malcolm Walter. b 26. Cheshunt Coll Cam 59 Ely Th Coll 63. **d** 64 **p** 65. C Bromsgrove St Jo *Worc* 64-67; V Blockley w Aston Magna *Glouc* 67-82; P-in-c Churchdown 82; V 82-92; rtd 92; Perm to Offic *Ban* from 92. *5 Maethlon Close, Tywyn LL36 0BN* Tel (01654) 710123

NORTHAM, Cavell Herbert James Cavell. *See* CAVELL-NORTHAM, Canon Cavell Herbert James

NORTHAM, Mrs Susan Jillian. b 36. Oak Hill Th Coll 87. **d** 89. NSM Enfield Ch Ch Trent Park *Lon* 89-91; Par Dn 91-94; C 94-97; rtd 97; Perm to Offic *Lon* from 02. *5 Beech Hill Avenue, Barnet EN4 0LW* Tel and fax (020) 8440 2723 E-mail jillandjohn.northam@btinternet.com

NORTHAMPTON, Archdeacon of. *See* ALLSOPP, The Ven Christine

NORTHCOTT, Canon Michael Stafford. b 55. St Chad's Coll Dur BA76 MA77 Sunderland Univ PhD81. St Jo Coll Dur 80. **d** 81 **p** 82. C Chorlton-cum-Hardy St Clem *Man* 81-84; USPG 84-89; Malaysia 84-89; Sen Lect Chr Ethics New Coll Edin Univ 89-91; NSM Edina Old St Paul 89-91; NSM Edin St Jas from 91; TV Edin St Marg 93-96; Can Th Liv Cathl from 05. *8 Dudley Gardens, Edinburgh EH6 4PY* Tel 0131-554 1651 E-mail m.northcott@ed.ac.uk

NORTHCOTT, William Mark. b 36. Clifton Th Coll 61. **d** 64 **p** 65. C Walthamstow St Luke *Chelmsf* 64-68; C Idle *Bradf* 68-70; N Sec CMJ 70-79; V Withnell *Blackb* 79-90; P-in-c Glenrothes *St And* 90-91; Asst Dioc Supernumerary 90-91; Perm to Offic *Blackb* and *Liv* from 91. *34 Welsby Road, Leyland PR25 1JB* Tel (01772) 493932

NORTHERN, Elaine Joy. *See* TIPP, Mrs Elaine Joy

NORTHEY, Edward Alexander Anson. b 81. Trin Coll Bris BA08. Wycliffe Hall Ox 09. **d** 11. C Barrow St Mark *Carl* from 11. *36 Thorncliffe Road, Barrow-in-Furness LA14 5PZ* Tel (01229) 826487 Mobile 07952-938797 E-mail edwardnorthey@gmail.com

NORTHEY (née GANT), Mrs Joanna Elizabeth. b 75. Dur Univ BSc96 Ox Univ PGCE97. Trin Coll Bris BA09. **d** 09 **p** 10. C Swindon Ch Ch *Bris* 09-11; C Barrow St Mark *Carl* from 11. *36 Thorncliffe Road, Barrow-in-Furness LA14 5PZ* Tel (01229) 826487 Mobile 07807-188912 E-mail jonorthey@hotmail.com

NORTHFIELD, Stephen Richmond. b 55. Lon Univ BSc77 Southn Univ BTh84. Sarum & Wells Th Coll 79. **d** 82 **p** 83. C Colchester St Jas, All SS, St Nic and St Runwald *Chelmsf* 82-85; C Chelmsf All SS 85-89; V Ramsey w Lt Oakley and Wrabness 89-95; V Hatfield Peverel w Ulting from 95. *The Vicarage, Church Road, Hatfield Peverel, Chelmsford CM3 2LE* Tel (01245) 380958 E-mail srnorthfield@aol.com

NORTHING, Ross. b 58. St Steph Ho Ox 92. **d** 94 **p** 95. CA from 87; C Up Hatherley *Glouc* 94-98; C Cheltenham St Steph 94-95; C Cheltenham Em w St Steph 95-98; V Stony Stratford *Ox* from 98; R Calverton from 98. *St Mary and St Giles Vicarage, 14 Willow Lane, Stony Stratford, Milton Keynes MK11 1FG* Tel (01908) 562148 Fax 565132 E-mail r.northing@btinternet.com

NORTHOLT, Archdeacon of. *Vacant*

NORTHOVER, Kevin Charles. b 57. Coll of Resurr Mirfield 89. **d** 91 **p** 92. C Kingston upon Hull St Alb *York* 91-94; V Moorends *Sheff* 94-00; R Guernsey St Michel du Valle *Win* from 00; Vice-Dean Guernsey from 07; Chapl HM Pris Guernsey from 00; CMP from 99. *The Rectory, L'Abbaye, Vale, Guernsey GY3 5SF* Tel (01481) 244088 E-mail frkevin@cwgsy.net

NORTHRIDGE, Herbert Aubrey Hamilton. b 16. TCD BA40 MA43. **d** 41 **p** 42. C Londonderry Ch Ch *D & R* 41-45; P-in-c Convoy 45-47; I 47-50; I Derg 50-70; I Derg w Termonamongan 70-81; Can Derry Cathl 72-81; rtd 81. *Goblusk, Ballinamallard BT94 2LW* Tel (028) 6638 8676

NORTHUMBERLAND, Archdeacon of. *See* MILLER, The Ven Geoffrey Vincent

NORTON, Andrew. *See* NORTON, John Colin

NORTON, Anthony Bernard. b 40. Man Univ BA62. Linc Th Coll 63. **d** 65 **p** 66. C Westbury-on-Trym H Trin *Bris* 65-68; C Bris St Agnes w St Simon 68-70; P-in-c Bris St Werburgh 70-72; TV Bris St Agnes and St Simon w St Werburgh 72-77; V Lakenham St Alb *Nor* 77-85; TV Trunch 85-93; TV Halesworth w Linstead, Chediston, Holton etc *St E* 93-99; TV Blyth Valley 99-05; RD Halesworth 98-01; rtd 05; Perm to Offic *St E* 06-08; P-in-c Heveningham from 08. *6 Bramblewood Way, Halesworth IP19 8JT* Tel (01986) 875374 E-mail anthonynorton@btinternet.com

NORTON, Benjamin James. b 80. Hull Univ BTh05. St Jo Coll Nottm 06. **d** 07 **p** 08. C Bridlington Em *York* from 07. *40 Georgian Way, Bridlington YO15 3TB* Tel (01262) 678133 Mobile 07780-606314 E-mail thepartycanstart@yahoo.co.uk

NORTON, Howard John. b 41. Fitzw Coll Cam BA64 MA68. S'wark Ord Course 78 St Jo Coll Nottm 79. **d** 80 **p** 81. C Sutton Ch Ch *S'wark* 80-82; C Morden 82-84; V Motspur Park 84-88; Perm to Offic *Chich* from 03. *Gladstone House, 8 Coburg Place, Hastings TN34 3HY*

NORTON, James Herbert Kitchener. b 37. Qu Coll Birm 78. **d** 81 **p** 82. NSM Donnington Wood *Lich* 81-83; C Matson *Glouc* 83-86; V New Mills *Derby* 86-96; RD Glossop 93-96; TR Buxton w Burbage and King Sterndale 96-02; RD Buxton 99-02; rtd 02; Perm to Offic *Derby* from 02; P-in-c Lt Drayton *Lich* 04-09; TV Cen Telford 09-11; C Tong from 11. *Heather Glen, 11 Ellis Peter's Drive, Telford TF3 1AW* Tel (01952) 595343 Mobile 07879-470172 E-mail jhknorton@lineone.net

NORTON, John Colin (Andrew). b 25. Magd Coll Ox BA50 MA54. Cuddesdon Coll 50. **d** 52 **p** 53. C Bris St Mary Redcliffe w Temple 52-57; C Bitterne Park *Win* 57-61; C-in-c Bishopwearmouth St Mary V w St Pet CD *Dur* 63-68; V Clifton All SS w Tyndalls Park *Bris* 68-78; Hon Can Bris Cathl 77-80; V Clifton All SS w St Jo 78-80; V Penistone *Wakef* 80-83; CR from 85; rtd 95. *House of the Resurrection, Stocks Bank Road, Mirfield WF14 0BN* Tel (01924) 494318

NORTON (or HARCOURT-NORTON), Michael Clive Harcourt. b 34. Selw Coll Cam BA58 MA60 Union Th Sem (NY) STM69 Univ of NSW MCom81 MACE84. Wells Th Coll 56 Bossey Ecum Inst Geneva 57. **d** 58 **p** 59. C Gt Ilford St Jo *Chelmsf* 58-62; NSW Sec Aus Coun Chs Australia 62-68; C Manhattan St Steph USA 68-69; C-in-c Mortdale Australia 69-77; R 77-79; Assoc Chapl and Hd RS Cranbrook Sch Sydney 79-85; R Hunter's Hill 85-00; rtd 00. *7 Dulwich Road, Chatswood NSW 2067, Australia* Tel (0061) (2) 9411 8606 Fax 9410 2069 Mobile 417-041779 E-mail chnorton@bigpond.com

NORTON, Michael James Murfin. b 42. Lich Th Coll 66. **d** 67 **p** 68. C W Bromwich St Fran *Lich* 67-70; C Wellington Ch Ch 70-72; C Norwood All SS *Cant* 72-76; V Elstow *St Alb* 76-82; Asst Chapl HM Pris Wakef 82-83; Chapl HM Pris Camp Hill 83-86; Parkhurst 86-88; Win 88-93; V Somborne w Ashley *Win* 93-03; rtd 03. *Bryneirian, Penparc, Cardigan SA43 1RG* Tel (01239) 623512 E-mail revmnorton@aol.com

NORTON, Paul James. b 55. Oak Hill Th Coll BA86. **d** 86 **p** 87. C Luton St Fran *St Alb* 86-89; C Bedworth *Cov* 89-95; TV Hitchin *St Alb* 95-02; V Portsdown *Portsm* 03-07; rtd 07. *23 Oxford Road, Southsea PO5 1NP*

NORTON, Canon Peter Eric Pepler. b 38. TCD BA61 G&C Coll Cam PhD64. Cranmer Hall Dur 78. **d** 80 **p** 81. C Ulverston St Mary w H Trin *Carl* 80-83; P-in-c Warcop, Musgrave, Soulby and Crosby Garrett 83-84; R 84-90; OCF 83-90; V Appleby and R Ormside *Carl* 90-04; P-in-c Kirkby Thore w Temple Sowerby and Newbiggin 01-04; RD Appleby and Hon Can Carl Cathl 00-04; rtd 04; Perm to Offic *Nor* 05-08. *Ard na Cree, Church Hill, Wicklow, Co Wicklow, Republic of Ireland* Tel (00353) (404) 62648 Mobile 07802-334575 E-mail pepnorton@gmail.com

NORTON, Sam Charles. b 70. Trin Coll Ox BA92 MA99 Heythrop Coll Lon MA00. Westcott Ho Cam 97. **d** 99 **p** 00. C Stepney St Dunstan and All SS *Lon* 99-02; R W w E Mersea *Chelmsf* 03-10; P-in-c Peldon w Gt and Lt Wigborough 03-10; R W w E Mersea, Peldon, Gt and Lt Wigborough from 10. *93 Kingsland Road, West Mersea, Colchester CO5 8AG* Tel (01206) 385635 E-mail elizaphanian@hotmail.com

NORTON (née FISHER), Mrs Susan Alexandra. b 54. Man Univ BA75 Hughes Hall Cam PGCE76. NEOC 01. **d** 04 **p** 05. NSM York St Olave w St Giles and York St Helen w St Martin 04-09. *21 Wentworth Road, York YO24 1DG* Tel (01904) 634911 E-mail s.norton@tinyworld.co.uk

NORTON, William Fullerton. b 23. Selw Coll Cam BA46 MA52. Wycliffe Hall Ox 46. **d** 48 **p** 49. C Leic H Apostles 48-52; C Singapore St Matt 52-54; Miss Selangor Malaya 54-56; Miss Kampong Tawas 56-60; V Ipoh St Pet 60-63; R Manila St Steph Philippines 63-66; C Smethwick St Luke *Lon* 67; C Tooting Graveney St Nic *S'wark* 68-71; V Hanley Road St Sav w St Paul *Lon* 71-89; rtd 89. *Charlesworth Nursing Home, 37 Beaconsfield Villas, Brighton BN1 6HB* Tel (01273) 565511

NORWICH, Archdeacon of. See McFARLANE, The Ven Janet Elizabeth

NORWICH, Bishop of. See JAMES, The Rt Revd Graham Richard

NORWICH, Dean of. See SMITH, The Very Revd Graham Charles Morell

NORWOOD, Andrew David. b 65. Lon Bible Coll BA91. Cranmer Hall Dur 92. **d** 94 **p** 95. C Headingley *Ripon* 94-97; C Handsworth St Mary *Birm* 97-00; Perm to Offic *Lon* 01-02; Chapl Chelsea Coll from 02; Perm to Offic *S'wark* from 06. *11 Ormonde Mansions, 106 Southampton Row, London WC1B 4BP* Tel (020) 7242 7533 or 7514 6230 E-mail a.norwood@arts.ac.uk or a.norwood@csm.linst.ac.uk

NORWOOD, David John. b 40. SS Paul & Mary Coll Cheltenham BEd82. Linc Th Coll 65. **d** 68 **p** 69. C Hitchin St Mary *St Alb* 68-71; P-in-c Luanshya Zambia 72-76; C Littlehampton St Jas *Chich* 76-77; P-in-c Chacewater *Truro* 77-79; Chapl R Cornwall Hosp Treliske 77-79; Hd RE Red Maids Sch Bris 82-85; Appeals Organiser Children's Soc 86-94; P-in-c Clarkston Glas *Glas* 96-99; R Dalbeattie 99-05; rtd 05. *Dove Cottage, Wellfield Terrace, Ferryside SA17 5SD* Tel (01267) 267125 E-mail norwoods@talktalk.net

NORWOOD, Paul James. b 71. **d** 08 **p** 09. OLM S Lynn *Nor* from 08. *46 Tennyson Avenue, King's Lynn PE30 2QJ* Tel (01553) 777455 Mobile 07720-806318 E-mail pjandcas.norwood@virgin.net

NORWOOD, Canon Philip Geoffrey Frank. b 39. Em Coll Cam BA62 MA66. Cuddesdon Coll 63. **d** 65 **p** 66. C New Addington *Cant* 65-69; Abp's Dom Chapl 69-72; V Hollingbourne 72-78; P-in-c Wormshill and Huckinge 74-78; V St Laur in Thanet 78-88; RD Thanet 86-88; V Spalding *Linc* 88-98; RD Elloe W 96-98; R Blakeney w Cley, Wiveton, Glandford etc *Nor* 98-05; RD Holt 02-05; Hon Can Nor Cathl 03-05; rtd 05. *30 Home Close Road, Houghton-on-the-Hill, Leicester LE7 9GT* Tel 0116-241 0255 E-mail philipandannenorwood@hotmail.com

NORWOOD, Robert William. b 38. Keble Coll Ox BA71 MA71 Lon Univ TCert64 Lambeth STh83. **d** 01 **p** 03. NSM St Pancras H Cross w St Jude and St Pet *Lon* from 01; Perm to Offic *Chelmsf* from 08. *Carlton Court, 11A Hermon Hill, London E11 2AR* Tel (020) 8530 2493

NORWOOD, Timothy. b 70. Aber Univ BD94. Westcott Ho Cam 95. **d** 97 **p** 98. C Upton cum Chalvey *Ox* 97-00; TV Watling Valley 00-10; AD Milton Keynes from 06; C Milton Keynes from 11. *3 Daubeney Gate, Shenley Church End, Milton Keynes MK5 6EH* Tel (01908) 505812 E-mail tim@thenorwoods.fsnet.co.uk

NOTLEY, Michael James. b 41. St Edm Hall Ox BA63 MA68 DipEd64. EMMTC 84. **d** 87 **p** 88. NSM Oadby *Leic* 87-96; P-in-c Holbeach Marsh *Linc* 96-06; P-in-c Lutton w Gedney Drove End, Dawsmere 96-06; rtd 06. *33 St John's Drive, Corby Glen, Grantham NG33 4NG* Tel (01476) 550721

NOTT, Canon George Thomas Michael. b 34. Ex Coll Ox BA58 MA62 Birm Univ MEd88 Cov Univ PhD95. Coll of Resurr Mirfield. **d** 60 **p** 61. C Solihull *Birm* 60-69; Chapl K Sch Worc and Min Can Worc Cathl 69-77; P-in-c Worc St Nic and Children's Officer 77-87; P-in-c Worc St Andr and All SS w St Helen 82-84; Droitwich Spa 87-89; V Broadheath, Crown East and Rushwick 89-04; Chapl Worc Coll of HE 89-96; RD Martley and Worc W 95-03; Hon Can Worc Cathl 99-04; P-in-c Worc St Mich 00-01; rtd 04. *17 Wirlpiece Avenue, Worcester WR4 0NF* Tel (01905) 729494 E-mail mnott17@btinternet.com

✠NOTT, The Rt Revd Peter John. b 33. Fitzw Ho Cam BA61 MA65. Westcott Ho Cam 58. **d** 61 **p** 62 **c** 77. C Harpenden St Nic *St Alb* 61-64; Chapl Fitzw Coll Cam 64-69; Fell 66-69; Chapl New Hall Cam 66-69; R Beaconsfield *Ox* 69-76; TR 76-77; Preb Wells Cathl 77-85; Suff Bp Taunton 77-85; Bp Nor 85-99; rtd 99; Hon Asst Bp Ox from 99. *Westcot House, Westcot, Wantage OX12 9QA* Tel (01235) 751233 E-mail peternott@btinternet.com

NOTT, Philip James. b 69. Nottm Trent Univ BA92. Ridley Hall Cam 95. **d** 98 **p** 99. C Kersal Moor *Man* 98-01; C Ealing St Mary *Lon* 01-04; Chapl Thames Valley Univ 01-04; P-in-c Broxtowe *S'well* 04-06; P-in-c Easton H Trin w St Gabr and St Lawr and St Jude *Bris* from 06; Min Inner City Partnership from 06. *St Anne's Vicarage, 75 Greenbank Road, Greenbank, Bristol BS5 6HD* Tel 0117-955 4255 E-mail rev@ecfc.org.uk

NOTTAGE, Preb Terence John. b 36. Oak Hill Th Coll. **d** 65 **p** 66. C Finchley St Paul Long Lane 65-68; C Edgware 68-72; V Harlesden St Mark 72-86; V Kensal Rise St Mark and St Martin 86; TR Plymouth Em w Efford *Ex* 86-92; P-in-c Laira 88-92; TR Plymouth Em, St Paul Efford and St Aug 93-96; Preb Ex Cathl from 96; Adv for Voc and Dioc Dir of Ords 96-01; rtd 01. *4 Keyberry Close, Newton Abbot TQ12 1DA* Tel (01626) 332277 E-mail terry.nottage@tesco.net

NOTTINGHAM, Archdeacon of. See HILL, The Ven Peter

NOVELL, Jill. b 49. Bris Univ BA72 Open Univ MA89 St Martin's Coll Lanc PGCE77. CBDTI 01. **d** 04 **p** 05. NSM Silverdale *Blackb* 04-11. *29 Hall Park, Lancaster LA1 4SH* E-mail riverlunelancaster@yahoo.co.uk

NOVIS, Timothy Wellington George. b 70. Trin Coll Toronto BA93 MDiv96. **d** 96 **p** 96. C Guelph St Geo Canada 96-98; R Hornby St Steph 98-05; Chapl Ridley Coll 05-08; Chapl Wellington Coll Berks from 08. *Chapel Hill, Wellington College, Crowthorne RG45 7PT* Tel (01344) 444104 E-mail twgn@wellingtoncollege.org.uk

NOWAK, Jurek Anthony (George). b 47. NTMTC 04. **d** 07. NSM Edmonton St Mary w St Jo *Lon* from 07. *138 Dysons Road, London N18 2DJ* Tel (020) 8884 0903 Mobile 07944-854617 E-mail jurek-n@dysons.demon.co.uk

NOWELL, Canon John David. b 44. AKC67. **d** 68 **p** 69. C Lindley *Wakef* 68-70; C Lightcliffe 70-72; V Wyke *Bradf* 72-80; V Silsden 80-92; V Baildon from 92; Hon Can Bradf Cathl from 00. *The Vicarage, Baildon, Shipley BD17 6NE* Tel and fax (01274) 594941 E-mail john.nowell@bradford.anglican.org

NOWEN, Lars Fredrik. b 71. Summit Pacific Coll BC BTh93 Regent Coll Vancouver MCS98. **d** 98 **p** 99. Dn Halifax St Geo Canada 98-99; P-in-c Meadow Lake and Loon Lake 99-04; C Pelton and W Pelton *Dur* 04-07; P-in-c St Bees *Carl* 07-10; Chapl St Bees Sch Cumbria 07-10. *Flat 3, 1 Compayne Gardens, London NW6 3DG* Tel (020) 7328 5347 E-mail lcnowen@gmail.com

NOY, Frederick William Vernon. b 47. Sarum Th Coll 67. **d** 71 **p** 72. C Swindon St Jo *Bris* 71-75; Chapl to the Deaf *Sarum* 75-80; P-in-c Stinsford, Winterborne Came w Whitcombe etc 76-80; Perm to Offic 80-08. *54 Casterbridge Road, Dorchester DT1 2AG* Tel (01305) 264269

NOYCE, Colin Martley. b 45. Brasted Th Coll 73 Ridley Hall Cam 74. **d** 76 **p** 77. C Cambridge St Jas *Ely* 76-78; Chapl RN 78-82; R Mistley w Manningtree *Chelmsf* 82-86; Miss to Seamen Kenya 86-89; Trinidad and Tobago 89-90; V Four Marks *Win* 90-99; Chapl Pilgrims Hospices E Kent 99-01; Chapl and Dir Ch Ch and Ras Morbat Clinics Yemen 01-03; Chapl Limassol St Barn and Miss to Seafarers 03-05; rtd 05; Perm to Offic *Chelmsf* 06-09 and *Portsm* from 08. *64 Whitwell Road, Southsea PO4 0QS* Tel (023) 9275 3517 E-mail candinoyce@sky.com

NOYCE, Graham Peter. b 62. Bedf Coll Lon BSc84. Trin Coll Bris BA92. **d** 92 **p** 93. C Sketty *S & B* 92-94; C Swansea St Jas 94-96; C Kensal Rise St Mark and St Martin Lon 96-04; TV 04-11; V Kensal Rise St Martin from 11. *26 Ashburnham Road, London NW10 5SD* Tel (020) 8960 6211 Mobile 07515-702862 E-mail graham@noycefamily.co.uk

NOYES, Roger. b 39. Linc Th Coll 65. **d** 67 **p** 68. C Adel *Ripon* 67-70; Chapl Aldenham Sch Herts 70-74; V Aldborough w Boroughbridge and Roecliffe *Ripon* 74-89; Rural Min Adv 89-90; Perm to Offic from 91; rtd 04. *Rose Cottage, Moor End, Nun Monkton, York YO26 8EN* Tel (01423) 330846 E-mail r.noyes1@btinternet.com

NSENGA-NGOY, Lusambo. b 77. Cranmer Hall Dur. **d** 08 **p** 09. C Staplehurst *Cant* from 08. *5 Oliver Road, Staplehurst, Tonbridge TN12 0TE* Tel (01580) 892324 E-mail lusansenga@gmail.com

NSHIMYE, Stephen Kamegeri. b 60. Bp Lutaya Th Coll Uganda 88. **d** 90 **p** 91. C Kamusemene Uganda 90-91; C Kigalama 92-93; C Nyagatovu Rwanda 94-99; Perm to Offic *S'wark* 02-05. *58 Hickin Close, London SE7 8SH* Tel (020) 8858 0624 Mobile 07950-346477

✠**NTAHOTURI, The Most Revd Bernard.** b 48. St Jo Coll Cam MA. Bp Tucker Coll Mukono 68. **d** 73 **c** 97. Burundi from 73; Bp Matana from 97; Abp Burundi from 05. *BP 447, Bujumbura, Burundi* Tel (00257) (2) 70361 Fax 29129 E-mail ntahober@cbinf.com

NTEGE, Nathan Kasolo. b 59. **d** 87 **p** 89. C St Paul's Cathl Namirembe Uganda 87-91; Bp Tucker Coll Mukono 91-94; V Luzira and Kabowa 94-96; Perm to Offic *S'wark* 97-02; P-in-c Thornton Heath St Jude w St Aid 02-07; V from 07. *St Jude's Vicarage, 11 Dunheved Road North, Thornton Heath CR7 6AH* Tel (020) 8665 5564 Mobile 07904-197329

NTOYIMONDO, Samuel. b 54. Wolv Univ BA05. Butare Th Sch Rwanda 80 All Nations Chr Coll BA02. **d** 84 **p** 87. Pastor Mutunda Rwanda 84-87; Pastor Butare 87-92; Dioc Sec Kigeme 92-94; Germany 96-99; Perm to Offic *Birm* 08-11; Chapl HM Pris Wellingborough from 11. *HM Prison, Millers Park, Wellingborough NN8 2NH* Tel (01933) 232700 Mobile 07908-207085 E-mail finasando@yahoo.co.uk

NUDDS, Douglas John. b 24. St Aid Birkenhead 48. **d** 51 **p** 52. C E Dereham w Hoe *Nor* 51-55; C Birstall *Leic* 55-58; V Bardon Hill 58-62; V Belgrave St Mich 62-68; Chapl Leic R Infirmary 68-72; High Royds Hosp Menston 72-79; V Bradf St Wilfrid Lidget Green 79-84; Lic to Offic *St Alb* 84-93; Chapl Shenley Hosp Radlett Herts 84-89; rtd 89; Perm to Offic *Nor* from 89. *Longview, Southgate Close, Wells-next-the-Sea NR23 1HG* Tel (01328) 711926

NUGENT, Canon Alan Hubert. b 42. Dur Univ BA65 MA78. Wycliffe Hall Ox 65 United Th Coll Bangalore 66. **d** 67 **p** 68. C Mossley Hill St Matt and St Jas *Liv* 67-71; C Bridgnorth St Mary *Heref* 71-72; Chapl Dur Univ 72-78; P-in-c Bishopwearmouth Ch Ch 78-85; P-in-c Brancepeth 85-94; Dioc Dir of Educn 85-97; Hon Can Dur Cathl 86-97; Dir of Miss and Tr Development Forum *Linc* 97-03; Can and Preb Linc Cathl 98-03; Can Res and Subdean Linc Cathl from 03. *The Subdeanery, 18 Minster Yard, Lincoln LN2 1RU* Tel (01522) 521932 *or* 523113 E-mail subdean@lincolncathedral.com

NUGENT, David Richard. b 54. MInstPS84 Liv Poly BA87. Oak Hill Th Coll BA95. **d** 95 **p** 96. C Birkenhead St Jas w St Bede *Ches* 95-99; V Blundellsands St Mich *Liv* 99-02; Asst Chapl Wirral and W Cheshire Community NHS Trust 02-03; Asst Chapl Cheshire and Wirral Partnerships NHS Trust from 03. *Chaplains' Office, Clatterbridge Hospital, Clatterbridge Road, Wirral CH63 4JY* Tel 0151-334 4000 E-mail dave.nugent@whnt.nhs.uk

NUGENT, Eric William. b 26. Bps' Coll Cheshunt 56. **d** 58 **p** 59. C Rochford *Chelmsf* 58-61; C Eastwood 61-62; C-in-c Eastwood St Dav CD 62-66; V Eastwood St Dav 66-79; P-in-c Weeley 79-81; V Lt Clacton 80-81; R Weeley and Lt Clacton 81-93; rtd 93; Perm to Offic *Chelmsf* from 93. *1 King's Court, King's Road, Dovercourt, Harwich CO12 4DS* Tel (01255) 552640

NUNN, Ms Alice Candida. b 52. Ripon Coll Cuddesdon 95. **d** 97 **p** 98. C Margate St Jo *Cant* 97-01; V Winterton Gp *Linc* from 01. *The Vicarage, High Street, Winterton, Scunthorpe DN15 9PU* Tel (01724) 732262

NUNN, Canon Andrew Peter. b 57. Leic Poly BA79 Leeds Univ BA82. Coll of Resurr Mirfield 80. **d** 83 **p** 84. C Manston *Ripon* 83-87; C Leeds Richmond Hill 87-91; Chapl Agnes Stewart C of E High Sch Leeds 87-95; V Leeds Richmond Hill *Ripon* 91-95; Personal Asst to Bp S'wark 95-99; Hon PV S'wark Cathl 95-99; Sub-Dean, Prec and Can Res S'wark Cathl from 99; Dioc Warden of Readers from 01. *73 St George's Road, London SE1 6ER* Tel (020) 7735 8322 *or* 7367 6727 Fax 7367 6725 Mobile 07961-332051 E-mail andrew.nunn@southwark.anglican.org

NUNN, Mrs Christine Jane. b 47. **d** 05 **p** 06. NSM Kesgrave *St E* from 05. *37 Bracken Avenue, Kesgrave, Ipswich IP5 2PP* Tel (01473) 622363

NUNN, Peter. b 32. Kelham Th Coll 53. **d** 57 **p** 58. C Wigan St Geo *Liv* 57-60; C Warrington St Elphin 60-62; V Warrington St Pet 62-65; Chapl Winwick Hosp Warrington 65-90; rtd 90; Perm to Offic *Liv* from 90. *9 Derby House, Scholes, Wigan WN1 3RN* Tel (01942) 235407

NUNN, Canon Peter Michael. b 38. MBE98. Sarum Th Coll 64. **d** 66 **p** 67. C Hornsey St Geo *Lon* 66-71; C Cleator Moor w Cleator *Carl* 71-72; V Carl St Luke Morton 72-79; V Wotton St Mary *Glouc* 79-02; Offg Chapl RAF 80-97; RD Glouc City 88-94; Hon Can Glouc Cathl 90-02; rtd 02; Perm to Offic *Chich* from 02. *87 South Street, Tarring, Worthing BN14 7ND* Tel (01903) 233748

NUNN, Peter Rawling. b 51. St Cath Coll Ox BA73 Sheff Univ MSc74. Oak Hill Th Coll BA85. **d** 85 **p** 86. C Bispham *Blackb* 85-87; C-in-c Anchorsholme 87-89; V 89-08; P-in-c Preston Risen Lord from 08. *St Matthew's Vicarage, 20 Fishwick View, Preston PR1 4YA* Tel (01772) 794312 E-mail peter@therisenlordpreston.org.uk

NUNN, Richard Ernest. b 38. SAOMC 96. **d** 99 **p** 00. NSM Maidenhead St Luke *Ox* 99-02; NSM Waltham St Lawrence 02-07; rtd 07; Perm to Offic *Ox* from 07 and Win from 08. *5 Glebe Fields, Milford on Sea, Lymington SO41 0WW* Tel (01590) 643118

NUNNERLEY, William John Arthur. b 27. Univ of Wales (Lamp) BA54. St Chad's Coll Dur. **d** 56 **p** 57. C Tredegar St Geo *Mon* 56-60; Chapl RN 60-81; QHC from 79; R Barnoldby le Beck *Linc* 81-92; R Waltham 81-92; rtd 92; Perm to Offic *B & W* from 00. *Juniper Cottage, 82B Lower Street, Merriott TA16 5NW* Tel (01460) 76049

NUNNEY, Sheila Frances. b 49. SRN74 RSCN74 SCM75. Oak Hill Th Coll BA92. **d** 92 **p** 94. C Swaffham *Nor* 92-96; Chapl Asst Norfolk and Nor Health Care NHS Trust 96-00; Chapl 00-01; Chapl Norfolk Primary Care Trust 01-09; Chapl Norfolk & Waveney Mental Health NHS Foundn Trust 03-09; rtd 09; Perm to Offic *Nor* from 09. *43A Chestnut Hill, Eaton, Norwich NR4 6NL* Tel (01603) 507110 E-mail sfn60@btinternet.com

NURSER, Canon John Shelley. b 29. Peterho Cam BA50 MA54 PhD58. Wells Th Coll 58. **d** 58 **p** 59. C Tankersley *Sheff* 58-61; Dean Trin Hall Cam 61-68; Australia 68-74; R Freckenham w Worlington *St E* 74-76; Can Res and Chan Linc Cathl 76-92; Can and Preb Linc Cathl 92-94; P-in-c Shudy Camps *Ely* 92-94; rtd 94; Perm to Offic *St E* from 94 and *Ely* 00-10. *68 Friars Street, Sudbury CO10 2AG* Tel (01787) 378595 E-mail jsnurser@btinternet.com

NURSEY (née HYLTON), Mrs Jane Lois. b 56. Leeds Univ BA78. **d** 07 **p** 08. OLM Dereham and Distr *Nor* from 07; Chapl Norfolk and Nor Univ Hosp NHS Trust from 11. *Chaplaincy Department, Norfolk and Norwich University Hospital, Colney Lane, Norwich NR4 7UY* Tel (01603) 287470 E-mail jane.nursey@nnuh.nhs.uk *or* nursey1@btinternet.com

NURTON, Robert. b 44. Univ of Wales (Lamp) BA67. Ridley Hall Cam 67. **d** 69 **p** 70. C Bris St Andr Hartcliffe 69-73; C Ipswich St Mary at Stoke w St Pet etc *St E* 73-77; Chapl RN 77-99; Chapl Morden Coll Blackheath 99-09; rtd 09; Perm to Offic *St E* from 11. *The Thatched Cottage, High Road, Great Finborough, Stowmarket IP14 3AQ* Tel (01449) 674396

NUTH, Stephen William. b 55. St Jo Coll Nottm 93. **d** 95 **p** 96. C Wadhurst and Stonegate *Chich* 95-99; R Marks Tey and Aldham *Chelmsf* 99-01; Perm to Offic *St E* 01-04; P-in-c Woburn w Eversholt, Milton Bryan, Battlesden etc *St Alb* 04-08; V from 08. *The Vicarage, Park Street, Woburn, Milton Keynes MK17 9PG* Tel (01525) 290225 E-mail stephen.nuth@googlemail.com

NUTT, Angela Karen. b 66. Homerton Coll Cam BEd89. STETS 08. **d** 11. C Totton *Win* from 11; C Copythorne from 11. *The Vicarage, Romsey Road, Cadnam, Southampton SO40 2NN* Tel (023) 8081 1929 Mobile 07740-424143 E-mail revdangi@gmail.com

NUTT, Susan Mary. b 45. **d** 99 **p** 00. OLM Blackbourne *St E* from 99; Hon Chapl St Nic Hospice Bury St Edmunds from 08. *Portelet, Blacksmith Lane, Barnham, Thetford IP24 2NE* Tel (01842) 890409 E-mail revdsuenutt@tiscali.co.uk

NUTTALL, George Herman. b 31. St Jo Coll Dur BA59. Cranmer Hall Dur 59. **d** 61 **p** 62. C Eccleshill *Bradf* 61-65; V Oldham St Barn *Man* 65-70; Area Sec CMS *Derby* and Linc 70-81; V Derby St Aug 81-84; Chapl Bournemouth and Poole Coll of FE *Sarum* 85-97; Chapl Dorset Inst of HE 85-90; Chapl

Bournemouth Poly *Win* 90-92; Chapl Bournemouth Univ 92-97; rtd 97; Perm to Offic *Sarum* 97-03 and *Carl* from 03. *Orchard End, 91 Silverdale Road, Arnside, Carnforth LA5 0EH*   Tel (01524) 760001

NUTTALL, Michael John Berkeley. b 36. K Coll Lon AKC60. St Boniface Warminster 61. **d** 61 **p** 62. C Chapel Allerton *Ripon* 61-64; C Stanningley St Thos 64-68; V Leeds Gipton Epiphany 68-76; P-in-c Stainby w Gunby *Linc* 76-83; R N Witham 76-83; R S Witham 76-83; TV Bottesford w Ashby 83-88; I Adare w Kilpeacon and Croom *L & K* 88-94; I Adare and Kilmallock w Kilpeacon, Croom etc 94-01; Chapl Limerick Univ 88-95; Adn Limerick 92-01; rtd 01. *29 Dulverton Hall, Esplanade, Scarborough YO11 2AR*   Tel (01723) 340129
E-mail adnmichaelnuttall@yahoo.com

NUTTER, Ms Tracy Jane. NTMTC. **d** 10 **p** 11. NSM Prittlewell St Steph *Chelmsf* from 10. *8 Ailsa Road, Westcliff-on-Sea SS0 8BL*

NUZUM, Daniel Robert. b 73. TCD BTh99 RGN94. **d** 99 **p** 00. C Bandon Union *C, C & R* 99-01; I Templebreedy w Tracton and Nohoval 02-09; Chapl Cork Univ Hosp from 09. *Cork University Hospital, Wilton, Cork, Republic of Ireland*   Tel (00353) (21) 454 6400

NWAEKWE, Augustine Ugochukwu. b 75. Leuven Univ Belgium MA07. St Paul's Univ Coll Awka Nigeria 95. **d** 98 **p** 00. Lic to Offic Dio Mbaise Nigeria 98-04; Asst Chapl Brussels *Eur* from 06. *rue Capitaine Crespel 29, 1050 Brussels, Belgium*   Tel (0032) (2) 511 7183   Fax 511 1028   Mobile 48-499 5790
E-mail augustine.nwaekwe@htbrussels.com

NYATSANZA, Petros Hamutendi. b 69. Redcliffe Coll Glouc BA04. Bp Gaul Th Coll Harare 95. **d** 95 **p** 96. Zimbabwe 95-01; C Greendale St Luke 95-96; C Highfields St Paul 96-97; R Mufakose St Luke 97-01; Perm to Offic *Glouc* 02-04; P-in-c Rounds Green *Birm* 04-08; V Goodmayes All SS *Chelmsf* from 08. *All Saints' Vicarage, 38 Broomshill Road, Ilford IG3 9SJ*   Tel (020) 8590 1476   Mobile 07877-841643
E-mail petrosnyatsanza@yahoo.co.uk

NYE, Canon David Charles. b 39. K Coll Lon BD65 Glos Univ MA01. **d** 63 **p** 64. C Charlton Kings St Mary *Glouc* 63-67; C Yeovil St Jo w Preston Plucknett *B & W* 67-70; V Lower Cam *Glouc* 70-74; Min Can Glouc Cathl 74-79; Dir of Ords 74-79; Prin Glouc Th Course 74-79; V Glouc St Mary de Lode and St Nic 74-76; V Maisemore 76-79; Chapl Grenville Coll Bideford 79-81; V Leckhampton SS Phil and Jas w Cheltenham St Jas *Glouc* 81-95; Hon Can Glouc Cathl 88-04; RD Cheltenham 89-95; P-in-c Northleach w Hampnett and Farmington 95-00; P-in-c Cold Aston w Notgrove and Turkdean 95-00; R Northleach w Hampnett and Farmington etc 00-04; RD Northleach 99-04; rtd 04. *2 Old Burford Road, Bledington, Chipping Norton OX7 6US*   Tel (01608) 659140
E-mail tisnyes@tiscali.co.uk

NYIRONGO, David. b 79. Wycliffe Hall Ox. **d** 11. C Penketh *Liv* from 11. *7 Shanklin Close, Great Sankey, Warrington WA5 3JN*

O

OADES, Debbie Gaynor. b 63. Middx Univ BA06. NTMTC 03. **d** 06 **p** 07. C Hounslow W Gd Shep *Lon* 06-08; NSM Hampton Hill 08-11; C Maybush and Southampton St Jude *Win* from 11. *St Peter's Church House, Lockerley Crescent, Southampton SO16 4BP*   E-mail debbieoades@hotmail.com

OADES, Michael Anthony John. b 45. Brasted Th Coll 69 Sarum & Wells Th Coll 71. **d** 73 **p** 74. C Eltham Park St Luke *S'wark* 73-78; C Coulsdon St Andr 78-81; P-in-c Merton St Jas 81-86; V 86-87; V Benhilton 87-10; rtd 10. *Cranleigh, Penbothidno, Constantine, Falmouth TR11 5AU*   Tel (01326) 341304
E-mail michaelandsylvia@btinternet.com

OADES, Canon Peter Robert. b 24. Fitzw Ho Cam BA47 CertEd48 MA53. **d** 67 **p** 67. C Warblington w Emsworth *Portsm* 67-68; V Choral Sarum Cathl 68-74; Chapl Salisbury Cathl Sch 68-74; P-in-c Sturminster Newton and Hinton St Mary *Sarum* 74-75; V 75-81; R Stock and Lydlinch 75-81; RD Blackmore Vale 78-81; V Woodford Valley 81-89; Can and Preb Sarum Cathl 85-89; rtd 89; Hon Chapl to the Deaf *Sarum* 82-92; Perm to Offic *Sarum* and *Win* 89-10. *41 Green Haven Court, 84 London Road, Cowplain, Waterlooville PO8 8EW*   Tel (023) 9226 1199

OAKDEN, David. **d** 10 **p** 11. OLM Shere, Albury and Chilworth *Guildf* from 10. *102 New Road, Chilworth, Guildford GU4 8LU*   Tel (01483) 578230

OAKE, Canon Barry Richard. b 47. MRICS71. Ripon Coll Cuddesdon 83. **d** 85 **p** 86. C Wantage *Ox* 85-88; C Warlingham w Chelsham and Farleigh *S'wark* 88-91; R N w S Wootton *Nor* 91-05; R Thorpe St Andr from 05; Asst Chapl among Deaf and Hearing-Impaired People from 01; Hon Can Nor Cathl from 07. *The Rectory, 21A South Avenue, Norwich NR7 0EY*   Tel (01603) 439754

OAKES, Graham. b 42. Chich Th Coll 68. **d** 70 **p** 71. C Hulme Ascension *Man* 70-74; C Clifton All SS w Tyndalls Park *Bris* 74-76; P-in-c Chadderton St Mark *Man* 76-78; V 78-82; V King Cross *Wakef* 82-95; R Bath H Trin *B & W* 95-07; Chapl R United Hosp Bath NHS Trust 99-07; rtd 07. *3 Friary Close, Clevedon BS21 7QA*   Tel (01275) 343822
E-mail revd@goakes.fsbusiness.co.uk

OAKES, Miss Jennifer May. b 43. Trin Coll Bris 78. **dss** 82 **d** 87 **p** 94. Wilnecote *Lich* 82-85; Stoneydelph St Martin CD 82-85; Bentley 85-89; Par Dn 87-89; Par Dn Hixon w Stowe-by-Chartley 89-94; C 94-98; Par Dn Fradswell, Gayton, Milwich and Weston 93-94; C 94-98; P-in-c Standon and Cotes Heath 98-00; rtd 03; Hon C Alfrick, Lulsley, Suckley, Leigh and Bransford *Worc* 03-04; Perm to Offic *Lich* from 05. *Willow Rise, Ashbourne Road, Whiston, Stoke-on-Trent ST10 2JE*   Tel (01538) 260013   E-mail oaklud@supanet.com

OAKES, Canon Jeremy Charles. b 51. ACA75 FCA81. Westcott Ho Cam 75. **d** 78 **p** 79. C Evington *Leic* 78-81; C Ringwood *Win* 81-84; P-in-c Thurnby Lodge *Leic* 84-89; TV Oakdale *Sarum* 89-95; P-in-c Canford Cliffs and Sandbanks 95-03; V from 03; Can and Preb Sarum Cathl from 03. *The Vicarage, 14 Flaghead Road, Canford Cliffs, Poole BH13 7JW*   Tel and fax (01202) 700341   E-mail jeremy.oakes@virgin.net

OAKES, John Cyril. b 49. AKC71. St Aug Coll Cant 71. **d** 72 **p** 73. C Broseley w Benthall *Heref* 72-76; C Cannock *Lich* 76-79; TV 79-83; V Rough Hills 83-09; P-in-c Wolverhampton St Steph 94-09; rtd 09; Perm to Offic *Lich* from 09. *Glendower, Bull Street, Gornal Wood, Dudley DY3 2NQ*   Tel (01384) 232097
E-mail classfortyseven@hotmail.co.uk

OAKES, Canon Leslie John. b 28. AKC53. **d** 54 **p** 55. C Bedford Leigh *Man* 54-58; C Walsall St Matt *Lich* 58-60; Chapl Selly Oak Hosp Birm 60-64; V Longbridge *Birm* 64-93; Hon Can Birm Cathl 84-93; rtd 93; Perm to Offic *Birm* from 93. *108 Hole Lane, Birmingham B31 2DF*   Tel 0121-476 8514

OAKES, Melvin. b 36. Lich Th Coll 77. **d** 79 **p** 80. C Lt Ilford St Mich *Chelmsf* 79-82; V Highams Park All SS 82-96; rtd 96; Perm to Offic *Chelmsf* from 99. *115 Richmond Avenue, London E4 9RR*   Tel (020) 8527 0457

OAKES, Robert. b 47. Chan Sch Truro 79. **d** 82 **p** 83. NSM Probus, Ladock and Grampound w Creed and St Erme *Truro* 82-84; TV Bodmin w Lanhydrock and Lanivet 85-88; R S Hill w Callington 88-03; RD E Wivelshire 95-00; Bp's Adv on Healing Min 98-03; Hon Can Truro Cathl 01-03; C Calstock from 06; Chapl Cornwall and Is of Scilly Primary Care Trust from 09. *48 Boconnoc Avenue, Callington PL17 7TW*   Tel (01579) 389109   Mobile 07890-099248
E-mail robert@oakesrobert.wanadoo.co.uk

OAKEY-JONES, Ms Angela Jean. b 71. Keele Univ BA93. NTMTC BA08. **d** 08 **p** 09. C Rushmere *St E* 08-11; P-in-c Ipswich All Hallows from 11. *All Hallows' Vicarage, Reynolds Road, Ipswich IP3 0JH*   E-mail angela.oj@btinternet.com

OAKHAM, Archdeacon of. See PAINTER, The Ven David Scott

OAKLAND, Mrs Sarah Marie. b 54. UEA BEd85. EAMTC 99. **d** 02 **p** 03. C Diss *Nor* 02-06; V Chessington *Guildf* 06-11; R E w W Harling, Bridgham w Roudham, Larling etc *Nor* from 11. *The Rectory, Church Road, East Harling, Norwich NR16 2NB*   Tel (01953) 718231   E-mail sarahoakland@hotmail.com

OAKLEY, Barry Wyndham. b 32. TD72. SS Coll Cam BA53 MA57. Ridley Hall Cam 56. **d** 58 **p** 59. C Alverstoke *Portsm* 58-61; C Bermondsey St Mary w St Olave and St Jo *S'wark* 61-63; V Crofton *Portsm* 63-78; V Edmonton All SS *Lon* 78-82; P-in-c Edmonton St Mich 80-82; V Edmonton All SS w St Mich 82-97; rtd 97; Perm to Offic *Lon* from 98. *25 Queen's Road, Enfield EN1 1NF*   Tel (020) 8363 3199

OAKLEY, Hilary Robert Mark. b 53. Univ of Wales (Ban) BSc73 Ox Univ BA78 MA81 MCIPD91. Ripon Coll Cuddesdon 76. **d** 79 **p** 80. C Birm St Pet 79-82; C Cambridge Gt St Mary w St Mich *Ely* 82-86; Chapl Girton Coll Cam 82-86; Chapl Zürich w St Gallen and Winterthur *Eur* 86-88; NSM Lon 88-92; Perm to Offic *St Alb* from 92. *55 Southdown Road, Harpenden AL5 1PQ*   Tel (01582) 761514
E-mail hilary.oakley@talk21.com

OAKLEY, James Robert. b 75. St Edm Hall Ox BA96. Oak Hill Th Coll BA05. **d** 05 **p** 06. C Audley *Lich* 05-09; P-in-c Kemsing w Woodlands *Roch* from 09. *The Vicarage, High Street, Kemsing, Sevenoaks TN15 6NA*   Tel (01732) 762556   Mobile 07827-299342   E-mail vicar@kemsing.org

OAKLEY, Jeremy Steven. b 52. Birm Univ BA99. Trin Coll Bris 95. **d** 97 **p** 98. C Walsall *Lich* 97-02; V Penn Fields from 02. *St Philip's Vicarage, Church Road, Bradmore, Wolverhampton WV3 7EJ*   Tel (01902) 332749
E-mail jeremy@pennfieldsparish.co.uk

OAKLEY, Canon Mark David. b 68. K Coll Lon BD90 AKC90. St Steph Ho Ox 90. **d** 93 **p** 94. C St John's Wood *Lon* 93-96; Bp's Chapl 96-00; P-in-c Covent Garden St Paul 00-03; R 03-05; AD Westmr St Marg 04-05; Chapl RADA 03-05; Chapl Copenhagen and Adn Germany and N Eur 05-08; P-in-c Grosvenor Chpl *Lon* 08-10; Can Res St Paul's Cathl from 10; Dep P in O from 96. *6 Amen Court, London EC4M 7BU* Tel (020) 7248 8572 E-mail mark.chaplain@gmail.com

OAKLEY, Richard John. b 46. AKC69 St Aug Coll Cant 69. **d** 70 **p** 71. C Wythenshawe Wm Temple Ch *Man* 70-75; V Ashton H Trin 75-80; CR 80-93; Lic to Offic *Lon* 88-93; V Cantley *Sheff* 93-99; V Carl St Aid and Ch C from 99. *St Aidan's Vicarage, 6 Lismore Place, Carlisle CA1 1LX* Tel (01228) 522942 E-mail fr.oakley.staidan@virgin.net

OAKLEY, Robert Paul. b 51. Sheff Univ BScTech72 PGCE74. St Jo Coll Nottm. **d** 89 **p** 90. C Heatherlands St Jo *Sarum* 89-92; V Burton All SS w Ch Ch *Lich* 92-99; V Gt Wyrley 99-07; Tutor Wilson Carlile Coll of Evang from 07. *Wilson Carlile College of Evangelism, 50 Cavendish Street, Sheffield S3 7RZ* Tel 0114-279 5863 E-mail p.oakley@churcharmy.org.uk

OAKLEY, Robin Ian. b 37. Ripon Hall Ox 68. **d** 70 **p** 71. C Leighton Buzzard *St Alb* 70-73; C Watford St Mich 73-76; R Ickleford 76-80; R Ickleford w Holwell 80-02; rtd 02; Perm to Offic *St Alb* from 02 and *Win* from 03. *13 Anders Road, South Wonston, Winchester SO21 3LA* Tel (01962) 880613

OAKLEY, Susan Mary. See HENWOOD, Mrs Susan Mary

OAKLEY, Timothy Crispin. b 45. Qu Coll Cam BA66 MA70 Bris Univ PGCE69. St Jo Coll Nottm 73. **d** 76 **p** 77. C Bromley Common St Aug *Roch* 76-79; C Fairfield *Liv* 79-81; CMS Kenya 82-90; P-in-c Beaford, Roborough and St Giles in the Wood *Ex* 91-96; Chapl St Andr Sch Turi Kenya 96-98; V Woodford Halse w Eydon *Pet* 99-10; RD Brackley 03-05; rtd 10. *Sunny Bank, Clive Avenue, Church Stretton SY6 7BL* Tel (01694) 724225 E-mail tim@revoakley.freeserve.co.uk

OATES, Alan. b 32. S'wark Ord Course 79. **d** 80 **p** 81. NSM Rayleigh *Chelmsf* 80-87; TV Jarrow *Dur* 87-92; P-in-c Stella 92-95; R 95-97; rtd 97; Perm to Offic *Dur* from 98 and *Newc* from 00. *1 The Haven, North Shields NE29 6YH* Tel 0191-258 6984

OATES, Alexander John. b 38. Clifton Th Coll 63. **d** 67 **p** 68. C Brixton Hill St Sav *S'wark* 67-68; C Westcombe Park St Geo 68-71; C Stechford *Birm* 71-74; R Greenhithe St Mary *Roch* 74-77; Soc worker 77-02; rtd 03. *1 Fairlight Villas, North Road, Havering-atte-Bower, Romford RM4 1PP* Tel (01708) 760252

OATES, Douglas. b 39. Bolton Coll of Educn CertEd74 Ches Coll of HE BTh97. NOC 94. **d** 97 **p** 98. NSM Balderstone *Man* 97-01; NSM Oldham St Barn 01-06; P-in-c 03-06; P-in-c Waterhead 05-06; TV Medlock Head 06-09; rtd 09; Perm to Offic *Man* from 09. *43 Devonport Crescent, Royton, Oldham OL2 6JX* Tel (01706) 849929 E-mail doug.oates400.freeserve.co.uk

OATES, Jeanette Linda. b 50. SEN70. NEOC 05. **d** 08 **p** 09. NSM Bridlington Priory *York* from 08. *77 St Alban Road, Bridlington YO16 7SY* Tel (01262) 678534 E-mail jeanetteoates@tiscali.co.uk

OATES, Canon John. b 30. Kelham Th Coll 53. **d** 57 **p** 58. C Hackney Wick St Mary of Eton w St Aug *Lon* 57-60; Development Officer C of E Youth Coun 60-64; Sec C of E Coun Commonwealth Settlement 64-65; Gen Sec 65-72; Sec C of E Cttee on Migration & Internat Affairs 68-72; Hon Can Bunbury from 69; V Richmond St Mary *S'wark* 70-79; P-in-c Richmond St Jo 76-79; V Richmond St Mary w St Matthias and St Jo 79-84; RD Richmond and Barnes 79-84; R St Bride Fleet Street w Bridewell etc *Lon* 84-00; AD The City 97-00; Preb St Paul's Cathl 97-00; rtd 00; Perm to Offic *Lon* from 01 and *S'wark* from 03. *27 York Court, Albany Park Road, Kingston upon Thames KT2 5ST* Tel (020) 8974 8821 E-mail john.oates@blueyonder.co.uk

OATES, Michael Graham. b 62. Leic Poly BSc84. Aston Tr Scheme 87 Cranmer Hall Dur 89. **d** 92 **p** 93. C Enfield St Andr *Lon* 92-96; TV N Poole Ecum Team *Sarum* 96-07; Perm to Offic 07-08. *51 Ringwood Road, Poole BH14 0RE*

OATES (née ADAMS), Canon Ruth. b 47. Bris Univ BSc69. SEITE 97. **d** 00 **p** 01. C Rainham *Roch* 00-03; V Gravesend St Mary from 03; RD Gravesend from 09; Hon Can Roch Cathl from 11. *The Vicarage, 57 New House Lane, Gravesend DA11 7HJ* Tel (01474) 740565 E-mail ruth.oates@diocese-rochester.org

OATRIDGE, Andrew Philip. b 77. Sheff Univ MMath00. Oak Hill Th Coll MTh10. **d** 10 **p** 11. C Chapeltown *Sheff* from 10. *The Vicarage, Church Drive, Wentworth, Rotherham S62 7TW* Tel (01226) 805815 Mobile 07894-167070 E-mail andyzsofi@gmail.com

OBAN, Provost of. See MacCALLUM, The Very Revd Norman Donald

OBEDOZA, William. b 58. NTMTC 05. **d** 08 **p** 09. C Walthamstow St Sav *Chelmsf* from 08. *212 Markhouse Road, London E17 8EP* Tel (020) 8988 6323 Mobile 07916-281227 E-mail fr.williamobedoza@yahoo.com

O'BENEY, Robin Mervyn. b 35. Ely Th Coll 61. **d** 64 **p** 65. C Liss *Portsm* 64-65; C Portsea St Cuth 65-68; Hon C Wymondham

Nor 74-76; R Swainsthorpe w Newton Flotman 76-80; NSM Sparkenhoe Deanery *Leic* 87-90; V Billesdon and Skeffington 90-91; rtd 95. *19 Bridge Street, Kington HR5 3DL* Tel (01544) 230416

OBIN, Raymond Clive. b 63. Girton Coll Cam BA85 MA89. Wycliffe Hall Ox BTh. **d** 04 **p** 05. NSM Bucklebury w Marlston *Ox* from 04; NSM Bradfield and Stanford Dingley from 04. *Solfonn, Enborne Row, Wash Water, Newbury RG20 0LY* Tel (01635) 38212 E-mail raymond@2bsd.org.uk

OBIORA, Arthur Cuenyem. b 42. JP91. **d** 95 **p** 95. OLM Hatcham St Cath *S'wark* from 95. *126 Perry Hill, London SE6 4EY*

OBORNE, Mrs Martine Amelia. b 57. St Hilda's Coll Ox MA80. SEITE BA09. **d** 09 **p** 10. C Islington St Mary *Lon* from 09. *Corner House, 12 Highbury Place, London N5 1QZ* Tel (020) 7359 8701 Mobile 07842-199556 E-mail maoborne@hotmail.com

O'BOYLE, Liam Patrick Butler. b 66. Nottm Univ BA90 MA98. EMMTC 98. **d** 01 **p** 02. C Cinderhill *S'well* 01-06; TV Clifton 06-10; Dioc Partnerships Officer from 10; C Chilwell from 11; C Lenton Abbey from 11. *23 Fellows Road, Beeston, Nottingham NG9 1AQ* Tel 0115-943 1032 E-mail liam.oboyle@ntlworld.com

O'BRIEN, Andrew David. b 61. Nottm Univ BTh88. Linc Th Coll 85. **d** 88 **p** 89. C Clare w Poslingford *St E* 88-89; C Clare w Poslingford, Cavendish etc 89-91; V Belton *Linc* 91-97; P-in-c Melbourn *Ely* 97-99; V from 99; P-in-c Meldreth 97-99; V from 99. *The Vicarage, Vicarage Close, Melbourn, Royston SG8 6DY* Tel (01763) 260295 E-mail revobrien@ntlworld.com

O'BRIEN, David. b 62. Moorlands Th Coll BA99. CBDTI 01. **d** 04 **p** 05. C Bispham *Blackb* 04-08; C S Shore H Trin 08-10; P-in-c Shelton and Oxon *Lich* from 10. *The Vicarage, 10A Shelton Gardens, Bicton Heath, Shrewsbury SY3 5AG* Tel (01743) 232774

O'BRIEN, Donogh Smith. b 34. St Pet Hall Ox BA56 MA60. Ripon Hall Ox 56. **d** 57 **p** 58. C Gt Sankey *Liv* 57-63; C Farnworth 63-66; Lic to Offic 66-03; Asst Master Wade Deacon Gr Sch Widnes 66-99; rtd 99; Perm to Offic *Liv* from 03. *Fourways, 178 Lunts Heath Road, Widnes WA8 5AZ* Tel 0151-424 0147

O'BRIEN, Mrs Elaine. b 55. CITC 94. **d** 97 **p** 98. Aux Min Killyman *Arm* 97-00; Aux Min Gilnahirk *D & D* 00-06; Bp's C Clogherny w Seskinore and Drumnakilly *Arm* 06-08; R 08-11; I Whitehouse *Conn* from 11. *The Rectory, 283 Shore Road, Newtownabbey BT37 9SR* Tel (028) 9036 9955 Mobile 07703-618119 E-mail elaineobrien1@btinternet.com

O'BRIEN, George Edward. b 32. Clifton Th Coll 61. **d** 64 **p** 65. C Denton Holme *Carl* 64-68; V Castle Town *Lich* 68-88; Chapl St Geo Hosp Stafford 88-94; Chapl Kingsmead Hosp Stafford 88-94; Chapl Foundation NHS Trust Stafford 94-99; rtd 99; Perm to Offic *Lich* from 99. *Abily, 185 Tixall Road, Stafford ST16 3XJ* Tel (01785) 244261

O'BRIEN, Kevin Michael. b 60. Herts Univ BA82. St Steph Ho Ox BTh05. **d** 01 **p** 02. C Uppingham w Ayston and Wardley w Belton *Pet* 01-04; Asst Chapl Wellington Coll Berks 04-06; Bp's Chapl and Office Manager *Eur* 06-10; V Burgess Hill St Jo *Chich* from 10; RD Hurst from 11. *St John's Rectory, 68 Park Road, Burgess Hill RH15 8HG* Tel (01444) 232582

O'BRIEN, Mary. See GUBBINS, Mrs Mary

O'BRIEN, Shelagh Ann. See STACEY, Mrs Shelagh Ann

O'CATHAIN, Damien. **d** 08 **p** 09. C Bandon Union *C, C & R* 08-11; I Castlepollard and Oldcastle w Loughcrew etc *M & K* from 11. *St Michael's Rectory, Castlepollard, Co Westmeath, Republic of Ireland* Tel (00353) (44) 966 1123 E-mail churchinfo21@gmail.com

OCHOLA, George Otieno. b 58. Lon Sch of Th BTh02. St Jo Sch of Miss Kokise. **d** 88 **p** 89. Kenya 88-99; Perm to Offic *Lon* 00-08; NSM Watford St Mich *St Alb* 08-10; Chapl W Herts Hosps NHS Trust from 10. *Foundation Trust Office, Watford General Hospital, 60 Vicarage Road, Watford WD18 0HB* Tel (01923) 436280 Mobile 07866-359120 E-mail georgeochola@hotmail.com

OCKFORD, Paul Philip. b 46. St Chad's Coll Dur BA67. St Steph Ho Ox 68. **d** 70 **p** 71. C Streatham St Pet *S'wark* 70-74; C Cheam 74-77; P-in-c Eastrington *York* 77-79; TV Howden 80-83; R Sherburn and W and E Heslerton w Yedingham 83-92; V Bampton, Morebath, Clayhanger and Petton *Ex* 92-98; R Goodmanham *York* 98-04; V Market Weighton 98-04; V Sancton 98-04; rtd 04. *78 Wold Road, Pocklington, York YO42 2QG*

OCKWELL, Canon Herbert Grant. b 12. Kelham Th Coll 30. **d** 36 **p** 37. C Newington St Matt *S'wark* 36-40; CF (EC) 40-46; V Lambeth St Phil *S'wark* 46-52; V Surbiton St Andr 52-62; V Balham Hill Ascension 62-70; Hon Can S'wark Cathl 64-70; R Blendworth, Chalton and Idsworth *Portsm* 70-81; rtd 81; Perm to Offic *Portsm* 81-07 and *Chich* 82-07. *Manormead Nursing Home, Tilford Road, Hindhead GU26 6RA* Tel (01428) 602500

O'CONNELL, Miss Mary Joy. b 49. York Univ BA71 Leeds Univ CertEd74. Chich Th Coll 84. dss 86 **d** 87 **p** 94. Cinderhill *S'well* 86-87; Par Dn 87-94; C 94; P-in-c 94-98; V Linc St Giles from 98. *The Vicarage, 25 Shelley Drive, Lincoln LN2 4BY* Tel (01522) 527655 E-mail mjoconnell@lineone.net

O'CONNELL, William Anthony. b 61. STETS. **d** 10 **p** 11. C Milton *Win* from 10. *10 Spinacre, Barton on Sea, New Milton BH25 7DF* Tel (01425) 611907
E-mail william.a.oconnell.woc@googlemail.com

O'CONNOR, Alfred Stanley. b 20. TCD BA43 MA60. **d** 43 **p** 44. C Belfast St Mich *Conn* 43-45; C Urney Union *K, E & A* 45-49; I Killesher 49-54; I Roscrea *L & K* 54-62; I Camlough w Killeavy *Arm* 62-65; I Drumglass 65-85; Can Arm Cathl 83-85; rtd 85. *25 West Street, Stewartstown, Dungannon BT71 5HT* Tel (028) 8773 8784

O'CONNOR, Canon Brian Michael McDougal. b 42. St Cath Coll Cam BA67 MA69. Cuddesdon Coll 67. **d** 69 **p** 70. C Headington *Ox* 69-71; Sec Dioc Past and Redundant Chs Uses Cttees 72-79; P-in-c Merton 72-76; V Rainham *Roch* 79-97; RD Gillingham 81-88; Hon Can Roch Cathl 89-97; Dean Auckland New Zealand 97-00; Hon Can from 00; Perm to Offic *Ox* 00-02; P-in-c Lt Missenden 02-04; rtd 04. *1 Steadys Lane, Stanton Harcourt, Witney OX29 5RL* Tel (01865) 882776 Mobile 07740-702161 E-mail canonmichaeloc@aol.com

O'CONNOR, Canon Daniel. b 33. Univ Coll Dur BA54 MA67 St Andr Univ PhD81. Cuddesdon Coll 56. **d** 58 **p** 59. C Stockton St Pet *Dur* 58-62; C W Hartlepool St Aid 62-63; Cam Miss to Delhi 63-70; USPG India 70-72; Chapl St Andr Univ 72-77; R Edin Gd Shep 77-82; Prin Coll of Ascension Selly Oak 82-90; Dir Scottish Chs Ho (Chs Together in Scotland) 90-93; Can Res Wakef Cathl 93-96; Bp's Adv on Inter-Faith Issues 93-96; rtd 96. *15 School Road, Balmullo, St Andrews KY16 0BA* Tel (01334) 8⁄1326 E-mail danoconnor@btinternet.com

O'CONNOR, John Goodrich. b 34. Keble Coll Ox BA58 MA60. Lich Th Coll. **d** 61 **p** 62. C Blackpool St Steph *Blackb* 61-66; C Holbeck *Ripon* 66-68; C Hendon St Mary *Lon* 68-73; TV Thornaby on Tees *York* 73-79; TR 79-89; V Blyth St Cuth *Newc* 89-96; Chapl Wellesley Nautical Sch 89-96; V Feniscliffe *Blackb* 96-04; rtd 04; Hon C Lightbowne *Man* from 04. *The Rectory, 173 Kenyon Lane, Manchester M40 5HS* Tel 0161-681 1308

O'CONNOR, Michael. *See* O'CONNOR, Canon Brian Michael McDougal

O'CONNOR, Rosemary Irene. b 43. St Gabr Coll Lon TCert65. WMMTC 96. **d** 99 **p** 00. NSM Cannock *Lich* 99-01; TV 01-09; rtd 09; Perm to Offic *Lich* from 01. *Windyridge, 25 The Leasowe, Lichfield WS13 7HD* Tel (01543) 252675

ODA-BURNS, John Macdonald. b 31. AKC56. **d** 57 **p** 58. C St Marychurch *Ex* 57-59; S Africa 59-64; Bahamas 64-67; USA from 67; rtd 96. *611 La Mesa Drive, Portola Valley CA 94028-7416, USA* Tel and fax (001) (650) 854 2831
E-mail bussels@aol.com

ODDY, Canon Frederick Brian. b 29. Univ of Wales (Lamp) BA50. Linc Th Coll 50. **d** 52 **p** 53. C Preston *Em Blackb* 52-55; C St Annes St Thos 55-57; V Chorley St Jas 57-64; V Warton St Oswald 64-76; P-in-c Yealand Conyers 74-76; V Warton St Oswald w Yealand Conyers 76-98; RD Tunstall 84-90; Hon Can Blackb Cathl 89-98; rtd 98; Perm to Offic *Blackb* from 98. *9 Main Road, Nether Kellet, Carnforth LA6 1HG*

ODDY, Joan Winifred. b 34. **d** 97 **p** 98. OLM Kessingland w Gisleham *Nor* 97-99; OLM Kessingland, Gisleham and Rushmere 99-04; rtd 04; Perm to Offic *Nor* from 04. *Rose Cottage, Wash Lane, Kessingland, Lowestoft NR33 7QY* Tel (01502) 742001

ODDY-BATES, Mrs Julie Louise. b 61. SRN82 SCM85. Ridley Hall Cam 04. **d** 06 **p** 07. C Watton w Carbrooke and Ovington *Nor* 06-07; C Ashill, Carbrooke, Ovington and Saham Toney 07-09; P-in-c Gillingham w Geldeston, Stockton, Ellingham etc from 09; C Loddon, Sisland, Chedgrave, Hardley and Langley from 09. *The Rectory, 60 The Street, Geldeston, Beccles NR34 0LN* Tel (01502) 715898 E-mail jlo32@tiscali.co.uk

O'DELL, Colin John. b 61. WEMTC 03. **d** 06 **p** 07. C Bishop's Cleeve *Glouc* 06-09; Chapl RAF from 09. *Chaplaincy Services, Valiant Block, HQ Air Command, RAF High Wycombe HP14 4UE* Tel (01494) 496800 Fax 496343 Mobile 07779-126050 E-mail revdcolin@hotmail.co.uk

ODEN, Herl. b 74. Ex Univ BA97. Oak Hill Th Coll BA09. **d** 09 **p** 10. C Sevenoaks St Nic *Roch* from 09. *40 South Park, Sevenoaks TN13 1EJ* Tel (01732) 454221 Mobile 07840-180395 E-mail mjoden@tiscali.co.uk

ODEWOLE, Israel Oluwagbemiga Omoniyi. b 68. Immanuel Coll Ibadan 90 W Africa Th Sem Lagos MA02. **d** 97 **p** 98. Nigeria 97-06; Chapl and Co-ord Boys' Brigade and Girls' Guild 98-06; Sec Youth Bd Dioc Ondo 99-06; Perm to Offic *Man* from 06. *Address temp unknown* E-mail jesuoluwaobami340@yahoo.com

ODLING-SMEE, George William. b 35. K Coll Dur MB, BS59 FRCS68 FRCSI86. **d** 77 **p** 78. NSM Belfast St Thos *Conn* 77-90; NSM Belfast St Geo 90-02. *The Boathouse, 24 Rossglass Road South, Killough, Downpatrick BT30 7RA* Tel (028) 4484 1868 Fax 4484 1143 E-mail wodlingsmee@aol.com

O'DONNELL, Mrs Mollie. b 39. Portsm Poly BA91. STETS 97. **d** 00 **p** 03. NSM Calbourne w Newtown and Shalfleet *Portsm*

00-09; rtd 09; Perm to Offic *Portsm* from 09. *36 Medina Court, Old Westminster Lane, Newport PO30 5PW*

O'DONOGHUE, Mark Ronald. b 69. St Aid Coll Dur BA91 Solicitor 93. Oak Hill Th Coll BA04. **d** 04 **p** 05. C St Helen Bishopsgate w St Andr Undershaft etc *Lon* from 04. *22 Chisenhale Road, London E3 5QZ* Tel (020) 8980 9150
E-mail odonoghue_mark@hotmail.com

O'DONOVAN, Canon Oliver Michael Timothy. b 45. Ball Coll Ox BA68 MA71 DPhil75. Wycliffe Hall Ox 68. **d** 72 **p** 73. Tutor Wycliffe Hall Ox 72-77; Prof Systematic Th Wycliffe Coll Toronto 77-82; Regius Prof Moral and Past Th Ox Univ 82-06; Can Res Ch Ch *Ox* 82-06; Prof Chr Ethics Edin Univ from 06. *New College, Mound Place, Edinburgh EH1 2LX* Tel 0131-650 8900 E-mail oliver.odonovan@ed.ac.uk

O'DOWD SMYTH, Christine. CITC. **d** 09 **p** 10. NSM Lismore w Cappoquin, Kilwatermoy, Dungarvan etc *C & O* from 09. *Address temp unknown*

O'DWYER, John Francis Joseph. b 61. NOC 00. **d** 03 **p** 04. C Bury St Jo w St Mark *Man* 03-06; P-in-c Bury St Pet 06-10. *Address temp unknown* E-mail johntricia2000@yahoo.co.uk

OEHRING, Canon Anthony Charles. b 56. Sheff City Poly BA79 CQSW79 Kent Univ MA02. Ridley Hall Cam 86. **d** 88 **p** 89. C Gillingham *Sarum* 88-91; TV S Gillingham *Roch* 91-00; P-in-c Faversham *Cant* from 00; C Preston next Faversham, Goodnestone and Graveney from 02; P-in-c The Brents and Davington w Oare and Luddenham 03-06; AD Ospringe from 02; Hon Can Cant Cathl from 06. *The Vicarage, 16 Newton Road, Faversham ME13 8DY* Tel (01795) 532592
E-mail anthonyoehring@aol.com

OEPPEN, Canon John Gerard David. b 44. St D Coll Lamp. **d** 67 **p** 68. C-in-c Cwmmer w Abercregan CD *Llan* 67-70; TV Glyncorrwg w Afan Vale and Cymmer Afan 70-71; C Whitchurch 71-74; V Aberavon H Trin 74-78; V Bargoed and Deri w Brithdir 78-86; R Barry All SS 86-08; Can Llan Cathl 04-08; rtd 08. *Oak Cottage, 5 Heol Leubren, Barry CF63 1HG*

OESTREICHER, Canon Paul. b 31. OM(Ger)95. Univ of NZ BA53 MA56 Cov Poly Hon DLitt91 Sussex Univ Hon LLD05 Lambeth DD08 Otago Univ Hon DD09. Linc Th Coll 56. **d** 59 **p** 60. C Dalston H Trin w St Phil *Lon* 59-61; C S Mymms K Chas 61-68; Asst in Relig Broadcasting BBC 61-64; Assoc Sec Internat Affairs Dept BCC 64-69; V Blackheath Ascension *S'wark* 68-81; Dir of Tr 69-72; Hon Can S'wark Cathl 78-81; Asst Gen Sec BCC 81-86; Can Res Cov Cathl 86-97; Dir of Internat Min 86-97; Humboldt Fell Inst of Th Free Univ of Berlin 92-93; rtd 98; Perm to Offic *Cov* 98-10 and *Chich* from 03; Hon Chapl Sussex Univ 04-09. *97 Furze Croft, Furze Hill, Hove BN3 1PE* Tel (01273) 728033 E-mail paul_oestreicher@yahoo.co.uk

O'FARRELL, Anne Marie. b 08 **p** 09. NSM Dublin Sandford w Milltown *D & G* from 08. *138 Meadow Grove, Dundrum, Dublin 14, Republic of Ireland* Tel (1) 296 6222

O'FERRALL, Patrick Charles Kenneth. b 34. OBE89. New Coll Ox BA58 MA60. **d** 00 **p** 01. OLM Godalming *Guildf* 00-04; Perm to Offic from 04. *Catteshall Grange, Catteshall Road, Godalming GU7 1LZ* Tel (01483) 410134 Fax 414161
E-mail patrick@oferrall.co.uk

OFFER, The Ven Clifford Jocelyn. b 43. Ex Univ BA67 FRSA97. Westcott Ho Cam 67. **d** 69 **p** 70. C Bromley SS Pet and Paul *Roch* 69-74; TV Southampton (City Cen) *Win* 74-83; TR Hitchin *St Alb* 83-94; Adn Nor and Can Res Nor Cathl 94-08; rtd 08. *Chase House, Peterstow, Ross-on-Wye HR9 6JX* Tel (01989) 567874

OFFER, Mrs Jill Patricia. b 44. CertEd65. **d** 03 **p** 04. OLM Salisbury St Mark *Sarum* from 03. *11 Netheravon Road, Salisbury SP1 3BJ* Tel (01722) 334455
E-mail jill.offer@osser.wanadoo.co.uk

OGADA, John Ochieng. b 56. Nairobi Univ LLB83 Univ of Wales (Cardiff) LLM89. **d** 01. Perm to Offic *York* 01-02; NSM Hull St Martin w Transfiguration 02-03. *44 Kingston Road, Willerby, Hull HU10 6BH* Tel (01482) 653592

O'GARRO, Henry Roland Furlonge. b 30. Leeward Is TCert52. St Steph Ho Ox 00. **d** 00. NSM Kilburn St Aug w St Jo *Lon* 00-05; NSM Willesden St Mary from 05. *32 Cedar Road, London NW2 6SR* Tel (020) 8452 4530

OGBEDE, Ms Olufunke Oladunni. b 48. Lon Inst of SS Educn MA81. **d** 06. OLM S Lambeth St Anne and All SS *S'wark* from 05. *98 Plummer Road, London SW4 8HJ* Tel (020) 8678 7387 Mobile 07944-424931 E-mail fundunni@aol.com

OGDEN, Harry. b 30. AKC57. **d** 58 **p** 59. C Hollinwood *Man* 58-60; C Langley St Aid CD 60-61; R Lightbowne 61-69; V Farnworth and Kearsley 69-72; V Oldham St Steph and All Martyrs 72-79; R Moss Side Ch 79-95; rtd 95; Perm to Offic *Man* 95-98; *Worc* 01-05; *Blackb* from 06. *16 Fosbrooke House, Clifton Drive, Lytham St Annes FY8 5RQ*

OGILVIE, The Ven Gordon. b 42. Glas Univ MA64 Lon Univ BD67. ALCD66. **d** 67 **p** 68. C Ashtead *Guildf* 67-72; V New Barnet St Jas *St Alb* 72-80; Dir Past Studies Wycliffe Hall Ox 80-87; P-in-c Harlow New Town w Lt Parndon *Chelmsf* 87-89; R 89-94; TR Harlow Town Cen w Lt Parndon 94-96; Hon Can Chelmsf Cathl 94-96; Chapl Princess Alexandra Hosp Harlow

88-96; Adn Nottingham *S'well* 96-06; rtd 07; Lic to Offic *St And* from 07. *49 Argyle Street, St Andrews KY16 9BX* Tel (01334) 470185 E-mail gordon.ogilvie@virgin.net

OGILVIE, Ian Douglas. b 37. Em Coll Cam BA59 MA63. Linc Th Coll 59. **d** 61 **p** 62. C Clapham H Trin *S'wark* 61-63; C Cambridge Gt St Mary w St Mich *Ely* 63-66; Chapl Sevenoaks Sch 66-77; Hon C Sevenoaks St Nic *Roch* 67-77; Chapl Malvern Coll 77-84; Hd Master St Geo Sch Harpenden 84-87; Lic to Offic *St Alb* 84-87; Bp's Dom Chapl 87-89; P-in-c Aldenham 87-91; Appeals Dir Mind 89-91; Fund Raising Dir Br Deaf Assn 91-94; NSM Tring *St Alb* 92-94; Perm to Offic from 94; Fund Raising Dir R Nat Miss to Deep Sea Fishermen from 94. *The White House, 19 Lower Icknield Way, Marsworth, Tring HP23 4LN* Tel (01296) 661479

OGILVIE, Pamela. b 56. Brunel Univ MA89 CQSW82. Qu Coll Birm 01. **d** 03 **p** 04. C Hill *Birm* 03-07; V Billesley Common from 07. *Holy Cross Vicarage, 29 Beauchamp Road, Birmingham B13 0NS* Tel 0121-444 1737 E-mail church@holycrossbillesley.co.uk

OGLE, The Very Revd Catherine. b 61. Leeds Univ BA82 MPhil85 MA91 Fitzw Coll Cam BA87. Westcott Ho Cam 85. **d** 88 **p** 94. C Middleton St Mary *Ripon* 88-91; Relig Progr Ed BBC Radio Leeds 91-95; NSM Leeds St Marg and All Hallows 91-95; P-in-c Woolley *Wakef* 95-01; P-in-c Huddersfield St Pet and All SS 01-03; V Huddersfield St Pet 03-10; RD Huddersfield 09-10; Chapl Huddersfield Univ 03-06; Hon Can Wakef Cathl 08-10; Dean Birm from 10. *38 Goodby Road, Birmingham B13 8NJ* Tel 0121-262 1840 Fax 262 1860 E-mail cogleathome@aol.com *or* dean@birminghamcathedral.com

OGLESBY, Ms Elizabeth Jane. b 73. Roehampton Inst BA95 Man Univ BPhil98. Westcott Ho Cam 00. **d** 03 **p** 04. C S Dulwich St Steph *S'wark* 03-06; P-in-c Camberwell St Mich w All So w Em 06-07; V from 07. *St Michael's Vicarage, 128 Bethwin Road, London SE5 0YY* Tel (020) 7703 8686 Mobile 07790-219725

OGLESBY, Canon Leslie Ellis. b 46. Univ Coll Ox BA69 MA73 City Univ MPhil73 Fitzw Coll Cam BA73 MA77. Ripon Coll Cuddesdon 77. **d** 78 **p** 79. C Stevenage St Mary Shephall *St Alb* 78-80; Dir St Alb Minl Tr Scheme 80-87; V Markyate Street *St Alb* 80-87; Dir CME 87-94; Hon Can St Alb 93-01; TR Hitchin 94-01; Adult Educn and Tr Officer *Ely* 01-04; Dioc Dir Minl and Adult Learning from 04; Hon Can Ely Cathl from 04. *1A Church Road, Everton, Sandy SG19 2JY* Tel (01767) 699165 *or* (01353) 652713 E-mail les.oglesby@ely.anglican.org

OGLEY, James Edward. b 76. St Jo Coll Nottm BA07. **d** 07 **p** 08. C Bursledon *Win* from 07. *13 Redcroft Lane, Bursledon, Southampton SO31 8GS* Tel (023) 8040 4220 Mobile 07968-083744 E-mail james@jamesthevicar.com

OGLEY, John. b 40. Oak Hill Th Coll 62. **d** 65 **p** 66. C Ardsley *Sheff* 65-68; C Carlton-in-the-Willows *S'well* 68-71; P-in-c Tollerton 71-79; V Skegby 79-93; R Carlton in Lindrick 93-01; P-in-c Langold 98-01; rtd 01; Perm to Offic *S'well* from 01. *The Bungalow, Church Lane, Carlton-in-Lindrick, Worksop S81 9EG* Tel (01909) 732367

OGRAM, Mrs Ann. b 44. WEMTC 04. **d** 06 **p** 07. NSM Clun w Bettws-y-Crwyn and Newcastle *Heref* from 06. *Highbeech House, Mount Pleasant, Llwyn Road, Clun, Craven Arms SY7 8JU* Tel (01588) 640830 Mobile 07970-072836 E-mail ann@ogram.com

OGSTON, Russell James. b 71. La Sainte Union Coll BA94. Qu Coll Birm BD97. **d** 98 **p** 99. C Andover w Foxcott *Win* 98-01; C Southampton Maybush St Pet 01-03; Asst Chapl Homerton Univ Hosp NHS Trust Lon 03-05; Chapl 05-08; Chapl Pilgrims Hospice Thanet 08-09; Chapl Newham Univ Hosp NHS Trust 09-10; Egypt from 10. *Address temp unknown* Tel 07523-094689 (mobile)

OGUGUO, Barnabas Ahuna. b 47. Rome Univ BA70 BD74 Glas Univ MTh84 PhD90 Strathclyde Univ PGCE93. **d** 73 **p** 74. Nigeria 73-93; RE Teacher Lenzie Academy *Glas* 93-96; Bearsden Academy from 96; Hon C Lenzie 95-05; P-in-c Cumbernauld from 07. *32 Carron Crescent, Lenzie, Glasgow G66 5YH* Tel 0141-776 1321 *or* 942 2297 Fax 578 9802 E-mail boguguo@lycos.co.uk

OGUNSANYA, Olumuyiwa Adegboyega. b 67. Lagos Angl Dioc Sem 01. **d** 03 **p** 04. C Alapere Ch Ch Nigeria 04-05; Perm to Offic *S'wark* from 07. *222 Seabrook Rise, Grays RM17 6BL* Tel (01375) 369415 Mobile 07946-488595 E-mail revoolord2005@yahoo.com

OGUNYEMI, Dele Johnson. b 56. Obafemi Awolowo Univ BA90. SEITE 04. **d** 07 **p** 08. NSM Plumstead All SS *S'wark* 07-11; C Nunhead St Antony w St Silas from 11. *St Antony w St Silas Vicarage, Athenlay Road, London SE15 3EP* Tel 07957-425113 (mobile) E-mail djogunyemi@tiscali.co.uk

OH, Abraham (Taemin). b 75. St Steph Ho Ox 08. **d** 11. NSM Colchester St Jas and St Paul w All SS etc *Chelmsf* from 11. *Benson House, 13 Roman Road, Colchester CO1 1UR* Tel 07737-161317 (mobile) E-mail taemin.oh@gmail.com

OHEN, John. b 42. **d** 06 **p** 07. NSM Clapham St Jas *S'wark* from 06. *47 Kirkstall Gardens, London SW2 4HR* Tel (020) 8671 0028

OHS, Lt Comdr Douglas Fredrick. b 49. Saskatchewan Univ BA74. Em Coll Saskatoon LTh75. **d** 74 **p** 75. C Bridgwater St Mary w Chilton Trinity *B & W* 75-77; Canada from 77. *14-3505 Willowdale Crescent, Brandon MB R7B 3C5, Canada*

OJI, Erasmus Oluchukwu. b 43. Lon Univ BSc66 LRCP70 MRCS70 FRCS76. Oak Hill Th Coll 75. **d** 78 **p** 79. C Ealing Dean St Jo *Lon* 78-80; Nigeria 80-90; Asst Chapl Rotherham Distr Gen Hosp 90-91; Perm to Offic *Sheff* from 92. *369 Fulwood Road, Sheffield S10 3BS* Tel and fax (07092) 147747 E-mail erasmus@doctors.org.uk

OKE, Mrs Elizabeth Mary. b 43. SAOMC 96. **d** 99 **p** 00. NSM Woolhampton w Midgham and Beenham Valance *Ox* 99-08; NSM Aldermaston w Wasing and Brimpton 05-08; NSM Aldermaston and Woolhampton from 08. *Gladstone Cottage, 18 Windmill Road, Mortimer, Reading RG7 3RN* Tel 0118-933 2829

OKE, Michael John. b 42. Ox Min Course 89. **d** 92 **p** 93. NSM Stratfield Mortimer *Ox* 92-99; NSM Stratfield Mortimer and Mortimer W End etc 99-03; NSM Tilehurst St Geo from 03; NSM Tilehurst St Mary from 03. *Gladstone Cottage, 18 Windmill Road, Mortimer, Reading RG7 3RN* Tel 0118-933 2829

OKECHI, Patrick Otosio. b 62. Chas Univ Prague MTh94. **d** 95 **p** 98. Perm to Offic *Eur* 95-02; Asst P Angl Episc Congregation Czech Republic 02; V W Bromwich Gd Shep w St Jo *Lich* 02-08. *8 Drake Road, Birmingham B66 1TF* Tel 07951-814518 (mobile) E-mail pokechi1@btinternet.com

OKEKE, Christian. b 71. **d** 05 **p** 06. C Avondale Zimbabwe 05; C Glas St Silas 05-08; P-in-c Glas Gd Shep and Ascension from 08; Chapl Strathclyde Univ from 08. *31 Westfield Drive, Glasgow G52 2SG* Tel 0141-882 4996

✠**OKEKE, The Rt Revd Ken Sandy Edozie.** b 41. Nigeria Univ BSc67 Man Univ MA94. Igbaja Sem Nigeria. **d** 76 **p** 76 **c** 00. Nigeria 76-80 and 87-89; Chapl to Nigerians in UK and Irish Republic 80-87; Hon Can Kwara from 85; Hon Adn from 98; C Man Whitworth 89-95; Chapl Inst of Higher Learning Man 89-95; CMS 95-01; Perm to Offic *S'wark* 96-02; Bp on the Niger from 00. *PO Box 42, Onitsha, Nigeria* Tel (00234) (46) 411282 *or* 410337

OKELLO, Modicum. b 53. Trin Coll Bris BA90. St Paul's Coll Limuru 76 Wycliffe Hall Ox 86. **d** 78 **p** 79. Kenya 78-80; Uganda 80-86; NSM Goodmayes All SS *Chelmsf* 91-92; C Barking St Marg w St Patr 92-96; C Stratford St Jo and Ch Ch w Forest Gate St Jas 96-99; TV Forest Gate St Sav w W Ham St Matt 99-10; P-in-c Hall Green St Mich *Birm* from 10. *St Michael's Vicarage, 237 Lakey Lane, Birmingham B28 8QT* E-mail modicumokello@okello8726modicum.freeserve.co.uk

OLADUJI, Christopher Temitayo. b 57. Awosika Th Coll Nigeria 84. **d** 87 **p** 88. Nigeria 87-89; C Ilutitun Ebenezer 87; Asst P Ondo Cathl 88; NSM W Ham *Chelmsf* 89-93; NSM Peckham St Jo w St Andr *S'wark* 97-98; NSM E Ham St Geo *Chelmsf* 99-01; NSM Hackney Wick St Mary of Eton w St Aug *Lon* 02-04; NSM Smithfield St Bart Gt from 04. *Church House, Cloth Fair, London EC1A 7JQ* Tel (020) 7606 1575 Mobile 07985-465401 E-mail coladuji@yahoo.com

OLANCZUK, Jonathan Paul Tadeusz. b 49. EAMTC 94. **d** 96 **p** 97. C Haverhill w Withersfield *St E* 96-00; P-in-c Badingham w Bruisyard, Cransford and Dennington 00-04; P-in-c Rendham w Sweffling 00-04; R Upper Alde from 04. *The Rectory, 5 Orchard Rise, Badingham, Woodbridge IP13 8LN* Tel and fax (01728) 638823 Mobile 07766-953558 *or* 07944-186526 E-mail olanczuk@suffolkonline.net *or* jolanczuk@aol.com

OLD, Arthur Anthony George (Tony). b 36. Clifton Th Coll 69. **d** 71 **p** 72. C Clitheroe St Jas *Blackb* 71-73; C Bispham 73-77; V Haslingden St Jo Stonefold 77-81; TV Lowestoft and Kirkley *Nor* 81-83; Chapl to the Deaf *Cant* 83-01; P-in-c Hernhill 83-85; C Preston next Faversham, Goodnestone and Graveney 85-01; rtd 01; Perm to Offic *Cant* from 01. *62 Knaves Acre, Headcorn, Ashford TN27 9TJ* Tel (01622) 891498

OLDFIELD, Jonathan Thomas. b 54. Bede Coll Dur TCert76. NEOC 04. **d** 07 **p** 08. NSM Patrick Brompton and Hunton *Ripon* from 07; NSM Crakehall from 07; NSM Hornby from 07. *12 St Mary's Mount, Leyburn DL8 5JB* Tel (01969) 622958 E-mail jonathan@jonathanoldfield.wanadoo.co.uk

OLDFIELD, Canon Roger Fielden. b 45. Qu Coll Cam BA67 MA71 Lon Univ BD75. Trin Coll Bris 73. **d** 75 **p** 76. C Halliwell St Pet *Man* 75-80 and 03-10; V 80-03; AD Bolton 93-02; Hon Can Man Cathl 00-10; rtd 10; Perm to Offic *Man* from 11. *70 Eastgrove Avenue, Bolton BL1 7HA* Tel (01204) 305228 E-mail rogerandruth@googlemail.com

OLDHAM, Dale Raymond. b 40. NZ Coll of Pharmacy MPS63 Cant Univ (NZ) MA87. Ridley Hall Cam 64. **d** 67 **p** 68. C Woking St Mary *Guildf* 67-70; C Papanui New Zealand 71-73; CMS Miss Dodoma Tanzania 74-81; Sec Home CMS New Zealand 81-85; C Burnside 85-88; V Shirley St Steph 89-06; rtd 06. *58 Pitcairn Crescent, Papanui, Christchurch 8053, New Zealand* E-mail d.oldham@xtra.co.nz

OLDHAM, David Christian. b 76. Surrey Univ MSc07 RN98. Ripon Coll Cuddesdon 09. **d** 10 **p** 11. C Wymondham *Nor* from

10. *The Curatage, 43 Black Lane, Wymondham NR18 0LB* Tel (01953) 602954 Mobile 07860-700277 E-mail revdavidoldham@btinternet.com

OLDHAM, Susan. d 10. NSM Georgeham *Ex* from 10. *Twinney Park House, Darracott, Georgeham, Braunton EX33 1JY* Tel (01271) 891088

OLDNALL, Frederick Herbert. b 16. Ripon Hall Ox 56. **d** 57 **p** 58. C Radford *Cov* 57-59; C Stratford-on-Avon 59-62; V Rosliston w Coton in the Elms *Derby* 62-83; rtd 83; Perm to Offic *Cov* from 93. *4 Margetts Close, Kenilworth CV8 1EN* Tel (01926) 852417

OLDROYD, Preb Colin Mitchell. b 30. Down Coll Cam BA54 MA60. Wells Th Coll 60. **d** 61 **p** 62. C Elton All SS *Man* 61-63; C Ex St Dav 63-66; P-in-c Neen Sollars w Milson *Heref* 66-78; P-in-c Coreley w Doddington 66-78; R Cleobury Mortimer w Hopton Wafers 66-78; RD Ludlow 75-78; P-in-c Eastnor 78-81; R Ledbury 78-81; RD Ledbury 78-81; Chapl Ledbury Cottage Hosp *Heref* 79-95; R Ledbury w Eastnor *Heref* 81-95; Preb Heref Cathl 84-95; P-in-c Lt Marcle 85-95; rtd 95; Perm to Offic *Heref* from 96. *2 Hampton Manor Close, Hereford HR1 1TG* Tel (01432) 340569

OLDROYD, David Christopher Leslie. b 42. FRICS. S Dios Minl Tr Scheme. **d** 85 **p** 86. NSM Four Marks *Win* 85-90; Perm to Offic *Portsm* from 06 and *Guildf* from 08. *18 Rozeldene, Grayshott, Hindhead GU26 6TW* Tel (01428) 606620

OLDROYD, Mrs Sheila Margaret. b 40. Liv Univ BSc63. St Steph Ho Ox 98. **d** 99 **p** 00. NSM Cotgrave *S'well* 99-03; NSM Keyworth and Stanton-on-the-Wolds and Bunny etc 03-08; rtd 08; Perm to Offic *S'well* from 08. *27 Lowlands Drive, Keyworth, Nottingham NG12 5HG* Tel 0115-937 6344 E-mail margaretoldroyd@btinternet.com

OLDROYD, Trevor. b 33. Hatf Coll Dur BA55 Lon Univ BD60. Wycliffe Hall Ox 60. **d** 61 **p** 62. C Barnes St Mary *S'wark* 61-65; C Wimbledon 65-68; W Germany 68-73; Chapl Dudley Sch 73-80; Asst Chapl Wellington Coll Berks 80-82; P-in-c Rendcomb *Glouc* 82-86; Chapl Rendcomb Coll 82-86; Chapl Wrekin Coll Telford 86-90; V Deptford St Jo w H Trin *S'wark* 91-94; rtd 94; Perm to Offic *Sarum* 94-00 and *Guildf* from 02. *4 The Larches, Woking GU21 4RE* Tel (01483) 720398

OLEY, Mrs Carolyn Joan Macdonald. b 44. Ox Min Course 05. **d** 08 **p** 09. NSM Lambfold *Pet* from 08. *10 The Green, Evenley, Brackley NN13 5SQ* Tel (01280) 701311 Mobile 07808-776751 E-mail carolyn.oley@btinternet.com

OLHAUSEN, William Paul. b 67. Wycliffe Hall Ox BA97. **d** 98 **p** 99. C Reading Greyfriars *Ox* 98-01; Sub Chapl HM YOI Reading 98-01; C Cambridge H Trin *Ely* 01-04; I Carrigrohane Union *C, C & R* 04-08; Chapl Monkton Combe Sch Bath 08-11; I Killiney Ballybrack *D & G* from 11. *The Rectory, Killiney Avenue, Killiney, Co Dublin, Republic of Ireland* Tel (00353) (1) 285 2228 E-mail wolhausen@googlemail.com

OLIVE, Dan. b 29. ARIBA54. Sarum & Wells Th Coll 79. **d** 82 **p** 83. NSM Wells St Cuth w Wookey Hole *B & W* 82-85; C Yatton Moor 86-88; R Mells w Buckland Dinham, Elm, Whatley etc 88-97; RD Frome 93-97; rtd 97; Perm to Offic *B & W* from 97. *Roseleigh, Woodcombe, Minehead TA24 8SA* Tel (01643) 702218

OLIVER, Bernard John. b 31. CEng65 MIMechE. S'wark Ord Course 75. **d** 78 **p** 79. NSM Chipping Ongar *Chelmsf* 78-81; C Waltham Abbey 81-85; C High Ongar w Norton Mandeville 85-87; C Somerton w Compton Dundon, the Charltons etc *B & W* 87-88; rtd 96; Perm to Offic *Sarum* from 01. *1 Orchard Way, Mosterton, Beaminster DT8 3LT* Tel (01308) 868037

OLIVER, David Leath. b 41. **d** 96. Old Catholic Ch Germany 96-01; Perm to Offic *Eur* 10-11; NSM Helsinki from 11. *Purotie 6 AS 14, 65410 Sundom, Finland* Tel (00358) (6) 4602 3780 Mobile 407-325250 E-mail tuulandavid@yahoo.com

OLIVER, Canon David Ryland. b 34. Univ of Wales (Lamp) BA56 St Cath Coll Ox BA58 MA62. Wycliffe Hall Ox 56. **d** 58 **p** 59. C Carmarthen St Pet *St D* 58-61; C Llangyfelach and Morriston *S & B* 61-63; R Aberedw w Llandeilo Graban etc 63-66; R Llanbadarn Fawr, Llandegley and Llanfihangel etc 66-67; Lic to Offic *Llan* 68-70 and *Ban* 70-73; V Nefyn w Pistyll w Tudweiliog w Llandudwen etc *Ban* 73-74; V Abercraf and Callwen *S & B* 74-77; V Llangyfelach 77-79; R Llanllwchaearn and Llanina *St D* 79-83; V Cwmaman 83-94; Can St D Cathl from 90; RD Dyffryn Aman 93-94; V Cynwyl Gaeo w Llansawel and Talley 94-99; rtd 99. *Maes y Gelynen, 40 Heol Bryngwili, Cross Hands, Llanelli SA14 6LR* Tel (01269) 840146

OLIVER, Gordon. See OLIVER, Canon Thomas Gordon

OLIVER, Graham Frank. b 42. St Barn Coll Adelaide. **d** 68 **p** 69. Australia 68-86; C Ealing Ch the Sav *Lon* 86-93; Perm to Offic 94-97 and 00-08; Asst Chapl Ypres *Eur* 97-99; P-in-c 99-00; rtd 07. *2 Aldridge Court, 176A High Street, London W3 9NN* Tel (020) 8992 0332

OLIVER, John Andrew George. b 28. OBE83. St Jo Coll Dur BA53. **d** 55 **p** 56. C Bermondsey St Mary w St Olave and St Jo *S'wark* 55-58; C Dulwich St Barn 58-61; Chapl RN 61-83; QHC 79-83; R Guisborough *York* 83-89; Tutor and Chapl Whittington Coll Felbridge 89-93; rtd 93; Perm to Offic *Carl*

from 93. *Allandale, Thacka Lane, Penrith CA11 9HX* Tel (01768) 892096

OLIVER, John Graham Wyand. b 47. Ridley Hall Cam 76. **d** 78 **p** 79. C Shortlands *Roch* 78-81; C Hammersmith St Paul *Lon* 81-85; V Mazabuka Zambia 85-91; Adn S Zambia 89-91; R Cape Town St Mark S Africa from 95. *The Rectory, 35 Beresford Road, University Estate, Cape Town, 7925 South Africa* Tel (0027) (21) 705 5502 *or* 448 1006 Fax 448 8500 Mobile 82-733 3500 E-mail revjohn@iafrica.com

✠**OLIVER, The Rt Revd John Keith. b** 35. G&C Coll Cam BA59 MA63 MLitt65. Westcott Ho Cam 59. **d** 64 **p** 65 **c** 90. C Hilborough w Bodney *Nor* 64-68; Chapl Eton Coll 68-72; R S Molton w Nymet St George *Ex* 73-75; P-in-c Filleigh w E Buckland 73-75; P-in-c Warkleigh w Satterleigh and Chittlehamholt 73-75; P-in-c High Bray w Charles 73-75; TR S Molton, Nymet St George, High Bray etc 75-82; P-in-c N Molton w Twitchen 77-79; RD S Molton 74-80; TR Cen Ex 82-85; Adn Sherborne *Sarum* 85-90; P-in-c W Stafford w Frome Billet 85-90; Can Res Sarum Cathl 85-90; Bp Heref 90-03; rtd 03; Hon Asst Bp S & B from 04; Perm to Offic *Heref* from 05. *The Old Vicarage, Glascwm, Llandrindod Wells LD1 5SE* Tel and fax (01982) 570771

OLIVER, John Kenneth. b 47. Brunel Univ MA92 ALBC70. EAMTC 98. **d** 00 **p** 01. C E Ham St Paul *Chelmsf* 00-03; V Stratford New Town St Paul 03-05; TV Totton *Win* from 05. *Calmore Vicarage, Cooks Lane, Calmore, Southampton SO40 2RU* Tel (023) 8081 2702 E-mail revjohnoliver@btinternet.com

OLIVER, The Ven John Michael. b 39. Univ of Wales (Lamp) BA62. Ripon Hall Ox 62. **d** 64 **p** 65. C High Harrogate St Pet *Ripon* 64-67; C Bramley 67-72; V Low Harrogate St Mary 72-78; V Beeston 78-92; RD Armley 86-92; Adn Leeds 92-05; Hon Can Ripon Cathl 87-05; rtd 05; Perm to Offic *Ripon* from 05. *42A Chapel Lane, Barwick in Elmet, Leeds LS15 4EJ* Tel 0113-393 5019

OLIVER, The Ven John Rodney. b 31. Melbourne Univ BA53 Lon Univ MTh73. Bps' Coll Cheshunt 54. **d** 56 **p** 57. C Much Hadham *St Alb* 56-57; Chapl Ballarat Gr Sch Australia 58-69; C Thorley and Bishop's Stortford H Trin *St Alb* 70-73; V Aberfeldie Australia 74-77; Chapl Trin Coll Melbourne 77-81; I Dandenong 81-91; Adn Box Hill 87-00; I East Kew St Paul 91-00; rtd 00. *27 Asquith Street, Box Hill South Vic 3128, Australia* Tel (0061) (3) 9888 7517 Fax 9888 7598 E-mail rodley@smartchat.net.au

OLIVER, Jonathan Andrew. b 79. Cam Univ MPhil11. Ridley Hall Cam 08. **d** 11. C Sholing *Win* from 11. *39 Whites Road, Southampton SO19 7NR* Tel 07779-156691 (mobile) E-mail jonoliver@live.co.uk

OLIVER, Mrs Josephine May. b 48. Cranmer Hall Dur. **d** 01 **p** 02. C Buckrose Carrs *York* 01-04; P-in-c Bubwith w Skipwith 04-10; rtd 10. *23 Skirbeck Road, Hull HU8 0HR* Tel (01482) 784744 Mobile 07885-448331 E-mail jovicar@jovicar.plus.com

OLIVER (née TROMANS), Canon Judith Anne. b 54. Liv Univ BSc76 Lanc Univ PGCE77 Birm Univ MA07. WMMTC. **d** 96 **p** 97. C Old Swinford Stourbridge *Worc* 96-99; C Pensnett 99-01; Asst to Suff Bp Dudley 99-01; P-in-c Dudley Wood 01-08; V 08-10; TV Dudley from 10; Hon Can Worc Cathl from 11. *St Francis' Vicarage, 50 Laurel Road, Dudley DY1 3EZ* Tel (01384) 832164 Mobile 07903-104862 E-mail juditholiver@blueyonder.co.uk

OLIVER, Canon Paul Robert. b 41. Tyndale Hall Bris 63. **d** 66 **p** 67. C Virginia Water *Guildf* 66-70; Scripture Union (E Region) 70-74; TV Thetford *Nor* 75-83; V Earlham St Anne 83-98; RD Nor S 94-98; Hon Can Nor Cathl 96-98; rtd 98; Perm to Offic *Nor* from 98. *The Sanctuary, 35A Blofield Road, Brundall, Norwich NR13 5NU* Tel (01603) 712124 E-mail paulandliz.oliver@virgin.net

OLIVER, Canon Philip Maule. b 38. Birm Univ LLB59. Wells Th Coll 62. **d** 64 **p** 65. C Chesterton *Lich* 64-67; C Tettenhall Wood 67-71; V Milton 71-78; V Ixworth and Bardwell *St E* 78-92; P-in-c Honington w Sapiston and Troston 81-92; TR Blackbourne 92-08; RD Ixworth 85-94; Hon Can St E Cathl 00-08; rtd 08; Perm to Offic *St E* from 08. *25 Millfield Road, Barningham, Bury St Edmunds IP31 1DX*

OLIVER, Rodney. See OLIVER, The Ven John Rodney

OLIVER, Ryland. See OLIVER, Canon David Ryland

OLIVER, Simon Andrew. b 71. Mansf Coll Ox BA93 MA98 Peterho Cam BA97 MA00 PhD03. Westcott Ho Cam 95. **d** 98 **p** 99. NSM Teversham *Ely* 98-01; NSM Cherry Hinton St Andr 98-01; Chapl Hertf Coll Ox 01-05; Lect Univ of Wales (Lamp) *St D* 05; Sen Lect 06-09; Perm to Offic 05-09; Assoc Prof Nottm Univ from 09; Perm to Offic from 10; Can Th S'well Minster from 10. *Department of Theology, University of Nottingham, University Park, Nottingham NG7 2RD* Tel 0115-951 5853 Fax 951 5887 E-mail simon.oliver@nottingham.ac.uk

✠**OLIVER, The Rt Revd Stephen John. b** 48. AKC59. St Aug Coll Cant 70. **d** 71 **p** 72 **c** 03. C Clifton w Glapton *S'well* 71-75; P-in-c Newark Ch Ch 75-79; R Plumtree 79-85; Sen Producer BBC Relig Broadcasting Dept Lon 85-87; Chief Producer 87-91; TR

Leeds City *Ripon* 91-97; Can Res and Prec St Paul's Cathl 97-03; Area Bp Stepney 03-10; rtd 10. *Garden Cottage, Church Lane, Averham, Newark NG23 5RB* Tel (01636) 673861 E-mail stephen@btinternet.com

OLIVER, Mrs Susan Jacqueline. b 54. Univ Coll Lon LLB78 CQSW86. Qu Coll Birm 03. **d** 05 **p** 06. C Fladbury w Wyre Piddle and Moor etc *Worc* 05-09; TV Louth *Linc* from 09. *The Vicarage, Little Lane, Louth LN11 9DU* Tel (01507) 601250 Mobile 07843-750451 E-mail suejoliver@tiscali.co.uk

OLIVER, Suzanne Marie. *See* PATTLE, Mrs Suzanne Marie

OLIVER, Canon Thomas Gordon. b 48. Nottm Univ BTh72 DipAdEd80. St Jo Coll Nottm 68 ALCD72. **d** 72 **p** 73. C Thorpe Edge *Bradf* 72-76; C Woodthorpe *S'well* 76-80; V Huthwaite 80-85; Dir Past Studies St Jo Coll Nottm 85-94; Dir of Min and Tr *Roch* 94-09; R Meopham w Nurstead from 09; Hon Can Roch Cathl from 95. *The Rectory, Shipley Hills Road, Meopham, Gravesend DA13 0AD* Tel (01474) 812068 *or* 813106 E-mail canongordon.oliver@googlemail.com

OLIVER, Mrs Trudi. b 65. Brighton Univ BA09. Trin Coll Bris 09. **d** 11. C Southampton Lord's Hill and Lord's Wood *Win* from 11. *All Saints' House, 60 Brookwood Road, Southampton SO16 9AJ* Tel 07856-029765 (mobile) E-mail kerygmababe@gmail.com

OLIVER, Canon Wendy Louise. b 54. Aston Tr Scheme 93 Oak Hill Th Coll 94. **d** 96 **p** 97. C Walmsley *Man* 96-99; P-in-c Goodshaw and Crawshawbooth 99-08; AD Rossendale 04-08; V Harwood from 08; AD Walmsley from 10; Hon Can Man Cathl from 11. *The Vicarage, Stitch mi Lane, Bolton BL2 4HU* Tel (01204) 525196 E-mail wendyloliver@googlemail.com

OLIVEY, Hugh Charles Tony. b 35. St Mich Coll Llan *71.* **d** *79* **p** 80. C St Winnow *Truro* 79-81; C Lanhydrock 81-82; C Lostwithiel 81-82; C Lanivet 81-82; P-in-c 82-83; TV Bodmin w Lanhydrock and Lanivet 84-89; P-in-c St Neot 89-90; P-in-c Warleggan 89-90; R St Neot and Warleggan 90-99; P-in-c Cardynham 97-99; rtd 99; Perm to Offic *Truro* from 99; Hon Chapl Duchy Hosp Truro from 04. *The Bungalow, 2 Lower Hugus Road, Threemilestone, Truro TR3 6BD* Tel (01872) 223103

OLIVIER, Bertrand Maurice Daniel. b 62. Ecole des Cadres Paris BA84. S'wark Ord Course 93. **d** 96 **p** 97. C Walworth St Jo *S'wark* 96-00; V Southfields St Barn 00-05; RD Wandsworth 03-05; V All Hallows by the Tower etc *Lon* from 05. *The Residence, 43 Trinity Square, London EC3N 4DJ* Tel (020) 7488 4772 Mobile 07958-411529 E-mail bertrand@ahbtt.org.uk

OLLIER, Mrs Jane Sarah. b 60. Leeds Univ BA81 Ex Univ MA05. SWMTC 02. **d** 05 **p** 06. NSM Seaton and Beer *Ex* 05-07; C Ottery St Mary, Alfington, W Hill, Tipton etc 07-10; P-in-c Ex St Mark, St Sidwell and St Matt from 10. *St Mark's Rectory, 8 Lamacraft Drive, Exeter EX4 8QS* Tel (01392) 438448

OLLIER, Canon Christopher John Douglas. b 44. Trin Hall Cam BA66 MA69. Cuddesdon Coll 66. **d** 68 **p** 69. C Silksworth *Dur* 68-71; C St Marylebone w H Trin *Lon* 71-74; C Winlaton *Dur* 74-77; R Redmarshall and V Bishopton w Gt Stainton 77-88; P-in-c Grindon and Stillington 83-88; V Gainford and R Winston 88-00; AD Barnard Castle 88-00; P-in-c Egglescliffe 00-03; R from 03; AD Stockton 01-07; Hon Can Dur Cathl from 94. *The Rectory, 10 Butts Lane, Egglescliffe, Stockton-on-Tees TS16 9BT* Tel (01642) 780185 Fax 791886 E-mail tim.ollier@synergybroadband.co.uk

OLLIFF, Roland. b 61. Ex Coll Ox MA98. Coll of Resurr Mirfield 93. **d** 95 **p** 96. C Bickleigh and Shaugh Prior *Ex* 95-98; CF 98-07; Sen CF from 07. *c/o MOD Chaplains (Army)* Tel (01980) 615804 Fax 615800 E-mail olliff@hotmail.com

OLLIVE, Mrs Patricia Ann. b 55. St Luke's Coll Ex BA91. Ripon Coll Cuddesdon BTh05. **d** 05 **p** 06. C Backwell w Chelvey and Brockley *B & W* 05-09; P-in-c Shapwick w Ashcott and Burtle from 09; P-in-c W Poldens from 09. *The Vicarage, Vicarage Lane, Shapwick, Bridgwater TA7 9LR* Tel (01458) 210260 Mobile 07840-387121 E-mail trishollive@hotmail.com

OLNEY, Dorian Frederick. b 50. Kingston Poly BA71 Anglia Poly Univ MA03 MIL88 MCIPD88. Ridley Hall Cam 96. **d** 98 **p** 99. C Glenfield *Leic* 98-02; Chapl ATC 99-01; TV Newark *S'well* 02-07; P-in-c Shenstone *Lich* 07-09; P-in-c Stonnall 07-09; V Shenstone and Stonnall from 09. *The Vicarage, St John's Hill, Shenstone, Lichfield WS14 0JB* Tel (01543) 480286 E-mail fred.olney@webleicester.co.uk

O'LOUGHLIN, Mrs Kathryn. b 60. Man Univ BSc81 Win Univ MA08. STETS 06. **d** 99 **p** 00. NSM Basing *Win* 99-03; Perm to Offic 03-08; C N Hants Downs from 08; Tutor STETS 08-11. *The Parsonage, Gaston Lane, South Warnborough, Hook RG29 1RH* Tel 07796-411511 (mobile) E-mail kathy.oloughlin@gmail.com

OLSEN, Arthur Barry. b 37. Univ of NZ BA61 Melbourne Coll of Div BD73. ACT ThL64. **d** 64 **p** 64. New Zealand 64-81; C Nelson All SS 64-67; V Ahuara 67-69; V Motupiko 69-70; V Amuri 70-73; Maori Miss and C Dunedin St Matt 73-76; V Brooklyn 77-81; C Hersham *Guildf* 81-84; P-in-c Botleys and Lyne 84-95; V 95-03; P-in-c Long Cross 84-95; V 95-03; Chapl NW Surrey Mental Health Partnership NHS Trust 85-03; rtd 03;

Hon C Rotherfield Peppard and Kidmore End etc *Ox* from 03. *2 Priory Copse, Peppard Common, Henley-on-Thames RG9 5LH* Tel 0118-924 2812 E-mail barry.o22@virgin.net

OLSWORTH-PETER, Edward James. b 77. UWE BA99. Wycliffe Hall Ox BTh04. **d** 04 **p** 05. C Guildf Ch Ch w St Martha-on-the-Hill 04-07; C Upper Chelsea St Sav and St Simon *Lon* 07-10; V Sydenham H Trin and St Aug *S'wark* from 10. *Holy Trinity Vicarage, 1 Sydenham Park Road, London SE26 4DY* E-mail ed_olsworth@hotmail.com

OLUKANMI, Miss Stella Grace Oluwafunmilayo Olanrewaju. b 57. St Jo Coll Nottm BTh95 LTh92. **d** 96 **p** 97. C Gt Ilford St Jo *Chelmsf* 96-01; V Barkingside St Cedd from 01. *The Vicarage, 10 Marston Road, Ilford IG5 0LY* Tel (020) 8551 3406 E-mail revdsolukanmi@btinternet.com

OLUMIDE, The Ven Oluseye Abiola Abisogun Okikiade ('Seye). b 42. Bradf Univ BA89 MSc92. Clifton Th Coll 68. **d** 71 **p** 72. C Halliwell St Pet *Man* 71-72; C Salford St Phil w St Steph 72; P-in-c Wood Green St Mich *Lon* 73; C Stanmer w Falmer and Moulsecoomb *Chich* 73-76; C Hulme Ascension *Man* 76-77; Chapl Asst N Man Gen Hosp 77-80; Chapl St Bernard's and Ealing Hosps 80-86; Chapl Bradf R Infirmary 86-91; Chapl Lynfield Mt Hosp Bradf 86-91; Chapl St Luke's Hosp Bradf 86-91; Chapl Bradf Hosps NHS Trust 91-96; Chapl Co-ord Parkside Community Hosp *Lon* 96-01; rtd 01; Can Lagos Cathl from 98; Adn in Egba from 00. *11 Walters Road, Cwmllynfell, Swansea SA9 2FH* Tel (01639) 830900

O'MALLEY, Canon Brian Denis Brendan. b 40. Univ of Wales (Lamp) MA97 MHCIMA60. Oscott Coll (RC) 74 Coll of Resurr Mirfield 82. **d** 77 **p** 83. In RC Ch 77-81; Warden St Greg Retreat Rhandirmwyn *St D* 80-83; Chapl and Min Can St D Cathl 83-85; V Wiston w Ambleston, St Dogwells, Walton E etc 85-89; V Wiston w Clarbeston and Walton E 89; R Walton W w Talbenny and Haroldston W 89-98; Chapl Pembrokeshire Coll of FE 93-98; Chapl St D Coll Lamp 98-07; Can St D Cathl 01-07; rtd 07. *Millbank, North Road, Lampeter SA48 7HZ* Tel (01570) 422148

O'MEARA, Colette Margaret Mary. *See* THORNBOROUGH, Ms Colette Margaret Mary

OMOLE, Oluremi Richard. b 63. **d** 05 **p** 07. NSM Dur N from 05. *7 Frensham Way, Meadowfield, Durham DH7 8UR* Tel 0191-378 9756

OMOYAJOWO, Justus Akinwale. b 65. Obafemi Awolowo Univ BA87 Ibadan Univ Nigeria MA90 Bayreuth Univ PhD99. Vining Coll of Th 90. **d** 92 **p** 93. Nigeria 92-94; C Akure St Andr 92; Chapl Ondo-State Pris 93; Chapl Ondo-State Univ 94; Asst Lect Bayreuth Univ Germany 95-97; Perm to Offic *S'wark* 98-99 and 00-01; C Hatcham St Jas 99-00; Chapl Goldsmiths' Coll Lon 99-00; P-in-c Sutton New Town St Barn 01-03; P-in-c Yardley St Edburgha *Birm* 03-09; V Mildmay Grove St Jude and St Paul *Lon* from 09. *The Vicarage, 71 Marquess Road, London N1 2PT* Tel (020) 7226 5924 E-mail justus-omoyajowo1@tiscali.co.uk

OMUKU, Precious Sotonye. b 47. Ibadan Univ Nigeria BSc73. Lagos Angl Dioc Sem 00. **d** 02 **p** 03. V Ikoyi Nativity Nigeria 02-06; Lic to Offic *Lon* and Perm to Offic *S'wark* 07-08; Hon C Morden *S'wark* from 08. *4 Litchfield Avenue, Morden SM4 5QS* Tel (020) 8640 7311 Mobile 07790-593392 E-mail precious.omuku@yahoo.com

O'NEILL, Mrs Caroline Lois. b 55. CQSW. Trin Coll Bris BA00. **d** 00 **p** 01. C Bath St Sav w Swainswick and Woolley *B & W* 00-03; C Charlcombe w Bath St Steph 03-08; Chapl K Edw Sch Bath from 09; Chapl Partis Coll Bath 09-10. *28 Pera Place, Bath BA1 5NX*

O'NEILL, Christopher John. b 53. Worc Coll Ox BA75 MA80 Surrey Univ PhD03 CertEd91 ALAM LGSM. Ripon Coll Cuddesdon 77. **d** 78 **p** 79. Asst Chapl Rugby Sch 78-80; Chapl Charterhouse Sch Godalming 81-98; Hd of Counselling from 98. *14 Chapelfields, Charterhouse Road, Godalming GU7 2BF* Tel (01483) 414437 E-mail cbenedictoneill@hotmail.com

O'NEILL, Edward Daniel. b 42. Man Univ BA62 Bradf Univ MSc76. NOC 89. **d** 92 **p** 93. NSM Prenton *Ches* 92-94; NSM Newton 94-95; Perm to Offic *Liv* 97-98; NSM W Derby Gd Shep 98-99; V 99-02; V Stockbridge Village from 02. *1 The Cross, Stanley Road, Huyton, Liverpool L36 9XL* Tel 0151-449 3800 E-mail eddieoneill@blueyonder.co.uk

O'NEILL, Gary. b 57. K Coll Lon BD79 AKC79 Liv Univ MA06. Westcott Ho Cam 80. **d** 81 **p** 82. C Oldham *Man* 81-84; C Birch w Fallowfield 84-87; R Moston St Chad 87-97; Can Res Birm Cathl 97-07; Dir Studies for Ords *Ches* from 07. *10 Neston Close, Helsby, Frodsham WA6 0FH* Tel (01928) 723327 Mobile 07976-729449 E-mail gary.oneill@chester.anglican.org

O'NEILL, Irene. *See* CARTER, Mrs Irene

O'NEILL, Robert Patrick. b 66. Herts Univ BA96. Ridley Hall Cam 06. **d** 08 **p** 09. NSM Lt Berkhamsted and Bayford, Essendon etc *St Alb* 08-09; C Luton St Mary from 09. *20 Copthorne, Luton LU2 8RJ* Tel (01582) 721867 E-mail rob.oneill@gmx.com

ONIONS, Mrs Angela Ann. b 33. STETS 01. **d** 02. NSM Bradford-on-Avon H Trin *Sarum* 02-08. *27 Berryfield Road, Bradford-on-Avon BA15 1SX* Tel (01225) 309001 Mobile 07719-726461 E-mail r.a.onions@btinternet.com

ONIONS, Martin Giles. b 63. Bp Otter Coll Chich BA99 Univ Coll Chich MA02. Chich Th Coll 85. **d** 88 **p** 89. C Eastbourne St Mary *Chich* 88-91; C-in-c The Hydneye CD 91-96; V The Hydneye 96-97; V Findon Valley 97-01; V Willingdon from 01. *The Vicarage, 35A Church Street, Willingdon, Eastbourne BN20 9HR* Tel and fax (01323) 502079
E-mail martin.onions@btinternet.com

ONUNWA, The Ven Udobata Rufus. b 47. Univ of Nigeria BA78 MA82 PhD85. Trin Coll Umuahia 72. **d** 74 **p** 75. Chapl Owerri Cathl Nigeria 74-75; Chapl Univ of Nigeria 75-78 and 82-84; Chapl to Abp Nigeria and P-in-c Okebola St Paul 78-79; Lect Trin Th Coll Umuahia 79-81; Hon Can Okigwe-Orlu 84-89; Can Res Calabar 90-91; V Calabar St Jude 92-96; Adn Calabar 94-96; Tutor Crowther Hall CMS Tr Coll Selly Oak 97-02; NW Regional Dir Crosslinks 03-05; P-in-c Grange St Andr *Ches* 05-09; rtd 09. *238 Green Lanes, Wylde Green, Sutton Coldfield B73 5LX* Tel 0121-354 5425 Mobile 07766-724510
E-mail uonunwa@yahoo.co.uk

ONYEKWELU, Mrs Ada. b 54. Ibadan Univ Nigeria BSc83 SEN98. **d** 07 **p** 08. NSM Selsdon St Fran CD *S'wark* from 07. *80 Tedder Road, South Croydon CR2 8AQ* Tel (020) 8657 4018
E-mail a_onye@yahoo.co.uk

OOSTERHOF, Ms Liesbeth. b 61. Ripon Coll Cuddesdon 02. **d** 04 **p** 05. C E Bergholt and Brantham *St E* 04-07; R Shoreline from 07; Dioc Adv for Women's Min from 11. *The Rectory, Rectory Field, Chelmondiston, Ipswich IP9 1HY* Tel (01473) 781902 E-mail l.oosterhof@btinternet.com

OPPERMAN, Graham William. b 40. Th Ext Educn Coll 98. **d** 00 **p** 03. C Linden St John *S Africa* 00-04; NSM Aberdour *St And* 04; NSM Burntisland 04; NSM Inverkeithing 04; TV Jarrow *Dur* 05-10; rtd 10; Hon C Cwmbran *Mon* from 10. *The Vicarage, 30 Longhouse Green, Henllys, Cwmbran NP44 6HQ* Tel (01633) 861978 Mobile 07792-451622
E-mail graham.opperman@sky.com

ORAM, Canon Geoffrey William James. b 14. Em Coll Cam BA37 MA40. Ridley Hall Cam 36. **d** 38 **p** 39. C Tooting Graveney St Nic *S'wark* 38-40; C Rugby St Andr *Cov* 40-41; V Ipswich St Thos *St E* 41-49; R E Bergholt 49-64; Bp's Chapl 54-67; Hon Can St E Cathl 59-80; RD Samford 59-64; V Aldeburgh w Hazlewood 64-80; rtd 80; Perm to Offic *St E* 80-81 and from 86; P-in-c Ipswich St Mich 81-86. *2B Clarkson Court, Ipswich Road, Woodbridge IP12 4BF* Tel (01394) 380269

ORAM, John Ernest Donald. b 34. Open Univ BA74. Tyndale Hall Bris. **d** 61 **p** 62. C Cheetham Hill *Man* 61-64; C Gt Baddow *Chelmsf* 64-67; V Blackb St Barn 67-72; Bp's Chapl for Soc Resp *Sheff* 72-86; Chapl Psychotherapist 79-86; Perm to Offic from 86; rtd 99. *12 Montgomery Road, Sheffield S7 1LQ* Tel 0114-221 4982

ORAM, Roland Martin David. b 45. Trin Coll Cam BA68 ARCM70. Cranmer Hall Dur. **d** 78 **p** 79. C Aspley *S'well* 78-81; Chapl Alleyn's Sch Dulwich 81-88; Chapl Versailles w Grandchamp and Chevry *Eur* 88-92; Chapl Denstone Coll Uttoxeter 92-01; C Hanford and Trentham *Lich* 02-10; rtd 10; Perm to Offic *Lich* from 10. *12 Ash Grove, Rode Heath, Stoke-on-Trent ST7 3TD* Tel (01270) 747271
E-mail orammb@tiscali.co.uk

ORAM, Stephen John. b 58. **d** 84 **p** 85. C Kidderminster St Jo *Worc* 84-88; Chapl RAF 88-92; P-in-c Brislington St Anne 92-97; V Cricklade w Latton 97-04; Co-ord Chapl N Bris NHS Trust from 04. *North Bristol NHS Trust, Frenchay Park Road, Bristol BS16 1LE* Tel 0117-970 1212
E-mail stephen.oram@ntlworld.com

ORAM, Vincent Charles. b 55. Rhodes Univ BA78 Fort Hare Univ BTh84. St Paul's Coll Grahamstown. **d** 81 **p** 82. C King Williams Town H Trin S Africa 81-85; R Barkly East St Steph 85-90; Can Grahamstown Cathl 94-00; Adn East London South 97-99; P-in-c Shenley *St Alb* 00-05; TV Aldenham, Radlett and Shenley from 05; RD Aldenham 03-08. *The Rectory, 63 London Road, Shenley, Radlett WD7 9BW* Tel (01923) 855383
E-mail vincent.oram@ntlworld.com

ORAMS, Ronald Thomas. b 49. ACMA80. **d** 08 **p** 09. NSM Laxfield, Cratfield, Wilby and Brundish *St E* from 08. *Crane Lodge, Bickers Hill, Laxfield, Woodbridge IP12 8DP* Tel (01986) 798901 Mobile 07721-682183 E-mail ron.orams@care4free.net

O'RAW, Canon Neal John. b 02 **p** 03. C Killala w Dunfeeny, Crossmolina, Kilmoremoy etc *T, K & A* 02-05; Bp's C from 05; Can Tuam Cathl from 09. *The Rectory, The Boreen, Crossmolina, Co Mayo, Republic of Ireland* Tel (00353) (96) 31384
E-mail revdoraw@hotmail.com

ORCHARD, Canon George Richard. b 41. Ex Coll Ox BA62 BA64 MA66. Ripon Hall Ox 62. **d** 65 **p** 66. C Greenhill St Pet *Derby* 65-70; Member Ecum Team Min Sinfin Moor 70-78; V Sinfin Moor 76-78; TR Dronfield 78-86; Can Res Derby Cathl 86-92; Hon Can 92-06; P-in-c Baslow 92-93; P-in-c Curbar and Stoney Middleton 92-93; V Baslow w Curbar and Stoney Middleton 93-06; rtd 06; Perm to Offic *Cant* and *Chich* from 07. *7 Love Lane, Rye TN31 7NE* Tel (01797) 225916
E-mail richardorchard41@yahoo.co.uk

ORCHARD, Helen Claire. b 65. Sheff Univ BA87 PhD96 Em Coll Cam MPhil02. Westcott Ho Cam 01. **d** 03 **p** 04. C Merrow *Guildf* 03-06; Chapl and Fell Ex Coll Ox 06-11; TV Wimbledon *S'wark* from 11. *St Matthew's House, 10 Coombe Gardens, London SW20 0QU* Tel (020) 8286 4584
E-mail orchard.helen@gmail.com

ORCHARD, Nigel John. b 56. CertEd78. St Steph Ho Ox 82. **d** 85 **p** 86. C Tottenham St Paul *Lon* 85-89; C Is of Dogs Ch Ch and St Jo w St Luke 89-90; TV 90-92; P-in-c Southall Ch Redeemer 92-99; V from 99. *Christ The Redeemer Vicarage, 299 Allenby Road, Southall UB1 2HE* Tel (020) 8578 2711
E-mail nigel.orchard1@btinternet.com

ORCHARD, Richard. See ORCHARD, Canon George Richard

ORCHARD, Mrs Tryphena Jane. b 35. Westf Coll Lon BA57. S'wark Ord Course 87. **d** 92 **p** 94. NSM Shaston *Sarum* 92-01; rtd 01; Perm to Offic *Sarum* 01-08. *Dunscar Fold, Hawkesdene Lane, Shaftesbury SP7 8NU* Tel (01747) 855228

O'REILLY, Brian. **d** 07 **p** 08. C Seagoe *D & D* 07-10; I Rathcooney Union *C, C & R* from 10. *The Rectory, Fota View, Ballycurreen, Glounthaune, Co Cork, Republic of Ireland* Tel (00353) (21) 435 5208 Mobile 868-223 0271
E-mail brianor@eircom.net

O'REILLY, Clare Maria. See KING, Clare Maria

O'REILLY, Canon Philip Jonathon. b 66. Portsm Poly BSc87 Kent Univ MA97 MRICS. Westcott Ho Cam 93. **d** 93 **p** 94. C Selsdon St Jo w St Fran *S'wark* 93-96; TV Staveley and Barrow Hill *Derby* 96-01; V Wistow *Leic* from 01; Hon Can Leic Cathl from 10. *The Vicarage, 12 Saddington Road, Fleckney, Leicester LE8 8AW* Tel 0116-240 2215
E-mail philip.oreilly@leicester.anglican.org

ORFORD, Barry Antony. b 49. Univ of Wales (Ban) BA71 MTh97 PhD01. St Steph Ho Ox 71. **d** 73 **p** 74. C Monmouth 73-77; V Choral St As Cathl 77-81; CR 83-96; Perm to Offic *St As* from 97; Hon Asst Chapl Univ of Wales (Ban) 99-01; Lib Pusey Ho from 01. *Pusey House, St Giles, Oxford OX1 3LZ* Tel (01865) 278415

ORFORD, Canon Keith John. b 40. FCIT. EMMTC 76. **d** 79 **p** 80. NSM Matlock Bank *Derby* 79-99; NSM Wirksworth from 99; Hon Can Derby Cathl 00-10. *27 Lums Hill Rise, Matlock DE4 3FX* Tel and fax (01629) 55349
E-mail keith.orford@btinternet.com

ORGAN, Mrs Alma. b 45. Bordesley Coll of Educn CertEd66. WEMTC 08. **d** 09 **p** 10. NSM Worc St Barn w Ch Ch from 09. *14 Ongrils Close, Pershore WR10 1QE* Tel (01386) 554248 Mobile 07531-461810 E-mail piglet1723@btinternet.com

ORGAN, Peter. b 73. K Coll Lon BA97 Birm Univ MA01. Qu Coll Birm 99. **d** 01 **p** 02. C E Wickham *S'wark* 01-05; TV Thamesmead 05-11; V E Wickham from 11. *St Michael's Vicarage, Upper Wickham Lane, Welling DA16 3AP* Tel (020) 8304 1214 E-mail revpeterorgan@yahoo.co.uk

ORME, Christopher Malcolm. b 60. City Univ BSc83. Wycliffe Hall Ox 03. **d** 05 **p** 06. C Shrewsbury H Cross *Lich* 05-08; P-in-c Meanwood *Ripon* from 08. *Meanwood Vicarage, 9 Parkside Green, Leeds LS6 4NY* Tel 0113-275 7885
E-mail chris.orme@holytrinitymeanwood.org.uk

ORME, Mrs Delia. b 57. STETS 01. **d** 08 **p** 09. NSM Haslemere and Grayswood *Guildf* from 08. *Tarn House, 17 Critchmere Hill, Haslemere GU27 1LS* Tel (01428) 644853
E-mail dj.orme@btconnect.com

ORME, Edward John Gilbert. b 42. Man Univ BSc64. Ox Min Course 04. **d** 07 **p** 08. NSM Reading St Agnes w St Paul and St Barn *Ox* from 07. *288 Wokingham Road, Reading RG6 1JU* Tel 07901-528971 (mobile) E-mail eddie.orme@yahoo.co.uk

ORME, John. b 29. Sarum Th Coll 58. **d** 60 **p** 61. C Heald Green St Cath *Ches* 60-64; C Ellesmere Port 64-67; Chapl Harperbury Hosp Radlett 67-73; P-in-c Luton All SS w St Pet *St Alb* 73-79; V 79-87; V Oxhey St Matt 87-96; rtd 97; Perm to Offic *St Alb* from 97. *1 Alzey Gardens, Harpenden AL5 5SZ* Tel (01582) 761931 E-mail john.orme117.freeserve.co.uk

ORME, Sydney. b 27. Oak Hill Th Coll 54. **d** 58 **p** 59. C Halliwell St Pet *Man* 58-61; V Friarmere 61-73; V Knypersley *Lich* 73-92; rtd 92; Perm to Offic *Ches* from 92. *10 Elworth Road, Sandbach CW11 9HQ* Tel (01270) 759233

ORMEROD, Henry Lawrence. b 35. Pemb Coll Cam BA58 MA63. Qu Coll Birm. **d** 60 **p** 61. C Chigwell *Chelmsf* 60-64; C Thundersley 64-68; C Canvey Is 68-72; V Stanground *Ely* 72-77; TR Stanground and Farcet 77-81; TR Swindon St Jo and St Andr *Bris* 81-90; TR N Wingfield, Clay Cross and Pilsley *Derby* 90-97; rtd 97; Hon C Ironstone *Ox* 98-03; Perm to Offic from 03. *5 Waterloo Drive, Banbury OX16 3QN* Tel (01295) 278483 E-mail henryormerod@aol.com

ORMESHER, David Rodney. b 39. **d** 05 **p** 06. OLM Delaval *Newc* from 05. *14 The Crest, Seaton Sluice, Whitley Bay NE26 4BG* Tel 0191-237 1104 E-mail david.ormesher.fslife.co.uk

ORMISTON, Albert Edward. b 26. AMCT46. Oak Hill Th Coll 53. **d** 56 **p** 57. C Worksop St Jo *S'well* 56-58; P-in-c Everton St Polycarp *Liv* 58-59; V 59-63; Org Sec SAMS 63-67; R Gateacre *Liv* 67-73; V Tonbridge St Steph *Roch* 73-86; V Dent w Cowgill *Bradf* 86-91; rtd 91; Perm to Offic *Ches* 91-00; *Glouc* from 02. *30 Capel Court, The Burgage, Prestbury, Cheltenham GL52 3EL* Tel (01242) 518625

ORMROD, Jonathan. d 11. C Llantrisant from 11. *Address temp unknown*

ORMROD, Paul William. b 57. Liv Univ BA80 MTh08. Westcott Ho Cam 80. **d** 83 **p** 84. C Prescot *Liv* 83-86; TV Padgate 86-95; V Formby St Pet from 95. *St Peter's Vicarage, Cricket Path, Formby, Liverpool L37 7DP* Tel (01704) 873369

ORMSBY, Robert Daly. b 22. CCC Ox BA42 MA48. Sarum & Wells Th Coll 77. **d** 78 **p** 79. Hon C Lydford and Brent Tor *Ex* 78-96; Hon C Peter Tavy, Mary Tavy, Lydford and Brent Tor from 96. *Lipscliffe, Coryton, Okehampton EX20 4AB* Tel (01822) 860344

ORMSTON, Derek. b 43. **d** 67 **p** 68. C Ogley Hay *Lich* 67-70; C Tettenhall Regis 70-74; P-in-c Leek All SS 74-79; TV Leek and Meerbrook 79-83; Youth Chapl *Bris* 83-87; R Brinkworth w Dauntsey from 87; Chapl New Coll Swindon from 87. *The Rectory, Brinkworth, Chippenham SN15 5AF* Tel (01666) 510207

ORMSTON, Canon Richard Jeremy. b 61. Southlands Coll Lon BA83 Brunel Univ MTh98. Oak Hill Th Coll BA87. **d** 87 **p** 88. C Rodbourne Cheney *Bris* 87-91; R Collingtree w Courteenhall and Milton Malsor *Pet* 91-01; RD Wootton 96-01; R Oundle w Ashton and Benefield w Glapthorn from 01; RD Oundle from 03; Can Pet Cathl from 03. *The Vicarage, 12 New Street, Oundle, Peterborough PE8 4EA* Tel (01832) 273595
E-mail ormston4@aol.com

✠**OROMBI, The Most Revd Henry Luke. b** 49. Bp Tucker Coll Mukono 75 St Jo Coll Nottm BTh83. **d** 79 **p** 79 **c** 93. Dioc Youth Officer Madi/W Nile Uganda 79-86; Adn Goli 87-93; Bp Nebbi 93-03; Abp Uganda and Bp Kampala from 03. *PO Box 14123, Kampala, Uganda* Tel (00256) (41) 270218, 270219 or 271138 Mobile 77-476476 Fax (41) 251925 *or* 245597
E-mail orombih@yahoo.com *or* couab@uol.co.ug

O'ROURKE, Brian Joseph Gerard. b 58. TCD BA82 HDipEd83. CITC 89. **d** 92 **p** 93. Chapl Glendalough Sch 90-96; C Newcastle w Newtownmountkennedy and Calary *D & G* 92-96; Bp's C 96-98; I 98-00; I Cork St Ann's Union *C, C & R* from 00; Hon Chapl Miss to Seafarers from 00. *The Rectory, 49 Ard na Laoi, Montenotte, Co Cork, Republic of Ireland* Tel and fax (00353) (21) 450456 *or* 455 2605 Mobile 86-807 9452
E-mail bjgorourke@gmail.com

O'ROURKE, Shaun. b 58. NOC 02. **d** 05 **p** 06. C Gorton and Abbey Hey *Man* 05-08; P-in-c Heaton Reddish from 08; Borough Dean Stockport from 10. *The Rectory, 8 St Mary's Drive, Stockport SK5 7AX* Tel 0161-477 6702 Mobile 07914-361905 E-mail sorourke@freezone.co.uk

ORPIN, Mrs Gillian. b 32. SRN53. Oak Hill Th Coll 82. **d** 87 **p** 95. Par Dn Passenham *Pet* 87-92; rtd 92; NSM Oban St Jo *Arg* 92-95; Dioc Chapl 95-98; Perm to Offic *St Alb* from 98. *11 Berwick Way, Sandy SG19 1TR* Tel (01767) 680629

ORR, Andrew Dermot Harman. b 66. Sheff Univ BSc89. CITC BTh92. **d** 92 **p** 93. C Ballymacash *Conn* 92-95; I Castlecomer w Colliery Ch, Mothel and Bilboa *C & O* 95-00; Dioc Registrar 95-00; I Castleknock and Mulhuddart w Clonsilla *D & G* 00-09; I Tullow w Shillelagh, Aghold and Mullinacuff *C & O* from 09. *The Rectory, Tullow, Co Carlow, Republic of Ireland* Tel and fax (00353) (59) 915 1481 E-mail greenorr@esatclear.ie

ORR, David Cecil. b 33. TCD BA56 MA68. **d** 57 **p** 58. C Drumragh *D & R* 57-60; I Convoy 60-70; I Maghera 70-80; I Drumragh w Mountfield 80-84; Dean Derry 84-97; I Templemore 84-97; Miss to Seamen 84-97; rtd 97. *Kilrory, 11 Broomhill Court, Londonderry BT47 6WP* Tel (028) 7134 8183
E-mail dcecilorr@btopenworld.com

ORR, Donald Macrae. b 50. Humberside Poly BA73 Glas Univ BD02 MTh04 PhD08. TISEC 02. **d** 04 **p** 05. C Greenock *Glas* 04-07; P-in-c Johnstone from 07; P-in-c Renfrew from 07. *16 Neilston Road, Barrhead, Glasgow G78 1TY* Tel 0141-881 1372 E-mail donaldorr@lycos.co.uk

ORR, Robert Vernon. b 50. Westmr Univ 80 MIQA89. Wycliffe Hall Ox 96. **d** 98 **p** 99. C Cowley St Jo *Ox* 98-01; P-in-c Reading St Agnes w St Paul 01-02; R Reading St Agnes w St Paul and St Barn from 02. *The Vicarage, 290 Northumberland Avenue, Reading RG2 8DD* Tel 0118-987 4448
E-mail vernon.orr@lineone.net

ORR, William James Craig. TCD BTh01. CITC 98. **d** 01 **p** 02. C Lurgan Ch the Redeemer *D & D* 01-07; I Muckamore *Conn* from 07; I Killead w Gartree from 07. *2 Greenmill, Muckamore, Antrim BT41 4SR* Tel (028) 9442 9019
E-mail william-orr@sky.com

ORR-EWING, Francis Ian Lance (Frog). b 75. Regent's Park Coll Ox BA97. Wycliffe Hall Ox MTh00. **d** 00 **p** 01. C Ox St Aldate 00-03; V Camberwell All SS *S'wark* 03-10; Perm to Offic *Ox* from 10. *Old Rowney, 35 Woodside Road, Beaconsfield HP9 1JW* Tel 07979-594762 (mobile) E-mail rector@latiminster.org

ORRIDGE, Harriet Grace. b 72. St Jo Coll Nottm. **d** 09 **p** 10. C Ironstone Villages *Leic* from 09. *18 Windsor Road, Waltham on the Wolds, Melton Mowbray LE14 4AS* Tel (01664) 464452

ORTON, Peter Joseph. b 57. **d** 03 **p** 04. OLM Burton St Chad *Lich* 03-10; NSM Burton St Aid and St Paul from 10.

237 Wetmore Road, Burton-on-Trent DE14 1RB Tel (01283) 537574 E-mail lightcommunity@yahoo.co.uk

ORTON, Canon Richard. b 33. Keble Coll Ox BA56 MA60 Leeds Univ. Lich Th Coll 60. **d** 61 **p** 64. C Penistone w Midhope *Wakef* 61-62; Hon C Meltham 62-69; Hon C Horsforth *Ripon* 69-72; C Far Headingley St Chad 72-75; V Hellifield *Bradf* 75-80; RD Bowland 78-80; R Hutton *Chelmsf* 80-87; R Wallasey St Hilary *Ches* 87-00; Dioc Ecum Officer 92-99; RD Wallasey 96-99; Hon Can Ches Cathl 97-00; rtd 00; C Gt Sutton *Ches* 01-05; Perm to Offic from 05. *137 Brimstage Road, Barnston, Wirral CH60 1XF* Tel 0151-348 4911

OSBORN, Miss Anne. b 40. Reading Univ BA62 MA64 Lon Univ PGCE67. Oak Hill NSM Course 87. **d** 92. Chapl Lon Univ 92-94; Chapl Lon Guildhall Univ 94-96; Chapl Univ of Westmr 94-95; Assoc Tutor NTMTC 97-03; Adv on Women's Min Edmonton Area *Lon* from 03. *8 Beaufort House, Talbot Road, London N15 4DR* Tel (020) 8801 0115

OSBORN, David Ronald. b 42. Bris Univ BA66 Leeds Univ CertEd77 Bath Univ MEd80. Clifton Th Coll 62. **d** 66 **p** 67. C Farndon *S'well* 66-69; P-in-c W Bridgford 69-72; Asst Dioc Dir Educn *Carl* 72-77; P-in-c Kirkandrews-on-Eden w Beaumont and Grinsdale 72-77; Hd RE and Chapl Dauntsey's Sch Devizes 77-83; V Southbroom *Sarum* 83-86; Hd RE Bexhill High Sch 86-93; TV Langtree *Ox* 93-95; TR 95-97; TR Bracknell 97-06; rtd 06; P-in-c Llantilio Crossenny w Penrhos, Llanvetherine etc *Mon* from 06. *The Vicarage, Llantilio Crossenny, Abergavenny NP7 8SU* Tel (01600) 780240 Mobile 07803-618464
E-mail davidosborn@ntlworld.com

OSBORN, David Thomas. b 58. K Coll Lon BD79 AKC79 PGCE80. Linc Th Coll 82. **d** 83 **p** 84. C Bearsted w Thurnham *Cant* 83-86; Chapl RAF 86-90; R Bassingham *Linc* 90-91; V Aubourn w Haddington 90-91; V Carlton-le-Moorland w Stapleford 90-91; R Thurlby w Norton Disney 90-91; Chapl RAF from 91. *Chaplaincy Services, Valiant Block, HQ Air Command, RAF High Wycombe HP14 4UE* Tel (01494) 496800 Fax 496343

OSBORN, Mrs Diana Marian. b 52. R Holloway Coll Lon BSc74 Birm Univ PGCE75. NEOC 81. **dss** 84 **d** 87 **p** 94. Malden St Jo *S'wark* 84-89; Par Dn 87-89; Par Dn Brampton *Ely* 89-92; Par Dn Richmond H Trin and Ch Ch *S'wark* 92-93; Chapl Ridley Hall Cam 94-96; Chapl Milton Children's Hospice 96-98; Chapl E Anglia's Children's Hospices 98-01; Perm to Offic *Ely* 01-07 and *Guildf* from 08. *25 Beech Hanger Road, Grayshott, Hindhead GU26 6LS* Tel (01428) 606308

OSBORN, Preb John Geoffrey Rowland. b 33. Jes Coll Cam BA55 MA59. Wells Th Coll 63. **d** 65 **p** 66. C Easthampstead *Ox* 65-68; Lic to Offic *Blackb* 68-70; Brunei 70-75; Asst Dir RE *Blackb* 75-77; V Tockholes 75-77; Dir RE *B & W* 77-83; Dir and Sec Lon Dioc Bd for Schs 83-95; Preb St Paul's Cathl 86-95; rtd 96. *4 Musson Close, Abingdon OX14 5RE* Tel (01235) 528701

OSBORNE, Alexander Deas. b 34. Liv Univ BSc54 PhD57. Oak Hill NSM Course 78. **d** 81 **p** 82. NSM Redbourn *St Alb* 81-98; rtd 98; Perm to Offic *Ely* from 00 and *St Alb* 00-08. *6 Cam Farm, North End, Meldreth, Royston SG8 6NT* Tel (01763) 260456 E-mail alexanderosborne@tiscali.co.uk

OSBORNE, Anthony Russell. b 47. Sarum & Wells Th Coll 77. **d** 79 **p** 80. C Heref St Martin 79-81; TV 82-86; TV Hanley H Ev *Lich* 86-92; Can Heref Cathl and Dioc Soc Resp Officer *Heref* 92-97; TR Cannock and V Hatherton *Lich* 97-06; V Penkhull 06-07; P-in-c Hartshill 06-07; P-in-c Trent Vale 06-07; TR Hartshill, Penkhull and Trent Vale 07-11; rtd 11. *1 Tulip Grove, Newcastle ST5 0SH* Tel (01782) 747669
E-mail osborne06@btinternet.com

OSBORNE, Canon Brian Charles. b 38. St Andr Univ MA61. Clifton Th Coll 61. **d** 63 **p** 64. C Skirbeck H Trin *Linc* 63-68; V 80-03; P-in-c New Clee 68-71; V 71-75; V Derby St Aug 75-80; Chapl Pilgrim Hosp Boston 84-88; RD Holland E *Linc* 85-95; Can and Preb Linc Cathl 92-03; rtd 03; Chapl to The Queen 97-08. *3 Newlands Road, Haconby, Bourne PE10 0UT* Tel (01778) 570818 E-mail revbrianosborne@ukonline.co.uk

OSBORNE, Christopher Hazell. b 60. Aston Tr Scheme 89 Sarum & Wells Th Coll 91. **d** 93 **p** 94. C Paignton St Jo *Ex* 93-96; C Hooe 96-97; TV Plymstock and Hooe 97-01; V Ivybridge w Harford from 01. *The Vicarage, Blachford Road, Ivybridge PL21 0AD* Tel (01752) 690193
E-mail osborne2001@btinternet.com

OSBORNE, Preb David Robert. b 50. Birm Univ BSc71 MEd86 Bris Univ PGCE73. St Jo Coll Dur 78. **d** 80 **p** 81. C Penkridge w Stretton *Lich* 80-85; R Longdon-upon-Tern, Rodington, Uppington etc 85-94; R Pilton w Croscombe, N Wootton and Dinder *B & W* from 94; RD Shepton Mallet 01-07; Sub-Dean and Preb Wells Cathl from 11. *The Rectory, Pilton, Shepton Mallet BA4 4DX* Tel (01749) 890423
E-mail drosborne@btinternet.com

OSBORNE, David Victor. b 36. Dur Univ BA59 Univ of Wales MA99. Cranmer Hall Dur. **d** 62 **p** 63. C Kennington Cross St Anselm *S'wark* 62-66; C Sandal St Helen *Wakef* 66-67; R Ancoats *Man* 67-73; V Claremont H Angels 73-80; R Breedon cum Isley Walton and Worthington *Leic* 80-87; V Beaumont

Leys 87-92; V Billesdon and Skeffington 92-01; rtd 01; Perm to Offic *Leic* and *Pet* from 02. *Rose Cottage, 12 Barlows Lane, Wilbarston, Market Harborough LE16 8QB* Tel (01536) 770400

OSBORNE, Canon Derek James. b 32. Tyndale Hall Bris 53. **d** 57 **p** 58. C Weymouth St Mary *Sarum* 57-60; C Southgate *Chich* 60-63; V Croydon Ch Ch Broad Green *Cant* 63-71; V Cromer *Nor* 71-83; P-in-c Gresham w Bessingham 71-83; Hon Can Nor Cathl 77-83; V Northwood Em *Lon* 83-94; Chapl Lee Abbey 94-97; rtd 97; Perm to Offic *Nor* from 97. *50 Clifton Park, Cromer NR27 9BG* Tel (01263) 511272

OSBORNE, Gerald Edward Richard. b 63. Ch Ch Ox MA85 Wye Coll Lon MSc86. **d** 99 **p** 00. OLM Pewsey and Swanborough *Sarum* 99-10; OLM Vale of Pewsey from 10. *Lawn Farm, Milton Lilbourne, Pewsey SN9 5LQ* Tel (01672) 563459 Fax 564271 Mobile 07798-942118 E-mail gerald.osborne@valeofpewsey.org.uk

OSBORNE, Gillian Margaret. b 54. Open Univ BA90 UEA PGCE93. **d** 07 **p** 08. OLM Stratton St Mary w Stratton St Michael etc *Nor* from 07. *5 Welford Court, The Street, Long Stratton, Norwich NR15 2XL* E-mail d-gosborne@btinternet.com

OSBORNE, Graham Daking. b 51. City Univ ACII74 FCII77. Cuddesdon Coll 94. **d** 96 **p** 97. C Cirencester *Glouc* 96-00; V Glouc St Cath 00-09; AD Glouc City 03-08; R Leatherhead and Mickleham *Guildf* from 09. *The Rectory, 3 St Mary's Road, Leatherhead KT22 8EZ* Tel and fax (01372) 372313 E-mail gdosborne@bigfoot.com

OSBORNE, The Ven Raymond John. b 48. New Coll Ox BA70 MA73. Westcott Ho Cam 71. **d** 73 **p** 74. C Bromley SS Pet and Paul *Roch* 73-77; C Halesowen *Worc* 77-80; TV 80-83; TR Worc St Barn w Ch Ch 83-88; V Moseley St Mary *Birm* 88-01; AD Moseley 94-01; Hon Can Birm Cathl 00-01; Adn Birm from 01; P-in-c Allens Cross 08-09. *23 Carisbrooke Road, Birmingham B17 8NN* Tel 0121-420 3299 *or* 426 0441 Fax 428 1114 E-mail archdeaconofbham@birmingham.anglican.org

OSBORNE, Jonathan Lloyd. b 62. Ripon Coll Cuddesdon 95. **d** 97 **p** 98. C Mill End and Heronsgate w W Hyde *St Alb* 97-00; Asst Chapl Ealing Hosp NHS Trust 00-03; Chapl Team Ldr 03-10; Asst Chapl W Middx Univ Hosp NHS Trust 00-03; Chapl Team Ldr 03-10; Chapl Team Ldr Meadow House Hospice 03-10; Chapl W Lon Mental Health NHS Trust 03-10; Sen Chapl Metrop Police *Lon* from 10; Hon Chapl S'wark Cathl from 03. *2 St Alphege House, Pocock Street, London SE1 0BJ* Tel (020) 7928 9203

OSBORNE, The Very Revd June. b 53. Man Univ BA74. St Jo Coll Nottm. dss 80 **d** 87 **p** 94. Birm St Martin 80-84; Old Ford St Paul and St Mark *Lon* 84-95; Par Dn Old Ford St Paul w St Steph and St Mark 87-94; P-in-c Old Ford St Paul and St Mark 94-95; Can Res and Treas Sarum Cathl 95-04; Bp's Dom Chapl 95-97; Dean Sarum from 04. *The Deanery, 7 The Close, Salisbury SP1 2EF* Tel (01722) 555176 Fax 555177 E-mail thedean@salcath.co.uk

OSBORNE, Malcolm Eric (Max). b 64. EN(G)87 RMN92. St Jo Coll Nottm 94. **d** 96 **p** 97. C Walton *St E* 96-99; C Ipswich St Matt 99-02; Soc Resp Adv 99-02; V Newmarket All SS from 02. *All Saints' Vicarage, 32 Warrington Street, Newmarket CB8 8BA* Tel (01638) 662514 E-mail max.osborne@stedmundsbury.anglican.org

OSBORNE, Mrs Marianne Lily-May. St Mich Coll Llan. **d** 09 **p** 10. C Tenby *St D* from 09. *The Vicarage, Penally, Tenby SA70 7PN* Tel (01834) 842035

OSBORNE, Mark William. b 67. Univ of Wales BA89 Lon Univ MTh06. Coll of Resurr Mirfield 94. **d** 94 **p** 95. C Goldthorpe w Hickleton *Sheff* 94-97; C-in-c Southey St Bernard CD 97-01; P-in-c Walham Green St Jo w St Jas *Lon* from 01. *The Vicarage, 40 Racton Road, London SW6 1LP* Tel and fax (020) 7385 3676 *or* 7385 7634 E-mail mark.osborne5@btinternet.com

OSBORNE, Norma. b 36. **d** 97 **p** 03. NSM Upper Tooting H Trin *S'wark* 02-03; NSM Tooting St Aug 02-03; NSM Wandsworth St Mich 03-06; NSM Wandsworth St Mich w St Steph 06-07; Perm to Offic from 07. *Garden Flat, 21A Trinity Crescent, London SW17 7AG* Tel (020) 8682 0423

OSBORNE, Ralph. b 38. Bernard Gilpin Soc Dur 62 Clifton Th Coll 63. **d** 66 **p** 67. C Harpurhey Ch Ch *Man* 66-68; C Chorlton on Medlock St Sav 68-71; C Wilmington *Roch* 71-74; V St Mary Cray and St Paul's Cray 74-85; P-in-c Bath St Steph *B & W* 85-88; P-in-c Charlcombe 86-88; R Charlcombe w Bath St Steph 88-03; rtd 03. *406 Bath Road, Saltford, Bristol BS31 3DH* Tel (01225) 872536 E-mail ralph.osborne@ic24.net

OSBORNE, Canon Robin Orbell. b 29. Leeds Univ BA54. Coll of Resurr Mirfield 52. **d** 54 **p** 55. C Wellingborough All Hallows *Pet* 54-58; C Oxhey St Matt *St Alb* 60-61; V Woburn and Battlesden and Pottesgrove 61-65; V Cheshunt 65-82; RD Cheshunt 70-81; Hon Can St Alb 76-82; V Penzance St Mary w St Paul *Truro* 82-88; Can Res and Treas Truro Cathl 88-94; rtd 94; Perm to Offic *B & W* from 94 and *S'wark* from 05. *The College of St Barnabas, Blackberry Lane, Lingfield RH7 6NJ* Tel (01342) 872833 Mobile 07776-081564 E-mail orbellosborne@gmail.com

OSBORNE, Mrs Sandra Anne. b 53. SRN74 SCM76. STETS 09. **d** 11. NSM Denmead *Portsm* from 11. *45 Wallisdean Avenue, Portsmouth PO3 6HA* Tel (023) 9236 2591 Mobile 07891-432667 E-mail sandie.osborne@btinternet.com

OSBOURNE, David John. b 56. Linc Th Coll 78. **d** 79 **p** 80. C Houghton le Spring *Dur* 79-82; C Spalding St Jo *Linc* 82-83; C Spalding St Jo w Deeping St Nicholas 83-84; V Swineshead 84-94; RD Holland W 86-92; P-in-c Boultham 94-01; R from 01; RD Christianity from 08. *The Rectory, 2A St Helen's Avenue, Lincoln LN6 7RA* Tel and fax (01522) 682026 E-mail davidosbourne@tiscali.co.uk

OSBOURNE, Steven John. b 59. St Jo Coll Nottm 92. **d** 94 **p** 95. C Bushbury *Lich* 94-98; C Tamworth 98-03; V Caverswall and Weston Coyney w Dilhorne from 03; RD Cheadle from 07. *8 Vicarage Crescent, Caverswall, Stoke-on-Trent ST11 9EW* Tel (01782) 388037 *or* 312570 E-mail steve.osbourne@btopenworld.com

OSEI, Robert Emmanuel. b 56. **d** 76 **p** 77. Ghana 76-83; C Hangleton *Chich* 83-84; Perm to Offic *S'wark* 00-02. *8 Plummer Court, London SE13 6RA*

OSGERBY, John Martin. b 34. Sheff Univ BSc56 PhD59. Linc Th Coll 75. **d** 77 **p** 78. C Rotherham *Sheff* 77-80; C-in-c W Bessacarr CD 80-84; V W Bessacarr 84-87; Warden of Readers 86-99; R Fishlake w Sykehouse and Kirk Bramwith etc 87-99; RD Snaith and Hatfield 93-99; rtd 99; Perm to Offic *Sheff* from 99 and *Linc* 00-02. *4 Marlborough Avenue, Haxey, Doncaster DN9 2HL* Tel (01427) 754815 E-mail jmosgerby.hax@virgin.net

OSGOOD, Graham Dean. b 39. Lon Univ BSc62 ALCD71. St Jo Coll Nottm 71. **d** 71 **p** 72. C Bebington *Ches* 71-76; V Gee Cross 76-05; rtd 05. *4 Lower Close, Bodicote, Banbury OX15 4DZ* Tel (01295) 266848 E-mail graham.htgx@btinternet.com

OSGOOD, Sylvia Joy. b 47. QUB BSc68 Lon Univ BD78 Man Univ PhD92. St Jo Coll Nottm MA98. **d** 97 **p** 98. NSM Bredbury St Mark *Ches* 97-01; Tutor and Chapl Spurgeon's Coll from 01. *4 Lower Close, Bodicote, Banbury OX15 4DZ* Tel (01295) 266848 E-mail j.osgood@spurgeons.ac.uk

O'SHAUGHNESSY, Mrs Janice Florence. b 51. STETS 95. **d** 98 **p** 99. NSM Bembridge *Portsm* 98-02; Asst Chapl Isle of Wight Healthcare NHS Trust 99-02; C Catherington and Clanfield *Portsm* 02-07; P-in-c Arreton 07-09; V from 09; P-in-c Newchurch 07-09; V from 09; P-in-c Gatcombe 07-09. *The Vicarage, High Street, Newchurch, Sandown PO36 0NN* Tel (01983) 865504

O'SHEA, Mrs Helen Mary. b 55. Univ of Wales (Abth) BA77 SRN79. Llan Ord Course 94. **d** 98 **p** 99. NSM Skewen *Llan* 98-01; C Llangynwyd w Maesteg 01-02; P-in-c Cwmafan from 02. *The Vicarage, 11 Tabernacle Terrace, Cwmavon, Port Talbot SA12 9HS* Tel (01639) 681890

OSLER, Philip. b 55. SEITE 99. **d** 02 **p** 03. NSM Staplehurst *Cant* 02-07; C Thurlestone, S Milton, W Alvington etc *Ex* 07-09; P-in-c from 09. *The Rectory, Thurlestone, Kingsbridge TQ7 3LF* Tel (01548) 560967 E-mail philip.osler@btinternet.com

OSMAN, David Thomas. b 49. Bradf Univ BTech72 Newc Univ MA93. Trin Coll Bris 75. **d** 78 **p** 79. C Stranton *Dur* 78-81; C Denton Holme *Carl* 81-84; V Preston on Tees *Dur* 84-97; P-in-c Hebburn St Jo from 97; P-in-c Jarrow Grange from 00. *St John's Vicarage, 23 St John's Avenue, Hebburn NE31 2TZ* Tel 0191-422 7505

OSMAN, Ernest. b 35. St Aid Birkenhead 61. **d** 64 **p** 65. C Heaton Ch Ch *Man* 64-68; V Farnworth St Pet 68-77; V St Martin's *Lich* 77-85; V Endon w Stanley 85-00; rtd 01; Hon C Llanyblodwel and Trefonen *Lich* 01-05; Perm to Offic from 05. *The Paddock, Silverdale Drive, Trefonen, Oswestry SY10 9DW* Tel (01691) 654184 E-mail paddock6@btinternet.com

OSMAN, Stephen William. b 53. Matlock Coll of Educn CertEd74 Teesside Poly CQSW80. St Jo Coll Dur 88. **d** 90 **p** 91. C Newbarns w Hawcoat *Carl* 90-93; TV Marfleet *York* 93-00; P-in-c Gotham *S'well* 00-10; P-in-c Barton in Fabis 02-10; P-in-c Thrumpton 02-10; P-in-c Kingston and Ratcliffe-on-Soar 02-10; P-in-c Herrington, Penshaw and Shiney Row *Dur* from 10. *23 Barnwell View, Herrington Burn, Houghton le Spring DH4 7FB* Tel 0191-584 5657 E-mail steveosman500@aol.com

OSMASTON, Canon Amiel Mary Ellinor. b 51. Ex Univ BA73 St Jo Coll Dur BA84. Cranmer Hall Dur 82. dss 84 **d** 87 **p** 94. Chester le Street *Dur* 84-88; Par Dn 87-88; Dir Miss and Past Studies Ridley Hall Cam 89-96; Min Development Officer *Ches* 96-03; C Lache cum Saltney 00-03; Min Development Officer *Carl* from 03; C Penrith w Newton Reigny and Plumpton Wall from 03; Hon Can Carl Cathl from 05. *The New Vicarage, Plumpton, Penrith CA11 9PA* Tel (01768) 885756 *or* (01228) 522573 Fax (01768) 885773 E-mail ministry.dev@carlislediocese.org.uk

✠**OSMERS, The Rt Revd John Robert.** b 35. Cant Univ (NZ) MA58. Coll of Resurr Mirfield 59. **d** 61 **p** 62 **c** 95. C Rawmarsh w Parkgate *Sheff* 61-65; Lesotho 65-81; Dar P Quthing 65-73; R Masite Miss 73-81; Botswana 81-88; Asst P H Cross Cathl 82-87; R Molepolole 82-88; Zambia from 88; Chapl ANC 88-91; Dioc Tr Chapl Lusaka 90-95; Bp E Zambia 95-03; Asst Bp Lusaka

03-07; R St Jo Angl Sem Kitwe from 07. *St John's Anglican Seminary, Mindolo Ecumenical Foundation, PO Box 20369, Kitwe, Zambia* Tel (00260) (2) 210960 Mobile 97-841215 E-mail josmers@zamnet.zm

OSMOND, Andrew Mark. b 62. Leeds Univ LLB85. Wycliffe Hall Ox 02. **d** 02 **p** 09. C Cheltenham St Mary, St Matt, St Paul and H Trin *Glouc* 02-03; NSM Cheltenham St Mark from 09. *40 Priors Road, Cheltenham GL52 5AA* Tel (01242) 253859 Mobile 07906-314463 E-mail andysueosmond@googlemail.com

OSMOND, David Methuen. b 38. Qu Coll Birm 75. **d** 77 **p** 78. C Yardley St Edburgha *Birm* 77-80; V Withall 80-89; R W Coker w Hardington Mandeville, E Chinnock etc *B & W* 89-95; Perm to Offic 96-98; rtd 98; Hon C Castle Town *Lich* 01-03; Perm to Offic *Blackb* 05-10. *25 Franklin Gardens, Hitchin SG4 0BS*

OSMOND, Mrs Heather Christine. b 44. ABSM64 ARCM65 Birm Poly CertEd65. Qu Coll Birm 83. **dss** 84 **d** 87 **p** 97. Brandwood *Birm* 84-85; Withall 85-89; Par Dn 87-89; Perm to Offic *B & W* 89-01; P-in-c Castle Town *Lich* 01-03; Perm to Offic *Blackb* 05-09. *25 Franklin Gardens, Hitchin SG4 0BS*

OSMOND, Oliver Robert. b 44. Ch Coll Cam BA66 MA70. Cuddesdon Coll 66 Trin Coll Toronto STB69. **d** 69 **p** 70. C Toronto St Jo York Mills 69-71; R N Essa 71-74; R Westmorland 74-77; P-in-c Lower Sackville 77-81; V Mill Hill Jo Keble Ch *Lon* 81-09; rtd 09. *PO Box 211, Lunenburg NS B0J 2C0, Canada* Tel (001) (902) 766 4318

OSMOND, Tobias Charles. b 74. Plymouth Univ BSc96. Ripon Coll Cuddesdon BTh99. **d** 99 **p** 00. C Wilton *B & W* 99-02; C Bath Abbey w St Jas 02-05; I Craighurst, Midhurst and Minesing Canada 05-11; P-in-c Wells St Thos w Horrington *B & W* from 11; P-in-c Chewton Mendip w Ston Easton, Litton etc from 11. *The Vicarage, 94 St Thomas Street, Wells BA5 2UZ* Tel (01749) 672193 E-mail tobieosmond@gmail.com

OSSORY AND LEIGHLIN, Archdeacon of. *See* MURRAY, The Ven John Grainger

OSSORY, Dean of. *See* POULTON, The Very Revd Katharine Margaret

OSTLER, Mrs Christine Anne. b 46. Bp Otter Coll CertEd68. Westcott Ho Cam 07. **d** 09 **p** 10. NSM Gt w Lt Harrowden and Orlingbury and Isham etc *Pet* from 09. *19B Castle Street, Wellingborough NN8 1LW* Tel (01933) 226730 E-mail c.ostler@btinternet.com

OSTLI-EAST (formerly EAST), Peter Alan. b 61. Southn Univ LLB82. Cranmer Hall Dur 90. **d** 93 **p** 94. C Combe Down w Monkton Combe and S Stoke *B & W* 93-97; Perm to Offic *Bris* 06-09; TV Bourne Valley *Sarum* from 09; C Salisbury St Fran and Stratford sub Castle from 09. *The Vicarage, Winterbourne Earls, Salisbury SP4 6HA* Tel (01980) 611350 Mobile 07805-581269 E-mail ostlieast@googlemail.com

O'SULLIVAN, Mrs Hazel. b 50. S Dios Minl Tr Scheme 91. **d** 94 **p** 95. C Cove St Jo *Guildf* 94-98; TV Headley All SS 98-02; V Bordon 02-04; Chapl Whiteley Village 04-11; rtd 11. *21 West Mount, The Mount, Guildford GU2 4HL* Tel (01932) 827428 E-mail hazel@revd.fsnet.co.uk

O'SULLIVAN, Helen Louise. b 68. Westmr Coll Ox BTh96. St Steph Ho Ox 06. **d** 08 **p** 09. C Chinnor, Sydenham, Aston Rowant and Crowell *Ox* from 08. *11 Elm Drive, Chinnor OX39 4HQ* Tel (01844) 354821 E-mail helenosullivan@o2.co.uk

O'SULLIVAN, Richard Norton. b 59. Glas Coll of Tech BSc80. Gregorian Univ Rome PhB85 STB88 STL90. **d** 89 **p** 90. In RC Ch 89-96; NSM Clarkston *Glas* 00-02; P-in-c Glas St Oswald 02-06; P-in-c Peterhead *Ab* from 06. *19 York Street, Peterhead AB42 1SN* Tel (01779) 472217 E-mail dick@osullivan53.fsnet.co.uk

OSWALD, John Edward Guy. b 39. Qu Coll Cam BA63 MA67. Ridley Hall Cam. **d** 68 **p** 69. C Chippenham St Paul w Langley Burrell *Bris* 68-72; C Hengrove 72-75; P-in-c Hardenhuish 75-79; P-in-c Kington St Michael 75-79; TV Chippenham St Paul w Hardenhuish etc 79-82; P-in-c Gt w Lt Somerford and Seagry 82-86; P-in-c Corston w Rodbourne 84-86; R Gt Somerford, Lt Somerford, Seagry, Corston etc 86-09; rtd 09; Perm to Offic *Bris* from 09. *Chauffeur Cottage, 26 Draycot Cerne, Chippenham SN15 5LG* Tel (01249) 720182

OSWIN, Frank Anthony (Tony). b 43. Chich Th Coll 69. **d** 71 **p** 72. C Radford *Cov* 71-74; C Shrub End *Chelmsf* 74-76; V Layer de la Haye 76-80; V Eastwood St Dav 80-93; TR Withycombe Raleigh *Ex* 93-10; rtd 10. *39 West Cliff Park Drive, Dawlish EX7 9ER* Tel (01626) 888897

OTTER, Anthony Frank. b 32. Kelham Th Coll 54. **d** 59 **p** 60. C Bethnal Green St Jo w St Simon *Lon* 59-63; C Aylesbury *Ox* 63-68; V Hanslope w Castlethorpe 68-77; P-in-c N w S Moreton 77-79; P-in-c Aston Tirrold w Aston Upthorpe 77-79; R S w N Moreton, Aston Tirrold and Aston Upthorpe 79-97; rtd 97; Perm to Offic *Ox* 97-09. *4 Emden House, Barton Lane, Headington, Oxford OX3 9JU* Tel (01865) 765447

OTTER, Martin John. b 65. Liv Poly BSc87 Leeds Univ BA11. Yorks Min Course 08. **d** 11. NSM Sherburn in Elmet w Saxton *York* from 11. *The Old Post Office, Main Street, Barkston Ash,*

Tadcaster LS24 9PR Tel (01937) 557254 Mobile 07842-106044 E-mail martin@theottersholt.plus.com

OTTEY, Canon John Leonard. b 34. AKC60 Nottm Univ BA70. **d** 61 **p** 62. C Grantham St Wulfram *Linc* 61-64; R Keyworth *S'well* 70-85; P-in-c Stanton-on-the-Wolds 71-85; P-in-c E Retford 85-87; V 87-99; P-in-c W Retford 85-87; R 87-99; Hon Can S'well Minster 93-99; rtd 99; Perm to Offic *Linc* from 00 and *S'well* from 04. *1 The Orchards, Grantham NG31 9GW* Tel (01476) 578762

OTTLEY, David Ronald. b 57. Lanc Univ BA78. Sarum & Wells Th Coll 79. **d** 81 **p** 82. C Urmston *Man* 81-85; Lect Bolton St Pet 85-87; P-in-c Halliwell St Thos 87-88; V Bolton St Thos 88-98; TR Halliwell 98-03; P-in-c Goostrey *Ches* 03-05; V Goostrey w Swettenham 05-09; rtd 09; Perm to Offic *Man* from 10. *77 Ravenscroft, Holmes Chapel, Crewe CW4 7HJ*

OTTO, Andrew James. b 63. St Pet Coll Ox BA86 MA90 Bris Univ BA01. Trin Coll Bris 99. **d** 01 **p** 02. C Trowbridge H Trin *Sarum* 01-05. *2 Swallow Drive, Trowbridge BA14 9TW* Tel (01225) 776325

OTTO, Francis James Reeve. b 42. New Coll Ox BA64 BA68. St Steph Ho Ox 66 Wells Th Coll 68. **d** 69 **p** 70. C St Stephen by Saltash *Truro* 69-72; C Newquay 72-73; V Lanteglos by Fowey 73-79; V St Goran w Caerhays 79-82; Chapl St Mary's Hall Brighton 82-88; Chapl Reading Sch 88-90; Chapl Lic Victuallers' Sch Ascot 91-93; Lic to Offic *Ox* 89-95; C Boyne Hill 95; P-in-c Cocking, Bepton and W Lavington *Chich* 95-99; Chapl Heathfield Sch Ascot 99-05; Perm to Offic *Ox* 05-06; C Parkham, Alwington, Buckland Brewer etc *Ex* from 06. *7 Shepherds Meadow, Abbotsham, Bideford EX39 5BP* Tel (01237) 477227 E-mail corporaljones@tiscali.co.uk

OUGH, John Christopher. b 51. Lon Univ CertEd74 Open Univ BA82. SWMTC 91. **d** 94 **p** 95. C Plymouth Em, St Paul Efford and St Aug *Ex* 94-97; P-in-c Diptford, N Huish, Harberton and Harbertonford 97-01; P-in-c Halwell w Moreleigh 97-01; R Diptford, N Huish, Harberton, Harbertonford etc from 01; C Ermington and Ugborough from 10. *The Rectory, Diptford, Totnes TQ9 7NY* Tel (01548) 821148 E-mail john@diptfordough.freeserve.co.uk

OULD, Julian Charles. b 57. MHCIMA77. Coll of Resurr Mirfield 80. **d** 83 **p** 84. C Hebburn St Cuth *Dur* 83-86; C Pet H Spirit Bretton 86-90; R Peakirk w Glinton 90-95; R Peakirk w 98-06; TR Totnes w Bridgetown, Berry Pomeroy etc *Ex* from 06. *The Rectory, Northgate, Totnes TQ9 5NX* Tel (01803) 865615 E-mail ypj69@dial.pipex.com

OULD, Peter. b 74. Man Univ BA96. Wycliffe Hall Ox BTh05. **d** 05 **p** 06. C Ware Ch Ch *St Alb* 05-11. *8 Westerham Close, Canterbury CT2 7TZ* E-mail mail@peter-ould.net

OULESS, John Michael. b 22. AKC49. Ridley Hall Cam 49. **d** 50 **p** 51. C Dallington *Pet* 50-55; C Evesham *Worc* 55-56; R Halewood *Liv* 56-62; V Southwick w Glapthorn *Pet* 62-71; Chapl Glapthorn Road Hosp Oundle 63-71; R Cogenhoe *Pet* 71-89; R Whiston 71-89; rtd 89; Perm to Offic *Win* 92-06 and *Pet* from 07. *3 St Peters Way, Cogenhoe, Northampton NN7 1NU* Tel (01604) 891104

OUTEN (née BAILEY), Mrs Joyce Mary Josephine. b 33. St Gabr Coll Lon CertEd69. S'wark Ord Course 80. **dss** 83 **d** 87 **p** 94. Par Dn Woolwich St Mary w St Mich *S'wark* 87-89; Par Dn Rusthall *Roch* 89-94; C 94-97; rtd 97; Asst Chapl Kent and Cant Hosps NHS Trust 97-99; Asst Chapl E Kent Hosps NHS Trust 99-00; TV Whitstable *Cant* 00-07; Perm to Offic from 07. *10 Foxgrove Road, Whitstable CT5 1PB* Tel (01227) 273643 E-mail joyceouten@tiscali.co.uk

OUTHWAITE, Stephen Anthony (Tony). b 35. Wells Th Coll 62. **d** 64 **p** 65. C Bitterne Park *Win* 64-67; C-in-c N Tadley CD 67-71; R Milton 71-93; RD Christchurch 82-90; V Win St Cross w St Faith 93-04; Master St Cross Hosp 93-04; rtd 04; Perm to Offic *B & W* from 05. *Wason House, Upper High Street, Castle Cary BA7 7AT* Tel (01963) 350302 Mobile 07940-389946

OUTRAM, David Michael. b 42. Univ of Wales (Ban) BA77 BD79. Coll of Resurr Mirfield 79. **d** 80 **p** 81. C Llandegfan and Beaumaris w Llanfaes w Penmon etc *Ban* 80-82; Chapl Prebendal Sch Chich 82-86; PV Chich Cathl 82-86; Asst Chapl Wellington Coll Berks 86-89; Hd Div 87-03; Chapl 89-03; V Dwygyfylchi *Ban* from 03; Hon Succ Ban Cathl from 08. *The Vicarage, Church Road, Penmaenmawr LL34 6BN* Tel (01492) 621276

OVENDEN, Canon John Anthony. b 45. LVO07. Open Univ BA80 BA93 K Coll Lon MA96. Sarum & Wells Th Coll 71. **d** 74 **p** 75. C Handsworth *Sheff* 74-77; C Isfield *Chich* 77-80; C Uckfield 77-80; P-in-c Stuntney *Ely* 80-85; Min Can, Prec and Sacr Ely Cathl 80-85; V Primrose Hill St Mary w Avenue Road St Paul *Lon* 85-98; Can Windsor and Chapl in Windsor Gt Park 98-11; rtd 11; Dir English Hymnal Co from 93; Chapl to The Queen from 02. *Little Croft, Great Rissington, Cheltenham GL54 2LN* E-mail johnovenden@btinternet.com

OVEREND, Alan. b 53. Sheff Univ BA75. Oak Hill Th Coll 84. **d** 86 **p** 87. C Aughton St Mich *Liv* 86-89; P-in-c Eccleston Park

89-92; V 92-99; V Ainsdale 99-07; V Billinge from 07. *5 Lostock Close, Billinge, Wigan WN5 7TQ* Tel (01744) 892210

OVEREND, Barry Malcolm. b 49. K Coll Lon BD71 AKC71. St Aug Coll Cant 71. **d** 72 **p** 73. C Nailsworth *Glouc* 72-74; C High Harrogate Ch Ch *Ripon* 75-78; V Collingham w Harewood 78-87; V Far Headingley St Chad 87-10; rtd 10. *4 Cherington Court, Burley in Wharfedale, Ilkley LS29 7BP* E-mail bmochad@aol.com

OVEREND, Paul. b 66. Coll of Ripon & York St Jo BA88 Hull Univ MA97 Univ of Wales (Cardiff) PhD04. Coll of Resurr Mirfield 88. **d** 93 **p** 94. C Cayton w Eastfield *York* 93-96; Asst Chapl Univ of Wales (Cardiff) *Llan* 96; Sen Chapl 97-03; Tutor 03-04; Tutor St Mich Coll Llan 03-04; Teaching Fell Liv Hope Univ 04-05; Dir Initial Minl Formation *Sarum* 05-07; Vice Prin Sarum OLM Scheme 05-07; Prin OLM 07-08; Tutor STETS and Co-ord for Locally Deployable Ord Min 08-09; Tutor STETS from 11. *STETS, 19 The Close, Salisbury SP1 2EE* Tel (01722) 424825 E-mail poverend@stets.ac.uk

OVERINGTON, Canon David Vernon. b 34. ALCD60. **d** 60 **p** 61. C Penge Ch Ch w H Trin *Roch* 60-62; C Lenton *S'well* 62-65; PC Brackenfield w Wessington *Derby* 65-71; P-in-c Cubley w Marston Montgomery 71-76; R Bridgetown Australia 76-79; Par P Denmark 79-85; Can Bunbury 84-85; R E Fremantle w Palmyra 85-90; Field Officer Angl Dept of Educn 90-93; R Wembley 93-99; Hon Can Perth from 96; rtd 99; P-in-c Longside *Ab* 99-03; P-in-c New Pitsligo 99-03; P-in-c Old Deer 99-03; P-in-c Strichen 99-03; Perm to Offic *Roch* from 04. *223 Ralph Perring Court, Stone Park Avenue, Beckenham BR3 3LX* Tel (020) 8650 5291 E-mail david.overington@diocese-rochester.org

OVERTHROW, Royston John. b 45. Southn Univ BTh94. Portsm Dioc Tr Course 84. **d** 85. NSM Portsm Cathl 85-91; Perm to Offic 91-94; Bp's Dom Chapl *Sarum* 94-02; NSM Marlborough 02-04; rtd 04. *19 Bratton Avenue, Devizes SN10 5BA* Tel (01380) 722404 E-mail liznroyuk@supanet.com

OVERTON, Charles Henry. b 51. CCC Ox BA74 MA77 Fitzw Coll Cam PGCE75 BA79 MA85. Ridley Hall Cam 77. **d** 80 **p** 81. C Tonbridge SS Pet and Paul *Roch* 80-84; Asst Chapl St Lawr Coll Ramsgate 84-87; P-in-c Aythorpe w High and Leaden Roding *Chelmsf* 88-95; P-in-c Hughenden *Ox* 95-01; P-in-c Chalfont St Peter 05-08; R from 08. *The Vicarage, 4 Austenway, Chalfont St Peter, Gerrards Cross SL9 8NW* Tel (01753) 882389 E-mail charlesoverton@hotmail.com

OVERTON, David Malcolm. b 52. Surrey Univ BA97. Chich Th Coll. **d** 84 **p** 85. C Ches H Trin 84-86; C Woodchurch 86-88; C Coppenhall 88-91; C Croydon St Jo *S'wark* 91-94; Perm to Offic *Lon* 97-00; C Selsey *Chich* 98-02; Miss P Ribbleton *Blackb* 02-07; Hon C Preston St Jo and St Geo 07-09. *42 Altcar Road, Formby, Liverpool L37 8DT*

OVERTON, Keith Charles. b 28. EAMTC 78. **d** 81 **p** 82. NSM Duxford *Ely* 81-84; NSM Whittlesford 84-88; P-in-c 88-94; P-in-c Pampisford 88-90; Perm to Offic *Bris* from 94. *86 Pittsfield, Cricklade, Swindon SN6 6AW* Tel (01793) 750321 E-mail keith@overton.org.uk

OVERTRON, Thomas Vincent Edersheim. b 34. New Coll Ox BA58 MA61. Wycliffe Hall Ox 58. **d** 60 **p** 61. C W Hampstead Trin *Lon* 60-63; C Leeds St Geo *Ripon* 63-67; Perm to Offic *Lon* 68-71; Thailand 71-78; R Knossington and Cold Overton *Leic* 78-81; V Owston and Withcote 78-81; R Bedford St Jo and St Leon *St Alb* 81-90; V Leigh *Roch* 91-99; rtd 99; Perm to Offic *B & W* 90-91 and *Lon* from 99. *14 The Broadwalk, Northwood HA6 2XD* Tel (01923) 829612

OVERTON-BENGE, Mrs Angela Margaret. b 46. UEA BA99 Anglia Poly Univ MA04. EAMTC 94. **d** 97 **p** 98. NSM Moulsham St Jo *Chelmsf* 97-01; Ind Chapl 01-04; C Aveley and Purfleet 01-04; Bp's Soc and Ind Adv *Bris* from 04; C Swindon All SS w St Barn from 06; C Swindon St Aug from 06. *St Augustine's Vicarage, Morris Street, Swindon SN2 2HT* Tel (01793) 618986

OVERY, Arthur William. b 19. JP. Nor Ord Course 73. **d** 76 **p** 77. NSM Lowestoft St Marg *Nor* 76-78; NSM Lowestoft and Kirkley 79-89; Perm to Offic from 89. *The Hollies, Warren Road, Lowestoft NR32 4QD* Tel (01502) 561289 E-mail bill@wovery.fsnet.co.uk

OVEY, Michael John. b 58. Ball Coll Ox BA81 BCL82 ACT MTh00 Lon Univ PhD04. Ridley Hall Cam 88. **d** 91 **p** 92. C Crowborough *Chich* 91-95; Australia 95-98; Kingham Hill Fell Oak Hill Th Coll 98-07; Prin from 07. *Oak Hill Theological College, Chase Side, London N14 4PS* Tel (020) 8449 0467 ext 248 E-mail mikeo@oakhill.ac.uk

OWEN, Bryan Philip. b 47. Keswick Hall Coll CertEd70. Cant Sch of Min 83. **d** 86 **p** 87. NSM Deal St Geo *Cant* 86-87; C Herne 87-89; R Clarkston *Glas* 89-93; Warden Scottish Chs Ho (Chs Together in Scotland) 93-96; V Cuddington *Guildf* 96-01; rtd 01; Perm to Offic *Glas* from 01. *Columcille, 10 Waverley Park, Kirkintilloch, Glasgow G66 2BP* Tel 0141-776 0407 Mobile 07796-155560 E-mail owen.owen@virgin.net

OWEN, Mrs Carole Janice. b 55. **d** 01 **p** 02. NSM Cley Hill Warminster *Sarum* 01-07; NSM Warminster St Denys and

Upton Scudamore from 07. *11 Stuart Green, Warminster BA12 9NU* Tel (01985) 214849 E-mail richardowen50@hotmail.com

OWEN, Caroline Ann. b 59. Univ of Wales (Abth) BA80 PGCE81. St Mich Coll Llan 03. **d** 05 **p** 06. NSM Bangor 05-09; V Cadoxton-juxta-Neath and Tonna *Llan* from 09. *St Catwg's Vicarage, Glebeland Street, Cadoxton, Neath SA10 8AY* Tel (01639) 643777

OWEN, Christine Rose. b 62. Univ of Wales (Ban) BA83 PGCE84. Qu Coll Birm 86. **d** 88 **p** 94. C Ynyscynhaearn w Penmorfa and Porthmadog *Ban* 88-90; Chapl Lon Univ 90-96; Hon C St Marylebone w H Trin 94-96; Min Can and Prec Worc Cathl 96-00; R Llansantffraid Glan Conwy and Eglwysbach *St As* from 00; AD Llanrwst from 09. *The Rectory, 16 Y Bryn, Glan Conwy, Colwyn Bay LL28 5NJ* Tel (01492) 583099 E-mail revdchristine@btinternet.com

OWEN, Clifford. *See* OWEN, Phillip Clifford

OWEN, Dafydd Gwyn. b 62. St Steph Ho Ox 95. **d** 97 **p** 98. C Whitchurch *Bris* 97-01; V Bris Ch the Servant Stockwood from 01; AD Bris S from 06; Hon Min Can Bris Cathl from 04. *The Vicarage, Goslet Road, Stockwood, Bristol BS14 8SP* Tel (01275) 831138 E-mail christtheservant@blueyonder.co.uk

OWEN, Daniel James. b 71. Anglia Poly Univ BSc94 TCD BTh00. CITC 97. **d** 00 **p** 01. C Belfast St Donard *D & D* 00-03; I Rathcooney Union *C, C & R* 03-09; I Kilgariffe Union from 09. *The Rectory, Gullanes, Clonakilty, Co Cork, Republic of Ireland* Tel (00353) (23) 883 3357 E-mail daniel.sonja@eircom.net

OWEN, David Cadwaladr. b 56. Grey Coll Dur BSc77 Univ Coll Worc PGCE99. WEMTC 00. **d** 03 **p** 04. NSM Pershore w Pinvin, Wick and Birlingham *Worc* 03-07; TV Droitwich Spa from 07; P-in-c Salwarpe and Hindlip w Martin Hussingtree from 10. *1 Ombersley Close, Droitwich WR9 8JY* Tel (01905) 771516 Mobile 07837-800009 E-mail david.droitwich@gmail.com

OWEN, Canon David William. b 31. Down Coll Cam BA55 MA58. Linc Th Coll 55. **d** 57 **p** 58. C Salford St Phil w St Steph *Man* 57-61; C Grantham St Wulfram *Linc* 61-65; V Messingham 65-70; V Spilsby w Hundleby 70-77; R Aswarby w Sausthorpe 71-77; R Langton w Sutterby 71-77; R Halton Holgate 73-77; P-in-c Firsby w Gt Steeping 75-77; P-in-c Lt Steeping 75-77; TR Louth 77-92; Chapl Louth Co Hosp 77-92; RD Louthesk *Linc* 82-89; Can and Preb Linc Cathl 85-92; TR Swan *Ox* 92-97; RD Claydon 94-96; rtd 97. *19 Stephen Road, Headington, Oxford OX3 9AY* Tel (01865) 766585

OWEN, Derek Malden. b 29. Oak Hill Th Coll 74. **d** 76 **p** 77. C Eastbourne H Trin *Chich* 76-78; C Walthamstow St Mary w St Steph *Chelmsf* 78-81; R Ditcheat w E Pennard and Pylle *B & W* 81-83; Warden Shaftesbury Housing Assn 86-94; rtd 94; Hon C Fairlight, Guestling and Pett *Chich* 94-97; P-in-c Llanishen w Trellech Grange and Llanfihangel etc *Mon* from 00. *The Vicarage, Llanishen, Chepstow NP16 6QE* Tel (01600) 860845

OWEN, Edgar. b 26. WMMTC. **d** 82 **p** 83. NSM Garretts Green *Birm* 82-88; NSM Stechford 88-94; rtd 94; Perm to Offic *Birm* from 94. *36 Colbourne Court, 116 Frederick Road, Stechford, Birmingham B33 8AE* Tel 0121-783 5603

OWEN, Emyr. b 69. Lancs Poly BSc91. Westcott Ho Cam BA94. **d** 95 **p** 96. C Llanbeblig w Caernarfon and Betws Garmon etc *Ban* 95-96; C Llanberis w Llanrug 96-98; TV Bangor 98-02; P-in-c Llandygai and Maes y Groes 98-02; V Nefyn w Tudweiliog w Llandudwen w Edern 02-07; Perm to Offic *St As* 08-10; TV Wrexham from 10. *Westview House, Hanmer, Whitchurch SY13 3BS* Tel (01948) 830074 E-mail emyr_owen@hotmail.com

OWEN, Eric Cyril Hammersley. b 46. Liv Univ LLB68 Barrister 69. St As Minl Tr Course 95. **d** 97 **p** 98. NSM Gresford w Holt *St As* 97-03; NSM Rhosymedre w Penycae 03-04. *Thistle Patch, 28 Wynnstay Lane, Marford, Wrexham LL12 8LG* Tel (01978) 856495 E-mail eowen@lineone.net

OWEN, Gary John. b 72. City Univ BSc93 Fitzw Coll Cam BA97 MA01. Ridley Hall Cam 95. **d** 98 **p** 99. C Welshpool w Castle Caereinion *St As* 98-01; TV Wrexham 01-10; R Eynsford w Farningham and Lullingstone *Roch* from 10. *The Rectory, Pollyhaugh, Eynsford, Dartford DA4 0HE* Tel (01322) 863050 Mobile 07947-358050 E-mail eflrector@googlemail.com

OWEN, Geoffrey Neill. b 55. Chich Th Coll. **d** 85 **p** 86. C Streatham St Pet *S'wark* 85-89; C Battersea Ch Ch and St Steph 89-91; TV Surbiton St Andr and St Mark 91-97; V Merton St Jas 97-08; V Battersea Ch Ch and St Steph from 08; RD Battersea from 10. *Christ Church Vicarage, Candahar Road, London SW11 2PU* Tel (020) 7228 1225

OWEN, Glyn John. b 56. Open Univ BA91 Nottm Univ MSc93 St Jo Coll Dur BA05. Cranmer Hall Dur 01. **d** 03 **p** 04. C Whiston *Sheff* 03-07; V Rudston w Boynton, Carnaby and Kilham *York* from 07; P-in-c Burton Fleming w Fordon, Grindale etc from 07. *The Vicarage, Rudston, Driffield YO25 4XA* Tel (01262) 420313 E-mail revglynowen@btinternet.com

OWEN, Graham Anthony. b 54. Birm Univ BA77. Trin Coll Bris 92. **d** 94 **p** 95. C Wiveliscombe w Chipstable, Huish

Champflower etc *B & W* 94-98; R 98-09; V Frome H Trin from 09. *Holy Trinity Vicarage, Orchard Street, Frome BA11 3BX* Tel (01373) 462586 E-mail graham-owen@hotmail.co.uk

OWEN, Graham Wynne. b 46. Lon Inst of Educn MA81 GTCL67 FTCL70. Cant Sch of Min 90. d 93 p 94. C Eltham H Trin *S'wark* 93-97; P-in-c Shooters Hill Ch Ch 97-00; V 00-01; TV Sole Bay *St E* 01-04; P-in-c Framlingham w Saxtead from 04; RD Loes from 05. *The Rectory, St Michael's Close, Framlingham, Woodbridge IP13 9BJ* Tel and fax (01728) 621082 E-mail gowen.mowen@btinternet.com

OWEN, Gwyn. *See* OWEN, Dafydd Gwyn

OWEN, Harry Dennis. b 47. Oak Hill Th Coll 73. d 76 p 77. C Fulham Ch Ch *Lon* 76-81; V Byker St Mark *Newc* 81-89; V Plumstead All SS *S'wark* from 89; RD Plumstead from 03. *All Saints' Vicarage, 106 Herbert Road, London SE18 3PU* Tel (020) 8854 2995 E-mail h.d.owen@talk21.com

OWEN, James Thomas. *See* McNAUGHTAN-OWEN, James Thomas

OWEN, John Edward. b 52. Middx Poly BA75. Sarum & Wells Th Coll BTh81. d 81 p 82. C S Ashford Ch Ch *Cant* 81-85; TV Bemerton *Sarum* 85-91; V St Leonards and St Ives *Win* 91-95; R N Stoneham 95-09; V Steep and Froxfield w Privett *Portsm* from 09. *The Vicarage, 77 Church Road, Steep, Petersfield GU32 2DF* Tel (01730) 264282 *or* 260169 E-mail revjohnowen@gmail.com

OWEN, Keith Robert. b 57. Warwick Univ BA Ox Univ BA MA85 Hull Univ MA(Ed)89. St Steph Ho Ox 79. d 82 p 83. C Headingley *Ripon* 82-85; Chapl Grimsby Colls of H&FE 85-90; Chapl for Educn *Linc* 85-90; P-in-c Linc St Botolph 90-95; Chapl to Caring Agencies Linc City Cen 90-95; V Steeton *Bradf* 95-01; Chapl Airedale NHS Trust 95-01; P-in-c Penzance St Mary w St Paul *Truro* 01-02; P-in-c Penzance St Jo 01-02; TR Penzance St Mary w St Paul and St Jo from 02. *St Mary's Vicarage, Chapel Street, Penzance TR18 4AP* Tel (01736) 363079 E-mail keith@gresley.f9.co.uk

OWEN, Kenneth Phillip. b 56. Liv Univ BA77 PGCE78. NOC 92. d 95 p 96. C Heswall *Ches* 95-01; V Frankby w Greasby from 01. *The Vicarage, 14 Arrowe Road, Greasby, Wirral CH49 1RA* Tel 0151-678 6155 E-mail greasby@office.fsworld.co.uk

OWEN, Mark. b 63. RMN. St Mich Coll Llan 03. d 05 p 06. C Tredegar *Mon* 05-08; V Rhymney from 08. *7 Rhymney Walk, Rhymney, Tredegar NP22 5BL* Tel (01685) 840500

OWEN, Paul Jonathan. b 59. S Bank Poly BSc81 Anglia Poly Univ MA03. Ridley Hall Cam 00. d 02 p 03. C Seaford w Sutton *Chich* 02-06; R Denton w S Heighton and Tarring Neville from 06; V Seaford w Sutton from 11. *The Vicarage, 46 Sutton Road, Seaford BN25 1SH* Tel (01323) 893508 E-mail revpowen@gmail.com

OWEN, Peter Russell. b 35. St Mich Coll Llan. d 63 p 64. C Wrexham *St As* 63-64; C Connah's Quay 64-65; Asst Chapl Miss to Seamen 66-69; P-in-c Upper Norwood All SS w St Marg *Cant* 69-72; C Hawarden *St As* 72-75; V Cilcain and Nannerch 75-79; R Cilcain and Nannerch and Rhydymwyn 79-83; V Brymbo and Bwlchgwyn 83-87; R Llangynhafal and Llanbedr Dyffryn Clwyd 87-99; P-in-c Llanychan 87-99; rtd 00. *Telpyn Forge, Rhewl, Ruthin LL15 1TP* Tel (01824) 704051

OWEN, Phillip Clifford. b 42. G&C Coll Cam BA65 MA69 Birm Univ PhD07. Ridley Hall Cam 71. d 73 p 74. C Stowmarket *St E* 73-76; C Headley All SS *Guildf* 76-81; TV 81-89; P-in-c Clifton-on-Teme, Lower Sapey and the Shelsleys *Worc* 89-97; R 97-02; Dioc Ecum Officer 89-02; P-in-c Corfu *Eur* 03-08; P-in-c Ostend from 08. *The English Church, Langestraat 101, 8400 Oostende, Belgium* Tel 07887-745632 (mobile) E-mail clavis@hotmail.com

OWEN, Mrs Phyllis Elizabeth. b 48. NTMTC. d 05 p 06. NSM Southend *Chelmsf* from 05. *42 Harcourt Avenue, Southend-on-Sea SS2 6HU* Tel (01702) 313312 E-mail thephiz@blueyonder.co.uk

OWEN, Raymond Philip. b 37. Man Univ BScTech60 AMCST60. Chich Th Coll 65. d 67 p 68. C Elland *Wakef* 67-70; C Lindley 70-73; V Bradshaw 73-80; Ind Chapl *Dur* 80-91; TR Hanley H Ev *Lich* 91-99; Bp Stafford's Past Aux 03-04; rtd 04; Perm to Offic *Lich* 04-07; C Alton w Bradley-le-Moors and Denstone etc from 07. *The Vicarage, Church Lane, Mayfield, Ashbourne DE6 2JR* Tel 07747-601379 (mobile) E-mail revrayowen@hotmail.com

OWEN, Canon Richard Llewelyn. b 27. Univ of Wales (Lamp) BA51. St Mich Coll Llan 51. d 53 p 54. C Holyhead w Rhoscolyn w Llanfair-yn-Neubwll *Ban* 53-57; C Porthmadog 57-59; R Llanfechell w Bodewryd, Rhosbeirio etc 59-67; Youth Chapl 66-67; V Penrhyndeudraeth and Llanfrothen 67-77; R Llangefni w Tregaean and Llangristiolus etc 77-89; Can Ban Cathl 82-93; Hon Can from 93; Treas 86-93; Can Missr and V Bangor Cathl Par 89-93; RD Arfon 92-93; rtd 93; Perm to Offic *Ban* from 93. *Bodowen, Great Orme's Road, Llandudno LL30 2BF* Tel (01492) 872765

OWEN, Richard Matthew. b 49. Sheff Univ BA70 Leeds Univ CertEd73. NOC 84. d 87 p 88. NSM Chorlton-cum-Hardy St Werburgh *Man* 87-89; C N Reddish 89-91; Perm to Offic *York* 91-96 and 97-03; NSM York St Olave w St Giles 96-97. *12 Sandrock House, Sandrock Road, Tunbridge Wells TN2 3PZ* Tel (01892) 516106 E-mail owen_rm@hotmail.com

OWEN, Robert Glynne. b 33. St Mich Coll Llan 56. d 58 p 59. C Machynlleth and Llanwrin *Ban* 58-62; C Llanbeblig w Caernarfon 62-65; V Carno and Trefeglwys 65-69; Hon C Dorking w Ranmore *Guildf* 69-75; Perm to Offic *St As* 75-94; V Broughton 94-99; rtd 99. *Briarcroft, Minera Road, Cefn y Bedd, Wrexham LL12 9TR* Tel (01978) 750134

OWEN, Robert Lee. b 56. Univ of Wales (Cardiff) BD79. Qu Coll Birm 79. d 81 p 82. C Holywell *St As* 81-84; Perm to Offic *Birm* 85-87; Chapl Blue Coat Sch Birm 85-87; Chapl St Elphin's Sch Matlock 87-94; Chapl Qu Marg Sch York from 94. *Queen Margaret's School, Escrick Park, Escrick, York YO19 6EU* Tel (01904) 728261

OWEN, Ronald Alfred. b 44. Wilson Carlile Coll 73 Sarum & Wells Th Coll 80. d 81 p 82. C Wotton St Mary *Glouc* 81-83; CF 83-97; P-in-c Salcombe *Ex* 97-02; V Salcombe and Malborough w S Huish 02-06; RD Woodleigh 00-03; rtd 07; Perm to Offic *B & W* from 07. *9 Reedmoor Gardens, Bridgwater TA6 3SL* Tel (01278) 433801 Mobile 07917-853901 E-mail revraowen@gmail.com

OWEN, Stuart James. b 68. Sunderland Poly BA91. Ripon Coll Cuddesdon BTh00. d 00 p 01. C Hendon St Mary *Lon* 00-01; C Hendon St Mary and Ch Ch 01-04; P Missr Edmonton St Mary w St Jo 04-08; V Edmonton All SS w St Mich from 08. *All Saints' Vicarage, 43 All Saints' Close, London N9 9AT* Tel (020) 8803 9199 E-mail fr.stuart@gmail.com

OWEN, Mrs Susan Margaret. b 38. St Andr Univ MA61 Univ of Wales (Swansea) MPhil91 Univ of Wales (Ban) BD93. Qu Coll Birm 94. d 95 p 96. NSM Shrewsbury St Geo *Lich* 95-98; P-in-c Penrhyndeudraeth w Llanfrothen w Beddgelert *Ban* 98-99; V Penrhyndeudraeth and Llanfrothen w Maentwrog etc 99-06; V Penrhyndeudraeth and Llanfrothen w Maentwrog etc 06-07; rtd 08. *Coed Helyg, Lower Moranedd, Criccieth LL52 0LA*

OWEN-JONES, Mrs Ingrid. b 41. Local Minl Tr Course 10. d 11. NSM W Hallam and Mapperley w Stanley *Derby* from 11. *Bridge Cottage, 63 Derby Road, Stanley, Ilkeston DE7 6EX* Tel 0115-932 0764 Mobile 07977-808041 E-mail ingridoj@talktalk.net

OWEN-JONES, Peter Charles. b 57. Ridley Hall Cam 92. d 94 p 95. C Leverington and Wisbech St Mary *Ely* 94-97; R Haslingfield w Harlton and Gt and Lt Eversden 97-05; P-in-c Glynde, W Firle and Beddingham *Chich* from 05. *The Vicarage, The Street, Firle, Lewes BN8 6NP* Tel (01273) 858005 Mobile 07973-265953 E-mail poj@lineone.net

OWEN-JONES, Peter John. b 47. RMCS BScEng68 CEng84 MIMechE84 MBIM87. EMMTC 85. d 88 p 89. NSM Holbrook and Lt Eaton *Derby* 88-00; NSM W Hallam and Mapperley w Stanley from 01. *Bridge Cottage, 63 Derby Road, Stanley, Ilkeston DE7 6EX* Tel 0115-932 0764 E-mail jowenjones@aol.com

OWEN-MOORE, Ms Petra Davine. b 65. Liv Univ BA87 Lanc Univ PGCE88. St Jo Coll Nottm MA97 MA98. d 98 p 99. C Brampton St Thos *Derby* 98-01; C Federal Way Gd Shep USA 01-05; NSM Ecclesall Deanery *Sheff* 06-08; TV N Wingfield, Clay Cross and Pilsley *Derby* 08-09. *Address temp unknown*

OWENS, Canon Ann Lindsay. b 47. St Hild Coll Dur CertEd68 Man Univ BA94. NOC 92. d 95 p 96. Chapl St Jas Sch Farnworth 94-97; NSM New Bury *Man* 95-97; C Heywood St Luke w All So 97-98; C Heywood 98-99; P-in-c Chadderton St Matt 99-04; P-in-c Chadderton St Luke 03-04; V Chadderton St Matt w St Luke 04-05; V Hurst from 05; Hon Can Man Cathl from 10. *St John's Vicarage, 155 Kings Road, Ashton-under-Lyne OL6 8EZ* Tel 0161-330 1935 E-mail ann-lindsay.owens@virgin.net

OWENS, Christopher Lee. b 42. SS Mark & Jo Coll Chelsea 61 Lon Inst of Educn TCert. Linc Th Coll 66. d 69 p 70. C Dalston H Trin w St Phil *Lon* 69-72; C Portsea N End St Mark *Portsm* 72-81; TV E Ham w Upton Park *Chelmsf* 81-92; C Is of Dogs Ch Ch and St Jo w St Luke *Lon* 92-98; P-in-c Chingford St Edm *Chelmsf* 98-02; V 02-07; rtd 07; Perm to Offic *Chelmsf* from 08. *67 Disraeli Road, London E7 9JU* Tel (020) 8555 6337 E-mail christopher@owenseaster.freeserve.co.uk

OWENS, Mrs Margaret Jean. b 49. Man Univ BSc70 Birm Univ MSc72. St Jo Coll Nottm 99. d 01 p 02. NSM Hurdsfield *Ches* 01-07; V Disley from 07. *Disley Vicarage, Red Lane, Disley, Stockport SK12 2NP* Tel (01663) 762068 Mobile 07775-801613 E-mail mowens44@hotmail.com

OWENS, Patricia Margaret. d 07 p 08. NSM Buckley *St As* from 07. *The Clappers, Pont-y-Capel Lane, Gresford, Wrexham LL12 8RS* Tel (01978) 854855 E-mail p.owens@liv.ac.uk

OWENS, Philip Roger. b 47. Wells Th Coll 71. d 71 p 72. C Colwyn Bay *St As* 71-74; C Wrexham 74-77; TV 77-80; P-in-c Yoxford *St E* 80-85; Asst Stewardship and Resources Adv 80-85; R Bangor Monachorum and Worthenbury *St As* 85-98; Sec Dioc Stewardship Cttee 89-98; RD Bangor Isycoed 92-98; R Flint 98-03; AD Holywell 02-03; rtd 06. *101 Thingwall Road, Wirral CH61 3UD* Tel 0151-648 3940 Mobile 07808-167147 E-mail philipowens653@btinternet.com

OWENS, Stephen Graham Frank. b 49. Ch Coll Cam BA71 MA75 CertEd72. Qu Coll Birm 73. d 75 p 76. C Stourbridge

St Mich Norton *Worc* 75-80; Tanzania 80-88; V Dudley Wood *Worc* 88-99; P-in-c Mamble w Bayton, Rock w Heightington etc 99-02; V from 02. *The Vicarage, Church Lane, Rock, Kidderminster DY14 9TT* Tel (01299) 266580 E-mail stephen.owens@ffvicarage.fsnet.co.uk

OWERS, Ian Humphrey. b 46. Em Coll Cam BA68 MA72. Westcott Ho Cam 71. **d** 73 **p** 74. C Champion Hill St Sav *S'wark* 73-77; V Peckham St Sav 77-82; P-in-c E Greenwich Ch Ch w St Andr and St Mich 82-83; V 83-94; P-in-c Westcombe Park St Geo 85-94; RD Greenwich 92-94; Perm to Offic *St E* 01-07; *Bradf* from 03; *Ripon* from 05; *Sheff* from 10. *St Aidan's Vicarage, 4 Manor Lane, Sheffield S2 1UF* Tel 0114-272 4676 Mobile 07808-613252 E-mail ianowers@ianowers.co.uk

OXBORROW, Alison Louise. b 68. Nottm Univ BA90 Lon Sch of Th BA04 Solicitor 92. St Jo Coll Nottm 08. **d** 11. C Didsbury St Jas and Em *Man* from 11. *99 Mellington Avenue, Didsbury, Manchester M20 5WF* Tel 07870-917710 (mobile) E-mail alioxborrow@hotmail.com

OXBROW, Canon Mark. b 51. Reading Univ BSc72 Fitzw Ho Cam BA75 MA79. Ridley Hall Cam 73. **d** 76 **p** 77. C Luton Ch Ch *Roch* 76-80; TV Newc Epiphany 80-88; Chapl Newc Mental Health Unit 80-88; Regional Sec Eur CMS 88-01; Communication Resources Sec 94-97; Internat Miss Dir 01-03; Asst Gen Sec 03-08; Internat Co-ord Faith2Share Network from 08; Hon Can Brussels Cathl from 98. *Faith2Share Network, Watlington Road, Oxford OX4 6BZ* Tel (01865) 787440 E-mail mark.oxbrow@faith2share.net

OXENFORTH, Colin Bryan. b 45. St Chad's Coll Dur BA67. **d** 69 **p** 70. C Bromley St Andr *Roch* 69-72; C Nunhead St Antony *S'wark* 72-76; V Toxteth St Marg *Liv* 76-89; V Brixton St Matt *S'wark* 89-00; V Pemberton St Jo *Liv* 00-10; rtd 10; Perm to Offic *Liv* from 10. *Flat 3, 5 Walmer Road, Liverpool L22 5NL* Tel 0151-721 2018 E-mail colinoxenforth@sky.com

OXFORD (Christ Church), Dean of. *See* LEWIS, The Very Revd Christopher Andrew

OXFORD, Archdeacon of. *Vacant*

OXFORD, Bishop of. *See* PRITCHARD, The Rt Revd John Lawrence

OXLEY, Canon Christopher Robert. b 51. Sheff Univ BA73 PGCE74. Wycliffe Hall Ox BA78 MA83. **d** 79 **p** 80. C Greasbrough *Sheff* 79-82; C Doncaster St Leon and St Jude 82-84; Asst Chapl Brussels *Eur* 84-87; V Humberstone *Leic* 87-93; V Beaumont Leys 93-05; RD Christianity S 98-01; P-in-c Leic St Anne 05-09; P-in-c Leic St Paul and St Aug 05-09; V Leic St Anne, St Paul and St Aug from 09; Dir Post-Ord Tr from 04; Hon Can Leic Cathl from 10. *St Anne's Vicarage, 76 Letchworth Road, Leicester LE3 6FH* Tel 0116-285 8452 E-mail oxley@leicester.anglican.org *or* oxleycr@btopenworld.com

OXLEY, David William. b 63. TCD BA85 BTh89. CITC 85. **d** 89 **p** 90. C Dublin Ch Ch Cathl Gp 89-92; Clerical V Ch Ch Cathl Dublin 90-92; I Templebreedy w Tracton and Nohoval *C, C & R* 92-96; Min Can Cork Cathl 95-96; I Tullow w Shillelagh, Aghold and Mullinacuff *C & O* 96-02; I Dublin Santry w Glasnevin and Finglas *D & G* from 02. *The Rectory, Church Street, Finglass, Dublin 11, Republic of Ireland* Tel (00353) (1) 834 1015 Mobile 86-881 6486 E-mail revdwo@hotmail.com

OXLEY, Martin Neil. b 65. Birm Univ BA86 Edin Univ BD95. Edin Th Coll 92. **d** 95 **p** 96. C Glas St Mary 95-97; C Glas St Matt 95-97; C Clydebank 95-97; P-in-c Glas St Matt 97-00; Dir Studies Edin Th Coll 97-00; R Lerwick *Ab* 00-05; P-in-c Burravoe 00-05. *1 Church Avenue, Beckenham BR3 1DT* Tel (020) 8658 1846 Mobile 07970-266578 E-mail frmartin@globalnet.co.uk

OXLEY, Paul. b 80. Chelt & Glouc Coll of HE BSc01 Glos Univ PGCE02. Trin Coll Bris BTh09. **d** 09 **p** 10. C Upper Sunbury St Sav *Lon* from 09. *41 Wolsey Road, Sunbury-on-Thames TW16 7TY* Tel (01932) 781995 Mobile 07985-937117 E-mail pauloxo@gmail.com

OXLEY, Mrs Paula Jane. b 51. Sheff Univ BA74 Nottm Univ MA00 PGCE75. EMMTC 93. **d** 93 **p** 94. NSM Birstall and Wanlip *Leic* 93-95; C Beaumont Leys 95-05; NSM Leic St Anne, St Paul and St Aug from 05. *St Anne's Vicarage, 76 Letchworth Road, Leicester LE3 6FH* Tel 0116-285 8452 E-mail oxleyp@btopenworld.com

OXTOBY, David Antony. b 72. Huddersfield Univ BSc98. Ridley Hall Cam 08. **d** 10 **p** 11. C Stamford St Geo w St Paul *Linc* from 10. *14 Queen Street, Stamford PE9 1QS* Tel 07595-387652 (mobile) E-mail fynesys@gmail.com

OYET, The Ven Julius Isotuk. b 34. Concordia Coll (USA) MA79. Immanuel Coll Ibadan 66. **d** 70 **p** 72. Nigeria 70-90 and from 96; Provost St Steph Cathl Bonny 81-85; Hon Can Ondo from 88; Miss Partner CMS 91-96; C Warblington w Emsworth *Portsm* 91-95; C Kirkby *Liv* 95-96; V Port Harcourt St Cypr 97-99; rtd 99; Dioc Dir Tr Niger Delta 97-05; Adn Bonny 01-05. *1 Panama Street, Abuloma GRA, Trans-Amadi Annex, PO Box 13608, Port Harcourt, Nigeria* Tel (00234) (803) 338 7403 (mobile) E-mail jisotuawaji@yahoo.com

P

PACEY, Graham John. b 52. Open Univ BA81 Leeds Univ CertEd74 Teesside Poly AdDipEd85. NEOC 90. **d** 93 **p** 94. C Kirkleatham *York* 93-96; V Middlesbrough St Agnes 96-00; R Skelton w Upleatham 00-09; V Boosbeck and Lingdale 07-09; R Guisborough from 09; RD Guisborough from 11. *The Rectory, Church Street, Guisborough TS14 6BS* Tel (01287) 632588 E-mail graham.pacey@ntlworld.com

PACEY, Michael John. b 28. **d** 96 **p** 97. NSM Tamworth *Lich* 96-09; Perm to Offic from 09. *1 Benson View, Tamworth B79 8TD* Tel (01827) 700410

PACKER, Catherine Ruth. *See* PICKFORD, Mrs Catherine Ruth

PACKER, Prof James Innell. b 26. CCC Ox BA48 MA52 DPhil55. Wycliffe Hall Ox 49. **d** 52 **p** 53. C Harborne Heath *Birm* 52-54; Lect Tyndale Hall Bris 55-61; Lib Latimer Ho Ox 61-62; Warden 62-69; Prin Tyndale Hall Bris 70-72; Assoc Prin Trin Coll Bris 72-79; Prof Hist Th Regent Coll Vancouver 79-89; Prof Th from 89; rtd 91. *6017 Holland Street, Vancouver BC V6N 2B2, Canada* Tel (001) (604) 266 6722

✠**PACKER, The Rt Revd John Richard.** b 46. Keble Coll Ox BA67 MA. Ripon Hall Ox 67. **d** 70 **p** 71 **c** 96. C St Helier *S'wark* 70-73; Chapl Abingdon St Nic *Ox* 73-77; Tutor Ripon Hall Ox 73-75; Tutor Ripon Coll Cuddesdon 75-77; V Wath-upon-Dearne w Adwick-upon-Dearne *Sheff* 77-86; RD Wath 83-86; TR Sheff Manor 86-91; RD Attercliffe 90-91; Adn W Cumberland *Carl* 91-96; P-in-c Bridekirk 93-96; Suff Bp Warrington *Liv* 96-00; Bp Ripon and Leeds from 00. *Hollin House, Weetwood Avenue, Headingley, Leeds LS16 5NG* Tel 0113-224 2789 Fax 230 5471 E-mail bishop@riponleeds-diocese.org.uk

PACKER, Peter Aelred. b 48. St Jo Coll Dur BA70 St Chad's Coll Dur PhD79 Strathclyde Univ MBA00. Ven English Coll Rome 95. **d** 96 **p** 97. SSM 91-98; Hon C S Lambeth St Anne and All SS *S'wark* 96-98; OSB and Lic to Offic *Ox* 98-99; Bp's Adv in Miss and Resources *Glas* 99-00; Perm to Offic *S'wark* 08-09; Hon C Deptford St Paul 09-10; P-in-c Peckham St Jo w St Andr from 10. *St John's Vicarage, 10A Meeting House Lane, London SE15 2UN* Tel (020) 7639 0084 E-mail admin@stjohnspeckham.org.uk

PACKER, Preb Roger Ernest John. b 37. ARCO59 Pemb Coll Cam BA60 MA64. Cuddesdon Coll 60. **d** 62 **p** 63. C Chippenham St Andr w Tytherton Lucas *Bris* 62-65; C Caversham *Ox* 65-70; R Sandhurst 70-91; V Bridgwater St Mary, Chilton Trinity and Durleigh *B & W* 91-00; RD Bridgwater 94-00; Preb Wells Cathl 96-00; rtd 00; Perm to Offic *Chelmsf* from 00. *3 Kreswell Grove, Harwich CO12 3SZ* Tel (01251) 502239

PACKHAM, Ms Elizabeth Daisy. b 33. Goldsmiths' Coll Lon BSc54 CertEd55. NOC. **dss** 83 **d** 87 **p** 94. Fairfield *Derby* 83-84; Buxton w Burbage and King Sterndale 84-95; Par Dn 87-94; C 94-95; P-in-c Chinley w Buxworth 95-98; Perm to Offic from 98; rtd 98. *100 Manchester Road, Chapel-en-le-Frith, Stockport SK23 9TP* Tel (01298) 812921

PACKMAN, James Morley. b 76. SS Hild & Bede Coll Dur MSci99. Oak Hill Th Coll BA04. **d** 04 **p** 05. C Eastbourne All SS *Chich* 04-08; R Frant w Eridge from 08. *The Rectory, Church Lane, Frant, Tunbridge Wells TN3 9DX* Tel (01892) 750638

PADDICK, Graham. b 47. S'wark Ord Course. **d** 89 **p** 90. C St Helier *S'wark* 89-93; P-in-c Thornton Heath St Paul 93-96; V 96-98; V Dormansland from 98; Chapl MU 03-08; AD Godstone from 08; Dir Ords Croydon Area from 96. *St John's Vicarage, The Platt, Dormansland, Lingfield RH7 6QU* Tel (01342) 832391 E-mail stjohndor@btinternet.com

PADDISON, Mrs Jennifer Sheila. b 70. Cranmer Hall Dur. **d** 07 **p** 08. C Newc H Cross from 07. *2A Lanercost Drive, Newcastle upon Tyne NE5 2DE* Tel 0191-274 9574 E-mail jenny@paddisons.plus.com

PADDISON, Canon Michael David William. b 41. Oak Hill Th Coll 75. **d** 77 **p** 78. C Gt Warley Ch Ch *Chelmsf* 77-80; C Rayleigh 80-83; R Scole, Brockdish, Billingford, Thorpe Abbots etc *Nor* 83-95; RD Redenhall 89-94; R Reepham, Hackford w Whitwell, Kerdiston etc 95-06; RD Sparham 00-05; Hon Can Nor Cathl 02-06; rtd 06; Perm to Offic *Nor* from 06. *4 North Street, Castle Acre, King's Lynn PE32 2BA*

PADDISON, Robert Michael. b 70. Cranmer Hall Dur. **d** 07 **p** 08. C Whorlton *Newc* from 07; P-in-c Barrow upon Soar w Walton le Wolds *Leic* from 11; P-in-c Wymeswold and Prestwold w Hoton from 11. *The Rectory, 27 Cotes Road, Barrow upon Soar, Loughborough LE12 8JP* E-mail rob@paddisons.plus.com

PADDOCK, The Very Revd John Allan Barnes. b 51. Liv Univ BA74 MA91 Ox Univ BA77 MA81 Glas Univ PhD05 Man Univ PGCE75 FRSA94. St Steph Ho Ox 75. **d** 80 **p** 81. C Matson *Glouc* 80-83; Asst Chapl Madrid *Eur* 82-83; Chapl R Gr Sch Lanc 83-86; Hon C Blackb Ch Ch w St Matt 83-86; Chapl RAF 86-91; Offg Chapl RAF 92-94; Chapl St Olave's Gr Sch Orpington 91-94; Perm to Offic *Blackb* 94-97; Chapl R Russell

Sch Croydon 97-00; Hon C Bickley *Roch* 97-00; V Folkestone St Pet *Cant* 00-03; Hon Min Can Cant Cathl 01-03; V Glouc St Geo w Whaddon 03-08; Dean Gib *Eur* from 08. *The Deanery, Bomb House Lane, Gibraltar* Tel (00350) 200 78377 Fax 78463 E-mail deangib@gibraltar.gi

PADDOCK, Susan. b 54. NTMTC 03. **d** 06 **p** 07. NSM Upper Holloway *Lon* from 06. *53 Morland Mews, London N1 1HN* Tel (020) 7609 1299 E-mail susie.paddock@lcbroadband.co.uk

PADFIELD, Stephen James. b 68. Ex Univ BA90 Univ Coll Dur PGCE92. Trin Coll Bris BA00 MA01. **d** 01 **p** 02. C Luton Ch Ch *Roch* 01-05; Chapl R Russell Sch Croydon from 05. *The Royal Russell School, Coombe Lane, Croydon CR9 5BX* Tel (020) 8657 4433 Mobile 07747-775385 E-mail stevepadfield@tiscali.co.uk

PADLEY, Miss Karen. b 68. RGN89. St Jo Coll Nottm MA00. **d** 00 **p** 01. C Broxtowe *S'well* 00-04; V Marlpool *Derby* from 04. *All Saints' Vicarage, 85 Ilkeston Road, Heanor DE75 7BP* Tel (01773) 712097 E-mail karen@hpadley.fsnet.co.uk

PADLEY, Kenneth Peter Joseph. b 78. Ex Coll Ox BA00 MA04 Ox Univ MSt04. Ripon Coll Cuddesdon BA03. **d** 04 **p** 05. C Cen Swansea *S & B* 04-07; Warden of Ch Hostel and Chapl Ban Univ from 07; Dir of Ords from 11. *Church Hostel, Prince's Road, Ffordd y Tyw, Bangor LL57 2BD* Tel (01248) 370566 E-mail kenneth_padley@hotmail.com

PADMORE, Lynn Beverley. b 51. EMMTC. **d** 06 **p** 07. NSM Beaumont Leys *Leic* 06-09; TV Ascension TM from 09. *122 Colby Drive, Thurmaston, Leicester LE4 8LB* Tel 0116-260 1584 E-mail lynnpadmore@btopenworld.com

PAGAN, Canon Keith Vivian. b 37. St Jo Coll Dur BA60 MA66. Chich Th Coll 60. **d** 62 **p** 63. C Clacton St Jas *Chelmsf* 62-64; C Wymondham *Nor* 64-70; P-in-c Guestwick 70-80; P-in-c Kettlestone 70-79; V Hindolveston 70-80; R Islay *Arg* 80-98; R Campbeltown 80-98; Miss to Seamen 80-98; Can St Jo Cathl Oban 85-98; Can Cumbrae 85-98; Hon Can from 99; rtd 98. *Mariefield, Southend, Campbeltown PA28 6RW* Tel (01586) 830310

PAGE, Alan Richard Benjamin. b 38. Univ of Wales (Lamp) BA60 BSc. St Mich Coll Llan 60. **d** 62 **p** 63. C Cardiff St Andr and St Teilo *Llan* 62-64; C Newport St Julian *Mon* 64-67; C Hoxton H Trin w St Mary *Lon* 67-69; C Winchmore Hill H Trin 69-71; V Camden Town St Mich w All SS and St Thos 71-98; Public Preacher 98-02; rtd 02. *7 Four Ash Street, Usk NP15 1BW*

PAGE, David. b 48. Bris Univ BA70 Leic Univ MA74 Southn Univ PGCE74. St Jo Coll Nottm 81. **d** 83 **p** 84. C Morden *S'wark* 83-86; V Wimbledon St Luke 86-91; P-in-c Clapham Common St Barn 91-92; V 92-08; rtd 08. *Rye View, The Strand, Winchelsea TN36 4JY* Tel (01797) 226524 E-mail david@ryeview.net

PAGE, David James. b 62. Liv Univ BSc83 Qu Coll Ox DPhil87. Trin Coll Bris BA93 MA95. **d** 96 **p** 97. C Knutsford St Jo and Toft *Ches* 96-99; R Elworth and Warmingham from 99. *The Rectory, 2 Taxmere Close, Sandbach CW11 1WT* Tel (01270) 762415 E-mail page.stpeter@tinyworld.co.uk

PAGE, Mrs Dorothy Jean. b 29. Portsm Poly CertEd50. Ox NSM Course 84. **d** 87 **p** 94. NSM Wantage Downs *Ox* from 87. *11 North Street, Marcham, Abingdon OX13 6NG* Tel (01865) 391462

PAGE, The Ven Gilbert Alfred Derek. b 35. **d** 93 **p** 94. C Launceston St Jo Australia 94-95; P-in-c George Town 95-98; Chapl Miss to Seamen Bell Bay 95-98; Adn Burnie 97-00; R Devonport 98-01; Miss Support Officer 01; rtd 01. *Unit 32/4 Brereton Street, Nowra NSW 2541, Australia* Tel (0061) (02) 4422 3403 Mobile 41-924 1950 E-mail gandrpage@shoal.net.au

PAGE, Gillian Fiona. b 55. Hull Coll of Educn CertEd76. Cranmer Hall Dur 08. **d** 10 **p** 11. C W Bolton *Man* from 10. *7 Mowbray Street, Bolton BL1 5JP* Tel (01204) 770523 Mobile 07866-936323 E-mail gill91@btopenworld.com

PAGE, Mrs Irene May. b 38. Birm Univ BA58. NEOC 85. **d** 87 **p** 94. Par Dn Cockfield *Dur* 87-90; Par Dn Waterloo St Jo w St Andr *S'wark* 90-94; C 94-95; R Old Charlton St Thos 95-02; C Charlton 02-03; rtd 03. *40 Wolverton Road, Rednal, Birmingham B45 8RN* Tel 0121-460 1745

PAGE, Jacqueline Anne. b 57. SAOMC 96. **d** 99 **p** 00. NSM Stevenage H Trin *St Alb* 99-03; NSM Benington w Walkern 03-06; P-in-c Ardeley and Cottered w Broadfield and Throcking 06-08; Perm to Offic from 08. *5 Sinfield Close, Stevenage SG1 1LQ* Tel (01438) 368502

PAGE, Jean. See PAGE, Mrs Dorothy Jean

PAGE, John Jeremy. b 56. Keble Coll Ox BA79 MA82 New Coll Edin BD86. Edin Th Coll 83. **d** 86 **p** 87. C Wetherby *Ripon* 86-89; TV Wrexham *St As* 89-92; Chapl Hymers Coll Hull 92-98; Chapl Charterhouse Sch Godalming 98-03; TR Hale w Badshot Lea *Guildf* 03-10; R Elstead from 10; V Thursley from 10. *The Rectory, Thursley Road, Elstead, Godalming GU8 6DG* Tel (01252) 702640 E-mail rev.john@elsteadandthursley.org.uk

PAGE, John Laurance Howard. b 40. ALCD. **d** 65 **p** 66. C Spitalfields Ch Ch w All SS *Lon* 65-69; C Win Ch Ch 69-72; C Ringwood 72-76; V Lockerley and E Dean w E and W Tytherley 76-89; V Lord's Hill 89-97; P-in-c Darby Green 97-02; V 02-05;

RD Romsey 85-89; rtd 05; Perm to Offic *Ely* from 05. *2 Champions Close, Fowlmere, Royston SG8 7TR* Tel (01763) 208214 E-mail jgpage@tiscali.co.uk

PAGE, Jonathan Michael. b 58. Ripon Coll Cuddesdon 97. **d** 99 **p** 00. C Littlemore *Ox* 99-02; V Chaddesden St Phil *Derby* 02-09; P-in-c Derby St Mark 07-09; V Chaddesden St Phil w Derby St Mark 09-10; RD Derby N 06-10; P-in-c Belper Ch Ch w Turnditch from 10; C Ambergate and Heage from 10; RD Duffield from 10. *Christ Church Vicarage, Bridge Street, Belper DE56 1BA* Tel (01773) 824974 E-mail frjonathan@philipandmary.org.uk

PAGE, Judy. b 42. Keele Univ DipEd63 BA63 Westmr Coll Ox BTh02. TISEC 03. **d** 05 **p** 06. C Paisley H Trin *Glas* from 05; C Paisley St Barn from 05. *36 Langside Drive, Kilbarchan, Johnstone PA10 2EW* Tel (01505) 703122 E-mail judypage@btinternet.com

PAGE, Lynda Christina. b 55. STETS 04. **d** 07 **p** 08. NSM Blackmoor and Whitehill *Portsm* from 07. *Willow Bank, Hawkley, Liss GU33 6NF* Tel (01730) 827334 Mobile 07790-494296 E-mail lyn.page@eds.com

PAGE, Mathew James. b 77. WEMTC. **d** 09 **p** 10. NSM Cainscross w Selsley *Glouc* from 09. *23 Regent Street, Stonehouse GL10 2AA*

PAGE, Canon Michael John. b 42. K Coll Lon BD66 AKC66. **d** 67 **p** 68. C Rawmarsh w Parkgate *Sheff* 67-72; C-in-c Gleadless Valley CD 72-74; TR Gleadless Valley 74-77; V Lechlade *Glouc* 77-86; RD Fairford 81-86; V Winchcombe, Gretton, Sudeley Manor etc 86-02; Hon Can Glouc Cathl 91-02; RD Winchcombe 94-99; Chapl E Glos NHS Trust 94-02; rtd 02; Perm to Offic *Sheff* from 03. *18 Brocco Bank, Sheffield S11 8RR* Tel 0114-266 3798 E-mail pages.brocco18@btinternet.com

PAGE, Owen Richard. b 53. FIBMS83. Linc Th Coll 89. **d** 91 **p** 92. C Gt Bookham *Guildf* 91-94; V Kings Heath *Pet* 94-99; TR Daventry, Ashby St Ledgers, Braunston etc 99-07; RD Daventry 00-07; ACUPA Link Officer 00-07; CUF Project Officer 00-05; Can Pet Cathl 07; V Todmorden *Wakef* from 07; Asst Dioc Dir of Ords from 09. *The Vicarage, 7 Fern Valley Chase, Todmorden OL14 7HB* Tel (01706) 813180 E-mail owen@owenpage.plus.com

PAGE, Canon Richard Dennis. b 23. G&C Coll Cam BA48 MA50. Ridley Hall Cam 48. **d** 50 **p** 51. C Ecclesfield *Sheff* 50-52; Chapl St Lawr Coll Ramsgate 52-58; Chapl Dean Close Sch Cheltenham 58-60 and 62-64; Chapl Netherton Tr Sch Morpeth 60-62; V Ecclesfield *Sheff* 64-71; RD Ecclesfield 66-71; P-in-c Holkham w Egmere and Waterden *Nor* 71-78; R Wells next the Sea 71-78; RD Burnham and Walsingham 72-78; V Hemsby 78-83; P-in-c Brooke w Kirstead 83-85; P-in-c Mundham w Seething 83-85; P-in-c Thwaite 83-85; R Brooke, Kirstead, Mundham w Seething and Thwaite 85-89; Hon Can Nor Cathl 87-89; rtd 90; Perm to Offic *Nor* from 90. *39 Bircham Road, Reepham, Norwich NR10 4NG* Tel (01603) 870886

PAGE, Teehan Dawson. b 61. Ch Ch Ox BA83 MA87 K Coll Lon MA96. St Steph Ho Ox 91. **d** 93 **p** 94. C Surbiton St Andr and St Mark *S'wark* 93-96; Chapl Reed's Sch Cobham 96-99; Asst Chapl Tonbridge Sch 99-00; Sen Chapl from 00. *1 Dry Hill Road, Tonbridge TN9 1LT* Tel (01732) 353468 E-mail tdp@tonbschl.demon.co.uk

PAGE, Thomas William. b 57. Sarum & Wells Th Coll 84. **d** 87 **p** 88. C Caterham *S'wark* 87-91; C Cheam 91-95; P-in-c Cranham *Chelmsf* 95-04; Dioc NSM Officer from 99; R Chingford SS Pet and Paul from 04. *The Rectory, 2 The Green Walk, London E4 7ER* Tel (020) 8529 1291 E-mail frtompage@priest.com

PAGE, Canon Trevor Melvyn. b 41. Dur Univ BA63 Fitzw Coll Cam BA67 MA72. Westcott Ho Cam 64. **d** 67 **p** 68. C Millhouses H Trin *Sheff* 67-69; Chapl Sheff Univ 69-74; V Doncaster Intake 74-82; Can Res Sheff Cathl 82-00; Dioc Dir of In-Service Tr 82-95; Dioc Dir of Ords and Post-Ord Tr 82-00; R Bradfield 00-06; Hon Can Sheff Cathl 01-06; rtd 06. *39 Benty Lane, Sheffield S10 5NF* Tel 0114-268 3879

PAGE, William George. b 42. Linc Th Coll 83. **d** 85 **p** 86. C Boston *Linc* 85-89; V Sibsey w Frithville 89-97; RD Holland E 95-97; rtd 07; Perm to Offic *York* from 08. *20 Marshall Drive, Pickering YO18 7JT* Tel (01751) 476915

PAGE-CHESTNEY, Michael William. b 47. Linc Th Coll 80. **d** 82 **p** 83. C Barton upon Humber *Linc* 82-85; TV Gt Grimsby St Mary and St Jas 85-91; V E Stockwith 91-96; V Blyton w Pilham and Laughton w Wildsworth 91-93; V Corringham and Blyton Gp 93-03; P-in-c Immingham from 03; P-in-c Habrough Gp from 03; P-in-c Keelby Gp from 03. *The Vicarage, 344 Pelham Road, Immingham DN40 1PU* Tel (01469) 572560 E-mail mike@page-chestney.co.uk

PAGE-CHESTNEY, Mrs Susan Valerie. b 49. EMMTC. dss 86 **d** 87 **p** 94. NSM Gt Grimsby St Mary and St Jas *Linc* 86-91; NSM Blyton w Pilham and Laughton w Wildsworth 91-93; NSM Corringham and Blyton Gp 93-03; Chapl W Lindsey NHS Trust 94-99; Chapl Linc and Louth NHS Trust 99-01; Chapl United Lincs Hosps NHS Trust 01-03; NSM Immingham *Linc*

from 03; NSM Habrough Gp from 03. *The Vicarage, 344 Pelham Road, Immingham DN40 1PU* Tel (01469) 572560 E-mail sue@heavenlyhugs.com
PAGE-CLARK, Howard David. b 53. Fitzw Coll Cam MA77. **d** 97 **p** 98. OLM Lytchett Minster *Sarum* 97-10; OLM The Lytchetts and Upton from 10. *37 Gorse Lane, Poole BH16 5RR* Tel (01202) 620239 E-mail hdpc@talktalk.net
PAGE DAVIES, David John. b 36. St Cath Soc Ox BA58 MA62. St D Coll Lamp 58. **d** 60 **p** 61. C Rhosddu *St As* 60-68; Chr Aid Area Sec (Glos, Herefords and Worcs) 68-85; Midl Regional Co-ord 78-85; Area Co-ord (Devon and Cornwall) 86-01; Lic to Offic *Truro* 80-01; Perm to Offic from 01; rtd 01. *3 Chyenhal Cottages, Buryas Bridge, Penzance TR19 6AN* Tel (01736) 732466 E-mail johnp-d@tiscali.co.uk
PAGE-TURNER, Canon Edward Gregory Ambrose Wilford. b 31. Qu Coll Birm 57. **d** 60 **p** 61. C Helmsley *York* 60-64; C Kensington St Phil Earl's Court *Lon* 64-67; C Walton-on-Thames *Guildf* 67-70; V Seend *Sarum* 70-71; V Seend and Bulkington 71-79; R Bladon w Woodstock *Ox* 79-87; P-in-c Begbroke 80-86; P-in-c Shipton-on-Cherwell 80-86; P-in-c Hampton Gay 80-85; RD Woodstock 84-87; P-in-c Wootton by Woodstock 85-87; R Patterdale *Carl* 87-89; R Askerswell, Loders and Powerstock *Sarum* 89-01; RD Lyme Bay 92-98; RD Beaminster 94-98; Can and Preb Sarum Cathl 99-01; rtd 01; Perm to Offic *Sarum* from 01; *B & W* 02-05; *Eur* 02-06. *The Old School House, 9 School House Close, Beaminster DT8 3AH* Tel (01308) 861410
PAGET, Alfred Ivor. b 24. St Aid Birkenhead 56. **d** 59 **p** 60. C Hoylake *Ches* 59-62; Chapl Miss to Seamen Hong Kong 62-63; Melbourne Australia 63-64; C Hyde St Geo *Ches* 64-66; R Gt and Lt Henny w Middleton *Chelmsf* 66-74; C Gt Holland 74-79; V Holland-on-Sea 79-92; rtd 92; Perm to Offic *S'wark* 92-98; *Lon* 96-02; *Chelmsf* 99-05. *6 Bary Close, Cheriton Fitzpaine, Crediton EX17 4JY* Tel (01363) 860069
PAGET, Richard Campbell. b 54. Collingwood Coll Dur BA76 Rob Coll Cam BA87. Ridley Hall Cam 85. **d** 88 **p** 89. C Gipsy Hill Ch Ch *S'wark* 88-92; R Chatham St Mary w St Jo *Roch* 92-98; P-in-c Brenchley 99-00; V from 00; RD Paddock Wood 06-10. *The Vicarage, 8 Broadoak, Brenchley, Tonbridge TN12 7NN* Tel (01892) 722140
PAGET, Robert James Innes. b 35. AKC59. **d** 60 **p** 61. C Attenborough w Bramcote *S'well* 60-63; C Cheltenham St Mark *Glouc* 63-72; P-in-c Pilsley *Derby* 72-73; TV N Wingfield, Pilsley and Tupton 73-89; R Pinxton 89-97; P-in-c Ambergate and Heage 97-05; rtd 06; Perm to Offic *Derby* from 06. *1A Jeffries Lane, Crich, Matlock DE4 5DT* Tel (01773) 852072
PAGET-WILKES, The Ven Michael Jocelyn James. b 41. ALCD69. **d** 69 **p** 70. C Wandsworth All SS *S'wark* 69-74; V Hatcham St Jas 74-82; V Rugby St Matt *Cov* 82-90; Adn Warwick 90-09; rtd 09. *64 Tarlton, Cirencester GL7 6PA* Tel (01285) 770553 E-mail michael.pw@btinternet.com
PAGETT, Andrew Stephen. b 45. Bris & Glouc Tr Course. **d** 82 **p** 83. NSM Swindon New Town *Bris* 82-01; C Paignton St Jo *Ex* 01-04; V Lifton, Broadwoodwidger, Stowford etc 04-10; rtd 10. *Yarde Villa, Peters Marland, Torrington EX38 8QA* E-mail a.pagett@tiscali.co.uk
PAICE, Michael Antony. b 35. Kelham Th Coll 55. **d** 60 **p** 61. C Skegby *S'well* 60-62; C Carlton 62-66; V Misterton and W Stockwith 66-81; V Olveston and P-in-c Littleton on Severn w Elberton *Bris* 81-83; Deputation Appeals Org CECS *Bris* and *Glouc* 83-84; *Bris, Glouc* and *B & W* 84-89; R Sutton St Nicholas w Sutton St Michael *Heref* 89-96; R Withington w Westhide 89-96; rtd 96. *Frankhurst, Sutton St Nicholas, Hereford HR1 3BN* Tel (01432) 880279 Mobile 07713-906554
PAICE, Richard James Rowland. b 72. Ch Ch Ox BA94 MA99. Oak Hill Th Coll BA00. **d** 00 **p** 01. C Eastbourne All So *Chich* 00-03; Chapl Bp Bell Sch 00-03; P-in-c Warbleton and Bodle Street Green *Chich* 03-08; V Wimbledon Park St Luke *S'wark* from 08. *St Luke's Vicarage, 28 Farquhar Road, London SW19 8DA* Tel (020) 3002 0962 E-mail warblebodle@yahoo.co.uk
PAILING, Crispin Alexander. b 75. Qu Coll Ox BA98 MA01 Birm Univ PhD08. Ripon Coll Cuddesdon BA02. **d** 03 **p** 04. C Four Oaks *Birm* 03-06; P-in-c Perry Barr 06-10; V from 10. *The Vicarage, Church Road, Perry Barr, Birmingham B42 2LB* Tel 0121-356 7998 E-mail crispin.pailing@queens.oxon.org
PAILING, Rowena Fay. b 77. Qu Coll Ox BA99 MA02 Birm Univ PhD08. Ripon Coll Cuddesdon BA02. **d** 03 **p** 04. C Four Oaks *Birm* 03-04; C Gravelly Hill 04-07; P-in-c Handsworth St Mich from 07. *The Vicarage, Church Road, Perry Barr, Birmingham B42 2LB* Tel 0121-356 7998 E-mail rowena.pailing@queens.oxon.org
PAIN, Canon David Clinton. b 36. K Coll Lon 56. **d** 64 **p** 64. Lic to Offic Benin 64-67; Lic to Offic Accra Ghana 67-86; Hon Can Accra from 80; V Kemp Town St Mary *Chich* 86-93; Chapl St Mary's Hall Brighton 88-93; V Billingshurst *Chich* 93-05; RD Horsham 98-02; rtd 05; P-in-c Chidham *Chich* from 05. *The Vicarage, Cot Lane, Chidham, Chichester PO18 8TA* Tel (01243) 573147

PAIN, Michael Broughton George. b 37. Dur Univ BA61. Wycliffe Hall Ox 61. **d** 63 **p** 64. C Downend *Bris* 63-67; C Swindon Ch Ch 67-70; V Alveston 70-78; V Guildf Ch Ch 78-90; TR Melksham *Sarum* 90-98; Chapl Melksham Hosp 90-98; TR Redhorn *Sarum* 98-03; rtd 03; Perm to Offic *Sarum* from 03. *Framfield, 10 Marie Road, Dorchester DT1 2LE* Tel (01305) 213469
PAIN, The Ven Richard Edward. b 56. Bris Univ BA79 Univ of Wales (Cardiff) BD84. St Mich Coll Llan 81. **d** 84 **p** 85. C Caldicot *Mon* 84-86; P-in-c Cwmtillery 86-88; V 88-91; V Six Bells 88-91; V Risca 91-98; V Overmonnow w Wonastow and Michel Troy 98-03; V Monmouth w Overmonnow etc 03-08; Adn Mon from 08; P-in-c Mamhilad w Monkswood and Glascoed Chapel from 08; Dioc Warden of Ord from 01; Can St Woolos Cathl from 03. *The Archdeaconry, 7 Lansdown Drive, Abergavenny NP7 6AW* Tel (01873) 856742 E-mail archdeacon.monmouth@churchinwales.org.uk
PAINE, Alasdair David MacConnell. b 60. Trin Coll Cam BA82 MA86 MSc84. Wycliffe Hall Ox 94. **d** 96 **p** 97. C Ex St Leon w H Trin 96-01; V Westbourne Ch Ch Chpl *Win* 02-11; V Cambridge H Sepulchre *Ely* from 11. *The Round Church Vicarage, Manor Street, Cambridge CB1 1LQ* E-mail alasdair@claranet.co.uk
PAINE, Peter Stanley. b 46. K Coll Lon BD69 AKC69. Cuddesdon Coll 69. **d** 71 **p** 72. C Leeds St Aid *Ripon* 71-74; C Harrogate St Wilfrid 74-78; V Beeston Hill H Spirit 78-82; TV Seacroft 82-90; V Martham w Repps w Bastwick *Nor* 90-94; V Martham and Repps with Bastwick, Thurne etc 94-04; P-in-c Foremark and Repton w Newton Solney *Derby* 04-08; V from 08. *St Wystan's Vicarage, Willington Road, Repton, Derby DE65 6FH* Tel (01283) 703317
PAINE, William Barry. b 58. CITC. **d** 84 **p** 85. C Glendermott *D & R* 84-86; C Lurgan St Jo *D & D* 86-88; I Kilbarron w Rossnowlagh and Drumholm *D & R* 88-91; CF 91-00; I Tynan w Middletown and Aghavilly *Arm* 00-09; I Ballinderry, Tamlaght and Arboe from 09. *The Rectory, 24 Circular Road, Moneymore, Magherafelt BT45 7PY* Tel (028) 8674 7615 E-mail bpaine.888@hotmail.co.uk
PAINE DAVEY, Nathan Paul. b 64. Barrister-at-Law 88 Birm Poly LLB86. St Steph Ho Ox 89. **d** 92 **p** 93. C Palmers Green St Jo *Lon* 92-95; C Kentish Town St Silas 95-98; C Haverstock Hill H Trin w Kentish Town St Barn 95-98; C Kentish Town St Silas and H Trin w St Barn 98-01; Perm to Offic 01-05. *Address temp unknown*
PAINTER, Christopher Mark. b 65. Cranmer Hall Dur. **d** 00 **p** 01. C Melksham *Sarum* 00-03; Chapl Wilts and Swindon Healthcare NHS Trust 02-03; TV Eccles *Man* 03-07. *Address temp unknown* E-mail ckpainter@blueyonder.co.uk
PAINTER, The Ven David Scott. b 44. Worc Coll Ox BA68 MA72 LTCL65. Cuddesdon Coll 68. **d** 70 **p** 71. C Plymouth St Andr *Ex* 70-73; Chapl Plymouth Poly 71-73; C St Marylebone All SS *Lon* 73-76; Abp's Dom Chapl and Dir of Ords *Cant* 76-80; V Roehampton H Trin *S'wark* 80-91; RD Wandsworth 85-90; PV Westmr Abbey 81-91; Can Res and Treas S'wark Cathl 91-00; Dioc Dir of Ords 91-00; Adn Oakham *Pet* from 00; Can Res Pet Cathl from 00. *The Diocesan Office, The Palace, Peterborough PE1 1YBS* Tel (01733) 891360 or 887017 Fax 555271 E-mail david.painter@peterborough-diocese.org.uk
PAINTER, John. b 25. Selw Coll Cam BA48 MA53. Ripon Hall Ox 48. **d** 50 **p** 51. C Stoke Newington St Mary *Lon* 50-55; C Woodside Park St Barn 55-56; C Llangiwg *S & B* 56-59; C-in-c Swansea St Jo 59-60; R Chipstable w Raddington *B & W* 61-64; V Audenshaw St Steph *Man* 64-66; V Sandown Ch Ch *Portsm* 66-72; R Keinton Mandeville *B & W* 72-77; P-in-c Lydford-on-Fosse 76-77; R Keinton Mandeville w Lydford on Fosse 77-90; RD Cary 81-90; RD Bruton 82-85; rtd 90; Perm to Offic *B & W* 90-05 and *Sarum* from 96. *2 Juniper Gardens, Gillingham SP8 4RF* Tel (01747) 823818
PAINTING, Stephen Nigel. b 60. Trin Coll Bris 01. **d** 03 **p** 04. C Heanton Punchardon w Marwood *Ex* 03-08; TV Beaconsfield *Ox* 08-11; Chapl Lee Abbey from 11. *Lee Abbey Fellowship, Lee Abbey, Lynton EX35 6JJ* Tel (01598) 752621 E-mail s.painting@btinternet.com
PAIRMAN, David Drummond. b 47. GGSM CertEd. Chich Th Coll 82. **d** 84 **p** 85. C Cowes St Mary *Portsm* 84-87; C Marshwood Vale *Sarum* 87-90; C Hawkchurch 87-90; C Marshwood Vale 90-95; rtd 95. *Chestnut Cottage, Old Pinn Lane, Exeter EX1 3RF* Tel (01392) 464448
PAISEY, Gerald Herbert John. b 31. Wm Booth Memorial Coll 51 Leic Univ CertEd62 Nottm Univ DipAdEd70 MPhil77 Lanc Univ MA78 K Coll Lon PhD91. St Alb Minl Tr Scheme 80. **d** 88 **p** 90. NSM Montrose *Bre* 88-90; NSM Inverbervie 88-90; Lect Robert Gordon Univ 89-97; P-in-c Stonehaven and Catterline *Bre* 90-01; rtd 01; Tutor Open Univ 95-00; Perm to Offic *Bre* 03-07; Lic to Offic *Edin* from 08. *40 South Middleton, Uphall, Broxburn EH52 5GB* Tel (01506) 865937
PAISEY, Canon Jeremy Mark. b 58. Aber Univ LLB81 Solicitor 83. Coates Hall Edin 92. **d** 94 **p** 95. C Turriff *Ab* 94-97; C Buckie 94-97; C Banff 94-97; C Cuminestown 94-97; C Portsoy 94-97; P-in-c Buckie from 97; P-in-c Portsoy from 97; P-in-c Banff from 98; Can St Andr Cathl from 08. *All Saints' Rectory, 14 Cluny*

Square, Buckie AB56 1HA Tel (01542) 832312 Mobile 07817-261435 E-mail jpaisey@aol.com

PAISLEY, Canon Samuel Robinson (Robin). b 51. Man Univ BSc72. Edin Th Coll BD91. **d** 91 **p** 92. C St Mary's Cathl 91-95; P-in-c Bishopbriggs 95-06; Teaching Consultant Glas Univ 95-99; Chapl Stobhill NHS Trust 95-99; Bp's Adv in Min *Glas* 99-07; R Dumfries from 06; Chapl NHS Dumfries and Galloway from 06; Can St Mary's Cathl from 06. *8 Newall Terrace, Dumfries DG1 1LW* Tel (01387) 254126 E-mail rector@episcopaldumfries.org

PAJUNEN, Mika Kari Tapani. b 76. Helsinki Univ MTh00. **p** 01. C Helsinki *Eur* 02-04; Asst Chapl from 05. *Kivikarintie 3, 21570 Sauvo, Finland* E-mail mika.pajunen@helsinki.fi

PAKENHAM, Charles Wilfrid. b 18. Trin Coll Ox BA40 MA52. Wycliffe Hall Ox 40. **d** 41 **p** 42. C Sutton *Liv* 41-44; CMS 44-49; Nigeria 44-49; C Cheltenham St Mary *Glouc* 49-52; V Litherland Ch Ch *Liv* 52-84; rtd 84; Perm to Offic *Sarum* from 90; P-in-c W Woodhay w Enborne, Hampstead Marshall etc *Ox* 91-92; Perm to Offic 92-00. *15 Cook Road, Marlborough SN8 2EG* Tel (01672) 540531 E-mail cepak@btinternet.com

PALIN, Elizabeth. b 62. Hull Univ BA85. WEMTC 08. **d** 11. NSM N Cheltenham *Glouc* from 11; Dir Glenfall Ho from 08. *Glenfall House, Mill Lane, Charlton Kings, Cheltenham GL54 4EP* Tel (01242) 583654 E-mail liz@glenfallhouse.org

PALIN, Roy. b 34. Man Univ BA56. Ripon Hall Ox 65. **d** 67 **p** 68. C Ilkeston St Mary *Derby* 67-70; C Wollaton *S'well* 70-71; V Harby w Swinethorpe 71-79; V Thorney w Wigsley and Broadholme 71-79; P-in-c N Clifton 75-79; R Harby w Thorney and N and S Clifton 79-80; V Tuxford 80-81; P-in-c Laxton 80-81; P-in-c Markham Clinton 80-81; P-in-c Weston 80-81; Tuxford w Weston and Markham Clinton 81-90; R Nuthall 90-99; rtd 99; Perm to Offic *Nor* from 00. *31 Pine Walk, Weybourne, Holt NR25 7HJ* Tel (01263) 588146

PALK, Deirdre Elizabeth Pauline. b 41. Reading Univ BA63 Lon Univ MA94 Leic Univ PhD02 AIL77 FIOSH96 FRHistS06. S'wark Ord Course 81. **dss** 84 **d** 87. Wanstead H Trin Hermon Hill *Chelmsf* 84-88; Hon Par Dn 87-88; Hon Par Dn Walthamstow St Pet 88-93; Hon Chapl UPA Projects 93-97; Tutor NTMTC 97-01; rtd 01. *3 Ashdon Close, Woodford Green IG8 0EF* Tel (020) 8498 0649

PALLANT, Canon Roger Frank. b 35. Trin Coll Cam BA57 MA61. Wells Th Coll 57. **d** 59 **p** 60. C Stafford St Mary *Lich* 59-62; C Ipswich St Mary le Tower *St E* 62-65; Dioc Youth Chapl 62-65; Development Officer C of E Youth Coun 65-70; Hon C Putney St Mary *S'wark* 66-71; Org Sec New Syn Gp 70-71; R Hintlesham w Chattisham *St E* 71-80; V Ipswich All Hallows 80-88; Hon Can St E Cathl 85-00; P-in-c Sproughton w Burstall 88-00; Dioc Officer for OLM 88-00; RD Samford 93-99; rtd 00; Perm to Offic *St E* from 00. *163 Fircroft Road, Ipswich IP1 6PT* Tel (01473) 461148

PALLENT, Ian. b 70. Newc Poly BA91. Ridley Hall Cam 05. **d** 07 **p** 08. C Bayston Hill *Lich* 07-10; R Jersey St Ouen w St Geo *Win* from 10. *The Rectory, La Route du Marais, St Ouen, Jersey JE3 2GG* Tel (01534) 481800 Mobile 07870-630433 E-mail ianpallent@hotmail.com

PALLETT, Ian Nigel. b 59. Leeds Univ BA80. Linc Th Coll 81. **d** 84 **p** 85. C Halesowen *Worc* 84-88; C Mansfield Woodhouse *S'well* 88-91; R Morton and Stonebroom *Derby* 91-98; P-in-c Heanor 98-01; V 01-03; P-in-c Dingwall *Mor* from 03; P-in-c Strathpeffer from 03. *The Parsonage, 4 Castle Street, Dingwall IV15 9HU* Tel (01349) 862244 E-mail pallett3000@btinternet.com

PALLIS, Mrs Maria. b 60. NOC 96. **d** 99 **p** 00. C Chapel Allerton *Ripon* 99-03; P-in-c Collingham w Harewood 03-11; P-in-c Spofforth w Kirk Deighton 07-11; V Banstead *Guildf* from 11. *The Vicarage, 21 Court Road, Banstead SM7 2NQ* Tel (01737) 351134 E-mail mariapallis@hotmail.com

PALMER, Alister Gordon. b 46. Univ of Tasmania BA73 DipEd74. Trin Coll Bris 76 Ridley Hall Cam 78. **d** 80 **p** 81. C Patchway *Bris* 80-83; C Bushbury *Lich* 83-86; V Wednesfield Heath 86-93; NSM Independent Ch Community Work 93-98; Dioc Officer for Min Tas Australia 98-02; Dir Angl Miss 99-02; C Smestow Vale *Lich* 02-03; V Knowle St Barn *Bris* 03-07; P-in-c Inns Court H Cross 05-07; V Filwood Park from 07. *St Barnabas' Vicarage, Daventry Road, Bristol BS4 1DQ* Tel 0117-966 4139 E-mail agpal46@btopenworld.com

PALMER, Angus Douglas. b 40. St Chad's Coll Dur BA62. **d** 63 **p** 64. C Wallsend St Pet *Newc* 63-66; C Newc H Cross 66-69; C Bottesford *Linc* 69-70; R Penicuik *Edin* 70-84; R W Linton 77-84. *6 Hackworth Gardens, Wylam NE41 8EJ* Tel (01661) 853786

PALMER, Christopher John Ingamells. b 71. **d** 98 **p** 99. C Emscote *Cov* 98-02; TV Mortlake w E Sheen *S'wark* 02-10; AD Richmond and Barnes 05-10; TR Merton Priory from 10. *The Vicarage, 1 Trinity Road, London SW19 8QT* Tel (020) 8542 2313 E-mail christopherpalmer@blueyonder.co.uk

PALMER, David Michael. b 53. QUB BA95 MSc. CITC 95. **d** 97 **p** 98. C Glenageary *D & G* 97-99; C Agherton *Conn* 99-00; I Ramoan w Ballycastle and Culfeightrin 00-10; I Magherally w

Annaclone D & D from 10. *Magherally Rectory, 46 Kilmacrew Road, Banbridge BT32 4EP* Tel (028) 4062 5625 Mobile 07591-382599 E-mail david.palmer@cantab.net

PALMER, David Philip. b 50. Sarum & Wells Th Coll. **d** 84 **p** 85. C St Ives *Ely* 84-86; C Luton All SS w St Pet *St Alb* 86-88; V Stocksbridge *Sheff* 88-97; P-in-c Seaton Hirst *Newc* 97-98; TR 98-08; R from 08; Chapl Northd Coll from 99. *The Vicarage, Newbiggin Road, Ashington NE63 0TQ* Tel (01670) 813218 E-mail davidseahirst@aol.com

PALMER, Derek James. b 54. Man Univ BA77. Qu Coll Birm 77. **d** 79 **p** 80. C Leek *Lich* 79-83; CF 83-92; R Riviera Beach St Geo USA 92-95; C S Ockendon and Belhus Park *Chelmsf* 95-98; V Walthamstow St Mich 98-00; Chapl Salford Univ 00-06; AD Salford 02-03; P-in-c Droylsden St Andr 06-09; TR Oldham 09-11; V Oldham St Mary w St Pet from 11; Bp's Adv on New Relig Movements from 02. *The Rectory, Prince Charlie Street, Oldham OL1 4HJ* Tel 0161-633 4847 Mobile 07504-953670 E-mail derek.palmer@hotmail.co.uk

PALMER, Elizabeth. *See* BLATCHLEY, Ms Elizabeth

PALMER, Preb Francis Harvey. b 30. Jes Coll Cam BA52 MA56. Wycliffe Hall Ox 53. **d** 55 **p** 56. C Knotty Ash St Jo *Liv* 55-57; C Southgate *Chich* 58-60; Chapl Fitzw Ho Cam 60-64; V Cambridge H Trin *Ely* 64-71; Chapl to Cam Pastorate 64-71; Prin Ridley Hall Cam 71-72; R Worplesdon *Guildf* 72-80; Bp's Ecum Officer 74-80; P-in-c Blymhill w Weston-under-Lizard *Lich* 80-82; Dioc Missr and Sec to Bd for Miss and Unity 80-90; Preb Lich Cathl 86-89; TV Walsall 87-90; rtd 90; Perm to Offic *Lich* 90-99; *Heref* 93-09; *Glouc* from 93. *c/o Mrs M S Palmer, 14 Hazeldine Court, Longden Coleham, Shrewsbury SY3 7BS* Tel (01743) 240798 E-mail francis@palmerfh.freeserve.co.uk

PALMER, Graham. b 31. Em Coll Cam BA53 MA57. Qu Coll Birm 56. **d** 58 **p** 59. C Camberwell St Giles *S'wark* 58-61; C Kilburn St Aug *Lon* 61-67; P-in-c Fulham St Alb 67-73; V 73-92; V Fulham St Alb w St Aug 92-97; rtd 97; Perm to Offic *Lon* from 97. *7 Wellington Court, 116 Knightsbridge, London SW1X 7PL* Tel (020) 7584 4036

PALMER, Hugh. b 50. Pemb Coll Cam BA72 MA76. Ridley Hall Cam 73. **d** 76 **p** 77. C Heigham H Trin *Nor* 76-80; Bp's Chapl for Tr and Miss 80-84; C St Helen Bishopsgate w St Andr Undershaft etc *Lon* 85-95; C Fulwood *Sheff* 95-97; V 97-05; Hon Can Sheff Cathl 01-05; R Langham Place All So *Lon* from 05. *12 Weymouth Street, London W1W 5BY* Tel (020) 7580 6029 E-mail hugh.palmer@allsouls.org

PALMER, Hugh Maurice Webber. b 28. Magd Coll Cam BA51 MA55. Cuddesdon Coll 51. **d** 53 **p** 54. C Bitterne Park *Win* 53-57; N Rhodesia 57-62; V Owslebury w Morestead *Win* 62-65; C Headbourne Worthy *Win* 70-71; P-in-c Rhodesia 65-70; C Headbourne Worthy *Win* 70-71; P-in-c Stratton Strawless *Nor* 72-77; R Hainford 72-77; R Haynford w Stratton Strawless 77-80; Chapl HM Pris Stafford 80-82; Chapl HM Pris Standford Hill 82-89; Sub-Chapl HM Pris Nor 89-91; rtd 91. *29 Mayfield Way, North Walsham NR28 0DQ* Tel (01692) 403664

PALMER, Ian Stanley. b 50. K Coll Lon BD71. Cranmer Hall Dur 73. **d** 75 **p** 76. C Huyton St Mich *Liv* 75-78; Chapl Dur Univ 78-83; V Collierley w Annfield Plain 83-90; Dir Evang Newc Australia 90-92; R Belmont N and Redhead 93-00; Adn Upper Hunter and R Muswellbrook 00-05; R Queanbeyan from 05. *39 Rutledge Street, PO Box 103, Queanbeyan NSW 2620, Australia* Tel (0061) (2) 6299 3920 or 6299 3917 Fax 6299 1360 Mobile 411-242596 E-mail palmeris@hunterlink.net.au

PALMER, John Richard Henry. b 29. AKC52. **d** 53 **p** 54. C Englefield Green *Guildf* 53-57; P-in-c Brewarrina Australia 57-62; C Wareham w Arne *Sarum* 62-63; PC Derby St Jo 63-66; Chapl Holloway Sanatorium Virginia Water 66-70; Chapl Brookwood Hosp Woking 70-94; rtd 94; Perm to Offic *Truro* from 94. *Lightning Ridge, Pentreath Road, The Lizard, Helston TR12 7NY* Tel (01326) 290654 E-mail vsp@oldlizardhead.freeserve.co.uk

PALMER, Ms Joy. NTMTC. **d** 10 **p** 11. NSM Becontree St Thos *Chelmsf* from 10. *15 Felhurst Crescent, Dagenham RM10 7XT* Tel (020) 8596 0577

PALMER, Judith Angela. b 47. Bris Univ MB, ChB71. NOC 02. **d** 05 **p** 06. NSM Strensall *York* from 05. *20 Bedern, York YO1 7LP* Tel (01904) 613356 E-mail j.palmer@phonecoop.coop

PALMER, Mrs Julia Elizabeth. b 57. Hull Univ BA80. St Jo Coll Nottm MA98. **d** 99 **p** 00. C Snodland All SS w Ch Ch *Roch* 99-03; P-in-c Sutton Bonington w Normanton-on-Soar *S'well* 03-08; P-in-c Sutton in Ashfield St Mary 08-11. *Address temp unknown* E-mail revjuliap@msn.com

PALMER, Mrs June Ann. b 42. EMMTC 02. **d** 11. NSM Elmton *Derby* from 11; NSM Whitwell from 11. *22 Field Drive, Shirebrook, Mansfield NG20 8BN* Tel (01623) 744835

PALMER, Kevin Anthony. b 59. St Steph Ho Ox. **d** 01 **p** 02. C Tunstall *Lich* 01-04; CMP from 02; R Wednesbury St Jas and St Jo *Lich* from 04. *The Rectory, 1 Hollies Drive, Wednesbury WS10 9EQ* Tel 0121-505 1188 or 505 1568

PALMER, Malcolm Leonard. b 46. Sarum & Wells Th Coll 80. **d** 82 **p** 83. C Cannock *Lich* 82-85; Chapl RAF 85-89; Asst Chapl

HM Pris Dur 89-90; Chapl HM YOI Hewell Grange 90-93; Chapl HM Rem Cen Brockhill 90-93; Chapl HM Pris Blakenhurst 93-01; Miss P Kugluktuk Canada 01-04; R Meadows from 04. *Box 3631, RR 2, Corner Brook NL A2H 6B9, Canada* Tel (001) (709) 783 2194 Fax 783 3093
E-mail atanck@excite.com

PALMER, Marc Richard. b 72. St Jo Coll Dur BA96. Cranmer Hall Dur 93. **d** 98 **p** 99. C Chester le Street *Dur* 98-03; TV Bensham 03-08; V Bensham and Teams 08-10; V Norwich St Mary Magd w St Jas from 10. *St Mary Magdalene Vicarage, 10 Crome Road, Norwich NR3 4RQ* Tel (01603) 661381
E-mail emnk@talktalk.net

PALMER, Marion Denise. b 42. Open Univ BA82 SRN64 SCM66. Linc Th Coll 84. **dss** 86 **d** 87 **p** 94. Par Dn 87-90; Par Dn Gillingham St Mary *Roch* 90-94; C 94-96; C Farnborough 96-02; rtd 02; Perm to Offic *St E* from 04. *14 Prestwick Avenue, Felixstowe IP11 9LF* Tel (01394) 671588

PALMER, Canon Maureen Florence. b 38. Qu Eliz Coll Lon BSc60 PhD64. Ripon Coll Cuddesdon. **dss** 85 **d** 87 **p** 94. Tupsley *Heref* 85-88; C 87-88; Par Dn Talbot Village *Sarum* 88-91; Chapl Birm Cathl 91-96; Can Pastor and Can Res Guildf Cathl 96-06; Sub-Dean 99-06; rtd 06; Perm to Offic *Heref* from 06. *28A Green Street, Hereford HR1 2QG* Tel (01432) 353771
E-mail drmaureenpalmer@btinternet.com

PALMER, Michael Christopher. b 43. MBE00. AKC67 CQSW76. **d** 68 **p** 69. C Easthampstead *Ox* 68-71; Miss to Seamen 71-73; Hong Kong 73; Lic to Offic *Ox* 76-79 and *Truro* 79-83; Dioc Soc Resp Adv *Truro* 83-98; Bp's Dom Chapl 85-87; V Devoran 87-98; rtd 98; Perm to Offic *Chich* 98-08 and *Ox* 08-10. *5 Little Drove, Singleton, Chichester PO18 0HD* Tel (01243) 811540

PALMER, Norman Ernest. b 28. Lon Univ BD59. Roch Th Coll 66. **d** 67 **p** 67. C Chipping Norton *Ox* 67-69; V Bozeat w Easton Maudit *Pet* 69-90; rtd 90; Perm to Offic *Chich* 90-94. *13 Gracey Court, Woodland Road, Broadclyst, Exeter EX5 3GA*

PALMER, Mrs Patricia. STETS. **d** 09 **p** 10. NSM Basingstoke *Win* from 09. *97 Packenham Road, Basingstoke RG21 8YA* Tel (01256) 412986 E-mail pat.palmer@ntlworld.com

PALMER, Canon Peter Malcolm. b 31. Chich Th Coll 56. **d** 59 **p** 60. C Leighton Buzzard *St Alb* 59-63; C Apsley End 63-65; C Hitchin H Sav 65-69; R Ickleford 69-76; V Oxhey St Matt 76-86; V Kensworth, Studham and Whipsnade 86-96; Hon Can St Alb 94-96; rtd 97; Perm to Offic *St Alb* from 97; Bp's Retirement Officer 97-10. *4 Sefton Close, St Albans AL1 4PF* Tel (01727) 763196

PALMER, Peter Parsons. b 27. **d** 59 **p** 61. SSJE from 59; Miss at Bracebridge Canada 59-79; Perm to Offic *Leic* 80-86 and *Lon* 86-94; Lic to Offic *Lon* 94-02. *College of St Barnabas, Blackberry Lane, Lingfield RH7 6NJ*

PALMER, Philip Edward Hitchen. b 35. St Jo Coll Cam MA61 DipAdEd74. Ridley Hall Cam 61 EAMTC 87. **d** 90 **p** 91. NSM Gt Oakley w Wix *Chelmsf* 90-96; NSM Gt Oakley w Wix and Wrabness 96-00; Perm to Offic from 00. *Glebe House, Wix Road, Great Oakley, Harwich CO12 5BJ* Tel (01255) 880737

PALMER, Robert William. b 28. Wells Th Coll 63. **d** 65 **p** 66. C Earlsdon *Cov* 65-69; P-in-c Cov St Mark 69-71; Chapl Cov and Warks Hosp 69-71; Hon C Binley *Cov* 72-76; V Sheff St Paul 76-84; V Deepcar 84-93; rtd 93; Perm to Offic *Sheff* from 93. *Moorlands, 26 Coal Pit Lane, Stocksbridge, Sheffield S36 1AW*

PALMER, Canon Stephen Charles. b 47. Portsm Univ PhD04 FRGS98 FLS01. Oak Hill Th Coll 71. **d** 74 **p** 75. C Crofton *Portsm* 74-77; Bp's Dom Chapl 77-80; Chapl RNR 78-91; R Brighstone and Brooke w Mottistone *Portsm* 80-91; P-in-c Shorwell w Kingston 82-86; RD W Wight 87-91; R Falkland Is 91-96; V Portsdown *Portsm* 96-02; V Newport St Jo 02-09; V Newport St Thos 02-09; Bp's Ecological Adv 00-07; Hon Can Portsm Cathl 91-09; rtd 09; Chapl to The Queen from 08. *Fintry Schoolhouse, Fintry, Turriff AB53 5RN* Tel (01888) 551367 Mobile 07799-412512 E-mail palmers@fintry.plus.com

PALMER, Steven Roy. b 51. Birm Univ BSc71. WMMTC 91. **d** 94 **p** 95. C Sheldon *Birm* 94-97; P-in-c Duddeston w Nechells 97-99; V Nechells 99-03; R Billing *Pet* from 03; RD Northn 06-07. *The Rectory, 25 Church Walk, Great Billing, Northampton NN3 4ED* Tel (01604) 788508 Fax 401641
E-mail stevenrpalmer@hotmail.com

PALMER, Canon Terence Henry James. b 34. Univ of Wales (Lamp) BA55 LTh57 St Edm Hall Ox BA65 MA69 FRSA08. **d** 57 **p** 58. C Griffithstown *Mon* 57-60; Min Can and C St D Cathl 60-63; Perm to Offic *B & W* and *Ox* 63-65; C Monmouth 65-69; C-in-c St Hilary Greenway CD 69-72; R Roggiett w Llanfihangel Roggiett 72-80; R Portskewett and Rogiet w Llanfihangel Rogiet 80-00; RD Netherwent 89-00; Dir NSM Studies 91-99; Can St Woolos Cathl 96-00; rtd 00; Perm to Offic *Eur* from 99; Lic to Offic *Mon* from 00; P-in-c Newport St Teilo from 03. *Terleen, 12 Windsor Park, Magor, Caldicot NP26 3NJ* Tel (01633) 881927 E-mail kathypalmer.1@virgin.net

PALMER FINCH, Barry Marshall. b 23. Hertf Coll Ox BA47 MA48. Westcott Ho Cam 47. **d** 49 **p** 50. C Alrewas *Lich* 49-52; C Wychnor 49-52; C Birchington w Acol *Cant* 52-56; R

Harrietsham 56-66; Chapl Westmr Hosp *Lon* 66-73; V Chipping Sodbury and Old Sodbury *Glouc* 73-88; rtd 88; Perm to Offic *Glouc* and *Bris* 90-06; *Lon* 90-00. *Finch's Folly, 45 Hay Street, Marshfield, Chippenham SN14 8PF* Tel (01225) 891096

PAMMENT, Gordon Charles. b 31. TCD BA54. Linc Th Coll 56. **d** 58 **p** 60. C Hemel Hempstead *St Alb* 58-63; C Gedney Drove End *Linc* 63-65; I Macroom Union *C, C & R* 65-72; I Rathcormac Union 72-78; I Fermoy Union 78-91; Can Ross Cathl 89-91; Can Cork Cathl 89-91; rtd 91. *Magoola, Dripsey, Co Cork, Republic of Ireland* Tel (00353) (21) 451 6532

PAMPLIN, Canon Richard Lawrence. b 46. Lon Univ BScEng68 Dur Univ BA75 NY Th Sem DMin85. Wycliffe Hall Ox 75. **d** 77 **p** 78. C Greenside *Dur* 77-80; C Sheff St Barn and St Mary 80-84; R Wombwell 84-90; P-in-c Madeley *Heref* 90-91; TR 91-01; Chapl Berne w Neuchâtel *Eur* 01-07; Can Gib Cathl 04-07; Chapl Viña del Mar w Valparaiso Chile from 07. *Casilla 676, Viña del Mar, Chile* Tel (0056) (32) 239 7771
E-mail richard.l.pamplin@gmail.com

PANG, Mrs Heather Marian. b 46. St Jo Coll Nottm BA08. SNWTP 09. **d** 11. NSM Gt Saughall *Ches* from 11. *20 Oakland Drive, Wirral CH49 6JL* Tel 0151-677 2690
E-mail wingonheather@gmail.com

PANG, Wing-On. b 43. Manitoba Univ BA67 SOAS Lon MA70. Oak Hill Th Coll 85. **d** 87 **p** 88. C Pennycross *Ex* 87-91; TV Mildenhall *St E* 91-96; Assoc P Kowloon St Andr Hong Kong 96-08; rtd 08; Perm to Offic from 09. *20 Oakland Drive, Wirral CH49 6JL* Tel 0151-677 2690
E-mail wingonheather@gmail.com

PANGBOURNE, John Godfrey. b 36. Ridley Hall Cam 82. **d** 84 **p** 85. C Ashtead *Guildf* 84-88; V Ore Ch Ch *Chich* 88-03; rtd 03; Perm to Offic *Ex* 04-06; Hon C Ottery St Mary, Alfington, W Hill, Tipton etc from 06. *Meon Croft, Toadpit Lane, West Hill, Ottery St Mary EX11 1TR* Tel (01404) 812393

PANKHURST, Donald Araunah. b 28. Qu Coll Birm. **d** 64 **p** 65. C Pemberton St Jo *Liv* 64-68; V Aspull 68-76; R Newchurch 76-88; R Winwick 88-94; rtd 94; Perm to Offic *Carl* from 94. *Hunters Hill, Spooner Vale, Windermere LA23 1AU* Tel (01539) 446390

PANKHURST, Ian Charles. b 50. Trin Coll Cam BA72 Lon Inst of Educn PGCE88. SAOMC 01. **d** 04 **p** 05. C Watford St Luke *St Alb* 04-10; P-in-c Watford St Andr from 10. *3 Albert Road North, Watford WD17 1QE* Tel (01923) 249139
E-mail ian_pankhurst@btinternet.com

PANNETT, Peter George. b 44. **d** 11. NSM Brighton St Geo w St Anne and St Mark *Chich* from 11. *Flat 4, 20 Bristol Road, Brighton BN2 1AP* Tel (01273) 694023
E-mail peter.pannett712@gmail.com

PANNETT, Philip Anthony. b 36. Brighton Poly MPS59 MRPharmS59. K Coll Lon AKC63 St Boniface Warminster 63. **d** 64 **p** 65. C Stanmer w Falmer and Moulsecoomb *Chich* 64-68; C Hangleton 68-72; Teacher Finchden Manor Sch Tenterden 72-74; Teacher Bodiam Manor Sch 74-76; Perm to Offic from 76; rtd 01. *1 Fitzjohns Road, Lewes BN7 1PP* Tel (01273) 472804

PANTER, The Ven Richard James Graham. b 48. Oak Hill Th Coll 73. **d** 76 **p** 77. C Rusholme H Trin *Man* 76-80; C Toxteth St Cypr w Ch Ch *Liv* 80-85; V Clubmoor 85-96; P-in-c Litherland St Jo and St Jas 96-02; AD Bootle 99-02; V Orrell Hey St Jo and St Jas 02-11; Adn Liv from 02. *St John and St James Vicarage, 2A Monfa Road, Bootle L20 6BQ* Tel and fax 0151-922 3758 E-mail archdeaconricky@blueyonder.co.uk

PANTER MARSHALL, Canon Susan Lesley. b 49. Portsm Poly BSc72. S Dios Minl Tr Scheme 88. **d** 91 **p** 94. NSM Southover *Chich* 91-95; C Iford w Kingston and Rodmell 95-98; C Hollington St Jo 98-02; P-in-c Herstmonceux and Wartling 02-07; R 07-10; Can and Preb Chich Cathl 07-10; rtd 10. *Address temp unknown*

PANTING, Nigel Roger. b 47. St Pet Coll Ox BA69 PGCE70. Local Minl Tr Course 06. **d** 11. NSM Ruskington Gp *Linc* from 11. *The Cottage, Roxholm, Sleaford NG34 8NE* Tel (01526) 832020 Mobile 07866-808737
E-mail nigelpanting@yahoo.co.uk

PANTLING, Rosemary Caroline. b 60. Ex Coll Ox BA83 MA89 Anglia Poly Univ MA03 Birm Univ PGCE84. EAMTC 98. **d** 01 **p** 02. NSM Bishop's Tachbrook *Cov* 01-08; P-in-c Cubbington 08-10; Perm to Offic from 10. *22 Touchstone Road, Heathcote, Warwick CV34 6EE* Tel 07846-220974 (mobile)

PANTON, Alan Edward. b 45. K Coll Lon BD67 AKC67. **d** 68 **p** 69. C Eltham St Jo *S'wark* 68-73; C Horley 73-78; V Dallington *Pet* 78-07; rtd 07; Perm to Offic *Pet* from 09. *28 Riverside Way, Northampton NN4 9QY* Tel (01604) 755421
E-mail rev.panton@virgin.net

PANTRY, John Richard. b 46. Oak Hill NSM Course 90. **d** 93 **p** 94. NSM Alresford *Chelmsf* 93-04; NSM W w E Mersea 04-10; NSM W w E Mersea, Peldon, Gt and Lt Wigborough from 10. *48 Empress Avenue, West Mersea, Colchester CO5 8EX* Tel and fax (01206) 386910 E-mail johnpantry@fsmail.net

PAPADOPULOS, Nicholas Charles. b 66. G&C Coll Cam BA88 MA92 Barrister-at-Law (Middle Temple) 90. Ripon Coll Cuddesdon. **d** 99 **p** 00. C Portsea N End St Mark *Portsm* 99-02; Bp's Dom Chapl *Sarum* 02-07; Hon Chapl 07-10; V Pimlico

St Pet w Westmr Ch Ch *Lon* from 07. *1 St Peter's House, 119 Eaton Square, London SW1W 9AL* Tel (020) 7235 4242 Mobile 07903-620018 E-mail vicar@stpetereatonsquare.co.uk
PAPANTONIOU, Ms Frances Caroline. b 52. S Dios Minl Tr Scheme 89. **d** 92 **p** 94. Par Dn Harrow Weald All SS *Lon* 92-94; C 94-95; C Preston Ascension 95-98; Assoc V Wembley Park 98-99; TV 99-04; V Horton Kirby and Sutton-at-Hone *Roch* from 04. *The Vicarage, 51A Main Road, Sutton at Hone, Dartford DA4 9HQ* Tel (01322) 862253
E-mail fran.papantoniou@diocese-rochester.org
PAPE, David. b 54. **d** 98 **p** 99. OLM S'wark St Geo w St Alphege and St Jude from 98; OLM Waterloo St Jo w St Andr from 98. *10 Stopher House, Webber Street, London SE1 0RE* Tel (020) 7928 3503
PAPE, Timothy Vernon Francis. b 39. OBE. Lon Univ BSc63. Wells Th Coll 63. **d** 65 **p** 66. C Pershore w Wick *Worc* 65-69; Perm to Offic *Bris* 69-73; NSM Southbroom *Sarum* 75-08; Hd Master Chirton Primary Sch Wilts from 81; Dir Gen Shaw Trust from 90. *Mallards, Chirton, Devizes SN10 3QX* Tel (01380) 840593
PAPUA NEW GUINEA, Archbishop of. *See* AYONG, The Most Revd James Simon
PAPWORTH, Daniel John. b 69. Plymouth Poly BSc90. Trin Coll Bris BA98 MA00. **d** 99 **p** 00. C Gabalfa *Llan* 99-02; Perm to Offic *B & W* 03-04; Asst Chapl Dudley Gp of Hosps NHS Trust 04-07; Chapl R Devon and Ex NHS Foundn Trust 07-08; TV N Cheltenham *Glouc* from 08. *The Rectory, Tatchley Lane, Prestbury, Cheltenham GL52 3DQ* Tel (01242) 575649
PAPWORTH, John. b 21. Lon Univ BSc(Econ). **d** 75 **p** 76. Zambia 76-81; Hon C Paddington St Sav *Lon* 81-83; Hon C St Marylebone St Mark Hamilton Terrace 85-97; Perm to Offic *Bris* from 01. *The Fourth World, The Close, 26 High Street, Purton, Swindon SN5 4AE* Tel (01793) 772214 Fax 772521
PAPWORTH, Miss Shirley Marjorie. b 33. CA Tr Coll. **d** 88 **p** 94. Par Dn Hornchurch H Cross *Chelmsf* 88-93; rtd 93; Chapl Havering Primary Care Trust 93-08; NSM Hornchurch St Andr *Chelmsf* 93-08; Perm to Offic from 08. *4 Gosport Drive, Hornchurch RM12 6NU* Tel (01708) 524348
PARAGUAY, Bishop of. *See* BARTLETT, The Rt Revd Peter
PARBURY, Mrs Heather Christina Winifred. b 56. **d** 01 **p** 02. C Long Compton, Whichford and Barton-on-the-Heath *Cov* 01-05; C Barcheston 01-05; C Cherington w Stourton 01-05; C Wolford w Burmington 01-05; TV Cherwell Valley *Ox* 05-08; P-in-c Pangbourne w Tidmarsh and Sulham 08-10; R from 10; Chapl MU from 10. *The Rectory, St James's Close, Pangbourne, Reading RG8 7AP* Tel 0118-984 2928
E-mail parbury@btinternet.com
PARE, Stephen Charles. b 53. Sussex Univ BEd75. St Mich Coll Llan 78. **d** 80 **p** 81. C Cardiff St Jo *Llan* 80-83; P-in-c Marcross w Monknash and Wick 83; TV Llantwit Major 83-91; V Penmark w Porthkerry 91-06; P-in-c Llansantffraid, Bettws and Aberkenfig from 06; Chapl Cardiff Wales Airport from 93. *St Bride's Rectory, Heol Persondy, Aberkenfig, Bridgend CF32 9RH* Tel (01656) 720274 E-mail scpare@googlemail.com
PARES, John. b 57. Bedf Coll Lon BA79. Westcott Ho Cam 08. **d** 10 **p** 11. C Diss *Nor* from 10. *7 De Lucy Close, Diss IP22 4YL* Tel 07972-075459 (mobile) E-mail j.pares@virginmedia.com
PARFFETT, Allan John. b 51. Open Univ BA97 CQSW76. Qu Coll Birm MA00. **d** 98 **p** 99. C Hall Green Ascension *Birm* 98-00; Soc Worker 00-09; rtd 09. *20 Kiln Close, Corfe Mullen, Wimborne BH21 3UR* Tel (01202) 690164
PARFITT, Anthony Colin. b 44. Ox Univ Inst of Educn CertEd66 Open Univ BA71 Plymouth Poly MPhil84. SWMTC 93. **d** 96 **p** 97. NSM Langport Area *B & W* 96-00; NSM Bruton and Distr 01-06; Perm to Offic from 07. *Tile Hill Cottage, North Brewham, Bruton BA10 0JT* Tel (01749) 850177
E-mail tonyparfitt@btinternet.com
PARFITT, Brian John. b 49. Ex Coll Ox BA71 MA76. Wycliffe Hall Ox 71. **d** 74 **p** 75. C Newport St Mark *Mon* 74-78; R Blaina 78-83; R Blaina and Nantyglo 83-86; Chapl Blaina and Distr Hosp Gwent 83-86; Regional Consultant (W Midlands and Wales) CPAS 86-95; V Magor w Redwick and Undy *Mon* 95-98; TR Magor 98-06; Local Min Officer *Glouc* from 06. *9 Red Admiral Drive, Abbeymead, Gloucester GL4 5EA* Tel (01452) 835543 Mobile 07847-359062
E-mail brianparfitt@btinternet.com
PARFITT, David George. b 65. De Montfort Univ Leic BA87. Wycliffe Hall Ox BTh92. **d** 95 **p** 96. C Malpas *Mon* 95-98; C Bassaleg 98-00; TV 00-01; V Malpas from 01. *The Vicarage, Malpas Road, Newport NP20 6GQ* Tel (01633) 852047
PARFITT, George Rudolf William. b 54. WMMTC 96. **d** 99 **p** 00. OLM Highnam, Lassington, Rudford, Tibberton etc *Glouc* 99-08; NSM Hardwicke and Elmore w Longney from 08. *66 Holbeach Drive, Kingsway, Quedgeley, Gloucester GL2 2BF* Tel (01452) 728180 E-mail george.parfitt@btinternet.com
PARFITT, Graeme Stephen. b 36. Qu Coll Birm 77. **d** 79 **p** 80. C Fishponds St Jo *Bris* 79-82; V Southmead 82-91; V Stockwell St Mich *S'wark* 91-01; rtd 01; Perm to Offic *Bris* from 02. *Brook End, Rectory Gardens, Bristol BS10 7AQ* Tel 0117-959 0293

PARFITT, Preb John Hubert. b 29. Southn Univ MA72 BPhil. Qu Coll Birm 78. **d** 80 **p** 81. C Fladbury, Wyre Piddle and Moor *Worc* 80-82; C Malvern Link w Cowleigh 82; V Hanley Castle, Hanley Swan and Welland 82-83; Dir RE *B & W* 84-93; Preb Wells Cathl from 85; rtd 93; Perm to Offic *B & W* from 93; Master Hugh Sexey's Hosp Bruton 95-05. *3 Willow Farm Cottages, Brister End, Yetminster, Sherborne DT9 6NH* Tel (01935) 873260 E-mail passitatwillow@btinternet.com
PARFITT, Canon Keith John. b 44. K Coll Lon BD68 AKC68. St Aug Coll Cant 69. **d** 70 **p** 71. C Kettering St Andr *Pet* 70-74; Asst Soc and Ind Adv *Portsm* 74-89; RD Alverstoke 79-86; C-in-c Bridgemary CD 81-82; V Bridgemary 82-89; Dioc UPA Officer *Blackb* 89-97; Can Res Blackb Cathl 94-97; Dir Is of Wight Rural Community Coun from 97. *Address temp unknown*
PARFITT, Susan Mary. b 42. Bris Univ BA63 CertEd68. Bris Minl Tr Scheme 82. **dss** 84 **d** 87 **p** 94. Assoc Dir of Ords *Bris* 84-86; CME Officer 87-91; Dir Past Care and Counselling *S'wark* 91-01; rtd 01; Perm to Offic *Bris* from 02. *Brook End, Rectory Gardens, Bristol BS10 7AQ* Tel 0117-959 0293
PARGETER, Canon Muriel Elizabeth. b 28. St Mich Ho Ox 53. **dss** 82 **d** 87 **p** 95. Hd Dss *Roch* 82-87; Dioc Dir of Ords 87-90; Hon Can Roch Cathl 87-90; rtd 90; Hon C Worthing Ch the King *Chich* 95-03; Perm to Offic from 03. *63 Pavilion Road, Worthing BN45 7EE* Tel (01903) 214476
PARISH, Mrs Mary Eileen. b 48. Nottm Univ BA70. STETS BTh98. **d** 98 **p** 99. NSM Worthing Ch the King *Chich* 98-08; NSM Worthing St Matt from 08. *The Heritage, 10 Winchester Road, Worthing BN11 4DJ* Tel (01903) 236909
E-mail frmary@theheritage.freeserve.co.uk
PARISH, Canon Nicholas Anthony. b 58. Oak Hill Th Coll BA84 Kingston Univ MA97. Ridley Hall Cam 84. **d** 86 **p** 87. C Eltham H Trin *S'wark* 86-89; C Barnes St Mary 89-91; V Streatham St Paul 91-96; Ind Chapl *Ox* 96-07; P-in-c Bracknell from 07; AD Bracknell from 04; Hon Can Ch Ch from 08. *1 Old Lands Hill, Bracknell RG12 2QX* Tel and fax (01344) 641498 *or* tel 867383 E-mail nick.parish@ntlworld.com
PARISH, Stephen Richard. b 49. Liv Univ MTh05. Oak Hill Th Coll 74. **d** 77 **p** 78. C Chadderton Ch Ch *Man* 77-81; C Chell *Lich* 81-82; TV 82-88; V Warrington St Ann *Liv* from 88; P-in-c Warrington H Trin from 06. *St Ann's Vicarage, 1A Fitzherbert Street, Warrington WA2 7QG* Tel (01925) 631781
E-mail bloovee@ntlworld.com
PARK, Christopher John. b 62. Sheff Poly BA83. Cranmer Hall Dur 00. **d** 02 **p** 03. C Didsbury St Jas and Em *Man* 02-08; P-in-c Alne *York* from 08; P-in-c Brafferton w Pilmoor, Myton-on-Swale etc from 08. *Monk Green House, Main Street, Alne, York YO61 1TB* Tel (01347) 838122
E-mail pastaparko@tiscali.co.uk
PARK, John Charles. b 55. St Pet Coll Ox BA77 St Mary's Coll Newc PGCE81. Cranmer Hall Dur 00. **d** 02 **p** 03. C Morpeth *Newc* 02-06; R Bothal and Pegswood w Longhirst from 06. *Bothal Rectory, Longhirst Road, Pegswood, Morpeth NE61 6XF* Tel (01670) 510793 E-mail jjat@parks2002.fsnet.co.uk
PARK, Tarjei Erling Alan. b 64. W Lon Inst of HE BA88 Lanc Univ MA89 Pemb Coll Ox DPhil96. Ripon Coll Cuddesdon 92. **d** 94 **p** 95. C Lancaster St Mary *Blackb* 94-98; V Enfield St Mich *Lon* 98-01; Asst Dir Post-Ord Tr 98-03; V Golders Green 01-06; C St Pancras w St Jas and Ch Ch 06-08; rtd 09. *30A Hadley Street, London NW1 8SS* Tel (020) 7482 1170
E-mail tarjeipark@aol.co.uk
PARK, Trevor. b 38. MBE05. Lon Univ BA64 Open Univ PhD90 Lambeth STh81. Linc Th Coll 64. **d** 66 **p** 67. C Crosthwaite Kendal *Carl* 66-68; Asst Chapl Solihull Sch 69-71; Chapl St Bees Sch and V St Bees *Carl* 71-77; V Dalton-in-Furness 77-84; V Natland 84-97; Hon Can Carl Cathl 86-97; RD Kendal 89-94; Chapl Oslo w Bergen, Trondheim and Stavanger *Eur* 97-05; rtd 05; P-in-c St Petersburg *Eur* 06-07. *20 Seacroft Drive, St Bees CA23 0AF*
PARKER, Angus Michael Macdonald. b 53. Bris Univ BSc74. St Jo Coll Nottm 80. **d** 83 **p** 84. C Northampton St Giles *Pet* 83-86; C Attenborough *S'well* 86-96; V Pennycross *Ex* 96-09; P-in-c Bitterne *Win* from 09. *The Vicarage, 2 Bursledon Road, Southampton SO19 7LW* Tel (023) 8044 0493
E-mail angus@mmparker.wanadoo.co.uk
PARKER, Mrs Ann Jacqueline. b 41. Dur Inst of Educn TCert63 Sunderland Poly TCert65 Open Univ BA82. WEMTC 91. **d** 95 **p** 96. NSM Pilning w Compton Greenfield *Bris* 95-98; NSM Almondsbury and Olveston 98-03; Asst Chapl N Bris NHS Trust from 98. *Wyngarth, Easter Compton, Bristol BS35 5RA* Tel (01454) 632329 E-mail annatdibley@aol.com
PARKER, Anne Margaret. *See* HINDLE, Anne Margaret
PARKER, Mrs Brenda. b 36. **d** 00 **p** 01. OLM Eccleston Ch Ch *Liv* 00-06; rtd 06. *22 Selkirk Drive, Eccleston, St Helens WA10 5PE* Tel (01744) 757495
PARKER, Brian William. b 39. Ulster Univ BA88. CITC 99. **d** 01 **p** 02. NSM Knock *D & D* 01-02; NSM Glencraig from 02. *7 Cairnsville Park, Bangor BT19 6EW* Tel (028) 9145 4549 Fax 9147 1804 E-mail bwparker@ukgateway.net

PARKER, David Anthony. b 38. St Chad's Coll Dur BA62. **d** 64 **p** 65. C Palmers Green St Jo *Lon* 64-65; C Kenton 65-71; C W Hyde St Thos *St Alb* 71-75; P-in-c Brinksway *Ches* 76-80; V 80-83; V Weston 83-92; NSM Cheadle Hulme All SS 97-98; C Offerton 98-00; TV Crosslacon *Carl* 00-02; rtd 02; C Cheadle Hulme All SS *Ches* from 02. *77 Station Road, Cheadle Hulme, Cheadle SK8 7BG* Tel 0161-485 4451

PARKER, David Charles. b 53. St Andr Univ MTheol75 Univ of Leiden DTh90. Ridley Hall Cam 75. **d** 77 **p** 78. C Hendon St Paul Mill Hill *Lon* 77-80; C Bladon w Woodstock *Ox* 80-85; C-in-c Shipton-on-Cherwell 80-85; C-in-c Begbroke 80-85; C-in-c Hampton Gay 80-85; Lect Qu Coll Birm 85-93 and 89-93; Lect Birm Univ 93-96; Sen Lect 96-98; Reader in NT Textual Criticism and Palaeography from 98. *Dumbleton Cottage, 24 Church Street, Bromyard HR7 4DP* Tel 0121-415 2415 E-mail d.c.parker@bham.ac.uk

PARKER, Canon David John. b 33. St Chad's Coll Dur BA55 Hull Univ MA85. Linc Th Coll 57. **d** 59 **p** 60. C Tynemouth Ch Ch *Newc* 59-60; C Ponteland 60-63; C Byker St Mich 63-64; C-in-c Byker St Martin CD 64-69; V Whorlton 69-73; TR 73-80; Ind Chapl *Linc* 80-84; Master Newc St Thos Prop Chpl 84-89; Exec Officer Dioc Bd for Ch and Soc *Man* 90-98; Lic Preacher 90-98; Hon Can Man Cathl 97-98; rtd 98; Perm to Offic *Newc* from 98. *4 The Kylins, Morpeth NE61 2DJ* Tel (01670) 516218 E-mail davidparker12@sky.com

PARKER, Canon David Louis. b 47. Lon Univ LLB70. Wycliffe Hall Ox BA79 MA82. **d** 80 **p** 81. C Broadwater St Mary *Chich* 80-84; TR Ifield 84-97; R Lavant from 97; RD Chich 01-06; Can and Preb Chich Cathl from 03. *The Rectory, Pook Lane, Lavant, Chichester PO18 0AH* Tel (01243) 527313

PARKER, David William. b 21. SEN CQSW MBASW. Glouc Th Course 77 Sarum & Wells Th Coll 81. **d** 81 **p** 81. Chapl HM Pris Leyhill 81-84; NSM Cromhall w Tortworth *Glouc* 81-83; NSM Wickwar w Rangeworthy 83-87; Perm to Offic 88-01. *22 Durham Road, Charfield, Wotton-under-Edge GL12 8TH* Tel (01454) 260253

PARKER, George William. b 29. Univ of K Coll Halifax NS BS53 BD57 Lon Univ PGCE67. **d** 53 **p** 54. C Calgary Cathl 53-55; I Cardston 55-59; C W Hackney St Barn *Lon* 59-61; V Haggerston St Mary w St Chad 61-68; Teacher St Adele Canada 68-71; C Portsea N End St Mark *Portsm* 72-75; V Darlington St Jo *Dur* 75-78; R Des Monts Canada 78-81; R Digby 81-87; R Rawdon 87-91; rtd 91. *clo T Parker Esq, 7 McNeil Street, Dartmouth NS B2Y 2H2, Canada*

PARKER, Hugh James. b 30. ACP55 TCD MA57 Ulster Univ DASE74. **d** 63 **p** 64. Lic to Offic *Conn* 63-70 and 96-01; Dioc C 70-96; Hd Master Larne High Sch 71-92; rtd 96. *25 Ballykillaire Terrace, Bangor BT19 1GS* Tel (028) 9185 7142

PARKER, Janet Elizabeth. b 54. Cranmer Hall Dur 05. **d** 07 **p** 08. C Sale St Anne *Ches* 07-10; V High Lane from 10. *35 Martlet Avenue, Disley, Stockport SK12 2JH* Tel (01663) 764519 E-mail janetparker1@homecall.co.uk

PARKER, Mrs Joanna Caroline. b 63. UEA BA95 Leeds Univ MA07 RGN85 RM92. NOC 04. **d** 07 **p** 08. C Pocklington Wold *York* 07-11; V Hyde St Geo *Ches* from 11. *The Vicarage, 85 Edna Street, Hyde SK14 1DR* Tel 0161-478 2608 E-mail joanna.parker@tinyworld.co.uk

PARKER, John. See PARKER, Linsey John Owen

PARKER, John Bristo. b 26. Edin Th Coll 61. **d** 64 **p** 65. C Barrow St Jo *Carl* 64-68; V Sledmere *York* 68-74; V Sledmere and Wetwang w Cowlan 74-79; R Cowlam 68-74; P-in-c Wetwang 69-74; V Kirkby Ireleth *Carl* 79-83; V Rillington w Scampston, Wintringham etc *York* 83-87; R Bishop Wilton w Full Sutton, Kirby Underdale etc 87-91; rtd 91; Perm to Offic *York* 91-11. *East Lodge, Sledmere, Driffield YO25 3XQ* Tel (01377) 236325

PARKER, John David. b 61. Ridley Hall Cam 00. **d** 02 **p** 03. C Aston cum Aughton w Swallownest and Ulley *Sheff* 02-06; TV Rugby *Cov* from 06. *The Vicarage, 63A Lower Hillmorton Road, Rugby CV21 3TQ* Tel (01788) 544381 E-mail jdparkeruk@aol.com

PARKER, Julian Roderick. b 57. Essex Univ BA80. Sarum & Wells Th Coll 91. **d** 93 **p** 94. C Gillingham *Sarum* 93-97; V N Bradley, Southwick and Heywood 97-08; V N Bradley, Southwick, Heywood and Steeple Ashton from 08. *The Vicarage, 62 Church Lane, North Bradley, Trowbridge BA14 0TA* Tel (01225) 752635 E-mail julian@roderick17.freeserve.co.uk

PARKER, Linsey John Owen. b 70. Oriel Coll Ox BA91 Lon Univ PGCE94. Oak Hill Th Coll 02. **d** 05 **p** 06. C Arborfield w Barkham *Ox* from 05. *7 Sheerlands Road, Arborfield, Reading RG2 9ND* Tel 0118-976 0245 E-mail johnandmim@bigfoot.com

PARKER, Lynn. b 54. SS Mark & Jo Univ Coll Plymouth BEd94. SWMTC 04. **d** 07 **p** 08. NSM S Hill w Callington *Truro* 07-10; P-in-c Torpoint from 10; P-in-c Antony w Sheviock from 10. *The Vicarage, 3 Grove Park, Torpoint PL11 2PP* Tel (01752) 815412 E-mail parker30@hotmail.com

PARKER, Miss Margaret. b 27. Lightfoot Ho Dur 54. **dss** 60 **d** 87 **p** 94. Ryhope *Dur* 56-61; Monkwearmouth St Andr 61-79; Adv for Accredited Lay Min 74-87; Adv for Accredited Lay Min

Newc 79-87; Newc St Geo 79-87; C 87; rtd 87; Perm to Offic *Dur* and *Newc* from 87; Tutor Cranmer Hall Dur 87-92; Hon C Dur Cathl 87-94; Min Can Dur Cathl 94-97; Chapl St Mary's Coll Dur 95-98. *clo P Davies Esq, 16 The College, Durham DH1 3EQ*

PARKER, Margaret Grace. See TORDOFF, Mrs Margaret Grace

PARKER, Matthew John. b 63. Man Univ BA85 SS Coll Cam BA88. Ridley Hall Cam 85. **d** 88 **p** 89. C Twickenham St Mary *Lon* 88-91; Chapl Stockport Gr Sch 91-94; C Stockport St Geo *Ches* 91-93; P-in-c Stockport St Mark 93-94; TV Stockport SW 94-00; TR Leek and Meerbrook *Lich* from 00; RD Leek from 03. *St Edward's Vicarage, 24 Ashenhurst Way, Leek ST13 5SB* Tel (01538) 382515 or 388134 E-mail matpark01@aol.com

PARKER, Michael. b 54. **d** 07. C Ebbw Vale *Mon* 07-09; Hon C Llanhilleth w Six Bells 09-10; Hon C Abertillery w Cwmtillery w Llanhilleth etc from 10. *43 Drysiog Street, Ebbw Vale NP23 6DE* Tel (01495) 304193 E-mail naso.01@btinternet.com

PARKER, Michael Alan. b 70. St Jo Coll Dur BA91. CITC BTh93. **d** 96 **p** 97. C Dundela St Mark *D & D* 96-00; I Carnalea from 00. *St Gall's Rectory, 171 Crawfordsburn Road, Bangor BT19 1BT* Tel (028) 9185 3366 or 9185 3810 E-mail carnalea@down.anglican.org *or* stgalloffice@btconnect.com

PARKER, Michael John. b 54. Cam Coll of Art and Tech BA76 Lon Univ BD85. Trin Coll Bris 82. **d** 85 **p** 86. C Leic H Trin w St Jo 85-88; P-in-c Edin Clermiston Em 88-90; R Edin St Thos 90-03; Can St Mary's Cathl 94-03; NSM Edin St Paul and St Geo 03-06; Gen Sec Evang Alliance Scotland 03-06; Middle E Dir Middle E Chr Outreach 06-09; Sen Min All SS Cathl Cairo from 09. *Middle East Christian Outreach, 22 Culverden Park Road, Tunbridge Wells TN4 9RA* Tel (01892) 521541 E-mail mikeparker@f2s.com

PARKER, Canon Michael John. b 57. BSc Nottm Univ MA04. Wycliffe Hall Ox 80. **d** 83 **p** 84. C Heigham H Trin *Nor* 83-86; C Muswell Hill St Jas w St Matt *Lon* 86-90; R Bedford St Jo and St Leon *St Alb* 90-98; V Knowle *Birm* from 98; AD Solihull from 04; Hon Can Birm Cathl from 05. *The Vicarage, 1811 Warwick Road, Knowle, Solihull B93 0DS* Tel and fax (01564) 773666 or tel 778802 Fax 779123 E-mail vicar@knowleparishchurch.org.uk

PARKER, Nigel Howard. b 69. St Jo Coll Dur BSc90. CITC BTh97. **d** 97 **p** 98. C Holywood *D & D* 97-00; Outreach Development Officer Think Again 00-04; I Bangor St Comgall from 04. *The Rectory, 2 Raglan Road, Bangor BT20 3TL* Tel (028) 9146 0712 E-mail bangorparish@btconnect.com

PARKER, Peter Edward. b 32. Edin Univ MA55 Lon Univ PGCE56 FRSA. Sarum & Wells Th Coll 73. **d** 74 **p** 75. C Kirkby Lonsdale w Mansergh *Carl* 74-76; C Kingston All SS w St Jo *S'wark* 76-80; Chapl S Bank Poly 80-85; Ind Chapl *Chelmsf* 85-90; Chapl Chelmsf Cathl 85-90; R Mistley w Manningtree and Bradfield 90-97; rtd 97; Perm to Offic *Ely* from 97. *2 Waterside, Ely CB7 4AZ* Tel (01353) 614103

PARKER, Philip Vernon. b 60. Birm Univ BSc82 PGCE83 Heythrop Coll Lon MA09. Wycliffe Hall Ox BA89. **d** 90 **p** 91. C Walkergate *Newc* 90-93; Chapl Shiplake Coll Henley 93-96; C Lindfield *Chich* 97-99; Scripture Union 99-04; Chapl Cranleigh Sch Surrey from 04; CF (TA) 97-05. *Cranleigh School, Horseshoe Lane, Cranleigh GU6 8QQ* Tel (01483) 542028 E-mail pvp@cranleigh.org

PARKER, Ramon Lewis (Brother Raphael). b 36. Kelham Th Coll 56. **d** 61 **p** 62. C Tonge Moor *Man* 61-64; C Clerkenwell H Redeemer w St Phil *Lon* 64-65; V Prestwich St Hilda *Man* 65-71; SSF from 71; Chapl Univ of Wales (Lamp) *St D* 81-86; Lic to Offic *Sarum* from 87; rtd 97. *clo Brother Samuel SSF, The Friary, Hilfield, Dorchester DT2 7BE* Tel (01300) 341345

PARKER, Canon Richard Bryan. b 64. Sheff Poly BA87. Coll of Resurr Mirfield 92. **d** 95 **p** 96. C Norton *Sheff* 95-98; C Hoyland 98-00; V Moorends 00-08; V Hoyland from 08; Dioc Warden of Readers from 10; Hon Can Sheff Cathl from 10. *The Vicarage, 104 Hawshaw Lane, Hoyland, Barnsley S74 0HH* Tel (01226) 749231 E-mail r.b.parker@btinternet.com

PARKER, Richard Frederick. b 36. Oak Hill Th Coll 72. **d** 74 **p** 75. C Wootton *St Alb* 74-76; C Hove Bp Hannington Memorial Ch *Chich* 76-81; R Northwood *Portsm* 81-88; V W Cowes H Trin 81-88; V Aldershot H Trin *Guildf* 88-98; R Spaxton w Charlynch, Goathurst, Enmore etc *B & W* 98-03; rtd 03. *47 Banneson Road, Nether Stowey, Bridgwater TA5 1NS* Tel (01278) 733883

PARKER, Robert. b 43. Lon Univ BSc65. Cuddesdon Coll. **d** 67 **p** 68. C Sheff St Cuth 67-70; Asst Chapl Cheltenham Coll 70-74; R Yate *Glouc* 74-76; R Yate Bris 76-77; TR Yate New Town 77-80; C of E Development Officer 80-83; NSM Pool Quay *St As* 99-07; P-in-c 99-04; Perm to Offic *Lich* from 08. *Tedsmore Hall, Tedsmore, West Felton, Oswestry SY11 4HD* Tel (01691) 610628 E-mail rgparker@tedsmorehall.co.uk

PARKER, Robert Lawrence. b 34. ALCD59. **d** 59 **p** 60. C Chippenham St Paul *Bris* 59-61; C Swindon Ch Ch 61-63; New Zealand 63-71; P-in-c Over Stowey w Aisholt *B & W* 71-73; V Nether Stowey 71-73; V Nether Stowey w Over Stowey 73-93;

RD Quantock 87-93; V Pitminster w Corfe 93-99; rtd 99; Perm to Offic *B & W* from 00. *Oratia, 9 Brookfield Way, Street BA16 0UE* Tel (01458) 442906

PARKER, Robert Nicolas. b 71. Nottm Univ BA93 PGCE95. Ridley Hall Cam 95. **d** 98 **p** 99. C Yardley St Edburgha *Birm* 98-02; Asst P Eugene St Mary USA 02-05; P-in-c Coleshill *Birm* 05-08; V from 08; P-in-c Maxstoke 05-08; V from 08. *The Vicarage, High Street, Coleshill, Birmingham B46 3BP* Tel (01675) 462188 E-mail nickthevicparker@btinternet.com

PARKER, Robert William. b 18. Linc Th Coll 81. **d** 81 **p** 82. NSM Mablethorpe w Trusthorpe *Linc* 81-83; NSM Alford w Rigsby 83-86; NSM Bilsby w Farlesthorpe 85-86; NSM Ford and Alberbury w Cardeston *Heref* 87-90; NSM Westbury 87-88; Perm to Offic *Linc* 90-99 and *Derby* 06-08. *Tedsmore Hall, West Felton, Oswestry SY11 4HD* Tel (01691) 610628 E-mail rgparker@tedsmorehall.co.uk

PARKER, Roger Thomas Donaldson. b 55. Simon Fraser Univ BC BA80 Univ of Wales (Cardiff) LLB84 Univ Coll Lon LLM85. Coll of Resurr Mirfield 95. **d** 95 **p** 96. C Swinton and Pendlebury *Man* 95-02; V Burnley St Cath w St Alb and St Paul *Blackb* from 02. *St Catherine's Parsonage, 156 Todmorden Road, Burnley BB11 3ER* Tel (01282) 424587 Fax 458579 Mobile 07977-291166 E-mail frrogerparker@aol.com

PARKER, Roland John Graham. b 48. AKC72 Hull Univ BA(Ed)83. St Aug Coll Cant 71. **d** 74 **p** 75. C Linc St Faith and St Martin w St Pet 74-78; V Appleby 78-84; Ind Chapl 78-84; V N Kelsey 84-92; V Cadney 84-92; P-in-c Waddington 92-97; R from 97. *The Rectory, Rectory Lane, Waddington, Lincoln LN5 9RS* Tel (01522) 720323 E-mail rolapark2@btinternet.com

PARKER, Russell Edward. b 48. Man Univ BA80. St Jo Coll Nottm MTh82. **d** 81 **p** 82. C Walmsley *Man* 81-85; V Coalville and Bardon Hill *Leic* 85-90; Dir Acorn Chr Foundn from 90. *Acorn Christian Foundation, Whitehill Chase, Bordon GU35 0AP* Tel (01420) 478121 E-mail rparker@acornchristian.org

PARKER, Stephen George. b 65. Birm Univ BEd89 MA97 PhD03. Qu Coll Birm 96. **d** 98. Teaching Asst Westhill Coll of HE Birm 98-01; Sen Lect Th Univ Coll Ches 01-04; Hd RS Cadbury Sixth Form Coll 04-08; Hd Postgraduate Studies in Educn Worc Univ from 08. *University of Worcester, Henwick Grove, Worcester WR2 6AJ* Tel (01905) 542165 E-mail s.parker@worc.ac.uk

PARKER, Stephen John. **d** 10 **p** 11. OLM Werrington and Wetley Rocks *Lich* from 10. *11 Tollbar Road, Werrington, Stoke-on-Trent ST9 0JG* Tel (01782) 851933 E-mail stephen.parker690@ntlworld.com

PARKER, Thomas Henry Louis. b 16. Em Coll Cam BA38 MA42 BD50 DD61. Lon Coll of Div 38. **d** 39 **p** 40. C Chesham St Mary *Ox* 39-42; C Cambridge St Phil *Ely* 42-43; C Cambridge St Andr Less 43-45; C Luddesdowne *Roch* 45-48; V Brothertoft *Linc* 48-55; R Lt Ponton w Stroxton 55-59; R Lt Ponton 59-61; R Gt Ponton 58-61; V Oakington *Ely* 61-71; Lect Dur Univ 71-81; rtd 81; Perm to Offic *Ely* 97-00. *Ceriogh, Flaggoners Green, Bromyard HR7 4QR* Tel (01885) 489307

PARKER, Thomas Richard. b 52. Imp Coll Lon BScEng73 Keele Univ MEd83. Cranmer Hall Dur. **d** 94 **p** 95. C Chadkirk *Ches* 94-08; RD Chadkirk 04-08; P-in-c Stalybridge H Trin and Ch Ch 08-11; V from 11. *277 Mottram Road, Stalybridge SK15 2RT* E-mail tom_parker@ntlworld.com

PARKER, Timothy James. b 82. Ch Ch Ox MPhys05. Wycliffe Hall Ox BA09. **d** 10 **p** 11. C Gamston and Bridgford *S'well* from 10. *9 Fountains Close, West Bridgford, Nottingham NG2 6LL* Tel 07719-268509 (mobile) E-mail timparker@gmx.net

PARKER, Timothy Percy. b 58. Man Univ BA. St Jo Coll Nottm. **d** 85 **p** 86. C Pitsmoor Ch Ch *Sheff* 85-87; C Kimberworth 87-89; C Brightside w Wincobank 89-91; C Upper Armley *Ripon* 91-95; TV Billingham St Aid *Dur* 95-97; V Billingham St Luke from 97. *17 Shadforth Drive, Billingham TS23 3PW* Tel (01642) 561870 E-mail timparker@ntlworld.com

PARKER-McGEE, Robert Thomas. b 78. Leeds Univ BA10. Coll of Resurr Mirfield 07. **d** 10 **p** 11. C Gornal and Sedgley *Worc* from 10. *2a The Straits, Lower Gornal, Dudley DY3 3AB* Tel (01384) 860525 Mobile 07588-801593 E-mail thepms@btinternet.com

PARKERSON, Trevor Richard. b 46. Qu Coll Birm 06. **d** 08 **p** 09. NSM Ashby-de-la-Zouch and Breedon on the Hill *Leic* from 08. *36 Ashby Road, Woodville, Swadlincote DE11 7BY* Tel (01283) 225408 E-mail trp@gofast.co.uk

PARKES, Mrs Celia Anne. b 50. STETS 06. **d** 09 **p** 10. NSM Bursledon *Win* from 09. *5 Cambrian Close, Bursledon, Southampton SO31 8GW* Tel (023) 8040 6363

PARKES, Edward Patrick. b 58. Crewe & Alsager Coll BEd80 Ban Univ MTh11. SWMTC 10. **d** 11. NSM Dawlish *Ex* from 11. *12 Ford Farm Court, Mamhead Road, Kenton, Exeter EX6 8LZ* Tel (01626) 899053 Mobile 07960-102001 E-mail ppp@tearfund.org

PARKES, Kevin. b 62. Trent Poly BA84. Sarum & Wells Th Coll BTh90. **d** 88 **p** 89. C Wandsworth St Anne *S'wark* 88-92; USPG 92-95; Trinidad and Tobago 93-95; Kingston Area Miss Team

S'wark 95-01; V Wandsworth Common St Mary 01-09; AD Tooting 07-09; Chapl Univ Coll Lon Hosps NHS Foundn Trust from 09. *UCLH NHS Foundation Trust, 235 Euston Road, London NW1 2BU* Tel 08451-555000 E-mail kevin.parkes@uclh.nhs.uk

PARKES, Patrick. *See* PARKES, Edward Patrick

PARKHILL, Alan John. b 43. TCD BA66. CITC 68. **d** 67 **p** 68. C Knockbreda *D & D* 67-70; Asst Warden Elswick Lodge Newc 71-72; C Bangor St Comgall 73-78; Bp's C Kilmore 78-82; I Kilmore and Inch 82-86; I Clonfeacle w Derrygortreavy *Arm* 86-09; rtd 09. *1 Rodney Park, Bangor BT19 6FN* Tel and fax (028) 9147 3916 E-mail aparkhill1@btinternet.com

PARKIN, Christopher. *See* PARKIN, Melvyn Christopher

PARKIN, George David. b 37. Cranmer Hall Dur BA60. **d** 62 **p** 63. C Balderstone *Man* 62-65; C Tunstead 65-67; C Gateshead Fell *Dur* 69-73; CMS Nigeria 74-76; V Walton Breck *Liv* 80-92; V Rawtenstall St Mary *Man* 92-07; P-in-c Constable Lee 02-07; rtd 07; Perm to Offic *Man* 07. *174 Bury Road, Rawtenstall, Rossendale BB4 6DJ* E-mail pamandco@googlemail.com

PARKIN, Mrs Jennifer Anne. b 47. Nene Coll Northn BEd85. WMMTC 95. **d** 98 **p** 99. C Northampton St Alb *Pet* 98-02; P-in-c Ecton 02-07; P-in-c Wootton w Quinton and Preston Deanery from 07; Chapl Cynthia Spencer Hospice 02-07; Warden of Past Assts *Pet* 06-10. *The Rectory, 67 Water Lane, Wootton, Northampton NN4 6HH* Tel (01604) 761891 E-mail parkinjen@btinternet.com

PARKIN, Canon John Edmund. b 44. Open Univ BA73. St Jo Coll Nottm 83. **d** 85 **p** 86. C Aberavon *Llan* 85-90; R Eglwysilan 90-01; P Missr Merthyr Tydfil Ch Ch 01-09; Hon Can Llan Cathl 09; rtd 09. *12 Heol Scwrfa, Merthyr Tydfil CF48 1HE*

PARKIN, John Francis. b 40. Linc Th Coll 65. **d** 68 **p** 69. C Cullercoats St Geo *Newc* 68-72; C Stony Stratford *Ox* 72-73; TV Lt Coates *Linc* 73-76; Perm to Offic 88-93; NSM Horncastle w Low Toynton 93-06; NSM High Toynton 93-06; NSM Horncastle Gp from 06. *The Firs, 68 Louth Road, Horncastle LN9 5LJ* Tel (01507) 523208

PARKIN, Jonathan Samuel. b 73. La Sainte Union Coll BTh95 Birm Univ MA97. Qu Coll Birm 98. **d** 98 **p** 99. C Skegness and Winthorpe *Linc* 98-01; Chapl Leic Coll of FE 01-03; Chapl De Montfort Univ 04-07; Chapl Leic Cathl 01-07; TV Market Harborough and The Transfiguration etc 07-11; P-in-c Welham, Glooston and Cranoe and Stonton Wyville 07-11; C Branston w Nocton and Potterhanworth *Linc* from 11; C Metheringham w Blankney and Dunston from 11. *The Rectory, 19 Abel Smith Gardens, Branston, Lincoln LN4 1NN* Tel (01522) 794275 E-mail parkin@tiscali.co.uk

PARKIN, Melvyn Christopher. b 57. NEOC 99. **d** 02 **p** 03. NSM Boston Spa *York* 02-03; C Elvington w Sutton on Derwent and E Cottingwith 03-06; R Howardian Gp from 06. *The Rectory, Terrington, York YO60 6PU* Tel (01653) 648226

PARKIN, Canon Trevor Kinross. b 37. MCMI. Cranmer Hall Dur 63. **d** 66 **p** 67. C Kingston upon Hull St Martin *York* 66-69; C Reading St Jo *Ox* 69-73; Ind Chapl *Lon* 73-80; Hon C Langham Place All So 73-80; Ind Chapl *Ely* 80-82; V Maidenhead St Andr and St Mary *Ox* 82-02; Hon Can Buckm from 00; rtd 02; Perm to Offic *Guildf* 03-07. *5 Hardwick Road, Eastbourne BN21 4NY* Tel (01323) 642287 E-mail trevorparkin@fsmail.net

PARKINSON, Alan. *See* PARKINSON, Thomas Alan

PARKINSON, Andrew. b 56. Keble Coll Ox BA77 MA80. Westcott Ho Cam 78. **d** 80 **p** 81. C S Shore H Trin *Blackb* 80-85; V Lea 85-94; V Longton from 94. *Longton Vicarage, Birchwood Avenue, Hutton, Preston PR4 5EE* Tel (01772) 612179 E-mail andrew.parkinson@talktalk.net

PARKINSON, Andrew. b 74. St Steph Ho Ox. **d** 01 **p** 02. C Lancaster Ch Ch *Blackb* 01-04; P-in-c Yarnton w Begbroke and Shipton on Cherwell *Ox* 04-05; TV Blenheim from 05. *The Rectory, 26 Church Lane, Yarnton, Kidlington OX5 1PY* Tel (01865) 375749

PARKINSON, Miss Brenda. b 40. Lancs Poly CQSW. Dalton Ho Bris 65. **dss** 74 **d** 87 **p** 94. Ribbleton *Blackb* 75-80; Ingol 82-88; Par Dn 87-88; Par Dn Ashton-on-Ribble St Mich 88-92; Par Dn Gt Marsden 92-94; C 94-98; C Gt Marsden w Nelson St Phil 99-00; rtd 00; Perm to Offic *Blackb* from 01. *18 Thorn Hill Close, Blackburn BB1 1YE* Tel (01254) 678367

PARKINSON, David Thomas. b 42. Linc Th Coll 77. **d** 79 **p** 80. C Yate New Town *Bris* 79-82; TV Keynsham *B & W* 82-88; R Bleadon 88-07; rtd 07. *Sherwell Court, 48 Old Church Road, Uphill, Weston-super-Mare BS23 4UP* E-mail dtparkinson@aol.com

PARKINSON, Derek Leslie. b 29. Ripon Hall Ox 64. **d** 66 **p** 67. C Guildf Ch Ch 66-69; P-in-c Preston St Sav *Blackb* 69-74; P-in-c Preston St Jas 69-74; P-in-c Fontmell Magna *Sarum* 74-81; P-in-c Ashmore 74-81; P-in-c Kingswood w Alderley and Hillesley *Glouc* 81-82; R 82-94; rtd 94. *25 Fountain Crescent, Wotton-under-Edge GL12 7LD*

PARKINSON, Francis Wilson. b 37. Open Univ BA80 MBACP. St Aid Birkenhead 59. **d** 62 **p** 63. C Monkwearmouth St Andr *Dur* 62-64; C Speke All SS *Liv* 64-67; CF 67-92; Perm to Offic *Ox* from 92. *9 Priory Mead, Longcot, Faringdon SN7 7TJ* Tel (01793) 784406

PARKINSON, Ian Richard. b 58. Dur Univ BA79 Lon Univ BD84. Wycliffe Hall Ox 80. **d** 83 **p** 84. C Hull St Jo Newland *York* 83-86; C Linthorpe 86-92; V Saltburn-by-the-Sea 92-01; V Marple All SS *Ches* from 01. *The Vicarage, 155 Church Lane, Marple, Stockport SK6 7LD* Tel and fax 0161-449 0950 *or* tel 427 2378 E-mail ian.parkinson7@ntlworld.com

PARKINSON, John Reginald. b 32. Qu Coll Birm 79. **d** 81 **p** 82. NSM Catshill *Worc* 81-85; C Knightwick w Doddenham, Broadwas and Cotheridge 85-88; C Martley and Wichenford 85-88; P-in-c Berrow w Pendock and Eldersfield 88-89; R Berrow w Pendock, Eldersfield, Hollybush etc 89-97; rtd 97; Perm to Offic *Glouc* and *Worc* from 97. *8 Glebe Close, Stow on the Wold, Cheltenham GL54 1DJ* Tel (01451) 830822

PARKINSON, Leslie. *See* PARKINSON, Derek Leslie

PARKINSON, Nicholas John. b 46. FCCA75 Cranfield Inst of Tech MBA85. St Alb Minl Tr Scheme 92. **d** 95 **p** 96. NSM Woburn Sands *St Alb* 95-98; NSM Westoning w Tingrith 98-01; NSM Woburn Sands from 01. *Thornbank House, 7 Church Road, Woburn Sands, Milton Keynes MK17 8TE* Tel (01908) 583397

PARKINSON, Peter. b 23. Roch Th Coll 61. **d** 63 **p** 64. C Linc St Mary-le-Wigford w St Martin 63-65; C Skegness 65-68; R Kettlethorpe 68-73; V Newton-on-Trent 68-73; V Grainthorpe w Conisholme 73-83; V Marshchapel 74-83; R N Coates 74-83; V Bicker 83-88; rtd 88. *11 Waltham Road, Lincoln LN6 0SD* Tel (01522) 680604

PARKINSON, Richard Duncan. ERMC. **d** 07 **p** 08. NSM Leverington, Newton and Tydd St Giles *Ely* 07-11; NSM Wisbech St Mary and Guyhirn w Ring's End etc from 11. *166 Leverington Common, Leverington, Wisbech PE13 5BP* Tel (01945) 465818 E-mail rykp@bigfoot.com

PARKINSON, Richard Francis. b 76. Cranmer Hall Dur. **d** 10 **p** 11. C Ilkley All SS *Bradf* from 10. *3 Low Beck, Ilkley LS29 8UN* Tel (01943) 604149 E-mail richard@poiema.co.uk

PARKINSON, Mrs Sarah Kathryn Rachel. b 80. Trin Coll Ox MMath02. Ripon Coll Cuddesdon BA06. **d** 07 **p** 08. NSM Steeple Aston w N Aston and Tackley *Ox* 07-10; Perm to Offic from 10; Chapl HM Pris Bullingdon 05-08; Manager Relig Affairs Campsfield Ho Immigration Removal Cen from 08. *Campsfield House, Langford Lane, Kidlington OX5 1RE* Tel (01865) 233000 E-mail sparkinson@thegeogroupinc.co.uk

PARKINSON, Simon George Denis. b 39. Univ of Wales (Lamp) BA66. Westcott Ho Cam 65. **d** 67 **p** 68. C Rothwell *Ripon* 67-70; Chapl RAF 70-73; C Leeds St Pet *Ripon* 74-75; V Horbury Junction *Wakef* 76-83; V Hanging Heaton 83-92; P-in-c Upper Hopton 92; V Eastthorpe and Upper Hopton 92-02; rtd 02. *126 Edge Lane, Dewsbury WF12 0HB* Tel (01924) 508885 E-mail sgdparkinson@hotmail.com

PARKINSON, Thomas Alan. b 40. St Jo Coll York CertEd61. NW Ord Course 75. **d** 78 **p** 79. NSM Sheff St Cecilia Parson Cross 78-82; NSM Goldthorpe w Hickleton 82-90; C Cantley 90-01; Dioc RE and Worship Adv 93-04; V Ryecroft St Nic 02-10; rtd 10; Perm to Offic *Sheff* from 10; CMP from 00. *40 South Street, Rawmarsh, Rotherham S62 5RG* Tel (01709) 525654

PARKINSON, Vivian Leslie. b 54. St Luke's Coll Ex CertEd76 Brighton Poly BEd87. St Jo Coll Nottm. **d** 94 **p** 95. C Cowbridge *Llan* 94-97; V Llantrisant from 97; AD Pontypridd 06-10. *The Vicarage, Coed yr Esgob, Llantrisant, Pontyclun CF72 8EL* Tel (01443) 223356 *or* 237983 Fax 230631 E-mail vivparkinson@parishofllantrisant.org.uk

PARKMAN, Mrs Michelle Joy. b 77. SS Mark & Jo Univ Coll Plymouth BA00. Trin Coll Bris BA08. **d** 08 **p** 09. C Nailsea H Trin *B & W* from 08. *3 St Mary's Grove, Nailsea, Bristol BS48 4NQ* Tel 07740-366597 (mobile) E-mail mparkman@hotmail.co.uk

PARKS, Paul. b 59. K Coll Lon BA96. St Jo Coll Nottm MA97. **d** 98 **p** 99. C S Molton w Nymet St George, High Bray etc *Ex* 98-04; P-in-c Hurst *Ox* 04-05; C Wokingham St Sebastian 05-07; TV Wednesfield *Lich* 07-11; V Hoddesdon *St Alb* from 11. *The Vicarage, 11 Oxenden Drive, Hoddesdon EN11 8QF* Tel (01992) 302008 E-mail revpaulparks@virginmedia.com

PARMENTER, Canon Deirdre Joy. b 45. EAMTC 91. **d** 94 **p** 95. C Ipswich St Aug *St E* 94-97; P-in-c Haughley w Wetherden 97-00; V Haughley w Wetherden and Stowupland 00-07; RD Stowmarket 99-05; Bp's Chapl 07-10; Dioc Adv for Women's Min 08-10; Hon Can St E Cathl 03-10; rtd 10; Perm to Offic *St E* from 10; Dioc Warden of Readers from 10. *Avalon, Marlesford Road, Campsea Ashe, Woodbridge IP13 0QG* Tel (01728) 748145 E-mail deirdre@stedmundsbury.anglican.org

PARNELL, Bryan Donald. b 38. JP. DipEd88. Chich Th Coll 66. **d** 69 **p** 70. C Lewisham St Jo Southend S'wark 69-72; Asst Chapl Colleg Sch of St Pet Australia 72-76; R Angaston 76-78; Chapl RAN 78-88; R Edwardstown 89-02; rtd 02. *PO Box 6619, Halifax Street, Adelaide SA 5000, Australia* Tel (0061) (8) 4100337 Mobile 414-692340 E-mail trinitas@senet.com.au

PARR, Mrs Anne Patricia. b 38. Nottm Univ CertEd59. **d** 07 **p** 08. OLM Penistone and Thurlstone *Wakef* from 07. *7 Rydal Close, Penistone, Sheffield S36 8HN* Tel (01226) 764490 Mobile 07971-513301 E-mail mail@anneparr.co.uk

PARR (née JOHNSON), Mrs Claire Elisabeth. b 83. Wheaton Coll Illinois BA05. Ridley Hall Cam 08. **d** 10 **p** 11. C Melksham *Sarum* from 10; C Broughton Gifford, Gt Chalfield and Holt from 10. *The Rectory, Canon Square, Melksham SN12 6LX* Tel (01225) 703262 E-mail claire.e.johnson@gmail.com

PARR, Clive William. b 41. FCIS. WEMTC 02. **d** 03 **p** 04. NSM Evesham w Norton and Lenchwick *Worc* 03-07; NSM Hampton w Sedgeberrow and Hinton-on-the-Green from 07; Bp's Health Service Adv from 08. *Grace Cottage, Mill Lane, Elmley Castle, Pershore WR10 3HP* Tel (01386) 710700 Fax 761214 Mobile 07801-820006

PARR, David Jonathan. b 77. Chelt & Glouc Coll of HE BA98. Trin Coll Bris BA04. **d** 04 **p** 05. C Whitchurch *Ex* 04-08; C Shepton Mallet w Doulting *B & W* 08-10; TV Melksham *Sarum* from 10. *The Rectory, Canon Square, Melksham SN12 6LX* Tel (01225) 703262 E-mail davejparr@yahoo.co.uk

PARR, Frank. b 35. Nottm Univ BCombStuds82 Lanc Univ MA86. Linc Th Coll 79. **d** 82 **p** 83. C Padiham *Blackb* 82-85; P-in-c Accrington St Andr 85-88; V Oswaldtwistle Immanuel and All SS 88-96; V Tunstall w Melling and Leck 96-01; rtd 01; Perm to Offic *Blackb* from 01 and *Bradf* from 04. *1 Bank View, Burton Road, Lower Bentham, Lancaster LA2 7DZ* Tel (015242) 61159 E-mail frank_parr@lineone.net

PARR, Jeffrey John. b 48. FCA73. EMMTC 03. **d** 06 **p** 07. NSM Bassingham Gp *Linc* 06-09; NSM Claypole 09-10; Lic to Offic from 10. *3 Manor Paddocks, Bassingham, Lincoln LN5 9GW* Tel (01522) 789869 Mobile 07785-281215 E-mail jparr@chesapeake.co.uk

PARR, John. b 53. St Edm Hall Ox BA74 MA87 Lon Univ BD79 Sheff Univ PhD90. Trin Coll Bris 75. **d** 79 **p** 80. C Gt Crosby St Luke *Liv* 79-82; C Walton St Mary 82-84; V Ince St Mary 84-87; Tutor and Lect Ridley Hall Cam 87-95; Chapl 87-93; Dir Studies 93-95; CME Officer *Ely* 95-99; P-in-c Harston w Hauxton 95-99; P-in-c Newton 97-99; Can Res and CME Officer *St E* 99-09; Perm to Offic 06-09; TR Bury St Edmunds All SS w St Jo and St Geo from 09. *All Saints' Vicarage, 59 Bennett Avenue, Bury St Edmunds IP33 3JJ* Tel (01284) 701063 E-mail parr28@btinternet.com

PARR, Mabel Ann. b 37. CBDTI 07. **d** 07 **p** 08. NSM Bentham *Bradf* 07-10; Perm to Offic *Blackb* from 10. *1 Bank View, Burton Road, Lower Bentham, Lancaster LA2 7DZ* Tel (015242) 61159 E-mail f.parr207@btinternet.com

PARR, Miss Vanessa Caroline. b 78. Lanc Univ BA00. Trin Coll Bris BA07. **d** 08 **p** 09. C Hoddesdon *St Alb* 08-11; C Edin St Paul and St Geo from 11. *Flat 11, 52 East Fettes Avenue, Edinburgh EH4 1FJ* Tel 07811-444435 (mobile) E-mail vanessa_parr@yahoo.co.uk

PARRATT, Dennis James. b 53. Glos Coll of Art & Design BA74. St Steph Ho Ox 82. **d** 84 **p** 85. C Cainscross w Selsley *Glouc* 84-88; C Old Shoreham and New Shoreham *Chich* 88-91; Perm to Offic *Glouc* 01-08. *11 Millbrook Gardens, Cheltenham GL50 3RQ* Tel (01242) 525730 E-mail djparratt@hotmail.co.uk

PARRETT, Mrs Mary Margaret. b 42. Shenstone Coll of Educn DipEd63. St Alb Minl Tr Scheme 86. **d** 98 **p** 99. NSM Barton-le-Cley w Higham Gobion and Hexton *St Alb* 98-06; Perm to Offic from 06; NSM Officer Bedford Adnry from 10. *49 Manor Road, Barton-le-Clay, Bedford MK45 4NP* Tel (01582) 883089 E-mail mary.parrett@btinternet.com

PARRETT, Mrs Rosalind Virginia. b 43. Ox Brookes Univ MTh02. Cant Sch of Min 84. **d** 87 **p** 94. NSM Selling w Throwley, Sheldwich w Badlesmere etc *Cant* 87-91; Asst Chapl Cant Hosp 87-91; Par Dn Stantonbury and Willen *Ox* 91-94; TV 94-96; P-in-c Owlsmoor 96-98; V 98-03; rtd 03; Perm to Offic *Cant* 03-04; Hon C Faversham 04-11; Hon C Goodnestone St Bart and Graveney 04-10; Perm to Offic from 11. *16 Hilton Close, Faversham ME13 8NN* Tel (01795) 530380 Mobile 07881-788155 E-mail revros@talktalk.net

PARRETT, Simon Christopher. b 60. Sarum & Wells Th Coll. **d** 87 **p** 88. C Ifield *Chich* 87-91; Chapl to the Deaf *Sarum* 91-94; NSM Bournemouth H Epiphany *Win* 94-96; Asst Chapl Poole Hosp NHS Trust 96-03; Chapl Dorothy House Hospice Winsley 01-04. *252 The Common, Holt, Trowbridge BA14 6QN* Tel (01225) 783163

PARRETT, Stephen. b 65. Cant Ch Ch Univ Coll BA96. **d** 07 **p** 08. OLM Herne Bay Ch Ch *Cant* from 07. *1 Birkdale Gardens, Herne Bay CT6 7TS* Tel (01227) 360139 Mobile 07742-439563 E-mail stephenparrett@lycos.co.uk

PARRI, Emyr. Univ of Wales BA96 FRAS. Ban & St As Minl Tr Course 98. **d** 98 **p** 99. NSM Tregarth *Ban* 98-04; Bp's Chapl 04-07. *Bryn Awel, Sling, Tregarth, Bangor LL57 4RH* Tel (01248) 602176

PARRISH, Ian Robert. b 62. SEITE 05. **d** 09 **p** 10. C Kingsnorth and Shadoxhurst *Cant* 09-10; C Maidstone St Paul from 11. *5 Furfield Chase, Boughton Monchelsea, Maidstone ME17 4GD* Tel (01622) 763363 E-mail ian.parrish@lenham.com

PARRISH, Robert Carey. b 57. St Steph Ho Ox 89. **d** 91 **p** 92. C Abington *Pet* 91-94; C Leckhampton SS Phil and Jas w Cheltenham St Jas *Glouc* 94-97; PV Llan Cathl 97-02; R Merthyr

Dyfan from 02. *Merthyr Dyfan Rectory, 10 Buttrills Road, Barry CF62 8EF* Tel (01446) 735943

PARROTT, David Wesley. b 58. Univ of Wales (Cardiff) LLM01. Oak Hill Th Coll BA. **d** 84 **p** 85. C Thundersley *Chelmsf* 84-87; C Rainham 87-89; P-in-c Heydon w Gt and Lt Chishill 89-90; P-in-c Chrishall 89-90; P-in-c Elmdon w Wendon Lofts and Strethall 89-90; R Heydon, Gt and Lt Chishill, Chrishall etc 91-96; R Rayleigh 96-00; TR 00-04; RD Rochford 02-04; Barking Area CME Adv 04-09; C Hornchurch St Andr 05-09; Hon Can Chelmsf Cathl 07-09; V St Lawr Jewry *Lon* from 09. *St Lawrence Jewry Vicarage, Church Passage, London EC2V 5AA* Tel (020) 7600 9478 E-mail dwparrott01@aol.com

PARROTT, George. b 37. Leeds Univ BA61. Bps' Coll Cheshunt 61. **d** 63 **p** 64. C Lower Mitton *Worc* 63-65; C-in-c Fairfield St Rich CD 65-68; Zambia 68-70; C Cleethorpes *Linc* 70-75; R Withern 75-80; P-in-c Gayton le Marsh 76-80; P-in-c Strubby 76-80; P-in-c Authorpe 76-80; P-in-c Belleau w Aby and Claythorpe 76-80; P-in-c N and S Reston 76-80; P-in-c Swaby w S Thoresby 76-80; R Withern 80-90; V Reston 80-90; V Messingham 90-93; P-in-c Fincham *Ely* 95-02; P-in-c Marham 95-02; P-in-c Shouldham 95-02; P-in-c Shouldham Thorpe 95-02; rtd 02; Perm to Offic *Linc* from 03. *8 Anson Close, Skellingthorpe, Lincoln LN6 5TH* Tel (01522) 694417

PARROTT, Canon Gerald Arthur. b 32. St Cath Coll Cam BA56 MA60. Chich Th Coll. **d** 58 **p** 59. C Ashington *Newc* 58-61; C Brighton St Pet *Chich* 61-63; V Leeds St Wilfrid *Ripon* 63-68; R Lewisham St Jo Southend *S'wark* 69-73; TR Catford (Southend) and Downham 73-77; RD E Lewisham 75-77; Can Res and Prec S'wark Cathl 77-88; TR Wimbledon 88-95; rtd 95; Perm to Offic *Chich* from 95. *10 Palings Way, Fernhurst, Haslemere GU27 3HJ* Tel (01428) 641533

PARROTT, Martin William. b 57. Keele Univ BA79 Lon Univ PGCE80. Ripon Coll Cuddesdon 82. **d** 85 **p** 86. C Birchfield *Birm* 85-88; Chapl Lon Univ 88-93; P-in-c Univ Ch Ch the K Lon 90-93; V Hebden Bridge *Wakef* 93-01; Asst Chapl Pinderfields and Pontefract Hosps NHS Trust 01-02; Chapl Calderdale and Huddersfield NHS Trust from 02. *The Royal Infirmary, Acre Street, Lindley, Huddersfield HD3 3EA* Tel (01484) 342000 E-mail martin.parrott@cht.nhs.uk

PARRY, Canon Alfred Charles Ascough. b 37. Natal Univ BA58. Westcott Ho Cam 59. **d** 61 **p** 62. C E Ham w Upton Park *Chelmsf* 61-63; C Durban N St Martin S Africa 63-64; R Newcastle H Trin 64-70; Dir Chr Educn Kloof 70-76; Sub Dean Pietermaritzburg 76-81; R Estcourt 81; Adn N Natal 81-85; R Kloof 86-93; R Berea 93-98; Hon Can Pietermaritzburg from 86; Sen Asst Min Hornchurch St Andr *Chelmsf* 99-04; C Furze Platt *Ox* 04-05; Hon C 05-07; rtd 05. *45 Windmill Drive, Croxley Green, Rickmansworth WD3 3FF* Tel (01923) 771037

PARRY, Andrew Martyn. b 61. Witwatersrand Univ BA81 MBA91 Open Univ BSc04. Ox Min Course 06. **d** 09 **p** 10. NSM Horton and Wraysbury *Ox* from 09. *2 Pennylets Green, Stoke Poges, Slough SL2 4BT* Tel (01753) 644239 E-mail andrew@vamparry.eclipse.co.uk

PARRY, Canon Bryan Horace. b 33. St Mich Coll Llan 65. **d** 67 **p** 68. C Holyhead w Rhoscolyn w Llanfair-yn-Neubwll *Ban* 67-71; TV 71-73; P-in-c Small Heath St Greg *Birm* 73-78; V 78-80; V Perry Barr 80-94; RD Handsworth 83-91; P-in-c Kingstanding St Luke 86-92; Hon Can Birm Cathl 87-94; rtd 94; Perm to Offic *Nor* from 94. *St Seiriol, Old Crown Yard, Walsingham NR22 6BU* Tel (01328) 820019

PARRY, Charles. See PARRY, Canon Alfred Charles Ascough

PARRY, David Allan. b 62. Bris Univ BSc83 Univ of Wales (Cardiff) CQSW88. Trin Coll Bris. **d** 94 **p** 95. C Withywood *Bris* 94-98; P-in-c Litherland St Phil *Liv* 98-02; V 02-06; Hon Chapl to the Deaf 00-05; AD Bootle 02-05; Hon Can Liv Cathl 03-05; Dioc Dir of Ords from 05; V Toxteth Park Ch Ch and St Mich w St Andr from 06. *St Michael's Vicarage, St Michael's Church Road, Liverpool L17 7BD* Tel 0151-286 2411

PARRY, David Thomas Newton. b 45. Selw Coll Cam BA67 MA71. Lambeth STh76 Cuddesdon Coll 67. **d** 69 **p** 70. C Oldham St Mary w St Pet *Man* 69-73; C Baguley 73-74; Tutor Sarum & Wells Th Coll 74-78; V Westleigh St Pet *Man* 78-88; TR E Farnworth and Kearsley 88-97; TR Chambersbury *St Alb* 97-03; V Blackbird Leys w Llangurig 89-01; rtd 11. *32 Barry Road, Pontypridd CF37 1HY* E-mail davidparry912@btinternet.com

PARRY, Denis. b 34. Sarum & Wells Th Coll 83. **d** 85 **p** 86. C Hubberston w Herbrandston and Hasguard etc *St D* 85-89; P-in-c Herbrandston and Hasguard w St Ishmael's 89-90; R 90-99; Dioc RE Adv 89-99; rtd 99; Perm to Offic *Heref* from 99. *Mayfield, 33 Mill Street, Kington HR5 3AL* Tel (01544) 230550

PARRY, Canon Dennis John. b 38. Univ of Wales (Lamp) BA60. St Mich Coll Llan 60. **d** 62 **p** 63. C Caerphilly *Llan* 62-64; C Aberdare St Fagan 64-67; Miss at Povungnituk Canada 67-69; R Gelligaer *Llan* 69-75; V Llanwnnog and Caersws w Carno *Ban* 75-89; V Llanidloes w Llangurig 89-01; RD Arwystli 89-01; Hon Can Ban Cathl 90-01; Can Cursal 97-01; rtd 02; Perm to Offic *Ban* from 02. *Lock Cottage, Groesfford, Brecon LD3 7UY* Tel (01874) 665400 E-mail dj519@btinternet.com

PARRY, Derek Nugent Goulding. b 32. Ely Th Coll 60. **d** 63 **p** 64. C Fareham SS Pet and Paul *Portsm* 63-67; C Portsea N End St Mark 67-74; P-in-c Piddletrenthide w Plush, Alton Pancras etc *Sarum* 74-92; rtd 92; Perm to Offic *Sarum* from 92. *Farthing Cottage, 12 Fordington Green, Dorchester DT1 1LU* Tel (01305) 269794

PARRY, Gordon Martyn Winn. b 47. Down Coll Cam BA68 MA70 Univ Coll Chich MA02. **d** 04 **p** 05. NSM Turners Hill *Chich* 04-07; NSM E Grinstead St Swithun from 07. *36 Hocken Mead, Crawley RH10 3UL* Tel 07802-432398 (mobile) E-mail gordonmwparry@btinternet.com

PARRY, Jane. See PARRY, Mrs Patricia Jane

PARRY, John Gareth. b 61. Univ of Wales (Abth) BA83 Univ of Wales (Ban) PGCE84. Westcott Ho Cam 94. **d** 96 **p** 97. C Holyhead *Ban* 96-99; C-in-c Llandinorwig w Penisa'r-waen 99-00; Perm to Offic from 00; Asst Master Bodedern Secondary Sch 00-01; Hd RE Pensby High Sch for Boys Wirral 02; Chapl and Hd RE Tettenhall Coll Wolv 03-09; Chapl Prestfelde Sch Shrewsbury 09-11; Chapl Oswestry Sch from 11. *34 Merton Park, Penmaenmawr LL34 6DH* Tel (01492) 622671 E-mail penmaen86@hotmail.com

PARRY, Keith Melville. b 31. MRICS65. S'wark Ord Course 80. **d** 83 **p** 84. NSM Bexley St Jo *Roch* 83-88; C Orpington All SS 88-96; rtd 96; Perm to Offic *Roch* from 96. *5 Greenside, Bexley DA5 3PA* Tel (01322) 555425

PARRY, Canon Kenneth Charles. b 34. Ripon Hall Ox 56. **d** 58 **p** 59. C Stoke *Cov* 58-61; Chapl RN 61-65; V Cradley *Worc* 65-70; V Gt Malvern H Trin 70-83; RD Malvern 74-83; Hon Can Worc Cathl 80-83; V Budleigh Salterton *Ex* 83-91; Can Res and Prec Ex Cathl 91-00; rtd 00. *Brook Cottage, Pye Corner, Kennford, Exeter EX6 7TB* Tel (01392) 832767 E-mail kcparry@ic24.net

PARRY, Ms Manon Ceridwen. b 69. Poly of Wales BA90 Selw Coll Cam BA93 MA97. Ridley Hall Cam. **d** 94 **p** 97. C Llandudno *Ban* 94-98; P-in-c Glanogwen w St Ann's w Llanllechid 98-99; V 99-05; V Pentir 04-05; Dir of Ords 02-05; C Llanrhos *St As* 05-07; Dioc Dir Lifelong Learning 05-08; R Llanddulas and Llysfaen from 08. *The Rectory, 2 Rhoddfa Wen, Llysfaen, Colwyn Bay LL29 8LE* Tel (01492) 516728 E-mail manon.parry@sky.com

PARRY, Canon Marilyn Marie. b 46. W Coll Ohio BA68 Man Univ MA77 PhD00. Episc Th Sch Cam Mass 68 Gilmore Ho 76. **dss** 79 **d** 87 **p** 94. Westleigh St Pet *Man* 78-85; Chapl Asst N Man Gen Hosp 85-90; Tutor NOC 90-97; Dir Studies 91-97; Lic Preacher *Man* 90-94; Hon C E Farnworth and Kearsley 94-97; Nat Adv for Pre-Th Educn and Selection Sec Min Division Abps' Coun 97-01; Public Preacher *St Alb* 98-01; Can Res Ch Ch *Ox* from 01; Dioc Dir of Ords 01-10; IME Officer 10-11; rtd 11. *32 Barry Road, Pontypridd CF37 1HY* Tel 07952-309667 (mobile) E-mail marilyn@parsonage.org.uk

PARRY, Nicholas John Sinclair. b 56. Sarum & Wells Th Coll 82. **d** 85 **p** 86. C Hendon St Mary *Lon* 85-87; C Verwood *Sarum* 87-90; TV Witney *Ox* 90-96; V Costessey *Nor* from 96. *The Vicarage, Folgate Lane, Costessey, Norwich NR8 5DP* Tel (01603) 742818 E-mail nicholas.parry@btinternet.com

PARRY, Mrs Olwen Margaret. b 45. Cardiff Coll of Educn CertEd67. Llan Dioc Tr Scheme 88. **d** 92 **p** 97. NSM Newcastle *Llan* 92-04; NSM Llansantffraid, Bettws and Aberkenfig from 04. *17 Wernlys Road, Bridgend CF31 4NS* Tel (01656) 721860

PARRY, Owen Benjamin. b 42. St As Minl Tr Course 99. **d** 01 **p** 02. C Llangollen w Trevor and Llantysilio *St As* 01-07; rtd 07; C-in-c Pradoe *Lich* from 09. *Fairways, Halton, Chirk, Wrexham LL14 5BD* Tel (01691) 778484

PARRY, Mrs Patricia Jane. b 54. Liv Univ BTh99. NOC 97. **d** 99 **p** 00. C Wilmslow *Ches* 99-03; V Baddiley and Wrenbury w Burleydam 03-08; V Alderley Edge from 08. *The Vicarage, Church Lane, Alderley Edge SK9 7UZ* Tel (01625) 583249 E-mail formidocornicarum@hotmail.com

PARRY, Peter John. b 42. Westmr Coll Ox BTh99. EAMTC 99. **d** 01 **p** 02. NSM Montreux w Gstaad *Eur* 01-06; Perm to Offic *Pet* from 05. *Forge House, Church Road, Hargrave, Wellingborough NN9 6BQ* E-mail phwparry@btinternet.com

PARRY, Miss Violet Margaret. b 30. Selly Oak Coll 53. **dss** 82 **d** 87. W Kilburn St Luke w St Simon and St Jude *Lon* 82-83; St Marylebone St Mary 83-86; Stamford All SS w St Jo *Linc* 86-90; C 87-90; rtd 90; Perm to Offic *Linc* 90-01 and *Leic* from 03. *2 Stuart Court, High Street, Kibworth, Leicester LE8 0LR* Tel 0116-279 6858

PARRY-JENNINGS, Christopher William. b 34. Lon Coll of Div 57. **d** 60 **p** 62. C Claughton cum Grange *Ches* 60-63; C Folkestone H Trin w Ch Ch *Cant* 63-67; New Zealand from 67; V Lincoln 67-72; Chapl Cant Univ 68-72; V Riccarton St Jas 72-88; V Heathcote Mt Pleasant 88-96; First Gen Sec SPCK (NZ) 89-90; P Asst Upper Riccarton St Pet from 96. *22 Ambleside Drive, Burnside, Christchurch 8053, New Zealand* Tel and fax (0064) (3) 358 9304 E-mail chpj@globe.net.nz

PARRY JONES, Leonard. b 29. Univ of Wales (Ban) BA52. St Mich Coll Llan 52. **d** 54 **p** 55. C Newtown w Llanllwchaiarn w Aberhafesp *St As* 54-58; C Abergele 58-60; V Pennant, Hirnant and Llangynog 60-65; V Llanynys w Llanychan 65-71; V Brynymaen w Trofarth 71-94; RD Rhos 77-94; rtd 94. *The Cottage, Kerry, Newtown SY16 4NU* Tel (01686) 670822

PARSELL, Howard Vivian. b 60. Univ of Wales (Lamp) BA87 Univ of Wales (Swansea) PGCE88. St Mich Coll Llan 93. **d** 94 **p** 95. C Builth and Llanddewi'r Cwm w Llangynog etc *S & B* 94-96; C Swansea St Thos and Kilvey 96-98; P-in-c Swansea St Jude 98-09; V Swansea St Jude w St Nic from 09; Chapl to the Deaf from 98; AD Swansea from 04. *St Nicholas' Vicarage, 58A Dyfed Avenue, Townhill, Swansea SA1 6NG* Tel (01792) 473154

PARSELLE, Stephen Paul. b 53. Univ of Wales (Cardiff) MTh06. St Jo Coll Nottm. **d** 82 **p** 83. C Boscombe St Jo *Win* 82-86; CF 86-05; Dir of Ords 02-05; Chapl RN 05-08. *11 Southbourne Overcliff Drive, Bournemouth BH6 3TE* Tel (01202) 433858 Mobile 07711-017282 E-mail parselle@aol.com

PARSONAGE, Robert Hugh. b 55. Nottm Trent Univ BSc78. Trin Coll Bris BA97. **d** 97 **p** 98. C Chell *Lich* 97-01; R Poringland *Nor* from 01; RD Loddon from 10. *The Rectory, Rectory Lane, Poringland, Norwich NR14 7SL* Tel (01508) 492215 E-mail rector@poringland-benefice.org.uk

PARSONS, Andrew David. b 53. UEA BA74 Fitzw Coll Cam BA77 MA81. Westcott Ho Cam 75. **d** 78 **p** 79. C Hellesdon *Nor* 78-82; C Eaton 82-85; P-in-c Burnham Thorpe w Burnham Overy 85-87; R Burnham Sutton w Burnham Ulph etc 85-87; R Burnham Gp of Par 87-93; P-in-c Wroxham w Hoveton and Belaugh 93; R 93-07; RD St Benet 99-07; V Old Catton from 07. *St Margaret's Vicarage, 1 Parkside Drive, Norwich NR6 7DP* Tel (01603) 425615 E-mail 2andrew@andrewparsons.fsnet.co.uk

PARSONS, Christopher Paul. b 58. EAMTC 01. **d** 04 **p** 05. C Pakenfield *Nor* 04-08; P-in-c Kenwyn w St Allen *Truro* from 08. *The Vicarage, Kenwyn Church Road, Truro TR1 3DR* Tel (01872) 263015 E-mail chris@cpp1.freeserve.co.uk

PARSONS, David Norman. b 39. FCIB83. Trin Coll Bris 92. **d** 94 **p** 95. NSM Swindon Dorcan *Bris* 94-03; Perm to Offic *Glouc* from 03. *31 Couzens Close, Chipping Sodbury, Bristol BS37 6BT* Tel (01454) 323070 E-mail david.parsons1@virgin.net

PARSONS, Mrs Deborah Anne. b 66. Surrey Univ BA87. STETS 04. **d** 07. C Goodrington *Ex* 07-11; TV Totnes w Bridgetown, Berry Pomeroy etc from 11. *St John's Vicarage, Crosspark, Totnes TQ9 5BQ* Tel (01803) 840113 E-mail d.a.parsons@btinternet.com

PARSONS, Desmond John. b 25. Coll of Resurr Mirfield 55. **d** 66 **p** 67. C Purley St Mark *S'wark* 66-70; V W Dulwich All SS and Em 71-83; R Limpsfield and Titsey 83-95; rtd 95; Perm to Offic *Guildf* and *S'wark* from 96. *Priors House, The Court, Croft Lane, Crondall, Farnham GU10 5QF* Tel (01252) 851137

PARSONS, Geoffrey Fairbanks. b 35. Trin Coll Cam BA58 MA68. Ridley Hall Cam 59. **d** 61 **p** 62. C Over St Chad *Ches* 61-64; C Heswall 64-69; V Congleton St Steph 69-75; V Weaverham 75-94; P-in-c Backford and Capenhurst 94-00; R 00-01; rtd 01; Perm to Offic *Ches* from 02. *28 Springcroft, Parkgate, South Wirral CH64 6SE* Tel 0151-336 3354

PARSONS, George Edward. b 35. St D Coll Lamp BA60 Ripon Hall Ox 60. **d** 62 **p** 63. C Leominster *Heref* 62-66; NSM Bromfield 67-72; NSM Culmington w Onibury 67-72; NSM Stanton Lacy 67-72; NSM Ludlow 72-77; P-in-c Caynham 77-79; NSM Bishop's Cleeve *Glouc* 79-91; Sub-Chapl HM Pris Glouc 88-91; P-in-c Hasfield w Tirley and Ashleworth 91-00; P-in-c Maisemore 91-00; rtd 00; Perm to Offic *Glouc* 00-02 and *Blackb* from 02. *Ballalona, 2 The Meadows, Hollins Lane, Forton, Preston PR3 0AF* Tel (01524) 792656

PARSONS, George Horace Norman. b 19. S'wark Ord Course 65. **d** 68 **p** 69. C Hatcham St Cath *S'wark* 68-72; C Horley 72-76; P-in-c S Wimbledon All SS 76-78; P-in-c Caterham 78-81; C Caterham and Chapl St Lawr Hosp Caterham 82-84; RAChD 72-84; rtd 85; Perm to Offic *S'wark* from 85. *15 Whitgift House, 76 Brighton Road, Croydon CR2 6AB* Tel (020) 8680 0028

PARSONS, Canon Jennifer Anne. b 53. Univ of Wales (Lamp) BA76 MA78 Jes Coll Cam PhD90. Westcott Ho Cam 92. **d** 94 **p** 95. C Halesowen *Worc* 94-97; TV Worc St Barn w Ch Ch 97-04; R Matson *Glouc* from 04; Hon Can Glouc Cathl from 07; Asst Dean of Women Clergy 09-11. *The Rectory, Matson Lane, Gloucester GL4 6DX* Tel (01452) 522598 E-mail jeni@hencity.fsnet.co.uk

PARSONS, Jeremy Douglas Adam. b 80. Ox Univ MA. Ridley Hall Cam. **d** 09 **p** 11. NSM Cambridge St Martin *Ely* from 09. *8A Saxon Street, Cambridge CB2 1HN* Tel (01223) 665420 Mobile 07980-016974 E-mail jdap@parsonses.co.uk

PARSONS, Canon John Banham. b 43. Selw Coll Cam BA65 MA68. Ridley Hall Cam 65. **d** 67 **p** 68. C Downend *Bris* 67-71; Public Preacher Withywood LEP 71-77; P-in-c Hengrove 77-78; V 78-85; V Letchworth St Paul w Willian *St Alb* 85-94; P-in-c Barking St Marg w St Patr *Chelmsf* 94-98; TR 98-04; RD Barking and Dagenham 00-04; P-in-c Hornchurch H Cross 04-09; RD Havering 04-08; Hon Can Chelmsf Cathl 01-09; rtd 09. *8 Pound Close, Upper Caldecote, Biggleswade SG18 9AU* Tel (01767) 315285 E-mail j.parsons986@btinternet.com

PARSONS, Canon Marlene Beatrice. b 43. Wilson Carlile Coll. dss 76 **d** 87 **p** 94. Coulsdon St Jo *S'wark* 76-79; Hill *Birm* 79-86;

Dioc Lay Min Adv 80-90; Vice Prin WMMTC 86-90; Dioc Dir of Ords *Birm* 90-04; Dean of Women's Min 90-04; Hon Can Birm Cathl 89-04; rtd 04; Perm to Offic *Birm* from 04. *20 Copperbeech Close, Birmingham B32 2HT* Tel 0121-427 2632

PARSONS, Miss Mary Elizabeth. b 43. Wilson Carlile Coll 65. dss 78 **d** 87 **p** 94. Chapl Asst Chu Hosp Ox 78-89; Chapl 89-93; rtd 93; NSM Sandford-on-Thames *Ox* 94-00. *20 Copperbeech Close, Birmingham B32 2HT* Tel 0121-426 4527

PARSONS, Michael. b 46. Open Univ BA84. SWMTC 05. **d** 08 **p** 09. NSM Boscastle w Davidstow *Truro* from 08. *2 Penally Terrace, Boscastle PL35 0HA* Tel (01840) 250625 E-mail mike@2penally.co.uk

PARSONS, Canon Michael William Semper. b 47. St Cath Coll Ox BA69 MA74 DPhil74 Selw Coll Cam BA77 MA81. Ridley Hall Cam 75. **d** 78 **p** 79. C Edmonton All SS *Lon* 78-81; SPCK Research Fell Dur Univ 81-84; Hon Lect Th 84-85; SPCK Fell N of England Inst for Chr Educn 84-85; P-in-c Derby St Aug 85-95; TR Walbrook Epiphany 95-96; Dioc Voc Adv 86-96; P-in-c Hempsted *Glouc* 96-00; Dir of Ords 96-04; Dir Curates' Tr 00-04; Prin WEMTC from 04; Prin Lect Glos Univ from 09; Hon Can Glouc Cathl from 03. *6 Spa Villas, Montpellier, Gloucester GL1 1LB* Tel (01452) 524550 or (01242) 714846 E-mail mparsons@wemtc.org.uk or mwsp@btinternet.com

PARSONS, Canon Robert Martin. b 43. Qu Coll Cam BA65 MA69. ALCD68. **d** 68 **p** 69. C Chapeltown *Sheff* 68-71; C Sheff St Jo 71-75; V Swadlincote *Derby* 75-91; RD Repton 81-91; P-in-c Gresley 82-86; R Etwall w Egginton 91-93; Can Res Derby Cathl 93-98; Hon Can 98-09; P-in-c Belper 98-03; V 03-09; Jt P-in-c Ambergate and Heage 06-09; rtd 09; Hon C Bicton, Montford w Shrawardine and Fitz *Lich* from 09; Hon C Leaton and Albrighton w Battlefield from 09. *The Vicarage, Baschurch Road, Bomere Heath, Shrewsbury SY4 3PN* Tel (01939) 291494 E-mail canonparsons@tiscali.co.uk

PARSONS, Roger John. b 37. Sarum Th Coll 62. **d** 65 **p** 66. C Bitterne Park *Win* 65-69; C Clerkenwell H Redeemer w St Phil *Lon* 69-72; C Willesden St Andr 72-76; C St Laur in Thanet *Cant* 76-81; Chapl Luton and Dunstable Hosp 81-86; Chapl St Mary's Hosp Luton 81-86; C Luton All SS w St Pet *St Alb* 81-86; TV E Dereham *Nor* 86-88; TV E Dereham and Scarning 89; Perm to Offic 89-93. *6 Ellastone Court, 1 Salisbury Road, Sheringham NR26 8EA* Tel (01263) 821241

PARSONS, Stephen Christopher. b 45. Keble Coll Ox BA67 MA72 BLitt78. Cuddesdon Coll 68. **d** 70 **p** 71. C Whitstable All SS *Cant* 70-71; C Croydon St Sav 71-74; Perm to Offic *Ox* 74-76; C St Laur in Thanet *Cant* 76-79; V Lugwardine w Bartestree and Weston Beggard *Heref* 79-87; V Lechlade *Glouc* 87-03; R Edin St Cuth 03-10; rtd 10. *15 St Andrews Road, Hexham NE46 2EY* Tel (01434) 600301 E-mail stephen@parsons252262.freeserve.co.uk

PARSONS, Stephen Drury. b 54. Qu Mary Coll Lon BSc76 CCC Cam MSc79. Westcott Ho Cam 79. **d** 82 **p** 83. C Stretford All SS *Man* 82-85; C Newton Heath All SS 85-86; V Ashton St Jas 86-90; Perm to Offic *Man* 90-09. *150 Henrietta Street, Ashton-under-Lyne OL6 8PH* Tel 0161-308 2852

PARSONS, Mrs Susan Catherine. b 60. SWMTC 06 ERMC 08. **d** 09 **p** 10. NSM Oakham, Ashwell, Braunston, Brooke, Egleton etc *Pet* from 09. *4 Quorn Crescent, Cottesmore, Oakham LE15 7NB* Tel (01572) 813848 E-mail susie.parsons@hotmail.co.uk

PARSONS, Thomas James. b 74. K Coll Lon BMus97 LRAM96. Oak Hill Th Coll BA06. **d** 06 **p** 07. C Hensingham *Carl* 06-10; V Sidcup Ch Ch *Roch* from 10. *The Vicarage, 16 Christchurch Road, Sidcup DA15 7HE* Tel (020) 8308 0835 Mobile 07960-944287 E-mail tjparsons@tiscali.co.uk

PARTINGTON, The Ven Brian Harold. b 36. OBE02. St Aid Birkenhead 60. **d** 63 **p** 64. C Barlow Moor *Man* 63-66; C Deane 66-68; V Patrick *S & M* 68-96; Bp's Youth Chapl 68-77; RD Peel 76-96; P-in-c German St Jo 77-78; V P-in-c Foxdale 77-78; V 78-96; Can St German's Cathl 85-96; Adn Man 96-05; V Douglas St Geo 96-04; rtd 04. *Brambles, Patrick Village, Peel, Isle of Man IM5 3AH* Tel (01624) 844173 E-mail bpartington@mcb.net

PARTINGTON, John. See PARTINGTON, Peter John

PARTINGTON, Kenneth. b 41. Lanc Univ MA86. Ripon Hall Ox. **d** 70 **p** 71. C Atherton *Man* 70-72; C Kippax *Ripon* 72-75; V Cartmel Fell *Carl* 75-95; V Crosthwaite Kendal 75-95; V Witherslack 75-95; V Winster 78-95; rtd 01; Perm to Offic *Carl* from 01 and *Blackb* from 03. *Kilvert Heights, 9 Castle Park, Kendal LA9 7AX* Tel (01539) 723963

PARTINGTON, Canon Kevin. b 51. Huddersfield Poly BA73. St Jo Coll Nottm 91. **d** 93 **p** 94. C Salterhebble All SS *Wakef* 93-96; V Pontefract All SS 96-03; TR Dewsbury from 03; Hon Can Wakef Cathl from 09. *The Rectory, 16A Oxford Road, Dewsbury WF13 4JT* Tel (01924) 465491 or 457057 E-mail kevin.partington@btopenworld.com

PARTINGTON, Canon Peter John. b 57. Peterho Cam MA. St Jo Coll Nottm. **d** 81 **p** 82. C Cov H Trin 81-85; C Woking St Jo *Guildf* 85-87; C 94-99; R Busbridge 87-94; Dir of Ords 94-03; P-in-c Winchcombe, Gretton, Sudeley Manor etc *Glouc* 03-05; TR

Winchcombe from 05. *The Rectory, Langley Road, Winchcombe, Cheltenham GL54 5QP* Tel (01242) 602368 E-mail revpjp@aol.com

PARTON, John Michael. b 44. Bradf & Ilkley Community Coll MA93. **d** 04 **p** 05. NSM Horbury w Horbury Bridge *Wakef* 04-10; NSM Dewsbury Deanery from 10. *106 Lennox Drive, Wakefield WF2 8LF* Tel and fax (01924) 360395 E-mail johnmparton@btinternet.com

PARTRIDGE, Alan Christopher. b 55. Thames Poly BA77 Ex Univ PGCE78. St Jo Coll Nottm MA00. **d** 00 **p** 01. C Woking St Jo *Guildf* 00-03; C Ely 03-08; TV Ely 08-09; P-in-c Sawston from 09; P-in-c Babraham from 09. *The Vicarage, Church Lane, Sawston, Cambridge CB22 3JR* Tel (01223) 832248 E-mail a.partridge7@ntlworld.com

PARTRIDGE, Anthony John. b 38. Univ of Wales (Lamp) BA61 Linacre Ho Ox BA63 K Coll Lon PhD77. St Steph Ho Ox 61. **d** 64 **p** 65. C Sydenham All SS *S'wark* 64-67; Hon C 68-74; Lic to Offic 74-08; Perm to Offic from 08; Lect Woolwich Poly 67-70; Thames Poly 70-74; Prin Lect 75-92; Greenwich Univ 92-03; rtd 03. *40 Upwood Road, London SE12 8AN* Tel (020) 8318 9901

PARTRIDGE, Mrs Bryony Gail. b 51. St Anne's Coll Ox BA72 MA76 Ox Univ PGCE73 Leeds Univ BA11. Yorks Min Course 09. **d** 11. NSM Oakworth *Bradf* from 11. *New House Farm, Oakworth, Keighley BD22 7JW* Tel (01535) 643206 E-mail geraldandbryony@hotmail.com

PARTRIDGE, Canon David John Fabian. b 36. Ball Coll Ox BA60 MA. Westcott Ho Cam 60. **d** 62 **p** 63. C Halliwell St Thos *Man* 62-65; C St Martin-in-the-Fields *Lon* 65-69; R Warblington w Emsworth *Portsm* 69-01; Hon Can Portsm Cathl 84-01; rtd 03. *3 Frarydene, Prinsted, Emsworth PO10 8HU* Tel (01865) 558630

PARTRIDGE, Ian Starr. b 36. Linc Th Coll 87. **d** 89 **p** 90. C Barton upon Humber *Linc* 89-92; P-in-c Barkwith Gp 92-97; R 97-02; rtd 02; Perm to Offic *Linc* from 02; RD Calcewaithe and Candleshoe 03-05. *Altair, 4 Thames Street, Louth LN11 7AD* Tel (01507) 600398 E-mail ian@altair.org.uk

PARTRIDGE, Miss Margaret Edith. b 35. Gilmore Ho 63. dss 85 **d** 87 **p** 94. Amblecote *Worc* 85-89; Par Dn 87-89; C Borehamwood *St Alb* 89-94; TV 94-00; rtd 00; Perm to Offic *Birm* from 01. *4 Cornerstone, Maryland Drive, Birmingham B31 2AT* Tel 0121-476 0854

PARTRIDGE, Martin David Waud. b 38. Ox NSM Course 86. **d** 89 **p** 90. NSM Wargrave *Ox* 89-97; NSM Schorne 97-05; rtd 05; Perm to Offic *Ox* from 05. *Barnes House, St James Street, Eastbury, Hungerford RG17 7JL* Tel (01488) 670281

PARTRIDGE, Michael John. b 61. St Edm Hall Ox BA83 MA89 St Jo Coll Dur BA86. Cranmer Hall Dur 84. **d** 87 **p** 88. C Amington *Birm* 87-90; C Sutton Coldfield H Trin 90-93; P-in-c W Exe 93-01; RD Tiverton 96-00; V Tiverton St Geo and St Paul 01-06; P-in-c Pinhoe and Broadclyst from 06; P-in-c Aylesbeare, Rockbeare, Farringdon etc from 06. *The Rectory, 9 Church Hill, Pinhoe, Exeter EX4 9ER* Tel (01392) 466257 E-mail m.partridge@talktalk.net

PARTRIDGE, Ronald Malcolm. b 49. Bris Bapt Coll LTh74 Cuddesdon Coll 74. **d** 75 **p** 76. C Bris St Andr Hartcliffe 75-78; C E Bris 78-82; V Easton All Hallows 82-85; TV Brighton St Pet w Chpl Royal and St Jo *Chich* 85-86; TV Brighton St Pet and St Nic w Chpl Royal 86-88; C-in-c Bermondsey St Hugh CD *S'wark* 88-90; Asst Chapl Gt Ormond Street Hosp for Sick Children *Lon* 91-94; Asst Chapl Gt Ormond Street Hosp for Children NHS Trust 94-97. *29 All Saints Street, Hastings TN34 3BJ* Tel (01424) 715219

PARTRIDGE, Ronald William. b 42. Shimer Coll Illinois BA64. Cant Sch of Min 93. **d** 96 **p** 97. NSM Upchurch w Lower Halstow *Cant* from 96. *4 The Green, Lower Halstow, Sittingbourne ME9 7DT* Tel (01795) 842007 Mobile 07779-789039 E-mail revdron.partridge@virgin.net

PARTRIDGE, Mrs Sarah Mercy. b 59. SEITE 04. **d** 07 **p** 08. NSM Tunbridge Wells K Chas *Roch* from 07. *Long Hedges, Station Road, Rotherfield, Crowborough TN6 3HP* Tel (01892) 853451 E-mail spartridge@partridges59.fsnet.co.uk

PARTRIDGE, Canon Timothy Reeve. b 39. Lon Univ BSc60 AKC60. Wells Th Coll 60. **d** 62 **p** 63. C Glouc St Cath 62-65; C Sutton St Nicholas *Linc* 65-74; R Bugbrooke *Pet* 74-95; R Bugbrooke w Rothersthorpe 95-04; RD Daventry 81-88; Can Pet Cathl 83-04; Warden of Par Ev 96-02; rtd 04. *54 Thorney Leys, Witney OX28 5LS* Tel (01993) 864926 E-mail tim.partridge39@tiscali.co.uk

PASCOE, Mrs Caroline Elizabeth Alice. **d** 08 **p** 09. NSM Ewenny w St Brides Major *Llan* 08-10; Lay Development Officer *Heref* from 10. *Address temp unknown*

PASCOE, Michael Lewis. b 43. **d** 99 **p** 00. OLM Crowan and Treslothan *Truro* 99-02; C from 02; OLM Penponds 01-02; C from 02. *Genesis, Bosparva Lane, Leedstown, Hayle TR27 6DN* Tel (01736) 850425 E-mail revdmike@supanet.com

PASHLEY, Howard Thomas. b 47. Kent Univ MSc85 Keele Univ PGCE71 ARIC70. **d** 06 **p** 07. OLM Sandwich *Cant* from 06. *8 Dover Road, Sandwich CT13 0BN* Tel (01304) 612018 E-mail howardpashley@yahoo.co.uk

PASK, Howard. b 54. St Jo Coll Nottm. **d** 99 **p** 00. C Todmorden *Wakef* 99-02; P-in-c Hebden Bridge 02-03; P-in-c Heptonstall 02-03; V Hebden Bridge and Heptonstall from 03. *The Vicarage, 12 Becketts Close, Heptonstall, Hebden Bridge HX7 7LJ* Tel (01422) 842138 Mobile 07779-243176 E-mail howardpask@btinternet.com

PASKETT, Ms Margaret Anne. b 45. Northd Coll of Educn CertEd67 York Univ BSc81 Leeds Univ MEd83. NEOC 84. **d** 87 **p** 94. Par Dn Marske in Cleveland *York* 87-91; C 92-96; Dioc Adv for Diaconal Mins 92-96; P-in-c Hemingbrough and Tr Officer (York Adnry) 96-05; rtd 06. *15 Hubert Street, York YO23 1EF* Tel (01904) 626521 E-mail annepaskett62@btinternet.com

PASKINS, David James. b 52. Univ of Wales (Lamp) BA73 Trin Hall Cam BA76 MA81. Westcott Ho Cam 74. **d** 77 **p** 78. C St Peter-in-Thanet *Cant* 77-80; C Swanage *Sarum* 80-82; R Waldron *Chich* 82-92; R Bere Ferrers *Ex* 92-96; V Lockerley and E Dean w E and W Tytherley *Win* 96-03; R Cranborne w Boveridge, Edmondsham etc *Sarum* from 03. *The Rectory, Grugs Lane, Cranborne, Wimborne BH21 5PX* Tel (01725) 517232

PASSANT, Keith. b 39. St Jo Coll Dur BA62 CertEd70. St Alb Minl Tr Scheme 77. **d** 87 **p** 88. C Hatfield Hyde *St Alb* 87-93; rtd 93; Perm to Offic *St Alb* from 93. *26 Monk's Rise, Welwyn Garden City AL8 7NF* Tel (01707) 332869

PASSEY, Miss Rhona Margaret. b 52. St Jo Coll Nottm BTh96. EMMTC 06. **d** 09 **p** 10. NSM Hugglescote w Donington, Ellistown and Snibston *Leic* from 09. *14 Atherstone Road, Measham, Swadlincote DE12 7EG* Tel (01530) 270823 Mobile 07787-573731 E-mail rhona.passey@btinternet.com

PATCHELL, Miss Gwendoline Rosa. b 49. Goldsmiths' Coll Lon BA69 TCert70. Trin Coll Bris 90. **d** 92 **p** 94. C Ashton-upon-Mersey St Mary Magd *Ches* 92-98; TV Hemel Hempstead *St Alb* 98-06; P-in-c Kirkby in Ashfield *S'well* from 06. *The Rectory, 12 Church Street, Kirkby-in-Ashfield, Nottingham NG17 8LE* Tel (01623) 720030

PATCHING, Colin John. b 47. Linc Th Coll 84. **d** 86 **p** 87. C Farnley *Ripon* 86-89; C Didcot St Pet *Ox* 89-92; P-in-c Steventon w Milton 92-97; R from 98. *The Vicarage, 73 Field Gardens, Steventon, Abingdon OX13 6TF* Tel (01235) 831243

PATE, Barry Emile Charles. b 50. NE Lon Poly BA80 CQSW80. S'wark Ord Course 85. **d** 88 **p** 89. NSM E Dulwich St Jo *S'wark* 88-92; C Farnborough *Roch* 92-94; C Broxbourne w Wormley *St Alb* 94-00; V Wilbury from 00. *Church House, 103 Bedford Road, Letchworth Garden City SG6 4DU* Tel and fax (01462) 623119 E-mail b.pate@ntlworld.com

PATEL, Jitesh Krisnakavi. b 82. Jes Coll Ox MPhys04 Kellogg Coll Ox PGCE06. Wycliffe Hall Ox BA09 MA09. **d** 10 **p** 11. C Abingdon *Ox* from 10. *33 Mattock Way, Abingdon OX14 2PQ* Tel (01235) 524159 E-mail bioneural@hotmail.com

PATEMAN, Edward Brian. b 29. Leeds Univ BA51. Qu Coll Birm 51. **d** 53 **p** 54. C Stockton St Pet *Dur* 53-57; Lect Bolton St Pet 57-58; V Coxhoe 58-65; V Dalton le Dale 65-93; RD Houghton 72-75; R Hawthorn 88-93; rtd 93. *27 Atherton Drive, Houghton le Spring DH4 6TA* Tel 0191-385 3168

PATEN, Richard Alfred. b 32. Ch Coll Cam BA56 MA60 CEng60 MICE60. Ripon Hall Ox 61. **d** 63 **p** 64. C Oadby *Leic* 63-67; C Pet St Mark 67-71; Chapl Community Relns 71-95; Bp's Dioc Chapl 73-85; rtd 97; Perm to Offic *Pet* from 93. *19 The Lindens, 86 Lincoln Road, Peterborough PE1 2SN* Tel (01733) 562089

PATERNOSTER, Canon Michael Cosgrove. b 35. Pemb Coll Cam BA59 MA63. Cuddesdon Coll 59. **d** 61 **p** 62. C Surbiton St Andr *S'wark* 61-63; Chapl Qu Coll Dundee 63-68; Dioc Supernumerary *Bre* 63-68; Chapl Dundee Univ 63-68; Sec Fellowship of SS Alb and Sergius 68-71; R Dollar *St And* 71-75; R Stonehaven *Bre* 75-90; Hon Can St Paul's Cathl Dundee from 81; R Aberdeen St Jas 90-00; rtd 00; Perm to Offic *B & W* from 00. *12 Priest Row, Wells BA5 2PY*

PATERSON, Alan (Brother Alan Michael). b 64. **d** 06 **p** 07. NSM Bartley Green *Birm* 06-10; V Cowgate *Newc* from 10. *St Peter's Vicarage, Druridge Drive, Newcastle upon Tyne NE5 3LP* Tel 0191-286 9913

PATERSON (née SOAR), Mrs Angela Margaret. b 59. Aston Univ MSc81 MCIPD82. SAOMC 97. **d** 00 **p** 01. NSM Icknield *Ox* from 00. *86 Hill Road, Watlington OX49 5AF* Tel (01491) 614034 E-mail angela@patersonlink.co.uk

PATERSON, David. b 33. Ch Ch Ox BA55 MA58. Linc Th Coll 56. **d** 58 **p** 59. C Kidderminster St Mary *Worc* 58-60; C Wolverhampton St Geo *Lich* 60-64; V Loughborough St Pet *Leic* 64-04; rtd 04; Perm to Offic *Ox* from 05. *487 Marston Road, Marston, Oxford OX3 0JQ* Tel (01865) 726842 E-mail davidpaterson129@hotmail.com

PATERSON, Douglas Monro. b 30. Em Coll Cam BA54 MA57. Tyndale Hall Bris 55. **d** 57 **p** 58. C Walcot *B & W* 57-60; C Portman Square St Paul *Lon* 60-62; Lect Oak Hill Th Coll 60-62; Min Hampstead St Jo Downshire Hill Prop Chpl *Lon* 62-65; Lect All Nations Chr Coll Ware 62-65; Rwanda 67-73; C Edin St Thos 73-75; Lect Northumbria Bible Coll 73-94; Perm to Offic *Edin* 75-94; Lic to Offic *Newc* 76-94; rtd 94; Perm to Offic

Ox 94-10 and *York* from 10. *8 Dulverton Hall, Esplanade, Scarborough YO11 2AR* Tel (01723) 340108

PATERSON, Geoffrey Gordon. b 45. Cant Univ (NZ) LTh69. **d** 69 **p** 70. C Linwood New Zealand 69-71; C Belfast-Redwood 71-76; V Mayfield Mt Somers 76-78; P-in-c Astwood Bank w Crabbs Cross *Worc* 78-80; V Halswell-Prebbleton New Zealand 80-87; Chapl Sunnyside Hosp 87-95. *19 Ridder Place, Christchurch 8025, New Zealand* Tel (0064) (3) 322 7787 *or* 365 3211 E-mail geoffpat@xtra.co.nz

PATERSON, James Beresford. b 21. DSC42. St Andr Univ MPhil85 FRSA93. Westcott Ho Cam 59. **d** 61 **p** 62. C Woodbridge St Mary *St E* 61-64; R Broughty Ferry *Bre* 64-72; Dioc Supernumerary 72-75; Sec Scottish Ch Action for World Development 72-79; P-in-c Glencarse 76-84; Dioc Sec 79-84; Hon Can St Paul's Cathl Dundee 79-89; rtd 84; Perm to Offic *Bre* and *St E* from 84. *67 Ipswich Road, Woodbridge IP12 4BT* Tel (01394) 383512

PATERSON, Mrs Jennifer Ann. b 49. Brooklands Tech Coll 69. S Dios Minl Tr Scheme 85. **d** 88 **p** 95. C Hale *Guildf* 88-92; NSM Seale, Puttenham and Wanborough 95-01; rtd 01; Perm to Offic *Guildf* 94-95 and from 01; rtd 09. *4 St George's Close, Badshot Lea, Farnham GU9 9LZ* Tel (01252) 316775
E-mail ja.paterson@btinternet.com

✠**PATERSON, The Rt Revd John Campbell.** b 45. Auckland Univ BA66. St Jo Coll Auckland. **d** 69 **p** 70 **c** 95. C Whangarei New Zealand 69-71; V Waimate Maori N Pastorate 71-76; Co-Missr Auckland Maori Miss 76; Chapl Qu Victoria Sch 76-82; CF 76-84; Sec Bishopric of Aotearoa 78-87; Prov Sec 86-92; Gen Sec Angl Ch in Aotearoa, NZ and Polynesia 92-95; Bp Auckland from 95; Presiding Bp and Primate New Zealand 98-04. *PO Box 37-242, Parnell, Auckland 1033, New Zealand* Tel (0064) (9) 302 7202 Fax 302 7217 E-mail bishop.auckland@xtra.co.nz

PATERSON, Michael Séan. b 61. Heythrop Coll Lon BD89 MA95 Univ of Wales (Lamp) MMin04. **d** 04 **p** 05. C Stonehaven *Bre* 04-05; C Arbroath 05-06; C Edin Ch Ch 06-08; Chapl St Andr Hospice Airdrie from 08. *St Andrew's Hospice, 1 Henderson Street, Airdrie ML6 6DJ* Tel (01236) 766951 Fax 748787 E-mail rev.pilgrim@btinternet.com

PATERSON, Mrs Moira. b 53. Edin Univ BA74 Lon Univ BA91. TISEC 07. **d** 10 **p** 11. C St Andr Cathl from 10. *31 Gladstone Place, Aberdeen AB10 6UX* Tel (01224) 321714 Mobile 07528-774046 E-mail moira.paterson1@virgin.net

PATERSON, Nigel John Merrick. b 53. Lanc Univ BEd75 Open Univ MA89. **d** 01 **p** 02. OLM N Walsham and Edingthorpe *Nor* from 01. *Marshgate Cottage, Marshgate, North Walsham NR28 9LG* Tel (01692) 406259 Mobile 07786-381361
E-mail nigel-paterson@tiscali.co.uk

PATERSON, Rex Douglas Trevor. b 27. AKC54. **d** 55 **p** 56. C Maidenhead St Luke *Ox* 55-58; C Littlehampton St Mary *Chich* 58-62; V Woodingdean 62-73; V Ferring 73-94; rtd 94; Perm to Offic *Chich* from 94. *14 Hurst Avenue, Worthing BN11 5NY* Tel (01903) 504252

✠**PATERSON, The Rt Revd Robert Mar Erskine.** b 49. St Jo Coll Dur BA71 MA82. Cranmer Hall Dur. **d** 72 **p** 73 **c** 08. C Harpurhey St Steph and Harpurhey Ch Ch *Man* 72-73; C Sketty *S & B* 73-78; R Llangattock and Llangyndir 78-83; V Gabalfa *Llan* 83-94; TR Cowbridge 94-00; Prin Officer Ch in Wales Coun for Miss and Min 00-06; Metrop Can 04-08; Abp's Chapl and Researcher *York* 06-08; Bp S & M from 08. *Thie yn Aspick, The Falls, Tromode Road, Douglas, Isle of Man IM4 4PZ* Tel (01624) 622108 Fax 672890 E-mail bishop@sodorandman.im

PATERSON, Robin Fergus (Robert). b 32. Moore Th Coll Sydney 83. **d** 87 **p** 89. Singapore 87-88; NSM Crieff *St And* 88-92; NSM Comrie 88-92; R Dunkeld 93-98; R Strathtay 93-98; rtd 98; Lic to Offic *St And* and *Eur* from 98. *1 Corsiehill House, Corsiehill, Perth PH2 7BN* Tel (01738) 446621
E-mail robinatcorsie@talktalk.net

PATERSON, Robin Lennox Andrew. b 43. NOC 84. **d** 87 **p** 88. C Manston *Ripon* 87-91; P-in-c Leeds All So 91-95; V 95-98; V Middleton St Mary 98-08; rtd 08. *22 Manston Way, Leeds LS15 8BR* Tel 07778-860178 (mobile)
E-mail rlap@ntlworld.com

PATERSON, Rodney John. b 62. Keele Univ BA84. St Jo Coll Nottm MA98. **d** 98 **p** 99. C Huddersfield H Trin *Wakef* 98-01; P-in-c Charlton Kings H Apostles *Glouc* from 01; TR Cheltenham St Mark from 11. *The Vicarage, Langton Grove Road, Charlton Kings, Cheltenham GL52 6JA* Tel (01242) 512254

PATERSON, Stuart Maxwell. b 37. Kelham Th Coll 57 Lich Th Coll 58. **d** 60 **p** 61. C Ilkeston St Mary *Derby* 60-64; V Somercotes 64-70; R Wingerworth 70-73; P-in-c Hawick *Edin* 92-95; R 95-00; rtd 00; Perm to Offic *Ab* 05-08; P-in-c Aberdeen St Jas from 08. *31 Gladstone Place, Aberdeen AB10 6UX* Tel (01224) 321714 E-mail max.stjames@btinternet.com

PATERSON, Mrs Susan Ann. b 57. St Hilda's Coll Ox MA84. EMMTC 92. **d** 95 **p** 96. NSM Evington *Leic* 95-98; C Humberstone 98-03; TV Melton Mowbray 03-09; P-in-c Ab Kettleby and Holwell w Asfordby from 09. *The Rectory, 2*

Church Lane, Asfordby, Melton Mowbray LE14 3RU* Tel (01664) 813130 E-mail spaterson@leicester.anglican.org

PATIENT, Terence Ian. b 35. Open Univ BA83. **d** 96 **p** 97. OLM Old Catton *Nor* 96-05; Perm to Offic from 05. *8 Players Way, Norwich NR6 7AU* Tel (01603) 427899
E-mail mandt.patient@virgin.net

PATO, Luke Luscombe Lungile. b 49. Fort Hare Univ BA76 Manitoba Univ MA80. St Bede's Coll Umtata. **d** 73 **p** 75. S Africa 73-81 and from 92; Canada 81-90; Tutor Coll of Ascension Selly Oak 90-92. *PO Box 62098, Marshalltown, 2107 South Africa* Tel (0027) (11) 763 2510 *or* 492 1380 Mobile 83-367 3961 E-mail luke@cpsa.org.za

PATON, David. *See* PATON, Preb John David Marshall

PATON, Canon Ian James. b 57. Jes Coll Cam MA78 PGCE79. Westcott Ho Cam MA81. **d** 82 **p** 83. C Whitley Ch Ch *Ox* 82-84; Bp's Dom Chapl 84-86; Chapl Wadh Coll Ox 86-90; C Ox St Mary V w St Cross and St Pet 86-90; Can and Vice Provost St Mary's Cathl Edin 90-94; R Edin St Mary 90-94; R Haddington and Dunbar 94-97; R Edin Old St Paul from 97; Can St Mary's Cathl from 04. *Lauder House, 39 Jeffrey Street, Edinburgh EH1 1DH* Tel 0131-556 3332 Mobile 07751-510594
E-mail rector@osp.org.uk

PATON, Preb John David Marshall. b 47. Barrister-at-Law (Middle Temple) 71. St Steph Ho Ox 81. **d** 83 **p** 84. C Bethnal Green St Matt w St Jas the *Gt Lon* 83-86; P-in-c St Geo-in-the-East St Mary 86-89; V 89-92; P-in-c Bethnal Green St Barn 92-96; AD Tower Hamlets 92-96; Dir Post-Ord Tr 92-99; P-in-c St Vedast w St Mich-le-Querne etc 97-06; P-in-c St Botolph without Bishopgate 97-06; AD The City 00-06; Preb St Paul's Cathl from 04; Master R Foundn of St Kath in Ratcliffe from 06. *The Royal Foundation of St Katharine, 2 Butcher Row, London E14 8DS* Tel (020) 7790 3540 Fax 7702 7603
E-mail enquiries@stkatharine.org.uk

PATON, John William Scholar. b 52. Mert Coll Ox BA74 MA95. St Steph Ho Ox 93. **d** 95 **p** 96. C Sherborne w Castleton and Lillington *Sarum* 95-98; Succ S'wark Cathl 98-01; Chapl Medical and Dental Students K Coll Lon 98-01; P-in-c Purley St Mark 01-07; P-in-c Purley St Swithun 05-07; Prec Ch Ch Ox from 07. *Christ Church, Oxford OX1 1DP* Tel (01865) 276150
E-mail john_w_s_paton@msn.com

PATON, The Ven Michael John Macdonald. b 22. Magd Coll Ox BA49 MA54. Linc Th Coll 52. **d** 54 **p** 55. C Gosforth All SS *Newc* 54-57; V Norton Woodseats St Chad *Sheff* 57-67; Sen Chapl Sheff United Hosps 67-70; Chapl Weston Park Hosp Sheff 70-78; V Sheff St Mark Broomhall 70-78; adn Sheff 78-87; Can Res Sheff Cathl 78-87; rtd 88; Perm to Offic *Sheff* 88-10. *43 Hinbush Court, Queens Crescent, Southsea PO5 3HY*

PATON-WILLIAMS, Canon David Graham. b 58. Warwick Univ BA81 Selw Coll Cam BA86 MA90 Newc Univ MA92. Ridley Hall Cam 84. **d** 87 **p** 88. C S Westoe *Dur* 87-90; C Newton Aycliffe 90-91; TV 91-93; Chapl Univ Coll of Ripon and York St Jo 93-98; Min Can Ripon Cathl 93-98; R Bedale 98-02; P-in-c Leeming 98-02; R Bedale and Leeming 03-08; P-in-c Thornton Watlass 07-08; R Bedale and Leeming and Thornton Watlass 08; AD Wensley 05-08; V Roundhay St Edm from 08; Hon Can Ripon Cathl from 11. *St Edmund's Vicarage, 5A North Park Avenue, Leeds LS8 1DN* Tel 0113-266 4532
E-mail davidpw@onetel.net

PATRICIA, Sister. *See* PERKINS, Patricia Doris

PATRICIA ANN, Sister. *See* GORDON, Sister Patricia Ann

PATRICK, Charles. *See* PATRICK, Peter Charles

PATRICK, Hugh Joseph. b 37. TCD BA62 MA66. **d** 63 **p** 64. C Dromore Cathl 63-66; C Lurgan Ch the Redeemer 66-70; C Rothwell *Ripon* 70-73; V Thurnscoe St Hilda *Sheff* 73-78; V Wales 78-02; P-in-c Thorpe Salvin 78-82; RD Laughton 93-98; rtd 02; Perm to Offic *Sheff* from 02. *5 Fairfax Avenue, Worksop S81 7RH* Tel (01909) 477622 E-mail hughpatrick@sky.com

PATRICK, James Harry Johnson. b 67. Birm Poly LLB88 Barrister 89. STETS 96 St Steph Ho Ox 99. **d** 99 **p** 00. Hon C Clifton All SS w St Jo *Bris* 99-10. *4 Clifton Park Road, Bristol BS8 3HL* Tel 0117-908 0460 Fax 930 3813 Mobile 07768-340344 E-mail jp@guildhallchambers.co.uk

PATRICK, Canon John Andrew. b 62. St Jo Coll Dur BA84. Ripon Coll Cuddesdon 87. **d** 89 **p** 90. C Frankby w Greasby *Ches* 89-92; Lect Boston *Linc* 92-95; P-in-c Grafhoe Gp 95-97; R 97-02; P-in-c New Sleaford from 02; P-in-c Kirkby Laythorpe from 10; RD Lafford from 08; Can and Preb Linc Cathl from 07. *The Vicarage, Market Place, Sleaford NG34 7SH* Tel (01529) 302177 E-mail japatrick1@btinternet.com

PATRICK, John Peter. b 23. AKC. **d** 52 **p** 53. C S Westoe *Dur* 52-55; C Woodhouse *Wakef* 55-58; C Batley All SS 58-59; V Upperthong 59-75; V Slaithwaite w E Scammonden 75-80; V Donington *Linc* 80-92; rtd 92; Perm to Offic *Linc* 92-01. *Little Paddock, 140 Main Road, Hundleby, Spilsby PE23 5NQ* Tel (01790) 752304

PATRICK, Peter Charles. b 64. Leeds Univ BA86 Fitzw Coll Cam BA91 MA95. Ridley Hall Cam 89. **d** 92 **p** 93. C Barton upon Humber *Linc* 92-96; TV Gt Grimsby St Mary and St Jas 96-03; RD Grimsby and Cleethorpes 99-03; R Middle Rasen Gp from

03; P-in-c Barkwith Gp from 07. *The Vicarage, North Street, Middle Rasen, Market Rasen LN8 3TS* Tel (01673) 842249 E-mail charles.batrick@talk21.com

PATSTON, Raymond Sidney Richard. b 26. Kelham Th Coll 47. d 51 p 52. C Hammersmith H Innocents *Lon* 51-53; C Acton Green St Pet 53-56; Area Sec E Counties UMCA 56-62; C Chesterton St Luke *Ely* 56-59; R Downham Market w Bexwell 61-71; V Clee *Linc* 71-97; rtd 97. *Ashlea Court Care Home, Church Lane, Waltham, Grimsby DN37 0ES* Tel (01472) 822666

PATTEN (*née* STARNS), Mrs Helen Edna. b 43. St Hilda's Coll Ox BA65 Maria Grey Coll Lon CertEd70. Trin Coll Bris 73 Oak Hill Th Coll 81. dss 82 d 87 p 94. Tunbridge Wells St Jo *Roch* 82-86; Patcham *Chich* 86-91; Par Dn 87-91; Par Dn Eckington w Handley and Ridgeway *Derby* 91-94; C 94-95; TV 95-98; Chapl St Mich Hospice 98-03; rtd 03; Hon C Fairlight, Guestling and Pett *Chich* from 04. *Holyoak, Workhouse Lane, Westfield, Hastings TN35 4QJ* Tel (01424) 752052

PATTEN, Miss Ruth Janet. b 72. Roehampton Inst BA94 Goldsmiths' Coll Lon MMus98. Westcott Ho Cam 08. d 10 p 11. C Witham *Chelmsf* from 10. *23 Forest Road, Witham CM8 2PS* E-mail ruthjpatten@googlemail.com

PATTENDEN, Mrs Alison Margaret. b 53. Eastbourne Tr Coll CertEd75 Sussex Univ BEd76. St Steph Ho Ox 04. d 06 p 07. C Goring-by-Sea *Chich* 06-10; P-in-c Amberley w N Stoke and Parham, Wiggonholt etc from 10. *The New Vicarage, School Road, Amberley, Arundel BN18 9NA* Tel (01798) 831500 E-mail alison.pattenden@btinternet.com

PATTERSON, Alfred Percy. d 85 p 87. NSM Aghalee *D & D* 85-91; C Gilford 91-93; Bp's C 93-95; I 95-00; rtd 00. *Brookdale, 723 Upper Newtownards Road, Belfast BT4 3NU* Tel (028) 9029 4741 E-mail revap.patterson@ntlworld.com

PATTERSON, Andrew John. b 56. Master Mariner 85. Qu Coll Birm 85. d 88 p 89. C Newc St Phil and St Aug 88-92; Chapl Hunter's Moor Hosp 91-92; Asst Chapl R Victoria Infirmary Newc 92-96; V Whitley *Newc* from 96; Chapl Hexham Gen Hosp from 96. *The Vicarage, Whitley, Hexham NE46 2LA* Tel (01434) 673379

PATTERSON, Anthony. b 43. Moore Th Coll Sydney BTh82. d 83 p 83. Australia 83-91; C Darfield *Sheff* 91-94; TR Marfleet York 94-99; TV Heeley and Gleadless Valley *Sheff* 99-04; TR 04-10; AD Attercliffe 04-10; rtd 11. *20 Tennyson Avenue, Bridlington YO15 2EP* E-mail tonypatterson1@gmail.com

PATTERSON, Charles David Gilliat. b 40. Oak Hill Th Coll 71. d 74 p 75. C Brompton H Trin *Lon* 74-77; C Spring Grove St Mary 77-80; V Bures *St E* 80-92; R Bath Weston St Jo w Kelston *B & W* 92-01; rtd 01; Perm to Offic *Ox* from 02. *Grove Mill, Mill Lane, Grove, Wantage OX12 7HU* Tel (01235) 772013

PATTERSON, Colin Hugh. b 52. St Pet Coll Ox MA77 Univ of Wales (Cardiff) MPhil90 CertEd75. Trin Coll Bris. d 87 p 88. C Blackb Sav 87-90; C Haughton le Skerne *Dur* 90-93; Adult Educn Adv 93-05; Asst Dir Bridge Builders from 05; NSM Dur St Nic from 05. *24 Monks Crescent, Durham DH1 1HD* Tel 0191-386 1691 E-mail colinpatterson@menno.org.uk

PATTERSON, Colin Peter Matthew. b 62. Newc Poly BA84. St Steph Ho Ox 92. d 94 p 95. C Cullercoats St Geo *Newc* 94-97; Shrine P Shrine of Our Lady of Walsingham 97-99; P-in-c Harlow St Mary Magd *Chelmsf* 99-00; V 00-09; V Willesden Green St Andr and St Fran *Lon* from 09; CMP from 97. *The Clergy House, 4 St Andrew's Road, London NW10 2QS* Tel (020) 8459 2670 E-mail cpmp1@btinternet.com

PATTERSON, Mrs Diane Rosemary. b 46. WMMTC 88. d 91 p 94. C Hill *Birm* 91-95; Perm to Offic 95-96; C Shottery St Andr *Cov* 96-01; C Hunningham from 01; C Wappenbury w Weston under Wetherley from 01; C Long Itchington and Marton from 01; C Offchurch from 01; RD Southam 02-08. *The Vicarage, School Lane, Hunningham, Leamington Spa CV33 9DS* Tel (01926) 633630

PATTERSON, Hugh John. b 38. Southn Univ MPhil76. AKC63. d 64 p 65. C Epsom St Martin *Guildf* 64-65; Chapl Ewell Coll 65-68; Asst Chapl and Lect Bp Otter Coll Chich 68-71; Lect Dudley Coll of Educn 71-77; Lect Wolv Poly 77-92; Wolv Univ 92-00; Chapl 89-00; rtd 01; Hon C Morville w Aston Eyre *Heref* from 82; Hon C Upton Cressett w Monk Hopton from 82; Hon C Acton Round from 82. *6 Victoria Road, Bridgnorth WV16 4LA* Tel (01746) 765298

PATTERSON, John. See PATTERSON, Norman John

PATTERSON, John. b 27. MBIM76. Bps' Coll Cheshunt 60. d 61 p 62. C Maidenhead St Luke *Ox* 61-65; Chapl RAF 65-72; V Ashton St Jas *Man* 72-78; USA 78-90; R Somercotes and Grainthorpe w Conisholme *Linc* 90-92; rtd 92; Perm to Offic *Linc* from 92. *9 Simpson Close, Barrow-upon-Humber DN19 7BL* Tel (01469) 30867

PATTERSON, John Norton. b 39. TCD BA64 MA68. d 65 p 66. C Belfast St Paul *Conn* 65-68; C Larne and Inver 68-72; I Ballintoy w Rathlin and Dunseverick 72-05; Miss to Seafarers 72-05; Can Belf Cathl 97-05; Adn Dalriada *Conn* 01-05; rtd 05. *31 Moycraig Road, Dunseverick, Bushmills BT57 8TB* Tel (028) 2073 0654

PATTERSON, Marjorie Jean. See BROWN, Mrs Marjorie Jean

PATTERSON, Neil Sydney. b 79. BNC Ox BA00 MA04. Ripon Coll Cuddesdon BA03. d 04 p 05. C Cleobury Mortimer w Hopton Wafers etc *Heref* 04-08; TV Ross 08; P Ariconium from 08. *The Rectory, Weston under Penyard, Ross-on-Wye HR9 7QA* Tel (01989) 567229 E-mail pattersonneil@hotmail.com

PATTERSON, Norman John. b 47. Peterho Cam BA69 ALCD. St Jo Coll Nottm 70. d 73 p 74. C Everton St Ambrose w St Tim *Liv* 73-74; C Everton St Pet 74-78; TV 79-84; C Aigburth and Dioc Adv for Past Care and Counselling 84-92; V Gt Crosby All SS 92-04; Crosslinks Uganda 05-09. *51 Shobnall Street, Burton-on-Trent DE14 2HH* E-mail john.patterson60@hotmail.com

PATTERSON, Patric Douglas MacRae. b 51. Wycliffe Hall Ox 73. d 76 p 77. C Bebington *Ches* 76-79; Canada from 79. *The Rectory, PO Box 10, Milford ON K0K 2P0, Canada*

PATTERSON, The Ven Philip Fredrick. b 50. Ulster Univ BSc QUB BD. d 82 p 83. C Lurgan Ch the Redeemer *D & D* 82-86; I Carrowdore w Millisle 86-89; I Knockbreda from 89; Preb Down Cathl from 00; Dioc Registrar 00-07; Adn Down from 07. *Knockbreda Rectory, 69 Church Road, Newtownbreda, Belfast BT8 4AN* Tel and fax (028) 9064 1493 E-mail pfpatterson@hotmail.com

PATTERSON, Scott Robert. b 71. GTCL92. Oak Hill Th Coll 07. d 09 p 10. C Newton Tracey, Horwood, Alverdiscott etc *Ex* from 09. *The Rectory, Beaford, Winkleigh EX19 8NN* Tel (01805) 603223 Mobile 07973-139092 E-mail scottr.patterson@btinternet.com

PATTERSON, Susan Margaret. b 48. Otago Univ BA71 BD89 PhD92. Knox Coll Dunedin 84. d 88 p 89. C Dunedin St Martin New Zealand 88-91; Tutor Otago Univ and Knox Coll 89-91; USA 91-92; Assoc P Hawke's Bay New Zealand 92-96; Lect Trin Coll Bris 97-00; I Kildallon w Newtowngore and Corrawallen *K, E & A* 00-04; I Killala w Dunfeeny, Crossmolina, Kilmoremoy etc *T, K & A* 04-10; Dean Killala 05-10; Sen Lect and Registrar Bishopdale Th Coll New Zealand from 10. *Bishop Eaton House, 30 Vanguard Street, PO Box 100, Nelson 7040, New Zealand* Tel (0064) (3) 548 8785

PATTERSON, Trevor Harold. b 60. QUB BA82 Stranmillis Coll PGCE83. Trin Coll Bris 91. d 93 p 94. C Ashtead *Guildf* 93-98; V Richmond H Trin and Ch Ch S'wark from 98. *Holy Trinity Vicarage, Sheen Park, Richmond TW9 1UP* Tel (020) 8404 1114 E-mail trevor.patterson@htrichmond.org.uk

PATTIMORE, Daniel James. b 64. Nottm Univ MEng88 Lon Bible Coll BA94. Wycliffe Hall Ox 97. d 99 p 00. C Charlesworth and Dinting Vale *Derby* 99-03; NSM Norley, Crowton and Kingsley *Ches* 03-04; P-in-c Heanor *Derby* from 04. *The Vicarage, 1A Mundy Street, Heanor DE75 7EB* Tel (01773) 719800 Mobile 07973-406022 E-mail dan.pattimore@tiscali.co.uk

PATTIMORE (*née* GORDON), Mrs Kristy. b 72. Leeds Univ BA94 Newc Univ PGCE95. Wycliffe Hall Ox 98. d 01 p 02. C Hallwood *Ches* 01-04; NSM Heanor *Derby* from 04. *The Vicarage, 1A Mundy Street, Heanor DE75 7EB* Tel (01773) 719800

PATTINSON, Christine Brodie. b 43. Darlington Tr Coll CertEd64. d 06 p 07. OLM Chertsey, Lyne and Longcross *Guildf* from 06. *28 Moorfields Close, Staines TW18 3LU* Tel (01784) 457260 E-mail cbpattinson@btinternet.com

PATTINSON, Rhobert James. St Mich Coll Llan. d 04 p 05. C Llanelli *St D* 04-07; TV Dewisland 07-10; V Llanegwad w Llanfihangel Uwch Gwili from 10; Min Can St D Cathl from 07. *Y Ficerdy, Cos y Myrtwydd, Nantgaredig, Carmarthen SA32 7LT* Tel (01267) 290142

PATTINSON, Richard Clive. b 46. Keble Coll Ox BA68 MA84. CBDTI 98. d 00 p 01. C Hesket-in-the-Forest and Armathwaite Carl 00-04; C Inglewood Gp 04-05; P-in-c Dacre from 05; TV Gd Shep TM from 10. *Dacre Vicarage, 12 Keld Close, Stainton, Penrith CA11 0EJ* Tel (01768) 890530

PATTISON, Prof George Linsley. b 50. Edin Univ MA72 BD77 Dur Univ PhD. Edin Th Coll 74. d 77 p 78. C Benwell St Jas *Newc* 77-80; P-in-c Kimblesworth *Dur* 80-83; R Badwell Ash w Gt Ashfield, Stowlangtoft etc *St E* 83-91; Dean of Chpl K Coll Cam 91-01; Lect Aarhus Univ Denmark 01-04; Lady Marg Prof Div Ox Univ from 04; Can Res Ch Ch Ox from 04. *Christ Church, Oxford OX1 1DP* Tel (01865) 276247 E-mail george.pattison@theology.ox.ac.uk

PATTISON, Stephen Bewley. b 53. Selw Coll Cam BA76. Edin Th Coll 76. d 78 p 80. C Gosforth All SS *Newc* 78-79; NSM St Nic Hosp Newc 78-82; Hon C Newc St Thos Prop Chpl 80-82; Chapl Edin Th Coll 82-83; Lect Past Studies Birm Univ 83-88; Perm to Offic *Birm* 83-86 and 87-00; Hon C Moseley St Mary 86-87. *11A Salisbury Road, Moseley, Birmingham B13 8JS* Tel 0121-449 3023

PATTLE (*née* OLIVER), Mrs Suzanne Marie. b 66. LMH Ox BA88 SSEES Lon MA91. Trin Coll Bris BTS03. d 03 p 04. C Rainham *Roch* 03-07; P-in-c Gillingham St Mary from 07. *The Vicarage, 27 Gillingham Green, Gillingham ME7 1SS* Tel (01634) 850529 Mobile 07971-073093 E-mail suzanne.pattle@diocese-rochester.org

PATTMAN, Andrew. b 53. Didsbury Coll Man BEd75. Westcott Ho Cam. **d** 95 **p** 96. C Washington *Dur* 95-98; Children's Work Adv *St Alb* 98-02; Perm to Offic 04-05. *110 Marshalswick Lane, St Albans AL1 4XE* Tel (01727) 841201

PAUL, Brother. *See* SINGLETON, Ernest George

PAUL, Ian Benjamin. b 62. St Jo Coll Ox BA84 MA88 Southn Univ MSc85 Nottm Univ BTh91 PhD98. St Jo Coll Nottm 89. **d** 96 **p** 97. C Longfleet *Sarum* 96-00; NSM 00-04; Visiting Lect Trin Coll Bris 00-01; Th Adv Dioc Bd of Min *Sarum* 00-04; Tutor Sarum OLM Scheme 00-04; Visiting Lect STETS 00-04; Dir Partnership Development St Jo Coll Nottm 04-05; Dean of Studies from 05. *St John's College, Chilwell Lane, Bramcote, Nottingham NG9 3DS* Tel 0115-925 1114 ext 254 E-mail ian.paul@stjohns-nottm.ac.uk *or* editor@grovebooks.co.uk

PAUL, John Matthew. b 61. K Coll Lon BA82 Fitzw Coll Cam BA88 MA92 FRSA06. Westcott Ho Cam 86. **d** 89 **p** 90. C Writtle w Highwood *Chelmsf* 89-94; Min Can and Chapl St Paul's Cathl 94-96; Min Can and Sacr St Paul's Cathl 96-99; V Winchmore Hill St Paul 99-09; AD Enfield 04-09; Perm to Offic from 09. *Meon Place, Selworth Lane, Soberton, Southampton SO32 3PX* Tel 07800-606555 (mobile) E-mail jm.paul@virgin.net

PAUL, Naunihal Chand (Nihal). b 40. Allahabad Univ MA. Bangalore Th Coll BD. **d** 69 **p** 70. C Simla Ch Ch India 69-70; V Kangra w Dharamsala 70-74; C Urmston *Man* 75-77; P-in-c Farnworth St Pet 77-80; TV E Farnworth and Kearsley 80-83; TV Laindon St Martin and St Nic w Nevendon *Chelmsf* 83-90; R Laindon w Dunton 90-05; rtd 05; Perm to Offic *Chelmsf* from 06. *3 Wellstye Green, Basildon SS14 2SR* E-mail rupriwas@aol.com

PAUL, Roger Philip. b 53. Clare Coll Cam BA74 MA88 CertEd76 Open Univ PhD98. Westcott Ho Cam 78. **d** 81 **p** 82. C Coventry Caludon 81-85; R Warmington w Shotteswell and Radway w Ratley 85-98; R Kirkby Stephen w Mallerstang etc *Carl* 98-08; Nat Adv (Unity in Miss) Coun for Chr Unity from 08. *Council for Christian Unity, Church House, Great Smith Street, London SW1P 3AZ* Tel (020) 7898 1473 E-mail roger.paul@churchofengland.org

PAUL, Rosalind Miranda. b 53. Man Univ BA74 Bris Univ PGCE77 Paris Univ LèsL86 Open Univ MBA95. Ripon Coll Cuddesdon 05. **d** 07 **p** 08. C Budock and Mawnan *Truro* 07-09; R Higham, Holton St Mary, Raydon and Stratford *St E* from 09. *The Rectory, Raydon, Ipswich IP7 5LH* Tel (01473) 310677 Mobile 07715-535748 E-mail rosalind.paul@yahoo.co.uk

PAUL, Simon Nicholas. b 56. Hull Univ BA81 PGCE82. Trin Coll Bris BA95. **d** 95 **p** 96. C Cranleigh *Guildf* 95-99; P-in-c Broughton and Duddon *Carl* 99-04; Chapl Ranby Ho Sch Retford 04-09; Chapl Chigwell Sch Essex from 09. *Chigwell School, High Road, Chigwell IG7 6QF* Tel (020) 8501 5700

PAULUS, Garrett Keith. b 76. Marymount Coll California BA98 Yale Univ MA00 Regent Coll Vancouver MA08. **d** 05 **p** 06. C Albuquerque St Mark on the Mesa USA 05-09; NSM N Ferriby *York* from 09. *9 Woodgates Close, North Ferriby HU14 3JS* Tel (01482) 634294 E-mail gadosii@aol.com

PAVEY, Canon Angela Mary. b 55. Hull Univ BA77 Nottm Univ BCombStuds84 Univ of Wales (Lamp) MA06. Linc Th Coll 81. **dss** 84 **d** 87 **p** 94. Linc St Faith and St Martin w St Pet 84-86; Chapl Boston Coll of FE 87-95; Asst Min Officer *Linc* 89-95; C Birchwood 95-97; Dioc Dir of Ords 97-07; P-in-c Linc St Faith and St Martin w St Pet from 07; Chapl Lincs Partnership NHS Foundn Trust from 07; Can and Preb Linc Cathl from 07. *The Vicarage, 165C Carholme Road, Lincoln LN1 1RU* Tel (01522) 829385 E-mail a.pavey1@ntlworld.com

PAVEY, John Bertram. b 51. Keele Univ BA73 Hull Univ PGCE74 MEd95. Linc Th Coll 81. **d** 83 **p** 84. C Boultham *Linc* 83-86; R Fishtoft 86-95; P-in-c Birchwood 95-01; V from 01. *St Luke's Vicarage, Jasmin Road, Lincoln LN6 0YR* Tel (01522) 688665 E-mail j.pavey@ntlworld.com

PAVLOU, Michael. b 55. St Jo Coll Nottm BA. **d** 06 **p** 07. C Woodside Park St Barn *Lon* 06-10; C Wandsworth St Mich w St Steph *S'wark* from 10. *St Stephen's Vicarage, 2A Oakhill Road, London SW15 2QU* Tel 07956-573217 (mobile) E-mail mike.pavi@talktalk.net

PAVYER, Jennifer Elizabeth. *See* FENNELL, Mrs Jennifer Elizabeth

PAWLEY, Adam Richard. St Mich Coll Llan. **d** 10 **p** 11. C Llanllwchaiarn and Newtown w Aberhafesp *St As* from 10. *10 Meadow Lane, Newtown SY16 2DU* E-mail adampawley2003@hotmail.com

PAWSON (née ROYLE), Mrs Gillian Mary. b 57. Kingston Univ BA79 Roehampton Inst PGCE82. SEITE 99. **d** 02 **p** 03. C Wimbledon *S'wark* 02-06; P-in-c Merton St Jo 06-09; P-in-c Colliers Wood Ch Ch 06-09; TV Merton Priory 09; Perm to Offic from 10. *The Big Boat, Harts Boatyard, Portsmouth Road, Surbiton KT6 4HJ* E-mail revgillypawson@btinternet.com

PAWSON, John. b 66. Moorlands Th Coll BA00. Wycliffe Hall Ox. **d** 02 **p** 03. C Bursledon *Win* 02-06; P-in-c Sway from 06. *The*

Vicarage, Station Road, Sway, Lymington SO41 6BA Tel (01590) 682358 Mobile 07762-246947 E-mail john@pawson1.wanadoo.co.uk

PAWSON, Preb John Walker. b 38. Kelham Th Coll 58. **d** 63 **p** 64. C N Hull St Mich *York* 63-67; C Lower Gornal *Lich* 67-70; V Tipton St Jo 70-78; V Meir Heath 78-03; RD Stoke 88-98; Preb Lich Cathl 93-03; rtd 03; Perm to Offic *Nor* from 03. *39 Runton Road, Cromer NR27 9AT* Tel (01263) 511715 E-mail pawson.meirton@virgin.net

PAXON, Robin Michael Cuninghame. b 46. St Jo Coll Dur BA69. Westcott Ho Cam 69. **d** 71 **p** 72. C Croydon St Pet S End *Cant* 71-77; C Saffron Walden w Wendens Ambo and Littlebury *Chelmsf* 77-80; P-in-c Plaistow St Mary 80-83; TV Plaistow 83-89; TV Dovercourt and Parkeston 90-95; rtd 95. *20 Park Road, Harwich CO12 3BJ* Tel (01255) 551139

PAXTON, John Ernest. b 49. Ex Univ BA71. Westcott Ho Cam 74. **d** 74 **p** 75. C Redditch St Steph *Worc* 74-77; UAE 77-81; C Bolton St Pet *Man* 81-91; Ind Missr 81-91; TV Southampton (City Cen) *Win* 91-96; R S'wark Ch Ch 96-03; Sen Chapl S Lon Ind Miss 96-03; Adv to Bd of Soc Resp *Worc* from 03. *57 Drovers Way, Worcester WR3 8QD* Tel (01905) 456793 *or* 732819 E-mail jpaxton@cofe-worcester.org.uk

PAXTON, William Neil. b 60. Brunel Univ BSc88 MA90. Ripon Coll Cuddesdon 02. **d** 04 **p** 05. C Camberwell St Geo *S'wark* 04-08; TV Southend *Chelmsf* from 08. *All Saints' Vicarage, 1 Sutton Road, Southend-on-Sea SS2 5PA* Tel (01702) 613440 E-mail neil.paxton@blueyonder.co.uk

PAY, Norman John. b 50. St Jo Coll Dur BA72. Cranmer Hall Dur. **d** 74 **p** 75. C S Moor *Dur* 74-78; C Rawmarsh w Parkgate *Sheff* 78-80; C-in-c New Cantley CD 80-82; V New Cantley 82-89; V Doncaster St Leon and St Jude from 89; Asst Clergy In-Service Tr Officer 90-93. *St Leonard's Vicarage, Barnsley Road, Doncaster DN5 8QE* Tel (01302) 784858

PAYN, Peter Richard. b 33. Moore Th Coll Sydney LTh59. **d** 60 **p** 60. C Pittwater Australia 60-61; C Kensington St Matt 61-63; C Melbourne St Jas w St Jo 63-65; V E Geelong St Matt 65-79; C Blackb Ch Ch w St Matt 79-81; V Lowestoft Ch Ch *Nor* 81-92; P-in-c Tunbridge Wells St Pet *Roch* 92-96; V 96-03; rtd 03. *Vincent, 24190 Neuvic, France* Tel (0033) 5 53 81 13 56 E-mail richardpayn@aol.com

PAYNE, Alan. *See* PAYNE, Canon Kenneth Alan

PAYNE, Arthur Edwin. b 37. K Alfred's Coll Win TCert59. St Mich Coll Llan 86. **d** 87 **p** 88. C Swansea St Gabr *S & B* 87-90; Chapl Univ of Wales (Swansea) 87-90; V Brynmawr 90-91; TV Wickford and Runwell *Chelmsf* 91-94; Chapl Runwell Hosp Wickford 91-94; P-in-c Wraxall *B & W* 94-95; Perm to Offic 95-97; V Rhymney *Mon* 97-98; rtd 98. *4 Villa Rosa, Shrubbery Road, Weston-super-Mare BS23 2JB*

PAYNE, Cyril Gordon. b 26. Bris Univ BA53. Linc Th Coll 53. **d** 55 **p** 56. C Southall H Trin *Lon* 55-58; C Christchurch *Win* 58-63; V Otterbourne 63-75; V Milford 75-90; rtd 90; Perm to Offic *Win* from 90. *11 Oaklands, Lymington SO41 3TH* Tel (01590) 671274

PAYNE, David Charles. b 62. Univ of Wales (Abth) BLib84. St Jo Coll Nottm MA95. **d** 95 **p** 96. C Horncastle w Low Toynton *Linc* 95-99; V Metheringham w Blankney and Dunston 99-04; Chapl Sherwood Forest Hosps NHS Trust 04-06; R Standon and The Mundens w Sacombe *St Alb* from 06. *The Vicarage, Kents Lane, Standon, Ware SG11 1PJ* Tel (01920) 821390 E-mail davidandjoanna.payne@virgin.net

PAYNE, David James. b 31. Clare Coll Cam BA54 MA61. Wycliffe Hall Ox 60. **d** 62 **p** 63. C Gt Faringdon w Lt Coxwell *Ox* 62-63; C Guildf Ch Ch 63-66; R Shackleford 66-73; R Peper Harow 66-73; R Odell *St Alb* 73-78; V Pavenham 73-78; Warden Home of Divine Healing Crowhurst 78-84; R Wraxall *B & W* 84-92; rtd 92; Perm to Offic *Glouc* 92-08; *Bris* 00-08; *Ely* from 07; Hon C Finchley St Mary *Lon* 93-95. *29 Hatley Drive, Burwell, Cambridge CB25 0AY* Tel (01638) 741448

PAYNE, David Ronald. b 49. Open Univ BA87. St Mich Coll Llan 88. **d** 90 **p** 91. C Oystermouth *S & B* 90-93; V Penllergaer 93-02; TV Llanelli *St D* 02-10; V Gwendraeth Fawr from 10. *The Vicarage, 56 Llannon Road, Pontyberem, Llanelli SA15 5LY* Tel (01269) 870744

PAYNE, Elizabeth. b 50. Univ Coll Lon BSc92. St Mich Coll Llan 96. **d** 98 **p** 99. C Cyncoed *Mon* 98-03; TV 03-04. *Address temp unknown*

PAYNE, Frederick Gates (Eric). b 19. Jes Coll Cam BA40 MA43. Lon Coll of Div 40. **d** 42 **p** 43. C Walcot *B & W* 42-45; CF (EC) 45-48; Hd CMJ Miss Ethiopia 48-67; SW Org Sec CMJ 68-85; rtd 84; Perm to Offic *B & W* from 85 and Truro from 91. *8 Penn Lea Road, Bath BA1 3RQ* Tel (01225) 423092

PAYNE, James John Henry. b 36. MBE69. St Pet Hall *Ox* MA59. Tyndale Hall Bris 48 Linc Th Coll 53. **d** 53 Chapl Mersey Miss to Seamen 53-55; C Stoneycroft 55-57; Chapl Igboli Coll Yaba Nigeria 57-62; V St Sav 62-88; Dir Lagos Ord Course 81-87; Hon 71-88; rtd 88; Perm to Offic *Ox* 88-93 and from Uffington, Shellingford, Woolstone and

1 Timberyard Cottages, Church Street, Shellingford, Faringdon SN7 7QA Tel (01367) 710274
E-mail james@payne2277.freeserve.co.uk
PAYNE, Jeffery Mark. b 68. Lon Sch of Th BTh99. Wycliffe Hall Ox 06. d 08 p 09. C Southall St Geo *Lon* 08-11; R Norwood St Mary from 11. *Norwood Rectory, 26 Tentelow Lane, Southall UB2 4LE* Tel (020) 8574 1362 Mobile 07827-965798
E-mail jeff.payne5@btinternet.com
PAYNE, Mrs Joanna Nicola. b 72. Liv Univ BA93 Homerton Coll Cam PGCE95. Trin Coll Bris BA00 MA01. d 01 p 02. C Chislehurst St Nic *Roch* 01-06. *15 Nursery Lane, Costessey, Norwich NR8 5BU* Tel (01603) 745792 Mobile 07958-598145
E-mail joanna.payne@hotmail.com
PAYNE, John. See PAYNE, Victor John
PAYNE, John Percival. b 49. Nottm Univ BA70. Cuddesdon Coll 70. d 72 p 73. C Tilehurst St Mich *Ox* 72-76; C Cross Green St Sav and St Hilda *Ripon* 76-79; Chapl St Hilda's Priory Whitby 79-83; V Leeds Belle Is St Jo and St Barn *Ripon* 83-88; Chapl St Hilda's Sch Whitby 88-97; R Loftus and Carlin How w Skinningrove *York* 97-99; Chapl OHP 99-01; Teacher Qu Mary's Sch Thirsk 02-11; Chapl 03-11; rtd 11; P-in-c Milan w Lake Como and Genoa *Eur* from 11. *All Saints', via Solferino 17, 20121 Milan, Italy* Tel (0039) (02) 655 2258
E-mail johnp.virgil@gmail.com
PAYNE, John Rogan. b 44. Episc Th Coll São Paulo. d 78 p 79. Brazil 78-86; C Ilkley All SS *Bradf* 86-88; R Elvington w Sutton on Derwent and E Cottingwith *York* 88-94. *Manor Farm House, East Flotmanby Road, Muston, Filey YO14 0HX* Tel (01723) 513969
PAYNE, Canon Joseph Marshall. b 17. TCD BA38 MA52. d 40 p 41. C Belfast St Aid *Conn* 40-43; C Ballynafeigh St Jude *D & D* 43-44; Chapl RAF 44-65; Asst Chapl-in-Chief RAF 65-72; QHC 70-72; V Malew *S & M* 72-82; RD Castletown 77-82; Can St German's Cathl 78-84; Treas 80-84; rtd 82; Perm to Offic *S & M* from 84. *8-11 Stanley View, Douglas, Isle of Man IM2 3JA*
PAYNE, Julia Kathleen. See PEATY, Canon Julia Kathleen
PAYNE, Canon Kenneth Alan. b 45. Pemb Coll Ox BA68 MA71. Qu Coll Birm 71. d 74 p 74. Hon C Perry Barr *Birm* 74-78; Hon C Ruislip Manor St Paul *Lon* 78-79; C Hawksworth Wood *Ripon* 79-84; R Stanningley St Thos 84-94; TR Kippax w Allerton Bywater 94-00; AD Whitkirk 95-00; P-in-c Lambley and Dioc Min Development Adv *S'well* 00-09; Dioc Dir of Min 02-09; Hon Can S'well Minster 06-09; rtd 10; Perm to Offic *York* from 10. *Fern Cottage, 2 Gladstone Terrace, Thornton Dale, Pickering YO18 7SS* Tel (01751) 476243 E-mail alanlambley@mac.com
PAYNE, Leonard John. b 49. St Jo Coll Nottm 93. d 95 p 96. C Trimley *St E* 95-98; TV Sole Bay 98-09; P-in-c Wrentham, Covehithe w Benacre etc from 09. *The Vicarage, 59 Southwold Road, Wrentham, Beccles NR34 7JE* Tel (01502) 675208 Mobile 07879-457902 E-mail leonard.payne@ireverend.com
PAYNE, Canon Mark James Townsend. b 69. Van Mildert Coll Dur BA90. Ridley Hall Cam 92. d 94 p 95. C Angmering *Chich* 94-98; Dioc Ev and C Prestonville St Luke 98-04; P-in-c Scaynes Hill 04-10; R Chich St Pancras and St Jo from 10; Can and Preb Chich Cathl from 08. *1 Lower Walls Walk, Chichester PO19 7BH* Tel (01243) 699718
PAYNE, Matthew Charles. b 62. Ex Univ LLB85 All Nations Chr Coll BA95 Solicitor 89. Oak Hill Th Coll 99. d 01 p 02. C Angmering *Chich* 01-05; V Lowestoft St Ch Ch *Nor* from 05. *The Vicarage, 16 Corton Road, Lowestoft NR32 4PL* Tel (01502) 572444 E-mail matthew@christ-church.info
PAYNE, Michael Frederick. b 49. St Jo Coll Nottm 81. d 83 p 84. C Hyson Green *S'well* 83-86; P-in-c Peckham St Mary Magd *S'wark* 86-90; V 90-05; Hon C Chenies and Lt Chalfont, Latimer and Flaunden *Ox* 05-09; P-in-c Tollerton *S'well* from 09. *The Rectory, Tollerton Lane, Tollerton, Nottingham NG12 4FW* Tel 0115-937 2349 E-mail mikefpayne@hotmail.com
PAYNE, Mrs Norma. b 48. Bris Univ BA70 Homerton Coll Cam PGCE71. STETS 98. d 01 p 02. NSM Cley Hill Warminster *Sarum* 01-04; TV 04-07; R Cley Hill Villages from 07. *The Vicarage, 6 Homefields, Longbridge Deverill, Warminster BA12 7DQ* Tel (01985) 841321
PAYNE, Mrs Penelope Kenward. b 42. LGSM64. Bp Otter Coll 94. d 94 p 98. NSM Portsea N End St Mark *Portsm* 94-05; NSM S Hayling from 05. *35 Saltmarsh Lane, Hayling Island PO11 0JT* Tel and fax (023) 9246 5259 *or* tel 9266 5753
E-mail pennie@ppayne.f9.co.uk
PAYNE, Philip John. b 56. Warwick Univ BA77 UMIST MSc94. Westcott Ho Cam 09. d 11. C Bury St Edmunds All SS w St Jo and St Geo *St E* from 11. *28 Philip Road, Bury St Edmunds IP32 6DR* Tel (01284) 719264 Mobile 07871-090557
E-mail revphilippayne@hotmail.com
PAYNE, Mrs Priscilla Mary. b 40. d 04 p 05. NSM Ditton *Roch* from 04. *7 Cobdown Close, Ditton, Aylesford ME20 6SZ* Tel (01732) 841257 E-mail priscilla.payne@diocese-rochester.org
PAYNE, Preb Robert Christian. b 42. St Mich Coll Llan. d 65 ɒ 66. C Charlton Kings St Mary *Glouc* 65-69; C Waltham Cross *4lb* 69-71; V Falfield *Glouc* 71-72; P-in-c Rockhampton 71-72;

V Falfield w Rockhampton 72-76; Chapl HM Det Cen Eastwood Park 71-76; Chapl HM Borstal Everthorpe 76-79; Chapl HM YOI Glen Parva 79-85; Pris Service Chapl Tr Officer 85-88; Chapl HM Pris Swinfen Hall 85-88; Asst Chapl Gen of Pris 88-02; rtd 02; Sessional Chapl HM YOI Stoke Heath 02-06; Sessional Chapl HM Pris Swinfen Hall from 05; Sessional Chapl HM Pris Foston Hall 06-08; Preb Lich Cathl from 05. *HM Prison Swinfen Hall, Swinfen, Lichfield WS14 9QS* Tel (01543) 484125 E-mail bob.payne@ukgateway.net
or bob.payne@hmps.gsi.gov.uk
PAYNE, Robert Harold Vincent. b 44. St Jo Coll York CertEd69. St Jo Coll Nottm 77. d 79 p 80. C Didsbury St Jas *Man* 79-80; C Didsbury St Jas and Em 80-83; V Southchurch Ch Ch *Chelmsf* 83-90; P-in-c Charles w Plymouth St Matthias *Ex* 90-94; Warden Lee Abbey 94-02; R Thorley *St Alb* from 02. *The Rectory, Vicerons Place, Bishop's Stortford CM23 4EL* Tel (01279) 659152 Fax 755179
E-mail bobpayne@stjamesthorley.freeserve.co.uk
PAYNE, Robert Sandon. b 48. Reading Univ BSc69 MRICS72. Ripon Coll Cuddesdon 77. d 80 p 81. C Bridgnorth, Tasley, Astley Abbotts and Oldbury *Heref* 80-83; P-in-c Wistanstow 83-92; P-in-c Acton Scott 86-92; P-in-c Dorrington 92-94; P-in-c Leebotwood w Longnor 92-94; P-in-c Smethcott w Woolstaston 92-94; P-in-c Stapleton 92-94; R Dorrington w Leebotwood, Longnor, Stapleton etc 94-11; rtd 11. *6 Clun Road, Aston-on-Clun, Craven Arms SY7 8EW* Tel (01588) 661008
E-mail robert.payne49@btinternet.com
PAYNE, Rosemary Ann. b 46. LSE LLB68. SAOMC 97. d 00 p 01. NSM Wooburn *Ox* 00-05; NSM Hedsor and Bourne End from 05; Bp's NSM Officer (Bucks) 05-09. *30 Goddington Road, Bourne End SL8 5TZ* Tel (01628) 521677
PAYNE, Stephen Michael. b 55. d 03 p 04. C Plymouth Em, St Paul Efford and St Aug *Ex* 03-10; TV Plymstock and Hooe from 11. *The Vicarage, 9 St John's Drive, Plymouth PL9 9SD* Tel (01752) 213358 E-mail spayne5@live.co.uk
PAYNE, Mrs Trudy. b 48. K Coll Lon BA66 Lon Inst of Educn PGCE73. d 04 p 05. OLM Clapham Park St Steph *S'wark* 04-06; Hon C Telford Park 06-09; Hon C Mitcham St Barn from 09. *6 Clarence Road, Croydon CR0 2EN* Tel (020) 8689 5857
E-mail paynetrudy@hotmail.com
PAYNE, Victor John. b 45. Open Univ BA81. St Mich Coll Llan. d 70 p 71. C Ystrad Mynach *Llan* 70-72; C Whitchurch 72-75; CF (TA) 74-75; CF 75-93; V Talgarth and Llanelieu *S & B* 93-95; Chapl Mid-Wales Hosp 85-87; C Bassaleg *Mon* 93-96; TV 96-01; V Tongwynlais *Llan* 01-11; AD Llan 08-10; rtd 11. *2 Spencer David Way, St Mellons, Cardiff CF3 0QB*
E-mail jaypay1960@yahoo.co.uk
PAYNE COOK, Canon John Andrew Somerset. b 43. St Pet Coll Ox BA65 MA65. Coll of Resurr Mirfield 65. d 68 p 69. C St Mary-at-Latton *Chelmsf* 68-71; C Gt Berkhamsted *St Alb* 71-76; C-in-c N Brickhill CD 76-82; V N Brickhill and Putnoe 83-85; TR Tring 85-99; RD Berkhamsted 92-97; Hon Can St Alb 98-99; USPG 99-03; P-in-c Sandy Pt St Anne St Kitts-Nevis 00-03; P-in-c Ickleford w Holwell *St Alb* 03-05; P-in-c Pirton 03-05; R Holwell, Ickleford and Pirton 05-10; Hon Can St Alb 03-10; rtd 10. *4 Lancotbury Close, Totternhoe, Dunstable LU6 1RQ* Tel (01582) 699485
PAYNTER, Stephen Denis. b 59. Bath Univ BSc82 CertEd82. Trin Coll Bris BA89. d 89 p 90. C Nailsea Ch Ch *B & W* 89-92; C Farnborough *Guildf* 92-97; TV N Farnborough 97-98; V Ealing St Mary *Lon* from 98. *11 Church Place, London W5 4HN* Tel (020) 8567 0414 *or* 8579 7134 Fax 8840 4534
E-mail steve.paynter@stmarysealing.org.uk
PAYNTON, Paul Alexander. b 42. Linc Th Coll 72. d 74 p 75. C Uppingham w Ayston *Pet* 74-77; R Teigh w Whissendine 77-79; P-in-c Market Overton w Thistleton 77-79; R Teigh w Whissendine and Market Overton 79-95; V Irchester 95-00; rtd 04. *11 Mount Street, Lincoln LN1 3JE* Tel (01522) 560428
PAYTON, Paul John. b 59. Middx Poly MA90 LRAM79 GRSM80. Ripon Coll Cuddesdon. d 05 p 06. C Lancaster St Mary w St John and St Anne *Blackb* 05-08; P-in-c Leeds Gipton Epiphany *Ripon* from 08. *Epiphany Vicarage, 227 Beech Lane, Leeds LS9 6SW* E-mail paytonpj@hotmail.com
PEABODY, Anthony John. b 43. St Cuth Soc Dur BSc64 MSc67 Surrey Univ PhD82 MIBiol82 CBiol82. Cuddesdon Coll 08. d 08. NSM Sulhamstead Abbots and Bannister w Ufton Nervet *Ox* from 08. *Blackberries, 29 Woodlands Avenue, Burghfield Common, Reading RG7 3HU* Tel 0118-983 2491
E-mail pisumcorporum@tinyworld.co.uk
PEACE, Brian. b 38. St Jo Coll Nottm 90. d 92 p 93. C Huddersfield H Trin *Wakef* 92-95; R Cheswardine, Childs Ercall, Hales, Hinstock etc *Lich* 95-00; TR 00-03; RD Hodnet 00-03; rtd 03; Perm to Offic *Ches* from 03. *2 Mouldsworth Close, Northwich CW9 8FT* Tel (01606) 333013
E-mail brian@peaceb.freeserve.co.uk
PEACE, Stuart Vaughan. d 04 p 05. OLM Dorking w Ranmore *Guildf* from 04. *95 Ashcombe Road, Dorking RH4 1LW* Tel (01306) 883002 E-mail stuart@peaces.freeserve.co.uk

PEACH, Malcolm Thompson. b 31. St Chad's Coll Dur BA56. Sarum Th Coll 56. **d** 58 **p** 59. C Beamish *Dur* 58-61; Chapl Dur Univ 61-65; NE England Sec SCM 61-65; C-in-c Stockton St Mark CD *Dur* 65-72; P-in-c Bishopwearmouth St Nic 72-81; V 81-85; V S Shields St Hilda w St Thos 85-95; Hon Chapl Miss to Seamen 85-95; P-in-c S Shields St And w St Steph *Dur* 92-95; rtd 95; Perm to Offic *Dur* from 95. *116 Mount Road, Sunderland SR4 7QD* Tel 0191-522 6216

PEACHELL, David John. b 45. Oak Hill Th Coll 85. **d** 86 **p** 87. C Prescot *Liv* 86-89; CF 89-98; P-in-c Hockering, Honingham, E and N Tuddenham *Nor* 98-02; rtd 02. *21 Brentwood, Eaton, Norwich NR4 6PN* Tel (01603) 880121

PEACOCK, Canon David. b 39. Liv Univ BA61 Lanc Univ MA71 Univ of the South (USA) Hon DD00 FRSA95. Westcott Ho Cam 84. **d** 84 **p** 85. Prin Lect St Martin's Coll Lanc 81-85; Hon C Lancaster St Mary *Blackb* 84-85; Prin Whitelands Coll 85-00; Pro Rector Surrey Univ 93-00; Hon C Roehampton H Trin *S'wark* 85-92; Hon C Putney St Mary 92-00; Hon Can S'wark Cathl 97-00; Perm to Offic *Blackb* from 00. *The Old Dairy, Keerside, Arkholme, Carnforth LA6 1AP* Tel (01524) 221706 E-mail keersidecowshed@aol.com

PEACOCK, John. b 34. ALCD60. **d** 60 **p** 61. C Addiscombe St Mary *Cant* 60-62; C Felixstowe St Jo *St E* 62-65; Chapl RAF 65-70; C Panania Australia 71-74; R Strathfield 74-80; Chapl Gladesville Hosp Sydney 81-94; Chapl Angl Retirement Villages Sydney 94-99; rtd 99. *511/6 Tarragal Glen Avenue, Erina NSW 2250, Australia* Tel (0061) (2) 4367 0936

PEACOCK, Mrs Kate Rebecca. b 78. Hatf Coll Dur BA00. Westcott Ho Cam 01. **d** 03 **p** 04. C Cambridge Ascension *Ely* 03-07; C Three Rivers Gp from 07. *The Vicarage, 24 Mildenhall Road, Fordham, Ely CB7 5NR* Tel (01638) 723960 E-mail kate.peacock@btopenworld.com

PEACOCK, Nicholas James. b 76. CCC Cam BA99 MA02. Ripon Coll Cuddesdon BA06. **d** 07 **p** 08. C Clapham Ch Ch and St Jo *S'wark* 07-10; V Wandsworth Common St Mary from 10. *The Vicarage, 291 Burntwood Lane, London SW17 0AP* Tel (020) 8874 4804 Mobile 07837-425792 E-mail revd.nick@btinternet.com

PEAKE, Ms Sue. b 42. K Coll Dur BA63. SEITE 99. **d** 02 **p** 03. NSM Clapham Ch Ch and St Jo *S'wark* from 02. *20 Gauden Road, London SW4 6LT* Tel (020) 7627 4060

PEAL, Jacqueline. b 46. MCSP70. Cant Sch of Min 88. **d** 91 **p** 94. NSM Bexley St Jo *Roch* 91-97; NSM Crayford 91-94; C 94-97 and 00-01; C Dartford H Trin 97-00; Hon C Ash 01-11; Asst Chapl Thames Gateway NHS Trust 01-11; Chapl Wisdom Hospice 04-11; rtd 11. *9 Crescent Rise, Thakeham, Pulborough RH20 3NB* E-mail peal@btinternet.com

PEAL, John Arthur. b 46. K Coll Lon BD70 AKC. **d** 71 **p** 72. C Portsea All SS w St Jo Rudmore *Portsm* 71-74; C Westbury *Sarum* 74-77; V Borstal *Roch* 77-82; Chapl HM Pris Cookham Wood 78-82; V Erith Ch Ch *Roch* 82-91; P-in-c Erith St Jo 86-91; V Bexley St Jo 91-00; Chapl Erith and Distr Hosp 82-90; R Ash *Roch* from 00; R Ridley from 00; rtd 11. *9 Crescent Rise, Thakeham, Pulborough RH20 3NB* E-mail peal@btinternet.com

PEAL, William John. b 26. K Coll Lon BSc47 AKC PhD52. St Jo Coll Nottm 79. **d** 80 **p** 81. C Coalville and Bardon Hill *Leic* 80-83; TV Melton Mowbray w Thorpe Arnold 83-86; TV Melton Gt Framland 86-90; rtd 90; Perm to Offic *Lich* 91-09 and *Ches* 91-99. *20 Conway Road, Knypersley, Stoke-on-Trent ST8 7AL* Tel (01782) 513580

PEALL, Mrs Linda Grace. b 66. Westmr Coll Ox BEd88. EAMTC 99. **d** 02 **p** 03. NSM Blackwell All SS and Salutation *Dur* 02-04; C Darlington H Trin 04-07; Chapl Co Durham and Darlington NHS Foundn Trust 05-10; Chapl Basildon & Thurrock Univ Hosps NHS Foundn Trust from 10. *Basildon University Hospital, Nethermayne, Basildon SS16 5NL* (01268) 524900 *or* 08451-553111 E-mail linda.peall@btopenworld.com

PEARCE, Adrian Francis. b 55. Westmr Coll Ox BTh05. S Dios Minl Tr Scheme 02. **d** 95 **p** 96. NSM Jersey St Jas *Win* from 95; NSM Jersey St Luke from 95; NSM Jersey St Mary from 01. *2 La Carriethe, Les Vaux, St Saviour, Jersey JE2 7US* Tel (01534) 873115 E-mail afpear@jerseymail.co.uk

PEARCE, Andrew John. b 66. Ex Univ BA89 Homerton Coll Cam PGCE93. St Mich Coll Llan 94. **d** 96 **p** 97. C Llansamlet *S & B* 96-99; C Clydach 99-00; P-in-c Knighton, Norton, Whitton, Pilleth and Cascob 00-02; V 02-06; V Bishopston w Penmaen and Nicholaston from 06. *The Rectory, 4 Portway, Bishopston, Swansea SA3 3JR* Tel (01792) 232140

PEARCE, Mrs Angela Elizabeth. b 36. K Coll Lon BSc58 CertEd59 BD79 AKC79. dss 79 **d** 87. Chapl Raines Sch 79-97; Homerton St Barn w St Paul *Lon* 79-85; Upper Chelsea St Simon 85-89; Hon Par Dn 87-89; Hon Par Dn Limehouse 89-97; Perm to Offic *St E* from 97. *50 Crown Street, Bury St Edmunds IP33 1QX* Tel (01284) 760016

PEARCE, Canon Brian Edward. b 39. Kelham Th Coll 59. **d** 64 **p** 65. C Smethwick St Matt *Birm* 64-68; C Kings Norton 68-72; TV 73-80; TR Swindon Dorcan *Bris* 80-91; Min Withywood CD

91-94; V Withywood 94-98; V Fishponds All SS 98-05; RD Bedminster 92-98; Hon Can Bris Cathl 97-05; rtd 05. *32 Brook Estate, Monmouth NP25 5AW* Tel (01600) 716057 E-mail rev.pearce@tesco.net

PEARCE, Preb Clive. b 40. Univ of Wales (Lamp) BA63 Heythrop Coll Lon MA01. St Steph Ho Ox 63. **d** 65 **p** 66. C Acton Green St Pet *Lon* 65-67; C Eastcote St Lawr 67-73; V Hatch End St Anselm from 73; Preb St Paul's Cathl from 08. *Hatch End Vicarage, 50 Cedar Drive, Pinner HA5 4DE* Tel and fax (020) 8428 4111 Mobile 07710-900545 E-mail ecclesiaenavis@aol.com

PEARCE, Colin James. b 51. Trin Coll Bris 94. **d** 96 **p** 97. C Kingswood *Bris* 96-00; TV Bedminster 00-07; Canada from 07. *189 Lafferty Avenue, Lasalle, Windsor ON N9J 1K1, Canada* Tel (001) (519) 734 1476 E-mail colinjpearce@hotmail.com

PEARCE, Daniel. *See* PEARCE, William Philip Daniel

PEARCE, Desmond. b 30. Univ of Wales (Abth) BA52. EMMTC 85. **d** 88 **p** 89. NSM Chellaston *Derby* 88-90; NSM Walsall St Gabr Fulbrook *Lich* 90; C Stoke Lacy, Moreton Jeffries w Much Cowarne etc *Heref* 91-97; Perm to Offic *Mon* 98-00; P-in-c New Tredegar 00-03. *56 Bedwellty Road, Cefn Forest, Blackwood NP12 3HB* Tel (01443) 833015

PEARCE, Elizabeth. *See* PEARCE, Mrs Janet Elizabeth

PEARCE, Canon Gerald Nettleton. b 25. St Jo Coll Dur BA49. **d** 51 **p** 52. C Bury St Edmunds St Mary *St E* 51-54; C Attenborough w Bramcote and Chilwell *S'well* 54-56; V Selston 56-61; R Wilford 61-73; RD Bingham 73-84; P-in-c Holme Pierrepont w Adbolton 73-84; V Radcliffe-on-Trent 73-84; V Shelford 73-84; Hon Can S'well Minster 77-84; R Sigglesthorne and Rise w Nunkeeling and Bewholme *York* 84-91; RD N Holderness 86-90; Perm to Offic from 91; rtd 91; Rtd Clergy and Widows Officer (E Riding) *York* from 91. *Sutherland Bridge, Cropton, Pickering YO18 8EU* Tel (01751) 417420

PEARCE, Mrs Iris Rose. b 27. **d** 00 **p** 03. OLM Parkstone St Pet and St Osmund w Branksea *Sarum* 00-03; Chapl Asst Poole Hosp NHS Trust 00-03; Hon Asst Chapl from 03. *Flat 1 Pelham, 34 Lindsay Road, Poole BH13 6AY* Tel (01202) 769301 E-mail iris1pelham@aol.com

PEARCE, Mrs Janet Elizabeth. b 49. Somerville Coll Ox BA72 MA76 CertEd74. NOC 85. **d** 88 **p** 94. Par Dn Helsby and Dunham-on-the-Hill *Ches* 88-94; C 94-96; C Norley, Crowton and Kingsley 96-06; Dioc Adv in Spirituality 02-06; R Llanfair Mathafarn Eithaf w Llanbedrgoch *Ban* 06-11; TR Bangor from 11. *St Peter's Vicarage, Penrhos Road, Bangor LL57 2LX* Tel (01248) 355037

PEARCE, Preb John Frederick Dilke. b 32. Ex Coll Ox BA55 MA59. Westcott Ho Cam. **d** 57 **p** 58. C Dalston St Mark w St Bart *Lon* 57-60; C Chelsea Ch Ch 60-63; R Lower Homerton St Paul 63-81; P-in-c Clapton Park All So 72-77; V 77-84; RD Hackney 74-79; R Homerton St Barn w St Paul 81-85; TR Hackney Marsh 85; P-in-c Upper Chelsea St Simon 85-89; AD Chelsea 88-89; R Limehouse 89-97; Preb St Paul's Cathl 70-97; rtd 97; Perm to Offic *St E* from 97. *50 Crown Street, Bury St Edmunds IP33 1QX* Tel (01284) 760016 Fax 756306 E-mail john@jfdp.freeserve.co.uk

PEARCE, Jonathan. b 55. St Jo Coll Nottm BTh85. **d** 85 **p** 86. C Gt Chesham *Ox* 85-89; C Newport Pagnell w Lathbury and Moulsoe 89-93; TV Waltham H Cross *Chelmsf* 93-07; R Gt Totham and Lt Totham w Goldhanger from 07. *The Vicarage, 1 Hall Road, Great Totham, Maldon CM9 8NN* Tel and fax (01621) 893150 E-mail revdjpearce@aol.com

PEARCE, Kenneth Jack. b 25. CIPFA. Linc Th Coll 62. **d** 63 **p** 64. C Wootton Bassett *Sarum* 63-66; C Broad Town 63-66; P-in-c Derby St Andr 66-68; V Derby St Mark 68-87; rtd 87; Perm to Offic *St E* from 91. *117 Oaks Cross, Stevenage SG2 8LT* Tel (01438) 317385

PEARCE, Michael Hawkins. b 29. Sarum Th Coll 61. **d** 62 **p** 63. C Bedminster St Aldhelm *Bris* 62-65; C Bishopston 65-68; R Jacobstow w Warbstow *Truro* 68-74; V Treneglos 68-74; V St Teath 74-94; rtd 94; Perm to Offic *Truro* from 94. *32 Trenant Road, Tywardreath, Par PL24 2QJ* Tel (01726) 813658

PEARCE, Neville John Lewis. b 33. CBIM88 Leeds Univ LLB53 LLM54. Trin Coll Bris 90. **d** 91 **p** 92. NSM Bath Walcot *B & W* 91-93; P-in-c Swainswick w Langridge and Woolley 93-98; Perm to Offic from 98. *Penshurst, Weston Lane, Bath BA1 4AB* Tel (01225) 426925 E-mail nevillepearce@tiscali.co.uk

PEARCE, Robert John. b 47. GLCM LLCM72 Birm Univ PGCE73. Ripon Coll Cuddesdon 79. **d** 82 **p** 83. C Broseley w Benthall *Heref* 82-83; C Kington w Huntington, Old Radnor, Kinnerton etc 83-85; R Westbury 85-94; R Yockleton 85-94; V Gt Wollaston 85-94; V Gwersyllt *St As* 94-99; V Northop 99-03; P-in-c Cerrigydrudion w Llanfihangel Glyn Myfyr etc from 03. *The Rectory, Cerrigydrudion, Corwen LL21 0RU* Tel (01490) 420900

PEARCE, Sacha Jane. b 64. Reading Univ BA92. RGN86 Ripon Coll Cuddesdon. **d** 00 **p** 01. C Tisbury *Sarum* 00-01; C Nadder Valley 01-04; V Seend, Bulkington and Poulshot 04-09; Chapl Plymouth Hosps NHS Trust from 09. *Derriford Hospital, Derriford Road, Plymouth PL6 8DH* Tel (01752) 792022 E-mail sacha.pearce@nhs.net

PEARCE, Mrs Susan Elizabeth. b 44. NEOC 03. **d** 06 **p** 07. NSM Pannal w Beckwithshaw *Ripon* 06-11; NSM High Harrogate St Pet from 11. *56 Beckwith Crescent, Harrogate HG2 0BH* Tel (01423) 565954 E-mail sue.pearce56@btopenworld.com

PEARCE, Trevor John. b 27. FSR57. Roch Th Coll 65. **d** 67 **p** 68. C Cheriton Street *Cant* 67-69; C Willesborough w Hinxhill 69-73; V Devonport St Barn *Ex* 73-79; Chapl N Devon Healthcare NHS Trust 79-83; V Derby St Andr w St Osmund 83-84; Chapl Derbyshire R Infirmary 83-92; Lic to Offic *Derby* 84-92; rtd 92; Perm to Offic *Derby* from 92. *4 Morrell Wood Drive, Belper DE56 0JD* Tel (01773) 828450

PEARCE, Valerie Olive. b 46. Whitelands Coll Lon CertEd67. SEITE 96. **d** 97 **p** 98. CSC 77-04; Lic to Offic *S'wark* 97-04. *13 Helder Street, South Croydon CR2 6HT* Tel (020) 8688 4082 E-mail v.pearce@homecall.co.uk

PEARCE, William Philip Daniel. b 26. Stanford Univ BA48 Leeds Univ CertEd64 MA75. Cuddesdon Coll 54. **d** 56 **p** 57. USA 56-60; CR 60-84; C St Geo-in-the-East w St Paul *Lon* 84-86; USA from 86; rtd 02. *1037 Olympic Lane, Seaside CA 93955-6226, USA* Tel (001) (831) 393 2176 E-mail danielp@mbay.net

PEARKES, Nicholas Robin Clement. b 49. Ex Univ BA. Linc Th Coll. **d** 82 **p** 83. C Plymstock *Ex* 82-85; P-in-c Weston Mill 85-86; TV Devonport St Boniface and St Phil 86-99; R Broadhempston, Woodland, Staverton etc from 99. *The Rectory, Broadhempston, Totnes TQ9 6AU* Tel (01803) 813754 E-mail nicholaspearkes@hotmail.com

PEARMAIN, Anthony Neil. b 55. K Coll Lon BD79 AKC79. Ridley Hall Cam 79. **d** 81 **p** 82. C Cranleigh *Guildf* 81-84; P-in-c Frimley 85-86; C 86-87. *4 Laurel Close, Farnborough GU14 0PT*

PEARMAIN, Brian Albert John. b 34. Lon Univ BD68. Roch Th Coll 63. **d** 66 **p** 67. C Shirley St Jo *Cant* 66-69; C Selsdon St Jo w St Fran 69-73; P-in-c Louth H Trin *Linc* 73-75; TV Louth 75-79; R Scartho 79-97; RD Grimsby and Cleethorpes 89-94; Can and Preb Linc Cathl 94-97; rtd 97; Perm to Offic *Linc* 00-07 and *Bradf* from 08. *20 Red Lion Street, Earby, Barnoldswick BB18 6RD* Tel (01282) 842680 Mobile 07944-675321

PEARMAN, Mrs Barbara Elizabeth Anne. b 48. RGN69 RHV72. ERMC 07. **d** 09 **p** 10. NSM E Marshland *Ely* from 09. *Rambles, 8 School Road, Tilney All Saints, King's Lynn PE34 4RS* Tel (01553) 828808 Mobile 07946-348744 E-mail barbarapearman@hotmail.com

PEARS, Anthony John. b 58. Ripon Coll Cuddesdon 00. **d** 02 **p** 03. C Watton w Carbrooke and Ovington *Nor* 02-05; R Northanger *Win* from 05. *The Rectory, Gaston Lane, Upper Farringdon, Alton GU34 3EE* Tel (01420) 588398 E-mail tony.pears@virgin.net

PEARSE, Andrew George. b 46. Wycliffe Hall Ox 71. **d** 74 **p** 75. C Homerton St Luke *Lon* 74-77; C Chadderton Em *Man* 77-81; R Collyhurst 81-89; Area Sec (NE, E Midl and Scotland) SAMS 89-03; rtd 03; Chapl Co-ord St Leon Hospice York 03-11; Perm to Offic *York* from 11. *9 Troutsdale Avenue, York YO30 5TR* Tel (01904) 332373 E-mail tarvethecurkey@yahoo.co.uk

PEARSE, Ronald Thomas Hennessy. b 26. AKC52. **d** 53 **p** 54. C Leic St Pet 53-55; C Hanwell St Thos *Lon* 55-58; R Asfordby *Leic* 58-84; P-in-c Scalford w Wycombe and Chadwell 75-76; R Thurcaston 84-89; rtd 89; Perm to Offic *Leic* 89-90. *15 Burton Street, Loughborough LE11 2DT* Tel (01509) 215478

PEARSON, Canon Andrew George Campbell. b 41. Qu Coll Ox BA63 BA66. Wycliffe Hall Ox 63. **d** 71 **p** 72. C Gillingham St Mark *Roch* 71-72; C Billingshurst *Chich* 72-77; C Ches Square St Mich w St Phil *Lon* 77-82; Co-ord Busoga Trust 82-02; Dir from 02; Hon Can Busoga from 98; P-in-c St Marg Pattens *Lon* 90-06; Hon C Kensington St Mary Abbots w St Geo 96-06; rtd 06. *Denecroft, Little East Street, Billingshurst RH14 9PN* Tel (01403) 782080 E-mail busogatrust@hotmail.com

PEARSON, Andrew John. b 59. Westcott Ho Cam 86. **d** 89 **p** 90. C Knaresborough *Ripon* 89-92; C Wetherby 92-94; P-in-c Hunslet Moor St Pet and St Cuth 94-96; V 96-01; V Hawksworth Wood 01-06; Dioc Environment Officer 96-07; P-in-c Oulton w Woodlesford from 06; P-in-c Methley w Mickletown from 06. *The Vicarage, 44 Holmsley Lane, Woodlesford, Leeds LS26 8RY* Tel 0113-282 0411 E-mail lindrew@pearley.fsnet.co.uk

PEARSON, Andrew Michael. b 54. Univ of Wales (Ban) BTh10 Solicitor 77. **d** 07 **p** 08. OLM Shere, Albury and Chilworth *Guildf* from 07. *Owl House, Shophouse Lane, Albury, Guildford GU5 9ET* Tel (01483) 203220 Mobile 07815-049950 E-mail rev.a.m.pearson@btinternet.com

PEARSON, Ms Brenda Elizabeth Frances (Brandy). b 51. SEITE 00. **d** 03 **p** 04. NSM Finsbury Park St Thos *Lon* 03-07; C Acton Green from 07. *276 Osborne Road, London W3 8SR* Tel (020) 8993 3237 E-mail brandy@brandypearson.wanadoo.co.uk

PEARSON, Canon Brian Robert. b 35. Leeds Univ BA59. Coll of Resurr Mirfield 59. **d** 61 **p** 62. C Chesterfield St Mary and All SS *Derby* 61-66; P-in-c Derby St Jo 66-72; P-in-c Derby St Anne 66-72; R Thorpe St Andr *Nor* 72-90; Hon Can Nor Cathl 85-90; RD Nor E 86-90; V Harrogate St Wilfrid *Ripon* 90-00; rtd 00; Perm to Offic *York* from 00 and *Bradf* from 04. *Green Garth, 13 Cedar Glade, Dunnington, York YO19 5QZ* Tel (01904) 481232

PEARSON, Canon Brian William. b 49. FHSM Brighton Poly BSc71 City Univ MSc80 Westmr Coll Ox MTh94. S'wark Ord Course & Clapham Ord Scheme 76. **d** 79 **p** 80. Hon C Plumstead All SS *S'wark* 79-81; Perm to Offic *Chich* 81-83; Hon C Broadwater St Mary 83-88; Bp's Research and Dioc Communications Officer *B & W* 88-90; Dioc Missr 91; Abp's Officer for Miss and Evang and Tait Missr *Cant* 91-97; Abp's Dioc Chapl 91-97; Hon Prov Can Cant Cathl 92-97; Gen Dir CPAS 97-00; P-in-c Leek Wootton and Dioc Officer for OLM *Cov* 00-06. *Woodspring, Northfields, Somerton TA11 6SL* Tel (01458) 274360 E-mail brian@bwpvic.fslife.co.uk

PEARSON, Mrs Béatrice Levasseur. b 53. Sorbonne Univ Paris LèsL74 MèsL75 Lon Inst of Educn PGCE76. Ripon Coll Cuddesdon 01. **d** 03 **p** 04. C Easthampstead *Ox* 03-06; TV Loddon Reach from 06. *The Vicarage, 11 Clares Green Road, Spencers Wood, Reading RG7 1DY* Tel 0118-988 3215 Mobile 07981-462145 E-mail bea.acumen@zetnet.co.uk

PEARSON, Christian David John (Brother Christian). b 42. Open Univ BA76 CCC Cam BA79 MA83. AKC65. **d** 66 **p** 67. C Pallion *Dur* 66-68; C Peterlee 68-71; SSF from 71; Lic to Offic *Sarum* 71-73; Tanzania 74-75; Lic to Offic *Ely* 75-90; Asst Chapl Keble Coll Ox 82-83; Chapl St Cath Coll Cam 83-86; Chapl Down Coll Cam 86-90; Lic to Offic *Lon* from 90; Dep Warden and Chapl Lon Goodenough Trust 90-95. *St Mary's House, Neasden Lane, London NW10 2TS* Tel (020) 8459 5834

PEARSON, Christopher John. b 49. GRSM LRAM ARCM. Oak Hill NSM Course 81. **d** 84 **p** 85. NSM Barton Seagrave w Warkton *Pet* 84-86; C Kettering St Andr 86-88; V Nassington w Yarwell and Woodnewton 88-91; V Pet St Mark 91-03; P-in-c Gt Doddington and Wilby from 03; P-in-c Ecton from 07. *The Vicarage, 72 High Street, Great Doddington, Wellingborough NN29 7TH* Tel and fax (01933) 226711 E-mail c.pearson1@homecall.co.uk

PEARSON, Christopher William. b 56. Univ Coll Ox MA. St Jo Coll Nottm 07. **d** 09 **p** 10. C Norton St Mary and Stockton St Chad *Dur* 09-11; P-in-c Easington and Easington Colliery from 11. *The Rectory, 5 Tudor Grange, Easington Village, Peterlee SR8 3DF* Tel 0191-527 1486 E-mail cwpearson@fastmail.fm

PEARSON, Colin Graham. b 58. St Jo Coll Nottm 01. **d** 04 **p** 05. C Mickleover All SS *Derby* 04-09; C Breadsall 09-10; P-in-c Alvaston from 10. *The Vicarage, 8 Church Street, Alvaston, Derby DE24 0PR* Tel (01332) 571143 E-mail colin_pearson@tiscali.co.uk

PEARSON, David. See PEARSON, James David

PEARSON, David. b 57. Man Poly BA78. Trin Coll Bris 85. **d** 88 **p** 89. C Shawbury *Lich* 88-91; C Morton 88-91; C Stanton on Hine Heath 88-91; R Mattishall w Mattishall Burgh, Welborne etc *Nor* 91-00; RD Dereham in Mitford 98-00; Asst P Tawa Linden New Zealand 00-04; V Levin from 04. *120 Cambridge Street, Levin 5500, New Zealand* Tel (0064) (6) 368 5955 E-mail vicar.levinanglicans@xtra.co.nz

PEARSON, Fergus Tom. b 58. Middx Poly BA81 Moore Th Coll Sydney MA98. Oak Hill Th Coll BA95. **d** 92 **p** 93. C Mildmay Grove St Jude and St Paul *Lon* 92-95; Australia 96-98; C Heatherlands St Jo *Sarum* 98-03; V Hensingham *Carl* from 03. *St John's Vicarage, Egremont Road, Hensingham, Whitehaven CA28 8QW* Tel (01946) 692822 E-mail fpe@rson.justbrowsing.com

PEARSON, Geoffrey Charles. b 49. Imp Coll Lon BSc70 ARCS. Oak Hill Th Coll 80. **d** 82 **p** 83. C Ford St Jo *Cant* 82-86; V Ramsgate St Luke 86-93; Chapl to People at Work in Cam *Ely* 93-01; Co-ord Chapl HM Pris Chelmsf 01-07; rtd 07; Perm to Offic *Cant* from 08. *99 Cherry Drive, Canterbury CT2 8ER* Tel and fax (01227) 379451 Mobile 07890-808739 E-mail pearsongeoff@hotmail.co.uk

✠**PEARSON, The Rt Revd Geoffrey Seagrave.** b 51. St Jo Coll Dur BA72. Cranmer Hall Dur 72. **d** 74 **p** 75 **c** 06. C Kirkheaton *Wakef* 74-77; C-in-c Blackb Redeemer 77-82; V 82-85; Asst Home Sec Gen Syn Bd for Miss and Unity 85-89; Hon C Forty Hill Jes Ch *Lon* 85-89; Exec Sec BCC Evang Cttee 86-89; V Roby *Liv* 89-06; AD Huyton 02-06; Hon Can Liv Cathl 03-06; Suff Bp Lancaster *Blackb* from 06; C Ellel w Shireshead from 08. *Shireshead Vicarage, Whinney Brow, Forton, Preston PR3 0AE* Tel (01524) 799900 Fax 799901 E-mail bishoplancaster@gmail.com

PEARSON, George Michael. b 31. FCA FBCS MIMC. Qu Coll Birm 86 Coll of Resurr Mirfield 89. **d** 88 **p** 90. NSM Solihull Birm 88-95; Perm to Offic from 95. *The Parsonage, 67A Hampton Lane, Solihull B91 2QD* Tel 0121-705 0288 E-mail parsonpearson@pearwood.org.uk

PEARSON, Canon Henry Gervis. b 47. Mansf Coll Ox BA72 MA76. St Jo Coll Nottm 72. **d** 74 **p** 75. C Southgate *Chich* 74-76; TV 76-82; V Debenham w Aspall and Kenton *St E* 82-91; Chapl to Suffolk Fire Service 88-91; RD Loes 89-91; TR Marlborough *Sarum* 91-02; RD Marlborough 94-02; Can and Preb Sarum Cathl from 99; Chapl Savernake Hosp Marlborough 91-94; Chapl E Wilts Health Care NHS Trust from 94; R Queen Thorne *Sarum* from 02; P-in-c Gifle Valley from 10; RD

Sherborne from 04. *The Rectory, Trent, Sherborne DT9 4SL* Tel (01935) 851049 E-mail canonhenry@btinternet.com
PEARSON, Ian. b 49. Liv Univ BA71. S'wark Ord Course 79. **d** 82 **p** 83. Archivist USPG 82-85; Archivist Nat Soc 85-91; NSM Lavender Hill Ascension *S'wark* 82-84; Lic to Offic *Lon* 84-86 and 88-90; NSM Westmr St Matt 86-88; Perm to Offic *S'wark* 85-90 and *St Alb* 90-91; C Chesterfield St Mary and All SS *Derby* 91-95; R Bengeo *St Alb* 95-04; P-in-c Worc City St Paul and Old St Martin etc 04-06; R Worc City 06-10; rtd 10. *7 Rosedale Walk, Frome BA11 2JH* Tel (01373) 469739 E-mail ianandlizpearson@waitrose.com
PEARSON, James David. b 51. Cape Town Univ BSocSc74. St Paul's Coll Grahamstown 76. **d** 78 **p** 79. C St Geo Cathl Cape Town 78-80; R Caledon H Trin 80-84; R Tristan da Cunha St Mary 84-86; R Camps Bay St Pet 86-89; R Kuruman St Mary-le-Bourne w Wrenchville St Pet 89-91; R Amalinda Ch 92-96; Asst P Cambridge St Mark 96-98; Asst P-in-c Kidds Beach St Mary and St Andr 99; C Prittlewell St Steph *Chelmsf* 00-04; TV Barking St Marg w St Patr 04-09; P-in-c Hornchurch H Cross from 09. *Holy Cross Vicarage, 260 Hornchurch Road, Hornchurch RM11 1PX* Tel (01708) 447976 E-mail david pearson@dsl.pipex.com
PEARSON, James William. b 20. FCA59. Qu Coll Birm 75. **d** 78 **p** 79. NSM Beoley *Worc* 78-90; Perm to Offic from 90. *Ringwood, Rowney Green, Alvechurch, Birmingham B48 7QE* Tel (01527) 66952
PEARSON, Miss Joanna Ruth. b 76. St Hilda's Coll Ox BA97 PGCE98 St Jo Coll Dur BA05 MA09. Cranmer Hall Dur 03. **d** 06 **p** 07. C Leeds St Geo *Ripon* 06-10; TV from 10. *18 Weetwood Road, Leeds LS16 5LP* Tel 0113-230 7113 E-mail joanna.pearson@stgeorgesleeds.org.uk
✠**PEARSON, The Rt Revd Kevin.** b 54. Leeds Univ BA75 Edin Univ BD79. Edin Th Coll 76. **d** 79 **p** 80 **c** 11. C Horden *Dur* 79-81; Chapl Leeds Univ 81-87; R Edin St Salvador 87-93; Chapl Napier Poly 88-92; Chapl Napier Univ 92-94; Dioc Dir of Ords 90-95; Prov Dir of Ords from 91; Assoc R Edin Old St Paul 93-94; P-in-c Linlithgow 94-95; R Edin St Mich and All SS 95-11; Can St Mary's Cathl 03-11; Dean Edin 04-10; Bp Arg from 11. *St Moluag's Diocesan Centre, Croft Avenue, Oban PA34 5JJ* Tel (01631) 570870 E-mail bishop@argyll.anglican.org
PEARSON, Mrs Lindsey Carole. b 61. Cov Poly BA85 CQSW85. Westcott Ho Cam 86. **d** 89 **p** 94. Par Dn High Harrogate St Pet *Ripon* 89-93; Par Dn Moor Allerton 93-94; C 94-96; TV Seacroft 96-04; World Development Officer 99-04; Area Co-ord (N and W Yorks) Chr Aid 04-07; P-in-c Swillington *Ripon* from 07. *The Vicarage, 46 Holmsley Lane, Woodlesford, Leeds LS26 8RY* Tel 0113-282 0411 E-mail lindrew@pearley.fsnet.co.uk
PEARSON, Michael Carden. b 38. Guy's Hosp Medical Sch MB63 BChir63 Down Coll Cam MA64 Lon Univ MSc94 FRCR75 FRCP94. St Steph Ho Ox 96. **d** 98 **p** 99. NSM Horsted Keynes *Chich* 98-99; NSM Worth 99-00; Chapl Gtr Athens *Eur* 00-01; Perm to Offic *Chich* 04-05; P-in-c Stapleford Common 05-08; rtd 08. *Bleak House, Station Road, Horsted Keynes, Haywards Heath RH17 7ED* Tel (01825) 790617 E-mail michaelpearson@coxlesspair.demon.co.uk
PEARSON, Michael John. b 53. Southn Univ BTh78. Sarum Th Coll 74. **d** 78 **p** 79. C Paignton St Jo *Ex* 78-82; TV Ilfracombe, Lee, Woolacombe, Bittadon etc 82-86; TV Barnstaple 86-08; Chapl N Devon Healthcare NHS Trust 86-96; RD Barnstaple *Ex* 97-01; C Shaldon, Stokeinteignhead, Combeinteignhead etc 08-09; rtd 09. *Mira Ceti, Salty Lane, Shaldon, Teignmouth TQ14 0AP* Tel (01626) 872443 E-mail fathermichaelpearson@googlemail.com
PEARSON, Nigel Hetley Allan. b 45. Fitzw Coll Cam BA67 MA87. EMMTC 04. **d** 06 **p** 07. NSM Papworth *Ely* from 06. *Manor Farm House, 53 Ermine Street, Caxton, Cambridge CB23 3PQ* Tel (01954) 719750 Fax 718566 Mobile 07713-639928 E-mail njfarm@gmail.com
PEARSON, Pauline Hilary. b 54. BA77 PhD88 RN77 RHV79. NEOC 02. **d** 05 **p** 06. NSM Denton *Newc* 05-10; NSM Newc St Geo and St Hilda from 10. *3 Belle Grove Place, Newcastle upon Tyne NE2 4LH* Tel 0191-232 5980 Mobile 07753-744349 E-mail pauline.pearson@northumbria.ac.uk
PEARSON, Mrs Priscilla Dawn. b 45. Oak Hill Th Coll BA90. **d** 90 **p** 94. Par Dn Stanford-le-Hope w Mucking *Chelmsf* 90-94; C 94; C Colchester St Jo 94-96; Hon C Woking St Jo *Guildf* 03-05; rtd 10. *Talywain Cottage, Shop Road, Cwmavon, Pontypool NP4 7RU* Tel (01495) 774132 E-mail priscillapearson@btinternet.com
PEARSON, Raymond Joseph. b 44. AKC71. St Aug Coll Cant 71. **d** 72 **p** 73. C Wetherby *Ripon* 72-75; C Goring-by-Sea *Chich* 75-77; C Bramley *Ripon* 77-82; V Patrick Brompton and Hunton 82-94; V Crakehall 82-94; V Hornby 82-94; World Miss Officer 88-94; RD Wensley 92-94; V Bardsey 94-09; rtd 09; Perm to Offic *York* from 09. *7 St George's Croft, Bridlington YO16 7RW* Tel (01262) 424332
PEARSON, Robert James Stephen. b 52. Cov Poly BA74. St Steph Ho Ox 85. **d** 87 **p** 88. C Stoke Newington St Mary *Lon*

87-90; C Haggerston All SS 90-97; C Dalston H Trin w St Phil and Haggerston All SS 97-98; Chapl HM Pris Wandsworth 98-02; Chapl HM Pris Pentonville 02-07; Perm to Offic *Lon* from 07. *276 Osborne Road, London W3 8SR* Tel (020) 8993 3237 E-mail ahjay@hotmail.co.uk
PEARSON, Robert Lyon. b 57. St Jo Coll Nottm 90. **d** 92 **p** 93. C Netherton *Liv* 92-96; V Woolston 96-02; V Highfield from 02. *St Matthew's Vicarage, Billinge Road, Wigan WN3 6BL* Tel (01942) 222121 Fax 211332 E-mail vicar@stmatthewhighfield.org.uk
PEARSON, Preb Roy Barthram. b 35. K Coll Lon 56. **d** 60 **p** 61. C Brookfield St Mary *Lon* 60-64; C St Marylebone St Cypr 64-70; V Tottenham All Hallows from 70; AD E Haringey 95-00; Preb St Paul's Cathl from 96. *The Priory, Church Lane, London N17 7AA* Tel (020) 8808 2470
PEARSON-GEE, William Oliver Clinton. b 61. Wycliffe Hall Ox 04. **d** 06 **p** 07. C Ox St Andr 06-10; R Buckingham from 10. *The Rectory, 8 Aris Way, Buckingham MK18 1FX* Tel (01280) 830221 E-mail rector@buckinghambenefice.org.uk
PEARSON-MILES, David. b 37. St Jo Coll Nottm 74. **d** 76 **p** 77. C Hazlemere *Ox* 76-79; R Waddesdon w Over Winchendon and Fleet Marston 79-82; CF 82-92; P-in-c Barcombe *Chich* 92-94; R 94-00; rtd 00. *The Coach House, Holme Place, Oakford, Tiverton EX16 9DH* Tel (01398) 351495
PEART, John Graham. b 36. Bps' Coll Cheshunt 65. **d** 68 **p** 69. C Cheshunt *St Alb* 68-70; C St Alb St Pet 70-73; R Hunsdon and Widford 73-76; Ind Chapl 76-82; Chapl St Geo Hosp and Distr Gen Hosp Stafford 82-87; Chapl Qu Eliz Hosp and Bensham Hosp Gateshead 87-89; Chapl Garlands Hosp 89-94; P-in-c Cotehill and Cumwhinton *Carl* 89-94; V Irthington, Crosby-on-Eden and Scaleby 94-98; rtd 98; Chapl Douglas MacMillan Hospice Stoke-on-Trent 98-01; P-in-c Salt and Sandon w Burston *Lich* 01-02; TV Mid Trent 02-03; Perm to Offic *Lich* 04-07 and *Eur* from 07. *Taljovagen 2, SE-184-92 Taljo, Akersberga, Sweden* Tel (0046) (8) 5402 1214 E-mail johnpeart@hotmail.co.uk
PEART, Patricia Isidora. b 55. Westcott Ho Cam 97. **d** 99. C Holland-on-Sea *Chelmsf* 99-00; C Shrub End 00-01. *6 Whitsand Road, Manchester M22 4ZA*
PEAT, Mrs Ann Kathleen. b 40. TCert60. **d** 98 **p** 99. OLM Brumby *Linc* from 98. *36 Glover Road, Scunthorpe DN17 1AS* Tel (01724) 852609
PEAT, David James. b 62. Leeds Univ BA84 Dur Univ MA91. Cranmer Hall Dur 86. **d** 89 **p** 90. C Wetherby *Ripon* 89-92; C Beeston 92-95; Chapl St Lawr Coll Ramsgate 95-06; Hd Relig Educn Eastbourne Coll from 06. *Eastbourne College, Old Wish Road, Eastbourne BN21 4JY* Tel (01323) 452244 E-mail djpeat@eastbourne-college.co.uk
PEAT, David William. b 37. Clare Coll Cam MA59 PhD62 FRAS63. Westcott Ho Cam 72. **d** 75 **p** 76. C Chesterton St Andr *Ely* 75-77; Chapl Univ Coll of Ripon and York St Jo 77-83; V E Ardsley *Wakef* 83-87; Prin Willesden Min Tr Scheme 87-94; NSM Headingley *Ripon* 94-; P-in-c from 06; Research Lect Leeds Univ from 94. *12 North Grange Mews, Headingley, Leeds LS6 2EW* Tel 0113-275 3179 E-mail phy6dwp@phys-irc.leeds.ac.uk
PEAT, The Ven Lawrence Joseph. b 28. Linc Th Coll 55. **d** 58 **p** 59. C Bramley *Ripon* 58-61; V 65-73; R Heaton Norris All SS *Man* 61-65; P-in-c Southend St Erkenwald *Chelmsf* 73-74; TR Southend St Jo w St Mark, All SS w St Fran etc 74-79; V Skelsmergh w Selside and Longsleddale *Carl* 79-86; RD Kendal 84-89; TV Kirkby Lonsdale 86-89; Hon Can Carl Cathl 88-95; Adn Westmorland and Furness 89-95; rtd 95; Perm to Offic *Carl* 95-09. *22 Links View, Frobisher Drive, Lytham St Annes FY8 2TW* E-mail lawrie.peat@fsmail.net
PEAT, Matthew. b 71. Bradf and Ilkley Coll BA97. Ripon Coll Cuddesdon BTh03. **d** 03 **p** 04. C Walney Is *Carl* 03-06; C Barrow St Matt 06-08; TR 08-10; TR N Barrow from 10. *St Matthew's Vicarage, Highfield Road, Barrow-in-Furness LA14 5NZ* Tel (01229) 823569
PEATMAN (née HUGHES), Mrs Debbie Ann. b 62. SS Hild & Bede Coll Dur BA83 St Jo Coll Dur BA89. Cranmer Hall Dur 87. **d** 90 **p** 94. C Edin Old St Paul 90-91; NSM Greasley *S'well* 92-94; NSM Whitley *Cov* 94-02; C Lancaster St Thos *Blackb* 02-09; Co Ecum Development Officer for Churches Together in Lancs from 09. *The Rectory, Church Walk, Morecambe LA4 5PR* Tel 07806-643097 (mobile) E-mail debbie.peatman@ctlancashire.org.uk
PEATMAN, Michael Robert. b 61. Keble Coll Ox BA85 MA89 St Jo Coll Dur BA89 Lanc Univ MA06. Cranmer Hall Dur 87. **d** 90 **p** 91. C Greasley *S'well* 90-94; P-in-c Whitley *Cov* 94-02; Dio Stewardship Adv 94-02; Sen Chapl St Martin's Coll *Blackb* 02-07; Sen Chapl Cumbria Univ 07-09; P-in-c Poulton-le-Sands w Morecambe St Laur from 09; AD Lancaster and Morecambe from 10. *The Rectory, Church Walk, Morecambe LA4 5PR* Tel and fax (01524) 410941 E-mail mikepeat@sky.com
PEATTIE, The Ven Colin Hulme Reid. b 39. Natal Univ BSc59. Ripon Hall Ox 61. **d** 63 **p** 64. C Belmont *Lon* 63-65; S Africa 65-83 and from 85; R Durban St Columba 65-69; R Dundee

St Jas 69-72; Chapl St Andr Sch Bloemfontein 72-76; R Pietermaritzburg St Alphege 76-83; V S Ossett *Wakef* 83-85; R York-cum-Ravensworth 85-93; R Stanger All SS 93-96; R Umhlali All So from 96; Adn N Coast from 01. *PO Box 222, Salt Rock, 4391 South Africa* Tel and fax (0027) (32) 947 2001 Mobile 82-413 8650 E-mail cpeattie@absamail.co.za

PEATY, Canon Julia Kathleen. b 53. Salford Univ BSc75. STETS 96. **d** 99 **p** 00. NSM E Grinstead St Swithun *Chich* from 99; RD E Grinstead from 10; Can and Preb Chich Cathl from 10. *15 Overton Shaw, East Grinstead RH19 2HN* Tel (01342) 322386 E-mail julia@peaty.net

PEBERDY (*née* GARNETT), Mrs Alyson Susan. b 48. Trevelyan Coll Dur BA69 Reading Univ MA75. Ox Min Course 95. **d** 96 **p** 97. C New Windsor *Ox* 96-99; V Brockley Hill St Sav *S'wark* from 99; P-in-c Perry Hill St Geo 00-01; P-in-c Forest Hill St Aug 00-02; Adv Women's Min Woolwich Area from 10. *St Saviour's Vicarage, 5 Lushner Hill, London SE23 1PZ* Tel (020) 8690 2499 E-mail alysonpeberdy@aol.com

PECK, Christopher Wallace. b 49. UEA BA72 Lon Bible Coll BA75 Ches Coll of HE MTh96. Ripon Coll Cuddesdon 10. **d** 11. C Abington *Pet* from 11. *10 Sharplands, Grendon, Northampton NN7 1JL* Tel (01933) 665965 Mobile-07505 253096 E-mail revchrispeck@hotmail.co.uk

PECK, David Warner. b 66. American Univ (Washington) BA88 Selw Coll Cam BA94 MA99. Westcott Ho Cam 92. **d** 95 **p** 96. C Weybridge *Guildf* 95-99; Bp's Chapl 99-05; Abp's Sec for Internat Development *Cant* 05-08; R Lancaster St Jas USA from 08. *The Rectory, 115 North Duke Street, Lancaster PA 17602, USA* Tel and fax (001) (717) 397 4858

PECK, Kay Margaret. b 51. Milton Keynes Coll of Ed BEd76. Ox Min Course 04. **d** 07 **p** 08. NSM Swan *Ox* 07-10; NSM Lenborough from 11. *21 Beamish Way, Winslow, Buckingham MK18 3EU* E-mail kmpeck@btinternet.com

PECK, Robert John. b 49. Bath Univ BSc72. STETS 00. **d** 03 **p** 04. NSM Stoke-next-Guildf 03-08; V Camberley St Martin Old Dean from 08. *St Martin's Vicarage, 2A Hampshire Road, Camberley GU15 4DW* Tel (01276) 23958 E-mail bob@stmartinolddean.com *or* rpeck@btinternet.com

PECKETT, Desmonde Claude Brown. b 19. Ex & Truro NSM Scheme. **d** 77 **p** 78. NSM Charlestown *Truro* 77-89; Perm to Offic from 89. *Smugglers, Porthpean, St Austell PL26 6AY* Tel (01726) 72768

PECKHAM, Richard Graham. b 51. Sarum & Wells Th Coll 84. **d** 86 **p** 87. C Bishop's Cleeve *Glouc* 86-89; TV Ilfracombe, Lee, Woolacombe, Bittadon etc *Ex* 89-96; TV Sidmouth, Woolbrook, Salcombe Regis, Sidbury etc from 96; RD Ottery 98-02; Hon Chapl ATC from 98. *The Vicarage, Harcombe Lane, Sidford, Sidmouth EX10 9QN* Tel (01395) 514522 E-mail rikpeckham@btinternet.com

PEDDER, Brian. b 38. Carl Dioc Tr Inst 88. **d** 91 **p** 92. NSM Wigton *Carl* 91-93; C Cleator Moor w Cleator 93-96; P-in-c Grayrigg, Old Hutton and New Hutton 96-04; rtd 04. *5 Scholars Green, Wigton CA7 9QW* Tel (016973) 45346

PEDLAR, Canon John Glanville. b 43. Ex Univ BA68 De Montfort Univ Hon MA06. St Steph Ho Ox 68. **d** 70 **p** 71. C Tavistock and Gulworthy *Ex* 70-73; Prec Portsm Cathl 74-77; Prec St Alb Abbey 77-81; V Redbourn 81-98; V Bedford St Paul from 98; PV Westmr Abbey 87-04; Hon Can St Alb from 06. *St Paul's Vicarage, 12 The Embankment, Bedford MK40 3PD* Tel (01234) 364638 E-mail johnpedlar@btinternet.com

PEDLEY, Canon Betty. b 49. Ripon Coll of Educn CertEd70 Leeds Univ BEd71 ALCM78. NOC 85. **d** 88 **p** 03. Par Dn Sowerby *Wakef* 88-92; Par Educn Adv and Youth Chapl 92-03; P-in-c Luddenden w Luddenden Foot 03-08; P-in-c Norland 06-08; Hon Can Wakef Cathl 00-08; rtd 08; Perm to Offic *Wakef* from 08. *7 Ogden View Close, Halifax HX2 9LY* Tel (01422) 882127

✠**PEDLEY, The Rt Revd Geoffrey Stephen.** b 40. Qu Coll Cam BA64 MA67. Cuddesdon Coll 64. **d** 66 **p** 67 **c** 98. C Liv Our Lady and St Nic 66-69; C Cov H Trin 69-71; P-in-c Kitwe Zambia 71-77; P-in-c Stockton H Trin *Dur* 77-83; V Stockton St Pet 77-88; Chapl to The Queen 84-98; R Whickham *Dur* 88-93; Can Res Dur Cathl 93-98; Suff Bp Lancaster *Blackb* 98-05; Hon Can Blackb Cathl 98-05; rtd 05. *The Blue House, Newbrough, Hexham NE47 5AN* Tel (01434) 674238

PEDLEY, Nicholas Charles. b 48. CQSW75. Qu Coll Birm 88. **d** 90 **p** 91. C Stafford St Jo and Tixall w Ingestre *Lich* 90-93; C Kingswinford St Mary *Worc* 93-96; TV 96-97; C Cheswardine, Childs Ercall, Hales, Hinstock etc *Lich* 97-99; Chapl HM YOI Stoke Heath 97-99; rtd 99; Perm to Offic *Worc* from 00. *33 Comber Grove, Kinver, Stourbridge DY7 6EN* Tel (01384) 877219 E-mail nick@npedley48.freeserve.co.uk

PEDLEY, Simon David. b 56. Lon Univ BSc98 ARCS98. Oak Hill Th Coll BA10. **d** 10 **p** 11. C St Helen Bishopsgate w St Andr Undershaft etc *Lon* from 10. *2 St Andrew's Mansions, Dorset Street, London W1 4EQ* Tel and fax (020) 7629 5885 Mobile 07713-897991 E-mail simon.pedley@christchurchmayfair.org

PEDLOW, Henry Noel. b 37. QUB BA59. **d** 61 **p** 62. C Belfast St Phil *Conn* 61-66; C Belfast St Nic 66-70; I Eglantine 70-82; I

Kilkeel *D & D* 82-89; I Belfast St Donard 89-03; rtd 03. *8 Old Mill Dale, Dundonalad, Belfast BT16 1WG* Tel (028) 9048 5416

PEEBLES, David Thomas. b 64. Bris Univ BA85 St Chad's Coll Dur PGCE86 Man Univ MA94. Coll of Resurr Mirfield 90. **d** 90 **p** 91. C Crewe St Andr *Ches* 90-93; Lect and Asst Dir Studies Mirfield 93-95; Chapl Qu Mary and Westf Coll Lon 95-00; P-in-c Bethnal Green St Matt w St Jas the Gt 97-99; Chapl LSE 00-10; R Bloomsbury St Geo w Woburn Square Ch Ch from 10; Bp's Adv on New Relig Movements from 01. *The Rectory, 6 Gower Street, London WC1E 6DP* Tel (020) 7580 4010 E-mail d.peebles@lse.ac.uk

PEEK, Alan Nicholas. b 65. Ridley Hall Cam 02. **d** 04 **p** 05. C Much Woolton *Liv* 04-08; I Derg w Termonamongan *D & R* from 08. *The Rectory, 13 Strabane Road, Castlederg BT81 7HZ* Tel (028) 8167 1362 E-mail rev.al@sky.com

PEEK, John Richard. b 51. Bris Univ BSc72 Nottm Univ BA75. St Jo Coll Nottm. **d** 76 **p** 77. C Hebburn St Jo *Dur* 76-78; C Dunston 78-81; R Armthorpe *Sheff* 81-86; RE Teacher K Edw VI Sch Southn 87-88; Chapl and Hd RE Casterton Sch Cumbria 89; Teacher Furze Platt Comp Sch Berks 89-90; Chapl Bearwood Coll Wokingham 96-97; Teacher K Manor Sch Guildf 97-98; Teacher Stowford Coll Sutton 98-08; Teacher Ryde Sch w Upper Chine 08-09; Perm to Offic *Portsm* from 08. *St Lawrence House, 59 Albert Street, Ventnor PO38 1EU* Tel (01983) 853328

PEEL, Mrs Christine Mary. b 44. Whitelands Coll Lon CertEd66. Portsm Dioc Tr Course. **d** 90. NSM Sheet *Portsm* 90-03; Perm to Offic *York* from 03. *11 Whiteoak Avenue, Easingwold, York YO61 3GB* Tel (01347) 823548 E-mail iw.peel@homecall.co.uk

PEEL, Canon David Charles. b 41. AKC75. St Aug Coll Cant 75. **d** 76 **p** 77. C Tynemouth Cullercoats St Paul *Newc* 76-79; C Tynemouth St Jo 79-84; Ldr Cedarwood Project 84-88 and from 91; Warden Communicare Ho 89-91; Min Killingworth 89-91; Hon Can Newc Cathl 08-11; rtd 11. *116 Grey Street, North Shields NE30 2EG* Tel 0191-272 8743

PEEL, Derrick. b 50. Open Univ BA82. Linc Th Coll 75. **d** 78 **p** 79. C Otley *Bradf* 78-82; V Shelf 82-94; P-in-c Buttershaw St Aid 89-94; TR Shelf w Buttershaw St Aid 94-95; V E Crompton *Man* 95-05; V Ware St Mary *St Alb* from 05. *St Mary's Vicarage, 31 Thunder Court, Ware SG12 0PT* Tel (01920) 464817

PEEL, John Bruce. b 30. TCD BA54 MA68. Wells Th Coll 69. **d** 70 **p** 71. C Wilmslow *Ches* 70-75; V Weston 75-83; V Henbury 83-95; Chapl Parkside Hosp Ches 83-95; rtd 95; Perm to Offic *Ches* from 95. *Winneba, 29 Hungerford Terrace, Crewe CW1 6HF* Tel (01270) 587464

PEEL, Capt Jonathan Sidney. b 37. CBE95 MC57 DL75. St Jo Coll Cam BA70 MA75. **d** 00 **p** 01. NSM Ashmanhaugh, Barton Turf etc *Nor* 00-07; rtd 07; Perm to Offic *Nor* from 07. *Barton Hall, Barton Turf, Norwich NR12 8AU* Tel (01692) 536250 Fax 536135

PEEL, Michael Jerome. b 31. Bris Univ BA55 MLitt73 Man Univ BD65 K Coll Lon PhD88. Wycliffe Hall Ox 57. **d** 59 **p** 60. C Stretford St Matt *Man* 59-61; C Chorlton upon Medlock 61-62; Chapl Man Univ 61-62; C Chorlton-cum-Hardy St Clem 62-65; V Chirbury *Heref* 65-68; P-in-c Marton 65-68; R Iver Heath *Ox* 68-87; V Linslade 87-95; rtd 95; Warden Coll of St Barn Lingfield 95-00; Lic to Offic *S'wark* 95-00; Perm to Offic *Chich* and *Roch* 95-00; *St E* from 00; *Chelmsf* from 01. *Poplar Meadow, Thedwastre Road, Thurston, Bury St Edmunds IP31 3QY* Tel (01359) 270296

PEELING, Mrs Pamela Mary Alberta. b 44. Oak Hill Th Coll 83. **dss** 86 **d** 87 **p** 94. NSM Moulsham St Luke *Chelmsf* 86-88; NSM N Springfield 88-95; C Basildon St Martin 95-97; TV Grays Thurrock 97-05; rtd 05; Perm to Offic *St E* from 05. *4 Heron Road, Saxmundham IP17 1WR* Tel (01728) 604584 E-mail ppeeling@freebie.net

PEER, Charles Scott. b 69. Bris Univ BSc91 PGCE94 Ex Univ MA05. Trin Coll Bris BA02. **d** 02 **p** 03. C Dawlish *Ex* 02-05; P-in-c Kea *Truro* from 05. *The Vicarage, Killiow, Truro TR3 6AE* Tel (01872) 272850 E-mail vicar@stkea.org.uk

✠**PEERS, The Most Revd Michael Geoffrey.** b 34. Univ of BC BA56. Trin Coll Toronto LTh59 Hon DD78. **d** 59 **p** 60 **c** 77. C Ottawa St Thos 59-61; C Ottawa Trin 61-65; Chapl Carleton Univ 61-66; R Winnipeg St Bede 66-72; R Winnipeg St Martin w Middlechurch St Paul 72-74; Adn Winnipeg 69-74; R St Paul's Cathl Regina and Dean Qu'Appelle 74-77; Bp Qu'Appelle 77-82; Abp Qu'Appelle and Metrop Rupert's Land 82-86; Primate Angl Ch of Canada 86-04; rtd 04. *195 Westminster Avenue, Toronto ON M6R 1N9, Canada*

PEERS, Michael John. b 65. SS Paul & Mary Coll Cheltenham BA86. Ripon Coll Cuddesdon 88. **d** 91 **p** 92. C Birstall and Wanlip *Leic* 91-94; C Leic St Marg and All SS 94-96; TV The Abbey Leic 96-00; P-in-c Langley Park *Dur* 00-01; V from 01; P-in-c Esh 00-01; V 01-11; P-in-c Hamsteels 00-01; V 01-11; V Esh and Hamsteels from 11; P-in-c Waterhouses 00-01; V from 01. *The Vicarage, Church Street, Langley Park, Durham DH7 9TZ* Tel 0191-373 3110 E-mail mjpeers@aol.com

PEERS, Richard Charles. b 65. K Alfred's Coll Win BEd88 Lon Inst of Educn MA05. Chich Th Coll BTh93. **d** 93 **p** 94. C

Grangetown *York* 93-95; C Portsea St Mary *Portsm* 95-97; Dep Hd Emsworth Primary Sch 97-01; Hon Chapl Portsm Cathl 01-03; Chapl St Luke's Sch Southsea 01-03; Dep Hd Ch Sch Richmond 03-06; Chapl Abp Tenison's Sch Kennington 06-08; Headmaster Trin Sch Lewisham from 08; Hon C Earlsfield St Andr *S'wark* 06-11; Hon C Blackheath All SS from 11. *Trinity Church of England School, Taunton Road, London SE12 8PD* Tel (020) 8852 3191 E-mail richard.peers1@btopenworld.com

PEET, Derek Edwin. b 26. Sheff Univ BA51 DipEd52. Qu Coll Birm 66. **d** 67 **p** 68. C Hebden Bridge *Wakef* 67-70; V Darton 70-79; TR Gleadless Valley *Sheff* 79-85; V Kirk Hallam *Derby* 85-96; rtd 96; Perm to Offic *Ripon* from 96. *44 Parkways Grove, Woodlesford, Leeds LS26 8TP* Tel 0113-282 3079 Mobile 07960-450038

PEET, John Christopher. b 56. Oriel Coll Ox BA80 MA83 Clare Coll Cam BA82 MA87. Ridley Hall Cam 80. **d** 83 **p** 84. C Menston w Woodhead *Bradf* 83-86; C Prenton *Ches* 86-89; V Harden and Wilsden *Bradf* 89-97; V Cononley w Bradley from 97. *The Vicarage, 3 Meadow Close, Cononley, Keighley BD20 8LZ* Tel (01535) 634369 E-mail john.peet@bradford.anglican.org

PEGG, Brian Peter Richard (Bill). b 30. Ox NSM Course 77 Sarum & Wells Th Coll 82. **d** 83 **p** 84. C Furze Platt *Ox* 83-85; V Ashbury, Compton Beauchamp and Longcot w Fernham 85-94; Chapl Málaga *Eur* 94-97; rtd 97; Hon C Shere, Albury and Chilworth *Guildf* 98-02; Perm to Offic *Eur* from 98 and *Linc* from 03. *31 King Street, Winterton, Scunthorpe DN15 9TP* Tel (01724) 734860

PEGLER, Mrs Eve Charlotte. b 73. Cheltenham & Glouc Coll of HE BSc95. Ridley Hall Cam 05. **d** 07 **p** 08. C Hullavington, Norton and Stanton St Quintin *Bris* 07-10; C Sherston Magna, Easton Grey, Luckington etc 07-10; TV Shaftesbury *Sarum* from 10. *The Vicarage, Bittles Green, Motcombe, Shaftesbury SP7 9NX* Tel (01747) 851442 E-mail evepegler@gmail.com

PEGLER, Frederic Arthur. b 19. Selw Coll Cam BA46 MA48. Qu Coll Birm 46. **d** 47 **p** 48. C Crawley *Chich* 47-49; C Rickmansworth *St Alb* 49-50; V Sark *Win* 50-52; PV S'well Minster 52-55; Canada 55-84 and from 86; rtd 84; Perm to Offic *St Alb* 84-85. *302 Goodwin Manor, 1148 Goodwin Street, Victoria BC V8S 5H2, Canada* Tel (001) (250) 370 9300

PEILOW, Lynda Elizabeth Anne. b 74. CITC BTh97. **d** 97 **p** 98. C Castleknock and Mulhuddart w Clonsilla *D & G* 97-00; C Dublin St Ann and St Steph 00-01; Min Can St Patr Cathl Dublin 00-01; I Clonsast w Rathangan, Thomastown etc *M & K* from 01. *The Rectory, Monasterois, Edenderry, Co Offaly, Republic of Ireland* Tel (00353) (46) 973 1585 E-mail lpeilow@oceanfree.net *or* edenderry@kildare.anglican.org

PEIRCE, John. b 35. Worc Coll Ox BA59 MA64 Kent Univ MA96. Wycliffe Hall Ox 59. **d** 61 **p** 62. C Brompton H Trin *Lon* 61-64; C Wareham w Arne *Sarum* 64-68; V Sturminster Newton and Hinton St Mary 68-74; V Kingswood *Bris* 74-79; Dir Coun Chr Care *Ex* 79-89; Public Preacher 89-92; NSM Hackney *Lon* 90-94; NSM St Botolph Aldgate w H Trin Minories from 94; Co-ord Ch Action on Disability 90-98; Perm to Offic *Ex* 92-98. *3 Mile End Place, London E1 4BH* Tel (020) 7790 9418

PEIRCE, Canon John Martin. b 36. Jes Coll Cam BA59 MA65. Westcott Ho Cam 65. **d** 66 **p** 67. C Croydon St Jo *Cant* 66-70; C Fareham H Trin *Portsm* 70-71; TV 71-76; TR Langley Marish *Ox* 76-85; RD Burnham 78-82; Dir of Ords and Post-Ord Tr 85-01; Can Res Ch Ch 87-01; rtd 01. *8 Burwell Meadow, Witney, Oxford OX28 5JQ*

PEIRIS, Lionel James Harold (Brother Lionel). b 45. Serampore Coll BD71. Bp's Coll Calcutta 67. **d** 70 **p** 71. P Lect Colombo Coll Sri Lanka 71-76 and 78-95; C Shirley *Birm* 76-78; P Brother SSF Auckland New Zealand 96-97; Asst Chapl and Past Asst Annerley Hosp Australia 97-98; Hon C Annerley St Phil 97-98; P-in-c from 99. *115 Cornwall Street, Annerley Qld 4103, Australia* Tel (0061) (7) 3391 3915 Fax 3391 3916

PELHAM, John. b 36. New Coll Ox BA61 MA65. **d** 79 **p** 80. NSM Balerno *Edin* 79-91; NSM W Linton and Penicuik 91-94; Dioc Supernumerary from 94; NSM Lanark *Glas* 03-07; Lic to Offic *Edin* from 08. *2 Horsburgh Bank, Balerno EH14 7DA* Tel 0131-449 3934 E-mail john@pelham21.fsnet.co.uk

PELL, Charles Andrew. b 54. Leeds Univ CertEd77. Aston Tr Scheme 87 St Jo Coll Nottm 87. **d** 89 **p** 90. C Mottram in Longdendale w Woodhead *Ches* 89-90; C Handforth 90-93; P-in-c Walton Breck *Liv* 93-94; V Hey *Man* 94-01; P-in-c Glyndyrdwy and Llansantfraid Glyn Dyfrdwy *St As* 96-01; V Rhodes *Man* 01-07; CF (ACF) 93-07; rtd 07; Perm to Offic *Man* 09-10. *Auf der Hude 21, 33175 Bad Lippspringe, Germany* E-mail padre@milnet.uk.net

PELLEY, John Lawless. b 34. Oak Hill Th Coll 67. **d** 69 **p** 70. C Fareham St Jo *Portsm* 69-72; C Frogmore *St Alb* 72-76; V Standon 76-96; RD Bishop's Stortford 91-95; rtd 96; Perm to Offic *Ely* from 96. *7 Home Close, Histon, Cambridge CB24 9JL* Tel (01223) 234636

PELLING, Nicholas Philip. b 48. EMMTC 05. **d** 07 **p** 08. C S Cluster S'well Deanery 07-10; V Oldbury, Langley and

Londonderry *Birm* from 10. *The Vicarage, 2 St John's Road, Oldbury B68 9RP* Tel 0121-552 5005 Mobile 07804-326416 E-mail nick@nickandju.plus.com

PELLY, Mrs Elizabeth Wigram (Lulu). b 52. Bris Univ BA73. ERMC 05. **d** 08 **p** 09. NSM Towcester w Caldecote and Easton Neston etc *Pet* from 08. *Home Farm, Wakefield Lodge, Potterspury, Towcester NN12 7QX* Tel (01327) 811218 Mobile 07723-604316 E-mail lulu.pelly@farming.co.uk

PELLY, Raymond Blake. b 38. Worc Coll Ox BA61 MA63 Geneva Univ DTh71. Linc Th Coll 61 Bossey Ecum Inst Geneva 62. **d** 63 **p** 64. C Gosforth All SS *Newc* 63-65; C N Lynn w St Marg and St Nic *Nor* 69-70; Vice-Prin Westcott Ho Cam 71-76; Warden St Jo Coll Auckland New Zealand 77-85; Visiting Lect Univ of Mass Boston USA 86-88 and 96; Chapl Victoria Univ of Wellington New Zealand 90-94; Asst P Wellington St Pet 92-94 and from 96; rtd 03. *12 Kio Crescent, Hataitai, Wellington 6021, New Zealand* Tel (0064) (4) 386 3972 Mobile 21-486200 Fax (4) 386 3729 E-mail raymond.pelly@xtra.co.nz

PEMBERTON, Anthony Thomas Christie (Chris). b 57. BA. Cranmer Hall Dur 82. **d** 84 **p** 85. C Maidstone St Luke *Cant* 84-88; Chapl Ox Pastorate 88-98; V Cant St Mary Bredin 98-09; Tr Dir New Wine from 09. *59 Cromwell Road, Canterbury CT1 3LE* Tel 03000-406205 E-mail chrisp@nwtp.org.uk

PEMBERTON, Carrie Mary. b 55. St Hilda's Coll Ox BA78 Cam Univ PGCE82 Leeds Univ MA92 Newnham Coll Cam PhD98. Cranmer Hall Dur 83 NEOC 84. **dss** 86 **d** 87 **p** 94. NSM Leeds St Geo *Ripon* 86-87; Miss Partner CMS and Dir Women's Studies Angl Th Inst Zaïre 87-91; Perm to Offic *Pet* 92-94; NSM Bourn and Kingston w Caxton and Longstowe *Ely* 94-99; TV Elsworth w Knapwell 99; Miln Cambourne LEP 00-01, Perm to Offic 01-07; Cen Chapl Yarlswood Immigration and Detention Cen 01-03; Chief Exec CHASTE 04-08; Development Officer Cam Cen for Applied Research in Human Trafficking from 08. *9 South End, Bassingbourn, Royston SG8 5NJ* Tel (01763) 252866 E-mail carrie@ccarht.org

PEMBERTON, Crispin Mark Rugman. b 59. St Andr Univ MTheol83. St Steph Ho Ox 84. **d** 86 **p** 87. C Acton Green *Lon* 86-90; C Leckhampton SS Phil and Jas w Cheltenham St Jas *Glouc* 90-93; V Tuffley 93-97; RE Teacher Cheltenham Coll Jun Sch 97-00. *3 Langdon Road, Cheltenham GL53 7NZ* Tel (01242) 526188

PEMBERTON, Elizabeth Joan. b 70. Univ of W Aus BA90. ACT. **d** 98. Field Officer Bible Soc Australia 98-09; Perm to Offic *Lich* from 09. *17 The Spinney, Finchfield, Wolverhampton WV3 9HE*

PEMBERTON, Canon Jeremy Charles Baring. b 56. Mert Coll Ox MA77 Fitzw Ho Cam BA80 Leeds Univ MA92. Ridley Hall Cam 78. **d** 81 **p** 82. C Stranton *Dur* 81-84; C Leeds St Geo *Ripon* 84-87; CMS Miss Partner and Dir Angl Th Inst Zaïre 87-91; V Irchester *Pet* 92-94; R Bourn and Kingston w Caxton and Longstowe *Ely* 94-00; P-in-c Elsworth w Knapwell 99-00; P-in-c Boxworth 99-00; TR Papworth 00-07; RD Bourn 98-03; Hon Can Ely Cathl 05-07; Community Chapl Notts Co Teaching Primary Care Trust 08-11; Dep Sen Chapl United Lincs Hosps NHS Trust from 11; Hon Can Boga from 05. *Department of Pastoral Care, Lincoln County Hospital, Greetwell Road, Lincoln LN2 5QY* Tel (01522) 597717 Mobile 07920-274719 E-mail jeremy.pemberton@ulh.nhs.uk *or* jeremy.pemberton@live.co.uk

PENBERTHY, Joanna Susan. b 60. Newnham Coll Cam BA81 MA85 St Jo Coll Nottm MTh84. Cranmer Hall Dur 83. **dss** 84 **d** 87 **p** 97. Haughton le Skerne *Dur* 84-85; Llanishen and Lisvane 85-89; NSM 87-89; NSM Llanwddyn and Llanfihangel-yng-Nghwynfa etc *St As* 89-93; NSM Llansadwrn w Llanwrda and Manordeilo *St D* 93-95; Prov Officer Div for Par Development Ch in Wales 94-99; P-in-c Cynwyl Gaeo w Llansawel and Talley *St D* 99-01; V 01-10; Dioc Adult Educn Officer 01-02; Warden of Readers 02-10; Can St D Cathl 07-10; P-in-c Charlton Musgrove, Cucklington and Stoke Trister *B & W* from 10. *The Rectory, Cucklington, Wincanton BA9 9PY* Tel (01747) 840230 E-mail cmstbcrectory@btinternet.com

PENDLEBURY, Stephen Thomas. b 50. ACA78 Southn Univ BSc73. Ridley Hall Cam 86. **d** 88 **p** 89. C Birkenhead St Jas w St Bede *Ches* 88-91; V 91-00; V Ches St Paul from 00. *St Paul's Vicarage, 10 Sandy Lane, Chester CH3 5UL* Tel (01244) 351377 E-mail spendleby@aol.com

PENDORF, Canon James Gordon. b 45. Drew Univ New Jersey BA67. Episc Th Sch Cam Mass STB71. **d** 71 **p** 71. V Newark St Greg USA 71-76; V Colne H Trin *Blackb* 76-80; Sen Dioc Stewardship Adv *Chelmsf* 80-83; Dioc Sec *Birm* 83-95; P-in-c Highgate 95-97; V 97-04; Dioc Stewardship Adv 95-04; AD Birm City Cen 96-02; Hon Can Birm Cathl 90-04; Par Resources Adv and Chapl St Nic Ch Cen *St E* from 04; NSM Holbrook, Stutton, Freston, Woolverstone etc from 05. *Little Park, Main Road, Woolverstone, Ipswich IP9 1AR* Tel (01473) 780295 *or* 298501 Mobile 07973-265037 E-mail jim@stedmundsbury.anglican.org

PENFOLD, Brian Robert. b 54. Lon Univ BSc75 Bris Univ PGCE77. Oak Hill Th Coll BA84. **d** 84 **p** 85. C Norwod

St Luke S'wark 84-88; C Rayleigh Chelmsf 88-92; V New Barnet St Jas St Alb 92-08; V Worthing St Geo Chich from 08. 14 Pendine Avenue, Worthing BN11 2NB Tel (01903) 203309 Mobile 07753-680839 E-mail brian@brpenfold.freeserve.co.uk

PENFOLD, Colin Richard. b 52. St Pet Coll Ox BA74 MA78. Ridley Hall Cam 81. d 84 p 85. C Buckhurst Hill Chelmsf 84-87; C Greenside Dur 87-90; V Cononley w Bradley Bradf 90-97; P-in-c Shipley St Paul and Frizinghall 97; V Shipley St Paul 98-08; P-in-c Gt Harwood Blackb from 08. St Bartholomew's Vicarage, Church Lane, Great Harwood, Blackburn BB6 7PU Tel (01254) 884039 E-mail colin@thepenfolds.org.uk

PENFOLD, Marion Jean. b 49. NEOC 96. d 99 p 00. NSM Lesbury w Alnmouth Newc 99-02; C 02-03; NSM Longhoughton w Howick 99-02; C 02-03; TV N Tyne and Redesdale 03-11; TV Glendale Gp from 11. Eglingham Vicarage, The Village, Eglingham, Alnwick NE66 2TX Tel (01665) 578250 E-mail marion.penfold@btinternet.com

PENFOLD, Canon Susan Irene. b 52. York Univ BA73 Bris Univ PhD77 Selw Coll Cam BA83 MA87. Ridley Hall Cam 81. dss 84 d 87 p 94. Buckhurst Hill Chelmsf 84-87; Hon C Greenside Dur 87-90; Hon C Cononley w Bradley Bradf 90-97; Assoc Dioc Dir of Ords 96-01; Hon C Shipley St Paul 97-00; Perm to Offic from 00; Dir of Ords and CME Officer Wakef 01-03; Dir of Ords and Dean of Min 03-08; Hon Can Wakef Cathl 04-08; Can Res Blackb Cathl from 08; Dir of Min from 08. The Vicarage, Church Lane, Great Harwood, Blackburn BB6 7PU Tel (01254) 503085 Mobile 07753-987977 E-mail sue.penfold@blackburn.anglican.org

PENGELLEY, Peter John. b 22. Sarum & Wells Th Coll 72. d 74 p 75. C Midsomer Norton B & W 74-78; R Stogursey w Fiddington 78-88; Ind Chapl 80-88; rtd 88; Perm to Offic B & W from 89. Rosslyn Cottage, Roadwater, Watchet TA23 0RB Tel (01984) 640798

PENGELLY, Canon Geoffrey. b 50. Oak Hill Th Coll 86. d 88 p 89. C Redruth w Lanner and Treleigh Truro 88-91; TV Bolventor 91-92; V Egloskerry, N Petherwin, Tremaine, Tresmere etc from 92; RD Trigg Major 04-10; Hon Can Truro Cathl from 03. The Vicarage, Egloskerry, Launceston PL15 8RX Tel (01566) 785365

PENISTAN, Richard Luke. See PENNYSTAN, Richard Luke

PENMAN, John Bain. b 67. Aber Univ BD89 New Coll Edin MTh93. Edin Th Coll 91. d 93 p 94. C Glas St Ninian 93-96; C Ealing Ch the Sav Lon 96-98; P-in-c Kirkcaldy and Kinghorn St And 98-04; R Falkirk Edin from 04. 55 Kerse Lane, Falkirk FK1 1RX Tel (01324) 623709 Mobile 07713-254660 E-mail jpenmanfct@btconnect.com

PENMAN, Miss Margaret Heather. b 50. St Martin's Coll Lanc CertEd71 Lanc Univ DipEd82 FRSA95. Carl Dioc Tr Inst 90. d 93 p 94. Headteacher Hesketh w Becconsall All SS C of E Sch 85-00; RE/Schools Adv Liv 00-09; NSM Lostock Hall Blackb 93-95; NSM Leyland St Jas from 95. 9 Oakfield Drive, Leyland PR26 7XE Tel (01772) 435927 Mobile 07968-315755 E-mail heather.penman@blueyonder.co.uk

PENMAN, Robert George. b 42. St Jo Coll Auckland LTh66. d 65 p 66. C Mt Roskill New Zealand 65-68; C Henderson 69-70; V Glen Innes 71-72; C Alverstoke Portsm 73-74; CF 74-77; C Bridgwater St Mary w Chilton Trinity B & W 77-80; P-in-c Haselbury Plucknett w N Perrott 80-81; P-in-c Misterton 80-81; V Haselbury Plucknett, Misterton and N Perrott 81-89; P-in-c Appleton Ox 89-07; P-in-c Besselsleigh w Dry Sandford 89-00; P-in-c Besselsleigh 00-07; rtd 07; Perm to Offic Ox from 07. 31 High Street, Sherington, Newport Pagnell MK16 9NU Tel (01908) 611838 E-mail penman298@btinternet.com

PENN, Barry Edwin. b 46. Univ of Wales (Swansea) BA72 Trin Coll Bris MA04. 32 St Jo Coll Nottm 77. d 79 p 80. C New Barnet St Jas St Alb 79-83; TV Preston St Jo Blackb 83-92; V Patchway Bris 92-01; Perm to Offic from 01. 50 Eastfield Road, Westbury-on-Trym, Bristol BS9 4AG Tel 0117-962 2862 E-mail barrypenn@aol.com

PENN, Christopher Francis. b 34. ACII63. Wells Th Coll 68. d 70 p 71. C Andover w Foxcott Win 70-72; C Odiham w S Warnborough 72-75; C Keynsham B & W 75-76; TV 76-82; R Chilcompton w Downside and Stratton on the Fosse 82-87; RD Midsomer Norton 84-86; V Bathford 87-90; V Avonmouth St Andr Bris 90-96; Ind Chapl 90-96; rtd 96; Perm to Offic B & W and Bris from 96. 53 Caernarvon Road, Keynsham, Bristol BS31 2PF Tel 0117-986 2367

PENN, Christopher Wilson. b 60. Cranmer Hall Dur 98. d 00 p 01. C Wrockwardine Deanery Lich 00-03; P-in-c Llanyblodwel and Trefonen 03-07; P-in-c Llanymynech 03-07; P-in-c Morton 03-07; R Llanyblodwel, Llanymynech, Morton and Trefonen from 07; Rural Officer (Salop Adnry) from 08. The Rectory, Rectory Lane, Pant, Oswestry SY10 9RA Tel (01691) 831211 E-mail bordergroupadmin@hotmail.co.uk

PENN, Jane Rachel. ERMC. d 10 p 11. NSM Orton Longueville w Bottlebridge Ely from 10. 39 Riseholme, Orton Goldhay, Peterborough PE2 5SP Tel (01733) 237549 E-mail janepenn@hotmail.com

PENN, Mrs Jennifer Anne. b 61. Imp Coll Lon BEng84 Leeds Univ BA07. NOC 04. d 07 p 08. C Halliwell St Pet Man 07-10; TV New Bury w Gt Lever from 10. 130 Green Lane, Bolton BL3 2HX Tel (01204) 524298 E-mail j.penn@homecall.co.uk

PENNAL, David Bernard. b 37. Ripon Hall Ox 64. d 67 p 68. C Moseley St Mary Birm 67-71; C Bridgwater St Mary w Chilton Trinity B & W 71-73; P-in-c Hilton w Cheselbourne and Melcombe Horsey Sarum 73-76; R Milton Abbas, Hilton w Cheselbourne etc 76-78; P-in-c Spetisbury w Charlton Marshall 78-88; R Spetisbury w Charlton Marshall etc 89-00; rtd 00. 11 High Street, Wicken, Ely CB7 5XR

PENNANT, David Falconer. b 51. Trin Coll Cam MA73. Trin Coll Bris BD84 PhD88. d 86 p 87. C Bramcote S'well 86-88; C Woking St Jo Guildf 88-93. 30 Oriental Road, Woking GU22 7AW Tel (01483) 768055 E-mail david.pennant@ntlworld.com

PENNELL (formerly COFFIN), Ms Pamela. b 45. EAMTC 94. d 97 p 98. NSM Moulsham St Luke Chelmsf 97-98; NSM Writtle w Highwood 98-00; Perm to Offic 01-04; NSM Gt Waltham w Ford End 04-06; Perm to Offic 06-08; P-in-c Sandon from 08; P-in-c E Hanningfield from 08. 33 Birch Lane, Stock, Ingatestone CM4 9NA Tel (01277) 841270 E-mail pencof.pam@btinternet.com

PENNELLS, David Malcolm Benedict. b 56. Leeds Univ BA11 CQSW80. Coll of Resurr Mirfield 09. d 11. C Kennington St Jo w St Jas S'wark from 11. 96 Vassall Road, London SW9 6JA Tel (020) 7840 0100 E-mail fatherdavid@btinternet.com

PENNEY, David Richard John. b 39. St Jo Coll Dur BA63. Cranmer Hall Dur 63. d 67 p 68. C Chilvers Coton w Astley Cov 67-70; C Styvechale 70-72; P-in-c Shilton w Ansty 72-77; P-in-c Withybrook 74-77; R Easington w Liverton York 77-85; Dir Soc Resp Sarum 85-93; Perm to Offic Blackb 93-02; rtd 01. Noyna House, 2 Noyna Street, Colne BB8 0PE Tel (01282) 870076 Mobile 07966-157697

PENNEY, William Affleck. b 41. MBIM75 FRSA91. K Coll Lon BD63 AKC63 St Boniface Warminster 65. d 66 p 67. C Chatham St Steph Roch 66-70; Ind Chapl 70-77; P-in-c Bredhurst 70-72; Hon C S Gillingham 72-74; Hon C Eynsford w Farningham and Lullingstone 74-77; Bp's Dom Chapl 74-88; Hon Ind Chapl 77-88; Hon C Balham St Mary and St Jo S'wark 89-91; Perm to Offic St Alb 91-94; Hon C Bushey 94-05; rtd 05. 6 Devonshire Court, 26A Devonshire Street, London W1G 6PJ Tel (020) 7486 1227 E-mail wpenney@btconnect.com

PENNICEARD, Clifford Ashley. b 42. Monash Univ Aus BA65 DipEd71 Linacre Coll Ox BA67 Ox Univ MA70. St Steph Ho Ox 65. d 68 p 69. C S Leamington St Jo Cov 68-70; P-in-c Wantirna Australia 74; Assoc P N Brighton 76-80; P-in-c Euroa 84-91; P-in-c Nagumbie 93-95; P-in-c Cudal 96-98; R Manly St Paul 98-04; P-in-c Cen Goulburn from 04. 1700 Euroa-Strathbogie Road, Kithbrook VIC 3666, Australia Tel (0061) 41-617 7732 (mobile) E-mail cliffpenn@dodo.com.au

PENNIECOOKE, Dorothy Victoria. b 45. Dioc OLM tr scheme 97. d 00 p 01. NSM Balham Hill Ascension S'wark from 00. 56 Lysias Road, London SW12 8BP Tel (020) 8673 0037

PENNINGTON, Mrs Catherine Prudence. b 56. Man Poly BSc82 Sussex Univ MSc87 Flinders Univ Aus BTh00. Adelaide Coll of Div 96. d 00 p 01. C Glenelg Australia 00-01; NSM American Cathl Paris 01-02; C Is of Dogs Ch Ch and St Jo w St Luke Lon 02-03; C De Beauvoir Town St Pet 03-04; P-in-c Nazeing Chelmsf from 05; P-in-c Roydon 05-09. The Vicarage, Betts Lane, Nazeing, Waltham Abbey EN9 2DB Tel (01992) 893167 Mobile 07800-822297 E-mail pennington@hotmail.com

PENNINGTON, Edward Francis Quentin. b 76. G&C Coll Cam BA97 MA01 Birm Univ MSc98. Oak Hill Th Coll BTh04. d 04 p 05. C Moulton Pet 04-07; C Fulwood Sheff from 07. 14 Dobbin Hill, Sheffield S11 7JB Tel 0114-263 1511 or 268 1795 Mobile 07743-942931 E-mail efqpennington@hotmail.com or ed@endcliffechurch.co.uk

PENNINGTON, Emma Louise. b 71. Ex Univ BA92 Kent Univ MA96. Ripon Coll Cuddesdon BA00. d 00 p 01. C Shepperton Lon 00-03; Chapl Worc Coll Ox 03-08; TV Wheatley Ox from 08. Garsington Rectory, 17 Southend, Garsington, Oxford OX44 9DH Tel (01865) 361381 E-mail emma.pennington@worc.ox.ac.uk

PENNINGTON, John Kenneth. b 27. Man Univ LLB48. Linc Th Coll 51. d 52 p 53. C Wavertree H Trin Liv 52-56; C Rotherham Sheff 56-59; P-in-c Kanpur All So India 59-63; V Nelson St Phil Blackb 64-66; Area Sec USPG Derby, Leic and S'well 66-71; Derby and Sheff 71-75; C Nottingham St Mary S'well 75-78; C Nottingham St Mary and St Cath 78-92; rtd 93; Perm to Offic S'well from 93. 3 St Jude's Avenue, Nottingham NG3 5FG Tel 0115-962 3420

PENNOCK, Mrs Christine. b 48. Bp Grosseteste Coll BEd71 Leeds Univ PGCE94 Teesside Univ PGDE95. NEOC 98. d 01 p 02. C Crowland Linc 01-05; P-in-c Ruskington Gp from 05; P-in-c Leasingham from 09; P-in-c Cranwell from 11. The Rectory, All Saints' Close, Ruskington, Sleaford NG34 9FP Tel (01526) 832463 Mobile 07813-954043 E-mail chris@cpennock.fsnet.co.uk

PENNY, Alexander Stuart Egerton. b 52. Wolv Art Coll BA75. Ridley Hall Cam MA00. **d** 00 **p** 01. C Uttoxeter Area *Lich* 00-03; V Crosthwaite Keswick *Carl* from 03. *Crosthwaite Vicarage, Vicarage Hill, Keswick CA12 5QB* Tel (01768) 772509 E-mail stuartpenny@onetel.com

PENNY, David Roy. b 67. Wilson Carlile Coll 89 NOC 00. **d** 03 **p** 04. C Hey and Waterhead *Man* 03-05; V Chadderton St Matt w St Luke from 05; AD Oldham W from 09. *St Matthew's Vicarage, Mill Brow, Chadderton, Oldham OL1 2RT* Tel 0161-624 8600 E-mail dpennyca@aol.com

PENNY, Diana Eleanor. b 51. Open Univ BA87 Birm Univ DipEd96. Nor Ord Course 87. **d** 89 **p** 94. NSM Gillingham w Geldeston, Stockton, Ellingham etc *Nor* 89-93; NSM Upton St Leonards *Glouc* 93-97; NSM Stiffkey and Cockthorpe w Morston, Langham etc *Nor* 97-03; NSM Stiffkey and Bale 03-04; C Lowestoft St Marg 04-06; V E Marshland *Ely* 06-10; rtd 10; Perm to Offic *Ely* from 10. *Hibiscus, 33 Church Drove, Outwell, Wisbech PE14 8RH* Tel (01945) 771978 E-mail dep451@btinternet.com

PENNY, Edwin John. b 43. Leeds Univ BA64. Coll of Resurr Mirfield 64. **d** 66 **p** 67. C Acocks Green *Birm* 66-69; C Wombourne *Lich* 69-71; C Wednesbury St Paul Wood Green 71-74; V Kingshurst *Birm* 74-79; Chapl All Hallows Convent Norfolk 79-82; Hon Chapl Overgate Hospice Yorkshire 82-84; Hon C Raveningham *Nor* 84-90; All Hallows Hosp Nor Past Team 90-93; P-in-c Upton St Leonards *Glouc* 93-97; Dioc Communications Officer 93-97; P-in-c Stiffkey and Cockthorpe w Morston, Langham etc *Nor* 97-03; P-in-c Gunthorpe w Bale w Field Dalling, Saxlingham etc 99-03; R Stiffkey and Bale 03-04; rtd 04; Perm to Offic *Nor* from 04 and *Ely* from 08; RD Wisbech Lynn Marshland *Ely* from 09. *Hibiscus, 33 Church Drove, Outwell, Wisbech PE14 8RH* Tel (01945) 771978 E-mail noakhillpupil@dialstart.net

PENNY, Michael John. b 36. Linc Th Coll 78. **d** 80 **p** 81. C Knighton St Mary Magd *Leic* 80-83; TV Leic Resurr 83-85; V Blackfordby 85-95; V Blackfordby and Woodville 95-00; RD Akeley W 88-93; rtd 00; Perm to Offic *Nor* from 00. *15 Sarah's Road, Hunstanton PE36 5PA* Tel (01485) 534957

PENNY, Stuart. See PENNY, Alexander Stuart Egerton

PENNYSTAN, Richard Luke. b 74. Newc Univ BA97 St Jo Coll Cam BA02. Ridley Hall Cam 00. **d** 03 **p** 04. C E Twickenham St Steph *Lon* 03-06; C Fulham Ch Ch 06-11. *Address temp unknown* Tel 07971-663129 (mobile)

PENRITH, Suffragan Bishop of. See FREEMAN, The Rt Revd Robert John

PENTELOW, Mrs Ysmena Rachael. b 73. St Andr Univ BD96 MLitt99. EAMTC 01. **d** 03 **p** 04. C Stevenage H Trin *St Alb* 03-06; P-in-c Langleybury St Paul from 06; Dioc CME Officer from 06. *The Vicarage, 1 Langleybury Lane, Kings Langley WD4 8QQ* Tel (01923) 270634 Mobile 07798-654194 E-mail pentelow@waitrose.com

PENTLAND, The Ven Raymond Jackson. b 57. Wm Booth Memorial Coll CertEd79 Open Univ BA90 Westmr Coll Ox MTh02. St Jo Coll Nottm 86. **d** 88 **p** 89. C Nottingham St Jude *S'well* 88-90; Chapl RAF 90-05; Command Chapl RAF 05-06; Adn RAF from 06; Chapl-in-Chief RAF from 09; QHC from 06; Can and Preb Linc Cathl from 06. *Chaplaincy Services, Valiant Block, HQ Air Command, RAF High Wycombe HP14 4UE* Tel (01494) 497595 Fax 496343 E-mail ray.pentland929@mod.uk

PENTREATH, Canon Harvey. b 29. Wells Th Coll 54. **d** 57 **p** 58. C Bris St Ambrose Whitehall 57-60; C Leatherhead *Guildf* 60-63; C Haslemere 63-65; R Elstead 65-72; V Cuddington 73-80; Hon Can Guildf Cathl 80; V Helston *Truro* 80-85; RD Kerrier 84-86; TR Helston and Wendron 85-92; Hon Can Truro Cathl 88-92; rtd 93; Perm to Offic *Truro* from 93. *Penmarr, 15 Penarwyn Crescent, Heamoor, Penzance TR18 3JU* Tel (01736) 360133

PEOPLES, James Scott. b 59. TCD BA BTh90. **d** 85 **p** 86. C Carlow w Urglin and Staplestown *C & O* 85-90; Chapl Kilkenny Coll 90-91; I Portarlington w Cloneyhurke and Lea *M & K* 91-99; Dioc Youth Officer (Kildare) 92-99; I Lucan w Leixlip *D & G* from 99. *5 Uppercross, Ballyowen Lane, Ballydowd, Lucan, Co Dublin, Republic of Ireland* Tel (00353) (1) 624 9147

PEOPLES, Mervyn Thomas Edwards. b 53. Open Univ BA88. CITC 03. **d** 06 **p** 07. NSM Raphoe w Raymochy and Clonleigh *D & R* 06-09; NSM Clooney w Strathfoyle from 09. *29 Dunnalong Road, Magheramason, Londonderry BT47 2RU* Tel (028) 7184 1416 E-mail mervynpeoples@hotmail.com

PEPPER, David Reginald. b 50. Lon Bible Coll. St Alb Minl Tr Scheme 89. **d** 92 **p** 93. NSM Cheshunt *St Alb* 92-95; NSM Bengeo 06-08; NSM Hertford from 08. *36 Salisbury Road, Hoddesdon EN11 0HX* Tel (01992) 427385 E-mail davidpepper2@yahoo.co.uk

PEPPER, Leonard Edwin. b 44. Ex Univ BA71. Ripon Hall Ox 71. **d** 73 **p** 74. C Cottingham *York* 73-76; C Kingsbury *Birm* 76-79; Dir Past Studies St Steph Ho Ox 80-89; TV Aylesbury w Bierton and Hulcott *Ox* 89-91; TV High Wycombe 91-96; rtd 96. *19 Gardiner Street, Oxford OX3 7AW* Tel (01865) 66191

PEPPIATT, Martin Guy. b 33. Trin Coll Ox BA57 MA60. Wycliffe Hall Ox 57. **d** 59 **p** 60. C St Marylebone All So w SS Pet and Jo *Lon* 59-63; Kenya 65-69; V E Twickenham St Steph *Lon* 69-96; rtd 96. *Pipers Cottage, East End, North Leigh, Witney OX29 8ND* Tel (01993) 883001

PEPPIATT, Quintin Brian Duncombe. b 63. Ex Univ BSc85 St Luke's Coll Ex PGCE86. Ripon Coll Cuddesdon 89 Ch Div Sch of the Pacific (USA) 90. **d** 92 **p** 93. C Gt Ilford St Clem and St Marg *Chelmsf* 92-95; TV E Ham w Upton Park from 95. *1 Norman Road, London E6 6HN* Tel (020) 8471 8751 E-mail quintinpeppiatt@aol.com

PERCIVAL, Brian Sydney. b 37. Univ of Wales (Ban) BA61. NOC 81. **d** 84 **p** 85. NSM Norbury *Ches* 84-88; P-in-c Werneth 88-04; RD Chadkirk 00-04; rtd 04; Perm to Offic *Ches* from 04. *21 Holly Road, High Lane, Stockport SK6 8HW* Tel (01663) 810217

PERCIVAL, James Edward Charles. b 50. NOC 92. **d** 95 **p** 96. C Broughton *Blackb* 95-99; P-in-c Blackb St Steph 99-03; P-in-c Freckleton from 03; Chapl Blackb, Hyndburn and Ribble Valley NHS Trust 99-03. *Holy Trinity Vicarage, 3 Sunnyside Close, Freckleton, Preston PR4 1YJ* Tel (01772) 632209 E-mail jamesperc2005@aol.com

PERCIVAL, James Frederick. b 74. New Coll Ox BA96 MA01 Barrister-at-Law (Middle Temple) 99. Ripon Coll Cuddesdon MA02. **d** 03 **p** 04. C Redhill St Matt *S'wark* 03-06; TV Sanderstead from 06. *St Mary's Vicarage, 85 Purley Oaks Road, South Croydon CR2 0NY* Tel (020) 8657 1725 E-mail james@sanderstead-parish.org.uk

PERCIVAL, Joanna Vèra. b 52. Univ of San Francisco BA87. Ch Div Sch of Pacific MDiv94. **d** 94 **p** 94. Asst R Almaden USA 94-95; NSM Ockham w Hatchford *Guildf* 95-96; C Cobham 96-00; Dioc Spirituality Adv 00-02; V Weston 02-06; Perm to Offic *Lon* and *S'wark* 06-07; *S & B* 07-08; Chapl Southn Univ Hosps NHS Trust from 08. *Southampton General Hospital, Tremona Road, Shirley, Southampton SO16 6YD* Tel (023) 8079 6745 E-mail joanna.percival@btinternet.com

PERCIVAL, Mrs Kathryn Janet. b 54. St Hilda's Coll Ox BA95 MA01 ARCM89 Barrister-at-Law (Lincoln's Inn) 98. Ripon Coll Cuddesdon 08. **d** 10 **p** 11. C Purley St Mark *S'wark* from 10; C Purley St Swithun from 10. *St Mary's Vicarage, 85 Purley Oaks Road, South Croydon CR2 0NY* Tel (020) 8405 9657 Mobile 07985-272437 E-mail kathryn.percival@blueyonder.co.uk

PERCIVAL, Martin Eric. b 45. Lon Univ BSc66 Linacre Coll Ox BA70 MA74. Wycliffe Hall Ox 67. **d** 70 **p** 71. C Anfield St Marg *Liv* 70-73; C Witney *Ox* 73-74; TV Bottesford w Ashby *Linc* 74-76; TV Grantham 76-80; R Coningsby w Tattershall 80-82; P-in-c Coleford w Holcombe *B & W* 82-83; V 83-84; Chapl Rossall Sch Fleetwood 84-88; Chapl Woodbridge Sch 88-02; R Downham w S Hanningfield *Chelmsf* 02-05; P-in-c Ramsden Bellhouse 02-05; P-in-c Leiston *St E* from 05. *18 Culcott Close, Yoxford, Saxmundham IP17 3GZ* Tel (01728) 668537 E-mail revmepercival@lycos.co.uk

PERCIVAL, Patricia Anne. b 52. SEITE 03. **d** 06 **p** 07. NSM Footscray w N Cray *Roch* 06-10; NSM Blendon from 10. *31 Collindale Avenue, Sidcup DA15 9DN* Tel (020) 8302 9754 E-mail pat@thepercies.freeserve.co.uk

PERCIVAL, Richard Thomas. b 33. MRICS59 MRTPI67 FRICS71. Edin Dioc NSM Course 79. **d** 91 **p** 98. S Africa 91-94; RD Adnry of Kokstad 93-94; NSM Edin St Ninian 94-01; rtd 01; Perm to Offic *Edin* from 01. *2/1 Fettes Rise, Edinburgh EH4 1QH* Tel 0131-552 5271 E-mail rpercival@freeukisp.co.uk

PERCIVAL, Robert Standring. b 27. Sheff Univ BSc55. Qu Coll Birm 57. **d** 59 **p** 60. C Lightbowne *Man* 59-62; C Prestwich St Marg 62-63; V Pendlebury St Aug 63-68; Lect Glos Coll of Arts and Tech 68-93; NSM Glouc St Mary de Crypt w St Jo and Ch Ch 68-82; Perm to Offic 82-97 and from 01; rtd 92. *5 Firwood Drive, Gloucester GL4 0AB* Tel (01452) 522739

PERCY, Brian. b 34. **d** 93 **p** 94. OLM Walton *St E* 93-00; OLM Walton and Trimley 00-04; rtd 04; Perm to Offic *St E* from 04. *16 Lynwood Avenue, Felixstowe IP11 9HS* Tel (01394) 286782

PERCY, Christopher. See HEBER PERCY, Canon Christopher John

PERCY, Mrs Emma Margaret. b 63. Jes Coll Cam BA85 MA89 St Jo Coll Dur BA89. Cranmer Hall Dur 87. **d** 90 **p** 94. C Bedford St Andr *St Alb* 90-94; Chapl Anglia Poly Univ 94-97; P-in-c Millhouses H Trin *Sheff* 97-03; V 03-04; Chapl Trin Coll Ox from 05. *2 Orchard View, High Street, Cuddesdon, Oxford OX44 9HP* Tel (01865) 876211 E-mail emma.percy@pmb.ox.ac.uk

PERCY, Gordon Reid. b 46. St Jo Coll Dur BA68. Cranmer Hall Dur 69. **d** 71 **p** 72. C Flixton St Jo *Man* 71-76; C Charlesworth *Derby* 76-77; P-in-c 77-87; P-in-c Dinting Vale 80-87; V Long Eaton St Jo 87-98; RD Ilkeston 92-98; R Torquay St Matthias, St Mark and H Trin *Ex* from 98. *The Rectory, Wellswood Avenue, Torquay TQ1 2QE* Tel (01803) 293280 or 214175 E-mail gordonpercy@minister.com *or* stmathiaschurch@minister.com

PERCY, Prof Martyn William. b 62. Bris Univ BA84 K Coll Lon PhD92 Sheff Univ MEd. Cranmer Hall Dur 88. **d** 90 **p** 91. C Bedford St Andr *St Alb* 90-94; Chapl and Dir Th and RS Ch Coll Cam 94-97; Dir Th and RS SS Coll Cam 95-97; Dir Linc Th Inst 97-04; Hon C Millhouses H Trin *Sheff* 97-04; Hon Can Sheff Cathl 97-04; Can Th from 04; Sen Lect Relig and Soc Sheff Univ 97-00; Reader 00-02; Reader Man Univ 02-04; Prof Th and Min Hartford Sem Connecticut 02-07; Prin Ripon Coll Cuddesdon from 04; Prof Th Educn K Coll Lon from 04; Prin Ox Min Course from 06; Can and Preb Sarum Cathl from 09. *Ripon College, Cuddesdon, Oxford OX44 9EX* Tel (01865) 874404 Fax 875431 Mobile 07941-072542 E-mail mpercy@ripon-cuddesdon.ac.uk

PERDUE, Ernon Cope Todd. b 30. TCD BA52 MA BD56 MEd73 UCD MPsychSc80. TCD Div Sch 53. **d** 54 **p** 55. C Dublin Drumcondra w N Strand *D & G* 54-58; C Dublin Booterstown w Carysfort 58-60; Dean of Res TCD 60-68; C-in-c Dublin St Mark *D & G* 66-68; C-in-c Dublin St Steph 68-69; I Rathmichael 69-76; Careers Counsellor Wicklow Voc Sch 76-82; I Limerick *L & K* 82-87; Can Limerick Cathl 82-87; Dean Killaloe, Kilfenora and Clonfert 87-95; I Killaloe w Stradbally 87-95; rtd 95. *18 The Mageough, Cowper Road, Rathmines, Dublin 6, Republic of Ireland* Tel and fax (00353) (1) 491 4867 Mobile 86-278 0354 E-mail ernonandheather@hotmail.com

PEREIRA, Alwyn Antonio Basilio. b 63. Trin Coll Bris. **d** 11. C Sea Mills *Bris* from 11. *20 Ridgehill, Bristol BS9 4SB* Tel 0117-307 0120 Mobile 07767-702094 E-mail alwynper@googlemail.com

PEREIRA, Melvyn Christopher. b 52. Oak Hill Th Coll BA04. **d** 04 **p** 05. C Kettering Ch the King *Pet* 04-07; Min Gleneagles CD from 07; Warden of Par Ev from 10. *20 Ribble Close, Wellingborough NN8 5XJ* Tel (01933) 673437 Mobile 07810-816744 E-mail melvyn.pereira@gleneagleschurch.co.uk

PERERA, Ms Chandrika Kumudhini. b 61. Qu Coll Birm. **d** 03 **p** 04. C Luton All SS w St Pet *St Alb* 03-07; TV Hemel Hempstead from 07. *St Paul's Vicarage, 23 Saturn Way, Hemel Hempstead HP2 5NY* Tel (01442) 255023 E-mail chandy.perera@btinternet.com

PERERA, George Anthony. b 51. Edin Univ BD74. Linc Th Coll 74. **d** 76 **p** 77. Chapl Mabel Fletcher Tech Coll Liv 76-79; C Wavertree H Trin *Liv* 76-79; TV Maghull 79-94; V Hunts Cross 94-04; Chapl Park Lane Hosp Maghull 79-89; Asst Chapl Ashworth Hosp Maghull 89-04; Chapl R Liverpool and Broadgreen Univ Hosps NHS Trust from 05. *Broadgreen Hospital, Thomas Drive, Liverpool L14 3LB* Tel 0151-282 6000 Fax 254 2070

✠**PERHAM, The Rt Revd Michael Francis.** b 47. Keble Coll Ox BA74 MA78. Cuddesdon Coll 74. **d** 76 **p** 77 **c** 04. C Addington *Cant* 76-81; Bp's Dom Chapl *Win* 81-84; Sec C of E Doctrine Commn 79-84; TR Oakdale *Sarum* 84-92; Prec and Can Res Nor Cathl 92-98; Provost Derby 98-00; Dean Derby 00-04; Bp Glouc from 04. *Bishopscourt, Pitt Street, Gloucester GL1 2BQ* Tel (01452) 410022 ext 271 Fax 308324 E-mail bshpglos@glosdioc.org.uk

PERKES, Brian Robert Keith. b 46. St Andr Univ BSc68. NOC 91. **d** 94 **p** 95. NSM Witton *Ches* 94-98; Bp's Chapl 98-00; P-in-c Ashton Hayes from 98; P-in-c Delamere from 00. *The Vicarage, Church Road, Ashton, Chester CH3 8AB* Tel (01829) 751265 E-mail brkperkes@tinyworld.co.uk

PERKIN, Jonathan Guy. b 52. Westmr Coll Ox BEd76. Trin Coll Bris 89. **d** 91 **p** 92. C Cullompton *Ex* 91-96; C Ashtead *Guildf* 96-01; V Egham 01-05; V Churchdown *Glouc* from 05. *The Vicarage, 5 Vicarage Close, Churchdown, Gloucester GL3 2NE* Tel (01452) 713203 E-mail jjperkin@btconnect.com

PERKIN, Paul John Stanley. b 50. Ch Ch Ox BA71 MA75 CertEd. Wycliffe Hall Ox 78. **d** 80 **p** 81. C Gillingham St Mark *Roch* 80-84; C Brompton H Trin w Onslow Square St Paul *Lon* 84-87; P-in-c Battersea Rise St Mark *S'wark* 87-92; V from 92; P-in-c Battersea St Pet and St Paul from 00. *St Mark's Vicarage, 7 Elsynge Road, London SW18 2HW* Tel (020) 8874 6023 or 7223 6188 E-mail mark.mail@ukonline.co.uk

PERKINS, Barnaby Charles Rudolf. b 80. Peterho Cam BA08 MPhil10. Ridley Hall Cam 06. **d** 10 **p** 11. C Guildf St Nic from 10. *St Catherine's House, 72 Wodeland Avenue, Guildford GU2 4LA* E-mail barnaby.perkins@cantab.net

PERKINS, Colin Blackmore. b 35. FCII65. Lon Coll of Div 68. **d** 70 **p** 71. C Hyson Green *S'well* 70-73; V Clarborough w Hayton 73-79; P-in-c Cropwell Bishop 79-84; P-in-c Colston Bassett 79-84; P-in-c Granby w Elton 79-84; P-in-c Langar 79-84; V Tithby w Cropwell Butler 79-84; R Cropwell Bishop w Colston Bassett, Granby etc 84-94; P-in-c Sutton Bonington w Normanton-on-Soar 94-01; rtd 01; Perm to Offic *Newc* from 01. *6 Ravensmede, Alnwick NE66 2PX* Tel (01665) 510445 E-mail cperk68836@aol.com

PERKINS, Canon David. b 51. Sarum & Wells Th Coll. **d** 87 **p** 88. C New Mills *Derby* 87-90; V Marlpool 90-95; P-in-c Turnditch 95-02; Min in charge Belper Ch Ch and Milford 95-02; V Belper Ch Ch w Turnditch 02-09; Jt P-in-c Ambergate and Heage 06-09; RD Duffield 97-09; Chapl Derbyshire Mental Health Services

NHS Trust 95-09; Can Res Derby Cathl from 09. *24 Kedleston Road, Derby DE22 1GU* Tel (01332) 343523 E-mail revdaveperkins@aol.com

PERKINS, David John Elmslie. b 45. Dur Univ BA66 ATII75. Cranmer Hall Dur 66. **d** 69 **p** 70. C Wadsley *Sheff* 69-71; C Shortlands *Roch* 71-73; Perm to Offic *Lon* 76-78; *B & W* 78-80 and from 02; Lic to Offic 80-02; rtd 02. *Rainbow's End, Montacute Road, Stoke-sub-Hamdon TA14 6UQ* Tel (01935) 823314

PERKINS, John Everard. b 47. SEITE 04. **d** 06 **p** 07. NSM Speldhurst w Groombridge and Ashurst *Roch* 06-10; NSM Tonbridge St Steph from 10. *25 Northfields, Speldhurst, Tunbridge Wells TN3 0PN* Tel (01892) 863239

PERKINS, Miss Julia Margaret. b 49. Linc Th Coll 85. **d** 87 **p** 94. Par Dn Owton Manor *Dur* 87-89; Par Dn Leam Lane 89-94; C 94; P-in-c Stockton St Chad 94-96; V 96-00; C Eppleton and Hetton le Hole 00-06; C Heworth St Mary 06-11; rtd 11. *19 Lauder Way, Gateshead NE10 0BG* Tel 0191-469 2866

PERKINS, Julian John. b 67. Southn Univ BSc90 MSc92. Trin Coll Bris BA00 MPhil03. **d** 01 **p** 02. C Thornbury *Glouc* 01-04; C Tewkesbury w Walton Cardiff and Twyning 04-07; P-in-c Crosland Moor *Wakef* 07-08; P-in-c Linthwaite 07-08; V Crosland Moor and Linthwaite 08-10; Perm to Offic *Man* from 11. *Pike Low, Stubbins Lane, Chinley, High Peak SK23 6EB* E-mail julian.perkins@zen.co.uk

PERKINS, Malcolm Bryan. b 20. SS Coll Cam BA41 MA45. Wycliffe Hall Ox 41. **d** 43 **p** 44. C Rainham *Roch* 43-47; C Bexley St Jo 47-50; P-in-c Chalk 50-51; V 51-56; V Borstal 56-61; Chapl St Bart Hosp Roch 59-74; P-in-c Strood St Mary *Roch* 61-65; R Wouldham 65-73; Chapl Medway Hosp Gillingham 65-67; Ioc H Staff Padre (SE Region) 73-85; Hon C Roch 74-85; rtd 85; Perm to Offic *Roch* 85-05 and *Cant* 85-04. *Roke Cottage, 3 Belgrave Terrace, Laddingford, Maidstone ME18 6BP* Tel (01622) 871774

PERKINS, Patricia Doris (Sister Patricia). b 29. Gilmore Ho 60. dss 73 **d** 87. CSA from 71; Sherston Magna w Easton Grey *Bris* 73-75; Cant St Martin and St Paul 76-78; Kilburn St Aug w St Jo *Lon* 80-84; Abbey Ho Malmesbury 84-87; Hon Par Dn Bayswater 87-94; Chapl St Mary's Hosp Praed Street Lon 88-89; Chapl St Chas Hosp Ladbroke Grove 88-89; Dean of Women's Min *Lon* from 89; Dioc Dir of Ords 90-94; Hon Par Dn St Olave Hart Street w All Hallows Staining etc 94-01. *St Mary's Convent and Nursing Home, Burlington Lane, London W4 2QF*

PERKINS, Sheila Barbara. b 50. SEITE BA07. **d** 07 **p** 08. NSM Tonbridge St Steph *Roch* from 07. *25 Northfields, Speldhurst, Tunbridge Wells TN3 0PN* Tel (01892) 863239 Mobile 07952-354478 E-mail perkins25@btinternet.com

PERKINSON, Neil Donald. b 46. Wycliffe Hall Ox 84. **d** 85 **p** 86. C Workington St Jo *Carl* 85-88; TV Cockermouth w Embleton and Wythop 88-93; TV St Laur in Thanet *Cant* 93-01; P-in-c Darlaston All SS and Ind Chapl Black Country Urban Ind Miss *Lich* 01-08; rtd 08; V Whangamata New Zealand from 08. *103 Durrant Drive, Whangamata, Waikato 3620, New Zealand* E-mail neil@perkinson.org.uk

PERKINTON, Keith Glyn. b 61. Humberside Poly BA83 Leeds Univ BA92. Coll of Resurr Mirfield 93. **d** 93 **p** 94. C Knowle H Nativity *Bris* 93-97; TV Brighton Resurr *Chich* 97-05; P-in-c Hangleton 05-07; V from 07; RD Hove 10. *The Vicarage, 127 Hangleton Way, Hove BN3 8ER* Tel (01273) 413044

PERKS, David Leonard Irving. b 38. Avery Hill Coll TCert61 Sussex Univ MA76. S Dios Minl Tr Scheme 84. **d** 87 **p** 88. NSM Lewes All SS, St Anne, St Mich and St Thos *Chich* 87-91; Chapl HM Pris Lewes 91-94; NSM Deanery of Lewes and Seaford *Chich* 94-96; C Peacehaven and Telscombe Cliffs 96-00; C Telscombe w Piddinghoe and Southease 96-00; rtd 00; Asst to RD Lewes and Seaford *Chich* from 00; Chapl S Downs Health NHS Trust from 01. *45 Fitzjohns Road, Lewes BN7 1PR* Tel (01273) 478719 E-mail danddperks@btopenworld.com

PERKS, Edgar Harold Martin. b 31. Open Univ BA87. Glouc Sch of Min 85. **d** 88 **p** 89. NSM Bromfield *Heref* 88-89; NSM Culmington w Onibury 88-89; NSM Stanton Lacy 88-89; NSM Culmington w Onibury, Bromfield etc 90-98; Perm to Offic from 98. *The Oaklands, Bromfield Road, Ludlow SY8 1DW* Tel (01584) 875525

PERRETT, David Thomas. b 48. Cranmer Hall Dur 80. **d** 82 **p** 83. C Stapleford *S'well* 82-86; V Ollerton 86-87; P-in-c Boughton 86-87; V Ollerton w Boughton 87-93; V Winklebury 93-05; P-in-c Gresley *Derby* 05-10; V from 10. *The Vicarage, 120 Church Street, Church Gresley, Swadlincote DE11 9NR* Tel (01283) 222966 E-mail dtp@dperrett.freeserve.co.uk

PERRETT, Mrs Jill. b 59. Trent Poly BA80 CQSW82. STETS 99. **d** 02 **p** 03. C Mere w W Knoyle and Maiden Bradley *Sarum* 02-07; P-in-c Atworth w Shaw and Whitley 07-11; V from 11; C Melksham from 07; C Broughton Gifford, Gt Chalfield and Holt from 07; Chapl Melksham Oak Community Sch from 11. *The Vicarage, Corsham Road, Shaw, Melksham SN12 8EH* Tel (01225) 703498 E-mail revjperrett@tiscali.co.uk

PERRETT (formerly ROWE), Mrs Vanda Sheila. b 63. STETS 95. **d** 98 **p** 99. C Marlborough *Sarum* 98-01; TV Pewsey and

Swanborough 01-06; TR Bourne Valley from 06; C Salisbury St Fran and Stratford sub Castle from 09; RD Alderbury from 06. *The Rectory, High Street, Porton, Salisbury SP4 0LH* Tel (01980) 610305 E-mail rev.vandaperrett@googlemail.com

PERRICONE, Vincent James. b 50. Connecticut Univ BA74 Pontifical Univ Rome STB88 STL90 Glas Univ PhD98. **d** 90 **p** 90. In RC Ch 89-94; C Glas St Mary 94-95; P-in-c Glas All SS and Glas H Cross 95-03; USA 03-08; Asst Chapl Florence w Siena *Eur* 08-09. *Address temp unknown*

PERRIN, Bruce Alexander. b 72. Birm Univ BSc94 MSc96. St Jo Coll Nottm 08. **d** 09 **p** 10. C Marple All SS *Ches* from 09. *66 Brindley Avenue, Marple, Stockport SK6 7NH* Tel 0161-427 6273 Mobile 07914-211376 E-mail bruce.perrin7@ntlworld.com

PERRIN, Michael Leonard. b 47. Shenstone Coll of Educn CertEd66 Lanc Univ BEd71. Dioc OLM tr scheme 97. **d** 01 **p** 02. OLM Aspull St Eliz *Liv* 01-06; OLM Haigh and Aspull from 06. *21 Firs Park Crescent, Aspull, Wigan WN2 2SJ* Tel (01942) 257418 E-mail mikeperrin99@hotmail.com

PERRINS, Christopher Neville. b 68. St Steph Ho Ox 01. **d** 03 **p** 04. C Warrington St Elphin *Liv* 03-08; TV Walton-on-the-Hill from 08. *St Nathanael's Vicarage, 65 Fazakerley Road, Liverpool L9 2AJ* E-mail revdcnperrins@aol.com

PERRINS, Mrs Lesley. b 53. St Hugh's Coll Ox BA74. S Dios Minl Tr Scheme 90. **d** 93 **p** 95. NSM Stoneleigh *Guildf* 93-94; NSM Haxby w Wigginton *York* 94-00; Asst Chapl York Health Services NHS Trust 99-00. *37 St John's Rise, Woking GU21 7PN* Tel (01483) 761427

PERRINS, Preb Anthony. b 48. Univ of Wales (Abth) BSc69 Selw Coll Cam BA76 MA79. Ridley Hall Cam 74. **d** 77 **p** 78. C Sandal St Helen *Wakef* 77-80; C Plymouth St Andr w St Paul and St Geo *Ex* 80-87; TV Yeovil *B & W* 87-88; V Preston Plucknett from 88; RD Yeovil from 06; Preb Wells Cathl from 11. *St James's Vicarage, 1 Old School Close, Yeovil BA21 3UB* Tel (01935) 429398 E-mail antonyperris@yahoo.com

PERRIS, Mrs Jocelyn Clare. b 69. Surrey Univ BSc91. ERMC 08. **d** 11. C St Alb St Pet *St Alb* from 11. *155 Toms Lane, Kings Langley WD4 8PA* Tel (01923) 263733 Mobile 07979-590480 E-mail josperris@aol.com

PERRIS, John Martin. b 44. Liv Univ BSc66. Trin Coll Bris 69. **d** 72 **p** 73. C Sevenoaks St Nic *Roch* 72-76; C Bebington *Ches* 76-79; V Redland *Bris* 79-97; RD Horfield 91-97; R Barton Seagrave w Warkton *Pet* 97-09; rtd 09. *3 Old Myse, Storth, Milnthorpe LA7 7HQ* Tel (01539) 564446

PERRY, Alan David. b 64. Avery Hill Coll BA86 Lon Inst of Educn PGCE87 Greenwich Univ MA99. NTMTC 01. **d** 03 **p** 04. NSM Romford St Edw *Chelmsf* 03-08; Hd Teacher St Edw C of E Sch Havering from 08; Public Preacher from 08. *1A Lyndhurst Drive, Hornchurch RM11 1JL* Tel (01708) 437852 Mobile 07946-730291 E-mail alan.perry80@ntlworld.com

PERRY, Andrew John. b 65. St Steph Ho Ox BTh00. **d** 00 **p** 01. C Southwick St Mich *Chich* 00-03; P-in-c Upper St Leonards St Jo 03; R from 03. *St John's Rectory, 53 Brittany Road, St Leonards-on-Sea TN38 0RD* Tel (01424) 423367 Mobile 07900-981345 E-mail perry.rickard@virgin.net

PERRY, Andrew Nicholas. b 62. Westmr Coll Ox BA86. Trin Coll Bris MA91. **d** 91 **p** 92. C Bath Weston All SS w N Stoke *B & W* 91-93; C Bath Weston All SS w N Stoke and Langridge 93-95; P-in-c Longfleet *Sarum* 95-00; V from 00. *The Vicarage, 2 Twemlow Avenue, Poole BH14 8AN* Tel (01202) 723359 *or* tel and fax 253527 E-mail andrew.perry@smlpoole.org.uk

PERRY, Andrew William. b 44. MRAC65. WMMTC 91. **d** 94 **p** 95. NSM Redmarley D'Abitot, Bromesberrow, Pauntley etc *Glouc* from 94; Perm to Offic *Heref* from 05. *Rye Cottage, Broomsgreen, Dymock GL18 2DP* Tel (01531) 890489 E-mail aw@perry.net

PERRY, Anthony Henry. b 54. Leic Univ BA76. Aston Tr Scheme 89 Linc Th Coll 93. **d** 93 **p** 94. C Bartley Green *Birm* 93-97; V Bearwood from 97; AD Warley from 06. *St Mary's Vicarage, 27 Poplar Avenue, Birmingham B17 8EG* Tel 0121-429 2165 E-mail trinity20@btopenworld.co.uk

PERRY, David William. b 42. St Chad's Coll Dur BA64. **d** 66 **p** 67. C Middleton St Mary *Ripon* 66-69; C Bedale 69-71; C Marton-in-Cleveland *York* 71-75; V Skirlaugh w Long Riston 75-05; V Skirlaugh w Long Riston, Rise and Swine 05-07; N Humberside Ecum Officer 84-07; RD N Holderness 06-07; rtd 07. *11 Middle Garth Drive, South Cave, Brough HU15 2AY* Tel (01430) 421412 E-mail perrydr@dsl.pipex.com

PERRY, Edward John. b 35. AKC62. **d** 63 **p** 64. C Honicknowle *Ex* 63-65; C Ashburton w Buckland-in-the-Moor 65-70; V Cornwood 70-92; Asst Dir of Educn 71-92; Chapl Moorhaven Hosp 91-93; V Ermington and Ugborough *Ex* 92-00; rtd 00; Perm to Offic *Ex* from 01. *32 Finches Close, Elburton, Plymouth PL9 8DP* Tel (01752) 405364

PERRY, Mrs Elizabeth Ann. b 59. WEMTC 04. **d** 07 **p** 08. NSM Soundwell *Bris* from 07; Chapl HM Pris Ashfield from 11. *HM Prison Ashfield, Shortwood Road, Pucklechurch, Bristol BS16 9QJ* Tel 0117-303 8000

PERRY, James Marcus. b 71. Ridley Hall Cam 02. **d** 04 **p** 05. C Cen Wolverhampton *Lich* 04-07; TV Tettenhall Regis from 07. *St Paul's Vicarage, 1 Talaton Road, Wolverhampton WV9 5LS* E-mail jimperry@operamail.com

PERRY, Mrs Joanna Teresa. b 60. K Coll Lon BD82. Trin Coll Bris. **d** 96 **p** 00. C Thornbury *Glouc* 96-97; C Winchcombe, Gretton, Sudeley Manor etc 97-99; Sub Chapl HM Pris and YOI New Hall 99-06; Chapl HM Pris and YOI Warren Hill from 06; Chapl HM Pris Hollesley Bay from 06. *HM Prison Hollesley Bay, Hollesley, Woodbridge IP12 3JW* Tel (01394) 412400

✠**PERRY, The Rt Revd John Freeman.** b 35. Lon Coll of Div MPhil86 ALCD59. **d** 59 **p** 60 **c** 89. C Woking Ch Ch *Guildf* 59-62; C Chorleywood Ch Ch *St Alb* 62; Min Chorleywood St Andr CD 63-66; V Chorleywood St Andr 66-77; RD Rickmansworth 72-77; Warden Lee Abbey 77-89; RD Shirwell *Ex* 80-84; Hon Can Win Cathl 89-96; Suff Bp Southampton 89-96; Bp Chelmsf 96-03; rtd 03; Hon Asst Bp *B & W* from 11. *8 The Firs, Bath BA2 5ED* Tel (01225) 833987

PERRY, John Neville. b 20. Leeds Univ BA41. Coll of Resurr Mirfield 41. **d** 43 **p** 44. C Poplar All SS w St Frideswide *Lon* 43-50; V De Beauvoir Town St Pet 50-63; V Feltham 63-75; RD Hounslow 67-75; Adn Middx 75-82; R Orlestone w Snave and Ruckinge w Warehorne *Cant* 82-86; rtd 86; Perm to Offic *Chich* from 90. *73 Elizabeth Crescent, East Grinstead RH19 3JG* Tel (01342) 315446

PERRY, John Walton Beauchamp. b 43. Ex Coll Ox BA64 Sussex Univ MA67. EAMTC 82 Westcott Ho Cam 84. **d** 85 **p** 86. C Shrewsbury St Chad w St Mary *Lich* 85-89; V Batheaston w St Cath *B & W* 89-99; V Milborne Port w Goathill etc 99-09; rtd 09. *67 Stevenmn New Road, Ludlow SY8 1JY* Tel (01584) 873755 E-mail jwbperry@hotmail.com

PERRY, Jonathan Robert. b 55. Cranmer Hall Dur. **d** 82 **p** 83. C Filey *York* 82-84; C Rayleigh *Chelmsf* 84-88; Asst Chapl St Geo Hosp Linc 88-90; Chapl Gateshead Hosps NHS Trust 90-98; Chapl Gateshead Health NHS Trust from 98. *Queen Elizabeth Hospital, Sheriff Hill, Gateshead NE9 6SX* Tel 0191-403 2072 *or* 482 0000 ext 2072

PERRY, Lesley Anne. b 52. K Coll Lon BA73 MIPR99. SEITE 96. **d** 99 **p** 00. NSM Fulham All SS *Lon* 99-07; NSM Kensington St Mary Abbots w Ch Ch and St Phil from 07. *Flat 3, 76 Philbeach Gardens, London SW5 9EY* Tel (020) 7373 3085 *or* 7419 5404 E-mail lesley.perry@universitiesuk.ac.uk

PERRY, Mrs Lynne Janice. b 48. **d** 90 **p** 97. NSM Llanfair Mathafarn Eithaf w Llanbedrgoch *Ban* 90-97; C Bangor 97-99; TV 99-05; V Tregarth 04-05; V Tregarth and Llandygai and Maes y Groes 05-09; AD Ogwen 02-07; rtd 09; C Ogwen Deanery 09-10; Hon Chapl Ban Cathl from 10. *Cwm Collen, 39 Tal y Cae, Tregarth, Bangor LL57 4AE* Tel (01248) 600997

PERRY, Mark. b 71. K Alfred's Coll Win BA97 Homerton Coll Cam PGCE Regent's Park Coll Ox 02. Trin Coll Cuddesdon 10. **d** 10. C Bourne Valley *Sarum* 10-11; C Iwerne Valley from 11. *Glen View, Church Lane, Sutton Waldron, Blandford Forum DT11 8PB* Tel (01747) 811284 E-mail revmarkperry@googlemail.com

PERRY, Martin Herbert. b 43. Cranmer Hall Dur 66. **d** 70 **p** 71. C Millfield St Mark *Dur* 70-74; C Haughton le Skerne 74-77; V Darlington St Matt 77-79; V Darlington St Matt and St Luke 79-84; TR Oldland *Bris* 84-91; V 91-01; rtd 01. *Address withheld by request*

PERRY, Martyn. b 57. Coll of Resurr Mirfield 89. **d** 90 **p** 91. In Bapt Ch 85-89; C Hornsey St Mary w St Geo *Lon* 90-93; V Pontlottyn w Fochriw *Llan* 93-97; R Cilybebyll from 97. *The Rectory, 7 Cwmnantllwyd Road, Gellinudd, Pontardawe, Swansea SA8 3DT* Tel (01792) 862118 E-mail father martyn@tiscali.co.uk

PERRY, Canon Michael Charles. b 33. Trin Coll Cam BA55 MA59 Lambeth DD03. Westcott Ho Cam 56. **d** 58 **p** 59. C Baswich *Lich* 58-60; Chapl Ripon Hall Ox 61-63; Chief Asst Home Publishing SPCK 63-70; Can Res Dur Cathl 70-98; Adn Dur 70-93; Bp's Sen Chapl 93-98; rtd 98. *57 Ferens Park, Durham DH1 1NU* Tel 0191-386 1891 E-mail mandmperry@totalserve.co.uk

PERRY, Michael James Matthew. b 66. Bris Univ BSc87 MSc89 PhD93. Trin Coll Bris BA99. **d** 99 **p** 00. C Keynsham *B & W* 99-03; R Cam Vale from 03. *The Rectory, Englands Lane, Queen Camel, Yeovil BA22 7NN* Tel (01935) 850326 E-mail mikepqc-crockfords@yahoo.co.uk

PERRY, Nicholas Charles. **d** 07 **p** 08. NSM Ebbw Vale *Mon* 07-10; R Blaina and Nantyglo from 10. *The Rectory, Station Road, Blaina NP13 3BW* Tel (01495) 290130 E-mail nick.perry1@btinternet.com

PERRY, Russell Lee. b 38. Worc Coll Ox BA60 MA64. CBDTI 98. **d** 98 **p** 99. NSM Grasmere *Carl* 98-01; rtd 01; Perm to Offic *S'well* from 01. *Dumble Howe, 3 Byron Gardens, Southwell NG25 0DW* Tel (01636) 815813

PERRY, Timothy Richard. b 64. Trin Coll Bris BA93. **d** 93 **p** 95. C Abingdon *Ox* 93-97; New Life Outreach/Fit Lives 97-01; Mountaintop Life Coaching Canada 01-09; Chapl Cothill Ho Sch from 10; Chapl Cothill Trust from 11; Hon C Wootton and

Dry Sandford *Ox* from 11. *6 Oakthorpe Road, Oxford OX2 7BE* Tel (01865) 318922 E-mail perry.tim@sky.com
PERRY, Valerie Evelyn. b 39. Southn Univ CertEd59. S'wark Ord Course 82. **dss** 85 **d** 87 **p** 94. NSM Romford St Edw *Chelmsf* 85-89; Par Dn 89-91; Asst Chapl Middx Hosp Lon 92-94; Chapl S Kent Hosps NHS Trust 94-98; Hon C Aylesham w Adisham *Cant* 98-00; Hon C Nonington w Wymynswold and Goodnestone etc 98-00; rtd 99; Perm to Offic *Truro* from 01. *115 Century Close, St Austell PL25 3UZ* Tel (01726) 68075
PERRY, William Francis Pitfield. b 61. Keble Coll Ox BA84 MA87. Ripon Coll Cuddesdon 94. **d** 96 **p** 97. C Brockworth *Glouc* 96-01; P-in-c Millbrook *Win* from 01. *58 Shirley Avenue, Shirley, Southampton SO15 5NJ* Tel (023) 8070 1896 E-mail fr.will@icxc.org
PERRY-GORE, Canon Walter Keith. b 34. Univ of Wales (Lamp) BA59. Westcott Ho Cam 60. **d** 61 **p** 62. C St Austell *Truro* 61-64; R H Innocents Barbados 64-71; Canada from 71; R New Carlisle 71-74; R N Hatley 74-96; rtd 96. *1115 Rue Massawippi, North Hatley QC J0B 2C0, Canada* Tel (001) (819) 842 4665 Fax 842 2176
PERRYMAN, Preb David Francis. b 42. Brunel Univ BSc64. Oak Hill Th Coll 74. **d** 76 **p** 77. C Margate H Trin *Cant* 76-80; R Ardingly *Chich* 80-90; V Bath St Luke *B & W* 90-07; RD Bath 96-03; Preb Wells Cathl 01-07; rtd 07. *Treetops, Upper Froyle, Alton GU34 4JH* Tel (01420) 520647 E-mail david@perrypeople.co.uk
PERRYMAN, Graham Frederick. b 56. Southn Univ BA78 Reading Univ PGCE80. Aston Tr Scheme 90 Trin Coll Bris 92. **d** 94 **p** 95. C Hamworthy *Sarum* 94-98; P-in-c Moreton and Woodsford w Tincleton 98-02; R 02-04; TV Melbury 04-06; TR from 06. *The Vicarage, Tollerford Lane, Higher Frome Vauchurch, Dorchester DT2 0AT* Tel and fax (01300) 320284 E-mail revgfp@btopenworld.com
PERRYMAN, James Edward. b 56. Lon Bible Coll BA85. Oak Hill Th Coll 86. **d** 88 **p** 89. C Gidea Park *Chelmsf* 88-91; C Becontree St Mary 91-94; Chapl Lyon *Eur* 94-00; R Allington and Maidstone St Pet *Cant* 00-08; Dioc Ecum Officer 02-08; P-in-c Stoneleigh w Ashow *Cov* from 08. *The Vicarage, 4 Hill Wootton Road, Leek Wootton, Warwick CV35 7QL* Tel (01926) 854832 E-mail jim@me16.com
PERRYMAN, Canon John Frederick Charles. b 49. Mert Coll Ox BA71 MA74 MInstGA98. Ridley Hall Cam 72. **d** 74 **p** 75. C Shortlands *Roch* 74-78; Asst Chapl St Geo Hosp Lon 78-82; Chapl Withington Hosp Man 83-94; Chapl S Man Univ Hosps NHS Trust 94-09; Hon Can Man Cathl 00-09; rtd 09; Perm to Offic *Man* from 09. *24 Alan Road, Manchester M20 4WG* Tel 0161-445 4769
PERSSON, Matthew Stephen. b 60. Dundee Univ BSc82 Bris Univ MA98. Wycliffe Hall Ox 88. **d** 91 **p** 92. C Bath Twerton-on-Avon *B & W* 91-94; Chapl HM Pris Shepton Mallet 94-97; Perm to Offic *B & W* 97-98; C Shepton Mallet w Doulting 98-00. *Grange Farm, Fair Place, West Lydford, Somerton TA11 7DN* Tel (01963) 240024
✠**PERSSON, The Rt Revd William Michael Dermot.** b 27. Oriel Coll Ox BA51 MA55. Wycliffe Hall Ox 51. **d** 53 **p** 54 **c** 82. C S Croydon Em *Cant* 53-55; C Tunbridge Wells St Jo *Roch* 55-58; V S Mimms Ch Ch *Lon* 58-67; R Bebington *Ches* 67-79; V Knutsford St Jo and Toft 79-82; Suff Bp Doncaster *Sheff* 82-92; rtd 93; Hon Asst Bp B & W from 93. *Ryalls Cottage, Burton Street, Marnhull, Sturminster Newton DT10 1PS* Tel (01258) 820452
PERTH (AUSTRALIA), Dean of. See SHEPHERD, The Very Revd John Harley
PERTH, Provost of. See FARQUHARSON, The Very Revd Hunter Buchanan
PERU, Bishop of. See GODFREY, The Rt Revd Harold William
PERUMBALATH, John. b 66. Calicut Univ BA86 Union Bibl Sem Pune BD90 Osmania Univ Hyderabad MA93 NW Univ S Africa PhD07. Serampore Th Coll MTh93. **d** 94 **p** 95. C Calcutta St Jo India 94-95; V Calcutta St Jas 95-00; V Calcutta St Thos 00-01; C Beckenham St Geo *Roch* 02-05; TV Northfleet and Rosherville 05-08; V Perry Street from 08; Dioc CUF Link Officer from 08. *All Saints' Vicarage, Perry Street, Gravesend DA11 8RD* Tel (01474) 534398 E-mail jperumbalath@btopenworld.com
PESCOD, John Gordon. b 44. Leeds Univ BSc70. Qu Coll Birm. **d** 72 **p** 73. C Camberwell St Geo S'wark 72-75; Chapl R Philanthropic Soc Sch Redhill 75-80; P-in-c Nunney w Wanstrow and Cloford *B & W* 80-84; R Nunney and Witham Friary, Marston Bigot etc 84-87; R Milverton w Halse and Fitzhead 87-93; V Frome St Jo and St Mary 93-00; V Frome St Jo 01; V Woodlands 93-01; RD Frome 97-01; V Castle Cary w Ansford 01-09; rtd 09. *32 Churchfield Drive, Castle Cary BA7 7LA* E-mail jjpescod@tiscali.co.uk
PESKETT, Richard Howard. b 42. Selw Coll Cam BA64 MA67. Ridley Hall Cam 64. **d** 68 **p** 69. C Jesmond H Trin *Newc* 68-71; Lect Discipleship Tr Cen Singapore 71-76; Dean 76-86; Lect Coll of SS Paul and Mary Cheltenham 86-87; Research Dir OMF 88-91; Tutor Trin Coll Bris 91-06; Vice-Prin 98-06; rtd 07; Perm

to Offic *Truro* 06-08; Hon C Penzance St Mary w St Paul and St Jo from 08; RD Penwith from 08. *7 North Parade, Penzance TR18 4SH* Tel (01736) 362913 E-mail howard.peskett@btinternet.com
PESKETT, Timothy Lewis. b 64. St Kath Coll Liv BA86. Chich Th Coll BTh90. **d** 90 **p** 91. C Verwood *Sarum* 90-91; C Southsea H Spirit *Portsm* 91-95; TV Burgess Hill St Jo w St Edw *Chich* 95-00; V Burgess Hill St Edw 00-05; R Felpham from 05. *The Rectory, 24 Limmer Lane, Felpham, Bognor Regis PO22 7ET* Tel (01243) 842522
PESTELL, Robert Carlyle. b 54. Aston Tr Scheme 89 Linc Th Coll 91. **d** 93 **p** 94. C Matson *Glouc* 93-97; P-in-c Charfield 97-01; R Charfield and Kingswood 02-06; P-in-c Cheltenham St Mich from 06; P-in-c Cheltenham St Luke and St Jo from 06. *St Michael's Vicarage, 1 Severn Road, Cheltenham GL52 5QA* Tel (01242) 694985 E-mail stmichaelsvicarage@blueyonder.co.uk
PETCH, Canon Douglas Rodger. b 57. Nottm Univ BSc79. St Jo Coll Nottm MA96. **d** 94 **p** 94. C Vom Nigeria 94-95; C Pendleton *Man* 96-98; P-in-c Werneth and C Oldham St Paul 98-03; CMS Nigeria 03-07; Hon Can Jos from 05; TV Halliwell *Man* 07-11; TV W Bolton from 11; AD Bolton from 10. *101 Cloister Street, Bolton BL1 3HA* Tel (01204) 842627 Mobile 07837-423501 E-mail rodgerpetch@yahoo.co.uk
PETER, Christopher Javed. b 51. Peshawar Univ BA75. Qu Coll Birm 94. **d** 96 **p** 97. C Darwen St Pet w Hoddlesden *Blackb* 96-98; C Accrington 98-99; C Burnley St Andr w St Marg and St Jas 99-05; Chapl R Liverpool and Broadgreen Univ Hosps NHS Trust from 05. *Royal Liverpool University Hospital, Prescot Street, Liverpool L7 8XP* Tel 0151-706 2826 E-mail christopher.peter@rlbuht.nhs.uk
PETER DOUGLAS, Brother. See NEEDHAM, Brother Peter Douglas
PETERBOROUGH, Bishop of. See ALLISTER, The Rt Revd Donald Spargo
PETERBOROUGH, Dean of. See TAYLOR, The Very Revd Charles William
PETERKEN, Canon Peter Donald. b 28. K Coll Lon BD51 AKC51 Open Univ BA09. **d** 52 **p** 53. C Swanley St Mary *Roch* 52-55 and 62-65; C Is of Dogs Ch Ch and St Jo w St Luke *Lon* 55-57; R S Perrott w Mosterton and Chedington *Sarum* 57-59; Br Guiana 59-62; R Killamarsh *Derby* 65-70; V Derby St Luke 70-90; RD Derby N 79-90; Hon Can Derby Cathl 85-95; R Matlock 90-95; rtd 95; Perm to Offic *Derby* from 95. *64 Brayfield Road, Littleover, Derby DE23 6GT* Tel (01332) 766285 E-mail peter.peterken@ntlworld.com
PETERS, Bill. See PETERS, Canon Cyril John
PETERS, Carl Richard. b 62. Ripon Coll Cuddesdon 95. **d** 97 **p** 98. C Coventry Caludon 97-01; V Gt Grimsby St Andr w St Luke and All SS *Linc* 01-02; TV Leek and Meerbrook *Lich* from 02. *All Saints Vicarage, Compton, Leek ST13 5PT* Tel (01538) 382588 E-mail carljackie@petersc.freeserve.co.uk
PETERS, Miss Carole Jean. b 61. Ripon Coll Cuddesdon 07. **d** 09 **p** 10. C Ivinghoe w Pitstone and Slapton and Marsworth *Ox* from 09. *5 The Crescent, Marsworth, Tring HP23 4LP* Tel (01296) 668238 Mobile 07710-128859 E-mail carolepeters@aol.com
PETERS, The Very Revd Christopher Lind. b 56. Oak Hill Th Coll. **d** 82 **p** 83. C Knockbreda *D & D* 82-84; C Lisburn Ch Ch Cathl 84-87; I Kilmocomogue C, C & R 87-93; P-in-c Beara 92-93; I Killiney Ballybrack *D & G* 93-98; Dean Ross *C, C & R* from 98; Chan Cork Cathl from 98; I Ross Union from 98. *The Deanery, Rosscarbery, Co Cork, Republic of Ireland* Tel (00353) (23) 48166 E-mail candjpeters@eircom.net
PETERS, Canon Cyril John (Bill). b 19. Fitzw Ho Cam BA42 MA45. Chich Th Coll 40. **d** 42 **p** 43. C Brighton St Mich *Chich* 42-45 and 47-50; C(E) 45-47; Hon CF from 47; Chapl Brighton Coll 50-69; R Uckfield *Chich* 69-96; R Isfield 69-96; R Lt Horsted 69-96; RD Uckfield 73-96; Can and Preb Chich Cathl 81-89; rtd 96; Perm to Offic *Chich* from 96. *Canon's Lodge, 9 Calvert Road, Uckfield TN22 2DB* Tel (01825) 766397
PETERS, David Alexander. b 72. K Coll Lon BA94. St Steph Ho Ox BA98 MA08. **d** 99 **p** 00. C Paddington St Jas *Lon* 99-03; PV Westmr Abbey from 01; V Reading H Trin and Reading St Mark *Ox* 03-08; Asst Chapl Tonbridge Sch from 08. *20 Manor Grove, Tonbridge TN10 3DT* Tel (01732) 364476 E-mail frpeters@hotmail.com
PETERS, David Lewis. b 38. Ch Ch Ox BA62 MA66. Westcott Ho Cam 63. **d** 65 **p** 66. C Oldham St Mary w St Pet *Man* 65-69; C Stand 70-74; P-in-c Hillock 70-74; V 74-82; V Haslingden w Haslingden Grane *Blackb* 82-88; rtd 88; Perm to Offic *Blackb* and *Man* 88-09. *37 Cyprus Road, Faversham ME13 8HB* Tel (01795) 537917
PETERS, Geoffrey John. b 51. BCom BSc MDiv MInstC(Glas). Oak Hill Th Coll 85. **d** 87 **p** 88. C Forest Gate St Sav w W Ham St Matt *Chelmsf* 87-90; C Wembley St Jo *Lon* 90-92; Chapl Wembley Hosp 90-92; TV Manningham *Bradf* 92-97; Res Scheme Manager Anchor Trust 02-04; NSM York St Clem w St Mary Bishophill from 07. *15 Cameron Walker Court,*

Bishopthorpe Road, York YO23 1LD Tel (01904) 638632 Mobile 07990-644779 E-mail geoffpeters04@aol.com
PETERS, Mrs Helen Elizabeth. b 67. Qu Marg Coll Edin BSc88. Ox Min Course 08. **d** 11. NSM Hughenden *Ox* from 11. *Boundary House, Missenden Road, Great Kingshill, High Wycombe HP15 6EB* Tel (01494) 716772 E-mail helen.peters@peters-research.com
PETERS, Mrs Jane Elisabeth. b 48. Kent Univ BA08. **d** 08 **p** 09. NSM Shortlands *Roch* from 08. *27 The Gardens, Beckenham BR3 5PH* Tel (020) 8650 5986 E-mail jane@beckenham.eclipse.co.uk
PETERS, John Peter Thomas. b 63. Keble Coll Ox BL85. Wycliffe Hall Ox BA91. **d** 95 **p** 96. C Brompton H Trin w Onslow Square St Paul *Lon* 95-99; P-in-c Bryanston Square St Mary w St Marylebone St Mark 00-04; R from 04. *13 Chomeley Crescent, London N6 5EZ* Tel (020) 7258 5042
PETERS, John Thomas. b 58. Connecticut Univ BA80. St Jo Coll Nottm 84. **d** 87 **p** 88. C Virginia Water *Guildf* 87-93; R Grand Rapids Ch Ch USA 93-00; R Eden Prairie St Alb from 00. *14434 Fairway Drive, Eden Prairie MN 557344-1904, USA* E-mail johnpeters@isd.net
PETERS, Canon Kenneth. b 54. Newport Univ Tokyo MBA88 Greenwich Univ MA02 MIW96. St Mich Coll Llan 74. **d** 77 **p** 78. C Mountain Ash *Llan* 77-80; Asst Chapl Mersey Miss to Seamen 80-82; Chapl Miss to Seamen Japan 82-89; Hon Can Kobe from 85; Chapl Supt Mersey Miss to Seamen 89-93; Justice and Welfare Sec 94-09; Dir Justice and Welfare from 09; Hon C St Mich Paternoster Royal *Lon* from 94. *The Mission to Seafarers, St Michael Paternoster Royal, College Hill, London EC4R 2RL* Tel (020) 7248 5202 Fax 7248 4761 E-mail justice@missiontoseafarers.org
PETERS, Malcolm John. b 71. Leic Univ BA92. Oak Hill Th Coll BA03. **d** 03 **p** 04. C Braintree *Chelmsf* 03-06; C Hull St Jo Newland *York* 06-09; P-in-c High Ongar w Norton Mandeville *Chelmsf* from 09. *The Rectory, The Street, High Ongar, Ongar CM5 9NQ* Tel (01277) 362593 E-mail malcolm.peters892@btinternet.com
PETERS, Preb Marilyn Ann. b 49. Open Univ BA90. Qu Coll Birm 96. **d** 98 **p** 99. C Blakenall Heath *Lich* 98-01; TV Cen Telford 01-05; TR from 05; Preb Lich Cathl from 09. *The Rectory, 20 Burlington Close, Dawley, Telford TF4 3TD* Tel (01952) 595915 Mobile 07754-435272 E-mail marilynpeters@waitrose.com
PETERS, Canon Michael. b 41. Chich Th Coll 75. **d** 77 **p** 78. C Redruth *Truro* 77-79; TV 79-80; TV Redruth w Lanner 80-82; R St Mawgan w St Ervan and St Eval 82-86; Chapl HM Pris Liv 86-87; Chapl HM Pris Bris 87-01; Hon Can Bris Cathl 96-01; P-in-c Middlezoy and Othery and Moorlinch *B & W* 01-08; rtd 08. *Archway House, North Lane, Othery, Bridgwater TA7 0QG* Tel (01823) 690208 E-mail mikesandra@ukgateway.net
PETERS, Rebecca Ann. b 76. St Hilda's Coll Ox MPhys98 St Cross Coll Ox PGCE99. Wycliffe Hall Ox 06. **d** 08 **p** 09. C Roxeth *Lon* from 08. *18 Welland Avenue, Didcot OX11 7QN* Tel 07967-598115 (mobile)
PETERS, Robert David. b 54. BA76. Oak Hill Th Coll 78. **d** 79 **p** 80. C Hyde St Geo *Ches* 79-83; C Hartford 83-86; V Lindow 86-96; V Throop *Win* 96-10; P-in-c Bournemouth H Epiphany 08-10; AD Bournemouth 03-08; Hon Can Win Cathl 08-10; V Plas Newton w Ches Ch Ch from 10. *St Michael's Vicarage, 22 Plas Newton Lane, Chester CH2 1PA* Tel (01244) 319677 E-mail rob.peters@tiscali.co.uk
PETERS, Stephen Eric. b 45. Westcott Ho Cam 74. **d** 77 **p** 78. C Wanstead St Mary *Chelmsf* 77-79; C Leigh-on-Sea St Marg 79-81; P-in-c Purleigh 81-82; P-in-c Cold Norton w Stow Maries 81-82; R Purleigh, Cold Norton and Stow Maries 83-84; V Bedford Park *Lon* 84-87; Perm to Offic *Ex* 87-88 and 93-08; TR Totnes and Berry Pomeroy 88-90; Chapl Ex Sch and St Marg Sch 91-93. *6 Armada Court, East Bracklesham Drive, Bracklesham Bay, Chichester PO20 8JS* E-mail stephen.e.peters@gmail.com
PETERS-WOTHERSPOON, Ann Margaret. b 48. Lon Univ BD84 Open Univ MA95 UEA EdD05. ERMC 05. **d** 07 **p** 08. NSM Somersham w Pidley and Oldhurst and Woodhurst *Ely* 07-11; Perm to Offic from 11. *14 Twentypence Road, Cottenham, Cambridge CB24 8SP* Tel (01954) 250694 E-mail ann_m_peters@hotmail.com
PETERSEN, Miss Jennifer Elizabeth. b 55. Aus Nat Univ BA78. Moore Th Coll Sydney BTh82 Wycliffe Hall Ox 92. **d** 94 **p** 95. C Elloughton and Brough w Brantingham *York* 94-96; C Ealing St Mary *Lon* 96-00; Chapl Thames Valley Univ 96-00; Chapl Qu Mary and Westf Coll from 00. *24 Sidney Square, London E1 2EY* Tel (020) 7791 1973 *or* 7882 3179 E-mail j.e.petersen@qmul.ac.uk
PETERSON, David Gilbert. b 44. Sydney Univ BA65 MA74 Lon Univ BD68 Man Univ PhD78. Moore Th Coll Sydney ThL68. **d** 68 **p** 69. C Manly St Matt Australia 68-70; Lect Moore Th Coll 71-75; C Cheadle *Ches* 75-78; Sen Can and R Wollongong Cathl Australia 80-84; Lect Moore Th Coll 84-96; Prin Oak Hill Th Coll 96-07; Perm to Offic *Lon* and *St Alb* 96-07; Research Fell

Moore Th Coll Australia from 07; rtd 09. *1 Vista Street, Belrose NSW 2085, Australia* E-mail davidandlesleypeterson@gmail.com
PETERSON, Dennis. b 25. Oak Hill Th Coll 51. **d** 54 **p** 55. C Leyton All SS *Chelmsf* 54-56; C Leeds St Geo *Ripon* 56-58; V E Brixton St Jude *S'wark* 58-91; rtd 91; Perm to Offic *Chelmsf* from 91. *79 Cavendish Gardens, Westcliff-on-Sea SS0 9XP* Tel (01702) 334400
PETERSON, Canon John Louis. b 42. Concordia Coll (USA) BA65 Harvard Div Sch STB68 Chicago Th Sem ThD76 Virginia Th Sem Hon DD93. **d** 76 **p** 77. V Plainwell St Steph USA 76-82; Dean St Geo Coll Jerusalem 82-94; Can Res 82-94; Hon Can from 95; Hon Can Kalamazoo from 82; Hon Prov Can Cant Cathl from 95; Sec Gen ACC 95-04; Hon Can Kaduna from 99; Hon Can St Paul's Cathl 00-05. *Episcopal Church House, Mount St Alban, Washington DC 20016, USA*
PETERSON, Paul John. b 67. Trin Coll Bris 94. **d** 97 **p** 98. C Burney Lane *Birm* 97-01; C-in-c Bradley Stoke N CD *Bris* 01-10; C Downend from 10. *15 Glendale, Bristol BS16 6EQ* Tel 0117-330 7673 E-mail paul@petersonp.freeserve.co.uk
PETFIELD, Bruce le Gay. b 34. FHA. NEOC 76. **d** 79 **p** 80. NSM Morpeth *Newc* 79-86; C Knaresborough *Ripon* 86-87; V Flamborough *York* 87-94; V Bempton 87-94; rtd 94; Perm to Offic *York* from 94. *36 Maple Road, Bridlington YO16 6TE* Tel (01262) 676028 E-mail bruce.petfield@talktalk.net
PETIT, Andrew Michael. b 53. Em Coll Cam MA78. Trin Coll Bris. **d** 83 **p** 84. C Stoughton *Guildf* 83-87; C Shirley *Win* 87-92; V Cholsey *Ox* 92-04; C Streatley w Moulsford 03-04; V Cholsey and Moulsford from 04; Chapl W Berks Priority Care Services NHS Trust 92-03. *The Vicarage, Church Road, Cholsey, Wallingford OX10 9PP* Tel (01491) 651216 Mobile 07986-005618 E-mail apetit@lineone.net
PETITT, Michael David. b 53. BCombStuds. Linc Th Coll 79. **d** 82 **p** 83. C Arnold *S'well* 82-86; Asst Chapl HM Youth Cust Cen Glen Parva 86-87; V Blaby *Leic* 87-94; V Leagrave *St Alb* 94-98; R Badby w Newham and Charwelton w Fawsley etc *Pet* 98-08; Dioc Voc Adv 00-08; Dir Tr for Past Assts 01-03; P-in-c Guilsborough w Hollowell and Cold Ashby 08-10; P-in-c Cottesbrooke w Gt Creaton and Thornby 08-10; C W Haddon w Winwick and Ravensthorpe 08-10; P-in-c Spratton 08-10; V Ilkeston St Mary *Derby* from 10. *St Mary's Vicarage, 63B Manners Road, Ilkeston DE7 5HB* Tel 0115-932 4725 E-mail michael.dp@virgin.net
PETRIE, Alistair Philip. b 50. Fuller Th Sem California DMin99. Oak Hill Th Coll 76. **d** 76 **p** 77. C Eston *York* 76-79; P-in-c Prestwick *Glas* 79-81; R 81-82; Canada from 82. *PO Box 25103, Kelowna BC V1W 3 Y7, Canada* Tel (001) (250) 764 8590 Fax 656 3298 E-mail alistair@partnershipministries.org
PETRIE, Ian Robert (Eric). b 53. Avery Hill Coll PGCE84 Oak Hill Th Coll BA83. Qu Coll Birm 93. **d** 95 **p** 96. C Sedgley All SS *Worc* 95-98; P-in-c Salwarpe and Hindlip w Martin Hussingtree 98-08; Co-ord Chapl W Mercia Police 98-08; rtd 08. *100 Highbridge Road, Burnham-on-Sea TA8 1LW* Tel (01278) 787402 E-mail eric@petrierev.freeserve.co.uk
PETRINE, Andrei Anatolievich. b 73. St Jo Coll Dur BA05. Cranmer Hall Dur 02. **d** 05 **p** 06. C Hounslow H Trin w St Paul *Lon* 05-08; Perm to Offic 08-09; P-in-c Greensted-juxta-Ongar w Stanford Rivers etc *Chelmsf* from 09; Chapl Russian Community *Lon* from 09. *52 Epping Road, Toot Hill, Ongar CM5 9SQ* Tel 07723-026925 (mobile) E-mail a.petrine@mac.com
PETTENGELL, Ernest Terence. b 43. Ex Univ MA98. K Coll *Lon* 65. **d** 69 **p** 70. C Chesham St Mary *Ox* 69-72; C Farnborough *Guildf* 72-75; Asst Master K Alfred Sch Burnham-on-Sea 75-78; C Bishop's Cleeve *Glouc* 78-80; Chapl Westonbirt Sch 80-85; P-in-c Shipton Moyne w Westonbirt and Lasborough *Glouc* 80-85; V Berkeley w Wick, Breadstone and Newport 85-92; TV Weston-super-Mare Cen Par *B & W* 92-95; P-in-c Weston super Mare Em 96-99; Chapl Staffs Univ 99-03; V Douglas All SS and St Thos *S & M* 03-07; rtd 07; Perm to Offic *Ox* from 09. *3 Rushall Road, Thame OX9 3TR* Tel (01844) 216298
PETTERSEN, Canon Alvyn Lorang. b 51. TCD BA73 Dur Univ BA75 PhD81. Sarum & Wells Th Coll 78. **d** 81 **p** 82. Chapl Clare Coll Cam 81-85; Fell and Chapl Ex Coll Ox 85-92; Research Fell Linc Coll Ox 92-93; V Frensham *Guildf* 93-02; Can Res Worc Cathl from 02. *2 College Green, Worcester WR1 2LH* Tel (01905) 732900 E-mail alvynpettersen@worcestercathedral.org.uk
PETTET, Christopher Farley. b 54. Ox Univ BEd78. St Jo Coll Nottm 87. **d** 90 **p** 91. C Luton St Mary *St Alb* 90-93; C Fawley *Win* 93-97; P-in-c Amport, Grateley, Monxton and Quarley 97-09; TV Portway and Danebury from 09. *The Vicarage, Amport, Andover SP11 8BE* Tel (01264) 772950 E-mail cpettet@btinternet.com
PETTIFER, Bryan George Ernest. b 32. Qu Coll Cam BA55 MA59 Bris Univ MEd74. Wm Temple Coll Rugby 56 Ridley Hall Cam 57. **d** 59 **p** 60. C Attercliffe w Carbrook *Sheff* 59-61; C Ecclesall 61-65; Chapl City of Bath Tech Coll 65-74; Adult Educn Officer *Bris* 75-80; Dir Past Th Sarum & Wells Th Coll

80-85; Can Res St Alb 85-92; Prin St Alb Minl Tr Scheme 85-92; Prin Ox Area Chr Tr Scheme 92-94; Min and Deployment Officer/Selection Sec ABM 94-97; rtd 97; Perm to Offic *Glouc* 98-00; *Sarum* and *Bris* from 98; *B & W* 02-05; Rtd Clergy Officer Malmesbury Adnry *Bris* from 04. *23 Curlew Drive, Chippenham SN14 6YG* Tel (01249) 659823

PETTIFER, John Barrie. b 38. Linc Th Coll 63. **d** 65 **p** 66. C Stretford St Matt *Man* 65-67; C Stand 67-71; V Littleborough 71-00; rtd 00. *Littleborough Christian Centre, 43 Todmorden Road, Littleborough OL15 9EL* Tel (01706) 374074

PETTIFOR, Canon David Thomas. b 42. Ripon Coll Cuddesdon 78. **d** 81 **p** 82. C Binley *Cov* 81-84; P-in-c Wood End 84-88; V 88-92; V Finham 92-98; TV Coventry Caludon 98-07; Hon Can Cov Cathl 04-07; rtd 07. *8 Austin Edwards Drive, Warwick CV34 5GW* Tel (01926) 498736
E-mail david@dtpettifor.fsnet.co.uk

PETTIGREW, Stanley. b 27. TCD BA49 MA62. Div Test. **d** 50 **p** 51. C Newcastle *D & D* 50-53; C Dublin Clontarf *D & G* 53-57; I Derralossary 57-62; Miss to Seamen 62-92; I Wicklow w Killiskey *D & G* 62-92; Can Ch Ch Cathl Dublin 87-92; rtd 92. *Corr Riasc, Bollarney South, Wicklow, Republic of Ireland* Tel (00353) (404) 69755

PETTINGELL, Hubert. b 32. ACA54 FCA65 AKC58. **d** 59 **p** 60. C Mansfield SS Pet and Paul *S'well* 59-61; CMS Iran 61-66; C Wellington w W Buckland and Nynehead *B & W* 67-68; Warden Student Movement Ho Lon 68-69; R Holywell w Needingworth *Ely* 69-71; Dir Finance WCC 80-96; Perm to Offic *Eur* from 94; rtd 97. *chemin du Pommier 22, CH-1218 Le Grand Saconnex, Geneva, Switzerland* Tel (0041) (22) 798 8586
E-mail hpettingell@hotmail.com

PETTIT, Mrs Alice Hazel Lester. b 78. St Mellitus Coll. **d** 11. C Teynham w Lynsted and Kingsdown *Cant* from 11. *19 Nobel Court, Faversham ME13 7SD* Tel (01795) 533153
E-mail alicepettit1@gmail.com

PETTIT, Anthony David. b 72. Univ of Cen England in Birm BA94 MA95 St Jo Coll Dur BA01. Cranmer Hall Dur 98. **d** 01 **p** 02. C Gt Malvern St Mary *Worc* 01-04; P-in-c Cradley 04-05; TV Halas 05-10; P-in-c Paget St Paul Bermuda from 10. *PO Box PG290, Paget PG BX, Bermuda* Tel (001) (441) 236 5880 Fax 236 8224 E-mail stpaulsoffice@logic.bm

PETTIT, James. b 78. Lon Bible Coll BA00 MA03. Ox Min Course 07. **d** 09 **p** 10. C Faversham *Cant* from 09. *Heronsmere, 19 Nobel Court, Faversham ME13 7SD* Tel (01795) 533153
E-mail jamesthemonk@gmail.com

PETTITT, Maurice. b 13. Clare Coll Cam BA35 MA57 MusBac37. Lich Th Coll 56. **d** 57 **p** 58. Asst Chapl Wellingborough Sch 57-62; R Rounton w Welbury *York* 62-69; V Riccall 69-78; RD Escrick 73-78; rtd 78; Perm to Offic *York* from 78. *Holbeck House, Low Street, Lastingham, York YO62 6TJ* Tel (01751) 417517

PETTITT, Robin Adrian. b 50. MRTPI79 Newc Univ BA77. St Steph Ho Ox 81. **d** 83 **p** 84. C Warrington St Elphin *Liv* 83-87; C Torrisholme *Blackb* 87-93; P-in-c Charnock Richard 93-00; Dioc Par Development Officer 93-98; Sec Dioc Adv Cttee for the Care of Chs 98-99; C Broughton 00-01; rtd 01; Perm to Offic *Liv* from 03. *The Vicarage, 169 Church Road, Haydock, St Helens WA11 0NJ* Tel (01942) 727956

PETTMAN, Mrs Hilary Susan. b 45. STETS 99. **d** 02 **p** 03. NSM Shottermill *Guildf* 02-08. *Stacey's Farm Cottage, Thursley Road, Elstead, Godalming GU8 6DG* Tel (01252) 703217
E-mail hilarypettman@tiscali.co.uk

PETTS, Mrs Anna Carolyn. b 44. St Mich Coll Sarum CertEd65. STETS 00. **d** 03 **p** 04. NSM Hordle *Win* 03-11; NSM NW Hants from 11. *The Clergy House, 2 Flexford Close, Highclere, Newbury RG20 9PE* Tel (01635) 255143
E-mail carolynpetts@tiscali.co.uk

PETTY, Alicia Christina Margaret. b 64. Wycliffe Hall Ox 01. **d** 03 **p** 04. C Ockbrook *Derby* 03-07; P-in-c Sawley 07-10; R from 10; Dean of Women's Min from 11. *The Rectory, 561 Tamworth Road, Long Eaton, Nottingham NG10 3FB* Tel 0115-973 4900
E-mail sawleyrector-alicia@yahoo.co.uk

PETTY, Brian. b 34. Man Univ BA90. St Aid Birkenhead 59. **d** 62 **p** 63. C Meole Brace *Lich* 62-65; Chapl RAF 65-69; Australia 70-75; P-in-c Kimbolton w Middleton-on-the-Hill *Heref* 76-79; P-in-c Pudleston-cum-Whyle w Hatfield, Docklow etc 76-79; P-in-c Haddenham *Ely* 79-80; V 80-84; V Fairfield *Derby* 84-90; Chapl St Geo Sch Ascot 90-93; TR Sampford Peverell, Uplowman, Holcombe Rogus etc *Ex* 93-99; RD Cullompton 95-99; rtd 99; Perm to Offic *Ex* 99-02; Hon C Diptford, N Huish, Harberton, Harbertonford etc from 02. *Woodrising, Fortescue Road, Sidmouth EX10 9QB* Tel (01395) 514203

PETTY, Duncan. *See* PETTY, William Duncan

PETTY, The Very Revd John Fitzmaurice. b 35. Trin Hall Cam BA59 MA65. Cuddesdon Coll. **d** 66 **p** 67. C Sheff St Cuth 66-69; C St Helier *S'wark* 69-75; V Hurst *Man* 75-88; AD Ashton-under-Lyne 83-87; Hon Can Man Cathl 86-88; Provost Cov 88-00; Dean Cov 00; rtd 00; Perm to Offic *Lich* from 01. *4 Granville Street, Copthorne, Shrewsbury SY3 8NE* Tel (01743) 231513

PETTY, Neil. b 40. Coll of Resurr Mirfield 04. **d** 04 **p** 05. NSM N Thornaby *York* from 04. *28 Bader Avenue, Thornaby, Stockton-on-Tees TS17 0HQ* Tel (01642) 761588 Mobile 07985-760490 E-mail neilpetty@hotmail.com

PETTY, Capt Stuart. b 56. Chich Th Coll 91. **d** 93 **p** 94. CA from 88; C W Bromwich St Andr w Ch Ch *Lich* 93-96; Asst Chapl Ldr R Wolv Hosps NHS Trust 96-00; Sen Chapl 00-03; Chapl Team Ldr R Wolv Hosps NHS Trust 03-08; Sen Chapl York Hosps NHS Foundn Trust from 08. *York Hospital, Wigginton Road, York YO31 8HE* Tel (01904) 631313

PETTY, William Duncan. b 55. Ex Univ BSc76 Leic Univ PGCE77. Oak Hill Th Coll 97. **d** 99 **p** 00. C Burscough Bridge *Liv* 99-04; Min Tanhouse The Oaks CD from 04. *181 Ennerdale, Skelmersdale WN8 6AH* Tel (01704) 892444
E-mail duncan@thepettys.freeserve.co.uk

PETZER, Garth Stephen. MBE99. Rhodes Univ BTh95. St Paul's Coll Grahamstown. **d** 88 **p** 91. C Queenstown St Mich S Africa 88-89; C E London St Sav 90-93; R E London St Martin 93-95; Chapl RN 96-03 and 04-07; CF 03-04; rtd 07; Perm to Offic *Nor* 04-07. *46 Crystal Way, Waterlooville PO7 8NB* Tel 07801-637205 (mobile)
E-mail petzeggs@hotmail.com

PETZSCH, Hugo Max David. b 57. Edin Univ MA79 BD83 PhD95 FSAScot91. Edin Th Coll 80. **d** 83 **p** 84. C Dollar *St And* 83-86; New Zealand 86-90; P-in-c Alyth, Blairgowrie and Coupar Angus *St And* 90-91; Chapl Glenalmond Coll 91-98; Dep Headmaster Benenden Sch from 99. *Benenden School, Cranbrook Road, Benenden, Cranbrook TN17 4AA* Tel (01580) 240592

PEVERELL, Canon Paul Harrison. b 57. Hull Univ BA80. Ripon Coll Cuddesdon. **d** 82 **p** 83. C Cottingham *York* 82-85; V Middlesbrough St Martin 85-93; V Gt Ayton w Easby and Newton under Roseberry from 93; Hon Can Ho Ghana from 04. *The Vicarage, Low Green, Great Ayton, Middlesbrough TS9 6NN* Tel (01642) 722333 E-mail revpev@btinternet.com

✠**PEYTON, The Rt Revd Nigel.** b 51. JP87. Edin Univ MA73 BD76 Lanc Univ PhD09. Union Th Sem (NY) STM77 Edin Th Coll 73. **d** 76 **p** 77 **c** 11. Chapl St Paul's Cathl Dundee 76-82; Dioc Youth Chapl 76-85; Chapl Invergowrie 79-82; P-in-c 82-85; Chapl Univ Hosp Dundee 82-85; V Nottingham All SS *S'well* 85-91; P-in-c Lambley 91-99; Chapl Bluecoat Sch Nottm 90-92; Dioc Min Development Adv *S'well* 91-99; Adn Newark 99-11; Bp Bre from 11; Hon Teaching Fell Lanc Univ from 10. *Bishop's House, 5 Glamis Drive, Dundee DD2 1QG* Tel (01382) 641586 *or* 562244 E-mail bishop@brechin.anglican.org

PEYTON JONES, Mrs Dorothy Helen. b 58. LMH Ox BA79 MPhil80 DipSW02. Trin Coll Bris 84. dss 86 **d** 87 **p** 94. W Holloway St Luke *Lon* 86-89; Par Dn 87-89; C Glas St Oswald 89-92; NSM Drumchapel 92-98; Perm to Offic *Ely* 98-03; NSM Chesterton St Andr from 03; Ind Chapl from 09. *71 Humberstone Road, Cambridge CB4 1JD* Tel (01223) 523485 Mobile 07503-746520 E-mail dorothypj@ntlworld.com

PHAIR, Neal David Stewart. b 70. Limerick Univ BA98 UCD HDipEd99 TCD MPhil02. CITC 99. **d** 02 **p** 03. C Ballymena w Ballyclug *Conn* 02-05; I Ballintoy w Rathlin and Dunseverick 05-07; Chapl Dub Inst of Tech 07-10; R Cherbury w Gainfield *Ox* from 10. *The Rectory, Church Lane, Longworth, Abingdon OX13 5DX* Tel (01865) 821277 E-mail nealphair@hotmail.com

PHARAOH, Carol Helen. b 63. Preston Poly BTech84. St Jo Coll Dur 96. **d** 98 **p** 99. C Heaton Ch Ch *Man* 98-02; TV Walkden and Lt Hulton 02-09; P-in-c E Farnworth and Kearsley 09-10; TR Farnworth, Kearsley and Stoneclough from 10. *The Rectory, 55 Church Street, Farnworth, Bolton BL4 8AQ* Tel (01204) 572819 E-mail pharaohingham@o2.co.uk

PHARAOH, Douglas William. b 18. MSHAA56. Worc Ord Coll 68. **d** 69 **p** 70. C Gt Malvern Ch Ch *Worc* 69-71; Area Sec Leprosy Miss 71-72; P-in-c Gateshead St Cuth *Dur* 72-73; V New Seaham 73-76; P-in-c Wymeswold *Leic* 76-78; V Wymeswold and Prestwold w Hoton 78-80; P-in-c Grandborough w Willoughby and Flecknoe *Cov* 80-81; V 81-83; rtd 83; Perm to Offic *Cov* from 83. *11 Margetts Close, Kenilworth CV8 1EN* Tel (01926) 779026

PHEELY, William Rattray. b 35. EN(M)88. Edin Th Coll 57. **d** 60 **p** 61. C Glas St Mary 60-63; C Salisbury St Martin *Sarum* 63-66; Guyana 66-82; V Bordesley St Oswald *Birm* 82-86; Perm to Offic *Birm* 86-00 and *Ex* 00-03; rtd 00. *Flat 2, 16 Westcliffe Road, Birkdale, Southport PR8 2BN* Tel (01704) 563346

PHELAN, Thomas Sylvester Patrick. b 36. CQSW79. Chich Th Coll 72. **d** 94 **p** 95. C Somers Town *Lon* 94-96; C Old St Pancras w Bedford New Town St Matt 96-97; Chapl Camden and Islington Community Health NHS Trust 96-97; OSB 97-09; Lic Preacher *Ox* 97-02; Hon C Nor St Jo w St Julian 02-06; Perm to Offic from 06. *7 Chaplain's House, The Great Hospital, Bishopgate, Norwich NR1 4EL* Tel (01603) 305522

PHELPS, Canon Arthur Charles. b 26. St Cath Coll Cam BA50 MA55. Ridley Hall Cam 51. **d** 53 **p** 54. C Kirkdale St Lawr *Liv* 53-56; C Rainham *Chelmsf* 56-60; Min Collier Row St Jas CD 60-65; V Collier Row St Jas 65-75; R Thorpe Morieux w Preston and Brettenham *St E* 75-84; R Rattlesden w Thorpe Morieux and Brettenham 84-90; Hon Can St E Cathl 89-90; rtd 90; Perm to Offic *Truro* 90-00 and *St E* from 01. *8 Northfield Court, Aldeburgh IP15 5LU* Tel (01728) 454772

PHELPS, Ian James. b 29. Oak Hill Th Coll 53. **d** 56 **p** 57. C Peckham St Mary *S'wark* 56-59; R Gaddesby w S Croxton *Leic* 59-67; R Beeby 59-67; Asst Dioc Youth Chapl and Rural Youth Adv 65-67; CF (TA) 60-67; CF (R of O) 67-84; Youth Chapl *Leic* 67-85; Dioc Adult Educn Officer 85-91; Past Asst to Bp and Adn *Leic* 91-94; rtd 94; Perm to Offic *Leic* 94-99 and *S'wark* from 99. *6 Montague Graham Court, Kidbrooke Gardens, London SE3 0PD* Tel (020) 8305 2150

PHELPS, Ian Ronald. b 28. Lon Univ BSc53 PhD57 FLS58. Chich Th Coll 57. **d** 59 **p** 60. C Brighton Gd Shep Preston *Chich* 59-61; C Sullington 62-64; C Storrington 62-64; R Newtimber w Pyecombe 64-68; V Brighton St Luke 68-74; TV Brighton Resurr 74-76; V Peacehaven 76-94; rtd 94; Perm to Offic *Chich* from 94. *2 Kingston Green, Seaford BN25 4NB* Tel (01323) 899511

PHENNA, Timothy Peter. b 69. Ridley Hall Cam BTh01. **d** 01 **p** 02. C Woodseats St Chad *Sheff* 01-04; USA from 04. *2051 Braun Drive, Golden CO 80401, USA* E-mail tpphenna@aol.com

PHILBRICK, Canon Gary James. b 57. Southn Univ BA78 K Alfred's Coll Win CertEd79 MA(Theol)00 Edin Univ BD86. Edin Th Coll 83. **d** 86 **p** 87. C Southampton Maybush St Pet *Win* 86-90; R Fawley 90-00; P-in-c Swaythling 00-04; V from 04; AD Southampton from 07; Hon Can Win Cathl from 09. *Swaythling Vicarage, 357 Burgess Road, Southampton SO16 3AD* Tel (023) 8055 4231 *or* 8067 9787 E-mail gary.philbrick@dsl.pipex.com

PHILBRICK, Miss Leah Karen. b 79. Gordon Coll Mass BA01. Ridley Hall Cam 09. **d** 11. C Sutton *S'wark* from 11. *37 St Barnabas Road, Sutton SM1 4NS* Tel 07952-640885 (mobile) E-mail l.philbrick@btinternet.com

PHILIP, Mathew. b 54. Leeds Univ BSc77 MSc78 PhD83 Surrey Univ BA05. STETS 02. **d** 05 **p** 06. NSM Patcham *Chich* from 05. *Hillside Lodge, 76 Redhill Drive, Brighton BN1 5FL* Tel (01273) 883726 Mobile 07760-158043 E-mail paluvalil@aol.com

PHILIP, Peter Wells. b 35. Ridley Hall Cam 64. **d** 67 **p** 68. C Tollington Park St Mark w St Anne *Lon* 67-70; C Battersea St Pet *S'wark* 70-72; Hon C Kennington St Mark 72-73; V Titirangi New Zealand 74-80; Hon C Blockhouse Bay 80-92; Past Dir Chr Advance Min 80-84; Dir Evang Fellowship of NZ 87-90; C Finchley Ch Ch *Lon* 92-93; V Frankton New Zealand 94-00; rtd 00. *608 Rolleston Street, Thames 3500, New Zealand* Tel (0064) (7) 868 5028 E-mail peterp@xnet.co.nz

PHILIP BARTHOLOMEW, Brother. See KENNEDY, Brother Philip Bartholomew

PHILIPPINES, Prime Bishop of the Episcopal Church in the. See MALECDAN, The Most Revd Edward Pacyaya

PHILLIP, Isaiah Ezekiel. b 59. Univ of W Indies BA88. Codrington Coll Barbados 85. **d** 88 **p** 89. C St Jo Cathl Antigua 88-91; R St Geo Dominica 91-96; R All SS Antigua 96-01; P-in-c Handsworth St Mich *Birm* 02-05; V Basseterre St Kitts from 05. *St Peter's Rectory, PO Box 702, Basseterre, St Kitts, West Indies* Tel (001869) (465) 2774 E-mail phillipisaiah@hotmail.com

PHILLIPS, Mrs Adele. b 59. Newc Univ LLB84. NEOC 04. **d** 07 **p** 08. NSM Gateshead *Dur* from 07. *47 Blackstone Court, Blaydon NE21 4HH* Tel 0191-414 0955 Mobile 07752-325736 E-mail jophillips06@aol.com

PHILLIPS, Andrew Graham. b 58. Ex Univ BSc79. Chich Th Coll 84. **d** 87 **p** 88. C Frankby w Greasby *Ches* 87-89; C Liv St Chris Norris Green 89-92; CF 92-97; Chapl RN from 00. *Royal Naval Chaplaincy Service, Mail Point 1-2, Leach Building, Whale Island, Portsmouth PO2 8BY* Tel (023) 9262 5655 Fax 9262 5134

PHILLIPS, Canon Anthony Charles Julian. b 36. Lon Univ BD63 AKC63 G&C Coll Cam PhD67 St Jo Coll Ox MA75 DPhil80. Coll of Resurr Mirfield 66. **d** 66 **p** 67. C-in-c Chesterton Gd Shep CD *Ely* 66-69; Dean, Chapl and Fell Trin Hall Cam 69-74; Hon Bp's Chapl *Nor* 70-71; Chapl and Fell St Jo Coll Ox 75-86; Lect Th Jes Coll Ox 75-86; Lect Th Hertf Coll Ox 84-86; Hd Master K Sch Cant 86-96; Hon Can Cant Cathl 87-96; Can Th Truro Cathl 86-02; Perm to Offic from 02; rtd 01. *10 St Peter's Road, Flushing, Falmouth TR11 5TP* Tel (01326) 377217

PHILLIPS, Mrs Audrey Katherine. b 32. Lorain Coll Ohio BS73. Ox Min Course 88. **d** 91 **p** 94. NSM Princes Risborough w Ilmer *Ox* 91-94; P Assoc Marco Is St Mark USA 94-98; NSM Akeman *Ox* 98-00; Perm to Offic from 08. *1 The Chestnuts, Kirtlington, Kidlington OX5 3UB* Tel (01869) 350194

PHILLIPS, Benjamin Guy. b 75. Wycliffe Hall Ox. **d** 02 **p** 03. C Cockermouth w Embleton and Wythop *Carl* 02-05; V Stanwix from 05. *Stanwix Vicarage, Dykes Terrace, Carlisle CA3 9AS* Tel (01228) 511430 E-mail benphillips@uk2k.com

PHILLIPS, Benjamin Lambert Meyrick. b 64. K Coll Cam BA86 MA90. Ridley Hall Cam 87. **d** 90 **p** 91. C Wareham *Sarum* 90-94; P-in-c Osmington w Poxwell *Sarum* 90-94; C Crowthorne *Ox* 94-96; V Bodicote *Ox* from 96; AD Deddington 05-10. *The Vicarage, Wykham Lane, Bodicote, Banbury OX15 4BW* Tel (01295) 270174

PHILLIPS, Beryl. See PHILLIPS, Mrs Elizabeth Beryl
PHILLIPS, Bill. See PHILLIPS, Edward Leigh Bill
PHILLIPS, Mrs Brenda. b 41. St Hugh's Coll Ox BA63 MA68. **d** 04 **p** 05. OLM Sherborne w Castleton, Lillington and Longburton *Sarum* 04-11; rtd 11; Perm to Offic *Sarum* from 11. *2 West Hall Cottages, Longburton, Sherborne DT9 5PF* Tel (01963) 210072 E-mail brendaphillips@courthousedairyfarm.freeserve.co.uk

PHILLIPS, Brian Edward Dorian William. b 36. Bris Univ BA58. Ripon Hall Ox 58. **d** 60 **p** 61. C Ross *Heref* 60-64; Chapl RAF 64-68; Hon C Fringford w Hethe and Newton Purcell *Ox* 68-73; Chapl Howell's Sch Denbigh 73-76; C Cleobury Mortimer w Hopton Wafers *Heref* 76-80; V Dixton 80-02; rtd 02; Perm to Offic *Heref* from 02. *37 Duxmere Drive, Ross-on-Wye HR9 5UW* Tel (01989) 562993 Mobile 07712-071558 E-mail brianphillips@u-genie.co.uk

PHILLIPS, Canon Brian Robert. b 31. Clare Coll Cam BA53 MA57. Linc Th Coll 54. **d** 56 **p** 57. C Tuffley *Glouc* 56-59; C Southgate Ch Ch *Lon* 59-62; R Luckington w Alderton *Bris* 62-69; V Highworth w Sevenhampton and Inglesham etc 69-84; Hon Can Bris Cathl 84-90; P-in-c Long Newnton 84-87; P-in-c Crudwell w Ashley 84-87; R Ashley, Crudwell, Hankerton, Long Newnton etc 87-90; rtd 90; Perm to Offic *Portsm* and *Win* from 90. *Hannington, Hospital Road, Shirrell Heath, Southampton SO32 2JR* Tel (01329) 834547

PHILLIPS, Mrs Caroline Jill. b 80. Nottm Univ BA02 Man Univ MA04. Qu Coll Birm 07. **d** 10 **p** 11. C Ollerton w Boughton *S'well* from 10. *Glebe House, Church Road, Boughton, Newark NG22 9JR* Tel (01623) 869560 E-mail caroline_phillips@ymail.com

PHILLIPS, David Arthur. b 36. S Dios Minl Tr Scheme 90. **d** 94 **p** 95. NSM Canford Magna *Sarum* 94-06; rtd 06. *32 Lynwood Drive, Wimborne BH21 1UG* Tel (01202) 880262

PHILLIPS, David Gordon. b 60. Toronto Univ BASc82. Wycliffe Coll Toronto MDiv95. **d** 94 **p** 95. R Kawawachikamach Canada 94-99; Exec Adn Price Albert 99-03; R Petite Riviere and New Dublin 04-09; P-in-c Palermo w Taormina *Eur* from 10. *Holy Cross, via Mariano Stabile 118b, 90139 Palermo, Italy* Tel (0039) (091) 772 4470 Mobile (0039) 338-612 3018 E-mail revdgphillips@hotmail.com

PHILLIPS, David Keith. b 61. New Coll Ox MA90 St Jo Coll Dur BA90. Cranmer Hall Dur 88. **d** 91 **p** 92. C Denton Holme *Carl* 91-94; C Chadderton Ch Ch *Man* 94-98; Gen Sec Sec Ch Soc 98-11; Public Preacher *St Alb* 98-11; V Chorley St Jas *Blackb* from 11. *St James's Vicarage, St James's Place, Chorley PR6 0NA* Tel (01257) 233714 E-mail vicar@stjameschorley.org

PHILLIPS, David Thomas. b 47. NEOC 03. **d** 05 **p** 06. NSM Gt and Lt Driffield *York* 05-06; C Elloughton and Brough w Brantingham 06-10; rtd 11; P-in-c Vernet-les-Bains *Eur* from 11. *Address temp unknown* E-mail dphill9590@yahoo.co.uk

PHILLIPS, Edward Leigh Bill. b 12. St Edm Hall Ox BA34 MA47. Wycliffe Hall Ox 33. **d** 35 **p** 36. Asst Chapl Dean Close Sch Cheltenham 35-37; C Highfield *Ox* 37-41; C Marcham Ch Ch the K CD *Chich* 39-41; CF (EC) 41-46; R Ide Hill *Roch* 46-49; V Moulsecoomb *Chich* 49-52; V Kingston w Iford 52-75; V Iford w Kingston and Rodmell 75-78; RD Lewes 65-77; rtd 78; Perm to Offic *Glouc* from 78. *35 Woodland Green, Upton St Leonards, Gloucester GL4 8BD* Tel (01452) 619894

PHILLIPS, Edwin George. b 35. N Wales Baptist Coll 64. **d** 03 **p** 03. NSM Morriston *S & B* 03-08; rtd 09. *146 Lingfield Avenue, Port Talbot SA12 6QA* Tel (01639) 886784 Mobile 07815-969913

PHILLIPS, Mrs Elizabeth Beryl. b 34. **d** 94 **p** 95. C N Farnborough *Guildf* 94-99; rtd 99; Perm to Offic *Sarum* from 00. *8 Byron Road, Wimborne BH21 1NX* Tel (01202) 883328

PHILLIPS, Mrs Emma Catharine. b 62. St Anne's Coll Ox BA84. Trin Coll Bris BA99. **d** 99 **p** 00. C Shawbury *Lich* 99-01; C Moreton Corbet 99-01; C Stanton on Hine Heath 99-01; C Cen Telford 01-02; TV 03-07; Perm to Offic 07-09; NSM Cen Telford from 09; Chapl Severn Hospice from 09. *11 Stocking Park Road, Lightmoor, Telford TF4 3QZ* Tel (01952) 502878

PHILLIPS, Geoffrey Clarke. b 50. SWMTC 94. **d** 96 **p** 97. NSM Georgeham *Ex* 96-98; Chapl HM YOI Huntercombe and Finnamore 99-00; Chapl HM Pris Shepton Mallet 01-03; Chapl Children's Hospice SW from 07. *Children's Hospice South West, Little Bridge House, Redlands Road, Fremington, Barnstaple EX31 2PZ* Tel (01271) 325270

PHILLIPS, Canon Geoffrey John. b 23. BNC Ox BA47 MA56. Ridley Hall Cam 54. **d** 56 **p** 57. C Kettering St Andr *Pet* 56-59; C Tideswell *Derby* 59-62; Ceylon 62-65; R Gillingham w Geldeston and Stockton *Nor* 65-70; V Eaton 70-81; RD Nor S 71-81; Hon Can Nor Cathl 78-81; Chapl Vienna w Budapest and Prague *Eur* 81-87; rtd 87; Perm to Offic *Nor* from 87. *Fieldside, Threadneedle Street, Bergh Apton, Norwich NR15 1BJ* Tel (01508) 480656

PHILLIPS, Ms Gillian. b 44. EMMTC 07. **d** 10. NSM Old Brampton and Great Barlow and Loundsley Green *Derby* 10-11. *78 Lawley Gate, Telford TF4 2NZ*

PHILLIPS, Ivor Lynn. b 44. Leeds Univ BA70. Cuddesdon Coll 69. **d** 71 **p** 72. C Bedlinog *Llan* 71-73; C Roath 73-77; TV

Wolverhampton All SS *Lich* 77-78; TV Wolverhampton 78-81; Chapl Charing Cross Hosp Lon 81-91; Chapl Milan w Genoa and Lugano *Eur* 91-94; C Hampstead St Jo *Lon* 95-00; V Whitton St Aug 00-09; rtd 09; Perm to Offic *S'wark* from 10. *Brooklyn Cottage, Church Street, East End, Earlston TD4 6HS* E-mail i.lyn@virgin.net

PHILLIPS, Mrs Janet Elizabeth. b 37. Bp Grosseteste Coll CertEd57. EMMTC 81. **dss** 84 **d** 87 **p** 94. Wisbech St Aug *Ely* 84-86; Cambridge St Jas 86-91; Par Dn 87-91; Par Dn Wisbech SS Pet and Paul 91-94; C 94-02; rtd 02; Hon C Elm and Friday Bridge w Coldham *Ely* 03-07; Hon C Leverington, Newton and Tydd St Giles 07-10; Perm to Offic from 10. *41 Mountbatten Drive, Leverington, Wisbech PE13 5AF* Tel (01945) 589034

PHILLIPS, Jason Paul. b 73. Man Metrop Univ BA95 CertEd95 PhD05. Ripon Coll Cuddesdon 07. **d** 09 **p** 10. C Mid Trent *Lich* from 09. *St Basil's House, 20 Sandalwood Drive, Stafford ST16 3FX* E-mail paxstbasils@fastmail.co.uk

PHILLIPS (*née* LANGLEY), **Mrs Jean.** b 52. St Mary's Coll Chelt CertEd73. WEMTC 03. **d** 06 **p** 07. NSM Bishop's Cleeve *Glouc* 06-08; NSM Bishop's Cleeve and Woolstone w Gotherington etc from 08. *3 St Nicholas Drive, Cheltenham GL50 4RY* Tel (01242) 673612 E-mail bcparishoffice@btinternet.com

PHILLIPS, Jeffery Llewellyn. b 32. Sarum & Wells Th Coll. **d** 87 **p** 88. C Ringwood *Win* 87-90; V Somborne w Ashley 90-93; rtd 93; Perm to Offic *Win* from 93. *Queen's Acre, 3 Solent Avenue, Lymington SO41 3SD* Tel (01590) 673955

PHILLIPS, Mrs Jennifer Jean. b 36. Guildf Dioc Min Course 98. **d** 01 **p** 02. OLM New Haw *Guildf* 01-07; Perm to Offic from 07. *20 Lindsay Road, New Haw, Addlestone KT15 3BD* Tel (01932) 429689 E-mail jennifer.phillips73@ntlworld.com

PHILLIPS, John. b 50. ACIB74. NOC 01. **d** 04. NSM Wavertree H Trin *Liv* from 04. *12 Montclair Drive, Liverpool L18 0HA* Tel 0151-722 2542 E-mail jpipps@aol.com

PHILLIPS, John David. b 29. G&C Coll Cam BA50 MA54 CertEd69. SWMTC 85. **d** 87 **p** 88. NSM St Martin w E and W Looe *Truro* 87-88; NSM St Merryn 88-94; rtd 94; Perm to Offic *Truro* from 94. *Restings, Plaidy, Looe PL13 1LF* Tel (01503) 262121

PHILLIPS, John Eldon. b 50. Univ of Wales (Cardiff) BEd85 MEd92. St Mich Coll Llan. **d** 90 **p** 91. NSM Merthyr Cynog and Dyffryn Honddu etc *S & B* 90-94; Lic to Offic *St D* 94-99; NSM Ystradgynlais *S & B* 95-99; Chapl Trin Coll Carmarthen 95-99; P-in-c Llanrhidian w Llanmadoc and Cheriton *S & B* 99-05; Dioc Press Officer from 02; NSM Burry Port and Pwll *St D* from 07. *2 Gerddi Glasfryn, Llanelli SA15 3LL* Tel (01554) 744770 E-mail reveldon@btinternet.com

PHILLIPS, John Reginald. b 64. St Steph Ho Ox BTh93. **d** 96 **p** 97. C Bognor *Chich* 96-99; TV Moulsecoomb 99-00; C Hove 00-05; P-in-c Mackworth St Fran *Derby* 05-10; V from 10. *St Francis's Vicarage, 78 Cuffingham Gardens, Derby DE22 4FQ* Tel (01332) 224264 E-mail frjohnphillips@aol.com

PHILLIPS, Judith Mary. b 46. Reading Univ BA67 Cardiff Coll of Educn PGCE86. St Mich Coll Llan 93. **d** 95 **p** 97. Lect Neath Coll 84-00; NSM Clydach *S & B* 95-00; Dep Chapl HM Pris Bris 00-01; Chapl HM Pris Eastwood Park from 01. *HM Prison, Eastwood Park, Falfield, Wotton-under-Edge GL12 8DB* Tel (01454) 382105 or 382100 Fax 382101 E-mail judith.phillips@hmps.gsi.gov.uk

PHILLIPS, Canon Kenneth John. b 37. Coll of Resurr Mirfield 67. **d** 67 **p** 68. C Blackb St Jas 67-69; C-in-c Lea CD 70-80; V Lea 80-84; P-in-c Priors Hardwick, Priors Marston and Wormleighton *Cov* 85-02; Sec Dioc Adv Cttee 85-99; RD Southam 89-95; Hon Can Cov Cathl 94-02; Dioc Rural Chs Officer 00-02; rtd 02; Hon C Gisburn *Bradf* 02-08; Hon C Hellifield 02-08; Perm to Offic from 08. *7 Temperance Square, Hellifield, Skipton BD23 4LG* Tel (01729) 850340 E-mail kcanonic@aol.com

PHILLIPS, Lamont Wellington Sanderson. b 33. S'wark Ord Course 73. **d** 76 **p** 78. NSM Tottenham St Paul *Lon* 76-83; P-in-c Upper Clapton St Matt 83-88; V 88-97; rtd 98. *24 Berkshire Gardens, London N18 2LF* Tel (020) 8807 7025

PHILLIPS, Lynn. See PHILLIPS, Ivor Lynn

PHILLIPS, Canon Martin Nicholas. b 32. Em Coll Cam BA57 MA61. Linc Th Coll 57. **d** 59 **p** 60. C Stocking Farm CD *Leic* 59-63; V Sheff Gillcar St Silas 63-71; V Birstall *Leic* 72-82; R Wanlip 72-82; V Birstall and Wanlip 82-88; TR Loughborough Em and St Mary in Charnwood 88-96; Hon Can Leic Cathl 90-96; rtd 96; Perm to Offic *Leic* from 96. *Foxhollow, 40A Lodge Close, Barrow upon Soar, Loughborough LE12 8ZL* Tel (01509) 416361

PHILLIPS, Mary Alice. b 53. Ripon Coll Cuddesdon 97. **d** 99 **p** 00. C Addiscombe St Mildred *S'wark* 99-02; TV Basingstoke *Win* from 02. *219 Paddock Road, Basingstoke RG22 6QP* Tel (01256) 464393 E-mail map13@tinyworld.co.uk

PHILLIPS, Michael John. b 54. JP. Trent Poly BA77. Sarum & Wells Th Coll 78. **d** 81 **p** 82. C Killay *S & B* 81-83; C Treboeth 83-85; Hong Kong 85-88; Japan 88-91; TR Is of Scilly *Truro*

91-95; TR Cwmbran *Mon* from 95. *The Rectory, Clomendy Road, Cwmbran NP44 3LS* Tel (01633) 489718

PHILLIPS, Michael Thomas. b 46. CQSW81. Linc Th Coll 89. **d** 90 **p** 91. C Hyson Green *S'well* 90-91; C Basford w Hyson Green 91-93; Chapl HM Pris Gartree 93-99; Chapl HM Pris Nottm 99-08; rtd 08; Hon C Radford All So and St Pet *S'well* from 08. *12 Edgbaston Gardens, Aspley, Nottingham NG8 5AY* Tel 0115-929 7029 E-mail bigviola@hotmail.com

PHILLIPS, Mrs Patricia. b 45. Glouc Sch of Min 83. **dss** 86 **d** 87 **p** 94. Newent and Gorsley w Cliffords Mesne *Glouc* 86-95; C 87-95; P-in-c Childswyckham w Aston Somerville, Buckland etc 95-97; R 97-00; R Redmarley D'Abitot, Bromesberrow, Pauntley etc 00-10; rtd 10. *5 Freemans Orchard, Newent GL18 1TX* Tel (01531) 828444 E-mail revpp@tesco.net

PHILLIPS, Miss Pauline. b 54. **d** 96 **p** 97. OLM Mossley *Man* from 96. *32 Mountain Street, Mossley, Ashton-under-Lyne OL5 0EZ* Tel (01457) 832363

PHILLIPS, Percy Graham. b 26. St Aid Birkenhead 46. **d** 51 **p** 52. C Wallasey St Hilary *Ches* 51-54; C Thrybergh *Sheff* 54-58; C Guernsey St Michel du Valle *Win* 58-60; V Heytesbury w Tytherington and Knook *Sarum* 60-65; V Stonebridge St Mich *Lon* 65-70; R Vernham Dean w Linkenholt *Win* 70-78; C Farnham *Guildf* 78-82; TV Cove St Jo 82-89; rtd 89. *22 Charts Close, Cranleigh GU6 8BH* Tel (01483) 272936

PHILLIPS, Peter. b 26. Oak Hill Th Coll 63. **d** 65 **p** 66. C Eastbourne All SS *Chich* 65-69; C St Alb St Paul *St Alb* 69-73; V Riseley w Bletsoe 73-84; R Arley *Cov* 84-91; rtd 91; Perm to Offic *B & W* 91-04; Clergy Retirement and Widows' Officer 99-04; Perm to Offic *Guildf* from 09. *1 Manormead, Tilford Road, Hindhead GU26 6RA* Tel (01428) 601501

PHILLIPS, Peter Miles Lucas. b 44. Reading Univ BA66 QUB DipEd69 Univ of Wales (Cardiff) MEd88 Bris Univ MA07. St Mich Coll Llan 90. **d** 92 **p** 93. Dep Hd Teacher Dynevor Sch 82-96; NSM Llangyfelach *S & B* 92-96; Dep Chapl HM Pris Liv 96-97; Chapl HM Pris Usk and Prescoed 97-01; Chapl HM Pris Bris 01-04; rtd 04; Perm to Offic *Bris* from 04; Chapl Wesley Coll Bris from 07. *7 St Lucia Close, Bristol BS7 0XS* Tel 0117-952 5859 E-mail revdpeterphillips@yahoo.co.uk

PHILLIPS, Ms Rachel Susan. b 64. Newnham Coll Cam BA86 MA90 Solicitor 89. St Jo Coll Nottm 04. **d** 07 **p** 08. C Eastcote St Lawr *Lon* 07-10; P-in-c Northaw and Cuffley *St Alb* from 10. *Northaw Vicarage, 58 Hill Rise, Cuffley, Potters Bar EN6 4RG* Tel (01707) 874126 E-mail revrachelphillips@gmail.co.uk

PHILLIPS, Miss Rebecca Jane. b 82. Birm Univ BA04 Clare Coll Cam BTh10. Ridley Hall Cam. **d** 10 **p** 11. C Childwall All SS *Liv* from 10. *80 Green Lane North, Liverpool L16 8NL* Tel 0151-737 2214 Mobile 07764-747611 E-mail curate.allsaints@uwclub.net

PHILLIPS, Richard Paul. b 76. Man Univ BA08. Trin Coll Bris 09. **d** 11. C Kingston upon Hull St Aid Southcoates *York* from 11. *9 Lorenzos Way, Hull HU9 3HS* Tel 07944-541968 (mobile) E-mail rich.phillips76@gmail.com

PHILLIPS, Robin Michael. b 33. AKC58. **d** 59 **p** 60. C Hanwell St Mellitus *Lon* 59-61; C St Margaret's-on-Thames 61-64; C Hangleton *Chich* 64-68; V Mellor *Derby* 68-95; RD Glossop 89-93; rtd 95; Hon C Bridekirk *Carl* 95-96. *30 Fosbrooke House, 8 Clifton Drive, Lytham St Annes FY8 5RQ*

PHILLIPS, Mrs Sandra Georgina. b 49. STETS 01. **d** 04 **p** 05. NSM Portsdown *Portsm* from 04. *14 Forest End, Waterlooville PO7 7AB* Tel (023) 9226 7740 Mobile 07778-921624

PHILLIPS, Canon Stephen. b 38. QUB BA60. Linc Th Coll 60. **d** 62 **p** 63. C Waddington *Linc* 62-65; C Gt Grimsby St Jas 65-72; V Kirmington 72-97; V Limber Magna w Brocklesby 73-97; V Brocklesby Park and R Croxton 97-04; RD Yarborough 92-00; Can and Preb Linc Cathl from 98; rtd 04. *The Stables, 14 Church Lane, Keelby, Grimsby DN41 8ED* Tel (01469) 561395 E-mail canstephil@glimreho.freeserve.co.uk

PHILLIPS, Thomas Wynford. b 15. Univ of Wales BA37 BD40. St Mich Coll Llan. **d** 43 **p** 44. C Shotton *St As* 43-46; C Rhyl 46-50; C Hall Green Ascension *Birm* 50-52; R Shustoke 52-55; P-in-c Maxstoke 52-55; V Clay Cross *Derby* 55-68; R Upton Magna *Lich* 68-73; V Withington 68-73; R Roche *Truro* 73-80; R Withiel 73-80; RD St Austell 76-80; rtd 80; Perm to Offic *Truro* from 80. *Brynawelon, Wheal Quoit Avenue, St Agnes TR5 0SJ* Tel (01872) 552862

PHILLIPS, Timothy Leo. b 72. Bris Univ BSc95 PhD99. Trin Coll Bris BA01 MA02. **d** 02 **p** 03. C Leic H Trin w St Jo 02-05; TV Ashby-de-la-Zouch and Breedon on the Hill from 05. *Holy Trinity Vicarage, 1 Trinity Close, Ashby-de-la-Zouch LE65 2GQ* Tel (01530) 412339

PHILLIPS, Wayne. **d** 10 **p** 11. NSM Pontefract All SS *Wakef* from 10. *16 Maple Walk, Knottingley WF11 0PU* Tel (01977) 678024 E-mail wayne.phillips16@btinternet.com

PHILLIPS-LAST, Martin. b 68. **d** 10 **p** 11. C Beccles St Mich and St Luke *St E* from 10. *The New House, Queens Road, Beccles NR34 9DU* Tel (01502) 712500 Mobile 07746-278390 E-mail rev.phillips-last@sky.com

PHILLIPS-SMITH, Edward Charles. b 50. AKC71. **d** 73 **p** 74. C Wolverhampton *Lich* 73-76; Chapl St Pet Colleg Sch Wolv 77-87; Hon C Wolverhampton *Lich* 78-87; V Stevenage St Pet

Broadwater *St Alb* 87-89; Chapl Millfield Jun Sch Somerset 89-95; Chapl Papplewick Sch 95-08; rtd 08. *5 Hampton Drive, Kings Sutton, Banbury OX17 3QR* Tel (01295) 811220 E-mail email@ecp-s.eclipse.co.uk

PHILLIPSON (*née* **MACKAY**), **Alison.** b 62. Teesside Univ BA00. NEOC 01. **d** 04 **p** 05. C Stokesley w Seamer *York* 04-08; P-in-c Cosby *Leic* 08-09; P-in-c Whetstone 08-09; V Coatham and Dormanstown *York* from 09. *Coatham Vicarage, 9 Blenheim Terrace, Redcar TS10 1QP* Tel (01642) 493661 E-mail alisonphillipson@aol.com

PHILLIPSON, Hugh Brian. b 41. Birm Univ BSc62 Qu Univ Kingston Ontario MSc64. **d** 96 **p** 97. Chapl Hong Kong Cathl 96-04; Perm to Offic *Ox* 05-06; NSM Ox St Mary V w St Cross and St Pet 06-08. *Address temp unknown* E-mail huruphillipson@yahoo.co.uk

PHILLIPSON-MASTERS, Miss Susan Patricia. b 52. Sussex Univ CertEd73 K Alfred's Coll Win BEd81 Leeds Univ MA04 Glos Univ MA09 FIST76 ACP80. Trin Coll Bris 86. **d** 89 **p** 95. C Saltford w Corston and Newton St Loe *B & W* 89-94; C Uphill 94-97; C Nailsea Ch Ch w Tickenham 97-98; P-in-c Tredington and Darlingscott w Newbold on Stour *Cov* 98-00; P-in-c The Stanleys *Glouc* 00-11; Chapl Wycliffe Prep Sch 07-11; rtd 11. *c/o I Phillipson-Masters Esq, 30 The Paddocks, Thornbury, Bristol BS35 2HP* E-mail sue.pm112@btinternet.com

PHILLPOT, Donald John. b 27. St Jo Coll Dur BA53. **d** 55 **p** 56. C Southmead *Bris* 55-60; C Brislington St Luke 60-63; R Stapleton *Heref* 63-68; V Dorrington 63-68; P-in-c Astley Abbotts 68-78; R Bridgnorth w Tasley 68-78; V Lillington *Cov* 78-92; rtd 92; Perm to Offic *Glouc* from 92. *22 Williams Orchard, Highnam, Gloucester GL2 8EL* Tel (01452) 306044

PHILP (*née* **NOBLE**), **Canon Ann Carol.** b 42. Sarum Dioc Tr Coll CertEd63 Southn Univ MA(Ed)89 MCIPD. S Dios Minl Tr Scheme 93. **d** 95 **p** 96. Dir Sarum Chr Cen 93-98; Chapl Sarum Cathl 95-02; Dioc NSM Officer 98-02; P-in-c Woodford Valley w Archers Gate from 02; Dioc Dir of Ords 02-07; Bp's Dom Chapl from 07; Can and Preb Sarum Cathl from 05. *The Vicarage, Middle Woodford, Salisbury SP4 6NR* Tel (01722) 782310 or 411944 E-mail ann.philp@tiscali.co.uk

PHILPOTT, Barbara May. *See* **WILKINSON,** Canon Barbara May

PHILPOTT, Canon John David. b 43. Leic Univ BA64. Trin Coll Bris 69. **d** 72 **p** 73. C Knutsford St Jo *Ches* 72-75; C Toft 72-75; C Bickenhill w Elmdon *Birm* 75-79; V Birm St Luke 79-91; RD Birm City 83-88; Hon Can Birm Cathl 89-91; V Chilvers Coton w Astley *Cov* 91-00; RD Nuneaton 95-00; Hon Can Cov Cathl 96-00; P-in-c Prague *Eur* 00-08; rtd 08. *2 Portland Court, 1 Portland Avenue, Exmouth EX8 2DJ* Tel (01395) 225044 E-mail jamphilpott@yahoo.com

PHILPOTT, John Wilfred. b 44. K Coll Lon BD67 AKC67. **d** 68 **p** 69. C Norbury St Steph *Cant* 68-71; C Addiscombe St Mildred 71-75; V Whitfield w Guston 75-01; rtd 02; Perm to Offic *Cant* from 02. *9 Mannering Close, River, Dover CT17 0UD* Tel (01304) 825875

PHILPOTT, Jonathan Mark. b 76. Chelt & Glouc Coll of HE BA98. Trin Coll Bris BA06 MA10. **d** 07 **p** 08. C Lydney *Glouc* 07-10; P-in-c By Brook *Bris* from 10; P-in-c Colerne w N Wraxall from 10. *By Brook Rectory, 3 Church Farm, Yatton Keynell, Chippenham SN14 7FD* Tel (01249) 782663 E-mail philpott.jonathan@gmail.com

PHILPOTT, Ronald. b 38. IPFA69. Cranmer Hall Dur 88. **d** 89 **p** 90. NSM S Ossett *Wakef* 89-93; R Clitheroe St Jas *Blackb* 93-03; rtd 03; Perm to Offic *York* from 03. *8 Headland Close, Haxby, York YO32 3HW* Tel (01904) 758697

PHILPOTT, Preb Samuel. b 41. Kelham Th Coll 60. **d** 65 **p** 66. C Swindon New Town *Bris* 65-70; C Torquay St Martin Barton *Ex* 70-73; TV Withycombe Raleigh 73-76; V Shaldon 76-78; P-in-c Plymouth St Pet 78-80; V 80-09; RD Plymouth Devonport 86-93 and 95-01; Preb Ex Cathl 91-09; rtd 09; P-in-c Plymouth St Pet and H Apostles *Ex* from 09. *21 Plaistow Crescent, Plymouth PL5 2EA* Tel (01752) 298502 E-mail frphilpott@aol.com

PHILPOTT-HOWARD, John Nigel. b 54. Univ of Wales Coll of Medicine MB, BCh77 FRCPsych83. SEITE 99. **d** 02 **p** 03. NSM Shooters Hill Ch Ch *S'wark* 02-11. *80 Charlton Road, London SE7 7EY* Tel (020) 8858 4692 E-mail jphilpotth@cs.com

PHILPS, Mark Seymour. b 51. Worc Coll Ox BA73 MA78 Lon Univ MA75 Nottm Univ BA79. St Jo Coll Nottm 77. **d** 80 **p** 81. C Chadwell Heath *Chelmsf* 80-83; C Woodford Wells 83-87; V Tipton St Matt *Lich* 87-02; TV Roxeth *Lon* 02-03; TR 03-11; V from 11. *Christ Church Vicarage, Roxeth Hill, Harrow HA2 0JN* Tel (020) 8423 3168 E-mail mark.philps@roxethteam.org

PHILSON, James Alexander Summers (Hamish). b 20. Edin Th Coll 48. **d** 51 **p** 52. C Falkirk *Edin* 51-53; R Dunblane *St And* 53-62; Australia from 62; R Beverley 62-64; R Victoria Park 64-75; R Cottesloe 75-85; rtd 85. *38 Allenswood Road, Greenwood WA 6024, Australia* Tel (0061) (8) 9447 9523 Mobile 0416-001620 E-mail jasp@smartchat.net.au

PHIPPS, David John. b 46. Bris Univ BSc68 Ex Univ PhD94 Nottm Univ PGCE69. Trin Coll Bris 75. **d** 78 **p** 79. C Madron w Morvah *Truro* 78-80; C Kenilworth St Jo *Cov* 80-83; TV

Barnstaple *Ex* 83-95; I Abercraf w Callwen w Capel Coelbren *S & B* 95-02; P-in-c Gulval and Madron *Truro* 02-05; rtd 05. *11 Walton Way, Barnstaple EX32 8AE* Tel (01271) 349746 E-mail phippsdv@dialstart.net

PHIPPS, Canon Frederick George. b 30. Kelham Th Coll 50. **d** 54 **p** 55. C Staveley *Derby* 54-59; Korea 59-65; Australia from 65; Can Ballarat Ch Ch Cathl 84-95; rtd 95. *240 Lava Street, PO Box 297, Warrnambool Vic 3280, Australia* Tel (0061) (3) 5562 6738

PHIZACKERLEY, The Ven Gerald Robert. b 29. Univ Coll Ox BA52 MA56. Wells Th Coll 52. **d** 54 **p** 55. C Carl St Barn 54-57; Chapl Abingdon Sch 57-64; R Gaywood, Bawsey and Mintlyn *Nor* 64-78; RD Lynn 68-78; Hon Can Nor Cathl 75-78; Hon Can Derby Cathl 78-96; P-in-c Ashford w Sheldon 78-90; Adn Chesterfield 78-96; rtd 96; Perm to Offic *Derby* and *Cov* from 96. *Archway Cottage, Hall Road, Leamington Spa CV32 5RA* Tel (01926) 332740 E-mail phizleam@yahoo.co.uk

PHOEBE, Sister. *See* HANMER, Sister Phoebe Margaret

PHYPERS, David John. b 39. Leic Univ BA60 CertEd61 Lon Univ BD65. Linc Th Coll 76. **d** 78 **p** 79. NSM Normanton *Derby* 78-80; NSM Sinfin 80-87; Lic to Offic 87-88; P-in-c Denby and Horsley Woodhouse 88-00; P-in-c Wormhill, Peak Forest w Peak Dale and Dove Holes 00-07; Adv for Chr Giving 00-07; rtd 07; Perm to Offic *Derby* from 07. *15 Albert Road, Chaddesden, Derby DE21 6SL* Tel (01332) 239134 E-mail david@phypers.co.uk

PICK, David. b 44. Linc Th Coll 85. **d** 87 **p** 88. C Howden *York* 87-90; P-in-c Sledmere and Cowlam w Fridaythorpe, Fimer etc 90-91; V 91-96; rtd 96; Perm to Offic *York* from 96. *Westwood Close, 16 North Street, Nafferton, Driffield YO25 4JW* Tel (01377) 240360

PICKARD, Canon Frank Eustace. b 31. Lon Univ BScEcon52 St Cath Soc Ox BA56 MA63. St Steph Ho Ox. **d** 57 **p** 58. C Haydock St Jas *Liv* 57-59; C Davenham *Ches* 59-60; Asst Master St Dunstan's Sch Lon 60-63; Min Can Pet Cathl 63-72; P-in-c Newborough 67-68; V 68-72; R Isham w Pytchley 72-76; R Abington 76-96; Can Pet Cathl 80-02; rtd 96; P-in-c Wappenham w Weedon Lois and Plumpton 96-02; Perm to Offic *Pet* from 02. *19 Watersmeet, Northampton NN1 5SQ* Tel (01604) 239667 E-mail margaret.pickard1@btinternet.com

PICKARD, Mrs Patricia Anne. b 44. **d** 04 **p** 05. NSM Ovenden *Wakef* from 04. *46 Crag Lane, Halifax HX2 8NU* Tel (01422) 346948 E-mail patricia-anne.pickard@sky.com

✠**PICKARD, The Rt Revd Stephen Kim.** b 52. Newc Univ Aus BCom74 Van Mildert Coll Dur PhD90. Melbourne Coll of Div BD79 St Jo Coll Morpeth 77. **d** 80 **p** 80 **c** 07. C Singleton Australia 80-82; C Dur St Cuth 82-84; Chapl Van Mildert Coll Dur 84-90; Chapl Trev Coll Dur 84-90; Lect United Th Coll Sydney Australia 91-97; Dir St Mark's Nat Th Cen 98-06; Assoc Prof and Hd Th Chas Sturt Univ 99-06; Asst Bp Adelaide 07-10; Adn The Port 07-09; Visiting Fell Ripon Coll Cuddesdon 10-11; Dir Ox Cen for Ecclesiology and Practical Th 10-11. *11 High Street, Cuddesdon, Oxford OX44 9HP* Tel (01865) 875904 E-mail s.k.pickard@gmail.com

PICKARD, William Priestley. b 31. MCIPD72. Clifton Th Coll 56. **d** 59 **p** 60. C Upper Tulse Hill St Matthias *S'wark* 59-63; Asst Warden Shaftesbury Crusade Bris 64; rtd 96. *45 Totterdown Road, Weston-super-Mare BS23 4LJ* Tel (01934) 628994

PICKEN, Canon David Anthony. b 63. Lon Univ BA84 Kent Univ PGCE85 Nottm Univ MA96. Linc Th Coll 87. **d** 90 **p** 91. C Worth *Chich* 90-93; TV Wordsley *Worc* 93-97; TR 97-04; RD Kingswinford 01-04; TR High Wycombe *Ox* from 04; AD Wycombe from 07; Hon Can Ch Ch from 11. *The Rectory, 6 Priory Avenue, High Wycombe HP13 6SH* Tel (01494) 525602 E-mail dap@dircon.co.uk

PICKEN, James Hugh. b 51. Victoria Univ (BC) BMus75 ARCT73. Ripon Coll Cuddesdon BA79 MA94. **d** 80 **p** 81. C Jarrow *Dur* 80-83; SSF 83-93; Perm to Offic *Sarum* 86-92; Guardian Almmouth Friary 92-94; Lic to Offic *Newc* 92-94; Canada from 94. *929 4th Street NW, Calgary AB T2N 1P4, Canada* Tel (001) (403) 270 9661

PICKERING, Alastair David. b 72. Newc Univ BA94. Wycliffe Hall Ox 03. **d** 05 **p** 06. C Silverhill St Matt *Chich* 05-09; P-in-c S Malling 09-10; R Lewes St Jo sub Castro and S Malling from 10. *The Vicarage, Church Lane, Lewes BN7 2JA* Tel (01273) 474387 Mobile 07976-449896 E-mail al@thepickerings.net

PICKERING, David Arthur Ashley. b 67. G&C Coll Cam BA89. Wycliffe Hall Ox BTh06. **d** 06 **p** 07. C Hornchurch H Cross *Chelmsf* 06-09; P-in-c Fyfield w Tubney and Kingston Bagpuize Ox from 09. *1 Oxford Road, Kingston Bagpuize, Abingdon OX13 5FZ* Tel (01865) 820451 E-mail picklesnpip@mac.com

PICKERING, Canon David Colville. b 41. Kelham Th Coll 61. **d** 66 **p** 67. C Chaddesden St Phil *Derby* 66-70; C New Mills 70-72; C Buxton 72-74; V Chesterfield St Aug 74-90; R Whittington 90-99; P-in-c Hathersage 99; P-in-c Bamford 99; R Hathersage w Bamford and Derwent 00-06; Hon Can Derby Cathl 05-06; rtd 06; Perm to Offic *Derby* from 06. *Les Chênes Verts, Chemin de St Laurent, Le Rang, 84750 Viens, France* Tel (0033) 4 90 74 68 55 Mobile 6 33 84 95 86 E-mail pickport@gmail.com

PICKERING, Geoffrey Craig. b 40. Leic Univ CertEd62. S Dios Minl Tr Scheme 90. **d** 93 **p** 94. C Horsham *Chich* 93-97; V Heathfield 97-08; rtd 08. *3 Bedlam Green, West End, Hertsmonceux, Hailsham BN27 4NW* Tel (01323) 833325 E-mail pickeringgeoff@aol.com

PICKERING, John Alexander. b 41. TCD BA63 MA66. CITC 65. **d** 65 **p** 66. C Magheralin *D & D* 65-67; C-in-c Outeragh *K, E & A* 67-68; I 68-71; Deputation Sec Hibernian Bible Soc 71-74; C-in-c Drumgoon and Ashfield 74-80; I Keady w Armaghbreague and Derrynoose 80-83; I Drumcree 83-07; rtd 07. *25 Twinem Court, Portadown, Craigavon BT63 5FH* Tel 07752-339558 (mobile)

PICKERING, John David. b 38. **d** 86 **p** 86. NSM Ellon *Ab* 86-88; NSM Cruden Bay 86-88; Ind Chapl *Dur* 88-97; TV Jarrow 91-97; P-in-c Newton Hall 97-02; TV Dur N 02-03; rtd 03. *14 Denholm Avenue, Cramlington NE23 3FT* Tel (01670) 716619

PICKERING, John Michael Staunton. b 34. Sarum & Wells Th Coll 71. **d** 72 **p** 73. C Gaywood, Bawsey and Mintlyn *Nor* 72-77; P-in-c Foulsham 77-81; R Foulsham w Hindolveston and Guestwick 81-88; P-in-c Bacton w Edingthorpe w Witton and Ridlington 88-98; rtd 98; Perm to Offic *Nor* from 04. *The Brambles, School Lane, Neatishead, Norwich NR12 8XH* Tel (01692) 630818

PICKERING, Malcolm. b 37. Sarum Th Coll 65. **d** 68 **p** 69. C Milton *Portsm* 68-70; C Stanmer w Falmer and Moulsecoomb *Chich* 70-75; Chapl Brighton Coll of Educn 71-75; V Hooe and R Ninfield *Chich* 75-80; V Ventnor H Trin and Ventnor St Cath *Portsm* 80-88; Chapl St Cath Sch Ventnor 87-88; V Marton *Blackb* 88-97; P-in-c Badingham w Bruisyard, Cransford and Dennington *St E* 97-99; V Leiston 99-04; rtd 04; Perm to Offic *B & W* 04-07; Hon C Drybrook, Lydbrook and Ruardean *Glouc* 07-08. *38 Lethbridge Road, Wells BA5 2FW* Tel (01749) 676526 E-mail malcolm@totland-a.freeserve.co.uk

PICKERING, Mark Penrhyn. b 36. Liv Univ BA59 St Cath Coll Ox BA62 MA67. Wycliffe Hall Ox 60. **d** 63 **p** 64. C Claughton cum Grange *Ches* 63-67; C Newland St Jo *York* 67-72; TV Marfleet 72-76; V Kingston upon Hull St Nic 76-85; V Elloughton and Brough w Brantingham 85-88; Chapl R Hull Hosps NHS Trust 88-01; Perm to Offic *York* from 01. *14 Sykes Close, Swanland, North Ferriby HU14 3GD* Tel (01482) 634892

PICKERING, Mrs Maureen Anne. b 46. Man Univ CertEd67 Open Univ BA88 MA93 Leeds Univ MA07. NOC 04. **d** 07 **p** 08. NSM Ches St Mary from 07. *Curzon Cottage, 2A Curzon Park South, Chester CH4 8AB* Tel (01244) 677352 Mobile 07966-409404

PICKERING, Michael. *See* PICKERING, John Michael Staunton

PICKERING, William Stuart Frederick. b 22. K Coll Lon BD49 AKC49 PhD58 Manitoba Univ Hon DCL81. **d** 50 **p** 51. C Frodingham *Linc* 50-53; Lic to Offic Guildf & Linc 55-56; Tutor K Coll Lon 53-56; Canada 58-66; Lic to Offic *Newc* 66-87; rtd 87; Perm to Offic *Ely* 87-97 and from 03. *1 Brookfield Road, Coton, Cambridge CB23 7PT* Tel (01954) 210525

PICKETT, Brian Laurence. b 48. Reading Univ BA70 Qu Coll Birm BA73 MA77. Ripon Coll Cuddesdon. **d** 88 **p** 88. C Highcliffe w Hinton Admiral *Win* 88-91; P-in-c Colbury 91-01; P-in-c W End 01-04; V from 04. *St James's Vicarage, Elizabeth Close, Southampton SO30 3LT* Tel (023) 8047 2180 Fax 8047 7661

PICKETT, David. b 65. MBE99. Leeds Univ BA11. Coll of Resurr Mirfield 09. **d** 11. C Edenham w Witham on the Hill and Swinstead *Linc* from 11. *14 St John's Drive, Corby Glen, Grantham NG33 4NG* Tel (01476) 552457 Mobile 07916-825465 E-mail daipickett@hotmail.co.uk

PICKETT, Ms Joanna Elizabeth. b 53. Leic Univ BA74 MA80 Lon Univ MTh95. Wycliffe Hall Ox 87. **d** 89 **p** 94. Chapl Southn Univ 89-94; C N Stoneham 94-95; NSM Colbury 97-01; NSM W End from 01. *St James's Vicarage, Elizabeth Close, Southampton SO30 3LT* Tel (023) 8047 2180 Fax 8047 7661

PICKETT, Mark William Leslie. b 60. Westhill Coll Birm BEd84. Trin Coll Bris 93. **d** 95 **p** 96. C Hellesdon *Nor* 95-98; TV Thetford 98-03; R Clitheroe St Jas *Blackb* from 03. *The Rectory, Woone Lane, Clitheroe BB7 1BJ* Tel (01200) 423608 E-mail rector@stjamesclitheroe.co.uk

PICKETT, Peter Leslie. b 28. Guy's Hosp Medical Sch LDS52. S Dios Minl Tr Scheme 83. **d** 86 **p** 87. NSM Eastbourne H Trin *Chich* 86-88; P-in-c Danehill 88-93; rtd 93; Perm to Offic *Chich* from 93. *Springfield, 76 Meads Road, Eastbourne BN20 7QJ* Tel (01323) 731709 Mobile 07733-090957 E-mail pjpickett@btinternet.com

PICKFORD (*née* PACKER), **Mrs Catherine Ruth.** b 76. Nottm Univ BA97 Anglia Poly Univ MA00. Westcott Ho Cam MA00. **d** 00 **p** 01. C Gosforth All SS *Newc* 00-04; NSM Benwell 04-09; TR from 09. *56 Dunholme Road, Newcastle upon Tyne NE4 6XE* Tel 0191-273 5356 E-mail catherine.p@blueyonder.co.uk

PICKLES, Mark Andrew. b 62. Edin Univ BA83. Cranmer Hall Dur 85. **d** 88 **p** 89. C Rock Ferry *Ches* 88-91; C Hartford 91-93; V Wharton 93-00; P-in-c Duffield *Derby* 00-05; V Duffield and Lt

Eaton from 05. *St Alkmund's Vicarage, Vicarage Lane, Duffield, Belper DE56 4EB* Tel (01332) 841168 *or* 840536 Fax 842595 E-mail pickles465@btinternet.com

PICKSTONE, Charles Faulkner. b 55. BNC Ox BA77 MA81 Leeds Univ BA80. Coll of Resurr Mirfield 78. **d** 81 **p** 82. C Birkenhead Priory *Ches* 81-84; Chapl Paris St Geo *Eur* 84; C Camberwell St Giles w St Matt *S'wark* 84-89; V Catford St Laur from 89; Asst RD E Lewisham 92-99. *St Laurence's Vicarage, 31 Bromley Road, London SE6 2TS* Tel (020) 8698 2871 *or* 8698 9706 E-mail charlston@mailbox.co.uk

PICKTHORN, Canon Charles Howard. b 25. Linc Coll Ox BA48 MA52. Sarum Th Coll 48. **d** 50 **p** 51. C High Harrogate Ch Ch *Ripon* 50-54; C Cheam *S'wark* 54-60; R Bourton-on-the-Water w Clapton *Glouc* 60-91; Chapl RAF 60-76; RD Stow *Glouc* 67-90; P-in-c Gt Rissington 68-81; Hon Can Glouc Cathl from 77; rtd 91; Perm to Offic *Glouc* from 91. *clo Mrs S P Stiggers, 23 Sutherland Close, Warwick CV34 5UJ*

PICKUP, Harold. b 17. St Pet Hall Ox BA39 MA46. Ridley Hall Cam 46. **d** 47 **p** 48. C Middleton *Man* 47-50; V Gravesend St Mary *Roch* 51-57; Australia from 57; rtd 82. *7 Farview Avenue, Riverside Tas 7250, Australia* Tel (0061) (3) 6327 4891

PIDGEON, Warner Mark. b 68. Trin Coll Bris 00. **d** 02 **p** 03. C Fair Oak *Win* 02-06; TV Billericay and Lt Burstead *Chelmsf* from 06. *10 Chestwood Close, Billericay CM12 0PB* Tel (01277) 652659 Mobile 07927-348741 E-mail warner@billericaychurches.org

PIDOUX, Ian George. b 32. Univ Coll Ox BA55 MA60. Coll of Resurr Mirfield 54. **d** 57 **p** 58. C Aldbrough All SS *York* 57-60; C Haggerston St Aug w St Steph *Lon* 60-62; C Aylesford *Roch* 80-81; TV Rye *Chich* 81-84; P-in-c Bridgwater St Jo *B & W* 84-86; V 86-98; Chapl Bridgwater Hosp 91-98; rtd 98; Perm to Offic *B & W* from 98. *18 Alexandra Road, Bridgwater TA6 3HE* Tel (01278) 452882 E-mail igsepidoux@btinternet.com

PIDSLEY, Preb Christopher Thomas. b 36. ALCD61. **d** 61 **p** 62. C Enfield Ch Ch Trent Park *Lon* 61-66; C Rainham *Chelmsf* 66-70; V Chudleigh *Ex* 70-98; RD Moreton 86-91; Preb Ex Cathl 92-98; rtd 98. *Bellever, Shillingford Abbot, Exeter EX2 9QF* Tel (01392) 833588

PIENAAR, Joseph. b 77. Birm Chr Coll MA09. **d** 09 **p** 10. C Romiley *Ches* from 09. *6 Etherow Avenue, Romiley, Stockport SK6 4HA* Tel 0161-427 6731 Mobile 07854-179087 E-mail joe@romileylifecentre.co.uk

PIERARD, Canon Beaumont Harold. b 21. MBE72 JP68. St Jo Coll Auckland 94-81. New Zealand 46-53; Chapl Hurstpierpoint Coll 53-54; Chapl Worksop Coll North 54-57; New Zealand from 57; Hon Can St Peter's Cathl Waikato 64-82. *287 Peachgrove Road, Hamilton 3214, New Zealand* Tel (0064) (7) 855 7000

PIERCE, Alan. b 46. St Mark & St Jo Coll Lon TCert68 Southlands Coll Lon BEd75 K Coll Lon MA85. NOC 89. **d** 92 **p** 93. NSM Bolton St Thos *Man* 92-98; NSM Halliwell 98-00; NSM Bolton Breightmet St Jas 00-06; NSM Leverhulme from 06. *3 Astley Road, Bolton BL2 4BR* Tel (01204) 300071 Fax 401556

✠**PIERCE, The Rt Revd Anthony Edward.** b 41. Univ of Wales (Swansea) BA63 Linacre Coll Ox BA65 MA71. Ripon Hall Ox 63. **d** 65 **p** 66 **c** 99. C Swansea St Pet *S & B* 65-67; C Swansea St Mary and H Trin 67-74; Chapl Univ of Wales (Swansea) 71-74; V Llwynderw 74-92; P-in-c Swansea St Barn 92-96; Dioc Dir of Educn 93-96; Can Brecon Cathl 93-99; Adn Gower 95-99; V Swansea St Mary w H Trin 96-99; Bp S & B 99-08; rtd 08. *2 Coed Ceirios, Swansea Vale, Swansea SA7 0NU* Tel (01792) 790258

PIERCE, Brian William. b 42. St Steph Ho Ox 86. **d** 88 **p** 89. C Cudworth *Wakef* 88-93; TV Manningham *Bradf* 93-98; V Tipton St Jo *Lich* 98-07; rtd 07; Perm to Offic *Blackb* from 08. *53 St Patricks Road North, Lytham St Annes FY8 2HB* Tel (01253) 711247 E-mail loggos@btinternet.com

PIERCE, Bruce Andrew. b 58. TCD BBS80 BTh89 Dub City Univ MA99 MA02. CITC 86. **d** 89 **p** 90. C Raheny w Coolock *D & G* 89-92; C Taney 92-93; I Lucan w Leixlip 93-98; Chapl Adelaide and Meath Hosp Dublin 98-02; C Haarlem *Eur* 02-03; Chapl Toronto Gen Hosp Canada 03-04; Chapl Princess Marg Hosp Toronto 04-05; Supervisor (Assoc) Kerry Gen Hosp 06-08; Dir Educn St Luke's Home Mahon from 08. *6 East Avenue, Frankfield, Douglas, Cork, Republic of Ireland* Tel (00353) (21) 489 7511 *or* 435 9444 ext 507 Fax 435 9450 E-mail bruapierce@hotmail.com *or* bruce.pierce@slukeshome.ie

PIERCE, Christopher Douglas. b 61. Middle Tennessee State Univ BSc95 Covenant Th Sem St Louis MA96. Asbury Th Sem Kentucky 92. **d** 08 **p** 09. C St Jo Cathl Antigua 08-10; I Clondehorkey w Cashel *D & R* from 10. *Ballymore Rectory, Port-na-Blagh, Letterkenny, Co Donegal, Republic of Ireland* Tel (00353) (74) 913 6185 E-mail revcdp@gmail.com

PIERCE, David. *See* PIERCE, Thomas David Benjamin

PIERCE, Jeffrey Hyam. b 29. Chelsea Coll Lon BSc51 FBIM80. Ox NSM Course 86. **d** 88 **p** 89. NSM Gt Missenden w Ballinger and Lt Hampden *Ox* 88-93; NSM Penn 93-97; rtd 97; Perm to

Offic *Ox* from 97. *Glebe Cottage, Manor Road, Penn, High Wycombe HP10 8HY* Tel (01494) 817179

PIERCE, Jonathan Douglas Marshall. b 70. UCD BA91. CITC BTh96. **d** 96 **p** 97. C Knockbreda *D & D* 96-99; L'Arche Community Dublin 99-00; C Taney *D & G* 00-03; I Kilmore and Inch *D & D* 03-09; I Cregagh from 09. *St Finnian's Rectory, 3 Upper Knockbreda Road, Belfast BT6 9QH* Tel (028) 9079 3822 E-mail jonopierce@btinternet.com

PIERCE, Roderick Martin. b 52. ACIB74. **d** 06 **p** 07. OLM Guildf H Trin w St Mary from 06. *Appledore, 18 Blackwell Avenue, Guildford GU2 8LU* Tel (01483) 505816 E-mail ann.rodpierce@ntlworld.com

PIERCE, Stephen Barry. b 60. Birm Univ BA81 MA82. Cranmer Hall Dur. **d** 85 **p** 86. C Huyton St Mich *Liv* 85-89; V Walton Breck Ch Ch 89-00; P-in-c Walton Breck 98-00; Resources Officer 00-08; Perm to Offic from 01. *39 Duke Street, Formby, Liverpool L37 4AP* Tel (01704) 833725

PIERCE, Thomas David Benjamin. b 67. Ulster Univ BA88. Oak Hill Th Coll BA94. **d** 94 **p** 95. C Cromer *Nor* 94-97; C Belfast St Donard *D & D* 97-99; C Holywood 99-00; I Kilwarlin Upper w Kilwarlin Lower from 00. *Kilwarlin Rectory, 9 St John's Road, Hillsborough BT26 6ED* Tel (028) 9268 3299

PIERCE, William Johnston. b 32. NOC. **d** 89 **p** 90. NSM Gt Crosby St Luke *Liv* 89-96; Perm to Offic from 96. *1 Forton Lodge, Blundellsands Road East, Liverpool L23 8SA* Tel 0151-924 2400

PIERCE-JONES, Alan. b 74. Coll of Ripon & York St Jo BA98. St Mich Coll Llan 98. **d** 00 **p** 01. C Port Talbot St Theodore *Llan* 00-02; TV Neath 02-05; V Lt Marsden w Nelson St Mary and Nelson St Bede *Blackb* 05-10, C W Burnley All SS 10; C Burnley St Mark 10; Chapl HM YOI Lanc Farms from 10; Chapl HM Pris Lanc Castle from 10. *HM YOI Lancaster Farms, Stone Row Head, Quernmore Road, Lancaster LA1 3QZ* Tel (01524) 563450 E-mail alan.pierce-jones@hmps.gsi.gov.uk

PIERCY, Elizabeth Claire. See FRANCE, Mrs Elizabeth Claire

PIERPOINT, The Ven David Alfred. b 56. **d** 86 **p** 88. NSM Athboy w Ballivor and Killallon *M & K* 86-88; NSM Killiney Ballybrack *D & G* 88-89; NSM Narraghmore and Timolin w Castledermot etc 89-91; Chan V St Patr Cathl Dublin 90-96; C Dublin St Patr Cathl Gp 92-95; V Dublin Ch Ch Cathl Gp from 95; Can Ch Ch Cathl Dublin from 95; Adn Dublin from 04. *The Vicarage, 30 Phibsborough Road, Dublin 7, Republic of Ireland* Tel (00353) (1) 830 4601 Mobile 87-263 0402 E-mail pierpoint.david@gmail.com

PIGGOTT, Alan Robert Lennox. b 62. Peterho Cam BA84 MA88. Westcott Ho Cam 00. **d** 02 **p** 03. C Dalston H Trin w St Phil and Haggerston All SS *Lon* 02-04; C Stoke Newington St Mary 04-05; P-in-c Hackney Wick St Mary of Eton w St Aug 05-10. *Address temp unknown* Tel 07743-294532 (mobile) E-mail alan.piggott@btinternet.com

PIGGOTT, The Ven Andrew John. b 51. Qu Mary Coll Lon BSc(Econ)72. St Jo Coll Nottm 83. **d** 86 **p** 87. C Dorridge *Birm* 86-89; TV Kidderminster St Geo *Worc* 89-94; V Biddulph *Lich* 94-99; Min and Voc Adv CPAS 99-01; Patr Sec 01-05; Adn Bath and Preb Wells Cathl from 05. *56 Grange Road, Saltford, Bristol BS31 3AG* Tel (01225) 873609 Fax 874110 E-mail adbath@bathwells.anglican.org

PIGGOTT, Clive. b 47. St Luke's Coll Ex CertEd69. **d** 96 **p** 97. OLM Malden St Jas *S'wark* from 96. *84 Manor Drive North, New Malden KT3 5PA* Tel (020) 8337 0801

PIGOTT, Graham John. b 44. Lon Bible Coll BD73 Nottm Univ MPhil84 MEd94 Lon Inst of Educn PGCE74. St Jo Coll Nottm 79. **d** 81 **p** 82. C Beeston *S'well* 81-84; P-in-c W Bridgford 84-88; V Wilford Hill 88-09; AD W Bingham 97-04; Hon Can S'well Minster 04-09; rtd 09; Perm to Offic *Derby* from 09. *Tanner's House, 3 Upperfields Cottages, Grindleford, Hope Valley S32 2HG* Tel (01433) 639641 E-mail graham.pigott@btinternet.com

PIGOTT, Nicholas John Capel. b 48. Qu Coll Birm 75. **d** 78 **p** 79. C Belmont *Dur* 78-79; C Folkestone St Sav *Cant* 79-82; C Birm St Geo 82-85; V Stevenage St Hugh and St Jo *St Alb* 85-91; TV Totnes w Bridgetown, Berry Pomeroy etc *Ex* 91-02; Asst P 02-04; rtd 04. *27 Croft Road, Ipplepen, Newton Abbot TQ12 5SS* Tel (01803) 813664 E-mail njsa@pigott.freeserve.co.uk

PIGREM, Terence John (Tim). b 39. Middx Univ BA97 MA01. Oak Hill Th Coll 66. **d** 69 **p** 70. C Islington St Andr w St Thos and St Matthias *Lon* 69-73; C Barking St Marg w St Patr *Chelmsf* 73-75; TV 75-76; C W Holloway St Luke *Lon* 76-79; V 79-95; P-in-c Abbess Roding, Beauchamp Roding and White Roding *Chelmsf* 95-96; R S Rodings 96-07; RD Dunmow 97-02; rtd 07; Perm to Offic *Chelmsf* from 08. *96 Vicarage Lane, Great Baddow, Chelmsford CM2 8JB* Tel (01245) 471878 E-mail pigrem@btinternet.com

PIIR, The Very Revd Gustav Peeter. b 61. St Olaf Coll Minnesota BA83 Saskatchewan Univ MDiv86. **p** 88. Asst Toronto St Pet Canada 88-92; Asst Chas Ch Tallinn Estonia 92-95; R Tallinn H Spirit from 95; Dean Tallinn from 99; P-in-c Tallinn SS Tim and Titus *Eur* from 00. *Pühavaimu 2, Tallinn 10123, Estonia* Tel (00372) 646 4430 Mobile 51-76159 Fax 644 1487 E-mail praost@hot.ee

PIKE, Mrs Amanda Shirley Gail. b 69. Cranmer Hall Dur 99. **d** 01 **p** 02. C Boston Spa *York* 01-03; C Elloughton and Brough w Brantingham 03-05; P-in-c Eggleston and Middleton-in-Teesdale w Forest and Frith *Dur* 05-08; TV Bosworth and Sheepy Gp *Leic* 08-11; C Nailstone and Carlton w Shackerstone 08-11; P-in-c Elmton *Derby* from 11; P-in-c Whitwell from 11. *The Vicarage, 1 Elmton Road, Creswell, Worksop S80 4HD* Tel (01909) 808975 Mobile 07968-543569 E-mail amanda@ichthos.me.uk

PIKE, David Frank. b 35. BA Lon Univ TCert CEng MIMechE. S Dios Minl Tr Scheme 82. **d** 85 **p** 86. NSM Lancing w Coombes Chich 85-88; R Albourne w Sayers Common and Twineham 88-94; V Wisborough Green 94-04; rtd 04. *42 Greenoaks, Lancing BN15 0HE* Tel (01903) 766209

PIKE, George Richard. b 38. Birm Univ BSc57. WMMTC 79. **d** 82 **p** 83. NSM Edgbaston St Bart *Birm* 82-89; NSM S Yardley St Mich 89-06; Perm to Offic from 06. *138 Charlbury Crescent, Birmingham B26 2LW* Tel and fax 0121-783 2818 E-mail kepi@geopi.fsnet.co.uk

PIKE, James. b 22. TCD 66. **d** 68 **p** 69. C Clooney *D & R* 68-72; I Ardstraw 72-76; I Ardstraw w Baronscourt 76-86; I Ardstraw w Baronscourt, Badoney Lower etc 76-92; Can Derry Cathl 90-92; rtd 92. *19 Knockgreenan Avenue, Omagh BT79 0EB* Tel (028) 8224 9007

PIKE, Paul Alfred. b 38. Bognor Regis Coll of Educn CertEd58 MIL88. Wycliffe Hall Ox 83. **d** 84 **p** 85. C Penn Fields *Lich* 84-89; OMF Internat Japan 89-03; rtd 03; Perm to Offic *Bris* from 03. *18 Silverlow Road, Nailsea, Bristol BS48 2AD* Tel (01275) 856270 E-mail papike@attglobal.net

PIKE, Peter John. b 23. Southn Univ BTh86 Lanc Univ PhD00 Sarum & Wells Th Coll 81. **d** 84 **p** 85. C Broughton *Blackb* 84-88; V Woodplumpton 88-93; Asst Dir of Ords and Voc Adv 89-93; P-in-c Barnacre w Calder Vale 93-98; Tutor CBDTI 93-98; V Briercliffe *Blackb* 98-04; AD Burnley 01-04; V Bempton w Flamborough, Reighton w Speeton *York* from 04; RD Bridlington from 08. *The Vicarage, Church Street, Flamborough, Bridlington YO15 1PE* Tel (01262) 851370 E-mail revpeterpike@hotmail.com

PIKE, Robert James. b 47. Kelham Th Coll 66. **d** 70 **p** 71. C Cov St Pet 70-74; C Bilton 74-76; P-in-c Southall St Geo *Lon* 76-81; V S Harrow St Paul 81-86; C Hillingdon St Jo 86-88; Chapl Hillingdon Hosp & Mt Vernon Hosp Uxbridge 88-90; Perm to Offic 91-96. *6 Salt Hill Close, Uxbridge UB8 1PZ* Tel (01895) 235212

PIKE, Timothy David. b 68. Collingwood Coll Dur BA90 Leeds Univ BA94. Coll of Resurr Mirfield 92. **d** 95 **p** 96. C Owton Manor *Dur* 95-98; C Old St Pancras w Bedford New Town St Matt *Lon* 98-03; CMP from 98; Warden from 05; CR 03-04; P-in-c Hornsey H Innocents *Lon* 04-07; V from 07; C Stroud Green H Trin from 04; P-in-c Harringay St Paul from 10; AD W Haringey 06-11. *99 Hillfield Avenue, London N8 7DG* Tel (020) 8340 1300 E-mail father timpike@hotmail.com

PILCHER, Mrs Jennifer. b 42. **d** 04 **p** 05. OLM Eastry and Northbourne w Tilmanstone etc *Cant* from 04. *1 Long Drive, Church Street, Eastry, Sandwich CT13 0HN* Tel (01304) 611472 E-mail jennifer.p@torview1.freeserve.co.uk

PILGRIM, Canon Colin Mark. b 56. BA77. Westcott Ho Cam 81. **d** 84 **p** 85. C Chorlton-cum-Hardy St Clem *Man* 84-87; C Whitchurch *Bris* 87-89; V Bedminster Down 89-95; Dioc Youth Officer 95-01; Hon C Stoke Bishop 96-01; V Henleaze from 01; AD Bris W from 06; Hon Can Bris Cathl from 09. *St Peter's Vicarage, 17 The Drive, Henleaze, Bristol BS9 4LD* Tel 0117-962 0636 or 962 3196 E-mail markpilgrimis@aol.com

PILGRIM, Donald Eric. b 55. Cant Univ (NZ) BA80 LTh87. St Jo Coll Auckland 81. **d** 81 **p** 82. New Zealand 81-85 and from 86; C Southampton Maybush St Pet *Win* 85-86. *212 Hoon Hay Road, Hoon Hay, Christchurch 8025, New Zealand* Tel and fax (0064) (3) 338 4277 E-mail pilgrimspalace@paradise.net.nz

PILGRIM, Ms Judith Mary. b 44. Westcott Ho Cam 88. **d** 90 **p** 94. C Probus, Ladock and Grampound w Creed and St Erme *Truro* 90-94; C Nottingham All SS *S'well* 94-97; Asst Chapl to the Deaf 94-97; Perm to Offic *S'well* 97-00 and *Ox* 00-01; P-in-c Zennor and Towednack *Truro* 02-06; rtd 06. *6 Cape Terrace, St Just, Penzance TR19 7JF* Tel (01736) 787371

PILGRIM, Kenneth George. b 49. Lon Univ BEd77 Kent Univ MA94. **d** 01 **p** 02. OLM Alkham w Capel le Ferne and Hougham *Cant* 01-03; Perm to Offic *Nor* 04-05; NSM E Dereham and Scarning 05-06; NSM Swanton Morley w Beetley w E Bilney and Hoe 05-06; NSM Dereham and Distr from 06; Bp's Officer for Wholeness and Healing from 10. *Sunny Oak, 27 Fakenham Road, Beetley, Dereham NR20 4BT* Tel (01362) 861265 E-mail kenpilgrim@btinternet.com

PILGRIM, Mark. See PILGRIM, Canon Colin Mark

PILKINGTON, Miss Anne. b 57. Aston Tr Scheme 88 NOC 90. **d** 93 **p** 94. C Wythenshawe Wm Temple Ch *Man* 93-96; P-in-c 96-99; TV Wythenshawe 99-06; P-in-c Didsbury Ch Ch 06; R W Didsbury and Withington St Chris from 06. *Christ Church Rectory, 35 Darley Avenue, Manchester M20 2ZD* Tel 0161-445 4152 E-mail anne@christchurchdidsbury.org.uk

PILKINGTON, Charles George Willink. b 21. Trin Coll Cam BA42 MA64. Westcott Ho Cam. **d** 63 **p** 64. C Pendleton St Thos *Man* 63-65; C Brindle Heath 63-65; C Chorlton-cum-Hardy St Clem 65-68; R Withington St Chris 68-88; rtd 88; Perm to Offic *Man* from 88. *32 Rathen Road, Withington, Manchester M20 9GH* Tel 0161-434 5365

PILKINGTON, Edward Russell. b 39. ALCD65. **d** 65 **p** 66. C Eccleshill *Bradf* 65-68; C Billericay St Mary *Chelmsf* 68-72; V New Thundersley 72-78; R Theydon Garnon 78-82; V Gidea Park 82-04; rtd 04. *19 Tryon Close, Swindon SN3 6HG* Tel (01793) 433495

PILKINGTON, John Rowan. b 32. Magd Coll Cam BA55 MA59. Ridley Hall Cam. **d** 59 **p** 60. C Ashtead *Guildf* 59-61; C Wimbledon *S'wark* 62-65; R Newhaven *Chich* 65-75; R Farlington *Portsm* 75-89; V Darlington St Mark w St Paul *Dur* 89-97; rtd 97; Perm to Offic *Portsm* from 98. *38 Main Road, Emsworth PO10 8AU* Tel (01243) 375830

PILKINGTON, Canon Timothy William. b 54. Nottm Univ BA85 Univ of Wales (Lamp) MA09. Linc Th Coll 82. **d** 85 **p** 86. C Newquay *Truro* 85-88; C Cockington *Ex* 88-91; R St John w Millbrook *Truro* 91-97; V Northampton St Matt *Pet* 97-02; TR Solihull *Birm* from 02; Hon Can Birm Cathl from 06. *The Rectory, St Alphege Close, Church Hill Road, Solihull B91 3RQ* Tel 0121-705 0069 or 705 5350 Fax 704 0646 E-mail rector@solihullparish.org.uk

PIMENTEL, Peter Eric. b 55. Lon Bible Coll BA79 MA94. Ridley Hall Cam. **d** 82 **p** 83. C Gt Ilford St Andr *Chelmsf* 82-85; Chapl Basingstoke Distr Hosp 85-88; TV Grays Thurrock *Chelmsf* 88-96; P-in-c Barton *Portsm* 96-99; V from 99; Dioc Ecum Officer 96-02. *St Paul's Vicarage, Staplers Road, Newport PO30 2HZ* Tel (01983) 522075 Mobile 07949-366625 Fax 08701-303386 E-mail peter@pimentel.freeserve.co.uk

PIMM, Robert John. b 57. Bris Univ BA78 ACIB82. Trin Coll Bris 92. **d** 94 **p** 95. C Long Benton *Newc* 94-98; TV Bath Twerton-on-Avon *B & W* from 98. *Ascension Vicarage, 35A Claude Avenue, Bath BA2 1AG* Tel (01225) 405354 E-mail robertpimm@tiscali.co.uk

PINCHBECK, Canon Caroline Rosamund. b 70. Hatf Coll Dur BA93. Wesley Ho Cam MA00. **d** 02 **p** 03. C Mawnan *Truro* 02-06; C Budock 03-06; P-in-c Eastling w Ospringe and Stalisfield w Otterden *Cant* 06-11; Communities and Partnership Exec Officer from 11; Rural Life Adv *Cant* and *Roch* from 06; Hon Can Cant Cathl from 11. *The Rectory, Newnham Lane, Eastling, Faversham ME13 0AS* Tel (01795) 890487 E-mail caroline.pinchbeck575@btinternet.com

PINCHES, Donald Antony. b 32. Pemb Coll Cam BA55 MA60 Linacre Coll Ox BA67. Wycliffe Hall Ox 64. **d** 67 **p** 68. C Aylesbury *Ox* 67-71; C Compton Gifford *Ex* 71-74; TV Lydford, Brent Tor, Bridestowe and Sourton 74-77; V Shiphay Collaton 77-97; rtd 97; Perm to Offic *Ex* from 98. *3 Malderek Avenue, Preston, Paignton TQ3 2RP* Tel (01803) 698003

PINDER, Canon John Ridout. b 43. Peterho Cam BA65 MA69. Cuddesdon Coll 65. **d** 73 **p** 74. C Leavesden *St Alb* 73-76; Gen Sec Melanesian Miss 77-89; P-in-c Harpsden *Ox* 82-89; R Farlington *Portsm* 89-02; R Liss 02-09; RD Portsm 96-01; Hon Can Portsm Cathl 01-09; rtd 09; P-in-c Stapleford *Ely* from 09. *The Vicarage, 43 Mingle Lane, Stapleford, Cambridge CB22 5SY* Tel (01223) 840256 E-mail johnpinder@waitrose.com

PINDER-PACKARD, John. b 47. Lon Univ BSc. NOC 81. **d** 84 **p** 85. NSM Mosbrough *Sheff* 84-85; C Norton 85-88; V New Whittington *Derby* 88-04; P-in-c Newbold and Gt Barlow 99-00; Chapl Whittington Hall Hosp 88-04; R Barlborough and Renishaw *Derby* 04-09; P-in-c Clowne 05-09; rtd 09. *1 Great Common Close, Barlborough, Chesterfield S43 4SY* E-mail packards@tiscali.co.uk

PINE, David Michael. b 41. Lich Th Coll 68. **d** 71 **p** 72. C Northam *Ex* 71-74; R Toft w Caldecote and Childerley *Ely* 74-80; R Hardwick 74-80; V Ipswich St Andr *St E* 80-84; P-in-c Hazelbury Bryan w Stoke Wake etc *Sarum* 84-91; R Hazelbury Bryan and the Hillside Par 91-93; V Steep and Froxfield w Privett *Portsm* 93-00; rtd 00; Perm to Offic *Portsm* 07-11. *3 Nansen Close, Bembridge PO35 5QD* Tel (01983) 872939

PINES, Christopher Derek. b 65. Lon Univ MB, BS89. Oak Hill Th Coll BA93 MA01. **d** 93 **p** 94. C Heref St Pet w St Owen and St Jas 93-97; Min Can and Chapl St Alb Abbey 97-03; Chapl St Alb Sch from 03. *1 Fishpool Street, St Albans AL3 4RS* Tel (01727) 846508 E-mail cdpines@st-albans.herts.sch.uk

PINFIELD, Leslie Arthur. b 57. Birm Univ BMus79. St Steph Ho Ox 92. **d** 94 **p** 95. C Bath Bathwick *B & W* 94-98; TV Swindon New Town *Bris* 98-07; P-in-c Huddersfield All SS and St Thos *Wakef* from 07; Bp's Adv on Inter-Faith Issues from 07. *The Vicarage, 17 Cross Church Street, Paddock, Huddersfield HD1 4SN* Tel (01484) 864266 E-mail frleslie@btopenworld.com

PINK, Canon David. b 34. Qu Coll Cam BA58 MA62. Linc Th Coll 58. **d** 60 **p** 61. C Lt Ilford St Mich *Chelmsf* 60-63; Lect Boston 63-65; V Kirton in Holland *Linc* 65-71; V Spittlegate 71-77; Ecum Officer Lincs and S Humberside from 77-85; P-in-c Canwick 77-87; R Washingborough w Heighington 87-88; R Washingborough w Heighington and Canwick 88-90; Can and Preb Linc Cathl 77-05; rtd 90; Perm to Offic *Linc* from 90. *The Old School, Swarby, Sleaford NG34 8TG*

PINKERTON, Ms Patricia Edith. b 38. California Univ BA72 MA75 BTh80. Ch Div Sch of the Pacific (USA). **d** 81 **p** 82. USA 81-88; C Coleford w Staunton *Glouc* 88-92; Dn-in-c St Briavels w Hewelsfield 92-94; P-in-c 94-97; rtd 97; Perm to Offic *Glouc* 97-09. *97 Kingsgate Road, Apt H-21, Lake Oswego OR 97035-2371, USA*

PINNELL (formerly ALLEN), Ms Beverley Carole. b 52. Ch Ch Coll Cant CertEd74 Open Univ BA91. Sarum Th Coll 93. **d** 96 **p** 97. NSM Ruislip Manor St Paul *Lon* from 96. *127 Cobden Close, Uxbridge UB8 2YH* E-mail revbev@tiscali.co.uk

PINNELL, George. b 39. NTMTC 96. **d** 99 **p** 00. NSM Hillingdon St Jo *Lon* from 99; Chapl Heathrow Airport from 08. *127 Cobden Close, Uxbridge UB8 2YH* Tel 07951-124976 (mobile) E-mail pinneg@tiscali.co.uk

PINNER, Mrs Cheri Lee. b 36. Marietta Coll (USA) BA59. **d** 07 **p** 08. C Greytown New Zealand 07-10; P-in-c Whaley Bridge *Ches* from 10. *5 The Sidings, Whaley Bridge, High Peak SK23 7HE* Tel (01663) 719535 Mobile 07889-796020 E-mail cheri.pinner@mac.com

PINNER, John Philip. b 37. K Coll Lon BA59 AKC59 Lon Inst of Educn PGCE60. Westcott Ho Cam 69. **d** 71 **p** 72. C Dover St Mary *Cant* 71-74; Chapl Felsted Sch 74-81; Chapl Rathkeale Coll New Zealand 81-02; P-in-c Greytown St Luke 04-08; rtd 10; Hon C Whaley Bridge *Ches* from 10. *5 The Sidings, Whaley Bridge, High Peak SK23 7HE* Tel (01663) 719535 E-mail cheri.john.pinner@xtra.co.nz

PINNER, Canon Terence Malcolm William. b 35. Southn Univ MA89. AKC59. **d** 60 **p** 61. C Eltham St Barn *S'wark* 60-64; S Africa 64-67 and 69-74; USPG 67-69; Sec for Home Affairs Conf of Br Miss Socs 74-76; P-in-c Hinstock *Lich* 76-79; Adult Educn Officer 76-79; Adult RE Officer 79-83; Chapl Southn Univ 83-88; Tutor S Dios Minl Tr Scheme 88-92; Dioc Dir of Ords *Win* 88-98; Hon Can Win Cathl 92-00; P-in-c Old Alresford and Bighton 93-00; rtd 00; Perm to Offic *Win* from 01. *47 Buriton Road, Winchester SO22 6JF* Tel (01962) 884215 Mobile 07889-177203

PINNINGTON, Mrs Gillian. b 59. St Kath Coll Liv BEd81 Ches Coll of HE BTh02. NOC 99. **d** 02 **p** 03. C Roby *Liv* 02-06; TV Speke St Aid from 06. *62 East Millwood Road, Liverpool L24 6SQ* Tel 0151-425 3388 E-mail pinny@supanet.com

PINNINGTON, Suzanne Jane. b 66. MBE10. Trevelyan Coll Dur BA89. St Steph Ho Ox 95. **d** 97 **p** 98. C Oakham, Hambleton, Egleton, Braunston and Brooke *Pet* 97-00; V Cottingley *Bradf* 00-08; Hon Can Bradf Cathl 04-08; R Houghton le Spring *Dur* from 08. *The Rectory, 5 Lingfield, Houghton le Spring DH5 8QA* Tel 0191-584 3487 E-mail rectorstmichaels@btinternet.com

PINNOCK, Martyn Elliott. b 47. Linc Th Coll 93. **d** 93 **p** 94. C Fordingbridge *Win* 93-97; V St Minver *Truro* 97-01; P-in-c Luray Ch Ch USA 01-02; V Steeton *Bradf* 02-05; P-in-c Scottsville USA 05-08; rtd 09. *26 Kirby Road, Truro TR1 3PH* Tel (01872) 273553 E-mail martynpinnock@aol.com

PINSENT, Ewen Macpherson. b 30. Edin Th Coll 67. **d** 69 **p** 70. C Holt *Nor* 69-72; R Kelso *Edin* 72-82; R Blendworth w Chalton w Idsworth etc *Portsm* 82-90; R Blendworth w Chalton w Idsworth 90-92; rtd 92; Perm to Offic *Sarum* from 94. *The Cross House, The Cross, Child Okeford, Blandford Forum DT11 8ED* Tel (01258) 860803

PIPER, Canon Andrew. b 58. Magd Coll Ox BA79 MA83. Chich Th Coll 80. **d** 83 **p** 84. C Eastbourne St Mary *Chich* 83-88; TV Lewes All SS, St Anne, St Mich and St Thos 88-93; TR Worth 93-03; Can Res and Prec Heref Cathl from 03. *1 The Close, Hereford HR1 2NG* Tel (01432) 266193 Fax 374220 E-mail precentor@herefordcathedral.org

PIPER, The Very Revd Clifford John. b 53. Moray Ord Course 91. **d** 93 **p** 94. C Invergordon St Ninian *Mor* 93-96; P-in-c 00-03; NSM Tain 96-98; P-in-c 98-03; P-in-c Forres from 03; Can St Andr Cathl Inverness 00-09; Dean Mor from 09. *St John's Rectory, Victoria Road, Forres IV36 3BN* Tel (01309) 672856 Fax 08712-422221 Mobile 07895-105104 E-mail cliffpiper@tiscali.co.uk

PIPER, Gary Quentin David. b 42. Nottm Coll of Educn TCert65 Maria Grey Coll Lon DipEd71. Oak Hill Th Coll 75. **d** 78 **p** 79. NSM Fulham St Matt *Lon* 78-85; V from 85; AD Hammersmith 86-92; AD Hammersmith and Fulham from 06. *St Matthew's Vicarage, 2 Clancarty Road, London SW6 3AB* Tel (020) 7731 3272 E-mail revgarypiper@hotmail.com

PIPER, Graham. b 58. Southn Univ BTh91. Chich Th Coll 88. **d** 91 **p** 92. C Horsham *Chich* 91-94; TV Haywards Heath St Wilfrid 94-99; Dioc Voc Adv 96-99; V Bamber Bridge St Aid *Blackb* 99-04; V Hawes Side and Marton Moss from 04. *The Vicarage, Hawes Side Lane, Blackpool FY4 5AH* Tel (01253) 697937 Mobile 07816-525843 E-mail fathergraham@fsmail.net

PIPPEN, Canon Brian Roy. b 50. St D Coll Lamp. **d** 73 **p** 74. C Maindee Newport *Mon* 73-77; TV Cwmbran 77-84; V Newport Ch Ch 84-90; R Pontypool from 90; AD Pontypool 98-08; Can

St Woolos Cathl from 01. *The Vicarage, Trevethin, Pontypool NP4 8JF* Tel (01495) 762228

PIRET, Michael John. b 57. State Univ NY BA79 Univ of Michigan MA80 PhD91 Mert Coll Ox MLitt89. Edin Th Coll 90. **d** 92 **p** 93. C St Andr Cathl Inverness 92-94; Dean of Div and Chapl Magd Coll Ox from 94. *Magdalen College, Oxford OX1 4AU* Tel (01865) 276027

PIRRIE, Stephen Robin. b 56. Kent Univ BA79 Cam Univ MA83 Barrister 80. EAMTC 94. **d** 97 **p** 98. C King's Lynn St Marg w St Nic *Nor* 97-99; C Bideford, Northam, Westward Ho!, Appledore etc *Ex* 99-00; TV 00-03. *Address withheld by request*

PITCHER, Canon David John. b 33. Ely Th Coll 55. **d** 58 **p** 59. C Kingswinford St Mary *Lich* 58-61; C Kirkby *Liv* 61-66; R Ingham w Sutton *Nor* 66-72; V Lakenham St Jo 72-76; R Framlingham w Saxtead *St E* 76-91; RD Loes 82-89; Hon Can St E Cathl 85-99; R Woodbridge St Mary 91-99; rtd 99; Perm to Offic *St E* from 00. *25 Coucy Close, Framlingham, Woodbridge IP13 9AX* Tel (01728) 621580

PITCHER, George Martell. b 55. Birm Univ BA77 Middx Univ BA05. NTMTC 02. **d** 05 **p** 06. NSM St Bride Fleet Street w Bridewell etc *Lon* from 05. *Culverwood, Little London Road, Cross in Hand, Heathfield TN21 0AX* Tel (01435) 865377 Mobile 07778-917182 E-mail george@pitcher.com

PITCHER, Robert Philip. b 47. Westhill Coll Birm DipEd70. Trin Coll Bris 90. **d** 92 **p** 93. C Llansamlet *S & B* 92-96; V Cwmgarreithin 96-02; V Llanidloes w Llangurig *Ban* 02-10; AD Arwystli 04-10; rtd 10. *22 Dysart Terrace, Canal Road, Newtown SY16 2JL* E-mail bob.pitcher@openworld.com

PITCHER, Ronald Charles Frederick. b 21. AKC50. **d** 51 **p** 52. C Burnage St Marg *Man* 51-53; C Heywood St Jas 53-55; C Newall Green CD 55-61; V Newall Green St Fran 61-73; Chapl Wythenshawe Hosp Man 64-73; C-in-c Danesholme CD *Pet* 73-81; V Estover *Ex* 81-91; rtd 91; Perm to Offic *Sarum* 92-10. *50 Townhill Drive, Broughton, Brigg DN20 0HG* Tel (01652) 653561

PITCHER, Simon John. b 63. Reading Univ BA85. Ridley Hall Cam 00. **d** 02 **p** 03. C Lightcliffe *Wakef* 02-05; P-in-c Heckmondwike 05-10; C Liversedge w Hightown 05-10; C Roberttown w Hartshead 05-10; RD Birstall 08-10; TR Sole Bay *St E* from 10; RD Halesworth from 11; RD Beccles and S Elmham from 11. *The Vicarage, Gardner Road, Southwold IP18 6HJ* E-mail revsimon@talktalk.net

PITHERS, Canon Brian Hoyle. b 34. Chich Th Coll 63. **d** 66 **p** 67. C Wisbech SS Pet and Paul *Ely* 66-70; V Fenstanton 70-75; V Hilton 70-75; V Habergham Eaves St Matt *Blackb* 75-85; P-in-c Habergham Eaves H Trin 78-85; V Burnley St Matt w H Trin 85-86; TR Ribbleton 86-92; V Torrisholme 92-00; Hon Can Blackb Cathl 97-00; rtd 01; Perm to Offic *Blackb* from 01. *37 Dallam Avenue, Morecambe LA4 5BB* Tel (01524) 424786 E-mail brianpithers@talktalk.net

PITKETHLY (née CHEVILL), Elizabeth Jane. b 65. Colchester Inst of Educn BA86 K Coll Lon MMus87 PhD93 Warwick Univ BPhil00 AKC89 Lon Inst of Educn PGCE91. Wycliffe Hall Ox MSt04 MLitt08. **d** 08 **p** 09. C Blackheath St Jo *S'wark* 08-11. *Address temp unknown* Tel 07952-024571 (mobile) E-mail elizabethchevill@tiscali.co.uk

PITKIN, James Mark. b 62. Man Univ BSc83 MRAeS90 CEng90 Glos Univ BA(Theol)03. STETS. **d** 99 **p** 00. C Chilworth w N Baddesley *Win* 99-03; V Lockerley and E Dean w E and W Tytherley from 03. *The Vicarage, The Street, Lockerley, Romsey SO51 0JF* Tel (01794) 340635 Fax 08701-674691 Mobile 07931-736166 E-mail jamespitkin@priest.com

PITKIN, Mrs Susan Margaret. b 60. Man Univ BA84 Surrey Univ BA03. STETS 00. **d** 03 **p** 04. C Southampton Maybush St Pet *Win* 03-06; C Maybush and Southampton St Jude 06-09; Asst Chapl Southn Univ Hosps NHS Trust from 09. *The Vicarage, The Street, Lockerley, Romsey SO51 0JF* Tel (01794) 340635 Mobile 07906-027042 E-mail suepitkin@minister.com

PITMAN, Jessica. b 62. Newton Park Coll Bath BEd85. STETS 07. **d** 10 **p** 11. C Langport Area *B & W* from 10. *Westerleigh, Newtown, Langport TA10 9SE* Tel (01458) 251489 E-mail jessicapitman@aol.com

PITMAN, Roger Thomas. b 64. St Mich Coll Llan BTh00. **d** 00 **p** 01. C Caerphilly *Llan* 00-02; C Coity w Nolton 02-07; P-in-c Llanharry from 07; Chapl Pontypridd and Rhondda NHS Trust from 07. *The Rectory, Llanharry, Pontyclun CF72 9LH* Tel (01443) 223140 E-mail way-follower@hotmail.com

PITT, Mrs Beatrice Anne. b 50. I M Marsh Coll of Physical Educn Liv CertEd71 Open Univ BA01. Trin Coll Bris 80. **d** 82 **p** 97. C Rhyl w St Ann *St As* 82-86; CMS 86-92; Jt Co-ord Dioc Bible Schs Bukavu Zaïre 88-92; NSM Penycae *St As* 92-98; Hon Rep for CMS *St As* and *Ban* 93-98; NSM Killesher K, E & A 98-01; P-in-c Killinagh w Kiltyclogher and Innismagrath 98-01; P-in-c Firbank, Howgill and Killington *Bradf* 01-05; rtd 05. *20 Thornsbank, Sedbergh LA10 5LF* Tel (01539) 622095 E-mail anne@pitt.euro1net.com

PITT, George. b 52. QUB BD79 MTh88. CITC 81. **d** 81 **p** 82. C Belfast St Mary *Conn* 81-86; CMS 86-92; Zaïre 88-92; V Penycae *St As* 92-98; I Killesher K, E & A 98-01; Educn Adv Ch of

Ireland Bps' Appeal 01-03; Perm to Offic *Bradf* 04-06; Chapl HM Pris Moorland from 06. *HM Prison Moorland, Bawtry Road, Hatfield Woodhouse, Doncaster DN7 6BW* Tel (01302) 523000

PITT, Karen Lesley Finella. See TIMMIS, Mrs Karen Lesley Finella

PITT, Robert Edgar. b 37. Chich Th Coll 70. **d** 73 **p** 74. C Knowle *Bris* 73-77; C Wells St Cuth w Coxley and Wookey Hole *B & W* 77-81; TV Wellington and Distr 81-94; V Burnham 94-02; Chapl Taunton and Somerset NHS Trust 94-02; rtd 02; Perm to Offic *Sarum* from 03. *Redmaye, 119 High Street, Burbage, Marlborough SN8 3AA* Tel (01672) 810651

PITT, Canon Trevor. b 45. Hull Univ BA66 MA69 Open Univ DipEd91. Linc Th Coll 68 Union Th Sem (NY) STM70. **d** 70 **p** 71. C Sheff St Geo 70-74; TV Gleadless Valley 74-78; TR 78-79; P-in-c Elham *Cant* 79-82; V Elham w Denton and Wootton 82-91; Vice Prin Cant Sch of Min 81-91; Six Preacher Cant Cathl 85-91; Prin NEOC *Newc* 91-10; Hon Can Newc Cathl 91-10; rtd 10; Perm to Offic *Ripon* and *York* from 91. *Green View House, Hamsterley, Bishop Auckland DL13 3QF* Tel (01388) 488898 E-mail trevorpitt@aol.com

PITT, Mrs Valerie. b 55. Liv Univ BA77. STETS 02. **d** 05 **p** 06. NSM Oxshott *Guildf* 05-09; NSM Meole Brace *Lich* from 09. *Address temp unknown*

PITTARIDES, Renos. b 62. Surrey Univ BA85. **d** 07 **p** 08. OLM Cobham and Stoke D'Abernon *Guildf* from 07. *46 Freelands Road, Cobham KT11 2ND* Tel and fax (01932) 887996 E-mail renosp@gmail.com

PITTIS, Canon Stephen Charles. b 52. Sheff Univ MA01. Oak Hill Th Coll. **d** 76 **p** 77. C Win Ch Ch 76-79; Chapl Dorset Inst of HE and Bournemouth and Poole Coll of FE *Sarum* 79-84; V Woking St Paul *Guildf* 84-97; Dir of Faith Development *Win* 97-09; Dioc Missr and Can Res Win Cathl from 09. *60 Upper Brook Street, Winchester SO23 8DG* Tel (01962) 854133

PITTS, Canon Evadne Ione (Eve). b 50. Qu Coll Birm. **d** 89 **p** 94. C Bartley Green *Birm* 89-93; TD Kings Norton 93-94; TV 94-98; P-in-c Highters Heath 98-00; V 00-09; P-in-c Birchfield from 09; Hon Can Birm Cathl from 05. *Holy Trinity Vicarage, 213 Birchfield Road, Birmingham B20 3DG* Tel 0121-356 4241 E-mail blackuhru@aol.com

PITTS, The Very Revd Michael James. b 44. Worc Coll Ox BA66 Worc Coll of Educn MA69. Qu Coll Birm 67. **d** 69 **p** 70. C Pennywell St Thos and Grindon St Oswald CD *Dur* 69-72; C Darlington H Trin 72-74; Chapl Dunkerque w Lille Arras etc Miss to Seamen *Eur* 74-79; V Tudhoe *Dur* 79-81; Chapl Helsinki w Moscow *Eur* 81-85; Chapl Stockholm 85-88; Hon Can Brussels Cathl 87-88; Hon Chapl Miss to Seafarers Canada from 88; R Montreal St Cuth 88-91; Dean Ch Ch Cathl Montreal 91-09; rtd 09; P-in-c Montreal St Ignatius from 09. *3279 rue Gariepy RR4, Sainte Julienne QC J0K 2T0, Canada* Tel (001) (450) 834 2956 E-mail michael.pitts@worc.oxon.org

PITYANA, Prof Nyameko Barney. b 45. K Coll Lon BD81 Cape Town Univ PhD95 Trin Coll Hartford (USA) Hon DD96. Ripon Coll Cuddesdon 82. **d** 82 **p** 83. C Woughton *Ox* 82-85; V Highters Heath *Birm* 85-88; Dir Progr to Combat Racism WCC 88-92; Hon C Geneva *Eur* 88-92; S Africa from 93; Sen Lect RS Cape Town Univ 93-95; Chair Human Rights Commission 95-01; Prin and Vice Chan UNISA from 01; FKC 06; R Coll of Transfiguration Grahamstown from 11; Can of Prov from 11. *College of the Transfiguration, PO Box 77, Grahamstown, 6140 South Africa* Tel (0027) (46) 622 3332 Fax 622 3877 E-mail rector@cott.co.za

PIX, Mrs Sarah Anne Louise. b 71. Southn Univ BSc92 Birkbeck Coll Lon MSc97. Ridley Hall Cam 02. **d** 06 **p** 07. C W Slough *Ox* 06-08; C Britwell 08-09; TV Hampreston *Sarum* from 09. *9 Pinewood Road, Ferndown BH22 9RW* Tel (01202) 890798 E-mail revsarahpix@yahoo.co.uk

PIX, Stephen James. b 42. Ex Coll Ox BA64 MA68 Univ of Wales (Cardiff) LLM97. Clifton Th Coll 66. **d** 68 **p** 69. C St Helens St Helen *Liv* 68-71; Lic to Offic *S'wark* 71-76; Hon C Wallington 76-84; V Osmotherley w E Harlsey and Ingleby Arncliffe *York* 84-89; V Ox St Mich w St Martin and All SS 89-01; rtd 01; Perm to Offic *St E* 01-07 and *Ox* from 07. *10 Cadogan Park, Woodstock OX20 1UW* Tel (01993) 812473

PIZZEY, Canon Lawrence Roger. b 42. Dur Univ BA64. Westcott Ho Cam 65. **d** 67 **p** 68. C Bramford *St E* 67-71; Tutor Woodbridge Abbey 71-77; Asst Chapl Woodbridge Sch 71-77; P-in-c Flempton w Hengrave and Lackford *St E* 77-85; R Culford, W Stow and Wordwell 77-85; P-in-c Acton w Gt Waldingfield 85-89; V 89-95; P-in-c Sudbury and Chilton 95-98; R 98-07; RD Sudbury 96-06; Hon Can St E Cathl 00-07; rtd 07; Perm to Offic *St E* from 07. *9 Constable Road, Bury St Edmunds IP33 3UQ* Tel (01284) 762863 E-mail lrp.sudbury@virgin.net

PLACE, Rodger Goodson. b 37. St Chad's Coll Dur BA60. **d** 62 **p** 63. C Pontesbury I and II *Heref* 62-65; C Heref St Martin 65-68; V Ditton Priors 68-75; R Neenton 68-75; P-in-c Aston Botterell w Wheathill and Loughton 69-75; P-in-c Burwarton w N Cleobury 69-75; P-in-c Dacre w Hartwith *Ripon* 75-76; V 76-82; V Wyther 82-92; P-in-c Roundhay St Jo 92-97; V 97-00;

rtd 00; Perm to Offic *York* from 00. *72 Field Lane, Thorpe Willoughby, Selby YO8 9FL* Tel (01757) 703174

PLACE, Thomas Richard. b 59. Ridley Hall Cam 93. **d** 93 **p** 94. C Huyton St Geo *Liv* 93-97; CF 97-07; Sen CF from 07. *clo MOD Chaplains (Army)* Tel (01980) 615804 Fax 615800

PLAISTER, Keith Robin. b 43. K Coll Lon BD65 AKC65. **d** 66 **p** 67. C Laindon w Basildon *Chelmsf* 66-71; V Gt Wakering 71-78; V Gt Wakering w Foulness 78-90; C Witham 91-94; TV 94-99; P-in-c Sandon and E Hanningfield 99-08; rtd 08. *118 Maldon Road, Great Baddow, Chelmsford CM2 7DH* Tel (01245) 473135 E-mail keithplaister@hotmail.com

PLANT, Caroline Mary. b 56. Ripon Coll Cuddesdon 01. **d** 03 **p** 04. C Gnosall *Lich* 03-06; C Gnosall and Moreton 06-07; TV Penkridge from 07. *The Vicarage, Top Road, Acton Trussell, Stafford ST17 0RQ* Tel (01785) 711154 E-mail carolineplant@yahoo.co.uk

PLANT, Mrs Edith Winifred Irene (Ewith). b 31. Liv Univ BEd71. Cranmer Hall Dur 81. **dss** 83 **d** 87. Countesthorpe w Foston *Leic* 83-86; Loughborough All SS and H Trin 86-90; Par Dn 87-90; Par Dn Thurnby Lodge 90-91; rtd 91; Perm to Offic *Leic* 91-96 and *Ab* from 96. *clo Mrs J Wallis, Upper Braikley Cottage, Methlick, Ellon AB41 7HD* Tel (01651) 806209

PLANT, Miss Elizabeth Bowers. b 48. Westf Coll Lon BA70 Man Univ PGCE71. **d** 08 **p** 09. OLM Deane *Man* from 08. *25 Kintyre Drive, Bolton BL3 4PE* Tel (01204) 63730 E-mail eplant@supanet.com

PLANT, Mrs Glenys. b 49. ALA71. EMMTC 95. **d** 98 **p** 99. C Allestree *Derby* 98-01; rtd 01; Perm to Offic *Derby* from 01. *3 Stoodley Pike Gardens, Allestree, Derby DE22 2TN* Tel (01332) 552697

PLANT, John Frederick. b 61. Man Univ BA82 MEd95. Qu Coll Birm 83. **d** 85 **p** 86. C Kersal Moor *Man* 85-88; Chapl Aston Univ 88-94; TR Market Bosworth, Cadeby w Sutton Cheney etc *Leic* 94-00; P-in-c The Sheepy Gp 98-00; TR Bosworth and Sheepy Gp from 00; P-in-c Nailstone and Carlton w Shackerstone from 04. *The Rectory, Park Street, Market Bosworth, Nuneaton CV13 0LL* Tel (01455) 290239 E-mail jplant@leicester.anglican.org

PLANT, Michael Ian. b 47. Man Univ MEd85 GNSM68. St Jo Coll Nottm 97. **d** 99 **p** 00. NSM St D Cathl 99-01; NSM Dewisland from 01. *Lower Treginnis, St Davids, Haverfordwest SA62 6RS* Tel (01437) 720840 Fax 721350

PLANT, Michelle. NEOC. **d** 08. NSM Burley *Ripon* from 08. *20 Lakeland Crescent, Leeds LS17 7PR* Tel 0113-261 4757

PLANT, Nicholas. See PLANT, Richard George Nicholas

PLANT, Nicholas. b 58. MAAT87. SAOMC 95. **d** 98 **p** 99. OLM W Slough *Ox* 98-04; OLM Burnham w Dropmore, Hitcham and Taplow 04-08; NSM Taplow and Dropmore 08-09; C The Cookhams from 09. *St John's House, Spring Lane, Cookham Dean, Maidenhead SL6 9PN* Tel (01628) 475672 Mobile 07802-363835 E-mail fr.nick@ymail.com

PLANT, Richard. b 41. Open Univ BSc93. Qu Coll Birm 88. **d** 90 **p** 91. C Skelmersdale St Paul *Liv* 90-93; R Golborne 93-00; R Hesketh w Becconsall *Blackb* 00-07; rtd 07; Perm to Offic *Blackb* from 07. *12 Granville Avenue, Hesketh Bank, Preston PR4 6AH* Tel (01772) 815257 E-mail richard.plant1@btinternet.com

PLANT, Richard George Nicholas. b 45. Man Univ BA67. Coll of Resurr Mirfield 68. **d** 71 **p** 72. C Cleckheaton St Jo *Wakef* 71-74; P-in-c Adel *Ripon* 74-78; V Ireland Wood 78-82; V Armley w New Wortley 82-92; R Garforth 92-08; rtd 08; Perm to Offic *York* from 08. *3 Holman Avenue, Garforth, Leeds LS25 1HU* Tel 0113-287 6064 E-mail nick.plant@tiscali.co.uk

PLANT, Robert David. b 28. Birm Univ BSc49 Ch Ch Coll Cant MA98. St Deiniol's Hawarden 74. **d** 76 **p** 80. NSM Llandrillo-yn-Rhos *St As* 76-79; NSM St Nicholas at Wade w Sarre and Chislet w Hoath *Cant* from 79. *4 Sandalwood Drive, St Nicholas-at-Wade, Birchington CT7 0PE* Tel (01843) 847276

PLANT, Stephen John. b 64. Birm Univ BA86 Fitzw Coll Cam PhD93. ERMC 10. **d** 11 **p** 11. NSM Cambridge St Jas *Ely* from 11; Dean Trin Hall Cam from 11. *Trinity Hall, Cambridge CB2 1TJ* Tel (01223) 241169 Mobile 07824-835199 E-mail sjp27@cam.ac.uk

PLATT, Andrew Martin Robert. b 41. Oak Hill Th Coll 74. **d** 76 **p** 77. C St Alb St Paul *St Alb* 76-79; V Gazeley w Dalham and Moulton *St E* 79-85; V Gazeley w Dalham, Moulton and Kentford 85-86; RD Mildenhall 84-86; P-in-c Saxmundham 86-89; R 89-97; P-in-c Sudbury w Ballingdon and Brundon 97-98; V 98-04; rtd 04; Co Ecum Officer *Nor* 04-09; Perm to Offic *Nor* and *St E* from 04. *21 Homefield Paddock, Beccles NR34 9NE* Tel (01502) 717744

PLATT, Anthea Kate Helen. b 71. **d** 08 **p** 09. NSM Thorley *St Alb* from 08. *St Barnabas Centre, Church Lane, Thorley, Bishop's Stortford CM23 4BE* Tel (01279) 506753 E-mail antheaplatt@hotmail.com

PLATT, David. See PLATT, William David

PLATT, Mrs Jane Marie. b 54. Westhill Coll Birm CertEd76 Open Univ BA90. Qu Coll Birm 05. **d** 08 **p** 09. NSM Quinton Road W St Boniface *Birm* from 08. *39 Richmond Road, Rubery, Rednal, Birmingham B45 9UN* Tel 0121-453 3035 E-mail janeplatt@onetel.com

PLATT, John Dendy. b 24. Magd Coll Cam BA49 MA55. Wells Th Coll 50. **d** 52 **p** 53. C Headley All SS *Guildf* 52-56; C Haslemere 56-58; R Skelton w Hutton-in-the-Forest *Carl* 59-71; rtd 89. *17 Primula Drive, Norwich NR4 7LZ* Tel (01603) 504272

PLATT, John Emerson. b 36. Pemb Coll Ox BA59 MA65 DPhil77 Hull Univ MTh72. Cuddesdon Coll 59. **d** 61 **p** 62. C Adlington *Blackb* 61-64; C Sutton St Mich *York* 64-68; C Ox St Giles 68-71; Asst Chapl Pemb Coll Ox 68-69; Chapl 69-02; rtd 02. *Apple Tree Cottage, 2 Church Road, Wilmcote, Stratford-upon-Avon CV37 9XD* Tel (01789) 770127

PLATT, Mrs Katherine Mary. b 29. Sheff Univ BA51 ARIBA51. Westcott Ho Cam 76. **dss** 79 **d** 87. Chesterton Gd Shep *Ely* 78-84; Whitton St Aug *Lon* 84-86; Dean of Women's Min 86-94; Hampton St Mary 86-94; Par Dn 87-94; rtd 94; Perm to Offic *Ches* 94-11. *Pine Cottage, Portloe, Truro TR2 5RB*

PLATT, Michael Robert. b 39. SS Coll Cam BA61 MA65 Nottm Univ PGCE62. Cuddesdon Coll 62. **d** 64. C Far Headingley St Chad *Ripon* 64-65; Asst Master Belmont Coll Barnstaple 65-68; Asst Master Qu Coll Taunton 68-00; Ho Master 72-83; Hd Geography 89-00; rtd 00. *8 Court Hill, Taunton TA1 4SX* Tel and fax (01823) 270687

PLATT, William David. b 31. St Chad's Coll Dur BA54. Coll of Resurr Mirfield 54. **d** 56 **p** 57. C Bethnal Green St Jo w St Simon *Lon* 56-60; C Pinner 60-65; V N Hammersmith St Kath 65-72; V Woodham *Guildf* 72-88; Chapl Community of St Mary V Wantage 88-96; rtd 96; NSM Blewbury, Hagbourne and Upton *Ox* 96-03. *14 Radley House, Marston Ferry Road, Oxford OX2 7EA* Tel (01865) 556019

PLATTEN, Aidan Stephen George. b 76. Ripon Coll Cuddesdon BTh03. **d** 03 **p** 04. C Woodbridge St Mary *St E* 03-06; Bp's Chapl *Glouc* 06-11; Hon Min Can Glouc Cathl 09-11; V St Marylebone St Mark Hamilton Terrace *Lon* from 11. *St Mark's Vicarage, Hamilton Terrace, London NW8 9UT* Tel (020) 7328 4373

PLATTEN, Gregory Austin David. b 78. Worc Coll Ox BA00 Ox Univ MTh05. Ripon Coll Cuddesdon 01. **d** 03 **p** 04. C St John's Wood *Lon* 03-07; Chapl Linc Coll Ox from 07; Hon C Ox St Mich w St Martin and All SS from 07. *14 Newton Road, Oxford OX1 4PT* E-mail gregoryplatten@ukonline.co.uk

✠**PLATTEN, The Rt Revd Stephen George.** b 47. Lon Univ BEd72 Trin Coll Ox BD03 UEA Hon DLitt03. Cuddesdon Coll 72. **d** 75 **p** 76 **c** 03. C Headington *Ox* 75-78; Chapl and Tutor Linc Th Coll 78-83; Can Res Portms Cathl and Dir of Ords 83-89; Abp's Sec for Ecum Affairs *Cant* 90-95; Hon Can Cant Cathl 90-95; Dean Nor 95-03; Bp Wakef from 03; Hon Can Musoma from 08. *Bishop's Lodge, Woodthorpe Lane, Wakefield WF2 6JL* Tel (01924) 255349 Fax 255202 E-mail bishop@bishopofwakefield.org.uk

PLATTIN, Miss Darleen Joy. b 63. Oak Hill Th Coll BA94. ERMC 04. **d** 07 **p** 08. C Barnham Broom and Upper Yare *Nor* 07-10; P-in-c Easton, Colton, Marlingford and Bawburgh from 10. *The Vicarage, 107 Dereham Road, Easton, Norwich NR9 5ES* E-mail darleenplattin@btinternet.com

PLATTS, Anthony Russell. b 41. Qu Coll Birm. **d** 08 **p** 09. NSM Hill *Birm* from 08. *Tree Tops, 200 Hill Village Road, Sutton Coldfield B75 5JN* Tel 0121-308 4478

PLATTS, Mrs Hilary Anne Norrie. b 60. K Coll Lon BD85 AKC85 SRN81. Ripon Coll Cuddesdon 86. **d** 88 **p** 94. C Moulsham St Jo *Chelmsf* 88-90; Chapl Reading Univ 90-99; C Calcot 90-92; NSM Reading Deanery 99-00; Perm to Offic *Birm* 00-07; Chapl Birm Specialist Community Health NHS Trust 01-07; Chapl N Warks NHS Trust 03-07; Perm to Offic *Chelmsf* from 07; Adv for Women's Min (Colchester Area) from 08; Chapl Colchester Hosp Univ NHS Foundn Trust from 09. *The Vicarage, Church Road, Elmstead, Colchester CO7 7AW* Tel (01206) 822431 E-mail hilaryplatts@googlemail.com

PLATTS, Timothy Caradoc. b 61. LMH Ox BA83 MA88 St Cross Coll Ox DPhil88. Ripon Coll Cuddesdon 87. **d** 89 **p** 90. C Whitley Ch Ch Ox 89-95; P-in-c Earley St Nic 95-98; V 98-00; V Four Oaks *Birm* 00-07; P-in-c Elmstead *Chelmsf* from 07; Chapl to Bp Colchester from 07. *The Vicarage, Church Road, Elmstead, Colchester CO7 7AW* Tel (01206) 822431 E-mail timatthevicarage@googlemail.com

PLAXTON, Canon Edmund John Swithun. b 36. AKC60. **d** 61 **p** 62. C Crofton Park St Hilda w St Cypr *S'wark* 61-65; C Coulsdon St Jo 65-69; V Forest Hill St Paul 69-80; V Belmont 80-93; V Lingfield and Crowhurst 93-01; Hon Can S'wark Cathl 97-01; rtd 01. *Tynymaes, Y Fron, Upper Llandwrog, Caernarfon LL54 7BW* Tel (01286) 880188 E-mail edmundrachel@aol.com

PLAYER, Leslie Mark. b 65. Ridley Hall Cam 92. **d** 95 **p** 96. C Belper *Derby* 95-98; C Hamworthy *Sarum* 98-03; R W Downland from 03. *The Rectory, 97 Mill End, Damerham, Fordingbridge SP6 3HU* Tel (01725) 518642

PLAYLE, Ms Merrin Laura. b 58. Univ of Wales (Swansea) BSc79. Ridley Hall Cam 99. **d** 01 **p** 02. C Haslemere and Grayswood *Guildf* 01-05; V E Ham St Paul *Chelmsf* from 05. *St Paul's Vicarage, 227 Burges Road, London E6 2EU* Tel (020) 8472 5531 E-mail merrin.playle@btopenworld.com

PLEDGER, Miss Alison Frances. b 56. Univ of Wales (Cardiff) BA79 K Alfred's Coll Win PGCE80. Linc Th Coll 89. **d** 91 **p** 94. Par Dn Soham *Ely* 91-94; C Ely 94-96; C Rusthall *Roch* 97-00; V Alkborough *Linc* from 00; P-in-c Flixborough w Burton upon Stather from 09. *The Vicarage, Back Street, Alkborough, Scunthorpe DN15 9JJ* Tel (01724) 721126

PLEDGER, Mrs Nicola. b 55. Lon Bible Coll BA94. SAOMC 99. **d** 01 **p** 02. C Ware Ch Ch *St Alb* 01-05; Perm to Offic from 05. *132 Quickley Lane, Chorleywood, Rickmansworth WD3 5PQ* Tel (01923) 283220 *or* 447111 E-mail nicky@thepledgers.co.uk

PLESSIS, John Kenneth. b 69. Univ of Wales (Cardiff) BSc91 BA05 Univ of Wales (Swansea) PhD03 PGCE92. St Mich Coll Llan 03. **d** 05 **p** 06. C Haverfordwest St Mary and St Thos w Haroldston *St D* 05-08; C Abergavenny St Mary w Llanwenarth Citra *Mon* 08-10. *4 Holywell Close, Abergavenny NP7 5LN* Tel (01873) 850128 Mobile 07868-750228

PLIMLEY, Canon William. b 17. St Aid Birkenhead 50. **d** 52 **p** 53. C Norbury *Ches* 52-55; V Laisterdyke *Bradf* 55-83; RD Calverley 65-78; Hon Can Bradf Cathl 67-83; rtd 83; Perm to Offic Bradf from 83. *465 Bradford Road, Pudsey LS28 8ED* Tel (01274) 664862

PLIMMER, Wayne Robert. b 64. St Chad's Coll Dur BA85 Leeds Univ MA07. St Steph Ho Ox 86. **d** 88 **p** 89. C Cockerton *Dur* 88-91; C Poulton-le-Fylde *Blackb* 91-93; V Darton *Wakef* 93-06; P-in-c Cawthorne 04-06; V Beeston *S'well* from 06. *The Vicarage, Middle Street, Beeston, Nottingham NG9 1GA* Tel 0115-925 4571 E-mail wplimmer@tiscali.co.uk

PLOWMAN, Richard Robert Bindon. b 38. Solicitor 61. Ridley Hall Cam 76. **d** 78 **p** 79. C Combe Down w Monkton Combe *B & W* 78-81; C Combe Down w Monkton Combe and S Stoke 81-83; V Coxley w Godney, Henton and Wookey 83-03; RD Shepton Mallet 95-01; rtd 03; Perm to Offic *B & W* from 04. *Hyland House, Lower Rudge, Frome BA11 2QE* Tel (01373) 831316

PLOWS, Jonathan. b 57. Warwick Univ BA79 Homerton Coll Cam PGCE80 Birkbeck Coll Lon MSc85. STETS BA07. **d** 07 **p** 08. NSM Salisbury St Thos and St Edm *Sarum* from 07. *171 Castle Road, Salisbury SP1 3RX* Tel (01722) 331647 Fax 410941 E-mail jonplows@aol.com

PLUCK, Richard. b 60. Southn Univ BTh90. Aston Tr Scheme 84 Sarum & Wells Th Coll 86. **d** 90 **p** 91. C Harpenden St Nic *St Alb* 90-94; CF from 94. *c/o MOD Chaplains (Army)* Tel (01264) 381140 Fax 381824

PLUMB, Gordon Alan. b 42. Leeds Univ BA. Sarum & Wells Th Coll. **d** 82 **p** 83. C Biggleswade *St Alb* 82-86; TV Grantham *Linc* 86-95; P-in-c Saxby All Saints 95-97; R 97-07; P-in-c Bonby 95-97; V 97-07; P-in-c Horkstow 95-97; V 97-07; P-in-c S Ferriby 95-97; R 97-07; P-in-c Worlaby 95-97; V 97-07; rtd 07. *Ingham House, 45A Dam Road, Barton-upon-Humber DN18 5BT* Tel (01652) 636445 E-mail gplumb2000@aol.com

PLUMB, Miss Valerie Isabelle Dawn Frances. b 69. Ripon Coll Cuddesdon BTh02. **d** 01 **p** 02. C Newport St Andr *Mon* 01-03; C Monmouth w Overmonnow etc 03-06; TV By Brook and Colerne w N Wraxall *Bris* 06-09; R Quantock Towers *B & W* from 09. *The Rectory, Yellow Road, Stogumber, Taunton TA4 3TL* Tel (01984) 656585 E-mail revd_val@yahoo.co.uk

PLUMLEY, Paul Jonathan. b 42. St Jo Coll Nottm 71. **d** 74 **p** 75. C Mile Cross *Nor* 74-77; P-in-c Wickham Skeith *St E* 77-79; P-in-c Stoke Ash, Thwaite and Wetheringsett 77-79; Assoc Min Woodbridge St Jo 80-81; Chapl RAF 81-86; Perm to Offic *Roch* 86-95; R Hever, Four Elms and Mark Beech 95-00; Sen Chapl Maidstone and Tunbridge Wells NHS Trust 00-07; rtd 07; Perm to Offic *Roch* from 08. *4 Cedar Ridge, Tunbridge Wells TN2 3NX* Tel (01892) 514499 Mobile 07925-615601 E-mail pauljplumley@gmail.com

PLUMMER, Miss Anne Frances. b 36. Bedf Coll Lon BA57. S'wark Ord Course 79. dss 82 **d** 87 **p** 94. NSM Salfords *S'wark* 82-06; Dean MSE (Croydon) 97-02; Perm to Offic 06-07. *50 Park View Road, Salfords, Redhill RH1 5DN* Tel (01293) 785852

PLUMMER, Mrs Deborah Ann. b 49. St Hugh's Coll Ox BA71 MA75. St Alb Minl Tr Scheme 82. dss 85 **d** 87 **p** 94. Ickenham *Lon* 85-88; Par Dn 87-88; C Northolt St Mary 88-92; Chapl Lee Abbey 92-95; P-in-c Kintbury w Avington *Ox* 95-01; Lect Bolton St Pet *Man* 01-07; P-in-c Prestwich St Marg from 07; C Prestwich St Mary from 10; C Prestwich St Gabr from 10; AD Radcliffe and Prestwich from 09. *St Margaret's Vicarage, 2 St Margaret's Road, Prestwich, Manchester M25 2QB* Tel 0161-773 2698 Mobile 07939-916315 E-mail prestwichplummers@btinternet.com

PLUMMER, Miss June Alice. b 29. Bris Univ BA50 CertEd51. Sarum & Wells Th Coll 89. **d** 89 **p** 94. NSM Hanham *Bris* 89-97; rtd 97; Perm to Offic *Bris* from 97. *11 Glenwood Drive, Oldland Common, Bristol BS30 9RZ* Tel 0117-949 8667

PLUMMER, Lee Richard. b 77. Liv Univ BA98 Birm Univ PGCE00. St Jo Coll Nottm LTh10. **d** 10. C Newchapel *Lich* from 10. *21 Powderham Close, Stoke-on-Trent ST6 6XN* Tel 07590-606425 (mobile) E-mail lee@leeandbeckyplummer.co.uk

PLUMPTON, Paul. b 50. Keble Coll Ox BA72 MA76. St Steph Ho Ox 72. **d** 74 **p** 75. C Tonge Moor *Man* 74-76; C Atherton

76-79; V Oldham St Jas 79-99; V Oldham St Jas w St Ambrose from 99. *The Vicarage, Yates Street, Oldham OL1 4AR* Tel 0161-633 4441

PLUNKETT, Michael Edward. b 38. MBE04. Leeds Univ BSc61. Ely Th Coll 61. **d** 63 **p** 64. C Kirkby *Liv* 63-68; Lect Stockton-on-Tees 68-72; Lic to Offic *Dur* 72-73; TV Stockton 73-75; V Cantril Farm *Liv* 75-81; Soc Resp Officer 81-89; V Melling 81-91; TR Speke St Aid 91-04; rtd 04; Perm to Offic *Heref* from 04. *1 The Ridge, Bishops Castle SY9 5AB* Tel (01588) 630018

PLUNKETT, Canon Peter William. b 30. Oak Hill Th Coll. **d** 61 **p** 62. C Fazakerley *Em Liv* 61-64; C St Helens St Mark 64-68; V Kirkdale St Paul N Shore 68-79; P-in-c Bootle St Mary w St Jo 77-79; V Bootle St Mary w St Paul 79-81; V Goose Green 81-89; V W Derby St Jas 89-98; Hon Can Liv Cathl 97-98; rtd 98. *50 Trinity Crescent, West Shore, Llandudno LL30 2PQ* Tel (01492) 872109

PLYMING, Philip James John. b 74. Rob Coll Cam BA96 St Jo Coll Dur BA00 Edin Univ PhD08. Cranmer Hall Dur 98. **d** 01 **p** 02. C Chineham *Win* 01-06; V Claygate *Guildf* from 06. *The Vicarage, Church Road, Claygate, Esher KT10 0JP* Tel (01372) 463603 E-mail philipplyming@holytrinityclaygate.org.uk

PLYMOUTH, Archdeacon of. See CHANDLER, The Ven Ian Nigel

PLYMOUTH, Suffragan Bishop of. See FORD, The Rt Revd John Frank

PNEMATICATOS, Nicholas Peter Anthony. b 59. N Lon Univ BA92 Lon Univ MA93. Ripon Coll Cuddesdon 93. **d** 95 **p** 96. C Yeovil St Mich *B & W* 95-98; Chapl Yeovil Coll 95-96; Chapl RN 98-02; Chapl RAF 02-08; P-in-c Mill End and Heronsgate w W Hyde *St Alb* 08-10. *5 St Joseph's House, 42 Brook Green, London W6 7BW* Tel 07703-566787 (mobile) E-mail delvillewood@aol.com

POARCH, Canon John Chilton. b 30. Bris Univ BA54. Ridley Hall Cam 54. **d** 56 **p** 57. C Swindon Ch Ch *Bris* 56-59; C Corsham 59-61; R Praslin Seychelles 61-63; V Brislington St Cuth 63-69; Adn Seychelles and R St Paul's Cathl Mahé 69-72; V Warmley 72-86; R Syston 72-86; RD Bitton 79-85; P-in-c Bitton 80-86; Hon Can Bris Cathl 82-95; P-in-c Langley Fitzurse 86-94; Dioc Dir of Ords 86-94; Dir Ord Tr 94-95; P-in-c Draycot Cerne 87-94; rtd 95; Perm to Offic *Bris* from 95 and *B & W* 98-01; Officer for the Welfare of Rtd Mins Bris Adnry from 01; Dioc Convenor Rtd Clergy Assn from 01. *16 Norley Road, Bristol BS7 0HP* Tel 0117-951 7970

POCOCK, Mrs Gillian Margaret. b 35. Nottm Univ BA57. Cranmer Hall Dur 82. dss 83 **d** 87 **p** 94. Bearpark *Dur* 83-88; Hon Par Dn 87-88; Par Dn S Hetton w Haswell 88; Asst RD Dur 89-90; Chapl St Aid Coll Dur 89-93; Par Dn Esh *Dur* 90-92; P-in-c 92-99; P-in-c Hamsteels 97-99; P-in-c Langley Park 98-99; rtd 99. *11 Cooke's Wood, Broom Park, Durham DH7 7RL* Tel 0191-386 1140 E-mail gillian.pocock@lineone.net

POCOCK, Lynn Elizabeth. b 48. Coll of Wooster Ohio BA69 CertEd71. Qu Coll Birm 73. dss 82 **d** 87 **p** 94. Gleadless *Sheff* 82-85; Thorpe Hesley 85-92; Par Dn 87-92; NSM Ribbesford w Bewdley and Dowles *Worc* 92-03; Perm to Offic from 03. *2 Waterworks Road, Worcester WR1 3EX* Tel (01905) 612634

POCOCK, Canon Nigel John. b 47. Lon Univ BSc68 Birm Univ MA83 Lambeth STh78. Oak Hill Th Coll 69. **d** 72 **p** 73. C Tunbridge Wells St Jas *Roch* 72-75; C Heatherlands St Jo *Sarum* 75-78; V Leic St Chris 78-83; R Camborne *Truro* 83-97; RD Carnmarth N 91-96; Hon Can Truro Cathl 92-97; V Old Windsor *Ox* 97-09; rtd 09. *23 Culm Valley Way, Uffculme, Cullompton EX15 3XZ* Tel (01884) 849198 E-mail njpoc@tiscali.co.uk

PODGER, Richard Philip Champeney. b 38. K Coll Cam BA61 MA66. Cuddesdon Coll 62. **d** 64 **p** 65. C Doncaster St Geo *Sheff* 64-68; C Orpington All SS *Roch* 68-74; W Germany 76-88; Chapl Kassel *Eur* 83-88; TV Whitstable *Cant* 88-94; Perm to Offic from 95; Chapl E Kent NHS and Soc Care Partnership Trust 02-06; Chapl Kent & Medway NHS and Soc Care Partnership Trust 06-10. *3 Alcroft Grange, Tyler Hill, Canterbury CT2 9NN* Tel and fax (01227) 462038 *or* tel (01233) 616082 E-mail podger@centrespace.freeserve.co.uk

POGMORE, Canon Edward Clement. b 52. Sarum & Wells Th Coll 76. **d** 79 **p** 80. C Calne and Blackland *Sarum* 79-82; TV Oakdale 82-89; Min Creekmoor LEP 82-89; Chapl Geo Eliot Hosp Nuneaton 89-94; Chapl Nuneaton Hosps 89-94; Chapl Geo Eliot Hosp NHS Trust Nuneaton from 94; Chapl Co-ord for N Warks from 94; Perm to Offic *Leic* from 91; Hon Can Cov Cathl from 00. *The Chaplaincy, George Eliot Hospital, College Street, Nuneaton CV10 7DJ* Tel (024) 7686 5046, 7686 5281 *or* 7635 1351 ext 3528 E-mail edpog@hotmail.com *or* edward.pogmore@geh-tr.wmids.nhs.uk

✠**POGO, The Most Revd Sir Ellison Leslie.** b 47. KBE01. Bp Patteson Th Coll (Solomon Is) St Jo Coll Auckland LTh79. **d** 79 **p** 80 **c** 81. Asst P Anderson's Bay New Zealand 79-81; Bp Ysabel Solomon Is from 81; Abp Melanesia and Bp Cen Melanesia 94-08; rtd 08. *Address temp unknown* E-mail epogo@comphq.org.sb

POINTS, John David. b 43. Qu Coll Birm 78. **d** 80 **p** 81. C Wednesbury St Paul Wood Green *Lich* 80-85; V 93-01; V Sedgley St Mary 85-93; TR Wednesfield 01-08; AD Wolverhampton 03-08; rtd 08. *13 Oldcastle Avenue, Guilsfield, Welshpool SY21 9PA* Tel (01938) 552092

POLASHEK, Miss Stella Christine. b 44. Leic Poly MA85. EMMTC 92. **d** 95 **p** 96. NSM Appleby Gp *Leic* 95-08; NSM Woodfield 08-10; Chapl Leic Gen Hosp NHS Trust 99-00; Chapl Univ Hosps Leic NHS Trust 00-10; rtd 10. *38 Mawbys Lane, Appleby Magna, Swadlincote DE12 7AA* Tel (01530) 272707 E-mail polashek@applebymagna.freeserve.co.uk

POLE, David John. b 46. Bath Academy of Art BA72. Trin Coll Bris 84. **d** 86 **p** 87. C Bris St Mary Redcliffe w Temple etc 86-90; V Alveston 90-98; V Alveston and Littleton-on-Severn w Elberton from 98. *The Vicarage, Gloucester Road, Alveston, Bristol BS35 3QT* Tel and fax (01454) 414810 E-mail david.pole@dial.pipex.com

POLE, Francis John Michael. b 42. FRSA64 MInstTA00 CQSW74 MCM199. St Jo Sem Wonersh 62. **d** 67 **p** 68. In RC Ch 67-75; NSM Walthamstow St Pet *Chelmsf* 75; NSM Penge Lane H Trin *Roch* 76-77; NSM Shirley St Jo *Cant* 77-79; Assoc Chapl The Hague *Eur* 79-83; V Norbury St Steph and Thornton Heath *Cant* 83-84; S'wark 85-00; Sen Dioc Police Chapl 95-00; Sen Chapl Sussex Police 00-03; Nat Co-ord Police Chapl 00-04; Sen Chapl Sussex Ambulance Service 04-06; Co-ord Chapl SE Coast Ambulance Service from 06; TV Crawley *Chich* from 00; Chapl to People at Work from 00. *35 Turnpike Place, Crawley RH11 7UA* Tel (01293) 513264 Mobile 07764-752608 E-mail francis.pole@virgin.net

POLIHILL, Mrs Christine. b 46. Nottm Coll of Educn CertEd67 Qu Coll Birm BA00. St Alb Minl Tr Scheme 81. **dss** 84 **d** 87 **p** 94. St Alb St Mary Marshalswick *St Alb* 84-94; Hon Par Dn 87-94; C Cottered w Broadfield and Throcking 94-96; P-in-c 96-99; C Ardeley 94-96; P-in-c 96-99; C Weston 94-96; Perm to Offic *Lich* 99-00; C Lich St Mich w St Mary and Wall 00-06; rtd 06; Lic to Offic *Lich* from 06. *Little Hayes, Beaudesert Park, Cannock Wood, Rugeley WS15 4JJ* Tel (01543) 674474 E-mail christine@reflectiongardens.org.uk

POLITT, Robert William. b 47. ARCM LGSM68. Oak Hill Th Coll 73. **d** 76 **p** 77. C Bexleyheath St Pet *Roch* 76-82; TV Southgate *Chich* 82-90; Chapl N Foreland Lodge Sch Basingstoke 90-98; R Sherfield-on-Loddon and Stratfield Saye etc *Win* from 98; P-in-c Bramley from 10. *The Rectory, 33 Northfield Road, Sherfield-on-Loddon, Hook RG27 0DR* Tel (01256) 882209 E-mail 113225.103@compuserve.com

POLKINGHORNE, Canon John Charlton. b 30. KBE97. Trin Coll Cam BA52 PhD55 MA56 ScD74 FRS74. Westcott Ho Cam 79. **d** 81 **p** 82. NSM Chesterton St Andr *Ely* 81-82; C Bedminster St Mich *Bris* 82-84; V Blean *Cant* 84-86; Dean Trin Hall Cam 86-89; Pres Qu Coll Cam 89-96; Can Th Liv Cathl from 94; rtd 95; Six Preacher Cant Cathl from 96; Perm to Offic *Ely* from 96. *74 Hurst Park Avenue, Cambridge CB4 2AF* Tel (01223) 360743

POLL, Martin George. b 61. Kent Univ BA83. Ripon Coll Cuddesdon 84. **d** 87 **p** 88. C Mill Hill Jo Keble Ch *Lon* 87-90; Chapl RN from 90. *Royal Naval Chaplaincy Service, Mail Point 1-2, Leach Building, Whale Island, Portsmouth PO2 8BY* Tel (023) 9262 5055 Fax 9262 5134 E-mail martin.poll791@mod.uk

POLLARD, Adrian. *See* POLLARD, James Adrian Hunter

POLLARD, Mrs Ann Beatrice. b 46. **d** 03 **p** 04. NSM Mirfield *Wakef* 03-10; NSM Dewsbury from 10. *9 Manor Drive, Mirfield WF14 0ER* Tel (01924) 495322 Mobile 07751-630609 E-mail ann.pollard@o2.co.uk

POLLARD, Mrs Christine Beryl. b 45. NOC 86. **d** 89 **p** 94. Par Dn Ingrow w Hainworth *Bradf* 89-94; C Nuneaton St Nic *Cov* 94-98; P-in-c Bourton w Frankton and Stretton on Dunsmore etc 98-07; C Leam Valley 06-07; rtd 07. *9 Overberry Orchard, Leamington Spa CV33 9SJ* Tel (01926) 832053

POLLARD, Canon Clifford Francis. b 20. AKC49. **d** 50 **p** 51. C Leominster *Heref* 50-53; C Luton St Mary *St Alb* 53-56; V Stopsley 56-60; Chapl Toc H (Kent and Sussex) 60-64; R Mersham *Cant* 64-68; Asst Dir of Educn 68-69; Dir of Educn 69-87; Hon Can Cant Cathl 72-91; rtd 87; Perm to Offic *Cant* from 03. *11 Mulberry Court, Stour Street, Canterbury CT1 2NT* Tel (01227) 761674

POLLARD, David. b 55. LSE BSc77. Trin Coll Bris 78. **d** 80 **p** 81. Canada 81-84; C-in-c Hillsfield and Monkspath LEP *Birm* 85-89; BCMS 89-93; Crosslinks 93-95; Spain 89-94; V Doncaster St Jas *Sheff* 95-98; rtd 98. *6 Mulberry Way, Armthorpe, Doncaster DN3 3UE* Tel (01302) 833404

POLLARD, David John Athey. b 44. ACP74 Culham Coll Ox CertEd69. St Jo Coll Nottm LTh88. **d** 88 **p** 89. C Illogan *Truro* 88-91; R Roche and Withiel 91-95; TV Maidstone St Martin *Cant* 95-97; C Parkwood CD 95-97; R Lanreath *Truro* 97-99; V Pelynt 97-99; R Lanreath, Pelynt and Bradoc 99-03; rtd 03. *Melyn Brea, 11 Mill Hill, Lostwithiel PL22 0HB* Tel (01208) 871541 E-mail david.pollard@totalise.co.uk

POLLARD, Eric John. b 43. Chich Th Coll 83. **d** 85 **p** 86. C Brighton St Matthias *Chich* 85-90; C E Grinstead St Swithun 90-96; C Hove 96-00; P-in-c Brighton St Matthias from 00. *St Matthias's Vicarage, 45 Hollingbury Park Avenue, Brighton BN1 7JQ* Tel and fax (01273) 508178 E-mail eric.pollard@btinternet.com

POLLARD, James Adrian Hunter. b 48. St Jo Coll Nottm BTh78. **d** 78 **p** 79. C Much Woolton *Liv* 78-81; CMS 81-84; V Toxteth Park Ch Ch *Liv* 85-90; CF 90-09; rtd 09; Perm to Offic *Sarum* from 09. *Horwood House, 80 Boreham Road, Warminster BA12 9JW*

POLLARD, John Edward Ralph. b 40. ALCD68. **d** 67 **p** 68. C Ollerton *S'well* 67-71; C Walton H Trin *Ox* 71-74; P-in-c Cuddington w Dinton 74-77; V Haddenham 74-77; V Kingsey 75-77; V Haddenham w Cuddington and Kingsey 77-85; RD Aylesbury 80-85; V Haddenham w Cuddington, Kingsey etc 85-87; V Furze Platt 87-96; rtd 97. *Waldren Close, Poole BH15 1XS* Tel (01202) 681494

POLLARD, Mrs Judith Mary. b 56. Westcott Ho Cam 09. **d** 11. C Newark w Coddington *S'well* from 11. *St Leonard's Vicarage, Lincoln Road, Newark NG24 2DQ* Tel 07852-257734 (mobile) E-mail wotzpollard@aol.com

POLLARD, Matthew Rupert. b 66. St Jo Coll Nottm. **d** 03 **p** 04. C Huddersfield St Pet *Wakef* 03-07; Asst Chapl Huddersfield Univ 03-07; P-in-c Rastrick St Matt 07-08; P-in-c Rastrick St Jo 07-08; V Rastrick from 08. *St Matthew's Vicarage, 1 Vicarage Gardens, Ogden Lane, Brighouse HD6 3HD* Tel (01484) 713386 E-mail matthewpollard@btinternet.com

POLLARD, Mrs Patricia Julie. b 46. Open Univ BA97. Cant Sch of Min 93. **d** 96 **p** 97. NSM Eastling w Ospringe and Stalisfield w Otterden *Cant* 96-04; rtd 04; Perm to Offic *Cant* from 04. *65 Princes Gardens, Margate CT9 3AS* Tel (01843) 280814 E-mail norman.pollard@tesco.net

POLLARD, Roger Frederick. b 32. Sheff Univ BSc52 K Coll Lon PGCE55 Lanc Univ MA78. Linc Th Coll 56. **d** 58 **p** 59. C Catford St Laur *S'wark* 58-63; Ghana 63-66; C Fulford *York* 66-67; C Camberwell St Geo *S'wark* 67; Asst Master Roch Valley Sch Milnrow 68-69; S Craven Sch Cross Hills 69-91; rtd 91; Perm to Offic *Bradf* 69-93 and *B & W* 93-06. *Little Garth, Rectory Lane, Dowlish Wake, Ilminster TA19 0NX* Tel (01460) 52594

POLLARD, Samuel David. b 84. Nottm Univ BA06 MA08. Trin Coll Bris MPhil11. **d** 11. C Loughton St Mary *Chelmsf* from 11. *49 The Drive, Loughton IG10 1HG* Tel (020) 8502 4680 E-mail samuel.d.pollard@gmail.com

POLLARD, Stephen. b 59. Coll of Resurr Mirfield 96. **d** 98 **p** 99. C Lt Lever *Man* 98-02; P-in-c Westleigh St Pet 02-10; P-in-c Westleigh St Paul 08-10; P-in-c Rosebud w McCrae Australia from 10. *120 Fifth Avenue, Rosebud, Victoria 3939, Australia* E-mail fatherstephenpollard@googlemail.com

POLLARD (née RAMSBOTTOM), Mrs Susan Elizabeth. b 56. Trin Coll Bris BD79. Qu Coll Birm 06. **d** 09 **p** 10. NSM Warndon St Nic *Worc* from 09. *5 Falmouth, Worcester WR4 0TE* Tel (01905) 759214 E-mail suepollard2610@hotmail.com

POLLARD, Vaughan. b 59. Aston Tr Scheme 88 Trin Coll Bris 90. **d** 92 **p** 93. C Nailsea H Trin *B & W* 92-95; C Acomb St Steph *York* 95-97; P-in-c Moldgreen *Wakef* 97-99; P-in-c Rawthorpe 97-99; V Moldgreen and Rawthorpe 99-07; C Spalding St Paul *Linc* from 07. *C* Spalding from 07. *18 Maple Grove, Spalding PE11 2LE* Tel (01775) 725637 E-mail pollard247@ntlworld.com

POLLINGER (née WHITFORD), Canon Judith. b 41. Ex Univ TCert78 BEd79. SWMTC 92. **d** 95 **p** 96. NSM St Endellion w Port Isaac and St Kew *Truro* from 95; NSM St Minver from 07; Convenor Bp's Gp for Min of Healing from 04; Hon Can Truro Cathl from 10. *4 Marshalls Way, Trelights, Port Isaac PL29 3TE* Tel (01208) 880181 E-mail rev.judith@btinternet.com

POLLINGTON, Miss Ann Elizabeth Jane. b 56. Univ Coll Chich BA00. Ripon Coll Cuddesdon 00. **d** 02 **p** 03. C Honiton, Gittisham, Combe Raleigh, Monkton etc *Ex* 02-07; P-in-c St Ippolyts *St Alb* 07-10; P-in-c Gt and Lt Wymondley 07-10; R St Ippolyts w Gt and Lt Wymondley from 10. *The Vicarage, Stevenage Road, St Ippolyts, Hitchin SG4 7PE* Tel (01462) 457552 E-mail annpolly@freeuk.com

POLLIT, Preb Michael. b 30. Worc Coll Ox BA54 MA58. Wells Th Coll 54. **d** 56 **p** 57. C Cannock *Lich* 56-59; C Codsall 59-62; V W Bromwich St Pet 62-67; R Norton in the Moors 67-76; RD Leek 72-76; V Shrewsbury St Chad 76-87; V Shrewsbury St Chad w St Mary 87-95; Preb Lich Cathl 81-95; P-in-c Shrewsbury St Alkmund 91-95; rtd 95; Perm to Offic *Heref* from 96. *Prenthreyling House, Churchstoke, Montgomery SY15 6HU* Tel (01588) 620273

POLLIT, Ruth Mary. *See* LILLINGTON, Mrs Ruth Mary

POLLITT, Graham Anthony. b 48. BA79. Oak Hill Th Coll 76. **d** 79 **p** 80. C Rusholme H Trin *Man* 79-82; TV Southgate *Chich* 82-83; C Burgess Hill St Andr 83-86; Chapl St Martin's Coll of Educn *Blackb* 86-90; Chapl Cheltenham and Glouc Coll of HE 90-98; Perm to Offic *Glouc* 98-99; C Bispham *Blackb* 99-04; P-in-c Caton w Littledale from 04. *The Vicarage, 153 Brookhouse Road, Brookhouse, Lancaster LA2 9NX* Tel (01524) 770300

POLLOCK, Christopher John. b 62. TCD BTh89 QUB BD. CITC 86. **d** 89 **p** 90. C Agherton *Conn* 89-91; C Ballymoney w Finvoy and Rasharkin 91-93; I Derryvolgie 93-03; I Saintfield *D & D* from 03. *The Vicarage, 11 Lisburn Road, Saintfield, Ballynahinch BT24 7AL* Tel (028) 9751 0286 E-mail chriswanda@talk21.com

POLLOCK, Duncan James Morrison. b 54. MBE95 QGM75. Nottm Univ BCombStuds83. Linc Th Coll 80. **d** 83 **p** 84. C Folkestone St Mary and St Eanswythe *Cant* 83-85; CF 85-98; R Broughton, Bossington, Houghton and Mottisfont *Win* 98-00; I Groomsport *D & D* from 00. *22 Sandringham Drive, Bangor BT20 5NA* Tel (028) 9146 4476 E-mail duncanjmpollock@btinternet.com

POLLOCK, James Colin Graeme. b 53. St Chad's Coll Dur BA76. Ripon Coll Cuddesdon 77. **d** 78 **p** 79. C Hartlepool St Oswald *Dur* 78-81; C Hartlepool St Aid 81-84; V Dawdon 84-05; V Seaham Harbour 03-05; TV S Shields All SS from 05. *The Vicarage, St Oswin's Street, South Shields NE33 4SE* Tel 0191-455 3072

POLLOCK, John Charles. b 23. Trin Coll Cam BA46 MA48 Samford Univ (USA) Hon DLitt02. Ridley Hall Cam 49. **d** 51 **p** 52. C Portman Square St Paul *Lon* 51-53; Ed *The Churchman* 53-58; R Horsington *B & W* 53-58; Perm to Offic *Ex* 61-98 and from 00; rtd 88. *8 Deans Park, South Molton EX36 3DY* Tel (01769) 572104

POLOMSKI, Elias Robert Michael. b 42. **d** 85 **p** 86. In RC Ch 85-90; C Headington Quarry *Ox* 91-94; Chapl St Alb Abbey 94-97; Chapl St Alb Sch 94-97; P-in-c Streatley w Moulsford *Ox* 97-03; C 03-04; P-in-c Streatley 04-07; rtd 07. *The Hermitage, 1 Bremilham Road, Malmesbury SN16 0DQ* Tel (01666) 825607

POMERY, David John. b 45. SS Mark & Jo Coll Chelsea CertEd67. Chich Th Coll 75. **d** 77 **p** 78. C Coseley Ch Ch *Lich* 77-79; C Stocksbridge *Sheff* 79-81; V Bentley 81-87; Asst Master Radlett Prep Sch 87-03; P-in-c Barton Bendish w Beachamwell and Shingham *Ely* 03-09; P-in-c Fincham 03-09; P-in-c Marham 03-09; P-in-c Shouldham 03-09; P-in-c Shouldham Thorpe 03-09; V Edstaston, Fauls, Prees, Tilstock and Whixall *Lich* from 09. *The Vicarage, Church Street, Prees, Whitchurch SY13 2EE* Tel (01948) 840243 E-mail rev-djpomery@supanet.com

POMFRET, Albert. b 23. Univ of Wales (Cardiff) BSc57 MTh95 Lon Univ MA69 FCP83 Potchefstroom Univ PhD02. Oak Hill NSM Course 72. **d** 75 **p** 76. NSM Dartford Ch Ch *Roch* 75-80; Perm to Offic 80-92; Perm to Offic *Ex* 92-08. *8 Wilshere Court, 43 Queen Street, Hitchin SG4 9TF* Tel (01462) 420821

POND, Canon Geraldine Phyllis. b 53. SRN74 HVCert75. St Jo Coll Nottm MA97. **d** 97 **p** 98. C Ancaster Wilsford Gp *Linc* 97-01; P-in-c Harlaxton Gp 01-07; Chapl Linc Distr Healthcare NHS Trust 01-07; P-in-c Ashbourne w Mapleton *Derby* from 07; P-in-c Clifton from 09; P-in-c Norbury w Snelston from 09; Asst Dir of Ords 08-09; Dioc Dir of Ords from 09; Hon Can Derby Cathl from 10. *The Vicarage, 61 Belle Vue Road, Ashbourne DE6 1AT* Tel (01335) 343129 E-mail geraldine@geraldinepond.com

POND, Nigel Peter Hamilton. b 40. AKC65. **d** 66 **p** 67. C E Dereham w Hoe *Nor* 66-69; C Chapl RN 69-85; TR Woughton *Ox* 85-93; Chapl Milton Keynes Gen Hosp 85-93; RD Milton Keynes *Ox* 90-93; R Olney w Emberton 93-97; R Olney 97-03; rtd 03. *11 Gippingstone Road, Bramford, Ipswich IP8 4DR* Tel (01473) 741887 E-mail nigel@npond.freeserve.co.uk

PONSONBY, Simon Charles Reuben. b 66. Bris Univ MLitt96. Trin Coll Bris BA94. **d** 95 **p** 96. C Thorpe Edge *Bradf* 95-98; Pastorate Chapl Ox St Aldate from 98. *St Aldate's Parish Centre, 40 Pembroke Street, Oxford OX1 1BP* Tel (01865) 254800 Fax 201543 E-mail simon.ponsonby@staldates.org.uk

PONT, Gordon John Harper. b 35. Glas Univ BSc56 BD65. Edin Th Coll 56. **d** 59 **p** 60. C Dunfermline *St And* 59-62; C Motherwell *Glas* 62-65; R Largs 65-68; Dioc Supernumerary *Bre* 68-71; Chapl Dundee Univ 68-73; R Dundee St Luke 71-74; NSM Dundee St Paul and Hon Chapl St Paul's Cathl Dundee 74-99; Dioc Sec 96-02; rtd 02. *Dalhousie, 11 West Moulin Road, Pitlochry PH16 5EA* Tel (01796) 472745 E-mail gordon.pont1@tesco.net

PONTEFRACT, Archdeacon of. See TOWNLEY, The Ven Peter Kenneth

PONTEFRACT, Suffragan Bishop of. See ROBINSON, The Rt Revd Anthony William

PONTER, John Arthur. b 37. Univ of Wales (Abth) BA61 Linacre Coll Ox BA63 MA68 UEA PhD81. Wycliffe Hall Ox 61. **d** 63 **p** 64. C Gidea Park *Chelmsf* 63-67; C-in-c Colchester St Anne CD 67-69; V Colchester St Anne 69-72; Chapl UEA *Nor* 72-78; Chapl Chelmsf Cathl 78-79; Chapl Chelmsf Cathl Cen 78-84; V Moulsham St Jo 79-85; Dir Man Chr Inst and Chr Leadership Course 85-92; Educn Officer N Federation for Tr in Min 85-92; TR Stantonbury and Willen *Ox* 92-02; rtd 02. *3 The Croft, 43A East Street, Wareham BH20 4NW* Tel (01929) 558286 E-mail ponter@msn.com

PONTIN, Colin Henry. b 37. Trin Coll Bris. **d** 83 **p** 84. C Downend *Bris* 83-86; C Riverside *Ox* 86-88; V Eton w Eton Wick and Boveney 88-90; TV Riverside 91-95; V Churt *Guildf*

95-02; rtd 02; Perm to Offic *Win* from 03. *22 Shearsbrook Close, Bransgore, Christchurch BH23 8HF* Tel (01425) 673918 Mobile 07989-173259 E-mail colinpontin@lineone.net

POOBALAN, Canon Isaac Munuswamy. b 62. RGN84 Edin Univ BD94 MTh97 Aber Univ MPhil98. Edin Th Coll 91. **d** 94 **p** 95. C Edin St Pet 94-97; P-in-c Aberdeen St Clem 97-01; R Aberdeen St Jo from 01; P-in-c Aberdeen St Pet from 04; Can St Andr Cathl from 06. *The Rectory, 15 Ashley Road, Aberdeen AB10 6RU* Tel (01224) 591527 E-mail aipoobalan@btinternet.com *or* rector@st-johns-aberdeen.org

POODHUN, Canon Lambert David. b 30. Natal Univ BA53. Edin Th Coll 54. **d** 56 **p** 57. C Durban St Aidan 56-60; P-in-c Pietermaritzburg St Paul 60-64; R 64-67; R Overport 67-74; Adn Durban 75-76; C Upton cum Chalvey *Ox* 77-80; Chapl Kingston Hosp Surrey 80-81; Chapl Tooting Bec Hosp Lon 81-84; Chapl Hurstwood Park Hosp Haywards Heath 84-01; Chapl St Fran Hosp Haywards Heath 84-94; Chapl Mid Sussex NHS Trust 94-01; Can and Preb Chich Cathl from 93; Hon C Haywards Heath St Rich from 01. *8 Nursery Close, Haywards Heath RH16 1HP* Tel (01444) 440938 E-mail lambertpoodhun@aol.com

POOLE, Andrew John. b 52. EMMTC 98. **d** 01 **p** 02. NSM Scraptoft *Leic* from 01. *64 Scalborough Close, Countesthorpe, Leicester LE8 5XH* Tel 0116-277 4949 E-mail andrew@aptrainingonline.co.uk

POOLE, Clifford George. b 36. Keble Coll Ox BA61 MA65 Lon Univ PGCE75. S'wark Ord Course 83. **d** 86 **p** 87. C W Dulwich All SS and Em *S'wark* 86-90; Chapl Luxembourg *Eur* 90-02; rtd 02; P-in-c Alderton, Gt Washbourne, Dumbleton etc *Glouc* 02-05; TV Winchcombe 05-08. *11 Berwyn Road, London SE24 9BD* Tel (020) 8674 3369 E-mail poole_clifford@yahoo.co.uk

POOLE, David. b 54. **d** 02 **p** 04. OLM Chase Terrace *Lich* from 02. *435 Littleworth Road, Cannock WS12 1HZ* Tel (01543) 422218 E-mail dave.poole54@sky.com

POOLE, Canon Denise June. b 49. Leic Univ BSc70 Bradf and Ilkley Coll DipAdEd85. NOC 90. **d** 93 **p** 94. C Horton and Bradf St Oswald Chapel Green 93-97; Chapl Co-ord Bradf Hosps NHS Trust 97-00; V Bradf St Aug Undercliffe 00-06; Dioc Dir of Ords 01-06; Bp's Dom Chapl from 06; Hon Can Bradf Cathl from 06. *23 Leylands Lane, Bradford BD9 5PX* Tel (01274) 401679 *or* 545414 E-mail denise.poole@bradford.anglican.org

POOLE, Edward John. b 53. Hull Univ BA81 Heythrop Coll Lon MA04. St Steph Ho Ox 81. **d** 83 **p** 84. C Stevenage St Andr and St Geo *St Alb* 83-86; Tutor St Paul's Th Coll Madagascar 86-88; V Weston and P-in-c Ardeley *St Alb* 88-96; P-in-c Cottered w Broadfield and Throcking 94-96; Chapl Bucharest w Sofia *Eur* 96-98; Chapl HM Pris Lewes 98-03; Chapl HM Pris Featherstone 03-09; R York, Beverley-Brookton and Quairading Australia from 09. *St Mary's Rectory, 64 John Street, Beverley WA 6304, Australia* Tel (0061) (8) 9646 1112 Mobile 43-704 0950 E-mail jpoole4@bigpond.com

POOLE, Helen Margaret. b 39. SRN. SWMTC. **d** 94 **p** 95. NSM Ludgvan *Truro* 94-97; NSM Paul 97-02; NSM St Buryan, St Levan and Sennen 02-04; rtd 04. *Underhill Farmhouse, St Levan, Penzance TR19 6JS* Tel (01736) 810842 Fax 810858

POOLE, Ian Richard Morley. b 62. Birm Univ MB, ChB85 MRCGP90. St Jo Coll Nottm MTh02. **d** 02 **p** 03. C Willenhall H Trin *Lich* 02-06; TV Bushbury from 06. *131 Taunton Avenue, Wolverhampton WV10 6PN* Tel (01902) 788151 E-mail woodchipper@blueyonder.co.uk

POOLE, James Christopher. b 73. Peterho Cam BA94 MA98. Aston Tr Scheme 96 Wycliffe Hall Ox 97. **d** 00 **p** 01. C Wimbledon Park St Luke *S'wark* 00-04; Miss Partner Crosslinks 04-07; Kenya 05-07; C Cambridge H Sepulchre *Ely* from 07. *64 St Albans Road, Cambridge CB4 2HG* Tel (01223) 700429 E-mail james.poole@stag.org

POOLE, Miss Joan Wendy. b 37. Sarum Dioc Teacher Tr Coll CertEd57 Trin Coll Bris 86. **d** 87 **p** 94. Par Dn Longfleet *Sarum* 87-89; Par Dn Hamworthy 89-94; C 94-97; rtd 97; Perm to Offic *Sarum* from 97. *35 Borley Road, Poole BH17 7DT* Tel (01202) 256377

POOLE, John. See POOLE, Edward John

POOLE, Martin Bryce. b 59. Reading Univ BSc80. St Jo Coll Nottm 81. **d** 87 **p** 88. NSM Tulse Hill H Trin and St Matthias *S'wark* 87-99; NSM Hove *Chich* 00-01; Perm to Offic 01-10; P-in-c Prestonville St Luke from 10. *St Luke's Vicarage, 64A Old Shoreham Road, Brighton BN1 5DD* Tel and fax (01273) 557772 E-mail martin@stlukesonline.co.uk

POOLE, Martin Ronald. b 59. Aston Univ BSc81 Leeds Univ BA86. Coll of Resurr Mirfield 84. **d** 87 **p** 88. C Sheff St Cath Richmond Road 87-90; C W Hampstead St Jas *Lon* 90-94; V Colindale St Matthias 94-06; V Munster Square Ch Ch and St Mary Magd from 06. *8 Laxton Place, London NW1 3PT* Tel (020) 7388 3095 Fax 08701-289048 E-mail martin@mpoole57.freeserve.co.uk

POOLE, Peter William. b 35. St Pet Hall Ox BA59 MA63. Wells Th Coll 59. **d** 61 **p** 62. C Cheriton Street *Cant* 61-64; C Birchington w Acol 64-67; V Newington 67-73; P-in-c Lower Halstow 72-73; V Bearsted 73-76; V Lane End w Cadmore End *Ox* 84-89; R Chalfont St Giles 89-99; rtd 99; Perm to Offic *Guildf* from 01. *Primrose Cottage, St Nicholas Avenue, Cranleigh GU6 7AQ* Tel (01483) 272703

POOLE, Richard Eric. b 65. Huddersfield Poly BEng87. Trin Coll Bris BA98. **d** 98 **p** 99. C Sandal St Helen *Wakef* 98-01; TV Southgate *Chich* from 01. *St Andrew's Vicarage, Weald Drive, Crawley RH10 6NU* Tel (01293) 531828

POOLE, Roy John. b 26. Lon Univ BD54. St Jo Coll Lon LTh54. **d** 54 **p** 55. C Benwell St Aid *Newc* 54-57; Bush Brotherhood of St Paul Australia 57-59; C Warwick 59-61; R Bradford cum Beswick *Man* 61-66; Area Sec Chr Aid Dept BCC 66-68; Regional Supervisor (S and E England) Chr Aid 68-74; Exec Officer Angl Health and Welfare Services Australia 74-77; Gen Sec W Australia Coun of Ch 77-83; Lic to Offic 84; R Carine w Cuncraig 85-91; rtd 91. *Unit 14, St Davids Retirement Centre, 17-19 Lawley Crescent, Mt Lawley, WA 6050, Australia* E-mail roy@poole.com.au

POOLE, Stuart. b 33. Lon Univ BScEng55 Man Univ MSc76 CEng65 FIEE85. **d** 91 **p** 92. NSM Cheadle *Ches* 91-03; Perm to Offic from 03. *1 Dene House, Green Pastures, Stockport SK4 3RB* Tel and fax 0161-432 6426 E-mail stuart.poole@ukgateway.net

POOLE, Wendy. See POOLE, Miss Joan Wendy

POOLEY, Clifford Russell. b 48. Glos Univ BA03. WEMTC 08. **d** 09 **p** 10. NSM Coberley, Cowley, Colesbourne and Elkstone *Glouc* from 09. *8A Salterley Grange, Leckhampton Hill, Cheltenham GL53 9QW* Tel (01242) 243981 E-mail cliff.pooley@btinternet.com

POOLEY, Peter Owen. b 32. Kelham Th Coll 54. **d** 58 **p** 59. C Paddington St Mary Magd *Lon* 58-62; R Rockland St Mary w Hellington *Nor* 62-67; Asst Master Thos Lethaby Sch 67-70; St Phil Gr Sch Edgbaston 70-74; Lordswood Gr Sch 74-80; Hon C Edgbaston St Geo *Birm* 77-80; R Elton *Ely* 80-01; P-in-c Stibbington and Water Newton 80-01; R Elton w Stibbington and Water Newton 01-02; rtd 02; Perm to Offic *Linc* from 03. *1 Warrenne Keep, Stamford PE9 2NX* Tel (01780) 751646

POOLMAN, Alfred John. b 46. K Coll Lon BD69 AKC69. St Aug Coll Cant 69. **d** 70 **p** 71. C Headingley *Ripon* 70-74; C Moor Allerton 75-78; C Monk Bretton *Wakef* 78-80; V Copley and Chapl Halifax Gen Hosp 80-90; R Llanfynydd *St As* 90-06; P-in-c 06-10; rtd 10. *The Rectory, Llanfynydd, Wrexham LL11 5HH* Tel (01978) 762304 E-mail john.poolman@tesco.net

POOLMAN, Mrs Carole Margaret. b 53. St As & Ban Minl Tr Course 98. **d** 01 **p** 02. NSM Pontblyddyn *St As* 01-06; P-in-c from 06. *The Rectory, Llanfynydd, Wrexham LL11 5HH* Tel (01978) 762304 E-mail carole.poolman@tesco.net

POOLTON, Martin Ronald. b 60. Kingston Poly BSc81 Salford Univ MSc83 Bp Grosseteste Coll PGCE85 FRGS81. Cuddesdon Coll 95. **d** 97 **p** 98. C Penzance St Mary w St Paul *Truro* 97-99; C Northampton St Matt *Pet* 99-01; R Jersey St Pet *Win* from 01. *The Rectory, La Rue du Presbytère, St Peter, Jersey JE3 7ZH* Tel and fax (01534) 481805 E-mail poolton@onetel.com

POPE, Preb Charles Guy. b 48. AKC70. St Aug Coll Cant 70. **d** 71 **p** 72. C Southgate Ch Ch *Lon* 71-74; C N St Pancras All Hallows 74-77; C Hampstead St Steph 74-77; V New Southgate St Paul 77-86; V Brookfield St Mary from 86; P-in-c Brookfield St Anne, Highgate Rise 88-99; AD S Camden 95-00; Preb St Paul's Cathl from 04. *St Mary's Vicarage, 85 Dartmouth Park Road, London NW5 1SL* Tel (020) 7267 5941 Fax 7482 2136 Mobile 07770-693435 E-mail guypope@blueyonder.co.uk

POPE, David Allan. b 20. Oriel Coll Ox BA45 MA72. Ely Th Coll 45. **d** 47 **p** 48. C Folkestone St Mary and St Eanswythe *Cant* 47-51; V Tovil 51-54; R E Horsley *Guildf* 54-63; R Ivychurch w Old Romney and Midley *Cant* 63-65; P-in-c Brenzett w Snargate and Snave 64-65; P-in-c Newchurch 64-65; P-in-c St Mary in the Marsh 64-65; P-in-c Burmarsh 64-65; R Broadstairs 65-73; P-in-c Berwick *Chich* 73-75; P-in-c Arlington 73-75; P-in-c Selmeston w Alciston 74-76; R Berwick w Selmeston and Alciston 76; P-in-c Rusper 76-79; R Colsterworth *Linc* 79-81; P-in-c Ingworth 81-85; P-in-c Alby w Thwaite *Nor* 81-85; P-in-c Erpingham w Calthorpe 81-85; P-in-c Aldborough w Thurgarton 83-85; rtd 85; Perm to Offic *Nor* from 85. *Burgate Lodge, Saddle Bow, King's Lynn PE34 3AR* Tel (01553) 617599

POPE, Donald Keith. b 35. Sarum & Wells Th Coll 81. **d** 76 **p** 77. Hon C Caerleon *Mon* 76-82; C 82-83; V Pontypool 83-86; R Grosmont and Skenfrith and Llangattock etc 86-98; RD Abergavenny 93-98; rtd 98. *24 Incline Way, Ridgewood Gardens, Saundersfoot SA69 9LX* Tel (01834) 812039

POPE, Miss Elizabeth Mercy. b 51. Man Univ BSc73 Ex Univ PGCE74. Trin Coll Bris 99. **d** 01 **p** 02. C Bardsley *Man* 01-05; P-in-c Oldham St Paul 05-08; P-in-c Denton St Lawr from 08. *St Lawrence's Rectory, 131 Town Lane, Denton, Manchester M34 2DJ* Tel 0161-320 4895 E-mail elizabeth@mpope.plus.com

POPE, Guy. See POPE, Preb Charles Guy

POPE, Michael John. b 37. Sarum Th Coll 62. **d** 65 **p** 66. C Broseley w Benthall *Heref* 65-68; C Shrewsbury St Giles *Lich* 68-71; P-in-c Shrewsbury St Geo 71-75; V 75-79; V Gnosall 79-00; RD Eccleshall 92-00; rtd 00; Perm to Offic *Lich* from 01. *Rivendell, 2 Dark Lane, Broseley TF12 5LH* Tel (01952) 883960

POPE, Michael Ronald. b 41. Bps' Coll Cheshunt 65. **d** 68 **p** 69. C Lyonsdown H Trin *St Alb* 68-72; C Seaford w Sutton *Chich* 72-76; R Hurstpierpoint 76-80; rtd 99. *34 Wilton Road, Shanklin PO37 7BZ* Tel (01983) 863602

POPELY, David Charles. K Coll Lon BA00. SEITE 00. **d** 03. NSM Catford St Laur *S'wark* 03-05. *83 Bower Hinton, Martock TA12 6LA* Tel (01935) 829376 Mobile 07957-825714 E-mail davidcpopely@hotmail.co.uk

POPHAM, Neil Andrew. b 69. Trin Coll Ox BA91 DPhil96 MA05 St Jo Coll Dur BA05. Cranmer Hall Dur 03. **d** 05 **p** 06. C Quarry Bank *Worc* 05-07; C Brierley Hill 07-09; P-in-c Kirkby in Ashfield St Thos *S'well* from 09. *The Vicarage, 109 Diamond Avenue, Kirkby-in-Ashfield, Nottingham NG17 7LX* E-mail thepophams@talktalk.net

POPP, Miss Julia Alice Gisela. b 45. Univ of BC BA71. St Jo Coll Nottm 78. **dss** 81 **d** 87 **p** 94. Woking St Mary *Guildf* 81-83; Hornsey Rise St Mary w St Steph *Lon* 83-87; Par Dn Hornsey Rise Whitehall Park Team 87-91; Par Dn Sutton St Nic *S'wark* 91-94; C 94-98; Missr Sutton Town Cen 91-98; TV Hackney Marsh *Lon* 98-05; rtd 05; Perm to Offic *Ely* from 06. *32 Regatta Court, Oyster Row, Cambridge CB5 8NS* Tel (01223) 350164 E-mail j.popp@btinternet.com

POPPE, Andrew Nils. b 60. NE Lon Poly BSc83. STETS 08. **d** 11. C Clarendon *Sarum* from 11. *28 Firs Road, Firsdown, Salisbury SP5 1SJ* Tel 07539-235000 (mobile) E-mail andrew.poppe@clarendonteam.org

POPPLETON, Julian George. b 63. St Chad's Coll Dur BA85 PGCE86 Surrey Univ BA02. STETS 99. **d** 02 **p** 03. NSM Harnham *Sarum* from 02; Chapl K Edw VI Sch Southn from 02. *19 Thompson Close, Salisbury SP2 8QU* Tel (01722) 334272 or (023) 8070 4561 E-mail jgp@kes.hants.sch.uk

POPPLEWELL, Andrew Frederick. b 53. St Jo Coll Dur BA75. Wycliffe Hall Ox 76. **d** 78 **p** 79. C Clifton *York* 78-81; C Lich St Chad 82-84; V Laisterdyke *Bradf* 84-99. *Clifton, 210A Leeds Road, Eccleshill, Bradford BD2 3JU* Tel (01274) 637651

PORT, Mrs Betty Anne. b 50. Univ of W Indies BA71 Open Univ MA93. STETS BA10. **d** 10 **p** 11. NSM Preston w Sutton Poyntz and Osmington w Poxwell *Sarum* from 10. *68 Mellstock Avenue, Dorchester DT1 2BQ* Tel (01305) 263058 E-mail betty.port@which.net

PORT MORESBY, Bishop of. See RAMSDEN, The Rt Revd Peter Stockton

PORTEOUS, Michael Stanley. b 35. S'wark Ord Course 70. **d** 73 **p** 74. C Barnes St Mich *S'wark* 73-76; Chapl Greycoat Hosp Sch 76-78; C Brighton Annunciation *Chich* 78-80; Chapl Ch Hosp Horsham 80-85; TV Moulsecoomb *Chich* 85-88; R W Blatchington 88-99; rtd 99; Perm to Offic *Chich* from 99. *15 Mariners Close, Shoreham-by-Sea BN43 5LU*

PORTER, Andrew William. b 69. Bris Univ BSc91 BA01 PGCE94. Trin Coll Bris 98. **d** 01 **p** 02. C Ipsley *Worc* 01-04; V Fairfield *Liv* 04-10; P-in-c Liv St Phil w St Dav 08-10; V Liv All SS from 11. *St John's Vicarage, 19 Lockerby Road, Liverpool L7 0HG* Tel 0151-263 4001 E-mail andrew.porter@bigfoot.com

PORTER, Anthony. See PORTER, Canon David Anthony

✠**PORTER, The Rt Revd Anthony.** b 52. Hertf Coll Ox BA74 MA78 Fitzw Ho Cam BA76 MA80. Ridley Hall Cam 74. **d** 77 **p** 78 **c** 06. C Edgware *Lon* 77-80; C Haughton St Mary *Man* 80-83; P-in-c Bacup Ch Ch 83-87; V 87-91; R Rusholme H Trin 91-06; Hon Can Man Cathl 04-06; Suff Bp Sherwood *S'well* from 06; Hon Can S'well Minster from 06. *Dunham House, Westgate, Southwell NG25 0JL* Tel (01636) 819133 Fax 819085 E-mail bishopsherwood@southwell.anglican.org

PORTER, Barbara Judith. See JEAPES, Mrs Barbara Judith

PORTER, Brian John Henry. b 33. SWMTC 78. **d** 81 **p** 82. NSM Plymouth St Andr w St Paul and St Geo *Ex* 81-85; Perm to Offic 85-87; NSM Devonport St Barn 87-90; C Brampton St Thos *Derby* 90-95; Asst Chapl Amsterdam w Den Helder and Heiloo *Eur* 95-97; rtd 97; Perm to Offic *Glouc* 99-00 and 05-08; *Ex* from 09. *Cornerstone, Burrator Road, Dousland, Yelverton PL20 6NE* Tel (01822) 853478

PORTER, Brian Meredith. b 39. Monash Univ Aus BA66 Trin Hall Cam BA75 MA79 New England Univ NSW BLitt79 MLitt85 ACT ThD01. Cuddesdon Coll 68. **d** 68 **p** 71. C Kew Australia 68-69; K Sch Parramatta 70-73; Perm to Offic *Ely* 73-75; Chapl Canberra Gr Sch Australia 75-82; Chapl Ivanhoe Gr Sch 83-97; Sen Chapl Melbourne Gr Sch 98-05; Chapl Brighton Gr Sch from 05. *4 Fairholme Grove, Camberwell Vic 3124, Australia* Tel (0061) (3) 9882 8740 E-mail bmporter@comcen.com.au

PORTER (née RICHARDSON), Mrs Catherine Elisabeth. b 75. Edge Hill Coll of HE BA96 Trin Coll Bris BA99 MA01. SNWTP 07. **d** 08. NSM Fairfield *Liv* 08-10; NSM Liv All SS from 11. *St John's Vicarage, 19 Lockerby Road, Liverpool L7 0HG* Tel 0151-263 2681 E-mail cathy.porter@bigfoot.com

PORTER, Damian Michael. b 66. Linc Th Coll BTh92. **d** 92 **p** 93. C Pelsall *Lich* 92-96; V Greenlands *Blackb* 96-00; V St Annes St Anne 00-09; AD Kirkham 06-09; P-in-c Warton St Oswald w Yealand Conyers 09-11; V from 11. *St Oswald's Vicarage, Warton, Carnforth LA5 9PG* Tel (01524) 732946 E-mail fatherd@btinternet.com

PORTER, Canon David Anthony (Tony). b 34. Wycliffe Hall Ox 73. **d** 75 **p** 76. C Watford St Luke *St Alb* 75-78; C Worting *Win* 78-81; V Snettisham *Nor* 81-82; P-in-c Ingoldisthorpe 81-82; C Fring 81-82; R Snettisham w Ingoldisthorpe and Fring 82-84; Chapl Asst Colchester Gen Hosp 87-88; Chapl Maidstone Hosp 88-94; Chapl Mid Kent Healthcare NHS Trust 94-98; Hon Can Cant Cathl 97-98; rtd 98. *The Greys, 12 Hawthorn Close, Watlington, King's Lynn PE33 0HD* Tel (01553) 811301 E-mail daporter7985@btinternet.com

PORTER, David Michael. b 37. Coll of Ripon & York St Jo BA88. Ely Th Coll 61. **d** 64 **p** 65. C Clun w Chapel Lawn *Heref* 64-67; C Scarborough St Mary w Ch St, St Paul and St Thos *York* 67-69; C Fulford 69-71; V Strensall 71-78; Chapl Claypenny and St Monica's Hosps 78-91; V Easingwold w Raskelfe *York* 78-91; TR York All SS Pavement w St Crux and St Martin etc 91-97; R York All SS Pavement w St Crux and St Mich 97-02; rtd 02; Perm to Offic *York* from 02. *10 Hall Rise, Haxby, York YO32 3LP* Tel (01904) 769823

PORTER, David Michael. b 46. Nottm Univ BMedSci80 BM82 BS82. EMMTC 94. **d** 97 **p** 98. NSM Edwinstowe *S'well* 97-99. *Gorsethorpe Cottage, Edwinstowe, Mansfield NG21 9HJ* Tel (01623) 844657

PORTER, David Rowland Shelley. b 46. City of Liv Coll of HE CertEd69. STETS 00. **d** 03 **p** 04. NSM Whitehawk *Chich* from 03. *33 Warleigh Road, Brighton BN1 4NT* Tel (01273) 703499 E-mail davejanera@aol.com

PORTER, Howard. b 56. S Glam Inst HE CertEd78. St Mich Coll Llan 99. **d** 01 **p** 02. C Maindee Newport *Mon* 01-05; TV Aberystwyth *St D* 05-09. *21 Gwalch y Penwaig, Barry CF62 5AG*

PORTER, James Richard. b 53. Lon Univ BMedSci97 MB, BS98. Oak Hill Th Coll MTh05. **d** 05 **p** 06. C Cromer *Nor* 05-09; R W Horsley *Guildf* from 09. *The Rectory, 80 East Lane, West Horsley, Leatherhead KT24 6LQ* Tel (01483) 286879 E-mail jamestherector@yahoo.co.uk

PORTER, John Dudley Dowell. b 33. St Edm Hall Ox BA60 MA61. Qu Coll Birm 57. **d** 59 **p** 60. C Londonderry *Birm* 59-62; C Tettenhall Regis *Lich* 62-65; Chapl RAF 65-69; V Wombourne *Lich* 69-75; V Rickerscote 75-81; P-in-c Chapel Chorlton 81-85; P-in-c Maer 81-85; P-in-c Whitmore 81-85; R Chapel Chorlton, Maer and Whitmore 85-92; TR Wednesfield 92-00; rtd 00; P-in-c Haughton St Anne *Man* 00-03; P-in-c Nord Pas de Calais *Eur* 04-06. *37 Rue Principale, 62130 Framecourt, France* Tel (0033) 3 21 04 36 35 E-mail jddporter@hotmail.co.uk

PORTER, Miss Joy Dove. b 50. Lon Bible Coll BA81 Lon Univ PGCE83. Wycliffe Hall Ox 89. **d** 91 **p** 94. Par Dn Chalgrove w Berrick Salome *Ox* 91-92; Par Dn Chipping Norton 92-94; C 94-95; Hong Kong 96-97; P-in-c Rouen All SS and Chapl Rouen Miss to Seamen *Eur* 97-00; Hon C Warfield *Ox* from 03. *Warfield Church Office, Church Lane, Warfield, Bracknell RG42 6EG* Tel (01344) 886900 E-mail admin@warfield.org.uk

PORTER, Malcolm Derek. b 53. BSc. NTMTC. **d** 05 **p** 06. C Woodford Wells *Chelmsf* 05-09; NSM from 10. *121 Beatyville Gardens, Ilford IG6 1JZ* Tel (020) 8550 8161 E-mail thoseporters@aol.com

PORTER, Mrs Marie-Jeanne. b 60. EMMTC 95. **d** 98 **p** 99. NSM Warsop *S'well* 98-04. *Gorsethorpe Cottage, Edwinstowe, Mansfield NG21 9HJ* Tel (01623) 844657

PORTER, Matthew James. b 69. Nottm Univ BA90. Wycliffe Hall Ox BTh93. **d** 96 **p** 97. C Dore *Sheff* 96-00; V Woodseats St Chad 00-09; C York St Mich-le-Belfrey 09-10; V from 10. *The Parsonage, 12 Muncastergate, York YO31 9LA* Tel (01904) 412057 Mobile 07985-645844 E-mail matthew.porter@stmichaelsyork.org

PORTER, Canon Michael Edward. b 44. Trin Coll Bris 75. **d** 77 **p** 78. C Corby St Columba *Pet* 77-81; C Rainham *Chelmsf* 81-82; TV 82-92; P-in-c S Hornchurch St Jo and St Matt 92-95; V Anerley *Roch* 95-09; TR 09; AD Beckenham 05-09; Hon Can Roch Cathl 09; rtd 09; Perm to Offic *Roch* from 10. *20 Park Lane, Wymondham NR18 9BG* Tel (01953) 602708 E-mail mike@porterfamily.freeuk.com

PORTER, Nigel Jonathan. b 58. Sunderland Univ BEd90 Portsm Univ MPhil99 PhD05. STETS MA10. **d** 10 **p** 11. C Sandown Ch Ch *Portsm* from 10; C Lower Sandown St Jo from 10. *70 Perowne Way, Sandown PO36 9DR* Tel (01983) 404584 Mobile 07533-394043 E-mail nigel.porter6@btopenworld.com

PORTER, Raymond John. b 43. Worc Coll Ox BA66 MA70 Wycliffe Hall Ox MPhil93 FRAS93. **d** 06 **p** 07. Dir World Miss Studies Oak Hill Th Coll from 06; Perm to Offic *St Alb* from 07 and Ely from 11. *24 Bevington Way, Eynesbury, St Neots PE19 2HQ* Tel (01480) 211839 *or* (020) 8449 0467 Mobile 07976-753822 E-mail ray@wiradanuprojo.f2s.com *or* rayp@oakhill.ac.uk

PORTER, Mrs Susan Patricia June. b 53. STETS 00. **d** 03. NSM Wilton w Netherhampton and Fugglestone *Sarum* 03-05; NSM Sarum Cathl 05-08; Perm to Offic 08-09; NSM Wilton w Netherhampton and Fugglestone from 09. *24 Belle Vue Road, Salisbury SP1 3YG* Tel (01722) 331314 E-mail rev.porter@tesco.net

PORTER, William Albert. b 28. Univ of NZ BA51 MA52. Coll of Resurr Mirfield 53. **d** 55 **p** 56. C Perry Barr *Birm* 55-58; V Port Chalmers NZ 59-61; V Warrington 61-62; Tutor St Jo Coll Suva Fiji 62-63; Asst Supt Melanesian Miss 62-64; Supt 64-67; Can and Prec H Trin Cathl Suva 65-67; C Wimbledon *S'wark* 68; Asst Chapl HM Pris Liv 69-70; Chapl HM Pris Brixton 70-74; Long Lartin 74-79; Nottm 87-90; P-in-c Sneinton St Matthias *S'well* 90-93; rtd 94; Perm to Offic *Glouc* from 01. *40 Duke Street, Cheltenham GL52 6BP* Tel (01242) 262198

PORTER-PRYCE, Ms Julia Frances. b 57. Man Univ BA78 Leic Univ MPhil94. NTMTC 93. **d** 96 **p** 97. C Stoke Newington Common St Mich *Lon* 96-99; C Is of Dogs Ch Ch and St Jo w St Luke 99-02; V De Beauvoir Town St Pet from 02; AD Hackney from 09. *St Peter's Vicarage, 86 De Beauvoir Road, London N1 5AT* Tel (020) 7254 5670 E-mail juliap@freeuk.com

PORTEUS, Canon James Michael. b 31. Worc Coll Ox BA55 MA58. Cuddesdon Coll. **d** 57 **p** 58. C Fleetwood St Pet *Blackb* 57-60; C Ox St Mary V 60-62; Staff Sec SCM Ox 60-62; Chapl Chicago Univ USA 62-65; Chapl Bryn Mawr, Haverford and Swarthmore Colls 62-65; Chapl Lon Univ 69-74; V Hampstead Garden Suburb 74-86; Chapl Arizona Univ USA 86-91; Min Livingston LEP *Edin* 91-96; rtd 96; P-in-c Portree *Arg* 96-05; Hon Can Cumbrae from 06; Perm to Offic *Truro* from 09. *Triskelo, Rinsey, Ashton, Helston TR13 9TS* Tel (01736) 761870

PORTEUS, Canon Robert John Norman. b 50. TCD BA72 MA76. CITC 75. **d** 75 **p** 76. C Portadown St Mark *Arm* 75-79; I Ardtrea w Desertcreat 79-83; I Annaghmore 83-98; I Derryloran from 98; Can Arm Cathl from 98; Preb from 01. *Derryloran Rectory, 13 Loy Street, Cookstown BT80 8PZ* Tel and fax (028) 8676 2261 E-mail rector@derryloran.com

PORTHOUSE, Canon John Clive. b 32. Lon Univ BD58. Tyndale Hall Bris 55 Oak Hill Th Coll 58. **d** 60 **p** 61. C Leyton All SS *Chelmsf* 60-62; C Kendal St Thos *Carl* 62-64; V Flimby 64-68; V Sidcup St Andr *Roch* 68-74; V Beckenham St Jo 74-86; RD Beckenham 80-86; V Southborough St Pet w Ch Ch and St Matt 86-96; TR 96-97; Hon Can Roch Cathl 96-97; rtd 97; Perm to Offic *Carl* from 98. *234 Ralph Perring Court, Stone Park Avenue, Beckenham BR3 3LX* Tel (020) 3441 4259 E-mail clive.porthouse@virgin.net

PORTHOUSE, Roger Gordon Hargreaves. b 39. Tyndale Hall Bris 66. **d** 69 **p** 70. C Wellington w Eyton *Lich* 69-71; C Cheadle *Ches* 71-75; R Frettenham w Stanninghall *Nor* 75-81; R Spixworth w Crostwick 75-81; V Hailsham *Chich* 81-04; RD Dallington 96-03; rtd 05. *19 Cornmill Gardens, Polegate BN26 5NJ* Tel (01323) 487372 E-mail rporthouse@btclick.com

PORTLOCK, John Anthony. b 37. RIBA. WMMTC 96. **d** 99 **p** 00. NSM Lyddington w Stoke Dry and Seaton etc *Pet* 99-07; NSM Bulwick, Blatherwycke w Harringworth and Laxton 05-07; rtd 07; Perm to Offic *Pet* from 08. *7 Chestnut Close, Uppingham, Oakham LE15 9TQ* Tel (01572) 823225 E-mail portlocklydd@aol.com

PORTSDOWN, Archdeacon of. See READER, The Ven Trevor Alan John

PORTSMOUTH, Bishop of. See FOSTER, The Rt Revd Christopher Richard James

PORTSMOUTH, Dean of. See BRINDLEY, The Very Revd David Charles

PORTWOOD, Prof Derek. b 31. Keele Univ MA69 PhD79. ALCD57. **d** 57 **p** 58. C Laisterdyke *Bradf* 57-60; C-in-c Westlands St Andr CD *Lich* 60-66; V Westlands St Andr 66-69; rtd 96; Perm to Offic *Ely* 96-00. *51 River Lane, Cambridge CB5 8HP* Tel and fax (01223) 311044

POSKITT, Mark Sylvester. b 63. Loughb Univ BSc84. St Jo Coll Nottm MA95. **d** 97 **p** 98. C Brigg, Wrawby and Cadney cum Howsham *Linc* 97-00; TV Howden *York* 00-09; P-in-c Barnsley St Edw *Wakef* from 09; P-in-c Gawber from 09. *The Vicarage, Church Street, Gawber, Barnsley S75 2RL* Tel (01226) 207140 E-mail rev.markp@tiscali.co.uk

POST, David Charles William. b 39. Jes Coll Cam BA61 MA65. Oak Hill Th Coll 61. **d** 63 **p** 64. C Orpington Ch Ch *Roch* 63-66; C Fulwood *Sheff* 66-68; V Lathom *Liv* 68-75; V Poughill *Truro* 75-78; V Braddan and Santan *S & M* 78-79; Dioc Missr 78-79; V Sherburn in Elmet *York* 79-91; P-in-c Kirk Fenton 84-85; V Thornthwaite cum Braithwaite and Newlands *Carl* 91-93; R Wheldrake w Thorganby *York* 93-04; P-in-c Elvington w Sutton on Derwent and E Cottingwith 03-04; rtd 04. *Cheviot, 5 Mayfield Crescent, Middle Rasen, Market Rasen LN8 3UA* Tel (01673) 843388

POST, Oswald Julian. b 48. Derby Lonsdale Coll BEd79. EMMTC. **d** 84 **p** 85. Travelling Sec Ruanda Miss 79-89; Hon C Hulland, Atlow, Bradley and Hognaston *Derby* 84-89; V Wormhill, Peak Forest w Peak Dale and Dove Holes 89-99; P-in-c Youlgreave, Middleton, Stanton-in-Peak 99-09; rtd 09.

Rose Cottage, Hulland Village, Ashbourne DE6 3EP Tel (01335) 370285 E-mail ossiepost@hotmail.com

POSTILL, John Edward. b 35. Oak Hill Th Coll 64. **d** 67 **p** 68. C Southgate *Chich* 67-70; C Bowling St Jo *Bradf* 70-74; TV Winfarthing w Shelfanger *Nor* 74-79; R Slaugham *Chich* 79-97; C Busbridge and Hambledon *Guildf* 97-03; rtd 03. *Dora Cottage, Beech Hill, Hambledon, Godalming GU8 4HL* Tel (01428) 687968 E-mail jandjpostill@talk21.com

POSTILL, Canon Richard Halliday. b 37. Hull Univ BSc59. Westcott Ho Cam 66. **d** 68 **p** 69. C Wylde Green *Birm* 68-72; C Kingswinford St Mary *Lich* 72-76; V Yardley Wood *Birm* 76-86; V Acocks Green 86-02; AD Yardley 93-00; Hon Can Birm Cathl 99-02; rtd 02; Perm to Offic *Birm* from 03. *32 Longmore Road, Shirley, Solihull B90 3DY* Tel 0121-744 6217 E-mail richardh@postill.fsbusiness.co.uk

POSTLES, Donald. b 29. MPS51 Birm Univ MA65. Qu Coll Birm 56. **d** 59 **p** 60. C Southport H Trin *Liv* 59-62; C Prescot 62-63; V Wigan St Steph 63-71; V Farnworth 71-84; V Mossley Hill St Barn 84-92; rtd 93. *43 The Broadway, Abergele LL22 7DD* Tel (01745) 826165

POSTON, Jonathan David. b 59. Ches Coll of HE MTh05. NOC 01. **d** 04 **p** 05. C Prestwich St Marg *Man* 04-10; Perm to Offic from 10; NSM Matlock Bank and Tansley *Derby* from 10; NSM Dethick, Lea and Holloway from 10. *96 Smedley Street, Matlock DE4 3JJ* Tel 07754-517797 (mobile) E-mail jont.post@talk21.com

POTHEN, Canon Simon John. b 60. Westmr Coll Ox BA86. Ripon Coll Cuddesdon 86. **d** 88 **p** 89. C Southgate Ch Ch *Lon* 88-91; C Tottenham St Mary 91-93; TV Gt Grimsby St Mary and St Jas *Linc* 93-96; R Friern Barnet St Jas *Lon* 96-02; V Pinner 02-07; Prec and Can Res Chelmsf Cathl from 07. *1A Harlings Grove, Chelmsford CM1 1YQ* Tel (01245) 491599 Mobile 07939-523366 E-mail precentor@chelmsfordcathedral.org.uk

POTIPHER, John Malcolm Barry. b 42. St Alb Minl Tr Scheme 79. **d** 82 **p** 83. Chapl Herts Fire Brigade 82-91; NSM Chambersbury *St Alb* 82-84; NSM Hemel Hempstead 84-86; NSM Digswell and Panshanger 86-92; P-in-c Pirton 92-95; rtd 95; Perm to Offic *St Alb* from 95. *66 Peartree Lane, Welwyn Garden City AL7 3UH* Tel (01707) 886953 E-mail jmbpot@ntlworld.com

POTTER, Mrs Anne Mary. b 57. Open Univ BA92 Chich Coll PGCE96. Qu Coll Birm 09. **d** 11. NSM Badsey w Aldington and Offenham and Bretforton *Worc* from 11. *Post Office, Main Street, Offenham, Evesham WR11 8RL* Tel (01386) 424429 Mobile 07783-711665 E-mail annemary.potter@virgin.net

POTTER, Charles Elmer. b 42. Georgetown Univ (USA) BS65 Valparaiso Univ JD73. Wycliffe Coll Toronto MDiv81. **d** 81 **p** 82. C Southport Ch Ch *Liv* 81-84; Chapl Lee Abbey 84-87; P-in-c Westmeadows and Bulla Australia 87-93; P-in-c Aldingham and Dendron and Rampside and Urswick 96-99; V Bexley St Mary *Roch* 99-07; rtd 07. *20 Bromley College, London Road, Bromley BR1 1PE* Tel 07951-780869 (mobile) E-mail charles.potter@tiscali.co.uk

POTTER, The Very Revd Christopher Nicholas Lynden. b 49. Leeds Univ BA71. St As Minl Tr Course 90. **d** 93 **p** 94. C Flint *St As* 93-96; V Llanfair DC, Derwen, Llanelidan and Efenechtyd 96-01; Dean and Lib St As Cathl from 01; V St As 01-03; TR from 03. *The Deanery, Upper Denbigh Road, St Asaph LL17 0RL* Tel (01745) 583597 E-mail chris_potter@btinternet.com

POTTER, Clive Geoffrey. b 55. Aston Tr Scheme 88 Sarum & Wells Th Coll 90. **d** 92 **p** 93. C Epsom Common Ch Ch *Guildf* 92-97; TV Westborough 97-98; TR 98-07; V Milford from 07. *The New Vicarage, Milford Heath, Milford, Godalming GU8 5BX* Tel (01483) 414710 E-mail milfordvicarage@gmail.com

POTTER, Desmond. b 54. St Paul's Coll Grahamstown 85. **d** 88 **p** 88. C Benoni S Africa 88-90; C Springs 90-91; C Linden 91-93; R Kempton Park 93-97; V Newton *Ches* 98-06; C Toowoomba Australia 06-08; R Callide Valley from 08. *76 Kariboe Street, PO Box 69, Biloela Qld 4715, Australia* Tel (0061) (7) 4992 1545 Fax 4992 3644 Mobile 41-975 5979 E-mail thesapotters@bigpond.com

POTTER, Harry Drummond. b 54. Em Coll Cam BA76 MA79 MPhil81 LLB92 Barrister 93. Westcott Ho Cam 79. **d** 81 **p** 82. C Deptford St Paul *S'wark* 81-84; Chapl Selw Coll Cam 84-87; Chapl Newnham Coll Cam 84-87; Chapl HM Pris Wormwood Scrubs 87-88; Chapl HM YOI Aylesbury 88-93; NSM Camberwell St Giles w St Matt *S'wark* 93-03; Perm to Offic 03-07. *19 Dobell Road, London SE9 1HE* Tel (020) 7067 1500 E-mail tuahousis@hotmail.com

POTTER, Canon James David. b 35. AKC66. **d** 67 **p** 68. C Longbridge *Birm* 67-70; Lic to Offic 71-73; V N Harborne 73-78; V Smethwick H Trin w St Alb 78-83; V Blurton *Lich* 83-90; V Dordon *Birm* 90-98; RD Polesworth 91-96; Hon Can Birm Cathl 96-98; rtd 98; Perm to Offic *Birm* from 98. *49 Winstanley Road, Stechford, Birmingham B33 8UH* Tel 0121-783 2734

POTTER, John Daniel. b 29. Sydney Univ BA50. St Jo Coll Morpeth ThL51. **d** 51 **p** 53. Australia 52-65 and from 71; C High Harrogate Ch Ch *Ripon* 65-66; Chapl St Mary's Sch Wantage 66-68; Chapl St Jo Sch and NSM St Andr Cathl Singapore 68-71; OCF 68-71; rtd 95; Lic to Offic *Eur* 95-97. *200 Castella Road, Toolangi Vic 3777, Australia* Tel (0061) (3) 5962 9449

POTTER, John Dennis. b 39. Ealing Tech Coll. S Dios Minl Tr Scheme 92. **d** 94 **p** 95. NSM Box w Hazlebury and Ditteridge *Bris* 94-98; Perm to Offic *B & W* from 06. *87A Southdown Road, Bath BA2 1HL* Tel (01225) 316656 E-mail johnpotter.j@tinyworld.co.uk

POTTER, John Ellis. b 45. Sarum & Wells Th Coll 82. **d** 84 **p** 85. C Wootton Bassett *Sarum* 84-88; TV Swindon New Town *Bris* 88-96; V Milber *Ex* from 96. *St Luke's Vicarage, 10 Laburnum Road, Newton Abbot TQ12 4LQ* Tel (01626) 365837

POTTER, Canon John Henry. b 26. Lon Univ BA50. Oak Hill Th Coll 50. **d** 52 **p** 53. C Islington St Mary *Lon* 52-55; C Kinson *Sarum* 55-58; V Upper Holloway St Jo *Lon* 58-65; R Illogan *Truro* 65-69; P-in-c Ilfracombe SS Phil and Jas *Ex* 69-72; V 72-76; R Poole *Sarum* 76-87; RD Poole 80-85; Can and Preb Sarum Cathl 83-91; P-in-c Charmouth and Catherston Leweston 87-91; rtd 91; Perm to Offic *Sarum* 91-99 and *Win* 91-00. *11 Park Terrace, Tenby SA70 7LY* Tel (01834) 843647

POTTER, Mrs Judith Anne. b 46. Rolle Coll CertEd68. **d** 05 **p** 06. OLM Shere, Albury and Chilworth *Guildf* from 05; Chapl Birtley Ho Bramley from 08. *3 Bank Terrace, Gomshall Lane, Shere, Guildford GU5 9HB* Tel (01483) 203352 Fax 202077 E-mail judyp@btopenworld.com

POTTER, Kenneth Benjamin. b 39. Open Univ BA GLCM. NEOC 84. **d** 87 **p** 88. NSM Ryton w Hedgefield *Dur* 87-95; P-in-c Harby w Thorney and N and S Clifton *S'well* 95-09; rtd 10. *Address withheld by request* E-mail kenneth.b.potter@btinternet.com

POTTER, Mrs Linda. b 47. Cranmer Hall Dur 92. **d** 94 **p** 95. C Shildon ·w Eldon *Dur* 94-98; P-in-c Castleside 98-04; TR Gt Aycliffe from 04. *St Clare's Rectory, St Cuthbert's Way, Newton Aycliffe DL5 5NT* Tel (01325) 313613 E-mail linda.potter@durham.anglican.org

POTTER, Malcolm Emmerson. b 48. Bedf Coll Lon BSc70. St Jo Coll Nottm. **d** 75 **p** 76. C Upton (Overchurch) *Ches* 76-78; CPAS Staff 78-84; Development Officer St Jo Coll Nottm 84-86; P-in-c Wellington All SS w Eyton *Lich* 86-95; V 95-06; Preb Lich Cathl 99-06; Membership Development Manager Age Concern 06-07; Chapl Shropshire Co Primary Care Trust from 07. *2 Barns Green, Shrewsbury SY3 9QB* Tel (01743) 641251 E-mail malcolmepotter@blueyonder.co.uk

POTTER, Neil John. b 63. **d** 11. NSM Chacewater w St Day and Carharrack *Truro* from 11; NSM St Stythians w Perranarworthal and Gwennap from 11; NSM Feock from 11; NSM Devoran from 11. *Strawberry Bank, Carn, Stithians, Truro TR3 7AW* Tel 07539-593684 (mobile) E-mail neilpotter@talktalk.net

POTTER, The Ven Peter Maxwell. b 46. Univ of Wales (Swansea) BA69 Univ of BC MA71. Sarum & Wells Th Coll 83. **d** 85 **p** 86. C Bradford-on-Avon H Trin *Sarum* 85-88; C Harnham 88-91; P-in-c N Bradley, Southwick and Heywood 91-96; V Sale St Anne *Ches* 96-00; R Largs *Glas* 00-08; Chapl Berne w Neuchâtel *Eur* from 08; Adn Switzerland from 09. *St Ursula, Jubiläumsplatz 2, 3005 Berne, Switzerland* Tel (0041) (31) 352 8567 Fax 351 0548 E-mail peshar@bluewin.ch *or* berne@anglican.ch

POTTER, Canon Phillip. b 54. Stirling Univ BA75. Trin Coll Bris 82. **d** 84 **p** 85. C Yateley *Win* 84-88; V Haydock St Mark *Liv* 88-07; Dir Pioneer Min from 07; C Haydock St Mark 07-09; Hon Can Liv Cathl from 03. *202 Alexandra Towers, 19 Princes Parade, Liverpool L3 1BJ*

POTTER, Richard Antony. b 36. K Coll Cam BA60 MA64. Ridley Hall Cam 60. **d** 62 **p** 63. C Luton w E Hyde *St Alb* 62-72; V Lyonsdown H Trin 72-85; R Broxbourne w Wormley 85-02; rtd 02; C Thorverton, Cadbury, Upton Pyne etc *Ex* 02-09. *Rivermead, 6 Colyford Road, Seaton EX12 2DF* Tel (01297) 21178

POTTER, Miss Sharon Jane. b 63. Suffolk Coll BSc96 K Coll Lon MSc00 RGN91. **d** 04 **p** 05. OLM Ipswich All Hallows *St E* 04-06; OLM Ipswich St Helen, H Trin, and St Luke from 07. *7 Vicarage Gardens, Debenham, Stowmarket IP14 6SH* Tel (01728) 861323 Mobile 07795-168600 E-mail revsharon@btinternet.com

POTTER, Stephen Michael. b 55. Oak Hill Th Coll 93. **d** 95 **p** 96. C Chesterfield H Trin and Ch Ch *Derby* 95-99; P-in-c S Normanton from 99. *The Rectory, Church Street, South Normanton, Alfreton DE55 2BT* Tel (01773) 811273 E-mail stephen@potter55.fsnet.co.uk

POTTER, Timothy John. b 49. Bris Univ BSc71. Oak Hill Th Coll 73. **d** 76 **p** 77. C Wallington *S'wark* 76-79; C Hampreston *Sarum* 79-81; TV Stratton St Margaret w S Marston etc *Bris* 81-87; P-in-c Hatfield Heath *Chelmsf* 87-89; P-in-c Sheering 87-89; R Hatfield Heath and Sheering 90-09; P-in-c Gt Hallingbury and Lt Hallingbury 06-09; RD Harlow 07-09; Hon Can Chelmsf

Cathl 02-09; rtd 09. *Redcott, 91 High Street, Dunmow CM6 1AF* E-mail tim.potter1@btinternet.com
POTTIER, Ronald William. b 36. S'wark Ord Course 73. d 76 p 77. NSM Lower Sydenham St Mich *S'wark* 76-98; NSM Sydenham All SS 98-05; Perm to Offic from 05. *12 Neiderwald Road, London SE26 4AD* Tel (020) 8699 4375
POTTINGER, Justin Charles Edward. b 82. Keble Coll Ox BA03 Ox Brookes Univ PGCE04. STETS 05 Ripon Coll Cuddesdon 07. d 08 p 09. C Devizes St Jo w St Mary *Sarum* 08-11; Chapl Clayesmore Sch Blandford from 11. *Clayesmore School, Iwerne Minster, Blandford DT11 8LL* Tel (01747) 813111
E-mail justinpottinger@msn.com
POTTS, Heather Dawn. See BUTCHER, Mrs Heather Dawn
POTTS, James. b 30. K Coll Lon BD56 AKC56. d 57 p 58. C Brighouse *Wakef* 57-59; Tanganyika 59-64; Tanzania 64-71; C-in-c Athersley and New Lodge CD *Wakef* 71-73; V Athersley 73-77; V Madeley *Lich* 77-85; V Baswich 85-93; RD Stafford 88-95; rtd 93; Perm to Offic *Lich* from 05. *16A Christchurch Lane, Lichfield WS13 8BA* Tel (01543) 418808
POTTS, Mrs Jill. b 46. Open Univ BA89. STETS 02. d 05 p 06. NSM Corfe Mullen *Sarum* 05-07; NSM Grantham, Manthorpe *Linc* from 07. *104 Longcliffe Road, Grantham NG31 8DY* Tel (01476) 578553 E-mail jill@jpotts.me.uk
POULARD, Christopher. b 39. FCA64. Ridley Hall Cam 82. d 84 p 85. C N Walsham w Antingham *Nor* 84-86; C Oulton Broad 86-90; TV Raveningham 90-94; R Raveningham Gp 94-99; RD Loddon 98-99; Perm to Offic *Chelmsf* from 99; rtd 04. *Cuddington, Colam Lane, Little Baddow, Chelmsford CM3 4SY* Tel (01245) 224221 Fax 221394 E-mail chris@poulard.org.uk
POULSON, Anna Louise. b 73. Univ Coll Dur BA94 K Coll Lon MA97 PhD06. Ridley Hall Cam 98. d 02 p 03. C Ealing St Mary *Lon* 02-06; NSM Southall Green St Jo from 11. *St John's Vicarage, Church Avenue, Southall UB2 4DH* Tel (020) 8571 3027 Mobile 07929-348621
E-mail annapoulson@btinternet.com
POULSON, Mark Alban. b 63. Bath Coll of HE BEd86 Anglia Poly Univ MA03. Ridley Hall Cam. d 00 p 01. C Alperton *Lon* 00-03; P-in-c Southall Green St Jo 03-06; V from 06. *St John's Vicarage, Church Avenue, Southall UB2 4DH* Tel (020) 8574 2055
POULTNEY, Andrew Timothy. b 68. K Coll Lon MA03. St Paul's Th Cen Lon 06. d 08 p 09. C Collier Row St Jas and Havering-atte-Bower *Chelmsf* from 08. *56 Parkside Avenue, Romford RM1 4ND* Tel (01708) 734418 Mobile 07903-112599
E-mail barkingandy@btconnect.com
POULTNEY, David Elis. b 73. Loughb Univ BEng96 CEng97. Trin Coll Bris 07. d 09 p 10. C Luton Lewsey St Hugh *St Alb* from 09. *247 Leagrave High Street, Luton LU4 0ND* Tel 07712-005449 (mobile) E-mail david_poultney@hotmail.com
POULTON, Arthur Leslie. b 28. K Coll Lon BA53 AKC53 BD60 Leic Univ MA85. Tyndale Hall Bris 53. d 55 p 56. C New Catton St Luke *Nor* 55-56; C Earlham St Anne 56-58; C Chorleywood Ch Ch *St Alb* 58-61; R E Barnet 61-64; Ches Coll of HE 64-87; Chapl 64-84; Sen Lect 66-87; Dir of Studies Course in Chr Studies *Chelmsf* 87-94; P-in-c Gt Canfield 87-94; rtd 94; Perm to Offic *Ches* from 96. *2 The Cloisters, Rhos on Sea, Colwyn Bay LL28 4PW* Tel (01493) 549473
POULTON, Canon Ian Peter. b 60. Lon Univ BSc(Econ)83 Open Univ BA94. d 86 p 87. C Newtownards *D & D* 86-89; I Bright w Ballee and Killough 89-96; Relig Adv Downtown Radio 91-96; I Larne and Inver *Conn* 96-99; I Killiney Ballybrack *D & G* 99-10; I Clonenagh w Offerlane, Borris-in-Ossory etc *C & O* from 10; Can St Patr Cathl Dublin from 11. *Clonenagh Rectory, Portlaoise Road, Mountrath, Co Laois, Republic of Ireland* Tel (00353) (57) 873 2146 E-mail poulton@oceanfree.net
POULTON, The Very Revd Katharine Margaret. b 61. Man Univ BA83. d 87 p 91. C Bangor St Comgall *D & D* 87-91; C Seagoe 91-96; C Kilwaughter w Cairncastle and Craigy Hill *Conn* 96-99; C Greystones *D & G* 99-00; Bp's C Dublin St Geo and St Thos 00-10; Can Ch Ch Cathl Dublin 07-10; Dean Ossory *C & O* from 10; Can Leighlin Cathl from 10; I Kilkenny w Aghour and Kilmanagh from 10. *The Deanery, The Close, Coach Road, Kilkenny, Republic of Ireland* Tel (00353) (56) 772 1516 Fax 775 1817 E-mail katharinepoulton@gmail.com
POULTON, Neville John. b 48. STETS. d 02. NSM Portsea St Cuth *Portsm* 02-07. *18 Belgravia Road, Portsmouth PO2 0DX* Tel (023) 9236 1104 Mobile 0768-661796
POUNCE, Alan Gerald. b 34. Lon Univ BSc55. Wycliffe Hall Ox 57. d 59 p 60. C Wednesfield Heath *Lich* 59-61; C Heref St Pet w St Owen 61-63; R Gt w Lt Dunham *Nor* 63-69; Asst Master Windsor Boys' Sch 69-94; rtd 94; Perm to Offic *Ox* 69-99; Lic to Offic from 99. *38 Longdown Road, Sandhurst GU47 8QG* Tel (01344) 772870
POUNCEY, Christopher Michael Godwin. b 52. Reading Univ BSc74 Wycliffe Hall Ox BA77 MA. SWMC 03. d 04 p 05. NSM S Molton w Nymet St George, High Bray etc *Ex* from 04. *Brightley Barton, Umberleigh EX37 9AL* Tel (01769) 540405 Mobile 07977-930045 E-mail cmgpouncey@hotmail.com

POUND, Canon Keith Salisbury. b 33. St Cath Coll Cam BA54 MA58. Cuddesdon Coll 55. d 57 p 58. C St Helier *S'wark* 57-61; Tr Officer Hollowford Tr and Conf Cen Sheff 61-64; Warden 64-67; R S'wark H Trin 68-74; P-in-c Newington St Matt 68-74; R S'wark H Trin w St Matt 74-78; RD S'wark and Newington 73-78; TR Thamesmead 78-86; Sub-Dean Woolwich 84-86; RD Greenwich 85-86; Hon Can S'wark Cathl 85-86; Chapl Gen of Pris 86-93; Chapl to The Queen 88-03; Chapl HM Pris Grendon and Spring Hill 93-98; rtd 98; Perm to Offic *Chich* from 99. *1 Sinnock Square, Hastings TN34 3HQ* Tel (01424) 428330
POVEY, William Peter. b 36. JP85. Man Univ MSc82 MRCS61 LRCP61 FFPH79 FRIPH HonFChS. NOC 90. d 93 p 94. Dioc Drug Liaison Officer *Ches* 93-01; NSM Latchford Ch Ch 93-00; NSM Daresbury 00-03; rtd 03; Perm to Offic *Ches* from 04 and *Ex* from 04. *Applebrook House, 4 Trinnicks Orchard, Ugborough, Ivybridge PL21 0NX* E-mail povey.peter@googlemail.com
POW, Canon Joyce. b 29. RGN55 SCM57 RSCN60 RNT73. St Jo Coll Nottm 88. d 88 p 94. Hon Par Dn Largs *Glas* 88-94; Hon C 94-00; Hon Can Cumbrae *Arg* from 09. *15 Shuna Court, Skelmorlie PA17 5EJ* Tel (01475) 520289
E-mail joycepow@yahoo.co.uk
POWDRILL, Penelope Anne. b 47. Lon Univ BSc69 PGCE71 Birm Univ MEd77. WEMTC 10. d 11. OLM Goodrich, Marstow, Welsh Bicknor, Llangarron etc *Heref* from 11; OLM Dixton, Wyesham, Bishopswood, Whitchurch etc from 11. *Homebush, Lower Prospect Road, Osbaston, Monmouth NP25 3HS* Tel (01600) 714096
E-mail pennypowdrill@btinternet.com
POWE, David James Hector. b 50. Wycliffe Hall Ox 88. d 90 p 91. C Ventnor St Cath *Portsm* 90-92; Chapl HM Pris Belmarsh 93-94; Chapl 98-04; Chapl HM Pris Lewes 94-97; Chapl HM Pris Bris from 04. *The Chaplain's Office, HM Prison, Cambridge Road, Bristol BS7 8PS* Tel 0117-372 3246 or 372 3100
POWELL, Canon Anthony James. b 51. Sarum & Wells Th Coll 78. d 79 p 80. C Larkfield *Roch* 79-83; C Leybourne 79-83; V Borough Green from 83; Hon Can Roch Cathl from 04. *The Vicarage, 24 Maidstone Road, Borough Green, Sevenoaks TN15 8BD* Tel and fax (01732) 882447
POWELL, Charles David. b 38. St Pet Coll Saltley CertEd61 ACP74. SAOMC 96. d 99 p 00. NSM Ampthill w Millbrook and Steppingley *St Alb* 99-04; Perm to Offic from 05; RD Ampthill 03-08. *33 Putnoe Heights, Bedford MK41 8EB* Tel (01234) 345020 Mobile 07811-260675
E-mail rev.davidpowell@btinternet.com
POWELL, Christopher John. b 71. K Coll Lon BA94 AKC94. Coll of Resurr Mirfield 95. d 97 p 98. C Botley *Portsm* 97-01; C Portsea N End St Mark 01-05; P-in-c Clayton w Keymer *Chich* from 05. *The Rectory, 1 The Crescent, Hassocks BN6 8RB* Tel (01273) 843570 E-mail christopherpowell@supanet.com
POWELL, Colin Arthur. b 32. Hatf Coll Dur BA53. Oak Hill Th Coll 56. d 58 p 59. C Leyland St Andr *Blackb* 58-61; C Lancaster St Thos 61-64; C Tranmere St Cath *Ches* 64-65; R Cheetham Hill *Man* 65-81; TV Oldham 81-86; TV Rochdale 86-97; Chapl Rochdale Healthcare NHS Trust 94-97; rtd 97; Perm to Offic *Man* from 97. *103 Parsonage Road, Withington, Manchester M20 4NU* Tel 0161-434 2409
POWELL, David. See POWELL, Charles David
POWELL, Mrs Diane. b 41. SWMTC 85. d 88 p 94. Hon C St Merryn *Truro* 88-92; Dn-in-c Gerrans w St Anthony in Roseland 92-94; P-in-c 94-00; Asst Chapl R Cornwall Hosps Trust 00-05; rtd 05; Perm to Offic *Truro* from 05. *Windsway, Sandy Common, Constantine Bay, Padstow PL28 8JL* Tel (01841) 521610 E-mail diannick@msn.com
POWELL, Dudley John. b 44. Tyndale Hall Bris 65. d 69 p 70. C Blackb Sav 69-71; C Rodbourne Cheney *Bris* 71-74; P-in-c Kingsdown 74-79; V 79-80; V Stoke Gifford 80-90; TR 90-91; Ancient World Outreach Albania 91-03; Perm to Offic *Bris* 91-03 and *Win* from 03; rtd 09. *30 Homechurch House, 31 Purewell, Christchurch BH23 1EH* Tel (01202) 481379
E-mail dudleyberat@tesco.net
POWELL, Eleanor Ann. b 55. Univ of Wales BA82 Leeds Univ MA06 Gwent Coll Newport CertEd76. Qu Coll Birm 82. d 83 p 94. C Caereithin *S & B* 83-86; C Bishopston 86-88; Dioc Children's Officer *Glouc* 88-94; Dioc Adv for Women's Min 94-01; P-in-c The Edge, Pitchcombe, Harescombe and Brookthorpe 94-00; V Churchdown St Jo 00-01; Hon Can Glouc Cathl 94-01; Chapl United Bris Healthcare NHS Trust 01-06; Chapl N Glam NHS Trust from 06. *Park Farm Lodge, The Legar, Langattock, Crickhowell NP8 1HH* Tel (01873) 811355
E-mail eleanor.powell@nglam-tr.wales.nhs.uk
POWELL, Elizabeth Mary. d 09 p 10. OLM The Bourne and Tilford *Guildf* from 09. *13 Woodcut Road, Wrecclesham, Farnham GU10 4QF* Tel (01252) 725933
E-mail powellliz@hotmail.com
POWELL, Eric Michael. b 46. St As Minl Tr Course. d 04 p 10. NSM Gwersyllt *St As* 04-06; NSM Welshpool w Castle Caereinion 06-08; NSM Welshpool, Castle Caereinion and Pool Quay from 08. *The Vicarage, Llansantffraid SY22 6TZ* Tel (01691) 828244 E-mail mikepowell4680@yahoo.co.uk

POWELL, Preb Frank. b 29. AKC52. **d** 53 **p** 54. C Stockingford *Cov* 53-56; C Netherton St Andr *Worc* 56-60; P-in-c W Bromwich St Jo *Lich* 60-66; C W Bromwich Gd Shep w St Jo 60-66; V 66-69; V Bilston St Leon 69-76; P-in-c Hanbury 76-82; V Hanbury w Newborough 83-86; V Basford 86-92; Preb Lich Cathl 87-92; rtd 92; Perm to Offic *Ches* from 92. *Pippins, 15 Jubilee Terrace, Nantwich CW5 7BT* Tel (01270) 610688 E-mail frank@fjpowell.fsnet.co.uk

POWELL, Gareth. b 78. Brunel Univ BA00 Pemb Coll Cam MPhil08. Westcott Ho Cam 07. **d** 11. C Solihull *Birm* from 11. *17 Church Hill Close, Solihull B91 3SB* Tel 07917-624177 (mobile) E-mail garethpowell@me.com

POWELL, Gary Charles. b 62. UWIST BSc84. Coll of Resurr Mirfield 92. **d** 95 **p** 96. C Roath *Llan* 95-00; V Llansawel, Briton Ferry 00-09; V Dafen *St D* from 09. *The Vicarage, Bryngwyn Road, Llanelli SA14 8LW* Tel (01554) 774730

POWELL, John. b 44. St Luke's Coll Ex CertEd66 Univ of Wales (Lamp) MA02. Glouc Sch of Min 81. **d** 84 **p** 85. NSM Stroud and Uplands w Slad *Glouc* 84-89; Chapl Eliz Coll Guernsey 89-92; C Llandudno *Ban* 92-93; TV 94-96; V Dwygyfylchi 96-02; V Cardigan w Mwnt and Y Ferwig w Llangoedmor *St D* 02-10; rtd 10; P-in-c Llangrannog w Llandysiliogogo w Penbryn *St D* 10-11. *Crud yr Haul, 12 Maesydderwen, Cardigan SA43 1PE* E-mail parchjohnpowell@btinternet.com

POWELL, John Keith Lytton. b 52. S Dios Minl Tr Scheme 91. **d** 94 **p** 95. NSM Bridgwater H Trin *B & W* 94-97; P-in-c Hatch Beauchamp w Beercrocombe, Curry Mallet etc 97-02; P-in-c Staple Fitzpaine, Orchard Portman, Thurlbear etc 97-02; R Beercrocombe w Curry Mallet, Hatch Beauchamp etc 02-05; P-in-c Exford, Exmoor, Hawkridge and Withypool 05-09; P-in-c Middlezoy and Othery and Moorlinch from 09; P-in-c Greinton from 09; Dioc Renewal Adv from 06. *The Vicarage, High Street, Othery, Bridgwater TA7 0QA* Tel (01823) 690100 E-mail jill.powell3@googlemail.com

POWELL, Miss Katherine. b 56. Sydney Univ BSS79. Wycliffe Hall Ox 84. **dss** 86 **d** 87 **p** 94. Broadwater St Mary *Chich* 86-87; Par Dn 87-91; Asst Chapl Ch Hosp Horsham 91-96; Australia from 96; Chapl Glennie Sch from 97. *The Glennie School, Herries Street, Toowoomba Qld 4350, Australia* Tel (0061) (7) 4637 9359 *or* 4688 8808 Fax 4688 8848 E-mail powellk@glennie.qld.edu.au

POWELL, Kelvin. b 49. Wycliffe Hall Ox 71. **d** 74 **p** 75. C Prescot *Liv* 74-77; C Ainsdale 77-79; V Bickershaw 79-85; R Hesketh w Becconsall *Blackb* 85-99; Perm to Offic *Ox* from 03. *43 Sharman Beer Court, Southern Road, Thame OX9 2DD*

POWELL, Mark. b 57. Bath Univ BSc78 PhD81. Ripon Coll Cuddesdon BA84 MA88. **d** 85 **p** 86. C Evesham *Worc* 85-88; V Exhall *Cov* 88-96; V Leavesden St Alb 96-00; V Ealing St Pet Mt Park *Lon* from 00; V Melbourne, Ticknall, Smisby and Stanton *Derby* from 11. *The Vicarage, Church Square, Melbourne, Derby DE73 8JH* Tel (01332) 864741 E-mail mark.powell4@btinternet.com

POWELL, Martin. b 71. St Steph Ho Ox BTh00. **d** 00 **p** 01. C Caterham *S'wark* 00-03; V New Addington from 03. *St Edward's Vicarage, Cleves Crescent, Croydon CR0 0DL* Tel (01689) 845588

POWELL, Michael. See POWELL, Eric Michael

POWELL, Pamela. b 56. Univ of Wales BEd79 Goldsmiths' Coll Lon MA82. St As Minl Tr Course 00. **d** 03 **p** 04. C Wrexham *St As* 03-06; P-in-c Llansantffraid-ym-Mechain and Llanfechain 06-08; V from 08; Dir Lay Min from 10; AD Llanfyllin from 11. *The Vicarage, Llansantffraid SY22 6TZ* Tel (01691) 828244 Mobile 07711-053565 E-mail pampowell@micro-plus-web.net

POWELL, Patricia Mary. STETS. **d** 03 **p** 04. NSM Woodford Valley *Sarum* 03-09; NSM Tidworth, Ludgershall and Faberstown from 09. *Hawthorn Cottage, Great Durnford, Salisbury SP4 6AZ* Tel (01722) 782546 E-mail patricia powell@btinternet.com

POWELL, Ralph Dover. b 49. ARMCM70. Chich Th Coll 71. **d** 74 **p** 75. C Coppenhall *Ches* 74-77; C Heref H Trin 77-80; V Crewe St Barn *Ches* from 80. *St Barnabas' Vicarage, West Street, Crewe CW1 3AX* Tel (01270) 212418

POWELL, Richard Penry. b 15. Dur Univ LTh38. St Aid Birkenhead 34. **d** 38 **p** 39. C Brierley Hill *Lich* 38-42; C Derby St Chad 42-45; C Uttoxeter w Bramshall *Lich* 45-47; V Alton 47-60; V Bradley-in-the-Moors 48-60; R Drayton Bassett 60-64; Min Canwell CD 60-64; V Wrockwardine 64-80; V Uppington 64-80; rtd 80; Perm to Offic *Lich* from 80. *34 Herbert Avenue, Wellington, Telford TF1 2BS* Tel (01952) 242528

POWELL, Robert John. b 65. Trin Coll Bris BA92. **d** 92 **p** 93. C Biggin Hill *Roch* 92-95; C Edgware *Lon* 95-01; Area Sec SAMS (NW England and N Wales) 01-04; TV Upper Holloway *Lon* from 04. *The Vicarage, 43 Dresden Road, London N19 3BG* Tel (020) 7686 2293

POWELL, Roger Roy. b 68. Thames Poly BSc91. Ripon Coll Cuddesdon BTh94. **d** 94 **p** 95. C Leic St Jas 94-98; C The Abbey Leic 98-00; TV 00-05; P-in-c Leic St Paul 01-05; Youth Chapl 98-05; P-in-c Ridgeway *Sarum* 05-10; R from 10. *The Rectory, 3 Butts Road, Chiseldon, Swindon SN4 0NN* Tel (01793) 740369 E-mail revd.rpowell@btopenworld.com

POWELL, Stuart William. b 58. K Coll Lon BD80 AKC80. Ripon Coll Cuddesdon 86. **d** 88 **p** 89. C Horden *Dur* 88-90; C Northolt Park St Barn *Lon* 90-93; V Castle Vale St Cuth *Birm* 93-00; V Stockland Green 00-11; P-in-c Rough Hills *Lich* from 11; P-in-c Wolverhampton St Steph from 11. *St Martin's Vicarage, Dixon Street, Wolverhampton WV2 2BG* Tel (01902) 341030 Mobile 07889-887358 Pager 07336-734456 E-mail spowell.t21@btinternet.com

POWER, Alan Edward. b 26. Worc Coll Ox BA50 MA53. Lich Th Coll. **d** 57 **p** 58. C Summerfield *Birm* 57-60; C Oldbury 60-63; V Short Heath 63-97; rtd 97; Perm to Offic *Birm* from 97. *8 Southam Drive, Sutton Coldfield B73 5PD* Tel 0121-355 8923

POWER, David Michael. b 56. BA81 BEd. Oak Hill Th Coll. **d** 81 **p** 82. C Warblington w Emsworth *Portsm* 81-84; C-in-c Hartplain CD 84-88; V Hartplain 88-91; Adv in Evang 91-97; V Portsea St Cuth from 97. *St Cuthbert's Vicarage, 2 Lichfield Road, Portsmouth PO3 6DE* Tel and fax (023) 9282 7071

POWER, Ivor Jonathan. b 43. Lambeth STh87. CITC 66. **d** 69 **p** 70. C Dromore Cathl 69-71; C Enniscorthy *C & O* 71-74; I Youghal *C, C & R* 74-78; I Youghal Union 78-81; I Athlone w Benown, Kiltoom and Forgney *M & K* 81-98; Can Meath 87-98; Dir of Ords (Meath) 91-97; I Dublin Crumlin w Chapelizod *D & G* 98-08; Can Ch Ch Cathl Dublin 05-08; rtd 08. *62 Maudlin Street, Kilkenny, Republic of Ireland*

POWER, James Edward. b 58. Nottm Univ BSc81 Leeds Univ BA85. Coll of Resurr Mirfield 83. **d** 86 **p** 87. C Cadoxton-juxta-Barry *Llan* 86-89; Chapl Harrow Sch from 89. *35 West Street, Harrow HA1 3EG* Tel (020) 8872 8234 E-mail jep@harrowschool.org.uk

POWER, Mrs Jeanette. b 57. Oak Hill Th Coll BA81. **dss** 82 **d** 87 **p** 94. Warblington w Emsworth *Portsm* 82-84; Hartplain CD 84-87; Hon C Hartplain 87-91; Community Mental Health Chapl Havant and Petersfield from 91; NSM Wickham 93-97; NSM Portsea St Cuth from 97; Team Chapl Portsm Hosps NHS Trust from 01. *St Cuthbert's Vicarage, 2 Lichfield Road, Portsmouth PO3 6DE* Tel and fax (023) 9282 7071 E-mail jeanettepower@ntlworld.com

POWIS, Michael Ralph. b 63. St Jo Coll Nottm BTh95. **d** 95 **p** 96. C Dibden *Win* 95-00; V Hedge End St Luke 00-09; Adult Discipleship and Evang Tr Officer from 09. *8 Juniper Close, Winchester SO22 4LU* Tel (01962) 621471 E-mail mike.powis@ukgateway.net

POWLES, Charles Anthony. b 39. EAMTC. **d** 88 **p** 89. NSM Hemsby *Nor* 88-93; NSM Bradwell 01-07; Perm to Offic from 07. *94 Winifred Way, Caister-on-Sea, Great Yarmouth NR30 5PE* Tel (01493) 720096 E-mail charles.powles@btinternet.com

POWLES, Michael Charles. b 34. Reading Univ BSc56 Lon Univ PGCE83. Qu Coll Birm. **d** 60 **p** 61. C Goodmayes All SS *Chelmsf* 60-65; C Surbiton St Matt *S'wark* 65-78; Lect Woolwich Coll 79-99; rtd 99. *Spring Cottage, 3 Rushett Close, Thames Ditton KT7 0UH* Tel (020) 8398 9654

POWLEY, Miss Julia Hodgson. b 55. St Andr Univ MA77 FCA80. Ridley Hall Cam 07. **d** 09 **p** 10. C Carl H Trin and St Barn from 09. *Holy Trinity Vicarage, 25 Wigton Road, Carlisle CA2 7BB* Tel (01228) 522938 Mobile 07765-217335 E-mail julia@powley.plus.com

POWLEY, Mark Thomas. b 75. Nottm Univ BA96 Birm Univ PGCE98. Wycliffe Hall Ox 01. **d** 03 **p** 04. C Addiscombe St Mary Magd w St Martin *S'wark* 03-06; C Hammersmith St Paul *Lon* 06-09; TV Leeds St Geo *Ripon* from 10. *2 Moor Drive, Leeds LS6 4BY* Tel 0113-278 5902 E-mail mark.powley@stgeorgesleeds.org.uk

POWLEY, Canon Robert Mallinson. b 39. Fitzw Coll Cam MA65. Ridley Hall Cam 61. **d** 63 **p** 64. C Bermondsey St Mary w St Olave, St Jo etc *S'wark* 63-67; C Moseley St Anne *Birm* 67-69; Lic to Offic *Man* 72-77; Hon C Walshaw Ch Ch 77-88; V Prestwich St Gabr 88-94; Bp's Dom Chapl 88-94; P-in-c Hargrave *Ches* 94-05; Exec Officer Bd for Soc Resp 94-05; Hon Can Ches Cathl 00-05; rtd 05; Perm to Offic *Ban* 05-11; Hon C Bangor from 11. *76 Fordd Cynan, Bangor LL57 2NS* Tel (01248) 364292

POWNALL, Miss Hilary Frances. b 54. SEITE 08. **d** 11. NSM Eastbourne St Mary *Chich* from 11. *Foundlings, 34A Broomfield Street, Eastbourne BN20 8LQ* Tel (01323) 411816 Mobile 07985-714201 E-mail hfpownall@hfpownall.plus.com

POWNALL, Lydia Margaret. See HURLE, Mrs Lydia Margaret

POWNALL, Stephen. b 56. St Jo Coll Nottm BA02. **d** 02 **p** 03. C Herne Hill *S'wark* 02-06; TV Westborough *Guildf* from 06. *St Clare's Vicarage, 242 Cabell Road, Guildford GU2 8JW* Tel (01483) 301349 E-mail steve@sbpownall.fsworld.co.uk

POWNALL-JONES, Timothy William. b 79. Univ of Wales (Cardiff) BD00 MTh02. Trin Coll Bris 04. **d** 06 **p** 07. C Newark w Coddington *S'well* 06-10; Chapl N Notts Coll of FE 10-11; Lic to Offic from 10. *The Vicarage, 3 Maple Drive, Elkesley, Retford DN22 8AX* Tel 07837-630005 (mobile) E-mail t_pownall_jones@hotmail.com

POWNE, Peter Rebbeck Lamb. b 23. Sarum & Wells Th Coll 80. **d** 83 **p** 84. C Calne and Blackland *Sarum* 83-86; V Netheravon w

Fittleton and Enford 86-93; rtd 93; Perm to Offic *Sarum* from 93. *2 Oak Lane, Figheldean, Salisbury SP4 8JS* Tel (01980) 670356

✠**POYNTZ, The Rt Revd Samuel Greenfield.** b 26. TCD BA48 MA51 BD53 PhD60 Ulster Univ Hon DLitt95. TCD Div Sch Div Test50. **d** 50 **p** 51 **c** 78. C Dublin St Geo *D & G* 50-52; C Bray 52-55; C Dublin St Michan w St Paul 55-59; Sec and Sch Insp Ch Educn Soc for Ireland 56-75; I Dublin St Steph 59-67; I Dublin St Ann 67-70; I Dublin St Ann w St Steph 70-78; Adn Dublin 74-78; Bp C, C & R 78-87; Bp Conn 87-95; rtd 95. *3 The Gables, Ballinteer Road, Dundrum, Dublin 16, Republic of Ireland* Tel (00353) (1) 296 6748

PRADELLA, Henry. b 54. St Mary's Coll Twickenham BEd78. NTMTC 97. **d** 00 **p** 01. NSM Hainault *Chelmsf* 00-04; C Romford Gd Shep 04-06; R Rainham w Wennington from 06. *The Vicarage, 73 Lake Avenue, Rainham RM13 9SG* Tel (01708) 559157 E-mail pradfam@btinternet.com

PRAGNELL, John William. b 39. Lon Univ BD65. Lambeth STh87 LTh88. **d** 65 **p** 66. C Bitterne *Win* 65-68; C Hatfield Hyde *St Alb* 68-73; Kuwait 73-75; Chapl Leavesden Hosp and Abbots Langley Hosp 75-88; Chapl Watford Gen Hosp 86-88; V St Alb St Steph *St Alb* 88-95; RD St Alb 91-95; P-in-c Copythorne *Win* 95-02; Dioc Ecum Officer 95-02; Hosp Chapl Adv (Bournemouth Adnry) 00-02; rtd 02; Perm to Offic *Sarum* 03-07. *10 Palmers Court, Southwell NG25 0JG*

PRAGNELL, Michael John. b 40. Down Coll Cam BA62 PhD65 MA66 FIQA81 MRSC CChem MSOSc88. Ox NSM Course 81. **d** 84 **p** 85. NSM High Wycombe *Ox* 84-98; C Beercrocombe w Curry Mallet, Hatch Beauchamp etc *B & W* 98-05; rtd 05; Perm to Offic *B & W* from 05. *2 Listers Court, Listers Hill, Ilminster TA19 0DF* Tel (01460) 54212

PRAGNELL, Ms Sandra Ann. b 53. Hull Univ BA75 TCD BTh01 Dub City Univ MA04. CITC 98. **d** 01 **p** 02. C Castleknock and Mulholdart w Clonsilla *D & G* 01-05; PV Ch Ch Cathl Dublin 03-05; I Dundalk w Heynestown *Arm* from 05; I Ballymascanlan w Creggan and Rathcor from 05. *The Rectory, Old Golf Links Road, Blackrock, Co Louth, Republic of Ireland* Tel (00353) (42) 932 1402 Mobile 87-265 8592 E-mail dundalk@armagh.anglican.org

PRAILL, David William. b 57. York Univ BA79 FRGS90. Cranmer Hall Dur 81. **d** 82 **p** 83. C Digswell and Panshanger *St Alb* 82-84; CMS 84-89; Course Dir St Geo Coll Jerusalem 85-89; Dir McCabe Educn Trust 90-91; Dir St Luke's Hospice Harrow and Wembley 91-98; Chief Exec Help the Hospices from 98. *Hospice House, 34-44 Britannia Street, London WC1X 9JG* Tel (020) 7520 8200 Fax 7278 1021

PRANCE, Robert Penrose. b 47. Southn Univ BTh73. Sarum & Wells Th Coll 69. **d** 72 **p** 73. C Gillingham and Fifehead Magdalen *Sarum* 72-76; P-in-c Edmondsham 76-80; P-in-c Woodlands 76-80; P-in-c Wimborne St Giles 76-80; P-in-c Cranborne 77-80; R Cranborne w Boveridge, Edmondsham etc 80-83; Chapl Sherborne Sch 83-93; Asst Dir of Ords *Sarum* 76-86; V Stoke Gabriel and Collaton *Ex* 93-99; Dep PV Ex Cathl 95-99; Chapl Shiplake Coll Henley 99-09; Chapl St Edm Sch Cant 09-10; Perm to Offic *Ox* from 09. *The Orchards, Hazel Gardens, Sonning Common, Reading RG4 9TF*

PRASADAM, Goruganthula Samuel Narayanamurthy. b 34. Andhra Univ India BA57. Bangalore Th Coll BD65 Union Th Sem (NY) STM68. **d** 62 **p** 65. In Ch of S India 62-74; C Llanbeblig w Caernarfon and Betws Garmon etc *Ban* 75-76; C Norbury *Ches* 77-78; V Aberaman and Abercwmboi *Llan* 78-83; N Sec CMS 83-87; V Luton All SS w St Pet *St Alb* 87-96; rtd 99. *306 Raaga Apartments, 10-5-34 Masabtank, Hyderabad 500 0028, India*

PRASADAM, Canon Jemima. b 39. MBE05. BD61 BA87. Cranmer Hall Dur 86. **d** 87 **p** 94. Par Dn Luton All SS w St Pet *St Alb* 87-94; C 94-96; P-in-c Lozells St Paul and Silas *Birm* 96-07; V 07-09; P-in-c from 09; rtd 09; Hon Can Birm Cathl from 05. *St Silas's Vicarage, 103 Heathfield Road, Birmingham B19 1HE* Tel 0121-523 5645

PRASADAM, Madhu Smitha. b 64. Qu Coll Birm. **d** 03 **p** 04. C Blackheath *Birm* 03-07; V Hamstead St Paul from 07. *Hamstead Vicarage, 840 Walsall Road, Birmingham B42 1ES* Tel 0121-357 8941

PRASADAM, Samuel. See PRASADAM, Goruganthula Samuel Narayanamurthy

PRATT, Basil David. b 38. Ripon Hall Ox 64. **d** 67 **p** 68. C Lewisham St Jo Southend *S'wark* 67-68; C Caterham Valley 68-70; CF 70-93; Perm to Offic *Glas* from 08. *St Michael's, Bankend Road, Dumfries DG1 4AL* Tel (01387) 267933

PRATT, Christine Fiona. See BLACKMAN, Christine Fiona

PRATT, Edward Andrew. b 39. Clare Coll Cam BA61 MA65. Clifton Th Coll 63. **d** 66 **p** 67. C Southall Green St Jo *Lon* 66-69; C Drypool St Columba w St Andr and St Pet *York* 69-71; P-in-c Radbourne *Derby* 71-74; R Kirk Langley 71-78; V Mackworth All SS 71-78; V Southsea St Simon *Portsm* 78-97; rtd 97; Perm to Offic *Sarum* from 97. *7 Bay Close, Swanage BH19 1RE*

PRATT, Mrs Janet Margaret. b 40. Herts Coll BEd78. St Alb Minl Tr Scheme 78. **dss** 81 **d** 87 **p** 94. High Wych and Gilston w Eastwick *St Alb* 81-89; Hon Par Dn 87-89; Par Dn Histon *Ely*

89-94; C 94-97; Par Dn Impington 89-94; C 94-97; R Bardney *Linc* 97-07; rtd 07; Perm to Offic *Ely* and *St Alb* from 08. *26 Stamford Avenue, Royston SG8 7DD* Tel (01763) 243508 E-mail janetmpratt99@yahoo.com

PRATT, John. b 37. **d** 99 **p** 00. OLM St Enoder *Truro* 99-05; rtd 06. *Chyteg, Newquay Road, St Columb Road, St Columb TR9 6PY* Tel and fax (01726) 860747

PRATT, John Anthony. b 38. Selw Coll Cam BA61 MA65. Qu Coll Birm. **d** 66 **p** 67. C Harrow Weald All SS *Lon* 66-69; C St Pancras w St Jas and Ch Ch 69-74; C Saffron Walden *Chelmsf* 74-75; TV Saffron Walden w Wendens Ambo and Littlebury 75-79; V St Mary-at-Latton 79-88; Chapl Princess Alexandra Hosp Harlow 82-88; RD Harlow *Chelmsf* 83-88; R Tolleshunt Knights w Tiptree and Gt Braxted 88-03; rtd 03; Perm to Offic *Cov* from 03. *2 Erica Drive, Whitnash, Leamington Spa CV31 2RS* Tel (01926) 428609

PRATT, Michael. See HARRIS, Michael

PRATT, The Ven Richard David. b 55. Linc Coll Ox BA77 MA81 Birm Univ PhD01 Nottm Univ BCombStuds84. Linc Th Coll 81. **d** 84 **p** 85. C Wellingborough All Hallows *Pet* 84-87; TV Kingsthorpe w Northampton St Dav 87-92; V Northampton St Benedict 92-97; Dioc Communications Officer *Carl* from 97; P-in-c Carl St Cuth w St Mary 97-08; Hon Can Carl Cathl 02-08; Adn W Cumberland from 09. *50 Stainburn Road, Stainburn, Workington CA14 1SN* Tel (01900) 66190 E-mail archdeacon.west@carlislediocese.org.uk

PRATT, Samuel Charles. b 40. ALAM59. Oak Hill Th Coll 69. **d** 71 **p** 72. C Upper Holloway St Jo *Lon* 71-73; C Bucknall and Bagnall *Lich* 73-76; V Liv St Mich 76-80; Chapl R Liv Hosp 80-94; Chapl R Liv Univ Hosp NHS Trust 94-01; V Billinge *Liv* 01-06; rtd 06. *15 Billinge Road, Wigan WN5 9JW* Tel (01942) 731346 Mobile 07957-367114 E-mail sp001f3678@blueyonder.co.uk

PRATT, Stephen Samuel. b 67. Univ Coll Ches BA88 Keele Univ PGCE89. Oak Hill Th Coll BA00. **d** 00 **p** 01. C Goodmayes All SS *Chelmsf* 00-03; TV Chell *Lich* 03-07; P-in-c 07-08; V from 08; CF(V) from 05. *The Rectory, 203 St Michael's Road, Stoke-on-Trent ST6 6JT* Tel (01782) 838708 E-mail stephen_pratt@sky.com

PRATT, Canon William Ralph. b 47. Keble Coll Ox BA69 MA73. Linc Th Coll 70. **d** 72 **p** 73. C Ifield *Chich* 72-78; TV 78; C Brighton St Pet w Chpl Royal and St Jo 79-83; P-in-c Hove St Jo 83-87; Dioc Communications Officer 87-00; V Ringmer from 00; Can and Preb Chich Cathl from 90. *The Vicarage, Vicarage Way, Ringmer, Lewes BN8 5LA* Tel (01273) 812243 E-mail wrpratt@btinternet.com

PRECIOUS, Sally Joanne. See WRIGHT, Sally Joanne

PREECE, Barry Leslie. b 48. Lich Th Coll 68. **d** 71 **p** 72. C Ewell *Guildf* 71-74; C York Town St Mich 75-77; P-in-c Ripley 77-81; Chapl HM Det Cen Send 77-81; V Cuddington *Guildf* 81-88; V Cobham 88-03; R E and W Clandon from 03. *The Rectory, The Street, West Clandon, Guildford GU4 7RG* Tel and fax (01483) 222573 E-mail rev.preece@btinternet.com

PREECE, Canon Colin George. b 51. Bernard Gilpin Soc Dur 71 Chich Th Coll 72. **d** 75 **p** 76. C Upper Gornal *Lich* 75-78; C Wednesbury St Paul Wood Green 78-81; V Oxley 81-89; V Kennington *Cant* 89-03; RD E Charing 92-98; P-in-c Ashford from 03; Hon Can Cant Cathl from 08. *The College, Church Yard, Ashford TN23 1QG* Tel (01233) 620672 E-mail cpreece@globalnet.co.uk

PREECE, Mrs Jill Annette. b 58. Bp Otter Coll BEd79. SEITE 08. **d** 11. NSM Eastbourne St Elisabeth *Chich* from 11. *2 Osborne Road, Eastbourne BN20 8JL* Tel (01323) 638020 Mobile 07742-655986

PREECE, Joseph. b 23. Univ of Wales (Ban) BA50. NW Ord Course 73. **d** 73 **p** 74. C Claughton cum Grange *Ches* 73-74; C Barnston 74-75; R Aldford and Bruera 75-80; V Wincle and Wildboarclough 80-82; P-in-c Cleeton w Silvington *Heref* 82-86; P-in-c Farlow 82-86; V Stottesdon 82-86; R Stottesdon w Farlow, Cleeton and Silvington 86-88; rtd 88; Perm to Offic *Heref* 91-10. *Lingholm, Woodhall Drive, Hanwood, Shrewsbury SY5 8JU* Tel (01743) 860946

PREECE, Mark Richard. b 61. St Paul's Coll Chelt BA85. Linc Th Coll 85. **d** 87 **p** 88. C Coity w Nolton *Llan* 87-89; C Penarth w Lavernock 89-92; V Ewenny w St Brides Major 92-99; V Canton St Luke 99-02; TR Canton Cardiff from 02; AD Cardiff from 08. *Canton Rectory, 12 Thompson Avenue, Cardiff CF5 1EY* Tel and fax (029) 2056 2022 E-mail mp@mandm6162.plus.com

PREECE, Roger Martin Howell. b 64. Imp Coll Lon BSc86 FRSA96. St Steph Ho Ox BA05. **d** 06 **p** 07. C Marple All SS *Ches* 06-08; V Bowdon from 08. *The Vicarage, Church Brow, Bowdon, Altrincham WA14 2SG* Tel 0161-928 2468 E-mail preece@europe.com

PREECE, Ronald Alexander. b 29. Lon Univ BD56. ALCD55. **d** 56 **p** 57. C Rusholme H Trin *Man* 56-59; Teacher Kidbrooke Sch Lon 59-60; Chapl Pernambuco Brazil 60-63; Perm to Offic *Cant* 63-70; Teacher Abp's Sch Cant 64-70; OMF 70-94; SW Regional Dir 76-94; rtd 94; Perm to Offic *Cant* from 98. *5 Tonford Lane, Canterbury CT1 3XU* Tel (01227) 471061

PREMRAJ, Deborah Devashanthy. b 66. Bangalore Univ BSc87 BEd92 Serampore Univ BD91. United Th Coll Bangalore 87. **d** 96 **p** 97. Deacon Vedal India 96-97; Presbyter Madurantakam 97-02; Perm to Offic *S'wark* 02-05; C Battersea Fields 05-06; Presbyter St Geo Cathl Chennai India from 06. *St George's Cathedral, 224 Cathedral Road, Chennai 600 086, India* Tel (0091) (44) 2811 4261
E-mail premraj@csistgeorgescathedral.org

PREMRAJ, Dhanaraj Charles. b 63. Madras Univ BA86 MA88 Heythrop Coll Lon MTh03. United Th Coll Bangalore BD92. **d** 93 **p** 94. India 93-02; Perm to Offic *S'wark* 02-05; C Battersea Fields 05-06; Presbyter St Geo Cathl Chennai India from 06. *St George's Cathedral, 224 Cathedral Road, Chennai 600 086, India* Tel (0091) (44) 2811 4261
E-mail premraj@csistgeorgescathedral.org

PRENTICE, Brian. b 40. St Jo Coll Nottm 81. **d** 83 **p** 84. C W Bromwich All SS *Lich* 83-86; C Tettenhall Wood 86-89; TV 89-90; V Essington 90-98; TR Willenhall H Trin 98-05; P-in-c Bentley 05; AD Wolverhampton 03-05; rtd 05; Perm to Offic *Lich* from 05. *3 Hamilton Gardens, Bushbury, Wolverhampton WV10 8AX* Tel (01902) 564603

PRENTICE, Mark Neil. b 73. Ex Univ BA94. Wycliffe Hall Ox MTh00. **d** 00 **p** 01. C Tulse Hill H Trin and St Matthias *S'wark* 00-04; C Langham Place All So *Lon* from 04. *25 Fitzroy Street, London W1T 6DR* Tel (020) 7387 1360 *or* 7580 3745

PRENTICE, Paul Frederick. b 68. SEITE 04. **d** 07 **p** 08. C Bromley SS Pet and Paul *Roch* 07-10; P-in-c Orpington St Andr from 10. *The Vicarage, Anglesea Road, Orpington BR5 4AN* Tel and fax (01689) 823775 Mobile 07949-059993
E-mail paul.prentice2@btinternet.com

PRENTIS, Calvert Clayton. b 62. Aston Tr Scheme 93 St Jo Coll Nottm 95. **d** 97 **p** 98. C Wood End *Cov* 97-00; TV Leeds St Geo *Ripon* 00-05; Asst Dioc Dir of Ords 02-05; P-in-c Huddersfield H Trin *Wakef* 05-07; V from 07; Asst Dioc Dir of Ords from 09. *Holy Trinity Vicarage, 132 Trinity Street, Huddersfield HD1 4DT* Tel (01484) 422998 E-mail holytvicar@btinternet.com

PRENTIS, Richard Hugh. b 36. Ch Coll Cam BA60 MA64. Sarum Th Coll 69. **d** 71 **p** 72. C Bath Bathwick St Mary *B & W* 71-76; Bp's Dom Chapl *Lich* 76-80; PV Lich Cathl 76-80; V Longton St Mary and St Chad 80-84; V Shifnal 84-94; P-in-c Badger 84-85; P-in-c Ryton 84-85; P-in-c Beckbury 84-85; rtd 94. *23A The Close, Lichfield WS13 7LD* Tel (01543) 411234

PRESCOTT, David Anthony. b 62. Univ of Wales (Lamp) BA84 Coll of Ripon & York St Jo PGCE85. Ripon Coll Cuddesdon MTh07. **d** 07 **p** 08. C W Heref 07-10; TV Burrington, Chawleigh, Cheldon, Chulmleigh etc *Ex* from 10. *The Vicarage, The Square, Witheridge, Tiverton EX16 8AE* Tel (01884) 860768 Mobile 07779-588619 E-mail david.prescott@ripon.oxon.org

PRESCOTT, David John. b 51. St Kath Coll Liv BEd73. NOC 00. **d** 03 **p** 04. C Southport Em *Liv* 03-07; P-in-c Birchwood from 07. *The Vicarage, Admiral's Road, Birchwood, Warrington WA3 6QG* Tel (01925) 811906 Mobile 07762-943138

PRESCOTT, Thomas Robert. b 41. St Mich Coll Llan 93. **d** 95 **p** 96. C Abertillery w Cwmtillery w Six Bells *Mon* 95-99; V Llanhilleth 99-03; rtd 03. *70 Glandwr Street, Abertillery NP13 1TZ* Tel (01495) 216782

PRESCOTT, William Allan. b 57. ACIS87. Sarum & Wells Th Coll 91. **d** 93 **p** 94. C Horsell *Guildf* 93-98; R Guernsey St Sav *Win* 98-08; P-in-c Guernsey St Marguerite de la Foret 98-08; Chapl Guernsey Airport 08; R Compton, Hursley, and Otterbourne from 08. *The Rectory, Kiln Lane, Otterbourne, Winchester SO21 2EJ* Tel (01962) 714551

PRESS, Richard James. b 45. Southn Univ CertEd67. Sarum & Wells Th Coll 92. **d** 92 **p** 93. C Bradford-on-Avon H Trin *Sarum* 92-95; P-in-c Rowde and Poulshot 95-98; R Rowde and Bromham 98-01; Chapl Wilts and Swindon Healthcare NHS Trust 98-00; P-in-c Chickerell w Fleet *Sarum* 01-07; R from 07; P-in-c Abbotsbury, Portesham and Langton Herring from 09. *The Rectory, East Street, Chickerell, Weymouth DT3 4DS* Tel (01305) 784915 E-mail revrichardpress@yahoo.co.uk

PRESS, William John. b 72. QUB MEng94 BTh. **d** 99 **p** 00. C Knockbreda *D & D* 99-03; C Dundonald 03-05; I Annalong from 05. *Kilhorne Rectory, 173 Kilkeel Road, Annalong, Newry BT34 4TN* Tel (028) 4376 8246

PREST, Ms Deborah Ann. b 56. Leeds Univ BA77 Man Univ PGCE98. SNWTP 07. **d** 10 **p** 11. C Timperley *Ches* from 10. *57 Heyes Lane, Timperley, Altrincham WA15 6DZ* Tel 0161-282 8981 E-mail deborahprest@virginmedia.com

PRESTIDGE, Colin Robert. b 58. W Sussex Inst of HE BEd86 Open Univ BA01. STETS 01. **d** 04 **p** 05. NSM Crofton *Portsm* from 04; Asst Chapl E Hants Primary Care Trust from 04. *96 Titchfield Road, Stubbington, Fareham PO14 2JB* Tel (01329) 664375 E-mail colin@prestidge.org.uk

PRESTNEY, Canon Patricia Christine Margaret. b 49. UEA BEd94. Oak Hill Th Coll 84. **d** 87 **p** 94. NSM Lawford *Chelmsf* 87-95; Chapl Benenden Sch 95-97; Chapl St Jo Coll Ipswich 97-00; R Lawford *Chelmsf* 00-10; Hon Can Chelmsf Cathl 09-10; rtd 10; Perm to Offic *Chelmsf* from 11. *2 Cedar Way, Great Bentley, Colchester CO7 8LT* Tel (01206) 255319
E-mail patprestney@yahoo.com

PRESTON, David Francis. b 50. BNC Ox BA72 MA78. St Steph Ho Ox 72. **d** 74 **p** 75. C Beckenham St Jas *Roch* 74-79; C Hockley *Chelmsf* 81-83; C Lamorbey H Redeemer *Roch* 83-89; V Gillingham St Barn 89-00; Perm to Offic 00-11. *103 High Street, Kirkcudbright DG6 4JG* Tel (01557) 330650
E-mail d.preston.347@btinternet.com

PRESTON, Mrs Deborah Anne. b 46. GTCL67. CBDTI 01. **d** 04 **p** 06. OLM Kirkby Lonsdale *Carl* 04-06; NSM Old Hutton and New Hutton from 06; NSM Crosscrake from 06. *The Old Schoolhouse, Kirkby Lonsdale, Carnforth LA6 2DX* Tel (015242) 72509 Mobile 07799-246380
E-mail deborah@jpreston83.freeserve.co.uk

PRESTON, Donald George. b 30. St Alb Minl Tr Scheme 77. **d** 80 **p** 81. NSM Elstow *St Alb* 80-87; NSM Goldington 87-94; Perm to Offic from 95. *106 Putnoe Street, Bedford MK41 8HJ* Tel (01234) 267313

PRESTON, Frederick John. b 32. MBE72. Oak Hill Th Coll 54. **d** 57 **p** 58. C Hove Bp Hannington Memorial Ch *Chich* 57-59; C-in-c Knaphill *Guildf* 60-62; CF 62-69 and 71-79; V Otterton *Ex* 69-71; NSM 79-84; Chapl ICS 84-89; rtd 89; Perm to Offic *Nor* 96-98 and *Chich* from 98. *10 Cliff House, 57 Chesterfield Road, Eastbourne BN20 7NU* Tel (01323) 638212

PRESTON, Jack. b 32. Th Ext Educn Coll 78. **d** 81 **p** 82. C Borrowdale Ch Ch Zimbabwe 81-85; C Mabelreign St Pet 85-87; C Belvedere St Eliz 87-94; C Harrismith St Jo S Africa 94-96; Lic to Offic Dio Harare Zimbabwe 96-09; Perm to Offic *Blackb* from 10. *12 St Clements Court, Barrowford, Nelson BB9 8QU* Tel (01282) 695306

PRESTON, James Martin. b 31. Trin Coll Cam MA55 Ch Ch Ox MA57. Virginia Th Sem 57 S'wark Ord Course 87. **d** 88 **p** 88. NSM Blackheath Ascension *S'wark* 88-95; NSM Lewisham St Mary 95-97; NSM Catford St Laur 97-99; Perm to Offic *Chich* 99-08 and *S'wark* from 08. *14 Curness Street, London SE13 6JY* Tel (020) 8690 0993
E-mail prestonjm@btopenworld.com

PRESTON, John Baker. b 23. Lon Univ BA49. Oak Hill Th Coll 46. **d** 51 **p** 52. C Fazakerley Em *Liv* 51-55; C Eastbourne H Trin *Chich* 55-57; V Blackheath St Jo *S'wark* 57-65; Perm to Offic *Cant* 69-91; rtd 88. *43 Wedgwood Drive, Poole BH14 8ES*

PRESTON, John Michael. b 40. K Coll Lon BD63 AKC63 Lon Univ BA81 Southn Univ PhD91. St Boniface Warminster. **d** 65 **p** 66. C Heston *Lon* 65-67; C Northolt St Mary 67-72; Trinidad and Tobago 72-74; P-in-c Aveley *Chelmsf* 74-78; V 78-82; C Eastleigh *Win* 82-84; C-in-c Boyatt Wood CD 84-87; V W End 87-00; P-in-c Newton Valence, Selborne and E Tisted w Colemore 00-03; rtd 03; Perm to Offic *Portsm* from 03; Chapl SSB from 03. *29 Selsmore Road, Hayling Island PO11 9JZ* Tel (023) 9263 7673 E-mail john.preston@ukgateway.net

PRESTON, Mrs Junko Monica. b 38. Aoyama Gakuin Tokyo BA. **d** 92 **p** 93. C St Paul's Cathl Wellington from 92. *60A Messines Road, Karori, Wellington 6012, New Zealand* Tel (0064) (4) 476 7902

PRESTON, Martin. *See* PRESTON, James Martin

PRESTON, Michael Christopher. b 47. Hatf Coll Dur BA68. Ripon Coll Cuddesdon 75. **d** 78 **p** 79. C Epsom St Martin *Guildf* 78-82; C Guildf H Trin w St Mary 82-86; V Epsom St Barn from 86. *St Barnabas' Vicarage, Hook Road, Epsom KT19 8TU* Tel (01372) 722874 E-mail rev@m-c-preston.org.uk

PRESTON, Canon Percival Kenneth. b 16. Ch Ch Ox BA38 MA48. Cuddesdon Coll 38. **d** 40 **p** 45. C Jersey St Helier *Win* 40-46; C Ox SS Phil and Jas 46-48; C Westbury-on-Trym H Trin *Bris* 48-50; Min Lawrence Weston CD 50-55; V Horfield St Greg 55-81; Hon Can Bris Cathl 74-82; RD Horfield 76-81; rtd 81; Perm to Offic *Bris* from 82 and *Glouc* from 83. *56 Gloucester Road, Rudgeway, Bristol BS35 3RT* Tel (01454) 612794

PRESTON, Reuben James. b 65. York Univ BSc86 MEng87 Birm Univ PGCE97. Westcott Ho Cam 88. **d** 91 **p** 92. C Weoley Castle *Birm* 91-94; TV Malvern Link w Cowleigh *Worc* 94-96; Perm to Offic *Birm* 96-99; C Bordesley St Benedict 99-07; Perm to Offic *Portsm* 07-08; Hon C Portsea St Sav and Portsea St Alb 08; P-in-c Bridgemary from 08; Chapl Bridgemary Community Sports Coll from 08; Chapl HM Pris Kingston (Portsm) from 08. *St Matthew's Vicarage, 7 Duncton Way, Gosport PO13 0FD* Tel (01329) 829883 E-mail rjp@reubenjamespreston.co.uk

PRESTON, William. b 25. St Cath Coll Cam BA46 MA50 Reading Univ MSc79. Oak Hill Th Coll 48. **d** 50 **p** 51. C Hyson Green *S'well* 50-52; C Lenton 52-55; Lic to Offic Kenya 55-59; Asst Master Thika High Sch 59-62; Bethany Sch Goudhurst 62-69; Cranbrook Sch Kent 69-90; Perm to Offic *Cant* 64-10 and *Roch* from 66; rtd 90. *29 Orchard Way, Horsmonden, Tonbridge TN12 8LA* Tel (01892) 722616

PRESTWOOD, James Anthony. b 78. York Univ BSc99 K Coll Lon MA03. St Mellitus Coll BA11. **d** 11. C Tollington *Lon* from 11. *St Saviour's Vicarage, Hanley Road, London N4 3DQ* E-mail jim.prestwood@gmail.com

PRESTWOOD, Ms Jayne Marie. b 64. Man Univ BA86 MA50 Univ MA93. Linc Th Coll MA94. **d** 94 **p** 95. C Reddish *Man* 94-98; Dioc Drugs Misuse Project Worker 98-00; P-in-c Reddish 00-04; P-in-c Haughton St Anne 04-06; Tr Officer for

Reader Tr 04-06; Vice Prin Dioc Reader and OLM Schemes from 06. *Church House, 90 Deansgate, Manchester M3 2GH* Tel 0161-828 1456 E-mail jprestwood@manchester.anglican.org

PRETT, Alan. b 39. **d** 05 **p** 06. OLM Styvechale *Cov* from 05. *55 Watercall Avenue, Coventry CV3 5AX* Tel (024) 7641 5357 E-mail alanprett@btinternet.com

PRETTY, John Leslie. d 10 **p** 11. OLM Draycott-le-Moors w Forsbrook *Lich* from 10. *29 Havensfield Drive, Tean, Stoke-on-Trent ST10 4RR* Tel (01538) 723561 E-mail angelaparty_145@hotmail.com

PREUSS-HIGHAM, Mrs Margaret. b 56. STETS 07. **d** 10 **p** 11. NSM Bridport *Sarum* from 10. *70 Alexandra Road, Bridport DT6 5AL* Tel (01308) 424234 Mobile 07817-161687 E-mail margaret.higham@hotmail.com

PREVETT, Mark Norman. b 59. Univ of Wales (Cardiff) BD88. St Mich Coll Llan 85. **d** 88 **p** 89. C Brynmawr *S & B* 88-90; C Bassaleg *Mon* 90-92; R Blaina and Nantyglo 92-97; TV Halas *Worc* 97-04; RD Dudley 00-04; TR Totton *Win* from 04. *The Rectory, 92 Salisbury Road, Totton, Southampton SO40 3JA* Tel (023) 8086 5103 E-mail tottonrectory@sky.com

PREVITÉ, Anthony Michael Allen. b 41. CITC 85. **d** 88 **p** 89. C Galway w Kilcummin *T, K & A* 88-91; I Omey w Ballynakill, Errislannan and Roundstone 91-93; Dean Tuam 93-96; I Tuam w Cong and Aasleagh 93-96; Adn Tuam and Can Tuam Cathl 96-06; I Omey w Ballynakill, Errislannan and Roundstone 96-06; rtd 06. *Oldchapel, Oughterard, Co Galway, Republic of Ireland* Tel and fax (00353) (91) 552126

PREWER, Dennis. b 30. Kelham Th Coll 50. **d** 54 **p** 55. C Stockport St Thos *Ches* 54-58; C Gt Grimsby St Mary and St Jas *Linc* 58-62; V Gt Harwood St Jo *Blackb* 62-64; V Scarcliffe *Derby* 64-70; Org Sec CECS 70-92; Dios Liv, Ban and St As 70-78; Dio Man 78-92; Lic to Offic *Ches* 70-92; Perm to Offic *Man* 78-96; rtd 92; Perm to Offic *Ches* from 92. *19 Alan Drive, Marple, Stockport SK6 6LN* Tel 0161-427 2827

PRICE, Alan John. b 48. Wilson Carlile Coll 69. **d** 08 **p** 08. P-in-c Charlesworth and Dinting Vale *Derby* 08-11; rtd 11. *2 Cloy Cottages, High Street, Fortrose IV10 8TA* Tel (01381) 622438 E-mail alan@alanprice.me.uk

PRICE, Alison Jane. *See* DOBELL, Mrs Alison Jane

PRICE, Alison Jean. b 50. Man Univ BSc71 Open Univ MA93 Kellogg Coll Ox DPhil01 PGCE89. Ox Min Course 06. **d** 09. NSM Marston w Elsfield *Ox* 09-11. *The Vicarage, Elsfield Road, Marston, Oxford OX3 0PR* Tel (01865) 721399 E-mail aprice@brookes.ac.uk

PRICE, Mrs Alison Mary. b 48. K Alfred's Coll Win CertEd69. **d** 01. Par Dn Magor *Mon* from 01. *Greenwillow, Church Road, Undy, Caldicot NP26 3EN* Tel (01633) 880557

PRICE, Alun. b 60. Bradf Univ BSc82 Loughb Univ MSc88 Univ Coll Ches BTh04 CSci. NOC 01. **d** 04 **p** 05. NSM Bramley *Sheff* 04-05; NSM Wath-upon-Dearne 05-07; P-in-c Wadworth w Loversall from 07. *The Vicarage, Vicarage Drive, Wadworth, Doncaster DN11 9AN* Tel (01302) 851974 Mobile 07958-685393 E-mail fatheralun@hotmail.com

PRICE, Alun Huw. b 47. MBE91. St D Coll Lamp. **d** 70 **p** 71. C Carmarthen St Dav *St D* 70-73; V Betws Ifan 73-77; CF 77-03. *Bryn Seion, Llynyfran Road, Llandysul SA44 4JW*

PRICE, Anthony Ronald. b 49. Linc Coll Ox BA71 MA83 St Jo Coll Dur BA78. **d** 79 **p** 80. C St Alb St Paul *St Alb* 79-81; C Wootton 81-85; C Lydiard Millicent w Lydiard Tregoz *Bris* 85-86; TV The Lydiards 86-91; V Marston *Ox* 91-95; V Marston w Elsfield from 95; RD Cowley 97-02. *The Vicarage, Elsfield Road, Marston, Oxford OX3 0PR* Tel (01865) 247034 E-mail tony@godspell.org.uk

PRICE, Carol Ann. b 46. St Jo Coll Nottm 02. **d** 03 **p** 04. NSM Derby St Alkmund and St Werburgh 03-04; NSM Charlesworth and Dinting Vale 04-11; rtd 11. *2 Cloy Cottages, High Street, Fortrose IV10 8TA* Tel (01381) 622438 Mobile 07787-522127 E-mail carol@carolprice.me.uk

PRICE, Christine. b 66. Leic Univ BA94. EAMTC 98. **d** 01 **p** 02. C Jersey St Helier *Win* 01-06; NSM Jersey St Sav from 10. *7 Le Geyt Close, La Rue de Deloraine, St Saviour, Jersey JE2 7NY* Tel (01534) 737575 Mobile 07971-026711 E-mail christineriss@jerseymail.co.uk

PRICE, Mrs Christine Janice. b 45. Sarum & Wells Th Coll 83. **dss** 86 **d** 87 **p** 94. Roxbourne St Andr *Lon* 86-90; NSM 87-90; NSM Roxeth Ch Ch and Harrow St Pet 90-93; C Roxeth 93-96; C Costessey *Nor* 96-98; rtd 98; Perm to Offic *Nor* 98-05. *31 Russell Court, Chesham HP5 3JH* Tel (01494) 773263 E-mail chrisjpri@aol.com

PRICE, Canon Clive Stanley. b 42. ALCD69. **d** 69 **p** 70. C Chenies and Lt Chalfont *Ox* 69-75; R Upper Stour *Sarum* 75-79; C-in-c Panshanger CD *St Alb* 79-82; TV Digswell and Panshanger 82-86; P-in-c St Oswald in Lee w Bingfield *Newc* 86-07; Dioc Ecum Officer 86-07; Hon Can Newc Cathl 97-07; AD Bellingham 00-06; rtd 07. *Ubbanford Bank Cottage, Norham, Berwick-upon-Tweed TD15 2JZ* Tel (01289) 382051

PRICE, David. b 27. Wycliffe Hall Ox 61. **d** 63 **p** 64. C Bucknall and Bagnall *Lich* 63-67; C Abingdon w Shippon *Ox* 67-76; Warden Stella Carmel Conf Cen Haifa Israel 76-80; Dir Israel Trust of the Angl Ch and R Jerusalem 80-84; V S Kensington St Luke *Lon* 84-92; P-in-c S Kensington St Jude 88-92; rtd 92; Hon C Hordle *Win* 92-97; Perm to Offic *Win* 97-98 and *Worc* 98-07. *16 Masefield Avenue, Ledbury HR8 1BW* Tel (01531) 634831

PRICE, David Derek. b 53. St Edm Hall Ox BA75 Southn Univ PhD80. ERMC 07. **d** 10 **p** 11. NSM Aldenham, Radlett and Shenley *St Alb* from 10. *34 Vanda Crescent, St Albans AL1 5EX*

PRICE, David Gareth Michael. b 64. Ex Univ BA86 Kent Univ MA87 FSS. Wycliffe Hall Ox BTh94. **d** 97 **p** 98. C Godalming *Guildf* 97-00; C-in-c Elvetham Heath LEP 00-02; Min from 02. *Church House, 30 Chineham Close, Fleet GU51 1BF* Tel (01252) 695067 Fax 695068 E-mail minister@churchontheheath.org.uk

PRICE, Canon David Rea. b 39. St Aid Birkenhead 61. **d** 63 **p** 64. C Green Street Green *Roch* 63-66; C Gillingham St Mary 66-69; C New Windsor St Jo *Ox* 69-72; V Winkfield 72-80; RD Bracknell 78-86; V Sunningdale 80-86; TR Wimborne Minster and Holt *Sarum* 86-96; R Wimborne Minster 96-01; Chapl Wimborne Hosp 86-01; RD Wimborne 88-98; Can and Preb Sarum Cathl 92-01; P-in-c Witchampton, Stanbridge and Long Crichel etc 00-01; rtd 01; Perm to Offic *Ex* from 01; RD Aylesbeare from 11. *14 The Broadway, Exmouth EX8 2NW* Tel (01395) 269811 E-mail rea@14broadway.eclipse.co.uk

PRICE, Canon David Trevor William. b 43. Keble Coll Ox BA65 MA69 MEHS79 FRHistS79 FSA95. Sarum & Wells Th Coll 72. **d** 72 **p** 73. Lect Univ of Wales (Lamp) *St D* 70-87; Sen Lect 87-97; Chapl 79-80; Dean of Chpl 90-91; Public Preacher 72-86; Dioc Archivist 82-98; P-in-c Betws Bledrws 86-97; Hon Can St D Cathl 90-92; Can 92-00; V Cydweli and Llandyfaelog 97-00; P-in-c Myddle and Broughton *Lich* 00-08; P-in-c Loppington w Newtown 02-08; rtd 08; Perm to Offic *St As* from 01 and *Lich* from 08. *57 Kynaston Drive, Wem, Shrewsbury SY4 5DE* Tel (01939) 234777 Mobile 07811-712911 E-mail williamprice@talktalk.net

PRICE, Dawson. b 31. OBE. Peterho Cam BA52. Oak Hill NSM Course 88. **d** 91 **p** 92. NSM Harpenden St Nic *St Alb* 91-99; rtd 99; Perm to Offic *Win* from 99. *8 Kimberley Close, Fair Oak, Eastleigh SO50 7EE* Tel (023) 8069 2273

PRICE, Derek Henry. b 51. Trin Coll Bris BA98. **d** 98 **p** 99. C Bayston Hill *Lich* 98-02; R Barrow St Paul *Carl* from 02. *St Paul's Rectory, 353 Abbey Road, Barrow-in-Furness LA13 9JY* Tel (01229) 821546 E-mail dh.price@virgin.net

PRICE, Canon Derek William. b 27. St Pet Hall Ox BA51 MA55. Qu Coll Birm 51. **d** 53 **p** 54. C St Marylebone St Mark Hamilton Terrace *Lon* 53-57; C Stevenage *St Alb* 57-63; Jamaica 63-67; R Bridgham and Roudham *Nor* 67-80; R E w W Harling 69-80; Hon Can Nor Cathl 75-92; RD Thetford and Rockland 76-86; P-in-c Kilverstone 80-87; P-in-c Croxton 80-87; TR Thetford 80-87; R Castleacre w Newton, Rougham and Southacre 87-92; Perm to Offic 92-99 and from 00; P-in-c Easton w Colton and Marlingford 99-00. *Fourways, King's Road, Dereham NR19 2AG* Tel (01362) 691660

PRICE, Chan Desmond. b 23. St D Coll Lamp BA50. **d** 51 **p** 52. C Llwynypia *Llan* 51-52; C Ystradyfodwg 52-54; C Watford Ch Ch *St Alb* 54-56; Chapl RAF 56-68; R Dinas and Llanllawer *St D* 68-72; V Llandeilo Fawr w Llandyfeisant 72-79; V Llandeilo Fawr and Taliaris 79-91; Can St D Cathl 83-91; Chan 89-91; RD Llangadog and Llandeilo 90-91; rtd 91; Hon Can St D Cathl from 91. *24 Diana Road, Llandeilo SA19 6RS* Tel (01558) 824039

PRICE, Canon Edward Glyn. b 35. Univ of Wales (Lamp) BA55. Ch Div Sch of the Pacific (USA) BD58. **d** 58 **p** 59. C Denbigh *St As* 58-65; V Llanasa 65-76; V Buckley 76-91; Dioc RE Adv 77-88; RD Mold 86-91; Can St As Cathl 87; Preb and Sacr from 95; V Llandrillo-yn-Rhos 91-00; rtd 00. *7 Rhodfa Criccieth, Bodelwyddan, Rhyl LL18 5WL* Tel (01745) 571286

PRICE, Frank Lea. b 69. SS Coll Cam BA92 Solicitor 96. Oak Hill Th Coll BA99. **d** 99 **p** 00. C Hinckley H Trin *Leic* 99-04; C Cambridge H Sepulchre *Ely* 04-08; P-in-c Cambridge St Matt from 08. *St Matthew's Vicarage, 24 Geldart Street, Cambridge CB1 2LX* Tel (01223) 363545 Fax 512304 E-mail frankprice@stmatthews.uk.net

PRICE, Frederick Leslie. b 30. Oak Hill Th Coll 59. **d** 61 **p** 62. C Hougham in Dover Ch Ch *Cant* 61-64; R Plumbland and Gilcrux *Carl* 64-95; rtd 95; Perm to Offic *Carl* from 98. *1 Beech Hill, Oughterside, Aspatria, Carlisle CA7 2QA* Tel (01697) 320255

PRICE, Geoffrey David Gower. b 46. Oak Hill Th Coll. **d** 83 **p** 84. C Gt Baddow *Chelmsf* 83-86; C Hampreston *Sarum* 86-88; TV 88-93; P-in-c Drayton in Hales *Lich* 93-97; V 97-99; P-in-c Adderley and Moreton Say 93-97; R Ipswich St Helen, H Trin, and St Luke *St E* 99-05; V E Bedfont *Lon* from 05. *St Mary's Vicarage, 9 Hatton Road, Bedfont, Feltham TW14 8JR* Tel (020) 8751 0088

PRICE, Gerald Andrew. b 31. NEOC. **d** 84 **p** 85. C Monkseaton St Mary *Newc* 84-87; V Cowgate 87-94; C Beltingham w Henshaw 94-96; C Haydon Bridge 94-96; rtd 96; Perm to Offic *Newc* from 96. *39 Primlea Court, Aydon Road, Corbridge NE45 5ES* Tel (01434) 634919

PRICE, Glyn. See PRICE, Canon Edward Glyn

PRICE, Ian Arthur. b 57. Yorks Min Course 09. **d** 11. NSM Eckington and Ridgeway *Derby* from 11. *118 Shakespeare Crescent, Dronfield S18 1ND* Tel (01246) 410892 Mobile 07929-716502 E-mail ianaprice@btinternet.com

PRICE, Iorwerth Meirion Rupert. b 68. Univ of Wales (Lamp) BA92 SOAS Lon MA93 Greenwich Univ PGCE97. SEITE 05 WEMTC 07. **d** 08 **p** 09. C Heref S Wye 08-10; C Woodford Valley w Archers Gate *Sarum* from 10; CF (TA) from 10. *Wilderness Cottage, Shady Bower, Salisbury SP1 2RE* Tel (01722) 430518 E-mail iorwerthprice@btinternet.com

PRICE, Mrs Jean Amelia. b 44. SAOMC 99. **d** 02 **p** 03. OLM N Buckingham *Ox* 02-06; NSM Beercrocombe w Curry Mallet, Hatch Beauchamp etc *B & W* 06-11; rtd 11. *Address temp unknown* E-mail jeanaprice@aol.com

PRICE, John Francis. b 32. Qu Coll Cam BA54 MA. Ridley Hall Cam 54. **d** 56 **p** 57. C Leic H Apostles 56-60; V Forest Gate St Mark *Chelmsf* 60-71; V Harold Hill St Geo 72-79; R Loughton St Mary 79-83; TR Loughton St Mary and St Mich 83-88; R Kirby-le-Soken w Gt Holland 88-92; rtd 92; Perm to Offic *Chelmsf* from 00. *97 Kings Parade, Holland-on-Sea, Clacton-on-Sea CO15 5JH* Tel (01255) 813202

PRICE, John Joseph. b 44. Ridley Hall Cam 89. **d** 92 **p** 93. C Glenfield *Leic* 92-97; Relig Affairs Adv BBC Radio Leics 93-97; Midl Regional Co-ord Crosslinks 97-05; NSM Werrington *Pet* 04-05; P-in-c Pet St Mark and St Barn 05-11; rtd 11; Chapl Peterborough and Stamford Hosps NHS Foundn Trust from 11. *Copper Beeches, 59A Peterborough Road, Castor, Peterborough PE5 7AL* Tel (01733) 380025 Mobile 07729-360524 E-mail johnjprice@tiscali.co.uk

PRICE, John Newman. b 32. St Alb Minl Tr Scheme 80. **d** 83 **p** 84. NSM Bedford St Pet w St Cuth *St Alb* 83-88; C Lt Berkhamsted and Bayford, Essendon etc 88-92; P-in-c Benington w Walkern 92-99; rtd 99; Perm to Offic *St Alb* from 00. *Abbott House, Glapthorn Road, Oundle, Peterborough PE8 4JA*

PRICE, Canon John Richard. b 34. Hull Univ Co BA58 MA62. Westcott Ho Cam 58. **d** 60 **p** 61. C Man St Aid 60-63; C Bramley *Ripon* 63-67; V Leeds All Hallows w St Simon 67-74; P-in-c Wrangthorn 73-74; V Claughton cum Grange *Ches* 74-78; V Mottram in Longdendale w Woodhead 78-88; R Nantwich 88-99; RD Mottram 79-88; Hon Can Ches Cathl 86-99; rtd 99; Perm to Offic *Bradf* from 99. *21 Mill Croft, Cowling, Keighley BD22 0AJ* Tel (01535) 637699

PRICE, Joseph Roderick. b 45. St Mich Coll Llan 74. **d** 75 **p** 76. C Fleur-de-Lis *Mon* 75-79; CF 79-99; Rtd Officer Chapl RAChD 99-05; Chapl Limassol St Barn Cyprus 06-08; rtd 08; Perm to Offic Cyprus and the Gulf from 08. *Flamingo Villa, Pine Bay Villas, PO Box 59426, Pissouri Village, 4607 Limassol, Cyprus* Tel (00357) (25) 222213 Mobile 99-965663 E-mail bodberyl@hotmail.com

PRICE, Julie Elizabeth. b 60. STETS. **d** 10 **p** 11. NSM Hambledon *Portsm* from 10. *39 Horndean Road, Emsworth PO10 7PU*

PRICE, Preb Lawrence Robert. b 43. LICeram71. St Jo Coll Dur 76. **d** 78 **p** 79. C Harlescott *Lich* 78-80; C Cheddleton 80-83; P-in-c Caulton, Cauldon, Grindon and Waterfall 83-84; R 85-88; P-in-c Kingsley 95-01; R Kingsley and Foxt-w-Whiston 01-07; C Alton w Bradley-le-Moors and Oakamoor w Cotton 06-07; RD Cheadle 98-07; Preb Lich Cathl 00-08; rtd 08; P-in-c Cheddleton *Lich* from 07. *The Vicarage, Hollow Lane, Cheddleton, Leek ST13 7HP* Tel (01538) 360226 E-mail preblrprice@btinternet.com

PRICE, Leslie. See PRICE, Frederick Leslie

PRICE, Canon Mari Josephine. b 54. St Hugh's Coll Ox BA65 Ox Univ MA69 DipEd66. Llan Dioc Tr Scheme 93. **d** 97 **p** 98. NSM Lisvane *Llan* 97-02; NSM Roath 02-03; Hon Chapl Llan Cathl from 03; Hon Can from 11. *23 Ty Draw Road, Roath, Cardiff CF23 5HB* Tel (029) 2045 6757 Mobile 07850-019883

PRICE, Martin Randall Connop. b 45. Lon Univ BSc71 Fitzw Coll Cam BA75 MA79 Univ of Wales (Swansea) PhD02. Ridley Hall Cam 73. **d** 76 **p** 77. C Keynsham *B & W* 76-79; Ind Chapl *Sheff* 79-83; V Wortley 79-83; R Hook Norton w Gt Rollright, Swerford etc *Ox* 83-91; V Shiplake w Dunsden 91-03; P-in-c Harpsden 02-03; R Shiplake w Dunsden and Harpsden 03-09; rtd 09. *Coniston, 20 Eastfield Road, Ross-on-Wye HR9 5JY* Tel (01989) 565975

PRICE (née ALDERTON), Mrs Mary Louise. b 54. Nottm Univ BSc71 IPFA87. EAMTC 02. **d** 05 **p** 06. NSM Melbourn *Ely* from 05; NSM Meldreth from 05. *4 Barrons Green, Shepreth, Royston SG8 6QN* Tel (01763) 261569 E-mail mary@price10051.fsnet.co.uk

PRICE, Michael Graham. b 62. Ex Coll Ox BA84. Linc Th Coll 84. **d** 86 **p** 87. C Salford St Phil w St Steph *Man* 86-90; R Man Gd Shep 90-95; V Netherton St Andr *Worc* 95-99; Chapl Bloxham Sch from 00. *Bloxham School, Bloxham, Banbury OX15 4PQ* Tel (01295) 720222

PRICE, Morris John. b 39. **d** 03 **p** 04. OLM Gt Wyrley *Lich* from 03. *42 Huthill Lane, Walsall WS6 6PB* Tel (01922) 412846 E-mail normoss@talktalk.net

PRICE, Norman. See PRICE, William Norman

PRICE, Canon Norman Havelock. b 28. Univ of Wales (Lamp) BA52. St Mich Coll Llan 52. **d** 54 **p** 55. C Maindee Newport *Mon* 54-58; V Llantilio Crossenny and Llanfihangel Ystern etc 58-64; V Mon St Thos-over-Monnow 64-65; V Mon St Thos-over-Monnow and Wonastow 65-71; V Overmonnow w Wonastow and Michel Troy 71-93; RD Monmouth 84-93; Can St Woolos Cathl 91-93; rtd 93; Hon Can St Woolos Cathl 93-96; Lic to Offic from 93. *17 Cinderhill Street, Monmouth NP25 5EY* Tel (01600) 714587

✠**PRICE, The Rt Revd Peter Bryan.** b 44. Redland Coll of Educn CertEd66. Oak Hill Th Coll 72. **d** 74 **p** 75 **c** 97. C Portsdown *Portsm* 74-78; Chapl Scargill Ho 78-80; P-in-c Addiscombe St Mary *Cant* 80-81; V Addiscombe St Mary *S'wark* 85-88; Can Res and Chan S'wark Cathl 88-92; Gen Sec USPG 92-97; Area Bp Kingston *S'wark* 97-02; Bp B & W from 02. *The Palace, Wells BA5 2PD* Tel (01749) 672341 Fax 679355 E-mail bishop@bathwells.anglican.org

PRICE, Peter Charles. b 27. Angl Th Coll (BC). **d** 61 **p** 62. Canada 61-66; C St Mary-at-Latton *Chelmsf* 66-68; C Bearsted *Cant* 68-74; TV Ebbw Vale *Mon* 74-77; V Llanfihangel Crucorney w Oldcastle etc 77-87; V St Paul's Cathl St Helena 87-90; V Llanishen w Trellech Grange and Llanfihangel etc *Mon* 90-94; rtd 94; Perm to Offic *Heref* from 95. *1 Kynaston, Much Marcle, Ledbury HR8 2PD* Tel (01531) 670687

PRICE, Raymond Francklin. b 30. Wycliffe Hall Ox 61. **d** 62 **p** 63. C Bilston St Leon *Lich* 62-67; C Keighley *Bradf* 67-70; V Mangotsfield *Bris* 70-79; Ind Chapl *Birm* 79-86; C Birm St Martin 84-85; C Birm St Martin w Bordesley St Andr 85-86; V Edgbaston St Aug 86-99; rtd 99; Perm to Offic *Birm* from 00. *35 Middle Park Road, Selly Oak, Birmingham B29 4BH* Tel 0121-475 4458

PRICE, Roderick. See PRICE, Joseph Roderick

PRICE, Roland Kendrick. b 41. Cam Univ MA64 Essex Univ PhD69. SAOMC 92. **d** 95 **p** 96. NSM Cholsey *Ox* 95-97; Asst Chapl The Hague *Eur* from 99. *Bentinckstraat 129, 2582 ST Den Haag, The Netherlands* Tel (0031) (15) 215 1871 *or* (70) 355 5359 Fax (70) 354 1023 E-mail rolandprice@ziggo.nl

PRICE, Stanley George. b 32. FRICS69. Trin Coll Bris 84. **d** 85 **p** 86. C Newport w Longford and Chetwynd *Lich* 85-88; V Ipstones w Berkhamsytch and Onecote w Bradnop 88-97; rtd 98; Perm to Offic *B & W* 98-03; P-in-c Rodney Stoke w Draycott 03-08. *St Aidan, Rectory Way, Lympsham, Weston-super-Mare BS24 0EN* Tel (01934) 750323 E-mail rev.price@tiscali.co.uk

PRICE, Steven Albert. b 68. Brunel Univ BSc90 CEng95. Oak Hill Th Coll BTh06. **d** 06 **p** 07. C New Borough and Leigh *Sarum* 06-09; C Loose *Cant* 09-11; P-in-c from 11. *The Vicarage, 17 Linton Road, Loose, Maidstone ME15 0AG* Tel (01622) 745882 E-mail steveandhelenprice@yahoo.co.uk

PRICE, Timothy Fry. b 51. CQSW. St Jo Coll Nottm 85. **d** 87 **p** 88. C Church Stretton *Heref* 87-91; V Sinfin *Derby* 91-00; Regional Adv (SW) CMJ 00-03; Nat Field Co-ord 03-05; Perm to Offic *B & W*, *Bris* and *Glouc* 01-05; V Chaffcombe, Cricket Malherbie etc *B & W* from 06. *The Vicarage, 3 Home Farm, Tatworth, Chard TA20 2SH* Tel (01460) 220237 *or* tel and fax 220404 E-mail pricetf@aol.com

PRICE, Victor John. b 35. Oak Hill Th Coll 62. **d** 65 **p** 66. C Rainham *Chelmsf* 65-70; V Dover St Martin *Cant* 70-78; V Madeley *Heref* 78-90; P-in-c Derby St Pet and Ch Ch w H Trin 90-91; V 91-96; P-in-c Morley w Morley 96-00; rtd 00; Perm to Offic *S'well* from 03. *4 Holmefield, Farndon, Newark NG24 3TZ* Tel (01636) 611788

PRICE, William. See PRICE, Canon David Trevor William

PRICE, William Norman. b 52. GRNCM73. NOC 86. **d** 89 **p** 90. C Lower Broughton Ascension *Man* 89-91; Min Can and Succ St E Cathl 92-96; Prec 94-96; V Par *Truro* 96-00; V Musbury *Blackb* 00-06; rtd 06; Perm to Offic *Man* from 06. *5 Lower Drake Fold, Westhoughton, Bolton BL5 2RE* Tel 07071-299999 E-mail golfsierra999@rcsb.co.uk

PRICE-ROBERTS, Mervyn. b 29. Trin Coll Carmarthen TCert51 Univ of Wales BEd79. Ban Ord Course 84. **d** 87 **p** 88. NSM Bangor 87-89; V Llandygai w Tregarth 89-97; rtd 97; Perm to Offic *Ban* from 97. *17 Parc Hen Blas Estate, Llanfairfechan LL33 0RW* Tel (01248) 680305

PRIDAY, Gerald Nelson. b 35. Glouc Th Course. **d** 89 **p** 88. NSM Eardisland *Heref* 85-91; NSM Aymestrey and Leinthall Earles w Wigmore etc 85-91; NSM Kingsland 85-91; NSM Eye, Croft w Yarpole and Lucton 91-94; NSM Heref All SS 94-96; NSM Letton w Staunton, Byford, Mansel Gamage etc 96-98; rtd 98; Perm to Offic *Heref* from 99. *4 Lime Close, Ludlow SY8 2PP* Tel (01584) 876910

PRIDDIN, Mrs Maureen Anne. b 46. Leeds Univ BA67 Nottm Univ DipEd68. EMMTC 82. **dss** 85 **d** 87 **p** 94. Mickleover St Jo *Derby* 85-11; Hon Par Dn 87-94; Hon C 94-06; P-in-c 06-11; Hon C Mickleover All SS 06-11; Dioc World Development Officer 87-90; rtd 11. *7 Portland Close, Mickleover, Derby DE3 9BZ* Tel (01332) 513672 E-mail mpriddin@ntlworld.com

✠**PRIDDIS, The Rt Revd Anthony Martin.** b 48. CCC Cam BA69 MA73 New Coll Ox MA75. Cuddesdon Coll 69. **d** 72 **p** 73 **c** 96.

C New Addington *Cant* 72-75; Chapl Ch Ch Ox 75-80; TV High Wycombe *Ox* 80-86; P-in-c Amersham 86-90; R 90-96; RD Amersham 92-96; Hon Can Ch Ch 95-96; Suff Bp Warw *Cov* 96-04; Hon Can Cov Cathl 96-04; Bp Heref from 04. *The Bishop's House, The Palace, Hereford HR4 9BN* Tel (01432) 271355 Fax 373346 E-mail bishop@hereford.anglican.org
PRIDEAUX, Humphrey Grevile. b 36. CCC Ox BA59 MA63 Birm Univ CertEd66 Lon Univ DipEd73 Open Univ BA87. Linc Th Coll 59. **d** 61 **p** 62. C Northampton St Matt *Pet* 61-62; C Milton *Portsm* 62-65; Perm to Offic *Birm* 65-66; Hd of RE Qu Mary's Gr Sch Walsall 66-69; Lect St Martin's Coll Lanc 69-80; Perm to Offic *Portsm* 80-86; Hon C Fareham H Trin 86-87; Hon C Bishop's Waltham 87-94; NSM P-in-c W Meon and Warnford 94-03. *6 Rectory Close, Alverstoke, Gosport PO12 2HT* Tel (023) 9250 1794
PRIDGEON, Paul Garth Walsingham. b 45. Sussex Univ BA69 CertEd. Glouc Sch of Min 87. **d** 87 **p** 88. NSM Cirencester *Glouc* 87-97; NSM Northleach w Hampnett and Farmington etc 97-03; Perm to Offic from 03. *4 Abbey Way, Cirencester GL7 2DT* Tel (01285) 656860
PRIDIE, William Raleigh. b 49. Bris Univ BEd72 ACP82 FCollP83. SWMTC 90. **d** 93 **p** 94. C Kingstone w Clehonger, Eaton Bishop etc *Heref* 93-96; P-in-c Kimbolton w Hamnish and Middleton-on-the-Hill 96-97; P-in-c Bockleton w Leysters 96-97; CME Officer 96-00; TV Leominster 97-00; R Fownhope w Mordiford, Brockhampton etc 00-10; rtd 11. *64 Bargates, Leominster HR6 8EY* E-mail wpridie365@waitrose.com
PRIDMORE, John Stuart. b 36. Nottm Univ BA67 Lon Inst of Educn PhD00. Ridley Hall Cam 62. **d** 65 **p** 66. C Camborne *Truro* 65-67; Tutor Ridley Hall Cam 67-68; Chapl 68-71; Asst Chapl K Edw Sch Witley 71-75; Chapl 75-86; Tanzania 86-88; Angl Chapl Hengrave Hall Cen 88-89; C St Martin-in-the-Fields *Lon* 89-95; TR Hackney 95-03; R St John-at-Hackney 03-06; rtd 06. *Flat 2, 3 Palmeira Square, Hove BN3 2JA* Tel (01273) 720654 E-mail john.pridmore@btinternet.com
PRIEST, Richard Mark. b 63. Oak Hill Th Coll BA90. **d** 90 **p** 91. C Okehampton w Inwardleigh *Ex* 90-94; C Okehampton w Inwardleigh, Bratton Clovelly etc 94; CF from 94. *c/o MOD Chaplains (Army)* Tel (01264) 381140 Fax 381824
PRIEST, Richard Philip. b 52. WEMTC 08. **d** 10. NSM Frome Valley *Heref* from 10. *Idalilian, Burley Gate, Hereford HR1 3QS* Tel (01432) 820170 Mobile 07717-132896 Fax (01885) 490615 E-mail richard@allegro.co.uk
PRIESTLEY, Canon Alan Charles. b 41. Lon Univ BD69. Kelham Th Coll 64 Wm Temple Coll Rugby 65. **d** 65 **p** 66. C Edgbaston St Aug *Birm* 65-68; C Chelmsley Wood 68-72; TV 72-76; V Hazelwell from 76; Dioc Communications Officer 83-94; Bp's Press Officer from 85; Hon Can Birm Cathl from 87. *The Vicarage, 316 Vicarage Road, Birmingham B14 7NH* Tel 0121-444 4469 Fax 444 8184 Mobile 07720-936729 E-mail apriestley@waitrose.com
PRIESTLEY, Mandy. b 65. **d** 11. NSM Broughton w Loddington and Cransley etc *Pet* from 11; C from 11. *The Maples, 15 Loddington Way, Mawsley, Kettering NN14 1GE* Tel (01536) 790140 E-mail priestleymandy@mac.com
PRIESTLEY, Richard Allan. b 63. Ridley Hall Cam 07. **d** 09 **p** 10. C Broughton w Loddington and Cransley etc *Pet* from 09. *The Maples, 15 Loddington Way, Mawsley, Kettering NN14 1GE* Tel (01536) 790140 Mobile 07725-190782 E-mail rpriestley@mac.com
PRIESTLEY, Rosemary Jane. *See* LAIN-PRIESTLEY, Ms Rosemary Jane
PRIESTNER, Hugh. b 45. Nottm Univ BTh75. Linc Th Coll 71. **d** 75 **p** 76. C Seaton Hirst *Newc* 75-78; C Longbenton St Bart 78-81; P-in-c Glendale Gp 81-82; TV 83-88; Chapl Stafford Acute Hosps 88-89; Tr Co-ord W Cumberland Hosp 89-92; Chapl Fair Havens Hospice 94-98; Chapl Walsgrave Hosps NHS Trust 98-00; Chapl Team Ldr Univ Hosps Cov and Warks NHS Trust from 00. *Walsgrave General Hospital, Clifford Bridge Road, Coventry CV2 2DX* Tel (024) 7696 7515 E-mail hugh.priestner@uhcw.nhs.uk
PRIGG, Patrick John. b 53. K Coll Lon BD82. Sarum & Wells Th Coll 89. **d** 92 **p** 93. C Wavertree St Mary *Liv* 92-96; Chapl Sandown Coll 92-96; P-in-c Glemsford, Hartest w Boxted, Somerton etc *St E* 96-99; R from 99. *The Rectory, 6 Lion Road, Glemsford, Sudbury CO10 7RF* Tel (01787) 282164 E-mail revpat@glem-valley.org.uk
PRIMROSE, David Edward Snodgrass. b 55. St Jo Coll Cam MA80. Trin Coll Bris BA92. **d** 87 **p** 92. Pakistan 87-89; C Glouc St Paul 92-96; R Badgeworth, Shurdington and Witcombe w Bentham 96-03; V Thornbury and Oldbury-on-Severn w Shepperdine 03-10; AD Hawkesbury 04-09; Dir Transforming Communities *Lich* from 10. *33 Teddesley Way, Huntington, Cannock WS12 4UX* E-mail primrose@blueyonder.co.uk
PRINCE, Alastair. b 76. Nottm Univ BSc99 SS Coll Cam BTh06. Westcott Ho Cam 03. **d** 06 **p** 07. C Toxteth Park Ch Ch and St Mich w St Andr *Liv* 06-09; V Croxteth Park from 09.

St Cuthbert's Vicarage, 1 Sandicroft Road, Liverpool L12 0LX Tel 0151-549 2202 Mobile 07732-489424 E-mail alastairprince@hotmail.com
PRINCE (née RUMBLE), Mrs Alison Merle. b 49. Surrey Univ BSc71. Trin Coll Bris BA89. **d** 89 **p** 94. Par Dn Willesden Green St Gabr *Lon* 89-91; Par Dn Cricklewood St Gabr and St Mich 92; Par Dn Herne Hill *S'wark* 92-94; C 94-95; Chapl Greenwich Healthcare NHS Trust 95-96; TV Sanderstead All SS *S'wark* 97-03; TV Kegworth, Hathern, Long Whatton, Diseworth etc *Leic* 04-09; rtd 09. *23 Grangefields Drive, Rothley, Leicester LE7 7ND*
PRINCE (née GRIFFITHS), Caroline Heidi Ann. b 66. Ex Univ BA88. Linc Th Coll 90. **d** 90 **p** 97. C Newport St Woolos and Chapl St Woolos Cathl 90-94; C Abergavenny Deanery 94-96; TV Cwmbran 96-97; V Llantilio Crossenny w Penrhos, Llanvetherine etc 97-06. *24 Cae Porth, Llangynidr, Crickhowell NP8 1NL*
PRINCE, Helena. b 23. Lightfoot Ho Dur 59. dss 66 **d** 87 **p** 94. W Derby St Mary *Liv* 65-85; rtd 85; Perm to Offic *Liv* 85-04. *c/o E B Harvey Esq, 3 Blackwood Court, 236 Woolton Road, Childwall, Liverpool L16 8NE* Tel 0151-722 5745
PRINCE, Mrs Melanie Amanda. b 71. St D Coll Lamp BA92 Univ of Wales (Cardiff) MPhil93. St Mich Coll Llan 96. **d** 98 **p** 99. C Aberavon *Llan* 98-01; C Gabalfa 01-08; TV Llantwit Major from 08. *The Rectory, 1 Rectory Drive, St Athan, Barry CF62 4PD* Tel (01446) 751241
PRINCE, Penelope Ann. b 46. SWMTC 96. **d** 99 **p** 00. NSM Halsetown *Truro* 99-02; P-in-c Breage w Godolphin and Germoe from 02. *The Vicarage, Breage, Helston TR13 9PN* Tel (01326) 573449 Mobile 07929-152234
PRING, Althon Kerrigan (Kerry). b 34. AKC58. **d** 59 **p** 60. C Limehouse St Anne *Lon* 59-61; C Lt Stanmore St Lawr 61-64; C Langley Marsh *Ox* 64-68; P-in-c Radnage 68-72; P-in-c Ravenstone w Weston Underwood 72-75; P-in-c Stoke Goldington w Gayhurst 72-75; R Gayhurst w Ravenstone, Stoke Goldington etc 75-85; P-in-c 85-86; RD Newport 78-80; TV Woughton 86-90; P-in-c Nash w Thornton, Beachampton and Thornborough 90-94; R 94-96; rtd 96; Perm to Offic *Ox* 99-07. *Kingsmead, 9 Malting Close, Stoke Goldington, Newport Pagnell MK16 8NX* Tel (01908) 551345
PRINGLE, The Ven Cecil Thomas. b 43. TCD BA65. CITC 66. **d** 66 **p** 67. C Belfast St Donard *D & D* 66-69; I Cleenish *Clogh* 69-80; I Mullaghdun 78-80; I Rossorry 80-08; P-in-c Drumkeeran w Templecarne and Muckross from 08; Preb Clogh Cathl 86-89; Adn Clogh from 89. *31 Station Road, Letterbreen, Enniskillen BT74 9FD* Tel 07742-516188 (mobile)
PRINGLE, Graeme Lindsley. b 59. St Cath Coll Cam BA81 MA85. St Jo Coll Nottm 92. **d** 94 **p** 95. C Binley *Cov* 94-99; V Allesley Park and Whoberley from 99. *St Christopher's Vicarage, 99 Buckingham Rise, Coventry CV5 9HF* Tel (024) 7667 2879 E-mail graeme@stchristopher.org.uk
PRINGLE, Miss Janyce Mary. b 32. Ex Univ DipAdEd70 MPhil85 ARCM53 LRAM54. SWMTC 83. dss 86 **d** 87 **p** 94. NSM Torquay St Matthias, St Mark and H Trin *Ex* 86-98; Chapl Asst Torbay Hosp Torquay 86-89; Perm to Offic *Ex* from 98. *Pendower, Wheatridge Lane, Torquay TQ2 6RA* Tel (01803) 607136
PRINGLE, Margaret Brenda. b 49. CITC. **d** 05 **p** 06. NSM Clogh w Errigal Portclare from 05. *Rawdeer Park, Clones, Co Monaghan, Republic of Ireland* Tel (00353) (47) 51439 E-mail margaretpringle@eircom.net
PRINGLE, Richard John. b 55. Lon Univ AKC76 CertEd77 Open Univ BA84. Chich Th Coll 78. **d** 78 **p** 79. C Northampton St Matt *Pet* 78-81; C Delaval *Newc* 81-84; V Newsham from 84; RD Bedlington 93-98. *St Bede's Vicarage, Newcastle Road, Newsham, Blyth NE24 4AS* Tel and fax (01670) 352391
PRINS, Canon Stanley Vernon. b 30. TD76. Dur Univ BSc54 MA69. Ripon Hall Ox 56. **d** 58 **p** 59. C Benwell St Jas *Newc* 58-61; Asst Chapl Newc Univ 61-65; CF (TA) from 64; C-in-c Whorlton H Nativity Chpl Ho Estate *Newc* 65-72; TV Whorlton 73-76; V Humshaugh 76-83; P-in-c Simonburn 82-83; P-in-c Wark 82-83; RD Bellingham 83-93; R Humshaugh w Simonburn and Wark 83-96; Hon Can Newc Cathl 88-96; rtd 96; Perm to Offic *Newc* from 96. *Woodside Cottage, Scrogwood, Bardon Mill, Hexham NE47 7AA* Tel (01434) 344876
PRIOR, Adam Phillip. b 72. Cen Lancs Univ BA94 K Coll Lon MA05. Ridley Hall Cam. **d** 08 **p** 09. NSM Watford St Pet *St Alb* from 08. *57 Brighton Road, Watford WD24 5NH* Tel 07931-896750 (mobile) E-mail aprior@soulsurvivorwatford.co.uk
PRIOR, David Clement Lyndon. b 40. Trin Coll Ox BA63 MA66. Ridley Hall Cam 65. **d** 67 **p** 68. C Reigate St Mary *S'wark* 67-72; C Kenilworth Ch Ch S Africa 72-76; R Wynberg 76-79; Can Cape Town 76-79; C Ox St Aldate w H Trin 79-82; C Ox St Aldate w St Matt 82-84; USA 84-85; V Ches Square St Mich w St Phil *Lon* 85-95; P-in-c Mayfair Ch Ch 85-95; Public Preacher 95-97; P-in-c St Botolph without Aldersgate 97-00; rtd 05; Perm to Offic *Chich* from 05. *2 North Lane, Wiston, Steyning BN44 3DQ* Tel (01903) 893566 E-mail dclraprior@hotmail.com

PRIOR

PRIOR (*née* CHIUMBU), **Esther Tamisa.** b 73. Univ of Zimbabwe BSc95. Trin Coll Bris BA02 MA07. **d** 03 **p** 04. NSM Redland *Bris* 03-05; C Deptford St Jo w H Trin and Ascension *S'wark* 05-08; Chapl Blackheath Bluecoat C of E Sch 08-09; Chapl HM Pris Cookham Wood 10-11; TV Cove St Jo *Guildf* from 11. *Fircroft, 21 St John's Road, Farnborough GU14 9RL* Tel (01252) 373301 E-mail esthertj@yahoo.com

PRIOR, Gregory Stephen. b 68. Geo Whitfield Coll S Africa BTh90. **d** 95 **p** 96. In C of E in S Africa 95-01; Min for Miss Muswell Hill St Jas w St Matt *Lon* 01-04; P-in-c Wandsworth All SS *S'wark* 04-06; V from 06. *Wandsworth Vicarage, 11 Rusholme Road, London SW15 3JX* Tel (020) 8788 7400 E-mail greg@wandsworthparish.co.uk

PRIOR, Canon Ian Graham. b 44. Lon Univ BSc(Econ)71. Oak Hill Th Coll 78. **d** 80 **p** 81. C Luton Ch Ch *Roch* 80-83; TV Southgate *Chich* 83-93; V Burgess Hill St Andr 93-09; RD Hurst 98-04; Can and Preb Chich Cathl 03-09; rtd 09. *5 Chestnut Walk, Worthing BN13 3QL* Tel (01903) 830127 E-mail ian@priorjane.wanadoo.co.uk

PRIOR, Ian Roger Lyndon. b 46. St Jo Coll Dur BA68. Lon Coll of Div 68. **d** 70 **p** 71. C S Croydon Em *Cant* 70-73; Perm to Offic *S'wark*; Dir Overseas Personnel TEAR Fund 73-79; Dep Dir 79-83; Fin and Admin Dir CARE Trust and CARE Campaigns 85-92; NSM New Malden and Coombe *S'wark* 85-11; Perm to Offic from 11; Dir Careforce from 92. *39 Cambridge Avenue, New Malden KT3 4LD* Tel (020) 8949 0912 *or* 8942 3331

PRIOR, James Murray. b 39. Edin Univ BCom64. St And Dioc Tr Course 85. **d** 90 **p** 91. NSM Kirriemuir *St And* 90-02; NSM Forfar 90-02; NSM Dundee St Jo and Dundee St Ninian *Bre* 02-10; rtd 10. *Naughton Lodge, Balmerino, Newport-on-Tay DD6 8RN* Tel (01382) 330132 E-mail ham.prior@tiscali.co.uk

PRIOR, Preb John Miskin. b 27. Lon Univ BSc(Econ)48. Westcott Ho Cam 49. **d** 51 **p** 52. C Bedminster St Fran *Bris* 51-55; C Sherston Magna w Easton Grey 55-57; C Yatton Keynell 57-61; C Castle Combe 57-61; C Biddestone w Slaughterford 57-61; V Bishopstone w Hinton Parva 61-66; V Marshfield w Cold Ashton 66-82; P-in-c Tormarton w W Littleton 68-82; RD Bitton 73-79; R Trull w Angersleigh *B & W* 82-91; RD Taunton 84-90; Preb Wells Cathl 90-91; Chapl Huggens Coll Northfleet 91-97; rtd 92; Hon PV Roch Cathl from 98; Perm to Offic from 99. *21 St Catherines Court, Star Hill, Rochester ME1 1GA* Tel (01634) 403499

PRIOR, Jonathan Roger Lyndon. b 74. Trin Coll Ox BA95 MA99 K Coll Lon PGCE96. Wycliffe Hall Ox 07. **d** 09 **p** 10. C Elworth and Warmingham *Ches* from 09. *80 Abbey Road, Elworth, Sandbach CW11 3HB* Tel (01270) 762555 E-mail j.prior@yahoo.co.uk

PRIOR, Canon Kenneth Francis William. b 26. St Jo Coll Dur BA49. Oak Hill Th Coll 46. **d** 49 **p** 50. C S Mimms Ch Ch *Lon* 49-52; C Eastbourne H Trin *Chich* 52-53; V Onslow Square St Paul *Lon* 53-65; V Hove Bp Hannington Memorial Ch *Chich* 65-70; R Sevenoaks St Nic *Roch* 70-87; Hon Can Roch Cathl 82-87; C-in-c Hampstead St Jo Downshire Hill Prop Chpl *Lon* 87-90; rtd 89; Perm to Offic *Ex* from 01. *22 Barnfield Road, Torquay TQ2 6TN* Tel (01803) 606760

PRIOR, Matthew Thomas. b 74. Rob Coll Cam BA97 MA00. Trin Coll Bris BA04 MA05. **d** 05 **p** 06. C Deptford St Jo w H Trin and Ascension *S'wark* 05-08; P-in-c Borstal *Roch* 08-11. *Fircroft, 21 St John's Road, Farnborough GU14 9RL* Tel (01252) 373301 E-mail mprior28@gmail.com

PRIOR, Nigel John. b 56. Bris Univ BA78 Chich Univ MA09. Westcott Ho Cam 79. **d** 81 **p** 82. C Langley All SS and Martyrs *Man* 81-82; C Langley and Parkfield 82-84; C Bury St Jo w St Mark 84-87; R Man Clayton St Cross w St Paul 87-99; P-in-c Mark Cross *Chich* 99-00; V Mayfield from 99. *The Vicarage, High Street, Mayfield TN20 6AB* Tel (01435) 873180 E-mail stdunstan@tiscali.co.uk

PRIOR, Stephen Kenneth. b 55. Rhode Is Coll (USA) BA78. Wycliffe Hall Ox 79. **d** 82 **p** 83. C Aberavon *Llan* 82-85; P-in-c New Radnor and Llanfihangel Nantmelan etc *S & B* 85-86; R 86-90; V Llansamlet 90-94; P-in-c Chester le Street *Dur* 94-96; R 96-01; R Caldbeck, Castle Sowerby and Sebergham *Carl* 01-09; Dir of Ords 04-08; R Rushden St Mary w Newton Bromswold *Pet* from 09. *The Rectory, Rectory Road, Rushden NN10 0HA* Tel (01933) 312554 E-mail sprior@toucansurf.com

PRIORY, Barry Edwin. b 44. FCIS Open Univ BA81. Qu Coll Birm 84. **d** 86 **p** 87. C Boldmere *Birm* 86-89; C Somerton w Compton Dundon, the Charltons etc *B & W* 89-93; R Porlock and Porlock Weir w Stoke Pero etc 93-08; RD Exmoor 97-03; rtd 08. *Dove Cottage, Moor Road, Minehead TA24 5RX* Tel (01643) 706808 E-mail barry.priory@virgin.net

PRISTON, David Leslie. b 28. Lon Bible Coll 49 Oak Hill Th Coll 66. **d** 66 **p** 67. C Heref St Pet w St Owen 66-71; R Beeby *Leic* 72-88; R Gaddesby w S Croxton 72-88; R S Croxton Gp 88-93; rtd 93; Perm to Offic *S'well* 93-08. *14 Gracey Court, Woodland Road, Broadclyst, Exeter EX5 3GA*

PRITCHARD, Andrew James Dunn. b 57. Van Mildert Coll Dur BSc79 Ch Ch Ox PGCE80. Wycliffe Hall Ox 07. **d** 09 **p** 10. C Cogges and S Leigh *Ox* from 09; C N Leigh from 09. *7 Barleyfield Way, Witney OX28 1AA* Tel 07944-522098 (mobile) E-mail andrewjdp@yahoo.co.uk

PRITCHARD, Antony Robin. b 53. Van Mildert Coll Dur BSc74 SS Paul & Mary Coll Cheltenham CertEd75. St Jo Coll Nottm. **d** 84 **p** 85. C Desborough *Pet* 84-87; C Rushden w Newton Bromswold 87-91; R Oulton St Mich *Nor* from 91. *The Rectory, Christmas Lane, Oulton, Lowestoft NR32 3JX* Tel (01502) 565722 E-mail robinpritchard925@btinternet.com

PRITCHARD, Brian James. Open Univ BA05 ACIS85. SAOMC 99. **d** 01 **p** 02. NSM Newbury *Ox* 01-06; V Billingshurst *Chich* from 06; Perm to Offic *St D* from 05. *The Vicarage, East Street, Billingshurst RH14 9PY* Tel (01403) 785303 *or* 782332 E-mail vicar.billingshurst@gmail.com

PRITCHARD, Brian James Pallister. b 27. CCC Cam BA51 MA66. Westcott Ho Cam 51. **d** 53 **p** 54. C Attercliffe w Carbrook *Sheff* 53-58; V New Bentley 58-60; Chapl Park Hill Flats Sheff 60-67; P-in-c Sheff St Swithun 67-72; V Welton *Linc* 72-92; RD Lawres 86-92; rtd 92; Perm to Offic *Derby* from 92. *Bridgeways, Milford Lane, Bakewell DE45 1DX* Tel (01629) 813553

PRITCHARD, Mrs Carol Sandra. b 52. St Aid Coll Dur BA74 Bris Univ PGCE75. EAMTC 96. **d** 99 **p** 00. NSM Oulton St Mich *Nor* from 99. *The Rectory, Christmas Lane, Oulton, Lowestoft NR32 3JX* Tel (01502) 565722 E-mail carolpritchard3@btinternet.com

PRITCHARD, Colin Wentworth. b 38. K Coll Lon 59 St Boniface Warminster 59. **d** 63 **p** 64. C Putney St Marg *S'wark* 63-67; C Brixton St Matt 67-70; C Milton *Portsm* 70-74; V Mitcham St Mark *S'wark* 74-82; R Long Ditton 82-94; V Earlsfield St Andr 94-03; RD Wandsworth 98-03; rtd 03. *38 Hartfield Road, Seaford BN25 4PW* Tel (01323) 894899 E-mail colin.pritchard@gmx.co.uk

PRITCHARD, Mrs Coral. b 37. F L Calder Coll Liv TCert58 Lanc Univ BA97. CBDTI 99. **d** 02 **p** 03. OLM Stalmine w Pilling *Blackb* 02-07; NSM 07-11; rtd 11; Perm to Offic *Blackb* from 11. *Heyswood House, Head Dyke Lane, Pilling, Preston PR3 6SJ* Tel (01253) 790335 E-mail coralpritchard@btinternet.com

PRITCHARD, Canon David Paul. b 47. Newc Univ BA68 Em Coll Cam PGCE69 LTCL70 FRCO72. Wycliffe Hall Ox 80. **d** 82 **p** 83. C Kidlington *Ox* 82-84; P-in-c Marcham w Garford 84-85; V 86-96; RD Abingdon 91-96; R Henley w Remenham 96-04; Can Res Ely Cathl from 04; Vice Dean and Pastor from 08. *The Black Hostelry, The College, Ely CB7 4DL* Tel (01353) 660302 E-mail david.pritchard@cathedral.ely.anglican.org

PRITCHARD, John Anthony. b 74. Ripon Coll Cuddesdon BTh07. **d** 07 **p** 08. C Gt Berkhamsted, Gt and Lt Gaddesden etc *St Alb* 07-11; C St Marylebone All SS *Lon* from 11. *6 Margaret Street, London W1W 8RQ* Tel (020) 7636 1788 E-mail johnapritchard@hotmail.co.uk

✠**PRITCHARD, The Rt Revd John Lawrence.** b 48. St Pet Coll Ox BA70 MA73 Dur Univ MLitt93. Ridley Hall Cam 70. **d** 72 **p** 73 **c** 02. C Birm St Martin 72-76; Asst Dir RE *B & W* 76-80; Youth Chapl 76-80; P-in-c Wilton 80-88; Dir Past Studies Cranmer Hall Dur 89-93; Warden 93-96; Adn Cant and Can Res Cant Cathl 96-02; Suff Bp Jarrow *Dur* 02-07; Bp Ox from 07. *Diocesan Church House, North Hinksey Lane, Botley, Oxford OX2 0NB* Tel (01865) 208222 E-mail bishopoxon@oxford.anglican.org

PRITCHARD, Jonathan Llewelyn. b 64. Edin Univ MA87 Leeds Univ MA89 PhD99. Ripon Coll Cuddesdon 98. **d** 00 **p** 01. C Skipton H Trin *Bradf* 00-04; P-in-c Keighley All SS from 04; P-in-c Thwaites Brow from 06. *All Saints' Vicarage, 21 View Road, Keighley BD20 6JN* Tel (01535) 665312 E-mail jonathan.pritchard@bradford.anglican.org

PRITCHARD, Miss Kathryn Anne. b 60. St Cath Coll Ox MA. St Jo Coll Dur. **d** 87. Par Dn Addiscombe St Mary *S'wark* 87-90; CPAS Staff 90-92; Perm to Offic *Cov* 92-95; Producer Worship Progr BBC Relig Broadcasting 94-99; Publicity Manager Hodder & Stoughton Relig Books 99-01; Commissioning and Product Development Manager Ch Ho Publishing 01-09. *Address temp unknown*

PRITCHARD, Kenneth John. b 30. Liv Univ BEng51. NW Ord Course 72. **d** 74 **p** 75. C Ches 74-78; Miss to Seamen 78-84; V Runcorn St Jo Weston *Ches* 78-84; V St Meols 84-98; rtd 98; Perm to Offic *Ches* and *Liv* from 99. *13 Fieldlands, Scarisbrick, Southport PR8 5HQ* Tel (01704) 514600 E-mail kjp@talk21.com

PRITCHARD, Malcolm John. b 55. Bradf Univ BA85 CQSW85. St Jo Coll Nottm 86. **d** 88 **p** 89. C Peckham St Mary Magd *S'wark* 88-93; V Luton St Matt High Town *St Alb* from 93. *St Matthew's Vicarage, 85 Wenlock Street, Luton LU2 0NN* Tel (01582) 732320 E-mail b4mjp2c@ntlworld.com

PRITCHARD, Michael Owen. b 49. Trin Coll Carmarthen CertEd71. St Mich Coll Llan 71. **d** 73 **p** 74. C Conwy w Gyffin *Ban* 73-76; TV Dolgellau w Llanfachreth and Brithdir etc 76-78; Dioc Children's Officer 77-86; V Betws y Coed and Capel Curig 78-83; CF (TAVR) from 79; V Betws-y-Coed and Capel Curig w Penmachno etc *Ban* 83-86; Chapl Claybury Hosp Woodford

Bridge 86-96; Chapl Team Leader Forest Healthcare NHS Trust Lon 96-01; Chapl Team Leader NE Lon Mental Health Tr from 01. *The Chaplaincy, Whipps Cross Hospital, Whipps Cross Road, London E11 1NR* Tel (020) 8539 5522 ext 5005 *or* 8989 3813 E-mail mopritchard@hotmail.com

PRITCHARD, Mrs Norma Kathleen. b 32. Birm Univ BA53 CertEd54. EMMTC 81. **dss** 84 **d** 87 **p** 94. Derby St Alkmund and St Werburgh 84-90; Par Dn 87-90; Par Dn Derby St Andr w St Osmund 90-94; C 94-96; Assoc Min Alvaston 96-02; rtd 02; Perm to Offic *Derby* and *S'wark* from 02. *44 Evans Avenue, Allestree, Derby DE22 2EN* Tel (01332) 557702

PRITCHARD, Peter Benson. b 30. FPhS60 LCP68 Univ of Wales (Lamp) BA51 Lon Univ PGCE68 DipEd70 Liv Univ MEd74 PhD81. Ripon Hall Ox 55. **d** 58 **p** 59. C Wavertree H Trin *Liv* 58-60; C Sefton 60-61; C-in-c Thornton CD 61-64; Chapl Liv Coll Boys' Sch 64-70; Hon C Wavertree St Bridget 70-89; Lect CF Mott Coll of Educn 70-76; Sen Lect Liv Coll of HE 76-83; Liv Poly 83-87; Perm to Offic Liv 90-96 and *Ches* from 90; Chapl St Jo Hospice Wirral from 93; Tutor Open Univ 90-95; rtd 95. *68 Gleggside, West Kirby, Wirral CH48 6EA* Tel 0151-625 8093

PRITCHARD, Peter Humphrey. b 47. Univ of Wales (Ban) BA70 MA98 Liv Univ PGCE73. Qu Coll Birm 85. **d** 87 **p** 88. C Llanbeblig w Caernarfon and Betws Garmon etc *Ban* 87-90; R Llanberis w Llanrug 90-94; R Llanfaethlu w Llanfwrog and Llanrhuddlad etc 94-99; R Llanfair Mathafarn Eithaf w Llanbedrgoch 99-05; rtd 05. *4 Penlon Gardens, Bangor LL57 1AQ*

PRITCHARD, Simon Geraint. b 61. Coll of Ripon & York St Jo BA85 Ex Univ PGCE88. Cranmer Hall Dur 98. **d** 00 **p** 01. C Heysham *Blackb* 00-01; C Morecambe St Barn 01-03; C Standish 03-06; V Haigh and Aspull *Liv* from 06. *The Vicarage, Copperas Lane, Haigh, Wigan WN2 1PA* Tel (01942) 830356 E-mail s.pritchard41@btinternet.com

PRITCHARD, Thomas James Benbow. b 47. St Paul's Coll Chelt CertEd69 Univ of Wales (Cardiff) BEd79 MSc85 Ex Univ BTh08. SWMTC 96. **d** 99 **p** 00. NSM St Enoder *Truro* 99-01; P-in-c Roche and Withiel 01-05; V Llangollen w Trevor and Llantysilio *St As* 05-06; P-in-c Mylor w Flushing *Truro* 06-07; rtd 07. *Suncot, Short Cross Road, Mount Hawke, Truro TR4 8DU* Tel (01209) 891766 E-mail thms_pritchard@yahoo.co.uk

PRITCHARD, The Ven Thomas William. b 33. Keele Univ BA55 DipEd55 Univ of Wales (Cardiff) LLM94. St Mich Coll Llan 55. **d** 57 **p** 58. C Holywell *St As* 57-61; C Ruabon 61-63; V 77-87; R Pontfadog 63-71; R Llanferres, Nercwys and Eryrys 71-77; Dioc Archivist 76-98; Can St As Cathl 84-98; RD Llangollen 86-87; Adn Montgomery 87-98; V Berriew and Manafon 87-98; rtd 98. *4 Glynne Way, Hawarden, Deeside CH5 3NL* Tel (01244) 538381

PRITCHETT, Antony Milner. b 63. Kent Univ BA86. Westcott Ho Cam 96. **d** 98 **p** 99. C Broughton Astley and Croft w Stoney Stanton *Leic* 98-02; V Gawber *Wakef* 02-08; Chapl Barnsley Hospice 02-08; P-in-c Pickering w Lockton and Levisham *York* from 08; V from 11. *The Vicarage, Whitby Road, Pickering YO18 7HL* Tel (01751) 472983 E-mail vicar@pickeringchurch.com

PRITCHETT, Mrs Beryl Ivy. b 48. Worc Coll of Educn TCert69. WMMTC 02. **d** 05 **p** 06. NSM Brockmoor *Worc* 05-07; NSM Brierley Hill from 07. *7 Muirville Close, Wordsley, Stourbridge DY8 5NR* Tel (01384) 271470 Mobile 07790-563479 E-mail beryl.pritchett@btinternet.com

PRIVETT, Peter John. b 48. Qu Coll Birm 75. **d** 78 **p** 79. C Moseley St Agnes *Birm* 78-81; V Kingsbury 81-87; P-in-c Dilwyn and Stretford *Heref* 87-90; Dioc Children's Adv 87-01; TV Leominster 90-98; NSM 98-05; Dioc Millennium Officer 98-01; Perm to Offic *Heref* 05-07 and *Cov* 07-09; C Rugby *Cov* from 09. *38 Oakfield Road, Rugby CV22 6AU* Tel (01788) 570332 E-mail pet.ros@btopenworld.com

PROBART, Raymond. b 21. Sarum Th Coll 49. **d** 51 **p** 52. C Padiham *Blackb* 51-54; C Burnley St Pet 54-56; V Heyhouses 56-60; V Douglas 60-88; rtd 88; Perm to Offic *B & W* 88-98; *Glouc* from 03. *6 Capel Court, The Burgage, Prestbury, Cheltenham GL52 3EL* Tel (01242) 235771

PROBERT, Beverley Stuart. b 42. **d** 01 **p** 02. OLM Canford Magna *Sarum* from 01. *Blaenafon, 102 Knights Road, Bournemouth BH11 9SY* Tel (01202) 571731

PROBERT, Christopher John Dixon. b 54. Univ of Wales (Ban) BTh95 MTh97. St Mich Coll Llan 74. **d** 78 **p** 79. C Aberdare St Fagan *Llan* 78-79; C Cadoxton-juxta-Barry 79-81; R Llanfynydd *St As* 81-84; V Gosberton Clough and Quadring *Linc* 84-86; TV Coventry Caludon 86-88; V Llanrhian w Llanhywel and Llanrheithan *St D* 88-91; V Tregaron w Ystrad Meurig and Strata Florida 91-93; Chapl Tregaron Hosp 91-93; Tutor St D NSM Course 89-93; V Betws-y-Coed and Capel Curig w Penmachno etc *Ban* 93-98; Warden of Readers 96-98; V Lt Drayton *Lich* 98-04; P-in-c North Hill and Lewannick *Truro* 04-10; C Lezant w Lawhitton and S Petherwin w Trewen 04-10; R Three Rivers 10-11. *La Haudiardière, 50640 Heusse, France* Tel (0033) (2) 33 61 35 82 E-mail cjdprobert@gmail.com

PROBERT, Canon Edward Cleasby. b 58. St Cath Coll Cam BA80 MA84. Ripon Coll Cuddesdon BA84. **d** 85 **p** 86. C Esher *Guildf* 85-89; V Earlsfield St Andr *S'wark* 89-94; V Belmont 94-04; Can Res and Chan Sarum Cathl from 04. *24 The Close, Salisbury SP1 2EH* Tel (01722) 555193 E-mail chancellor@salcath.co.uk

PROBETS, Canon Desmond. b 26. AKC50. **d** 51 **p** 52. C Finsbury St Clem *Lon* 51-52; C Kenton 52-62; Sub Warden St Pet Th Coll Siota Solomon Is 62-64; Hd Master All Hallows Sch Pawa Ugi 64-69; Hon Can Honiara from 67; Dean 69-72; V Timperley *Ches* 72-92; RD Bowdon 77-87; Hon Can Ches Cathl 82-92; rtd 92; Perm to Offic *Wakef* from 92. *24 Shelley Close, Penistone, Sheffield S36 6GT* Tel (01226) 766402

PROCTER, Andrew David. b 52. St Jo Coll Ox BA74 MA BA86. Trin Coll Bris 74. **d** 77 **p** 78. C Barnoldswick w Bracewell *Bradf* 77-80; P-in-c Kelbrook 80-82; V 82-87; V Heaton St Barn 87-93; V Swanley St Paul *Roch* 93-07; R Shipbourne w Plaxtol from 07. *The Rectory, The Street, Plaxtol, Sevenoaks TN15 0QG* Tel (01732) 811081 Mobile 07963-943524 E-mail a.procter@live.co.uk

PROCTER, Nicholas Jonathan. b 59. Liv Univ BVSc84 MRCVS84. LCTP 06. **d** 09 **p** 10. NSM Leyland St Jo *Blackb* from 09. *23 Regents Way, Euxton, Chorley PR7 6PG* Tel (01257) 241927 E-mail n.r.procter@btinternet.com

PROCTER, Robert Henry. b 31. Trin Hall Cam BA54 MA58. Edin Dioc NSM Course 88. **d** 93 **p** 94. NSM Edin Ch Ch 93-94; TV 94-07. *2 Braid Avenue, Edinburgh EH10 6DR* Tel 0131-447 1140 E-mail hendy@procters.plus.com

PROCTOR, Kenneth Noel. b 33. St Aid Birkenhead 61. **d** 63 **p** 64. C Oldham St Paul *Man* 63-66, C Davyhulme St Mary 66-69, V Norden w Ashworth 69-00; rtd 00. *4 Bankscroft, Hopwood, Heywood OL10 2NG* Tel (01706) 364197

PROCTOR, Michael John. b 59. Cranmer Hall Dur 93. **d** 93 **p** 94. C Leatherhead *Guildf* 93-98; V Henlow and Langford *St Alb* 98-01; V Marton-in-Cleveland *York* from 01; Min Coulby Newham LEP from 03. *The Vicarage, Stokesley Road, Marton-in-Cleveland, Middlesbrough TS7 8JU* Tel (01642) 326305 E-mail mike@stcuthbertmarton.org.uk

PROCTOR, Canon Michael Thomas. b 41. Ch Ch Ox BA65 MA67. Westcott Ho Cam 63. **d** 65 **p** 66. C Monkseaton St Mary *Newc* 65-69; Pakistan 69-72; C Willington *Newc* 72-77; TV Willington 77-79; Ed Sec Nat Soc 79-84; P-in-c Roxwell *Chelmsf* 79-84; Bp's Ecum Officer 85-00; Dir of Miss and Unity 85-94; P-in-c Gt Waltham w Ford End 94-00; Hon Can Chelmsf Cathl 85-00; rtd 00; Dir Chelmsf Counselling Foundn from 00. *Claremont, South Street, Great Waltham, Chelmsford CM3 1DP* E-mail mtproctor@lineone.net

PROCTOR, Nicholas Jonathan. See PROCTER, Nicholas Jonathan

PROCTOR, Canon Noel. b 30. MBE93. St Aid Birkenhead 62. **d** 64 **p** 65. C Haughton le Skerne *Dur* 64-67; R Byers Green 67-70; Chapl HM Pris Eastchurch 70-74; Dartmoor 74-79; Man 79-95; Hon Can Man Cathl 91-95; rtd 95; Perm to Offic *Man* from 95. *222 Moor Lane, Salford M7 3PZ* Tel 0161-792 1284

PROCTOR, Canon Susan Katherine. b 44. **d** 89 **p** 94. Par Dn Beighton *Sheff* 89-91; Par Dn Aston cum Aughton and Ulley 91-93; Par Dn Aston cum Aughton w Swallownest, Todwick etc 93-94; TV 94-96; P-in-c Aston cum Aughton w Swallownest and Ulley 01-02; TR 02-05; R Dinnington 96-01; AD Laughton 98-03; Hon Can Sheff Cathl 98-05; rtd 05. *69 Ings Mill Avenue, Clayton West, Huddersfield HD8 9QG* Tel (01484) 866189 Mobile 07768-293588 E-mail sueproctor@lineone.net

PROFIT, David Hollingworth. b 17. Man Univ BA38. Cuddesdon Coll 40. **d** 41 **p** 42. C Kings Heath *Birm* 41-43; S Africa from 43. *Braehead House, 1 Braehead Road, Kenilworth, 7708 South Africa* Tel (0027) (21) 762 6041

PROSSER, Gillian Margaret. b 40. Lon Inst of Educn TCert61. **d** 99. OLM Cwmbran *Mon* 99-10. *25 Forest Close, Coed Eva, Cwmbran NP44 4TE* Tel (01633) 866716

PROSSER, Hugh. See PROSSER, Richard Hugh Keble

PROSSER, Jean. b 40. MBE10. Open Univ BA84 Surrey Univ PhD94. **d** 02 **p** 05. NSM Grosmont and Skenfrith and Llangattock etc *Mon* from 02; P-in-c from 09. *Yew Tree Farm, Llangattock Lingoed, Abergavenny NP7 8NS* Tel (01873) 821405 E-mail jean.prosser@talk21.com

PROSSER, Canon Rhys. b 51. BA74 Southn Univ BTh83 Hull Univ MA93 Bris Univ CertEd75. Sarum & Wells Th Coll 77. **d** 80 **p** 81. C Wimbledon *S'wark* 80-83; C St Helier 83-88; TV Gt and Lt Coates w Bradley *Linc* 88-95; P-in-c Saxilby Gp 95-97; R from 97; RD Corringham from 00; Can and Preb Linc Cathl from 03. *69 Mill Lane, Saxilby, Lincoln LN1 2HN* Tel (01522) 702427 E-mail rs.prosser@virgin.net

PROSSER, Richard Hugh Keble. b 31. Trin Coll Cam BA53 MA57 Leeds Univ PGCE63. Cuddesdon Coll 55. **d** 57 **p** 58. C Wigan All SS *Liv* 57-60; CR 62-87; St Aug Miss Penhalonga Zimbabwe 64-90; R Pocklington and Owsthorpe and Kilnwick Percy etc *York* 90-00; rtd 00; Perm to Offic *Sarum* from 02. *26 Fleur de Lis, Middlemarsh Street, Poundbury, Dorchester DT1 3GX* Tel (01305) 260329

PROSSER, Stephanie. b 42. Linc Th Coll 94. **d** 96 **p** 99. NSM Linc St Nic w St Jo Newport 96-99; NSM Saxilby Gp from 99. *The Vicarage, 69 Mill Lane, Saxilby, Lincoln LN1 2HN* Tel (01522) 702427

PROTHERO, Brian Douglas. b 52. St Andr Univ MTheol75 Dundee Univ CertEd77. Linc Th Coll 84. **d** 86 **p** 87. C Thornbury *Glouc* 86-89; V Goodrington *Ex* 89-04; R Weybridge *Guildf* from 04; Chapl Sam Beare Hospice from 06. *The Rectory, 3 Churchfields Avenue, Weybridge KT13 9YA* Tel (01932) 842566 Mobile 07715-364389 E-mail brianprothero@btinternet.com

PROTHERO, David John. b 43. St Pet Coll Ox BA66 MA70. St Steph Ho Ox 68. **d** 70 **p** 71. C Kirkby *Liv* 70-72; C St Marychurch *Ex* 72-74; V Marldon 74-83; Chapl HM Pris Channings Wood 78-83; V Torquay St Martin Barton *Ex* 83-91; P-in-c Bath Bathwick *B & W* 91-93; R from 93. *Bathwick Rectory, Sham Castle Lane, Bath BA2 6JL* Tel (01225) 460052 E-mail david@prothero.fsnet.co.uk

PROTHERO, John Martin. b 32. Oak Hill Th Coll 64. **d** 66 **p** 67. C Tipton St Martin *Lich* 66-69; C Wednesfield Heath 69-72; Distr Sec BFBS 72-85; Lic to Offic *S'well* 73-86; Hon C Gedling 73; V Willoughby-on-the-Wolds w Wysall and Widmerpool 86-97; rtd 98. *The Elms, Vicarage Hill, Aberaeron SA46 0DY* Tel (01545) 570568

PROTHEROE, Rhys Illtyd. b 50. St D Coll Lamp. **d** 74 **p** 75. C Pen-bre *St D* 74-76; C Carmarthen St Dav 76-78; V Llanegwad 78-79; V Llanegwad w Llanfynydd 79-82; V Gors-las 82-95; RD Dyffryn Aman 94-95; V Llan-llwch w Llangain and Llangynog from 95. *The New Vicarage, Millbank Lane, Johnstown, Carmarthen SA31 3HW* Tel (01267) 236805

PROTHEROE, Canon Robin Philip. b 33. St Chad's Coll Dur BA54 MA60 Nottm Univ MPhil75 Ox Univ DipEd62. **d** 57 **p** 58. C Roath *Llan* 57-60; Asst Chapl Culham Coll Abingdon 60-64; Sen Lect RS Trent (Nottm) Poly *S'well* 64-84; Perm to Offic 64-66; Lic to Offic 66-84; P-in-c Barton in Fabis 70-73; P-in-c Thrumpton 70-73; Dir of Educn *Bris* 84-98; Hon Can Bris Cathl 85-98; Capitular Can Bris Cathl 01-07; Perm to Offic *Bris* 98-10 and *Chich* from 10. *58 Stroudley Road, Brighton BN1 4BH* Tel (01273) 687822 E-mail rpprotheroe@gmail.com

✠**PROUD, The Rt Revd Andrew John.** b 54. K Coll Lon BD79 AKC79 SOAS Lon MA01. Linc Th Coll 79. **d** 80 **p** 81 **c** 07. C Stansted Mountfitchet *Chelmsf* 80-83; TV Borehamwood *St Alb* 83-90; C Bp's Hatfield 90-92; R E Barnet 92-01; Chapl Adis Ababa St Matt Ethiopia 02-07; Area Bp Ethiopia and Horn of Africa 07-11; Area Bp Reading *Ox* from 11. *Bishop's House, Tidmarsh Lane, Tidmarsh, Reading RG8 8HA* Tel 0118-984 1216 Fax 984 1218 E-mail bishopreading@oxford.anglican.org

PROUD, David John. b 56. Leeds Univ BA77 Dur Univ CertEd78. Ridley Hall Cam 85. **d** 88 **p** 89. C Lindfield *Chich* 88-91; TV Horsham 91-97; V Ware Ch *St Alb* 97-10; RD Hertford and Ware 04-10; Chapl E Herts NHS Trust 97-00; Chapl E and N Herts NHS Trust 00-06; R Bedhampton *Portsm* from 10. *The Rectory, Bidbury Lane, Bedhampton, Havant PO9 3JG*

PROUD, George. b 43. Newc Univ BDS71 MB, BS71 MD81 FRCS. Lindisfarne Regional Tr Partnership 10. **d** 11. OLM Riding Mill *Newc* from 11. *Cartref, Marchburn Lane, Riding Mill NE44 6DN* Tel (01434) 682393 Mobile 07990-970202 E-mail george.proud.1@btinternet.com

PROUDFOOT (*née* BLACKBURN)**, Mrs Jane Elizabeth.** b 66. Lanc Univ BA88 St Martin's Coll Lanc PGCE93 Leeds Univ BA09. NOC 06. **d** 09 **p** 10. C Stockton Heath *Ches* from 09. *36 Senna Lane, Comberbach, Northwich CW9 6BQ* Tel (01606) 892418 E-mail janeproudfoot@tiscali.co.uk

PROUDLEY, Sister Anne. b 38. Edin Univ BSc60. SAOMC 97. **d** 00 **p** 01. CSJB from 00; NSM Blackbird Leys *Ox* 00-04; Lic to Offic 04-11; Chapl to the Homeless 05-11; NSM Blenheim from 11. *Priory House, 25 Woodstock Road West, Begbroke, Kidlington OX5 1RJ* Tel (01865) 855331 E-mail annecsjb@csjb.org.uk

PROUDLOVE, Lee Jason. b 70. Lon Bible Coll BA94. Trin Coll Bris MA01. **d** 01 **p** 02. C Morden *S'wark* 01-04; CMS Philippines 05-08; P-in-c W Bridgford *S'well* from 08. *The Rectory, 86 Bridgford Road, West Bridgford, Nottingham NG2 6AX* Tel 0115-981 1112 E-mail rector@stgilesparish.com

PROUDMAN, Canon Colin Leslie John. b 34. K Coll Lon BD60 MTh63. Wells Th Coll 60. **d** 61 **p** 62. C Radlett *St Alb* 61-64; Canada from 64; Hon Can Toronto from 86; Dean Div Toronto Div Coll 90-92; rtd 97. *1802-77 Maitland Place, Toronto ON M4Y 2V6, Canada* Tel (001) (416) 923 4235

PROUT, Mrs Joan. b 42. Gipsy Hill Coll of Educn TCert63. **d** 97 **p** 98. OLM Whitton *Sarum* 97-06. *22 Ermin Close, Baydon, Marlborough SN8 2JQ* Tel (01672) 540445 E-mail joan.prout@genie.co.uk

PROVOST, Ian Keith. b 47. CA Tr Coll IDC73 Ridley Hall Cam 91. **d** 93 **p** 94. C Verwood *Sarum* 93-97; P-in-c Redlynch and Morgan's Vale 97-02; TV Plymstock and Hooe *Ex* 02-10; rtd 10. *8 Larkhall Rise, Plymouth PL3 6LY* E-mail ian.provost17@gmail.com

PROWSE, Mrs Barbara Bridgette Christmas. b 41. R Holloway Coll Lon BA62. **d** 91 **p** 94. C Kingsthorpe w Northampton St Dav *Pet* 91-97; V Northampton St Jas 97-02; rtd 02; Perm to Offic *Truro* from 02. *36 Carn Basavern, St Just, Penzance TR19 7QX* Tel (01736) 787994 E-mail bbc@prowseb.freeserve.co.uk

PRUDOM, William Haigh. b 26. STh79 APhS81 Hull Univ MPhil88. St D Coll Lamp 60. **d** 62 **p** 63. C Aylesford *Roch* 62-63; C Margate St Jo *Cant* 63-66; V Long Preston *Bradf* 66-73; C Darlington St Cuth *Dur* 73-75; V Ticehurst *Chich* 75-79; P-in-c Flimwell 78-79; V Ticehurst and Flimwell 79-81; R Spennithorne w Finghall and Hauxwell *Ripon* 81-91; rtd 91; Perm to Offic *Ripon* from 91. *9 Sydall's Way, Catterick Village, Richmond DL10 7ND* Tel (01748) 818604

PRUEN, Canon Edward Binney. b 56. K Coll Lon BD77 AKC77. St Jo Coll Nottm 78. **d** 79 **p** 80. C Kidderminster St Mary *Worc* 79-82; C Woking St Jo *Guildf* 82-84; Chapl Asst R Marsden Hosp Lon and Surrey 84-86; C Stapleford *S'well* 86-88; Min Winklebury CD 88; V Winklebury 88-93; Chapl Ld Mayor Treloar Coll Alton 93-09; Hon Can Win Cathl 05-09; Can Res S'well Minster from 09. *5 Vicars Court, Southwell NG25 0HP* Tel (01636) 819848 E-mail edpruen@btconnect.com *or* edpruen@southwellminster.org.uk

PRUST, Mrs Judith Ann. b 46. St Mich Coll Llan 05. **d** 07. NSM Llanrhaeadr ym Mochnant etc *St As* from 07. *Minffordd, Llangynog, Oswestry SY10 0HD* Tel (01691) 860420 E-mail judithprust@yahoo.co.uk

PRYCE, Donald Keith. b 36. Man Univ BSc. Linc Th Coll 69. **d** 71 **p** 72. C Heywood St Jas *Man* 71-74; P-in-c 74-75; V 75-86; R Ladybarn 86-06; Chapl S Man Coll 87-06; Chapl Christie Hosp NHS Trust Man 93-06; rtd 06; Perm to Offic *Ches* and *Man* from 06. *62 Belmont Road, Gatley, Cheadle SK8 4AQ* E-mail donaldpryce@hotmail.com

PRYCE, Robin Mark. b 60. Sussex Univ BA82 Cam Univ MA94. Westcott Ho Cam 84 United Th Coll Bangalore 85. **d** 87 **p** 88. C W Bromwich All SS *Lich* 87-90; Chapl Sandwell Distr Gen Hosp 90; Chapl and Fell CCC Cam 90-02; Tutor 92-02; Dean of Chpl 96-02; V Smethwick *Birm* 02-06; Bp's Adv for Clergy CME from 06. *175 Harborne Park Road, Birmingham B17 0BH* Tel 0121-426 0430 E-mail m.pryce@birmingham.anglican.org

PRYCE, William Robert. b 28. MBE91. **d** 79 **p** 80. NSM Leverstock Green *St Alb* 79-80; Perm to Offic *Sheff* 80-84; NSM Sheff St Barn and St Mary 84-90; NSM Alveley and Quatt *Heref* 91-93; Perm to Offic 93-03. *5 Wren Way, Bicester OX26 6UJ*

PRYCE-WILLIAMS, Jean. b 48. **d** 10 **p** 11. NSM Cumnor *Ox* from 10. *118 Oxford Road, Cumnor, Oxford OX2 9PQ* Tel (01865) 865687 E-mail j.pryce-williams@pippins.myzen.co.uk

PRYKE, Jonathan Justin Speaight. b 59. Trin Coll Cam BA80 MA85. Trin Coll Bris BD85. **d** 85 **p** 86. C Corby St Columba *Pet* 85-88; C Jesmond Clayton Memorial *Newc* from 88. *15 Lily Avenue, Newcastle upon Tyne NE2 2SQ* Tel 0191-281 9854

PRYOR, Derek John. b 29. Lon Univ BD63 Birm Univ MEd74. Linc Th Coll 79 Chich Th Coll 79. **d** 80 **p** 81. Hon C Youlgreave *Derby* 80-82; Hon C Stanton-in-Peak 80-82; Hon C Ingham w Cammeringham w Fillingham *Linc* 82-87 and 92-99; Chapl Bp Grosseteste Coll Linc 83-84; Dioc Schs Officer *Linc* 87-92; rtd 92. *Walnut Cottage, Chapel Lane, Fillingham, Gainsborough DN21 5BP* Tel (01427) 668276 Fax 667956 E-mail john.pryor@btinternet.com

PRYOR, William Lister Archibald. b 39. Trin Coll Cam BA67 MA69 DipEd68. Ox NSM Course 72. **d** 75 **p** 90. NSM Summertown *Ox* from 75; Perm to Offic *Nor* 93-04 and from 09. *23 Harbord Road, Oxford OX2 8LH* Tel and fax (01865) 515102

PRYS, Deiniol. b 53. Univ of Wales (Ban) BTh91. St Mich Coll Llan 82. **d** 83 **p** 84. C Llanbeblig w Caernarfon and Betws Garmon etc *Ban* 83-86; TV Amlwch 86-88; V Llanerch-y-medd 89-92; R Llansadwrn w Llanddona and Llaniestyn etc 92-11; Lic to Offic from 11. *The Rectory, Llansadwrn, Menai Bridge LL59 5SL* Tel (01248) 810534 Mobile 07740-541316

PRYSE, Hugh Henry David. b 58. St Chad's Coll Dur BA81 SS Coll Cam PGCE82 K Coll Lon MA96. St Steph Ho Ox 94. **d** 96 **p** 97. C Branksome St Aldhelm *Sarum* 96-00; TV Hove *Chich* 00-05; R Ex St Jas from 05. *The Rectory, 45 Thornton Hill, Exeter EX4 4NR* Tel (01392) 431297 or 420407 E-mail henry.pryse@blueyonder.co.uk

PRYSOR-JONES, John Glynne. b 47. Heythrop Coll Lon MA94 Leeds Metrop Univ BSc05 CQSW73. Westcott Ho Cam 88. **d** 90 **p** 91. C Mitcham St Mark *S'wark* 90-93; V Dudley St Fran *Worc* 93-99; R Woodchurch *Ches* 99-01; Hd Past Care Services Chorley and S Ribble NHS Trust and Preston Acute Hosps NHS Trust 01-02; Hd Past Care Services Lancs Teaching Hosps NHS Trust 02-06. *Bryn-y-Mor, St John's Park, Penmaenmawr LL34 6NE* Tel (01492) 622515

PRYTHERCH, David. b 30. Down Coll Cam BA54 MA58 Lon Univ CertEd68 DipAdEd71. Coll of Resurr Mirfield 55. **d** 56 **p** 57. C Blackpool St Steph *Blackb* 56-61; R Matson *Glouc* 61-65; Chapl St Elphin's Sch Matlock 65-85; V Thornton-le-

Fylde *Blackb* 85-94; RD Poulton 91-94; rtd 94; Perm to Offic *Ches* from 96. *8A Dunraven Road, West Kirby, Wirral CH48 4DS*

PRZESLAWSKI, Maria Christina. EMMTC. **d** 10 **p** 11. NSM Wilne and Draycott w Breaston *Derby* from 10. *9 Holmes Road, Breaston, Derby DE72 3BT* Tel (01332) 874480 E-mail maria.9@btinternet.com

PRZYWALA, Karl Andrzej. b 63. Univ Coll Dur BA85 Chas Sturt Univ NSW BTh04. St Mark's Nat Th Cen Canberra 01. **d** 04 **p** 05. C Houghton le Spring *Dur* 04-05; C Chester le Street 05-07; P-in-c Whatton w Aslockton, Hawksworth, Scarrington etc *S'well* from 07. *The Vicarage, Main Street, Aslockton, Nottingham NG13 9AL* Tel (01949) 850523 E-mail karl_sydney@yahoo.co.uk

PUCKRIN, Christopher. b 47. Oak Hill Th Coll. **d** 82 **p** 83. C Heworth H Trin *York* 82-84; C Sherburn in Elmet 84-85; P-in-c Kirk Fenton 85-86; P-in-c Kirkby Wharfe 85-86; V Kirk Fenton w Kirkby Wharfe and Ulleskelfe 86-87; C York St Mich-le-Belfrey 87-94; P-in-c Barnstaple *Ex* 94-97; TV 97-00; V Woodside *Ripon* 00-07; C Holbeck 07-09; V Bardsey from 09. *The Vicarage, Woodacre Lane, Bardsey, Leeds LS17 9DG* Tel (01937) 579590

PUDDEFOOT, John Charles. b 52. St Pet Coll Ox BA74 Edin Univ BD78. Edin Th Coll 76. **d** 78 **p** 79. C Darlington H Trin *Dur* 78-81; Ind Chapl *Chich* 81-84; Asst Master Eton Coll from 84; Hd Mathematics from 93. *Eton College, Windsor SL4 6DB* Tel (01753) 671320 E-mail j.puddefoot@etoncollege.org.uk

PUDGE, Mark Samuel. b 67. K Coll Lon BD90 AKC90 Heythrop Coll Lon MA99. Ripon Coll Cuddesdon 91. **d** 93 **p** 94. C Thorpe Bay *Chelmsf* 93-96; TV Wickford and Runwell 97-00; Management Consultant Citizens' Advice Bureau from 00; Hon C Paddington St Jo w St Mich *Lon* from 03. *Flat 2, 12 Connaught Street, London W2 2AF*

PUDNEY, Malcolm Lloyd. b 48. SEITE 99. **d** 01 **p** 02. NSM S Nutfield w Outwood *S'wark* 01-06; P-in-c Woodham Mortimer w Hazeleigh and Woodham Walter *Chelmsf* 06-10; P-in-c Lurgashall, Lodsworth and Selham *Chich* from 10; P-in-c N Chapel w Ebernoe from 10. *The Rectory, Northchapel, Petworth GU28 9HP* Tel (01428) 707373 Mobile 07860-464836 E-mail yenduptoo@madasafish.com

PUERTO RICO, Bishop of. *See* ALVAREZ-VELAZQUEZ, The Rt Revd David Andres

PUGH, Brian. *See* PUGH, William Bryan

PUGH, Geoffrey William. b 47. Ox Min Course 09. **d** 09 **p** 10. NSM Ruscombe and Twyford *Ox* from 09. *3 Willow Drive, Twyford, Reading RG10 9DB* Tel 0118-934 5482 Mobile 07934-420303 E-mail revgeoff@familypugh.com

PUGH, Harry. b 48. K Coll Lon BD70 AKC71 Lanc Univ MA89. **d** 72 **p** 73. C Milnrow *Man* 72-75; P-in-c Rochdale Gd Shep 75-78; TV Rochdale 78-79; Perm to Offic *Liv* 79-82; C Darwen St Cuth *Blackb* 82-85; C Darwen St Cuth w Tockholes St Steph 85-86; V Burnley St Steph 86-93; R Hoole 93-01; P-in-c Porthleven w Sithney *Truro* from 01. *The Vicarage, Pendeen Road, Porthleven, Helston TR13 9AL* Tel (01326) 562419

PUGH, Lynda. b 49. Man Univ BSocSc93 MA96 PhD04. Ripon Coll Cuddesdon 07. **d** 09 **p** 10. C Glen Gp *Linc* from 09. *78 Gallery Walk, Pinchbeck, Spalding PE11 3XJ* Tel (01775) 710904 Mobile 07775-660081 E-mail lynda.pugh@hemscott.net

PUGH, Ronald Keith. b 32. Jes Coll Ox BA54 MA57 DPhil57. Ripon Hall Ox 56. **d** 59 **p** 60. C Bournemouth St Mich *Win* 59-61; Asst Chapl Bryanston Sch 61-66; Chapl Cranleigh Sch Surrey 66-68; Lect K Alfred Coll Winchester 68-97; rtd 97; Hon Sec and Treas Win and Portsm Dioc Clerical Registry 97-06. *6 Windermere Gardens, Alresford SO24 9NL* Tel (01962) 732879 E-mail rk.pugh@btinternet.com

PUGH, Stephen Gregory. Southn Univ BEd77. Linc Th Coll 85. **d** 87 **p** 88. C Harpenden St Nic *St Alb* 87-90; C Stevenage All SS Pin Green 90-93; V Stotfold and Radwell 93-00; V Gt Ilford St Marg and St Clem *Chelmsf* from 00. *The Vicarage, 70 Brisbane Road, Ilford IG1 4SL* Tel (020) 8554 7542 Mobile 07910-395925 E-mail stephenpugh@waitrose.com

PUGH, Miss Wendy Kathleen. b 48. Newnham Coll Cam BA69 MA75. Trin Coll Bris 93. **d** 95 **p** 96. C Hailsham *Chich* 95-99; C Frimley *Guildf* 99-07; Hon C Chertsey, Lyne and Longcross from 07. *The Vicarage, Lyne Lane, Lyne, Chertsey KT16 0AJ* Tel (01932) 874405 E-mail wkpugh@aol.com

PUGH, William Bryan (Brian). b 34. Ridley Hall Cam 59. **d** 61 **p** 62. C Oseney Crescent St Luke w Camden Square St Paul *Lon* 61-64; C N Wembley St Cuth 64-67; CF 67-88; QHC 85-88; Chapl Heathfield Sch Ascot 88-95; rtd 99; Perm to Offic *Ox* and *Guildf* from 99. *3 College Close, Windlesham GU15 4JU* Tel (01276) 503702 E-mail w.pugh@ntlworld.com

PUGMIRE, Canon Alan. b 37. Tyndale Hall Bris 61. **d** 64 **p** 65. C Islington St Steph w St Bart and St Mark *Lon* 64-66; C St Helens St Mark *Liv* 66-71; R Stretford St Bride *Man* 71-82; R Burnage St Marg 82-02; AD Heaton 88-98; Hon Can Man Cathl 98-02; rtd 02; Perm to Offic *Man* from 02. *20 Shortland Crescent, Manchester M19 1SZ* Tel and fax 0161-431 3476 E-mail alan.pugmire@tiscali.co.uk

---

PUGSLEY, Anthony John. b 39. ACIB. Oak Hill Th Coll 89. **d** 90 **p** 91. C Chadwell *Chelmsf* 90-94; P-in-c Gt Warley Ch Ch 94-01; V Warley Ch Ch and Gt Warley St Mary 01-04; rtd 04. *3 Southcliffe Court, Southview Drive, Walton on the Naze CO14 8EP* Tel (01255) 850967 E-mail revtony@aol.com

PULESTON, Mervyn Pedley. b 35. K Coll Lon BD60 AKC60. **d** 61 **p** 62. C Gt Marlow *Ox* 61-65; P Missr Blackbird Leys CD 65-70; V Kidlington 70-85; R Hampton Poyle 78-85; TR Kidlington w Hampton Poyle 85-86; Chapl Geneva *Eur* 86-92; TV Dorchester *Ox* 92-00; rtd 00. *55 Benmead Road, Kidlington OX5 2DB* Tel (01865) 372360 E-mail mpuleston@aol.com

PULFORD, Christopher. b 59. Pemb Coll Ox BA81 MA87. Trin Coll Bris 82. **d** 84 **p** 85. C Parr *Liv* 84-87; Chapl Berkhamsted Colleg Sch Herts 87-92; Development Dir React from 92. *c/o React, St Luke's House, 270 Sandycombe Road, Kew, Richmond TW9 3NA* Tel (020) 8940 2575 Fax 8940 2050

PULFORD, John Shirley Walter. b 31. Jes Coll Cam BA55 MA59. Cuddesdon Coll 55. **d** 57 **p** 58. C Blackpool St Steph *Blackb* 57-60; N Rhodesia 60-63; V Newington St Paul *S'wark* 63-68; C Seacroft *Ripon* 68-70; Chapl HM Pris Liv 70-72; Chapl HM Pris Linc 72-73; Student Cllr Linc Colls of Art and Tech 73-79; Cam Univ Counselling Service 79-96; Dir 82-96; rtd 96. *59 Cromer Road, North Walsham NR28 0HB* Tel (01692) 404320

PULFORD, Canon Stephen Ian. b 25. Clifton Th Coll 53. **d** 56 **p** 57. C Heref St Jas 56-58; R Coberley w Cowley *Glouc* 58-94; P-in-c Colesborne 75-94; Hon Can Glouc Cathl 84-94; RD Cirencester 88-89; rtd 94; Perm to Offic *Glouc* from 94. *16 Bafford Grove, Charlton Kings, Cheltenham GL53 9JE* Tel (01242) 524261

PULLAN, Ben John. b 43. Univ of Wales (Cardiff) MSc(Econ)83. Bris Minl Tr Scheme 74. **d** 77 **p** 78. NSM Westbury-on-Trym St Alb *Bris* 77-91; NSM Henleaze 91-03; NSM Bishopston and St Andrews from 03. *28 Hobhouse Close, Bristol BS9 4LZ* Tel 0117-962 4190 E-mail ben@bpullan.wanadoo.co.uk

PULLAN, Lionel Stephen. b 37. Keble Coll Ox BA58 MA62 ARCO58 FIST77. Cuddesdon Coll 58. **d** 60 **p** 61. C Tranmere St Paul *Ches* 60-63; C Higher Bebington 63-64; Perm to Offic 64-70; Hon C Luton St Chris Round Green *St Alb* 70-72; Hon C Hitchin H Sav 72-73; Hon C Welwyn 73-75; Hon C Welwyn w Ayot St Peter 75-78; Hon C Kimpton w Ayot St Lawrence 78-82; Hon C Stevenage St Andr and St Geo 82-85; Deputation Appeals Org CECS 85-90; V Sundon *St Alb* 90-03; rtd 03; Perm to Offic *St Alb* from 03; Chapl ATC from 92. *139 Turnpike Drive, Luton LU3 3RB* Tel (01582) 573236

PULLEN, Adam William. b 73. Univ of Wales (Abth) BSc97. St Jo Coll Nottm 03. **d** 06 **p** 07. C Swansea St Pet *S & B* 06-09; C Swansea St Thos and Kilvey 09-10; I Ballisodare w Collooney and Emlaghfad *T, K & A* from 10. *The Rectory, Ballisodare, Co Sligo, Republic of Ireland* Tel (00353) (71) 913 3217 Mobile 87-682 9627 E-mail adam.pullen@googlemail.com

PULLEN, James Stephen. b 43. Lon Univ BSc64 PGCE65 Linacre Coll Ox BA68. St Steph Ho Ox 66. **d** 68 **p** 69. C Chorlton-cum-Hardy St Clem *Man* 68-71; C Doncaster St Leon and St Jude *Sheff* 72-73; Chapl St Olave's Gr Sch Orpington 73-75; Chapl Haileybury Coll 75-01; Second Master 99-01; V St Ives *Ely* 01-10; rtd 10. *12 Broad Leas, St Ives PE27 5QB* Tel (01480) 300070 E-mail pullen846@btinternet.com

PULLEN, Roger Christopher. b 43. Lon Univ BSc65 PGCE90. Wells Th Coll 65. **d** 67 **p** 68. C S w N Hayling *Portsm* 67-69; C Farlington 69-73; V Farington *Blackb* 73-80; V Chorley All SS 80-83; V Kingsley *Ches* 83-92; R Cilcain and Nannerch and Rhydymwyn *St As* 92-99; Dioc MU Admin *Guildf* 99-02; Hon C Bramley and Grafham 99-00; Perm to Offic *Guildf* 00-02 and *Chich* from 03. *Ewhurst, 6 Chichester Way, Selsey, Chichester PO20 0PJ* Tel (01243) 601684 Mobile 07989-732729 E-mail roger.pullen@lineone.net

PULLEN, Canon Timothy John. b 61. BNC Ox BA84 St Jo Coll Dur MA96. Cranmer Hall Dur 93. **d** 96 **p** 97. C Allesley *Cov* 96-00; V Wolston and Church Lawford 00-08; Can Res Cov Cathl from 08; Sub-Dean from 10. *18 Ranulf Croft, Coventry CV3 5FB* Tel (024) 7650 2844 *or* 7652 1230 Mobile 07974-007665 E-mail tim.pullen@coventrycathedral.org.uk

PULLIN, Andrew Eric. b 47. Kelham Th Coll 67 Linc Th Coll 71. **d** 73 **p** 74. C Pershore w Pinvin, Wick and Birlingham *Worc* 73-77; TV Droitwich 77-80; V Woburn Sands *St Alb* 80-85; Perm to Offic *B & W* 85-87. *85 Weymouth Road, Frome BA11 1HJ* Tel (01373) 472170 E-mail a.pullin@talktalk.net

PULLIN, Canon Christopher. b 56. St Chad's Coll Dur BA77 Heythrop Coll Lon MA04. Ripon Coll Cuddesdon 78 Ch Div Sch of Pacific 79. **d** 80 **p** 81. C Tooting All SS *S'wark* 80-85; V New Eltham All SS 85-92; V St Jo in Bedwardine *Worc* 92-08; RD Martley and Worc W 03-08; Hon Can Worc Cathl 07-08; Can Res and Chan Heref Cathl from 08. *2 Cathedral Close, Hereford HR1 2NG* Tel (01432) 341905 Fax 374220 E-mail chancellor@herefordcathedral.org

PULLIN, Peter Stanley. b 29. MA MSc CEng. Trin Coll Bris 87. **d** 88 **p** 89. NSM Rugby *Cov* 88-90; NSM Aylesbeare, Rockbeare, Farringdon etc *Ex* 90-98; Perm to Offic *Ex* 99-04 and *B & W*

from 05. *25 Ashley Road, Bathford, Bath BA1 7TT* Tel (01225) 852050

PULLIN, Rebecca. See CLARKE, Kathleen Jean Rebecca

PULLIN, Stephen James. b 66. S Bank Univ BEng89 Open Univ MBA98. Trin Coll Bris BA04. **d** 04 **p** 05. C Soundwell *Bris* 04-07; P-in-c Stapleton from 07; C Frenchay and Winterbourne Down from 07; Bp's Adv for Deliverance Min from 10. *The Rectory, 21 Park Road, Stapleton, Bristol BS16 1AZ* Tel 0117-958 4714 Mobile 07866-700881 E-mail stephenjpullin@aol.com

PULLINGER, Mrs Catherine Ann. b 54. York Univ BA76. Oak Hill Th Coll 91. **d** 93 **p** 97. NSM Luton St Paul *St Alb* 93-99; NSM Luton Lewsey St Hugh 99-11; P-in-c Woodside from 11. *52 Wheatfield Road, Luton LU4 0TR* Tel (01582) 606996 Fax 472726 E-mail cathy@pullinger.net

PULLINGER, Ian Austin. b 61. Oak Hill Th Coll. **d** 96 **p** 97. C Weston *Win* 96-00; TV The Ortons, Alwalton and Chesterton *Ely* from 00. *Christ Church House, 1 Benstead, Orton Goldhay, Peterborough PE2 5JJ* Tel (01733) 394185 E-mail ianpullinger@btinternet.com

PULLINGER, Peter Mark. b 53. Heythrop Coll Lon MA97. Ridley Hall Cam 01. **d** 03 **p** 04. C Clapham Park St Steph *S'wark* 03-06; C Telford Park 06-07; TV Sutton from 07. *Christ Church Vicarage, 14C Christchurch Park, Sutton SM2 5TN* Tel (020) 8642 2757 Mobile 07796-956774 E-mail mark@pullinger.net

PULMAN, John. b 34. EMMTC 78. **d** 81 **p** 82. NSM Mansfield SS Pet and Paul *S'well* 81-83; C Mansfield Woodhouse 83-86; V Flintham 86-99; R Car Colston w Screveton 86-99; Chapl HM YOI Whatton 87-90; Chapl HM Pris Whatton 90-99; rtd 99; Perm to Offic *S'well* from 99 and *Derby* from 00. *101 Ling Forest Road, Mansfield NG18 3NQ* Tel (01623) 474707

PUMFREY (née CERRATTI), Canon Christa Elisabeth. b 54. Wycliffe Hall Ox 94. **d** 97 **p** 98. C Chipping Norton *Ox* 97-00; P-in-c Lavendon w Cold Brayfield, Clifton Reynes etc 00-08; R from 08; R Gayhurst w Ravenstone, Stoke Goldington etc from 08; Deanery Youth Co-ord from 00; AD Newport from 06; Hon Can Ch Ch from 11. *The New Rectory, 7A Northampton Road, Lavendon, Olney MK46 4EY* Tel (01234) 240013

PUMPHREY, Norman John Albert. b 21. Nor Ord Course 76. **d** 77 **p** 78. NSM Aylsham *Nor* 77-94; Chapl St Mich Hosp Aylsham 88-99; Perm to Offic *Nor* from 94. *12 Buxton Road, Aylsham, Norwich NR11 6JD* Tel (01263) 733207

PUNSHON, Carol Mary. See BRENNAND, Ms Carol Mary

PUNSHON, George Wilson. b 30. Bris Univ BSc Michigan State Univ MSc DipEd. Ripon Hall Ox 71. **d** 73 **p** 74. C Knighton St Mary Magd *Leic* 73-76; V Donisthorpe and Moira w Stretton-en-le-Field 76-82; R Gt Bowden w Welham, Glooston and Cranoe 82-86; Zimbabwe 87-89 and 00-04; Perm to Offic *Pet* 96-00; V Ascension Is 97-98; Chapl Peterho Sch Marondera 00-04. *101 The Downs, Nottingham NG11 7EA*

PUNSHON, Canon Keith. b 48. Jr. Jes Coll Cam BA69 MA73 Birm Univ MA77. Qu Coll Birm 71. **d** 73 **p** 74. C Yardley St Edburgha *Birm* 73-76; Chapl Eton Coll 76-79; V Hill *Birm* 79-86; CF (TA) from 79; V S Yardley St Mich *Birm* 86-96; Can Res Ripon Cathl from 96. *St Peter's House, Minster Close, Ripon HG4 1QP* Tel (01765) 604108 E-mail postmaster@riponcathedral.org.uk

PURCHAS, Canon Catherine Patience Ann. b 39. St Mary's Coll Dur BA61. St Alb Minl Tr Scheme 77. **dss** 80 **d** 87 **p** 94. RE Resource Cen 80-81; Relig Broadcasting Chiltern Radio 81-87; Wheathampstead *St Alb* 81-00; Hon Par Dn 87-94; Hon C 94-00; Relig Broadcasting Beds Radio from 88; Bp's Officer for Women 93-07; Bp's Officer for NSMs and Asst Dir of Ords 93-00; Assoc Dioc Dir of Ords 00-03; Hon Can St Alb 96-00; rtd 03; Dir of Ords *St Alb* from 10. *14 Horn Hill, Whitwell, Hitchin SG4 8AS* Tel and fax (01438) 871668 E-mail patiencepurchas@hotmail.com

PURCHAS, Canon Thomas. b 35. Qu Coll Birm 59. **d** 62 **p** 63. C Bp's Hatfield *St Alb* 62-71; R Blunham 71-78; P-in-c Tempsford w Lt Barford 71-78; R Blunham w Tempsford and Lt Barford 78-80; R Wheathampstead 80-00; RD Wheathampstead 92-99; Hon Can St Alb 99-00; rtd 00; RD Hitchin 00-02; Perm to Offic *St Alb* from 00. *14 Horn Hill, Whitwell, Hitchin SG4 8AS* Tel and fax (01438) 871668

PURDY, Canon John David. b 44. Leeds Univ BA65 MPhil76. Coll of Resurr Mirfield 72. **d** 75 **p** 76. C Marske in Cleveland *York* 75-78; C Marton-in-Cleveland 78-80; V Newby 80-87; V Kirkleatham 87-95; V Kirkbymoorside w Gillamoor, Farndale etc 95-09; RD Helmsley 99-09; rtd 09; P-in-c Fylingdales and Hawsker cum Stainsacre *York* from 10; Can and Preb York Minster from 98. *St Stephen's House, Laburnum Avenue, Robin Hood's Bay, Whitby YO22 4RR* E-mail david.purdy@virgin.net

PURNELL, Marcus John. b 75. Ridley Hall Cam 07. **d** 09 **p** 10. C Northampton St Benedict *Pet* from 09. *44 Barn Owl Close, East Hunsbury, Northampton NN4 0UA* Tel (01604) 765060 Mobile 07535-639915 E-mail marcuspurnell@hotmail.com

PURSER, Alan Gordon. b 51. Leic Univ BSc73. Wycliffe Hall Ox 74. **d** 77 **p** 78. C Beckenham Ch Ch *Roch* 77-81; TV Barking St Marg w St Patr *Chelmsf* 81-84; R Kensington S Africa 84-88; Min Hadley Wood St Paul Prop Chpl *Lon* 88-03; UK Team Ldr

Crosslinks from 03. *18 Salmon Lane, London E14 7LZ* Tel (020) 7702 8741 Mobile 07802-888439 E-mail apurser@crosslinks.org

PURSER, Alec. **d** 10. NSM Abbeyleix w Ballyroan etc *C & O* from 10. *The Kennels, Moyle Big, Carlow, Republic of Ireland* Tel (00353) (59) 914 8829 Mobile 87-923 2694 E-mail familypurser@eircom.net

PURVEY-TYRER, Neil. b 66. Leeds Univ BA87 MA88. Westcott Ho Cam 88. **d** 90 **p** 91. C Denbigh and Nantglyn *St As* 90-92; Chapl Asst Basingstoke Distr Hosp 92-95; TV Cannock *Lich* 95-99; V Northampton H Sepulchre w St Andr and St Lawr *Pet* 99-02; Dioc Co-ord for Soc Resp 99-03; TR Duston 02-08; Chapl St Andr Hosp Northn 08-09; Sen Chapl from 09; Past Care and Counselling Adv *Pet* from 10. *St Andrew's Healthcare, Billing Road, Northampton NN1 5DG* Tel (01604) 616379 E-mail ntyrer@standrew.co.uk

PURVIS, Canon Colin. b 19. Kelham Th Coll 37. **d** 44 **p** 45. C Hebburn St Cuth *Dur* 44-47; C Sunderland 47-50; C Darlington St Cuth 50-53; C-in-C Humbledon St Mary V CD 53-58; C-in-c Bishopwearmouth St Mary V w St Pet CD 58-62; V Heworth St Mary 62-76; RD Gateshead 69-76; R Egglescliffe 76-84; Hon Can Dur Cathl 83-92; rtd 84. *c/o The Revd Canon J E Sadler, 26 Crompton Road, Newcastle upon Tyne NE6 5QL*

PURVIS, Lynn. b 58. St Jo Coll Dur BA97. Cranmer Hall Dur 94. **d** 98 **p** 99. C Gt Aycliffe *Dur* 98-02; Chapl N Tees and Hartlepool NHS Trust from 02. *University Hospital of North Tees, Hardwick Road, Stockton-on-Tees TS19 8PE* Tel (01642) 624714 E-mail lpurvis@nth.nhs.uk

PURVIS, Ms Sandra Anne. b 56. Univ Coll Ches BTh01. NOC 98. **d** 01 **p** 02. C Blackpool St Jo *Blackb* 01-06; P-in-c Gt Harwood 06-08; Chapl Pennine Acute Hosps NHS Trust from 08. *North Manchester General Hospital, Delaunays Road, Crumpsall, Manchester M8 5RB* Tel 0161-795 4567 Mobile 07967-136992 E-mail sandraapurvis@aol.com

PURVIS, Canon Stephen. b 48. AKC70. **d** 71 **p** 72. C Peterlee *Dur* 71-75; Dioc Recruitment Officer 75-79; V Stevenage All SS Pin Green *St Alb* 79-88; TR Borehamwood 88-00; RD Aldenham 94-98; V Leagrave from 00; Hon Can St Alb from 02; RD Luton from 07. *St Luke's Vicarage, High Street, Leagrave, Luton LU4 9JY* Tel and fax (01582) 572737 E-mail stephen.purvis@yahoo.co.uk

PUSEY, Canon Ian John. b 39. Sarum Th Coll 69. **d** 71 **p** 72. C Waltham Abbey *Chelmsf* 71-75; TV Stantonbury *Ox* 75-80; P-in-c Bletchley 80-84; R 84-00; RD Milton Keynes 96-00; P-in-c Lamp 00-06; AD Newport 04-06; Hon Can Ch Ch 06; rtd 06. *16 Gussiford Lane, Exmouth EX8 2SF* Tel (01395) 275549 E-mail ian.pusey@virgin.net

PUTNAM, Mrs Gillian. b 43. WEMTC 00. **d** 02 **p** 03. NSM Milton *B & W* 02-09; NSM Milton and Kewstoke from 09. *6 Miller Close, Weston-super-Mare BS23 2SQ* Tel (01934) 416917 E-mail gillianputnam@yahoo.co.uk

PUTNAM, Jeremy James. b 76. Ripon Coll Cuddesdon 09. **d** 11. C Portishead *B & W* from 11. *25 Lambourne Way, Portishead, Bristol BS20 7LQ* Tel (01275) 844137 Mobile 07894-628405 E-mail jeremyputnam@live.com

PUTT, Thomas David. b 83. Loughb Univ BEng05. Oak Hill Th Coll BA11. **d** 11. C Kirk Ella and Willerby *York* from 11. *24 Redland Drive, Kirk Ella, Hull HU10 7UZ* Tel (01482) 653251 Mobile 07824-337885 E-mail tomputt@witty.com

✠**PWAISIHO, The Rt Revd William Alaha.** b 48. Bp Patteson Th Coll (Solomon Is) 71. **d** 74 **p** 75 **c** 81. Solomon Is 74-76; New Zealand 78-79; Solomon Is 79-95; Dean Honiara 80-81; Bp Malaita 81-89; Hon Asst Bp Ches from 97; C Sale St Anne 97-99; R Gawsworth from 99. *The Rectory, Church Lane, Gawsworth, Macclesfield SK11 9RJ* Tel (01260) 223201 Mobile 07711-241625 E-mail bishop.gawsworth@virgin.net

PYATT, Noel Watson. b 34. AKC57. **d** 58 **p** 59. C Prenton *Ches* 58-61; C Cheadle Hulme All SS 61-63; P-in-c Hattersley 63-66; V 66-70; V Ches St Paul 70-99; rtd 99; Perm to Offic *Sheff* 99-02. *273 School Road, Sheffield S10 1GQ* Tel 0114-266 9944

PYBURN, Canon Alan. b 29. G&C Coll Cam BA51 MA55. Westcott Ho Cam 53. **d** 55 **p** 56. C Barnard Castle *Dur* 55-57; Chapl G&C Coll Cam 57-60; V Dallington *Pet* 60-72; V Ox St Giles 72-79; P-in-c Remenham 79-94; R Henley 79-94; RD Henley 84-94; Hon Can Ch Ch 90-95; R Henley w Remenham 94-95; rtd 95. *Pippin Cottage, Well Hill, Finstock, Chipping Norton OX7 3BU* Tel (01993) 868651

PYBUS, Antony Frederick. b 54. Birm Univ BA77. St Jo Coll Dur 78. **d** 81 **p** 82. C Ches H Trin 81-84; C W Hampstead St Jas *Lon* 84-89; V Alexandra Park St Andr 89-93; V Alexandra Park from 93. *The Vicarage, 34 Alexandra Park Road, London N10 2AB* Tel (020) 8883 3181 *or* 8444 6898 E-mail office@alexandrapark.org *or* vicar@alexandrapark.org

PYE, Alexander Frederick. b 61. St Mich Coll Llan 93. **d** 95 **p** 96. C Griffithstown *Mon* 95-97; P-in-c Bistre *St As* 97-99; P-in-c Penmaen and Crumlin *Mon* 99-00; V 00-02; R Govilon w Llanfoist w Llanelen 02-09; V Beguildy and Heyope and Llangynllo and Bleddfa *S & B* from 09. *The Vicarage, Beguildy, Knighton LD7 1YE* Tel (01547) 510080

PYE, Canon Allan Stephen. b 56. Univ of Wales (Lamp) BA78 Lanc Univ MA85 MPhil87. Westcott Ho Cam 79. **d** 81 **p** 82. C Scotforth *Blackb* 81-85; C Oswaldtwistle All SS 85-87; V Wrightington 87-91; Chapl Wrightington Hosp 87-91; P-in-c Hayton St Mary *Carl* 91-93; V Hayton w Cumwhitton 93-98; RD Brampton 96-98; Hon Can Carl Cathl from 97; P-in-c Hawkshead and Low Wray w Sawrey 98-03; V Hawkshead and Low Wray w Sawrey and Rusland etc 03-06; V Keswick St Jo from 06. *St John's Vicarage, Ambleside Road, Keswick CA12 4DD* Tel (017687) 72130 E-mail stephen.pye@virgin.net

PYE, Mrs Gay Elizabeth. b 46. RN67 RM68. Trin Coll Bris BD73. **d** 96 **p** 96. NSM Castle Church *Lich* 96-00; Asst Chapl HM Pris Stafford 96-97; Chapl HM Pris Shrewsbury 97-00; Regional Manager Bible Soc 00-06; NSM Upper Derwent *Carl* from 06. *The Vicarage, Borrowdale, Keswick CA12 5XQ* Tel (017687) 77238 Mobile 07901-837813 E-mail gay.pye@gmail.com

PYE, James Timothy. b 58. Oak Hill Th Coll BA90. **d** 90 **p** 91. C Normanton *Derby* 90-94; R Talke *Lich* 94-04; R Knebworth *St Alb* from 04. *The Rectory, 15 St Martin's Road, Knebworth SG3 6ER* Tel (01438) 817396 E-mail jim@jimpye.plus.com

PYE, Joseph Terence Hardwidge. b 41. MRICS64. Trin Coll Bris 70. **d** 73 **p** 74. C Blackb Ch Ch 73-76; OMF 77-90; Korea 77-90; V Castle Church *Lich* 90-06; rtd 06. *The Vicarage, Borrowdale, Keswick CA12 5XQ* Tel (017687) 77238 E-mail terry.pye@gmail.com

PYE, Michael Francis. b 53. New Coll Ox BA75 MA78 DPhil78. STETS 97. **d** 00 **p** 01. C Fareham H Trin *Portsm* 00-07; V Portsea All SS from 07. *All Saints' Vicarage, 51 Staunton Street, Portsmouth PO1 4EJ* Tel (023) 9287 2815 E-mail mike@pye229.freeserve.co.uk

PYE, Nicholas Richard. b 62. Univ Coll Lon BA84 Man Univ PGCE87 Anglia Poly Univ MA03. Ridley Hall Cam 95. **d** 98 **p** 99. C Epsom Common Ch Ch *Guildf* 98-01; C Harrow Trin St Mich Lon 01-03; V Finchley St Paul and St Luke from 03. *St Paul's Vicarage, 50 Long Lane, London N3 2PU* Tel (020) 8346 8729 E-mail revpye@xalt.co.uk

PYE, Mrs Paula Jayne. b 67. St Jo Coll Dur BA09 RGN90. Cranmer Hall Dur 07. **d** 09 **p** 10. C Cockermouth Area *Carl* from 09. *139 The Parklands, Cockermouth CA13 0XJ* Tel 07805-411936 (mobile) E-mail thepyes@hotmail.co.uk

PYE, Sandra Anne. *See* ELLISON, Ms Sandra Anne

PYE, Stephen. *See* PYE, Canon Allan Stephen

PYKE, Alan. b 37. Trin Coll Bris BA87. **d** 87 **p** 88. C A 58-87; C Ipswich St Mary at Stoke w St Pet *St E* 87-90; C St Mary, Creeting St Peter etc 90-98; C S Trin Broads *Nor* 98-02; rtd 03; Perm to Offic *Nor* 03-08. *29 Stuart Court, High Street, Kibworth, Leicester LE8 0LR* Tel 0116-279 0113 E-mail alanpyke@scs-datacom.co.uk

PYKE, Barry John. b 62. Qu Mary Coll Lon BSc84 Southn Univ BTh94 Open Univ BA96 FGS84. Sarum & Wells Th Coll 91. **d** 94 **p** 95. C Bengeworth *Worc* 94-96; C Worc City St Paul and Old St Martin etc 96-99; R Chipping Ongar w Shelley *Chelmsf* 99-06; RD Ongar 04-06; R Hinderwell, Roxby and Staithes etc *York* from 06. *The Rectory, 1 The High Street, Hinderwell, Saltburn-by-the-Sea TS13 5JX* Tel (01947) 840249 E-mail bpyke@care4free.net

PYKE, Mrs Marion. b 41. **d** 10 **p** 11. OLM Caversham Thameside and Mapledurham *Ox* from 10. *26 Priest Hill, Caversham, Reading RG4 7RZ* Tel 0118-947 5834

PYKE, Richard Ernest. b 50. Sarum & Wells Th Coll. **d** 82 **p** 83. C Bushey *St Alb* 82-85; C Gt Berkhamsted 85-89; V St Alb St Mary Marshalswick 89-00; TR Bp's Hatfield 00-05; TR Bp's Hatfield, Lemsford and N Mymms from 05; RD Welwyn Hatfield from 03. *The Rectory, 1 Fore Street, Hatfield AL9 5AN* Tel and fax (01707) 262072 E-mail richard50pyke@tiscali.co.uk

PYKE, Mrs Ruth Cheryl. b 56. Bath Coll of HE BA78 W Lon Inst of HE PGCE80. SAOMC 95. **d** 98 **p** 99. C Leavesden *St Alb* 98-02; C St Alb St Steph 02-06; P-in-c Caddington from 06; Bedfordshire Area Children's Work Adv from 06. *The Vicarage, Collings Wells Close, Caddington, Luton LU1 4BG* Tel (01582) 731692 E-mail ruth.pyke@tesco.net

PYKE, Thomas Fortune. b 62. St Chad's Coll Dur BA85 Fitzw Coll Cam BA88. Ridley Hall Cam 86. **d** 89 **p** 90. C Hitchin *St Alb* 89-94; Chapl Aston Univ 94-99; V Birm St Paul 99-06; Ind Chapl 01-06; Th Ecum Officer Birm Bd for Miss 01-06; V Is of Dogs Ch Ch and St Jo w St Luke Lon from 06. *Christ Church Vicarage, Manchester Road, London E14 3BN* Tel (020) 7538 1766 Mobile 07753-616499 E-mail tom.pyke@parishiod.org.uk

PYLE, John Alan. b 31. Qu Coll Birm. **d** 69 **p** 70. C Fenham St Jas and St Basil *Newc* 69-72; C Monkseaton St Pet 72-74; C Morpeth 74-78; R Bothal 78-83; TV Willington 83-91; R Chollerton w Birtley and Thockrington 91-97; rtd 97; Perm to Offic *Newc* from 97. *37 Ullswater Drive, Killingworth, Newcastle upon Tyne NE12 6GX* Tel 0191-268 6044

PYM, David Pitfield. b 45. Nottm Univ BA65 Ex Coll Ox DPhil68. Ripon Hall Ox 66. **d** 68 **p** 69. C Nottingham St Mary *S'well* 68-72; Chapl RN 72-76 and 79-84; Chapl Worksop Coll

Notts 76-79; R Avon Dassett w Farnborough and Fenny Compton *Cov* 84-07; rtd 07; Perm to Offic *Ox* from 07. *Sunrise, Bury Court Lane, Shotteswell, Banbury OX17 1JA* Tel (01295) 738948 E-mail davidpym@lineone.net

PYM, Gordon Sydney. b 19. Worc Ord Coll 59. **d** 61 **p** 62. C Highweek *Ex* 61-63; C Plymouth Em 63-66; V Kilnhurst *Sheff* 66-69; V Owston 69-72; V Hensall 72-75; rtd 75; Perm to Offic *Sheff* from 75. *6 Greno Road, Swinton, Mexborough S64 8RP* Tel (01709) 586884

PYMBLE, Adam Oliver James. b 79. **d** 11. C Lindfield *Chich* from 11. *2 Church Close, Francis Road, Lindfield, Haywards Heath RH16 2JB* E-mail adampymble@gmail.com

PYNE, Robert Leslie. b 51. Lanchester Poly Cov BA72 Solicitor 75. Coll of Resurr Mirfield 76. **d** 79 **p** 80. C Clifton All SS w St Jo *Bris* 79-81; Bp's Dom Chapl *Ox* 81-84; TV High Wycombe 84-90; Chapl RN 90-11; rtd 11; Perm to Offic *S'wark* from 11. *Holy Trinity Vicarage, 59 Southwell Crescent, London SE9 2SD* Tel (020) 8850 1246 E-mail rlp1951@tiscali.co.uk

PYNN, Catherine. b 45. Reading Univ BSc67. SAOMC 93. **d** 96 **p** 97. NSM Caversham St Pet and Mapledurham etc *Ox* 96-03; NSM Aldermaston w Wasing and Brimpton 03-06; NSM Woolhampton w Midgham and Beenham Valance 05-06; Chapl Bradfield Coll Berks 00-06; NSM Kintbury w Avington *Ox* 06-11; NSM W Woodhay w Enborne, Hampstead Marshall etc 06-11; NSM Walbury Beacon from 11. *The Vicarage, 3 Elizabeth Gardens, Kintbury, Newbury RG17 9TB* Tel (01488) 658243 Mobile 07717-726410

PYNN, David Christopher. b 47. Trin Coll Cam MA70 Cam Inst of Educn CertEd69. NOC 06. **d** 08 **p** 09. NSM Scalby *York* from 08; NSM Scarborough St Luke from 08. *6 Stepney Drive, Scarborough YO12 5DH* Tel 07530-753187 (mobile) E-mail davidpynn12@aol.com

✠**PYTCHES, The Rt Revd George Edward David.** b 31. Bris Univ BA54 Nottm Univ MPhil84. Tyndale Hall Bris 51. **d** 55 **p** 56 **c** 70. C Ox St Ebbe 55-58; C Wallington *S'wark* 58-59; Chile 59-77; Suff Bp Valparaiso 70-72; Bp Chile, Bolivia and Peru 72-77; V Chorleywood St Andr *St Alb* 77-96; rtd 96; Perm to Offic *St Alb* from 96. *Red Tiles, Homefield Road, Chorleywood, Rickmansworth WD3 5QJ* Tel (01923) 282764 Fax 283762

PYTCHES, Preb Peter Norman Lambert. b 32. Lon Univ BD57 Bris Univ MLitt67 Southn Univ PhD81 K Coll Lon MA00 Potchefstroom Univ MTh03 Open Univ MPhil06 Lambeth STh74. Tyndale Hall Bris 53. **d** 57 **p** 58. C Heatherlands St Jo *Sarum* 57-61; C Cromer *Nor* 61-63; V Plymouth St Jude *Ex* 63-71; V Heatherlands St Jo *Sarum* 71-76; Dir Past Tr Oak Hill Th Coll 76-81; V Finchley Ch Ch *Lon* 81-91; AD Cen Barnet 86-91; V Forty Hill Jes Ch 91-97; Preb St Paul's Cathl 92-97; rtd 97; Perm to Offic *Lon* from 98. *25 Weardale Gardens, Enfield EN2 0BA* Tel and fax (020) 8366 5126

Q

QUANCE, John David. b 42. Kelham Th Coll 61. **d** 67 **p** 68. C Southgate Ch Ch *Lon* 67-70; C Norbury St Phil *Cant* 70-73; Asst Chapl Middx Hosp Lon 73-80; R Failsworth St Jo *Man* 80-95; Australia 84-85; P-in-c Healey *Man* 95-04; V Islamabad Pakistan 00-01; rtd 07; Perm to Offic *Man* from 04. *4 Elm Grove, Rochdale OL11 3RZ* Tel (01706) 343473 Mobile 07876-742189

QUARMBY, David John. b 43. St Jo Coll Dur BA64 Lon Univ CertEd70 Man Univ MEd89 Sheff Univ MA99. Ridley Hall Cam 65. **d** 67 **p** 68. C Bournville *Birm* 67-71; V Erdington St Chad 71-73; Lic to Offic *Blackb* 73-83; Perm to Offic *Man* 83-90 and from 98; C Oldham St Paul 90-98; Hon C from 98; Cllr Huddersfield Poly 90-92; Huddersfield Univ 92-01; Prin Adult Psychotherapist Hyndburn Community Mental Health Team from 00; Sen Cllr Blackb and Darwen Primary Care Trust 01-08. *30 College Avenue, Oldham OL8 4DS* Tel 0161-626 2771 E-mail david.quarmby@zen.co.uk

QUARRELL, John Beck. b 39. Hull Coll of Educn CertEd59. Chich Th Coll 67. **d** 70 **p** 71. C Horbury *Wakef* 70-71; C Sowerby 71-73; V Brotherton 74-80; Chapl Pontefract Gen Hosp 78-80; V Staincliffe *Wakef* 80-88; Chapl Staincliffe Hosp 82-88; R Farndon w Thorpe, Hawton and Cotham *S'well* 89-09; rtd 09. *3 Dr Caldwell Drive, Newark NG24 4JS* Tel (01636) 612833 E-mail jbq339@yahoo.co.uk

QUARTON, Robert Edward. b 43. Wilson Carlile Coll 64 EMMTC 84. **d** 87 **p** 88. C Gresley *Derby* 87-88; C Clay Cross 88-90; C N Wingfield, Clay Cross and Pilsley 90-91; R Darley 91-10; P-in-c S Darley, Elton and Winster 03-10; RD Wirksworth 03-08; rtd 10. *12 Blenheim Avenue, Swannick DE55 1PQ* Tel (01773) 605766 E-mail robertquarton@uwclub.net

QUASH, Canon Jonathan Ben. b 68. Peterho Cam BA90 MA94 PhD99. Westcott Ho Cam 91. **d** 95 **p** 96. NSM Cambridge St Mary Less *Ely* 95-96; Asst Chapl Peterho Cam 95-96; Chapl Fitzw Coll Cam 96-99; Fell 98-99; Tutor Wesley Ho Cam 96-99; Fell and Dean Peterho Cam 99-07; Prof K Coll Lon from 07; Can Th Cov Cathl from 04. *King's College London, Strand, London WC2R 2LS* Tel (020) 7848 2336 Fax 7848 2255 E-mail ben.quash@kcl.ac.uk

✠**QUASHIE, The Rt Revd Kobina Adduah.** b 34. ACIS60 Univ of Ghana LLB71 LLM74. **d** 78 **p** 78 **c** 92. Ghana 78-80 and 92-02; Chapl Middx Hosp Lon 80; Funding Officer USPG 80-92; Hon Can Kumasi from 86; Hon Can Koforidua from 86; Hon Can Accra from 87; Bp Cape Coast 92-02; rtd 02. *32 Chandos Road, London NW2 4LU* Tel (020) 8452 5721

QUAYLE, Margaret Grace. b 28. Gipsy Hill Coll of Educn TCert48 Lon Univ BA53 Liv Univ MPhil78. **d** 98 **p** 99. OLM Gt Crosby St Luke *Liv* 98-03; Perm to Offic from 03. *Clwyd, 9 Myers Road West, Liverpool L23 0RS* Tel 0151-924 1659

QUIBELL, Edward Villiers. b 71. Anglia Poly BSc93 Hughes Hall Cam PGCE94. Trin Coll Bris BA03. **d** 03 **p** 04. C Swindon Ch Ch *Bris* 03-06; Perm to Offic *Lon* 06-08; TV Broadwater Chich from 08. *The Vicarage, 53 Lavington Road, Worthing BN14 7SL* Tel (01903) 236363 E-mail revted@hotmail.co.uk

QUIBELL, Mrs Susan Elizabeth. b 50. **d** 03 **p** 04. OLM Aldridge *Lich* from 03. *29 Lingmoor Grove, Aldridge, Walsall WS9 8BY* Tel (01922) 744205 E-mail s.quibell@googlemail.com

QUICK, John Michael. b 46. N Counties Coll Newc TCert68 Birkbeck Coll Lon BSc73 FRGS70. SAOMC 97. **d** 00 **p** 01. OLM New Windsor *Ox* from 00. *White Roses, 45 York Road, Windsor SL4 3PA* Tel (01753) 865557 Mobile 07977-754822 E-mail littlefrquick@aol.com

QUICK, Roger Aelfred Melvin Tricquet. b 55. Leeds Univ BA79 PGCE81. Coll of Resurr Mirfield BA94. **d** 96 **p** 97. C Chapel Allerton *Ripon* 96-00; C Ireland Wood 00-03; Hon C 03-04; Chapl Strathallan Sch from 04. *Jacaranda, Strathallan School, Forgandenny, Perth PH2 9EN* Tel (01738) 813509 Mobile 07762-159047 E-mail father@priest.com

QUIGLEY, Adam. d 03 p 04. NSM Castlerock w Dunboe and Fermoyle *D & R* from 03. *41 Queens Park, Coleraine BT51 3JS* Tel (028) 7035 5191

QUIGLEY, Andrew. b 72. New Coll Ox BA96 Bris Univ PGCE98. St Jo Coll Nottm MTh03. **d** 04 **p** 05. C Burbage w Aston Flamville *Leic* 04-07; TV Market Harborough and The Transfiguration etc from 07. *The Vicarage, 49 Ashley Road, Market Harborough LE16 7XD* Tel (01858) 463441 E-mail a.quigley@ntlworld.com

QUIGLEY, Donna Maree. Ulster Univ BEd BTh. **d** 01 **p** 02. C Portadown St Columba *Arm* 01-03; I Derryvolgie *Conn* 04-09. *Address temp unknown* E-mail donna quigley@yahoo.co.uk

QUIGLEY, John Christopher. b 41. Pontifical Lateran Univ STL68. **d** 67 **p** 68. P-in-c N Bersted *Chich* 03-08; rtd 08; P-in-c Lyminster *Chich* from 11. *The Vicarage, The Paddock, Lyminster, Littlehampton BN17 7QH* Tel 07792-718875 (mobile) E-mail john.quigley4@btinternet.com

QUIGLEY, William. b 46. Ulster Univ BA86. CITC BTh98. **d** 98 **p** 99. C Ballymoney w Finvoy and Rasharkin *Conn* 98-01; I Eglish w Killylea *Arm* 01-11; rtd 11. *15 Castlerocklands, Carrickfergus BT38 8FY* E-mail williamquigley@btinternet.com

QUILL, Andrew Thomas Edward. b 67. Heriot-Watt Univ BArch91. Uganda Chr Univ 05. **d** 05 **p** 07. Dioc Co-ord Community Health Empowerment Uganda 05-06; C Drumragh w Mountfield *D & R* 06-09; I Kinawley w H Trin *K, E & A* from 09; Dioc Communications Officer from 10. *The Rectory, 144A Main Street, Cloghan, Derrylin, Enniskillen BT92 9LD* Tel (028) 6774 8994 Mobile 07738-960707 E-mail quills155@btinternet.com *or* kinawley@kilmore.anglican.org

QUILL, Walter Paterson. b 35. MBE. **d** 60 **p** 61. C Glendermott *D & R* 60-63; I Kilbarron 63-66; I Kilcronaghan w Ballynascreen 66-81; I Derg w Termonamongan 81-07; Can Derry Cathl 89-07; Preb Howth St Patr Cathl Dublin 94-07; rtd 07; P-in-c Clondevaddock w Portsalon and Leatbeg *D & R* from 09. *1 University Gardens, Coleraine BT52 1JT* Tel (028) 7035 2114 E-mail wquill@btinternet.com

QUILLIAM, Miss Anne Eleanor Scott. b 31. Bedf Coll Lon BA54 CertEd55. Dalton Ho Bris 59. **d** 87. Par Dn Toxteth St Philemon w St Gabr and St Cleopas *Liv* 87-92; rtd 92; Perm to Offic *S & M* from 92. *Brough Fort, Santon, Isle of Man IM4 2HX* Tel (01624) 611777

QUIN, David Christopher. b 42. SAOMC 97. **d** 00 **p** 01. NSM Blunham, Gt Barford, Roxton and Tempsford etc *St Alb* 00-06; rtd 06. *16 Beceshore Close, Moreton-in-Marsh GL56 9NB* Tel (01608) 651571 Mobile 07867-664924 E-mail davidcquin@aol.com

QUIN, Eric Arthur. b 22. Magd Coll Cam BA46 MA48 Lon Univ BD56. Bps' Coll Cheshunt 46. **d** 48 **p** 49. C Luton St Andr *St Alb*

48-50; C Barnoldswick w Bracewell *Bradf* 50-52; PC Bradf St Sav 52-57; P-in-c Gt w Lt Wymondley *St Alb* 57-58; P-in-c St Ippolyts 57-58; V 58-70; RD Hitchin 68-70; V Haynes 70-87; rtd 87; Perm to Offic *Ches* from 87. *Annabel's Cottage, The Lydiate, Wirral CH60 8PR* Tel 0151-342 8650

QUIN, John James Neil. b 31. Ox Univ MA DipEd53. Qu Coll Birm 61. **d** 63 **p** 64. C Cannock *Lich* 63-68; V Sneyd Green 68-78; V Stafford St Paul Forebridge 78-90; TV Tettenhall Regis 90-98; rtd 98; Perm to Offic *Ex* from 00. *Watcombe House, 28 Barnpark Road, Teignmouth TQ14 8PN* Tel (01626) 772525

QUINE, Christopher Andrew. b 38. St Aid Birkenhead 61. **d** 64 **p** 65. C Hunts Cross *Liv* 64-67; C Farnworth and C-in-c Widnes St Jo 67-71; V Clubmoor 71-78; V Formby H Trin 78-99; V Arbory and Santan *S & M* 99-03; rtd 03. *15 Sandringham Road, Formby, Liverpool L37 6EG* Tel 07963-588332 (mobile) E-mail chris.quine@googlemail.com

QUINE, David Anthony. b 28. Qu Coll Cam BA52 MA59. Ridley Hall Cam 53. **d** 55 **p** 56. C Beckenham Ch Ch *Roch* 55-59; C Normanton *Derby* 59-60; V Low Elswick *Newc* 60-66; V Houghton *Carl* 66-68; Lic to Offic *York* 68-71; Chapl Monkton Combe Sch Bath 71-85; rtd 85; Perm to Offic *Carl* from 85. *Briar Cragg, Gale Rigg, Ambleside LA22 0AZ* Tel (01539) 433563

✠**QUINLAN, The Rt Revd Alan Geoffrey.** b 33. Kelham Th Coll 54. **d** 58 **p** 59 **c** 88. C Bedford Leigh *Man* 58-61; R Bloemfontein St Marg S Africa 61-68; R Sasolburg 68-70; R Parys 70-72; Warden CR and Chapl Teachers Tr Coll Grahamstown 72-76; R Plumstead All SS 76-88; Can Cape Town 80-88; Suff Bp Cape Town (Cen Region) 88-98; rtd 98. *132 Woodley Road, Plumstead, Cape Town, 7800 South Africa* Tel and fax (0027) (21F) 705 1452

QUINN, Canon Arthur Hamilton Riddel. b 37. TCD BA60 MA64 BD67. **d** 61 **p** 62. C Belfast H Trin *Conn* 61-63; C Belfast St Mary Magd 63-64; Chapl Hull Univ 64-69; Chapl Keele Univ 69-74; P-in-c Keele 72-74; V Shirley St Jo *Cant* 74-84; V Shirley St Jo S'wark 85-06; RD Croydon Addington 95-04; Hon Can S'wark Cathl 03-06; rtd 06; Perm to Offic *S'wark* from 06. *23 Eden Road, Croydon CR0 1BB* E-mail quinncanon@aol.com

QUINN, Canon Derek John. b 55. TCD BTh88. **d** 88 **p** 89. C Mossley *Conn* 88-91; I Cappagh w Lislimnaghan *D & R* from 91; Bp's Dom Chapl from 00; Dioc Warden of Readers from 04; Can Derry Cathl from 07. *Erganagh Rectory, 1 Erganagh Road, Omagh BT79 7SX* Tel (028) 8224 2572

QUINN, Eugene Frederick. b 35. Allegheny Coll (USA) AB57 Univ of California MA66 MA69 PhD70. Vancouver Sch of Th 71. **d** 74 **p** 75. C Washington St Columba USA 74-75 and 78-81; Chapl Prague *Eur* 75-78; C Chevy Chase All SS USA 81-82 and 86-90; Chapl Nat Cathl Washington 81-82 and from 95; C Washington Epiphany 83 and 86-89; V Bowie St Jas 83-84; Chapl Warsaw 93-95. *5702 Kirkside Drive, Chevy Chase MD 20815-7116, USA* E-mail efquinn@msn.com

QUINN, George Bruce. b 23. MBE05. **d** 82 **p** 83. NSM Douglas St Ninian *S & M* 82-05. *85 Port-e-Chee Avenue, Douglas, Isle of Man IM2 5EZ* Tel (01624) 674080

QUINN, John James. b 46. TCD BA70 PhD76. St Jo Coll Nottm. **d** 81 **p** 82. C Gorleston St Andr *Nor* 81-84; R Belton 84-90; R Burgh Castle 84-90; R Belton and Burgh Castle 90-10; rtd 10; Perm to Offic *Nor* from 10. *23 Wren Drive, Bradwell, Great Yarmouth NR31 8JW* Tel (01493) 718634 E-mail johnjquinn@lineone.net

QUINN, Kenneth Norman. b 40. QUB BSc62 CEng MICE. CITC 80. **d** 85 **p** 86. NSM Seapatrick *D & D* 85-09; rtd 09. *4 Knollwood, Seapatrick, Banbridge BT32 4PE* Tel (028) 4062 3515 E-mail ken.quinn@nireland.com

QUINN, Marjorie. d 94 p 97. NSM Hawarden *St As* 94-05; Lic to Offic from 05. *21 Hawarden Way, Mancot, Deeside CH5 2EL* Tel (01244) 531639

QUINNELL, Peter Francis. b 48. St Steph Ho Ox 93. **d** 95 **p** 96. C Tewkesbury w Walton Cardiff *Glouc* 95-99; R Stratton, N Cerney, Baunton and Bagendon 99-08; AD Cirencester 06-08; R Whitewater *Win* from 08. *The Rectory, London Road, Hook RG27 9EG* Tel (01256) 760377 E-mail quinnell708@btinternet.com

QUINT, Mrs Patricia Mary. b 51. Milton Keynes Coll of Ed CertEd76 Open Univ BA77 Lon Univ MA99. St Alb Minl Tr Scheme 90. **d** 93 **p** 94. C Hertford St Andr *St Alb* 93-96; C Bromham w Oakley and Stagsden 96-00; V Stotfold and Radwell from 00. *The Vicarage, 61 Church Road, Stotfold, Hitchin SG5 4NE* Tel and fax (01462) 730218 E-mail revquint@ntlworld.com

QUIREY, Mrs Edith. b 56. CITC 98. **d** 01 **p** 02. Aux Min Belfast St Mich *Conn* 01-05; P-in-c Belfast St Steph w St Luke 05-07; Bp's C 07-09; I from 09. *42 Lansdowne Road, Belfast BT15 4AB* Tel (028) 9077 4119 E-mail edith.quirey@tesco.net

QUIST, Ms Frances Buckurel. NTMTC BA09. **d** 09 **p** 10. C E Ham w Upton Park *Chelmsf* from 09. *2 Norman Road, London E6 6HN* Tel (020) 8471 3214 Mobile 07734-711929 E-mail francesquist@btinternet.com

R

✠RABENIRINA, The Rt Revd Remi Joseph. b 38. Antananarivo Univ LèsL83. St Paul's Coll Ambatoharanana 61 St Chad's Coll Dur 64 Bossey Ecum Inst Geneva. **d** 67 **p** 68 **c** 84. Dn Toamasina St Jas Madagascar 67; R St Matt Pro-Cathl Antsiranana 68-73; R Ambohimangakely St Jo 73-84; Angl Chapl Antananarivo Univ 73-84; Bp Antananarivo 84-08; Abp Indian Ocean 95-06; rtd 08. *Address temp unknown* Tel (00261) 3311-20827 (mobile)

RABIN, Peter David. b 62. Southlands Coll Lon BA86. Aston Tr Scheme 88 Ripon Coll Cuddesdon BTh93. **d** 93 **p** 94. C Hornsey St Mary w St Geo *Lon* 93-97; V Cricklewood St Pet 97-07; C S Ockendon and Belhus Park *Chelmsf* from 07. *The Rectory, North Road, South Ockendon RM15 6QJ* Tel (01708) 855321 E-mail frrabin@sky.com

RABJOHNS, Alan. b 40. Leeds Univ BA62. Coll of Resurr Mirfield 62. **d** 64 **p** 65. C Ashington *Newc* 64-67; C Upton cum Chalvey *Ox* 67-76; V Roath St Sav *Llan* 76-08; AD Cardiff 03-08; rtd 08. *40 Cwmgelli Close, Treboeth, Swansea SA5 9BY* Tel (01792) 561157

RABJOHNS, Benjamin Thomas. **d** 11. C Aberavon *Llan* from 11. *Address temp unknown*

RABLEN, Antony Ford. b 52. St Jo Coll Nottm. **d** 82 **p** 83. C Clifton *York* 82-85; TV Marfleet 85-92; P-in-c Welton w Melton 92-00; TR Sutton St Jas and Wawne 00-05; Chapl R Brompton and Harefield NHS Trust 05-08; Chapl Oxon & Bucks Mental Health Partnership NHS Trust from 06. *St Andrew's Vicarage, Malvern Avenue, Harrow HA2 9ER* Tel (020) 8422 3633 E-mail antonym@rablen.fsnet.co.uk

RABLEN, Mrs Christine Mary. b 52. Trevelyan Coll Dur BA74 Hull Univ BA92. NOC 94. **d** 02 **p** 03. C Sutton St Mich *York* 02-05; V Roxbourne St Andr *Lon* from 05; V Leyton St Mary w St Edw and St Luke *Chelmsf* from 11. *Leyton Vicarage, 4 Vicarage Road, London E10 5EA* Tel (020) 8539 7882 E-mail christinerablen@dsl.pipex.com

RABY, Malcolm Ernest. b 47. St Jo Coll York BEd73. NOC 81. **d** 84 **p** 85. NSM Chadkirk *Ches* 84-88; Consultant E England CPAS 88-94; C Ely 94-96; TV Ely 96-98; P-in-c Over from 98; Dioc Adv in Miss and Evang from 98; P-in-c Long Stanton w St Mich from 02. *The Vicarage, Horseware, Over, Cambridge CB24 5NX* Tel and fax (01954) 230329 E-mail mission@ely.anglican.org

RACE, Canon Alan. b 51. Bradf Univ BTech73 Birm Univ MA82. Ripon Coll Cuddesdon 73. **d** 76 **p** 77. C Tupsley *Heref* 76-79; Asst Chapl Kent Univ 79-84; Dir Studies S'wark Ord Course 84-94; R Aylestone St Andr w St Jas *Leic* 94-07; P-in-c Leic St Phil from 07; Hon Can Leic Cathl 07-11; R Lee St Marg S'wark from 11. *St Margaret's Rectory, Brandram Road, London SE13 5EA* E-mail alan.race@ntlworld.com

RACE, Christopher Keith. b 43. St Paul's Coll Grahamstown 76. **d** 78 **p** 80. Angl Chapl Stellenbosch Univ S Africa 79-81; R Kalk Bay 81-83; Dioc Admin Botswana and Personal Asst to Abp Cen Africa 83-86; C E Kalahari 83-86; V Tanworth St Patr Salter Street *Birm* 86-96; P-in-c Rothiemurchus *Mor* 96-01; Perm to Offic *Glouc* 02-03; P-in-c Kemble, Poole Keynes, Somerford Keynes etc 03-04; R 04-06; Prin Tutor and Lect Cant Ch Ch Univ 06-08; rtd 08. *c/o the Revd S P Race, The Vicarage, Green Road, Dodworth, Barnsley S75 3RT* Tel 07866-585973 (mobile) E-mail ck.race@gmail.com

RACE, John Arthur. b 37. SAOMC 95. **d** 98 **p** 99. OLM Haddenham w Cuddington, Kingsey etc *Ox* 98-08; Perm to Offic from 08. *8 The Closes, Haddenham, Aylesbury HP17 8JN* Tel (01844) 290180

RACE, Canon Stephen Peter. b 69. SS Hild & Bede Coll Dur BA93. St Steph Ho Ox MTh03. **d** 02 **p** 03. C Wigton *Carl* 02-05; V Dodworth *Wakef* from 05; Asst Dioc Dir of Ords 05-09; Dir from 09; RD Barnsley from 09; Hon Can Wakef Cathl from 11. *The Vicarage, Green Road, Dodworth, Barnsley S75 3RT* Tel (01226) 206276 E-mail stephen.race@wakefield.anglican.org

RACTLIFFE, Dudley John. b 38. Man Univ BA62. Ridley Hall Cam 63. **d** 66 **p** 67. C Radford *Cov* 66-68; C Haslemere *Guildf* 69-73; V Perry Beeches *Birm* 73-78; V Worle *B & W* 78-88; Dioc Ecum Officer and R Dowlishwake w Kingstone, Chillington etc 88-93; TR Swanage and Studland *Sarum* 93-01; rtd 01; Perm to Offic *B & W* from 02. *12 Sid Lane, Sidmouth EX10 9AN* Tel (01395) 579712

RADCLIFFE, Canon Albert Edward. b 34. Lon Univ BD63. St Aid Birkenhead Ch Div Sch of the Pacific (USA) 61. **d** 62 **p** 63. C Knotty Ash St Jo *Liv* 62-64; C Blundellsands St Nic 64-66; Chapl Haifa St Luke Israel 66-69; V Tonge w Alkrington *Man* 69-77; R Ashton St Mich 77-91; AD Ashton-under-Lyne 87-91; Can Res Man Cathl 91-00; rtd 00; Perm to Offic *Man* from 01. *26 St Chad's Road, Withington, Manchester M20 4WH* Tel 0161-445 1327

RADCLIFFE, David Jeffrey. b 52. Linc Th Coll 77. **d** 79 **p** 80. C Poulton-le-Fylde *Blackb* 79-84; V Ingol 84-88; R Lowther and Askham *Carl* 88-96; R Lowther and Askham and Clifton and Brougham 96-06; R Upton-on-Severn, Ripple, Earls Croome etc *Worc* 06-11; P-in-c W Preston *Blackb* from 11. *St Michael's Vicarage, 2 Egerton Road, Ashton-on-Ribble, Preston PR2 1AJ* Tel (01772) 726157 E-mail revjeffradcliffe@hotmail.co.uk

RADCLIFFE, Eileen Rose. b 54. Carl Dioc Tr Inst 92. **d** 95 **p** 96. NSM Gt Salkeld w Lazonby *Carl* 95-96; NSM Dacre 99-02; Perm to Offic *Carl* 02-06 and *Worc* 06-08; NSM Upton-on-Severn, Ripple, Earls Croome etc *Worc* 08-11; Perm to Offic *Blackb* and *Worc* from 11. *St Michael's Vicarage, 2 Egerton Road, Ashton-on-Ribble, Preston PR2 1AJ* Tel (01772) 726157

RADCLIFFE, James. b 75. Rob Coll Cam MA98. Oak Hill Th Coll BA08. **d** 08 **p** 09. C Hove Bp Hannington Memorial Ch *Chich* from 08. *47 Nevill Avenue, Hove BN3 7NB* Tel 07941-248213 (mobile) E-mail radders@eb1000.fsnet.co.uk

RADCLIFFE, John Frederick. b 39. **d** 01 **p** 02. OLM Meltham *Wakef* from 01. *13 Orchard Close, Meltham, Huddersfield HD9 4EG* Tel (01484) 348806 E-mail johnandenid@yahoo.com

RADCLIFFE, Robert Mark. b 63. Cranmer Hall Dur 05. **d** 08 **p** 09. C Welling *Roch* from 08. *52 Clifton Road, Welling DA16 1QD* Tel (020) 8306 1829 E-mail markradcliffe@msn.com

RADCLIFFE, Mrs Rosemary. b 45. SWMTC 87. **d** 90 **p** 94. NSM Devoran *Truro* 90-93; Dn-in-c N Newton w St Michaelchurch, Thurloxton etc *B & W* 93-94; P-in-c 94-00; Chapl to the Deaf 93-96; P-in-c Whipton *Ex* 00-01; rtd 01; Perm to Offic *Truro* from 03. *76 Upland Crescent, Truro TR1 1NE* Tel (01872) 273906

RADCLIFFE, Rosie. See RADCLIFFE, Eileen Rose

RADFORD, Vincent Arthur. b 45. Ches Coll of HE CertEd69. **d** 05 **p** 06. OLM Westhoughton and Wingates *Man* from 05. *64 Molyneux Road, Westhoughton, Bolton BL5 3EU* Tel (01942) 790091 E-mail vincent.radford@ntlworld.com

RADLEY, Mrs Jean Frances. b 40. Man Univ RGN62 Univ Coll Lon RSCN65 Cen Lancs Univ BSc95. **d** 00 **p** 01. OLM Kendal St Geo *Carl* 00-07; OLM Beacon from 07. *7 Castle Grove, Kendal LA9 7AY* Tel (01539) 740811 Mobile 07714-020189 E-mail jeanradley@btconnect.com

RADLEY, Richard Brian. b 68. St Jo Coll Nottm 02. **d** 04 **p** 05. C Utley *Bradf* 04-08; P-in-c Doncaster St Mary *Sheff* 09-10; P-in-c Wheatley Park 09-10; V Doncaster St Mary and St Paul from 10. *St Mary's Vicarage, 59 St Mary's Road, Doncaster DN1 2NR* Tel (01302) 342565 E-mail radley@radleyfamily.fsnet.co.uk

RADLEY, Stephen John. b 68. St Jo Coll Nottm BTh96. **d** 96 **p** 97. C Boulton *Derby* 96-00; Chapl RAF from 00. *Chaplaincy Services, Valiant Block, HQ Air Command, RAF High Wycombe HP14 4UE* Tel (01494) 496800 Fax 496343

RAE, Stephen Gordon. b 65. AGSM87. Oak Hill Th Coll BA09. **d** 09 **p** 10. C Danehill *Chich* from 09. *Marten Cottage, Coach and Horses Lane, Danehill, Haywards Heath RH17 7JF* Tel 07776-147212 (mobile) E-mail stephen@raefamily.net

RAE SMITH, Tristram Geoffrey. b 57. Clare Coll Cam BA79 MA83 St Jo Coll Dur BA04. Cranmer Hall Dur 02. **d** 04 **p** 05. C Bradford-on-Avon Ch *Sarum* 04-08; C Westwood and Wingfield 04-08; R Camelot Par *B & W* from 08; C Bruton and Distr from 08. *The Rectory, 6 The Close, North Cadbury, Yeovil BA22 7DX* Tel (01963) 440585 Mobile 07751-306272

RAFFAY, Julian Paul. b 60. Stirling Univ BSc84. Cranmer Hall Dur 88. **d** 90 **p** 91. C Adel *Ripon* 90-93; C Leeds Halton St Wilfrid 93-95; Asst Chapl S Derbys Mental Health NHS Trust 95-97; TV Gleadless *Sheff* 97-01; V Deepcar 01-07; Chapl Team Ldr Sheff Care Trust from 07. *Chaplaincy, Sheffield Care Trust, Longley Centre, Longley Grange Drive, Sheffield S5 7AU* Tel 0114-226 1675 E-mail julian.raffay@sct.nhs.uk

RAGAN, Mrs Jennifer Mary. b 39. Linc Th Coll 71. **dss** 80 **d** 87 **p** 94. Hackney *Lon* 80-84; Hornchurch St Andr *Chelmsf* 84-88; Par Dn 87-88; Par Dn Ingrave St Steph CD 88-90; Par Dn Gt Parndon 90-94; C 94-99; TV 99-07; Perm to Offic *Chelmsf* and *St E* from 07. *18 Holme Oaks Court, 50 Cliff Lane, Ipswich IP3 0PE* Tel (01473) 213577 E-mail revjenniferragan@btinternet.com

RAGBOURNE, Miss Pamela Mary. b 27. CertEd47. Dalton Ho Bris 53. **dss** 76 **d** 87 **p** 94. CPAS Staff 68-79; Tottenham St Jo *Lon* 79-81; Gt Cambridge Road St Jo and St Jas 82-84; Camberley St Paul *Guildf* 84-86; rtd 87; Perm to Offic *Glouc* 87-93 and 97-05; NSM Winchcombe, Gretton, Sudeley Manor etc 93-97. *14 Crispin Close, Winchcombe, Cheltenham GL54 5JY* Tel (01242) 603469

RAGGETT, Anita Jane. b 56. NOC. **d** 07 **p** 08. C Gomersal *Wakef* 07-10; C Cleckheaton St Jo 08-10; P-in-c Lepton from 10; Chapl Huddersfield Univ from 10. *The Vicarage, 138 Wakefield Road, Lepton, Huddersfield HD8 0LU* Tel (01484) 606126 E-mail daraggett@hotmail.com

RAHI, Hakim Banta Singh. b 36. Union Bibl Sem Yavatmal BD71. **d** 74 **p** 74. India 74-83; In URC 83-88; Perm to Offic *Birm* 88-93; Ecum Evang Asian Community 88-93. *Flat 5, 12 Taverners Gree, Birmingham B20 2JJ*

RAHILLY, Philip James. b 54. Univ of Wales (Cardiff) BD86. Wycliffe Hall Ox 86. **d** 88 **p** 89. C Knightwick w Doddenham, Broadwas and Cotheridge *Worc* 88; C Martley and Wichenford, Knightwick etc 89-91; C Worc St Barn w Ch Ch 91-92; TV Kidderminster St Mary and All SS w Trimpley etc 92-95; P-in-c Childe Okeford, Okeford Fitzpaine, Manston etc *Sarum* 95-00; P-in-c Shilling Okeford 99-00; R Okeford 00-06; P-in-c Stogursey w Fiddington *B & W* 06-07; R Quantock Coast from 07. *The Rectory, High Street, Stogursey, Bridgwater TA5 1PL* Tel (01278) 732884

RAI, Mrs Mary Anne. b 61. La Sainte Union Coll BTh83 PGCE84. Trin Coll Bris 85. **dss** 86 **d** 87 **p** 99. Bury St Edmunds St Mary *St E* 86-89; Par Dn 87-89; Perm to Offic 90-93; Perm to Offic *Cov* 94-99 and from 02; NSM Styvechale 99-01. *61 Malthouse Lane, Kenilworth CV8 1AD* Tel (01926) 732223 E-mail kal.rai@virgin.net

RAIKES, Miss Gwynneth Marian Napier. b 51. Somerville Coll Ox MA72 Lon Univ BD81. Trin Coll Bris 79. **dss** 81 **d** 98 **p** 98. Asst Chapl Bris Poly 81-86; Beckenham Ch Ch *Roch* 86-98; C 98-00; Dean of Women and Dir Past Tr Oak Hill Th Coll from 00; Perm to Offic *Lon* from 03 and *Ely* from 07. *Oak Hill College, Chase Side, London N14 4PS* Tel (020) 8449 0467 Mobile 07866-651272 E-mail marianr@oakhill.ac.uk

RAIKES, Canon Peter. b 37. St Mich Coll Llan 78. **d** 80 **p** 81. C Roath *Llan* 80-82; V Resolven 82-86; V Resolven w Tonna 86-92; RD Neath 89-01; V Skewen 92-02; Can Llan Cathl 97-02; rtd 02. *2 Kennedy Drive, Pencoed, Bridgend CF35 6TW* Tel (01656) 862317

RAIKES, Robert Laybourne. b 32. Wells Th Coll 59. **d** 61 **p** 62. C Poplar All SS w St Frideswide *Lon* 61-66; C Grendon Underwood w Edgcott *Ox* 66-68; C Swan 68-71; V Whitchurch Canonicorum w Wooton Fitzpaine etc *Sarum* 71-81; P-in-c Branksome St Aldhelm 81-82; V 82-91; V Pitminster w Corfe *B & W* 91-92; rtd 92; Chapl Madeira *Eur* 93-95; Perm to Offic *Glouc* 95-98; Hon C Broadwell, Evenlode, Oddington, Adlestrop etc 98-01; Lic to Offic *Eur* from 02; Perm to Offic *Chelmsf* from 09. *The College of St Barnabas, Blackberry Lane, Lingfield RH7 6NJ* Tel (01342) 872826

RAILTON, David James. b 66. Bradf Univ BPharm89. EMMTC 06. **d** 08 **p** 09. C Melbourne, Ticknall, Smisby and Stanton *Derby* from 08. *1 Blackthorn Close, Melbourne, Derby DE73 8LY* Tel (01332) 862383 E-mail davidrailton@gmail.com

RAILTON, John Robert Henry. b 45. Reading Univ BSc68 PhD82 FCIB79. S Dios Minl Tr Scheme 82. **d** 85 **p** 86. NSM Wickham *Portsm* 85-89; C Bridgemary 89-90; V 90-96; TR Ridgeway *Sarum* 96-02; TR Whitton 02-08; rtd 08. *20 Baileys Way, Wroughton, Swindon SN4 9AH* Tel (01793) 814162 E-mail john.railton@btinternet.com

RAILTON, Sandra. b 46. S Dios Minl Tr Scheme 82. **dss** 85 **d** 87 **p** 94. Catherington and Clanfield *Portsm* 85-86; Lee-on-the-Solent 86-89; C 87-89; Par Dn Burnham w Dropmore, Hitcham and Taplow *Ox* 89-94; TV Wallingford w Crowmarsh Gifford etc 94-98; Dioc Dir Ords (OLM) Berks 96-99; TV Ridgeway *Sarum* 98-02; Dioc Voc Adv 99-02; TV Whitton 02-08; RD Marlborough 04-08; rtd 08. *20 Baileys Way, Wroughton, Swindon SN4 9AH* Tel (01793) 814162

RAILTON-CROWDER, Mrs Mary. b 51. Luton Univ BA96 RN72 RM91 MIOSH93. SAOMC 98. **d** 01 **p** 02. NSM Elstow *St Alb* 01-04; Chapl De Montford Univ 02-04; C Douglas All SS and St Thos *S & M* 04-07; P-in-c Birchencliffe *Wakef* 07-08; V Birkby and Birchencliffe from 08; RD Huddersfield from 10. *The Vicarage, 4 Brendon Drive, Huddersfield HD2 2DF* Tel (01484) 546966 E-mail revmrc@yahoo.com

RAINBIRD, Ms Ruth Patricia. b 40. SRN62. **d** 01 **p** 02. OLM Limpsfield and Titsey *S'wark* 01-10; Perm to Offic from 10. *73 Stoneleigh Road, Oxted RH8 0TP* Tel (01883) 713683

RAINE, Alan. b 49. NEOC 92. **d** 95 **p** 96. NSM Jarrow *Dur* 95-05; Chapl S Tyneside Coll 95-05; V Leam Lane *Dur* from 05. *St Andrew's Vicarage, Whinbrooke, Gateshead NE10 8HR* Tel 0191-489 3042 E-mail alanraine49@aol.com

RAINE, David. b 58. Dur Univ MBA96 Open Univ BA96 MCIM99 MCIPD03. NEOC 01. **d** 04 **p** 05. NSM N Wearside *Dur* 04-06; NSM Millfield St Mary from 06; NSM Bishopwearmouth Gd Shep from 06. *5 Maydown Close, Sunderland SR5 3DZ* Tel 0191-549 7262 E-mail davidraine@dunelm.org.uk

RAINE, Patrick John Wallace. b 21. DFC. Sarum & Wells Th Coll 72. **d** 74 **p** 75. C Chandler's Ford *Win* 74-76; R Highclere and Ashmansworth w Crux Easton 76-84; R Copythorne and Minstead 84-87; rtd 87; P-in-c Breamore *Win* 91-95; Perm to Offic *Win* 95-03; *Sarum* 98-03; *Cov* from 03. *23 Willis House, Hilditch Way, Nuneaton CV11 4LW* Tel (024) 7634 9871

RAINE, Stephen James. b 49. Sheff Poly BA80. NOC 85. **d** 86 **p** 87. C Cottingham *York* 86-90; V Dunscroft Ch Ch *Sheff* 90-92; V Dunscroft St Edwin 92-96; V Kettering St Mary *Pet* 96-08; P-in-c Ipswich St Mary at the Elms *St E* from 08; Chapl Ipswich Hosp NHS Trust from 08. *The Vicarage, 68 Black Horse Lane, Ipswich IP1 2EF* Tel (01473) 216484 E-mail evangelist24@aol.com

RAINER, John Charles. b 54. Ex Univ BA76 CertEd78 Hull Univ MBA02. St Jo Coll Nottm 86. **d** 88 **p** 89. C Fletchamstead *Cov* 88-94; V Leic H Apostles 94-03; V Shipley St Pet *Bradf* from 03. *The Vicarage, 2 Glenhurst Road, Shipley BD18 4DZ* Tel (01274) 584488 E-mail john.rainer@bradford.anglican.org

RAINES, Mrs Gisela Rolanda. b 58. Groningen Univ Kandidaats 80. K Coll Lon BD83. **dss** 84 **d** 87 **p** 94. Charlton St Luke w H Trin *S'wark* 84-87; Par Dn 87; Chapl Imp Coll *Lon* 87-91; Hon C Birch w Fallowfield *Man* 94-95; P-in-c Withington St Chris 95-03; C Man St Ann 03-10; R Withington St Paul from 10. *197 Old Hall Lane, Manchester M14 6HJ* Tel 0161-224 6643 E-mail revgisela@btinternet.com

RAINES, William Guy. b 46. Lon Univ BSc69 MSc70 Ox Univ BA80. Ripon Coll Cuddesdon 78. **d** 81 **p** 82. C W Drayton *Lon* 81-84; C Charlton St Luke w H Trin *S'wark* 84-87; Chapl K Coll Lon 87-94; Chapl Imp Coll 91-94; P-in-c Birch w Fallowfield *Man* 94-95; R from 95. *197 Old Hall Lane, Manchester M14 6HJ* Tel 0161-224 1310 E-mail wraines@btinternet.com

RAINEY, Graeme Norman. b 66. Van Mildert Coll Dur BA88 Reading Univ MA01. Ridley Hall Cam 93. **d** 93 **p** 94. C Maltby *Sheff* 93-96; Chapl Reading Univ 96-04; Chapl Downe Ho Sch Berks 04-10; Asst Chapl Roedean Sch Brighton from 11. *Roedean School, Roedean Way, Brighton BN2 5RQ* Tel (01273) 667500

RAINFORD, Robert Graham. b 55. Lanc Univ CertEd76 BEd77. St Steph Ho Ox 81. **d** 83 **p** 84. C Burnley St Cath w St Alb and St Paul *Blackb* 83-86; C-in-c Hawes Side St Chris CD 86-89; V Hawes Side 89-03; P-in-c Marton Moss 01-03; AD Blackpool 00-03; Hon Can Blackb Cathl 01-03; Sen Chapl to Bp Dover *Cant* 03-05; P Admin Upper Chelsea H Trin *Lon* 05-08; Asst P from 08; Perm to Offic from 08. *Holy Trinity Church, Sloane Street, London SW1X 9BZ* Tel (020) 7730 7270 E-mail priest@holytrinitysloanesquare.co.uk

RAINSBURY, Mark James. b 56. NE Lon Poly BA79. Oak Hill Th Coll BA87. **d** 88 **p** 89. C Tonbridge St Steph *Roch* 88-95; C Hampreston *Sarum* 95-97; TV 97-99; Perm to Offic *Win* from 03. *Old Orchard, Church Lane, West Parley, Ferndown BH22 8TS* Tel (01202) 590042

RAINSFORD, Peter John. b 31. FCP72. Qu Coll Birm 75. **d** 77 **p** 78. Hon C Lich St Chad 77-81; C 82; C Coseley Ch Ch 82-84; V Wednesbury St Bart 84-91; Chapl Sandwell Distr Gen Hosp 89-91; rtd 91; Perm to Offic *Lich* from 91. *157 Broadway, Walsall WS1 3HD* Tel (01922) 624526 E-mail p.j.rainsford@tinyonline.co.uk

RAISTRICK, Brian. b 38. St Paul's Coll Chelt TCert60 Ex Univ AdDipEd68 Newc Univ MEd76 UEA PhD86. Westcott Ho Cam 92. **d** 93 **p** 94. C Haverhill w Withersfield, the Wrattings etc *St E* 93-95; P-in-c Horringer cum Ickworth 95-02; P-in-c Risby w Gt and Lt Saxham and Westley 99-02; P-in-c Chevington w Hargrave and Whepstead w Brockley 00-02; R Horringer 02; RD Thingoe 99-01; rtd 03; Perm to Offic *St E* from 03. *Greenways, Westwood, Great Barton, Bury St Edmunds IP31 2SF* Tel (01284) 787372 or 747372 E-mail brian@raistrick.freeserve.co.uk

RAISTRICK, Tulo Dirk. b 69. SEITE. **d** 11. C Telford Park *S'wark* from 11. *12A Salford Road, London SW2 4BH* Tel (020) 8678 7130 E-mail tulo.raistrick@hotmail.co.uk

RAITT, Derek. b 41. K Coll Lon BD63 AKC63. **d** 64 **p** 65. C Blackb St Jas 64-67; C Burnley St Pet 67-69; V Foulridge 69-74; V Euxton 74-91; V Penwortham St Mary 91-00; P-in-c Halton w Aughton 00-06; rtd 06; Perm to Offic *Blackb* from 06. *84 Lymm Avenue, Lancaster LA1 5HR* E-mail draitt@wightcablenorth.net

RAJ-SINGH, Reji. b 52. Sidney Webb Coll of Educn CertEd79 N Lon Poly BEd90 Heythrop Coll Lon MA02. SAOMC 02. **d** 05 **p** 06. NSM Paddington St Jas *Lon* from 05. *27 Kendal Steps, St Georges Fields, London W2 2YE* Tel (020) 7262 4261 Mobile 07983-430050

RAJA, John Joshva. b 65. Serampore Coll MTh93 Leic Univ MA96 New Coll Edin 96. **d** 93 **p** 94. India 93-95; Hon C Leic H Spirit 95-96; Hon C Edin H Cross 96-99. *43 Scotland Street, Edinburgh EH3 6PY* Tel and fax 0131-557 3797 E-mail j.raja@sms.ed.ac.uk

RAJKOVIC, Michael. b 52. Sheff Univ BMet74 MMet75 PhD79 St Jo Coll Nottm MA95 Lon Bible Coll MPhil03. Cranmer Hall Dur 93. **d** 95 **p** 96. C Harrow Weald All SS *Lon* 95-98; C Woodford Wells *Chelmsf* 98-02; V Bricket Wood *St Alb* from 02. *20 West Riding, Bricket Wood, St Albans AL2 3QP* Tel (01923) 681107 E-mail mrajk30852@aol.com

RAJKUMAR, Peniel Jesudason Rufus. b 77. Sri Venkateswara Univ India BA98 MA02 BD03. **d** 05 **p** 06. NSM Upper Holloway *Lon* 05-08; Tutor United Th Coll Bangalore from 08. *63 Millers Road, Benson Town Post, Bangalore, 560 046, India* E-mail rufus_peniel@rediffmail.com

RAKE, David John. b 47. Nottm Univ BA68 PhD73. Wycliffe Hall Ox 73. **d** 74 **p** 75. C Radcliffe-on-Trent *S'well* 74-77; P-in-c Upwell St Pet *Ely* 77-79; P-in-c Outwell 77-79; Chapl Warw Univ 79-86; V Kenilworth St Nic 86-98; P-in-c Tintagel *Truro* 98-08; Bp's Adv on Spiritual Formation 98-03; Dioc Adv 03-08; rtd 08;

Perm to Offic *Truro* from 09. *The Old Vicarage, Zennor, St Ives TR26 3BY* Tel (01736) 796955
RALPH, Brian Charles. b 66. St Steph Ho Ox 89. **d** 92 **p** 93. C Yeovil St Mich *B & W* 92-95; TV St Jo on Bethnal Green *Lon* 95-01; P-in-c Bethnal Green St Barn 01-03; V from 03. *12 Chisenhale Road, London E3 5TG* Tel (020) 8983 3426, 8806 4130 *or* 7247 1448 E-mail brianralph@btinternet.com
RALPH, Ms Caroline Susan. b 60. Birm Univ BA81 UWE LLM98. Westcott Ho Cam 04. **d** 06 **p** 07. C Crediton, Shobrooke and Sandford etc *Ex* 06-10; V Harborne St Pet *Birm* from 10. *The Vicarage, Old Church Road, Harborne, Birmingham B17 0BB* Tel 0121-681 5446 E-mail csralph@ukonline.co.uk
RALPH, Canon Nicholas Robert. b 63. Lanc Univ BSc85 Trin Coll Cam BA91. Westcott Ho Cam 89. **d** 92 **p** 93. C Fareham H Trin *Portsm* 92-95; C Portsea St Cuth 95-96; V Hayling Is St Andr 96-03; V N Hayling St Pet 96-03; Soc Resp Adv 03-06; Hd Miss and Soc Down 06; Hon Can Portsm Cathl 06-09; Can Res from 09. *101 St Thomas's Street, Portsmouth PO1 2HE* Tel (023) 9289 9674 E-mail nick@ralphy.org *or* nick.ralph@portsmouth.anglican.org
RALPH, Richard Gale. b 51. Pemb Coll Ox BA73 MA78 DPhil78 FRSA90. S Dios Minl Tr Scheme 84. **d** 87 **p** 88. NSM St Leonards Ch Ch and St Mary *Chich* from 87; NSM St Pancras H Cross w St Jude and St Pet *Lon* 87-94; Prin Westmr Coll Ox 96-00. *St Alban, 11 The Mount, St Leonards-on-Sea TN38 0HR* Tel (01424) 422722 E-mail wea@nildram.co.uk
RALPHS, John Eric. b 26. St Cath Coll Ox BA52 MA56 MBAP66. Wycliffe Hall Ox 53. **d** 53 **p** 54. C Wolvercote *Ox* 53-55; Chapl Asst Radcliffe Infirmary Ox 54-62; Chapl Dragon Sch Ox 55-68; Asst Chapl HM Pris Ox 58-61; Jun Chapl Mert Coll Ox 59-62; Chapl St Hugh's Coll Ox 62-67; Priest-Psychotherapist from 68; Lic to Offic *Ox* from 83; rtd 91. *209 Woodstock Road, Oxford OX2 7AB* Tel (01865) 515550
RALPHS, Robert Brian. b 31. Qu Coll Birm 75. **d** 78 **p** 79. Hon C Wednesbury St Jo *Lich* 78-80; Hon C Wednesbury St Paul Wood Green 80-81; Perm to Offic 81-96 and from 97; Hon C W Bromwich Gd Shep w St Jo 96. *204 Bromford Lane, West Bromwich B70 7HX* Tel 0121-553 0119
RALPHS, Sharon Ann. *See* SIMPSON, Mrs Sharon Ann
RAMPTON, Paul Michael. b 47. St Jo Coll Dur BA69 MA73 K Coll Lon PhD85 Westmr Coll Ox MTh99. Wycliffe Hall Ox 72. **d** 73 **p** 74. C Folkestone H Trin w Ch Ch *Cant* 73-77; P-in-c Ringwould w Oxney 77-79; P-in-c Kingsdown 77-79; R Ringwould w Kingsdown 79-83; V Maidstone St Paul 83-88; V Maidstone St Martin 88-95; V Steyning *Chich* from 95; R Ashurst from 95; RD Storrington 99-03. *St Andrew's Vicarage, Station Road, Steyning BN44 3YL* Tel and fax (01903) 813256
RAMPTON, Canon Valerie Edith. b 41. Nottm Univ BSc63 MSc66 BA79. Gilmore Course 78. **dss** 82 **d** 87 **p** 94. Sneinton St Chris w St Phil *S'well* 80-87; Par Dn 87-88; Par Dn Stapleford 88-93; Dioc Adv on Women in Min 90-01; Dn-in-c Kneesall w Laxton and Wellow 93-94; V 94-02; Hon Can S'well Minster 97-02; rtd 02; Perm to Offic *Linc* and *S'well* from 02. *Tansy Cottage, Hillside, Beckingham, Lincoln LN5 0RQ* Tel (01636) 626665 E-mail valerie.rampton@btinternet.com
RAMSARAN (or COOPER), Susan Mira. b 49. K Coll Lon BA70 Univ Coll Lon MA72 PhD78. Ripon Coll Cuddesdon BA92. **d** 93 **p** 94. C Selling w Throwley, Sheldwich w Badlesmere etc *Cant* 93-97; P-in-c Shipbourne *Roch* 97-99; P-in-c Plaxtol 97-99; R Shipbourne w Plaxtol 99-06; RD Shoreham 01-06; TR N Tyne and Redesdale *Newc* from 06. AD Bellingham from 06. *The Rectory, Bellingham, Hexham NE48 2JS* Tel (01434) 220019 E-mail smramsaran@aol.com
RAMSAY, Alan Burnett. b 34. AKC62. **d** 63 **p** 64. C Clapham H Trin *S'wark* 63-67; C Warlingham w Chelsham and Farleigh 67-71; P-in-c Stockwell St Mich 71-78; V Lingfield 78-85; P-in-c Crowhurst 83-85; V Lingfield and Crowhurst 85-92; RD Godstone 88-92; V Mitcham St Mark 92-00; Hon Can S'wark Cathl 93-00; rtd 00; Perm to Offic *Cant* from 00. *Kent House, 9 Scotton Street, Wye, Ashford TN25 5BU* Tel (01233) 813730 E-mail aramsay@talktalk.net
RAMSAY, Preb Carl Anthoney St Aubyn. b 55. WMMTC 88. **d** 90 **p** 91. C Wednesfield Heath *Lich* 90-94; V Willenhall St Anne 94-03; V Pelsall from 03; Preb Lich Cathl from 04. *The Vicarage, 39 Hall Lane, Pelsall, Walsall WS3 4JN* Tel (01922) 682098 E-mail spreeboy@talk21.com
RAMSAY, Christopher. b 68. St Jo Coll Dur BA90. Wycliffe Hall Ox BTh94. **d** 97 **p** 98. C Cricklewood St Gabr and St Mich *Lon* 97-01; P-in-c Southall St Geo 01-06; V from 06; AD Ealing from 10. *1 Lancaster Road, Southall UB1 1NP* Tel (020) 8574 1876 E-mail christopher.ramsay@btinternet.com
RAMSAY, Eric Nicolson. b 29. **d** 94 **p** 95. C Forfar *St And* 94-99 and 00-09; C Kirriemuir 94-99 and 00-09; Asst Chapl Gtr Athens *Eur* 99-00. *4 Beechwood Place, Kirriemuir DD8 5DZ* Tel (01575) 572029 E-mail ericaileenramsay@tinyworld.co.uk
RAMSAY, James Anthony. b 52. Wadh Coll Ox BA75 MA. **d** 86 **p** 87. C Olney w Emberton 86-89; V Blackbird Leys 89-02; Chapl Bucharest w Sofia *Eur* 02-05; P-in-c Lt Ilford St Barn *Chelmsf* 05-10; V from 10; Chapl E Lon Univ from 05.

St Barnabas' Vicarage, Browning Road, London E12 6PB Tel (020) 8472 2777 E-mail ramsay.jas@gmail.com
RAMSAY, Kenneth William. b 18. ALCD48. **d** 52 **p** 53. C Southall Green St Jo *Lon* 52-57; Asst Chapl Lee Abbey 57-60; Perm to Offic *Portsm* 69-80 and *Sarum* 77-87; rtd 87; Hon C Burstow *S'wark* 87-98; Perm to Offic 98-07. *3 Park Close, Strood Green, Betchworth RH3 7JB* Tel (01737) 843470 E-mail ramsay@iname.com
RAMSAY, Kerry. *See* TUCKER, Kerry
RAMSAY, Max Roy MacGregor. b 34. Ball Coll Ox MA58. Qu Coll Birm 82. **d** 84 **p** 85. C Hale *Ches* 84-86; C Nantwich 87; V Haslington w Crewe Green 87-91; P-in-c Dunham Massey St Marg and St Mark 92-95; rtd 95; Perm to Offic *Ches* from 95. *6 Comber Way, Knutsford WA16 9BT* Tel (01565) 632362 E-mail max@rmramsay.fsnet.co.uk
RAMSBOTTOM, Mrs Julie Frances. b 54. Trevelyan Coll Dur BA76. S'wark Ord Course 88. **d** 91 **p** 94. Par Dn Bray and Braywood *Ox* 91-94; C 94-97; R W Woodhay w Enborne, Hampstead Marshall etc 97-11; P-in-c Kintbury w Avington 05-11; R Walbury Beacon from 11. *The Rectory, Enborne, Newbury RG20 0HD* Tel (01635) 34427 E-mail julie.ramsbottom@talk21.com
RAMSBURY, Area Bishop of. *Vacant*
RAMSDEN, Canon Arthur Stuart. b 34. Kelham Th Coll 56. **d** 61 **p** 62. C Featherstone *Wakef* 61-63; C Barnsley St Pet 63-67; V Charlestown 67-70; V Middlestown 70-77; V Purston cum S Featherstone 77-04; Hon Can Wakef Cathl 95-04; rtd 04. *31 Barnsley Road, Cawthorne, Barnsley S75 4HW* Tel (01226) 790696
RAMSDEN, The Rt Revd Peter Stockton. b 51. Univ Coll Lon BSc74 Leeds Univ MA92. Coll of Resurr Mirfield 74. **d** 77 **p** 78 **c** 07. C Houghton le Spring *Dur* 77-80; C S Shields All SS 80-83; Papua New Guinea 83-90 and 93-96; P-in-c Micklefield *York* 90-93; V Long Benton *Newc* 96-07; Bp Port Moresby from 07. *PO Box 6491, Boroko, NCD, Papua New Guinea* Tel (00675) 323 2489 E-mail psramsden.pomanglican@gmail.com
RAMSDEN, Raymond Leslie. b 49. Open Univ BA86. **d** 78 **p** 79. C Greenhill St Jo *Lon* 78-85; C Staines St Mary and St Pet 85-90; V Hounslow St Steph from 90. *St Stephen's Vicarage, Parkside Road, Hounslow TW3 2BP* Tel (020) 8570 3056 E-mail revrramsden@hotmail.com
RAMSDEN, Stuart. *See* RAMSDEN, Canon Arthur Stuart
RAMSEY, Alan Edward. b 72. Wycliffe Hall Ox. **d** 08 **p** 09. C Ox St Aldate 08-11; C Ox St Giles and SS Phil and Jas w St Marg from 11. *St Margaret's Church, St Margaret's Road, Oxford OX2 6RX* E-mail alanramsey@yahoo.com
RAMSEY, Christopher John. b 76. St Jo Coll Nottm BA07. **d** 07 **p** 08. C Saxmundham w Kelsale cum Carlton *St E* 07-10; V Gt Cornard from 10. *The Vicarage, 95 Bures Road, Great Cornard, Sudbury CO10 0JE* Tel (01787) 376293 E-mail revchrisramsey@gmail.com
RAMSHAW, Marcus John. b 71. St Andr Univ MTheol93 York Univ MA94. Cranmer Hall Dur 94. **d** 96 **p** 97. C Hythe *Cant* 96-00; Chapl Down Coll Cam 01-03; NSM Cam St Edw *Ely* from 03. *19 Grantchester Road, Cambridge CB3 9ED* Tel 07793-064455 (mobile)
RANCE, Eleanor Jane. b 72. K Coll Lon BA93 AKC93 St Jo Coll Dur MA96. Cranmer Hall Dur 94. **d** 96 **p** 97. C Barnes St Mary *S'wark* 96-97; C Barnes 97-99; Chapl RAF 99-10; Perm to Offic *Blackb* from 10. *Address temp unknown*
RANDALL, Anthony. *See* RANDALL, James Anthony
RANDALL, Bernard Charles. b 72. St Andr Univ MA95 Edin Univ MSc97 Man Univ PhD04. St Steph Ho Ox BA06. **d** 06 **p** 07. C Bury St Mary *Man* 06-07; C Atherton and Hindsford w Howe Bridge 07-09; C Sale St Paul *Ches* 09-11. *Address temp unknown* E-mail bernard.randall@hotmail.co.uk
RANDALL, Colin Anthony. b 57. SS Paul & Mary Coll Cheltenham BEd78. Trin Coll Bris BD84. **d** 84 **p** 85. C Denton Holme *Carl* 84-87; C Brampton RD 87-90; R Hanborough and Freeland *Ox* 90-99; P-in-c Croglin *Carl* 99-09; P-in-c Holme Eden 99-05; P-in-c Wetheral w Warwick 99-05; R Holme Eden and Wetheral w Warwick 05-09; RD Brampton 05-09; Hon Can Carl Cathl 08-09; P-in-c Barrow *Ches* 09-10; R from 10; Dioc Worship Adv from 09. *The Rectory, Mill Lane, Great Barrow, Chester CH3 7JF* Tel (01829) 740263 E-mail carandall@freeuk.com
RANDALL, Preb Colin Michael Sebastian. b 50. Aston Univ BSc72. Qu Coll Birm 72. **d** 75 **p** 76. C Tonge w Alkrington *Man* 75-78; C Elton All SS 78-82; P-in-c Bridgwater H Trin *B & W* 82-86; V 86-90; V Bishops Hull 90-98; TR Wellington and Distr from 00; Preb Wells Cathl from 05. *The Rectory, 72 High Street, Wellington TA21 8RF* Tel (01823) 662248 E-mail colinms.randall@virgin.net
RANDALL, Elizabeth. *See* BILLETT, Mrs Elizabeth Nicola
RANDALL, Evelyn. **d** 10. NSM Dormansland *S'wark* from 10. *58 Hickmans Close, Godstone RH9 8EB* Tel (01883) 742751
RANDALL, Gareth John. b 49. Southn Univ BA72 PGCE73 ACP80. Oak Hill Th Coll 90. **d** 93 **p** 94. Dir of Studies Dame Alice Owen's Sch Potters Bar 84-95; Dir of Personnel 95-00; Asst

Hd 00-07; NSM S Mymms K Chas *St Alb* 93-98; NSM Potters Bar 98-07; P-in-c Dinard *Eur* from 07. *No 7 Résidence Victor Hugo, 6 ave Georges Clemenceau, 35800 Dinard, France* Tel (0033) 2 99 46 77 00

RANDALL, Gordon Charles. STETS. **d** 11. NSM Chineham *Win* from 11. *37 Belvedere Gardens, Chineham, Basingstoke RG24 8GB* Tel (01256) 364940
E-mail gordon.randall@sky.com

RANDALL, Ian Neville. b 39. Oriel Coll Ox BA62 MA65. St Steph Ho Ox 62. **d** 65 **p** 66. C Perivale *Lon* 65-68; C Fulham St Jo Walham Green 68-73; C Cowley St Jas *Ox* 73-79; TV 79-82; V Didcot St Pet 82-93; P-in-c Clewer St Andr 93-04; rtd 04. *12 Westmead Road, Fakenham NR21 8BL* Tel (01328) 862443

RANDALL, James Anthony. b 36. ACIB69. Ridley Hall Cam 68. **d** 70 **p** 71. C Rusthall *Roch* 70-74; V Shorne 74-79; V Bexleyheath Ch Ch 79-89; R Stone 89-98; rtd 98; Perm to Offic *Roch* from 99. *6 Sandling Way, St Mary's Island, Chatham ME4 3AZ* Tel (01634) 890603

RANDALL, Canon John Terence. b 29. St Cath Coll Cam BA52 MA59. Ely Th Coll 52. **d** 54 **p** 55. C Luton Ch Ch *St Alb* 54; C Dunstable 54-57; C Ely 57-60; C March St Jo 60-62; Area Sec (S Midl) UMCA 62-64; Area Sec USPG *Birm* and *Cov* 65-76; P-in-c Avon Dassett w Farnborough *Cov* 76-78; P-in-c Fenny Compton 76-78; R Avon Dassett w Farnborough and Fenny Compton 78-84; V New Bilton 84-94; RD Rugby 89-94; Hon Can Cov Cathl 93-94; rtd 94; Perm to Offic *Cov* and *Pet* from 94; *Leic* from 96. *52 Cymbeline Way, Rugby CV22 6LA* Tel (01788) 816659

RANDALL, Jonathan Aubrey. b 64. Bris Univ BSc85. Ridley Hall Cam 04. **d** 06 **p** 07. C Hemingford Abbots and Hemingford Grey *Ely* 06-09; V Yaxley and Holme w Conington from 09; P-in-c Farcet Hampton from 09. *The Vicarage, Church Street, Yaxley, Peterborough PE7 3LH* Tel (01733) 240339
E-mail jon.randall@yfh.org.uk

RANDALL, Julian Adrian. b 45. Open Univ BA78 Stirling Univ MSc94 St Andr Univ PhD01 MCIPD. St Jo Sem Wonersh 68. **d** 70 **p** 71. Asst P Mortlake w E Sheen *S'wark* 71-72; Asst P Welling 72-74; Asst P Tunbridge Wells H Trin w Ch Ch *Roch* 74-79; NSM Dunfermline *St And* 96-98; P-in-c Elie and Earlsferry 98-03; P-in-c Pittenweem 98-03; Asst P St Andrews St Andr 03-05; Dir Progr Business Sch St Andr Univ 03-05; Sen Lect Aber Univ from 05. *Flat D, 10 Shearwater Crescent, Dunfermline KY11 8JX* Tel (01382) 554546
E-mail jrandall@randall.co.uk *or* julian.randall@abdn.ac.uk

RANDALL, Kelvin John. b 49. JP80. K Coll Lon BD71 AKC71 Birm Univ PGCE72 Trin Coll Carmarthen MPhil97 Univ of Wales (Ban) PhD00. St Jo Coll Nottm 73. **d** 74 **p** 75. C Peckham St Mary Magd *S'wark* 74-78; C Portsdown *Portsm* 78-81; C-in-c Crookhorn Ch Cen CD 81-82; R Bedhampton 82-90; Bp's Chapl for Post-Ord Tr 84-89; RD Havant 87-89; P-in-c Bournemouth St Jo w St Mich *Win* 90-94; V 94-97; Chapl Talbot Heath Sch Bournemouth 90-94; Research Fell Trin Coll Carmarthen 97-00; C Portswood St Denys *Win* 00-02; P-in-c from 02; Visiting Research Fell Glyndwr Univ from 10. *The Vicarage, 54 Whitworth Crescent, Southampton SO18 1GD* Tel (023) 8067 2108 Fax 8067 1757 E-mail st.denys@tiscali.co.uk

RANDALL, Mrs Lynda Lorraine. b 44. Sarum & Wells Th Coll 89. **d** 91 **p** 94. Par Dn Chesterton St Andr *Ely* 91-94; C 94-95; C Linton 95-96; TV Linton 96-99; R Byfield w Boddington and Aston le Walls *Pet* 99-10; rtd 10. *14 Smithland Court, Greens Norton, Towcester NN12 8DA* Tel (01327) 350203
E-mail lynda@chrislyn.demon.co.uk

RANDALL, Miss Marian Sally. b 49. Trin Coll Bris 75. dss 80 **d** 87 **p** 94. Peckham St Mary Magd *S'wark* 80-83; Sutton Ch Ch 83-97; Par Dn 87-94; C 94-97; P-in-c S Merstham 97-08; rtd 08; Perm to Offic *Cant* from 09. *5 Cheeselands, Biddenden, Ashford TN27 8HJ* Tel (01580) 291684

RANDALL, Martin Trevor. b 51. St Jo Coll Dur BA74. Trin Coll Bris 74. **d** 77 **p** 78. C Ashton-upon-Mersey St Mary Magd *Ches* 77-80; C Everton St Sav w St Cuth *Liv* 80-82; V W Derby Gd Shep 82-91; P-in-c Toxteth Park Ch Ch 91-94; P-in-c Toxteth Park St Bede 91-94; V Toxteth Park Ch Ch w St Bede 95-97; Chapl HM Pris Altcourse 97-07; Perm to Offic *Liv* from 07. *HM Prison Altcourse, Higher Lane, Liverpool L9 7LH* Tel 0151-522 2000 ext 2397 E-mail martin.randall@gslglobal.com

RANDALL, Canon Samuel Paul. b 59. Leeds Univ MA90. Ridley Hall Cam 84. **d** 87 **p** 88. C Kingston upon Hull St Nic *York* 87-89; CF 89-93; TV Bramley *Ripon* 93-96; Dioc Ecum Officer *Dur* 97-01; P-in-c Holmside 97-01; Bp's Officer for Ch in the World *Bradf* from 02; Hon Can Bradf Cathl from 04. *The Vicarage, Morton Lane, East Morton, Keighley BD20 5RS* Tel (01274) 561640 Mobile 07967-120070
E-mail sam.randall@bradford.anglican.org

RANDALL, David Peter. b 48. Trin Coll Bris BA88. **d** 92 **p** 93. C Wells St Cuth w Wookey Hole *B & W* 92-95; TV Wellington and Distr 95-05; R Chenderit *Pet* from 05. *The Rectory, Marston St Lawrence, Banbury OX17 2DB* Tel (01295) 712279
E-mail revrandell@supanet.com

RANDALL, Phillip John. b 45. Lon Univ BD73 CertEd. Linc Th Coll 67. **d** 68 **p** 69. C Henbury *Bris* 68-71; C Summertown *Ox* 71-73; C Liskeard w St Keyne *Truro* 73-75; Chapl Coll of SS Mark and Jo Plymouth 75-79; Tutor St Mark's Th Coll Dar es Salaam 80-82; R Alvescot w Black Bourton, Shilton, Holwell etc *Ox* 82-87; R St Gennys, Jacobstow w Warbstow and Treneglos *Truro* 87-97; rtd 97; Perm to Offic *Truro* from 01. *14 Merlin's Way, Tintagel PL34 0BP* Tel (01840) 770559

RANDOLPH-HORN, David Henry. b 47. Nottm Univ BA69 CQSW71. Qu Coll Birm 80. **d** 82 **p** 83. C Hamstead St Paul *Birm* 82-84; V Aston St Jas 84-94; Hon C Leytonstone H Trin and St Aug Harrow Green *Chelmsf* 93-99; Sec Inner Cities Relig Coun 94-99; Assoc Dir Leeds Ch Inst 99-07; P-in-c Heptonstall *Wakef* 99-02; Hon C Farnley *Ripon* 03; Hon C Leeds St Marg and All Hallows from 07. *23 Spencer Place, Leeds LS7 4DQ* Tel 0113-229 7546 E-mail david.hrh@virgin.net

RANGER, Keith Brian. b 34. Down Coll Cam BA58 MA63. Glas NSM Course 58. **d** 81 **p** 82. OMF Internat 81-99; Ethnic Min Co-ord 90-99; Hong Kong 81-89; Perm to Offic *Ches* 89-93 and from 99; *Man* 93-99; rtd 99. *144 Newton Street, Macclesfield SK11 6RW* Tel (01625) 439184
E-mail keithcath@ranger144.fsnet.co.uk

RANKIN, John. *See* RANKIN, Canon William John Alexander

RANKIN, John Cooper. b 24. Glas Univ MA44 Lon Univ BD53. Edin Th Coll 48. **d** 50 **p** 51. C Dundee St Mary Magd *Bre* 50-52; Chapl R Merchant Navy Sch Bearwood 53-60; Min Can Bris Cathl 60-66; Lic to Offic *Lich* 66-69; Prin Lect Bp Otter Coll Chich 69-84; rtd 84. *Address temp unknown*
E-mail johnrankin@cs.com

RANKIN, Joyce. **d** 03 **p** 04. C Dublin St Ann and St Steph *D & G* 03-09; I Bailieborough w Knockbride, Shercock and Mullagh *K, E & A* from 09. *The Rectory, Baillieborough, Co Cavan, Republic of Ireland* Tel (00353) (42) 966 6794
E-mail fejoycer@eircom.net

RANKIN, Stephen Brian. b 65. Salford Univ BSc88. Trin Coll Bris 95. **d** 97 **p** 98. C Ashton-upon-Mersey St Mary Magd *Ches* 97-06; V from 06. *St Mary's Vicarage, 20 Beeston Road, Sale M33 5AG* Tel 0161-973 5118 E-mail srankin@uk2.net

RANKIN, Canon William John Alexander. b 45. Van Mildert Coll Dur BA68 Fitzw Coll Cam BA73 MA77. Westcott Ho Cam 71. **d** 74 **p** 75. C St John's Wood *Lon* 74-78; Chapl Clifton Coll Bris 78-86; P-in-c The Claydons *Ox* 86-91; R 91-93; R Clare w Poslingford, Cavendish etc *St E* 93-04; R Stour Valley 04-10; Hon Can St E Cathl 05-10; rtd 10; Perm to Offic *St E* from 10 and *Pet* from 11. *12 Hawthorn Drive, Uppingham, Oakham LE15 9TA* Tel (01572) 822180
E-mail elizabeth@rankin4736.fsnet.co.uk

RANKINE, Christopher Barry. b 66. Portsm Poly BA88. Linc Th Coll BTh93. **d** 93 **p** 95. C Farlington *Portsm* 93-96; C Alverstoke 96-98; C Romsey *Win* 98-00; P-in-c W Andover 00-09; TR Portway and Danebury from 09. *The Vicarage, 17 Millway Road, Andover SP10 3EU* Tel (01264) 392541
E-mail chris.rankine@lineone.net

RANN, Preb Harry Harvey. b 18. Sarum Th Coll 47. **d** 50 **p** 51. C Victoria Docks Ascension *Chelmsf* 50-52; C Christchurch *Win* 52-56; C Mill Hill Jo Keble Ch *Lon* 56-57; V Woolfold *Man* 57-62; Dean's Chapl and PV Ex Cathl 62-77; Sacr 65-77; Succ 73-77; V Colyton 77-84; R Colyton and Southleigh 84-86; RD Honiton 84-86; Preb Ex Cathl 84-87; TR Colyton, Southleigh, Offwell, Widworthy etc 86-87; rtd 87; Perm to Offic *Ex* from 87. *19 Betjeman Drive, Exmouth EX8 5ST* Tel (01395) 265995

RANN, Ruth Margaret. b 32. Bris Univ BA54. **d** 03 **p** 04. NSM Exminster and Kenn 03-04; C Kenton, Mamhead, Powderham, Cofton and Starcross 04-10; rtd 10. *19 Betjeman Drive, Exmouth EX8 5ST* Tel (01395) 265995 E-mail r.rann@tiscali.co.uk

RANSFORD, Elizabeth Ann. b 49. Sussex Univ BSc70 Leeds Univ MA99 Whitelands Coll Lon PGCE71. Cranmer Hall Dur 07. **d** 08 **p** 09. OLM York St Thos w St Maurice from 08. *17 St Mary's, York YO30 7DD* Tel (01904) 672332 Mobile 07525-210572 E-mail liz.ransford@ntlworld.com

RANSON, Canon Arthur Frankland. b 50. St Jo Coll Dur BA73. Wycliffe Hall Ox 73. **d** 75 **p** 76. C Bare *Blackb* 75-78; C Scotforth 78-81; V Leyland St Ambrose 81-02; AD Leyland 96-02; P-in-c Blackb St Silas from 02; Hon Can Blackb Cathl from 00. *St Silas's Vicarage, Preston New Road, Blackburn BB2 6PS* Tel (01254) 671293 E-mail arthur.ranson@ntlworld.com

RANSON, Terence William James. b 42. AKC64 MTh87 STM88 AFAIM91. St Boniface Warminster 64. **d** 65 **p** 66. C Walton St Mary *Liv* 65-69; C Ipswich St Mary le Tower *St E* 69-71; Chapl Mersey Miss to Seamen 71-74; V N Keyham *Ex* 74-79; Ind Chapl 76-79; Australia 79-91; Sen Chapl and State Sec Fremantle Miss to Seamen 79-91; V N Mymms *St Alb* 91-04; rtd 04; Perm to Offic *Heref* from 04. *23 Pennine Close, Hereford HR4 0TE* Tel and fax (01432) 278363
E-mail terry.ranson42@googlemail.com

RANYARD, Michael Taylor. b 43. Nottm Univ BTh74. Linc Th Coll 71. **d** 74 **p** 75. C Sutton in Ashfield St Mary *S'well* 74-76; Hon C Lewisham St Mary *S'wark* 76-77; C Rushmere *St E* 77-79; R Hopton, Market Weston, Barningham etc 79-83; Chr

Educn and Resources Adv *Dur* 83-93; Prin Adv to Dioc Bd of Educn *Blackb* 93-98; Asst P Blackb Cathl 98-99; rtd 99; Perm to Offic *Heref* from 99. *72 Wyedean Rise, Belmont, Hereford HR2 7XZ* Tel and fax (01432) 355452 E-mail smranyard@xalt.co.uk

RAO, Norma Ruoman. b 63. Westmr Coll Ox BTh97. Westcott Ho Cam 99. **d** 01 **p** 02. C Endcliffe *Sheff* 01-04; C Rotherham 04-08; R Rossington from 08. *The Rectory, Sheep Bridge Lane, Rossington, Doncaster DN11 0EZ* Tel (01302) 867597 E-mail normarowe@btinternet.com

RAPHAEL, Brother. *See* PARKER, Ramon Lewis

RAPHAEL, The Ven Timothy John. b 29. Leeds Univ BA53. Coll of Resurr Mirfield. **d** 55 **p** 56. C Westmr St Steph w St Jo *Lon* 55-60; V Welling *S'wark* 60-63; New Zealand 63-72; Dean Dunedin 65-72; V St John's Wood *Lon* 72-83; AD Westmr St Marylebone 82-83; Adn Middx 83-96; rtd 96; Perm to Offic *Glouc* from 96. *121 Hales Road, Cheltenham GL52 6ST* Tel (01242) 256075

RAPHOE, Archdeacon of. *See* HARTE, The Ven Matthew Scott

RAPHOE, Dean of. *See* HAY, The Very Revd John

RAPKIN, Kevern. b 39. St D Coll Lamp BA62 Univ of Wales BD72. Lich Th Coll 63. **d** 65 **p** 66. C Hanley w Hope *Lich* 65-68; C Woodchurch *Ches* 68-70; C Abbots Langley *St Alb* 70-73; R Mt Pleasant Australia 73-80; R Rockingham and Safety Bay 80-90; R Lesmurdie 90-00; C Sholing *Win* 00-04; rtd 04; Australia from 04. *15 Gamage Way, Lockridge WA 6054, Australia* Tel (0061) (8) 9377 0332

RAPLEY, Frederick Arthur. b 27. Roch Th Coll 67. **d** 69 **p** 70. C Tenterden St Mildred w Smallhythe *Cant* 69-75; P-in-c Sittingbourne H Trin w Bobbing 75-85; V 85-89; rtd 89; Hon C Luton St Andr *St Alb* 89-92; Perm to Offic *St Alb* 92-98; Cant 98-02; *St E* from 02. *26 Angela Close, Martlesham, Woodbridge IP12 4TG* Tel (01473) 622922

RAPLEY, Mrs Joy Naomi. b 41. Portsm Poly CertEd63 Open Univ BA79. Sarum & Wells Th Coll 87. **d** 89 **p** 94. Par Dn Welwyn Garden City *St Alb* 89-92; Chapl S Beds Community Healthcare Trust 92-98; C Wilbury *St Alb* 98-99; NSM St Mary's Bay w St Mary-in-the-Marsh etc *Cant* 98-02; NSM New Romney w Old Romney and Midley 98-02; Asst Chapl E Kent NHS and Soc Care Partnership Trust 99-02; P-in-c Clopton w Otley, Swilland and Ashbocking *St E* 02-08; Perm to Offic from 08. *26 Angela Close, Martlesham, Woodbridge IP12 4TG* Tel (01473) 622922 E-mail revraps@aol.com

RAPSEY, Preb Peter Nigel. b 46. K Coll Lon BD68 AKC68. St Boniface Warminster. **d** 69 **p** 70. C Walton-on-Thames *Guildf* 69-73; C Fleet 73-77; P-in-c The Collingbournes and Everleigh *Sarum* 77-79; TV Wexcombe 79-84; R Wokingham St Paul *Ox* 84-93; Chapl Warminster Sch 93-96; V Frome Ch Ch *B & W* 96-04; P-in-c Evercreech w Chesterblade and Milton Clevedon 04-11; RD Frome 01-03; Dir of Ords 03-11; Preb Wells Cathl 04-11; rtd 11. *3A Saxon Close, Crediton EX17 3DS* E-mail peter.rapsey@btinternet.com

RASHBONE, Alan Victor. b 42. S'wark Ord Course. **d** 75 **p** 76. Hon C Woking St Mary *Guildf* 75-83. *Hope Cottage, Robin Hood Lane, Sutton Green, Guildford GU4 7QG* Tel (01483) 762760

RASON, Frederick George. b 26. Qu Coll Birm 68. **d** 69 **p** 70. C Weymouth H Trin *Sarum* 69-72; P-in-c Yatesbury 72-73; P-in-c Cherhill 72-73; R Oldbury 73-76; R W Parley 76-91; rtd 91; Perm to Offic *Sarum* from 91 and *Win* from 92. *4 Knoll Gardens, St Ives, Ringwood BH24 2LW* Tel (01425) 475761

RASON, Stuart Paul. Trin Coll Bris BA08. **d** 08 **p** 09. C Downs Benefice *Win* from 08. *The Rectory, The Street, Chilbolton, Stockbridge SO20 6BA* Tel (01264) 860258 E-mail stuartrason@hotmail.com

RASTALL, Preb Thomas Eric. b 19. St Aid Birkenhead 62. **d** 63 **p** 64. C Leek St Luke *Lich* 64-67; V Brown Edge 67-74; P-in-c Croxden 74-78; V Denstone 74-81; P-in-c Ellastone 78-81; V Denstone w Ellastone and Stanton 81-91; RD Uttoxeter 87-91; Preb Lich Cathl 89-91; rtd 91; Perm to Offic *Cov* 91-01. *10 Vicarage Close, Burton, Carnforth LA6 1NP* Tel (01524) 782386

RATCLIFF, Canon David William. b 37. Edin Th Coll 59. **d** 62 **p** 63. C Croydon St Aug *Cant* 62-65; C Selsdon St Jo w St Fran 65-69; V Milton Regis St Mary 69-75; Hon Min Can Cant Cathl 75-91; Asst Dir of Educn 75-91; Dioc Adv in Adult Educn and Lay Tr 75-91; Hon Pres Protestant Assn for Adult Educn in Eur 82-88; Chapl Frankfurt-am-Main 91-98; Adn Scandinavia *Eur* 96-05; Chapl Stockholm w Gävle and Västerås 98-02; rtd 05; Perm to Offic *Cant* from 02. *9 The Orchards, Elham, Canterbury CT4 6TR* Tel (01303) 840624 Fax 840871

RATCLIFF, Paul Ronald. b 62. Univ Coll Lon BSc83 Leic Univ MSc84 PhD85 FRAS MInstP. SEITE 05. **d** 09 **p** 10. C Cant St Martin and St Paul from 09. *Glebe House, Military Road, Canterbury CT1 1PA* Tel (01227) 463505 E-mail pr.ratcliff@googlemail.com

RATCLIFFE, Canon Michael David. b 43. Lon Univ BSc65 Southn Univ PGCE67 Lon Univ BA75 Lanc Univ MA84. Cranmer Hall Dur 75. **d** 77 **p** 78. C Blackpool St Thos *Blackb* 77-81; V Oswaldtwistle St Paul 81-10; RD Accrington 97-03;

Hon Can Blackb Cathl 00-10; rtd 10; Perm to Offic *Blackb* from 10. *8 Stanhill Road, Oswaldtwistle, Accrington BB5 4PP* E-mail mratossy@tiscali.co.uk

RATCLIFFE, Peter Graham Bruce. St Mich Coll Llan. **d** 08 **p** 09. C Carmarthen St Pet *St D* 08-09; C E Carmarthen 09-10; P-in-c Llanpumsaint w Llanllawddog from 10. *The Vicarage, Llanpumsaint, Carmarthen SA33 6BZ* Tel (01267) 253205

RATCLIFFE, Peter William Lewis. b 30. Birm Univ BSc55 Lon Univ BD58. Tyndale Hall Bris 55. **d** 58 **p** 59. C Cambridge St Andr Less *Ely* 58-61; R Wistow 61-74; R Bury 61-74; V Rainham *Chelmsf* 74-85; R Wennington 75-85; V Heacham *Nor* 85-87; P-in-c Sedgeford w Southmere 85-87; V Heacham and Sedgeford 87-95; rtd 95; Perm to Offic *Nor* from 95. *22 Birchfield Gardens, Mulbarton, Norwich NR14 8BT* Tel (01508) 570511 E-mail prate@mulb.fsnet.co.uk

RATCLIFFE, Mrs Roosevelta (Rosie). b 60. K Coll Lon BA97 MA99. SEITE 98. **d** 01 **p** 02. C Croydon St Matt *S'wark* 01-04; Hon C Sanderstead 05-06; Chapl S Lon and Maudsley NHS Foundn Trust from 04. *Bethlem Royal Hospital, Monks Orchard Road, Beckenham BR3 3BX* Tel (020) 8777 6611 Fax 8777 1668

RATHBAND, The Very Revd Kenneth William. b 60. Edin Univ BD86. Edin Th Coll 82. **d** 86 **p** 87. C Dundee St Paul *Bre* 86-88; TV Dundee St Martin 88-89; C Edin SS Phil and Jas 90-91; R Alyth *St And* from 91; R Blairgowrie from 91; R Coupar Angus from 91; Dean St Andr from 07. *10 Rosemount Park, Blairgowrie PH10 6TZ* Tel (01250) 872431 *or* 874583 E-mail krathband@btinternet.com

RATHBONE, Mrs Elizabeth. b 51. Lon Univ MB, BS76 MRCGP80, MMMTC 03. **d** 03 **p** 04. C Tettenhall Regis *Lich* 03-06; TV from 06. *76 Tyninghame Avenue, Wolverhampton WV6 9PW* Tel (01902) 753562 E-mail liz.rathbone@blueyonder.co.uk

RATHBONE, Mrs Isobel. b 48. Girton Coll Cam MA70 Leeds Univ MA02 Solicitor 81. NEOC 02. **d** 05 **p** 06. NSM Moor Allerton *Ripon* 05-08; NSM Hooe and Ninfield *Chich* 08-09; NSM Guiseley w Esholt *Bradf* from 10. *1 Tranfield Close, Guiseley, Leeds LS20 8LT* Tel 07775-656257 (mobile) E-mail isobel.rathbone@lmh.ox.ac.uk

RATHBONE, Paul. b 36. BNC Ox BA58 MA62. Wycliffe Hall Ox 58. **d** 60 **p** 61. C Carl St Jo 60-63; C Heworth w Peasholme St Cuth *York* 63-68; V Thorganby w Skipwith and N Duffield 68-83; V Bishopthorpe and Acaster Malbis 83-01; rtd 01; Perm to Offic *York* from 01. *12 Whitelass Close, Thirsk YO7 1FG* Tel (01845) 523347

RATHBONE, Stephen Derek. b 61. Wycliffe Hall Ox. **d** 00 **p** 01. C W Kirby St Bridget *Ches* 00-03; P-in-c Rainow w Saltersford and Forest 03-10; V from 10. *The Vicarage, Pedley Hill, Rainow, Macclesfield SK10 5TZ* Tel (01625) 572013 E-mail steve.rathbone@virgin.net

RATINGS, Canon John William. b 37. St Pet Coll Ox BA62 MA71. Cuddesdon Coll 62. **d** 64 **p** 65. C Langley All SS and Martyrs *Man* 64-68; C Easthampstead *Ox* 68-71; V Wargrave 71-02; V Wargrave w Knowl Hill 02-08; RD Sonning 88-98; Hon Can Ch Ch from 97; Provost Woodard Corp (S Division) 00-06; rtd 08; Perm to Offic *Ox* from 08. *18 Autumn Walk, Wargrave, Reading RG10 8BS* Tel 0118-940 1363 E-mail jratings@sky.com

RATTENBERRY, Christopher James. b 59. York Univ BA80 Solicitor. St Jo Coll Nottm 91. **d** 93 **p** 94. C Porchester *S'well* 93-98; P-in-c Daybrook 98-04; V 04-06; AD Nottingham N 01-05; P-in-c Ravenshead from 06. *St Peter's Vicarage, 55 Sheepwalk Lane, Ravenshead, Nottingham NG15 9FD* Tel (01623) 405203 E-mail chris.rattenberry@ntlworld.com

✠**RATTERAY, The Rt Revd Alexander Ewen.** b 42. Codrington Coll Barbados 61. **d** 65 **p** 66 **c** 96. C S Kirkby *Wakef* 66-68; C Sowerby St Geo 68-71; V Airedale w Fryston 71-80; Bermuda 80-08; Adn Bermuda 94-96; Bp Bermuda 96-08; rtd 08. *PO Box HM 2021, Hamilton HM CX, Bermuda* E-mail bishopratteray@ibl.bm

RATTIGAN, Paul Damian. b 61. Reading Univ BSc87 Liv Hope MA00 Sussex Univ PGCE88. Qu Coll Birm 93. **d** 95 **p** 96. C Parr *Liv* 95-99; P-in-c St Helens St Matt Thatto Heath 99-01; V 01-05; Dioc Voc Adv 02-05; P-in-c Boldmere *Birm* 05-08; V from 08. *209 Station Road, Sutton Coldfield B73 5LE* Tel 0121-354 4501 E-mail paul@stmichaels.org.uk

RATTUE, James. b 69. Ball Coll Ox BA91 MA04 Leic Univ MA93. St Steph Ho Ox 03. **d** 05 **p** 06. C Weybridge *Guildf* 05-08 and 09; C Englefield Green 08-09; R Farncombe from 09. *The Rectory, 38 Farncombe Hill, Godalming GU7 2AU* Tel (01483) 860709 Mobile 07952-615499 E-mail jamesrattue@hotmail.com

RAVALDE, Canon Geoffrey Paul. b 54. St Cuth Soc Dur BA76 SS Coll Cam BA86 MA90 Lon Univ MTh91 Barrister 78. Westcott Ho Cam 84. **d** 87 **p** 88. C Spalding *Linc* 87-91; P-in-c Wigton *Carl* 91-92; V from 92; P-in-c Thursby from 10; RD Carl 95-00; Hon Can Carl Cathl from 96. *The Vicarage, Longthwaite Road, Wigton CA7 9JR* Tel (01697) 342337

RAVEN, Ann. *See* GURNER, Mrs Margaret Ann

RAVEN, Barry. b 48. Sarum & Wells Th Coll 69. **d** 72 **p** 73. C Henbury *Bris* 72-76; P-in-c S Marston w Stanton Fitzwarren 76-78; TV Stratton St Margaret w S Marston etc 78-80; P-in-c Coalpit Heath 80-84; V 84-91; R Ashley, Crudwell, Hankerton and Oaksey from 91; P-in-c Ashton Keynes, Leigh and Minety from 07; RD N Wilts 99-06. *The Rectory, 1 Days Court, Crudwell, Malmesbury SN16 9HG* Tel (01666) 577118 E-mail barry@deanery.org.uk

RAVEN, Margaret Hilary. b 45. Dur Univ BA67 Man Univ MEd73. Wesley Th Sem Washington MDiv95. **d** 96 **p** 97. USA 96-01; Asst R Martinsburg Trin Ch 96-99; Assoc R Toms River Ch Ch 99-00; Perm to Offic *Edin* 02-06; NSM Edin Ch Ch from 06. *32 Montpelier Park, Edinburgh EH10 4NJ* Tel 0131-228 4790 E-mail mthrraven@btopenworld.com

RAVEN, Tony. b 39. Garnett Coll Lon CertEd65 CEng72 MIET72. SAOMC 94. **d** 97 **p** 98. NSM Lt Berkhamsted and Bayford, Essendon etc *St Alb* 97-01; P-in-c Lt Hadham w Albury 01-05; rtd 05; Hon C Hazelbury Bryan and the Hillside Par *Sarum* 07-11. *1 Church View, Wonston, Hazelbury Bryan, Sturminster Newton DT10 2DF* E-mail t raven@btopenworld.com

RAVENS, David Arthur Stanley. b 30. Jes Coll Ox BA53 MA61 Lon Univ BD63. Wells Th Coll 61. **d** 63 **p** 64. C Seacroft *Ripon* 63-70; TV 70-73; Teacher Sir Wm Borcase's Sch Marlow 73-87; rtd 95. *44 Arthursdale Grange, Scholes, Leeds LS15 4AW* Tel 0113-273 6648

RAVENSCROFT, Avril Shirley. b 46. **d** 11. NSM Prestbury *Ches* from 11. *2 Castlegate Mews, Prestbury, Macclesfield SK10 4BP* Tel (01625) 820041

RAVENSCROFT, The Ven Raymond Lockwood. b 31. Leeds Univ BA53. Coll of Resurr Mirfield 54. **d** 55 **p** 56. C Goodwood S Africa 55-57; C St Jo Cathl Bulawayo S Rhodesia 57-59; R Francistown Bechuanaland 59-62; C St Ives *Truro* 62-64; V Falmouth All SS 64-68; V St Stephens by Launceston 68-73; P-in-c Launceston St Thos 68-73; V Launceston St Steph w St Thos 73-74; TR Probus, Ladock and Grampound w Creed and St Erme 74-88; RD Powder 77-81; Hon Can Truro Cathl 82-88; P-in-c St Erme 84-85; Adn Cornwall and Can Lib Truro Cathl 88-96; rtd 96; Perm to Offic *Truro* from 96 and *Ex* from 00. *19 Montpelier Court, St David's Hill, Exeter EX4 4DP* Tel (01392) 430607

RAWDING, Andrew. b 70. Cranmer Hall Dur 00. **d** 02 **p** 03. C Enfield St Andr *Lon* 02-05; Hon C Arm St Mark 05-07; Chapl RN from 08. *Royal Naval Chaplaincy Service, Mail Point 1-2, Leach Building, Whale Island, Portsmouth PO2 8BY* Tel (023) 9262 5055 Fax 9262 5134

RAWDON-MOGG, Timothy David. b 45. St Jo Coll Dur BA76. Cuddesdon Coll 75. **d** 77 **p** 78. C Wotton St Mary *Glouc* 77-80; C Ascot Heath *Ox* 80-82; V Woodford Halse w Eydon *Pet* 82-88; V Shrivenham w Watchfield and Bourton *Ox* 88-00; R Horsted Keynes *Chich* 00-08; rtd 08. *Stone Cottage, The Bog, Minsterley, Shrewsbury SY5 0NJ* Tel (01743) 792073

RAWE, Alan Charles George. b 29. ALCD56. **d** 56 **p** 57. C W Kilburn St Luke w St Simon and St Jude *Lon* 56-59; Lect Watford St Mary *St Alb* 59-61; R Ore St Helen and St Barn *Chich* 61-69; R Moreton Ches 69-80; V Coppull *Blackb* 80-83; Miss to Seamen 83-94; Felixstowe Seafarers' Cen 88-94; rtd 94; Perm to Offic *Blackb* from 94. *15 Starfield Close, Lytham St Annes FY8 4QA* Tel (01253) 733647

RAWLING, Miss Jane Elizabeth. b 51. Birm Univ BSc73 St Jo Coll York CertEd75. St Jo Coll Nottm 81. **dss** 84 **d** 87 **p** 94. Southsea St Jude *Portsm* 84-88; C 87-88; C St Paul's Cray St Barn *Roch* 88-91; Hon C from 91; SE Regional Co-ord BCMS Crosslinks 91-01; Sec for Bps' Selection Conf and CME Sec Min Division 01-07. *50 Batchwood Green, Orpington BR5 2NF* Tel (01689) 871467

RAWLING, Preb Stephen Charles. b 43. Man Univ BSc64 Bris Univ MSc71. Sarum & Wells Th Coll 71. **d** 73 **p** 74. C Bris St Andr Hartcliffe 73-76; C Westlands St Andr *Lich* 76-78; R Darlaston St Lawr 78-90; TR Bloxwich 90-08; Preb Lich Cathl 07-08; rtd 08; Perm to Offic *Lich* from 09. *31 Stowe Street, Lichfield WS13 6AQ* Tel (01543) 262917

RAWLINGS, Canon Brenda Susan. b 48. Sussex Univ CertEd69. Oak Hill Th Coll 85. **d** 87 **p** 94. Par Dn Green Street Green *Roch* 87-90; Par Dn Collier Row St Jas and Havering-atte-Bower *Chelmsf* 90-94; C Greenstead Nor 98; R 98-00; TR Greenstead w Colchester St Anne 00-06; Hon Can Chelmsf Cathl 05-06; rtd 06; Perm to Offic *Nor* and *St E* from 07. *10 Sorrel Drive, Thetford IP24 2YJ* Tel (01842) 752881

RAWLINGS, Elizabeth. b 66. Nottm Univ BSc96 RGN87. St Jo Coll Nottm 04. **d** 06 **p** 07. C Derby St Alkmund and St Werburgh 06-07; C Walbrook Epiphany 07-10; Min Hamilton CD *Leic* from 10; Warden Past Assts from 11. *2 Cransley Close, Hamilton, Leicester LE5 1QQ* E-mail lizrawlings66@yahoo.co.uk

RAWLINGS, Gayle Ann Mary. b 53. Toronto Univ MD76 BA88 K Coll Lon MA89 FRCP(C)81. Westcott Ho Cam 01. **d** 03 **p** 04. C Ex St Thos and Em 03-07; Chapl Univ Coll of SS Mark and Jo Plymouth 07-09; Canada from 09. *Address temp unknown*

RAWLINGS, The Ven John Edmund Frank. b 47. AKC69. St Aug Coll Cant 69. **d** 70 **p** 71. C Rainham *Roch* 70-73; C Tattenham Corner and Burgh Heath *Guildf* 73-76; Chapl RN 76-92; V Tavistock and Gulworthy *Ex* 92-05; Chapl Kelly Coll Tavistock 93-02; RD Tavistock *Ex* 97-02; Preb Ex Cathl from 99; Adn Totnes from 06. *Blue Hills, Bradley Road, Bovey Tracey, Newton Abbot TQ13 9EU* Tel (01626) 832064 Fax 834947 E-mail archdeacon.of.totnes@exeter.anglican.org

RAWLINGS, Canon Philip John. b 53. St Jo Coll Nottm BTh83 **d** 83 **p** 84. C Blackley St Andr *Man* 83-87; C Halliwell St Pe 87-93; R Old Trafford St Bride from 93; AD Stretford 98-05; Borough Dean Trafford 10-11; Hon Can Man Cathl from 04. *St Bride's Rectory, 29 Shrewsbury Street, Old Trafford Manchester M16 9BB* Tel 0161-226 6064 E-mail philjr@zetnet.co.uk

RAWLINGS, Susan. *See* RAWLINGS, Canon Brenda Susan

RAWLINS, Clyde Thomas. b 28. **d** 02. NSM Leeds St Aid *Ripon* from 02. *26 Gledhow Wood Close, Leeds LS8 1PN* Tel 0113-266 7731

RAWLINSON, Curwen. b 32. MBE73. Leeds Univ CertEd55 Man Univ DipEd56 Open Univ BA80. Sarum Th Coll 59. **d** 61 **p** 62. C Wigan St Mich *Liv* 61-63; CF 63-78; Dep Asst Chap Gen 78-80; Asst Chapl Gen 80-85; QHC 83-98; R Uley w Owlpen and Nympsfield *Glouc* 85-98; RD Dursley 89-96; rtd 98 Perm to Offic *Glouc* from 98; Sub Chapl HM Pris Glouc from 02 *Cark House, 6 Groves Place, Fairford GL7 4BJ* Tel (01285 711009

RAWLINSON, James Nigel. b 56. Em Coll Cam BA77 MB BCh80 FRCSE86 FFAEM98. WMMTC 95. **d** 98 **p** 99. NSM Bath Weston All SS w N Stoke and Langridge *B & W* from 98 Perm to Offic *Bris* from 98; Consultant Bris R Infirmary from 99. *Glen Boyd House, 38 Court View, Wick, Bristol BS30 5QI* Tel 0117-303 9220 E-mail nigel.rawlinson@bristol.ac.uk

RAWLINSON, John. b 47. Guy's Hosp Medical Sch BSc67 MB BS71 MRCS. EAMTC 89. **d** 92 **p** 93. NSM Tilbrook *Ely* 92-05 NSM Covington 92-05; NSM Catworth Magna 92-05; NSM Keyston and Bythorn 92-05; Chapl Chu Coll Cam from 98. *The Malt House, 42 Stonely, Huntingdon PE28 0EH* Tel (01480 860263 Fax 861590 E-mail dingleberry@lineone.net *or* jr338@cam.ac.uk

RAWSON, Canon Michael Graeme. b 62. York Univ BA84 St Steph Ho Ox BA88. **d** 89 **p** 90. C Brighouse St Martin *Wake* 89-92; C Brighouse and Clifton 92-93; V Gomersal 93-04; Bp's Dom Chapl and Publicity Officer 04-07; Can Res Wakef Cath from 07. *3 Cathedral Close, Margaret Street, Wakefield WF1 2DP* Tel (01924) 379743 *or* 373923 E-mail michael.rawson@wakefield-cathedral.org.uk

RAY, Mrs Joanna Zorina. b 55. AIMLS78 K Coll Lon BSc77 Garnett Coll Lon PGCE80 Lon Inst of Educn MA92. S'wark Ord Course 84. **d** 87 **p** 94. NSM Carshalton *S'wark* 87-91 NSM Sutton New Town St Barn 91-93; NSM Knighton St Mary Magd *Leic* 93-94; C Leic H Spirit 94-98; Chapl for Deaf People 94-98; Chapl St Andr Hosp Northn 99-03; Perm to Offic *S'well* from 04. *37 Torvill Drive, Nottingham NG8 2BU* Tel 07802-300799 (mobile) E-mail revdjoannaray@aol.com

RAY, John Mead. b 28. OBE79. St Andr Univ MA50 DipEd51 CMS Tr Coll Chislehurst 60. **d** 70 **p** 71. Miss Partner CMS 70-95 C Sparkhill St Jo *Birm* 87-90; C Sparkbrook Em 87-90; C Sparkhill w Greet and Sparkbrook 90; Deanery Missr 90-95; rtd 95; Perm to Offic *Birm* from 95. *190 Sarehole Road, Birmingham B28 8EF* Tel 0121-777 6143 E-mail cath.john@blueyonder.co.uk

RAY, Robin John. b 44. Sarum & Wells Th Coll 72. **d** 74 **p** 75. C Bourne Valley *Sarum* 74-78; P-in-c Dilton's-Marsh 78-82; V 82-87; V Taunton Lyngford *B & W* 87-93; R Exford, Exmoor Hawkridge and Withypool 93-04; ACORA Link Officer and Rural Affairs Officer 93-04; rtd 04; Perm to Offic *B & W* from 04 RD Glastonbury from 09. *Leigholt Farm, Somerton Road, Street BA16 0SU* Tel (01458) 841281

RAYBOULD, James Clive Ransford. b 37. Wolv Univ BSc62 Anglia Poly Univ MBA94 PhD01. Cranmer Hall Dur 81. **d** 83 **p** 84. C Cannock *Lich* 83-86; P-in-c Leek Wootton *Cov* 86-89 Dioc Tr Adv 86-89; TV Cannock *Lich* 89; Assoc Lect Anglia Ruskin Univ from 90; rtd 00. *29 Greystones, Bromham Chippenham SN15 2JT* Tel (01380) 859623

✠**RAYFIELD, The Rt Revd Lee Stephen.** b 55. Southn Univ BSc78 Lon Univ PhD81 SOSc95. Ridley Hall Cam 93. **d** 93 **p** 94 **c** 05. C Woodford Wells *Chelmsf* 93-97; P-in-c Furze Platt *Ox* 97-05; AD Maidenhead and Windsor 00-05; Suff Bp Swindon *Bris* from 05. *Mark House, Field Rise, Swindon SN1 4HP* Te (01793) 538654 Fax 525181 E-mail bishop.swindon@bristoldiocese.org

RAYMENT, Andrew David. b 45. Univ of Wales (Lamp) BA68 Univ of Wales (Abth) MA70 Nottm Univ PhD06. Ridley Hal Cam 78. **d** 80 **p** 81. C Costessey *Nor* 80-83; C Earlham St Anne 83-90; V Old Catton 90-96; Perm to Offic *Pet* 00-11; Mir Partnership Development Officer 04-11; Adult Educn Officer (CME and Min Partnership) 05-11; rtd 11; P-in-c Ketton Collyweston, Easton-on-the-Hill etc *Pet* from 11. *The Vicarage, 4*

Edmonds Drive, Ketton, Stamford PE9 3TH Tel (01780) 729052
E-mail andrew-rayment2010@hotmail.co.uk

RAYMENT, Mrs Helen Elizabeth. b 46. Keswick Hall Coll
CertEd67. EAMTC 92. **d** 95 **p** 96. NSM Old Catton *Nor* 95-96;
Perm to Offic *Pet* 01-02; P-in-c Weedon Bec w Everdon and
Dodford 02-03; V 03-11; rtd 11. *The Vicarage, 4 Edmonds Drive,
Ketton, Stamford PE9 3TH* Tel (01780) 729052
E-mail h.rayment@btinternet.com

RAYMER, Victoria Elizabeth. b 46. Wellesley Coll (USA) BA68
Harvard Univ MA69 JD78 PhD81. St Steph Ho Ox BA86 Qu
Coll Birm 88. **d** 89 **p** 94. Par Dn Bushey *St Alb* 89-94; C Eaton
Socon 94-98; V Milton Ernest, Pavenham and Thurleigh 98-01;
Dir Studies Westcott Ho Cam from 01. *1 Short Street,
Cambridge CB1 1LB* Tel (01223) 352922 *or* tel and fax 741011
E-mail ver21@cam.ac.uk

RAYMOND, The Very Revd Walter. b 49. **d** 92 **p** 93. OGS from
93; C Willowdale All So Canada 92-94; Chapl H Trin Sch
Toronto 94-99; Dean and R H Trin Cathl Quebec 99-07; Chapl
Monte Carlo *Eur* from 08. *St Paul's House, 22 avenue de Grande-
Bretagne, 98000 Monte Carlo, Monaco* Tel (00377) 9330 7106
Fax 9330 5039 E-mail wraymond@ogs.net

RAYMONT, Philip Richard. b 56. Univ of Qld BA79 BEdSt86
Melbourne Univ MEd00 Cam Univ PhD05 MACE. **d** 04 **p** 09.
Asst Chapl Selw Coll Cam 04-07; Perm to Offic *Ely* 07-09; Sen
Chapl Guildford Gr Sch Australia from 09. *Guildford Grammar,
11 Terrace Road, Guildford WA 6935, Australia* Tel (0061) (8)
9377 9245 E-mail praymont@ggs.wa.edu.au

RAYNER, Canon George Charles. b 26. Bps' Coll Cheshunt 50.
d 52 **p** 53. C Rowbarton *B & W* 52-56; V Taunton H Trin 56-63;
Chapl Taunton and Somerset Hosp 60-63, V Lower Sandown
St Jo *Portsm* 63-69; R Wootton 69-89; Hon Can Portsm Cathl
84-89; rtd 89; Perm to Offic *B & W* 89-92 and *Portsm* from 98;
P-in-c Six Pilgrims *B & W* 93-02. *The Bungalow, 1 Alresford
Road, Shanklin PO37 6HX* Tel (01983) 867304

RAYNER, Mrs Karen June. b 54. ERMC 11. **d** 11. NSM Ormesby
St Marg w Scratby, Ormesby St Mich etc *Nor* from 11. *29 Old
Market Close, Acle, Norwich NR13 3EY* Tel (01493) 751227
E-mail kjrayner23@hotmail.com

RAYNER, Michael John. b 55. Magd Coll Ox BA78 DPhil85.
Ox Min Course 04. **d** 07 **p** 08. Dir Br Heart Foundn
Health Promotion Research Gp from 94; NSM Ox St Matt
from 07. *198 Marlborough Road, Oxford OX1 4LT* Tel (01865)
289244 Mobile 07871-758745
E-mail mike.rayner@dph.ox.ac.uk

RAYNER, Paul Anthony George. b 39. Dur Univ BA60 Lon Univ
BD68 Cape Town Univ MA79. Lon Coll of Div 65. **d** 68 **p** 69. C
Crookes St Thos *Sheff* 68-72; P-in-c Diep River St Luke S Africa
72-79; P-in-c S Shoebury *Chelmsf* 80-84; R 84-97; V Loughton
St Mich 97-04; rtd 04; Perm to Offic *Chelmsf* from 04 and *Eur*
from 08. *36 Amberley Road, Buckhurst Hill IG9 5QW* Tel (020)
8504 7434 E-mail prayner@globalnet.co.uk

RAYNER, Richard Noel. b 24. Lon Univ BD51. Oak Hill Th Coll
50. **d** 52 **p** 53. C Plymouth St Jude *Ex* 52-55; V Walthamstow
St Luke *Chelmsf* 55-61; V Romford Gd Shep 61-65; V Slough *Ox*
65-72; V Heworth w Peasholme St Cuth *York* 72-75; V Heworth
H Trin 75-81; V Okehampton w Inwardleigh *Ex* 81-89; RD
Okehampton 87-89; rtd 89; Perm to Offic *Ex* 90-98 and *B & W*
90-06. *Redlands, 5 Ladymeade, Ilminster TA19 0EA* Tel (01460)
52491

RAYNER, Mrs Shirley Christine. b 54. SEITE BA08. **d** 05 **p** 06. C
S Croydon St Pet and St Aug *S'wark* 05-09; C Carew *St D* 09-11;
TV from 11. *The Vicarage, Manorbier, Tenby SA70 7TN* Tel
(01834) 871617 E-mail revshirley@btinternet.com

RAYNER, Stewart Leslie. b 39. St Jo Coll Dur BA61 MA73.
Cranmer Hall Dur. **d** 67 **p** 68. C Whiston *Sheff* 67-70; C
Doncaster St Geo 70-74; Chapl Doncaster R Infirmary 70-74; R
Adwick-le-Street *Sheff* 74-85; V Totley 85-91; Asst Chapl
Pastures Hosp Derby 91-94; Asst Chapl Kingsway Hosp Derby
91-94; Asst Chapl S Derby Mental Health Services 91-94; P-in-c
Etwall w Egginton *Derby* 94-99; R 99-08; RD Longford 96-01;
rtd 09. *26 Lawn Avenue, Etwall, Derby DE65 6JB* Tel (01283)
736079 E-mail stewart.rayner37@googlemail.com

RAYNES, Canon Andrew. b 60. R Holloway Coll Lon BA83.
Wycliffe Hall Ox 93. **d** 95 **p** 96. C Crowborough *Chich* 95-99; V
Blackb Ch Ch w St Matt from 99; AD Blackb and Darwen from
03; Hon Can Blackb Cathl from 10. *The Vicarage, Brandy House
Brow, Blackburn BB2 3EY* Tel (01254) 56292
E-mail andrewraynes@btopenworld.com

RAYNHAM, Mrs Penelope Anne. b 44. SWMTC 97. **d** 00 **p** 01.
OLM S Hill w Callington *Truro* from 00. *Bramblings, Honicombe
Corner, Harrowbarrow, Callington PL17 8JN* Tel (01822) 833065
E-mail penny@bramvista.co.uk

RAYNOR, Duncan Hope. b 58. Ex Coll Ox MA80 MA82 Birm
Univ PGCE88 MLitt93. Qu Coll Birm 82. **d** 84 **p** 85. C Kings
Heath *Birm* 84-87; Perm to Offic from 87; Hd of RE Alderbrook
Sch Solihull 88-94; Chapl K Edw Sch Birm from 94. *134 Addison
Road, Birmingham B14 7EP* Tel 0121-684 3407 *or* 472 1672
E-mail dhr@kes.bham.sch.uk

RAYNOR, Michael. b 53. Lanc Univ BA74 MSc75. Ripon Coll
Cuddesdon BA84 MA99. **d** 85 **p** 86. C Gt Crosby St Faith *Liv*
85-88; V Warrington St Barn 88-97; V Orford St Andr from 97;
AD Warrington 99-05; Hon Can Liv Cathl 03-05. *St Andrew's
Vicarage, Poplars Avenue, Orford, Warrington WA2 9UE* Tel
(01925) 631903 E-mail mjraynor@care4free.net

RAZZALL, Charles Humphrey. b 55. Worc Coll Ox BA76 MA81
Qu Coll Cam BA78. Westcott Ho Cam 76. **d** 79 **p** 80. C Catford
(Southend) and Downham *S'wark* 79-83; V Crofton Park
St Hilda w St Cypr 83-87; UPA Officer 87-92; TV Oldham *Man*
87-01; AD Oldham 92-99; Hon Can Man Cathl 98-01; R
Coppenhall *Ches* from 01. *The Rectory, 198 Ford Lane, Crewe
CW1 3TN* Tel (01270) 215151

REA, Simon William John. b 60. G&C Coll Cam MA Victoria
Univ Wellington MA Liv Univ BTh07 Univ of Wales (Ban)
PGCE. Ridley Hall Cam 02. **d** 04 **p** 05. C Moreton *Ches* 04-08; C
Edgware *Lon* from 08. *St Peter's Vicarage, Stonegrove, Edgware
HA8 8AB* Tel 07905-699185 (mobile)
E-mail simonrea@gmx.net

READ, Andrew Gordon. b 40. Nottm Univ BA69 MRICS63
FRICS86. Cuddesdon Coll 70. **d** 70 **p** 71. C E Retford *S'well*
70-72; C Woodthorpe 72-76; P-in-c Newark St Leon 76-78; Perm
to Offic *Roch* 79-91. *The Gables, 148 Hastings Road, Battle
TN33 0TW* Tel (01424) 773044

READ, Charles William. b 60. Man Univ BA81 MPhil95 Man
Poly PGCE82. St Jo Coll Nottm 86. **d** 88 **p** 89. C Oldham *Man*
88-90; C Urmston 90-94; P-in-c Broughton St Jas w St Clem and
St Matthias 94-96; TV Broughton 96-99; Lect Cranmer Hall
Dur 99-06; Dir Studies Dioc Min Scheme *Dur* 00-06; Teacher
Dur Seh 06; Vice Prin and Dir Studies Nor Dioc Min Course
from 07. *42 Heigham Road, Norwich NR2 3AU* Tel (01603)
660824 E-mail charlesread@norwich.anglican.org

READ, Geoffrey Philip. b 61. Bris Univ LLB82 Spurgeon's Coll
MTh04. Wycliffe Hall Ox 85. **d** 88 **p** 89. C Dorking St Paul
Guildf 88-92; TV Westborough 92-97; TR 97-98; Chapl Basle
Eur from 98; P-in-c Freiburg-im-Breisau 98-01. *St Johanns-Ring
92, CH-4056 Basle, Switzerland* Tel (0041) (61) 321 7477 Fax 321
7476 E-mail admin@anglicanbasel.ch

READ, James Arthur. b 51. Nottm Coll of Educn BEd74.
EMMTC 84. **d** 87 **p** 88. C Weoley Castle *Birm* 87-91; C W
Smethwick 91-92; TV Atherton *Man* 92-97; P-in-c Facit 97-00; V
Whitworth w Facit 00-08; P-in-c Royton St Anne from 08.
St Anne's Vicarage, St Anne's Avenue, Royton, Oldham OL2 5AD
Tel 0161-652 3090 E-mail revjames.read@btinternet.com

READ, John. b 33. Worc Coll Ox BA56 MA60. Chich Th Coll 56.
d 58 **p** 59. C Babbacombe *Ex* 58-60; C Heavitree 60-63; V
Swimbridge 63-69; V Ex St Matt 69-80; P-in-c Ex St Sidwell
79-80; R Ex St Sidwell and St Matt 80-83; Chapl Warneford
Hosp Leamington Spa 83-89; Chapl S Warks Hosps 83-89;
Chapl Dur and Ches le Street Hosps 89-95; Chapl Dryburn
Hosp 89-95; rtd 95; NSM Tamworth *Lich* 95-98; Perm to Offic
Cov from 02. *8 Newsholme Close, Warwick CV34 5XF* Tel
(01926) 411598

READ, John du Sautoy. CITC. **d** 66 **p** 67. V Choral Derry Cathl
66-67; Dean's V Derry Cathl 67; S Africa from 69. *8 Allison
Road, Scottsville, 3209 South Africa* Tel (0027) (33) 342 0262
E-mail woeber@lantic.net

READ, John Samuel. b 33. Fitzw Ho Cam BA56. Clifton Th Coll
62. **d** 64 **p** 65. C Sneinton St Chris w St Phil *S'well* 64-67; C
Huyton St Geo *Liv* 67-70; Lic to Offic *Blackb* 70-72; V
Moldgreen *Wakef* 72-84; V Rawtenstall St Mary *Man* 84-91;
Chapl Rossendale Gen Hosp 84-91; R Earsham w Alburgh and
Denton *Nor* 91-98; P-in-c Ditchingham, Hedenham and Broome
94-98; rtd 98; Perm to Offic *Nor* and *St E* from 98. *7 Pine Tree
Close, Worlingham, Beccles NR34 7EE* Tel (01502) 712585

READ, Mrs Julie Margaret. b 61. Keble Coll Ox BA82 Univ of
Wales (Ban) PGCE83. WEMTC 97. **d** 00 **p** 01. C Bishop's Castle
w Mainstone, Lydbury N etc *Heref* 00-03; R Pembridge w Moor
Court, Shobdon, Staunton etc from 03. *The Rectory, Manley
Crescent, Pembridge, Leominster HR6 9EB* Tel (01544) 388998

READ, Maureen Elizabeth. b 52. Man Metrop Univ BEd93 Ches
Coll of HE BTh99. NOC 95. **d** 98 **p** 99. NSM Leesfield Man
98-99; C 99-02; TV Heywood 02-09; V Meltham *Wakef* from 09.
*The Vicarage, 150 Huddersfield Road, Meltham, Holmfirth
HD9 4AL* Tel (01484) 850500
E-mail maureen.read09@btinternet.com

READ, Michael Antony. b 75. Lanc Univ BA99 St Jo Coll Dur
BA01. Cranmer Hall Dur 99. **d** 02 **p** 03. C Stanley *Liv* 02-05;
P-in-c Lowton St Luke 05-11; P-in-c Sudden and Heywood All
So *Man* from 11. *26 Heywood Hall Road, Heywood OL10 4UU*
Tel (01706) 360693 E-mail revmikeread@yahoo.co.uk

READ, Nicholas George. b 51. Chelsea Coll Lon BSc72 PhD81.
SEITE 97. **d** 00 **p** 01. NSM Beckenham St Jo *Roch* 00-03; P-in-c
Penge Lane H Trin 03-09; V from 09. *Holy Trinity Vicarage, 64
Lennard Road, London SE20 7LX* Tel (020) 8778 8113 Mobile
07904-317488 E-mail nicholas.read@diocese-rochester.org
or hancompro@aol.com

READ, Nicholas John. b 59. OBE99. Keble Coll Ox BA81 MSc82
MA85. Ox Min Course 92. **d** 95 **p** 96. NSM Charlbury w

Shorthampton Ox 95-98; Dir Rural Stress Information Network 96-00; Chapl for Agric Heref 98-11. The Rectory, Manley Crescent, Pembridge, Hereford HR6 9EB Tel (01544) 388998

READ, Canon Robert Edgar. b 47. Kelham Th Coll 66. d 70 p 71. C Harton Colliery Dur 70-75; C Wilmslow Ches 76-80; V Gatley 80-92; V Offerton 92-06; RD Stockport 00-05; V Newton 06-07; P-in-c Gatley 07-10; V from 10; Hon Can Ches Cathl from 03. 14 Elm Road, Gatley, Cheadle SK8 4LY Tel 0161-428 4764 E-mail reread@btinternet.com

READ, Victor. b 29. Lon Univ BD58. ALCD57. d 58 p 59. C Wimbledon S'wark 58-61; C Lt Marlow Ox 61-64; V Wootton Linc 64-67; R Croxton 64-67; V Ulceby 64-67; V Linc St Pet in Eastgate w St Marg 67-73; V W Wimbledon Ch Ch S'wark 73-94; rtd 94; Perm to Offic Pet from 94. 27 Nightingale Drive, Towcester NN12 6RA Tel (01327) 352027

✠**READE, The Rt Revd Nicholas Stewart.** b 46. Leeds Univ BA70. Coll of Resurr Mirfield 70. d 73 p 74 c 04. C Coseley St Chad Lich 73-75; C Codsall 75-78; V Upper Gornal 78-82; V Mayfield Chich 82-88; RD Dallington 82-88; V Eastbourne St Mary 88-97; RD Eastbourne 88-97; Can and Preb Chich Cathl 90-97; Can 97-04; Min The Hydneye CD 91-93; Adn Lewes and Hastings 97-04; Bp Blackb from 04. Bishop's House, Ribchester Road, Blackburn BB1 9EF Tel (01254) 248234 Fax 246668 E-mail bishop@bishopofblackburn.org.uk

READE, Richard Barton. b 53. Wolv Poly BA88. Ripon Coll Cuddesdon BA91 MA97. d 92 p 93. C Wilnecote Lich 92-96; C Penkridge 96-98; P-in-c Basford 98-04; P-in-c Matlock Bank Derby 04-11; V Matlock Bank and Tansley from 11. All Saints' Vicarage, Smedley Street, Matlock DE4 3JG Tel (01629) 584107 E-mail richardreade3@supanet.com

READER, Christine Sarah. b 44. STETS. d 00 p 01. NSM N Waltham and Steventon, Ashe and Deane Win from 00. 5 Church Farm Close, North Waltham, Basingstoke RG25 2BN Tel (01256) 397503

READER, John. b 53. Trin Coll Ox BA75 MA79 Man Univ MPhil91 Univ of Wales (Ban) PhD02. Ripon Coll Cuddesdon 76. d 78 p 79. C Ely 78-80; C Baguley Man 80-83; TV Kirkby Lonsdale Carl 83-86; V Lydbury N Heref 86-89; P-in-c Hopesay w Edgton 86-89; R Lydbury N w Hopesay and Edgton 89-90; Tutor Glouc Sch for Min 86-88; Vice-Prin 88-90; Dir Past Th Sarum & Wells Th Coll 90-92; P-in-c Elmley Lovett w Hampton Lovett and Elmbridge etc Worc 92-07; Assoc Tr and Educn Officer 92-02; Ind Chapl 01-07; P-in-c Chelford w Lower Withington and Dioc Rural Officer Ches 07-09; R Ironstone Ox from 09. The Rectory, Church Street, Wroxton, Banbury OX15 6QE Tel (01795) 730346 E-mail drjohnreader@hotmail.co.uk

READER, The Ven Trevor Alan John. b 46. Lon Univ BSc68 MSc70 Portsm Poly PhD72. S Dios Minl Tr Scheme 83. d 86 p 87. C Alverstoke Portsm 86-89; P-in-c Hook w Warsash 89-95; V 95-98; P-in-c Blendworth w Chalton w Idsworth 98-03; Dioc Dir NSM 98-04; Adn Is of Wight 03-06; Adn Portsdown from 06; Bp's Liaison Officer for Pris from 03. 5 Brading Avenue, Southsea PO4 9QJ Tel and fax (023) 9229 8788 or tel 9243 2693

READING, Glenn Thomas. b 76. Staffs Univ BSc98. Ripon Coll Cuddesdon 07. d 09 p 10. C Horninglow Lich from 09. 10 Field Rise, Burton-on-Trent DE13 0NR Tel 07964-282278 (mobile) E-mail glenn.reading@googlemail.com

READING, Mrs Lesley Jean. b 49. GNSM70 Trent Park Coll of Educn CertEd71. NOC 98. d 01 p 02. NSM Eccles Man 01-05; P-in-c Heywood St Jas 05-11; rtd 11. 21 Sunny Bower Street, Tottington, Bury BL8 3HL Tel (01204) 886108 E-mail readinglesley@hotmail.com

READING, Miss Siân Jacqueline Mary. b 64. Westcott Ho Cam 92. d 95 p 96. C Northampton St Alb Pet 95-98; TV Duston 98-05; P-in-c Gretton w Rockingham and Cottingham w E Carlton from 05. The Vicarage, Station Road, Gretton, Corby NN17 3BU Tel (01536) 770237 E-mail sjmr216@btinternet.com

READING, Area Bishop of. See PROUD, The Rt Revd Andrew John

REAGON, Darrol Franklin. b 46. St Mich Coll Llan 74. d 76 p 77. C Llandrillo-yn-Rhos St As 76-78; C Hawarden 78-81; V Northwich St Luke and H Trin Ches 81-85; V Moulton Linc 85-91; V Scunthorpe Resurr 91-92; P-in-c Branston 92-94; R Branston w Nocton and Potterhanworth 94-07; rtd 07. 17 Wessex Avenue, New Milton BH25 6NG Tel (01425) 613622 E-mail revddarrol@btinternet.com

REAKES, Richard Frank. b 68. STETS 02. d 05 p 06. NSM Shepton Mallet w Doulting B & W 05-09; NSM Evercreech w Chesterblade and Milton Clevedon from 09. Ashdene, Frome Road, Doulting, Shepton Mallet BA4 4QQ Tel (01749) 880086 Fax 880105 E-mail reakes4@aol.com

REAKES-WILLIAMS, Gordon Martin. b 63. St Cath Coll Cam BA86 MA89. St Jo Coll Dur BA90. d 91 p 92. C Oxford Wood Chelmsf 91-94; Chapl Leipzig Eur from 95. Hillerstrasse 3, 04109 Leipzig, Germany Tel (0049) (341) 302 7951 Fax 215 3666 Mobile 177-240 4207 E-mail earwig@t-online.de

REALE, Mrs Kathleen. b 38. Carl Dioc Tr Course 83. dss 86 d 8? p 94. Dalston Carl 86-87; Par Dn 87-90; Par Dn Westward Rosley-w-Woodside and Welton 87-90; Par Dn Thursby 89-90; Dn-in-c Gt Salkeld w Lazonby 90-94; P-in-c 94-97; rtd 97; Perm to Offic Carl from 98. 4 Low Moorlands, Carlisle CA5 7NX Te (01228) 711749

REANEY, Mrs Beverly Jane. b 58. Nottm Univ BA81. S Wales Ord Course 06. d 03 p 04. NSM Llanharry 03-11; NSM Llangynwyd w Maesteg from 11. 10 Upper Street, Maesteg CF34 9DU Tel (01656) 734142 E-mail beverly.j.reaney@rhondda-cynon-taf.gov.uk

REANEY, Christopher Thomas. b 60. Univ of Wales (Lamp) BA82. St Mich Coll Llan. d 85 p 86. C Maindee Newport Mor 85-87; C Griffithstown 88-89; V Treherbert w Treorchy Llan 89-99; V Treorchy and Treherbert 99-02; R Llanfabon 02-11; V Troedrhiwgarth from 11. 10 Upper Street, Maesteg CF34 9DU Tel (01656) 734142 E-mail chris.reaney@virgin.net

REAPER-BROWN, Graham Stanley. b 51. Sarum & Wells Th Coll 82. d 84 p 85. C Crediton and Shobrooke Ex 84-87; Chapl RAF 87-93 and 99-06; R Elgin w Lossiemouth Mor 93-98; R Castle Douglas Glas 98-99; Chapl Sherwood Forest Hosps NHS Trust 06-09; Chapl Univ Hosps Bris NHS Foundn Trust 09-11 rtd 11. 11 Severn Road, Shirehampton, Bristol BS11 9TE Tel 0117-3821 748 E-mail padregsbrown@aol.com

REARDON, Mrs Catherine Barbara. b 57. d 10 p 11. C Bradley Wakef from 10; C Fixby and Cowcliffe from 10. 10 The Dell Huddersfield HD2 2FD Tel (01484) 304457 E-mail cathyreardon@virginmedia.com

REAST, Eileen Joan. See BANGAY, Mrs Eileen Joan

REAVLEY, Cedric. b 51. Lon Univ BPharm73. d 05 p 06. OLM Burford w Fulbrook, Taynton, Asthall etc Ox from 05. 124 High Street, Burford OX18 4QR Tel (01993) 823957 Fax 824887 E-mail cedric reavley@lineone.net

RECORD, John. b 47. St Chad's Coll Dur BA71. Westcott Ho Cam 71. d 73 p 74. C Paddington St Jo w St Mich Lon 73-75; C Witney Ox 75-78; P-in-c Lt Compton and Chastleton 78-80; R Lt Compton w Chastleton, Cornwell etc 80-83; V Hawkhurst Cant 83-97; RD W Charing 89-95; Hon Can Cant Cathl 96-97 P-in-c Devizes St Jo w St Mary Sarum 97-07; P-in-c Devizes St Pet 00-04; RD Devizes 98-07; Can and Preb Sarum Cath 02-07; V Hammersmith St Pet Lon from 07. 17 Ravenscour Road, London W6 0UH Tel (020) 8748 1781 E-mail vicar@stpetersw6.org

RECORD, Sister Marion Eva. b 25. MRCS50 LRCP50 Leeds Univ FFARCS57 Lon Univ BD79. dss 78 d 87 p 94. OHP from 72; Chapl Hull Univ 72-78; Chapl York Univ 78-80; Lic to Offic 80-95; Perm to Offic from 95; rtd 96. St Hilda's Priory, Sneator Castle, Whitby YO21 3QN Tel (01947) 602079

REDDIN, Mrs Christine Emily. b 46. Essex Univ BA67. STETS 01. d 04 p 05. NSM Burpham Guildf 04-10; rtd 11. The Corner House, Sutton Green Road, Guildford GU4 7QD Tel (01483 714708 Mobile 07764-677898 E-mail c.reddin@sky.com

REDDING, Benjamin James. b 73. K Coll Lon BSc94 PGCE95 Oak Hill Th Coll BA05. d 05 p 06. C Angmering Chich from 05 7 Beech View, Angmering, Littlehampton BN16 4DE Tel (01903 784459 E-mail benjamesredding@yahoo.co.uk

REDDING, Roger Charles. b 45. Chich Th Coll 87. d 89 p 90. C Yeovil St Mich B & W 89-93; P-in-c Salisbury St Mark Sarun 93-94; Lic to Offic 94-96; TV Chalke Valley from 96; Chapl to Travelling People from 02. The Vicarage, May Lane, Ebbesbourne Wake, Salisbury SP5 5JL Tel (01722) 780408

REDDINGTON, Gerald Alfred. b 34. S'wark Ord Course 76. d 79 p 79. NSM St Vedast w St Mich-le-Querne etc Lon 79-85; Di Past Support Gp Scheme 83-86; Hon C St Marylebone All SS 85-90; V Ealing St Barn 90-99; rtd 99; Perm to Offic Portsm from 88 and Lon from 02. The Orange Tree, Madeira Road, Seaview PO34 5BA Tel (01983) 617026 E-mail rev.redd@btinternet.com

REDEYOFF, Neil Martyn. b 69. St Jo Coll Nottm BA01. d 0: p 02. C Grange St Andr and Runcorn H Trin Ches 01-04; R Darfield Sheff 04-08; P-in-c Finningley w Auckley 08-10; R from 10; AD W Doncaster from 11. The Rectory, Rectory Lane Finningley, Doncaster DN9 3DA Tel (01302) 770240 E-mail neilredeyoff1@btinternet.com

REDFEARN, James Jonathan. b 62. Newc Univ BA83 PGCE89 Cranmer Hall Dur 95. d 95 p 96. C Kidsgrove Lich 95-97 56 Holly Avenue, Jesmond, Newcastle upon Tyne NE2 2QA Te 0191-281 9046 E-mail jaredfearn@compuserve.com

REDFEARN, Michael. b 42. Open Univ BA78 Hull Univ MA84 BA86. St Aid Birkenhead 64. d 68 p 69. C Bury St Pet Mar 68-71; C Swinton St Pet 71-74; Ind Chapl Bris 74-79 and 80-81 Ind Chapl Australia 79-80; Ind Chapl York 83-96; V Southill and Course Dir St Alb Minl Tr Scheme 86-93; Dep Chapl HM Pri: Wandsworth 94; Chapl HM YOI and Rem Cen Feltham 94-97 Chapl HM YOI Aylesbury 97-02; rtd 02; Asst Chapl Palma de Mallorca Eur 04-10. Dju-Auve-Nous, North Street, Haselbury Plucknett, Crewkerne TA18 7RJ E-mail michaelredfearn18@hotmail.com

REDFEARN, Ms Tracy Anne. b 66. Heythrop Coll Lon BD88 Ripon Coll Cuddesdon 91. d 93 p 94. C Haslemere Guildf 93-97

TV Gt Grimsby St Mary and St Jas *Linc* 97-00; P-in-c Legbourne 00-01; P-in-c Raithby 00-01; P-in-c Wold-Marsh Gp 00-01; V Legbourne and Wold Marsh 01-05; C Brumby 05-08; rtd 08. *674 Firskill Crescent, Sheffield S4 7DR*
E-mail tracy.redfearn@btopenworld.com

⊕REDFERN, The Rt Revd Alastair Llewellyn John. b 48. Ch Ch Ox BA70 MA74 Trin Coll Cam BA74 MA79 Bris Univ PhD01. Westcott Ho Cam 72 Qu Coll Birm 75. **d** 76 **p** 77 **c** 97. C Tettenhall Regis *Lich* 76-79; Tutor Ripon Coll Cuddesdon 79-87; Hon C Cuddesdon *Ox* 83-87; Can Res Bris Cathl 87-97; Dioc Dir Tr 91-97; Suff Bp Grantham *Linc* 97-05; Dean Stamford 98-05; Can and Preb Linc Cathl 00-05; Bp Derby from 05. *The Bishop's House, 6 King Street, Duffield, Belper DE56 4EU* Tel (01332) 840132 Fax 842743 E-mail bishop@bishopofderby.org
REDFERN, Paul. b 48. Ulster Univ BA88. CITC BTh94. **d** 94 **p** 95. C Belfast St Aid *Conn* 94-97; I Belfast St Mark 97-03; I Kilbride from 03. *Kilbride Rectory, 7 Rectory Road, Doagh, Ballyclare BT39 0PT* Tel (028) 9334 0225
REDFIELD, David Peter. b 80. Anglia Ruskin Univ BA10. Ridley Hall Cam 07. **d** 10 **p** 11. C Grays Thurrock *Chelmsf* from 10. *11 Conrad Gardens, Grays RM16 2TN* Tel (01375) 460054
E-mail revdredfield@gmail.com
REDGERS, Brian. b 42. St Jo Coll Dur BA65 Keswick Hall Coll PGCE75. Westcott Ho Cam 65. **d** 67 **p** 68. C Rushmere *St E* 67-73; Lic to Offic from 73. *44 Belvedere Road, Ipswich IP4 4AB* Tel (01473) 273829
REDGRAVE, Christine Howick. b 50. AIAT73. Trin Coll Bris 75. **dss** 78 **d** 87 **p** 94. Watford *St Alb* 78-83; Maidenhead St Andr and St Mary *Ox* 83-85; Bracknell 85-96; Par Dn 87-94; TV 94-96, P-in-c Woollhampton w Midgham and Beenham Valance 96-04; Asst Dir of Ords 95-04; Dir of Ords (Reading and Dorchester) 04-10; Hon Can Ch Ch 00-10; C Yoxmere *St E* from 10. *1 Oakwood Park, Yoxford, Saxmundham IP17 3JU* Tel and fax (01728) 667095 E-mail credgrave7@gmail.com
REDHOUSE, Edward. b 30. St Deiniol's Hawarden 60. **d** 63 **p** 64. C Mottram in Longdendale w Woodhead *Ches* 63-67; V Rivington *Man* 67-72; V Bloxwich *Lich* 72-75; Hon C Lich St Chad 82-84; P-in-c Bromfield w Waverton *Carl* 84-85; V 85-90; P-in-c W Newton 84-85; V 85-90; R Harrington 90-93; rtd 93. *Tigh-na-Mara, 2-3 Caroy, Struan, Isle of Skye IV56 8FQ* Tel (01470) 572338
REDHOUSE, Mark David. b 67. Oak Hill Th Coll BA94. **d** 94 **p** 95. C Fulham St Mary N End *Lon* 94-96; C Hove Bp Hannington Memorial Ch *Chich* 96-01; V Horam 01-10; RD Dallington 04-07; V Eastbourne All So from 10. *All Souls Vicarage, 53 Susans Road, Eastbourne BN21 3TH* Tel (01323) 727033 E-mail markredhouse@aol.com
REDKNAP, Clive Douglas. b 53. Trin Coll Bris BA95. **d** 95 **p** 96. C Patcham *Chich* 95-00; C Wadhurst and Stonegate 00-03; P-in-c Hollington St Jo 03-05; V 05-10. *Address temp unknown*
REDMAN, Anthony James. b 51. Reading Univ BSc72 Anglia Ruskin Univ MA05 FRICS95. EAMTC 01. **d** 03 **p** 04. NSM Bury St Edmunds All SS w St Jo and St Geo *St E* 03-06; NSM Blackbourne from 06. *The Cottage, Great Livermere, Bury St Edmunds IP31 1JG* Tel (01359) 269335 Fax (01284) 704734
E-mail tony@theredmans.co.uk
REDMAN, Canon Arthur Thomas. b 28. Dur Univ BA52 PGCE. Ridley Hall Cam 62. **d** 63 **p** 64. C Heaton St Barn *Bradf* 63-66; C Hitchin St Mary *St Alb* 66-70; P Missr 72-75; Hd RE Stopsley High Sch Luton 66-70; Hd Humanities and Modern Studies Hewett Sch Nor 70-72; Perm to Offic *Nor* 70-72; V Swanwick and Pentrich *Derby* 75-80; Warden of Readers 78-97; Dir Bp's Cert 78-88; V Allestree 80-96; P-in-c Morley 82-85; Hon Can Derby Cathl 86-96; RD Duffield 88-96; rtd 96; Hon C Bretby w Newton Solney *Derby* 96-97; Chapl and Development Officer Children in Distress 97-01; Dir St Barn Project Romania from 01. *9 Ludgate Walk, Mackworth, Derby DE22 4HQ* Tel (01332) 521733 Fax 551569
REDMAN, Canon Douglas Stuart Raymond. b 35. MCIOB64. Roch Th Coll 66. **d** 68 **p** 69. C Shortlands *Roch* 68-71; V 80-00; R Kingsdown 71-76; R Chatham St Mary w St Jo 76-80; RD Beckenham 90-00; Hon Can Roch Cathl 93-00; rtd 00; Perm to Offic *Cant* from 01. *25 Hovendens, Sissinghurst, Cranbrook TN17 2LA* Tel and fax (01580) 714600
REDMAN, Julia Elizabeth Hithersay. See WHITE, Mrs Julia Elizabeth Hithersay
REDMAN, Michael John. b 52. St Jo Coll Ox BA74 Solicitor 86. NTMTC 04. **d** 06 **p** 07. NSM St Marylebone St Paul *Lon* from 06. *8 Brynaston Mews West, London W1H 2DD* Tel (020) 7723 7407
REDPARTH, Paul Robert. b 58. Open Univ BSc97 K Coll Lon PhD01. Westcott Ho Cam 04. **d** 06 **p** 07. C Roughey *Chich* 06-09; C Forest Row 09-11; P-in-c Kirdford from 11. *The Vicarage, Kirdford, Billingshurst RH14 0LU* Tel (01403) 820601
REDSELL, Corin Michael. b 69. Homerton Coll Cam BEd92. Ridley Hall Cam 09. **d** 11. C Lordsbridge *Ely* from 11. *St Peter's Parsonage, 70 High Street, Coton, Cambridge CB23 7PL*
REDSHAW, Mrs Alison Janet. EMMTC. **d** 10 **p** 11. NSM Crich and S Wingfield *Derby* from 10. *7 Chapel Close, Blackwell,*

Alfreton DE55 5BL Tel (01773) 819673 Mobile 07522-265336 E-mail rev-alison-r@hotmail.co.uk
REDWOOD, Canon David Leigh. b 32. Glas Univ DipSW78. Edin Th Coll 57. **d** 59 **p** 60. C Stirling *Edin* 59-61; C Glas Ch Ch 61-64; P-in-c Glas Ascension 64-66; R 66-69; R Hamilton 69-74; R Callander *St And* 74-76; Hon C 76-78; R Lochearnhead 74-76; R Killin 74-76; Hon C Doune 76-78; Hon C Aberfoyle 78-85; R Dunfermline 85-97; TR W Fife Team Min 85-97; Can St Ninian's Cathl Perth 90-97; Syn Clerk 93-97; rtd 97. *8 Strathmore Avenue, Dunblane FK15 9HX* Tel and fax (01786) 825493 E-mail david.redwood1@btinternet.com
REDWOOD, Marion. b 47. **d** 00 **p** 09. NSM Abercarn and Cwmcarn *Mon* from 00. *30 John Street, Cwmcarn, Crosskeys, Newport NP11 7EH* Tel (01495) 271910
REECE, Donald Malcolm Hayden. b 36. CCC Cam BA58 MA62. Cuddesdon Coll 58. **d** 60 **p** 61. C Latchford St Jas *Ches* 60-63; C Matlock and Tansley *Derby* 63-67; C-in-c Hackenthorpe Ch Ch CD 67-70; C Salisbury Cathl Rhodesia 70-73; V Leic St Pet 74-82; V Putney St Marg *S'wark* 82-91; Home Sec Coun for Chr Unity 92-97; Hon C Wandsworth St Anne 94-97; V Shepherd's Bush St Steph w St Thos *Lon* 97-04; rtd 04; Perm to Offic *Ox* from 05. *8 Lamarsh Road, Oxford OX2 0LD* Tel (01865) 792678
REECE, Paul Michael. b 60. Southn Univ BA81. Coll of Resurr Mirfield 83. **d** 85 **p** 86. C Borehamwood *St Alb* 85-89; C Potters Bar 89-92; R Lt Stanmore St Lawr *Lon* from 92; AD Harrow 97-02; Chapl R Nat Orthopaedic Hosp NHS Trust from 92. *Whitchurch Rectory, St Lawrence Close, Edgware HA8 6RB* Tel (020) 8952 0019 Fax 8537 0547 Mobile 07860-690503
E-mail paul.reece@london.anglican.org
REECE, Roger Walton Arden. b 56. **d** 00 **p** 01. OLM Chadderton St Luke *Man* 00-04; OLM Chadderton St Matt w St Luke 04-08; NSM 08-09; C Ashton from 09; Chapl HM Pris Buckley Hall from 08. *HM Prison Buckley Hall, Buckley Hall Road, Rochdale OL12 9DP* Tel (01706) 514300 Mobile 07904-078901
E-mail roger.reece@ntlworld.com
REED, Adam Michael Frederick. b 73. Humberside Univ BA95. Cranmer Hall Dur 96. **d** 99 **p** 00. C Northallerton w Kirby Sigston *York* 99-03; R Middleton, Newton and Sinnington 03-11; V Saltburn-by-the-Sea from 11. *The Vicarage, Greta Street, Saltburn-by-the-Sea TS12 1LS*
E-mail bilpot@btinternet.com
REED, Alan Ronald. b 44. Sarum Th Coll 66. **d** 68 **p** 70. C Ifield *Chich* 68-71; C Perivale *Lon* 71-72; C Ruislip St Martin 72-75; C Burgess Hill St Jo *Chich* 76-78; V Shoreham Beach 78-80; V Roughey 80-97; P-in-c Rusper 84-97; V Hove St Barn and St Agnes 97-10; rtd 10; Perm to Offic *Nor* from 10. *Candlemass Lodge, 12 Clarendon Road, Fakenham NR21 9HG* Tel (01328) 855919
REED, Ms Annette Susan. b 54. Birm Univ BA76 CQSW78. Qu Coll Birm 84. **d** 87 **p** 94. C Churchover w Willey *Cov* 89-92; C Clifton upon Dunsmore and Newton 89-92; C Walsgrave on Sowe 92-95; C Cov E 92-95; C Burbage w Aston Flamville *Leic* 95-98; C Hinckley St Mary 95-98; C The Sheepy Gp 98-00; TV Bosworth and Sheepy Gp 00-06; V The Paxtons w Diddington *Ely* from 06; RD St Neots from 07. *The Vicarage, 24 St James's Road, Little Paxton, St Neots PE19 6QW* Tel (01480) 211048
E-mail rev.reed@btinternet.com
REED, Brian. b 43. Bris Univ BSc65. Linc Th Coll 73. **d** 76 **p** 77. C S Ashford Ch Ch *Cant* 76-78; C Spring Park 78-83; V Barming Heath from 83. *St Andrew's Vicarage, 416 Tonbridge Road, Maidstone ME16 9LW* Tel (01622) 726245 Mobile 07759-620502
REED, Christopher John. b 42. Selw Coll Cam BA64 MA68. Cranmer Hall Dur 64. **d** 67 **p** 68. C Gt Ilford St Andr *Chelmsf* 67-70; P-in-c Bordesley St Andr *Birm* 70-72; V 72-80; V Crofton St Paul *Roch* 80-98; V Yalding w Collier Street 98-08; RD Paddock Wood 01-06; rtd 08; Perm to Offic *Roch* from 09. *66 Willow Park, Otford, Sevenoaks TN14 5NG* Tel (01959) 523439 E-mail chris.reed@diocese-rochester.org
REED, Colin. See REED, Matthew Colin
REED, Colin Bryher. b 58. York Univ BA80 RGN86. Ridley Hall Cam 93. **d** 95 **p** 96. C Grays North *Chelmsf* 95-99; Chapl Plymouth Hosps NHS Trust 99-02; Hd Chapl Services Norfolk and Nor Univ Hosp NHS Trust 02-09; Asst RD Ingworth *Nor* 10-11; TR High Oak, Hingham and Scoulton w Wood Rising from 11. *The Rectory, Attleborough Road, Hingham, Norwich NR9 4HP* Tel 07773-360262 (mobile)
E-mail revcolinreed@computekmail.co.uk
REED, Colin Charles Gilmour. b 40. LCP75 FCP86 St Luke's Coll Ex TCert63 La Trobe Univ Vic MA94 ACT ThD06. Tyndale Hall Bris 67. **d** 69 **p** 70. C Weston-super-Mare Ch Ch *B & W* 69-71; Asst Master St Andr Sch Turi Kenya 71-79; Chapl Brighton Coll Jun Sch 79-80; Australia 80-99 and from 06; R Corrimal 80-84; Educn Sec CMS 84-99; Lect Amani Inst Tanzania 99-06; rtd 06. *7 Camden Street, Wingello NSW 2579, Australia* (Tel) (2) 4884 4551
E-mail wendyreed2@hotmail.com *or* cwreed@cms.org.au
REED, David. See REED, Richard David

REED, Mrs Elizabeth Christine. b 43. Lon Bible Coll Lon Univ BD65. WMMTC 95. d 97 p 98. NSM Ledbury *Heref* from 97; Chapl Bromsgrove Sch 99-06. *The Old Barn, Perrystone Hill, Ross-on-Wye HR9 7QX* Tel (01989) 780439

REED, Ethel Patricia Ivy. *See* WESTBROOK, Mrs Ethel Patricia Ivy

REED, Geoffrey **Martin**. b 51. Univ of Wales (Cardiff) BA73 Open Univ PGCE98. Oak Hill Th Coll 73. d 76 p 77. C Swansea St Nic *S & B* 76-78; C Sketty 78-84; V Glasbury and Llowes 84-86; V Glasbury and Llowes w Clyro and Betws 86-01; R Teme Valley S *Worc* 01-04. *2 Lyons Lodge, Colesbourne Road, Withington, Cheltenham GL54 4BH* Tel (01242) 890134 Mobile 07977-229103 E-mail martin.reed@reedboats.co.uk

REED, Mrs Gillian **Yvonne**. b 44. CBDTI 04. d 07 p 10. NSM Blackb St Thos w St Jude 07-09; NSM Blackb St Mich w St Jo and H Trin 07-09; NSM Ospringe Deanery 09-10; NSM Faversham *Cant* from 10. *18 Four Horseshoes Park, Seasalter Road, Graveney, Faversham ME13 9DE* Tel (01795) 534059 E-mail gill.pete@talktalk.net

REED, Harvey. *See* REED, William Harvey

REED, The Ven John **Peter Cyril**. b 51. BD78 AKC78. Ripon Coll Cuddesdon 78. d 79 p 80. C Croydon St Jo *Cant* 79-82; Prec St Alb Abbey 82-86; R Timsbury and Priston *B & W* 86-93; Chapl Rural Affairs Bath Adnry 87-93; P-in-c Ilminster w Whitelackington 93-94; TR Ilminster and Distr 94-99; Adn Taunton from 99. *2 Monkton Heights, West Monkton, Taunton TA2 8LU* Tel (01823) 413315 Fax 413384 E-mail adtaunton@bathwells.anglican.org

REED, John **William**. b 57. Sussex Univ BSc79. NOC 95. d 97 p 98. C Padgate *Liv* 97-99; C Orford St Marg 99-01; V 01-08; P-in-c Golborne from 08. *St Thomas's Rectory, Church Street, Golborne, Warrington WA3 3TH* Tel (01942) 728305 E-mail john.reed@liverpool.anglican.org

REED (*née* McCARTHY), Mrs Lorraine **Valmay**. b 52. Birm Univ CertEd73 Univ of Wales (Ban) BA95 MTh97 LGSM82. SNWTP 09. d 11. NSM Middlewich w Byley *Ches* from 11. *1 Douglas Close, Hartford, Northwich CW8 1SH* Tel (01606) 781071 Mobile 07711-379339 E-mail reed.blackbird77@tiscali.co.uk

REED, Malcolm **Edward**. Graduate Soc Dur MSc75. Yorks Min Course 08. d 10 p 11. NSM Hoylandswaine and Silkstone w Stainborough *Wakef* from 10. *Clough Cottage, Cathill, Hoylandswaine, Sheffield S36 7JB* Tel (01226) 767328 Mobile 07803-031199 E-mail cathillreed@btinternet.com

REED, Matthew **Colin**. b 50. Edin Univ BD82. Edin Th Coll 72. d 84 p 85. C Edin St Pet 84-87; P-in-c Linlithgow 87-94; P-in-c Bathgate 87-91; Chapl HM Pris Polmont 91-94; R Motherwell *Glas* 94-97; R Wishaw 94-97; Hon Asst P Edin St Fillan from 00; Chapl HM Pris Edin from 02. *HM Prison Edinburgh, 33 Stenhouse Road, Edinburgh EH11 3LN* Tel 0131-444 3115 E-mail colin.reed@sps.gov.uk

REED, Matthew **Graham**. b 68. Nottm Univ BEng89 Roehampton Inst MSc03. Ripon Coll Cuddesdon BA92 MA97. d 93 p 94. C Oxton *Ches* 93-97; TV Gt Marlow w Marlow Bottom, Lt Marlow and Bisham *Ox* 97-02; Hd Lon and SE Team Chr Aid 02-04; C and Community Dir 04-08; Marketing Dir 08-10; Chief Exec Officer Cystic Fibrosis Trust from 10. *11 London Road, Bromley BR1 1BY* Tel (020) 8464 7211 E-mail mreed@cftrust.org.uk

REED, Canon Pamela **Kathleen**. b 38. EMMTC. dss 84 d 87 p 94. Cambridge Ascension *Ely* 84-88; Par Dn 87-88; Par Dn Cherry Hinton St Andr 88-90; C 91-95; C Teversham 91-95; V Chesterton St Geo 95-04; Hon Can Ely Cathl 00-04; rtd 04; Perm to Offic *Ely* from 04. *17 Woodland Road, Sawston, Cambridge CB22 3DT* Tel (01223) 832571 E-mail pamk.reed@hotmail.com

REED, Richard **David**. b 32. K Alfred's Coll Win CertEd54 Ex Univ MA02. Trin Coll Carmarthen. d 91 p 92. NSM Dale and St Brides w Marloes *St D* 91-96; P-in-c Blisland w St Breward Truro 96-99; rtd 99; Perm to Offic Truro from 99 and St D from 02. *5 Smokehouse Quay, Milford Haven SA73 3BD* Tel (01646) 663819 E-mail davidreed456@btinternet.com

REED, Canon Robert **Chase**. b 47. Emerson Coll Boston (USA) BSc70 TCD HDipEd72. d 87 p 88. Aux Min Taney *D & G* 87-97; Res Hd Master Wesley Coll Dub from 87; Succ St Patr Cathl Dublin 93-97; Treas 96-01; Prec from 01. *Embury House, Wesley College, Dublin 16, Republic of Ireland* Tel and fax (00353) (1) 296 8010 *or* 299 1140 E-mail canrcr@gmail.com

REED, Simon **John**. b 63. Trin Coll Ox BA86 MA90. Wycliffe Hall Ox BA90. d 91 p 92. C Walton H Trin *Ox* 91-96; P-in-c Hanger Hill Ascension and W Twyford St Mary *Lon* 96-01; V from 01. *The Ascension Vicarage, Beaufort Road, London W5 3EB* Tel and fax (020) 8566 9920 E-mail coa@surfaid.org

REED, William **Harvey**. b 47. K Coll Lon BD69 AKC69. St Aug Coll Cant 69. d 70 p 71. C Stockton St Mark CD *Dur* 70-72; C Billingham St Cuth 72-76; C S Westoe 76-79; V Chilton Moor 79-87; R Hutton *Chelmsf* 87-95; V Hullbridge 95-10; C Rawreth w Rettendon 06-10; V Rettendon and Hullbridge from 10. *The*

Vicarage, 93 Ferry Road, Hullbridge, Hockley SS5 6EL* Tel (01702) 232017 E-mail revharveyreed@whsmithnet.co.uk

REEDER, Angela **Lilian**. d 99 p 00. OLM Eastington, Frocester, Haresfield etc *Glouc* 99-04; Perm to Offic from 04. *St Loy Cottage, West End, Stonehouse GL10 3SL* Tel (01453) 827446

REEDER, Michael **William Peter**. b 58. Wilson Carlile Coll 84. d 09 p 10. Chapl St Luke's Hospice Sheff from 07; Hon C Sheff Cathl from 09. *St Luke's Hospice, Little Common Lane, Sheffield S11 9NE* Tel 0114-236 9911 Mobile 07947-706256 E-mail m.reeder@hospicesheffield.co.uk

REES (*née* HOLDER), Ms Adèle **Claire**. b 76. Luton Univ BSc97 Sheff Univ MTh03. Ripon Coll Cuddesdon 04. d 07 p 08. C Hill *Birm* 07-10; C Hatcham St Jas *S'wark* from 10; Chapl Goldsmiths' Coll Lon from 10. *3 St Michael's Centre, Desmond Street, London SE14 6JF* Tel (020) 8691 4335 Mobile 07841-640974 E-mail adelerees@yahoo.co.uk

REES, Andrew **Richard Akeroyd**. b 76. Sydney Univ BEc. Moore Th Coll Sydney BD. d 04. C Kellyville Australia 04-06; C Fulwood *Sheff* from 07. *1 Silver Birch Avenue, Sheffield S10 3TA* Tel 0114-230 1588 *or* 229 5567 E-mail andrew@fulwoodchurch.co.uk

REES, Anthony **John**. b 49. St Jo Coll Dur BA72 MA77 Man Univ MEd89 MPhil07. d 74 p 75. C Smethwick St Matt w St Chad *Birm* 74-77; C Bolton St Pet *Man* 77-80; R Cheetham St Mark 80-88; V Mottram in Longdendale w Woodhead *Ches* 88-93; V Mottram in Longdendale 93-02; V Chirk *St As* from 02. *The Vicarage, Trevor Road, Chirk, Wrexham LL14 5HD* Tel (01691) 778519

REES, **Antony**. *See* REES, Percival Antony Everard

REES, Canon **Brian**. b 48. McGill Univ Montreal BA74 St Andr Univ BD76 PhD80. Montreal Dioc Th Coll 76. d 80 p 81. Canada 80-85; C Montreal St Jas and Chapl Concordia Univ 80-82; R Rawdon Ch Ch 82-85; Chapl Bedford Sch 85-92; Hd Master Bedford Prep Sch 92-97; Hd Master Pilgrims' Sch from 97; Hon Can Win Cathl from 11. *The Pilgrims' School, 3 The Close, Winchester SO23 9LT* Tel (01962) 854189 E-mail hmsecretary@pilgrims-school.co.uk

REES, **Ceirion James**. b 80. Glam Univ BA01 Trin Coll Bris BA10. St Mich Coll Llan 10. d 10 p 11. C Coity, Nolton and Brackla *Llan* from 10. *2 Fenwick Drive, Brackla, Bridgend CF31 2LD* E-mail cei@cnb-parish.org.uk

REES, **Celia Pamela**. b 48. St D Coll Lamp BA70. d 98 p 99. OLM Leominster *Heref* from 98. *Rivendell, 50 Oldfields Close, Leominster HR6 8TL* Tel (01568) 616581 *or* 612124

REES, Mrs **Christine Deryn Irving**. b 57. Nottm Univ BSc Sheff Univ MA. Qu Coll Birm. d 00 p 01. NSM Astwood Bank *Worc* 00-01; C 01-03; TV Dronfield w Holmesfield *Derby* from 03. *43 Firthwood Road, Dronfield S18 3BW* Tel (01246) 411251 *or* 413893 E-mail christine.rees@dwhparish.org.uk

REES, **Christopher John**. b 40. Dur Univ BA62. Ridley Hall Cam 62. d 64 p 65. C Wilmslow *Ches* 64-70; C Birkenhead St Pet w St Matt 70-75; V Lostock Gralam 75-83; R Davenham 83-96; P-in-c Aldford and Bruera 96-05; rtd 05; Perm to Offic *Ches* from 05. *15 Chapel Close, Comberbach, Northwich CW9 6BA* Tel (01606) 891366 E-mail cjrees@surfaid.org

REES, Canon **David Frederick**. b 21. SS Coll Cam BA48 MA52. Sarum Th Coll 48. d 50 p 51. C Blackb St Luke 50-53; C St Annes St Thos 53-55; V Choral York Minster 55-62; V Penwortham St Mary *Blackb* 62-90; RD Leyland 70-84; Hon Can Blackb Cathl 79-90; rtd 90; Perm to Offic *Blackb* from 91. *24 Fosbrooke House, 8 Clifton Drive, Lytham St Annes FY8 5RQ* Tel (01253) 667024

REES, **David Grenfell**. b 18. St D Coll Lamp BA40 Qu Coll Birm 42. d 43 p 44. C Llangeinor 43-47; C Cadoxton-juxta-Barry 47-53; C St Andrews Major 53-60; V Dyffryn 60-84; rtd 84; Perm to Offic *Llan* from 84. *10 Tyn-yr-Heol Road, Bryncoch, Neath SA10 7EA* Tel (01639) 644488

REES, Canon **David Philip Dunn Hugh**. b 38. Jes Coll Ox BA60 MA64 Ox Univ DipEd67. Westcott Ho Cam 62. d 64 p 65. C Salford St Phil w St Steph *Man* 64-66; Perm to Offic *St A* 66-67 and *Derby* 67-74; Chapl St Marg C of E High Sch Aigburth Liv 74-83; V Meliden and Gwaenysgor *St As* 84-08; Dioc Adv for Schs 85-91; Warden of Readers 89-91; Dioc Dir of Ords 91-00; Hon Can St As Cathl 93-95; Can Cursal 95-08; Chan 96-08; rtd 08. *Y Cae Gwyn, Ffordd Teilia, Gwaenysgor, Rhyl LL18 6EQ* Tel (01745) 889927

REES, **David Richard**. b 60. St Mich Coll Llan. d 84 p 85. C Llanstadwel *St D* 84-86; C Carmarthen St Dav 86-91; V Llanrhian w Llanhywel and Carnhedryn etc 91-99; V Spittal w Trefgarn and Ambleston w St Dogwells from 99. *The Vicarage, Spittal, Haverfordwest SA62 5QP* Tel (01437) 741505

REES, Ms **Diane Eluned**. b 61. Univ of Wales (Ban) BSc82 Em Coll Cam PGCE83 Univ of Wales (Swansea) MEd87 CPsychol AFBPsS. St Jo Coll Nottm BTh95 MA96. d 96 p 97. C Hall Green St Pet *Birm* 96-00; P-in-c Bozeat w Easton Maudit *Pet* 00-03; C Putney St Mary *S'wark* 03-04; TV 04-05; Asst Dir of Min and Tr *Roch* 06-09; Perm to Offic from 09. *59 Hayes Wood Avenue, Bromley BR2 7BG* E-mail dereeswdt@aol.com

REES, Miss Emma Louise. b 79. Univ of Wales (Abth) BTh01. St Mich Coll Llan MTh11. **d** 11. C Barry All SS *Llan* from 11. *4 Alwen Drive, Barry CF52 7LH* Tel (01446) 401792 E-mail reverendemma@gmail.com

REES, Glyn. b 63. St Bede's Coll Umtata 85. **d** 87 **p** 87. C Turffontein S Africa 87-88; Chapl S African Defence Force 89-90; P-in-c Nigel 91-92; C Kempton Park and Edenvale 92-93; TR Secunda 94-98; R Brakpan 99-00; R Whitwell *Derby* 00-05; R Wodonga Australia from 05. *225 Beechworth Road, Wodonga Vic 3690, Australia* Tel (0061) (2) 6056 5795 *or* tel and fax 6024 2053

REES, Grenfell. See REES, David Grenfell

REES, Mrs Helen. b 78. Univ of Wales (Cardiff) BD99 MTh10. St Mich Coll Llan 07. **d** 09 **p** 10. NSM Penarth All SS *Llan* 09-10; NSM Llandrindod w Cefnllys and Disserth *S & B* from 10. *The Rectory, Broadway, Llandrindod Wells LD1 5HT* Tel (01597) 822739 E-mail helenv.rees@virgin.net

REES, Ian Kendall. b 66. St Mich Coll Llan 98. **d** 00 **p** 01. C Barry All SS *Llan* 00-03; Assoc P Grangetown 03-05; P-in-c Pyle w Kenfig 05-10; R Llandrindod w Cefnllys and Disserth *S & B* from 10. *The Rectory, Broadway, Llandrindod Wells LD1 5HT* Tel (01597) 822739 E-mail ianrees66@gmail.com

REES, Ivor. See REES, The Rt Revd John Ivor

REES, Jennifer Mary. See MORRELL, Mrs Jennifer Mary

REES, Joanna Mary. See STOKER, Canon Joanna Mary

REES, John. See REES, Canon Vivian John Howard

REES, The Rt Revd John Ivor. b 26. Univ of Wales (Abth) BA50. Westcott Ho Cam 50. **d** 52 **p** 53 **c** 88. C Fishguard w *Llanvchar St D* 52-55; C Llangathen w Llanfihangel Cilfargen 55-57; P-in-c Uzmaston and Boulston 57-59; V Slebech and Uzmaston w Boulston 59-65; V Llangollen and Trevor *St As* 65-74; RD Llangollen 70-74; TR Wrexham 74-76; Can St As Cathl 75-76; Dean Ban 76-88; V Ban Cathl 79-88; Asst Bp St D 88-91; Adn St D 88-91; Bp St D 91-95; rtd 95; Hon Fell Univ of Wales (Trin St Dav) from 96. *Llys Dewi, 45 Clover Park, Haverfordwest SA61 1UE* Tel (01437) 764846

REES, John Martin Rawlins Gore. b 30. St D Coll Lamp BA53. **d** 55 **p** 57. C Mold *St As* 55-56; C Broughton 56-59; C Newtown 59-61; V Penycae 61-73; V Northop 73-83; V Bickerton w Bickley *Ches* 83-91; Lic to Offic 91-95; rtd 95. *Hafod, 9 High Park, Gwernaffield, Mold CH7 5EE* Tel (01352) 740412

REES, John Nigel. b 58. Derby Lonsdale Coll BCombStuds79 Coll of Ripon & York St Jo PGCE80. STETS 03. **d** 06 **p** 07. NSM Broad Blunsdon and Highworth w Sevenhampton and Inglesham etc *Bris* 06-10; P-in-c Rowde and Bromham *Sarum* from 10. *The Rectory, High Street, Bromham, Chippenham SN15 2HA* Tel (01380) 859646 Mobile 07912-503267 E-mail reesfam@btinternet.com

REES, Canon John Philip Walford. b 41. St D Coll Lamp BA62 Linacre Coll Ox BA64 MA69 Univ of Wales (Cardiff) BD72. Wycliffe Hall Ox 62. **d** 64 **p** 65. C Reading St Jo *Ox* 64-67; V Patrick *S & M* 67-68; C Pontypool *Mon* 68-70; Area Sec CMS *Glouc, Heref* and *Worc* 70-75; V Bream *Glouc* 75-91; Team Ldr Ichthus Chr Fellowship 91-96; TV Glyncorrwg w Afan Vale and Cymmer Afan *Llan* 96-99; R Llandogo and Tintern *Mon* 99-00; R Llandogo w Whitebrook Chpl and Tintern Parva 00-07; AD Monmouth 02-06; Hon Can St Woolos Cathl 01-07; rtd 07. *Sparrow Cottage, The Narth, Monmouth NP25 4QG* Tel (01600) 869194

REES, Canon Judith Margaret. b 39. Southn Univ BTh89. **dss** 86 **d** 87 **p** 94. Sanderstead All SS *S'wark* 86-87; Par Dn 87; Dir Cottesloe Chr Tr Progr *Ox* 89-99; Par Dn Gt Horwood 89-91; Par Dn Winslow w Gt Horwood and Addington 91-94; C 94-99; RD Claydon 96-99; Hon Can Ch 97-99; rtd 99; Perm to Offic *Sarum* from 01. *Sidney Cottage, 111 Lower Road, Salisbury SP2 9NH* Tel (01722) 410050

REES, Leslie. b 49. Leeds Univ LLB72. NOC 03. **d** 06 **p** 07. NSM Swinton H Rood *Man* 06-08; NSM Eccles 08-09; NSM Hanbury, Newborough, Rangemore and Tutbury *Lich* from 09. *The New Vicarage, Church Lane, Hanbury, Burton-on-Trent DE13 8TF* Tel (01283) 813357 E-mail leslie.rees@virgin.net

REES, The Rt Revd Leslie Lloyd. b 19. Kelham Th Coll 36. **d** 42 **p** 43 **c** 80. C Roath St Sav *Llan* 42-45; Asst Chapl HM Pris Cardiff 42-45; Chapl HM Pris Dur 45-48; V Princetown *Ex* 48-55; Chapl HM Pris Dartmoor 48-55; Chapl HM Pris Win 55-62; Chapl Gen of Pris 62-80; Hon Can Cant Cathl 66-80; Chapl to The Queen 71-80; Suff Bp Shrewsbury *Lich* 80-87; rtd 86; Hon Asst Bp Win from 87. *c/o G H Rees Esq, 31 Collin Road, Kendal LA9 5LH*

REES, Matthew Haydn Brinley. b 69. Wycliffe Hall Ox. **d** 03 **p** 04. C Ox St Aldate 03-06; C Ox St Clem 06-08; Lic to Offic 08-10; NSM Cowley St Jo from 10. *58 Magdalen Road, Oxford OX4 1RB* Tel 07811-149305 (mobile) E-mail matt@home-online.org

REES, Michael. See REES, Canon Richard Michael

REES, Canon Michael Lloyd. b 51. St D Coll Lamp. **d** 74 **p** 75. C Cardigan w Mwnt and Y Ferwig *St D* 74-77; Min Can St D Cathl 77-81; TV Aberystwyth 81-83; Dioc Children's Adv 83-92;

V Pen-boyr 83-88; V Henfynyw w Aberaeron and Llanddewi Aberarth 88-99; RD Glyn Aeron 95-99; V Gors-las from 99; AD Dyffryn Aman from 07; Hon Can St D Cathl from 09. *The Vicarage, 56 Black Lion Road, Cross Hands, Llanelli SA14 6RU* Tel (01269) 842561

REES (née CURREY), Mrs Pauline Carol. b 46. WMMTC 94. **d** 98 **p** 99. OLM Leominster *Heref* from 98. *Crossways Cottage, Leysters, Leominster HR6 0HR* Tel (01568) 750300 *or* 612124 E-mail rees.crossways@btinternet.com

REES, Percival Antony Everard. b 35. Pemb Coll Ox BA56 MA59. Clifton Th Coll 58. **d** 60 **p** 61. C Heatherlands St Jo *Sarum* 60-65 and 69-70; India 65-69; V W Hampstead St Luke *Lon* 70-82; Lect Oak Hill Th Coll 82-86; V Enfield Ch Ch Trent Park *Lon* 87-00; rtd 00; Perm to Offic *Chelmsf* from 00. *10 Winchester Road, Frinton-on-Sea CO13 9JB* Tel (01255) 852464

REES, Philip. See REES, Canon John Philip Walford

REES, Canon Richard John Edward Williams. b 36. Univ of Wales (Lamp) BA58. St Mich Coll Llan 58. **d** 60 **p** 61. C St Issells *St D* 60-64; C Llanedy 64-67; V Whitchurch w Solva and St Elvis 67-77; V Whitchurch w Solva and St Elvis w Brawdy etc 77-01; RD Dewisland and Fishguard 73-01; Can St D Cathl 87-01; Treas Cathl 97-01. *The Smithy, Cheriton, Stackpole, Pembroke SA71 5BZ* Tel (01646) 672235

REES, Canon Richard Michael. b 35. St Pet Hall Ox BA57 MA61. Tyndale Hall Bris 57. **d** 59 **p** 60. C Crowborough *Chich* 59-62; C Clifton Ch Ch w Em *Bris* 62-64; V Clevedon Ch Ch *B & W* 64-72; V Cambridge H Trin *Ely* 72-84; Chief Sec CA 84-90; Can Res Ches Cathl 90-00; Vice-Dean 93-00; Dioc Missr 90-00; Cheshire Co Ecum Officer 91-99; rtd 00; Perm to Offic *Nor* from 01. *65 Tennyson Avenue, King's Lynn PE30 2QJ* Tel (01553) 691982

REES, Ronald Benjamin Dennis. b 44. Univ of Wales (Ban) BTh00. St Mich Coll Llan 00. **d** 00 **p** 01. C Llanbedrog w Llannor and Llangian *Ban* 00-02; P-in-c Llanllyfni 02-03; R 03-05; R Dolgellau w Llanfachreth and Brithdir etc from 05; AD Ystumaner from 10. *The Rectory, Pencefn Road, Dolgellau LL40 2YW* Tel (01341) 422225

REES, Stephen Philip. b 70. St Luke's Coll Ex BA. Oak Hill Th Coll BA03. **d** 03 **p** 04. C Moreton-in-Marsh w Batsford, Todenham etc *Glouc* 03-06; P-in-c Lt Heath *St Alb* from 06. *The Vicarage, Thornton Road, Potters Bar EN6 1JJ* Tel (01707) 654414 E-mail zipyzac@global.net

REES, Miss Susan Mary. b 61. Univ of Wales (Cardiff) BSc82 Ox Univ BTh05. Ripon Coll Cuddesdon 00. **d** 02 **p** 03. C Penarth All SS *Llan* 02-05; C Roath 05-08; P-in-c Eglwysilan from 08. *The Rectory, Brynhafod Road, Abertridwr, Caerphilly CF83 4BH* Tel (029) 2083 0220 E-mail susanmrees@hotmail.com

REES, Canon Vivian John Howard. b 51. Southn Univ LLB72 Ox Univ BA79 MA84 Leeds Univ MPhil84. Wycliffe Hall Ox 76. **d** 79 **p** 80. C Moor Allerton *Ripon* 79-82; Sierra Leone 82-86; Lic to Offic *Ox* from 86; Jt Dioc Reg from 98; Dep Prov Reg 98-00; Prov Reg from 00; Legal Adv ACC from 98; Hon Prov Can Cant Cathl from 01. *Oxford Diocesan Registry, 16 Beaumont Street, Oxford OX1 2LZ* Tel (01865) 297214 Fax 726274 E-mail jrees@wslaw.co.uk

REES, William David Cledwyn. b 25. FRGS54 Qu Coll Cam BA49 DipEd50 MA52 Univ of Wales MA75 PhD81. St Deiniol's Hawarden 63. **d** 65 **p** 66. Hon C Rhyl w St Ann *St As* 65-72; Chapl and Lect St Mary's Coll Ban 77-73; Lic to Offic *Ban* 72-77; Lect Ban Univ from 77; Chapl Univ of Wales (Ban) 77-84; Sec Dioc Schs Cttee 84-86. *Anwylfa, Fron Park Avenue, Llanfairfechan LL33 0AS* Tel (01248) 680054

REES-JONES, Diana Mary. b 58. Ridley Hall Cam. **d** 07 **p** 08. C Ness Gp *Linc* 07-09; Asst Chapl Oundle Sch from 09. *17 Milton Road, Oundle, Peterborough PE8 4AB* Tel (01832) 270926 E-mail diana.reesjones@btinternet.com

REESE, Preb John David. b 49. Cuddesdon Coll 73. **d** 76 **p** 77. C Kidderminster St Mary *Worc* 76-81; Malaysia 81-85; V Bishop's Castle w Mainstone *Heref* 85-91; RD Clun Forest 87-91; V Tupsley 91-93; P-in-c Hampton Bishop and Mordiford w Dormington 91-93; V Tupsley w Hampton Bishop 93-08; RD Heref City 96-02; TR Heref S Wye from 08; Preb Heref Cathl from 96. *1 Prinknash Close, Belmont, Hereford HR2 7XA*

REEVE, Canon Brian Charles. b 36. Lon Univ BSc57 BD60. Tyndale Hall Bris 58. **d** 61 **p** 62. C Eccleston St Luke *Liv* 61-63; C Upton (Overchurch) *Ches* 63-65; C Pemberton St Mark Newtown *Liv* 65-68; V Macclesfield Ch Ch Ches 68-74; V Stone Ch Ch *Lich* 74-84; RD Trentham 77-84; V Hoole *Ches* 84-94; Chapl Ches City Hosp 84-91; P-in-c Alderley *Ches* 94-01; Dioc Warden of Readers 94-00; Hon Can Ches Cathl 94-01; rtd 01; Perm to Offic *Ches* from 02. *73 Spring Gardens, Leek ST13 8DD* Tel (01538) 387321

REEVE, David Michael. b 44. St Cath Coll Cam BA67 MA71. Coll of Resurr Mirfield 68. **d** 70 **p** 71. C Willingdon *Chich* 70-73; C Hove All SS 73-76; C Moulsecoomb 76-80; R Singleton and V E and W Dean 80-90; R Hurstpierpoint 90-99; R Kingston Buci 99-05; rtd 05; Perm to Offic *Cant* from 06; Clergy Widows Officer

Cant Adnry from 09. *11 Wells Avenue, Canterbury CT1 3YB* Tel (01227) 478446

REEVE, John Richard. b 65. Southn Univ BA86 La Sainte Union Coll PGCE88. Ripon Coll Cuddesdon 95. **d** 97 **p** 98. C Hale w Badshot Lea *Guildf* 97-00; TV Totton *Win* from 00; P-in-c Copythorne from 11. *The Vicarage, Ringwood Road, Woodlands, Southampton SO40 7GX* Tel (023) 8066 3267 E-mail johnreeve6@aol.com

REEVE, Kenneth John. b 42. Sarum & Wells Th Coll 91. **d** 93 **p** 94. C Thorpe St Matt *Nor* 93-96; P-in-c S Lynn 96-99; Perm to Offic 03-04; P-in-c Gt and Lt Ellingham, Rockland and Shropham etc 04-11; RD Thetford and Rockland 09-11; rtd 11. *Hillmora Cottage, Tabernacle Lane, Forncett St Peter, Norwich NR16 1LE* E-mail kenreeve@btinternet.com

REEVE, Michael. See REEVE, David Michael

REEVE, Richard Malcolm. b 64. Reading Univ BSc85. Trin Coll Bris BA92. **d** 92 **p** 93. C Northolt St Mary *Lon* 92-95; C Acton Green 95-98; V Hayes St Edm 98-08; TR Tettenhall Regis *Lich* from 08. *The Rectory, 2 Lloyd Road, Tettenhall, Wolverhampton WV6 9AU* Tel (01902) 742801 E-mail richardmreeve@aol.com

REEVE, Richard Noel. b 29. MB, ChB. St Deiniol's Hawarden. **d** 84 **p** 85. Hon C Norton *Ches* 84-85; C Filey *York* 85-87; TV Brayton 87-90; rtd 90; Perm to Offic *Man* 90-93 and *Lich* from 99; Res Min Bicton, Montford w Shrawardine and Fitz *Lich* 97-99. *26 Windsor Road, Stafford ST17 4PA* Tel (01785) 252607

REEVE, Preb Roger Patrick. b 42. Fitzw Coll Cam BA65 MA68. Coll of Resurr Mirfield. **d** 67 **p** 68. C Barnstaple St Pet w H Trin *Ex* 67-74; V Ernesettle 74-78; V Braunton 78-05; RD Barnstaple 85-93 and 01-03; Preb Ex Cathl from 92; rtd 05. *27 Westacott Meadow, Barnstaple EX32 8QX* Tel (01271) 326927 E-mail rogerreeve@cwcom.net

REEVE, Mrs Sally Ann. b 55. SEITE 07. **d** 10 **p** 11. C Ringmer *Chich* from 10. *53 Springett Avenue, Ringmer, Lewes BN8 5QT* Tel (01273) 812114 E-mail sally.reeve@btinternet.com

REEVES, Christopher. b 30. Nottm Univ BA53. Wells Th Coll 53. **d** 55 **p** 56. C Rowbarton *B & W* 55-59; C Cant St Greg 59-61; Chapl Schiedam Miss to Seamen *Eur* 61-67; V Barkingside H Trin *Chelmsf* 67-97; rtd 97; Perm to Offic *Truro* from 00. *3 Albany Close, Goonown, St Agnes TR5 0XE* Tel (01872) 552976

REEVES, David Eric. b 46. Sarum Th Coll 68. **d** 71 **p** 72. C Guildf H Trin w St Mary 71-74; C Warmsworth *Sheff* 74-78; V Herringthorpe 78-90; V Cleveleys *Blackb* from 90; RD Poulton 94-00. *The Vicarage, Rough Lea Road, Thornton-Cleveleys FY5 1DP* Tel (01253) 852153

REEVES, Donald St John. b 34. Qu Coll Cam BA57 MA61 Lambeth MLitt03. Cuddesdon Coll 62. **d** 63 **p** 64. C Maidstone All SS w St Phil *Cant* 63-65; Bp's Dom Chapl *S'wark* 65-68; V St Helier 69-80; R Westmr St Jas *Lon* 80-98; Dir Soul of Eur Project from 98; rtd 98; Perm to Offic *Ex* from 00. *The Coach House, Church Street, Crediton EX17 2AQ* Tel (01363) 775100 Fax 773911 E-mail donalreeve@aol.com

REEVES, Elizabeth Anne. See THOMAS, Mrs Elizabeth Anne

REEVES, Gillian Patricia. b 46. S'wark Ord Course 87. **d** 90 **p** 94. Par Dn Shirley St Geo *S'wark* 90-94; C 94-96; C Caterham 96-98; TV from 98. *St Luke's Vicarage, 8 Whyteleafe Hill, Whyteleafe CR3 0AA* Tel (020) 8660 4015

REEVES, Graham. b 65. Southn Univ BTh94 Univ Coll Chich MA04. Chich Th Coll 91. **d** 94 **p** 95. C Cardiff St Mary and St Steph w St Dyfrig etc *Llan* 94-95; C Roath 95-98; Chapl Sussex Weald and Downs NHS Trust 98-02; Chapl W Sussex Health and Soc Care NHS Trust from 02. *45 Abbottsbury, Bognor Regis PO21 4RT* Tel (01243) 815310 or 623576

REEVES, John Graham. b 44. Kelham Th Coll 64. **d** 69 **p** 71. C Aston cum Aughton *Sheff* 69-71; C Ribbleton *Blackb* 72-74; C Cleveleys 74-75; P-in-c Huncoat 75-77; V 77-82; V Knuzden 82-92; V Sandylands 92-09; rtd 09. *51 Parkfield Drive, Lancaster LA1 4BT* Tel (01524) 411299 E-mail revjgr@tiscali.co.uk

REEVES, Ms Karen Susan. b 66. Bris Univ BA78. Ripon Coll Cuddesdon 02. **d** 05 **p** 07. C De Beauvoir Town St Pet *Lon* 05-06; C Islington St Jas w St Pet 06-08; Chapl Frimley Park Hosp NHS Foundn Trust 08-09; NSM Frimley *Guildf* 08-09; Chapl Milton Keynes Hosp NHS Foundn Trust 09-10; TV Coventry Caludon from 10. *Holy Cross Vicarage, 14 St Austell Road, Coventry CV2 5AE* E-mail karen.reeves6@btinternet.com

REEVES, Kenneth William. b 38. TCD 67. **d** 69 **p** 70. C Killowen *D & R* 69-70; I Ardara 70-76; TV Quidenham *Nor* 76-81; V Swaffham 81-86; Chapl Nor City Coll of F&HE 86-91; P-in-c Lakenham St Alb 86-91; rtd 92; Perm to Offic *Nor* 92-98 and from 05; P-in-c Nerja and Almuñécar *Eur* 03-04. *15 Morris Close, Stoke Holy Cross, Norwich NR14 8LL* Tel (01508) 494583 E-mail revkenn@btinternet.com

REEVES, Maria Elizabeth Ann. See COULTER, Mrs Maria Elizabeth Ann

REEVES, Michael Richard Ewert. b 74. Girton Coll Cam MA00. Oak Hill Th Coll 98. **d** 02 **p** 03. NSM Langham Place All So *Lon* 02-05; Th Adv UCCF from 05. *UCCF, 38 De Montfort Street, Leicester LE1 7GP* Tel 0116-255 1700 Fax 255 5672 E-mail mreeves@dsl.pipex.com

REEVES, Nicholas John Harding. b 44. Open Th Coll BA99 Nottm Univ MA02. ALCD69. **d** 69 **p** 70. C Upton (Overchurch *Ches* 69-72; C Woodlands *Sheff* 72-74; C-in-c Cranham Park CD *Chelmsf* 74-79; V Cranham Park 79-88; R Aldridge *Lich* 88-02 Dioc Officer for Evang *Carl* 03-10; C Eden, Gelt and Irthing 03-09; rtd 09. *The New Vicarage, Irthington, Carlisle CA6 4N₂* Tel (01697) 741864 Mobile 07714-245506 E-mail the7reeves@aol.com

REGAN, Brian. b 46. MBIM80. WMMTC 88. **d** 91 **p** 92. C Cov St Jo 91-94; V Tile Hill 94-09; rtd 09; Perm to Offic *Cov* from 09 *160 Ansley Road, Nuneaton CV10 8NU* Tel (024) 7673 424₀ Mobile 07766-721837 E-mail brianregan32@hotmail.com

REGAN, Noel Henry Likely. b 49. **d** 99 **p** 00. Aux Min Cloonclare w Killasnett, Lurganboy and Drumlease *K, E & A* 99-06; Dioc and P-in-c Garrison w Slavin and Belleek *Clogh* from 06. *Gurteen Farm, Cliffoney, Co Sligo, Republic of Ireland* Tel (00353) (71) 916 6253 Mobile 86-887 5714 E-mail revnoelregan@hotmail.com

REGAN, Paul John. b 67. Southn Univ BA88 PhD96 St Jo Coll Dur BA98. Cranmer Hall Dur 96. **d** 99 **p** 00. C St Alb St Pet *St Alb* 99-03; TV Smestow Vale *Lich* 03-09; Chapl Trevelyan Coll *Dur* from 09; Chapl Van Mildert Coll from 09; C Dur St Oswald and Shincliffe from 09. *20 Dickens Wynd, Elvet Moor, Durham DH1 3QT* Tel 0191-334 7037

REGAN, Philip. b 49. Qu Mary Coll Lon BSc MSc. Wycliffe Hall Ox 81. **d** 83 **p** 84. NSM Scotforth *Blackb* 83-89; P-in-c Combe St Nicholas w Wambrook *B & W* 89-01; V 01-08; P-in-c Whitestaunton 89-01; R 01-08; rtd 08. *1 Blackmoor Road, Wellington TA21 8ED* Tel (01823) 662193 E-mail pregan@ukonline.co.uk

REGINALD, Brother. See BOX, Reginald Gilbert

REID, Amanda Joy. See MARRIOTT, Mrs Amanda Joy

REID, Andrew John. b 47. Birm Univ BEd70 Man Univ MEd76. S'wark Ord Course 88. **d** 88 **p** 89. NSM Westerham *Roch* 88-90; Chapl Abp Tenison's Sch Kennington 90-05; Perm to Offic *Roch* from 05. *12 Westways, Westerham TN16 1TT* Tel (01959) 561428

REID, Andrew John. b 58. Thames Poly BA90. Trin Coll Bris 09. **d** 11. C Chorleywood St Andr *St Alb* from 11. *Wick Cottage, 36 Quickley Lane, Chorleywood, Rickmansworth WD3 5AF* Tel 07876-773387 (mobile) E-mail kaleidos@inbox.com

REID, Christopher Jason. b 69. Trin Coll Bris 01. **d** 03 **p** 04. C Woodley *Ox* 03-07; V Selby St Jas *York* from 07. *St James's Vicarage, 14 Leeds Road, Selby YO8 4HX* Tel (01757) 702861 E-mail cjasonreid@hotmail.com

REID, Canon Colin Guthrie. b 30. **d** 56 **p** 57. C Kendal St Thos *Carl* 56-59; C Crosthwaite Keswick 59-60; R Caldbeck w Castle Sowerby 60-76; R/D Wigton 69-70; P-in-c Sebergham 75-76; R Caldbeck, Castle Sowerby and Sebergham 76-93; Hon Can Carl Cathl 88-93; rtd 93; Perm to Offic *Carl* from 93. *Mellbreak, Longthwaite Road, Wigton CA7 9JR* Tel (01697) 345625

REID, David Graham. b 78. Hatf Coll Dur BSc00. Wycliffe Hall Ox BTh09. **d** 09 **p** 10. NSM Ox St Ebbe w H Trin and St Pet from 09. *24 East Avenue, Oxford OX4 1XP* Tel (01865) 240438 E-mail dave.reid@stebbes.org.uk

REID, Mrs Diane Mary. b 73. Lanc Univ BMus94 Huddersfield Univ PGCE98. Trin Coll Bris BA04. **d** 04 **p** 05. C Reading St Agnes w St Paul and St Barn *Ox* 04-07. *St James's Vicarage, 14 Leeds Road, Selby YO8 4HX* Tel (01757) 702861 E-mail dianem_clark@hotmail.com

REID, Donald. b 58. Glas Univ LLB79 Pemb Coll Ox MPhil81 Edin Univ BD85. Edin Th Coll 82. **d** 85 **p** 86. C Greenock *Glas* 85-88; C Baillieston 88-91; R 91-95; C Glas St Serf 88-91; R 91-95; Chapl Glas Univ 89-00; Chapl Glas Caledonian Univ 89-00; Chapl Strathclyde Univ 89-00; TP Glas St Mary 95-00; Assoc P 00-04; C Edin St Jo from 04. *11A Cornwall Street, Edinburgh EH1 2EQ* Tel 0131-466 2461 *or* 229 7565 E-mail donald.reid@stjohns-edinburgh.org.uk

REID, Gareth McEwan. b 82. Univ of Wales (Abth) BA03 St Mich Coll Llan BTh10. **d** 10 **p** 11. C Dewisland *St D* from 10. *The Vicarage, Whitchurch, Solva, Haverfordwest SA62 6UD* Tel (01437) 721281 E-mail garethmreid@googlemail.com

✠**REID, The Rt Revd Gavin Hunter.** b 34. OBE00. K Coll Lon BA56. Oak Hill Th Coll 56. **d** 60 **p** 61 **c** 92. C E Ham St Paul *Chelmsf* 60-63; C Rainham 63-66; Publications Sec CPAS 66-71; Hon C St Paul's Cray St Barn *Roch* 68-71; Ed Sec USCL 71-74; Hon C Woking St Jo *Guildf* 72-92; Sec for Evang CPAS 74-92; Consultant Missr CPAS and BMU Adv 90-92; Suff Bp Maidstone *Cant* 92-00; Six Preacher Cant Cathl 92-97; rtd 00 Perm to Offic *Nor* and *St E* from 00; Hon Asst Bp St E from 00 *Furzefield, 17 Richard Crampton Road, Beccles NR34 9HN* Tel (01502) 717042 Fax 710739 Mobile 07941-770549 E-mail gavin@reids.org

REID, Geraldine Felicity (Jo). b 47. RGN69. EMMTC 95. **d** 98 **p** 99. NSM Skellingthorpe w Doddington *Linc* 98-02; NSM Hykeham from 02. *Tol Peden, Monson Park, Skellingthorpe, Lincoln LN6 5UE* Tel (01522) 828402 *or* 828403 E-mail tolpedn@ntlworld.com

REID, Gordon. See REID, Canon William Gordon

REID, Herbert Alan. b 31. AKC55. **d** 56 **p** 57. C Penwortham St Mary *Blackb* 56-59; C-in-c Penwortham St Leon CD 59-63; V Brierfield 63-72; V Warton St Paul 72-79; V Read in Whalley 79-98; rtd 98; Perm to Offic *Blackb* from 98. *Paslew House, 6 The Sands, Whalley, Blackburn BB7 9TL* Tel (01254) 824620

REID, James. b 46. Strathclyde Univ BSc69. WMMTC 88. **d** 91 **p** 92. C Attleborough *Cov* 91-95; V Walsall Pleck and Bescot *Lich* 95-99; TR Chell 99-06; rtd 06. *22 St Ives Way, Nuneaton CV11 6FR* Tel (024) 7634 2264

REID, Jason. See REID, Christopher Jason

REID, Jo. See REID, Geraldine Felicity

REID, Joanne. b 68. St Mich Coll Llan 08. **d** 10 **p** 11. C Brize Norton and Carterton *Ox* from 10. *39 Bluebell Way, Carterton OX18 1JY* Tel (01993) 843173 E-mail joreid185@btinternet.com

REID, Lucinda Jane. b 57. Dur Univ BA78. Ripon Coll Cuddesdon 79. **dss** 81 **d** 85 **p** 85. Birtley *Dur* 81-84; Canada from 84. *5551 West Saanich Road, Victoria BC V9E 2G1, Canada* E-mail lreid@uoguelpha.ca

REID, Miss Margaret Patricia. b 41. Hull Univ BSc62 Leeds Univ MA07. Yorks Min Course 09. **d** 10 **p** 11. NSM Ilkley All SS *Bradf* from 10. *1 Chestnut Close, Ilkley LS29 8PX* E-mail pat.reid29@btinternet.com

REID, Mark. **d** 07 **p** 08. NSM Glenavy w Tunny and Crumlin *Conn* from 07. *12B Carmavy Road, Nutts Corner, Crumlin BT29 4TF* Tel (028) 9445 4725

REID, Mrs Pauline Ann. b 57. EAMTC 00. **d** 03 **p** 04. C Silverstone and Abthorpe w Slapton etc *Pet* 03-07; P-in-c Raddesley Gp *Ely* from 07. *The Rectory, 23 Stetchworth Road, Dullingham, Newmarket CB8 9UJ* Tel (01638) 508990 Mobile 07812-831869 E-mail revpauline@btinternet.com

REID, Peter Ivor. b 30. Qu Coll Cam BA53 MA72. St Mich Coll Llan 78. **d** 80 **p** 81. C Llantwit Major and St Donat's 80-83; C Llantwit Major 83-84; V Laleston w Tythegston 84; V Laleston w Tythegston and Merthyr Mawr 84-88; V Roath 88-98; rtd 98. *18 Woolaston Avenue, Cardiff CF23 5AD* Tel (029) 2075 3306

REID, Robert. See McLEAN-REID, Robert

REID, Roderick Andrew Montgomery. b 80. Brunel Univ BSc01 Trin Hall Cam BTh10. Westcott Ho Cam 08. **d** 11. C Waltham H Cross *Chelmsf* from 11. *8 Flagstaff Road, Waltham Abbey EN9 1JE* Tel 07799-734898 (mobile) E-mail rod.a.reid@gmail.com

REID, Stewart Thomas. b 45. Liv Hope MA01. Oak Hill Th Coll 66. **d** 70 **p** 71. C Normanton *Derby* 70-73; C Leyland St Andr *Blackb* 73-78; V Halliwell St Luke *Man* 78-95; V Southport Ch Ch *Liv* from 95. *The Vicarage, 12 Gloucester Road, Southport PR8 2AU* Tel (01704) 565120

REID, Canon William Gordon. b 43. Edin Univ MA63 Keble Coll Ox BA66 MA72. Edin Th Coll 63 Cuddesdon Coll 66. **d** 67 **p** 68. C Edin St Salvador 67-69; Chapl and Tutor Sarum Th Coll 69-72; R Edin St Mich and All SS 72-84; Provost St Andr Cathl Inverness 84-87; Chapl Ankara *Eur* 87-89; Chapl Stockholm w Gävle and Västerås 89-92; V Gen to Bp Eur 92-02; Can Gib Cathl 92-98; Adn in Eur 96-98; P-in-c St Mich Cornhill w St Pet le Poer etc *Lon* 97-98; Dean Gib *Eur* 98-00; Adn Italy and Malta 00-03; Chapl Milan w Genoa and Varese 00-03; R Philadelphia St Clem USA from 04. *2013 Appletree Street, Philadelphia PA 19103-1409, USA* Tel (001) (215) 563 1876 Fax 563 7627 E-mail gordonrr@earthlink.net

REIDE, Susannah Louise Court. b 69. Clare Coll Cam BA91. Trin Coll Bris BA04. **d** 04 **p** 05. C Marlborough *Sarum* 04-08; TV Cowley St Jas *Ox* 08-11. *96 Cricket Close, Oxford OX4 3DJ* Tel (01865) 401439 E-mail sr@reide.plus.com

REIGATE, Archdeacon of. See KAJUMBA, The Ven Daniel Steven Kimbugwe

REILLY, Frederick James. b 29. CITC 70. **d** 73 **p** 74. C Agherton *Conn* 73-75; C Ballymena 75-82; I Ballyscullion *D & R* 82-04; Can Derry Cathl 03-04; rtd 04. *11 Swilly Drive, Portstewart BT55 7FJ* Tel (028) 7083 5788

REILLY, Thomas Gerard. b 38. **d** 64 **p** 64. In RC Ch 64-73; Hon C Clapton Park All So *Lon* 73-76; Hon C Haggerston All SS 76-78; Hon C Walthamstow St Sav *Chelmsf* 78-85; P-in-c Forest Gate Em w Upton Cross 85-89; V 89-92; V Chaddesden St Phil *Derby* 92-01; RD Derby N 95-00; rtd 01; Perm to Offic *B & W* from 01. *8 Victoria Square, Poples Well, Crewkerne TA18 7ES* Tel (01460) 72613 E-mail ger_mon@totalise.co.uk

REILY, Jacqueline Estelle. b 61. Oak Hill Th Coll BA84. ERMC 08. **d** 11. C Rayleigh *Chelmsf* from 11. *15 The Limes, Rayleigh SS6 8TH* Tel (01268) 770058 Mobile 07580-114641 E-mail jackie@reily.co.uk

REILY, Paul Alan. b 59. UEA BA81. St Jo Coll Nottm MA92. **d** 92 **p** 93. C Westcliff St Mich *Chelmsf* 92-96; P-in-c Barkingside St Cedd 96-98; V 98-01; V Leyton St Cath and St Paul 01-11; AD Waltham Forest 04-07. *15 The Limes, Rayleigh SS6 8TH* Tel (01268) 770058 Mobile 07967-977115 E-mail paul@reily.co.uk

REINDORP, David Peter Edington. b 52. TD05. Trin Coll Cam BA82 MA86 CQSW77. Westcott Ho Cam 79. **d** 83 **p** 84. C

Chesterton Gd Shep *Ely* 83-85; C Hitchin *St Alb* 85-88; R Landbeach and V Waterbeach *Ely* 88-97; OCF 88-97; CF(V) from 92; RD Quy *Ely* 94-97; V Cherry Hinton St Jo 97-06; RD Cambridge 04-06; Hon Can Ely Cathl 05-06; V Chelsea All SS *Lon* from 06; AD Chelsea from 11. *2 Old Church Street, London SW3 5DQ* Tel (020) 7352 5627 E-mail david.reindorp@talk21.com

REINDORP, Canon Michael Christopher Julian. b 44. Trin Coll Cam BA67 MA70 K Coll Lon MA99. Cuddesdon Coll 67 United Th Coll Bangalore 68. **d** 69 **p** 70. C Poplar *Lon* 69-74; V Chatham St Wm *Roch* 74-84; R Stantonbury *Ox* 84-87; TR Stantonbury and Willen *Ox* 87-92; P-in-c Richmond St Mary w St Matthias and St Jo *S'wark* 92-95; TR 96-09; Hon Can S'wark Cathl 03-09; rtd 09. *10 Alpha Road, Teddington TW11 0QG* Tel (020) 8614 6800

REISS, Prof Michael Jonathan. b 58. Trin Coll Cam BA78 MA82 PhD82 PGCE83 FIBiol90 Open Univ MBA02. EAMTC 87. **d** 90 **p** 91. Lect Cam Univ 88-94; Reader 94-00; NSM Comberton *Ely* 90-94; NSM Deanery of Bourn 94-96 and 99-00; P-in-c Boxworth and Elsworth w Knapwell 96-99; Perm to Offic 99-03; Prof Science Educn Inst of Educn Lon Univ from 01; NSM Toft w Caldecote and Childerley *Ely* 03-10; NSM Lordsbridge from 10. *Institute of Education, University of London, 20 Bedford Way, London WC1H 0AL* Tel (020) 7947 9522 E-mail m.reiss@ioe.ac.uk

REISS, Canon Peter Henry. b 62. Hertf Coll Ox BA85 MA91 Natal Univ MA95. St Jo Coll Nottm 95. **d** 95 **p** 96. C Sherwood *S'well* 95-00; TV Bestwood 00-03; V Bestwood Park w Rise Park 03-04; Tr Officer CME and Laity Development *Man* 04-06; Dir Discipleship and Min Tr from 06; Hon Can Man Cathl from 11. *Discipleship and Ministry Training, 5th Floor, Church House, 90 Deansgate, Manchester M3 2GJ* Tel 0161-828 1455 Fax 828 1485 E-mail preiss@manchester.anglican.org

REISS, Canon Robert Paul. b 43. Trin Coll Cam BA67 MA71. Westcott Ho Cam 67. **d** 69 **p** 70. C St John's Wood *Lon* 69-73; Bangladesh 73; Chapl Trin Coll Cam 73-78; Selection Sec ACCM 78-85; Sen Selection Sec 83; TR Grantham *Linc* 86-96; RD Grantham 92-96; Adn Surrey and Hon Can Guildf Cathl 96-05; Can Westmr Abbey from 05. *1 Little Cloister, London SW1P 3PL* Tel (020) 7654 4804 Fax 7654 4811 E-mail robert.reiss@westminster-abbey.org

REITH, Robert Michael. b 55. Oak Hill Th Coll BA83. **d** 83 **p** 84. C Kendal St Thos *Carl* 83-87; C Leyland St Andr *Blackb* 87-92; V Leyland St Jo 92-94; TR Dagenham *Chelmsf* 94-03; V from 03. *The Vicarage, Church Lane, Dagenham RM10 9UL* Tel (020) 8215 2962 Mobile 07595-303023 E-mail mikereith@me.com

RENDALL, Canon John Albert. b 43. Hull Univ BTh84 MA89. Ripon Hall Ox 65. **d** 68 **p** 69. C Southsea St Simon *Portsm* 68-71; C Wallington *S'wark* 71-77; P-in-c Rufforth w Moor Monkton and Hessay *York* 77-79; R 79-08; P-in-c Long Marston 77-79; R 79-08; RD New Ainsty 85-97; P-in-c Healaugh w Wighill, Bilbrough and Askham Richard 02-08; P-in-c Tockwith and Bilton w Bickerton 03-08; Can and Preb York Minster 94-08; Chapl Purey Cust Nuffield Hosp 82-04; rtd 08; Perm to Offic *York* from 09. *5 Wains Road, York YO24 2TP* Tel (01904) 778764 E-mail canjohnrendall@aol.com

RENDALL, Richard John. b 54. Wadh Coll Ox BA76 LLB78 MA92 Solicitor 78. Wycliffe Hall Ox 90. **d** 92 **p** 93. C Heswall *Ches* 92-98; R High Ongar w Norton Mandeville *Chelmsf* 98-04; R Broadwell, Evenlode, Oddington, Adlestrop etc *Glouc* from 04. *The Rectory, Broadwell, Moreton-in-Marsh GL56 0TU* Tel (01451) 831866 E-mail rendalls@talk21.com

RENDELL, Jason. b 68. **d** 09. Chapl to Bp Stepney *Lon* 05-07; NSM Clerkenwell H Redeemer 06-07; NSM Clerkenwell St Mark 06-07; Min Can and Succ St Paul's Cathl 07-09; Min Can and Sacr St Paul's Cathl from 09. *8A Amen Court, London EC4M 7BU* Tel (020) 7246 8338

RENDLE, Graham Barton. b 40. **d** 99 **p** 00. OLM Rougham, Beyton w Hessett and Rushbrooke *St E* 99-10; rtd 10; Perm to Offic *St E* from 10. *Appletrees, Bury Road, Beyton, Bury St Edmunds IP30 9AB* Tel (01359) 270924

RENFREY, Edward Donald John-Baptist. b 53. ACT. **d** 76 **p** 77. C Naracoorte Australia 76-77; P-in-c Kingston w Robe 78-81; R 81-84; Chapl RN 84-99; Chapl R Aus Navy from 99. *5/7 Buoyant Street, Fannie Bay NT 0820, Australia* Tel (0061) (8) 409-662823 (mobile) E-mail edwardrenfrey@hotmail.com.au

RENGERT, Keith Alan Francis. b 67. RGN92. Ripon Coll Cuddesdon 07. **d** 09 **p** 10. C N Walsham and Edingthorpe *Nor* from 09. *8 Plumbly Close, North Walsham NR28 9YB* Tel (01692) 500028 Mobile 07796-607649 E-mail k.rengert@btinternet.com

RENISON, Canon Gary James. b 62. SS Hild & Bede Coll Dur BA83. Ridley Hall Cam 84. **d** 86 **p** 87. C Stapenhill w Cauldwell *Derby* 86-89; C Cheadle Hulme St Andr *Ches* 89-92; Min Cheadle Hulme Em CD 92-95; P-in-c Bar Hill *Ely* 95-05; V Childwall All SS *Liv* from 05. Hon Can Liv Cathl from 11. *All Saints' Vicarage, Childwall Abbey Road, Liverpool L16 0JW* Tel 0151-737 2169 E-mail vicar.allsaints@uwclub.net

RENNARD, Edward Lionel. b 51. CertEd72 Nottm Univ BTh80. Linc Th Coll 76. **d** 80 **p** 81. C Old Brumby *Linc* 80-82; C-in-c Gt Grimsby St Matt Fairfield CD 82-86; V Fairfield St Matt 86-88; V Hykeham 88-91; TR 91-00; TR Blyth Valley *St E* from 00. *The Rectory, Highfield Road, Halesworth IP19 8SJ* Tel (01986) 872602 Mobile 07958-191975 E-mail edward.rennard@btinternet.com

RENNARD, Margaret Rose. b 49. CertEd75. Linc Th Coll 76. **dss** 80 **d** 87 **p** 94. C Fairfield St Matt *Linc* 87-88; C Hykeham 88-00; Chapl HM Pris Morton Hall 91-00; Asst Chapl HM Pris Blundeston 00-01; Asst Chapl HM Pris Hollesley Bay from 01; Chapl Allington NHS Trust 00-01; Perm to Offic *St E* from 00. *The Rectory, Highfield Road, Halesworth IP19 8SJ* Tel (01986) 872602 E-mail edward.rennard@btinternet.com

RENNIE, Iain Hugh. b 43. Ripon Coll Cuddesdon 88. **d** 90 **p** 91. C Poulton-le-Sands w Morecambe St Laur *Blackb* 90-94; V Hornby w Claughton 94-02; V Hornby w Claughton and Whittington etc 02-11; rtd 11. *65 Ashton Drive, Lancaster LA1 2LQ* Tel (01524) 382926

RENNIE, John Aubery. b 47. Lon Univ MB, BS70 FRCS75. SEITE 04. **d** 06 **p** 07. NSM Melbury *Sarum* 06-10; NSM Sherborne w Castleton, Lillington and Longburton from 10. *Rectory House, 2 Fore Street, Evershot, Dorchester DT2 0JW* Tel (01935) 83003 Mobile 07826-447432 E-mail johnrennie40@hotmail.com

RENNIE, Paul Antony. b 58. Heriot-Watt Univ BSc82 Edin Univ LTh. **d** 87 **p** 88. C Nairn *Mor* 87-90; C Forres 87-90; C Edin St Pet 90-92; Dep Chapl HM Pris Leeds 92; Chapl HM YOI Hindley 93-95; Chapl HM Pris Liv 95-97; Chapl RAF from 97. *Chaplaincy Services, HQ Personnel and Training Command, RAF High Wycombe HP14 4UE* Tel (01494) 496800 Fax 496343

RENNISON, Mrs Patricia Elinor. b 46. **d** 11. OLM Shilbottle *Newc* from 11. *8 The Crescent, Shilbottle, Alnwick NE66 2UU* Tel (01665) 575686 E-mail patriciarennison983@btinternet.com

RENNIX, Raymond Latham. b 37. QUB BTh02. CITC 00. **d** 03 **p** 04. NSM Killaney w Carryduff *D & D* 03-08; NSM Glencraig from 08. *5 Brompton Court, Dromara, Dromore BT25 2DQ* Tel (028) 9753 3167 Mobile 07977-584053 E-mail r.rennix@btinternet.com

RENSHAW, Mrs Anne-Marie Louise. b 71. St Hilda's Coll Ox MA96 Fitzw Coll Cam BA97. Ridley Hall Cam 95. **d** 98 **p** 99. C Norton *St Alb* 98-02; TV Borehamwood 02-05; TV Elstree and Borehamwood from 05; P-in-c Tolleshunt Knights w Tiptree and Gt Braxted *Chelmsf* from 11. *The Rectory, Rectory Road, Tiptree, Colchester CO5 0SX* Tel (01621) 815260 E-mail amlrenshaw@btinternet.com

RENSHAW, Anthony. b 40. Montreal Dioc Th Coll 83. **d** 87 **p** 88. Canada 87-90; P-in-c Ainsdale *Liv* 90-91; V 91-98; V Singleton w Weeton *Blackb* 98-03; rtd 03; Perm to Offic *Man* from 03. *20 The Windrush, Rochdale OL12 6DY* Tel (01706) 341420 E-mail tonyrenshaw@tiscali.co.uk

RENSHAW, David William. b 59. Oak Hill Th Coll BA85. **d** 85 **p** 86. C Shawbury *Lich* 85-88; V Childs Ercall and R Stoke upon Tern 88-92; V Stoneleigh *Guildf* 92-97; RD Epsom 95-97; Chapl Scarborough and NE Yorks Healthcare NHS Trust 97-99; Chapl St Cath Hospice Scarborough 97-99; R Meppershall w Campton and Stondon *St Alb* 99-01; C Bedford St Andr 02; Perm to Offic *Chich* 05-06; Hon C Bexhill St Pet 06; TV Rye 09-11; P-in-c Lynch w Iping Marsh and Milland from 11. *Linch Rectory, Fernhurst Road, Milland, Liphook GU30 7LU* Tel (01428) 741285 E-mail renshaw221@btinternet.com

RENSHAW, Susan Kathryn. b 55. Shenstone Coll of Educn CertEd77. WMMTC 99. **d** 02 **p** 03. C Sedgley All SS *Worc* 02-05; C Gornal and Sedgley 05-06; V Eckington from 06; V Defford w Besford from 06; C Overbury w Teddington, Alstone etc from 09. *The Vicarage, Drakes Bridge Road, Eckington, Pershore WR10 3BN* Tel (01386) 750203 E-mail revsusan@btinternet.com

RENSHAW, Timothy John. b 65. Trin Coll Carmarthen BA86. St Jo Coll Nottm MA97. **d** 97 **p** 98. C Calverton *S'well* 97-01; C Epperstone 97-01; C Gonalston 97-01; C Oxton 97-01; P-in-c Shireoaks 01-05; Dioc Adv on Notts Coalfield 01-05; Project Manager Cathl Breakfast and Archer Projects *Sheff* from 05. *The Cathedral, 4-7 East Parade, Sheffield S1 2ET* Tel 0114-275 1650 or 279 7042

RENWICK, Canon Colin. b 30. St Aid Birkenhead. **d** 59 **p** 60. C Drypool St Columba w St Andr and St Pet *York* 59-62; C Wigan St Cath *Liv* 62-64; Min Thornton CD 64-77; V Thornton 77-97; RD Bootle 83-89; Hon Can Bauchi from 93; rtd 97; Perm to Offic *Ches* from 97. *27 Briar Drive, Heswall, Wirral CH60 5RN* Tel 0151-342 3308

RENYARD, Christopher. b 52. Open Univ BA87. Coll of Resurr Mirfield 81. **d** 84 **p** 85. C Heckmondwike *Wakef* 84-88; V Harpenden St Nic *St Alb* 88-95; Asst Chapl Salisbury Health Care NHS Trust 95-01; Chapl Team Ldr Salisbury NHS Foundn Trust from 01. *The Chaplain's Office, Salisbury District Hospital, Salisbury SP2 8BJ* Tel (01722) 429271 E-mail chaplains.department@shc-tr.swest.nhs.uk

RENYARD, Paul Holmwood. b 42. K Coll Lon BD65 AKC65. **d** 66 **p** 67. C Croydon St Aug *Cant* 66-69; C Farnham *Guildf* 69-72; V Capel 72-78; Asst Dir RE 72-78; Asst Dir RE *Roch* 78-83; Hon C Roch 78-83; V Holdenhurst *Win* 83-95; V Pennington 95-07; rtd 07. *53 Scarf Road, Poole BH17 8QJ* Tel (01202) 682460 E-mail renyard@tiscali.co.uk

RENZ, Thomas. b 69. Freie Theologische Akademie Giessen MA93 Chelt & Glouc Coll of HE PhD97. Coll of Resurr Mirfield 09. **d** 09. C Highgate St Mich *Lon* from 09. *17 Bishan Gardens, London N6 6DJ* Tel (020) 8341 0568 Mobile 07933-073692 E-mail thomas.renz@gmail.com

REPATH, George David. b 43. Kellogg Coll Ox MSt96. St D Coll Lamp. **d** 68 **p** 69. C Cardiff St Jo *Llan* 68-73; C Gt Stanmore *Lon* 73-77; V Stratfield Mortimer *Ox* 77-85; RD Bradfield 82-85 P-in-c Mortimer W End w Padworth 83-85; V Bray and Braywood 85-07; rtd 07. *8 Summerfields, Findon, Worthing BN14 0TU* Tel (01903) 877366

REPATH, John Richard. b 48. St Mich Coll Llan 72. **d** 75 **p** 76. C Canton St Jo *Llan* 75-79; C Burghclere w Newtown and Ecchinswell w Sydmonton *Win* 80-83; R Bewcastle and Stapleton *Carl* 83-88; P-in-c Kirklinton w Hethersgill and Scaleby 86-88; R Bewcastle, Stapleton and Kirklinton etc 88-97; rtd 97; P-in-c New Galloway *Glas* from 97. *The Rectory Kenbridge Road, New Galloway, Castle Douglas DG7 3RP* Tel (01644) 420235

REPTON, Suffragan Bishop of. See SOUTHERN, The Rt Revd Humphrey Ivo John

RESCH, Colin Ernst. b 67. Trin Coll Bris 04. **d** 06 **p** 07. C Highley w Billingsley, Glazeley etc *Heref* 06-10; P-in-c Stottesdon w Farlow, Cleeton St Mary etc from 10. *The Rectory, Stottesdon Kidderminster DY14 8UE* Tel (01746) 718297 E-mail colin@godstuff.org.uk

RESCH, Michael Johann. b 63. NTMTC 96. **d** 99 **p** 00. C Cullompton *Ex* 99-01; C Cullompton, Willand, Uffculme Kentisbeare etc 01-03; P-in-c Sittingbourne H Trin w Bobbing *Cant* from 03. *88 Albany Road, Sittingbourne ME10 1EL* Tel (01795) 473393 Mobile 07967-771231 E-mail mikeresch@aol.com

RESTALL, Miss Susan Roberta. b 45. MSc. Sarum & Wells Th Coll 79. **dss** 82 **d** 87 **p** 94. Dorchester *Sarum* 82-84; Portland All SS w St Pet 84-87; Par Dn 87; TD Yate New Town *Bris* 87-94 TV 94-95; Chapl Birm Heartlands and Solihull NHS Trust 95-01; rtd 01; Perm to Offic *Birm* from 03. *12 Croft Road Yardley, Birmingham B26 1SG* Tel 0121-783 3325

REUSS, Nathanael. b 76. Ballarat Univ BAppSc98. St Jo Coll Nottm MA(MM)11. **d** 11. C Ripley *Derby* from 11 *31 Porterhouse Road, Ripley DE5 3FL* Tel (01773) 57001 Mobile 07840-343525 E-mail nat.reuss@allsaintsripley.org.uk

REVELEY, James Stewart. b 69. Goldsmiths' Coll Lon BMus92 Ch Div Sch of the Pacific (USA) 95 Ripon Coll Cuddesdor BA97. **d** 96 **p** 97. C Goldington *St Alb* 96-00; C Harpender St Nic 00-04; V Boxmoor St Jo from 04. *St John's Vicarage, 10 Charles Street, Hemel Hempstead HP1 1JH* Tel and fax (01442) 255382 E-mail revjumble@aol.com

REVELEY, Mrs Valerie Mary. b 39. Lon Inst of Educn BEd77 SAOMC 96. **d** 99 **p** 00. OLM Olney *Ox* 99-05; Perm to Offic from 11. *56 Hipwell Court, Olney MK46 5QB* Tel (01234) 712352

REVELL, Patrick Walter Millard. b 32. Wells Th Coll 65. **d** 67 **p** 68. C Leic St Jas 67-74; V Quorndon 74-82; TR Camelot Par *B & W* 82-90; RD Cary and Bruton 90-96; V Castle Cary w Ansford 90-97; rtd 97; Perm to Offic *B & W* and *Sarum* from 97 *80 Sheepland Lane, Sherborne DT9 4BP* Tel (01935) 813083

REVERA, Susan Mary. See LEATHLEY, Susan Mary

REW, Eric Malcolm. b 63. UEA BSc84 PGCE89. Qu Coll Birm 98. **d** 00 **p** 01. C Shepshed *Leic* 00-04; TV Kingsthorpe w Northampton St Dav *Pet* from 04; Chapl Northants Police from 07. *The Vicarage, 42 Fallow Walk, Northampton NN2 8DE* Tel (01604) 843465 E-mail rev.rew@mypostoffice.co.uk

REX, Keith Leslie Herbert. b 30. K Coll Lon and St Boniface Warminster AKC53. **d** 55 **p** 56. C Shepton Mallet *B & W* 55-58 C Cheshunt *St Alb* 58-60; V Weston-super-Mare St Andr Bournville *B & W* 60-67; R Charlton Adam w Charlton Mackrell 67-69; rtd 90. *46 Petherton Gardens, Hengrove, Bristo BS14 9BS* Tel (01275) 891574

REYNISH, David Stuart. b 52. Nottm Univ BEd75. Linc Th Col 72. **d** 77 **p** 78. C Boston *Linc* 77-80; C Chalfont St Peter *Ox* 80-84; V Thursby *Carl* 84-88; R Iver Heath *Ox* 88-03; V Kelvedon and Feering *Chelmsf* from 03. *The Vicarage, Churcl Street, Kelvedon, Colchester CO5 9AL* Tel (01376) 571172

REYNOLDS, Alan Martin. b 53. Sarum & Wells Th Coll 73. **d** 77 **p** 78. C Glan Ely *Llan* 77-84; V Pontyclun w Talygarn 84-97 Perm to Offic from 97. *The Orchards, Stow Hill, Newpor NP20 4EA* Tel (01633) 215841 E-mail martin.reynolds1@virgin.net

REYNOLDS, Alan Thomas William. b 43. Lon Univ BSc64. Line Th Coll 64. **d** 66 **p** 67. C Leic St Pet 66-70; C Huntington *York* 70-72; R Darliston Jamaica 72-76; V Stechford *Birm* 76-83 Chapl E Birm Hosp 76-83; P-in-c Hampton in Arden *Birm* 83-86; V 87-93; Chapl Parkway Hosp Solihull 83-93; V Moseley St Anne *Birm* 93-02; Chapl Moseley Hall Hosp Birm 93-02; V

Kerry, Llanmerewig, Dolfor and Mochdre *St As* 02-08; AD Cedewain 03-08; rtd 08; Perm to Offic *Lich* from 08. *49 Gittin Street, Oswestry SY11 1DU* Tel (01691) 680416 E-mail robbie.reynolds1@btinternet.com

REYNOLDS, Mrs Angela Heather. b 44. Wye Coll Lon BSc66 Birm Univ CertEd67. EAMTC 94. **d** 97 **p** 98. NSM Barnham Broom *Nor* 97-99; C Easton w Colton and Marlingford 99-00; P-in-c Easton, Colton, Marlingford and Bawburgh 00-09; rtd 09; Perm to Offic *Nor* from 09. *26 Clickers Road, Norwich NR3 2DD* E-mail angela@ecmb.wanadoo.co.uk

REYNOLDS, David Hammerton. b 39. St Jo Coll Dur BA62. Qu Coll Birm 63. **d** 65 **p** 66. C N Ormesby *York* 65-68; C Hessle 68-71; V Sherburn in Elmet 71-79; V Fulford 79-87; Resp for Clergy In-Service Tr York Area 82-87; TV Bolventor *Truro* 87-90; TR Brayton *York* 90-06; RD Selby 04-06; rtd 06; Perm to Offic *Sheff* from 06 and *York* from 08. *42A George Street, Snaith, Goole DN14 9HZ* Tel (01405) 869352 E-mail dhrey@btopenworld.com

REYNOLDS, David James. b 48. St Jo Coll Dur BA72 Lanc Univ MA85. Cranmer Hall Dur 69. **d** 73 **p** 74. C Formby H Trin *Liv* 73-77; P-in-c Widnes St Paul 77-80; V Southport St Paul 80-87; P-in-c Mawdesley *Blackb* 87-91; R from 91; P-in-c Croston and Bretherton from 06; Chapl Derian Ho Children's Hospice 93-97. *Mawdesley Rectory, Green Lane, Ormskirk L40 3TH* Tel (01704) 822203 E-mail rectordavid@hotmail.co.uk

REYNOLDS, Gordon. b 42. Sarum & Wells Th Coll 71. **d** 72 **p** 73. C Tunstall *Lich* 72-74; USPG Zambia 75-88; C Southmead *Bris* 88-90; rtd 07. *78 William Bentley Court, Graiseley Lane, Wolverhampton WV11 1QW* Tel (01902) 730381

REYNOLDS, Hannah Claire. b 67. Kingston Univ MBA95. St Steph Ho Ox BTh09. **d** 06 **p** 07. C Twickenham All Hallows *Lon* 06-09; P-in-c Hanworth All SS from 09. *All Saints' Vicarage, Uxbridge Road, Feltham TW13 5EE* Tel (020) 8894 9330 Mobile 07981-981493 E-mail hcreynolds@hotmail.co.uk

REYNOLDS, Ms Helen Tracy. b 65. Huddersfield Univ BA. Cranmer Hall Dur 03. **d** 06 **p** 07. C Ryton *Dur* 06-11. *292 Wingrove Road North, Newcastle upon Tyne NE4 9EE* E-mail tracyreynolds@gmail.com

REYNOLDS, Canon John Lionel. b 34. JP. Westmr Coll Ox MTh00. Chich Th Coll 58. **d** 61 **p** 62. C Whitkirk *Ripon* 61-64; C Tong *Bradf* 64-68; V Chisledon and Draycot Foliatt *Sarum* 68-74; TR Ridgeway 74-76; RD Marlborough 74-76; V Calne and Blackland 76-89; RD Calne 77-84; Can and Preb Sarum Cathl 80-02; V Woodford Valley 89-02; rtd 02; Perm to Offic *Sarum* from 02 and *Win* from 03. *St Edmund, 21 New Road, Romsey SO51 7LL* Tel (01794) 516349

REYNOLDS, Mandy Elizabeth. b 54. NTMTC 99. **d** 02 **p** 03. NSM Wembley St Jo *Lon* 02-04; CF from 04. *c/o MOD Chaplains (Army)* Tel (01264) 381140 Fax 381824 E-mail mandyreynoldsuk@yahoo.co.uk

REYNOLDS, Marion. b 49. Chelmer Inst of HE CertEd84. STETS 04. **d** 06 **p** 07. NSM Quantock Towers *B & W* 06-07; NSM Shelswell *Ox* from 07. *10C St Michael's Close, Fringford, Bicester OX27 8DW* Tel (01869) 278972 Mobile 07834-062268 E-mail marion.reynolds2@btopenworld.com

REYNOLDS, Martin. *See* REYNOLDS, Alan Martin

REYNOLDS, Michael. *See* REYNOLDS, Richard Michael

REYNOLDS, Mrs Michelle Angela. b 70. Ridley Hall Cam 02. **d** 04 **p** 05. C Hoddesdon *St Alb* 04-07; TV Grays Thurrock *Chelmsf* from 07. *Wendover Vicarage, College Avenue, Grays RM17 5UW* Tel (01375) 373468 E-mail michellea_reynolds@hotmail.com

REYNOLDS, Paul Andrew. b 57. BA86. Trin Coll Bris 83. **d** 86 **p** 87. C Reading St Jo *Ox* 86-90; C Drayton *Birm* 90-95; TV Riverside *Ox* 95-06; R Beercrocombe w Curry Mallet, Hatch Beauchamp etc *B & W* from 06. *The Rectory, Stoke St Mary, Taunton TA3 5BX* Tel (01823) 444023

REYNOLDS, Paul Frederick. b 56. St Jo Coll Nottm 90. **d** 92 **p** 93. C Hyde St Geo *Ches* 92-96; P-in-c Delamere 96-00; Asst Dir Par Support and Development 96-98; Acting Dir 98-00; V Handforth 00-07; P-in-c Bramcote *S'well* from 07. *The Vicarage, Moss Drive, Bramcote, Beeston NG9 3NF* Tel 0115-922 9600 E-mail vicar@bramcoteparishchurch.com

REYNOLDS, Philip Delamere. b 53. Leeds Univ CertEd74 Nottm Univ BCombStuds82. Linc Th Coll 79. **d** 82 **p** 83. C Huddersfield St Jo *Wakef* 82-85; C Barkisland w W Scammonden 85-87; P-in-c Skelmanthorpe from 87. *St Aidan's Vicarage, Radcliffe Street, Skelmanthorpe, Huddersfield HD8 9AF* Tel (01484) 863232 E-mail life.draw@virgin.net

REYNOLDS, Raymond Ernest. b 29. Nottm Univ MPhil89. Lambeth STh84 CA Tr Coll 50 Chich Th Coll 58. **d** 60 **p** 61. C Leeds St Marg *Ripon* 60-62; C Beeston *S'well* 62-64; R Farnley *Ripon* 64-76; R Higham-on-the-Hill w Fenny Drayton *Leic* 76-81; R Higham-on-the-Hill w Fenny Drayton and Witherley 81-90; V Sutton *Ely* 90-94; R Witcham w Mepal 90-94; rtd 94; C Nantwich *Ches* 94-96; Perm to Offic from 96. *4 St Alban's Drive, Nantwich CW5 7DW* Tel (01270) 623534

REYNOLDS, Richard Michael. b 42. St Steph Ho Ox 65. **d** 67 **p** 68. C Kidderminster St Mary *Worc* 67-70; Guyana 70-73; TV

N Creedy *Ex* 73-80; R Holsworthy w Hollacombe 80-86; R Holsworthy w Hollacombe and Milton Damerel from 86; Chapl N Devon Healthcare NHS Trust from 94. *The Rectory, Bodmin Street, Holsworthy EX22 6BH* Tel (01409) 253435 E-mail michael@rnlds85.freeserve.co.uk

REYNOLDS, Roderick Bredon (Rory). b 58. Man Univ BA80. Ripon Coll Cuddesdon 93. **d** 95 **p** 96. C Hitchin *St Alb* 95-98; C Stevenage St Andr and St Geo 98-00; P-in-c High Wych and Gilston w Eastwick 00-06; TV Plaistow and N Canning Town *Chelmsf* 06-10; Chapl S Lon and Maudsley NHS Foundn Trust from 10. *Chaplaincy, Bethlem Royal Hospital, Monks Orchard Road, Beckenham BR3 3BX* Tel (020) 3228 4361 Mobile 07515-353456 E-mail roryreynolds@mac.com

REYNOLDS, Mrs Rosemary Joan. b 46. WMMTC 00. **d** 03 **p** 04. NSM Brandwood *Birm* from 03. *23 Chanston Avenue, Birmingham B14 5BD* Tel 0121-444 7015 E-mail hello@frankandrosemary.freeserve.co.uk

REYNOLDS, Simon Andrew. b 65. UEA MA00 ARCM85. Westcott Ho Cam 98. **d** 00 **p** 01. C Ex St Thos and Em 00-03; Min Can and Succ St Paul's Cathl 03-07; Warden Coll Min Cans 04-07; P-in-c Darton *Wakef* from 07; P-in-c Cawthorne from 07. *The Vicarage, 6 Jacob's Hall Court, Darton, Barnsley S75 5LY* Tel (01226) 384596 E-mail frsimonreynolds@btinternet.com

REYNOLDS, Stephen Paul. **d** 08 **p** 09. NSM Cannock *Lich* 08-09; NSM Heath Hayes from 09. *4 Harebell Close, Cannock WS12 3XA* Tel (01543) 270940 E-mail stevereyno@tiscali.co.uk

REYNOLDS, Tracy. *See* REYNOLDS, Ms Helen Tracy

RHOADES, Andrew Craig. b 56. Hatf Poly BSc79 CEng84 MIEE84. St Jo Coll Nottm MTh09. **d** 09 **p** 10. C Hexagon Leic from 09. *The Rectory, Dag Lane, North Kilworth, Lutterworth LE17 6HA* Tel (01858) 882099 Mobile 07531-121145 E-mail acrhoades@cheerful.com

RHODES, Adrian Michael. b 48. K Coll Lon BD71 AKC71. Qu Coll Birm 71. **d** 72 **p** 73. C Bury St Jo *Man* 73-75; Chapl N Man Gen Hosp 75-77; C Crumpsall *Man* 75-77; Chapl Walsall Manor and Bloxwich Hosps 77-83; Chapl Walsall Gen Hosp 81-83; Chapl Man R Infirmary 83-94; Chapl St Mary's Hosp Man 83-94; Chapl Man R Eye Hosp 83-94; Chapl Cen Man Healthcare NHS Trust 94-00; Perm to Offic *Man* 00-08. *58 Errwood Road, Burnage, Manchester M19 2QH* Tel 0161-224 1739 E-mail adrian@rhodes.net

RHODES, Mrs Amanda Louise. b 63. Leeds Univ BA07. NOC 04. **d** 07 **p** 08. C Kippax w Allerton Bywater *Ripon* 07-11; P-in-c Lofthouse from 11. *The Vicarage, 8 Church Farm Close, Lofthouse, Wakefield WF3 3SA* Tel (01924) 823286 Mobile 07971-998621 E-mail revmac63@googlemail.com

RHODES, Anthony John. b 27. Mert Coll Ox BA50 MA53. St Steph Ho Ox 52. **d** 54 **p** 55. C Northampton St Alb *Pet* 54-57; C Oakham 57-60; P-in-c S Queensferry *Edin* 60-74; V Mitcham St Olave *S'wark* 74-81; V Owston *Linc* 81-92; V W Butterwick 81-92; rtd 92. *1 Trentside, Owston Ferry, Doncaster DN9 1RS* Tel (01427) 728237

RHODES, Arthur. b 31. Dur Univ BA58. Cranmer Hall Dur 57. **d** 59 **p** 60. C Kirkdale St Lawr *Liv* 59-61; C Litherland St Phil 61-64; V St Helens St Matt Thatto Heath 64-67; V Samlesbury *Blackb* 67-79; Lic to Offic 80-01; Perm to Offic from 01. *88 Deborah Avenue, Fulwood, Preston PR2 9HU* Tel (01772) 712212

RHODES, Benjamin. b 71. Portsm Univ BSc93 Heythrop Coll Lon MA10. Westcott Ho Cam 94. **d** 97 **p** 98. C Upminster *Chelmsf* 97-01; Asst Chapl Lewisham Hosp NHS Trust 01-05; Sen Chapl Barts and The Lon NHS Trust 05-08; Lead Chapl 08-10; Lead Chapl Tower Hamlets Primary Care Trust 08-10; Spiritual Care Lead and Chapl Team Ldr King's Coll Hosp NHS Trust from 10; NSM St Bart Less *Lon* 05-07; Bp's Adv for Healthcare Chapl Stepney Area 08-10. *The Chaplaincy, King's College Hospital, Denmark Hill, London SE5 9RS* Tel (020) 3299 3522 E-mail benrhodes@nhs.net

RHODES, Mrs Caroline Laura. b 66. Bath Univ BPharm87 K Coll Lon MSc91. Ripon Coll Cuddesdon 08. **d** 10 **p** 11. C Allestree St Edm and Darley Abbey *Derby* from 10. *25 Church Lane, Darley Abbey, Derby DE22 1EE* Tel (01332) 554759 E-mail caroline@cgrhodes.myzen.co.uk

RHODES, Christine. *See* RHODES, Lois Christine

RHODES, David George. b 45. Univ of Wales (Abth) BA66. Trin Coll Bris 83. **d** 85 **p** 86. C Brinsworth w Catcliffe *Sheff* 85-89; V Mortomley St Sav *Sheff* 89-90; V Mortomley St Sav High Green 90-99; V Totley 99-11; rtd 11. *12 Sheards Close, Dronfield Woodhouse, Sheffield S18 8NJ* E-mail drhodes@toucansurf.com

RHODES, Duncan. b 35. Leeds Univ BSc56. **d** 93 **p** 94. OLM Saddleworth *Man* 93-05; rtd 05; Perm to Offic *Man* from 06. *Holden Cottage, 21 Spurn Lane, Diggle, Oldham OL3 5QP* Tel (01457) 872399 E-mail dunrhodes@aol.com

RHODES, Heather. b 32. **d** 88. Par Dn Purley St Mark *S'wark* 89-94; C 94-98; rtd 98; Hon C Purley St Mark *S'wark* 00-05; Perm to Offic from 05. *24 Highfield Road, Purley CR8 2JG* Tel (020) 8660 1486

RHODES, Canon John Lovell. b 33. MBE81. Lon Univ BD59. St Aid Birkenhead 55. **d** 59 **p** 60. C Bradf St Clem 59-61; C Heeley *Sheff* 61-66; Ind Chapl *Linc* 66-81; Sen Ind Chapl 81-98; RD Grimsby and Cleethorpes 76-83; Can and Preb Linc Cathl 77-98; Chapl Franklin Coll 92-98; rtd 98; Perm to Offic *Linc* 98-01. *19 Augusta Close, Grimsby DN34 4TQ* Tel (01472) 343167

RHODES, Jonathan Peter. b 69. Coll of Ripon & York St Jo BA96. NOC 01. **d** 04 **p** 05. C High Harrogate Ch Ch *Ripon* 04-08; P-in-c Hartlepool St Aid and St Columba *Dur* from 08. *39 Chichester Close, Hartlepool TS25 2QT* Tel (01429) 871009

RHODES, Lois Christine. b 34. Lon Univ BSc61. Glouc Sch of Min 84. **d** 87 **p** 94. NSM Weobley w Sarnesfield and Norton Canon *Heref* 87-92; NSM Letton w Staunton, Byford, Mansel Gamage etc 87-92; Chapl Asst Heref Hosps NHS Trust from 93. *Bellbrook, Bell Square, Weobley, Hereford HR4 8SE* Tel (01544) 318410 *or* (01432) 355444

RHODES, Matthew Ivan. b 66. Bris Univ BA89 Birm Univ MPhil95 PhD05. Qu Coll Birm BD93. **d** 94 **p** 95. C Willenhall H Trin *Lich* 94-97; Chapl Maadi St Jo Egypt 97-00; P-in-c Middleton *Birm* 00-07; P-in-c Wishaw 00-07; P-in-c Curdworth 05-07; R Curdworth, Middleton and Wishaw 07-11; P-in-c Maney from 11; AD Sutton Coldfield from 06. *The Vicarage, Maney Hill Road, Sutton Coldfield B72 1JJ* Tel 0121-354 2426 E-mail catmat30@hotmail.com

RHODES, Robert George. b 41. Man Univ BSc62. Ripon Hall Ox 72. **d** 74 **p** 75. C Banbury *Ox* 74-77; TV Banbury 77-81; P-in-c Long Horsley and Adult Educn Adv *Newc* 81-86; TR Wolverton *Ox* 86-97; P-in-c Bledlow w Saunderton and Horsenden 97-98; TV Risborough 98-02; Warden of Readers 97-02; USPG Miss Belize 02-06; rtd 06; Perm to Offic *Derby* from 07. *3 China House Yard, St Mary's Gate, Wirksworth, Matlock DE4 4DQ* Tel (01629) 823623 E-mail bandjrhodes@hotmail.com

RHODES-WRIGLEY, James. b 35. AKC59. **d** 60 **p** 61. C S Harrow St Paul *Lon* 60-66; V Hendon Ch Ch 66-71; V Northolt Park St Barn 71-92; rtd 92; Hon C Whyke w Rumboldswhyke and Portfield *Chich* from 96. *4 Gordon Avenue, Donnington, Chichester PO19 8QY* Tel (01243) 781664

RHYDDERCH, David Huw. b 48. St Mich Coll Llan 70. **d** 73 **p** 74. C Gelligaer *Llan* 73-76; C Penarth All SS 76-78; V Resolven 78-81; V Ystrad Rhondda w Ynyscynon 81-93; RD Rhondda 89-93; R St Andrews Major w Michaelston-le-Pit from 93. *The Rectory, Lettons Way, Dinas Powys CF64 4BY* Tel (029) 2051 2555

RICE, David. b 57. Nottm Univ BA79. Ripon Coll Cuddesdon 80. **d** 82 **p** 83. C Cirencester *Glouc* 82-86; R Theale and Englefield *Ox* 86-00; TR Wallingford from 00. *The Rectory, 22 Castle Street, Wallingford OX10 8DW* Tel (01491) 202188

RICE, Franklin Arthur. b 20. FRICS49. St Alb Minl Tr Scheme 77. **d** 80 **p** 81. NSM Hoddesdon *St Alb* 80-84; Perm to Offic *Guildf* from 85. *27 Mead Court, 281 Station Road, Addlestone KT15 2PR* Tel (01932) 846462

RICE, John Leslie Hale. b 38. Lon Univ BScEng60 BD68 FCMI. EMMTC 73. **d** 76 **p** 77. NSM Allestree St Nic *Derby* 76-90; Lic to Offic from 90. *14 Gisborne Crescent, Allestree, Derby DE22 2FL* Tel (01332) 557222

RICE, Lt Cdr Peter Langford. b 49. STETS 97. **d** 00 **p** 01. NSM Salisbury St Fran and Stratford sub Castle *Sarum* 00-03; P-in-c W Highland Region *Arg* 03-08. *The Old Manse, Lochgair, Argyll PA31 8SB* Tel (01546) 886674 Mobile 07776-105279 E-mail fynesinbosun@aol.com

RICE-OXLEY, John Richard. b 44. Keble Coll Ox BA66 MA69 Dur Univ MA85. Lon Coll of Div 68. **d** 70 **p** 71. C Eastwood *S'well* 70-73; Youth Adv CMS 73-78; V Mansfield St Jo *S'well* 78-82; P-in-c Thornley *Dur* 82-85; P-in-c Darlington St Matt and St Luke 85-87; V 87-98; V Hornsea w Atwick *York* 98-06; P-in-c Aldbrough, Mappleton w Goxhill and Withernwick 05-06; rtd 06; Perm to Offic *York* from 07. *The Vicarage, Carlton Drive, Aldbrough, Hull HU11 4SF* Tel (01964) 529032 E-mail richardriceoxley@gmail.com

RICE-OXLEY, Mrs Sylvia Jeanette Kathleen. b 48. **d** 08 **p** 09. C Aldbrough, Mappleton w Goxhill and Withernwick *York* 08-11; P-in-c from 11. *The Vicarage, Carlton Drive, Aldbrough, Hull HU11 4SF* Tel (01964) 529032 E-mail sylviariceoxley@gmail.com

RICH, Brian John. b 49. Reading Univ BSc70. Guildf Dioc Min Course 94. **d** 97 **p** 98. OLM Stoke Hill *Guildf* from 97. *Roewen, 1 Trentham Crescent, Woking GU22 9EW* Tel (01483) 829541 E-mail btrich@ntlworld.com

RICH, Canon Christopher Robin. b 49. LSE MSc(Econ)95. Brasted Th Coll 70 Sarum & Wells Th Coll 72. **d** 74 **p** 75. C Sholing *Win* 74-76; C Southampton Maybush St Pet 76-79; R Fawley 79-90; Ind Chapl 83-90; Dir Soc Resp 90-99; Hon Can Win Cathl 96-99; Dir Soc Resp *Blackb* 99-05; Dir Soc Resp *Guildf* from 06. *Diocesan House, Quarry Street, Guildford GU1 3XG* Tel (01483) 571826 E-mail chris.rich@cofeguildford.org.uk

RICH, Nicholas Philip. b 49. St Cuth Soc Dur BA74 PGCE75 Coll of Ripon & York St Jo CertEd83. Linc Th Coll 86. **d** 88 **p** 89. C W Acklam *York* 88-91; Chapl St Geo Sch Harpenden 91-95; rtd 95. *36 Park Hill, Ampthill, Bedford MK45 2LF* Tel (01525) 403445 E-mail maggie.rich@phonecoop.coop

RICH, Paul Michael. b 36. OBE87. Sarum Th Coll 62. **d** 65 **p** 66. C Woodbridge St Mary *St E* 65-68; C W Wycombe *Ox* 68-70. CF 70-88; Lic to Offic *S & B* 88-90; V Crondall and Ewshot *Guildf* 91-05; rtd 05. *The Firs, The Street, Binsted, Alton GU34 4PF* Tel (01420) 525302

RICH, Peter Geoffrey. b 45. Oak Hill Th Coll 74. **d** 77 **p** 78. C Blackheath St Jo *S'wark* 77-80; C Surbiton St Matt 80-87; V St Alb St Luke *St Alb* 87-98; V Gravesend St Aid *Roch* 98-10; rtd 11; P-in-c Stone w Dinton and Hartwell *Ox* from 11. *10 Badgers Rise, Stone, Aylesbury HP17 8RR* Tel (01296) 748068 E-mail angela_richuk@yahoo.co.uk

RICH, Thomas. b 52. St Jo Coll Nottm 86. **d** 88 **p** 89. C Netherton *Liv* 88-91; P-in-c Bootle Ch Ch 91-93; V from 93. *Christ Church Vicarage, 1 Breeze Hill, Bootle L20 9EY* Tel 0151-525 2565 Mobile 07958-784313 E-mail tom@richchurch.freeserve.co.uk

RICHARDS, Alan Grenville. b 41. Kelham Th Coll. **d** 69 **p** 70. C Northolt St Mary *Lon* 69-75; V Fatfield *Dur* 75-84; V Beighton *Sheff* 84-91; V Endcliffe 91-94; Deputation Appeals Org Children's Soc 94-98; V Cheriton All So w Newington *Cant* 98-06; rtd 06; Hon C Cheriton All So w Newington *Cant* 06-07; Hon C Cheriton St Martin 06-07; Perm to Offic from 07. *82 Capel Street, Capel-le-ferne, Folkestone CT18 7HF* Tel (01303) 243999

RICHARDS, Andrew David Thomas. b 55. St Jo Coll Dur BA76 Roehampton Inst PGCE84 FRSA96. St Steph Ho Ox 76. **d** 78 **p** 79. C Shirley *Birm* 78-80; C Cowley St Jo Ox 80-82; Perm to Offic *Win* 84-88; and *Sarum* 88-92; NSM Hazelbury Bryan and the Hillside Par *Sarum* 92-94; Chapl Rossall Sch Fleetwood 94-99; Min Can Ely Cathl and Chapl K Sch Ely 99-03; Sen Chapl and Hd RS Wellington Coll Berks 03-08; Chapl Duke of York's R Mil Sch Dover from 08. *Duke of York's Royal Military School, Dover CT15 5EQ* Tel (01304) 245023 Mobile 07757-601244 E-mail andrew.richards@doyrms.com

RICHARDS, Anne. b 42. Man Univ BSc63. S Dios Minl Tr Scheme 82. **dss** 85 **d** 87 **p** 94. Catherington and Clanfield *Portsm* 85-89; C 87-89; C E Meon and Langrish 89-95; Chapl Portsm Hosps NHS Trust 92-95; P-in-c Blackmoor and Whitehill *Portsm* 95-98; V 98-05; RD Petersfield 99-04; rtd 05. *6 Burrows Vale, Brixworth, Northampton NN6 9US* Tel (01604) 882230 E-mail aprilrichards@waitrose.com

RICHARDS, Mrs Anne Maria. b 54. Wolv Poly CertEd88 HCIMA83. Qu Coll Birm 08. **d** 11. OLM Fletchamstead *Cov* from 11. *2 Farthing Walk, Coventry CV4 8GR* Tel (024) 7646 8660 Mobile 07769-943019

RICHARDS, Anthony Francis. b 26. Edin Univ 45 Wadh Coll Ox BA51 MA54. Ridley Hall Cam 50. **d** 52 **p** 53. C Finchley Ch Ch *Lon* 52-55; C Maidenhead St Andr and St Mary Ox 55-59; Lect All Nations Chr Coll Ware 58-59; V High Wycombe Ch Ch *Ox* 59-63; P-in-c 63-66; V Terriers 63-73; USA 70-71; V Cinderford St Steph w Littledean *Glouc* 73-80; V Clacton St Paul *Chelmsf* 80-93; New Zealand 88-89; rtd 93. *Montrichards, Mont, 58230 Ouroux-en-Morvan, France* Tel (0033) 3 86 78 24 44 E-mail anthony.richards@libertysurf.fr

RICHARDS, Mrs April Deborah. b 42. Man Univ BSc63. S Dios Minl Tr Scheme 82. **dss** 85 **d** 87 **p** 94. Catherington and Clanfield *Portsm* 85-89; C 87-89; C E Meon and Langrish 89-95; Chapl Portsm Hosps NHS Trust 92-95; P-in-c Blackmoor and Whitehill *Portsm* 95-98; V 98-05; RD Petersfield 99-04; rtd 05. *6 Burrows Vale, Brixworth, Northampton NN6 9US* Tel (01604) 882230 E-mail aprilrichards@waitrose.com

RICHARDS, Brian. b 39. Open Univ BA78 BSc05. St Deiniol's Hawarden 94. **d** 94 **p** 94. C St Mellons and Michaelston-y-Fedw *Mon* 94-96; P-in-c Michaelston-y-Fedw 96-02; P-in-c Haarlem *Eur* 02-06; rtd 06; P-in-c Llangwm Uchaf and Llangwm Isaf w Gwernesney etc *Mon* 06-07. *32 Monnow Keep, Monmouth NP25 3EX* Tel (01600) 772824

RICHARDS, Brian William. b 45. Spurgeon's Coll Lon BA88 MTh99. Guildf Dioc Min Course 01. **d** 03 **p** 04. NSM Howell Hill w Burgh Heath *Guildf* from 03. *2 Canford Court, 88A Epsom Road, Sutton SM3 9ES* Tel (020) 8330 1196 E-mail brianr@saintpauls.co.uk

RICHARDS, Christopher Mordaunt. b 40. New Coll Ox BA63 MA72 Bris Univ MB, ChB72. Cuddesdon Coll 63. **d** 65 **p** 81. C Bris St Mary Redcliffe w Temple etc 65-66; Perm to Offic 66-72; Hon C Keynsham *B & W* 81-90; Perm to Offic 90-93. *4 St Ronans Avenue, Bristol BS6 6EP* Tel 0117-974 4062

RICHARDS, Daniel James. b 40. St D Coll Lamp. **d** 66 **p** 67. C Kingswinford H Trin *Lich* 66-69; C Banbury *Ox* 69-71; C Aylesbury 71-73; C-in-c Stoke Poges St Jo Manor Park CD 73-78; R W Slough 78-80; R Ilchester w Northover, Limington Yeovilton etc *B & W* 80-90; RD Ilchester 81-91; RD Martock 89-91; TR Bruton and Distr 90-97; R Axbridge w Shipham and Rowberrow 97-04; rtd 04; Perm to Offic *B & W* from 05; Co-ord Clergy Retirement and Widows' Officer from 06. *1 Quaperlake Street, Bruton BA10 0HA* Tel (01749) 812386 E-mail revdanrich@mbzonline.net

RICHARDS, Daniel Michael Hamilton. b 79. Man Univ BA02. Cranmer Hall Dur 05. **d** 07 **p** 08. C Bury St Jo w St Mark *Man* 07-08; C Tonge w Alkrington 08-11; Chapl Cov Univ from 11. *Coventry University, Priory Street, Coventry CV1 5FB* Tel (024) 7688 7688 E-mail dogcollar@tiscali.co.uk

RICHARDS, Canon David. b 30. Bris Univ BA52. St Mich Coll Llan 52. **d** 54 **p** 55. C Llangynwyd w Maesteg 54-56; Iran 57-61 and 62-66; C Skewen *Llan* 61-62; V Cwmbach 66-76; Warden of Ords 71-77; R Coity w Nolton 76-96; Can Llan Cathl 88-96; rtd 96; Perm to Offic *Llan* and *Mon* from 96. *Inglewood, 5 Hopewell Close, Bulwark, Chepstow NP16 5ST* Tel (01291) 628912

RICHARDS, David Arnold. b 56. Wycliffe Hall Ox 76. **d** 81 **p** 82. C Skewen *Llan* 81-84; C Barking St Marg w St Patr *Chelmsf* 84-85; TV 85-90; Chapl Barking Hosp 87-88; P-in-c Stratford St Jo and Ch Ch w Forest Gate St Jas *Chelmsf* 90-97; V Stratford St Jo w Ch Ch and St Jas from 97. *Stratford Vicarage, 20 Deanery Road, London E15 4LP* Tel (020) 8534 8388 *or* 8503 1913 E-mail office@stjohnse15.freeserve.co.uk

RICHARDS, David Gareth. b 60. Hull Univ BA83. Qu Coll Birm 89. **d** 92 **p** 93. C Knowle *Birm* 92-96; Assoc R Edin St Paul and St Geo 96-00; R from 00. *11 East Fettes Avenue, Edinburgh EH4 1DN* Tel 0131-332 3904 *or* 556 1355 Fax 556 0492 E-mail dave@pandgchurch.org.uk

RICHARDS, Dennis. b 48. St Mich Coll Llan 95. **d** 97 **p** 98. C Cwmbran *Mon* 97-00; TV 00-06; TV Caldicot from 06. *The Rectory, 19 Main Road, Portskewett, Caldicot NP26 5SG* Tel (01291) 420313 E-mail den.richards@btinternet.com

RICHARDS, Mrs Glenys Heather. b 51. SEN73. **d** 06 **p** 07. OLM Heatons *Man* from 06. *61 All Saints Road, Heaton Norris, Stockport SK4 1QA* Tel 0161-477 2137 E-mail glh@123.com

RICHARDS, Gwilym David Marshall. b 56. SEITE. **d** 09 **p** 10. NSM Southgate *Chich* from 09. *11 Duncton Close, Crawley RH11 0AX* Tel (01293) 547809

RICHARDS, James Johnston. b 59. Solicitor 84 Lon Bible Coll BA90 Dur Univ MA97. Cranmer Hall Dur 90. **d** 92 **p** 93. C Harrow Trin St Mich *Lon* 92-95; C Kendal H Trin *Carl* 95-99; R Windermere from 99; RD Windermere from 10. *The Rectory, Longlands Road, Bowness-on-Windermere, Windermere LA23 3AS* Tel (01539) 443063 E-mail rector@stmartin.org.uk

RICHARDS, Mrs Jane Valerie. b 43. Westf Coll Lon BA64 Birm Univ CertEd65. S Dios Minl Tr Scheme 84. **d** 87 **p** 94. NSM Locks Heath *Portsm* 87-90; Asst Chapl Qu Alexandra Hosp Portsm 90-92; Chapl Portsm Hosps NHS Trust 92-95; Asst to RD Fareham *Portsm* 95-96; C Locks Heath 95-96; Chapl Southn Univ Hosps NHS Trust 96-03; rtd 03; Perm to Offic *Portsm* from 97 and *Win* 03-06. *16 Lodge Road, Locks Heath, Southampton SO31 6QY* Tel (01489) 573891 E-mail revjane.richards@btinternet.com

RICHARDS, Preb John Francis. b 37. Dur Univ BA61. Wells Th Coll 61. **d** 63 **p** 64. C Sherwood *S'well* 63-67; C Bishopwearmouth St Mich *Dur* 67-69; C Egg Buckland *Ex* 69-75; CF (ACF) 72-02; V Plymouth St Jas Ham *Ex* 75-83; V Plympton St Mary 83-02; RD Plymouth Moorside 88-93 and 96-01; Preb Ex Cathl 91-07; rtd 02; Clergy Widow(er)s Officer *Ex* from 02. *24 Trewithy Drive, Plymouth PL6 5TY* Tel (01752) 214442 E-mail jfr-sjr@blueyonder.co.uk

RICHARDS, John George. b 48. Qu Coll Birm 87. **d** 89 **p** 90. C Acocks Green *Birm* 89-92; TV Shirley 92-96; P-in-c Yardley Wood 96-00; V from 00. *Christ Church Vicarage, School Road, Yardley Wood, Birmingham B14 4EP* Tel 0121-436 7726 E-mail rev.johnrichards@btinternet.com

RICHARDS, John Henry. b 34. CCC Cam BA57 MA75. St Mich Coll Llan BD77. **d** 77 **p** 78. C Llangynwyd w Maesteg 77-79; C Cardiff St Jo 79-82; Asst Chapl Univ of Wales (Cardiff) 79-82; V Penmark w Porthkerry 82-83; R Stackpole Elidor w St Petrox *St D* 83-85; R St Petrox w Stackpole Elidor and Bosherston etc 85-99; rtd 99. *20 Williamson Street, Pembroke SA71 4ER* Tel (01646) 672472

RICHARDS, John Michael. b 53. Coll of Ripon w York St Jo TCert76 Open Univ BA81. Cranmer Hall Dur 93. **d** 93 **p** 94. C Wath-upon-Dearne *Sheff* 93-95; R Warmsworth 95-01; R Sprotbrough 01-10; P-in-c Barningham w Hutton Magna and Wycliffe *Ripon* from 10; P-in-c Gilling and Kirkby Ravensworth from 10. *The Rectory, Barningham, Richmond DL11 7DW* Tel (01833) 621259 E-mail johnmr1953@talk21.com

RICHARDS, John William. b 29. Southn Univ BSc55. Sarum & Wells Th Coll 78. **d** 81 **p** 82. NSM Woking St Mary *Guildf* 81-85; C Addlestone 85-87; C S Gillingham *Roch* 87-89; Hon C W Byfleet *Guildf* 91-95; rtd 94; Perm to Offic *Sarum* from 95. *16 Normandy Way, Poundbury Whitfield, Dorchester DT1 2PP* Tel (01305) 251529

RICHARDS, Julian. b 25. Wycliffe Hall Ox 71. **d** 73 **p** 74. C Hessle *York* 73-76; P-in-c Rowley 76-82; Chapl HM Pris Hull 79-82; P-in-c Boldre *Win* 82-83; P-in-c Boldre w S Baddesley 83; V 83-93; rtd 93; RD Alton *Win* 93-98; Perm to Offic *Portsm* and *Win* from 98; Clergy Widows Officer (Win Adnry) 00-04. *Manor End, Worldham Hill, East Worldham, Alton GU34 3AX* Tel (01420) 86894 E-mail manorend134@btinternet.com

RICHARDS, Keith David. b 50. Didsbury Coll of Educn CertEd72. S'wark Ord Course 79. **d** 82 **p** 83. NSM Walworth *S'wark* 82-85; Chapl Derbyshire Coll of HE 85-87; V Rottingdean *Chich* 87-93; TR Crawley 93-97; V Arundel w Tortington and S Stoke 97-07; RD Arundel and Bognor 04-07; Can and Preb Chich Cathl 07; V Selby Abbey *York* 07-10; P-in-c Hove St Barn and St Agnes *Chich* from 10; RD Hove from 11. *St Barnabas' Vicarage, 88 Sackville Road, Hove BN3 3HE* Tel (01273) 732427

RICHARDS, Kelvin. b 58. Univ of Wales (Abth) BSc80 MA88. Ripon Coll Cuddesdon BA82. **d** 83 **p** 84. C Killay *S & B* 83-86; C Morriston 86-89; R Llangattock and Llangynidr from 89; AD Crickhowell from 02. *The Rectory, Llangattock, Crickhowell NP8 1PH* Tel (01873) 810270

RICHARDS, Llewelyn. b 15. St Deiniol's Hawarden 73. **d** 75 **p** 76. NSM Corwen and Llangar *St As* 75-85; Past Care Gwyddelwern 78-85; rtd 85. *120 Maesyfallen, Corwen LL21 9AD* Tel (01490) 412195

RICHARDS, Mrs Mary Edith. b 33. SWMTC 85. **d** 87 **p** 94. NSM Kea *Truro* 87-88; Asst Chapl Bris Poly 88-91; C E Clevedon and Walton w Weston w Clapton *B & W* 91-96; rtd 96; Hon C Probus, Ladock and Grampound w Creed and St Erme *Truro* from 97; Mental Health Chapl Cornwall Healthcare NHS Trust 97-01. *62 Midway Drive, Uplands Park, Truro TR1 1NQ* Tel (01872) 277556

RICHARDS, Norman John. b 47. BSc. Ridley Hall Cam. **d** 83 **p** 84. C Luton St Fran *St Alb* 83-86; R Aspenden and Layston w Buntingford 86-95; P-in-c Westmill 94-95; R Aspenden, Buntingford and Westmill 95-08; rtd 09; Hon Chapl Stansted Airport *Chelmsf* from 09. *Gardners Cottage, Hare Street, Buntingford SG9 0DY* Tel (01763) 289720 E-mail nrichardsvic@aol.com

RICHARDS, Robert Graham. b 42. St Jo Coll Nottm 77. **d** 80 **p** 81. C Radipole and Melcombe Regis *Sarum* 80-83; TV Billericay and Lt Burstead *Chelmsf* 84-91; UK Dir CMJ 91-95; Chief Exec Nat Bibl Heritage Cen Ltd Trust 95-97; C Chorleywood St Andr *St Alb* 97-00; Chapl Lee Abbey 02-05; rtd 05; Perm to Offic *Sarum* from 05. *33 Stowell Crescent, Wareham BH20 4PT* Tel (01929) 552174 E-mail robandannar@tiscali.co.uk

RICHARDS, Simon Granston. b 47. St Jo Coll Nottm BTh72 ALCD72. **d** 72 **p** 73. C Waltham Abbey *Chelmsf* 72-77; TV Basildon St Martin w H Cross and Laindon etc 77-80; V Grayshott *Guildf* 80-88; V Eccleston Ch Ch *Liv* 88-92; V Berkeley w Wick, Breadstone and Newport *Glouc* 92-02; P-in-c Stone w Woodford and Hill 99-02; V Berkeley w Wick, Breadstone, Newport, Stone etc 02-05; RD Dursley 96-02; Chapl Severn NHS Trust 94-05; V Bisley, Chalford, France Lynch, and Oakridge *Glouc* from 05; AD Bisley 06-08. *The Vicarage, Cheltenham Road, Bisley, Stroud GL6 7BJ* Tel (01452) 770056 E-mail simongr@tiscali.co.uk

RICHARDS, Stephen. b 51. Bris Univ BSc72 Maria Grey Coll Lon PGCE73 Birm Univ MEd77. STETS 07. **d** 10 **p** 11. NSM Corfe Mullen *Sarum* from 10. *Trevilling, Blandford Road, Corfe Mullen, Wimborne BH21 3HH* Tel (01202) 698567 Mobile 07801-461117 E-mail richards.steve@btinternet.com

RICHARDS, Stuart Anthony. b 70. K Coll Lon BA92 AKC92 Keble Coll Ox BA97 MA02. St Steph Ho Ox MTh02. **d** 99 **p** 00. C Reading All SS *Ox* 99-02; C Solihull *Birm* 02-06; Deanery P Handsworth 06-07; CF from 07. *c/o MOD Chaplains (Army)* Tel (01264) 381140 Fax 381824

RICHARDS, Terence David. b 43. Trin Coll Carmarthen DipEd64 Open Univ BA73 Magd Coll Ox MSc83. Ox Min Course 04. **d** 07 **p** 08. NSM Chenderit *Pet* from 07. *11 Portway Drive, Croughton, Brackley NN13 5NA* Tel (01869) 811251 E-mail tasker1@btinternet.com

RICHARDS, Canon Thomas John Wynzie. b 25. St D Coll Lamp BA49. **d** 51 **p** 52. C Llandybie *St D* 51-53; V 71-87; C Llandegai Ban 53; R Llanymawddwy 56-57; Chapl Nat Nautical Sch Portishead 57-71; RD Dyffryn Aman *St D* 78-85; Can St D Cathl 83-92; Treas St D Cathl 89-92; V Pencarreg and Llancrwys 87-92; rtd 92. *Maes Teifi, Cwmann, Lampeter SA48 8DT* Tel (01570) 423354

RICHARDS, Tony Benjamin. b 48. STETS. **d** 09 **p** 10. NSM Sandown Ch Ch *Portsm* from 09; NSM Lower Sandown St Jo from 09. *Abbotsford Lodge, Cliff Bridge, Shanklin PO37 6QJ* Tel (01983) 863607

RICHARDS, Canon William Hughes. b 37. St D Coll Lamp BA58. **d** 60 **p** 61. C Llandysul *St D* 60-63; C Llanelli 63-65; V Llanddewi Brefi w Llanbadarn Odwyn 65-73; V Pen-bre 73-83; V Llangunnor w Cwmffrwd 83-88; V Cardigan w Mwnt and Y Ferwig 88-99; V Cardigan w Mwnt and Y Ferwig w Llangoedmor 99-01; Can St D Cathl 89-01; Treas 01; rtd 01. *Hafan Gobaith, 6 Cwrt y Gloch, Peniel, Carmarthen SA32 7HW* Tel (01267) 235995

RICHARDS, Canon William Neal. b 38. ALCD63. **d** 63 **p** 64. C Otley *Bradf* 63-65; C Leamington Priors St Mary *Cov* 65-67; CMS 67-69; Kenya 69-74; Asst Provost and Can Res Nairobi 70-74; V Gt Malvern St Mary *Worc* 74-86; Chapl Kidderminster

Health Distr 86-91; RD Kidderminster *Worc* 89-91; R Martley and Wichenford, Knightwick etc 91-01; rtd 01; Perm to Offic *Worc* from 01. *Bay Tree Cottage, 32 Pump Street, Malvern WR14 4LU* Tel (01684) 569658

RICHARDSON, Aidan. *See* RICHARDSON, James Aidan

RICHARDSON, Ms Alison Mary. b 63. Leic Univ BSc84 St Jo Coll Dur BA09. Cranmer Hall Dur 07. **d** 09 **p** 10. C Spennymoor and Whitworth *Dur* 09-11; C Upper Skerne from 11. *1 Broad Oaks, Bishop Middleham, Ferryhill DL17 9BW* Tel 07873-596164 (mobile) E-mail arichardson2@btinternet.com

RICHARDSON, Andrew Edward John. b 75. St Andr Univ BD97. TISEC 04. **d** 06 **p** 07. C Dundee St Mary Magd *Bre* 06-09; Hon Chapl Dundee Univ 07-09; P-in-c Glas E End from 09. *Flat 1/1, 25 Queensborough Gardens, Glasgow G12 9QP* E-mail aejrichardson@hotmail.com

RICHARDSON, Andrew John. b 44. Ex Univ CertEd69. Trin Coll Bris 83. **d** 82 **p** 83. Kenya 82-87; Dioc Educn Sec Maseno N 83-87; Chapl Brentwood Sch Essex 88; Chapl Scarborough Coll 88-01; TV Parkham, Alwington, Buckland Brewer etc *Ex* 01-09; RD Hartland 03-09; rtd 09. *La Retraite, 3 Park Avenue, Bideford EX39 2QH* Tel (01237) 478324 E-mail rev.andy-ros@care4free.net

RICHARDSON, Miss Ann. b 72. Leeds Univ BA94. Trin Coll Bris BA10. **d** 10 **p** 11. C Bromley St Mark *Roch* from 10. *25 Matfield Close, Bromley BR2 9DY* Tel (020) 8325 0282 Mobile 07710-160972 E-mail ann_r@btinternet.com

RICHARDSON, Aubrey. *See* RICHARDSON, John Aubrey

RICHARDSON, Canon Charles Leslie Joseph. b 54. St Jo Coll Dur BA76. Coll of Resurr Mirfield 76. **d** 79 **p** 80. C Folkestone St Mary and St Eanswythe *Cant* 79-83; C Maidstone St Martin 83-86; Selection Sec and Voc Adv ACCM 86-91; PV Westmr Abbey 87-91; R Hastings St Clem and All SS *Chich* 91-98; RD Hastings 92-97; V E Dulwich St Jo *S'wark* from 98; Dioc Voc Adv from 99; Hon Can S'wark Cathl from 10. *St John's Vicarage, 62 East Dulwich Road, London SE22 9AU* Tel (020) 7639 3807 *or* 8693 3897 E-mail stjohnsse22@hotmail.com

RICHARDSON, Clive John. b 57. Oak Hill Th Coll BA83 Bris Univ MA00. **d** 83 **p** 84. C Woking St Pet *Guildf* 83-86; C Worplesdon 86-90; V Rowledge 90-03; V Rowledge and Frensham from 03. *The Vicarage, Church Lane, Rowledge, Farnham GU10 4EN* Tel (01252) 792402 E-mail rowvicar@aol.com

RICHARDSON, David. b 71. Edin Univ MA93 Stranmillis Coll PGCE94 QUB PhD98. CITC BTh02. **d** 02 **p** 03. C Coleraine *Conn* 02-06; Chapl RAF from 06. *Chaplaincy Services, Valiant Block, HQ Air Command, RAF High Wycombe HP14 4UE* Tel (01494) 496800 Fax 496343 E-mail richardsons05@hotmail.co.uk

RICHARDSON, David Anthony. b 41. Kelham Th Coll 57. **d** 66 **p** 67. C Tong *Bradf* 66-68; C Richmond St Mary *S'wark* 68-71; C Sanderstead All SS 71-74; TV 74-78; R Beddington 78-92; V Dormansland 92-98; RD Godstone 95-98; Assoc R Tucson St Phil in the Hills USA 98-03; R Lake Havasu City from 04. *3111 Silver Saddle Drive, Lake Havasu City AZ 86406-6284, USA* Tel (001) (928) 855 5397 Fax 855 2508 E-mail medart1@frontiernet.net

RICHARDSON, Canon David Gwynne. b 39. FIMMM09. K Coll Lon 60. **d** 64 **p** 65. C Birtley *Dur* 64-67; Bp's Soc and Ind Adv 67-77; TV Brayton *York* 78-92; Ind Chapl 78-92; R Monk Fryston and S Milford 92-04; RD Selby 93-04; Can and Preb York Minster 03-04; rtd 04; Perm to Offic *York* from 04; Chapl IMinE 85-02; Chapl IMMM from 02. *14 Beechcroft, Brayton, Selby YO8 9EP* Tel (01757) 704121 E-mail d.gwynne.richardson@homecall.co.uk

RICHARDSON, David John. b 50. MA LLB FCIArb. S'wark Ord Course. **d** 85 **p** 86. NSM S Croydon Em *S'wark* 85-06; Perm to Offic 06-07. *20 Hurst View Road, South Croydon CR2 7AG* Tel (020) 8688 4947 *or* 8688 6676 E-mail richardsonhome@blueyonder.co.uk

RICHARDSON, The Very Revd David John Leyburn. b 46. Univ of Qld BA69. St Barn Coll Adelaide ACT ThL70 Melbourne Coll of Div BD75. **d** 70 **p** 71. C Maryborough Australia 71-73; C Ipswich and C-in-c E Heights 74-75; Perm to Offic *Birm* 75-76; C Cambridge Gt St Mary w St Mich *Ely* 76-79; Tutor St Barn Th Coll Adelaide 79-80; Sub-Warden 80-82; R St Lucia 82-88; R Adelaide Cathl 88-89; Dean Adelaide 89-99; Dean Melbourne 99-08; Dir Angl Cen Rome from 08; Hon Prov Can Cant Cathl from 10. *Palazzo Doria Pamphilj, Piazza del Collegio Romano 2, 00186 Rome, Italy* Tel (0039) 066 780 302 Fax 066 780 674 E-mail director@anglicancentre.it

RICHARDSON, Preb Douglas Stanley. b 23. Bps' Coll Cheshunt 55. **d** 57 **p** 58. C Hampton St Mary *Lon* 57-61; V W Twyford 61-69; V Notting Hill St Pet 69-78; V Staines St Pet 78-83; P-in-c Staines St Mary 81-83; V Staines St Mary and St Pet 83-92; AD Spelthorne 83-92; Preb St Paul's Cathl 92; rtd 92; Perm to Offic *Win* from 92. *22 Rooks Down Road, Badgers Farm, Winchester SO22 4LT* Tel (01962) 863687

RICHARDSON, Edward John. b 39. Westmr Coll Ox MTh98. Lich Th Coll 62. **d** 65 **p** 66. C Chessington *Guildf* 65-70; TV

Trunch *Nor* 70-75; V Stoneleigh *Guildf* 75-79; Perm to Offic *S'wark* 92-94; Hon C Kingston All SS w St Jo 94-99; C 99-04; rtd 04; Perm to Offic *S'wark* 04-05; P-in-c Burpham *Chich* 05-09. *3 Westways, Epsom KT19 0PH* Tel (0208) 393 3648 E-mail rev.johnrichardson@tiscali.co.uk

RICHARDSON (née WOOD), Elaine Mary. b 51. SRN74. SEITE 00. **d** 03 **p** 04. C Hythe *Cant* 03-06; C Folkestone Trin 06-07; V Herne from 07. *The New Vicarage, Herne Street, Herne Bay CT6 7HE* Tel (01227) 374328 E-mail elaine.longview@virgin.net

RICHARDSON, Mrs Elizabeth Rosalind. b 54. STETS 05. **d** 08 **p** 09. NSM Ewell St Fran *Guildf* from 08. *1 Stewart, Tadworth KT20 5TU* Tel (01737) 379859 E-mail liz@servercity.co.uk

RICHARDSON, Canon Eric Hatherley Humphrey. b 12. Qu Coll Ox BA35 MA46. Westcott Ho Cam 35. **d** 36 **p** 37. C Stoke Newington St Mary *Lon* 36-39; S Africa from 39. *PO Box 2289, Cramerview, 2060 South Africa* Tel (0027) (11) 787 7813 E-mail ceric@kon.co.za

RICHARDSON, Geoffrey Stewart. b 47. St Jo Coll Ox BA69 MA73. St Steph Ho Ox 70. **d** 72 **p** 73. C Roxbourne St Andr *Lon* 72-75; C Woodford St Barn *Chelmsf* 75-80; V Goodmayes St Paul 80-87; R Stow in Lindsey *Linc* 87-92; P-in-c Coates 87-92; P-in-c Willingham 87-92; R Stow Gp 92-01; RD Corringham 93-00; R Shaldon, Stokeinteignhead, Combeinteignhead etc *Ex* from 01. *The Rectory, Torquay Road, Shaldon, Teignmouth TQ14 0AX* Tel (01626) 872396

RICHARDSON, Graeme James. b 75. Oriel Coll Ox BA97. Ripon Coll Cuddesdon MPhil02. **d** 03 **p** 04. C Hatfield Hyde *St Alb* 03-06; Chapl BNC Ox from 06. *Brasenose College, Oxford OX1 4AJ* Tel (01865) 277833 Fax 277822 E-mail graeme.richardson@theology.ox.ac.uk

RICHARDSON, Gwynne. *See* RICHARDSON, Canon David Gwynne

RICHARDSON, Hedley. *See* RICHARDSON, John Hedley

RICHARDSON, Mrs Jacqueline Ann. b 61. **d** 10 **p** 11. OLM Walton-on-Thames *Guildf* from 10. *61 Braycourt Avenue, Walton-on-Thames KT12 2BA* Tel (01932) 228883 Mobile 07787-445272 E-mail jackie.richardson@uwclub.net

RICHARDSON, James Aidan. b 28. St Chad's Coll Dur BA51. **d** 54 **p** 55. C Ferryhill *Dur* 54-56; C Stirling *Edin* 56-58; P-in-c Bo'ness 58-64; P-in-c Linlithgow 58-64; V Linthwaite *Wakef* 64-79; RD Blackmoorfoot 77-79; V Clifton 79-92; P-in-c Hartshead 83-88; rtd 92; Perm to Offic *Wakef* 92-04. *10B Brooke Street, Cleckheaton BD19 3RY* Tel (01274) 874587

RICHARDSON, Canon James John. b 41. OBE07. Hull Univ BA63 Sheff Univ DipEd64 FRSA91. Cuddesdon Coll 66. **d** 69 **p** 70. C Wolverhampton St Pet *Lich* 69-72; P-in-c Hanley All SS 72-75; R Nantwich *Ches* 75-82; Hon Can Ripon Cathl 82-88; V Leeds St Pet 82-88; Exec Dir Coun of Chrs and Jews 88-92; P-in-c Brington w Whilton and Norton *Pet* 93-96; P-in-c Church Brampton, Chapel Brampton, Harleston etc 94-96; TR Bournemouth St Pet w St Swithun, H Trin etc *Win* 96-08; P-in-c Bournemouth St Aug 01-08; rtd 09; Hon C Sherborne w Castleton, Lillington and Longburton *Sarum* from 09. *67 Acreman Street, Sherborne DT9 3PH* Tel (01935) 814984 E-mail canonrichardson@btinternet.com

RICHARDSON, John. *See* RICHARDSON, Edward John

RICHARDSON, John. b 41. Qu Coll Birm 69. **d** 72 **p** 73. C Ormskirk *Liv* 72-74; C Doncaster St Geo *Sheff* 74-77; R Hemsworth *Wakef* 77-79; V Penallt *Mon* 79-85; R Amotherby w Appleton and Barton-le-Street *York* 85-89; P-in-c Hovingham 86-89; P-in-c Slingsby 86-89; TR Street 89-90; R Skelton w Shipton and Newton on Ouse 90-93; V Alsager St Mary *Ches* 93-96; V Grangetown *York* 96-00; V E Coatham 00-02; V St Nic 04-06; rtd 06; Chapl Castle Howard from 06. *Beech House, Coneysthorpe, York YO60 7DD* Tel (01653) 648359 E-mail johnrichardson02@aol.com

RICHARDSON, John. b 47. Linc Th Coll 78. **d** 80 **p** 81. C Keighley St Andr *Bradf* 80-83; V Hugglescote w Donington *Leic* 83-84; V Hugglescote w Donington-le-Heath and Ellistown 84-86; TR Hugglescote w Donington, Ellistown and Snibston 86-97; RD Akeley S 87-96; Chapl ATC 84-97; R Hallaton w Horninghold, Allexton, Tugby etc *Leic* 97-00; Rural Officer (Leic Adnry) 97-00; rtd 00; Perm to Offic *Pet* 00-05; P-in-c Fylingdales and Hawsker cum Stainsacre *York* 05-09; C Alton w Bradley-le-Moors and Denstone etc *Lich* from 09. *The Vicarage, Bennion Grove, Denstone, Uttoxeter ST14 5EZ* Tel (01889) 590266

RICHARDSON, John. b 55. Lon Univ BEd BD Kent Univ MA. St Steph Ho Ox. **d** 83 **p** 84. C Thornbury *Glouc* 83-86; C Sheff St Cecilia Parson Cross 86-87; C Clacton St Jas *Chelmsf* 87-90; R Gt and Lt Tey w Wakes Colne and Chappel from 90. *The Rectory, Brook Road, Great Tey, Colchester CO6 1JF* Tel (01206) 211481 E-mail revjohn.richardson@virgin.net

RICHARDSON, John Aubrey. b 33. NEOC 90. **d** 93 **p** 94. NSM Warkworth and Acklington *Newc* 93-03; Perm to Offic from 03. *Harvest Lodge, 27 Acklington Village, Morpeth NE65 9BL* Tel (01670) 760761

RICHARDSON, John Hedley. b 45. Leeds Univ BA72. Qu Coll Birm 72. **d** 74 **p** 75. C Chaddesden St Phil *Derby* 74-76; Perm to Offic 76-86; TV Old Brampton and Loundsley Green 86-91; R Caston w Griston, Merton, Thompson etc *Nor* 91-95; RD Breckland 94-99; P-in-c Hockham w Shropham Gp of Par 94-95; R Caston, Griston, Merton, Thompson etc 95-02; P-in-c Clifton St Jas *Sheff* 02-03; V 03-08; rtd 08; Perm to Offic *Nor* from 11. *2 Admirals Court, Swaffham PE37 7TE* Tel (01760) 722698 E-mail hedleyrichardson@aol.com

✠**RICHARDSON, The Rt Revd John Henry.** b 37. Trin Hall Cam BA61 MA65. Cuddesdon Coll 61. **d** 63 **p** 64 **c** 94. C Stevenage *St Alb* 63-66; C Eastbourne St Mary *Chich* 66-68; V Chipperfield St Paul *St Alb* 68-75; V Rickmansworth 75-86; RD Rickmansworth 77-86; V Bishop's Stortford St Mich 86-94; Hon Can St Alb 87-94; Suff Bp Bedford 94-02; rtd 02; Hon Asst Bp Carl from 03; Hon Asst Bp Newc from 03. *The Old Rectory, Bewscastle, Carlisle CA6 6PS* Tel (01697) 748389

RICHARDSON, John Humphrey. b 33. Dur Univ BA57. Chich Th Coll 57. **d** 59 **p** 60. C Bexhill St Barn *Chich* 59-61; C Stanmer w Falmer and Moulsecoomb 61-64; C Ifield 64-70; R Earnley and E Wittering 70-79; V Stamford All SS w St Pet *Linc* 79-81; R Stamford St Jo w St Clem 79-81; V Stamford All SS w St Jo 81-92; RD Aveland and Ness w Stamford 80-87; P-in-c Metheringham w Blankney 92-94; V Metheringham w Blankney and Dunston 94-98; rtd 98; Perm to Offic *Chich* from 99. *68 Bishopsgate Walk, Chichester PO19 6FQ* Tel (01243) 536864

RICHARDSON, John Malcolm. b 39. Glas Univ MA60 BD63 Andover Newton Th Coll STM65. Edin Th Coll 84. **d** 84 **p** 85. C Edin Old St Paul 84-86; R Leven *St And* 86-90; R Newport-on-Tay 90-96, R Tayport 90-96, R Forfar 96-07, Can St Ninian's Cathl Perth 93-07; rtd 07; Lic to Offic *St And* from 07. *14 Chewton Road, Thornton, Kirkcaldy KY1 4AZ* Tel and fax (01592) 775133

RICHARDSON, John Peter. b 50. Keele Univ BA72. St Jo Coll Nottm 73. **d** 76 **p** 77. C Blackheath *Birm* 76-81; P-in-c Sparkbrook Ch Ch 81-83; Chapl NE Lon Poly *Chelmsf* 83-92; Chapl E Lon Univ 92-99; Hon C Stratford St Jo w Ch Ch and St Jas 83-99; C 99-00; C Henham and Elsenham w Ugley from 00. *39 Oziers, Elsenham, Bishop's Stortford CM22 6LS* Tel (01279) 813703 Mobile 07931-506913 E-mail john.richardson@heuchurch.f9.co.uk

RICHARDSON, John Stephen. b 50. Southn Univ BA71. St Jo Coll Nottm 72. **d** 74 **p** 75. C Bramcote *S'well* 74-77; C Radipole and Melcombe Regis *Sarum* 77-80; P-in-c Stinsford, Winterborne Came w Whitcombe etc 80-83; Asst Dioc Missr 80-83; V Nailsea Ch Ch *B & W* 83-90; Adv on Evang 86-90; Provost Bradf 90-00; Dean Bradf 00-01; V Wye w Brook and Hastingleigh etc *Cant* 01-09; P-in-c Eastwell w Boughton Aluph 04-09; C Mersham w Hinxhill and Sellindge 08-09; AD W Bridge 03-09; Chapl Wye Coll Kent *Lon* 01-09; P-in-c Margate H Trin *Cant* from 09. *The Vicarage, 5 Devonshire Gardens, Cliftonville, Margate CT9 3AF* Tel (01843) 294129 E-mail vicarjohnsrichardson@googlemail.com

RICHARDSON, Canon John Stuart. b 46. Trin Coll Ox BA68 MA71 DPhil73 FRSE96. **d** 79 **p** 80. NSM St Andrews St Andr *St And* 79-87; Chapl St Andr Univ 80-87; Prof Classics Edin Univ from 87; TV Edin St Columba from 87; Hon Can St Mary's Cathl from 00. *29 Merchiston Avenue, Edinburgh EH10 4PH* Tel 0131-228 3094 E-mail j.richardson@ed.ac.uk

RICHARDSON, John Thandule. b 49. Bradf and Ilkley Coll BSc80 Lanc Univ MA97. CBDTI 94. **d** 97 **p** 98. NSM Lea *Blackb* 97-02; NSM Broughton 02-04; NSM Lanercost, Walton, Gilsland and Nether Denton *Carl* 04-05; C Preston Risen Lord from 09; Chapl Preston Coll 09-11. *65 Lower Bank Road, Fulwood, Preston PR2 8NU* Tel (01772) 787689 Mobile 07769-716861 E-mail johntr123@aol.com

RICHARDSON, Laurence Leigh. b 71. Trin Coll Carmarthen BA92 PGCE93 Univ of Wales (Cardiff) BTh97 FGMS04. St Mich Coll Llan 94. **d** 97 **p** 98. C Carmarthen St Pet *St D* 97-01; Chapl Carmarthenshire Coll 99-01; P-in-c Abergwili w Llanfihangel-uwch-Gwili etc *St D* 01-03; V 03-09; TV E Carmarthen 09-10; TR from 10; AD Carmarthen from 09; CF(V) from 01. *St Peter's Vicarage, Church Street, Carmarthen SA31 1GW* Tel (01267) 237117 E-mail landcat10a@aol.com *or* rector@stpeterscarmarthen.org

RICHARDSON, Mrs Linda Joan. b 58. Univ of Wales BSc80. SAOMC 01. **d** 04 **p** 05. NSM W Wycombe w Bledlow Ridge, Bradenham and Radnage *Ox* from 04. *Long Acre, Greenend Road, Radnage, High Wycombe HP14 4BY* Tel (01494) 484607 Fax 484608 E-mail linda.richardson@long-acre.co.uk

RICHARDSON, Malcolm. *See* RICHARDSON, John Malcolm

RICHARDSON, Preb Neil. b 46. Southn Univ BTh83. Sarum & Wells Th Coll 71. **d** 74 **p** 75. C Oldham St Mary w St Pet *Man* 74-77; C-in-c Holts CD 77-82; R Greenford H Cross *Lon* from 82; Preb St Paul's Cathl from 02. *The Rectory, Oldfield Lane South, Greenford UB6 9JS* Tel (020) 8578 1543 E-mail neil@holycross.ndo.co.uk

RICHARDSON, Canon Paul. b 58. Univ of Wales (Cardiff) BSc80. Ridley Hall Cam 81. **d** 84 **p** 85. C Stanwix *Carl* 84-87; Ind

Chapl 87-89; Staff P Dalton-in-Furness 87-89; V Marton Moss *Blackb* 89-95; P-in-c Prestwich St Gabr *Man* 95-00; Bp's Dom Chapl 95-00; V Westbury *Sarum* 00-02; TR White Horse 02-07; RD Heytesbury 04-07; R Devizes St Jo w St Mary from 07; Can and Preb Sarum Cathl from 07; RD Devizes 10-11. *The Rectory, Brandon House, Potterne Road, Devizes SN10 5DD* Tel (01380) 829616 E-mail paul.richardson8@btinternet.com

RICHARDSON, Pauline Kate. *See* JENKINS, Pauline Kate

RICHARDSON, Robin John. b 71. Bris Univ BA01 Loughb Univ BEng92 PGCE93. Trin Coll Bris 98. **d** 01 **p** 02. C Sidmouth, Woolbrook, Salcombe Regis, Sidbury etc *Ex* 01-04; CF from 04. *clo MOD Chaplains (Army)* Tel (01264) 381140 Fax 381824 E-mail strangways@xalt.co.uk

RICHARDSON, Simon James. b 51. Loughb Univ BSc82 Nottm Univ MA99. EMMTC 96. **d** 99 **p** 00. C Market Harborough and The Transfiguration etc *Leic* 99-02; C Loughborough All SS w H Trin 02-04; Chapl Loughb Univ from 02. *13 Spinney Hill Drive, Loughborough LE11 3LB* Tel (01509) 237761 *or* 223741 Fax 223740 E-mail s.j.richardson@lboro.ac.uk

RICHARDSON, Simon John. b 56. Univ of Wales (Ban) BA77. Ridley Hall Cam 81. **d** 84 **p** 85. C Luton St Mary *St Alb* 84-88; C Middleton *Man* 88-91; Sweden from 91. *Enebacken, Racksätter, 732 97 Arboga, Sweden* Tel (0046) (589) 70103

RICHARDSON, Simon Kay Caoimhin. b 74. St Jo Coll Dur BA96 Cant Ch Ch Univ MA10. Wycliffe Hall Ox 01. **d** 03 **p** 04. C Folkestone Trin *Cant* 03-06; C Hillsborough *D & D* 06-08; I 08-11; C Holywood from 11. *51 Princess Gardens, Holywood BT18 0PN* Tel 07875-514431 (mobile) E-mail simonkcr@gmail.com

RICHARDSON, Miss Susan. b 58. Cranmer Hall Dur. **d** 87 **p** 94. Par Dn Stokesley *York* 87-91; Par Dn Beverley St Nic 91-94; P-in-c Cloughton 94-97; V Cloughton and Burniston w Ravenscar etc 97-99; V Middlesbrough St Oswald 99-10; P-in-c Middlesbrough St Chad 09-10; V Middlesbrough St Oswald and St Chad from 10; Tr Officer E Riding Adnry from 94. *St Oswald's Vicarage, Lambton Road, Middlesbrough TS4 2RG* Tel (01642) 816156 E-mail sue.richardson3@btinternet.com

RICHBOROUGH, Suffragan Bishop of (Provincial Episcopal Visitor). *See* BANKS, The Rt Revd Norman

RICHERBY, Canon Glynn. b 51. K Coll Lon BD73 AKC73. St Aug Coll Cant 73. **d** 74 **p** 75. C Weston Favell *Pet* 74-78; Prec Leic Cathl 78-81; V Glen Parva and S Wigston 81-93; V Leic St Jas from 93; Dir Post-Ord Tr 86-95; Dir CME from 95; Hon Can Leic Cathl from 98. *St James the Greater Vicarage, 216 London Road, Leicester LE2 1NE* Tel 0116-254 4113 E-mail vicar.stjames@ntlworld.com

RICHES, Canon John Kenneth. b 39. CCC Cam BA61 MA65. Kirchliche Hochschule Bethel 61 Westcott Ho Cam 62. **d** 65 **p** 66. C Costessey *Nor* 65-68; Chapl and Fell SS Coll Cam 68-72; Lect Glas Univ 72-86; Sen Lect 86-91; Prof Div and Bibl Criticism Glas Univ 91-02; Hon Research Prof from 02; Lic to Offic *Glas* from 85; Can St Mary's Cathl from 01. *Viewfield House, Balmore, Torrance, Glasgow G64 4AE* Tel (01360) 620254 E-mail randj.riches@virgin.net *or* j.riches@divinity.gla.ac.uk

RICHES, Malcolm Leslie. b 46. St Jo Coll Nottm 92. **d** 94 **p** 95. C Swaythling *Win* 94-97; P-in-c Boldre w S Baddesley 97-01; V 01-03; V Ellingham and Harbridge and Hyde w Ibsley 03-11; rtd 11; Hon C Caldbeck, Castle Sowerby and Sebergham *Carl* from 11. *The Rectory, Brewery House, Caldbeck, Wigton CA7 8EW* Tel and fax (016974) 78233 Mobile 07968-139851 E-mail malcolm.l.riches@googlemail.com

RICHES, Nichola. b 72. Homerton Coll Cam BEd95 R Holloway & Bedf New Coll Lon MA96. SEITE 05. **d** 08 **p** 09. NSM Purley St Mark and Purley St Swithun *S'wark* 08-11. *5 Hambledon Road, Caterham CR3 5EZ*

RICHEUX, Marc Stephen. b 66. Man Univ BA89. Trin Coll Bris BA00. **d** 00 **p** 01. C Plumstead St Jo w St Jas and St Paul *S'wark* 00-04; V Streatham Park St Alb from 04. *St Alban's Vicarage, 5 Fayland Avenue, London SW16 1SR* Tel (020) 8677 4521 *or* 8769 5415 E-mail mricheux@clara.co.uk

✠**RICHMOND, The Rt Revd Francis Henry Arthur.** b 36. TCD BA59 MA66 Strasbourg Univ BTh60 Linacre Coll Ox MLitt64. Wycliffe Hall Ox 60. **d** 63 **p** 64 **c** 86. C Woodlands *Sheff* 63-66; Chapl Sheff Cathl 66-69; V Sheff St Geo 69-77; Chapl Sheff Univ 74-77; Warden Linc Th Coll 77-86; Can and Preb Linc Cathl 77-86; Suff Bp Repton *Derby* 86-98; Hon Can Derby Cathl 86-98; rtd 98; Hon Asst Bp *Ox* from 99. *39 Hodges Court, Oxford OX1 4NZ* Tel (01865) 790466

RICHMOND, Gordon Hazlewood. b 33. Launde Abbey 77. **d** 79 **p** 80. C Leic St Paul 79-81; C Shepshed 81-84; V Ryhall w Essendine *Pet* 84-91; RD Barnack 89-91; V Gretton w Rockingham 91-98; rtd 98; Perm to Offic *Pet* from 98 and *Leic* from 99. *Malvern, 2 Linwal Avenue, Houghton-on-the-Hill, Leicester LE7 9HD* Tel 0116-241 7638

RICHMOND, Patrick Henry. b 69. Ball Coll Ox BA90 Green Coll Ox MA94 DPhil94. Wycliffe Hall Ox BA96. **d** 97 **p** 98. C Leic Martyrs 97-01; Chapl and Fell St Cath Coll Cam 01-07; Dean of Chpl 06-07; V Eaton Ch Ch *Nor* from 07.

161 Newmarket Road, Norwich NR4 6SY Tel (01603) 250844
E-mail phr@eatonparish.com
RICHMOND, Peter James. b 54. Ex Univ PGCE95 Cant Ch Ch
Univ MSc07. St Jo Coll Nottm. **d** 80 **p** 81. C Ogley Hay *Lich*
80-83; C Trentham 83-85; P-in-c Wolverhampton St Jo 85-89;
P-in-c Loppington w Newtown 89-93; P-in-c Edstaston 89-93;
Perm to Offic *Ex* 94-95; P-in-c Weston Zoyland w Chedzoy
B & W 95-03; Chapl Somerset Partnership NHS and Soc Care
Trust 97-03; Lead Chapl E Kent NHS and Soc Care Partnership
Trust 03-06; Lead Chapl Kent & Medway NHS and Soc Care
Partnership Trust from 06; Hon C St Nicholas at Wade w Sarre
and Chislet w Hoath *Cant* 04-10. *St Martin's Hospital,
Littlebourne Road, Canterbury CT1 1TD* Tel (01227) 812047
E-mail peter.richmond@ekentmht.nhs.uk
RICHMOND, Canon Yvonne Lorraine. b 63. Sheff Univ MA07.
WEMTC 96. **d** 99 **p** 00. NSM Magor *Mon* 99-00; NSM
Kenilworth St Jo *Cov* 00-05; Chapl for Evang Cov Cathl 05-06;
Can Res for Miss 06-09; Can for Development Birm Cathl from
09. *Hope House, Sixpence Close, Coventry CV4 8HL* Tel
0121-262 1840
E-mail canonfordevelopment@birminghamcathedral.com
RICHMOND, Archdeacon of. *See* HENDERSON, The Ven
Janet
RICKARDS, Bruce Walter. b 69. NTMTC 98. **d** 01 **p** 02. NSM
St Marg Lothbury and St Steph Coleman Street etc *Lon* 01-06;
NSM Wimbledon *S'wark* 06-09; C from 09. *85A Toynbee Road,
London SW20 8SJ* Tel (020) 8540 4150 Mobile 07850-655102
E-mail byrickards@btinternet.com
RICKETTS, Allan Fenn. b 46. Open Univ BA76. Cranmer Hall
Dur 68. **d** 71 **p** 72. C Rowley Regis *Birm* 71-72; C The Quinton
72-74; C Brierley Hill *Lich* 74-77; TV Chelmsley Wood *Birm*
77-82; TV Ross w Brampton Abbotts, Bridstow and Peterstow
Heref 82-88; R Linton w Upton Bishop and Aston Ingham
88-96; rtd 06. *13 Falaise Close, Ross-on-Wye HR9 5UT* Tel
(01989) 565077 E-mail allanricketts@fsmail.net
RICKETTS, Mrs Diane. b 54. NTMTC 98. **d** 01 **p** 02. NSM
Nazeing and Roydon *Chelmsf* 01-06; R Laindon w Dunton from
06. *38 Claremont Road, Basildon SS15 5PZ* Tel (01268) 411190
E-mail revd diane ricketts@hotmail.com
RICKETTS, Canon Kathleen Mary. b 39. Southlands Coll Lon
TCert59 Univ of W Aus BA79. Westcott Ho Cam 81. **dss** 83 **d** 87
p 94. All Hallows by the Tower etc *Lon* 83-88; C 87-88; C Hall
Green Ascension *Birm* 88-91; Chapl Birm Children's Hosp
91-94; Chapl Birm Children's Hosp NHS Trust 94-99; Hon Can
Birm Cathl 96-99; rtd 99; Perm to Offic *Birm* from 00. *22 Holly
Drive, Birmingham B27 7NF* Tel 0121-706 1087
RICKETTS, Mrs Linda Elizabeth. b 52. RNMH85. EAMTC 98.
d 01 **p** 02. C Loddon, Sisland, Chedgrave, Hardley and Langley
Nor 01-05; V Gorleston St Mary from 05. *The Vicarage, 41
Nuffield Crescent, Gorleston, Great Yarmouth NR31 7LL* Tel
(01493) 661741 E-mail l.ricketts787@btinternet.com
RICKMAN, Peter Alan. b 68. Ripon Coll Cuddesdon BTh97.
d 97 **p** 98. C Bitterne Park *Win* 97-01; Chapl St Paul's Colleg Sch
Hamilton NZ 01-04; Sub Chapl HM Pris Win 04-05; P-in-c
Bransgore *Win* 05-09; P-in-c Bransgore and Hinton Admiral
from 09. *St Mary's Vicarage, Ringwood Road, Bransgore,
Christchurch BH23 8JH* Tel (01425) 672327 Mobile 07789-
684481 E-mail pizzarev@aol.com
RIDDEL, Robert John. b 37. CITC 65. **d** 68 **p** 69. C Derryloran
Arm 68-74; I Keady w Armaghbreague and Derrynoose 74-80; I
Mullaghdun *Clogh* 80-84; I Cleenish 80-84; I Fivemiletown
84-05; Can Clogh Cathl 91-05; Preb Donaghmore St Patr Cathl
Dublin 95-05; rtd 05. *9 Coolcrannel Square, Maguiresbridge,
Enniskillen BT94 4RE* Tel (028) 6772 3199
E-mail riddel.r.j@btinternet.com
RIDDELL, Morris Stroyan. b 34. Lon Univ BD69. Tyndale Hall
Bris 57. **d** 60 **p** 60. S Africa 60-63; C Mowbray 60-62; V
Addington Ch Ch 62-63; V N Grimston w Wharram Percy and
Wharram-le-Street *York* 63-67; V Kirby Grindalythe 63-67;
P-in-c Weaverthorpe w Helperthorpe and Luttons 65-67; P-in-c
Settrington 65-67; P-in-c Wintringham 65-67; P-in-c Thorpe
Bassett 65-67; R Bris St Jo w St Mary-le-Port 67-70; Dir Bris
Samaritans 67-70; Chapl HM Pris Long Lartin 71-74; Chapl
HM Pris Brixton 74-78; Chapl Cane Hill Hosp Coulsdon 78-85;
Chapl HM Rem Cen Latchmere Ho 85-89; rtd 96. *Flat 5, 30
Montpelier Crescent, Brighton BN1 3JJ* Tel (01273) 329229
RIDDELSDELL, Canon John Creffield. b 23. Selw Coll Cam
BA47 MA52 Lon Univ BD70. Ridley Hall Cam 47. **d** 49 **p** 50. C
Kilburn St Mary *Lon* 49-52; Kenya 52-77; V Gt Ilford St Andr
Chelmsf 77-88; rtd 88; Perm to Offic *Chelmsf* from 88. *Waverley,
Mill Lane, Walton on the Naze CO14 8PE* Tel (01255) 850213
RIDDING, George. b 24. Oriel Coll Ox BA50 MA57. Wells Th
Coll 60. **d** 61 **p** 62. C Countess Wear *Ex* 61-62; Chapl Ex Sch
62-64; India 64-68; Hd Master W Buckland Sch Barnstaple
68-78; USPG 78-82; P-in-c Broadhembury w Payhembury *Ex*
82-83; P-in-c Plymtree 82-83; R Broadhembury, Payhembury
and Plymtree 83-89; rtd 89; Perm to Offic *Sarum* 89-99. *The
College of St Barnabas, Blackberry Lane, Lingfield RH7 6NJ* Tel
(01342) 872821

RIDDING, William Thomas. b 54. Southn Univ BTh. Sarum &
Wells Th Coll 80. **d** 83 **p** 84. C Verwood *Sarum* 83-86; TV
Gillingham 86-01; RD Blackmore Vale 95-01; P-in-c Stalbridge
01-02; R Stalbridge and Stock 02-07; R Spire Hill from 07; C
Hazelbury Bryan and the Hillside Par from 08; C Okeford from
08. *The Rectory, Church Hill, Stalbridge, Sturminster Newton
DT10 2LR* Tel (01963) 362859
RIDDLE, Kenneth Wilkinson. b 20. St Cath Soc Ox BA42 MA46.
Ripon Hall Ox 42. **d** 43 **p** 44. C Lowestoft St Marg *Nor* 43-47; C
Luton St Mary *St Alb* 47-49; V Sundon w Streatley 49-52; R
Pakefield *Nor* 52-59; V Nor St Pet Mancroft 59-60; R E w W
Harling 60-65; P-in-c Bridgham and Roudham 60-61; R 61-65;
R Lowestoft St Marg 65-68; rtd 85. *9 Clare Court, Clarence
Road, Fleet GU51 3XX* Tel (01252) 617460
RIDEOUT, Canon Gordon Trevor. b 38. BA87 Westmr Coll Ox
MTh96. Lon Coll of Div 58. **d** 62 **p** 63. C Southgate *Chich* 62-65;
Chapl Dr Barnardo's Barkingside and Woodford Bridge 65-67;
CF 67-73; V Nutley *Chich* 73-79; V Eastbourne All SS and
Chapl Moira Ho Sch 79-03; Chapl Brighton Poly 80-92; Chapl
Brighton Univ 92-03; rtd 03; Can and Preb Chich Cathl from 90;
RD Eastbourne 97-06. *9 Filching Close, Polegate BN26 5NU* Tel
(01323) 482660 Fax 640033
RIDER, Andrew. b 62. RMN85 Nottm Univ BTh90 K Coll Lon
MA96. Aston Tr Scheme 85 St Jo Coll Nottm 87. **d** 90 **p** 91. C
Luton Ch Ch *Roch* 90-93; C w resp for Clubhouse Langham
Place All So *Lon* 93-03; P-in-c Spitalfields Ch Ch w All SS 03-04;
R from 04. *The Rectory, 2 Fournier Street, London E1 6QE* Tel
(020) 7247 0790 *or* 7247 7202 Fax 7247 5921
E-mail arider@clara.co.uk
RIDER, Canon Dennis William Austin. b 34. St Aid Birkenhead
58. **d** 61 **p** 62. C Derby St Aug 61-64; C Sutton *Liv* 64-67; R
Stiffkey w Morston, Langham Episcopi etc *Nor* 67-71; V Buxton
w Oxnead 71-79; R Lammas w Lt Hautbois 72-79; R Gaywood,
Bawsey and Mintlyn 79-91; RD Lynn 89-91; Hon Can Nor
Cathl 90-99; R E Dereham and Scarning 91-98; TR 98-99; RD
Dereham in Mitford 95-98; rtd 99; Perm to Offic *Nor* 01-08; C
Litcham w Kempston, E and W Lexham, Mileham etc 08-09;
C Gt and Lt Dunham w Gt and Lt Fransham and Sporle 08-09;
C Foulsham, Guestwick, Stibbard, Themelthorpe etc from 10.
37A Holt Road, Fakenham NR21 8BW Tel (01328) 856018
E-mail dandprider@btinternet.com
RIDER, Geoffrey Malcolm. b 29. Selw Coll Cam BA53 MA56
Lon Inst of Educn PGCE68. Coll of Resurr Mirfield 53. **d** 55
p 56. C S Elmsall *Wakef* 55-60; C Barnsley St Mary 60-63; V
Cleckheaton St Jo 63-67; Public Preacher *S'wark* 67-92; rtd 92;
Succ Kimberley Cathl S Africa 92-95; Perm to Offic *S'wark*
95-03; Chapl and Hon Min Can Ripon Cathl from 04. *35 Kirkby
Road, Ripon HG4 2EY* Tel (01765) 690517
E-mail geoffrey.rider@btinternet.com
RIDER, Neil Wilding. b 35. St Jo Coll Dur BA59 Univ of Wales
(Lamp) MA00. Cranmer Hall Dur 59. **d** 62 **p** 63. C Blackb
St Barn 62-64; C Chadderton Em *Man* 64-69; C Deane 69-72; V
Coldhurst 72-75; Perm to Offic *Ely* 76-78; C Didsbury Ch Ch
Man 78-80; Perm to Offic *St D* from 80; rtd 00. *Caergrawnt,
Llandovery Road, Cwmann, Lampeter SA48 8EL* Tel (01570)
422921
RIDGE, Aubrey. b 25. Oak Hill Th Coll 67. **d** 68 **p** 69. C Gorleston
St Andr *Nor* 68-70; C Hamworthy *Sarum* 70-75; P-in-c Pitsea
Chelmsf 75-78; R 78-81; P-in-c Stoke Ash, Thwaite and
Wetheringsett *St E* 81-85; P-in-c Bedingfield and Thorndon w
Rishangles 81-85; P-in-c Thorndon w Rishangles, Stoke Ash,
Thwaite etc 85-86; P-in-c Risby w Gt and Lt Saxham and
Westley 86-90; rtd 90; Perm to Offic *Sarum* 90-93; Hon C
Milford *Win* 93-96; Perm to Offic 96-99. *7 Cherry Tree Court,
Station Road, New Milton BH25 6LP*
RIDGE, Haydn Stanley. b 24. Univ of Wales (Lamp) BA51 Bris
Univ CertEd52. Qu Coll Birm 56. **d** 56 **p** 57. C Blackheath *Birm*
56-60; Div Master Guernsey Gr Sch 60-75; Perm to Offic *Win*
60-62; Hon C Guernsey St Steph 62-96; Dep Hd Master St Peter
Port Sch 75-80; Hd Master St Sampson Sch 75-87; rtd 91; Perm
to Offic *Win* 96-00. *St David, Les Cherfs, Castel, Guernsey
GY5 7HG* Tel (01481) 56209
RIDGE, James Scott. b 77. Ex Univ BSc99 Selw Coll Cam
BTh05. Westcott Ho Cam 02. **d** 05 **p** 06. C Halstead Area
Chelmsf 05-09; C Bocking St Pet 09; Chapl HM Pris Chelmsf
from 09. *HM Prison Chelmsford, 200 Springfield Road,
Chelmsford CM2 6LQ* Tel (01245) 552000
E-mail james.ridge@hmps.gsi.gov.uk
RIDGE, Michael Anthony. b 70. Collingwood Coll Dur BSc91
Dur Sch of Educn PGCE93. St Jo Coll Nottm 07. **d** 09. C
Formby St Luke *Liv* from 09. *17 Moor Coppice, Liverpool
L23 2XJ* Tel 07980-242401 (mobile)
E-mail michaelridge@hotmail.co.uk
RIDGEWAY, David. b 59. St Chad's Coll Dur BSc80 Cam Univ
CertEd81. Ripon Coll Cuddesdon 84. **d** 87 **p** 88. C Kempston
Transfiguration *St Alb* 87-90; C Radlett 90-95; P-in-c Heath and
Reach 95-98; V 98-01; V St Alb St Steph from 01; RD St Alb
from 05. *St Stephen's Vicarage, 14 Watling Street, St Albans
AL1 2PX* Tel (01727) 862598 Fax 07092-109111
E-mail davidridgeway@btinternet.com

RIDGEWELL, Miss Mary Jean. b 54. Dur Univ BA76 PGCE77. Ridley Hall Cam 89. d 91 p 94. Par Dn Trowbridge St Jas *Sarum* 91-94; C 94-95; Chapl Lee Abbey 95-96; NSM Bradford Peverell, Stratton, Frampton etc *Sarum* 96-97; Chapl HM Pris and YOI Guys Marsh from 97. *HM Prison and YOI, Guy's Marsh, Shaftesbury SP7 0AH* Tel (01747) 853344 ext 325 Fax 851584 E-mail mary@jridgewell.fsnet.co.uk

RIDGWAY, David. b 28. Trin Hall Cam BA54 MA58. Westcott Ho Cam 54. d 56 p 57. C Milton *Portsm* 56-59; CF 59-63; R Gosforth *Carl* 63-70; V Walney Is 70-76; P-in-c Irthington 76-78; P-in-c Crosby-on-Eden 77-78; V Irthington, Crosby-on-Eden and Scaleby 79-93; rtd 93. *11 Woodleigh, Walton, Brampton CA8 2DS* Tel (01697) 73252

RIDGWAY, Mrs Janet Elizabeth Knight. b 40. St Alb Minl Tr Scheme 83. dss 86 d 87 p 94. Tring *St Alb* 86-87; Hon Par Dn 87-94; Hon C 94-05; rtd 05. *Barleycombe, Trooper Road, Aldbury, Tring HP23 5RW* Tel and fax (01442) 851303 E-mail rev.j.ridgway@breathemail.net

RIDGWELL, Graham Edgar Charles. b 46. LGSM71 Open Univ BA82 Leeds Univ MA04. d 02 p 03. NSM Whitby w Aislaby and Ruswarp *York* 02-05; Hon TV Linton *Ely* from 05. *The Vicarage, Park Lane, Castle Camps, Cambridge CB21 4SR* Tel (01799) 584545 E-mail gecridgwell@googlemail.com

RIDING, Pauline Alison. *See* BICKNELL, Mrs Pauline Alison

RIDINGS, Neil Arthur. b 66. Man Poly BEd90. St Jo Coll Nottm 01. d 01 p 02. C Holyhead *Ban* 01-05; TV 05-07; R Valley w Llechylched and Caergeiliog from 07. *The Rectory, London Road, Valley, Holyhead LL65 3DP* Tel (01407) 741242

RIDLEY, Alfred Forbes. b 34. Bps' Coll Cheshunt 62. d 65 p 66. C Prittlewell St Mary *Chelmsf* 65-69; R Paulerspury *Pet* 69-73; P-in-c Wicken 71-73; V W Haddon w Winwick 73-83; RD Brixworth 80-83; R Guernsey St Philippe de Torteval *Win* 83-92; R Guernsey St Pierre du Bois 83-92; R Blakesley w Adstone and Maidford etc *Pet* 92-99; rtd 99; Perm to Offic *Pet* 99-07. *7 Alchester Court, Towcester NN12 6RL* Tel (01327) 358664

RIDLEY, Andrew Roy. b 55. St Pet Coll Ox BA77. Ripon Coll Cuddesdon 78. d 79 p 80. C Bollington St Jo *Ches* 79-83; V Runcorn St Mich 83-94; Dioc Chapl to MU 92-98; RD Frodsham 94-98; V Helsby and Dunham-on-the-Hill 94-98; P-in-c Alvanley 94-98; R Whitchurch *Lich* from 98; RD Wem and Whitchurch 01-06; V Barton under Needwood w Dunstall and Tatenhill from 11. *The Vicarage, 3 Church Lane, Barton under Needwood, Burton-on-Trent DE13 8HU* E-mail arceridley@btinternet.com

RIDLEY, David Gerhard. b 60. Southn Univ BSc82 Bath Univ PGCE83. Qu Coll Birm 91. d 93 p 94. C Faversham *Cant* 93-97; Min Folkestone St Aug CD 97-01; V Dover St Mary from 01; P-in-c Guston from 02; AD Dover 06-11. *The Vicarage, Taswell Street, Dover CT16 1SE* Tel and fax (01304) 206842 Mobile 07887-880272 E-mail davidridley@bigfoot.com

RIDLEY, Derek. b 40. Newc Univ BSc74. Cranmer Hall Dur 75. d 78 p 79. C Upperby St Jo *Carl* 78-81; C Penrith w Newton Reigny 81; C Penrith w Newton Reigny and Plumpton Wall 81-82; TV 82-86; V Cadishead *Man* 86-99; R Asfordby and P-in-c Ab Kettleby Gp *Leic* 99-02; P-in-c Old Dalby and Nether Broughton 99-01; rtd 02. *32 Carleton Place, Penrith CA11 8LW* Tel (01768) 890676

RIDLEY, Jay. b 41. Birm Univ BA63. St Steph Ho Ox 63. d 65 p 66. C Woodford St Mary *Chelmsf* 65-67; C Prittlewell St Mary 67-70; C-in-c Dunscroft CD *Sheff* 70-74; Asst Chapl HM Pris Wormwood Scrubs 75-77; Chapl HM Rem Cen Ashford 77-84; Chapl HM YOI Feltham 84-91; Chapl HM Pris Ashwell 91-00; C Oakham, Hambleton, Egleton, Braunston and Brooke *Pet* 00-11; rtd 11. *11 Ramsay Hall, 9-13 Byron Road, Worthing BN11 3HN* Tel (01903) 210224 E-mail jay.ridley@hotmail.co.uk

RIDLEY, Mrs Lesley. b 46. Cranmer Hall Dur 75. dss 78 d 87 p 94. Upperby St Jo *Carl* 78-81; Penrith w Newton Reigny and Plumpton Wall 81-86; Cadishead *Man* 86-99; Par Dn 87-94; C 94-99; C Asfordby and Ab Kettleby Gp *Leic* 99-02; rtd 02. *32 Carleton Place, Penrith CA11 8LW* Tel (01768) 890676

RIDLEY, Louise. *See* COLLINS, Louise Ridley

RIDLEY, Canon Michael Edward. b 37. Ex Univ MA90. St Boniface Warminster AKC62. d 63 p 64. C Chapel Allerton *Ripon* 63-67; C Epsom St Martin *Guildf* 67-70; C Claxby w Normanby-le-Wold etc *Linc* 70-72; V Leake 72-75; R Harlaxton w Wyville and Hungerton 75-80; R Stroxton 76-80; Dioc Stewardship Adv *Portsm* 80-86; P-in-c Rowlands Castle 80-82; C Blendworth w Chalton w Idsworth etc 83-86; TV N Creedy *Ex* 86-90; R W Downland *Sarum* 90-02; RD Chalke 92-97 and 98-00; Can and Preb Sarum Cathl 00-02; rtd 02; Perm to Offic *Truro* from 03. *6 Cole Moore Meadow, Tavistock PL19 0ES* Tel (01822) 610799

RIDLEY, Michael Laurence. b 59. BA81. Ripon Coll Cuddesdon 81. d 83 p 84. C Bollington St Jo *Ches* 83-88; V Thelwall 88-95; V Weaverham 95-05; RD Middlewich 99-05; V Stockton Heath from 05. *12 Melton Avenue, Walton, Warrington WA4 6PQ* Tel (01925) 261396

RIDLEY, Peter John. b 39. Keble Coll Ox BA61. Tyndale Hall Bris 61. d 63 p 64. C Clifton Ch Ch w Em *Bris* 63-67; C Lambeth St Andr w St Thos *S'wark* 67-69; V W Hampstead St Cuth *Lon* 69-77; V Eynsham *Ox* 77-85; RD Woodstock 82-84; V Nicholforest and Kirkandrews on Esk *Carl* 85-96; P-in-c E Knoyle, Semley and Sedgehill *Sarum* 96-04; rtd 04. *The Castle, Castle Street, Hilton, Appleby-in-Westmorland CA16 6LX* Tel (017683) 51682

RIDLEY, Simon. b 33. Magd Coll Ox BA54 MA58 BD66. Linc Th Coll 54. d 57 p 58. C St John's Wood *Lon* 57-60; Abp's Dom Chapl *Cant* 60-61; V N Wootton *B & W* 61-66; Lect Wells Th Coll 61-65; Hong Kong 66-70; TR Basingstoke *Win* 70-73; rtd 96; Perm to Offic *Cant* from 96. *Oxney House, The Street, Wittersham, Tenterden TN30 7ED* Tel (01797) 270215

RIDLEY, Stephen James. b 57. St Pet Coll Ox MA83. Ripon Coll Cuddesdon 80. d 82 p 83. C Heald Green St Cath *Ches* 82-85; Chapl Ches Coll 85-90; Dioc Press Officer 85-90; Chapl Birkenhead Sch Merseyside 90-96; Lic to Offic *Ches* 90-96; Chapl Barnard Castle Sch from 96. *3 Old Courts, Barnard Castle School, Newgate, Barnard Castle DL12 8UN* Tel (01833) 690222

RIDLEY, Stewart Gordon. b 47. K Coll Lon AKC72. St Aug Coll Cant 72. d 73 p 74. C Armley w New Wortley *Ripon* 73-77; C Hawksworth Wood 77-79; C Rothwell w Lofthouse 79-81; R Whitwood *Wakef* 81-87; R Ingoldmells w Addlethorpe *Linc* 87-92; RD Calcewaithe and Candleshoe 89-92; V Settle *Bradf* 92-05; C Bolton by Bowland w Grindleton 05-07; P-in-c Hurst Green and Mitton 05-07; P-in-c Waddington 05-07; rtd 07; Perm to Offic *York* from 09. *12 Bramblefields, Northallerton DL6 1ST* Tel (01609) 775857 E-mail stewartridley@uwclub.net

RIDLEY, Vic. *See* RIDLEY, David Gerhard

RIDOUT, Canon Christopher John. b 33. K Coll Lon BD57 AKC57 MA92. d 58 p 59. C Roxeth Ch Ch *Lon* 58-62; CMS 62-63; Kenya 63-75; C Gt Malvern St Mary *Worc* 75-79; R Bredon w Bredon's Norton 79-98; RD Pershore 91-97; Hon Can Worc Cathl 92-98; rtd 98; Perm to Offic *Glouc* from 98. *5 Belworth Drive, Hatherley, Cheltenham GL51 6EL* Tel (01242) 231765

RIDYARD, Preb John Gordon. b 33. St Aid Birkenhead 59. d 62 p 63. C Lancaster St Mary *Blackb* 62-65; C Bushbury *Lich* 65-68; V Darlaston All SS 68-76; TV Wolverhampton St Mark 76-78; TV Wolverhampton 78-82; V Bishopswood 82-89; V Brewood 82-89; RD Penkridge 83-89; R Newcastle w Butterton 89-98; Preb Lich Cathl 82-03; rtd 98; Perm to Offic *Lich* 98-11. *Upper Flat, Vicars' Hall, Beacon Street, Lichfield WS13 7AD* Tel (01543) 306297

RIEM, Canon Roland Gerardus Anthony. b 60. St Chad's Coll Dur BSc82 Kent Univ PhD86 Heythrop Coll Lon MA99. St Jo Coll Nottm 86. d 89 p 90. C Deal St Leon and St Rich and Sholden *Cant* 89-92; Sen Chapl Nottm Univ 92-98; Dir Min STETS 98-05; Can Res Win Cathl from 05. *5A The Close, Winchester SO23 9LS* Tel (01962) 857216 or 857239 Fax 857201 E-mail roland.riem@winchester-cathedral.org.uk

RIESS, Trevor William. b 54. Down Coll Cam MA76 CertEd77. St Jo Coll Nottm 84. d 86 p 87. C Stainforth *Sheff* 86-88; Chapl St Jas Choir Sch Grimsby 89; C Lowestoft and Kirkley *Nor* 89-90; TV 90-94; TV Lowestoft St Marg 94-95; Chapl Lothingland Hosp 90-95; V Gorleston St Mary *Nor* 95-05; P-in-c Scole, Brockdish, Billingford, Thorpe Abbots etc from 05. *The Rectory, Norwich Road, Scole, Diss IP21 4DB* Tel (01379) 742762

RIGBY, Francis Michael. b 29. Glouc Sch of Min. d 90 p 91. NSM Alvescot w Black Bourton, Shilton, Holwell etc *Ox* 90-92; P-in-c Gt w Lt Tew 92-95; P-in-c Bishop's Frome w Castle Frome and Fromes Hill *Heref* 96-99; P-in-c Acton Beauchamp and Evesbatch 96-99; Perm to Offic 00-07. *Address temp unknown*

RIGBY, Harold. b 34. Nottm Univ BA56 St Cath Soc Ox BA58 MA62 Man Poly PGCE77. Ripon Hall Ox 56. d 58 p 59. C Didsbury St Jas and Em *Man* 58-61; C Bury St Jo 61-64; P-in-c Lostock St Thos and St Jo 64-76; Hon C Davyhulme St Mary 76-79; Lic Preacher 79-10; Perm to Offic from 10. *17 Atwood Road, Didsbury, Manchester M20 0TA* Tel 0161-445 7454

RIGBY, Joseph. b 37. Open Univ BA72. Ox NSM Course. d 78 p 79. NSM Earley St Pet *Ox* 78-80; C Penzance St Mary w St Paul *Truro* 80-82; V Mevagissey 82-85; P-in-c St Ewe 83; R Mevagissey and St Ewe 83-90; rtd 90; Perm to Offic *Truro* 90-09. *Flat 5, Manormead, Tilford Road, Hindhead GU26 6RA* Tel (01428) 601505

RIGBY, Michael. *See* RIGBY, Francis Michael

RIGBY, William. b 51. Leic Univ BSc(Econ)72 Newc Poly BSc82. Cranmer Hall Dur 86. d 88 p 89. C Morpeth *Newc* 88-92; R St John Lee 92-00; Chapl to the Deaf *Newc* 92-00; P-in-c Chapel House 00-08; V Bywell and Mickley from 08. *Bywell Vicarage, Meadowfield Road, Stocksfield NE43 7PY* Tel (01661) 842272 E-mail bill.rigby1@btopenworld.com

RIGELSFORD, Mrs Anne Catharina (Ank). b 44. EAMTC 99. d 02 p 03. NSM Cambridge H Cross *Ely* 02-06; NSM Cambridge Ascension from 06. *19 Clare Street, Cambridge CB4 3BY* Tel (01223) 368150 Mobile 07932-846395 E-mail ank1@btinternet.com

RIGLIN, Keith Graham. b 57. Lon Inst of Educn BEd80 Regent's Park Coll Ox BA83 MA86 Heythrop Coll Lon MTh85 Birm Univ ThD08 FRSA09. Westcott Ho Cam 06. **d** 08 **p** 08. In Bapt Union 83-96; in URC 97-08; C Notting Dale St Clem w St Mark and St Jas *Lon* from 08. *St Clement's Vicarage, 95 Sirdar Road, London W11 4EQ* Tel (020) 7313 4674 E-mail kgr23@cam.ac.uk

RIGNEY, Mrs Cindy Joanne. b 65. Coll of Ripon & York St Jo BA89. CBDTI 03. **d** 06 **p** 07. C Poulton Carleton and Singleton *Blackb* 06-10; P-in-c Dolphinholme w Quernmore and Over Wyresdale from 10; V from 11. *St Mark's Vicarage, Dolphinholme, Lancaster LA2 9AH* Tel (01524) 793125 E-mail revcinders@hotmail.co.uk

RIGNEY, The Very Revd James Thomas. b 59. Sydney Univ BA82 MA88 Pemb Coll Ox DPhil95 CCC Cam BA00 MA04. Westcott Ho Cam 98. **d** 01 **p** 02. C Cambridge St Jas *Ely* 01-04; Chapl and Fell Magd Coll Cam 05-09; Dean Newcastle Australia from 09. *The Deanery, 46 Newcomer Street, Newcastle NSW 2300, Australia* E-mail jamesrigney@hotmail.com

RILEY, David Leo. b 51. S Bank Univ MSc95. Dioc OLM tr scheme 97. **d** 00 **p** 01. NSM Bellingham St Dunstan *S'wark* from 00. *117 Whitefoot Lane, Bromley BR1 5SB* Tel (020) 8516 4544 E-mail driley3020@aol.com

RILEY, John Graeme. b 55. St Jo Coll Dur BA78. Trin Coll Bris 79. **d** 81 **p** 82. C Hensingham *Carl* 81-84; C Preston St Cuth *Blackb* 84-87; V Blackb Ch Ch w St Matt 87-98; Chapl Qu Park Hosp Blackb 87-94; V Shevington *Blackb* 98-04; V Euxton from 04. *The Vicarage, Wigan Road, Euxton, Chorley PR7 6JH* Tel (01257) 262102 E-mail john.riley@uwclub.net

RILEY, Canon John Martin. b 37. St D Coll Lamp BA62. **d** 63 **p** 64. C Conwy w Gyffin *Ban* 63-68; P-in-c Llanfachraeth 68-70; TV Dolgellau, Llanfachreth, Brithdir etc 70-72; V Beddgelert and Dioc Youth Chapl 72-78; V Tywyn 78-82; V Tywyn w Aberdyfi 82-95; V Llanegryn w Aberdyfi w Tywyn 95-03; AD Ystumaner 87-03; Can Ban Cathl 90-97; Preb 97-03; rtd 03; Perm to Offic *Ban* from 03; AD Cyfeiliog and Mawddwy from 10. *Llwyncelyn, Chapel Street, Corris, Machynlleth SY20 9SP* Tel (01654) 761769

RILEY, The Very Revd Kenneth Joseph. b 40. OBE03. Univ of Wales BA61 Linacre Ho Ox BA64 MA68. Wycliffe Hall Ox 61. **d** 64 **p** 65. C Fazakerley Em *Liv* 64-66; Chapl Brasted Place Coll Westerham 66-69; Chapl Oundle Sch 69-74; Chapl Liv Cathl 74-75; Chapl Liv Univ 74-93; V Mossley Hill St Matt and St Jas 75-83; RD Childwall 82-83; Can Res Liv Cathl 83-93; Treas 83-87; Prec 87-93; Dean Man 93-05; rtd 05. *145 Turning Lane, Southport PR8 5HZ*

RILEY, Mrs Lesley Anne. b 54. Totley Thornbridge Coll TCert75. Trin Coll Bris. **dss** 81 **d** 87 **p** 98. Hensingham *Carl* 81-84; Preston St Cuth *Blackb* 84-87; Hon Par Dn Blackb Ch Ch w St Matt 87-98; Asst Dir of Ords 96-00; Dir of Ords 00-05; Hon C Shevington 98-04; Hon C Whittle-le-Woods 06-07; Resources Co-ord Dioc Bd of Educn from 07. *The Vicarage, Wigan Road, Euxton, Chorley PR7 6JH* Tel (01257) 276718 E-mail lesley.riley@uwclub.net

RILEY, Linda. See RILEY-DAWKIN, Mrs Linda

RILEY, Martin. See RILEY, Canon John Martin

RILEY, Martin Shaw. b 47. Selw Coll Cam BA71 MA75 Cam Univ CertEd72. Sarum & Wells Th Coll 85. **d** 87 **p** 88. C Tuffley *Glouc* 87-91; Hon Min Can Glouc Cathl from 88; P-in-c Barnwood 91-94; V 94-99; P-in-c Highnam, Lassington, Rudford, Tibberton etc 99-04; R 04-06; Chapl Glos Hosps NHS Foundn Trust from 06. *61 Kingsholm Road, Gloucester GL1 3BA, or Gloucestershire Royal Hospital, Great Western Road, Gloucester GL1 3NN* Tel (01452) 417337 *or* 08454-222222

RILEY, Michael Charles. b 57. Ball Coll Ox BA79 MA83 Ex Univ CertEd80. Edin Th Coll 84. **d** 86 **p** 87. C Newc St Geo 86-89; C Chiswick St Nic w St Mary *Lon* 89-90; V Chiswick St Paul Grove Park from 90. *St Paul's Vicarage, 64 Grove Park Road, London W4 3SB* Tel (020) 8987 0312 E-mail michaelc.riley@virgin.com

RILEY, Preb Patrick John. b 39. Leeds Univ BA62. Coll of Resurr Mirfield 62. **d** 64 **p** 65. C Rowbarton *B & W* 64-72; P-in-c Farleigh Hungerford w Tellisford 72-73; P-in-c Rode, Rode Hill and Woolverton 72-73; R Rode Major 73-85; RD Frome 78-85; V Glastonbury w Meare and W Pennard 85-01; Preb Wells Cathl 90-01; rtd 01; Perm to Offic *Sarum* from 02. *24 Tanyard Lane, Shaftesbury SP7 8HW* Tel (01747) 850361

RILEY, Peter Arthur. b 23. Kelham Th Coll 40. **d** 51 **p** 52. C Aston cum Aughton *Sheff* 51-53; C Doncaster Ch Ch 53-55; Trinidad and Tobago 55-59; C-in-c Leic St Chad CD 59-62; Jamaica 62-77; V Abertillery *Mon* 77-83; R Panteg 83-88; rtd 88; Hon C Dartmouth *Ex* 88-99; Lic to Offic *Mon* from 99. *The Bungalow, Clewer Court, Newport NP20 4LQ* Tel (01633) 766870

RILEY, Sidney David. b 43. Birm Univ BA. Ridley Hall Cam 69. **d** 71 **p** 72. C Herne Bay Ch Ch *Cant* 71-74; C Croydon St Sav 74-77; C-in-c Aylesham CD 77; P-in-c Aylesham 77-78; V 78-82; V Tudeley w Capel *Roch* 82-97; Asst Chapl Pembury Hosp 83-86; P-in-c Morley St Paul *Wakef* 97-00; rtd 00; Perm to Offic *York* 07-09. *18 Wheatlands Drive, Beverley HU17 7HR*

RILEY, Canon William. b 24. St Aid Birkenhead 48. **d** 51 **p** 52. C Edgehill St Dunstan *Liv* 51-53; C Halsall 53-57; V Prestolee *Man* 57-62; P-in-c Ringley 60-62; R Tarleton *Blackb* 62-92; RD Leyland 84-89; Hon Can Blackb Cathl 90-92; rtd 92; Perm to Offic *Blackb* from 92. *114 Liverpool Road, Hutton, Preston PR4 5SL* Tel (01772) 614267

RILEY-BRALEY, Robert James. b 57. Ch Ch Ox BA82 Ch Ch Ox MA82 Down Coll Cam BA83 MA87 K Coll Lon MA98 Surrey Univ PGCE92. Ridley Hall Cam 81. **d** 84 **p** 85. C Thames Ditton *Guildf* 84-87; C Gravesend St Geo *Roch* 87-91; Perm to Offic *Lon* 91-92; *Blackb* 92-95; S'wark 95-02; C Stevenage St Mary Shephall w Aston *St Alb* 02-08; P-in-c Croxley Green St Oswald from 08. *St Oswald's Vicarage, 159 Baldwins Lane, Croxley Green, Rickmansworth WD3 3LL* Tel (01923) 332244 E-mail ril.bral@virgin.net

RILEY-DAWKIN, Mrs Linda. b 67. St Jo Coll Nottm BA00. **d** 00 **p** 01. C Ince Ch Ch *Liv* 00-06; Chapl Knowsley Community Coll 06-08; V Ditton St Mich w St Thos *Liv* from 08. *339 Ditchfield Road, Widnes WA8 8XR* Tel 0151-420 4963 Mobile 07932-038443 E-mail revlin.riley@btinternet.com

RIMELL, Gilbert William. b 22. Llan Dioc Tr Scheme 76. **d** 81 **p** 82. NSM Laleston w Tythegston and Merthyr Mawr *Llan* 81-94; rtd 94; Perm to Offic *Llan* from 94. *75 Bryntirion Hill, Bridgend CF31 4BY* Tel (01656) 658002

RIMMER, Andrew Malcolm. b 62. Magd Coll Cam BA84 MA88. Wycliffe Hall Ox 86. **d** 88 **p** 89. C Romford Gd Shep *Chelmsf* 88-92; C Hazlemere *Ox* 92-97; V Crookhorn *Portsm* 97-05; TV Canford Magna *Sarum* from 05. *The Vicarage, 359 Sopwith Crescent, Wimborne BH21 1XQ* Tel (01202) 883630 E-mail a.rimmer@tesco.net

RIMMER, Canon David Henry. b 36. Ex Coll Ox BA60 MA65. Linc Th Coll 62. **d** 64 **p** 65. C Liv Our Lady and St Nic 64-66; C Daybrook *S'well* 66-69; Chapl St Mary's Cathl 69-71; R Kirkcaldy *St And* 71-78; R Haddington *Edin* 78-83; R Dunbar 79-83; R Edin Gd Shep 83-01; Hon Can St Mary's Cathl 98-01; rtd 01; Lic to Offic *Edin* from 01. *3 Southbank Court, Easter Park Drive, Edinburgh EH4 6SH* Tel 0131-539 0283 E-mail rimmerdh@blueyonder.co.uk

RIMMER, Janet. See SPICER, Dorothy Janet Rosalind

RIMMER, Mrs Margaret. b 55. St Jo Coll Dur BA05 SRN77 SCM78. Cranmer Hall Dur 00. **d** 02 **p** 03. C Aysgarth and Bolton cum Redmire *Ripon* 02-06; V Gt and Lt Ouseburn w Marton cum Grafton etc 06-10; P-in-c Lostock Hall and Farington Moss *Blackb* from 10. *St James's Vicarage, 76A Brownedge Road, Lostock Hall, Preston PR5 5AD* Tel (01772) 463842 E-mail margaret.rimmer1@tesco.net

RIMMER, Paul Nathanael. b 25. Jes Coll Ox BA48 MA50. Wycliffe Hall Ox 48. **d** 50 **p** 51. C Douglas St Thos *S & M* 50-52; C Windermere St Martin *Carl* 52-55; Ch of S India 55-59; V Marston *Ox* 59-90; RD Cowley 69-73; rtd 90. *32 Ulfgar Road, Wolvercote, Oxford OX2 8AZ* Tel (01865) 352567

RIMMER, Peter Anthony. b 39. St As Minl Tr Course 90. **d** 96 **p** 97. NSM Abergele *St As* 96-00; C Bodelwyddan 00-09; rtd 09. *St Mary's, 25 Lon Caradog, Abergele LL22 7DE* Tel (01745) 833222

RIMMINGTON, Gerald Thorneycroft. b 30. Lon Univ BSc56 PhD64 Leic Univ MA59 Nottm Univ MEd72 PhD75 FCP66. **d** 76 **p** 78. C Sackville and Dorchester Canada 76-79; Prof of Educn Mt Allison Univ 76-79; Lic to Offic *Leic* 79-80; R Paston Pet 81-86; V Cosby *Leic* 86-90; Dir CME 87-90; R Barwell w Potters Marston and Stapleton 90-95; rtd 95; Perm to Offic *Leic* from 95; RD Guthlaxton 1 03-04. *7 Beechings Close, Countesthorpe, Leicester LE8 5PA* Tel 0116-277 7155

RINDL, Antony William. b 64. St Jo Coll Nottm 97. **d** 99 **p** 00. C Syston *Leic* 99-03; TV Colne and Villages *Blackb* 03-08; TR from 08; P-in-c Brierfield from 10; AD Pendle from 05. *The Vicarage, Skipton Road, Foulridge, Colne BB8 7NP* Tel (01282) 870959 E-mail tony.rindl@googlemail.com

RINGER, Philip James. b 47. Ox Min Course 88. **d** 91 **p** 92. NSM Chalfont St Peter *Ox* 91-95; TV Combe Martin, Berrynarbor, Lynton, Brendon etc *Ex* 96-03; R Wriggle Valley *Sarum* 03-08; rtd 08; Perm to Offic *Sarum* from 08. *7 Wanderwell Farm Lane, Bridport DT6 4JW* Tel (01308) 425774 E-mail philipringer@aol.com

RINGLAND, Tom Laurence. b 61. SS Hild & Bede Coll Dur BSc83. Trin Coll Bris BA89. **d** 89 **p** 90. C Southgate *Chich* 89-92; C Polegate 92-96; P-in-c Coalville and Bardon Hill *Leic* 96-98; V 98-06; TR Kirby Muxloe from 06. *The Rectory, 6 Station Road, Kirby Muxloe, Leicester LE9 2EJ* Tel 0116-238 6822 *or* 238 6811 E-mail tringland@aol.com

RINGROSE, Brian Sefton. b 31. Clare Coll Cam BA54 MA58 Lon Univ PGCE55. Tyndale Hall Bris 56. **d** 58 **p** 59. C Ox St Ebbe 58-60; C Erith St Paul *Roch* 60-61; India 61-75; P-in-c Ox St Matt 75-78; Interserve (Scotland) 78-96; Perm to Offic Glas 78-96; rtd 96; Lic to Offic *Edin* 96-10. *Corner Stores, Tetbury Lane, Crudwell, Malmesbury SN16 9HD* Tel (01666) 577667 E-mail brianringrose@aol.com

RINGROSE, The Ven Hedley Sidney. b 42. Open Univ BA79. Sarum Th Coll 65. **d** 68 **p** 69. C Bishopston *Bris* 68-71; C Easthampstead *Ox* 71-75; V Glouc St Geo w Whaddon 75-88; RD Glouc City 83-88; Hon Can Glouc Cathl 86-09; V Cirencester 88-98; RD Cirencester 89-97; Adn Cheltenham 98-09; rtd 10. *131 North Street, Calne SN11 0HL* Tel (01249) 821215 E-mail hedleyringrose@talktalk.net

RINK, Pamela Rosemary. b 56. **d** 10. NSM E Malling, Wateringbury and Teston *Roch* from 10. *27 Water Lane, West Malling ME19 6HH* Tel (01732) 870279
E-mail pam.rink@gmail.com

RINTAMÄKI, Juha Matti Sakari. b 69. **d** 02. Chapl Finnish Ch in Lon from 03; Lic to Offic *S'wark* from 04. *The Finnish Church in London, 33 Albion Street, London SE16 7HZ* Tel (020) 7237 1261 Fax 7237 1245 Mobile 07768-870614
E-mail juha.rintamaki@finnishchurch.org.uk

RIOCH, Mrs Wenda Jean. b 35. Sarum & Wells Th Coll 84. **d** 87 **p** 94. Par Dn Basingstoke *Win* 87-91; Par Dn Catshill and Dodford *Worc* 91-94; C 94-98; TV Ottery St Mary, Alfington, W Hill, Tipton etc *Ex* 98-05; rtd 05. *76 Gardeners Green, Shipton Bellinger, Tidworth SP9 7TA* Tel (01980) 842334
E-mail wrioch@aol.com

RIORDAN, Sean Charles. b 67. Loughb Univ BA89. St Jo Coll Nottm MA98 LTh99. **d** 99 **p** 00. C Ockbrook *Derby* 99-03; Asst Chapl Tervuren *Eur* 03-08; C Woodley *Ox* from 08. *171 Hurricane Way, Woodley, Reading RG5 4UH* Tel 0118-375 3718 E-mail sean.riordan907@gmail.com

RIPLEY, Preb Geoffrey Alan. b 39. Dur Univ BA62. St Aid Birkenhead. **d** 64 **p** 65. C E Herrington *Dur* 64-67; Hon C Hodge Hill *CD Birm* 68-70; Youth Chapl *Liv* 70-73; Chapl Liv Cathl 70-78; Bp's Dom Chapl 75-78; V Wavertree St Bridget 78-87; Lay Tr Adv *B & W* 87-95; Dioc Chapl MU 92-01; R S Petherton w the Seavingtons 95-01; Chapl E Somerset NHS Trust 95-01; Preb Wells Cathl 97-01; rtd 02; Perm to Offic *B & W* from 02. *20 Overleigh, Street BA16 0TL* Tel (01458) 446766

RIPLEY, Gordon. b 48. SWMTC 03. **d** 06 **p** 07. NSM Torquay St Matthias, St Mark and H Trin *Ex* 06-10; NSM Timsbury w Priston, Camerton and Dunkerton *B & W* from 10. *The Rectory, Skinners Hill, Camerton, Bath BA2 0PU* Tel (01761) 470249
E-mail gordonripley@blueyonder.co.uk

RIPON AND LEEDS, Bishop of. *See* PACKER, The Rt Revd John Richard

RIPON, Dean of. *See* JUKES, The Very Revd Keith Michael

RISBY, John. b 40. Lambeth STh82. Oak Hill Th Coll 64. **d** 67 **p** 68. C Fulham Ch Ch *Lon* 67-68; C Ealing St Mary 68-70; C Chitts Hill St Cuth 70-73; C Hove Bp Hannington Memorial Ch *Chich* 73-76; V Islington St Jude Mildmay Park *Lon* 76-82; P-in-c Islington St Paul Ball's Pond 78-82; V Mildmay Grove St Jude and St Paul 82-84; R Hunsdon w Widford and Wareside *St Alb* 84-05; RD Hertford 91-96; rtd 05; Perm to Offic *Chelmsf* from 06. *1 Pilgrim Close, Great Chesterford, Saffron Walden CB10 1QG* Tel (01799) 530232 E-mail jjrisby@tiscali.co.uk

RISDON, John Alexander. b 42. Clifton Th Coll 66. **d** 68 **p** 69. C Ealing Dean St Jo *Lon* 68-72; C Heref St Pet w St Owen 72-74; Ord Cand Sec CPAS and Hon C Bromley Ch Ch *Roch* 74-77; TV Cheltenham St Mary, St Matt, St Paul and H Trin *Glouc* 77-86; R Stapleton *Bris* 86-00; R Bedhampton *Portsm* 00-09; rtd 09. *10 St Margarets Road, Gloucester GL3 3BP* Tel (01452) 372702 Mobile 07719-460991 E-mail sue.risdon@care4free.net

RISHTON, Mrs Tracy Jane. b 67. St Jo Coll Nottm 01. **d** 04 **p** 05. C Earby *Bradf* 04-07; C Kelbrook 04-07; C Cross Roads cum Lees 07-09; Area Missr S Craven Deanery 07-09. *Hovland, 4389 Vikesa, Norway* E-mail tracy@rishton.info

RITCHIE, Canon Angus William Mark. b 74. Magd Coll Ox BA94 BPhil96 MA98. Westcott Ho Cam 96. **d** 98 **p** 99. C Plaistow and N Canning Town *Chelmsf* 98-02; TV 02-04; Dir Contextual Th Cen R Foundn of St Kath in Ratcliffe from 05; Hon C Gt Ilford St Luke from 05; Fells' Chapl Magd Coll Ox from 05; Chapl E Lon Univ from 08; Hon Can Worc Cathl from 11. *The Royal Foundation of St Katharine, 2 Butcher Row, London E14 8DS* Tel (020) 7790 3540 Fax 7702 7603
E-mail director@theology-centre.org

RITCHIE, Brian Albert. b 34. Open Univ BA80 Birm Univ MA84. Qu Coll Birm 60. **d** 63 **p** 64. C S Leamington St Jo *Cov* 63-67; C-in-c Canley CD 67-70; Perm to Offic 71-80; Hon C Cov H Trin 82-88; R Hatton w Haseley, Rowington w Lowsonford etc 88-97; rtd 97; Perm to Offic *Cov* from 98. *10 Margetts Close, Kenilworth CV8 1EN*

RITCHIE, David John Rose. b 48. St Jo Coll Dur BA72. Cranmer Hall Dur. **d** 74 **p** 75. C Harold Wood *Chelmsf* 74-79; TV Ipsley *Worc* 79-84; Chapl Vevey w Château d'Oex and Villars *Eur* 84-93; V Stoke Bishop *Bris* from 93. *The Vicarage, Mariner's Drive, Bristol BS9 1QJ* Tel 0117-968 1858 *or* 968 7449
E-mail churchmanager@stmarymagdalenestokebishop.org.uk

RITCHIE, Canon David Philip. b 60. Hatf Coll Dur BA85. Wycliffe Hall Ox 85. **d** 87 **p** 88. C Chadwell *Chelmsf* 87-90; C Waltham H Cross 90-94; TV Becontree W 94-98; TR 98-01; Lay Tr Officer 01-11; C Lt Waltham 02-05; C Gt and Lt Leighs and Lt Waltham 05-11; Dir Lay Min Studies NTMTC 06-11; TR Gt

Baddow *Chelmsf* from 11; Hon Can Chelmsf Cathl from 09. *The Rectory, 12 Church Street, Great Baddow, Chelmsford CM2 7HZ* Tel (01245) 471995 Mobile 07738-815761
E-mail dpritchie1@gmail.com

RITCHIE, Miss Jean. b 30. Lon Univ CertEd51. Trin Coll Bris 77. **dss** 79 **d** 87 **p** 94. Ox St Ebbe w H Trin and St Pet 79-87; Par Dn 87-91; rtd 91; Perm to Offic *B & W* 91-94 and from 96; NSM Clevedon St Andr and Ch Ch 94-96. *63 Holland Road, Clevedon BS21 7YJ* Tel (01275) 871762

RITCHIE, Philip. *See* RITCHIE, Canon David Philip

RITCHIE, Philip Simon James. b 68. Man Univ BA90 Sussex Univ MA98 Leeds Univ MA01 Man Metrop Univ PGCE92. Coll of Resurr Mirfield 99. **d** 01 **p** 02. C Brighton St Nic *Chich* 01-04; P-in-c Chich St Wilfrid 04-08; P-in-c Hove 08-10; V Hove All SS from 10. *The Vicarage, Wilbury Road, Hove BN3 3PB* Tel (01273) 733331 E-mail office@allsaintshove.org

RITCHIE, Robert Peter. b 57. St Pet Coll Ox BA81 St Jo Coll Cam MPhil83. SEITE 97. **d** 00 **p** 01. NSM Kingston All SS w St Jo *S'wark* 00-11; Perm to Offic from 11. *7 Gibbon Road, Kingston upon Thames KT2 6AD* Tel (020) 8546 5964
E-mail robert@rsritchie.freeserve.co.uk

RITCHIE, Canon Samuel. b 31. Lon Coll of Div 65. **d** 67 **p** 68. C Westlands St Andr *Lich* 67-70; V Springfield H Trin *Chelmsf* 70-82; Chapl HM Pris Chelmsf 70-82; Brixton 82-84; Hull 84-86; Sen Chapl HM Prison Wymott 86-95; NW Area Chapl Co-ord 86-95; rtd 95; P-in-c Helmingham w Framsden and Pettaugh w Winston *St E* 96-97; Perm to Offic from 03. *Hillcrest, 3 Highfield Drive, Claydon, Ipswich IP6 0EY* Tel (01473) 833798

RITCHIE, William James. b 62. TCD MA84. CITC. **d** 86 **p** 87. C Enniscorthy *C & O* 86-89; Asst Chapl Alexandria Egypt 89-91; Bp's C Kells Gp *C & O* 91-92; I Kells Union *M & K* 92-99; Warden of Readers 93-97; Dioc Ecum Officer 97-99; Min Can St Patr Cathl Dublin 97-99; I Clondehorkey w Cashel *D & R* 99-00; I Dublin St Bart w Leeson Park *D & G* 00-04; I Tullow w Shillelagh, Aghold and Mullinacuff *C & O* 04-08; Warden of Readers 05-08; Perm to Offic *Lon* from 08. *St Alban's Clergy House, 18 Brooke Street, London EC1N 7RD* Tel (020) 7405 1831

RITSON, Canon Gerald Richard Stanley (Bill). b 35. CCC Cam BA59 MA63. Linc Th Coll 59. **d** 61 **p** 62. C Harpenden St Jo *St Alb* 61-65; C Goldington 65-69; R Clifton 69-76; Sec to Dioc Past Cttee and P-in-c Aldenham 76-87; Hon Can St Alb 80-87; Can Res St Alb 87-00; rtd 00; Perm to Offic *S'wark* from 00 and *Lon* from 04. *97 Mitre Road, London SE1 8PT* Tel (020) 7633 0012

RITTMAN, Margaret. STETS. **d** 11. NSM Knight's Enham and Smannell w Enham Alamein *Win* from 11. *24 Stoke Road, Winchester SO23 7ET* Tel (01962) 878390
E-mail mgtritt@me.com

RIVERS, David John. b 51. St Jo Coll Nottm. **d** 84 **p** 85. C Woodthorpe *S'well* 84-88; C Hyson Green St Paul w St Steph 88; Asst Chapl Colchester Gen Hosp 89-91; Chapl Leeds Teaching Hosps NHS Trust 91-05; rtd 05; Perm to Offic *Ripon* from 05. *28 Palace Road, Ripon HG4 1ET* Tel (01765) 606227 Mobile 07810-430245 E-mail woollrivers@msn.com

RIVERS, John Arthur. b 21. EAMTC 79. **d** 81 **p** 82. NSM Blakeney w Cley, Wiveton, Glandford etc *Nor* 81-86; Hon C Cromer 86-87; Perm to Offic 87-06. *Address temp unknown*

RIVETT, Canon Peter John. b 42. St Jo Coll Dur BA71. Cranmer Hall Dur. **d** 72 **p** 73. C Newland St Jo *York* 72-76; TV Marfleet 76-82; V Oxhey All SS *St Alb* 82-93; TR Swanborough *Sarum* 93-98; TV Pewsey and Swanborough 98-01; USPG Zambia 01-07; Adn S Zambia 03-10; Hon Can Lusaka 10; rtd 10. *9 Church View, Bewdley DY12 2BZ* Tel (01299) 402768
E-mail peter.rivett280@btinternet.com

RIVIERE, Jonathan Byam Valentine. b 54. Cuddesdon Coll. **d** 83 **p** 84. C Wymondham *Nor* 83-88; TV Quidenham 88-94; P-in-c Somerleyton w Ashby, Fritton and Herringfleet 94; R Somerleyton, Ashby, Fritton, Herringfleet etc 95-03; R Sandringham w W Newton and Appleton etc from 03; P-in-c Castle Rising 03-11; R from 11; P-in-c Hillington 03-11; R from 11; Dom Chapl to The Queen from 03; Chapl to The Queen from 07. *The Rectory, Sandringham PE35 6EH* Tel (01485) 540587 E-mail jonathan@riviere.co.uk

RIVIERE, Mrs Tanagra June. b 41. S Dios Minl Tr Scheme 88. **d** 91. NSM Medstead w Wield *Win* 91-94; NSM Bishop's Sutton and Ropley and W Tisted 94-96. *The Drey, Paice Lane, Medstead, Alton GU34 5PT* Tel and fax (01420) 563330

RIX, Patrick George. b 30. Magd Coll Ox BA54 MA57 DipEd55. Ridley Hall Cam 58. **d** 60 **p** 61. C Dur St Nic 60-62; Asst Chapl Wrekin Coll Telford 62-70; Asst Chapl Gresham's Sch Holt 70-80; Chapl Bloxham Sch 80-86; rtd 86; P-in-c Swanton Abbott w Skeyton *Nor* 89; Perm to Offic 89-08. *c/o Miss C Rix, 195 Earlham Road, Norwich NR2 3RQ*

ROACH, Jason O'Neale. b 77. Guy's Hosp Medical Sch BSc98 K Coll Lon MB, BS02 St Mary's Coll Twickenham MA05. Oak Hill Th Coll MTh10. **d** 10 **p** 11. C St Helen Bishopsgate w St Andr Undershaft etc *Lon* from 10. *11 Heron House, Searles*

Close, London SW11 4RJ Tel (020) 7223 0273 Mobile 07957-473507 E-mail joroach@gmail.com
ROACH, Kenneth Thomas. b 43. St Andr Univ BD69 Fitzw Coll Cam BA71 MA76. Westcott Ho Cam 69. **d** 71 **p** 72. C Glas St Marg 71-73; CF 73-76; R Johnstone *Glas* 76-85; R Bearsden 85-96; TR Bearsden w Milngavie 96-08; CF (TA) 86-08; rtd 08. *Flat 1, 3 St John's Court, Pollokshields, Glasgow G41 5ED* Tel 0141-429 1064 Mobile 07774-814052 E-mail kenroach@freeuk.co.uk
ROACH, Lynne Elisabeth. See DAVIES, Mrs Lynne Elisabeth
ROACHE, Anthony. b 60. Nazarene Th Coll Man BA78. **d** 99 **p** 00. C Bury St Mary *Man* 99-02; P-in-c Ringley w Prestolee 02-06; Voc Adv 04-06; CF(V) 03-06; CF from 06. *c/o MOD Chaplains (Army)* Tel (01264) 381140 Fax 381824 E-mail roachefamily@ntlworld.com
ROAKE, Anthony Richard Garrard. b 52. Keble Coll Ox BA75 MA80. Wycliffe Hall Ox 75. **d** 77 **p** 78. C Clifton *S'well* 77-80; V Lapley w Wheaton Aston *Lich* 80-86; V Bournemouth St Andr *Win* 86-98; V Fernhurst *Chich* 98-07; Chapl The Hague *Eur* from 07. *Riouwstraat 2, 2585 HA Den Haag, The Netherlands* Tel (0031) (70) 355 5359 E-mail tonyrgr@gmail.com
ROAN, Canon William Forster. b 21. St Chad's Coll Dur BA47. **d** 49 **p** 50. C Barrow St Jas *Carl* 49-52; C-in-c Westf St Mary CD 52-58; V Westfield St Mary 58-61; R Greystoke 61-69; V Workington St Jo 70-86; Hon Can Carl Cathl 72-86; RD Solway 77-84; rtd 86; Perm to Offic *Carl* from 86. *41 Chiswick Street, Carlisle CA1 1HJ* Tel (01228) 521756
ROBARTS, Mrs Freda Margaret. b 43. Open Univ BA86. St As Minl Tr Course 98. **d** 04 **p** 06. NSM Berriew *St As* 04-06; P-in-c Llansilin w Llangadwaladr and Llangedwyn 06-09; rtd 09. *Bryn Awel, Llanrhaedr ym Mochnant, Oswestry SY10 0DJ*
ROBB, Ian Archibald. b 48. K Coll Lon 68. **d** 72 **p** 73. C E Ham w Upton Park *Chelmsf* 72-74; C Leckhampton SS Phil and Jas w Cheltenham St Jas *Glouc* 74-79; P-in-c Cheltenham St Mich 79-90; V Lower Cam w Coaley from 90. *St Bartholomew's Vicarage, 99 Fairmead, Cam, Dursley GL11 5JR* Tel (01453) 542679 E-mail ia_jdr@lineone.net
ROBB, Robert Hammond Neill. b 46. Open Univ BA89 Man Univ 66. St Deiniol's Hawarden 87. **d** 87 **p** 88. C Lache cum Saltney *Ches* 87-89; V Norley and Crowton 89-97; P-in-c Kingsley 95-97; V Norley, Crowton and Kingsley 97-98; V Neston from 98. *The Vicarage, High Street, Neston CH64 9TZ* Tel 0151-353 1000 E-mail celtic.robb@btopenworld.com
ROBB, Timothy Simon. b 72. Cant Univ (NZ) BMus94 LTCL94 Lon Bible Coll BTh98. Trin Coll Bris MA03. **d** 03 **p** 04. C Bedford Ch Ch *St Alb* 03-07; Chapl De Montford Univ 05-07; V Eaton Socon from 07. *St Mary's Vicarage, 34 Drake Road, Eaton Socon, St Neots PE19 8HS* Tel (01480) 212219 E-mail vicar@stmaryseatonsocon.org.uk
ROBBIE, James Neil. b 68. Strathclyde Univ BEng90. Oak Hill Th Coll BTh02. **d** 05 **p** 06. C Wolverhampton St Luke *Lich* 05-09; V W Bromwich H Trin from 09. *Holy Trinity Vicarage, 1 Burlington Road, West Bromwich B70 6LF* Tel 0121-525 3595 E-mail rev.robbie@btinternet.com
ROBBINS, Angela Mary. See WEAVER, Canon Angela Mary
ROBBINS, David Leslie. b 43. Univ Coll Lon BSc65 Nottm Univ CertEd66. EMMTC 96. **d** 00 **p** 01. NSM Newark *S'well* 00-04; NSM S'well H Trin from 04. *21 Woodland View, Southwell NG25 0AG* Tel (01636) 812641 Mobile 07773-361042 E-mail dlrobbins1@hotmail.com
ROBBINS, David Ronald Walter. b 47. Sarum & Wells Th Coll 85. **d** 87 **p** 88. C Meir Heath *Lich* 87-89; C Collier Row St Jas and Havering-atte-Bower *Chelmsf* 89-93; C Tamworth *Lich* 93-97; P-in-c Hulland, Atlow, Bradley and Hognaston *Derby* 97-98; P-in-c Kniveton 97-98; R Hulland, Atlow, Kniveton, Bradley and Hognaston 98-02; R Widford *Chelmsf* from 02. *The Rectory, 3 Canuden Road, Widford, Chelmsford CM1 2SU* Tel (01245) 346329 Fax 346365 E-mail robbinsdrw@btinternet.com
ROBBINS, Mrs Janet Carey. b 41. LMH Ox BA63 MA95 Nôtre Dame Coll Bearsden PGCE81. St D Dioc Tr Course 96. **d** 98 **p** 99. NSM Llanfihangel Ystrad and Cilcennin w Trefilan etc *St D* 98-01; NSM Quantock Towers B & W 02-03; rtd 03; Hon C Bro Teifi Sarn Helen *St D* 08-11. *Rhydyfran, Cribyn, Lampeter SA48 7NH* Tel (01570) 470349 E-mail revdjanet@tiscali.co.uk
ROBBINS, Martin Charles. b 68. Thames Valley Univ BA91. Ripon Coll Cuddesdon BTh00. **d** 00 **p** 01. C Thatcham *Ox* 00-03; CF 03-08; Chapl Heathfield St Mary's Sch Ascot 08-11; Asst Chapl K Sch Cant from 11. *The King's School, 25 The Precincts, Canterbury CT1 2ES* Tel (01227) 595501
ROBBINS, Peter Tyndall. b 25. Magd Coll Ox BA46 MA51. Westcott Ho Cam 48. **d** 50 **p** 51. C Bury St Paul *Man* 50-53; C Swinton St Pet 53-55; V Prestwich St Hilda 55-59; V Lower Halstow Chart 59-63; V Charing w Lt Chart 63-73; V Basing *Win* 73-83; V Kingsclere 83-90; rtd 90; Perm to Offic *Birm* 91-00; Asst RD Tamworth *Lich* 91-95; Perm to Offic from 95. *St John's Hospital, St John Street, Lichfield WS13 6PB* Tel (01543) 415197 E-mail robbinspt@tiscali.co.uk
ROBBINS, The Ven Stephen. b 53. K Coll Lon BD74 AKC74. St Aug Coll Cant 75. **d** 76 **p** 77. C Tudhoe Grange *Dur* 76-80; C-in-c Harlow Green CD 80-84; V Gateshead Harlow Green

84-87; CF 87-97; Sen CF 97-01; Chapl R Memorial Chpl Sandhurst 01-02; Asst Chapl Gen 02-07; Dep Chapl Gen 07-09; Chapl Gen 08-11; Adn for the Army 04-11; QHC 05-11; rtd 11; Can and Preb Sarum Cathl from 07. *c/o MOD Chaplains (Army)*
ROBBINS, Walter. b 35. **d** 72 **p** 73. Argentina 73-82; Adn N Argentina 80-82; C Southborough St Pet w Ch Ch and St Matt *Roch* 82-86; V Sidcup St Andr 86-95; V Grain w Stoke 95-00; rtd 00; Perm to Offic *Roch* from 00 and *Cant* 01-09. *Mariners, Imperial Avenue, Minster on Sea, Sheerness ME12 2HG* Tel (01795) 876588
ROBBINS-COLE, Adrian Peter. b 62. LSE BSc(Econ)84 K Coll Lon MA96. Ch Div Sch of the Pacific (USA) 90 Ripon Coll Cuddesdon BA92. **d** 93 **p** 94. C S Dulwich St Steph *S'wark* 93-97; V Motspur Park 97-04; RD Merton 01-04; R Peterborough All SS USA from 04. *49 Concord Street, Peterborough NH 03458-1510, USA* Tel (001) (603) 924 3202 E-mail allsaintsnh@verizon.net
ROBBINS-COLE, Ms Sarah Jane. b 68. Vermont Univ BA90 K Coll Lon MA00. Ch Div Sch of the Pacific (USA) 92 Ripon Coll Cuddesdon BA95. **d** 95 **p** 96. C W Dulwich All SS *S'wark* 95-98; Chapl K Coll Sch Wimbledon 98-04; Hon C Motspur Park *S'wark* 98-04; Asst P Peterborough All SS USA from 04. *49 Concord Street, Peterborough NH 03458-1510, USA* Tel (001) (603) 924 3202 E-mail allsaintsnh@verizon.net
ROBERT, Brother. See ATWELL, The Rt Revd Robert Ronald
ROBERT HUGH, Brother. See KING-SMITH, Philip Hugh
ROBERTS, Aelwyn. See ROBERTS, Joseph Aelwyn
ROBERTS, Alan Moss. b 39. CEng68 MIMechE68 MIMarEST68. St Jo Coll Nottm 77. **d** 79 **p** 80. C Bromsgrove St Jo *Worc* 79-83; C Edgbaston St Germain *Birm* 83-89; R Broadhembury, Payhembury and Plymtree *Ex* 89-96; rtd 06. *8 Oakleigh, Sheldon, Honiton EX14 4QT* Tel (01404) 841358 E-mail alanmossroberts@lineone.net
ROBERTS, Allen. b 47. Trin Coll Ox MA72 Warwick Univ MA74 PhD79 Wolv Univ LLM99. Qu Coll Birm 06. **d** 07 **p** 09. NSM Tettenhall Regis *Lich* from 07. *11 Grosvenor Court, Lime Tree Avenue, Wolverhampton WV6 8HB* Tel (01902) 765741 Mobile 07885-341540 E-mail allen.roberts1@btinternet.com
ROBERTS, Mrs Andrea Joan. b 46. Liv Poly ALA68 St Jo Coll Dur BA73 PGCE74. Cranmer Hall Dur 70 CBDTI 03. **d** 04 **p** 05. NSM Garstang St Thos *Blackb* from 04. *The Vicarage, 5 Lancaster Road, Cockerham, Lancaster LA2 0EB* Tel and fax (01524) 791390 E-mail andrea.j.roberts@ukonline.co.uk
ROBERTS, Preb Andrew Alexander. b 49. Open Univ BA75. Bp Otter Coll CertEd70 Sarum & Wells Th Coll 76. **d** 80 **p** 81. NSM Dorchester *Sarum* 80-85; C Swanage and Studland 85-87; TV 87-94; TR Bridgnorth, Tasley, Astley Abbotts, etc *Heref* 94-09; P-in-c Morville w Aston Eyre 08-09; P-in-c Acton Round 08-09; P-in-c Upton Cressett w Monk Hopton 08-09; RD Bridgnorth 05-09; Preb Heref Cathl 03-09; rtd 09. *Quaywalk Cottage, 2 Cliff Place, Swanage BH19 2PL* Tel (01929) 424324 E-mail andyaroberts@talk21.com
ROBERTS, Andrew John. b 55. Newc Univ BA77. EMMTC 00. **d** 03 **p** 04. NSM Church Langton cum Tur Langton etc *Leic* 03-07; Chapl HM Pris Linc from 07. *The Chaplains' Office, HM Prison, Greetwell Road, Lincoln LN2 4BD* Tel (01522) 663090 E-mail andrewroberts28@aol.com
ROBERTS, Anne Judith. b 44. CertEd65 DipEd78 Open Univ BA82. S Dios Minl Tr Scheme 86. **d** 89 **p** 94. Hon Par Dn S Kensington H Trin w All SS *Lon* 89-92; NSM Barnes *S'wark* from 92; S'wark OLM Scheme 98-04. *5 Avenue Gardens, London SW14 8BP* Tel (020) 8878 5642 E-mail revjr@blueyonder.co.uk
ROBERTS, Mrs Anne Marie. b 55. York Univ BA77. St Jo Coll Nottm 80 WMMTC 93. **d** 96 **p** 97. NSM Meole Brace *Lich* 96-08; Chapl Robert Jones/Agnes Hunt Orthopaedic NHS Trust 98-00; Chapl Prestfelde Sch Shrewsbury 99-08; Chapl N Cumbria Univ Hosps NHS Trust from 11. *2 The Abbey, Carlisle CA3 8TZ*
ROBERTS, Anthony. See ROBERTS, John Anthony Duckworth
ROBERTS, Barrie Moelwyn Antony. b 43. RN Coll Dartmouth 63 Trin Coll Carmarthen CertEd70 Birm Poly BA83. Qu Coll Birm 00. **d** 04 **p** 05. NSM Bartley Green *Birm* from 04. *34 Wheats Avenue, Harborne, Birmingham B17 0RJ* Tel 0121-426 2501 E-mail b.roberts@lineone.net
ROBERTS, Barry. See ROBERTS, Ronald Barry
ROBERTS, Brian David. b 44. Ball Coll Ox BA66 Univ of Wales (Ban) BTh06 FRSA00. **d** 03 **p** 04. OLM Guildf H Trin w St Mary from 03. *Risby, Upper Guildown Road, Guildford GU2 4EZ* Tel (01483) 570556 Fax (020) 7631 6224 Mobile 07979-766471 E-mail b.roberts4u@ntlworld.com
ROBERTS, Bryan Richard. b 55. Univ of Wales (Cardiff) BD80. St Mich Coll Llan 78. **d** 80 **p** 81. C Finham *Cov* 80-83; Asst Youth Officer *Nor* 83-86; R N and S Creake w Waterden 86-91; P-in-c E w N and W Barsham 86-91; Chapl Epsom Coll 91-01; Chapl Gresham's Sch Holt from 01. *10 Kelling Road, Holt NR25 6RT* Tel (01263) 713234
ROBERTS, Carol Susan Butler. b 63. Univ of Wales (Ban) BA84 MTh99 MPhil02 PhD05. Ban Ord Course 06. **d** 07 **p** 08. NSM

Bangor 07-10; C from 10. *Tu Hwnt I'r Afon, 55 Braichmelyn, Bethesda, Bangor LL57 3RD* Tel (01248) 600420 E-mail davecas@tesco.net
ROBERTS, Charles Richard Meyrick. b 53. Huddersfield Poly BA75 ARCM75. St Paul's Coll Grahamstown 89. **d** 92 **p** 92. C Lansdowne St Aidan S Africa 92-93; C Claremont St Sav 93-94; C Bath Abbey w St Jas *B & W* 94-98; P-in-c Chew Magna w Dundry 98-00; R Chew Magna w Dundry and Norton Malreward 00-10; R Chew Magna w Dundry, Norton Malreward etc from 10; P-in-c Chew Stoke w Nempnett Thrubwell from 03. *The Rectory, Tunbridge Close, Chew Magna, Bristol BS40 8SU* Tel (01275) 332199 E-mail chewrector@hotmail.com
ROBERTS, Christopher Michael. b 39. Man Univ DipAE79. Qu Coll Birm 62. **d** 64 **p** 65. C Milton next Gravesend Ch Ch *Roch* 64-68; C Thirsk w S Kilvington *York* 68-69; V Castleton *Derby* 69-75; TV Buxton w Burbage and King Sterndale 75-79; Perm to Offic 84-87; NSM Marple All SS *Ches* 87-90; Chapl Asst St Helens Hosp Liv 90-91; Chapl Asst Whiston Co Hosp Prescot 90-91; Chapl Asst Rainhill Hosp Liv 90-91; Chapl R United Hosp Bath 91-94; Chapl R United Hosp Bath NHS Trust 94-99; Sen Chapl Birm Children's Hosp NHS Trust 99-04; rtd 04; Perm to Offic Birm from 04. *6 Myring Drive, Sutton Coldfield B75 7RZ* Tel 0121-329 2547 E-mail chrismirob@aol.com
ROBERTS, Colin Edward. b 50. Sarum & Wells Th Coll. **d** 83 **p** 84. C Harton *Dur* 83; C S Shields All SS 83-85; C Thamesmead *S'wark* 85-87; TV 87-89; C Streatham St Pet 89-90 and 92; Zimbabwe 90-92; V Earlsfield St Jo *S'wark* from 92. *St John's Vicarage, 40 Atheldene Road, London SW18 3BW* Tel (020) 8874 2837 Fax 08088-742816 E-mail viva.stjohns@btinternet.com
ROBERTS, Canon Cyril. b 41. St Deiniol's Hawarden. **d** 84 **p** 85. C Maltby *Sheff* 84-86; TR Gt Snaith from 86; AD Snaith and Hatfield 03-11; Hon Can Sheff Cathl from 05. *The Orchard, Pontefract Road, Snaith, Goole DN14 9JS* Tel (01405) 860866 Mobile 07702-004870 E-mail cyrilroberts@hotmail.co.uk
ROBERTS, David. b 44. Ex Univ BA65. St Steph Ho Ox 65. **d** 67 **p** 68. C Southwick St Columba *Dur* 67-72; C-in-c Southwick St Cuth CD 72-79; R Alyth *St And* 79-84; R Blairgowrie 79-84; R Coupar Angus 79-84; P-in-c Taunton St Jo *B & W* from 84; rtd 09; Chapl Somerset Coll of Arts and Tech 84-10. *17 Henley Road, Taunton TA1 5BW* Tel (01823) 284176 E-mail scat.chap@virgin.net
ROBERTS, David Alan. b 38. Open Univ BA82. Ripon Hall Ox 71. **d** 73 **p** 74. C W Bridgford *S'well* 73-77; V Awsworth w Cossall 77-82; V Oxclose *Dur* 82-94; P-in-c New Seaham 94-04; rtd 04. *8 Hazel Road, Gateshead NE8 2EP* Tel 0191-460 9919
ROBERTS, David Charles. b 53. Poly of Wales CertEd76 Open Univ BA82 BA93 Univ of Wales MEd87. St Mich Coll Llan 96. **d** 98 **p** 99. C Whitchurch *Llan* 98-00; Chapl Univ of Wales Inst Cardiff 00-05; Mental Health Chapl Gwent Healthcare NHS Trust from 05. *6 Gwaun Llwyfen, Nelson, Treharris CF46 6HY* Tel (01443) 450995
ROBERTS, Preb David Henry. b 38. St Chad's Coll Dur BA60. Qu Coll Birm. **d** 62 **p** 63. C Stonehouse *Glouc* 62-65; C Hemsworth *Wakef* 65-69; V Newsome 69-76; R Pontesbury I and II *Heref* 76-03; RD Pontesbury 83-93; Preb Heref Cathl from 85; rtd 03; Perm to Offic *Heref* from 03. *14 Beaconsfield Park, Ludlow SY8 4LY* Tel (01584) 878568 E-mail dhroberts@lineone.net
ROBERTS, Canon David John. b 36. Man Univ BSc58. St D Coll Lamp 65. **d** 67 **p** 68. C Rhosllannerchrugog *St As* 67-70; R Cerrigydrudion w Llanfihangel Glyn Myfyr etc 70-75; R Llanrwst and Llanddoget 75-77; R Llanrwst and Llanddoget and Capel Garmon 77-84; RD Llanrwst 77-84; V Abergele 84-01; RD Rhos 94-00; Hon Can St As Cathl 95-96; Can Cursal St As Cathl 96-01; rtd 01. *21 Lowther Court, Bodelwyddan, Rhyl LL18 5YG* Tel (01745) 798604
ROBERTS, Mrs Deryn Anne. b 49. Nottm Univ TCert70 BEd71. SWMTC 04. **d** 07 **p** 08. C Lanteglos by Camelford w Advent Truro from 07; C St Teath from 07. *11 Cambeak Close, Crackington Haven, Bude EX23 0PE* Tel (01840) 230493 Mobile 07977-318589
ROBERTS, Dewi. b 57. LWCMD77 Cyncoed Coll CertEd78. St Mich Coll Llan. **d** 84 **p** 85. C Clydach *S & B* 84-88; V Glantawe 88-94; V Loughor 94-06; V Gowerton from 06; AD Llwchwr from 10. *The Vicarage, 14 Church Street, Gowerton, Swansea SA4 3EA* Tel (01792) 872266
ROBERTS, Dewi James Llewelyn. b 63. United Th Coll Abth 83. **d** 96 **p** 97. C Llandudno *Ban* 96-02; C Llanfachraeth and Llechgynfarwy 99-02; C Llanfaethlu w Llanfwrog and Llanrhuddlad etc 99-02; V Newcastle Emlyn w Llandyfriog and Troedyraur etc *St D* from 02. *The Vicarage, Terra Cotta, Station Road, Newcastle Emlyn SA38 9BX* Tel (01239) 710154 E-mail dewi44@googlemail.com
ROBERTS, Diane. b 45. Bris Univ CertEd66 BEd82. STETS 02. **d** 05 **p** 06. NSM Kinson and W Howe *Sarum* from 05. *21 Highfield Road, Bournemouth BH9 2SE* E-mail robertsdiane1@aol.com

ROBERTS, Dilwyn Carey. b 38. St Deiniol's Hawarden 74. **d** 76 **p** 77. C Glanadda *Ban* 76-77; TV Amlwch, Rhosybol, Llandyfrydog etc 77-81; V Llanllechid 81-85; V Caerhun w Llangelynin 85-87; V Caerhun w Llangelynin w Llanbedr-y-Cennin 87-92; rtd 93. *67 St Georges Drive, Conwy LL31 9PR*
ROBERTS, Donald James. b 26. Sarum & Wells Th Coll 83. **d** 86 **p** 87. NSM Corfe Castle, Church Knowle, Kimmeridge etc *Sarum* 86-88 and 91-95; C Broadstone 88-91; rtd 91; Perm to Offic *Sarum* 95-98 and *St E from 01. 42 Priory Court, Nacton, Ipswich IP10 0JU* Tel (01473) 711242
ROBERTS, Edward. *See* ROBERTS, Canon Henry Edward
ROBERTS, Edward John Walford. b 31. Trin Coll Carmarthen CertEd. St D Dioc Tr Course. **d** 79 **p** 80. NSM Burry Port and Pwll *St D* 79-98; NSM Swansea St Jas *S & B* 98-02; Lic to Offic from 02. *Hen Parc Cottage, Hen Par Lane, Upper Killay, Swansea SA2 7JL*
ROBERTS, Edward Mark. b 68. **d** 07 **p** 08. OLM Droylsden St Mary *Man* 07-10; P-in-c Blackley St Paul from 10; P-in-c Blackley St Pet from 10. *14 Hill Lane, Blackley, Manchester M9 6PE* Tel 0161-740 2124 E-mail eddie@eddieroberts.net
ROBERTS, Canon Edward Owen. b 38. K Coll Lon BD63 AKC63. **d** 64 **p** 65. C Auckland St Andr and St Anne *Dur* 64-67; C Cheltenham St Paul *Glouc* 67-68; Asst Master Colne Valley High Sch Linthwaite 69-71; V Meltham Mills *Wakef* 71-75; R Emley 75-88; RD Kirkburton 80-88; V Huddersfield H Trin 88-04; RD Huddersfield 89-99; Hon Can Wakef Cathl 92-04; rtd 04; Perm to Offic *York* from 04. *2B Queen Street, Filey YO14 9HB* Tel (01723) 515535
ROBERTS, Mrs Elizabeth Rose. **d** 11. NSM Llanfihangel Ysgeifiog w Llangristiolus etc *Ban* from 11. *10 Y Fron, Aberffraw, Ty Croes LL63 5EQ* Tel (01407) 840605 E-mail cushlarose@btinternet.com
ROBERTS, Eric. b 40. Ban Ord Course 90 St Mich Coll Llan 92. **d** 93 **p** 94. Min Can Ban Cathl 93-97; R Llanllyfni 97-02; V Llandysul w Bangor Teifi w Henllan etc *St D* 02-11; AD Emlyn 04-11; rtd 11. *Gerallt, Erw Wen, Caeathro, Caernarfon LL55 2TW* Tel (01286) 671861
ROBERTS, Erica Jane. MB, ChB MRCP. STETS. **d** 10 **p** 11. *Brookvale Cottage, Highfield Lane, Southampton SO17 1NQ* Tel (02380) 556887 E-mail erica@samotto.demon.co.uk
ROBERTS, Graham Miles. b 59. Open Univ BA95. Trin Coll Bris 90. **d** 92 **p** 93. C Charles w Plymouth St Matthias *Ex* 92-96; Chapl Plymouth Univ 92-94; TV Liskeard, St Keyne, St Pinnock, Morval etc *Truro* 96-99; P-in-c Bournemouth St Andr *Win* 99-04; V from 04. *St Andrew's Vicarage, 53 Bennett Road, Bournemouth BH8 8QQ* Tel (01202) 396022 E-mail graham roberts@ntlworld.com
ROBERTS, Gregory Stephen. b 64. St Chad's Coll Dur BSc86 PGCE87 CPhys95. Ripon Coll Cuddesdon 08. **d** 10 **p** 11. C Kettering SS Pet and Paul from 10. *2 Moorhouse Way, Kettering NN15 7LX* Tel (01536) 525591 E-mail gregroberts81@hotmail.com
ROBERTS, Canon Henry Edward (Ted). b 28. Oak Hill Th Coll 53. **d** 56 **p** 57. C Edgware *Lon* 56-58; C Bedworth *Cov* 58-61; V Bethnal Green St Jas Less *Lon* 61-73; V Old Ford St Mark Victoria Park 61-73; V Bethnal Green St Jas Less w Victoria Park 73-78; RD Tower Hamlets 76-78; Can Res Bradf Cathl 78-82; Dioc Dir Soc Resp 78-82; V Bermondsey St Jas w Ch Ch *S'wark* 82-90; P-in-c Bermondsey St Anne 82-90; Hon Can S'wark Cathl 90-93; Gen Adv for Inner City Min 90-93; rtd 93. *12 Bromeswell Road, Ipswich IP4 3AS* Tel (01473) 288956
ROBERTS, James. *See* ROBERTS, William James
ROBERTS, Jane Elizabeth. b 53. SEITE 98. **d** 01 **p** 02. NSM Mitcham Ascension *S'wark* from 01. *39 Castleton Road, Mitcham CR4 1NZ* Tel (020) 8764 6423 Mobile 07790-703710 E-mail janeroberts@nasuwt.net
ROBERTS, Miss Janet Lynne. b 56. Trin Coll Bris 76. **dss** 82 **d** 87 **p** 94. Dagenham *Chelmsf* 82-86; Huyton St Mich *Liv* 86-91; Par Dn 87-91; C Aughton Ch Ch 91-98; TV Parr 98-05; TR from 05. *St Paul's Vicarage, 75 Chain Lane, St Helens WA11 9QF* Tel and fax (01744) 734335 E-mail rovingrector@btinternet.com
ROBERTS, Mrs Jasmine Cynthia. b 46. Cant Sch of Min 88. **d** 91. NSM Sandwich *Cant* from 91; Asst Dir of Ords 02-09. *The Rectory, Knightrider Street, Sandwich CT13 9ER* Tel and fax (01304) 613138 E-mail jasmineroberts@supanet.com
ROBERTS, Ms Jeanette. b 67. RMHN00. Cranmer Hall Dur 07. **d** 09 **p** 10. C Todmorden *Wakef* from 09. *12 Phoenix Court, Todmorden OL14 5SJ* Tel (01706) 813165 E-mail jay.roberts@hotmail.co.uk
ROBERTS, John Anthony Duckworth. b 43. K Coll Lon BD65 AKC65. St Boniface Warminster 65. **d** 66 **p** 67. C Wythenshawe Wm Temple Ch CD *Man* 66-69; C Bradford-on-Avon H Trin *Sarum* 69-72; Chapl Dauntsey's Sch Devizes 72-73; CF 73-77; P-in-c Verwood *Sarum* 77-81; V All Hallows, St Mary Blackb 86-97; R Paget St Paul Bermuda 97-03; rtd 03. *The Old Coach House, Forwood, Minchinhampton, Stroud GL6 9AB* Tel (01453) 835811

ROBERTS, John Charles Welch. b 39. UMIST BSc60. Oak Hill NSM Course 91 SWMTC 92. **d** 94 **p** 95. NSM Washfield, Stoodleigh, Withleigh etc *Ex* from 94. *East Sidborough, Loxbeare, Tiverton EX16 8DA* Tel and fax (01884) 256302 E-mail john@sidborough.eclipse.co.uk

ROBERTS, Canon John Hugh. b 42. K Alfred's Coll Win CertEd72 Open Univ BA75. Wells Th Coll 65. **d** 67 **p** 68. C Wareham w Arne *Sarum* 67-70; C Twyford *Win* 70-72; Asst Teacher Rawlins Sch Leics 72-74; V Nassington w Yarwell *Pet* 74-77; Asst Teacher Sponne Sch Towcester 78-92; RD Brackley 94-03; P-in-c Helmdon w Stuchbury and Radstone etc 93-03; P-in-c Weedon Lois w Plumpton and Moreton Pinkney etc 02-03; R Astwell Gp 03-05; Can Pet Cathl 01-05; rtd 05; Perm to Offic Pet from 05; Chapl to Retired Clergy and Clergy Widows' Officer 08-10. *Pimlico House, Pimlico, Brackley NN13 5TN* Tel (01280) 850378 E-mail rev.roberts@virgin.net

ROBERTS, Canon John Mark Arnott. b 54. AKC75 CertEd76. Chich Th Coll 77. **d** 77 **p** 78. C Ashford *Cant* 77-82; V St Mary's Bay w St Mary-in-the-Marsh etc 82-91; R Sandwich from 91; AD Sandwich 00-06; Hon Can Cant Cathl from 03; C Woodnesborough w Worth and Staple from 04; P-in-c Eastry and Northbourne w Tilmanstone etc from 10. *The Rectory, Knightrider Street, Sandwich CT13 9ER* Tel and fax (01304) 613138 E-mail revdmarkroberts@supanet.com

ROBERTS, Canon John Victor. b 34. St Edm Hall Ox BA58 MA62. Tyndale Hall Bris 58. **d** 60 **p** 61. C Southport Ch Ch *Liv* 60-62; C Pemberton St Mark Newtown 62-65; V Blackb Sav 65-71; Chapl Blackb and Lancs R Infirmary and Park Lee Hosp 65-71; V Parr *Liv* 71-73; TR 73-80; R Much Woolton 80-02; RD Childwall 84-89; AD Liv S 89-00; Hon Can Liv Cathl 95-02; rtd 02; Perm to Offic *Liv* from 02; Hon Chapl Liv Cathl from 04. *8 Cherry Vale, Liverpool L25 5PX* Tel and fax 0151-428 8290 E-mail canonjvr@hotmail.com

ROBERTS, John Victor. b 40. GIPE61. Qu Coll Birm 83. **d** 85 **p** 86. C Ludlow *Heref* 85-89 and 92-93; P-in-c Coreley w Doddington 89-92; P-in-c Knowbury 89-92; TV Ludlow, Ludford, Ashford Carbonell etc 93-02; rtd 02; Perm to Offic *Heref* from 02. *Carwood, 16 Stretton Farm Road, Church Stretton SY6 6DX* Tel (01694) 723164

ROBERTS, Jonathan George Alfred. b 60. Lon Univ BD. Qu Coll Birm. **d** 84 **p** 85. C Shepshed *Leic* 84-86; C Braunstone 86-87; Dioc Youth Adv *Dur* 88-92; Nat Youth Officer Gen Syn Bd of Educn 92-94; P-in-c Washington *Dur* 94-95; R 95-99; Regional Co-ord for Community Work Assessment Consortium for the NE 99-03; Sen Lect Teesside Univ from 03; Perm to Offic *Dur* from 99 and *Newc* from 01. *10 Brierville, Durham DH1 4QE* Tel 0191-383 9148 E-mail j.roberts@tees.ac.uk

ROBERTS, Joseph Aelwyn. b 18. Univ of Wales (Lamp) BA40. St Mich Coll Llan 41. **d** 42 **p** 43. C Llanllyfni *Ban* 42-44; Min Can Ban Cathl 44-52; V Llandegai 52-88; Dioc Dir for Soc Work 73-88; rtd 88; Perm to Offic *Ban* from 88. *The Vicarage, Llandygai, Bangor LL57 4LA* Tel (01248) 353711

ROBERTS, Judith. *See* ROBERTS, Anne Judith

ROBERTS, Judith. *See* ABBOTT, Ms Judith

ROBERTS, Mrs Kathleen Marie. b 50. Th Ext Educn Coll 94. **d** 00 **p** 01. S Africa 00-02; C Crediton, Shobrooke and Sandford etc *Ex* 03-05; P-in-c Black Torrington, Bradford w Cookbury etc from 05. *The Rectory, Black Torrington, Beaworthy EX21 5PU* Tel (01409) 231279

ROBERTS, Keith Mervyn. b 55. St Pet Coll Birm CertEd76 LGSM78 GMus78. Qu Coll Birm 89. **d** 91 **p** 92. C Hall Green St Pet *Birm* 91-95; TV Warwick *Cov* 95-00; P-in-c Bishop's Tachbrook 00-09; Dioc Communications Officer 03-04; Dir Communications 04-09; Relig Affairs Correspondent BBC Radio Cov & Warw 95-01; Presenter/Producer 01-09; Hon Can Cov Cathl 07-09; TR Godalming *Guildf* from 09. *The Rectory, Westbrook Road, Godalming GU7 1ET* Tel and fax (01483) 860594 E-mail mervynrob@aol.com *or* mervyn.roberts@godalming.org.uk

ROBERTS, The Ven Kevin Thomas. b 55. Qu Coll Cam BA78 MA82 Nottm Univ BA82. St Jo Coll Nottm 80. **d** 83 **p** 84. C Beverley Minster *York* 83-86; C Woodley St Jo the Ev *Ox* 86-91; V Meole Brace *Lich* 91-09; RD Shrewsbury 98-08; Preb Lich Cathl 02-08; Adn Carl and Can Res Carl Cathl from 09. *2 The Abbey, Carlisle CA3 8TZ* Tel (01228) 523026 E-mail archdeacon.north@carlislediocese.org.uk

ROBERTS, Laurence James. b 51. Sussex Univ BEd73. Sarum & Wells Th Coll 75. **d** 78 **p** 79. C Rotherhithe St Mary w All SS *S'wark* 78-81; Public Preacher 81-84; Ind Chapl 81-84; Hon P Nunhead St Silas 82-84; TV Plaistow *Chelmsf* 84-89; Chapl Newham Gen Hosp and Plaistow Hosp 84-96; Tutor Community Nursing Services 89-96; Tutor Westmr Past Foundn from 90; Lect E Lon Univ from 92. *40 Boleyn Road, London E7 9QE* Tel (020) 8472 2430 E-mail laurence.roberts@virgin.net

ROBERTS, Canon Leanne Kelly. b 74. St Hilda's Coll Ox BA95 MA02 Em Coll Cam BA01 MA05. Westcott Ho Cam 99. **d** 02 **p** 03. C Hampton All SS *Lon* 02-05; Chapl Hertf Coll Ox 05-11; Can Res and Treas S'wark Cathl from 11; Dioc Dir of Ords

from 11. *Trinity House, 4 Chapel Court, London SE1 1HW* Tel (020) 7939 9400 Fax 7939 9468 E-mail leanne.roberts@southwark.anglican.org

ROBERTS, Miss Marguerite Mary Grace. b 43. Keswick Hall Coll CertEd65 Sussex Univ BEd74 UEA MA86. EAMTC 97. **d** 00 **p** 01. Hon C Cambridge St Mark *Ely* from 00. *5 Eachard Road, Cambridge CB3 0HZ* Tel (01223) 359167

ROBERTS, Mark. *See* ROBERTS, Canon John Mark Arnott

ROBERTS, Martin Meredith Edward. b 62. Univ of Wales (Abth) BSc85. **d** 06 **p** 07. OLM Woodbridge St Jo and Bredfield *St E* from 06. *64 Victoria Road, Woodbridge IP12 1EL* Tel (01394) 388140 E-mail martin.me.roberts@bt.com

ROBERTS, Martin Vincent. b 53. Birm Univ BA76 MA77 PhD82 LRAM72. Ripon Coll Cuddesdon 76. **d** 78 **p** 79. C Perry Barr *Birm* 78-81; Sen Chapl and Lect W Sussex Inst of HE 81-86; Leic Poly 86-92; Sen Chapl De Montfort Univ 92-95; TV Leic H Spirit 86-89; TR 89-95; V Baswich *Lich* 95-01; V Selly Oak St Mary *Birm* 01-08; rtd 08. *89 Sargent House, Symphony Court, Birmingham B16 8AF* Tel 0121-472 0250 E-mail martin@mroberts48.fsnet.co.uk

ROBERTS, Mervyn. *See* ROBERTS, Keith Mervyn

ROBERTS, Michael Brian. b 46. Oriel Coll Ox BA68 MA72 St Jo Coll Dur BA73. Cranmer Hall Dur 71. **d** 74 **p** 75. C St Helens St Helen *Liv* 74-76; C Goose Green 76-78; C Blundellsands St Nic 78-80; V Fazakerley St Nath 80-87; V Chirk *St As* 87-01; V Cockerham w Winmarleigh and Glasson *Blackb* from 01. *The Vicarage, 5 Lancaster Road, Cockerham, Lancaster LA2 0EB* Tel and fax (01524) 791390 E-mail michael.andrea.r@ukonline.co.uk

ROBERTS, Michael Frederick. b 46. Sarum Th Coll 86. **d** 88 **p** 89. C Reading St Matt *Ox* 88-91; NSM Douglas St Geo and St Barn *S & M* 91-93; V Malew 93-11; rtd 11. *Rose Cottage, St Mary's Road, Port Erin, Isle of Man IM9 6JL* E-mail revroberts@manx.net

ROBERTS, Michael Graham Vernon. b 43. Keble Coll Ox BA65. Cuddesdon Coll 65 Ch Div Sch of the Pacific (USA) BD67. **d** 67 **p** 68. C Littleham w Exmouth 67-70; Chapl Clare Coll Cam 70-74; V Bromley St Mark *Roch* 74-79; Tutor Qu Coll Birm 79-85; TR High Wycombe *Ox* 85-90; Vice-Prin Westcott Ho Cam 90-93; Prin 93-06; Hon Can Ely Cathl 04-06; rtd 06. *La Herviais, 22100 Trévron, France* Tel 08446-176806 E-mail michael.su.roberts@orange.fr

ROBERTS, Nia Wyn. *See* MORRIS, Nia Wyn

ROBERTS, Nicholas John. b 47. Lon Univ BD70 AKC70 MTh78 Surrey Univ MSc93. St Aug Coll Cant 70. **d** 71 **p** 72. C Trivdale *Lich* 71-74; C St Pancras H Cross w St Jude and St Pet *Lon* 74-76; C Camberwell St Giles *S'wark* 76-78; Chapl Ch Coll Cam 78-82; V Kingstanding St Luke *Birm* 82-85; Chapl St Chas Hosp Ladbroke Grove 85-96; Chapl Princess Louise Hosp Lon 85-96; Chapl Paddington Community Hosp 85-96; Chapl Cen Middx Hosp NHS Trust 96-99; Chapl St Mary's NHS Trust Paddington 99-04; Chapl CSC 04-10; rtd 10; Perm to Offic *S'wark* from 10. *183 Dukes Avenue, Richmond TW10 7YH* Tel (020) 8940 5504 Mobile 07946-243660 E-mail n.roberts7@homecall.co.uk

ROBERTS, Mrs Patricia Frances. b 62. Roehampton Inst BEd85. Trin Coll Bris 93. **d** 96 **p** 97. NSM Buckhurst Hill *Chelmsf* 96-99; NSM Gt Baddow 99-07; NSM W Swindon and the Lydiards *Bris* from 11. *The Vicarage, The Butts, Lydiard Millicent, Swindon SN5 3LR* Tel (01793) 772417 E-mail tudorandtricia@btinternet.com

ROBERTS, Paul Carlton. b 57. Worc Coll Ox BA78 MA86 CertEd. St Jo Coll Nottm 84. **d** 87 **p** 88. C Hazlemere *Ox* 87-91; C Woodley St Jo the Ev 91-92; TV Woodley 92-03; R Coulsdon St Jo *S'wark* from 03. *The Rectory, 232 Coulsdon Road, Coulsdon CR5 1EA* Tel and fax (01737) 552152 E-mail proberts8@toucansurf.com

ROBERTS, Paul John. b 60. Man Univ BA82 PhD91 Man Poly PGCE83. St Jo Coll Nottm 83. **d** 85 **p** 86. C Burnage St Marg *Man* 85-88; Tutor Trin Coll Bris 88-00; V Cotham St Sav w St Mary and Clifton St Paul *Bris* 00-08; Hon Can Bris Cathl 06-08; Dean Non-Res Tr St Mich Coll Llan 09-10; Dir Angl Formation and Tutor Trin Coll Bris from 10. *30 Seymour Avenue, Bristol BS7 9HN, or Trinity College, Stoke Hill, Bristol BS9 1JP* Tel 0117-908 0332 *or* 968 0267 E-mail paul.roberts@trinity-bris.ac.uk

ROBERTS, Peter Francis. b 59. N Illinois Univ BSc81 Leeds Univ BA87. Coll of Resurr Mirfield 85. **d** 88 **p** 89. C Leeds All So *Ripon* 88-92; Asst Dioc Youth Chapl 91-92; USPG Belize 92-94; V Collingham w Harewood *Ripon* 95-01; World Miss Officer 95-01; Chapl Dubai and Sharjah w N Emirates 01-03; R Merritt Is USA from 03. *PO Box 541025, Merritt Island FL 32953, USA* Tel (001) (321) 452 5260 E-mail stlukes1@bellsouth.net

ROBERTS, Peter Reece. b 43. Chich Th Coll 73. **d** 75 **p** 76. C Cadoxton-juxta-Barry *Llan* 75-79; C Brixham w Churston Ferrers *Ex* 79-81; C Bexhill St Pet *Chich* 81-84; R Heene w Worthing 89-97. *Heene Rectory, 4 Lansdowne Road, Worthing BN11 4LY* Tel (01903) 202312 E-mail revp.roberts@btinternet.com

ROBERTS, Philip Alan. b 59. Chich Th Coll 85. **d** 88 **p** 89. C Friern Barnet St Jas *Lon* 88-93; C Farnham Royal w Hedgerley *Ox* 93-02; TV Southend *Chelmsf* from 02. *39 St John's Road, Westcliff-on-Sea SS0 7JY* Tel (01702) 433327
ROBERTS, Philip Anthony. b 50. St Jo Coll Dur BA73. Wycliffe Hall Ox 75. **d** 77 **p** 78. C Roby *Liv* 77-79; C Ainsdale 79-80; C Pershore w Pinvin, Wick and Birlingham *Worc* 80-83; Chapl Asst Radcliffe Infirmary Ox 83-88; John Radcliffe and Littlemore Hosps Ox 83-88; Chapl R Victoria and Bournemouth Gen Hosps 88-91; Chapl Heref Co Hosp 91-94; Chapl Heref Hosps NHS Trust from 94. *The County Hospital, Union Walk, Hereford HR1 2ER* Tel (01432) 364139 *or* 355444
ROBERTS, The Ven Raymond Harcourt. b 31. CB84. St Edm Hall Ox BA54 MA58. St Mich Coll Llan 54. **d** 56 **p** 57. C Bassaleg *Mon* 56-59; Chapl RNR 57-59; Chapl RN 59-84; Chapl of the Fleet and Adn for the RN 80-84; QHC 80-84; Hon Can Gib Cathl 80-84; Gen Sec JMECA 85-89; C Hale *Guildf* 85-89; Hon Chapl Llan Cathl 90-95; Lic to Offic from 95. *8 Baynton Close, Llandaff, Cardiff CF5 2NZ* Tel (029) 2057 8044
ROBERTS, Miss Rebecca Mary. b 71. Glam Univ BA92 Chelt & Glouc Coll of HE PGCE93. Qu Coll Birm BA02 MA03. **d** 03 **p** 04. C Greenstead w Colchester St Anne *Chelmsf* 03-06; Perm to Offic *Win* 06-10; NSM Southampton (City Cen) from 10. *Southampton City Centre Parish, 135 St Mary's Street, Southampton SO14 1NX* Tel 07727-154234 (mobile) E-mail bricklanebek@hotmail.com
ROBERTS, Canon Richard Stephanus Jacob (Steph). b 28. TCD BA51 MA57. TCD Div Sch Div Test51. **d** 51 **p** 52. C Orangefield *D & D* 51-54; Miss to Seamen 51-94; Portuguese E Africa 51-65; Ceylon 65-68; Chapl Miss to Seamen Dublin 68 72; Chapl Miss to Seamen Southn 72-94; Sen Chapl Ch on the High Seas 72-94; Hon Can Win Cathl 82-94; rtd 94; Perm to Offic *Win* from 94. *25 Bassett Crescent West, Southampton SO16 7EB* Tel (023) 8079 0734
ROBERTS, Ronald Barry. b 40. S Dios Minl Tr Scheme 80. **d** 83 **p** 85. NSM Wedmore w Theale and Blackford *B & W* 83-85; C Odd Rode *Ches* 85-87; V Eaton and Hulme Walfield 87-04; rtd 04; Perm to Offic *Ches* from 04. *Iona, 8 Belmont Avenue, Sandbach CW11 1BX* Tel (01270) 766124 E-mail barryroberts@uwclub.net
ROBERTS, Mrs Rosamunde Mair. b 58. RN80. STETS 98. **d** 01 **p** 02. C Farnham *Guildf* 01-04; C Fleet 04-08; V Lenborough *Ox* from 08. *The Vicarage, Thornborough Road, Padbury, Buckingham MK18 2AH* Tel (01280) 813162 E-mail rosm.roberts@dsl.pipex.com
ROBERTS, Mrs Rosanne Elizabeth. b 51. Glouc Sch of Min 85. **d** 88 **p** 94. NSM Charlton Kings St Mary *Glouc* 88-93; C Leckhampton SS Phil and Jas w Cheltenham St Jas 93-96; R Ashchurch 96-08; R Ashchurch and Kemerton from 08. *The Rectory, Ashchurch Road, Tewkesbury GL20 8JZ* Tel (01684) 293729
ROBERTS, Miss Sandra June. b 58. Univ Coll Ches BA96. Qu Coll Birm 98. **d** 98 **p** 99. C Mold *St As* 98-01; V Llandrillo and Llandderfel from 01; P-in-c Betws Gwerful Goch w Llangwm w Llawrybetws from 05; AD Penllyn and Edeirnion 04-10. *The Vicarage, Llandrillo, Corwen LL21 0SW* Tel (01490) 440224
ROBERTS, Mrs Sharon. b 56. **d** 11. OLM Amersham on the Hill *Ox* from 11. *25 Longfield Drive, Amersham HP6 5HD* Tel (01494) 433853 E-mail robertsn1@btinternet.com
ROBERTS, Stephanus. *See* ROBERTS, Canon Richard Stephanus Jacob
ROBERTS, Stephen Bradley. b 66. K Coll Lon BD90 Heythrop Coll Lon MA03 PhD11. Wycliffe Hall Ox 89. **d** 91 **p** 92. C W Hampstead St Jas *Lon* 91-94; TV Uxbridge 94-98; Chapl Brunel Univ 98-04; Vice Prin St Mich Coll Llan from 04. *St Michael and All Angels' College, 54 Cardiff Road, Llandaff, Cardiff CF5 2YJ* Tel (029) 2083 8004 *or* 2055 1780 E-mail sr@stmichaels.ac.uk
ROBERTS, The Ven Stephen John. b 58. K Coll Lon BD81 Heythrop Coll Lon MTh99. Westcott Ho Cam. **d** 83 **p** 84. C Riverhead w Dunton Green *Roch* 83-86; C St Martin-in-the-Fields *Lon* 86-89; Warden Trin Coll Cen Camberwell 89-99; V Camberwell St Geo *S'wark* 89-99; RD Camberwell 97-99; Treas and Can Res S'wark Cathl 00-05; Sen Dioc Dir of Ords 00-05; Adn Wandsworth from 05; P-in-c Upper Tooting H Trin w St Aug 10-11. *2 Alma Road, London SW18 1AB* Tel (020) 8874 8567 *or* 8545 2440 Fax 8545 2441 E-mail stephen.roberts@southwark.anglican.org
ROBERTS, Preb Susan Emma. b 60. La Sainte Union Coll BTh93. St Steph Ho Ox 94. **d** 96 **p** 97. C Petersfield *Portsm* 96-00; P-in-c Ashprington, Cornworthy and Dittisham *Ex* 00-04; TV Totnes w Bridgetown, Berry Pomeroy etc 04-06; RD Totnes 03-06; TR Honiton, Gittisham, Combe Raleigh, Monkton etc from 06; Preb Ex Cathl from 06; RD Honiton from 07. *The Rectory, Rookwood Close, Honiton EX14 1BH* Tel (01404) 42925 E-mail revdsue@btinternet.com
ROBERTS, Sydney Neville Hayes. b 19. K Coll Lon 38. Cuddesdon Coll 45. **d** 47 **p** 48. C Aylesbury *Ox* 47-52; CF 52-69; R Theale w N Street *Ox* 69-76; R Theale and Englefield 76-85; rtd 85; Perm to Offic *Ox* from 89. *34 Stonebridge Road, Steventon, Abingdon OX13 6AU* Tel (01235) 834777

ROBERTS, Mrs Sylvia Ann. b 40. Stockwell Coll Lon TCert60. S Dios Minl Tr Scheme 81. **dss** 84 **d** 87 **p** 94. Crookhorn *Portsm* 84-88; Hon Par Dn Bedhampton 88-89; Par Dn Southampton (City Cen) *Win* 89-91; TD 91-94; TV 94-96; V Merton St Jo *S'wark* 96-06; P-in-c Colliers Wood Ch Ch 01-06; rtd 06; Perm to Offic *Portsm* from 07. *16 Bramble Road, Petersfield GU31 4HL* E-mail sylkenco@hotmail.com
ROBERTS, Canon Tegid. b 47. **d** 87 **p** 88. Lic to Offic *Ban* 87-93; NSM Llandinorwig w Penisa'r-waen 93-99; Lic to Offic 99-00; Dioc Officer for Children and Schs from 00; Min Can Ban Cathl 00-05; V Llandwrog and Llanwnda 05-11; Hon Can Ban Cathl 07-11; Can Res from 11. *Arwel, Llanrug, Caernarfon LL55 3BA* Tel (01286) 870760 E-mail tr@roberts485.freeserve.co.uk
ROBERTS, Terry Harvie. b 45. Sarum & Wells Th Coll 87. **d** 89 **p** 90. C Weymouth H Trin *Sarum* 89-93; TV Basingstoke *Win* 93-98; P-in-c Win St Barn 98-10; rtd 10. *1 Poulner Park, Ringwood BH24 1TZ* Tel (01425) 470232
ROBERTS, Tudor Vaughan. b 58. Newc Univ BA81. All Nations Chr Coll 91 Trin Coll Bris BA94. **d** 96 **p** 97. C Buckhurst Hill *Chelmsf* 96-99; TV Gt Baddow 99-07; TV W Swindon and the Lydiards *Bris* from 07. *The Vicarage, The Butts, Lydiard Millicent, Swindon SN5 3LR* Tel (01793) 772417 E-mail tudorandtricia@btinternet.com
ROBERTS, Tunde. *See* ROBERTS, Vincent Akintunde
ROBERTS, Vaughan Edward. b 65. Selw Coll Cam BA88 MA91. Wycliffe Hall Ox 89. **d** 91 **p** 92. C Ox St Ebbe w H Trin and St Pet 91-95; Student Pastor 95-98; R from 98. *St Ebbe's Rectory, 2 Roger Bacon Lane, Oxford OX1 1QE* Tel (01865) 248154 E-mail vroberts@stebbes.org.uk
ROBERTS, Vaughan Simon. b 59. Univ of Wales (Ban) BA80 Bath Univ PhD99. McCormick Th Sem Chicago MA82 Westcott Ho Cam 83. **d** 85 **p** 86. C Bourne *Guildf* 85-89; Chapl Phyllis Tuckwell Hospice Farnham 88-89; Chapl Bath Univ 89-96; NSM Bath Ch Ch Prop Chpl 90-96; P-in-c 92-96; P-in-c Chewton Mendip w Ston Easton, Litton etc 96-03; Dioc Voc Adv 96-99; Dir of Ords 99-03; TR Warwick *Cov* from 03. *St Mary's Vicarage, The Butts, Warwick CV34 4SS* Tel and fax (01926) 492909 E-mail vaughan.roberts@btinternet.com
ROBERTS, Vincent Akintunde (Tunde). b 55. Kingston Poly BA(Econ)81. S'wark Ord Course. **d** 91 **p** 92. Hon C Brixton Road Ch Ch *S'wark* 91-96; C Mitcham St Barn 96-99; P-in-c Stoke Newington St Olave *Lon* 99-03; V from 03; P-in-c Stoke Newington St Andr from 06; P-in-c Upper Clapton St Matt from 08. *St Olave's Vicarage, Woodberry Down, London N4 2TW* Tel and fax (020) 8800 1374 E-mail tunde.roberts@talk21.com
ROBERTS, Vivian Phillip. b 35. Univ of Wales BD78. St D Coll Lamp 57. **d** 60 **p** 61. C Cwmaman *St D* 60-64; R Puncheston, Lt Newcastle and Castle Bythe 64-72; V Brynamman 72-77; V Brynaman w Cwmllynfell 77-83; V Pen-bre 83-00; rtd 00. *40 New Road, Llanelli SA15 3DR* Tel (01554) 755506
ROBERTS, Wallace Lionel. b 31. Univ of Wales (Lamp) BA58. St D Coll Lamp 55. **d** 59 **p** 60. C Astley Bridge *Man* 59-61; Asst Master Stand Gr Sch 61-66; Hon C Stand 61-66; Hon CF Aden 66-67; Lect Stockport Tech Coll 67-70; Hon C Heaton Moor *Man* 67-70; Chapl Qu Sch Rheindahlen 70-76; Hon CF 70-76; Swaziland 76-85; Chapl Oporto *Eur* 86-89; Chapl Hordle Ho Sch Milford-on-Sea 89-90; C Portishead *B & W* 91-96; rtd 96; Perm to Offic *B & W* from 96. *17 Clockhouse News, Portishead, Bristol BS20 7HS* Tel (01275) 845944
ROBERTS, William James (Jim). b 55. Lon Bible Coll BA77 Hughes Hall Cam PGCE78. NEOC 92. **d** 94 **p** 95. NSM York St Mich-le-Belfrey from 94; Chapl Pocklington Sch from 06. *12 Bishop's Way, York YO10 5JG* Tel (01904) 413479 E-mail roberts.jim@talk21.com
ROBERTS, Wynne. b 61. Univ of Wales (Ban) BTh92. Ridley Hall Cam 85. **d** 87 **p** 88. Min Can Ban Cathl and C Ban Cathl 87-90; V Ynyscynhaearn w Penmorfa and Porthmadog 90-94; TV Bangor 94-04; Chapl NW Wales NHS Trust from 99. *North West Wales NHS Trust, Ysbyty Gwynedd, Penrhosgarnedd, Bangor LL57 2PW* Tel (01248) 384384 Fax 370629 E-mail wynne.roberts@nww-tr.wales.nhs.uk
ROBERTSHAW, John Sean. b 66. Cranmer Hall Dur 90. **d** 93 **p** 94. C Morley St Pet w Churwell *Wakef* 93-96; TV Upper Holme Valley 96-01; TR from 01; CF (TA) from 98. *The Vicarage, Kirkroyds Lane, New Mill, Holmfirth HD9 1LS* Tel and fax (01484) 683375 Mobile 07980-289727 E-mail revsean@tiscali.co.uk
ROBERTSHAW, Jonathan Kempster Pickard Sykes. b 41. AKC65. **d** 66 **p** 67. C Perranzabuloe *Truro* 66-69; Miss to Seamen 69-76; Hong Kong 69-72; Namibia 73-76; TV Probus, Ladock and Grampound w Creed and St Erme *Truro* 76-79; TV N Hill w Altarnon, Bolventor and Lewannick 79-80; P-in-c Lansallos 80-84; R 84-96; P-in-c Talland 80-84; V 84-96; C Madron 96-01; P-in-c Gulval 99-01; V Gulval and Madron 01; rtd 01; Hon C Penzance St Mary w St Paul and St Jo *Truro* 09-11; Hon Chapl R Cornwall Hosps Trust from 09; Hon Chapl Miss to Seafarers from 09. *38 Treasswe Road, Penzance TR18 2AU* Tel (01736) 330612

ROBERTSON, Agnes Muriel Hodgson. b 20. Edin Univ MA41. St And NSM Tr Scheme. d 91 p 94. NSM Lochgelly *St And* 91-92; Par Dn Glenrothes 92-94; NSM 94-98; NSM Leven 94-01; NSM St Andrews St Andr 94-01; NSM Lochgelly 94-01; rtd 98; P Cupar *St And* 01-04. *8 Bathgate Court, Cupar KY15 4LP* Tel (01334) 653543

ROBERTSON, Ms Beverley Ann. b 57. Qu Coll Birm 98. d 01 p 02. C Sutton Coldfield H Trin *Birm* 01-05; C Portsea N End St Mark *Portsm* 05-06; TV 06-10; P-in-c Bromsgrove All SS *Worc* from 10; C Catshill and Dodford from 10. *All Saints' Vicarage, 20 Burcot Lane, Bromsgrove B60 1AE* Tel (01527) 578297 E-mail bev_robertson@yahoo.com

ROBERTSON, Brian Ainsley. b 50. Warwick Univ BSc72. St Jo Coll Nottm 94. d 94 p 95. C Leic Martyrs 94-97; C Oadby 97-98; TV 98-02; P-in-c Ashby-de-la-Zouch St Helen w Coleorton 02-05; P-in-c Breedon cum Isley Walton and Worthington 03-05; TR Ashby-de-la-Zouch and Breedon on the Hill from 05; RD NW Leics from 07. *The Rectory, 4 Upper Packington Road, Ashby-de-la-Zouch LE65 1EF* Tel (01530) 414404 E-mail barobertson@tesco.net

ROBERTSON, Charles Kevin. b 64. Virginia Poly & State Univ BA85 Dur Univ PhD99. Virginia Th Sem MDiv93. d 93 p 94. P-in-c USA 93-96; NSM Neville's Cross St Jo CD *Dur* 96-97; NSM Esh 97-99; R Milledgeville St Steph USA from 99. *Box 309, Milledgeville GA 31059-0309, USA* Tel (01334) 40599 E-mail rector@ststephensga.org

ROBERTSON, Charles Peter. b 57. Aston Tr Scheme 92 Linc Th Coll 94. d 96 p 97. C Holbeach Linc 96-99; C S Lafford 01-03; P-in-c from 03. *The Rectory, 16 West Street, Folkingham, Sleaford NG34 0SW* Tel (01529) 497617

ROBERTSON, David John. b 54. Sheff Univ BA76. Ridley Hall Cam 77. d 79 p 80. C Downend *Bris* 79-83; C Yate New Town 83-85; TV 85-87; TV High Wycombe *Ox* 87-97; RD Wycombe 91-97; P-in-c Haley Hill *Wakef* 97-99; V Ovenden 97-11; V S Ossett from 11. *South Ossett Vicarage, 36 Manor Road, Ossett WF5 0AU* Tel (01924) 263311 E-mail rev.d.robertson@gmail.com

ROBERTSON, Douglas Laurence. b 52. St Edm Hall Ox MA75. SEITE 04. d 07 p 08. C Roch 07-11; V Pembury from 11. *The Vicarage, 4 Hastings Road, Pembury, Tunbridge Wells TN2 4PD* Tel (01892) 824761 E-mail dlrobertson@btinternet.com

ROBERTSON, Mrs Elizabeth Mary. b 60. Cam Univ BA82 MA86 ACA85 FCA95. SEITE 03. d 06 p 07. NSM Fawkham and Hartley *Roch* from 06. *58 Redhill Wood, New Ash Green, Longfield DA3 8QP* Tel (01474) 874144 E-mail robertem@supanet.com

ROBERTSON, Miss Fiona Jane. b 76. Birm Univ BA98. Wycliffe Hall Ox BA05. d 06 p 07. C Aston SS Pet and Paul *Birm* 06-08; C Aston St Jas 06-08; C Nechells 06-08; C Aston and Nechells 08-10; P-in-c Girlington *Bradf* from 10; C Manningham from 10. *The Vicarage, 27 Baslow Grove, Bradford BD9 5JA* Tel (01274) 544987 E-mail fiona.robertson@bradford.anglican.org

ROBERTSON, Iain Michael. b 67. Trin Coll Bris 03. d 05 p 06. C E Clevedon w Clapton in Gordano etc *B & W* 05-09; TV Salter Street and Shirley *Birm* 09-11; P-in-c Heanton Punchardon w Marwood *Ex* from 11. *The Rectory, Heanton, Barnstaple EX31 4DG* Tel (01271) 817448 E-mail reviain@hotmail.com

ROBERTSON, Canon James Alexander. b 46. Ox Univ MTh99. Sarum & Wells Th Coll 72. d 75 p 76. C Monkseaton St Pet *Newc* 75-78; C Prudhoe 78-79; TV Brayton *York* 79-84; V Redcar 84-93; V Selby Abbey 93-96; V Monkseaton St Pet *Newc* 96-11; AD Tynemouth 98-09; V Whittingham and Edlingham w Bolton Chapel from 11; AD Alnwick from 11; Hon Can Newc Cathl from 05. *The Vicarage, Whittingham, Alnwick NE66 4UP* Tel (01665) 574704 E-mail jim.a.robertson@blueyonder.co.uk

ROBERTSON, James Macaulay. b 51. St Jo Coll Dur BA73. Oak Hill Th Coll. d 00 p 01. C Holdenhurst and Iford *Win* 00-04; V Marden *Cant* 04-11; R Holwell, Ickleford and Pirton *St Alb* from 11. *The Vicarage, Crabtree Lane, Pirton, Hitchin SG5 3QE* Tel (01462) 712230 E-mail revjr@btinternet.com

ROBERTSON, Canon John Charles. b 61. St Pet Coll Ox BA81 Trin Coll Cam BA89. Ridley Hall Cam 87. d 90 p 91. C Kenilworth St Jo *Cov* 90-94; Chapl York Univ 94-00; V Grove *Ox* from 00; RD Wantage from 09; Hon Can Ch Ch from 11. *The Vicarage, Main Street, Grove, Wantage OX12 7LQ* Tel (01235) 766484 E-mail vicargrove@tiscali.co.uk

ROBERTSON (née PEGG), Mrs Josephine Anne. b 51. Lon Univ CertEd72 Ch Ch Coll Cant BSc91. d 02 p 03. OLM Folkestone H Trin w Ch Ch *Cant* 02-06; Chapl Dover Coll 02-05; C Sandgate St Paul w Folkestone St Geo *Cant* 05-06; C Folkestone Trin 06-10; C Wingham w Elmstone and Preston w Stourmouth from 10. *St Mary's House, St Mary's Meadow, Wingham, Canterbury CT3 1DF* Tel (01227) 721530 Mobile 07905-954504 E-mail jo.robertson@btinternet.com

ROBERTSON, Kathryn. b 58. Leeds Univ BA05. NOC 02. d 05 p 06. C Dewsbury *Wakef* 05-08; TV from 08. *The Vicarage, 68 Staincliffe Road, Dewsbury WF13 4ED* Tel (01924) 438302 E-mail kathycurate@drobertson99.wanadoo.co.uk

ROBERTSON, Mrs Linda Margaret. b 51. Somerville Coll Ox BA71 MA76 Aber Univ MSc72. STETS 00. d 03 p 04. NSM Ampfield *Win* 03-08; NSM Totton from 08; TV from 10. *35 Winnington, Fareham PO15 6HP* Tel (01329) 239857 E-mail revlindarob@yahoo.co.uk

ROBERTSON, Muriel. See ROBERTSON, Agnes Muriel Hodgson

ROBERTSON, Canon Paul Struan. b 45. St Jo Coll Dur BA73 Newc Univ Aus BEdSt79 MA95. d 72 p 73. C Chester le Street *Dur* 72-73; Australia 73-88 and from 89; C Hamilton 73-77; C Cessnock 77-79; R Scone 79-88; V Collierley w Annfield Plain *Dur* 88-89; R New Lambton from 89; AD Newc W from 96; Lect St Jo Coll Morpeth from 97; Can Newc Cathl from 01. *122 St James Road, PO Box 292, New Lambton NSW 2305, Australia* Tel (0061) (2) 4957 1173 *or* 4952 2218 Fax 4957 1788 E-mail saints@idl.net.au

ROBERTSON, Philip Stuart. b 55. Newc Univ BA77 BArch80. Oak Hill Th Coll BA07. d 07 p 08. C Woking St Jo *Guildf* 07-11; V Wolverhampton St Jude *Lich* from 11. *St Jude's Vicarage, St Jude's Road, Wolverhampton WV6 0EB* E-mail philip_r_is@hotmail.com

ROBERTSON, Mrs Priscilla Biddulph. b 25. St And Dioc Tr Course 87. d 90 p 94. C St Andrews St Andr *St And* from 90; P-in-c Pittenweem 04-06. *8 Balrymonth Court, St Andrews KY16 8XT* Tel (01334) 474976

ROBERTSON (née OWEN), Sally Ann. b 68. New Hall Cam BA89. Ox Min Course 07. d 10 p 11. NSM Purley *Ox* from 10. *Melyn, Colyton Way, Purley on Thames, Reading RG8 8BL* Tel 0118-962 5978 E-mail sally.a.robertson@ntlworld.com

ROBERTSON, Scott. b 64. Edin Univ BD90 Open Univ MA02 Glas Univ PhD08. Edin Th Coll 86. d 90 p 91. C Glas Gd Shep and Ascension 90-92; P-in-c 92-97; P-in-c Ardrossan 97-10; P-in-c Dalry 97-10; P-in-c Irvine St Andr LEP 97-10; R Glas St Marg from 10. *Address temp unknown* Tel 07703-709176 (mobile) E-mail revscottrobertson@btinternet.com

ROBERTSON, Mrs Sheila Jean. b 40. d 99 p 01. OLM Chase *Sarum* 99-09; rtd 09. *Church Mead, Harley Lane, Gussage All Saints, Wimborne BH21 5HD* Tel (01258) 840182 E-mail ross@churchmead.wanadoo.co.uk

ROBERTSON, Stephen Andrew. b 60. Strathclyde Univ BSc82. Trin Coll Bris 90. d 92 p 93. C Vange *Chelmsf* 92-96; R Creeksea w Althorne, Latchingdon and N Fambridge 96-06; R Downham w S Hanningfield from 06. *The Rectory, Castledon Road, Downham, Billericay CM11 1LD* Tel (01268) 710370 E-mail stephen.r@quista.net

ROBERTSON, Stuart Lang. b 40. Glas Univ MA63 Edin Univ MTh97. St Jo Coll Nottm 72. d 75 p 76. C Litherland St Jo and St Jas *Liv* 75-78; C Edin St Thos 78-81; Chapl Edn Univ and C Edin St Pet 81-83; R Edin St Jas 83-91; Miss to Seamen 83-91; Crosslinks 91-05; Hon Chapl St Petersburg *Eur* 93-98; Chapl Warsaw 98-04; Asst Chapl Barcelona 04-05; rtd 05. *3 Pentland Villas, Juniper Green EH14 5EQ* Tel 0131-453 4755 E-mail stur067@yahoo.co.uk

ROBERTSON, William Robert Wilson. b 48. Glas Univ MA71 MPhil74 Strathclyde Univ PGCE72. TISEC 03. d 05 p 06. C Edin St Mich and All SS 05-08; Chapl Dioc Boys' Sch Kowloon Hong Kong from 08. *Diocesan Boys' School, 131 Argyle Street, Mongkok, Kowloon, Hong Kong, China* Tel (00852) 2711 5191 *or* 2711 5192 E-mail bill.robertson1@tiscali.co.uk

ROBIN, Peter Philip King. b 23. Trin Coll Cam BA48 MA81. Cuddesdon Coll 49. d 51 p 52. C Bethnal Green St Matt *Lon* 51-54; Papua New Guinea 54-75; R Elsing w Bylaugh *Nor* 76-85; R Lyng w Sparham 76-85; P-in-c Holme Cultram St Mary *Carl* 85-88; rtd 88; Perm to Offic *Carl* 88-99 and from 02. *191 Brampton Road, Carlisle CA3 9AX* Tel (01228) 545293

ROBINS, Christopher Charles. b 41. St Mich Coll Llan 66. d 68 p 69. C Bideford *Ex* 68-71; C Dawlish 71-74; V Laira 74-81; P-in-c Dodbrooke 81-83; P-in-c Churchstow w Kingsbridge 81-83; R Kingsbridge and Dodbrooke 83-06; rtd 07. *26 Brownings Walk, Ogwell, Newton Abbot TQ12 6YR* Tel (01626) 331366

ROBINS, Canon Douglas Geoffrey. b 45. Open Univ BA90. Ex & Truro NSM Scheme. d 81 p 83. NSM Kenwyn *Truro* 81-84; Public Preacher 84-00; NSM Truro St Paul and St Clem 00-04; P-in-c Gerrans w St Anthony-in-Roseland and Philleigh 04-08; P-in-c Veryan w Ruan Lanihorne from 08; Hon Can Truro Cathl from 09. *The Vicarage, Veryan, Truro TR2 5QA* Tel (01872) 501618 E-mail fatherdougrobins@talktalk.net

ROBINS, Ian Donald Hall. b 28. K Coll Lon BD51 AKC51 Lanc Univ MA74. d 52 p 53. C Heyhouses on Sea *Blackb* 52-55; C Clitheroe St Mary 55-57; V Trawden 57-67; Hd of RE St Chris C of E Sch Accrington 67-76; P-in-c Hugill *Carl* 76-82; Asst Adv for Educn 76-82; Chapl St Martin's Coll of Educn *Blackb* 82-86; V St Annes St Marg 86-91; rtd 91; Perm to Offic *Blackb* from 91 and *Bradf* from 08. *33 Manorfields, Whalley, Clitheroe BB7 9UD* Tel (01254) 824930

ROBINS, Mrs Mary Katherine. b 34. FRGS Bris Univ BSc55 CertEd56. St Alb Minl Tr Scheme. dss 84 d 87 p 94. N Mymms *St Alb* 84-92; Hon Par Dn 87-92; NSM Northaw 92-95; NSM Hon C

Westmr St Jas *Lon* 95-00; Perm to Offic *St Alb* from 95. *15 Bluebridge Road, Brookmans Park, Hatfield AL9 7UW* Tel (01707) 656670 E-mail maryrob@eclipse.co.uk

ROBINS, Terrence Leslie. b 38. CEng67 FIMechE78. NOC 99. **d** 00 **p** 01. Bp's Adv for Elderly People in Res Care *Wakef* 98-01; Hon C Cumberworth, Denby and Denby Dale 00-03; P-in-c 03-08; rtd 08; Perm to Offic *Wakef* from 08. *Cruck Cottage, Cumberworth Lane, Denby Dale, Huddersfield HD8 8RU* Tel and fax (01484) 866000 E-mail robinslt@aol.com

ROBINS, Canon Wendy Sheridan. b 56. Lanc Univ BA77. EAMTC 93. **d** 93 **p** 94. Dir Communications and Resources *S'wark* from 92; NSM Walthamstow St Pet *Chelmsf* 93-02; Hon C S'wark Cathl from 02; Hon Can S'wark Cathl from 08. *17 Hillcrest Road, London E17 4AP,* or *Trinity House, 4 Chapel Court, Borough High Street, London SE1 1HW* Tel (020) 8523 0016 *or* 7403 8686 Fax 7403 4770 E-mail wendy.s.robins@southwark.anglican.org

ROBINSON, Alan Booker. b 27. Keble Coll Ox BA51 MA56. Sarum Th Coll 51. **d** 53 **p** 54. C Leeds All So *Ripon* 53-56; C Ilkley St Marg *Bradf* 57-59; V Carlton *Wakef* 59-66; OCF 66-92; V Hooe *Ex* 66-95; RD Plympton 81-83; RD Plymouth Sutton 86-91; rtd 95; Perm to Offic *Ripon* from 95. *1 Charlton Court, Knaresborough HG5 0BZ* Tel (01423) 860884 E-mail robalb@ntlworld.com

ROBINSON, Alison Jane. b 55. WEMTC 99. **d** 02 **p** 03. C Bishop's Cleeve *Glouc* 02-06; P-in-c Meysey Hampton w Marston Meysey and Castle Eaton 06-08; TV Fairford Deanery 09-10; rtd 10. *Orchard House, High Street, Meysey Hampton, Cirencester GL7 5JT* Tel (01285) 851854 Mobile 07773-721238 E-mail alisonjane.robinson@btinternet.com

ROBINSON, Andrew David. b 61. St Cath Coll Ox BA84 MA01 RMN89. Trin Coll Bris 97. **d** 02 **p** 08. C Southmead *Bris* 02-03; C Kington St Michael and Chippenham St Paul w Hardenhuish etc 03-04; NSM Barlby w Riccall *York* 05-10; P-in-c Ledsham w Fairburn from 10. *The Vicarage, 11 Main Street, Ledston, Castleford WF10 2AA* Tel (0977) 553591 Mobile 07896-506321 E-mail andrewrobinson9@hotmail.com

ROBINSON, Canon Andrew Nesbitt. b 43. AKC67. **d** 68 **p** 69. C Balsall Heath St Paul *Birm* 68-71; C Westmr St Steph w St Jo *Lon* 71-75; Chapl Sussex Univ from 75; Chapl Brighton Poly 75-92; Chapl Brighton Univ 92-93; P-in-c Stanmer w Falmer from 80; Can and Preb Chich Cathl from 98. *St Laurence House, Park Street, Brighton BN1 9PG* Tel (01273) 606928 *or* 606755 E-mail goretti.uk@yahoo.co.uk

ROBINSON, Andrew Stephen. b 49. Lanc Univ BA71 Worc Coll of Educn PGCE72. St Mich Coll Llan 90. **d** 95 **p** 96. NSM Llangattock and Llangynidr *S & B* 95-04; P-in-c Llanfeugan w Llanthetty etc from 04. *The Hollies, Station Road, Talybont-on-Usk, Brecon LD3 7JE* Tel (01874) 676584

✠**ROBINSON, The Rt Revd Anthony William.** b 56. CertEd. Sarum & Wells Th Coll. **d** 82 **p** 83 **c** 02. C Tottenham St Paul *Lon* 82-85; TV Leic Resurr 85-89; TR 89-97; RD Christianity N 92-97; P-in-c Belgrave St Pet 94-95; Hon Can Leic Cathl 94-97; Adn Pontefract *Wakef* 97-03; Suff Bp Pontefract from 02; Can Res Wakef Cathl from 05. *Pontefract House, 181A Many-gates Lane, Sandal, Wakefield WF2 7DR* Tel (01924) 250781 Fax 240490 E-mail bishop.pontefract@wakefield.anglican.org

ROBINSON, Arthur Robert Basil. b 32. ACP67 St Jo Coll Dur BA56 Bradf Univ MA84. Wycliffe Hall Ox 56. **d** 58 **p** 59. C Pemberton St Mark Newtown *Liv* 58-62; CF 62-65; Asst Master Colne Valley High Sch Linthwaite 65-69; Asst Chapl HM Pris Man 69; Chapl HM Borstal Rochdale 69-74; Peru 74-77; V Golcar *Wakef* 77-83; Admin Sheff Fam Conciliation Service 84-91; Warden St Sampson's Cen York 91-00; rtd 00. *Morangie, 2A Brecksfield, Skelton, York YO30 1YD* Tel (01904) 470558

ROBINSON, Arthur William. b 35. Dur Univ BSc60. Clifton Th Coll 60. **d** 62 **p** 63. C Ox St Clem 62-65; Chile 65-77; V Hoxton St Jo w Ch Ch *Lon* 78-88; TV Gateacre *Liv* 88-00; rtd 00; Perm to Offic *Liv* from 00. *86 Kingsthorne Park, Liverpool L25 0QS* Tel 0151-486 2588 E-mail arthelrob@aol.com

ROBINSON, Brian John Watson. b 33. St Cath Coll Cam BA56 MA60. Westcott Ho Cam 57. **d** 58 **p** 59. C Whitworth w Spennymoor *Dur* 58-62; India 62-66; P-in-c Preston St Steph *Blackb* 66-72; V Ashton-on-Ribble St Andr 72-79; Lic to Offic 79-82; V Preston St Jude w St Paul 82-97; Chapl N Tyneside Health Care NHS Trust 94-97; rtd 97; Perm to Offic *Blackb* from 97. *50 Greenacres, Fulwood, Preston PR2 7DB* Tel (01772) 861516 E-mail jandjrobbo@hotmail.co.uk

ROBINSON, Canon Bryan. b 32. Fitzw Ho Cam BA56. Ely Th Coll 56. **d** 58 **p** 59. C Fleetwood St Pet *Blackb* 58-65; V Burnley St Andr 65-74; V Burnley St Marg 65-74; V Burnley St Andr w St Marg 74-97; RD Burnley 85-91; P-in-c Burnley St Jas 92-97; Hon Can Blackb Cathl 94-97; rtd 97; Perm to Offic *Blackb* from 97. *50 Fountains Avenue, Simonstone, Burnley BB12 7PY* Tel (01282) 776518

ROBINSON, Mrs Christine. b 50. Nottm Univ BA71. EAMTC 01. **d** 04 **p** 05. NSM Prittlewell St Pet w Westcliff St Cedd *Chelmsf* from 04. *Pasadena, St John's Road, Benfleet SS7 2PT* Tel (01702) 557000 E-mail crrob75@aol.com

ROBINSON (née KILCOOLEY), Mrs Christine Margaret Anne. b 59. K Coll Lon BA05. SEITE 06. **d** 07 **p** 08. C Notting Hill St Pet *Lon* 07-10; V Belmont from 10. *St Anselm's Vicarage, Ventnor Avenue, Stanmore HA7 2HU* Tel (020) 8907 3186 E-mail xtinerob@googlemail.com

ROBINSON, Christopher Gordon. b 49. Ridley Hall Cam. **d** 82 **p** 83. C Stanton *St E* 82-85; C Lawshall 85-86; P-in-c Lawshall w Shimplingthorne and Alpheton 86-89; TV Oakdale *Sarum* 89-99; V Easton H Trin w St Gabr and St Lawr and St Jude *Bris* 99-05; C S Molton w Nymet St George, High Bray etc *Ex* from 05. *The Rectory, Parsonage Lane, South Molton EX36 3AX* Tel (01769) 572411

ROBINSON, Christopher James. b 52. St Pet Coll Birm CertEd74. OLM course 97. **d** 99 **p** 00. OLM Wilnecote *Lich* from 99. *55 Sycamore, Wilnecote, Tamworth B77 5HB* Tel (01827) 282331 E-mail chrisrobinson55@hotmail.co.uk

ROBINSON, Christopher Mark Scott. b 83. Warwick Univ BSc04. Ridley Hall Cam 06. **d** 09 **p** 10. C S Hartismere *St E* from 09. *4 Yaxley Road, Mellis, Eye IP23 8DP* Tel (01379) 788430 Mobile 07789-772024 E-mail tifferrobinson@gmail.com

ROBINSON, Daffyd Charles. b 48. Qu Coll Birm 77. **d** 80 **p** 85. C Abington *Pet* 80-82; C Immingham *Linc* 85-90; R Willoughby from 90. *The Rectory, Station Road, Willoughby, Alford LN13 9NA* Tel and fax (01507) 462045 E-mail rector@willoughby-lincs.org.uk

ROBINSON, Mrs Danielle Georgette Odette. b 47. SEITE 98. **d** 01 **p** 02. NSM Reigate St Mary *S'wark* from 01; Chapl Surrey and Sussex Healthcare NHS Trust from 01; Perm to Offic *Chich* from 01. *1 Chandler Way, Dorking RH5 4GA* Tel (01306) 883947 *or* (01293) 600300 ext 3141 E-mail daniellerobinson@uwclub.net *or* danielle.robinson@sash.nhs.uk

ROBINSON, David. b 42. Sarum & Wells Th Coll. **d** 82 **p** 83. C Billingham St Cuth *Dur* 82-86; V Longwood *Wakef* 86-94; C Athersley 94-97; P-in-c Brotherton 97-02; rtd 02; Perm to Offic *York* from 03. *The Vicarage, Market Weighton Road, Holme-on-Spalding-Moor, York YO43 4AG* Tel (01430) 860379

ROBINSON, Canon David Hugh. b 47. Linc Th Coll 76. **d** 79 **p** 80. C Bulkington *Cov* 79-82; P-in-c Whitley 82-87; Chapl Whitley, Gulson & Cov and Warks Hosp 82-87; Chapl Walsgrave Hosp Cov 87-97; Hon Can Cov Cathl 92-98; Succ 00-05; Perm to Offic 97-00 and 05-07; P-in-c Cov St Mary 07-10; rtd 10. *95 Potters Green Road, Coventry CV2 2AN* Tel (024) 7662 2683 Mobile 07947-023888 E-mail drx2robinson@talktalk.net

ROBINSON, David Mark. b 55. Univ Coll Dur BSc76 Leic Univ MA80 CQSW80. Cranmer Hall Dur 86. **d** 88 **p** 89. C Shipley St Pet *Bradf* 88-92; P-in-c Ingrow w Hainworth 92-97; V Bramhope *Ripon* 97-05; V Chapel Allerton from 05. *The Vicarage, Wood Lane, Chapel Allerton, Leeds LS7 3QF* Tel 0113-268 3072

ROBINSON, David Michael Wood. See WOOD-ROBINSON, David Michael

ROBINSON, Deborah Veronica. b 73. St Andr Univ MTheol95 Hull Univ MA97. NEOC 05. **d** 08 **p** 09. NSM Darlington St Hilda and St Columba *Dur* from 08. *14 Yoredale Avenue, Darlington DL3 9AN* Tel (01325) 265434 Mobile 07971-549439 E-mail deborah.robinson5@ntlworld.com

ROBINSON, Capt Denis Hugh. b 53. SS Mark & Jo Univ Coll Plymouth CertEd75. Sarum & Wells Th Coll 88. **d** 91 **p** 92. NSM Bisley and W End *Guildf* from 91; Asst Chapl Gordon's Sch Woking 91-94; Chapl from 94. *2A Queen's Road, Bisley, Woking GU24 9AN* Tel (01276) 857624 E-mail steviedenrob@aol.com

ROBINSON, Dennis Winston. b 42. QUB BScEng68. CITC. **d** 88 **p** 89. NSM Mullavilly *Arm* 88-92; NSM Arm St Mark 92-95; C Portadown St Mark 95-98; I Aghavea *Clogh* 98-10; Preb Clogh Cathl 06-10; rtd 10. *29A Snowhill Road, Beagho, Lisbellaw, Enniskillen BT94 5FY* E-mail dw.robinson@btopenworld.com

ROBINSON, Derek Charles. b 43. S'wark Ord Course 91. **d** 94 **p** 95. NSM Abbey Wood *S'wark* from 94. *19 Silverdale Road, Bexleyheath DA7 5AB* Tel (01322) 523870

ROBINSON, Dorothy Ann. b 50. Cranmer Hall Dur 05. **d** 07 **p** 08. NSM Tynemouth Priory *Newc* from 07. *57 Millview Drive, North Shields NE30 2QD* Tel and fax 0191-257 0980 E-mail dottirobinson@hotmail.com

ROBINSON, Douglas. b 48. Nottm Univ BEd70 Lon Univ BD74 Union Th Sem Virginia MA75. **d** 75 **p** 76. C Southport Ch Ch *Liv* 75-78; V Clubmoor 78-85; Chapl Epsom Coll 85-88; Chapl Dauntsey's Sch Devizes 89-95; Perm to Offic *Eur* from 95. *Im Grünen Weg 1, Hangen Wiesheim 55234, Germany* Tel (0049) (6375) 941575 E-mail reverendrobinson@t-online.de

ROBINSON, Elizabeth Carole Lesley. b 67. CITC 99. **d** 02 **p** 03. Aux Min Clonfert Gp *L & K* 02-06; Aux Min Roscrea w Kyle, Bourney and Corbally from 06. *St Cronan's Rectory, Roscrea, Co Tipperary, Republic of Ireland* Tel and fax (00353) (505) 21725 Mobile 87-909 1561 E-mail kandlrobinson@eircom.net

ROBINSON, Eric Charles. b 47. Lon Univ BD71 Lanc Univ MA97. CBDTI 94. **d** 97 **p** 98. NSM Carl St Cuth w St Mary 97-99; C Kendal H Trin 99-01; P-in-c Arthuret 01-07; P-in-c

Nicholforest and Kirkandrews on Esk 01-07; R Arthuret w Kirkandrews-on-Esk and Nicholforest 07-08; P-in-c Kendal H Trin 08-10; rtd 10. *15 Caldew Maltings, Bridge Lane, Carlisle CA2 5SW* Tel (01228) 590602

ROBINSON, Frank. *See* ROBINSON, John Francis Napier

ROBINSON, George. b 27. Oak Hill Th Coll 59. d 61 p 62. C Branksome St Clem *Sarum* 61-64; Australia from 64; rtd 80. *24 Abingdon Road, Roseville NSW 2069, Australia* Tel (0061) (2) 9416 4330 Fax 9416 9936 E-mail mandgrobinson@ozemail.com.au

ROBINSON, Mrs Hazel. b 61. RGN83 RSCN83. St Jo Coll Nottm 02. d 04 p 05. C Toton *S'well* 04-09; P-in-c Blidworth w Rainworth from 09. *The Vicarage, 27 St Peter's Drive, Rainworth, Mansfield NG21 0BE* Tel (01623) 475135 E-mail haze.rob@btopenworld.com

ROBINSON, Canon Ian. b 57. Nottm Univ BTh87 MA97. Linc Th Coll 84. d 87 p 88. C Bottesford w Ashby *Linc* 87-90; TV 90-95; P-in-c Caistor w Clixby 95-00; P-in-c Grasby 95-00; P-in-c Searby w Owmby 95-00; V Caistor Gp from 00; RD W Wold from 01; Can and Preb Linc Cathl from 07. *3 Spa Top, Caistor, Market Rasen LN7 6RB* Tel (01472) 851339 E-mail revianrobinson@tiscali.co.uk

ROBINSON, Ian Cameron. b 19. OBE72. Em Coll Cam BA40 MA44. Linc Th Coll 71. d 72 p 73. C Ipswich St Aug *St E* 72-74; V Darsham 74-84; V Westleton w Dunwich 74-84; RD Saxmundham 79-83; rtd 84; Perm to Offic *St E* 84-03. *Corner House, Rectory Street, Halesworth IP19 8BS* Tel (01986) 873573

ROBINSON, Ian Christopher. b 63. Hull Univ BSc84 Leeds Univ MA10 ACMA. Yorks Min Course 07. d 10 p 11. C New Malton *York* from 10. *6 Pinfold Garth, Malton YO17 7XQ* Tel (01653) 696566 Mobile 07538-239068 E-mail curate@stmichaelsmalton.org.uk

ROBINSON, Ian Morgan. b 53. Lanc Univ BA08 CEng86 MCIBSE86. CBDTI 05. d 08 p 09. NSM Askrigg w Stallingbusk *Ripon* from 08; NSM Hawes and Hardraw from 09. *Tom Gill House, Thoralby, Leyburn DL8 3SU* Tel (01969) 663159 Mobile 07801-657988 E-mail revrobbo@btinternet.com

ROBINSON, Mrs Jane Hippisley. b 41. Somerville Coll Ox MA66 K Coll Lon PGCE. S Dios Minl Tr Scheme 88. d 91. NSM Ealing St Pet Mt Park *Lon* 91-96; NSM N Acton St Gabr 96-00; Perm to Offic from 00. *40 Brentham Way, London W5 1BE* Tel (020) 8991 0206

ROBINSON, Mrs Janet. b 34. Milton Keynes Coll of Ed CertEd77 Open Univ BA78. WMMTC 89. d 92 p 94. NSM Roade and Ashton w Hartwell *Pet* 92-94; NSM Potterspury, Furtho, Yardley Gobion and Cosgrove 94-99; rtd 99; Perm to Offic *Pet* from 99. *73 Eastfield Crescent, Yardley Gobion, Towcester NN12 7TT* Tel (01908) 542331 E-mail revjandrewrobinson@btinternet.com

ROBINSON, Mrs Jean Anne. b 50. Lon Univ BPharm72 MRPharmS73 Southn Univ BTh98. STETS 95. d 98 p 99. NSM Frimley *Guildf* 98-03; NSM Worplesdon 03-05; NSM Egham Hythe 05-07; C Woodham from 07; Chapl Surrey and Borders Partnership NHS Trust from 05; Chapl Alpha Hosp Woking from 06. *8 Westfield Avenue, Woking GU22 9PH* Tel (01483) 727589 E-mail revjar@yahoo.co.uk

ROBINSON, Jennifer Elizabeth. b 53. Sheff Hallam Univ BA96. NOC 01. d 04 p 06. NSM Fishlake w Sykehouse and Kirk Bramwith etc *Sheff* 04-08; Perm to Offic from 08. *Address temp unknown* E-mail jenny@ardyne.freeserve.co.uk

ROBINSON, John Francis Napier (Frank). b 42. St Edm Hall Ox BA64 MA68. Clifton Th Coll 65. d 68 p 69. C Southport Ch Ch *Liv* 68-71; C Coleraine *Conn* 71-74; Deputation Sec (Ireland) BCMS 74-76; TV Marfleet *York* 76-81; V Yeadon St Jo *Bradf* 81-95; P-in-c Rounds Green *Birm* 95-00; V 00-02; rtd 02; Perm to Offic *Derby* and *S'well* from 03. *61 Clumber Avenue, Beeston, Nottingham NG9 4BH* Tel 0115-922 1704

ROBINSON, The Very Revd John Kenneth. b 36. K Coll Lon BD61 AKC61. d 62 p 63. C Poulton-le-Fylde *Blackb* 62-65; C Lancaster St Mary 65-66; Chapl HM Pris Lanc 65-66; Chapl St Jo Sch Singapore 66-68; V Colne H Trin *Blackb* 68-71; Dir Educn Windward Is 71-74; V Skerton St Luke *Blackb* 74-81; Area Sec (E Anglia) USPG 81-91; Hon Min Can St E Cathl 82-91; Chapl Gtr Lisbon *Eur* 91-00; Adn Gib 94-02; Can Gib Cathl 94-00; Dean Gib 00-03; rtd 03; Perm to Offic *Blackb* from 03. *9 Poplar Drive, Coppull, Chorley PR7 4LS* Tel (01257) 470042

ROBINSON, John Leonard William. b 23. Lon Univ BA50. Bps' Coll Cheshunt 50. d 52 p 53. C Victoria Docks Ascension *Chelmsf* 52-55; C Kilburn St Aug *Lon* 55-63; C Westmr St Jas 63-81; V Compton, the Mardens, Stoughton and Racton *Chich* 81-93; V Stansted 85-93; rtd 93; Perm to Offic *St Alb* from 93 and *Lon* from 96. *19 Greenhill Park, Barnet EN5 1HQ* Tel (020) 8449 3984

ROBINSON, Jonathan William Murrell. b 42. Univ of Wales (Lamp) MA01. Sarum Th Coll 63. d 68 p 69. C Tooting All SS *S'wark* 68-71; C Bourne *Guildf* 71-76; Dir Grail Trust from 76; Dir Grail Trust Chr Community Cen Burtle *B & W* 78-82; Hon C Willesden Green St Gabr *Lon* 78-82; V Stoke St Gregory w

Burrowbridge and Lyng *B & W* 82-90; Dir Grail Retreat Cen from 90; NSM Aymestrey and Leinthall Earles w Wigmore etc *Heref* 92-96; rtd 01; Perm to Offic *Heref* from 01 and *St D* 05-07. *The Liberty, Poole Road, Arthurs Gate, Montgomery SY15 6QU* Tel (01686) 668502

ROBINSON, Kathryn Elizabeth. b 55. Hull Univ BA76 K Coll Lon MSc86 St Hilda's Coll Ox PGCE77. NTMTC 03. d 05 p 06. NSM Leytonstone St Jo *Chelmsf* from 05. *54 Corbett Road, London E17 3JZ* Tel (020) 8520 3771 E-mail kthrynrbnsn@aol.com

ROBINSON, Kenneth. *See* ROBINSON, The Very Revd John Kenneth

ROBINSON, Kenneth Borwell. b 37. Lon Univ BA62. Ridley Hall Cam 68. d 70 p 71. C Walthamstow St Jo *Chelmsf* 70-74; P-in-c Becontree St Alb 74-78; P-in-c Heybridge w Langford 78-84; TV Horley *S'wark* 84-98; C Oxted and Tandridge 98-02; rtd 02; Perm to Offic *Portsm* from 03. *49 Osborne Road, East Cowes PO32 6RZ* Tel (01983) 295736

ROBINSON, Kevan John. b 63. Chich Univ BA09. SEITE 07. d 10 p 11. NSM Southbourne w W Thorney *Chich* from 10. *3 Trafalgar Close, Emsworth PO10 8HQ* Tel (01243) 376359 Mobile 07757-122446 E-mail k.robinson275@btinternet.com

ROBINSON, Lesley. *See* ROBINSON, Elizabeth Carole Lesley

ROBINSON, Leslie. b 31. St Aid Birkenhead 56. d 59 p 60. C Hugglescote w Donington *Leic* 59-61; C Greenside *Dur* 61-63; C-in-c New Cantley CD *Sheff* 63-66; V Choral Heref Cathl 66-67; R Easton-on-the-Hill *Pet* 67-69; Hon Min Can Pet Cathl 68-69; C Weston-super-Mare St Jo *B & W* 69-70; V Winkleigh *Ex* 70-72; V Thorpe Acre w Dishley *Leic* 72-78; V Cloughton *York* 78-79; V Iledon w Paull 79-81; V Bywell *Newc* 81-86; V Wymeswold and Prestwold w Hoton *Leic* 86-97; rtd 97; Perm to Offic *Leic* 97-98. *16 Victoria Road, Oundle, Peterborough PE8 4AY* Tel (01832) 275048

ROBINSON, Miss Margaret. b 32. S'wark Ord Course 83. dss 86 d 87 p 94. Finsbury St Clem w St Barn and St Matt *Lon* 86-87; Par Dn St Giles Cripplegate w St Bart Moor Lane etc 87-94; C 94-95; rtd 95; Perm to Offic *Win* 95-00 and *Portsm* from 00; Hon Chapl Win Cathl 98-00. *32 Madeline Road, Petersfield GU31 4AL* Tel (01730) 268056

ROBINSON, Margaret Ann. b 50. d 10 p 11. NSM Erdington Ch the K *Birm* from 10. *3 Hepburn Edge, Birmingham B24 9JW* Tel 0121-681 8283

ROBINSON, Monica Dorothy. b 40. SAOMC 99. d 01 p 02. NSM Bedford St Andr *St Alb* 01-10. *Shoyswell, Radwell Road, Milton Ernest, Bedford MK44 1RY* Tel (01234) 824366 E-mail mdrobinson@btopenworld.com

ROBINSON, Norman Leslie. b 50. Liv Univ BSc71. Lon Bible Coll BA78 Wycliffe Hall Ox 78. d 80 p 81. C Bebington *Ches* 80-83; C St Helens St Helen *Liv* 83-90; P-in-c Westward, Rosley-w-Woodside and Welton *Carl* from 90; P-in-c Thursby 98-10; P-in-c Caldbeck, Castle Sowerby and Sebergham from 10. *The Vicarage, Rosley, Wigton CA7 8AU* Tel (01697) 343723 E-mail normalrevs@aol.com

ROBINSON, Paul Andrew. b 68. Hull Univ MBA09. d 09 p 10. OLM Royton St Anne *Man* from 09. *19 Dorchester Drive, Royton, Oldham OL2 5AU* Tel 0161-628 9019 Mobile 07984-938393 E-mail paul@nomoreproblems.co.uk

ROBINSON, Canon Paul Leslie. b 46. Dur Univ BA67. Linc Th Coll 71. d 74 p 75. C Poynton *Ches* 74-76; C Prenton 76-78; V Seacombe 78-88; V Stalybridge St Paul 88-00; P-in-c Walkalane St Hilary 00-04; R 04-10; Urban Min Officer 96-00; Hon Can *Ches* Cathl 98-10; P-in-c E and W Tilbury and Linford *Chelmsf* from 10. *St Catherine's Rectory, 24 Somerset Road, Linford, Stanford-le-Hope SS17 0QA* Tel (01375) 842220 E-mail paul@canonrobinson.plus.com

ROBINSON, Paul Leslie. b 65. St Steph Ho Ox 95. d 97 p 98. C Upholland *Liv* 97-01; V Lydiate and Downholland 01-08; P-in-c Halsall 00-08; R Halsall, Lydiate and Downholland from 08. *The Vicarage, Church Lane, Lydiate, Liverpool L31 4HL* Tel 0151-526 0512 E-mail frpaul.robinson@btopenworld.com

ROBINSON, Paula Patricia. b 50. Man Univ MEd83 TCD BTh94. d 94 p 95. C Killala w Dunfeeny, Crossmolina, Kilmoremoy etc *T, K & A* 94-97; I Crosspatrick Gp *C & O* 97-00; R Leonardtown St Andr USA 00-09; P-in-c Tockwith and Bilton w Bickerton *York* from 09; P-in-c Rufforth w Moor Monkton and Hessay from 09; P-in-c Healaugh w Wighill, Bilbrough and Askham Richard from 09; P-in-c Long Marston from 09. *The Vicarage, Wetherby Road, Rufforth, York YO23 3QF* Tel (01904) 738262 E-mail revpaula@supanet.com

ROBINSON, Canon Peter Charles. b 53. Open Univ BA83. Oak Hill Th Coll 85. d 87 p 88. C Nottingham St Ann w Em *S'well* 87-89; C Worksop St Anne 89-92; V S Ramsey St Paul *S & M* 92-99; Can St German's Cathl 98-99; P-in-c Goostrey and Dioc Dir of Ords *Ches* 99-03; P-in-c Aldeburgh w Hazlewood *St E* 03-04; C Arbory *S & M* 05-06; V from 06; C Santan 05-06; V from 06; RD Castletown and Peel from 08; Hon Can St German's Cathl from 09. *The Vicarage, Arbory Road, Castletown, Isle of Man IM9 1ND* Tel (01624) 823509 Mobile 07941-202524 E-mail pcrwoodbridge@aol.com

ROBINSON, Peter Edward Barron. b 40. Open Univ BSc99. Sarum & Wells Th Coll 76. **d** 78 **p** 79. C Petersfield w Sheet *Portsm* 78-82; R Bentworth and Shalden and Lasham *Win* 82-88; R W Horsley *Guildf* 88-00; rtd 00; Perm to Offic *B & W* from 01. *14 Lyndhurst Grove, Martock TA12 6HW* E-mail peb.robinson@ntlworld.com

ROBINSON, The Ven Peter John Alan. b 61. St Jo Coll Cam BA83 MA87 St Jo Coll Dur BA92 PhD97. Cranmer Hall Dur 90. **d** 95 **p** 96. C N Shields *Newc* 95-99; P-in-c Byker St Martin 99-08; P-in-c Byker St Mich w St Lawr 01-08; Hon Can Newc Cathl 07-08; Adn Lindisfarne from 08. *4 Acomb Close, Morpeth NE61 2YH* Tel (01670) 503810 Fax 510469 E-mail p.robinson@newcastle.anglican.org

ROBINSON, Peter McCall. b 24. Worc Coll Ox BA48 MA50. Wells Th Coll 48. **d** 50 **p** 51. C Durban St Thos S Africa 50-54; C Stoke Poges *Ox* 55-57; Asst Chapl Michaelhouse Sch S Africa 57-58; V Ixopo 58-65; R Margate 65-71; V Payhembury *Ex* 71-79; R Cheriton w Tichborne and Beauworth *Win* 79-81; Perm to Offic Natal 81-82; V Marystowe, Coryton, Stowford, Lewtrenchard etc *Ex* 82-85; V Blackawton and Stoke Fleming 85-88; rtd 88; Perm to Offic *Ex* 89-09. *2 Langwells Court, Blackawton, Totnes TQ9 7BG* Tel (01803) 712827

ROBINSON, Philip. b 38. S Dios Minl Tr Scheme 88. **d** 91 **p** 92. NSM Ickenham *Lon* 91-95; P-in-c 95-04; P-in-c Hayes St Anselm 98-99; P-in-c Harlington 98-00; AD Hillingdon 97-03; rtd 04; Perm to Offic *Lon* and *Eur* from 04. *5 Preston Court, 4 Fairfield Road, Uxbridge UB8 1DQ* Tel (01895) 200303 *or* (0033) (4) 93 04 75 11 E-mail philip@stjean.fslife.co.uk

ROBINSON, Philip John. b 50. St Luke's Coll Ex CertEd71 Leeds Univ BA07. NOC 04. **d** 06 **p** 07. NSM Macclesfield Team *Ches* 06-09; P-in-c Rostherne w Bollington from 09. *The Vicarage, Rostherne Lane, Rostherne Village, Knutsford WA16 6RZ* Tel (01565) 830595 E-mail p.robinson233@btinternet.com

ROBINSON, Raymonde Robin. b 43. St Jo Coll Dur BA66. Chich Th Coll 67. **d** 70 **p** 71. C Ealing St Barn *Lon* 70-72; C Pinner 72-75; C Clerkenwell H Redeemer w St Phil 75-80; TV Kingsthorpe w Northampton St Dav *Pet* 80-89; R Letchworth *St Alb* 89-95; V Noel Park St Mark *Lon* 95-06; rtd 06. *12 West Hill Street, Brighton BN1 3RR* Tel (01273) 728778

ROBINSON, Richard Hugh. b 35. St Jo Coll Cam BA58 MA62. Ridley Hall Cam 58. **d** 60 **p** 81. C Cheadle Hulme St Andr *Ches* 60-62; Hon C Alvanley 62-64; Perm to Offic *York* 64-80; Hon C Elloughton and Brough w Brantingham 80-86; C 86-87; Exit Dir CMJ 87-88; NSM Appleby *Carl* 91-93; Perm to Offic *Carl* and *York* 93-98; rtd 00; Perm to Offic *Ely* 01-04 and from 10. *26 Paradise Street, Cambridge CB1 1DR* Tel (01223) 328833 Fax 328838

ROBINSON, Canon Roger George. b 24. Qu Coll Cam BA46 MA50. Ridley Hall Cam 46. **d** 48 **p** 49. C Gorleston St Andr *Nor* 48-51; C Drypool St Andr and St Pet *York* 51-54; P-in-c Kingston upon Hull St Aid Southcoates 54-55; V 55-60; V Clifton 60-70; Chapl Clifton Hosp York 61-70; V Far Headingley St Chad *Ripon* 70-81; RD Headingley 72-81; Hon Can Ripon Cathl 81; R Drayton w Felthorpe *Nor* 81-91; rtd 91; Perm to Offic *Ripon* from 91. *24 St Matthew's Walk, Leeds LS7 3PS* Tel 0113-269 6307

ROBINSON, Ronald Frederick. b 46. Ian Ramsey Coll Brasted 72 Oak Hill Th Coll 74. **d** 76 **p** 77. C Pennington *Man* 76-77; C Bedhampton *Portsm* 77-79; C Portsea N End St Mark 79-82; V 90-92; R Rowner 82-90; Perm to Offic *Portsm* 93-02; P-in-c Bury and Houghton *Chich* 96-97; P-in-c Coldwaltham and Hardham 96-97; P-in-c Bury w Houghton and Coldwaltham and Hardham 97-98; V 98; Past Sec Ch Union 98-02; P-in-c Portsea Ascension *Portsm* 02-05; V 05-09; rtd 10. *28 Haleybridge Walk, Tangmere, Chichester PO20 2HG* Tel (01243) 533768 E-mail fr.robinson@tiscali.co.uk

ROBINSON, Roy David. b 35. AKC59. **d** 60 **p** 61. C Acocks Green *Birm* 60-62; C Shirley 62-65; C Haslemere *Guildf* 65-70; R Headley w Box Hill 70-85; V Hinchley Wood 85-00; rtd 00; Perm to Offic *Guildf* from 02. *1 Park Road, Slinfold, Horsham RH13 0SD* Tel (01403) 791640

ROBINSON, Prof Simon John. b 51. Edin Univ MA72 PhD89 Ox Univ BA77. Wycliffe Hall Ox 75. **d** 78 **p** 79. C Haughton le Skerne *Dur* 78-81; Chapl Asst N Tees Hosp Stockton-on-Tees 81-83; C Norton St Mary *Dur* 81-83; Chapl Heriot-Watt Univ 83-90; R Dalmahoy 83-90; Chapl Leeds Univ 90-04; P-in-c Leeds Em 90-04; Prof Ethics Leeds Metrop Univ from 04; NSM Leeds City from 05. *42 Woodside Avenue, Meanwood, Leeds LS7 2UL* Tel 0113-283 7440 Mobile 07931-916381 E-mail s.j.robinson@leedsmet.ac.uk

ROBINSON, Steven Paul. b 65. Roehampton Univ BEd89. Oak Hill Th Coll BA05 NTMTC 08 K Coll Lon 08. **d** 10 **p** 11. C Perranzabuloe and Crantock w Cubert *Truro* from 10. *37 Tywarnhayle Road, Perranporth TR6 0DX* Tel (01872) 858786 Mobile 07813-324148 E-mail forchurch@hotmail.com

✠**ROBINSON, The Rt Revd Stuart Peter.** b 59. Moore Th Coll Sydney BTh85. ACT. **d** 87 **p** 87 **c** 09. C Miranda Australia 87-89; Asst Min Doonside and Quakers Hill 89-91; C-in-c Quakers Hill 91-97; Perm to Offic *Ox* 96; Chapl Tervuren *Eur* 98-01; P-in-c Liège 98-00; Sen Assoc Ev Dept Evang Min Australia 01-09; R Chatswood 05-09; Bp Canberra and Goulburn from 09. *GPO Box 1981, Canberra ACT 2601, Australia* Tel (0061) (2) 6248 0811 Fax 6247 6829

ROBINSON, Mrs Teresa Jane. b 56. SAOMC 98. **d** 01 **p** 02. OLM The Cookhams *Ox* 01-08; NSM Maidenhead St Luke from 08. *7 Golden Ball Lane, Maidenhead SL6 6NW* Tel (01628) 634107 E-mail terrie@7goldenball.freeserve.co.uk

ROBINSON, Tiffer. See ROBINSON, Christopher Mark Scott

ROBINSON, Timothy. b 56. Hull Univ BSc78 Liv Univ PhD83 St Jo Coll Dur BA07 FGA86. Cranmer Hall Dur 05. **d** 07 **p** 08. C Nantwich *Ches* 07-10; V Stalybridge St Paul from 10. *St Paul's Vicarage, Huddersfield Road, Stalybridge SK15 2PT* Tel 0161-304 7123 Mobile 07981-108779 E-mail timrobbo@aol.com

ROBINSON, Timothy James. b 59. Middx Poly BA84 Coll of Ripon & York St Jo PGCE00. St Steph Ho Ox 88. **d** 91 **p** 92. C W Acklam *York* 91-95; P-in-c N Ormesby 95-96; V 96-99; Teacher Hall Garth Sch Middlesbrough 00-10; Perm to Offic *Ripon* 99-02; Tutor NEOC 02-09; P-in-c Helmsley *York* from 10; P-in-c Upper Ryedale from 10. *14 High Street, Helmsley, York YO62 5AG* Tel (01439) 770983 E-mail timr.helmsley@gmail.com

ROBINSON, Miss Tracy. b 75. Univ of Zimbabwe BSc98. Wycliffe Hall Ox 03 Ripon Coll Cuddesdon MA09. **d** 09 **p** 10. C Fordingbridge and Breamore and Hale etc *Win* from 09. *19 Falconwood Close, Fordingbridge SP6 1TB* Tel (01425) 657516 *or* 653112 E-mail team.curate@googlemail.com

ROBINSON-MULLER, Mrs Ank. b 75. Radboud Univ Nijmegen MA04. ERMC 07. **d** 09. C E Netherlands *Eur* 09-10; C Rotterdam from 10; Chapl Vlissingen (Flushing) Miss to Seafarers from 10. *Ritthemsestraat 498, 4389 PA Vlissingen, The Netherlands* Tel (0031) (118) 467063 E-mail ank_muller@yahoo.com *or* ank.muller@mtsmail.org

ROBOTTOM, David Leonard Douglas. b 40. Qu Coll Birm 80 Sarum & Wells Th Coll 81. **d** 83 **p** 84. C Uppingham w Ayston and Wardley w Belton *Pet* 83-87; TV Sidmouth, Woolbrook and Salcombe Regis *Ex* 87-91; TV Sidmouth, Woolbrook, Salcombe Regis, Sidbury etc 91-95; R Bradninch and Clyst Hydon 95-10; RD Cullompton 03-10; rtd 10. *86 Queen Elizabeth Drive, Crediton EX12 2EJ* Tel (01363) 773028 E-mail su2312@eclipse.co.uk

ROBSON, Alan. See ROBSON, Gilbert Alan

ROBSON, Angus William. b 13. Kelham Th Coll 32. **d** 38 **p** 39. C Regent Square St Pet *Lon* 38-40; C Mill End *St Alb* 40-45; CF 43-45; P-in-c Luton St Pet 45; Perm to Offic *St Alb* 45-46; V Sark *Win* 46-50; V Jersey St Jas 50-75; Chapl HM Pris Jersey 60-75; rtd 78; Perm to Offic *Win* 78-98. *Lakeside Care Home, La Rue de la Commune, St Peter, Jersey JE3 7BN*

ROBSON, Claire English. b 62. Middx Poly BEd88. Westcott Ho Cam 96. **d** 99 **p** 00. C Dorchester *Sarum* 99-02; C Kilburn St Mary w All So and W Hampstead St Jas *Lon* 02-04; Min Can and Chapl St Paul's Cathl 04-09; C Bath Abbey w St Jas *B & W* from 09. *5 Sunnybank, Bath BA2 4NA* Tel (01225) 484469 E-mail clairerobson@clara.net

ROBSON, Gilbert Alan. b 30. St Pet Hall Ox BA53 MA57. Linc Th Coll 56. **d** 57 **p** 58. C Chatham St Mary w St Jo *Roch* 57-59; Sub Warden Roch Th Coll 59-62; Min Can Roch Cathl 59-62; Bp's Dom Chapl 61-64; Chapl Roch Th Coll 62-64; R Wouldham *Roch* 62-64; Chapl Nor Coll of Educn 65-68; Sen Lect in Div 68-72; V Shotwick *Ches* 72-74; Dioc Dir of Ords 72-74; Bp's Dom Chapl 72-74; Hd of Div Eton Coll Windsor 74-89; R Wrotham *Roch* 89-95; rtd 95; Perm to Offic *Nor* from 95. *3 Staden Park, Trimingham, Norwich NR11 8HX* Tel (01263) 834887

ROBSON, Howard. See ROBSON, John Howard

ROBSON, Preb Ian Leonard. b 32. K Coll Lon MA00. Bps' Coll Cheshunt 61. **d** 63 **p** 64. C Croxley Green All SS *St Alb* 63-65; C Harpenden St Nic 65-68; V Redbourn 68-72; V Ashford St Matt *Lon* 72-77; V Kensington St Mary Abbots w St Geo 77-97; AD Kensington 94-97; Preb St Paul's Cathl 96-97; rtd 97; Perm to Offic *Chich* from 97. *Wepham Lodge, Wepham, Arundel BN18 9RA* Tel (01903) 884667 E-mail robsonoblate@aol.com

ROBSON, James Edward. b 65. Pemb Coll Ox BA88 Middx Univ PhD05. Wycliffe Hall Ox 91. **d** 94 **p** 95. C Enfield Ch Ch Trent Park *Lon* 94-98; C Oakwood St Thos 98-00; Tutor Oak Hill Th Coll 00-09; Tutor Wycliffe Hall Ox from 09. *Wycliffe Hall, 54 Banbury Road, Oxford OX2 6PW* Tel (01865) 274200

ROBSON, John Howard. b 60. Newc Univ BA81 ACIB87. Cranmer Hall Dur 98. **d** 00 **p** 01. C Hethersett w Canteloff w Lt and Gt Melton *Nor* 00-04; R Brooke, Kirstead, Mundham w Seething and Thwaite from 04. *The Vicarage, 105 The Street, Brooke, Norwich NR15 1JU* Tel (01508) 550378

ROBSON, John Phillips. b 32. LVO99. St Edm Hall Ox. AKC58. **d** 59 **p** 60. C Huddersfield SS Pet and Paul *Wakef* 59-62; Asst Chapl Ch Hosp Horsham 62-65; Chapl 65-80; Sen Chapl Wellington Coll Berks 80-89; Chapl to RVO and Qu Chpl of the Savoy 89-02; Chapl to The Queen 93-02; rtd 02; Extra Chapl to

The Queen from 02. *Charterhouse, Charterhouse Square, London EC1M 6AN* Tel (020) 7253 1591

ROBSON, Mrs Margery June. b 44. Darlington Tr Coll CertEd65. St Steph Ho Ox 92. **d** 94 **p** 95. C Tuffley *Glouc* 94-98; V Darlington St Mark w St Paul *Dur* 98-03; Chapl Metro Cen Gateshead 03-06; rtd 06. *23 Carr House Mews, Consett DH8 6FD* Tel (01207) 581270

ROBSON, Martin Douglas. b 62. St Andr Univ MTheol85 Cam Univ PGCE88 Edin Univ MTh94. Edin Th Coll 92. **d** 94 **p** 95. C Perth St Ninian *St And* 94-97; P-in-c Lockerbie *Glas* 97-01; P-in-c Moffat 97-01; R Edin St Fillan from 01. *St Fillan's Rectory, 8 Buckstone Drive, Edinburgh EH10 6PD* Tel 0131-445 2942 E-mail stfillan@blueyonder.co.uk

ROBSON, Pamela Jean. b 44. STETS 94. **d** 97 **p** 98. NSM W Ewell *Guildf* 97-01; NSM Wotton and Holmbury St Mary from 02. *The Rectory, Horsham Road, Holmbury St Mary, Dorking RH5 6NL* Tel (01306) 730285
E-mail pamrobson@waitrose.com

ROBSON, Canon Patricia Anne. b 40. MBE99. CertEd60. SWMTC 85. **d** 87 **p** 94. Dioc Youth Officer *Truro* 87-92; Hon C Paul 87-92; Hon C Kenwyn St Geo 88-92; Dn-in-c St Enoder 92-94; P-in-c 94-05; P-in-c Newlyn St Newlyn 03-05; Hon Can Truro Cathl 98-05; RD Pydar 02-03; rtd 05; P-in-c St Goran w Caerhays *Truro* 06-09. *Mill Cottage, Mill Lane, Grampound, Truro TR2 4RU* Tel (01726) 882366 E-mail intercelt@aol.com

ROBSON, Paul Coutt. b 37. Leeds Univ BA60. Coll of Resurr Mirfield 63. **d** 64 **p** 65. C Stokesay *Heref* 64-66; C St Geo Cathl Cape Town 66-68; R Roodebloem All SS 68-70; Chapl HM Pris Man 70-71; Chapl HM Borstal Feltham 71-74; Hollesley Bay 74-78; Chapl HM Pris Grendon and Spring Hill 78-85; Norwich 85-92; Chapl HM YOI and Remand Cen Brinsford 92-99; rtd 99; Perm to Offic *Heref* 00-01 and from 04; P-in-c Wistanstow 01-04. *Pilgrims, Henley Common, Church Stretton SY6 6RS* Tel (01694) 781221 E-mail smrpcr@lineone.net

ROBSON, Peter. b 58. Leeds Univ BEd80. Cranmer Hall Dur 05. **d** 07 **p** 08. C Bishopwearmouth St Gabr *Dur* 07-11. *35 Charter Drive, Sunderland SR3 3PG* Tel 0191-528 2848
E-mail peterpoprobson@aol.co.uk

ROBSON, Peter Cole. b 45. Clare Coll Cam BA66 MA70 Oriel Coll Ox BLitt69 MLitt70. Coll of Resurr Mirfield 70. **d** 71 **p** 72. C Gt Grimsby St Mary and St Jas *Linc* 71-73; Chapl BNC Ox 73-76; R Timsbury *B & W* 76-79; P-in-c Blanchland w Hunstanworth *Newc* 80-83; rtd 87. *c/o J W T Robson Esq, 54 Linkfield Road, Mountsorrel, Leicester LE12 7DL*

ROBSON, Stephen Thomas. b 54. Chich Th Coll 84. **d** 86 **p** 87. C Newc St Fran 86-89; C Gateshead St Cuth w St Paul *Dur* 89-91; TV Stanley 91-96; V Sugley *Newc* from 96. *Sugley Vicarage, Lemington, Newcastle upon Tyne NE15 8RD* Tel 0191-267 4633

ROBSON, William. b 34. FCIS66 FCCA80. Sarum & Wells Th Coll 77. **d** 79 **p** 80. C Lymington *Win* 79-81; CF 81-93; V Barton Stacey and Bullington etc *Win* 93-98; rtd 98; Hon C Knaresborough *Ripon* 98-01; Perm to Offic *Newc* 03-04; Hon C Barrow upon Soar w Walton le Wolds *Leic* 04-07; Hon C Wymeswold and Prestwold w Hoton 04-07. *27 St James Road, Scawby, Brigg DN20 9BD* Tel (01652) 600922
E-mail knotsbarn@hotmail.co.uk

ROBUS, Keith Adrian. b 59. Heythrop Coll Lon MA01 MHCIMA82. Chich Th Coll 85. **d** 88 **p** 89. C Greenhill St Jo *Lon* 88-92; C Willesden St Matt 92-02; V N Acton St Gabr 02-09; Chapl RN from 09. *Royal Naval Chaplaincy Service, Mail Point 1-2, Leach Building, Whale Island, Portsmouth PO2 8BY* Tel (023) 9262 5055 Fax 9262 5134
E-mail keith@robus.demon.co.uk

ROBY, Richard James. b 33. Imp Coll Lon BSc54 Lon Inst of Educn PGCE55. St Alb Minl Tr Scheme 82. **d** 85 **p** 86. NSM Bushey *St Alb* 85-92; NSM Wootton 92-00; rtd 00; Perm to Offic *St Alb* from 00. *5 Powis Mews, Flitwick, Bedford MK45 1SU* Tel (01525) 718529 E-mail richard.roby@ntlworld.com

ROCHDALE, Archdeacon of. See VANN, The Ven Cherry Elizabeth

ROCHE, Miss Alison Mary. b 70. Man Univ BSc91 Nottm Univ PGCE94. St Jo Coll Nottm MA00. **d** 01 **p** 02. C Leic Martyrs 01-05; P-in-c Leic St Chris 05-09; V from 09. *256 Milligan Road, Leicester LE2 8FD* Tel 0116-283 0510 Mobile 07918-642567 E-mail vicar@stchristophers.info

ROCHE, Barry Robert Francis. b 40. Lon Univ BD66 Ox Univ MTh93. Clifton Th Coll 63. **d** 68 **p** 69. C Beckenham Ch Ch *Roch* 68-72; C Chester le Street *Dur* 72-74; C-in-c N Bletchley CD *Ox* 74-78; R Luton Ch Ch *Roch* 78-92; Chapl All SS Hosp Chatham 78-92; TR Glascote and Stonydelph *Lich* 92-99; RD Tamworth 95-99; V Oulton Broad *Nor* 99-05; rtd 05; Perm to Offic *S & B* from 06. *24 Lakeside Close, Nantyglo, Ebbw Vale NP23 4EG* Tel (01495) 311048

ROCHESTER, Thomas Robson. b 33. NEOC 85. **d** 90 **p** 91. NSM Glendale Gp *Newc* 90-03; rtd 03; Perm to Offic *Newc* from 03. *Cushat Law, Thropton, Morpeth NE65 7HX* Tel (01669) 62079 E-mail trochester2@aol.com

ROCHESTER, Archdeacon of. See BURTON-JONES, The Ven Simon David

ROCHESTER, Bishop of. See LANGSTAFF, The Rt Revd James Henry

ROCHESTER, Dean of. *Vacant*

ROCK, Mrs Jean. b 37. Gilmore Course 76. **dss** 79 **d** 87 **p** 97. Douglas St Matt *S & M* 79-81; Marown 81-83; Chapl Asst Oswestry and Distr Hosp 83-87; Oswestry St Oswald *Lich* 83-90; Par Dn 87-90; C-in-c Pont Robert and Pont Dolanog *St As* 90-97; V 97; rtd 97; Perm to Offic *Lich* from 99. *10 Wharf Cottages, Rhoswiel, Weston Rhyn, Oswestry SY10 7TD* Tel (01691) 773766

ROCKALL, Miss Valerie Jane. b 42. City of Cov Coll CertEd63. St Alb Minl Tr Scheme 78. **dss** 81 **d** 87 **p** 94. Asst Hd Wigginton Sch Tring 73-90; Boxmoor St Jo *St Alb* 81-87; NSM Hemel Hempstead 87-90; Par Dn Ampthill w Millbrook and Steppingley 90-93; TD Southampton (City Cen) *Win* 93-94; TV 94-99; P-in-c Aveley and Purfleet *Chelmsf* 99-10; rtd 10. *29 Astway Way, Tring HP23 5DY* Tel (01442) 891386
E-mail rockallv@aol.com

ROCKEY, Antony Nicolas. b 65. Kingston Poly BEng89 CEng94 MICE94 MCIWEM95. CBDTI 02. **d** 05 **p** 06. C Cockermouth Area *Carl* 05-09; P-in-c Fernhurst *Chich* from 09. *The Vicarage, Church Road, Fernhurst, Haslemere GU27 3HZ* Tel (01428) 652229

ROCKS, James Anthony. b 82. Trin Coll Bris BA10. **d** 11. C Stoke Gifford *Bris* from 11. *8 Somerset Crescent, Stoke Gifford, Bristol BS34 8PP* Tel 07786-034993 (mobile)
E-mail jimmy@st-michaels-church.org.uk

RODD, Philip Rankilor. b 60. Ex Univ BA79 K Coll Lon PGCE85. Ridley Hall Cam 03. **d** 05 **p** 06. C Heigham H Trin *Nor* 05-08; V Eaton St Andr from 08. *The Vicarage, 210 Newmarket Road, Norwich NR4 7LA* Tel (01603) 455778

RODD, Susan Eleanor. **d** 10 **p** 11. NSM Whitton *Sarum* from 10. *16 The Garlings, Aldbourne, Marlborough SN8 2DT*

RODDY, Keith Anthony. b 67. Leic Univ BA89. Oak Hill Th Coll BA09. **d** 09 **p** 10. C Chesterton *Lich* from 09. *17 Checkley Road, Newcastle ST5 7TN* Tel (01782) 560721 Mobile 07986-903110
E-mail keitharoddy@googlemail.com

RODE, Margaret. **d** 08. NSM Hedsor and Bourne End *Ox* from 08. *35 Shelley Road, High Wycombe HP11 2UW* Tel 07855-952237 (mobile) E-mail maggie.rode@ntlworld.com

RODE, Nigel. **d** 08. NSM Chalfont St Peter *Ox* from 08. *35 Shelley Road, High Wycombe HP11 2UW*
E-mail nigel.rode@ntlworld.com

RODEL, Mark Neil. b 71. Southn Univ BA96. STETS 02. **d** 05 **p** 06. C Southsea St Jude *Portsm* 05-08; C Portsea St Luke from 08. *39 St Andrews Road, Portsmouth PO5 1ER* Tel 07748-272360 (mobile) Pager 07654-325425
E-mail curate@stjudes-southsea.org.uk

RODEN, Jo. See LOVERIDGE, Ms Joan Margaretha Holland

RODEN, John Michael. b 37. St Jo Coll York CertEd64 Open Univ BA82 MA92 York Univ DPhil96. Ripon Hall Ox 71. **d** 73 **p** 74. C Saltburn-by-the-Sea *York* 73-77; Chapl St Pet Sch York 77-82; Warden Marrick Priory *Ripon* 83; Hon C Appleton Roebuck w Acaster Selby *York* 84-85; P-in-c 86-03; Youth Officer 86-91; Sen Chapl Selby Coalfield Ind Chapl 96-03; rtd 03; Perm to Offic *York* from 03. *Ebor Cottage, 8 Copmanthorpe Grange, Copmanthorpe, York YO23 3TN* Tel (01904) 744826
E-mail rodenjohn@lineone.net

RODEN, Michael Adrian Holland. b 60. Birm Univ MA03. Ripon Coll Cuddesdon 82. **d** 85 **p** 86. C S Lambeth St Anne and All SS *S'wark* 85-88; C Wandsworth St Paul 88-90; C Ox St Mary V w St Cross and St Pet 90-94; Chapl Wadh Coll Ox 90-94; R Steeple Aston w N Aston and Tackley *Ox* 94-02; TR Hitchin *St Alb* from 02; P-in-c St Paul's Walden from 10; RD Hitchin from 07. *The Rectory, 21 West Hill, Hitchin SG5 2HZ* Tel (01462) 434017 or 452758
E-mail michaelroden@btinternet.com

RODERICK, Philip David. b 49. Univ of Wales (Swansea) BA70 Univ of Wales (Abth) BD77 Lon Univ CertEd71. Linc Th Coll 80. **d** 80 **p** 81. C Llanfair-is-gaer and Llanddeiniolen *Ban* 80-82; TV Holyhead w Rhoscolyn w Llanfair-yn-Neubwll 82-84; Chapl and Lect Th Univ of Wales (Ban) 84-88; Warden Angl Chapl Cen 84-88; Prin Bucks Chr Tr Scheme *Ox* 88-94; Dir Chiltern Chr Tr Progr 88-94; Dir Quiet Garden Trust from 92; Dir The Well Inst from 96; V Amersham on the Hill *Ox* 96-04; Ldr Contemplative Fire from 04; Bp's Adv in Spirituality *Sheff* from 10; Chapl Whirlow Grange Conf Cen Sheff from 10. *23 Hill Turrets Close, Sheffield S11 9RE* Tel 0114-262 0655 or 235 3704
E-mail philiproderick@btinternet.com

RODFORD, Canon Brian George. b 50. Hatf Poly BEd84. **d** 79 **p** 80. NSM St Alb St Steph *St Alb* 79-85; Chapl St Mary's Sch 81-90; Sen Teacher 83-90; Hon C Hendon St Mary and Golders Green *Lon* 85-90; Hon C Winchmore Hill H Trin 90-95; V Ponders End St Matt 95-02; Dir Chain Foundn Uganda from 02; Can All SS Cathl Kampala from 02; Perm to Offic *St Alb* 04-05. *Simon's Acre, 17 Pagasvlei Road, Constantia, 7806 South Africa* Tel (0027) (21) 794 8940 *or* (01727) 850382
E-mail brodford chain@hotmail.com

RODGER, Canon Raymond. b 39. Westmr Coll Ox MTh93. Bps' Coll Cheshunt 62. **d** 63 **p** 64. C Frodingham *Linc* 63-66; Asst Chapl St Geo Hosp Lon 66-69; C Waltham *Linc* 69-73; V Nocton 73-86; P-in-c Potter Hanworth 74-86; P-in-c Dunston 77-86; RD Graffoe 81-92; Can and Preb Linc Cathl from 85; V Nocton w Dunston and Potterhanworth 86-92; Bp's Dom Chapl 92-05; Gen Preacher 92-05; rtd 05. *13 Lupin Road, Lincoln LN2 4GB* Tel (01522) 536723 Mobile 07803-123975 E-mail canrod@hotmail.com

RODGERS, Canon Cyril George Hooper. b 20. Qu Coll Birm 50. **d** 52 **p** 53. C Bishop's Cleeve *Glouc* 52-56; V Nailsworth 56-61; Chapl Longford's Approved Sch Minchinhampton 56-57; CF (TA) 58-62; R Upwell Christchurch *Ely* 61-66; CF (TA - R of O) 62-87; V Wiggenhall St Germans and Islington *Ely* 66-76; RD Lynn Marshland 68-76; R Woolpit *St E* 76-84; RD Lavenham 78-87; Hon Can St E Cathl 84-87; R Woolpit w Drinkstone 84-87; rtd 87; Perm to Offic *St E* 87-11. *The Cottage, Upper Linney, Ludlow SY8 1EF*

RODGERS, David. b 26. Sarum Th Coll 63. **d** 65 **p** 66. C Combe Down *B & W* 65-68; V Leigh Woods 68-76; R Wellow w Foxcote and Shoscombe 76-79; C Wells St Cuth w Coxley and Wookey Hole 79-82; P-in-c Wookey w Henton 79-82; V Ercall Magna *Lich* 82-89; V Rowton 82-89; RD Wrockwardine 84-88; rtd 89; Perm to Offic *B & W* from 98. *6 The Cloisters, South Street, Wells BA5 1SA*

RODGERS, Eamonn Joseph. b 41. QUB BA63 PhD70. TISEC 04. **d** 05 **p** 06. NSM Glas St Ninian from 05. *4 Albert Drive, Glasgow G73 3RT* Tel 0141-583 6949 Mobile 07910-262983 E-mail eamonn.rodgers@mac.com *or curate@stniniansglasgow.org.uk*

RODGERS, Preb Frank Ernest. b 46. Tyndale Hall Bris 68. **d** 71 **p** 72. C Madeley *Heref* 71-74; C Littleover *Derby* 74-77; V Clodock and Longtown w Craswell and Llanveynoe *Heref* 77-79; P-in-c St Margaret's w Michaelchurch Eskley and Newton 77-79; V Clodock and Longtown w Craswall, Llanveynoe etc 79-10; RD Abbeydore 90-96; Preb Heref Cathl 96-10; rtd 10. *Thorneyglatt Cottage, Didley, Hereford HR2 9DA* Tel (01981) 570629

RODGERS, John Terence Roche. b 28. TCD BA53 MA57 ACII. Bps' Coll Cheshunt. **d** 57 **p** 58. C Templecorran *Conn* 57-60; C Derriaghy 60-61; C Antrim All SS 62-64; I Belfast St Steph 64-79; I Dunmurry 79-94; Can Belf Cathl 92-94; rtd 94. *8 Aberdelghy Park, Lambeg, Lisburn BT27 4QF* Tel (028) 9266 0430

RODGERS, Richard Thomas Boycott. b 47. Lon Univ MB, BS70 FRCS81. St Jo Coll Nottm. **d** 77 **p** 78. C Littleover *Derby* 77-80; Lect Birm St Martin w Bordesley St Andr 89-90; Perm to Offic from 90. *63 Meadow Brook Road, Birmingham B31 1ND* Tel 0121-476 0789

RODHAM, The Ven Morris. b 59. Hatf Coll Dur BA81 St Jo Coll Dur PGCE85. Trin Coll Bris MA93. **d** 93 **p** 94. C New Milverton *Cov* 93-97; V Leamington Priors St Mary 97-10; RD Warwick and Leamington 06-09; Adn Missr from 10; Adn Warwick from 10. *Cathedral and Diocesan Office, 1 Hill Top, Coventry CV1 5AB* Tel (02476) 521337 Mobile 07929-861233 E-mail morris.rodham@covcofe.org

RODLEY, Ian Tony. b 48. Open Univ BA08. Qu Coll Birm 77. **d** 80 **p** 81. C Baildon and Dioc Children's Adv *Bradf* 80-85; V Bradf St Wilfrid Lidget Green 85-90; Chapl to the Deaf 88-90; V Otley 90-98; C Wolverton *Ox* 98-03; TR Bramley *Ripon* from 03. *St Peter's Vicarage, 8 Hough Lane, Leeds LS13 3NE* Tel 0113-255 5180 E-mail ianrod@clara.co.uk

RODLEY, James William Eric. b 66. SS Hild & Bede Coll Dur BA86 ACA89. St Steph Ho Ox 07. **d** 09 **p** 10. C Pokesdown All SS *Win* from 09; C Bournemouth St Clem from 09. *The Vicarage, St Clement's Road, Bournemouth BH1 4DZ* E-mail jwerodley@yahoo.co.uk

RODRIGUEZ-VEGLIO, Francis Bonny. b 33. Sarum Th Coll 62. **d** 64 **p** 65. C Alnwick St Paul *Newc* 64-68; V Horton w Piddington *Pet* 68-79; P-in-c Preston Deanery 68-79; CF (ACF) 75-82; TV Is of Scilly *Truro* 79-82; Hon Chapl Miss to Seamen 79-82; Perm to Offic *Pet* 86-88; C Leic Ch Sav 88-91; V Kirkwhelpington, Kirkharle, Kirkheaton and Cambo *Newc* 91-95; Perm to Offic *Pet* 99-01 and from 10. *Gemacq Cottage, 14 Daventry Road, Norton, Daventry NN11 2ND* Tel (01327) 872030 E-mail francis.andree@tiscali.co.uk

RODWELL, Barry John. b 39. Birm Univ CertEd59 Cam Univ DipAdEd77. Ridley Hall Cam 67. **d** 70 **p** 71. C Sudbury St Greg and St Pet *St E* 70-73; Hd RE Hedingham Sch 73-80; R Sible Hedingham *Chelmsf* 80-85; RE Adv 85-93; V Gt Burstead 93-00; rtd 00; Perm to Offic *Nor* 00-07. *The Nutshell, 11 Filbert Road, Loddon, Norwich NR14 6LW* Tel (01508) 522949 E-mail nutshell@tesco.net

RODWELL, Mrs Helen. WEMTC. **d** 09 **p** 10. NSM Forest of Dean Ch Ch w English Bicknor *Glouc* from 09. *The Other House, English Bicknor, Coleford GL16 7PD* Tel (01594) 860205

RODWELL (née VINCENT), Mrs Jacqueline Margaret. b 59. Glos Univ BA04. WEMTC 01. **d** 04 **p** 05. NSM Cheltenham St Mark *Glouc* 04-08; NSM Cheltenham Em w St Steph 08-09;

NSM S Cheltenham from 10. *Emmanuel Vicarage, 25 Hatherley Court Road, Cheltenham GL51 3AG* Tel (01242) 697541 E-mail emmanuel.church@btconnect.com

RODWELL, Canon John Stanley. b 46. Leeds Univ BSc68 Southn Univ PhD74. Cuddesdon Coll 71. **d** 74 **p** 75. Hon C Horfield H Trin *Bris* 74-75; Hon C Skerton St Luke *Blackb* 75-77; Lic to Offic from 77; Hon Can Blackb Cathl from 03. *7 Derwent Road, Lancaster LA1 3ES* Tel (01524) 62726

ROE, Mrs Caroline Ruth. b 57. Birm Univ BA80 PGCE93. Wycliffe Hall Ox 81. **dss** 84 **d** 87 **p** 96. Olveston *Bris* 84-87; Par Dn 87; NSM Alveley and Quatt *Heref* 87-94; Bp's Voc Officer 90-94; Hon C Loughborough Em and St Mary in Charnwood *Leic* 97-98; C Hathern, Long Whatton and Diseworth w Belton etc 98-00; Perm to Offic 01-04; Chapl Univ Hosps Leic NHS Trust 04-07; Lead Chapl from 07. *4 John's Lee Close, Loughborough LE11 3LH* Tel (01509) 260217 or 0116-258 5487

ROE, Daniel Cameron. b 84. Ball Coll Ox BA05. Oak Hill Th Coll MTh10. **d** 10 **p** 11. C Clifton *York* from 10. *5 Manor Park Close, York YO30 5UZ* Tel (01904) 345746 Mobile 07778-572928 E-mail daniel.roe@balliol.oxon.org or daniel.c.roe@gmail.com

ROE, Frank Ronald. b 31. Brasted Th Coll Westcott Ho Cam 55. **d** 57 **p** 58. C S w N Hayling *Portsm* 57-61; Hong Kong 61-77; Sen Chapl St Jo Cathl 61-66; Asst Chapl 77; Sen Chapl Miss to Seamen 66-69; Hon Chapl Miss to Seamen Australia 77-06; rtd 96. *2004-699 Cardero Street, Vancouver BC VG6 E3H, Canada* Tel (001) (604) 325 5591 E-mail revfrank@bigpond.com

ROE, Canon Joseph Thorley. b 22. AKC49 DipAdEd Hull Univ PhD90. K Coll Lon 46. **d** 50 **p** 51. C Methley *Ripon* 50-53; C Richmond 53-55; V Leeds Gipton Epiphany 55-60; C of E Youth Coun Tr Officer 60 64; Sec Youth Dept BCC 64-67; Prin Lect Bretton Hall Coll Wakef 67-74; Sec for Miss and Unity *Ripon* 74-78; Dioc Missr and Bp's Dom Chapl 75-78; Can Res Carl Cathl 78-82; Dioc Dir of Tr 78-82; Dioc Adult Educn Officer *Wakef* 82-88; Hon Can Wakef Cathl 83-88; Dir Educn 85-88; rtd 88; Perm to Offic *Wakef* 88-08. *2 Fosbrook House, 8 Clifton Drive, Lytham St Annes FY8 5RQ* Tel (01253) 667052

ROE, Peter Harold. b 37. K Coll Lon BD62 AKC62. **d** 63 **p** 64. C Knowle St Barn *Bris* 63-65; C Leckhampton St Pet *Glouc* 65-68; V Shaw Hill *Birm* 68-73; V Hobs Moat 73-90; V Packwood w Hockley Heath 90-99; rtd 99; Perm to Offic *Blackb* from 99. *14 Worcester Avenue, Garstang, Preston PR3 1EY* Tel (01995) 605775

ROE, Robert Henry. b 22. LCP57. Westcott Ho Cam 72. **d** 74 **p** 75. Hd Master St Mary's Primary Sch Saffron Walden 74-83; NSM Saffron Walden w Wendens Ambo and Littlebury *Chelmsf* 75-86; Perm to Offic *Nor* from 86. *Larchmount, High Street, Cley, Holt NR25 7RG* Tel (01263) 740369 E-mail robertroe@ukf.net

ROE, Thorley. See ROE, Canon Joseph Thorley

ROEMMELE, Michael Patrick. b 49. TCD BA72 MA76. **d** 73 **p** 74. C Portadown St Columba *Arm* 73-77; C Drumachose *D & R* 77-80; Bahrain 79-83; Cyprus 79-83; Chapl RAF 83-00; CF 00-07; I Camus-juxta-Bann *D & R* from 07. *30 Drumrane Road, Limavady BT49 9LB* Tel (028) 7776 3554 Mobile 07977-239863 E-mail mproemmele@googlemail.com *or macosquin@derry.anglican.org*

ROESCHLAUB, Robert Friedrich. b 39. Purdue Univ BSc63. Berkeley Div Sch MDiv66. **d** 66 **p** 66. USA 66-77; Hon C Tilehurst St Cath *Ox* 78-79; Hon C Tilehurst St Mich 79-82; P-in-c Millom H Trin w Thwaites *Carl* 82-85; P-in-c Millom 85-89; R Dunstall w Rangemore and Tatenhill *Lich* 89-93; rtd 94; Perm to Offic *Carl* from 98 and *Lich* from 02. *20 Pannatt Hill, Millom LA18 5DB* Tel (01229) 772185

ROEST, Wilma. b 62. Utrecht Univ MA88 Roehampton Inst PGCE92. SEITE 96. **d** 99 **p** 00. C Merton St Mary *S'wark* 99-02; TV N Lambeth 02-06; P-in-c Balham St Mary and St Jo 06-10; V from 10; AD Tooting from 09. *St Mary's Vicarage, 218A Balham High Road, London SW12 9BS* Tel (020) 8673 1188 E-mail vicar@stmarybalham.org.uk

ROFF, Andrew Martin. b 42. Bede Coll Dur BSc65. Westcott Ho Cam 65. **d** 70 **p** 71. C Ches St Mary 70-73; Min Can Blackb Cathl 73-76; P-in-c Blackb St Jo 74-75; V Longton 76-81; Chapl Trin Coll Glenalmond 82-83; R Allendale w Whitfield *Newc* 83-92; V Gosforth St Nic 92-97; Dioc Supernumerary *Mor* 01-07; Lic to Offic from 08. *Rowan Glen, Upper Braefindon, Culbokie, Dingwall IV7 8GY* Tel (01349) 877762 E-mail martin@roff-rowanglen.co.uk

ROFF, Canon John Michael. b 47. St Chad's Coll Dur BSc69. Westcott Ho Cam 70. **d** 72 **p** 73. C Lancaster St Mary *Blackb* 72-75; C Dronfield *Derby* 75-76; TV N Wingfield, Pilsley and Tupton 80-85; V Ilkeston St Mary 85-90; V Stockport St Geo *Ches* 90-94; TR Stockport SW 94-00; RD Stockport 95-00; Dioc Ecum Officer 92-99; Hon Can Ches Cathl 98-00; Can Res 00-04; rtd 04; Perm to Offic *Ches* and *Blackb* from 05. *14 Westbourne Road, Lancaster LA1 5DB* Tel (01524) 841621 E-mail roff@roff.org.uk

ROGAN, Canon John. b 28. St Jo Coll Dur BA49 MA51 Open Univ BPhil81. **d** 54 **p** 55. C Ashton St Mich *Man* 54-57; C Sharrow St Andr *Sheff* 57-61; Ind Chapl 57-61; Sec C of E Ind

Cttee 61-66; V Leigh St Mary *Man* 66-78; RD Leigh 71-78; Hon Can Man Cathl 75-78; Provost St Paul's Cathl Dundee 78-83; R Dundee St Paul 78-83; Soc Resp Adv *Bris* 83-93; Can Res Bris Cathl 83-93; rtd 93; Perm to Offic *Bris* from 93. *84 Concorde Drive, Bristol BS10 6PX* Tel 0117-950 5803

ROGERS, Mrs Angela. b 52. d 00 p 01. OLM Bridgnorth, Tasley, Astley Abbotts, etc *Heref* 00-08; TV from 08. *18 St Nicholas Road, Bridgnorth WV15 5BW* Tel (01746) 762013 E-mail angelam@rogers4949.freeserve.co.uk

ROGERS, Brian Robert. b 36. Open Univ BA80. St Jo Coll Nottm 70. d 72 p 73. C Ealing St Mary *Lon* 72-74; C Greenside *Dur* 74-75; Lic to Offic 75-85; Perm to Offic *Lich* 85-95; rtd 97; Perm to Offic *Sarum* from 97. *71 Alderney Avenue, Poole BH12 4LF* Tel (01202) 772103

ROGERS, Brian Victor. b 50. Trin Coll Bris 75. d 78 p 79. C Plumstead St Jo w St Jas and St Paul *S'wark* 78-83; P-in-c Gayton *Nor* 83-85; P-in-c Gayton Thorpe w E Walton 83-85; P-in-c Westacre 83-85; P-in-c Ashwicken w Leziate 83-85; R Gayton Gp of Par 85-91; R Rackheath and Salhouse 91-96; P-in-c Warmington, Tansor, Cotterstock and Fotheringhay *Pet* 96-97; V Warmington, Tansor and Cotterstock etc from 97. *The Vicarage, Church Street, Warmington, Peterborough PE8 6TE* Tel (01832) 280263 Mobile 07733-124719 E-mail bvictorr@hotmail.co.uk

ROGERS, Christopher Antony. b 47. NOC 79. d 81 p 82. C Chesterfield St Aug *Derby* 81-84; C Chaddesden St Phil 84-86; R Whitwell 86-95; V W Burnley All SS *Blackb* 95-01; V Ashford St Hilda *Lon* from 01. *St Hilda's Vicarage, 8 Station Crescent, Ashford TW15 3HH* Tel (01784) 254237 or 245712 E-mail christopher.rogers@london.anglican.org

ROGERS, Christopher Ian. b 79. Trin Coll Bris BA01. K Coll Lon MA05. d 07 p 08. NSM Roxeth *Lon* 07-10; C Shadwell St Paul w Ratcliffe St Jas from 10; C Bromley by Bow All Hallows from 10. *All Hallows' Rectory, Devons Road, London E3 3PN* Tel (020) 7538 9756 Mobile 07974-371418 E-mail revcrisrogers@me.com

ROGERS, Clive Trevor Thorne. b 49. SAOMC 02. d 05 p 06. NSM Beaconsfield *Ox* from 05. *23 Stratton Road, Beaconsfield HP9 1HR* Tel (01494) 675298 E-mail clive_rogers@btinternet.com

ROGERS, Clive William. b 62. Selw Coll Cam BA83 MA87 MEng93 Southn Univ BTh90. Chich Th Coll 87. d 90 p 91. C Leic St Aid 90-93; P-in-c Ryhall w Essendine *Pet* 93-94; Lic to Offic *Ely* 94-03; Perm to Offic 00-04; Lic to Offic *Sarum* from 04. *4 The Sidings, Downton, Salisbury SP5 3QZ* Tel (01725) 512141 Mobile 07909-992548 E-mail bill@billrogers.info

ROGERS, Cyril David. b 55. Birm Univ BA76 BTheol. Sarum & Wells Th Coll 80. d 83 p 84. C Leagrave *St Alb* 83-87; TV Langtree *Ox* 87-97; R Ballaugh *S & M* from 97; V Michael from 97. *The Rectory, Ballacrosha, Ballaugh, Isle of Man IM7 5AQ* Tel (01624) 897873

ROGERS, Damon. b 66. Cov Univ BEng92 Wolv Univ PGCE94 Warwick Univ BPhil02. Cranmer Hall Dur 01. d 03 p 04. C Heigham St Thos *Nor* 03-06; R Freethorpe, Wickhampton, Halvergate etc from 06. *The Rectory, Church Road, Reedham, Norwich NR13 3TZ* Tel (01493) 700268 E-mail therogers5@ukonline.co.uk

ROGERS, Canon David. b 48. Univ of Wales (Ban) BA69. Westcott Ho Cam 70. d 72 p 73. C Rainbow Hill and Tolladine *Worc* 72-75; C Astwood Bank w Crabbs Cross 75-79; V Cradley 79-90; V Beoley 90-08; RD Bromsgrove 00-06; TR Redditch H Trin from 08; Hon Can Worc Cathl from 07. *The Vicarage, Church Hill, Beoley, Redditch B98 9AR* Tel (01527) 63976 E-mail davidrogers@santiago.plus.com

ROGERS, David Alan. b 55. City of Lon Poly BA77 MCIT82. Linc Th Coll 88. d 90 p 91. C Kingston upon Hull St Nic *York* 90-93; P-in-c Kingston upon Hull St Mary 93-96; N Humberside Ind Chapl 93-02; Dir Leeds Ch Inst *Ripon* 02-04; Chief Officer Hull Coun for Voluntary Service from 04; Perm to Offic *York* from 07. *Hull Council for Voluntary Service, The Strand, 75 Beverley Road, Hull HU3 1XL* Tel (01482) 324474 Fax 580565 E-mail davidrogers@santiago.plus.com

ROGERS, The Ven David Arthur. b 21. Ch Coll Cam BA47 MA52. Ridley Hall Cam 47. d 49 p 50. C Stockport St Geo *Ches* 49-53; R Levenshulme St Pet *Man* 53-59; V Sedbergh *Bradf* 59-74; P-in-c Cautley w Dowbiggin 59-60; V 60-74; P-in-c Garsdale 59-60; V 60-74; V Sedbergh, Cautley and Garsdale 74-79; P-in-c Firbank, Howgill and Killington 73-77; RD Sedbergh 59-73; RD Ewecross 73-77; Hon Can Bradf Cathl 67-77; Adn Craven 77-86; rtd 86; Lic to Offic *Blackb* 87-06; Perm to Offic *Blackb* 87-06 and *Carl* 89-06. *24 Towns End Road, Sharnbrook, Bedford MK44 1HY* Tel (01234) 782650

ROGERS, David Barrie. b 46. S Dios Minl Tr Scheme 89. d 93. NSM Old Alresford and Bighton *Win* 93-96; Dep Warden Dioc Retreat Ho (Holland Ho) Cropthorne *Worc* 96-98; Warden Stacklands Retreat Ho W Kingsdown 98-03; Hon C Kingsdown *Roch* 98-03; Warden St Pet Bourne Cen from 03. *St Peter's Bourne Centre, 40 Oakleigh Park South, London N20 9JU*

ROGERS, David Martyn. b 56. Univ of Wales (Lamp) BA77 K Coll Lon BD79 AKC79 St Kath Coll Liv DipEd86 Liv Univ BPhil94 MA07. Chich Th Coll 79. d 80 p 81. C Hockerill *St Alb*

80-85; Perm to Offic *St As* 85-87; C Kilburn St Mary *Lon* 87-90; V New Longton *Blackb* from 90; Chapl Lancs Constabulary from 90. *All Saints' Vicarage, Station Road, New Longton, Preston PR4 4LN* Tel (01772) 613347

ROGERS, George Hutchinson. b 51. Windsor Univ Ontario BSW75. Wycliffe Coll Toronto MDiv78. d 78 p 78. C Victoria St Matthias Canada 78-81; R Cobble Hill and Cowichan Station 81-86; I Vancouver St Matthias 86-97; Hon C Vancouver St Helen 97-98; C Tonbridge SS Pet and Paul *Roch* 99-03; V Werrington *Pet* from 03. *The Vicarage, 51 The Green, Werrington, Peterborough PE4 6RT* Tel (01733) 571649 E-mail ghrogers@nildram.co.uk

ROGERS, George Michael Andrew. b 69. Yale Div Sch MDiv95. d 99 p 99. C Brant Lake St Paul USA 99-00; C New York St Thos 00-03; C Pelham Ch Ch 03-10; C Staines *Lon* from 10. *Christ Church Vicarage, Kenilworth Gardens, Staines TW18 1DR* Tel (01784) 451923 Mobile 07527-746060 E-mail george@stainesparish.org

ROGERS, Howard. Ripon Coll Cuddesdon. d 09 p 09. NSM Southgate Ch Ch *Lon* from 09. *48 Twisden Road, London NW5 1DN* E-mail hrogers442@aol.com

ROGERS, Ian Colin. b 73. Wolv Univ BA95. Coll of Resurr Mirfield BA99. d 00 p 01. C Lon Docks St Pet w Wapping St Jo 00-03; P-in-c Hammersmith St Luke 03-08; P-in-c Tangmere and Oving *Chich* from 08. *St Andrew's Vicarage, 21 Gibson Road, Tangmere, Chichester PO20 2JA* Tel (01243) 785089 E-mail fr.ianrogers@ntlworld.com

ROGERS, The Very Revd John. b 34. Univ of Wales (Lamp) BA55 Oriel Coll Ox BA58 MA61. St Steph Ho Ox 57. d 59 p 60. C Roath St Martin *Llan* 59-63; Br Guiana 63-66; Guyana 66-71; V Caldicot *Mon* 71-77; V Monmouth 77-84; RD Monmouth 81-84; TR Ebbw Vale 84-93; RD Blaenau Gwent 86-93; Can St Woolos Cathl 88-93; Dean Llan 93-99; V Llandaff w Capel Llanilltern 93-99; rtd 99. *Fron Lodge, Llandovery SA20 0LJ* Tel (01550) 720089

ROGERS, John. b 61. St Jo Coll Nottm 03. d 05 p 06. C Otley *Bradf* 05-08; V Oakworth from 08. *The Vicarage, 18 Sunhurst Drive, Oakworth, Keighley BD22 7RG* Tel (01274) 408354 E-mail john.rogers@bradford.anglican.org

ROGERS, John Arthur. b 47. MBIM. Edin Dioc NSM Course 90. d 92. C Middlesbrough St Martin *York* 92-93; NSM The Trimdons *Dur* 00-05; NSM Upper Skerne 05-07; R Tilehurst St Mich *Ox* from 07. *Tilehurst Rectory, Routh Lane, Reading RG30 4JY* Tel 0118-941 1127 E-mail rogj8@aol.com

ROGERS, John Robin. b 36. St Alb Minl Tr Scheme 78. d 81 p 82. NSM Digswell and Panshanger *St Alb* 81-84; C Welwyn w Ayot St Peter 85-92; R Wilden w Colmworth and Ravensden 92-99; rtd 99; Perm to Offic *St Alb* 99-02 and *Heref* from 03. *37 The Birches, Shobdon, Leominster HR6 9NG* Tel (01568) 708903

ROGERS, John William Trevor. b 28. Qu Coll Birm. d 85 p 86. NSM Dunchurch *Cov* 85-95; Perm to Offic 95-07. *15 Hillyard Road, Southam, Leamington Spa CV47 0LD* Tel (01926) 813469

ROGERS, Mrs Kathleen. b 56. Open Univ BA93 Leeds Univ BA07. NOC 04. d 07 p 08. Sen Resources Officer *Liv* 93-09; NSM Formby H Trin 07-09; C from 09. *2 Castle Drive, Formby, Liverpool L37 6EH* Tel (01704) 873545

ROGERS, Mrs Kathleen Anne. b 54. d 08 p 09. C Machynlleth w Llanwrin and Penegoes *Ban* 08-11; P-in-c from 11. *30 Tregarth, Machynlleth SY20 8HU* Tel (01654) 702961 E-mail kathleenrogers@hotmail.com

ROGERS, Canon Kenneth. b 33. Cuddesdon Coll 68. d 69 p 70. C Perranzabuloe *Truro* 69-71; C Truro St Paul 71-74; P-in-c Kenwyn St Geo 74-87; RD Powder 81-88; Hon Can Truro Cathl 87-98; TR Bodmin w Lanhydrock and Lanivet 87-98; RD Trigg Minor and Bodmin 89-93; rtd 98; Perm to Offic *Truro* from 98. *28 Lowen Court, Quay Street, Truro TR1 2GA* Tel (01872) 261169

ROGERS, Leon James. b 83. St Andr Univ MTheol06. Qu Coll Birm 07. d 09 p 10. C E Darlington *Dur* from 09. *239 Parkside, Darlington DL1 5TG* Tel 07714-354771 (mobile) E-mail lnrgrs@gmail.com

ROGERS, Canon Llewelyn. Univ of Wales (Lamp) BA59. St Mich Coll Llan. d 61 p 62. C Holywell *St As* 61-64; C Hawarden 64-70; R Bodfari 70-73; V Rhosymedre 73-78; V Llansantffraid-ym-Mechain 77-83; V Llansantffraid-ym-Mechain and Llanfechain 83-98; RD Llanfyllin 84-88; V Pont Robert, Pont Dolanog, Garthbeibio etc 98-01; Can St As Cathl 98-01; rtd 01; Perm to Offic *Lich* from 02. *17 Maes-y-Berllan, Llanymynech SY22 6PJ* Tel (01691) 839920

ROGERS, Mrs Lynne Rosemary. b 49. CITC 00. d 03 p 04. Aux Min Ferns w Kilbride, Toombe, Kilcormack etc *C & O* 03-06; Aux Min Gorey w Kilnahue, Leskinfore and Ballycanew 06-07; P-in-c New w Old Ross, Whitechurch, Fethard etc 07-11; C Bridge Camt from 11. *Address temp unknown* E-mail lynnerogers@eircom.net

ROGERS, Malcolm Dawson. b 63. SS Hild & Bede Coll Dur BA84 Selw Coll Cam BA88. Ridley Hall Cam 86. d 89 p 90. C Ipswich St Jo *St E* 89-93; CMS Russia 93-95; C Holloway St Mary Magd *Lon* 95-97; V 97-05; V Bury St Edmunds St Mary

St E from 05. *St Mary with St Peter Vicarage, 78 Hardwick Lane, Bury St Edmunds IP33 2RA* Tel (01284) 763416
E-mail malcolmrogers@onetel.com

ROGERS, Malcolm Kenneth. b 72. Liv Inst of Educn BA93. St Jo Coll Nottm MA95 LTh96. **d** 96 **p** 97. C W Derby St Luke *Liv* 96-00; V Huyton Quarry from 00. *St Gabriel's Vicarage, 2 St Agnes Road, Huyton, Liverpool L36 5TA* Tel 0151-489 2688
E-mail malcolm.rogers@huytondeanery.org

ROGERS, Mark James. b 64. Univ of Wales (Lamp) BA. Qu Coll Birm. **d** 89 **p** 90. C Dudley St Aug Holly Hall *Worc* 89-93; C Worc St Barn w Ch Ch 93-94; TV 94-97; USPG Belize 97-00; R Montreal St Columba Canada from 00. *4020 Hingston Avenue, Montreal QC H4A 2J7, Canada* Tel (001) (514) 486 1753
E-mail mrogers@montreal.anglican.ca

ROGERS, Martin Brian. b 53. **d** 92 **p** 93. OLM Collyhurst *Man* from 92. *8 Greenford Road, Crumpsall, Manchester M8 0NW* Tel 0161-740 4614

ROGERS, Maurice George Walden. b 23. AKC51. **d** 52 **p** 53. C Bedford All SS *St Alb* 52-56; C Southfields St Barn *S'wark* 56-58; C Chingford SS Pet and Paul *Chelmsf* 58-61; V Gt Ilford St Luke 61-72; V Woodford St Barn 72-89; rtd 89; Perm to Offic *Chelmsf* from 89 and *Win* from 93. *The Coach House, 13 Bodorgan Road, Bournemouth BH2 6NQ* Tel (01202) 291034

ROGERS, Michael Andrew. b 47. OBE91. FRAeS96. Ripon Coll Cuddesdon. **d** 01 **p** 02. C Bromsgrove St Jo *Worc* 01-04; R Berrow w Pendock, Eldersfield, Hollybush etc from 04. *The Vicarage, Berrow, Malvern WR13 6JN* Tel (01684) 833230
E-mail mandmrogers@btinternet.com

ROGERS, Michael Ernest. b 34. Sarum & Wells Th Coll 83. **d** 85 **p** 86. C Rochampton H Trin *S'wark* 85-88; V Ryhill *Wakef* 88-94; V S Elmsall 94-00; rtd 00; Perm to Offic *Derby* from 00. *The Willows, 49 Main Street, Weston-on-Trent, Derby DE72 2BL* Tel (01332) 700273

ROGERS, Michael Hugh Walton. b 52. K Coll Lon BD73 AKC73. St Aug Coll Cant 74. **d** 75 **p** 76. C Eastbourne St Andr *Chich* 75-78; C Uppingham w Ayston *Pet* 78-82; V Eye 82-90; R Cottesmore and Barrow w Ashwell and Burley 90-04; C 04-09; C Greetham and Thistleton w Stretton and Clipsham 01-05; P-in-c 05-09; C Empingham and Exton w Horn w Whitwell 06-09; RD Rutland 95-00; Can Pet Cathl 01-09; Bp's Adv for Min of Healing 05-09; P-in-c Ilfracombe SS Phil and Jas w W Down *Ex* from 09. *The Vicarage, Kingsley Avenue, Ilfracombe EX34 8ET* Tel (01271) 863519
E-mail mhwrogers@btinternet.com

ROGERS, Mrs Pamela Rose. b 46. Keswick Hall Coll CertEd68. S Dios Minl Tr Scheme 92. **d** 95 **p** 96. NSM Axbridge w Shipham and Rowberrow *B & W* 95-11; Bp's Officer for Ord NSM (Wells Adnry) 02-11; rtd 11. *28 Beech Road, Shipham, Winscombe BS25 1SB* Tel (01934) 842685
E-mail pam.rogers@care4free.net

ROGERS, Mrs Patricia Anne. b 54. Lon Univ BD. Trin Coll Bris. **d** 87 **p** 94. Hon C Gayton Gp of Par *Nor* 87-91; Hon C Rackheath and Salhouse 91-96; Chapl to the Deaf 91-96; Chapl to the Deaf *Pet* 96-00; Visual Communications from 00. *1-2 Lees Cottages, Poole Lane, Thornton-le-Moors, Chester CH2 4JE*
E-mail visiblecommunication@lineone.net

ROGERS, Philip John. b 52. Univ of Wales CertEd74 Nottm Univ BTh79. St Jo Coll Nottm 76. **d** 79 **p** 80. C Stretford St Bride *Man* 79-84; P-in-c Plumstead St Jo w St Jas and St Paul *S'wark* 84-85; V from 85. *St John's Vicarage, 176 Griffin Road, London SE18 7QA* Tel (020) 8855 1827
E-mail philipjrogers@ukonline.co.uk

ROGERS (née GOLDER), Mrs Rebecca Marie (Beki). b 71. Brunel Univ BA94. Trin Coll Bris BA02. **d** 02 **p** 03. C Short Heath *Birm* 02-05; Dir Faith Willesden Area *Lon* from 05; NSM Roxeth 05-10; NSM Bromley by Bow All Hallows from 10. *All Hallows' Rectory, Devons Road, London E3 3PN* Tel (020) 7538 9756 E-mail beki.rogers@hotmail.com

ROGERS, Richard Anthony. b 46. Ex Coll Ox BA69. Qu Coll Birm 70. **d** 71 **p** 72. C Shirley *Birm* 71-74; Chapl Solihull Sch 74-78; Hon C Cotteridge *Birm* 78-84; Hon C Hill 84-93; Hd RE Kings Norton Girls' Sch 93-05; Perm to Offic *Birm* from 93. *4 Byron House, Belwell Place, Sutton Coldfield B74 4AY* Tel 0121-308 0310 E-mail richardrogers154@hotmail.com

ROGERS, Richard Jonathan. b 64. Trin Coll Bris BTh96. **d** 96 **p** 97. C Carterton *Ox* 96-00; Crosslinks 00-03; Perm to Offic *B & W* 00-06. *11 East End Avenue, Warminster BA12 9NF* Tel (01985) 214123

ROGERS, Canon Robert. b 42. Bernard Gilpin Soc Dur 66 St Aid Birkenhead 67 Ridley Hall Cam 69. **d** 70 **p** 71. C Childwall St Dav *Liv* 70-73; C Huntington *York* 73-76; TR Brayton 76-89; RD Selby 84-89; V New Malton 89-98; RD Bulmer and Malton 97-98; Asst Chapl York Health Services NHS Trust 98-99; Sen Chapl York Hosps NHS Foundn Trust 99-08; Can and Preb York Minster 03-08; rtd 08; Perm to Offic *York* from 08. *Tabgha, 9 Middlecave Drive, Malton YO17 7BB* Tel (01653) 699469
E-mail bob.jacqui@btinternet.com

ROGERS, Robert Charles. b 55. St Pet Coll Birm CertEd77 Warwick Univ MA99. St Jo Coll Nottm 87. **d** 89 **p** 90. C

Wellesbourne *Cov* 89-93; R Bourton w Frankton and Stretton on Dunsmore etc 93-97; Behaviour Support Teacher Warks LEA from 98; Lic to Offic 98-07; NSM Rugby from 07. *18 Waring Way, Dunchurch, Rugby CV22 6PH* Tel (01788) 817361
E-mail rob.rogers@talktalk.net

ROGERS, Robin. See ROGERS, John Robin

ROGERS, Ryder Rondeau. b 44. Lon Bible Coll 62. **d** 08 **p** 08. In Bapt Min 68-04; NSM Bride Valley *Sarum* from 08. *Stonehaven, 25 Bindbarrow Road, Burton Bradstock, Bridport DT6 4RG* Tel (01308) 897780

ROGERS, Ms Sally Jean. b 54. Univ of Wales (Lamp) BA77 Nottm Univ BTh87. Linc Th Coll 84. **d** 87 **p** 94. Par Dn Bris St Mary Redcliffe w Temple etc 87-90; Par Dn Greenford H Cross *Lon* 90-94; C 94-96; TV Hemel Hempstead *St Alb* 96-02; Development Worker Changing Attitude 03-06; Chapl R Holloway and Bedf New Coll *Guildf* 06-10; R Petryal and Betws yn Rhos *St As* from 10. *The Rectory, Llanfairtalhaiarn, Abergele LL22 8ST* Tel (01745) 720273

ROGERS, Sarah Ann. b 73. York Univ BSc94 Univ of Wales (Cardiff) PhD98. St Mich Coll Llan BA09. **d** 09 **p** 10. C Caerphilly *Llan* from 09. *Church House, 71 Bartlett Street, Caerphilly CF83 1JT* Tel (029) 2088 2695

ROGERS, Trevor. See ROGERS, John William Trevor

ROGERS, Valentine Hilary. b 48. NUI BA68. St Columban's Coll Navan 65. **d** 71 **p** 72. C Dandenong Australia 88-89; P-in-c Eltham 89-92; I 92-96; C Dublin Ch Ch Cathl Gp and PV Ch Ch Cathl Dublin 96-97; I Armadale H Advent Australia 98-09; I Aughaval w Achill, Knappagh, Dugort etc *T, K & A* from 09. *The Rectory, Newport Road, Westport, Co Mayo, Republic of Ireland* Tel (00353) (98) 25127 Mobile 87-147 3397

ROGERS, William. See ROGERS, Clive William

ROGERS, William Arthur. b 41. Lon Univ BA64 CertEd. Chich Th Coll 79. **d** 81 **p** 82. C Chandler's Ford *Win* 81-84; R Bentley and Binsted 84-94; P-in-c The Lulworths, Winfrith Newburgh and Chaldon *Sarum* 94-99; rtd 99. *Greenways, 6 Shaves Lane, New Milton BH25 5DJ* Tel (01425) 638751

ROGERS, William John. b 71. SEITE 07. **d** 10 **p** 11. C Wimbledon Park St Luke *S'wark* from 10. *All Saints' Vicarage, 10 Deburgh Road, London SW19 1DX* Tel (020) 8542 3881 Mobile 07879-084321 E-mail william.j.rogers@btinternet.com

ROGERSON, Anthony Carroll. b 37. Trin Coll Ox BA59 MA63 MCIPD92. SAOMC 96. **d** 98 **p** 99. NSM Radley and Sunningwell *Ox* 98-02; Perm to Offic from 02. *Noggins, 35 Lower Radley, Abingdon OX14 3AY* Tel (01235) 550214
E-mail tonyrogerson@cygnet.org.uk

✠**ROGERSON, The Rt Revd Barry.** b 36. Leeds Univ BA60 Bris Univ Hon LLD93. Wells Th Coll 60. **d** 62 **p** 63 **c** 79. C S Shields St Hilda w St Thos *Dur* 62-65; C Bishopwearmouth St Nic 65-67; Lect Lich Th Coll 67-71; Vice-Prin 71-72; Lect Sarum & Wells Th Coll 72-74; V Wednesfield St Thos *Lich* 75-79; TR Wednesfield 79; Suff Bp Wolverhampton 79-85; Bp Bris 85-02; rtd 02; Hon Asst Bp *B & W* from 03. *Flat 2, 30 Albert Road, Clevedon BS21 7RR* Tel (01275) 541964
E-mail barry.rogerson@blueyonder.co.uk

ROGERSON, Colin Scott. b 30. St Andr Univ MA55. Edin Th Coll. **d** 57 **p** 58. C Byker St Ant *Newc* 57-59; C Newc St Geo 59-63; C Wooler 63-67; V Tynemouth St Aug 67-75; C Dur St Marg 75-88; P-in-c Hebburn St Jo 88-95; rtd 95; Perm to Offic *Dur* from 95. *6 Edlingham Road, Durham DH1 5YS* Tel 0191-386 1956

ROGERSON, Canon Ian Matthew. b 45. Bede Coll Dur CertEd67 Open Univ BA76. Oak Hill Th Coll. **d** 83 **p** 84. C Haughton St Mary *Man* 83-86; V Ramsbottom St Andr 86-05; P-in-c Edenfield and Stubbins 04-05; TR Ramsbottom and Edenfield 05-10; AD Bury 96-05; Hon Can Man Cathl 04-10; rtd 10; Perm to Offic *Man* from 10. *Cae Banc, Broadway, Laugharne, Carmarthen SA33 4NT* Tel (01994) 427664

ROGERSON, Prof John William. b 35. Man Univ BD61 DD75 Linacre Ho Ox BA63 MA67 Aber Univ Hon DD98 Friedrich Schiller Univ DrTheol05 Freiburg Univ DrTheol06. Ripon Hall Ox 61. **d** 64 **p** 66. C Dur St Oswald 64-67; Tutor Dur Univ 64-75; Sen Lect 75-79; Lic to Offic *Dur* 67-79; Lic to Offic *Sheff* from 79; Prof Bibl Studies Sheff Univ 79-94; Hd of Dept 79-94; Hon Can Sheff Cathl 82-95. *60 Marlborough Road, Sheffield S10 1DB* Tel 0114-268 1426

ROLAND, Andrew Osborne. b 45. Mert Coll Ox BA66 St Jo Coll Dur BA84. Cranmer Hall Dur. **d** 84 **p** 85. C Streatham St Leon *S'wark* 84-87; C Kingston All SS w St Jo 87-94; P-in-c Hackbridge and Beddington Corner 94-06; V from 06. *All Saints' Vicarage, New Road, Mitcham CR4 4JL* Tel (020) 8648 3650

ROLFE, Charles Edward. b 34. Wells Th Coll 68. **d** 70 **p** 71. C Bath Twerton-on-Avon *B & W* 70-79; TV Wellington and Distr 79-85; P-in-c Frome Ch 85-89; V 89-94; Chapl Victoria Hosp Frome 85-94; Chapl St Adhelm's Hosp Frome 88-94; rtd 94; NSM Fordingbridge and Breamore and Hale etc *Win* 95-05. *29 Ayleswade Road, Salisbury SP2 8DW* Tel (01722) 335601
E-mail charles@rolfe14.freeserve.co.uk

ROLFE, Joseph William. b 37. Qu Coll Birm 78. **d** 81 **p** 82. NSM Tredington and Darlingscott w Newbold on Stour *Cov* 81-91; NSM Brailes from 91; NSM Sutton under Brailes from 91; NSM Shipston Deanery from 98. *35 Manor Lane, Shipston-on-Stour CV36 4EF* Tel (01608) 661737

ROLFE, Paul Douglas. b 46. MIBC90. NOC 90. **d** 93 **p** 94. C Urmston *Man* 93-96; V Lawton Moor 96-03; P-in-c Burnage St Nic 03-07; Sen Chapl Costa Blanca *Eur* 07-08; P-in-c Mellor *Blackb* from 09; P-in-c Balderstone from 09. *The Vicarage, Church Lane, Mellor, Blackburn BB2 7JL* Tel (01254) 812324 E-mail paul.d.rolfe@btinternet.com

ROLFE, Mrs Susan Margaret. b 58. Man Univ BA81. ERMC 05. **d** 08 **p** 09. NSM Pet Ch Carpenter 08-11; NSM Paston from 11. *1 Woodfield Road, Peterborough PE3 6HD* Tel (01733) 567509 E-mail susan.m.rolfe@btinternet.com

ROLLETT, Robert Henry. b 39. Leeds Univ BA61 Leic Univ CertEd62. Linc Th Coll 77. **d** 79 **p** 80. C Littleport *Ely* 79-82; P-in-c Manea 82-83; V 83-85; P-in-c Wimblington 82-83; R 83-85; V Thorney Abbey 85-93; P-in-c The Ramseys and Upwood 93-94; TR 94-99; rtd 99; P-in-c Scalford w Goadby Marwood and Wycombe etc *Leic* 99-00; Perm to Offic *Pet* 01-05. *2 Stockerston Crescent, Uppingham, Oakham LE15 9UB* Tel (01572) 823685

ROLLINS, David. b 65. De Montfort Univ BA98. St Steph Ho Ox 99. **d** 01 **p** 02. C Leic St Aid 01-05; P-in-c Corringham *Chelmsf* 05-10; P-in-c Fobbing 05-10; R Corringham and Fobbing from 10. *The Rectory, Church Road, Corringham, Stanford-le-Hope SS17 9AP* Tel (01375) 673074 E-mail drollins@drollins.freeserve.co.uk

ROLLS, Miss Pamela Margaret. b 59. **d** 10 **p** 11. OLM Harwell w Chilton *Ox* from 10. *15 Elderfield Crescent, Chilton, Didcot OX11 0RY* Tel (01235) 834475 E-mail pamrolls@tiscali.co.uk

ROLLS, Peter. b 40. Leeds Inst of Educn CertEd. NOC 80. **d** 83 **p** 84. NSM Meltham *Wakef* from 83. *14 Heather Road, Meltham, Huddersfield HD7 3EY* Tel (01484) 340342 E-mail p.c.rolls@hotmail.com

ROLPH, Reginald Lewis George. b 29. Open Univ BA74. Bps' Coll Cheshunt 55. **d** 58 **p** 59. C Perivale *Lon* 58-61; C Wokingham St Paul *Ox* 61-63; C Letchworth *St Alb* 63-78; Perm to Offic from 78; rtd 93. *22 Souberie Avenue, Letchworth Garden City SG6 3JA* Tel (01462) 684596

ROLSTON, Cyril Willis Matthias. b 29. CITC 66. **d** 68 **p** 69. C Portadown St Mark *Arm* 68-71; I Loughgilly w Clare 71-81; Dir of Ords from 72; Asst Chapl Craigavon Area Hosp Gp Trust 80-96; I Moy w Charlemont *Arm* 81-96; Preb Arm Cathl 92-96; rtd 96; Chapl Armagh and Dungannon Health and Soc Services from 96. *19 Lower Parklands, Dungannon BT71 7JN* Tel (028) 8772 5910 Mobile 07742-421886 E-mail cyril.rolston@btinternet.com

ROLSTON, John Ormsby. b 28. TCD BA51 MA59 BD63. CITC 51. **d** 51 **p** 52. C Belfast St Mary Magd *Conn* 51-55; C Knock *D & D* 55-59; P-in-c Gilnahirk 59-63; I 63-66; I Belfast St Jas *Conn* 66-79; I Belfast St Jas w St Silas 79-96; Can Belf Cathl 82-96; Prec Belf Cathl 88-96; Adn Conn 88-96; rtd 96; Dioc C *Conn* 96-98. *5 Springburn Park, Lisburn BT27 5QZ* Tel (028) 9267 8932 E-mail j.o.rolston@lineone.net

ROLT (formerly SHARPLES), Mrs Jean. b 37. Padgate Coll of Educn TCert58. **d** 04 **p** 05. NSM Gerrans w St Anthony-in-Roseland and Philleigh *Truro* 04-08; NSM St Just-in-Roseland and St Mawes 05-08; rtd 08. *Tregear Vean Farmhouse, St Mawes, Truro TR2 5AB* Tel (01326) 270954 Mobile 07840-567933 E-mail revjeanrolt@mac.com

ROLTON, Patrick Hugh. b 49. Sarum & Wells Th Coll 72. **d** 74 **p** 75. C Roch 74-79; C Edenbridge 79-81; R N Cray 81-97; rtd 97. *45 Chalk Pit Avenue, Orpington BR5 3JJ* Tel (01689) 872916

ROM, Norman Charles. b 24. S'wark Ord Course 63. **d** 66 **p** 67. C Leatherhead *Guildf* 66-71; Chapl HM Pris Cant 71-74; Pentonville 74-85; Stocken 85-87; P-in-c Empingham *Pet* 85-87; R Empingham and Exton w Horn w Whitwell 87-94; rtd 94; Perm to Offic *Pet* 94-09 and *Linc* 03-09. *6 Church View, Clowne, Chesterfield S43 4LN* Tel (01246) 575795

ROMANIS, Adam John Aidan. b 57. Pemb Coll Ox BA78 MA83. Westcott Ho Cam 81. **d** 84 **p** 85. C Northfield *Birm* 84-88; TV Seaton Hirst *Newc* 88-93; V Newc Ch Ch w St Ann 93-99; V Cowley St Jo *Ox* from 99. *The Vicarage, 271 Cowley Road, Oxford OX4 2AJ* Tel (01865) 242396 E-mail adamox4@aol.com

ROMANO, Paul. b 56. Glas Univ MA77 LLB79 Open Univ BA91. TISEC. **d** 05. NSM Glas St Marg from 05. *63 Westfield Drive, Glasgow G52 2SG* Tel 0141-882 7026 E-mail paul.romano@btinternet.com

ROMER, William Miller. b 35. Brown Univ Rhode Is BA57. MDiv60. **d** 60 **p** 60. P-in-c Lake Luzerne St Mary USA 60-64; Asst Min Hanover St Andr 64-65; V New York St Boniface 65-70; P-in-c Troy St Luke 70-71; R Rochester Redeemer 98-03; P-in-c Rathkeale w Askeaton, Kilcornan and Kilnaughtin *L & K* 03-08; rtd 08. *Address temp unknown* Tel (00353) 87-236 8552 (mobile) E-mail molroms@aol.com

ROMO-GARCIA, Brother Gerardo. b 66. **d** 04 **p** 05. Mexico 04-07; SSF from 08; Perm to Offic *Cant* from 09. *The Master's Lodge, 58 St Peter's Street, Canterbury CT1 2BE* Tel (01227) 479364 E-mail amici 91401@hotmail.com

RONAYNE, Peter Henry. b 34. FCA68. Oak Hill Th Coll 64. **d** 66 **p** 67. C Chesham St Mary *Ox* 66-69; C Worthing H Trin *Chich* 69-74; V Shoreditch St Leon w St Mich *Lon* 74-82; P-in-c Norwood St Luke *S'wark* 82-85; V 85-94; V W Norwood St Luke 94-99; RD Streatham 87-91; rtd 99; Perm to Offic *S'wark* 00-04. *54 Maywater Close, South Croydon CR2 0LS* Tel (020) 8651 9743 E-mail pronayne@onetel.com

RONCHETTI, Quentin Marcus. b 56. Ripon Coll Cuddesdon 79. **d** 80 **p** 81. C Eastbourne St Mary *Chich* 80-83; C Moulsecoomb 83-85; TV 85-90; V Findon Valley 90-97; V Shoreham Beach 97-07; V Midhurst from 07. *The Vicarage, June Lane, Midhurst GU29 9EW* Tel (01730) 813339

RONE, The Ven James. b 35. St Steph Ho Ox 79. **d** 80 **p** 81. C Stony Stratford *Ox* 80-82; P-in-c Fordham St Pet *Ely* 82-83; V 83-89; P-in-c Kennett 82-83; R 83-89; Can Res Ely Cathl 89-95; Treas 92-95; Adn Wisbech 95-02; Hon Can Ely Cathl 95-02; Bp's Adv for Hosp Chapl 96-02; rtd 03; Perm to Offic *Ely* from 03. *Little Housing, 32 Lumley Close, Ely CB7 4FG* Tel (01353) 667088

RONGONG, Tembu Namderr. b 76. St Andr Univ MA98. TISEC. **d** 06 **p** 07. C Dunfermline *St And* 06-08; R Edin SS Phil and Jas from 08. *Church of St Philip and St James, 57B Inverleigh Road, Edinburgh EH5 5PX* Tel 0131-624 7777 E-mail tembu.rongong@btinternet.com

ROOKE, James Templeman. b 43. Saltley Tr Coll Birm CertEd65. EMMTC 79. **d** 84 **p** 85. NSM Bassingham *Linc* 84-89; NSM Hykeham 89-94; Sub Chapl HM Pris Morton Hall 94; P-in-c Borrowdale *Carl* 94-97; Chapl Keswick Sch 94-95; NSM Hykeham *Linc* 97-02; Sub Chapl HM Pris Morton Hall 97-00; CF (ACF) 00-08; NSM Swinderby *Linc* from 02. *The Chestnuts, Main Street, Norton Disney, Lincoln LN6 9JU* Tel (01522) 788315

ROOKE, John George Michael. b 47. St Jo Coll Dur BA72. Cranmer Hall Dur 71. **d** 74 **p** 75. C Skelmersdale St Paul *Liv* 74-78; TV Speke St Aid 78-81; Ind Chapl 81-85; V Knotty Ash St Jo 85-08; rtd 08. *clo Fairway Golf Shops Ltd, Units 1 & 2, Victoria Forge, Victoria Street, Windermere LA23 1AD*

✠**ROOKE, The Rt Revd Patrick William.** b 55. Open Univ BA85 TCD MPhil04. Sarum & Wells Th Coll 75. **d** 78 **p** 79 **c** 11. C Mossley *Conn* 78-81; C Ballywillan 81-83; I Craigs w Dunaghy and Killagan 83-88; I Ballymore *Arm* 88-94; Asst Prov and Dioc Registrar 92-94; Hon V Choral Arm Cathl 93-94; I Agherton *Conn* 94-06; Preb and Can Conn Cathl 01-06; Adn Dalriada 05-06; Dean Arm and Keeper of Public Lib 06-11; Bp T, K & A from 11. *The Bishop's House, Knockglass, Crossmolina, Co Mayo, Republic of Ireland* Tel (00353) (96) 31317 Fax 31775 E-mail bptuam@iol.ie *or* rooke59@hotmail.com

ROOKWOOD, Colin John. b 40. TCD BA64 MA66 SS Mark & Jo Coll Chelsea PGCE66. Clifton Th Coll 67. **d** 70 **p** 71. C Eccleston Ch Ch *Liv* 70-75; V Penge St Jo *Roch* 75-82; V Childwall All SS *Liv* 82-91; Chapl Bethany Sch Goudhurst 91-03; rtd 03; Perm to Offic *Roch* 01-10. *2 Glenthorn Grove, Sale M33 3AG* Tel 0161-962 0003 Mobile 07541-426440 E-mail colinrookwood120@btinternet.com

ROOM, Canon Frederick John. b 24. St Jo Coll Ox BA49 MA53. Wells Th Coll 49. **d** 51 **p** 52. C Bradford cum Beswick *Man* 51-54; C Halliwell St Marg 54-56; C Farnham Royal *Ox* 56-58; C-in-c Farnham Royal S CD 58-70; TV Thetford *Nor* 70-89; Sen Ind Missr 75-89; Hon Can Nor Cathl 77-89; rtd 89; Perm to Offic *Nor* from 89. *61 Beechwood Drive, Thorpe St Andrew, Norwich NR7 0LN* Tel (01603) 435930

ROOME, Mrs Alison Morag Venessa. b 48. Bp Lonsdale Coll TCert71. EMMTC 98. **d** 01 **p** 02. NSM Alfreton *Derby* 01-07; P-in-c 05-07; NSM Belper Ch Ch w Turnditch from 07. *55 Dovedale Crescent, Belper DE56 1HJ* Tel (01773) 825635 E-mail aliroome@lineone.net

ROOMS, (née JONES), Mrs Karen Sheila Frances. b 61. Bris Univ BA82. St Jo Coll Nottm MTh06. **d** 06 **p** 07. C Hyson Green and Forest Fields *S'well* 06-09; P-in-c Nottingham St Ann w Em from 09. *St Ann's Vicarage, 17 Robin Hood Chase, Nottingham NG3 4EY* Tel 0115-950 5471 E-mail vyumba@yahoo.co.uk

ROOMS, Canon Nigel James. b 60. Leeds Univ BSc81 Nottm Univ MA95 Birm Univ ThD08 CEng86 MIChemE86. St Jo Coll Nottm 87. **d** 90 **p** 91. C Chell *Lich* 90-94; Min Moshi St Marg Tanzania 94-01; Dir Th Educn by Ext 94-01; Hon Can Arusha from 01; Dioc Dir of Tr *S'well* 02-07; Assoc Dir Practical Th 07-10; P-in-c Basford St Leodegarius 07-09; Dir Min and Miss from 10; C Bestwood Park w Rise Park from 10. *St Ann's Vicarage, 17 Robin Hood Chase, Nottingham NG3 4EY* Tel 0115-950 5471 E-mail nigel.rooms@southwell.anglican.org

ROOSE-EVANS, James Humphrey. b 27. St Benet's Hall Ox BA52 MA56. **d** 81 **p** 81. NSM Kington and Weobley *Heref* 81-05; NSM Primrose Hill St Mary w Avenue Road St Paul *Lon* 82-97; Perm to Offic *Lon* from 97; *Heref* from 05; *S & B* from 07. *Waterloo Lodge, Knighton LD7 1NA*

ROOT, Preb John Brereton. b 41. Lon Univ BA64 Em Coll Cam BA66 MA. Ridley Hall Cam 64. **d** 68 **p** 69. C Harlesden St Mark *Lon* 68-73; C Lower Homerton St Paul 73-76; Chapl Ridley Hall Cam 76; Vice-Prin 76-79; V Alperton *Lon* 79-11; AD Brent 95-00; Preb St Paul's Cathl 01-11; rtd 11. *42 Newlyn Road, London N17 6RX* Tel 07723-033831 (mobile)

ROOTES, William Brian. b 44. St And NSM Tr Scheme 88. **d** 91. NSM Auchterarder *St And* 91-97; NSM Muthill 91-97; Dioc Sec 98-00; Treas Action of Chs Together in Scotland 01-06; Lic to Offic from 06. *Drummond Park Farm, Logiealmond, Perth PH1 3TJ* Tel (01738) 880477 Fax 880709 E-mail w.rootes77@btinternet.com

ROOTHAM, Gerald Raymond. b 47. **d** 02 **p** 03. OLM Mattishall and the Tudd Valley *Nor* 02-10; C from 10. *8 Burgh Lane, Mattishall, Dereham NR20 3QW* Tel (01362) 858533 E-mail grootham@yahoo.co.uk

ROPER, Canon David John. b 53. St Steph Ho Ox 93. **d** 95 **p** 96. C Hunstanton St Mary w Ringstead Parva etc *Nor* 95-98; TV E Dereham and Scarning 98-00; R Barham w Bishopsbourne and Kingston *Cant* 00-08; C Nonington w Wymynswold and Goodnestone etc 00-08; AD E Bridge 01-08; P-in-c Broadstairs from 08; AD Thanet 00-09; P-in-c St Peter-in-Thanet 10-11; Hon Min Can Cant Cathl 03-08; Hon Can from 08. *The Rectory, Nelson Place, Broadstairs CT10 1HQ* Tel (01843) 862921 E-mail roper995@btinternet.com

ROPER, Glenn. b 51. York Univ MA91 Caerleon Coll of Educn CertEd73. **d** 04 **p** 05. NSM Ovenden *Wakef* from 04. *113 Meadow Drive, Halifax HX3 5JZ* Tel (01422) 368086 E-mail glennroper@fsmail.net

ROPER, Mrs Joan. b 49. **d** 10 **p** 11. NSM Newport w Longford, Chetwynd and Forton *Lich* 10-11; NSM Newport w Longford, and Chetwynd from 11. *19 Gilbert Close, Newport TF10 7UU*

ROPER, Michael Darwin Alston. b 66. Leeds Univ BA03. Coll of Resurr Mirfield 01. **d** 03 **p** 04. C Mortlake w E Sheen *S'wark* 03-07; P-in-c Egham Hythe *Guildf* from 07. *St Paul's Vicarage, 214 Wendover Road, Staines TW18 3DF* Tel (01784) 453625 E-mail gore_lodge@yahoo.co.uk

ROPER, Terence Chaus. b 35. K Coll Lon 56. St Boniface Warminster 59. **d** 60 **p** 61. C Forton *Portsm* 60-63; C Arlington St Alban USA 63-65; C Dallas St Thos 65-67; R Dallas Our Lady of Grace 67-73; R Irving Redeemer 73-76; R Dallas Transfiguration 76-99; R Philadelphia H Trin from 99. *1815 John F Kennedy Boulevard #2308, Philadelphia PA 19103-1731, USA* Tel (001) (215) 587 6873 *or* 567 1267

ROPER, Canon Timothy Hamilton. b 34. Qu Coll Cam BA57 MA61. Sarum Th Coll 57. **d** 59 **p** 60. C Kingsthorpe *Pet* 59-62; C Kirkby *Liv* 62-65; Chapl Rossall Sch Fleetwood 65-84; R Arthingworth, Harrington w Oxendon and E Farndon *Pet* 84-99; RD Brixworth 89-94; Can Pet Cathl 94-99; rtd 99. *47 Cromwell Crescent, Market Harborough LE16 8JN* Tel (01858) 468032

ROSAMOND, Derek William. b 49. Linc Th Coll 87. **d** 89 **p** 90. C Coventry Caludon 89-93; Urban Regeneration Chapl S Tyneside *Dur* 93-96; TV Sunderland 96-04; Community P SW Stockton from 04; P-in-c Stockton St Paul from 04. *65 Bishopton Road, Stockton-on-Tees TS18 4PE* Tel (01642) 895868 E-mail derekrosamond@hotmail.com

ROSBOROUGH, Mrs Rachel Claire. b 76. Anglia Poly Univ BA00. St Jo Coll Nottm 06. **d** 08 **p** 09. C Charlton Kings H Apostles *Glouc* from 08; R Bourton-on-the-Water w Clapton etc from 11. *The Rectory, School Hill, Bourton-on-the-Water, Cheltenham GL54 2AW* E-mail rachelrosborough@hotmail.com

ROSCOE, David John. b 64. UEA BA87 Selw Coll Cam BA93. Aston Tr Scheme 89 Westcott Ho Cam 91. **d** 94 **p** 95. C Ditton St Mich *Liv* 94-98; TV Kirkby 98-99; V Wigan St Steph 99-03; Jt P-in-c Aspull and New Springs 02-03; V New Springs and Whelley and Chapl Wrightington Wigan and Leigh NHS Trust 03-10; P-in-c Feniscowles *Blackb* from 10. *The Vicarage, 732 Preston Old Road, Feniscowles, Blackburn BB2 5EN* Tel (01254) 201236

ROSCOE, Simon Nicolas. b 51. SEITE 02. **d** 04 **p** 06. C Whitstable *Cant* 04-05; C Faversham 05-09; V Southchurch Ch Ch *Chelmsf* from 09. *Christ Church Vicarage, 58 Colbert Road, Southend-on-Sea SS1 3BP* Tel (01702) 582585 E-mail simonsccc@aol.com

ROSE, Andrew David. b 45. BA81. Oak Hill Th Coll 78. **d** 81 **p** 82. C Northwood Em *Lon* 81-86; V Iver *Ox* 86-95; R Frinton *Chelmsf* 95-07; TV Washfield, Stoodleigh, Withleigh etc *Ex* 07-10; rtd 10. *3 Corinda House, 14 Queens Road, Frinton-on-Sea CO13 9JA* E-mail andrewandjen@eclipse.co.uk

ROSE (née ARDLEY), Annette Susan. b 68. SEITE 01. **d** 04 **p** 05. C Barham w Bishopsbourne and Kingston *Cant* 04-07; P-in-c Wingham w Elmstone and Preston w Stourmouth 07-09; P-in-c New Eltham All SS *S'wark* 09-10; V from 10. *All Saints' Vicarage, 22 Bercta Road, London SE9 3TZ* Tel (020) 8850 0374 E-mail revannette.rose@btinternet.com

ROSE, Anthony James. b 47. Trin Coll Bris BD72. **d** 73 **p** 74. C Halliwell St Pet *Man* 73-76; CF 76-94; R Colchester Ch Ch w

St Mary V *Chelmsf* 94-01; RD Colchester 98-01; P-in-c Boreham 01-06; rtd 06; Perm to Offic *Chelmsf* from 06. *19 Holm Oak, Colchester CO2 8QA* Tel (01206) 576532 E-mail ajrose@dsl.pipex.com

ROSE, Anthony John. b 53. Birm Univ BA79. Trin Coll Bris 84. **d** 86 **p** 87. C The Quinton *Birm* 86-90; R Abbas and Templecombe w Horsington *B & W* 90-98; V New Thundersley *Chelmsf* from 98. *St George's Vicarage, 89 Rushbottom Lane, Benfleet SS7 4DN* Tel (01268) 792088 E-mail stgvicar@blueyonder.co.uk

ROSE, Canon Barry Ernest. b 35. Chich Th Coll 58. **d** 61 **p** 62. C Forest Gate St Edm *Chelmsf* 61-64; Antigua 64-66; Dominica 66-69; V St Mary-at-Latton *Chelmsf* 69-79; V Stansted Mountfitchet 79-88; V Halstead St Andr w H Trin and Greenstead Green 88-00; RD Halstead and Coggeshall 91-95; RD Hinckford 95-98; Hon Can Chelmsf Cathl 96-00; rtd 00; Perm to Offic *Chelmsf* from 00. *26 Gurton Road, Coggeshall CO6 1QA* Tel (01376) 563988 Mobile 07984-546638 E-mail jbrose@talk21.com

ROSE, Canon Bernard Frederick. b 47. **d** 91 **p** 92. OLM Ipswich St Thos *St E* 91-09; P-in-c Somersham w Flowton and Offton w Willisham from 09; P-in-c Ringshall w Battisford, Barking w Darmsden etc from 09; Hon Can *St E* Cathl from 05. *The Rectory, Main Road, Willisham, Ipswich IP8 4SP* Tel (01473) 657153 E-mail holy-rose@supanet.com

ROSE, Charles. *See* ROSE, Westmoreland Charles Edward

ROSE, Christopher John. b 66. Edin Univ BSc88. EAMTC 97. **d** 00 **p** 01. NSM Cambridge St Paul *Ely* 00-07; NSM All Hallows Lon Wall from 07. *6 Montreal Road, Cambridge CB1 3NP* Tel (01223) 511241 *or* (020) 7588 8922 Fax 566092 E-mail chris@amostrust.org

ROSE, David. *See* ROSE, John David

ROSE, Eve. b 63. Leeds Univ BA85. Qu Coll Birm 99. **d** 01 **p** 02. C Seacroft *Ripon* 01-04; Chapl Hull and E Riding Community Health NHS Trust 04-06; Mental Health Chapl Humber Mental Health Teaching NHS Trust from 06; Hon C Hessle *York* 06-11. *Humber Mental Health NHS Trust, Beverley Road, Willerby, Hull HU10 6ED* Tel (01482) 223191 Fax 303900 Mobile 07771-851725

ROSE, Miss Geraldine Susan. b 47. Trin Coll Bris BD78. dss 78 **d** 87 **p** 94. Tonbridge St Steph *Roch* 78-80; Littlemore *Derby* 80-88; Par Dn 87-88; Par Dn Wombwell *Sheff* 88-94; C 94-96; rtd 96; Perm to Offic *Sheff* from 96. *5 Wheatcroft, Conisbrough, Doncaster DN12 2BL* Tel (01709) 867761 E-mail sroserhodon@onetel.net.uk

ROSE, Harry. *See* ROSE, Lionel Stafford Harry

ROSE, Ingrid Elizabeth. b 57. Univ of Wales (Abth) BA78 DipEd79. Trin Coll Carmarthen 84. **d** 87 **p** 01. NSM Ysbyty Cynfyn w Llantrisant and Eglwys Newydd *St D* 87-90 and 92-95; NSM to Adn Cardigan 00-03; NSM Grwp Bro Ystwyth a Mynach from 06. *Frongoch Newydd, Trisant, Aberystwyth SY23 4RL*

ROSE, John Clement Wansey. b 46. New Coll Ox BA71 MA72. Ripon Hall Ox 70. **d** 72 **p** 73. C Harborne St Pet *Birm* 72-76; TV Kings Norton 76-81; V Maney 81-02; R Condover w Frodesley, Acton Burnell etc *Heref* from 02. *The Vicarage, Condover, Shrewsbury SY5 7AA* Tel (01743) 872251

ROSE, John David. b 40. Dioc OLM tr scheme 97. **d** 00 **p** 01. OLM Prescot *Liv* from 00. *18 Eccleston Gardens, St Helens WA10 3BL* Tel (01744) 736168 Mobile 07808-350859 Fax 0151-426 5121

ROSE, Jonathan Graham. b 75. Leeds Univ BA72 Birm Univ MEd83 Ex Univ MA08 FRSA97 MCIPD03. STETS 10. **d** 11. NSM Quantock Towers *B & W* from 11. *Latchets, 81 Staplegrove Road, Taunton TA1 1DN* Tel (01823) 332685 Mobile 07969-008091 E-mail jonrose 59@fsmail.net

ROSE, Judith Barbara. b 51. TCert72. SAOMC 96. **d** 99 **p** 00. OLM Stantonbury and Willen *Ox* 99-11; Perm to Offic from 11. *16 Runnymede, Giffard Park, Milton Keynes MK14 5QL* Tel and fax (01908) 618634

ROSE, The Ven Kathleen Judith. b 37. Lon Bible Coll BD73 St Mich Ho Ox 64. dss 76 **d** 87 **p** 94. Leeds St Geo *Ripon* 76-81; Bradf Cathl 81-85; S Gillingham *Roch* 85-87; Par Dn 87-90; RD Gillingham 88-90; Bp's Dom Chapl 90-95; Asst Dir of Ords 90-95; Hon Can Roch Cathl 93-02; Acting Adn Tonbridge 95-96; Adn Tonbridge 96-02; rtd 02; Perm to Offic *B & W* from 03. *47 Hill Lea Gardens, Cheddar BS27 3JH* Tel (01934) 741708 Mobile 07736-616382 E-mail rosegwyer@btinternet.com

ROSE, Lionel Stafford Harry. b 38. MBE93. Wells Th Coll 69. **d** 71 **p** 72. C Minchinhampton *Glouc* 71-73; C Thornbury 73-75; R Ruardean 75-80; V Whiteshill 80-84; CF 84-93; Chapl HM Pris Kirkham 93-95; Wymott 95-01; Rye Hill 01; rtd 01; Perm to Offic *Ely* from 02. *4 Samian Close, Highfield, Caldecote, Cambridge CB23 7GP*

ROSE, Mrs Lynda Kathryn. b 51. Ex Univ BA73 Barrister-at-Law (Gray's Inn) 81. Wycliffe Hall Ox BA86. **d** 87 **p** 94. C Highfield *Ox* 87-88; C Ox St Clem 89-93; Dir Anastasis Min 93-99; NSM Ambrosden w Merton and Piddington 94-99. *14 Scholar Mews, Marston Ferry Road, Oxford OX2 7GY* Tel (01865) 554421 E-mail lyndarose2000@yahoo.co.uk

ROSE, Michael Mark. b 63. Hull Univ BA04. Westcott Ho Cam 07. **d** 09 **p** 10. C Linc St Nic w St Jo Newport 09-10; C Boultham from 10. *74 Roman Wharf, Lincoln LN1 1SR* Tel 07846-601141 (mobile) E-mail mikeredrose63@hotmail.com

ROSE, Mrs Pamela Inneen. b 49. Hull Univ BSc71 Moray Ho Coll of Educn PGCE72. **d** 06 **p** 07. OLM Stow Gp *Linc* from 06. *Daisy Cottage, 16-18 Grange Lane, Willingham by Stow, Gainsborough DN21 5LB* Tel (01427) 787578 E-mail pamrose@worldshare.org.uk

ROSE, Canon Paul Rosamond. b 32. Trin Hall Cam BA56 MA60. Westcott Ho Cam 57. **d** 59 **p** 60. C Wandsworth St Anne *S'wark* 59-61; C Tormohun *Ex* 61-64; P-in-c Daramombe Rhodesia 64-67; Min Can, Prec and Sacr Pet Cathl 67-72; V Paddington St Jo w St Mich *Lon* 72-79; PV Westmr Abbey 74-79; Min Can and Prec Cant Cathl 79-84; V Rothwell w Orton *Pet* 84-87; R Rothwell w Orton, Rushton w Glendon and Pipewell 87-97; Can Pet Cathl 94-97; rtd 97; Heidelberg *Eur* 98; Perm to Offic *Pet* from 97; *Lon* and *Eur* from 98; *Ely* from 03. *15 Standish Court, Campaign Avenue, Peterborough PE2 9RR* Tel (01733) 553272 E-mail canons.rose@virgin.net

ROSE, Robert Alec Lewis. b 41. Man Univ BSc64. Wycliffe Hall Ox 85. **d** 87 **p** 88. C Vange *Chelmsf* 87-91; C Langdon Hills 91-94; P-in-c Bentley Common 94-00; P-in-c Kelvedon Hatch 94-00; P-in-c Navestock 94-00; R Bentley Common, Kelvedon Hatch and Navestock 00-08; rtd 08; Perm to Offic *St E* from 09. *47 High Street, Wickham Market, Woodbridge IP13 0HE* Tel (01728) 748199 E-mail robdaphnerose@btinternet.com

ROSE, Susan. *See* ROSE, Miss Geraldine Susan

ROSE, Mrs Susan Margaret. b 59. Westmr Coll of Educn BEd81. SAOMC 95. **d** 98 **p** 99. C N Petherton w Northmoor Green *B & W* 98-01; P-in-c 01-03; P-in-c N Newton w St Michaelchurch, Thurloxton etc 01-03; R Alfred Jewel 03-09; RD Sedgemoor 06-09; P-in-c Cheddar from 09; P-in-c Rodney Stoke w Draycott from 09. *The Vicarage, Station Road, Cheddar BS27 3AH* Tel (01934) 740394 E-mail rev.suerose@virgin.net

ROSE, Miss Susan Mary. b 36. TCert56. Dalton Ho Bris 68 Trin Coll Bris 74. **dss** 81 **d** 87 **p** 94. Brinsworth w Catcliffe *Sheff* 75-77; Scargill Ho 77-83; Netherthorpe *Sheff* 83-87; Tutor Trin Coll Bris 87-96; V Normanton *Wakef* 96-01; rtd 01; Perm to Offic *Sheff* from 01 and *Wakef* from 02. *23 Kendal Vale, Worsborough Bridge, Barnsley S70 5NL* Tel (01226) 771590

ROSE, Timothy Edward Francis. b 72. Univ of Wales (Cardiff) BD93 MA95 K Coll Lon PhD98. Wycliffe Hall Ox MTh03. **d** 01 **p** 02. C Jesmond H Trin and Newc St Barn and St Jude 01-04; Chapl R Holloway and Bedf New Coll Lon 04-06; C Farnham *Guildf* 06-09; P-in-c Stanford in the Vale w Goosey and Hatford *Ox* from 09. *The Vicarage, Church Green, Stanford in the Vale, Faringdon SN7 8HU* Tel (01252) 737771 Mobile 07709-722325 E-mail tim.rose1@btinternet.com

ROSE, Timothy Mark. b 77. Luton Univ BA98. St Mellitus Coll BA10. **d** 10 **p** 11. C Upper Sunbury St Sav *Lon* from 10. *73 Kenyngton Drive, Sunbury-on-Thames TW16 7RT* Tel (01932) 782800 Mobile 07966-031432 E-mail tim@st-saviours-sunbury.org.uk

ROSE, Westmoreland Charles Edward. b 32. St Jo Coll Nottm 85. **d** 87 **p** 88. C Fairfield *Derby* 87-90; V Linton and Castle Gresley 90-01; rtd 01; Perm to Offic *Derby* 01-08. *Lavender Lodge Nursing Home, 48-50 Stafford Street, Derby DE1 1JL* Tel (01332) 298388

ROSE-CASEMORE, Claire Pamela. b 63. St Paul's Coll Chelt BA84 St Luke's Coll Ex PGCE85 Anglia Poly Univ MA02. Ridley Hall Cam 95. **d** 97 **p** 98. Par Dn Kingsthorpe w Northampton St Dav *Pet* 97-98; C 98-01; TV Daventry, Ashby St Ledgers, Braunston etc 01-10; P-in-c Bideford, Northam, Westward Ho!, Appledore etc *Ex* from 10. *The Rectory, Abbotsham Road, Bideford EX39 3AB* Tel (01237) 475765 E-mail clairerc@btopenworld.com

ROSE-CASEMORE, John. b 27. Chich Th Coll. **d** 55 **p** 56. C Epsom Common Ch Ch *Guildf* 55-58; C Hednesford *Lich* 58-60; V Dawley 60-65; R Puttenham and Wanborough *Guildf* 65-72; R Frimley 72-83; RD Surrey Heath 76-81; R Ludgershall and Faberstown *Sarum* 83-86; R Tidworth, Ludgershall and Faberstown 86-92; rtd 92; Perm to Offic *Ex* from 93. *5 Culvery Close, Woodbury, Exeter EX5 1LZ* Tel (01395) 233426

ROSE-CASEMORE, Miss Penelope Jane. b 56. Bris Univ CertEd77 BEd78. Westcott Ho Cam 83. **dss** 85 **d** 87 **p** 94. Waterloo St Jo w St Andr *S'wark* 85-87; Par Dn 87-88; Asst Chapl St Ormond Street Hosp for Sick Children Lon 88-90; Par Dn Balham St Mary and St Jo *S'wark* 90-94; C 94-96; Par Dn Upper Tooting H Trin 90-94; C 94-96; TV Clapham Team 96-01; V Clapham Ch Ch and St Jo from 02; AD Lambeth N 05-10. *Christchurch Vicarage, 39 Union Grove, London SW8 2QJ* Tel and fax (020) 7622 3552 E-mail penny@christchurchstjohn.com

ROSEDALE, John Richard. b 54. Leeds Univ BA05. NOC 02. **d** 05 **p** 06. NSM Hadfield *Derby* 05-10; TV Saddleworth *Man* from 10. *Friarmere Vicarage, 1 Coblers Hill, Delph, Oldham OL3 5HT* Tel (01457) 874209

ROSENTHAL, Canon James Milton. b 51. **d** 07 **p** 09. Dir Communications Angl Communion Office 89-09; NSM All Hallows by the Tower etc *Lon* from 07. *8 Margaret Street, London W1W 8JG* Tel 07595-888751 (mobile) E-mail james.rosenthal@gmail.com

ROSENTHAL, Sheila. b 57. Warwick Univ BA81 MA95. Ripon Coll Cuddesdon 04. **d** 06 **p** 07. C Worc SE 06-09; Asst Chapl St Richard's Hospice Worc from 09; Chapl Worcs Primary Care Trust from 10. *Springwood Cottage, Bourton on the Hill, Moreton-in-Marsh GL56 9AE* Tel (01386) 700530 E-mail mrsr@quista.net

ROSEWEIR, Clifford John. b 43. Glas Univ MA64 MCIPD81. S'wark Ord Course 83. **d** 84 **p** 85. NSM Redhill H Trin *S'wark* 84-89; P-in-c Croydon St Martin 89-92; Perm to Offic 92-93; Hon C Wallington 93-94; V Croydon Ch Ch 94-97; Perm to Offic from 06. *206 Bridle Road, Croydon CR0 8HL* Tel (020) 8777 2820 Mobile 07850-480058 E-mail rosewec@hotmail.com

ROSIE, James Robert. b 78. Leeds Univ BA08. Coll of Resurr Mirfield 08. **d** 10 **p** 11. C Kingston upon Hull St Alb *York* from 10. *223 Cottingham Road, Hull HU5 4AU* Tel (01482) 343182 Mobile 07931-120897 E-mail james.rosie1@googlemail.com

⊁**ROSIER, The Rt Revd Stanley Bruce.** b 28. Univ of W Aus BSc48 Ox Univ BA52 MA56. Westcott Ho Cam 53. **d** 54 **p** 55 **c** 67. C Ecclesall *Sheff* 54-57; R Wyalkatchem Australia 57-64; R Kellerberrin 64-67; Can Perth 66-67; Adn Narrogin 67-70; Bp Willochra 70-87; Asst Bp 90-92; R Parkside 87-94; rtd 94. *5A Fowler's Road, Glenunga SA 5064, Australia* Tel (0061) (8) 8379 5213 E-mail bfrosier@senet.com.au

ROSKELLY, James Hereward Emmanuel. b 57. BSc ACSM80. Cranmer Hall Dur 83. **d** 86 **p** 87. C Dunster, Carhampton and Withycombe w Rodhuish *B & W* 86-90; C Ealing St Mary *Lon* 90-93; Chapl R Marsden Hosp Lon and Surrey 93-95; CF 95-03; TV Rayleigh *Chelmsf* 03-10; R Dickleburgh and The Pulhams *Nor* from 10. *The Rectory, Station Road, Pulham Market, Diss IP21 4TE* Tel (01379) 676256 Mobile 07989-442434 E-mail jamesroskelly@btinternet.com

ROSKILLY, John Noel. b 33. Man Univ MB, ChB58 MRCGP68. St Deiniol's Hawarden 74. **d** 75 **p** 76. NSM Bramhall *Ches* 75-86; V Capesthorne w Siddington and Marton 86-91; Dioc Dir of Counselling 84-93; Bp's Officer for NSM 87-93; NSM Macclesfield St Paul 92-93; rtd 93; Perm to Offic *Ches* from 93. *North View, Hawkins Lane, Rainow, Macclesfield SK10 5TL* Tel (01625) 501014

ROSKROW, Neil. b 27. FBCO80. St Alb Minl Tr Scheme 82. **d** 85 **p** 86. NSM Digswell and Panshanger *St Alb* 85-90; P-in-c Gt Gaddesden 90-95; P-in-c Lt Gaddesden 92-95; rtd 96; Perm to Offic *St Alb* 96-05. *Jevinda, 5 Phillips Terrace, North Roskear, Camborne TR14 8PJ* Tel (01209) 711761

ROSKROW, Mrs Pamela Mary. b 25. St Alb Minl Tr Scheme. **dss** 85 **d** 87 **p** 94. Digswell and Panshanger *St Alb* 85-90; Hon Par Dn 87-90; Hon Par Dn Gt Gaddesden 90-94; Hon C 94-95; Hon Par Dn Lt Gaddesden 92-94; Hon C 94-95; Perm to Offic 96-05. *Jevinda, 5 Phillips Terrace, North Roskear, Camborne TR14 8PJ* Tel (01209) 711761

ROSS, Alexander. *See* ROSS, David Alexander

ROSS, Canon Anthony McPherson. b 38. OBE. Univ of Wales (Lamp) BA60 Lon Univ BD63. St Mich Coll Llan 60. **d** 61 **p** 62. C Gabalfa *Llan* 61-65; Chapl RN 65-93; QHC 89-93; P-in-c Coln St Aldwyns, Hatherop, Quenington etc *Glouc* 93-95; V 95-08; RD Fairford 96-04; rtd 08; Bp's Adv on Deliverance Min *Glouc* from 08; Hon Can Glouc Cathl from 02. *Rowan Tree Cottage, Ampney Crucis, Cirencester GL7 5RY* Tel (01285) 851410 E-mail tonyrosstsst@talktalk.net

ROSS, Mrs Audrey Ruth. b 42. Herts Coll BA86. SAOMC 99. **d** 02 **p** 03. NSM Leavesden *St Alb* 02-06; NSM Storrington Chich from 06. *9 Longland Avenue, Storrington, Pulborough RH20 4HY* Tel (01903) 746231 E-mail revross@supanet.com

ROSS, David Alexander. b 46. Oak Hill Th Coll 73. **d** 75 **p** 76. C Northwood Em *Lon* 75-80; R Eastrop *Win* 80-86; V Hove Bp Hannington Memorial Ch Chich 86-93; V Muswell Hill St Jas w St Matt *Lon* 93-97; rtd 07; Hon C S Tottenham St Ann *Lon* 07-11; Perm to Offic *Ox* from 11. *4 Glissard Way, Bradwell Village, Burford OX18 4XD* Tel (01993) 824871 E-mail alexlynne.ross@googlemail.com

ROSS, Preb Duncan Gilbert. b 48. Lon Univ BSc70. Westcott Ho Cam 75. **d** 78 **p** 79. C Stepney St Dunstan and All SS *Lon* 78-84; V Hackney Wick St Mary of Eton w St Aug 84-95; P-in-c Bow Common 95-03; V from 03; Preb St Paul's Cathl from 95. *St Paul's Vicarage, Leopold Street, London E3 4LA* Tel and fax (020) 7987 4941 E-mail duncan.ross5@btinternet.com

ROSS, Frederic Ian. b 34. Man Univ BSc56. Westcott Ho Cam 58. **d** 62 **p** 63. C Oldham *Man* 62-65; Sec Th Colls Dept SCM 65-69; Teacher Man Gr Sch 69-84; V Shrewsbury H Cross *Lich* 84-02; rtd 02; Perm to Offic *Heref* and *Lich* from 02. *The Paddock, Pealey Road, Annscroft, Shrewsbury SY5 8AN* Tel (01743) 860327

ROSS, Frederick Kenneth Wilson. b 29. **d** 99 **p** 00. C Margate S Africa 99-02; Perm to Offic *S & M* from 04. *116 Saddle Mews, Douglas, Isle of Man IM2 1HU* Tel (01624) 672591 Mobile 07624-477279 E-mail kaross@manx.net

ROSS, Henry Ernest. b 40. NW Ord Course 70. **d** 73 **p** 74. NSM Litherland St Phil *Liv* 73-75; C Newton-le-Willows 75-77; P-in-c Walton St Luke 77-79; V 79-10; RD Walton 84-89; rtd 10. *Blue Haven, 46 Somerset Drive, Southport PR8 3SN* Tel (01704) 571287 E-mail harry.ross@hotmail.co.uk

ROSS, John. b 41. Wells Th Coll 66. **d** 69 **p** 70. C Newc St Gabr 69-71; C Prudhoe 71-75; Hon C Shotley 75-87; Hon C Whittonstall 75-87; P-in-c Wallsend St Pet 93-94. *11 Weston Avenue, Whickham, Newcastle upon Tyne NE16 5TS* Tel 0191-488 1546 E-mail rossj41@blueyonder.co.uk

ROSS, John Colin. b 50. Oak Hill Th Coll 84. **d** 86 **p** 87. C Stowmarket *St E* 86-89; C Wakef St Andr and St Mary 89-91; R Gt and Lt Whelnetham w Bradfield St George *St E* 91-94; V Newmarket All SS 94-02; V Erith St Paul *Roch* 02-04; P-in-c Combs and Lt Finborough *St E* from 04. *The Rectory, 135 Poplar Hill, Combs, Stowmarket IP14 2AY* Tel (01449) 612076 Mobile 07904-124227 E-mail revjohnross@dsl.pipex.com

ROSS (née YOUNG), Mrs Karen Heather. b 66. Nottm Univ BA01. Westcott Ho Cam 02. **d** 05 **p** 07. C Airedale w Fryston *Wakef* 05-06; Hon C Ravenshead *S'well* 07-09; Mental Health Chapl Notts Healthcare NHS Trust 08-09. *Address temp unknown*

ROSS, Malcolm Hargrave. b 37. Dur Univ BSc58. Westcott Ho Cam 63. **d** 64 **p** 65. C Armley St Bart *Ripon* 64-67; USPG 67-71; Trinidad and Tobago 67-71; V New Rossington *Sheff* 71-75; Bp's Missr in E Lon 75-82; P-in-c Haggerston All SS 75-82; V Bedford Leigh *Man* 82-85; Area Sec USPG *Bris* and *Glouc* 85-90; Bp's Officer for Miss and Evang *Bris* 90-94; P-in-c Lacock w Bowden Hill 90-94; V Sherston Magna, Easton Grey, Luckington etc 94-06; rtd 06. *132 Larecombe Road, St Austell PL25 3EZ* E-mail m-eross@tiscali.co.uk

ROSS, Oliver Charles Milligan. b 58. Lon Univ BA80 St Edm Ho Cam BA85. Ridley Hall Cam 84. **d** 87 **p** 88. C Preston St Cuth *Blackb* 87-90; C Paddington St Jo w St Mich *Lon* 90-95; V Hounslow H Trin w St Paul 95-06; P-in-c Isleworth St Mary 01-02; R St Olave Hart Street w All Hallows Staining etc from 06; P-in-c St Kath Cree from 06; AD The City from 09. *St Olave's Rectory, 8 Hart Street, London EC3R 7NB* Tel (020) 7702 0244 E-mail ocmross@mac.com

ROSS, Ms Rachel Anne. b 64. York Univ BSc85 SS Coll Cam PGCE86 Sheff Univ MA97 Coll of Ripon & York St Jo MA00. NOC 97. **d** 00 **p** 01. C Pendleton *Man* 00-04; P-in-c Salford Ordsall St Clem 03-04; P-in-c Salford St Ignatius and Stowell Memorial 03-04; R Ordsall and Salford Quays 04-07; P-in-c Loughborough All SS w H Trin *Leic* 07-08; R Loughborough All SS w H Trin from 08; Bp's NSM Officer from 10. *The Rectory, 60 Westfield Drive, Loughborough LE11 3QL* Tel (01509) 212780 Mobile 07884-371688 E-mail rachelross@tiscali.co.uk

ROSS, Canon Raymond John. b 28. Trin Coll Cam BA52 MA57. St Steph Ho Ox 52. **d** 54 **p** 55. C Clifton All SS *Bris* 54-58; C Solihull *Birm* 58-66; C-in-c Hobs Moat CD 66-67; V Hobs Moat 67-72; R Newbold w Dunston *Derby* 72-95; RD Chesterfield 78-91; Hon Can Derby Cathl 86-95; rtd 96; Perm to Offic *Derby* 96-09. *20 Stuart Court, High Street, Kibworth, Leicester LE8 0LR* Tel (0116) 2793874

ROSS (née FAIRWEATHER), Mrs Sally Helen. b 69. St Hilda's Coll Ox BA91. Cranmer Hall Dur 94. **d** 97 **p** 98. C Illingworth *Wakef* 97-01; Warden H Rood Ho and C Thirsk *York* 01-02; Chapl Northallerton Health Services NHS Trust 01-02; C Sheff St Mark Broomhill 02-04; Mental Health Chapl Sheff Care Trust from 04. *40 Bents Green, Sheffield S11 9RP* Tel 0114-235 1652 E-mail sh.ross@tiscali.co.uk

ROSS, Vernon. b 57. Portsm Poly BSc79 RGN86. Trin Coll Bris 89. **d** 91 **p** 92. C Fareham St Jo *Portsm* 91-94; P-in-c Witheridge, Thelbridge, Creacombe, Meshaw etc *Ex* 94-00; TR Barnstaple 00-08; P-in-c Fyfield, Moreton w Bobbingworth etc *Chelmsf* from 08. *6 Forest Drive, Fyfield, Ongar CM5 0TP* Tel (01277) 899886 E-mail vfsd.ross1@btinternet.com

ROSS-McCABE, Mrs Philippa Mary Seton. b 63. Natal Univ BA83 HDipEd86 Bris Univ BA01. Trin Coll Bris 99. **d** 01 **p** 02. C Burpham *Guildf* 01-05; Lic to Offic 05-06; C Wisley w Pyrford 06-08; Tutor Local Min Progr from 06; Hon C Byfleet from 09. *The Rectory, 81 Rectory Lane, Byfleet, West Byfleet KT14 7LX* Tel (01932) 342374 E-mail p.rossmccabe@btinternet.com

ROSS-McNAIRN, Jonathon Edward. b 73. Sheff Univ LLB95 Solicitor 98. St Mellitus Coll BA11. **d** 11. C Hucclecote *Glouc* from 11. *St Philip and St James Church Office, Larkhay Road, Hucclecote, Gloucester GL3 3QH* Tel (01452) 372177 E-mail jonathonrossm@yahoo.co.uk

ROSS, Dean of. See PETERS, The Very Revd Christopher Lind

✠**ROSSDALE, The Rt Revd David Douglas James.** b 53. Westmr Coll Ox MA91 Surrey Univ MSc01 K Coll Lon MSc10. Chich Th Coll 80. **d** 81 **p** 82 **c** 00. C Upminster *Chelmsf* 81-86; V Moulsham St Luke 86-90; V Cookham *Ox* 90-00; RD Maidenhead 91-00; Hon Can Ch Ch 99-00; Suff Bp Grimsby *Linc* from 00; Can and Preb Linc Cathl from 00. *Bishop's House, Church Lane, Irby, Grimsby DN37 7JR* Tel (01472) 371715 Fax 371716 E-mail rossdale@btinternet.com

ROSSETER, Miss Susan Mary. b 46. Man Univ BA67 Edin Univ DASS71. St Jo Coll Nottm LTh84. **d** 87 **p** 94. Par Dn Bromley Common St Aug *Roch* 87-88; C Pudsey St Lawr and St Paul *Bradf* 88-95; C Haughton le Skerne *Dur* 95-00; C Wilnecote *Lich* 00-11; rtd 11. *5 Avill, Hockley, Tamworth B77 5QE* Tel (01827) 701075 E-mail s.rosseter@ntlworld.com

ROSSITER, Donald William Frank. b 30. **d** 80 **p** 81. NSM Abergavenny St Mary w Llanwenarth Citra *Mon* 80-96; NSM Govilon w Llanfoist w Llanelen 92-05; Perm to Offic from 05. *10 Meadow Lane, Abergavenny NP7 7AY* Tel (01873) 855648

ROSSITER, Gillian Alice. b 56. SRN75 RSCN75. NOC 98. **d** 01 **p** 02. C Neston *Ches* 01-06; P-in-c Gt Meols 06-09; V from 09; RD Wirral N from 08. *St John's Vicarage, 142 Birkenhead Road, Meols, Wirral CH47 0LF* Tel 0151-632 1661

ROSSITER, Paul Albert. b 55. Leeds Univ BA06. NOC 03. **d** 06 **p** 07. NSM Wallasey St Nic w All SS *Ches* from 06. *St John's Vicarage, 142 Birkenhead Road, Meols, Wirral CH47 0LF* Tel 0151-632 1661 E-mail p.a.rossiter@liverpool.ac.uk

ROSSITER, Raymond Stephen David. b 22. MBE99. St Deiniol's Hawarden 75. **d** 76 **p** 77. NSM Sale St Anne *Ches* 76-90; Perm to Offic from 90; rtd 91. *75 Temple Road, Sale M33 2FQ* Tel 0161-962 3240

ROSSLYN SMITH, Mrs Katherine Dorothy Nevill. b 40. STETS 97. **d** 00 **p** 01. NSM Tisbury *Sarum* 00-01; NSM Nadder Valley 01-03; NSM Chalke Valley 03-06; rtd 06. *The Old School House, Church Street, Bowerchalke, Salisbury SP5 5BE* Tel (01722) 780011

ROSSLYN-SMITH, Mrs Kirsten Louise. b 73. Nottm Trent Univ BA96. St Jo Coll Nottm MTh05. **d** 05 **p** 06. C Tunbridge Wells St Jas *Roch* 05-10; V Stoke Hill *Guildf* from 10. *St Peter's Church House, 37 Hazel Avenue, Guildford GU1 1NP* Tel (01483) 572078

ROSTILL, Brian. b 50. K Alfred's Coll Win BTh00. Cranmer Hall Dur 01. **d** 03 **p** 04. C Knight's Enham and Smannell w Enham Alamein *Win* 03-07; P-in-c Boyatt Wood 07-09; V from 09. *St Peter's Church House, 53 Sovereign Way, Eastleigh SO50 4SA* Tel (023) 8064 2188 E-mail rostill@tiscali.co.uk

ROSTRON, Derek. b 34. St Mich Coll Llan 65. **d** 67 **p** 68. C Morecambe St Barn *Blackb* 67-70; C Ribbleton 70-72; V Chorley All SS 72-79; C Woodchurch *Ches* 79-80; V Audlem 80-03; RD Nantwich 87-97; rtd 04; Perm to Offic *Lich* 01-06 and *Ches* 04-06. *30 St Matthew's Drive, Derrington, Stafford ST18 9LU* Tel (01785) 246349

ROTERS, Craig Lawrence. b 81. St Jo Coll Dur BA03 Man Metrop Univ PGCE06. Coll of Resurr Mirfield 08. **d** 10 **p** 11. C High Crompton *Man* from 10. *6 Norfolk Close, Shaw, Oldham OL2 7ER* Tel (01706) 666575 E-mail c.l.roters@dunelm.org.uk

ROTH, Jill Marie. b 61. Ox Min Course 07. **d** 10 **p** 11. NSM Flackwell Heath *Ox* from 10. *White Cottage, Hay Lane, Fulmer, Slough SL3 6HJ* Tel (01753) 663181 Mobile 07985-945990 E-mail jillroth@dsl.pipex.com

ROTHERHAM, Eric. b 36. Clifton Th Coll 63. **d** 67 **p** 68. C Gt Crosby St Luke *Liv* 67-69; C Sutton 69-71; V Warrington St Paul 72-79; Lic to Offic 79-80; Perm to Offic *Ches* and *Liv* from 80. *7 Paul Street, Warrington WA2 7LE* Tel (01925) 633048

ROTHERY, Jean. b 44. **d** 98 **p** 99. NSM Purley *Ox* from 98. *Oak Lea, Tidmarsh Road, Tidmarsh, Reading RG8 8ER* Tel 0118-984 3625

ROTHERY, Robert Frederick (Fred). b 34. Lon Coll of Div 67. **d** 69 **p** 70. C Burscough Bridge *Liv* 69-72; C Chipping Campden *Glouc* 72-75; P-in-c Didmarton w Oldbury-on-the-Hill and Sopworth 75-77; R Boxwell, Leighterton, Didmarton, Oldbury etc 77-83; R Stow on the Wold 83-00; RD Stow 90-99; rtd 00. *12 Phillips Road, Marnhull, Sturminster Newton DT10 1LF* Tel (01258) 820668

ROTHWELL, Canon Bryan. b 60. St Edm Hall Ox BA81 MA85. Trin Coll Bris. **d** 85 **p** 86. C Carl St Jo 85-88; C Ulverston St Mary w H Trin 88-90; P-in-c Preston St Mary *Blackb* 90-96; P-in-c St John's-in-the-Vale in the Vale w Wythburn *Carl* 96-99; R St John's-in-the-Vale, Threlkeld and Wythburn from 99; Warden Dioc Youth Cen 96-11; RD Derwent 05-10; TR Solway Plain from 11; Hon Can Carl Cathl from 08. *The Vicarage, Wigton Road, Silloth, Carlisle CA7 4NJ* E-mail bryan.rothwell@btinternet.com

ROTHWELL, Edwin John. b 53. Lanc Univ BA74 PhD79. Sarum & Wells Th Coll 88. **d** 90 **p** 91. C Malvern Link w Cowleigh *Worc* 90-94; R Bowbrook N 94-00; Asst Chapl Swindon and Marlborough NHS Trust 00-03; Chapl E Somerset NHS Trust from 03. *Chaplain's Office, Yeovil District Hospital, Higher Kingston, Yeovil BA21 4AT* Tel (01935) 475122 E-mail john.rothwell@ydh.nhs.uk

ROTHWELL, Mrs Emma. b 73. Liv Univ BSc Cam Univ MEd. ERMC. **d** 10 **p** 11. C Papworth *Ely* from 10. *The Rectory, 3A Stocks Lane, Gamlingay, Sandy SG19 3JP* Tel (01767) 650568 Mobile 07793-954603 E-mail emma.rothwell@ely.anglican.org

ROTHWELL, Harold. b 34. AKC58. K Coll Lon St Boniface Warminster. **d** 59 **p** 60. C Old Brumby *Linc* 59-62; P-in-c Sheff St Steph w St Phil and St Ann 62-64; V Caistor w Holton le Moor and Clixby *Linc* 67-77; Chapl Caistor Hosp 67-77; Org Sec

CECS *Ex* and *B & W* 77-81; P-in-c Deeping Fen *Linc* 78-81; C Boston 86-88; C Spilsby w Hundleby 88-91; C Bracebridge Heath 91-94; rtd 94; Perm to Offic *Linc* 94-05. *c/o S H Rothwell Esq, 38 Park Road, Spalding PE11 1NH*

ROTHWELL, Michael John Hereward. See HEREWARD-ROTHWELL, Canon Michael John

ROTHWELL, Steven. b 68. Roehampton Inst BA99 Cam Univ MA02. Westcott Ho Cam 00. **d** 02 **p** 03. C Chesterton Gd Shep *Ely* 02-06; R Gamlingay and Everton from 06. *The Rectory, 3A Stocks Lane, Gamlingay, Sandy SG19 3JP* Tel (01767) 650568 E-mail s.rothwell3@btinternet.com

ROTHWELL-JACKSON, Christopher Patrick. b 32. St Cath Soc Ox BA58 MA61 Bris Univ PGCE66. St Steph Ho Ox 55. **d** 59 **p** 60. C E Clevedon All SS *B & W* 59-62; C Midsomer Norton 62-65; Asst Teacher St Pet Primary Sch Portishead 66-68; Clevedon Junior Sch 68-72; Dep Hd Clevedon All SS Primary Sch 72-75; Hd Master Bp Pursglove Sch Tideswell 75-90; rtd 90; Perm to Offic *Ex* from 95. *Rosedale, Hookway, Crediton EX17 3PU* Tel (01363) 772039

ROUCH, David Vaughan. b 36. Oak Hill Th Coll 67. **d** 69 **p** 70. C Denton Holme *Carl* 69-74; V Litherland St Jo and St Jas *Liv* 74-95; V Pemberton St Mark Newtown 95-06; P-in-c Wigan St Barn Marsh Green 03-06; rtd 06; Perm to Offic *Lich* from 07. *16 Parrs Lane, Baysdon Hill, Shrewsbury SY3 0JS* Tel (01743) 873800 E-mail drouchatjennyr@blueyonder.co.uk

ROUCH, The Ven Peter Bradford. b 66. BNC Ox MA87 Peterho Cam MA99 Man Univ PhD05. Westcott Ho Cam 96. **d** 99 **p** 00. C E Dulwich St Jo *S'wark* 99-02; Jun Research Fell St Steph Ho Ox 02-04; Chapl St Jo Coll Ox 03-04; P-in-c Man Apostles w Miles Platting 05-11; Hon Research Fell Man Univ 07-11; Adn Bournemouth *Win* from 11. *Glebe House, 22 Bellflower Way, Chandler's Ford, Eastleigh SO53 4HN* Tel and fax (023) 8026 0955 E-mail peter.rouch@winchester.anglican.org

ROULSTON, Joseph Ernest. b 52. BNC Ox BA74 MA78 Lon Univ PhD81 FRSC86 FLS94 FIBiol01 FRCPath01 CSci04. Edin Dioc NSM Course 83. **d** 86 **p** 87. C Edin St Hilda 86-88; C Edin St Fillan 86-88; NSM Edin St Mich and All SS 88-97; Dioc Chapl Gen from 96; Assoc P Roslin (Rosslyn Chpl) 99-07; P-in-c from 07. *16 Summerside Street, Edinburgh EH6 4NU* Tel 0131-554 6382 *or* 242 9225 Mobile 07903-969698 E-mail j.e.roulston@ed.ac.uk

ROUND, Keith Leonard. b 49. Sarum & Wells Th Coll 88. **d** 90 **p** 91. C Meir *Lich* 90-95; V Burslem St Werburgh from 95. *The Presbytery, Haywood Road, Stoke-on-Trent ST6 7AH* Tel (01782) 837582

ROUND, Malcolm John Harrison. b 56. Lon Univ BSc77 BA81. Oak Hill Th Coll. **d** 81 **p** 82. C Guildf St Sav w Stoke-next-Guildford 81-85; C Hawkwell *Chelmsf* 85-88; R Balerno *Edin* from 88. *53 Marchbank Drive, Balerno EH14 7ER* Tel 0131-449 4127

ROUNDHILL, Andrew (John). b 65. CCC Cam BA87. Ripon Coll Cuddesdon BTh93. **d** 93 **p** 94. C Lancaster Ch Ch w St Jo and St Anne *Blackb* 93-97; Chapl Loretto Sch Musselburgh 97-02; Chapl Hong Kong Cathl from 02. *D2 On Lee, 2 Mount Davis Road, Pok Fu Lam, Hong Kong, China* Tel (00852) 2817 8774 *or* 2523 4157 E-mail roundhill@netvigator.com

ROUNDTREE, James Clabern (Clay). b 75. Oklahoma Univ BFA98 York Univ MA00. St Steph Ho Ox BA02. **d** 03 **p** 04. C Yarm *York* 03-07; V Ingleby Barwick from 07. *St Francis's House, Barwick Way, Ingleby Barwick, Stockton-on-Tees TS17 0WD* Tel (01642) 760171 E-mail clayroundtree@hotmail.com

ROUNDTREE, Samuel William. b 19. TCD BA42 MA54. CITC 43. **d** 43 **p** 44. C Waterford Ch Ch *C & O* 44-47; I Tallow w Kilwatermoy 47-51; I Kiltegan w Stratford (and Rathvilly from 60) 51-62; Treas Leighlin Cathl 62-78; Preb Ossory Cathl 62-78; I Dunleckney 62-82; Chan Ossory and Leighlin Cathls 78-80; Prec 80-82; I New w Old Ross, Whitechurch, Fethard etc 82-88; Adn Ferns 86-88; rtd 88. *Greystones Nursing Home, Church Road, Greystones, Co Wicklow, Republic of Ireland*

ROUNTREE, The Ven Richard Benjamin. b 52. NUI BA73. CITC 76. **d** 76 **p** 77. C Orangefield *D & D* 76-80; C Dublin Zion Ch *D & G* 80-83; I Dalkey St Patr 83-97; I Powerscourt w Kilbride from 97; Dioc Dir Decade of Evang 90-96; Can Ch Ch Cathl Dublin from 92; Treas from 04; Dioc Dir Lay Min 05-09; Adn Glendalough from 09. *Powerscourt Rectory, Enniskerry, Bray, Co Wicklow, Republic of Ireland* Tel and fax (00353) (1) 286 3534 Mobile 87-276 7564 E-mail rbrountree@gmail.com

ROUSE, Graham. b 58. Sheff City Coll of Educn CertEd79 Leic Univ DipEd84. Cranmer Hall Dur 90. **d** 92 **p** 93. C Longridge *Blackb* 92-96; P-in-c Fairhaven 96-97; V 97-07; P-in-c Blackpool St Mary 07-10; P-in-c S Shore St Pet 07-10; P-in-c S Shore H Trin 08-10; Perm to Offic from 10. *36 Canterbury Street, Chorley PR6 0LN* Tel (01257) 265996 E-mail revg.rouse@btinternet.com

ROUT, Thomas. b 78. Univ Coll Lon BA02. Wycliffe Hall Ox BA10. **d** 11. C Rothley *Leic* from 11. *11 Oldfield Lane, Rothley, Leicester LE7 7QD* Tel 07791-122331 (mobile) E-mail tomrout@gmail.com

ROUTH, Canon Eileen Rosemary. b 41. Cant Sch of Min 82. **dss** 85 **d** 87 **p** 94. Folkestone St Sav *Cant* 85-90; Par Dn 87-90; Par Dn Woodnesborough w Worth and Staple 90-91; Dn-in-c 91-94; V 94-96; V Maidstone St Martin 96-99; Hon Can Cant Cathl 99; rtd 99; Perm to Offic *Cant* from 00. *121 Rough Common Road, Canterbury CT2 9DA* Tel (01227) 464052

ROUTH, William John. b 60. Magd Coll Ox BA81 MA92. Ripon Coll Cuddesdon 93. **d** 95 **p** 96. C Longton *Blackb* 95-99; V Sutton Coldfield St Chad *Birm* 99-06; P-in-c from 06; P-in-c Sutton Coldfield H Trin from 06. *Holy Trinity Rectory, 5 Broome Gardens, Sutton Coldfield B75 7JE* Tel 0121-311 0474 E-mail john.routh@btinternet.com

ROUTLEDGE, Christopher Joseph. b 78. Keele Univ BSc99 SS Mark & Jo Univ Coll Plymouth PGCE01. Oak Hill Th Coll BA08. **d** 08. C Tiverton St Geo and St Paul *Ex* from 08. *St George's Vicarage, St Andrew Street, Tiverton EX16 6PH*

ROUTLEDGE, Christopher Simon Bruce. b 73. Southn Univ BA94. Ripon Coll Cuddesdon 09. **d** 11. C Northfleet and Rosherville *Roch* from 11. *St Mark's Vicarage, 123 London Road, Northfleet, Gravesend DA11 9NH* Tel (01474) 535814 Mobile 07837-177571 E-mail rev.chrisr73@gmail.com

ROW, Mrs Pamela Anne. b 54. Open Univ BA86 MA92 Homerton Coll Cam BEd75. NOC 94. **d** 96 **p** 97. NSM Neston *Ches* 96-01; Chapl Heref Cathl Sch from 02; Min Can Heref Cathl from 04. *4 Harley Court, Hereford HR1 2NA* Tel (01432) 363508 *or* 363522 Fax 363525

ROWAN, Nicholas Edward. b 76. Essex Univ BA. Trin Coll Bris. **d** 06 **p** 07. C Rayleigh *Chelmsf* 06-10; TV from 10. *St Michael's House, Sir Walter Raleigh Drive, Rayleigh SS6 9JB* Tel (01268) 784426 E-mail nickrowan@btinternet.com

ROWBERRY, Christopher Michael. b 58. Univ of Wales (Lamp) MA04 CQSW85. Qu Coll Birm 94. **d** 96 **p** 97. C Lytchett Minster *Sarum* 96-00; TV Totton *Win* 00-10; V Hedge End St Jo from 10. *The Vicarage, Vicarage Drive, Hedge End, Southampton SO30 4DU* Tel (01489) 789578 E-mail chrisrow@btopenworld.com

ROWBERRY, Mrs Karen. b 57. Ex Univ BEd79. STETS 07. **d** 10 **p** 11. NSM Eastleigh *Win* from 10. *The Vicarage, Vicarage Drive, Hedge End, Southampton SO30 4DU* Tel (01489) 789578 Mobile 07976-232259 E-mail karenrow@btinternet.com

ROWBERRY, Michael James. b 46. Sussex Univ BA74. Edin Th Coll 85. **d** 87 **p** 92. C Wolvercote w Summertown *Ox* 87-88; NSM Cov St Fran N Radford 91-95; Perm to Offic 95-98; C Doncaster Intake and Doncaster H Trin *Sheff* 98-00; C-in-c St Edm Anchorage Lane CD 00-06; C Doncaster St Geo from 06. *69 Chequer Road, Doncaster DN1 2AN* Tel (01302) 323392

ROWDON, John Michael Hooker. b 27. Witwatersrand Univ BA52. Ridley Hall Cam 52. **d** 54 **p** 55. C Broadwater St Mary *Chich* 54-56; C Streatham Immanuel w St Anselm *S'wark* 56-59; Nigeria 60-62; C All Hallows Lon Wall 62-66; Warden Toc H Tower Hill 64-66; Australia from 66; rtd 92. *PO Box 678, Ballarat Vic 3350, Australia*

ROWE, Andrew Gidleigh Bruce. b 37. AKC62. St Boniface Warminster. **d** 63 **p** 64. C Midsomer Norton *B & W* 63-68; Chapl RN 68-84; Chapl Heathfield Sch Ascot 84-86; Hon C Winkfield and Cranbourne *Ox* 84-86; TV Wellington and Distr *B & W* 86-95; R Chewton Mendip w Ston Easton, Litton etc 95-96; Perm to Offic *Ex* from 96; rtd 99. *19 Greenway, Crediton EX17 3LP* Tel (01363) 772262

ROWE, Andrew Robert. b 64. Westmr Coll Ox BA85 PGCE86. Ridley Hall Cam 93. **d** 95 **p** 96. C Broadheath *Ches* 95-99; C Ardsley *Wakef* 99-06; Chapl HM Pris Wakef from 06. *HM Prison, 5 Love Lane, Wakefield WF2 9AG* Tel (01924) 246000 Pager 01523-472096 E-mail andyrowe@uwclub.net

ROWE, Canon Bryan. b 50. Carl Dioc Tr Course 87. **d** 90 **p** 91. C Kells *Carl* 90-93; P-in-c Aspatria w Hayton 93-02; R Workington St Mich from 02; P-in-c Distington 06-08; RD Solway 99-08; Hon Can Carl Cathl from 99. *St Michael's Rectory, Dora Crescent, Workington CA14 2EZ* Tel (01900) 602311

ROWE, Christine Elizabeth. b 55. Southn Univ BEd77. Ripon Coll Cuddesdon 83. **dss** 86 **d** 87 **p** 94. Denham *Ox* 86-87; Par Dn 87-89; Par Dn Aylesbury 89; Par Dn Aylesbury w Bierton and Hulcott 89-93; NSM Caversham St Jo 93-99; Chapl HM Pris Reading 93-98; Chapl MU 95-00; Chapl R Berks and Battle Hosps NHS Trust 96-00; P-in-c Vancouver St Thos Canada 00-01; R 01-04; Adn Burrard 04-06; R N Vancouver St Cath from 06. *1062 Ridgewood Drive, North Vancouver BC V7R 1H8, Canada* Tel (001) (604) 987 6307 *or* 985 0666 Fax 980 3868 E-mail stcatherinecr@aol.com

ROWE, David Brian. b 58. Trin Coll Bris 80. **d** 83 **p** 84. C Radipole and Melcombe Regis *Sarum* 83-86; C Cranham Park *Chelmsf* 86-88; Assoc Min and Par Missr Eastrop *Win* 88-92; P-in-c Arborfield w Barkham *Ox* 92-97; Asst Dioc Adv in Evang *S'well* 97-02; P-in-c Wilford 00-06; R 06-08; Warden Lee Abbey from 08. *Garden Lodge, Lee Abbey, Lynton EX35 6JJ* Tel (01598) 752621 *or* 754204 Fax 752619 E-mail warden@leeabbey.org.uk

ROWE, Geoffrey Lewis. b 44. Univ of Wales (Lamp) BA. Ripon Coll Cuddesdon 80. **d** 82 **p** 83. C Milber *Ex* 82-84; TV Withycombe Raleigh 84-90; R Clyst St Mary, Clyst St George etc

90-08; rtd 08. *Odle Hill Cottage, Abbotskerswell, Newton Abbot TQ12 5NW* Tel (01626) 366143

ROWE, George William. b 36. K Alfred's Coll Win CertEd64 BEd82. **d** 07 **p** 08. NSM Week St Mary Circle of Par *Truro* 07-11. *Tanglewood, Long Park Drive, Widemouth Bay, Bude EX23 0AN* Tel (01288) 361712 Mobile 07970-186038 E-mail george@rowe.gs.go-plus.net

ROWE, Miss Joan Patricia. b 54. Trin Coll Bris BA87. **d** 88 **p** 94. C Radstock w Writhlington *B & W* 88-92; C Nailsea H Trin 92-96; P-in-c Shapwick w Ashcott and Burtle 96-07; Master St Jo Hosp Bath 07-09; Perm to Offic *Liv* 10-11; P-in-c Westbury *Heref* from 11; P-in-c Yockleton from 11; P-in-c Worthen from 11. *The Rectory, Westbury, Shrewsbury SY5 9QX* Tel (01743) 885318 E-mail j.rowe91@btinternet.com

ROWE, John Goring. b 23. McGill Univ Montreal BA48 BD51 Selw Coll Cam BA53. Montreal Dioc Th Coll LTh51. **d** 51 **p** 52. C N Clarendon Canada 51; C Trumpington *Ely* 51-53; Hon C Bow Common *Lon* 53-84; rtd 88. *10 Cordelia Street, London E14 6DZ* Tel (020) 7515 4681

ROWE, Peter Anthony. b 46. Univ Coll Dur BA68 Birkb Coll Lon MA91 Heythrop Coll Lon MTh02 St Andr Univ PhD11 Barrister 78 Solicitor 85. SEITE 95. **d** 98 **p** 99. NSM Ashford *Cant* 98-03; Perm to Offic from 04. *22 Blue Field, Ashford TN23 5HP* Tel (01233) 637769 E-mail peterrowe@madasafish.com

ROWE, Philip William. b 57. Southn Univ BSc78 Lambeth STh86. Trin Coll Bris 82. **d** 85 **p** 86. C Tooting Graveney St Nic *S'wark* 85-89; V Abbots Leigh w Leigh Woods *Bris* 89-96; V Almondsbury 96-98; P-in-c Littleton on Severn w Elberton 96-98; V Almondsbury and Olveston from 98, P-in-c Pilning w Compton Greenfield from 10; AD Bris W 00-06. *The Vicarage, Sundays Hill, Almondsbury, Bristol BS32 4DS* Tel (01454) 613223 E-mail office@stmaryssevernside.org.uk

ROWE, Shiela. *See* JOHNSON, Mrs Shiela

ROWE, Canon Stanley Hamilton. b 18. St Pet Hall Ox BA48 MA52. ALCD50. **d** 50 **p** 51. C Leyton St Paul *Chelmsf* 50-52; CMS Nigeria 52-65; P-in-c Becontree St Cedd *Chelmsf* 65-67; Hd of RE Jo Hampden Sch High Wycombe 67-83; Perm to Offic *Ox* 67-84 and from 86; rtd 83; Hon P-in-c Aston Rowant w Crowell *Ox* 84-86; Hon Can Oke-Osun from 94. *37 Greenwood Avenue, Chinnor OX39 4HW* Tel (01844) 351278 E-mail stanleyhrowe@googlemail.com

ROWE, The Ven Stephen Mark Buckingham. b 59. SS Mark & Jo Univ Coll Plymouth BA81. Ripon Coll Cuddesdon 83. **d** 86 **p** 87. C Denham *Ox* 86-89; C Aylesbury w Bierton and Hulcott 89-90; TV 90-93; V Caversham St Jo 93-00; Canada from 00; Sen Chapl Miss to Seafarers 00-01; P-in-c Surrey Epiphany 01-02; R 02-07; Adn Fraser from 07. *1062 Ridgewood Drive, North Vancouver BC V7R 1H8, Canada* Tel (001) (604) 987 6307 *or* tel and fax 588 4511 E-mail rowesmb@aol.com

ROWE, Vanda Sheila. *See* PERRETT, Mrs Vanda Sheila

ROWELL, Canon Alan. b 50. Lon Univ BSc71 AKC71. Trin Coll Bris. **d** 75 **p** 76. C W Hampstead St Cuth *Lon* 75-78; C Camborne *Truro* 78-81; V Pendeen w Morvah from 81; Hon Can Truro Cathl from 03. *The Vicarage, Pendeen, Penzance TR19 7SE* Tel (01736) 788777

✠**ROWELL, The Rt Revd Douglas Geoffrey.** b 43. CCC Cam BA64 MA68 PhD68 Keble Coll Ox DD97. Cuddesdon Coll. **d** 68 **p** 69 **c** 94. Asst Chapl New Coll Ox 68-72; Chapl Keble Coll Ox 72-94; Wiccamical Preb Chich Cathl 81-01; Suff Bp Basingstoke *Win* 94-01; Bp Eur from 01. *Bishop's Lodge, Church Road, Worth, Crawley RH10 7RT, or 14 Tufton Street, London SW1P 3QZ* Tel (01293) 883051 *or* (020) 7898 1155 Fax (01293) 884479 *or* (020) 7898 1166 E-mail bishop.europe@churchofengland.org

ROWELL, Mrs Gillian Margaret. b 56. Lon Bible Coll BA96. SAOMC 97. **d** 99 **p** 00. NSM The Lee *Ox* 99-04; NSM Hawridge w Cholesbury and St Leonard 99-14. *81 Eskdale Avenue, Chesham HP5 3AY* Tel (01494) 772833

ROWETT, David Peter. b 55. Univ Coll Dur BA76. Ripon Coll Cuddesdon 82. **d** 84 **p** 85. C Yeovil *B & W* 84-88; C Yeovil St Mich 88-89; V Fairfield St Matt *Linc* 89-05; P-in-c Barton upon Humber 05-10; V from 10; R Saxby All Saints from 10; V Horkstow from 10; R S Ferriby from 10. *The Vicarage, Beck Hill, Barton-upon-Humber DN18 5EY* Tel (01652) 632202 E-mail david.rowett@aol.com

ROWETT, Mrs Margaret Pettigrew Coupar. b 33. Sarum & Wells Th Coll 84. **dss** 86 **d** 87 **p** 95. Widley w Wymering *Portsm* 86-88; C 87-88; Par Dn Plympton St Mary *Ex* 88-91; rtd 91; NSM St Mewan *Truro* 94-96; Perm to Offic from 97. *Epiphany Cottage, 9 Socotra Drive, Trewoon, St Austell PL25 5SQ* Tel (01726) 71450

ROWLAND, Andrew John William. b 60. STETS 98. **d** 01 **p** 02. C Verwood *Sarum* 01-06; V W Moors from 06. *The Vicarage, 57 Glenwood Road, West Moors, Ferndown BH22 0EN* Tel (01202) 893197

ROWLAND, Prof Christopher Charles. b 47. Ch Coll Cam BA69 MA73 PhD75. Ridley Hall Cam 72. **d** 75 **p** 76. Lect RS Newc Univ 74-79; Hon C Benwell St Jas 75-78; Hon C Gosforth All SS 78-79; Dean Jes Coll Cam 79-91; Asst Lect Div Cam Univ 83-85; Lect Div 85-91; Lic to Offic *Ely* 79-91; Prof of Exegesis of H Scripture Ox Univ from 91; Fell Qu Coll Ox from 91; Can Th Liv Cathl from 05. *Queen's College, Oxford OX1 4AW* Tel (01865) 279120

ROWLAND, Ms Dawn Jeannette. b 38. RSCN61 RGN63. S'wark Ord Course 81. **dss** 84 **d** 87 **p** 94. Par Dn Croydon H Sav *S'wark* 84-89; NSM Riddlesdown 89-08; Perm to Offic from 08. *9 Hartley Hill, Purley CR8 4EP* Tel (020) 8660 6270

ROWLAND, Derek John. b 47. St Jo Coll Nottm 84. **d** 86 **p** 87. C Porchester *S'well* 86-89; V Fairfield *Liv* 89-96; V Buckfastleigh w Dean Prior *Ex* from 96. *The Vicarage, Glebelands, Buckfastleigh TQ11 0BH* Tel (01364) 644228

ROWLAND, Eric Edward James. b 35. Leeds Univ BA62. Coll of Resurr Mirfield 61. **d** 63 **p** 64. C S Kirkby *Wakef* 63-65; C Headingley *Ripon* 65-70; V Osmondthorpe St Phil 70-79; R Sandy *St Alb* 79-00; RD Biggleswade 85-94; rtd 00; Perm to Offic *Ely* from 01. *3 Tower Road, Ely CB7 4HW* Tel (01353) 664359 E-mail erowland@tiscali.co.uk

ROWLAND, Geoffrey Watson. b 17. **d** 55 **p** 56. BCMS Burma 55-65; C Blackheath Park St Mich *S'wark* 65-71; V W Bromwich St Paul *Lich* 71-76; Chapl Community Relns *Lon* 77-83; C Southall Green St Jo 83; rtd 83; Perm to Offic *Lon* 83-05. *3 Amber Court, Longford Avenue, Southall UB1 3QR* Tel (020) 8574 3442

ROWLAND, Jennifer Norah. b 48. Worc Coll of Educn CertEd70 Open Univ BA83 ACIB. WMMTC 96. **d** 99 **p** 00. C Stratford-upon-Avon, Luddington etc *Cov* 99-03; P-in-c Ditton Priors w Neenton, Burwarton etc *Heref* from 03. *The Vicarage, Ditton Priors, Bridgnorth WV16 6SQ* Tel (01746) 712636 E-mail jenny@rowland.entadsl.org

ROWLAND, Mrs June Mary. b 46. SRN67. EMMTC 03. **d** 05 **p** 06. NSM Grantham *Linc* from 05; Chapl United Lincs Hosps NHS Trust from 06. *St Anne's Vicarage, Harrowby Road, Grantham NG31 9ED* Tel (01476) 572380 Mobile 07710-455379 E-mail junerowlandhome@aol.com

ROWLAND, Canon Robert William. b 51. Birm Univ BA72. St Mich Coll Llan 72. **d** 74 **p** 75. C Connah's Quay *St As* 74; C Shotton 74-76; C Llanrhos 76-81; V Dyserth and Trelawnyd and Cwm from 81; AD St As 94-10; Hon Can St As Cathl 08-11; Can Cursal from 11. *The Vicarage, Dyserth, Rhyl LL18 6DB* Tel (01745) 570750

ROWLAND, Sally Margaret. b 58. SEITE. **d** 10 **p** 11. C Melton Mowbray *Leic* from 10. *1 Palmerston Road, Melton Mowbray LE13 0SS* Tel (01664) 564734

ROWLAND, Stanley George. b 48. Middx Univ BA86. NTMTC 95. **d** 98 **p** 99. NSM Enfield St Geo *Lon* 98-02; C Grantham *Linc* 02-03; V Grantham, Earlesfield from 03; P-in-c Grantham St Anne New Somerby and Spitalgate from 10. *St Anne's Vicarage, Harrowby Road, Grantham NG31 9ED* Tel (01476) 572380 E-mail sgrathome@aol.com

ROWLAND JONES, Sarah Caroline. b 59. LVO93 OBE03. Newnham Coll Cam BA80 MA84. St Jo Coll Nottm BTh98. **d** 99 **p** 00. C Wrexham *St As* 99-02; S Africa from 02. *Bishopshaven, PO Box 420, Malmesbury, 7299 South Africa* E-mail sarahrj@surfaid.org *or* justusmm@xsinet.co.za

ROWLANDS, Mrs Alison Mary. b 51. **d** 06 **p** 07. OLM Redland *Bris* from 06. *24 Northumberland Road, Bristol BS6 7BB* Tel 0117-924 3528 Mobile 07749-044041 E-mail alisrow@blueyonder.co.uk

ROWLANDS, The Ven Emyr Wyn. b 42. St Mich Coll Llan 69. **d** 70 **p** 71. C Holyhead w Rhoscolyn *Ban* 70-74; V Bodedern w Llechgynfarwy and Llechylched etc 74-88; R Machynlleth and Llanwrin 88-97; R Machynlleth w Llanwrin and Penegoes 97-10; AD Cyfeiliog and Mawddwy 96-10; Can Ban Cathl 97-03; Can and Preb Ban Cathl 03-10; Adn Meirionnydd 04-10; rtd 10. *2 Ffordd Meillion, Llangristiolus, Bodorgan LL62 5DQ* Tel (01248) 750148

ROWLANDS, Forrest John. b 25. LSE BSc(Econ)51. Chich Th Coll 54. **d** 56 **p** 57. C Hove St Phil *Chich* 56-58; C Haywards Heath St Wilfrid 58-62; R Kingston by Sea 62-74; rtd 90. *11 Granville Terrace, Yeadon, Leeds LS19 7UW* Tel 0113-250 0208

ROWLANDS, Gareth Richard. b 70. Univ of Wales BA93. St Steph Ho Ox BTh93. **d** 96 **p** 97. C Shotton *St As* from 96; TV Wrexham and Chapl Maelor Hosp 00-03; Chapl Co-ord Ches and Ellesmere Port Hosps 03-05; Lead Chapl Princess Alexandra Hosp NHS Trust 05-07; Chapl Papworth Hosp NHS Foundn Trust from 07; Bp's Adv for Health Chapl *Ely* from 09. *Papworth Hospital, Papworth Everard, Cambridge CB3 8RE* Tel (01480) 830541 E-mail gareth.rowlands@papworth.nhs.uk

ROWLANDS, Graeme Charles. b 53. K Coll Lon BD74 AKC74. St Aug Coll Cant 75. **d** 76 **p** 77. C Higham Ferrers w Chelveston *Pet* 76-79; C Gorton Our Lady and St Thos *Man* 79-81; C Reading H Trin *Ox* 81-89; P-in-c Kentish Town St Silas *Lon* 89-92; V 92-98; P-in-c Haverstock Hill H Trin w Kentish Town St Barn 93-98; V Kentish Town St Silas and H Trin w St Barn from 98. *St Silas's House, 11 St Silas's Place, London NW5 3QP* Tel (020) 7485 3727 E-mail ssmktw@gmail.com

ROWLANDS, Mrs Jacqueline Adèle. b 43. Golds Coll Lon CertEd65 BEd72. St Alb Minl Tr Scheme 82. **dss** 85 **d** 87 **p** 05. Bromham w Oakley *St Alb* 85-88; Par Dn 87-88; Par Dn Bromham w Oakley and Stagsden 88-89; Perm to Offic 04-05; Hon C Bedford St Andr from 05. *2A Rosemary Drive, Bromham, Bedford MK43 8PL* Tel (01234) 403841

ROWLANDS, Canon John Henry Lewis. b 47. Univ of Wales (Lamp) BA68 Magd Coll Cam BA70 MA74 Dur Univ MLitt86. Westcott Ho Cam 70. **d** 72 **p** 73. C Aberystwyth *St D* 72-76; Chapl Univ of Wales (Lamp) 76-79; Youth Chapl 76-79; Dir Academic Studies St Mich Coll Llan 79-84; Sub-Warden 84-88; Warden 88-97; Lect Univ of Wales (Cardiff) *Llan* 79-97; Asst Dean 81-83; Dean 93-97; Dean of Div Univ of Wales 91-95; Dir of Ords 85-88; V Whitchurch 97-02; TR from 02; Hon Can Llan Cathl 90-97; Can from 97; Chan from 02; Chapl Cardiff Community Healthcare NHS Trust from 97. *The Vicarage, 6 Penlline Road, Cardiff CF14 2AD* Tel and fax (029) 2062 6072 E-mail office@parishofwhitchurch.freeserve.co.uk

ROWLANDS, Canon Joseph Haydn. b 36. Univ of Wales (Lamp) BA61. **d** 63 **p** 64. C Llanfairisgaer *Ban* 63-68; R Maentwrog w Trawsfynydd 68-75; V Henfynyw w Aberaeron and Llanddewi Aberarth *St D* 75-80; R Trefdraeth *Ban* 80-84; V Llandysul *St D* 84-98; V Llandysul w Bangor Teifi w Henllan etc 98-01; Hon Can St D Cathl 88-90; Can St D Cathl from 90; RD Emlyn 92-01; rtd 01. *1 Llys Ystrad, Johnstown, Carmarthen SA31 3PU*

ROWLANDS, Kenneth Albert. b 41. MA DipAE. NW Ord Course 70. **d** 73 **p** 74. NSM Hoylake *Ches* 73-80; NSM Oxton 80-82; Perm to Offic 82-00; C Stoneycroft All SS *Liv* 92-94; V Mossley Hill St Barn 94-03; rtd 03. *77 Queens Avenue, Meols, Wirral CH47 0LT* Tel 0151-632 3033

ROWLANDS, Marc Alun. b 62. Univ of Wales (Abth) BSc84 St D Coll Lamp MPhil89 PhD95. Wycliffe Hall Ox 97. **d** 99 **p** 00. C Betws w Ammanford *St D* 99-01; C Carmarthen St Pet 01-02; P-in-c Llanpumsaint w Llanllawddog 02-05; TV Cwm Gwendraeth 06-10; TR Trisant from 10. *The Vicarage, 32A Heol y Bryn, Upper Tumble, Llanelli SA14 6DR* Tel (01269) 841358 E-mail marc rowlands@hotmail.com

ROWLANDS, Michael Huw. b 62. Birm Univ BA85 Univ of Wales (Cardiff) BD88. St Mich Coll Llan 85. **d** 88 **p** 89. C Penarth All SS *Llan* 88-91; V Martletwy w Lawrenny and Minwear etc *St D* 91-99; CF 99-02; P-in-c Nolton w Roch *St D* 02-04; R Nolton w Roch and St Lawrence w Ford etc from 04. *Calbern, Simpson Cross, Haverfordwest SA62 6EP* Tel (01437) 710209

ROWLANDS, Robert. b 31. Roch Th Coll. **d** 68 **p** 69. C Hooton *Ches* 68-71; V Stretton 71-88; P-in-c Appleton Thorn and Antrobus 87-88; V Stretton and Appleton Thorn 88-00; rtd 00; Perm to Offic *Carl* from 01. *Uplands, Redhills Road, Arnside, Carnforth LA5 0AS* Tel (01524) 761612

ROWLANDS, Simon David. b 66. **d** 99 **p** 00. C St Peter-in-Thanet *Cant* 99-03; Chapl Cant Ch Ch Univ 03-06; V Bridge *Cant* from 07. *The Vicarage, 23 High Street, Bridge, Canterbury CT4 5JZ* Tel (01227) 830250

ROWLANDS, Mrs Valerie Christine. b 54. St As Minl Tr Course 99. **d** 02 **p** 03. NSM Llanbedr DC w Llangynhafal, Llanychan etc *St As* 02-04; Chapl St As Cathl from 04; TV St As from 06. *Cefn Coed, Upper Denbigh Road, St Asaph LL17 0RR* Tel (01745) 583264

ROWLES, Mrs Carol. **d** 06 **p** 07. NSM Worcester Park Ch Ch w St Phil *S'wark* from 06. *23 Delcombe Avenue, Worcester Park KT4 8NY* Tel (020) 8330 2068

ROWLEY, Preb Christopher Francis Elmes. b 48. St Jo Coll Dur BA70 St Luke's Coll Ex PGCE71. St Steph Ho Ox 76. **d** 78 **p** 79. C Parkstone St Pet w Branksea and St Osmund *Sarum* 78-81; TV 82-85; P-in-c Chard Gd Shep Furnham *B & W* 85-89; P-in-c Dowlishwake w Chaffcombe, Knowle St Giles etc 88-89; R Chard, Furnham w Chaffcombe, Knowle St Giles etc 89-91; V Stoke St Gregory w Burrowbridge and Lyng 91-04; RD Taunton 01-04; TV Wellington and Distr from 04; RD Tone from 07; Preb Wells Cathl from 09. *All Saints' Vicarage, 62 Rockwell Green, Wellington TA21 9BX* Tel (01823) 662742 E-mail christopherrowley@uwclub.net

ROWLEY, David Michael. b 39. NOC 87. **d** 90 **p** 91. C Stainland *Wakef* 90-93; V Hayfield *Derby* 93-99; P-in-c Chinley w Buxworth 98-99; V Glossop 99-04; RD Glossop 96-04; rtd 04; Perm to Offic *Derby* from 04. *8 Weavers Close, Belper DE56 0HZ* Tel (01773) 882690

ROWLEY, Jennifer Jane Elisabeth. b 61. LMH Ox BA84 MA92. EAMTC 99. **d** 02 **p** 03. C Kingsthorpe w Northampton St Dav *Pet* 02-04; C Kettering SS Pet and Paul 04-06; P-in-c Nettleham *Linc* from 06; P-in-c Welton and Dunholme w Scothern from 10. *The Vicarage, 2 Vicarage Lane, Nettleham, Lincoln LN2 2RH* Tel (01522) 754752 E-mail jennyrowley@waitrose.com

ROWLEY, John. b 47. **d** 05 **p** 06. OLM Mitford and Hebron *Newc* from 05. *Thistledene, Fulbeck, Morpeth NE61 3JU* Tel (01670) 515915 E-mail john.rowley1@btinternet.com

ROWLEY, Mrs Susan. b 49. **d** 01 **p** 02. OLM Fazeley *Lich* 01-11; rtd 11. *137 Reindeer Road, Fazeley, Tamworth B78 3SP* Tel (01827) 250431 *or* 289414 E-mail s.rowley2@sky.com

ROWLEY-BROOKE, Canon Marie Gordon. b 46. ARIAM69. Ripon Coll Cuddesdon 00. **d** 02 **p** 03. C Leckhampton SS Phil and Jas w Cheltenham St Jas *Glouc* 02-05; I Nenagh *L & K* from 05; Can Limerick Cathl from 10. *St Mary's Rectory, Church Road, Nenagh, Co Tipperary, Republic of Ireland* Tel (00353) (67) 32598 E-mail revdmarie@eircom.net

ROWLING, Canon Catherine. b 55. Man Poly BEd77. Westcott Ho Cam 83 NEOC 85. **dss** 86 **d** 87 **p** 94. Gt Ayton w Easby and Newton-in-Cleveland *York* 86-89; Par Dn 87-89; Chapl Teesside Poly 89-92; Chapl Teesside Univ 92-96; Dioc Adv for Diaconal Mins 96-98; Dean of Women's Min 98-08; Co Dir of Ords 98-05; Dioc Dir of Ords 05-09; Dioc Moderator Reader Tr 99-04; Dir Reader Studies 05-09; Can and Preb York Minster 01-09; Prin Lindisfarne Regional Tr Partnership from 09; Perm to Offic *York* from 09. *The Rectory, Cemetery Road, Thirsk YO7 1PR* Tel (01845) 522258 Mobile 07714-052282 E-mail cathyrowling@dunelm.org.uk

ROWLING, Canon Richard Francis. b 56. BA. Westcott Ho Cam. **d** 84 **p** 85. C Stokesley *York* 84-87; C Stainton-in-Cleveland 87-90; V New Marske 90-96; V Wilton 92-96; P-in-c Ingleby Greenhow w Bilsdale Priory, Kildale etc 96-98; V 98-03; R Thirsk from 03; Abp's Adv for Rural Affairs from 98; RD Mowbray from 04; Can and Preb York Minster from 10. *The Rectory, Cemetery Road, Thirsk YO7 1PR* Tel (01845) 523183 E-mail richardrowling@dunelm.org.uk

ROWNTREE, Peter. b 47. St D Coll Lamp BA68 Univ of Wales (Cardiff) MA70. St Steph Ho Ox 70. **d** 72 **p** 73. C Stanwell *Lon* 72-75; C Northolt St Mary 75-79; Chapl Ealing Gen Hosp 79-83; Chapl Cherry Knowle Hosp Sunderland 83-87; Chapl Ryhope Hosp Sunderland 83-87; Chapl Ealing Gen Hosp 87-94; Chapl Ealing Hosp NHS Trust 94-99; Chapl W Lon Healthcare NHS Trust 94-99; Sen Co-ord Chapl Univ Coll Lon Hosps NHS Foundn Trust 99-08; rtd 08; Perm to Offic *Nor* from 08. *4 Chapel Court, Chapel Street, King's Lynn PE30 1EG*

ROWSELL, Canon John Bishop. b 25. Jes Coll Cam BA49 MA55. Ely Th Coll 49. **d** 51 **p** 52. C Hackney Wick St Mary of Eton w St Aug *Lon* 51-55; C Is of Dogs Ch Ch and St Jo w St Luke 55-56; C Reading St Mary V *Ox* 56-59; V Hightown *Wakef* 59-69; R Harlton *Ely* 69-81; V Haslingfield 69-81; V Methwold 81-95; RD Feltwell 81-95; R Northwold 82-95; Hon Can Ely Cathl 84-99; P-in-c Hockwold w Wilton 95-99; P-in-c Weeting 95-99; Perm to Offic from 00. *Reed House, High Street, Hilgay, Downham Market PE38 0LH* Tel (01366) 387662

ROWSON, Frank. b 40. CEng67 MIStructE67. Sarum & Wells Th Coll 87. **d** 90 **p** 91. NSM Ore Ch Ch *Chich* 90-98; NSM Fairlight, Guestling and Pett 98-00; rtd 00; Perm to Offic *Chich* from 01. *149 Priory Road, Hastings TN34 3JD* Tel (01424) 439802

ROWSON, Mrs Rhoda Lyn. b 63. RGN86. Qu Coll Birm 06. **d** 09 **p** 10. NSM Coseley Ch Ch *Worc* from 09. *54 Grenville Road, Dudley DY1 2NE* Tel (01384) 829868 E-mail lyn63@blueyonder.co.uk

✠**ROWTHORN, The Rt Revd Jeffery William.** b 34. Ch Coll Cam BA57 MA62 Union Th Sem (NY) BD61 Oriel Coll Ox BLitt72 Berkeley Div Sch DD87. Cuddesdon Coll 61. **d** 62 **p** 63 **c** 87. C Woolwich St Mary w H Trin *S'wark* 62-65; R Garsington *Ox* 65-68; Chapl and Dean Union Th Sem NY USA 68-73; Assoc Prof Past Th Yale and Berkeley Div Schs 73-87; Suff Bp Connecticut 87-93; Bp in Charge Convocation of American Chs in Eur 94-01; Asst Bp Eur 95-01; Asst Bp Spain 97-01; Asst Bp Portugal 97-01; rtd 01. *17 Woodland Drive, Salem CT 06420-4023, USA* Tel (001) (860) 859 3377 E-mail jefferyrowthorn@yahoo.com

ROXBY, Gordon George. b 39. Lon Univ BSc61. Coll of Resurr Mirfield 61. **d** 63 **p** 64. C Fleetwood St Pet *Blackb* 63-66; C Kirkham 66-68; V Runcorn St Jo Weston *Ches* 68-78; R Moston St Chad *Man* 78-86; V Bury St Pet 86-99; AD Bury 86-96; Hon Can Man Cathl 97-99; V Sandiway *Ches* 99-05; Initial Minl Tr Officer 99-04; rtd 05; Perm to Offic *Ches* from 05. *16 St Joseph's Way, Nantwich CW5 6TE* Tel (01270) 619898 E-mail gordon@roxbylife.org.uk

ROY, Jennifer Pearl. *See* DREW, Mrs Jennifer Pearl

ROYALL, Preb Arthur Robert. b 19. Lambeth MA. Qu Coll Birm 51. **d** 53 **p** 54. C Ashford St Matt *Lon* 53-56; V Heap Bridge *Man* 56-59; V Whitton St Aug *Lon* 59-64; R Poplar All SS w St Frideswide 64-71; P-in-c Bromley St Mich 64-71; P-in-c Poplar St Sav w St Gabr and St Steph 68-71; R Poplar 71-73; R Bow w Bromley St Leon 73-76; P-in-c Mile End Old Town H Trin 73-76; P-in-c Bethnal Green St Barn 73-75; RD Poplar 65-66; RD Tower Hamlets 68-76; Preb St Paul's Cathl 73-86; Clergy Appts Adv 76-85; Perm to Offic *Nor* 77-98, *Ely* 78-98 and *Lon* 86-91; rtd 86. *4 Manormead Nursing Home, Tilford Road, Hindhead GU26 6RA* Tel (01428) 608755 E-mail arthur@royall.co.uk

ROYDEN, Charles. b 60. Wycliffe Hall Ox BA86 MA91. **d** 87 **p** 88. C Bidston *Ches* 87-91; V N Brickhill and Putnoe *St Alb* 91-92; V Bedf St Mark from 93. *The Vicarage, Calder Rise, Bedford MK41 7UY* Tel and fax (01234) 342613 *or* tel 309175 Mobile 07973-113861 E-mail vicar@thisischurch.com

ROYDEN, Eric Ramsay. b 29. St Deiniol's Hawarden 75. **d** 77 **p** 78. Hon C Tranmere St Paul w St Luke *Ches* 77-81; C Eastham 81; V New Brighton All SS 81-95; P-in-c 95-97; rtd 95; Perm to Offic *Ches* 97-07. *84 Asgard Drive, Bedford MK41 0UT* Tel (01234) 294496 E-mail eroyden@googlemail.com

ROYDEN, Ross Eric. b 55. Lon Bible Coll BA77 Nottm Univ MTh82. Wycliffe Hall Ox 79. **d** 81 **p** 82. C Moreton *Ches* 81-84; Chapl and Tutor Bedf Coll of HE *St Alb* 84-93; R Banchory *Ab* 93-00; R Kincardine O'Neil 93-00; V Kowloon Tong Ch Ch Hong Kong from 00. *Christ Church Vicarage, 2 Derby Road, Kowloon Tong, Kowloon, Hong Kong* Tel (00852) 2338 4433 Fax 2338 8422 E-mail rossroyden@aol.com

ROYLANCE, Mrs Margaret. b 47. St Mary's Coll Chelt CertEd68. Cant Sch of Min 93. **d** 96 **p** 97. NSM Tenterden and Smallhythe *Cant* from 96; Chapl Ashford Sch 96-10. *5 Southgate Road, Tenterden TN30 7BS* Tel (01580) 762332 Fax 765267 E-mail johnsroylance@btopenworld.com

ROYLE, Antony Kevan. b 50. Lon Univ BSc71 FIA76. Trin Coll Bris 76. **d** 79 **p** 80. C Chell *Lich* 79-82; C Leyland St Andr *Blackb* 82-86; V Blackb Sav 86-95; Chapl Blackb R Infirmary and Park Lee Hosp 86-95; Chapl E Lancs Hospice 86-95; TR Walton H Trin *Ox* 95-01; NSM Wendover Deanery from 01. *4 Darley Close, Aylesbury HP21 7EA* Tel (01296) 582470 Mobile 07796-143905

ROYLE, Michael Arthur. b 38. Univ of Wales (Ban) BSc61. St Jo Coll Nottm 81. **d** 82 **p** 83. C Boulton *Derby* 82-85; C Belper 85-87; P-in-c Smalley and Morley 87-95; RD Heanor 89-94; V Charlesworth and Dinting Vale 95-02; rtd 02; Perm to Offic *Ches* from 02 and *Derby* from 03. *Kaiama, 55 Cross Lane, Marple, Stockport SK6 7PZ* Tel 0161-427 6453

ROYLE, Canon Peter Sydney George. b 34. K Coll Lon BD57 AKC57. **d** 58 **p** 59. C St Helier *S'wark* 58-62; C Alice Springs Australia 62-63; R 63-68; Can Darwin 68; P-in-c Sydenham St Phil *S'wark* 69-72; V Leigh Park *Portsm* 72-85; RD Havant 77-82; V S w N Hayling 85-96; V S Hayling 96-97; Hon Can Portsm Cathl 95-97; rtd 97; Perm to Offic *Ex* 97-06 and *Sarum* from 06. *12 Jackson Close, Devizes SN10 3AP* Tel (01380) 720405 E-mail george.royle.1@btinternet.com

ROYLE, Canon Roger Michael. b 39. AKC61 Lambeth MA90. **d** 62 **p** 63. C Portsea St Mary *Portsm* 62-65; C St Helier *S'wark* 65-68; Succ S'wark Cathl 68-71; Warden Eton Coll Dorney Par Project *Ox* 71-74; Conduct Eton Coll 74-79; Lic to Offic *S'wark* 79-90; Chapl Ld Mayor Treloar Coll Alton 90-92; Hon C Froyle and Holybourne *Win* 90-92; Hon Can and Chapl S'wark Cathl 93-99; Perm to Offic from 99; rtd 04. *Address withheld by request*

ROYLE, Canon Stanley Michael. b 43. K Coll Lon BD69 AKC69 Man Univ MA75. St Aug Coll Cant 71. **d** 72 **p** 73. C Timperley *Ches* 72-76; Perm to Offic 76-81; R Milton Abbas, Hilton w Cheselbourne etc *Sarum* 81-86; Dir of Ords 86-01; Adv on CME 86-98; Can and Preb Sarum Cathl from 89; Bp's Dom Chapl 98-01; Lic to Offic from 01. *Three Firs, Blandford Road, Sturminster Marshall, Wimborne BH21 4AF* Tel (01258) 857326

RUAHA, Bishop of. See MTETEMELA, The Rt Revd Donald Leo

RUCK, John. b 47. Bris Univ BSc68 Birm Univ MPhil92. All Nations Chr Coll MA03. **d** 80 **p** 83. OMF Internat from 78; Indonesia 80-86 and 87-91; Perm to Offic *Birm* 86-87 and 91-98; Lic to Offic from 03; Lect Crowther Hall CMS Tr Coll Selly Oak 00-04; CMS from 04. *121 Bournbrook Road, Birmingham B29 7BY* Tel 0121-415 4036 E-mail johnnane@ruckja.freeserve.co.uk

RUDALL, Mark Edward. b 53. Regent's Park Coll Ox BA80 MA84. Ripon Coll Cuddesdon 00. **d** 01 **p** 02. In Bapt Min 80-00; C Wallingford *Ox* 01-03; Dioc Dir Communications *Guildf* from 04. *Diocesan House, Quarry Street, Guildford GU1 3XG* Tel (01483) 790310 Fax 790311 Mobile 07779-654975 E-mail mark.rudall@cofeguildford.org.uk *or* mark.rudall@ntlworld.com

RUDD, Carl Nigel. b 71. Salford Univ BSc93 PhD97. Trin Coll Bris BA06. **d** 06 **p** 07. C Whitstable *Cant* 06-10; C Penn Fields *Lich* from 10. *100 Bellencroft Gardens, Wolverhampton WV3 8DU* Tel (01902) 766929 E-mail carl.rudd@googlemail.com

RUDD, Charles Robert Jordeson. b 34. TCD BA56 MA65 BD65. **d** 57 **p** 58. C Lurgan Redeemer *D & D* 57-61; C Lisburn Ch Ch Cathl 61-62; C Willowfield *D & D* 62-66; I Drumgooland w Kilcoo 66-75; I Moira 75-95; I Magherally w Annaclone 95-02; Can Belf Cathl 90-02; rtd 02. *12 Thorn Heights, Banbridge BT32 4BF* Tel (028) 4062 8995

RUDD, Colin Richard. b 41. AKC64. **d** 65 **p** 66. C N Stoneham *Win* 65-70; V Rotherwick, Hook and Greywell 70-74; R Hook w Greywell 74-78; Toc H 78-89; V Buckland *Ox* 89-98; V Littleworth 89-98; R Pusey 89-98; R Gainfield 98-99; RD Vale of White Horse 96-99; rtd 99; Perm to Offic *B & W* from 06. *Alcudia, Bilbrook, Minehead TA24 6HE* Tel (01984) 640021

RUDD, Robert. See RUDD, Charles Robert Jordeson

RUDD, Robert Arthur. b 33. ALCD60. **d** 60 **p** 61. C Blackb Sav 60-63; C Huyton St Geo *Liv* 63-65; V Bickershaw 65-72; Asst Chapl HM Pris Liv 72-73; Birm 73-78; Parkhurst 78-86; Camp

Hill 86-92; Chapl St Mary's Hosp Newport 92-95; rtd 95; Perm to Offic *Portsm* from 95. *The Elms, 13 Horsebridge Hill, Newport PO30 5TJ* Tel (01983) 524415

RUDD, Mrs Sonia Winifred. b 44. Nottm Univ BSc66 Leeds Univ MSc68. Ox Min Course 92. **d** 94 **p** 95. NSM Ox St Andr 94-96; C Buckland 96-99; Perm to Offic *B & W* from 06. *Alcudia, Bilbrook, Minehead TA24 6HE* Tel (01984) 640021 Mobile 07886-451743 E-mail soniahall55@aol.com

RUDDICK, David Mark. b 76. Pemb Coll Cam BA98 Homerton Coll Cam PGCE99. Oak Hill Th Coll BA09. **d** 09 **p** 10. C Elmswell *St E* from 09. *25 Crown Mill, Elmswell, Bury St Edmunds IP30 9GF* Tel (01359) 241277 Mobile 07761-320736 E-mail davidruddick.online@googlemail.com

RUDDLE, Canon Donald Arthur. b 31. MBE04. Linc Th Coll 64. **d** 66 **p** 67. C Kettering SS Pet and Paul 66-70; V Earlham St Anne *Nor* 70-79; V E Malling *Roch* 79-95; RD Malling 84-93; Hon Can Roch Cathl 88-95; Chapl Nord Pas de Calais *Eur* 95-98; rtd 98; Perm to Offic *Eur* from 98 and *Cant* from 05. *Sycamore Lodge, 5 Windmill Lane, Faversham ME13 7GT* Tel (01795) 533461 E-mail don.ruddle@talktalk.net

RUDDOCK, Brian John. b 45. Dur Univ BA66 Nottm Univ MEd91. Westcott Ho Cam 67. **d** 69 **p** 70. C Ross *Heref* 69-72; C Kettering SS Pet and Paul 72-75; P-in-c Colchester St Steph *Chelmsf* 75-77; TR Colchester St Leon, St Mary Magd and St Steph 77-84; R March St Pet *Ely* 84-89; R March St Mary 84-89; RD March 87-89; Bp's Officer for Unemployment *Sheff* 89-94; Resource and Development Officer CCWA 96-02; Lic to Offic from 96; Perm to Offic *Sarum* from 07; rtd 09. *5 Springers Close, Devizes SN10 3SG* E-mail brianjruddock@btinternet.com

RUDDOCK, Bruce. See RUDDOCK, Canon Reginald Bruce

RUDDOCK, Charles Cecil. b 28. TCD Div Sch. **d** 57 **p** 58. C Belfast St Mary *Conn* 57-59; C Carnmoney 59-61; C Belfast St Aid 61-63; I Kiltegan w Rathvilly *C & O* 63-69; C Newtownards *D & D* 69-72; R Beaconsfield w Exeter Australia 72-77; R Sandford 77-83; I Mallow Union *C, C & R* 83-89; I Fenagh w Myshall, Aghade and Ardoyne *C & O* 89-95; Can Ossory and Leighlin Cathls 92-95; rtd 95; Perm to Offic *Glouc* 95-05. *11 Bevis Court, Bibra Lake, Perth WA 6163, Australia*

RUDDOCK, Edgar Chapman. b 48. St Jo Coll Dur BA70 MA76. Cranmer Hall Dur 70. **d** 74 **p** 75. C Birm St Geo 74-78; R 78-83; Dir Tr Dio St Jo S Africa 83-86; P-in-c Mandini 86-87; Prov Dir Tr 88-91; TR Stoke-upon-Trent *Lich* 91-02; Internat Relns Sec USPG from 03. *USPG, 200 Dover Street, London SE1 4YB* Tel (020) 7378 5678 E-mail edrud@cix.co.uk

RUDDOCK, Kenneth Edward. b 30. TCD BA52 QUB MTh79. CITC 53 Div Test. **d** 53 **p** 54. C Ballymena *Conn* 53-56; C Belfast St Thos 56-60; I Tomregan w Drumlane *K, E & A* 60-68; I Belfast St Luke *Conn* 68-80; Miss to Seamen 80-96; I Whitehead and Islandmagee *Conn* 80-96; Can Lisburn Cathl 90-96; Dioc Info Officer from 90; Chan Conn Cathl 96; rtd 96; Dioc C *Conn* from 98. *24 Fourtowns Manor, Aghoghill, Ballymena BT42 1RS* Tel (028) 2587 8966 Mobile 07970-639067

RUDDOCK, Leonard William. b 58. CITC 90. **d** 94 **p** 95. NSM Roscrea w Kyle, Bourney and Corbally *L & K* 94-06; C Stillorgan w Blackrock *D & G* 06-08; I Blessington w Kilbride, Ballymore Eustace etc from 08. *The Rectory, 13 Ashton, Blessington, Co Wicklow, Republic of Ireland* Tel (00353) (45) 865178 Mobile 87-764 3296 E-mail leonardruddock@gmail.com

RUDDOCK, Canon Reginald Bruce. b 55. AGSM72. Chich Th Coll. **d** 83 **p** 84. C Felpham w Middleton *Chich* 83-86; C Portsea St Mary *Portsm* 86-88; P-in-c Barnes St Mich *S'wark* 88-95; Dir Angl Cen Rome 95-99; Hon Can American Cathl Paris from 96; Can Res Worc Cathl 99-04; Can Res Pet Cathl from 04; Liturg Officer from 04; Chapl to The Queen from 08. *The Chapter Office, Minster Precincts, Peterborough PE1 1XS* Tel (01733) 343342 *or* 355310 Fax 355316 E-mail bruce.ruddock@peterborough-cathedral.org.uk

RUDEN, Lars Olav. b 43. **d** 00 **p** 01. OLM Bamford *Man* 00-05; P-in-c Healey from 05. *Healey Vicarage, 10 Healey Avenue, Rochdale OL12 6EG* Tel (01706) 657386 Mobile 07743-509193 E-mail larsruden.norge@virgin.net

RUDGE, Colin. b 48. Open Univ BA04. Wilson Carlile Coll 96 SEITE 08. **d** 10 **p** 11. C Hollington St Jo *Chich* from 10. *227 Hillside Road, Hollington, Hastings TN34 2QY* Tel (01424) 751799 Mobile 07967-778765 E-mail colin.rudge@gmail.com

RUDGE, Miss Susannah Mary. b 84. Trin Coll Ox BA05 MA10 Jes Coll Cam MPhil10. Westcott Ho Cam 08. **d** 10 **p** 11. C Bournville *Birm* from 10. *63 Linden Road, Bournville, Birmingham B30 1JT* E-mail susannah.rudge@gmail.com

RUDIGER, David John. b 42. MCMI91. Ox Min Course 91. **d** 94 **p** 95. NSM Woughton *Ox* 94-11; rtd 11. *56 Kirtlington, Downhead Park, Milton Keynes MK15 9AZ* Tel (01908) 668474 E-mail david@rudiger2.freeserve.co.uk

RUDKIN, Simon David. b 51. Bradf Univ BA74 K Coll Lon BD77 AKC77. Coll of Resurr Mirfield 77. **d** 78 **p** 79. C Flixton St Mich *Man* 78-81; C Atherton 81-84; V Lever Bridge 84-91; P-in-c Pennington w Lindal and Marton *Carl* 91-96; P-in-c

721

Pennington and Lindal w Marton and Bardsea 96-00; V Morland, Thrimby, Gt Strickland and Cliburn 00-09; P-in-c Kirkby Thore w Temple Sowerby and Newbiggin 04-07; P-in-c Bolton and Crosby Ravensworth 05-09; R Bedale and Leeming and Thornton Watlass *Ripon* 09-11; R The Thorntons and The Otteringtons *York* from 11; Chapl N Yorks Police from 11. *The Vicarage, 4 Endican Lane, Thornton le Moor, Northallerton DL7 9FB* Tel (01609) 761806
E-mail sd.rudkin@btinternet.com

RUDMAN, Preb David Walter Thomas. b 48. Oak Hill Th Coll BD72. **d** 72 **p** 73. C Plymouth St Jude *Ex* 72-75; C Radipole *Sarum* 76-77; Warden St Geo Ho Braunton 77-03; R Georgeham *Ex* 88-03; Dioc Adv in Adult Tr 97-03; TV S Molton w Nymet St George, High Bray etc from 03; Dioc Adv in OLM from 03; Preb Ex Cathl from 09. *The Rectory, Kingsnymphton, Umberleigh EX37 9ST* Tel (01769) 580457
E-mail davidrudman@ntlworld.com

RUE, Kenneth. TCD BBS75. **d** 10. NSM Powerscourt w Kilbride *D & G* from 10. *9 Kingston Crescent, Dundrum, Dublin 16, Republic of Ireland* Tel (00353) (1) 298 9497 Mobile 87-656 5698
E-mail krue@eircom.net

RUEHORN, Eric Arthur. b 33. St Aid Birkenhead 58. **d** 61 **p** 62. C Harpurhey Ch Ch *Man* 61-65; V Roughtown 65-74; V Hawkshaw Lane 74-99; rtd 99; Perm to Offic *Man* from 00. *29 Hunstanton Drive, Bury BL8 1EG* Tel 0161-761 3983

RUFF, Brian Chisholm. b 36. Lon Univ BD66 ACA60 FCA70. Oak Hill Th Coll 63. **d** 67 **p** 68. C Cheadle *Ches* 67-72; Educn and Youth Sec CPAS 72-76; V New Milverton *Cov* 76-90; V Westbourne Ch Ch Chpl *Win* 90-01; rtd 02; Perm to Offic *Win* from 02 and *Sarum* from 03. *19 Hardy Road, West Moors, Wimborne BH22 0EX* Tel (01202) 868733
E-mail bcr@ruffys.fsnet.co.uk

RUFF, Michael Ronald. b 49. K Coll Lon BD72 AKC72 Ch Ch Coll Cant PGCE77. St Aug Coll Cant 72. **d** 73 **p** 74. C Old Shoreham *Chich* 73-76; Chapl Ellesmere Coll 77-81; Chapl Grenville Coll Bideford 81-87; Chapl Stamford Sch 87-06; P-in-c Stamford St Mary and St Martin *Linc* from 06; Confrater Browne's Hosp Stamford from 11. *3 Baxters Lane, Easton on the Hill, Stamford PE9 3NH* Tel (01780) 766567

RUFFLE, Preb John Leslie. b 43. ALCD66. **d** 66 **p** 67. C Eastwood *S'well* 66-70; C Keynsham w Queen Charlton *B & W* 70-75; P-in-c Weston-super-Mare Em 75; TV Weston-super-Mare Cen Par 75-84; V Yatton Moor 84-91; TR 91-98; P-in-c Chew Stoke w Nempnett Thrubwell 98-03; Dioc Adv in Past Care and Counselling 03-06; rtd 06; Perm to Offic *B & W* from 06; Preb Wells Cathl from 97. *52 Highbridge Road, Burnham-on-Sea TA8 1LN* Tel (01278) 788322
E-mail john-ruffles01.freeserve.co.uk

RUFFLE, Wendy Ann. **d** 10 **p** 11. NSM Tewkesbury w Walton Cardiff and Twyning *Glouc* from 10. *High Bank, Gambles Lane, Cleeve Hill, Cheltenham GL52 3QA* Tel (01242) 674103
E-mail wendyruffle@btinternet.com

RUFLI, Alan John. b 63. TCD BA89. **d** 91 **p** 92. C Donaghcloney w Waringstown *D & D* 91-94; C Knock 94-95; I Rathcoole *Conn* 95-01; I Holmpatrick w Balbriggan and Kenure *D & G* 01-10; I Clondalkin w Rathcoole from 10. *St John's Rectory, 5 Monastery Road, Clondalkin, Dublin 22, Republic of Ireland* Tel (00353) (1) 459 2160 Mobile 78-997 2401 E-mail rufrev@aol.com

RUGEN, Peter. b 60. Crewe & Alsager Coll BEd86. Trin Coll Bris MA00. **d** 00 **p** 01. C Shipley St Pet *Bradf* 00-04; P-in-c Riddlesden and Morton St Luke 04-08; P-in-c Norley, Crowton and Kingsley Ches from 08. *St John's House, Pike Lane, Kingsley, Frodsham WA6 8EH* Tel (01928) 787180
E-mail peter.rugen1@tiscali.co.uk

RUGG, Andrew Philip. b 47. Kent Univ BA82. Sarum & Wells Th Coll 83. **d** 85 **p** 86. C Harlesden All So *Lon* 85-90; TV Benwell *Newc* 90-97; V Weetslade 97-00; rtd 00; Perm to Offic *York* from 00. *36 Whenby Grove, York YO31 9DS* Tel and fax (01904) 652567 Mobile 07980-390051

RUGG, Christopher James McTeer. b 75. St Jo Coll Dur BSc97. Trin Coll Bris 06. **d** 08 **p** 09. C Week St Mary Circle of Par *Truro* 08-11; USA from 11. *4104 Tiffany Lane, Redding CA 96002, USA* Tel (001) (503) 233 3833 E-mail cjmrugg@gmail.com

RUGMAN, Mrs Hazel. b 47. R Holloway Coll Lon BA68 ACIS89. NOC 01. **d** 03 **p** 04. NSM Sandbach *Ches* 03-06; NSM Crewe St Andr w St Jo from 06; NSM Crewe Ch Ch from 07. *High Trees, 157 Sandbach Road North, Alsager, Stoke-on-Trent ST7 2AX* Tel (01270) 876386 Fax 883737 Mobile 07762-706120
E-mail hazelrugman@btinternet.com

✠**RUHUMULIZA, The Rt Revd Jonathan.** b 56. Makumira Univ Coll Tanzania BD89. Butare Th Sch Rwanda 78. **d** 82 **p** 83 **c** 91. C Kigeme Rwanda 82-84; Manager and Chapl Kigeme High Sch 83-86 and 90-91; Manager and Chapl Kigeme Hosp 89-90; Asst Bp Butare 91-92; Prov Sec 92-93; Asst Bp Kigali 93; Coadjutor Bp 93-95; Bp 95-97; Miss Bp Cameroon 98-04; Hon Asst Bp *Worc* 05-06; Hon Asst Bp *Worc* from 05. *6 Riverside Way, Droitwich, Worcester WR9 8UP* Tel (01905) 799329
E-mail bspjrmuliza@yahoo.co.uk

RUITERS, Ivan John. b 61. Coll of Transfiguration Grahamstown 94. **d** 96 **p** 97. C Berea S Africa 96-00; R Maidstone 00-01; R Newlands 02-07; I Killesher *K, E & A* from 07. *The New Rectory, Tully, Enniskillen BT92 1FN* Tel (028) 6634 8235 Mobile 07902-174219
E-mail ivanruiters@yahoo.com

✠**RUMALSHAH, The Rt Revd Munawar Kenneth (Mano).** b 41. Punjab Univ BSc60 Serampore Coll BD65 Karachi Univ MA68 Homerton Coll Cam PGCE88. Bp's Coll Calcutta 62. **d** 65 **p** 66 **c** 94. C H Trin Cathl Karachi Pakistan 65-69; C Roundhay St Edm *Ripon* 70-73; Area Sec and Asst Home Sec CMS 73-78; Educn Sec BCC 78-81; P-in-c Southall St Geo *Lon* 81-88; Lect Edwardes Coll Peshawar Pakistan 89-94; Bp Peshawar 94-99 and 03-07; Gen Sec USPG and Hon Asst Bp *S'wark* 99-03; rtd 07. *62 Stapleton Close, Marlow SL7 1TZ* Tel (01628) 475889
E-mail bishopmanodop@hotmail.com

RUMBALL, William Michael. b 41. Surrey Univ BSc63 Birm Univ PhD66 Open Univ BA75 MIM66 MINucE73 FIMMM03. Wycliffe Hall Ox 78. **d** 80 **p** 81. C S Molton, Nymet St George, High Bray etc *Ex* 80-83; V S Hetton w Haswell *Dur* 83-90; V S Wingfield and Wessington *Derby* 90-99; rtd 99; Hon C Brailsford w Shirley and Osmaston w Edlaston *Derby* 01-03; Perm to Offic *Derby* from 03; Curch from 08; *B & W* from 10. *Flat 6, 97 Lansdown Lane, Bath BA1 4NB* Tel (01225) 421037
E-mail wm.rumball@gmail.com

RUMBLE, Alison Merle. *See* PRINCE, Mrs Alison Merle

RUMBOLD, Bernard John. b 43. **d** 73 **p** 75. Hon C Alotau Papua New Guinea 73-76; C Gt Burstead *Chelmsf* 76-77; Chapl RAF 77-93; Chapl HM Pris Featherstone 93-95; C Wordsley *Worc* 95-96; TV 96-99; Chapl Dudley Gp of Hosps NHS Trust 96-99; R Teme Valley N *Worc* 99-02; P-in-c Brompton Regis w Upton and Skilgate *B & W* 03-08; P-in-c Gt w Lt Tew and Over w Nether Worton *Ox* 08-10; rtd 11. *6 St David's Drive, Evesham WR11 2AU* E-mail bernardrumbold@btinternet.com

RUMBOLD, Graham Charles. b 44. Open Univ BA79. S Dios Minl Tr Scheme 76. **d** 79 **p** 80. NSM Widley w Wymering *Portsm* 79-82; Chapl Cynthia Spencer Unit Manfield Hosp 82-94; Chapl Northampton Community Healthcare NHS Trust 94-01; Chapl Northants Healthcare NHS Trust 01-04; NSM Weston Favell *Pet* 93-95; NSM Northampton St Matt from 98. *3 Calstock Close, Northampton NN3 3BA* Tel (01604) 627389
E-mail graham.rumbold@yahoo.com

RUMENS, Canon John Henry. b 21. AKC49. **d** 50 **p** 51. C Wareham w Arne *Sarum* 50-54; V Alderholt 54-59; R Salisbury St Edm 59-72; RD Salisbury 69-72; R Trowbridge H Trin 72-79; P-in-c Sturminster Marshall 79-83; V 83-85; Can and Preb Sarum Cathl 72-85; rtd 85; Perm to Offic *Sarum* from 85. *20 Constable Way, Salisbury SP2 8LN* Tel (01722) 334716

RUMENS, Ms Katharine Mary. b 53. UEA BEd76. Westcott Ho Cam 90. **d** 92 **p** 94. Par Dn E Ham w Upton Park *Chelmsf* 92-94; C 94-95; C Waterloo St Jo w St Andr *S'wark* 95-00; Chapl S Bank Cen and Chapl Lon Weekend TV 95-00; R St Giles Cripplegate w St Bart Moor Lane etc *Lon* from 00. *The Rectory, 4 The Postern, Wood Street, London EC2Y 8BJ* Tel and fax (020) 7588 3013 *or* tel 7638 1997
E-mail rumens@stgileschurch.com

RUMING, Canon Gordon William. b 27. Kelham Th Coll 45. **d** 52 **p** 53. C Baildon *Bradf* 52-55; C Prestbury *Glouc* 55-60; C Penzance St Mary *Truro* 60-61; R Calstock 61-92; Hon Can Truro Cathl 79-92; RD E Wivelshire 85-91; rtd 92; Perm to Offic *Truro* from 92 and *Ex* from 99. *3 Derry Avenue, Plymouth PL4 6BH* Tel (01752) 661986

RUMSEY, Andrew Paul. b 68. Reading Univ BA89. Ridley Hall Cam MA98. **d** 97 **p** 98. C Harrow Trin St Mich *Lon* 97-01; V Gipsy Hill Ch Ch *S'wark* 01–11; R Oxted and Tandridge from 11. *Oxted Rectory, 29 Chichele Road, Oxted RH8 0AE* E-mail andrew.rumsey@btinternet.com

RUMSEY, Ian Mark. b 58. Van Mildert Coll Dur BSc79 St Jo Coll Dur BA89. Cranmer Hall Dur 87. **d** 90 **p** 91. C Dalston *Carl* 90-94; C Wreay 92-94; TV Cockermouth w Embleton and Wythop 94-04; Adv for Post-Ord Tr 97-00; V Hurdsfield *Ches* from 04. *197A Hurdsfield Road, Macclesfield SK10 2PX* Tel (01625) 424587

RUNCORN, David Charles. b 54. BA77. St Jo Coll Nottm 77. **d** 79 **p** 80. C Wealdstone H Trin *Lon* 79-82; Chapl Lee Abbey 82-87; C Ealing St Steph Castle Hill *Lon* 89-90; V 90-96; Dir Past and Evang Studies Trin Coll Bris 96-03; Dir Min Development *Lich* 03-08; Perm to Offic *Derby* from 03; Tutor St Jo Coll Nottm from 08. *The Vicarage, 35 Church Street, Littleover, Derby DE23 6GF* Tel (01332) 272184 Mobile 07870-331337
E-mail davidruncorn@mac.com

RUNCORN, Jacqueline Ann. *See* SEARLE, Canon Jacqueline Ann

RUNDELL, Simon Philip. b 67. Univ of N Lon BSc95 Leeds Univ BA01 KGN90. Coll of Resurr Mirfield 99. **d** 01 **p** 02. C Southsea H Spirit *Portsm* 01-04; P-in-c Elson 04-09; V from 09. *St Thomas's Vicarage, 21 Elson Road, Gosport PO12 4BL* Tel (023) 9258 2824 E-mail simon@rundell.org.uk

RUNDLE, Mrs Beryl Rosemary. b 28. Bris Univ BA49 CertEd50. S Dios Minl Tr Scheme 83. **dss** 86 **d** 87. Tangmere *Chich* 86-87; Hon Par Dn 87-92; Boxgrove 86-87; Hon Par Dn 87-92; Hon Par Dn Eastbourne St Sav and St Pet 92-98; Perm to Offic *Portsm* from 98. *22 Sovereign Drive, Southsea PO4 8XX* Tel (01705) 826859

RUNDLE, Hilary. *See* WONG, Hilary

RUNDLE, Nicholas John. b 59. Southn Univ BA80. St Steph Ho Ox BTh84. **d** 84 **p** 85. C E Preston w Kingston *Chich* 84-87; Chapl RAF 87-91; Assoc P Magill Australia 91-93; R Grange 93-98; R Hawthorn 98-02; Chapl Past Care Co-ord Mission Australia from 03. *Mission Australia, PO Box 6626, Adelaide SA 5000, Australia* Tel (0061) (8) 8370 3583 *or* 8223 5428 Fax 8223 6425 Mobile 403-183005 E-mail rundlen@mission.com.au

RUNDLE, Penelope Anne. b 36. St Hugh's Coll Ox MA59. S Dios Minl Tr Scheme 85. **d** 88 **p** 94. Hon Par Dn Mere w W Knoyle and Maiden Bradley *Sarum* 88-91; Hon Par Dn Upper Stour 91-94; Hon C 94-02; rtd 02; Perm to Offic *Sarum* 02-08. *7 Prospect Place, Ann Street, Salisbury SP1 2EA* Tel (01722) 411774

RUNNACLES, Ms Jasmine Celine Leweston. b 47. Lon Bible Coll BA75 RN68. STETS 05. **d** 08 **p** 09. NSM Burpham *Guildf* from 08. *Chydham Cottage, Maybury Hill, Woking GU22 8AF* Tel and fax (01483) 765239 Mobile 07774-171818 E-mail jclrunnacles@tiscali.co.uk

RUSCHMEYER, Henry Cassell. b 44. Union Coll NY BA66 Bank St Coll of Ed NY MEd73 NY Univ MA88. Gen Th Sem (NY) MD78. **d** 78 **p** 79. USA 78-89 and from 97; NSM Wilton Place St Paul *Lon* 89-97. *PO Box 25012, Sarasota FL 34217-2012, USA*

RUSCOE, Canon John Ernest. b 32. Dur Univ BA57. Qu Coll Birm 57. **d** 59 **p** 60. C Jarrow St Paul *Dur* 59-63; C Whitburn 63-65; V S Hylton 65-10; Hon Can Dur Cathl 85-10; rtd 10. *17 Marina Avenue, Sunderland SR6 9AL* Tel 0191-549 8371

RUSDELL-WILSON, Arthur Neville. b 43. Lon Univ BScEng65 Linacre Coll Ox BA70 MA74. St Steph Ho Ox 68. **d** 71 **p** 72. C Whitton St Aug *Lon* 71-73; C Chiswick St Nic w St Mary 73-76; C Littlehampton St Jas *Chich* 76-81; C Littlehampton St Mary 76-81; C Wick 76-81; V Whitworth St Bart *Man* 81-88; V Shaw 88-98; rtd 03. *21 Fairview Avenue, Goring-by-Sea, Worthing BN12 4HT* Tel (01903) 242561

RUSH, Paul Andrew. b 57. Lon Bible Coll BA79 Anglia Poly Univ MA03. Ridley Hall Cam 98. **d** 00 **p** 01. C Bar Hill *Ely* 00-03; Dioc Evang Officer *Leic* 03-06; Adv in Evang and Par Development *Bris* from 06. *5 Gold View, Swindon SN5 8ZG* Tel (01793) 872853 E-mail rev.paul.rush@ntlworld.com

RUSH, Miss Shan Elizabeth. b 64. RGN86 RSCN86. Yorks Min Course 07. **d** 10. NSM Sheff St Mark Broomhill from 10. *28 Rivelin Street, Sheffield S6 5DL* Tel 07598-156817 (mobile) E-mail sh@stmarkssheffield.co.uk

RUSHER, James Victor Francis. b 28. RMA. Ridley Hall Cam 58. **d** 60 **p** 61. C Kensington St Helen w H Trin *Lon* 60-63; C Edgbaston St Bart *Birm* 63-66; V Summerfield 66-71; V Knowle 71-82; Perm to Offic from 82; Chapl Parkway Hosp Solihull 85-93; rtd 93. *4 Froxmere Close, Solihull B91 3XG* Tel 0121-705 4514

RUSHFORTH, Richard Hamblin. b 40. Keble Coll Ox BA62 MA71. Chich Th Coll 62. **d** 64 **p** 65. C St Leonards Ch *Chich* 64-79; Org Sec Fellowship of St Nic 79-81; V Portslade St Nic and St Andr from 81; Min Portslade Gd Shep CD 88-89. *The Vicarage, South Street, Portslade, Brighton BN41 2LE* Tel (01273) 418090

RUSHOLME, Susan. b 53. Leeds Univ BA10. Yorks Min Course 07. **d** 10 **p** 11. NSM Chapel Allerton *Ripon* from 10. *71 Eaton Hill, Leeds LS16 6SE* Tel 0113-261 2913 Mobile 07504-880199 E-mail susan.rusholme@btinternet.com

RUSHTON, Christopher John. b 54. JP89. LBIPP93. **d** 11. OLM Hartshill, Penkhull and Trent Vale *Lich* from 11. *The School House, Vicarage Road, Hartshill, Stoke-on-Trent ST4 7NL* Tel (01782) 410011 E-mail church@chrisrushton.co.uk

RUSHTON, David William. b 70. St Chad's Coll Dur BA96. St Steph Ho Ox. **d** 98 **p** 99. C Hornsey St Mary w St Geo *Lon* 98-01; C Thamesmead *S'wark* 01-02; Asst Chapl King's Coll Hosp NHS Trust 02-04; Chapl 04-10; Lead Chapl and Hospitaller Barts and The Lon NHS Trust from 10. *The Chaplain's Office, The Royal London Hospital, PO Box 59, London E1 1BB* Tel (020) 7377 7385 E-mail david.rushton@bartsandthelondon.nhs.uk

RUSHTON, Canon James David. b 39. Dur Univ BA61. Cranmer Hall Dur. **d** 64 **p** 65. C Upper Armley *Ripon* 64-67; C Blackpool Ch Ch *Blackb* 67-70; V Preston Ch Ch 70-79; V Denton Holme *Carl* 79-96; P-in-c Preston All SS *Blackb* 96-00; V 00-04; AD Preston 98-03; Hon Can Blackb Cathl 00-04; rtd 04; Perm to Offic *Blackb* from 04. *1 Stable Mews, Fleetwood Road, Thornton-Cleveleys FY5 1SQ* Tel (01253) 820402 E-mail james@jamesrushton.wanadoo.co.uk

RUSHTON, Ms Janet Maureen. b 46. Keele Univ BA68 Leic Univ PGCE69. Wycliffe Hall Ox BTh94. **d** 94 **p** 95. C Harrow St Mary *Lon* 94-98; C Putney St Mary *S'wark* 98-02; P-in-c

Wolvercote w Summertown *Ox* 02-07; P-in-c Summertown 07-11; rtd 11. *20 Harvard Court, Honeybourne Road, London NW6 1HJ* Tel (020) 7431 4606 E-mail janrushton@lineone.net

RUSHTON, Malcolm Leslie. b 47. Bris Univ BSc69 Birm Univ PhD72 Fitzw Coll Cam BA74. Ridley Hall Cam 72. **d** 75 **p** 76. C Cullompton *Ex* 75-79; Chapl Univ Coll Lon 79-87; Chapl R Veterinary Coll Lon 87-90; Chapl R Free Medical Sch 87-90. *Flat 3, 13 Belsize Grove, London NW3 4UX* Tel and fax (020) 7722 1989

RUSHTON, Matthew John. b 75. St Anne's Coll Ox BA96 MA01 Solicitor 01. Ripon Coll Cuddesdon 07. **d** 09 **p** 10. C Nettleham *Linc* from 09. *23 Kingsway, Nettleham, Lincoln LN2 2QA*

RUSHTON, Philip William. b 38. Open Univ BA87. Clifton Th Coll 62. **d** 65 **p** 66. C Brixton St Paul *S'wark* 65-67; C Aldridge *Lich* 67-69; C Bushbury 69-71; Chapl Nat Nautical Sch Portishead 71-72; Chapl RAF 72-79; P-in-c Bolton on Swale *Ripon* 79-87; P-in-c The Cowtons 80-82; V 82-89; CF (TA) from 88; R Litcham, Kempston, Lexham, Mileham, Beeston etc *Nor* 89-95; P-in-c Tittleshall w Godwick 93-95; R Litcham w Kempston, E and W Lexham, Mileham etc 95-96; P-in-c Scole, Brockdish, Billingford, Thorpe Abbots etc 96-98; R 98-01; rtd 01; Perm to Offic *St E* and *Carl* from 01. *Helm Lea, Kirkby Thore, Penrith CA10 1UA* Tel and fax (01768) 361597 E-mail philipwrushton@hotmail.com

RUSHTON, Mrs Samantha Jayne. b 65. St Hilda's Coll Ox MA87. Trin Coll Bris BA05. **d** 05 **p** 06. C Highworth w Sevenhampton and Inglesham etc *Bris* 05-08; C Broad Blunsdon 05-08; Dioc Adv for Lic Min from 08; C Chippenham St Paul w Hardenhuish etc from 08; C Kington St Michael from 08; Warden of Readers from 11. *33 Fallow Field, Chippenham SN14 6YA* Tel (01249) 660451 E-mail sam.rushton@bristoldiocese.org

RUSHTON, Mrs Susan Elizabeth. b 44. Univ of Wales (Cardiff) BA65. Bris Sch of Min 83. **dss** 86 **d** 87 **p** 94. Westbury-on-Trym H Trin *Bris* 86-91; Hon Par Dn 87-91; C Wotton St Mary *Glouc* 91-94; P-in-c Frampton Cotterell *Bris* 94-07; Chapl United Bris Healthcare NHS Trust 94-98; P-in-c Iron Acton 98-07; rtd 07; Perm to Offic *York* from 08. *9 Lime Avenue, Heworth, York YO31 1BT* Tel (01904) 410363 E-mail susan.rushton@onetel.net

RUSHTON, Mrs Valerie Elizabeth Wendy. b 40. Birm Univ BSocSc62. WMMTC 86. **d** 89 **p** 94. C Nuneaton St Nic *Cov* 89-93; C Stockingford 93-96; TV Watling Valley *Ox* 96-01; rtd 02; Perm to Offic *Ox* from 02. *106 Moreton Road, Buckingham MK18 1PW* Tel (01280) 824942

RUSK, The Very Revd Frederick John. b 28. QUB BA50 TCD 52. **d** 53 **p** 54. C Ballymoney *Conn* 53-56; C Belfast St Nic 56-59; I Broomhedge 59-65; RE Insp 64-66; I Belfast St Simon 65-78; I Ballymena w Ballyclug 78-88; I Belfast St Nic 88-98; Preb Conn Cathl 84-86; Treas 86-90; Prec 90; Chan Conn Cathl 90-95; Dean Conn 95-98; rtd 98. *28 Banbridge Road, Lurgan, Craigavon BT66 7EQ* Tel (028) 3832 9763

RUSK, Canon Michael Frederick. b 58. Cam Univ BA MA Dur Univ MA98. Westcott Ho Cam 81. **d** 84 **p** 85. C Altrincham St Geo *Ches* 84-87; Chapl Collingwood and Grey Coll *Dur* 87-90; Lect Dur Univ 89-99; C-in-c Neville's Cross St Jo CD 90-99; TR Oadby *Leic* from 99; RD Gartree II from 00; RD Gartree I from 07; Hon Can Leic Cathl from 06. *The Rectory, 31 Hill Field, Oadby, Leicester LE2 4RW* Tel 0116-271 2135 E-mail m.f.rusk@leicester.anglican.org

RUSS, Canon Timothy John. b 41. AKC64. Sarum Th Coll 66. **d** 66 **p** 67. C Walthamstow St Pet *Chelmsf* 66-70; C Epping St Jo 70-73; C Stepney St Dunstan and All SS *Lon* 73-75; Youth Officer 75-79; Tutor YMCA Nat Coll Walthamstow 79-84; Hon C St Botolph Aldgate w H Trin Minories *Lon* 82-89; Selection Sec ACCM 84-89; Dir St Marylebone Healing and Counselling Cen 89-92; Gen Sec Inst of Relig and Medicine 89-92; Hon C Hoxton St Anne w St Columba *Lon* 90-92; P-in-c St Dennis *Truro* 92-96; Par Development Adv 92-99; Dioc Dir Minl Tr 99-06; Hon Can Truro Cathl 01-06; rtd 06. *Russet Cottage, 26 St Francis Meadow, Mitchell, Newquay TR8 5DB* Tel (01872) 519142 E-mail timruss@tesco.net

RUSSELL, Adrian Camper. b 45. Chich Th Coll 79. **d** 81 **p** 82. C Marton *Blackb* 81-84; C Haslemere *Guildf* 84-85; V Hartlepool H Trin *Dur* 85-89; P-in-c Cornforth 89-94; R Auckerarder and Muthill *St And* 94-97; P-in-c Kenton Ascension *Newc* 97-07; rtd 07. *23 Lambley Avenue, North Shields NE30 3SL* Tel 0191-280 9552 E-mail acr26682@blueyonder.co.uk

RUSSELL, Alexandra Blaise. b 58. St Steph Ho Ox 96. **d** 98 **p** 99. C Gt Bookham *Guildf* 98-03; R Long Ditton 03-07; Perm to Offic *Win* 07-08; P-in-c Pennington from 08. *19 Stanley Road, Lymington SO41 3SJ* Tel (01590) 610963 E-mail revdalexrussell@hotmail.co.uk

RUSSELL, Andrea. b 64. K Coll Lon LLB86 Nottm Univ BA04 MA05 PhD10. EMMTC 08. **d** 10 **p** 11. NSM Sherwood *S'well* from 10. *12 Barleylands, Nottingham NG11 6JG* Tel 0115-921 7051 E-mail russelland@ntlworld.com

RUSSELL, Ms Anne. b 66. Man Univ BA(Econ)88. LCTP 06. **d** 11. C Kendal H Trin *Carl* from 11. *4 Millbeck, New Hutton,*

Kendal LA8 0BD Tel (01539) 737008 Mobile 07528-572072 E-mail anne@stridingedgecom.co.uk

✠RUSSELL, The Rt Revd Anthony John. b 43. St Chad's Coll Dur BA65 Trin Coll Ox DPhil71. Cuddesdon Coll 65. **d** 70 **p** 71 **c** 88. C Hilborough w Bodney *Nor* 70-73; P-in-c Preston-on-Stour w Whitchurch *Cov* 73-76; P-in-c Atherstone on Stour 73-76; V Preston on Stour and Whitchurch w Atherstone 77-88; Can Th Cov Cathl 77-88; Chapl Arthur Rank Cen 73-82; Dir 83-88; Chapl to The Queen 83-88; Area Bp Dorchester *Ox* 88-00; Bp Ely 00-10; rtd 10. *Lye Hill House, Holton, Oxford OX33 1QF* Tel (01865) 876415

RUSSELL, The Ven Brian Kenneth. b 50. Trin Hall Cam BA73 MA76 Birm Univ MA77 PhD83. Cuddesdon Coll 74. **d** 76 **p** 77. C Redhill St Matt *S'wark* 76-79; Dir Studies NEOC 79-83; P-in-c Merrington *Dur* 79-83; Dir of Studies and Lect Linc Th Coll 83-86; Selection Sec and Sec Cttee for Th Educn ABM 86-93; Bp's Dir for Min *Birm* 93-05; Adn Aston from 05; Hon Can Birm Cathl from 99. *26 George Road, Edgbaston, Birmingham B15 1PJ* Tel 0121-454 5525 *or* 426 0437 Fax 455 6085 *or* 428 1114 E-mail b.russell@birmingham.anglican.org

RUSSELL, Brian Robert. b 61. QUB BA BD92. CITC. **d** 85 **p** 86. C Dublin Drumcondra w N Strand *D & G* 85-87; C Carrickfergus *Conn* 87-90; I Kilmegan w Maghera *D & D* 90-96; I Bailieborough w Knockbride, Shercock and Mullagh *K, E & A* 96-00; I Kilbarron w Rossnowlagh and Drumholm *D & R* from 00. *The Rectory, Lisminton, Ballintra, Co Donegal, Republic of Ireland* Tel and fax (00353) (74) 973 4025 E-mail bestrussell@eircom.net

RUSSELL, Bruce Harley. b 57. Ch Ch Ox BA79 Roehampton Inst PGCE80. Ripon Coll Cuddesdon. **d** 99 **p** 00. C Bracknell *Ox* 99-03; TV Langley Marish from 03. *St Francis's Vicarage, 21 Lynward Avenue, Slough SL3 7BJ* Tel (01753) 557150 E-mail bhrussell@supanet.com

RUSSELL, Christopher Ian. b 68. St Jo Coll Dur BA91 St Edm Coll Cam MPhil96. Ridley Hall Cam 93. **d** 96 **p** 97. C Deptford St Jo w H Trin *S'wark* 96-99; Soul Survivor Watford *St Alb* 99-01; C Reading St Mary w St Laur *Ox* from 01. *9 Mansfield Road, Reading RG1 6AL* Tel 0118-956 0559 E-mail chris@belindarussell.freeserve.co.uk

RUSSELL, Clive Phillip. b 61. Ridley Hall Cam 04. **d** 06 **p** 07. C High Ongar w Norton Mandeville *Chelmsf* 06-09; V Grays North from 09. *St John's Vicarage, 8A Victoria Avenue, Grays RM16 2RP* Tel (01375) 372101 E-mail russell-family@tiscali.co.uk

RUSSELL, David John. b 57. Sarum & Wells Th Coll BTh94. **d** 94 **p** 95. C Glouc St Geo w Whaddon 94-98; P-in-c Wickwar w Rangeworthy 98-01; R Wickwar, Rangeworthy and Hillesley 02-11; R Charfield and Kingswood w Wickwar etc from 11. *The Rectory, 75 High Street, Wickwar, Wotton-under-Edge GL12 8NP* Tel (01454) 294267 E-mail davidrussell@gmx.com

RUSSELL, David John Timothy. b 75. Oak Hill Th Coll. **d** 09 **p** 10. C Padiham w Hapton and Padiham Green *Blackb* from 09. *5 St John's Road, Padiham, Burnley BB12 7BN* Tel (01282) 773219 E-mail drjaz@hotmail.com

RUSSELL, David Robert. b 43. Brasted Th Coll 66 Sarum Th Coll 68. **d** 70 **p** 71. C Leintwardine *Heref* 70-73; C Bridgnorth w Tasley 73-75; R Lockridge and Eden Hill Australia 75-80; R Bellevue and Darlington 80-87; Asst Chapl Dept of Corrective Services 87-93; Sen Chapl 93-95; R Carlisle and Rivervale 95-03; E Deanery Miss Development P 03-04; R Kondinin and Corrigin 05-08; rtd 08. *Unit 403, 34 Robinson Street, Inglewood WA 6052, Australia* Tel (0061) (8) 6106 1070 Mobile 42-754 5560 E-mail davrobrus@virginbroadband.com.au

RUSSELL, Canon Derek John. b 30. St Pet Hall Ox BA54 MA58. Qu Coll Birm 54. **d** 56 **p** 57. C Boxley *Cant* 56-59; C Whitstable All SS 59-63; Chapl HM Pris Wormwood Scrubs 63-65 and 71-89; Chapl HM Pris Stafford 65-69; Pentonville 70; SE Regional Chapl 74-81; Chapl HM Rem Cen Latchmere Ho 74-77; Asst Chapl Gen of Pris 81-83; Dep 83-90; Hon Can Cant Cathl 86-90; rtd 90; Perm to Offic *Cant* from 90. *25 Pier Avenue, Whitstable CT5 2HQ* Tel (01227) 276654

RUSSELL, Ms Elizabeth Marilyn Vivia. b 50. LRAM70 GRSM72. Westcott Ho Cam 95. **d** 97 **p** 98. C Alton St Lawr *Win* 97-01; C St Martin-in-the-Fields *Lon* 01-08; P-in-c S Kensington H Trin w All SS from 08; Dir of Ords Two Cities Area from 08. *5 Aldwyn House, Davidson Gardens, London SW8 2HX* Tel (020) 7498 5623 E-mail erussell101@btinternet.com

RUSSELL, Eric Watson. b 39. FCA76. Clifton Th Coll 66. **d** 69 **p** 70. C Kinson *Sarum* 69-73; C Peckham St Mary Magd *S'wark* 73-77; TV Barking St Marg w St Patr *Chelmsf* 77-82; V Lozells St Paul and St Silas *Birm* 82-95; RD Aston 89-94; P-in-c Barston and C Knowle 95-04; I Kells Union *M & K* 04-09; rtd 09. *20 Slater Road, Bentley Heath, Solihull B93 8AG* Tel (01564) 779709 E-mail ericandjoan@uwclub.net

RUSSELL, Gary William Algernon. b 64. Ripon Coll Cuddesdon 04. **d** 06 **p** 07. C Harpenden St Nic *St Alb* 06-09; P-in-c St Alb St Mary Marshalswick from 09; Chapl ATC from 07. *The Vicarage, 1A Sherwood Avenue, St Albans AL4 9QA* Tel (01727) 851544 E-mail moreteavicar@hotmail.co.uk

RUSSELL, The Ven Harold Ian Lyle. b 34. Lon Coll of Div ALCD59 BD60. **d** 60 **p** 61. C Iver *Ox* 60-63; C Fulwood *Sheff* 63-67; V Chapeltown 67-75; RD Tankersley 73-75; V Nottingham St Jude *S'well* 75-89; AD Nottingham Cen 86-89; Hon Can S'well Minster 88-89; Adn Cov 89-00; rtd 01; Chapl to The Queen 97-04; Perm to Offic *S'well* from 01. *5 Old Acres, Woodborough, Nottingham NG14 6ES* Tel 0115-965 3543

RUSSELL, Ms Isoline Lucilda (Lyn). b 41. **d** 03 **p** 04. OLM Camberwell St Giles w St Matt *S'wark* from 03. *124 Hindman's Road, London SE22 9NH* Tel (020) 8299 4431

RUSSELL, James Anthony Tomkins. b 67. Oak Hill Th Coll BA99. **d** 99 **p** 00. C Chadwell *Chelmsf* 99-03; C Patcham *Chich* 03-07; P-in-c N Mundham w Hunston and Merston from 07. *The Rectory, Church Lane, Hunston, Chichester PO20 1AJ* Tel (01243) 782003 E-mail jamesandannabel@aol.com

RUSSELL, Mrs Janet Mary. b 53. Univ of Wales BSc74 BArch76. Ox Min Course 91. **d** 94 **p** 95. C Watlington w Pyrton and Shirburn *Ox* 94-97; C Icknield 97-98; TV Wallingford 98-05; Par Development Adv (Berks) 05-11; Dir Miss *S & B* from 11. *The Rectory, Talybont-on-Usk, Brecon LD3 7UX* Tel (01874) 676494 E-mail janetrussell@churchinwales.org.uk

RUSSELL, Canon John Arthur. b 29. AKC62. **d** 63 **p** 64. C Fareham H Trin *Portsm* 63-67; R Greatham w Empshott 67-79; V Ham St Andr *S'wark* 79-87; P-in-c Battersea St Luke 87-92; V 92-96; Hon Can S'wark Cathl 95-96; rtd 97; Perm to Offic *S'wark* 97-03. *Toni Llido 4, 2, apt 5, 03730 Puerto de Javea (Alicante), Spain* Tel (0034) 965 790 587 E-mail jarussell@ya.com

RUSSELL, John Bruce. b 56. Ripon Coll Cuddesdon. **d** 95 **p** 96. C Newport Pagnell w Lathbury and Moulsoe *Ox* 95-98; P-in-c Wing w Grove 98-03; AD Mursley 02-03; Perm to Offic *St Alb* 08-10; TV Gt Berkhamsted, Gt and Lt Gaddesden etc from 10. *St John's Vicarage, Pipers Hill, Great Gaddesden, Hemel Hempstead HO1 3BY* Tel (01442) 214898 E-mail john_russell@live.co.uk

RUSSELL, John Graham. b 35. G&C Coll Cam BA58 MA62. Westcott Ho Cam 59. **d** 61 **p** 62. C Durleigh *B & W* 61-66; C Bridgwater St Mary w Chilton Trinity 61-66; C Far Headingley St Chad *Ripon* 66-72; P-in-c Leeds St Matt Lt London 72-79; V Rowley Regis *Birm* 79-84; V Hall Green Ascension 84-95; Deanery P Warley Deanery 95-00; rtd 01; Perm to Offic *Birm* from 01. *1 Stapylton Avenue, Harborne, Birmingham B17 0BA* Tel 0121-426 4529 E-mail pmr@russellp21.fsnet.co.uk

RUSSELL, John Richard. b 53. Westmr Coll Ox MTh01 FRSA02. Spurgeon's Coll 77 Ripon Coll Cuddesdon 01. **d** 01 **p** 02. Hon C St Mary le Strand w St Clem Danes *Lon* 01-02; Chapl RAF 02-08; Perm to Offic *Chelmsf* from 09. *18 Wambrook, Shoeburyness, Southend-on-Sea SS3 8BW* Tel (01702) 580545

RUSSELL, Canon Jonathan Vincent Harman. b 43. K Coll Lon 68. **d** 69 **p** 70. C Addington *Cant* 69-73; C Buckland in Dover w Buckland Valley 73-76; P-in-c Selling 76-85; P-in-c Throwley w Stalisfield and Otterden 79-85; R Selling w Throwley, Sheldwich w Badlesmere etc 85-95; Hon Min Can Cant Cathl 83-94; RD Ospringe 90-95; P-in-c Elham w Denton and Wootton 95-01; V 01-08; Hon Can Cant Cathl 94-08; rtd 08; Perm to Offic *Cant* from 08. *Kirkella, Goodwin Road, St Margaret's Bay, Dover CT15 6ED* Tel (01304) 852811 Mobile 07702-314865

RUSSELL, Jonathan Wingate. b 55. Newc Univ BSc76. St Jo Coll Nottm BA83. **d** 84 **p** 85. C Southsea St Jude *Portsm* 84-87; P-in-c Shorwell w Kingston 87-92; V 92-06; P-in-c Gatcombe 87-92; R 92-06; P-in-c Chale 89-92; R 92-06; RD W Wight 96-01; R Allendale w Whitfield *Newc* from 06. *The Rectory, 16 Forstersteads, Allendale, Hexham NE47 9AS* Tel and fax (01434) 618607 E-mail rector@allendalechurch.co.uk

RUSSELL, Lyn. *See* RUSSELL, Ms Isoline Lucilda

RUSSELL, Madeleine. b 41. Pargau Teacher Tr Coll Switzerland TDip62. **d** 04 **p** 05. NSM Halifax H Trin and St Jude *Wakef* from 04. *Holy Trinity Vicarage, 9 Love Lane, Halifax HX1 2BQ* Tel (01422) 352446

RUSSELL, Mrs Marion. b 54. Glas Univ BEd75 Jordanhill Coll Glas TCert75. CBDTI 03. **d** 06 **p** 07. NSM Altham w Clayton le Moors *Blackb* 06-10; Chapl Trin Academy Halifax from 10. *470 Revidge Road, Blackburn BB1 8DF* Tel (01254) 692522 E-mail marion1.russell@googlemail.com

RUSSELL, Martin Christopher. b 48. St Jo Coll Dur BA70. Coll of Resurr Mirfield 72. **d** 74 **p** 75. C Huddersfield St Pet *Wakef* 74-77; Trinidad and Tobago 78-85; V S Crosland *Wakef* 86-00; P-in-c Helme 86-00; P-in-c Halifax H Trin 00-02; P-in-c Halifax St Jude 00-02; V Halifax H Trin and St Jude from 02. *Holy Trinity Vicarage, 9 Love Lane, Halifax HX1 2BQ* Tel (01422) 352446

RUSSELL, Michael John. b 38. Clifton Th Coll 68. **d** 68 **p** 69. C Cranham Park CD *Chelmsf* 68-70; C Bucknall and Bagnall *Lich* 70-77; P-in-c Tintwistle *Ches* 77-79; V 79-86; New Zealand from 86; rtd 03. *144 Winchester Street, Ashhurst 4810, New Zealand* Tel (0064) (6) 326 8547

RUSSELL, Canon Neil. b 47. EMMTC 78. **d** 81 **p** 82. NSM Wyberton *Linc* 81-84; C 84-85; V Frampton 85-93; Agric Chapl and Countryside Officer 88-93; P-in-c Stamford All SS w St Jo

93-97; V 97-08; RD Aveland and Ness w Stamford 00-06; Warden Sacrista Prebend Retreat Ho *S'well* 08-10; Can and Preb Linc Cathl 02-10; rtd 10. *11 Gleneagles Drive, Greylees, Sleaford NG34 8GH* Tel (01529) 488225 Mobile 07730-403630 E-mail canonneilrussell@yahoo.co.uk

RUSSELL, Mrs Noreen Margaret. b 39. Man Univ BA60 Lon Univ PGCE61 BD66. WMMTC 90. **d** 91 **p** 94. NSM Swynnerton and Tittensor *Lich* 91-97; C Draycott-le-Moors w Forsbrook 97-06; rtd 06; Perm to Offic *Lich* from 06. *40 Old Road, Barlaston, Stoke-on-Trent ST12 9EQ* Tel (01782) 372992

RUSSELL, the Ven Norman Atkinson. b 43. Chu Coll Cam BA65 MA69 Lon Univ BD70. Lon Coll of Div 67. **d** 70 **p** 71. C Clifton Ch Ch w Em *Bris* 70-74; C Enfield Ch Ch Trent Park *Lon* 74-77; R Harwell w Chilton *Ox* 77-84; P-in-c Gerrards Cross 84-88; P-in-c Fulmer 85-88; R Gerrards Cross and Fulmer 88-98; Hon Can Ch 95-98; RD Amersham 96-98; Adn Berks from 98. *Foxglove House, Love Lane, Donnington, Newbury RG14 2JG* Tel (01635) 552820 Fax 522165 E-mail archdber@oxford.anglican.org

RUSSELL, Peter Richard. b 60. Ch Ch Coll Cant BA99. SEITE 02. **d** 05 **p** 06. NSM Margate All SS and Westgate St Sav *Cant* 05-08; Chapl St Lawr Coll Ramsgate from 09. *St Lawrence College, College Road, Ramsgate CT11 7AE* Tel (01843) 572900 E-mail minnisbay@hotmail.com

RUSSELL, Richard Alexander. b 44. Univ of Wales (Abth) BA65 McMaster Univ Ontario MA67 Bris Univ MA73 PGCE74 MEd76. Trin Coll Bris 79. **d** 82 **p** 83. C Hartlepool St Paul *Dur* 82-85; P-in-c Bath Widcombe *B & W* 85-88; V 88-00; rtd 00. *76 Waterside Way, Radstock, Bath BA3 3YQ* Tel (01761) 433217 E-mail 113135.2044@compuserve.com

RUSSELL, Roger Geoffrey. b 47. Worc Coll Ox BA69 MA73. Cuddesdon Coll 70. **d** 72 **p** 73. C Anlaby Common St Mark *York* 72-75; C Wilton Place St Paul *Lon* 75-86; R Lancing w Coombes *Chich* from 86; RD Worthing 97-05. *The Vicarage, 63 Manor Road, Lancing BN15 0EY* Tel (01903) 753212

RUSSELL, William Warren. b 52. QUB BSocSc74. CITC 74. **d** 77 **p** 78. C Agherton *Conn* 77-79; C Lisburn Ch Ch Cathl 79-83; I Magheradroll *D & D* from 83; Treas Dromore Cathl from 08. *The Rectory, 18 Church Road, Ballynahinch BT24 8LP* Tel (028) 9756 2289 Mobile 07810-222906 E-mail rev_wwrussell@hotmail.com

RUSSELL GRANT, Julia Rosalind. b 45. **d** 11. OLM Layer de la Haye and Layer Breton w Birch etc *Chelmsf* from 11. *Heath House, Crayes Garden, Layer Breton, Colchester CO2 0PN* Tel (01206) 330235 E-mail julia@bretonheath.me.uk

RUSSELL-SMITH, Mark Raymond. b 46. New Coll Edin MTh91. St Jo Coll Dur BA71 Cranmer Hall Dur. **d** 72 **p** 73. C Upton (Overchurch) *Ches* 72-75; C Deane *Man* 75-77; UCCF Travelling Sec 77-80; Lic to Offic *York* 78-81; BCMS 81-92; Kenya 81-92; P-in-c Slaidburn *Bradf* from 92; P-in-c Long Preston w Tosside from 97. *The Rectory, Slaidburn, Clitheroe BB7 3ER* Tel (01200) 446238 E-mail mark.russell-smith@bradford.anglican.org

RUST, Alison Theresa (Tessa). St Mellitus Coll. **d** 11. NSM W Ealing St Jo w St Jas *Lon* from 11. *14 Gloucester Road, London W5 4JB* Tel (020) 8567 1047 E-mail tessa@gtrust.fsnet.co.uk

RUST, Jonathan Kenneth. b 62. Reading Univ BSc84. Ridley Hall Cam. **d** 00 **p** 01. C Holloway St Mary Magd *Lon* from 00. *59 Bride Street, London N7 8RN* Tel (020) 7607 1316 E-mail j.rust@tiscali.co.uk

RUSTED, Mrs Mary Elizabeth. b 44. **d** 00 **p** 01. OLM Mildenhall *St E* 00-10; rtd 10; Perm to Offic *St E* from 10. *3 Ford Close, West Row, Bury St Edmunds IP28 8NR* Tel (01638) 715054 E-mail maryrusted@hotmail.com

RUSTELL, Anthony Christopher. b 77. Ch Ch Ox BA98 MSt01 MA02 Keble Coll Ox DPhil07. St Steph Ho Ox 98. **d** 01 **p** 02. NSM Ox St Barn and St Paul 01-04; P-in-c N Hinksey and Wytham 04-10; P-in-c Ox St Frideswide w Binsey 09-10; R Osney from 10. *The Vicarage, 81 West Way, Oxford OX2 9JY* Tel (01865) 242345 E-mail acrustell@tiscali.co.uk

RUTHERFORD, Anthony Richard. b 37. Culham Coll Ox TCert62 Sussex Univ MA77. S'wark Ord Course 83. **d** 86 **p** 87. Hon C Tunbridge Wells St Luke *Roch* 86-88; C Bromley SS Pet and Paul 88-90; V Wragby *Linc* 90-94; Asst Min Officer 90-94; V Penge Lane H Trin *Roch* 94-02; rtd 02; Perm to Offic *Roch* from 03. *6 Ashley Gardens, Tunbridge Wells TN4 8TY* Tel (01892) 541009 E-mail arrutherford@f2s.com

RUTHERFORD, Arthur Ernest. b 26. Saltley Tr Coll Birm CertEd53 DLC54 Loughb Univ Hon BSc09. Sarum & Wells Th Coll 91. **d** 92 **p** 93. NSM Lilliput *Sarum* 92-96; rtd 96; Perm to Offic *Sarum* from 96. *9 Park View, 53 Parkstone Road, Poole BH15 2NX* Tel (01202) 669019 E-mail aerutherford@btinternet.com

RUTHERFORD, Daniel Fergus Peter. b 65. Hatf Coll Dur BA86 CertEd87. Ridley Hall Cam 88. **d** 90 **p** 91. C Harold Wood *Chelmsf* 90-94; C Hove Bp Hannington Memorial Ch *Chich* 94-97; Chapl City of Lon Freemen's Sch from 97. *City of London Freemen's School, Park Lane, Ashtead KT21 1ET* Tel (01372) 277933 Fax 276728

RUTHERFORD, Ian William. b 46. Univ of Wales (Lamp) BA68. Cuddesdon Coll 68. **d** 70 **p** 71. C Gosforth All SS *Newc* 70-72; C Prestbury *Glouc* 73-76; Chapl RN 76-93; CMP from 93; TV Redruth w Lanner and Treleigh *Truro* 93-94; V Paulsgrove *Portsm* 94-99; V Leeds Belle Is St Jo and St Barn *Ripon* 99-11; rtd 11. *Flat 12, 27-29 St Simons Road, Southsea PO5 2PE* E-mail fatherian@onetel.com

RUTHERFORD, Janet Elizabeth. b 37. S'wark Ord Course 86. **d** 89. NSM Plaistow St Mary *Roch* 89-90; NSM Linc St Botolph 91-93. *6 Ashley Gardens, Tunbridge Wells TN4 8TY* Tel (01892) 541009

RUTHERFORD, Canon John Bilton. b 23. Qu Coll Birm 49. **d** 52 **p** 53. C Newc H Cross 52-57; C Longbenton St Bart 57-60; V High Elswick St Phil 60-66; V Walker 66-74; I Benwell St Jas 74-81; Hon Can Newc Cathl 80-90; V Lesbury w Alnmouth 81-90; RD Alnwick 86-89; Perm to Offic from 90; rtd 90. *68 Worcester Way, Woodlands Park, Wideopen, Newcastle upon Tyne NE13 6JD* Tel 0191-236 4785

RUTHERFORD, Peter George. b 34. Nor Ord Course 73. **d** 76 **p** 77. NSM New Catton Ch Ch *Nor* 76-79; NSM Eaton 79-80; NSM Nor St Steph 81-92; Perm to Offic 92-94 and from 99; P-in-c Earlham St Mary 94-99; RD Nor S 98-99; rtd 99. *126 Colman Road, Norwich NR4 7AA* Tel and fax (01603) 457629 E-mail petergrutherford@btinternet.com

RUTHERFORD, Peter Marshall. b 57. St Andr Univ MTheol81 Ulster Univ MA96. CITC 83. **d** 83 **p** 84. C Stormont *D & D* 83-85; CF 85-01; Asst Chapl Gen 01-02; Asst Chapl Milan w Genoa and Varese *Eur* 03-04; I Castlepollard and Oldcastle w Loughcrew etc *M & K* 04-10; I Julianstown and Colpe w Drogheda and Duleck from 10; Dioc Dir of Ords from 05. *The Rectory, Laytown Road, Julianstown, Co Meath, Republic of Ireland* Tel (00353) (41) 982 9831 E-mail peterrutherford@me.com

RUTHERFORD (née ERREY), Ms Rosalind Elisabeth. b 52. St Hugh's Coll Ox BA74 Surrey Univ BA02 Goldsmiths' Coll Lon PGCE78. STETS 99. **d** 02 **p** 03. C Earley St Pet *Ox* 02-06; TV Basingstoke *Win* from 06. *45 Beaconsfield Road, Basingstoke RG21 3DG* Tel (01256) 464616 E-mail revrosalind@btinternet.com

RUTLEDGE, Canon Christopher John Francis. b 44. Lon Univ BSc67 Univ of Wales MPhil94 PhD99 TCert80. Sarum Th Coll 67. **d** 70 **p** 71. C Birm St Pet 70-73; C Calne and Blackland *Sarum* 73-76; P-in-c Derry Hill 76-78; V 78-81; P-in-c Talbot Village 81-82; V 82-10; Can and Preb Sarum Cathl 95-10; Chapl Talbot Heath Sch Bournemouth 04-09; rtd 10; Perm to Offic *Sarum* from 10. *48 Wollaton Road, Ferndown BH22 8QY* Tel (01202) 895116 E-mail christopher.rutledge@talktalk.net

RUTLEDGE, Francis George. b 62. TCD BA83 BTh90. **d** 86 **p** 87. C Holywood *D & D* 86-89; C Willowfield 89-91; I Kilmakee *Conn* 91-97; I Carrigrohane Union *C, C & R* 97-04; I Donacavey w Barr *Clogh* 04-05; Bp's C Bangor Primacy *D & D* from 05. *4 Glendown Way, Bangor BT19 7SP* Tel (028) 9185 9731 E-mail francis.rutledge@btinternet.com

RUTT, Mrs Celia Mary Avril. b 43. Cranmer Hall Dur. **d** 02 **p** 03. NSM Heworth H Trin *York* 02-05; NSM Acomb St Steph 05-09; NSM Clifton 09-11; rtd 11; Perm to Offic *York* from 11. *226 Shipton Road, York YO30 5RZ* Tel (01904) 627384 E-mail celia.rutt@tiscali.co.uk

RUTT, Canon Denis Frederic John. b 17. Kelham Th Coll 34. **d** 41 **p** 42. C Luton Ch Ch *St Alb* 41-44; Bp's Youth Chapl 44-48; R Empangeni S Africa 48-54; R Yaxham and Welborne *Nor* 54-61; R Kirkley 61-71; RD Lothingland 65-71; R N Lynn w St Marg and St Nic 71-76; Can Res and Prec Lich Cathl 76-83; rtd 83; Perm to Offic *Bradf* 83-99. *5 Manormead, Tilford Road, Hindhead GU26 6RA* Tel (01428) 604415

RUTT-FIELD, Benjamin John. b 48. Chich Th Coll. **d** 90 **p** 91. C Wickford and Runwell *Chelmsf* 90-94; V Goodmayes St Paul from 94. *St Paul's Vicarage, 20 Eastwood Road, Ilford IG3 8XA* Tel (020) 8590 6596 E-mail bjrf@nildram.co.uk

RUTTER, Canon Allen Edward Henry (Claude). b 28. Qu Coll Cam BA52 MA56. Cranmer Hall Dur. **d** 59 **p** 60. C Bath Abbey w St Jas *B & W* 59-60; C E Dereham w Hoe *Nor* 60-64; R Cawston 64-69; Chapl Cawston Coll 64-69; P-in-c Felthorpe w Haveringland 64-69; R Gingindhlovu S Africa 69-73; P-in-c Over and Nether Compton, Trent etc *Sarum* 73-80; RD Sherborne 77-87; P-in-c Oborne w Poyntington 79-80; P-in-c Queen Thorne 80-96; Can and Preb Sarum Cathl 86-96; rtd 96; Perm to Offic *B & W* 98-99 and from 00; P-in-c Thorncombe w Winsham and Cricket St Thomas 99; C Chard and Distr 99-00. *Home Farm, Chilson, South Chard, Chard TA20 2NX* Tel (01460) 221368

RUTTER, Graham Piers. b 77. St Jo Coll Dur BSc98 PhD03 Liv Univ MSc99. St Jo Coll Nottm 06. **d** 08 **p** 09. C Wellington All SS w Eyton *Lich* from 08. *1 Stile Rise, Telford TF5 0LR* Tel (01952) 641229 E-mail graham_rutter@yahoo.co.uk

RUTTER, John Edmund Charles. b 53. Qu Coll Cam MA76. St Jo Coll Nottm MA93. **d** 93 **p** 94. C Penge St Jo *Roch* 93-97; Bp's C Bangor Primacy *D & D* 97-04; I Glenavy w Tunny and

Crumlin *Conn* from 04. *The Vicarage, 30 Crumlin Road, Glenavy, Crumlin BT29 4LG* Tel and fax (028) 9442 2361 E-mail glenavy@connor.anglican.org

RUTTER, John Smiles. b 49. Hertf Coll Ox BA71 PGCE72. NEOC 02. **d** 07 **p** 08. NSM Ripon H Trin from 07; NSM Ripon Cathl from 11. *17 Church Lane, Ripon HG4 2ES* Tel (01765) 605638

RUTTER, Martin Charles. b 54. Wolv Poly BSc75 Southn Univ BTh81. Sarum & Wells Th Coll 76. **d** 79 **p** 80. C Cannock *Lich* 79-82; C Uttoxeter w Bramshall 82-86; V W Bromwich St Jas 86-97; P-in-c W Bromwich St Paul 89-97; V W Bromwich St Jas w St Paul 97-02; RD W Bromwich 94-02; V Gt Barr from 02; RD Walsall from 10. *St Margaret's Vicarage, Chapel Lane, Great Barr, Birmingham B43 7BD* Tel 0121-357 1390

RUTTER, Michael. b 75. Trin Coll Bris BA06. **d** 07 **p** 08. C Dudley Wood *Worc* 07-10; TV Halas from 10. *2 Stennels Avenue, Halesowen B62 8QJ*

RUTTER, Michael John. **d** 10 **p** 11. NSM York St Paul from 10. *23 Lidgett Grove, York YO26 5NE* Tel (01904) 788445 E-mail mike@rutterworld.com

RUTTER, Ronald. b 47. SS Hild & Bede Coll Dur TCert71 Open Univ BA81 CMath MIMA. CBDTI. **d** 00 **p** 01. NSM Heversham and Milnthorpe *Carl* from 00. *Ellerslie, Woodhouse Lane, Heversham, Milnthorpe LA7 7EW* Tel and fax (01539) 564260 E-mail ron_rutter@hotmail.com

RUXTON, Charles. b 58. Van Mildert Coll Dur BSc79 CGeol FGS MCIWEM. **d** 06 **p** 07. OLM Meole Brace *Lich* from 06. *New Place, Westbury, Shrewsbury SY5 9RY* Tel (01743) 891636 E-mail c.ruxton@btinternet.com

RWANDA, Archbishop of. *See* KOLINI, The Most Revd Emmanuel Musaba

RYALL, John Francis Robert. b 30. New Coll Ox BA52 MA57. Westcott Ho Cam 52. **d** 54 **p** 55. C Petersfield w Sheet *Portsm* 54-56; C Portsea St Mary 56-62; C Warblington w Emsworth 62-65; C Freshwater 65-67; R Frating w Thorrington *Chelmsf* 67-73; R Gt Yeldham 74-76; P-in-c Lt Yeldham 75-76; R Gt w Lt Yeldham 76-80; P-in-c Thorley *Portsm* 80-82; P-in-c Shalfleet 80-82; V 82-95; V Calbourne w Newtown 82-95; rtd 95; Perm to Offic *Portsm* from 95. *Weald House, Main Road, Wellow, Yarmouth PO41 0SZ* Tel (01983) 760783

RYALL, Michael Richard. b 36. TCD BA58 MA65. TCD Div Sch Div Test58. **d** 58 **p** 59. C Dublin St Geo *D & G* 58-62; CF 62-65 and 68-90; CF (TAVR) 67-68; C Dublin Rathmines *D & G* 65-66; Asst Master Dungannon Secondary Sch 66-68; R Yardley Hastings, Denton and Grendon etc *Pet* 90-01; rtd 01; Perm to Offic *Chich* from 02; *Pet* 06-09; *St D* from 07; P-in-c Mayland *Chelmsf* from 08. *31 Imperial Avenue, Mayland, Chelmsford CM3 6AH* Tel (01621) 740943 Mobile 07968-111258 E-mail michaelryall@waitrose.com

RYALLS, Craig James. b 74. Bris Univ BA96 Peterho Cam BA01. Ridley Hall Cam 99. **d** 02 **p** 03. C Bearsted w Thurnham *Cant* 02-06; C Woking Ch Ch *Guildf* from 06. *4 Orchard Drive, Woking GU21 4BN* Tel (01483) 771551 *or* 740897 E-mail craig.ryalls@christchurchwoking.org

RYAN, Alan John. b 57. SWMTC. **d** 09 **p** 10. C Fremington, Instow and Westleigh *Ex* 09-11; C Whitchurch from 11. *1 St Andrews Road, Tavistock PL19 9BY* Tel (01822) 61339 E-mail alanryan1957@btinternet.com

RYAN, David Peter. b 64. Aston Univ BSc86. Linc Th Coll BTh94. **d** 94 **p** 95. C Horsforth *Ripon* 94-97; C Bedale 97-98; P-in-c Startforth and Bowes and Rokeby w Brignall 98-00; V 00-04; P-in-c Warndon St Nic *Worc* from 04; Dioc Ecum Officer from 04. *The Vicarage, 4 Daty Croft, Home Meadow, Worcester WR4 0JB* Tel (01905) 616109 E-mail davidryannow@netscapeonline.co.uk

RYAN, Graham William Robert (Gregg). b 51. CITC 90. **d** 93 **p** 94. NSM Clonsast w Rathangan, Thomastown etc *M & K* 93-97; Dioc Communications Officer 96-97; Press Officer from 97; Dioc C from 97. *Millicent Hall, Millicent South, Sallins, Naas, Co Kildare, Republic of Ireland* Tel (00353) (45) 879464 Fax 875173 E-mail gregg.ryan@irishrail.ie

RYAN, James Francis. b 47. Surrey Univ BSc. St Jo Coll Nottm. **d** 83 **p** 84. C Littleover *Derby* 83-86; C Chipping Sodbury and Old Sodbury *Glouc* 86-89; V Pype Hayes *Birm* 89-99; R W Winch w Setchey, N Runcton and Middleton *Nor* from 99. *The Rectory, Rectory Lane, West Winch, King's Lynn PE33 0NR* Tel (01553) 840835

RYAN, Canon Maureen. **d** 98 **p** 99. C Tuam w Cong and Aasleagh *T, K & A* from 98; Preb Kilmactalway St Patr Cathl Dublin 01-09; Can Tuam Cathl from 05. *Marshal's Park, Rinville, Oranmore, Galway, Republic of Ireland* Tel and fax (00353) (91) 794599 E-mail ryans@iol.ie

RYAN, Robert Lloyd. b 65. Warwick Univ BA(QTS)87. SEITE 05. **d** 08 **p** 09. C Roch Cathl from 08. *68 Montrose Avenue, Chatham ME5 7HX* Tel (01634) 856598 E-mail robryan68@blueyonder.co.uk

RYAN, Roger John. b 47. Lon Bible Coll BA79 Surrey Univ MA00 St Pet Coll Ox DPhil06 Univ Coll Lon MA09. Oak Hill Th Coll 79. **d** 80 **p** 81. C Luton St Fran *St Alb* 80-83; R Laceby

Linc 83-88; V Summerstown *S'wark* from 88. *St Mary's Vicarage, 46 Wimbledon Road, London SW17 0UQ* Tel (020) 8946 9853 E-mail rogerryan307@hotmail.com

RYAN, Canon Stephen John. b 49. Univ of Wales (Swansea) BA70. Sarum & Wells Th Coll 70. **d** 73 **p** 74. C Llantrisant 73-77; V Treherbert w Treorchy 77-89; Youth Chapl 80-85; RD Rhondda 84-89; V Aberdare St Fagan 89-02; RD Cynon Valley 97-02; TR Neath from 02; Can Llan Cathl from 02; AD Neath 04-10. *The Rectory, 23 London Road, Neath SA11 1LE* Tel (01639) 644612 E-mail rectorneath@btinternet.com

RYCRAFT, Andrew George. b 48. FRICS94. Wycliffe Hall Ox 02 SAOMC 04. **d** 06 **p** 07. NSM Ray Valley *Ox* 06-07 and from 09. *St Mary's House, High Street, Charlton on Otmoor, Kidlington OX5 2UQ* Tel (01865) 331124 E-mail andrew.rycraft@ntlworld.com

RYCRAFT, Mrs Rosemary Ives Stewart. b 49. Westmr Coll Ox BTh00 SRN72 SCM74. SAOMC 00. **d** 03 **p** 04. NSM New Marston *Ox* 03-07; TV Aylesbury w Bierton and Hulcott 07-11; rtd 11; Perm to Offic *Ox* from 11. *St Mary's House, High Street, Charlton on Otmoor, Kidlington OX5 2UQ* Tel (01865) 331124

RYCROFT, Alistair John. b 79. St Cath Coll Ox BA01 Fitzw Coll Cam BA08 Ox Brookes Univ PGCE02. Ridley Hall Cam 06. **d** 09 **p** 10. C York St Mich-le-Belfrey from 09. *157 Haxby Road, York YO31 8JL* Tel (01904) 341979 E-mail al.rycroft@stmichaelsyork.org

RYDER, Canon Derek Michael. b 36. St Cath Coll Cam BA60 MA64. Tyndale Hall Bris 61. **d** 63 **p** 64. C Hampreston *Sarum* 63-66; Asst Chapl Brentwood Sch Essex 66-72; Chapl Ipswich Sch 72-77; Home Sec CMJ 77-87; TR Wexcombe *Sarum* 87-99; RD Pewsey 89-99; Can and Preb Sarum Cathl 97-99; rtd 99; Perm to Offic *Ox* and *Sarum* from 00. *31 The Green, Calne SN11 8DJ* Tel (01249) 821797

RYDER, Jennifer Ann. *See* HAYNES, Mrs Jennifer Ann

RYDER, John Merrick. b 55. Natal Univ BA75 BA77. St Pet Coll Natal 81. **d** 82 **p** 83. S Africa 84-88; St Helena 88-91; C Havant *Portsm* 91-95; P-in-c Godshill 95-99; V from 99; P-in-c Wroxall *Portsm* 99-02. *The Vicarage, Church Hill, Godshill, Ventnor PO38 3HY* Tel (01983) 840895 E-mail johnmryder@btinternet.com

RYDER, Lisle Robert Dudley. b 43. Selw Coll Cam BA68 MA72. Sarum Th Coll 69. **d** 71 **p** 72. C Lowestoft St Marg *Nor* 71-75; Chapl Asst Oxon Area HA 76-79; C Littlehampton St Jas *Chich* 79-85; C Littlehampton St Mary 79-85; C Wick 79-85; Chapl Worc R Infirmary 85-94; Chapl Worc R Infirmary NHS Trust 94-00; Chapl Worcs Acute Hosps NHS Trust 00-03; Hon Can Worc Cathl 89-04; P-in-c Pyworthy, Pancrasweek and Bridgerule *Ex* 04-08; rtd 08. *Little Appleton, 3 Lumley Terrace, Newton le Willows, Bedale DL8 1SS* Tel (01677) 450180 E-mail lisle@safehaven.me.uk

RYDER, Oliver Hugh Dudley. b 74. UEA BA98. Ridley Hall Cam 05. **d** 07 **p** 08. C Tollington *Lon* 07-10; C Kensal Rise St Mark and St Martin 10-11; V Kensal Rise St Mark from 11. *Kensal Rise Vicarage, 93 College Road, London NW10 5EU* Tel (020) 8969 4598 Mobile 07963-580242 E-mail oliver.ryder@gmail.com

RYDER-WEST, Keith. b 63. Sunderland Poly BSc86 Leeds Univ BTh95. Chich Th Coll 92 Coll of Resurr Mirfield. **d** 95 **p** 96. C Rawmarsh w Parkgate *Sheff* 95-96; C Armley w New Wortley *Ripon* 96-99; V Altofts *Wakef* 99-06; V Sheff St Cecilia Parson Cross from 06. *St Cecilia's Priory, 98 Chaucer Close, Sheffield S5 9QE* Tel 0114-232 1084

RYDINGS, Donald. b 33. Jes Coll Ox BA57 MA61. Linc Th Coll 57. **d** 59 **p** 60. C Poulton-le-Fylde *Blackb* 59-62; C Ox St Mary V 62-66; Staff Sec SCM 62-66; C-in-c Bourne End St Mark CD *Ox* 66-74; R Hedsor and Bourne End 74-76; P-in-c Gt Missenden w Ballinger and Lt Hampden 76-93; RD Wendover 79-89; V Gt Missenden w Ballinger and Lt Hampden 93-02; rtd 02. *16 Marroway, Weston Turville, Aylesbury HP22 5TQ* Tel (01296) 612281

RYELAND, John. b 58. K Coll Lon BD80 AKC80 Lon Sch of Th MA09. Linc Th Coll 80. **d** 81 **p** 82. C Enfield St Jas *Lon* 81-84; C Coulsdon St Andr *S'wark* 84-87; C-in-c Ingrave St Steph CD *Chelmsf* 87-97; Dir Chr Healing Miss from 97. *8 Cambridge Court, 210 Shepherd's Bush Road, London W6 7NJ* Tel (020) 7603 8118 Fax 7603 5224 E-mail chm@healingmission.org

RYLANDS, Preb Amanda Craig. b 52. Homerton Coll Cam CertEd75. Trin Coll Bris 83. **dss** 85 **d** 87 **p** 94. Chippenham St Andr w Tytherton Lucas *Bris* 85-87; Par Dn Stockport St Geo *Ches* 87-91; Par Dn Acton and Worleston, Church Minshull etc 91-94; C 94-97; Dioc Adv for Min Among Children 95-97; NSM Langport Area *B & W* 97-98 and 99-01; TV 98-99; Asst Dioc Voc Adv 00-01; Perm to Offic *Ex* 02-03; C Tedburn St Mary, Whitestone, Oldridge etc 04-05; Dioc Dir of Ords 05-09; Bp's Adv for Women in Min 06-09; Preb Ex Cathl 08-09; Perm to Offic *Lich* from 10. *Athlone House, 68 London Road, Shrewsbury SY2 6PG* Tel (01743) 235867

✠**RYLANDS, The Rt Revd Mark James.** b 61. SS Hild & Bede Coll Dur BA83. Trin Coll Bris BA87. **d** 87 **p** 88 **c** 09. C Stockport St Geo *Ches* 87-91; V Acton and Worleston, Church Minshull etc 91-97; TR Langport Area *B & W* 97-02; Dioc Missr and Can

Res Ex Cathl 02-09; Area Bp Shrewsbury *Lich* from 09. *Athlone House, 68 London Road, Shrewsbury SY2 6PG* Tel (01743) 235867 Fax 242296
E-mail bishop.shrewsbury@lichfield.anglican.org
RYLE, Denis Maurice. b 16. OBE70. St Aid Birkenhead 35. **d** 39 **p** 40. C Parr *Liv* 39-42; C Widnes St Paul 42-44; C Much Woolton 44-45; CF 45-58; Sen CF 58-65; Dep Asst Chapl Gen 65-73; P-in-c Latimer w Flaunden *Ox* 73-85; rtd 85; Perm to Offic *York* 90-11. *5 Church Close, Wheldrake, York YO19 6DP* Tel (01904) 898124
RYLEY, Canon Patrick Macpherson. b 30. Pemb Coll Ox BA54 Lon Univ BD56. Clifton Th Coll 54. **d** 56 **p** 57. C Ox St Clem 56-59; Burma 60-66; Kenya 68-75; V Lynn St Jo *Nor* 76-92; V King's Lynn St Jo the Ev 92-95; RD Lynn 78-83; Hon Can Nor Cathl 90-95; rtd 95; Perm to Offic *Bradf* 95-11. *12 Green End, Denton, Manchester M34 7PU*
RYLEY, Timothy Patrick. b 64. Man Univ BA86. St Jo Coll Nottm MA93. **d** 93 **p** 94. C Pendlebury St Jo *Man* 93-97; P-in-c Norris Bank 97-01; Age Concern from 01; Perm to Offic *Man* from 09. *12 Green End, Denton, Manchester M34 7PU*
RYMER, David John Talbot. b 37. Chich Th Coll 63. **d** 66 **p** 67. C Tuffley *Glouc* 66-69; Rhodesia 69-79; P-in-c S Kensington St Jude *Lon* 79-82; V 82-88; P-in-c Ambergate *Derby* 88-91; P-in-c Heage 88-91; R Ambergate and Heage 91-96; P-in-c Findern 96-01; V 01-03; P-in-c Willington 96-01; V 01-03; rtd 03; Perm to Offic *Derby* from 03. *2 Glebe Close, Long Lane, Dalbury Lees, Ashbourne DE6 5BJ* Tel (01332) 824165
E-mail david.rymer@amserve.net
RYRIE, Alexander Crawford. b 30. Edin Univ MA52 BD55 Glas Univ MLitt75. New Coll Edin 52 Union (NY) STM56. **d** 83 **p** 83. Hon C Edin St Mary 83-85; R Jedburgh 85-95; rtd 95. *Boisils, Bowden, Melrose TD6 0ST* Tel (01835) 823226
E-mail sandyryrie@googlemail.com
RYRIE, Mrs Isabel. b 31. Edin Univ MA51 Glas Univ MEd70 ABPsS73 CPsychol88. **d** 89 **p** 94. Bp's Dn *Edin* 89-91; NSM Edin St Mary 91-98; rtd 98. *Boisils, Bowden, Melrose TD6 0ST* Tel (01835) 823226 E-mail isabel.ryrie@virgin.net

S

SABAN, Ronald Graham Street. b 28. Bps' Coll Cheshunt 60. **d** 62 **p** 63. C Maidstone St Martin *Cant* 62-66; C Croydon St Sav 66; rtd 94. *34 Kingsway, Caversham, Reading RG4 6RA* Tel 0118-947 9454
SABELL, Michael Harold. b 42. Open Univ BA78 Surrey Univ MSc. Sarum & Wells Th Coll 77. **d** 80 **p** 81. NSM Shirley *Win* 80-82; NSM Finham *Cov* 82-85; Chapl to the Deaf *Win* 81-82; *Cov* 82-85; Sheff 85-89; Lich 89-96; P-in-c Gt and Lt Wymondley *St Alb* 96-01; R Ingoldsby *Linc* 01-04; R Old Somerby 01-04; R Ropsley 01-04; R Sapperton w Braceby 01-04; rtd 04; Perm to Offic *Lich* 05-08 and from 10; P-in-c Muchalls *Bre* 08-10. *35 Charlemont Avenue, West Bromwich B71 3BY* Tel 0121-588 6185 E-mail michaelhsabell@btinternet.com
SABEY-CORKINDALE, Charmaine Clare. b 58. SROT87. SAOMC. **d** 02 **p** 03. NSM St Ippolyts *St Alb* 02-03; C Hitchin 03-05; TV from 05. *5 Lavender Way, Hitchin SG5 2LU* Tel (01462) 435497
SABINE WILLIS, Anthony Charles. *See* WILLIS, Anthony Charles Sabine
SACH, Andrew. b 75. Oak Hill Th Coll. **d** 07. C St Helen Bishopsgate w St Andr Undershaft etc *Lon* from 07. *St Helen's Church, Great St Helen's, London EC3A 6AT* Tel (020) 7283 2231
SACHS, Andrew James. b 73. Reading Univ BSc94 Kingston Univ PGCE96. Wycliffe Hall Ox BTh05. **d** 05 **p** 06. C Upper Sunbury St Sav *Lon* 05-08; C E Twickenham St Steph from 08. *308 Richmond Road, Twickenham TW1 2PD* Tel (020) 8892 5258 E-mail andysachs@freeuk.com
SACKLEY (née WITT), Mrs Caroline Elizabeth. b 51. Surrey Univ BSc04. STETS 02. **d** 05 **p** 06. C Graffoe Gp *Linc* 05-08; P-in-c W Meon and Warnford *Portsm* from 08. *The Rectory, Doctors Lane, West Meon, Petersfield GU32 1LR* Tel (01730) 829226 E-mail sackleys@btopenworld.com
SADDINGTON, Mrs Jean. b 53. Bournemouth Univ BSc02 Cant Ch Ch Univ PGCE04. STETS 05. **d** 08. Lic to RD Dorchester from 08. *9 Conway Walk, Dorchester DT1 2EJ* Tel (01305) 250334 E-mail jean.saddington@hotmail.co.uk
SADDINGTON, Peter David. b 42. Cranmer Hall Dur. **d** 84 **p** 85. C Tudhoe Grange *Dur* 84-86; C Monkwearmouth St Andr

86-88; V Burnopfield 88-94; P-in-c Greenside 94-96; V 96-04; rtd 04. *19 The Lawns, Ryton Village, Ryton NE40 3QN* Tel 0191-413 6881
SADGROVE, The Very Revd Michael. b 50. Ball Coll Ox BA71 MA75. Trin Coll Bris 72. **d** 75 **p** 76. Lic to Offic *Ox* 75-77; Tutor Sarum & Wells Th Coll 77-82; Vice-Prin 80-82; V Alnwick *Newc* 82-87; Vice-Provost, Can Res and Prec Cov Cathl 87-95; Provost Sheff 95-00; Dean Sheff 00-03; Dean Dur from 03. *The Deanery, The College, Durham DH1 3EQ* Tel 0191-384 7500 Fax 386 4267
E-mail michael.sadgrove@durhamcathedral.co.uk
SADLER, The Ven Anthony Graham. b 36. Qu Coll Ox BA60 MA64. Lich Th Coll 60. **d** 62 **p** 63. C Burton St Chad *Lich* 62-65; V Rangemore and Dunstall 65-72; V Abbots Bromley 72-79; V Pelsall 79-90; RD Walsall 82-90; P-in-c Uttoxeter w Bramshall 90-97; P-in-c Stramshall 90-97; P-in-c Kingstone w Gratwich 90-97; P-in-c Checkley 90-97; P-in-c Marchington w Marchington Woodlands 90-97; P-in-c Leigh 93-97; TR Uttoxeter Area 97; Adn Walsall 97-04; Preb Lich Cathl 87-04; rtd 04. *Llidiart Newydd, Llanrhaeadr-ym-Mochnant, Oswestry SY10 0ED* Tel (01691) 780276
SADLER, Canon John Ernest. b 45. Nottm Univ BTh78. Linc Th Coll 74. **d** 78 **p** 79. C Brampton St Thos *Derby* 78-81; TV Coventry Caludon 81-85; V Newc St Phil and St Aug 86-94; P-in-c Newc Epiphany 94-99; Perm to Offic from 00; Ch Development Worker from 01; Hon Can Newc Cathl from 08. *26 Crompton Road, Heaton, Newcastle upon Tyne NE6 5QL* Tel 0191-262 1680 E-mail jjsadler@btinternet.com
or john@umtp.org
SADLER, Michael Stuart. b 57. Wycliffe Hall Ox 78. **d** 81 **p** 82. C Henfynyw w Aberaeron and Llanddewi Aberarth *St D* 81-88; V Llanddewi Rhydderch w Llangattock-juxta-Usk etc *Mon* 88-09; V Llandeilo Fawr and Taliaris *St D* from 09. *The Vicarage, 10 Carmarthen Road, Llandeilo SA19 6RS* Tel (01558) 823862
SAFFORD, Jeremy. b 66. Ox Brookes Univ BA02. Ridley Hall Cam 08. **d** 09 **p** 10. C Collingtree w Courteenhall and Milton Malsor *Pet* from 09. *The Rectory, Barn Corner, Collingtree, Northampton NN4 0NF* Tel (01604) 705620 Mobile 07512-856732 E-mail jez.safford@ntlworld.com
SAGAR, Brian. b 39. Sarum & Wells Th Coll 78. **d** 80 **p** 81. C Radcliffe St Thos and St Jo *Man* 80-82; P-in-c Charlestown 82-85; R Gt Lever 85-89; Chapl Cov Ch Housing Assn 89-92; V Wing w Grove *Ox* 92-97; P-in-c Diddington, Lt Paxton and Southoe *Ely* 97-00; P-in-c Lever Bridge *Man* 00-05; rtd 05; Perm to Offic *Man* from 05. *6 Loweswater Road, Farnworth, Bolton BL4 0PL* Tel (01204) 574200 E-mail b.sagar@ntlworld.com
SAGE, Canon Andrew George. b 58. Univ Coll Chich BA99. Chich Th Coll 83. **d** 85 **p** 86. C Rawmarsh w Parkgate *Sheff* 85-87; C Fareham SS Pet and Paul *Portsm* 87-89; C Southsea H Spirit 89-91; P-in-c Nuthurst *Chich* 91-93; R 93-95; V Hangleton 95-04; Chapl Worthing and Southlands Hosps NHS Trust 01-04; V Blackpool St Steph *Blackb* from 04; Warden Whalley Abbey 08-10; Hon Can Blackb Cathl from 08. *The Vicarage, St Stephen's Avenue, Blackpool FY2 9RB* Tel (01253) 351484
E-mail andrewsage@aol.com
SAGE, Canon Jesse. b 35. Trin Hall Cam BA61 MA65. Chich Th Coll 61. **d** 63 **p** 64. C Feltham *Lon* 63-67; C Port Elizabeth St Mary S Africa 67; P-in-c Port Elizabeth Ch the K and St Mark 68-72; R Abbas and Temple Combe *B & W* 72-75; R Abbas and Templecombe w Horsington 76-77; Chapl Agric and Rural Soc in Kent *Cant* 78-95; Hon Can Cant Cathl 90-95; R Gonubie St Martin by the Sea S Africa 96-00; P-in-c Komga St Paul 98-00; rtd 00; Hon Can Grahamstown from 02. *180 Crewe Road, Willaston, Nantwich CW5 6NF* Tel 07955-251312 (mobile) E-mail jessesage@qwest.co.za
SAGOVSKY, Canon Nicholas. b 47. CCC Ox BA69 St Edm Ho Cam PhD81. St Jo Coll Nottm BA73. **d** 74 **p** 75. C Newc St Gabr 74-77; C Cambridge Gt St Mary w St Mich *Ely* 81; Vice-Prin Edin Th Coll 82-86; Dean of Chpl Clare Coll Cam 86-97; Wm Leech Prof Fell Newc Univ 97-02; Liv Hope Univ Coll 02-04; Can Westmr Abbey 04-11; rtd 11. *Address temp unknown*
SAID, Yazeed. b 75. Hebrew Univ Jerusalem BA96 CCC Cam BA99 MA03 MPhil05 PhD10. Westcott Ho Cam 97. **d** 99 **p** 01. Chapl Ch Ch Sch Nazareth 99-00; Chapl to Bp Jerusalem 00-02; C St Geo Cathl 00-04; Acting Dean 02-04; Asst Chapl CCC Cam 04-08; Perm to Offic *Ely* from 08. *Faculty of Religious Studies, 3520 University Street, Montreal QC H3A 2A7, Canada* E-mail yazeed.said@gmx.net *or* yazid.said@mcgill.ca
SAIET, Timothy Robin. b 65. Wycliffe Hall Ox 06. **d** 08 **p** 09. NSM Stanley St Paul *Lon* 08-11; Chapl Philip Trust from 11. *16 Butler Avenue, Harrow HA1 4EH* Tel (01923) 287777 Mobile 07973-136968 E-mail timsaiet@btinternet.com
SAINSBURY, Peter Donald. b 67. K Coll Lon MA04. Ridley Hall Cam 98. **d** 00 **p** 01. C Longfleet *Sarum* 00-04; Chapl Glos Univ 04-08; V Summerfield *Birm* from 08. *Christ Church Vicarage, 64 Selwyn Road, Birmingham B16 0SW* Tel 0121-454 2689 E-mail cec.summerfield@yahoo.co.uk
✠**SAINSBURY, The Rt Revd Roger Frederick.** b 36. Jes Coll Cam BA58 MA62. Clifton Th Coll. **d** 60 **p** 61 **c** 91. C Spitalfields

Ch Ch w All SS *Lon* 60-63; Missr Shrewsbury Ho Everton *Liv* 63-74; P-in-c Everton St Ambrose w St Tim 67-74; Warden Mayflower Family Cen Canning Town *Chelmsf* 74-81; P-in-c Victoria Docks St Luke 78-81; V Walsall *Lich* 81-87; TR 87-88; Adn W Ham *Chelmsf* 88-91; Area Bp Barking 91-02; Moderator Ch's Commn for Racial Justice 99-02; rtd 02; Hon Asst Bp B & W from 03. *Abbey Lodge, Battery Lane, Portishead, Bristol BS20 7JD* Tel (01275) 847082
E-mail bishoproger.abbey@btopenworld.com

SAINT, David Gerald. b 45. Sarum & Wells Th Coll 72. **d** 75 **p** 76. C Wellingborough All Hallows *Pet* 75-79; R Kislingbury w Rothersthorpe 79-83; V Kings Heath 83-85; Relig Progr Producer BBC Radio Northn from 85; Perm to Offic *Pet* from 86; rtd 10. *71 Stanwell Way, Wellingborough NN8 3DD* Tel (01933) 675995 E-mail words@davidsaint.co.uk

ST ALBANS, Archdeacon of. *See* SMITH, The Ven Jonathan Peter

ST ALBANS, Bishop of. *See* SMITH, The Rt Revd Alan Gregory Clayton

ST ALBANS, Dean of. *See* JOHN, The Very Revd Jeffrey Philip Hywel

ST ANDREWS, DUNKELD AND DUNBLANE, Bishop of. *See* CHILLINGWORTH, The Most Revd David Robert

ST ANDREWS, DUNKELD AND DUNBLANE, Dean of. *See* RATHBAND, The Very Revd Kenneth William

ST ASAPH, Archdeacon of. *See* THOMAS, The Ven Elwyn Bernard

ST ASAPH, Bishop of. *See* CAMERON, The Rt Revd Gregory Kenneth

ST ASAPH, Dean of. *See* POTTER, The Very Revd Christopher Nicholas Lynden

ST DAVIDS, Archdeacon of. *See* SMALLDON, The Ven Keith

ST DAVIDS, Bishop of. *See* EVANS, The Rt Revd John Wyn

ST DAVIDS, Dean of. *See* LEAN, The Very Revd David Jonathan Rees

ST EDMUNDSBURY AND IPSWICH, Bishop of. *See* STOCK, The Rt Revd William Nigel

ST EDMUNDSBURY, Dean of. *See* WARD, The Very Revd Frances Elizabeth Fearn

ST GERMANS, Suffragan Bishop of. *See* SCREECH, The Rt Revd Royden

ST HELENA, Bishop of. *See* FENWICK, The Rt Revd Richard David

ST JOHN-CHANNELL, Canon Michael Alister Morrell. b 53. Bris Univ BEd76 MA01. Ripon Coll Cuddesdon 76. **d** 78 **p** 79. C Portsea St Mary *Portsm* 78-81; PV Linc Cathl 82-85; P-in-c Linc St Mary-le-Wigford w St Benedict etc 82-85; R Cranford *Lon* 85-92; V Staines St Mary and St Pet 92-99; V Cirencester *Glouc* 99-06; RD Cirencester 01-06; Can Res Win Cathl from 06. *8 The Close, Winchester SO23 9LS* Tel (01962) 856236 or 857211 E-mail mstjc@hotmail.com

ST JOHN NICOLLE, Jason Paul. b 66. Mert Coll Ox BA88 Called to the Bar (Inner Temple) 95. Ripon Coll Cuddesdon 01. **d** 04 **p** 05. C Kidlington w Hampton Poyle *Ox* 04-08; R The Churn from 08. *The Rectory, Church End, Blewbury, Didcot OX11 9QH* Tel (01235) 850267

SALA, Kuabuleke Meymans. b 68. **d** 08 **p** 09. C Edmonton All SS w St Mich *Lon* from 08. *60 Tillotson Road, London N9 9AH* Tel (020) 8887 9369 E-mail smeymans@hotmail.com

SALES, Canon Patrick David. b 43. K Coll Lon AKC68 BD74 Kent Univ MA00. **d** 69 **p** 70. C Maidstone All SS w St Phil *Cant* 69-72; C Chart next Sutton Valence 72-74; C Birchington w Acol 75-77; V Boughton under Blean w Dunkirk 77-83; V Herne 83-03; P-in-c Hoath 98-03; TV Whitstable 03-06; Hon Min Can Cant Cathl 83-01; Hon Can 01-06; RD Reculver 86-92; AD 01-06; Dioc Adv in Liturgy 00-06; rtd 06. *The Well House, South Lane, Dallington, Heathfield TN21 9NJ* Tel (01435) 830194 Mobile 07803-257283 E-mail patrick@sales64.freeserve.co.uk

SALFORD, Archdeacon of. *See* SHARPLES, The Ven David John

SALISBURY, Anne Ruth. b 37. Dalton Ho Bris 63. **d** 87 **p** 94. C Harrow Trin St Mich *Lon* 87-98; C Paddington Em and W Kilburn St Luke w St Simon and St Jude 99-03; rtd 03. *clo Crockford, Church House, Great Smith Street, London SW1P 3AZ* Tel 07986-868667 (mobile)

SALISBURY, Harold Gareth. b 21. St Pet Hall Ox BA42 MA46. Wycliffe Hall Ox 42. **d** 44 **p** 45. C Pet St Mark 44-46; India 47-63; Lect Bp's Coll Calcutta 47-49; Chapl St Andr Cathl Nasik 49-51; Chapl Aurangabad 51-53; Chapl Thana and Agripada 53-57; Chapl Union Th Coll Poona 58-62; V Norham *Newc* 63-70; V Duddo 63-70; V Norham and Duddo 70-78; V Snaith *Sheff* 78-86; P-in-c Cowick 78-86; TR Gt Snaith 86; rtd 86; Perm to Offic *Pet* from 87. *33 Nightingale Drive, Towcester NN12 6RA* Tel (01327) 353674 E-mail gareth.salisbury@btopenworld.com

SALISBURY, Peter Brian Christopher. b 58. UMIST BSc80 MBCS85. Sarum & Wells Th Coll BTh92. **d** 92 **p** 93. C Stanmore *Win* 92-95; V Chilworth w N Baddesley 95-05; V Lymington from 05. *The Vicarage, Grove Road, Lymington SO41 3RF* Tel (01590) 673847

SALISBURY, Canon Roger John. b 44. Lon Univ BD67. Lon Coll of Div 66. **d** 68 **p** 69. C Harold Wood *Chelmsf* 68-73; V Dorking St Paul *Guildf* 73-82; R Rusholme H Trin *Man* 82-90; TR Gt Chesham *Ox* 90-06; RD Amersham 98-04; Hon Can Ch Ch 02-06; C Langham Place All So *Lon* 06-11; rtd 11; Sec Ch Patr Trust from 06; Sec Peache Trustees from 11. *6 Church Street, Widcombe, Bath BA2 6AZ*

SALISBURY, Canon Tobias. b 33. Em Coll Cam BA60. Ripon Hall Ox 60. **d** 62 **p** 63. C Putney St Mary *S'wark* 62-65; C Churchdown St Jo *Glouc* 65-67; V Urchfont w Stert *Sarum* 67-73; R Burton Bradstock w Shipton Gorge and Chilcombe 73-79; P-in-c Long Bredy w Lt Bredy and Kingston Russell 75-79; TR Bride Valley 79-86; V Gt and Lt Bedwyn and Savernake Forest 86-97; Can and Preb Sarum Cathl 92-98; rtd 98; Perm to Offic *B & W* from 98. *Anfield, Hayes Lane, Compton Dundon, Somerton TA11 6PB* Tel (01458) 274459

SALISBURY, Bishop of. *See* HOLTAM, The Rt Revd Nicholas Roderick

SALISBURY, Dean of. *See* OSBORNE, The Very Revd June

SALMON, Alan Clive. b 63. Bris Univ BA84. St Mich Coll Llan 84. **d** 86 **p** 87. C Llanelli *St D* 86-88; C Roath St German *Llan* 88-90; V Nevern and Y Beifil w Eglwyswrw and Meline etc *St D* 90-92; In RC Ch 92-99; Perm to Offic *S'wark* 99-00; Hon C Lavender Hill Ascension etc 00-01; TP Glas E End 01-03; P-in-c Mathry w St Edren's and Grandston etc *St D* from 08. *The Rectory, St Nicholas, Goodwick SA64 0LG* Tel (01348) 891230 Mobile 07763-133775

SALMON, Canon Andrew Ian. b 61. St Jo Coll Nottm BTh88. **d** 88 **p** 89. C Collyhurst *Man* 88-92; P-in-c Pendleton St Ambrose 92-95; TV Pendleton 95-99; TR 99-04; P-in-c Salford Sacred Trin and St Phil from 04; AD Salford from 06; Hon Can Man Cathl from 10. *St Philip's Rectory, 6 Encombe Place, Salford M3 6FJ* Tel 0161-834 2041 E-mail rev.andy@btinternet.com

SALMON, Andrew Meredith Bryant. b 30. Jes Coll Cam BA54 MA58. Ridley Hall Cam 54. **d** 56 **p** 57. C Enfield Ch Ch Trent Park *Lon* 56-58; Chapl Monkton Combe Sch Bath 58-71; Chapl Milton Abbey Sch Dorset 71-89; TV Bride Valley *Sarum* 89-96; rtd 97; Perm to Offic *Sarum* from 97. *1 Barnhill Road, Wareham BH20 5BD* Tel (01929) 554039

SALMON, Anthony James Heygate. b 30. CCC Ox BA53 MA57. Cuddesdon Coll 54. **d** 56 **p** 57. C S Norwood St Mark *Cant* 56-59; S Africa 59-69; Chapl USPG Coll of the Ascension Selly Oak 69-74; P-in-c Frinsted 74-78; R Harrietsham *Cant* 74-85; P-in-c Ulcombe 81-85; V Chobham w Valley End *Guildf* 85-95; rtd 95; Perm to Offic *St Alb* from 95. *24 Elmwood, Welwyn Garden City AL8 6LE* Tel (01707) 333694

SALMON, Mrs Constance Hazel. b 25. R Holloway Coll Lon BSc46. Lon Bible Coll 66 Gilmore Course 71. **dss** 80 **d** 87 **p** 96. Sidcup St Andr *Roch* 80-88; NSM 87-88; Perm to Offic 88-96; NSM Eynsford w Farningham and Lullingstone from 96. *43 Old Mill Close, Eynsford, Dartford DA4 0BN* Tel (01322) 866034

SALMON, Jonathan. b 66. Univ Coll of Swansea BSc(Econ)88 Sussex Univ MA95 MPhil95. Wycliffe Hall Ox 01. **d** 03 **p** 04. C Bowling St Jo *Bradf* 03-07; P-in-c Earley Trin *Ox* from 07. *Trinity Church House, 15 Caraway Road, Earley, Reading RG6 5XR* Tel 0118-986 9798 Mobile 07840-494072 E-mail salmonj@btinternet.com

SALMON, Mrs Margaret. b 37. Leeds Univ BA59 CertEd60. SWMTC 85. **d** 88 **p** 94. NSM Yelverton, Meavy, Sheepstor and Walkhampton *Ex* from 88. *5 Manor Park, Dousland, Yelverton PL20 6LX* Tel (01822) 853310 E-mail peggy@littlegidding.eclipse.co.uk

SALMON, Mark Harold. b 62. Trin Coll Bris. **d** 00 **p** 01. C Bath Weston All SS w N Stoke and Langridge *B & W* 00-04; P-in-c Harlescott *Lich* 04-07; V from 07. *Harlescott Vicarage, Meadow Farm Drive, Shrewsbury SY1 4NG* Tel (01743) 362883 E-mail mark.salmon@xalt.co.uk

SALMON, Paul Richard. **d** 06 **p** 07. OLM Humberston *Linc* from 06. *47 Tetney Road, Humberstone, Grimsby DN36 4JQ* Tel (01472) 814550 E-mail paulsal@stayfree.co.uk

SALMON, Philip John. b 63. Oak Hill Th Coll 96. **d** 98 **p** 99. C Kington w Huntington, Old Radnor, Kinnerton etc *Heref* 98-02; TV Radipole and Melcombe Regis *Sarum* from 02. *The Vicarage, 74 Field Barn Drive, Weymouth DT4 0EF* Tel (01305) 778995 Mobile 07771-688226 E-mail vicar@emmanuelwey.co.uk

SALMON, Richard Harold. b 35. Fitzw Ho Cam BA57. Clifton Th Coll 57. **d** 59 **p** 60. C Blackheath Park St Mich *S'wark* 59-61; C St Alb St Paul *St Alb* 61-63; Malaysia 63-75; OMF 63-65; C Telok Anson St Luke 63-65; V Kuantan Pehang Epiphany 65-75; P-in-c March St Wendreda *Ely* 75-76; R 76-85; V Congresbury w Puxton and Hewish St Ann *B & W* 85-00; rtd 00; Perm to Offic *Truro* 00-01 and *B & W* from 02. *2 Wisteria Avenue, Hutton, Weston-super-Mare BS24 9QF* Tel (01934) 813733 E-mail richard.salmon@talk21.com

SALMON, The Very Revd Thomas Noel Desmond Cornwall. b 13. TCD BA35 MA49 BD42. TCD Div Sch 35. **d** 37 **p** 38. C Bangor St Comgall *D & D* 37-40; C Belfast St Jas *Conn* 40-41; C Larne and Inver 42-44; Clerical V Ch Ch Cathl Dublin 44-45;

Lect TCD 45-89; C Dublin Rathfarnham *D & G* 45-50; Hon Clerical V Ch Ch Cathl Dublin 45-63; I Tullow 50-62; I Dublin St Ann 62-67; Preb Dunlavin St Patr Cathl Dublin 63-67; Dean Ch Ch Cathl Dublin 67-89; I Dublin Ch Ch Cathl Gp 76-89; rtd 89. *clo Mrs I Sherwood, Hillcrest, Kilmolin, Enniskerry, Co Wicklow, Republic of Ireland*

SALMON, William John. b 50. Lon Univ BSc72 DipEd73. Cranmer Hall Dur 76. **d** 79 **p** 80. C Summerstown *S'wark* 79-81; C Hampreston *Sarum* 81-86; V Sundon *St Alb* 86-90; Dep Chapl HM Young Offender Inst Glen Parva 90-91; Chapl HM Pris Whitemoor 91-95; Chapl HM Pris Blundeston 95-04 and from 07; Chapl HM Pris Belmarsh 04-07. *HM Prison Blundeston, Lowestoft NR32 5BG* Tel (01502) 734500 Fax 734501 E-mail william.salmon@hmps.gsi.gov.uk

SALMON, Mrs Yvonne Delysia. b 40. Cant Sch of Min 00. **d** 03 **p** 04. OLM Boughton Monchelsea *Cant* 03-10; Perm to Offic from 11. *Elderden Farm Cottage, Maidstone Road, Staplehurst, Tonbridge TN12 0RN* Tel (01622) 842598 E-mail y.salmon@tesco.net

SALONIA, Ivan. b 38. Open Univ BA81 N Lon Poly MA85 CQSW78. Milan Th Coll (RC) 60. **d** 63 **p** 64. In RC Ch Hong Kong 64-73; Hon C Woolwich St Thos *S'wark* 89-91; C Greenwich St Alfege w St Pet and St Paul 91-93; C Kidbrooke St Jas 93-95; TV 95-02; rtd 02; Perm to Offic *S'wark* from 03. *247 Hook Lane, Welling DA16 2NZ* Tel (020) 8306 2862 *or* 8298 1309 Fax 8306 6859 Mobile 07946-085065 E-mail ivanus_magnus@hotmail.com

SALOP, Archdeacon of. See THOMAS, The Ven Paul Wyndham

SALT, Canon David Christopher. b 37. Univ of Wales (Lamp) BA59. Sarum Th Coll 59. **d** 61 **p** 62. C Kidderminster St Mary *Worc* 61-66; Ind Chapl 66-72; R Knightwick w Doddenham, Broadwas and Cotheridge 72-82; Chapl Worc Coll of HE 72-82; V Redditch St Steph *Worc* 82-02; P-in-c Tardebigge 84-88; RD Bromsgrove 91-00; Hon Can Worc Cathl 92-02; rtd 02; Perm to Offic *Worc* from 03 and Cov from 05. *7 Longmoor Close, Redditch B97 6SX* Tel (01527) 68735

SALT, David Thomas Whitehorn. b 32. K Coll Lon AKC56 BD57. **d** 57 **p** 58. Chapl Torgil Girls' Sch Aoba New Hebrides 57-59; Warden Catechist Coll Lolowai 59-63; Prin St Andr Coll Guadalcanal Solomon Is 63-66; C Hawley H Trin *Guildf* 66-68; V Shelf *Bradf* 68-73; R Checkendon *Ox* 73-81; RD Henley 78-84; TR Langtree 81-84; V Hungerford and Denford 84-89; Chapl Hungerford Hosp 84-89; P-in-c Harpsden *Ox* 89-95; Gen Sec Melanesian Miss 89-95; rtd 95; Perm to Offic *Guildf* and *Win* from 06. *18 Manormead, Tilford Road, Hindhead GU26 6RA* Tel (01428) 601518 E-mail dtwsalt@gmail.com

SALT, Jeremy William. St Mellitus Coll. **d** 11. NSM Ingatestone w Fryerning *Chelmsf* from 11. *13 Covenbrook, Brentwood CM13 2TR*

✠SALT, The Rt Revd John William. b 41. Kelham Th Coll 61. **d** 66 **p** 67 **c** 99. C Barrow St Matt *Carl* 66-70; C Mohale's Hoek Lesotho 70-71; Asst Chapl St Agnes Sch Teyateyaneng 71-72; C Maseru Cathl 73-77; S Africa 77-99; OGS from 81; Superior 96-05; Dean Eshowe Cathl and Adn S Zululand 89-99; Bp St Helena 99-11; rtd 11. *Palmers, 5 Common Place, Walsingham NR22 6BW* Tel (01328) 820823 E-mail jsalt@ogs.net

SALT, Leslie. b 29. Linc Th Coll 68. **d** 69 **p** 69. C Alford w Rigsby *Linc* 69-75; V Torksey 75-94; R Kettlethorpe 77-94; V Marton 77-94; V Newton-on-Trent 77-94; rtd 94; Perm to Offic *Linc* 94-97. *2 Holdenby Close, Lincoln LN2 4TQ*

SALT, Neil. b 64. Univ of Wales (Ban) BA85 New Coll Edin BD89 Man Metrop Univ BSc97. Edin Th Coll 86. **d** 89 **p** 90. C Stretford All SS *Man* 89-93; V Smallbridge and Wardle 93-94; Perm to Offic *Wakef* 94-01; Hon C Ripponden and Barkisland w W Scammonden 01-06; Chapl Rishworth Sch Ripponden 02-05; V Thornton-le-Fylde *Blackb* from 06. *The Vicarage, Meadows Avenue, Thornton-Cleveleys FY5 2TW* Tel (01253) 855099 E-mail nsalt@waitrose.com

SALTER, Arthur Thomas John. b 34. TD88. AKC60. **d** 61 **p** 62. C Ealing St Pet Mt Park *Lon* 61-65; C Shepherd's Bush St Steph w St Thos 65-66; C Holborn St Alb w Saffron Hill St Pet 66-70; P-in-c Barnsbury St Clem 70-77; P-in-c Islington St Mich 70-77; V Pentonville St Silas w All SS and St Jas 70-00; CF (TAVR) from 75; Gen Sec Angl and E Chs Assn from 76; Chmn from 90; P-in-c St Dunstan in the West *Lon* 79-99; rtd 00. *1 St James's Close, Bishop Street, London N1 8PH* Tel (020) 7359 0250

SALTER, Christopher. See SALTER, Nigel Christopher Murray

SALTER, David Whitton. b 69. Bris Univ BEng00. Trin Coll Bris 06. **d** 08 **p** 09. C Eynsham and Cassington *Ox* from 08. *Jovonne, Bell Lane, Cassington, Witney OX29 4DS* Tel (01865) 881434 Mobile 07768-582285 E-mail david.w.salter@btinternet.com

SALTER, George Alfred. b 25. TCD BA47 MA. CITC 49. **d** 49 **p** 50. C Rathdowney *C & O* 49-51; C Cork St Luke *C, C & R* 51-53; I Fermoy Union 53-55; I Cork St Luke w St Ann 55-73; Can Ross Cathl 69-88; Can Cork Cathl 69-88; Treas 88-94; I Cork St Luke Union 73-94; Preb Tymothan St Patr Cathl Dublin 88-94; rtd 94. *Mount Vernon House, 66 Wellington Road, Cork, Republic of Ireland* Tel (00353) (21) 450 6844

SALTER, Janet Elizabeth. b 48. Leeds Univ CertEd69. SWMTC 92. **d** 95 **p** 98. C Coleshill *Birm* 95-97; Hon C St Dennis *Truro* 97-00; TV Gillingham *Sarum* 00-04; V Stour Vale 04-11; rtd 11. *6 Maple Close, St Columb TR9 6SL* Tel (01637) 881552 E-mail vicarjan@tiscali.co.uk

SALTER, John. See SALTER, Arthur Thomas John

SALTER, Canon John Frank. b 37. Dur Univ BA62. Cranmer Hall Dur 62. **d** 64 **p** 65. C Bridlington Priory *York* 64-67; Travelling Sec IVF 67-70; V Stoughton *Guildf* 70-02; RD Guildf 89-94; Hon Can Guildf Cathl 99-02; rtd 03. *7 Aldershot Road, Guildford GU2 8AE* Tel (01483) 511165 E-mail j.salter@btinternet.com

SALTER, Canon John Leslie. b 51. AKC76 Heythrop Coll Lon MA05. Coll of Resurr Mirfield 77. **d** 78 **p** 79. C Tottenham St Paul *Lon* 78-82; P-in-c Castle Vale *Birm* 82-83; TV Curdworth w Castle Vale 83-90; V Castle Vale St Cuth 90-92; V Wantage *Ox* from 93; AD Wantage 01-08; Hon Can Ch Ch from 06. *The Vicarage, The Cloisters, Wantage OX12 8AQ* Tel (01235) 762214

SALTER, Nigel Christopher Murray. b 46. Loughb Univ BTech. Ripon Coll Cuddesdon 79. **d** 81 **p** 82. C Glouc St Aldate 81-84; C Solihull *Birm* 84-88; V Highters Heath 88-97; Asst Chapl Greenwich Healthcare NHS Trust 97-01; Asst Chapl Qu Eliz Hosp NHS Trust 01-03; P-in-c Leaton and Albrighton w Battlefield *Lich* 03-06; rtd 06. *621 Vista Building, 30 Calderwood Street, London SE18 6JG* Tel (020) 8465 7854 E-mail chris@princehal.freeserve.co.uk

SALTER, Roger John. b 45. Trin Coll Bris 75. **d** 79 **p** 80. C Bedminster St Mich *Bris* 79-82; C Swindon Ch Ch 82-84; V Bedminster Down 84-89; P-in-c Northwood *Portsm* 89-93; P in c W Cowes H Trin 89-92; V Cowes H Trin and St Mary 92-94; USA from 94; rtd 10. *1300 Panorama Drive, Vestavia Hill AL 35216-3032, USA* Tel (001) (1) 205 7967 E-mail salter.roger@gmail.com

SALTMARSH, Philip. b 71. Keele Univ MA05. SNWTP 09. **d** 11. NSM Grassendale *Liv* from 11. *24 Kintore Road, Liverpool L19 0NL* Tel 0151-427 2512 E-mail philsaltmarsh@aol.com

SALTWELL, Ms Kathleen. b 48. Edin Univ BD00 Cam Univ MA02. Westcott Ho Cam 00. **d** 02 **p** 03. C Worc SE 02-06; Teacher Amity Foundn China from 07. *3 Chiserley Stile, Hebden Bridge HX7 8SB* Tel (01422) 842532 E-mail kathsaltwell@tiscali.co.uk

SALWAY, Canon Donald Macleay. b 31. St Pet Hall Ox BA54 MA59. Oak Hill Th Coll 54. **d** 56 **p** 57. C Holloway St Mary w St Jas *Lon* 56-67; V Cambridge St Phil *Ely* 67-81; V Mile Cross *Nor* 81-96; RD Nor N 89-95; Hon Can Nor Cathl 91-96; rtd 96; Perm to Offic *B & W* from 96; C Langport Area 98-00. *2 Hodges Barton, Somerton TA11 6QD* Tel (01458) 274640

SAMBROOK, Kenneth Henry. b 42. NOC 04. **d** 05 **p** 06. NSM Wistaston *Ches* from 05. *6 Westfield Drive, Wistaston, Crewe CW2 8ES* Tel (01270) 662454 E-mail kensambrook@beeb.net

SAMMÉ, Raymond Charles. b 50. Anglia Poly Univ MA03 St Andr Univ MLitt08 MIBiol80 CBiol80. Oak Hill Th Coll 85. **d** 87 **p** 88. C Holmer w Huntington *Heref* 87-90; C Derby St Alkmund and St Werburgh 90-93; V Romford Gd Shep *Chelmsf* 93-08; P-in-c Swanley St Paul *Roch* from 08. *3 Holt Close, Sidcup DA14 5EQ* Tel (020) 8302 5491 E-mail ray.samme@btinternet.com

SAMMON, Helen Mary. b 57. Newnham Coll Cam MA79 Bris Univ MB, ChB82 MRCGP98. WEMTC 00. **d** 03 **p** 04. NSM Painswick, Sheepscombe, Cranham, The Edge etc *Glouc* 03-07; P-in-c Stroud from 07. *St Barnabas' Vicarage, 200 Reservoir Road, Gloucester GL4 6SB* Tel (01452) 543738 E-mail helen.sammon@doctors.org.uk

SAMMONS, Elizabeth Mary. See SLATER, Mrs Elizabeth Mary

SAMPFORD, John Alfred. b 36. Lich Th Coll 58. **d** 61 **p** 62. C Lambeth St Phil *S'wark* 61-65; C Beddington 65-69; V Hampstead Ch Ch *Lon* 69-79; V Enfield Chase St Mary 79-02; rtd 02; Perm to Offic *Ches* from 02. *Ellisland, Bryn Gwyn Lane, Northop Hall, Mold CH7 6JT* Tel (01244) 810635

SAMPLE, Mrs Fiona Jean. b 55. **d** 08 **p** 09. OLM Bolam w Whalton and Hartburn w Meldon *Newc* from 08; OLM Nether Witton from 08. *South Middleton, Scots Gap, Middleton, Morpeth NE61 4EB* Tel (01670) 774245 Mobile 07905-207117

SAMPSON, Brian Andrew. b 39. **d** 94 **p** 95. C Glemsford, Hartest w Boxted, Somerton etc *St E* 94-96; C Pentlow, Foxearth, Liston and Borley *Chelmsf* 96-97; P-in-c 97-04; C N Hinckford 04-09; rtd 09. *4 Friars Court, Edgworth Road, Sudbury CO10 2TG* Tel (01787) 371529 E-mail captainbrianca@waitrose.co.uk

SAMPSON, Clive. b 38. St Jo Coll Cam BA61 MA64. Ridley Hall Cam 63. **d** 65 **p** 66. C Tunbridge Wells St Jo *Roch* 65-69; Travelling Sec Scripture Union 69-79; V Maidstone St Luke *Cant* 79-94; rtd 98. *108 Bure Homage Gardens, Christchurch BH23 4DR* Tel (01425) 279029

SAMPSON, Desmond William John. b 25. FRICS60. Roch Th Coll 63. **d** 65 **p** 66. C Hythe *Cant* 65-70; V Alkham w Capel le Ferne and Hougham 70-76; V Wingham w Elmstone and Preston w Stourmouth 76-86; RD E Bridge 81-86; C Hythe 86-91; rtd 91; Perm to Offic *Cant* from 91. *25 Albert Road, Hythe CT21 6BP* Tel (01303) 268457

SAMPSON, Jeremy John Egerton. b 23. Dur Univ BSc45. Wells Th Coll 46. **d** 48 **p** 49. C Longbenton St Bart *Newc* 48-51; V N Perak Singapore 51-52; P-in-c Johore Bahru 52-57; V Ipoh St Jo 57-62; V Killingworth *Newc* 62-76; V Consett *Dur* 76-90; RD Lanchester 80-85; rtd 90; Perm to Offic *Dur* and *York* 90-06. *3 Ferens House, Sherburn Hospital, Durham DH1 2SE*

SAMPSON, Julian Robin Anthony. b 78. St D Coll Lamp BA00. St Steph Ho Ox 01. **d** 03. C Notting Hill All SS w St Columb *Lon* 03-04; C Staines and Asst Chapl HM Pris Bronzefield 04-07; Chapl HM Pris Birm from 07. *HM Prison, Winson Green Road, Birmingham B18 4AS* Tel 0121-345 2500
E-mail jrasampson@yahoo.co.uk

SAMPSON, Mrs Susan Ann. b 57. Bedf Coll Lon BA81 St Mary's Coll Twickenham PGCE98. Ripon Coll Cuddesdon 09. **d** 11. C Haywards Heath Ascension *Chich* from 11. *74 Updown Hill, Haywards Heath RH16 4GD* Tel (01444) 452547 Mobile 07780-907467 E-mail sue@suesabode.freeserve.co.uk

SAMPSON, Terence Harold Morris. b 41. ACA64 FCA75. Bps' Coll Cheshunt 64. **d** 67 **p** 68. C Penrith St Andr *Carl* 67-72; V Carl St Barn 72-80; TR Carl H Trin and St Barn 80-84; Chapl Cumberland Infirmary 83-84; R Workington St Mich *Carl* 84-01; Hon Can Carl Cathl 89-01; RD Solway 90-95; Perm to Offic *Carl* from 02 and *Eur* from 03. *Edificio Balcon de San Miguel, Avenida de Alicante 17/19, 03193 San Miguel de Salinas, (Alicante) Spain* Tel 07775-683275 (mobile)
E-mail terenceandmargaret@hotmail.co.uk

SAMS, Mrs Jacqueline. b 53. Open Univ BA82 St Osyth Coll of Educn CertEd74. NTMTC BA10. **d** 10 **p** 11. NSM Colchester Ch Ch w St Mary V *Chelmsf* from 10. *17 Chestnut Avenue, Colchester CO2 0AL* Tel (01206) 530586

SAMS, Michael Charles. b 34. FCA62. Ox NSM Course 81. **d** 84 **p** 85. NSM Abingdon *Ox* 84-92 and 99-04; P-in-c Shippon 92-99; Perm to Offic from 04. *13 Hound Close, Abingdon OX14 2LU* Tel (01235) 529084

SAMS, Raymond Victor. b 51. Goldsmiths' Coll Lon TCert73. ERMC 03. **d** 06 **p** 07. NSM Colchester Ch Ch w St Mary V *Chelmsf* 06-10; P-in-c Cressing w Stisted and Bradwell etc from 10. *18 Munnings Road, Colchester CO3 4QG* Tel (01206) 560691
E-mail ray@issachar.freeserve.co.uk

SAMSON, Hilary Lynn. b 50. SWMTC. **d** 03 **p** 04. NSM St Agnes and Mithian w Mount Hawke *Truro* 03-06; P-in-c St Enoder from 06; P-in-c Newlyn St Newlyn from 06. *The Rectory, Penhale View, My Lords Road, Fraddon, St Columb TR9 6LX* Tel (01726) 860514
E-mail hilarysamson@lineone.net

SAMSON, Mrs Susan Mary. b 52. Southn Univ BA73. **d** 09 **p** 10. OLM Sittingbourne H Trin w Bobbing *Cant* from 09. *60 Rock Road, Sittingbourne ME10 1JG* Tel (01795) 478635
E-mail suesamson@sky.com

SAMUEL, Adrian Frank Graham. b 68. Essex Univ BA94 PhD02 Warwick Univ MA95. NTMTC 04. **d** 07 **p** 08. C Twickenham St Mary *Lon* 07-10. *11 Mary's Terrace, Twickenham TW1 3JB* Tel 07766-664345 (mobile) E-mail adriansamuel@msn.com

SAMUEL, Alwin John. b 55. **d** 81 **p** 83. Pakistan 81-03; Interfaith Worker and Dioc Adv *Ox* 03-05; Inter Faith Adv Cowley Deanery from 05. *63 Copperfields, High Wycombe HP12 4AN* Tel 07956-882588 (mobile)

SAMUEL, Brother. *See* DOUBLE, Richard Sydney

SAMUEL, Canon James Louis. b 30. Birm Poly CQSW72 Open Univ BA77. Sarum Th Coll 59. **d** 61 **p** 62. C Dursley *Glouc* 61-63; C Matson 63-65; C Leckhampton SS Phil and Jas 65-66; C Blakenall Heath *Lich* 67-69; P-in-c Dudley St Aug Holly Hall *Worc* 81-86; V 86-94; RD Dudley 87-93; Hon Can Worc Cathl 88-94; rtd 94; Perm to Offic *Worc* 94-96 and from 98; C Kidderminster St Mary and All SS w Trimpley etc 96-98. *44 Broadwaters Drive, Kidderminster DY10 2RY* Tel (01562) 68533 E-mail jimsam@sagainternet.co.uk

SAMUEL, Kerry Jay. b 71. Nottm Univ BA92 Hughes Hall Cam PGCE93 K Coll Lon PhD07. NTMTC 05. **d** 07 **p** 08. C Twickenham St Mary *Lon* 07-10. *11 Mary's Terrace, Twickenham TW1 3JB* Tel 07717-470403 (mobile)
E-mail kerrysamuel@hotmail.com

✠**SAMUEL, The Most Revd Kunnumpurathu Joseph.** b 42. Union Bibl Sem Yavatmal BRE68 Texas Chr Univ MDiv86. **d** 68 **c** 90. Ch of S India from 68; Bp E Kerala from 90; Moderator Ch of S India 99-04. *CSI Bishop's House, Melukavumattom PO, Kottayam 686 652, Kerala State, India* Tel (0091) (482) 291026 Fax 291044

SAMUEL, Luther Fiaz. b 47. Karachi Univ BA83. St Thos Th Coll Karachi BTh88. **d** 88 **p** 89. Pakistan 88-96; Oman 96-03; Perm to Offic *Lich* 03-04; NSM Walsall St Matt from 04; Minority Ethnic Angl Concerns Officer 04-05; Asian Missr from 05. *16 Bescot Drive, Walsall WS2 9DF* Tel (01543) 631814 Mobile 07901-718371 E-mail revlfs@hotmail.com

SAMUEL, Mrs Mary Rose. b 42. Newc Univ BA65 CQSW67. STETS 95. **d** 98 **p** 99. C Waltham on the Wolds, Stonesby, Saxby etc *Leic* 98-01; P-in-c Wymondham w Edmondthorpe, Buckminster etc 01-04; R S Framland 04-08; rtd 08; Hon C Barrow upon Soar w Walton le Wolds *Leic* from 08; Hon C

Wymeswold and Prestwold w Hoton from 08. *13A Lenham Road West, Rottingdean, Brighton BN2 7GJ*
E-mail mary.rosesamuel@tiscali.co.uk

SAMUEL, Oliver Harold. b 53. **d** 05 **p** 07. OLM Old Trafford St Bride *Man* from 05. *115 Northumberland Road, Old Trafford, Manchester M16 9PY* Tel 0161-876 5055

SAMUEL, Stuart. b 48. AKC70. St Aug Coll Cant 70. **d** 71 **p** 72. C Golcar *Wakef* 71-77; V Brampton St Mark *Derby* 77-79; P-in-c Hathern *Leic* 79-83; R Hathern, Long Whatton and Diseworth 83-90; R Hathern, Long Whatton and Diseworth w Belton etc 90-97; RD Akeley E 92-96; P-in-c Waltham on the Wolds, Stonesby, Saxby etc 97-02; P-in-c Wymondham w Edmondthorpe, Buckminster etc 97-01; P-in-c High Framland Par 97-01; P-in-c Helpringham w Hale *Linc* 02-10. *6 Seabank Road, Rhyl LL18 1EA* E-mail stuart@marymag.freeserve.co.uk

SAMUELS, Canon Ann Elizabeth. b 51. Birm Univ BA73 CertEd74. Trin Coll Bris 85. **d** 87 **p** 94. Par Dn Moreton *Ches* 87-91; Par Dn Halton 91-94; C 94-03; Bp's Adv for Women in Min 94-96; Asst Dir of Ords 96-03; RD Frodsham 99-03; Chapl Halton Gen Hosp NHS Trust 99-03; V Higher Bebington *Ches* from 03; Hon Can Ches Cathl from 01. *The Vicarage, King's Road, Bebington, Wirral CH63 8LX* Tel 0151-609 0943
E-mail vicar@higher.bebington.fsnet.co.uk

SAMUELS, Canon Christopher William John. b 42. AKC66. **d** 67 **p** 68. C Kirkholt *Man* 67-72; C-in-c Houghton Regis St Thos CD *St Alb* 72-76; R Tarporley *Ches* 76-83; R Ches St Mary 83-05; RD Ches 95-02; Hon Can Ches Cathl 97-05; Chapl to The Queen from 01; rtd 05; Perm to Offic *Ches* from 07. *Riverleigh House, Station Road, Rossett, Wrexham LL12 0HE* Tel (01244) 579097 E-mail cwjsamuels@tiscali.co.uk

SAMUELS, Raymond John. b 49. Qu Mary Coll Lon BSc73 Essex Univ CertEd74. Trin Coll Bris 85. **d** 87 **p** 88. C Moreton *Ches* 87-91; V Halton 91-02; Dioc Dir of Ords from 03. *The Vicarage, King's Road, Bebington, Wirral CH63 8LX* Tel 0151-609 0942 *or* (01244) 346945
E-mail ray.samuels@chester.anglican.org

SAMWAYS, Denis Robert. b 37. Leeds Univ BA62. Coll of Resurr Mirfield 62. **d** 64 **p** 65. C Clun w Chapel Lawn *Heref* 64-69; C Pocklington w Yapham-cum-Meltonby, Owsthorpe etc *York* 69-71; C Millington w Gt Givendale 69-71; R Hinderwell w Roxby 71-76; Hon C 80-91; Hon C Loftus 76-80; V Boosbeck w Moorsholm 91-95; R Kirby Misperton w Normanby, Edston and Salton 95-02; rtd 02. *7 High Street, Gatehouse of Fleet, Castle Douglas DG7 2HR* Tel (01557) 814095

SAMWAYS, John Feverel. b 44. BA. Trin Coll Bris 81. **d** 83 **p** 84. C Patcham *Chich* 83-86; C Ox St Aldate w St Matt 86-94; R Ox St Matt 95-97; TR Keynsham *B & W* 97-09; rtd 09. *9 Newland Gardens, Frome BA11 1PN* Tel (01373) 454047
E-mail john.samways@blueyonder.co.uk

✠**SAN SI HTAY, The Most Revd Samuel.** BA. **d** 67 **c** 89. Asst Pastor Indaw Burma 67-69; P-in-c Mawbi 70-76; Prin H Cross Coll 76-91; Asst Bp Yangon 91-93; Gen Sec Myanmar 93-01; Abp Myanmar and Bp Yangon from 01. *Bishopscourt, 140 Pyidaungsu Yeiktha Road, Dagon, Yangon 11191, Myanmar* Tel (0095) (1) 246813 Fax 251405
E-mail cpm.140@mptmail.net.mm

✠**SANANA, The Rt Revd Rhynold Ewaruba.** b 39. Newton Th Coll 60 St Barn Coll Adelaide 71 St Aug Coll Cant 75. **d** 67 **p** 67 **c** 76. Papua New Guinea 67-72, 73-90 and from 92; Asst P Dogura Cathl 67-69; Asst P Popondetta Resurr 69-70; St Barn Coll Adelaide Australia 72-73; Dean Dogura and Adn E Region 74-76; Asst Bp New Guinea 76-77; Bp Dogura 77-89; Asst P Lakenham St Mark *Nor* 90-92; rtd 99. *Diocesan Office, PO Box 26, Popondetta, Oro Province, Papua New Guinea*

SANDAY, Robert Ward. b 55. Sarum & Wells Th Coll 89. **d** 91 **p** 92. C Swindon Ch Ch *Bris* 91-94; V Lyddington and Wanborough and Bishopstone etc 94-00; Chapl to the Deaf *Portsm* and *Win* from 00; V Southampton Lord's Hill and Lord's Wood from 10. *1 Tangmere Drive, Southampton SO16 8GY* Tel (023) 8073 1091 E-mail robertsandays@talktalk.net

SANDBERG, Canon Peter John. b 37. Lon Univ LLB59. Lon Coll of Div 67. **d** 69 **p** 70. C Hailsham *Chich* 69-72; C Billericay St Mary *Chelmsf* 72-77; TV Billericay and Lt Burstead 77-83; R Thundersley 83-02; RD Hadleigh 90-02; Hon Can Chelmsf Cathl 00-02; rtd 02; Perm to Offic *Chelmsf* from 02. *Hethersett, School Road, Pentlow, Sudbury CO10 7JR* Tel (01787) 281006 E-mail psandberg@talktalk.net

SANDELLS-REES, Kathy Louise. *See* JONES, Ms Kathy Louise

SANDER, Thomas William. b 87. Westcott Ho Cam. **d** 11. C Sharnbrook, Felmersham and Knotting w Souldrop *St Alb* from 11. *The Old Manse, Kennell Hill, Sharnbrook, Bedford MK44 1PS* E-mail thomas.william.sander@gmail.com

SANDERS, Mrs Alexandra Jane. b 58. Ex Univ BA80 Leeds Univ MA09. NOC 06. **d** 09 **p** 10. NSM Tarporley *Ches* 09-10; C Acton and Worleston, Church Minshull etc from 11. *Woodstock, Hill Close, Bunbury, Tarporley CW6 9QJ* Tel and Fax (01829) 262494 Mobile 07813-326313 E-mail alex@oftheriver.com

SANDERS, Colin Anthony Wakefield. b 26. Wadh Coll Ox MA55. Ox NSM Course 89. **d** 90 **p** 91. NSM Eynsham and

Cassington *Ox* 90-95; NSM Bladon w Woodstock 95-05; NSM Blenheim from 05. *Little Firs, 41 Bladon Road, Woodstock OX20 1QD* Tel (01993) 813357

SANDERS, Diana Faye. b 46. Auckland Univ MA68 LSE PhD75 Anglia Ruskin Univ PhD10. Westcott Ho Cam 02. **d** 04 **p** 05. NSM Cottenham *Ely* 04-08; P-in-c Farley Hill St Jo *St Alb* from 08. *The Vicarage, 47 Rotheram Avenue, Luton LU1 5PP* Tel (01582) 729466 E-mail revdsanders@googlemail.com

SANDERS, Diana Louise. b 59. Southn Univ BSc80 ACA83. STETS 95. **d** 98 **p** 99. NSM Alderbury Team *Sarum* 98-01; NSM Clarendon 01-08. *Address temp unknown* E-mail diana@ds1999.force9.co.uk

SANDERS, Graham Laughton. b 32. Kelham Th Coll 52. **d** 56 **p** 57. C Glouc St Paul 56-60; India 61-68; V Heaton St Martin *Bradf* 68-76; V Gt Waltham *Chelmsf* 76-79; V Gt Waltham w Ford End 79-87; Sec Dioc Liturg Cttee 78-87; TR Guiseley w Esholt *Bradf* 87-94; rtd 97. *77 Malletts Close, Stony Stratford, Milton Keynes MK11 1DG* Tel (01908) 265290 Mobile 07808-123165 E-mail sanders966@btinternet.com

SANDERS, Canon Hilary Clare. b 57. Hull Univ BA79 UEA CertEd81. EAMTC 83. **dss** 85 **d** 87 **p** 94. Haverhill w Withersfield, the Wrattings etc *St E* 85-87; Hon Par Dn Melton 87-94; Hon C 94-99; Dioc Dir Educn (Schools) 88-99; P-in-c Earl Soham w Cretingham and Ashfield 99-05; P-in-c Boulge w Burgh, Grundisburgh and Hasketon from 05; Dioc Adv for Women's Min from 10; RD Woodbridge from 11; Hon Can St E Cathl from 04. *The Rectory, Woodbridge Road, Grundisburgh, Woodbridge IP13 6UF* Tel (01473) 735183 E-mail revclaresanders@tiscali.co.uk

SANDERS, James Alexander. b 29. **d** 65 **p** 66. Australia 65-78 and from 81; C Enfield St Jas *Lon* 78-81; rtd 94. *Apt 8, 82 Sandy Bay Road, Battery Point Tas 7004, Australia*

SANDERS, Canon Mark. b 57. Hull Univ BA79 Cam Univ BA82. Westcott Ho Cam 80. **d** 83 **p** 84. C Haverhill w Withersfield, the Wrattings etc *St E* 83-87; P-in-c Melton 87-91; R 91-98; Dioc Dir Post-Ord Tr from 97; Asst Dioc Dir of Ords 98-99; Dioc Dir of Ords from 99; Dioc Dir of CME 99-01; Hon Can St E Cathl from 01. *The Rectory, Woodbridge Road, Grundisburgh, Woodbridge IP13 6UF* Tel and fax (01473) 735182 E-mail mark@stedmundsbury.anglican.org

SANDERS, Michael Barry. b 45. Fitzw Coll Cam BA67 MA71 Lon Univ BD71. St Jo Coll Nottm 68 Lon Coll of Div. **d** 71 **p** 72. C Ashtead *Guildf* 71-74; Chapl St Jo Coll Cam 75-79; V Dorridge *Birm* 79-89; TR Walsall *Lich* 89-01; Preb Lich Cathl 97-01; Chapl The Hague *Eur* 01-07; P-in-c Kemble, Poole Keynes, Somerford Keynes etc *Glouc* from 07. *The Rectory, Coates, Cirencester GL7 8NR* Tel (01285) 770235

SANDERS, Nigel Wilding. b 29. Mert Coll Ox MA55. Ox Min Course 91. **d** 92 **p** 93. NSM Maidenhead St Andr and St Mary *Ox* 92-97; NSM Furze Platt 97-04; rtd 04; Perm to Offic *B & W* from 05. *48 Hapil Close, Sandford, Winscombe BS25 5AA* Tel (01934) 820136 E-mail nigelisan@btinternet.com

SANDERS, Mrs Nora Irene. b 29. Lon Univ BA50 CertEd51. WMMTC 74. **dss** 78 **d** 87 **p** 94. Dorridge *Birm* 78-90; Par Dn 87-90; rtd 90; Hon C Tanworth *Birm* 94-96; Perm to Offic from 96. *10 Dove House Court, Warwick Grange, Solihull B91 1EW* Tel 0121-704 1765

SANDERS (née SHAW), Mrs Pamela Joyce. b 54. Liv Univ BA76. WEMTC 02. **d** 05 **p** 06. C Leominster *Heref* 05-09; R Crathorne *York* from 09; V Kirklevington w Picton, and High and Low Worsall from 09; V Rudby in Cleveland w Middleton from 09. *The Vicarage, 2 Langbaurgh Road, Hutton Rudby, Yarm TS15 0HL* Tel (01642) 700223 E-mail pam.notsanders@googlemail.com

SANDERS, Roderick David Scott. b 58. Southn Univ BA80 CertEd81. Cranmer Hall Dur 85. **d** 88 **p** 89. C Luton St Mary *St Alb* 88-93; P-in-c Clovelly *Ex* 93-94; P-in-c Woolfardisworthy and Buck Mills 93-94; TV Parkham, Alwington, Buckland Brewer etc 94-98; NSM Cove St Jo *Guildf* 98-03; NSM Guildf Ch Ch w St Martha-on-the-Hill 03-10. *Address temp unknown* Tel 07720-856460 (mobile) E-mail rod.sanders@ntlworld.com

SANDERS (née COLLINGRIDGE), Mrs Susan Rachel. b 61. St Mary's Coll Dur BA83. Cranmer Hall Dur 85. **d** 88 **p** 94. Par Dn Luton St Mary *St Alb* 88-93; Perm to Offic *Ex* 93-94; NSM Parkham, Alwington, Buckland Brewer etc 94-98; TV Cove St Jo *Guildf* 98-03; V Guildf Ch Ch w St Martha-on-the-Hill 03-11. *Address temp unknown* Tel 07913-840820 (mobile)

SANDERS, Mrs Wendy Elizabeth. b 49. Carl Dioc Tr Course 87. **d** 90 **p** 94. NSM Bampton w Mardale *Carl* 90-92; C Walney Is 92-94; C Stanwix 94-98; TV Chippenham St Paul w Hardenhuish etc *Bris* 98-03; TV Kington St Michael 98-03; RD Chippenham 99-03; TR Cockermouth Area *Carl* from 03; RD Derwent from 11. *The Rectory, Lorton Road, Cockermouth CA13 9DU* Tel and fax (01900) 823269 Mobile 07980-598892 E-mail wendy@cateam.org.uk

SANDERS, William John. b 48. Liv Inst of Educn BA80. Wycliffe Hall Ox 81. **d** 83 **p** 84. C Netherton *Liv* 83-87; P-in-c Wavertree St Bridget 87-97; V Wavertree St Bridget and St Thos from 97. *The Vicarage, Ashfield, Wavertree, Liverpool L15 1EY* Tel 0151-733 1117

SANDERSON, Colin James. b 54. Univ of Wales (Cardiff) MA95 SEN76 RGN. St Mich Coll Llan 85. **d** 87 **p** 88. C Merthyr Dyfan *Llan* 87-90; C Cadoxton-juxta-Barry 90-91; V Llangeinor 91-99; Lic to Offic 04-10; V Congleton St Jas *Ches* from 10; Chapl Mid Cheshire Hosps Trust from 11. *St James's Vicarage, 116 Holmes Chapel Road, Congleton CW12 4NX* Tel (01260) 408203 *or* (01270) 255141 Mobile 07713-742365 E-mail cjsanderson2005@hotmail.com

SANDERSON, Daniel. b 40. AKC66. **d** 67 **p** 68. C Upperby St Jo *Carl* 67-72; V Addingham 72-75; V Ireleth w Askam 75-02; C Dalton-in-Furness and Ireleth-with-Askam 02-05; Hon Can Carl Cathl 95-05; RD Furness 01-04; rtd 05. *52 Parklands Drive, Askam-in-Furness LA16 7JP* Tel (01229) 463018

SANDERSON, Canon Gillian. b 47. Cranmer Hall Dur 80. **dss** 82 **d** 87 **p** 94. Allesley *Cov* 82-86; Warwick 86-00; C 87-94; TV 94-00; Hon Can Cov Cathl 94-00; Perm to Offic from 00. *17 Marlborough Drive, Leamington Spa CV31 1XY* Tel (01926) 459749 Mobile 07714-193776 E-mail gillian-7 wine@tiscali.co.uk

SANDERSON, Paul. b 59. Univ of Wales (Abth) BSc80 Ches Coll of HE PGCE81 Man Univ MEd92. **d** 05 **p** 06. OLM Bury St Jo w St Mark *Man* 05-10; OLM Walmersley Road, Bury from 10. *261 Walmersley Road, Bury BL9 6NX* Tel 0161-764 3452 E-mail paul261@fsmail.net

SANDERSON, Canon Peter Oliver. b 29. St Chad's Coll Dur BA52. **d** 54 **p** 55. C Houghton le Spring *Dur* 54-59; R Linstead Jamaica 59-63; Chapl RAF 63-67; P-in-c Winksley cum Grantley and Aldfield w Studley *Ripon* 67-68; V 68-74; V Leeds St Aid 74-84; Can and Provost St Paul's Cathl Dundee 84-91; R Dundee St Paul 84-91; USA from 91, rtd 94, Interim Dean Trin Cathl Iowa 05-06; Asst to the Dean 06-07. *410 Brentwood Drive, Alamogordo NM 88310-5439, USA* E-mail petersanderson@q.com

SANDERSON, Scott. b 42. Oak Hill Th Coll. **d** 82 **p** 83. C Galleywood Common *Chelmsf* 82-88; P-in-c Newport w Widdington 88-92; V Newport 92-98; V Walton le Soken 98-05; rtd 05; Perm to Offic *Chelmsf* from 07. *The Bungalow, 2 Captains Road, West Mersea, Colchester CO5 8QS* Tel (01206) 385571 E-mail scott.sanderson@lineone.net

SANDERSON, Timothy. b 68. York Univ BSc89 Glos Univ BA03 St Jo Coll Dur MA09. Cranmer Hall Dur 07. **d** 09 **p** 10. C Jesmond H Trin *Newc* from 09; C Newc St Barn and St Jude from 09. *52 Fern Avenue, Jesmond, Newcastle upon Tyne NE2 2QX* Tel 07724-136581 (mobile)

SANDES, The Very Revd Denis Lindsay. b 46. CITC BTh86. **d** 89 **p** 90. C Bandon Union *C, C & R* 89-92; I Kells Gp *C & O* 92-07; Can Leighlin Cathl 03-07; I Omey w Ballynakill, Errislannan and Roundstone *T, K & A* from 07; Can Tuam Cathl 08-11; Provost Tuam from 10. *The Rectory, Clifden, Co Galway, Republic of Ireland* Tel (00353) (95) 21147 Mobile 86-647 5056 E-mail revdlsandes@gmail.com

SANDFORD, Nicholas Robert. b 63. Kent Univ BA84 Univ of Wales (Cardiff) BD87. St Mich Coll Llan 84. **d** 87 **p** 88. C Neath w Llantwit 87-90; C Cardiff St Jo 90-94; R Cilybebyll 94-97; Chapl HM Pris Swansea 95-97; Chapl HM Pris Parc (Bridgend) 97-04; Chapl HM Pris Usk and Prescoed from 04. *HM Prison Usk, 47 Maryport Street, Usk NP15 1XP* Tel (01291) 671600

SANDFORD, Paul Richard. b 47. Em Coll Cam BA69 MA73. Wycliffe Hall Ox 72. **d** 75 **p** 76. C Upper Holloway St Pet *Lon* 75-77; C Finchley St Paul Long Lane 77-81; Ind Chapl *Newc* 81-88; TV Cramlington 81-88; TV Dronfield *Derby* 88-90; TV Dronfield w Holmesfield 90-02; P-in-c Sinfin 02-10; V from 10; RD Derby S 02-10. *St Stephen's Vicarage, 313 Sinfin Lane, Derby DE24 9GP* Tel (01332) 760135 E-mail prsandford@ntlworld.com

SANDHAM, Daniel Paul. b 82. St Chad's Coll Dur BA05. St Steph Ho Ox BA09. **d** 09 **p** 10. C Hendon St Mary and Ch Ch *Lon* from 09. *St Mary's Cottage, 48 Church End, London NW4 4JT* E-mail danielsandham@hotmail.com

SANDHAM, Shaun Graham. b 60. Cranmer Hall Dur 02. **d** 04 **p** 05. C Workington St Mich *Carl* 04-08; TV Sutton St Jas and Wawne *York* from 08. *11 Sovereign Way, Kingswood, Hull HU7 3JG* Tel (01482) 838486 Mobile 07778-334356 E-mail pillar@pillar.karoo.co.uk

SANDHAM, Stephen McCourt. b 41. K Coll Lon BD65 AKC65. **d** 66 **p** 67. C Stockton St Pet *Dur* 66-69; C Bishopwearmouth Gd Shep 69-71; C Bishopwearmouth St Mich w St Hilda 71-75; V Darlington St Mark w St Paul 75-82; P-in-c Sunderland St Chad 82-87; R Shincliffe 87-98; P-in-c 98-06; rtd 06; Chapl Sherburn Hosp Dur 98-07. *21 Hill Meadows, High Shincliffe, Durham DH1 2PE* E-mail stephensandham@yahoo.co.uk

SANDOM, Miss Carolyn Elizabeth. b 63. Homerton Coll Cam BEd85. Wycliffe Hall Ox BTh93. **d** 94. C St Helen Bishopsgate w St Andr Undershaft etc *Lon* 94-96; C Cambridge H Sepulchre *Ely* 96-05. *Address temp unknown* E-mail carrie@sandom63.freeserve.co.uk

SANDS, Colin Robert. b 38. JP84. Ches Coll of HE CertEd64. NOC 82. **d** 85 **p** 86. Hd Master St Andr Magull Primary Sch

80-00; NSM Bootle Ch Ch *Liv* 85-94; NSM Maghull 94-01; rtd 01; Perm to Offic *Carl* 01-07 and *Liv* from 01. *16 Strafford Drive, Bootle L20 9JW* Tel 0151-525 8709 *or* (01768) 863968

SANDS, Frederick William. b 25. St Deiniol's Hawarden 86. **d** 87 **p** 88. Chapl Asst Leic Gen Hosp 87-89; Chapl 89-95; rtd 95; Perm to Offic *Leic* from 95. *Cobblestones, Laughton, Lutterworth LE17 6QD* Tel 0116-240 3163

SANDS, Nigel Colin. b 39. Dur Univ BA64 MA68. Oak Hill Th Coll 65. **d** 67 **p** 68. C Skelmersdale St Paul *Liv* 67-71; C Childwall All SS 71-72; V Wavertree St Bridget 72-78; P-in-c Welford w Wickham and Gt Shefford *Ox* 78-86; P-in-c Boxford w Stockcross and Speen 84-86; R Welford w Wickham and Gt Shefford, Boxford etc 86-09; rtd 09; Perm to Offic *Ox* from 09. *Applemead, Chilton Way, Hungerford RG17 0JR* Tel (01488) 680618

SANDS, William James. b 55. Nottm Univ LTh83 Birm Univ MA99. St Jo Coll Nottm 80. **d** 83 **p** 84. C St Mary-at-Latton *Chelmsf* 83-86; R Mvurwi Zimbabwe 86-87; C-in-c Barkingside St Cedd *Chelmsf* 87-89; C Woodford St Mary w St Phil and St Jas 87-89; P-in-c Elmsett w Aldham *St E* 89-92; P-in-c Kersey w Lindsey 89-92; R Esigodini Zimbabwe 92-96; Sub Dean Harare 97; Chapl Algarve *Eur* 98-00; V Castle Bromwich St Clem *Birm* 00-09; P-in-c Yardley St Edburgha 09-11; V from 11. *49 Vicarage Road, Yardley, Birmingham B33 8PH* Tel 0121-784 6556 E-mail williamsands123@btinternet.com

SANER-HAIGH, Robert James. b 73. Birm Univ BA94 MPhil98. Wycliffe Hall Ox BA04 MA08. **d** 05 **p** 06. C Appleby *Carl* 05-07; Bp's Dom Chapl and C Dalston w Cumdivock, Raughton Head and Wreay 07-10; Officer for IME 4-7 07-08; Dir of Ords 08-10; P-in-c Kendal H Trin from 10. *Holy Trinity Vicarage, 2 Lynngarth Drive, Kendal LA9 4JA* Tel (01539) 729403

SANGSTER, Andrew. b 45. K Coll Lon BD67 AKC67 BA71 MA84 Lon Inst of Educn MPhil93 LLB97 FCollP. St Boniface Warminster. **d** 69 **p** 70. C Aylesford *Roch* 69-72; C Shirley *Win* 73-76; V Woolston 76-79; Prov Youth Chapl Ch in Wales 79-82; Chapl Collegiate Sch New Zealand 82-89; Chapl Eton Coll 89-92; Hd Master St Edm Sch Hindhead 92-96; Hd Thos Day Schs Lon 96-99; V Ormesby St Marg w Scratby, Ormesby St Mich etc *Nor* 99-04; Chapl Bromley Coll 04-10; rtd 10; Perm to Offic *Nor* from 10. *10 Harvey Lane, Norwich NR7 0BQ* Tel (01603) 437402 E-mail asangster666@btinternet.com

SANKEY, Julian. b 52. Qu Coll Ox BA74 MA79. St Jo Coll Nottm 84. **d** 86 **p** 87. C New Barnet St Jas *St Alb* 86-89; C Mansfield SS Pet and Paul *S'well* 89-94; Chapl St Luke's Hospice Sheff 94-07. *Address temp unknown*

SANKEY, Terence Arthur Melville. b 51. Trin Coll Bris 87. **d** 89 **p** 90. C Chalke Valley W *Sarum* 89-93; NSM Chalke from 93; Chapl HM Pris Dorchester from 99. *HM Prison Dorchester, 7 North Square, Dorchester DT1 1JD* Tel (01305) 266021 E-mail terry@rkhaye.globalnet.co.uk

SANLON, Peter Thomas. b 80. Wycliffe Hall Ox BA01 St Cath Coll Cam MPhil07 PhD10. Ridley Hall Cam 05. **d** 10 **p** 11. C S Tottenham St Ann *Lon* from 10; Lect Oak Hill Th Coll from 10. *3 Farm Lane, London N14 4PP* Tel 07961-053781 (mobile) *or* (020) 8449 0467 ext 231 E-mail petersanlon@gmail.com *or* peters@oakhill.ac.uk

SANSBURY, Canon Christopher John. b 34. Peterho Cam BA57 MA. Westcott Ho Cam 58. **d** 59 **p** 60. C Portsea N End St Mark *Portsm* 59-63; C Weeke *Win* 63-71; V N Eling St Mary 71-78; R Long Melford *St E* 78-00; P-in-c Shimpling and Alpheton 98-00; Hon Can St E Cathl 97-00; rtd 00; Perm to Offic *St E* from 00. *2 Deacon's Close, Lavenham, Sudbury CO10 9TT* Tel (01787) 248068

SANSOM, John Reginald. b 40. St Jo Coll Nottm 73. **d** 75 **p** 76. C Ipswich St Marg *St E* 75-79; P-in-c Emneth *Ely* 79-85; P-in-c Hartford 85-86; TV Huntingdon 86-91; R Sawtry 91-97; R Sawtry and Glatton 97-99; TV Ely 99-05; rtd 05; Perm to Offic *Ely* from 06. *77 St Ovins Green, Ely CB6 3AW* Tel (01353) 614913 E-mail johnjudysansom@ntlworld.com

SANSOM, Canon Michael Charles. b 44. Bris Univ BA66 St Jo Coll Dur PhD74. Cranmer Hall Dur 68. **d** 72 **p** 73. C Ecclesall *Sheff* 72-76; Lic to Offic *Ely* 76-88; Dir of Studies Ridley Hall Cam 76-88; Vice-Prin 79-88; Dir of Ords *St Alb* 88-10; Can Res St Alb 88-10; rtd 10. *101 Churchfields Drive, Bovey Tracey, Newton Abbot TQ13 9QZ* Tel (01626) 836773 E-mail michaelsansom@btinternet.com

SANSOM, Robert Arthur. b 29. St Aid Birkenhead 60. **d** 62 **p** 63. C Sutton in Ashfield St Mary *S'well* 62-65; V Holbrooke *Derby* 65-70; R North Saanich St Andr and H Trin Canada 70-80; R Oak Bay St Mary 80-84; R Saanichton St Mary 84-89; rtd 89. *1-9871 Resthaven Drive, Sidney BC V8L 3E9, Canada*

SANSOME, Geoffrey Hubert. b 29. Man Univ BA53. Qu Coll Birm. **d** 62 **p** 63. C Prenton *Ches* 62-68; P-in-c Liscard St Thos 68-72; V Kingsley 72-83; V Wybunbury w Doddington 83-91; V Marbury 91-99; rtd 99; Perm to Offic *Blackb* from 00 and *Ches* from 01. *21 Ash Drive, Warton, Preston PR4 1DD* Tel (01772) 633799

SANSUM, Canon David Henry. b 31. Bris Univ BA52 MA63. St Aid Birkenhead 54. **d** 56 **p** 57. C Henleaze *Bris* 56-59; C

Stratton St Margaret 59-60; C Stoke Bishop 60-64; V Stechford *Birm* 64-76; V Ashbourne w Mapleton *Derby* 76-98; P-in-c Thorpe 77-83; V Ashbourne St Jo 81-98; RD Ashbourne 91-98; Hon Can Derby Cathl 95-98; rtd 98; Perm to Offic *Bris* and *Glouc* from 98. *Greenleaze, Main Road, Easter Compton, Bristol BS35 5SQ* Tel (01454) 632563

✠**SANTER, The Rt Revd Mark.** b 36. Qu Coll Cam BA60 MA64 Lambeth DD99. Westcott Ho Cam. **d** 63 **p** 64 **c** 81. Tutor Cuddesdon Coll 63-67; C Cuddesdon *Ox* 63-67; Fell and Dean Clare Coll Cam 67-72; Tutor 68-72; Prin Westcott Ho Cam 73-81; Hon Can Win Cathl 78-81; Area Bp Kensington *Lon* 81-87; Bp Birm 87-02; rtd 02; Hon Asst Bp *Worc* from 02 and *Birm* from 03. *81 Clarence Road, Kings Heath, Birmingham B13 9UH* Tel 0121-441 2194

SANTORINI, Melanie Yvonne. b 62. St Aid Coll Dur BA84 Victoria Univ (BC) MA85 Hertf Coll Ox DPhil89. WMMTC 91. **d** 94 **p** 95. C Penn *Lich* 94-97; TV Wolverhampton 97-98; TV Cen Wolverhampton 98-99; rtd 10. *Tanydderwen, Corris, Machynlleth SY20 9SH* Tel (01654) 761260 E-mail melanie.clayton@virginmedia.com

SANTRA, Jagat Ranjan. b 54. Utkal Univ BA74 Serampore Univ BD81 MTh88. **d** 00 **p** 02. NSM Edin Old St Paul 00-06; Lect Union Bibl Sem Pune India from 06. *Union Biblical Seminary, PO Box 1425, Bibwewadi, Pune, India* Tel (0091) (20) 2421 1747, 2421 1203, *or* 2421 8670 Fax 2421 5471 E-mail jagat_s@hotmail.com

SANTRAM, Philip James. b 27. MA Delhi Univ BSc48 Serampore Univ BD53. Bp's Coll Calcutta 48. **d** 52 **p** 54. India 52-66; Lect Bp's Coll Calcutta 61-65; R Delhi St Martin w H Trin and Gurgaon Epiphany 65-66; Ethiopia 66-68; C Horton *Bradf* 68-71; C Whitley Ch Ch *Ox* 71-72; P Missr Tilehurst St Mary CD 72-76; V Tilehurst St Mary 76-78; R Lakefield Canada 78-82; R Chomedey-Bordeaux 82-97; rtd 97; Hon C Oakville Epiphany from 00. *2336 Adirondak Trail, Oakville ON L6M 0E9, Canada* Tel (001) (905) 827 6327 E-mail rpsantram@aol.com

SAPWELL, Mrs Lynette Lilian. b 51. Sussex Univ BEd73 Middx Univ BA03. NTMTC 00. **d** 03 **p** 04. NSM Rochford *Chelmsf* 03-07; P-in-c Appleton *Ox* from 07; P-in-c Besselsleigh from 07. *The Rectory, Oakesmere, Appleton, Abingdon OX13 5JS* Tel (01865) 862458 E-mail lynsapwell@sky.com

SARALIS, Preb Christopher Herbert. b 34. Univ of Wales BA54 St Cath Coll Ox BA56 MA60. Wycliffe Hall Ox. **d** 57 **p** 58. C Abergavenny St Mary w Llanwenarth Citra *Mon* 57-61; C Bridgwater St Mary w Chilton Trinity *B & W* 61-65; V Berrow 65-72; R Berrow and Breane 72-76; RD Burnham 72-76; V Minehead 76-92; RD Exmoor 80-86; Preb Wells Cathl 84-92; V Bovey Tracey SS Pet, Paul and Thos w Hennock *Ex* 92-99; rtd 99; Perm to Offic *B & W* from 99. *1 Broadway Road, Horton, Ilminster TA19 9RX* Tel (01460) 52416

SARAPUK, Susan. b 59. Lon Univ BA80 Univ of Wales PGCE81. St Mich Coll Llan. **d** 90 **p** 97. C Morriston *S & B* 90-94; C Swansea St Pet 94-97; P-in-c Llangyfelach 97-98; V 98-02; C Sketty 02-08. *13 Edison Crescent, Clydach, Swansea SA6 5JF* Tel (01792) 843521

SARGANT, John Raymond. b 38. CCC Cam BA61 MA70. Westcott Ho Cam 64 Harvard Div Sch 66. **d** 67 **p** 68. C Croydon St Jo *Cant* 67-72; Sec Zambia Angl Coun 72-75; P-in-c Bradford-on-Avon Ch Ch *Sarum* 76-81; V 81-90; TV Marlborough 90-03; Dioc Inter-Faith Adv 90-00; Can and Preb Sarum Cathl 92-01; rtd 03. *48 Summerhill Road, Lyme Regis DT7 3DT* Tel (01297) 445922

SARGEANT, Prof Anthony John. b 44. Goldsmiths' Coll Lon BEd70 Univ Coll Leic BSc73 LSHTM PhD76. Westcott Ho Cam 99. **d** 00 **p** 01. NSM Goostrey w Swettenham *Ches* 00-08; TV Rye *Chich* 08-09. *The Vicarage, 21 Fair Meadow, Rye TN31 7NL* Tel (01797) 227621 E-mail a.j.sargeant@hotmail.com

✠**SARGEANT, The Rt Revd Frank Pilkington.** b 32. St Jo Coll Dur BA55. Cranmer Hall Dur 57. **d** 58 **p** 59 **c** 84. C Gainsborough All SS *Linc* 58-62; C Gt Grimsby St Jas 62-66; V Hykeham 66-73; Dir In-Service Tr and Adult Educn *Bradf* 73-84; Can Res Bradf Cathl 73-77; Adn Bradf 77-84; Suff Bp Stockport *Ches* 84-94; Bp at Lambeth (Hd of Staff) *Cant* 94-99; rtd 99; Hon Asst Bp *Eur* 99-07; Perm to Offic *Ches* from 99. *32 Brotherton Drive, Trinity Gardens, Salford M3 6BH* Tel 0161-839 7045 E-mail franksargeant68@hotmail.com

SARGEANTSON, Kenneth William. b 30. **d** 90 **p** 91. NSM The Marshland *Sheff* 90-93; NSM Goole 93-97; Perm to Offic 97-06; NSM The Marshland from 06; Hon Chapl Miss to Seafarers from 95. *97 High Street, Swinefleet, Goole DN14 8AH* Tel (01405) 704256 E-mail kensargeantson@yahoo.co.uk

SARGENT, Miss Ann. b 65. **d** 98 **p** 99. C Bris St Andr Hartcliffe 98-01; P-in-c Flax Bourton *B & W* 01-09; P-in-c Barrow Gurney 01-09; P-in-c Long Ashton 05-09; R Long Ashton w Barrow Gurney and Flax Bourton from 09. *The Vicarage, 7 Church Lane, Long Ashton, Bristol BS41 9LU* Tel (01275) 393194

SARGENT, Benjamin Charles. b 83. K Coll Lon BA05 MA07 AKC05 Ox Univ DPhil11. Wycliffe Hall Ox MTh09. **d** 09 **p** 10.

C Warblington w Emsworth *Portsm* from 09. *1 Godwin Close, Emsworth PO10 7XT* Tel 07990-695830 (mobile) E-mail benjamin.sargent@wycliffe.ox.ac.uk

SARGENT, Charles Edward. b 68. K Coll Lon BD89 Leeds Univ MA96. Coll of Resurr Mirfield 94. **d** 96 **p** 97. C Notting Dale St Clem w St Mark and St Jas *Lon* 96-00; P-in-c S Kensington St Aug 00-04; Chapl Imp Coll 00-04; Chapl Brunel Univ 04-10; Perm to Offic *S'wark* from 11. *4 Spinnakers, Pentire Avenue, Newquay TR7 1TT* Tel (01637) 859934 E-mail charles.sargent@sky.com

SARGENT, David Gareth. b 63. Sheff Univ BA85 St Jo Coll Dur BA96. Cranmer Hall Dur 93. **d** 96 **p** 97. C Norbury *Ches* 96-01; V Hooton 01-06; TR Penrith w Newton Reigny and Plumpton Wall *Carl* from 06. *The Rectory, 3 Lamley Gardens, Penrith CA11 9LR* Tel (01768) 863000 E-mail revdave.sargent@talk21.com

SARGENT, Derek Connor. b 66. TCD BTh99. CITC 96. **d** 99 **p** 00. C Waterford w Killea, Drumcannon and Dunhill *C & O* 99-01; V 01-03; I Dublin Clontarf *D & G* from 03. *The Rectory, 15 Seafield Road West, Clontarf, Dublin 3, Republic of Ireland* Tel (00353) (1) 833 1181 E-mail clontarf@dublin.anglican.org

SARGENT, Mrs Janet. b 54. **d** 07 **p** 08. OLM Birchencliffe *Wakef* 07-08; OLM Birkby and Birchencliffe from 08. *11 Kirkwood Drive, Huddersfield HD3 3WA* Tel (01484) 650390

SARGENT, Preb Richard Henry. b 26. Man Univ BA50. Ridley Hall Cam 50. **d** 52 **p** 53. C Rusholme H Trin *Man* 52-54; C Cheadle *Ches* 54-59; V Cheadle Hulme St Andr 59-67; V Bushbury *Lich* 67-73; V Castle Church 73-89; RD Stafford 81-88; Preb Lich Cathl 87-89; rtd 89; Perm to Offic *Lich* from 90. *5/ Deanshill Close, Stafford ST16 1BW* Tel (01705) 605335

SARGISSON, Conrad Ralph. b 24. Keble Coll Ox BA46 MA50. Wells Th Coll 48. **d** 50 **p** 51. C Charlton Kings St Mary *Glouc* 50-53; C Prestbury 53-55; V St Briavels 55-58; V Lanteglos by Fowey *Truro* 58-62; V Penzance St Mary 62-73; RD Penwith 72-73; V Westbury-on-Trym H Trin *Bris* 73-79; P-in-c Blisland w St Breward *Truro* 79-83; V Mylor w Flushing 83-91; rtd 91; Perm to Offic *Heref* 91-93; P-in-c St Hilary *Truro* 93-96; Perm to Offic from 96. *8 Halgavor Park, Bodmin PL31 1DL* Tel (01208) 264938

SARMEZEY, George Arpad. b 61. Qu Mary Coll Lon BA83 Goldsmiths' Coll Lon PGCE86. Westcott Ho Cam 89. **d** 92 **p** 93. C Eastville St Anne w St Mark and St Thos *Bris* 92-94; C Stratton St Margaret w S Marston etc 94-97; Asst Chapl Northn Gen Hosp NHS Trust 97-00; Sen Chapl from 00. *Northampton General Hospital, Billing Road, Northampton NN1 5BD* Tel (01604) 545773 Fax 544608 E-mail george.sarmezey@ngh.nhs.uk

SARUM, Archdeacon of. *See* JEANS, The Ven Alan Paul

SARVANANTHAN, Sudharshan. b 70. Trin Coll Bris 06. **d** 08 **p** 09. C Heart of Eden *Carl* from 08. *92 Rivington Park, Appleby-in-Westmorland CA16 6HU* Tel (01768) 354099 Mobile 07879-656492 E-mail sudharshan@sarva.info

SASADA, Benjamin John. b 33. EAMTC. **d** 82 **p** 83. NSM Dickleburgh, Langmere, Shimpling, Thelveton etc *Nor* 82-88; NSM Diss 88-95; P-in-c Dickleburgh, Langmere, Shimpling, Thelveton etc 95-99; rtd 99; Perm to Offic *St E* from 84 and *Nor* from 99. *The Grange, Walcott Green, Diss IP22 5SS* Tel (01379) 642174 E-mail benjamin@sasada2.freeserve.co.uk

SASSER, Col the Revd Canon Howell Crawford. b 37. Maryland Univ BA72 Geo Mason Univ Virginia MA74 Westmr Coll Ox MTh97. Washington Dioc Course 75. **d** 77 **p** 78. W Germany 77-80; Somalia 80-83; Cyprus 84-92; Chapl Montreux w Gstaad *Eur* 92-97; Chapl Oporto 97-05; Adn Gib 02-05; Bp's Chapl and Research Asst 05-06; rtd 06. *11944 Perry Drive, Fairfax VA 22030-6710, USA* Tel (001) (703) 631 0466

SATKUNANAYAGAM, Kuhan. b 76. St Jo Coll Dur BSc01 BA11 Univ of E Lon MSc06 PsychD08. Cranmer Hall Dur 09. **d** 11. C Leatherhead and Mickleham *Guildf* from 11. *52 Woodbridge Avenue, Leatherhead KT22 7QN* Tel (01372) 372203 Mobile 07957-293907 E-mail kuhan@dunelm.org.uk

SATTERLY, Gerald Albert. b 34. Lon Univ BA56 Ex Univ Hon BA. Wycliffe Hall Ox 58. **d** 60 **p** 61. C Southborough St Pet *Roch* 60-63; C S Lyncombe *B & W* 63-66; V Sheff St Barn 66-69; R Adwick-le-Street 69-73; V Awre and Blakeney *Glouc* 73-82; P-in-c Newnham 80-82; V Newnham w Awre and Blakeney 82-90; R Instow *Ex* 90-98; V Westleigh 90-98; rtd 98; Perm to Offic *Ex* from 98. *Tryst Lea, 2 Cameron Close, Maer Lane, Bude EX23 8SP* Tel (01288) 359256

✠**SATTERTHWAITE, The Rt Revd John Richard.** b 25. CMG91. Leeds Univ BA46. Coll of Resurr Mirfield 48. **d** 50 **p** 51 **c** 70. C Carl St Barn 50-53; C Carl St Aid and Ch Ch 53-55; Asst Gen Sec C of E Coun on Foreign Relns 55-59; C St Mich Paternoster Royal *Lon* 55-59; P-in-c 59-65; Gen Sec C of E Coun on Foreign Relns from 59; V St Dunstan in the West *Lon* 59-70; Hon Can Cant Cathl 63-70; Gen Sec Abp's Commn on RC Relns 65-70; Suff Bp Fulham *Lon* 70-80; Bp Gib 70-80; Bp Eur 80-93; P-in-c Warsaw 90-93; rtd 93; Hon Asst Bp Carl 94-01 and from 04; Perm to Offic 01-04. *25 Spencer House, St Paul's Square, Carlisle CA1 1DG* Tel (01228) 594055

SAUL, Norman Stanley. b 30. St Aid Birkenhead 51. **d** 54 **p** 55. C S Shore H Trin *Blackb* 54-57; C Poulton-le-Fylde 57-59; PC Freckleton 59-66; V Blackb St Luke 66-68; V Barton 68-72; V Foxdale *S & M* 72-77; V Maughold 77-90; CF (ACF) 80-86; rtd 90; Perm to Offic *Blackb* from 90. *15 Croft Meadow, Bamber Bridge, Preston PR5 8HX* Tel (01772) 314475

SAUNDERS, Andrew Vivian. b 44. Leeds Univ BA65. Coll of Resurr Mirfield 66. **d** 68 **p** 69. C Goodmayes St Paul *Chelmsf* 68-71; C Horfield H Trin *Bris* 71-75; C Oldland 75-77; Ind Chapl *B & W* 77-80; P-in-c Buckland Dinham w Elm, Orchardleigh etc 77-78; P-in-c Buckland Dinham 78-80; V Westfield 80-90; R Clutton w Cameley 90-99; C Christchurch *Win* 99-05; rtd 05; Perm to Offic *B & W* from 06. *8 Mill House Court, Willow Vale, Frome BA11 1BG* Tel (01373) 467683

SAUNDERS, Barry. *See* SAUNDERS, John Barry

SAUNDERS, Brian Gerald. b 28. Pemb Coll Cam BA49 MA53. Cuddesdon Coll 63. **d** 66 **p** 67. NSM Gt Berkhamsted *St Alb* 66-87; P-in-c Lt Gaddesden 87-92; rtd 92; Perm to Offic *Ox* 92-94; *St Alb* 92-02; *Linc* from 01; Hon C Newton Longville w Stoke Hammond and Whaddon 94-01. *2 Bruce Close, Lincoln LN2 1SL* Tel (01522) 523193

SAUNDERS, Canon Bruce Alexander. b 47. St Cath Coll Cam BA68 MA72. Cuddesdon Coll 68. **d** 71 **p** 72. C Westbury-on-Trym H Trin *Bris* 71-74; Hon C Clifton St Paul 74-78; Asst Chapl Bris Univ 74-78; TV Fareham H Trin *Portsm* 78-84; TR Mortlake w E Sheen *S'wark* 84-97; RD Richmond and Barnes 89-94; Can Missr for Ch in Soc 97-03; Can Res S'wark Cathl from 03; C-in-c Bermondsey St Hugh CD from 03. *7 Temple West Mews, West Square, London SE11 4TJ* Tel (020) 7735 0143 *or 7367 6706* Fax 7367 6725 E-mail bruce.saunders@southwark.anglican.org

SAUNDERS, David. b 28. Keble Coll Ox BA50 MA59. Cuddesdon Coll 51. **d** 53 **p** 54. C Mexborough *Sheff* 53-56; C Sheff St Cuth 56-60; V New Bentley 60-67; V Grimsby All SS *Linc* 67-78; V Caistor w Clixby 78-88; P-in-c Grasby 78-94; Chapl Caistor Hosp 78-94; P-in-c Searby w Owmby *Linc* 79-94; V Dunholme 88-92; P-in-c Welton and Dunholme w Scothern 92-94; rtd 94; Perm to Offic *Linc* from 94. *2 Oundle Close, Washingborough, Lincoln LN4 1DR* Tel (01522) 793164

SAUNDERS, Gareth John McKeith. b 71. St Andr Univ BD93 Edin Univ MTh99. TISEC 99. **d** 99 **p** 00. C Inverness St Andr *Mor* 99-03; C Edin St Salvador and Edin Gd Shep 03-06. *45 Lindsay Berwick Place, Anstruther KY10 3YP* Tel (01333) 310140 Mobile 07732-356123 E-mail gareth@garethjmsaunders.co.uk

SAUNDERS, Geoffrey David. b 51. Bris Univ BSc73. **d** 01 **p** 02. OLM Rockland St Mary w Hellington, Bramerton etc *Nor* 01-07; NSM from 07. *13 The Street, Rockland St Mary, Norwich NR14 7ER* Tel (01508) 538550 E-mail geoffsaunders@waitrose.com

SAUNDERS, Graham Howard. b 53. Hatf Poly BSc77. Trin Coll Bris BA86. **d** 86 **p** 87. C Birm St Martin w Bordesley St Andr 86-89; C Olton 89-96; TV Bedminster *Bris* 96-02; P-in-c Farnham Royal w Hedgerley *Ox* 02-08; R from 08. *The Rectory, Victoria Road, Farnham Common, Slough SL2 3NJ* Tel (01753) 643233 Fax 644130

SAUNDERS, Ivor John. b 37. Wolv Poly CQSW81. **d** 04 **p** 05. OLM Wolverhampton St Jude *Lich* from 04. *34 Wrottesley Road, Wolverhampton WV6 8SF* Tel (01902) 751162 E-mail ivor.wendy@talktalk.net

SAUNDERS, James Benedict John. b 72. St Aid Coll Dur BA93 St Jo Coll Cam PhD97 St Jo Coll Dur BA00. Cranmer Hall Dur 98. **d** 01 **p** 02. C Sole Bay *St E* 01-04; P-in-c Teigh w Whissendine and Market Overton *Pet* 04-09; Asst Chapl HM Pris Ashwell 04-07; Chapl Uppingham Sch from 09. *Pentire, 48 High Street West, Uppingham, Oakham LE15 9QD* Tel (01572) 829934 E-mail jbjs@uppingham.co.uk

SAUNDERS, Mrs Joan Mary (Jo). b 44. Univ Coll Lon BA66 PGCE67. EAMTC 00. **d** 03 **p** 04. NSM Gt and Lt Casterton w Pickworth and Tickencote *Pet* 03-05; P-in-c from 09; P-in-c Castle Bytham w Creeton *Linc* 05-09; Hon C Ketton, Collyweston, Easton-on-the-Hill etc *Pet* from 09. *Mellstock, Bourne Road, Essendine, Stamford PE9 4LH* Tel (01780) 480479 E-mail revjosaunders@live.co.uk

SAUNDERS, John Barry. b 40. Chich Th Coll. **d** 83 **p** 84. C St Breoke *Truro* 83-84; C St Breoke and Egloshayle 84-87; V Treverbyn 87-96; RD St Austell 91-96; V Perranzabuloe 96-03; rtd 03; Perm to Offic *Truro* from 04. *48 Cormorant Drive, St Austell PL25 3BA* Tel (01726) 71994

SAUNDERS, Canon John Michael. b 40. Brasted Th Coll 66 Clifton Th Coll 68. **d** 70 **p** 71. C Homerton St Luke *Lon* 70-74; SAMS Brazil 74-91; P-in-c Horsmonden *Roch* 91-97; Area Sec (SE England) SAMS 91-97; V Gillingham St Mark *Roch* 97-08; rtd 08; Hon C Newton Longville, Mursley, Swanbourne etc *Ox* from 08. *The Rectory, Drayton Road, Newton Longville, Milton Keynes MK17 0BH* Tel (01908) 647694 E-mail jandjsaunders@aol.com

SAUNDERS, Kenneth John. b 35. Linc Th Coll 73. **d** 75 **p** 76. C Boultham *Linc* 75-79; V Swinderby 79-87; V Cherry Willingham w Greetwell 87-95; P-in-c S Kelsey Gp 95-98; P-in-c N Kelsey 95-98; P-in-c Kelsey Gp 98-00; rtd 00; Perm to Offic *Linc* from 01. *Pew End, 17 Wentworth Drive, Dunholme, Lincoln LN2 3UH* Tel (01673) 862930

SAUNDERS, Malcolm Walter Mackenzie. b 34. Em Coll Cam BA58 MA62. Wycliffe Hall Ox 58. d 60 p 61. C Northampton St Giles *Pet* 60-63; C Northampton St Alb 63-66; V Corby St Columba 66-84; Nat Dir Evang Explosion 84-91; V Ketton *Pet* 91-92; R Ketton w Tinwell 92-01; rtd 01; Perm to Offic *Pet* from 01. *35 Main Street, Barrowden, Oakham LE15 8EQ* Tel (01572) 747036

SAUNDERS, Mrs Margaret Rose. b 49. Newnham Coll Cam BA71 St Jo Coll York PGCE72. St Alb Minl Tr Scheme 85. d 88 p 94. Hon Par Dn Gt Berkhamsted *St Alb* 88-90; Hon Chapl Asst Gt Ormond Street Hosp for Sick Children Lon 88-90; Asst Chapl Aylesbury Vale HA 90-92; Chapl Milton Keynes Gen NHS Trust 92-98; Chapl Milton Keynes Community NHS Trust 92-98; C Newport Pagnell w Lathbury and Moulsoe *Ox* 98-01; TV Grantham *Linc* 01-02; P-in-c Grantham, Manthorpe 02-04; Chapl United Lincs Hosps NHS Trust from 01. *2 Bruce Close, Lincoln LN2 1SL* Tel (01522) 523193 *or* 537403 E-mail margaret@saunderstd.fsnet.co.uk

SAUNDERS, Mark Richard. *See* VASEY-SAUNDERS, Mark Richard

SAUNDERS, Martin Paul. b 54. K Coll Lon BD76 AKC76 Univ of Northumbria at Newc DipSW96. Westcott Ho Cam 77. d 78 p 79. C Seaton Hirst *Newc* 78-81; Regional Chapl Hong Kong Miss to Seamen 81; C Egglescliffe *Dur* 81-82; Chapl to Arts and Recreation 81-84; C Jarrow 82-84; TV 84-88; V Southwick St Columba 88 94; Perm to Offic from 94. *55 The Meadows, Burnopfield, Newcastle upon Tyne NE16 6QW* Tel (01207) 271242 Mobile 07710-325197 E-mail martinsaunders@derwentheights.freeserve.co.uk

SAUNDERS, Martyn Leonard John. b 69. Magd Coll Cam MEng92. Wycliffe Hall Ox BA97. d 98 p 99. C Quinton Road W St Boniface *Birm* 98-02; TV Barnsbury *Lon* 02-10; V Chatham St Phil and St Jas *Roch* from 10. *The Vicarage, 139 Sussex Drive, Walderslade, Chatham ME5 0NR* Tel (01634) 861108

SAUNDERS, Michael. b 38. Charing Cross Hosp Medical Sch MB, BS62 FRCPEd74 FRCP78 MSOSc84. NEOC 82. d 84 p 85. Lic to Offic *York* 84-92; Tutor NEOC 84-93; NSM Stokesley *York* 92-93; C Ripon Cathl 93-95; Perm to Offic *York* from 93; NSM Gt and Lt Ouseburn w Marton cum Grafton etc *Ripon* 95-02; NSM Masham and Healey from 02. *College Grove, 2 College Lane, Masham, Ripon HG4 4HE* Tel (01765) 688306 Mobile 07711-567160 E-mail michael.saunders@btinternet.com

SAUNDERS, Michael Walter. b 58. Grey Coll Dur BSc79 CChem MRSC84. Wycliffe Hall Ox 86. d 89 p 90. C Deane *Man* 89-93; TV Eccles 93-02; Chapl Eccles Sixth Form Coll 96-02; Dioc Adv on Evang *Man* 98-02; C Yateley and Eversley *Win* 02-06; P-in-c Darby Green 05-06; V Darby Green and Eversley from 06. *The Rectory, Glaston Hill Road, Eversley, Hook RG27 0LX* Tel 0118-973 6595 E-mail mikethevicar@thesaunders.plus.com

SAUNDERS, Moira Ruth Forbes. b 76. Birm Univ BA99. Ridley Hall Cam 02. d 04 p 05. C Welling *Roch* 04-08. *Address temp unknown*

SAUNDERS, Canon Reginald Frederick. b 15. St And NSM Tr Scheme 76. d 79 p 79. NSM Perth St Ninian *St And* from 79; NSM Stanley from 79; Hon Can St Ninian's Cathl Perth from 04. *31 Muirend Road, Perth PH1 1JU* Tel (01738) 626217

SAUNDERS, Canon Richard Charles Hebblethwaite. b 17. Qu Coll Ox BA40 MA42. Westcott Ho Cam 41. d 42 p 43. C Darnall *Sheff* 42-45; India 46-49; V Thornton-le-Street w Thornton-le-Moor etc *York* 49-52; V Eastwood *Sheff* 52-62; V Bris St Ambrose Whitehall 62-75; P-in-c Easton All Hallows 65-68; TR E Bris 75-77; P-in-c Colerne 77-82; P-in-c N Wraxall 77-82; RD Chippenham 80-82; Hon Can Bris Cathl 82; rtd 82; Hon C Honiton, Gittisham, Combe Raleigh, Monkton etc *Ex* from 85. *St Michael's Cottage, Gittisham, Honiton EX14 3AH* Tel (01404) 850634 E-mail richard.saunders01@mypostoffice.co.uk

SAUNDERS, Richard George. b 54. BNC Ox BA76 MA81. St Jo Coll Nottm 82. d 85 p 86. C Barrow St Mark *Carl* 85-89; C Cranham Park *Chelmsf* 89-97; TV Kinson *Sarum* 97-00; TR Kinson and W Howe from 00. *St Philip's Vicarage, 41 Moore Avenue, Kinson, Bournemouth BH11 8AT* Tel and fax (01202) 581135 *or* fax 581485 E-mail dick.saunders@ntlworld.com

SAUNDERS, Ronald. b 37. St Pet Coll Birm CertEd62 Memorial Univ Newfoundland CertEd80 Columbia Univ MA82 BD87 ACP67. Sarum Th Coll 69. d 68 p 70. Lic to Offic Malawi 68-70; C Blantyre 71-72; C Kensington St Mary Abbots w St Geo *Lon* 72-73; C Bournemouth St Fran *Win* 73-75; I Twillingate Canada 76; Lic to Offic 77-81; C Gt Marlow *Ox* 81-82; Area Org Leprosy Miss 82-85; V Penycae *St As* 85-87; TV Wrexham 87-89; Lic to Offic *Ox* 90-91; Chapl Morden Coll Blackheath 91-97; Master Wyggeston's Hosp Leic 97-03; P-in-c Nerja and Almuñécar *Eur* 05-07. *Barrio San Isidro 92, 18830 Huescar (Granada), Spain* E-mail ron1937uk@hotmail.co.uk

SAUNDERS, Sheila Lilian. b 42. d 03 p 04. OLM Walworth St Pet *S'wark* 03-07; NSM from 07. *9 Wooler Street, London SE17 2ED* Tel (020) 7252 5045 E-mail sheila.saunders3@btopenworld.com

SAUNDERS (née CORNWALL), Valerie Cecilia. b 40. Bedf Coll Lon BSc62 Lon Inst of Educn PGCE63. Scottish Chs Open Coll 96. d 03 p 04. NSM Dingwall *Mor* from 03; NSM Strathpeffer from 03. *Chessbury, 12 Firthview, Dingwall IV15 9PF* Tel (01349) 865445 Mobile 07747-066993 E-mail valeriestj@btopenworld.com

SAUNDERS, Ms Wendy Jennifer. b 49. S'wark Ord Course 86. d 95 p 96. Bp's Adv for Urban Min and Leadership *S'wark* 90-91; C Thamesmead 95-98; P-in-c Eltham St Sav from 98. *St Saviour's Vicarage, 98 Middle Park Avenue, London SE9 5JH* Tel (020) 8850 6829 Mobile 07802-603754 E-mail wendy.saunders@sunday.surfaid.org

SAUNT, James Peter Robert. b 36. Chich Th Coll 73. d 75 p 76. C Portland All SS w St Pet *Sarum* 75-78; P-in-c Bratton 78-81; V 81-94; Chapl HM Pris Erlestoke 80-94; P-in-c Oldbury *Sarum* 94-99; R 99-01; rtd 01; Perm to Offic *Sarum* from 02. *Elms, Waddon, Portesham, Weymouth DT3 4ER* Tel (01305) 871553

SAUSBY, John Michael. b 39. AKC. d 63 p 64. C Crosland Moor *Wakef* 63-65; C Halifax St Jo Bapt 65-67; V Birkby 67-77; V Holmfirth 77-89; TR Upper Holme Valley 89-01; rtd 01; Perm to Offic *Wakef* from 04. *15 River Holme View, Brockholes, Huddersfield HD9 7BP* Tel (01484) 667228

SAVAGE, Andrew Michael. b 67. Wye Coll Lon BSc89 Cranfield Inst of Tech MSc91. Wycliffe Hall Ox 93. d 96 p 97. C Ecclesall *Sheff* 96-99; TV Kirk Ella and Willerby *York* 99-06; Chapl Kingham Hill Sch from 06. *Kingham Hill School, Kingham, Chipping Norton OX7 6TH* Tel (01608) 658999

SAVAGE, Canon Christopher Marius. b 46. Hull Univ MA94 FRSA99. Bps' Coll Cheshunt 66 Qu Coll Birm 68. d 70 p 71. C Battersea St Luke *S'wark* 70-75; TV Newbury *Ox* 75-80; R Lich St Mary w St Mich 80-85; V Chessington *Guildf* 85-91; Ind Chapl *Win* 91-00; Chapl Basingstoke Coll of Tech 91-00; V Newc Ch Ch w St Ann 00-07; Team Ldr Chapl to People at Work in Cam *Ely* from 07. *31 Thornton Close, Girton, Cambridge CB3 0NF* Tel (01223) 279145 *or* 276657 Mobile 07788-741489 E-mail chris.savage@workplacechaplaincy.org.uk

SAVAGE, Graham John. b 47. Univ of Wales (Ban) BSc69 PhD78. CITC 89. d 92 p 94. Lic to Offic *D & D* from 92; NSM Down Cathl 94-97; NSM Lecale Gp from 97. *7 Cedar Grove, Ardglass, Downpatrick BT30 7UE* Tel (028) 4484 1501

SAVAGE, Helen. b 55. Birm Univ BA76 Dur Univ BA82 MA90 Newc Univ MLitt83 Dur Univ PhD05. Cranmer Hall Dur 80. d 83 p 84. C Newc St Gabr 83-86; Adult Educn Adv 86-94; V Bedlington 94-04. *22 Cecil Street, North Shields NE29 0DH* Tel 0191-257 8111 E-mail helensavage1@gmail.com

SAVAGE, Mrs Hilary Linda. b 48. RGN71 RM86. WMMTC 89. d 92 p 94. C Quinton Road W St Boniface *Birm* 92-96; P-in-c Edgbaston SS Mary and Ambrose 96-01; V 01-02; TV Cramlington *Newc* 02-10; R Eckington and Ridgeway *Derby* from 10. *The Rectory, 17 Church Street, Eckington, Sheffield S21 4BG* Tel (01246) 432196 E-mail hilarysavage@hotmail.com

SAVAGE, Mrs Jennifer Anne. b 52. CertEd73. NOC 96. d 99 p 00. C Haworth *Bradf* 99-02; R 02-09; P-in-c Cross Roads cum Lees 07-09; P-in-c Thornton in Lonsdale w Burton in Lonsdale from 09. *The Vicarage, Low Street, Burton in Lonsdale, Carnforth LA6 3LF* Tel (01524) 261579 E-mail jenny.savage@bradford.anglican.org *or* revdjenny@aol.com

SAVAGE, John. b 48. Bris Univ BEd76. SWMTC 94. d 97 p 98. C Falmouth K Chas *Truro* 97-00; P-in-c Mabe from 00; Chapl Miss to Seafarers 00-07. *1 Willow Close, Mylor Bridge, Falmouth TR11 5SG* Tel (01326) 259739

SAVAGE, Jonathan Mark. b 57. Kingston Poly BSc79 MSc89 Roehampton Inst PGCE80. Ridley Hall Cam 94. d 96 p 97. C Ely 96-99; TV Huntingdon 99-07; C Gt w Lt Stukeley 04-07; TV Huntingdon w the Stukeleys from 07. *The Vicarage, 3A Longstaff Way, Hartford, Huntingdon PE28 7XT* Tel (01480) 434463 E-mail mark.savage@ely.anglican.org

SAVAGE, Michael Atkinson. b 33. St Pet Hall Ox BA57 MA61. Tyndale Hall Bris 57. d 59 p 60. C Rugby St Matt *Cov* 59-62; C Welling *Roch* 62-66; V Bowling St Steph *Bradf* 66-73; V Ben Rhydding 73-92; RD Otley 87-92; TR Quidenham *Nor* 92-97; R Quidenham Gp 97-99; rtd 99; Perm to Offic *Bradf* from 00. *42 Hollins Lane, Utley, Keighley BD20 6LT* Tel (01535) 606790 E-mail damsav@talktalk.net

SAVAGE, Paul James. b 58. Liv Univ BA81. Wycliffe Hall Ox 88. d 91 p 92. C Litherland St Phil *Liv* 91-94; CMS from 94. *CMS, PO Box 1799, Oxford OX4 9BN* Tel 08456-201799

SAVEGE, Timothy Michael. b 38. d 00 p 01. OLM Blyth Valley *St E* 00-05; OLM Bury St Edmunds St Mary 05-09; Perm to Offic *Chelmsf* from 09. *2 Chequer Square, Bury St Edmunds IP33 1QZ* Tel (01284) 728041 E-mail tim.savege@btinternet.com

SAVIGEAR, Miss Elfrida Beatrice. b 49. Wye Coll Lon BSc71 Bath Univ MSc85 Lambeth STh94. Ridley Hall Cam 91. **d** 93 **p** 94. C Ross w Brampton Abbotts, Bridstow, Peterstow etc *Heref* 93-97; P-in-c Butlers Marston and the Pillertons w Ettington *Cov* 97-99; P-in-c Alderminster and Halford 97-99; P-in-c Bicknoller w Crowcombe and Sampford Brett *B & W* 99-00; P-in-c Stogumber w Nettlecombe and Monksilver 99-00; R Quantock Towers 00-08; C Darlington H Trin *Dur* 08-11; rtd 11. *Manderley, Dodhams Lane, Bridport DT6 3DY* Tel (01308) 424031

SAVILL, David. b 27. TD69 and Bar 75. Em Coll Cam BA49 MA52. Ridley Hall Cam 50. **d** 52 **p** 53. Chapl St E Cathl 52-54; C St Martin-in-the-Fields *Lon* 54-57; V Sunbury 57-67; V Heston 67-73; Hon C Mettingham w Ilketshall St John *St E* 73-79; Hon C Mettingham 79-80; Chapl Felixstowe Coll 80-90; rtd 90; Perm to Offic *B & W* 90-11 and *St E* from 11. *14 St Anne's Close, Beccles NR34 9SD* Tel (01502) 716380 E-mail david.savill886@btinternet.com

SAVILLE, Andrew. b 66. Worc Coll Ox BA92 MA92 Cov Univ PhD00. Wycliffe Hall Ox. **d** 95 **p** 96. C Tonbridge SS Pet and Paul *Roch* 95-99; NSM Bromley Ch Ch 99-03; Dir Bromley Chr Tr Cen 99-03; C Fordham *Chelmsf* 03-10; V Laleham *Lon* from 10. *Erasmus House, Church Square, Shepperton TW17 9JY* Tel (01932) 247695 E-mail andy@savilles.org.uk

SAVILLE, Preb David James. b 39. Ch Ch Ox BA60 MA64. Clifton Th Coll 61. **d** 63 **p** 64. C Darfield *Sheff* 63-66; C St Leonards St Leon *Chich* 66-68; Cand Sec CPAS 69-74; Hon C Bromley Ch Ch *Roch* 69-74; V Taunton St Jas *B & W* 74-80; RD Taunton N 78-80; V Chorleywood Ch Ch *St Alb* 80-90; RD Rickmansworth 86 90; Adv for Evang Edmonton *Lon* 91-96; Dioc Adv for Evang 96-01; TR Hackney Marsh 01-07; Preb St Paul's Cathl 97-07; rtd 07; Perm to Offic *Ox* from 08. *22 Latimer Road, Headington, Oxford OX3 7PF* Tel (01865) 766431 E-mail david.j.saville@tesco.net

SAVILLE, Edward Andrew. b 47. Leeds Univ CertEd70 Open Univ BA75. Carl Dioc Tr Inst. **d** 90 **p** 91. C Accrington St Jo w Huncoat *Blackb* 90-93; C Standish 93-95; V Brierfield 95-09; P-in-c 09-10; Hon C from 10; AD Pendle 98-05; Lead Officer Dioc Bd for Soc Resp from 09. *The Vicarage, 5 Reedley Farm Close, Reedley, Burnley BB10 2RB* Tel and fax (01282) 613235 Mobile 07912-227144 E-mail ed.saville@blackburn.anglican.org

SAVILLE (née McCULLAGH), Mrs Elspeth Jane Alexandra. b 68. Man Univ BSc90. Wycliffe Hall Ox BTh95. **d** 95 **p** 96. C Huddersfield H Trin *Wakef* 95-98; NSM Tonbridge SS Pet and Paul *Roch* 98-99; NSM Bromley Ch Ch 99-03; NSM Fordham *Chelmsf* 03-07. *Erasmus House, Church Square, Shepperton TW17 9JY* Tel (01932) 247695

SAVILLE, Mrs Margaret. b 46. SWMTC 93. **d** 94 **p** 95. C Over St Chad *Ches* 94-98; V Crewe All SS and St Paul 98-05; P-in-c Helsby and Dunham-on-the-Hill from 05. *St Paul's Vicarage, Vicarage Lane, Helsby, Frodsham WA6 9AB* Tel (01928) 722151 E-mail thesavilles@tiscali.co.uk

SAWARD, Canon Michael John. b 32. Bris Univ BA55. Tyndale Hall Bris. **d** 56 **p** 57. C Croydon Ch Ch Broad Green *Cant* 56-59; C Edgware *Lon* 59-64; Sec Liv Coun of Chs 64-67; Radio and TV Officer CIO 67-72; Hon C Beckenham St Jo *Roch* 70-72; V Fulham St Matt *Lon* 72-78; V Ealing St Mary 78-91; AD Ealing E 79-84; P-in-c Ealing St Paul 86-89; Preb St Paul's Cathl 85-91; Can Res and Treas St Paul's Cathl 91-00; rtd 01; Perm to Offic *Lon* from 02. *6 Discovery Walk, London E1W 2JG* Tel (020) 7702 1130 E-mail michaelsaward@googlemail.com

SAWLE, Martin. b 49. Solicitor 74 Dundee Univ LLB70. NOC 87. **d** 90 **p** 91. NSM Longton *Blackb* 90-92; P-in-c Hoghton 92-04; Perm to Offic from 04. *38 Chepstow Gardens, Garstang, Preston PR3 1TJ* E-mail martin@sawleandco.com

SAWYER, Andrew William. b 49. AKC71 St Aug Coll Cant 71. **d** 72 **p** 73. C Farnham *Guildf* 72-75; C Dawlish *Ex* 75-78; R Colkirk w Oxwick, Whissonsett and Horningtoft *Nor* 78-82; R Colkirk w Oxwick w Pattesley, Whissonsett etc 82-90; V Hungerford and Denford *Ox* from 90. *The Vicarage, Parsonage Lane, Hungerford RG17 0JB* Tel (01488) 682844

SAWYER, Derek Claude. b 33. ALCD58. **d** 58 **p** 59. C Kirby Muxloe *Leic* 58-60; C Braunstone 60-65; R Vacoas St Paul Mauritius 65-68; V Knighton St Mich *Leic* 68-82; Chapl Kifissia *Eur* 82; Lic to Offic *Glouc* 85-87; V Glouc St Aldate 87-01; rtd 01; R Capisterre w Dieppe St Kitts 01-08; Lic to Offic 09; P-in-c Roseau w Portsmouth Dominica 09-11. *Rawlins Ground, St Paul's Village, St Kitts, St Kitts and Nevis* Tel (001) (869) 466 2773 E-mail derekcsawyer@gmail.com

SAX, Ms Katharine Margaret. b 50. Ripon Coll Cuddesdon. **d** 03 **p** 06. NSM Pokesdown All SS and Southbourne St Chris *Win* 04-05; C Swaythling 06-09; Ecum Officer (Wilts Area) *Sarum* 09-11; P-in-c Churchill and Langford *B & W* from 11. *Park View, Maysmead Lane, Langford, Bristol BS40 5HX* Tel 07733-442476 (mobile) E-mail katharine.sax@kinkiizi.fsnet.co.uk

✠SAXBEE, The Rt Revd John Charles. b 46. Bris Univ BA68 St Jo Coll Dur PhD74. Cranmer Hall Dur 68. **d** 72 **p** 73 **c** 94. C Compton Gifford *Ex* 72-77; P-in-c Weston Mill 77-80; V 80-81;

TV Cen Ex 81-87; Jt Dir SWMTC 81-92; Preb Ex Cathl 88-92; Adn Ludlow *Heref* 92-01; Preb Heref Cathl 92-01; P-in-c Wistanstow 92-94; P-in-c Acton Scott 92-94; Suff Bp Ludlow 94-01; Bp Linc 01-11; rtd 11. *22 Shelley Road, Priory Park, Haverfordwest SA61 1RX* Tel (01437) 768918

SAXBY, Canon Martin Peter. b 52. St Jo Coll Dur BA77. Cranmer Hall Dur 74. **d** 78 **p** 79. C Peckham St Mary Magd *S'wark* 78-81; C Ramsey *Ely* 81-84; P-in-c Mattishall w Mattishall Burgh *Nor* 84-89; P-in-c Welborne 84-89; P-in-c Yaxham 84-89; R Mattishall w Mattishall Burgh, Welborne etc 89-90; V Rugby St Matt *Cov* 90-07; V Rugby W from 08; RD Rugby from 06; Hon Can Cov Cathl from 11. *St Matthew's Vicarage, 7 Vicarage Road, Rugby CV22 7AJ* Tel (01788) 330442 or 330447 Fax 07053-480079 E-mail martinpa@stmatthews.org.uk

SAXBY, Steven Michael Paul. b 70. Fitzw Coll Cam BA98 MA02 Heythrop Coll Lon MA05 Univ Coll Lon MA08. Aston Tr Scheme 92 Linc Th Coll 94 Westcott Ho Cam 95. **d** 98 **p** 01. C E Ham w Upton Park *Chelmsf* 98-00; C Barking St Marg w St Patr 00-02; Waltham Forest Deanery Development Worker 02-07; NSM Walthamstow 02-03; V Walthamstow St Pet 03-09; P-in-c Walthamstow St Barn and St Jas Gt from 09; RD Waltham Forest from 07. *St Barnabas' Vicarage, St Barnabas Road, London E17 8JZ* Tel (020) 8520 5323 E-mail stevensaxby@btinternet.com

SAXTON, James. b 54. Lanc Univ BEd77 Hull Univ MEd85. Linc Th Coll 84. **d** 86 **p** 87. C Moor Allerton *Ripon* 86-90; C Knaresborough 90-92; TV Seacroft 92-95; V Ireland Wood 95-00; TV Becontree S *Chelmsf* 02-09; C Camberwell St Geo *S'wark* from 09; Chapl S Lon and Maudsley NHS Foundn Trust from 09. *131 Coleman Road, London SE5 7TF* Tel (020) 7703 2704 E-mail james.saxton@talktalk.net

SAYER, Derek John. b 32. St Steph Ho Ox 55. **d** 58 **p** 58. C Tottenham All Hallows *Lon* 58-61; C Letchworth *St Alb* 61-63; Chapl RADD 63-64 and 66-82; C Lancing St Mich *Chich* 64-66; C Dorking w Ranmore *Guildf* 89-92; V Holmwood 92-95; Perm to Offic 95-04; rtd 97. *Richeldis, 24 Chalkpit Lane, Dorking RH4 1ER* Tel (01306) 882610

SAYER, Penelope Jane. b 59. Newc Univ BA80 Open Univ BA93. SEITE 04. **d** 07 **p** 08. NSM Upper St Leonards St Jo *Chich* 07-10; TR Becontree S *Chelmsf* from 10. *St Alban's Vicarage, Vincent Road, Dagenham RM9 6AL* Tel (020) 8595 1042 Mobile 07729-372996 E-mail penny.st.john@btinternet.com

SAYER, Simon Benedict. b 59. Man Univ BA07. St Steph Ho Ox 09. **d** 10 **p** 11. C Hollinwood and Limeside *Man* from 10. *19 Milford Avenue, Oldham OL8 3UP* Tel 0161-478 8363 Mobile 07754-100845 E-mail fr.simon@tiscali.co.uk

SAYER, Canon William Anthony John. b 37. St Mich Coll Llan 60. **d** 64 **p** 65. C Gorleston St Andr *Nor* 64-67; P-in-c Witton w Ridlington 67-71; P-in-c Honing w Crostwight 67-71; V Bacton w Edingthorpe 67-71; CF 71-84; Miss to Seafarers from 84; R Holkham w Egmere w Warham, Wells and Wighton *Nor* 84-02; RD Burnham and Walsingham 87-92; Hon Can Nor Cathl 97-02; rtd 02; Perm to Offic *Nor* from 02. *Greenway Lodge, Mill Road, Wells-next-the-Sea NR23 1RF* Tel (01328) 711224

SAYERS, Karen Jane. See GARDINER, Mrs Karen Jane

SAYERS, Simon Philip. b 59. Cam Univ MA81. Oak Hill Th Coll 83. **d** 85 **p** 86. C Alperton *Lon* 85-89; C Hornsey Rise Whitehall Park Team 89-90; TV 90-96; Min Panshanger CD *St Alb* 96-02; R Warblington w Emsworth *Portsm* from 02. *The Rectory, 20 Church Path, Emsworth PO10 7DP* Tel (01243) 372428 E-mail simonsayers@hotmail.com

SAYERS, Susan. b 46. Bp Otter Coll Chich BEd69 Middx Univ BA02. NTMTC 99. **d** 02 **p** 03. NSM Southend *Chelmsf* from 02; TV from 05; Asst Chapl HM Pris Bullwood Hall 02-06. *17 Claremont Close, Westcliff-on-Sea SS0 7UA* Tel (010702) 431843 Mobile 07765-857320 E-mail susansayers@yahoo.com

SAYLE, Philip David. b 61. Nottm Univ BA98. St Jo Coll Nottm 92. **d** 94 **p** 95. C Helston and Wendron *Truro* 94-97; R St Stephen in Brannel 97-00; R Kenwyn w St Allen 00-06; V Upton Ascension *Ches* from 06. *49 Heath Road, Upton, Chester CH2 1HT* Tel (01244) 381181 E-mail pdsayle@btinternet.com

SAYWELL, Philip. b 33. Linc Th Coll 57. **d** 60 **p** 61. C Stepney St Dunstan and All SS *Lon* 60-63; C Calstock *Truro* 63-66; V Lanteglos by Fowey 66-73; Iran 73-77; R Cockley Cley w Gooderstone *Nor* 78-81; V Didlington 78-81; R Gt and Lt Cressingham w Threxton 78-81; R Hilborough w Bodney 78-81; R Oxborough w Foulden and Caldecote 78-81; UAE 81-84; Perm to Offic *Chich* 84-88; Nat Co-ord (UK) SOMA UK 85-88; rtd 93. *Riverside, Exford, Minehead TA24 7PX* Tel (01643) 831619 Fax 831416 E-mail philip.saywell@virgin.net

SCAIFE, Andrew. b 50. Ex Coll Ox BA73 MA76. Wycliffe Hall Ox 74. **d** 77 **p** 78. C Everton St Geo *Liv* 77-81; P-in-c Liv St Mark 81; TV St Luke in the City 81-86; V Litherland St Phil 86-96; Sen Chapl Cheshire and Wirral Partnerships NHS Trust from 96. *Arrowe Park Hospital, Upton, Wirral CH49 5PE* Tel 0151-678 5111 ext 2275 or 632 0646 E-mail andrew.scaife@whnt.nhs.uk

SCALES, Barbara Marion. b 24. S'wark Ord Course. **dss** 82 **d** 87 **p** 94. St Helier *S'wark* 82-87; Hon Par Dn 87-89; Chapl Asst

St Helier Hosp Carshalton 82-88; NSM Cheam Common St Phil *S'wark* 89-95; rtd 95; Perm to Offic *S'wark* 95-04. *Address temp unknown*

SCAMMAN (*née* **BEWES**), **Mrs Helen Catherine.** b 71. Leeds Univ BA94 York Univ PGCE95 Cam Univ BA01. Ridley Hall Cam 99. **d** 02 **p** 03. C Win Ch Ch 02-06; NSM 06-07; Perm to Offic *Ely* 07-10 and *Blackb* from 10. *St Thomas's Vicarage, 33 Belle Vue Terrace, Lancaster LA1 4TY* Tel (01524) 590410 E-mail scampersons@yahoo.com

SCAMMAN, Jonathan Leitch. b 73. St Andr Univ MA96 Ex Coll Ox MPhil98 Cam Univ BA01. Ridley Hall Cam 99. **d** 02 **p** 03. C Win Ch Ch 02-07; C Cambridge St Barn *Ely* 07-10; P-in-c Lancaster St Thos *Blackb* from 10. *St Thomas's Vicarage, 33 Belle Vue Terrace, Lancaster LA1 4TY* Tel (01524) 590410 E-mail scampersons@yahoo.com

SCAMMAN, Peter Fletcher. b 80. SS Hild & Bede Coll Dur MEng03. Oak Hill Th Coll BA09. **d** 10 **p** 11. C Ox St Andr from 10. *5 Stanchey Lane, Oxford OX2 7LD* Tel (01865) 580315 Mobile 07917-714939 E-mail petescamman@hotmail.com

SCAMMELL, Frank. b 56. Cam Univ MA. St Jo Coll Nottm BA83. **d** 82 **p** 83. C Stapenhill w Cauldwell *Derby* 82-86; TV Swanage and Studland *Sarum* 86-92; Min Southgate LEP *St E* 92-03; V Stoughton *Guildf* from 03; RD Guildf from 11. *Stoughton Vicarage, 3 Shepherds Lane, Guildford GU2 9SJ* Tel (01483) 561603

SCANLAN, Helen Tracy. b 66. Dioc OLM tr scheme 06. **d** 09 **p** 10. NSM Heaton Reddish *Man* 09-11; C Heaton Ch Ch w Halliwell St Marg from 11. *6 Glenfield Road, Stockport SK4 2QP* E-mail helen.scanlan@btinternet.com

SCANLON, Geoffrey Edward Leyshon. b 44. Coll of Resurr Mirfield. **d** 76 **p** 77. C Beamish *Dur* 76-79; C-in-c Bishopwearmouth St Mary V w St Pet CD 79-81; V Laurens Epiphany USA 81-85; V Columbia St Dav 85-87; R Danville H Trin 87-09; rtd 09. *2910 Stone Creek Boulevard, Urbana IL 61802-9420, USA* Tel (001) (217) 344 1174

SCANTLEBURY, James Stanley. b 48. St Jo Coll Dur BA69 Heythrop Coll Lon MTh80. Westcott Ho Cam 70. **d** 72 **p** 73. C Upperby St Jo *Carl* 72-75; C Guildf H Trin w St Mary 75-77; Order of St Aug 77-86; Chapl Austin Friars Sch Carl 80-86; Chapl Mayfield Coll E Sussex 86-88; Chapl H Trin Sen Sch Halifax 88-90; NSM Ripponden *Wakef* 88-90; V Torpenhow *Carl* 91-94; V Allhallows 91-94; V Falmouth All SS *Truro* 94-98; V Harden and Wilsden *Bradf* 98-02; rtd 03. *5 Westhill Avenue, Cullingworth, Bradford BD13 5BB* Tel (01535) 272980

SCARGILL, Christopher Morris. b 57. UEA BA79 York Univ MA81 Leeds Univ CertEd81 Nottm Univ BTh89. Linc Th Coll 86. **d** 89 **p** 90. C Desborough and Brampton Ash w Dingley and Braybrooke *Pet* 89-92; C Buxton w Burbage and King Sterndale *Derby* 92-93; TV 93-98; V Ipstones w Berkhamsytch and Onecote w Bradnop *Lich* 98-09; RD Alstonfield 08-09; Local Min Adv (Stafford) 07-09; Sen Chapl Torrevieja *Eur* from 09. *Apartado 3257, Torre la Mata, 03188 Torrevieja (Alicante), Spain* Tel (0034) 966 925 205 E-mail revdcms@gmail.com

SCARISBRICK, Mrs Helen. b 60. Sheff Univ BA81 Sheff Poly PGCE82 Ches Coll of HE BTh99. NOC 97. **d** 99 **p** 00. C Norbury *Ches* 99-03; P-in-c Cheadle Heath 03-07; C Edgeley and Cheadle Heath 07-09; V Broadheath from 09. *The Vicarage, Lindsell Road, West Timperley, Altrincham WA14 5NX* Tel 0161-928 4820 E-mail helenscarisbrick@btinternet.com

SCARR, Mrs Hazel Anne. b 44. SAOMC. **d** 00 **p** 01. NSM Adderbury w Milton *Ox* 00-04; NSM Chadlington and Spelsbury, Ascott under Wychwood 04-05; NSM Hardington Vale *B & W* 05-07; NSM Hook Norton w Gt Rollright, Swerford etc *Ox* 07-10; Perm to Offic from 11. *Wooden Hill Farm, Barford Road, Bloxham, Banbury OX15 4LP* Tel (01295) 72022 E-mail hazel@jandhscarr.sagehost.co.uk

SCARTH, John Robert. b 34. Leeds Univ BSc55 CertEd. Cranmer Hall Dur 63. **d** 65 **p** 66. C Dewsbury All SS *Wakef* 65-68; V Shepley 68-72; Asst Master Kingston-upon-Hull Gr Sch 72-78; St Mary's C of E Sch Hendon 78-81; V Ossett cum Gawthorpe 81-88; R Tarrington w Stoke Edith, Aylton, Pixley etc *Heref* 88-96; rtd 96; Perm to Offic *Wakef* 96-09 and *S'wark* from 10. *3 Russet Drive, Croydon CR0 7DS* Tel 07867-505615 (mobile)

SCARTH, Maurice John. b 31. MInstPS AMBIM. St Deiniol's Hawarden 81. **d** 83 **p** 84. C Llandrillo-yn-Rhos *St As* 83-87; V Rhosymedre 87-91; V Kerry and Llanmerewig and Dolfor 91-93; rtd 93. *Homelands, 11A Compton Way, Abergele LL22 7BL* Tel (01745) 833783

SCEATS, Preb David Douglas. b 46. Ch Coll Cam BA68 MA72 Bris Univ MA71. Clifton Th Coll 68. **d** 71 **p** 72. C Cambridge St Paul *Ely* 71-74; Lect Trin Coll Bris 74-83; V Shenstone *Lich* 83-86; Dioc Tr Officer 86-91; P-in-c Colton 86-90; Dir Local Min Development 91-98; Warden of Readers 91-96; C Lich St Chad 94-98; Dioc Board of Min Team Ldr 96-98; Preb Lich Cathl 96-98; Prin NTMTC 99-07; Preb St Paul's Cathl 02-07; P-in-c Selkirk *Edin* from 07. *St John's Rectory, Viewfield Park, Selkirk TD7 4LH* Tel (01750) 21364 E-mail d-sceats@sky.com

SCHAEFER, Carl Richard. b 67. Coll of Resurr Mirfield 91. **d** 94 **p** 95. C Ribbleton *Blackb* 94-98; V Blackb St Thos w St Jude 98-08; P-in-c Blackb St Mich w St Jo and H Trin 03-08; V Goldthorpe w Hickleton *Sheff* from 08. *Goldthorpe Presbytery, Lockwood Road, Goldthorpe, Rotherham S63 9JY* Tel (01709) 898426 E-mail carl@schaeferc.freeserve.co.uk

SCHARF, Brian Howard. b 39. Alberta Univ BA60. Trin Coll Toronto 60 Coll of Resurr Mirfield 61. **d** 63 **p** 65. C Vancouver St Faith Canada 63-65; C Broadstairs *Cant* 65-68. *3236 Robinson Road, North Vancouver BC V7J 3E9, Canada* Tel (001) (604) 987 0219 E-mail brianscharf@shaw.ca

SCHARF, Ulrich Eduard Erich Julian. b 35. Melbourne Univ BA59 MA67 Linacre Coll Ox BA67 MA72 Lon Univ PhD81. Ripon Hall Ox 65. **d** 67 **p** 68. C Hackney St Jo *Lon* 68-71; Chapl to Bp Stepney 71-75; P-in-c Shadwell St Paul w Ratcliffe St Jas 75-90; R St Geo-in-the-East w St Paul 79-86; P-in-c W Ham *Chelmsf* 90-95; V 95-05; rtd 05; Perm to Offic *Chelmsf* from 06. *c/o Miss N C Scharf, 19 Felltor Close, Liverpool L25 6DP*

SCHARIAH, Canon Zechariah. b 43. Zürich Univ BD87. Baptist Th Sem Rueschlikon 83. **d** 93 **p** 93. Chapl to Miss to Minorities from 93; Perm to Offic *Eur* from 95; Can Dar-es-Salaam from 00. *Schaubhus 7, 6020 Emmenbrücke, Switzerland* E-mail karibumade@hotmail.com

SCHATZ, Stefani. b 62. Mills Coll Oakland (USA) BA84. Episc Div Sch Cam Mass MDiv01. **d** 01 **p** 02. C Hermosa Beach USA 01-04; C Brookline All SS 04-06; Perm to Offic *Man* 06-07; TV Gorton and Abbey Hey 07-08; R Reno Trin USA from 08. *1644 Shadow Wood Road, Reno NV 89523-1244, USA* Tel (001) (775) 329 4279 E-mail stefani@trinityreno.org

SCHEMANOFF, Ms Natasha Anne. b 50. CertEd71. **d** 96 **p** 97. C Freshford, Limpley Stoke and Hinton Charterhouse *B & W* 96-99; TV Worle 99-00; V Kewstoke w Wick St Lawrence 00-07; Bp's Adv for Racial Justice 00-07; rtd 07; Perm to Offic *Truro* from 97. *Hallane End, 4 The Terrace, Lostwithiel PL22 0DT* Tel (01208) 871330

SCHIBILD, Nigel Edmund David. b 47. Oak Hill Th Coll BA81. **d** 81 **p** 82. C Eccleston Ch Ch *Liv* 81-85; P-in-c Sydenham H Trin *S'wark* 85-87; V 87-91; Chapl Mildmay Miss Hosp 91-98; Assoc V Beirut All SS Lebanon 99-04; C Westminster St Jas the Less *Lon* 05-07; Chapl John Taylor Hospice Birm from 07. *John Taylor Hospice, 76 Grange Road, Erdington, Birmingham B24 0DF* Tel 0121-465 2000 E-mail nigel.schibild@benpct.nhs.uk

SCHILD, John. b 38. ALCD64. **d** 64 **p** 65. C Cheltenham Ch Ch *Glouc* 64-67; Area Sec CMS *Sheff* and *S'well* 67-73; Area Sec CMS *Chelmsf* and *St Alb* 73-76; V Lt Heath *St Alb* 76-88; R Bedford St Pet w St Cuth 88-94; P-in-c King's Walden and Offley w Lilley 94-98; V 98-03; rtd 03. *Trenarren, St Cleer, Liskeard PL14 5DN* Tel (01579) 347047 E-mail john@schild.demon.co.uk

SCHLEGER, Ms Maria Francesca. b 57. LSE BA78 SS Coll Cam BA84 MA89. Westcott Ho Cam 82. **dss** 85 **d** 87 **p** 94. De Beauvoir Town St Pet *Lon* 85-90; Par Dn 87-90; TD Bow H Trin and All Hallows 90-94; Dean of Women's Min (Stepney Area) 90-94; Perm to Offic *Birm* 94-98; NSM Stepney St Dunstan and All SS *Lon* 99-03; Chapl Mildmay Miss Hosp from 03. *75 Lansdowne Drive, London E8 3EP* Tel (020) 7683 0051 *or* 7613 6300 ext 6170 E-mail schleger@waitrose.com *or* chaplain@mildmay.org

SCHLUTER, Nathaniel David. b 71. Pemb Coll Ox BA93 MA97 Green Coll Ox DPhil98. Wycliffe Hall Ox BA. **d** 00 **p** 01. C Gerrards Cross and Fulmer *Ox* 00-05; Prin Johannesburg Bible Coll S Africa from 05. *PO Box 374, Auckland Park, 2006 South Africa* E-mail info@johannesburgbiblecollege.org

SCHMIDT, Mrs Karen Rosemarie. b 48. Surrey Univ BSc70 Solicitor 76. STETS 96. **d** 99 **p** 00. NSM Lee-on-the-Solent *Portsm* 99-05; P-in-c Purbrook 05-06; V 06-09; rtd 09; Bp's Dom Chapl *Portsm* from 09. *43 Deal Close, Fareham PO14 2LZ* Tel (023) 9223 0143 Mobile 07990-518541 E-mail karenrschmidt@yahoo.co.uk

SCHNAAR, Howard William. b 71. Wilson Carlile Coll 95. **d** 08. C Worthing H Trin w Ch Ch *Chich* from 08. *5 Christchurch Road, Worthing BN11 1JH* Tel (01903) 202433

SCHOFIELD, Andrew Thomas. b 47. K Coll Lon BD70 AKC71 PGCE72. St Aug Coll Cant 70. **d** 81 **p** 82. C Whittlesey *Ely* 81-84; C Ramsey 84-87; P-in-c Ellington, Grafham, Easton and Spaldwick w Barham and Woolley 87-94; R March St Jo 94-05; P-in-c Duxford 05-09; P-in-c Hinxton 05-09; P-in-c Ickleton 05-09; rtd 09; P-in-c Beetham *Carl* from 09. *The Parsonage, Stanley Street, Beetham, Milnthorpe LA7 7AS* Tel (01539) 562216 E-mail atschofield@msn.com

SCHOFIELD, David. b 43. Linc Th Coll 74. **d** 75 **p** 76. C Gainsborough All SS *Linc* 75-78; R Bolingbroke w Hareby 78-79; P-in-c Hagnaby 78-79; P-in-c Hagworthingham w Asgarby and Lusby 78-79; P-in-c Mavis Enderby w Raithby 78-79; P-in-c E Kirkby w Miningsby 78-79; R Bolingbroke 79-81; C-in-c Stamford Ch CD 81-90; V Crowle 90-97; V Crowle Gp 97-07; rtd 07. *19 Station Road, Hadfield, Glossop SK13 1BQ* Tel (01457) 857885 E-mail david@schofield1.freeserve.co.uk

SCHOFIELD, David Leslie. b 40. MISM89. EMMTC 98. **d** 01 **p** 02. NSM Derby St Mark 01-04; P-in-c Dukinfield St Luke *Ches* from 07. *72 Bromley Cross Road, Bromley Cross, Bolton BL7 9LT* Tel (01204) 303137

SCHOFIELD, Gary. b 64. Ripon Coll Cuddesdon 97. **d** 99 **p** 00. C Exhall *Cov* 99-02; V Wales *Sheff* from 02; P-in-c Harthill and Thorpe Salvin from 08; AD Laughton from 11. *The Vicarage, Manor Road, Wales, Sheffield S26 5PD* Tel (01909) 771111 E-mail gary.schofield@sheffield.anglican.org

SCHOFIELD, John Martin. b 47. Selw Coll Cam BA69 MA73. St Steph Ho Ox 70. **d** 72 **p** 73. C Palmers Green St Jo *Lon* 72-75; C Friern Barnet St Jas 75-80; V Luton St Aug Limbury *St Alb* 80-89; V Biddenham and Dir CME 89-94; Dir Minl Tr *Guildf* 94-99; Can Res Guildf Cathl 95-99; Perm to Offic 03-05; Dir Dioc Min Course 05-09; rtd 09. *3 Despenser Road, Tewkesbury GL20 5TP* E-mail johnscho@ntlworld.com

SCHOFIELD, John Verity. b 29. Jes Coll Ox BA52 MA56. Cuddesdon Coll 53. **d** 55 **p** 56. C Cirencester *Glouc* 55-59; R Stella *Dur* 59-67; Kenya 67-69; Asst Chapl St Paul's Sch Barnes 69-70; Chapl 71-80; Australia 81-83; Gen Sec Friends of Elderly & Gentlefolk's Help 83-94; Perm to Offic *Sarum* from 83; rtd 94. *Bishops Barn, Foots Hill, Cann, Shaftesbury SP7 0BW* Tel (01747) 853852

SCHOFIELD, Canon Nigel Timothy. b 54. Dur Univ BA76 Nottm Univ BCombStuds83 FRCO. Linc Th Coll 80. **d** 83 **p** 84. C Cheshunt *St Alb* 83-86; V Colyton, Southleigh, Offwell, Widworthy etc *Ex* 86-94; V Seaton 94-03; P-in-c Beer and Branscombe 01-03; V Seaton and Beer 03-06; RD Honiton 99-03; Can Res Chich Cathl from 06, *4 Vicars Close, Chichester PO19 1PT* Tel (01243) 813589 E-mail precentor@chichestercathedral.org.uk

SCHOFIELD, Ruth Elizabeth. b 65. Imp Coll Lon BEng87. STETS 06. **d** 09 **p** 10. NSM Botley *Portsm* from 09; NSM Curdridge from 09; NSM Durley from 09. *5 Myers Close, Swanmore, Southampton SO32 2RN* Tel (01489) 895824 E-mail rschofield@f2s.com

SCHOFIELD, Ms Sarah. b 70. Man Univ BA95. Qu Coll Birm 95. **d** 97 **p** 98. C Longsight St Luke *Man* 97-02; Tutor (Man Ho) Westcott Ho Cam 00-04; P-in-c Gorton St Phil *Man* 02-06; P-in-c Abbey Hey 04-06; TV Cen Wolverhampton *Lich* from 06. *All Saints Vicarage, 2A Vicarage Road, Wolverhampton WV2 1DT* Tel (01902) 452584 E-mail sarahschof@aol.com

SCHOFIELD, Timothy. See SCHOFIELD, Canon Nigel Timothy

SCHOFIELD, Mrs Victoria Louise. b 56. Liv Poly BSc88 Liv Univ PGCE91. Wycliffe Hall Ox BTh05. **d** 02 **p** 03. C Hattersley *Ches* 02-05; P-in-c Runcorn St Mich 05-06; V from 06. *145 Greenway Road, Runcorn WA7 4NR* Tel (01928) 500993

SCHOLEFIELD, John. b 27. Leeds Univ BSc50. Wells Th Coll 51. **d** 53 **p** 54. C Ossett cum Gawthorpe *Wakef* 53-56; C Hebden Bridge 56-58; V Sowerby St Geo 58-64; V Darton 64-70; V Stoke Gabriel *Ex* 70-84; P-in-c Collaton St Mary 82-84; V Stoke Gabriel and Collaton 84-92; rtd 92; Perm to Offic *Ex* 92-09. *25 Droridge, Dartington, Totnes TQ9 6JQ* Tel (01803) 863192

SCHOLEFIELD, Mrs Judith Lenore. b 45. RN66 Open Univ BA97. WEMTC 99. **d** 04 **p** 05. OLM Ledbury *Heref* from 04. *Oakland Lodge, The Homend, Ledbury HR8 1AR* Tel (01531) 632279

SCHOLES, Ms Victoria Prichard. b 68. Man Univ BSc89. St Jo Coll Nottm 97. **d** 00 **p** 01. C Macclesfield St Jo *Ches* 00-02; NSM 02-03; Perm to Offic from 03. *87B Gawsorth Road, Macclesfield SK11 8UF* Tel (01625) 425049

SCHOLEY, Michael. **d** 10. NSM Staincross *Wakef* from 10. *8 Croft Close, Mapplewell, Barnsley S75 6FN* Tel (01226) 386173 E-mail michael.scholey@virgin.net

SCHOLLAR, Canon Pamela Mary. b 39. Southn Univ DipEd80. S Dios Minl Tr Scheme 89. **d** 92 **p** 94. NSM Bournemouth St Andr *Win* 92-94; NSM Pokesdown St Jas from 94; Hon Can Win Cathl from 02. *22 Bethia Road, Bournemouth BH8 9BD* Tel (01202) 397925 E-mail schollar@ukgateway.net

SCHOLZ, Terence Brinsley. b 44. St Martin's Coll Lanc MA98. CBDTI 94. **d** 97 **p** 98. NSM St Annes St Thos *Blackb* 97-01; NSM Broughton 01-02; Perm to Offic 02-04; NSM Freckleton from 04. *14 Further Ends Road, Freckleton, Preston PR4 1RL* Tel (01772) 632966 Mobile 07989-931909 E-mail tbscholz@btinternet.com

SCHOOLING, Bruce James. b 47. Rhodes Univ BA73. St Paul's Coll Grahamstown 76. **d** 76 **p** 77. C Rondebosch St Thos S Africa 76-79; C St Geo Cathl Cape Town 79-83; R Malmesbury 83-86; C Wanstead St Mary *Chelmsf* 87-90; V Leigh-on-Sea St Jas 90-04; Perm to Offic from 05; rtd 07. *249 Woodrange Drive, Southend-on-Sea SS1 2SQ* Tel (01702) 613429 Mobile 07710-208476 E-mail b.schooling@btinternet.com

SCHRIMSHAW, Angela Anna Violet. b 51. SRN73 SCM76 Hull Univ BSc98. NEOC 01. **d** 04 **p** 05. NSM Welton w Melton *York* from 04. *22 Bricknell Avenue, Hull HU5 4JS* Tel (01482) 446609 E-mail schrim@schrim.karoo.co.uk

SCHRODER, Edward Amos. b 41. Cant Univ (NZ) BA64. Cranmer Hall Dur. **d** 67 **p** 68. C St Marylebone All So w SS Pet and Jo *Lon* 67-71; Dean Gordon Coll USA and C Hamilton Ch Ch 71-76; Can Missr and Asst to Bp Florida 76-79; R Orange Park Grace Ch 79-86; R San Antonio Ch Ch 86-00; Chapl Amelia Plantation Chpl 00-06; rtd 06. *15 Hickory Lane, Amelia Island FL 32034-5064, USA* Tel (001) (904) 277 6752 Fax 277 8323 E-mail tschroder@ameliachapel.com

SCHRYVER, Mrs Linda Jean. b 56. Ch Ch Coll Cant BSc00. SEITE 00. **d** 03 **p** 04. NSM Willesborough *Cant* 03-09. *2 Church Cottages, Canterbury Road, Godmersham, Canterbury CT4 7DS* Tel (01227) 730750 Mobile 07768-566372 E-mail linda.schryver@mariecurie.org.uk

SCHULD DE VERNY, Dietrich Gustave. See DE VERNY, David Dietrich Schuld

SCHUMAN, Andrew William Edward. b 73. Birm Univ BA95 MSc96 Bris Univ PhD00 FRGS02. Trin Coll Bris BA03 MA04. **d** 04 **p** 05. C Shirehampton *Bris* 04-08; C Bris Ch the Servant Stockwood from 08; Partnership P Bris S from 08. *69 Bifield Road, Bristol BS14 8TT* Tel (01275) 830944 E-mail andrewschuman@me.com

SCHUNEMANN, Bernhard George. b 61. K Coll Lon BD86 AKC86 LRAM83. Ripon Coll Cuddesdon 88. **d** 90 **p** 91. C Kirkby *Liv* 90-93; C St Martin-in-the-Fields *Lon* 93-97; Chapl Br Sch of Osteopathy 93-97; P-in-c Littlemore *Ox* 97-06; V S Dulwich St Steph *S'wark* from 06. *St Stephen's Vicarage, 111 College Road, London SE21 7HN* Tel (020) 8693 3797 *or* 8766 7281 Fax 8693 7194 E-mail bschunemann@compuserve.com

SCHUTTE, Ms Margaret Ann. b 50. Natal Univ BA71. SAOMC. **d** 04 **p** 05. C Overbury w Teddington, Alstone etc *Worc* 04-07; Chapl HM Pris Hewell from 07. *HM Prison Hewell, Hewell Lane, Redditch B97 6QS* Tel (01527) 785000 E-mail schuttefamily@tesco.net

SCHWIER, Paul David. b 55. **d** 96 **p** 97. OLM Pulham Market, Pulham St Mary and Starston *Nor* 96-99; OLM Dickleburgh and The Pulhams from 99. *Street Farm, Pulham Market, Diss IP21 4SP* Tel (01379) 676240

SCHWIER, Peter Andrew. b 52. **d** 91 **p** 92. NSM Fressingfield, Mendham etc *St E* from 91. *Valley Farm, Metfield, Harleston IP20 0JZ* Tel (01379) 586517

SCLATER, Jennifer. b 44. TISEC. **d** 02 **p** 04. Par Dn Elgin w Lossiemouth *Mor* 02-04; NSM from 04. *82 Pluscarden Road, Elgin IV30 1SU* Tel (01343) 549442 E-mail jenny@sclater.com

SCLATER, John Edward. b 46. Nottm Univ BA68 St Edm Hall Ox CertEd71. Cuddesdon Coll 69. **d** 71 **p** 72. C Bris St Mary Redcliffe w Temple etc 71-75; Chapl Bede Ho Staplehurst 75-79; Chapl Warw Sch 79; P-in-c Offchurch *Cov* 79-80; Belgium 81-89; Willen Priory 89-91; C Linslade *Ox* 91-94; P-in-c Hedsor and Bourne End 94-02; rtd 02; Perm to Offic *B & W* from 03. *3 East Court, South Horrington Village, Wells BA5 3HL* Tel (01749) 671349 E-mail john@jes07.freeserve.co.uk

SCOBIE, Geoffrey Edward Winsor. b 39. Bris Univ BSc62 MSc68 Birm Univ MA70 Glas Univ PhD78 FRSA96 AFBPsS. Tyndale Hall Bris 62. **d** 65 **p** 66. C Summerfield *Birm* 65-66; C Moseley St Anne 66-67; Lect Psychology Glas Univ 67-04; Hon C Glas St Silas 70-83; P-in-c 83-84; Hon R 84-85; TR 85-86; Team Chapl 86-88; Hon Asst Team Chapl 88-99; Assoc P Bishopbriggs 99-08; P-in-c Lenzie from 06. *3 Norfolk Crescent, Bishopbriggs, Glasgow G64 3BA* Tel 0141-722 2907 *or* 330 4699 E-mail gscobie@ntlworld.com

SCOONES, Roger Philip. b 48. Trin Coll Bris. **d** 82 **p** 83. C Childwall All SS *Liv* 82-85; Bradf Cathl 85-90; V Congleton St Pet *Ches* 90-96; P-in-c Congleton St Steph 94-96; R Stockport St Mary from 96. *St Mary's Rectory, 24 Gorsey Mount Street, Stockport SK1 4DU* Tel 0161-429 6564 *or* 480 1815 Fax 429 6564 E-mail roger@scoones9.freeserve.co.uk

SCORER, Canon John Robson. b 47. Westcott Ho Cam 73. **d** 75 **p** 76. C Silksworth *Dur* 75-78; C Newton Aycliffe 78-82; V Sherburn 82-83; V Sherburn w Pittington 83-89; P-in-c Croxdale 89-93; Chapl Dur Constabulary from 89; Chapl Dur Police Tr Cen 93-05; Hon Can Dur Cathl from 04. *1 Vicarage Close, Howden le Wear, Crook DL15 8RB* Tel and fax (01388) 764938

SCOTFORD, Bethan Lynne. b 44. Univ of Wales (Cardiff) BA67 PGCE68. St As Minl Tr Course 95. **d** 99 **p** 00. Fieldworker (Wales) USPG 98-11; C Guilsfield w Pool Quay *St As* 99-02; R Corwen and Llangar w Gwyddelwern and Llawrybetws 02-11; rtd 11. *7 Fairview Avenue, Guilsfield, Welshpool SY21 9NE* Tel (01938) 555153 Mobile 07802-656607 E-mail bscotford@toucansurf.com

SCOTLAND, Nigel Adrian Douglas. b 42. McGill Univ Montreal MA71 Aber Univ PhD75 CertEd75 Bris Univ MLitt85. Gordon-Conwell Th Sem MDiv70 Lon Coll of Div ALCD66 LTh74. **d** 66 **p** 67. C Harold Wood *Chelmsf* 66-69; USA 69-70; R Lakefield Canada 70-72; Lic to Offic *Ab* 72-75; Chapl and Lect St Mary's Coll Cheltenham 75-79; Sen Lect 77-79; Chapl and Sen Lect Coll of St SS Paul and Mary Cheltenham 79-84; NSM Cheltenham St Mark *Glouc* 85-92; Field Chair RS Cheltenham and Glouc Coll of HE 89-01; Field Chair Glos Univ 01-05; Prin Lect 96-08; Research Fell from 08; Perm to Offic *Glouc* from 92;

Tutor Trin Coll Bris from 06; Lic to Offic *Bris* from 07; Tutor Bris Univ from 09. *23 School Road, Charlton Kings, Cheltenham GL53 8BG* Tel (01242) 529167
E-mail nigel.scotland@btopenworld.com

SCOTLAND, Primus of the Episcopal Church in. *See* CHILLINGWORTH, The Most Revd David Robert

SCOTT, Adam. b 47. OBE08 TD78. Ch Ch Ox BA68 MA72 City Univ MSc79 St Andr Univ PhD10 Barrister 72 FRSA95 CEng81 MIET81 FIEE94. S'wark Ord Course 73. **d** 75 **p** 76. MSE Blackheath Park St Mich *S'wark* from 75; Dean for MSE, Woolwich from 90; Prof Fell St Andr Univ 96-97 and from 98; Perm to Offic from 96. *19 Blackheath Park, London SE3 8RW* Tel (020) 8852 3286 Fax 8852 6247
E-mail adam.scott@btinternet.com

SCOTT, Preb Allan George. b 39. Man Univ BA61. Coll of Resurr Mirfield 61. **d** 63 **p** 64. C Bradford cum Beswick *Man* 63-66; P-in-c 66-72; Hon C Bramhall *Ches* 72-74; Hon C Tottenham St Jo *Lon* 74-76; Hon C Bush Hill Park St Steph 76-79; R Stoke Newington St Mary 79-92; P-in-c Brownswood Park 95-97; Preb St Paul's Cathl 91-04; rtd 04. *8 West Hackney House, 15 Northwold Road, London N16 7HJ* Tel (020) 7923 0153

SCOTT, Andrew Charles Graham. b 28. Mert Coll Ox BA57 MA. Wells Th Coll 57. **d** 59 **p** 60. C Bangor St Andr *Cov* 59-64; Chapl RN 64-68; C Prenton *Ches* 68-71; V Tow Law *Dur* 71-81; RD Stanhope 77-81; V Bampton w Clanfield *Ox* 81-95; rtd 95; Perm to Offic *Ex* from 95. *99 Speedwell Crescent, Plymouth PL6 5SZ* Tel (01752) 773570

SCOTT, Barrie. b 63. Birm Univ BA85 Goldsmiths' Coll Lon PGCE86. St Steph Ho Ox 93. **d** 95 **p** 96. C Tilehurst St Mich *Ox* 95-98; Perm to Offic *Birm* from 98. *3 Old Langley Hall, Ox Leys Road, Sutton Coldfield B75 7HP* Tel 0121-351 2050
E-mail barrie@waitrose.com

SCOTT, Basil John Morley. b 34. Qu Coll Cam BA59 Banaras Hindu Univ MA65. Ridley Hall Cam 58. **d** 60 **p** 61. C Woking St Pet *Guildf* 60-63; India 63-83; TR Kirby Muxloe *Leic* 83-89; Asian Outreach Worker (Leic Martyrs) 89-95; Derby Asian Chr Min Project 95-00; rtd 00; Perm to Offic *Ely* from 00. *14 Scotsdowne Road, Trumpington, Cambridge CB2 9HU* Tel (01223) 476565 E-mail basil.scott2@ntlworld.com

SCOTT, Mrs Beryl May. b 28. Lon Univ BD91 Westmr Coll Ox MTh00. **d** 02 **p** 04. NSM Dalbeattie *Glas* from 02. *Islecroft House, Mill Street, Dalbeattie DG5 4HE* Tel (01556) 610283
E-mail berylm.scott@virgin.net

SCOTT, Brian. b 35. CCC Ox BA58. Coll of Resurr Mirfield 59. **d** 61 **p** 65. C Carl St Aid and Ch Ch 61-62; Asst Master Hutton Gr Sch 63-65; Perm to Offic *Leic* 65-67; Lic to Offic 67-70; V Lubenham and P-in-c Theddingworth 71-78; Asst Chapl Oundle Sch 78-83; R Barrowden and Wakerley w S Luffenham *Pet* 83-98; rtd 98; Perm to Offic *Leic* and *Pet* from 98. *The Cedars, 3 Glaston Road, Preston, Oakham LE15 9NH* Tel (01572) 737242

SCOTT, Charles Geoffrey. b 32. St Jo Coll Cam BA54 MA58. Cuddesdon Coll 56. **d** 58 **p** 59. C Brighouse *Wakef* 58-61; C Bathwick w Woolley *B & W* 61-64; V Frome Ch Ch 64-78; R Winchelsea *Chich* 78-93; R Winchelsea and Icklesham 93-95; rtd 95; Perm to Offic *Chich* from 95. *Hickstead, Main Street, Iden, Rye TN31 7PT* Tel (01797) 280096

SCOTT, Christopher. *See* DAVIES, Christopher

SCOTT, Christopher John Fairfax. b 45. Magd Coll Cam BA67 MA71. Westcott Ho Cam 68. **d** 70 **p** 71. C Nor St Pet Mancroft 70-73; Chapl Magd Coll Cam 73-79; V Hampstead Ch Ch *Lon* 79-94; rtd 00. *49 St Barnabas Road, Cambridge CB1 2BX* Tel (01223) 359421

SCOTT, Canon Christopher Michael. b 44. SS Coll Cam BA66 MA70. Cuddesdon Coll 66. **d** 68 **p** 69. C New Addington *Cant* 68-73; C Westmr St Steph w St Jo *Lon* 73-78; V Enfield St Mich 78-81; V Effingham w Lt Bookham *Guildf* 81-87; R Esher 87-98; RD Emly 91-96; R Bude Haven and Marhamchurch *Truro* 98-08; Hon Can Truro Cathl 03-08; rtd 08. *Lantyan, Poughill, Bude EX23 9EU* Tel (01288) 350741
E-mail chriscott98@yahoo.co.uk

SCOTT, Christopher Stuart. b 48. Surrey Univ BA92 MBPsS92. Sarum & Wells Th Coll 79. **d** 81 **p** 82. C Enfield Chase St Mary *Lon* 81-82; C Coalbrookdale, Iron-Bridge and Lt Wenlock *Heref* 82-86; P-in-c Breinton 86-89; Chapl Hickey's Almshouses Richmond 89-01; Perm to Offic *S'wark* from 06; Chapl Richmond Charities' Almshouses from 08. *164 Sheen Road, Richmond TW9 1XD* Tel (020) 8940 6560

SCOTT, Claude John. b 37. Qu Mary Coll Lon BSc60 PhD64 Lon Inst of Educn PGCE61 FRSA94. EAMTC 88. **d** 91 **p** 92. NSM Heigham H Trin *Nor* 91-98; Perm to Offic from 98. *26 The Pastures, Blakeney, Holt NR25 7LY* Tel (01263) 740573
E-mail cjscott@talktalk.net

SCOTT, Colin. b 32. Dur Univ BA54. Coll of Resurr Mirfield 58. **d** 60 **p** 61. C Wallsend St Pet *Newc* 60-64; C Seaton Hirst 64-68; C Longbenton St Bart 68-70; V Benwell St Aid 70-77; V Sleekburn 77-89; P-in-c Cambois 89-96; V Longhoughton w Howick 89-96; rtd 96; Perm to Offic *Newc* from 96. *Pele Cottage, Hepple, Morpeth NE65 7LH* Tel (01669) 640258

✠SCOTT, The Rt Revd Colin John Fraser. b 33. Qu Coll Cam BA56 MA60. Ridley Hall Cam 56. **d** 58 **p** 59 **c** 84. C Clapham Common St Barn *S'wark* 58-61; C Hatcham St Jas 61-64; V Kennington St Mark 64-71; RD Lambeth 68-71; Vice-Chmn Dioc Past Cttee 71-77; Hon Can S'wark Cathl 73-84; TR Sanderstead All SS 77-84; Suff Bp Hulme *Man* 84-98; Chmn CCC 94-98; rtd 99; Hon Asst Bp Leic from 99; Perm to Offic *Derby* from 00. *The Priest House, Prior Park Road, Ashby-de-la-Zouch LE65 1BL* Tel (01530) 564403

SCOTT, David. b 40. Rhodes Univ BA63. St Paul's Coll Grahamstown LTh65. **d** 65 **p** 66. C Pietermaritzburg St Pet S Africa 66-67; C Durban N St Martin-in-the-Fields 68; R Harding 69; R Newcastle H Trin 70-75; R Bellair 76-78; R Kabega Park All SS 79-87; Chapl Port Elizabeth Univ 88-91; TV Cheltenham St Mark *Glouc* 92-96; R Swanscombe *Roch* 96-10; rtd 10. *103 Hillside Avenue, Gravesend DA12 5QN* Tel (01474) 248735 E-mail david.40scott@btinternet.com

SCOTT, Canon David Victor. b 47. St Chad's Coll Dur BA69. Cuddesdon Coll 69. **d** 71 **p** 72. C St Mary-at-Latton *Chelmsf* 71-73; Chapl Haberdashers' Aske's Sch Elstree 73-80; V Torpenhow *Carl* 80-91; V Allhallows 80-91; R Win St Lawr and St Maurice w St Swithun 91-10; Warden Sch of Spirituality Win 91-10; Hon Can Win Cathl 02-10; rtd 10. *2 Sunnyside, Kendal LA9 7DJ* Tel (01539) 583887 E-mail scott.d.v@live.com

SCOTT, Mrs Erica Jane. b 58. Trin Coll Bris BA02. **d** 02 **p** 03. C Ilminster and Distr *B & W* 02-05; C Nailsea Ch Ch w Tickenham 05-07; P-in-c Whitchurch *Bris* 07-08; Perm to Offic *S & M* from 09. *Coral Cottage, 37 The Promenade, Castletown, Isle of Man IM9 1BG* E-mail reverica@btinternet.com

SCOTT, Francis Richard. b 63. St Jo Coll Dur BA85 Selw Coll Cam PGCE86. St Jo Coll Nottm MA02. **d** 00 **p** 01. C Huntington *York* 00-03; TV 03-09; V Swanland from 09. *The Vicarage, St Barnabas Drive, Swanland, North Ferriby HU14 3RL* Tel (01482) 631271 E-mail fandfscott@aol.com

SCOTT, Gary James. b 61. Edin Univ BD87. Edin Th Coll 85. **d** 87 **p** 88. C Edin St Cuth 87-90; R Peebles 90-92; P-in-c Innerleithen 92-96; R Penicuik 96-98; R W Linton 96-98; Sen Chapl ACF 98-06; Lic to Offic *Edin* from 98. *3 Crossburn Farm Road, Peebles EH45 8EG* Tel (01721) 721886

SCOTT, Geoffrey. *See* SCOTT, Charles Geoffrey

SCOTT, Canon Gordon. b 30. Man Univ BA51. St Jo Coll Dur 51. **d** 53 **p** 54. C Monkwearmouth St Andr *Dur* 53-55; C Stranton 55-56; C Chester le Street 56-59; V Marley Hill 59-62; Chapl Forest Sch Snaresbrook 62-66; Chapl Dunrobin Sch Sutherland 66-72; Chapl Pocklington Sch York 72-74; V Barton w Pooley Bridge *Carl* 74-80; RD Penrith 79-82; P-in-c Lazonby 80; R Gt Salkeld w Lazonby 80-90; Hon Can Carl Cathl 83-94; P-in-c Patterdale 90-94; rtd 94; Perm to Offic *Carl* 94-97. *48 Lakeland Park, Keswick CA12 4AT* Tel (01768) 775862

SCOTT, Guy Charles. b 61. Coll of Resurr Mirfield. **d** 00 **p** 01. C Abington *Pet* 00-03; P-in-c Mullion *Truro* 03-07; C Cury and Gunwalloe 03-07; R Is of Scilly 07-10; P-in-c Biggleswade *St Alb* from 10. *The Vicarage, Shortmead Street, Biggleswade SG18 0AT* Tel (01767) 312243
E-mail g.c.scott@btinternet.com

SCOTT, Mrs Helen Ruth. b 59. Surrey Univ BA97 K Coll Lon MA99 SRN81 RM85. S'wark Ord Course 89. **d** 92 **p** 94. NSM Richmond St Mary w St Matthias and St Jo *S'wark* 92-01; Chapl Hickey's Almshouses Richmond 01-08; Perm to Offic *S'wark* from 08; Chapl Ch Sch Richmond from 09. *164 Sheen Road, Richmond TW9 1XD* Tel (020) 8940 6560

SCOTT, Ian Michael. b 25. Bris Univ BA50 Leic Univ DipEd51 Open Univ MA99. Bps' Coll Cheshunt 52. **d** 53 **p** 54. C Rotherhithe St Mary w All SS *S'wark* 53-55; C Lavender Hill Ascension 55-59; C Camberwell St Mich w All So w Em 59-60; C Kettering St Mary *Pet* 60-63; V Haverstock Hill H Trin w Kentish Town St Barn *Lon* 63-93; rtd 93; Perm to Offic *Nor* 93-96. *Los Molinos 8, 03726 Benitachell (Alicante), Spain* Tel (0034) 965 741 342 E-mail ian.benitachell@yahoo.co.uk

SCOTT, Mrs Inez Margaret Gillette. b 26. St Alb Minl Tr Scheme 76. **dss** 79 **d** 87 **p** 94. Preston w Sutton Poyntz and Osmington w Poxwell *Sarum* 83-86; Dorchester 86-96; Par Dn 87-88; NSM 88-96; rtd 88; Perm to Offic *Sarum* 96-08. *14 Came View Road, Dorchester DT1 2AE* Tel (01305) 267547

SCOTT, James Alexander Gilchrist. b 32. Linc Coll Ox BA56 MA60. Wycliffe Hall Ox 56. **d** 58 **p** 59. C Shipley St Paul *Bradf* 58-61; Abp's Dom Chapl *York* 61-65; Brazil 65-68; V Grassendale *Liv* 68-77; V Thorp Arch w Walton *York* 77-89; RD Tadcaster 78-86; Chapl HM Pris Rudgate 77-82; Askham Grange 82-87; V Kirk Ella 89-92; TR 92-97; rtd 97; Perm to Offic *York* from 98. *2 Keld CLose, Pickering YO18 9NJ* Tel (01751) 476226

SCOTT, James William. b 39. S Dios Minl Tr Scheme 84. **d** 88 **p** 89. NSM Bremhill w Foxham and Hilmarton *Sarum* 88-94; NSM Derry Hill w Bremhill and Foxham 94-09. *14 Bremhill, Calne SN11 9LA* Tel (01249) 813114
E-mail james@bremhill.force9.co.uk

SCOTT, Canon Janice Beasant. b 44. MCSP66. EAMTC 89. **d** 93 **p** 94. NSM Fakenham w Alethorpe *Nor* 92-95; C Eaton 95-99; R

Dickleburgh and The Pulhams 99-09; RD Redenhall 03-06; Hon Can Nor Cathl 08-09; rtd 09; Perm to Offic *Nor* from 09. *2 Reve Crescent, Blofield, Norwich NR13 4RX* Tel (01603) 712428 Mobile 07905-039243 E-mail janice@janice-scott.com
SCOTT, John. See SCOTT, William John
SCOTT, John. b 54. QUB BD79. CITC 80. **d** 81 **p** 82. C Willowfield *D & D* 81-83; C Newtownards 83-85; I Kilskeery w Trillick *Clogh* 85-90; Lic to Offic *D & D* 90-96; I Bright w Ballee and Killough 96-01; Perm to Offic from 01. *Ash Tree House, Moor Road, Ballyward, Castlewellan BT31 9TY* Tel (028) 4065 0908 E-mail john@ashtreehouse.net
SCOTT, John. b 54. Heriot-Watt Univ BA76 Leeds Univ BA97 Heythrop Coll Lon MA05. Coll of Resurr Mirfield 95. **d** 97 **p** 98. C Bethnal Green St Matt w St Jas the Gt *Lon* 97-00; Asst Chapl Qu Mary and Westf Coll 97-00; C Heston 00-04; Inter-Faith Adv 00-05; USA from 06. *The Old Pottery, Baptist Hill, St Mary Bourne, Andover SP11 6BQ* Tel (01264) 738972 Mobile 07889-977593 E-mail absalom1662@yahoo.co.uk
SCOTT, John Eric. b 16. St Cath Coll Ox BA38 MA42 FSA. Ripon Hall Ox 39. **d** 40 **p** 41. C Heworth St Alb *Dur* 40-43; C Gateshead St Mary 43-45; Chapl and Sacr Ch Ch *Ox* 45-47; Ho Master Forest Sch Snaresbrook 55-81; P-in-c St Mich Cornhill w St Pet le Poer etc *Lon* 81-85; rtd 85. *17 Harman Avenue, Woodford Green IG8 9DS* Tel (020) 8505 7093
SCOTT, John Harold. b 46. Univ of Wales (Cardiff) BSc69. St Steph Ho Ox 69. **d** 72 **p** 73. C Skewen *Llan* 72-74; C Port Talbot St Theodore 74-77; P-in-c Bedlinog 77-78; V 78-85; R Penderyn w Ystradfellte and Pontneathvaughan *S & B* 85-04; R Penderyn Mellte from 04. *The Vicarage, Ystradfellte, Aberdare CF44 9JE* Tel (01639) 720405 Mobile 07711-961667 E-mail jhs46@tesco.net
SCOTT, John Peter. b 47. Open Univ BA80. Lambeth STh81 K Coll Lon 69 St Aug Coll Cant 74. **d** 75 **p** 76. C Dartford St Alb *Roch* 75-78; C-in-c Goring-by-Sea *Chich* 78-81; Chapl Wells and Meare Manor Hosps 81-86; CF (TAVR) 82-90; Chapl Pangbourne Coll 86-90; Min Reigate St Phil CD *S'wark* 90-92; P-in-c Reigate St Phil from 92; Chapl St Bede's Ecum Sch Reigate from 90. *The Parsonage, 102A Nutley Lane, Reigate RH2 9HA* Tel (01737) 244542
SCOTT, John Vickers. b 48. Open Univ BA88 MCIOB81. CBDTI 02. **d** 05 **p** 06. NSM Penwortham St Leon *Blackb* 05-09; P-in-c Chipping and Whitewell from 09. *The Vicarage, Garstang Road, Chipping, Preston PR3 2QH* Tel (01995) 61252 Mobile 07875-895354 E-mail frjohn.chipping@btinternet.com
SCOTT (née GOLDIE), Canon Katrina Ruth. b 76. Fitzw Coll Cam MA97 MPhil00 MA01. Westcott Ho Cam 98. **d** 00 **p** 01. C Cov E 00-04; V Willenhall from 04; Dioc Adv for Women's Min 06-10; Dean Women's Min from 10; Hon Can Cov Cathl from 10. *Willenhall Vicarage, Robin Hood Road, Coventry CV3 3AY* Tel (024) 7630 3266 E-mail krgscott@hotmail.com
SCOTT, Keith Brounton de Salve. b 55. QUB BD. **d** 83 **p** 84. C Belfast St Matt *Conn* 83-87; I Ardclinis and Tickmacrevan w Layde and Cushendun 87-01; CMS 02-09; P-in-c Rathkeale w Askeaton, Kilcornan and Kilnaughtin *L & K* from 09. *The Rectory, Church Street, Askeaton, Co Limerick, Republic of Ireland* Tel (00353) (61) 398647 E-mail kbs16355@gmail.com *or* rathkeale@limerick.anglican.org
SCOTT, Kenneth James. b 46. Bris Univ BA68. Trin Coll Bris 71. **d** 73 **p** 74. C Illogan *Truro* 73-76; C Camberley St Paul *Guildf* 76-81; R Bradford Peverell, Stratton, Frampton etc *Sarum* 81-08; RD Dorchester 95-99; rtd 08; Perm to Offic *St E* from 09. *2 Fir Close, Wickham Market, Woodbridge IP13 0UB* Tel (01728) 747232 E-mail kenscott@surfaid.org
SCOTT, Kevin Francis. b 51. Peterho Cam MA Mert Coll Ox DPhil76 CChem MRSC. Wycliffe Hall Ox BA83. **d** 83 **p** 84. C Ox St Ebbe w H Trin and St Pet 83-86; P-in-c Prestonpans *Edin* 86-93; R Musselburgh 86-93; R Edin SS Phil and Jas 93-08. *Kirklands, Craigend Road, Stow, Galashiels TD1 2RJ* Tel 0131-208 0402 E-mail drkfs@aol.com
SCOTT, Kevin Peter. b 43. Coll of Resurr Mirfield 93. **d** 93 **p** 94. C Rushall *Lich* 93-97; P-in-c Goldenhill 97-10; rtd 10. *St John's Vicarage, Drummond Street, Stoke-on-Trent ST6 5RF* Tel (01782) 782736
SCOTT, Kevin Willard. b 53. Open Univ BA96 Glos Univ MA03. Linc Th Coll 92. **d** 92 **p** 93. C Walton-on-Thames *Guildf* 92-97; R Matson *Glouc* 97-03; RD Glouc City 01-03; V Malden St Jo *S'wark* from 03; AD Kingston 05-09. *5 Vicarage Close, Worcester Park KT4 7LZ* Tel (020) 8337 8830 E-mail kevinwscott@btinternet.com
SCOTT, Laurence Stanley. b 33. Open Univ BSc09. **d** 05 **p** 06. NSM Calstock *Truro* from 05. *88 Priory Close, Tavistock PL19 9DG* Tel (01822) 613227
SCOTT, Lester Desmond Donald. NUI BA89. CITC BTh92. **d** 92 **p** 93. C Killeshandra w Killegar and Derrylane *K, E & A* 92-95; C Kilmore w Ballintemple 92-95; I Fenagh w Myshall, Aghade and Ardoyne *C & O* from 95. *The Glebe House, Ballon, Co Carlow, Republic of Ireland* Tel and fax (00353) (59) 915 9367 Mobile 87-250 4322 E-mail lestersscott@oceanfree.net

SCOTT (née CURRELL), Mrs Linda Anne. b 62. K Alfred's Coll Win BEd84. Trin Coll Bris BA92. **d** 92 **p** 94. Par Dn Tunbridge Wells St Mark *Roch* 92-94; C 94-97; TV Walthamstow *Chelmsf* 97-02; Perm to Offic *Chelmsf* 02-04 and *S'wark* from 05. *35 Oswin Street, London SE11 4TF* Tel (020) 7735 4077 E-mail scottlindatim@aol.com
SCOTT, Canon Malcolm Kenneth Merrett. b 30. ACA53 FCA64. Clifton Th Coll 56. **d** 58 **p** 59. C Highbury Ch Ch *Lon* 58-60; CMS 60-61; Uganda 61-74; V Sunnyside w Bourne End *St Alb* 74-90; V Clapham 90-95; rtd 95; Perm to Offic *Lich* from 96. *10 The Ring, Little Haywood, Stafford ST18 0TP* Tel (01889) 881464
SCOTT, Nicholas Charles Andrew. b 74. Univ of Wales (Ban) BD95. Westcott Ho Cam 97. **d** 99 **p** 00. C Ryde H Trin and Swanmore St Mich *Portsm* 99-01; C Burbage w Aston Flamville *Leic* 01-04; Perm to Offic *Cov* 04-08; NSM Willenhall from 08. *Willenhall Vicarage, Robin Hood Road, Coventry CV3 3AY* Tel (024) 7630 3266 E-mail ncascott@hotmail.com
SCOTT, Paul Malcolm. b 57. Sheff City Poly BA79 CPFA85. Ripon Coll Cuddesdon 98. **d** 00 **p** 01. C N Shields *Newc* 00-03; V Shiremoor from 03. *St Mark's Vicarage, Brenkley Avenue, Shiremoor, Newcastle upon Tyne NE27 0PP* Tel 0191-253 3291 E-mail paulmcscott@3.freeserve.co.uk
SCOTT, Mrs Pauline Claire Michalak. b 55. St Anne's Coll Ox BA77 MA82 Dur Univ PGCE78. TISEC 98. **d** 01 **p** 02. NSM Papworth *Ely* 01-05; TV Ely 05-09; P-in-c Alresford *Chelmsf* 09-10; P-in-c Frating w Thorrington 09-10; V Alresford and Frating w Thorrington from 10. *The Rectory, St Andrew's Close, Alresford, Colchester CO7 8BL* Tel (01206) 822088 Mobile 07855-395840 E-mail paulmecm.scott@tiscali.co.uk
SCOTT, Peter Crawford. b 35. Ch Ch Ox BA56 MA61. Cuddesdon Coll 60. **d** 62 **p** 63. C Broseley w Benthall *Heref* 62-66; P-in-c Hughenden *Ox* 66-71; C Hykeham *Linc* 71-73; P-in-c Stottesdon *Heref* 73-76; Australia from 76; rtd 97. *33 Church Street, Coleraine Vic 3315, Australia* Fax (0061) (3) 5575 2491
SCOTT, Peter James Douglas Sefton. b 59. OBE03. Edin Univ BD83. Edin Th Coll 81. **d** 83 **p** 84. C Helensburgh *Glas* 83-86; C-in-c Glas St Oswald 86-89; R 89-91; Chapl RN from 91. *Royal Naval Chaplaincy Service, Mail Point 1-2, Leach Building, Whale Island, Portsmouth PO2 8BY* Tel (023) 9262 5055 Fax 9262 5134
SCOTT, Peter Lindsay. b 29. Keble Coll Ox BA54 MA58. Linc Th Coll 54. **d** 56 **p** 57. C Weston-super-Mare St Sav *B & W* 56-59; C Knowle H Nativity *Bris* 59-61; P-in-c Glas St Pet 61-63; V Heap Bridge *Man* 63-73; V Rochdale St Geo w St Alb 73-86; R Droylsden St Andr 86-94; rtd 94; Perm to Offic *Man* from 94. *2 Chancel Place, Rochdale OL16 1FB* Tel (01706) 523270
SCOTT, Ruth. See SCOTT, Mrs Helen Ruth
SCOTT, Sara Rosamund. b 49. Portsm Poly BSc70 Plymouth Poly MPhil74. SEITE 97. **d** 00 **p** 01. NSM Rotherhithe H Trin *S'wark* 00-04; NSM Sydenham H Trin and St Aug from 04. *147 Jerningham Road, London SE14 5NJ* Tel (020) 7639 6311 Fax 7639 1842 E-mail sarascott@btinternet.com
SCOTT, Simon James. b 65. Ch Ch Ox BA87 MA90. Wycliffe Hall Ox 87. **d** 91 **p** 92. C Cheadle All Hallows *Ches* 91-95; Scripture Union 95-98; C Cambridge H Sepulchre *Ely* 98-05; R Lt Shelford from 05. *The Rectory, 2 Manor Road, Little Shelford, Cambridge CB22 5HF* Tel (01223) 841998 Mobile 07739-984323 E-mail simonjscott1965@btinternet.com
SCOTT, Canon Terence. b 56. QUB BSc77. CITC 77. **d** 80 **p** 81. C Ballymena *Conn* 80-83; C Antrim All SS 83-85; P-in-c Connor w Antrim St Patr 85-88; I Magherafelt *Arm* from 88; Hon V Choral Arm Cathl 95-06; Can Arm Cathl from 06. *The Rectory, 1 Churchwell Lane, Magherafelt BT45 6AL* Tel (028) 7963 2365 Mobile 07904-894529 E-mail terryscott123@btinternet.com
SCOTT, Canon Theresa Anne. b 53. Bris Univ BSc75 Lon Univ PGCE76. Ox Min Course 89. **d** 92 **p** 94. NSM Wickham Bishops w Lt Braxted *Chelmsf* 92-93; NSM Drayton St Pet (Berks) *Ox* 94-01; NSM Convenor (Berks) 97-01; Bp's Officer for NSM 98-01; Bp's Adv for Women in Ord Min 01-05; P-in-c Hurley and Stubbings 01-02; V Burchetts Green 02-08; AD Maidenhead and Windsor 05-07; TR Bicester w Bucknell, Caversfield and Launton from 08; Hon Can Ch Ch from 05. *The Rectory, 6 Tinkers Lane, Bicester OX26 6ES* Tel (01869) 241361 E-mail theresa.scott@driftway.co.uk
SCOTT, Timothy Charles Nairne. b 61. Ex Univ BA83. Westcott Ho Cam 84. **d** 87 **p** 88. C Romford St Edw *Chelmsf* 87-89; Community Priest 89-94; P-in-c Leytonstone H Trin and St Aug Harrow Green 94-97; V 97-02; Educn and Tr Adv (Bradwell Area) 02-04; R S'wark Ch Ch from 04. *35 Oswin Street, London SE11 4TF* Tel (020) 7735 4077 E-mail tim.scott@southwark.anglican.org
SCOTT, Trevor Ian. b 57. Culham Coll Ox CertEd79. EAMTC 97. **d** 98 **p** 99. NSM Waltham H Cross *Chelmsf* from 98. *Hartland Villas, 208 High Road, Broxbourne EN10 6QF* Tel (01992) 420376 or 450321 E-mail trevor.scott2@ntlworld.com
SCOTT, Vernon Malcolm. b 30. TCD BA57 MA60. TCD Div Sch Div Test56 Ridley Hall Cam 58. **d** 58 **p** 59. C Limehouse St Anne

SCOTT, *Lon* 58-62; C N St Pancras All Hallows 62-66; V Enfield St Mich 66-77; R Tansor w Cotterstock and Fotheringhay *Pet* 77-81; R Barby w Onley 81-83; V Kilsby 81-83; R Barby w Kilsby 83-90; R Coxford Gp *Nor* 90-94; P-in-c S Raynham, E w W Raynham, Helhoughton, etc 94-96; R E and W Rudham, Houghton-next-Harpley etc 95-96; rtd 96; Perm to Offic *Nor* 96-11. *The College of St Barnabas, Blackberry Lane, Lingfield RH7 6NJ* Tel (01342) 870260

SCOTT, William. b 20. MBE97. St Chad's Coll Dur BA46 Leeds Univ DipEd53. d 60 p 61. CR 60-99; C Wolborough w Newton Abbot *Ex* 60-63; Chapl St Cath Sch Bramley 63-67; Chapl St Mary and St Anne's Sch Abbots Bromley 67-76; Perm to Offic *Cant* 77-90; Chapl Boulogne-sur-Mer w Calais and Lille *Eur* 87-90; Chapl Lille 90-97; rtd 97; Perm to Offic *Eur* from 97. *42 Westgate Court Avenue, Canterbury CT2 8JR* Tel (01227) 456277

SCOTT, William John. b 46. TCD BA70. CITC. d 71 p 72. C Bangor St Comgall *D & D* 71-74; C Holywood 74-80; Dioc Min of Healing Team from 75; I Carnalea 80-90; N Ireland Wing Chapl ATC from 80; I Seapatrick *D & D* 90-11; Treas Dromore Cathl 02-08; Adn Dromore 05-11; rtd 11. *Address temp unknown*

SCOTT, Preb William Sievwright. b 46. Edin Th Coll 67. d 70 p 71. C Glas St Ninian 70-73; C Bridgwater St Fran *B & W* 73-77; R Shepton Beauchamp w Barrington, Stocklinch etc 77-81; P-in-c Cossington and Woolavington 82-84; Chapl Community of All Hallows Ditchingham 84-91; V Pimlico St Mary Bourne Street *Lon* 91-02; P-in-c Pimlico St Barn 97-01; V 01-02; AD Westmr St Marg 97-04; Preb St Paul's Cathl from 00; Chapl to RVO and Qu Chpl of the Savoy 02-07; Chapl to The Queen 03-07; Sub-Dean HM Chpls R and Dep Clerk of the Closet from 07; Sub-Almoner and Dom Chapl to The Queen from 07. *The Queen's Chapel, Marlborough Road, St James's Palace, London SW1A 1BG* Tel (020) 7024 5576 *or* 7930 9996 Mobile 07941-470399 E-mail william.scott@royal.gsx.gov.uk

SCOTT-BROMLEY, Mrs Deborah Joan. b 58. Surrey Univ BA01 Open Univ BA96. STETS 98. d 01 p 02. C Hale w Badshot Lea *Guildf* 01-05; V Bordon from 05. *St Mark's Vicarage, 58 Forest Road, Bordon GU35 0BP* Tel (01420) 477550 Mobile 07855-704849 E-mail d.scott.bromley@ntlworld.com

SCOTT-DEMPSTER, Canon Colin Thomas. b 37. Em Coll Cam BA65 MA68. Cuddesdon Coll 64. d 66 p 67. C Caversham *Ox* 66-69; Chapl Coll of SS Mark and Jo Chelsea 69-73; V Chieveley w Winterbourne and Oare *Ox* 73-02; RD Newbury 77-98; Hon Can Ch Ch 90-02; rtd 02. *Old Faskally House, Killiecrankie, Pitlochry PH16 5LG* Tel (01796) 473575 E-mail colin@faskally25.freeserve.co.uk

SCOTT-GARNETT, Linda. b 44. d 07 p 08. NSM Bermondsey St Hugh CD *S'wark* from 07. *1 Strood House, Manciple Street, London SE1 4LR* Tel (020) 7642 1367 E-mail lindag@bulldoghome.com

SCOTT-HAMBLEN, Shane. b 66. Webster Univ (USA) BMus89 St Thos Aquinas Univ Rome STB94 MA96 STL96. d 94 p 95. In RC Ch 94-97; C Staines St Mary and St Pet *Lon* 97-99; USA from 99; R Highlands St Mary from 02. *The Episcopal Church of St Mary, 1 Chestnut Street, Cold Spring NY 10516, USA* Tel (001) (845) 265 2539

✠SCOTT-JOYNT, The Rt Revd Michael Charles. b 43. K Coll Cam BA65 MA68 Win Univ Hon DD10. Cuddesdon Coll 65. d 67 p 68 c 87. C Cuddesdon *Ox* 67-70; Tutor Cuddesdon Coll 67-71; Chapl 71-72; TV Newbury St Nic *Ox* 72-75; P-in-c Bicester 75-79; P-in-c Caversfield 75-79; P-in-c Bucknell 76-79; TR Bicester w Bucknell, Caversfield and Launton 79-81; RD Bicester and Islip 76-81; Can Res St Alb 82-87; Dir of Ords and Post-Ord Tr 82-87; Suff Bp Stafford *Lich* 87-92; Area Bp Stafford 92-95; Bp Win 95-11; rtd 11. *Easter House, Funtington, Chichester PO18 9LJ* Tel (01243) 575762 E-mail lousj@ukgateway.net

SCOTT-THOMPSON, Ian Mackenzie. b 57. Ch Ch Ox BA78. St Jo Coll Nottm BA82. d 83 p 84. C Hartley Wintney, Elvetham, Winchfield etc 83-85; C Bitterne 85-89; V Iford 89-99; P-in-c Holdenhurst 95-99; TR Cove St Jo *Guildf* 99-06; RD Aldershot 03-06; V Wonersh w Blackheath 06-10; P-in-c Marks Tey and Aldham *Chelmsf* from 10. *17 North Lane, Marks Tey, Colchester CO6 1EG* Tel (01206) 215772 E-mail ian.scott-thompson@virgin.net

SCRACE, Canon David Peter. b 46. Sarum & Wells Th Coll 79. d 81 p 82. C Abbots Langley *St Alb* 81-85; TV Chippenham St Paul w Hardenhuish etc *Bris* 85-91; P-in-c Harnham *Sarum* 91-99; V from 99; RD Salisbury 93-98; Can and Preb Sarum Cathl from 10. *The Vicarage, Old Blandford Road, Salisbury SP2 8DQ* Tel (01722) 333564 E-mail d.scrace@btopenworld.com

SCRAGG, Michael John. b 39. Griffith Univ Brisbane BA93 MA01 Jas Cook Univ Townsville BCommWelf97. ACT. d 74 p 75. C Camp Hill w Carina Australia 74-77; C Chesterton Gd Shep *Ely* 77-79; C Maryborough Australia 79-80; V Biggenden 80-85; Chapl Wolston Park Hosp 85-91; P-in-c Taroom 91-96; C Willunga w Seaford Ecum Miss 96-97; Lic to Offic 97-98; rtd 98; Perm to Offic Brisbane 98-05; Guardian Community of the Epiphany from 05. *Clarendon Spence, 18/79 Spence Street, PO Box 5143, Cairns Qld 4870, Australia* Tel (0061) (7) 4041 5707 Mobile 41-876 4567 E-mail hapy5859@yahoo.com.au

SCRASE-FIELD, Edward Fraser Austin Longmer. b 76. Aber Univ BSc98 Man Univ PhD04 Cam Univ BA07. Ridley Hall Cam 05. d 08 p 09. C Denton Holme *Carl* 08-11; C Cheadle *Ches* from 11. *1 Warren Avenue, Cheadle SK8 1NB* Tel 07730-514074 (mobile)

SCREECH, Prof Michael. b 26. Ordre national du Mérite 83 Chevalier Légion d'Honneur 92. Univ Coll Lon BA50 Birm Univ DLitt59 Univ Coll Lon DLitt82 All So Coll Ox MA84 DLitt90 Ex Univ Hon DLitt93 Geneva Univ Hon DD98 FBA81 FRSL87. Ox Min Course 92. d 93 p 94. NSM Ox St Giles and SS Phil and Jas w St Marg 93-02; Perm to Offic from 02; Extraordinary Fell Wolfs Coll Ox from 93; Chapl and Fell All So Coll Ox 01-03. *5 Swanston Field, Whitchurch on Thames, Reading RG8 7HP* Tel and fax 0118-984 2513

✠SCREECH, The Rt Revd Royden. b 53. K Coll Lon BD74 AKC74. St Aug Coll Cant 75. d 76 p 77 c 00. C Hatcham St Cath *S'wark* 76-80; V Nunhead St Antony 80-87; P-in-c Nunhead St Silas 82-87; RD Camberwell 83-87; V New Addington 87-94; Selection Sec ABM 94-97; Sen Selection Sec Min Division Abps' Coun 97-00; Suff Bp St Germans *Truro* from 00. *32 Falmouth Road, Truro TR1 2HX* Tel (01872) 273190 Fax 277883 E-mail bishop@stgermans.truro.anglican.org

SCRINE, Ralph. b 19. Bris Univ BA40 Fitzw Ho Cam BA46 MA60 Lon Univ MPhil81. Westcott Ho Cam 45. d 46 p 47. C Moorfields *Bris* 46-51; P-in-c Biddestone w Slaughterford 51-52; P-in-c Lockleaze CD 52-60; V St Jas Less 60-65; Chapl Eliz Coll Guernsey 60-65; Lect Div Ch Ch Coll Cant 65-68; Chapl Ch Ch Coll of HE Cant 68-75; Sen Lect Ch Ch Coll Cant 68-84; rtd 84; Perm to Offic *Cant* 84-03. *14 Riverdale, Harbertonford, Totnes TQ9 7TJ* Tel (01803) 731046

✠SCRIVEN, The Rt Revd Henry William. b 51. Sheff Univ BA72. St Jo Coll Nottm 73. d 75 p 76 c 95. C Wealdstone H Trin *Lon* 75-79; SAMS Argentina 79-82; USA 82-83; SAMS Spain 84-90; Chapl Madrid w Bilbao *Eur* 90-95; Suff Bp Eur 95-02; Dean Brussels 95-97; Dir of Ords 97-02; Asst Bp Pittsburgh USA 02-08; Miss Dir for S America SAMS / CMS from 09; Hon Asst Bp Ox from 09. *16 East St Helen Street, Abingdon OX14 5EA* Tel (01235) 536607 *or* (01865) 787500 E-mail henry.scriven@cms-uk.org

SCRIVEN, Hugh Alexander. b 59. Trin Coll Cam BA80. Cranmer Hall Dur 81. d 84 p 85. C Pudsey St Lawr and St Paul *Bradf* 84-87; C Madeley *Heref* 87-91; TV 91-00; V Edgbaston St Germain *Birm* from 00. *St Germain's Vicarage, 180 Portland Road, Birmingham B16 9TD* Tel 0121-429 3431

SCRIVENER, John Glenfield (Glen). b 78. Ball Coll Ox BA96. Oak Hill Th Coll BTh07. d 07 p 08. C Eastbourne All So *Chich* 07-11; Evang Revival Media from 11. *84 Susans Road, Eastbourne BN21 3TH* Tel (01323) 644054 Mobile 07876-031734 E-mail glen@christthetruth.org.uk

SCRIVENER, Robert Allan. b 54. Nottm Univ BEd78 Hull Univ BTh98 De Montfort Univ Leic MA99 Huddersfield Univ BA03. Linc Th Coll 79. d 80 p 81. C Sherwood *S'well* 80-83; C Burghclere w Newtown and Ecchinswell w Sydmonton *Win* 83-86; TV Hemel Hempstead *St Alb* 86-93; V Kingston upon Hull St Nic *York* 93-03; V Mansfield Woodhouse *S'well* from 03. *The Vicarage, 7 Butt Lane, Mansfield Woodhouse, Mansfield NG19 9JS* Tel (01623) 621875 E-mail allan.scrivener@virginmedia.com

SCRIVENS, Mrs Elaine. b 53. TCert74 Man Univ BEd75. NEOC. d 00 p 01. NSM E Coatham *York* 00-02; NSM Coatham and Dormanstown 02-04; Chapl Ven Bede Sch Ryhope 04-10; P-in-c Bishop's Tachbrook *Cov* from 10. *The Vicarage, 24 Mallory Road, Bishops Tachbrook, Leamington Spa CV33 9QX* Tel (01926) 426922

SCROGGIE, Mrs Felicity Marie-Louise. b 62. Pemb Coll Ox BA86 St Andr Univ MPhil87. STETS BTh99. d 99 p 00. C Brondesbury St Anne w Kilburn H Trin *Lon* 99-02; V Sudbury St Andr from 02; AD Brent from 10. *St Andrew's Vicarage, 956 Harrow Road, Wembley HA0 2QA* Tel (020) 8904 4016 E-mail felicity.scroggie@london.anglican.org

SCUFFHAM, Canon Frank Leslie. b 30. AKC56. d 57 p 58. C Kettering SS Pet and Paul 57-59; Ind Chapl *Sheff* 60-61; Ind Chapl *Pet* 61-95; Can Pet Cathl 72-95; RD Corby 76-79; P-in-c Stoke Albany w Wilbarston 79; R 79-95; rtd 95; Perm to Offic *St E* from 95. *The Orchard, Earlsford Road, Mellis, Eye IP23 8EA* Tel (01379) 783378 E-mail fscuff@yahoo.co.uk

SCULLY, Hazel Mary. RGN NCA 02. d 06 p 07. Aux Min Portarlington w Cloneyhurke, Lea etc *M & K* 01-06; Chapl Wilson's Hosp Sch Multyfarnham from 06; NSM Mullingar, Portnashangan, Moylisear, Kilbixy etc from 11. *Wilson's Hospital School, Multyfarnham, Co Westmeath, Republic of Ireland* Tel (00353) (44) 937 1115 Mobile 87-281 3956

SCULLY, Kevin John. b 55. NIDA BDA96. St Steph Ho Ox 91. d 93 p 94. C Stoke Newington St Mary *Lon* 93-97; C Stepney St Dunstan and All SS 97-00; Dir of Ords and Voc Adv 97-00;

P-in-c Bethnal Green St Matt w St Jas the Gt 00-02; R from 02. *The Rectory, Hereford Street, London E2 6EX* Tel and fax (020) 7739 7586 E-mail revkev@onetel.com

SCURR, David. b 54. Wilson Carlile Coll 98 SAOMC 05. **d** 05 **p** 06. C Thatcham *Ox* 05-08; P-in-c Farndon and Coddington *Ches* from 08. *The Vicarage, Church Lane, Farndon, Chester CH3 6QD* Tel and fax (01829) 270270 E-mail david.scurr@tinyworld.co.uk

SCUTTER, Canon James Edward. b 36. OBE91. AKC59 St Boniface Warminster 59. **d** 60 **p** 61. C Tilbury Docks *Chelmsf* 60-63; Bechuanaland 63-65; Rhodesia 65-70; New Zealand 70-79; Singapore 79-81; New Zealand from 81; Prin Chapl NZ Defence Force 84-91; QHC from 84; Hon Can Wellington from 87. *32 Waitaheke Road, RD1, Otaki 5581, New Zealand* Tel (0064) (4) 364 3260 E-mail jandhscutter@asiaonline.net.nz

SEABRIGHT, Mrs Elizabeth Nicola. b 52. SRN73. WEMTC 01. **d** 04 **p** 05. NSM Ledbury *Heref* from 04. *The Grove Cottage, Fromes Hill, Ledbury HR8 1HP* Tel (01531) 640252 E-mail nicky.seabright@tesco.net

SEABROOK, Alan Geoffrey. b 43. ALCD65. **d** 66 **p** 67. C Bethnal Green St Jas Less *Lon* 66-70; C Madeley *Heref* 70-73; V Girlington *Bradf* 74-80; P-in-c Abdon w Clee St Margaret *Heref* 80-83; R Bitterley 80-83; P-in-c Cold Weston 80-83; P-in-c Hopton Cangeford 80-83; P-in-c Stoke St Milburgh w Heath 80-83; R Bitterley w Middleton, Stoke St Milborough etc 83-08; RD Ludlow 01-05; rtd 08. *Penhope House, Ballhurst, Bromyard HR7 4EF* Tel (01885) 482184

SEABROOK, Alistair William. b 78. CCC Ox BA99 MA03. Oak Hill Th Coll MTh06. **d** 06 **p** 07. C The Ortons, Alwalton and Chesterton *Ely* 06-09; C Elton w Stibbington and Water Newton 06-09; C Gladesville Australia from 09. *Address temp unknown* E-mail alistair.seabrook@yahoo.co.uk

SEABROOK, Paul. b 60. Univ of Wales (Cardiff) BA81 Nottm Univ PGCE82. Ridley Hall Cam 01. **d** 03 **p** 04. C Wimborne Minster *Sarum* 03-07; R Taverham *Nor* from 07. *The Rectory, 173 Taverham Road, Taverham, Norwich NR8 6SG* Tel (01603) 868217 E-mail seabrooktribe@telco4u.net

SEABROOK, Mrs Penelope Anne. b 56. Hertf Coll Ox BA77 K Coll Lon MA98. SEITE 00. **d** 03 **p** 04. C Southfields St Barn *S'wark* 03-08; NSM 03-07; C Fulham All SS *Lon* from 08. *8 Deodar Road, London SW15 2NN* Tel 07985-108541 (mobile) E-mail pennyseabrook@hotmail.com

SEABROOK, Richard Anthony. b 68. Southn Univ BTh92. Chich Th Coll 92. **d** 92 **p** 93. C Cottingham *York* 92-94; C Hawley H Trin *Guildf* 94-98; V Hockley *Chelmsf* 98-05; R Benalla Australia from 05. *Holy Trinity Rectory, 77 Arundel Street, Benalla Vic 3672, Australia* Tel (0061) (3) 5762 2061 Fax 5762 7009

SEACH, Gregory John. b 65. Sydney Univ BA88 DipEd88 Clare Coll Cam PhD09. Trin Coll Melbourne BD02. **d** 02 **p** 02. C Camberwell St Jo Australia 02-04; Perm to Offic *Ely* 05-08; Dean Clare Coll Cam from 08. *Clare College, Cambridge CB2 1TL* Tel (01223) 333240 E-mail gjs32@cam.ac.uk

SEAFORD, The Very Revd John Nicholas. b 39. Dur Univ BA67. St Chad's Coll Dur 68. **d** 68 **p** 69. C Bush Hill Park St Mark *Lon* 68-71; C Stanmore *Win* 71-73; V N Baddesley 73-76; V Chilworth w N Baddesley 76-93; V Highcliffe w Hinton Admiral 78-93; RD Christchurch 90-93; Hon Can Win Cathl 93-05; Dean Jersey and R Jersey St Helier 93-05; Angl Adv Channel TV 93-05; Chapl Jersey Airport 98-00; Chapl HM Pris La Moye 03-05; rtd 05; Perm to Offic *Sarum* and *Win* from 05. *Claremont, Buffetts Road, Sturminster Newton DT10 1DZ* Tel (01258) 471479

SEAGO, Timothy Paul. b 59. Ripon Coll Cuddesdon 06. **d** 08 **p** 09. C Marlborough *Sarum* from 08. *The Firs, Salisbury Road, Marlborough SN8 4AE* Tel 07772-809136 (mobile) E-mail timseago@btinternet.com

SEAGRAVE, Katherine Victoria. b 81. Wycliffe Hall Ox. **d** 09 **p** 10. C Balham Hill Ascension *S'wark* from 09. *107B Ramsden Road, London SW12 8RD* Tel 07905-342802 (mobile)

SEAL, Nicholas Peter. b 57. Ex Univ BA. Linc Th Coll 81. **d** 83 **p** 84. C Wareham *Sarum* 83-87; Chapl K Alfred Coll *Win* 87-91; V Stanmore 91-01; P-in-c Win St Matt 01-10; R from 10; RD Win 99-07; Chapl Peter Symonds Coll *Win* from 01. *The Rectory, 44 Cheriton Road, Winchester SO22 5AY* Tel and fax (01962) 854849 E-mail peter.seal@ntlworld.com

SEAL, Philip Trevor. b 32. AKC55. **d** 56 **p** 57. C Godalming *Guildf* 56-60; C Tamworth *Lich* 60-61; V Lich St Chad 61-73; Chapl HM Youth Cust Cen Swinfen Hall 66-73; R Shere *Guildf* 74-88; RD Cranleigh 76-81; V Abbotsbury, Portesham and Langton Herring *Sarum* 88-97; rtd 97; Perm to Offic *Ex* 01-08. *Llys Helyg, Llwyncoed Road, Blaenannerch, Cardigan SA43 2AN*

SEAL (formerly MILLER), Mrs Rosamund Joy. b 56. R Holloway Coll Lon BSc77 Whitelands Coll Lon PGCE80. EMMTC 89. **d** 94 **p** 96. NSM Grantham *Linc* 94-96; C Stamford All SS w St Jo 96-00; C Spalding 00-05; P-in-c Moulton *Linc* from 09; RD Elloe W from 09. *All Saints' Vicarage, 34 Church Lane, Moulton, Spalding PE12 6NP* Tel (01406) 370791 E-mail rosamund@sealatmoulton.co.uk

SEAL, William Christopher Houston. b 50. Occidental Coll (USA) BA72. Ch Div Sch of the Pacific (USA) MDiv81. **d** 81 **p** 82. USA 81-88 and from 94; R Etton w Helpston *Pet* 88-94. *The Rectory, 171 Grove Street, Nevada City CA 95959-2601, USA* Tel (001) (530) 265 8836

SEALE, William Arthur. b 62. NUI BA84. CITC. **d** 87 **p** 88. C Drumragh w Mountfield *D & R* 87-90; I from 01; I Drumragh w Drumgooland and Clonduff *D & D* 90-01. *The Rectory, 8 Mullaghmenagh Avenue, Omagh BT78 5QH* Tel and fax (028) 8224 2130 E-mail waseale@btinternet.com *or* drumragh@derry.anglican.org

SEALY, Daniel O'Neill. b 21. Oak Hill Th Coll 62. **d** 64 **p** 65. C Walcot *B & W* 64-67; Chapl RN 67-73; Nigeria 73-79; Libya 79-82; Tunisia 82-86; rtd 86; I Kilgariffe Union *C, C & R* 87-92. *Swanhill, Culver Street, Newent GL18 1JA*

SEALY, Canon Gordon William Hugh. b 27. Leeds Univ BA53 MA64. Coll of Resurr Mirfield 53. **d** 55 **p** 56. C Greenford H Cross *Lon* 55-58; Br Honduras 58-68; R Tarrant Gunville, Tarrant Hinton etc *Sarum* 68-74; V Leic St Paul 74-96; Hon Can Leic Cathl 86-96; rtd 96. *12 Kingfisher Court, West Bay, Bridport DT6 4HQ* Tel (01308) 422045

SEALY, Stephen. b 52. K Coll Lon BD86 AKC86. Linc Th Coll 86. **d** 88 **p** 89. C Bordey *Portsm* 88-91; Min Can and Prec Cant Cathl 91-96; V Pembury *Roch* 96-04; V Sidcup St Jo from 04; AD Sidcup from 08. *St John's Vicarage, 13 Church Avenue, Sidcup DA14 6BU* Tel and fax (020) 8300 0383 E-mail stephen.sealy@diocese-rochester.org

SEAMAN, Christopher Robert. b 34. St Jo Coll Ox BA58 MA74 Solicitor 62. Ox Min Course 92 SAOMC 94. **d** 95 **p** 96. NSM Watlington w Pyrton and Shirburn *Ox* 95-97; NSM Icknield 97-98; Perm to Offic 98-99 and from 05; Hon C Shippon 99-04. *5 Curtyn Close, Abingdon OX14 1SE* Tel (01235) 520380

SEAMAN, John. *See* SEAMAN, Robert John

SEAMAN, Miss Miranda Kate. b 66. Univ Coll Lon BSc88 Solicitor 90. EAMTC 02. **d** 05 **p** 06. NSM S Weald *Chelmsf* 05-08; NSM Ingatestone w Fryerning 08-10; NSM Downham w S Hanningfield from 10. *Hollyhock Cottage, 25 Common Lane, Stock, Ingatestone CM4 9LP* Tel (01277) 841921 *or* 210021 Mobile 07909-522763 E-mail seaman-young@tiscali.co.uk

SEAMAN, Paul Robert. b 61. Bp Grosseteste Coll BEd82. Chich Th Coll 83. **d** 86 **p** 87. C Tilehurst St Mich *Ox* 86-91; TV Moulsecoomb *Chich* 91-95; R Whyke w Rumboldswhyke and Portfield 95-06; V E Grinstead St Mary from 06. *St Mary's Vicarage, Windmill Lane, East Grinstead RH19 2DS* Tel (01342) 323439

SEAMAN (née HEWLINS), Mrs Pauline Elizabeth. b 47. Lon Univ BD68 AKC. Ox Min Course 93. **d** 96 **p** 97. NSM Radley and Sunningwell *Ox* 96-99; NSM Shippon 99-09; P-in-c 06-09; Chapl SS Helen and Kath Sch Abingdon 96-04; Chapl SW Oxon Primary Care Trust 05-07; Perm to Offic *Ox* from 09. *5 Curtyn Close, Abingdon OX14 1SE* Tel (01235) 520380

SEAMAN, Robert John. b 44. Glos Univ BA04 Newland Park Teacher Tr Coll DipEd69 ACP84. EAMTC 84. **d** 84 **p** 85. NSM Downham Market w Bexwell *Ely* 84-90; V Southea w Murrow and Parson Drove 90-97; V Guyhirn w Ring's End 90-97; V Newnham w Awre and Blakeney *Glouc* 97-08; AD Forest N 04-08; rtd 08; Hon C Whitwick, Thringstone and Swannington *Leic* 08-11. *The Vicarage, 37 North Street, Whitwick, Coalville LE67 5HB* Tel (01530) 813268 E-mail seaman437@btinternet.com

SEAMER, Stephen James George. b 50. AKC73. Ridley Hall Cam 74. **d** 75 **p** 76. C Rustington *Chich* 75-78; C Bulwell St Jo *S'well* 78-79; P-in-c Camber and E Guldeford *Chich* 79-80; TV Rye 80-83; V Knowle *Birm* 83-87; Assoc Chapl Brussels Cathl 87-88; P-in-c Tervuren 88-94; Chapl 94-98; P-in-c Liège 90-98; V Tonbridge SS Pet and Paul *Roch* 98-06; Chapl Düsseldorf *Eur* from 06. *Mulvany House, Rotterdamer Strasse 135, 40474 Düsseldorf, Germany* Tel (0049) (211) 452759 E-mail christchurch@online.de

SEAR, Mrs Julie Anne Caradoc. b 61. Trin Coll Bris 08. **d** 10 **p** 11. C Ashington, Washington and Wiston w Buncton *Chich* from 10. *1 Crackers Cottages, Hole Street, Wiston, Steyning BN44 3DJ* Tel 07840-021909 (mobile) E-mail juliesear@googlemail.com

SEAR, Peter Lionel. b 49. Ex Univ BA72. Linc Th Coll 72. **d** 74 **p** 75. C Sheldon *Birm* 74-77; C Caversham *Ox* 77-81; C Caversham St Pet and Mapledurham etc 81-85; TR Thatcham 85-98; V Castle Cary w Ansford *B & W* 98-00; rtd 00; Perm to Offic *B & W* from 03. *Plumtree Cottage, 1 Rodmore Road, Evercreech, Shepton Mallet BA4 6JL* Tel (01749) 838843 E-mail peter@knowlecottage.wanadoo.co.uk

SEAR, Terence Frank. b 39. LDS62 Univ Coll Lon BDS63. Portsm Dioc Tr Course 88. **d** 89. NSM Ryde H Trin *Portsm* 89-98; NSM Swanmore St Mich w Havenstreet 89-92; NSM Swanmore St Mich 92-98; NSM Wroxall 99-00; NSM Godshill 99-01; Perm to Offic from 02. *34 Whitehead Crescent, Wootton Bridge, Ryde PO33 4JF* Tel (01983) 883560

SEARE, Mrs Janice Mae. b 48. SEN. STETS 99. **d** 02 **p** 03. NSM Holdenhurst and Iford *Win* from 02. *Wood Farm, Holdenhurst Village, Bournemouth BH8 0EE* Tel (01202) 302468 Fax 391281

SEARL, John. b 37. Southn Univ BSc58 Edin Univ PhD69. **d** 00 **p** 01. NSM Edin St Cuth 00-03; Asst P Poolewe and Kishorn *Mor* 05-08; Lic to Offic from 08. *Tulach Ard, Badachro, Gairloch IV21 2AA* Tel (01445) 741231 E-mail m.jsearl@tiscali.co.uk

SEARLE, Alan Mansfield. b 47. SEITE 04. **d** 07 **p** 08. NSM E Malling, Wateringbury and Teston *Roch* from 07. *6 Cobbs Close, Wateringbury, Maidstone ME18 5NJ* Tel (01622) 814443 E-mail alan.searle8@btinternet.com

SEARLE, Anthony Miles. b 76. Univ of Wales (Abth) BSc98 PGCE99. Westcott Ho Cam 98. **d** 10 **p** 11. C Bishop's Stortford St Mich *St Alb* from 10. *Cowell House, 24 Apton Road, Bishop's Stortford CM23 3SN* Tel 07785-357562 (mobile) E-mail asearle76@googlemail.com

SEARLE, Charles Peter. b 20. Selw Coll Cam BA48 MA53. Ridley Hall Cam. **d** 50 **p** 51. C Becontree St Mary *Chelmsf* 50-53; P-in-c Bedford St Jo *St Alb* 53-56; R 56-60; V Weston-super-Mare Ch Ch *B & W* 60-70; V Woking Ch Ch *Guildf* 70-85; rtd 85; Perm to Offic *Ex* 85-07. *17 Woodlands Court, The Mount, St Johns, Woking GU21 7FA* Tel (01483) 773577 E-mail asearle@dialstart.net

SEARLE, David William. b 37. MASI89 ACIOB98. **d** 99 **p** 00. OLM E Bergholt and Brantham *St E* 99-07; rtd 07; Perm to Offic *St E* from 07. *46 Chaplin Road, East Bergholt, Colchester CO7 6SR* Tel (01206) 298932

SEARLE, Canon Hugh Douglas. b 35. St Cath Coll Cam BA59 MA63 Cranfield Inst of Tech MSc85. Oak Hill Th Coll 59. **d** 61 **p** 62. C Islington H Trin Cloudesley Square *Lon* 61-64; Chapl HM Pris Lewes 64-65; Chapl HM Borstal Roch 65-69; Chapl HM Youth Cust Cen Hollesley Bay Colony 70-74; Chapl HM Pris Parkhurst 74-78; P-in-c Barton *Ely* 78-84; V 84-00; P-in-c Coton 78-84; R 84-00; RD Bourn 81-92; Hon Can Ely Cathl 97-00; rtd 00; Perm to Offic *Ely* from 00. *38 Field End, Witchford, Ely CB6 2XE* Tel (01353) 659749 E-mail hugdoug@talktalk.net

SEARLE, Canon Jacqueline Ann. b 60. Whitelands Coll Lon BEd82 Bris Univ MA01. Trin Coll Bris 90. **d** 92 **p** 94. Par Dn Roxeth *Lon* 92-94; C Ealing St Steph Castle Hill 94-96; Tutor and Dean of Women Trin Coll Bris 96-03; P-in-c Littleover *Derby* 03-04; V from 04; RD Derby S from 10; Hon Can Derby Cathl from 11. *The Vicarage, 35 Church Street, Littleover, Derby DE23 6GF* Tel (01332) 767802 E-mail j.searle80@ntlworld.com *or* jackie@stpeterlittleover.org.uk

SEARLE, John Francis. b 42. OBE98. FRCA70 FRSM84 Lon Univ MB, BS66. SWMTC 92. **d** 95 **p** 96. NSM Ex St Leon w H Trin 95-03; Assoc Staff Member SWMTC from 03; Perm to Offic *Truro* from 03. *Belle Isle Lodge, Belle Isle Drive, Exeter EX2 4RY* Tel (01392) 432153 E-mail johnlizex@aol.com

SEARLE, Mark Robin. b 73. Cen Sch Speech & Drama BA94. Trin Coll Bris BA03. **d** 03 **p** 04. C Cant St Mary Bredin 03-07; C Ashtead *Guildf* 07-10; C Upton *Ex* from 10. *Upton Rectory, Furzehill Road, Torquay TQ1 3JG* Tel (01803) 201119 E-mail revmarksearle@gmail.com

SEARLE, Michael Stanley. b 38. AMIQ63. NOC 93. **d** 95 **p** 96. NSM Hoole *Ches* 95-99; P-in-c Marbury 99-06; P-in-c Tushingham and Whitewell 02-06; R Marbury w Tushingham and Whitewell 06; rtd 06. *2 Meadow Close, Farndon, Chester CH3 6PP* Tel (01829) 271198 Mobile 07850-720120 E-mail mike.s.searle@btinternet.com

SEARLE, Michael Westran. b 47. Leeds Univ LLB68. Cuddesdon Coll 69. **d** 71 **p** 72. C Norton St Mary *Dur* 71-74; C Westbury-on-Trym H Trin *Bris* 74-77; V Bedminster Down 77-84; V Bris Ch the Servant Stockwood 84-88; Dir of Tr *York* 88-00; R Dunnington 00-07; rtd 07. *Lamorna Vean, Lamorna, Penzance TR19 6NY* Tel (01736) 810218 E-mail msearle@yorktrain.demon.co.uk

SEARLE, Peter. *See* SEARLE, Charles Peter

SEARLE, Philip Robert. b 67. Westcott Ho Cam. **d** 95 **p** 96. C Plymstock *Ex* 95-97; C Plymstock and Hooe 97-98; TV Stoke-upon-Trent *Lich* 98-10; Perm to Offic from 10. *164 Vicarage Gardens, Plymouth PL5 1LJ* E-mail phil.hairetic@hotmail.co.uk

SEARLE, Ralph Alan. b 57. G&C Coll Cam BA79 MA83. Coll of Resurr Mirfield 81. **d** 83 **p** 84. C Cockerton *Dur* 83-86; C S Shields All SS 86-88; TV 88-96; Assoc P Worksop Priory *S'well* 96-97; Assoc P Paignton St Jo *Ex* 97-01; V Horfield St Greg *Bris* 01-03; Hon Min Can Bris Cathl 02-03. *2 Temple Gate, Temple End, High Wycombe HP13 5DY* Tel (01494) 437012 E-mail fr.ralph@tinyonline.co.uk

SEARLE-BARNES, Albert Victor. b 28. Sheff Univ BA48 Lon Univ BD53. ALCD53. **d** 53 **p** 54. C Iver *Ox* 53-55; C Attenborough w Bramcote *S'well* 55-59; C Bramcote 59-65; R Cratfield w Heveningham and Ubbeston *St E* 59-64; R Wick w Doynton *Bris* 64-70; Perm to Offic 70-72; V Downend 73-78; V Market Rasen *Linc* 78-86; R Linwood 79-86; V Legsby 79-86; R Green's Norton w Bradden *Pet* 86-88; V Hambledon *Portsm* 88-92; rtd 92; Perm to Offic *Glouc* 92-09. *30 Gracey Court, Woodland Road, Exeter EX5 3GA* Tel (01392) 462613

SEARLE-BARNES, Belinda Rosemary. b 51. Lon Univ MA93 ARCM72 GRSM73. Sarum Th Coll 93. **d** 96 **p** 97. NSM Pimperne, Stourpaine, Durweston and Bryanston *Sarum* 96-00; Asst Par Development Adv 98-00; Asst Chapl Bryanston Sch 98-00; TV Southampton (City Cen) *Win* 00-04; Chapl Godolphin Sch 04-07; P-in-c Winslow w Gt Horwood and Addington *Ox* 07-08; R from 08. *The Vicarage, 19 Vicarage Road, Winslow, Buckingham MK18 3BJ* Tel (01296) 712564 E-mail bsbwinslow@fsmail.net

SEARS, Helen. *See* THAKE, Ms Helen

SEARS, Jacqueline Isabella. SRN69. NTMTC 95. **d** 99 **p** 00. NSM Hanwell St Mellitus w St Mark *Lon* 99-03; Asst Chapl Essex Rivers Healthcare NHS Trust 03-04; Chapl 04-06; C Ipswich St Matt *St E* 04-06; C Triangle, St Matt and All SS 06-10; rtd 10; Perm to Offic *St E* from 10. *4 Woodward Close, Ipswich IP2 0EA* Tel (01473) 214125 Mobile 07984-077990 E-mail jackie@jbsears.com

SEARS, Jeanette. b 59. Man Univ BA80 PhD84 Lon Univ PGCE85. Wycliffe Hall Ox 90. **d** 92 **p** 94. NSM Ox St Aldate 92-96; Perm to Offic *Lon* 98-01 and *Ox* 01-04; Tutor Trin Coll Bris from 04. *1 Little Stoke Road, Bristol BS9 1HQ* Tel 0117-968 6810 Mobile 07950-047476 E-mail jeanette.sears@trinity-bris.ac.uk

SEARS, Michael Antony. b 50. Birm Univ BSc71 PGCE72. Linc Th Coll 78. **d** 80 **p** 81. C Willenhall H Trin *Lich* 80-83; C Caldmore 83-84; P-in-c 84-86; V 86-89; Abp Ilsley RC Sch Birm 89-97; TV Solihull *Birm* 98-02; R Castle Bromwich SS Mary and Marg 02-07; R Wroxham w Hoveton and Belaugh *Nor* from 07. *The Vicarage, 11 Church Lane, Wroxham, Norwich NR12 8SH* Tel (01603) 784536 E-mail rectorwhb@googlemail.com

SEATON, Christopher Charles. **d** 10 **p** 11. C St Andrews Major w Michaelston-le-Pit *Llan* from 10. *13 Hillside Close, Barry CF63 2QP* Tel (01446) 747541 E-mail chris.c.seaton@fsmail.net

SEATON, Canon James Bradbury. b 29. Ch Coll Cam BA53 MA57. Westcott Ho Cam 53. **d** 55 **p** 56. C Derby St Werburgh 55-58; C Darlington St Cuth *Dur* 58-64; V Preston on Tees 64-72; TV Stockton H Trin 72-73; TV Cen Stockton 73-75; R Anstey *Leic* 75-89; RD Sparkenhoe III 81-89; Hon Can Leic Cathl 87-94; R Market Harborough Transfiguration 89-94; rtd 94; Perm to Offic *Glouc* from 94. *Wayside, Sheep Street, Chipping Campden GL55 6DW* Tel (01386) 841753

SEATON-BURN, Paul Simon. b 70. Ex Univ BA92. St Jo Coll Nottm MTh06. **d** 06 **p** 07. C Broughton w Loddington and Cransley etc *Pet* 06-09; P-in-c Desborough, Brampton Ash, Dingley and Braybrooke from 09. *The Vicarage, Lower Street, Desborough, Kettering NN14 2NP* Tel (01536) 760324 E-mail paulsburn@btinternet.com

SEBER, Derek Morgan. b 43. Man Poly MA87 Man Metrop Univ MPhil96. Oak Hill Th Coll 71. **d** 73 **p** 74. C Collyhurst *Man* 73-76; C Radcliffe St Thos and St Jo 76-77; Ind Missr 77-89; P-in-c Hulme St Geo 77-83; Hon C Moss Side St Jas w St Clem 83-96; Project Officer Linking Up 89-96; Lic Preacher 90-96; P-in-c Cheetham St Jo 97; P-in-c Thornton Hough *Ches* 97-05; V 05-08; Ind Chapl 97-05; rtd 08. *8 Hillside, Hawarden, Deeside CH5 3HQ* Tel (01244) 533583 E-mail derek@morganseber.freeserve.co.uk

SECCOMBE, Marcus John. b 34. Oak Hill Th Coll 60. **d** 63 **p** 64. C Woodthorpe *S'well* 63-67; C Doncaster St Mary *Sheff* 67-72; V Owston 72-90; R Rossington 90-99; rtd 99; Perm to Offic *Sheff* from 99. *39 Marlborough Road, Doncaster DN2 5DF* Tel (01302) 321505 E-mail mark@secco9.freeserve.co.uk

SECOMBE, Preb Frederick Thomas. b 18. St D Coll Lamp BA40 St Mich Coll Llan 40. **d** 42 **p** 43. C Swansea St Mark *S & B* 42-44; C Knighton 44-46; C Machen *Mon* 46-49; C Newport St Woolos 49-52; Chapl St Woolos Hosp Newport 49-52; V Llanarth w Clytha, Llansantffraed and Bryngwyn *Mon* 52-54; R Machen and Rudry 54-59; V Swansea St Pet *S & B* 59-69; R Hanwell St Mary *Lon* 69-83; AD Ealing W 78-82; Preb St Paul's Cathl 81-83; rtd 83. *30 Westville Road, Penylan, Cardiff CF23 5AG* Tel (029) 2048 3978

SECRETAN, Ms Jenny Ruth. b 54. St Aid Coll Dur BA76 Ex Univ PGCE77 Dur Univ MA97. Linc Th Coll 81 Cranmer Hall Dur 83. dss 84 **d** 87 **p** 94. Asst Chapl Newc Poly 84-86; Sunderland St Chad *Dur* 84-86; Bordesley St Oswald *Birm* 86-91; Par Dn 87-91; Assoc Soc Resp Officer *Dur* 92-95; Perm to Offic *Dur* and Newc 95-99. *14 Southwood Gardens, Newcastle upon Tyne NE3 3BU*

SEDANO, Juan Antonio. b 55. Centro de Discipulado Lima 85. **d** 88 **p** 88. Peru 88-90; Crosslinks 91-94; SAMS from 95; NSM Ingrave St Steph CD *Chelmsf* from 95. *5 The Chase, Middle Road, Ingrave, Brentwood CM13 3QT* Tel (01277) 810907 E-mail esedano@btinternet.com

SEDDON, Mrs Carol Susan. b 44. ARCM63 GNSM66 Man Univ CertEd67. Ripon Coll Cuddesdon. **d** 05 **p** 06. NSM Alsager St Mary *Ches* 05-08; Asst Chapl HM YOI Stoke Heath 05-08; V Northwich St Luke and H Trin *Ches* from 08. *1 Tall Trees Close, Northwich CW8 4YA* Tel (01606) 74632 Mobile 07973-737038 E-mail carol.seddon@hotmail.com

SEDDON, Ernest Geoffrey. b 26. Man Univ MA85 ARIBA51. St Deiniol's Hawarden 80. **d** 80 **p** 81. C Dunham Massey St Marg *Ches* 80-83; P-in-c Warburton 82-87; P-in-c Dunham Massey St Mark 85-86; V 86-92; rtd 92; Perm to Offic *Ches* from 92. *7 Colwyn Place, Llandudno LL30 3AW* Tel (01492) 547639 *or* 642107

SEDDON, Philip James. b 45. Jes Coll Cam BA68 MA71 Birm Univ MPhil01. Ridley Hall Cam 67. **d** 70 **p** 71. C Tonge w Alkrington *Man* 70-74; CMS Nigeria 74-78; Lect St Jo Coll Nottm 78-79; Lic to Offic *Ely* 79-85; Chapl Magd Coll Cam 79-85; Lect Bibl Studies Selly Oak Colls 86-00; Lic to Offic *Birm* 87-05; Lect Th Birm Univ 00-05; Dir Min STETS 05-10; rtd 10. *6 Beech Close, Porton, Salisbury SP4 0NP* Tel (02980) 619104 E-mail philipjseddon@gmail.com

SEDEN, Martin Roy. b 47. Man Univ MSc Salford Univ PhD. EMMTC 79. **d** 82 **p** 83. NSM Knighton St Mary Magd *Leic* 82-07; NSM Rutland Deanery from 08. *60 Leicester Road, Uppingham, Oakham LE15 9SD* Tel (01572) 822244 Mobile 07806-940407 E-mail rseden@googlemail.com

SEDGEWICK, Clive Malcolm. b 56. Loughb Univ BSc78 UEA MA92 PGCE79. SAOMC 00. **d** 04 **p** 05. NSM High Harrogate Ch Ch *Ripon* from 04. *11 Bogs Lane, Harrogate HG1 4DY* Tel (01423) 548548 *or* 817553 Mobile 07903-326053 E-mail clives@brleducationteam.org.uk

SEDGLEY, Mrs Jean. b 41. Whitelands Coll Lon CertEd63. S Dios Minl Tr Scheme 92. **d** 95 **p** 96. NSM Haywards Heath St Wilfrid *Chich* 95-01; NSM Cuckfield 01-09; rtd 09. *25 Pasture Hill Road, Haywards Heath RH16 1LY* Tel (01444) 413974

SEDGLEY, Canon Timothy John. b 42. St Jo Coll Ox BA63 MA68. Westcott Ho Cam 64. **d** 66 **p** 67. C Nor St Pet Mancroft 66-70; V Costessey 70-79; RD Nor N 75-79; V Walton-on-Thames *Guildf* 79-05; RD Emly 86-91; Hon Can Guildf Cathl 86-05; Dir OLMs and NSMs 93-05; rtd 05. *6 St Paul's Court, Moreton-in-Marsh, Gloucester GL56 0ET* E-mail timsedgley@hotmail.com

SEDGWICK, Jonathan Maurice William. b 63. BNC Ox BA85 MA89 Leeds Univ BA88. Coll of Resurr Mirfield 86. **d** 89 **p** 90. C Chich St Paul and St Pet 89-91; Dean of Div and Chapl Magd Coll Ox 91-94; Perm to Offic *S'wark* 97-00; Hon C E Dulwich St Jo 00-11; Hon C Walworth St Chris from 11. *46 Wood Vale, London SE23 3EE* Tel (020) 8693 8129 E-mail jonathan@woodvale46.freeserve.co.uk

SEDGWICK, Peter Humphrey. b 48. Trin Hall Cam BA70 Dur Univ PhD83. Westcott Ho Cam 71. **d** 74 **p** 75. C Stepney St Dunstan and All SS *Lon* 74-77; P-in-c Pittington *Dur* 77-79; Lect Th Birm Univ 79-82; Hon C The Lickey *Birm* 79-82; Th Consultant for NE Ecum Gp *Dur* 82-88; Lect Th Hull Univ 88-94; Abp's Adv on Ind Issues *York* 88-94; Vice-Prin Westcott Ho Cam 94-96; Asst Sec Abps' Coun Bd for Soc Resp 96-04; NSM Pet St Barn 96-98; Prin St Mich Coll Llan from 04; Can Llan Cathl from 06. *St Michael and All Angels' College, 54 Cardiff Road, Llandaff, Cardiff CF5 2YJ* Tel (029) 2056 3379 E-mail revgould@virgin.net

SEDLMAYR, Peter. b 53. Univ Coll Chich BA01. **d** 04. NSM Littlehampton and Wick *Chich* from 04. *83 Joyce Close, Wick, Littlehampton BN17 7JG* Tel (01903) 714968 Mobile 07941-921263 E-mail peterpaul@sedlmayr83.freeserve.co.uk

SEED, Richard Edward. b 55. UNISA BTh86 Westmr Coll Ox MEd. Kalk Bay Bible Inst S Africa. **d** 80 **p** 81. S Africa 80-85 and 87-89; Zimbabwe 85-87; Asst Chapl Kingham Hill Sch Oxon 89-90; C Beckenham Ch Ch *Roch* 90-95; Chapl Düsseldorf *Eur* 96-00; CMS from 00. *CMS, PO Box 1799, Oxford OX4 9BN* Tel 08456-201799

SEED, the Ven Richard Murray Crosland. b 49. Leeds Univ MA91. Edin Th Coll 69. **d** 72 **p** 73. C Skipton Ch Ch *Bradf* 72-75; C Baildon 75-77; Chapl HM Det Cen Kidlington 77-80; TV Kidlington *Ox* 77-80; V Boston Spa *York* 80-99; P-in-c Newton Kyme 84-85; P-in-c Clifford 89-99; P-in-c Thorp Arch w Walton 98-99; Chapl Martin House Hospice for Children Boston Spa 85-99; RD New Ainsty *York* 79-99; Adn York from 99; R York H Trin Micklegate from 00; Can Res York Minster from 11. *Holy Trinity Rectory, Micklegate, York YO1 6LE* Tel (01904) 623798 Fax 628155 E-mail archdeacon.of.york@yorkdiocese.org

SEEL, Richard Malcolm. b 45. **d** 04 **p** 05. OLM Bacton w Edingthorpe w Witton and Ridlington *Nor* 04-07; OLM Happisburgh, Walcott, Hempstead w Eccles etc 04-07; NSM Loddon, Sisland, Chedgrave, Hardley and Langley from 07. *31 Hillside, Chedgrave, Norwich NR14 6HZ* Tel (01508) 521938 Mobile 07711-069680 E-mail richard@emerging-church.org

SEELEY, Jutta. *See* BRUECK, Ms Jutta

SEELEY, Canon Martin Alan. b 54. Jes Coll Cam BA76 MA79. Ripon Coll Cuddesdon 76 Union Th Sem (NY) STM78. **d** 78 **p** 79. C Bottesford w Ashby *Linc* 78-80; USA 80-90; Selection Sec ABM 90-96; Sec for Continuing Minl Educn 90-96; V Is of Dogs Ch Ch and St Jo w St Luke *Lon* 96-06; Prin Westcott Ho Cam from 06; Hon Can Ely Cathl from 08. *St James's Vicarage, 110 Wulfstan Way, Cambridge CB1 8QJ* Tel (01223) 241791 *or* 741010 Fax 741002 E-mail mas209@cam.ac.uk

SEGAL, Mrs Marie. b 57. Leeds Univ BEd78. NTMTC BA07. **d** 07 **p** 08. NSM Gt Ilford St Andr *Chelmsf* 07-10; P-in-c from 10. *St Andrew's Vicarage, St Andrew's Road, Ilford IG1 3PE* Tel (020) 8554 3858 Mobile 07787-188449 E-mail segal.marie@btinternet.com

SEGGAR, Jennifer Mary. b 63. Open Univ PGCE01. **d** 05 **p** 06. OLM Bildeston w Wattisham and Lindsey, Whatfield etc *St E* 05-09; C Sudbury and Chilton 09-11; P-in-c Bramford from 11. *The Vicarage, Vicarage Lane, Bramford, Ipswich IP8 4AE* Tel (01473) 748914 E-mail jmseggar@aol.com

SEGRAVE-PRIDE, Mrs Philippa Louise. b 73. Westhill Coll Birm BTh96. Ripon Coll Cuddesdon 97. **d** 99 **p** 00. C Harborne St Pet *Birm* 99-02; TV Tring *St Alb* 02-04; TV Bp's Hatfield, Lemsford and N Mymms 04-09; P-in-c Harpenden St Jo from 09. *St John's Vicarage, 5 St John's Road, Harpenden AL5 1DJ* Tel (01582) 467168 E-mail philippa@segrave-pride.freeserve.co.uk

SELBY, Benjamin. b 75. Ripon Coll Cuddesdon 08. **d** 10. C Clifton *S'well* from 10. *1 Osprey Close, Nottingham NG11 8SX* Tel 07527-994313 (mobile) E-mail bselbyrev@aol.com

SELBY, Miss Carole Janis. b 50. Chelsea Coll of Physical Educn CertEd71 Sussex Univ BEd72 K Coll Lon MA03. Westcott Ho Cam 93. **d** 95 **p** 96. C Worc St Barn w Ch Ch 95-99; Min Turnford St Clem CD *St Alb* 99-08; TV Cheshunt from 08; RD Cheshunt from 04. *St James Vicarage, St James Road, Goffs Oak, Waltham Cross EN7 6TP* Tel (01707) 872328 E-mail c_selby@talk21.com

✠**SELBY, The Rt Revd Peter Stephen Maurice.** b 41. St Jo Coll Ox BA64 MA67 Episc Th Sch Cam Mass BD66 K Coll Lon PhD75 Birm Univ Hon DD07. Bps' Coll Cheshunt 66. **d** 66 **p** 67 **c** 84. C Queensbury All SS *Lon* 66-69; C Limpsfield and Titsey *S'wark* 69-77; Assoc Dir of Tr 69-73; Vice-Prin S'wark Ord Course 70-72; Asst Dioc Missr *S'wark* 73-77; Dioc Missr *Newc* 77-84; Can Res Newc Cathl 77-84; Suff Bp Kingston *S'wark* 84-91; Area Bp 91-92; Wm Leech Prof Fell Dur 92-97; Asst Bp Dur and Newc 92-97; Bp Worc 97-07; Hon Prof Univ Coll Worc from 98; Bp HM Pris 01-07; rtd 07; Pres Nat Coun Ind Monitoring Boards from 08; Hon Asst Bp Portsm 08-11; Hon Asst Bp S'wark from 11; Visiting Prof K Coll Lon from 08. *57 Girton Road, London SE26 5DJ* E-mail peterselby@onetel.com

SELBY-BOOTHROYD, Richard George. b 46. SWMTC. **d** 09 **p** 10. NSM St Illogan *Truro* from 09. *4 Brunel Close, Angarrack, Hayle TR27 5LL* Tel (01736) 752789 E-mail selbyboothroyd@btinternet.com

SELBY, Suffragan Bishop of. *See* WALLACE, The Rt Revd Martin William

SELDON, Francis Peter. b 58. St Jo Coll Nottm 98. **d** 00 **p** 01. C Styvechale *Cov* 00-02; C Cheylesmore 02-04; V from 04. *Christ Church Vicarage, 11 Frankpledge Road, Coventry CV3 5GT* Tel (024) 7650 2770

SELF, Canon David Christopher. b 41. Toronto Univ BSc62 MA64 K Coll Lon BD68 AKC68. **d** 69 **p** 70. C Tupsley *Heref* 69-73; Chapl Dur Univ 73-78; TV Southampton (City Cen) *Win* 78-84; TR Dunstable *St Alb* 84-95; RD Dunstable 90-91; TR Bris St Paul's 95-06; RD Bris City 98-99; AD City 99-03; Hon Can Bris Cathl 99-06; rtd 06. *3 Shannon Court, Thornbury, Bristol BS35 2HN* Tel (01454) 418006 E-mail dcself@btinternet.com

SELF, John Andrew. b 47. Trin Coll Bris 74 CMS Tr Coll Crowther Hall 76. **d** 81 **p** 83. CMS Pakistan 77-91; Assoc V Bath Weston All SS w N Stoke *B & W* 91-92; V Sparkhill St Jo *Birm* from 92. *St John's Vicarage, 15 Phipson Road, Birmingham B11 4JE* Tel and fax 0121-444 4566 *or* 753 1415 E-mail john.self@stjohnsparkhill.org

SELF, Peter Allen. b 41. S Dios Minl Tr Scheme 84. **d** 87 **p** 98. NSM Wilton *B & W* 87-91; NSM Taunton Lyngford 91-96; Asst Chapl Taunton and Somerset NHS Trust 96-08; rtd 08. *20 Dyers Close, West Buckland, Wellington TA21 9JU* Tel (01823) 663408 Fax 663448

SELFE, John Ronald. b 41. EMMTC 85. **d** 95 **p** 96. OLM Mid Marsh Gp *Linc* from 95. *Bookend, 236 Eastgate, Louth LN11 8DA* Tel (01507) 603809 E-mail john.dorothyselfe@tiscali.co.uk

SELIM, Claes Eric. b 48. Uppsala Univ MA73 BD76. **p** 77. C Rasbo Sweden 77-80; P-in-c Hablingbo 81-85; P-in-c Öja and Huddunge 85-89; Dep Lect Uppsala Univ 81-89; Lect 89-95; V Öja 89-92; V Vänge 95-00; C Holbeach *Linc* 00-02; R Guernsey Ste Marie du Castel *Win* from 02; V Guernsey St Matt from 02. *Castel Rectory, La Rue de la Lande, Castel, Guernsey GY5 7EJ* Tel (01481) 256793

SELLER, Prof Mary Joan. b 40. Qu Mary Coll Lon BSc61 Lon Univ PhD64 DSc82. S'wark Ord Course 89. **d** 91 **p** 94. NSM Hurst Green *S'wark* 91-10; Perm to Offic from 10. *11 Home Park, Oxted RH8 0JS* Tel (01883) 715675

SELLER, Timothy John. b 46. Qu Mary Coll Lon BSc67 Lon Univ PhD71. **d** 08 **p** 09. OLM Ewhurst *Guildf* from 08. *Kerne Hus, Walliswood, Dorking RH5 5RD* Tel (01306) 627548 Mobile 07845-192041 E-mail t.seller@dsl.pipex.com

SELLERS, Anthony. b 48. Southn Univ BSc71 PhD76. Wycliffe Hall Ox 84. **d** 86 **p** 87. C Luton St Mary *St Alb* 86-90; V Luton St Paul from 90. *St Paul's Vicarage, 37A Arthur Street, Luton LU1 3SG* Tel (01582) 481796 E-mail tsellers@route56.co.uk

SELLERS, George William. b 35. NOC. **d** 89 **p** 90. NSM Rothwell *Ripon* 89-05; rtd 05. *16 Thornegrove, Rothwell, Leeds LS26 0HP* Tel 0113-282 3522

SELLERS, Robert. b 58. Coll of Resurr Mirfield 90. **d** 92 **p** 93. C Wotton St Mary *Glouc* 92-95; TV Redruth w Lanner and Treleigh *Truro* 95-98; P-in-c Devoran 98-03; Bp's Dom Chapl 98-03; R Fountains Gp *Ripon* 03-11; TR Withycombe Raleigh *Ex* from 11. *The Rectory, 74 Withycombe Village Road, Exmouth EX8 3AE* Tel (01395) 270206 E-mail robert.sellers@ukonline.co.uk

SELLERS, Mrs Rosalind April. b 48. Liv Univ MA77. SWMTC 06. **d** 09 **p** 11. NSM Cannington, Otterhampton, Combwich and Stockland *B & W* 09-10; NSM Puriton and Pawlett from 10. *1 St Mary's Crescent, North Petherton, Bridgwater TA6 6RA* Tel (01278) 661279 Mobile 07794-666247 E-mail rosalind.sellers@virgin.net

SELLERS, Warren John. b 43. Bp Otter Coll Chich TCert73 W Sussex Inst of HE DipAdEd88. K Coll Lon 63 Sarum Th Coll 65. **d** 68 **p** 69. C Guildf H Trin w St Mary 68-72; Hon C Chich St Paul and St Pet 72-73; C Epping St Jo *Chelmsf* 73-76; Hon C Pulborough *Chich* 76-90; Hon C Fleet *Guildf* 90-92; Teacher 73-89; Waltham Abbey St Lawr and H Cross Schs Essex 73-76; Pulborough St Mary, Easeboure & Bp Tuffnell Schs 76-89; Hd Teacher St Pet Jun Sch Farnborough 90-92; TV Upper Kennet *Sarum* 92-95; TR 95-03; rtd 03. *71 Bay Crescent, Swanage BH19 1RD* E-mail wjandmjs27@btinternet.com

SELLEY, Paul Edward Henry. b 47. Bris Univ BEd70 ALCM67 LTCL87. Sarum Th Coll 93. **d** 96 **p** 97. C Swindon Dorcan *Bris* 96-00; V Ashton Keynes, Leigh and Minety 00-07; rtd 07. *577 Dorchester Road, Weymouth DT3 5BT* Tel (01305) 814948 E-mail paul.selley@which.net

SELLGREN, Eric Alfred. b 33. AKC61. **d** 62 **p** 63. C Ditton St Mich *Liv* 62-66; V Hindley Green 66-72; V Southport St Paul 72-80; Warden Barn Fellowship Winterborne Whitchurch 80-86; V The Iwernes, Sutton Waldron and Fontmell Magna *Sarum* 86-98; rtd 98; Perm to Offic *Sarum* from 98. *16 The Limes, Motcombe, Shaftesbury SP7 9QL* Tel (01747) 850747

SELLICK, Peter James. b 67. Wadh Coll Ox BA89. Edin Th Coll BD94. **d** 94 **p** 95. C Kippax w Allerton Bywater *Ripon* 94-97; C Stanningley St Thos 97-02; C W Bromwich All SS *Lich* from 02; Ind Chapl Black Country Urban Ind Miss from 02. *7 Hopkins Drive, West Bromwich B71 3RR* Tel 0121-588 3744

SELLIN, Deborah Mary. b 64. St Andr Univ MA86. STETS 04. **d** 07 **p** 08. NSM Guildf St Sav 07-10; V Wonersh w Blackheath from 10. *The Vicarage, The Street, Wonersh, Guildford GU5 0PF* Tel (01483) 894805 E-mail d.sellin@ntlworld.com

SELLIX, Mrs Pamela Madge. b 47. Lon Univ BA68 PGCE68. SWMTC 00. **d** 04 **p** 05. NSM Saltash *Truro* from 04. *Farthings, Quarry Road, Pensilva, Liskeard PL14 5NT* Tel (01579) 363464

SELLORS, Glenys Margaret. b 43. NOC. **d** 07 **p** 08. NSM Offerton *Ches* from 07. *36 Brookside Avenue, Stockport SK2 5HR* E-mail glenys.sellors@virgin.net

SELMAN, Michael Richard. b 47. Sussex Univ BA68 Bris Univ MA70. Coll of Resurr Mirfield 71. **d** 73 **p** 74. C Hove All SS *Chich* 73-74; C Horfield H Trin *Bris* 74-78; P-in-c Landkey *Ex* 78-79; C Barnstaple and Goodleigh 78-79; TV Barnstaple, Goodleigh and Landkey 79-82; TR 82-84; P-in-c Sticklepath 83-84; TR Barnstaple 85; RD Barnstaple 83-85; TR Cen Ex 85-00; Chapl Aquitaine *Eur* 00-08; Partnership P E Bris from 08. *St Aidan's Vicarage, 2 Jockey Lane, Bristol BS5 8NZ* Tel 0117-904 2830 Mobile 07735-499920

SELMES, Brian. b 48. Nottm Univ BTh74 Dur Univ MA97. Linc Th Coll 70. **d** 74 **p** 75. C Padgate *Liv* 74-77; C Sydenham St Bart *S'wark* 77-80; Chapl Darlington Memorial Hosp from 80; Chapl Darlington Memorial Hosp NHS Trust 94-98; Chapl S Durham Healthcare NHS Trust 98-02; Chapl Co Durham and Darlington NHS Foundn Trust from 02. *Darlington Memorial Hospital, Hollyhurst Road, Darlington DL3 6HX* Tel (01325) 743029 *or* 359688 E-mail brian.selmes@cddah.nhs.uk

SELVARATNAM, Christian Nathan. b 68. Warwick Univ BSc90. Cranmer Hall Dur 06. **d** 08 **p** 09. NSM York St Mich-le-Belfrey from 08. *11/12 Minster Yard, York YO1 7HH* Tel (01904) 624190 Mobile 07773-784728 E-mail christian.selvaratnam@gmail.com

SELVEY, Canon John Brian. b 33. Dur Univ BA54. Cuddesdon Coll 56. **d** 58 **p** 59. C Lancaster St Mary *Blackb* 58-61; C Blackb Cathl 61-65; Cathl Chapl 64-65; V Foulridge 65-69; V Walton-le-Dale 69-82; V Cleveleys 82-89; Hon Can Bloemfontein Cathl from 88; V Slyne w Hest *Blackb* 89-97; Hon Can Blackb Cathl 93-97; rtd 97; Perm to Offic *Carl* from 98. *Low Quietways, Borrowdale Road, Keswick CA12 5UP* Tel (01768) 773538

SELWOOD, Michael. b 40. Oak Hill Th Coll BA91. **d** 91 **p** 92. Canada 91-95; P-in-c Sherborne, Windrush, the Barringtons etc *Glouc* 95-07; rtd 07. *17 Croft Holm, Moreton-in-Marsh GL56 0JH* Tel (01608) 812384 E-mail 106631.11@compuserve.com

SELWOOD, Robin. b 37. ALCD61. **d** 61 **p** 62. C Lenton *S'well* 61-63; C Norbury *Ches* 63-66; V Newton Flowery Field 66-75; V Kelsall 75-89; V Sale St Paul 89-02; rtd 02; P-in-c Langtoft w Foxholes, Butterwick, Cottam etc *York* 02-06. *16 Harewood Avenue, Bridlington YO16 7PY* Tel (01262) 603078

SELWOOD, Timothy John. b 45. Lon Univ LLB66. Sarum Th Coll. **d** 83 **p** 84. NSM Colbury *Win* 83-85; NSM Copythorne and Minstead 85-90; Perm to Offic from 98. *Monks Barn, Knapp Lane, Ampfield, Romsey SO51 9BT* E-mail tim_selwood@btinternet.com

SELWYN, David Gordon. b 38. MEHS Clare Coll Cam BA62 MA66 DD New Coll Ox MA66. Ripon Hall Ox 62. **d** 64 **p** 65. C Ecclesall *Sheff* 64-65; Asst Chapl New Coll Ox 65-68; Lect Univ of Wales (Lamp) 68-98; Reader 98-05; Perm to Offic 68-05. *62A Swiss Valley, Llanelli SA14 8BT* Tel (01554) 773983

SEMEONOFF, Canon Jean Mary Agnes. b 36. Leic Coll of Educn BSc56 PGCE57. EMMTC 84. **d** 87 **p** 94. Par Dn Leic H Spirit 87 and 89-94; Chapl for Deaf People *Derby* 87-89; Chapl for Deaf People *Leic* 89-94; Hon Can Leic Cathl 92-99; rtd 94; Bp's Adv for Women's Min *Leic* 93-97; Min for Special Past Duties 94-99; Perm to Offic from 99. *7 Sunnycroft Road, Leicester LE3 6FU* Tel 0116-285 8854 E-mail rjsem@tiscali.co.uk

SEMPER, The Very Revd Colin Douglas. b 38. Keble Coll Ox BA62. Westcott Ho Cam 61. **d** 63 **p** 64. C Guildf H Trin w St Mary 63-67; Sec ACCM 67-69; Producer Relig Broadcasting Dept BBC 69-75; Overseas Relig Broadcasting Org BBC 75-79; Hd Relig Progr BBC Radio 79-82; Hon Can Guildf Cathl 80-82; Provost Cov 82-87; Can and Treas Westmr Abbey 87-97; Steward 87-90; rtd 97; Perm to Offic *Sarum* 97-03; Hon C Rowledge and Frensham *Guildf* 03-06. *Beech House, 1 Twycross Road, Godalming GU7 2HH* Tel (01483) 422790 E-mail sempers@freezone.co.uk

SEMPLE, Henry Michael. b 40. K Coll Lon BSc62 Birkbeck Coll Lon PhD67 CMath FIMA FCMI FRSA. S Dios Minl Tr Scheme. **d** 87 **p** 88. NSM Steyning *Chich* 87-91; Perm to Offic *Guildf* 87-91 and *Linc* 92-93; NSM Linc Cathl 93-99; TR Headley All SS *Guildf* 99-02; R 02-10; rtd 10; Perm to Offic *Chich* from 11. *12 St Michael's Road, Worthing BN11 4SD* Tel (01903) 520691 E-mail michael.semple@hotmail.co.uk

SEMPLE, Studdert Patrick. b 39. TCD BA66. CITC 66. **d** 67 **p** 68. C Orangefield *D & D* 67-70; USA 70-71; I Stradbally *C & O* 71-82; Ch of Ireland Adult Educn Officer 82-88; I Donoughmore and Donard w Dunlavin *D & G* 88-96; Bp's C Dublin St Geo and St Thos 96-99; Chapl Mountjoy Pris and Mater Hosps 96-99; rtd 99. *49 Richmond Park, Monkstown, Co Dublin, Republic of Ireland* Tel (00353) (1) 230 1712 E-mail pat.semple@gmail.com

SEN, Arani. b 61. R Holloway Coll Lon BA84 St Martin's Coll Lanc PGCE86 Open Univ MA94 Fitzw Coll Cam BA98 MA02. Ridley Hall Cam 96. **d** 99 **p** 00. C Mildmay Grove St Jude and St Paul Lon 99-02; C-in-c Southall Em CD 02-06; V Southall Em 06-08; V Upper Armley *Ripon* from 08. *22 Hill End Crescent, Leeds LS12 3PW* Tel 0113-263 8788 E-mail rev.sen@virgin.net

SENIOR, Brian Stephen. b 55. Brighton Coll of Educn CertEd76. Oak Hill Th Coll 91. **d** 93 **p** 94. C Hildenborough *Roch* 93-98; TV Tunbridge Wells St Jas w St Phil 98-04; V Tunbridge Wells St Phil from 04; RD Tunbridge Wells from 07. *St Philip's Vicarage, Birken Road, Tunbridge Wells TN2 3TE* Tel (01892) 512071 *or* 531031 E-mail brian.senior@diocese-rochester.org

SENIOR, David John. b 47. Oak Hill Th Coll. **d** 82 **p** 83. C Market Harborough *Leic* 82-85; TV Marfleet *York* 85-91; R Desford and Peckleton w Tooley *Leic* 91-96; P-in-c Hall Green Ascension *Birm* 96-99; V from 99; P-in-c Gospel Lane St Mich 97-03; AD Shirley from 10. *The Vicarage, 592 Fox Hollies Road, Birmingham B28 9DX* Tel 0121-777 3689 E-mail david@ascensionhallgreen.fsnet.co.uk

SENIOR, John Peter. b 23. Lon Univ BSc48. Edin Th Coll 63. **d** 65 **p** 66. C Marton *Blackb* 65-68; C Heysham 68-71; V Blackpool St Mich 71-79; V Heddon-on-the-Wall *Newc* 79-88; rtd 88; Perm to Offic *Wakef* from 88. *56 Thorpe Lane, Huddersfield HD5 8TA* Tel (01484) 530466

SENIOR, Mrs Lisa Elaine. b 65. Leeds Univ BA09. NOC 06. **d** 09 **p** 10. C Dewsbury *Wakef* from 09. *The Vicarage, 24 Intake Lane, Brownhill, Batley WF17 0BT* Tel (01924) 471999 E-mail lisasenior24@fsmail.net

SENIOR, Patrick Nicolas Adam. b 63. Univ of Wales (Ban) BA86. Trin Coll Bris BA94. **d** 94 **p** 95. C Derringham Bank *York* 94-98; V Brownhill *Wakef* from 98. *The Vicarage, 24 Intake Lane, Brownhill, Batley WF17 0BT* Tel and fax (01924) 471999 E-mail patrick.senior@sky.com

✠**SENTAMU, The Most Revd and Rt Hon John Tucker Mugabi.** b 49. Makerere Univ Kampala LLB71 Selw Coll Cam BA76 MA MPhil79 PhD84. Ridley Hall Cam. **d** 79 **p** 79 **c** 96. Chapl HM Rem Cen Latchmere Ho 79-82; C Ham St Andr *S'wark*

79-82; C Herne Hill St Paul 82-83; P-in-c Tulse Hill H Trin 83-84; V Upper Tulse Hill St Matthias 83-84; V Tulse Hill H Trin and St Matthias 85-96; P-in-c Brixton Hill St Sav 87-89; Hon Can S'wark Cathl 93-96; Area Bp Stepney *Lon* 96-02; Bp Birm 02-05; Abp York from 05. *Bishopthorpe Palace, Bishopthorpe, York YO23 2GE* Tel (01904) 707021 Fax 709204
E-mail office@archbishopofyork.org

SENTAMU BAVERSTOCK, Mrs Grace Kathleen Nabanja. b 75. Nottm Univ BA96 Selw Coll Cam BTh10. Ridley Hall Cam 06. **d** 10 **p** 11. C Watford St Luke *St Alb* from 10. *St Andrew's Vicarage, 18 Park Road, Watford WD17 4QN* Tel (01923) 442870 E-mail grace-sentamu@baverstock.org.uk

SEPHTON, Mrs Jacqueline Ann Driscoll. b 46. RGN67. **d** 10 **p** 11. OLM Stoke by Nayland w Leavenheath and Polstead *St E* from 10. *12 Highlands Road, Hadleigh, Ipswich IP7 5HU* Tel (01473) 810072 E-mail jackie.sephton@tiscali.co.uk

SEPHTON, John. b 43. **d** 01 **p** 02. OLM Newburgh w Westhead *Liv* from 01; Asst Chapl HM Pris Risley 02-09. *37 Brighouse Close, Ormskirk L39 3NA* Tel (01695) 576774
E-mail johnsephton@postmaster.co.uk

SEPPALA, Christopher James. b 59. St Jo Coll Dur BA82 Ch Ch Coll Cant CertEd92. Chich Th Coll 83. **d** 85 **p** 86. C Whitstable *Cant* 85-88; C S Ashford Ch Ch 88-91; Perm to Offic from 01. *2 The Briars, Long Reach Close, Whitstable CT5 4QF* Tel (01227) 282622 E-mail xpristopheros@netscapeonline.co.uk

SERBUTT, Rita Eileen. b 33. Man Univ BA54 Univ of Wales (Cardiff) DipEd56 FRSA94. Dioc OLM tr scheme 98. **d** 01 **p** 02. OLM Balham St Mary and St Jo *S'wark* from 01. *5 Veronica Road, London SW17 8QL* Tel (020) 8772 1031
E mail eileen.serbutt@virgin.net

SERGEANT, John Richard Arthur. b 43. K Coll Dur BA65 Newc Univ DipEd66 DAES87. **d** 06 **p** 07. NSM Cullercoats St Geo *Newc* from 06. *5 Jedburgh Close, North Shields NE29 9NU* Tel 0191-259 1752 E-mail sergeantjra@aol.com

SERJEANT, Frederick James. b 28. Lon Inst of Educn BEd77. AKC53 St Boniface Warminster 53. **d** 54 **p** 55. C Leytonstone St Marg w St Columba *Chelmsf* 54-58; C Parkstone St Pet w Branksea *Sarum* 58-59; V Reigate St Luke S Park *S'wark* 59-65; V Battersea St Pet 65-71; C-in-c Battersea St Paul 67-71; V W Mersea *Chelmsf* 71-73; P-in-c E Mersea 71-73; R W w E Mersea 73-75; rtd 93. *3 Church Hill View, Sydling, Dorchester DT2 9SY* Tel (01300) 341670

SERJEANT, Mrs Heather Faith. b 60. Stirling Univ BSc80 Ox Univ BTh04. Ripon Coll Cuddesdon 00. **d** 02 **p** 03. C Caversham St Pet and Mapledurham *Ox* 02-06. *4A The Mount, Caversham, Reading RG4 7RU* Tel 0118-947 2729
E-mail heatherserjeant@aol.com

SERJEANTSON, John Cecil Mylles. b 36. Bp's Univ Lennoxville BA63 McGill Univ Montreal BD66. Montreal Dioc Th Coll LTh66. **d** 66 **p** 67. C Westmount St Matthias Canada 66-68; R Huntingdon w Ormstown 68-72; C Gt and Lt Driffield *York* 72-76; V Bilton St Pet 76-79; R Brome Canada 79-01; rtd 01. *103 St Patrick Boulevard, Cowansville QC J2K 1M4, Canada* Tel (001) (450) 263 0454

SERMON, Michael John. b 61. Univ of Cen England in Birm ACIB85. Qu Coll Birm BA98 MA99. **d** 99 **p** 00. C W Heath *Birm* 99-03; V Blackheath from 03. *St Paul's Vicarage, 83 Vicarage Road, Halesowen B62 8HX* Tel 0121-559 1000
E-mail mike@mikesermon.co.uk

SERTIN, John Francis. b 22. Fitzw Ho Cam BA50 MA54. Tyndale Hall Bris. **d** 45 **p** 46. C Sidcup Ch Ch *Roch* 45-47; Chapl Fitzw Ho Cam 47-50; C-in-c St Paul's Cray St Barn CD *Roch* 50-59; V Chitts Hill St Cuth *Lon* 59-62; Sec Ch Soc 62-67; P-in-c Woburn Square Ch Ch *Lon* 67-77; R Holborn St Geo w H Trin and St Bart 67-80; R Donyatt w Horton, Broadway and Ashill *B & W* 80-92; rtd 92; Perm to Offic *B & W* 92-02. *23 Birstan Gardens, Andover SP10 4NY* Tel (01264) 334544

SERVANT, Canon Alma Joan. b 51. Nottm Univ BA76. Westcott Ho Cam 83. dss 85 **d** 87 **p** 94. Ordsall *S'well* 85-88; Par Dn 87-88; Par Dn Man Whitworth 88-94; TV 94-96; Chapl Man Poly 88-92; Chapl Man Metrop Univ 92-96; P-in-c Heaton Norris St Thos 96-00; P-in-c Hulme Ascension 00-05; R from 05; Hon Can Man Cathl from 02. *The Rectory, Royce Road, Hulme, Manchester M15 5FQ* Tel 0161-226 5568

SERVANTE, Kenneth Edward. b 29. AKC55. **d** 56 **p** 57. C Chaddesden St Phil *Derby* 56-58; C Brampton St Thos 58-61; C Whitfield 61-63; V Derby St Paul 63-70; V Elmton 70-81; P-in-c Winster 81-82; P-in-c Elton 81-82; R S Darley, Elton and Winster 82-94; rtd 94; Perm to Offic *Derby* from 94. *13 Chestnut Avenue, Belper DE56 1LY* Tel (01773) 820513

SESSFORD, Canon Alan. b 34. Bps' Coll Cheshunt 65. **d** 66 **p** 67. C Highcliffe w Hinton Admiral *Win* 66-69; C Minehead *B & W* 70; C Chandler's Ford *Win* 70-73; V Burton and Sopley 73-00; RD Christchurch 93-98; Hon Can Win Cathl 98-00; rtd 00; Perm to Offic *Win* from 00; Chapl R Bournemouth and Christchurch Hosps NHS Trust from 01. *4 Benson Close, Bransgore, Christchurch BH23 8HX* Tel (01425) 673412

SETTERFIELD, Nicholas Manley. b 63. Colchester Inst of Educn BA89. St Steph Ho Ox 89. **d** 92 **p** 93. C Prestbury *Glouc*

92-96; R Letchworth *St Alb* 96-03; V Northampton St Matt *Pet* from 03. *St Matthew's Vicarage, 30 East Park Parade, Northampton NN1 4LB* Tel (01604) 604412
E-mail vicar@stmatthews-northampton.org

SETTIMBA, John Henry. b 52. Nairobi Univ BSc78 Leeds Univ MA91. Pan Africa Chr Coll BA78. **d** 78 **p** 80. Kenya 78-81; Uganda 81-85; C Allerton *Bradf* 86-87; C W Ham *Chelmsf* 87-91; C-in-c Forest Gate All SS 91-94; P-in-c 94-96; TV Hackney *Lon* 96-02; rtd 07. *63 Belvedere Court, Upper Richmond Road, London SW15 6HZ* Tel (020) 8789 8376

SEVILLE, Thomas Christopher John. b 57. Trin Hall Cam MA80. Coll of Resurr Mirfield 87. **d** 89 **p** 90. C Knowle *Bris* 89-93; CR from 93. *House of the Resurrection, Stocks Bank Road, Mirfield WF14 0BN* Tel (01924) 483315
E-mail tseville@mirfield.org.uk

SEWARD, Jolyon Frantom. b 57. Univ of Wales (Cardiff) BA81. Chich Th Coll 83. **d** 86 **p** 87. C Llanblethian w Cowbridge and Llandough etc 86-88; C Newton Nottage 88-93; Dioc Children's Officer 88-98; V Penyfai w Tondu 93-01; TV Heavitree and St Mary Steps *Ex* from 01. *St Lawrence's Vicarage, 36 Lower Hill Barton Road, Exeter EX1 3EH* Tel (01392) 466302 *or* 677152 E-mail frjolyon@eurobell.co.uk

SEWARD, Nicholas. b 70. Imp Coll Lon BEng91 St Jo Coll Dur BA96 MA98. Cranmer Hall Dur 94. **d** 98 **p** 99. C Bearsted w Thurnham *Cant* 98-02; Chapl and Hd RS Magd Coll Sch Ox 02-08; Hd Kingham Hill Sch from 08. *Kingham Hill School, Kingham, Chipping Norton OX7 6TH* Tel (01608) 658999
E-mail n.seward@kingham-hill.oxon.sch.uk

SEWELL, Andrew. *See* SEWELL, John Andrew Clarkson

SEWELL, Canon Andrew William. b 61. Nottm Univ BSc83. St Jo Coll Nottm 93. **d** 93 **p** 94. C Adel *Ripon* 93-96; C Far Headingley St Chad 96-98; Asst Dioc Missr 96-98; P-in-c Otham w Langley *Cant* 98-01; R 01-10; P-in-c Maidstone St Paul from 10; AD Maidstone from 10; Hon Can Cant Cathl from 11. *St Paul's Vicarage, 130 Boxley Road, Maidstone ME14 2AH* Tel (01622) 691926 E-mail andrew@asewell.plus.com

SEWELL, Barry. *See* SEWELL, John Barratt

SEWELL, Miss Elizabeth Jill. b 56. Reading Univ BSc77. Trin Coll Bris BA97. **d** 97 **p** 98. C Rothley *Leic* 97-01; TV Market Harborough and The Transfiguration etc 01-07; RD Gartree I 06-07; TR Knaresborough *Ripon* from 07; P-in-c Nidd from 11. *The Rectory, High Bond End, Knaresborough HG5 9BT* Tel (01423) 865273 E-mail ejsewell@btinternet.com

SEWELL, John Andrew Clarkson. b 58. Aston Tr Scheme 93 Ripon Coll Cuddesdon 95. **d** 97 **p** 98. C Horsham *Chich* 97-99; C Cleobury Mortimer w Hopton Wafers etc *Heref* 99-01; R 01-03; TV Ludlow, Ludford, Ashford Carbonell etc 03-04; Chapl Shropshire's Community NHS Trust 03-04; Ld Chapl ChAT (Weston-super-Mare Chapl About Town) *B & W* from 05; Hon C Weston super Mare St Jo 06-07; P-in-c Westbury sub Mendip w Easton 07-09. *Chaplaincy About Town, 67 Meadow Street, Weston-super-Mare BS23 1QL* Tel (01934) 643533
E-mail enquiries@westonchat.org.uk
or andy.sewell@tiscali.co.uk

SEWELL, John Barratt (Barry). b 39. St Bart Hosp Medical Coll MB, BS63. Ridley Hall Cam. **d** 92 **p** 93. C Ulverston St Mary w H Trin *Carl* 92-94; Asst Chapl R Cornwall Hosps Trust 94-98; Chapl 98-99; P-in-c Gerrans w St Anthony-in-Roseland and Philleigh *Truro* 00-03; rtd 03; Perm to Offic *Truro* from 04. *Greenacre, Zelah, Truro TR4 9HS* Tel (01872) 540747
E-mail barry@cleswyth.freeserve.co.uk

SEWELL, Jonathan William. b 60. Lanc Univ BA82 BTh86. Linc Th Coll 83. **d** 86 **p** 87. C Ilkeston St Mary *Derby* 86-89; C Enfield Chase St Mary *Lon* 89-92; Chapl Youth Officer *Win* 92-97; P-in-c Headington St Mary *Ox* 98-10; V 10-11. *Hartley House, Hartley, Kirkby Stephen CA17 4JJ* Tel (017683) 71456
E-mail jonathan.sewell@ntlworld.com

SEWELL, Peter Alexis. b 35. Lon Univ BSc61 PhD67 FRSC86. Cyprus & Gulf Ord Course 92. **d** 94 **p** 95. Cyprus and the Gulf 94-97; NSM Ormskirk *Liv* 97-01; Perm to Offic from 01. *Shakelady Hey, Sandy Lane, Lathom, Ormskirk L40 5TU* Tel and fax (01695) 572095

SEWELL, Richard Michael. b 62. Birm Univ BA84. SEITE 99. **d** 02 **p** 03. C Putney St Mary *S'wark* 02-05; TV Wimbledon 05-10; TR Barnes from 10. *The Rectory, 25 Glebe Road, London SW13 0DZ* E-mail sewell4321@btinternet.com

SEWELL, Robin Warwick. b 42. Trin Coll Bris 80. **d** 82 **p** 83. C Hinckley H Trin *Leic* 82-85; C Broadwater St Mary *Chich* 85-89; Chapl Barcelona *Eur* 89-02; V Braintree St Paul *Chelmsf* from 02. *St Paul's Vicarage, Hay Lane, Braintree CM7 3DY* Tel (01376) 325095 E-mail robin@sewellgospel.fsnet.co.uk

SEWELL, Miss Sarah Frances. b 61. Wycliffe Hall Ox 87. **d** 91 **p** 94. C Binley *Cov* 91-94; Asst Chapl Derriford Hosp Plymouth 94-96; Chapl Stoke Mandeville Hosp NHS Trust 96-00; Chapl R Marsden NHS Foundn Trust 00-05; Chapl Team Ldr Epsom and St Helier Univ Hosps NHS Trust 05-07; Sen Co-ord Chapl from 07. *The Chaplains' Office, Epsom General Hospital, Dorking Road, Epsom KT18 7EG* Tel (01372) 735322
E-mail sarah.sewell@epsom-sthelier.nhs.uk

SEXTON, Canon Michael Bowers. b 28. SS Coll Cam BA52 MA56. Wells Th Coll 52. **d** 54 **p** 55. C Miles Platting St Luke *Man* 54-57; C Bradford cum Beswick 57-58; C-in-c Oldham St Chad Limeside CD 58-62; R Filby w Thrigby w Mautby *Nor* 62-72; P-in-c Runham 67-72; P-in-c Stokesby w Herringby 68-72; R Hethersett w Canteloff 72-85; V Ketteringham 73-84; RD Humbleyard 81-86; Hon Can Nor Cathl 85-93; R Hethersett w Canteloff w Lt and Gt Melton 85-86; V Hunstanton St Mary w Ringstead Parva, Holme etc 86-93; rtd 94; Perm to Offic *Nor* from 94. *3 Forge Close, Poringland, Norwich NR14 7SZ* Tel (01508) 493885

SEYMOUR, Dom Anthony Nicholas. b 39. QUB BA61. **d** 96 **p** 97. Community of Our Lady and St John 86-01; Perm to Offic *Win* from 01. *Alton Abbey, Abbey Road, Beech, Alton GU34 4AP* Tel (01420) 562145 or 563575 Fax 561691

SEYMOUR, Brian Anthony. b 45. **d** 07 **p** 08. OLM Ottershaw *Guildf* from 07. *50 Rowtown, Addlestone KT15 1HQ* Tel (01932) 705260 E-mail brianandchrisseymour@yahoo.co.uk

SEYMOUR, David. b 43. Kelham Th Coll 60. **d** 68 **p** 69. C Cowley St Jas *Ox* 68-73; TV Lynton, Brendon, Countisbury, Lynmouth etc *Ex* 73-77; C-in-c Luton (Princes Park) CD *Roch* 78-79; V Rosherville 79-90; rtd 90. *3 Fosbrooke House, 8 Clifton Drive, Lytham St Annes FY8 5RQ* E-mail markbeech@boltblue.com

SEYMOUR, David Raymond Russell. b 56. Keble Coll Ox BA79 MA88. St Steph Ho Ox 79. **d** 81 **p** 82. C Tilehurst St Mich *Ox* 81-85; TV Parkstone St Pet w Branksea and St Osmund *Sarum* 85-91; V Bradford-on-Avon Ch Ch 91-01; P-in-c Sturminster Newton and Hinton St Mary 01-02; V Sturminster Newton, Hinton St Mary and Lydlinch from 02; C Hazelbury Bryan and the Hillside Par from 08; C Okeford from 08; RD Blackmore Vale from 08. *The Vicarage, Church Street, Sturminster Newton DT10 1DB* Tel (01258) 471276 E-mail drrseymour@hotmail.co.uk

SEYMOUR, Ian. See SEYMOUR, Robert Ian

SEYMOUR, John. b 73. Bris Univ BSc95 MB, ChB98 Heythrop Coll Lon MA03 Trin Coll Cam BA05. Westcott Ho Cam 03. **d** 06 **p** 07. C Poplar Lon 06-09; Chapl Twyford C of E High Sch Acton from 09. *St Edward's House, 12A Medway Drive, Greenford UB6 8LN* Tel (020) 8930 9305 E-mail john.seymour@london.anglican.org

SEYMOUR, John Anthony. b 46. SWMTC. **d** 08 **p** 09. NSM Carbis Bay w Lelant *Truro* 08-11; P-in-c from 11. *The Vicarage, Porthrepta Road, Carbis Bay, St Ives TR26 2LD* E-mail tonyseymour@talktalk.net

SEYMOUR, Canon John Charles. b 30. Oak Hill Th Coll 51 and 55 Wycliffe Coll Toronto 54. **d** 57 **p** 58. C Islington St Andr w St Thos and St Matthias *Lon* 57-60; C Worthing St Geo *Chich* 60-63; V Thornton *Leic* 63-70; R Kirby Muxloe 70-81; TR 81-83; RD Sparkenhoe I 83-88; R Market Bosworth w Shenton 83-87; TR Market Bosworth, Cadeby w Sutton Cheney etc 87-93; RD Sparkenhoe W 89-92; Hon Can Leic Cathl 82-93; rtd 93. *56 Wyggeston Hospital, Hinkley Road, Leicester LE3 0UX* Tel 0116-254 8295 E-mail jams56@btinternet.com

SEYMOUR, Nicholas. See SEYMOUR, Dom Anthony Nicholas

SEYMOUR, Paul Edward. b 62. Humberside Univ BA92. St Jo Coll Nottm 01. **d** 03 **p** 04. C Ingleby Barwick *York* 03-07; C Hatfield Hyde *St Alb* 07-10; P-in-c Stevenage All SS Pin Green from 10. *All Saints' Vicarage, 100 Derby Way, Stevenage SG1 5TJ* Tel (01438) 358108 Mobile 07815-729831 E-mail revpaulseymour@btinternet.com

SEYMOUR, Robert Ian. b 63. Ox Min Course 08. **d** 11. OLM Wokingham St Sebastian *Ox* from 11. *24 Booth Drive, Finchampstead, Wokingham RG40 4HL* Tel 0118-973 1857 E-mail ian.seymour@btinternet.com

SEYMOUR-JONES, Michael D'Israeli. b 37. **d** 09. OLM Shiplake w Dunsden and Harpsden *Ox* from 09. *6 Heathfield Close, Binfield Heath, Henley-on-Thames RG9 4DS* Tel 0118-947 8632 E-mail m.seymour-jones@btinternet.com

SEYMOUR-WHITELEY, Ms Alison. b 51. City of Lon Poly MA90 Homerton Coll Cam PGCE95. CITC 04. **d** 07 **p** 08. Lic to Offic *Clogh* 07-11; Chapl HM Pris Morton Hall from 11. *HM Prison Morton Hall, Swinderby, Lincoln LN6 9PT* Tel (01522) 666700 E-mail alisonsw@hotmail.co.uk

SEYMOUR-WHITELEY, Richard Dudley. b 59. Leic Poly BSc80. Linc Th Coll 82. **d** 85 **p** 86. C Bushey *St Alb* 85-89; C Stevenage St Mary Shephall w Aston 89-93; P-in-c Blunham w Tempsford and Lt Barford 93-99; P-in-c The Stodden Churches 99-01; I Grey Abbey w Kircubbin *D & D* 01-06; I Galloon w Drummully and Sallaghy *Clogh* 06-11; P-in-c Bilsthorpe *S'well* from 11; P-in-c Farnsfield from 11; P-in-c Eakring from 11; P-in-c Kirklington w Hockerton from 11; P-in-c Maplebeck from 11; P-in-c Winkburn from 11. *The Vicarage, Beck Lane, Farnsfield, Newark NG22 8ER* Tel (01623) 882076 Mobile 07789-550508

SHACKELL, Daniel William. b 42. **d** 95 **p** 96. Dir Spires Cen *S'wark* 93-06; OLM Streatham St Leon *S'wark* 95-99; Lic to Offic 99-06; rtd 07; Perm to Offic *Sarum* from 09. *Wynways, 146*

West Bay Road, Bridport DT6 4AZ Tel (01308) 426514 Mobile 07818-808249 E-mail danshackell@hotmail.com

SHACKELL, Kenneth Norman. b 26. S'wark Ord Course 66. **d** 69 **p** 70. NSM Greenwich St Alfege w St Pet and St Paul *S'wark* 69-95; Perm to Offic *Sarum* 95-03. *17 Portman Drive, Child Okeford, Blandford Forum DT11 8HU* Tel and fax (01258) 861583

SHACKERLEY, Canon Albert Paul. b 56. K Coll Lon MA97 Sheff Univ PhD07. Chich Th Coll 91. **d** 93 **p** 94. C Harlesden All So *Lon* 93-96; P-in-c Chelmsf All SS 96-98; V 98-02; Can Res Sheff Cathl 02-09; Vice Dean 05-09; Hon Can from 10; V Doncaster St Geo from 10. *The Vicarage, 98 Thorne Road, Doncaster DN2 5BJ* Tel (01302) 323665 E-mail paul_shackerley@btinternet.com

SHACKLADY, Mrs Thelma. b 38. Liv Univ BA60. St Alb Minl Tr Scheme 89. **d** 92 **p** 94. NSM Luton St Andr *St Alb* 92-96; NSM Luton All SS w St Pet 96-03; Perm to Offic from 03. *45 Lilly Hill, Olney MK46 5EZ* Tel (01234) 712997 E-mail bill.shacklady@virgin.net

SHACKLEFORD, Richard Neal. b 40. Univ of Denver BA64 Univ of N Colorado MA74. St Steph Ho Ox 84. **d** 86 **p** 87. C Poulton-le-Fylde *Blackb* 86-88; Can St Jo Cathl Colorado USA 88-92; C Denver St Mich 92-96; R Lindenhurst St Boniface from 96. *100 46th Street, Lindenhurst NY 11747-2009, USA* Tel (001) (631) 957 2666 Fax 957 2665

SHACKLETON, Canon Alan. b 31. Sheff Univ BA53. Wells Th Coll 54. **d** 56 **p** 57. C Ladybarn *Man* 56-58; C Bolton St Pet 58-61; V Middleton Junction 61-70; V Heywood St Luke 70-84; AD Rochdale 82-92; Hon Can Man Cathl 84-97; V Heywood St Luke w All So 85-86; TV Rochdale 86-91; TR 91-97; rtd 97; Perm to Offic *Man* from 97. *28 Taunton Avenue, Rochdale OL11 5LD* Tel (01706) 645335 E-mail alan@shackletong.demon.co.uk

SHACKLETON, Anthea. b 42. **d** 07. OLM Ravensthorpe and Thornhill Lees w Savile Town *Wakef* 07-10; OLM Ossett and Gawthorpe from 10. *1 Fearnley Drive, Ossett WF5 9EU* Tel (01924) 270830 Mobile 07815-445757 E-mail ant.shackleton@talktalk.net

SHACKLETON, Ian Roderick. b 40. St Fran Coll Brisbane 69. **d** 72 **p** 72. C Toowoomba Australia 72-74; P-in-c Milmerran 74-75; R 75-78; C Birch St Agnes *Man* 79-80; P-in-c Newton Heath St Wilfrid and St Anne 80-87; NSM W Derby St Jo *Liv* 87-90; C 90-94; P-in-c Southport St Luke 94-05; Asst Chapl HM Pris Liv 94-05; rtd 06; Perm to Offic *Cant* from 06. *31 The Shrubbery, Walmer, Deal CT14 7PZ* Tel (01304) 379773

SHACKLEY, Prof Myra Lesley. b 49. Southn Univ BA70 PhD75 Nottm Univ MA99 FRGS. EMMTC 96. **d** 99 **p** 00. NSM Ordsall *S'well* 99-02; Dioc Tourism Adv 02-08; PV *S'well* Minster 02-06; P-in-c N and S Muskham 06-08; P-in-c Averham w Kelham 06-08; Hon C Spofforth w Kirk Deighton *Ripon* from 08. *The Rectory, Church Lane, Spofforth, Harrogate HG3 1AF* Tel (01937) 590770 Mobile 07889-691504

SHAFTO, Robert James. b 38. FCA61. OLM course 96. **d** 99 **p** 00. NSM W Dulwich All SS *S'wark* 99-07; rtd 07; Perm to Offic *S'wark* from 08. *46 Cedar Close, London SE21 8HX* Tel (020) 8761 7395 E-mail bob@shafto46.wanadoo.co.uk

SHAHZAD, Sulaiman. b 60. BA. Oak Hill Th Coll BA93. **d** 96 **p** 97. C Winchmore Hill St Paul *Lon* 96-00; TV Digswell and Panshanger *St Alb* 00-10; V Bostall Heath *Roch* from 10. *St Andrew's Parsonage, 276 Brampton Road, Bexleyheath DA7 5SF* Tel (020) 8303 9332 E-mail sulishahzad@tiscali.co.uk

SHAKESPEARE, James Douglas Geoffrey. b 71. Fitzw Coll Cam BA93 MA97 Man Univ MA96. Westcott Ho Cam 97. **d** 99 **p** 00. C Cherry Hinton St Jo *Ely* 99-02; Bp's Chapl and Policy Adv *Leic* 02-05; P-in-c Birstall and Wanlip 05-09; V 09-10; NSM Market Harborough and The Transfiguration etc 10-11; TV from 11. *The Vicarage, Dingley Road, Great Bowden, Market Harborough LE16 7ET* Tel (01858) 469109 E-mail jshakespeare@btinternet.com

SHAKESPEARE, Steven. b 68. CCC Cam BA89 PhD94. Westcott Ho Cam 93. **d** 96 **p** 97. C Cambridge St Jas *Ely* 96-99; V Endcliffe and Chapl Sheff Hallam Univ 99-03; Chapl Liv Hope Univ from 03. *Anglican Chaplaincy, Hope Park, Taggart Avenue, Liverpool L16 9JD* Tel 0151-291 3545 E-mail shakess@hope.ac.uk

SHAMBROOK, Roger William. b 46. Sarum & Wells Th Coll 78. **d** 83 **p** 84. OSP 76-82; C Southbourne St Kath *Win* 83-86; TV Bridport *Sarum* 86-01; Chapl Bridport Community Hosp 86-94; Chapl Dorset Community NHS Trust 94-01; P-in-c Torre All SS *Ex* from 01. *All Saints' Vicarage, 45 Barton Road, Torquay TQ1 4DT* Tel (01803) 328865

SHAND, Brian Martin. b 53. Univ Coll Lon BA76 PhD82. St Steph Ho Ox 85. **d** 87 **p** 88. C Uxbridge St Marg *Lon* 87-89; C Uxbridge 88-90; C Worplesdon *Guildf* 90-94; Relig Affairs Producer BBC Radio Surrey 90-94; V Weston 94-01; V Witley from 01. *The Vicarage, Petworth Road, Witley, Godalming GU8 5LT* Tel and fax (01428) 681872 E-mail allsaints.witley@btinternet.com

SHANKS, Canon Robert Andrew Gulval. b 54. Ball Coll Ox BA75 G&C Coll Cam BA79 Leeds Univ PhD90. Westcott Ho Cam 77. **d** 80 **p** 81. C Potternewton *Ripon* 80-83; C Stanningley St Thos 84-87; Lect Leeds Univ 87-91; Teaching Fell Lanc Univ 91-95; Research Fell in Th Cheltenham and Glouc Coll of HE 95-96; NSM Leeds City *Ripon* 95-96; P-in-c Upper Ryedale and CME Officer Cleveland Adnry *York* 97-04; Can Res Man Cathl from 04. *3 Booth Clibborn Court, Salford M7 4PJ* Tel 0161-792 8820 E-mail ragshanks@hotmail.com

SHANNON, Mrs Annette Denise. b 61. Hatf Poly BSc83 Anglia Poly Univ CertEd99. ERMC 05. **d** 08 **p** 09. C St Edm Way *St E* from 08. *53 Raynsford Road, Great Welnetham, Bury St Edmunds IP30 0TN* Tel (01284) 386115 E-mail revannettes@aol.com

SHANNON, Helen Louise. b 68. NTMTC 07. **d** 10. C Woodside Park St Barn *Lon* from 10. *24 Stable Walk, London N2 9RD* Tel (020) 8883 7450 Mobile 07866-507609 E-mail helenshannon@stbarnabas.co.uk

SHANNON, The Ven Malcolm James Douglas. b 49. TCD BA72 MA75. CITC 75. **d** 75 **p** 76. C Clooney *D & R* 75-78; I Kilcolman w Kiltallagh, Killorglin, Knockane etc *L & K* 78-09; Adn Ardfert and Aghadoe 88-09; Adn Limerick 04-09; Treas Limerick Cathl 88-09; Dir of Ords 91-09; rtd 09. *Cloonfad More, Carrick-on-Shannon, Co Leitrim, Republic of Ireland*

SHANNON, Canon Trevor Haslam. b 33. Wele Coll Cam BA57 MA61 Lon Univ BD69. Westcott Ho Cam 57. **d** 59 **p** 60. C Moss Side Ch Ch *Man* 59-62; V Woolfold 62-66; Chapl Forest Sch Snaresbrook 66-80 and 87-88; V St Ilford St Marg *Chelmsf* 88-90; TR St Ilford St Clem and St Marg 90-96; V 96-99; RD Redbridge 90-95; Hon Can Chelmsf Cathl 93-99; rtd 99; Perm to Offic Nor from 00. *Honeysuckle Cottage, Chubbs Lane, Wells-next-the-Sea NR23 1DP* Tel (01328) 711409

SHAPLAND, David Edward. b 26. Cuddesdon Coll 51. **d** 53 **p** 54. C Cranbrook *Cant* 53-55; Chapl St Cath Coll Cam 55-61; R Fittleworth *Chich* 62-65; Warden Bede Ho Staplehurst 65-69; Warden Llanerchwen Trust 70-91; Lic to Offic *S & B* 70-79; Perm to Offic *Chich* 79-91; rtd 91. *6 The Stables, Flete House, Ermington, Ivybridge PL21 9NZ* Tel (01752) 830308

SHARKEY, Philip Michael. b 50. York Univ BA73 MA08 CQSW78. ERMC 06. **d** 08 **p** 09. NSM Shingay Gp *Ely* from 08. *23 Cherry Drive, Royston SG8 7DL* Tel (01763) 221284 Mobile 07917-619124 E-mail sharkey_phil@yahoo.co.uk

SHARLAND, Canon Marilyn. b 40. City of Birm Coll CertEd61. Oak Hill Th Coll 84. dss 86 **d** 87 **p** 94. Barkingside St Laur *Chelmsf* 86-88; Hon Par Dn Hucclecote *Glouc* 88-89; C Coney Hill 89-98; P-in-c Tuffley 98-99; V 99-06; Hon Can Glouc Cathl 02-06; rtd 06. *51 Lynmouth Road, Hucclecote, Gloucester GL3 3JD*

SHARP, Alfred James Frederick. b 30. Oak Hill Th Coll 62. **d** 64 **p** 65. C Hanley Road St Sav w St Paul *Lon* 64-68; P-in-c Leverton *Linc* 68-84; Chapl Pilgrim Hosp Boston 76-84; P-in-c Benington w Leverton *Linc* 84; V Ch Broughton w Boylestone amd Sutton on the Hill *Derby* 84-89; R Ch Broughton w Barton Blount, Boylestone etc 89-94; rtd 94. *14 Edgefield, Weston, Spalding PE12 6RQ* Tel (01406) 370376

SHARP, Canon Andrew Timothy. b 58. K Alfred's Coll Win BA79. Wycliffe Hall Ox 82. **d** 85 **p** 86. C Scarborough St Mary w Ch Ch and H Apostles *York* 85-89; C Luton St Fran *St Alb* 89-90; V 90-98; P-in-c Guernsey St Jo *Win* 98-01; V from 01; Vice-Dean Guernsey from 01; Hon Can Win Cathl from 11. *St John's Vicarage, Les Amballes, St Peter Port, Guernsey GY1 1WY* Tel and fax (01481) 720879

SHARP, Mrs Barbara Elaine. b 52. Open Univ BA84. Ripon Coll Cuddesdon 01. **d** 03. C Timperley *Ches* 03-06; P-in-c Lostock Gralam from 06. *The Vicarage, Station Road, Lostock Gralam, Northwich CW9 7PS* Tel (01606) 43477 E-mail barbara@sharp6152.fsnet.co.uk

SHARP, Brian Phillip. b 48. Cant Sch of Min 85. **d** 88 **p** 89. C S Ashford Ch Ch *Cant* 88-92; C St Laur in Thanet 92-96; V Margate St Jo from 96; P-in-c Margate All SS from 09. *The Vicarage, 24 St Peter's Road, Margate CT9 1TH* Tel (01843) 230766 or 223144 E-mail vicarpfstjohns@yahoo.co.uk

SHARP, Canon David Malcolm. b 33. Hertf Coll Ox BA56 MA59. Cuddesdon Coll 56. **d** 58 **p** 59. C Bris St Mary Redcliffe w Temple 58-65; V Henleaze 65-75; V Nor St Pet Mancroft 75-82; R Nor St Pet Mancroft w St Jo Maddermarket 82-98; Hon Can Nor Cathl 86-98; Dioc Eur Contact 91-09; rtd 98; Perm to Offic Nor from 98. *The Pines, Field Lane, Fakenham NR21 9QX* Tel (01328) 864121 E-mail dmsharp22@btinternet.com

SHARP, Harold. b 41. JP90. FCCA76. CITC 03. **d** 06 **p** 07. Aux Min Larne and Inver *Conn* from 06; Aux Min Glynn w Raloo from 06. *110 Dreen Road, Cullybackey, Ballymena BT42 1EE* Tel (028) 2588 0461 E-mail sharpharold@aol.com

SHARP, Mrs Hazel Patricia. b 39. Qu Eliz Coll Lon BSc61. SWMTC 05. **d** 06 **p** 07. NSM St Merryn and St Issey w St Petroc Minor *Truro* 06-09; rtd 09. *The Coppice, Vicarage Gardens, St Issey, Wadebridge PL27 7QB* Tel (01841) 540334 E-mail hh.psharp@btinternet.com

SHARP, Mrs Heather Karin. b 48. **d** 04 **p** 05. OLM Blackrod *Man* 04-10; Perm to Offic from 10. *27 Hill Lane, Blackrod, Bolton BL6 5JW* Tel (01204) 693609 E-mail heatherksharp@hotmail.com

SHARP, James Michael. b 65. **d** 11. C Southbourne St Kath *Win* from 11. *1 Gervis Road, Bournemouth BH1 3ED* Tel (01202) 293933 E-mail sharpcity@gmail.com

SHARP (née BROWN), Mrs Jane Madeline. b 54. **d** 97 **p** 98. C Aylestone St Andr w St Jas *Leic* 97-00; NSM Knighton St Mary Magd 00-08; NSM Leic St Jas from 08. *10 St Mary's Road, Leicester LE2 1XA* Tel 0116-270 6002 E-mail a.sharp53@ntlworld.com

SHARP, Mrs Janice Anne. b 54. Aston Tr Scheme 91 NOC 93. **d** 96 **p** 97. C Skipton H Trin *Bradf* 96-00; V But!ershaw St Paul 00-02; Chapl Hull and E Yorks Hosps NHS Trust from 02; Hon C Patrington w Hollym, Welwick and Winestead *York* from 07. *The Hull Royal Infirmary, Anlaby Road, Hull HU3 2JZ* Tel (01482) 328541

SHARP, Nicholas Leonard. b 64. Grey Coll Dur BA85. St Jo Coll Nottm MA95. **d** 95 **p** 96. C Oakwood St Thos *Lon* 95-99; TV N Farnborough *Guildf* 99-05; Chapl Farnborough Sixth Form Coll 01-05; P-in-c Lt Amwell *St Alb* 05-08; TV Hertford from 08. *The Vicarage, 17 Barclay Close, Hertford Heath, Hertford SG13 7RW* Tel (01992) 589140 E-mail nick.sharp@xalt.co.uk

SHARP, Philip Paul Clayton. b 66. Open Univ BSc97. Trin Coll Bris 04. **d** 06 **p** 07. C Liskeard and St Keyne *Truro* from 06. *The New Vicarage, Maddever Crescent, Liskeard PL14 3PT* Tel (01579) 347145

SHARP, Preb Robert. b 36. FLCM58. St Aid Birkenhead 64. **d** 67 **p** 68. C Shipley St Paul *Bradf* 67-70; C-in-c Thwaites Brow CD 70-74; V Thwaites Brow 74-77; P-in-c Alberbury w Cardeston *Heref* 77-78; V 78-87; V Ford 77-87; V Claverley w Tuckhill 87-97; RD Bridgnorth 89-96; Preb Heref Cathl 91-97; rtd 97; Perm to Offic *Heref* 97-99 and from 01; C Stoke Lacy, Moreton Jeffries w Much Cowarne etc 99-00. *62 Biddulph Way, Ledbury HR8 2HN* Tel (01531) 631972

SHARP, Miss Sarah Elizabeth. b 67. Bp Otter Coll Chich BA89 Anglia Poly Univ MA00 Coll of Ripon & York St Jo PGCE90. Westcott Ho Cam 98. **d** 00 **p** 01. C Ross *Heref* 00-03; R Lower Windrush *Ox* from 03. *The Rectory, Main Road, Stanton Harcourt, Witney OX29 5RP* Tel (01865) 880249 E-mail s550sharp@btinternet.com

SHARPE, Canon Bruce Warrington. b 41. JP88. Ely Th Coll 62 St Steph Ho Ox 64. **d** 65 **p** 66. C Streatham St Pet *S'wark* 65-67; C Castries St Lucia 67-68; Hon C Leic St Matt and St Geo 68-69; Hon C Catford St Laur *S'wark* 69-70; Hon C Deptford St Paul 70-75; Hon C Lamorbey H Redeemer *Roch* 76-83; Hon C Sidcup St Andr 88-99; Locum Chapl Morden Coll Blackheath 98-08; Perm to Offic *Roch* 83-88 and 99-01; *Lon* 97-06; *S'wark* 98-11; *Ex* from 09; Hon C Bickley *Roch* 01-11; Hon Can Windward Is from 01. *3 Taddyforde Court Mansions, New North Road, Exeter EX4 4AS* Tel (01392) 277706 E-mail canonbruce1@aol.com

SHARPE, Cecil Frederick. b 23. Edin Th Coll 52. **d** 54 **p** 55. C Falkirk *Edin* 54-56; C Kings Norton *Birm* 56-58; V Withall 58-80; Perm to Offic from 80; rtd 88. *clo R J S Palmer Esq, 5 Belton Close, Hockley Heath, Solihull B94 6QU*

SHARPE, David Francis. b 32. Ex Coll Ox BA56 MA59. St Steph Ho Ox 57. **d** 60 **p** 61. C Hunslet St Mary and Stourton *Ripon* 60-63; C Notting Hill St Jo *Lon* 63-68; V Haggerston St Mary w St Chad 68-78; P-in-c Haggerston St Aug w St Steph 73-78; V Haggerston St Chad 78-83; V Mill Hill St Mich 83-98; rtd 98; Chapl St Raphaël *Eur* 98-02; Perm to Offic *Lon* 02-09. *10 Up The Quadrangle, Morden College, London SE3 0PW* Tel (020) 8853 5104 E-mail davidsharpe32@waitrose.com

SHARPE, Derek Martin Brereton (Pip). b 29. Birkbeck Coll Lon BA60. NEOC 90. **d** 90 **p** 91. NSM Scarborough St Luke *York* 90-92; Asst Chapl Scarborough Distr Hosp 90-92; P-in-c Sherburn and W and E Heslerton w Yedingham *York* 92-99; Hon C Buckrose Carrs 99; rtd 99; Perm to Offic *York* from 00. *Byland Lodge, 68A Low Moorgate, Rillington, Malton YO17 8JW* Tel (01723) 759063

SHARPE, Gerard John. b 23. Westcott Ho Cam. **d** 64 **p** 65. C Thetford St Cuth w H Trin *Nor* 64-70; V Holme *Ely* 70-76; R Conington 70-76; V Holme w Conington 76-93; R Glatton 74-93; RD Yaxley 82-88; rtd 93; Perm to Offic *Ely* 93-00. *24 St Margaret's Road, Girton, Cambridge CB3 0LT* Tel (01223) 574246

SHARPE, Miss Joan Valerie. b 33. EMMTC 73. dss 84 **d** 88 **p** 94. Hon Par Dn Warsop *S'well* 88-94; Hon C 94-98; rtd 98; Perm to Offic *S'well* from 04. *1 Forest Court, Eakring Road, Mansfield NG18 3DP* Tel (01623) 424051

SHARPE, Canon John Edward. b 50. St Jo Coll Dur BSc72. Cranmer Hall Dur 73. **d** 76 **p** 77. C Woodford Wells *Chelmsf* 76-79; C Ealing St Mary *Lon* 79-83; Min Walsall St Martin *Lich* 83-87; TV Walsall 87-96; R Glenfield *Leic* from 96; AD Sparkenhoe E 03-11; Hon Can Leic Cathl from 10. *The Rectory, Main Street, Glenfield, Leicester LE3 8DG* Tel 0116-287 1604 E-mail jesharpe@leicester.anglican.org

SHARPE, The Ven Kenneth William. b 40. Univ of Wales (Lamp) BA61. Sarum Th Coll 61. d 63 p 64. C Hubberston St D 63-71; TV Cwmbran Mon 71-74; Dioc Children's Adv 72-82; Dioc Youth Chapl 74-82; V Dingestow and Llangovan w Penyclawdd and Tregaer 74-82; V Newport St Mark 82-97; Chapl Alltyryn Hosp Gwent 83-97; RD Newport Mon 93-97; Can St Woolos Cathl 94-08; Adn Newport 97-08; rtd 08. 27 Incline Way, Saundersfoot SA69 9LX Tel (01834) 813674

SHARPE, Mrs Margaret Joy. b 43. Qu Coll Birm. d 09 p 10. OLM Bilton Cov from 09. 60 Cymbeline Way, Bilton, Rugby CV22 6LA Tel (01788) 810794

SHARPE, Mrs Margaret Theresa. b 48. Man Univ BEd70. Cranmer Hall Dur 72 WMMTC 90. d 91 p 94. C W Bromwich H Trin Lich 91-96; Asst Chapl Glenfield Hosp NHS Trust Leic 96-99; Chapl 99-00; Chapl Univ Hosps Leic NHS Trust 00-04; Chapl Team Ldr from 04. Chaplains' Department, Glenfield Hospital, Groby Road, Leicester LE3 9QP Tel 0116-256 3413 or 287 1604 E-mail margaret.sharpe@uhl-tr.nhs.uk

SHARPE, Miss Mary. b 31. CQSW71. Dalton Ho Bris 58. dss 78 d 87 p 94. Upton (Overchurch) Ches 78-83; Harlescott Lich 83-84; New Brighton All SS Ches 85-89; Par Dn 87-89; rtd 89; Perm to Offic Ches from 89. 20 Winstanley Road, Little Neston, Neston CH64 0UZ

SHARPE, Mrs Mary Primrose. b 22. Coll of St Matthias Bris CertEd55. Gilmore Ho 51. dss 81 d 87. Coley Wakef 81-89; Hon Par Dn 87-89; rtd 89; Perm to Offic Bradf 89-99. 54 Bradford Road, Menston, Ilkley LS29 6BX Tel (01943) 877710

SHARPE, Peter Richard. b 55. Salford Univ BSc76 ACIB81. STETS 98. d 01 p 02. C Fx St Jas 01-04; R S Hill w Callington Truro from 04; C St Ive and Pensilva w Quethiock from 09; P-in-c Linkinhorne from 10; P-in-c Stoke Climsland from 10; RD E Wivelshire from 11. The Rectory, Liskeard Road, Callington PL17 7JD Tel (01579) 383341 Mobile 07767-251136 E-mail prshome@clara.net

SHARPE, Pip. See SHARPE, Derek Martin Brereton

SHARPE, Richard Gordon. b 48. Birm Univ BA69. St Jo Coll Nottm BA74. d 75 p 76. C Hinckley H Trin Leic 75-78; C Kingston upon Hull H Trin York 78-85; Chapl Marston Green Hosp Birm 85-88; Chapl Chelmsley Hosp Birm 86-88; TV Chelmsley Wood Birm 85-88; P-in-c Dosthill 88-93; V 93-97; R Desford and Peckleton w Tooley Leic from 97. The Rectory, 27 Church Lane, Desford, Leicester LE9 9GD Tel (01455) 822276 E-mail sharpeblackhorse@aol.com

SHARPE, Canon Roger. b 35. TCD BA60 MA63. Qu Coll Birm 60. d 62 p 63. C Stockton H Trin Dur 62-64; C Oakdale St Geo Sarum 64-68; V Redlynch and Morgan's Vale 68-86; RD Alderbury 82-86; V Warminster St Denys 86-88; R Upton Scudamore 86-88; V Horningsham 86-88; R Warminster St Denys, Upton Scudamore etc 88-95; Can and Preb Sarum Cathl 89-00; RD Heytesbury 89-95; Chmn Dioc Assn for Deaf from 91; P-in-c Corsley 92-95; TR Cley Hill Warminster 95-00; rtd 00; Perm to Offic Sarum from 01. Woodside, Bugmore Lane, East Grimstead SP5 3SA Tel (01722) 712753

SHARPE, William Wilberforce. b 62. d 05 p 06. NSM Brixton St Matt w St Jude S'wark 05-10; NSM Tulse Hill H Trin and St Matthias from 10; Chapl Guy's and St Thos' NHS Foundn Trust from 08. 1D Lovelace Road, London SE21 8JY Tel and fax (020) 8761 8539 Mobile 07956-546394 E-mail sharpeww@aol.com

SHARPLES, Canon Alfred Cyril. b 09. Man Univ BA33. Linc Th Coll 33. d 35 p 36. C Rochdale Man 35-39; C Ashton St Mich 39-42; R Cheetham St Mark 42-46; V Tonge w Alkrington 46-51; V Hope St Jas 51-76; Hon Can Man Cathl 74-76; rtd 76; Perm to Offic Ches from 77 and Man 77-08. 30 Greenbank Drive, Bollington, Macclesfield SK10 5LW Tel 0161-207 5073

SHARPLES, Angela (Ella). b 65. d 07 p 08. C Timperley Ches 07-09; C Congleton 09-11. The Rectory, Astbury, Congleton CW12 4RQ Tel (01260) 272625 E-mail ella_sharples@hotmail.com

SHARPLES, David. b 41. Linc Th Coll 71. d 73 p 74. C Reddish Man 73-75; C Prestwich St Mary 76-78; V Ashton St Jas 78-86; V Hope St Jas 86-06; rtd 06; Perm to Offic Man 06-08. 18 Holly Avenue, Worsley, Manchester M28 3DW Tel 0161-950 8675

SHARPLES, The Ven David John. b 58. Lon Univ BD81 AKC81. Coll of Resurr Mirfield. d 82 p 83. C Prestwich St Mary Man 82-87; V Royton St Anne 87-02; AD Tandle 94-02; Dir of Ords from 02; Hon Can Man Cathl from 06; Adn Salford from 09. 2 The Walled Gardens, Swinton, Manchester M27 0FR Tel 0161-794 2401 Fax 794 2411 E-mail ddo@bishopscourt.manchester.anglican.org

SHARPLES, Derek. b 35. SS Paul & Mary Coll Cheltenham CertEd57 Liv Univ DipEd63 Man Univ MEd66 Bath Univ PhD72 Open Univ BA79 FCollP86. WMMTC 83. d 86 p 87. NSM Malvern H Trin and St Jas Worc 86-90; C St Jo in Bedwardine 90-92; R Belbroughton w Fairfield and Clent 92-00; rtd 00; Perm to Offic Worc from 00. Witton, 16 Moorlands Road, Malvern WR14 1VA Tel (01684) 575742 E-mail witton@clara.co.uk

SHARPLES, Ella. See SHARPLES, Angela

SHARPLES, Jean. See ROLT, Mrs Jean

SHARPLES, Jonathan David. b 65. Lon Bible Coll BA95. Wycliffe Hall Ox 03. d 05 p 06. C Ashton-upon-Mersey St Mary Magd Ches 05-09; R Astbury and Smallwood from 09. The Rectory, Astbury, Congleton CW12 4RQ Tel (01260) 272625 E-mail jonsharples@hotmail.com

SHARPLEY, The Ven Roger Ernest Dion. b 28. Ch Ch Ox BA52 MA56. St Steph Ho Ox 52. d 54 p 55. C Southwick St Columba Dur 54-60; V Middlesbrough All SS York 60-81; P-in-c Middlesbrough St Hilda w St Pet 64-72; P-in-c Middlesbrough St Aid 79; V 79-81; RD Middlesbrough 70-81; Can and Preb York Minster 74-81; V St Andr Holborn Lon 81-92; Adn Hackney 81-92; rtd 92; Perm to Offic Dur from 92; Chapl Grey Coll Dur 96-01. 2 Hill Meadows, High Shincliffe, Durham DH1 2PE Tel 0191-386 1908

SHAVE, Neil Christopher. b 82. Bris Univ MSc05 Clare Coll Cam BA09. Westcott Ho Cam 07. d 10 p 11. C Prestwich St Marg Man from 10. 8 Kenyon Lane, Prestwich, Manchester M25 1HY Tel 0161-773 6021 Mobile 07828-190206 E-mail neil_shave@yahoo.co.uk

SHAVE, Norman Rossen. b 60. G&C Coll Cam BA82 MA95 Newc Univ MB, BS85 MRCGP90. Cranmer Hall Dur 98. d 00 p 01. C Preston on Tees Dur 00-03; C Preston-on-Tees and Longnewton 03-04; V Norton St Mary from 04; P-in-c Stockton St Chad from 04. 2 Brambling Close, Norton, Stockton-on-Tees TS20 1TX Tel (01642) 558888

SHAW, Alan Taylor. b 52. Sarum & Wells Th Coll 88. d 90 p 91. C Beeston Ripon 90-93; C Stanningley St Thos 93-96; TV Seacroft 96-98; V Ryhill Wakef 98-02; rtd 03; Perm to Offic Wakef from 04. 65 Hollingthorpe Avenue, Hall Green, Wakefield WF4 3NP Tel (01924) 255210

SHAW, Alan Walter. b 41. TCD BA63 BAI63 Chu Coll Cam MSc66. d 94 p 95. NSM Drumcliffe w Kilnasoolagh L & K 94-97; NSM Kenmare w Sneem, Waterville etc 97-09; Can Limerick Cathl 07-09; rtd 09. 22 Ceann Mara Court, Pairc na Gloine, Kenmare, Co Kerry, Republic of Ireland Tel (00353) 87-678 8700 (mobile) E-mail shawa@eircom.net

✠SHAW, The Rt Revd Alexander Martin. b 44. AKC67. d 68 p 69 c 04. C Glas St Oswald 68-70; C Edin Old St Paul 70-75; Chapl K Coll Cam 75-77; C St Marylebone All SS Lon 77-78; R Dunoon Arg 78-81; Succ Ex Cathl 81-83; Dioc Miss and Ecum Officer 83-89; TV Cen Ex 83-87; Can Res St E Cathl 89-04; Prec 96-04; Bp Arg 04-09; rtd 09; Hon Asst Bp Ex from 10. 11 Russell Terrace, Exeter EX4 4HX Tel (01392) 663511 Mobile 07801-549615 E-mail alexandermartin.shaw@virgin.net

SHAW, Mrs Alison Barbara. b 55. Open Univ BA92. SWMTC 98. d 01 p 02. NSM St Breoke and Egloshayle Truro 01-03; C Bodmin w Lanhydrock and Lanivet 03-05; TV 05-10; P-in-c Devonport St Boniface and St Phil Ex from 10. The Vicarage, 1 Normandy Way, Plymouth PL5 1SW Tel (01752) 369140 E-mail alishaw2001@yahoo.co.uk

SHAW, Alison Ruth. b 66. RGN86. SNWTP 08. d 11. C Ormskirk Liv from 11. 2 Greenfield Road, Scarisbrick, Southport PR8 5LX Tel (01704) 888993 Mobile 07757-978041 E-mail revali.shaw@gmail.com

SHAW, Andrew James. b 54. York Univ MA97 Cumbria Univ BA10. LCTP 07. d 10 p 11. NSM Fleetwood St Dav Blackb from 10; NSM Fleetwood St Pet from 10. 5 Taywood Road, Thornton-Cleveleys FY5 2RT Tel (01253) 852209 Mobile 07876-571978 E-mail shaw-family@tiscali.co.uk

SHAW, Andrew Jonathan. b 50. Wycliffe Hall Ox 85. d 87 p 88. C Witton w Brundall and Braydeston Nor 87-89; C Brundall w Braydeston and Postwick 89-90; C Grayswood Guildf 90-91; P-in-c 91-99; Chapl RN Sch Haslemere 90-96; V Hendon St Paul Mill Hill Lon from 99. St Paul's Vicarage, Hammers Lane, London NW7 4EA Tel (020) 8959 1856 or tel and fax 8906 3793 E-mail parishoffice@stpaulsmillhill.freeserve.co.uk

SHAW, Ms Anne Lesley. b 50. SRN SCM. Linc Th Coll 77. dss 80 d 87 p 94. Camberwell St Luke S'wark 80-85; Chapl Asst Lon Hosp (Whitechapel) 85-90; Chapl Lewisham Hosp 90-94; Chapl Hither Green Hosp 90-94; Chapl Sydenham Childrens' Hosp 90-94; Chapl Lewisham Hosp NHS Trust 94-10; rtd 10. 54 Nutcroft Road, London SE15 1AF Tel (020) 7639 4031 E-mail shawpowell@hotmail.co.uk

SHAW, Anne Patricia Leslie. b 39. MB, BS63 MRCS63 LRCP63. Qu Coll Birm 79. dss 81 d 87 p 94. Pinner Lon 81-84; Rickmansworth St Alb 84-09; NSM 87-09; rtd 09; Perm to Offic St Alb from 09. 37 Sandy Lodge Road, Moor Park, Rickmansworth WD3 1LP Tel (01923) 827663 E-mail anneshaw@doctors.net.uk

SHAW, Anthony Keeble. b 36. K Alfred's Coll Win CertEd60 Birkbeck Coll Lon CPsychol98. SWMTC 78. d 81 p 82. Hd Teacher Wolborough C of E Primary Sch 73-87; NSM E Teignmouth Ex 81-83; NSM Highweek and Teigngrace 83-87; Sub Chapl HM Pris Channings Wood 85-87; C Southbourne St Kath Win 87-89; Teaching 89-96; NSM Regent's Park St Mark Lon 93-96; P-in-c Winthorpe and Langford w Holme S'well 96-01; Dioc Chief Insp of Schs 96-01; rtd 01; Perm to Offic

Win from 01. *Manlea Cottage, Centre Lane, Everton, Lymington SO41 0JP* Tel (01590) 645451

SHAW, Clive Ronald. b 54. UEA BA75 Hatf Coll Dur PGCE76. CBDTI 99. **d** 02 **p** 03. C Westfield St Mary *Carl* 02-06; V Aspatria w Hayton and Gilcrux from 06. *St Kentigern's Vicarage, King Street, Aspatria, Wigton CA7 3AL* Tel (01697) 320398 E-mail c.shaw@rowan1.fslife.co.uk

SHAW, David George. b 40. Lon Univ BD64 MA03. Tyndale Hall Bris 58. **d** 65 **p** 66. C Kirkdale St Lawr *Liv* 65-68; C Bebington *Ches* 68-70; V Swadlincote *Derby* 70-75; R Eyam 75-04; rtd 04. *86 Higher Street, Okeford Fitzpaine, Blandford Forum DT11 0RQ* Tel (01258) 860571

SHAW, David Michael. b 61. Univ Coll Dur BA83 Bris Univ BA97. Trin Coll Bris 91. **d** 93 **p** 94. C Wotton-under-Edge w Ozleworth and N Nibley *Glouc* 93-97; P-in-c Jersey St Clem *Win* 97-98; R from 98. *The Rectory, La rue du Presbytere, St Clement, Jersey JE2 6RB* Tel (01534) 851992 E-mail st.clement@jerseymail.co.uk

SHAW, David Parlane. b 32. CITC. **d** 69 **p** 70. Bp's C Lower w Upper Langfield *D & R* 69-75; R Chedburgh w Depden and Rede *St E* 75-78; R Chedburgh w Depden, Rede and Hawkedon 79-82; R Desford *Leic* 82-83; R Desford and Peckleton w Tooley 84-91; P-in-c Ramsden Crays w Ramsden Bellhouse *Chelmsf* 91-95; rtd 95; Perm to Offic *Leic* from 95. *9 Hambleton Close, Leicester Forest East, Leicester LE3 3NA* Tel 0116-224 6507 E-mail david.shaw15@ntlworld.com

SHAW, David Thomas. b 45. Open Univ BA78. WMMTC 87. **d** 90 **p** 91. C Sheldon *Birm* 90-93; R Chelmsley Wood 93-02; TR Broughton Astley and Croft w Stoney Stanton *Leic* 02-10; rtd 10. *39 Orchard Way, Stretton on Dunsmore, Rugby CV23 9HP* Tel (024) 7654 2036 E-mail davidshaw139@btinternet.com

SHAW, Dennis Alfred Arthur. b 24. Wells Th Coll 64. **d** 65 **p** 66. C Redditch St Steph *Worc* 65-70; R Addingham *Bradf* 70-92; rtd 92; Perm to Offic *Bradf* from 92. *67 Crowther Avenue, Calverley, Pudsey LS28 5SA* Tel (01274) 611454

SHAW, Mrs Felicity Mary. b 46. UEA BSc67 MSc68. NOC 88. **d** 91 **p** 94. Par Dn Benchill *Man* 91-94; C 94-95; TV E Farnworth and Kearsley 95-98; TR 98-03; V Woodhall *Bradf* 03-07; rtd 07; Perm to Offic *Man* from 08. *99 Pennine Road, Horwich, Bolton BL6 7HW* Tel (01204) 696851 E-mail rev.fmshaw@tesco.net

SHAW, Gerald Oliver. b 32. K Coll Lon 56. **d** 60 **p** 61. C Burnley St Cuth *Blackb* 60-62; C Heysham 62-65; C-in-c Oswaldtwistle All SS CD 65-66; V Oswaldtwistle All SS 66-69; Chapl Leavesden Hosp Abbots Langley 69-75; Chapl Broadmoor Hosp Crowthorne 75-88; C Easthampstead *Ox* 88-92; P-in-c Beech Hill, Grazeley and Spencers Wood 92-97; rtd 97; Lic to Offic *Ox* from 99; Perm to Offic *Win* from 02. *1 Mortimer House Cottage, Mortimer Lane, Mortimer, Reading RG7 3PR* Tel 0118-933 3660

SHAW, Graham. b 44. Worc Coll Ox BA65. Cuddesdon Coll. **d** 69 **p** 70. C Esher *Guildf* 69-73; R Winford *B & W* 73-78; Chapl Ex Coll Ox 78-85; R Farnborough *Roch* 88-95; rtd 04. *21 Oliver Court, Albany Park Road, Kingston upon Thames KT2 5SS*

SHAW, Graham Lister. b 81. Fitzw Coll Cam BA04. Wycliffe Hall Ox 05. **d** 07 **p** 08. C Camberley St Paul *Guildf* from 07. *Cornerways, 3 Upper Gordon Road, Camberley GU15 2HJ* Tel (01276) 700210 E-mail glshaw@gmail.com

SHAW, Canon Grahame David. b 44. Lich Th Coll 65. **d** 68 **p** 69. C Grange St Andr *Ches* 68-73; TV E Runcorn w Halton 73-74; TV Thamesmead *S'wark* 74-79; V Newington St Paul from 79; S'wark Adnry Ecum Officer from 90; RD S'wark from 07. *The Vicarage, Lorrimore Square, London SE17 3QU* Tel (020) 7735 2947 or 7735 3506 E-mail grahame@leat.org.uk

SHAW, Mrs Irene. b 45. Gilmore Course 80 NEOC 82. **dss** 83 **d** 87 **p** 94. Elloughton and Brough w Brantingham *York* 83-86; Westborough *Guildf* 86-88; C 87-88; C Shottermill 88-91; C Lamorbey H Redeemer *Roch* 91-97; V Belvedere All SS 97-02; TV Em TM *Wakef* 02-05; rtd 05; Perm to Offic *York* from 07. *10 Rowan Avenue, Beverley HU17 9UN* Tel (01482) 871005

SHAW, The Very Revd Jane Alison. b 63. Ox Univ BA85 MA91 Harvard Div Sch MDiv88 Univ of California Berkeley PhD94. SAOMC 96. **d** 97 **p** 98. Fell Regent's Park Coll Ox 94-01; Dean 98-01; Hon Cathl Chapl Ch Ch Ox 00-10; Fell, Chapl and Dean of Div New Coll Ox 01-10; NSM Ox St Mary V w St Cross and St Pet 97-01; Hon Can Ch Ch 05-10; Can Th Sarum Cathl 07-10; Dean Grace Cathl San Francisco USA from 10. *Grace Cathedral, 1100 California Street, San Francisco CA 94108, USA* Tel (001) (415) 749 6321 E-mail janes@gracecathedral.org

SHAW, Miss Jane Elizabeth. b 47. New Hall Cam BA68 MA72 Brunel Univ MPhil79. NEOC 98. **d** 01 **p** 02. NSM Moor Allerton *Ripon* 01-05; Chapl Bp Rocky Chpl Raiwind Pakistan from 06. *Diocese of Raiwind, 17 Warris Road, Lahore, Pakistan* E-mail shawjane2005@yahoo.co.uk

SHAW, Mrs Jane Louise Claridge. b 66. Birm Poly BA87. WMMTC 00. **d** 03 **p** 04. C Longbridge *Birm* 03-07; V Dosthill from 07. *The Vicarage, 1 Church Road, Dosthill, Tamworth B77 1LU* Tel (01827) 281349 E-mail louiseshaw6@yahoo.co.uk

SHAW, Mrs Janet Elaine. b 53. EMMTC 94. **d** 97 **p** 98. C Cleveleys *Blackb* 97-01; P-in-c Blackpool St Paul 01-03; V from

03. *St Paul's Vicarage, 253 Warbreck Hill Road, Blackpool FY2 0SP* Tel (01253) 350007 E-mail mail@vicstp.fsnet.co.uk

SHAW, Mrs Jayne. St Mich Coll Llan. **d** 08 **p** 09. NSM Tonyrefail w Gilfach Goch *Llan* from 08. *11 Portreeve Close, Llantrisant, Pontyclun CF72 8DU* Tel (01443) 238356

SHAW, John Boyde. b 52. St Jo Coll Nottm BA00. **d** 00 **p** 01. C Gorleston St Andr *Nor* 00-04; P-in-c Rockland St Mary w Hellington, Bramerton etc 04-06; R from 06. *The Rectory, 2 Rectory Lane, Rockland St Mary, Norwich NR14 7EY* Tel (01508) 538619 E-mail revjohnshaw@gmail.com

SHAW, Jonathan. *See* SHAW, Andrew Jonathan

SHAW, Keith Arthur. b 51. **d** 10 **p** 11. NSM Baswich *Lich* from 10; Chapl S Staffs Healthcare NHS Trust from 10. *3 Newhall Gardens, Cannock Road, Cannock WS11 5EA* Tel (01543) 572255 E-mail keith.shaw@sssft.nhs.uk

SHAW, Kenneth James. b 36. St Jo Coll Nottm 85 Edin Th Coll 88. **d** 87 **p** 89. NSM Troon *Glas* 87-89; C Glas St Mary 89-90; R Lenzie 90-01; Warden of Readers 96-01; rtd 01; Hon C Glas St Mary 02-06. *19 Mailerbeg Gardens, Moodiesburn, Glasgow G69 0JP* Tel (01236) 873987 E-mail ken@kjshaw.fsnet.co.uk

SHAW, Louise. *See* SHAW, Mrs Jane Louise Claridge

SHAW, Malcolm. b 46. Trin Coll Bris. **d** 01 **p** 02. C Bolsover *Derby* 01-05; R Brimington 05-10; P-in-c Chelford w Lower Withington *Ches* from 10. *The New Vicarage, Chelford, Macclesfield SK11 9AH* Tel (01625) 861231 Mobile 07713-624005 E-mail malcolmshaw238@btinternet.com

SHAW, Malcolm Roy. b 47. Lon Univ BA69 CQSW76. NEOC 03. **d** 05 **p** 06. NSM Hunmanby w Muston *York* 05-08; NSM Rufforth w Moor Monkton and Hessay from 08; NSM Long Marston from 08; NSM Healaugh w Wighill, Bilbrough and Askham Richard from 08; NSM Tockwith and Bilton w Bickerton from 08. *32 Westfield Road, Tockwith, York YO26 7PY* Tel (01423) 359003 E-mail revroytockwith@btinternet.com

SHAW, Mrs Margaret Ann. b 58. Bp Otter Coll Chich BA80 SS Paul & Mary Coll Cheltenham PGCE81. EAMTC 00. **d** 03 **p** 04. C Langdon Hills *Chelmsf* 03-06; TV Basildon St Andr w H Cross from 06; RD Basildon from 10. *St Andrew's Vicarage, 3 The Fremnells, Basildon SS14 2QX* Tel (01268) 520516 E-mail sh.ma@btinternet.com

SHAW, Martin. *See* SHAW, The Rt Revd Alexander Martin

SHAW, Michael. *See* SHAW, Ralph Michael

SHAW, Michael Howard. b 38. Leeds Univ BSc61. Linc Th Coll 64. **d** 66 **p** 67. C W Hartlepool St Paul *Dur* 66-68; Asst Master Stockbridge Co Sec Sch 68; Totton Coll 69; Gravesend Boys' Gr Sch 70-72; Maidstone Gr Sch 72-94; Perm to Offic *Cant* and *Roch* from 70; rtd 03. *2 Bredgar Close, Maidstone ME14 5NG* Tel (01622) 673415

SHAW, Neil Graham. b 61. St Jo Coll Nottm 89. **d** 91 **p** 92. C Leamington Priors St Paul *Cov* 91-95; TV Bestwood *S'well* 95-99; Chapl HM YOI Thorn Cross 99-01; Chapl HM Pris Hindley 01-07; Chapl HM Pris Liv from 07. *HM Prison Liverpool, 68 Hornby Road, Liverpool L9 3DF* Tel 0151-530 4127

SHAW, Norman. b 33. Cranmer Hall Dur. **d** 82 **p** 83. C Beamish *Dur* 82-84; P-in-c Craghead 84-88; V Cleadon 88-98; rtd 98. *3 St Mary's Drive, Sherburn Village, Durham DH6 1RL* Tel 0191-372 2540 E-mail normandcon@aol.com

SHAW, Peter Anthony. b 49. **d** 10 **p** 11. NSM Burwash *Chich* from 10. *3 Rother View, Church Lane, Etchingham TN19 7AS*

SHAW, Peter Hawksworth. Qu Coll Birm BA39 MA65. Worc Ord Coll 65. **d** 67 **p** 68. C S Kensington St Jude *Lon* 67-69; V Alderney *Win* 69-78; V Disley *Ches* 78-82; rtd 82; Chapl Athens w Kifissia, Patras and Corfu *Eur* 82-85; Hon C Las Palmas 84-85; Hon C Breamore *Win* 85-89; Perm to Offic *Pet* from 07. *24 Hanover Court, Dulverton TA22 9HZ* Tel (01398) 323740

SHAW, Ralph. b 38. Man Univ MEd70. Sarum & Wells Th Coll 78. **d** 80 **p** 81. C Consett *Dur* 80-84; P-in-c Tanfield 84-88; V 88-97; R S Shields St Aid and St Steph 97-05; rtd 05. *10 Shipley Court, Gateshead NE8 4EZ* Tel 0191-420 5137

SHAW, Ralph Michael. b 46. DipAdEd. Lich Th Coll 68. **d** 70 **p** 71. C Dewsbury All SS *Wakef* 70-75; TV Redcar w Kirkleatham *York* 75-76; Dioc Youth Officer *St Alb* 76-91; Chief Exec Jo Grooms 91-08; Team Ldr Workplace Min *St Alb* 08-10; rtd 10; Perm to Offic *St Alb* from 10. *18 Wyton, Welwyn Garden City AL7 2PF* Tel (01707) 321813 E-mail revmshaw@yahoo.co.uk

SHAW, Richard. b 46. **d** 89 **p** 90. NSM Porchester *S'well* 89-91; NSM Daybrook 04-06; P-in-c Basford St Aid 06-11; P-in-c Basford St Leodegarius 09-11; V Basford St Leodegarius and St Aid from 11. *The Vicarage, 152 Perry Road, Nottingham NG5 1GL* Tel 0115-829 2369

SHAW, Preb Richard Tom. b 42. AKC69. St Aug Coll Cant 69. **d** 70 **p** 71. C Dunston St Nic *Dur* 70-73; C Maidstone All SS w St Phil and H Trin *Cant* 73-75; Chapl RN 75-79; V Barrow-on-Humber *Linc* 79-83; V Linc St Faith and St Martin w St Pet 83-91; V Clun w Bettws-y-Crwyn and Newcastle *Heref* 91-11; P-in-c Hopesay 98-11; rtd 11; RD Clun Forest *Heref* 94-05 and from 08; Preb Heref Cathl from 02. *The Vicarage, Vicarage Raod, Clun, Craven Arms SY7 8JG* Tel (01588) 640809 E-mail richard@rick-shaw.co.uk

SHAW, Robert Christopher. b 34. Man Univ BA BD. Union Th Sem (NY) STM. **d** 82 **p** 83. C Sharlston *Wakef* 82-83; C Scissett St Aug 83-85; R Cumberworth w Denby Dale 85-90; P-in-c Denby 85-90; R Bolton w Ireby and Uldale *Carl* 90-95; rtd 95; Perm to Offic *York* from 95. *Stonecroft, Sproxton, York YO62 5EF* Tel (01439) 770178

SHAW, Canon Robert William. b 46. Lon Univ BD69. St Aug Coll Cant 69. **d** 70 **p** 71. C Hunslet St Mary and Stourton *Ripon* 70-71; C Hunslet St Mary 71-74; C Hawksworth Wood 74-76; R Stanningley St Thos 76-84; V Potternewton 84-94; V Manston 94-02; P-in-c Beeston Hill H Spirit 02-04; P-in-c Hunslet Moor St Pet and St Cuth 02-04; V Beeston Hill and Hunslet Moor from 04; Hon Can Ripon Cathl from 08. *St Peter's Vicarage, 139 Dewsbury Road, Leeds LS11 5NW* Tel 0113-277 2464 E-mail bobshaw46@hotmail.co.uk

SHAW, Roderick Kenneth. b 37. MBIM77. Moray Ord Course 88. **d** 92 **p** 95. Hon C Grantown-on-Spey *Mor* 92-96; Hon C Rothiemurchus 92-00; P Companion Missr from 00. *The Cottage, Balliefurth, Grantown-on-Spey PH26 3NH* Tel (01479) 821496

SHAW, Mrs Rosemary Alice. b 44. CertEd65 CQSW78 Heythrop Coll Lon MA96 MA04. S'wark Ord Course 87. **d** 89 **p** 94. Par Dn Walworth *S'wark* 89-92; Par Dn E Dulwich St Jo 92-95; NSM 95-96; Eileen Kerr Mental Health Fell Maudsley Hosp 95-96; Chapl King's Healthcare NHS Trust 96-01; Sen Chapl Guy's and St Thos' NHS Foundn Trust 02-07; Hon C E Dulwich St Jo *S'wark* from 96. *19 Scutari Road, London SE22 0NN* Tel (020) 8693 6325 E-mail stjohnsenq33@black1.org.uk

SHAW, Roy. *See* SHAW, Malcolm Roy

SHAW, Stewart James. b 64. Wilson Carlile Coll 97 NTMTC BA07. **d** 07 **p** 08. C Hounslow H Trin w St Paul *Lon* 07-09; Chapl RAF from 09. *Chaplaincy Services, Valiant Block, HQ Air Command, RAF High Wycombe HP14 4UE* Tel (01494) 496800 Fax 496343 E-mail stewchaplain82@blueyonder.co.uk

SHAW, Wendy Jane. b 54. Shenstone Coll of Educn CertEd75 Man Univ MEd90. EAMTC 01. **d** 05 **p** 06. C Thurton *Nor* 05-08; Bp's Officer for Visual Arts from 08. *The Rectory, 2 Rectory Lane, Rockland St Mary, Norwich NR14 7EY* Tel (01508) 537045 Mobile 07830-306384 E-mail wendyjane.shaw@virgin.net

SHAYLER-WEBB, Peter. b 57. Bath Univ BSc81 BArch83. Ripon Coll Cuddesdon 93. **d** 95 **p** 96. C Bedford St Paul *St Alb* 95-99; C Dorking w Ranmore *Guildf* 99-04; R Sherwood Australia from 04. *PO Box 107, Sherwood Qld 4075, Australia* Tel (0061) (7) 3278 2498 *or* 3379 3437 Fax 3278 2048 E-mail psw5957@bigpond.net.au

SHEA, Martyn Paul Leathley. b 66. City Univ BSc89. Wycliffe Hall Ox. **d** 00 **p** 01. C Ches Square St Mich w St Phil *Lon* 00-03; C Stamford St Geo w St Paul *Linc* 03-08; P-in-c Jersey St Mark *Win* 08-10; V from 10. *The Vicarage, St Mark's Road, St Helier, Jersey JE2 4LY* Tel (01534) 720595 Mobile 07976-869467 E-mail martyn.shea@stmarksjersey.org

SHEAD, John Frederick Henry. b 38. ACP74 FCP81. Westcott Ho Cam 72. **d** 74 **p** 75. Hd Master Thaxted Co Primary Sch 70-85; Hon C Thaxted *Chelmsf* 74-85; C Saffron Walden w Wendens Ambo and Littlebury 86-88; P-in-c Wethersfield w Shalford 88-96; P-in-c Finchingfield and Cornish Hall End 94-96; V Finchingfield and Cornish Hall End etc 96-04; RD Braintree 95-00; rtd 04. *55 Kenworthy Road, Braintree CM7 1JJ* Tel (01376) 321783 E-mail j.shead@tiscali.co.uk

SHEARCROFT, Sister Elizabeth Marion. b 57. SRN76. **d** 94 **p** 95. CA from 84; NSM Margate H Trin *Cant* 94-98; Chapl Thanet Healthcare NHS Trust 94-98; Chapl E Kent Hosps NHS Trust 99-02; C Kendal H Trin *Carl* 02-05; V Streatham Immanuel and St Andr *S'wark* from 05. *Immanuel Vicarage, 51A Guildersfield Road, London SW16 5LS* Tel (020) 8764 5103 E-mail liz@thekingfishery.co.uk

SHEARD, Andrew Frank. b 60. York Univ BA81. St Jo Coll Nottm 92. **d** 94 **p** 95. C Uxbridge *Lon* 94-96; TV 96-99; P-in-c 99-01; TR from 01. *St Margaret's Vicarage, 72 Harefield Road, Uxbridge UB8 1PL* Tel (01895) 237853 *or* 258766 Fax 812194 E-mail andrewf.sheard@btinternet.com

SHEARD, Gillian Freda. *See* COOKE, Ms Gillian Freda

SHEARD, Preb Michael Rowland. b 42. K Coll Lon BA Man Univ PhD. **d** 95 **p** 95. World Miss Officer *Lich* 86-09; TV Willenhall H Trin *Lich* 95-09; Preb Lich Cathl 99-09; rtd 09. *9 Queen Street, Kirton Lindsey, Gainsborough DN21 4NS* Tel (01652) 648846 Mobile 07711-541983 E-mail michael.sheard@btinternet.com

SHEARER, John Frank. b 35. Ex Univ BSc60. Tyndale Hall Bris 62. **d** 63 **p** 64. C Blackheath St Jo *S'wark* 63-67; R Nuffield *Ox* 67-06; rtd 06. *Denbeigh Spring Gardens, Oak Street, Lechlade GL7 3AY* Tel (01367) 252806

SHEARING, Michael James. b 39. Lanc Univ BA71. Linc Th Coll. **d** 66 **p** 67. NSM Hartlepool St Paul *Dur* 66-76; Asst Master Dyke Ho Comp Sch Hartlepool 76-87; C Houghton le Spring 87; P-in-c Wheatley Hill 87-95; V Bishopwearmouth St Nic

95-97; R Cockfield and V Lynesack 97-04; rtd 04. *83 Welham Road, Norton, Malton YO17 9DS* Tel (01653) 694928

SHEARLOCK, The Very Revd David John. b 32. FRSA91 Birm Univ BA55. Westcott Ho Cam 56. **d** 57 **p** 58. C Guisborough *York* 57-60; C Christchurch *Win* 60-64; V Kingsclere 64-71; V Romsey 71-82; Dioc Dir of Ords 77-82; Hon Can Win Cathl 78-82; Dean Truro 82-97; R Truro St Mary 82-97; Chapl Cornwall Fire Brigade 91-97; rtd 98; Perm to Offic *Sarum* from 98. *3 The Tanyard, Shadrack Street, Beaminster DT8 3BG* Tel (01308) 863170

SHEARMAN, Michael Alan. b 22. Down Coll Cam BA44 MA48. Coll of Resurr Mirfield 46. **d** 48 **p** 49. C Bounds Green *Lon* 48-53; C Wembley Park St Aug 53-58; V Enfield St Luke 58-87; rtd 87; Perm to Offic *Nor* 87-02. *18 Thompson Avenue, Holt NR25 6EN* Tel (01263) 713072

SHEARN, Andrew William. b 43. Ex Univ BA65. WMMTC 04. **d** 06 **p** 07. NSM Wellesbourne *Cov* 06-09; NSM Studley from 10; NSM Spernall, Morton Bagot and Oldberrow from 10. *32 Birmingham Road, Alcester B49 5EP* Tel (01789) 763348 E-mail andy.shearn@hotmail.com

SHEARS, Canon Michael George Frederick. b 33. Pemb Coll Cam BA57 MA68. St Steph Ho Ox 57. **d** 59 **p** 60. C Grantham St Wulfram *Linc* 59-68; R Waltham 68-80; R Barnoldby le Beck 74-80; RD Haverstoe 78-80; V Soham *Ely* 80-99; RD Fordham 83-95; Hon Can Ely Cathl 94-99; rtd 99; Perm to Offic *Nor* from 00. *Woodcutter's Cottage, 19 High Street, Wicklewood, Wymondham NR18 9QE* Tel (01953) 605535

SHEATH, Allan Philip. b 48. MWMTC 04. **d** 98 **p** 99. NSM Tiverton St Pet and Chevithorne w Cove *Ex* 98-03; C Honiton, Gittisham, Combe Raleigh, Monkton etc 03-04; TV 04-11; rtd 11. *11 Fairfield, Sampford Peverell, Tiverton EX16 7DE* Tel (01884) 820136 E-mail allan.sheath@gmail.com

SHEDD, Mrs Christine Elizabeth. b 49. City of Birm Coll CertEd70 St Jo Coll York MA02. NOC 02. **d** 04 **p** 05. C Thornton St Jas *Bradf* 04-07; TV Oakenshaw, Wyke and Low Moor from 07; Warden of Readers from 09. *Holy Trinity Vicarage, Park House Road, Low Moor, Bradford BD12 0HR* Tel (01274) 678859 Mobile 07814-958919 E-mail c.shedd@btinternet.com

SHEDDEN, Mrs Valerie. b 56. Ripon Coll of Educn CertEd77. Cranmer Hall Dur 81. **dss** 84 **d** 87 **p** 94. Tudhoe Grange *Dur* 84-85; Whitworth w Spennymoor 85-91; Par Dn 87-91; Par Dn E Darlington 91-94; P-in-c Bishop Middleham 94-00; Dioc RE Adv 94-00; V Heworth St Mary 00-10; AD Gateshead 06-10; P-in-c Consett from 10. *The Vicarage, 10 Aynsley Terrace, Consett DH8 5NF* Tel (01207) 500996 E-mail val.shedden@talk21.com

SHEEHAN, Patrick Edward Anthony. b 37. Campion Ho Middx 58 English Coll Lisbon 62. **d** 67 **p** 69. In RC Ch 67-73; C Clapham H Spirit *S'wark* 73-75; P-in-c Wimbledon 75-77; R Balga Good Shep Australia 77-80; R Melville H Cross 80-85; Chapl R Newcastle Hosp 85-91; Chapl Jo Hunter Hosp 91-97; R Terrigal 97-01; rtd 01. *22 Abby Crescent, Ashmore Qld 4214, Australia* Tel (0061) (7) 5564 7064

SHEEHY, Jeremy Patrick. b 56. Magd Coll Ox BA78 MA81 New Coll Ox DPhil90. St Steph Ho Ox 78. **d** 81 **p** 82. C Erdington St Barn *Birm* 81-83; C Small Heath St Greg 83-84; Dean Div, Fell and Chapl New Coll Ox 84-90; V Leytonstone St Marg w St Columba *Chelmsf* 90-96; P-in-c Leytonstone St Andr 93-96; Prin St Steph Ho Ox 96-06; TR Swinton and Pendlebury *Man* from 06; AD Eccles from 11. *St Peter's Rectory, Vicarage Road, Swinton, Manchester M27 0WA* Tel 0161-794 1578

SHEEKEY, Raymond Arthur. b 23. Chich Th Coll 51. **d** 53 **p** 54. C Ramsgate St Geo *Cant* 53-56; C Birchington w Acol 56-61; V Brabourne w Smeeth 61-79; RD N Lympne 75-78; R Lenham w Boughton Malherbe 79-88; Chapl Lenham Hosp 79-88; rtd 88; Perm to Offic *Bris* 88-97 and *Glouc* 98-99. *41 Barleycorn, Leybourne, West Malling ME19 5PS* Tel (01732) 847722

SHEEN, David Kenneth. b 70. Cov Univ BSc95 Univ of Wales (Cardiff) BA04 MA08. St Mich Coll Llan 01. **d** 04 **p** 05. C Cowbridge *Llan* 04-07; C Penarth and Llandough 07-10; P-in-c Pwllgwaun and Llanddewi Rhondda from 10; Warden of Readers from 10. *The Vicarage, Lanelay Crescent, Pontypridd CF37 1JB* Tel (01443) 402417 E-mail dks101@mac.com

SHEEN, Canon John Harold. b 32. Qu Coll Cam BA54 MA58. Cuddesdon Coll 56. **d** 58 **p** 59. C Stepney St Dunstan and All SS *Lon* 58-62; V Tottenham St Jo 62-68; V Wood Green St Mich 68-78; P-in-c Southgate St Mich 77-78; R Kirkbride *S & M* 78-97; Chapl Ramsey Cottage Hosp 80-98; V Lezayre St Olave Ramsey 80-98; RD Ramsey 88-97; Can St German's Cathl 91-98; Dir of Ords 93-01; rtd 98; Perm to Offic *S & M* from 99. *Kentraugh Mill, Colby, Isle of Man IM9 4AU* Tel (01624) 832406

SHEEN, Canon Victor Alfred. b 17. Tyndale Hall Bris 47. **d** 49 **p** 50. Uganda 49-56; C Cheltenham St Mark *Glouc* 56-58; V W Streatham St Jas *S'wark* 58-65; V Clapham St Jas 65-86; RD Clapham and Brixton 75-82 and 85-86; Hon Can S'wark Cathl 80-86; rtd 86; Perm to Offic *Chich* from 86. *10 Porters Way, Polegate BN26 6AP* Tel (01323) 487487

SHEERAN, Antony. b 58. Birm Poly BA80. SEITE 02. **d** 05 **p** 06. NSM Mildmay Grove St Jude and St Paul *Lon* 05-09; NSM Dalston St Mark w St Bart 09-10. *26 Harcombe Road, London N16 0SA* Tel (020) 7275 9190 Mobile 07881-811586 E-mail tony.sheeran@hotmail.com

SHEFFIELD, Julia. b 55. MCSP78 SRP78. NTMTC BA05. **d** 05 **p** 06. NSM Yiewsley *Lon* 05-09; Chapl Mid-Essex Hosp Services NHS Trust from 09. *Latton Vicarage, The Gowers, Harlow CM20 2JP* Tel (01279) 423609 E-mail julishef@hotmail.co.uk *or* julia.sheffield@meht.nhs.uk

SHEFFIELD, Michael Julian. b 53. Brentwood Coll of Educn CertEd. Sarum & Wells Th Coll 76. **d** 79 **p** 80. C Locks Heath *Portsm* 79-83; C Ryde All SS 83-86; P-in-c Ryde H Trin 86-92; V 92-96; P-in-c Swanmore St Mich w Havenstreet 86-92; V Swanmore St Mich 92-96; V W Leigh 96-04; V Waterlooville from 04. *The Vicarage, 5 Deanswood Drive, Waterlooville PO7 7RR* Tel (023) 9226 2145 Mobile 07818-031902 E-mail mikejs99@hotmail.com

SHEFFIELD AND ROTHERHAM, Archdeacon of. *See* SNOW, The Ven Martyn James

SHEFFIELD, Bishop of. *See* CROFT, The Rt Revd Steven John Lindsey

SHEFFIELD, Dean of. *See* BRADLEY, The Very Revd Peter Edward

SHEGOG, Preb Eric Marshall. b 37. City Univ MA88 FRSA92. Lich Th Coll 64. **d** 65 **p** 66. C Benhilton *S'wark* 65-68; Asst Youth Adv 68-70; V Abbey Wood 70-76; Chapl Sunderland Town Cen 76-83; C Bishopwearmouth St Mich w St Hilda *Dur* 76-83; Hd Relig Broadcasting IBA 84-90; Perm to Offic *Lon* 85-90 and *St Alb* 85-89; Hon C Harpenden St Nic *St Alb* 89-97; Dir Communications for C of E 90-97; Dir Communications *Lon* 97-00; Preb St Paul's Cathl 97-00; Acting Dioc Gen Sec 99; rtd 00; Perm to Offic *St Alb* from 00. *The Coach House, 7A High Street, Clophill, Bedford MK45 4AB* Tel (01234) 381089

SHEHADI, Nabil Faouzi. b 58. Wycliffe Hall Ox 00. **d** 02 **p** 03. C Cobbold Road St Sav w St Mary *Lon* 02-05; V Internat Congregation Beirut All SS Lebanon from 05. *All Saints' Church, PO Box 11-2211, Riad El Solh, Beirut 1107 2100, Lebanon* Tel (00961) (4) 530551 E-mail nabilshehadi@hotmail.com

SHELDON, Jennifer Christine. b 43. K Coll Lon BA99. NTMTC 00. **d** 02 **p** 03. NSM Poplar *Lon* from 02. *23 Lancaster Drive, London E14 9PT* Tel (020) 7538 2375 *or* 7538 9198 Fax 7538 1551 E-mail jensheldon@aol.com

SHELDON, Jonathan Mark Robin. b 59. Cam Univ MA83. Ridley Hall Cam 81. **d** 83 **p** 84. C Dulwich St Barn *S'wark* 83-86; C Worle *B & W* 86-88; V Chesterton St Andr *Ely* 88-97. *21 Chancery Lane, Thrapston, Kettering NN14 4JL* Tel (01832) 731173 E-mail jsheldon@agnet.co.uk

SHELDON, Martin David. b 67. Sussex Univ BA89. St Jo Coll Nottm MTh01. **d** 01 **p** 02. C Milton *Win* 01-05; V Lightwater *Guildf* 05-11; Chapl RAF from 11. *Chaplaincy Services, Valiant Block, HQ Air Command, RAF High Wycombe HP14 4UE* Tel (01494) 496800 Fax 496343 E-mail martinsheldon@me.com

SHELDRAKE, Philip John William. b 74. Bedfordshire Univ BA96. Trin Coll Bris BA11. **d** 11. C Maidstone St Faith *Cant* from 11. *St Faith's Vicarage, Moncktons Lane, Maidstone ME14 2PY* Tel (01622) 851822 E-mail revdphilsheldrake@gmail.com

SHELDRAKE, Mrs Varlie Ivy. b 39. SRN64 SCM65. **d** 03 **p** 04. OLM E w W Harling, Bridgham w Roudham, Larling etc *Nor* 03-09; rtd 09; Perm to Offic *Nor* from 09. *Springfield, Lopham Road, East Harling, Norwich NR16 2PX* Tel (01953) 717404 E-mail varlie@eastharling.com

SHELLEY, Ms Catherine Jean. b 65. Down Coll Cam BA88 MA93 Barrister 91 Solicitor 00. Westcott Ho Cam 08. **d** 10 **p** 11. C Kersal Moor *Man* from 10. *94 Woodward Road, Prestwich, Manchester M25 9TY* Tel 0161-773 9859 Mobile 07711-611201 E-mail cjts08@email.com

SHELLEY, Derrick Sydney David. b 38. Lon Univ LLB60 AKC65. Linc Th Coll 66. **d** 68 **p** 69. C Weybridge *Guildf* 68-72; Chapl Red Bank Schs 71-76; Perm to Offic *Blackb* 76-96; rtd 96; Perm to Offic *Truro* 96-03 and *Lich* 04-09. *57 Kenilworth Road, Lytham St Annes FY8 1LB* Tel (01253) 780298 E-mail notatmyage@ntlworld.com

SHELLEY, Robin Arthur. b 34. CEng MIMechE. St Jo Coll Nottm 85. **d** 87 **p** 88. C Countesthorpe w Foston *Leic* 87-90; V Enderby w Lubbesthorpe and Thurlaston 90-00; rtd 00; Perm to Offic *Leic* 00-03; *York* from 02. *10 West Leys Park, Swanland, North Ferriby HU14 3LS* Tel (01482) 637603

SHELLEY, Rupert Harry. b 78. Bris Univ BSc00. Wycliffe Hall Ox BTh10. **d** 10 **p** 11. C Wimbledon Em Ridgway Prop Chpl *S'wark* from 10. *207 Cottenham Park Road, London SW20 0SY* Tel (020) 8947 9612 Mobile 07956-914123 E-mail rupertshelley@hotmail.com

SHELLS, Canon Charles Harry. b 15. St Chad's Coll Dur BA38 MA43. **d** 39 **p** 40. C Almondbury *Wakef* 39-42; C Camberwell St Geo *S'wark* 42-47; V Newington St Paul 47-54; V

Wandsworth St Anne 54-65; RD Wandsworth 63-65; R Trunch w Swafield *Nor* 65-71; R Bradfield 65-71; P-in-c Gimingham 65-71; P-in-c Trimingham 65-71; P-in-c Antingham w Thorpe Market 65-71; P-in-c Felmingham 65-68; P-in-c Suffield 65-68; P-in-c Gunton St Pet 65-71; RD Tunstead 65-68; Can Res Bris Cathl 71-81; rtd 81; Lic to Offic *B & W* 81-96 and *Sarum* from 81; Perm to Offic *Bris* 81-02 and *B & W* 88-07. *9 Immacolata House, Portway, Langport TA10 0NQ*

SHELTON, Ian Robert. b 52. BEd74 Lon Univ MA79. Ripon Coll Cuddesdon BA81 MA90. **d** 82 **p** 83. C Wath-upon-Dearne w Adwick-upon-Dearne *Sheff* 82-86; TV Grantham *Linc* 86-93; P-in-c Waltham 93-97; R 97-11; P-in-c Barnoldby le Beck 93-97; R 97-11; RD Haverstoe 01-11; RD Grimsby and Cleethorpes 10-11; Can and Preb Linc Cathl 05-11; V Rowley Regis *Birm* from 11. *St Giles' Vicarage, 192 Hanover Road, Rowley Regis, Warley B65 9EQ* Tel 0121-559 1251 E-mail robertshelton954@hotmail.com

SHELTON, Ms Pauline Mary. b 52. K Coll Lon BA73. NOC 96. **d** 99 **p** 00. C Baswich *Lich* 99-02; TV Stoke-upon-Trent 02-06; Dioc OLM Course Ldr 06-10; Prin OLM and Reader Tr from 10. *Dray Cottage, Cheadle Road, Draycott, Stoke-on-Trent ST11 9RQ* Tel (01782) 388834 E-mail rev.pauline@virgin.net

SHEMILT, Lisa. b 69. St Jo Coll Nottm 03. **d** 05 **p** 06. C Walton St Jo *Derby* from 05. *8 Birkdale Drive, Chesterfield S40 3JL* Tel (01246) 207939 E-mail lisa@shemilt.fslife.co.uk

SHENTON, Canon Brian. b 43. Chich Th Coll 73. **d** 75 **p** 76. C Mill Hill Jo Keble Ch *Lon* 75-78; C New Windsor *Ox* 78-81; TV 81-82; P-in-c Cherbury 82-83; V Calcot 83-89; R Reading St Mary w St Laur from 89; P-in-c Reading St Matt 96-00; RD Reading from 95; Hon Can Ch Ch from 98. *Hamelsham, Downshire Square, Reading RG1 6NJ* Tel 0118-956 8163 *or* 957 1057 Mobile 07710-490250 E-mail stmaryshouserdg@waitrose.com

SHENTON, David. b 57. Aston Tr Scheme 91 Ripon Coll Cuddesdon 93. **d** 95 **p** 96. C Thurmaston *Leic* 95-98; C Melton Mowbray 98-99; TV 99-01; Perm to Offic *Linc* 08-10; C Gt Grimsby St Mary and St Jas 10-11; TV from 11. *62A Brighowgate, Grimsby DN32 0QW* Tel (01472) 241725 E-mail davidshenton257@btinternet.com

SHEPHARD, Brian Edward. b 34. Magd Coll Cam BA56 MA60 Ox Univ CertEd71. Wycliffe Hall Ox 58. **d** 60 **p** 61. C Wigan St Cath *Liv* 60-62; C Kidderminster St Geo *Worc* 62-65; Lect CA Tr Coll Blackheath 65-70; Lect Hamilton Coll of Educn 70-77; Chapl Buchan Sch Castletown 77-88; Tutor Wilson Carlile Coll of Evang 88-89; C Andreas St Jude *S & M* 89-91; C Jurby 89-91; V Lezayre 91-02; rtd 02; Perm to Offic *S & M* from 02. *Keayn Ard, Queens Road, Port St Mary, Isle of Man IM9 5EP* Tel (01624) 833315 E-mail kyriosvoskos@manx.net

SHEPHEARD-WALWYN, John. b 16. Oriel Coll Ox BA38 MA44. Wells Th Coll 38. **d** 40 **p** 42. C Roch St Pet w St Marg 41-44; C Lamorbey H Redeemer 44-49; C Edenbridge 49-56; V Rosherville 56-61; R Horwood and V Westleigh *Ex* 61-78; P-in-c Harberton w Harbertonford 78-82; rtd 82; Perm to Offic *Bris* 82-05. *5 Holly Road, Bramhall, Stockport SK7 1HH* Tel 0161-439 9458

SHEPHERD, Canon Anthony Michael. b 50. Em Coll Cam BA72 MA76. Westcott Ho Cam 72. **d** 74 **p** 75. C Folkestone St Mary and St Eanswythe *Cant* 74-79; Bp's Dom Chapl *Ripon* 79-87; Dioc Communications Officer 79-87; V High Harrogate St Pet from 87; Hon Can Ripon Cathl from 99; Chapl to The Queen from 09. *St Peter's Vicarage, 13 Beech Grove, Harrogate HG2 0ET* Tel (01423) 500901 E-mail ashepherd@onetel.net

SHEPHERD, Mrs Bridget. b 76. Open Univ BSc01 K Coll Lon MA04. Trin Coll Bris BA08. **d** 08 **p** 09. C S Croydon Em *S'wark* from 08. *12 Hurst View Road, South Croydon CR2 7AG* Tel (020) 8688 6676 Mobile 07977-555135 E-mail shoesnbags_addict@yahoo.co.uk

SHEPHERD, Christopher Francis Pleydell. b 44. St Steph Ho Ox 68. **d** 69 **p** 70. C Milber *Ex* 69-72; C Ex St Thos 72-74; TV Ilfracombe, Lee and W Down 74-78; TV Ilfracombe, Lee, W Down, Woolacombe and Bittadon 78-80; P-in-c Tregony w St Cuby and Cornelly *Truro* 80-83; R 83-96; rtd 04. *2 Cherry Meadow, Cheriton Fitzpaine, Crediton EX17 4JX* Tel (01363) 866896

SHEPHERD, David. b 42. St Jo Coll Dur BA65 MA68 MLitt76. Edin Th Coll 66. **d** 68 **p** 69. Chapl St Paul's Cathl Dundee 68-79; Chapl Dundee Univ 73-79; R Dundee St Mary Magd from 79; Hon Chapl Abertay Univ from 01. *14 Albany Terrace, Dundee DD3 6HR* Tel (01382) 223510

SHEPHERD, David Mark. b 59. Reading Univ BA81 Nottm Univ BTh86. Linc Th Coll 83. **d** 86 **p** 87. C Wilmslow *Ches* 86-89; C Bromborough 89-92; V Leasowe 92-97; V Oxhey St Matt *St Alb* from 97. *The Vicarage, St Matthew's Close, Eastbury Road, Watford WD19 4ST* Tel (01923) 241420 E-mail davidshepherd@matts52.fsnet.co.uk

SHEPHERD, Ernest John Heatley. b 27. TCD BA48 BD53. **d** 50 **p** 51. C Belfast St Mary Magd *Conn* 50-54; I Whitehouse 54-96; Can Conn Cathl 86-90; Co-ord Aux Min 87-96; Treas Conn

Cathl 90; Prec Conn Cathl 90-96; rtd 96. *15 Downshire Gardens, Carrickfergus BT38 7LW* Tel (028) 9336 2243

SHEPHERD, Miss Jayne Elizabeth. b 57. Reading Univ BA78. Cranmer Hall Dur 79. **dss** 82 **d** 87 **p** 94. Wombourne *Lich* 82-85; Harlescott 85-90; Par Dn 87-90; Chapl Asst Qu Medical Cen Nottm Univ Hosp NHS Trust 90-97; Asst Chapl Cen Notts Healthcare NHS Trust 90-97; Chapl Pet Hosps NHS Trust 97-02; Chapl St Helens and Knowsley Hosps NHS Trust 02-08; V Knutsford St Cross *Ches* from 08. *The Vicarage, Mobberley Road, Knutsford WA16 8EL* Tel (01565) 640702
E-mail j.shepherd57@ntlworld.com

SHEPHERD, Joan Francis Fleming. See STENHOUSE, Joan Frances Fleming

SHEPHERD, The Very Revd John Harley. b 42. Melbourne Univ BA64 Union Th Sem (NY) MSacMus73 St Cath Coll Cam PhD84. Trin Coll Melbourne ThL66. **d** 67 **p** 68. C W Footscray Australia 67-68; C Brunswick 69-70; C Stretford St Matt *Man* 71; Asst P Sayville Long Is USA 72-77; C Cherry Hinton St Andr *Ely* 78-80; Chapl Ch Ch Ox 80-88; Chapl Univ W Australia 88-90; Dean Perth from 90. *St George's Cathedral, 38 St George's Terrace, Perth WA 6000, Australia* Tel (0061) (8) 9325 5766 *or* 9322 7265 Fax 9325 5242
E-mail thedean@perthcathedral.org

SHEPHERD, John Martin. b 68. St Jo Coll Cam BA90. Oak Hill Th Coll BA96. **d** 96 **p** 97. C Rusholme H Trin *Man* 96-00; SAMS Brazil 00-03; TV Gt Chesham *Ox* from 03. *14A Manor Way, Chesham HP5 3BG* Tel (01494) 771471
E-mail john@theshepherds.org.uk

SHEPHERD, Canon John Michael. b 42. BNC Ox BA63 MA72. Coll of Resurr Mirfield 64. **d** 66 **p** 67. C Clapham H Spirit *S'wark* 66-69; C Kingston All SS 69-72; V Upper Tooting H Trin 73-80; V Wandsworth St Paul 80-90; P-in-c Mitcham SS Pet and Paul 90-92; V 92-97; RD Merton 96-97; V Battersea St Luke 97-07; RD Battersea 01-04; Hon Can S'wark Cathl 01-07; rtd 07; Perm to Offic *Portsm* from 08. *15 Whitehaven, Waterlooville PO8 0DN* Tel (023) 9259 8130
E-mail johnshepherd@waitrose.com

SHEPHERD, Mrs Julie Margaret. b 37. **d** 03 **p** 04. OLM Halliwell *Man* 03-08; Perm to Offic from 08. *Apple Cottage, 16 Grove Street, Bolton BL1 3PG* Tel (01204) 844508 Mobile 07742-667903 E-mail julie.shepherd@care4free.net

SHEPHERD, Keith Frederick. b 42. EMMTC 86. **d** 89 **p** 90. NSM Stocking Farm *Leic* 89-93; NSM Church Langton w Tur Langton, Thorpe Langton etc 93-99; TV Syston 99-07; rtd 07; Perm to Offic *Leic* from 07. *57 Fielding Road, Birstall, Leicester LE4 3AG* Tel 0116-267 4172
E-mail keithshepherd55@btinternet.com

SHEPHERD, Michael John. b 54. St Chad's Coll Dur BA75 St Paul Univ Ottawa LCL81 Ottawa Univ MCL81. Ushaw Coll Dur 73. **d** 77 **p** 78. In RC Ch 77-93; NSM Evesham *Worc* 95-97; NSM Evesham w Norton and Lenchwick 97-99; NSM Badsey w Aldington and Offenham and Bretforton 99-03; R Ab Kettleby and Holwell w Asfordby *Leic* 03-08; TV Beacon *Carl* from 08. *St George's Vicarage, 3 Firbank, Sedbergh Road, Kendal LA9 6EG* Tel (01539) 723039
E-mail rev.shepherd@btinternet.com

SHEPHERD, Mrs Pauline. b 53. Stockwell Coll of Educn TCert73. WMMTC 00. **d** 03 **p** 04. C Walsall Pleck and Bescot *Lich* 03-08; P-in-c Yoxall 08; rtd 09; Perm to Offic *Lich* from 10. *7 Vicar's Close, Lichfield WS13 7LE* Tel (01543) 418451 Mobile 07814-680304 E-mail p.shepherd140@btinternet.com

SHEPHERD, Canon Peter William. b 48. Reading Univ BA71 Lon Univ BD80 Brighton Poly MPhil87 Lanc Univ MA94 Open Univ PhD04. Chich Th Coll 77. **d** 80 **p** 81. NSM Eastbourne St Sav and St Pet *Chich* 80-82; NSM Clitheroe St Mary *Blackb* from 82; Hd Master Wm Temple Sch Preston 83-88; Hd Master Canon Slade Sch Bolton 89-06; rtd 06; Perm to Offic *Man* from 89; Hon Can Man Cathl from 06. *Homestead, Eastham Street, Clitheroe BB7 2HY* Tel and fax (01200) 425053
E-mail pws.canonslade@btconnect.com

✠**SHEPHERD, The Rt Revd Ronald Francis.** b 26. Univ of BC BA48. AKC52 St Jo Coll Winnipeg Hon DD89. **d** 52 **p** 53 **c** 85. C Westmr St Steph w St Jo Lon 52-57; Canada from 57; Dean Edmonton 65-70; Dean Montreal 70-82; Bp BC 85-92; rtd 92; Hon V St Barn Miss San Diego USA 95-00. *Easter Hill, 110 Ensilwood Road, Salt Spring Island BC V8K 1N1, Canada* Tel (001) (250) 537 1399

SHEPHERD, Thomas. b 52. Man Univ BA79 Didsbury Coll Man PGCE83 SRN74. NOC 92. **d** 95 **p** 96. C Baguley *Man* 95-99; C Timperley *Ches* 99-03; V Sale St Paul 03-08; V Sandbach from 08. *The Vicarage, 15 Offley Road, Sandbach CW11 1GY* Tel (01270) 762379 E-mail revts@mac.com

SHEPHERD, Timothy Roy. b 34. Selw Coll Cam BA58. Linc Th Coll 62. **d** 64 **p** 65. C Selly Oak St Mary *Birm* 64-67; C Stockland Green 67-72; V Perry Common 72-76; V Holton-le-Clay *Linc* 76-84; V Habrough Gp 84-93; P-in-c Uffington 93-95; R Uffington Gp 95-99; rtd 99; Perm to Offic *Pet* 99-01 and *Linc* 00-01. *Chapelside, Chapel Hill, Wootton, Woodstock OX20 1DX* Tel (01993) 813319

SHEPHERDSON, Mrs Maria Thérèse. b 65. STETS. **d** 07 **p** 08. C Warmley, Syston and Bitton *Bris* 07-11; P-in-c Upper Kennet *Sarum* from 11. *The Rectory, 27 High Street, Avebury, Marlborough SN8 1RF* Tel (01672) 539643
E-mail m.shep@upkennet.eclipse.co.uk

SHEPPARD, Derrick Richard Adam. b 44. **d** 07 **p** 08. OLM Quidenham Gp *Nor* from 07; OLM Guiltcross from 07. *Orchard House, Back Street, Garboldisham, Diss IP22 2SD* Tel (01953) 681445 E-mail derrick.sheppard@btconnect.com

SHEPPARD, Evelyn Anne Frances. **d** 08 **p** 09. OLM Hanbury, Newborough, Rangemore and Tutbury *Lich* from 08. *Melbourne House, Knightsfield Road, Hanbury, Burton-on-Trent DE13 8TH* Tel (01283) 575551 E-mail frances@melbourne-house.com

SHEPPARD, Ian Arthur Lough. b 33. Sarum & Wells Th Coll 71. **d** 74 **p** 75. C Bishop's Cleeve *Glouc* 74-77; Chapl RAF 77-81; V Gosberton *Linc* 81-87; V Leven Valley *Carl* 87-90; Deputation and Gen Appeals Org Children's Soc 90-98; rtd 98. *57 Seymour Grove, Eaglescliffe, Stockton-on-Tees TS16 0LE* Tel (01642) 791612 E-mail ials@btopenworld.com

SHEPPARD, Canon Martin. b 37. Hertf Coll Ox BA61 MA65. Chich Th Coll 63. **d** 65 **p** 66. C N Hull St Mich *York* 65-68; C Hove St Jo *Chich* 68-71; V Heathfield St Rich 71-77; V New Shoreham and Old Shoreham 77-94; TR Rye 94-03; RD Rye 95-02; Can and Preb Chich Cathl 02-03; rtd 03; Perm to Offic *Chich* from 03. *62 St Pancras Road, Lewes BN7 1JG* Tel (01273) 474999

SHEPPARD, Norman George. b 32. Wolv Teacher Tr Coll CertEd73. St D Coll Lamp 57. **d** 59 **p** 60. C Burry Port and Pwll *St D* 59-64; SAMS Chile 64-68; C Madeley *Heref* 68-69; Asst Master Madeley Court Sch 73-75; Gilbert Inglefield Sch Leighton Buzzard 75-80; USPG 80-81; Argentina from 80; rtd 95. *Doering 528, Capilla del Monte 5184, Provincia de Cordoba, Argentina*

SHEPPARD, Roger Malcolm. b 47. Aston Univ MBA86 Wolv Poly PGCE88 Solicitor 74. WMMTC 98. **d** 01 **p** 02. NSM Castle Vale w Minworth *Birm* 01-07; NSM Four Oaks from 08; Chapl CF(V) from 07. *193 Dower Road, Sutton Coldfield B75 6SY* Tel 0121-682 3976 *or* 308 8850
E-mail roger_m_sheppard@hotmail.com

SHEPPARD, Stanley Gorton. b 18. St Jo Coll Dur 46. **d** 62 **p** 63. C Leic St Mark 62-65; R Cole Orton 65-75; V Ashby Folville and Twyford w Thorpe Satchville 75-88; rtd 88; Perm to Offic *Ex* from 89. *1 Peak Coach House, Cotmaton Road, Sidmouth EX10 8SY* Tel (01395) 516124

SHEPPARD, Mrs Susan. b 59. Ex Univ BA80 MA99 SS Hild & Bede Coll Dur PGCE81. SWMTC 95. **d** 98 **p** 99. NSM Stoke Canon, Poltimore w Huxham and Rewe etc *Ex* 98-01; Chapl St Pet High Sch Ex 99-06; Tutor SWMTC from 05; NSM Brampford Speke, Cadbury, Newton St Cyres etc *Ex* from 08. *Autumn Haze, Rewe, Exeter EX5 4HA* Tel and fax (01392) 841284 E-mail suesheppard@supanet.com

SHEPTON, Robert Leonard McIntyre. b 35. Jes Coll Cam BA58 MA61. Oak Hill Th Coll 59. **d** 61 **p** 62. C Weymouth St Jo *Sarum* 61-63; Boys' Ldr Cam Univ Miss Bermondsey 63-66; Warden Ox-Kilburn Club 66-69; Chapl St D Coll Llandudno 69-77; Chief Instructor Carnoch Outdoor Cen 77-80; Chapl Kingham Hill Sch Oxon 80-92; rtd 92. *Innisfree, Duror, Appin PA38 4DA* Tel (01631) 730437 Fax 730382
E-mail bob@innisfree.free-online.co.uk

SHER, Falak. b 65. Coll of Resurr Mirfield. **d** 07 **p** 08. C Radcliffe *Man* 07-10; TV Gorton and Abbey Hey from 10. *St Philip's Rectory, Lavington Grove, Manchester M18 7EQ* Tel 07930-573624 (mobile) E-mail falakfalak@hotmail.com

SHERBORNE, Archdeacon of. See TAYLOR, The Ven Paul Stanley

SHERBORNE, Area Bishop of. See KINGS, The Rt Revd Graham Ralph

SHERBOURNE, Gloria. b 49. STETS 00. **d** 03 **p** 04. NSM Jersey St Brelade *Win* 03-10; Asst Chapl Jersey Gp of Hosps 03-04 and 05-10. *11 Iter Court, Bow, Crediton EX17 6BZ* Tel (01363) 881240 E-mail gsherbourne@gmail.com

SHERCLIFF, Elizabeth Ann. b 56. Salford Univ BSc79 Open Univ MA96. St Jo Coll Nottm 08. **d** 09 **p** 10. Dir of Studies for Readers *Ches* from 09; NSM Marple All SS from 09. *56 Ernocroft Road, Marple Bridge, Stockport SK6 5DY* Tel 07515-633856 (mobile) E-mail lizshercliff@hotmail.com

SHERDLEY, Mrs Margaret Ann. b 46. Ches Coll of HE BTh03. NOC 00. **d** 03 **p** 04. NSM Fellside Team *Blackb* from 03; Chapl Myerscough Coll 06-11; rtd 11. *Home Barn, Hollowforth Lane, Woodplumpton, Preston PR4 0BD* Tel (01772) 691101 Mobile 07931-592787 E-mail m.sherdley@sky.com

SHERIDAN, Andrew Robert (Drew). b 61. Edin Univ MA83 Jordanhill Coll Glas PGCE86. TISEC 95. **d** 98 **p** 99. C Glas St Mary 98-01; R Greenock from 01; P-in-c Gourock from 06. *The Rectory, 96 Finnart Street, Greenock PA16 8HL* Tel (01475) 732441 E-mail drew@frsheridan.fsnet.co.uk

SHERIDAN, Mrs Deborah Jane. b 47. Kent Univ BA69 ALA73. WMMTC 90. **d** 93 **p** 94. NSM Lich St Chad 93-03; NSM The Ridwares and Kings Bromley from 03; Voc Educn Officer from

06; Chapl St Giles Hospice Lich from 98. *45 High Grange, Lichfield WS13 7DU* Tel (01543) 264363 *or* 416595 E-mail d.sheridan@postman.org.uk

SHERIDAN, Peter. b 37. Saltley Tr Coll Birm CertEd59 Leic Poly BEd82. NOC 89. **d** 92 **p** 93. NSM Braunstone *Leic* 92-95; NSM Ratby cum Groby 95-98; NSM Newtown Linford 95-98; TV Bradgate Team 98-00; Perm to Offic 00-01 and from 06; NSM Woodhouse, Woodhouse Eaves and Swithland 01-06. *16 Turnpike Way, Markfield LE67 9QT* Tel (01530) 245166

SHERIDAN, Stephen Anthony. b 62. RMN87. SEITE 04. **d** 07 **p** 08. NSM Bexhill St Pet *Chich* 07-08; NSM Stone Cross St Luke w Ninfield from 08. *14 Chailey Close, Hastings TN34 2RG* Tel 07871-727743 (mobile) E-mail steveasheridan@btinternet.com

SHERIFF (*née* WORRALL), **Canon Suzanne.** b 63. Trin Coll Bris BA86. **d** 87 **p** 94. Par Dn Kingston upon Hull St Nic *York* 87-91; Par Dn Kingston upon Hull St Aid Southcoates 91-94; C 94-96; TV Marfleet 96-00; TR 00-07; V Tadcaster w Newton Kyme from 07; P-in-c Kirk Fenton w Kirkby Wharfe and Ulleskelfe from 10; Can and Preb York Minster from 01. *The Vicarage, 78 Station Road, Tadcaster LS24 9JR* Tel (01937) 833394 E-mail sue.sheriff@virgin.net

SHERLOCK, Mrs Barbara Lee Kerney. b 48. Dur Univ PhD07. Westcott Ho Cam. **d** 05 **p** 06. C Norton St Mary and Stockton St Chad *Dur* 05-07; P-in-c Newport and Widdington *Chelmsf* 07-11; V Barrow *St E* from 11. *The Rectory, Barrow, Bury St Edmunds IP29 5BA* Tel (01284) 810929 E-mail barbara_sherlock@btinternet.com

SHERLOCK, Charles Patrick. b 51. New Coll Ox BA73 MA76 Open Univ MBA00. Ripon Coll Cuddesdon 75. **d** 77 **p** 78. C Ashtead *Guildf* 77-81; Ethiopia 81-82; Chapl Belgrade w Zagreb *Eur* 82-84; USPG Ethiopia 84-91; R Dollar *St And* 91-97; Bursar Fistula Hosp Ethiopia 97-00; P-in-c Crieff *St And* 01-04; R 04-07; P-in-c Comrie 01-04; R 04-07; P-in-c Lochearnhead 01-04; R 04-07; Perm to Offic from 07; Assoc Chapl Addis Ababa St Matt Ethiopia from 07. *The Ibert, Monzie, Crieff PH7 3LL* Tel (01764) 652619 *or* 656222 Mobile 07740-981951 E-mail cpsherlock@msn.com

SHERLOCK, Canon Thomas Alfred. b 40. Aux Course 87. **d** 90 **p** 91. NSM Kilmallock w Kilflynn, Kilfinane, Knockaney etc *L & K* 90-94; C Templemore w Thurles and Kilfithmone *C & O* 95-98; I 98-00; I Castlecomer w Colliery Ch, Mothel and Bilboa from 00; Preb Ossory Cathl from 05. *The Rectory, Castlecomer, Co Tipperary, Republic of Ireland* Tel and fax (00353) (56) 444 1677 E-mail castlecomer@ossory.anglican.org

SHERMAN, Cornelia. b 70. STETS 06. **d** 09 **p** 10. C Portchester *Portsm* from 09. *24 Jute Close, Fareham PO16 8EZ* Tel (01329) 510432 E-mail connie.27@hotmail.co.uk

SHERRATT, David Arthur. b 60. Univ of Wales (Lamp) BA82 Leeds Univ BA91. Coll of Resurr Mirfield 92. **d** 92 **p** 93. C St Jo on Bethnal Green *Lon* 92-95; C W Hampstead St Jas 95-98; V Abbey Wood *S'wark* from 98. *St Michael's Vicarage, 1 Conference Road, London SE2 0YH* Tel (020) 8311 0377

SHERRED, Peter William. b 47. Kent Univ BA69. SEITE 96. **d** 99 **p** 00. NSM Dover St Mary *Cant* 99-02; Perm to Offic from 02. *Copthorne, Dover Road, Guston, Dover CT15 5EN* Tel (01304) 203548 Fax 206950 E-mail copthorne@talk21.com

SHERRING, Patrick. b 55. Trent Park Coll of Educn BEd73 CertEd77. Ridley Hall Cam 95. **d** 97 **p** 98. C Leyton St Mary w St Edw and St Luke *Chelmsf* 97-01; P-in-c Ingatestone w Buttsbury 01-04; V Ingatestone w Fryerning from 04. *The Rectory, 1 Rectory Close, Fryerning Lane, Ingatestone CM4 0DB* Tel (01277) 352562 E-mail patrick.sherring@ingatestoneparishchurch.org.uk

SHERRING, Toby Bruce. b 76. Ex Univ BA97 St Luke's Coll Ex PGCE98. St Steph Ho Ox MTh04. **d** 02 **p** 03. C W Derby St Jo *Liv* 02-05; Chapl St Hilda's Sch for Girls Perth Australia from 06. *St Hilda's, Bay View Terrace, Mosman Park WA 6012, Australia* Tel (0061) (8) 9285 4100

SHERRINGTON, Penelope. b 51. Kent Univ BA11. SEITE 08. **d** 11. Chapl Gt Ormond Street Hosp for Children NHS Trust from 11. *Little Granta, Godstone Road, Bletchingley, Redhill RH1 4PL* Tel (01883) 744991 E-mail martinpenny012000@yahoo.com

SHERSBY, Brian Alfred. b 41. Clifton Th Coll 68. **d** 71 **p** 72. C Stoughton *Guildf* 71-74; C Heref St Pet w St Owen 75-79; V Earlham St Mary *Nor* 79-91; R Murston w Bapchild and Tonge *Cant* 91-07; rtd 07. *4 Blenheim Gardens, Chichester PO19 7XE*

SHERWIN, David Royston. b 56. St Jo Coll Nottm 84. **d** 89 **p** 90. C Conisbrough *Sheff* 89-95; V Wheatley Park and Dioc Adv for Evang 95-01; P-in-c Martley and Wichenford, Knightwick etc *Worc* 01-08; TR Worcs W from 09. *The Rectory, Martley, Worcester WR6 6QA* Tel and fax (01886) 888664 E-mail davidwin56@aol.com

SHERWIN, Mrs Jane. b 41. Sarum Th Coll 93. **d** 96 **p** 97. NSM Brightling, Dallington, Mountfield etc *Chich* 96-02; P-in-c Waldron 02-09; rtd 09; Perm to Offic *St E* from 10. *Treetops at Merlins, Uckfield Road, Ringmer, Lewes BN8 5RU* Tel (01273) 812173 E-mail jane.sherwin@virgin.net

SHERWIN, Canon Margaret Joyce. b 65. NOC BTh99. **d** 99 **p** 00. C Litherland St Phil *Liv* 99-03; V Hindley Green from 03; AD Wigan from 08; Hon Can Liv Cathl from 08. *3 Green Lane, Hindley Green, Wigan WN2 4HN* Tel (01942) 255833 E-mail revmarg@btopenworld.com

SHERWIN, Miss Margaret Miriam. b 32. dss 83 **d** 87 **p** 94. Holborn St Alb w Saffron Hill St Pet *Lon* 83-88; Par Dn 87-88; Par Dn Highgate St Mich 88-93; rtd 93; Hon C Purbrook *Portsm* 93-99; Perm to Offic from 99. *16 Lombard Court, Lombard Street, Portsmouth PO1 2HU* Tel (023) 9283 8429

SHERWIN, Mrs Philippa Margaret. b 46. Lon Univ BDS70 LDS70. **d** 99 **p** 00. OLM Queen Thorne *Sarum* 99-08; rtd 08; Perm to Offic *Sarum* from 08. *Haycroft, Sandford Orcas, Sherborne DT9 4RP* Tel (01963) 220380 E-mail p.sherwin@virgin.net

SHERWOOD, David Charles. b 56. LRPS94. WEMTC 98. **d** 01 **p** 02. C Taunton Lyngford *B & W* 01-05; P-in-c Hemyock w Culm Davy, Clayhidon and Culmstock *Ex* 05-11; P-in-c Ashburton, Bickington, Buckland in the Moor etc from 11. *The Rectory, Copperwood Close, Ashburton, Newton Abbot TQ13 7JQ* Tel (01364) 652968 E-mail revdcs@yahoo.co.uk

SHERWOOD, David James. b 45. Univ of Wales (Cardiff) LLM94 Solicitor 69. St Steph Ho Ox 81. **d** 83 **p** 84. C Westbury-on-Trym H Trin *Bris* 83-85; C Corringham *Chelmsf* 85-87; V Hullbridge 87-94; V Kenton *Lon* 94-06; rtd 06. *130 St Helens Road, Hastings TN34 2EJ* Tel (01424) 719768 Mobile 07891-783719 E-mail canddsherwood@aol.co.uk

SHERWOOD, Canon Ian Walter Lawrence. b 57. TCD BA80. **d** 82 **p** 84. C Dublin St Patr Cathl Gp 82-83; Chapl Billinge Hosp Wigan 83 86; C Orrell *Liv* 83 86; Chapl Ruoharoot w Sofia *Eur* 86-89; Chapl Istanbul w Moda from 89; Can Malta Cathl from 97. *c/o FCO (Istanbul), King Charles Street, London SW1A 2AH* Tel (0090) (212) 251 5616 Fax 243 5702 E-mail parson@tnn.net

SHERWOOD, Mrs Jane. b 62. Ripon Coll Cuddesdon 05. **d** 07 **p** 08. NSM Ox St Matt from 07. *36 Canning Crescent, Oxford OX1 4XB* Tel (01865) 250672 E-mail jane@sherwoodz.plus.com

SHERWOOD, Kenneth Henry. b 37. CITC 90. **d** 93 **p** 94. NSM Malahide w Balgriffin *D & G* 93-96 and from 04; NSM Castleknock and Mulhuddart w Clonsilla 96-97; NSM Leighlin w Grange Sylvae, Shankill etc *C & O* 97-04. *6 Beverton Way, Donabate, Co Dublin, Republic of Ireland* Tel (00353) (1) 843 5287 E-mail kensherwood07@eircom.net

SHERWOOD, Nigel John Wesley. b 58. CITC 86. **d** 86 **p** 87. C Kilmore w Ballintemple, Kildallan etc *K, E & A* 86-89; I Tullow w Shillelagh, Aghold and Mullinacuff *C & O* 89-95; I Arklow w Inch and Kilbride *D & G* from 95; Sec SPCK Glendalough from 98. *The Rectory, Emoclew Road, Arklow, Co Wicklow, Republic of Ireland* Tel (00353) (402) 32439

SHERWOOD, Suffragan Bishop of. *See* PORTER, The Rt Revd Anthony

SHEWAN, Alistair Boyd. b 44. Open Univ BA83 BSc95. Edin Th Coll 63. **d** 67 **p** 68. Prec St Andr Cathl Inverness 67-69; C Shepherd's Bush St Steph w St Thos *Lon* 70-72; Hon C Edin St Mich and All SS 73-75; Perm to Offic 75-81; Hon C Edin Old St Paul 81-86; NSM Edin St Columba 87-91; Asst Dioc Supernumerary from 91; C Edin St Ninian 95-08. *Limegrove, High Street, Gifford, Haddington EH41 4QU* Tel (01620) 810402

SHEWAN, James William. b 36. Sarum Th Coll 61. **d** 63 **p** 64. C Rainbow Hill St Barn *Worc* 63-64; C Newton Aycliffe *Dur* 64-66; C Harton 66-69; V S Moor 69-72; CF 72-77; CF(V) from 81; P-in-c Benwell St Aid *Newc* 77-79; V Longhoughton w Howick 79-88; V Spittal and Scremerston 88-00; RD Norham 96-00; rtd 00; Perm to Offic *Newc* 00-04; Hon C Norham and Duddo 04-08; Hon C Cornhill w Carham 04-08; Hon C Branxton 04-08. *36 Askew Crescent, Spittal, Tweedmouth, Berwick-upon-Tweed TD15 2AU* Tel (01289) 309771

SHEWRING (*née* SMITH), **Mrs Susan Helen.** b 51. Univ of Cen England in Birm BEd87 Warwick Univ PGDE90. WMMTC 01. **d** 04 **p** 05. NSM Billesley Common *Birm* 04-07; Asst Chapl Univ Hosp Birm NHS Foundn Trust from 07. *48 St Helens Road, Solihull B91 2DA* Tel 0121-705 1845 E-mail sue_shewring@yahoo.co.uk

SHIELD, Barry Graham. b 39. Univ of Qld BA79 Univ of New England DipEd83 MLitt86 Kent Univ MA95 Washington Univ PhD00. **d** 83 **p** 84. Australia 83-00 and from 01; P-in-c Haselbury Plucknett, Misterton and N Perrott *B & W* 00-01. *107 Molesworth Street, Tenterfield NSW 2372, Australia* Tel (0061) (2) 6736 1405 E-mail barryshield1@bigpond.com

SHIELD, Graham Friend. b 63. Ripon Coll Cuddesdon. **d** 00 **p** 01. C Camborne *Truro* 00-03; P-in-c St Mawgan w St Ervan and St Eval 03-11; C St Columb Major w St Wenn 09-11. *Burtree Cottage, Little Crakehall, Bedale DL8 1LB* Tel (01677) 427970 Mobile 07980-524774 E-mail grahamshield@btinternet.com

SHIELD, Ian Thomas. b 32. Hertf Coll Ox BA56 MA60 BLitt60. Westcott Ho Cam 59. **d** 61 **p** 62. C Shipley St Paul *Bradf* 61-64; Tutor Lich Th Coll 64-71; Chapl 67-71; V Dunston w Coppenhall *Lich* 71-79; TV Wolverhampton 79-86; rtd 87; Perm to Offic *Lich* from 87. *13 Duke Street, Penn Fields,*

Wolverhampton WV3 7DT Tel (01902) 337037
E-mail ianshield@aol.com
SHIELDS, Dennis. Brighton Coll of Educn CertEd72 Brighton
Poly DipEd84 Roehampton Inst MA87. **d** 05 **p** 06. NSM
Meltham *Wakef* from 05. *11 The Hollow, Meltham, Holmfirth
HD9 5LA* Tel (01484) 850074 Fax 326222 Mobile
07974-146120 E-mail dennis_shields@btinternet.com
SHIELDS, Mrs Jennifer Jill. b 39. Heref Coll of Educn
CertEd74. SAOMC 99. **d** 02 **p** 03. OLM Lenborough *Ox* from
02. *8 West Furlong, Padbury, Buckingham MK18 2BP* Tel
(01280) 814474
SHIELDS, Canon Michael Penton. b 30. Bps' Coll Cheshunt. **d** 64
p 65. C Kingsbury St Andr *Lon* 64-67; C Friern Barnet All SS
67-69; V Colindale St Matthias 69-76; V Sevenoaks St Jo *Roch*
76-95; RD Sevenoaks 84-95; Chapl Sevenoaks Hosp 78-94;
Chapl St Mich Sch Otford 90-95; Hon Can Roch Cathl 94-95;
rtd 95; CMP from 79; Hon PV Roch Cathl 96-05; Perm to Offic
from 05. *16 Bromley College, London Road, Bromley BR1 1PE*
Tel and fax (020) 8464 7906 E-mail pentonhook@tiscali.co.uk
SHILL, Kenneth Leslie. b 49. Leic Univ BA70 Lon Univ BD73.
Ridley Hall Cam 75. **d** 77 **p** 78. C Harborne Heath *Birm* 77-83; V
Mansfield St Jo *S'well* 83-93; Bp's Adv on Healing 89-93; Chapl
Amsterdam w Heiloo *Eur* 93-95; TR Bath Twerton-on-Avon
B & W 95-04; V Arnold *S'well* from 04. *St Mary's Vicarage,
Church Lane, Arnold, Nottingham NG5 8HJ* Tel 0115-926 2946
E-mail shill1@tinyworld.co.uk
SHILLAKER, Mrs Christine Frances. b 39. Gilmore Ho 74.
dss 86 **d** 87 **p** 94. Colchester St Leon, St Mary Magd and
St Steph *Chelmsf* 86-89; Par Dn 87-89; Par Dn Colchester, New
Town and The Hythe 89-94; C 94-96; P-in-c Ramsey w Lt
Oakley 96-02; rtd 02; Perm to Offic *Chelmsf* from 02. *21 Nelson
Road, Colchester CO3 9AP* Tel (01206) 570234
SHILLAKER, John. b 34. K Coll Lon BD60 AKC60. **d** 61 **p** 62. C
Bush Hill Park St Mark *Lon* 61-65; C Milton *Win* 65-69; C-in-c
Moulsham St Luke CD *Chelmsf* 69-78; V Moulsham St Luke
78-85; P-in-c Colchester St Leon, St Mary Magd and St Steph
85-86; R 86-89; R Colchester, New Town and The Hythe 89-96;
rtd 96; Perm to Offic *Chelmsf* from 00. *21 Nelson Road,
Colchester CO3 9AP* Tel (01206) 570234 Mobile 07889-816264
SHILLING, Ms Audrey Violet. b 26. Dur Univ BA69. CA Tr Coll
51 Cranmer Hall Dur 66. **d** 87 **p** 94. CA from 53; NSM
Gillingham H Trin *Roch* 87-93; NSM Rainham 94-96; Perm to
Offic from 96. *13 Guardian Court, London Road, Rainham,
Gillingham ME8 7HQ* Tel (01634) 233654
E-mail audrey.shilling@diocese-rochester.org
SHILLINGFORD, Brian. b 39. Lich Th Coll 65. **d** 68 **p** 69. C
Lewisham St Swithun *S'wark* 68-71; C Godstone 71-75; TV
Croydon St Jo *Cant* 75-81; TV N Creedy *Ex* 81-93; TR 93-05; rtd
05. *Lyndbank, Albert Road, Crediton EX17 2BZ* Tel (01363)
877221 E-mail brianandkajshil@aol.com
SHILSON-THOMAS, Mrs Annabel Margaret. b 60. Jes Coll Ox
BA82. Westcott Ho Cam 87. **d** 89 **p** 98. Par Dn Sydenham
St Bart *S'wark* 89-93; Journalist CAFOD 95-03; Hon C
Kingston All SS w St Jo *S'wark* 97-98; Perm to Offic *Ely* 00-03;
Chapl Anglia Poly Univ 03-04; C Kingston All SS w St Jo *S'wark*
04-05; Spirituality Consultant CAFOD from 05; C Cambridge
Gt St Mary w St Mich *Ely* from 07. *28 Fulbrooke Road,
Cambridge CB3 9EE* Tel (01223) 729475
E-mail ams94@cam.ac.uk
SHILSON-THOMAS, Canon Hugh David. b 64. Ex Coll Ox
BA86 MA98 K Coll Lon MA99. Westcott Ho Cam 87. **d** 89
p 90. C Sydenham All SS *S'wark* 89-92; C Lower Sydenham
St Mich 89-92; Ecum Chapl Kingston Univ 93-98; Chapl Rob
Coll Cam 98-03; Nat Adv for HE/Chapl Abps' Coun 03-08;
Chapl and Dean of Chpl Selw Coll Cam from 08; Chapl
Newnham Coll Cam from 08; Chapter Can Ely Cathl from 10.
28 Fulbrooke Road, Cambridge CB3 9EE Tel (01223) 729475 *or*
335846 E-mail hds21@cam.ac.uk
SHILVOCK, Geoffrey. b 47. Univ of Wales (Lamp) BA69. Sarum
Th Coll 70. **d** 72 **p** 73. C Kidderminster St Mary *Worc* 72-78;
P-in-c Gt Malvern Ch Ch 78-85; V Wolverley and Cookley from
85; RD Kidderminster 95-01. *The Vicarage, Wolverley,
Kidderminster DY11 5XD* Tel (01562) 851133
E-mail geoffshilvock@hotmail.com
SHIMWELL, Robert John. b 46. ARCM65. Trin Coll Bris 75.
d 78 **p** 79. C Richmond H Trin *S'wark* 78-79; C Cullompton and
Kentisbeare w Blackborough *Ex* 79-81; V S Cave and Ellerker w
Broomfleet *York* 81-87; Chapl Lee Abbey 87-88; R Glas St Silas
88-94; V Upton (Overchurch) *Ches* 94-05; RD Wirral N 97-98;
Hon Can Ches Cathl 02-05; V Lee St Mildred *S'wark* from 05.
The Vicarage, 1A Helder Grove, London SE12 0RB Tel (020)
8857 5205 E-mail rob@shimwell.org
SHIN, Beom Jin (Stephen). b 80. Kyung Hee Univ Korea BA03
Univ Coll Lon MSc08. St Steph Ho Ox 08. **d** 11. C Banbury *Ox*
from 11. *38 Hightown Road, Banbury OX16 9BT* Tel (01295)
550369 Mobile 07830-707012 E-mail bjmonani@gmail.com
SHINE, Canon Ann Aisling. RGN SCM. **d** 03 **p** 04. Aux Min
Dublin Drumcondra w N Strand *D & G* 03-05; Aux
Min Clondalkin w Rathcoole from 05; Can Ch Ch Cathl Dublin

from 10. *1 Roselawn Grove, Castleknock, Dublin 15, Republic of
Ireland* Tel (00353) (1) 820 1797 Mobile 87-239 7902
E-mail aislingshine@hotmail.com
SHINER, Michael Joseph. b 21. Chich Th Coll 51. **d** 53 **p** 54. C
Weymouth H Trin *Sarum* 53-56; V Stanbridge w Tilsworth
St Alb 56-63; V Powerstock w W Milton, Witherstone and N
Poorton *Sarum* 67-73; V Knutsford St Cross *Ches* 73-75; Area
Sec Age Concern Cornwall 75-86; Co Org W Sussex 80-86; rtd
86. *55 Tennyson Drive, Malvern WR14 2UL* Tel (01684) 563269
SHINKINS, Pamela Mhairi. b 41. Leeds Univ BSc62 Open Univ
BA84. TISEC 05. **d** 07 **p** 08. Lic to Offic *Mor* from 08. *Homelea,
7 Blair, Poolewe, Achnasheen IV22 2LP* Tel (01445) 781346
E-mail pam.shinkins@btinternet.com
SHINN, William Raymond. b 22. Sarum & Wells Th Coll 71. **d** 73
p 74. C Letchworth St Paul *St Alb* 73-75; C Dunstable 76-78; TV
78-80; V Luton St Chris Round Green 80-88; rtd 88; Perm
to Offic *St Alb* from 88. *31 Coleridge Close, Hitchin SG4 0QX*
Tel (01462) 641883
SHINTON, Bertram David. b 41. WMMTC 95. **d** 98 **p** 99. NSM
Broseley w Benthall, Jackfield, Linley etc *Heref* from 98.
Gestiana, Woodlands Road, Broseley TF12 5PU Tel (01952)
882765 *or* 0121-311 2104
SHIPLEY, Christopher John. b 44. Leeds Univ BSc65 MSc70
BA72. Coll of Resurr Mirfield 70. **d** 73 **p** 74. C Preston St Jo
Blackb 73-77; Chapl Lancs (Preston) Poly 75-77; V Blackb
St Mich w St Jo 77-81; P-in-c Blackb H Trin 78-81; V Blackb
St Mich w St Jo and H Trin 81-82; V Walthamstow St Pet
Chelmsf 82-85; Gen Sec Mary Feilding Guild Lon 85-86; Org
Waltham Forest Coun for Voluntary Service 86-89; Gen Sec Hull
89-91; Dir Grimsby and Cleethorpes 91; Teacher Upbury Manor
High Sch Gillingham 92-94; Hd of Science 94-02; Teacher
Whitstable Community Coll 02-03; Hd of Science Cheyne
Middle Sch Sheerness 03-09; Team Ldr Science Is of Sheppey
Academy from 09; Hon C Minster-in-Sheppey *Cant* from 10.
2 St Peter's Close, Minster-on-Sea, Sheerness ME12 3DD
E-mail chrisshply@googlemail.com
SHIPLEY, June Patricia. *See* ASQUITH, June Patricia
SHIPLEY, Canon Stephen Edwin Burnham. b 52. Univ Coll Dur
BA74. Westcott Ho Cam 85. **d** 87 **p** 88. C Ipswich St Marg *St E*
87-90; P-in-c Stuntney *Ely* 90-95; Min Can, Prec and Sacr Ely
Cathl 90-95; Producer Worship Progr BBC Relig Broadcasting
from 95; Lic to Offic *Derby* from 96; Hon Can Derby Cathl from
09. *21 Devonshire Road, Buxton SK17 6RZ* Tel (01298) 78383 *or*
0161-244 3292 Mobile 07808-403812 Fax 0161-244 3290
E-mail stephen.shipley@bbc.co.uk
SHIPP, Miss Elizabeth Ann. b 81. Leic Univ BA02 Ox Brookes
Univ MA09. Ripon Coll Cuddesdon BA06. **d** 07 **p** 08. C
Wymondham *Nor* 07-11; Bp's Chapl *Worc* from 11. *The Old
Palace, Deansway, Worcester WR1 1AH* Tel (01905) 731603
Mobile 07554-013547
E-mail lizzie.shipp@cofe-worcester.org.uk
SHIPP, Linda Mary. b 49. Cranmer Hall Dur 00. **d** 02 **p** 03. Chapl
among Deaf People *York* from 02; C Kirkleatham 02-05; V
Whorlton w Carlton and Faceby from 05. *Whorlton Vicarage, 18
Church Lane, Swainby, Northallerton DL6 3EA* Tel (01642)
701777 Fax 706131 Mobile 07970-908517
E-mail revlmshipp@btinternet.com
SHIPP, Susan. *See* HOLLINS, Patricia Susan
SHIPSIDES, Brian Kenneth. b 56. Reading Univ BA. Westcott
Ho Cam 79. **d** 82 **p** 83. C Bramley *Ripon* 82-85; C Notting Dale
St Clem w St Mark and St Jas *Lon* 85-90; Chapl N Lon Poly
90-92; Chapl Univ of N Lon 92-97; P-in-c Forest Gate All SS
and St Edm *Chelmsf* from 97. *The Vicarage, 79 Claremont Road,
London E7 0QA* Tel (020) 8534 7463 *or* 8472 8584
SHIPTON, Canon Andrew James. b 60. Leeds Univ BA82 Univ
of Northumbria at Newc MEd99 Leeds Univ MPhil06.
Cranmer Hall Dur 83. **d** 85 **p** 86. C Fishponds St Jo *Bris* 85-88; C
Gosforth All SS *Newc* 88-91; V Long Benton St Mary 91-96;
Chapl Northumbria Univ 96-06; TV Ch the King 06-07; TR
from 07; Dioc Development Officer for Youth Work from 06;
Hon Can Newc Cathl from 07. *60 Barmoor Drive, Newcastle
upon Tyne NE3 5RG* Tel 0191-236 3788
E-mail andrewshipton085@aol.com
SHIPTON, Linda Anne. *See* GREEN, Mrs Linda Anne
SHIPTON (née WILSON), Mrs Marjorie Jayne. b 59. Hull Univ
BA80 Leeds Univ MA01 K Alfred's Coll Win PGCE81.
Cranmer Hall Dur 85. **dss** 86 **d** 87 **p** 94. Ormesby *York* 86-89; Par
Dn 87-89; Chapl Asst Newc Gen Hosp 89-91; Chapl 91-95; Dep
Hd Chapl Newcastle upon Tyne Hosps NHS Foundn Trust from
95; NSM Whorlton *Newc* 94-97. *Royal Victoria Infirmary, Queen
Victoria Road, Newcastle upon Tyne NE1 4LP* Tel 0191-232
5131 *or* 266 6172
SHIRES, Alan William. b 36. Lon Univ BA60. Oak Hill Th Coll
57. **d** 61 **p** 62. C York St Paul 61-64; C Southgate *Chich* 64-67; V
Doncaster St Mary *Sheff* 67-75; Perm to Offic *Portsm* 75-96;
Student Counsellor Portsm Poly 75-88; Hd Student Services
Portsm Poly 88-96; rtd 96. *15 Broomfield Road, Admaston,
Wellington TF5 0AR*

SHIRESS, Canon David Henry Faithfull. b 27. St Cath Coll Cam
BA49 MA53. Ridley Hall Cam 51. **d** 53 **p** 54. C Southport Ch
Ch *Liv* 53-55; C St Helens St Mark 55-58; V Shrewsbury
St Julian *Lich* 58-67; V Blackheath Park St Mich *S'wark* 67-93;
Sub-Dean Greenwich 81-90; RD Greenwich 90-91; Hon Can
S'wark Cathl 89-93; rtd 93; Perm to Offic *Sarum* from 93.
35 Rempstone Road, Wimborne BH21 1SS Tel (01202) 887845
SHIRLEY, Gary Ronald. b 57. Wilson Carlile Coll 96 SWMTC
06. **d** 09 **p** 10. C Devonport St Budeaux *Ex* from 09. *The
Vicarage, Bridwell Lane North, Plymouth PL5 1AN* Tel (01752)
369489 E-mail gary.shirley2@btinternet.com
SHIRLEY, Valerie Joy. b 42. **d** 96 **p** 97. OLM Sydenham H Trin
S'wark 96-07; OLM Sydenham H Trin and St Aug from 07.
9 Faircroft, 5 Westwood Hill, London SE26 6BG Tel (020) 8778
2551
SHIRRAS, The Ven Edward Scott. b 37. St Andr Univ BSc61.
Clifton Th Coll 61. **d** 63 **p** 64. C Surbiton Hill Ch Ch *S'wark*
63-66; C Jesmond Clayton Memorial *Newc* 66-68; CPAS 68-75;
Hon C Wallington *S'wark* 69-75; V Roxeth Ch Ch *Lon* 75-82; V
Roxeth Ch Ch and Harrow St Pet 82-85; AD Harrow 82-85; Adn
Northolt 85-92; V Win Ch Ch 92-01; rtd 01; Perm to Offic *Ox*
01-02 and from 09; P-in-c Marcham w Garford 02-09. *4 Culham
Close, Abingdon OX14 2AS* Tel (01235) 553129
E-mail epshirras@aol.com
SHIRRAS, Mrs Pamela Susan. b 41. St Andr Univ BSc62 Brunel
Univ PGCE80. Wycliffe Hall Ox 04. **d** 05 **p** 06. NSM Marcham
w Garford *Ox* 05-09; Perm to Offic 09; NSM Abingdon from 09.
4 Culham Close, Abingdon OX14 2AS Tel (01235) 553129
E-mail epshirras@aol.com
SHIRRAS, Rachel Joan. *See* COLLINS, Rachel Joan
SHOCK, Rachel Alexandra. b 63. Nottm Trent Univ LLB94.
EMMTC 95. **d** 98 **p** 00. NSM Radford All So w Ch Ch and
St Mich *S'well* 98-99; NSM Lenton Abbey 99-02; NSM
Wollaton 02-08; Chapl Development Worker from 06. *1 May
Avenue, Wollaton, Nottingham NG8 2NE*
SHOESMITH (*née* HALL), **Mrs Judith Frances.** b 64. SS Coll
Cam BA85 MA89 MEng94 BTh02 CEng97. Ridley Hall Cam
99. **d** 02 **p** 03. C Drayton in Hales *Lich* 02-05; Lic to Offic *Liv*
05-11; TV Walthamstow *Chelmsf* from 11. *11 Sylvan Road,
London E17 7QR* Tel 07505-126167 (mobile)
E-mail frances@walthamstowchurch.org.uk
SHOESMITH, Ms Kathia Andree. b 64. Leeds Univ BA08
RN98. Coll of Resurr Mirfield 06. **d** 08 **p** 09. C Ripponden and
Barkisland w W Scammonden Wakef 08-11; V Bradshaw and
Holmfield from 11. *The Vicarage, Pavement Lane, Bradshaw,
Halifax HX2 9JJ* Tel (01422) 244330
E-mail zen27915@zen.co.uk
SHOKRALLA, Adel Salah Makar. b 75. Ain Shams Univ Cairo
BSc96. Alexandria Sch of Th 05 Trin Coll Bris MA10. **d** 10. C
Heavitree and St Mary Steps *Ex* from 10. *10 Sherwood Close,
Exeter EX2 5DX* Tel 07503-903323 (mobile)
E-mail adels2000@gmail.com
SHONE, The Very Revd John Terence. b 35. Selw Coll Cam BA58
MA64 Newc Univ MA92. Linc Th Coll 58. **d** 60 **p** 61. C
St Pancras w St Jas and Ch Ch *Lon* 60-62; Chapl Aber Univ
62-68; Chapl St Andr Cathl 62-65; V Gt Grimsby St Andr and
St Luke *Linc* 68-69; Chapl Stirling Univ 69-80; R Bridge of
Allan 69-86; P-in-c Alloa 77-85; Can St Ninian's Cathl Perth
80-89; P-in-c Dollar 81-86; Dean St Andr 82-89; Research and
Development Officer 86-89; Dioc Supernumerary 86-89; TV
Cullercoats St Geo *Newc* 89-00; rtd 00. *33D Grange Road, Alloa
FK10 1LR* Tel (01259) 721388 E-mail husnwif@aol.com
SHONE, Miss Ursula Ruth. b 34. Stirling Univ BA75 Open Univ
BPhil88. dss 81 **d** 86 **p** 94. Bridge of Allan *St And* 81-85;
Lochgelly 85-87; Chapl Cov Cathl 87-90; Ind Chapl 87-90; Par
Dn Ainsdale *Liv* 90-94; Dioc Science Adv 90-99; C Ainsdale
94-96; C Childwall St Dav 96-99; rtd 99; NSM Brechin from 00.
4 Park Road, Brechin DD9 7AF Tel (01356) 626087
SHOOTER, Philippa Margaret. b 49. Hull Univ BA70 Nottm
Univ MA72 CQSW72. NOC 04. **d** 06 **p** 07. NSM Fence-in-
Pendle and Higham *Blackb* 06-11; Hon C Coppull from 11; Hon
C Coppull St Jo from 11. *291 Spendmore Lane, Coppull, Chorley
PR7 5DF* Tel (01257) 792676
E-mail philippashooter@btinternet.com
SHOOTER, Robert David. b 44. Lon Univ BSc70 Lanc Univ
MA94 CQSW72 LRAM92. NOC 99. **d** 02 **p** 03. NSM Brierfield
Blackb 02-04; NSM Briercliffe and Extwistle 04-11; Perm to Offic from 09.
234 Briercliffe Road, Burnley BB10 2NZ Tel (01282) 412404
E-mail robertshooter@btinternet.com
SHOOTER, Ms Susan. b 58. Nottm Univ BA81 PGCE82. St Jo
Coll Nottm MA96. **d** 96 **p** 98. C Dartford H Trin *Roch* 96-97; C
Crayford 97-00; V Bostall Heath 00-09. *131 Pengelly, Delabole
PL33 9AT* Tel (01840) 213645 Mobile 07929-496942
E-mail shooter160@btinternet.com
SHORROCK, John Musgrave. b 29. TCD BA54 MA58. Bps'
Coll Cheshunt 54. **d** 56 **p** 57. C Fleetwood St Pet *Blackb* 56-59; C
Lancaster St Mary 59-61; C-in-c Blackpool St Wilfrid CD 61-65;
V Blackpool St Wilfrid 65-67; Min Can and Sacr Cant Cathl
67-70; V Chorley St Geo *Blackb* 71-78; P-in-c Bredgar w Bicknor
and Huckinge *Cant* 78-82; P-in-c Frinsted w Wormshill and

Milstead 78-82; R Bredgar w Bicknor and Frinsted w Wormshill
etc 82-92; rtd 92; Perm to Offic *Cant* 92-06; Clergy Widows
Officer Cant Adnry 97-06; Perm to Offic *Portsm* from 06.
55 Brook Gardens, Emsworth PO10 7JY Tel (01243) 389430
E-mail john_shorrock@talktalk.net
SHORT, Brian Frederick. b 29. St Jo Coll Nottm 70. **d** 72 **p** 73. C
Walton *St E* 72-75; P-in-c Barking w Darmsden and Gt Bricett
75-78; P-in-c Ringshall w Battisford and Lt Finborough 75-78;
TV Nor St Pet Parmentergate w St Jo 78-88; R Winfarthing w
Shelfanger w Burston w Gissing etc 88-90; rtd 90; Perm to Offic
Nor from 92. *31 Nursery Gardens, Blofield, Norwich NR13 4JE*
Tel (01603) 712396
SHORT, Bryan Raymond. b 37. Bris Univ BSc59 CertEd60. Dioc
OLM tr scheme 00. **d** 02 **p** 03. OLM Kirkheaton *Wakef* 02-09;
Perm to Offic from 09. *12 Bankfield Lane, Kirkheaton,
Huddersfield HD5 0JG* Tel (01484) 425832
E-mail bryan@b-s-short.fsnet.co.uk
SHORT, Ms Clare. b 50. Leic Univ BA72 St Mary's Coll
Twickenham PGCE73. S Dios Minl Tr Scheme 89. **d** 92 **p** 94.
NSM Horsham *Chich* 92-99; Perm to Offic *Newc* from 04.
Hedgelea, South Road, Lowick, Berwick-upon-Tweed TD15 2TX
Tel (01289) 389222
SHORT, Eileen. b 45. Ex Univ BA66. NOC 93. **d** 96 **p** 97. NSM
Castleton Moor *Man* 96-98; NSM Chorlton-cum-Hardy
St Clem 98-00; NSM Baguley 00-10; Perm to Offic from 10.
2 Netherwood Road, Northenden, Manchester M22 4BQ
SHORT, Mrs Heather Mary. b 50. LWCMD71 Cardiff Coll of
Educn CertEd72. WEMTC 98. **d** 01 **p** 02. C Heref S Wye 01-05;
P-in-c Bodenham, Felton and Preston Wynne from 05; P-in-c
Marden w Amberley and Wisteston from 05; P in c Sutton
St Nicholas w Sutton St Michael from 05. *The Vicarage,
Bodenham, Hereford HR1 3JX* Tel (01568) 797370
SHORT, Canon John Sinclair. b 33. Oak Hill Th Coll 64. **d** 66
p 67. C Islington St Mary *Lon* 66-70; V Becontree St Mary
Chelmsf 70-76; V New Malden and Coombe *S'wark* 76-90; RD
Kingston 79-84; Hon Can S'wark Cathl 83-90; P-in-c Peldon w
Gt and Lt Wigborough *Chelmsf* 90-93; rtd 93; Perm to Offic
S'wark 93-08. *22 Chart Lane, Reigate RH2 7BP* Tel (01737)
245244
SHORT, Canon John Timothy. b 43. Kelham Th Coll 63. **d** 68
p 69. C St Marylebone Ch Ch w St Barn *Lon* 68-70; C Southgate
Ch Ch 70-72; P-in-c Mosser and Dioc Youth Officer *Carl* 72-78;
R Heyford w Stowe Nine Churches *Pet* 78-87; V Northampton
St Jas 87-96; RD Wootton 88-96; TR Kingsthorpe w
Northampton St Dav 96-08; Can Pet Cathl 97-08; rtd 08; Perm
to Offic *Pet* from 09. *11 Cytringan Close, Kettering NN15 6GW*
Tel (01536) 310633 E-mail tim@johnshort.orangehome.co.uk
SHORT, Kenneth Arthur. b 33. Tyndale Hall Bris 64. **d** 67 **p** 68. C
E Twickenham St Steph *Lon* 67-71; C Paddock Wood *Roch*
71-74; SE Area Sec BCMS 74-82; Hon C Sidcup Ch Ch *Roch*
74-82; V Tollington Park St Mark w St Anne *Lon* 82-86; V
Holloway St Mark w Em 86-89; R Alfold and Loxwood *Guildf*
89-98; rtd 98; Perm to Offic *Roch* from 00 and *Lon* from 02.
*10 Montague Graham Court, Kidbrooke Gardens, London
SE3 0PD* Tel (020) 8858 8033
E-mail jukebox.short@btinternet.com
SHORT, Martin Peter. b 54. Peterho Cam BA77 MA81. Wycliffe
Hall Ox 77. **d** 79 **p** 80. C Shipley St Pet *Bradf* 79-82; C Becontree
St Mary *Chelmsf* 82-86; V Bolton St Jas w St Chrys *Bradf* 86-92;
Dioc Communications Officer 92-98; C Otley 92-98; Hd Media
Tr Communications Dept Abps' Coun 98-05; Hon C and Hon
Chapl Bradf Cathl 98-05; Chapl to Bp Dover *Cant* from 06; Hon
Min Can Cant Cathl from 06. *The Bishop's Office, The Old
Palace, The Precincts, Canterbury CT1 2EE* Tel (01227) 459382
E-mail martin.short@bishcant.org
SHORT, Martin Ronald. b 57. Crewe & Alsager Coll CertEd78
Leic Univ BEd85. St Jo Coll Nottm 93. **d** 93 **p** 94. C Frankby w
Greasby *Ches* 93-97; TV Horwich and Rivington *Man* 97-02; TV
Turton Moorland Min 02-08; P-in-c Rawtenstall St Mary from
08; P-in-c Constable Lee from 08; Borough Dean Rossendale
from 10. *St Paul's Vicarage, Hollin Lane, Rawtenstall, Rossendale
BB4 8HT* Tel (01706) 215585
E-mail martin.short1@btopenworld.com
SHORT, Canon Michael John. b 38. Univ of Wales (Lamp)
BA59. Sarum Th Coll 59. **d** 61 **p** 62. C Swansea St Nic *S & B*
61-64; C Oystermouth 64-69; V Merthyr Vale w Aberfan *Llan*
69-82; RD Merthyr Tydfil 76-82; R Caerphilly 82-08; RD
Caerphilly 83-04; Can Llan Cathl 89-08; Prec 02-08; rtd 08.
238 Abercynon Road, Abercynon, Mountain Ash CF45 4LU Tel
(01443) 742650 Mobile 07831-742515
SHORT, Neil Robert. b 58. Loughb Univ BSc81 St Jo Coll Dur
BA86. Cranmer Hall Dur 83. **d** 86 **p** 87. C Whitfield *Derby* 86-90;
C Bradf St Aug Undercliffe 90-96; V Burscough Bridge *Liv*
96-07; Pioneer Min Toxteth 07-09; V St Jas in the City from 09.
8 Lady Chapel Close, Liverpool L1 7BZ Tel 0151-708 8559
E-mail neil@theshorts.go-plus.net
SHORT, Mrs Patricia Ann (Pip). b 41. K Coll Lon BA62 AKC62.
d 00 **p** 01. NSM Etwall w Egginton *Derby* 00-10; NSM
Ashbourne St Jo from 10; NSM Ashbourne w Mapleton from
10; NSM Clifton from 10; NSM Norbury w Snelston from 10;

Chapl Asst Derby Hosps NHS Foundn Trust from 00; Perm to Offic *Lich* 05-09. *Ivy Cottage, 19 Monk Street, Tutbury, Burton-on-Trent DE13 9NA* Tel (01283) 813640 *or* (01332) 347141 Mobile 07711-823082 Fax (01283) 814373 E-mail pip.short@derbyhospitals.nhs.uk

SHORT, Robert Leslie. b 48. Em Coll Cam BA70 MA76. Wycliffe Hall Ox 87. **d** 92 **p** 92. Mexico 92-93; Chapl Repton Sch Derby 93-04; P-in-c Ibiza *Eur* from 04. *Capellania Anglicana de Ibiza, Apartado 547, 07820 San Antonio, Ibiza (Baleares), Spain* Tel and fax (0034) 971 343 383 E-mail chaplainibiza@netscape.net

SHORT, Stephen Timothy. b 71. Cheltenham & Glouc Coll of HE BA96. Ripon Coll Cuddesdon 05. **d** 07 **p** 08. C Tewkesbury w Walton Cardiff and Twyning *Glouc* 07-11; P-in-c Clowne *Derby* from 11; C Barlborough and Renishaw from 11. *The New Rectory, Church Street, Barlborough, Chesterfield S43 4EP* Tel (01246) 813569 Mobile 07801-357612 E-mail stephen.short71@btinternet.com

SHORT, Timothy. *See* SHORT, Canon John Timothy

SHORT, Vincent Charles. b 57. Oak Hill Th Coll 95. **d** 97 **p** 98. C Chatham St Phil and St Jas *Roch* 97-01; V Istead Rise 01-11; V New Beckenham St Paul from 11. *St Paul's Vicarage, Brackley Road, Beckenham BR3 1RB* Tel 07913-473142 (mobile) E-mail vcshort@o2.co.uk *or* vince.short@diocese-rochester.org

SHORTER, Mrs Anne Roberta. b 56. Edin Univ BA77. Westcott Ho Cam 07. **d** 09 **p** 10. C Brackley St Pet w St Jas from 09. *36 Prices Way, Brackley NN13 6NR* Tel (01280) 701561 E-mail anne.shorter@btinternet.com

SHORTER, Robert Edward. b 48. Ripon Coll Cuddesdon 89. **d** 91 **p** 92. C Braunton *Ex* 91-94; C Bishopsnympton, Rose Ash, Marianslegh etc 94-96; TV 96-98; P-in-c E w W Harptree and Hinton Blewett *B & W* 98-03; Dioc Ecum Officer 98-03; rtd 03. *Pen-y-Bryn, Dolau, Llandrindod Wells LD1 5TW* Tel (01597) 850132 E-mail robertshorter@live.co.uk

SHORTHOUSE, Raymond Trevor. b 34. DipAdEd Warwick Univ DPhil00. Ridley Hall Cam 68. **d** 70 **p** 71. C Gt Ilford St Andr *Chelmsf* 70-73; C Ludlow *Heref* 73-75; P-in-c Cressage w Sheinton 76-80; P-in-c Harley w Kenley 76-80; P-in-c Denby *Derby* 80-84; Adult Educn Officer 80-85; RD Heanor 83-84; V Chellaston 84-88; P-in-c Breadsall 88-98; Dioc Dir of Studies 88-96; rtd 98; P-in-c Symondsbury *Sarum* 99-04. *6 Heatherwood, Forden, Welshpool SY21 8LQ* E-mail justin@shorthouse.netlineuk.net

SHORTT, Noel Christopher. b 36. Open Univ BA76 Ulster Univ MA DPhil91. Bps' Coll Cheshunt 63. **d** 63 **p** 64. C Belfast St Mary *Conn* 63-66; C Agherton 66-68; Chapl RAF 68-69; I Duneane w Ballyscullion *Conn* 69-79; I Belfast St Steph w St Luke 79-89; I Ballyrashane w Kildollagh 89-99; Can Belfast St Anne 96-99; rtd 99. *2 Woodview Park, Ballymoney BT53 6DJ*

SHOTLANDER, Lionel George. b 27. Cant Univ (NZ) BA49 MA51. **d** 51 **p** 52. New Zealand 51-58 and 60-74; C Southsea St Pet *Portsm* 58-60; V Curdridge 74-85; R Durley 79-85; V Twyford and Owslebury and Morestead *Win* 85-91; rtd 91; Perm to Offic *Win* and *Portsm* from 91. *Cambria, High Street, Shirrell Heath, Southampton SO32 2JN* Tel (01329) 832353

SHOTTER, The Very Revd Edward Frank. b 33. Univ of Wales (Lamp) BA58 FRSM74 Hon FRCP07. St Steph Ho Ox 58. **d** 60 **p** 61. C Plymouth St Pet *Ex* 60-62; Inter-Colleg Sec SCM (Lon) 62-66; Perm to Offic *Lon* 62-69; Dir Lon Medical Gp 63-89; Chapl Lon Univ Medical Students 69-89; Dir Inst of Medical Ethics 74-89; Preb St Paul's Cathl 77-89; Dean Roch 89-03; rtd 03; Perm to Offic *St E* from 04. *Hill House, School Road, Westhall, Halesworth IP19 8QZ* Tel (01502) 575364 E-mail tedshotter@hotmail.com

SHOULER, Mrs Margaret Fiona. b 55. Nottm Univ BEd78. St Jo Coll Nottm MTh03. **d** 01 **p** 02. C Sherwood *S'well* 01-06; P-in-c Selston from 06. *The Vicarage, 58 Church Lane, Selston, Nottingham NG16 6EW* Tel (01773) 813777 E-mail fionashouler@hotmail.com

SHOULER, Simon Frederic. b 54. Pemb Coll Cam MA79 FRICS89. EMMTC 82. **d** 85 **p** 86. NSM Asfordby *Leic* 85-89; Lic to Offic from 89. *1 West End, Long Clawson, Melton Mowbray LE14 4PE* Tel (01664) 822698 E-mail oldmanorhouse@shoulers.co.uk

SHREEVE, The Ven David Herbert. b 34. St Pet Hall Ox BA57 MA61. Ridley Hall Cam 57. **d** 59 **p** 60. C Plymouth St Andr *Ex* 59-64; V Bermondsey St Anne *S'wark* 64-71; V Eccleshill *Bradf* 71-84; RD Calverley 78-84; Hon Can Bradf Cathl 83-84; Adn Bradf 84-99; rtd 99; Perm to Offic *Bradf* from 99 and *Ripon* from 00. *26 Kingsley Drive, Harrogate HG1 4TJ* Tel (01423) 886479

SHREWSBURY, Preb Michael Buller. b 30. St Jo Coll Dur BA54. Linc Th Coll 54. **d** 56 **p** 57. C Salford St Phil w St Steph *Man* 56-60; Chapl RN 60-63; Chapl HM Pris Pentonville 64-67; Bermuda 67-70; V Dalston H Trin w St Phil *Lon* 70-86; AD Hackney 79-84; Preb St Paul's Cathl 86-92; R Stepney St Dunstan and All SS 86-92; rtd 92; Perm to Offic *Lon* from 92. *Flat 1, 150 Wapping High Street, London E1W 3PH* Tel (020) 7480 5479 E-mail mike.shrewsbury@btinternet.com

SHREWSBURY, Area Bishop of. *See* RYLANDS, The Rt Revd Mark James

SHRIMPTON, Mrs Sheila Nan. b 32. Qu Mary Coll Lon BA54 LSE CertSS55. St Chris Coll Blackheath 57. **dss** 83 **d** 87 **p** 94. Lic to Offic *B & W* 83-90; NSM Barkston and Hough Gp *Linc* 90-97; Asst Local Min Officer 90-97; C Brant Broughton and Beckingham 97-98; P-in-c Churchstanton, Buckland St Mary and Otterford *B & W* 98-02; rtd 02; Perm to Offic *B & W* from 03. *2 King William Mews, Church Street, Curry Rivel, Langport TA10 0HD* Tel (01458) 259293 E-mail nanshrimpton@aol.com

SHRINE, Robert Gerald. b 44. Birm Univ BA65 Univ of Zambia PGCE70 Lanc Univ MA74 Open Univ BA80. St Jo Coll Nottm MA97. **d** 97 **p** 98. C Blackpool St Thos *Blackb* 97-99; Dioc Chapl among Deaf People *Bradf* and *Wakef* from 99. *7 Russell Hall Lane, Queensbury, Bradford BD13 2AJ* Fax (01274) 889006 E-mail bob.shrine@bradford.anglican.org

SHRINE, Mrs Susan Elaine Walmsley. b 56. NOC. **d** 02 **p** 03. C Bradshaw and Holmfield *Wakef* 02-04; TV Shelf w Buttershaw St Aid *Bradf* 04-10; P-in-c Queensbury from 10. *7 Russell Hall Lane, Queensbury, Bradford BD13 2AJ* Tel (01274) 818280 E-mail sue.shrine@tiscali.co.uk

SHRISUNDER, David Shripat. b 29. Osmania Univ Hyderabad BA52 Serampore Univ BD59 Shivaji Univ Kolhapur MA69. Bp's Coll Calcutta 54. **d** 57 **p** 58. C Poona St Paul w Kirkee All SS India 57-58; P I Bombay Em 58-61; I Solapur Epiphany 61-71, 72-75 and 88-90; Lect Dayanand Coll Solapur 69-71, 72-75 and 78-79; C Batley All SS *Wakef* 71-72; C Skegness *Linc* 75-77; C Derringham Bank *York* 80-81; TV Grays Thurrock *Chelmsf* 81-85; R Uddingston *Glas* 85-88; R Cambuslang 85-88; P-in-c Sinfin Moor *Derby* 90-94; rtd 94; Perm to Offic *Wakef* 94-96 and from 98. *23 Foundry Street, Ravensthorpe, Dewsbury WF13 3HW* Tel (01924) 501336

SHRISUNDER, Romita Jones. b 78. Kolhapur Univ India BSc98 Leeds Univ BA03 MA10. St Steph Ho Ox 04. **d** 06 **p** 07. C Brighouse and Clifton *Wakef* 06-09; V Chaddesden St Phil w Derby St Mark from 11. *St Philip's Vicarage, Taddington Road, Chaddesden, Derby DE21 4JU* Tel (01332) 660072 E-mail romitashrisunder@yahoo.com

SHRIVES, Austen Geoffrey. b 28. Lon Univ BD68 MTh77. S'wark Ord Course. **d** 64 **p** 65. C Lower Sydenham St Mich *S'wark* 64-68; Miss to Seamen 68-74; V Epsom St Martin *Guildf* 74-84; V York Town St Mich 84-87; R Churchstanton, Buckland St Mary and Otterford *B & W* 87-93; rtd 93; Perm to Offic *Ex* 94-96 and *Heref* from 97. *16 Watling Street, Ross-on-Wye HR9 5UF* Tel (01989) 566237

SHUFFLEBOTHAM, Alastair Vincent. b 32. Nottm Univ CSocSc57. Lich Th Coll 63. **d** 65 **p** 66. C W Kirby St Bridget *Ches* 65-69; V Tranmere St Paul 69-71; V Tranmere St Paul w St Luke 71-78; V Neston 78-97; rtd 97. *Y-Clystyrau, 5 Tan-y-Bryn, Llanbedr Dyffryn Clwyd, Ruthin LL15 1AQ* Tel (01824) 704619

SHUKER, Linda Kathleen. b 56. Imp Coll Lon BSc77 PhD81. St Jo Coll Nottm 05. **d** 07 **p** 08. C Rothley *Leic* 07-11; R Birling, Addington, Ryarsh and Trottiscliffe *Roch* from 11. *The Vicarage, Birling Road, Ryarsh, West Malling ME19 5AW* Tel (01732) 842249 E-mail dlshuker@aol.com

SHUKMAN, Ann Margaret. b 31. Girton Coll Cam BA53 MA58 LMH Ox DPhil74. WMMTC 80. **dss** 84 **d** 92 **p** 94. Steeple Aston w N Aston and Tackley *Ox* 84-96; NSM 92-96; rtd 96; Perm to Offic *Ox* from 96; Hon C Dumfries *Glas* from 01. *Elshieshields Tower, Lockerbie DG11 1LY* Tel (01387) 810280 Fax 811777 E-mail ann.shukman@virgin.net

SHULER, Patricia Ann Margaret. b 52. Anglia Ruskin Univ MA08 Univ of Wales (Ban) BTh08. Ridley Hall Cam 02. **d** 05 **p** 06. C Ipswich St Aug *St E* 05-09; C Woodbridge St Jo and Bredfield from 09. *1 Anderson's Way, Woodbridge IP12 4EB* Tel (01394) 383162 E-mail tricia.shuler@gmail.com

SHUTT, Anthony John. b 57. Brunel Univ BSc79. Trin Coll Bris 87. **d** 89 **p** 90. C Epsom St Martin *Guildf* 89-95; P-in-c Send from 95. *St Mary's Vicarage, Vicarage Lane, Send, Woking GU23 7JN* Tel (01483) 222193

SHUTT, Laurence John. b 42. MPS64 MRPharmS88. St Steph Ho Ox 87 Llan Dioc Tr Scheme 80. **d** 84 **p** 85. NSM Whitchurch *Llan* 84-87; C Llanishen and Lisvane 88-90; V Middlestown *Wakef* 90-97; P-in-c Arnside *Carl* 97-04; Chapl RNR 89-04; rtd 04. *PO Box 59448, Pissouri, 4607 Limassol, Cyprus* Tel (00357) 2522 2507 Mobile 9913 8292 *or* 9913 9416 E-mail shasting@cytanet.com.cy

SHUTT, Nicholas Stephen. b 58. Qu Mary Coll Lon LLB80 Solicitor 83. SWMTC 91. **d** 94 **p** 95. NSM Yelverton, Meavy, Sheepstor and Walkhampton *Ex* from 94; P-in-c from 08. *12 Blackbrook Close, Walkhampton, Yelverton PL20 6JF* Tel (01822) 854653 E-mail nick.shutt@dsl.pipex.com

SHUTTLEWORTH, Alexander John. b 78. Lanc Univ LLB99 Barrister-at-Law (Middle Temple) 00 Solicitor 05. Trin Coll Bris BA10. **d** 10 **p** 11. C Redhill H Trin *S'wark* from 10. *3 Ringwood Avenue, Redhill RH1 2DY* Tel (01737) 766604 Mobile 07735-360901 E-mail alexshuttleworth@talk21.com

SIBANDA, Melusi Francis. b 72. Univ of Zimbabwe BSc96 BA99. St Martin's Coll Lanc MA06. Bp Gaul Th Coll Harare 97. **d** 98 **p** 99. C Bulawayo Cathl Zimbabwe 98-01; R Bulawayo St Marg 01-03; C Colne and Villages *Blackb* 03-06; P-in-c Rednal *Birm*

from 06. *St Stephen's Vicarage, Edgewood Road, Rednal, Birmingham B45 8SG* Tel 0121-453 3347 Mobile 07887-745427 E-mail mfsibanda@tiscali.co.uk

SIBBALD, Olwyn. *See* MARLOW, Mrs Olwyn Eileen

SIBLEY, Jonathan Paul Eddolls. b 55. Newc Univ BA77. Westcott Ho Cam 78 Ripon Coll Cuddesdon 85. d 87 p 88. C Waltham Cross *St Alb* 87-90; C Chalfont St Peter *Ox* 90-96; P-in-c Sulhamstead Abbots and Bannister w Ufton Nervet 96-02; P-in-c Sutton St Mary *Linc* from 02. *The Vicarage, Market Place, Long Sutton, Spalding PE12 9JJ* Tel and fax (01406) 362033 E-mail jonathan.sibley3@btinternet.com

SIBLEY, Peter Linsey. b 40. Selw Coll Cam BA61 MA63. Oak Hill Th Coll 79. d 81 p 82. C Crofton *Portsm* 81-84; TV Cheltenham St Mark *Glouc* 84-93; P-in-c Tewkesbury H Trin 93-96; V 96-05; RD Tewkesbury and Winchcombe 97-02; rtd 05. *14 Griffiths Avenue, Cheltenham GL51 7BH* Tel (01242) 514640 E-mail sibglos@aol.com

SIBSON, Canon Edward John. b 39. Brasted Th Coll 61 St Aid Birkenhead 63. d 65 p 66. C Gt Parndon *Chelmsf* 65-69; C Saffron Walden 69-72; P-in-c Colchester St Leon 72-77; Ind Chapl 72-80; TV Colchester St Leon, St Mary Magd and St Steph 77-80; V Layer de la Haye 80-90; R Chipping Ongar w Shelley 90-98; RD Ongar 94-98; P-in-c High and Gd Easter w Margaret Roding 98-04; P-in-c Gt Canfield w High Roding and Aythorpe Roding 02-04; Hon Can Chelmsf Cathl 01-04; rtd 04; Perm to Offic *Chelmsf* from 04. *73 Thaxted Road, Saffron Walden CB11 3AG* Tel (01799) 520007 E-mail john@trsw73.wanadoo.co.uk

SIBSON, Canon Robert Francis. b 46. Leeds Univ CertEd68. Sarum & Wells Th Coll 78. d 80 p 81. C Watford St Mich *St Alb* 80-83; TV Digswell and Panshanger 83-90; V Biggleswade 90-02; Chapl Bedford and Shires Health and Care NHS Trust 94-02; RD Biggleswade *St Alb* 96-01; Hon Can St Alb from 98; V Sawbridgeworth from 02. *The Vicarage, 144 Sheering Mill Lane, Sawbridgeworth CM21 9ND* Tel (01279) 723305 Fax 721541 E-mail robert.sibson@btinternet.com

SICHEL, Stephen Mackenzie. b 59. UEA BA80 Birm Univ MA95. Ripon Coll Cuddesdon 87. d 90 p 91. C Tottenham St James *Lich* 90-95; C Camberwell St Giles w St Matt *S'wark* 95-01; P-in-c Brixton St Matt 01-02; V Brixton St Matt w St Jude from 02; AD Lambeth N from 10. *The Vicarage, 5 St Matthew's Road, London SW2 1ND* Tel and fax (020) 7733 9605 E-mail sichel@freenet.co.uk

SIDAWAY, The Ven Geoffrey Harold. b 42. Kelham Th Coll 61. d 66 p 67. C Beighton *Derby* 66-70; C Chesterfield St Mary and All SS 70-72; P-in-c Derby St Bart 72-74; V 74-77; V Maidstone St Martin *Cant* 77-86; V Bearsted w Thurnham 86-00; RD Sutton 92-99; Hon Can Cant Cathl 94-00; Adn Glouc from 00; Can Res Glouc Cathl from 00. *Glebe House, Church Road, Maisemore, Gloucester GL2 8EY* Tel (01452) 528500 Fax 381528 E-mail archdglos@star.co.uk

SIDDALL, Canon Arthur. b 43. Lanc Univ MA81 Surrey Univ PGCE94 MCMI96. ALCD67. d 67 p 68. C Formby H Trin *Liv* 67-70; C Childwall All SS 70-72; CMS 72-77; Chapl Chittagong Ch Ch Bangladesh 74-77; V Clitheroe St Paul Low Moor *Blackb* 77-82; V Blackb St Gabr 82-90; Dep Gen Sec Miss to Seamen 90-93; Hon C Leatherhead *Guildf* 93-96; V Chipping and Whitewell *Blackb* 96-04; Rural Chapl 03-04; Chapl Naples w Sorrento, Capri and Bari *Eur* 04-07; Chapl Montreux w Anzere, Gstaad and Monthey 07-09; Adn Italy and Malta 05-09; Adn Switzerland 09-09; rtd 09. *24 Shaw Crescent, Liverpool L37 8DA* Tel 0151-929 2608

SIDDLE, Michael Edward. b 33. Dur Univ BA54. St Aid Birkenhead 55. d 57 p 58. C Fazakerley *Liv* 57-59; C Farnworth 59-62; V Swadlincote *Derby* 62-70; Distr Sec (Northd and Dur) BFBS 70-72; Yorkshire 72-82; V Bamber Bridge St Aid *Blackb* 82-87; V Horsforth *Ripon* 87-00; rtd 00; Perm to Offic *Ripon* from 00. *28 Carr Bridge Drive, Cookridge, Leeds LS16 7JY* Tel 0113-261 0498 Mobile 07941-209069 E-mail mirisiddle@aol.com

SIDEBOTHAM, Canon Stephen Francis. b 35. Qu Coll Cam BA58 MA80. Linc Th Coll 58. d 60 p 61. C Bitterne Park *Win* 60-64; Hong Kong 64-83; Dean 76-83; Archdeacon 78-83; Chapl Gravesend and N Kent Hosp 83-94; R Gravesend St Geo *Roch* 83-94; RD Gravesend 91-94; P-in-c Rosherville 91-94; Acorn Chr Foundn from 94; rtd 97; Perm to Offic *Ox* 97-98. *87 Aston Abbotts Road, Weedon, Aylesbury HP22 4NH* Tel (01296) 640098

SIDEBOTTOM, Andrew John. *See* DAVIES, Andrew John

SIDEBOTTOM, Susan. b 54. NSM Course. d 09 p 10. NSM Chesterton *Lich* from 09. *18 Leek Avenue, Newcastle ST5 7PN*

SIDWELL, Elizabeth Sarah. b 57. Girton Coll Cam BA79 MA83 Univ of Wales (Swansea) MSc94. Ripon Coll Cuddesdon 08. d 10 p 11. C Wells St Cuth w Wookey Hole *B & W* from 10. *25 Wood Close, Wells BA5 2GA* Tel (01749) 673447 E-mail essidwell@yahoo.ie

SIEBERT, Mrs Rosemary Clare. b 48. Solicitor 03. SEITE 99. d 08 p 09. NSM Folkestone St Mary, St Eanswythe and St Sav *Cant* from 08. *35 Warren Way, Folkestone CT19 6DT* Tel (01303) 244114 Mobile 07763-330113 E-mail rsiebert@btinternet.com

SIEJKOWSKI, Piotr Jan. *See* ASHWIN-SIEJKOWSKI, Piotr Jan

SIGRIST, Mrs Catherine Mary. b 55. Westcott Ho Cam. d 07 p 08. C Cheriton St Martin *Cant* 07-10; C Cheriton All So w Newington 07-10; R Ringwould w Kingsdown and Ripple etc from 10. *The Rectory, Upper Street, Kingsdown, Deal CT14 8BJ* Tel (01304) 373951 E-mail catherine.sigrist@btinternet.com

SIGRIST, Richard Martin. b 46. Bernard Gilpin Soc Dur 67 Sarum Th Coll 68. d 71 p 72. C Yeovil St Mich *B & W* 71-74; Chapl RN 74-84; TV Sidmouth, Woolbrook and Salcombe Regis *Ex* 84-86; TR 86-91; TR Sidmouth, Woolbrook, Salcombe Regis, Sidbury etc 91-94; RD Ottery 90-94; USA 94-99; P-in-c Devonport St Bart *Ex* 99-02; V 02-07; V Devonport St Bart and Ford St Mark 08-11; RD Plymouth Devonport 01-11; rtd 11. *4 Brue Crescent, Burnham-on-Sea TA8 1LR* Tel (01278) 780135 E-mail rmsigrist@hotmail.com

SILCOCK, Donald John. b 30. AKC59. d 60 p 61. C Hackney St Jo *Lon* 60-63; C-in-c Plumstead Wm Temple Ch Abbey Wood CD *S'wark* 63-68; C Felpham w Middleton *Chich* 68-74; R Ightham *Roch* 74-84; R Cliffe at Hoo w Cooling 84-92; RD Strood 85-91; rtd 92; Perm to Offic *Chich* from 92. *Puck's House, 26 Ancton Way, Bognor Regis PO22 6JN* Tel (01243) 582589

SILINS, Jacqueline. *See* JOHNSON, Ms Jacqueline

SILK, Canon Ian Geoffrey. b 60. Pemb Coll Cam BA81 MA85. Trin Coll Bris BA89. d 89 p 90. C Linc St Giles 89-93; P-in-c Linc St Geo Swallowbeck 93-98; V from 98; PV Linc Cathl from 01; Can and Preb Linc Cathl from 07. *St George's Vicarage, 87 Eastbrook Road, Lincoln LN6 7EW* Tel (01522) 870881

SILK, John Arthur. b 52. Selw Coll Cam BA73 MA77 K Coll Lon M1 h80. Westcott Ho Cam 75. d 77 p 78. C Banstead *Guildf* 77-80; C Dorking w Ranmore 80-84; R Ringwould w Kingsdown *Cant* 84-95; V Thames Ditton *Guildf* from 95. *The Vicarage, Summer Road, Thames Ditton KT7 0QQ* Tel (020) 8398 3446 E-mail johnsilk@tiscali.co.uk

SILK, Richard Trevor. b 67. St Steph Ho Ox 01. d 03 p 04. C St Marychurch *Ex* 03-06; P-in-c Bovey Tracey St Jo w Heathfield 06-09; V Hamilton Ch Ch Australia from 09. *The Rectory, 39 Griffin Street, Hamilton Vic 3300, Australia* Tel (0061) (3) 5571 1317 E-mail fr.richard@bigpond.com

SILK, Stuart Charles. b 76. SS Mark & Jo Univ Coll Plymouth BA99. Oak Hill Th Coll BA10. d 10 p 11. C Southbourne w W Thorney *Chich* from 10. *8 Hurstwood Avenue, Southbourne PO10 8LN* Tel (01243) 389743 Mobile 07866-487535 E-mail stuartcsilk@gmail.com

SILK, Timothy James. b 73. Ox Brookes Univ BSc96. Oak Hill Th Coll BA99. d 99 p 00. C Stamford St Geo w St Paul *Linc* 99-02; C Arborfield w Barkham *Ox* 02-07; Ireland Team Ldr Crosslinks 07-11; C Kill *D & G* 08-11; P-in-c Bris St Phil and St Jacob w Em from 11. *Parish Office, St Philip and St Jacob Church, Tower Hill, Bristol BS2 0ET* Tel 0117-929 3386 E-mail tsilk@crosslinks.org

SILKSTONE, Thomas William. b 27. St Edm Hall Ox BA51 MA55 BD67. Wycliffe Hall Ox 51. d 53 p 54. C Aston SS Pet and Paul *Birm* 53-56; Div Master Merchant Taylors' Sch Crosby 56-62; Lect K Alfred's Coll Win 62-65; Sen Lect 65-75; Prin Lect 75-85; Lic to Offic *Win* 62-85; Perm to Offic *Truro* from 82; rtd 92. *Trevalyon, Lansallos, Looe PL13 2PX* Tel (01503) 72110

SILLER, Canon James Robert William. b 44. Pemb Coll Ox BA65 MA70. Westcott Ho Cam 67. d 70 p 71. C Spring Grove St Mary *Lon* 70-73; C Leeds St Pet *Ripon* 73-77; P-in-c Quarry Hill 73-77; V Gilling and Kirkby Ravensworth 77-82; P-in-c Melsonby 77-82; R Farnley 82-94; V Potternewton 94-05; Hon Can Ripon Cathl 99-05; rtd 05; Perm to Offic *York* from 06. *1 Sandhill Oval, Leeds LS17 8EB* Tel 0113-268 0014

SILLETT, Angela Veronica Isabel. *See* BERNERS-WILSON, Preb Angela Veronica Isabel

SILLEY, Canon Michael John. b 48. Ripon Coll Cuddesdon 82. d 84 p 85. C Frodingham *Linc* 84-87; V Ingham w Cammeringham w Fillingham 87-96; R Aisthorpe w Scampton w Thorpe le Fallows etc 87-96; RD Lawres 92-96; P-in-c N w S Carlton 93-96; P-in-c Brigg 96-97; V Brigg, Wrawby and Cadney cum Howsham 97-04; RD Yarborough 01-02; Bp's Dom Chapl from 05; Gen Preacher from 05; Can and Preb Linc Cathl from 09. *Bishop's House, Eastgate, Lincoln LN2 1QQ* Tel (01522) 534701 E-mail michael.silley@lincoln.anglican.org

SILLIS, Andrew Keith. b 66. Wolv Poly BSc87. Aston Tr Scheme 91 Westcott Ho Cam 93. d 96 p 97. C Boyne Hill *Ox* 96-99; C Hayes St Nic CD *Lon* 99-00; C-in-c 00-05; V N Hayes St Nic 05-09; V Cuddington *Guildf* from 09. *St Mary's Vicarage, St Mary's Road, Worcester Park KT4 7JL* Tel (020) 8337 4704 E-mail asillis@aol.com

SILLIS, Eric Keith. b 41. NW Ord Course 75. d 78 p 79. C Blackpool St Steph *Blackb* 78-82; V Huncoat 82-86; V Blackpool St Wilfrid 86-95; V Fleetwood St Dav 95-06; Dioc Chapl MU 99-06; rtd 06; Perm to Offic *Blackb* from 06. *23 Fernwood Avenue, Thornton-Cleveleys FY5 5EU* Tel (01253) 865449 E-mail ksillis@stdavid.freeserve.co.uk *or* ksillis@fsnet.co.uk

SILLIS, Graham William. b 46. S'wark Ord Course 73. d 76 p 77. C Palmers Green St Jo *Lon* 76-79; C Dawlish *Ex* 79-81; V Ipswich St Thos *St E* 81-87; V Babbacombe *Ex* 87-95; C Tividale *Lich* 98-00; R Winchelsea and Icklesham *Chich* 00-03; V Derby St Luke from 03. *St Luke's Vicarage, 48 Peet Street, Derby DE22 3RF* Tel (01332) 345720 E-mail graham.sillis@freezone.co.uk

SILLITOE, William John. b 37. Lich Th Coll 67. d 69 p 70. C Ettingshall *Lich* 69-71; C March St Jo *Ely* 72-74; P-in-c Kennett 74-77; V Fordham St Pet 74-77; V Castle Bromwich St Clem *Birm* 77-00; rtd 00; Perm to Offic *Birm* 00-04. *St Clement's Croft, 11 Wood Green Road, Wednesbury WS10 9AX* Tel 0121-505 5954 E-mail mwm@fort34.freeserve.co.uk

SILLS, Canon Peter Michael. b 41. Nottm Univ BA63 LLM68 Kent Univ PhD00 Barrister 76. S'wark Ord Course 78. d 81 p 82. C W Wimbledon Ch Ch *S'wark* 81-85; P-in-c Barnes H Trin 85-93; Wandsworth Adnry Ecum Officer 90-93; V Purley St Mark 93-00; Can Res Ely Cathl 00-08; rtd 08; Perm to Offic *Chich* from 08. *The Coach House, Keymer Road, Hassocks BN6 8JR* Tel (01273) 842760

SILVA, Peter John. b 47. Rhodes Univ BA73 HDipEd77 BEd79. St Paul's Coll Grahamstown 68. d 74 p 74. C Bloemfontein Cathl S Africa 74-75; Chapl Dioc Sch for Girls Grahamstown 75-79 and 89-95; Lect Rhodes Univ 79-81; Dir Academic Support Services Natal Univ 81-85; Regional Manager Performance and Educn Services 86; Dir Tape Aids for the Blind 87; R Overport Ch Ch 88-89; Dir Educn Projects Grahamstown Foundn 95-98; TV Abingdon *Ox* 99-02; Chief Exec Officer Peers Early Educn Partnership 02-11; P-in-c Gt w Lt Tew *Ox* from 11; P-in-c Over w Nether Worton from 11. *The Vicarage, New Road, Great Tew, Chipping Norton OX7 4AG* Tel (01608) 683263 Mobile 07980-264472 E-mail silvapete@gmail.com

SILVERMAN, Prof Bernard Walter. b 52. Jes Coll Cam BA73 MA76 PhD78 ScD89 Southn Univ BTh00 FRS97. STETS 97. d 99 p 00. Prof Statistics Bris Univ 93-03; Prof Statistics Ox Univ from 03; Master St Pet Coll Ox 03-09; Hon C Cotham St Sav w St Mary and Clifton St Paul *Bris* 99-05; Lic to Offic *Ox* 05-09; Hon C Ox St Giles and SS Phil and Jas w St Marg from 09. *St Margaret's Church, 19 St Margaret's Road, Oxford OX2 6RX* E-mail bernard.silverman@smithschool.ox.ac.uk

SILVERSIDES, Mark. b 51. Lon Univ BD73. St Jo Coll Nottm 74. d 76 p 77. C Hornchurch St Andr *Chelmsf* 76-80; P-in-c Becontree St Thos 80-85; TR Becontree W 85-86; CPAS Staff 86-92; New Media Producer from 92. *15 Glenhurst Drive, Whickham, Newcastle upon Tyne NE16 5SH* Tel 0191-488 1937 E-mail msilversides@ambitnewmedia.com

SILVERTHORN, Alan. b 37. St Mich Coll Llan 62. d 65 p 66. C Machen and Rudry *Mon* 65-71; V New Tredegar 71-83; V Llanfrechfa and Llanddewi Fach w Llandegfeth 83-04; rtd 04. *14 Davies Street, Ystrad Mynach, Hengoed CF82 8AD* Tel (01443) 816649

SILVESTER, Christine. b 51. WMMTC 02. d 05 p 06. NSM Walsall Wood *Lich* 05-08; NSM Shelfield and High Heath from 08; Chapl R Wolv Hosps NHS Trust from 08. *31 Field Lane, Pelsall, Walsall WS4 1DN* E-mail silvesterchristine@hotmail.com

SILVESTER, David. b 59. Qu Mary Coll Lon BSc80 Nottm Univ BCombStuds85. Linc Th Coll 82. d 85 p 86. C Walthamstow St Mary w St Steph *Chelmsf* 85-90; TV Barking St Marg w St Patr 90-96; V Mildmay Grove St Jude and St Paul *Lon* 96-08; AD Islington 03-07; TR Hackney Marsh from 08. *St Barnabas' Rectory, 111 Homerton High Street, London E9 6DL* Tel (020) 8533 1156 E-mail dsilve5737@aol.com

SILVESTER, Stephen David. b 59. Chu Coll Cam BA80 MA83 Man Univ PGCE82. St Jo Coll Nottm 88. d 91 p 92. C Nottingham St Jude *S'well* 91-96; V Gamston and Bridgford 96-08; AD W Bingham 04-07; P-in-c Nottingham St Nic from 08; P-in-c Sneinton St Chris w St Phil from 10. *37 Lyme Park, West Bridgford, Nottingham NG2 7TR* Tel 0115-982 0407

SIM, David Hayward. b 29. Qu Coll Birm 57. d 59 p 60. C Foleshill St Laur *Cov* 59-62; C Kenilworth St Nic 62-64; V Devonport St Aubyn *Ex* 64-69; V Frampton *Linc* 69-74; V Gainsborough St Geo 74-82; V Sturminster Newton and Hinton St Mary *Sarum* 82-89; R Stock and Lydlinch 82-89; Dorchester 89-94; Chapl HM Pris Dorchester 89-94; rtd 95; Perm to Offic *Sarum* from 95. *12 Eldridge Close, Dorchester DT1 2JS* Tel (01305) 269262

SIMCOX, Stephen Roy. b 59. Ridley Hall Cam 02. d 04 p 05. C The Ramseys and Upwood *Ely* 04-07; P-in-c Tyseley *Birm* 07-10; V from 10; P-in-c Sparkbrook Ch Ch from 07. *St Edmund's Vicarage, 277 Reddings Lane, Tyseley, Birmingham B11 3DD* Tel 0121-777 2433 E-mail rev.stevesimcox@tiscali.co.uk

SIMESTER, Paul Stephen. b 57. Oak Hill Th Coll 97. d 99 p 00. C Branksome Park All SS *Sarum* 99-03; TV Wareham 03-07. *27 Weyman's Avenue, Bournemouth BH10 7JR* Tel (01202) 574995 E-mail psimester@hotmail.com *or* paul@church2.freeserve.co.uk

SIMISTER, Charles Arnold. b 19. MM44. Edin Th Coll 49. d 52 p 53. C Glas Ch Ch 52-57; C Worsley *Man* 57-60; V Downton *Sarum* 60-63; CF 63-84; R Kirkcudbright *Glas* 63-84; R Gatehouse of Fleet 63-84; rtd 84; Perm to Offic *Glas* from 84. *98 High Street, Kirkcudbright DG6 4JQ* Tel (01557) 330747

SIMISTER, Norman Harold. b 39. Bris Univ BSc60. d 93 p 94. OLM Wainford *St E* 93-09; Perm to Offic from 10. *Romaine, 1 School Road, Ringsfield, Beccles NR34 8NZ* Tel (01502) 715549

SIMM, Michael Keith. b 63. Trin Coll Bris BA. d 00 p 01. C Ipswich St Matt *St E* 00-03; C Gorleston St Andr *Nor* from 03. *283 Lowestoft Road, Gorleston, Great Yarmouth NR31 6JW* Tel (01493) 667914 E-mail mike simm@talk21.com

SIMMONDS, David Brian. b 38. Selw Coll Cam BA62 MA66 Heidelberg Univ 62. Ridley Hall Cam 63. d 65 p 66. C Newcastle w Butterton *Lich* 65-69; V Branston 69-97; RD Tutbury 95-97; rtd 97; Perm to Offic *Pet* 97-00 and 04-10; P-in-c Easton on the Hill, Collyweston w Duddington etc 00-02; Hon C Ketton, Collyweston, Easton-on-the-Hill etc 03-04. *8 Plover Road, Essendine, Stamford PE9 4UR* Tel (01780) 751967 E-mail david937@sky.com

SIMMONDS, Edward Alan. b 32. St Edm Hall Ox MA60. Ripon Coll Cuddesdon 88. d 89 p 90. NSM Ox St Mich w St Martin and All SS 89-92; NSM Ox St Mary V w St Cross and St Pet 92-94; Chapl Lugano *Eur* 94-98; rtd 98; Perm to Offic *Ex* from 98. *Rokesdown, Higher Duryard, Pennsylvania Road, Exeter EX4 5BQ* Tel (01392) 270311 E-mail asimmonds@eclipse.co.uk

SIMMONDS, John. b 24. Sheff Univ BA50. Ridley Hall Cam 50. d 52 p 53. C Portsdown *Portsm* 52-55; C-in-c Fareham St Jo Ev CD 55-65; V W Streatham St Jas *S'wark* 65-73; V Congresbury B & W 73-75; P-in-c Puxton w Hewish St Ann and Wick St Lawrence 73-75; V Congresbury w Puxton and Hewish St Ann 75-84; Warden Home of Divine Healing Crowhurst 84-89; rtd 89. *Beach Villa, 14 The Beach, Clevedon BS21 7QU* Tel (01275) 342295

SIMMONDS, Paul Andrew Howard. b 50. Nottm Univ BSc73. Trin Coll Bris 75. d 78 p 79. C Leic H Trin w St Jo 78-82; SW Regional Co-ord CPAS 83-86; Hd Adult Tr and Resources CPAS 86-95; Hon C Wolston and Church Lawford *Cov* from 89; Dioc Miss Adv 95-03; Research Dir Forward Vision 03-05; Team Ldr Foundations21 BRF from 05; Ind Chapl *Cov* from 08. *31 John Simpson Close, Wolston, Coventry CV8 3HX* Tel (024) 7654 3188 E-mail paul@workcare.org

SIMMONDS, Canon Paul Richard. b 38. AKC63. d 64 p 65. C Newington St Mary *S'wark* 64-67; C Cheam 68-73; P-in-c Stockwell Green St Andr 73-87; V 87-03; Hon Can S'wark Cathl 97-03; rtd 03. *Timbers, 37 Ocean Drive, Ferring, Worthing BN12 5QP* Tel (01903) 242679 E-mail paulangela@hotmail.com

SIMMONDS, Robert John. b 58. Aston Tr Scheme 92 Ripon Coll Cuddesdon 94. d 96 p 97. C Southampton Thornhill St Chris *Win* 96-00; TV Basingstoke 00-05; Chapl Co-ord HM Pris Peterborough 05-08; Chapl W Lon Mental Health NHS Trust 08-11; Sen Chapl R Berks NHS Foundn Trust from 11. *Royal Berkshire Hospital Foundation Trust, London Road, Reading RG1 5AN* Tel 0118-322 5111 E-mail bob.simmonds@royalberkshire.nhs.uk

SIMMONDS, Robert William. b 52. Nottm Univ BTh77. Linc Th Coll 72. d 80 p 81. C Roehampton H Trin *S'wark* 80-83; TV Hemel Hempstead *St Alb* 83-90; V S Woodham Ferrers *Chelmsf* 90-94; rtd 94; Perm to Offic *Cant* from 03. *21 Copperfield Court, Rectory Road, Broadstairs CT10 1HE* Tel (01843) 863564 E-mail bobwsimmonds@tiscali.co.uk

SIMMONS, Mrs Ann. b 56. WMMTC 04. d 07 p 08. C Blackheath *Birm* 07-11; V Dordon from 11. *The Vicarage, Watling Street, Dordon, Tamworth B78 1TE* Tel (01827) 892294 E-mail annbsimmons@aol.com

SIMMONS, Barry Jeremy. b 32. Leeds Univ BA54 MA62. Ridley Hall Cam 61. d 63 p 64. C Buttershaw St Aid *Bradf* 63-65; Jamaica 65-68; V Earby *Bradf* 68-73; Hong Kong 73-74; Bahrain 75-79; Chapl Luxembourg *Eur* 80-91; V Shoreham *Roch* 91-00; rtd 00; Perm to Offic *Glouc* and *Worc* from 01. *Touchdown, 57 Griffin Close, Stow on the Wold, Cheltenham GL54 1AY* Tel (01451) 831637

SIMMONS, Bernard Peter. b 26. CA Tr Coll 48 S'wark Ord Course 86. d 88 p 88. C Chatham St Wm *Roch* 88-91; rtd 91; P-in-c Underriver and Seal St Lawr *Roch* 91-95; Perm to Offic *Pet* 95-11. *5 Sycamore Drive, Desborough, Kettering NN14 2YH* Tel (01536) 763302 E-mail mail@petersimmons.me.uk

SIMMONS, Canon Brian Dudley. b 35. Master Mariner. St Steph Ho Ox 62. d 64 p 65. C Bournemouth St Pet *Win* 64-67; Miss to Seamen 67-71; Hon C Milton next Gravesend w Denton *Roch* 67-70; Hon C Gravesend St Geo 70-71; V Lamorbey H Trin 71-90; R Hever w Mark Beech 90-93; P-in-c Four Elms 90-93; R Hever, Four Elms and Mark Beech 93-94; V Langton Green 94-01; Hon Can Roch Cathl 91-01; rtd 01; Perm to Offic *Roch* from 04. *17 Chancellor House, Mount Ephraim, Tunbridge Wells TN4 8BT* Tel (01892) 617262

SIMMONS, Canon Christopher John. b 49. Mert Coll Ox MA77. NEOC 88. **d** 90 **p** 91. C Kirkleatham *York* 90-93; P-in-c Barlby 93-95; V Barlby w Riccall 95-02; RD Derwent 98-01; R Pocklington and Owsthorpe and Kilnwick Percy etc 02-08; P-in-c Burnby 06-08; P-in-c Londesborough 06-08; P-in-c Nunburnholme and Warter and Huggate 06-08; P-in-c Shiptonthorpe and Hayton 06-08; P-in-c Skirlaugh w Long Riston, Rise and Swine from 08; RD N Holderness from 09; Can and Preb York Minster from 08; C Brandesburton and Leven w Catwick from 11. *105 Main Street, Brandesburton, Driffield YO25 8RG* Tel (01964) 541593
E-mail chris@csimmons.plus.com

SIMMONS, Eric. b 30. Leeds Univ BA51. Coll of Resurr Mirfield 51. **d** 53 **p** 54. C Chesterton St Luke *Ely* 53-57; Chapl Keele Univ 57-61; CR from 63; Warden Hostel of the Resurr Leeds 66-67; Superior CR 74-87; R Foundn of St Kath in Ratcliffe 89-92; Prior St Mich Priory 93-97; rtd 98. *House of the Resurrection, Stocks Bank Road, Mirfield WF14 0BN* Tel (01924) 494318   Fax 490489

SIMMONS, Gary David. b 59. Trin Coll Bris BA86. **d** 87 **p** 88. C Ecclesfield *Sheff* 87-90; Min Stapenhill Immanuel CD *Derby* 90-96; V Stapenhill Immanuel 97-98; R Slaugham *Chich* 98-10; P-in-c Staplefield Common 08-10; R Slaugham and Staplefield Common from 10. *The Rectory, Brighton Road, Handcross, Haywards Heath RH17 6BU* Tel (01444) 400221

SIMMONS, Godfrey John. b 39. Open Univ BA81. St And NSM Tr Scheme 71 Edin Th Coll 77. **d** 74 **p** 74. Dioc Supernumerary *St And* 74-75 and 80-81; C Strathtay and Dunkeld 75 77; C Bridge of Allan and Alloa 77-80; Asst Chapl Stirling Univ 77-80; Chapl 80; Min Crieff, Muthill and Comrie 80-81; R 81-85; Chapl HM Pris Perth 80-85; R Kirkwall and Stromness *Ab* 85-91; R Strichen 91-94; R Longside, Old Deer and Peterhead 91-94; Chapl HM Pris Peterhead 91-94; Miss to Seafarers 85-02; Hon Chapl (Scotland) 85-90; Hon Area Chapl (Scotland) 90-94; Chapl Supt Mersey Miss to Seafarers 94-02; TV Ch the K *Dur* 02-06; rtd 06; Perm to Offic *Glas* from 07. *11/13 High Street, Lochmaben, Lockerbie DG11 1NG* Tel (01387) 810490
E-mail joandjohnsimmons@aol.com

SIMMONS, John. b 53. Carl Dioc Tr Course 82. **d** 85 **p** 86. C Wotton St Mary *Glouc* 85-88; P-in-c Amberley 88-92; R Burton Latimer *Pet* 92-98; RD Kettering 94-98; R Paston 98-01; V Irchester from 01. *The Vicarage, 19 Station Road, Irchester, Wellingborough NN29 7EH* Tel (01933) 312674
E-mail vicar@stkatharinesirchester.com

SIMMONS, John Graham. b 54. Westf Coll Lon BSc75 Man Univ PGCE76. NOC 89. **d** 92 **p** 93. C Thame w Towersey *Ox* 92-97; R Heydon, Gt and Lt Chishill, Chrishall etc *Chelmsf* 97-05; V Chadderton Ch Ch *Man* from 05. *The Vicarage, Block Lane, Chadderton, Oldham OL9 7QB* Tel 0161-652 2950
E-mail john@christchurchchadderton.co.uk

SIMMONS, John Harold. b 46. FCCA. Sarum & Wells Th Coll 86. **d** 89 **p** 90. NSM The Iwernes, Sutton Waldron and Fontmell Magna *Sarum* 89-01; NSM Iwerne Valley from 01. *Fourways, Frog Lane, Iwerne Courtney, Blandford Forum DT11 8QL* Tel (01258) 860515   E-mail john@fourways.plus.com

SIMMONS, Ms Margaret Irene. Cov Univ BSc02 RGN RSCN. **d** 08 **p** 09. NSM Leam Valley *Cov* 08-10; NSM Hillmorton from 10. *76 Bilton Road, Rugby CV22 7AL* Tel (01788) 574497

SIMMONS, Ms Marion. b 45. NOC 95. **d** 98 **p** 99. NSM Stoneycroft All SS *Liv* 98-99; C 00-01; TV Fazakerley Em 01-08; TR from 08. *St Paul's Vicarage, Formosa Drive, Liverpool L10 7LB* Tel 0151-521 3344   E-mail marionstpauls@aol.com

SIMMONS, Canon Maurice Samuel. b 27. St Chad's Coll Dur BA50 Newc Univ MA99 MPhil02. **d** 52 **p** 53. C S Shields St Hilda *Dur* 52-58; Youth Chapl 56-60; R Croxdale 58-81; Soc and Ind Adv to Bp Dur 61-70; Gen Sec Soc Resp Gp 70-75; Hon Can Dur Cathl from 71; Sec Dioc Bd for Miss and Unity 75-82; V Norton St Mary 81-92; RD Stockton 85-92; rtd 92. *11 Roecliffe Grove, Stockton-on-Tees TS19 8JU* Tel (01642) 618880   E-mail m.simmons1@ntlworld.com

SIMMONS, Peter. See SIMMONS, Bernard Peter

SIMMONS, Peter Maurice. b 51. ERMC 10. **d** 11. NSM Kettering Ch the King Pet from 11. *43 Walsingham Avenue, Kettering NN15 5ER* Tel (01536) 510715
E-mail peter2112@live.co.uk

SIMMONS, Richard Andrew Cartwright. b 46. Trin Coll Bris 73. **d** 75 **p** 76. C Worting *Win* 75-80; R Six Pilgrims *B & W* 80-92; R Bincombe w Broadwey, Upwey and Buckland Ripers *Sarum* from 92. *The Rectory, 526 Littlemoor Road, Weymouth DT3 5PA* Tel (01305) 812542   E-mail rac simmons@lineone.net

SIMMS, Miss Melanie Laura. b 73. Trin Coll Bris 06. **d** 08. C Southway *Ex* from 08. *16 Southway Lane, Plymouth PL6 7DH* Tel 07984-316812 (mobile)
E-mail revmelaniesimms@hotmail.co.uk

SIMMS, William Michael. b 41. Open Univ BA87 BSc01 ACIS70 MCIPD75. NEOC 84. **d** 87 **p** 88. C Croft and Eryholme and Middleton Tyas and Melsonby *Ripon* 87-88; C Headingley

88-90; C Richmond w Hudswell and C-in-c Downholme and Marske 90-93; V Hawes and Hardraw 93-09; rtd 09. *56 Ronaldshay Drive, Richmond DL10 5BW* Tel (01748) 826702

SIMON, Brother. See BROOK, Peter Geoffrey

SIMON, David Sidney. b 49. Univ of Wales (Abth) BSc(Econ)70 Hull Univ MA83 Lanc Univ MA05. NEOC 84. **d** 87 **p** 88. NSM Beverley St Mary *York* 87-94; NSM Beverley Deanery 94-98; Lect Humberside Coll of HE 87-90; Humberside Poly 90-92; Humberside Univ 92-96; Lincs and Humberside Univ 96-98; Admin Rydal Hall *Carl* 98-01; Perm to Offic 01-02; NSM Cartmel Peninsula from 02; Dioc Officer for NSM from 08. *3 Kent's Bank House, Kentsford Road, Grange-over-Sands LA11 7BB* Tel (01539) 536762
E-mail davidsimon@ktdbroadband.com

SIMON, Fiona Elizabeth. b 64. Bradf Univ BEng86. STETS 06. **d** 09 **p** 10. C Stoke-next-Guildf from 09. *35 Woking Road, Guildford GU1 1QD* Tel (01483) 569862
E-mail fiona@stjohnstoke.com

SIMON, Frederick Fairbanks. b 42. Ripon Coll Cuddesdon 74. **d** 77 **p** 78. C Cheddleton *Lich* 77-79; C Woodley St Jo the Ev *Ox* 79-82; V Spencer's Wood 82-85; P-in-c Steventon w Milton 85-87; Chapl Grenville Coll Bideford 87-95; rtd 96; Perm to Offic *Ex* 96-04. *Fairview Cottage, Link Road, Pillowell, Lydney GL15 4QY* Tel (01594) 560308

SIMON, Haydn Henry England. See ENGLAND-SIMON, Haydn Henry

SIMON, Oliver. b 45. Dur Univ BA67 Sussex Univ MA68 Sheff Univ MMinTheol94 Lon Univ DMin09. Cuddesdon Coll 69. **d** 71 **p** 72. C Kidlington *Ox* 71-74; C Bracknell 74-78; V Frodsham *Ches* 78-88; R Easthampstead *Ox* 88-00; Chapl Ripon Coll Cuddesdon 00-05; Chapl Community of St Mary V Wantage 00-05; Chapl Pemb Coll Ox 03-04; TV Rugby *Cov* 05-10; OLM Officer and Dir Studies 06-10; OLM Tutor Qu Foundn Birm 07-10; rtd 10. *Colcombe Mill Cottage, Colyton EX24 6EU* Tel (01297) 552860
E-mail oliversimon@dunelm.org.uk

SIMONS, Miss Christine. b 40. RGN62 RM64 RHV69. St Jo Coll Nottm 82. **dss** 84 **d** 87 **p** 94. Claygate *Guildf* 84-87; C Camberley St Paul 87-93; NSM 93-99; C Woking Ch Ch 99-05; rtd 05. *25 Kingsway, Blackwater, Camberley GU17 0JW* Tel (01276) 503174   E-mail chris.simons2@ntlworld.com

SIMONS, Preb John Trevor. b 34. Lon Univ BD67. ALCD66. **d** 67 **p** 68. C Becontree St Mary *Chelmsf* 67-71; V Cranham Park 71-78; P-in-c Nailsea H Trin *B & W* 78-83; R 83-97; Sen Asst P 97-99; Preb Wells Cathl 90-99; rtd 99; Nat Dir Crosswinds Prayer Trust from 97; Perm to Offic *B & W* from 99. *11 Spring Hill, Weston-super-Mare BS22 9AP* Tel and fax (01934) 624302
E-mail crosswinds@btopenworld.com

SIMONS, Mark Anselm. b 38. ARCM60. Oak Hill Th Coll 62. **d** 65 **p** 66. C Nottingham St Ann *S'well* 65-68; C N Ferriby *York* 68-75; P-in-c Sherburn 75-78; V Gt and Lt Driffield 78-93; Perm to Offic from 95; rtd 03. *7 Royal Crescent, Scarborough YO11 2RN* Tel (01723) 378056
E-mail m&f@bibleschool.go-plus.net

SIMONS, William Angus. b 18. Keble Coll Ox BA39 MA47. Cuddesdon Coll 40. **d** 41 **p** 42. C Poplar All SS w St Frideswide *Lon* 44-44 and 47-48; RAChD 44-47; C Is of Dogs Ch Ch and St Jo w St Luke *Lon* 48-54; V Fulham St Jas Moore Park 54-62; Ind Chapl *Worc* 62-63; Ind Missr R Foundn of St Kath in Ratcliffe 63-65; Chapl Hammersmith Hosp Lon 65-68; Chapl St Edm Hosp Northn 68-88; Chapl Northn Gen Hosp 68-72; P-in-c Northampton St Lawr *Pet* 72-76; C Northampton H Sepulchre w St Andr and St Lawr 76-81; rtd 81; Northants Past Coun Service from 76; Founder Dir 76-84; Supervisor from 84; Perm to Offic *Pet* from 81. *54 Park Avenue North, Northampton NN3 2JE* Tel (01604) 713767

SIMONSON, Canon Juergen Werner Dietrich. b 24. Lon Univ BD52. ALCD52. **d** 52 **p** 53. C W Kilburn St Luke w St Simon and St Jude *Lon* 52-56; Nigeria 57-63; Chapl CMS Tr Coll Chislehurst 64-65; Vice-Prin 65-67; Prin CMS Tr Coll Chislehurst 67-69; V Putney St Marg *S'wark* 69-81; RD Wandsworth 74-81; Hon Can S'wark Cathl 75-90; R Barnes St Mary 81-90; rtd 90; Perm to Offic *Win* from 90. *Elm Cottage, Horseshoe Lane, Ibthorpe, Andover SP11 0BY* Tel (01264) 736381

SIMPER, Rachel Dawn. See WATTS, Rachel Dawn

SIMPKINS, Canon Lionel Frank. b 46. UEA BSc68 Lambeth STh77. St Jo Coll Nottm LTh74. **d** 73 **p** 74. C Leic H Apostles 73-77; C Bushbury *Lich* 77-80; V Sudbury w Ballingdon and Brundon *St E* 80-96; Chapl Sudbury Hosps 80-96; RD Sudbury 88-96; V Ipswich St Aug from 96; Hon Can St E Cathl from 94; Warden of Readers 03-10. *St Augustine's Vicarage, 2 Bucklesham Road, Ipswich IP3 8TJ* Tel (01473) 728654
E-mail lionel.staug@btconnect.com

SIMPKINS, Susan Carol. b 58. St Steph Ho Ox 03. **d** 05. NSM Ruislip St Martin *Lon* from 05. *70 Park Avenue, Ruislip HA4 7UJ* Tel (01895) 630170
E-mail sue.simpkins@btopenworld.com

SIMPSON, Alan Eric. b 52. Ch Ch Ox BA73 MA77 Birm Univ PhD77 Dur Univ MA01 CPhys77 MInstP77. Cranmer Hall Dur 96. d 98 p 99. C Long Benton *Newc* 98-02; P-in-c Cresswell and Lynemouth 02-06; V from 06. *The Vicarage, 33 Till Grove, Ellington, Morpeth NE61 5ER* Tel (01670) 860242 E-mail fr.alan@talk21.com

SIMPSON, Alexander. b 31. Oak Hill Th Coll 74. d 76 p 77. Hon C Lower Homerton St Paul *Lon* 76-81; Hon C Homerton St Barn w St Paul 81-85; TV Hackney Marsh 85-87; V Kensington St Helen w H Trin 87-97; rtd 97; Perm to Offic *Derby* 01-07 and *Nor* from 08. *2 Ferndale Close, Norwich NR6 5SD* Tel (01603) 443412

SIMPSON, Canon Alison Jane. b 60. St Andr Univ BSc83 BD86 Princeton Univ MTh87. d 99 p 99. C Ellon *Ab* 99-02; R Huntly *Mor* 02-09; R Keith 02-09; R Aberchirder 02-09; P-in-c Fochabers 04-09; R Nairn from 09; Can St Andr Cathl Inverness from 09. *The New Rectory, 3 Queen Street, Nairn IV12 4AA* Tel (01667) 452458 Mobile 07548-230745 E-mail revalison433@btinternet.com

SIMPSON, Andrew. b 48. Liv Univ BEng69. Sarum Th Coll 83. d 86 p 87. NSM Canford Magna *Sarum* from 86. *17 Sopwith Crescent, Wimborne BH21 1SH* Tel (01202) 883996 E-mail andrew.simpson6@virgin.net

SIMPSON, Andrew Charles. b 65. NEOC 06. d 09 p 10. C Hessle *York* from 09. *167 First Lane, Hessle HU13 9EY* Tel (01482) 645745 E-mail andy@allsaintshessle.karoo.co.uk

SIMPSON, Charles Michael. b 38. St Cath Coll Cam MA64 Campion Hall Ox MA65 Heythrop Coll Lon STL69 K Coll Lon PhD71. d 68 p 69. Lect Th Lon Univ 72-84; Chapl Prince of Peace Community Greenwich 85-87; Retreat Dir St Beuno's Clwyd 87-91; P-in-c Selkirk *Edin* 91-94; P-in-c Offchurch *Cov* 94-96; Warden Offa Retreat Ho and Dioc Spirituality Adv 94-00; P-in-c Stoke Canon, Poltimore w Huxham and Rewe etc *Ex* 00-04; Dioc Adv in Adult Tr 00-04; rtd 04; Perm to Offic *Cov* from 05. *15 Shepherds Way, Stow on the Wold, Cheltenham GL54 1EA* Tel (01451) 831028 E-mail michaelsharon@shepherdsway.wanadoo.co.uk

SIMPSON, Christine. d 07 p 08. OLM Drayton in Hales *Lich* from 07. *18 Mortimer Road, Buntingsdale Park, Market Drayton TF9 2EP* Tel (01630) 638794 E-mail christine@simpson12.plus.com

SIMPSON, Colin George. b 63. Qu Coll Birm 06. d 08 p 09. C Astwell Gp *Pet* 08-11; P-in-c Brigstock w Stanion and Lowick and Sudborough 08-11; P-in-c Weldon w Deene from 11. *The Rectory, 12 Church Street, Brigstock, Kettering NN14 3EX* E-mail revcolinsimpson@btinternet.com

SIMPSON, David Charles Edward. b 51. NEOC 02. d 05 p 06. NSM York St Chad 05-09; Perm to Offic from 09. *98 Brunswick Street, York YO23 1ED* Tel (01904) 635085 E-mail david@simpson5000.fslife.co.uk

SIMPSON, David John. b 61. Univ Coll Dur BA85. Sarum & Wells Th Coll 89. d 91 p 92. C Selby Abbey *York* 91-94; C Romsey *Win* 94-97; Chapl Southn Univ 97-05; Chapl RN from 05. *Royal Naval Chaplaincy Service, Mail Point 1-2, Leach Building, Whale Island, Portsmouth PO2 8BY* Tel (023) 9262 5055 Fax 9262 5134

SIMPSON, Derek John. b 59. Oak Hill Th Coll BA89. d 89 p 90. C Alperton *Lon* 89-95; TR Brentford from 95; AD Hounslow from 02. *The Rectory, 3 The Butts, Brentford TW8 8BJ* Tel (020) 8568 6502 *or* 8568 7442 E-mail derek.simpson@btinternet.com

SIMPSON, Mrs Eleanor Elizabeth Mary. b 77. Univ of Wales (Ban) BA98 MTh00 Leeds Univ MA10 PGCE99. Yorks Min Course 08. d 10 p 11. C Stainforth *Sheff* from 10. *10 Grange Close, Hatfield, Doncaster DN7 6QR* Tel (01302) 841088 Mobile 07742-696363 E-mail eleanorbox@yahoo.co.uk

SIMPSON, Mrs Elizabeth Ann. b 59. Lon Bible Coll BA80 Trin Coll Bris 84. dss 86 d 97 p 98. Thornbury *Glouc* 86-87; Beckenham Ch Ch *Roch* 87-90; Heydon, Gt and Lt Chishill, Chrishall etc *Chelmsf* 90-93; Shirwell, Loxhore, Kentisbury, Arlington, etc *Ex* 93-97; NSM S Molton w Nymet St George, High Bray etc 97-99; C 99-03; P-in-c W Buckingham *Ox* from 03. *The Vicarage, Orchard Place, Westbury, Brackley NN13 5JT* Tel (01280) 704964

SIMPSON, Geoffrey Sedgwick. b 32. Hamilton Coll (NY) BA54 Wisconsin Univ MA Pemb Coll Cam PhD70. Gen Th Sem (NY) STB57. d 57 p 57. USA 57-77; Chapl Birm Univ 77-80; V Shoreham *Roch* 80-90; TR Street *York* 90-02; rtd 02; Perm to Offic *Sarum* from 03. *The Laurels, Queen Street, Yetminster, Sherborne DT9 6LL* Tel (01935) 872915

SIMPSON, Mrs Georgina. b 46. Westmr Coll Ox BTh93 Birm Univ MA95 DipEd98. SAOMC 95. d 97 p 98. NSM Littlemore *Ox* 97-98; C Ox St Giles and SS Phil and Jas w St Marg 98-09; Perm to Offic from 09. *85 Church Road, Sandford-on-Thames, Oxford OX4 4YA* Tel (01865) 775160 E-mail georgio-simpson1@gmail.com

SIMPSON, Godfrey Lionel. b 42. Sarum Th Coll 63. d 66 p 67. C Leintwardine *Heref* 66-70; C Leominster 70-73; P-in-c Whitbourne 73-79; V Barlaston *Lich* 79-02; RD Trentham 85-00;

P-in-c The Guitings, Cutsdean and Farmcote *Glouc* 02-03; P-in-c Upper and Lower Slaughter w Eyford and Naunton 02-03; R The Guitings, Cutsdean, Farmcote etc 03-09; rtd 09. *Rectory Cottage, Rendcomb, Cirencester GL7 7EZ* Tel (01285) 831358 E-mail godfreysimpson@waitrose.com

SIMPSON, Herbert. b 20. Carl Dioc Tr Course. d 82 p 83. NSM Barrow St Aid *Carl* 82; NSM Barrow St Jo 82-90; rtd 90; Perm to Offic *Carl* 90-07. *3 Glenridding Drive, Barrow-in-Furness LA14 4PE* Tel (01229) 823707

SIMPSON, Mrs Janet Mary. b 42. New Coll Edin LTh94. EAMTC 99. d 00 p 01. C Aldringham w Thorpe, Knodishall w Buxlow etc *St E* 00-03; R Elmsett w Aldham, Hintlesham, Chattisham etc 03-06; rtd 06. *8 Meadow Close, Wootton Basset, Swindon SN4 7JL* Tel (01793) 848006 E-mail revjanelmsett@tiscali.co.uk

SIMPSON, The Very Revd John Arthur. b 33. OBE01. Keble Coll Ox BA56 MA60. Clifton Th Coll 56. d 58 p 59. C Low Leyton *Chelmsf* 58-59; C Orpington Ch Ch *Roch* 59-62; Tutor Oak Hill Th Coll 62-72; V Ridge *St Alb* 72-79; P-in-c 79-81; Dir of Ords and Post-Ord Tr 75-81; Hon Can St Alb 77-79; Can Res St Alb 79-81; Adn Cant and Can Res Cant Cathl 81-86; Dean Cant 86-00; rtd 00; Perm to Offic *Cant* from 01. *Flat D, 9 Earls Avenue, Folkestone CT20 2HW* Tel (01303) 211868

SIMPSON, Canon John Bernard. b 40. St Paul's Coll Chelt CertEd62 Ox Univ MTh95 ACP66. d 93 p 93. In URC 63-93; Asst to RD Lothingland *Nor* 93-94; RD 99-10; C Hopton w Corton 93-94; P-in-c 94-99; TR Lowestoft St Marg 99-10; Hon Can Nor Cathl 01-10; rtd 10; P-in-c Publow w Pensford, Compton Dando and Chelwood *B & W* from 10. *The Rectory, Old Road, Pensford, Bristol BS39 4BB* Tel (01761) 490227 Mobile 07905-013183 E-mail canonjohn@btinternet.com

SIMPSON, Canon John Lawrence. b 33. DL04. SS Coll Cam BA55 MA59 ARCM60 UWE Hon MMus. Wells Th Coll 63. d 65 p 66. Chapl Win Cathl 65-66; C Win St Bart 65-69; Chapl Repton Sch Derby 69-71; Hd of RE Helston Sch 71-78; P-in-c Curry Rivel *B & W* 79-80; R Curry Rivel w Fivehead and Swell 80-86; V Tunbridge Wells K Chas *Roch* 86-89; Can Res Bris Cathl 89-99; rtd 99; Perm to Offic *B & W* from 00. *Yardes Cottage, Windmill Hill, Ilminster TA19 9NT* Tel (01823) 480593

SIMPSON, John Peter. b 39. ALCD66. d 66 p 67. C Woodside *Ripon* 66-69; C Burnage St Marg *Man* 69-72; V Rochdale Deeplish St Luke 72-80; R Lamplugh w Ennerdale *Carl* 80-04; rtd 04. *8 Queens Avenue, Seaton, Workington CA14 1DN* Tel (01900) 604215 E-mail revpetersim@supanet.com

SIMPSON, John Raymond. b 41. Univ of S Aus DipEd92. Chich Th Coll 65. d 67 p 68. C Scarborough St Martin *York* 67-71; C Grangetown 71-72; Youth Chapl Bermuda 72-75; C Lewisham St Mary *S'wark* 76; C Albany Australia 76-78; R Carey Park 78-84; Chapl RAN 84-90; Chapl RAAF 90-99; Grace Cathl San Francisco USA 99-00; Chapl RANSR from 00. *44/19 Oakleigh Drive, Erskine Grove, Erskine WA 6210, Australia* Tel (0061) (8) 9586 4144 E-mail simpsonjohnr@googlemail.com

SIMPSON, John Verrent. b 68. Univ of Wales (Cardiff) BScEcon93. Ripon Coll Cuddesdon BTh98. d 98 p 99. C Cardiff St Jo *Llan* 98-00; C Cen Cardiff 00-01; C Upper Chelsea H Trin *Lon* 01-04; P-in-c Lt Missenden *Ox* from 05. *The Vicarage, Little Missenden, Amersham HP7 0RA* Tel (01494) 862008 Mobile 07919-551614 E-mail office@littlemissendenparish.org.uk

SIMPSON, Kevin Gordon. b 54. QPM02. Univ of Wales BEd96 MCIPD94. St Mich Coll Llan. d 02 p 03. NSM Llantwit Fardre from 02. *95 St Anne's Drive, Pontypridd CF38 2PB* Tel (01443) 207033 Mobile 07870-397494 E-mail k.g.simpson@btinternet.com

SIMPSON, Miss Margery Patricia. b 36. SRN57 SCM59. Oak Hill Th Coll BA86. dss 86 d 87 p 94. Rodbourne Cheney *Bris* 86-87; Par Dn 87-90; Par Dn Warmley 90-94; C Warmley, Syston and Bitton 94-95; TV Yate New Town 95-96; rtd 97; Perm to Offic *Sarum* from 97. *19 Wentworth Park, Stainburn, Workington CA14 1XP* Tel (01900) 61523

SIMPSON, Mark Lawrence. b 73. Oak Hill Th Coll BA03. d 03 p 04. C Leyland St Andr *Blackb* from 03. *45 Westgate, Leyland PR25 2LX* Tel (01772) 622446 E-mail mark.simpson@standrewsleyland.org.uk

SIMPSON, Michael. *See* SIMPSON, Charles Michael

SIMPSON, Peter. *See* SIMPSON, John Peter

SIMPSON, Canon Peter Wynn. b 32. Birm Univ BA53. Ripon Hall Ox 55. d 57 p 58. C Leamington Priors H Trin *Cov* 57-60; C Croydon St Jo *Cant* 60-63; V Foleshill St Laur *Cov* 63-70; V Radford 70-79; RD Cov N 76-79; V Finham 79-91; RD Cov S 82-88; Hon Can Cov Cathl 83-91; rtd 91; Perm to Offic *Cov* from 91. *Faith Cottage, 118 Main Street, Wolston, Coventry CV8 3HP* Tel (024) 7654 3965

SIMPSON, Philip Alexander. b 54. Keele Univ BA79 CQSW79 Sunderland Univ MSc03. CMS Tr Coll Selly Oak 85. d 89 p 07. CMS from 85; Pakistan 85-98; Regional Dir for Eurasia from 98; Perm to Offic *Guildf* 06-07; NSM Woking Ch Ch from 07. *CMS, PO Box 1799, Oxford OX4 9BN* Tel 08456-201799 E-mail phil.simpson@cms-uk.org

SIMPSON, Raymond James. b 40. Lon Coll of Div ALCD63 LTh74. **d** 63 **p** 64. C Longton St Jas *Lich* 64-68; C Upper Tooting H Trin *S'wark* 68-71; BFBS Distr Sec E Anglia 71-77; C-in-c Bowthorpe CD *Nor* 78-84; V Bowthorpe 84-96; Perm to Offic *Newc* from 96; Guardian Community of Aid and Hilda from 96. *White House, Fenkle Street, Holy Island, Berwick-upon-Tweed TD15 2SR* Tel (01289) 389145 E-mail raysimpson@ndirect.co.uk

SIMPSON, Richard Lee. b 66. Keble Coll Ox BA88 MPhil91 Westmr Coll Ox PGCE89. Wycliffe Hall Ox 91. **d** 93 **p** 94. C Newc St Gabr 93-97; P-in-c Jesmond H Trin 97-06; P-in-c Newc St Barn and St Jude 97-06; P-in-c Brancepeth *Dur* from 06; Dir IME 4-7 *Dur* and *Newc* 06-10. *The Rectory, Brancepeth, Durham DH7 8EL* Tel 0191-380 0440 Mobile 07867-802671 E-mail ricksimpson300@btinternet.com

SIMPSON, Canon Robert Charles. b 46. Ridley Hall Cam. **d** 85 **p** 86. C Eastwood *S'well* 85-88; V Yardley St Cypr Hay Mill *Birm* 88-93; P-in-c Newent and Gorsley w Cliffords Mesne *Glouc* 93-95; R 95-05; Dioc Ecum Officer 04-05; P-in-c Glouc St Jas and All SS 05-10; V Glouc St Jas and All SS and Ch H from 10; AD Glouc City from 08; Hon Can Glouc Cathl from 10. *The Vicarage, 1 The Conifers, Gloucester GL1 4LP* Tel (01452) 422349 E-mail revrobertcsimpson@blueyonder.co.uk

SIMPSON, Robert David. b 61. Fitzw Coll Cam BA83 MA87 Bris Univ MLitt94. Trin Coll Bris 85. **d** 87 **p** 88. C Beckenham Ch Ch *Roch* 87-90; C Heydon w Gt and Lt Chishill *Chelmsf* 90; C Chrishall 90; C Elmdon w Wendon Lofts and Strethall 90; C Heydon, Gt and Lt Chishill, Chrishall etc 91-93; TV Shirwell, Loxhore, Kentisbury, Arlington, etc *Ex* 93-97; TR S Molton w Nymet St George, High Bray etc 97-03. *The Vicarage, Orchard Place, Winford, Brackley NN13 5JT* Tel (01280) 782893 E-mail revsimpson@supanet.com

SIMPSON, Robert John. NUU BA PGCE. **d** 03 **p** 04. NSM Ballymoney w Finvoy and Rasharkin *Conn* 03-08; NSM Ballywillan from 08. *28 Willowfield Park, Coleraine BT52 2NF* Tel (028) 7035 8552 E-mail robert@robertheather.fsnet.co.uk

SIMPSON, Robert Theodore. b 34. Linc Coll Ox BA58 MA61 K Coll Lon PhD71 UNISA MEd85. Chich Th Coll 58. **d** 60 **p** 61. C Ellesmere Port *Ches* 60-63; CR 63-66; S Africa 68-88; Prin St Pet Coll 72-75; Pres Federal Th Sem 73-75; Sen Lect Th Swaziland Univ 83-87; Assoc Prof Th 87-88; Chapl and Lect Coll of SS Mark and Jo Plymouth 88-90; Tutor Simon of Cyrene Th Inst 90-92; Perm to Offic *S'wark* 91-92; P-in-c Shadwell St Paul w Ratcliffe St Jas *Lon* 92-01; rtd 01. *36 Whitton Dene, Hounslow TW3 2JT* E-mail theo@cologon.org

SIMPSON, Canon Roger Westgarth. b 51. Lon Univ BSc72. St Jo Coll Nottm 77. **d** 79 **p** 80. C St Marylebone All So w SS Pet and Jo *Lon* 79-85; R Edin St Paul and St Geo 85-95; R Vancouver H Trin Canada 95-99; V York St Mich-le-Belfrey 99-10; C from 10; Abp's Evangelist from 10; Can and Preb York Minster from 10. *St Barnabas' Vicarage, Jubilee Terrace, York YO26 4YZ* Tel (01904) 654214 *or* 628539 E-mail roger.simpson@stmichaelsyork.org

SIMPSON, Samuel. b 26. TCD BA55 MA69 Div Test56. TCD Div Sch. **d** 56 **p** 57. C Coleraine *Conn* 56-60; I Donagh w Cloncha and Clonmany *D & R* 60-64; I Ballyscullion 64-81; Can Derry Cathl 78-96; I Errigal w Garvagh 81-96; Adn Derry 89-96; rtd 96. *53 Magheramenagh Drive, Atlantic Road, Portrush BT56 8SP* Tel (028) 7082 4292

SIMPSON (*née* RALPHS), Mrs Sharon Ann. b 55. St Mary's Coll Dur BA77. Cranmer Hall Dur 81. **dss** 83 **d** 87 **p** 94. Caverswall *Lich* 83-87; Par Dn 87-89; Asst Dioc Officer for Minl Tr *St As* 90-91; NSM Selkirk *Edin* 91-94; C Offchurch *Cov* 94-96; Warden Offa Retreat Ho and Dioc Spirituality Adv 94-00; C Stoke Canon, Poltimore w Huxham and Rewe etc *Ex* 00-04; Dioc Adv in Adult Tr 00-04; rtd 04; Perm to Offic *Cov* from 05. *15 Thornbury Way, Stow on the Wold, Cheltenham GL54 1EA* Tel (01451) 831028 E-mail michaelandsharon@shepherdsway.wanadoo.co.uk

SIMPSON, Susan Fiona. b 67. Herts Univ BSc. ERMC. **d** 11. C Soham and Wicken *Ely* from 11. *5 Adelaide Close, Soham, Ely CB7 5FJ* Tel (01353) 723229

SIMPSON, Mrs Susie Alexandra. b 58. Hertf Coll Ox BA81. St Steph Ho Ox BA98. **d** 99 **p** 00. C High Wycombe *Ox* 99-03; TV 03-08; Chapl HM YOI Roch 09-10; Chapl HM Pris Isis from 10. *HM Prison Isis, 1 Belmarsh Road, London SE28 0EB* Tel (020) 8331 4400 E-mail susie.simpson@hmps.gsi.gov.uk

SIMPSON, Ursula Lucy. b 51. St Anne's Coll Ox MA73 Leeds Univ MA05. NOC 02. **d** 05 **p** 06. NSM York St Paul 05-10; P-in-c York St Barn from 10. *St Barnabas' Vicarage, Jubilee Terrace, York YO26 4YZ* Tel and fax (01904) 654214 E-mail u.simpson@btinternet.com

SIMS, Bernard David. b 40. Bath Univ BSc66. Ox Min Course 91. **d** 94 **p** 95. NSM Beedon and Peasemore w W Ilsley and Farnborough *Ox* 94-98; TV Blakenall Heath *Lich* 98-10; rtd 10; Perm to Offic *Lich* from 10. *2 March Way, Walsall WS9 8SG* E-mail sims@beechdale.fsnet.co.uk

SIMS, The Ven Christopher Sidney. b 49. Wycliffe Hall Ox 74. **d** 77 **p** 78. C Walmley *Birm* 77-80; V Yardley St Cypr Hay Mill

80-88; V Stanwix *Carl* 88-96; RD Carl 89-95; Hon Can Carl Cathl 91-95; P-in-c Bassenthwaite, Isel and Setmurthy 96-00; P-in-c Bolton w Ireby and Uldale 96-00; P-in-c Allhallows 96-00; P-in-c Torpenhow 96-00; TR Binsey 00-03; V Shrewsbury H Cross *Lich* 03-09; RD Shrewsbury 08-09; Adn Walsall from 09. *55B Highgate Road, Walsall WS1 3JE* Tel (01922) 620153

SIMS, James Henry. b 35. St Jo Coll Nottm 87. **d** 89 **p** 91. NSM Bangor Abbey *D & D* 89-93; C Holywood 93; Bp's C Kilbroney 93-01; Min Can Belf Cathl 99-09; P-in-c Clonallon w Warrenpoint *D & D* 01-09; Can Dromore Cathl 03-09; rtd 09. *7 Prior's Lea, Holywood BT18 9QW* Tel (028) 9042 4360 E-mail jim.sims321@tiscali.co.uk

SIMS, Mrs Julia Mary Heaton. b 56. STETS 04. **d** 07 **p** 08. NSM Winscombe and Sandford *B & W* 07-11; Past Co-ord St Monica Trust Sandford Station from 11. *7 Round Oak Grove, Cheddar BS27 3BW* Tel (01934) 740120 E-mail jms125@hotmail.co.uk

SIMS, Ruth. b 06 **p** 07. NSM Alveley and Quatt *Heref* from 06. *Church Farm House, Alveley, Bridgnorth WV15 6ND*

SIMS, Sidney. b 20. Wycliffe Hall Ox. **d** 64 **p** 65. C Attenborough w Bramcote *S'well* 64-67; V Ramsey St Mary's w Ponds Bridge *Ely* 67-70; V Cambridge St Matt 70-85; Algeria 85-86; rtd 86; Perm to Offic *Nor* from 86. *Cockley Cottage, 66 Morston Road, Blakeney, Holt NR25 7BE* Tel (01263) 740184

SIMS, Vickie Lela. b 56. Iowa State Univ BA79. Ripon Coll Cuddesdon 00. **d** 02 **p** 03. C Grantham *Linc* 02-05; P-in-c Coulsdon St Andr *S'wark* 05-11; V from 11; Jt Dir of IME Croydon Area from 09. *99A St Andrew's Road, Coulsdon CR5 3HG* Tel (020) 8676 2827 E-mail simstabbat@hotmail.com

SINCLAIR, Andrew John McTaggart. b 50. Ex Univ BA80. Westcott Ho Cam 81. **d** 84 **p** 85. C Aston cum Aughton and Ulley *Sheff* 84-87; C Rotherham 87-88; TV Edin Old St Paul 88-93; Hon Angl Chapl Edin Univ and Moray Ho Coll 89-93; TV Dunstable *St Alb* 93-00; V Verwood *Sarum* from 00. *The Vicarage, 34 Dewlands Way, Verwood BH31 6JN* Tel (01202) 822298 *or* 813256 E-mail ansinclair@aol.com

SINCLAIR, Canon Arthur Alfred. b 46. **d** 87 **p** 89. Hon C St Andr Cathl Inverness 87-92; C 93-97; Chapl Asst Inverness Hosp 87-89; Dioc Chapl 87-89; NSM Culloden St Mary-in-the-Fields 89-92; P-in-c from 93; P-in-c Inverness St Jo from 93; Edin Th Coll 92-93; Chapl Raigmore Hosp NHS Trust Inverness from 93; Can St Andr Cathl Inverness from 05. *St John's Rectory, Southside Road, Inverness IV2 3BG* Tel (01463) 716288 E-mail sinclairstjohns@aol.com

SINCLAIR, Charles Horace. b 19. Keble Coll Ox BA40 MA44. Linc Th Coll 41. **d** 42 **p** 43. C Upper Norwood St Jo *Cant* 42-45; Chapl K Coll Auckland 46-50; Hd Master Prebendal Sch Chich 51-53; PV Chich Cathl 51-53; Chapl and Sen Tutor Brookland Hall Welshpool 53-57; Hd Master St Aid Sch Denby Dale 57-64; Perm to Offic *Wakef* 58-64; rtd 84; Perm to Offic *Cant* 84-09. *21 St Andrews, The Durlocks, Folkestone CT19 6AW* Tel (01303) 250882 Mobile 07974-294886

SINCLAIR, Colin. b 52. Ch Ch Ox MA. **d** 84 **p** 85. NSM Ramoan w Ballycastle and Culfeightrin *Conn* 84-92. *4 Bushfoot Cottages, Portballintrae, Bushmills BT57 8RN* Tel (028) 2073 1551

✠SINCLAIR, The Rt Revd Gordon Keith. b 52. Ch Ch Ox MA. Cranmer Hall Dur. **d** 84 **p** 85 **c** 08. C Summerfield *Birm* 84-88; V Aston SS Pet and Paul 88-01; AD Aston 00-01; Hon Can Birm Cathl 00-01; V Cov H Trin 01-07; Suff Bp Birkenhead *Ches* from 07. *Bishop's Lodge, 67 Bidston Road, Prenton CH43 6TR* Tel 0151-652 2741 Fax 651 2330 E-mail bpbirkenhead@chester.anglican.org

SINCLAIR, Horace. See SINCLAIR, Charles Horace

SINCLAIR, The Ven Jane Elizabeth Margaret. b 56. St Hugh's Coll Ox BA78 MA80. St Jo Coll Nottm BA82. **dss** 83 **d** 87 **p** 94. Herne Hill St Paul *S'wark* 83-86; Chapl and Lect St Jo Coll Nottm 86-93; Can Res Sheff Cathl 93-03; Hon Can Stow 03-07; V Rotherham 03-07; Adn Stow *Linc* from 07; Adn Lindsey from 07. *Sanderlings, Willingham Road, Market Rasen LN8 3RE* Tel (01673) 849896 E-mail archdeacon.stowlindsey@lincoln.anglican.org

SINCLAIR, Canon John Robert. b 58. Oak Hill Th Coll 90. **d** 92 **p** 93. C Ponteland *Newc* 92-96; V Long Benton St Mary 96-01; V Newburn from 01; AD Newc W from 07; Hon Can Newc Cathl from 08. *The Vicarage, High Street, Newburn, Newcastle upon Tyne NE15 8LQ* Tel 0191-229 0522 Fax 267 0582 E-mail john.r.sinclair@lineone.net

SINCLAIR, Keith. See SINCLAIR, The Rt Revd Gordon Keith

✠SINCLAIR, The Rt Revd Maurice Walter. b 37. Nottm Univ BSc59 Leic Univ PGCE60. Tyndale Hall Bris 62 Nashotah Ho Hon DD01. **d** 64 **p** 65 **c** 90. C Boscombe St Jo *Win* 64-67; SAMS 67-02; Argentina 67-78; Personnel Sec 79-83; Asst Gen Sec 83-84; Prin Crowther Hall CMS Tr Coll Selly Oak 84-90; Bp N Argentina 90-02; Primate of S Cone 95-02; rtd 02; Hon Asst Bp Birm from 02. *55 Selly Wick Drive, Birmingham B29 7JQ* Tel 0121-471 2617 E-mail mandg@sinclair401.fsnet.co.uk

SINCLAIR, Michael David Bradley. b 42. NOC Coll of Resurr Mirfield. **d** 97 **p** 98. NSM Settrington w N Grimston, Birdsall w Langton *York* 97-99; R W Buckrose 99-08; rtd 08; NSM

Helmsley *York* from 09; NSM Upper Ryedale from 09. *Witham Cottage, Langton, Malton YO17 9QP* Tel (01653) 658360

SINCLAIR, Nigel Craig. b 65. Teesside Poly BA87 Coll of Ripon & York St Jo MA00. St Jo Coll Dur BA93. d 94 p 95. C Marton-in-Cleveland *York* 94-97; TV Thirsk 97-02; V Pannal w Beckwithshaw *Ripon* from 02; AD Harrogate from 09. *St Robert's Vicarage, 21 Crimple Meadows, Pannal, Harrogate HG3 1EL* Tel (01423) 870202
E-mail nigelsinclair@btinternet.com

SINCLAIR, Peter. b 44. Oak Hill Th Coll. d 88 p 89. C Darlington H Trin *Dur* 88-91; C-in-c Bishop Auckland Woodhouse Close CD 91-98; P-in-c Consett 98-09; rtd 09. *16 Deanery View, Lanchester, Durham DH7 0NH*

SINCLAIR, Peter Monteith. b 52. St Andr Univ BSc73. NEOC. d 01 p 02. NSM Darlington St Cuth *Dur* 01-05; Hon Min Can Dur Cathl from 05. *Sundial Cottage, 7 Haughton Green, Darlington DL1 2DD* Tel (01325) 358424 Fax 361572 Mobile 07710-017625 E-mail peter@psld.co.uk

SINCLAIR, Reginald William. b 53. Wolv Poly BSc77 CEng MIMechE. Man OLM Scheme 04. d 07 p 08. OLM Atherton and Hindsford w Howe Bridge *Man* 07-09; TV from 09. *Bumbles, 23 Millers Lane, Atherton, Manchester M46 9BW* Tel (01942) 892996 Mobile 07707-419642
E-mail reg.sinclair@tiscali.co.uk

SINCLAIR, Robert Charles. b 28. Liv Univ LLB49 QUB LLM69 PhD82. Ely Th Coll 58. d 60 p 61. C Glenavy *Conn* 60-63; Chapl RN 63-67; C Cregagh *D & D* 67-68; Perm to Offic *Conn* from 69. *Juniper Cottage, 11A Glen Road, Glenavy, Crumlin BT29 4LT* Tel (028) 9445 3126

SINCLAIR, Robert Michael. b 41. CQSW81. Edin Th Coll 63. d 66 p 67. C Dunfermline *St And* 66-68; C Edin Old St Paul 68-72; P-in-c Edin St Dav 72-77; Hon Dioc Supernumerary 77-96. *121/19 Comiston Drive, Edinburgh EH10 5QU* Tel 0131-447 5068

SINDALL, Canon Christine Ann. b 42. ALA69. EAMTC 84. d 87 p 94. NSM Sutton *Ely* 87-89; C Cambridge Ascension 89-94; TV 94-96; R Cheveley 96-07; R Ashley w Silverley 96-07; V Kirtling 96-07; V Wood Ditton w Saxon Street 96-07; RD Linton 01-07; Hon Can Ely Cathl 01-07; rtd 07. *9 East Moor, Longhoughton, Alnwick NE66 3JB* Tel (01665) 572287
E-mail csindall@btinternet.com

SINGAPORE, Bishop of. See CHEW, The Most Revd John Hiang Chea

SINGH, Balwant. b 32. BA60. Saharanpur Th Coll 50. d 53 p 58. India 53-67 and 71-73; Hon C Handsworth St Jas *Birm* 67-71; Hon C N Hinksey *Ox* 73-80; Lic to Offic 80-81; Hon C S Hinksey 82-05; Perm to Offic from 05. *9 Jersey Road, Oxford OX4 4RT* Tel (01865) 717277

SINGH, Graham Andrew. b 77. Huron Coll Ontario BA00 LSE MSc01. Ridley Hall Cam 06. d 08 p 09. C W Hampstead Trin *Lon* 08-10; Perm to Offic Kensington Area from 10. *198 Broom Road, Teddington TW11 9PQ* Tel 07940-385688 (mobile)
E-mail graham@stjohnshamptonwick.org

SINGH, Thomas Balwant. b 62. Westmr Coll Ox BTh98. Wycliffe Hall Ox 98. d 00 p 01. C Houghton Regis *St Alb* 00-04; V Biscot from 04. *The Vicarage, 161 Bishopscote Road, Luton LU3 1PD* Tel (01582) 579410 E-mail thomassingh@hotmail.com

SINGH, Timon Balwant. b 60. Ripon Coll Cuddesdon. d 08 p 09. C Waterlooville *Portsm* from 08. *5 Chilsdown Way, Waterlooville PO7 5DT* Tel (023) 9225 2315 E-mail timon ox@hotmail.com

SINGH, Vivian Soorat. b 30. Trin Coll Cam BA MA53. Westcott Ho Cam 54. d 55 p 56. C Yardley Wood *Birm* 55-57; C Birm St Paul 57-59; Asst Master Framlingham Coll 59-72; Chapl 60-72; Chapl Wymondham Coll 72-75; Dep Hd Litcham High Sch 75-88; rtd 88; Perm to Offic *Nor* from 88. *Manor Cottage, Wendling Road, Longham, Dereham NR19 2RD* Tel (01362) 687382

SINGLETON, David Brinley. b 59. St Steph Ho Ox. d 00 p 01. C Soham *Ely* 00-01; C Soham and Wicken 02-04; P-in-c Capel St Mary w Lt and Gt Wenham *St E* 04-08; R from 08; RD Samford from 10. *The Rectory, Days Road, Capel St Mary, Ipswich IP9 2LE* Tel (01473) 310759
E-mail brin.singleton@ukgateway.net

SINGLETON, Mrs Editha Mary. b 27. WMMTC 85. dss 84 d 87 p 94. Lich St Chad 84-90; Hon Par Dn 87-90; Hon Par Dn Beaulieu and Exbury and E Boldre *Win* 90-94; Hon C 94-97; Perm to Offic from 97. *The Peregrine, The Lane, Fawley, Southampton SO45 1EY* Tel (023) 8089 4364

SINGLETON, Ernest George (Paul). b 15. St Aug Coll Cant 38. d 41 p 42. C Portsea N End St Mark *Portsm* 41-46; C Hendon St Mary *Lon* 46-48; C Lic to Offic *Wakef* 49-51; Lic to Offic *Lon* 52-56; S Africa 56-60; Prior St Teilo's Priory Cardiff 61-68; Perm to Offic *Lon* 68-91 and 93-95; rtd 80; Hon C Twickenham St Mary *Lon* 91-93. *Suite 268, Postnet X31, Saxonwold, Johannesburg, 2132 South Africa* Tel (0027) (11) 880 2982 Fax 447 5144

SINGLETON, Kenneth Miller. b 58. Oak Hill Th Coll 89. d 91 p 92. C Grove *Ox* 91-95; P-in-c Ashbury, Compton Beauchamp and Longcot w Fernham 95-99; C Kirkheaton *Wakef* 99-04.

34 Arlington Way, Huddersfield HD5 9TF Tel (01484) 319592 E-mail kensingleton@hotmail.com

SINGLETON, Mary. See SINGLETON, Mrs Editha Mary

SINNAMON, Canon William Desmond. b 43. TCD BA65 MA80 MPhil95. CITC 66. d 66 p 67. C Seapatrick *D & D* 66-70; C Arm St Mark 70-74; V Choral Arm Cathl 73-74; I Ballinderry 75-80; I Dublin St Patr Cathl Gp 80-83; Preb Tipperkevin St Patr Cathl Dublin 80-83; I Taney *D & G* from 83; Can St Patr Cathl Dublin from 91; Treas 91-96; Chan from 96. *Taney Rectory, 6 Stoney Road, Dundrum, Dublin 14, Republic of Ireland* Tel (00353) (1) 298 4497 *or* tel and fax 298 5491
E-mail taney@dublin.anglican.org
or parishoftaney@eircom.net

SINTON, Bernard. b 43. Leic Univ BSc66. Sarum & Wells Th Coll 87. d 90 p 91. NSM Horsham *Chich* from 90. *The Vicarage, Red Lane, Shipley, Horsham RH13 8PH* Tel (01403) 741238

SINTON, Mrs Patricia Ann. b 41. RGN62 SCM64. STETS 95. d 98 p 99. NSM Horsham *Chich* 98-01; P-in-c Shipley from 01. *The Vicarage, Red Lane, Shipley, Horsham RH13 8PH* Tel (01403) 741238 E-mail pa.sinton@tesco.net

SINTON, Vera May. b 43. Somerville Coll Ox BA65 MA69 Bris Univ CertEd66. Trin Coll Bris 79. dss 81 d 87 p 94. Broxbourne w Wormley *St Alb* 81-87; Hon Par Dn 87; Tutor All Nations Chr Coll Ware 81-87; Chapl St Hilda's Coll Ox 87-90; Tutor Wycliffe Hall Ox 87-98; NSM Ox St Clem 99-09; Tutor Ox Cen for Youth Min 01-04; rtd 09; Perm to Offic *Ox* from 09. *Rookhurst, West End, Gayle, Hawes DL8 3RT* E-mail vera.sinton@ntlworld.com

SIRCAR, Deepak Debchandan. b 46. Lon Hosp BDS72 Leeds Univ BA06. NOC 03. d 06 p 07. NSM Doncaster St Geo *Sheff* 06-10; NSM Bath Widcombe *B & W* from 10. *The Orchard, Forefield Rise, Bath BA2 4PL* Tel 07768-830393 (mobile)
E-mail deepak.sircar@sky.com

SIRMAN, Allan George. b 34. Lon Univ BA58. Oak Hill Th Coll 55. d 59 p 60. C Uphill *B & W* 59-61; C Morden *S'wark* 61-65; R Chadwell *Chelmsf* 65-75; V Wandsworth All SS *S'wark* 75-95; rtd 95; Perm to Offic *Ripon* from 95. *Marydale, Kingsley Drive, Middleham, Leyburn DL8 4PZ* Tel (01969) 624582
E-mail sirmans@freeuk.com

SIRR, John Maurice Glover. b 42. TCD BA63. CITC 65. d 65 p 66. C Belfast St Mary *Conn* 65-68; C Finaghy 68-69; I Drumcliffe w Lissadell and Munninane *K, E & A* 69-87; Preb Elphin Cathl 87-87; Dean Limerick and Ardfert *L & K* 87-11; I Limerick City 87-11; Chapl Limerick Pris 87-11; rtd 11. *17A Knockhill, Ennis Road, Limerick, Republic of Ireland* Tel (00353) 87-254 1121 (mobile)

SISTIG, Andreas. b 75. St Geo Th Sem Frankfurt 96. d 04 p 05. C Hillcrest S Africa 04-08; C Fleet *Guildf* from 08. *38 Oasthouse Drive, Fleet GU51 2UL* Tel (01252) 621139 Mobile 07595-542143 E-mail andreas@parishoffleet.org.uk

SISTIG (*née* STEWART), Mrs Jennifer Jane. b 71. Urban Univ Rome STB00. St Jos Th Inst Cedara BTh00. d 99 p 00. C Kirby-Hilton S Africa 99-00; C Scottsville 00-01; R Woodlands-Montclair-cum-Yellowwood Park 01-05; R Hillcrest 05-08; NSM Fleet *Guildf* from 08; Chapl St Geo Sch Ascot from 10. *38 Oasthouse Drive, Fleet GU51 2UL* Tel (01252) 621139 Mobile 07546-120844 E-mail jennifer@parishoffleet.org.uk

SITCH, Keith Frank. b 40. Ex Univ BA63 Lon Univ MA95. S'wark Ord Course 72. d 75 p 76. NSM Romford St Edw *Chelmsf* 75-78; NSM Kidbrooke St Jas *S'wark* 78-10; Perm to Offic from 10. *92 Kidbrooke Park Road, London SE3 0DX* Tel (020) 8856 3843

SITWELL, Mrs Mary Elizabeth. b 49. Brighton Coll of Educn DipEd71 Sussex Univ BEd72. d 03. NSM Bishopstone *Chich* 03-06; NSM Alfriston w Lullington, Litlington and W Dean 06-09; Chapl Roedean Sch Brighton 03-09; rtd 09. *49 Fitzgerald Avenue, Seaford BN25 1AZ* Tel (01323) 892424
E-mail isla.sitwell@btinternet.com

SIXSMITH, David. b 39. Lon Univ BD66. d 97 p 98. OLM Narborough w Narford *Nor* 97-99; OLM Pentney St Mary Magd w W Bilney 97-99; OLM Westacre 97-99; OLM Castleacre w Newton and Southacre 97-99; C Hunstanton St Mary w Ringstead Parva etc 99-01; P-in-c Foulsham w Hindolveston and Guestwick 01-06; P-in-c N Elmham w Billingford and Worthing 02-05; rtd 06; Perm to Offic *Nor* from 06. *Old Mill Cottage, Broadmeadow Common, Castle Acre, King's Lynn PE32 2BU* Tel (01760) 755703 *or* 577253

SIXTUS, Bernd (Bernard). b 68. German Armed Forces Univ BA(Ed)93 Hamburg Univ PhD02 Leeds Univ MA03. Coll of Resurr Mirfield 01. d 03 p 04. C Paris St Geo *Eur* 03-07; C Abergavenny St Mary w Llanwenarth Citra *Mon* from 07; C Abergavenny H Trin from 07. *Holy Trinity Vicarage, Baker Street, Abergavenny NP7 5BH* Tel (01873) 851062
E-mail frbernard@gmx.com

SIZER, Stephen Robert. b 53. Sussex Univ BA Ox Univ MTh94. Trin Coll Bris 80. d 83 p 84. C St Leonards St Leon *Chich* 83-86; C Guildf St Sav w Stoke-next-Guildford 86-89; R Stoke-next-Guildf 89-97; V Virginia Water from 97. *Christ Church Vicarage, Callow Hill, Virginia Water GU25 4LD* Tel and fax (01344) 842374 Mobile 07970-789549
E-mail stephen.sizer@btinternet.com *or* stephen@sizers.org

SKELDING, Mrs Hazel Betty. b 25. LGSM66 CertEd45. Gilmore Course 80. **dss** 83 **d** 87 **p** 94. Hinstock and Sambrook *Lich* 83-84; Asst Children's Adv RE 86-91; Hon Par Dn Alderbury Team *Sarum* 91-94; C 94-96; rtd 96; Perm to Offic *Sarum* 96-01 and *Truro* 01-06. *308 Grafton Road, Thames 3500, New Zealand* Tel (0064) (7) 868 3231

SKELLEY, Mrs Janice Ann. b 66. St Jo Coll Nottm 04. **d** 06 **p** 07. C Barnard Castle w Whorlton *Dur* 06-08; C Hedworth from 09. *Boldon Rectory, 13 Rectory Green, West Boldon NE36 0QD* Tel 0191-536 5037 E-mail jas66@hotmail.com

SKELTON, Beresford. b 52. St Chad's Coll Dur BA74. Chich Th Coll 74. **d** 76 **p** 77. CMP from 77; C Byker St Ant *Newc* 76-80; C Newc St Jo 80-82; Chapl Asst Newc Gen Hosp 80-81; Chapl Asst Freeman Hosp Newc 81-82; V Cresswell and Lynemouth *Newc* 82-88; P-in-c Millfield St Mary *Dur* 88-93; V from 93; P-in-c Bishopwearmouth Gd Shep from 04. *St Mary Magdalene's Vicarage, Wilson Street, Sunderland SR4 6HJ* Tel and fax 0191-565 6318

SKELTON, Mrs Caroline. **d** 11. NSM Baildon *Bradf* from 11. *2 Highfield Mews, Baildon, Shipley BD17 5PF* Tel (01274) 582224

SKELTON, Dennis Michael. b 33. K Coll Lon BSc55. NEOC 76. **d** 79 **p** 80. NSM Pennywell St Thos and Grindon St Oswald *CD Dur* 79-84; V Heatherycleugh 84-99; V St John in Weardale 84-99; V Westgate 84-99; rtd 99; Perm to Offic *Dur* from 99. *52 Vicarage Close, New Silksworth, Sunderland SR3 1JF* Tel 0191-523 7135

SKELTON, Melvyn Nicholas. b 38. St Pet Coll Ox BA61 MA65 Selw Coll Cam BA63 MA68. Ridley Hall Cam 62. **d** 64 **p** 65. C St Marychurch *Ex* 64-66; C Bury St Edmunds St Mary *St E* 66-69; Hon C 69-78; Lic to Offic 78-08; Perm to Offic from 09. *Milburn House, The Street, Moulton, Newmarket CB8 8RZ* Tel (01638) 750563

SKELTON, Canon Pamela Dora. b 38. Hull Coll of Educn DipEd60. Edin Th Coll 80. **dss** 78 **d** 86 **p** 94. Edin St Barn 78-86; Dn-in-c 86-90; Dioc Youth Chapl 83-90; Min Edin Ch Ch 91-97; Chapl Lothian Primary Healthcare NHS Trust 91-96; Lic to Offic *Edin* from 06; Hon Can St Mary's Cathl from 00. *112 St Alban's Road, Edinburgh EH9 2PG* Tel 0131-667 1280 E-mail pdskelton@yahoo.com *or* pdskelton@blueyonder.co.uk

SKEPPER, Mrs Suzanne. b 63. Trin Coll Bris BA09. **d** 09 **p** 10. C Wotton St Mary *Glouc* from 09. *30 Simon Road, Longlevens, Gloucester GL2 0TP* Tel (01452) 528065 Mobile 07981-429259 E-mail troppusrekrow@hotmail.com

SKETCHLEY, Edward Sydney. b 20. Qu Coll Birm. **d** 49 **p** 50. C Bakewell *Derby* 49-53; PC Ridgeway 53-57; PC Abbey Dale 57-65; V Walsgrave on Sowe *Cov* 65-73; V Hound *Win* 73-90; rtd 90; Perm to Offic *Win* 90-05 and *Portsm* 02-05. *107A Lenthay Road, Sherborne DT9 6AQ*

SKIDMORE (née CANNINGS), Karen Rachel. b 75. Nottm Univ BA96. Ridley Hall Cam 04. **d** 06 **p** 07. C Pitsmoor Ch Ch *Sheff* 06-10; P-in-c Herringthorpe from 10. *The Vicarage, 493 Herringthorpe Valley Road, Rotherham S60 4LB* Tel (01709) 836052 E-mail karen.skidmore@yahoo.co.uk

SKIDMORE, Michael Anthony. b 38. **d** 98 **p** 99. NSM Rainworth and Blidworth *S'well* 98-00; P-in-c Basford St Leodegarius 00-05; P-in-c Willoughby-on-the-Wolds w Wysall and Widmerpool 05-07; NSM Carlton-in-the-Willows, Porchester and Woodthorpe 07-09; rtd 09. *11 Graveney Gardens, Arnold, Nottingham NG5 6QW* Tel 0115-926 0773 E-mail mike.skidmore@breathemail.net

SKIDMORE, Mrs Sheila Ivy. b 36. **d** 87 **p** 94. Hon Par Dn Leic Resurr 87-91; Par Dn Clarendon Park St Jo w Knighton St Mich 91-94; TV 94-01; rtd 01; Perm to Offic *Leic* from 01. *15 School Lane, Birstall, Leicester LE4 4EA* Tel 0116-267 3318 E-mail revd.sheila@theskidmores.f9.co.uk

SKILLEN, John Clifford Tainish. b 50. NUU BA72 MA82 TCD BTh89 QUB DipEd73. CITC 86. **d** 89 **p** 90. C Bangor Abbey *D & D* 89-92; I Kilwarlin Upper w Kilwarlin Lower 92-96; I Finaghy *Conn* 96-09; Asst Ed *The Church of Ireland Gazette* from 99; Bp's Sen Dom Chapl from 08. *25 Berkeley Hall Square, Lisburn BT27 5TB* Tel (028) 9267 0257 Mobile 07740-553926

SKILLINGS, Martyn Paul. b 46. St Chad's Coll Dur BA68. Linc Th Coll 68. **d** 70 **p** 71. C Stanley *Liv* 70-72; C Warrington St Elphin 72-75; Ind Chapl 75-76; V Surfleet *Linc* 88-92; V Burton St Chad *Lich* 92-08; R Calton, Cauldon, Grindon, Waterfall etc from 08; RD Alstonfield from 10. *The Vicarage, Waterfall Lane, Waterhouses, Stoke-on-Trent ST10 3HT* Tel (01538) 308506 Mobile 07887-854525 E-mail paul_skillings@talktalk.net

SKILTON, The Ven Christopher John. b 55. Magd Coll Cam BA76 MA80. Wycliffe Hall Ox 77. **d** 80 **p** 81. C Ealing St Mary *Lon* 80-84; C New Borough and Leigh *Sarum* 84-88; TV Gt Baddow *Chelmsf* 88-95; TR Sanderstead All SS *S'wark* 95-04; P-in-c Sanderstead St Mary 02-04; RD Croydon S 00-04; Adn Lambeth from 04; P-in-c Kennington St Mark 08-09. *7 Hoadly Road, London SW16 1AE* Tel (020) 8769 4384 *or* 8545 2440 Fax 8677 2854 *or* 8545 2441 E-mail christopher.skilton@southwark.anglican.org

SKILTON, Joseph Laurence. b 41. Univ of Wales TCert64 Murdoch Univ Aus BA90 Aus Pacific Coll MA93. St Mich Coll Llan. **d** 70 **p** 71. C Bicester *Ox* 71-73; C Shrewsbury St Chad *Lich* 73-76; V W Bromwich St Phil 76-80; Australia from 80; rtd 06. *11 Tillbrook Street, Glen Forrest WA 6071, Australia* Tel (0061) (8) 9298 9454 *or* 6188 6024 E-mail pax2u2@gmail.com

SKINGLEY, Christopher George. b 49. K Coll Lon MA98. Oak Hill Th Coll BA90 Qu Coll Birm. **d** 00 **p** 01. C Enfield St Jas *Lon* 00-03; V Ramsgate St Mark *Cant* from 03. *St Mark's Vicarage, 198 Margate Road, Ramsgate CT12 6AQ* Tel (01843) 581042 E-mail chris.skingley@btinternet.com

SKINNER, Arthur. b 38. **d** 97 **p** 98. NSM Selling w Throwley, Sheldwich w Badlesmere etc *Cant* 97-08; rtd 08; Perm to Offic *Cant* from 08. *Address temp unknown* E-mail askinner@lineone.net

✠SKINNER, The Rt Revd Brian Antony. b 39. Reading Univ BSc60. Tyndale Hall Bris 66. **d** 67 **p** 68 **c** 77. C Woking St Pet *Guildf* 67-70; Chile 70-86; Adn Valparaiso 76-77; Suff Bp Valparaiso 77-86; C Chorleywood St Andr *St Alb* 87-96; V Iver Ox 96-06; rtd 06. *10 Benton Drive, Chinnor OX39 4DP* Tel (01844) 353504 E-mail skinnerofiver@go-plus.net

SKINNER, Mrs Elaine Teresa (Terri). b 55. Bath Univ BSc78. EMMTC 99. **d** 02 **p** 03. NSM Whitwick St Jo the Bapt *Leic* 02-05; NSM Thorpe Acre w Dishley 05-10; P-in-c Leic St Theodore from 10. *St Theodore's House, 4 Sandfield Close, Leicester LE4 7RE* Tel 07810-241381 (mobile) E-mail terri.skinner@btopenworld.com

SKINNER, Graeme John. b 57. Southn Univ BSc79. Trin Coll Bris BA86. **d** 86 **p** 87. C Bebington *Ches* 86-90; V Ashton-upon-Mersey St Mary Magd 90-06; V Upton (Overchurch) from 06. *The Vicarage, 20 Church Road, Upton, Wirral CH49 6JZ* Tel 0151-677 4810 E-mail graeme@stm-upton.org.uk

SKINNER, Mrs Jane Mary. b 59. Leeds Univ BA81. Cranmer Hall Dur 82. **dss** 84 **d** 87 **p** 94. Chatham St Phil and St Jas *Roch* 84-87; Hon Par Dn Church Coniston *Carl* 87-91; Hon Par Dn Torver 87-91; NSM Dalton-in-Furness 91-97; Chapl HM Pris Haverigg 92-97; Chapl Carl Hosps NHS Trust 97-01; Chapl N Cumbria Acute Hosps NHS Trust 01-02; TV Carl H Trin and St Barn 98-02; Hon C W Swindon and the Lydiards *Bris* 02-09; Chapl Swindon and Marlborough NHS Trust 03-10; NSM Golden Cap Team *Sarum* 09-10; TV from 10. *The Vicarage, 4 Dragons Hill, Lyme Regis DT7 3HW* Tel (01297) 443763 E-mail sjmskinners@btinternet.com

SKINNER, Mrs Jean. b 47. Univ of Northumbria at Newc BA03 RN68 RM70. NEOC 93. **d** 96 **p** 97. NSM Ch the King *Newc* 96-03; NSM Newc St Thos Prop Chpl from 03; NSM City Cen Chapl 03-06; Dioc Child Protection Adv from 07. *32 Easedale Avenue, Melton Park, Newcastle upon Tyne NE3 5TB* Tel 0191-236 3474 E-mail revjeanskinner@yahoo.com

SKINNER, Preb John Cedric. b 30. Bris Univ BA55. Tyndale Hall Bris 55. **d** 57 **p** 58. C St Leonard *Ex* 57-62; Univ Sec IVF 62-68; V Guildf St Sav 68-76; R Stoke next Guildf St Jo 74-76; R Guildf St Sav w Stoke-next-Guildford 76-84; R Ex St Leon w H Trin 84-98; Chapl R W of England Sch for the Deaf 84-98; Preb Ex Cathl 92-98; rtd 98; Perm to Offic *Ex* from 00. *386 Topsham Road, Exeter EX2 6HE* Tel (01392) 876540

SKINNER, John Richard. b 45. NOC 84. **d** 87 **p** 88. C Allerton *Liv* 87-90; C Huyton St Mich 90-97; P-in-c Fairfield 97-03; rtd 04. *30 Duke Street, Formby, Liverpool L37 4AT* Tel (01704) 874989

SKINNER, John Timothy. b 55. Linc Th Coll 79. **d** 81 **p** 82. C Newton Aycliffe *Dur* 81-82; Perm to Offic *Newc* 95-01; Bermuda from 01. *St John's Church, PO Box HM 1856, Hamilton HM HX, Bermuda* Tel (001441) 292 6802

SKINNER, Leonard Harold. b 36. K Coll Lon BD62 AKC62. **d** 63 **p** 64. C Hackney Wick St Mary of Eton w St Aug *Lon* 63-66; C Palmers Green St Jo 66-70; V Grange Park St Pet 70-80; TV Hanley H Ev *Lich* 80-86; Chapl Sunderland Poly *Dur* 86-92; Chapl Sunderland Univ 92-93; P-in-c Hebburn St Oswald 93-01; rtd 01; Perm to Offic *Newc* from 01. *28 Brighton Grove, Whitley Bay NE26 1QH* Tel 0191-251 4891

SKINNER, Maurice Wainwright. b 30. St Jo Coll Ox BA53 MA59 FRSC70. Ox NSM Course. **d** 86 **p** 87. NSM Furze Platt *Ox* 86-94; NSM Hurley and Stubbings 94-00; rtd 00; Perm to Offic *Ox* from 00. *133 Beverley Gardens, Maidenhead SL6 6ST* Tel (01628) 624875

SKINNER, Michael Thomas. b 39. Open Univ BA88 BA90. S'wark Ord Course 73. **d** 78 **p** 79. NSM Orpington St Andr *Roch* 78-82; P-in-c 99-09; NSM Orpington All SS 82-99; Assoc Bp's Officer for NSMs 90-98; Bp's Officer for NSMs 98-09; rtd 09; Perm to Offic *S'wark* 02-05 and from 10. *16 Ambleside Gardens, South Croydon CR2 8SF* E-mail mikeskinner@messages.co.uk

SKINNER, Mrs Nicola Jayne. b 70. Birm Univ BA92. Cuddesdon Coll MTh. **d** 98 **p** 99. C Bartley Green *Birm* 98-01; Assoc Min Aurora Trin Ch Canada 01-06; P-in-c King City All SS from 06. *All Saints Church, 12935 Keele Street, King City ON L4G 1R3, Canada* Tel (001) (905) 833 5432 Fax 833 2597

SKINNER, Paul Anthony. b 35. RD. Sarum Th Coll. **d** 09 **p** 10. NSM Sixpenny Handley w Gussage St Andrew etc *Sarum* from 09. *11 The Parsonage, Sixpenny Handley, Salisbury SP5 5QJ* Tel (01785) 552785 E-mail paulofpaskin@rya-online.net

SKINNER, Peter William. b 47. Sarum & Wells Th Coll 85. **d** 87 **p** 88. C Latchford St Jas *Ches* 87-89; C Weymouth St Paul *Sarum* 89; Perm to Offic *Lon* 97-99; C Leic St Aid 99-01; TV Staveley and Barrow Hill *Derby* 01-04; V Middlesbrough St Thos *York* 04-06; rtd 06; Perm to Offic *York* from 11. *23 Adshead Road, Redcar TS10 5EX*

SKINNER, Philip Harold. b 30. **d** 97 **p** 98. OLM Tisbury *Sarum* 97-01; rtd 01; Perm to Offic *Sarum* 02-08; OLM Sixpenny Handley w Gussage St Andrew etc from 09. *Ladydown House, Vicarage Road, Tisbury, Salisbury SP3 6HY* Tel (01747) 870394

SKINNER, Raymond Frederick. b 45. St Jo Coll Dur BA67 Dur Univ MA93. Cranmer Hall Dur. **d** 70 **p** 71. C High Elswick St Paul *Newc* 70-76; V Newbottle *Dur* 76-87; Ind Chapl 81-87; RD Houghton 84-87; Oman 87-90; TR Morden *S'wark* from 90; Asst RD Merton from 91. *The Rectory, London Road, Morden SM4 5QT* Tel (020) 8648 3920 *or* 8658 0012 E-mail skinhicks@aol.com

SKINNER, Stephen John. b 52. Bris Univ BSc St Jo Coll Dur BA Dur Univ MLitt AIA. Cranmer Hall Dur. **d** 83 **p** 84. C Chatham St Phil and St Jas *Roch* 83-87; P-in-c Torver *Carl* 87-90; R 90-91; P-in-c Church Coniston 87-90; V 90-91; V Dalton-in-Furness 91-97; TR Carl H Trin and St Barn 97-02; TR W Swindon and the Lydiards *Bris* 02-09; TR Golden Cap Team *Sarum* from 09. *The Vicarage, 4 Dragons Hill, Lyme Regis DT7 3HW* Tel (01297) 443763 E-mail sjmskinners@btinternet.com

SKINNER, Terri. *See* SKINNER, Mrs Elaine Teresa

SKIPPER, Kenneth Graham. b 34. St Aid Birkenhead 65. **d** 68 **p** 69. C Newland St Aug *York* 68-71; C Newby 71-74; V Dormanstown 74-78; V Aldbrough, Mappleton w Goxhill and Withernwick 79-89; R Londesborough 89-96; R Burnby 90-96; R Nunburnholme and Warter 90-96; V Shiptonthorpe w Hayton 90-96; rtd 96. *18 Elder Crescent, Bowmore, Isle of Islay PA43 7HU* Tel (01496) 810321 Mobile 07776-373057 E-mail kgsbow@onetel.net

SKIPPON, Kevin John. b 54. St Steph Ho Ox 78. **d** 81 **p** 82. C Gt Yarmouth *Nor* 81-84; C Kingstanding St Luke *Birm* 84-86; V Smethwick SS Steph and Mich 86-92; Chapl Derbyshire R Infirmary 92-94; Chapl Derbyshire R Infirmary NHS Trust 94-98; Chapl S Derbyshire Acute Hosps NHS Trust 98-04; Chapl Derby Hosps NHS Foundn Trust 04-08; Hon C Upminster *Chelmsf* from 09; Chapl St Andr Healthcare from 11. *6 Gaynes Park Road, Upminster RM14 2HH* Tel (01708) 226004 E-mail kevin.skippon@asitis.me.uk

SKIPWORTH, Nicola Rachael. b 72. Southn Inst BA95. Trin Coll Bris BA01. **d** 01 **p** 02. C Bassaleg *Mon* 01-05; TV High Wycombe *Ox* from 05. *St James's Vicarage, Plomer Hill, High Wycombe HP13 5NB* Tel (01494) 526896 Mobile 07725-106529 E-mail nicky.skipworth@btinternet.com

SKIRROW, Paul Richard. b 52. Hull Univ BA82 Ches Coll of HE MTh00. NOC 97. **d** 00 **p** 01. C St Luke in the City *Liv* 00-03; V Ditton St Mich w St Thos 03-07; Asst Dir CME 03-07; rtd 07; Perm to Offic *Ely* from 10. Ferrar House, Little Gidding, Huntingdon PE28 5RJ Tel (01832) 293383 E-mail paulskirrow@googlemail.com

SKLIROS, Michael Peter. b 33. Clare Coll Cam BA57 MA62. Ridley Hall Cam 57. **d** 59 **p** 60. C Hornchurch St Andr *Chelmsf* 59-61; Asst Chapl Denstone Coll Uttoxeter 61-65; Chapl RAF 65-77; P-in-c Stowmarket *St E* 77-78; Lic to Offic 78-85; C St Finborough w Onehouse and Harleston 85-91; P-in-c 91; R Gt and Lt Bealings w Playford and Culpho 91-96; rtd 96; Hon Asst to Bp Brandon Canada from 03. *49 Almond Crescent, Brandon MB R7B 1A2, Canada* Tel (001) (204) 726 9144 E-mail pifont@westman.wave.ca

SKOYLES, John Alan. b 32. Breakspear Coll 50 Christleton Hall 53. **d** 58 **p** 59. In RC Ch 59-80; Soc worker 80-99; NSM The Hydneye *Chich* 99-00; C Kenton, Mamhead, Powderham, Cofton and Starcross *Ex* 00-01. *18 Bodiam Crescent, Eastbourne BN22 9HQ* Tel (01323) 504358

SKRINE, Charles Walter Douglas. b 75. Qu Coll Ox BA98. Oak Hill Th Coll BA03. **d** 03 **p** 04. C St Helen Bishopsgate w St Andr Undershaft etc *Lon* from 03. *73 Victoria Park Road, London E9 7NA* Tel (020) 7283 2231 E-mail charles@cwdskrine.freeserve.co.uk

SKUBLICS, Ernest. b 36. Sant' Anselmo Univ Rome STB62 Ottawa Univ MTh64 STL64 Nijmegen Univ DrTheol67. **d** 73 **p** 73. R Whitewood Canada 73-76; Chapl Manitoba Univ 76-77; Soc Worker 77-86; Registrar and Asst Prof Manitoba Univ 86-90; Assoc Dir Inst for Th Studies Seattle Univ USA 90-93; Dean Graduate Sch Mt Angel Sem Oregon 93-00; C Hawley H Trin *Guildf* 04-07; rtd 07; Perm to Offic *Bradf* from 08. *Broadfield House, Dent, Sedbergh LA10 5TG* Tel (015396) 25296 E-mail eskublics1@freeuk.com

SKUCE, Canon David. b 56. NUU BSc79 QUB PGCE80 TCD BTh89. CITC 87. **d** 89 **p** 90. C Templemore *D & R* 89-92; I Kilbarron w Rossnowlagh and Drumholm 92-99; I Urney w Sion Mills 99-06; Bp's Dom Chapl 94-06; I Maguiresbridge w Derrybrusk *Clogh* from 06; Preb Donaghmore St Patr Cathl Dublin from 11; Preb Clogh Cathl from 11. *The Rectory, Maguiresbridge, Enniskillen BT94 4PJ* Tel (028) 6772 1250

SKUSE, Anne Martha. CITC. **d** 09 **p** 10. NSM Kilmocomogue *C, C & R* from 09. *Westlands, Crossmahon, Bandon, Co Cork, Republic of Ireland* Tel (00353) (23) 884 4306

SLACK, Michael. b 53. St Jo Coll Dur BA74 Lon Univ PGCE79 RGN83. St Steph Ho Ox 74. **d** 76 **p** 77. C Wolverhampton St Steph *Lich* 76-77; NSM Bywell *Newc* 89-93; TV Cullercoats St Geo 93-98; TR 98-05. *8 Kittiwake Drive, Washington NE38 0DW* Tel 0191-416 6257

SLACK, Mrs Moira Elizabeth. b 52. Brunel Univ BTech74 Leeds Univ BA06. NOC 03. **d** 06 **p** 07. C Heaton Ch Ch *Man* 06-09; P-in-c Stretford All SS from 09. *The Rectory, 233 Barton Road, Stretford, Manchester M32 9RB* Tel 0161-865 1350 E-mail moslack@btinternet.com

SLADDEN, David. *See* SLADDEN, John David

SLADDEN, John David. b 49. RN Eng Coll Plymouth BSc74 St Edm Coll Cam MA86. Ridley Hall Cam 80. **d** 83 **p** 84. C St Bees *Carl* 83-85; Perm to Offic *Lich* 85-87; Miss Co-ord Down to Earth Evangelistic Trust 85-87; V Doncaster St Jas *Sheff* 87-94; Perm to Offic *Ely* from 07. *9 Teal Close, Chatteris PE16 6PR* Tel (01354) 694097

SLADE, Canon Adrian Barrie. b 47. K Alfred's Coll Win DipEd68. St Jo Coll Nottm BTh73 ALCD72. **d** 73 **p** 74. C Streatham Immanuel w St Anselm *S'wark* 73-76; C Chipping Barnet *St Alb* 76-78; C Chipping Barnet w Arkley 78-80; V Sundon 80-85; Soc Resp Officer *Glouc* from 86; Hon Can Glouc Cathl from 91. *16 Conway Road, Hucclecote, Gloucester GL3 3PL* Tel (01452) 372468 E-mail glossr@star.co.uk

SLADE, Alfred Laurence. b 12. ACII. Roch Th Coll 67. **d** 69 **p** 70. NSM Cliftonville *Cant* 69-71; NSM Westgate St Jas 71-75; Perm to Offic *Sarum* 75-81 and *Cant* 81-93. *21 McKinlay Court, The Parade, Birchington CT7 9QG* Tel (01843) 46882

SLADE, Michael John. b 55. Trin Coll Bris 94. **d** 96 **p** 97. C Blagdon w Compton Martin and Ubley *B & W* 96-99; V Winscombe and Sandford 99-10; RD Locking 05-08; R Chollerton w Birtley and Thockrington *Newc* from 10. *The Vicarage, Chollerton, Hexham NE46 4TF* Tel (01434) 681721 E-mail michaeljohnslade@aol.com

SLADE, Canon William Clifford. b 24. St Jo Coll Dur BA47 MA53. **d** 49 **p** 50. C Northallerton w Deighton and Romanby *York* 49-52; C Eston 52-54; V Anlaby Common St Mark 54-60; V Brompton w Snainton 60-67; R Stokesley 67-71; V Felixkirk w Boltby and Kirkby Knowle 71-82; Abp's Adv for Spiritual Direction 82-86; C Topcliffe w Dalton and Dishforth 82-86; Can and Preb York Minster 79-86; rtd 86; Perm to Offic *York* 86-11. *Bede House, Beck Lane, South Kilvington, Thirsk YO7 2NL* Tel (01845) 522915

SLADEN, Katharine Anne. b 78. St Mellitus Coll. **d** 11. C Easthampstead *Ox* from 11. *16 Blackcap Lane, Bracknell RG12 8AA* Tel (01344) 443245 E-mail kate@popvote.co.uk

SLATER, Canon Ann. b 46. Somerville Coll Ox BA67 MA71. WMMTC 92. **d** 95 **p** 96. C Northampton St Benedict *Pet* 95-99; TV Daventry, Ashby St Ledgers, Braunston etc 99-05; R Heyford w Stowe Nine Churches and Flore etc from 05; RD Daventry from 08; Can Pet Cathl from 10. *The Rectory, Church Lane, Nether Heyford, Northampton NN7 3LQ* Tel (01327) 342201 E-mail ann.slater@btinternet.com

SLATER, Christopher Richard. b 69. Oak Hill Th Coll BA08. **d** 08. C Rock Ferry *Ches* from 08; C Tranmere St Cath from 08. *21 Alpha Drive, Birkenhead CH42 1PH* Tel 0151-644 1018 Mobile 07899-807507 E-mail slater.cr@btinternet.com

SLATER, David. *See* SLATER, Canon Philip David

SLATER (née SAMMONS), Mrs Elizabeth Mary. b 71. RN94 RHV98. Wycliffe Hall Ox 03. **d** 05 **p** 06. C Stoke Gifford *Bris* 05-09; Perm to Offic from 09. *20 Railton Jones Close, Stoke Gifford, Bristol BS34 8BF* E-mail wizsammons@hotmail.com

SLATER, Ian Stuart. b 47. St Jo Coll Nottm BA07. **d** 04 **p** 05. NSM St Horton *Bradf* 04-11; P-in-c from 11. *Stable Cottage, 5 The Drive, Denholme, Bradford BD13 4DY* Tel (01274) 831437 E-mail revianslater@gmail.com

SLATER, James Richard David. b 61. New Univ of Ulster BA83 TCD BTh89 Univ of Ulster MA92. CITC 86. **d** 89 **p** 90. C Clooney w Strathfoyle *D & R* 89-93; I Aghadowey w Kilrea 93-05; I Cumber Upper w Learmount from 05; Bp's Dom Chapl from 07. *248B Glenshane Road, Killaloo, Londonderry BT47 3SN* Tel (028) 7130 1724

SLATER, John Ralph. b 38. Kent Univ BA90. Linc Th Coll 71. **d** 73 **p** 74. C S Hackney St Mich w Haggerston St Paul *Lon* 73-74; C Leytonstone St Marg w St Columba *Chelmsf* 74-77; C Whitstable All SS w St Pet *Cant* 77-80; V Gt Ilford St Alb *Chelmsf* 80-83; V Clipstone *S'well* 83-87; rtd 87. *4 Rowena Road, Westgate-on-Sea CT8 8NQ* Tel (01227) 831593

SLATER, Mark Andrew. b 56. ARCS79 Imp Coll Lon BSc79. Ridley Hall Cam 87. **d** 89 **p** 90. C Northampton St Giles *Pet* 89-92; C Stopsley *St Alb* 92-93; C-in-c Bushmead CD 93-99;

V St Alb St Luke from 99. *St Luke's Vicarage, 46 Cell Barnes Lane, St Albans AL1 5QJ* Tel (01727) 865399 Fax 865399 E-mail mark.slater@saint-lukes.co.uk

SLATER, The Ven Paul John. b 58. CCC Ox MA83 St Jo Coll Dur BA83. Cranmer Hall Dur 81. **d** 84 **p** 85. C Keighley St Andr *Bradf* 84-88; P-in-c Cullingworth and Dir Dioc Foundn Course 88-93; Bp's Personal Exec Asst 93-95; Warden of Readers 92-96; R Haworth 95-01; Bp's Officer for Min and Miss from 01; Adn Craven from 05. *Woodlands, Nethergyll Lane, Cononley, Keighley BD20 8PB* Tel (01535) 635113 *or* 650533 E-mail paul.slater@bradford.anglican.org

SLATER, Canon Philip **David**. b 27. K Coll Lon 58. **d** 60 **p** 61. C Havant *Portsm* 60-67; C Leigh Park 68-69; Hants Co RE Adv 69-74; Gosport and Fareham RE Adv 74-82; Hon C Bishop's Waltham 76-82; V Bulford, Figheldean and Milston *Sarum* 82-93; RD Avon 85-95; Can and Preb Sarum Cathl 91-95; V Avon Valley 93-95; rtd 95; V of Close Sarum Cathl 95-02; Chapl Godolphin Sch 95-04. *102 Coombe Road, Salisbury SP2 8BD* Tel (01722) 332529 E-mail voc@salcath.co.uk

SLATER, Robert Adrian. b 48. St Jo Coll Nottm 76. **d** 79 **p** 80. C Bedworth *Cov* 79-82; TV Billericay and Lt Burstead *Chelmsf* 82-88; V Rounds Green *Birm* 88-94; rtd 07. *11 Lewis Road, Birmingham B30 2SU* Tel 0121-689 2721 E-mail robslater@freeuk.com

SLATER, Thomas Ernest. b 37. Chelsea Coll Lon TCert60 Lon Univ BD71. ALCD66. **d** 67 **p** 68. C Bootle Ch Ch *Liv* 67-72; C Stapleford *S'well* 72-75; Supt Tower Hamlets Miss 75-77; Hon C Stepney St Pet w St Benet *Lon* 78-79; Asst Chapl The Lon Hosp (Whitechapel) 79-83; Chapl 83-89; NSM Poplar *Lon* 89-92 and 94-02; Perm to Offic 92-94; rtd 02. *11 Elgin House, Cordelia Street, London E14 6EG* Tel (020) 7987 4504

SLATER, Victoria Ruth. b 59. Hertf Coll Ox BA82 MA87 Selw Coll Cam BA89 MA94. Westcott Ho Cam 86. **d** 89 **p** 94. Chapl Asst Man R Infirmary 89-90; Chapl 90-94; Chapl St Mary's Hosp Man 90-94; Chapl Ox Radcliffe Hosp NHS Trust 94-97; Chapl Sir Michael Sobell Ho Palliative Care Unit 97-05; Asst Soc Resp Adv *Ox* from 05. *Diocesan Church House, North Hinksey Lane, Botley, Oxford OX2 0NB* Tel (01865) 208214

SLATER, Preb William Edward. b 51. Aston Tr Scheme 85 Oak Hill Th Coll 87. **d** 89 **p** 90. C Balderstone *Man* 89-94; V Newchapel *Lich* from 94; RD Stoke N 99-08; Preb Lich Cathl from 08. *The Vicarage, 32 Pennyfield Road, Newchapel, Stoke-on-Trent ST7 4PN* Tel (01782) 782837 E-mail willslater@tinyworld.co.uk

SLATTER, Barrie John. b 44. Nottm Univ BSc66 FRICS97. Dioc OLM tr scheme 97. **d** 00 **p** 01. OLM Hundred River *St E* 00-03; C Alde River 03-06; R from 06. *The Rectory, Stratford St Andrew, Saxmundham IP17 1LJ* Tel (01728) 603180 Mobile 07802-924738 E-mail rectory@barrieslatter.fsnet.co.uk

SLATTERY, Maurice Michael. b 43. Southlands Coll Lon TCert73 Lon Inst of Educn BEd74. S'wark Ord Course 91. **d** 94 **p** 95. NSM Malden St Jas *S'wark* 94-97; NSM Niton, Whitwell and St Lawrence *Portsm* 97-99; NSM Selsdon St Jo w St Fran *S'wark* 99-03; Perm to Offic *Portsm* 03-04 and 07-08 and from 09; P-in-c St Lawrence 04-06; NSM Clayton w Keymer *Chich* 08-09. *1 Woodland Mews, East Hill Road, Ryde PO33 1QU* E-mail jillslattery@btinternet.com

SLAUGHTER, Clive Patrick. b 36. St Paul's Coll Grahamstown. **d** 77 **p** 78. S Africa 77-87; R Thorley w Bishop's Stortford H Trin *St Alb* 87-90; R Thorley 90-01; RD Bishop's Stortford 96-01; rtd 01; Perm to Offic *St Alb* 01-03; P-in-c Much Hadham 03-04; P-in-c Braughing w Furneux Pelham and Stocking Pelham 04-05. *13 Mile High Street, Hunsdon, Ware SG12 8QB* Tel (01279) 844955 E-mail clive.slaughter@virgin.net

SLAUGHTER, Canon Maurice Basil. b 20. Leeds Univ BA42. Coll of Resurr Mirfield 42. **d** 44 **p** 45. C Kingswinford St Mary *Lich* 44-46; C Roch St Nic w St Clem 46-47; C Luton Ch Ch *St Alb* 47-50; V Birm St Marg Ladywood 50-52; V Newsome *Wakef* 52-60; V Queensbury *Bradf* 60-63; V Skipton Ch Ch 63-78; Hon Can Bradf Cathl 67-85; RD Skipton 73-82; P-in-c Bolton Abbey 78-85; P-in-c Rylstone 78-85; P-in-c Arncliffe w Halton Gill 79-82; rtd 85; Perm to Offic *Bradf* 85-99; *Wakef* 85-96; *Ely* 96-00. *Hawkhill House, 234 North Deeside Road, Milltimber AB13 0DQ* Tel (01224) 734609

SLEDGE, The Ven Richard Kitson. b 30. Peterho Cam BA52 MA57. Ridley Hall Cam 52. **d** 54 **p** 55. C Compton Gifford *Ex* 54-57; C Ex St Martin, St Steph, St Laur etc 57-63; V Dronfield *Derby* 63-76; TR 76-78; RD Chesterfield 72-78; Adn Huntingdon *Ely* 78-96; R Hemingford Abbots 78-89; Hon Can Ely Cathl 78-99; Bp's Dom Chapl *Ely* 96-99; Retired Clergy Officer 98-07; Asst (Huntingdon/Pet Area) from 07; Perm to Offic from 99. *7 Budge Close, Brampton, Huntingdon PE29 4PL* Tel (01480) 380284 *or* (01353) 662749 Fax (01480) 437789 E-mail rksledge@supanet.com

SLEDGE, Timothy Charles Kitson. b 64. Coll of Ripon & York St Jo BA87 York Univ MA88. Trin Coll Bris. **d** 95 **p** 96. C Huddersfield St Thos *Wakef* 95-98; V Luddenden w Luddenden Foot 98-03; P-in-c Sowerby 02-03; Dioc Miss Enabler *Pet* 03-08;

V Romsey *Win* from 08. *The Vicarage, Church Lane, Romsey SO51 8EP* Tel (01794) 513125 E-mail vicarofromsey@hotmail.co.uk

SLEE, John Graham. b 51. Brunel Univ BTech73. Oak Hill Th Coll 85. **d** 87 **p** 88. C St Columb Minor and St Colan *Truro* 87-91; R St Mawgan w St Ervan and St Eval 91-02; RD Pydar 93-95; P-in-c St Just-in-Roseland and St Mawes 02-07; rtd 07; Perm to Offic *Ox* from 08. *Oaklea, Manor Road, Great Bourton, Banbury OX17 1QP* E-mail john@nbepiphany.co.uk

SLEEMAN, Matthew Timothy. b 68. St Cath Coll Cam BA90 MA95 PhD96 K Coll Lon PhD07. Wycliffe Hall Ox BA97 MA07. **d** 98 **p** 99. C Eynsham and Cassington *Ox* 98-02; Perm to Offic *Lon* 03-06 and *St Alb* from 03; Lect Oak Hill Th Coll from 06. *Oak Hill College, Chase Side, London N14 4PS* Tel (020) 8449 0467

SLEGG, John Edward. b 36. St Pet Coll Ox BA62 MA66. Ridley Hall Cam 62. **d** 64 **p** 65. C Perranzabuloe *Truro* 64-66; CF 66-86; V Lyminster and Poling *Chich* 86-05; rtd 06. *4 Bakers Meadow, Billingshurst RH14 9GG* Tel (01403) 784362

SLEIGHT, Gordon Frederick. b 47. AKC69. St Aug Coll Cant 69. **d** 70 **p** 71. C Boston *Linc* 70-74; P-in-c Louth St Mich and Stewton 74; TV Louth 74-81; V Crosby 81-95; P-in-c Nettleham 95-97; V 97-05; RD Lawres,04-05; rtd 05; Lic to Offic *Mor* from 05. *Elderbank, Stoer, Lochinver, Lairg IV27 4JE* Tel (01571) 855207 E-mail gordon@gsleight.freeserve.co.uk

SLENNETT, Mrs Jane Alison. b 57. St Mich Coll Llan. **d** 08. NSM Aberavon *Llan* from 08. *42 Carlton Place, Porthcawl CF36 3ET* Tel (01656) 784840 E-mail deacon@parishofaberavon.org

SLIM, David Albert. b 49. Westhill Coll Birm CertEd72. Line Th Coll 90. **d** 90 **p** 91. C Walmley *Birm* 90-93; R Marchwiel and Isycoed *St As* 93-03; TV Wrexham 03-08; Chapl Ellesmere Coll from 08. *The Shippon, Ellesmere College, Ellesmere SY12 9BE* Tel (01691) 622380

SLIPPER, Charles Callan. b 55. Lanc Univ BA77 PhD84. S Dios Minl Tr Scheme 91. **d** 93 **p** 94. Focolare Movement from 77; NSM N Acton St Gabr *Lon* 93-96. *38 Audley Road, London W5 3ET* Tel (020) 8991 2022 *or* 8354 0763 Fax 8453 1621 E-mail callan@onetel.com

SLIPPER, Robert James. b 64. St Jo Coll Cam BA87 MA91. Wycliffe Hall Ox BA92. **d** 92 **p** 93. C Southgate *Chich* 92-95; C Stoughton *Guildf* 95-00; V Terrington St Clement *Ely* from 00. *The Vicarage, 27 Sutton Road, Terrington St Clement, King's Lynn PE34 4PQ* Tel (01553) 828430 E-mail rjslipper@dsl.pipex.com

SLOAN, William. b 49. Lanc Univ CertEd78 BEd79. CBDTI 04. **d** 07 **p** 08. NSM Croston and Bretherton *Blackb* 07-10; NSM Hoole 10-11. *5 Red House Lane, Eccleston, Chorley PR7 5RH* Tel (01257) 453665 Mobile 07721-923001 E-mail billsloan5@btinternet.com

SLOANE, Niall James. b 81. TCD BA03. CITC 03. **d** 05 **p** 06. C Agherton *Conn* 05-07; C Taney *D & G* from 07. *Church Lodge, 21 Taney Road, Dundrum, Dublin 14, Republic of Ireland* Tel (00353) (1) 295 1895 E-mail curate.taney@dublin.anglican.org

SLOGGETT, Donald George. b 49. Trin Coll Bris 81. **d** 83 **p** 84. C Horfield H Trin *Bris* 83-86; C Highworth w Sevenhampton and Inglesham etc 86-88; P-in-c Upavon w Rushall *Sarum* 88-90; R Upavon w Rushall and Charlton 90-01; R Stoulton w Drake's Broughton and Pirton etc *Worc* from 01. *The Rectory, Manor Farm, Stoulton, Worcester WR7 4RS* Tel (01905) 840528 E-mail donsloggett@zetnet.co.uk

SLOW, Leslie John. b 47. Liv Univ BSc68 MSc69. NOC 77. **d** 80 **p** 81. NSM Gt Horton *Bradf* 80-07; Perm to Offic *York* from 08. *21 Mile End Park, Pocklington, York YO42 2TH* Tel (01759) 303888

SLUMAN, Richard Geoffrey Davies. b 34. St Jo Coll Ox BA68 MA68. Sarum Th Coll 68. **d** 70 **p** 71. C Gt Yarmouth *Nor* 70-73; V Churchdown *Glouc* 73-82; P-in-c Blockley w Aston Magna 82-83; V Blockley w Aston Magna and Bourton on the Hill 83-94; rtd 94; Perm to Offic *Cov* 94-10. *21 Manor Farm Road, Tredington, Shipston-on-Stour CV36 4NZ* Tel (01608) 662317

SLUSAR, *(née* WOODLEY), Priscilla Elizabeth. b 54. Univ of Wales (Abth) BA75 Homerton Coll Cam PGCE76. Westcott Ho Cam 08. **d** 10 **p** 11. C Codsall *Lich* from 10. *9 Windsor Gardens, Codsall, Wolverhampton WV8 2EX* Tel (01902) 845238 Mobile 07812-851839 E-mail priscillaslusar@fsmail.net

SLY, Canon Christopher John. b 34. Selw Coll Cam BA58 MA62. Wycliffe Hall Ox. **d** 60 **p** 61. C Buckhurst Hill *Chelmsf* 60-64; V Berechurch 64-75; V Southend St Sav Westcliff 75-87; R Wickham Bishops w Lt Braxted 87-99; RD Witham 87-96; Hon Can Chelmsf Cathl 93-99; rtd 99. *Ludlow Cottage, Church Lane, Little Leighs, Chelmsford CM3 1PQ* Tel (01245) 361489

SLYFIELD, John David. b 32. TD67. Roch Th Coll 66. **d** 68 **p** 69. C St Mary in the Marsh *Cant* 68-71; P-in-c Steeple Claydon *Ox* 71-76; P-in-c Middle w E Claydon 71-76; RD Claydon 73-78; R The Claydons 76-78; V S Westoe *Dur* 78-82; V Tideswell *Derby* 82-92; RD Buxton 84-91; rtd 92; Perm to Offic *Derby* 92-02 and from 06; P-in-c Beeley and Edensor 02-06. *Stile Close, Main Road, Taddington, Buxton SK17 9TR* Tel (01298) 85507

SMAIL, Richard Charles. b 57. CCC Ox BA80 MA83. Ox Min Course 90. **d** 93 **p** 95. NSM Keble Coll Ox 93-96; Chapl, Fell and Lect BNC Ox 97-02; Perm to Offic Ox 02-05; P-in-c Rousham from 05. *5 Summerfield, Oxford OX1 4RU* Tel (01865) 245553 E-mail richardsmail@supanet.com

SMAIL, Canon Thomas Allan. b 28. Glas Univ MA49 Edin Univ BD52. **d** 79 **p** 79. Vice-Prin St Jo Coll Nottm 80-85; TR Sanderstead All SS *S'wark* 85-94; Hon Can S'wark Cathl 91-94; rtd 94; Perm to Offic *S'wark* from 94. *The College of St Barnabas, Blackberry Lane, Lingfield RH7 6NJ* Tel (01342) 872879 E-mail tasmail@blueyonder.co.uk

SMAILES, Ian Collingwood. b 46. Brighton Poly BSc71. NTMTC BA07. **d** 07 **p** 08. NSM Laleham *Lon* from 07. *Gadebridge House, 211 Thames Side, Staines TW18 1UF* Tel (01784) 461195

SMALE, Frederick Ronald. b 37. K Coll Lon BD60 AKC60. **d** 61 **p** 62. C Bearsted *Cant* 61-64; C Fishponds St Mary *Bris* 64-69; V Hartlip *Cant* 69-71; P-in-c Stockbury w Bicknor and Huckinge 69-71; V Hartlip w Stockbury 71-75; R River 75-85; V Birchington w Acol and Minnis Bay 85-00; rtd 00; Perm to Offic *Cant* from 01. *28 Margate Road, Broomfield, Herne Bay CT6 7BL* Tel (01227) 283880

SMALE, Ian Keith. b 53. Wycliffe Hall Ox 98. **d** 00 **p** 01. C Overton w Laverstoke and Freefolk *Win* 00-04; P-in-c E Dean w Friston and Jevington *Chich* 04-06; R 06-08; P-in-c Overton w Laverstoke and Freefolk *Win* from 08; P-in-c N Waltham and Steventon, Ashe and Deane from 11. *The Rectory, 54 Lordsfield Gardens, Overton, Basingstoke RG25 3EW* Tel (01256) 770207 E-mail iansue.smale@btinternet.co.uk

SMALE, Ian Stuart. b 49. **d** 07. NSM Chich Cathl from 07. *65 Stockbridge Road, Chichester PO19 8QE* Tel 07973-747694 (mobile)

SMALL, David Binney. b 39. Brasted Th Coll 61 Westcott Ho Cam 63. **d** 65 **p** 66. C Milton *Portsm* 65-69; CF 69-92; R Wickwar w Rangeworthy *Glouc* 92-97; RD Hawkesbury 94-97; rtd 97; Perm to Offic *Glouc* from 97; Sub Chapl HM Pris Glouc 98-01. *16 Wotton Road, Charfield, Wotton-under-Edge GL12 8TP* Tel and fax (01454) 261746

SMALL, Gordon Frederick. b 41. St Jo Coll Nottm 77. **d** 79 **p** 80. C Belper *Derby* 79-84; NSM Matlock Bath 90-91; C Ripley 91-93; TV Bucknall and Bagnall *Lich* 93-98; Assoc P Deal St Leon w St Rich and Sholden etc *Cant* 99-06; rtd 06. *10 Elmer Close, Malmesbury SN16 9UE* Tel (01666) 823722 E-mail gordon.small1@btopenworld.com

SMALL, Marcus Jonathan. b 67. Univ of Wales (Ban) BD94. Ripon Coll Cuddesdon 94. **d** 96 **p** 97. C Moseley St Mary *Birm* 96-99; TV Wenlock *Heref* 99-05; R Eardisley w Bollingham, Willersley, Brilley etc from 05. *Church House, Church Road, Eardisley, Hereford HR3 6NN* Tel (01544) 327440 E-mail rector@eardisleygroup.org.uk

SMALL, Mrs Shirley Maureen. b 45. WEMTC. **d** 09 **p** 10. NSM Pontesbury I and II *Heref* from 09. *Nills Farm House, Habberley Road, Pontesbury, Shrewsbury SY5 0TN* Tel (01743) 791885

SMALL, Simon William. b 57. Cuddesdon Coll. **d** 98 **p** 99. C Kidderminster St Mary and All SS w Trimpley etc *Worc* 98-01; Chapl to Bp Dudley 01-07; Perm to Offic from 08. *15 Chilkwell Street, Glastonbury BA6 8DQ* Tel (01458) 835503 E-mail simon@simonsmall.info

SMALLDON, The Ven Keith. b 48. Open Univ BA76 Newc Univ MA94. St Mich Coll Llan. **d** 71 **p** 72. C Cwmbran *Mon* 71-73; C Chepstow 73-75; Dioc Youth Adv *Bradf* 75-79; P-in-c Woolfold *Man* 82-85; Dioc Youth and Community Officer 82-90; P-in-c Thursby *Carl* 90-94; Dir of Clergy Tr 90-94; TR Daventry, Ashby St Ledgers, Braunston etc *Pet* 94-98; Chapl Danetre Hosp 94-98; TR Llantwit Major 98-03; Can Res Brecon Cathl 03-11; Dioc Dir of Min 03-11; P-in-c Swansea St Barn 08-11; Adn St D from 11; V Steynton from 11. *The Vicarage, Steynton, Milford Haven SA73 1AW* Tel (01646) 699343 E-mail archdeacon.stdavids@churchinwales.org.uk

SMALLEY, The Very Revd Stephen Stewart. b 31. Jes Coll Cam BA55 MA58 PhD79. Eden Th Sem (USA) BD57 Ridley Hall Cam. **d** 58 **p** 59. C Portman Square St Paul *Lon* 58-60; Chapl Peterho Cam 60-63; Dean 62-63; Lect RS Ibadan Univ Nigeria 63-69; Lect Th Man Univ 70-77; Can Res and Prec Cov Cathl 77-87; Vice-Provost 86-87; Dean Ches 87-01; rtd 01; Perm to Offic *Glouc* from 02. *The Old Hall, The Folly, Longborough, Moreton-in-Marsh GL56 0QS* Tel (01451) 830238 E-mail stephen@sssss.fsworld.co.uk

SMALLMAN, Miss Margaret Anne. b 43. Hull Univ BSc64 Bris Univ CertEd65. St Jo Coll Nottm. **dss** 83 **d** 87 **p** 94. Bromsgrove St Jo *Worc* 83-88; Par Dn 87-88; Par Dn Stoke Prior, Wychbold and Upton Warren 88-90; TD Tettenhall Wood *Lich* 91-94; TV 94-99; P-in-c W Bromwich H Trin 99-08; C W Bromwich Gd Shep w St Jo 99-08; RD W Bromwich 04-08; rtd 08; Perm to Offic *Lich* 08-09; Hon C Wellington All SS w Eyton from 09. *10 St Agatha's Close, Telford TF1 3QP* Tel (01952) 253643 E-mail mas@msmallman.fsnet.co.uk

SMALLMAN, Mrs Wilhelmina Tokcumboh. b 56. Cen Sch Speech & Drama BEd88 Middx Univ BA06. NTMTC 03. **d** 06

p 08. C S Harrow St Paul *Lon* 06-07; C Gt Stanmore 07-10; TV Barking St Marg w St Patr *Chelmsf* from 10. *Christ Church Vicarage, Bastable Avenue, Barking IG11 0NG* Tel (020) 8594 1505 E-mail minaexp@hotmail.com

SMALLS, Peter Harry. b 34. FCCA. **d** 97 **p** 98. OLM Narborough w Narford *Nor* 97-99; OLM Pentney St Mary Magd w W Bilney 97-99; OLM Castle Acre w Newton and Southacre 97-99; OLM Westacre 97-99; OLM Narborough w Narford and Pentney 99-02; Perm to Offic *Nor* from 03 and *St E* from 07. *Windward, Drapers Lane, Ditchingham, Bungay NR35 2JW* Tel (01986) 894667 E-mail peter@smalls6740.freeserve.co.uk

SMALLWOOD, Simon Laurence. b 58. St Jo Coll Dur BSc80. Cranmer Hall Dur 89. **d** 92 **p** 93. C Stapenhill w Cauldwell *Derby* 92-96; TV Dagenham *Chelmsf* 96-03; V Becontree St Geo from 03. *The Vicarage, 86 Rogers Road, Dagenham RM10 8JX* Tel (020) 8593 2760 E-mail thesmallies@ntlworld.com

SMART, Barry Anthony Ignatius. b 57. Lanc Univ BEd79. St Steph Ho Ox 85. **d** 88 **p** 89. C Wantage *Ox* 88-91; C Abingdon 91-93; TV 93-95; C Princes Risborough w Ilmer 95-97; C Kingstanding St Luke *Birm* 97-00; V Small Heath 00-09; Chapl Compton Hospice from 09. *Chaplain's Office, Compton Hospice, 4 Compton Road West, Wolverhampton WV3 9DH* Tel 08452-255497

SMART, Beryl. b 33. Sheff Univ BSc55 FCMI83. **d** 01 **p** 02. OLM Newchurch w Croft *Liv* from 01. *41 Culcheth Hall Drive, Culcheth, Warrington WA3 4PT* Tel (01925) 762655

SMART, Mrs Carol. b 45. SSF SRN67. S Dios Minl Tr Scheme 89. **d** 92 **p** 94. Chapl St Mary's Hosp NHS Trust 92-99; NSM Shorwell w Kingston *Portsm* 99-02; NSM Gatcombe 92-02; NSM Chale 92-02; Perm to Offic from 02. *20 Sydney Close, Shide, Newport PO30 1YG* Tel (01983) 526242 E-mail revcarolsmart@tiscali.co.uk

SMART, Clifford Edward James. b 28. Kelham Th Coll 48. **d** 53 **p** 54. C Blackb St Pet 53-56; Korea 56-65 and 66-93; C Birm St Aid Small Heath 65-66; rtd 93. *6045 Glennaire Drive, St Louis MO 63129-4761, USA* Tel (001) (314) 846 5927

SMART, Harry Gavin. b 67. St D Coll Lamp BA90 Sheff Hallam Univ MA06. Westcott Ho Cam 90. **d** 94 **p** 95. C Thirsk *York* 94-97; C Sheff St Leon Norwood 97-99; Mental Health Chapl Sheff Care Trust 99-06; Lead Mental Health Chapl Lincs Partnership NHS Foundn Trust from 07. *Lincolnshire Partnership NHS Foundation Trust, Witham Court, Fen Lane, North Hykeham, Lincoln LN6 8UZ* Tel (01522) 508310 E-mail harry.smart@lpft.nhs.uk

SMART, Canon Haydn Christopher. b 38. Wells Th Coll 66. **d** 69 **p** 70. C Hillmorton *Cov* 69-72; C Duston *Pet* 72-75; V Woodford Halse 75-79; V Woodford Halse w Eydon 79-82; V Wellingborough All SS 82-92; RD Wellingborough 87-92; V Longthorpe 92-03; Can Pet Cathl 92-03; RD Pet 96-01; rtd 03; P-in-c Madeira *Eur* 03-06; Perm to Offic *Pet* from 06; Chapl to Retired Clergy and Clergy Widows' Officer from 08. *4 Silvester Road, Castor, Peterborough PE5 7BA* Tel (01733) 380460 E-mail havenincastor@btinternet.com

SMART, Mrs Hilary Jean. b 42. SOAS Lon BA63. EMMTC 85. **d** 88 **p** 94. Par Dn Walsall Pleck and Bescot *Lich* 88-94; TV Sheff Manor 94-02; Bp's Ecum Officer 94-02; rtd 02; Chapl Compton Hospice 02-06. *77 Denton Drive, West Bridgford, Nottingham NG2 7FS* Tel 0115-923 1097

SMART, John Francis. b 36. Keble Coll Ox BA59 MA69. Cuddesdon Coll 59. **d** 61 **p** 66. C Cannock *Lich* 61-63; Hon C Gt Wyrley 63-66; C Wednesfield St Thos 66-70; V Brereton 70-85; R E Clevedon and Walton w Weston w Clapton *B & W* 85-02; Chapl Southmead Health Services NHS Trust 85-99; Chapl N Bris NHS Trust 99-02; rtd 02. *Sunnymead, Ford Cross, South Zeal, Okehampton EX20 2JL* Tel (01837) 840233 E-mail andrsmart@tiscali.co.uk

SMART, Neil Robert. b 61. Bris Univ BVSc84. Ridley Hall Cam 01. **d** 03 **p** 04. C Shirley *Win* 03-07; P-in-c Brockenhurst from 07; P-in-c Boldre w S Baddesley from 09. *The Vicarage, Meerut Road, Brockenhurst SO42 7TD* Tel (01590) 623309 E-mail somesmarts@btopenworld.com

SMART, Richard Henry. b 23. Lon Univ BA51. Oak Hill Th Coll. **d** 53 **p** 54. C Bedworth *Cov* 53-56; C New Malden and Coombe *S'wark* 56-59; V Hanley Road St Sav w St Paul *Lon* 59-71; V Plumstead All SS *S'wark* 71-88; rtd 88; Perm to Offic *Chich* from 88. *2 Annington Road, Eastbourne BN22 8NG* Tel (01323) 726850

SMART, Russell Martin. b 79. Moorlands Coll BA06. Ridley Hall Cam 09. **d** 11. C Romford Gd Shep *Chelmsf* from 11. *470 Mawney Road, Romford RM7 8QB* Tel (01708) 762159 E-mail russellsmart@hotmail.com *or* curategs@thegoodshepherd.co.uk

SMEATON, William Brian Alexander. b 37. CITC 69. **d** 71 **p** 72. C Belfast St Luke *Conn* 71-81; I Tullyaughnish w Kilmacrennan and Killygarvan *D & R* 81-02; Bp's Dom Chapl 87-02; Can Raphoe Cathl 88-02; Dioc Radio Officer 90-02; rtd 02. *Bearna Ghaoithe, Drumcavney, Trentagh, Letterkenny, Co Donegal, Republic of Ireland* Tel (0353) 74-913 7917 (mobile) E-mail smeaton@indigo.ie

SMEDLEY, Christopher John. b 62. Trent Poly BSc90. St Jo Coll Nottm MA98. **d** 98 **p** 99. C Cotmanhay *Derby* 98-02; R Wilne and Draycott w Breaston from 02. *The Rectory, 68 Risley Lane, Breaston, Derby DE72 3AU* Tel (01332) 872242

SMEDLEY, Paul Mark. b 59. Bris Univ BA80 Lanc Univ MA81. S Dios Minl Tr Scheme 89. **d** 92 **p** 93. NSM Acton St Mary *Lon* 92-08; Perm to Offic from 08. *12 Baldwyn Gardens, London W3 6HH* Tel (020) 8993 5527 *or* 8932 8497 Fax 8932 8315 E-mail paul@planningforum.co.uk

SMEETON (née GRESHAM), Mrs Karen Louise. b 75. Hull Univ LLB96. Ripon Coll Cuddesdon BA01. **d** 02 **p** 03. C Leesfield *Man* 02-05; V Hamer 05-11; P-in-c Spotland from 11; C Oakenrod and Bamford from 11. *13 Brooklands Court, Rochdale OL11 4EJ* E-mail therevdk-smeeton@yahoo.co.uk

SMEETON, Nicholas Guy. b 74. Trin Hall Cam MA99. Ripon Coll Cuddesdon BA03. **d** 04 **p** 05. C Ashton Ch Ch *Man* 04-07; P-in-c Oldham St Steph and All Martyrs 07-11; TV Oldham 07-11; V Coldhurst and Oldham St Steph from 11. *13 Brooklands Court, Rochdale OL11 4EJ* E-mail nick@smeeton100.freeserve.co.uk

SMEJKAL, Yenda Marcel. b 68. Van Mildert Coll Dur BA97. Coll of Resurr Mirfield 97. **d** 99 **p** 00. C S Shields All SS *Dur* 99-03; TV N Wearside 03-04; P-in-c Sundon *St Alb* from 04. *St Mary's Vicarage, 1 Selina Close, Luton LU3 3AW* Tel (01582) 583076 E-mail yenda.smejkal@virgin.net

SMETHAM, Abigail Laura. See THOMPSON, Abigail Laura

SMETHURST, David Alan. b 36. Lon Univ BD60 Man Univ MPhil84. Tyndale Hall Bris 57. **d** 61 **p** 62. C Burnage St Marg *Man* 61-63; P-in-c Whalley Range St Marg 63-65; R Haughton St Mary 65-74; R Warburton St Mary w H Trin *Carl* 74-87; Dean Hong Kong 87; Dir Acorn Chr Healing Trust Resource Cen 88-93; V Epsom St Martin *Guildf* 93-00; RD Epsom 97-00; rtd 01; Perm to Offic *Carl* from 01. *3 Friars Ground, Kirkby-in-Furness LA17 7YB* Tel and fax (01229) 889725 E-mail friarsground@yahoo.com

SMETHURST, Gordon McIntyre. b 40. Man Univ BA62 BD69. Wells Th Coll 70. **d** 70 **p** 71. C Sandal St Helen *Wakef* 70-73; P-in-c Whitwood and Smawthorpe 73-75; Hd RE Goole Gr Sch 75-79; S Hunsley Sch Melton 80-00; V Anlaby Common St Mark *York* 00-03; P-in-c Roos and Garton w Tunstall, Grimston and Hilston 03-07; rtd 07. *43 Ebor Manor, Keyingham, Hull HU12 9SN* Tel 07817-434209 (mobile) E-mail revsmev@hotmail.com

SMETHURST, Leslie Beckett. b 22. CEng. NW Ord Course 72. **d** 75 **p** 76. C Baguley *Man* 75-78; TV Droylsden St Mary 78-81; V Droylsden St Martin 81-86; rtd 87; Perm to Offic *Blackb* from 87. *27 Calf Croft Place, Lytham St Annes FY8 4PU* Tel (01253) 733159

SMILLIE, Linda Barbara. b 46. Oak Hill Th Coll 85. **d** 87 **p** 94. Par Dn Holloway St Mary w St Jas *Lon* 87-88; Par Dn Holloway St Mary Magd 88-90; Chapl W End Stores 90-91; C Holloway St Mark w Em 90-91; Hon C Islington St Mary 92-94; C-in-c Southall Em CD 95-01; rtd 01; Perm to Offic *Ox* 01-04; Hon C Hanger Hill Ascension and W Twyford St Mary *Lon* 04-07. *20 Wyvern Place, Warnham, Horsham RH12 3QU* Tel (01403) 273788 E-mail rsmillie@freenetname.co.uk

SMITH, Adrian Paul. b 73. Ches Coll of HE BA94. Cranmer Hall Dur 07. **d** 09 **p** 10. C Mablethorpe w Trusthorpe *Linc* from 09. *30 Trusthorpe Road, Sutton-on-Sea, Mablethorpe LN12 2LT* Tel (01507) 440888 Mobile 07773-581065 E-mail aksmith96@btopenworld.com

SMITH, Aidan John. b 54. Leic Univ BA76 Man Univ MBA81. STETS 04. **d** 07 **p** 08. NSM St Martin Ludgate *Lon* from 07. *4 Terrilands, Pinner HA5 3AJ* Tel (020) 3226 0061

✠**SMITH, The Rt Revd Alan Gregory Clayton.** b 57. Birm Univ BA78 MA79 Univ of Wales (Ban) PhD02. Wycliffe Hall Ox 79. **d** 81 **p** 82 **c** 01. C Pudsey St Lawr *Bradf* 81-82; C Pudsey St Lawr and St Paul 82-84; Chapl Lee Abbey 84-90; TV Walsall *Lich* 90-97; Dioc Missr 90-97; Adn Stoke 97-01; Area Bp Shrewsbury 01-09; Bp St Alb from 09. *Abbey Gate House, 4 Abbey Hill Lane, St Albans AL3 4HD* Tel (01727) 853305 Fax 846715 E-mail bishop@stalbans.anglican.org

SMITH, Alan Leonard. b 51. Madeley Coll of Educn CertEd72. Trin Coll Bris 93. **d** 95 **p** 96. C Taunton St Mary *B & W* 95-98; V Taunton Lyngford 98-07; RD Taunton 04-06; V Chatham St Steph *Roch* from 07. *St Stephen's Vicarage, 55 Pattens Lane, Chatham ME4 6JR* Tel (01634) 849791 E-mail revdalansmith@talktalk.co.uk

SMITH, Alan Pearce Carlton. b 52. Trin Hall Cam BA40 MA45 LLB46. Westcott Ho Cam 76. **d** 78 **p** 79. NSM Cherry Hinton St Jo *Ely* 78-82; P-in-c Madingley and Dry Drayton 82-83; P-in-c Swaffham Bulbeck 84-88; Perm to Offic *Ely* 88-03 and from 07. *38 Alpha Road, Cambridge CB4 3DG* Tel (01223) 358124

SMITH, Alan Thomas. b 35. Open Univ BA78 Sussex Univ DipEd79. Ridley Hall Cam 82. **d** 84 **p** 85. C Bedworth *Cov* 84-89; R Carlton Colville w Mutford and Rushmere *Nor* 89-97; rtd 97; Perm to Offic *Nor* from 01. *17 St Martins Gardens, New Buckenham, Norwich NR16 2AX* Tel (01953) 860550 Mobile 07811-229493

SMITH, Alec John. b 29. AKC53. **d** 54 **p** 55. C Charlton Kings St Mary *Glouc* 54-56; C-in-c Findon Valley CD *Chich* 56-57; V Viney Hill *Glouc* 57-65; V Churchdown St Jo 65-66; V Bishop's Cannings *Sarum* 66-69; CF 69-88; V Douglas St Thos *S & M* 88-92; rtd 92; Perm to Offic *S & M* 92-05. *17 Saddle Mews, Douglas, Isle of Man IM2 1JA* Tel (01624) 670093

SMITH, Alexander Montgomery. b 36. TCD BA59 MA64 BD65. TCD Div Sch Div Test60. **d** 61 **p** 62. C Knock *D & D* 61-64; C Belfast St Thos *Conn* 64-66; Lect St Kath Coll Liv 66-69; Sen Lect 69-98; Asst Chapl St Kath Coll *Liv* 66-69; Chapl 69-80; NSM Allerton 80-98; NSM Christchurch *Win* from 98. *Priory Cottage, 4 Quay Road, Christchurch BH23 1BU* Tel (01202) 476103

SMITH, Andrew. b 84. Southn Univ BSc06. Wycliffe Hall Ox 06. **d** 09. C Lymington *Win* from 09. *29 Ramley Road, Lymington SO41 8HF* Tel (01590) 674049 E-mail revandysmith@gmail.com

SMITH, Andrew Clifford. b 67. Ridley Coll Melbourne BMin00. **d** 01 **p** 01. C Clayton All SS Australia 01-03; C Gainsborough and Morton *Linc* 03-06; TV 06-08; P-in-c Woodhall Spa Gp from 08. *The Vicarage, Alverston Avenue, Woodhall Spa LN10 6SN* Tel (01526) 353973 E-mail bandasmiths@btinternet.com

SMITH, Andrew John. b 37. Leeds Univ BA61. Coll of Resurr Mirfield 61. **d** 63 **p** 64. C W Hackney St Barn *Lon* 63-65; Dir and Chapl Northorpe Hall Trust Yorkshire 65-72; Warden Ox Ho Bethnal Green 72-78; Dir and Chapl The Target Trust 78-86; P-in-c Gt Staughton *Ely* 86-88; Norfolk DTI Educn Adv 88-91; Perm to Offic *Ex* 92-96 and from 98; C Widecombe-in-the-Moor, Leusdon, Princetown etc 96-97; rtd 97. *Mountjoy, Rilla Mill, Callington PL17 7NT*

SMITH, Andrew John. b 46. Lon Univ BScEng67 PhD71 Bath Univ MEd88 CEng96 MIET96. Coll of Resurr Mirfield 74. **d** 76 **p** 77. C Swindon New Town *Bris* 76-78; C Southmead 78-79; Perm to Offic 79-91; rtd 11. *15 Dyrham Close, Bristol BS9 4TF* Tel 0117-942 8594 E-mail a3-smith@blueyonder.co.uk

SMITH, Andrew John. b 53. Loughb Univ BTech74. Lon Bible Coll 95 St Jo Coll Nottm MA98. **d** 99 **p** 00. C Hailsham *Chich* 99-02; P-in-c Worc St Mich 02-03; TV Almondbury w Farnley Tyas *Wakef* 03-07; V Woolston New Zealand 07-11. *211 Hampden Street, Nelson 7010, New Zealand* Tel (0064) (3) 545 7230 Mobile 21-0251 5716 E-mail ajsinz@xtra.co.nz

SMITH, Andrew John. b 59. Birm Univ BSc80 PhD81. WMMTC 89. **d** 91 **p** 92. C Lower Mitton *Worc* 91-92; C Stourport and Wilden 92-95; TV Redditch, The Ridge 95-05; P-in-c Redditch St Steph 02-05; Ind Chapl 95-05; Chapl Redditch and Bromsgrove Primary Care Trust 01-05; V W Bromwich All SS *Lich* from 05; RD W Bromwich from 08. *All Saints' Vicarage, 90 Hall Green Road, West Bromwich B71 3LB* Tel 0121-588 3698

SMITH, Andrew Lewis. b 60. Bris Univ BSc83 CEng89. Trin Coll Bris BA11. **d** 11. C E Dean w Friston and Jevington *Chich* from 11. *6 Summerdown Lane, East Dean, Eastbourne BN20 0LF* Tel (01323) 422528 Mobile 07974-795343 E-mail alsmithuk@hotmail.com

SMITH, Andrew Perry Langton. b 56. Sheff City Poly BSc79 Imp Coll Lon MSc80. Trin Coll Bris 89. **d** 91 **p** 92. C Littleover *Derby* 91-95; TV Walsall *Lich* 95-09; Ind Chapl Black Country Urban Ind Miss from 95; Hon C Walsall St Paul and Walsall Pleck and Bescot 05-09; Ecum Dean Telford Chr Coun from 10. *St Matthew's Vicarage, St George's Road, Donnington, Telford TF2 7NJ* Tel (01952) 604239 E-mail andysmith@telfordchristiancouncil.co.uk

SMITH, Angela Elisabeth. b 53. Southn Univ BA75 Bp Grosseteste Coll PGCE76. WEMTC 03. **d** 06 **p** 07. NSM Matson *Glouc* 06-09; NSM Glouc St Geo w Whaddon from 09. *St George's Vicarage, Grange Road, Gloucester GL4 0PE* Tel (01452) 520851 E-mail angela.draesmith@blueyonder.co.uk

SMITH, Mrs Anita Elisabeth. b 57. Westhill Coll Birm BEd79. Trin Coll Bris 85. **d** 88 **p** 94. Par Dn Bermondsey St Anne *S'wark* 88-92; Par Dn Brockley Hill St Sav 92-94; C 94-99; Miss Partner CMS Kenya from 99. *CMS, PO Box 40360, Nairobi, Kenya*

SMITH, Ann Veronica. b 38. Doncaster Coll of Educn DipEd. Edin Dioc NSM Course 88. **d** 95 **p** 96. NSM S Queensferry *Edin* 95-99; NSM Falkirk 99-10; rtd 10. *16 Mannerston, Linlithgow EH49 7ND* Tel (01506) 834361

SMITH (née JENNINGS), Mrs Anne. b 41. CertEd63 STh. Gilmore Ho 65. **dss** 71 **d** 87 **p** 94. Barton w Peel Green *Man* 71-76; Wythenshawe Wm Temple Ch 76-79; Rochdale 79-83; Chapl Rochdale Colls of FE 79-83; Hillock *Man* 83-88; Dn-in-c 87-88; Chapl Wakef Cathl 88-96; P-in-c Whitwell *Derby* 96-00; V Mansfield Woodhouse *S'well* 00-01; rtd 01; Perm to Offic *Carl* 02-05; *Blackb* and *Bradf* from 05. *20 Bendwood Close, Padiham, Burnley BB12 8RT* Tel (01282) 680372

SMITH, Canon Anthony Charles. b 43. Sarum & Wells Th Coll 90. **d** 92 **p** 93. C Dartford H Trin *Roch* 92-95; V Northfleet 95-05; TR Northfleet and Rosherville 05-07; Bp's Dom Chapl 07-10; Hon Can Roch Cathl 05-10; rtd 10. *24 The Forstal, Hadlow, Tonbridge TN11 0RT* Tel 07958-739301 (mobile) E-mail smithab@sky.com

SMITH, Anthony Cyril. b 40. K Coll Lon 65. **d** 69 **p** 70. C Crewkerne *B & W* 69-74; TV Hemel Hempstead *St Alb* 74-76; Asst Chapl K Coll Taunton 76-80; Chapl 80-02; rtd 02; Perm to Offic *B & W* from 03. *1 Castle Street, Stogursey, Bridgwater TA5 1TG* Tel (01278) 733577

SMITH, Anthony James. b 57. ACA Sheff Univ BA. Ridley Hall Cam 83. **d** 86 **p** 87. C Woking St Pet *Guildf* 86-90; C Reigate St Mary *S'wark* 90-94; CMS Kenya 94-00; Finance Team Ldr World Vision UK 00-05; NSM Walton Milton Keynes *Ox* from 10. *7 Shuttleworth Grove, Wavendon Gate, Milton Keynes MK7 7RX* Tel (01908) 586156
E-mail anthony.smith@summitskills.org.uk

SMITH, The Ven Anthony Michael Percival. b 24. G&C Coll Cam BA48 MA53. Westcott Ho Cam 48. **d** 50 **p** 51. C Leamington Priors H Trin *Cov* 50-53; Abp's Dom Chapl *Cant* 53-57; Chapl Norwood and Distr Hosp 57-66; V Norwood All SS 57-66; V Yeovil St Jo w Preston Plucknett *B & W* 66-72; RD Merston 68-72; Preb Wells Cathl 70-72; V Addiscombe St Mildred *Cant* 72-79; Adn Maidstone 79-89; Dir of Ords 80-89; Hon Can Cant Cathl 80-89; rtd 89; Perm to Offic *Cant* 90-06; *Chich* 89-91 and 93-06; RD Rye *Chich* 91-93. *3 Bourne Close, Tonbridge TN9 1LH*

SMITH, Antoinette. b 47. NTMTC 95. **d** 98 **p** 99. NSM Chigwell and Chigwell Row *Chelmsf* 98-02; TV 02-10; V Blackmore and Stondon Massey from 10; RD Ongar from 10. *The Vicarage, Church Street, Blackmore, Ingatestone CM4 0RN* Tel (01277) 821464 E-mail blackmore.vicarage@btinternet.com

SMITH, Miss Audrey. b 47. S'wark Ord Course 89. **d** 92 **p** 94. NSM Croydon St Aug *S'wark* 92-98; P-in-c Redmarley D'Abitot, Bromesberrow w Pauntley etc *Glouc* 98-00; Perm to Offic 05-06; NSM Newent and Gorsley w Cliffords Mesne 06-08; Chapl Hartpury Coll 06-08; NSM Brampton St Thos *Derby* 08-10; rtd 10. *Rose Cottage, Cotton Mill Hill, Holymoorside, Chesterfield S42 7EJ* Tel (01246) 569632

SMITH, Mrs Audrey Isabel. b 20. Lon Univ. Qu Coll Birm IDC79. **dss** 84 **d** 87 **p** 94. NSM Kingston All SS w St Jo *S'wark* 87-95; Perm to Offic *Truro* 95-08. *31 Copes Gardens, Truro TR1 3SN* Tel (01872) 261813

SMITH, Austin John Denyer. b 40. Worc Coll Ox BA62. Cuddesdon Coll 64. **d** 66 **p** 67. C Shepherd's Bush St Steph w St Thos Lon 66-69; C W Drayton 69-72; Chapl Sussex Univ 72-79; V Caddington *St Alb* 79-06; rtd 06. *209 Bedford Road, Hitchin SG5 2UE* Tel (01462) 437433
E-mail ajdsmith@waitrose.com

SMITH, Mrs Barbara Ann. b 56. SNWTP 07. **d** 10 **p** 11. NSM Liv St Chris Norris Green from 10. *25 Meadow Lane, Liverpool L12 5EA* Tel 0151-226 3534 Mobile 07957-963546
E-mail basmith@blueyonder.co.uk

SMITH, Mrs Barbara Jean. b 39. Bris Univ BA62 Surrey Univ PGCE93. S'wark Ord Course 83. **dss** 86 **d** 87 **p** 94. Hon Dss Chislehurst St Nic *Roch* 86; Hon Par Dn 87-90; Hon C Wrecclesham *Guildf* 90-94; Hon C Herriard w Winslade and Long Sutton etc 94-99; P-in-c 99-03; P-in-c Newnham w Nately Scures w Mapledurwell etc 99-03; rtd 03; Perm to Offic *Portsm* 06-07. *15 The Ridings, Paddock Wood, Tonbridge TN12 6YA* Tel (01892) 833564 E-mail barbarajsmith@btopenworld.com

SMITH, Mrs Barbara Mary. b 47. Doncaster Coll of Educn CertEd68. St Jo Coll Dur 82. **dss** 85 **d** 87 **p** 94. Beverley St Nic *York* 85-87; Par Dn 87; NSM S'wark H Trin w St Matt 89-90; Ind Chapl Teesside *York* 91-95; Hon C Middlesbrough St Chad 94-95; Perm to Offic *St Alb* 96-02; Locum Chapl Anglia Poly Univ 96-98; TV Linton 00-04; rtd 04. *Catref, Rookhope, Bishop Auckland DL13 2BG*

SMITH, Canon Barry. b 41. Univ of Wales (Lamp) BA62 Fitzw Ho Cam BA64 MA68 Man Univ MPhil91. Ridley Hall Cam. **d** 65 **p** 66. C Rhyl w St Ann *St As* 65-70; Chapl Scargill Ho 70-72; C Flint *St As* 72-74; V Broughton 74-86; Dioc Ecum Officer 82-86; RD Wrexham 82-86; TR Wrexham 86-92; Can Cursal St As Cathl 86-95; Chan 95; Perm to Offic *S'wark* 97-02. *1 Acorn Keep, Rowhills, Farnham GU9 9BL* Tel (01252) 322111

SMITH, Barry Roy. b 46. STETS. **d** 00 **p** 04. NSM Blandworth w Chalton w Idsworth *Portsm* 00-05; Asst Chapl Portsm Hosps NHS Trust 03-07; Team Chapl from 05; Perm to Offic *Portsm* 05-07 and from 09; NSM Blendworth w Chalton w Idsworth 07-09. *298 Milton Road, Cowplain, Waterlooville PO8 8JP* Tel (023) 9226 5620 E-mail barry.roy.smith@googlemail.com

SMITH, Beverley Anne. b 56. Univ of Wales Coll of Medicine MSc97 RN78 RM80 RHV87 Univ of Wales PGCE00. St Mich Coll Llan. **d** 05 **p** 06. NSM Whitchurch Llan 05-11; NSM Mynyddislwyn *Mon* from 11. *The Vicarage, Central Avenue, Oakdale, Blackwood NP12 0JS* Tel (01495) 225394 Mobile 07841-707525 E-mail beverley.anne@btinternet.com

SMITH, The Ven Brian. b 44. Westmr Coll Ox MTh95. Sarum & Wells Th Coll 71. **d** 74 **p** 75. C Pennywell St Thos and Grindon St Oswald CD *Dur* 74-77; Chapl RAF 77-95; P-in-c Keswick St Jo *Carl* 95-96; V 96-05; RD Derwent 98-05; Hon Can Carl Cathl 99-05; Adn Is of Man *S & M* from 05; V Douglas St Geo from 05. *St George's Vicarage, 16 Devonshire Road, Douglas, Isle of Man IM2 3RB* Tel (01624) 675430 Fax 616136
E-mail archd-sodor@mcb.net

✠**SMITH, The Rt Revd Brian Arthur.** b 43. Edin Univ MA66 Fitzw Coll Cam BA68 MA72 Jes Coll Cam MLitt73. Westcott Ho Cam 66. **d** 72 **p** 73 **c** 93. Tutor and Lib Cuddesdon Coll 72-75; Dir of Studies 75-78; Sen Tutor Ripon Coll Cuddesdon 78-79; C Cuddesdon *Ox* 76-79; Dir Tr *Wakef* 79-87; P-in-c Halifax St Jo 79-85; Hon Can Wakef Cathl 81-87; Adn Craven *Bradf* 87-93; Suff Bp Tonbridge *Roch* 93-01; Hon Can Roch Cathl 93-01; Bp Edin from 01. *3 Eglinton Crescent, Edinburgh EH12 5DH,* or *Bishop's Office, 21A Grosvenor Crescent, Edinburgh EH12 5EL* Tel 0131-226 5099 *or* 538 7044 Fax 538 7088 E-mail bishop@edinburgh.anglican.org

SMITH, Brian Godfrey. b 24. Chich Th Coll 63. **d** 65 **p** 66. C Newc H Cross 65-68; C Redcar *York* 68-72; C Kirkleatham 68-72; V Wortley de Leeds *Ripon* 72-76; Chapl Costa del S E *Eur* 76-82; Chapl Estoril 82-84; V Worfield *Heref* 84-89; rtd 89; Perm to Offic *Heref* from 92. *2 Pineway, Lodge Farm, Bridgnorth WV15 5DT* Tel (01746) 764088

SMITH, Brian Michael. b 42. Kelham Th Coll 69. **d** 69 **p** 70. C Somers Town *Lon* 70-74; C Stamford Hill St Jo 74-75; C Stamford Hill St Bart 75-84; P-in-c Edmonton St Pet w St Martin 84-92; V 92-07; rtd 07. *16 Hurst Rise, Matlock DE4 3EP* E-mail bms@sple.freeserve.co.uk

SMITH, Canon Bridget Mary. b 46. Bp Otter Coll CertEd67. S Dios Minl Tr Scheme 88. **d** 91 **p** 94. C Pet H Spirit Bretton 91-95; P-in-c Silverstone and Abthorpe w Slapton 95-03; R Silverstone and Abthorpe w Slapton etc 03-09; Warden of Past Assts 00-06; Can Pet Cathl 01-09; rtd 09. *2 Merryweather Close, Southwell NG25 0BN* Tel (01636) 812215 E-mail quickvic@lineone.net

SMITH, Mrs Carol. b 55. SEITE 01. **d** 04 **p** 05. C Epping Distr *Chelmsf* 04-07; Chapl Epping Forest Primary Care Trust 05-07; V Moulsham St Luke *Chelmsf* from 07. *St Luke's House, 24 Lewis Drive, Chelmsford CM2 9EF* Tel (01245) 354479 E-mail carolrev@gotadsl.co.uk

SMITH, Mrs Catherine Eleanor Louise. b 52. SAOMC 99. **d** 02 **p** 03. NSM Denham *Ox* 02-05; NSM Penn Street from 05; Chapl Heatherwood and Wexham Park Hosp NHS Trust from 05. *55 Penn Road, Beaconsfield HP9 2LW* Tel and fax (01494) 670389

SMITH, Charles Henry Neville. b 31. Nottm Univ BA52 MA65. Sarum Th Coll 55. **d** 57 **p** 58. C Thirsk w S Kilvington *York* 57-60; C Linthorpe 60-61; V Danby 61-66; Chapl United Cam Hosps 66-76; Chapl Lanc Moor Hosp 76-84; Hon Can Blackb Cathl 81-84; Asst Sec Gen Syn Hosp Chapl Coun 84-88; Hon C Lee St Marg *S'wark* 84-88; Chapl Guy's Hosp Lon 88-96; rtd 96; Hon Chapl S'wark Cathl from 96. *57 Belmont Park, London SE13 5BW* Tel (020) 8318 9993

SMITH, Charles Rycroft. b 46. Sarum & Wells Th Coll 76. **d** 78 **p** 79. C Heref St Martin 78-81; C Southampton Maybush St Pet *Win* 81-83; R The Candover Valley 83-99; RD Alresford 90-99; P-in-c Guernsey St Andr 99-01; R 01-07; Vice-Dean Guernsey 02-07; P-in-c Beaulieu and Exbury and E Boldre from 07. *The Rectory, Palace Lane, Beaulieu, Brockenhurst SO42 7YG* Tel (01590) 612242 E-mail ryc@beaulieu-rectory.org.uk

SMITH, Charles Septimus. b 23. Bris & Glouc Tr Course. **d** 79 **p** 80. NSM Bris St Agnes and St Simon w St Werburgh 79-86; C 86-87; C Bris St Paul's 87-89; rtd 89. *2432 Jarvis Street West, Mississauga ON L5C 2P6, Canada*

SMITH, Mrs Christine. b 46. NOC 94. **d** 97 **p** 98. C Salterhebble All SS *Wakef* 97-01; P-in-c Siddal 01-06; V Cornholme and Walsden from 06. *The Heights, 30 Cross Lee Road, Todmorden OL14 8EH* Tel (01706) 813604
E-mail c.waltonsmith@talktalk.net

SMITH, Christine Lydia. See CARTER, Mrs Christine Lydia

SMITH, The Ven Christopher Blake Walters. b 63. Univ of Wales (Cardiff) BMus84 BD88 LLM95. St Mich Coll Llan 85. **d** 88 **p** 89. C Aberdare *Llan* 88-93; V Tongwynlais 93-00; Dioc Dir Post-Ord Tr 95-05; Dom Chapl Bp Llan and Warden of Ords 01-07; Chapl to Abp Wales 03-07; Adn Morgannwg from 06; P-in-c Cwmbach from 07; Metrop Can from 04. *The Heights, Nant y Groes Drive, Tirfounder Road, Aberdare CF44 0BE* Tel (01685) 378455
E-mail archdeacon.morgannwg@churchinwales.org.uk

SMITH, Canon Christopher Francis. b 46. K Coll Lon BD68 AKC68. St Aug Coll Cant 69. **d** 70 **p** 71. C Norwood All SS *Cant* 70-72; Asst Chapl Marlborough Coll 72-76; C Deal St Leon w Sholden *Cant* 77-81; P-in-c Benenden 81-83; V 83-07; P-in-c Sandhurst w Newenden 04-07; Hon Can Cant Cathl 03-07; AD Tenterden 05-07; Chapl Benenden Sch 81-92; Chapl Benenden Hosp 91-07; rtd 07; Perm to Offic *Cant* from 07. *34 Richmond Road, Whitstable CT5 3PH* Tel (01227) 266569
E-mail christopherfrancissmith@yahoo.co.uk

SMITH, Christopher James. b 72. Newc Univ BSc94. Wycliffe Hall Ox BTh01. **d** 02 **p** 03. C Cambridge H Trin *Ely* 02-04; Assoc R Manchester Zion Ch USA 04-08; R Chevening *Roch* from 09. *Chevening Rectory, Homedean Road, Chipstead, Sevenoaks TN13 2RU* Tel (01732) 453555 E-mail revcjsmith@gmail.com

SMITH, Christopher Matthew. b 67. New Coll Ox BA89 MA93 Homerton Coll Cam PGCE90 LLB07. St Steph Ho Ox BA94. **d** 95 **p** 96. C Wantage *Ox* 95-99; Dom Chapl to Bp Horsham

Chich 99-01; V Beckenham St Mich w St Aug *Roch* 01-11; V Holborn St Alb w Saffron Hill St Pet *Lon* from 11. *St Alban's Clergy House, 18 Brooke Street, London EC1N 7RD* Tel (020) 7405 1831 Fax 7430 2551

SMITH, Canon Christopher Milne. b 44. Selw Coll Cam BA66. Cuddesdon Coll 67. **d** 69 **p** 70. C Liv Our Lady and St Nic 69-74; TV Kirkby 74-81; R Walton St Mary 81-91; Can Res Sheff Cathl 91-02; V Doncaster St Geo 02-10; Bp's Adv on the Paranormal 97-10; Hon Can Sheff Cathl 03-10; rtd 10; Perm to Offic *Sheff* from 10; Chapl to The Queen from 04. *14 Ravensdowne, Berwick-upon-Tweed TD15 1HX* Tel (01289) 330375 E-mail smith@rev.cm.fsnet.co.uk

SMITH, Clarice Mary. b 25. St Mich Coll Llan 76. **dss** 77 **d** 80. Llangiwg *S & B* 77-80; C Llwynderw 80-84; C Newton St Pet 84-88; rtd 88. *33 Sherringham Drive, Newton, Swansea SA3 4UG* Tel (01792) 367984

SMITH, Clifford. b 31. St Aid Birkenhead 59. **d** 61 **p** 62. C Limehouse St Anne *Lon* 61-63; C Ashtead *Guildf* 63-66; R Bromley All Hallows *Lon* 66-76; V Hillsborough and Wadsley Bridge *Sheff* 76-89; V Stainforth 89-96; rtd 96; Hon C Hurst *Ox* from 97. *33 King Street Lane, Winnersh, Wokingham RG41 5AX* Tel 0118-978 9453

SMITH, Clive Leslie. b 50. Leeds Univ BA72 MA03 Ch Coll Liv PGCE73. Coll of Resurr Mirfield 75. **d** 77 **p** 78. C Goldington *St Alb* 77-81; C Cheshunt 81-84; V Watford St Pet 84-89; Chapl Leavesden Hosp Abbots Langley 89-94; Chapl St Alb and Hemel Hempstead NHS Trust 94-00; Chapl W Herts Hosps NHS Trust 00-01; Sen Chapl Doncaster and Bassetlaw Hosps NHS Trust from 01; Perm to Offic *S'well* from 02. *Chaplaincy Department, Doncaster Royal Infirmary, Armthorpe Road, Doncaster DN2 5LT* Tel (01302) 381484 E-mail clive.smith2@dbh.nhs.uk

SMITH, Colin. b 39. MBE. Open Univ BA80 LRSC65 CChem88 FRSC88. NEOC 94. **d** 97 **p** 98. NSM Jesmond H Trin and Newc St Barn and St Jude 97-08; rtd 08. *1 Cayton Grove, Newcastle upon Tyne NE5 1HL* Tel 0191-267 9519 E-mail colinandevelyn@btopenworld.com

SMITH, Colin Graham. b 59. Hatf Poly BA82 CQSW82. Trin Coll Bris BA88. **d** 88 **p** 89. C Bermondsey St Jas w Ch Ch *S'wark* 88-92; V Brockley Hill St Sav 92-99; Miss Partner CMS Kenya from 99. *CMS, PO Box 40360, Nairobi, Kenya*

SMITH, Colin Richard. b 53. Liv Poly BA80 Liv Univ MTD83. Oak Hill Th Coll 84. **d** 86 **p** 87. C Ormskirk *Liv* 86-89; V Wigan St Cath 89-94; C St Helens St Helen 94-99; TV 99-10; P-in-c St Helens St Mark 06-10; TV St Helens Town Cen from 10. *14 Alpine Close, St Helens WA10 4EY* Tel (01744) 453681

SMITH, Mrs Corinne Anne. b 52. St Andr Univ MTheol91. SAOMC 95. **d** 97. C Abingdon *Ox* 97-02; Chapl Pemb Coll Ox 02-03; Chapl Ox Radcliffe Hosps NHS Trust 03-07; Chapl Portsm Hosps NHS Trust from 07. *Chaplaincy Office, De La Court House, Queen Alexandria Hospital, Portsmouth PO6 3LY* Tel (023) 9228 6000 E-mail corinne.smith@vizzavi.net

SMITH, Craig Philip. b 61. Sheff City Poly BA86. St Jo Coll Nottm 90. **d** 93 **p** 94. C Bramley and Ravenfield w Hooton Roberts etc *Sheff* 93-97; C Rainham w Wennington *Chelmsf* 97-00; TV Gainsborough and Morton *Linc* 00-03; V Catshill and Dodford *Worc* 03-07; New Zealand from 07. *PO Box 64, Culverden, North Canterbury 7345, New Zealand* Tel (0064) (3) 315 8210

SMITH, Daniel Bradley. b 69. Harris Man Coll Ox BTh05. St Steph Ho Ox 04. **d** 06 **p** 07. C Bexhill St Pet *Chich* 06-11; R W Blatchington from 11. *St Peter's Rectory, 23 Windmill Close, Hove BN3 7LJ* E-mail db.smith@alumni.oxon.net

SMITH, Darren John Anthony. b 62. Nottm Univ BCombStuds84. Linc Th Coll 84. **d** 86 **p** 87. C Leic Ascension 86-90; C Curdworth w Castle Vale *Birm* 90; C Castle Vale St Cuth 90-91; C Kingstanding St Luke 91-92; P-in-c 92-93; V 93-08; P-in-c Kingstanding St Mark 01-02; Gen Sec ACS from 08. *Gordon Browning House, 8 Spitfire Road, Birmingham B24 9PB* Tel 0121-382 5533 Fax 382 6999

SMITH, David. See SMITH, Terence David

SMITH, David Earling. b 35. AKC60. **d** 61 **p** 62. C Knebworth *St Alb* 61-63; C Chipping Barnet 64-66; C S Ormsby w Ketsby, Calceby and Driby *Linc* 66-69; R Claxby w Normanby-le-Wold 69-74; R Nettleton 69-74; R S Kelsey 69-74; R N Owersby w Thornton le Moor 69-74; R Stainton-le-Vale w Kirmond le Mire 69-74; V Ancaster 74-79; Warden and Chapl St Anne Bedehouses Linc 79-89; C Linc Minster Gp 79-89; rtd 89; Perm to Offic *Linc* 90-02. *17 Egerton Road, Lincoln LN2 4PJ* Tel (01522) 510336 E-mail david@limani17.fsnet.co.uk

✠**SMITH, The Rt Revd David James.** b 35. AKC58 FKC99. **d** 59 **p** 60 **c** 87. C Gosforth All SS *Newc* 59-62; C Newc St Fran 62-64; C Longbenton St Bart 64-68; V Longhirst 68-75; V Monkseaton St Mary 75-82; RD Tynemouth 80-82; Hon Can Newc Cathl 81-87; Adn Lindisfarne 81-87; V Felton 82-83; Suff Bp Maidstone *Cant* 87-92; Bp HM Forces 90-92; Bp Bradf 92-02; rtd 02; Hon Asst Bp York from 02; Hon Asst Bp Eur from 02. *34 Cedar Glade, Dunnington, York YO19 5QZ* Tel (01904) 481225 E-mail david@djmhs.force9.co.uk

SMITH, Canon David John. b 32. Goldsmiths' Coll Lon BA76 LSE MSc79. Lon Coll of Div 68. **d** 70 **p** 71. C Clerkenwell St Jas and St Jo w St Pet *Lon* 70-73; P-in-c Penge St Paul *Roch* 74-78; V 78-89; RD Beckenham 86-89; Chapl Bromley and Sheppard's Colls 90-97; Perm to Offic *S'wark* 90-97; Dioc Clergy Widows and Retirement Officer *Roch* 90-97; Hon Can Roch Cathl 95-97; rtd 98; Perm to Offic *St Alb* from 98 and *Lon* from 99. *13 Park Way, Rickmansworth WD3 7AU* Tel (01923) 775963

SMITH, David Leonard. b 37. St Alb Minl Tr Scheme 84. **d** 91 **p** 92. NSM Potton w Sutton and Cockayne Hatley *St Alb* 91-09. *Address temp unknown* E-mail davidlsmith@hotmail.com

SMITH, David Robert. b 44. Southn Univ BSc75 Loughb Univ MSc86 CEng84 MRAeS84. WEMTC 02. **d** 05 **p** 06. C Matson *Glouc* 05-09; P-in-c Glouc St Geo w Whaddon from 09. *St George's Vicarage, Grange Road, Gloucester GL4 0PE* Tel (01452) 520851 E-mail draesmith@blueyonder.co.uk

SMITH, David Roland Mark. b 46. Dur Univ BA68 ACP78 FRSA87. Edin Th Coll 68. **d** 70 **p** 71. C Southwick St Columba *Dur* 70-74 and 81-82; Asst Chapl Univ of Wales (Cardiff) *Llan* 74-76; Hon C E Bris 76-78; Hon C Filton 78-79; Min Leam Lane CD *Dur* 80-81; Co-ord Chapl Service Sunderland Poly 81-86; Chapl Birm Univ 86-95; Chapl Heathrow Airport *Lon* 95-00; rtd 00; Chapl Wolv Airport *Lich* 00-09. *5 The Keepings, 12 Priory Road, Dudley DY1 4AD* Tel (01384) 259540 Mobile 07778-876695 E-mail revdrmsmith@aol.com

SMITH, David Stanley. b 41. Ox NSM Course. **d** 84 **p** 85. NSM Burghfield *Ox* 84-86; NSM Stratfield Mortimer 86-88; NSM Mortimer W End w Padworth 86-88; C St Breoke and Egloshayle *Truro* 88-93; V Penwerris 93-07; rtd 07; Perm to Offic *Ox* 09-10. *51 Manchester Road, Reading RG1 3QL* Tel 0118-926 4104

SMITH, David Watson. b 31. Sarum Th Coll 63. **d** 65 **p** 66. C W Wimbledon Ch Ch *S'wark* 65-69; C Cheam 69-74; V Haslington *Ches* 74-83; V Haslington w Crewe Green 83-87; V Daresbury 87-98; rtd 98; Perm to Offic *Pet* from 98. *4 Wakefield Way, Nether Heyford, Northampton NN7 3LU* Tel (01327) 341561 E-mail rev.dw.smith@freeuk.com

SMITH, Canon David William. b 46. Sarum Th Coll 70. **d** 72 **p** 73. C Stokesley *York* 72-75; C Edin St Mich and All SS 75-77; R Galashiels 77-85; R Yarm *York* 85-00; TR Whitby w Ruswarp from 00; P-in-c Fylingdales and Hawsker cum Stainsacre 03-05; Can and Preb York Minster from 05. *The Rectory, Chubb Hill Road, Whitby YO21 1JP* Tel (01947) 602590

SMITH, Deborah Jane. b 62. Newc Poly BA83. STETS 00. **d** 03 **p** 04. C Dorchester *Sarum* 03-07; R Wyke Regis from 07. *The Rectory, 1 Portland Road, Weymouth DT4 9ES* Tel and fax (01305) 784649 Mobile 07870-560354 E-mail smithsmania@btopenworld.com

SMITH, Mrs Deborah Louise. b 56. WEMTC 02 NOC 03. **d** 05 **p** 06. C Honley *Wakef* 05-07; Chapl HM Pris and YOI New Hall 05-07; NSM Woolston New Zealand 07-11; Chapl Nelson Hosps from 11. *211 Hampden Street, Nelson 7010, New Zealand* Tel (0064) (3) 545 7230 E-mail dlsinz@xtra.co.nz

SMITH, Mrs Decia Jane. b 47. ALAM66. WMMTC 92. **d** 95 **p** 96. C Edgbaston St Germain *Birm* 95-99; P-in-c Abbots Leigh w Leigh Woods *Bris* from 00. *The Vicarage, 51 Church Road, Abbots Leigh, Bristol BS8 3QU* Tel (01275) 373996 Fax 371799 E-mail revdecia@yahoo.co.uk

SMITH, Declan. See SMITH, Godfrey Declan Burfield

SMITH, Denis Richard. b 53. MA. St Jo Coll Nottm 83. **d** 85 **p** 86. C Hersham *Guildf* 85-88; C Thatcham *Ox* 88-91; V Shefford *St Alb* 91-02; P-in-c Tilehurst St Cath *Ox* 02-07; V Tilehurst St Cath and Calcot from 07. *The Vicarage, Wittenham Avenue, Tilehurst, Reading RG31 5LN* Tel 0118-942 7786 E-mail revdenissmith@hotmail.com

SMITH, Mrs Denise. b 46. Didsbury Coll of Educn CertEd67. **d** 08 **p** 09. OLM Goodshaw and Crawshawbooth *Man* from 08. *122 Goodshaw Lane, Rossendale BB4 8DD* Tel (01706) 830251 Mobile 07954-645212 E-mail mrsbucket122@btinternet.com

SMITH, Dennis Austin. b 50. Lanc Univ BA71 Liv Univ PGCE72. NW Ord Course 74. **d** 77 **p** 78. NSM Seaforth *Liv* 77-83; NSM Gt Crosby St Faith 77-83; Hon C 83-98; Hon C Gt Crosby St Faith and Waterloo Park St Mary from 98; Asst Chapl Merchant Taylors' Sch Crosby 79-83; Chapl from 83. *16 Fir Road, Liverpool L22 4QL* Tel 0151-928 5065

SMITH, Derek Arthur. b 38. Chich Th Coll 63. **d** 66 **p** 67. C Cheadle *Lich* 66-70; C Blakenall Heath 70-72; P-in-c 76-77; TR 77-86; V Knutton 72-76; R Lich St Mary w St Mich 86-96; P-in-c Wall 90-96; R Lich St Mich w St Mary and Wall 96-98; V W Bromwich St Andr w Ch Ch 98-02; rtd 02; Perm to Offic *Lich* from 02. *20 Tiverton Drive, West Bromwich B71 1DA* Tel 0121-525 0260

SMITH, Derek Arthur Byott. b 26. Hull Univ MA89. S Dios Minl Tr Scheme 78. **d** 81 **p** 82. NSM Wimborne Minster and Holt *Sarum* 81-83; C Northampton St Alb *Pet* 83-85; Ind Chapl *York* 85-89; P-in-c Kingston upon Hull St Mary 88-89; P-in-c Newington w Dairycoates 89-93; rtd 93; Perm to Offic *York* from 93. *107 Cardigan Road, Bridlington YO15 3LP* Tel (01262) 678852 E-mail dabs@talktalk.net

SMITH, Derek Graham. b 52. St Cath Coll Cam BA74 MA77. Westcott Ho Cam 74. **d** 76 **p** 77. C Weymouth H Trin *Sarum* 76-79; P-in-c Bradpole 79; TV Bridport 79-84; R Monkton Farleigh, S Wraxall and Winsley 84-98; TR Melksham 98-09; C Atworth w Shaw and Whitley 07-09; C Broughton Gifford, Gt Chalfield and Holt 07-09; RD Bradford 01-08; Chapl Wilts and Swindon Healthcare NHS Trust 00-02; Can and Preb Sarum Cathl 03-09; Chapl Limassol St Barn from 09. *PO Box 51494, 3506 Limassol, Cyprus SN12 6LX* Tel (00357) (22) 671220 E-mail stbac@spidernet.com.cy

SMITH, Diana Linnet. b 47. Sheff Univ BSc69 Goldsmiths' Coll Lon MA83 Trin Coll Carmarthen PhD99. EAMTC 02. **d** 03 **p** 04. C Oundle w Ashton and Benefield w Glapthorn *Pet* 03-06; R Brundall w Braydeston and Postwick *Nor* from 06. *The Rectory, 73 The Street, Brundall, Norwich NR13 5LZ* Tel (01603) 715136

SMITH, Donald Edgar. b 56. Oak Hill Th Coll 89. **d** 91 **p** 92. C Holloway St Mark w Em *Lon* 91-92; C Tollington 92-95; TV W Ealing St Jo w St Jas 95-08; R Frinton *Chelmsf* from 08. *The Rectory, 22 Queens Road, Frinton-on-Sea CO13 9BL* Tel (01255) 674664 E-mail donthevic@btinternet.com

SMITH, The Ven Donald John. b 26. Univ of Wales (Cardiff) LLM96. Clifton Th Coll 50. **d** 53 **p** 54. C Edgware *Lon* 53-56; C Ipswich St Marg *St E* 56-58; V Hornsey Rise St Mary *Lon* 58-62; R Whitton and Thurleston w Akenham *St E* 62-75; Hon Can St E Cathl 73-91; Adn Suffolk 75-84; R The Rickinghalls 75-76; P-in-c Redgrave w Botesdale 75-76; R Redgrave cum Botesdale w Rickinghall 76-78; Adn Sudbury 84-91; rtd 91; Perm to Offic *Cov, Ox, St E* and *Worc* from 91; *Glouc* 91-96 and from 03. *1 Manor Lane, Shipston-on-Stour CV36 4EF*

✠**SMITH, The Rt Revd Donald Westwood.** b 28. Edin Th Coll 54 St D Coll Lamp 50. **d** 54 **p** 55 **c** 90. Asst Dioc Supernumerary *Ab* 54-55; Chapl St Andr Cathl 55-56; Canada 56-57; R Longside *Ab* 57-65; Mauritius 65-85; P-in-c St Geo-in-the-East St Mary *Lon* 85-86; Seychelles 86-87; Madagascar 87-99; Bp Toamasina 90-99. *Avenue Cote d'Emeraude, Morcellement Raffray, Albion, Mauritius* Tel (00230) 238 5966 E-mail tighdhonuil@hotmail.com

SMITH, Edward George. b 61. Surrey Univ BSc82 Cov Univ MSc95. Ox Min Course 06. **d** 09 **p** 10. NSM Aynho and Croughton w Evenley etc *Pet* from 09. *7 Chacombe Road, Middleton Cheney, Banbury OX17 2QS* Tel (01295) 711915 Mobile 07740-909756 E-mail eddie.smith@talk21.com

SMITH, Elaine Joan. See GARRISH, Elaine Joan

SMITH, Ms Elizabeth. b 46. Liv Inst of Educn CertEd67 Heythrop Coll Lon BD76 Lon Univ MPhil84. Westcott Ho Cam 90. **d** 92 **p** 94. Par Dn Moulsham St Jo *Chelmsf* 92-94; C 94-96; V Westcliff St Andr 96-00; V Sedgley St Mary *Worc* 00-09; rtd 09. *2 Buckstone Close, Leeds LS17 5EU* E-mail revdeliz@aol.com

SMITH (née HOWSE), Mrs Elizabeth Ann. b 39. Bath Academy of Art CertEd60 Warwick Univ BEd85. WMMTC 91. **d** 94 **p** 95. C Fletchamstead *Cov* 94-97; P-in-c Leamington Hastings and Birdingbury 97-03; P-in-c Grandborough w Willoughby and Flecknoe 97-03; V Leam Valley 03-05; rtd 05; Perm to Offic *Cov* from 05. *94 Abelia, Amington, Tamworth B77 4EZ* Tel (01827) 704930 E-mail beth@bethemail.co.uk

SMITH, Elizabeth Anne. See ETHERINGTON, Mrs Elizabeth Anne

SMITH, Miss Elizabeth Jane. b 50. Birm Univ BA72. Trin Coll Bris 88. **d** 90 **p** 95. C Lowestoft and Kirkley *Nor* 90-94; TV Rugby *Cov* 94-01; C Shepton Mallet w Doulting *B & W* 01-03; R 03-10; Chapl Mendip Primary Care Trust 01-06; Chapl Somerset Primary Care Trust 06-10; rtd 10. *19 Alcock Crest, Warminster BA12 8ND* E-mail revdlizsmith@btinternet.com

SMITH, Canon Elizabeth Marion. b 52. ACA76 FCA82. Carl Dioc Tr Inst 91. **d** 94 **p** 95. C Appleby *Carl* 94-98; P-in-c Hesket-in-the-Forest and Armathwaite 98-04; P-in-c Skelton and Hutton-in-the-Forest w Ivegill 98-04; R Inglewood Gp from 04; RD Penrith 06-09; Hon Can Carl Cathl from 08. *St Mary's Vicarage, High Hesket, Carlisle CA4 0HU* Tel (01697) 473320 Fax 473167 E-mail revdesmith@hotmail.com

SMITH, Eustace. b 20. St Pet Hall Ox BA43 MA46. Wycliffe Hall Ox 43. **d** 46 **p** 46. C Tiverton St Pet *Ex* 46-47; C Lenton *S'well* 47-49; C Aston SS Pet and Paul *Birm* 49-53; V Bermondsey St Anne *S'wark* 53-59; V Buckminster w Sewstern *Leic* 59-74; V Buckminster w Sewstern, Sproxton and Coston 74-82; R Algarkirk *Linc* 82-88; V Fosdyke 82-88; rtd 88; Perm to Offic *Leic* 89-00. *32 Wordsworth Way, Measham, Swadlincote DE12 7ER* Tel (01530) 273765

SMITH (née DAVIS), Felicity Ann. b 40. Bris Univ MB, ChB63. Qu Coll Birm 83. **dss** 86 **d** 87 **p** 94. NSM Dioc Bd for Soc Resp *Cov* 86-96; NSM Leamington Spa H Trin from 96. *14 Oakwood Grove, Warwick CV34 5TD* Tel (01926) 492452 E-mail felicity@fandi.me.uk

SMITH, Francis Christian Lynford. b 36. Padgate Coll of Educn TCert57. Cuddesdon Coll 72. **d** 74 **p** 75. C Catford St Laur *S'wark* 74-79; P-in-c Vacoas St Paul Mauritius 79-80; Chapl Dulwich Coll 81-91; Chapl St Mich Univ Sch Victoria Canada from 91; rtd 01. *Apartment 403, 2626 Blackwood Street, Victoria BC V8T 3W3, Canada* Tel (001) (250) 598 3459 E-mail smudge4147@hotmail.com

SMITH, Francis Malcolm. b 44. Open Univ BA82 FCMI ACIB69. EAMTC 90. **d** 93 **p** 94. NSM Prittlewell *Chelmsf* 93-08; Perm to Offic from 08. *14 St James Avenue, Southend-on-Sea SS1 3LH* Tel (01702) 586680 Fax 291166 E-mail franksmith44@hotmail.com

SMITH, Canon Frank. b 39. Nottm Univ CertEd65 Open Univ BA76. Paton Congr Coll Nottm 61 Cuddesdon Coll 69. **d** 69 **p** 70. C Davyhulme St Mary *Man* 69-72; PC Peak Forest and Wormhill *Derby* 72-78; R W Hallam and Mapperley 78-85; V Henleaze *Bris* 85-01; RD Clifton 93-99; Hon Can Bris Cathl 99-01; rtd 01; Perm to Offic *Derby* from 01. *4 Hall Court, The Village, West Hallam, Ilkeston DE7 6GS* Tel 0115-944 3474

SMITH, Mrs Gabrielle Lynette Claire. b 49. St Aid Coll Dur BA70 ARCM73. SAOMC 95. **d** 98 **p** 99. NSM Gt Marlow w Marlow Bottom, Lt Marlow and Bisham *Ox* from 98. *29 Bovingdon Heights, Marlow SL7 2JR* Tel (01628) 482923

SMITH (née SAMPSON), Ms Gail Simpson. b 49. Towson State Univ (USA) BA85. Virginia Th Sem MDiv93. **d** 93 **p** 94. Assoc R Ellicott City St Jo USA 93-99; Perm to Offic *S'wark* 00-01; Hon C Kew St Phil and All SS w St Luke 01-02 and 06-07; The Netherlands 02-06; USA from 07. *Address temp unknown* E-mail ukrevgss@aol.com

SMITH, Gareth Hugh St John. b 46. FCA69. SEITE BA06. **d** 06 **p** 07. NSM Tunbridge Wells St Phil *Roch* 06-08. *Hill View, Willetts Lane, Blackham, Tunbridge Wells TN3 9TU* Tel 07780-907066 (mobile) E-mail gareth.smith@diocese-rochester.org

SMITH, Gary Russell. b 56. Southn Univ BTh94 Ox Brookes Univ DipEd02. Cuddesdon Coll 94. **d** 96 **p** 97. C Southampton Maybush St Pet *Win* 96-00. *Soar Valley College, Gleneagles Avenue, Leicester LE4 7GY* Tel 0116-266 9625

SMITH, Gavin Craig. b 71. Ridley Hall Cam 02. **d** 04 **p** 05. C Heatons *Man* 04-07; CF from 07. *c/o MOD Chaplains (Army)* Tel (01264) 381140 Fax 381824 Mobile 07919-354796 E-mail gavinsmith1971@hotmail.com

SMITH, Geoffrey. See SMITH, Richard Geoffrey

SMITH, Geoffrey. b 45. Bernard Gilpin Soc Dur 65 Sarum Th Coll 66. **d** 69 **p** 70. C Hatfield *Sheff* 69-71; C Bolton St Pet *Man* 71-74; V Lt Hulton 74-78; P-in-c Newc St Andr and Soc Resp Adv *Newc* 78-87; Hon Can Newc Cathl 84-87; Dir Cen for Applied Chr Studies 87-91; Team Ldr Home Office Birm Drug Prevention Unit 91-93; Public Preacher *Birm* 87-93; C Brampton and Farlam and Castle Carrock w Cumrew *Carl* 93-96; ACUPA Link Officer 94-96; Can Res Bradf Cathl 96-00; Nat Dir Toc H 00-07; Perm to Offic *Ox* 00-02; Hon C Biddenham *St Alb* 02-07; rtd 07; Perm to Offic *Carl* and *Eur* from 07. *30 Waters Meet, Warwick Bridge, Carlisle CA4 8RT* Tel (01228) 560981 *or* 05602-231702 E-mail geoffsmith1@btinternet.com

SMITH, Canon Geoffrey Cobley. b 30. Bps' Coll Cheshunt 63. **d** 65 **p** 66. C Hockerill *St Alb* 65-68; C Evesham *Worc* 68-72; V Walberswick w Blythburgh *St E* 72-85; RD Halesworth 81-85; R Newmarket St Mary w Exning St Agnes 85-00; RD Mildenhall 86-00; Hon Can St E Cathl 87-00; rtd 00; Perm to Offic *St E* from 00. *78 Eastgate Street, Bury St Edmunds IP33 1YR* Tel (01284) 731061

SMITH, Geoffrey Keith. b 37. Lon Coll of Div 57. **d** 60 **p** 61. C Leek St Luke *Lich* 60-63; C Trentham 63-66; V Lilleshall 66-84; P-in-c Sheriffhales w Woodcote 83-84; V Lilleshall and Sheriffhales 84-87; P-in-c Haughton 87-91; R Derrington, Haughton and Ranton 91-03; RD Stafford 95-03; rtd 03; Perm to Offic *Lich* from 03. *19 Meadow Drive, Haughton, Stafford ST18 9HU* Tel (01785) 259076

SMITH, Geoffrey Raymond. b 49. AKC71. St Aug Coll Cant 71. **d** 72 **p** 73. C Hendon St Alphage *Lon* 72-75; C Notting Hill St Mich and Ch Ch 75-78; P-in-c Isleworth St Fran 78-83; P-in-c Chipping Ongar *Chelmsf* 83-84; R 84-86; R Shelley 84-86; R Chipping Ongar w Shelley 86-89; RD Ongar 88-89; P-in-c Harlow St Mary Magd 89-90; V 90-98; R Woodford St Mary w St Phil and St Jas 98-08; TR Loughton St Jo 08-09; R from 09. *The Rectory, Church Lane, Loughton IG10 1PD* Tel (020) 8508 1224

SMITH, George Frederick. b 35. AKC59. **d** 60 **p** 61. C Radford *Cov* 60-64; C Kenilworth St Nic 64-67; V Burton Dassett 67-71; OCF 67-71; CF 71-74; V Lapley w Wheaton Aston *Lich* 74-80; V Gt Wyrley 80-90; V Shareshill 90-95; rtd 95. *Brantome, North Road, Lampeter SA48 7JA*

SMITH, Canon George Robert Henry. b 24. Chich Th Coll 49. **d** 52 **p** 53. C Glouc St Steph 52-56; V Parkend 56-65; P-in-c Clearwell 60-62; V Tuffley 65-82; Hon Can Glouc Cathl 81-95; R Leckhampton St Pet 82-94; rtd 94; NSM Westcote w Icomb and Bledington *Glouc* 95-98; Perm to Offic from 98. *The Old Bakehouse, The Green, Bledington, Chipping Norton OX7 6XQ* Tel (01608) 659194

SMITH, Gerald. b 36. Sarum Th Coll 61. **d** 63 **p** 64. C Menston w Woodhead *Bradf* 63-66; Chapl RAF 66-70; C Hoylake *Ches* 70-72; R Inverurie *Ab* 72-74; R Kemnay 72-74; TV Hucknall

Torkard *S'well* 74-75; R Falkland Is 75-78; V Luddenden w Luddenden Foot *Wakef* 79-86; V Scopwick Gp *Linc* 86-94; P-in-c Leasingham 94-96; rtd 96; Perm to Offic *Ex* from 96 and *Truro* from 00. *Ivy Cottage, Woolsery, Bideford EX39 5QS* Tel and fax (01237) 431298

SMITH, Mrs Gillian. b 55. EAMTC 02. **d** 05 **p** 06. NSM Burwell w Reach *Ely* 05-09; P-in-c Potton w Sutton and Cockayne Hatley *St Alb* from 09. *The Rectory, Hatley Road, Potton, Sandy SG19 2RP* Tel (01767) 260782
E-mail gillsmith.pot@gmail.com

SMITH, Mrs Gillian Angela. b 39. RGN60 RM62. All Nations Chr Coll IDC65. **d** 94 **p** 95. NSM Haydock St Mark *Liv* 94-96; Perm to Offic *Ely* 96-02; rtd 99; Hon C Milton *Win* 02-03; Perm to Offic *Ely* 03-11; *Chelmsf* 04-11; *York* from 11. *3 Dulverton Hall, The Esplanade, Scarborough YO11 2AR* Tel (01723) 448560 E-mail gill.rev@gmail.com

SMITH, Godfrey Declan Burfield. b 42. TCD BA64 MA67 PGCE65. Sarum Th Coll. **d** 69 **p** 70. Zambia 70-75; Perm to Offic *D & G* 81-02; S Regional Sec (Ireland) CMS 81-99; Overseas Sec 87-93; Miss Personnel Sec 93-99; I Donoughmore and Donard w Dunlavin *D & G* from 02. *The Rectory, Donard, Co Wicklow, Republic of Ireland* Tel (00353) (45) 404631 Fax 404800 Mobile 87-298 7364 E-mail declansmith14@gmail.com *or* 3deesparish@gmail.com

SMITH, Graeme Richard. b 65. Leeds Univ BA87 MA91 Birm Univ PhD97. Qu Coll Birm 87. **d** 89 **p** 90. C Daventry *Pet* 89-92; Perm to Offic *Birm* 92-97; Lect Th Westmr Coll Ox 97-00; Co Ecum Officer *Ox* 97-00; Sen Lect Ox Brookes Univ 00-02; Dean Non-Res Tr St Mich Coll Llan 04-08; Sen Lect Chich Univ from 08. *37 Middleton Hall Road, Birmingham B30 1AB* Tel 0121 459 0565

SMITH, Graham. See SMITH, John Graham

SMITH, Graham. b 39. Univ of Wales (Ban) CertEd60 Lon Univ DipEd75. **d** 01 **p** 02. OLM Upper Holme Valley *Wakef* 01-05; NSM E Richmond *Ripon* 05-08; rtd 08. *15 Church Street, Denby Village, Ripley DE5 8PA* Tel (01332) 881324 Mobile 07918-025346 E-mail graham.smith50@btopenworld.com

SMITH, Graham Arthur James. b 43. MRICS68. STETS 98 Coll of Resurr Mirfield 01. **d** 01 **p** 02. NSM Broadstone *Sarum* 01-06; NSM Christchurch *Win* 06-10; rtd 10; Perm to Offic *Sarum* from 10. *5 Durlston Road, Poole BH14 8PQ* Tel 07710-328685 (mobile) E-mail fr.graham.smith@talk21.com

SMITH, The Very Revd Graham Charles Morell. b 47. St Chad's Coll Dur BA74. Westcott Ho Cam 74. **d** 76 **p** 77. C Tooting All SS *S'wark* 76-80; TV Thamesmead 80-87; TR Kidlington w Hampton Poyle *Ox* 87-97; RD Ox 89-95; TR Leeds City *Ripon* 97-04; Hon Can Ripon Cathl 97-04; Dean Nor from 04. *The Deanery, Cathedral Close, Norwich NR1 4EG* Tel (01603) 218308 Mobile 07798-916321
E-mail graham@gcmsmith.org.uk *or* dean@cathedral.org.uk

SMITH, Graham David Noel. b 37. Oak Hill Th Coll 72. **d** 73 **p** 74. C Southborough St Pet w Ch and St Matt *Roch* 73-76; C Bedworth *Cov* 76-79; R Treeton *Sheff* 79-84; V Riddlesden *Bradf* 84-96; RD S Craven 91-96; rtd 96; Hon C Ilkley All SS *Bradf* 97-03; Perm to Offic from 03. *26 Hawthorne Grove, Burley in Wharfdale, Ilkley LS29 7RF* Tel (01943) 864754
E-mail graham.smith@bradford.anglican.org

SMITH, Graham John. b 31. **d** 75 **p** 76. NSM Devonport St Mark Ford *Ex* 75-81; NSM Plympton St Maurice 81-90; V Ernesettle 90-03; P-in-c 03-08; rtd 08. *15 Abingdon Road, Plymouth PL4 6HZ* Tel (01752) 603812 Mobile 07974-815552
E-mail fathergrahamsmith@hotmail.com

SMITH, Graham John. b 60. Trin Coll Bris BA90 St Jo Coll Nottm MA00. **d** 90 **p** 91. C Herne Cant 90-93; Chapl RN 93-96; C Henfield w Shermanbury and Woodmancote *Chich* 96-98; Chapl Sussex Police 96-98; Chapl Portsm Hosps NHS Trust 98-00; P-in-c Cosham and Chapl Highbury Coll of FE Portsm 00-05; CME Officer *Portsm* 03-05; rtd 05; Perm to Offic *Portsm* from 06. *18 Poynings Place, Portsmouth PO1 2PB* Tel (023) 9229 1239 Mobile 07970-826160 E-mail gjsmith@first-web.co.uk

SMITH, Graham Russell. b 60. New Coll Ox BA81 MA89 Lon Univ BD89. Qu Coll Birm 02. **d** 04 **p** 05. C Yardley St Edburgha *Birm* 04-08; TV Bushbury *Lich* from 08. *The Good Shepherd Vicarage, 17 Goodyear Avenue, Wolverhampton WV10 9JX* Tel (01902) 731713 Mobile 07746-994186
E-mail grakime@talktalk.net

SMITH, Grahame Clarence. b 32. Lich Th Coll 58. **d** 60 **p** 61. C New Sleaford *Linc* 60-63; R Tydd 63-76; V Barholm w Stowe 76-81; V Tallington 76-81; R Uffington 76-81; P-in-c W Deeping 76-77; R 77-81; R Uffington 81-92; rtd 92; Perm to Offic *Linc* 92-95. *Keeper's Cottage, Careby Road, Aunby, Stamford PE9 4EG* Tel (01780) 66386

SMITH, Greg Peter. b 60. Warwick Univ BA86 Qu Coll Birm BA99. WMMTC 97. **d** 99 **p** 00. C Binley *Cov* 99-04; P-in-c E Green from 04. *St Andrew's Vicarage, Church Lane, Eastern Green, Coventry CV5 7BX* Tel (024) 7642 2856
E-mail gregsmith31760@aol.com

SMITH, Gregory James. See CLIFTON-SMITH, Gregory James

SMITH, Canon Guy Howard. b 33. Man Univ BA54. Coll of Resurr Mirfield 60. **d** 62 **p** 63. C Oswestry H Trin *Lich* 62-66; Chapl RNR 63-03; Prin St Aug Sch Betong Malaysia 66-69; V Willenhall St Anne *Lich* 69-79; P-in-c Willenhall St Steph 75-79; Tr Officer Dio Lake Malawi 79-82; Adn Lilongwe 80-82; V Tettenhall Wood *Lich* 82-89; TR 89-91; TR Kidderminster St Jo and H Innocents *Worc* 91-99; rtd 99; Perm to Offic *Worc* from 99; P-in-c St Petersburg *Eur* 05-06. *11 Church Walk, Stourport-on-Severn DY13 0AL* Tel (01299) 828120
E-mail mandgs36@tiscali.co.uk

SMITH, Mrs Gwendoline Anne. b 52. K Coll Lon BA97. SEITE 97. **d** 99 **p** 00. C Erith St Paul *Roch* 99-02; V Hadlow from 02; RD Paddock Wood from 10. *The Vicarage, Maidstone Road, Hadlow, Tonbridge TN11 0DJ* Tel (01732) 850238
E-mail gwen.smith@diocese-rochester.org

SMITH, Harold. See SMITH, Robert Harold

SMITH, Harold. b 20. Qu Coll Birm 77. **d** 80 **p** 81. NSM Gravelly Hill *Birm* 80-85; NSM Duddeston w Nechells 85-93; Perm to Offic from 93. *37 Dovey Tower, Duddeston Manor Road, Birmingham B7 4LE* Tel 0121-682 9417

SMITH, Harvey Jefferson. b 19. AMCT39 FIEE38 FIMechE52 FIPlantE67 ACIArb78. St Alb Minl Tr Scheme 81. **d** 88 **p** 97. NSM Hemel Hempstead *St Alb* 88-92 and 95-00; Perm to Offic 92-95 and from 00. *43 Garland Close, Hemel Hempstead HP2 5HU* Tel (01442) 266377

SMITH, Sister Hazel Ferguson Waide. b 33. Univ Coll Lon BA55. **dss** 64 **d** 87. CSA 58-77; St Etheldreda's Children's Home Bedf 64-85; Bedford St Paul *St Alb* 85-92; Par 92; rtd 92; Perm to Offic *St Alb* from 92; *Ox* 93-00; Assoc Sister CSA from 03. *Paddock House, 6 Linford Lane, Willen, Milton Keynes MK15 9DL* Tel and fax (01908) 397267 Mobile 07789-654881
E-mail hazel.s35@ukonline.co.uk

SMITH, Henry Robert. b 41. Lanchester Poly Cov BSc66. Qu Coll Birm 75. **d** 78 **p** 79. Hon C Hillmorton *Cov* 78-81; Lic to Offic *S'well* 81-85; Hon C Radcliffe-on-Trent and Shelford etc 85-89; C Sutton in Ashfield St Mary 89-92; P-in-c Forest Town 92-98; P-in-c Babworth w Sutton-cum-Lound 98-02; P-in-c Scofton w Osberton 98-02; R Babworth w Sutton-cum-Lound and Scofton etc 02-06; rtd 06. *61 Eldon Street, Tuxford, Newark NG22 0LG* Tel (01777) 872819 E-mail bobsmith@dircon.co.uk

SMITH, Howard Vincent. **d** 11. OLM Winterbourne *Bris* from 11. *15 Winchcombe Road, Frampton Cotterell, Bristol BS36 2AG* Tel (01454) 773817 Mobile 07793-906028
E-mail hvs@blueyonder.co.uk

SMITH, Howard Alan. b 46. St Jo Coll Dur BA73. Cranmer Hall Dur. **d** 74 **p** 75. C Brighton St Matthias *Chich* 74-77; C Henfield w Shermanbury and Woodmancote 77-80; R Northiam 80-87; Chapl St Ebba's Hosp Epsom 87-94; Chapl Qu Mary's Hosp Carshalton 87-94; Chapl Merton and Sutton Community NHS Trust 94-99; Chapl Epsom and St Helier Univ Hosps NHS Trust 99-08; rtd 08; Perm to Offic *S'wark* from 08; Chapl Wandsworth Primary Care Trust from 10. *72 Park Lane, Wallington SM6 0TL* Tel (020) 8643 3300 E-mail howard_a_smith2003@yahoo.co.uk

SMITH, Howard Gilbert. b 48. Leeds Univ BA69. St Steph Ho Ox BA71 MA75 Ridley Hall Cam 72. **d** 73 **p** 74. C Wallsend St Luke *Newc* 73-76; C Farnworth and Kearsley *Man* 76-77; P-in-c Farnworth All SS 77-78; TV E Farnworth and Kearsley 78-82; V Belfield 82-93; V Leesfield 93-04; V Northallerton w Kirby Sigston *York* from 04. *27 Mowbray Road, Northallerton DL6 1QT* Tel (01609) 770082
E-mail howardgsmith@tiscali.co.uk

SMITH, Ian. b 62. Hull Univ BA83. Oak Hill Th Coll BA88. **d** 88 **p** 89. C W Hampstead St Luke *Lon* 88-90; C Woking St Pet *Guildf* 90-95; V Leyland St Jo *Blackb* 95-02; C Goole *Sheff* 02-03; P-in-c Sheff St Paul from 03. *St Paul's Vicarage, Wheata Road, Sheffield S5 9FP* Tel 0114-246 8494
E-mail ian.smith@sheffield.anglican.org

SMITH, Canon Ian Walker. b 29. Leeds Univ BA52. Coll of Resurr Mirfield 52. **d** 54 **p** 55. C Moulsecoomb *Chich* 54-61; Chapl K Sch Cant 61-62; C Crawley *Chich* 62-79; TV 79-81; R Clenchwarton *Ely* 81-94; RD Lynn Marshland 84-94; Hon Can Ely Cathl 88-94; Perm to Offic *Nor* 88-94; rtd 94; Perm to Offic *Ely* from 94. *24 Jubilee Drive, Dersingham, King's Lynn PE31 6YA* Tel (01485) 540203

SMITH, Irene Lillian. b 47. **d** 99 **p** 00. OLM Moston St Chad *Man* from 99. *1 Walmersley Road, Manchester M40 3RS* Tel 0161-682 5927 E-mail irenel.smith@ukgateway.net

SMITH, Mrs Irene Mary. b 43. Shenstone Coll of Educn CertEd64 Lon Univ BD77. OLM course 96. **d** 99 **p** 00. OLM Uttoxeter Area *Lich* from 99. *16 Teanhurst Close, Tean, Stoke-on-Trent ST10 4NN* Tel (01538) 722975
E-mail irene.smith0@btinternet.com

SMITH, Miss Irene Victoria. b 45. SRN66 SCM69. **d** 03 **p** 04. OLM Lawton Moor *Man* from 03. *288 Wythenshawe Road, Manchester M23 9DA* Tel 0161-998 4100 Mobile 07889-116856

SMITH, James. See SMITH, Michael James

SMITH, James. See SMITH, Philip James

SMITH, James. b 26. NEOC 76. **d** 79 **p** 80. NSM Seaton Hirst *Newc* 79-82; NSM Cresswell and Lynemouth 82-88; NSM

Cambois 88-93; rtd 93; Perm to Offic *Newc* from 93. *140 Pont Street, Ashington NE63 0PX* Tel (01670) 816557

SMITH, James Edward. b 30. Chich Th Coll 57. **d** 58 **p** 59. C Ellesmere Port *Ches* 58-61; C W Bromwich All SS *Lich* 61-63; Chapl RN 63-65; V Walton St Jo *Liv* 65-71; V Anfield St Columba 71-79; V Altcar 79-92; rtd 92; Perm to Offic *Linc* 93-02. *The Hollies, 43 Carlton Road, Bassingham, Lincoln LN5 9HB* Tel (01522) 788260

SMITH, James Harold. b 31. Ch Coll Tasmania ThL61. **d** 61 **p** 61. Australia 61-63, 66-85 and 92-94; Canada 64-65; Chapl St Chris Hospice Lon 86-87; Asst Chapl Brook Gen Hosp Lon 87-92; Asst Chapl Greenwich Distr Hosp Lon 87-92; Perm to Offic *S'wark* 94-07. *Poplar Cottage, 80 Charlton Road, London SE7 7EY* Tel (020) 8858 4692

SMITH, James Henry. b 32. St Aid Birkenhead. **d** 65 **p** 66. C Wigan St Cath *Liv* 65-68; V Parkfield in Middleton *Man* 68-77; V Bolton Breightmet St Jas 77-97; rtd 97; Perm to Offic *Liv* from 97. *Flat 4, 14A Cropton Road, Formby, Liverpool L37 4AD* Tel (01704) 833682

SMITH, Janet. See SMITH, Ms Patricia Janet

SMITH, Mrs Janice Lilian. b 51. Open Univ BSc98. NOC 98. **d** 01 **p** 02. NSM Yeadon St Jo *Bradf* 01-06; P-in-c Bramhope *Ripon* from 06; P-in-c Ireland Wood from 09. *The Vicarage, 26 Leeds Road, Bramhope, Leeds LS16 9BQ* Tel 0113-203 7523 E-mail revjanice.smith@tiscali.co.uk

SMITH, Jeffery Donald Morris. b 23. **d** 53 **p** 54. C Gwelo St Cuth S Rhodesia 53-57; C St Patr 57-59; P-in-c 59-61; R Old Deer *Ab* 61-63; R Fraserburgh 63-68; C Kimberley Cathl S Africa 68-70; R Upington 70-73; P-in-c Bintree w Themelthorpe *Nor* 73-76; V Twyford w Guist 73-76; R Twyford w Guist and Bintry w Themelthorpe 76-80; RD Sparham 79-81; R Twyford w Guist w Bintry w Themelthorpe etc 81; TR Hempnall 81-84; R Catfield 84-89; R Ingham w Sutton 84-89; rtd 89; Perm to Offic *Nor* from 89. *27 Dale Road, Dereham NR19 2DD* Tel (01362) 697022

SMITH, Canon Jeffry Bradford. b 56. Pitzer Coll BA82. Ripon Coll Cuddesdon 83 Ch Div Sch of the Pacific (USA) MDiv85. **d** 86 **p** 87. C Visalia USA 86-87; C Frimley *Guildf* 87-91; R E and W Clandon 91-03; Chapl HM Pris Send 94-96; Chapl HM Pris Channings Wood 03-04; Bermuda 04-09; TV Glendale Gp *Newc* from 09. *2 Queens Road, Wooler NE71 6DR* Tel (01668) 281468 E-mail honesmith@talk21.com

SMITH, Mrs Jennifer Pamela. b 63. Girton Coll Cam BA85 MA88. Oak Hill Th Coll BA91. **d** 91 **p** 94. C Rawdon *Bradf* 91-93; Chapl Bradf Cathl 93-96; P-in-c Kelbrook 96-00; Asst Chapl Airedale NHS Trust from 01. *24 Greenacres, Skipton BD23 1BX* Tel (01756) 790852 E-mail jenny.smith@bradford.anglican.org

SMITH, Jeremy John Hawthorn. b 52. Birm Univ BSc73 Lanc Univ MA97. CBDTI 94. **d** 97 **p** 98. NSM Long Marton w Dufton and w Milburn *Carl* 97-00; NSM Hesket-in-the-Forest and Armathwaite 00-04; NSM Skelton and Hutton-in-the-Forest w Ivegill 00-04; NSM Ainstable 00-04; NSM Inglewood Gp from 04. *St Mary's Vicarage, High Hesket, Carlisle CA4 0HU* Tel (01697) 473320

SMITH, Jeremy Victor. b 60. Keble Coll Ox BA82. Chich Th Coll 83. **d** 85 **p** 86. C Alton St Lawr *Win* 85-88; C W Hampstead St Jas *Lon* 88-93; V St Geo-in-the-East St Mary 93-97. *18 The Grange, Grange Road, London W4 4DE* Tel (020) 8742 7104

SMITH, Jesse Lee. b 70. Man Univ BA93 Nottm Univ MA96. Linc Th Coll 94 Westcott Ho Cam 95. **d** 96 **p** 97. C Gomersal *Wakef* 96-00; C Penarth All SS *Llan* 00-02; TV Cen Cardiff 02-03; V Hartlepool H Trin *Dur* 03-08; V Caerau w Ely *Llan* from 08. *The Vicarage, Cowbridge Road West, Cardiff CF5 5BQ* Tel (029) 2056 32564 E-mail jls4hart@yahoo.co.uk

SMITH, John. See SMITH, Stephen John

SMITH, John. b 64. Bournemouth Univ BA92 Leeds Metrop Univ MSc01 Leeds Univ BA10 Huddersfield Univ CertEd89. Yorks Min Course 08. **d** 10 **p** 11. C Idle *Bradf* from 10. *33 Cavalier Drive, Apperley Bridge, Bradford BD10 0UF* Tel (01274) 921547 Mobile 07772-165722 E-mail jrs.smith@talktalk.net

SMITH, John Alec. b 37. Lon Coll of Div ALCD62 BD63. **d** 63 **p** 64. C Cromer *Nor* 63-66; C Barking St Marg *Chelmsf* 66-69; V Attercliffe *Sheff* 69-75; P-in-c Sheff St Barn 76-78; V Sheff St Barn and St Mary 78-89; Ind Chapl 78-89; RD Ecclesall 80-85; TR Chippenham St Paul w Hardenhuish etc *Bris* 89-00; V Kington St Michael 89-00; rtd 00. *82 Victoria Road, Bidford-on-Avon, Alcester B50 4AR* Tel (01789) 772072

SMITH, John Bartlett. b 50. St Chad's Coll Dur BA73 ACIPD. Cuddesdon Coll 73. **d** 76 **p** 77. C Heref St Martin 76-86; NSM Isleworth St Mary *Lon* 86-89; NSM Millom *Carl* 89-92; NSM Balham St Mary and St Jo *S'wark* 92-04; Perm to Offic *Ox* from 10. *The Lilacs, Longwater Lane, Finchampstead, Wokingham RG40 4NZ* Tel 07834-144055 (mobile) E-mail j29bs@yahoo.com

SMITH, John Denmead. b 44. Keble Coll Ox BA65 MA69 St Jo Coll Ox DPhil71. Coll of Resurr Mirfield 72. **d** 75 **p** 76. NSM Win St Lawr and St Maurice w St Swithun 75-80; Chapl Win Coll 75-04; Sen Chapl 04-06; rtd 06; Lect Uganda Chr Univ

Mukono from 06. *56D North Bar Without, Beverley HU17 7AB* Tel (01482) 865513 E-mail jds1000@gmail.com

SMITH, John Ernest. b 52. St Andr Univ MTheol77. Wycliffe Hall Ox 78. **d** 79 **p** 80. C Bermondsey St Mary w St Olave, St Jo etc *S'wark* 79-87; P-in-c Whyteleafe 87-97; RD Caterham 96-98; P-in-c Merstham and Gatton 98-10; TR Merstham, S Merstham and Gatton from 10. *The Rectory, Gatton Bottom, Merstham, Redhill RH1 3BH* Tel (01737) 643755 Fax 642954 E-mail revjohn.e.smith@btinternet.com

SMITH, John Graham. b 32. **d** 78 **p** 79. NSM Hordle *Win* 78-00; rtd 00; Perm to Offic *Win* from 00. *3 Marryat Road, New Milton BH25 5LW* Tel (01425) 615701

SMITH, John Lawrence. b 43. Birm Univ BSc65. Linc Th Coll 67. **d** 70 **p** 71. C Frodingham *Linc* 70-75; TV Gt Grimsby St Mary and St Jas 75-83; V Wolverhampton St Andr *Lich* from 83. *St Andrew's Vicarage, 66 Albert Road, Wolverhampton WV6 0AF* Tel (01902) 712935

SMITH, Canon John Leslie. b 44. Trin Coll Cam BA65 MA71. Ripon Coll Cuddesdon 79. **d** 81 **p** 82. C Ollerton *S'well* 81-84; P-in-c Farndon and Thorpe 84-88; P-in-c Winthorpe and Langford w Holme 88-95; Dioc Chief Insp Ch Schs 88-95; Dir of Educn *Pet* 95-99; P-in-c Cottingham w E Carlton 97-99; Dir of Educn *Roch* 99-10; Hon Can Roch Cathl 04-10; P-in-c Bredgar w Bicknor and Frinsted w Wormshill etc *Cant* 05-10; rtd 10; Perm to Offic *S'well* from 10. *Whiteways, Low Road, Besthorpe, Newark NG23 7HJ* Tel (01636) 894277 E-mail revcanjohn.smith@googlemail.com

SMITH, John Macdonald. b 29. Ch Coll Cam BA52 MA56. Wells Th Coll 56. **d** 58 **p** 59. C Westbury-on-Trym H Trin *Bris* 58-60; C Reading St Giles *Ox* 60-63; V Kidmore End 63-82; rtd 82. *38 Main Road, Norton, Evesham WR11 4TL* Tel (01386) 870918

SMITH, John Malcolm. b 36. ACIB60. NOC 81. **d** 84 **p** 85. NSM Bury St Pet *Man* 84-10; NSM Bury, Roch Valley from 10. *46 Ajax Drive, Bury BL9 8EF* Tel 0161-766 8378

SMITH, John Roger. b 36. Dur Univ BA59. Tyndale Hall Bris 59. **d** 61 **p** 62. C Chaddesden St Mary *Derby* 61-63; C Gresley 63-66; V Burton Ch *Lich* 66-76; V Doncaster St Mary *Sheff* 76-92; R Barnburgh w Melton on the Hill etc 92-01; rtd 01; Perm to Offic *Bradf* from 02. *2 Fieldhead Drive, Cross Hills, Keighley BD20 7RJ* Tel (01535) 634062

SMITH, John Simon. b 46. Middx Hosp MB, BS70 FRCGP91. Ripon Coll Cuddesdon 05. **d** 06 **p** 07. NSM Kettering SS Pet and Paul from 06. *34 Poplars Farm Road, Barton Seagrave, Kettering NN15 5AG* Tel (01536) 513786 E-mail john@poplarsfarm.org

SMITH, John Sydney. b 36. Lanc Univ MA97 ALA59 FLA68 FISM82. CBDTI 94. **d** 97 **p** 98. NSM Arthuret, Nicholforest and Kirkandrews on Esk *Carl* 97-02; rtd 02; Perm to Offic *Carl* from 01. *The Jays, 3 White House, Walton, Brampton CA8 2DJ* Tel (01697) 741114 E-mail johnandjill.thejays@btinternet.com

SMITH, John Thomas. b 29. Keele Univ DASE72 Wolv Poly MPhil81 PhD87. WMMTC 87. **d** 91 **p** 92. NSM Drayton in Hales *Lich* 91-96; NSM Cheswardine, Childs Ercall, Hales, Hinstock etc 96-98; rtd 98; Perm to Offic *Lich* from 98. *Red Bank House, Market Drayton TF9 1AY* Tel (01630) 652302

SMITH, John Thompson. b 30. Wycliffe Hall Ox 64. **d** 66 **p** 67. C Walsall *Lich* 66-69; V Stoke Prior *Worc* 69-75; Asst Gen Sec Red Triangle Club 75-85; R Tendring and Lt Bentley w Beaumont cum Moze *Chelmsf* 85-89; R Fairstead w Terling and White Notley etc 89-92; Chapl Heath Hosp Tendring 85-92; rtd 92; Perm to Offic *B & W* from 92. *1 Harvey Close, Weston-super-Mare BS22 7DW* Tel (01934) 514256

SMITH, John Trevor. b 47. GGSM. Coll of Resurr Mirfield 74. **d** 77 **p** 78. C Loughton St Jo *Chelmsf* 77-80; C Ruislip St Martin *Lon* 80-84; P-in-c Southall Ch Redeemer 84-91; V Kingsbury St Andr from 91. *St Andrew's Vicarage, 28 Old Church Lane, London NW9 8RZ* Tel (020) 8205 7447 Fax 8205 7652 E-mail standrews.kingsbury@london.anglican.org

SMITH, John William. b 51. EAMTC 00. **d** 03 **p** 04. NSM Erpingham w Calthorpe, Ingworth, Aldborough etc *Nor* 03-06; P-in-c Roughton and Felbrigg, Metton, Sustead etc from 06. *18 Pound Lane, Aylsham, Norwich NR11 6DR* Tel (01263) 734761 E-mail ajksmith@btinternet.com

SMITH, Jonathan Paul. b 56. Univ of Wales (Lamp) BA81. Wycliffe Hall Ox 82. **d** 84 **p** 85. C Baglan *Llan* 84-88; C Gabalfa 88-90; R Llangammarch w Llanganten and Llanlleonfel etc *S & B* 90-01; Dioc Missr 95-01; R Denbigh *St As* from 01; AD Denbigh from 09. *The Rectory, 5 St David's Court, Denbigh LL16 3EJ* Tel (01745) 812284 E-mail plwyfdinbych@googlemail.com

SMITH, The Ven Jonathan Peter. b 55. K Coll Lon BD77 AKC77 Cam Univ PGCE78. Westcott Ho Cam 79. **d** 80 **p** 81. C Gosforth All SS *Newc* 80-82; C Waltham Abbey *Chelmsf* 82-85; Chapl City Univ 85-88; R Harrold and Carlton w Chellington *St Alb* 88-97; Chapl Beds Police 90-97; V Harpenden St Jo 97-08; RD Wheathampstead 99-04; Adn St Alb from 08. *6 Sopwell Lane, St Albans AL1 1RR* Tel (01727) 818121 E-mail archdstalbans@stalbans.anglican.org

SMITH, Joseph Paul Tobias George. b 73. Ox Univ BTh95 Ex Univ MA97. **d** 08 **p** 09. OLM Talbot Village *Sarum* 08-11; NSM

Branksome St Aldhelm from 11. *16 Southlea Avenue, Bournemouth BH6 3AB* Tel (01202) 424148 E-mail sudibb1@aol.com

SMITH, Joyce Mary. b 52. Lon Hosp BDS74 Nottm Univ MMedSc77 Lon Univ PhD84 MCCDRCS89. EAMTC. **d** 00 **p** 01. C Harlow St Mary and St Hugh w St Jo the Bapt *Chelmsf* 00-02; C Waltham H Cross 02-03; TV 03-10; NSM from 10; RD Epping Forest from 10; Chapl St Clare Hospice from 10. *St Lawrence House, 46 Mallion Court, Waltham Abbey EN9 3EQ* Tel (01992) 767916 E-mail joyce@smith2767.fsnet.co.uk

SMITH, Miss Judith. b 74. SS Coll Cam BA95 MA98 PGCE97. Trin Coll Bris BA09. **d** 09 **p** 10. C Beeston *Ripon* from 09. *38 Beechcroft View, Leeds LS11 0LN* Tel 0113-277 0631 Mobile 07974-248841 E-mail jude@judesmith.me.uk

SMITH, Julian William. b 64. Liv Univ BSc85. Trin Coll Bris BA93. **d** 93 **p** 94. C Henfynyw w Aberaeron and Llanddewi Aberarth *St D* 93-97; V Llansantffraed and Llanbadarn Trefeglwys etc 97-05; V Llansantffraed w Llanrhystud and Llanddeiniol from 05. *The Vicarage, 11 Maes Wyre, Llanrhystud SY23 5AH* Tel (01974) 202336

SMITH, Mrs Katherine. b 42. Sussex Univ BA65. **d** 07 **p** 08. NSM Battersea St Luke *S'wark* from 07. *74 Alfriston Road, London SW11 6NW* Tel (020) 7228 3079 E-mail katherine.smith42@btopenworld.com

SMITH, Keith. b 46. ACIB. S Dios Minl Tr Scheme 85. **d** 87 **p** 88. NSM W Worthing St Jo *Chich* 87-94; NSM Maybridge 94-96; C Durrington 96-01; V Pagham 01-11; rtd 11. *20 Trent Road, Worthing BN12 4EL*

SMITH, Kenneth Robert. b 48. K Coll Lon BD75 AKC75. St Aug Coll Cant 75. **d** 76 **p** 77. C Birtley *Dur* 76-80; V Lamesley 80-90; R Whitburn from 90. *The Rectory, 51 Front Street, Whitburn, Sunderland SR6 7JD* Tel 0191-529 2232

SMITH, Kenneth Victor George. b 37. ALCD61 Lon Univ BD62. **d** 62 **p** 63. Hon C Bromley Common St Aug *Roch* 62-66; Hon C Streatham Immanuel w St Anselm *S'wark* 66-68; Perm to Offic 68-78; Chapl Whitgift Sch and Ho Croydon 78-97; Hon C Sanderstead All SS 78-91; Hon C Croydon St Jo 91-97; rtd 02. *Bridle Ways, Haling Grove, South Croydon CR2 6DQ* Tel (020) 8680 4460

SMITH, Kevin. b 66. Westmr Coll Ox BA89. Chich Th Coll 90. **d** 92 **p** 93. C Worksop Priory *S'well* 92-96; V New Cantley *Sheff* 96-03; P-in-c Horden *Dur* 03-06; V from 06. *The Vicarage, 4 Stapylton Drive, Peterlee SR8 4HY* Tel 0191-586 7110 E-mail ks.horden@btinternet.com

SMITH, Laurence Sidney. b 37. Sarum & Wells Th Coll 70. **d** 73 **p** 74. C Surbiton St Matt *S'wark* 73-76; C Horley 76-81; V W Ewell *Guildf* 81-90; V W Byfleet 90-02; rtd 02; Perm to Offic *Glouc* from 03. *Candlemill Cottage, Millbank, George Street, Nailsworth, Stroud GL6 0AG* Tel (01453) 836432

SMITH, Lawrence Paul. b 51. Southn Univ BTh81 Ch Ch Coll Cant CertEd72. Chich Th Coll 76. **d** 79 **p** 80. C Margate St Jo *Cant* 79-84; R Eythorne and Elvington w Waldershare etc 84-97; Par Min Development Adv Kensington Area *Lon* 97-09; NSM Isleworth St Fran 00-09; P-in-c 05-09; TR Northfleet and Rosherville *Roch* from 09. *St Botolph's Vicarage, The Hill, Northfleet, Gravesend DA11 9EU* Tel (01474) 566400

SMITH, Lewis Shand. b 52. Aber Univ MA74 Edin Univ BD78 FRSA00. Edin Th Coll 74. **d** 77 **p** 78. C Wishaw *Glas* 77-79; P-in-c 79-80; C Motherwell 77-79; P-in-c 79-80; R Lerwick and Burravoe *Ab* 80-00; Can St Andr Cathl 93-00; R Dumfries *Glas* 00-05; Miss to Seamen 80-00; Lic to Offic *Edin* from 08. *27 Abbotsford Court, Colinton Road, Edinburgh EH10 5EH* Tel 0131-447 2595 E-mail shand.smith@talk21.com

SMITH, Linda Jean. b 61. Ripon Coll Cuddesdon 97. **d** 99 **p** 00. C St Martin w Looe *Truro* 99-03; P-in-c Talland 03-09; C Lanreath, Pelynt and Bradoc 03-09; TV Langtree *Ox* from 09. *The Vicarage, Reading Road, Woodcote, Reading RG8 0QX* Tel (01491) 680979

SMITH, Linnet. See SMITH, Diana Linnet

SMITH, Miss Lorna Cassandra. b 43. Open Univ BA76. Cant Sch of Min 82. **dss** 86 **d** 87 **p** 94. Birchington w Acol and Minnis Bay *Cant* 86-92; Par Dn 87-92; C Addlestone *Guildf* 92-97; V Englefield Green 97-05; rtd 05; Perm to Offic *Guildf* from 05 and *Lon* from 08. *39 Simons Walk, Englefield Green, Egham TW20 9SJ* Tel (01784) 470800 E-mail revlcs@aol.com

SMITH, Mrs Lorna Rosalind. b 53. Oak Hill NSM Course 89. **d** 92 **p** 94. NSM Squirrels Heath *Chelmsf* 92-94; NSM Stanford-le-Hope w Mucking 94-97; P-in-c Fobbing 97-04; P-in-c Tillingham from 04. *The Vicarage, 6 Bakery Close, Tillingham, Southminster CM0 7TT* Tel (01621) 778017 E-mail lornads24@aol.com

SMITH, Lynford. See SMITH, Francis Christian Lynford

SMITH (née THORNTON), Magdalen Mary. b 69. Warwick Univ BA90. Qu Coll Birm BD95. **d** 96 **p** 97. C Kirkby *Liv* 96-98; C Birm St Martin w Bordesley St Andr 00-03; NSM Tilston and Shocklach *Ches* 03-08; C Wilmslow from 08. *15 Parkway, Wilmslow SK9 1LS* Tel (01625) 524717 E-mail revmagssmith@btinternet.com

SMITH, Margaret Elizabeth. b 46. Bretton Hall Coll CertEd67. NOC 85. **d** 88 **p** 94. Hon Par Dn Battyeford *Wakef* 88-89; Hon C Mirfield 89-91; Chapl HM Pris and YOI New Hall 90-95; Dn-in-c Flockton cum Denby Grange *Wakef* 91-94; P-in-c 94-96; V Scholes 96-01; P-in-c Buckden *Ely* 01-05; P-in-c Offord D'Arcy w Offord Cluny 01-05; R Buckden w the Offords 05-06; rtd 06; Perm to Offic *Bradf* from 06. *9 Bobbin Mill Court, Steeton, Keighley BD20 6PU* Tel (01535) 654721 E-mail memagsmith@tesco.net

SMITH, Mrs Marion Elizabeth. b 51. Bris Univ CertEd73 Middx Univ BA99. NTMTC. **d** 98 **p** 99. NSM Cowley *Lon* 98-00; P-in-c Harlington 00-08; R from 08. *The Rectory, St Peter's Way, Hayes UB3 5AB* Tel (020) 8759 9569 Mobile 07803-617509 E-mail marion.smith@tiscali.co.uk

SMITH, Mark Andrew. b 59. UNISA BA86. St Paul's Coll Grahamstown. **d** 85 **p** 86. P Port Elizabeth St Mary Magd S Africa 88-89; R Cradock St Pet 89-92; R Alexandra Plurality 93; Chapl St Andr Coll Grahamstown 94-01; Chapl Denstone Coll Uttoxeter 02-07; NSM Alton w Bradley-le-Moors and Oakamoor w Cotton *Lich* 06-07; NSM Denstone w Ellastone and Stanton 06-07; NSM Mayfield 06-07; Chapl K Coll Taunton from 07. *King's College, South Road, Taunton TA1 3LA* Tel (01823) 328211 or 328137 E-mail masmith@kings-taunton.co.uk

SMITH, Mark David. See LAYNESMITH, Mark David

SMITH, Mark Gordon Robert Davenport. b 56. St Jo Coll Dur BA77. Ridley Hall Cam 78. **d** 80 **p** 81. C Sheff St Jo 80-83; C Brightside w Wincobank 83-86; V Kimberworth Park 86-91; Consultant NE England CPAS 91-98; Nat Co-ord Cert in Evang Studies (CA) 98-01; Chapl for Deaf People *Derby* from 04. *6 Old Chester Road, Derby DE1 3SA* Tel (01332) 370905 Mobile 07702-269608 E-mail mark@deafchurch.co.uk

SMITH, Mark Graham. b 63. Ex Univ BA86 Lanc Univ PhD03. Westcott Ho Cam 87. **d** 90 **p** 91. C Cottingham *York* 90-92; C Guisborough 92-94; Sen Chapl St Martin's Coll *Blackb* 94-98; V Ashton-on-Ribble St Mich w Preston St Mark 98-03; V Scotforth 03-10; Dioc World Development Adv 00-10; P-in-c Vale of Belvoir *Leic* from 10. *The Rectory, 4 Rutland Lane, Bottesford, Nottingham NG13 0DG* Tel (01949) 843615 E-mail mark-smith23@sky.com

SMITH, Mark Peter. b 61. Reading Univ BA82 Open Univ BA93 MA97 Liv Univ MTh02 Keele Univ PGCE84. NOC 99. **d** 02 **p** 03. C Wingerworth *Derby* 02-06; TV Ex St Thos and Em 06-09; P-in-c Kingsteignton and Teigngrace from 09. *The Vicarage, Daws Meadow, Kingsteignton, Newton Abbot TQ12 3UA* Tel (01626) 355127 E-mail mark@mpsosb1.demon.co.uk

SMITH, Mark Winton. b 60. St Jo Coll Dur BA81 Barrister-at-Law (Middle Temple) 82. SEITE 01. **d** 04 **p** 05. NSM E Wickham *S'wark* from 04. *16 Watersmeet Way, London SE28 8PU* Tel and fax (020) 8310 5063 E-mail revdmarksmith@aol.com

SMITH, Martin David. b 52. Hull Univ BA75 LTCL. Cuddesdon Coll 75. **d** 78 **p** 79. C Brentwood St Thos *Chelmsf* 78-80; C Reading St Giles *Ox* 80-91; R Colkirk w Oxwick w Pattesley, Whissonsett etc *Nor* 91-95; P-in-c Gt and Lt Ryburgh w Gateley and Testerton 94-95; P-in-c Hempton and Pudding Norton 94-95; P-in-c Nor St Pet Parmentergate w St Jo 95-03; R Nor St Jo w St Julian from 03. *The Rectory, 8 Kilderkin Way, Norwich NR1 1RD* Tel (01603) 622509 Fax 628417 E-mail frmartinsmith@clara.net

SMITH, Martin Lee. b 47. Worc Coll Ox BA68 MA72. Cuddesdon Coll 68. **d** 70 **p** 71. C Digswell *St Alb* 70-71; C Cheshunt 71-73; Perm to Offic *Ox* 74-80; SSJE 76-02; USA from 81. *1245 4th Street SW E208, Washington DC 20024, USA* E-mail martin.l.smith@worldnet.att.net

SMITH, Martin Stanley. b 53. Univ of Wales (Abth) BScEcon75. STETS. **d** 99 **p** 00. NSM Woking Ch Ch *Guildf* from 99. *Brackenlea, Heather Close, Horsell, Woking GU21 4JR* Tel (01483) 714307 E-mail martin.wokingsmiffs@ntlworld.com

SMITH, Canon Martin William. b 40. K Coll Lon BD63 AKC63. **d** 64 **p** 65. C Ashford St Hilda CD *Lon* 64-67; R Labuan Sabah Malaysia 67-69; R Likas Sabah 69-71; V Lakenham St Mark *Nor* 72-85; V N Walsham w Antingham 85-01; P-in-c Neatishead, Barton Turf and Irstead 94-95; RD Tunstead 91-96; RD St Benet 96-99; Hon Can Nor Cathl 93-05; V Wymondham 01-05; rtd 06; Perm to Offic *Nor* from 06. *Dragon House, 72 Besthorpe Road, Attleborough NR17 2NQ* Tel (01953) 456003 E-mail martinsmith@nnvicarage.freeserve.co.uk

SMITH, Martyn. b 52. CertEd73. Oak Hill Th Coll BA81. **d** 81 **p** 82. C Halliwell St Pet *Man* 81-86; V Cambridge St Martin *Ely* 86-89; Vineyard Chr Fellowship from 89. *M V Centre, 1 Belmont House, Deakins Park, Blackburn Road, Egerton, Bolton BL7 9RP* Tel 08452-303321 E-mail admin@manchestervineyard.co.uk

SMITH, Megan Rachel. b 70. Man Univ MB, ChB94 Liv Univ MTh00 Univ of Wales Coll of Medicine MSc04 MRCP97 FRCPCH05. EMMTC 06. **d** 07 **p** 08. NSM Wilford *S'well* from 07. *112 Ruddington Lane, Nottingham NG11 7BZ* Tel 0115-981 2370 Mobile 07843-051960 E-mail megansmith@doctors.net.uk

SMITH, Melvyn. *See* SMITH, Canon William Melvyn

SMITH, Merrick Thomas Jack. b 37. CEng65 MCIBSE65. Oak Hill NSM Course 90. **d** 92 **p** 93. NSM Isleworth St Mary *Lon* 92-94; Perm to Offic *Birm* 94-96; NSM Warfield *Ox* 96-98; TV Wallingford 98-01; P-in-c Tredington and Darlingscott w Newbold on Stour *Cov* 01-03; rtd 03; Perm to Offic *Sarum* from 03; P-in-c Ilsington *Ex* 06-11. *Vale View, Carnon Crescent, Carnon Downs, Truro TR3 6HL* Tel (01872) 865649
E-mail smith.merrick@virgin.net

SMITH, Michael. *See* SMITH, The Ven Anthony Michael Percival

SMITH, Michael. b 54. Matlock Coll of Educn CertEd76 Nottm Univ BEd77. Ridley Hall Cam 87. **d** 89 **p** 90. C Ilkeston St Mary *Derby* 89-92; TV Wirksworth 92-98; RD Wirksworth 97-98; V Ashbourne w Mapleton 98-04; P-in-c Ashbourne St Jo 98-04; rtd 09. *4 Montford Road, Worksop S81 7RY*
E-mail mikesmith@belton77.wanadoo.co.uk

SMITH, Michael David. b 57. BA80. St Steph Ho *Ox* 81. **d** 83 **p** 84. C Beaconsfield *Ox* 83-87; V Wing w Grove 87-92; R Farnham Royal w Hedgerley 92-01; P-in-c Cookham 01-03; V The Cookhams from 03. *The Vicarage, Church Gate, Cookham, Maidenhead SL6 9SP* Tel (01628) 810345

SMITH, Michael Edward. b 69. STETS 08. **d** 11. C Chandler's Ford *Win* from 11. *St Martin's House, 50 Randall Road, Chandler's Ford, Eastleigh SO53 5AL* Tel (023) 8026 3483 Mobile 07799-730362 E-mail frmichael.smith@gmail.com

SMITH, Michael Ian Antony. b 69. Warwick Univ BSc91. Oak Hill Th Coll BA95. **d** 95 **p** 96. C Cheadle *Ches* 95-98; C Hollington St Leon *Chich* 98-01; C Hartford *Ches* 01-04; V from 04. *The Vicarage, 7 The Green, Hartford, Northwich CW8 1QA* Tel (01606) 77557 or 872255 E-mail mike@stjohnshartford.org.uk

SMITH, Michael James. b 47. AKC69. St Aug Coll Cant 70. **d** 71 **p** 72. C Corby St Columba *Pet* 71-78; V Collierley *Dur* 78-80; CPAS Evang 83-90. *56 Kingsmere, Chester le Street DH3 4DE* Tel 0191-209 2985

SMITH, Michael John. b 47. Kelham Th Coll 65. **d** 71 **p** 72. C Cov St Mary 71-75; Chapl RN 75-90; CF 90-95; R Lynch w Iping Marsh and Milland *Chich* 95-03; RD Midhurst 98-03; Community Chapl Bielefeld Station Germany from 03. *Community Chaplain's Office, 7 Regt RLC, Catterick Barracks, Bielefeld, BFPO 39* Tel (0049) (521) 9254 3118
E-mail revmjsmith@hotmail.com

SMITH, Michael Keith John. b 66. Thames Poly BSc88. Linc Th Coll BTh95. **d** 95 **p** 96. C Birch St Agnes w Longsight St Jo w St Cypr *Man* 95-99; TV Pendleton 99-06; P-in-c Lower Kersal 03-06; Bp's Chapl and Policy Adv *Leic* from 06. *Bishop's Lodge, 10 Springfield Road, Leicester LE2 3BD* Tel 0116-270 3390 Fax 270 3288 E-mail mike.smith@leccofe.org

SMITH, Michael Raymond. b 36. Qu Coll Cam BA59 MA63 ARCM56 ARCO56. Cuddesdon Coll 64. **d** 65 **p** 66. C Redcar *York* 65-70; V Dormanstown 70-73; Prec Worc Cathl 73-77; TR Worc St Barn w Ch Ch 77-83; RD Worc E 79-83; V Eskdale, Irton, Muncaster and Waberthwaite *Carl* 83-87; Chapl Uppingham Sch 87-93; P-in-c Stoke Lacy, Moreton Jeffries w Much Cowarne etc *Heref* 93-01; Dioc Schs Officer 93-03; rtd 01; Perm to Offic *Heref* from 04 and *Mon* from 10. *Upper House, Grosmont, Abergavenny NP7 8EP* Tel (01981) 240790
E-mail michael.smith365@btinternet.com

SMITH, Michael Richard Guy. b 55. Man Univ BA77. Ripon Coll Cuddesdon 88. **d** 90 **p** 91. C Wallasey St Hilary *Ches* 90-93; C Howden *York* 93-94; TV 94-97; V Gt and Lt Driffield 04-10; RD Harthill 08-10; Chapl Tenerife *Eur* from 10. *Apartado 68, Parque Taoro, 38400, Puerto de la Cruz, Tenerife, Canary Islands* Tel (0034) 922 372 292

SMITH, Neville. *See* SMITH, Charles Henry Neville

SMITH, Norman George. b 27. K Coll Lon BD52 AKC52. **d** 53 **p** 54. C Pennington *Man* 53-56; C Chorlton-cum-Hardy St Clem 56-57; V Heywood St Jas 57-63; R Bedhampton *Portsm* 63-81; V Win St Bart 81-92; RD Win 84-89; rtd 92; Perm to Offic *Win* from 92. *89 Priors Dean Road, Winchester SO22 6JY* Tel (01962) 883015

SMITH, Norman Jordan. b 30. Sarum Th Coll 57. **d** 60 **p** 61. C Parkend *Glouc* 60-61; C Clearwell 60-61; C W Tarring *Chich* 61-65; Australia 65-68; V Chidham *Chich* 68-94; rtd 95. *Potters Paradise, 82 Church Road, Hayling Island PO11 0NX*

SMITH, Preb Olwen. b 44. Birm Univ BA66. Selly Oak Coll 67. **d** 67 **p** 94. Ind Chapl Black Country Urban Ind Miss *Lich* 84-98; TV Cen Wolverhampton 94-10; Preb Lich Cathl 99-10; rtd 10; Perm to Offic *Lich* from 10. *St Andrew's Vicarage, 66 Albert Road, Wolverhampton WV6 0AF* Tel (01902) 712935
E-mail smitholwen@btinternet.com

SMITH, Mrs Pamela Christina. b 46. SAOMC 97. **d** 00 **p** 01. NSM Ironstone *Ox* and Chapl Kath Ho Hospice 00-10; Perm to Offic *Ox* from 10. *12 Grange Road, Banbury OX16 9AY* Tel (01295) 253038 E-mail pamela@banx.fsnet.co.uk

SMITH, Miss Pamela Frances. b 44. St Mary's Coll Chelt TCert65. WEMTC 91. **d** 94 **p** 95. NSM Badgeworth, Shurdington and Witcombe w Bentham *Glouc* 94-02; NSM The Lavingtons, Cheverells, and Easterton *Sarum* 02-05; C E Clevedon w Clapton in Gordano etc *B & W* 05-08; rtd 08.

58 Glebe Farm Court, Up Hatherley, Cheltenham GL51 3EB
E-mail pfsmith@freeuk.com

SMITH, Ms Pamela Jane Holden. b 56. Warwick Univ BA78 Lon Inst of Educn PGCE82. Qu Coll Birm BA04. **d** 04 **p** 05. C Coventry Caludon 04-08; NSM 04-06; Perm to Offic from 08; Web Pastor i-church *Ox* from 08. *34 Styvechale Avenue, Coventry CV5 6DX* Tel (024) 7667 2893
E-mail rev.pam.smith@gmail.com *or* webpastor@i-church.org

SMITH, Mrs Patricia. b 48. **d** 10 **p** 11. NSM Silsden *Bradf* from 10. *34 Lower Park Green, Silsden, Keighley BD20 9QE* Tel (01535) 653740 E-mail pat@smithcorner.co.uk

SMITH, Ms Patricia Janet. b 45. Oak Hill Th Coll 87. **d** 89 **p** 90. Canada 89-02; V Charminster and Stinsford *Sarum* from 02; P-in-c Bradford Peverell, Stratton, Frampton etc from 09; RD Dorchester from 09. *The Vicarage, Mill Lane, Charminster, Dorchester DT2 9QP* Tel (01305) 262477
E-mail plumsmith@tiscali.co.uk

SMITH, Paul. b 48. STETS 99. **d** 02 **p** 03. NSM Copthorne *Chich* from 02. *7 Heather Close, Copthorne, Crawley RH10 3PZ* Tel (01342) 714308 E-mail heatherclose@freenet.co.uk

SMITH, Paul. b 52. **d** 98 **p** 99. OLM Leominster *Heref* from 98. *32 The Meadows, Leominster HR6 8RF* Tel (01568) 615862 *or* 612124

SMITH, Paul Aidan. b 59. Birm Univ BA82. Wycliffe Hall Ox 82. **d** 85 **p** 86. C Selly Park St Steph and St Wulstan *Birm* 85-88; C Kensal Rise St Mark and St Martin *Lon* 88-91; V Water Eaton *Ox* 91-00; TR Hale w Badshot Lea *Guildf* 00-02; TV Stantonbury and Willen *Ox* 02-09; TR from 09. *2 Hooper Gate, Willen, Milton Keynes MK15 9JR* Tel (01908) 606689 Mobile 07930-308644 E-mail paul_a_smith@bigfoot.com

SMITH, Paul Allan. b 66. Ch Coll Cam BA88 MA00 PhD94. WMMTC 98 Ripon Coll Cuddesdon 99. **d** 00 **p** 01. C Moseley St Mary *Birm* 00-03; P-in-c Tilston and Shocklach *Ches* 03-08; Officer for Initial Min Tr 03-08; R Wilmslow from 08. *15 Parkway, Wilmslow SK9 1LS* Tel (01625) 524717
E-mail revpaulsmith@btinternet.com

SMITH, Paul Andrew. b 55. St Chad's Coll Dur BA76. Chich Th Coll 78. **d** 80 **p** 81. C Habergham Eaves St Matt *Blackb* 80-83; C Ribbleton 83-86; V Rishton 86-05; RD Whalley 95-01; R Cottingham *York* from 05; AD Cen and N Hull from 10. *The Rectory, Hallgate, Cottingham HU16 4DD* Tel (01482) 847668 E-mail dreadnoughtfam@aol.com

SMITH, Paul Anthony. b 66. Ripon Coll Cuddesdon. **d** 00 **p** 01. C Prestwood and Gt Hampden *Ox* 00-05; P-in-c W Leigh *Portsm* 05-06; V 06-10; TV Abingdon *Ox* from 10. *St Michael's Vicarage, Faringdon Road, Abingdon OX14 1BG* Tel (01235) 534654

SMITH, Preb Paul Gregory. b 39. Ex Univ BA61. St Steph Ho Ox 61. **d** 63 **p** 64. C Walthamstow St Mich *Chelmsf* 63-66; C Devonport St Mark Ford *Ex* 66-69; C Hemel Hempstead *St Alb* 69-71; TV 71-83; R Bideford *Ex* 83-96; TR Bideford, Northam, Westward Ho!, Appledore etc 96; Chapl Bideford and Torridge Hosps 83-96; P-in-c Ex St Jas 96-98; R 98-03; rtd 03; Preb Ex Cathl from 95. *Valrose, Broad Lane, Appledore, Bideford EX39 1ND* Tel (01237) 423513
E-mail fatherpaulsmith@aol.com

SMITH, Mrs Paula Mary. b 57. Sheff Poly BA79 Qu Coll Birm BA06. WMMTC 03. **d** 06 **p** 07. C Walsall *Lich* 06-10; P-in-c Donnington Wood from 10; Min Development Adv (Salop) from 10. *St Matthew's Vicarage, St George's Road, Donnington, Telford TF2 7NJ* Tel (01952) 604239
E-mail revdpaula@tiscali.co.uk

SMITH, Mrs Pauline Frances. b 37. Bris Univ BA58 Lon Univ CertEd59. Sarum & Wells Th Coll 87. **d** 90 **p** 94. C Cobham *Guildf* 90-96; P-in-c Lower Wylye and Till Valley *Sarum* 96-97; TV Wylye and Till Valley 97-03; RD Stonehenge 01-03; rtd 03; Perm to Offic *Glouc* from 04. *267B London Road, Charlton Kings, Cheltenham GL52 6YG* Tel (01242) 222810
E-mail panda.smith@talktalk.net

SMITH (formerly FLEMING), Penelope Rawling. b 43. Glas Univ MA63. Westcott Ho Cam 87. **d** 89 **p** 94. C Bourne *Guildf* 89-94; R Wotton and Holmbury St Mary 94-01; RD Dorking 99-01; Dioc Voc Adv 94-01; R Gt Bookham 01-07; rtd 07. *Westrip Farm House, Redhouse Lane, Westrip, Stroud GL6 6HA* Tel (01453) 757296

SMITH, Peter. b 36. Keele Univ BA60. Cuddesdon Coll 73. **d** 75 **p** 76. C Shrewsbury St Chad *Lich* 75-80; V Burton St Chad 80-90; P-in-c Berwick w Selmeston and Alciston *Chich* 90-91; R 91-02; rtd 02; Perm to Offic *Sarum* from 03. *40 Homefield, Child Okeford, Blandford Forum DT11 8EN* Tel (01258) 861833

SMITH, Peter. b 49. Ex Univ BSc69 PGCE73. Carl Dioc Tr Course. **d** 82 **p** 83. NSM Kendal H Trin *Carl* from 82. *55 Empson Road, Kendal LA9 5PR* Tel (01539) 721467
E-mail rev.p.smith@btinternet.com

SMITH, Peter Alexander. *See* GRAYSMITH, Peter Alexander

SMITH, Peter Denis Frank. b 52. Local Minl Tr Course. **d** 81 **p** 83. OLM Camberwell St Mich w All So w Em *S'wark* 81-95; OLM Croydon St Jo 95-04. *57 Alton Road, Croydon CR0 4LZ* Tel (020) 8760 9656

SMITH, Peter Francis Chasen. b 28. Leeds Univ BA54. Coll of Resurr Mirfield 54. **d** 56 **p** 57. C E Dulwich St Clem *S'wark* 56-59; C Sutton St Nic 59-62; C-in-c Wrangbrook w N Elmsall CD *Wakef* 62-68; Chapl St Aid Sch Harrogate 68-85; P-in-c Lower Nidderdale *Ripon* 85-93; rtd 93; Perm to Offic *Ripon* from 93 and *York* from 95. *Clematis Cottage, Main Street, Kilburn, York YO61 4AH* Tel (01347) 868394
E-mail peter.f.c.smith@btinternet.com

SMITH, Peter Harold. b 53. LCTP 07. **d** 10 **p** 11. NSM Euxton *Blackb* from 10. *15 Howard Road, Chorley PR7 3NJ* Tel (01257) 270411 Mobile 07708-657358 E-mail peter@smithers.plus.com

SMITH, Peter Henry. b 62. Bris Univ BA83. SEITE 96. **d** 99 **p** 00. C Romford St Edw *Chelmsf* 99-02; V Aldersbrook 02-10; TR Waltham H Cross from 10. *The Rectory, Highbridge Street, Waltham Abbey EN9 1DG* E-mail peterhxsmith@aol.com

SMITH, Peter Howard. b 55. St Andr Univ MTheol78. Trin Coll Bris 78. **d** 79 **p** 80. C Handforth *Ches* 79-82; C Eccleston St Luke *Liv* 82-85; V Leyton St Paul *Chelmsf* 85-91; V Darwen St Barn *Blackb* 91-99; TR Bushbury *Lich* 99-06; R Hawkwell *Chelmsf* from 06. *The Rectory, Ironwell Lane, Hawkwell, Hockley SS5 4JY* Tel (01702) 200620 E-mail peterhsmith@talktalk.net

SMITH, Peter James. b 55. St Jo Coll Dur BSc78 Selw Coll Cam BA82 MA85. Ridley Hall Cam 80. **d** 83 **p** 84. C Welling *Roch* 83-87; C Hubberston w Herbrandston and Hasguard etc *St D* 87-89; C Hubberston 89-91; V Canley *Cov* 91-00; V Burney Lane *Birm* 00-06; P-in-c 06-07; P-in-c Ward End 06-07; P-in-c Bordesley Green 06-07; V Ward End w Bordesley Green from 07; AD Yardley and Bordesley from 05. *Christ Church Vicarage, Burney Lane, Birmingham B8 2AS* Tel 0121-783 7455
E-mail peter@uebl.org.uk

SMITH, Peter James. b 23. K Coll Lon 49. **d** 53 **p** 54. C Atherton *Man* 53-55; C Wokingham All SS *Ox* 55-56; C Doncaster St Geo *Sheff* 56-59; V Whitgift w Adlingfleet 59-62; Chapl Highcroft Hosp Birm 62-71; C Wolborough w Newton Abbot *Ex* 71-74; C Furze Platt *Ox* 74-78; Travelling Sec Ch Coun for Health and Healing 78-81; P-in-c Bisham *Ox* 82-90; rtd 90; NSM Hindhead *Guildf* 90-96; Perm to Offic *Guildf* 96-97 and *Portsm* 97-07. *37 St Mary's Square, Gloucester GL1 2QT* Tel (01452) 330842

SMITH, Peter Michael. b 28. Open Univ BA75. K Coll Lon 52. **d** 56 **p** 57. C Pokesdown St Jas *Win* 56-59; C Weeke 59-63; V Hutton Roof *Carl* 63-69; V Barrow St Aid 69-72; V Preston Patrick 72-93; rtd 93; Chapl to the Deaf and Hard of Hearing *Carl* from 93; Perm to Offic from 93. *7 Green Road, Kendal LA9 4QR* Tel (01539) 726741 Mobile 07973-224289
E-mail peter@smith687.freeserve.co.uk

SMITH, Philip David. b 55. Shoreditch Coll Lon BEd78. Oak Hill Th Coll BA98. **d** 98 **p** 99. C Cheltenham St Mary, St Matt, St Paul and H Trin *Glouc* 98-03; TV Cheltenham St Mark from 03. *3 Deacon Close, Cheltenham GL51 3NY* Tel (01242) 528567

SMITH, Philip Hathway. b 66. St Andr Univ MTheol88. Coll of Resurr Mirfield 90. **d** 92 **p** 93. C Shrewsbury St Giles w Sutton and Atcham *Lich* 92-94; C Clayton 94-97; TV Hanley H Ev 97-02; C Croydon St Mich w St Jas *S'wark* 02-04; P-in-c Sydenham All SS from 04. *All Saints' Vicarage, 41 Trewsbury Road, London SE26 5DP* Tel (020) 8778 3065

SMITH, Philip James. b 32. St Alb Minl Tr Scheme. **d** 82 **p** 83. NSM Radlett *St Alb* 82-85; C 85-89; V Codicote 89-99; RD Hatfield 95-01; rtd 99; Perm to Offic *St Alb* from 00. *34 Cherry Tree Rise, Walkern, Stevenage SG2 7JL* Tel (01438) 861951

SMITH, Philip James. b 60. Imp Coll Lon BScEng82 Fitzw Coll Cam BA94. Ridley Hall Cam 92. **d** 95 **p** 96. C Aldborough w Boroughbridge and Roecliffe *Ripon* 95-99; V from 99. *The Vicarage, Church Lane, Boroughbridge, York YO51 9BA* Tel (01423) 322433 Mobile 07958-024689
E-mail vicar@aldwithbb.freeserve.co.uk

SMITH, Philip James. b 84. Dur Univ BA06. Westcott Ho Cam. **d** 10 **p** 11. C Darlington St Mark w St Paul *Dur* from 10. *242 North Road, Darlington DL1 2EN* Tel 07903-567894 (mobile) E-mail philbo.the.grey@gmail.com

SMITH, Philip Lloyd Cyril. b 22. Ch Coll Cam BA47 MA49. Wycliffe Hall Ox 47. **d** 49 **p** 50. C St Helens St Helen *Liv* 49-52; C Woking St Jo *Guildf* 52-56; R Burslem St Jo *Lich* 56-83; P-in-c Burslem St Paul 82-83; R Burslem 83-86; rtd 86; Perm to Offic *Sheff* 86-01. *Upper Treasurer's House, 42 Bromley College, London Road, Bromley BR1 1PE* Tel (020) 8290 1566

SMITH, Philip Raymond. b 56. **d** 11. NSM Farndon w Thorpe, Hawton and Cotham *S'well* from 11. *Dart Cottage, 4 Lancaster Road, Coddington, Newark NG24 2TA* Tel (01636) 703305
E-mail dartcottage@btinternet.com

SMITH, Ralston Antonio. b 28. St Pet Coll Jamaica 53. **d** 56 **p** 57. Jamaica 56-60 and from 72; C Ex St Thos 60-62; C Withycombe Raleigh 62-68; V Exwick 68-72; rtd 93. *PO Box 136, Anglican House, United Theological College, Kingston 7, Jamaica* Tel (001) (876) 977 6263

SMITH, Raymond Charles William. b 56. K Coll Lon BD78 AKC78. Coll of Resurr Mirfield 79. **d** 80 **p** 81. C Iffley *Ox* 80-83; C Wallingford w Crowmarsh Gifford etc 83-86; V Tilehurst St Mary 86-96; TR Haywards Heath St Wilfrid *Chich* 96-08; V from 08. *The Rectory, St Wilfrid's Way, Haywards Heath RH16 3QH* Tel (01444) 413300

SMITH, Canon Raymond Douglas. b 31. TCD BA53 MA56 BD56. **d** 54 **p** 55. C Belfast St Mich *Conn* 54-56; C Ballymacarrett St Patr *D & D* 56-58; CMS Tr Coll Chislehurst 58-60; Kenya (CMS) 60-71; Asst Gen Sec (Hibernian) CMS 71-74; Gen Sec CMS 74-86; CMS Ireland 76-86; Hon Can N Maseno from 78; I Powerscourt w Kilbride and Annacrevy *D & G* 86-96; Can Ch Cath Dublin 94-96; rtd 96. *Glencarrig Lodge, Kindlestown Upper, Delgany, Co Wicklow, Republic of Ireland* Tel (00353) (1) 287 3229

SMITH, Raymond Frederick. b 28. Lon Univ BSc51 Leeds Univ MA65. Oak Hill Th Coll 51. **d** 53 **p** 54. C Toxteth Park St Philemon *Liv* 53-56; C Halliwell St Pet *Man* 56-58; V Denton and Weston *Bradf* 58-66; V Normanton *Wakef* 66-81; RD Chevet 73-81; R Moreton *Ches* 81-90; rtd 90; Perm to Offic *Lich* from 03. *Cornerways, Station Road, Llanymynech SY22 6EG* Tel (01691) 839294

SMITH, Raymond George Richard. b 38. Univ of Wales (Ban) BSc61 MSc65. WMMTC 91. **d** 94 **p** 95. NSM Edgmond w Kynnersley and Preston Wealdmoors *Lich* 94-97; Chapl Princess R Hosp NHS Trust Telford 95-03; V Llandegfan w Llandysilio Ban 03-08; rtd 09; AD Tindaethwy and Menai *Ban* from 11. *41 Cae Mair, Beaumaris LL58 8YN* Tel (01248) 810032

SMITH, Raymond Horace David. b 30. Sir John Cass Coll Lon FIBMS61. Lon Coll of Div 64. **d** 67 **p** 68. C Shoreditch St Leon *Lon* 67-70; SAMS 71-73; Chile 71-80; P-in-c Castle Hedingham *Chelmsf* 80-83; P-in-c Cambridge St Phil *Ely* 83-86; V 86-91; Chapl Ibiza *Eur* 91-94; C Lowton St Mary *Liv* 94-96; rtd 96; Perm to Offic *Ely* 96-02 and 03-11; *Win* 02-03; *Chelmsf* 04-11; *York* from 11. *3 Dulverton Hall, Esplanade, Scarborough YO11 2AR* Tel (01723) 440560
E-mail rev.raysmith@gmail.com

SMITH, Richard Geoffrey. b 46. St Jo Coll Dur BA68 MA69. St Steph Ho Ox BA74 MA78. **d** 75 **p** 76. C Brentwood St Thos *Chelmsf* 75-78; C Corringham 78-81; R Shepton Beauchamp w Barrington, Stocklinch etc *B & W* 81-83; TV Redditch, The Ridge *Worc* 85-89; R Teme Valley N 89-98; Perm to Offic *Heref* 02-05; Hon C Cleobury Mortimer w Hopton Wafers etc from 05. *Churchbridge, Nash, Ludlow SY8 3AX* Tel (01584) 891329
E-mail churchbridge@tinyworld.co.uk

SMITH, Richard Harwood. b 34. Sarum Th Coll 57. **d** 59 **p** 60. C Kington w Huntington *Heref* 59-62; C Georgetown St Phil Br Guiana 62-64; C Kitty 64-65; V Mackenzie 65-69; C Broseley w Benthall 69-70; Area Sec USPG *Heref* and *Worc* 70-76; R Wigmore Abbey *Heref* 76-84; V Eye w Braiseworth and Yaxley *St E* 84-96; P-in-c Bedfield 84-96; P-in-c Occold 84-96; rtd 96. *33 Broad Street, Leominster HR6 8DD* Tel (01568) 610676

SMITH, Canon Richard Ian. b 46. Jes Coll Ox BA69 MA80. Ripon Hall Ox 69. **d** 70 **p** 71. C Eston *York* 70-76; TV E Ham w Upton Park *Chelmsf* 76-80; R Crook *Dur* 80-86; V Stanley 80-86; V Billingham St Cuth 86-11; AD Stockton 92-01; Hon Can Dur Cathl 98-11; rtd 11. *The Garth, 21A Upper Garth Gardens, Guisborough TS14 6HA* Tel (01287) 205012
E-mail richardismith57@hotmail.com

SMITH, Richard Keith. b 44. St Jo Coll Nottm. **d** 84 **p** 85. C Wirksworth w Alderwasley, Carsington etc *Derby* 84-87; R Hulland, Atlow, Bradley and Hognaston 87-96; P-in-c Long Compton, Whichford and Barton-on-the-Heath *Cov* 96-08; P-in-c Wolford w Burmington 97-08; P-in-c Cherington w Stourton 97-08; P-in-c Barcheston 97-08; R S Warks Seven Gp 08-09; RD Shipston 05-09; rtd 09; Perm to Offic *Cov* from 09. *12 Moreton Close, Stratford-upon-Avon CV37 7HB* Tel (01789) 296712 E-mail rkvjsmith@gmail.com

SMITH, Richard Michael. b 52. Lon Univ BA74. EAMTC 79. **d** 82 **p** 83. NSM Cambridge Ascension *Ely* 82-84; C Rainham *Roch* 84-88; V Southborough St Thos 88-96; P-in-c Lake *Portsm* 96-99; V 99-06; P-in-c Shanklin St Sav 96-99; V 99-06; V Eastney from 06. *St Margaret's Vicarage, 13 Cousins Grove, Southsea PO4 9RP* Tel (023) 9273 1316

SMITH, Robert Alfred William. b 53. **d** 08 **p** 09. OLM Withington St Paul *Man* from 08. *61 Burnside Drive, Burnage, Manchester M19 2NA* Tel 0161-225 2509
E-mail bob.smith@sumojo.co.uk

SMITH, Robert Harold. b 23. Lon Univ BA49. Oak Hill Th Coll 46. **d** 50 **p** 51. C Nottingham St Ann *S'well* 50-52; C-in-c Elburton CD *Ex* 52-57; V Lowestoft Ch Ch *Nor* 57-67; R Upton Ex 67-80; R Bressingham *Nor* 80-81; P-in-c N w S Lopham 80-81; P-in-c Fersfield 80-81; R Bressingham w N and S Lopham and Fersfield 81-87; rtd 87; Perm to Offic *Nor* from 87. *22 St Walstan's Road, Taverham, Norwich NR8 6NG* Tel (01603) 861285

✠**SMITH, The Rt Revd Robin Jonathan Norman.** b 36. Worc Coll Ox BA60 MA64. Ridley Hall Cam 60. **d** 62 **p** 63 **c** 90. C Barking St Marg *Chelmsf* 62-67; Chapl Lee Abbey 67-72; V Chesham St Mary *Ox* 72-80; RD Amersham 79-82; TR Gt Chesham 80-90; Hon Can Ch Ch 88-90; Suff Bp Hertford *St Alb* 90-01; rtd 01; Hon Asst Bp St Alb from 02. *7 Aysgarth Road, Redbourn, St Albans AL3 7PJ* Tel and fax (01582) 791964
E-mail bprobin@no7.me.uk

SMITH, Rodney Frederic Brittain. b 37. Jes Coll Cam BA61 MA64. St Steph Ho Ox 87. **d** 88 **p** 89. NSM Rainworth *S'well* 88-89; C Basford St Aid 89-91; C Sneinton St Cypr 91-94; P-in-c Sneinton St Matthias 94-96; V 96-02; P-in-c Sneinton St Steph w St Alb 01-02; rtd 02. *43 Cyprus Road, Nottingham NG3 5EB* Tel 0115-962 0378

SMITH, Roger. *See* SMITH, Canon Thomas Roger

SMITH, Roger. *See* SMITH, John Roger

SMITH, Roger Owen. b 50. Univ of Wales (Abth) BA72 St Chad's Coll Dur CertEd73 FRGS. S'wark Ord Course 84. **d** 87 **p** 88. NSM Nunhead St Antony w St Silas *S'wark* 87-91; NSM Forest Hill St Aug 91-98; NSM Crofton Park St Hilda w St Cypr 91-98; NSM Brockley Hill St Sav 91-98; NSM Camberwell St Giles w St Matt 98-00; Perm to Offic *Cant* 01-07; NSM Folkestone Trin from 07. *22 Wear Bay Road, Folkestone CT19 6BN* Tel (01303) 259896

SMITH, Canon Roger Stuart. b 41. Chich Th Coll 65. **d** 66 **p** 67. C Garforth *Ripon* 66-70; C Hilborough Gp *Nor* 70-73; TV 73-78; V Mendham w Metfield and Withersdale *St E* 78-89; P-in-c Fressingfield w Weybread 86-89; R Fressingfield, Mendham etc 90-91; RD Hoxne 86-91; R Kelsale-cum-Carlton, Middleton, Theberton etc 91-01; C Yoxmere Conf 01-04; RD Saxmundham 96-03; Hon Can St E Cathl 97-04; rtd 04; Perm to Offic *St E* from 04. *Rookery Nook, The Green, St Margaret South Elmham, Harleston IP20 0PN* Tel (01986) 782465 E-mail canonroger@middleton3112.freeserve.co.uk

SMITH, Roger William. b 48. Imp Coll Lon BSc70. EAMTC. **d** 00 **p** 01. NSM Rothwell w Orton, Rushton w Glendon and Pipewell *Pet* 00-11. *6A Kipton Close, Rothwell, Kettering NN14 6DR* Tel (01536) 710981 E-mail kipton@ntlworld.com

SMITH, Ronald Deric. b 21. Lon Univ BA46. Bps' Coll Cheshunt 59. **d** 61 **p** 62. C Crayford *Roch* 61-67; USA 67-68; C W Malling w Offham *Roch* 68-71; V Slade Green 71-78; V Bromley Common St Luke 78-91; rtd 91; Perm to Offic *S'wark* and *Roch* from 91. *5 Bromley College, London Road, Bromley BR1 1PE* Tel (020) 8464 0212

SMITH, Ronald Eric. b 43. EMMTC 93. **d** 93 **p** 94. NSM Wingerworth *Derby* 93-99; NSM Newbold w Dunston 99-01; NSM Loundsley Green 01-05; rtd 05; Perm to Offic *Derby* from 05 and *York* from 06. *20 Oak Tree Lane, Haxby, York YO32 2YH* Tel (01904) 767691 E-mail revron@btinternet.com

SMITH, Canon Ronald James. b 36. Linc Th Coll 73. **d** 75 **p** 76. C Bilborough St Jo *S'well* 75-78; P-in-c Colwick 78-81; R 81-85; P-in-c Netherfield 78-81; V 81-85; C Worksop Priory 85-90; TV Langley and Parkfield *Man* 90-95; P-in-c Barton w Peel Green 95-01; Hon Can Tamale from 01; rtd 01; Perm to Offic *Man* 01-08 and *Ches* from 03. *12 Bramhall Drive, Holmes Chapel, Crewe CW4 7EJ* Tel (01477) 544072 E-mail anne@vicarage01.freeserve.co.uk

SMITH, Ronald William. b 45. St Jo Coll York CertEd67. Chich Th Coll 70. **d** 73 **p** 74. C Scarborough St Martin *York* 73-76; C Stainton-in-Cleveland 76-80; V E Coatham 80-89; V Brookfield 89-10; rtd 10; Perm to Offic *York* from 11. *85 High Street, Marske by the Sea, Redcar TS11 6JL* Tel (01642) 282241 E-mail ronald.smith180@ntlworld.com

SMITH, Canon Rowan Quentin. b 43. AKC66. **d** 67 **p** 68. C Matroosfontein S Africa 67-69; C Bonteheuwel 70; C Plumstead All SS 71-72; P-in-c Grassy Park 72-77; CR 77-88; Chapl Cape Town Univ 88-90; Prov Exec Officer 90-95; Dean Cape Town 96-10; rtd 10. *30 Balers Way, Sunset Beach, Cape Town, 7441 South Africa*

SMITH, Preb Roy Leonard. b 36. Clifton Th Coll 63. **d** 66 **p** 67. C Clapham St Jas *S'wark* 66-70; C Kennington St Mark 70-74; C-in-c Southall Em CD *Lon* 74-83; V Stonebridge St Mich 83-06; Preb St Paul's Cathl 96-06; rtd 06; Hon C Kensal Rise St Mark and St Martin *Lon* 06-11; Hon C Kensal Rise St Mark from 11. *82 Herbert Gardens, London NW10 3BU* Tel (020) 8969 2875 E-mail prebroy@yahoo.co.uk

SMITH, Royston. b 55. EMMTC 87. **d** 90 **p** 91. NSM Shirland *Derby* 90-94; NSM Ashover and Brackenfield 95-00; Lic to Offic from 00. *Kirkdale Cottage, Oakstedge Lane, Milltown, Ashover, Chesterfield S45 0HA* Tel (01246) 590975 E-mail royston@kirkdalecottage.freeserve.co.uk

SMITH, Royston Burleigh. b 26. St Deiniol's Hawarden 76. **d** 79 **p** 80. C Prestatyn *St As* 79-83; V Kerry and Llanmerewig 83-90; C Rhyl w St Ann 90-91; rtd 91. *45 Clwyd Park, Kinmel Bay, Rhyl LL18 5EJ* Tel (01745) 337684

SMITH, Ruth. *See* SMITH, Ms Vivienne Ruth

SMITH, Rycroft. *See* SMITH, Charles Rycroft

SMITH, Mrs Sally Anne. b 63. RN85. St Jo Coll Nottm 07. **d** 09 **p** 10. C Stone St Mich and St Wulfad w Aston St Sav *Lich* from 09. *Covenant Cottage, Cotes Heath, Stafford ST21 6QU* Tel (01782) 791043 Mobile 07962-025659 E-mail silsmth@aol.com

SMITH, Sarah Anne Louise. *See* PIX, Mrs Sarah Anne Louise

SMITH, Scott Anthony. b 73. K Alfred's Coll Win BA99. Trin Coll Bris 08. **d** 10 **p** 11. C Clevedon St Andr and Ch Ch *B & W* from 10. *33 Ash Grove, Clevedon BS21 7JZ* Tel 07810-810313 (mobile) E-mail smithscott@hotmail.com

SMITH, Mrs Shirley Ann. b 46. RSCN68 RM82 RGN84 RHV86. Sarum & Wells Th Coll 89. **d** 93 **p** 94. C Totton *Win* 93-96; Chapl Portsm Hosps NHS Trust 96-98; V Lord's Hill *Win* 98-01; TV Beaminster Area *Sarum* 01-05; rtd 05; Perm to Offic *Sarum* 05-08; P-in-c Hazelbury Bryan and the Hillside Par 08-11; P-in-c Okeford 08-11. *3 Ash Croft, Ash, Martock TA12 6PH* Tel (01935) 508756 E-mail shirleywinch@aol.com

SMITH, Stephen. b 53. CQSW78. Sarum & Wells Th Coll 87. **d** 89 **p** 90. C Redcar *York* 89-92; C Leeds St Aid *Ripon* 92-96; R Langtoglos by Camelford w Advent *Truro* 96-99; Chapl Hull and E Yorks Hosps NHS Trust 99-01; V Leeds St Marg and All Hallows *Ripon* from 08; AD Headingley from 09. *All Hallows Vicarage, 24 Regent Terrace, Leeds LS6 1NP* Tel 0113-242 2205 E-mail simeve@ntlworld.com

SMITH, Stephen. b 60. Coll of Resurr Mirfield 02. **d** 04 **p** 05. C Burnley St Cath w St Alb and St Paul *Blackb* 04-07; C St Annes St Anne 07-10; Perm to Offic from 10. *7 Gayle Way, Accrington BB5 0JX* Tel 07898-301807 (mobile) E-mail stephen.smith6@o2.co.uk

SMITH, Stephen John. b 46. Kelham Th Coll 65. **d** 69 **p** 70. C Warsop *S'well* 69-73; C Heaton Ch Ch *Man* 73-75; V Bolton St Bede 75-78; R Bilborough w Strelley *S'well* 78-84; R E Leake 84-92; P-in-c Costock 84-92; P-in-c Rempstone 84-92; P-in-c Stanford on Soar 84-92; R E and W Leake, Stanford-on-Soar, Rempstone etc 92-97; RD W Bingham 92-97; V Swaffham *Nor* 97-11; C Gt and Lt Dunham w Gt and Lt Fransham and Sporle 03-11; RD Breckland 02-06; Chapl NW Anglia Healthcare NHS Trust 99-11; rtd 11. *338A Dysart Road, Grantham NG31 7LY* E-mail s-smith102@sky.com

SMITH, Stephen John. b 55. Lon Univ BD80. Trin Coll Bris 77. **d** 81 **p** 82. C Fulham St Matt *Lon* 81-86; C Stoke Gifford *Bris* 86-90; TV 90-01; rtd 01; Perm to Offic *Bris* from 01. *47 Saxon Way, Bradley Stoke, Bristol BS32 9AR* Tel (01454) 616429 E-mail steve@revsmith.freeserve.co.uk

SMITH, Canon Stephen John Stanyon. b 49. Sussex Univ BA81 Birm Univ MSocSc83. Westcott Ho Cam 83. **d** 85 **p** 86. C Four Oaks *Birm* 85-89; Asst P Cheyenne River Reservation USA 89-91; Miss P Rosebud Reservation 91-94; Assoc R Ivoryton and Essex 94-98; Can St Paul's Cathl Buffalo 98-04; Asst P Buffalo St Andr from 04. *3105 Main Street, Buffalo NY 14214, USA* Tel (001) (716) 834 9337 Fax 836 0558 E-mail sjsmith6@buffalo.edu

SMITH, Stephen Thomas. b 55. Westcott Ho Cam 95. **d** 97 **p** 98. C Kempston Transfiguration *St Alb* 97-01; C Bromham w Oakley and Stagsden 01-05; TV Elstow from 05. *St Michael's Vicarage, Faldo Road, Bedford MK42 0EH* Tel (01234) 266920

SMITH, Steven Barnes. b 60. Cov Poly BA83 Leeds Univ BA86 MSc02. Coll of Resurr Mirfield 84. **d** 87 **p** 88. C Darlington St Mark w St Paul *Dur* 87-89; C Prescot *Liv* 89-91; V Hindley Green 91-96; Asst Chapl Havering Hosps NHS Trust 96-98; Hd Multi-Faith Chapl Chelsea and Westmr Hosp NHS Foundn Trust 98-07; Perm to Offic *Lon* from 07. *9 Walham Grove, London SW6 1QP* Tel (020) 7385 1348 E-mail sbsmith01@aol.com

SMITH, Steven Gerald Crosland. b 48. Linc Th Coll 82. **d** 84 **p** 85. Chapl St Jo Sch Tilfield 84-87; C Towcester w Easton Neston *Pet* 84-87; P-in-c Kings Heath 87-89; V 89-93; TV N Creedy *Ex* 93-06; TR from 06; RD Cadbury from 02. *The Vicarage, Cheriton Fitzpaine, Crediton EX17 4JB* Tel (01363) 866352 E-mail stevengcsmith@aol.com

SMITH, Susan. b 48. FInstD87. Ox Min Course 93. **d** 96 **p** 97. C Burnham w Dropmore, Hitcham and Taplow *Ox* 96-00; TV Whitton *Sarum* 00-02; TV W Slough *Ox* 02-08; V Cippenham from 08. *St Andrew's House, Washington Drive, Slough SL1 5RE* Tel (01628) 661994

SMITH, Miss Susan Ann. b 50. Bris Univ BA72 St Jo Coll York PGCE73. Ripon Coll Cuddesdon 97. **d** 99 **p** 00. C Swaffham *Nor* 99-02; R King's Beck from 02. *The Rectory, Aylsham Road, Felmingham, North Walsham NR28 0LD* Tel (01692) 402382 E-mail revsusan@kingsbeck.fslife.co.uk

SMITH, Mrs Susan Elizabeth. b 53. Man Univ BSc94 Brunel Univ MSc98. SEITE 05. **d** 08 **p** 09. NSM Reigate St Mark *S'wark* from 08. *The Rectory, Gatton Bottom, Merstham, Redhill RH1 3BH* Tel (01737) 643755

SMITH, Mrs Susan Jennifer. b 52. MCIPD90. SAOMC 94. **d** 97 **p** 98. C Ascot Heath *Ox* 97-01; P-in-c Flixton St Mich *Man* 01-10; P-in-c Altcar and Hightown *Liv* from 10. *79 Greenloons Drive, Formby, Liverpool L37 2LX* Tel (01704) 833856 E-mail saxoncross@aol.com

SMITH, Terence. b 38. Brunel Univ BSc79 Cranfield Inst of Tech MSc80. Tyndale Hall Bris 67. **d** 69 **p** 70. C Cheylesmore *Cov* 69-71; C Leamington Priors St Paul 71-74; V Halliwell St Paul *Man* 74-75; Lect Uxbridge Coll 80-86; R Medstead w Wield *Win* 86-99; P-in-c Kennington *Ox* 99-03; V 03-08; rtd 08. *15 Grove Road, Seaford BN25 1TP* E-mail ter.s@btinternet.com

SMITH, Terence David. b 59. **d** 02. NSM Myddle *Lich* 02-08; NSM Broughton 02-08; NSM Loppington w Newtown 02-08; NSM Wem from 08; NSM Lee Brockhurst from 08. *Lamorna, Scholars' Lane, Loppington, Shrewsbury SY4 5RE* Tel 07703-183034 (mobile)

SMITH, Terrence Gordon. b 34. TD83. MCSP58 SRN60. St Mich Coll Llan 68. d 70 p 71. C Gelligaer Llan 70-73; CF (TA) 72-99; C Aberavon Llan 73-75; V Pontlottyn w Fochriw 75-77; V Kenfig Hill 77-84; V Dyffryn 84-99; rtd 99. 1 Gnoll Crescent, Neath SA11 3TF

SMITH, Canon Thomas Roger. b 48. Cant Sch of Min 77. d 80 p 81. NSM Folkestone St Sav Cant 80-82; NSM Lyminge w Paddlesworth, Stanford w Postling etc 82-85; Chapl Cant Sch of Min 82-91; R Biddenden and Smarden Cant 86-91; TR Totnes, Bridgetown and Berry Pomeroy etc Ex 91-96; P-in-c Haslingden w Grane and Stonefold Blackb 96-98; V from 98; P-in-c Musbury from 07; AD Accrington from 03; Hon Can Blackb Cathl from 08. St James's Vicarage, Church Street, Haslingden, Rossendale BB4 5QU Tel (01706) 215533 E-mail rsmith9456@aol.com

SMITH, Timothy. b 58. Trin Coll Bris 00. d 02 p 03. C Warminster Ch Ch Sarum 02-06; P-in-c Plymouth St Jude Ex from 06. St Jude's Vicarage, Knighton Road, Plymouth PL4 9BU Tel (01752) 224178 E-mail timmy.smith@virgin.net

SMITH, Timothy Brian. b 62. Brisbane Coll BA(Theol)92. d 92 p 92. Coff's Harbour Australia 92-94; C Heald Green St Cath Ches 94-96; R Mid Richmond Australia 96-01; P-in-c Belmont St Steph from 01. 42 Regent Street, Belmont Vic 3216, Australia Tel (0061) (3) 5243 2557 Mobile 412-673152 E-mail timsandy@turboweb.net.au

SMITH, Toni. See SMITH, Antoinette

SMITH, Trevor Andrew. b 60. St Jo Coll Dur BA86. Cranmer Hall Dur 83. d 87 p 88. C Guisborough York 87-90; C Northallerton w Kirby Sigston 90-95; R Middleton, Newton and Sinnington 95-01; Chapl St Luke's Hospice Plymouth from 01. St Luke's Hospice, Stamford Road, Plymouth PL9 9XA Tel (01752) 401172 or 316868 Fax 481878

SMITH, Trevor Bernard. b 33. Culham Coll of Educn CertEd70 Ox Poly BEd82. Oak Hill Th Coll 61. d 64 p 65. C Bispham Blackb 64-66; C Chesham St Mary Ox 66-68; Perm to Offic 90-94; rtd 96. 126 The Broadway, Herne Bay CT6 8HA Tel (01227) 362665

SMITH (née WOOD), Mrs Valerie Rosemary. b 53. Warwick Univ BA74. WEMTC 06. d 09 p 10. NSM Highley w Billingsley, Glazeley etc Heref from 09. 20 Yew Tree Grove, Highley, Bridgnorth WV16 6DG Tel (01746) 861966 E-mail keithandvals@aol.com

SMITH, Vernon Hemingway. b 33. St Alb Minl Tr Scheme 83. d 86 p 87. NSM Leighton Buzzard w Eggington, Hockliffe etc St Alb 86-98; NSM Newbury Ox 98-03; rtd 03. 41 Orion Way, Leighton Buzzard LU7 8XJ Tel (01525) 370304

SMITH, Mrs Virginia Jane. b 41. Nottm Univ BSc63. Guildf Dioc Min Course 04. d 09 p 10. NSM Surrey Weald Guildf from 09. Dove Cottage, 14 The Paddock, Westcott, Dorking RH4 3NT Tel (01306) 885349 E-mail virginia.smith@smartemail.co.uk

SMITH, Ms Vivienne Ruth. b 57. St Jo Coll Dur BA79. NOC 95. d 00 p 01. C Heckmondwike Wakef 00-03; TV Dewsbury 03-06. Address temp unknown

SMITH, Walter. b 37. Westcott Ho Cam 67. d 69 p 70. C N Hull St Mich York 69-72; C Whitby 72-74; V Newington w Dairycoates 74-77; P-in-c Skipton Bridge 77-78; P-in-c Baldersby 77-78; TV Thirsk 77-88; P-in-c Topcliffe w Dalton and Dishforth 82-87; V Lythe w Ugthorpe 88-97; rtd 97; Perm to Offic York 98-11. 102 Upgang Lane, Whitby YO21 3JW Tel (01947) 605456

SMITH, Miss Wendy Hamlyn. b 41. ALA70 Open Univ BA85. Ridley Hall Cam 85. d 87 p 94. C Stroud H Trin Glouc 87-90 and 91-92; Australia 90-91; TD Stoke-upon-Trent Lich 92-94; TV 94-97; V Pheasey 97-02; P-in-c Barlaston 02-06; Chapl Douglas Macmillan Hospice Blurton 04-06; rtd 07; Perm to Offic Lich 07-11 and Portsm from 11. 4 Brook House, Rufflers Way, Ryde PO33 3LX Tel (01983) 556701

SMITH, Mrs Wendy Patricia. b 60. d 10 p 11. OLM Walton and Trimley St E from 10. 12A Langley Avenue, Felixstowe IP11 2NA Tel (01394) 211755 Mobile 07708-597808 E-mail grannysmith57@hotmail.co.uk

SMITH, William Manton. b 64. Univ of Wales (Abth) LLB85 St Jo Coll Dur PGCE90. United Th Coll Abth BD89 St Jo Coll Nottm 91. d 93 p 94. C Coventry Caludon 93-97; V Exhall 97-09; TR Coventry Caludon from 09. Stoke Rectory, 365A Walsgrave Road, Coventry CV2 4BG Tel (024) 7663 5731 or 7644 3691 E-mail wms.smith@btinternet.com

SMITH, Canon William Melvyn. b 47. K Coll Lon BD69 AKC69 PGCE70. St Aug Coll Cant 71. d 71 p 72. C Kingswinford H Trin Lich 71-73; Hon C Coseley Ch Ch 73-74; C Wednesbury St Paul Wood Green 75-78; V Coseley St Chad 78-91; TR Wordsley 91-93; RD Himley 83-93; TR Wordsley Worc 93-96; RD Himley 93-96; Stewardship and Resources Officer 97-10; Hon Can Worc Cathl 03-10; Asst Chapl Palma de Mallorca Eur from 10. Nuñez de Balboa 6, Son Armadans, 07014 Palma de Mallorca, Spain Tel (0034) 971 737 279 Fax 971 454 492 E-mail melvynsm@aol.com

SMITH-CAMERON, Canon Ivor Gill. b 29. Madras Univ BA50 MA52. Coll of Resurr Mirfield. d 54 p 55. C Rumboldswyke

Chich 54-58; Chapl Imp Coll Lon 58-72; Dioc Missr S'wark 72-92; Can Res S'wark Cathl 72-94; C Battersea Park All SS 92-94; Hon C 94-96; Hon C Battersea Fields 96-05; Co-ord All Asian Chr Consultation 92-93; rtd 94; Chapl to The Queen 95-99; Perm to Offic S'wark from 05. 24 Holmewood Gardens, London SW2 3RS Tel (020) 8678 8977

SMITHAM, Ann. See HOWELLS, Mrs Elizabeth Ann

SMITHSON, Michael John. b 47. Newc Univ BA68 Lon Univ BD79 Dur Univ PGCE FRGS. Trin Coll Bris 76. d 79 p 80. C S Mimms Ch Ch Lon 79-81; Support and Public Relations Sec UCCF 82-84; R Frating w Thorrington Chelmsf 84-88; V Portsea St Luke Portsm 88-04. 52 Walmer Road, Portsmouth PO1 5AS Tel 07802-482584 (mobile)

SMITHSON, Philip George Allan. b 55. Bede Coll Dur TCert76 Open Univ BA82. d 07 p 08. OLM Monkwearmouth Dur from 07. 2 Sea View Gardens, Sunderland SR6 9PN E-mail philipsmithson@talktalk.net

SMITHURST, Jonathan Peter. b 54. FInstLEx81. EMMTC 91. d 94 p 95. NSM Bramcote S'well 94-03; NSM Attenborough 03-06; AD Beeston 99-06; P-in-c Everton, Mattersey, Clayworth and Gringley from 06; AD Bawtry 09-10. The Rectory, Abbey Road, Mattersey, Doncaster DN10 5DX Tel (01777) 817364

SMITS, Eric. b 29. d 61 p 62. C Thornaby on Tees St Paul York 61-66; R Brotton Parva 66-98; rtd 98. 7 Pikes Nurseries, Ludham, Great Yarmouth NR29 5NW Tel (01692) 678156

SMOUT, Francis David James. b 36. TD. d 03 p 04. NSM Eyemouth Edin from 03. Benedict House, Coldingham, Eyemouth TD14 5NE Tel (01890) 771220 E-mail mail@davidsmout.free-online.co.uk

SMOUT, Canon Michael John. b 37. St Pet Coll Ox BA61 MA75 Lon Univ BD64. Lon Coll of Div 62. d 64 p 65. C Toxteth Park St Philemon w St Silas Liv 64-69; C Everton St Sav 69-70; Missr E Everton Gp of Chs 70-74; V Everton St Sav w St Cuth 74-79; R Aughton St Mich 79-02; RD Ormskirk 82-89; AD 89-02; Hon Can Liv Cathl 92-02; rtd 02. 4 Victoria Road, Aughton, Ormskirk L39 5AU Tel (01695) 423054

SMYTH, Anthony Irwin. b 40. TCD BA63 MA66. Clifton Th Coll 64. d 66 p 67. C Worthing St Geo Chich 66-69; SAMS Chile 70-75; Dir Th Educn Valparaiso 72-75; C Woodley St Jo the Ev Ox 75-80; V St Leonards St Ethelburga Chich 80-93; R Stopham and Fittleworth 93-05; rtd 05; Perm to Offic Portsm and Chich from 05. 20 Grenehurst Way, Petersfield GU31 4AZ Tel (01730) 260370 E-mail anthony.smyth@btinternet.com

SMYTH, Canon Gordon William. b 47. Open Univ BA. St Jo Coll Nottm 81. d 83 p 84. C St Keverne Truro 83-86; V Landrake w St Erney and Botus Fleming 86-95; RD E Wivelshire 94-95; V Highertown and Baldhu from 95; Hon Can Truro Cathl from 06. All Saints' Vicarage, Highertown, Truro TR1 3LD Tel (01872) 261944 E-mail gordon@asht.org.uk

SMYTH, Kenneth James. b 44. TCD BA67 MA72. d 68 p 69. C Bangor Abbey D & D 68-71; C Holywood 71-74; I Gilnahirk 74-82; I Newtownards w Movilla Abbey 82-89; I Newtownards 89-11; Preb Wicklow St Patr Cathl Dublin 93-11; rtd 11. 3 Mount Royal, Bangor BT20 3BG Tel (028) 9145 8706 E-mail kennethjsmyth@o2.co.uk

SMYTH, Peter Charles Gordon. b 72. Univ of Wales (Ban) BA94 TCD BTh98. CITC. d 98 p 99. C Stillorgan w Blackrock D & G 98-01; R Thunder Bay St Mich Canada from 01. 2 Sydney Street, Thunder Bay ON P7B 1P7, Canada Tel (001) (807) 767 4711 Fax 768 0382 E-mail stmichaelsch@tbaytel.net

SMYTH, Peter Frederick. b 58. SNWTP. d 10 p 11. C Prescot Liv from 10. St Mary's House, 2 West Street, Prescot L34 1LQ Tel 0151-426 0716 Mobile 07847-846526

SMYTH, Robert Andrew Laine (Brother Anselm). b 30. Trin Coll Cam BA53 MA59 Lon Univ PGCE60 DipEd65. d 79 p 80. SSF from 53; Min Prov Eur Prov SSF 79-91; Lic to Offic Linc 84-92; P-in-c Cambridge St Benedict Ely 92-93; V 93-00; rtd 00. Glasshampton Monastery, Shrawley, Worcester WR6 6TQ Tel (01299) 896345

SMYTH, Trevor Cecil. b 45. Chich Th Coll 66. d 69 p 70. C Cookridge H Trin Ripon 69-73; C Middleton St Mary 73-75; C Felpham w Middleton Chich 75-78; P-in-c Wellington Ch Ch Lich 78-80; V 80-86; P-in-c W Wittering Chich 86; R W Wittering and Birdham w Itchenor 86-94; Perm to Offic 00; TV Withycombe Raleigh Ex from 01. All Saints' Vicarage, Church Road, Exmouth EX8 1RZ Tel (01395) 278534

SMYTH, William Richard Stephen. b 56. Cape Town Univ BA77. d 90 p 92. S Africa 90-07; C Ballyholme D & D from 09. 34 Beverley Gardens, Bangor BT20 4NQ Tel (028) 9127 1922 or 9127 4912 E-mail stephensmyth17@gmail.com

SMYTHE, Mrs Angela Mary. b 53. St Jo Coll Nottm 85. d 87 p 94. Par Dn Forest Town S'well 87-90; Dn-in-c Pleasley Hill 90-94; V 94-03; AD Mansfield 98-03; P-in-c Sneinton St Chris w St Phil 03-08; Chapl Qu Eliz Sch and Samworth Ch Academy from 08. Happy Days, 1A Main Street, Palterton, Chesterfield S44 6UJ E-mail angiesmythe@aol.com

SMYTHE, Peter John Francis. b 32. Lon Univ LLB56 Barrister-at-Law (Middle Temple) 76. Wells Th Coll 56. d 58 p 59. C Maidstone All SS Cant 58-62; V Barrow St Jo Carl 62-65;

V Billesdon w Goadby and Rolleston *Leic* 65-71; rtd 97. *The Gables, 16 Geraldine Road, Malvern WR14 3PA* Tel (01684) 573266

SNAITH, Bryan Charles. b 33. Univ of Wales BSc55. St Mich Coll Llan 61. **d** 61 **p** 62. C Bargoed w Brithdir *Llan* 61-62; C Llanishen and Lisvane 62-71; Ind Chapl *Dur* 71-76; Ind Chapl *Worc* 76-81; P-in-c Stone 76-81; C Chaddesley Corbett 77-81; Ind Chapl *Chelmsf* 81-03; TV Colchester St Leon, St Mary Magd and St Steph 81-86; rtd 03; Perm to Offic *Chelmsf* from 04. *4 Wren Close, Stanway, Colchester CO3 8ZB* Tel (01206) 767793 E-mail bryansnaith-colchester@msn.com

SNAPE, Gary John Stanley. b 50. STETS. **d** 05 **p** 06. NSM Fareham H Trin *Portsm* 05-09; NSM Whiteley CD from 09. *20 Sheridan Gardens, Whiteley, Fareham PO15 7DY* Tel (01489) 589205 E-mail gary.snape1@ntlworld.com

SNAPE, Harry. b 21. Qu Coll Birm 76. **d** 78 **p** 79. NSM Highters Heath *Birm* 78-82; NSM Stirchley 82-84; TV Corby SS Pet and Andr w Gt and Lt Oakley 84-89; rtd 89; Perm to Offic *Chich* 89-05. *16 Capel Court, The Burgage, Prestbury, Cheltenham GL52 3EL* Tel (01242) 513289

SNAPE, Mrs Lorraine Elizabeth. b 52. STETS. **d** 02 **p** 07. NSM Titchfield *Portsm* 02-06; C-in-c Whiteley CD from 06. *20 Sheridan Gardens, Whiteley, Fareham PO15 7DY* Tel (01489) 589205

SNAPE, Paul Anthony Piper. b 44. **d** 98 **p** 99. OLM Tettenhall Wood and Perton *Lich* 98-10; Perm to Offic from 10. *24 Windsor Gardens, Castlecroft, Wolverhampton WV3 8LY* Tel (01902) 763577 E-mail p-snape44@tiscali.co.uk

SNARE, Peter Brian. b 39. Cape Town Univ BSc63. SEITE 99. **d** 02 **p** 03. NSM Dymchurch w Burmarsh and Newchurch *Cant* 02-09; NSM New Romney w Old Romney and Midley 07-09; NSM St Mary's Bay w St Mary-in-the-Marsh etc 07-09; Perm to Offic from 09. *35 Shepherds Walk, Hythe CT21 6PW* Tel (01303) 269242 *or* (020) 7320 1701 E-mail peter.snare@btinternet.com

SNARES, Ian. b 68. Brunel Univ BEng91. Ridley Hall Cam 09. **d** 11. C Ilfracombe, Lee, Woolacombe, Bittadon etc *Ex* from 11; C Ilfracombe SS Phil and Jas w W Down from 11. *St Peter's House, Highfield Road, Ilfracombe EX34 9LH* Tel 07971-798191 (mobile) E-mail snares@me.com

SNASDELL, Canon Antony John. b 39. St Chad's Coll Dur BA63. **d** 65 **p** 66. C Boston *Linc* 65-70; Hon C Worksop Priory *S'well* 71-82; P-in-c Gt Massingham *Nor* 82-84; P-in-c Lt Massingham 82-84; P-in-c Harpley 82-84; R Gt and Lt Massingham and Harpley 84-91; R Thorpe St Andr 91-04; Hon Can Nor Cathl 03-04; rtd 04; Perm to Offic *Nor* from 05. *1 Speedwell Road, Wymondham NR18 0XQ* Tel (01953) 857509

SNEARY, Michael William. b 38. Brentwood Coll of Educn CertEd71 Open Univ BA79. Ely Th Coll 61. **d** 64 **p** 65. C Loughton St Jo *Chelmsf* 64-67; Youth Chapl 67-70; Hon C Ingrave 70-71; Teacher Harold Hill Gr Sch Essex 71-74; Ivybridge Sch 74-76; Coombe Dean Sch Plymouth 76-03; rtd 03. *The Lodge, 1 Lower Port View, Saltash PL12 4BY*

SNEATH, Canon Sidney Dennis. b 23. Leeds Univ BA50. Bps' Coll Cheshunt 50. **d** 52 **p** 53. C Nuneaton St Mary *Cov* 52-59; C-in-c Galley Common Stockingford CD 59-68; V Camp Hill from 68; Hon Can Cov Cathl from 80. *The Vicarage, Cedar Road, Nuneaton CV10 9DL* Tel (024) 7639 2523

✠**SNELGROVE, The Rt Revd Donald George.** b 25. TD72. Qu Coll Cam BA48 MA53 Hull Univ Hon DD97. Ridley Hall Cam. **d** 50 **p** 51 **c** 81. C Oakwood St Thos *Lon* 50-53; C Hatch End St Anselm 53-56; V Dronfield *Derby* 56-62; CF (TA) 60-73; V Hessle *York* 63-70; RD Hull 67-70 and 81-90; Can and Preb York Minster 69-81; Adn E Riding 70-81; R Cherry Burton 70-78; Suff Bp Hull 81-94; rtd 94; Hon Asst Bp Linc from 95. *Kingston House, 8 Park View, Barton-upon-Humber DN18 6AX* Tel (01652) 634484 E-mail donaldsnelgrove@aol.com

SNELL, Mrs Brigitte. b 43. BA85. EAMTC 86. **d** 89 **p** 94. NSM Cambridge Gt St Mary w St Mich *Ely* 89-91; Par Dn Cambridge St Jas 91-94; C 94-95; V Sutton 95-03; R Witcham w Mepal 95-03; rtd 03; Perm to Offic *Ely* from 05. *45 London Road, Harston, Cambridge CB22 7QQ* Tel (01223) 872839 E-mail brigittesnell@gmail.com

SNELL, Colin. b 53. Trin Coll Bris 94. **d** 96 **p** 97. C Martock w Ash *B & W* 96-00; TV Wilton 00-08; V Galmington from 08. *St Michael's House, 1 Comeytrowe Lane, Taunton TA1 5PA* Tel (01823) 326525

SNELLGROVE, Martin Kenneth. b 54. City Univ BSc77 CEng80 MICE84. Aston Tr Scheme 85 Ridley Hall Cam 87. **d** 89 **p** 90. C Four Oaks *Birm* 89-92; TV Wrexham *St As* 92-01; R Hope from 01; AD Hawarden 03-10. *The Rectory, Kiln Lane, Hope, Wrexham LL12 9PH* Tel (01978) 762127

SNELLING, Brian. b 40. **d** 69 **p** 70. C Slough *Ox* 69-72; C Hoole *Ches* 72-76; V Millbrook 76-80; V Homerton St Luke *Lon* 80-90; R Marks Tey w Aldham and Lt Tey *Chelmsf* 90-98; V Stebbing w Lindsell 98-04; V Stebbing and Lindsell w Gt and Lt Saling 04-05; rtd 05; Perm to Offic *Chelmsf* from 06. *69 Reymead Close, West Mersea, Colchester CO5 8DN* Tel (01206) 383717 E-mail revbrians@aol.com

SNELLING, Stephen Thomas. b 47. City of Lon Poly BA73. SEITE 08. **d** 10 **p** 11. NSM Seal SS Pet and Paul *Roch* from 10. *13 Glebelands, Bidborough, Tunbridge Wells TN3 0UQ* Tel (01892) 547199 E-mail curate@sealpeterandpaul.com

SNELSON, William Thomas. b 45. Ex Coll Ox BA67 Fitzw Coll Cam BA69 MA75. Westcott Ho Cam 67. **d** 69 **p** 70. C Godalming *Guildf* 69-72; C Leeds St Pet *Ripon* 72-75; V Chapel Allerton 75-81; V Bardsey 81-93; Dioc Ecum Officer 86-93; W Yorkshire Ecum Officer *Bradf* 93-97; Gen Sec Chs Together in England 97-08; rtd 08; Angl Cen Rome from 08; Perm to Offic *Ripon* from 09. *6 Abbey Crags Way, Knaresborough HG5 8EF* Tel (01423) 862660 Mobile 07917-663250 E-mail developmentuk@anglicancentre.it

SNOOK, Hywel Geraint. b 77. Aston Univ BSc99 Leeds Univ BA04. Coll of Resurr Mirfield 02. **d** 05 **p** 06. C Marton *Blackb* 05-06; C Chorley St Laur 06-09; P-in-c Lt Drayton *Lich* from 09. *The Vicarage, 1 Christ Church Copse, Christ Church Lane, Market Drayton TF9 1DY* Tel (01630) 652801 E-mail hywel.snook@tiscali.co.uk

SNOOK, Mrs Margaret Ann. b 41. S Dios Minl Tr Scheme. **d** 91 **p** 94. NSM Keynsham *B & W* 91-04; Chapl Univ Hosps Bris NHS Foundn Trust from 91; Perm to Offic *B & W* from 04. *32 Hurn Lane, Keynsham, Bristol BS31 1RS* Tel 0117-986 3439

SNOOK, Walter Currie. *See* CURRIE, Walter

SNOW, Campbell Martin Spencer. b 35. JP75. Roch Th Coll 65. **d** 67 **p** 68. C Dover St Mary *Cant* 67-72; C Birchington w Acol 72-74; V Reculver 74-80; P-in-c New Addington 80-81; V 81-84; V New Addington *S'wark* 85-87; P-in-c Caterham Valley 87-99; CF (ACF) 84-87; CF (TA) 87-92; OCF 92-95; rtd 99; Perm to Offic *S'wark* from 99; Widows' Officer 99-04. *28 The Crossways, Merstham, Redhill RH1 3NA* Tel (01737) 643388 E-mail csnow@talktalk.net

SNOW, Frank. b 31. Lon Univ BD57. **d** 83 **p** 84. Hon C Tweedmouth *Newc* 83-86; Hon C Berwick H Trin 86-89; Hon C Berwick St Mary 86-89; Hon C Berwick H Trin and St Mary 89-90; R Gt Smeaton w Appleton Wiske and Birkby etc *Ripon* 90-97; rtd 97; Perm to Offic *Ripon* from 97 and *Sheff* from 02. *11 The Green, Sheffield S17 4AT* Tel 0114-235 0024 E-mail frank@fcrsnow.freeserve.co.uk

SNOW, The Ven Martyn James. b 68. Sheff Univ BSc89. Wycliffe Hall Ox BTh95. **d** 95 **p** 96. C Brinsworth w Catcliffe and Treeton *Sheff* 95-97; CMS Guinea 98-01; V Pitsmoor Ch Ch *Sheff* 01-10; P-in-c Stocksbridge 07-08; AD Ecclesfield 07-10; Adn Sheff and Rotherham from 10. *34 Wilson Road, Sheffield S11 8TN* Tel 0114-327 6001 *or* (01709) 309110 Mobile 07729-104792 Fax (01709) 309107 E-mail archdeacons.office@sheffield.anglican.org

SNOW, Miss Patricia Margaret. b 21. Dub Bible Coll 45 St Mich Ho Ox 51. dss 72 **d** 87 **p** 96. W Ham *Chelmsf* 72-78; Acomb St Steph *York* 78-83; rtd 83; NSM Northfleet *Roch* 96-01; Perm to Offic from 01. *29 Huggens' College, College Road, Northfleet, Gravesend DA11 9DL* Tel (01474) 369463

SNOW, Peter David. b 37. St Jo Coll Cam BA61 MA67. Ridley Hall Cam 62. **d** 64 **p** 65. C Kingshurst *Birm* 64-66; C Santa Barbara All SS USA 67-71; Can Missr for Youth Los Angeles 71-75; R Jackson St Jo 75-81; Asst R Bellevue Resurr 81-85; R Redmond H Cross 89-01; rtd 01; P-in-c Edmonds SS Hilda and Patr 02-03. *927 36th Avenue, Seattle WA 98122-5216, USA* Tel (001) (206) 329 3784 E-mail peterorlisa@cs.com

SNOW, Richard John. b 57. Bris Univ BSc80 K Coll Lon MA05. **d** 90 **p** 91. C Preston Plucknett *B & W* 90-95; TV Stratton St Margaret w S Marston etc *Bris* 95-02; R Box w Hazlebury and Ditteridge 02-07; TR Kirkby Lonsdale *Carl* from 07. *The Rectory, Vicarage Lane, Kirkby Lonsdale, Carnforth LA6 2BA* Tel (01524) 272044 E-mail rector@therainbowparish.org

SNOWBALL, Miss Deborah Jane. b 67. Middx Poly BEd90. Ripon Coll Cuddesdon 02. **d** 04 **p** 05. C Sawbridgeworth *St Alb* 04-07; P-in-c Rickmansworth from 07. *The Vicarage, Bury Lane, Rickmansworth WD3 1ED* Tel (01923) 772627 E-mail vicar@stmarysrickmansworth.org.uk

SNOWBALL, Dorothy Margaret. b 52. Sunderland Univ BA98. NEOC 98. **d** 01 **p** 02. NSM Heworth St Mary *Dur* 01-07; P-in-c Eighton Banks from 07. *2 Oval Park View, Felling, Gateshead NE10 9DS* Tel 0191-469 5059 E-mail dsnowball@talk21.com

SNOWBALL, Michael Sydney. b 44. Dur Univ BA70 MA72. Cranmer Hall Dur. **d** 72 **p** 73. C Stockton St Pet *Dur* 72-75; C Dunston St Nic 75-77; C Dunston 77-78; C Darlington St Jo 78-81; V Chilton 81-91; V Brompton w Deighton *York* 91-09; rtd 09; Perm to Offic *York* from 10. *36 Woodford Close, Marske-by-the-Sea, Redcar TS11 6AJ* Tel (01642) 271147 E-mail mickthevic@aol.com

SNOWDEN, Miss Alice Isabel Glass. b 55. Lanc Univ BA77 Humberside Coll of Educn PGCE84. Ripon Coll Cuddesdon 91. **d** 94 **p** 95. C Mirfield *Wakef* 94-97; TV Guiseley w Esholt *Bradf* 97-02; V Bankfoot 02-09; P-in-c Leeds All So *Ripon* from 09. *All Souls' Vicarage, Blackman Lane, Leeds LS2 9EY* Tel 0113-212 0035 E-mail sobak@blueyonder.co.uk

SNOWDEN (née HALL), Mrs Elizabeth. b 58. Plymouth Poly BSc79 Birm Univ BA01 Lon Inst of Educn PGCE80. Qu Coll

Birm 98. **d** 01 **p** 02. C Burntwood *Lich* 01-04; C and Youth Work Co-ord Ogley Hay 04-10; P-in-c Bestwood Em w St Mark *S'well* from 10. *10 Church View Close, Arnold, Nottingham NG5 9QP* Tel 0115-920 8879 Mobile 07973-824934
E-mail revesnowden@yahoo.co.uk

SNUGGS, Canon David Sidney. b 49. Keble Coll Ox BA71 PGCE72 MA75. S Dios Minl Tr Scheme 89. **d** 92 **p** 93. C Bitterne *Win* 92-96; V Fair Oak from 96; Hon Can Win Cathl from 11. *The Vicarage, Fair Oak Court, Fair Oak, Eastleigh SO50 7BG* Tel (023) 8069 2238

SNYDER, Miss Susanna Jane. b 78. Em Coll Cam BA00 MA05. Qu Coll Birm BA04. **d** 05 **p** 06. C Brownswood Park and Stoke Newington St Mary *Lon* 05-08; Perm to Offic *Ox* 08-10; USA from 10. *Episcopal Divinity School, 99 Brattle Street, Cambridge MA 02138, USA* E-mail ssnyder@eds.edu

SNYDER GIBSON, Catherine. *See* GIBSON, Catherine Snyder

SOADY, Mark. b 60. RMN84 Univ of Wales BTh. St Mich Coll Llan 96. **d** 96 **p** 97. C Tenby *St D* 96-99; TV 99-03; Min Can St Woolos Cathl 03-08; P-in-c Newport All SS from 08; Chapl Univ of Wales (Newport) from 08; CF(V) from 98. *The Vicarage, Brynglas Road, Newport NP20 5QY* Tel (01633) 854657 Mobile 07968-753978 E-mail marksoady@btinternet.com

SOAR, Martin William. b 54. Wye Coll Lon BSc78. Wycliffe Hall Ox 86. **d** 88 **p** 89. C Henfynyw w Aberaeron and Llanddewi Aberarth *St D* 88-91; C Hubberston 91-93; P-in-c Low Harrogate St Mary *Ripon* 93-95; V 95-06; Chapl Old Swinford Hosp Sch Stourbridge from 06; C Kinver and Enville *Lich* from 10. *Westwood Lodge, Heath Lane, Stourbridge DY8 1QX* Tel (01384) 817300 Fax 441686 E-mail soars@blueyonder.co.uk *or* msoar@oshsch.com

✠**SOARES, The Rt Revd Fernando da Luz.** b 43. Univ of Porto. **d** 71 **p** 72 **c** 80. Bp Lusitanian Ch from 80; Hon Asst Bp Eur from 95. *Rua Elias Garcia 107-1 Dto, 4430-091 Vila Nova de Gaia, Portugal* Tel (00351) (22) 375 4646 Fax 375 2016 E-mail fernandols@netc.pt *or* ilcae@mail.telepac.pt

SOCHON, David Lomas Philipe. b 40. Univ Coll Lon BA62. **d** 07 **p** 08. OLM Newton Flotman, Swainsthorpe, Tasburgh, etc *Nor* from 07; RD Depwade from 09. *The Bungalow, Chapel Lane, Shotesham All Saints, Norwich NR15 1YP* Tel (01508) 558495 E-mail davids@tasvalley.org

SODADASI, David Anand Raj. b 63. Osmania Univ Hyderabad BCom85 MA99 Union Bibl Sem Pune BD95. United Th Coll Bangalore MTh00. **d** 01 **p** 02. C Jabalpur Cathl India 01-04; Lect Leonard Th Coll 00-04; Perm to Offic *Ox* 04-05; NSM Ray Valley 05-10; R Cusop w Blakemere, Bredwardine w Brobury etc *Heref* from 10. *The Rectory, Cusop, Hay-on-Wye, Hereford HR3 5RF* Tel (01497) 821656
E-mail anandsodadasi@hotmail.co.uk

SODOR AND MAN, Bishop of. *See* PATERSON, The Rt Revd Robert Mar Erskine

SOER, Patricia Kathleen Mary. b 40. Hull Coll of Educn CertEd61. **d** 99 **p** 00. OLM Deptford St Jo w H Trin *S'wark* 99-06; OLM Deptford St Jo w H Trin and Ascension 06-10; Perm to Offic from 10. *350 Wood Vale, London SE23 3DY* Tel (020) 8699 4616 E-mail pat@sjht.org.uk

SOFIELD, Martin. b 60. **d** 02 **p** 03. OLM Clifton *Man* 02-10. *21 Mariners View, Ardrossan KA22 8BF*
E-mail martin.sofield@ntlworld.com

SOGA, Hector Ian. b 47. Glas Univ MA70 BMus78 PhD90 Selw Coll Cam BA72 MA76. St And NSM Tr Scheme 87. **d** 88 **p** 89. NSM Dollar *St And* from 88. *2 Harviestoun Road, Dollar FK14 7HF* Tel (01259) 743169

SOKANOVIC (née HARRIS), Mrs Mary Noreen Cecily. b 58. Suffolk Coll BA97 RGN79 RN96. EAMTC 02. **d** 05 **p** 06. NSM Whitton and Thurleston w Akenham *St E* 05-10; Bp's Chapl from 10. *Bishop's House, 4 Park Road, Ipswich IP1 3ST* Tel (01473) 252829 *or* (01449) 760527
E-mail mary@stedmundsbury.anglican.org
or marysok@tiscali.co.uk

SOKOLOWSKI (née MAHON), Mrs Stephanie Mary. b 56. Liv Univ BSc80 SRN80 K Coll Lon BA00. S'wark Ord Course 91. **d** 94 **p** 95. C Warlingham w Chelsham and Farleigh *S'wark* 94-97; C Godstone and Blindley Heath 97-04; C Shere, Albury and Chilworth *Guildf* from 07. *The Vicarage, Brook Road, Chilworth, Guildford GU4 8ND* Tel (01483) 534293 Mobile 07731-783924 E-mail ssokolowski@btinternet.com

✠**SOLIBA, The Most Revd Ignacio Capuyan.** b 44. Univ of Philippines AB72. St Andr Th Sem Manila BTh73 MDiv88. **d** 73 **p** 74 **c** 91. Chapl St Paul's Memorial Sch Philippines 73-75; Officer-in-charge 75-76; P-in-c Balbalasang 74-76; V Balantoy 77-78 and 82-91; V Mt Data 79-81; Bp N Luzon 91-97; Prime Bp Philippines 97-08; rtd 09. *Address temp unknown*
E-mail soliba@edsamail.com.ph *or* soliba@hotmail.com

SOLMAN, Mrs Fiona Barbara. b 53. SRN75 RSCN75 RHV80. STETS 03. **d** 06 **p** 07. C Cottesmore and Barrow w Ashwell and Burley *Pet* 06-09; C Empingham and Exton w Horn w Whitwell 06-09; C Greetham and Thistleton w Stretton and Clipsham 06-09; R Etwall w Egginton *Derby* from 09. *Etwall Rectory,*

Rectory Court, Main Street, Etwall, Derby DE65 6LP Tel (01283) 732349 E-mail fionasolman@aol.com

SOMERS-EDGAR, Carl John. b 46. Otago Univ BA69. St Steph Ho Ox 72. **d** 75 **p** 76. C Northwood H Trin *Lon* 75-79; C St Marylebone All SS 79-82; V Liscard St Mary w St Columba *Ches* 82-85; V Caversham St Pet New Zealand 85-11; rtd 11. *32 Cole Street, Caversham, Dunedin 9012, New Zealand* Tel (0064) (3) 487 9877 E-mail paratus@xtra.co.nz

SOMERS HESLAM, Peter. *See* HESLAM, Peter Somers

SOMERVILLE, David. b 58. QUB BEd. **d** 00 **p** 01. C Lisburn Ch Ch *Conn* 00-03; I Drumgath w Drumgooland and Clonduff D & D from 03. *The Rectory, 29 Cross Road, Hilltown, Newry BT34 5TF* Tel (028) 4063 1171 Mobile 07811-916825
E-mail revds@btinternet.com

SOMERVILLE, John William Kenneth. b 38. St D Coll Lamp 60. **d** 63 **p** 64. C Rhosllannerchrugog *St As* 63-67; C Llangystennin 67-70; V Gorsedd 70-77; V Gorsedd w Brynford and Ysgeifiog 77-02; RD Holywell 96-02; rtd 02. *15 Bryn Marl Road, Mochdre, Colwyn Bay LL28 5DT*

SOMMERVILLE, Prof Robert Gardner. b 27. Glas Univ MB50 ChB50 MD60 FRCPGlas67 Lon Univ FRCPath68. **d** 96 **p** 96. NSM Blairgowrie *St And* 96-97; NSM Coupar Angus 96-97; NSM Alyth 96-97; P-in-c Killin 97-99; Perm to Offic 99-01; P-in-c Tayport from 01. *Monkmyre, Myreriggs Road, Coupar Angus, Blairgowrie PH13 9HS* Tel and fax (01828) 627131 E-mail rsommerville120@btinternet.com

SONG, James. b 32. Lon Coll of Div 57. **d** 60 **p** 61. C Virginia Water *Guildf* 60-63; C Portman Square St Paul *Lon* 63-66; V Matlock Bath *Derby* 66-76; V Woking St Jo *Guildf* 76-94; RD Woking 87-92; rtd 94; Perm to Offic *Guildf* from 94. *4 sh House, Churt, Farnham GU10 2JU* Tel and fax (01428) 714493

SONG, Leonardo. b 60. Angl Th Coll Seoul BA. Angl Th Sem Seoul MDiv. **d** 91 **p** 93. Korea 91-03; Fell Crowther Hall CMS Tr Coll Selly Oak 03-04; Consultant CMS 05-06; Chapl Angl Korean Community *Lon* from 07. *268C New Cross Road, London SE14 5PL* Tel (020) 7732 2377 Mobile 07834-831022 E-mail leonardosong@hotmail.com

SOOSAINAYAGAM, Xavier. b 50. Sri Lanka Nat Sem BPh73 St Paul's Sem Trichy BTh77 S'wark Ord Course 89. **d** 76 **p** 77. In RC Ch 76-89; C Streatham St Leon *S'wark* 89-94; C Merton St Jas 94-97; V Croydon H Sav from 97. *The Vicarage, 115 St Saviour's Road, Croydon CR0 2XF* Tel (020) 8684 1345 Mobile 07789-567842

SOPER, Jonathan Alexander James. b 64. Univ Coll Dur BA85. Wycliffe Hall Ox 94. **d** 96 **p** 97. C Bath Weston All SS w N Stoke and Langridge *B & W* 96-00; C Bryanston Square St Mary w St Marylebone St Mark *Lon* 00-04; Lic to Offic *Ex* from 07. *Church Office, 22 Southernhay West, Exeter EX1 1PR* Tel (01392) 434311 E-mail jon@enc.uk.net

SOPHIANOU, Neofitos Anthony. b 47. Sarum & Wells Th Coll 86. **d** 88 **p** 89. C St Peter-in-Thanet *Cant* 88-91; Perm to Offic *St Alb* 97-99; C Stevenage St Nic and Graveley 99-03; Perm to Offic 03-04; V Wheatley Park *Sheff* 04-07; V Goole 07-11; R Sprotbrough from 11; Bp's Urban Adv from 05. *The Rectory, 42A Spring Lane, Sprotborough, Doncaster DN5 7QG* Tel (01302) 857073 E-mail tony.sophianou@sheffield.anglican.org

SORENSEN, Ms Anna Katrine Elizabeth. b 58. Man Univ BA82 MPhil94 Open Univ PGCE95. Ripon Coll Cuddesdon 83. **d** 87 **p** 94. Par Dn Ashton H Trin *Man* 87-88; Asst Chapl St Felix Sch Southwold 89-90; Chapl 90-99; Hon Par Dn Reydon *St E* 89-92; Hon Par Dn Blythburgh w Reydon 92-94; Hon C 94-99; C Gislingham and Thorndon 99-03; P-in-c Billingborough Gp *Linc* from 03. *The Vicarage, 13 High Street, Billingborough, Sleaford NG34 0QG* Tel (01529) 240750 Mobile 07932-031479 E-mail anna.sor@yahoo.com

SOTONWA, Canon Oladapo Oyegbola. b 56. Ibadan Univ Nigeria BEd79 MEd81 PhD86. Immanuel Coll Ibadan 91. **d** 94 **p** 95. C Italupe Em Nigeria 94-95; V Egbeba All SS 95-03; V Simeon Adeyemi Ashiru Mem Ch 03-04; V Odogbondu St Pet 04-05; Hon Can Ijebu from 05; Perm to Offic *S'wark* 06-07 and from 11; Hon C W Dulwich Em 07-11; Chapl Guy's and St Thos' NHS Foundn Trust from 11; Chapl HM Pris Brixton from 11. *HM Prison Brixton, Jebb Avenue, London SW2 5XF* Tel 07904-866635 (mobile)
E-mail oladaposotonwa@yahoo.co.uk

SOULSBY, Canon Michael. b 36. Dur Univ BSc57. Westcott Ho Cam 61. **d** 62 **p** 63. C Selly Oak St Mary *Birm* 62-66; C Kings Norton 66-72; TV 73-76; TR Sutton *Liv* 76-88; RD Prescot 84-88; P-in-c Orton Longueville *Ely* 88-96; RD Yaxley 92-02; TR The Ortons, Alwalton and Chesterton 96-04; Hon Can Ely Cathl 94-04; rtd 04; Perm to Offic *Ely* from 05. *8 Leiston Court, Eye, Peterborough PE6 7WL* Tel (01733) 221124
E-mail m.soulsby@talk21.com

SOULT, Mrs Pamela Elizabeth. b 46. SNWTP. **d** 09 **p** 10. NSM Goostrey w Swettenham *Ches* from 09. *The Tower House, The Courtyard, Swettenham, Congleton CW12 2JZ* Tel (01477) 571844

SOUNDY, Mrs Philippa Clare. b 60. BNC Ox BA81. St Mellitus Coll BA10. **d** 10 **p** 11. NSM Amersham on the Hill *Ox* from 10;

CMS from 10. *3 Hoppers Way, Great Kingshill, High Wycombe HP15 6EY* Tel (01494) 714161 Mobile 07736-971243 E-mail pippa.soundy@cms-uk.org

SOUPER, Patrick Charles. b 28. K Coll Lon BD55 AKC55. d 57 p 58. Chapl Derby City Hosp 57-62; Chapl Derby Cathl 57-62; Asst Chapl Lon Univ 62-64; C St Marylebone w H Trin 64-65; Chapl St Paul's Sch Barnes 65-70; Lect in Educn Southn Univ 70-87; rtd 87. *Prines, Box 3726, 74100 Rethymno, Crete, Greece* Tel (0030) (831) 31521 Fax 31903 E-mail pigiaki@phl.uoc.gr

SOUPPOURIS, Ms Gail Camilla. b 52. Essex Univ BA75. SEITE 02. d 05 p 06. C W Wickham St Fran and St Mary S'wark 05-08; P-in-c Shoreham Beach *Chich* from 08. *The Vicarage, 1 West Beach, Shoreham-by-Sea BN43 5LF* Tel (01273) 453768 Mobile 07950-665051 E-mail revdgail.souppouris@ntlworld.com

SOURBUT, Catherine Ann. b 67. Bath Univ BA91 MSc93 PhD97. STETS MA07. d 07 p 08. C Saltford w Corston and Newton St Loe *B & W* from 07; P-in-c Bath St Barn w Englishcombe from 11. *The Vicarage, Mount Road, Southdown, Bath BA2 1JX* E-mail catherine.sourbut@tiscali.co.uk

SOURBUT, Philip John. b 57. Cam Univ BA MA. Cranmer Hall Dur BA. d 85 p 86. C Springfield All SS *Chelmsf* 85-88; C Roxeth Ch Ch and Harrow St Pet *Lon* 88-91; P-in-c Bath St Sav *B & W* 91-93; R Bath St Sav w Swainswick and Woolley 93-98; V Cullompton and R Kentisbeare w Blackborough *Ex* 98-01; TR Cullompton, Willand, Uffculme, Kentisbeare etc 01-09; Dioc Voc Development Officer from 09; Tutor SWMTC from 09; C Ex St Mark, St Sidwell and St Matt from 09. *45 Spicer Road, Exeter EX1 1TA* Tel (01392) 817296 E-mail psourbut@lineone.net

SOUTER, Ruth Rosemary. b 55. Dur Univ BEd77. EMMTC 00. d 03 p 04. C Braunstone Park CD *Leic* 03-07; V Erdington Ch the K *Birm* from 07. *St Margaret's Vicarage, Somerset Road, Erdington, Birmingham B23 6NQ* Tel 0121-373 9209 E-mail ruthsouter@yahoo.com

SOUTER, William Ewen Logan. b 66. Em Coll Cam BA88 Univ Coll Lon PhD93. Trin Coll Bris BA94 MA97. d 97 p 98. C Harborne Heath *Birm* 97-01; TV Horsham *Chich* from 01. *St John's House, Church Road, Broadbridge Heath, Horsham RH12 3ND* Tel (01403) 265238 Mobile 07889-612861 E-mail ewen@souter.me.uk

SOUTH, Gerald. d 09 p 10. NSM Limpsfield and Tatsfield *S'wark* from 09. *Clouds, Ricketts Hill Road, Tatsfield, Westerham TN16 2NB* Tel (01959) 577598

SOUTH, Gillian. See HARWOOD, Mrs Gillian

SOUTH EAST ASIA, Archbishop of. See CHEW, The Most Revd John Hiang Chea

SOUTHALL, Colin Edward. b 36. Lich Th Coll 63. d 65 p 82. C Wylde Green *Birm* 65-67; Perm to Offic *Birm* 68-73 and *Pet* 73-81; Hon C Linc St Faith and St Martin w St Pet 82-85; Hon C Gt Glen, Stretton Magna and Wistow etc *Leic* 85-93; Chapl Asst Leic R Infirmary 93-96; Hon C Fleckney and Kilby *Leic* 96-98; Perm to Offic from 99. *1 Spinney View, Great Glen, Leicester LE8 9EP* Tel 0116-259 2959

SOUTHAMPTON, Suffragan Bishop of. See FROST, The Rt Revd Jonathan Hugh

SOUTHEE, Mrs Sandra Margaret. b 43. EAMTC 97. d 00 p 01. NSM Galleywood Common *Chelmsf* 00-02; NSM Moulsham St Jo 02-06; Perm to Offic 06-07; NSM Gt Baddow from 07; Asst Chapl Mid-Essex Hosp Services NHS Trust from 02. *6 Hampton Road, Chelmsford CM2 8ES* Tel (01245) 475456 E-mail sandysouthee@hotmail.co.uk

SOUTHEND, Archdeacon of. See LOWMAN, The Ven David Walter

✠**SOUTHERN, The Rt Revd Humphrey Ivo John.** b 60. Ch Ch Ox BA82 MA86. Ripon Coll Cuddesdon 83. d 86 p 87 c 07. C Rainham *Roch* 86-90; C Walton St Mary *Liv* 90-92; C Walton-on-the-Hill 92; V Hale *Guildf* 92-96; TR 96-97; TR Hale w Badshot Lea 97-99; Dioc Ecum Officer 92-99; TR Tisbury *Sarum* 99-01; TR Nadder Valley 01-07; RD Chalke 00-07; Can and Preb Sarum Cathl 06-07; Suff Bp Repton *Derby* from 07; Warden of Readers from 09. *Repton House, Church Street, Lea, Matlock DE4 5JP* Tel (01629) 534644 Fax 534003 E-mail bishop@repton.free-online.co.uk

SOUTHERN, John Abbott. b 27. Leeds Univ BA47. Coll of Resurr Mirfield. d 51 p 52. C Leigh St Mary *Man* 51-55; C Gt Grimsby St Jas *Linc* 55-58; V Oldham St Jas *Man* 58-60; V Haigh *Liv* 60-75; V Pemberton St Jo 75-98; rtd 98; Perm to Offic *Liv* from 00. *145 Moor Road, Orrell, Wigan WN5 8SJ* Tel (01942) 732132

SOUTHERN, Mrs Lindsay Margaret. b 70. Univ of Wales (Abth) BA01 Reading Univ PGCE04 St Jo Coll Dur BA08. Cranmer Hall Dur 06. d 08 p 09. C Kirklington w Burneston and Wath and Pickhill *Ripon* from 08. *21 Meltowns Green, Pickhill, Thirsk YO7 4LL* Tel (01845) 567961 E-mail revlindsay@btinternet.com

SOUTHERN, Paul Ralph. b 48. Oak Hill Th Coll 85. d 87 p 88. C Chadwell Heath *Chelmsf* 87-91; P-in-c Tolleshunt D'Arcy and Tolleshunt Major 91-01; V 01-08; rtd 08; Perm to Offic *Chelmsf*

from 08. *12 Guisnes Court, Back Road, Tolleshunt D'Arcy, Maldon CM9 8TW* Tel (01621) 860381

SOUTHERN CONE OF AMERICA, Primate of. See VENABLES, The Most Revd Gregory James

SOUTHERTON, Kathryn Ruth. See TRIMBY, Canon Kathryn Ruth

SOUTHERTON, Canon Peter Clive. b 38. MBE01. Univ of Wales (Lamp) BA59. Qu Coll Birm. d 61 p 62. C Llandrillo-yn-Rhos *St As* 61-68; Bermuda 68-71; V Esclusham *St As* 72-82; V Prestatyn 82-04; Hon Can St As Cathl 96-04; rtd 04. *6 Llwyn Mesen, Prestatyn LL19 8NS* Tel (01745) 853176

SOUTHEY, George Rubidge. b 34. St Mich Coll Llan 84. d 86 p 87. C Hessle *York* 86-89; P-in-c Scarborough St Columba 89-92; V 92-99; rtd 99; Perm to Offic *Glouc* 00-06. *9 Smokey Glade, Doreen Vic 3754, Australia* Tel (0061) (3) 9717 5717 Mobile 43-833 9877 E-mail george.southey@bigpond.com

SOUTHGATE, Mrs Clair. b 67. Trin Coll Bris 09. d 11. OLM Box w Hazlebury and Ditteridge *Bris* from 11. *6 Queens Square, Box, Corsham SN13 8EA* Tel (01225) 743970 Mobile 07917-117644 E-mail meddling@tiscali.co.uk

SOUTHGATE, Graham. b 63. GIBiol85 NE Surrey Coll of Tech PhD89. Ripon Coll Cuddesdon BTh93. d 93 p 94. C Tisbury *Sarum* 93-97; TV Chalke Valley 97-03; R Bratton, Edington and Imber, Erlestoke etc from 03. *The Vicarage, Upper Garston Lane, Bratton, Westbury BA13 4SN* Tel (01380) 830374 E-mail grahamsouthgate63@hotmail.com

SOUTHGATE, Patricia. d 03 p 04. OLM Parkstone St Pet and St Osmund w Branksea *Sarum* from 03. *60 Orchard Avenue, Poole BH14 8AJ* Tel (01202) 745081 E-mail pat.southgate@virgin.net

SOUTHGATE, Stephen Martin. b 61. Lanc Univ BA83 St Martin's Coll Lanc PGCE84. Cranmer Hall Dur 96. d 98 p 99. C Witton *Ches* 98-01; R Backford and Capenhurst from 01. *The Vicarage, Grove Road, Mollington, Chester CH1 6LG* Tel (01244) 851071 E-mail mollingtonvicarage@tiscali.co.uk

SOUTHWARD, Douglas Ambrose. b 32. St Jo Coll Nottm LTh74 FBS02. ALCD57. d 57 p 58. C Otley *Bradf* 57-61; C Sedbergh 61-63; C Cautley w Dowbiggin 61-63; C Garsdale 61-63; PV Lich Cathl 63-65; V Hope *Derby* 65-72; V Crosby Ravensworth *Carl* 72-82; V Bolton 74-82; Sec Dioc Past and Redundant Chs Uses Cttees 78-82; RD Appleby 78-82; Hon Can Carl Cathl 81-95; R Asby 81-82; V Hawkshead and Low Wray w Sawrey 82-98; P-in-c Windermere St Jo 84-89; RD Windermere 84-89; P-in-c Satterthwaite 94-95; rtd 98; Perm to Offic *Carl* from 98. *Hawthorn House, Town End, Witherslack, Grange-over-Sands LA11 6RL* Tel (01539) 552078

SOUTHWARD, Canon James Fisher. b 57. St Martin's Coll Lanc BEd80. Chich Th Coll 83. d 86 p 87. C Woodford St Barn *Chelmsf* 86-89; TV Crawley *Chich* 89-95; V Higham and Merston *Roch* from 95; RD Strood from 02; Hon Can Roch Cathl from 09. *The Vicarage, Hermitage Road, Higham, Rochester ME3 7NE* Tel and fax (01634) 717360 E-mail james.southward@diocese-rochester.org

SOUTHWARK, Archdeacon of. See IPGRAVE, The Ven Michael Geoffrey

SOUTHWARK, Bishop of. See CHESSUN, The Rt Revd Christopher Thomas James

SOUTHWARK, Dean of. *Vacant*

SOUTHWELL, Peter John Mackenzie. b 43. New Coll Ox BA64 MA68. Wycliffe Hall Ox 66. d 67 p 68. C Crookes St Thos *Sheff* 67-70; Lect Sheff Univ 67-70; Sen Tutor Wycliffe Hall Ox 70-08; Chapl and Lect Qu Coll Ox 82-10; rtd 10; Lic to Offic *Ox* from 10. *The Queen's College, Oxford OX1 4AW* Tel (01865) 279120 E-mail peter.southwell@queens.ox.ac.uk

SOUTHWELL AND NOTTINGHAM, Bishop of. See BUTLER, The Rt Revd Paul Roger

SOUTHWELL, Dean of. See GUILLE, The Very Revd John Arthur

SOWDEN, Charles William Bartholomew. b 47. d 97 p 98. OLM Saxonwell *Linc* 97-06; NSM Metheringham w Blankney and Dunston 06-09; P-in-c Wyberton from 09; P-in-c Frampton from 09. *The Rectory, Church Lane, Wyberton, Boston PE21 7AF* Tel (01205) 353593 E-mail charles.sowden1@btinternet.com

SOWDEN, Geoffrey David. b 57. Kingston Poly BA79. Wycliffe Hall Ox 95. d 97 p 98. C Ware Ch Ch *St Alb* 97-02; V Highworth w Sevenhampton and Inglesham etc *Bris* from 02; P-in-c Broad Blunsdon from 05. *The Vicarage, 10 Stonefield Drive, Highworth, Swindon SN6 7DA* Tel (01793) 765554 E-mail the.sowdens@btinternet.com

SOWDON, Henry Lewis Malcolm. b 37. TCD BA. Bps' Coll Cheshunt. d 64 p 65. C Newport w Longford *Lich* 64-66; C Caverswall 66-69; Chapl Clayesmore Sch Blandford 69-72; Hon C Hornsey Ch Ch *Lon* 72-80; Chapl Gordon's Sch Woking 80-86; TV Hodge Hill *Birm* 86-91; Perm to Offic from 91; rtd 02. *157 Heathfield Road, Birmingham B19 1JD* Tel 0121-240 3557

SOWERBUTTS, Alan. b 49. Sheff Univ BSc70 PhD73 Qu Coll Cam BA75 MA79. Westcott Ho Cam 74. d 76 p 77. C Salesbury *Blackb* 76-80; V Lower Darwen St Jas 80-84; V Musbury 84-93; P-in-c Brindle 93-98; Sec Dioc Adv Cttee for the Care of Chs

93-98; V Read in Whalley from 98. *The Vicarage, George Lane, Read, Burnley BB12 7RQ* Tel (01282) 771361 E-mail anseres@tiscali.co.uk

SOWERBUTTS, Philip John. b 67. Ches Coll of HE BEd89 Edge Hill Coll of HE PGCE99. Oak Hill Th Coll BA03. **d** 03 **p** 04. C Kirk Ella and Willerby *York* 03-07; V Castle Church *Lich* from 07. *Castle Church Vicarage, 18 Castle Bank, Stafford ST16 1DJ* Tel (01785) 223673 Mobile 07957-122836 E-mail philip-claire@hotmail.com

SOWERBY, Geoffrey Nigel Rake. b 35. St Aid Birkenhead 56. **d** 60 **p** 61. C Armley St Bart *Ripon* 60-63; Min Can Ripon Cathl 63-65; V Thornthwaite w Thruscross and Darley 65-69; V Leeds All SS 69-73; V Leyburn w Bellerby 73-81; R Edin Old St Paul 81-86; V Hawes and Hardraw *Ripon* 86-92; Dioc Adv in Deliverance Min 91-92; rtd 92; Perm to Offic *Dur* and *Ripon* from 92. *6 Wycar Terrace, Bedale DL8 2AG* Tel (01677) 425860 Mobile 07749-229189 E-mail geoffreysowerby@onetel.com

✠**SOWERBY, The Rt Revd Mark Crispin Rake.** b 63. K Coll Lon BD85 AKC85 Lanc Univ MA94. Coll of Resurr Mirfield 85. **d** 87 **p** 88 **c** 09. C Knaresborough *Ripon* 87-90; C Darwen St Cuth w Tockholes St Steph *Blackb* 90-92; V Accrington St Mary 92-97; Chapl St Chris High Sch Accrington 92-97; Chapl Victoria Hosp Accrington 92-97; Asst Dir of Ords *Blackb* 93-96; Voc Officer and Selection Sec Min Division 97-01; V Harrogate St Wilfrid *Ripon* 01-04; TR 04-09; Asst Dir of Ords 05-09; Area Bp Horsham *Chich* from 09. *Bishop's House, 21 Guildford Road, Horsham RH12 1LU* Tel (01403) 211139 Fax 217349 E-mail bishop.horsham@diochi.org.uk

SOWTER, Colin Victor. b 35. Ball Coll Ox BA56 MA59 DPhil60. Oak Hill NSM Course 88. **d** 91 **p** 92. NSM Cranleigh *Guildf* 91-93; NSM Wonersh 93-98; NSM Wonersh w Blackheath 98-05; rtd 05; Perm to Offic *Guildf* from 05. *Hollycroft, Grantley Avenue, Wonersh Park, Guildford GU5 0QN* Tel (01483) 892094 Fax 892894 E-mail sowter@lineone.net

SOWTON, Mrs Alison. b 62. Qu Coll Birm. **d** 09 **p** 10. C Oxhey All SS *St Alb* from 09. *14 The Hoe, Watford WD19 5AY* Tel 07739-712548 (mobile) E-mail alisonsowton@live.com

SOX, Harold David. b 36. N Carolina Univ BA58. Union Th Sem (NY) MDiv61. **d** 61 **p** 61. USA 61-74; Hon C Richmond St Mary *S'wark* 74-79; Hon C Richmond St Mary w St Matthias and St Jo 79-82; Hon C Kensington St Mary Abbots w St Geo *Lon* 82-84 and 89-93; Perm to Offic 84-89; Hon C Beedon and Peasemore w W Ilsley and Farnborough *Ox* 93-94; Perm to Offic *Ox* 93-97 and *S'wark* 97-04. *20 The Vineyard, Richmond TW10 6AN* Tel (020) 8940 0094

SPACKMAN (née MORRISON), Mrs Ailsa. b 40. Qu Univ Kingston Ontario BA82. Montreal Dioc Th Coll. **d** 83 **p** 85. Canada 83-95; Dn Caspe 83-85; I Malbay Miss Par 85-92; Chapl Drummondville Penitentiary 92-93; rtd 93; Perm to Offic *Ex* from 99. *Cofton Lodge, Cofton Hill, Cockwood, Exeter EX6 8RB* Tel (01626) 891584

SPACKMAN, Canon Peter John. b 37. Southn Univ BSc60. Westcott Ho Cam 65. **d** 66 **p** 67. C Boxmoor St Jo *St Alb* 66-69; C Alnwick St Paul *Newc* 69-72; C-in-c Stewart Town Jamaica 72-74; Canada 74-95; I Sept-Iles 74-77; R Baie Comeau 77-80; R Gaspe 80-92; Adn Gaspe 88-92; R Richmond 92-94; Hon Can Quebec 92-94; Perm to Offic *Ex* 95-97; Hon C Kenton, Mamhead, Powderham, Cofton and Starcross 97-02; Perm to Offic from 02. *Cofton Lodge, Cofton Hill, Cockwood, Exeter EX6 8RB* Tel (01626) 891584 E-mail spackman1@btinternet.com

SPAIGHT, Robert George. b 45. Ridley Hall Cam. **d** 84 **p** 85. C St Columb Minor and St Colan *Truro* 84-87; C Worksop St Jo *S'well* 87-89; V Barlings *Linc* from 89. *The Vicarage, Station Road, Langworth, Lincoln LN3 5BB* Tel (01522) 754233

SPANNER, Handley James. b 51. Lanchester Poly Cov BSc73 BA. Oak Hill Th Coll 82. **d** 85 **p** 86. C Cov H Trin 85-89; V Rye Park St Cuth *St Alb* 89-01; V Colney Heath St Mark from 01. *St Mark's Vicarage, St Mark's Close, Colney Heath, St Albans AL4 0NQ* Tel (01727) 822040 E-mail jamesspanner@aol.com

SPARGO, Anne Elizabeth. b 51. Newnham Coll Cam MB76 BChir77 MA79. WEMTC 03. **d** 06 **p** 07. NSM Frampton on Severn, Arlingham, Saul etc *Glouc* 06-10; P-in-c from 10. *Ashleigh House, The Street, Frampton on Severn, Gloucester GL2 7ED* Tel (01452) 741147 E-mail anne.spargo@btinternet.com

SPARHAM, Canon Anthony George. b 41. St Jo Coll Dur BA69. Cranmer Hall Dur 66. **d** 71 **p** 72. C Bourne *Linc* 71-74; TV Tong *Bradf* 74-76; V Windhill 76-81; Dioc Dir of Educn *St E* 82-85; V Goostrey *Ches* 85-99; R Wilmslow 99-08; Dir Lay Tr 85-90; Jt Dir Lay Tr 90-97; Hon Can Ches Cathl 94-08; rtd 08; Perm to Offic *Lich* 08-11; Hon C Whittington and W Felton w Haughton from 11. *8 Sycamore Close, St Martins, Oswestry SY11 3EL* Tel (01691) 770320 E-mail tony.sparham@virgin.net

SPARKES, Donald James Henry. b 33. Oak Hill Th Coll. **d** 59 **p** 60. C Southall Green St Jo *Lon* 59-63; P-in-c Pitsmoor *Sheff* 63-70; V 70-73; P-in-c Wicker w Neepsend 70-73; V Pitsmoor w Wicker 73-79; V Pitsmoor w Ellesmere 79-86; V Pitsmoor Ch Ch 86-96; rtd 96; Perm to Offic *Derby* and *Sheff* from 96.

---

8 Grosvenor Mansions, Broad Walk, Buxton SK17 6JH Tel (01298) 25134

SPARKES, Mrs Lynne. b 55. Chelt & Glouc Coll of HE BEd96. WEMTC 06. **d** 09 **p** 10. NSM Barnwood *Glouc* from 09. *25 The Plantation, Abbeymead, Gloucester GL4 5TR* Tel (01452) 372988 E-mail lynnesparkes@googlemail.com

SPARKS, Christopher Thomas. b 29. Lanc Univ PGCE69 Birm Univ 81. St D Coll Lamp BA53 Lich Th Coll 53. **d** 55 **p** 56. C Macclesfield St Mich *Ches* 55-59; C W Kirby St Bridget 59-61; V Altrincham St Jo 61-68; Lic to Offic *Blackb* 68-79; C Lancaster St Mary 79-83; Chapl HM Pris Lanc 83-84; Perm to Offic *Blackb* from 84; rtd 94. *1 Yealand Drive, Scotforth, Lancaster LA1 4EW* Tel (01524) 67507

SPARKS, Ian. b 59. Lanc Univ BSc(Econ)81. Cranmer Hall Dur 94. **d** 96 **p** 97. C Bowdon *Ches* 96-00; V Chelford w Lower Withington 00-06; P-in-c Macclesfield St Jo from 06. *St John's Vicarage, 25 Wilwick Lane, Macclesfield SK11 8RS* Tel (01625) 424185 E-mail sparks.family@ntlworld.com

SPARROW, Miss Elisabeth Joy. b 70. Nottm Univ BEng94. Qu Coll Birm 11. **d** 11. C Bartley Green *Birm* from 11. *55 Brett Drive, Birmingham B32 3JU* E-mail lis.sparrow@gmail.com

SPARROW, Michael Kenneth. St Jo Coll Dur BA74. Coll of Resurr Mirfield 74. **d** 75 **p** 76. C N Hinksey *Ox* 75-78; C Portsea St Mary *Portsm* 78-85; V Midsomer Norton w Clandown *B & W* 85-93; Chapl Schiedam Miss to Seafarers *Eur* 93-03; Chapl Mombasa Kenya from 04. *Missions to Seamen, PO Box 80424, Mombasa, Kenya* Tel (00254) (41) 223 0027 Fax 223 0001 E-mail missions@wananchi.com

SPEAKMAN, Anthony Ernest. b 43. **d** 71 **p** 72. C Newtown *St As* 71-77; C Holywell 72-75; C St Marylebone w H Trin *Lon* 75-77; V Camberwell St Phil and St Mark *S'wark* 77-80; Lic to Offic *Lon* 94-96; NSM Kensington St Jo 96-05. *6A Park Place Villas, London W2 1SP* Tel (020) 7723 8920

SPEAKMAN, Joseph Frederick. b 26. NW Ord Course 75. **d** 78 **p** 79. NSM Wallasey St Hilary *Ches* 78; C 79-82; V Marthall w Over Peover 82-91; rtd 91; Perm to Offic *Ches* from 91. *1 Kinnaird Court, Cliff Road, Wallasey CH44 3AX* Tel 0151-637 0109 E-mail revjoe@talktalk.net

SPEAR, Andrew James Michael. b 60. Dur Univ BA81. Ridley Hall Cam 83. **d** 86 **p** 87. C Haughton le Skerne *Dur* 86-90; C Eastbourne H Trin *Chich* 90-95; C Patcham 95-02; V Oldland *Bris* from 02. *Oldland Vicarage, Grangeville Close, Longwell Green, Bristol BS30 9YJ* Tel 0117-932 7178 *or* 932 3291 E-mail andrewjmspear@hotmail.com

SPEAR, Miss Jennifer Jane. b 53. Westhill Coll Birm BEd76. Trin Coll Bris 82. dss 84 **d** 87 **p** 95. Reading St Jo *Ox* 84-90; Par Dn 87-90; Hon Par Dn Devonport St Barn *Ex* 90-91; Hon Par Dn Devonport St Mich 90-91; Par Dn Plymstock 91-94; C 94-97; TV Plymstock and Hooe 97-11; rtd 11. *69 Plymstock Road, Plymouth PL9 7PD* Tel (01752) 405202 E-mail jenniferspear@amserve.com

SPEAR, John Cory. b 33. Open Univ BA87. Ridley Hall Cam 68. **d** 70 **p** 71. C Gerrards Cross *Ox* 70-73; TV Washfield, Stoodleigh, Withleigh etc *Ex* 73-79; R Instow 79-90; V Westleigh 79-90; RD Hartland 82-89; V Pilton w Ashford 90-97; TR Barnstaple 97-99; rtd 99; Perm to Offic *Ex* from 00. *Abbots Lodge, Abbotsham Court, Abbotsham, Bideford EX39 5BH* Tel (01237) 476607

SPEAR, Sylvia Grace. b 36. St Chris Coll Blackheath 60. dss 76 **d** 87 **p** 94. S Wimbledon H Trin and St Pet *S'wark* 76-80; Lee Gd Shep w St Pet 80-95; Par Dn 87-94; C 94-95; rtd 95; Perm to Offic *Nor* from 95. *19 Grovelands, Ingoldisthorpe, King's Lynn PE31 6PG* Tel (01485) 543469

SPEARS, Reginald Robert Derek. b 48. Trin Coll Ox BA72 MA75. Cuddesdon Coll 72. **d** 75 **p** 76. C Hampton All SS *Lon* 75-79; C Caversham *Ox* 79-81; C Caversham St Pet and Mapledurham etc 81-84; V Reading St Matt 84-94; V Earley St Pet from 94. *St Peter's Vicarage, 129 Whiteknights Road, Reading RG6 7BB* Tel and fax 0118-926 2009 E-mail derekspears@compuserve.com

SPECK, Ms Jane Elisabeth. b 72. Univ of Cen England in Birm BA94 St Jo Coll Dur BA01 MA02. Cranmer Hall Dur 98. **d** 02 **p** 03. C Stourport and Wilden *Worc* 02-05; C N Lambeth *S'wark* 05-11; Chapl K Coll Lon from 05. *58 Salisbury Place, London SW9 6UW* E-mail janespeck@hotmail.com

SPECK, Preb Peter William. b 42. Univ of Wales (Ban) BSc64 Birm Univ BA66 MA71. Qu Coll Birm 64. **d** 67 **p** 68. C Rhosddu *St As* 67-71; C Wrexham 71-72; Asst Chapl United Sheff Hosps 72-73; Chapl N Gen Hosp Sheff 73-79; Chapl R Free Hosp Lon 79-95; Hon Sen Lect Sch of Med 87-95; Preb St Paul's Cathl 92-95; Chapl Southn Univ Hosps NHS Trust 95-02; rtd 02; Public Preacher *Win* from 02; Visiting Fell Southn Univ from 02; Hon Sen Research Fell and Hon Sen Lect K Coll Lon from 02. *22 The Harrage, Romsey SO51 8AE* Tel (01794) 516937

SPECK, Raymond George. b 39. Oak Hill Th Coll 64. **d** 67 **p** 68. C Stretford St Bride *Man* 67-70; C Roxeth Ch Ch *Lon* 70-74; V Woodbridge St Jo *St E* 74-85; R Jersey St Ouen w St Geo *Win* 85-98; rtd 98; Perm to Offic *Win* from 98. *Rosevale Lodge, rue du Craslin, St Peter, Jersey JE3 7BU* Tel (01534) 634987

SPEDDING, Clare. *See* FRYER-SPEDDING, Mrs Clare Caroline

SPEDDING, Geoffrey Osmond. b 46. Hull Univ BA67 Fitzw Coll Cam BA69 MA BD. d 70 p 71. C Bradf Cathl 70-73; C Sutton St Jas and Wawne *York* 73-76; TV Preston St Jo *Blackb* 76-82; TV Yate New Town *Bris* 82-87; TR Bestwood *S'well* 87-94; V Ravenshead 94-04; rtd 04; Estate Manager Scargill Ho 06-08; P-in-c Cullingworth *Bradf* 08-09; Hon C E Richmond *Ripon* from 09. *The Vicarage, St Paul's Drive, Brompton on Swale, Richmond DL10 7HQ*

SPEDDING, William Granville. b 39. Tyndale Hall Bris BD60. d 62 p 63. C Man Albert Memorial Ch 62-65; Hd RE Whitecroft Sch Bolton 65-71; Co-ord Humanities Hayward Sch Bolton 71-93; Perm to Offic 65-67 and from 02; NSM New Bury 67-79; NSM Bolton St Paul w Em 79-86; NSM Pennington 86-02. *26 Milverton Close, Lostock, Bolton BL6 4RR* Tel (01204) 841248 E-mail granvillespedding@ntlworld.com

SPEEDY (née BRINDLEY), Mrs Angela Mary. b 44. Oak Hill Th Coll 93 NOC 99. d 00 p 01. C Handforth *Ches* 00-03; R Whaley Bridge 03-05; rtd 05; Hon C Barthomley *Ches* from 07. *The Rectory, Rushy Lane, Barthomley, Crewe CW2 5PE* Tel (01270) 877112

SPEEDY, Canon Darrel Craven. b 35. St Chad's Coll Dur BA57. Wells Th Coll 57. d 59 p 60. C Frodingham *Linc* 59-63; V Heckington w Howell 63-71; V Barton upon Humber 71-79; R Tain *Mor* 79-85; Dioc Sec 82-85; Can St Andr Cathl Inverness 83-85; Syn Clerk 83-85; R Whaley Bridge *Ches* 85-01; RD Chadkirk 88-95; Hon Can Ches Cathl from 96; rtd 01; P-in-c Barthomley *Ches* from 01. *The Rectory, Rushy Lane, Barthomley, Crewe CW2 5PE* Tel (01270) 877112 E-mail darrel.speedy@btopenworld.com

SPEEKS, Mark William. b 62. Ex Univ BA82 Ex Coll Ox MSt83 Yale Univ MDiv02. d 02 p 02. C Los Angeles St Alban USA 02-03; NSM Kilburn St Mary w All So and W Hampstead St Jas *Lon* 04-08; NSM St Botolph Aldgate w H Trin Minories 08-10; CF from 10; NSM Belsize Park *Lon* from 10; NSM S Hampstead St Sav from 10. *c/o MOD Chaplains (Army)* Tel (01264) 381140 Fax 381824 Mobile 07843-518063 E-mail mspeeks@acuitycapital.co.uk

SPEERS, Canon Samuel Hall. b 46. TCD BA70 MA75. Cuddesdon Coll 70. d 73 p 74. C Boreham Wood All SS *St Alb* 73-76; Madagascar 76-88; Hon Can Antananarivo from 85; R S Lafford *Linc* 88-02; RD Lafford 96-02; TR Chipping Barnet *St Alb* from 02. *The Rectory, 38 Manor Road, Barnet EN5 2JJ* Tel (020) 8449 3894 E-mail hall.speers@talk21.com

SPENCE, Beth Ann. b 65. Smith Coll (USA) BA87 St Hilda's Coll Ox MA90. SAOMC 02. d 05 p 06. C Cowley St Jas *Ox* 05-08; Australia from 08. *Address temp unknown* E-mail beth.a.spence@googlemail.com

SPENCE, Brian Robin. b 39. St Chad's Coll Dur BA61. d 63 p 64. C Weston *Guildf* 63-67; Lesotho 67-68; C Chobham w Valley End *Guildf* 68-71; C Gt Yarmouth *Nor* 71-74; V Warnham *Chich* 74-81; V E Grinstead St Mary 81-86; V Crowthorne *Ox* 86-05; rtd 05; Hon C Theale and Englefield *Ox* from 05. *St Mark's House, Englefield, Reading RG7 5EP* Tel 0118-930 2227 E-mail brian@stmarkshouse.f9.co.uk

SPENCE, James Knox. b 30. Worc Coll Ox BA55 MA58. Ridley Hall Cam. d 57 p 58. C W Hampstead Trin *Lon* 57-60; C Ox St Ebbe w St Pet 61-64; Cand Sec CPAS 64-68; V Reading Greyfriars *Ox* 68-78; C St Helen Bishopsgate w St Andr Undershaft etc *Lon* 78-82; P-in-c Gt Baddow *Chelmsf* 82-86; V 86-88; TR 88-95; rtd 95; Hon C Wallingford *Ox* from 96. *15 High Street, Wallingford OX10 0BP* Tel (01491) 826814 E-mail jim@spence15.plus.com

SPENCE, Canon John Edis. b 24. St Edm Hall Ox BA46 MA48. Westcott Ho Cam 47. d 48 p 49. C Newland St Jo *York* 48-50; Australia 50-54; C Uckfield *Chich* 54-55; Chapl RN 55-59 and 60-65; V Thornton-le-Street w Thornton-le-Moor etc *York* 59-60; Chapl RNR 65-94; V St Germains *Truro* 65-73; V Tideford 65-73; P-in-c Sheviock 69-70; Perm to Offic 73-76; Dioc Chapl to Bp 76-78; C Newlyn St Newlyn 76-78; Chapl for Maintenance of the Min 78-87; Stewardship Adv 80-87; Hon Can Truro Cathl 84-89; Bp's Dom Chapl 87-89; P-in-c St Allen 87-89; rtd 89; Lic to Offic *Truro* 89-95; Perm to Offic *Ex* 91-98 and 04-09; Hon C Diptford, N Huish, Harberton, Harbertonford etc 98-04. *26 Kerries Road, South Brent TQ10 9DA* Tel (01364) 72578

SPENCE, Michael James. b 62. Sydney Univ BA85 LLB87 St Cath Coll Ox DPhil96. St Steph Ho Ox. d 06 p 07. NSM Cowley St Jas *Ox* 06-08; Vice-Chan Sydney Univ Australia from 08. *Address temp unknown* E-mail vice-chancellor@vcc.usyd.edu.au

SPENCE, Mrs Moira Joan. b 44. SAOMC 96. d 01 p 02. OLM Risborough *Ox* 01-06; NSM Ewenny w St Brides Major *Llan* from 07. *Ty Bara, 33 Main Road, Ogmore-by-Sea, Bridgend CF32 0PD*

SPENCE, Canon Philip Arthur. b 39. Lon Univ BD71 Open Univ BA76. Westcott Ho Cam 78. d 78 p 79. In Methodist Ch 67-78; C Walthamstow St Pet *Chelmsf* 78-80; Dioc Adv on Evang 80-87; Dep Dir Dept of Miss (Evang Division) 80-85; P-in-c

Greensted 80-86; Bp's Adv on Tourism 81-87; Asst Dir of Miss and Unity 85-87; R Greensted-juxta-Ongar w Stanford Rivers 86-87; V Cambridge St Mark *Ely* 87-95; Chapl Wolfs Coll Cam 87-95; Relig Adv Anglia TV 91-95; V Pet St Jo 95-01; Can Res and Warden Pet Cathl 97-01; Can 01-06; P-in-c Preston and Ridlington w Wing and Pilton 01-06; Adult Educn Officer 01-05; rtd 06; Perm to Offic *Pet* from 06. *20 Bayley Close, Uppingham, Oakham LE15 9TG* Tel (01572) 820199 E-mail monica.spence@virgin.net

SPENCELEY, Douglas. b 49. Edin Univ MA70 SS Mark & Jo Univ Coll Plymouth PGCE71. ERMC 07. d 09 p 10. NSM Arthingworth, Harrington w Oxendon and E Farndon *Pet* from 09; NSM Maidwell w Draughton, Lamport w Faxton from 09. *50 Orchard Hill, Little Billing, Northampton NN3 9AG* Tel (01604) 407977 E-mail dspenceley@lineone.net

SPENCELEY, Malcolm. b 40. Open Univ BA92 Dur Inst of Educn CertEd72. Cranmer Hall Dur 78. d 80 p 81. C Redcar *York* 80-85; V Middlesbrough Ascension 85-93; V Newby 93-05; rtd 05; Perm to Offic *York* from 06. *6 Tameside, Stokesley, Middlesbrough TS9 5PE* Tel (01642) 710443

SPENCER, Andrew. b 47. St Matthias Coll Bris BEd70 Univ of Wales (Ban) BTh05. d 04 p 05. Moderator for Reader Tr *Guildf* 01-06; OLM Busbridge and Hambledon from 04; Tutor Local Min Progr from 07. *24 Park Road, Godalming GU7 1SH* Tel (01483) 416333 E-mail andy.spencer@busbridgechurch.org

SPENCER, Antony Wade. b 50. Ridley Hall Cam 92. d 94 p 95. C Bury St Edmunds St Geo *St E* 94-96; Perm to Offic 96-97; C Rougham, Beyton w Hessett and Rushbrooke 97-99; TV Mildenhall 99-07; Dir Past Development Harborne Heath *Birm* from 07. *74 Croftdown Road, Birmingham B17 8RD* Tel 0121-426 6228 Mobile 07704-324444 E-mail antonyspencer@stjohns-church.co.uk

SPENCER, Christopher Graham. b 61. Magd Coll Cam BA83 MA87 Bath Univ MSc84. St Jo Coll Nottm 93. d 93 p 94. C Ore St Helen and St Barn *Chich* 93-97; V Deal St Geo *Cant* from 97. *The Vicarage, 8 St George's Road, Deal CT14 6BA* Tel (01304) 372587 E-mail vicar@stgeorgesdeal.org.uk *or* vicar.chris@macunlimited.net

SPENCER, David William. b 43. EAMTC 80. d 81 p 82. NSM Wisbech St Aug *Ely* 81-84; C Whittlesey 84-86; R Upwell Christchurch 86-90; R March St Pet and March St Mary 90-98; TV Stanground and Farcet 98-01; V Farcet 01-04; V Farcet Hampton 04-08; rtd 08; Perm to Offic *Ely* 08-10; P-in-c Elton w Stibbington and Water Newton from 10. *10 Hemingford Crescent, Peterborough PE2 8LL* E-mail davidspencer@freezone.co.uk

SPENCER, Derek Kenneth. b 67. St Jo Coll Nottm BA98. d 03 p 05. Storrington Deanery Youth Missr *Chich* 01-06; C Steyning 05-06; P-in-c Sullington and Thakeham w Warminghurst from 07. *The Rectory, The Street, Thakeham, Pulborough RH20 3EP* Tel (01798) 813121 Mobile 07734-330678 E-mail noba@btinternet.com

SPENCER, Mrs Gail. b 57. STETS. d 03 p 04. NSM Wilton w Netherhampton and Fugglestone *Sarum* 03-06; NSM Radcliffe-on-Trent and Shelford *S'well* 06-07; Chapl Qu Medical Cen Nottm Univ Hosp NHS Trust from 07. *2 Gatcombe Close, Radcliffe-on-Trent, Nottingham NG12 2GG* Tel 0115-933 6068 E-mail gailespencer@yahoo.co.uk

SPENCER, Geoffrey. b 50. Open Univ BA84 Nottm Univ CertEd78 ALCM76. Linc Th Coll 85. d 87 p 88. C Skegness and Winthorpe *Linc* 87-90; V Heckington 90-93; P-in-c Bottesford and Muston *Leic* 93-98; P-in-c Harby, Long Clawson and Hose 94-98; P-in-c Barkestone w Plungar, Redmile and Stathern 94-98; RD Framland 97-98; Perm to Offic *Linc* 03-05; Lic Preacher 05-06; P-in-c Church Langton cum Tur Langton etc *Leic* 07-10; P-in-c Mundford w Lynford *Nor* 10-11; P-in-c Ickburgh w Langford 10-11; P-in-c Cranwich 10-11; P-in-c W Tofts and Buckenham Parva 10-11; rtd 11. *Owl Cottage, 3 Manor Road, Burton Coggles, Grantham NG33 4JR* Tel (01476) 552432 E-mail gspencer22@btinternet.com

SPENCER, Canon Gilbert Hugh. b 43. Lon Univ BD67. ALCD66. d 67 p 68. C Bexleyheath Ch Ch *Roch* 67-73; C Bexley St Jo 73-76; P-in-c Bromley St Jo 76-78; V 78-81; R Chatham St Mary w St Jo 81-91; V Minster-in-Sheppey *Cant* 91-09; P-in-c Queenborough 99-05; AD Sittingbourne 94-00, 03-04 and 06-09; Hon Can Cant Cathl 99-09; Chapl Sheppey Community Hosp 91-98; Chapl Thames Gateway NHS Trust 98-09; rtd 09; Perm to Offic *Cant* from 09; Retirement Officer (Ashford Adnry) from 11. *75 Acorn Close, Kingsnorth, Ashford TN23 3HR* Tel (01233) 501774 Mobile 07961-545934 E-mail gilbert_spencer@hotmail.com

SPENCER, Gordon Thomas. b 45. ACA68. STETS 03. d 06 p 07. NSM W Tarring *Chich* from 06. *8 Thakeham Close, Goring-by-Sea, Worthing BN12 5BA* Tel (01903) 243998 E-mail gordon.spencer8@btinternet.com

SPENCER, Graham Lewis. b 48. St Jo Coll Nottm 80. d 82 p 83. C Leic St Anne 82-85; P-in-c Frisby-on-the-Wreake w Kirby Bellars 85-86; TV Melton Gt Framland 86-93; V Upper Wreake 93-99; V Glen Magna cum Stretton Magna etc 99-05; rtd 05;

Perm to Offic *Leic* from 05. *18 Chetwynd Drive, Melton Mowbray LE13 0HU* Tel (01664) 564266 E-mail grahamandtrish@talktalk.net

SPENCER, Ian John. b 61. Qu Coll Birm 03. **d** 05 **p** 06. C Gt Malvern St Mary *Worc* 05-08; Warden Dioc Retreat Ho (Holland Ho) Cropthorne from 08. *Holland House, Main Street, Cropthorne, Pershore WR10 3NB* Tel (01386) 860330 E-mail ian.spencer@talktalk.net

SPENCER, Joan. b 50. **d** 98 **p** 99. OLM Norwich St Mary Magd w St Jas from 98. *94 Mousehold Avenue, Norwich NR3 4RS* Tel (01603) 404471 E-mail joanspencer@talktalk.net

SPENCER, John Edward. b 36. Bris Univ BA60. Tyndale Hall Bris 60. **d** 61 **p** 62. C St Helens St Mark *Liv* 61-64; Japan 65-70; Area Sec CMS *Leic* and *Pet* 70-71; Warden and Chapl Rikkyo Japanese Sch Rudgwick 71-73; Hd Master and Chapl Pennthorpe Sch Rudgwick 74-96; NSM Rudgwick *Chich* 95-96; rtd 96; Perm to Offic *Chich* and *Guildf* 96-98; Hd Master Ardingly Coll Jun Sch Haywards Heath 97-98; Chapl Rowcroft Hospice Torquay 99-01; Hon C Bovey Tracey SS Pet, Paul and Thos w Hennock *Ex* from 99. *5 Anthony Cottages, Alfington Road, Alfington, Ottery St Mary EX11 1FE* Tel (01404) 850430

SPENCER, Mrs Margot Patricia Winifred. b 48. Coll of St Matthias Bris CertEd69. STETS 98. **d** 01 **p** 02. NSM Wonersh w Blackheath *Guildf* 01-05; NSM Busbridge and Hambledon from 05. *24 Park Road, Godalming GU7 1SH* Tel (01483) 416333 E-mail margotspencer@btinternet.com

SPENCER, Neil Richard. b 49. Leeds Univ BA70 ALA72. WEMTC 96. **d** 99 **p** 00. NSM Ludlow, Ludford, Ashford Carbonell etc *Heref* 99-02; C Letton w Staunton, Byford, Mansel Gamage etc 02-03; P-in-c Ormesby St Marg w Scratby, Ormesby St Mich etc *Nor* 05-07; V from 07. *The Rectory, 11 Church View, Ormesby, Great Yarmouth NR29 3PZ* Tel (01493) 730234 E-mail nspencer@revd.freeserve.co.uk

SPENCER, Peter Roy. b 40. CertEd. Sarum & Wells Th Coll 72. **d** 74 **p** 75. C Northampton St Alb *Pet* 74-77; TV Cov E 77-90; V Erdington St Barn *Birm* 90-02; TR Erdington 02-07; Chapl John Taylor Hospice Birm 90-07; rtd 07. *15 Poplar Road, Smethwick B66 4AW* Tel 0121-429 4514

SPENCER, Richard Dennis. b 50. Imp Coll Lon BSc71. NTMTC 93. **d** 96 **p** 97. C Leek and Meerbrook *Lich* 96-00; P-in-c Shrewsbury H Trin w St Julian 00-10; V from 10. *Holy Trinity Vicarage, Greyfriars Road, Shrewsbury SY3 7EP* Tel (01743) 244891 E-mail rds@htbv.org.uk

SPENCER, Richard Hugh. b 62. Univ of Wales (Cardiff) LLB84 BD88 Bris Univ MA92. St Mich Coll Llan 85. **d** 88 **p** 89. C Barry All SS *Llan* 88-90; Asst Chapl Univ of Wales (Cardiff) 90-92; Lect NT Studies 92-98; Tutor St Mich Coll Llan 92-98; R Llangenni and Llanbedr Ystrad Yw w Patricio *S & B* 98-00; Dir Post-Ord Tr 00; TV Cowbridge *Llan* 02-03; NSM 03-04; Hd of Th Trin Coll Carmarthen 03-04; P-in-c Kenfig Hill *Llan* 04-10; P-in-c Cardiff Ch Ch Roath Park from 10; Dioc Dir of Ords 10-11. *154 Lake Road East, Cardiff CF23 5NQ* Tel (029) 2075 7190 E-mail rhspencer7@btinternet.com

SPENCER, Richard William Edward. b 33. FSCA66. WMMTC 78. **d** 81 **p** 82. NSM The Lickey *Birm* 81-83; Area Sec (Warks and W Midl) Chr Aid 83-93; Perm to Offic *Worc* from 95 and *Heref* from 98. *Honey Hedge, 165 Godiva Road, Leominster HR6 8TB* Tel (01568) 620097

SPENCER, Robert. b 48. St Jo Coll Nottm. **d** 93 **p** 94. NSM Ellon *Ab* 93-95 and 99-09; NSM Cruden Bay 93-95; NSM Fraserburgh w New Pitsligo 95-99; P-in-c Oldmeldrum from 09. *12 Riverview Place, Ellon AB41 9NW* Tel (01358) 723193 Fax (01224) 248515 E-mail revbob.spencer@btinternet.com

SPENCER, Roy Primett. b 26. Oak Hill Th Coll 50. **d** 53 **p** 54. C Bedford St Pet *St Alb* 53-55; C Luton Ch Ch 55-58; C Nottingham St Mary *S'well* 58-60; V Middlestown *Wakef* 60-61; Chapl Crumpsall Hosp Man 61-66; R Fleet *Linc* 66-69; V Accrington St Paul *Blackb* 69-78; V Woodplumpton 78-83; P-in-c Preston St Luke 83-89; P-in-c Preston St Luke and St Oswald 89-90; Chapl Preston Hosp N Shields 83-91; rtd 91; Perm to Offic *Blackb* from 91. *5 Hollywood Avenue, Penwortham, Preston PR1 9AS* Tel (01772) 743783

SPENCER, Stephen Christopher. b 60. Ball Coll Ox BA82 DPhil90. Edin Th Coll 88. **d** 90 **p** 91. C Harlesden All So *Lon* 90-93; P-in-c Nyamandhlovu Zimbabwe 93-99; R Bulawayo All SS 96-99; V Caton w Littledale *Blackb* 99-03; Dep Prin CBDTI 99-03; Tutor NOC 03-08; Tutor Yorks Min Course from 08; Co-ord Yorks Regional Tr Partnership 08-10; P-in-c Brighouse and Clifton *Wakef* 10; V from 11. *2 St John Street, Brighouse HD6 1HN*, or *The Mirfield Centre, Stocks Bank Road, Mirfield WF14 0BW* Tel (01924) 481906 E-mail stephen@ymc.org.uk

SPENCER, Stephen Nigel Howard. b 53. Pemb Coll Ox BA75 MA03 Jes Coll Cam PGCE76. Trin Coll Bris 80. **d** 82 **p** 83. C Partington and Carrington *Ches* 82-85; C Brunswick *Man* 85-88; Chapl UEA *Nor* 88-92; rtd 92; Perm to Offic *Nor* 92-95. *43 College Lane, Norwich NR4 6TW* Tel (01603) 506815 E-mail stephen.spencer@btinternet.com

SPENCER, Stephen Robert. b 61. NTMTC BA08. **d** 08 **p** 09. C Langdon Hills *Chelmsf* from 08; V Eastwood from 11. *The*

Vicarage, Eastwoodbury Lane, Southend-on-Sea SS2 6UH* Tel (01702) 525272 E-mail stevelinda.spencer@btinternet.com

SPENCER, Steven Christopher. b 47. RGN69. NTMTC 98. **d** 98 **p** 99. NSM Chatham St Phil and St Jas *Roch* from 98; Asst Chapl Medway NHS Foundn Trust 04-09; Lead Chapl from 09. *Medway Hospital, Windmill Road, Gillingham ME7 5NY* Tel (01634) 830000 ext 5414 E-mail steven.spencer@medway.nhs.uk

SPENCER, Canon Susan. b 47. EMMTC 87. **d** 90 **p** 94. Par Dn Cotgrave *S'well* 90-94; C 94-98; P-in-c Rolleston w Fiskerton, Morton and Upton 98-10; Asst Warden of Readers 98-07; AD S'well 07-10; Jt AD S'well and Newark 08-09; Hon Can S'well Minster 08-10; rtd 10. *15 Cherry Avenue, Branston, Lincoln LN4 1UY* Tel (01522) 823947 E-mail suespencer47@googlemail.com

SPENCER, Mrs Susan Lesley. b 55. **d** 00 **p** 01. OLM Middleton and Thornham *Man* from 00. *1 Westbrook Close, Rochdale OL11 2XY* Tel (01706) 350668 E-mail suespencer@bigfoot.com

SPENCER, Sylvia. **d** 98. Chapl Grampian Univ Hosp NHS Trust from 98. *Aberdeen Royal Infirmary, Foresterhill, Aberdeen AB9 2ZB* Tel (01224) 681818

SPENCER-THOMAS, Canon Owen Robert. b 40. MBE08. Lon Univ BSc(Soc)70 Westmr Coll Lon DLitt10 LGSM96 MRTvS76. Westcott Ho Cam 70. **d** 72 **p** 73. C S Kensington St Luke Lon 72-76; Lect RS S Kensington Inst 74-76; Dir Lon Chs Radio Workshop & Relig Producer BBC 76-78; Relig Producer Anglia TV 78-95; Lic to Offic *Lon* 76-87; NSM Cambridge Ascension *Ely* 87-07; Chapl St Jo Coll Sch Cam 93-98; Chapl St Bede's Sch Cam 96-97; Chapl Ch Coll Cam 97 01; Dioc Dir of Communications *Ely* 02-07; Bp's Press Officer from 07; Hon Can Ely Cathl from 04. *52 Windsor Road, Cambridge CB4 3JN* Tel and fax (01223) 358448 Mobile 07801-492151 E-mail owenst@btinternet.com

SPENDLOVE, Mrs Lindsay Kate. b 55. Man Univ LLB77 Essex Univ BA88. EAMTC 89. **d** 92 **p** 94. NSM Lexden *Chelmsf* 92-94; NSM Colchester Ch Ch w St Mary V 94-96; NSM Pleshey 97-02; Perm to Offic *St E* from 02 and *Chelmsf* from 04. *Green Blade, The Street, Wenhaston, Halesworth IP19 9EF* Tel (01502) 478301 E-mail ikspendlove@supanet.com

SPERRING, Clive Michael. b 43. Oak Hill Th Coll 71. **d** 75 **p** 76. C Hawkwell *Chelmsf* 75-78; C-in-c Gt Baddow 78-82; Asst P Kohimarama New Zealand 82-85; V Orakei St Jas from 86. *132 Gowing Drive, Meadowbank, Auckland 1072, New Zealand* Tel (0064) (9) 528 4400 E-mail cmsperring@vodafone.co.nz

SPICER, David John. b 52. Sussex Univ BA76 Lon Univ MTh78. Westcott Ho Cam 77. **d** 79 **p** 80. C E Dulwich St Jo *S'wark* 79-82; C Richmond St Mary w St Matthias and St Jo 82-87; V Lewisham St Swithun 87-91; Chapl Community of All Hallows Ditchingham from 91. *St Edmund's House, All Hallows Convent, Ditchingham, Bungay NR35 2DZ* Tel (01986) 892139

SPICER (formerly RIMMER), Dorothy Janet Rosalind. b 49. Cen Sch of Art Lon BA72 Middx Poly ATD74 E Lon Univ MA98. Westcott Ho Cam. **d** 00 **p** 01. C Notting Hill St Jo and St Pet *Lon* 00-02; V Totternhoe, Stanbridge and Tilsworth *St Alb* from 02. *The Vicarage, Mill Road, Stanbridge, Leighton Buzzard LU7 9HX* Tel (01525) 210253 E-mail revjanetspicer@btinternet.com

SPICER, Leigh Edwin. b 56. Sarum & Wells Th Coll 78. **d** 81 **p** 82. C Harborne St Pet *Birm* 81-83; C Bloxwich *Lich* 83-87; Chapl RAF from 87. *Chaplaincy Services, Valiant Block, HQ Air Command, RAF High Wycombe HP14 4UE* Tel (01494) 496800 Fax 496343

SPICER, Nicolas. b 61. Univ of Wales (Lamp) BA84. Coll of Resurr Mirfield 84. **d** 86 **p** 87. C Westbury-on-Trym H Trin *Bris* 86-89; C Willesden Green St Andr and St Fran *Lon* 89-93; Chapl Asst Charing Cross Hosp Lon 93-94; Asst Chapl Hammersmith Hosps NHS Trust 94-97; R Ardleigh and The Bromleys *Chelmsf* 97-07; P-in-c Worksop Priory *S'well* from 07. *The Vicarage, Cheapside, Worksop S80 2HX* Tel (01909) 472180 E-mail nspicer@lineone.net

SPICER, Robert Patrick. b 39. FCA68. SAOMC 94. **d** 97 **p** 98. NSM Riverside *Ox* 97-01; NSM Beaconsfield 01-07. *16 Hayse Hill, Windsor SL4 5SZ* Tel (01753) 864697 E-mail spicerrevrob@aol.com

SPIERS, Canon Peter Hendry. b 61. St Jo Coll Dur BA82. Ridley Hall Cam 83. **d** 86 **p** 87. C W Derby St Luke *Liv* 86-90; TV Everton St Pet 90-95; V Everton St Geo 95-05; P-in-c Gt Crosby St Luke from 05; Hon Can Liv Cathl from 06. *St Luke's Vicarage, Liverpool Road, Crosby, Liverpool L23 5SE* Tel 0151-924 1737 E-mail pete@spiersfamily.eclipse.co.uk

SPIKIN, Simon John Overington. b 48. Nottm Univ BTh74. Linc Th Coll 70. **d** 75 **p** 76. C Sawbridgeworth *St Alb* 75-79; C Odiham w S Warnborough and Long Sutton *Win* 79-81; R Dickleburgh w Thelveton w Frenze and Shimpling *Nor* 81-82; P-in-c Rushall 81-82; R Dickleburgh, Langmere, Shimpling, Thelveton etc 82-96; rtd 96; Perm to Offic *Cant* from 01. *Marley Court, Kingston, Canterbury CT4 6JH* Tel (01227) 832405

SPILLER, Canon David Roger. b 44. St Jo Coll Dur BA70 Fitzw Coll Cam BA72 MA76 Nottm Univ DipAdEd80. Ridley Hall

Cam 70. **d** 73 **p** 74. C Bradf Cathl 73-77; C Stratford-on-Avon w Bishopton *Cov* 77-80; Chapl Geo Eliot Hosp Nuneaton 80-90; V Chilvers Coton w Astley *Cov* 80-90; RD Nuneaton 84-90; Prin Aston Tr Scheme 90-97; C Kings Norton *Birm* 98-99; C Shirley 99-00; Dir of Min and Dioc Dir of Ords *Cov* from 00; Hon Can Cov Cathl from 04. *The Parsonage, Sambourne Lane, Sambourne, Redditch B96 6PA* Tel (01527) 892372 *or* (024) 7671 0504 Fax (024) 7671 0550 E-mail rogerspiller@btinternet.com

SPILMAN, Derrick Geoffrey. b 27. Roch Th Coll 61. **d** 63 **p** 64. C Dover St Mary *Cant* 63-67; CF 67-71; Canada from 71; rtd 92. *5398 Walter Place, Burnaby BC V5G 4K2, Canada* Tel (001) (604) 294 6816

SPILSBURY, Stephen Ronald Paul. b 39. Nottm Univ BSc69 MPhil72 Bris Univ PhD99. Linc Th Coll 71. **d** 64 **p** 65. In RC Ch 64-71; C Cricklade w Latton *Bris* 72-75; P-in-c Swindon All SS 76-81; V Lawrence Weston 81-95; RD Westbury and Severnside 89-91; rtd 99; Perm to Offic *Bris* from 03. *10 Woodside Grove, Bristol BS10 7RF* Tel 0117-959 1079 E-mail paul.spilsbury@btinternet.com

SPINDLER, Miss Jane Diana. b 54. Southn Univ BA75 CertEd76. Wycliffe Hall Ox 87. **d** 89 **p** 94. C Bishopsworth *Bris* 89-93; C Brislington St Luke 93-94; rtd 95; Perm to Offic *Bris* from 95. *143 Highridge Road, Bishopsworth, Bristol BS13 8HT* Tel 0117-935 8137

SPINK, Mrs Diana. b 40. Ex Univ BA63 PGCE64. SAOMC 97. **d** 00 **p** 01. NSM Hemel Hempstead *St Alb* 00-10; rtd 10; Perm to Offic *St Alb* from 10. *39 Garland Close, Hemel Hempstead HP2 5HU* Tel (01442) 262133 Mobile 07808-184321 E-mail diana2spink@hotmail.com

SPINKS, Prof Bryan Douglas. b 48. St Chad's Coll Dur BA70 BD79 K Coll Lon MTh72 Dur Univ DD88 Yale Univ Hon MA98 FRHistS85. **d** 75 **p** 76. C Witham *Chelmsf* 75-78; C Clacton St Jas 78-79; Chapl Chu Coll Cam 80-97; Affiliated Lect Div Cam 82-97; Prof Liturg Studies Yale Univ and Fell Morse Coll 98-07; Prof Past Th Yale Univ from 07; Perm to Offic *Ely* from 02. *27 Egypt Lane, Clinton CT 06413, USA* E-mail bryan.spinks@yale.edu *or* bryspinkus@aol.com

SPINKS, Christopher George. b 53. Oak Hill Th Coll BA88. **d** 88 **p** 89. C Hove Bp Hannington Memorial Ch *Chich* 88-92; Travelling Sec UCCF 92-95; Itinerant Min 95-98; Chapl Martlets Hospice Hove 98-11; TV Hove *Chich* 99-10; V Polegate from 11. *35 St Heliers Avenue, Hove BN3 5RE* Tel (01273) 730027 E-mail chrisgpinks@hotmail.com

SPINKS, John Frederick. b 40. Westmr Coll Ox MTh97. Oak Hill Th Coll 79. **d** 82 **p** 83. NSM Roxbourne St Andr *Lon* 82-89; C Northwood H Trin 89-93; P-in-c Greenhill St Jo 93-96; V 96-04; rtd 04; Perm to Offic *Lon, Ox* and *St Alb* from 04. *Woodpecker Cottage, 232 Northwood Road, Harefield, Uxbridge UB9 6PT* Tel (01895) 822477 Mobile 07711-635199 E-mail woodpecker232@tiscali.co.uk

SPITTLE, Christopher Bamford. b 74. St Jo Coll Dur BA95. Ridley Hall Cam 97. **d** 99 **p** 00. C Netherton *Liv* 99-03; TR Sutton 03-11; P-in-c Skelmersdale St Paul from 11. *The Vicarage, Church Road, Skelmersdale WN8 8ND* Tel (01695) 722087

SPITTLE, Robin. b 57. St Jo Coll Nottm 84. **d** 86 **p** 87. C Ipswich St Fran *St E* 86-91; Min Shotley St Mary CD 91-92; R Shotley 92-99; P-in-c Copdock w Washbrook and Belstead 93-99; V Kesgrave from 99. *The Vicarage, 18 Bell Lane, Kesgrave, Ipswich IP5 1JQ* Tel (01473) 622181 E-mail robin.spittle@lineone.net

SPIVEY, Colin. b 35. ACII61. Oak Hill Th Coll 74. **d** 76 **p** 77. C Egham *Guildf* 76-79; C Edgware *Lon* 79-83; R Haworth *Bradf* 83-95; Sub Chapl HM Pris Leeds 94-99; V Thorpe Edge *Bradf* 95-00; rtd 01; Perm to Offic *Ripon* from 01. *2 Woodhill View, Wetherby LS22 6PP* Tel (01937) 581508 E-mail ca.spivey@virgin.net

SPOKES, David Lawrence. b 57. Nottm Univ BCombStuds85. Linc Th Coll 82. **d** 85 **p** 86. C Rushall *Lich* 85-89; TV Thornaby on Tees *York* 89-93; R Yardley Hastings, Denton and Grendon etc *Pet* from 02; Rural Adv Northn Adnry from 05. *The Rectory, 14 The Leys, Denton, Northampton NN7 1DH* Tel (01604) 891294 E-mail mail@davidspokes.com

SPOKES, Keith John. b 29. EAMTC. **d** 84 **p** 85. NSM Bury St Edmunds St Mary *St E* 84-89; P-in-c Helmingham w Framsden and Pettaugh w Winston 89-92; rtd 93; Perm to Offic *St E* from 93. *34 Southgate House, Rougham Road, Bury St Edmunds IP33 2RN* Tel (01284) 706742

SPONG, Bennett Jarod. b 49. Coll of Charleston (USA) BA74 Thames Poly PGCE87. **d** 05 **p** 06. OLM Charlton *S'wark* from 05. *10 Mayhill Road, London SE7 7JQ* Tel (020) 8853 4457 E-mail bjspong@hotmail.com

SPONG, Mrs Hilary Vida. b 44. Ex Univ BTh09. SWMTC 06. **d** 09 **p** 10. NSM St Stythians w Perranarworthal and Gwennap *Truro* from 09; NSM Feock from 11; NSM Devoran from 11. *Nansough Manor, Ladock, Truro TR2 4PB* Tel (01726) 883315 Mobile 07855-781134 E-mail hilaryspong@sent.com

SPONG, Terence John. See MESLEY-SPONG, Terence John

SPOONER, Anthony Patrick David. b 45. Univ Coll of Rhodesia Univ Coll of Nyasaland BA68. Linc Th Coll 71. **d** 74 **p** 75. C Glynde, W Firle and Beddingham *Chich* 74-77; Rhodesia 77-80;

Zimbabwe 80-86; P-in-c Clacton St Jas *Chelmsf* 86-90; V from 90. *St James's Vicarage, 44 Wash Lane, Clacton-on-Sea CO15 1DA* Tel (01255) 422007 E-mail revapdspooner@aol.com

SPOTTISWOODE, Anthony Derek. b 25. Solicitor 50 Pemb Coll Cam BA47 MA86. Sarum & Wells Th Coll 85. **d** 86 **p** 87. C Hampstead St Jo *Lon* 86-94; rtd 95; Perm to Offic *Lon* from 95. *Flat 6, 38-40 Eton Avenue, London NW3 3HL* Tel (020) 7435 6756

SPRAGGETT, Miss Agnes Louise. b 29. Bp Otter Coll Chich TCert55. CBDTI 06. **d** 06 **p** 07. NSM Embsay w Eastby *Bradf* from 06. *16 Millholme Rise, Embsay, Skipton BD23 6NU* Tel (01756) 793575 E-mail loutin@talktalk.net

SPRATLEY, Deryck Edward. b 30. BSc. Oak Hill Th Coll 62. **d** 64 **p** 65. C Ramsgate St Luke *Cant* 64-67; C W Holloway St Dav *Lon* 67-73; V Upper Holloway St Pet 73-79; V Upper Holloway St Pet w St Jo 79-82; P-in-c Dagenham *Chelmsf* 82-88; P-in-c Becontree St Geo 84-88; TR Dagenham 88-93; rtd 93; Perm to Offic *Chelmsf* 93-01. *c/o Mrs H Ursell, 9 Winchester Road, Frinton-on-Sea CO13 9JB* Tel (01255) 672973

SPRATT, Laurence Herbert. b 28. Linc Th Coll 76. **d** 78 **p** 79. C Mexborough *Sheff* 78-80; R Wrentham w Benacre, Covehithe, Frostenden etc *St E* 80-88; Perm to Offic *Arg* 89-90 and 91-98; P-in-c Inveraray 90-91; rtd 93. *19 Church Street, Ellesmere SY12 0HD*

SPRATT, Robert Percival. b 31. MBE08. FCIOB MRSH ABEng. Carl Dioc Tr Inst 84. **d** 87 **p** 88. NSM Kendal St Thos *Carl* 87-89; Chapl HM Pris Preston 89-96; Dir Miss to Pris from 96; Perm to Offic *Blackb* from 96 and *Carl* from 97; Asst Chapl HM Pris Haverigg from 06. *Missions to Prisons, PO Box 37, Kendal LA9 6GF* Tel and fax (01539) 720475

SPRAY, Canon Charles Alan Francis Thomas. b 27. Lon Univ BScEng51 ARSM51. Ridley Hall Cam 57. **d** 59 **p** 60. C Chich St Pancras and St Jo 59-63; V Shipley 63-69; R Ore St Helen and St Barn 70-85; V Burgess Hill St Andr 85-93; Can and Preb Chich Cathl 88-93; rtd 93; Perm to Offic *Chich* from 93. *6 Silverdale Road, Burgess Hill RH15 0EF* Tel (01444) 232149

SPRAY, John William. b 29. Sarum & Wells Th Coll 71. **d** 73 **p** 74. C Clayton *Lich* 73-77; V Hartshill 77-82; P-in-c Aston 82-83; P-in-c Stone St Mich 82-83; P-in-c Stone St Mich w Aston St Sav 83-84; R 84-90; rtd 90; Perm to Offic *Lich* from 90. *2 Belvoir Avenue, Trentham, Stoke-on-Trent ST4 8SY* Tel (01782) 644959

SPRAY, Mrs Josephine Ann. b 44. Nottm Coll of Educn TCert65. SAOMC 95. **d** 98 **p** 99. NSM Watford St Mich *St Alb* 98-02; P-in-c Turvey 02-10; rtd 11; Perm to Offic *St Alb* from 11. *121 High Street, Olney MK46 4EF* Tel (01234) 713726 E-mail jo-spray@sky.com

SPRAY, Mrs Karen. b 55. **d** 06 **p** 07. NSM Littleham w Exmouth 06-07; C Honiton, Gittisham, Combe Raleigh, Monkton etc 07-09; P-in-c Clyst St Mary, Clyst St George etc from 09; C Lympstone and Woodbury w Exton from 09; C Aylesbeare, Rockbeare, Farringdon etc from 09. *The Rectory, 40 Clyst Valley Road, Clyst St Mary, Exeter EX5 1DD* Tel (01392) 877400

SPRAY, Richard Alan. b 43. EMMTC 85. **d** 88 **p** 89. NSM Cotgrave *S'well* 88-96; P-in-c Barton in Fabis 96-01; P-in-c Thrumpton 96-01; P-in-c Kingston and Ratcliffe-on-Soar 96-01; P-in-c Blyth 01-02; P-in-c Scrooby 01-02; V Blyth and Scrooby w Ranskill 02-10; AD Bawtry 06-09; rtd 11. *Thorn Lea, Mattersey Road, Ranskill, Retford DN22 8ND* Tel 07971-637670 (mobile) E-mail revrich@talktalk.net

SPREADBRIDGE, Alison Margaret. b 50. Open Univ BSc96. SEITE 04. **d** 07 **p** 08. C Dartford St Edm *Roch* 07-11; P-in-c Gillingham H Trin from 11. *Holy Trinity Vicarage, 2 Waltham Road, Gillingham ME8 6XQ* Tel (01634) 231690 Mobile 07979-013559 E-mail a.spreadbridge9@btinternet.com

SPREADBRIDGE, Paul Andrew. b 49. Greenwich Univ CertEd02 Kent Univ BA05. SEITE 99. **d** 98 **p** 03. In RC Ch 98-01; NSM Chatham St Steph *Roch* 02-04; C Orpington All SS 04-07; V Bexley St Mary 07-11; R Chelsfield from 11. *The Rectory, Skibbs Lane, Chelsfield, Orpington BR6 7RH* Tel (01689) 825749 E-mail paul.spreadbridge@btinternet.com

SPREADBURY, Joanna Mary Magdalen. b 65. Magd Coll Ox BA90 MA93 K Coll Lon PhD99. Westcott Ho Cam MA99. **d** 99 **p** 00. C Watford St Mich *St Alb* 99-03; C Leavesden 03-06; V Abbots Langley from 06. *The Vicarage, 6 High Street, Abbots Langley WD5 0AS* Tel (01923) 263013

SPREADBURY, John Graham. b 59. **d** 99 **p** 00. OLM Billingborough Gp *Linc* from 99. *Osbourne House, 3-5 Low Street, Billingborough, Sleaford NG34 0QJ* Tel (01529) 240440

SPREDBURY, Mary Jane. b 59. Open Univ BA99. STETS 03. **d** 06 **p** 07. NSM Acton St Mary *Lon* from 06. *6 St Catherine's Court, Bedford Road, London W4 1UH* Tel (020) 8723 1035 Mobile 07803-759886 E-mail spredbury@btinternet.com

SPRENT, Michael Francis (Brother Giles). b 34. Ex Coll Ox BA58 MA62. Kelham Th Coll 58. **d** 61 **p** 62. C Plaistow St Andr *Chelmsf* 61-63; SSF from 61; Papua New Guinea 65-69; Hilfield Friary 69-74, 77-78, 97-02 and 03-04; Alnmouth Friary 74-76; Sweden 76-77; TV High Stoy *Sarum* 77-78; Harbledown Friary 78-82; Solomon Is 83-97; Zimbabwe 02-03; Stepney Friary

05-08; Canning Town Friary from 08. *St Matthias' Vicarage, 45 Mafeking Road, London E16 4NS* Tel (020) 7511 7848
E-mail gilesssf@franciscans.org.uk

SPRIGGS, John David Robert. b 36. BNC Ox BA58 MA63. S'wark Ord Course 73. **d** 75 **p** 76. Lic to Offic *Ox* 75-97; Chapl Pangbourne Coll 95-97; Perm to Offic *Linc* from 97. *Glen House, Great Ponton Road, Boothby Pagnell, Grantham NG33 4DH* Tel (01476) 585756

SPRINGATE, Paul Albert Edward. b 48. Oak Hill Th Coll 81. **d** 83 **p** 84. C Pennycross *Ex* 83-87; TV Sileby, Cossington and Seagrave *Leic* 87-96; Chapl and Warden Harnhill Healing Cen from 96; Bp's Adv on Healing *Glouc* from 03. *Centre of Christian Healing, Harnhill Centre, Harnhill, Cirencester GL7 5PX* Tel (01285) 850283 Fax 850519
E-mail office@harnhillcentre.org.uk

SPRINGBETT, John Howard. b 47. Pemb Coll Cam BA70 MA74. Ridley Hall Cam 70. **d** 72 **p** 73. C Ulverston St Mary w H Trin *Carl* 72-76; V Dewsbury Moor *Wakef* 76-84; V Hoddesdon *St Alb* 84-00; RD Cheshunt 94-00; TR Shelf w Buttershaw St Aid *Bradf* 00-03; V Woodford Bridge *Chelmsf* from 03. *St Paul's Vicarage, 4 Cross Road, Woodford Green IG8 8BS* Tel (020) 8504 3815
E-mail springbett25@hotmail.com

SPRINGETT, The Ven Robert Wilfred. b 62. Nottm Univ BTh89 Lon Univ MA92. Linc Th Coll 86. **d** 89 **p** 90. C Colchester St Jas, All SS, St Nic and St Runwald *Chelmsf* 89-92; C Basildon St Martin w Nevendon 92-94; P-in-c Belhus Park and S Ockendon 94-01; RD Thurrock 98-01; R Wanstead St Mary w Ch Ch 01-10; AD Redbridge 08-10; Hon Can Chelmsf Cathl 08-10, Adn Cheltenham *Glouc* from 10. *Abbey Cottage Stables, 1 Gloucester Road, Tewkesbury GL20 5SS* Tel (01684) 300067
E-mail archdchelt@glosdioc.org.uk

SPRINGETT, Simon Paul. b 56. Warwick Univ LLB78. Wycliffe Hall Ox 78. **d** 81 **p** 82. C Harlow St Mary and St Hugh w St Jo the Bapt *Chelmsf* 81-84; C Gt Clacton 84-86; R Rayne 86-91; Chapl RN from 91. *Royal Naval Chaplaincy Service, Mail Point 1-2, Leach Building, Whale Island, Portsmouth PO2 8BY* Tel (023) 9262 5055 Fax 9262 5134

SPRINGFORD, Patrick Francis Alexander. b 45. Wycliffe Hall Ox 71. **d** 74 **p** 75. C Finchley Ch Ch *Lon* 74-79; CF 79-06; Rtd Officer Chapl RAChD from 06. *c/o MOD Chaplains (Army)* Tel (01980) 615804 Fax 615800
E-mail patrick.springford@freenet.de

SPRINGHAM, Desmond John. b 32. Bris Univ BA56. Oak Hill Th Coll 56. **d** 58 **p** 59. C St Alb St Paul *St Alb* 58-61; C Reading St Jo *Ox* 61-66; R Worting *Win* 66-80; V Jersey St Andr 80-97; rtd 97; Perm to Offic *Sarum* from 97. *19 Balmoral Crescent, Dorchester DT1 2BN* Tel (01305) 268022

SPRINGTHORPE, Canon David Frederick. b 47. Open Univ BA. AKC72. **d** 73 **p** 74. C Dartford St Alb *Roch* 73-77; C Biggin Hill 77-80; R Ash 80-89; R Ridley 80-89; R Eynsford w Farningham and Lullingstone 89-94; V Barnehurst 94-04; RD Erith 98-04; R Keston from 04; Hon Can Roch Cathl from 02. *The Rectory, 24 Commonside, Keston BR2 6BP* Tel (01689) 853186 E-mail david.springthorpe@btopenworld.com

SPROSTON, Bernard Melvin. b 37. St Jo Coll Dur 77. **d** 79 **p** 80. C Westlands St Andr *Lich* 79-82; P-in-c Heage *Derby* 82-87; V Heath 87-02; rtd 02; Perm to Offic *Derby* from 02. *2 Upwood Close, Holmehall, Chesterfield S40 4UP* Tel (01246) 207401
E-mail bernel@hotmail.co.uk

SPROULE, Gerald Norman. b 26. TCD Div Sch. **d** 60 **p** 61. C Monaghan *Clogh* 60-62; I Cleenish 62-68; I Magheracross 68-73; Admin Sec (Ireland) BCMS 73-79; I Belfast St Aid *Conn* 79-86; I Magherally w Annaclone *D & D* 86-94; rtd 94. *4 Hilden Park, Lisburn BT27 4UG* Tel (028) 9260 1528

SPRY, Miss Elisabeth Roselie. b 47. Open Univ BA82. **d** 06 **p** 07. OLM Stratton St Mary w Stratton St Michael etc *Nor* from 06. *13 Whitehouse Drive, Long Stratton, Norwich NR15 2TD* Tel (01508) 530478 E-mail erspry@yahoo.co.uk

SPURGEON, Michael Paul. b 53. MIEx. Linc Th Coll 83. **d** 85 **p** 86. C Lillington *Cov* 85-89; C Min Can Ripon Cathl 89-95; R Lower Nidderdale from 95. *Lower Nidderdale Rectory, 6 Old Church Green, Kirk Hammerton, York YO26 8DL* Tel (01423) 331142 E-mail lowernidderdale@aol.com

SPURIN, Canon Richard Mark. b 28. Peterho Cam BA52 MA60. Wycliffe Hall Ox 54. **d** 55 **p** 56. C Foleshill St Laur *Cov* 55-58; C Atherstone 58-60; CMS 60-61; Kenya 61-73; C-in-c Ewell St Paul Howell Hill CD *Guildf* 73-82; V Netherton *Liv* 82-86; V Brandwood *Birm* 86-91; C Padiham *Blackb* 91-93; Hon Can Nambale Cathl Kenya from 92; rtd 93; Perm to Offic *Blackb* from 93. *11 Rosemount Avenue, Burnley BB11 2JU* Tel (01282) 421402

SPURR, Andrew. b 58. St Jo Coll Dur BA80. Qu Coll Birm 92. **d** 93 **p** 94. C Rainham *Roch* 93-96; C Stansted Mountfitchet *Chelmsf* 96; C Stansted Mountfitchet w Birchanger and Farnham 97; R 97-06; V Evesham w Norton and Lenchwick *Worc* from 06. *Church House, Market Place, Evesham WR11 4RW* Tel (01386) 446219
E-mail vicar@eveshamparish.com

SPURRELL, John Mark. b 34. CCC Ox BA57 MA61 FSA87. Linc Th Coll 58. **d** 60 **p** 61. C Tilbury Docks *Chelmsf* 60-65; C Boston *Linc* 65-76; R Stow in Lindsey 76-85; P-in-c Willingham 76-85; P-in-c Coates 76-85; P-in-c Brightwell w Sotwell *Ox* 85-97; rtd 97; Perm to Offic *B & W* from 97. *10 The Liberty, Wells BA5 2SU* Tel (01749) 678966

SPURRIER, Richard Patrick Montague. b 25. Bris Univ BA59. Wycliffe Hall Ox 59. **d** 61 **p** 62. C S Lyncombe *B & W* 61-63; C Weston St Jo 63-64; rtd 90. *48 Longford Road, Melksham SN12 6AU* Tel (01225) 707419

SPURWAY, Christine Frances. b 54. Cuddesdon Coll 96. **d** 98 **p** 99. C Coulsdon St Andr *S'wark* 98-02; P-in-c Riddlesdown 02-05; V from 05; RD Croydon S from 04. *St James's Vicarage, 1B St James's Road, Purley CR8 2DL* Tel (020) 8660 5436

SQUIRE, Geoffrey Frank. b 36. Ex & Truro NSM Scheme. **d** 83 **p** 84. NSM Barnstaple *Ex* 83-98; NSM Swimbridge w W Buckland and Landkey from 98. *Little Cross, Northleigh Hill, Goodleigh, Barnstaple EX32 7NR* Tel (01271) 344935

SQUIRE, Humphrey Edward. b 35. St Chad's Coll Dur BA55. Coll of Resurr Mirfield. **d** 57 **p** 58. C Newbold w Dunston *Derby* 57-59; C Thorpe St Andr *Nor* 59-61; Zanzibar 61-63; C Whittington *Derby* 63-64; R Drayton *Nor* 64-75; Chapl Dover Coll 75-83; TV Wareham *Sarum* 83-94; rtd 94; Perm to Offic *Sarum* from 94. *La Retraite, Burbidge Close, Lytchett Matravers, Poole BH16 6EG* Tel (01202) 623204

SQUIRES, John Anthony. b 50. CPFA78. LCTP. **d** 08 **p** 09. OLM Waterside Par *Blackb* from 08. *11 Carr Lane, Hambleton, Poulton-le-Fylde FY6 9BA* Tel (01253) 701895 Mobile 07704-659556 E-mail squiresja@aol.com

SQUIRES, John Wallace Howden. b 45. Sydney Univ BA67 DipEd68 MTh97 PhD05 Lon Univ BD75. Moore Th Coll Sydney ThL74. **d** 76 **p** 76. C Normanhurst Australia 76-78; Luton St Mary *St Alb* 78-79; Chapl Home of Divine Healing Crowhurst 79-80; C-in-c Putney Australia 80-82; R Longueville 83-97; Dir Inst for Values Univ of NSW 97-02; Dir Aus Human Rights Cen Univ of NSW 03-05. *22 Moorehead Street, Redfern NSW 2016, Australia* Tel (0061) (2) 9690 0206 *or* 9385 3637 Fax 9385 1778 Mobile 41-822 6976
E-mail j.squires@unsw.edu.au

SQUIRES, The Ven Malcolm. b 46. St Chad's Coll Dur BA72. Cuddesdon Coll 72. **d** 74 **p** 75. C Headingley *Ripon* 74-77; C Stanningley St Thos 77-80; V Bradshaw *Wakef* 80-85; V Ripponden 85-89; V Barkisland w W Scammonden 85-89; V Mirfield 89-96; TR Wrexham *St As* 96-02; Hon Can St As Cathl 00-01; Adn Wrexham 01-10; R Llandegla 02-10; Bp's Chapl 10-11; Can Cursal St As Cathl 10-11; rtd 11. *1A Penrhyn Park, Penrhyn Bay, Llandudno LL30 3HW* Tel (01492) 544560

SQUIRES, Miss Rachel Louise. b 79. Coll of Ripon & York St Jo BA00. Ripon Coll Cuddesdon MA07. **d** 07 **p** 08. C Alnwick *Newc* from 07. *2 Northumberland Street, Alnwick NE66 1LT* Tel (01665) 600888 E-mail rachelsquires@googlemail.com

SSERUNKUMA, Michael Wilberforce. b 54. Trin Coll Bris BA90. Bp Tucker Coll Mukono. **d** 77 **p** 78. Uganda 77-87; C Gabalfa *Llan* 90-94; TV Cyncoed *Mon* 94-95; R Canton St Jo *Llan* 95-01; Asst Chapl R Berks and Battle Hosps NHS Trust 01-02; Chapl Team Ldr R Berks NHS Foundn Trust 02-10; Hd Past Care W Middx Univ Hosp NHS Trust from 10. *West Middlesex University Hospital, Twickenham Road, Isleworth TW7 6AF* Tel (020) 8560 2121

STABLES, Courtley Greenwood. b 13. Keble Coll Ox BA49 MA54. St Steph Ho Ox 48. **d** 50 **p** 51. C Watlington *Ox* 50-51; C Bracknell 51-55; Br Honduras 55-57; C Guildf H Trin w St Mary 57-61; Chapl Bedford Modern Sch 61-63; Sen Lect Coll of All SS Tottenham 63-72; Chmn Coun of Ch Schs Co 68-87; C St Andr Undershaft w St Mary Axe *Lon* 64-72; Hon C Uckfield *Chich* 72-94; rtd 78; Perm to Offic *Chich* from 94. *c/o Ms B J Simson, Walnut Barn, Queen Street, Keinton Mandeville, Somerton TA11 6EG*

STABLES, Katharine Ruth. b 45. R Holloway Coll Lon BA67. WMMTC 90. **d** 93 **p** 94. NSM Knutton *Lich* 93-05; NSM Silverdale and Alsagers Bank 93-96; Soc Resp Officer 96-99; Officer for NSMs 03-05; P-in-c Startforth and Bowes and Rokeby w Brignall *Ripon* 05-09; rtd 10; Perm to Offic *Dur* from 10. *15 Greenbank, Eggleston, Barnard Castle DL12 0BQ* Tel (01833) 650006 E-mail kruth@btopenworld.com

STACE, Michael John. b 44. Open Univ BA80. SEITE 94. **d** 97 **p** 98. NSM Cant St Dunstan w St Greg 97-01; NSM Cant All SS 01-06; P-in-c Harbledown from 06. *124 St Stephen's Road, Canterbury CT2 7JS* Tel (01227) 451169 Fax 455627 Mobile 07831-174900
E-mail michaelstace@btconnect.com

STACEY, Graham John. b 68. Lon Bible Coll BA97. Ripon Coll Cuddesdon 05. **d** 08 **p** 09. C Beedon and Peasemore w W Ilsley and Farnborough *Ox* 08-10; C E Downland 10-11. *The Vicarage, Church Street, Shipton-under-Wychwood, Chipping Norton OX7 6BP* Tel (01993) 830257 Mobile 07753-687389
E-mail graham@thestaceys.tv

STACEY, Helen Norman. Edin Univ MB, ChB45 PhD49. S'wark Ord Course 82. **dss** 83 **d** 87 **p** 94. Notting Hill St Jo and St Pet *Lon* 83-85; Upper Kennet *Sarum* 85-93; Hon Par Dn 87-93;

Perm to Offic 93-04. *Greystones House, Green Street, Avebury, Marlborough SN8 1RE* Tel (01672) 539289

STACEY, Mrs Kate Elizabeth. b 73. Lon Bible Coll BTh97. Ripon Coll Cuddesdon 05. **d** 08 **p** 09. C E Downland *Ox* from 08; V Shipton-under-Wychwood w Milton, Fifield etc from 11. *The Vicarage, Church Street, Shipton-under-Wychwood, Chipping Norton OX7 6BP* Tel (01993) 830257
E-mail kate@wychwoodbenefice.org.uk

STACEY, La. *See* STACEY, Mrs Rosalind Ruth

STACEY, Nicolas David. b 27. St Edm Hall Ox BA51 MA55. Cuddesdon Coll 51. **d** 53 **p** 54. C Portsea N End St Mark *Portsm* 53-58; Bp's Dom Chapl *Birm* 58-59; R Woolwich St Mary w H Trin *S'wark* 59-68; Borough Dean Greenwich 65-68; Dep Dir Oxfam 68-70; Perm to Offic *Ox* 68-71; P-in-c Selling *Cant* 76-78; Perm to Offic 79-84 and from 90; Six Preacher Cant Cathl 84-89; rtd 92. *The Old Vicarage, Selling, Faversham ME13 9RD* Tel (01227) 752833 Fax 752889 E-mail nicolas@nstacey.fsnet.co.uk

STACEY, Mrs Rosalind Ruth (La). b 54. New Hall Cam MA81 Bulmershe Coll of HE PGCE94. Ripon Coll Cuddesdon 09. **d** 11. C Easthampstead *Ox* from 11. *Magdalene House, Crowthorne Road, Bracknell RG12 7ER* Tel (01344) 428518
E-mail revlastacey@aol.com

STACEY (*née* O'BRIEN), Mrs Shelagh Ann. b 55. RGN83 Bedf Coll Lon BSc77. NOC 89. **d** 92 **p** 94. Par Dn S Elmsall *Wakef* 92-94; C 94-95; C Carleton 95-97; P-in-c 97-99; C E Hardwick 95-97; P-in-c 97-99; V Carleton and E Hardwick from 99. *The Vicarage, 10 East Close, Pontefract WF8 3NS* Tel (01977) 702478

STACEY, Timothy Andrew. b 58. Imp Coll Lon BSc79 York Univ PGCE83. St Jo Coll Nottm 94. **d** 94 **p** 95. C Chorleywood St Chis *St Alb* 94-99; P-in-c Chalfont St Giles *Ox* 99-08; R from 08; Chapl Bucks New Univ from 99. *The Rectory, 2 Deanway, Chalfont St Giles HP8 4JH* Tel (01494) 872097
E-mail t.ands.stacey@virgin.net *or* tstace01@bcuc.ac.uk

STACEY, Canon Victor George. b 44. NUI BA69 QUB MTh. CITC 72. **d** 72 **p** 73. C Derriaghy *Conn* 72-76; C Knock *D & D* 76-79; I Ballymacarrett St Martin 79-86; I Dublin Santry w Glasnevin *D & G* 86-95; Bp's Dom Chapl from 90; I Dun Laoghaire from 95; Prov and Dioc Registrar from 95; Preb Maynooth St Patr Cathl Dublin from 97. *Christ Church Vicarage, 2 Park Road, Dun Laoghaire, Co Dublin, Republic of Ireland* Tel (00353) (1) 280 9537

STACY, Christine Rosemary. b 49. UEA BSc70 Keswick Hall Coll PGCE71 Univ of Wales (Ban) MSc75 Northumbria Univ PhD94. **d** 10 **p** 11. OLM Upper Coquetdale *Newc* from 10. *Ovenstone, Sharperton, Morpeth NE65 7AT* Tel (01669) 640382
E-mail rosie.stacy@virgin.net

STAFF, Mrs Jean. b 44. CertEd64. EMMTC 81. **dss** 84 **d** 87 **p** 94. Old Brumby *Linc* 84-88; C 87-88; C Gainsborough St Geo 88-91; Dn-in-c 91-94; P-in-c 94-96; P-in-c Haxey 96-97; P-in-c Owston 96-97; V Haxey 97-04; V Owston 97-04; rtd 04. *5 South Furlong Croft, Epworth, Doncaster DN9 1GB* Tel (01427) 871422

STAFF, Susan. *See* JACKSON, Mrs Susan

STAFFORD, Christopher James. b 67. Birm Univ BSc88 PhD92. St Jo Coll Nottm MA98. **d** 99 **p** 00. C Westbrook St Phil *Liv* 99-03; R Newchurch w Croft from 03. *Newchurch Rectory, 17 Jackson Avenue, Culcheth, Warrington WA3 4ED* Tel (01925) 766300 E-mail cjstaff@surfaid.org

STAFFORD, David George. b 45. Qu Coll Birm 75. **d** 77 **p** 78. C Chesterfield St Aug *Derby* 77-80; C Ranmoor *Sheff* 80-83; V Bolton-upon-Dearne 83-11; rtd 11. *4 Rylestone Court, Sheffield S12 4NJ* Tel 0114-248 0993
E-mail davidstaffordbod@yahoo.co.uk

STAFFORD, Canon John Ingham Henry. b 31. TCD BA52 MA58. **d** 53 **p** 55. C Clonallon *D & D* 53-56; C Belfast Malone St Jo *Conn* 56-59; Australia 59-64; Min Can Down Cathl 64-68; Hd of S Ch Miss Ballymacarrett 68-73; I Bright w Killough 73-83; C Bangor Primacy 83-92; Can Down Cathl 90-92; I Urney w Sion Mills *D & R* 92-98; rtd 98. *14 Cleland Park North, Bangor BT20 3EN* Tel (028) 9145 6311 Mobile 07709-978874
E-mail jihstafford@btinternet.com

STAFFORD, Mark Anthony. b 64. Huddersfield Univ BSc92. St Jo Coll Nottm MA98. **d** 98 **p** 99. C Stafford St Jo and Tixall w Ingestre *Lich* 98-01; C W Retford *S'well* 01; TV Retford 02-09; P-in-c Babworth w Sutton-cum-Lound and Scofton etc 08-09. *Address temp unknown*

STAFFORD, Matthew Charles. b 73. Wilson Carlile Coll 94 Ripon Coll Cuddesdon 99. **d** 99 **p** 00. C High Wycombe *Ox* 99-02; P-in-c Wrockwardine Wood *Lich* 02-04; R Oakengates and Wrockwardine Wood from 04. *The New Rectory, Church Road, Wrockwardine Wood, Telford TF2 7AH* Tel (01952) 613865 Mobile 07981-380226 E-mail oranconall@aol.com

STAFFORD, Canon Richard William. b 46. Ringsent Tech Inst TCert69. CITC 96. **d** 99 **p** 00. NSM Annagh w Drumgoon, Ashfield etc *K, E & A* 99-07; P-in-c Drumgoon from 07; Can Kilmore Cathl from 08. *12 Cherrymount, Keadue Lane, Cavan, Co Cavan, Republic of Ireland* Tel (00353) (49) 437 1173 Mobile 87-240 4630 E-mail rwstafford@yahoo.com

STAFFORD, Area Bishop of. *See* ANNAS, The Rt Revd Geoffrey Peter

STAFFORD-WHITTAKER, William Paul. b 69. Chich Th Coll 91. **d** 94 **p** 95. C Brighton Resurr *Chich* 94-97; C Holborn St Alb w Saffron Hill St Pet *Lon* 97-02; V Stanwell from 02. *Stanwell Vicarage, 1 Lord Knyvett Close, Stanwell, Staines TW19 7PF* Tel (01784) 252044 E-mail vicar.stanwell@btinternet.com

STAGG, Jeremy Michael. b 47. Leeds Univ BSc69 Fontainebleau MBA77. Sarum & Wells Th Coll 90. **d** 92 **p** 93. C Basing *Win* 92-96; P-in-c Barton, Pooley Bridge and Martindale *Carl* 96-99; Hon CMS Rep 96-99; C Burgh-by-Sands and Kirkbampton w Kirkandrews etc *Carl* 99-00; C Barony of Burgh 00-01; P-in-c Distington 01-05; Dioc Past Sec 00-05; TR Cheswardine, Childs Ercall, Hales, Hinstock etc *Lich* 05-10; RD Hodnet 06-11; rtd 10. *27 Fishers Lock, Newport TF10 7ST* Tel (01952) 813735

STAGG, Canon Michael Hubert. b 39. St Chad's Coll Dur 58. **d** 63 **p** 64. C Weston-super-Mare St Sav *B & W* 63-66; P-in-c Fosdyke *Linc* 66-71; R Brompton Regis w Upton and Skilgate *B & W* 71-78; P-in-c Kidderminster St Jo *Worc* 78-80; P-in-c Cannington *B & W* 80-84; R Cannington, Otterhampton, Combwich and Stockland 84-87; Dioc Communications Officer *Nor* 88-93; Bp's Chapl 88-93; R Sprowston w Beeston 93-01; P-in-c Nor St Andr 01-04; P-in-c Nor St Geo Colegate 01-04; RD Nor N 95-04; Hon Can Nor Cathl 98-04; rtd 05; Perm to Offic *Nor* from 05. *31 Ash Grove, Norwich NR3 4BE* Tel (01603) 444549 E-mail michaelstagg@waitrose.com

STAGG, Roy Ernest. b 48. **d** 01 **p** 02. OLM Birchington w Acol and Minnis Bay *Cant* 01-04; OLM St Laur in Thanet 04-05. *7 Minster Road, Acol, Birchington CT7 0JB* Tel (01843) 841551 Mobile 07802-406066 E-mail roystagg@hotmail.co.uk

STAGG, Russell James. b 69. SEITE 08. **d** 11. C Haggerston St Chad *Lon* from 11. *72 St Augustine's Road, Belvedere DA17 5HH* Tel (01322) 476195 Mobile 07834-735002
E-mail father.russell@rjstagg.co.uk

STAINER, David John. b 58. RCM BMus80. St Mellitus Coll BA11. **d** 11. NSM Collier Row St Jas and Havering-atte-Bower *Chelmsf* from 11. *29 Cormorant Walk, Hornchurch RM12 5HE* Tel (01708) 550053 Mobile 07870-820314
E-mail davidjstainer@hotmail.co.uk

STAINER, Helene Lindsay. b 59. SWMTC 01. **d** 04 **p** 05. NSM Ivybridge w Harford *Ex* 04-09; P-in-c Milverton w Halse and Fitzhead *B & W* 09-10; R Milverton w Halse, Fitzhead and Ash Priors from 10. *The Vicarage, Parsonage Lane, Milverton, Taunton TA4 1LR* Tel (01823) 400305
E-mail helene_stainer@aol.com

STAINER, Richard Bruce. b 62. Anglia Ruskin Univ MA09. Linc Th Coll 92. **d** 94 **p** 95. C N Walsham w Antingham *Nor* 94-97; R Cogenhoe and Gt and Lt Houghton w Brafield *Pet* from 97; RD Wootton 01-07. *The Rectory, Church Street, Cogenhoe, Northampton NN7 1LS* Tel and fax (01604) 891166
E-mail richard.stainer123@btinternet.com

STAINES, Edward Noel. b 26. Trin Coll Ox BA48 BSc49 MA52 MSc85. Chich Th Coll 51 57. **d** 57 **p** 58. C Eastbourne St Mary *Chich* 57-61; V Amberley w N Stoke 61-70; V Forest Row 70-75; V Bexhill St Aug 75-79; TR Ovingdean w Rottingdean and Woodingdean 79-85; V Rottingdean 85-86; Chapl Gtr Lisbon *Eur* 88; Chapl Marseille 90; rtd 90; Perm to Offic *Worc* 86-09. *16 Conningsby Drive, Pershore WR10 1QX* Tel (01386) 554382

STAINES, Michael John. b 28. Trin Coll Ox BA52 MA56. Wells Th Coll 62. **d** 64 **p** 65. C Southwick St Mich *Chich* 64-67; TV Harling Gp *Nor* 67-73; P Missr S Chilterns Gp *Ox* 74-75; R W Wycombe w Bledlow Ridge, Bradenham and Radnage 76-93; RD Wycombe 83-87; rtd 93; Perm to Offic *Heref* from 93 and *Worc* 93-06. *The Old Forge, Lyonshall, Kington HR5 3JW, or PO Box 28077, Kitwe, Zambia* Tel (01544) 340013

STAINSBY, Alan. b 48. NEOC 01. **d** 04 **p** 05. NSM Hart w Elwick Hall *Dur* 04-06; NSM Haswell, Shotton and Thornley from 06. *6 Church View, Shotton Colliery, Durham DH6 2YD* Tel 0191-526 5200 E-mail astainsbyshotton@aol.com

STALEY, Andrew. b 50. Rhode Is Univ BA83. Westcott Ho Cam 01. **d** 04 **p** 05. C Bridport *Sarum* 04-08; TV Nadder Valley from 08. *The Rectory, Park Road, Tisbury, Salisbury SP3 6LF* Tel (01747) 870312 E-mail rev.staley@googlemail.com

STALEY, John Colin George. b 44. Hull Univ MA83. Wycliffe Hall Ox 68. **d** 71 **p** 72. C Tinsley *Sheff* 71-73; C Slaithwaite w E Scammonden *Wakef* 73-75; V Wakef St Andr and St Mary 75-80; Warden Scargill Ho 80-82; P-in-c Macclesfield St Pet *Ches* 82-85; TV Macclesfield Team 85-99; Sen Ind Chapl 86-99; Hon Ind Chapl 99-02. *Greenhills, Swanscoe, Rainow, Macclesfield SK10 5SZ* Tel (01625) 421296 Mobile 07824-736383
E-mail jjstaley@hotmail.co.uk

STALKER, Harry. b 47. **d** 04 **p** 05. OLM Felixstowe SS Pet and Paul *St E* from 04. *2 Ascot Drive, Felixstowe IP11 9DW* Tel (01394) 210536 Mobile 07710-221275
E-mail aitchess@clara.net

STALKER, William John. b 49. NOC 89. **d** 91 **p** 92. C Formby H Trin *Liv* 91-94; V Stoneycroft All SS 94-03; Chapl R Liv Univ Hosp NHS Trust 94-03; P-in-c Lowton St Mary *Liv* from 03. *The Vicarage, 1 Barford Drive, Lowton, Warrington WA3 1DD* Tel (01942) 607705

STALLARD, John Charles. b 34. Selw Coll Cam BA58 MA62. Ripon Hall Ox 62. **d** 64 **p** 65. C Hall Green Ascension *Birm* 64-66; C Sutton Coldfield H Trin 66-68; C-in-c Brandwood CD 68-71; Chapl Dame Allan's Schs Newc 71-74; V Warley Woods *Birm* 75-84; TR Droitwich *Worc* 84-87; P-in-c Dodderhill 84-87; TR Droitwich Spa 87-94; V Pensnett 94-00; rtd 00; Perm to Offic *St D* 00-07. *Craigievar, Abbey Road, Llangollen LL20 8SN* Tel (01978) 860654 E-mail greengates@breathemail.net

STALLARD, Canon Mary Kathleen Rose. b 67. Selw Coll Cam BA88 Lon Inst of Educn PGCE90. Qu Coll Birm 91. **d** 93 **p** 97. C Newport St Matt *Mon* 93-96; P-in-c Ysbyty Cynfyn w Llantrisant and Eglwys Newydd *St D* 96-97; V 97-02; Min Can and Chapl St As Cathl 02-03; Can Res from 03; Dir of Ords and Co-ord of Minl Formation from 10. *The Vicarage, Abbey Road, Llangollen LL20 8SN* Tel (01978) 860231

STALLEY, Brian Anthony. b 38. Oak Hill Th Coll 60. **d** 63 **p** 64. C Summerstown *S'wark* 63-70; Surrey BFBS Sec 70-73; Manager Action Cen BFBS 73-76; R Branston *Linc* 76-91; rtd 91; Perm to Offic *Linc* from 91. *6 Sunningdale Grove, Washingborough, Lincoln LN4 1SP* Tel (01522) 794164 Fax 794663 Mobile 07941-508445 E-mail brian@bstalley.freeserve.co.uk

STAMFORD, Brian. b 37. **d** 91 **p** 92. CMS Uganda 88-95; P-in-c North Hill and Lewannick *Truro* 95-03; P-in-c Altarnon w Bolventor, Laneast and St Clether 03-07; rtd 07; Perm to Offic *Pet* from 08. *2 William Dalby House, South Street, Oakham LE15 6HY* Tel (01572) 723493 E-mail brianstamford@btopenworld.com

STAMFORD, Dean of. Vacant

STAMP, Andrew Nicholas. b 44. Ex Univ BA67. Sarum Th Coll 67. **d** 69 **p** 70. C S Beddington St Mich *S'wark* 69-73; Tutor Sarum & Wells Th Coll 73-76; Chapl RN 76-81; C-in-c W Leigh CD *Portsm* 81-82; V W Leigh 82-87; R Botley 87-95; V Curdridge and R Durley 94-95; P-in-c Compton, the Mardens, Stoughton and Racton *Chich* 95-08; P-in-c Stansted 95-08; Dioc Rural Officer *Chich* 00-08; rtd 08; Hon C Arlington, Berwick, Selmeston w Alciston etc *Chich* from 11. *The Vicarage, The Street, Wilmington, Polegate BN26 5SL* E-mail revastamp@aol.com

STAMP, Canon Ian Jack. b 47. Aston Tr Scheme 82 NOC 83. **d** 86 **p** 87. C Tonge w Alkrington *Man* 86-89; V Heywood St Marg 89-98; P-in-c Heywood St Luke w All So 96-98; TR Heywood 98-01; V Bury St Jo w St Mark 01-10; V Walmersley Road, Bury from 10; Borough Dean Bury from 10; Hon Can Man Cathl from 11. *St John's Vicarage, 270 Walmersley Road, Bury BL9 6NH* Tel and fax 0161-764 3412 E-mail ianstamp@tiscali.co.uk

STAMP, Philip Andrew. b 53. Linc Th Coll 86. **d** 88 **p** 89. C Barton w Peel Green *Man* 88-91; R Blackley H Trin from 91; P-in-c Lightbowne from 04. *Holy Trinity Rectory, Goodman Street, Manchester M9 4BW* Tel 0161-205 2879

STAMP, Richard Mark. b 36. St Chad's Coll Dur BA60. **d** 62 **p** 63. Australia 62-69 and from 72; C Greenhill St Jo *Lon* 69-72; rtd 01. *127 Hilda Drive, RMB Ravenswood, Harcourt Vic 3453, Australia* Tel and fax (0061) (3) 5435 3576 E-mail stamp@netcon.net.au

STAMPS, Canon Dennis Lee. b 55. Biola Univ (USA) BA78 Trin Evang Div Sch (USA) MDiv83 MA87 Dur Univ PhD95. Westcott Ho Cam 90. **d** 92 **p** 93. C Moseley St Mary *Birm* 92-96; Dir WMMTC 96-01; Dean Qu Coll Birm 01-02; Can Res St Alb from 02; Minl Development Officer from 02; Dir Min from 11. *7 Corder Close, St Albans AL3 4NH* Tel (01727) 841116 E-mail dstampsuk@aol.com

✠STANAGE, The Rt Revd Thomas Shaun. b 32. Pemb Coll Ox BA56 MA60 Nashotah Ho Wisconsin Hon DD86. Cuddesdon Coll 56. **d** 58 **p** 59 c 78. C Gt Crosby St Faith *Liv* 58-61; Min Orford St Andr CD 61-63; V Orford St Andr 63-70; S Africa from 70; Dean Kimberley 75-78; Suff Bp Johannesburg 78-82; Bp Bloemfontein 82-97; rtd 97; Acting Lect Th Univ of the Free State from 97. *PO Box 13598, Noordstad, Bloemfontein, 9301 South Africa* Tel (0027) (51) 436 7282

STANBRIDGE, The Ven Leslie Cyril. b 20. St Jo Coll Dur BA47 MA54. **d** 49 **p** 50. C Erith St Jo *Roch* 49-51; Tutor St Jo Coll Dur 51-55; Chapl 52-55; V Kingston upon Hull St Martin *York* 55-64; R Cottingham 64-72; Can and Preb York Minster 68-00; Succ Canonicorum from 88; RD Hull 70-72; Adn York 72-88; rtd 88; Perm to Offic *York* from 00. *39 Lucombe Way, New Earswick, York YO32 4DS* Tel (01904) 750812

✠STANCLIFFE, The Rt Revd David Staffurth. b 42. Trin Coll Ox BA65 MA68 Lambeth DD04. Cuddesdon Coll 65. **d** 67 **p** 68 c 93. C Armley St Bart *Ripon* 67-70; Chapl Clifton Coll Bris 70-77; Dir of Ords and Can Res Portsm Cathl 77-82; Provost Portsm 82-93; Bp Sarum 93-10; rtd 10; Hon Asst Bp Eur from 11. *Butts House, 15 The Butts, Stanhope, Bishop Auckland DL13 2UQ* Tel (01388) 526912 E-mail david.stancliffe@hotmail.com

STAND, Andrew George. b 68. St Jo Coll Dur BA06. Cranmer Hall Dur 04. **d** 06 **p** 07. C Bromsgrove St Jo *Worc* 06-09; TV Gornal and Sedgley from 09. *The Vicarage, 35 Eve Lane, Dudley DY1 3TY* Tel (01902) 883467

STANDEN, David Charles. b 68. K Coll Lon BA91 AKC91 PGCE92 Lon Univ PhD00. Westcott Ho Cam 01. **d** 03 **p** 04. C Prittlewell *Chelmsf* 03-07; P-in-c Stratton and Launcells *Truro* 07-11; P-in-c Bude Haven and Marhamchurch 09-11; R Edin St Mich and All SS from 11. *The Rectory, 203 Gilmore Place, Edinburgh EH3 9PN* Tel 0131-229 6368 E-mail d.c.standen@btinternet.com

STANDEN, Mark Jonathan. b 63. LMH Ox BA85 Cam Univ BA94 Barrister 86. Ridley Hall Cam 92. **d** 95 **p** 96. C Sevenoaks St Nic *Roch* 95-99; R Angmering *Chich* from 99; RD Arundel and Bognor from 08. *The Rectory, Rectory Lane, Angmering, Littlehampton BN16 4JU* Tel (01903) 784979

STANDEN McDOUGAL, Canon John Anthony Phelps. b 33. AKC58. **d** 59 **p** 60. C Ipswich St Marg *St E* 59-63; C Bury St Edmunds St Mary 63-65; C Wadhurst *Chich* 65-70; C Tidebrook 65-70; R Tollard Royal w Farnham *Sarum* 70-81; P-in-c Gussage St Michael and Gussage All Saints 71-76; R 76-81; RD Milton and Blandford 81-86; R Tollard Royal w Farnham, Gussage St Michael etc 82-86; Can and Preb Sarum Cathl 86-94; TR Bride Valley 86-94; rtd 94; Perm to Offic *Sarum* from 94. *Silverbridge Cottage, North Chideock, Bridport DT6 6LG* Tel (01297) 489408

STANDING, Victor. b 44. Lon Univ BMus66 FRCO67 Clare Coll Cam CertEd68. Ripon Coll Cuddesdon 75. **d** 78 **p** 79. C Wimborne Minster *Sarum* 78-80; TV Wimborne Minster and Holt 80-83; R Ex St Sidwell and St Matt 83-94; Dep PV Ex Cathl 83-01; Chapl R Devon and Ex Hosp 83-94; Chapl W of England Eye Infirmary Ex 83-94; P-in-c Tedburn St Mary, Whitestone, Oldridge etc *Ex* 94-96; P-in-c Dunsford and Doddiscombsleigh 95-96; P-in-c Cheriton Bishop 95-96; R Tedburn St Mary, Whitestone, Oldridge etc 96-01; RD Kenn 97-01; V New Shoreham *Chich* from 01; V Old Shoreham from 01; rtd 11; P-in-c Shanklin St Blasius *Portsm* from 11. *St Blasius Rectory, Rectory Road, Shanklin PO37 6NX* E-mail victorstanding@tiscali.co.uk

STANDISH, Derrick Edgar. b 41. Univ of Wales (Lamp) BA67. Wycliffe Hall Ox 68. **d** 68 **p** 69. C Brynmawr *S & B* 68-69; C Morriston 69-74; V Merthyr Cynog and Dyffryn Honddu 74-76; R Llanwenarth Ultra *Mon* 76-83; V Abersychan and Garndiffaith 83-91. *7 Intermediate Road, Brynmawr, Ebbw Vale NP23 4SF* Tel (01495) 312183

STANDRING, Rupert Benjamin Charles. b 68. Pemb Coll Ox BA90 MA99 Cam Univ BA94. Ridley Hall Cam 92. **d** 95 **p** 96. C Bromley Ch Ch *Roch* 95-99; Tutor Cornhill Tr Course 99-04; Hon C W Hampstead St Luke *Lon* 99-04; Perm to Offic 04-05; Min Mayfair Ch Ch 05-09; Lic Preacher 09-10; P-in-c Fulham St Pet from 10. *56 Langthorne Street, London SW6 6JY* Tel (020) 7385 4950 E-mail rupert.standring@googlemail.com

STANES, The Ven Ian Thomas. b 39. Sheff Univ BSc62 Linacre Coll Ox BA65 MA69. Wycliffe Hall Ox 63. **d** 65 **p** 66. C Leic H Apostles 65-69; V Broom Leys 69-76; Warden Marrick Priory *Ripon* 76-82; Officer Miss, Min and Evang Willesden Area *Lon* 82-92; CME Officer 82-92; Preb St Paul's Cathl 89-92; Adn Loughborough *Leic* 92-05; rtd 05. *192 Bath Road, Bradford-on-Avon BA15 1SP* Tel (01225) 309036

STANESBY, Derek Malcolm. b 31. Leeds Univ BA56 Man Univ MEd75 PhD84 SOSc. Coll of Resurr Mirfield 56. **d** 58 **p** 59. C Lakenham St Jo *Nor* 58-61; C Welling *S'wark* 61-63; V Bury St Mark *Man* 63-67; R Ladybarn 67-85; Can and Steward Windsor 85-97; rtd 97; Perm to Office *Leic* from 00 and *Pet* 00-07. *32 Elizabeth Way, Uppingham, Oakham LE15 9PQ* Tel (01572) 821298

STANFORD, Emma Joanne. b 72. Qu Coll Birm. **d** 11. C Wordsley *Worc* from 11. *St Clare's House, 1 Denleigh Road, Kingswinford DY6 8QB* Tel (01384) 359443

STANFORD, Canon Mark Roger. b 59. Cranmer Hall Dur 96. **d** 98 **p** 99. C Aughton Ch Ch *Liv* 98-02; TV Toxteth St Philemon w St Gabr and St Cleopas 02-11; TR from 11; AD Toxteth and Wavertree from 06; Hon Can Liv Cathl from 06; Chapl St Hilda's Priory and Sch Whitby from 03. *St Philemon's Vicarage, 40 Devonshire Road, Princes Park, Liverpool L8 3TZ* Tel 0151-727 1248 E-mail mark@stphilemons.org.uk

STANFORD, Timothy Charles. b 61. **d** 11. C Walton Breck *Liv* from 11. *Holy Trinity Vicarage, Richmond Park, Liverpool L6 5AD* Tel 0151-263 1538

STANGHAN, Eileen. b 40. Whitelands Coll Lon CertEd75. **d** 98 **p** 99. OLM Reigate St Phil *S'wark* 98-10; Perm to Office from 10. *20 Saxon Way, Reigate RH2 9DH* Tel (01737) 240920 *or* (01293) 430043

STANIER, Robert Sebastian. b 75. Magd Coll Ox BA98 Selw Coll Cam BA05. Westcott Ho Cam 03. **d** 06 **p** 07. C Perry Hill St Geo w Ch Ch and St Paul *S'wark* 06-09; Chapl Abp Tenison's Sch Kennington from 09; Hon C N Lambeth *S'wark* from 09. *28 Oval Mansions, Kennington Oval, London SE11 5SQ* Tel (020) 7627 3792 E-mail robertstanier@btinternet.com

STANIFORD, Canon Doris Gwendoline. b 43. Gilmore Course IDC79. **dss** 80 **d** 87 **p** 94. Hangleton *Chich* 80-82; Durrington 82-89; Par Dn 87-89; Chich Th Coll 83-89; C Crawley and Chapl Crawley Gen Hosp 89-97; Dioc Voc Adv and Chapl St Cath

Hospice 92-97; Asst Dir of Ords *Chich* from 97; C Southwick St Mich 97-99; TV Ifield from 99; Can and Preb Chich Cathl from 08. *St Alban's Vicarage, Gossops Drive, Crawley RH11 8LD* Tel (01293) 529848

STANIFORTH, Julian Martin. b 59. Aston Univ BSc82 MCIMA93. SEITE 07. **d** 10 **p** 11. C Herne *Cant* from 10. *69B Herne Bay Road, Whitstable CT5 2LP* Tel (01227) 639895 Mobile 07879-626115 E-mail julian.staniforth@gmail.com

STANLEY, Arthur Patrick. b 32. TCD BA54 Div Test55 MA64. **d** 55 **p** 56. C Waterford H Trin *C & O* 55-57; CF 58-74; Dep Asst Chapl Gen 74-83; USA 84-04; rtd 94; Perm to Offic *B & W* from 05. *10 Knights Court, Keyford, Frome BA11 1JD* Tel (01373) 301694 E-mail patnpaddy@hotmail.com

STANLEY, Baden Thomas. b 68. TCD BA91. CITC BTh94. **d** 94 **p** 95. C Seapatrick *D & D* 94-98; I Bray *D & G* from 98. *The Rectory, Church Road, Bray, Co Wicklow, Republic of Ireland* Tel and fax (00353) (1) 286 2968 Mobile 87-948 4407 E-mail christchurchbray@gmail.com

STANLEY, Canon John Alexander. b 31. OBE99. Tyndale Hall Bris. **d** 56 **p** 57. C Preston All SS *Blackb* 56-60; C St Helens St Mark *Liv* 60-63; V Everton St Cuth 63-70; P-in-c Everton St Sav 69-70; V Everton St Sav w St Cuth 70-74; V Huyton St Mich from 74; Hon Can Liv Cathl from 87; AD Huyton 89-02; Chapl to The Queen 93-01. *The Vicarage, Bluebell Lane, Liverpool L36 7SA* Tel 0151-449 3900 Fax 480 6002 Mobile 07740-621833 E-mail huytonchurch@btconnect.com

STANLEY, Mrs Nicola Vere. b 56. Surrey Univ BA07 MCIPD83. STETS 99. **d** 02 **p** 03. C Bedford Park *Lon* 02-06; V Twickenham All Hallows from 06; Asst Dir of Ords Kensington Area from 04. *All Hallows' Vicarage, 138 Chertsey Road, Twickenham TW1 1EW* Tel (020) 8892 1322 E-mail nvs@mosaicpublishing.co.uk

STANLEY, Patrick. See STANLEY, Arthur Patrick

STANLEY, Canon Simon Richard. b 44. Wells Th Coll 66. **d** 69 **p** 70. C Foleshill St Laur *Cov* 69-71; C Hessle *York* 71-75; P-in-c Flamborough 75-80; R Dunnington 80-92; P-in-c York St Barn 92-99; P-in-c York St Chad 99-09; P-in-c York All SS Pavement w St Crux and St Mich 03-09; P-in-c York St Denys 04-09; Can and Preb York Minster from 05; Relig Progr Producer BBC Radio York 94-03; rtd 09; NSM York St Chad from 09. *St Chad's Vicarage, 36 Campleshon Road, York YO23 1EY* Tel (01904) 674524 Mobile 07946-466364 E-mail simonstanley@clara.net

STANLEY-SMITH, James. b 29. Hatf Coll Dur BA54 DipEd55. S Dios Minl Tr Scheme 81. **d** 84 **p** 85. C Bournemouth St Jo w St Mich *Win* 84-87; R Hale w S Charford 87-94; rtd 94; Perm to Offic *Win* from 94. *10 Rownhams Way, Rownhams, Southampton SO16 8AE* Tel (023) 8073 2529 E-mail jstanley-smith@cwcom.net

STANNARD, Miss Beryl Elizabeth. b 36. SRN62 SCM64. Oak Hill Th Coll BA92. **d** 92 **p** 94. Par Dn Streatham Park St Alb *S'wark* 92-94; C 94-96; C Gerrards Cross and Fulmer *Ox* 96-01; rtd 01; Perm to Offic *Ox* from 02. *20 Wey Lane, Chesham HP5 1JH* Tel (01494) 774715

STANNARD, Brian. b 46. MICE71 MIStructE71. Cranmer Hall Dur 86. **d** 88 **p** 89. C Burnage St Marg *Man* 88-91; V Walmersley 91-03; TV Westhoughton and Wingates 03-04; rtd 04. *63 Portland Street, Southport PR8 5AF* Tel (01704) 534632 E-mail brian@stannardrev.fsnet.co.uk

STANNARD, The Ven Colin Percy. b 24. TD66. Selw Coll Cam BA47 MA49. Linc Th Coll 47. **d** 49 **p** 50. C St E Cathl 49-52; C-in-c Nunsthorpe CD *Linc* 52-55; CF (TA) 53-67; V Barrow St Jas *Carl* 55-64; V Upperby St Jo 64-70; R Gosforth 70-75; RD Calder 70-75; P-in-c Natland 75-76; V 76-84; RD Kendal 75-84; Hon Can Carl Cathl 75-84; Can Res Carl Cathl 84-93; Adn Carl 84-93; rtd 93; Perm to Offic *Carl* from 93. *51 Longlands Road, Carlisle CA3 9AE* Tel (01228) 538584

STANNARD, Canon Peter Graville. b 59. Univ of Wales (Abth) BSc(Econ)81. St Steph Ho Ox BA85 MA86. **d** 86 **p** 87. C Worksop Priory *S'well* 86-89; Prin St Nic Th Coll Ghana 89-96; Hon Can Koforidua from 93; TR Shelf w Buttershaw St Aid *Bradf* 96-99; P-in-c Heaton Norris St Thos *Man* 00-02; TV Heatons 02-08; P-in-c S Shields St Hilda w St Thos *Dur* from 08; P-in-c S Shields St Aid and St Steph from 08. *40 Lawe Road, South Shields NE33 2EU* Tel 0191-454 1414 E-mail frpeter@blueyonder.co.uk

STANNING (*née* CROMPTON), **Mrs Gillian Kay.** b 65. Univ of Wales (Ban) BA86 Homerton Coll Cam PGCE87. SNWTP 07. **d** 10 **p** 11. C Norley, Crowton and Kingsley *Ches* from 10. *Fullwood, Blakemere Lane, Norley, Frodsham WA6 6NS* Tel (01928) 788623 Mobile 07840-627725 E-mail g.stanning@btinternet.com

STANTON, Ms Angela. b 59. Loughb Univ BSc80 Ch Coll Liv PGCE81. Westcott Ho Cam 03. **d** 05 **p** 06. C Atherton and Hindsford w Howe Bridge *Man* 05-08; P-in-c Reddish from 08; Hon Assoc Dioc Dir of Ords from 10. *St Elisabeth's Rectory, 28 Bedford Street, Stockport SK5 6DJ* Tel 0161-432 3033 E-mail angiestanton27@yahoo.co.uk

STANTON, Miss Barbara. b 51. Whitelands Coll Lon TCert72 Lon Univ BD86. WMMTC 89. **d** 92 **p** 94. NSM Hinckley St Mary *Leic* 92-97; P-in-c Husbands Bosworth w Mowsley and Knaptoft etc 97-06; P-in-c Arnesby w Shearsby and Bruntingthorpe 02-06; Bp's Ecum Adv 97-03; Dioc Rural Officer 03-06; R Bildeston w Wattisham and Lindsey, Whatfield etc *St E* from 06. *7 Chamberlin Close, Bildeston, Ipswich IP7 7EZ* Tel (01449) 744190 E-mail barbarastanton@supanet.com

STANTON, Canon David John. b 60. St Andr Univ MTheol82 Exic Univ MA00 FSAScot89 FRSA98. Ripon Coll Cuddesdon 83. **d** 85 **p** 86. C Beckenham St Geo *Roch* 85-88; Asst Chapl Shrewsbury Sch 88-90; Hon C Shrewsbury All SS w St Mich *Lich* 88-90; P-in-c Abbotskerswell *Ex* 90-94; Chapl Plymouth Univ 92-97; P-in-c Bovey Tracey St Jo, Chudleigh Knighton etc 94-99; V Bovey Tracey St Jo w Heathfield 99-05; Dioc Voc Adv 95-05; Warden of Readers 96-03; Acting Dioc Dir of Ords 03-05; RD Moreton 98-05; Can Prec and Can Past Worc Cathl from 05. *15A College Green, Worcester WR1 2LH* Tel (01905) 732940 Fax 29119 E-mail davidstanton@worcestercathedral.org.uk

STANTON, Gregory John. b 47. Sarum & Wells Th Coll 84. **d** 86 **p** 87. C Willenhall H Trin *Lich* 86-89; C Plympton St Mary *Ex* 89-91; V Milton Abbot, Dunterton, Lamerton etc from 91. *The Vicarage, The Parade, Milton Abbot, Tavistock PL19 0NZ* Tel (01822) 612732 E-mail gjstanton31@hotmail.com

STANTON, John Maurice. b 18. Univ Coll Ox BA45 MA45. Wycliffe Hall Ox 51. **d** 52 **p** 53. C Tonbridge SS Pet and Paul *Roch* 52-54; Hd Master Blundell's Sch Tiverton 59-71; Public Preacher *Ex* 71-72; C Ex St Matt 72-73; R Chesham Bois *Ox* 73-83; rtd 83; Perm to Offic *Ox* from 83. *16 Emden House, Barton Lane, Headington OX3 9JU* Tel (01865) 765206

STANTON, Miss Julie Elizabeth. b 59. Matlock Coll of Educn CertEd80. EMMTC 00. **d** 03 **p** 04. NSM Matlock Bath and Cromford *Derby* 03-11. *35 Intake Lane, Cromford, Matlock DE4 3RH* Tel (01629) 822653 Fax 760903 Mobile 07769-748276 E-mail revjs@hotmail.com

STANTON, Ms Karen Janis. b 55. NOC 00. **d** 03 **p** 04. C Withington St Paul *Man* 03-04; C Urmston 04-07; TV Wythenshawe from 07. *St Luke's Vicarage, Brownley Road, Manchester M22 4PT* Tel 0161-998 2071 Mobile 07814-254744 E-mail kaz@thestantons.me.uk

STANTON, Thomas Hugh (Timothy). b 17. Trin Coll Cam BA38 MA45. Coll of Resurr Mirfield 46. **d** 47 **p** 48. C Camberwell St Geo *S'wark* 47-49; CR from 52; S Africa 54-87; rtd 87; Perm to Offic *Wakef* from 07. *House of the Resurrection, Stocks Bank Road, Mirfield WF14 0BN* Tel (01924) 494318

STANTON-HYDE, Mrs Marjorie Elizabeth. b 37. TCert58. Cranmer Hall Dur 86. **d** 88 **p** 94. Par Dn Elmley Lovett w Hampton Lovett and Elmbridge etc *Worc* 88-91; Par Dn Wilden 88-91; Par Dn Hartlebury 88-91; Dn-in-c 91-94; P-in-c 94-97; R Jes Hosp Cant 02-05; Chapl Worcs Community and Mental Health Trust from 05. *4 Severn Drive, Malvern WR14 2SZ* Tel (01684) 569589

STANTON-SARINGER, Maurice Charles. b 49. Bris Univ BSc71 PGCE72 Fitzw Coll Cam BA77 MA81. Ridley Hall Cam 75. **d** 78 **p** 79. C Gerrards Cross *Ox* 78-80; C Bletchley 80-83; Chapl Stowe Sch 83-91; R Sherington w Chicheley, N Crawley, Astwood etc *Ox* 91-06; RD Newport 95-04; TR Loddon Reach from 06. *The Vicarage, 12 The Manor, Shinfield, Reading RG2 9DP* Tel and fax 0118-988 3363 E-mail saringer@onetel.com

STANWAY, Peter David. b 48. K Coll Lon BD71. St Aug Coll Cant 72. **d** 73 **p** 74. C Maidstone All SS w St Phil and H Trin Cant 73-77; Canada 77-84; C Waterlooville *Portsm* 84-87; R Laughton w Ripe and Chalvington *Chich* 87-90; Chapl Witney Community Hosp 90-91; C Wheatley w Forest Hill and Stanton St John *Ox* 91-92; C Cowley St Jas 93-02; rtd 02. *22 Colleywood, Kennington, Oxford OX1 5NF* Tel (01865) 739342

STAPLE, Miss Patricia Ann. b 54. Birm Univ BA75. St Steph Ho Ox 00. **d** 02 **p** 05. C Dartmouth and Dittisham *Ex* 02-04; C Colyton, Musbury, Southleigh and Branscombe 04-07; V Athelney *B & W* from 07. *Athelney Rectory, Stoke Road, North Curry, Taunton TA3 6HN* Tel (01823) 490255 Mobile 07719-120908 E-mail tricia_staple@hotmail.com

STAPLEFORD, Robin Duncan. b 62. Aston Tr Scheme 92 St Jo Coll Nottm 94. **d** 96 **p** 97. C Evington *Leic* 96-99; TV Vale of Belvoir 00-08; R Upper Wensum Village Gp *Nor* from 08. *The Rectory, Market Hill, Colkirk, Fakenham NR21 7NU* Tel (01328) 864128 E-mail stapleford@tiscali.co.uk

STAPLES, David. b 35. Jes Coll Ox BA59 MA63 BD75. Linc Th Coll 59. **d** 61 **p** 62. C Kettering St Andr *Pet* 61-64; C Doncaster St Geo *Sheff* 64-66; Dioc Youth Chapl 66-71; V Mexborough 71-83; Chapl Montagu Hosp Mexborough 71-83; RD Wath *Sheff* 77-83; Hon Can Sheff Cathl 80-83; V W Haddon w Winwick *Pet* 83-88; RD Brixworth 83-89; V W Haddon w Winwick and Ravensthorpe 88-00; ACUPA Link Officer 90-00; rtd 00; Perm to Offic *Linc* from 00. *1 Sycamore Close, Bourne PE10 9RS* Tel (01778) 423121

STAPLES, Jeffrey Joseph. b 61. St Jo Coll Nottm 97. **d** 99 **p** 00. C Prenton *Ches* 99-03; P-in-c Wallasey St Nic 03-04; P-in-c New Brighton All SS 03-04; V Wallasey St Nic w All SS from 04. *St Nicholas' Vicarage, 22 Groveland Road, Wallasey CH45 8JY* Tel 0151-639 3589 E-mail jeffstaples4@hotmail.com

STAPLES, John Michael. b 45. STETS 94. **d** 97 **p** 98. C Tisbury *Sarum* 97-01; P-in-c Barford St Martin, Dinton, Baverstock etc 00-01; TV Nadder Valley 01-08; C Fovant, Sutton Mandeville and Teffont Evias etc 06-08; rtd 08. *Crabstone Cottage, Locarno Road, Swanage BH19 1HY* Tel (01929) 421421 E-mail john_staples@btinternet.com

STAPLES, John Wedgwood. b 42. Hertf Coll Ox BA64 MA. Wycliffe Hall Ox 64. **d** 66 **p** 67. C Yardley St Edburgha *Birm* 66-69; C Knowle 69-74; R Barcombe *Chich* 74-81; V Old Windsor *Ox* 81-96; P-in-c Pangbourne w Tidmarsh and Sulham 96-99; R 99-07; rtd 07. *6 Douglas Road, Bournemouth BH6 3ER* Tel (01202) 425859 E-mail revd_staples@yahoo.com

STAPLES, Peter. b 35. Jes Coll Ox BA59. Ripon Hall Ox 59. **d** 62 **p** 63. C Fairfield *Derby* 62-63; C Dore 63-66; C Wilne and Draycott w Breaston 66-71; The Netherlands from 72; Asst Chapl Utrecht w Zwolle *Eur* 94-08. *Doldersweg 39C, 3712 BN Huis Ter Heide, Utrecht, The Netherlands* Tel (0031) (30) 693 1928 Fax 253 3241

STAPLES, Canon Peter Brian. b 38. Bps' Coll Cheshunt 66. **d** 68 **p** 69. C Birkdale St Jas 68-71; C Sevenoaks St Jo *Roch* 71-74; V Treslothan *Truro* 74-80; V Truro St Paul and St Clem 80-02; Hon Can Truro Cathl 98-02; rtd 02; Perm to Offic *St E* from 03. *25 Osmund Walk, Bury St Edmunds IP33 3UU* Tel (01284) 760620

STAPLETON, The Very Revd Henry Edward Champnoys. b 32. MBE09. FSA74 Pemb Coll Cam BA54 MA58. Ely Th Coll 54. **d** 56 **p** 57. C York St Olave w St Giles 56-59; C Pocklington w Yapham-cum-Meltonby, Owsthorpe etc 59-61; R Seaton Ross w Everingham and Bielby and Harswell 61-67; RD Weighton 66-67; R Skelton by York 67-75; V Wroxham w Hoveton *Nor* 75-81; P-in-c Belaugh 76-81; Can Res and Prec Roch Cathl 81-88; Dean Carl 88-98; rtd 98; Perm to Offic *Wakef* from 98 and *York* from 03. *Rockland House, 20 Marsh Gardens, Honley, Huddersfield HD9 6AF* Tel (01484) 666629

STAPLETON, Leonard Charles. b 37. Chich Th Coll 75. **d** 77 **p** 78. C Crayford *Roch* 77-81; C Lamorbey H Redeemer 81-83; V Belvedere St Aug 83-89; V Beckenham St Jas 89-02; rtd 02; Perm to Offic *Roch* 03-04 and *Win* from 04. *14 Howlett Close, Lymington SO41 9LA* Tel (01590) 679414

STAPLETON, Robert Michael Vorley. b 25. ALCD51. **d** 51 **p** 52. C Plymouth St Andr *Ex* 51-56; Chapl RN 56-60; C Surbiton St Matt *S'wark* 60-64; R Chenies and Lt Chalfont *Ox* 64-87; P-in-c Latimer w Flaunden 86-87; R Chenies and Lt Chalfont, Latimer and Flaunden 87-92; rtd 92. *Woodside, Swannaton Road, Dartmouth TQ6 9RL* Tel (01803) 832972

STAPLETON, Robert Vauvelle. b 47. St Jo Coll Dur BA70. Cranmer Hall Dur. **d** 71 **p** 72. C Moreton *Ches* 71-73; C Monkwearmouth All SS *Dur* 73-76; C Stranton 76-79; P-in-c Kelloe 79-86; V New Shildon 86-96; R Stoke Albany w Wilbarston and Ashley etc *Pet* 96-04; P-in-c Somborne w Ashley *Win* from 04; Dioc Rural Officer from 04. *The New Vicarage, Romsey Road, Kings Somborne, Stockbridge SO20 6PR* Tel (01794) 388223 E-mail robertstapleton@hotmail.com

STARBUCK, Francis Tony. b 36. Kelham Th Coll 57. **d** 61 **p** 62. C Mansfield St Mark *S'well* 61-63; C Clifton H Trin CD 63-64; C Didcot *Ox* 67-71; P Missr California CD 71-75; R Barkham 74-75; V Hagbourne 75-82; V Maidenhead St Luke 82-87; V Te Puke St Jo New Zealand 87-96; Can Waiapu 90-94; V Clevedon All So 96-01; rtd 01; Chapl Selwyn Oaks Papakura from 01. *16 Selwyn Oaks, 21 Youngs Road, Papakura 2110, New Zealand*

STARES, Canon Brian Maurice William. b 44. St Deiniol's Hawarden 74. **d** 74 **p** 75. C Risca *Mon* 74-77; V Newport St Steph and H Trin 77-87; V Fleur-de-Lis 87-92; Chapl HM Pris Belmarsh 92-93; Chapl HM YOI Dover 93-98; Feltham 98-99; V Bishton *Mon* 99-09; Hon Can St Woolos Cathl 07-09; rtd 09. *25 Verona Court, Myers Lane, London SE14 5RX*

STARES, Mrs Olive Beryl. b 33. Sarum Th Coll 83. **dss** 86 **d** 87 **p** 94. Crofton *Portsm* 86-87; Hon C 87-01; rtd 01. *62 Mancroft Avenue, Hill Head, Fareham PO14 2DD* Tel (01329) 668540

STARK, Mrs Beverley Ann. b 52. Bp Otter Coll CertEd73 EMMTC 92. **d** 92 **p** 94. Par Dn Bulwell St Jo *S'well* 92-97; TV Bestwood 97-03; V Bestwood Em w St Mark 03-04; R Ironstone Villages *Leic* from 04; RD Framland 06-11. *The Rectory, 23 Melton Road, Waltham on the Wolds, Melton Mowbray LE14 4AJ* Tel (01664) 464600 E-mail beverley.stark@ntlworld.com

STARK, John Jordan. b 40. Hull Univ BA62. St Chad's Coll Dur. **d** 64 **p** 65. C Buxton *Derby* 64-67; C Wolborough w Newton Abbot *Ex* 67-74; R Belstone 74-79; P-in-c Plymouth St Gabr 79-80; V 80-10; rtd 10. *11 Warwick Orchard Close, Plymouth PL5 3NZ* Tel (01752) 787132

STARK, Margaret Alison. b 46. Univ of Wales BA70 BA71. St Mich Coll Llan. **d** 90 **p** 97. C Llanishen and Lisvane 90-93; C Llanishen 93-94; C Aberavon 94-98; R Llanfabon 98-01; rtd 01.

6 Alexandra House, Beach Road, Penarth CF64 1FN Tel (029) 2070 1303

STARK, Michael. b 35. Dur Univ BSc56 SEN58. Chich Th Coll 58. **d** 60 **p** 61. C Middlesbrough St Paul *York* 60-64; C S Bank 64-66; R Skelton in Cleveland 66-74; P-in-c Upleatham 66-67; R 67-74; Asst Chapl HM Pris Wormwood Scrubs 74-76; Liv 75-76; Chapl HM Pris Featherstone 76-83; Ex 83-89; Leic 89-97; rtd 97; Perm to Offic *Leic* and *S'well* from 99; P-in-c Rotterdam *Eur* 04-06. *28 St Peter's Road, Leicester LE2 1DA*

STARKEY, Gerald Dennis. b 34. Qu Coll Birm 79. **d** 82 **p** 83. C Wilnecote *Lich* 82-86; Min Stoke-upon-Trent 86-90; P-in-c W Bromwich St Pet 90-00; rtd 00; Perm to Offic *Lich* from 01. *6 Hazelwood Drive, Wednesfield, Wolverhampton WV11 1SH* Tel (01902) 726252

STARKEY, John Douglas. b 23. St Chad's Coll Dur BA47. **d** 48 **p** 49. C Horninglow *Lich* 48-52; C Lower Gornal 52-55; C-in-c W Bromwich Ascension CD 55-57; V Coseley Ch Ch 57-66; V Freehay 66-84; P-in-c Oakamoor w Cotton 78-84; R Dunstall w Rangemore and Tatenhill 84-88; rtd 88; Perm to Offic *Lich* 88-09 and *Derby* from 88. *34 Park Crescent, Doveridge, Ashbourne DE6 5NE* Tel (01889) 566384

STARKEY, Michael Stuart. b 63. LMH Ox BA85 Nottm Univ BTh92 MA93. St Jo Coll Nottm 90. **d** 93 **p** 94. C Ealing St Mary *Lon* 93-95; C Brownswood Park 95-97; P-in-c 97-01; V Twickenham Common H Trin 01-09; V Kennington St Mark *S'wark* 09-11; V Llanidloes w Llangurig *Ban* from 11. *The Vicarage, Trefeglwys Road, Llanidloes SY18 6HZ* Tel (01686) 412370 Mobile 07870-281055 E-mail revstarkey@yahoo.co.uk

STARKEY, Naomi Faith Ezitt (Ness). b 61. Lanc Univ BSc97 MA02 Leeds Univ MA07 RGN83 RM85. NOC 04. **d** 07 **p** 08. C Broughton *Blackb* 07-10; Lic to Offic from 10; C Braunschweig Germany from 10. *c/o Der Braunschweiger Dom, Domplatz 5, 38100 Braunschweig, Germany* Tel (0039) (531) 253350 E-mail ness.starkey@ic24.net

STARKEY, Patrick Robin. b 37. **d** 64 **p** 65. C Tonbridge SS Pet and Paul *Roch* 64-68; Asst Chapl Sherborne Sch 68-72; Scripture Union 73-85; rtd 99. *14 Heol Twrch, Lower Cwmtwrch, Swansea SA9 2TD*

STARKEY, Simon Mark. b 36. Liv Univ BA78 MA96. Clifton Th Coll 63. **d** 66 **p** 67. C Ox St Ebbe w St Pet 66-72; Community Chapl CPAS Kirkdale 72-75; TV Toxteth Park St Bede *Liv* 75-78; P-in-c 78-80; V 80-90; RD Toxteth 81-89; Chapl Ches Coll of HE 90-96; TV St Luke in the City *Liv* 96-03; rtd 03; Perm to Offic *Liv* from 03. *23 Merlin Street, Liverpool L8 8HY* Tel 0151-709 0208

STARKEY, Susan Anne. b 52. St Jo Coll Nottm. **d** 97 **p** 98. C Watford St Luke *St Alb* 97-02; C Oxhey All SS 02-04; V Findern *Derby* from 04; V Willington from 04. *The Vicarage, 66 Castle Way, Willington, Derby DE65 6BU* Tel (01283) 703928 E-mail susan.starkey@btopenworld.com

STARKINGS, Susan Anne. b 52. Kent Univ BSc82 Sheff City Poly MSc90 Punjab Univ PhD93. SEITE 08. **d** 11. NSM C Hothfield Benefice *Cant* from 11. *Stable Cottage, Church Lane, Hothfield, Ashford TN26 1EL* Tel (01233) 643497

STARNES, Peter Henry. b 19. St Jo Coll Cam BA42 MA47 Ch Ch Coll Cant PGCE72 LTCL74. Linc Th Coll 42. **d** 44 **p** 45. C Gillingham *Sarum* 44-50; C St Peter-in-Thanet *Cant* 50-52; CF 52-55; Hon CF from 55; R Hothfield *Cant* 56-60; V Westwell 56-65; R Eastwell w Boughton Aluph 60-65; rtd 84. *Whitebeams, High Halden, Ashford TN26 3LY* Tel (01233) 850245

STARNS, Helen Edna. See PATTEN, Mrs Helen Edna

STARR, Michael Richard. b 43. Sarum Th Coll 65. **d** 68 **p** 69. C Plymouth St Pet *Ex* 68-72; C Blackpool St Paul *Blackb* 72-74; V Burnley St Cuth 74-79; C Eastbourne St Mary *Chich* 79-84; P-in-c Eastbourne Ch Ch 84-87; V 87-88; R Guernsey Ste Marie du Castel *Win* 88-01; V Guernsey St Matt 94-01; Vice-Dean Guernsey 99-01; P-in-c Win St Bart 01-08; rtd 09. *62 Beresford Road, Chandler's Ford, Eastleigh SO53 2LY*

STARRS, Lindsey Carolyn. b 49. Alsager Coll of Educn CertEd70 Liv Inst of HE BEd85. Ripon Coll Cuddesdon 00. **d** 02 **p** 03. C Penkridge *Lich* 02-06; TV N Creedy *Ex* from 06. *The Rectory, Church Street, Morchard Bishop, Crediton EX17 6PJ* Tel (01363) 877221 E-mail starrs@lstarrs.fsnet.com

STARTIN, Nicola Gail. b 57. K Coll Lon LLB79. St Steph Ho Ox 88. **d** 90 **p** 96. C Wellingborough All SS *Pet* 90-92; NSM Pyle w Kenfig *Llan* 94-95; Asst Chapl Mid Kent Healthcare NHS Trust 95-97; Chapl HM Pris E Sutton Park 97-00; Chapl HM Pris Haslar 00-02; Chapl Haslar Immigration Removal Cen from 02. *Haslar Immigration Removal Centre, 2 Dolphin Way, Gosport PO12 2AW* Tel (023) 9260 4047 E-mail nicola.startin@hmps.gsi.gov.uk

STATHAM, Brian Edward. b 55. K Coll Lon MA AKC76. St Steph Ho Ox 77. **d** 78 **p** 79. C Ches H Trin 78-81; C Birkenhead Priory 81-82; TV 82-86; V Newton 86-91; SSF 91-94; TV Horsham *Chich* 95-99; Chapl Horsham Gen Hosp 95-99; TV Ches 99-03; P-in-c Stockport St Matt 03-07; C Edgeley and Cheadle Heath 07-10; V Milton *Lich* from 10. *The Vicarage, Baddeley Green Lane, Stoke-on-Trent ST2 7EY* Tel (01782) 534062 E-mail brianstatham@aol.com

STATHAM, John Francis. b 31. Kelham Th Coll 51. **d** 56 **p** 57. C Ilkeston St Mary *Derby* 56-58; C New Mills 58-59; V 69-81; C Newbold w Dunston 59-62; PC Ridgeway 62-69; RD Glossop 78-81; R Matlock 81-89; R Killamarsh 89-93; rtd 93; Perm to Offic *Derby* and *S'well* from 93. *33 Ackford Drive, The Meadows, Worksop S80 1YG* Tel (01909) 476031

STATHER, Thomas William John. b 79. Van Mildert Coll Dur BSc00. St Steph Ho Ox BTh04. **d** 04 **p** 05. C Colchester St Jas and St Paul w All SS etc *Chelmsf* 04-08; P-in-c Tunstall *Lich* 08-10; V Goldenhill and Tunstall from 10. *Christ Church Vicarage, 26 Stanley Street, Tunstall, Stoke-on-Trent ST6 6BW* Tel (01782) 838288 E-mail john_stather@hotmail.com

STATON, Preb Geoffrey. b 40. Wells Th Coll 64. **d** 66 **p** 67. C Wednesfield St Thos *Lich* 66-69; C Cannock 69-72; V Cheddleton 72-82; RD Leek 77-82; V Harlescott 82-90; TR Penkridge 90-05; rtd 05; C Colton, Colwich and Gt Haywood *Lich* 05-10; C Abbots Bromley, Blithfield, Colton, Colwich etc from 11; Preb Lich Cathl 87-10. *5 Hunters Close, Great Haywood, Stafford ST18 0GF* Tel (01889) 882081 Mobile 07971-016494 E-mail geoffrey.staton@virgin.net

STATTER, Ms Deborah Hilary. b 55. **d** 00 **p** 01. OLM Everton St Pet *Liv* 00-02; OLM Everton St Pet w St Chrys 02-04; C 04-08; P-in-c Netherton from 08. *St Oswald's Vicarage, 183 St Oswald's Lane, Bootle L30 5SR* Tel 0151-525 1882 Mobile 07952-105466

STAUNTON, Mrs Mary Provis. b 52. Leic Univ BSc74. EMMTC 05. **d** 07 **p** 08. NSM Mickleover All SS *Derby* from 07; NSM Mickleover St Jo from 07. *165A Pastures Hill, Littleover, Derby DE23 4AZ* Tel (01332) 510264

STAUNTON, Richard Steedman. b 25. Wadh Coll Ox BA49 MA50 BSc51. Cuddesdon Coll 63. **d** 64 **p** 65. C Wyken *Cov* 64-68; V Tile Hill 68-76; V Hillmorton 76-90; rtd 90; Perm to Offic *Ban* from 90. *2 Tan-y-fron, Corris Uchaf, Machynlleth SY20 9BN* Tel (01654) 761466

STAVELEY-WADHAM, Robert Andrew. b 43. ACII. Ridley Hall Cam 79. **d** 81 **p** 82. C Saffron Walden w Wendens Ambo and Littlebury *Chelmsf* 81-84; P-in-c Austrey and Warton *Birm* 84-87; Perm to Offic *Chich* 87-02; Ely 88-96; P-in-c Tillington 02-07; P-in-c Duncton 02-07; P-in-c Up Waltham 02-07; rtd 07. *2 Little Bognor Cottage, Little Bognor, Fittleworth, Pulborough RH20 1JT* Tel (01798) 865668 E-mail bobswpic@aol.com

STAVROU, Stephen Francis. b 83. St Jo Coll Cam BA05 MA09 MPhil09. Westcott Ho Cam 07. **d** 09 **p** 10. C Peterho Cam Bedford Park Lon from 09. *33 Quick Road, London W4 2BU* Tel (020) 8707 2078 Mobile 07528-930966 E-mail stephenfrancisstavrou@yahoo.co.uk

STEACY, William Leslie. b 59. UCD BAgrSc82 MAgrSc88 TCD BTh06. CITC 03. **d** 06 **p** 07. C Dunboyne and Rathmolyon *M & K* 06-10; I Kingscourt w Syddan from 10. *The Rectory, Kingscourt, Co Cavan, Republic of Ireland* Tel (00353) (42) 966 7255 E-mail williamsteacy@eircom.net

STEAD, Andrew Michael. b 63. BA84. Coll of Resurr Mirfield 84. **d** 87 **p** 88. C Wellingborough All Hallows *Pet* 87-90; Chapl St Alb Abbey 90-94; Chapl Aldenham Sch Herts 94-04; Ho Master 01-08; Teacher from 08; Perm to Offic *St Alb* from 04; Assoc Min St Alb Abbey from 05. *7 Wallingford Walk, St Albans AL1 2JL* Tel (01727) 764666 E-mail rev.amstead@gmail.com

STEAD, Philip John. b 60. Sheff Univ LLB82 City of Lon Poly ACII85. Linc Th Coll 95. **d** 95 **p** 96. C Warsop *S'well* 95-99; P-in-c Forest Town from 99; P-in-c Mansfield Oak Tree Lane from 07. *The Vicarage, Old Mill Lane, Forest Town, Mansfield NG19 0EP* Tel (01623) 622177

STEAD, Timothy James. b 60. Ex Univ BSc82. St Steph Ho Ox 93. **d** 95 **p** 97. C Broseley w Benthall, Jackfield, Linley etc *Heref* 95-99; TV Haywards Heath St Wilfrid *Chich* 99-07; P-in-c Headington Quarry *Ox* 07-10; V from 10. *The Vicarage, 46 Quarry Road, Headington, Oxford OX3 8NU* Tel (01865) 307939 or 762931 E-mail susieandtim@lycos.co.uk

STEADMAN, Mrs Gloria Ann. b 44. STETS BA04. **d** 04 **p** 05. NSM Farlington *Portsm* 04-08; NSM W Leigh from 08. *Lane End House, 63 Glamorgan Road, Waterlooville PO8 0TS* Tel (023) 9259 5561 E-mail gloria_nembles@yahoo.co.uk

STEADMAN, Mark John. b 64. Southn Univ LLB95 Ch Coll Cam BA01 MA05 Barrister-at-Law (Inner Temple) 96. Westcott Ho Cam 99. **d** 02 **p** 03. C Portsea St Mary *Portsm* 02-05; P-in-c Camberwell St Phil and St Mark *S'wark* 05-11; AD Bermondsey 08-11; Bp's Chapl from 11. *Trinity House, 4 Chapel Court, London SE1 1HW* Tel (020) 7939 9420 E-mail mark.steadman@southwark.anglican.org

STEADMAN, Mrs Wendy Anne Eleanor. b 35. Somerville Coll Ox MA56 MA61. **d** 06 **p** 07. NSM Lache cum Saltney *Ches* from 06. *32 Curzon Park South, Chester CH4 8AB* Tel (01244) 682989 E-mail wsteadman@tiscali.co.uk

STEADMAN-ALLEN, Miss Barbara. b 53. Trent Park Coll of Educn CertEd74 Birm Univ BMus77 ARCM83. Cranmer Hall Dur 88. **d** 90 **p** 94. C Chessington *Guildf* 90-94; C Chertsey 94-99; P-in-c Mickleham 99-01; C Leatherhead and Mickleham 01-04; Chapl Box Hill Sch 99-04; TV Surrey Weald *Guildf* from 04. *The*

Vicarage, Horsham Road, Holmwood, Dorking RH5 4JX Tel (01306) 889118 Mobile 07817-006254 E-mail bsa311@freenet.co.uk

STEADY, Miss Vilda May. b 51. Linc Th Coll 87. **d** 89 **p** 94. Par Dn Cannock *Lich* 89-91; Par Dn Hammerwich 91-94; C 94-95; Asst Chapl Eastbourne Hosps NHS Trust 95-97; Chapl Luton and Dunstable Hosp NHS Trust 97-01; Sen Chapl Jas Paget Healthcare NHS Trust 01-11; rtd 11. *4 Cliff Cottages, Warren Road, Hopton, Great Yarmouth NR31 9BN*

STEAR, Michael Peter Hutchinson. b 47. Goldsmiths' Coll Lon TCert68. Wycliffe Hall Ox 71. **d** 74 **p** 75. C Streatham Vale H Redeemer *S'wark* 74-77; C-in-c Ramsgate St Mark *Cant* 77-82; V 82-83; Min Jersey St Paul Prop Chpl *Win* 83-94; TR Radipole and Melcombe Regis *Sarum* 94-00; Chapl Weymouth Coll 94-97; rtd 00; Perm to Offic *Sarum* from 01. *132 Preston Road, Preston, Weymouth DT3 6BH*

STEAR, Mrs Patricia Ann. b 38. Birm Univ BSc60. **d** 97 **p** 98. OLM Bradford Peverell, Stratton, Frampton etc *Sarum* 97-09; rtd 09; Perm to Offic *Sarum* from 09. *Westwood House, Bradford Peverell, Dorchester DT2 9SE* Tel (01305) 889227 Fax 889718 E-mail patstear@saqnet.co.uk

STEBBING, Christopher Henry. b 64. G&C Coll Cam MEng87 MA90. Cranmer Hall Dur 98. **d** 00 **p** 01. C Malin Bridge *Sheff* 00-04; V Sheff St Jo from 04. *St John's Vicarage, 91 Manor Oaks Road, Sheffield S2 5EA* Tel 0114-272 7423 or 272 8678 E-mail chris@stebbingfamily.go-plus.net

STEBBING, Michael Langdale (Nicolas). b 46. Univ of Zimbabwe BA68 UNISA MTh86. Coll of Resurr Mirfield. **d** 74 **p** 75. C Borrowdale *Carl* 74-75; P-in-c Chikwaka Rhodesia 76-77; S Africa 79-86; CR from 80. *House of the Resurrection, Stocks Bank Road, Mirfield WF14 0BN* Tel (01924) 494318 E-mail nstebbing@mirfield.org.uk

STEDMAN, Barrie John. b 49. **d** 00 **p** 01. OLM Mildenhall *St E* 00-07. *The Cottage, Tudor Grange, Poy Street Green, Rattlesden, Bury St Edmunds IP30 0RX* Tel (01638) 750505 Mobile 07864-076896 E-mail barriestedman@aol.com

STEDMAN, Preb Michael Sydney. b 34. MRICS58. Clifton Th Coll 62. **d** 65 **p** 66. C Lindfield *Chich* 65-68; C Gt Baddow *Chelmsf* 68-73; TV Ashby w Thurton, Claxton and Carleton *Nor* 73-75; P-in-c 75-85; TV Rockland St Mary w Hellington 73-75; P-in-c 75-85; TV Framingham Pigot 73-75; P-in-c 75-85; TV Bramerton w Surlingham 73-75; P-in-c 75-85; TV Bergh Apton w Yelverton 73-75; P-in-c 75-85; RD Loddon 78-85; R Church Stretton *Heref* 85-99; RD Condover 88-96; Preb Heref Cathl 94-99; rtd 99; Perm to Offic *St E* from 00. *44 The Mowbrays, Framlingham, Woodbridge IP13 9DL* Tel (01728) 724479 E-mail michael@stedmann.freeserve.co.uk

STEDMAN, Robert Alfred. b 24. Qu Coll Birm 50. **d** 52 **p** 53. C Portchester *Portsm* 52-55; V Brighton St Anne *Chich* 55-61; V Salehurst 61-76; R Newhaven 76-90; rtd 90; Perm to Offic *Chich* 90-99. *12 Lady Wootton's Green, Canterbury CT1 1NG*

STEED, Christopher Denis. b 55. Lon Univ BD92 Ex Univ PGCE01 Bris Univ MSc03 Ex Univ EdD05. Sarum Th Coll 05. **d** 06 **p** 07. C Yatton Moor *B & W* 06-10; P-in-c Combe Martin, Berrynarbor, Lynton, Brendon etc *Ex* from 11. *The Rectory, Rectory Road, Combe Martin, Ilfracombe EX34 0NS* Tel (01271) 883203 Mobile 07704-138433 E-mail chrissteed@uwclub.net

STEED, Canon Helene. b 70. Uppsala Univ MDiv95. Past Inst Uppsala 95. **p** 96. C Stora Melby Sweden 96-97; TV Essunga 97-04; Dean's V Cork Cathl 04-08; I Clones w Killeevan *Clogh* from 08; Preb Clogh Cathl from 11. *The Rectory, Scotshouse, Clones, Co Monaghan, Republic of Ireland* Tel (00353) (47) 56962 E-mail helenesteed@yahoo.com

STEEL, Coralie Mary. b 47. Bedf Coll Lon BA69 Solicitor 73. St Mich Coll Llan 98. **d** 01 **p** 02. NSM Llangunnor w Cwmffrwd *St D* from 01. *Llwyn Celyn, 24 Picton Terrace, Carmarthen SA31 3BX* Tel (01267) 236369

STEEL, Graham Reginald. b 51. Cam Univ MA. Trin Coll Bris 80. **d** 83 **p** 84. C Gt Parndon *Chelmsf* 83-86; C Barking St Marg w St Patr 86-89; P-in-c Westcliff St Cedd 89-96; P-in-c Prittlewell St Pet 92-96; Chapl Southend Gen Hosp 89-92; V Prittlewell St Pet w Westcliff St Cedd *Chelmsf* 96-07; P-in-c S Trin Broads *Nor* 07-08; R from 08. *The Rectory, Main Road, Fleggburgh, Great Yarmouth NR29 3AG* Tel (01493) 368210 E-mail grahamsteel@tiscali.co.uk

STEEL, Leslie Frederick. b 34. Webster Univ Geneva MA88. St Jo Coll Auckland 57 LTh65. **d** 59 **p** 60. C Roslyn New Zealand 59-62; V Waimea Plains 62-69; CF 70-73; Singapore 72-73; V Dunstan New Zealand 74-81; Adn Otago 77-82; V Anderson's Bay and Chapl Police Force 82-86; Can Dunedin Cathl 82-85; Adn Dunedin 85-86; Hon C Geneva *Eur* 87-90; Chapl Lausanne 90-97; Perm to Offic *Pet* 98-99; P-in-c Potterspury, Furtho, Yardley Gobion and Cosgrove 99-02; R Potterspury w Furtho and Yardley Gobion etc 02-04; rtd 04. *14 Kaspar Street, Warkworth 0910, New Zealand* Tel (0064) (9) 422 2560 E-mail ehsteel@xtra.co.nz

STEEL, Norman William. b 53. Sarum & Wells Th Coll 85. **d** 87 **p** 88. C S Woodham Ferrers *Chelmsf* 87-91; V Woolavington w

Cossington and Bawdrip *B & W* 91-99; P-in-c Pitminster w Corfe 99-02; Chapl Huish Coll Taunton from 99; Perm to Offic *B & W* 02-05. *28 Wilton Street, Taunton TA1 3JR* Tel (01823) 368098 E-mail norman.steel@btinternet.com

STEEL, Richard John. b 57. Dur Univ BA79 Cam Univ MA86 Edin Univ MTh97. Ridley Hall Cam 81. **d** 84 **p** 85. C Hull St Jo Newland *York* 84-87; Relig Broadcasting Officer *Derby* 88-92; Dioc Communications Officer *Blackb* 92-97; Communication Dir CMS 97-05; NSM Stoke-next-Guildf 00-05; R Kirkheaton *Wakef* from 05; RD Almondbury from 06. *The New Rectory, Church Lane, Kirkheaton, Huddersfield HD5 0BH* Tel (01484) 532410 E-mail richard.steel@ntlworld.com

STEEL, Thomas Molyneux. b 39. Man Univ BA61. Ripon Hall Ox 61. **d** 63 **p** 64. C Newc H Cross 63-66; P-in-c Man St Aid 66-71; R Failsworth St Jo 71-79; P-in-c Farnham Royal *Ox* 79-81; P-in-c Hedgerley 80-81; R Farnham Royal w Hedgerley 81-91; V Prescot *Liv* 91-03; rtd 03; Perm to Offic *Lon* from 04. *20 Barnet Way, London NW7 3BH* Tel (020) 8906 0271

STEELE, Alan Christopher. b 63. Cape Town Univ BA85 Univ of Zimbabwe BA91. Gaul Ho Harare 89. **d** 91 **p** 93. C Harare St Mary Magd 91-93; C Harare St Luke 93-95; Chapl Ruzawi Sch 96-99; CF from 99. *c/o MOD Chaplains (Army)* Tel (01264) 381140 Fax 381824

STEELE, Alan Lindsay. b 44. **d** 09 **p** 10. OLM Billingborough Gp *Linc* from 09. *7 Paddock Estate, Horbling, Sleaford NG34 0PQ* Tel (01529) 240602

STEELE, Charles Edward Ernest. b 24. Cuddesdon Coll 72. **d** 74 **p** 75. C Rubery *Birm* 74-77; P-in-c Shaw Hill 77-79; V 79-82; C Curdworth 82-83; C Curdworth w Castle Vale 83-85; rtd 85; Perm to Offic *Birm* from 85. *3 Dominic Drive, Middleton Hall Road, Birmingham B30 1DW* Tel 0121-451 3372

STEELE, Derek James. b 53. St Jo Coll Nottm. **d** 97 **p** 98. Aux Min Ballywillan *Conn* from 97. *106 Mountsandel Road, Coleraine BT52 1TA* Tel (028) 7035 1633

STEELE, Edwin Harry. b 80. Mattersey Hall BA05. Ridley Hall Cam 06. **d** 08 **p** 09. C Ecclesall *Sheff* 08-11; P-in-c Greenhill from 11. *St Peter's Vicarage, Reney Avenue, Sheffield S8 7FN* Tel 0114-237 7422 E-mail edwinharrysteele@gmail.com

STEELE, Canon Gordon John. b 55. Kent Univ BA76 Worc Coll Ox BA82 MA87. Coll of Resurr Mirfield 82. **d** 84 **p** 85. C Greenhill St Jo *Lon* 84-88; C Uxbridge St Andr w St Jo 88; TV Uxbridge 88-94; V Northampton St Alb *Pet* 94-01; V Pet St Jo from 01; RD Pet 04-10; Can Pet Cathl from 04. *26 Minster Precincts, Peterborough PE1 1XZ* Tel (01733) 566265 E-mail gordon@gsteele.entadsl.com

STEELE, Keith Atkinson. b 28. CEng MIMechE FInstMC. Qu Coll Birm Oak Hill Th Coll 80. **d** 81 **p** 82. NSM Westoning w Tingrith *St Alb* 81-87; NSM Chalgrave 87-88; P-in-c 88-96; RD Dunstable 91-96; Perm to Offic from 96. *Mariner's Lodge, Church Road, Westoning, Bedford MK45 5JW* Tel (01525) 714111

STEELE, Peter Gerald. b 44. Bournemouth Tech Coll BSc67 Essex Univ MSc69. Sarum & Wells Th Coll 91. **d** 93 **p** 94. C Beaminster Area *Sarum* 93-97; P-in-c Aldermaston w Wasing and Brimpton *Ox* 97-08; P-in-c Woolhampton w Midgham and Beenham Valance 05-08; R Aldermaston and Woolhampton 08-10; AD Bradfield 07-10; rtd 10. *11 Mayfield Way, Ferndown BH22 9HP* Tel (01202) 895927 E-mail p.steele343@btinternet.com

STEELE, Canon Terence. b 54. Linc Th Coll 85. **d** 87 **p** 88. C New Sleaford *Linc* 87-90; V Cowbit 90-95; P-in-c Burgh le Marsh 95-97; V 97-06; P-in-c Orby 95-97; V 97-06; P-in-c Bratoft w Irby-in-the-Marsh 95-97; R 97-06; P-in-c Welton-le-Marsh w Gunby 95-97; R 97-06; R Burgh Gp from 06; RD Calcewaithe and Candleshoe from 05; Can and Preb Linc Cathl from 07. *The Vicarage, Glebe Rise, Burgh le Marsh, Skegness PE24 5BL* Tel (01754) 810216 E-mail father.terry@btclick.com

STEELE-PERKINS, Mrs Barbara Anita. b 46. Whitelands Coll Lon CertEd68 Spurgeon's Coll MTh98. STETS 99. **d** 01 **p** 02. Tutor Local Min Progr *Guildf* from 95; NSM Wisley w Pyrford 01-04; NSM Haslemere and Grayswood from 04. *Church House, Church Close, Grayswood, Haslemere GU27 2DB* Tel (01428) 656504 E-mail barbarasteeleperkins@tiscali.co.uk

STEELE-PERKINS, Richard De Courcy. b 36. Clifton Th Coll 61. **d** 64 **p** 65. C Stoke Damerel *Ex* 64-65; C Washfield 65-68; P-in-c Wimbledon *S'wark* 68-70; Chapl Lambeth Hosp 70-74; Asst Chapl St Thos Hosp Lon 70-74; P-in-c Tawstock *Ex* 74-75; R 75-81; P-in-c Sticklepath 74-75; R 75-81; V Buckfastleigh w Dean Prior 81-91; TR Camelot Par *B & W* 91-94; Asst Chapl R Surrey Co and St Luke's Hosps NHS Trust 94-99; Asst Chapl Heathlands Mental Health Trust Surrey 94-99; P-in-c Ockham w Hatchford *Guildf* 99-01; rtd 02; Hon C E Horsley and Ockham w Hatchford and Downside *Guildf* 02-04; Perm to Offic from 04. *Church House, Church Close, Grayswood, Haslemere GU27 2DB* Tel (01428) 656504 E-mail richard@steele-perkins.fsnet.co.uk

STEEN, Canon Jane Elizabeth. b 64. Newnham Coll Cam BA88 MA90 PhD92. Westcott Ho Cam 93. **d** 96 **p** 97. C Chipping Barnet w Arkley *St Alb* 96-99; Chapl and Personal Asst to Bp S'wark 99-05; Hon Chapl S'wark Cathl 00-05; Chan and Can Th

and Dir Min Tr from 05. *2 Harmsworth Mews, London SE11 4SQ* Tel (020) 7820 8079 *or* 7939 9449 E-mail jane.steen@southwark.anglican.org

STEER, Norman William. b 35. MBE00. SRN57. EAMTC 01. **d** 03 **p** 04. NSM Dickleburgh and The Pulhams *Nor* from 03. *Brook Cottage, Harleston Road, Starston, Harleston IP20 9NL* Tel (01379) 854245 Mobile 07941-473255 E-mail norman@nandrsteer.com

STEIN, Ms Ann Elizabeth. b 57. Loughb Univ BSc78 Liv Hope MA01. NOC 05. **d** 07 **p** 08. C Ormskirk *Liv* 07-11; P-in-c Abram from 11; P-in-c Bickershaw from 11. *The Rectory, 246 Slag Lane, Lowton, Warrington WA3 2ED* Tel (01942) 208828 E-mail annstein@sky.com

STEINBERG, Eric Reed (Joseph). b 65. Trin Coll Bris BA94. **d** 94 **p** 95. C Chigwell and Chigwell Row *Chelmsf* 94-99; Dir Y2000 99-00; Dir Jews for Jesus UK 00-05; Dir CMS from 05. *CMS, PO Box 1799, Oxford OX4 9BN* Tel 08456-201799 E-mail kosherjoe@mac.com

STELL, Peter Donald. b 50. Leeds Univ 74 Southn Univ BA81 Man Univ 93 MInstM. Sarum & Wells Th Coll 78. **d** 81 **p** 82. C Rothwell w Lofthouse *Ripon* 81-85; TV Brayton *York* 85-87; Chapl Asst Leybourne Grange Hosp W Malling 87-88; Chapl Asst Kent, Sussex and Pembury Hosps Tunbridge Wells 87-88; C Spalding St Jo w Deeping St Nicholas *Linc* 87-93; Chapl S Lincs HA Mental Handicap Unit 88-93; Chapl HM Pris Liv 93-94; Chapl HM Pris Wayland 94-99; Chapl HM Pris Grendon and Spring Hill 99-02; Chapl HM Pris Rye Hill 02-05; Chapl HM Pris N Sea Camp from 05. *HM Prison North Sea Camp, Croppers Lane, Freiston, Boston PE22 0QX* Tel (01205) 769300 Fax 769301

STENHOUSE, Joan Frances Fleming. b 45. RGN66. Ab Dioc Tr Course 82. **dss** 84 **d** 86 **p** 94. Ellon and Cruden Bay *Ab* 84-97; NSM 86-97; Bp's Chapl for Tr and Educn 95-97; Asst P Cuminestown 97-00; C Nova Scotia St Martin Canada from 00. *27 Birch Grove, Upper Tantallon NS B3Z 1L1, Canada* E-mail jstenhouse@bwr.eastlink.ca

STENTIFORD, Canon Pauline Cecilia Elizabeth. b 48. EAMTC 98. **d** 00 **p** 01. NSM Gt and Lt Bealings w Playford and Culpho *St E* 00-03; P-in-c from 03; RD Woodbridge 05-11; Hon Can *St E* Cathl from 08. *Sheepstor, Boyton, Woodbridge IP12 3LH* Tel (01394) 411469 E-mail pauline.stentiford@btopenworld.com

STEPHEN, Canon Kenneth George. b 47. Strathclyde Univ BA69 Edin Univ BD72. Edin Th Coll 69. **d** 72 **p** 73. C Ayr *Glas* 72-75; R Renfrew 75-80; R Motherwell 80-93; R Wishaw 80-93; R Kilmarnock 93-06; R Dalbeattie from 06; Can St Mary's Cathl from 87; Syn Clerk from 87. *The Rectory, 1 Alpine Terrace, Dalbeattie DG5 4HJ* Tel (01556) 610671 E-mail ken.stephen@tiscali.co.uk

STEPHEN, Robert. b 63. Lon Bible Coll BA85 Westmr Coll Ox MTh96 FSAScot01. EMMTC. **d** 04 **p** 05. In Bapt Min 85-97; NSM Burbage w Aston Flamville *Leic* from 04; Perm to Offic *Cov* from 05; Chapl K Henry VIII Sch Cov from 07. *Small Change, 4 Woodland Road, Hinckley LE10 1JG* Tel (01455) 615503 Mobile 07957-312832 E-mail revrstephen@ntlworld.com

STEPHENI, Frederick William. b 28. TD73. FSAScot81 FRSA82 Cranfield Inst of Tech MSc82. Lambeth STh83 Qu Coll Birm 54. **d** 55 **p** 56. C Arnold *S'well* 55-57; P-in-c 57-58; P-in-c Hucknall Torkard 58-59; Chapl Stoke-on-Trent City Gen Hosp 59-62; Chapl N Staffs R Infirmary Stoke-on-Trent 59-62; CF (TA) 60-88; Chapl K Coll Hosp Lon 62-63; R Cotgrave *S'well* 63-76; V Owthorpe 63-76; Chapl Addenbrooke's Hosp Cam 76-88; Lic to Offic *Ely* 76-99; rtd 88; Perm to Offic *York* from 00. *64A Scarborough Road, Norton, Malton YO17 8AE* Tel (01653) 694995

STEPHENS, Anthony Wayne. b 54. Surrey Univ BSc80. St Jo Coll Nottm 02. **d** 04 **p** 05. C Preston w Sutton Poyntz and Osmington w Poxwell *Sarum* 04-08; C Pioneer Min Weymouth Town Cen from 08. *16 Lynmoor Road, Weymouth DT4 7TW* Tel (01305) 780844

STEPHENS, Canon Archibald John. b 15. Selw Coll Cam BA37 MA44. Wells Th Coll 46. **d** 47 **p** 48. C Gt Malvern St Mary *Worc* 47-50; Nigeria 50-68 and 70-71; Hon Can Ondo 57-71; Hon Can Owerri from 71; C Swindon Ch Ch *Bris* 68-70; C-in-c Ash Vale CD *Guildf* 71-72; V Ash Vale 72-77; P-in-c Thursley 77-82; rtd 82; Perm to Offic *Guildf* 85-06. *26 Cruse Close, Sway, Lymington SO41 6AY* Tel (01590) 682097 E-mail resfernhill@aol.com

STEPHENS, Grahame Frank Henry. b 33. **d** 02 **p** 03. OLM Woolwich St Mary w St Mich *S'wark* 02-05; Perm to Offic from 05. *121 The Drive, Bexley DA5 3BY* Tel (020) 8303 3546 Fax 8306 2155 Mobile 07775-796896

STEPHENS, Canon Harold William Barrow. b 47. Lon Univ BEd71. S Dios Minl Tr Scheme 80. **d** 82 **p** 83. NSM Heytesbury and Sutton Veny *Sarum* 82-83; NSM Bishopstrow and Boreham 83-91; Dep Hd Master Westwood St Thos Sch Salisbury 91-99; P-in-c Market Lavington and Easterton 99-03; P-in-c W Lavington and the Cheverells 02-03; R The Lavingtons, Cheverells, and Easterton 03-07; TR Dorchester from 07; P-in-c

The Winterbournes and Compton Valence from 09; Can and Preb Sarum Cathl from 09. *The Rectory, 17A Edward Road, Dorchester DT1 2HL* Tel and fax (01305) 268434 E-mail harold.stephens@ukonline.co.uk

STEPHENS, James Charles. b 62. **d** 91 **p** 92. C Kilcolman w Kiltallagh, Killorglin, Knockane etc *L & K* from 91. *Kilderry, Miltown, Co Kerry, Republic of Ireland* Tel (00353) (66) 976 7735 Mobile 87-052 9107 E-mail stiofain.s@gmail.com *or* stephens.j@temmler.eu

STEPHENS, Mrs Jean. b 46. St As Minl Tr Course. **d** 89 **p** 97. NSM Gwernaffield and Llanferres *St As* 89-02 and 04-09; NSM Hawarden 02-04; NSM Cilcain, Gwernaffield, Llanferres etc from 09. *Noddfa, Pen-y-Fron Road, Pantymwyn, Mold CH7 5EF* Tel (01352) 740037

STEPHENS, Jill. See STEPHENS, Mrs Rosemary Jill

STEPHENS, Mrs Joan. b 38. Dioc OLM tr scheme 97. **d** 00 **p** 01. OLM Irlam *Man* from 00; OLM Cadishead from 09. *77 Baines Avenue, Irlam, Manchester M44 6AS* Tel 0161-775 7538

STEPHENS, Mrs Joanna Louise. b 69. St Jo Coll Nottm BA08. **d** 08 **p** 09. C Bramcote *S'well* 08-10; C Attenborough from 10; C Toton from 10. *22 Church Street, Bramcote, Nottingham NG9 3HD* Tel 0115-943 0177 Mobile 07890-385133 E-mail joke.stephens@talktalk.net

STEPHENS, John. See STEPHENS, Canon Archibald John

STEPHENS, John Michael. b 29. MRICS52. Lich Th Coll 62. **d** 64 **p** 65. C Birchington w Acol *Cant* 64-70; V Tovil 70-79; V Brabourne w Smeeth 79-94; RD N Lympne 87-94; rtd 94; Perm to Offic *York* from 94. *Southacre, Kirby Mills, Kirkbymoorside, York YO62 6NR* Tel (01751) 432766

STEPHENS *(née FLIPPANCE),* **Mrs Kim Sheelagh May.** b 64. RGN85 RM88. Trin Coll Bris 97. **d** 99 **p** 00. C Alderbury Team *Sarum* 99-01; C Clarendon 01-02; Asst Chapl Salisbury NHS Foundn Trust from 02. *The Chaplain's Office, Salisbury District Hospital, Salisbury SP2 8BJ* Tel (01722) 336262 E-mail chaplains.department@salisbury.nhs.uk

STEPHENS, Martin Nicholas. b 64. Brunel Univ BSc88 Nottm Univ MTh01. St Jo Coll Nottm 99. **d** 01 **p** 02. C Newchapel *Lich* 01-04; TV Bucknall from 04. *St John's Parsonage, 28 Greasley Road, Stoke-on-Trent ST2 8JE* Tel (01782) 542861

STEPHENS, Michael. See STEPHENS, John Michael

STEPHENS, Paul. b 53. AGSM73 Newton Park Coll Bath PGCE74. Trin Coll Bris 91. **d** 93 **p** 94. C S Molton w Nymet St George, High Bray etc *Ex* 93-97; R Norton Fitzwarren *B & W* 97-99; Chapl St Aug Sch Taunton 97-99; Chapl Monkton Combe Sch Bath 99-08; P-in-c Winford w Felton Common Hill *B & W* from 08. *The Rectory, 4 Parsonage Lane, Winford, Bristol BS40 8DG* Tel (01275) 474636

STEPHENS, Paul. b 74. Ridley Hall Cam 09. **d** 11. C Forest Row *Chich* from 11. *7 Westbrook, Priory Road, Forest Row RH18 5HX* Tel 07879-864611 (mobile) E-mail stephenspz@hotmail.com

STEPHENS, Mrs Penny Clare. b 60. St Anne's Coll Ox BA83 Lon Inst of Educn PGCE85. Oak Hill Th Coll. **d** 99 **p** 00. C Turnham Green Ch Ch *Lon* 99-03; P-in-c Brasted *Roch* 03-10; Perm to Offic from 10. *The Oast House, Forest Farm, Pembury Road, Tonbridge TN11 0ND* Tel (01732) 358208 E-mail pennystephens@btinternet.com

STEPHENS, Canon Peter John. b 42. Oriel Coll Ox BA64 MA67. Clifton Th Coll 63. **d** 68 **p** 68. C Lenton *S'well* 68-71; C Brixton Hill St Sav *S'wark* 71-73; P-in-c 73-82; TV Barnham Broom *Nor* 82-89; V Gorleston St Mary 89-94; RD Flegg (Gt Yarmouth) 92-94; P-in-c High Oak 94-97; RD Humbleyard 95-98; C Hingham w Wood Rising w Scoulton 96-97; TR High Oak, Hingham and Scoulton w Wood Rising 97-05; Hon Can Nor Cathl 99-05; rtd 05. *15 Church Row, Wootton, Bedford MK43 9HQ* Tel (01234) 765403 Mobile 07768-425349 *or* 07973-322513 E-mail peterstephens@aol.com

STEPHENS, Preb Peter Stanley. b 33. ALCD59. **d** 59 **p** 60. C Paignton St Paul Preston *Ex* 59-64; V Buckland Monachorum 64-74; RD Tavistock 70-74; V Compton Gifford 74-85; RD Plymouth Sutton 83-86; Preb Ex Cathl 84-05; TR Plymouth Em w Efford 85-86; R Thurlestone w S Milton 86-98; rtd 98. *Headland View, 14 Court Park, Thurlestone, Kingsbridge TQ7 3LX* Tel and fax (01548) 560891

STEPHENS, Richard William. b 37. Dur Univ BSc62. Cranmer Hall Dur 62. **d** 64 **p** 65. C Hensingham *Carl* 64-67; C Norbury *Ches* 67-71; R Elworth and Warmingham 71-79; V Bootle St Matt *Liv* 79-89; P-in-c Litherland St Andr 79-83; P-in-c Failsworth H Trin *Man* 89-93; R 93-02; P-in-c Oldham St Barn 01-02; AD Oldham 99-02; rtd 02; Hon C Dalbeattie *Glas* from 02. *Cloverstone, 3 Craignair Street, Dalbeattie DG5 4AX* Tel (01556) 610627 E-mail revrstephens@btinternet.com

STEPHENS, Robert Charles. b 46. Nottm Trent Univ BA03. EMMTC 08. **d** 10 **p** 11. NSM Daybrook *S'well* from 10. *3 Ashington Drive, Arnold, Nottingham NG5 8GH* Tel 0115-967 1684 Mobile 07757-422260 E-mail totonstephens@aol.com

STEPHENS, Mrs Rosemary Jill. b 46. SRN68. WEMTC 96. **d** 08. NSM Goodrich, Marstow, Welsh Bicknor, Llangarron etc *Heref* from 08; NSM Dixton, Wyeham, Bishopswood,

Whitchurch etc from 08. *Sunnyside Cottage, Coppett Hill, Goodrich, Ross-on-Wye HR9 6JG* Tel (01600) 890975 E-mail jill.stephens1@btinternet.com

STEPHENS, Canon Simon Edward. b 41. OBE97. Qu Coll Birm PhD80. Bps' Coll Cheshunt 63. **d** 67 **p** 68. C Cov St Mark 64-71; C Lillington 71-76; C-in-c Canley CD 76-79; V Canley 79-80; Chapl RN 80-97; Asst Chapl Menorca *Eur* 97-98; Chapl 98-99; Chapl Moscow from 99; Hon Can Malta Cathl from 01. *British Embassy - Moscow, FCO, King Charles Street, London SW1A 2AH* Tel and fax (007) (495) 629 0990 E-mail chaplain@standrewsmoscow.org

STEPHENS, Mrs Susanne Hilary. b 44. St Jo Coll Nottm. Guildf Dioc Min Course. **d** 00 **p** 01. OLM Camberley St Paul *Guildf* from 00. *St Paul's Church, Crawley Ridge, Camberley GU15 2AD* Tel (01276) 700210 E-mail suestephens@onetel.com

STEPHENS, Mrs Tessa. b 74. Leeds Univ BA97. St Jo Coll Nottm MTh10. **d** 10 **p** 11. C Hipswell *Ripon* from 10. *Sunset House, Hipswell, Catterick Garrison DL9 4BG* Tel (01748) 830774 Mobile 07944-302344 E-mail tessa.stephens@btinternet.com

STEPHENSON, David John. b 65. Bris Univ BSc(Soc)87 Dur Univ BA91. Cranmer Hall Dur 92. **d** 92 **p** 93. C Wickham Dur 92-94; C Sunderland Pennywell St Thos 94-97; V Stockton St Jo and Stockton St Jas 99-06; V W Dulwich All SS *S'wark* from 06. *All Saints' Vicarage, 165 Rosendale Road, London SE21 8LN* Tel (020) 8670 0826 E-mail vicar@all-saints.org.uk

STEPHENSON, Canon Eric George. b 41. Bede Coll Dur CertEd63. Qu Coll Birm. **d** 66 **p** 67. C Wakef St Jo 66-69; C Seaham w Seaham Harbour *Dur* 69-73; C Cockerton 73-75; Lic to Offic 75-85; V E Boldon 85-08; AD Jarrow 92-01; Hon Can Dur Cathl 93-08; rtd 08; Chapl to The Queen from 02. *39 Haversham Park, Sunderland SR5 1HW* Tel 0191-549 5278 E-mail ericgstephenson@googlemail.com

STEPHENSON, Ian Clarke. b 24. Tyndale Hall Bris 52. **d** 56 **p** 57. C Bedworth *Cov* 56-58; C Edgware *Lon* 58-65; R Biddulph Moor *Lich* 65-70; Hon C Biddulph 70-88; Hon C Burslem 85-88; New Zealand from 87; rtd 89. *5 Arthur Terrace, Balclutha 9230, New Zealand* Tel (0064) (3) 418 2657 E-mail clarkeia@es.co.nz

STEPHENSON, James Alexander. b 77. Hatf Coll Dur BSc00. Ripon Coll Cuddesdon 09. **d** 11. C N Poole Ecum Team *Sarum* from 11; Chapl Canford Sch from 11. *Canford School, Canford Magna, Wimborne BH21 3AD* Tel (01202) 841254 Mobile 07709-865590 E-mail jxstevo@hotmail.com

STEPHENSON, Mrs Jane Eleanor. b 50. Leeds Univ BA72 PGCE73. **d** 05 **p** 06. NSM Bunbury and Tilstone Fearnall *Ches* 05-09; Educn and Tr Officer 07-09; P-in-c Tilston and Shocklach from 09; Past Worker Tr Officer 06-10. *The Mount, Hobb Hill, Tilston, Malpas SY14 7DU* Tel (01829) 250249 *or* 250628 E-mail stephenson256@btinternet.com

STEPHENSON, John Joseph. b 35. St Jo Coll Dur BA74. Qu Coll Birm 75. **d** 76 **p** 77. C Whitworth w Spennymoor *Dur* 76-79; V Eppleton 79-96; rtd 96; Perm to Offic *Dur* from 96. *29 Launceston Drive, Sunderland SR3 3QB* Tel 0191-528 2144

STEPHENSON *(née BRYAN),* **Judith Claire.** b 57. Aston Univ BSc79 PhD82 Trent Poly PGCE83. St Jo Coll Nottm BTh94 LTh95. **d** 95 **p** 96. C Wolverhampton St Matt *Lich* 95-99; Chapl Hull Univ 99-08; Chapl W Lon YMCA from 08. *Chaplain, West London YMCA, 45 St Mary's Road, London W5 5RG* Tel 03001-111500 ext 6530

STEPHENSON, Juliet. b 69. St Jo Coll Dur BA05. Cranmer Hall Dur 03. **d** 05 **p** 06. C Retford *S'well* 05-08; V Newnham w Awre and Blakeney *Glouc* from 08. *The Vicarage, 1 Whetstones, Unlawater Lane, Newnham GL14 1BT* Tel (01594) 516690 E-mail juliet_stephenson@hotmail.com

STEPHENSON, Martin Woodard. b 55. St Cath Coll Cam BA77 MA82. Westcott Ho Cam 78. **d** 81 **p** 82. C Eastleigh *Win* 81-85; C Ferryhill *Dur* 85-87; Asst Dir of Ords 87-89; Chapl St Chad's Coll 87-89; TR Clarendon Park St Jo w Knighton St Mich *Leic* 89-98; P-in-c Hall Green St Pet *Birm* 98-99; V from 99. *St Peter's Vicarage, 33 Paradise Lane, Birmingham B28 0DY* Tel 0121-777 1935 E-mail martinw.stephenson@virgin.net

STEPHENSON, Norman Keith. b 62. St Jo Coll Cam MA88 Strathclyde Univ MBA91. NEOC 04. **d** 07 **p** 08. NSM Kingston upon Hull H Trin *York* 07-08; NSM Ealing St Pet Mt Park *Lon* from 08. *Flat B, Edenhall, Montpelier Road, London W5 2QT* Tel (020) 8991 9134 Mobile 07880-602577 E-mail n.k.stephenson@btinternet.com

STEPHENSON, Canon Robert. b 36. St Chad's Coll Dur BA58. **d** 60 **p** 61. C Whickham *Dur* 60-63; C Gateshead St Mary 63-65; PC Low Team 65-67; R Stella 67-74; V Comberton *Ely* 74-04; RD Bourn 94-97; P-in-c Dry Drayton 97-01; Hon Can Ely Cathl 01-04; rtd 04; Perm to Offic *Ely* from 04. *1 Porthmore Close, Highfields, Caldecote, Cambridge CB23 7ZR* Tel (01954) 210638 E-mail robert@stephenson.wanadoo.co.uk

STEPHENSON, Simon George. b 44. St Jo Coll Dur BA67. Trin Coll Bris 74. **d** 76 **p** 77. C Hildenborough *Roch* 76-82; C Bishopsworth *Bris* 82-85; C-in-c Withywood CD 85-90; TV Wreningham *Nor* 90-97; P-in-c Tasburgh w Tharston, Forncett and Flordon 94-97; TV High Oak, Hingham and Scoulton w

Wood Rising 98-05; rtd 05; Asst Chapl HM Pris Wayland 98-09; Perm to Offic *Nor* from 09. *7 Swanton Avenue, Dereham NR19 2HJ* Tel (01362) 699537

STEPNEY, Area Bishop of. *See* NEWMAN, The Rt Revd Adrian

STERLING, Anne. *See* HASELHURST, Mrs Anne

STERLING, John Haddon. b 40. Pemb Coll Cam BA62 MA66. Cuddesdon Coll 63. **d** 65 **p** 66. C Pretoria Cathl 65-69; Lic to Offic Natal 69-70; Chapl Bris Cathl 71-74; Member Dioc Soc and Ind Team 71-74; Ind Chapl *Linc* 74-87; Ind Chapl *Ripon* 87-92; TV Hanley H Ev and Min in Ind *Lich* 92-97; P-in-c Hixon w Stowe-by-Chartley 97-02; P-in-c Fradswell, Gayton, Milwich and Weston 97-02; TR Mid Trent 02-06; rtd 06; Perm to Offic *Lich* from 07. *10 Newquay Avenue, Stafford ST17 0EB* Tel (01785) 662870

STERRY, Christopher. b 54. K Coll Lon BD77 AKC77. Episc Sem Austin Texas 78 St Jo Coll Nottm 79. **d** 80 **p** 81. C Huddersfield St Jo *Wakef* 80-84; V Middlestown 84-89; Chapl and Tutor NOC 89-94; Lect Ches Coll of HE 93-94; NSM Padgate *Liv* 92-94; Bp's Dom Chapl *Blackb* 94-97; Chapl Whalley Abbey 94-97; Warden 97-04; V Whalley 97-09; P-in-c Sabden and Pendleton 07-09; C Colne and Villages from 09. *Christ Church Vicarage, Keighley Road, Colne BB8 7HF* Tel (01282) 859321 Mobile 07010-717992 E-mail colneteamchch@aol.com

STERRY, Timothy John. b 34. Oriel Coll Ox BA58 MA62. Wycliffe Hall Ox 58. **d** 60 **p** 61. C Cromer *Nor* 60-64; Chapl Oundle Sch 64-72; Teacher Cheam Prep Sch 72-75; Hd Master Temple Grove Sch E Sussex 75-80; Team Ldr Scripture Union Independent Schs 81-99; rtd 00; Perm to Offic *Sarum* from 02. *24 Darn Road, Broadstone BH18 8NJ* Tel (01202) 699299 E-mail tim@sterry.org

STEVEN, Canon David Bowring. b 38. AKC64. **d** 64 **p** 65. C Grantham St Wulfram *Linc* 64-68; C Kimberley St Cypr S Africa 68-71; R Mafeking 71-75; C Bramley *Ripon* 76-77; V Sutton Valence w E Sutton and Chart Sutton *Cant* 77-82; P-in-c Littlebourne and Warden of Readers 82-86; V Mansfield Woodhouse *S'well* 86-98; P-in-c Mullion *Truro* 98-03; RD Kerrier 01-03; rtd 03; Hon Can Truro Cathl 03-07; Perm to Offic from 03. *5 Guinea Port Parc, Wadebridge PL27 7BY* Tel (01208) 815393

STEVEN, James Henry Stevenson. b 62. CCC Cam MA84 St Jo Coll Dur BA87 K Coll Lon PhD99. Cranmer Hall Dur 84. **d** 87 **p** 88. C Welling *Roch* 87-91; C Bournemouth St Jo w St Mich *Win* 91-94; TV Bournemouth St Pet w St Swithun, H Trin etc 94-00; Chapl Bournemouth and Poole Coll of FE 94-00; Tutor Trin Coll Bris 00-08; Lect K Coll Lon from 08. *King's College London, Strand, London WC2R 2LS* Tel (020) 7848 3027 Fax 7848 3182 E-mail james.steven@kcl.ac.uk

STEVEN, John Brian. b 54. Oak Hill Th Coll BA99. **d** 99 **p** 01. Asst P Bluff Pt Australia 00-03; P-in-c Horsmonden *Roch* 04-09; Chapl HM Pris Blantyre Ho 05-09; Australia from 09. *Address temp unknown* E-mail ra-steven@hotmail.com

STEVENETTE, John Maclachlan. b 30. St Pet Coll Ox MA60. Ripon Hall Ox 60. **d** 61 **p** 62. C Newhaven *Chich* 61-66; R Lynch w Iping Marsh 66-74; R Birdham w W Itchenor 74-78; R Byfleet *Guildf* 78-86; V Whittlesey *Ely* 86-90; TR Whittlesey and Pondersbridge 91; R Itchen Valley *Win* 91-99; rtd 99; Perm to Offic *Bris* from 00. *35 Ballard Chase, Abingdon OX14 1XQ* Tel (01235) 526706

STEVENETTE, Simon Melville. b 62. Hull Univ BA83. Wycliffe Hall Ox 84. **d** 87 **p** 88. C Carterton *Ox* 87-90; C Keynsham *B & W* 90-91; TV 91-98; Chapl Keynsham Hosp Bris 92-98; V Swindon Ch Ch *Bris* from 98; AD Swindon from 11. *Christ Church Vicarage, 26 Cricklade Street, Swindon SN1 3HG* Tel and fax (01793) 529166 *or* tel 522832 Mobile 07880-710172 E-mail simon@stevenette.freeserve.co.uk

STEVENS, Andrew. *See* STEVENS, John David Andrew

STEVENS, Andrew Graham. b 54. BEd MA. Coll of Resurr Mirfield. **d** 83 **p** 84. C Leigh Park *Portsm* 83-87; TV Brighton Resurr *Chich* 87-94; V Plumstead St Nic *S'wark* from 94. *St Nicholas's Vicarage, 64 Purrett Road, London SE18 1JP* Tel (020) 8854 0461 Fax 8265 5065 E-mail frandrew@dircon.co.uk

STEVENS, Canon Anne Helen. b 61. Warwick Univ BA82 Fitzw Coll Cam BA90 MA94 Heythrop Coll Lon MTh99. Ridley Hall Cam 88. **d** 91 **p** 94. Par Dn E Greenwich Ch Ch w St Andr and St Mich *S'wark* 91-94; Chapl Trin Coll Cam 94-99; P-in-c Battersea St Mich *S'wark* 99-07; V from 07; Dir Readers' Tr from 99; Hon Can S'wark Cathl from 05. *93 Bolingbroke Grove, London SW11 6HA* Tel (020) 7228 1990 E-mail anne.stevens@southwark.anglican.org

STEVENS, Anthony Harold. b 46. CEng71 MIStructE71 FIStructE87 MICE75 FICE92. St Mich Coll Llan 94. **d** 95 **p** 96. C Cardiff St Jo *Llan* 95-98; TV Cowbridge 98-01; R Eglwysilan 01-08; R Gelligaer from 08; AD Caerphilly 04-10. *The Rectory, Church Road, Gelligaer, Hengoed CF82 8FW* Tel (01443) 830300 E-mail revtonystevens@sky.com

STEVENS, Brian Henry. b 28. Oak Hill Th Coll. **d** 69 **p** 70. C Chadwell *Chelmsf* 69-75; V Penge Ch Ch w H Trin *Roch* 75-85; V St Mary Cray and St Paul's Cray 85-93; rtd 93; Perm to Offic *Cant* from 93. *53 Middle Deal Road, Deal CT14 9RG*

STEVENS, Brian Henry. b 45. Open Univ BA80. S Dios Minl Tr Scheme 81. **d** 84 **p** 85. NSM S Malling *Chich* 84-86; C Langney 86-87; TV Wolverton *Ox* 87-88; V Welford w Sibbertoft and Marston Trussell *Pet* 88-91; V Hardingstone and Horton and Piddington 91-11; Chapl Northants Police 06-11; rtd 11. *30 Valentine Way, Great Billing, Northampton NN3 9XD* Tel (01604) 949042 Mobile 07710-207201 E-mail fr.brian@talktalk.net

STEVENS, Cyril David Richard. b 25. NZ Bd of Th Studies. **d** 59 **p** 60. New Zealand 59-65 and 67-68; V Playford w Culpho and Tuddenham St Martin *St E* 65-67; R Rendham w Sweffling and Cransford 69-73; RD Saxmundham 72-74; R Rendham w Sweffling 73-95; rtd 95; Perm to Offic *St E* from 95. *Meadow Cottage, Low Road, Marlesford, Woodbridge IP13 0AW* Tel (01728) 746013

STEVENS, David John. b 45. Bris Univ BA67. Clifton Th Coll. **d** 70 **p** 71. C Ex St Leon w H Trin 70-75; P-in-c Lt Burstead *Chelmsf* 75-77; TV Billericay and Lt Burstead 77-81; P-in-c Illogan *Truro* 81-83; R St Illogan 83-96; RD Carnmarth N 96; V Highworth w Sevenhampton and Inglesham etc *Bris* 96-01; P-in-c Constantine *Truro* 01-10; RD Kerrier 03-10; rtd 10. *Bede House, Primrose Hill, Goldsithney, Penzance TR20 9JR* Tel (01736) 719090

STEVENS, David Lynne. b 59. Poly of Wales BA81 York St Jo Coll MA06. NOC 99. **d** 02 **p** 03. C Horsforth *Ripon* 02-06; Chapl Abbey Grange High Sch Leeds 04-06; P-in-c Potternewton *Ripon* from 06. *St Martin's Vicarage, 2A St Martin's View, Leeds LS7 3LB* Tel 0113-262 4271 Mobile 07963-060911 E-mail davidstev1@aol.com

STEVENS, David Norman. b 44. QPM91. EAMTC 01. **d** 03 **p** 04. NSM Necton, Holme Hale w N and S Pickenham *Nor* 03-05; Asst Chapl HM Pris Wayland 04-06; New Zealand from 06. *Address temp unknown* E-mail david.sue.stevens@hotmail.co.uk

STEVENS, Douglas George. b 47. Lon Univ BA69. Westcott Ho Cam 69. **d** 72 **p** 73. C Portsea St Geo CD *Portsm* 72-75; C Portsea N End St Mark 75-79; Chapl NE Lon Poly *Chelmsf* 79-83; C-in-c Orton Goldhay CD *Ely* 83-87; V Elm 87-91; V Coldham 87-91; V Friday Bridge 87-91; R Woodston 91-98; P-in-c Fletton 94-98; rtd 98. *28 Francis Gardens, Peterborough PE1 3XX* Tel (01733) 755430

STEVENS, Frederick Crichton. b 42. K Coll Lon BD78 AKC78. St Steph Ho Ox 78. **d** 79 **p** 80. C Newquay *Truro* 79-81; C St Martin-in-the-Fields *Lon* 81-85; P-in-c Soho St Anne w St Thos and St Pet 85-93; R 93-98; R Lostwithiel, St Winnow w St Nectan's Chpl etc *Truro* 98-07; C Lanreath, Pelynt and Bradoc 03-07; rtd 07. *12 Penmare Court, Hayle TR27 4RD* Tel (01736) 757516 E-mail stevens.crich@tiscali.co.uk

STEVENS, Miss Gillian. b 51. K Alfred's Coll Win CertEd72. EAMTC 98. **d** 01 **p** 02. C March St Mary and March St Pet *Ely* 01-03; C Whittlesey, Pondersbridge and Coates 03-05; TV from 05. *8 The Grove, Whittlesey, Peterborough PE7 2RF* Tel and fax (01733) 200563 E-mail gill.stevens8@btinternet.com

STEVENS, James Anthony. b 47. Worc Coll Ox MA69. Trin Coll Bris 78. **d** 80 **p** 81. C Heref St Pet w St Owen and St Jas 80-84; C Lowestoft and Kirkley *Nor* 84-85; TV 85-89; V Dorridge *Birm* 89-05; AD Shirley 02-05; R Sarratt and Chipperfield *St Alb* from 05. *The Vicarage, The Street, Chipperfield, Kings Langley WD4 9BJ* Tel (01923) 265848 E-mail jimandjudy@6manor.fsnet.co.uk

STEVENS, Jane. *See* KRAFT, Mrs Jane

STEVENS, Janice Hazel. b 42. **d** 00 **p** 01. Hon C Warlingham w Chelsham and Farleigh *S'wark* from 00; Chapl S Lon and Maudsley NHS Foundn Trust 00-07. *7 Harrow Road, Warlingham CR6 9EY* Tel (01883) 626308 *or* (020) 8776 4361

STEVENS, John David Andrew. b 44. Wycliffe Hall Ox. **d** 68 **p** 69. C Standish *Blackb* 68-71; C Stonehouse *Glouc* 71-76; P-in-c Closworth *B & W* 76-77; P-in-c Barwick 76-77; TV Yeovil 77-80; R Chewton Mendip w Ston Easton, Litton etc 80-94; R Quantoxhead 94-07; RD Quantock 95-01; rtd 07. *Amberwell, Holywell Road, Edington, Bridgwater TA7 9LE* E-mail andrewstevens@zetnet.co.uk

STEVENS, Martin Leonard. b 35. St Jo Coll Dur BA60 MA72. Oak Hill Th Coll 60. **d** 62 **p** 63. C Low Elswick *Newc* 62-65; C S Croydon Em *Cant* 65-69; Hon C 69-74; S England Deputation Sec ICM 69-74; V Felling *Dur* 74-86; NSM Ches Square St Mich w St Phil *Lon* 92-96; rtd 95; Hon C Cullompton and Kentisbeare w Blackborough *Ex* 96-01; Perm to Offic *Cov* from 03. *11 Foxes Way, Warwick CV34 6AX* Tel (01926) 490864

STEVENS, Matthew. b 80. Cam Univ BTh07. Ridley Hall Cam 04. **d** 07 **p** 08. C Reading St Mary w St Laur *Ox* 07-11; Chapl RAF from 11. *Chaplaincy Services, Valiant Block, HQ Air Command, RAF High Wycombe HP14 4UE* Tel (01494) 496800 Fax 496343 E-mail rev.mattstevens@googlemail.com

STEVENS, Michael John. b 37. St Cath Coll Cam BA63. Coll of Resurr Mirfield 63. **d** 65 **p** 66. C Poplar All SS w St Frideswide *Lon* 65-71; Asst Chapl The Lon Hosp (Whitechapel) 71-74; Chapl St Thos Hosp Lon 75-96; Hospitaller St Barts Hosp Lon 96-05; P-in-c St Bart Less *Lon* 96-99; V 99-05; rtd 05; Perm to

Offic *Chelmsf* 03-10. *The Oaks, Toogood Way, Nursling, Southampton SO16 0XL* Tel (023) 8073 2234

STEVENS, Norman William. b 38. St Chad's Coll Dur BA61. d 63 p 99. C Wingate Grange *Dur* 63-64; NSM Ansty and Shilton *Cov* from 99. *60 Clinton Lane, Kenilworth CV8 1AT* Tel (01926) 858090 *or* (024) 7622 7597

STEVENS, Olive. b 48. Ex Univ BA04. SWMTC 01. d 04 p 05. C Camborne *Truro* from 04; RD Carnmarth N from 08. *Hideaway, The Square, Portreath, Redruth TR16 4LA* Tel (01209) 842372 E-mail oste621439@aol.com

STEVENS, Penelope Ann. See PRINCE, Penelope Ann

STEVENS, Peter David. b 36. MRICS. Oak Hill Th Coll 79. d 81 p 82. C Branksome St Clem *Sarum* 81-87; R Moreton and Woodsford w Tincleton 87-98; rtd 98; Hon C Hordle *Win* 98-02; Perm to Offic from 02. *34 Wisbech Way, Hordle, Lymington SO41 0YQ* Tel (01425) 628922

STEVENS, Philip Terence. b 55. MBE07. Man Univ BSc76 Lon Univ BD81 St Jo Coll Dur MA86. Cranmer Hall Dur 81. d 83 p 84. C Withington St Paul *Man* 83-86; C Middleton 86-88; V Saddleworth 88-92; V Sheff St Paul 93-96; TR Sheff Manor 96-00; Perm to Offic *Sheff* 00-07; Newc 07-09; *B & W* 09-10; P-in-c Bleadon *B & W* from 10; P-in-c Weston-super-Mare St Andr Bournville from 10. *The Rectory, 17 Coronation Road, Bleadon, Weston-super-Mare BS24 0PG* Tel (01934) 812978 E-mail philipstevens@tiscali.co.uk

STEVENS, Richard William. b 36. AKC59. St Boniface Warminster 59. d 60 p 61. C Greenhill St Jo *Lon* 60-63; Chapl RAF 63-79; CF 79-01; rtd 01; Perm to Offic *Cant* 02-10. *The Old Vicarage, Stockbury, Sittingbourne ME9 7UN* Tel (01795) 844891

STEVENS, Robin George. b 43. Leic Univ BA65. Cuddesdon Coll 74. d 74 p 75. C Hemel Hempstead *St Alb* 74-77; Chapl K Coll Sch Wimbledon 77-03; TV Wimbledon *S'wark* 98-08; rtd 09; Perm to Offic *S'wark* from 11. *329 Wimbledon Park Road, London SW19 6NS* Tel (020) 8788 4308

STEVENS, Simon Mark. b 72. Lon Univ BD Cam Univ MPhil. STETS 00. d 01 p 02. C Sholing *Win* 01-05; Chapl Southn Univ 05-10; Chapl Lough'b Univ from 10. *1 Holywell Drive, Loughborough LE11 3JU* E-mail simon.m.stevens@btinternet.com

STEVENS, Mrs Susan Ann. b 46. Lon Univ BEd85. St Mich Coll Llan. d 07 p 08. NSM Bargoed and Deri w Brithdir *Llan* 07-10; NSM Gelligaer from 10. *The Rectory, Church Road, Gelligaer, Hengoed CF82 8FW* Tel (01443) 830300 E-mail salutsue@aol.com

STEVENS, Mrs Susan Marjorie Earlam. b 52. RGN74. WMMTC 97. d 00 p 01. NSM Harborne St Faith and St Laur *Birm* 00-02; NSM Publow w Pensford, Compton Dando and Chelwood *B & W* from 03; Chapl R United Hosp Bath NHS Trust from 06. *Woollard Place, Woollard, Pensford, Bristol BS39 4HU* Tel (01761) 490898 E-mail smestevens@hotmail.co.uk

STEVENS, Thomas Walter. b 33. Bps' Coll Cheshunt. d 65 p 66. C Newc St Matt w St Mary 65-69; C Wallsend St Luke 69-70; C Cranford *Lon* 70-87; C Fulwell St Mich and St Geo 87-90; C Teddington SS Pet and Paul and Fulwell 90-91; rtd 92; Perm to Offic *S'wark* from 92. *23A Samos Road, London SE20 7UQ* Tel (020) 8776 7960

✠STEVENS, The Rt Revd Timothy John. b 46. Selw Coll Cam BA68 MA72. Ripon Coll Cuddesdon 75. d 76 p 77 c 95. C E Ham w Upton Park *Chelmsf* 76-80; TR Canvey Is 80-88; Dep Dir Cathl Cen for Research and Tr 82-84; Bp's Urban Officer 87-91; Hon Can Chelmsf Cathl 87-91; Adn W Ham 91-95; Suff Bp Dunwich *St E* 95-99; Bp Leic from 99. *Bishop's Lodge, 10 Springfield Road, Leicester LE2 3BD* Tel 0116-270 8985 Fax 270 3288 E-mail bishop.tim@leccofe.org

STEVENSON, Canon Alastair Rice. b 42. Open Univ BA78. Ripon Coll Cuddesdon 78. d 80 p 81. C Bexhill St Pet *Chich* 80-82; C Brighton St Matthias 82-84; C Swindon Ch Ch *Bris* 84-87; Bp's Soc and Ind Adv 87-97; P-in-c Swindon All SS w St Barn 97-01; V from 01; Hon Can Bris Cathl from 02. *The Vicarage, Southbrook Street, Swindon SN2 1HF* Tel and fax (01793) 612385 E-mail alastair@asteve.fsbusiness.co.uk

STEVENSON, Andrew James. b 63. IEng AMICE MIAT. SWMTC 94. d 97 p 98. NSM Highertown and Baldhu *Truro* 97-08; NSM Mylor w Flushing from 08. *31 Nansavallon Road, Truro TR1 3JU* Tel (01872) 241880 E-mail theblackstuff@sky.com

STEVENSON, Beaumont. See STEVENSON, Canon Frank Beaumont

STEVENSON, Bernard Norman. b 57. Kent Univ BA78 Fitzw Coll Cam BA81 MA86. Ridley Hall Cam. d 82 p 83. C Mortlake w E Sheen *S'wark* 82-84; C Kensal Rise St Martin *Lon* 84-88; C Headstone St Geo 88-90; V Worfield *Heref* 90-95; R Hutton *B & W* 95-07; RD Locking 04-05. *55 Smyth Road, Bristol BS3 2DS* E-mail bstevenson@clara.net

STEVENSON, Brian. See STEVENSON, Canon Robert Brian

STEVENSON, Brian. b 34. JP66. NW Ord Course 76. d 79 p 80. C Padiham *Blackb* 79-82; V Clitheroe St Paul Low Moor 82-89; V Blackb St Silas 89-01; rtd 01; Perm to Offic *Blackb* from 01.

1 Chatburn Close, Great Harwood, Blackburn BB6 7TL Tel (01254) 885051

STEVENSON, Christopher James. b 43. TCD BA65 MA73 Em Coll Cam BA69 MA73. Westcott Ho Cam 68. d 70 p 71. C Newc H Cross 70-72; C Arm St Mark 72-73; C Dublin Crumlin *D & G* 73-76; Hon Clerical V Ch Ch Cathl Dublin 75-76; C-in-c Appley Bridge All SS CD *Blackb* 76-82; P-in-c Appley Bridge 82-91; Bp's C Cloonclare w Killasnett, Lurganboy and Drumlease *K, E & A* from 91. *The Rectory, Manorhamilton, Co Leitrim, Republic of Ireland* Tel (00353) (71) 985 5041 Mobile 07982-262862

STEVENSON, David Andrew. b 60. Trin Coll Bris BA92. d 92 p 93. C Nottingham St Sav *S'well* 92-96; P-in-c Darlaston All SS and Ind Chapl Black Country Urban Ind Miss *Lich* 96-00; C Darlaston St Lawr 99-00; TV Broadwater *Chich* 00-08; P-in-c Eastwood *S'well* from 08; P-in-c Brinsley w Underwood from 09. *The Rectory, 5A Woodland Way, Eastwood, Nottingham NG16 3BU* Tel (01773) 710770

STEVENSON, David Eugene. b 66. Luton Univ BA02. St Steph Ho Ox 06. d 08 p 09. C Nor St Jo w St Julian from 08. *18 Kilderkin Way, Norwich NR1 1RD* Tel (01603) 661401 Mobile 07980-315534 E-mail rev.davidstevenson@googlemail.com

STEVENSON, Donald Macdonald. b 48. Lon Univ BSc(Econ)70 Leeds Univ MA72. Univ of Wales (Abth) PGCE73 Warwick Univ MEd78. Oak Hill Th Coll BA88. d 88 p 89. C Gt Malvern St Mary *Worc* 88-92; Chapl Bedford Sch 92-98; Sen Chapl 96-98; Perm to Offic *St Alb* 99-02. *94 Curlew Crescent, Bedford MK41 7HZ* Tel (01234) 217013 E-mail donstevenson100@hotmail.com

STEVENSON, Elizabeth. See STEVENSON, Miss Margaret Elizabeth Maud

STEVENSON, Canon Frank Beaumont. b 39. Duke Univ (USA) BA61 MInstGA. Episc Th Sch Harvard MDiv64. d 64 p 64. USA 64-66; Zambia 66-68; Lect Th Ox Univ from 68; Bp's Tr Officer *Ox* 69-70; Chapl Keble Coll Ox 71-72; Chapl Oxon Mental Healthcare NHS Trust 75-07; Officer for CME from 90; Dioc Adv Past Care from 90; Hon Can Ch Ch *Ox* from 98. *The School House, Wheatley Road, Stanton St John, Oxford OX33 1ET* Tel (01865) 351635 *or* 778911 E-mail 101531.3264@compuserve.com

STEVENSON, Gerald Ernest. b 35. S'wark Ord Course 80. d 83 p 84. NSM Eltham Park St Luke *S'wark* 83-88; Asst Chapl HM Pris Wormwood Scrubs 88-98; Perm to Offic *S'wark* 88-99; rtd 99; Hon C Eltham St Barn *S'wark* from 99. *7 Moira Road, London SE9 1SJ* Tel (020) 8850 2748

STEVENSON, James Christian William. b 79. New Coll Ox BA00. Trin Coll Bris 05. d 07 p 08. C Henbury *Bris* 07-10; P-in-c Bishopston and St Andrews from 10. *7 Kings Drive, Bishopston, Bristol BS7 8JW* Tel 0117-373 8450 E-mail revjamesstevenson@yahoo.co.uk

STEVENSON, John. b 39. Glas Univ MA64 Jordan Hill Coll Glas TCert65. St Jo Coll Nottm Edin Th Coll. d 87 p 88. NSM Moffat *Glas* 87-92; P-in-c Eastriggs 92-95; P-in-c Gretna 92-95; P-in-c Langholm 92-95; Israel 95-01; P-in-c Thurso and Wick *Mor* 01-06; rtd 06. *Hoppertitty, Beattock, Moffat DG10 9PJ* Tel (01683) 300164 Mobile 07958-307390 E-mail hoppertitty@msn.com

STEVENSON, John William. b 44. Salford Univ BSc66 UNISA BTh89. St Paul's Coll Grahamstown 84. d 87 p 87. S Africa 87-93; V Broom Leys *Leic* from 93. *St David's Vicarage, 7 Greenhill Road, Coalville LE67 4RL* Tel (01530) 836262 E-mail johnandrene@btinternet.com

STEVENSON, The Ven Leslie Thomas Clayton. b 59. TCD BA MPhil. d 83 p 84. C Dundela St Mark *D & D* 83-87; I Kilmore and Inch 87-92; R Donaghadee 92-99; I Portarlington w Cloneyhurke, Lea etc *M & K* from 99; Can Meath from 08; Can Kildare Cathl from 08; Adn Meath from 09; Adn Kildare from 09. *The Rectory, Portarlington, Co Laois, Republic of Ireland* Tel and fax (00353) (57) 864 0117 E-mail lesliestevenson@eircom.net

STEVENSON, Miss Margaret Elizabeth Maud. b 49. Stranmillis Coll CertEd70 Ulster Univ BEd86. CITC 07. d 10. NSM Drumglass w Moygashel *Arm* from 10. *1 Derrycaw Lane, Portadown, Craigavon BT62 1TW* Tel (028) 3885 1503 E-mail elizabethstevenson431@btinternet.com

STEVENSON, Michael Richard Nevin. b 52. Univ Coll Lon MA77. CITC. d 86 p 87. C Clooney w Strathfoyle *D & R* 86-89; CF from 89. *c/o MOD Chaplains (Army)* Tel (01264) 381140 Fax 381824

STEVENSON, Miss Pamela Mary. b 35. CQSW74. d 97 p 98. OLM Mitcham Ascension *S'wark* 97-05; Perm to Offic from 05; Retirement Officer Kingston Area from 08. *7 Robin Hood Close, Mitcham CR4 1JN* Tel (020) 8764 8331 Mobile 07702-928204

STEVENSON, Peter John. b 70. Southn Univ BSc91 MSc93. Wycliffe Hall Ox 00. d 02 p 03. C Watford St Luke *St Alb* 02-06; TV Hemel Hempstead from 06. *The Vicarage, 436 Warners End Road, Hemel Hempstead HP1 3QF* Tel (01442) 251897

STEVENSON, Richard Clayton. b 22. TCD BA48 MA56. CITC 48. d 48 p 49. C Belfast St Mary Magd *Conn* 48-51; C Bangor

St Comgall *D & D* 51-54; I Comber 54-60; I Belfast St Barn *Conn* 60-70; I Belfast St Nic 70-88; Adn Conn 79-88; rtd 88. *42 Malone Heights, Belfast BT9 5PG* Tel (028) 9061 5006

STEVENSON, Richard Hugh. b 45. Ex Univ BA68 Bexley Hall Rochester NY DMin83. Westcott Ho Cam 68. **d** 70 **p** 71. C Millhouses H Trin *Sheff* 70-74; Chapl Hong Kong Cathl 74-80; R Fairport St Luke USA 81-91; R Kenwood St Patr from 91. *610 Los Alamos Road, Santa Rosa CA 95409-4413, USA* Tel (001) (707) 833 4228 E-mail stpatskenwood@aol.com

STEVENSON, Robert. b 52. UWIST BSc73 MRTPI78 MCIM89. SEITE 03. **d** 05 **p** 06. NSM Woodnesborough w Worth and Staple *Cant* from 05. *The Old Rectory, 5 Cowper Road, Deal CT14 9TW* Tel (01304) 366003 E-mail robert@robstevenson.fsnet.co.uk

STEVENSON, Canon Robert Brian. b 40. QUB BA61 Qu Coll Cam BA67 MA71 Pemb Coll Ox BA69 BD76 MA76 Birm Univ PhD70. Cuddesdon Coll 69. **d** 70 **p** 71. C Lewisham St Jo Southend *S'wark* 70-73; C Catford (Southend) and Downham 73-74; Lect and Dir Past Studies Chich Th Coll 74-81; Acting Vice-Prin 80-81; V W Malling w Offham *Roch* 81-10; RD Malling 93-02; Hon Can Roch Cathl 98-10; rtd 10. *Michaelmas Cottage, Beech Farm, Stan Lane, West Peckham, Maidstone ME18 5JT* E-mail woolystevenson@yahoo.co.uk

STEVENSON, Sheila Reinhardt. *See* SWARBRICK, Mrs Sheila Reinhardt

STEVENSON, Trevor Donald. b 59. TCD Div Sch BTh. **d** 91 **p** 92. C Magheralin w Dollingstown *D & D* 91-95; CMS Uganda 95-98; Dir Fields of Life from 98. *Tree Tops, Brides Glen Road, Shankill, Dublin 18, Republic of Ireland* Tel and fax (00353) (1) 282 0150 E-mail fieldsoflife@oceanfree.net

STEVENTON, Canon June Lesley. b 61. Aston 'Ir Scheme 86 Sarum & Wells Th Coll BTh91. **d** 91 **p** 94. Par Dn Chatham St Steph *Roch* 91-94; C 94-96; Perm to Offic *York* 96-97 and *Liv* 97-00; V Abram *Liv* 00-10; V Bickershaw 00-10; P-in-c Winwick from 10; Hon Can Liv Cathl from 06. *The Rectory, Golborne Road, Winwick, Warrington WA2 8SZ* Tel (01925) 632760 E-mail june.steventon123@btinternet.com

STEVENTON, Kenneth. b 59. Cuddesdon Coll 94. **d** 96 **p** 97. C Spalding *Linc* 96-99; R Sutterton, Fosdyke, Algarkirk and Wigtoft 99-05; P-in-c Evenwood *Dur* 05-09; P-in-c Ingleton from 05; P-in-c Staindrop from 05. *St Mary's Vicarage, 7 Beechside, Staindrop, Darlington DL2 3PE* Tel (01833) 660237 E-mail revken@freeuk.co.uk

STEVINSON, Harold John Hardy. b 34. Selw Coll Cam BA57 MA61. Qu Coll Birm. **d** 59 **p** 60. C Bris St Mary Redcliffe w Temple 59-63; C Caversham *Ox* 63-73; Soc Resp Officer *Dur* 74-82; Sec Dioc Bd for Miss and Unity 82-88; P-in-c Croxdale 82-88; P-in-c Leamington Hastings and Birdingbury *Cov* 88-96; rtd 96; Perm to Offic *Cov* and *Glouc* from 96. *8 Greenways, Winchcombe, Cheltenham GL54 5LG* Tel (01242) 602195

STEVINSON, Mrs Josephine Mary. b 25. STh56. Cranmer Hall Dur 86. **dss** 86 **d** 87 **p** 94. Croxdale *Dur* 86-87; Lic to Offic 87-88; Lic to Offic *Cov* 88-96; NSM Leamington Hastings and Birdingbury 94-96; rtd 96; Perm to Offic *Glouc* from 96. *8 Greenways, Winchcombe, Cheltenham GL54 5LG* Tel (01242) 602195

STEWARD, Mrs Linda Christine. b 46. NE Lon Poly CQSW82. S'wark Ord Course 85. **d** 88 **p** 94. NSM E Ham w Upton Park *Chelmsf* 88-91; Chapl Newham Healthcare NHS Trust Lon 91-98; NSM Plaistow *Chelmsf* 91-96; NSM Plaistow and N Canning Town 96-98; P-in-c Rawreth w Rettendon 98-06; rtd 06. *2 Belfairs Park Close, Leigh-on-Sea SS9 4TR* Tel (01702) 525638 E-mail steward_linda@hotmail.com

STEWARDSON, Enid Joyce. **d** 11. OLM Heath Hayes *Lich* from 11. *Highfield House, 20 Highfield Road, Cannock WS12 2DX* Tel (01543) 279817 E-mail joyceestewa@aol.com

STEWART, Alan. *See* STEWART, Hugh Alan

STEWART, Alan Valentine. b 47. Univ Coll Galway BA98. **d** 97 **p** 98. NSM Mullingar, Portnashangan, Moyliscar, Kilbixy etc *M & K* 97-00; NSM Clane w Donadea and Coolcarrigan 00-05; NSM Dunboyne and Rathmolyon from 05. *Casteway, Baltrasna, Ashbourne, Co Meath, Republic of Ireland* Tel (00353) (1) 835 0997 *or* 814 0297 Mobile 87-179 3197 E-mail casteway@hotmail.com *or* alan.stewart@fas.ie

STEWART, Alice Elizabeth. b 42. **d** 00 **p** 01. C Cloughfern *Conn* from 00. *3 Fergus Court, Carrickfergus BT38 8HT* Tel (028) 9336 5721

STEWART, Alistair Charles. b 60. St Andr Univ MA83 Birm Univ PhD92. Qu Coll Birm 86. **d** 89 **p** 90. C Stevenage St Andr and St Geo *St Alb* 89-92; C Castle Vale St Cuth *Birm* 92-93; Tutor Codrington Coll Barbados 93-96; C Hanley H Ev *Lich* 97-98; Lect Gen Th Sem NY USA 98-01; V Bridge Par *Sarum* 01-10; C Sherborne w Castleton, Lillington and Longburton from 10. *The Rectory, Church Road, Thornford, Sherborne DT9 6QE* Tel (01935) 873838

STEWART (*née* BARBER), Mrs Anne Louise. b 71. QUB BA93 PGCE94. CITC 97. **d** 00 **p** 01. NSM Belfast Malone St Jo *Conn* 00-09; NSM Finaghy 09-11; from 11. *St George's Rectory, 6 Royal Lodge Park, Belfast BT8 7YP* Tel (028) 9070 1350 *or* 9029 2980 Mobile 07724-067547 E-mail stewartrevslb@yahoo.com

STEWART, Miss Betty. b 25. S'wark Ord Course 91. **d** 93 **p** 94. NSM Wandsworth Common St Mary *S'wark* 93-95; NSM Hampton Hill *Lon* 95-05. *71 Ormond Drive, Hampton TW12 2TL* Tel (020) 8979 2069

STEWART, Ms Brenda Alice. b 60. ERMC. **d** 09 **p** 10. C Abbots Ripton w Wood Walton *Ely* from 09; C Kings Ripton from 09; C Houghton w Wyton from 09. *The Rectory, 3 Rectory Lane, Wyton, Huntingdon PE28 2AQ* Tel (01480) 300152 E-mail bas@con-brio.com

STEWART, Brian. b 59. TCD BTh91. CITC 88. **d** 91 **p** 92. C Ballywillan *Conn* 91-94; I Belfast St Geo from 94. *St George's Rectory, 6 Royal Lodge Park, Belfast BT8 7YP* Tel (028) 9070 1350 Mobile 07902-792080

STEWART, Charles. b 55. St Jo Coll Cam BA77 MA81 CertEd79. Wycliffe Hall Ox 85. **d** 87 **p** 88. C Bowdon *Ches* 87-90; C Bath Abbey w St Jas *B & W* 90-94; Can Res, Prec and Sacr Win Cathl 94-06; V Walton-on-Thames *Guildf* from 06. *The Vicarage, 53 Ashley Park Avenue, Walton-on-Thames KT12 1EU* Tel (01932) 227184 E-mail vicar@waltonparish.org.uk

STEWART, Charles Michael. b 50. Ball Coll Ox MA82 K Coll Lon BA05 AKC05 MA07 FCA82. Ripon Coll Cuddesdon 06. **d** 07 **p** 08. NSM Leatherhead and Mickleham *Guildf* from 07. *Rickstones, Punchbowl Lane, Dorking RH5 4BN* Tel (01306) 884153 Mobile 07936-524152 E-mail mikestewart999@btinternet.com

STEWART, Ms Dorothy Elaine. b 51. Man Metrop Univ BA93 Bradf Univ MA98. Coll of Resurr Mirfield 08. **d** 10 **p** 11. C Potternewton *Ripon* from 10. *1B Southlands Avenue, Leeds LS17 5NU* Tel (0113) 226 2392 Mobile 07826-107049 E mail dotelartuna@hotmail.com

STEWART, Hugh Alan. b 67. Lon Inst BA91 Middx Univ BA03. NTMTC 00. **d** 03 **p** 04. C Gt Stanmore *Lon* 03-06; P-in-c Hertford St Andr *St Alb* 06-08; P-in-c Hertingfordbury 06-08; TV Hertford from 08. *St Andrew's Rectory, 7 Elizabeth Close, Hertford SG14 2DB* Tel (01992) 582726 E-mail h.alanstewart@tiscali.co.uk

STEWART, Ian Guild. b 43. Edin Th Coll 89. **d** 84 **p** 85. NSM Dundee St Mary Magd *Bre* 84-87; NSM Dundee St Jo 87-90; C 90-92; NSM Dundee St Martin 87-90; C 90-92; R Montrose 92-08; P-in-c Inverbervie 92-08; Can St Paul's Cathl Dundee 01-08; Dean Bre 07-08; rtd 08. *36 Forbes Road, Edinburgh EH10 4ED*

STEWART, James. *See* STEWART, Malcolm James

STEWART, James. b 32. Div Hostel Dub. **d** 69 **p** 70. C Belfast St Donard *D & D* 69-72; C Dundonald 72-74; I Rathmullan w Tyrella 74-80; I Belfast St Clem 80-97; I Moy w Charlemont *Arm* 97-04; rtd 04. *25 Barnish Road, Kells, Ballymena BT42 3PA* Tel (028) 2589 8787 Mobile 07833-791790 E-mail revj.stewart@subfish.com

STEWART, Canon James Patrick. b 55. Keele Univ BA77 Birm Univ MA78. Ridley Hall Cam 86. **d** 88 **p** 89. C Boulton *Derby* 88-91; C Cove St Jo *Guildf* 91-92; TV 92-97; TR Tunbridge Wells St Jas w St Phil *Roch* 97-04; V Tunbridge Wells St Jas from 04; RD Tunbridge Wells 99-07; Hon Can Roch Cathl from 05. *The Vicarage, 12 Shandon Close, Tunbridge Wells TN2 3RE* Tel (01892) 530687 *or* 521703 E-mail jpstewart4@googlemail.com

STEWART, James William. b 71. Selw Coll Cam BA92 MA96. Westcott Ho Cam 09 Yale Div Sch 10. **d** 11. C Gt Yarmouth *Nor* from 11. *1 Osborne Avenue, Great Yarmouth NR30 4EE* Tel 07986-839583 (mobile) E-mail jstewart1971@googlemail.com

STEWART, Mrs Janet Margaret. b 41. Roehampton Inst CertEd62. Cranmer Hall Dur 87. **d** 87 **p** 94. Hon Par Dn Oulton Broad *Nor* 87-94; Hon C 94-97; Chapl Lowestoft Hosp 94-97; Perm to Offic *B & W* 97-98; C Quidenham *Gp Nor* 98-01; Asst Chapl Norfolk and Nor Univ Hosp NHS Trust from 00. *30 St Joseph's Road, Sheringham NR26 8JA* Tel (01263) 824497

STEWART, Jennifer Jane. *See* SISTIG, Mrs Jennifer Jane

STEWART, John. b 39. Oak Hill Th Coll 75. **d** 77 **p** 78. C Accrington Ch Ch *Blackb* 77-79; TV Darwen St Pet w Hoddlesden 79-86; R Coppull St Jo 86-04; rtd 04; Perm to Offic *Blackb* from 05. *83 Regents Way, Euxton, Chorley PR7 6PG*

✠STEWART, The Rt Revd John Craig. b 40. Ridley Coll Melbourne LTh64. **d** 65 **p** 66 **c** 84. C Prospect Australia 65-67; C Mt Gambier 67-68; C Crawley *Chich* 68-70; I Frankston S Australia 74-79; Gen Sec CMS Vic 79-84; Asst Bp Melbourne 84-01; W Region 84-91; N Region 91-94; E Region 94-01; V Gen 88-01; R Woodend 01-04; rtd 04. *PO Box 928, Bacchus Marsh Vic 3440, Australia* Tel (0061) (3) 5367 0081 E-mail bishopjcstewart@bigpond.com

STEWART, Canon John Roberton. b 29. Sarum Th Coll 63. **d** 65 **p** 66. C Gillingham *Sarum* 65-70; R Langton Matravers 70-84; RD Purbeck 82-89; Can and Preb Sarum Cathl 83-90; R Kingston, Langton Matravers and Worth Matravers 84-90; Can Res Sarum Cathl 90-95; Treas 90-95; rtd 95; Perm to Offic *Sarum* from 95. *Wolfeton Manor Residential Home, 16 East Hill, Charminster, Dorchester DT2 9QL* Tel (01305) 262340

STEWART, Canon John Wesley. b 52. QUB BD76 TCD 76. **d** 77 **p** 78. C Seagoe *D & D* 77-79; C Lisburn Ch Ch *Conn* 79-85; I

Ballybay w Mucknoe and Clontibret *Clogh* 85-90; I Derryvullen S w Garvary from 90; Bp Dom Chapl 95-00; Glebes Sec from 95; Dioc Registrar from 98; Exam Can Clogh Cathl 98-00; Preb from 00. *The Rectory, 2 Ballylucas Road, Tullyharney, Enniskillen BT74 4PR* Tel (028) 6638 7236 E-mail jva.stewart@hotmail.co.uk

STEWART, Keith Malcolm Morris. b 45. d 08 p 09. OLM Stalybridge *Man* from 08. *10 Ladysmith Road, Stalybridge SK15 1HB* Tel 0161-303 7483

STEWART, Louise. See STEWART, Mrs Anne Louise

STEWART, Malcolm James. b 44. TD78. York Univ BA66 K Coll Lon MA68 Lon Inst of Educn PGCE69 Solicitor 79. NEOC 89. d 93 p 94. NSM Upper Nidderdale *Ripon* 93-95; C Fountains Gp 95-98; V Catterick 98-03; P-in-c Culmington w Onibury, Bromfield etc *Heref* 03-06; TV Ludlow 06-10; RD Ludlow 07-10; rtd 10. *3 Leadon Place, Ledbury HR8 2GD* Tel (01531) 630237

STEWART, Marcus Patrick Michael. b 66. Ox Univ BA89 MSc93 Cam Univ BA92. Ven English Coll Rome 89 Westcott Ho Cam 96. d 98 p 99. C Headington *Ox* 98-00; Hon C S Hinksey 00-01; CF 01-04; Chapl RN 04-07; Perm to Offic *Cant* 08-09; Chapl HM Pris Elmley 09-10; Hon C St Peter-in-Thanet *Cant* 09-10; Chapl Kent Police 09-10; Lead Chapl Peterborough and Stamford Hosps NHS Foundn Trust from 10. *Faith Centre, PO Box 016, Peterborough City Hospital, Bretton Gate, Peterborough PE3 9GZ* Tel 07948-218521 (mobile)

STEWART, Maxwell Neville Gabriel. b 33. Essex Univ MA68 Hertf Coll Ox BA58 MA59. Wycliffe Hall Ox 58. d 60 p 61. C Perry Beeches *Birm* 60-62; Chapl Rosenberg Coll St Gallen 62-64; Perm to Offic *Chelmsf* 64-70; Warden Leics Poly 70-92; De Montfort Univ Leic 92-93; Hon C Leic St Mary 74-79; rtd 93; Perm to Offic *Leic* from 79. *25 Sidney Court, Norwich Road, Leicester LE4 0LR*

STEWART, Michael. b 65. St Jo Coll Nottm LTh89. d 89 p 90. C Ealing St Paul *Lon* 89-93; P-in-c N Wembley St Cuth 93-98; V 98-02; Assoc P Abbotsford Canada from 02. *St Matthew's Anglican Church, 2010 Guilford Drive, Abbotsford BC V2S 5R2, Canada* Tel (001) (604) 853 2416 E-mail mikes@stmatthewsanglicanchurch.com

STEWART, Ms Monica Frances Ethel. b 35. RGN57 RM59. d 08. NSM Stamford Hill St Thos *Lon* from 08. *2 The Heights, 165 Mountview Road, London N4 4JU* Tel (020) 8340 4746 Mobile 07947-026297 E-mail monica.f.stewart@googlemail.com

STEWART, Canon Raymond John. b 55. TCD BA79 MA82. CITC Div Test77. d 79 p 80. C Clooney *D & R* 79-82; I Dunfanaghy 82-87; I Gweedore Union 85-87; Dioc Youth Adv 83-87; Bp's Dom Chapl 85-87; I Castledawson 87-03; I Tamlaght O'Crilly Upper w Lower from 03; Ed *D & R Dioc News* 89-93; Dioc Glebes Sec from 93; Stewardship Adv from 98; Can Derry Cathl from 99. *Hervey Hill Rectory, 16 Hervey Hill, Kilrea, Coleraine BT51 5TT* Tel and fax (028) 2954 0296 Mobile 07761-585412 E-mail raymondandpatricia@herveyhill.wanadoo.co.uk

STEWART, Stephen John. b 62. Oak Hill Th Coll. d 99 p 00. C Mile Cross *Nor* 99-04; TV Cove St Jo *Guildf* from 04. *Southwood Vicarage, 15 The Copse, Farnborough GU14 0QD* Tel (01252) 513422 E-mail stevestewartce@hotmail.com

STEWART, Susan Theresa. b 58. NOC 01. d 04 p 05. C Lodge Moor St Luke *Sheff* 04-08; V Mosbrough from 08. *The Vicarage, 25 Kelgate, Mosborough, Sheffield S20 5EJ* Tel 0114-248 6518 Mobile 07966-695095

STEWART, William. d 01 p 02. NSM Kilroot and Templecorran *Conn* from 01. *63 Victoria Road, Carrickfergus BT38 7JJ* Tel (028) 9336 2145

STEWART, William James. b 58. Ulster Poly BA82 Spurgeon's Coll Lon MTh10. CITC 80. d 83 p 84. C Glenageary *D & G* 83-86; Rostrevor Renewal Cen 86-87; I Naas w Kill and Rathmore *M & K* 87-93; Min Dublin Ch Ch Cathl Gp 93-04; CORE (St Cath Ch) 93-04; Min Can St Patr Cathl Dublin 00-04; Lic to Offic *C & O* 08-11; V Loddon, Sisland, Chedgrave, Hardley and Langley *Nor* from 11. *The Vicarage, 4 Market Place, Loddon, Norwich NR14 6EY* Tel (01508) 520659 Mobile 07582-873183 E-mail willijstewart@yahoo.co.uk

STEWART, William Jones. b 32. Trin Hall Cam BA55 MA59 Cam Univ CertEd56. Edin Th Coll 67. d 69 p 69. Chapl St Ninian's Cathl Perth 69-71; Bp's Dom Chapl *Ox* 71-75; V Lambourn 75-03; P-in-c Lambourne Woodlands 83-90; P-in-c Eastbury and E Garston 83-03; rtd 04. *9 Ascott Way, Newbury RG14 2FH* Tel (01635) 580244 E-mail stewart.clan4@btopenworld.com

STEWART-DARLING, Fiona Lesley. b 58. Kingston Poly GRSC79 Lon Univ PhD82 K Coll Lon MA99. Trin Coll Bris BA91. d 91 p 94. C Cirencester *Glouc* 91-94; Chapl Cheltenham and Glouc Coll of HE 94-97; Chapl Portsm Univ 97-04; Hon Chapl Portsm Cathl 97-04; Bp's Chapl in Docklands *Lon* from 04. *143 New Atlas Wharf, 3 Arnhem Place, London E14 3ST* Tel (020) 7477 1073 Mobile 07739-461090 E-mail fiona.stewart-darling@london.anglican.org

STEWART ELLENS, Gordon Frederick. *See* ELLENS, Gordon Frederick Stewart

STEWART-SYKES, Teresa Melanie. b 64. Bris Univ BA85. Qu Coll Birm 87. d 89. Par Dn Stevenage St Andr and St Geo *St Alb* 89-92; Perm to Offic *Birm* 92-93; Barbados 93-97; C Meir Heath *Lich* 97-98; USA 98-01. *Address temp unknown*

STIBBE, Mrs Hazel Mary. d 99 p 00. NSM Wolverhampton St Andr *Lich* 99-02; Lic to Offic *St As* 03-08; rtd 08. *Braemar, Kerry Street, Montgomery SY15 6PG* Tel (01686) 668912

STIBBE, Mark William Godfrey. b 60. Trin Coll Cam BA83 MA86 Nottm Univ PhD88. St Jo Coll Nottm 83. d 86 p 87. C Stapleford *S'well* 86-90; C Crookes St Thos *Sheff* 90-93; Lect Sheff Univ 90-97; V Grenoside 93-97; V Chorleywood St Andr *St Alb* 97-09; Ldr Father's Ho Trust from 09. *3rd Floor, 26 The Parade, Watford WD17 1AA* Tel (01923) 256352 E-mail markstibbe@aol.com

STICKLAND, David Clifford. b 44. Surrey Univ BA01 CPFA68 MAAT77 FCCA80. STETS 98. d 01 p 02. NSM Greatham w Empshott and Hawkley w Prior's Dean *Portsm* 01-05; NSM Petersfield and Buriton 05-10; rtd 10; Perm to Offic *Portsm* from 11. *14 Captains Row, Portsmouth PO1 2TT* Tel 07836-282561 (mobile) E-mail david_stickland.t21@btinternet.com

STICKLAND, Geoffrey John Brett. b 42. Open Univ BSc96. St D Coll Lamp. d 66 p 67. C Aberavon H Trin *Llan* 66-69; C-in-c Llanrumney CD *Mon* 69-72; C Tetbury w Beverston *Glouc* 72-75; V Hardwicke 75-82; R Hardwicke, Quedgeley and Elmore w Longney 82-98; V Quedgeley from 98; rtd 11. *19 Tai Cae Mawr, Llanwrtyd Wells LD5 4RJ* Tel (01591) 610701 E-mail geoffstickland@hotmail.com

STICKLEY (née BRAGG), Mrs Annette Frances. b 44. Chich Th Coll 97. d 00. NSM Worth *Chich* 00-06; Perm to Offic from 06. *14 Elmstead Park Road, West Wittering, Chichester PO20 8NQ* Tel (01243) 514619 E-mail annettestickley@talktalk.net

STIDOLPH, Canon Robert Anthony. b 54. GBSM76 ARCM75 FRSA92. St Steph Ho Ox 77. d 80 p 80. C Hove All SS *Chich* 80-84; TV Brighton Resurr 84-87; Chapl Cheltenham Coll 87-94; Sen Chapl and Hd RS Wellington Coll Berks 94-01; Chapl and Asst Master Radley Coll 01-05; Hon Can Ch Ch *Ox* 00-04; P-in-c Worth, Pound Hill and Maidenbower *Chich* 05-10; Chapl Peterho Zimbabwe from 10. *Peterhouse, Private Bag 3741, Marondera, Zimbabwe* E-mail anthony.stidolph@hotmail.co.uk

STIFF, Canon Derrick Malcolm. b 40. Lich Th Coll 69. d 72 p 73. C Cov St Geo 72-75; R Benhall w Sternfield *St E* 75-79; P-in-c Snape w Friston 75-79; V Cartmel *Carl* 79-87; R Sudbury and Chilton *St E* 87-94; P-in-c Lavenham 94-95; P-in-c Preston 94-95; R Lavenham w Preston 95-03; Min Can St E Cathl 90-00; Hon Can 00-03; RD Lavenham 95-03; rtd 03; Perm to Offic *St E* and *Sarum* from 03. *8 Keats Close, Saxmundham IP17 1WJ* E-mail canonstiff@hotmail.com

STILEMAN, William Mark Charles. b 63. Selw Coll Cam BA85 MA89 PGCE86. Wycliffe Hall Ox. d 91 p 92. C Ox St Andr 91-95; TV Gt Chesham 95-03; P-in-c Maidenhead St Andr and St Mary 03-04; V from 04. *St Mary's Vicarage, 14 Juniper Drive, Maidenhead SL6 8RE* Tel (01628) 624908

STILL, Colin Charles. b 35. Selw Coll Cam BA67 MA71 United Th Sem Dayton STM69. Cranmer Hall Dur 67. d 69 p 70. C Drypool St Columba w St Andr and St Pet *York* 69-72; Abp's Dom Chapl 72-75; Recruitment Sec ACCM 76-80; P-in-c Ockham w Hatchford *Guildf* 76-80; R 80-90; Can Missr and Ecum Officer 80-90; Perm to Offic *Chich* from 92; rtd 96. *Flat 9, 16 Lewes Crescent, Brighton BN2 1GB* Tel (01273) 686014

STILL (née STACEY), Mrs Gillian. b 53. SWMTC 94. d 99 p 98. NSM Peter Tavy, Mary Tavy, Lydford and Brent Tor *Ex* 97-06; C Abbotskerswell from 06; Chapl Rowcroft Hospice Torquay from 01. *The Vicarage, Church Path, Abbotskerswell, Newton Abbot TQ12 5NY* Tel (01626) 334445 *or* (01803) 210829 Mobile 07971-412511 E-mail gillstill@yahoo.co.uk

STILL, Jonathan Trevor Lloyd. b 59. Ex Univ BA81 Qu Coll Cam BA84 MA88. Westcott Ho Cam 82. d 85 p 86. C Weymouth H Trin *Sarum* 85-88; Chapl for Agric *Heref* 88-93; V N Petherton w Northmoor Green *B & W* 93-00; V The Bourne and Tilford *Guildf* 00-11; RD Farnham 05-10; V Buckland Newton, Cerne Abbas, Godmanstone etc *Sarum* from 11. *The Vicarage, 4 Back Lane, Cerne Abbas, Dorchester DT2 7JW* Tel (01300) 341251

STILL, Kenneth Donald. b 37. St Aid Birkenhead 64. d 67 p 95. C Ainsdale *Liv* 67-68; C Kirkby 68-69; C Sutton 96-98; TV 98-03; rtd 03. *The Cottage, Wash Road, Kirton, Boston PE20 1QG* Tel (01205) 724043

STILLWELL, Wayne Anthony. b 68. Univ of Greenwich BA91. Oak Hill Th Coll 94. d 96 p 97. C Necton, Holme Hale w N and S Pickenham *Nor* 96-98; C Eastbourne H Trin *Chich* 98-03; V Chaddesden St Mary *Derby* from 03. *The Vicarage, 133 Chaddesden Lane, Chaddesden, Derby DE21 6LL* Tel (01332) 280924 E-mail chaddesden.church@ntlworld.com

STILWELL, Malcolm Thomas. b 54. Coll of Resurr Mirfield 83. d 86 p 87. C Workington St Mich *Carl* 86-90; P-in-c Flimby 90-93; Perm to Offic 93-95; NSM Westfield St Mary from 95. *18 Moorfield Avenue, Workington CA14 4HJ* Tel (01900) 66757 E-mail stilwellstudio@supanet.com

STILWELL, Mrs Susan May. b 59. Herts Univ MA96. ERMC 08. **d** 11. NSM Bp's Hatfield, Lemsford and N Mymms *St Alb* from 11. *42 Barleycroft Road, Welwyn Garden City AL8 6JU* Tel (01707) 338304 E-mail susan.stilwell@clara.co.uk

STILWELL, Timothy James. b 65. Birm Univ BA87. Wycliffe Hall Ox 96. **d** 98 **p** 99. C Clifton Ch Ch w Em *Bris* 98-02; C Hammersmith St Paul *Lon* 02-05; V Fulham St Dionis from 05. *St Dionis' Vicarage, 18 Parson's Green, London SW6 4UH* Tel (020) 7731 1376 E-mail tim@stdionis.org.uk

STIMPSON, Nigel Leslie. b 60. St Martin's Coll Lanc BA92 Lanc Univ MA99. Coll of Resurr Mirfield 94. **d** 94 **p** 95. C Heyhouses on Sea *Blackb* 94-96; C Torrisholme 96-99; V Ravensthorpe and Thornhill Lees w Savile Town *Wakef* 99-05; TR Ribbleton *Blackb* from 05. *The Rectory, 238 Ribbleton Avenue, Ribbleton, Preston PR2 6QP* Tel and fax (01772) 791747 E-mail frnigel2005@btinternet.com

STINSON, William Gordon. b 29. Lon Univ BSc50. Ely Th Coll 51. **d** 52 **p** 53. C Kingston upon Hull St Alb *York* 52-56; Br Guiana 56-61; V E and W Ravendale w Hatcliffe *Linc* 61-67; R Beelsby 61-67; P-in-c Ashby w Fenby and Brigsley 62-66; R 66-67; V New Cleethorpes 67-76; RD Grimsby and Cleethorpes 73-76; P-in-c Dovercourt *Chelmsf* 76-83; TR Dovercourt and Parkeston 83-91; RD Harwich 87-91; V Gosfield 91-95; rtd 95; Perm to Offic *Chelmsf* and *St E* from 95. *14 The Columbines, Melford Road, Cavendish, Sudbury CO10 8AB* Tel (01787) 281381

STIRLING, Canon Christina Dorita (Tina). b 48. Lon Univ BEd73. Wycliffe Hall Ox 87. **d** 89 **p** 94. Par Dn Thame w Towersey *Ox* 89-94; C 94-98; P-in-c Brill, Boarstall, Chilton and Dorton 98; R Bernwode from 98, AD Aylesbury 05 10; Hon Can Ch Ch from 09. *The Vicarage, 7 High Street, Brill, Aylesbury HP18 9ST* Tel and fax (01844) 238325

STIRZAKER, Maureen Ann. b 51. **d** 08 **p** 09. NSM Chadderton St Matt w St Luke *Man* 08-11; NSM Aberdour *St And* from 11; NSM Burntisland from 11; NSM Inverkeithing from 11. *4 Morayvale, Aberdour, Burntisland KY3 0XE* Tel (01383) 861283 E-mail stirzaker776@btinternet.com

STOBART, Stuart Malcolm. b 64. Glos Univ BA07. Yorks Min Course 07. **d** 09 **p** 10. C Clayton *Bradf* from 09. *Claverings, Chrisharben Park, Clayton, Bradford BD14 6AE* Tel (01274) 881502 Mobile 07545-631387 E-mail stuart.stobart@yahoo.co.uk *or* curate@stjohnsclayton.org

STOBER, Brenda Jacqueline. b 57. Liv Univ BSc79 Leeds Univ BA08 Lanc Univ PGCE80. NOC 04. **d** 07 **p** 08. C Southport Em *Liv* 07-11; C Wavertree H Trin from 11. *20 Eardisley Road, Liverpool L18 0HS* Tel 0151-345 5695 Mobile 07812-471269 E-mail jacqstober@yahoo.co.uk

STOCK, Lionel Crispian. b 58. ACMA85 ACIS94. Linc Th Coll BTh94. **d** 94 **p** 95. C Preston w Sutton Poyntz and Osmington w Poxwell *Sarum* 94-97; P-in-c Stalbridge 97-00; Hon C Hillingdon All SS *Lon* 01-04; NSM Kendal H Trin *Carl* 04-10; Perm to Offic *Eur* and *Win* from 10. *84 Lapwing Way, Four Marks, Alton GU34 5FD* E-mail revlstock@hotmail.com

STOCK, Nigel. *See* STOCK, The Rt Revd William Nigel

STOCK, Miss Ruth Vaughan. b 51. Birkbeck Coll Lon BA79 MA85. Wycliffe Hall Ox 91. **d** 93 **p** 94. Par Dn Toxteth St Philemon w St Gabr and St Cleopas *Liv* 93-94; C 94-97; TV 97-10; Miss Development Min St Luke in the City from 10; TV Toxteth St Philemon w St Gabr and St Cleopas from 11. *2 Steble Street, Liverpool L8 6QH* Tel 0151-708 7751

STOCK, The Very Revd Victor Andrew. b 44. OAM02. AKC68 FRSA95. **d** 69 **p** 70. C Pinner *Lon* 69-73; Chapl Lon Univ 73-79; R Friern Barnet St Jas 79-86; R St Mary le Bow w St Pancras Soper Lane etc 86-02; P-in-c St Mary Aldermary 87-98; Dean Guildf from 02. *The Deanery, 1 Cathedral Close, Guildford GU2 7TL* Tel (01483) 560328 *or* 547861 Fax 303350 E-mail dean@guildford-cathedral.org

✠**STOCK, The Rt Revd William Nigel.** b 50. St Cuth Soc Dur BA72. Ripon Coll Cuddesdon. **d** 76 **p** 77 **c** 00. C Stockton St Pet *Dur* 76-79; Papua New Guinea 79-84; V Shiremoor *Newc* 85-91; TR N Shields 91-98; RD Tynemouth 92-98; Hon Can Newc Cathl 97-98; Can Res Dur Cathl 98-00; Chapl Grey Coll Dur 99-00; Suff Bp Stockport *Ches* 00-07; Bp St E from 07. *The Bishop's House, 4 Park Road, Ipswich IP1 3ST* Tel (01473) 252829 Fax 232552

STOCKBRIDGE, Alan Carmichael. b 33. MBE89. Keble Coll Ox BA55 MA62. Wycliffe Hall Ox 66. **d** 68 **p** 69. CF 68-78 and 82-92; Chapl Reading Sch 78-82; R Harrietsham w Ulcombe *Cant* 92-98; rtd 98; Perm to Offic *Eur* from 00 and *Cant* from 09. *Albrecht Dürerstrasse 4, 96106 Ebern, Germany* Tel and fax (0049) (9531) 942799 E-mail erikastockbridge@aol.com

STOCKER, David William George. b 37. Bris Univ BA58 CertEd. Qu Coll Birm 59. **d** 60 **p** 61. C Sparkhill St Jo *Birm* 60-64; C Keighley *Bradf* 64-66; V Grenoside *Sheff* 66-83; V Sandbach *Ches* 83-01; rtd 01; Perm to Offic *Ches* from 01. *18 Mill Bridge Close, Crewe CW1 5DZ* Tel (01270) 212865

STOCKER, John Henry. b 48. Cov Univ BSc71 Sheff Univ BEd81 ACP88. St Mich Coll Llan 01. **d** 04 **p** 05. NSM

Knighton, Norton, Whitton, Pilleth and Cascob *S & B* 04-06; NSM Irfon Valley 06-09; rtd 09. *1 Tai Cae Mawr, Llanwrtyd Wells LD5 4RJ* Tel (01592) 610231 Mobile 07891-086631

STOCKER, Rachael Ann. *See* KNAPP, Mrs Rachael Ann

STOCKING, Clifford Brian. b 67. Trin Coll Bris 08. **d** 10 **p** 11. C Hadlow *Roch* from 10. *45 The Cherry Orchard, Hadlow, Tonbridge TN11 0HU* Tel (01732) 851655 Mobile 07941-056237 E-mail c.stocking@btinternet.com

STOCKITT, Robin Philip. b 56. Liv Univ BA77 Crewe & Alsager Coll PGCE78. Ridley Hall Cam 95. **d** 97 **p** 98. C Billing *Pet* 97-01; P-in-c Freiburg-im-Breisau *Eur* from 01; Asst Chapl Basle from 01. *Talvogteistrasse 16, 79199 Kirchzarten Burg-Hofen, Freiburg, Germany* Tel (0049) (7661) 904693 Fax 967726 E-mail stockitt@t-online.de

STOCKLEY, Mrs Alexandra Madeleine Reuss. b 43. Cranmer Hall Dur 80 Carl Dioc Tr Inst. **dss** 84 **d** 87 **p** 94. Upperby St Jo *Carl* 84-89; Par Dn 87-89; Dn-in-c Grayrigg, Old Hutton and New Hutton 90-94; P-in-c 94-95; P-in-c Levens 95-03; rtd 03; Perm to Offic *Carl* from 03. *Crowberry, Ulpha, Broughton-in-Furness LA20 6DZ* Tel (01229) 716875

STOCKPORT, Suffragan Bishop of. *See* ATWELL, The Rt Revd Robert Ronald

STOCKS, Simon Paul. b 68. Rob Coll Cam BA89 MA93. Trin Coll Bris BA03 MPhil06. **d** 04 **p** 05. C Coulsdon St Jo *S'wark* from 04; Hon C from 07. *316 Coulsdon Road, Coulsdon CR5 1EB* Tel (01737) 553190 E-mail simon@spstocks.freeserve.co.uk

STOCKTON, Canon Ian George. b 49. Selw Coll Cam BA72 MA76 Hull Univ PhD90. St Jo Coll Nottm PGCE74. **d** 75 **p** 76. C Chell *Lich* 75-78; C Trentham 78-80; R Dalbeattie *Glas* 80-84; P-in-c Scotton w Northorpe *Linc* 84-88; Asst Local Min Officer 84-88; Local Min Officer and LNSM Course Prin 88-97; TR Monkwearmouth *Dur* 97-11; Can Res and Chan Blackb Cathl from 11. *St Francis House, St Francis Road, Blackburn BB2 2TZ* Tel (01254) 200720 E-mail ian.stockton@blackburncathedral.co.uk

STODDART, David Easton. b 36. K Coll Dur BSc60 PhD66 CEng66 MIMechE66 FCMI72 FIQA76. WEMTC 92. **d** 95 **p** 96. OLM Stroud H Trin *Glouc* 95-99; OLM Woodchester and Brimscombe 99-00; NSM 00-08; Jt Angl Chapl Severn NHS Trust 99-06; Jt Angl Chapl Glos Primary Care Trust 06-11; rtd 11; Perm to Offic *Glouc* from 08. *Woodstock, Hampton Green, Box, Stroud GL6 9AD* Tel (01453) 885338 E-mail stoddart@david-isabel.co.uk

STOKE-ON-TRENT, Archdeacon of. *See* STONE, The Ven Godfrey Owen

STOKER, Andrew. b 64. Coll of Ripon & York St Jo BA86. Coll of Resurr Mirfield 87. **d** 90 **p** 91. C Horton *Newc* 90-92; C Clifford *Newc* 92-96; P-in-c Cawood w Ryther 96-98; P-in-c Wistow 96-98; R Cawood w Ryther and Wistow 98-04; P-in-c York St Clem w St Mary Bishophill Senior 04-05; R York St Clem w St Mary Bishophill from 05. *13 Nunthorpe Avenue, York YO23 1PF* Tel (01904) 624425

STOKER, Howard Charles. b 62. Linc Th Coll BTh93. **d** 93 **p** 94. C Hessle *York* 93-96; C Richmond w Hudswell *Ripon* 96-99; C Downholme and Marske 96-99; R Holt w High Kelling *Nor* from 99; RD Holt from 05. *The Rectory, 11 Church Street, Holt NR25 6BB* Tel (01263) 712048 Fax 711397 E-mail holtrectory@dialstart.com

STOKER, Canon Joanna Mary. b 57. Leic Univ BA79 Nottm Univ BCombStuds83. Linc Th Coll 80. **dss** 83 **d** 87 **p** 94. Greenford H Cross *Lon* 83-87; Par Dn 87-89; Par Dn Farnham Royal w Hedgerley *Ox* 89-92; Dn-in-c Seer Green and Jordans 92-94; P-in-c 94-97; TV Stantonbury and Willen 97-03; TR Basingstoke *Win* from 03; Hon Can Win Cathl from 08. *The Rectory, Church Street, Basingstoke RG21 7QT* Tel (01256) 326654 E-mail jostoker@dsl.pipex.com

STOKES, Canon Andrew John. b 38. G&C Coll Cam BA60 MA64. Ripon Hall Ox 60. **d** 62 **p** 63. C Northampton All SS w St Kath *Pet* 62-65; C Endcliffe *Sheff* 65-68; Ind Missr 65-68; Sen Ind Chapl 69-74; P-in-c Bridport *Sarum* 75-79; TR 79-80; V Holbeach Marsh *Linc* 82-88; Bp's Dom Chapl 88-92; Can Res and Prec Linc Cathl 92-03; rtd 03; Perm to Offic *Linc* from 03. *2 Lupin Road, Lincoln LN2 4GD* Tel (01522) 537595 E-mail andrew.stokes@ntlworld.com

STOKES, Colin Arthur (Ted). b 59. Birm Univ BDS82. WEMTC 00. **d** 03 **p** 04. NSM Bromyard *Heref* 03-08; NSM Bromyard w Stoke Lacy from 09. *Solmor Paddocks, Linley Green Road, Whitbourne, Worcester WR6 5RE* Tel (01886) 821625

STOKES, David Francis Robert. b 53. Lon Inst of Educn PGCE76 Peterho Cam MA81 Trin Coll Bris BA87. Cranmer Hall Dur 01. **d** 03 **p** 04. C Salisbury St Mark *Sarum* 03-08; Perm to Offic from 08. *Address temp unknown* E-mail davidshelley.stokes@gmail.com

STOKES (née VASTENHOUT), Mrs Jeannetta Hermina. b 62. St Jo Coll Nottm BA07. **d** 07 **p** 08. C Newport w Longford, Chetwynd and Forton *Lich* 07-11; P-in-c Worfield *Heref* from 11. *The Vicarage, Hallon, Worfield, Bridgnorth WV15 5JZ* Tel (01746) 716698 Mobile 07985-923202 E-mail jeannetta.stokes@btopenworld.com

STOKES, Miss Mary Patricia. b 39. St Hilda's Coll Ox BA62 MA66 Lanc Univ MA80 Bris Univ CertEd63. EMMTC 78. **d** 87 **p** 94. Par Dn Pheasey *Lich* 87-93; C Walton-on-Thames *Guildf* 93-05; rtd 05. *21 Brittain Road, Walton-on-Thames KT12 4LR* Tel (01932) 248945 E-mail marystokes1@excite.co.uk

STOKES, Michael John. b 34. Lich Th Coll 63. **d** 65 **p** 66. C Worplesdon *Guildf* 65-68; Chapl RAF 68-84; Asst Chapl-in-Chief RAF 84-89; QHC 87-95; V Chesterton w Middleton Stoney and Wendlebury *Ox* 89-95; RD Bicester and Islip 90-95; Chapl Kyrenia St Andr Cyprus 95-00; rtd 00; Perm to Offic *Ox* from 00. *Keeper's Cottage, Manor Farm Lane, Chesterton, Bicester OX25 1UD* Tel and fax (01869) 248744

STOKES, Roger Sidney. b 47. Clare Coll Cam BA68 MA72. Sarum & Wells Th Coll 69. **d** 72 **p** 73. C Keighley *Bradf* 72-74; C Bolton St Jas w St Chrys 74-78; V Hightown *Wakef* 78-85; Dep Chapl HM Pris Wakef 85-87; Chapl HM Pris Full Sutton 87-89; Perm to Offic *Wakef* 92-95; P-in-c Carlinghow 95-99; P-in-c Bedford St Martin *St Alb* from 99. *St Martin's Vicarage, 76 Clapham Road, Bedford MK41 7PN* Tel (01234) 357862 E-mail r.s.stokes.65@cantab.net

STOKES, Canon Simon Colin. b 62. Nene Coll Northn BSc83. Ridley Hall Cam 89. **d** 92 **p** 93. C New Catton Ch Ch *Nor* 92-96; P-in-c King's Lynn St Jo the Ev 96-06; P-in-c Bowthorpe from 06; Chapl Coll of W Anglia 01-06; R Sprowston w Beeston *Nor* from 11; Hon Can Nor Cathl from 06. *The Vicarage, 2 Wroxham Road, Sprowston, Norwich NR7 8TZ* E-mail simon@simonstokes.co.uk

STOKES, Simon Jeremy. b 63. St Anne's Coll Ox BA86 MA90 Mass Inst of Tech SM88 Univ of Wales (Cardiff) LLM97 Solicitor 92. NTMTC BA08. **d** 08 **p** 09. NSM Clerkenwell H Redeemer *Lon* from 08. *10 Pensioners Court, Charterhouse, Charterhouse Square, London EC1M 6AU* Tel 077220-48110 (mobile) E-mail frsstokes@googlemail.com

STOKES, Ted. See STOKES, Colin Arthur

STOKES, Terence Harold. b 46. Open Univ BA89. Sarum & Wells Th Coll 71. **d** 73 **p** 74. C Blakenall Heath *Lich* 73-75; C Walsall Wood 75-78; C Northampton St Alb *Pet* 78-81; TV Swinton St Pet *Man* 81-85; V Daisy Hill 85-92; rtd 09; Perm to Offic *Blackb* from 09. *17 St John's Court, Chorley Road, Westhoughton, Bolton BL5 3WG* E-mail revthstokes@aim.com

STOKES, Preb Terence Walter. b 34. Bps' Coll Cheshunt 62. **d** 64 **p** 65. C Wanstead St Mary *Chelmsf* 64-67; C St Alb Abbey 67-70; Asst Dir RE *B & W* 70-75; Youth Chapl 70-75; P-in-c Yeovil 75-77; TV 77-82; TR Wellington and Distr 82-99; RD Tone 89-96; Preb Wells Cathl 90-99; rtd 99; Perm to Offic *B & W* 99-10. *16 Tadfield Road, Romsey SO51 5AJ* Tel (01794) 518396

STOKES-HARRISON, David Neville Hurford. b 41. FCA65 FCCA67 FInstM68. Qu Coll Birm 97. **d** 00 **p** 01. NSM Walsall *Lich* 00-07; NSM Edgmond w Kynnersley and Preston Wealdmoors from 07; NSM Tibberton w Bolas Magna and Waters Upton from 07. *The Rectory, Mill Lane, Tibberton, Newport TF10 8NL* Tel (01952) 551063 E-mail stokesharrison@btinternet.com

STOKOE, Prof Rodney James Robert. b 20. Dur Univ BSc46 BA48. Crozer Th Sem Pennsylvania ThM67 Atlantic Sch of Th Halifax (NS) Hon DD87. **d** 49 **p** 50. C W Hartlepool St Paul *Dur* 49-53; R Edin Ch Ch 53-57; P-in-c Bishopwearmouth St Gabr *Dur* 57-60; Prof Div K Coll NS Canada 60-71; Prof Past Th Atlantic Sch Th NS 71-85; rtd 85. *Fergus Hall C61, 378 Young Street, Truro NS B2N 7H2, Canada* Tel (001) (902) 843 8076 E-mail rodstokoe20@yahoo.ca

STOKOE, Wayne Jeffrey. b 56. Coll of Resurr Mirfield 94. **d** 96 **p** 97. C Sheff St Cath Richmond Road 96-99; V Edlington 99-09; P-in-c Doncaster H Trin 09-10; P-in-c New Cantley 09-10; V from 10. *St Hugh's House, Levet Road, Doncaster DN4 6JQ* Tel (01302) 371256 E-mail wjs56@live.co.uk

STOLTZ, Christopher Barry. b 76. St Olaf Coll Minnesota BA99. Concordia Th Sem Indiana MDiv03. **d** 06 **p** 07. C Highgate St Mich *Lon* 06-09; Chapl Trin Coll Cam from 09. *Trinity College, Cambridge CB2 1TQ* Tel (01223) 766327 E-mail cbstoltz@yahoo.com

STONE, Adrian Gordon. b 68. Trent Poly BSc89 Nottm Univ PGCE92. St Jo Coll Nottm 01. **d** 03 **p** 04. C Bayston Hill *Lich* 03-06; V Stafford St Jo and Tixall w Ingestre from 06. *St John's Vicarage, Westhead Avenue, Stafford ST16 3RP* Tel (01785) 253493 Mobile 07739-043709 E-mail adrian@the-stone-family.net

STONE, Albert John. b 44. Loughb Univ BTech67 BSc. Sarum & Wells Th Coll 83. **d** 85 **p** 86. C Plymstock *Ex* 85-88; P-in-c Whitestone 88-92; P-in-c Oldridge 88-92; P-in-c Holcombe Burnell 88-92; R Tedburn St Mary, Whitestone, Oldridge etc 93-94; P-in-c Yarcombe w Membury and Upottery 94; P-in-c Cotleigh 94; V Yarcombe, Membury, Upottery and Cotleigh 95-99; P-in-c Bampton, Morebath, Clayhanger and Petton 99-10; rtd 10. *9 Castle Park, Hemyock, Cullompton EX15 3SA* Tel (01823) 681459 E-mail ajstone@orpheusmail.co.uk

STONE, Miss Carol Ann. b 54. TD04. Leic Univ BA75 Qu Coll Cam BA77 MA81. Westcott Ho Cam 76. **d** 78 **p** 79. C Bradford-on-Avon H Trin *Sarum* 78-81; R Corsley 81-83; Chapl Dauntsey's Sch Devizes 83-88; V Studley *Sarum* 89-94; Chapl Cheltenham Coll 94-95; Venezuela 95-96; V Upper Stratton *Bris* from 96; P-in-c Penhill from 06; CF (ACF) 84-89; CF(V) 90-04. *The Vicarage, 67 Beechcroft Road, Swindon SN2 7RE* Tel (01793) 723095 Mobile 07702-342848 E-mail revcarolstone@btopenworld.com

STONE, Christopher. See STONE, Canon John Christopher

STONE, Christopher John. b 49. Lanc Univ MA89 Keele Univ MA92. Lambeth STh84 Linc Th Coll 78. **d** 81 **p** 82. C Bromley St Mark *Roch* 81-84; R Burgh-by-Sands and Kirkbampton w Kirkandrews etc *Carl* 84-89; Chapl N Staffs R Infirmary Stoke-on-Trent 89-93; Co-ord Staff Support Services N Staffs Hosp 93-09; rtd 09. *Coppers Nest, 37 The Village, Milton Abbot, Tavistock PL19 0PB* Tel (01822) 8870721 E-mail christopherstn550@googlemail.com

STONE, Christopher Martyn Luke. b 78. Glam Univ BA99. St Steph Ho Ox 99. **d** 02 **p** 03. C Merthyr Tydfil Ch Ch *Llan* 02-07; TV Bassaleg *Mon* from 07. *St John's Vicarage, Wern Terrace, Rogerstone, Newport NP10 9FG* Tel (01633) 893357 E-mail vicchris@waitrose.com

STONE, Canon David Adrian. b 56. Oriel Coll Ox BA78 MA83 BM, BCh83. Wycliffe Hall Ox 85. **d** 88 **p** 89. C Holborn St Geo w H Trin and St Bart *Lon* 88-91; C S Kensington St Jude 91-93; V 93-02; AD Chelsea 96-02; TR Newbury *Ox* 02-10; Can Res and Prec Cov Cathl from 10. *55 Cotswold Drive, Coventry CV3 6EZ* Tel 07973-215927 (mobile) E-mail david@dandb.org.uk

STONE, Elizabeth Karen Forbes. See FORBES STONE, Elizabeth Karen

STONE, Geoffrey. See STONE, John Geoffrey Elliot

STONE, The Ven Godfrey Owen. b 49. Ex Coll Ox BA71 MA75 W Midl Coll of Educn PGCE72. Wycliffe Hall Ox BA78. **d** 81 **p** 82. C Rushden w Newton Bromswold *Pet* 81-87; Dir Past Studies Wycliffe Hall Ox 87-92; TR Bucknall and Bagnall *Lich* 92-02; RD Stoke 98-02; Adn Stoke from 02; P-in-c Edensor 04-07. *Archdeacon's House, 39 The Brackens, Newcastle ST5 4JL* Tel (01782) 663066 Fax 711165 E-mail archdeacon.stoke@lichfield.anglican.org

STONE, Ian Matthew. b 72. Ox Univ BTh08. Ripon Coll Cuddesdon 03. **d** 05 **p** 06. C Hammersmith St Pet *Lon* 05-08; V Queensbury All SS from 08. *The Vicarage, 24 Waltham Drive, Edgware HA8 5PQ* Tel (020) 8952 4536 E-mail matthew.stone1@virgin.net

STONE, Jeffrey Peter. b 34. Nottm Univ TCert72 BEd73. Lich Th Coll 58. **d** 61 **p** 62. C Newark St Mary *S'well* 61-65; C Sutton in Ashfield St Mich 65-69; Robert Smyth Sch Market Harborough 72-89; R Waltham on the Wolds, Stonesby, Saxby etc *Leic* 90-96; rtd 96; Perm to Offic *Leic* from 99. *71 Redland Road, Oakham LE15 6PH* Tel (01572) 756842

STONE, John. See STONE, Albert John

STONE, John Anthony. b 46. Univ of Wales (Lamp) MA05. St Chad's Coll Dur BA68. **d** 69 **p** 70. C New Addington *Cant* 69-72; C Tewkesbury w Walton Cardiff *Glouc* 72-76; C-in-c Dedworth CD *Ox* 76-82; V Dedworth 82-86; TV Chipping Barnet w Arkley *St Alb* 86-95; R Baldock w Bygrave 95-03; R Ches H Trin 03-11; rtd 11. *4 Carpenter Avenue, Llandudno LL30 1YW* E-mail jastone@dunelm.org.uk

STONE, Canon John Christopher. b 53. Newc Univ BA74 Birkbeck Coll Lon MA77 MSTSD74 LGSM73 MIPR FRSA. Oak Hill NSM Course 89. **d** 92 **p** 93. NSM Southfleet *Roch* 92-07; Dioc Communications Officer 96-03; Chapl Univ of Greenwich 98-99; Hon Can Roch Cathl from 02; Bp's Dom Chapl 03-07; Bp's Media Adv 03-07; Bp's Communications Consultant from 07; R Gravesend St Geo from 07. *St George's Rectory, 54 The Avenue, Gravesend DA11 0LX* Tel (01474) 534965 E-mail chris.stone@rochester.anglican.org

STONE, John Geoffrey Elliot. b 20. Ch Coll Cam BA41 MA45. Ridley Hall Cam 47. **d** 49 **p** 50. C Wellingborough St Barn *Pet* 49-51; C Bexhill St Pet *Chich* 51-56; C Ifield 56-59; V Southwater 59-70; V Thornham w Titchwell *Nor* 70-74; R Copdock w Washbrook and Belstead *St E* 74-77; P-in-c Therfield *St Alb* 77-82; P-in-c Kelshall 77-82; C Littlehampton St Jas *Chich* 82-85; C Littlehampton St Mary 82-85; C Wick 82-85; TV Littlehampton and Wick 86; rtd 86; C Compton, the Mardens, Stoughton and Racton *Chich* 86-92; Perm to Offic *Nor* 92-96 and *Chich* from 96. *11 Ramsay Hall, Byron Road, Worthing BN11 3HN* Tel (01903) 212947

STONE, Martyn. See STONE, Christopher Martyn Luke

STONE, Matthew. See STONE, Ian Matthew

STONE, Michael Graham. b 33. FBCS. S Dios Minl Tr Scheme. **d** 83 **p** 84. NSM Chich St Paul and St Pet 83-95; NSM Chich 95-98; rtd 98; Perm to Offic *Chich* from 98. *125 Cedar Drive, Chichester PO19 3EL* Tel (01243) 784484

STONE, Michael John. b 33. Trin Hall Cam MA56 LLB58. EAMTC 78. **d** 80 **p** 81. NSM Whitton and Thurleston w Akenham *St E* 80-84; NSM Westerfield and Tuddenham w Witnesham 84-95; Dioc Chr Stewardship Adv 93-95; P-in-c Coddenham w Gosbeck and Hemingstone w Henley 95-98; Asst

P 98-02; Asst P Crowfield w Stonham Aspal and Mickfield 98-02; Dioc Voc Adv 95-99; rtd 02; Perm to Offic *St E* from 02. *10 Coppice Close, Melton, Woodbridge IP12 1RX* Tel (01394) 385810 E-mail emjaystone@aol.com

STONE, Nigel John. b 57. Bedf Coll Lon BSc82 Lon Bible Coll MA95. St Jo Coll Nottm 82. d 85 p 86. C Battersea Park St Sav *S'wark* 85-87; C Battersea St Sav and St Geo w St Andr 87-89; P-in-c Brixton St Paul 89-92; V 92-97; Adult Education and Tr Officer 97-09; Dioc Olympic Adv from 10; Par Support P Kingston Area from 10; Hon Chapl S'wark Cathl from 97. *11 Wilkinson Street, London SW8 1DD* Tel (020) 7582 6424 *or* 8545 2440 Fax 8545 2441 E-mail nigel.stone@southwark.anglican.org

STONE, Peter Jonathan Michael. b 71. Ripon Coll Cuddesdon 08. d 10 p 11. C Charminster and Stinsford *Sarum* from 10. *3 Ash Road, Charlton Down, Dorchester DT2 9UJ* Tel (01305) 265845 Mobile 09971-425889 E-mail petejmstone@tiscali.co.uk

STONE, Philip William. b 58. Ridley Hall Cam 85. d 88 p 89. C Hackney Marsh *Lon* 88-97; V Kensal Rise St Mark and St Martin 97-04; TR 04-10; AD Brent 03-10; Dir Scargill Ho from 10. *Scargill House, Kettlewell, Skipton BD23 5HU* Tel (01756) 761240 E-mail philstone@freenet.co.uk

STONEBANKS, David Arthur. b 34. Louvain Univ Belgium MA70. Coll of Resurr Mirfield 64. d 66 p 67. C Burgess Hill St Jo *Chich* 66-68; Chapl City Univ 70-73; Chapl Strasbourg w Stuttgart and Heidelberg *Eur* 73-80; Chapl Geneva 80-86; Chapl Zürich w St Gallen and Winterthur 86-89; R Horsted Keynes *Chich* 89-99; rtd 99; Perm to Offic *S'wark* from 01. *42 Home Park, Oxted RH8 0JU* Tel (01883) 732339

STONEHOLD, Wilfred Leslie. b 33. St Luke's Coll Ex TCert71. d 99 p 00. OLM Harlescott *Lich* 99-06; Perm to Offic from 06. *19 Wendsley Road, Harlescott Grange, Shrewsbury SY1 3PE* Tel (01743) 369237

STONES, John Graham. b 49. Southn Univ BSc72. SWMTC 91. d 94 p 95. C Okehampton w Inwardleigh, Bratton Clovelly etc *Ex* 94-97; TV Sidmouth, Woolbrook, Salcombe Regis, Sidbury etc 97-04; R Church Stretton *Heref* 04-07; TR Teignmouth, Ideford w Luton, Ashcombe etc *Ex* from 07. *The Rectory, 30 Dawlish Road, Teignmouth TQ14 8TG* Tel (01626) 774495 E-mail graham.stones@haldonteam.org.uk

STONESTREET, George Malcolm. b 38. MBE05. AKC61. d 62 p 63. C Leeds St Pet *Ripon* 62-64; C Far Headingley St Chad 64-67; V Askrigg w Stallingbusk 67-82; V Bramley 82-85; TR 85-94; V Eskdale, Irton, Muncaster and Waberthwaite *Carl* 94-03; rtd 03. *Northside, Grange, Keswick CA12 5UQ* Tel (01768) 777671 E-mail malcolm@dip.edi.co.uk

STONIER, Mrs Mary. b 56. d 09 p 10. OLM Crowle Gp *Linc* from 09. *28 Windsor Road, Crowle, Scunthorpe DN17 4ES* Tel (01724) 710900 E-mail mary.stonier@tiscali.co.uk

STOODLEY, Peter Bindon. b 47. Linc Th Coll 89. d 91 p 92. C Holbeck *Ripon* 91-94; P-in-c Osmondthorpe St Phil 94-99; V Sowerby Bridge *Wakef* 99-09; rtd 09; Perm to Offic *Wakef* 09-11. *1056 Bolton Road, Bradford BD2 4LH* Tel (01274) 405086 E-mail maverick.stoodley@tiscali.co.uk

STORDY, Richard Andrew. b 64. St Jo Coll Ox BA86 Barrister 86. Cranmer Hall Dur BA97. d 98 p 99. C Gt Horton *Bradf* 98-02; V Chapeltown *Sheff* from 02; AD Ecclesfield from 10. *St John's Vicarage, 23 Housley Park, Chapeltown, Sheffield S35 2UE* Tel 0114-257 0966

STOREY, Earl. See STOREY, William Earl Cosbey

STOREY, Gerard Charles Alfred. b 57. Thames Poly BSc80 Lon Univ PhD84 GRSC80. Wycliffe Hall Ox 84. d 87 p 88. C Broadwater *Chich* 92-97; TV 92-95; Chapl Northbrook Coll of Design and Tech 90-95; Oman 95-99; P-in-c Guernsey H Trin *Win* 99-01; V 01-07; P-in-c Bream *Glouc* from 07. *The Vicarage, Coleford Road, Bream, Lydney GL15 6ES* Tel (01594) 563579 E-mail gerardstorey@yahoo.co.uk

STOREY, Canon Michael. b 36. Chich Th Coll 73. d 75 p 76. C Illingworth *Wakef* 75-78; V Rastrick St Jo 78-87; V Crosland Moor 87-06; Hon Can Wakef Cathl 00-06; rtd 06; Perm to Offic *Wakef* from 07. *198 Healey Wood Road, Brighouse HD6 3RW* Tel (01484) 713663 E-mail mickthevic@googlemail.com

STOREY, Mrs Patricia Louise. b 60. TCD MA83. CITC BTh94. d 97 p 98. C Ballymena w Ballyclug *Conn* 97-00; C Glenavy w Tunny and Crumlin 00-04; I Londonderry St Aug *D & R* from 04. *St Augustine's Rectory, 4 Bridgewater, Londonderry BT47 6YA* Tel (028) 7134 7532 E-mail patriciastorey56@yahoo.co.uk

STOREY, Timothy. b 60. Trin Coll Bris 92. d 94 p 95. C Bath Weston St Jo w Kelston *B & W* 94-98; C Shirley *Win* 98-03; R Blandford Forum and Langton Long *Sarum* from 03. *The Rectory, 2 Portman Place, Blandford Forum DT11 7DG* Tel (01258) 480092 E-mail t.storey@btopenworld.com

STOREY, William Earl Cosbey. b 58. Kent Univ BA MPhil. CITC. d 82 p 83. C Drumglass w Moygashel *Arm* 82-86; I Crinken *D & G* 86-96; I Glenavy w Tunny and Crumlin *Conn* 98-04. *St Augustine's Rectory, 4 Bridgewater, Londonderry BT47 6YA* Tel (028) 7134 7532 E-mail es@cofire.freeserve.co.uk

STOREY, William Leslie Maurice. b 31. Oak Hill Th Coll 67. d 69 p 70. C Wembley St Jo *Lon* 69-71; C Ealing Dean St Jo 71-75; V W Derby St Luke *Liv* 75-80; V Hunts Cross 80-83; Hon C Brixton St Paul *S'wark* 83-86; P-in-c 87-88; P-in-c Brixton Hill St Sav 83-86; rtd 88; Perm to Offic *S'wark* 88-02. *124 Surbiton Hill Park, Surbiton KT5 8EP* Tel (020) 8390 2821

STORY, Victor Leonard. b 45. St Mark & St Jo Coll Lon TCert66 Brighton Poly BSc74 LIMA74. Ripon Coll Cuddesdon 80. d 81 p 82. C Evesham *Worc* 81-85; P-in-c Ilmington w Stretton on Fosse and Ditchford *Cov* 85-90; P-in-c Ilmington w Stretton-on-Fosse etc 90-96; Chapl Vlissingen (Flushing) Miss to Seamen *Eur* 96-97; Chapl Rotterdam Miss to Seamen 97-99; R Gt w Lt Milton and Gt Haseley *Ox* from 99. *The Rectory, Great Milton, Oxford OX44 7PN* Tel (01844) 279498

STOTE, Mrs Judith Ann. b 50. Qu Coll Birm 07. d 09 p 10. OLM Studley *Cov* from 09. *The Paddocks, Birmingham Road, Mappleborough Green, Studley B80 7DJ* Tel (01527) 852515 E-mail judy@ardenmarches.com

STOTE, Mrs Pamela Anne. b 49. Dudley Coll of Educn TCert70 Open Univ BA83. WMMTC 97. d 00 p 01. NSM Cov St Geo 00-03; NSM Whitley from 03. *St James's Church, 171 Abbey Road, Coventry CV3 4BG* Tel and fax (024) 7630 1617 Mobile 07905-230924 E-mail st.james@stote.force9.co.uk

STOTER, David John. b 43. MBE02. K Coll Lon AKC66. d 67 p 68. C Reading St Giles *Ox* 67-71; C Luton Lewsey St Hugh *St Alb* 71-73; Chapl Westmr Hosp Lon 73-79; Convenor of Chapls Notts Distr HA 79-94; Chapl Univ Hosp Nottm 79-94; Chapl Nottm Gen Hosp 79-02; Sen Chapl Qu Medical Cen Nottm Univ Hosp NHS Trust 94-02; Sen Chapl Notts Healthcare NHS Trust 94-02; Manager Chapl and Bereavement Services 94-02; R Gedling *S'well* 02-06; rtd 06; Perm to Offic w Bix, Highmoor, Pishill etc *Ox* 08-10. *7 Wentworth Drive, Bramhall, Stockport SK7 2LQ* E-mail david.stoter@yahoo.co.uk

STOTESBURY, Robert John. d 06 p 07. NSM Ferns w Kilbride, Toombe, Kilcormack etc *C & O* 06-10; NSM Enniscorthy w Clone, Clonmore, Monart etc from 10. *Croneyhorn, Carnew, Arklow, Co Wicklow, Republic of Ireland* Tel (00353) (53) 942 6300 Mobile 87-988 2507 E-mail rstotesbury@hotmail.com

STOTT, Andrew David. b 61. NOC 03. d 05 p 06. C Walton Breck *Liv* 05-09; P-in-c W Derby St Luke from 09. *St Luke's Vicarage, Princess Drive, West Derby, Liverpool L14 8XG* Tel 0151-259 8125 Mobile 07510-222374 E-mail andrew@stott401.fsnet.co.uk

STOTT, Antony. b 21. Bps' Coll Cheshunt 53. d 55 p 56. Australia 55-62; V Longbridge Deverill w Hill Deverill *Sarum* 62-66; V Bratton 66-74; R Marnhull 74-81; P-in-c Broad Chalke and Bower Chalke 81; P-in-c Ebbesbourne Wake w Fifield Bavant and Alvediston 81; P-in-c Berwick St John 81; V Chalke Valley W 81-87; rtd 87; Perm to Offic *Ex* from 87. *11 Luscombe Close, Ivybridge PL21 9TT* Tel (01752) 896142 E-mail revtony1@aol.com

STOTT, Christopher John. b 45. Lon Univ BD68. Tyndale Hall Bris. d 69 p 70. C Croydon Ch Ch Broad Green *Cant* 69-72; Ethiopia 73-76; Area Sec (SW) BCMS 76-78; Tanzania 78-85; R Harwell w Chilton *Ox* 85-10; RD Wallingford 91-95; rtd 10; Perm to Offic *Ox* from 10. *1 Dibleys, Blewbury, Didcot OX11 9PT* E-mail cjstott@freenetname.co.uk

STOTT, Eric. b 36. ALCD62. d 62 p 63. C Penn Fields *Lich* 62-65; C Normanton *Derby* 65-71; R Lower Broughton St Clem w St Matthias *Man* 71-79; V Chadderton Em 79-01; rtd 01; Perm to Offic *Glouc* from 01. *21 Laynes Road, Hucclecote, Gloucester GL3 3PU* Tel (01452) 534492

STOTT, Frederick. b 23. Portsm Univ MA05 CQSW71 TCert75. Sarum & Wells Th Coll 83. d 85 p 86. NSM Sholing *Win* 85-89; Perm to Offic *Portsm* 89-06; *Win* 90-06; *Sarum* 93-06; rtd 06. *35 Broadwater Road, Southampton SO18 2DW* Tel (023) 8055 7193

STOTT, Gary. b 69. Leeds Univ BA92 St Jo Coll Dur MA99. Cranmer Hall Dur 97. d 99 p 00. C Farnley *Ripon* 99-03; V Manston 03-06; Care Cen Manager St Geo Crypt Leeds 06-07; Chief Exec Officer 07-09; Dep Chairman Create Foundn from 09. *The Create Foundation, Moor View, Leeds LS11 9NF* Tel 0113-394 6120 E-mail gary.stott@createfoundation.com

STOTT, Jonathan. d 07 p 07. NSM Cheltenham H Trin and St Paul *Glouc* 07-09; Perm to Offic from 09. *29 Brizen Lane, Cheltenham GL53 0NG* Tel (01242) 228894 E-mail jonathan@glenfall.org.uk

STOTT, Jonathan Robert. b 76. Ripon Coll Cuddesdon 99. d 01 p 02. C Anfield St Columba *Liv* 01-05; V Dovecot 05-10; Chapl HM Pris Risley 10; P-in-c Dovecot *Liv* from 10. *Holy Spirit Vicarage, Dovecot Avenue, Liverpool L14 7QJ* Tel 0151-220 6611 E-mail frjonathan@btinternet.com

STOTT, Miss Teresa. b 57. Linc Th Coll 94. d 94 p 95. C Lee-on-the-Solent *Portsm* 94-97; C Spalding St Jo w Deeping St Nicholas *Linc* 97-98; P-in-c Freiston w Butterwick 98-99; R Freiston w Butterwick and Benington 99-03; R Freiston, Butterwick w Bennington, and Leverton 03-04; C-in-c

Cleethorpes St Fran CD 04-09; TV Gt and Lt Coates w Bradley from 09; Chapl Matthew Humberston Sch from 04; Chapl St Andr Hospice Grimsby from 06. *St Nicholas' Vicarage, Great Coates Road, Grimsby DN37 9NS* Tel (01472) 882495 E-mail stott145@btinternet.com

STOTT, Victoria. Wycliffe Hall Ox. **d** 09 **p** 10. NSM Battersea Rise St Mark *S'wark* from 09. *St Mark's Church, Battersea Rise, London SW11 1EJ* Tel (020) 7326 9423 E-mail viccy.stott@stmarks-battersea.org.uk

STOW, John Mark. b 51. Selw Coll Cam BA73 MA77. Linc Th Coll 76. **d** 78 **p** 79. C Harpenden St Jo *St Alb* 78-82; TV Beaminster Area *Sarum* 82-87; P-in-c Hawkchurch 87-90; P-in-c Marshwood Vale 87-88; TR Marshwood Vale 88-91; Past Co-ord Millfield Jun Sch from 93. *Chestnut House, Edgarley, Glastonbury BA6 8LL* Tel (01458) 832245

STOW, Peter John. b 50. Oak Hill Th Coll. **d** 89 **p** 90. C Forest Gate St Mark *Chelmsf* 89-94; V from 94. *St Mark's Vicarage, Tylney Road, London E7 0LS* Tel (020) 8555 2988 E-mail saintmarks@clara.co.uk

STOW, Archdeacon of. See SINCLAIR, The Ven Jane Elizabeth Margaret

STOWE, Brian. b 32. Trin Coll Cam BA55 BA56 MA59. Ridley Hall Cam 55. **d** 57 **p** 58. C New Catton St Luke *Nor* 57-59; Chapl R Masonic Sch Bushey 59-70; Tutor Rickmansworth Sch Herts 70-71; Chapl Alleyn's Foundn Dulwich 71-75; Hon C Dulwich St Barn *S'wark* 71-75; Chapl Ellerslie Sch Malvern 75-92; Chapl Malvern Coll 92-93; TV Malvern Link w Cowleigh *Worc* 93-94; rtd 95; P-in-c Malvern St Andr *Worc* 95-96; Perm to Offic from 96. *31 Park View, Grange Road, Malvern WR14 3HG* Tel 07792-515307 (mobile) E-mail bandmstowe2@onctel.com

STOWE, Mrs Katharine Elizabeth. b 78. Birm Univ BA01 PGCE02 Trin Coll Cam BA06. Westcott Ho Cam 04. **d** 07 **p** 08. C Salter Street and Shirley *Birm* from 07. *93 Baxters Road, Shirley, Solihull B90 2RS* Tel 0121-745 8896 E-mail katestowe@yahoo.com

STOWE, Nigel James. b 36. Bris Univ BSc57. Clifton Th Coll 59. **d** 61 **p** 62. C Ware Ch Ch *St Alb* 61-64; C Reigate St Mary *S'wark* 64-67; V Islington St Jude Mildmay Park *Lon* 67-75; V Penn Street *Ox* 75-01; rtd 01. *27 Snowdrop Way, Widmer End, High Wycombe HP15 6BL* Tel (01494) 717496

STOWE, Canon Rachel Lilian. b 33. Qu Coll Birm 79. **dss** 83 **d** 87 **p** 94. Dean w Yelden, Melchbourne and Shelton *St Alb* 82-87; Pertenhall w Swineshead 82-87; Bp's Officer for NSMs and Asst Dir of Ords 87-93; rtd 93; NSM The Stodden Churches *St Alb* 87-96; Hon Can St Alb 92-96; Convenor Dioc Adv Gp for Chr Healing *Ripon* 98-03; Perm to Offic *Ripon* from 97 and *York* from 98. *Preston Cottage, East Cowton, Northallerton DL7 0BD* Tel and fax (01325) 378173 Mobile 07860-618600 E-mail rachel@stowe2106.freeserve.co.uk

STOWELL, Ms Jody. b 75. Spurgeon's Coll BD09. Ridley Hall Cam 09. **d** 11. C Harrow Weald All SS *Lon* from 11. *17 Windsor Road, Harrow HA3 5PT* Tel 07940-432410 (mobile) E-mail jody@radical-disciple.org.uk

STRACHAN, Donald Philip Michael. b 37. St D Coll Lamp 60. **d** 62 **p** 63. C Aberdeen St Mary 62-64; P-in-c Aberdeen St Paul 64-66; Chapl St Andr Cathl 65-68; Itinerant Priest *Mor* 68-73; R Coatbridge *Glas* 73-85; Chapl HM Pris Glas (Barlinnie) 84-87; Dioc Supernumerary *Glas* 85-94; rtd 94; Perm to Offic *Arg* 87-06; Lic to Offic from 06. *Reul na Mara, Claddach Kirkibost, Isle of North Uist HS6 5EP* Tel (01876) 580392

STRACHAN, Mrs Gillian Lesley. b 44. Furzedown Coll of Educn TCert65 Open Univ BA77 Hatf Poly MA87. EAMTC 03. **d** 06 **p** 07. C Aquitaine *Eur* 06-10; Asst Chapl from 10. *La Gravette, 24150 Bayac, France* Tel and fax (0033) 5 53 58 12 58 Mobile 6 76 39 25 15 E-mail gillstrachan@wanadoo.fr

STRAFFORD, Mrs Elizabeth. **d** 09 **p** 10. NSM Dur N from 09. *41 The Orchard, Pity Me, Durham DH1 5DA* Tel 0191-384 9802

STRAFFORD, Nigel Thomas Bevan. b 53. Univ of Wales (Lamp) BA80. Sarum & Wells Th Coll 80. **d** 82 **p** 94. C Kidderminster St Mary *Worc* 82; C Kidderminster St Mary and All SS, Trimpley etc 82-83; Hon C Stockton St Mark *Dur* 84-86; Asst P Longwood *Wakef* 86-94; V Athersley 94-97; P-in-c Ferrybridge 97-03; P-in-c Holme and Seaton Ross Gp *York* 03-04; R from 04. *The Vicarage, Market Weighton Road, Holme-on-Spalding-Moor, York YO43 4AG* Tel (01430) 860379

STRAIN, Christopher Malcolm. b 56. Solicitor Southn Univ LLB77. Wycliffe Hall Ox 83. **d** 86 **p** 87. C Werrington *Pet* 86-89; C Broadwater *Chich* 89-94; TV Hampreston *Sarum* 94-00; P-in-c Parkstone St Luke 00-03; V from 03. *The Vicarage, 2 Birchwood Road, Parkstone, Poole BH14 9NP* Tel (01202) 741030

STRAIN, John Damian. b 49. Keele Univ BA72 Birkbeck Coll Lon MSc83 PhD89 AFBPsS89. STETS BTh00. **d** 00 **p** 01. NSM Hindhead *Guildf* 00-03; NSM Churt and Hindhead 03-09; P-in-c Compton, the Mardens, Stoughton and Racton *Chich* from 09; P-in-c Stansted from 09. *The Vicarage, Compton, Chichester PO18 9HD* Tel (023) 9263 1252 E-mail j.strain@surrey.ac.uk

STRAINE, Gillian Kathleen. b 79. Imp Coll Lon BSc00 PhD05. Ripon Coll Cuddesdon BA08. **d** 09 **p** 10. C Kidlington w

Hampton Poyle *Ox* from 09. *29 Andersons Close, Kidlington, Oxford OX5 1ST* Tel 07747-010249 (mobile) E-mail gstraine@yahoo.co.uk

STRANACK, The Very Revd David Arthur Claude. b 43. Chich Th Coll 65. **d** 68 **p** 69. C Forest Gate St Edm *Chelmsf* 68-69; C Colchester St Jas, All SS, St Nic and St Runwald 69-74; V Brentwood St Geo 74-82; V Nayland w Wiston *St E* 82-99; R Hadleigh 99-02; V Hadleigh, Layham and Shelley 02-08; Dean Bocking 99-08; RD Hadleigh 99-07; Hon Can St E Cathl 94-08; rtd 08; Perm to Offic *St E* from 08. *12 Sandy Lane, Sudbury CO10 7HG* Tel (01787) 881657

STRANACK, Canon Richard Nevill. b 40. Leeds Univ BA63. Coll of Resurr Mirfield 63. **d** 65 **p** 66. C Bush Hill Park St Mark *Lon* 65-68; C Brighton St Martin *Chich* 68-72; P-in-c Toftrees w Shereford *Nor* 72-74; V 74-81; P-in-c Pensthorpe 72-74; R 74-81; V Hempton and Pudding Norton 72-81; RD Burnham and Walsingham 78-81; V Par *Truro* 81-94; P-in-c St Blazey 87-91; Hon Chapl Miss to Seafarers from 81; V Stratton and Launcells *Truro* 94-06; RD Stratton 02-05; Chapl Cornwall Healthcare NHS Trust 97-02; Chapl N and E Cornwall Primary Care Trust 02-06; rtd 06; P-in-c Duloe, Herodsfoot, Morval and St Pinnock *Truro* 06-08; Hon Can Truro Cathl 98-08. *8 Sunwine Place, Exmouth EX8 2SE* Tel (01395) 225638 E-mail rnstranack@yahoo.co.uk

STRANG, Martin Guthrie. b 55. Bris Univ BSc76 Paisley Coll of Tech MSc83 MIMechE85. St Jo Coll Nottm 07. **d** 09 **p** 10. C Trowell, Awsworth and Cossall *S'well* from 09. *The Vicarage, The Lane, Awsworth, Nottingham NG16 2QP* Tel 0115-932 8143 Mobile 07908-995450

STRANGE, Canon Alan Michael. b 57. Pemb Coll Ox BA79 MA89. Wycliffe Hall Ox BA84. **d** 84 **p** 85. C York St Paul 84-87; Asst Chapl Brussels Cathl 87-91; Assoc Chapl 91-95; P-in-c Heigham H Trin *Nor* 95-99; R from 99; RD Nor S from 09; Hon Can Nor Cathl from 10. *The Rectory, 17 Essex Street, Norwich NR2 2BL* Tel (01603) 622225 E-mail rector@trinitynorwich.org *or* big1al@ntlworld.com

STRANGE, Bryan. b 26. Sarum & Wells Th Coll 73. **d** 75 **p** 76. C King's Worthy *Win* 75-78; C Wilton *B & W* 78-80; V Kewstoke w Wick St Lawrence 80-89; rtd 89; Perm to Offic *Ex* 90-09. *29 Bluebell Avenue, Tiverton EX16 6SX*

STRANGE, Malcolm. b 58. Westmr Coll Ox MTh95. Sarum & Wells Th Coll 82. **d** 85 **p** 86. C Seaton Hirst *Newc* 85-88; C Ridgeway *Sarum* 88-89; TV 89-91; TV Newbury *Ox* 91-98; TR Bideford, Northam, Westward Ho!, Appledore etc *Ex* 98-01; RD Hartland 99-01. *Address withheld by request*

✠**STRANGE, The Rt Revd Mark Jeremy.** b 61. Aber Univ LTh82. Linc Th Coll 87. **d** 89 **p** 90 c 07. C Worc St Barn w Ch Ch 89-92; V Worc St Wulstan 92-98; R Elgin w Lossiemouth *Mor* 98-07; P-in-c Dufftown 04-07; P-in-c Aberlour 04-07; Can St Andr Cathl Inverness 00-07; Syn Clerk 03-07; Bp Mor from 07. *Bishop's House, St John's, Arpafeelie, North Kessock, Inverness IV1 3XD* Tel (01463) 811333 E-mail bishop@moray.anglican.org

STRANGE, Canon Peter Robert. b 48. Univ Coll Lon BA69 Ex Coll Ox BA71 MA76. Cuddesdon Coll 71. **d** 72 **p** 73. C Denton *Newc* 72-74; C Newc St Jo 74-79; Chapl for Arts and Recreation 79-90; R Wallsend St Pet 79-86; Can Res Newc Cathl from 86; Angl Adv Tyne Tees TV from 90; Asst Dioc Dir of Ords *Newc* 94-98. *55 Queen's Terrace, Jesmond, Newcastle upon Tyne NE2 2PL* Tel 0191-281 0181 *or* 232 1939 Fax 230 0735 E-mail peterstrange@stnicnewcastle.co.uk

STRANGE, Preb Robert Lewis. b 45. Sarum & Wells Th Coll 72. **d** 74 **p** 75. C Walthamstow St Barn and St Jas Gt *Chelmsf* 74-77; C Wickford 77-80; P-in-c Treverbyn *Truro* 80-83; V 83-86; Asst Stewardship Adv 82-96; V Newlyn St Pet 86-10; Preb Trehaverock 94-10; rtd 10; Hon Chapl Miss to Seafarers from 86. *Michaelmas, Lelant Downs, Hayle TR27 6NJ* E-mail robert.sarov@tiscali.co.uk

STRANGE, The Ven William Anthony. b 53. Qu Coll Cam BA76 MA80 K Alfred's Coll Win CertEd77 Ox Univ DPhil89. Wycliffe Hall Ox 79. **d** 82 **p** 83. Tutor Wycliffe Hall Ox 82-87; C Aberystwyth *St D* 87; TV 87-91; V Llandeilo Fawr and Taliaris 91-96; Hd of Th and RS Trin Coll Carmarthen 96-01; V Carmarthen St Pet *St D* 03-09; AD Carmarthen 06-09; V Pencarreg and Llanycrwys from 09; Adn Cardigan from 09. *The Vicarage, Cwmann, Lampeter SA48 8DU* Tel (01570) 422385 E-mail archdeacon.cardigan@churchinwales.org.uk

STRANRAER-MULL, The Very Revd Gerald Hugh. b 42. AKC69. St Aug Coll Cant 69. **d** 70 **p** 71. C Hexham *Newc* 70-72; C Corbridge w Halton 72; R Ellon *Ab* 72-08; R Cruden Bay 72-08; Can St Andr Cathl 81-08; Dean Ab 88-08; P-in-c Peterhead 02-04; rtd 08. *75 The Cairns, Muir of Ord IV6 7AT* Tel (01463) 870986 E-mail stranraermull@btinternet.com

STRAPPS, Canon Robert David. b 28. St Edm Hall Ox BA52 MA56. Wycliffe Hall Ox 52. **d** 54 **p** 55. C Low Leyton *Chelmsf* 54-57; C Ox St Aldate w St Matt w Trin 57-60; V Sandal St Helen *Wakef* 60-94; RD Chevet 81-93; Hon Can Wakef Cathl 92-94; rtd 94; Perm to Offic *Wakef* 94-98; *Glouc* and *Worc* from 94. *Brookside, Hill Road, Kemerton, Tewkesbury GL20 7JN* Tel (01386) 725515

STRASZAK, Edmund Norman. b 57. Coll of Resurr Mirfield 88. **d** 90 **p** 91. C Adlington *Blackb* 90-93; C Harrogate St Wilfrid and St Luke *Ripon* 93-95; V Chorley All SS *Blackb* from 95. *All Saints' Vicarage, Moor Road, Chorley PR7 2LR* Tel (01257) 265665 E-mail edmund1@talktalk.net

STRATFORD, Mrs Anne Barbara. Southn Univ CertEd58 Ox Univ MTh99. Qu Coll Birm 88. **d** 91 **p** 94. Officer Dioc Bd of Soc Resp (Family Care) *Lich* 85-97; NSM Kinnerley w Melverley and Knockin w Maesbrook 91-95; Chapl Robert Jones and Agnes Hunt Orthopaedic Hosp 95-97; NSM Maesbury *Lich* 95-96; P-in-c 96-97; Chapl Moreton Hall Sch from 96; P-in-c Ford *Heref* 97-02; V 02-05; P-in-c Alberbury w Cardeston 97-02; V 02-05; rtd 05; Perm to Offic *Lich and St As* from 05. *Pentre Cleddar, Hengoed, Oswestry SY10 7AB* Tel (01691) 650469

STRATFORD, David. b 46. **d** 98 **p** 99. OLM Ditton St Mich w St Thos *Liv* 98-11. *96 Clincton View, Widnes WA8 8RW* Tel 0151-423 4912

STRATFORD, Niall. CITC. **d** 09. NSM Killiney Ballybrack *D & G* from 09. *Address temp unknown*

STRATFORD, Ralph Montgomery. b 30. TCD BA53 MA67. CITC 53. **d** 54 **p** 54. Dioc *C C & O* 54-55; C Waterford Ch Ch 55-56; I Ballisodare w Collooney 56-00; Adn Killala and Achonry *T, K & A* 69-00; Can Killala Cathl 69-00; Preb Kilmactalway St Patr Cathl Dublin 85-00; rtd 00. *Knoxpark House, Robinstown, Mullingar, Co Westmeath, Republic of Ireland* Tel (00353) (44) 933 5292

STRATFORD, Terence Stephen. b 45. Chich Th Coll 67. **d** 69 **p** 70. C Old Shoreham *Chich* 69-73; C New Shoreham 69-73; C Uckfield 73-75; C Lt Horsted 73-75; C Isfield 73-75; P-in-c Waldron 76-80; R 80-82; V Blacklands Hastings Ch Ch and St Andr 82-89; P-in-c Ovingdean 85-95; Dioc Ecum Officer 89-95; P-in-c Staplefield Common 95-00; Sussex Ecum Officer 95-01; V Ferring 00-08; C New Shoreham and Old Shoreham 08-11; P-in-c Kingston Buci from 11. *Kingston Buci Rectory, Rectory Road, Shoreham-by-Sea BN43 6EB* Tel (01273) 592591 E-mail terry.stratford@yahoo.co.uk

STRATFORD, Timothy Richard. b 61. York Univ BSc82 Sheff Univ PhD08. Wycliffe Hall Ox 83. **d** 86 **p** 87. C Mossley Hill St Matt and St Jas *Liv* 86-89; C St Helens St Helen 89-91; Bp's Dom Chapl 91-94; V W Derby Gd Shep 94-03; TR Kirkby from 03. *The Rectory, Old Hall Lane, Liverpool L32 5TH* Tel 0151-547 2155 Fax 08701-673589 E-mail tim.stratford@btinternet.com

STRATHIE, Duncan John. b 58. Heythrop Coll Lon MA02. Cranmer Hall Dur BA95. **d** 97 **p** 98. C Yateley *Win* 97-01; V Kempshott 01-07; Min Tr Officer from 07; Dioc Convener of Voc Adv from 03. *10 Pigeonhouse Field, Sutton Scotney, Winchester SO21 3NJ* Tel (01962) 760339 E-mail duncan@strathie.org

STRATON, Christopher James. b 46. **d** 93 **p** 94. Chapl Miss to Seamen S Africa 93-96; Asst P Gingindlovu All SS 97-99; R 99-00; P-in-c Tyldesley w Shakerley *Man* 00-06; TV Astley, Tyldesley and Mosley Common from 06. *11 Peel Hall Avenue, Tyldesley, Manchester M29 8TA* Tel (01942) 882914

STRATTA, Antony Charles. b 36. ACIS. S'wark Ord Course 82. **d** 85 **p** 86. C Southborough St Pet w Ch Ch and St Matt *Roch* 85-88; R Gt Mongeham w Ripple and Sutton by Dover *Cant* 88-96; rtd 96; Perm to Offic *St E* from 96. *Well House, The Great Yard, Rougham Green, Bury St Edmunds IP30 9JP* Tel (01284) 386140 E-mail antonystratta@btinternet.com

STRATTON, Mrs Anne Margaret. b 58. JP98. Nottm Univ BEng79. EMMTC 03. **d** 06 **p** 07. NSM Bradgate Team *Leic* 06-10; P-in-c Belper *Derby* from 10. *St Peter's Vicarage, 6 Chesterfield Road, Belper DE56 1FD* Tel (01773) 821323 Mobile 07773-076555 E-mail rev.annestratton@btinternet.com

STRATTON, Henry William. b 39. Bris Univ CertEd74 BEd75. Glouc Sch of Min 80. **d** 83 **p** 84. NSM Cainscross w Selsley *Glouc* 83-87; C Odd Rode *Ches* 87-92; V Runcorn H Trin 92-96; V Lostock Gralam 96-05; rtd 05; Perm to Offic *Ches* from 05. *10 The Beeches, Great Sutton, Ellesmere Port CH66 4UJ* Tel 0151-339 3715 E-mail harry@hstratton.fsnet.co.uk

STRATTON, John Jefferies. b 27. Bps' Coll Cheshunt 53. **d** 55 **p** 56. C Watford St Mich *St Alb* 55-60; C Stevenage 60-65; R Cottered w Broadfield and Throcking 65-82; RD Buntingford 75-82; V S Mimms St Mary and Potters Bar *Lon* 82-84; V Potters Bar *St Alb* 85-94; P-in-c Flamstead 94-96; rtd 94; Hon C Taunton H Trin *B & W* from 97. *17 The Fairways, Sherford, Taunton TA1 3PA* Tel (01823) 330564 E-mail jj.stratton@btinternet.com

STRAUGHAN, Prof Keith. b 60. Imp Coll Lon BSc81 Lon Univ PhD87 Imp Coll Lon ARCS81 CPhys87 MInstP87 Trin Coll Cam BA97 MA00. Westcott Ho Cam 94. **d** 97 **p** 98. C Abbots Langley *St Alb* 97-00; Fell SS Coll Cam 00-08; Chapl 00-03; Dean 03-05; Sen Tutor 05-08; Dean Univ Cen Milton Keynes 08; NSM Milton Keynes *Ox* from 11. *University Centre Milton Keynes, 200 Silbury Boulevard, Milton Keynes MK9 1LT* Tel 08458-380880 E-mail keith.straughan@ucmk.ac.uk

STRAW, Mrs Juliet Lesley. b 49. Univ of Wales (Ban) BA70 Leeds Univ PGCE71. SAOMC 00. **d** 03 **p** 04. NSM Stratfield Mortimer and Mortimer W End etc *Ox* 03-10; P-in-c Wymering *Portsm* from 10; P-in-c Cosham from 10. *Wymering Vicarage, Medina Road, Portsmouth PO6 3NH* Tel (023) 9238 1836 E-mail juliet.straw@btinternet.com

STRAWBRIDGE, Jennifer Ruth. b 78. Washington & Lee Univ BA01 Ox Univ MSt02. Yale Div Sch MDiv04. **d** 04 **p** 04. C New Haven Ch Ch USA 04-05; C Arlington St Mary 05-09; Asst Chapl Keble Coll Ox 09-10; Chapl from 10. *Keble College, Parks Road, Oxford OX1 3PG* Tel (01865) 272725 E-mail jennifer.strawbridge@keble.ox.ac.uk

STREATER, David Arthur. b 33. Oak Hill Th Coll 67. **d** 68 **p** 69. C Lindfield *Chich* 68-71; S Africa 71-86; R Kingham w Churchill, Daylesford and Sarsden *Ox* 86-91; Dir Ch Soc 91-98; Sec Ch Soc Trust 91-96; rtd 98; P-in-c Odell *St Alb* 98-03. *16 Linden Avenue, West Cross, Swansea SA3 5LE* Tel (01792) 406849 E-mail monty@ukgateway.net

STREATFEILD, Peter Michael Fremlyn. b 53. Newc Univ BSc77 St Jo Coll Dur BA03. Cranmer Hall Dur 00. **d** 03 **p** 04. C Solway Plain *Carl* 03-08; TV Binsey from 08. *The Vicarage, Bassenthwaite, Keswick CA12 4QH* Tel (017687) 76198 E-mail petermfs@hotmail.com

STREET, Anthony James. b 57. Trin Coll Bris 79. **d** 85 **p** 87. SAMS 85-95; C Temuco H Trin Chile 85-87; V Temuco St Matt 87-95; P-in-c Warley *Wakef* 96-99; V from 99; P-in-c Halifax St Hilda from 10. *The Vicarage, 466 Burnley Road, Warley, Halifax HX2 7LW* Tel (01422) 363623 E-mail familiastreet@btinternet.com

STREET, David. b 72. St Jo Coll Nottm. **d** 10 **p** 11. C Bucknall *Lich* from 10. *12 Tansey Close, Bucknall, Stoke-on-Trent ST2 9QX* Tel (01782) 283934 E-mail davestreet@xalt.co.uk

STREET, Matthew Graham. b 61. Regent's Park Coll Ox BA83. Wycliffe Hall Ox 99. **d** 01 **p** 02. C Combe Down w Monkton Combe and S Stoke *B & W* 01-05; P-in-c Peasedown St John w Wellow 05-10; V Peasedown St John w Wellow and Foxcote etc from 10. *The Vicarage, 18 Church Road, Peasedown St John, Bath BA2 8AA* Tel (01761) 432293 Fax 08701-307814 Mobile 07762-794371 E-mail mgstreet@me.com

STREET, Peter Jarman. b 29. K Coll Lon BD59 AKC59. **d** 59 **p** 60. C Highters Heath *Birm* 59-60; C Shirley 60-62; Lect Cheshire Coll of Educn 62-66; St Pet Coll of Educn Birm 66-70; RE Adv Essex Co Coun 70-92; Hon C Gt Dunmow *Chelmsf* 71-85; Sen Insp RE and Humanities 74-92; R Gt w Lt Yeldham 85-92; RD Belchamp 90-92; rtd 92; Perm to Offic *Chelmsf* from 92. *18 Jubilee Court, Great Dunmow CM6 1DY* Tel (01371) 876871

STREET, Philip. b 47. Lon Univ BPharm68. NW Ord Course 75. **d** 78 **p** 79. C Heaton St Barn *Bradf* 78-81; C Evington *Leic* 82-84; R Wymondham w Edmondthorpe, Buckminster etc 84-88; V Gosberton Clough and Quadring *Linc* 88-95; Asst Local Min Officer 88-95; V Buttershaw St Paul *Bradf* 95-99; P-in-c Gt and Lt Casterton w Pickworth and Tickencote *Pet* 99-04; R 04-09; P-in-c Exton w Horn 02-06; rtd 09; Perm to Offic *Pet* from 09. *35 Foundry Walk, Thrapston, Kettering NN14 4LS* Tel (01832) 731661 E-mail p.street08@btinternet.com

STREETER, Brian Thomas. b 68. Reading Univ BSc89. Ridley Hall Cam 05. **d** 08 **p** 09. C Windermere St Mary and Troutbeck *Carl* from 08. *4 St Mary's Park, Windermere LA23 1AY* Tel 07981-951882 (mobile) E-mail bts@rapport.ltd.uk

STREETER, Christine Mary. See HADDON-REECE, Mrs Christine Mary

STREETER, David James. b 42. Pemb Coll Cam BA64 MA68. Qu Coll Birm 65. **d** 67 **p** 68. C Saffron Walden *Chelmsf* 67-71; C Shrub End 71-73; R Rayne 73-79; V Highams Park All SS 79-82; P-in-c Stradbroke w Horham and Athelington *St E* 82-87; R Stradbroke, Horham, Athelington and Redlingfield from 87; RD Hoxne 91-00. *The Rectory, Doctors Lane, Stradbroke, Eye IP21 5HU* Tel (01379) 384363 Mobile 07798-784179 E-mail david.streeter@stedmundsbury.anglican.org

STREETING, John William. b 52. Cam Inst of Educn CertEd74 Birm Univ BEd77 Anglia Poly Univ MA99 FGMS98 FRSA98. St Steph Ho Ox 90. **d** 92 **p** 93. C Upminster *Chelmsf* 92-95; C Chingford SS Pet and Paul 95-97; Assoc V Chelsea St Luke and Ch Ch *Lon* 97-03; V Sheerness H Trin w St Paul *Cant* 03-10; P-in-c 10; P-in-c Queenborough 05-10; AD Sittingbourne 04-06; P-in-c Axminster, Chardstock, All Saints etc *Ex* from 10. *The Rectory, Church Street, Axminster EX13 5AQ* Tel (01297) 598213 E-mail axrector@talktalk.net

STREETING, Laurence Storey. b 14. VRD65. St Jo Coll Dur BA39 MA42. **d** 40 **p** 41. C Bishopwearmouth St Gabr *Dur* 40-46; Chapl RNVR 42-46; S Africa 46-49; Chapl Garden City Woodford Bridge 49-51; Chapl Village Home Barkingside 49-51; Chapl RAF 51-56; Chapl RNR 56-90; Asst Chapl Eliz Coll Guernsey 56-60; Chapl Eshton Hall Sch Gargrave 60-64; Perm to Offic *Cant* 64-65; R Guernsey St Sampson *Win* 65-71; St Vincent 72-76; Chapl Madeira *Eur* 76-80; rtd 80; Perm to Offic *Win* from 79. *Apartment 8, de Hubie Court, Les Cotils Christian Centre, St Peter Port, Guernsey GY1 1VV*

STRETCH, Richard Mark. b 53. d 93 p 94. OLM Stowmarket *St E* from 93. *91 Kipling Way, Stowmarket IP14 1TS* Tel (01449) 676219

STRETTON, Reginald John. b 37. MRPharmS63 CBiol70 MIBiol70 Man Univ BSc62 Nottm Univ PhD65. EMMTC 88. d 91 p 92. NSM Loughb Gd Shep *Leic* 91-94; P-in-c Burrough Hill Pars 94-02; rtd 02; Perm to Offic *Leic* and *S'well* from 02; *Derby* from 05. *19 Paddock Close, Quorn, Loughborough LE12 8BJ* Tel (01509) 412935 E-mail rstretton@leicester.anglican.org

STRETTON, Robert John. b 45. Kelham Th Coll. d 69 p 70. C Hendon St Ignatius *Dur* 69-73; C Middlesbrough St Thos *York* 73-77; OSB 77-78; V Brandon *Dur* 78-85; SSM from 85; Lic to Offic *Dur* 85-91; Tr in Evang Ch in Wales 91-94; Perm to Offic *S'wark* 94-01; Lesotho 01-05. *The Well, Newport Road, Willen, Milton Keynes MK15 9AA* Tel (01908) 242741

STREVENS, Brian Lloyd. b 49. St Jo Coll Dur BA70. Ripon Hall Ox 70. d 73 p 74. C Old Trafford St Jo *Man* 73-76; C Bolton St Pet 76-78; Org Sec Southn Coun of Community Service 78-92; Perm to Offic *Win* 82-86, 92-95 and from 01; Hon C Bitterne Park *Win* 86-92; Hon C N Stoneham 95-01. *186 Hill Lane, Southampton SO15 5DB* Tel (023) 8033 3301 E-mail hq@scaccs.org.uk

STREVENS, Richard Ernest Noel. b 34. Nottm Univ BA60. Linc Th Coll 60. d 62 p 63. C St Botolph Aldgate w H Trin Minories *Lon* 62-66; C Ealing St Steph Castle Hill 66-68; Hon C St Botolph without Bishopgate 68-76; V Clent *Worc* 76-86; V Pirbright *Guildf* 86-00; Perm to Offic *Ex* 69-98 and from 00; rtd 00. *83 Head Weir Road, Cullompton EX15 1NN* Tel (01884) 35823

STRIBLEY, William Charles Harold. b 29. SWMTC 84. d 87 p 88. NSM Kenwyn St Geo *Truro* 87-92; NSM Truro St Paul and St Clem 92-98; Perm to Offic from 99. *54 Chirgwin Road, Truro TR1 1TT* Tel (01872) 272958

STRICKLAND (née CUTTS), Mrs Elizabeth Joan Gabrielle. b 61. St Jo Coll Dur BA83. Westcott Ho Cam 87. d 90 p 94. C Cayton w Eastfield *York* 90-92; NSM Biggin Hill *Roch* 93-96; Perm to Offic *Ex* 96-00 and *Ely* 00-02; P-in-c Holywell w Needingworth *Ely* 02-07. *Windswept, Holywell, St Ives PE27 4TQ* Tel (01480) 495275 *or* 460107 E-mail epstrickland@ukonline.co.uk

STRICKLAND, Jonathan Edward Tully. b 56. Westf Coll Lon BSc78. Ridley Hall Cam 00. d 02 p 03. C Margate H Trin *Cant* 02-06; P-in-c Bawtry w Austerfield and Misson *S'well* from 07. *The Vicarage, Martin Lane, Bawtry, Doncaster DN10 6NJ* Tel (01302) 710298 E-mail strickers@tesco.net

STRIDE, Clifford George. b 58. Win Univ BA11. STETS 08. d 11. NSM Ampfield, Chilworth and N Baddesley *Win* from 11. *4 Dibble Drive, North Baddesley, Southampton SO52 9NF* Tel (023) 8073 9835 E-mail cgstride@btinternet.com

STRIDE, Clifford Stephen. b 21. Ex & Truro NSM Scheme. d 81 p 82. NSM Chulmleigh *Ex* 81-83; NSM Hardham *Chich* 87-93; NSM Coldwaltham and Hardham 93-97; NSM Sutton w Houghton and Coldwaltham and Hardham 97-05. *Ambleside, Sandy Lane, Watersfield, Pulborough RH20 1NF* Tel (01798) 831851

STRIDE, John David. b 46. Ex Univ BSc68. Oak Hill Th Coll 86. d 88 p 89. C Ashtead *Guildf* 88-96; V Lodge Moor St Luke *Sheff* 96-11; rtd 11; Perm to Offic *Sheff* from 11. *11 Blenheim Mews, Sheffield S11 9PR* Tel 0114-235 6220 E-mail john@jonjax.net

STRIDE, John Michael. b 48. Oak Hill Th Coll BA77. d 80 p 81. C Edmonton All SS *Lon* 80-82; C Edmonton All SS w St Mich 82-83; C Wembley St Jo 83-85; P-in-c Hockering *Nor* 85-89; R Hockering, Honingham, E and N Tuddenham 89-91; V Tuckswood 91-93; Chapl HM Pris Leeds 93-94; Chapl HM Pris Littlehey 94-96; V Heeley *Sheff* 96-99; TR Heeley and Gleadless Valley 99-04; AD Attercliffe 02-04; V Goole 04-06; Chapl Combined Courts 06-11; Hon C Darfield 07-11; V Ludham, Potter Heigham, Hickling and Catfield *Nor* from 11. *The Vicarage, Norwich Road, Ludham, Great Yarmouth NR29 5QA* E-mail johnmo@mojnst.plus.com

STRIKE, Maurice Arthur. b 44. FRSA66. Sarum & Wells Th Coll 85. d 87 p 88. C Chippenham St Andr w Tytherton Lucas *Bris* 87-91; R Corfe Castle, Church Knowle, Kimmeridge etc *Sarum* 91-04; R Guernsey St Philippe de Torteval *Win* from 04; R Guernsey St Pierre du Bois from 04. *The Rectory, St Pierre du Bois, Guernsey GY7 9SB* Tel (01481) 263544 E-mail mauricestrike@stpeters.wtb.co.uk

STRINGER, Adrian Nigel. b 60. Univ of Wales (Cardiff) BD82 Lanc Univ PGCE83. Sarum & Wells Th Coll 86. d 88 p 89. C Barrow St Matt *Carl* 88-92; TV Westhoughton *Man* 92-94; I Inver w Mountcharles, Killaghtee and Killybegs *D & R* 94-96; V Tuckingmill *Truro* 96-01; Chapl R Alexandra and Albert Sch Reigate 01-03; I Desertlyn w Ballyeglish *Arm* from 03. *The Rectory, 24 Cookstown Road, Moneymore, Magherafelt BT45 7QF* Tel (028) 8674 8200 E-mail adrianstringer@gatton-park.org.uk

STRINGER, Harold John. b 36. Peterho Cam BA58. Ripon Hall Ox 62. d 64 p 65. C Hackney St Jo *Lon* 64-68; C Roehampton H

Trin *S'wark* 68-71; P-in-c Southampton St Mich w H Rood, St Lawr etc *Win* 71-73; TV Southampton (City Cen) 73-82; Ind Chapl 77-82; V Notting Hill St Jo *Lon* 82-87; V Notting Hill St Pet 82-87; V Notting Hill St Jo and St Pet 87-01; AD Kensington 98-01; rtd 02; Perm to Offic *Lon* from 03. *56 Mountfield Road, London W5 2NQ* Tel (020) 8998 8049 E-mail mail@haroldandchristina.co.uk

STRINGER, Canon John Roden. b 33. AKC61. d 62 p 63. C Auckland St Helen *Dur* 62-63; C Hebburn St Cuth 63-67; V Cassop cum Quarrington 67-88; RD Sedgefield 84-88; V Lumley 88-98; Hon Can Dur Cathl 88-98; rtd 98; Perm to Offic *Dur* 98-03. *4 Darwin Road, Walsall WS2 7EW* Tel (01922) 649243

STROEBEL, Mrs Stephanie Suzanne. b 47. Middx Univ BA06. NTMTC 03. d 06 p 07. NSM Ashingdon w S Fambridge *Chelmsf* 06-08; NSM S Woodham Ferrers 08-10; P-in-c Woodham Mortimer w Hazeleigh from 10; P-in-c Woodham Walter from 10. *St Margaret's Rectory, Maldon Road, Woodham Mortimer, Maldon CM9 6SN* Tel (01621) 857501 Mobile 07930-105163 E-mail s.stroebel@virgin.net

STRØMMEN, Mrs Mary Natasha. b 52. Kent Univ BA73 Bp Otter Coll Chich PGCE74. EAMTC 00. d 03 p 04. NSM Oslo w Bergen, Trondheim and Stavanger *Eur* from 03. *Lykkestien 4, 7053 Ranheim, Norway* Tel (0047) 7391 3281 E-mail mary.strommen@c2i.net

STRONG, Christopher Patteson. b 43. Ridley Hall Cam. d 83 p 84. C Dalton-in-Furness *Carl* 83-87; V Wootton *St Alb* 87-02; RD Elstow 94-02; R Fowlmere, Foxton, Shepreth and Thriplow *Ely* 02-08; rtd 08. *Kiln Farm, Priory Road, Campton, Shefford SG17 5PG* Tel (01462) 819274 E-mail christopherpstrong@hotmail.com

STRONG, John. *See* STRONG, Capt William John Leonard

STRONG, Canon John David. b 34. Cuddesdon Coll 59. d 61 p 62. C Gosforth All SS *Newc* 61-65; Chapl Malvern Coll 65-71; R Welford w Weston on Avon *Glouc* 72-79; V Nailsworth 79-01; RD Tetbury 83-00; Hon Can Glouc Cathl 91-01; rtd 01. *Glebe House, The Meads, Leighterton, Tetbury GL8 8UW* Tel (01666) 890236 E-mail canondavid@penshouse.freeserve.co.uk

STRONG (formerly BULMAN), Ms Madeline Judith. b 61. K Coll Lon BD AKC Lon Metrop Univ MA. dss 86 d 87 p 94. Shepperton *Lon* 86-88; Par Dn 87-88; Par Dn Brentford 88-94; C 94-96; V Cobbold Road St Sav w St Mary 96-04; Dean of Women's Min 99-02; Chapl Stamford Ho Secure Unit 02-04; Spiritual Cllr PROMIS 04-07; Perm to Offic *Cant* 04-10; Hon C Stone Street Gp from 10. *The Vicarage, Pilgrims Way, Hastingleigh, Ashford TN25 5HP* Tel (01233) 750260 Mobile 07973-954802 E-mail expressiveart@idnet.uk

STRONG, Matthew John. b 60. Lon Univ BA81 Cam Univ BA84 MA89. Ridley Hall Cam 82. d 85 p 86. C Houghton *Carl* 85-89; C Hirwaun *Llan* 89-91; V Troedyrhiw w Merthyr Vale 91-95; Tutor Llan Ord Course 91-95. *22 Birch Lane, Oldbury B68 0NZ* Tel 0121-421 5978

STRONG, Rowan Gordon William. b 53. Victoria Univ Wellington BA76 Edin Univ PhD92 Melbourne Coll of Div ThM88. St Jo Coll (NZ) LTh80. d 77 p 78. C Kapiti New Zealand 77-79; C Palmerston N St Pet 79-81; V Shannon 81-83; Assoc P E Hill Australia 83-89; NSM Edin Old St Paul 89-92; Tutor Edin Univ 91-92; Lect Murdoch Univ Australia from 92; Sen Lect from 02. *150 George Street, East Fremantle WA 6158, Australia* Tel (0061) (8) 9339 0643 *or* 9360 6470 Fax 9360 6480 Mobile 439-988896 E-mail r.strong@murdoch.edu.au

STRONG, Capt William John Leonard. b 44. CA Tr Coll 64 Chich Th Coll 87. d 89 p 90. CA from 66; C Mayfield *Chich* 89-92; C Seaford w Sutton 92-94; V Crawley Down All SS 94-97; rtd 01. *21 Carroll Close, Poole BH12 1PL* Tel (01202) 733940 Mobile 07944-670125

STROUD, David Alan. b 74. Kent Univ BA96 Ch Ch Coll Cant PGCE95. Westcott Ho Cam 02. d 04 p 05. C Liss *Portsm* 04-08; Asst Chapl Cant Ch Ch Univ from 08. *Canterbury Christ Church University, North Holmes Road, Canterbury CT1 1QU* Tel (01227) 767700 E-mail david.stroud@canterbury.ac.uk

STROUD, The Ven Ernest Charles Frederick. b 31. St Chad's Coll Dur BA59. d 60 p 61. C S Kirkby *Wakef* 60-63; C Whitby *York* 63-66; C-in-c Chelmsf All SS CD 66-69; V Chelmsf All SS 69-75; V Leigh-on-Sea St Marg 75-83; Asst RD Southend 76-79; RD Hadleigh 79-83; Hon Can Chelmsf Cathl 82-83; Adn Colchester 83-97; rtd 97; Perm to Offic *Chelmsf* from 97. *St Therese, 67 London Road, Hadleigh, Benfleet SS7 2QL* Tel (01702) 554941 Fax 500789

STROUD, Canon Robert Owen. b 29. AKC56. d 57 p 58. C Aylesbury *Ox* 57-60; C Bexhill St Pet *Chich* 60-64; C Gosforth All SS *Newc* 64-66; V High Elswick St Phil 66-72; V Tynemouth Cullercoats St Paul 72-77; R Orlestone w Ruckinge w Warehorne *Cant* 77-81; RD N Lympne 79-81; V Folkestone H Trin w Ch Ch 81-83; TR Folkestone H Trin and St Geo w Ch Ch 83-90; V Folkestone H Trin w Ch Ch 90-93; RD Elham 90-93; Hon Can Cant Cathl 92-93; rtd 93; Perm to Offic *Ex* 94-02; *Cant* 02-06 and from 08. *27 Rochester Avenue, Canterbury CT1 3YE* Tel (01227) 767312

STROWGER, Mrs Patricia. b 45. Surrey Univ BA06. STETS 01. **d** 04 **p** 05. NSM The Lavingtons, Cheverells, and Easterton *Sarum* 04-11; C Bishop's Cannings, All Cannings etc from 11. *The Vicarage, The Street, Bishop's Cannings, Devizes SN10 2LD* Tel (01380) 860073 E-mail canningschurcheswilts@yahoo.com

✠**STROYAN, The Rt Revd John Ronald Angus.** b 55. St Andr Univ MTheol76. Qu Coll Birm 81 Bossey Ecum Inst Geneva 82. **d** 83 **p** 84 c 05. C Cov E 83-87; V Smethwick St Matt w St Chad *Birm* 87-94; V Bloxham w Milcombe and S Newington *Ox* 94-05; AD Deddington 02-05; Suff Bp Warw *Cov* from 05. *Warwick House, 139 Kenilworth Road, Coventry CV4 7AF* Tel (024) 7641 2627 Fax 7641 5254 E-mail bishop.warwick@covcofe.org

STRUDWICK, Canon Vincent Noel Harold. b 32. Nottm Univ BA59 DipEd Lambeth DD09. Kelham Th Coll 52. **d** 59 **p** 60. Tutor Kelham Th Coll 59-63; Sub-Warden 63-70; C Crawley *Chich* 70-73; Adult Educn Adv 73-77; R Fittleworth 73-77; Planning Officer for Educn Milton Keynes 77-80; Dir of Educn *Ox* 80-89; Hon Can Ch Ch from 82; Continuing Minl Educn Adv 85-89; Dir Dioc Inst for Th Educn 89-97; Prin Cov Min Course 89-94; Prin SAOMC 94-96; Fell and Tutor Kellogg Coll Ox 94-00; C Aylesbury w Bierton and Hulcott *Ox* 97-98. *31 The Square, Brill, Aylesbury HP18 9RP* Tel (01865) 280354 Fax 270309 E-mail vincent.strudwick@conted.ox.ac.uk

STRUGNELL, John Richard. b 30. Lon Univ BA52 Leeds Univ MA61 Univ of Qld PhD77. Wells Th Coll 54. **d** 56 **p** 57. C Leeds Halton St Wilfrid *Ripon* 56-59; C Moor Allerton 59-62; Australia from 65; rtd 95. *231 Grandview Road, Pullenvale Qld 4069, Australia* Tel (0061) (7) 3374 1776

STRUTT, Peter Edward. b 40. SAOMC 94. **d** 97 **p** 98. NSM Penn Street *Ox* 97-02; Perm to Offic from 02. *59 King's Ride, Penn, High Wycombe HP10 8BP* Tel (01494) 812418

STRUTT, Preb Susan. b 45. Glouc Sch of Min 87. **d** 90 **p** 94. NSM Eye, Croft w Yarpole and Lucton *Heref* 90-94; C Leominster 94-96; Hon Chapl RAF 94-96; P-in-c Bosbury w Wellington Heath etc *Heref* 96-98; TV Ledbury from 98; Dioc Adv on Women in Min 99-03; Preb Heref Cathl from 07. *The Vicarage, Bosbury, Ledbury HR8 1QA* Tel (01531) 640144 E-mail suestrutt@strutts.fsnet.co.uk

STUART, Angus Fraser. b 61. Bedf Coll Lon BA83 K Coll Lon PhD91 St Jo Coll Dur BA92. Cranmer Hall Dur 90. **d** 93 **p** 94. C Twickenham St Mary *Lon* 93-96; Sen Chapl Bris Univ 96-05; Hon C Bris St Mich and St Paul 96-98; P-in-c 98-00; Hon C Cotham St Sav w St Mary and Clifton St Paul 00-05; I W Vancouver St Fran in the Wood Canada from 05. *4773 South Piccadilly, West Vancouver BC V7W 1J8, Canada* Tel (001) (604) 922 3531

STUART, Sister Ann-Marie Lindsay. b 41. Westmr Coll Lon CertEd69 Kent Univ BA80 Univ of Wales (Lamp) MA03. Franciscan Study Cen 76. **d** 99 **p** 00. NSM Sherborne w Castleton and Lillington *Sarum* 99-01; TV Golden Cap Team 01-08; rtd 08; Hon C Crosslacon *Carl* 08-11; NSM Brigham, Gt Broughton and Broughton Moor from 11; Dioc Adv for Spirituality from 09. *The Benefice Vicarage, The Green, Little Broughton, Cockermouth CA13 0YG* Tel (01900) 825317 E-mail revams41@btinternet.com

STUART, Brother. See BURNS, The Rt Revd Stuart Maitland

STUART, Christopher John. b 74. Keble Coll Ox BA95 MA04 Loughb Univ MSc98 St Jo Coll Dur BA05 MA06. Cranmer Hall Dur 03. **d** 06 **p** 07. C Pershore w Pinvin, Wick and Birlingham *Worc* 06-09; P-in-c St Jo in Bedwardine from 09. *St John's Vicarage, 143 Malvern Road, Worcester WR2 4LN* Tel (01905) 429773 Mobile 07906-721060 E-mail chris.j.stuart@connectfree.co.uk

STUART, Francis David. b 32. Barrister-at-Law Lon Univ BA54 AKC57. Ridley Hall Cam 62. **d** 64 **p** 65. C Addiscombe St Mildred *Cant* 64-67; Chapl RN 67-71; Lic to Offic *Liv* 76-80; TV Oldham *Man* 84-89; Chapl Oldham and Distr Gen Hosp 84-89; Chapl Oldham R Infirmary 86-89; Chapl R Oldham Hosp 89-94; Chapl Oldham NHS Trust 94-98; rtd 97; Perm to Offic *Man* 00-03. *17 rue de la Villeneuve, 56150 Baud, France* Tel (0033) 2 97 51 11 38 E-mail davidetpam@orange.fr

STUART, Canon Herbert James. b 26. CB83. TCD BA48 MA55. **d** 49 **p** 50. C Sligo Cathl 49-53; C Dublin Rathmines *D & G* 53-55; Chapl RAF 55-73; Asst Chapl-in-Chief RAF 73-80; Chapl-in-Chief and Archdeacon for the RAF 80-83; Can and Preb Linc Cathl 81-83; R Cherbury *Ox* 83-87; Perm to Offic *Glouc* 87-97 and *Ox* 87-96; rtd 91. *1 Abbot's Walk, Lechlade GL7 3DB* Tel (01367) 253299

✠**STUART, The Rt Revd Ian Campbell.** b 42. New England Univ (NSW) BA70 CertEd70 Melbourne Univ DipEd77 MA92 MACE72 FAIM91. St Barn Coll Adelaide 84. **d** 85 **p** 85 c 92. Australia 85-99; Asst Bp N Queensland 96-99; Chapl Liv Hope Univ from 99; Hon Asst Bp Liv from 99. *The Chaplaincy, Liverpool Hope, Hope Park, Taggart Avenue, Liverpool L16 9JD* Tel 0151-291 3547 Fax 291 3873 E-mail stuarti@hope.ac.uk

STUART-BOURNE, Mrs Rona. b 67. Surrey Univ BSc89. Ripon Coll Cuddesdon 09. **d** 11. C Freshwater *Portsm* from 11; C

Yarmouth from 11. *Easterholme, Tennyson Road, Yarmouth PO41 0PR* Tel 07899-848434 (mobile) E-mail rona.stuartbourne@gmail.com

STUART-LEE, Nicholas Richard. b 54. Wycliffe Hall Ox. **d** 83 **p** 84. C Costessey *Nor* 83-85; TV Dewsbury *Wakef* 85-90; R Rowlands Castle *Portsm* 90-00; V Nottingham St Jude *S'well* 00-03; TR Thame *Ox* 03-07. *69 Harefields, Oxford OX2 8NR* Tel (01865) 511044 E-mail nrsl@ciloros.fsnet.co.uk

STUART-SMITH, David. b 36. St Pet Coll Ox BA61 MA65. Tyndale Hall Bris. **d** 63 **p** 64. C Tooting Graveney St Nic *S'wark* 63-67; C Richmond H Trin 67-70; Lic to Offic 70-74; NSM Canonbury St Steph *Lon* 70-74; Travelling Sec IVF 70-74; Bangladesh 74-79; V Clapham Park St Steph *S'wark* 79-95; RD Streatham 83-87; Chapl Wye Coll Kent 95-01; P-in-c Wye w Brook *Cant* 95-01; P-in-c Hastingleigh 00-01; rtd 01; Perm to Offic *Cant* 01-07 and *Lon* from 07. *42 Rennie Court, 11 Upper Ground, London SE1 9LP* Tel (020) 7261 1866

STUART-WHITE, Canon William Robert. b 59. Ox Univ BA. Trin Coll Bris BA. **d** 86 **p** 87. C Upper Armley *Ripon* 86-91; P-in-c Austrey *Birm* 91-92; P-in-c Warton 91-92; V Austrey and Warton 92-98; R Camborne *Truro* 98-06; P-in-c Stoke Climsland 06-09; P-in-c Linkinhorne 06-09; P-in-c St Breoke and Egloshayle from 09; Hon Can Truro Cathl from 09. *8 Winwell Field, Wadebridge PL27 6UJ* Tel (01208) 816431 E-mail wstuartwhi@aol.com

STUBBINGS, Frank Edward. b 20. Fitzw Coll Cam BA48 MA53. Worc Ord Coll 60. **d** 61 **p** 62. C Rowbarton *B & W* 61-64; V Catcott 64-74; V Burtle 64-74; Chapl St Cath Sch Bramley 74-83; R Barkestone w Plungar, Redmile and Stathern *Leic* 83-87; rtd 87; Perm to Offic *B & W* 88-91; Hon C Lostwithiel, St Winnow w St Nectan's Chpl etc *Truro* from 91. *Flat 8, Manormead, Tilford Road, Hindhead GU26 6RA*

STUBBS, Ian Kirtley. b 47. Man Univ DipAE90. Kelham Th Coll 66. **d** 70 **p** 71. C Chandler's Ford *Win* 70-75; C Farnham Royal *Ox* 75-80; Ind Chapl 75-80; Ind Chapl *Man* 81-86; TV Oldham 81-86; TR Langley and Parkfield 86-88; Community Work Officer Dioc Bd of Soc Resp 88-90; Dir Laity Development 90-96; Nat Adv in Adult Learning C of E Bd of Educn 97-02; V Stalybridge *Man* 02-11; P-in-c Glossop *Derby* from 11; C Hadfield from 11; C Charlesworth and Dinting Vale from 11. *The Vicarage, Church Street South, Glossop SK13 7RU* Tel (01457) 852146 Mobile 07712-451710 E-mail iks47@live.co.uk

STUBBS, Stanley Peter Handley. b 23. Lon Univ BD52 Lille 3 Univ MèsL82. Ely Th Coll 55. **d** 55 **p** 56. C Fletton *Ely* 55-58; Hon Min Can Pet Cathl 56-58; C Hounslow Heath St Paul *Lon* 58-63; CF (TA) 59-78; V Northampton St Alb *Pet* 63-76; R Brondesbury Ch Ch and St Laur *Lon* 76-93; rtd 93; Perm to Offic *Lon* from 93. *3 Westbury Lodge Close, Pinner HA5 3FG* Tel (020) 8868 8296

STUBBS, Canon Trevor Noel. b 48. AKC70. St Aug Coll Cant 73. **d** 74 **p** 75. C Heckmondwike *Wakef* 74-77; C Warwick Australia 77-80; V Middleton St Cross *Ripon* 80-89; R Wool and E Stoke *Sarum* 89-95; TR Bridport 95-09; RD Lyme Bay 06-09; rtd 09; Admin Bp Gwynne Th Coll Sudan from 09; Lic to Offic *Sarum* from 09; Can and Preb Sarum Cathl from 03. *1 Winford Grove, Bristol BS13 7DY* E-mail revtrev.stubbs@gmail.com

STUBENBORD, Jess William. b 48. BA72. Trin Coll Bris 75. **d** 78 **p** 79. C Cromer *Nor* 78-82; C Gorleston St Mary 82-85; P-in-c Saxthorpe and Corpusty 85-89; P-in-c Blickling 86-89; R Saxthorpe w Corpusty, Blickling, Oulton etc 89-93; P-in-c Mulbarton w Kenningham 93-97; P-in-c Flordon 94-97; P-in-c Wreningham 95-97; R Mulbarton w Bracon Ash, Hethel and Flordon from 98. *The Rectory, The Common, Mulbarton, Norwich NR14 8JS* Tel (01508) 570296 E-mail jess.stubenbord@btinternet.com

STUCKES, Stephen. b 62. Trin Coll Bris. **d** 96 **p** 97. C Dunster, Carhampton and Withycombe w Rodhuish *B & W* 96-00; V Alcombe from 00; RD Exmoor from 09. *The Vicarage, 34 Manor Road, Minehead TA24 6EJ* Tel (01643) 703285 E-mail sjstuckes@hotmail.com

STUDD, John Eric. b 34. Clare Coll Cam BA58 MA62. Coll of Resurr Mirfield 58. **d** 60 **p** 61. C Westmr St Steph w St Jo *Lon* 60-65; Australia 65-69; Hon C Kensington St Mary Abbots w St Geo *Lon* 70-71; P-in-c Monks Risborough *Ox* 72-77; P-in-c Gt and Lt Kimble 72-77; C Aylesbury 78; Chapl to the Deaf 78-82; Chapl Hants, Is of Wight and Channel Is Assn for Deaf 82-91; Chapl to the Deaf *Win* 91-99; rtd 99; Perm to Offic *Guildf* 82-96 and *Portsm* 82-99. *28 Elgin Way, Flagstaff Hill SA 5159, Australia* Tel (0061) (8) 8370 4707 Fax 8370 6517 E-mail jonea@senet.com.au

STUDDERT-KENNEDY, Andrew Geoffrey. b 59. Ch Ch Ox BA80 MA86. Ripon Coll Cuddesdon BA88. **d** 89 **p** 90. C Wimbledon *S'wark* 89-94; V Norbury St Oswald 94-02; RD Croydon N 99-02; TR Marlborough *Sarum* from 02; RD Marlborough from 09. *The Rectory, 1 Rawlingswell Lane, Marlborough SN8 1AU* Tel (01672) 514357 or 512357 E-mail andrew@studdert-kennedy.wanadoo.co.uk

STUDDERT-KENNEDY, Canon Christopher John. b 22. BNC Ox BA49 MA53. Wells Th Coll 49. **d** 51 **p** 52. C Bermondsey

St Mary w St Olave and St Jo *S'wark* 51-54; C Clapham H Trin 54-56; V Putney St Marg 56-66; R Godstone 66-91; RD Godstone 76-88; Hon Can S'wark Cathl 80-91; rtd 91; Perm to Offic *Chich* from 91. *Orchard House, The Street, Washington, Pulborough RH20 4AS* Tel (01903) 892774

STUDHOLME, Muriel Isabel. b 25. **d** 96. NSM Bromfield w Waverton *Carl* 96-02; NSM Solway Plain from 02. *Yew Tree Cottage, Dundraw, Wigton CA7 0HY* Tel (01697) 342506

STURCH, Richard Lyman. b 36. Ch Ch Ox BA58 MA61 DPhil70 Open Univ BSc06. Ely Th Coll. **d** 62 **p** 63. C Hove All SS *Chich* 62-65; C Burgess Hill St Jo 65-66; C Ox St Mich w St Martin and All SS 67-68; Tutor Ripon Hall Ox 67-71; Lect Univ of Nigeria 71-74; Lect Lon Bible Coll 75-80; TV Wolverton *Ox* 80-86; R Islip w Charlton on Otmoor, Oddington, Noke etc 86-01; rtd 01. *35 Broomfield, Stacey Bushes, Milton Keynes MK12 6HA* Tel (01908) 316779 E-mail rsturch@fsmail.net

STURMAN, Robert George. b 50. Nottm Univ BTh79. Linc Th Coll 75. **d** 79 **p** 80. C Cainscross w Selsley *Glouc* 79-83; TV Bottesford w Ashby *Linc* 83-88; V Prescot *Liv* 88-91; P-in-c Abenhall w Mitcheldean *Glouc* 93-97; R 97-10; AD Forest N 99-04 and 08-09; rtd 11. *2 Backney View, Greytree, Ross-on-Wye HR9 7JP* E-mail robertsturman@tiscali.co.uk

STURROCK, Marian Elizabeth. b 46. Westmr Coll Ox BTh97. St Mich Coll Llan 97. **d** 99 **p** 00. C Swansea St Pet *S & B* 99-03; Chapl Swansea NHS Trust 00-03; R Thundersley *Chelmsf* from 03. *St Peter's Rectory, Church Road, Thundersley, Benfleet SS7 3HG* Tel (01268) 566206 E-mail mariansturrock@sky.com

STURT, Mrs Rachel Caroline. b 60. Open Univ BSc03 RGN81. STETS 08. **d** 11. NSM Wrecclesham *Guildf* from 11. *14 Arthur Road, Farnham GU9 8PB* Tel (01252) 710968 E-mail rachelsturt@btopenworld.com

STURT, Rock André Daniel. b 56. Liv Univ BSc79 Lon Univ CertEd80. Oak Hill Th Coll BA88. **d** 88 **p** 89. Chapl St Bede's Sch Cam 88-90; Par Dn Cambridge St Martin *Ely* 88-90; C 90-91; P-in-c Alwalton and Chesterton 91-96; TV The Ortons, Alwalton and Chesterton 96-03; R Gravesend St Geo *Roch* 03-06. *51G Lower Higham Road, Gravesend DA12 2NQ*

STUTZ, Clifford Peter. b 25. **d** 83 **p** 84. OLM Cusop w Blakemere, Bredwardine w Brobury etc *Heref* 83-08. *Burnt House, Dorstone, Hereford HR3 5SX* Tel (01497) 831472

STUTZ, Mrs Sally Ann. b 64. Univ of Wales BSc88 Leeds Metrop Univ MSc93 Birm Univ BD95 SRD90. Qu Coll Birm 93. **d** 96 **p** 97. C Middleton St Mary *Ripon* 96-00; C Wilmslow *Ches* 00-03; Dioc Adv in Chr Worship 00-03; Perm to Offic from 03. *1 Arundel Close, Knutsford WA16 9BZ* Tel (01565) 650919 E-mail sally.stutz@stutzsanyal.fsnet.co.uk

STYLER, Jamie Cuming. b 36. Sarum & Wells Th Coll 70. **d** 72 **p** 73. C Whipton *Ex* 72-75; C Paignton St Jo 76-78; V Topsham 78-88; V Plymouth St Simon 88-01; Chapl Plymouth Community Services NHS Trust 94-01; rtd 01; Perm to Offic *Ex* from 01. *Drey House, 27 Langham Way, Ivybridge PL21 9BX* Tel (01752) 691592

STYLES, Charles Adam Mark. b 81. St Hild Coll Dur BA04. Oak Hill Th Coll 06. **d** 09 **p** 10. C Britwell *Ox* from 09. *19 Goodwin Road, Slough SL2 2ET* E-mail charliestyles@dunelm.org.uk

STYLES, Canon Lawrence Edgar. b 19. AM88. Pemb Coll Cam BA48 MA52. Ridley Hall Cam. **d** 50 **p** 51. C Bishop's Stortford St Mich *St Alb* 50-53; V Tyldesley w Shakerley *Man* 53-60; Australia from 60; Can Melbourne 82-86; rtd 86. *25 Carson Street, Kew Vic 3101, Australia* Tel and fax (0061) (3) 9853 9749 E-mail lstyles@co31.aone.net.au

SUART, Geoffrey Hugh. b 49. Man Univ BSc70 Nottm Univ PGCE71. Oak Hill Th Coll. **d** 83 **p** 84. C Ogley Hay *Lich* 83-86; TV Wenlock *Heref* 86-90; TR Kirby Muxloe *Leic* 90-04; RD Sparkenhoe E 99-03; R Snettisham w Ingoldisthorpe and Fring *Nor* from 04; Chapl Norfolk Hospice from 11. *The Vicarage, 18 Park Lane, Snettisham, King's Lynn PE31 7NW* Tel (01485) 541301 E-mail geoffsuart.t21@btinternet.com

SUCH, Colin Royston. b 62. UEA LLB83. Ripon Coll Cuddesdon 94. **d** 97 **p** 98. C Streetly *Lich* 97-00; P-in-c Wednesfield St Greg 00-04; V Rushall from 04; P-in-c Walsall St Pet from 08. *Rushall Vicarage, 10 Tetley Avenue, Walsall WS4 2HE* Tel (01922) 624677

SUCH, Howard Ingram James. b 52. Southn Univ BTh81 Lon Univ MA97. Sarum & Wells Th Coll 77. **d** 81 **p** 82. C Cheam *S'wark* 81-84; Prec Cant Cathl 84-91; V Borden 91-03; Hon Min Can Cant Cathl 84-03; AD Sittingbourne 00-03; Can Res and Prec Sheff Cathl 03-07; Warden St Barn Coll Lingfield *S'wark* from 07; Superior Soc of Retreat Conductors from 05. *The Lodge, The College of St Barnabas, Blackberry Lane, Lingfield RH7 6NJ* Tel (01342) 872805

SUCH, Paul Nigel. b 52. FGA72 BTh84. Chich Th Coll 79. **d** 84 **p** 85. C Handsworth St Andr *Birm* 84-87; C Rugeley *Lich* 87-88; TV 88-91; R Longton 91-02; R Cov St Jo from 02. *St John's Rectory, 9 Davenport Road, Coventry CV5 6QA* Tel and fax (024) 7667 3203

SUCH, Royston Jeffery. b 46. Solicitor Univ Coll Lon LLB67. Sarum & Wells Th Coll 83. **d** 83 **p** 84. NSM Ringwood *Win* 83-90; R Bishop's Sutton and Ropley and W Tisted from 90. *The*

Vicarage, Lyeway Lane, Ropley, Alresford SO24 0DW Tel (01962) 772205

SUCKLING, Keith Edward. b 47. CChem FRSC Darw Coll Cam PhD71 Liv Univ BSc87 DSc89. Oak Hill NSM Course 91. **d** 94 **p** 95. NSM Digswell and Panshanger *St Alb* from 94. *291 Knightsfield, Welwyn Garden City AL8 7NH* Tel (01707) 330022 E-mail keith@suckling291.freeserve.co.uk

SUDAN, Archbishop of the Episcopal Church of the. *See* MARONA, The Most Revd Joseph Biringi Hassan

SUDBURY, Archdeacon of. *See* JENKINS, The Ven David Harold

SUDDABY, Susan Eveline. b 43. Bedf Coll of Educn CertEd64. S'wark Ord Course 93. **d** 96 **p** 97. NSM Rusthall *Roch* 96-00; C Northfleet 00-02; Perm to Offic 03-06; P-in-c N Chapel w Ebernoe *Chich* 06-08; rtd 08; Perm to Offic *Chich* from 08. *54 Garden Wood Road, East Grinstead RH19 1JX* Tel (01342) 313042

SUDDARDS, John Martin. b 52. Trin Hall Cam BA74 MA77 Barrister-at-Law 75. Qu Coll Birm 86. **d** 89 **p** 90. C Halstead St Andr w H Trin and Greenstead Green *Chelmsf* 89-93; P-in-c Gt w Lt Yeldham 93-97; P-in-c Toppesfield and Stambourne 93-97; R Upper Colne 97-01; RD Hinckford 98-01; TR Witham 01-11; RD Witham 07-11; V Thornbury and Oldbury-on-Severn w Shepperdine *Glouc* from 11. *The Vicarage, 27 Castle Street, Thornbury, Bristol BS35 1HQ* Tel (01454) 418415 E-mail john@suddards.plus.com

SUDELL, Philip Henry. b 61. Thames Poly BScEng84 Lon Univ PGCE85. Wycliffe Hall Ox 89. **d** 92 **p** 93. C Worthing Ch the King *Chich* 92-96; C Muswell Hill St Jas w St Matt *Lon* 96-05; Lic to Offic from 05. *163 Colney Hatch Lane, London N10 1HA* Tel (020) 8883 7417 E-mail philip.sudell@gracech.org.uk

SUDRON, David Jeffrey. b 78. Univ Coll Dur BA99 MA00. St Steph Ho Ox 01. **d** 03 **p** 04. C Gt Grimsby St Mary and St Jas *Linc* 03-08; Min Can Dur Cathl from 08. *3 The College, Durham DH1 3EQ* Tel 0191-384 2481 E-mail david.sudron@dunelm.org.uk

SUDWORTH, Frank. b 43. Open Univ BA92. Oak Hill Th Coll. **d** 78 **p** 79. C Deane *Man* 78-81; C Worksop St Jo *S'well* 82-85; V Wollaton Park 85-90; P-in-c Lenton Abbey 85-86; V 86-90; V Upper Armley *Ripon* 90-97; RD Armley 92-95; Dep Chapl HM Pris Liv 97-98; P-in-c Low Moor H Trin *Bradf* 98-03; V Low Moor 03; P-in-c Wyke 03-05; TR Oakenshaw, Wyke and Low Moor 06-07; rtd 07; Perm to Offic *Blackb* from 07. *12 Brampton Avenue, Thornton-Cleveleys FY5 2JY* Tel (01253) 858377

SUDWORTH, Richard John. b 68. Leeds Univ LLB90 Spurgeon's Coll MTh05. Qu Coll Birm 05. **d** 10 **p** 11. C Sparkbrook Ch Ch *Birm* from 10; C Tyseley from 10. *65 Arden Road, Acocks Green, Birmingham B27 6AH* Tel 07891-635664 (mobile) E-mail suddy@blueyonder.co.uk

SUDWORTH, Timothy Mark. b 70. St Martin's Coll Lanc BA93 K Coll Lon MA03. St Paul's Th Cen Lon 06. **d** 08 **p** 09. NSM Egham *Guildf* from 08; Chapl Strode's Coll from 08. *25 Mead Close, Egham TW20 8JA* Tel (01784) 437935 E-mail timsudworth@btinternet.com

SUFFERN, Richard William Sefton. b 57. Reading Univ BSc79. Trin Coll Bris 88. **d** 90 **p** 91. C Radipole and Melcombe Regis *Sarum* 90-94; TV Cheltenham St Mark *Glouc* 94-99; R Whitnash Cov from 99. *St Margaret's Rectory, 2 Church Close, Whitnash, Leamington Spa CV31 2HJ* Tel (01926) 425070 E-mail rwss@talktalk.net

SUFFOLK, Archdeacon of. *See* HUNT, The Ven Judith Mary

SUGDEN, Charles Edward. b 59. Magd Coll Cam PGCE82 MA83. Trin Coll Bris 89. **d** 91 **p** 92. C Gidea Park *Chelmsf* 91-94; TV Melksham *Sarum* 94-01; NSM Poole 02-08; V Locks Heath *Portsm* from 08. *The Vicarage, 125 Locks Heath Park Road, Locks Heath, Southampton SO31 6LY* E-mail cesthevicar28@hotmail.com

SUGDEN, Canon Christopher Michael Neville. b 48. St Pet Coll Ox BA70 MA74 Nottm Univ MPhil74 Westmr Coll Ox PhD88. St Jo Coll Nottm 72. **d** 74 **p** 75. C Leeds St Geo *Ripon* 74-77; Assoc P Bangalore St Jo India 77-83; Lic to Offic *Ox* from 83; Can St Luke's Cathl Jos Nigeria from 00; Exec Dir Ox Cen for Miss Studies 01-04; Exec Sec Angl Mainstream Internat from 04. *Anglican Mainstream International, 21 High Street, Eynsham, Oxford OX29 4HE* Tel (01865) 883388 E-mail csugden@anglican-mainstream.net

SULLIVAN, Canon Julian Charles. b 49. Lon Univ BSc74 CertEd75. Wycliffe Hall Ox 80. **d** 83 **p** 84. C Southall Green St Jo *Lon* 83-87; C Wells St Cuth w Wookey Hole *B & W* 87-90; V Sheff St Barn and St Mary 90-91; V Sheff St Mary w Highfield Trin 91-95; V Sheff St Mary Bramall Lane from 95; P-in-c Endcliffe 04-07; Hon Can Sheff Cathl from 01; AD Ecclesall 01-06; Bp's Urban Adv from 05. *St Mary's Vicarage, 42 Charlotte Road, Sheffield S1 4TL* Tel 0114-272 4987 E-mail jandvsullivan@blueyonder.co.uk

SULLIVAN, The Ven Nicola Ann. b 58. SRN81 RM84. Wycliffe Hall Ox BTh95. **d** 95 **p** 96. C Earlham St Anne *Nor* 95-99; Assoc V Bath Abbey w St Jas *B & W* 99-02; Chapl R Nat Hosp for Rheumatic Diseases NHS Trust 99-02; Bp's Chapl and Past Asst

B & W 02-07; Sub-Dean and Preb Wells Cathl 03-07; Adn Wells and Can Res Wells Cathl from 07. *6 The Liberty, Wells BA5 2SU* Tel (01749) 685147 E-mail adwells@bathwells.anglican.org
SULLIVAN, Trevor Arnold. b 40. CITC 69. **d** 70 **p** 71. C Lurgan Ch the Redeemer *D & D* 71-72; C Tralee *L & K* 72-75; Irish Sch of Ecum 75-77; Ind Chapl *D & G* 77-80; I Ematris *Clogh* 80-84; I Aughrim w Ballinasloe etc *L & K* 84-07; Can Limerick and Killaloe Cathls 89-07; rtd 07. *4 Woodview, Ballinasloe, Co Galway, Republic of Ireland* Tel (00353) 87-241 2194 (mobile)
SULLY, Andrew Charles. b 67. Southn Univ BA88 Birm Univ MPhil95. Qu Coll Birm 90. **d** 93 **p** 94. C Maindee Newport *Mon* 93-96; V Llanfihangel w Llanafan and Llanwnnws etc *St D* 96-02; TV St As 03-06; PV St As Cathl 02-06; V Llangollen w Trevor and Llantysilio from 06; AD Llangollen from 10. *The Vicarage, Abbey Road, Llangollen LL20 8SN* Tel (01978) 860231
SULLY, Christine Ann. **d** 11. NSM Corringham and Blyton Gp *Linc* from 11; NSM Glentworth Gp from 11. *Hampden House, 6 Lancaster Green, Hemswell Cliff, Gainsborough DN21 5TQ*
SULLY, Martin John. b 44. AIAS. St Jo Coll Nottm 80. **d** 82 **p** 83. C Lindfield *Chich* 82-86; V Walberton w Binsted 86-01; R Lewes St Jo sub Castro 01-09; rtd 09. *5 Camden Avenue, Pembury, Tunbridge Wells TN2 4PQ* Tel (01892) 822033
SULTAN, Pervaiz. b 55. Punjab Univ BSc75 Ox Cen for Miss Studies PhD97. Gujranwala Th Sem MDiv80. **d** 80 **p** 84. Pakistan 80-11; Sec for Inter Faith Relns 89; Lect St Thos Th Coll Karachi 89-11; Vice Prin 93-95; Prin 95-11; V Murree H Trin 84-85; Assoc V Lahore St Andr 86-89; V Karachi St Andr 90-93 and 06-10; P-in-c Highgate *Birm* from 11; Chapl St Alb Academy from 11. *The Vicarage, 120 Stanhope Street, Birmingham B12 0XB* Tel 0121-440 4603 Mobile 07075 554543 E-mail sultanp35@yahoo.com
SUMARES, Manuel. b 43. Stonehill Coll USA BA66 Dominican Coll of Philosophy and Th Ottawa BPh74 Catholic Univ of Portugal PhD84 Westmr Coll Ox BTh99. **d** 97 **p** 99. Hon Asst Chapl Oporto *Eur* 97-05; P-in-c from 05. *Casa do Bárrio-Monsul, P-Pvoa de Lanhoso 4830, Portugal* Tel (00351) (253) 993067 E-mail op14089@mail.telepac.pt
SUMMERS, Alexander William Mark. b 75. Leic Univ BA98 MA00 Fitzw Coll Cam BTh09 Open Univ PGCE01. Westcott Ho Cam 07. **d** 09 **p** 10. C Chingford SS Pet and Paul *Chelmsf* from 09. *50 Mayfield Road, London E4 7JA* Tel (020) 8529 3963 Mobile 07717-575772 E-mail fr.alex@yahoo.co.uk
SUMMERS, Jeanne. *See* SUMMERS, Preb Ursula Jeanne
SUMMERS, John Ewart. b 35. MIMechE66 Ex Univ MA95. ALCD69. **d** 69 **p** 70. C Fulham St Matt *Lon* 69-72; Chapl RN 72-81; V Devonport St Barn *Ex* 81-98; V Devonport St Mich and St Barn 98-00; rtd 00; Perm to Offic *Ex* from 00. *Box Cottage, Aish, South Brent TQ10 9JH* Tel (01364) 72976
SUMMERS (née PASCOE), Mrs Lorraine Eve. b 51. SAOMC 98. **d** 01 **p** 02. NSM Sandon, Wallington and Rushden w Clothall *St Alb* 01-06; P-in-c Kimpton w Ayot St Lawrence from 06; Asst Chapl E and N Herts NHS Trust from 06. *The Vicarage, 11 High Street, Kimpton, Hitchin SG4 8RA* Tel (01438) 833419
SUMMERS, Neil Thomas. b 58. Roehampton Inst BA93 K Coll Lon MA94 St Mary's Coll Strawberry Hill PGCE95. SEITE 97. **d** 00 **p** 01. NSM Richmond St Mary w St Matthias and St Jo S'wark from 00. *2 Ravensbourne Road, Twickenham TW1 2DH* Tel (020) 8892 8313 E-mail ntsummers@aol.com
SUMMERS, Paul Anthony. b 53. St Jo Coll York CertEd75. Coll of Resurr Mirfield 77. **d** 80 **p** 81. C Manston *Ripon* 80-83; Min Can and Prec Ripon Cathl 83-88; Chapl Univ Coll of Ripon and York St Jo 84-88; V Whitkirk *Ripon* 88-95; R Lower Wharfedale 95-00; AD Harrogate 98-00; rtd 04; Perm to Offic *Bradf* from 05. *16 Beacon Street, Addingham, Ilkley LS29 0QX* Tel (01943) 839552 Mobile 07747-131731 E-mail paulsummers65@hotmail.com
SUMMERS, Canon Raymond John. b 41. Univ of Wales TCert63 Open Univ BA75. St Mich Coll Llan 77. **d** 77 **p** 78. NSM Mynyddislwyn *Mon* 77-81; NSM Abercarn 81-82; P-in-c 82-89; V 89-91; V Mynyddislwyn 91-95; TR 95-08; RD Bedwellty 93-04; Can St Woolos Cathl 01-08; rtd 08. *12A Maple Gardens, Risca, Newport NP11 6AR* Tel (01633) 613676
SUMMERS, Stephen Bruce. b 63. St Andr Univ MTheol95 Chich Univ PhD08. STETS 98. **d** 00 **p** 01. C Bishop's Waltham *Portsm* 00-02; R Farlington 02-09; Prin Local Min Progr *Guildf* from 09. *Diocesan House, Quarry Street, Guildford GU1 3XG* Tel (01483) 790319
SUMMERS, Preb Ursula Jeanne. b 35. Birm Univ BA56 Liv Univ CertEd57. Glouc Sch of Min. **dss** 85 **d** 87 **p** 94. Fownhope *Heref* 85-87; Hon C 87; Brockhampton w Fawley 85-87; Hon C 87; C Marden w Amberley and Wisteston 88-94; P-in-c 94-02; RD Heref Rural 93-99; P-in-c Moreton-on-Lugg 96-02; Preb Heref Cathl 96-02; rtd 02; Perm to Offic *Heref* from 02. *33 St Botolph's Green, Leominster HR6 8ER* Tel (01568) 617456 E-mail rolandandjeanne@yahoo.co.uk
SUMNER, Preb Gillian Mansell. b 39. St Anne's Coll Ox BA61 MA65 MLitt76. Wycliffe Hall Ox BA85. **dss** 86 **d** 87 **p** 94. Ox St Andr 86-91; Hon C 87-91; Tutor Wycliffe Hall Ox 86-89; Prin Ox Area Chr Tr Scheme 89-91; Vice-Prin Ox Min Course 89-91;

Assoc Prin 91-94; Hon C Kirtlington w Bletchingdon, Weston etc 91-94; Hon Can Ch Ch 94; Local Min Officer *Heref* 95-02; P-in-c Wistanstow 95-98; Preb Heref Cathl from 97; Adv for NSM 02-05; rtd 05. *Black Venn, Reeves Lane, Stanage, Knighton LD7 1NA* Tel (01547) 530281 E-mail gandmsumner@compuserve.com
SUMNER, John Gordon. b 46. CCC Cam BA68 MA72. Ridley Hall Cam 69. **d** 72 **p** 73. C Liskeard w St Keyne *Truro* 72-75; C Caversham *Ox* 75-81; V Swallowfield 81-93; Asst Chapl Reading Univ 81-93; C Glastonbury w Meare *B & W* 93-04; Ldr Quest Community 93-08; Chapl Laslett's *Worc* 04-08; Hon C Worcs W from 08; Bp's Adv on New Relig Movements from 08. *The Rectory, Church Road, Clifton-on-Teme, Worcester WR6 6DJ* E-mail johngordonsumner@tiscali.co.uk
SUMNERS, Ms Cristina Jordan. b 47. Vassar Coll (NY) BA73 BNC Ox MPhil85. Princeton Th Sem 73 Gen Th Sem (NY) MDiv76. **d** 78 **p** 82. USA 79-91 and from 02; Asst to R San Antonio St Dav 80-90; P-in-c Rockport Trin by Sea 90-91; Asst Chapl K Edw Sch Witley 93-95; Perm to Offic *Guildf* 93-96; NSM Guildf H Trin w St Mary 97-02; Educn Officer 98-00. *NDCBU 5798, Taos NM 87571, USA*
SUMPTER, Guy. b 60. Leic Univ BA01 PhD08. Ripon Coll Cuddesdon 09. **d** 11. C Brentwood St Thos *Chelmsf* from 11. *25 St Thomas Road, Brentwood CM14 4DF* Tel (01277) 204447 E-mail guysumpter@tinyworld.co.uk
SUMPTER, Timothy Mark. b 62. St Jo Coll Nottm BTh95 MA98. **d** 95 **p** 96. C Ockbrook *Derby* 95-98; C Wallington S'wark 98-01; V Ockbrook *Derby* from 01; CF (TA) from 09. *74 The Ridings, Ockbrook, Derby DE72 3SF* Tel (01332) 820084 Mobile 07900-023122 E-mail tmsumpter@btinternet.com
SUMSION, Paul Henry. b 74. UMIST BSc91. Trin Coll Bris BA03. **d** 04 **p** 05. C Hawkshaw Lane *Man* 04-08; P-in-c 08; C Holcombe 04-08; P-in-c 08; R Holcombe and Hawkshaw from 09; Chapl Bury Coll of FE 05-07. *St Mary's Vicarage, Bolton Road, Hawkshaw, Bury BL8 4JN* Tel (01204) 888064 E-mail paul@sumsion.org.uk
SUNDERLAND, Christopher Allen. b 52. BA75 St Pet Coll Ox MA80 DPhil80. Trin Coll Bris 84. **d** 86 **p** 87. C Stratton St Margaret w S Marston etc *Bris* 86-90; V Barton Hill St Luke w Ch Ch 90-98; RD Bris City 94-98; Perm to Offic from 98; Research Assoc Churches' Coun for Ind & Soc Resp from 98. *50 Guest Avenue, Emersons Green, Bristol BS16 7GA* Tel and fax 0117-957 4652 E-mail csunderland@pavilion.co.uk
SUNDERLAND, Preb Geoffrey. b 21. St Edm Hall Ox BA43 MA47. St Steph Ho Ox 46. **d** 48 **p** 49. C Clifton All SS *Bris* 48-51; C Elland *Wakef* 52-54; C Devonport St Mark Ford *Ex* 55-56; C-in-c Plymouth St Jas Ham CD 56-59; V Plymouth St Jas Ham 59-63; Chapl K Coll Taunton 63-65; C Clifton All SS *Bris* 65-68; V Plymstock *Ex* 68-86; RD Plympton 76-81; Preb Ex Cathl 82-89; rtd 86; Perm to Offic *B & W* and *Ex* 86-08. *30 Capel Court, The Burgage, Prestbury, Cheltenham GL52 3EL* E-mail geoffrey.sunderland@tiscali.co.uk
SUNDERLAND, Wendy Jillian. b 47. **d** 99 **p** 00. OLM Bury St Edmunds St Mary *St E* 99-08; rtd 08. *9 Crown Street, Bury St Edmunds IP33 1QU* Tel (01284) 766883 E-mail wendy.sunderland@btinternet.com
SUNDERLAND, Archdeacon of. *See* BAIN, The Ven John Stuart
SUNLEY, Denis John. b 50. **d** 02. OLM Cannock *Lich* 02-09; OLM Cannock and Huntington from 09; Chapl Walsall Hosps NHS Trust from 10. *22 Huntsman's Rise, Huntington, Cannock WS12 4PH* Tel (01543) 570572 E-mail dsunley@bigfoot.com
SURMAN, Malcolm Colin. b 48. Birm Univ CertEd72 Southn Univ BTh88. Sarum & Wells Th Coll 76. **d** 78 **p** 79. C Basingstoke *Win* 78-81; P-in-c Alton All SS 81-85; V 85-01; Chapl N Hants Loddon Community NHS Trust 84-01; P-in-c Burton and Sopley *Win* from 01. *The Vicarage, Preston Lane, Burton, Christchurch BH23 7JU* Tel (01202) 489807 Fax 475793 E-mail malcolm.surman@dsl.pipex.com
SURREY, Mrs Maureen. b 53. Man OLM Scheme 98. **d** 01 **p** 03. OLM Davyhulme Ch Ch *Man* 01-02; OLM Walkden and Lt Hulton 03-09; OLM Flixton St Jo from 09. *56 Abingdon Road, Urmston, Manchester M41 0GN* Tel 0161-748 3961 E-mail sidandmo@hotmail.com
SURREY, Archdeacon of. *See* BEAKE, The Ven Stuart Alexander
SURRIDGE, Mrs Faith Thomas. b 45. Open Univ BA75 Lon Univ PGCE76 BPhil(Ed)96. SWMTC 83. **dss** 85 **d** 87 **p** 94. St Breoke and Egloshayle *Truro* 85-87; NSM St Mawgan w St Ervan and St Eval 91-95; NSM St Columb Major w St Wenn 95-03; P-in-c 03-08. *The Gables, Union Hill, St Columb TR9 6AR* Tel (01637) 881197 E-mail faith@ftsurridge.wanadoo.co.uk
SURTEES, Brian Lawrence. b 44. NTMTC. **d** 01 **p** 02. NSM Hatfield Heath and Sheering *Chelmsf* 01-05; NSM Tye Green w Netteswell from 05; NSM Chipping Ongar w Shelley from 08. *13 Bowes Drive, Ongar CM5 9AU* Tel (01277) 363607 E-mail bsurtees@ntlworld.com
SURTEES, Timothy John de Leybourne. b 31. G&C Coll Cam BA54 MA58. Westcott Ho Cam 54. **d** 56 **p** 57. C Guisborough *York* 56-59; C Grantham St Wulfram *Linc* 59-61; V Cayton w

Eastfield *York* 61-72; R Cheam *S'wark* 72-96; rtd 96; Perm to Offic *Heref* from 96. *39 Campbell Road, Hereford HR1 1AD* Tel (01432) 371654

SUTCH, The Ven Christopher David. b 47. TD92. AKC69. St Aug Coll Cant 69. **d** 70 **p** 71. C Bris St Andr Hartcliffe 70-75; C Swindon Dorcan 75-78; TV 78-79; P-in-c Alveston 79-83; V 83-89; RD Westbury and Severnside 86-89; CF (TA) 80-03; TR Yate New Town *Bris* 89-99; RD Stapleton 95-99; V Cainscross w Selsley *Glouc* 99-07; AD Stonehouse 04-07; Chapl Costa del Sol E *Eur* from 07; Adn Gib from 08. *Edificio Jupiter 1, Avenida Nuestro Padre Jesus Cautivo, 74 Los Boliches, 29640 Fuengirola (Málaga),* Spain Tel and fax (0034) (95) 258 0600 E-mail frdavid@standrews-cofe-spain.com

SUTCH, Canon Christopher Lang. b 21. Oriel Coll Ox BA47 MA47. Cuddesdon Coll 47. **d** 49 **p** 50. C Westbury-on-Trym H Trin *Bris* 49-53; V Bedminster Down 53-58; V Hanham 58-74; R Brinkworth w Dauntsey 74-86; RD Malmesbury 79-85; Hon Can Bris Cathl 82-86; rtd 86; Hon C E Bris 86-91; Perm to Offic *Bris* 91-08 and *Glouc* 01-08. *14 Queen Anne Court, Quedgeley, Gloucester GL2 4JY* Tel (01452) 690040

SUTCLIFFE, Crispin Francis Henry. b 48. Keble Coll Ox BA69. Sarum & Wells Th Coll 73. **d** 74 **p** 75. C Truro St Paul 74-77; C St Jo Cathl Umtata S Africa 77-80; P-in-c Treslothan *Truro* 80-85; V 85-91; R Ilchester w Northover, Limington, Yeovilton etc *B & W* 91-11; rtd 11. *57 Wilbert Road, Beverley HU17 0AJ*

SUTCLIFFE, Howard Guest. b 44. Fitzw Coll Cam BA66 MA70 Birm Univ MA75. Westcott Ho Cam 73. **d** 74 **p** 75. C Chorlton-cum-Hardy St Clem *Man* 74-77; Chapl Chetham's Sch of Music 77-80; V Oldham St Paul *Man* 80-94; Co-ord Werneth and Freehold Community Development Project 94-06; Perm to Offic 94-09; rtd 09; Hon C Saddleworth *Man* from 09. *The Vicarage, Station Road, Uppermill, Oldham OL3 6HQ* Tel (01457) 872412 E-mail howardguestsutcliffe@yahoo.co.uk

SUTCLIFFE, Ian. b 31. Surrey Univ BSc69. Qu Coll Birm 61. **d** 63 **p** 65. C W Wimbledon Ch Ch *S'wark* 63-65; C Battersea St Phil 65-66; C Kingston Hill St Paul 71-73; Lic to Offic *Carl* 75-96; rtd 96. *42 Hill Street, Arbroath DD11 1AB*

SUTCLIFFE, John Leslie. b 35. Liv Univ BA56. Sarum Th Coll 58. **d** 60 **p** 61. C Lytham St Cuth *Blackb* 60-62; C Altham w Clayton le Moors 62-65; C-in-c Penwortham St Leon CD 65-71; Ind Chapl *Liv* 71-74; V Orford St Andr 74-79; V Burnley St Cuth *Blackb* 79-88; Bp's Adv on UPA *Ripon* 88-94; Hon C Leeds Gipton Epiphany 88-94; I Carrickmacross w Magheracloone Clogh 94-01; rtd 01; Perm to Offic *Blackb* from 02. *1 Beckside, Barley, Burnley BB12 9JZ* Tel (01282) 449687 E-mail sutcliffe287@btinternet.com

SUTCLIFFE, Peter John. b 58. BA. Linc Th Coll. **d** 82 **p** 83. C Skipton Ch Ch *Bradf* 82-85; C Tettenhall Regis *Lich* 85-86; TV 86-89; TV Warwick *Cov* 89-93; Relig Producer BBC Radio Cov and Warks 89-93; V Burley in Wharfedale *Bradf* 93-03; RD Otley 97-02; P-in-c Yeadon St Andr 03-06; V Lightcliffe *Wakef* 06-09; V Lesbury w Alnmouth *Newc* from 09; V Longhoughton w Howick from 09. *The Vicarage, Lesbury, Alnwick NE66 3AU* Tel (01665) 830281 E-mail peter.sutcliffe@btinternet.com

SUTER, Canon Richard Alan. b 48. Rhodes Univ BA72 St Jo Coll Dur BA74. Cranmer Hall Dur 72. **d** 75 **p** 76. C Darlington H Trin *Dur* 75-77; C Wrexham *St As* 77-82; R Llansantffraid Glan Conwy and Eglwysbach 82-87; V Broughton 87-92; RD Wrexham 90-97; V Rossett 92-04; V Holt, Rossett and Isycoed 04-09; V Rossett and Isycoed from 09; Hon Can St As Cathl from 11. *The Vicarage, Rossett, Wrexham LL12 0HE* Tel (01244) 570498 E-mail etsuterra1@googlemail.com

SUTHERLAND, Alistair Campbell. b 31. Lon Univ BSc50 Ex Univ BA77 CEng MIET. Wycliffe Hall Ox 77. **d** 78 **p** 79. C Nottingham St Jude *S'well* 78-81; R Barton in Fabis 81-96; P-in-c Thrumpton 81; V 81-96; RD W Bingham 87-92; Dioc Adv on Ind Society 92-96; NSM Gotham 93-96; NSM Kingston and Ratcliffe-on-Soar 93-96; rtd 96; Perm to Offic *S'wark* 88-01 and *Ex* 99-05. *36 Pyrton Lane, Watlington OX49 5LX* Tel (01491) 612705

SUTHERLAND, Mrs Elaine Anita. EMMTC 95 Moorlands Bible Coll 86. **d** 10 **p** 11. NSM Leic H Trin w St Jo from 10. *1 Anthony Drive, Thurnby, Leicester LE7 9RA* Tel 0116-241 7109 Mobile 07747-466865 E-mail elainesutherland@fsmail.net

SUTHERLAND, Mark Robert. b 55. Univ of NZ LLB77 Lon Inst of Educn MA95. Ripon Coll Cuddesdon 82. **d** 85 **p** 86. C Pinner *Lon* 85-88; C Sudbury St Andr 88-91; Chapl Maudsley Hosp Lon 91-94; Chapl Bethlem R Hosp Beckenham 91-94; Chapl Bethlem and Maudsley NHS Trust Lon 94-99; Presiding Chapl S Lon and Maudsley NHS Foundn Trust 99-10; USA from 10. *Address temp unknown*

SUTHERLAND, Robert. b 78. Newc Univ BA00 St Jo Coll Dur MA09 SS Hild & Bede Coll Dur PGCE01. Cranmer Hall Dur 05 Coll of Resurr Mirfield 08. **d** 09 **p** 10. C Morley *Wakef* from 09. *2 Bridge Court, Morley, Leeds LS27 0BD* Tel 0113-238 1984 Mobile 07751-306568 E-mail robb@priest.com

SUTTIE, Miss Jillian. b 53. ERMC. **d** 08 **p** 09. NSM Colney Heath St Mark *St Alb* from 08. *51 West Riding, Bricket Wood, St Albans AL2 3QE* Tel (01923) 662772

SUTTLE, Neville Frank. b 38. Reading Univ BSc61 Aber Univ PhD64. **d** 76 **p** 77. NSM Penicuik *Edin* from 76. *44 St James's Gardens, Penicuik EH26 9DU* Tel and fax (01968) 673819

SUTTON, Charles Edwin. b 53. Bris Univ BEd77 Ox Univ. Ripon Coll Cuddesdon 77. **d** 80 **p** 81. C Stanwix *Carl* 80-84; Warden Marrick Priory *Ripon* 84-88. *7 Beech Close, Baldersby, Thirsk YO7 4QB* Tel (01765) 640616

SUTTON, Colin Phillip. b 51. Birm Univ BA73. Chich Th Coll 73. **d** 75 **p** 76. C Penarth All SS *Llan* 75-77; C Roath 77-80; C Caerau w Ely 80-84; V Rhydyfelin 84-04; V Fairwater from 04. *St Peter's Parsonage, 211 St Fagans Road, Cardiff CF5 3DW* Tel (029) 2056 2551

SUTTON, David John. b 49. St Mich Coll Llan 97. **d** 99 **p** 00. C Maesglas and Duffryn *Mon* 99-05; Chapl Paphos Cyprus 05; R Luton Ch Ch *Roch* from 06. *Luton Rectory, Capstone Road, Chatham ME5 7PN* Tel (01634) 843780

SUTTON, David Robert. b 49. Birm Univ BA69 Ox Univ CertEd72. St Steph Ho Ox 70. **d** 72 **p** 73. C Clitheroe St Mary *Blackb* 72-75; C Fleetwood St Pet 75-78; V Calderbrook *Man* 78-88; V Winton 88-08; Chapl Salford Mental Health Services NHS Trust 92-08; Chapl Gtr Man W Mental Health NHS Foundn Trust from 08. *The Chaplaincy, Knowsley Building, Bury New Road, Prestwich, Manchester M25 3BL* Tel 0161-772 3833 Mobile 07770-737887 E-mail david.sutton@gmw.nhs.uk

SUTTON, Eves. See SUTTON, The Rt Revd Peter Eves

SUTTON, James William. b 41. Oak Hill Th Coll 81. **d** 84 **p** 85. NSM Chorleywood St Andr *St Alb* 84-06; Perm to Offic *Eur* 06-11; Dean's Chapl and Hon Min Can Gibraltar Cathl from 11. *1A Mediterranean Terrace, Library Ramp, Gibraltar* Tel (00350) 200 46796 E-mail sutton@gibtelecom.net

SUTTON, Jeremy John Ernest. b 60. Ridley Hall Cam 83. **d** 86 **p** 87. C Seacombe *Ches* 86-88; C Northwich St Luke and H Trin 88-90; TV Birkenhead Priory 90-94; V Over St Chad 94-01; V Dunham Massey St Marg and St Mark from 01. *St Margaret's Vicarage, Dunham Road, Altrincham WA14 4AQ* Tel and fax 0161-928 1609 E-mail jerrysutton@dunhamvicarage.fsnet.co.uk

SUTTON, Canon John. b 47. St Jo Coll Dur BA70. Ridley Hall Cam 70. **d** 72 **p** 73. C Denton St Lawr *Man* 72-77; R 77-82; V High Lane *Ches* 82-88; V Sale St Anne 88-96; V Timperley from 96; Hon Can Ches Cathl from 01; RD Bowdon from 03. *The Vicarage, 12 Thorley Lane, Timperley, Altrincham WA15 7AZ* Tel 0161-980 4330 E-mail jfsuttontimp@aol.com

SUTTON, John Stephen. b 33. Em Coll Cam BA57 MA61. Wycliffe Hall Ox 57. **d** 59 **p** 60. C Dagenham *Chelmsf* 59-62; C Bishopwearmouth St Gabr *Dur* 62-63; V Over Kellet *Blackb* 63-67; V Darwen St Barn 67-74; V Walthamstow St Jo *Chelmsf* 74-84; V Stebbing w Lindsell 84-98; RD Dunmow 94-98; rtd 98; Perm to Offic *Chich* from 98. *20 Firwood Close, Eastbourne BN22 9QL* Tel (01323) 504654

SUTTON, Canon John Wesley. b 48. Rolle Coll CertEd71. All Nations Chr Coll. **d** 76 **p** 77. Chile 76-77; Peru 79-84; Area Sec SAMS 84-88; Youth Sec 88-91; Personnel Sec and Asst Gen Sec 91-03; Gen Sec 03-09; Dir Strategic Partnerships and Miss Nationwide Chr Trust 09-10; C Hornchurch St Andr *Chelmsf* from 10; Hon Can Peru from 93. *3 Keswick Avenue, Hornchurch RM11 1XR* E-mail johnsutton.woodford99@ntlworld.com

✠**SUTTON, The Rt Revd Keith Norman.** b 34. Jes Coll Cam BA58 MA62. Ridley Hall Cam. **d** 59 **p** 60 **c** 78. C Plymouth St Andr *Ex* 59-61; Chapl St Jo Coll Cam 62-67; Chapl Bp Tucker Coll Uganda 68-72; Prin Ridley Hall Cam 73-78; Suff Bp Kingston *S'wark* 78-84; Bp Lich 84-03; rtd 03. *Afton Farmhouse, Newport Road, Freshwater PO40 9UE* Tel (01983) 756487

SUTTON, Kingsley James. b 70. TCD BTh94. **d** 97 **p** 98. C Belfast St Matt *Conn* 97-99; C Willowfield *D & D* 99-02; I Newry from 02. *Glebe House, Windsor Avenue, Newry BT34 1EQ* Tel (028) 3026 2621 E-mail revsutton@gmail.com

SUTTON, Canon Malcolm David. b 26. Selw Coll Cam BA47 MA52. Ridley Hall Cam 48. **d** 50 **p** 51. C Owlerton *Sheff* 50-52; C Kew *S'wark* 52-54; C Hornchurch St Andr *Chelmsf* 54-56; V Roxeth Ch Ch *Lon* 56-63; R Beccles St Mich *St E* 63-82; TR 82-94; RD Beccles 65-73; Hon Can St E Cathl 70-94; rtd 94; Perm to Offic *St E* from 94 and *Nor* 95-10. *Flat 2, Manormead, Tilford Road, Hindhead GU26 6RA*

SUTTON, Mrs Monica Rosalind. b 48. Sheff Hallam Univ MSc99 Leeds Univ BA09. Yorks Min Course. **d** 09 **p** 10. NSM Sheff St Cuth from 09. *4 Cyprus Terrace, Sheffield S6 3QH* Tel 0114-232 3559 E-mail monica_r_sutton@yahoo.com

SUTTON, Canon Peter Allerton. b 59. Ex Univ BA85. Linc Th Coll 85. **d** 87 **p** 88. C Fareham H Trin *Portsm* 87-90; C Alverstoke 90-93; Chapl HM Pris Haslar 90-93; V Lee-on-the-Solent *Portsm* from 93; Warden of Readers 96-00; RD Gosport 06-09; Hon Can Portsm Cathl from 09. *St Faith's Vicarage, Victoria Square, Lee-on-the-Solent PO13 9NF* Tel and fax (023) 9255 0269

✠**SUTTON, The Rt Revd Peter Eves.** b 23. CBE90. Wellington Univ (NZ) BA45 MA47. NZ Bd of Th Studies LTh48. **d** 47 **p** 48 **c** 65. C Wanganui New Zealand 47-50; C Bethnal Green St Jo *Lon* 50-51; C Bp's Hatfield *St Alb* 51-52; V Berhampore New

Zealand 52-58; V Whangarei 58-64; Adn Waimate 62-64; Dean St Paul's Cathl Dunedin 64-65; Bp Nelson 65-90; Acting Primate of New Zealand 85-86; rtd 90. *3 Ngatiawa Street, Nelson 7010, New Zealand* Tel and fax (0064) (3) 546 6591 E-mail bishop.sutton@xtra.co.nz

SUTTON, Philip Frank. b 55. SAOMC 92. d 95 p 96. NSM Akeman *Ox* 95-00; Chapl Ox Radcliffe Hosps NHS Trust 96-00; Sen Chapl R United Hosp Bath NHS Trust 00-07; Dioc Adv Hosp Chapl 04-07; Chapl Team Ldr Ox Radcliffe Hosps NHS Trust from 07. *The John Radcliffe, Headley Way, Headington, Oxford OX3 9DU* Tel (01865) 741166

SUTTON, Richard Alan. b 39. Reading Univ BSc61. Wycliffe Hall Ox 70. d 72 p 73. C Galleywood Common *Chelmsf* 72-76; Pakistan 76-79; C Walsall St Martin *Lich* 79-83; V Barton Hill St Luke w Ch Ch *Bris* 83-89; V Sidcup Ch Ch *Roch* 89-95; rtd 95; Perm to Offic *Roch* 95-98. *30 Mill Road Avenue, Angmering, Littlehampton BN16 4HS* Tel (01903) 856721

SUTTON, Richard John. b 45. Lon Inst of Educn CertEd68. St Alb Minl Tr Scheme 77 Linc Th Coll 81. d 82 p 83. C Royston *St Alb* 82-87; C Bp's Hatfield 87-95; P-in-c Kempston and Biddenham 95-05; P-in-c Rackheath and Salhouse *Nor* 05-08; rtd 08; Perm to Offic *Nor* from 08. *Augusta Cottage, 1 Old School Court, Upper Sheringham, Sheringham NR26 8UA* Tel (01263) 821918 E-mail sutton@greenbee.net

SUTTON, Ronald. b 27. FSCA. NW Ord Course 76. d 79 p 80. C Helsby and Dunham-on-the-Hill *Ches* 79-81; R Church Lawton 81-92; RD Congleton 91-92; rtd 92; Perm to Offic *Ches* from 92. *79 Thornton Avenue, Macclesfield SK11 7XL* Tel (01625) 430212

SWABEY, Brian Frank. b 44. BA. Oak Hill Th Coll 70. d 82 p 83. C Clapham St Jas *S'wark* 82-84; C Wallington 84-88; Chapl Mt Gould Hosp Plymouth 88-89; V Plymouth St Jude *Ex* 88-92; Chapl RN 92-99; V Penn Fields *Lich* 99-01; rtd 01; Perm to Offic *Ex* 01-09. *30 Treskewes Estate, St Keverne, Helston TR12 6RA* Tel (01326) 281168 E-mail brian@swabey.org

SWABY, Anthony. *See* SWABY, Leward Anthony Woodrow

SWABY, Desrene. SEITE 00. d 03 p 04. NSM S'wark St Geo w St Alphege and St Jude 03-09; NSM Camberwell St Mich w All So w Em from 09. *36 Gabriel House, 10 Odessa Street, London SE16 7HQ* Tel (020) 7231 9834

SWABY, Keith Graham. b 48. Southn Univ BA75. St Steph Ho Ox 75. d 77 p 78. C Lt Stanmore St Lawr *Lon* 77-80; C Hove All SS *Chich* 80-83; TV Haywards Heath St Wilfrid 83-95; C Clayton w Keymer 95-02; rtd 02. *3 Lonsdale Court, Penrith CA11 8LD* Tel (01768) 862453

SWABY, Leward Anthony Woodrow. b 60. Trin Coll Bris 86 Ripon Coll Cuddesdon 89. d 92 p 93. C Wembley St Jo *Lon* 92-95; C Northampton St Matt *Pet* 95-97; TV Kingsthorpe w Northampton St Dav 97-01; Asst Chapl Worcs Acute Hosps NHS Trust 01-05; P-in-c Willenhall St Anne *Lich* 05-09; Asst Chapl HM Pris Brinsford 06-09; P-in-c Farnsfield 09-10; P-in-c Eakring 09-10; P-in-c Kirklington w Hockerton 09-10; P-in-c Maplebeck 09-10; P-in-c Winkburn 09-10; Perm to Offic *Lich* from 11. *11 Wordsworth Street, West Bromwich B71 1EP* E-mail lawswaby@aol.com

SWADLING, Pamela Grace. b 45. SEITE 08. d 10. NSM Middleton *Chich* from 10. *66 Lane End Road, Middleton-on-Sea, Bognor Regis PO22 6LT* Tel (01243) 587979 E-mail pam_swadling@hotmail.co.uk

SWAIN, Allan. *See* SWAIN, Canon William Allan

SWAIN, David Noel. b 36. Wellington Univ (NZ) BA63 MA66. Coll of Resurr Mirfield 65. d 67 p 68. C Clapham H Trin *S'wark* 67-70; New Zealand 70-75; P-in-c Hermitage *Ox* 75-76; P-in-c Hampstead Norris 75-76; V Hermitage w Hampstead Norreys 76-80; TR Hermitage and Hampstead Norreys, Cold Ash etc 80-82; R Bingham *S'well* 82-94; rtd 94; Perm to Offic *S'well* 94-07 and *Ox* from 08. *9 Stephen Court, 3 Stephen Road, Headington, Oxford OX3 9AY* Tel (01865) 767068 E-mail swain936@btinternet.com

SWAIN, John Edgar. b 44. Lich Th Coll 67. d 69 p 70. C E Dereham w Hoe *Nor* 69-73; V Haugh *Linc* 73-74; R S Ormsby w Ketsby, Calceby and Driby 73-74; R Harrington w Brinkhill 73-74; R Oxcombe 73-74; R Ruckland w Farforth and Maidenwell 73-74; R Somersby w Bag Enderby 73-74; R Tetford and Salmonby 73-74; R Belchford 73-74; V W Ashby 73-74; C Attleborough *Nor* 74-78; Canada 78-90; P-in-c Oxford Cen w Eastwood and Princeton 78-84; P-in-c Oldcastle w Colchester N 84-90; P-in-c Kirton w Falkenham *St E* 90-95; Chapl Suffolk Constabulary 90-01; P-in-c Gt and Lt Whelnetham w Bradfield St George 95-01; P-in-c Lawshall 98-01; R Wawa w White River and Hawk Junction Canada 01-09; rtd 09. *70 Mosher Road, RR #2, Iron Bridge ON P0R 1H0, Canada* E-mail jswain@ontera.net

SWAIN, Canon John Roger. b 29. Fitzw Ho Cam BA55 MA59. Bps' Coll Cheshunt 55. d 57 p 58. C Headingley *Ripon* 57-60; C Moor Allerton 60-65; V Wyther 65-75; V Horsforth 75-86; P-in-c Roundhay St Edm 86-88; V 88-95; RD Allerton 89-94; Hon Can Ripon Cathl 89-95; rtd 95; Perm to Offic *Ripon* from 05.

3 Harlow Court, Park Avenue, Leeds LS8 2JH Tel 0113-246 1274

SWAIN, Preb Peter John. b 44. Sarum & Wells Th Coll 86. d 88 p 89. C Beaminster Area *Sarum* 88-92; P-in-c W Newton and Bromfield w Waverton *Carl* 92-98; Member Rural Life and Agric Team 93-96; Ldr 96-98; RD Solway 95-98; Hon Can Carl Cathl 96-98; TR Leominster *Heref* 98-05; RD Leominster 98-05; Preb Heref Cathl 03-05; rtd 05. *10 Market Hall Street, Kington HR5 3DP* Tel (01544) 230999

SWAIN, Ronald Charles Herbert. b 08. Dur Univ BA42 MA50. St Aug Coll Cant 29. d 32 p 33. C S Wimbledon H Trin *S'wark* 32-34; SPG China 34-40; Perm to Offic *Dur* and *Newc* 41-42; P-in-c Padgate Ch Ch *Liv* 42-46; Perm to Offic *S'wark* 46-47; Chapl RAF 47-54; CF 54-62; V Walsham le Willows *St E* 62-70; V Shipley *Chich* 70-74; rtd 74; Perm to Offic *St E* 74-02. *clo Rudlings Wakelam Solicitors, 14 Woolhall Street, Bury St Edmunds IP33 1LA*

SWAIN, Mrs Sharon Juanita. b 46. Sussex Univ BA75 CertEd76 Heythrop Coll Lon MA04. Glouc Sch of Min 81. dss 84 d 87 p 94. Upton St Leonards *Glouc* 84-88; C 87-88; Children's Officer *Worc* 88-95; Min Can Worc Cathl 94-95; V Hanley Castle, Hanley Swan and Welland 95-01; R E Bergholt and Brantham *St E* 01-06; RD Samford 01-06; TR Solway Plain *Carl* 06-10; rtd 10. *Selemat, Jameston, Tenby SA70 8QJ* Tel (01834) 871381 E-mail rev.s.swain@googlemail.com

SWAIN, Canon William Allan. b 38. Kelham Th Coll 63. d 68 p 69. C Welwyn Garden City *St Alb* 68-72; C Romsey *Win* 72-74; C Weeke 74-78; V Bournemouth H Epiphany 78-91; P-in-c Moordown 91-94; V 94-08; Hon Can Win Cathl 04-08; rtd 08. *20 Elizabeth Road, Wimborne BH21 1AX* E-mail canon.swain@talktalk.net

SWAINE, Judith Ann. b 55. STETS. d 09 p 10. C Portsea All SS *Portsm* from 09. *102 Copnor Road, Portsmouth PO3 5AL* Tel (023) 9266 0259

SWAINSON, Norman. b 38. Salford Univ MSc75. St Jo Coll Nottm 77. d 79 p 80. C Levenshulme St Pet *Man* 79-84; R Jarrow Grange *Dur* 84-97; rtd 97; Perm to Offic *Ches* from 98. *176 George Street, Compstall, Stockport SK6 5JD* Tel 0161-449 0551

SWALES, David James. b 58. Warwick Univ BA79. Cranmer Hall Dur 81. d 84 p 85. C Eccleshill *Bradf* 84-88; C Prenton *Ches* 88-92; V Oakworth *Bradf* 92-00; V Bolton St Jas w St Chrys 00-09; V Haughley w Wetherden and Stowupland *St E* from 09. *The Vicarage, The Folly, Haughley, Stowmarket IP14 3NS* Tel (01449) 675503 Mobile 07806-785714 E-mail david.swales@blueyonder.co.uk

SWALES, Peter. b 52. ACIB78 Open Univ BA99. Ridley Hall Cam 85. d 87 p 88. C Allestree *Derby* 87-91; P-in-c Horsley 91-99; RD Heanor 97-99; V Heckmondwike *Wakef* 99-03; V Chellaston *Derby* 03-10; rtd 10. *18 Kerry Drive, Smalley, Ilkeston DE7 6ER* Tel (01332) 881752 E-mail pasta.swales@gmail.com

SWALLOW, Mrs Alice Gillian. b 51. Birm Univ BA72 CertEd73. NEOC 82. dss 84 d 87 p 94. Morpeth *Newc* 84-86; Uttoxeter w Bramshall *Lich* 86-88; Par Dn 87-88; Par Dn Rocester 88; Chapl to the Deaf *Man* 88-90; Par Dn Goodshaw and Crawshawbooth 88-93; C Barkisland w W Scammonden *Wakef* 93-95; V Ripponden 95-97; rtd 97; Perm to Offic *Wakef* from 02. *22 Scholes Lane, Scholes, Cleckheaton BD19 6NR* Tel (01274) 875529 E-mail jill_swallow@yahoo.co.uk

SWALLOW, John Allen George. b 28. St Jo Coll Dur BA53. d 54 p 55. C Billericay St Mary *Chelmsf* 54-57; C Bishop's Stortford St Mich *St Alb* 57-59; V Roxwell *Chelmsf* 59-64; V S Weald 64-81; R W w E Mersea 81-93; rtd 93; Perm to Offic *Chelmsf* from 93 and *St E* from 95. *72 Rembrandt Way, Bury St Edmunds IP33 2LT* Tel (01284) 725136

SWALLOW, John Brian. b 36. Trent Poly 78. d 84 p 85. C Cleveleys *Blackb* 84-87; V Blackpool St Mich 87-93; P-in-c Burnley St Steph 93-98; V 98-01; RD Burnley 97-00; rtd 01; Perm to Offic *Dur* from 02. *6 Chichester Walk, Haughton-le-Skerne, Darlington DL1 2SG*

SWAN, Duncan James. b 65. Imp Coll Lon BSc88 SS Coll Cam BA91 MA95 K Coll Lon MA04. Ridley Hall Cam 89. d 92 p 93. C Stevenage St Andr and St Geo *St Alb* 92-95; C Harpenden St Nic 95-99; Chapl 96-00; TR Caterham *S'wark* from 06. *The Rectory, 5 Whyteleafe Road, Caterham CR3 5EG* Tel (01883) 373083 E-mail duncpen@hotmail.com

SWAN, Owen. b 28. ACP71. Edin Th Coll 56. d 59 p 60. C Lewisham St Jo Southend *S'wark* 59-64; CF (TA) from 60; V Richmond St Luke *S'wark* 64-82; C-in-c Darlington St Hilda and St Columba CD *Dur* 83-87; R Feltwell *Ely* 84-87; R Holywell w Needingworth 87-97; rtd 97; Perm to Offic *Ely* and *St E* from 02. *Primrose Cottage, Hawes Lane, Norton, Bury St Edmunds IP31 3LS* Tel (01359) 231108

SWAN, Philip Douglas. b 56. Wye Coll Lon BSc78 Qu Coll Cam MA81 CertEd81. St Jo Coll Nottm 86. d 88 p 89. C Birm St Martin w Bordesley St Andr 88-92; C Selly Park St Steph and St Wulstan 92-96; P-in-c The Lickey 96-98; V 98-10; Dir World

Miss *Lich* from 10. *38 Lyndhurst Road, Wolverhampton WV3 0AA* Tel (01902) 621148
E-mail swan@lickey30.freeserve.co.uk

SWAN, Preb Ronald Frederick. b 35. St Cath Coll Cam BA59 MA. Coll of Resurr Mirfield. **d** 61 **p** 62. C Staveley *Derby* 61-65; Chapl Lon Univ 65-72; C St Martin-in-the-Fields 72-77; V Ealing St Barn 77-88; V Ealing St Steph Castle Hill 81-88; AD Ealing E 84-88; V Harrow St Mary 88-97; AD Harrow 89-94; Preb St Paul's Cathl 91-06; Master R Foundn of St Kath in Ratcliffe 97-06; rtd 06. *8 Moat Lodge, London Road, Harrow HA1 3LU* Tel (020) 8864 4625

SWANBOROUGH, Alan William. b 38. Southn Univ BEd75. Sarum & Wells Th Coll 77. **d** 80 **p** 81. NSM Ventnor H Trin *Portsm* 80-85; NSM Ventnor St Cath 80-85; Chapl Upper Chine Sch Shanklin 85-94; Chapl Ryde Sch w Upper Chine 94-03; NSM Shanklin St Blasius *Portsm* 91-10; P-in-c 93-10; rtd 10; Perm to Offic *Portsm* from 10. *6 The Cambria, 32 Broadway, Sandown PO36 9BY* Tel (01983) 402686
E-mail a.swanborough38@btinternet.com

SWANEPOEL, David John. b 41. Rhodes Univ BA62 UNISA BA64 BTh84. **d** 75 **p** 76. S Africa 75-94; Dean George 85-89; NSM Hellingly and Upper Dicker *Chich* 94-99. *Providence House, Coldharbour Road, Upper Dicker, Hailsham BN27 3QE* Tel (01323) 843887

SWANN, Ms Anne Barbara. b 49. St Mich Coll Llan BTh07 MTh08. **d** 08 **p** 09. Hon C Peterston-super-Ely w St Brides-super-Ely *Llan* 08-10; Perm to Offic from 10. *19 Fairways Crescent, Cardiff CF5 3DZ* Tel (029) 2056 2641 Mobile 07810-798465 E-mail revdanne@live.co.uk

SWANN, Antony Keith. b 34. St Aid Birkenhead 58. **d** 61 **p** 62. C Bilston St Leon *Lich* 61-66; Sierra Leone 66-70; V W Bromwich St Phil *Lich* 70-75; Nigeria 76-78; R Church Lench w Rous Lench and Abbots Morton *Worc* 78-88; Chapl HM Pris Coldingley 88-90; Chapl HM Pris Leyhill 91-97; rtd 97; P-in-c Kemble, Poole Keynes, Somerford Keynes etc *Glouc* 97-02; Perm to Offic from 03. *30 Perry Orchard, Upton St Leonards, Gloucester GL4 8DQ*

SWANN, Deborah Jane. b 68. St Jo Coll Dur BA89 Brunel Univ MSc01 DipCOT92. St Mich Coll Llan 08. **d** 10 **p** 11. C Gwersyllt *St As* from 10. *Rosslyn, Station Road, Trevor, Llangollen LL20 7TP* Tel (01978) 821618 Mobile 07583-275053
E-mail debjswann@gmail.com

SWANN, Edgar John. b 42. TCD BA66 MA70 BD77 HDipEd80. CITC 68. **d** 68 **p** 69. C Crumlin *Conn* 68-70; C Howth *D & G* 70-73; I Greystones 73-08; Can Ch Ch Cathl Dublin 90-08; Adn Glendalough 93-08; rtd 09. *Noah's Ark, 4 Mount Haven, New Road, Greystones, Co Wicklow, Republic of Ireland* Tel (00353) (1) 255 7572 Mobile 87-255 7032
E-mail edgarjswann@eircom.net

SWANN, Frederick David. b 38. **d** 69 **p** 70. C Lurgan Ch the Redeemer *D & D* 69-77; I Ardmore w Craigavon 77-79; I Comber 79-85; I Drumglass w Moygashel *Arm* 85-06; Can Arm Cathl 96-06; Preb 98-01; Treas 01-06; rtd 06. *Branchfield, Ballymote, Co Sligo, Republic of Ireland* Tel (00353) (71) 919 7097 E-mail derickswann@eircom.net

SWANN, Paul David James. b 59. Ch Ch Ox BA81 MA88. St Jo Coll Nottm 87. **d** 90 **p** 91. C Old Hill H Trin *Worc* 90-94; V 94-02; C Worc City and Chapl Worc Tech Coll 02-09; rtd 09. *26 Knotts Avenue, Worcester WR4 0HZ* Tel (01905) 619339
E-mail paul@swannfamily.co.uk

SWANNACK, David Joseph. b 65. **d** 11. C Frodingham *Linc* from 11. *All Saints' Vicarage, 159 Vicarage Road, Scunthorpe DN16 1HH* Tel (01724) 860345

SWANSEA AND BRECON, Bishop of. See DAVIES, The Rt Revd John David Edward

SWANTON, John Joseph. b 61. Bradf and Ilkley Coll BA84 Univ of Wales (Ban) BTh10 MCIH89. S Dios Minl Tr Scheme 92. **d** 95 **p** 96. NSM Shalford *Guildf* 95-99; NSM Compton w Shackleford and Peper Harow 99-11; TV Fairford Deanery *Glouc* from 11. *The Rectory, Ampney Crucis, Cirencester GL7 5RY* Tel (01285) 851309 E-mail a.jo@swanton.plus.com

SWARBRICK (née PITE), Mrs Sheila Reinhardt. b 60. St Jo Coll Dur BA82 Nottm Univ MA98. Oak Hill Th Coll BA88. **d** 88 **p** 94. Par Dn Derby St Aug 88-92; C Brampton St Thos 92-95; Perm to Offic *St Alb* 95-96; P-in-c The Stodden Churches 96-98; Chapl Papworth Hosp NHS Trust 98-99; TV Braunstone *Leic* 99-02; P-in-c 02-07; Perm to Offic *Ex* 07-08; Hon C Cen Ex from 08; Asst Chapl R Devon and Ex NHS Foundn Trust from 09. *7 Lower Kings Avenue, Exeter EX4 6JT* Tel (01392) 438866
E-mail sheila.pite@cooptel.net

SWARBRIGG, David Cecil. b 42. TCD BA64 MA67. **d** 65 **p** 66. C Lisburn Ch Ch *Conn* 65-67; C Thames Ditton *Guildf* 72-76; Chapl Hampton Sch Middx 76-97; rtd 97. *39 Harefield, Hinchley Wood, Esher KT10 9TY* Tel and fax (020) 8398 3950

SWART-RUSSELL, Phoebe. b 58. Cape Town Univ BA79 MA82 DPhil88. Ox NSM Course 89. **d** 90 **p** 94. C Riverside *Ox* 90-95; Hon C Chenies and Lt Chalfont, Latimer and Flaunden 96-00. *The Rectory, Latimer, Chesham HP5 1UA* Tel (01494) 762281

SWARTZ, Clifford Robert. b 71. Trin Coll Connecticut BA92 Trin Coll Cam BA99. Ridley Hall Cam 97. **d** 00 **p** 01. C Kirk Ella *York* 00-03; Regional Dir FOCUS USA 03-11; Hon C Tariffville Trin Ch 03-11; P-in-c St Bees *Carl* from 11; Chapl St Bees Sch from 11. *The Vicarage, Priory Close, St Bees CA27 0DR* E-mail clifford.swartz@gmail.com

SWARTZ, The Very Revd Oswald Peter Patrick. b 53. St Paul's Coll Grahamstown 76. **d** 80 **p** 80. C Welkom St Matthias S Africa 80-81; R Heidedal 81-87; R Mafikeng 87-92; Adn Mafikeng 89-92; Bp's Exec Officer Kimberley and Kuruman 93-94; Sub-Dean Kimberley 94-96; Dioc Sec and Bp's Exec Officer 96-00; Can Kimberley from 93; Regional Desk Officer USPG 01-06; Hon Chapl S'wark Cathl 01-06; Dean Pretoria from 06. *St Alban's Cathedral, PO Box 3053, Pretoria, 0001 South Africa* Tel and fax (0027) (12) 322 7670 *or* tel 348 4955 E-mail cathedral@mail.ngo.za

SWAYNE, Jeremy Michael Deneys. b 41. Worc Coll Ox BA63 BM, BCh62 MRCGP71 FFHom91. **d** 00 **p** 01. NSM Fosse Trinity *B & W* 00-04; P-in-c 04-05; rtd 05; Perm to Offic *B & W* from 05. *Tanzy Cottage, Rimpton, Yeovil BA22 8AQ* E-mail jem.swayne@btinternet.com

SWEATMAN, John. b 44. Open Univ BA89. Bernard Gilpin Soc Dur 67 Oak Hill Th Coll 68. **d** 71 **p** 72. C Rayleigh *Chelmsf* 71-73; C Seaford w Sutton *Chich* 73-77; Chapl RN 77-82; CF 82-85; V Hellingly and Upper Dicker *Chich* 85-90; Hon C Mayfield 95-96; P-in-c Malborough w S Huish, W Alvington and Churchstow *Ex* 96-02; V Ash w Westmarsh *Cant* from 02; P-in-c Wingham w Elmstone and Preston w Stourmouth from 10; AD E Bridge 08-11. *The Vicarage, Queen's Road, Ash, Canterbury CT3 2BG* Tel (01304) 812296
E-mail thevicar@s8nicholas.org.uk

SWEED, John William. b 35. Bernard Gilpin Soc Dur 58 Clifton Th Coll 59. **d** 62 **p** 63. C Shrewsbury St Julian *Lich* 62-64; C Sheff St Jo 64-70; V Doncaster St Jas 70-79; V Hatfield 79-00; RD Snaith and Hatfield 84-93; rtd 00; Perm to Offic *Sheff* from 00. *21 The Oval, Tickhill, Doncaster DN11 9HF* Tel (01302) 743293

SWEENEY, Andrew James. b 61. Wycliffe Hall Ox 96. **d** 96 **p** 97. C Bladon w Woodstock *Ox* 96-99; C Coleraine *Conn* 99-02; V Cogges and S Leigh *Ox* from 02; V N Leigh from 09; AD Witney 07-08. *Cogges Priory, Church Lane, Witney OX28 3LA* Tel (01993) 702155 Mobile 07720-472556
E-mail sweeney@coggespriory.freeserve.co.uk

SWEENEY, Andrew John. b 59. Ripon Coll Cuddesdon 09. **d** 11. C Clapham Ch Ch and St Jo *S'wark* from 11. *49 Voltaire Road, London SW4 6DD* Tel (020) 7498 4625
E-mail andrew@theophilia.com

SWEENEY, Robert Maxwell. b 38. Ch Ch Ox BA63 MA66 Birm Univ MA78. Cuddesdon Coll 63. **d** 65 **p** 66. C Prestbury *Glouc* 65-68; C Handsworth St Andr *Birm* 68-70; Asst Chapl Lancing Coll 70-73; V Wotton St Mary *Glouc* 74-79; V Ox St Thos w St Frideswide and Binsey 79-03; Chapl Magd Coll Ox 82-88; rtd 03. *22 Park House, 39 Park Place, Cheltenham GL50 2RF* Tel (01242) 254028

SWEET, Miss Lynette Jessica. b 59. Kent Univ BA80. Westcott Ho Cam 03. **d** 05 **p** 06. C Wilton w Netherhampton and Fugglestone *Sarum* 05-09; P-in-c Marthall *Ches* from 09; Chapl David Lewis Cen for Epilepsy from 09. *The Vicarage, Sandlebridge Lane, Marthall, Knutsford WA16 7SB* Tel (01625) 860618 *or* (01565) 640000 ext 2776
E-mail lynettesweet753@btinternet.com

SWEET, Mrs Margaret Adelaide. b 33. Open Univ BA75 UEA MA83 FCollP83 FRSA89. St Steph Ho Ox BTh05. **d** 06 **p** 07. NSM Stratford-upon-Avon, Luddington etc *Cov* from 06. *5 Broad Street, Stratford-upon-Avon CV37 6HN* Tel (01789) 297395 E-mail sweetmargaret@btinternet.com

SWEET, Reginald Charles. b 36. Open Univ BA74. Ripon Hall Ox 61. **d** 62 **p** 63. C Styvechale *Cov* 62-65; Chapl RN 65-69 and 74-93; R Riddlesworth w Gasthorpe and Knettishall *Nor* 69-74; R Brettenham w Rushford 69-74; Perm to Offic 93-96; Chapl Miss to Seamen 96-99; rtd 99; Chapl Win St Cross w St Faith from 99. *The Chaplain's Lodge, The Hospital of St Cross, St Cross Road, Winchester SO23 9SD* Tel (01962) 853525 Mobile 07889-375085

SWEET, Preb Vaughan Carroll. b 46. Aston Univ BSc69 MSc70. Linc Th Coll 89. **d** 91 **p** 92. C Uttoxeter w Bramshall *Lich* 91-95; P-in-c Hadley 95-98; V 98-07; P-in-c Wellington Ch Ch 03-07; V Hadley and Wellington Ch Ch from 07; RD Telford from 00; RD Telford Severn Gorge *Heref* 00-03; Preb Lich Cathl from 05. *The Vicarage, 180 Holyhead Road, Wellington, Telford TF1 2DN* Tel and fax (01952) 254251 E-mail vaughan.sweet@virgin.net

SWEETING, David Charles. b 67. Nottm Univ BSc89. STETS 04. **d** 08 **p** 09. C Holbeach *Linc* from 08. *15 Greenwich Avenue, Holbeach, Spalding PE12 7JF* Tel (01406) 423963 Mobile 07973-841799 E-mail david@davidsweeting.orangehouse.co.uk

SWEETING, Paul Lee. b 68. Lanc Univ BSc90 St Martin's Coll Lanc PGCE92. Cranmer Hall Dur BA99. **d** 99 **p** 00. C Blackb St Gabr 99-03; R Falkland Is 03-06; Chapl Sedbergh Sch from

06. *4 The Leyes, Station Road, Sedbergh LA10 5DJ* Tel (015396) 22099 Mobile 07736-672016 E-mail sweeting.paul@googlemail.com

SWEETMAN (*née* BURNIE), Ms Judith. b 57. Leic Univ BA79 Anglia Ruskin Univ BA07. Westcott Ho Cam 05. d 07 p 08. C Coggeshall w Markshall *Chelmsf* 07-10; P-in-c Boxford, Edwardstone, Groton etc *St E* from 10. *The Rectory, School Hill, Boxford, Sudbury CO10 5JT* Tel (01787) 210091 E-mail rvdjudithboxriver@btinternet.com

SWENSSON, Sister Gerd Inger. b 51. Lon Univ MPhil85 Uppsala Univ 70. dss 74 d 87. In Ch of Sweden 74-75; Notting Hill *Lon* 75-77; CSA from 75; Abbey Ho Malmesbury 77-79; R Foundn of St Kath 79-81; Notting Hill All SS w St Columb *Lon* 81-84; Kensington St Mary Abbots w St Geo 85-89; C Bedford Park 91-95; Sweden from 95. *Christens Gård, Pl 8, St Slågarp, S-231 95 Trelleborg, Sweden* Tel and fax (0046) (40) 487059 Mobile 708-743994 E-mail tedeum@mail.bip.net

SWIFT, Ainsley Laird. b 56. Liv Univ BEd80. Ripon Coll Cuddesdon. d 94 p 95. C Prescot *Liv* 94-98; TV New Windsor *Ox* 98-01; P-in-c from 01. *The Vicarage, Hermitage Lane, Windsor SL4 4AZ* Tel (01753) 858720 *or* 855447 Fax 860839 E-mail ainsley@swift9485.fsnet.co.uk

SWIFT, Andrew Christopher. b 68. Edin Univ BEng90 Aber Univ MSc97. Ripon Coll Cuddesdon BTh05. d 07 p 08. C Glouc St Cath 07-10; P-in-c Dunoon *Arg* from 10; P-in-c Tighnabruaich from 10; P-in-c Rothesay from 10. *The Rectory, Kilbride Road, Dunoon PA23 7LN* Tel (01369) 702444 E-mail rev.andrew@familyswift.org.uk

SWIFT, Christopher James. b 65. Hull Univ BA86 Man Univ MA95 Sheff Univ PhD06. Westcott Ho Cam 89. d 91 p 92. C Longton *Blackb* 91-94; TV Chipping Barnet w Arkley *St Alb* 94-97; Chapl Wellhouse NHS Trust 97-98; Chapl Dewsbury Health Care NHS Trust 98-01; Hd Chapl Services Leeds Teaching Hosps NHS Trust from 01. *The Chaplaincy, St James's University Hospital, Beckett Street, Leeds LS9 7TF* Tel 0113-206 4658 Mobile 07866-563640 E-mail chris.swift@leedsth.nhs.uk

SWIFT, Christopher John. b 54. Linc Coll Ox BA76 MA Selw Coll Cam BA80. Westcott Ho Cam 79. d 81 p 82. C Portsea N End St Mark *Portsm* 81-84; C Alverstoke 84-87; V Whitton SS Phil and Jas *Lon* 87-94; R Shepperton 94-08; R Shepperton and Littleton from 08; AD Spelthorne 98-04. *The Rectory, Church Square, Shepperton TW17 9JY* Tel and fax (01932) 220511 E-mail christopher.swift@london.anglican.org

SWIFT (*formerly* LAKER), Mrs Grace. b 39. RN63. Sarum & Wells Th Coll BTh91. d 91 p 94. C Helston and Wendron *Truro* 91-95; Chapl Havering Hosps NHS Trust 95-02; NSM Rush Green *Chelmsf* 98-02; Bp Barking's Adv for Hosp Chapl 99-02; NSM Gt Burstead 06-08; P-in-c Purleigh 08-11. *21 New Court, Church Road, Cambridge CB4 1EF* E-mail graceswift@hotmail.com

SWIFT, Ian John Edward. b 46. NTMTC 99. d 02 p 03. NSM Basildon St Martin *Chelmsf* 02-06; C Vange from 06; Ind Chapl from 06; rtd 11; P-in-c Crosscrake *Carl* from 11. *The Vicarage, Shyreakes Lane, Crosscrake, Kendal LA8 0AB* Tel 07725-037680 (mobile) E-mail ijeswift@googlemail.com

SWIFT, Jessica Suzanne. b 75. Univ of New Brunswick BSc99. Wycliffe Hall Ox 99. d 02 p 03. C Islington St Mary *Lon* 02-05; C Mildmay Grove St Jude and St Paul 05-09; C Barnsbury from 09. *306B Amhurst Road, London N16 7UE* Tel (020) 7923 0114 Mobile 07812-676240 E-mail swift_jessica@hotmail.com

SWIFT, Ms Pamela Joan. b 47. Liv Univ BSc68. NEOC 85. d 88 p 94. Par Dn Bermondsey St Jas w Ch Ch *S'wark* 88-91; Par Dn Middleton St Cross *Ripon* 91-92; C Leeds All So and Dioc Stewardship Adv 92-95; TR Brampton 95-99; Miss Adv USPG *Blackb, Bradf, Carl* and *Wakef* 99-01; Hon C Kildwick *Bradf* 99-01; R and Community P Glas St Matt 01-05; rtd 05; Hon C Lanercost, Walton, Gilsland and Nether Denton *Carl* 06-08; Chapl N Cumbria Acute Hosps NHS Trust 06-08. *61 Axwell Park View, Newcastle upon Tyne NE15 6NR* Tel 0191-274 9482 Mobile 07833-938843 E-mail pam.swift@tiscali.co.uk

SWIFT, Richard Barrie. b 33. Selw Coll Cam BA58 MA64. Ripon Hall Ox. d 60 p 61. C Stepney St Dunstan and All SS *Lon* 60-64; C Sidmouth St Nic *Ex* 64-72; P-in-c W Hyde St Thos *St Alb* 72-77; V Mill End 72-77; V Mill End and Heronsgate w W Hyde 77-82; V Axminster *Ex* 82-83; P-in-c Chardstock 82-83; P-in-c Combe Pyne w Rousdon 82-83; TR Axminster, Chardstock, Combe Pyne and Rousdon 83-94; rtd 94; Perm to Offic *Ex* from 94. *28 Gracey Court, Broadclyst, Exeter EX5 3GA* Tel (01392) 469436

SWIFT, Sarah Jane. b 65. St Aid Coll Dur BSc88. St Jo Coll Nottm 05. d 06 p 07. C Wealdstone H Trin *Lon* 06-10. *Address temp unknown* E-mail sarah@sarahswift.org.uk

SWIFT, Selwyn. b 41. Trin Coll Bris 73. d 76 p 77. C Melksham *Sarum* 76-79; TV Whitton 81-84; V Everton w Mattersey w R Bunwell, Carleton Rode, Tibenham, Gt Moulton etc *Nor* 89-01; RD Depwade 97-01; rtd 01. *2 Kembold Close, Bury St Edmunds IP32 7EF* Tel (01284) 701258

SWIFT, Stanley. b 47. Open Univ BA86 ACIS71. Linc Th Coll 71. d 74 p 75. C Heaton St Barn *Bradf* 74-77; C Bexhill St Pet *Chich* 77-81; R Crowland *Linc* 81-86; RD Elloe W 82-86; R Upminster *Chelmsf* 86-95; P-in-c N Ockendon 94-95; V Rush Green 95-02; V Gt Burstead from 02. *The Vicarage, 111 Church Street, Billericay CM11 2TR* Tel (01277) 625947 E-mail stanswift@hotmail.com

SWINBANK, Mrs Anne Jennifer. b 52. SS Paul & Mary Coll Cheltenham BA90. St Steph Ho Ox 08. d 09. NSM N Cheltenham *Glouc* from 09. *5 Priory Mews, Sidney Street, Cheltenham GL52 6DJ* Tel (01242) 700128 E-mail jennifer.swinbank@northchelt.org.uk

SWINBURNE, Harold Noel. b 27. Univ Coll Lon BA49. St Chad's Coll Dur. d 53 p 54. C Cockerton *Dur* 53-57; C Wisbech St Aug *Ely* 57-59; V Chilton Moor *Dur* 59-71; Lect RS New Coll Dur 71-93; Lic to Offic *Dur* 71-85; V Bishopwearmouth St Nic 85-93; rtd 93. *39 Durham Moor Crescent, Durham DH1 5AS* Tel 0191-386 2603

SWINDELL, Anthony Charles. b 50. Selw Coll Cam BA73 MA77 Leeds Univ MPhil77 PhD07. Ripon Hall Ox 73. d 75 p 76. C Hessle *York* 75-78; P-in-c Litlington w W Dean *Chich* 78-80; Adult Educn Adv E Sussex 78-80; TV Heslington *York* 80-81; Chapl York Univ 80-81; R Harlaxton *Linc* 81-91; RD Grantham 85-90; R Jersey St Sav *Win* from 91; Perm to Offic *Nor* 93-96. *The Rectory, Rectory Lane, St Saviour's Hill, St Saviour, Jersey JE2 7NP* Tel (01534) 736679 E-mail anthonyswindell@aol.co.uk

SWINDELL, Brian. b 35. St Jo Coll Nottm 86. d 88 p 89. C Wombwell *Sheff* 88-91; V Brinsworth w Catcliffe 91-93; TR Brinsworth w Catcliffe and Treeton 93-99; rtd 99; Perm to Offic *S'well* from 04. *36 Wasdale Close, West Bridgford, Nottingham NG2 6RG* Tel 0115-914 1125

SWINDELL, Richard Carl. b 45. Didsbury Coll Man CertEd67 Open Univ BA73 Leeds Univ MEd86. NOC 79 Qu Coll Birm 77. d 82 p 83. Hd Teacher Moorside Jun Sch 78-96; NSM Halifax St Aug *Wakef* 82-92; NSM Huddersfield H Trin from 92; Family Life and Marriage Officer 96-02; Bp's Adv for Child Protection from 02. *13 Moor Hill Court, Laund Road, Salendine Nook, Huddersfield HD3 3GQ* Tel (01484) 640473 Mobile 07946-761364 E-mail rswin25004@aol.com

SWINDELLS, Jonathan Reid. b 66. Bp Otter Coll Chich BA90 Cam Univ PGCE93 Leeds Univ BA02. Coll of Resurr Mirfield 00. d 02 p 03. C Sherborne w Castleton and Lillington *Sarum* 02-05; TV Hove *Chich* 05-10; V Hove St Andr from 10. *The Vicarage, 17 Vallance Gardens, Hove BN3 2DB* Tel (01273) 734859 Mobile 07790-430070 E-mail jonathan@swindellsj.fsworld.co.uk

SWINDELLS, Philip John. b 34. St Edm Hall Ox BA56 MA60. Ely Th Coll 56. d 58 p 59. C Upton cum Chalvey *Ox* 58-62; C Bishops Hull St Jo *B & W* 62-66; C Stevenage St Geo *St Alb* 66-71; V Stevenage All SS Pin Green 71-78; R Clophill 78-00; P-in-c Upper w Lower Gravenhurst 83-93; P-in-c Shillington 96-99; rtd 00; Perm to Offic *Ely* from 00. *21 Wertheim Way, Huntingdon PE29 6UH* Tel (01480) 436886 Mobile 07980-093219 E-mail philip.swindells@btinternet.com

SWINDLEHURST, Canon Michael Robert Carol. b 29. Worc Coll Ox BA52 MA56. Cuddesdon Coll 61. d 63 p 64. C Havant *Portsm* 63-65; C Hellesdon *Nor* 66-69; V Brightlingsea *Chelmsf* 69-95; Miss to Seamen 69-95; RD St Osyth *Chelmsf* 84-94; Hon Can Chelmsf Cathl 89-95; rtd 95; Perm to Offic *Chelmsf* from 95 and *St Alb* 95-98. *9 Radwinter Road, Saffron Walden CB11 3HU* Tel (01799) 513788

SWINDON, Suffragan Bishop of. *See* RAYFIELD, The Rt Revd Lee Stephen

SWINGLER, Preb Jack Howell. b 19. St Jo Coll Cam BA41 MA47. Ridley Hall Cam 46. d 48 p 49. C Yeovil St Jo w Preston Plucknett *B & W* 48-53; V Henstridge 53-79; P-in-c Charlton Horethorne w Stowell 78-79; R Henstridge and Charlton Horethorne w Stowell 79-85; RD Merston 74-84; Preb Wells Cathl 79-05; rtd 85; Perm to Offic *B & W* from 85. *St Andrew's, March Lane, Galhampton, Yeovil BA22 7AN* Tel (01963) 440842

SWINHOE, John Robert. b 10. NSM Horton *Newc* from 10; Chapl Northd Fire and Rescue Service from 11. *37 Dene View Drive, Blyth NE24 5PT*

SWINHOE, Terence Leslie. b 49. Man Univ BA71 PGCE72 Lon Univ BD95. NOC. d 84 p 85. C Harborne St Pet *Birm* 84-87; V Warley *Wakef* 87-96; V Rastrick St Matt 96-06; P-in-c Greetland and W Vale from 06. *The Vicarage, 2 Goldfields Way, Greetland, Halifax HX4 8LA* Tel (01422) 372802 E-mail swinfam@aol.com

SWINN, Gerald Robert. b 40. Leeds Univ BSc60 Lon Univ BD70. Oak Hill Th Coll 63. d 66 p 67. C Weston-super-Mare Ch Ch *B & W* 66-69; C Harefield *Lon* 70-72; Lic to Offic *Sarum* from 72. *7 Witchampton Road, Broadstone BH18 8HY* Tel (01202) 249782 E-mail geraldswinn@ntlworld.com

SWINN, Philip Daniel. b 65. Oak Hill Th Coll BA01. d 01 p 02. C Harpenden St Nic *St Alb* 01-04; TV Bp's Hatfield 04-05; TV Bp's

Hatfield, Lemsford and N Mymms 05-10; R Cowra Australia from 10. *The Rectory, 131 Taragala Street, Cowra NSW 2794, Australia* E-mail pd_swinn@swinns.com

SWINNERTON, Ernest George Francis. b 33. Clare Coll Cam BA54 MA57. Linc Th Coll 56. **d** 58 **p** 59. C Kirkholt *Man* 58-61; C Swindon Ch *Bris* 61-67; C-in-c Walcot St Andr CD 67-75; P-in-c Chilton Foliat *Sarum* 76; TV Whitton 76-85; V Bolton St Matt w St Barn *Man* 85-95; rtd 95; Perm to Offic *Man* 95-08. *15 Orchard Close, Chelmsford CM2 9SL* Tel (01245) 491366

SWINNEY, Shawn Douglas. b 76. Oak Hill Th Coll BA01 Regent Coll Vancouver MA04. Ox Min Course 07. **d** 09 **p** 10. NSM Gerrards Cross and Fulmer *Ox* from 09. *Address temp unknown* Tel 07507-304902 (mobile) E-mail shawnswinney@hotmail.com

SWINTON, Garry Dunlop. b 59. SS Mark & Jo Univ Coll Plymouth BA81 CertEd82. Ripon Coll Cuddesdon 85. **d** 88 **p** 89. C Surbiton St Andr and St Mark *S'wark* 88-92; Succ S'wark Cathl 92-97; P-in-c Wandsworth St Faith 97-01; Chapl YMCA Wimbledon 97-01; Chapl Greycoat Hosp Sch from 01; Chapl Westmr City Sch from 01; PV Westmr Abbey from 06. *4 Greenham Close, London SE1 7RP* Tel (020) 7261 9321 Mobile 07961-422303 E-mail garry.swinton1@btinternet.com

SWIRES-HENNESSY, Matthew. b 81. Lon Sch of Th BA06. Wycliffe Hall Ox MTh10. **d** 09 **p** 10. C Luton St Fran *St Alb* from 09. *15 Lancing Road, Luton LU2 8JN* Tel (01582) 515834 Mobile 07803-928006 E-mail revd.msh@googlemail.com

SWITHINBANK, Kim Stafford. b 53. SS Coll Cam BA77 MA79. Cranmer Hall Dur 78. **d** 80 **p** 81. C Heigham H Trin *Nor* 80-83; Chapl Monkton Combe Sch Bath 83-85; C Langham Place All So *Lon* 85-89; R Stamford St Geo w St Paul *Linc* 90-02; Chapl NW Anglia Healthcare NHS Trust 90-02; V Falls Ch Virginia USA 02-05; Dir Alpha Network 05-07; V Muswell Hill St Jas w St Matt *Lon* from 08. *St James's Vicarage, 2 St James's Lane, London N10 3DB* Tel (020) 8883 6277 Fax 8883 4459 Mobile 07891-615984 E-mail kim.swithinbank@st-james.org.uk

SWITHINBANK, Mrs Penelope Jane. b 53. St Andr Univ MTheol74 Hughes Hall Cam PGCE75. Ridley Hall Cam 00. **d** 02 **p** 03. Dir Connections Falls Ch Virginia USA 02-07; R Johns Island Ch of Our Sav 07-08; Chapl St Mellitus Coll *Lon* from 08. *St James's Vicarage, 2 St James's Lane, London N10 3DB* Tel (020) 8442 2821 *or* 7481 9477 Mobile 07870-497365 E-mail penelope.swithinbank@st-james.org.uk

SWITZERLAND, Archdeacon of. See POTTER, The Ven Peter Maxwell

SWORD, Bernard James. b 46. **d** 04 **p** 05. NSM Millbrook *Ches* 04-07; P-in-c Bredbury St Barn from 07. *St Barnabas' Vicarage, Osborne Street, Lower Bredbury, Stockport SK6 2DA* Tel 0161-406 6569 Mobile 07866-446681 E-mail bernardsword1@aol.com

SWYER, David Martin. b 64. Univ of Wales (Abth) BA87 PGCE89. St Mich Coll Llan 89. **d** 91 **p** 92. C Killay *S & B* 91-93; C Newton St Pet 93-95; R Albourne w Sayers Common and Twineham *Chich* from 95. *The Rectory, 5 The Twitten, Albourne, Hassocks BN6 9DF* Tel (01273) 832129

SWYER (née HARRIS), Mrs Rebecca Jane. b 67. Univ of Wales (Lamp) BA88 Univ of Wales (Cardiff) MPhil93. St Mich Coll Llan 89. **d** 91. C Sketty *S & B* 91-95; Perm to Offic *Chich* 95-02; Lic to Offic from 02; Lect Th Chich Univ 97-09; Min Development Officer *Chich* from 09. *The Rectory, 5 The Twitten, Albourne, Hassocks BN6 9DF* Tel (01273) 832129

SWYNNERTON, Brian Thomas. b 31. JP77. Ox Univ Inst of Educn 56 NY Univ BA74 PhD75 FRGS62 LCP62. Lich Th Coll 67. **d** 69 **p** 70. C Swynnerton *Lich* 69-71; CF (TAVR) 70-80; C Eccleshall *Lich* 71-74; C Croxton w Broughton 74-80; Chapl and Lect Stafford Coll 80-84; Chapl Naples w Sorrento, Capri and Bari *Eur* 84-85; Perm to Offic *Lich* from 85; Chapl Rishworth Sch Ripponden 85-88; Chapl Telford City Tech Coll from 96. *Hales Farm, Market Drayton TF9 2PP* Tel (01630) 657156

SYDNEY, Archbishop of. See JENSEN, The Most Revd Peter Frederick

SYER, Mrs Angela. b 48. ARCM69 Philippa Fawcett Coll CertEd71. Qu Coll Birm. **d** 00 **p** 01. C Oakdale *Sarum* 00-04; P-in-c Coxley w Godney, Henton and Wookey *B & W* from 04. *The Vicarage, Vicarage Lane, Wookey, Wells BA5 1JT* Tel (01749) 676710 E-mail angelasyer@hotmail.com

SYKES, Alan Roy. b 53. Sheff Univ BA75. Dioc OLM tr scheme 05. **d** 08 **p** 09. NSM Richmond St Mary w St Matthias and St Jo *S'wark* from 08. *251 King's Road, Kingston upon Thames KT2 5JH* Tel (020) 8549 3887 E-mail alan.sykes10@btinternet.com

SYKES, Christine Virginia. b 07. NSM Castle Church *Lich* from 07. *18 Delamere Lane, Stafford ST17 9TL* Tel (01785) 240529 E-mail curate@castlechurch.co.uk

SYKES, Mrs Clare Mary. b 61. WMMTC 93. **d** 96 **p** 97. C Tupsley w Hampton Bishop *Heref* 96-01; NSM Bromyard 01-08; NSM Stanford Bishop, Stoke Lacy, Moreton Jeffries w Much Cowarne etc 01-08; NSM Bromyard and Stoke Lacy from 09;

NSM Frome Valley from 09; RD Bromyard from 05. *The Vicarage, 28 Church Lane, Bromyard HR7 4DZ* Tel (01885) 482438 E-mail clare@thesykes.plus.com

SYKES, Cynthia Ann. b 41. **d** 05 **p** 06. OLM Em TM *Wakef* from 05. *The Old Dairy, Parkhead Farm, Birdsedge, Huddersfield HD8 8XW* Tel (01484) 603894

SYKES, Mrs Emma Caroline Mary. b 75. Warwick Univ BA96. St Jo Coll Nottm 06. **d** 08 **p** 09. C Birm St Martin w Bordesley St Andr from 08. *159 Boldmere Road, Sutton Coldfield B73 5UL* Tel 0121-354 3130 Mobile 07859-066510 E-mail emmarsykes@hotmail.com

SYKES, Gerald Alfred. b 58. Univ of Wales (Abth) BSc79 PhD83 Univ of Wales (Cardiff) BD98. St Mich Coll Llan 95. **d** 98 **p** 99. C Cardigan w Mwnt and Y Ferwig w Llangoedmor *St D* 98-01; P-in-c Brechfa w Abergorlech etc 01-08; P-in-c Alverthorpe *Wakef* from 08; P-in-c Westgate Common from 08. *The Vicarage, St Paul's Drive, Wakefield WF2 0BT* Tel (01924) 383724 E-mail sykesga@bigfoot.com

SYKES, Graham Timothy Gordon. b 59. ACIB89. St Jo Coll Nottm BTh92. **d** 92 **p** 93. C Kington w Huntington, Old Radnor, Kinnerton etc *Heref* 92-95; C Breinton 95-97; TV W Heref 97-98; Dioc Co-ord for Evang 95-01; V Bromyard 01-08; P-in-c Stanford Bishop, Stoke Lacy, Moreton Jeffries w Much Cowarne etc 01-08; V Bromyard and Stoke Lacy from 09. *The Vicarage, 28 Church Lane, Bromyard HR7 4DZ* Tel (01885) 482438 E-mail vicar@stpetersbromyard.plus.com

SYKES, Ian. b 44. Leic Univ DipEd. Bris Bapt Coll 64 Ripon Coll Cuddesdon 84. **d** 85 **p** 86. In Bapt Min 64-84; C Headington *Ox* 85-88; TV Bourne Valley *Sarum* 88-97; R Peter Tavy, Mary Tavy, Lydford and Brent Tor *Ex* 97-07; Hon C 07-10. *Forge Cottage, East End, Damerham, Fordingbridge SP6 3HQ* Tel (01725) 518635

SYKES, James Clement. b 42. Keble Coll Ox BA64 MA71. Westcott Ho Cam 65. **d** 67 **p** 68. C Bishop's Stortford St Mich *St Alb* 67-71; Chapl St Jo Sch Leatherhead 71-73; Bermuda 74-79; V Northaw *St Alb* 79-87; Chapl St Marg Sch Bushey 87-98; R Guernsey St Sampson *Win* 99-07; rtd 07. *Petit Robinet, Rue de Bouverie, Castel, Guernsey GY5 7UA* Tel (01481) 256381 Mobile 07781-111459 E-mail jimandsue@cwgsy.net

SYKES, Miss Jean. b 45. Leeds Univ BA66 Bris Univ CertEd67. Ripon Coll Cuddesdon 86. **d** 88 **p** 94. C N Huddersfield *Wakef* 88-91; TV Rixby 93; TV Kippax w Allerton Bywater *Ripon* from 93; AD Whitkirk 05-09. *The Vicarage, 134 Leeds Road, Allerton Bywater, Castleford WF10 2HB* Tel 0113-286 9415 E-mail vicar@stmarykippax.org.uk

SYKES, Jeremy Gordon. b 63. Hull Univ BA85. St Alb Minl Tr Scheme 92 Ripon Coll Cuddesdon 97. **d** 99 **p** 00. C Ipswich St Mary-le-Tower *St E* 99-02; P-in-c Briston w Burgh Parva and Melton Constable *Nor* 02-06; P-in-c Briston, Burgh Parva, Hindolveston etc from 06. *The Vicarage, 1 Grange Close, Briston, Melton Constable NR24 2LY* Tel (01263) 860280 E-mail jeremy@sykes-uk.com

SYKES, Jeremy Jonathan Nicholas. b 61. Girton Coll Cam BA83 MA86. Wycliffe Hall Ox BA88. **d** 89 **p** 90. C Knowle *Birm* 89-92; Asst Chapl Oakham Sch 92-98; Chapl Giggleswick Sch 98-06; Hd Master Gt Walstead Sch from 06. *Great Walstead School, East Mascalls Lane, Lindfield, Haywards Heath RH16 2QL* Tel (01444)483528 Fax 482122 E-mail admin@greatwalstead.co.uk

SYKES, Canon John. b 39. Man Univ BA62. Ripon Hall Ox 61. **d** 63 **p** 64. C Heywood St Luke *Man* 63-67; C Bolton H Trin 67-71; Chapl Bolton Colls of H&FE 67-71; R Reddish *Man* 71-78; V Saddleworth 78-87; TR Oldham 87-04; Hon Can Man Cathl 91-04; rtd 04; Perm to Offic *Man* from 04; Chapl to The Queen 95-09. *53 Ivy Green Drive, Springhead, Oldham OL4 4PR* Tel 0161-678 6767 E-mail j.sykes@rdplus.net

SYKES, John Harold. b 50. Van Mildert Coll Dur BA71 K Coll Lon BD73 AKC74 MTh75 Linc Coll Ox MSc89 ALAM71 FRSA92. S'wark Ord Course 75. **d** 09 **p** 09. NSM Ashburnham w Penhurst *Chich* from 09. *Woodlands, Dorothy Avenue, Cranbrook TN17 3AL* Tel (01580) 712793

SYKES, Margaret. b 48. CITC 03. **d** 06 **p** 07. NSM Ardamine w Kiltennel, Glascarrig etc *C & O* 06-10; NSM Ferns w Kilbride, Toombe, Kilcormack etc from 10. *Friedland, Kilnahue, Gorey, Co Wexford, Republic of Ireland* Tel (00353) (53) 942 1958 Mobile 87-640 7627 E-mail margaretsykes@eircom.net

✠**SYKES, The Rt Revd Prof Stephen Whitefield.** b 39. St Jo Coll Cam BA61 MA65. Ripon Hall Ox 63. **d** 64 **p** 65. Fell and Dean St Jo Coll Cam 64-74; Asst Lect Div Cam Univ 64-68; Lect 68-74; Van Mildert Prof Div Dur Univ 74-85; Can Res Dur Cathl 74-85; Regius Prof Div Cam Univ 85-90; Hon Can Ely Cathl 85-90; Bp Ely 90-99; Prin St Jo Coll Dur 99-06; Hon Asst Bp Dur from 99. *Ingleside, Whinney Hill, Durham DH1 3BE* Tel 0191-384 6465

SYKES, William George David. b 39. Ball Coll Ox BA63 MA68. Wycliffe Hall Ox 63. **d** 65 **p** 66. Chapl Bradf Cathl 65-69; Chapl Univ Coll *Lon* 69-78; Chapl Univ Coll Ox 78-05; rtd 05. *Yew Tree Cottage, 6 Glebe Road, Cunnor, Oxford OX2 9QJ* Tel (01865) 861810

SYLVESTER, Jeremy Carl Edmund. b 56. Cape Town Univ BA78 HDipEd79. Coll of Resurr Mirfield 84. d 87 p 88. C St Cypr Cathl Kimberley S Africa 87-89; C Ganyesa 89-92; Chapl Informal Settlements Johannesburg 92-96; P-in-c Stoke Newington St Olave Lon 96-98; TV Plymouth Em, St Paul Efford and St Aug Ex 98-01; CMS 01-06; V Nether w Upper Poppleton York from 06. The Vicarage, 15 Nether Way, Upper Poppleton, York YO26 6JQ Tel (01904) 789522

SYLVIA, Keith Lawrence Wilfred. b 63. Chich Th Coll 85. d 88 p 89. C Newbold w Dunston Derby 88-91; C Heston Lon 91-95; V Brighton St Matthias Chich 95-00; C Hove St Patr 00-04; P-in-c Croydon St Andr S'wark from 04. St Andrew's Vicarage, 6 St Peter's Road, Croydon CR0 1HD Tel (020) 8688 6011 E-mail frkeithsylvia@hotmail.com

SYMCOX, Ms Caroline Jane. b 80. Keble Coll Ox BA01 MSt02 MLitt10. Ripon Coll Cuddesdon 09. d 11. C Amersham Ox from 11. 31 Piggott's End, Amersham HP7 0JF Tel 07811-212370 (mobile) E-mail carolinesymcox@googlemail.com

SYMES, Andrew John Barrington. b 66. Magd Coll Cam BA88 MA92. All Nations Chr Coll 90. d 00 p 00. C Walmer St Jo S Africa 00-02; Dir Ext Progr Bible Inst E Cape 02-06; P-in-c Kings Heath Pet from 07; C Northampton St Giles from 07. 95 Harlestone Road, Northampton NN5 7AB Tel (01604) 453598 Mobile 07726-796306 E-mail andrew.symes1@ntlworld.com

SYMES, Percy Peter. b 24. Leeds Univ BA50. Coll of Resurr Mirfield 50. d 52 p 53. C Ox St Barn 52-54; C Headington 54-56; C Abingdon w Shippon 56-61; V Reading St Luke 61-81; V Drayton St Pet (Berks) 81-89; rtd 89; Perm to Offic Ox 94-02. Merrileas, 23 Hollesley Road, Alderton, Woodbridge IP12 3BX Tel (01394) 410452

SYMES-THOMPSON, Hugh Kynard. b 54. Peterho Cam BA76 MA81. Cranmer Hall Dur. d 79 p 80. C Summerfield Birm 79-82; C Harlow New Town w Lt Parndon Chelmsf 82-83; Australia 84-89; TV Dagenham Chelmsf 89-95; R Cranfield and Hulcote w Salford St Alb from 95; Chapl Cranfield Univ from 02. The Rectory, Court Road, Cranfield, Bedford MK43 0DR Tel (01234) 750214 E-mail revhugh@symes-thom.freeserve.co.uk

SYMMONS, Roderic Paul. b 56. Chu Coll Cam BA77 MA81 Oak Hill Th Coll BA83 Fuller Th Sem California DMin90. d 83 p 84. C Ox St Aldate w St Matt 83-88; Lic to Offic LA USA 89-90; R Ardingly Chich 90-99; RD Cuckfield 95-99; P-in-c Redland Bris from 99; Tutor Trin Coll Bris 99-10. Redland Vicarage, 151 Redland Road, Bristol BS6 6YE Tel 0117-946 4691 Fax 946 6862 E-mail rod@redland.org.uk

SYMON, Canon John Francis Walker. b 26. Edin Univ MA50. Edin Th Coll 50. d 52 p 53. C Edin St Cuth 52-56; CF 56-59; R Forfar St And 59-68; R Dunblane 68-85; Can St Ninian's Cathl Perth 74-91; Can Emer St Andr from 00; Chapl Trin Coll Glenalmond 85-91; rtd 91; P-in-c Killin St And 95-98. 20 Cromlix Crescent, Dunblane FK15 9JQ Tel (01786) 822449 E-mail johnsymon@freeola.net

SYMON, Canon Roger Hugh Crispin. b 34. St Jo Coll Cam BA59. Coll of Resurr Mirfield 59. d 61 p 62. C Westmr St Steph w St Jo Lon 61-66; P-in-c Hascombe Guildf 66-68; Chapl Surrey Univ 66-74; V Paddington Ch Ch Lon 74-78; V Paddington St Jas 78-79; USPG 80-87; Abp Cant's Acting Sec for Angl Communion Affairs 87-94; Can Res Cant Cathl 94-02; rtd 02; Perm to Offic Glouc from 02. 5 Bath Parade, Cheltenham GL53 7HL Tel (01242) 700645 E-mail rogersymon@blueyonder.co.uk

SYMONDS, Alan Jeffrey. b 56. Ridley Hall Cam 93. d 95 p 96. C Bath St Luke B & W 95-99; R Abbas and Templecombe w Horsington 99-06; P-in-c Somerton w Compton Dundon, the Charltons etc from 06. Rosemount, Sutton Road, Somerton TA11 6QP Tel (01458) 272029

SYMONDS, James Henry. b 31. Ripon Coll Ox 67. d 69 p 70. C Southampton (City Cen) Win 69-71; CF 71-78; CF 79-90; P-in-c Arrington Ely 78-79; P-in-c Orwell 78-79; P-in-c Wimpole 78-79; P-in-c Croydon w Clopton 78-79; CF (R of O) 90-96; rtd 96; P-in-c Coughton, Spernall, Morton Bagot and Oldberrow Cov 99-02; Perm to Offic Lich from 00 and Cov from 02. Thimble Cottage, Kings Coughton, Alcester B49 5QD Tel (01789) 400814

SYMONS, Stewart Burlace. b 51. Keble Coll Ox BA55 MA59. Clifton Th Coll 55. d 57 p 58. C Hornsey Rise St Mary Lon 57-60; C Gateshead St Geo Dur 60-61; C Patcham Chich 61-64; R Stretford St Bride Man 64-91; V Waterloo St Jo Liv 71-83; R Ardrossan Glas 83-96; C-in-c Irvine St Andr LEP 83-96; Miss to Seamen 83-96; rtd 96; Perm to Offic Carl from 96. 8 Carlingdale, Burneside, Kendal LA9 6PW Tel (01539) 728750

SYMONS, Mrs Susannah Mary. b 59. LMH Ox BA81 La Sainte Union Coll PGCE94. STETS 02. d 05 p 06. C Nadder Valley Sarum 05-09; TV Beaminster Area from 09. The Vicarage, Orchard Mead, Broadwindsor, Beaminster DT8 3RA Tel (01308) 867472 E-mail sue.symons@btinternet.com

SYMS, Richard Arthur. b 43. Ch Coll Cam BA66 MA71. Wycliffe Hall Ox 66. d 68 p 69. C New Eltham All SS S'wark 68-72; Chapl to Arts and Recreation Dur 72-73; C Hitchin St Mary St Alb 73-76; TV Hitchin 77-78; Perm to Offic 78-97; P-in-c Datchworth 97-03; rtd 03; Perm to Offic Lon and St Alb from 03.

8 Lytton Fields, Knebworth SG3 6AZ Tel (01438) 811933 Mobile 07900-241470 E-mail richard.syms@sky.com

SYNNOTT, The Ven Alan Patrick Sutherland. b 59. d 85 p 86. C Lisburn Ch Ch Conn 85-88; CF 88-95; I Galloon w Drummully Clogh 95-01; I Monkstown Conn 01-04; Perm to Offic 04-09; I Skreen w Kilmacshalgan and Dromard T, K & A from 09; Adn Killala from 10; Can Killala Cathl from 10; Can Achonry Cathl from 10. The Rectory, Skreen, Co Sligo, Republic of Ireland Tel (00353) (71) 916 6941 Mobile 86-848 4924 E-mail alan.synnott@yahoo.ie or skreen@killala.anglican.org

T

TABER-HAMILTON, Nigel John. b 53. Univ of Wales (Ban) BA75. Qu Coll Birm Ch Div Sch of Pacific 77. d 78 p 81. C W Wimbledon Ch Ch S'wark 78-79; USA from 79; C Berkeley St Mark 79-81; C Bloomington H Trin 81-90 and 92-94; Interim R Crawfordsville St Jo 90-91; Interim R New Harmony St Steph 91-92; V Seymour All SS 94-00; R St Aug in-the-Woods from 00. PO Box 11, Freeland WA 98249, USA Tel (001) (360) 331 4887 Fax 331 1822 E mail rector@whidbey.com

TABERN, James. b 23. St Aid Birkenhead 57. d 59 p 60. C Garston Liv 59-61; V Litherland St Paul Hatton Hill 61-72; V Gillingham St Mark Roch 72-79; V Lindow Ches 79-85; rtd 85; Perm to Offic Liv 86-91 and from 98; Ches from 97. 12 Dickinson Road, Formby, Liverpool L37 4BX Tel (01704) 831131

TABERNOR, Brian Douglas. d 07 p 08. OLM Brereton and Rugeley Lich from 07. 31 Ashtree Bank, Rugeley WS15 1HN Tel (01889) 804587 E-mail brian.tabernor@ntlworld.com

TABOR, James Hugh. b 63. Univ of W Aus BA85. Ripon Coll Cuddesdon BTh06. d 04 p 05. C Alverstoke Portsm 04-07; Chapl RN from 07. Royal Naval Chaplaincy Service, Mail Point 1-2, Leach Building, Whale Island, Portsmouth PO2 8BY Tel (023) 9262 5055 Fax 9262 5134

TABOR, John Tranham. b 30. Ball Coll Ox BA56 MA58. Ridley Hall Cam 56. d 58 p 59. C Lindfield Chich 58-62; Tutor Ridley Hall Cam 62-63; Chapl 63-68; Warden Scargill Ho 68-75; R Berkhamsted St Mary St Alb 75-96; rtd 96; Perm to Offic St Alb from 96 and Ox 99-00. 2 Warwick Close, Aston Clinton, Aylesbury HP22 5JF Tel and fax (01296) 631562 E-mail johnttabor@yahoo.co.uk

TAFT, Mrs Janet Anne. b 59. Sheff Univ BA80 Wolv Univ PGCE82. Wycliffe Hall Ox 06. d 08 p 09. NSM Abingdon Ox from 08; Chapl SS Helen and Kath Sch Abingdon from 10. 9 The Chestnuts, Abingdon OX14 3YN Tel (01235) 200593 Mobile 07929-543626 E-mail janet.taft@ntlworld.com

TAGGART, William Joseph. b 54. d 85 p 86. C Belfast St Mich Conn 85-90; I Belfast St Kath from 90; Dioc Registrar from 06. St Katharine's Rectory, 24 Lansdowne Road, Belfast BT15 4DB Tel (028) 9077 7647 E-mail belfast.stkatharine@connor.anglican.org

TAGUE, Russell. b 59. Aston Tr Scheme 90 Linc Th Coll 92. d 94 p 95. C Astley Man 94-97; Chapl HM YOI Swinfen Hall 97-00; Chapl HM Pris Risley 00-05; TV Kirkby Liv 05-08; R Arthuret w Kirkandrews-on-Esk and Nicholforest Carl from 08. Arthuret Rectory, 1 Arthuret Drive, Longtown, Carlisle CA6 5SG Tel (01228) 791338 E-mail taguejosh@yahoo.co.uk

TAILBY, Ms Jane Dorothy. b 56. Culham Coll of Educn BEd79. WEMTC 01. d 04 p 05. NSM Frampton Cotterell and Iron Acton Bris 04-09; NSM Winterbourne and Frenchay and Winterbourne Down 08-09; TV Nadder Valley Sarum from 09. The Vicarage, 11A Tyndale's Meadow, Dinton, Salisbury SP3 5HU Tel (01722) 717883 E-mail jdtailby@aol.com

TAILBY, Peter Alan. b 49. Chich Th Coll 83. d 85 p 86. C Stocking Farm Leic 85-88; C Knighton St Mary Magd 88-90; P-in-c Thurnby Lodge 90-98; P-in-c W Molesey Guildf 98-05; V from 05. The Vicarage, 518 Walton Road, West Molesey KT8 2QF Tel (020) 8979 3846 E-mail ptailby@supanet.com

TAINTON, Mrs Carol Anne. b 50. EMMTC 96. d 99 p 00. NSM Gamston and Bridgford S'well 99-03; P-in-c Lowdham w Caythorpe, and Gunthorpe 03-04; V from 04. 4 Hazelas Drive, Gunthorpe, Nottingham NG14 7FZ Tel 0115-966 5922 E-mail revcaroltainton@ukonline.co.uk

TAIT, James Laurence Jamieson. b 47. St Jo Coll Dur 78. d 80 p 81. C Heyside Man 80-81; C Westhoughton 81-84; R Aldingham and Dendron and Rampside Carl 84-88; V Flookburgh 88-92; V Hunterville New Zealand 92-94; V Palmerston N from 94. PO Box 5134, Terrace End, Palmerston North 4441, New Zealand Tel (0064) (6) 358 9134 or tel and fax 358 5403 E-mail stpeters@inspire.net.nz

TAIT, Philip Leslie. b 52. Ex Univ BA73 Hull Univ PGCE74. NEOC 87. **d** 90 **p** 91. NSM Osbaldwick w Murton *York* 90-92; Chapl and Hd RS Berkhamsted Sch Herts 93-97; P-in-c Woodhorn w Newbiggin *Newc* 98; Chapl HM Pris Wolds 98-00; **TAIT** (*née* **DAVIS**), **Canon Ruth Elizabeth.** b 39. St Andr Univ MA62 Moray Ho Coll of Educn DipEd63. Moray Ord Course 89. **dss** 90 **d** 94 **p** 95. Elgin w Lossiemouth *Mor* 90-96; C 94-96; NSM Dufftown *Ab* 96-03; C Forres *Mor* 96-98; NSM Aberlour 98-03; Dioc Dir of Ords from 02; NSM Elgin w Lossiemouth from 04; Hon Can St Andr Cathl Inverness from 03. *Benmore, Burnbank, Birnie, Elgin IV30 8RW* Tel (01343) 862808 E-mail ruth.e.tait@btinternet.com

TAIT, Ms Valerie Joan. b 60. Open Univ BA96 SRN82 RSCN82. Trin Coll Bris 99. **d** 01 **p** 02. C W Heref 01-06; P-in-c Ford from 06; P-in-c Alberbury w Cardeston from 06; P-in-c Gt Wollaston from 10. *The Vicarage, Ford, Shrewsbury SY5 9LZ* Tel (01743) 850254

TALBOT, Alan John. b 23. BNC Ox BA49 MA55. Coll of Resurr Mirfield 49. **d** 51 **p** 52. C Hackney Wick St Mary of Eton w St Aug *Lon* 51-54; C Portsea St Sav *Portsm* 54-63; Chapl St Jo Coll Chidya Tanzania 63-65; P-in-c Namakambale 65-68; V Stepney St Aug w St Phil *Lon* 69-78; V Twickenham All Hallows 78-86; rtd 88; Perm to Offic S'wark from 88. *46 Brandon Street, London SE17 1NL* Tel (020) 7703 0719

TALBOT, Derek Michael (Mike). b 55. St Jo Coll Dur BSc77. St Jo Coll Nottm 84. **d** 87 **p** 88. C Rushden w Newton Bromswold *Pet* 87-90; C Barton Seagrave w Warkton 90-95; V Kettering Ch the King 95-02; V Northwood Em *Lon* from 02; AD Harrow 02-07. *Emmanuel Vicarage, 3 Gatehill Road, Northwood HA6 3QB* Tel (01923) 828914 *or* 845209 Fax 845209 Mobile 07767-763715 E-mail mike.talbot@lineone.net *or* mike.talbot@ecn.org.uk

TALBOT (*née* **THOMSON**), **Mrs Elizabeth Lucy.** b 74. Lanc Univ BA96 Bris Univ BA00 MA01. Trin Coll Bris 98. **d** 01 **p** 02. C Bitterne *Win* 01-05; Chapl Dean Close Sch Cheltenham from 05. *Dean Close School, Shelburne Road, Cheltenham GL51 6HE* Tel (01242) 258000 Mobile 07977-115923 E-mail libby@thomson74.fslife.co.uk

TALBOT, George Brian. b 37. Qu Coll Birm 78. **d** 80 **p** 81. C Heref St Martin 80-83; R Bishop's Frome w Castle Frome and Fromes Hill 83-90; P-in-c Acton Beauchamp and Evesbatch w Stanford Bishop 83-90; R Burstow S'wark 90-02; rtd 02. *Rose Barn, Elms Lane, West Wittering, Chichester PO20 8LW*

TALBOT, John Herbert Boyle. b 30. TCD BA51 MA57. CITC 52. **d** 53 **p** 54. C Dublin St Pet *D & G* 53-57; Chan Vicar St Patrick's Cathl Dub 56-61; C Dublin Zion Ch 57-61; Chapl Asst St Thos Hosp Lon 61-64; Min Can and Sacr Cant Cathl 64-67; R Brasted *Roch* 67-84; R Ightham 84-95; P-in-c Shipbourne 87-91; RD Shoreham 89-95; rtd 95; Perm to Offic *Roch* from 01. *12 Waterlakes, Edenbridge TN8 5BX* Tel (01732) 865729

TALBOT, John Michael. b 23. Lon Univ MD52 FRSM FRCPath68. S'wark Ord Course 75. **d** 78 **p** 79. NSM S Croydon Em *Cant* 78-81; Perm to Offic *Nor* 82-85 and from 96; NSM Hethersett w Canteloff w Lt and Gt Melton 85-96. *3 White Gates Close, Hethersett, Norwich NR9 3JG* Tel (01603) 811709 E-mail johnmtalbot@waitrose.com

TALBOT, Mrs June Phyllis. b 46. Ripon Coll of Educn CertEd67. NEOC 88. **d** 91 **p** 94. NSM Cleadon *Dur* 91-97; Dioc Voc Adv from 94; NSM Bishopwearmouth St Gabr from 97. *66 Wheatall Drive, Whitburn, Sunderland SR6 7HQ* Tel 0191-529 2265

TALBOT (*née* **KINGHAM**), **Canon Mair Josephine.** b 59. Univ Coll Lon BA84. Ridley Hall Cam 85. **d** 88 **p** 94. C Gt Yarmouth *Nor* 88-94; Sen Asst P Raveningham Gp 94-99; Chapl Norfolk Mental Health Care NHS Trust 94-02; Bp's Adv for Women's Min *Nor* 01-04; P-in-c Watton w Carbrooke and Ovington 02-06; Project Manager Magd Gp 06-10; Chapl Norfolk Primary Care Trust from 10; Hon Can Nor Cathl from 02. *Chaplain's Office, Colman Hospital, Unthank Road, Norwich NR2 2PJ* Tel (01603) 225720 E-mail mair.talbot@norfolk-pct.nhs.uk

TALBOT, Mrs Margaret Eileen Coxon. b 52. Whitelands Coll Lon TCert73. STETS 01. **d** 04 **p** 05. NSM Herstmonceux and Wartling *Chich* 04-06; C Seaford w Sutton 06-09; TV Ely from 09. *The Rectory, Main Street, Little Downham, Ely CB6 2ST* Tel (01353) 698410 Mobile 07792-140076 E-mail mectalbot@googlemail.com

TALBOT, Mrs Marian. b 25. Qu Coll Birm 76. **dss** 78 **d** 87 **p** 94. Droitwich *Worc* 78-87; Par Dn Droitwich Spa 87-88; Chapl Droitwich Hosps 83-88; Asst Chapl Alexandra Hosp Redditch 88-98; Perm to Offic 88-98; rtd 98; Perm to Offic *Truro* from 06. *Number Ten The Fairway, Mawnan Smith, Falmouth TR11 5LR* Tel (01326) 250035

TALBOT, Mike. See TALBOT, Derek Michael

TALBOT, Simon George Guy. b 79. Reading Univ BSc01. Oak Hill Th Coll BA07. **d** 07 **p** 08. C Ipswich St Marg *St E* 07-10; C Plymouth Em, St Paul Efford and St Aug *Ex* from 10. *28A Sefton Avenue, Plymouth PL4 7HB* Tel (01752) 245813 E-mail simon@thetalbots.org.uk

TALBOT, Stephen Richard. b 52. Portsm Poly BSc73. Trin Col Bris 81. **d** 84 **p** 85. C Tonbridge SS Pet and Paul *Roch* 84-89 P-in-c Hemingford Grey *Ely* 89-01; P-in-c Hemingford Abbot 89-96; P-in-c Ashburnham w Penhurst *Chich* 01-06; Perm tc Offic *Chich* 06-10 and *Ely* from 10. *The Rectory, Main Street Little Downham, Ely CB6 2ST* Tel (01353) 698410 Mobile 07792-139820 E-mail stephen.talbot@revivalmedia.org

TALBOT, Sister Susan Gabriel. b 46. Leeds Univ BA69 Man Poly CertEd70 Man Univ PhD00. NOC 91. **d** 94 **p** 95. C Wythenshawe St Martin *Man* 94-98; P-in-c Cheetham St Jo 98-02; Lic Preacher 02-04; C Wilmslow *Ches* 04-05; Dioc Adv Healing 06-08; NSM Bowdon from 06. *34 Eaton Road, Bowdon Altrincham WA14 3EH* Tel 0161-233 0630 E-mail susangabriel@btinternet.com

TALBOT-PONSONBY, Preb Andrew. b 44. Coll of Resurr Mirfield 66. **d** 68 **p** 70. C Radlett *St Alb* 68-70; C Salisbury St Martin *Sarum* 70-73; P-in-c Acton Burnell w Pitchford *Here*, 73-80; P-in-c Frodesley 73-80; P-in-c Cound 73-80; Asst Dioc Youth Officer 73-80; P-in-c Bockleton w Leysters 80-81; V 81-92 P-in-c Kimbolton w Middleton-on-the-Hill 80-81; V Kimboltor w Hamnish and Middleton-on-the-Hill 81-92; P-in-c Wigmore Abbey 92-96; R 97-98; RD Leominster 97-98; Public Preacher from 98; Warden of Readers from 02; Preb Heref Cathl from 87 rtd 09. *The Old Barn, Cleeve Lane, Ross-on-Wye HR9 7TB* Te (01989) 565003 E-mail andrew@talbot-ponsonby.org

TALBOT-PONSONBY, Mrs Gillian. b 50. Sarum & Wells Th Coll 89. **d** 91 **p** 94. C Leominster *Heref* 91-92; NSM Wigmore Abbey 92-98; Public Preacher from 98; Asst Dioc Adv or Women in Min 99-03; Dioc Adv from 03. *The Old Barn, Cleeve Lane, Ross-on-Wye HR9 7TB* Tel (01989) 565003 E-mail jill@talbot-ponsonby.org

TALBOTT, Brian Hugh. b 34. RD78. St Pet Hall Ox BA57 MA64. Westcott Ho Cam. **d** 59 **p** 60. C Newc H Cross 59-61; C Newc St Jo 61-64; Chapl RNR 63-91; Chapl Barnard Castle Sch 64-71; Chapl Bishop's Stortford Coll 71-96; Hon C Bishop's Stortford St Mich *St Alb* 71-96; rtd 96; Perm to Offic *B & W* from 96; Acting Chapl Wells Cathl Sch 97-98. *Four Seasons, Milton Lane, Wookey Hole, Wells BA5 1DG* Tel (01749) 679678

TALBOTT, Scott Malcolm. b 55. SAOMC 00. **d** 03 **p** 04. NSM Watford St Andr *St Alb* 03-10; Perm to Offic from 10. *Elmhurst, 40 Berks Hill, Chorleywood, Rickmansworth WD3 5AH* Te (01923) 282370 Mobile 07802-244877 E-mail scott.talbott@talk21.com

TALBOTT, Simon John. b 57. Pontifical Univ Maynooth BD81 **d** 81 **p** 82. In RC Ch 81-87; C Headingley *Ripon* 88-91; V Gt and Lt Ouseburn w Marton cum Grafton 91-97; Chapl Qu Ethelburga's Coll York 91-97; P-in-c Markington w S Stainley and Bishop Thornton *Ripon* 97-01; AD Ripon 97-01; P-in-c Epsom St Martin *Guildf* 01-02; V from 02; Chapl Univ for the Creative Arts from 06. *35 Burgh Heath Road, Epsom KT17 4LF* Tel (01372) 743336 Fax 749193 E-mail s.talbott@virgin.net

TALING, Johannes Albert (Hans). b 59. St Jo Coll Nottm 93. EAMTC 00. **d** 02 **p** 03. C Littleborough *Man* 02-05; P-in-c N Buckingham *Ox* 05-08; R from 08. *The Rectory, South Hall, Maids Moreton, Buckingham MK18 1QD* Tel (01280) 813246 E-mail family@taling.fsnet.co.uk

TALKS, David. b 57. Trin Hall Cam BA78 MA81. Trin Coll Bris BA06. **d** 06 **p** 07. C Colchester St Jo *Chelmsf* 06-11; P-in-c Lynchmere and Camelsdale *Chich* from 11. *The Vicarage, Schoo Road, Camelsdale, Haslemere GU27 3RN* Tel (01428) 652108 Mobile 07867-808207 E-mail rev.dave@btinternet.com *or* lynchcam.vicarage@btinternet.com

TALLANT, John. b 45. Edin Th Coll 86. **d** 88 **p** 89. C Cayton w Eastfield *York* 88-90; C N Hull St Mich 90-91; V Scarborough St Sav w All SS 91-93; V Fleetwood St Nic *Blackb* 93-99; P-in-c Sculcoates St Paul w Ch Ch and St Silas *York* 99-03; P-in-c Hull St Mary Sculcoates 99-03; P-in-c Hull St Steph Sculcoates 99-03; R Woldsburn 03-11; P-in-c Dunscroft St Edwin *Sheff* from 11. *The Vicarage, 162 Station Road, Dunscroft, Doncaster DN7 4JR* Tel (01302) 354356 E-mail john.tallant@homecall.co.uk

TALLINN, Dean of. See PIIR, The Very Revd Gustav Peeter

TALLON, Jonathan Robert Roe. b 66. Rob Coll Cam BA88 MA92 Nottm Univ MPhil07. St Jo Coll Nottm BTh94. **d** 97 **p** 98. C Bury St Jo w St Mark *Man* 97-01; P-in-c Cadishead 01-08; V 08-09; Tutor N Bapt Learning Community from 09. *Luther King House, Brighton Grove, Manchester M14 5JP* Te 0161-249 2546 E-mail jonathan.tallon@northern.org.uk

TALLOWIN (*née* **BOUDIER**), **Mrs Rosemary.** b 57. St Mellitus Coll BA11. **d** 11. NSM Colchester St Mich Myland *Chelmsf* from 11. *11 Tufnell Way, Colchester CO4 5AP* Tel (01206) 835039 E-mail rosie@mylandchurch.org.uk

TAMPLIN, Peter Harry. b 44. Sarum & Wells Th Coll 71. **d** 73 **p** 74. C Digswell *St Alb* 73-76; C Chesterton St Luke *Ely* 76-82; V Chesterton St Geo 82-95; R Durrington *Sarum* 95-07; rtd 07. *1 Gathorne Road, Bristol BS3 1LR* Tel 0117-963 9628 E-mail phtamplin@yahoo.co.uk

TAMPLIN, Roger Ian. b 41. K Coll Lon BD63 AKC63. St Boniface Warminster 60. **d** 64 **p** 65. C St Helier S'wark 64-68; C Camberwell St Giles 68-72; C Tanga St Aug Tanzania 72-73;

P-in-c Brent Pelham w Meesden *St Alb* 74-78; P-in-c Anstey 75-78; rtd 01. *31 Shackleton Spring, Stevenage SG2 9DF* Tel (01438) 316031 E-mail roger.tamplin@ic24.net

'AMS, Gordon Thomas Carl. b 37. Leeds Univ BA60 Newc Univ MLitt84 Reading Univ CertEd61 LLCM76. Edin Dioc NSM Course 83. **d** 90 **p** 91. NSM Kelso *Edin* 90-92; P-in-c Coldstream 92-02; rtd 02; Lic to Offic *Edin* from 06. *47 Lennel Mount, Coldstream TD12 4NS* Tel (01890) 882479 E-mail tamsga@btinternet.com

'AMS, Paul William. b 56. Huddersfield Poly CertEd77. EAMTC 87. **d** 90 **p** 91. NSM Mildenhall *St E* 90-93; NSM Brandon and Santon Downham w Elveden etc from 93. *38 Raven Close, Mildenhall, Bury St Edmunds IP28 7LF* Tel (01638) 715475 E-mail paultams@lineone.net

'AN (née MITCHELL), Mrs Sarah Rachel. b 79. Birm Univ BA00 Fitzw Coll Cam BA04. Westcott Ho Cam 02. **d** 05 **p** 06. C Reddal Hill St Luke *Worc* 05-08; Chapl HM Pris Wayland from 08. *HM Prison Wayland, Griston, Thetford IP25 6RL* Tel (01953) 804080 E-mail sarah.tan@hmps.gsi.gov.uk

'ANCOCK, Steven John. b 73. Westmr Coll Ox BTh01. St Steph Ho Ox 02. **d** 04 **p** 05. C Wincanton and Pen Selwood *B & W* 04-09; C Warren Park *Portsm* from 09; C Leigh Park from 09. *St Clare's House, Strouden Court, Havant PO9 4JX* E-mail rev.steve@btinternet.com

'ANN, Canon David John. b 31. K Coll Lon BD57 AKC57. **d** 58 **p** 59. C Wandsworth St Anne *S'wark* 58-60; C Sholing *Win* 60-64; Asst Chapl Lon Univ 64-65; C Fulham All SS 65-68; Hon C 72-82; Lic to Offic 68-72; Teacher Godolphin and Latymer Sch Hammersmith 68-73; Ealing Boys Gr Sch 69-73; Hd of RE Green Sch Isleworth 73-82, V Dudley St Jas *Worc* 82 95; Chapl Burton Road Hosp Dudley 83-95; Hon Can Worc Cathl 90-95; RD Dudley 93-95; rtd 95; Perm to Offic *Lon* from 97. *75 Parkview Court, Fulham High Street, London SW6 3LL* Tel (020) 7736 6018

'ANNER, Preb Alan John. b 25. OBE97. SS Coll Cam 43 Linc Coll Ox BA52 MA65. Coll of Resurr Mirfield 52. **d** 54 **p** 55. C Hendon St Mary *Lon* 54-58; V S Harrow St Paul 58-60; Dir Coun for Chr Stewardship 60-65; Sec Coun for Miss and Unity 65-80; V St Nic Cole Abbey 66-78; Sec Gtr Lon Chs' Coun 76-83; P-in-c St Ethelburga Bishopsgate 78-85; R St Botolph without Bishopsgate 78-97; P-in-c All Hallows Lon Wall 80-97; Bp's Ecum Officer 81-97; AD The City 90-97; Preb St Paul's Cathl 91-97; P-in-c St Clem Eastcheap w St Martin Orgar 93-97; P-in-c St Sepulchre w Ch Ch Greyfriars etc 93-97; P-in-c St Kath Cree 93-97; P-in-c Smithfield St Bart 94-95; rtd 97; Preacher Charterhouse 73-00; Perm to Offic *Lon* from 00; *B & W* 01-02; *Cant* from 03. *The White House, Derringstone Hill, Barham, Canterbury CT4 6QD* Tel (01227) 830356

'ANNER, Canon Frank Hubert. b 38. St Aid Birkenhead 63. **d** 66 **p** 67. C Ipswich St Marg *St E* 66-69; C Mansfield SS Pet and Paul *S'well* 69-72; V Huthwaite 72-79; Chapl to the Deaf 79-92; Hon Can S'well Minster 90-92; Chapl Northn and Rutland Miss to the Deaf 92-01; rtd 01; Perm to Offic *Truro* from 03. *The Tamarisks, Trenow Lane, Perranuthnoe, Penzance TR20 9NY* Tel (01736) 719426 E-mail franktanner@lineone.net

'ANNER, Leonard John. **d** 03 **p** 04. C Taney *D & G* 03-07; I Tullow from 07; Dioc Dir Lay Min from 09. *Tullow Rectory, Brighton Road, Carrickmines, Dublin 18, Republic of Ireland* Tel (00353) (1) 289 3154 Mobile 86-302 1376 E-mail tanner1@eircom.net

'ANNER, Mark Simon Austin. b 70. Ch Ch Ox BA92 MA96 St Jo Coll Dur BA98 Liv Univ MTh05. Cranmer Hall Dur 95. **d** 98 **p** 99. C Upton (Overchurch) *Ches* 98-01; V Doncaster St Mary *Sheff* 01-07; V Ripon H Trin 07-11; AD Ripon 09-11; Warden Cranmer Hall Dur from 11. *St John's College, 3 South Bailey, Durham DH1 3RJ* Tel 0191-334 3500 Fax 334 3501 E-mail m.s.a.tanner@durham.ac.uk

'ANNER, Canon Mark Stuart. b 59. Nottm Univ BA81. Sarum & Wells Th Coll. **d** 85 **p** 86. C Radcliffe-on-Trent *S'well* 85; C Radcliffe-on-Trent and Shelford etc 85-87; C Bestwood 88-89; TV 89-93; Bp's Research Officer 93-97; P-in-c S'well H Trin 93-98; V from 98; AD S'well 01-06; Hon Can S'well Minster from 07. *Holy Trinity Vicarage, Westhorpe, Southwell NG25 0NB* Tel (01636) 813243 E-mail mark.tanner@tesco.net

'ANNER, Martin Philip. b 54. Univ Coll Lon BSc(Econ)75. Ridley Hall Cam 79. **d** 82 **p** 83. C Bitterne *Win* 82-85; C Weeke 85-88; V Long Buckby w Watford *Pet* 88-96; P-in-c Desborough 96-97; R Desborough, Brampton Ash, Dingley and Braybrooke 97-08; P-in-c Drayton in Hales *Lich* from 08. *The Vicarage, Mount Lane, Market Drayton TF9 1AQ* Tel (01630) 652527 E-mail mp.tanner@btinternet.com

'ANSILL, Canon Derek Ernest Edward. b 36. Univ of Wales (Lamp) BA61. Ripon Hall Ox 61. **d** 63 **p** 64. C Chelsea St Luke *Lon* 63-67; C-in-c Saltdean CD *Chich* 67-69; V Saltdean 69-73; V Billingshurst 73-82; R Bexhill St Pet 82-85; RD Battle and Bexhill 84-86; V Horsham 85-86; TR 86-06; RD Horsham 77-82 and 85-93; Can and Preb Chich Cathl from 81; Chapl Chich Cathl from 06. *5 The Chantry, Canon Lane, Chichester PO19 1PZ* Tel (01243) 775596 E-mail derek@tansill.plus.com

TANSWELL, Stuart Keith. b 79. Reading Univ BSc01. Ripon Coll Cuddesdon BTh08. **d** 08 **p** 09. C St Blazey and Luxulyan and Tywardreath w Tregaminion *Truro* 08-11; V N Holmwood *Guildf* from 11. *The Vicarage, Willow Green, North Holmwood, Dorking RH5 4JB* Tel (01306) 882135 E-mail stuart@tanswell.net *or* vicar@stjohns-northholmwood.info

TAPHOUSE, Bryan George. b 50. STETS 95. **d** 98 **p** 99. NSM Romsey *Win* from 98. *2 Campion Drive, Romsey SO51 7RD* Tel (01794) 516022

TAPLIN, John. b 35. St Alb Minl Tr Scheme 78. **d** 81 **p** 82. NSM Knebworth *St Alb* 81-88; R Lt Hadham w Albury 88-00; rtd 00; Perm to Offic *St E* from 00. *77 Hepworth Road, Stanton, Bury St Edmunds IP31 2UA* Tel (01359) 250212 E-mail johntaplin@supanet.com

TAPLIN, Kim. b 58. Lon Bible Coll BA79 Homerton Coll Cam PGCE84. S Dios Minl Tr Scheme 94. **d** 94 **p** 95. C Sholing *Win* 94-97; P-in-c Rendcomb *Glouc* 97-00; Chapl Rendcomb Coll Cirencester 97-00; Chapl Clifton Coll Bris from 01. *The Chaplaincy, Clifton College, 83B Pembroke Road, Clifton BS8 3EA* Tel 0117-315 7257 *or* 315 7258

TAPLIN, Stewart Tennent Eaton. b 46. Melbourne Univ BEd92 MEd97. ACT ThL69. **d** 72 **p** 73. C Reservoir Australia 72-74; C Stocking Farm *Leic* 74-76; Lic to Offic *Carl* 76-77; Chapl Yarra Valley Sch Australia 78-82; Perm to Offic Melbourne 83-85; Asst Chapl St Mich Gr Sch 86-91; C Mornington 91-93; Chapl Tintern Girls' Gr Sch from 94. *2 Boston Street, Ashwood Vic 3147, Australia* Tel (0061) (3) 9888 3328 *or* 9845 7777 Fax 9845 7710 Mobile 40-208 0366 E-mail staplin@tintern.vic.edu.au

TAPPER, Canon John A'Court. b 42. FCA64. Sarum & Wells Th Coll 89. **d** 91 **p** 92. C Ashford *Cant* 91-94; P-in-c Folkestone H Trin w Ch 94-96; V 96-06; P-in-c Sandgate St Paul w Folkestone St Geo 01-06; V Folkestone Trin 06-07; AD Elham 00-05; Hon Can Cant Cathl 06-07; rtd 07; Perm to Offic *Cant* 07-08; Hon C Cranbrook from 08; Retirement Officer (Maidstone Adnry) 07-08. *Mill Cottage, Mill Lane, Sissinghurst, Cranbrook TN17 2HX* Tel (01580) 713836 E-mail johnliztapper@tesco.net

TARGETT, Kenneth. b 28. Qu Coll Birm 54. **d** 57 **p** 58. C Mansfield Woodhouse *S'well* 57-59; C Skipton Ch Ch *Bradf* 59-62; V Bradf St Jo 62-65; Perm to Offic 65-82; Australia 82-87; V Old Leake w Wrangle *Linc* 87-94; rtd 94; Perm to Offic *Linc* from 00. *The Sloop, Sea Lane, Old Leake, Boston PE22 9JA* Tel (01205) 871991 E-mail ken@thesloop.fsnet.co.uk

TARLETON, Peter. b 46. TCD BA72 MA80 HDipEd77. TCD Div Sch Div Test 73. **d** 73 **p** 74. C Cork St Luke w St Ann *C, C & R* 73-75; C Dublin Drumcondra *D & G* 75-77; I Limerick City *L & K* 77-82; I Drumgoon w Dernakesh, Ashfield etc *K, E & A* 82-85; Chapl HM YOI Hindley 85-89; Chapl HM Pris Lindholme 89-99; Hon Can Sheff Cathl 98-99; Chapl HM Pris Leeds 99-06; Chapl Lancs Teaching Hosps NHS Trust 08-11; Co-ord Chapl Southport and Ormskirk NHS Trust from 11. *Southport and Formby District General Hospital, Town Lane, Southport PR8 6PN* Tel (01704) 547471 E-mail peter.tarleton@hotmail.co.uk

TARLING, Matthew Paul. b 79. Nottm Univ MEng03. Oak Hill Th Coll BA09. **d** 09 **p** 10. C Blaydon and Swalwell *Dur* from 09. *21 Park Terrace, Dunston, Gateshead NE11 9PA* Tel 0191-460 6706 Mobile 07714-212374 E-mail mattandkatetarling@blueyonder.co.uk

TARLING, Preb Paul. b 53. Oak Hill Th Coll BA. **d** 85 **p** 86. C Old Hill H Trin *Worc* 85-89; V Walford w Bishopswood *Heref* 89-90; P-in-c Goodrich w Welsh Bicknor and Marstow 89-90; R Walford and St John w Bishopswood, Goodrich etc 90-96; RD Ross and Archenfield 95-96; P-in-c Kington w Huntington, Old Radnor, Kinnerton etc 96-00; R 00-08; RD Kington and Weobley 02-07; Preb Heref Cathl 07-08; rtd 08. *1 Alexandra Road, Llandrindod Wells LD1 5LT* E-mail revpt@yahoo.com

TARPER, Miss Ann Jennifer. b 47. SRN71 Nottm Univ BCombStuds82. Linc Th Coll 79. **dss** 83 **d** 87 **p** 96. Stamford All SS w St Jo *Linc* 82-85; Witham *Chelmsf* 85-90; Par Dn 87-90; Min and Educn Adv to Newmarch Gp Min *Heref* 90-93; Perm to Offic 93-95; Dep Chapl HM Pris Dur 95-97; Chapl HM Pris Foston Hall 97-00; Perm to Offic *Lich* 97-02; C W End *Win* 02-05; V Slade Green Roch from 05. *St Augustine's Vicarage, Slade Green Road, Erith DA8 2HX* Tel (01322) 332669 *or* 346258

TARR, James Robert. b 39. Bps' Coll Cheshunt 64. **d** 67 **p** 68. C Wortley de Leeds *Ripon* 67-69; C Hunslet St Mary and Stourton St Andr 70-73; V Moorends *Sheff* 73-77; V Cross Stone *Wakef* 77-83; V Chilworth w N Baddesley *Win* 83-90; V Andover St Mich 90-93; V Andover w Foxcott 93-02; Chapl Mojácar *Eur* 00-02; rtd 02. *Les Courades, 16350 Le Vieux-Cerier, France* Tel (0033) 5 45 30 00 39

TARRAN, Mrs Susan Ann. b 63. CPFA92. ERMC 08. **d** 11. NSM Bishop's Stortford *St Alb* from 11. *47 Church Manor, Bishop's Stortford CM23 5AF* Tel 07970-952228 (mobile) E-mail su.tarran@ntlworld.com

TARRANT, Canon Ian Denis. b 57. G&C Coll Cam BA MA. St Jo Coll Nottm 81. **d** 84 **p** 85. C Ealing St Mary *Lon* 84-87;

CMS Republic of Congo 88-98; Can Boga from 97; Sen Angl Chapl Nottm Univ 98-09; R Woodford St Mary w St Phil and St Jas *Chelmsf* from 09. *The Rectory, 8 Chelmsford Road, London E18 2PL* Tel (020) 8504 7981
E-mail rector@stmaryswoodford.org.uk

TARRANT, John Michael. b 38. St Jo Coll Cam BA59 MA63 Ball Coll Ox BA62 MA76. Ripon Hall Ox 60. **d** 62 **p** 63. C Chelsea All SS *Lon* 62-65; Chapl and Lect St Pet Coll Saltley 66-70; Belize 70-74; V Forest Row *Chich* 75-87; Perm to Offic *Heref* 93-99; NSM Ross 99-00; P-in-c Guilsborough w Hollowell and Cold Ashby *Pet* 00-08; Jt P-in-c Cottesbrooke w Gt Creaton and Thornby 00-08; P-in-c Ravensthorpe 03-08; P-in-c Spratton 07-08; rtd 08. *16 Windsor Road, Salisbury SP2 7DX* Tel (01722) 340058

TARREN, Eileen. b 46. Cranmer Hall Dur. **d** 02 **p** 03. NSM Shadforth and Sherburn *Dur* from 02. *St Mary's Vicarage, 89 Front Street, Sherburn Village, Durham DH6 1HD*

TARRIS, Canon Geoffrey John. b 27. Em Coll Cam BA50 MA55. Westcott Ho Cam 51. **d** 53 **p** 54. C Abbots Langley *St Alb* 53-55; Prec St E Cathl 55-59; V Bungay H Trin w St Mary 59-72; RD S Elmham 65-72; V Ipswich St Mary le Tower 72-78; V Ipswich St Mary le Tower w St Lawr and St Steph 78-82; Hon Can St E Cathl 74-82; Can Res 82-93; Dioc Dir of Lay Min and Warden of Readers 82-87; Dioc Dir of Ords 87-93; rtd 93; Perm to Offic *Nor* and *St E* from 93; Hon PV Nor Cathl from 94. *53 The Close, Norwich NR1 4EG* Tel (01603) 622136

TARRIS, Philip Geoffrey. Univ of Wales (Swansea) BSc76 Lon Univ MSc78. ERMC. **d** 10 **p** 11. NSM Gt Dunmow and Barnston *Chelmsf* from 10. *1 Hydes Gate Cottages, Thaxted, Dunmow CM6 3QB* Tel (01799) 586570

TARRY, Canon Gordon Malcolm. b 54. Leeds Univ BSc75 Lon Bible Coll BA83. Ridley Hall Cam. **d** 85 **p** 86. C Gt Ilford St Andr *Chelmsf* 85-89; C Rainham 89-92; C Rainham w Wennington 92-93; V Gt Ilford St Jo 93-06; RD Redbridge 01-06; TR Barking St Marg w St Patr from 06; Hon Can Chelmsf Cathl from 05. *20 Sandringham Road, Barking IG11 9AB* Tel (020) 8594 4513
E-mail gordontarry@yahoo.co.uk

TASH, Stephen Ronald. b 56. Warw Univ BEd79. WMMTC 88. **d** 91 **p** 92. C Studley *Cov* 91-95; P-in-c Salford Priors 95-09; Dioc Youth Officer 95-00; P-in-c Temple Grafton w Binton 00-09; P-in-c Exhall w Wixford 03-09; V Fulford *York* 09-11; rtd 11. *2 Little Pittern, Kineton, Warwick CV35 0LU* Tel (01926) 641211 E-mail stevetash@aol.com

TASKER, Harry Beverley. b 41. BA76. Wycliffe Hall Ox 64. **d** 67 **p** 68. C Withington St Paul *Man* 67-71; C Bingley All SS *Bradf* 71-72; Chapl RAF 72-76; R Publow w Pensford, Compton Dando and Chelwood *B & W* 76-84; V Long Ashton 84-04; RD Portishead 86-91; rtd 04. *The Malthouse, Manor Court, Manor Lane, Ettington, Stratford-upon-Avon CV37 7TW* Tel (01789) 748290

TASSELL, Mrs Stella Venetia. b 39. RGN60 RNT63 RMN66 RHV72. Guildf Dioc Min Course 91. **d** 01 **p** 02. OLM Woodham *Guildf* 01-09. *72 Sandy Lane, Woking GU2 8BH* Tel (01483) 762944 Mobile 07790-521567
E-mail stella.tassell@btinternet.com

TATE, David. b 44. Open Univ BA78 CIPFA70. **d** 02 **p** 03. OLM N w S Wootton *Nor* from 02. *36 The Birches, South Wootton, King's Lynn PE30 3JG* Tel (01553) 672474
E-mail revdavidtate@talktalk.net

TATE, Denis Steven. b 53. Lanc Univ MA76. LCTP 09. **d** 11. NSM Ellel w Shireshead *Blackb* from 11. *13 Meadowside, Lancaster LA1 3AQ* E-mail tated@ripley.lancs.sch.uk

TATE, Mrs Harriet Jane. b 62. Hull Univ BA84. **d** 02 **p** 03. OLM Heatons *Man* 02-10; Lic Preacher from 10. *70 Winchester Drive, Stockport SK4 2NU* Tel 0161-431 7051
E-mail harriettate@supanet.com

TATE, James. b 56. Oak Hill Th Coll 93. **d** 95 **p** 96. C Hammersmith St Simon *Lon* 95-98; C N Hammersmith St Kath 98-99; P-in-c from 99. *St Katherine's Vicarage, Primula Street, London W12 0RF* Tel (020) 8746 2213 *or* 8743 3951
E-mail jim@stkats.wanadoo.co.uk

TATE, John Robert. b 38. Dur Univ BA61 MA71. Cranmer Hall Dur. **d** 70 **p** 71. C Bare *Blackb* 70-73; V Over Darwen St Jas 73-81; V Caton w Littledale 81-98; rtd 98; Perm to Offic *Blackb* from 98. *19 Clifton Drive, Morecambe LA4 6SR* Tel (01524) 832840

TATE, Pauline Marilyn. b 42. Westcott Ho Cam 05. **d** 07 **p** 08. NSM Gt w Lt Addington and Woodford *Pet* from 07; NSM Irthlingborough from 11. *2 Manor Close, Great Addington, Kettering NN14 4BU* Tel (01536) 330740 Mobile 07803-455700
E-mail pmtate@hotmail.com

TATE, Robert John Ward. b 24. St Jo Coll Morpeth ThL48. **d** 49 **p** 50. Australia from 49; Chapl RN 53-79; QHC 76-79; rtd 79. *58 Skye Point Road, Carey Bay NSW 2283, Australia* Tel (0061) (2) 4959 2921

TATHAM, Andrew Francis. b 49. Grey Coll Dur BA71 K Coll Lon PhD84 AKC88 FBCartS96. S'wark Ord Course 87. **d** 92 **p** 93. NSM Headley w Box Hill *Guildf* 92-02; TV Ilminster and

---

Distr *B & W* 02-10; V Isle Valley from 10; RD Crewkerne and Ilminster from 07. *The Rectory, Broadway, Ilminster TA19 9RF* Tel (01460) 52559 E-mail aftatham@ukonline.co.uk

TATTERSALL, John Hartley. b 52. Ch Coll Cam BA73 MA76 FCA89. SEITE 04. **d** 07 **p** 08. NSM Wykeham *Ox* from 07. *Abingdon House, Park Lane, Swalcliffe, Banbury OX15 5EU* Tel (01295) 780283 Mobile 07711-733978
E-mail jhtatters@aol.com

TATTON-BROWN, Simon Charles. b 48. Qu Coll Cam BA70 MA78 Man Univ CQSW72. Coll of Resurr Mirfield 78. **d** 79 **p** 80. C Ashton St Mich *Man* 79-82; P-in-c Prestwich St Gabr 82-87; V 87-88; Bp's Dom Chapl 82-88; TR Westhoughton 88-96; TR Westhoughton and Wingates 97-00; V Chippenham St Andr w Tytherton Lucas *Bris* from 00; RD Chippenham 03-06. *The Vicarage, 54A St Mary Street, Chippenham SN15 3JW* Tel (01249) 656834 E-mail stbrown@ukip.co.uk

TATTUM, Ian Stuart. b 58. N Lon Poly BA79 Fitzw Coll Cam BA89. Westcott Ho Cam 87. **d** 90 **p** 91. C Beaconsfield *Ox* 90-94; C Bushey *St Alb* 94-96; P-in-c Pirton 96-01; P-in-c St Ippolyts 00-06; P-in-c Gt and Lt Wymondley 01-06; P-in-c Southfields St Barn *S'wark* 06-11; V from 11. *St Barnabas' Vicarage, 146A Lavenham Road, London SW18 5EP* Tel (020) 8480 2290
E-mail iantattum@gmail.com

TATTUM, Ruth Margaret. See LAMPARD, Ms Ruth Margaret

TAULTY, Mrs Eileen. b 45. **d** 03. OLM Pemberton St Mark Newtown *Liv* 03-07; OLM Marsh Green w Newtown from 08. *38 Alexandra Crescent, Wigan WN5 9JP* Tel (01942) 208021

TAUNTON, Archdeacon of. See REED, The Ven John Peter Cyril

TAUNTON, Suffragan Bishop of. See MAURICE, The Rt Revd Peter David

TAVERNER, Lorraine Dawn. See COLAM, Mrs Lorraine Dawn

TAVERNOR (née LLOYD), Mrs Eileen. b 50. FIBMS74. NOC 88. **d** 91 **p** 94. C Heref St Martin w St Fran 91-95; P-in-c Bucknell w Chapel Lawn, Llanfair Waterdine etc 95-01; V 01-09; rtd 09. *Froglands, Rosemary Lane, Leintwardine, Craven Arms SY7 0LP* Tel (01547) 540365

TAVERNOR, James Edward. b 23. Lich Th Coll 41 St D Coll Lamp BA49. **d** 50 **p** 51. C Monmouth 50-52; C Prestbury *Glouc* 52-53; C Newbold w Dunston *Derby* 53-55; C Buxton 67-69; Perm to Offic *Derby* 70-75; *Heref* 75-83; *St D* 83-91; rtd 88. *c/o Mrs E M Akers, 101 Stourport Road, Bewdley DY12 1BJ* Tel (01299) 404104

TAVERNOR, William Noel. b 16. Lich Th Coll 37. **d** 40 **p** 41. C Ledbury *Heref* 40-43; C Kidderminster St Mary *Worc* 43-46; V Bettws-y-Crwyn w Newcastle *Heref* 46-50; V Upton Bishop 50-57; V Aymestrey and Leinthall Earles 57-65; P-in-c Shobdon 58-65; V Canon Pyon w Kings Pyon and Birley 65-88; rtd 88; Perm to Offic *Heref* from 97. *Vine Cottage, Kingsland, Leominster HR6 9QS* Tel (01568) 708817

TAVINOR, The Very Revd Michael Edward. b 53. Univ Coll Dur BA75 Em Coll Cam CertEd76 K Coll Lon MMus77 AKC77 ARCO77 Univ of Wales (Lamp) MTh10. Ripon Coll Cuddesdon BA81 MA86. **d** 82 **p** 83. C Ealing St Pet Mt Park *Lon* 82-85; Min Can, Prec and Sacr Ely Cathl 85-90; P-in-c Stuntney 87-90; V Tewkesbury w Walton Cardiff *Glouc* 90-99; P-in-c Twyning 98-99; V Tewkesbury w Walton Cardiff and Twyning 99-02; Hon Can Glouc Cathl 97-02; Dean Heref from 02. *The Deanery, Cathedral Close, Hereford HR1 2NG* Tel (01432) 374203 Fax 374220
E-mail dean@herefordcathedral.org

TAWN, Andrew Richard. b 61. Trin Coll Cam BA83 Ox Univ BA88. Ripon Coll Cuddesdon 86. **d** 89 **p** 90. C Dovecot *Liv* 89-93; TV Dorchester *Ox* 93-98; Student Supervisor Cuddesdon Coll 93-98; R Addingham *Bradf* from 98. *The Rectory, Low Mill Lane, Addingham, Ilkley LS29 0QP* Tel and fax (01943) 830276
E-mail saintpeter@addinghamrectory.fsnet.co.uk

TAYLER, Raymond James. b 38. K Alfred's Coll Win TCert74 SWMTC 98. **d** 01 **p** 02. NSM Málaga *Eur* 01-07. *Casa Palomero, Oficina de Correos, 29714 Salares (Málaga), Spain* Tel (0034) 952 030 461 E-mail rjtayler@yahoo.co.uk

TAYLEUR, Mrs Gillian Sarah. b 61. Bedf Coll Lon BSc82. OLM course 05. **d** 08 **p** 09. NSM Herne Hill *S'wark* from 08. *27 Finsen Road, London SE5 9AX* Tel (020) 7737 1991
E-mail gill@hernehillparish.org

TAYLOR, Alan Clive. b 48. Southn Univ BTh79. Sarum Th Coll 69. **d** 74 **p** 75. C Watford St Pet *St Alb* 74-78; C Broxbourne w Wormley 78-83; Chapl to the Deaf 83-91; V Shefford 83-91; R Portishead *B & W* 91-02; TR 02-08; rtd 08. *Larkhill, The Green, Dauntsey, Chippenham SN15 4HY*
E-mail padreact@yahoo.co.uk

TAYLOR, Alan Gerald. b 33. Roch Th Coll 61 St Aid Birkenhead 61. **d** 63 **p** 64. C W Bridgford *S'well* 63-66; C E w W Barkwith *Linc* 66-69; V E Stockwith 69-76; V Morton 69-76; Countryside Officer 69-88; R Ulceby w Fordington 76-88; R Willoughby w Sloothby w Claxby 76-88; R Woolpit w Drinkstone *St E* 88-98; Rural Min Adv from 88; rtd 98; Perm to Offic *St E* from 01. *5 Finch Close, Stowmarket IP14 5BQ* Tel (01449) 614078

TAYLOR, Canon Alan Leonard. b 43. Chich Th Coll 67. **d** 69 **p** 70. C Walton St Mary *Liv* 69-73; C Toxteth St Marg 73-75; V

Stanley 75-83; V Leeds St Aid *Ripon* from 84; V Leeds Richmond Hill from 06; Hon Can Ripon Cathl from 97; AD Allerton from 08. *The Vicarage, Elford Place West, Leeds LS8 5QD* Tel and fax 0113-248 6992
E-mail alan.taylor@leeds.gov.uk

TAYLOR, Mrs Alison Isabella. b 76. d 10 p 11. C Sparkhill St Jo *Birm* from 10. *132 Oakwood Road, Sparkhill, Birmingham B11 4HD* Tel 0121-247 9428
E-mail tayloriali@googlemail.com

TAYLOR, Andrew David. b 58. Regent's Park Coll Ox BA81 MA86 Toronto Univ MDiv92 K Coll Lon MTh95. Westcott Ho Cam 85. d 87 p 89. C Leckhampton SS Phil and Jas w Cheltenham St Jas *Glouc* 87-91; P-in-c Swindon w Uckington and Elmstone Hardwicke 92-93; C Highgate St Mich *Lon* 94-97; Chapl R Holloway and Bedf New Coll *Guildf* 97-03; Public Preacher 04; Perm to Offic from 05. *8 Stable Mews, Coworth Park, London Road, Sunninghill, Ascot SL5 7SE* Tel (01344) 870319

TAYLOR, Ann. *See* TAYLOR, Margaret Ann

TAYLOR, Ms Anne Elizabeth. b 68. Ulster Univ BSc91 MA99. CITC BTh94. d 94 p 95. C Dublin Rathfarnham *D & G* from 94; Chapl Adelaide and Meath Hosp Dublin 01-03; Abp's Dom Chapl *D & G* from 03; Children's Min Officer Sunday Sch Soc of Ireland from 05. *The Rectory, 41 Rathfarnham Road, Terenure, Dublin 6W, Republic of Ireland* Tel and fax (00353) (1) 490 5543
E-mail sundayschoolsociety@ireland.anglican.org

TAYLOR, Arthur Alfred. b 32. Univ Coll Ox MA56. Ox NSM Course 80. d 83 p 84. NSM Monks Risborough *Ox* 83-96; NSM Aylesbury Deanery from 96, *9 Place Farm Way, Monks Risborough, Princes Risborough HP27 9JJ* Tel (01844) 347197

TAYLOR, Miss Averil Mary. b 36. Sarum Dioc Tr Coll TCert56 Westmr Coll Ox TCert (Mus) 66. WEMTC 99. d 00 p 01. OLM Longden and Annscroft w Pulverbatch *Heref* 00-08. *Sheaves, Lyth Bank, Lyth Hill, Shrewsbury SY3 0BE* Tel and fax (01743) 872071

TAYLOR, Avril Fiona. b 58. NEOC 02. d 05 p 06. NSM Byker St Silas *Newc* from 05. *20 Percy Gardens, Gateshead NE11 9RY* Tel 0191-420 7983 E-mail avriltaylor@blueyonder.co.uk

TAYLOR, Bernard Richmond Hartley. b 30. Reading Univ MEd. S Dios Minl Tr Scheme 82. d 85 p 86. NSM Englefield Green *Guildf* 85-90; NSM Lyddington w Stoke Dry and Seaton *Pet* 90-95; rtd 95; Perm to Offic *Guildf* from 96. *Middleton House, 40 Bond Street, Egham TW20 0PY* Tel (01784) 435886

TAYLOR, Brian. b 38. Bris Univ BA60 Liv Univ BA70 Southn Univ MA90. Ridley Hall Cam 60. d 66 p 66. Chapl Victoria Coll Ondo Nigeria 66-72; Perm to Offic *Derby* 74-78; Chapl Newbury Coll 76-94; P-in-c Shaw cum Donnington *Ox* 89-90; R 90-08; rtd 08; Perm to Offic *Ox* from 08. *39 Chaucer Crescent, Speen, Newbury RG14 1TP* Tel 07925-126761 (mobile)
E-mail brian_harker_taylor@yahoo.co.uk

TAYLOR, Brian. b 42. St Deiniol's Hawarden 78. d 80 p 81. C Mold *St As* 80-84; V Bagillt 84-08; rtd 08. *13 Bryn Awel, Pentre Halkyn, Holywell CH8 8JB* Tel (01352) 780744 Mobile 07803-305956 E-mail brian@prayers.freeserve.co.uk

TAYLOR, Brian. b 61. St Mich Coll Llan 91. d 94 p 95. C Aberdare *Llan* 94-97; V Cwmparc 97-07; V Pen Rhondda Fawr from 07. *The Vicarage, Vicarage Terrace, Cwmparc, Treorchy CF42 6NA* Tel (01443) 773303 E-mail frbtaylor@talktalk.net

TAYLOR, Brian John Chatterton. b 30. Trin Hall Cam BA53 Kent Univ MA57 Melbourne Univ BEd66 Lon Univ PhD84. Westcott Ho Cam 53. d 55 p 56. C Leigh St Jo *Man* 55-57; C Ashton Ch Ch 57-58; Australia from 58; Miss to Seamen 58-60; Vic State High Schs 60-71; Sen Lect Toorak Teachers' Coll 72-80; Prin Lect Inst of Cath Educn 80-88; Co-ord RE Tintern Angl Girls' Gr Sch 89-93; Supernumerary Asst Redhill St Geo from 90. *21 One Chain Road, Merricks North Vic 3926, Australia* Tel and fax (0061) (3) 5989 7564 Mobile 408-250630
E-mail sumptonv@surf.net

TAYLOR, Charles Derek. b 36. Trin Hall Cam BA59 MA62. Ripon Hall Ox 59. d 61 p 62. C Nottingham All SS *S'well* 61-64; C Binley *Cov* 64-67; C Stoke 67-70; R Purley *Ox* 70-74; V Milton B & W 74-93; RD Locking 86-87 and 90-93; V Wells St Cuth w Wookey Hole 93-98; rtd 98; Perm to Offic *Roch* from 00. *5 Banner Farm Road, Tunbridge Wells TN2 5EA* Tel (01892) 526825

TAYLOR, The Very Revd Charles William. b 53. Selw Coll Cam BA74 MA78. Cuddesdon Coll 74. d 76 p 77. C Wolverhampton *Lich* 76-79; Chapl Westmr Abbey 79-84; V Stanmore *Win* 84-90; R N Stoneham 90-95; Can Res and Prec Lich Cathl 95-07; Dean Pet from 07. *The Deanery, Minster Precincts, Peterborough PE1 1XS* Tel (01733) 562780 Fax 897874
E-mail deanpetoffice@aol.com

TAYLOR, Christopher Drewett. b 58. Qu Coll Birm 06. d 09 p 10. C Shepshed and Oaks in Charnwood *Leic* from 09. *12 Smithy Way, Shepshed, Loughborough LE12 9TQ* Tel (01509) 556014 Mobile 07946-763257 E-mail christaylor36beacon@msn.com

TAYLOR, Christopher Vincent. b 47. Cranmer Hall Dur 94. d 96 p 97. C Kendal St Geo *Carl* 96-99; TV Wheatley *Ox* 99-03; TV

Leeds City *Ripon* 03-06; rtd 06; Hon C Beacon *Carl* from 08. *78 Windermere Road, Kendal LA9 5EZ* Tel (01539) 727424

TAYLOR, Colin John. b 66. Witwatersrand Univ BCom87 BTh94. Wycliffe Hall Ox MTh97. d 97 p 98. C Denton Holme *Carl* 97-01; Bp's Dom Chapl 01-06; Dir CME 1-4 00-06; V Felsted and Lt Dunmow *Chelmsf* from 06. *The Vicarage, Bury Chase, Felsted, Dunmow CM6 3DQ* Tel (01371) 820242
E-mail vicar.felsted@btinternet.com

TAYLOR, Canon David. b 53. St Jo Coll Dur BA74 PGCE75 Liv Univ MTh04. Sarum & Wells Th Coll 91. d 93 p 94. C Cheadle Hulme All SS *Ches* 93-97; V Macclesfield St Jo 97-05; RD Macclesfield 03-05; TR Congleton from 05; RD Congleton from 08; Hon Can Ches Cathl from 09. *2 Hartley Gardens, Congleton CW12 3WA* Tel (01260) 273182
E-mail revddtaylor@hotmail.com

TAYLOR, David Christopher Morgan. b 56. Leeds Univ BSc77 Univ Coll Lon PhD80 Univ Coll Ches MEd96 SOSc MIBiol. NOC 91. d 94 p 95. Tutor Liv Univ from 86; NSM Waterloo Ch and St Mary 94-99; P-in-c Altcar 98-00; NSM Altcar and Hightown from 03. *20 Liverpool Road, Formby, Liverpool L37 4BW* Tel (01704) 873304 Fax 0151-794 5337
E-mail dcmt@liverpool.ac.uk *or* taylordcm@aol.com

TAYLOR, Derek. *See* TAYLOR, Charles Derek

TAYLOR, The Very Revd Derek John. b 31. Univ of Wales (Lamp) BA52 Fitzw Ho Cam BA54 MA58 Ex Univ CertEd70. St Mich Coll Llan 54. d 55 p 56. C Newport St Paul *Mon* 55-57; CF (TA) 57-59 and 62-64; CF 59-62; V Bettws *Mon* 62-64; V Exminster 64-70; Hd of RE Heathcote Sch Tiverton 70-71; W Germany 71-75; Chapl R Russell Sch Croydon 75-79; Chapl St Andr Sch Croydon 79-84, P-in-c Croydon St Andr *Cant* 79-81; V 81-84; Chapl Bromsgrove Sch 84-89; Provost St Chris Cathl Bahrain 90-97; Hon Chapl Miss to Seamen 90-97; NSM Droitwich Spa *Worc* 97-99; Asst P Finstall 99-00; P-in-c Milngavie *Glas* 00-03; Perm to Offic *Worc* from 04. *19 Warwick Hall Gardens, Bromsgrove B60 2AU* Tel and fax (01527) 872144 Mobile 07904-205669 E-mail dervaltaylor@talktalk.net

TAYLOR, Donald Alastair. b 26. Lon Univ BD Linc Coll Ox DPhil77. St Paul's Coll Mauritius. d 65 p 65. C Ware St Mary *St Alb* 65-66; Seychelles 66-78; SSJE from 68; Lect RS Middx Poly *Lon* 78-92. *74 Woodcote Road, Caversham, Reading RG4 7EX* Tel and fax 0118-946 3965
E-mail da.taylor3@ntlworld.com

TAYLOR, Edward Frank. b 23. Lon Univ BSc44. Chich Th Coll 50. d 52 p 53. C Manston *Ripon* 52-55; Chapl Chich Th Coll 55-59; PV Chich Cathl 57-59; C Ifield 59-63; V Hangleton 63-73; V Wivelsfield 73-88; rtd 88; Perm to Offic *Bradf* 88-00. *8 Linkway, Westham, Pevensey BN24 5JB*

TAYLOR, Elizabeth. *See* TAYLOR, Mrs Mary Elizabeth

TAYLOR, Garry Kenneth. b 53. Edin Univ BMus75 Southn Univ BTh81 Ch Ch Coll Cant PGCE95. Sarum & Wells Th Coll 76. d 79 p 80. C Southsea H Spirit *Portsm* 79-82; C Croydon St Jo *Cant* 82-84; C Croydon St Jo *S'wark* 85-86; V Choral S'well Minster 86-90; V Portsea St Alb *Portsm* 90-94; NSM Hamble le Rice *Win* 96-97; P-in-c Southampton St Jude 97-04; V Highcliffe w Hinton Admiral 04-09; V Highcliffe from 09. *The Vicarage, 33 Nea Road, Christchurch BH23 4NB* Tel (01425) 272761
E-mail garrykt@aol.com

TAYLOR, George James Trueman. b 36. Ripon Hall Ox 66. d 69 p 70. C Wavertree H Trin *Liv* 69-73; V Newton-le-Willows 73-79; V Stoneycroft All SS 79-83; V Haigh 83-04; Jt P-in-c Aspull and New Springs 02-03; rtd 04. *228 Wigan Road, Aspull, Wigan WN2 1DU* Tel (01942) 830430

TAYLOR, Canon Godfrey Alan. b 36. Oak Hill Th Coll. d 61 p 62. C Herne Bay Ch Ch *Cant* 61-64; C Tunbridge Wells St Jas *Roch* 64-68; V Guernsey H Trin *Win* 68-81; V Boscombe St Jo 81-03; Hon Can Win Cathl 96-03; AD Bournemouth 99-03; rtd 03; Perm to Offic *Truro* from 05. *Bosnoweth Vean, 21 Cullen View, Probus, Truro TR2 4NY* Tel (01726) 884493
E-mail canongmort@btinternet.com

TAYLOR, Canon Gordon. b 46. AKC68. St Aug Coll Cant 69. d 70 p 71. C Rotherham *Sheff* 70-74; P-in-c Brightside St Thos 74-79; P-in-c Brightside St Marg 77-79; V Brightside St Thos and St Marg 79-82; R Kirk Sandall and Edenthorpe 82-91; V Beighton 91-96; V Goole 96-03; AD Snaith and Hatfield 98-03; V Tickhill w Stainton 03-11; Hon Can Sheff Cathl 93-11; rtd 11. *96 Whitton Close, Doncaster DN4 7RD* Tel (01302) 533249
E-mail gordon.taylor89@btinternet.com

TAYLOR, Canon Graham Smith. b 70. TISEC 98. d 01 p 02. C Ellon, Cruden Bay and Peterhead *Ab* 01-04; P-in-c 04-06; R Aberdeen St Mary from 06; Dioc Dir Ords from 06; Can St Andr Cathl from 08. *St Mary's Rectory, 28 Stanley Street, Aberdeen AB10 6UR* Tel (01224) 584123 Mobile 07773-482174
E-mail revgraham@tiscali.co.uk

TAYLOR, Hugh Nigel James. b 43. MCMI FInstD. NTMTC 04. d 06 p 07. NSM Loughton St Mary *Chelmsf* from 06. *4 Twentyman Close, Woodford Green IG8 0EW* Tel and fax (020) 8504 8901 Mobile 07770-365255
E-mail hughnj@btinternet.com

✠**TAYLOR, The Rt Revd Humphrey Vincent.** b 38. Pemb Coll Cam BA61 MA66 Lon Univ MA70. Coll of Resurr Mirfield 61. **d** 63 **p** 64 **c** 91. C N Hammersmith St Kath *Lon* 63-64; C Notting Hill St Mark 64-66; USPG 67-71; Malawi 67-71; Chapl Bp Grosseteste Coll Linc 72-74; Sec Chapls in HE Gen Syn Bd of Educn 75-80; Gen Sec USPG 80-91; Sec Miss Progr 80-84; Hon Can Bris Cathl 86-91; Lic to Offic *S'wark* 89-91; Suff Bp Selby *York* 91-03; rtd 03; Hon Asst Bp *Glouc* and *Worc* from 03. *10 High Street, Honeybourne, Evesham WR11 7PQ* Tel (01386) 834846 E-mail humanne.taylor@virgin.net

TAYLOR, Iain William James. b 41. **d** 03 **p** 04. OLM Cant St Pet w St Alphege and St Marg etc from 03. *30 Deans Mill Court, The Causeway, Canterbury CT1 2BF* Tel (01227) 457711

TAYLOR, Ian. b 53. Saltley Tr Coll Birm CertEd75. **d** 95 **p** 96. OLM Heywood *Man* 95-10; OLM Sudden and Heywood All So from 10. *818A Edenfield Road, Rochdale OL12 7RB* Tel (01706) 355738

TAYLOR, Mrs Jacqueline Margaret. b 56. Trin Coll Bris 02. **d** 04 **p** 05. C Bath St Luke *B & W* 04-08; Chapl Univ Hosps Bris NHS Foundn Trust from 08. *United Bristol Healthcare NHS Trust, Trust Headquarters, Marlborough Street, Bristol BS1 3NU* Tel 0117-923 0000 E-mail wookeyjackie@hotmail.com

TAYLOR, Jamie Alexander Franklyn. b 73. Kent Univ BA95. Westcott Ho Cam. **d** 98 **p** 99. C Walton-on-Thames *Guildf* 98-02; C St Peter-in-Thanet *Cant* 02-08; Chapl E Kent NHS and Soc Care Partnership Trust 03-06; Chapl Kent & Medway NHS and Soc Care Partnership Trust 06-08; V Sonning *Ox* from 08. *The Vicarage, Thames Street, Sonning, Reading RG4 6UR* Tel 0118-969 3298 E-mail revjaft@yahoo.co.uk

TAYLOR, Jan William Karel. b 59. QUB BD82 MSocSc89. CITC. **d** 84 **p** 85. C Belfast St Simon w St Phil *Conn* 84-87; I Belfast St Paul 87-92; Chapl RAF from 92; Perm to Offic *Ban* from 97. *Chaplaincy Services, Valiant Block, HQ Air Command, RAF High Wycombe HP14 4UE* Tel (01494) 496800 Fax 496343

TAYLOR, Jane Suzanne. b 54. Ex Univ BA73. SEITE 96. **d** 99 **p** 00. NSM Knaphill w Brookwood *Guildf* 99-00; C Frimley Green and Mytchett 00-04; Perm to Offic *Ex* from 04. *Rocknell Manor Farm, Westleigh, Tiverton EX16 7ES* Tel (01884) 829000 E-mail janetaylor@millhouseretreats.co.uk

TAYLOR (*née* **MAYOR), Mrs Janet Hilary.** b 55. St Martin's Coll Lanc BA96 Open Univ PGCE98. LCTP 10. **d** 11. NSM Chorley St Laur *Blackb* from 11. *Woodlands, Highfield Road, Croston, Leyland PR26 9HH* Tel (01772) 603155 E-mail janet55@hotmail.co.uk

TAYLOR, Jason Victor. b 71. Lon Bible Coll BTh01 St Jo Coll Dur MA03. Cranmer Hall Dur 01. **d** 03 **p** 04. C Ripley *Derby* 03-07; TV Drypool *York* from 07; Chapl Abp Sentamu Academy Hull from 09. *Archbishop Sentamu Academy, Hopewell Road, Kingston-upon-Hull HU9 4HD* Tel (01482) 781912 Mobile 07825-408351 E-mail revjasontaylor@gmail.com

TAYLOR, Miss Jean. b 37. Nottm Univ TCert58. St Andr Coll Pampisford 62. **dss** 68 **d** 00 **p** 01. CSA 62-79; E Crompton *Man* 79-97; Chadderton St Luke 97-04; OLM 00-04; OLM Chadderton St Matt w St Luke 04-05; Warden Jes Hosp Cant 05-08; Perm to Offic *Cant* from 05. *7 Chantry Court, St Radigund's Street, Canterbury CT1 2AD* Tel (01227) 761652

TAYLOR, Mrs Jennifer Anne. b 53. Sussex Univ BEd75 Surrey Univ BA01 Win Univ MA09. STETS 98. **d** 01 **p** 02. Chapl Salisbury Cathl Sch from 01; NSM Salisbury St Thos and St Edm *Sarum* 01-09; TV Chalke Valley from 09. *27 Viking Way, Salisbury SP2 8TA* Tel and fax (01722) 503081 E-mail geoffrey.taylor5@ntlworld.com

TAYLOR, Sister Jennifer Mary. b 41. CA Tr Coll IDC65. **dss** 77 **d** 87 **p** 07. CA from 65; Chapl Asst HM Pris Holloway 75-79; Ho Mistress Ch Hosp Sch Hertf 78-79; Chapl Asst RAChD 80-90; Germany 90-96; rtd 96; Perm to Offic *Eur* from 96; *Nor* 06-07 and from 11; Hon C Dereham and Distr *Nor* 07-11. *4 Eckling Grange, Norwich Road, Dereham NR20 3BB* Tel (01362) 692547

TAYLOR, Jeremy Christopher. b 75. Birm Univ BA97. Oak Hill Th Coll BA07. **d** 07 **p** 08. C Chell *Lich* 07-10; P-in-c Enderby w Lubbesthorpe and Thurlaston *Leic* from 10. *The Rectory, 16A Desford Road, Leicester LE9 7TE* Tel (01455) 888679 Mobile 07787-514058 E-mail juneandjerry@btinternet.com

TAYLOR, Joanna Beatrice. See NEARY, Mrs Joanna Beatrice

TAYLOR, John. b 58. Aston Tr Scheme 94 Ripon Coll Cuddesdon 96. **d** 98 **p** 99. C Southport Em *Liv* 98-03; V Hindley All SS 03-09; R Yanchep Australia from 09. *Address temp unknown* E-mail johntaylor@supanet.com

TAYLOR, John Alexander. b 54. S Dios Minl Tr Scheme 89. **d** 92 **p** 93. NSM Abbotts Ann and Upper and Goodworth Clatford *Win* 92-99; Perm to Offic 99-00; NSM Hatherden w Tangley, Weyhill and Penton Mewsey 00-02; NSM W Andover 02-09; NSM Portway and Danebury from 09. *256 Weyhill Road, Andover SP10 3LR* Tel (01264) 359160 E-mail john@w256.fsnet.co.uk

TAYLOR, Canon John Andrew. b 53. Linc Th Coll 86. **d** 88 **p** 89. C Stanley *Liv* 88-91; V Wigan St Jas w St Thos 91-04; AD Wigan W 99-04; Hon Can Liv Cathl 03-04; V Prescot from 04; AD

Huyton from 06; Hon Can Liv Cathl from 07. *The Vicarage, Vicarage Place, Prescot L34 1LA* Tel 0151-426 6719

✠**TAYLOR, The Rt Revd John Bernard.** b 29. KCVO97. Ch Coll Cam BA50 MA54 Jes Coll Cam 52 Hebrew Univ Jerusalem 54. Ridley Hall Cam 55. **d** 56 **p** 57 **c** 80. C Morden *S'wark* 56-59; V Henham *Chelmsf* 59-64; V Elsenham 59-64; Sen Tutor Oak Hill Th Coll 64-65; Vice-Prin 65-72; V Woodford Wells *Chelmsf* 72-75; Dioc Dir of Ords 72-80; Adn W Ham 75-80; Bp St Alb 80-95; High Almoner 88-97; rtd 95; Hon Asst Bp Ely from 95; Hon Asst Bp Eur from 98. *22 Conduit Head Road, Cambridge CB3 0EY* Tel (01223) 313783 E-mail john.taylor6529@ntlworld.com

TAYLOR, Canon John Michael. b 30. St Aid Birkenhead 56. **d** 59 **p** 60. C Chorley St Jas *Blackb* 59-62; C Broughton 62-64; Chapl St Boniface Coll Warminster 64-68; V Altham w Clayton le Moors *Blackb* 68-76; RD Accrington 71-76; Can Res Blackb Cathl 76-96; Tutor CBDTI 88-96; rtd 96; Perm to Offic *Blackb* 96-11. *8 Fosbrooke House, Clifton Drive, Lytham St Annes FY8 5RQ*

✠**TAYLOR, The Rt Revd John Mitchell.** b 32. Aber Univ MA54. Edin Th Coll 54. **d** 56 **p** 57 **c** 91. C Aberdeen St Marg 56-58; R Glas H Cross 58-64; R Glas St Ninian 64-73; R Dumfries and Chapl Dumfries and Galloway R Infirmary 73-91; Can St Mary's Cathl 79-91; Bp Glas 91-98; rtd 98; Hon Asst Bp Glas from 99. *10 St Georges, Castle Douglas DG7 1LN* Tel and fax (01556) 502593

TAYLOR, John Porter. b 48. Ex Univ BA71 MA76. Cranmer Hall Dur 93. **d** 93 **p** 94. C Ossett cum Gawthorpe *Wakef* 93-96; R Crofton 96-02; Chapl Mid Yorks Hosps NHS Trust 03-06; Chapl Oakham Sch from 06. *69 Station Road, Oakham LE15 6QT* Tel (01572) 720665 E-mail jpt@oakham.rutland.sch.uk

TAYLOR, John Ralph. b 48. St Jo Coll Nottm BTh74. **d** 74 **p** 75. C Clitheroe St Jas *Blackb* 74-77; C Kidsgrove *Lich* 77-79; C Hawkwell *Chelmsf* 79-82; V Linc St Geo Swallowbeck 82-92; rtd 92. *16 Rosedale Close, Cherry Willingham, Lincoln LN3 4RE*

TAYLOR, Canon John Rowland. b 29. OBE74. St Mich Coll Llan 57. **d** 58 **p** 59. C Caerau St Cynfelin *Llan* 58-59; C Aberdare 59-61; Chapl Miss to Seamen 61-88; Dar-es-Salaam Tanzania 61-73; Adn Dar-es-Salaam 65-73; V-Gen 67-73; Hon Can Dar-es-Salaam from 73; V Bangkok Ch Ch Thailand 73-84; Chapl Rotterdam w Schiedam *Eur* 84-88; V Warnham *Chich* 88-98; rtd 98; Perm to Offic *Chich* 98-00; P-in-c Streat w Westmeston 00-07. *The Rectory, Streat Lane, Streat, Hassocks BN6 8RX* Tel (01273) 890607

TAYLOR, Jonathan Paul. b 74. Birm Univ BEng97 Birm Chr Coll BA05. Trin Coll Bris 07. **d** 11. C Coventry Caludon from 11. *9 Hulme Close, Coventry CV3 2XN* E-mail jonandsu@gmail.com

TAYLOR, Joseph Robin Christopher. b 34. St Aid Birkenhead 58. **d** 61 **p** 62. C Aldershot St Mich *Guildf* 61-64; C Fleet 64-68; R Manaton *Ex* 69-74; R N Bovey 69-74; V Dawlish 74-87; P-in-c Christow, Ashton, Trusham and Bridford 87-88; R 88-95; Perm to Offic *Ex* 95-98; *St E* from 98; rtd 99. *24 Edwin Panks Road, Hadleigh, Ipswich IP7 5JL* Tel (01473) 824262

TAYLOR, Julia Mary. b 73. Reading Univ LLB94. Ridley Hall Cam 06. **d** 08 **p** 09. C Penkridge *Lich* from 08. *31 Nursery Drive, Penkridge ST19 5SJ* Tel 07990-976859 (mobile) E-mail jules.m.taylor@googlemail.com

TAYLOR, Kane Matthew. b 70. Open Univ BSc04. Wycliffe Hall Ox 09. **d** 11. C Kettering St Andr *Pet* from 11. *80 Pollard Street, Kettering NN16 9RP* E-mail kane.taylor@hotmail.co.uk

TAYLOR, Kelvin John. b 53. Portsm Univ CertEd94 BA96. Trin Coll Bris 02. **d** 04 **p** 05. C Overton w Laverstoke and Freefolk *Win* 04-08; V Kempshott from 08. *The Vicarage, 191 Kempshott Lane, Kempshott, Basingstoke RG22 5LF* Tel (01256) 356400

TAYLOR, Kingsley Graham. b 55. Univ of Wales (Cardiff) BD93. St Mich Coll Llan 90. **d** 93 **p** 94. C Llanelli *St D* 93-97; V Whitland w Cyffig and Henllan Amgoed etc from 97. *The Vicarage, North Road, Whitland SA34 0BH* Tel (01994) 240494 E-mail ktaylor559@aol.com

TAYLOR, Luke Alastare John. b 68. Brunel Univ BA97. Oak Hill Th Coll BA00. **d** 00 **p** 01. C Hanworth St Rich *Lon* 00-04; C E Twickenham St Steph 04-10; C Dedworth *Ox* from 10; C Clewer St Andr from 10; C Sunningdale from 11. *11 The Close, Ascot SL5 8EJ* Tel 07939-526361 (mobile) E-mail lukeandgissy@talktalk.net

TAYLOR, Lynda Brigid. Man Univ BA Cam Univ PhD. ERMC. **d** 10 **p** 11. NSM Chesterton St Geo *Ely* from 10. *47 Montague Road, Cambridge CB4 1BU* Tel (01223) 575172 E-mail lynda_and_nigel_taylor@ntlworld.com

TAYLOR, Lyndon John. b 49. St Mich Coll Llan 92. **d** 95 **p** 96. NSM Swansea St Nic *S & B* 95-99; C Llwynderw 99-01; V Waunarllwydd 01-06; V Clydach from 08. *The Vicarage, Woodland Park, Ynystawe, Swansea SA6 5AR* Tel (01792) 843203

TAYLOR, Lynne. b 51. Sheff Univ BMet73 Salford Univ PhD80. Man OLM Scheme 98. **d** 01 **p** 02. OLM Turton Moorland Min *Man* 01-11; rtd 11; Perm to Offic *Man* from 11. *56 Station Road, Turton, Bolton BL7 0HA* Tel (01204) 852551

TAYLOR, Margaret Ann. b 46. **d** 98 **p** 99. OLM Newcastle w Butterton *Lich* from 98. *12 Silverton Close, Bradwell, Newcastle ST5 8LU* Tel (01782) 660174 E-mail revanntaylor@yahoo.co.uk

TAYLOR, Marian Alexandra. b 62. Newc Univ BA85. Qu Coll Birm 89. **d** 91 **p** 96. C Earls Barton *Pet* 91-93; NSM Wellingborough St Barn 95-96; NSM Beaumont Leys *Leic* 96-97; Perm to Offic *Pet* 99-00; NSM Kingsthorpe w Northampton St Dav 00-04; TV 04-09. *75 Kentstone Close, Northampton NN2 8UH* E-mail marian.taylor62@ntlworld.com

TAYLOR, Mark Frederick. b 62. N Ireland Poly BA84. CITC. **d** 87 **p** 88. C Ballymacarrett St Patr *D & D* 87-90; C Dundela St Mark 90-93; I Kilmore and Inch 93-02; I Whitehead and Islandmagee *Conn* from 02. *St Patrick's Rectory, 74 Cable Road, Whitehead, Carrickfergus BT38 9SJ* Tel and fax (028) 9337 3300

TAYLOR, Mark John. b 73. St Andr Univ MTheol99. Coll of Resurr Mirfield 01. **d** 03 **p** 04. C N Meols *Liv* 03-07; TV Sutton from 07. *40 Eaves Lane, St Helens WA9 3UB* E-mail mtaylor@ntlworld.com

TAYLOR, Martyn Andrew Nicholas. b 66. **d** 96 **p** 97. C Stamford St Geo w St Paul *Linc* 96-03; R from 03; P-in-c Stamford Ch Ch from 11. *St George's Rectory, 16 St George's Square, Stamford PE9 2BN* Tel (01780) 757343 *or* 481800 E-mail rector@stgeorgeschurch.net

TAYLOR, Mrs Mary Elizabeth. b 39. **d** 01 **p** 02. OLM Parr *Liv* from 01. *16 Hignett Avenue, St Helens WA9 2PJ* Tel (01744) 21086

TAYLOR, Matthew. b 62. NTMTC. **d** 11. C Rushden St Mary w Newton Bromswold *Pet* from 11. *50 Meadow Sweet Road, Rushden NN10 0GA* Tel (01933) 311164

TAYLOR, Mrs Maureen. b 36. Lon Bible Coll BTh90 MA94. **d** 97 **p** 98. NSM Borehamwood *St Alb* 97-00; NSM Radlett 00-05; Perm to Offic from 06. *57A Loom Lane, Radlett WD7 8NX* Tel (01923) 855197

TAYLOR, Michael. *See* TAYLOR, Canon John Michael

TAYLOR, Michael Alan. b 47. Bris Univ CertEd70 Lon Univ BD85. Trin Coll Bris 72. **d** 76 **p** 77. C Chilwell *S'well* 76-79; Chapl RAF 79-87; New Zealand from 87. *31 Kiteroa Place, Cashmere, Christchurch 8022, New Zealand* Tel (0064) (3) 352 331 8440 E-mail strategic@chch.planet.org.nz

TAYLOR, Michael Allan. b 50. Nottm Univ BTh80. St Jo Coll Nottm 76. **d** 80 **p** 81. C Bowling St Jo *Bradf* 80-82; C Otley 82-85; P-in-c Low Moor St Mark 85-92; P-in-c Bris St Andr w St Bart 92-96. *25 Cornfield Close, Bradley Stoke, Bristol BS32 9DN* Tel (01454) 618677

TAYLOR, Michael Andrew James. b 40. Univ Coll Ches BTh96. **d** 99 **p** 00. NSM Halliwell *Man* 99-11; TV 03-11; NSM W Bolton from 11; TV from 11. *123 Smithills Dean Road, Bolton BL1 6JZ* Tel (01204) 491503

TAYLOR, Michael Barry. b 38. Bps' Coll Cheshunt 63. **d** 65 **p** 66. C Leeds St Cypr Harehills *Ripon* 65-68; C Stanningley St Thos 68-70; V Hunslet Moor St Pet and St Cuth 70-78; V Starbeck 78-00; rtd 00; Perm to Offic *Leic* from 00. *11 Aulton Crescent, Hinckley LE10 0XA* Tel (01455) 442218

TAYLOR, Michael Frank Chatterton. b 30. St Aid Birkenhead 59. **d** 61 **p** 62. C Knighton St Jo *Leic* 61-65; V Briningham *Nor* 65-86; R Melton Constable w Swanton Novers 65-86; P-in-c Thornage w Brinton w Hunworth and Stody 85-86; R Lyng w Sparham 86-90; R Elsing w Bylaugh 86-90; R Lyng, Sparham, Elsing and Bylaugh 90-95; RD Sparham 92-95; rtd 95; Perm to Offic *Portsm* from 95. *The Rhond, 33 Station Road, St Helens, Ryde PO33 1YF* Tel and fax (01983) 873531 Mobile 07989-274848 E-mail mfct@tesco.net

TAYLOR, Michael John. b 50. **d** 07 **p** 08. OLM Went Valley *Wakef* 07-11; NSM Pontefract St Giles from 11. *19 Windsor Rise, Pontefract WF8 4PZ* Tel (01977) 702824 Mobile 07968-932135 E-mail michael@darringtonchurch.com

TAYLOR, Canon Michael Joseph. b 49. Gregorian Univ Rome STB72 PhL74 Birm Univ MA81 Nottm Univ PhD05. English Coll Rome 67. **d** 72 **p** 73. In RC Ch 72-83; Hon C Newport Pagnell w Lathbury *Ox* 83-86; TV Langley Marish 86-90; Vice Prin EMMTC *S'well* 90-97; Prin 97-06; R Gedling from 06; Hon Can *S'well* Minster from 00. *The Rectory, Rectory Drive, Gedling, Nottingham NG4 4BG* Tel 0115-961 3214

TAYLOR, Michael Laurence. b 43. Ch Coll Cam BA66 MA70 CertEd72 MPhil90 ARCM68. Cuddesdon Coll 66. **d** 68 **p** 69. C Westbury-on-Trym H Trin *Bris* 68-72; Asst Chapl Wellington Coll Berks 72-76; C St Helier *S'wark* 76-78; TV Bedminster *Bris* 78-82; P-in-c Chippenham St Andr w Tytherton Lucas 82-88; V 88-89; Dioc Ecum Officer *B & W* 89-90; P-in-c Rodney Stoke w Draycott 89-90. *The Paddock, Wells Road, Rodney Stoke, Cheddar BS27 3UU* Tel (01749) 870684 E-mail mendipadvolacy@btinternet.com

TAYLOR, Michael Noel. b 40. Leeds Univ BSc62 PGCE63. EMMTC 95. **d** 98 **p** 99. NSM Woodthorpe *S'well* 98-02; NSM Gedling Deanery 02-03; NSM Epperstone, Gonalston, Oxton and Woodborough from 03; NSM Calverton from 03. *16 Church*

Meadow, Calverton, Nottingham NG14 6HG Tel 0115-847 3718 Fax 912 7671 Mobile 07713-125771 E-mail michael.taylor21@ntlworld.com

TAYLOR, Michael Stewart. b 58. St Mich Coll Llan BTh91. **d** 91 **p** 92. C Llangunnor w Cwmffrwd *St D* 91-94; V Llansantffraed and Llanbadarn Trefeglwys etc 94-97; P-in-c Jersey St Andr *Win* 97-99; V from 99. *The Vicarage, St Andrew's Road, First Tower, St Helier, Jersey JE2 3JG* Tel and fax (01534) 734975 E-mail vicarmike@aol.com

TAYLOR, Mrs Monica. b 39. **d** 06 **p** 07. OLM Wyke *Guildf* from 06. *Glifada, Guildford Road, Normandy, Guildford GU23 2AR* Tel (01483) 234927 E-mail mrsmonicataylor@hotmail.com

TAYLOR, Nancy. b 49. SRN70 SCM72. Ox Min Course 88. **d** 91 **p** 94. Chapl Asst Stoke Mandeville Hosp Aylesbury 91-94; Asst Chapl Aylesbury Vale Community Healthcare NHS Trust 94-97; NSM Weston Turville *Ox* 91-99; Chapl Kneesworth Ho Hosp from 98. *Kneesworth House, Old North Road, Bassingbourn, Royston SG8 5JP* Tel (01763) 255700

TAYLOR, Canon Nicholas Hugh. b 63. Cape Town Univ BA83 MA87 Dur Univ PhD91 Ox Univ MTh07. **d** 96 **p** 97. Lect and Chapl Univ of Swaziland 95-98; Chapl St Mich Sch Manzini 96-98; Sen Lect Africa Univ Zimbabwe 98-01; Can Th Mutare Cathl from 99; Dioc Dir Th Educn Manicaland 99-01; R Penhalonga 00-01; Assoc Prof Pretoria Univ S Africa 02-04; R Pretoria St Hilda 02-03; R Pretoria N St Mary 03; Hon C Smithfield St Bart Gt *Lon* 04; Research Fell Univ of Zululand from 04; Hon Tutor Ripon Coll Cuddesdon 04-05; Lect K Coll Lon 06; Perm to Offic *Nor* from 04 and *Ox* 05-07; R Clarkston *Glas* from 09. *St Aidan's Rectory, 8 Golf Road, Clarkston, Glasgow G76 7LZ* Tel 0141-638 3080 Mobile 07944-091132 E-mail nhtaylor@dunelm.org.uk

TAYLOR, Preb Nicholas James. b 46. St Chad's Coll Dur BA67. **d** 69 **p** 70. C Beamish *Dur* 69-74; C Styvechale *Cov* 74-77; P-in-c Wilmcote w Billesley 77-79; P-in-c Aston Cantlow 77-79; V Aston Cantlow and Wilmcote w Billesley 79-87; V Cov St Fran N Radford 87-97; RD Cov N 93-97; V Wilton *B & W* 97-11; Preb Wells Cathl 08-11; rtd 11. *50 Summerlands Park Avenue, Ilminster TA19 9BT* Tel (01460) 929392 E-mail nickruthtaylor@gmail.com

TAYLOR, Nicholas John. b 48. Leeds Univ BSc69. St Mich Coll Llan BTh09. **d** 09 **p** 10. NSM Griffithstown *Mon* from 09. *82 Greenhill Road, Sebastopol, Pontypool NP4 5BQ* Tel (01495) 740189 Mobile 07860-507258 E-mail njt.littlebarton@btinternet.com

TAYLOR, Nigel James. b 73. Lanc Univ BA94. Trin Coll Bris BA11. **d** 11. C Risborough *Ox* from 11. *26 Summerleys Road, Princes Risborough HP27 9DT* Tel 07749-816265 (mobile) E-mail taylors18@tiscali.co.uk

TAYLOR, Nigel Thomas Wentworth. b 60. Bris Univ BA82 Ox Univ BA86. Wycliffe Hall Ox 84. **d** 87 **p** 88. C Ches Square St Mich w St Phil *Lon* 87-91; C Roxeth Ch Ch and Harrow St Pet 91-93; TV Roxeth 93-97; V S Mimms Ch Ch from 97; AD Cen Barnet 04-09. *Christ Church Vicarage, St Albans Road, Barnet EN5 4LA* Tel (020) 8449 0942 *or* 8449 0832 E-mail nigel.taylor@london.anglican.org

TAYLOR, Mrs Noelle Rosemary. b 58. NTMTC 02. **d** 05 **p** 06. C St Mary-at-Latton *Chelmsf* 05-08; TV Gt Parndon from 08. *80 Deer Park, Harlow CM19 4LF* E-mail noelletaylor@hotmail.com

TAYLOR, Norman. b 26. CCC Cam BA49 MA52. Cuddesdon Coll 49. **d** 51 **p** 52. C Clitheroe St Mary *Blackb* 51-54; C Pontesbury I and II *Heref* 54-55; R Lt Wilbraham *Ely* 55-71; Chapl St Faith's Sch Cam 71-86; Hon C Chesterton St Andr *Ely* 87-91; rtd 91; Perm to Offic *Sarum* 91-09 and *York* from 11. *Brook House, West End, Ampleforth, York YO62 4DY* Tel (01439) 787199

TAYLOR, Norman Adrian. b 48. St D Coll Lamp. **d** 73 **p** 74. C Fleur-de-Lis *Mon* 73-75; C W Drayton *Lon* 75-79; C-in-c Hayes St Edm CD 79-85; V Hayes St Edm 85-87; V Pilton w Ashford *Ex* 87-89; V Sidley *Chich* 89-02; Chapl Hastings and Rother NHS Trust 00-02; V Durrington *Chich* from 02. *Durrington Vicarage, Bramble Lane, Worthing BN13 3JE* Tel (01903) 693499 E-mail frnorman@nataylor.freeserve.co.uk

TAYLOR, Norman Wyatt. b 23. Wells Th Coll 58. **d** 60 **p** 61. C Lawrence Weston *Bris* 60-63; V 63-69; V Bishop's Cannings *Sarum* 69-77; V Bishop's Cannings, All Cannings etc 77-80; V W Moors 80-87; rtd 88; Perm to Offic *Ex* 89-98. *3 Kits Close, Chudleigh, Newton Abbot TQ13 0LG* Tel (01626) 852733

TAYLOR, Mrs Patricia Anne. b 56. TCD BTh05. CITC 03. **d** 05 **p** 06. C Wicklow w Killiskey *D & G* 05-10; TV Smestow Vale *Lich* from 10. *12 St John's Close, Swindon, Dudley DY3 4PQ* Tel (01384) 620626 E-mail patricia.taylor@gmail.com

TAYLOR, Patricia Mary. b 52. Goldsmiths' Coll Lon BEd80. Wycliffe Hall Ox 06. **d** 09 **p** 10. NSM Upper Holloway *Lon* from 09. *4 Anatola Road, London N19 5HN* Tel (020) 7272 8990 E-mail p.taylor2410@btinternet.com

TAYLOR, Patrick James. b 72. Magd Coll Cam BA96 MA99 MEng96. Ripon Coll Cuddesdon BA00. **d** 01 **p** 02. C Kenilworth

St Nic *Cov* 01-05; TV Solihull *Birm* from 05. *45 Park Avenue, Solihull B91 3EJ* Tel 0121-705 4927 *or* 705 5350 E-mail patrick@solihullparish.org.uk

TAYLOR, Paul. b 63. RGN85. Sarum & Wells Th Coll 92 Linc Th Coll BTh95. **d** 95 **p** 96. C Boultham *Linc* 95-98; C Ditton St Mich w St Thos *Liv* 98-00; V Bickerstaffe and Melling 00-06; TV N Meols 06-08; rtd 08. *139 Sussex Road, Southport PR8 6AF* Tel (01704) 500617 E-mail joandpaultaylor@talktalk.net

TAYLOR, Paul Frank David. b 60. Leic Poly BSc84 MRICS87. Trin Coll Bris BA91. **d** 91 **p** 92. C Edin St Thos 91-94; C Kempshott *Win* 94-98; C-in-c Hatch Warren CD 98-01; V Salisbury St Fran and Stratford sub Castle *Sarum* from 01; C Bourne Valley from 09. *The Vicarage, 52 Park Lane, Salisbury SP1 3NP* Tel (01722) 333762 E-mail paul@pfdt.freeserve.co.uk

TAYLOR, Paul Jeremy. b 72. Brunel Univ BSc96. Ridley Hall Cam 02. **d** 04 **p** 05. C Longfleet *Sarum* 04-08; V Hordle *Win* from 08. *The Vicarage, Stopples Lane, Hordle, Lymington SO41 0HX* Tel (01425) 614428 Mobile 07776-425621 E-mail pjtaylorsurfing@hotmail.com

TAYLOR, Paul Michael. b 66. EMMTC 03. **d** 05 **p** 05. C Derby St Pet and Ch Ch w H Trin 05-07; P-in-c Brailsford w Shirley and Osmaston w Edlaston 07-09; R Brailsford w Shirley, Osmaston w Edlaston etc from 09. *The Rectory, Church Lane, Brailsford, Derby DE6 3BX* Tel (01335) 361221

TAYLOR, The Ven Paul Stanley. b 53. Ox Univ BEd75 MTh98. Westcott Ho Cam. **d** 84 **p** 85. C Bush Hill Park St Steph *Lon* 84-88; Asst Dir Post Ord Tr Edmonton Episc Area 87-94; Dir Post Ord Tr 94-00 and 02-04; V Southgate St Andr 88-97; V Hendon St Mary 97-01; V Hendon St Mary and Ch Ch 01-04; AD W Barnet 00-04; Adn Sherborne *Sarum* from 04; Can and Preb Sarum Cathl from 04. *Aldhelm House, West Stafford, Dorchester DT2 8AB* Tel and fax (01305) 269074 *or* tel (01258) 859110 E-mail adsherborne@salisbury.anglican.org *or* ptatstmarys@aol.com

TAYLOR, Peter. b 35. Sussex Univ MA72. Wells Th Coll 58. **d** 60 **p** 61. C Godalming *Guildf* 60-62; C Epsom St Martin 62-65; R E Clandon and W Clandon 65-75; rtd 96; P-in-c Burpham *Chich* 96-04; Perm to Offic from 04. *Jordan's Bank, 20 Penfold Place, Arundel BN18 9SA* Tel (01903) 885706 E-mail pburpham@globalnet.co.uk

TAYLOR, Peter. b 51. St Jo Coll Cam BA72 MA76. Ridley Hall Cam 73. **d** 76 **p** 77. C Roch 76-79; Perm to Offic *Ely* 79-99 and 05-06; NSM Downham 99-05; P-in-c Coveney from 06; RD Ely from 09; Bp's Adv for Self-Supporting Min from 10. *Gravel Head Farm, Downham Common, Little Downham, Ely CB6 2TY* Tel (01353) 698714 Fax 699107 E-mail peter@taylormonroe.co.uk

TAYLOR, Peter David. b 38. FCA. NOC 77. **d** 80 **p** 81. C Penwortham St Mary *Blackb* 80-84; V Farington 84-92; V Euxton 92-04; rtd 04; Perm to Offic *Blackb* from 04. *33 Aspendale Close, Longton, Preston PR4 5LJ* Tel (01772) 614795

TAYLOR, Canon Peter David. b 47. Liv Univ BEd74 Man Univ MEd78 Lanc Univ MA88. NOC 78. **d** 81 **p** 82. C Formby H Trin *Liv* 81-84; V Stoneycroft All SS 84-91; Chapl St Kath Coll 91-96; Dioc RE Field Officer 91-96; Dioc Dir of Educn *Leic* 96-09; Hon Can Leic Cathl 98-09; Dir Operations Ch Academy Services Ltd *Pet* from 09; Perm to Offic *Leic* from 09. *87 Main Street, Humberstone, Leicester LE5 1AE* Tel 0116-220 1461 *or* (01733) 566575 E-mail peter.taylor@leccofe.org *or* peter@churchacademies.org.uk

TAYLOR, The Ven Peter Flint. b 44. Qu Coll Cam BA65 MA69. Lon Coll of Div BD70. **d** 70 **p** 71. C Highbury New Park St Aug *Lon* 70-73; C Plymouth St Andr w St Paul and St Geo *Ex* 73-77; V Ironville *Derby* 77-83; P-in-c Riddings 82-83; R Rayleigh *Chelmsf* 83-96; Chapl HM YOI Bullwood Hall 85-90; RD Rochford *Chelmsf* 89-96; Adn Harlow 96-09; rtd 09. *5 Springfield Terrace, Springfield Road, South Brent TQ10 9AP* Tel (01364) 73427 E-mail peterftaylor@lineone.net

TAYLOR, Peter John. b 40. Oak Hill Th Coll 62. **d** 65 **p** 66. C St Paul's Cray St Barn *Roch* 65-69; C Woking St Jo *Guildf* 69-77; R Necton w Holme Hale *Nor* 77-94; R Necton, Holme Hale w N and S Pickenham 95-05; RD Breckland 86-94; Hon Can Nor Cathl 98-03; rtd 05; Perm to Offic *Nor* from 05. *5 Starling Close, Aylsham, Norwich NR11 6XG* Tel (01263) 731964

TAYLOR, Peter John. b 60. New Coll Edin LTh87. Edin Th Coll 83. **d** 87 **p** 88. C Edin SS Phil and Jas 87-90; USA 90-92; R Glas St Oswald 92-97; R Kirkcudbright and Gatehouse of Fleet 97-07. *Address temp unknown* E-mail ptkbt@aol.com

TAYLOR, Peter John. b 71. St Andr Univ MA94 Sussex Univ PGCE99. Oak Hill Th Coll BA05. **d** 05 **p** 06. C Boscombe St Jo *Win* 05-09; P-in-c Heatherlands St Jo *Sarum* 09-11; V from 11. *St John's Vicarage, 72 Alexandra Road, Poole BH14 9EW* Tel (01202) 741172

TAYLOR, Peter Joseph. b 41. Bps' Coll Cheshunt 66. **d** 68 **p** 69. C Wollaton *S'well* 68-71; C Cockington *Ex* 71-74; V Broadhembury 74-79; V Broadhembury w Payhembury 79-81; V Gt Staughton *Ely* 81-86; V Gt Paxton and R Offord D'Arcy w Offord Cluny 86-01; Chapl HM YOI Gaynes Hall 81-91; rtd 01; Perm to Offic *Ely* from 01. *9 Park Way, Offord Cluny, St Neots PE19 5RW* Tel (01480) 811662

TAYLOR, Mrs Rachel Sara. b 60. Univ Coll Lon BA81. SEITE 98. **d** 01 **p** 02. C Wimbledon *S'wark* 01-05; V Motspur Park from 05. *The Vicarage, 2 Douglas Avenue, New Malden KT3 6HT* Tel (020) 8942 3117 E-mail rachel@taylortalk.fsnet.co.uk

TAYLOR (or URMSON-TAYLOR), Ralph Urmson. Tulsa Univ MA72 Man Coll of Educn DipEd74 TCert82. Kelham Th Coll. **d** 56 **p** 57. C Redcar *York* 57-59; C Bridlington Quay H Trin 59-62; C Sewerby w Marton 60-62; Asst P Tulsa H Trin USA 62-65; Sacr 93-02; Chapl Holland Hall Sch 65-93; rtd 93. *Via Porta Perlici 47A, 06081 Assisi PG, Italy*

TAYLOR, Raymond. b 34. Lon Coll of Div 62. **d** 65 **p** 66. C Pennington *Man* 65-70; P-in-c Wombridge *Lich* 70-80; R S Normanton *Derby* 80-88; RD Alfreton 86-88; V Youlgreave, Middleton, Stanton-in-Peak etc 88-98; rtd 99; Perm to Offic *Derby* from 98. *4 Jeffries Avenue, Crich, Matlock DE4 5DU* Tel (01773) 856845

TAYLOR, Raymond George. b 39. Bucknell Univ BS59 Univ of Penn MS65 EdD66 Penn State Univ MPA77 Maine Univ MBA85. Episc Th Sch Cam Mass BD62. **d** 62 **p** 63. C Chestnut Hill St Martin USA 62-66; V Warwick St Mary 70-77; Assoc P Smithfield St Paul 87-90; Assoc P Oriental St Thos 90-00; Superintendent of Schs Maine 77-86; Prof N Carolina State Univ 86-01; P-in-c Málaga *Eur* 04-06. *Cortijo Moya, 29710 Periana (Málaga), Spain* Tel and fax (0034) 609 885 479 Mobile 650 780 087 E-mail cortijomoya@terra.es

TAYLOR, Raymond Montgomery. b 43. Oak Hill Th Coll 77. **d** 80 **p** 81. Hon C Cricklewood St Pet *Lon* 80-85; Hon C Golders Green 85-87; V New Southgate St Paul 87-00; AD Cen Barnet 96-00; V Thaxted *Chelmsf* from 00. *The Vicarage, Watling Lane, Thaxted, Dunmow CM6 2QY* Tel and fax (01371) 830221 E-mail furor@scribendi.freeserve.co.uk

TAYLOR, Richard David. b 44. Worc Coll Ox BA67 MA70. Coll of Resurr Mirfield 67. **d** 69 **p** 70. C Barrow St Geo w St Luke *Carl* 69-73; C Gosforth All SS *Newc* 73-80; TR Newc Epiphany 80-83; V Tynemouth Priory 83-91; TR Benwell 91-98; P-in-c Blyth St Cuth 98-01; V 01-10; rtd 10. *38 Westbourne Avenue, Gosforth, Newcastle upon Tyne NE3 2HN* Tel 0191-284 6065 E-mail rdtaylor@metronet.co.uk

TAYLOR, Richard Godfrey. b 73. Pemb Coll Cam MA99. Oak Hill Th Coll BA00. **d** 00 **p** 01. C Brunswick *Man* 00-04; C Aldridge *Lich* 04-09; V Clapham Common St Barn *S'wark* from 09. *The Vicarage, 8 Lavender Gardens, London SW11 1DL* Tel (020) 7223 5953 E-mail fatboytaylor@hotmail.com

TAYLOR, Preb Richard John. b 21. Kelham Th Coll 38. **d** 45 **p** 46. C Tunstall Ch Ch *Lich* 45-48; C Uttoxeter w Bramshall 48-52; V Croxden 52-57; V Willenhall H Trin 57-68; R Edgmond 68-77; V Streetly 77-87; Preb Lich Cathl 78-87; rtd 87; Perm to Offic *Lich* from 87. *15 Covey Close, Lichfield WS13 6BS* Tel (01543) 268558

TAYLOR, Richard John. b 46. Ripon Coll Cuddesdon 85. **d** 85 **p** 86. C Moseley St Mary *Birm* 85-87; V Kingsbury 87-91; TR Hodge Hill 91-03; P-in-c 03-05; R Weston super Mare St Jo *B & W* from 05; RD Locking from 08. *The Rectory, Cecil Road, Weston-super-Mare BS23 2NF* Tel (01934) 623399

TAYLOR, Robert Ian. b 68. St Jo Coll Nottm. **d** 08 **p** 09. C Buttershaw St Paul *Bradf* from 08; Chapl Bradf Academy from 08. *52 Bowling Park Drive, East Bowling, Bradford BD4 7ES* Tel (01274) 788722 E-mail robtlr@aol.com

TAYLOR, Robert Stirling. b 62. Ball Coll Ox BA83 Leeds Univ PhD88 Nottm Trent Univ PGCE93. Cranmer Hall Dur 00. **d** 02 **p** 03. C Mansfield St Jo *S'well* 02-04; V Eastwood 04-06; Chapl Loughb Univ 06-09; R Kingsland w Eardisland, Aymestrey etc *Heref* from 10. *The Rectory, Kingsland, Leominster HR6 9QW* Tel (01568) 708255

TAYLOR, Robin. *See* TAYLOR, Joseph Robin Christopher

TAYLOR, Roger James Benedict. b 42. Glouc Sch of Min 89 WMMTC 95. **d** 96 **p** 97. NSM Cromhall w Tortworth and Tytherington *Glouc* 96-99; P-in-c Wistanstow *Heref* 99-01; Min Can Brecon Cathl 01-07; rtd 07. *The Chaplain's House, St Oswald's Hospital, Upper Tything, Worcester WR1 1HR* Tel (01905) 294380 E-mail roger.taylor36@btinternet.com

TAYLOR, Canon Roland Haydn. b 29. St Chad's Coll Dur BA53. **d** 55 **p** 56. C N Gosforth *Newc* 55-58; C Barnsley St Mary *Wakef* 58-61; V Brotherton 61-68; V Purston cum S Featherstone 68-76; RD Pontefract 74-94; R Badsworth 76-97; Hon Can Wakef Cathl 81-97; rtd 97. *57 Fairview, Carleton, Pontefract WF8 3NU* Tel (01977) 796564

TAYLOR, Rosemary Edith. b 47. Nottm Univ MA04 RGN68 RHV71. EMMTC 01. **d** 04 **p** 05. NSM Bassingham Gp *Linc* 04-08; P-in-c Sibsey w Frithville from 08; P-in-c Brothertoft Gp from 10. *The Vicarage, Vicarage Lane, Sibsey, Boston PE22 0RT* Tel (01205) 751674 E-mail natuna@btopenworld.com

TAYLOR, Roy. b 63. Ex Coll Ox BA86 Ox Univ MA89 York Univ PGCE87 Univ of Wales (Cardiff) BD97. St Mich Coll Llan 95. **d** 97 **p** 98. C Guisborough *York* 97-99; Chapl Rossall Sch Fleetwood 99-02; V Dolphinholme w Quernmore and Over Wyresdale *Blackb* 02-08; Chapl Geneva *Eur* from 08. *Rue de Montbrillant 84, #72, 1202 Geneva, Switzerland*

TAYLOR, Roy Partington. b 33. Birm Univ BA54 PGCE55 Bulmershe Coll of HE MPhil87. SAOMC 96. **d** 98 **p** 99. NSM Hurley and Stubbings *Ox* 98-02; NSM Burchetts Green 02-03; rtd 03; Perm to Offic *Ox* 03-04; Hon C Maidenhead St Andr and St Mary from 04; Lect Bp Hannington Inst Kenya 01-02; Prin from 04. *16 Highfield Road, Maidenhead SL6 5DF* Tel (01628) 625454 E-mail roy.taylor@telco4u.net

TAYLOR, Roy William. b 37. Ch Coll Cam BA61 MA64. Clifton Th Coll 61. **d** 63 **p** 64. C Blackb Sav 63-66; C Hensingham *Carl* 66-68; CMS Taiwan 69-79; TV Bushbury *Lich* 79-85; OMF 85-93; Hon C Wolverhampton St Jude *Lich* 93-94; P-in-c Torquay St Jo and Ellacombe *Ex* 94-99; R Instow and V Westleigh 99-03; RD Hartland 01-03; rtd 03. *31 Shore Road, Millisle, Newtownards BT22 2BT* Tel (028) 9186 2769

TAYLOR, Simon Dominic Kent. b 69. Surrey Univ BSc90 W Sussex Inst of HE PGCE91 Sussex Univ MA(Ed)99. Trin Coll Bris BA01. **d** 01 **p** 02. C Southgate *Chich* 01-04; TV 04-10; R Busbridge and Hambledon *Guildf* from 10. *Busbridge Rectory, Old Rectory Gardens, Godalming GU7 1XB* Tel (01483) 418820 E-mail simon@busbridgechurch.org.uk

TAYLOR, Simon John. b 72. Worc Coll Ox BA94 MPhil96 MA99 DPhil00. St Mich Coll Llan 00 Ven English Coll Rome 01. **d** 02 **p** 03. C Cotham St Sav w St Mary and Clifton St Paul *Bris* 02-06; P-in-c Bris St Mary Redcliffe w Temple etc from 06. *The Vicarage, 10 Redcliffe Parade West, Bristol BS1 6SP* Tel 0117-929 1962 E-mail simon.taylor@redcliffe.co.uk

TAYLOR, Mrs Stella Isabelle. b 31. S Dios Minl Tr Scheme 86. **d** 89 **p** 94. NSM Haworth *Bradf* 89-91; Par Dn Keighley St Andr 92-94; C 94-96; rtd 97; Perm to Offic *Bradf* 97-00. *8 The Linkway, Westham, Pevensey BN24 5JB*

TAYLOR, Stephen. b 53. St Edm Hall Ox BA75 Ex Univ PGCE78. WEMTC 05. **d** 08 **p** 09. NSM Highnam, Lassington, Rudford, Tibberton etc *Glouc* from 08. *Perrick's Farmhouse, Northwood Green, Westbury-on-Severn GL14 1NB* Tel (01452) 760568 E-mail sct@churchdown.gloucs.sch.uk

TAYLOR, Stephen. b 65. City Univ BSc87 Lon Univ PGCE90. NTMTC 95. **d** 98 **p** 99. Chapl Bp Stopford's Sch Enfield 98-02 and 03-06; NSM Enfield Chase St Mary *Lon* 98-02; Perm to Offic *Eur* 02-03; C Hornsey St Mary w St Geo *Lon* 03-06; P-in-c March St Jo *Ely* 06-08; Hon Asst Dir of Ords 07-08; P-in-c Enfield St Mich *Lon* from 08. *The Vicarage, 2 Gordon Hill, Enfield EN2 0QP* Tel (020) 8363 1063 Mobile 07711-559107 E-mail stephen.taylor@london.anglican.org

TAYLOR, Stephen Gordon. b 35. Bris Univ BA60. Ridley Hall Cam 60. **d** 62 **p** 63. C Gt Baddow *Chelmsf* 62-65; C Portsdown *Portsm* 65-69; P-in-c Elvedon *St E* 69-70; R 70-75; P-in-c Eriswell 69-70; R 70-75; P-in-c Icklingham *St E* 70-75; Chapl St Felix Sch Southwold 75-77; R Lt Shelford w Newton *Ely* 77-96; rtd 96; Perm to Offic *Ely* from 96. *15 Church Close, Whittlesford, Cambridge CB22 4NY* Tel (01223) 830461

TAYLOR, Stephen Graham. b 77. St Jo Coll Nottm. **d** 08. C Sparkhill St Jo *Birm* from 08. *132 Oakwood Road, Sparkhill, Birmingham B11 4HD* Tel 0121-247 9428 E-mail vicarsteve@googlemail.com

TAYLOR, Stephen James. b 48. Chich Th Coll 70. **d** 73 **p** 74. C Tottenham St Paul *Lon* 73-76; St Vincent 78-85; Grenada 85-88; C-in-c Hammersmith SS Mich and Geo White City Estate CD *Lon* 88-96; AD Hammersmith 92-96; P-in-c Hammersmith St Luke 94-96; USPG Brazil 96-08. *Rua Dr Boureau 127/203, Costa Azul, Salvador, BA 41 760-050, Brazil* Tel (0055) (71) 3341 6797 E-mail stephentaylor2001@hotmail.com

TAYLOR, The Ven Stephen Ronald. b 55. MBE09. Dur Univ MA99. Cranmer Hall Dur 80. **d** 83 **p** 84. C Chester le Street *Dur* 83-87; V Newbottle 87-92; V Stranton 92-00; TR Sunderland 00-07; Provost Sunderland Minster from 07; Hon Can Dur Cathl 06-11; Adn Maidstone *Cant* from 11; Hon Can Rift Valley Tanzania from 00; Hon Fell Sunderland Univ from 09. *267 Boxley Road, Maidstone ME14 2AE*

TAYLOR, Stewart. b 51. St Jo Coll Dur 74. **d** 77 **p** 78. C Norwood St Luke *S'wark* 77-81; C Surbiton Hill Ch Ch 81-91; V Cambridge St Phil *Ely* from 91. *St Philip's Vicarage, 252 Mill Road, Cambridge CB1 3NF* Tel (01223) 247652 or 414775 E-mail vicar@stphilipschurch.org.uk

TAYLOR, Canon Stuart Bryan. b 40. St Chad's Coll Dur BA64. **d** 66 **p** 67. C Portsea N End St Mark *Portsm* 66-70; C Epsom St Martin *Guildf* 70-76; Chapl Clifton Coll Bris 76-88; Dir Bloxham Project 88-93; Chapl Giggleswick Sch 93-95; Bp's Officer for Miss and Evang *Bris* 96-01; Bp's Adv for Past Care for Clergy and Families 01-10; Hon Min Can Bris Cathl 02-04; Chapl Bris Cathl Sch 01-09; Hon Can Bris Cathl 04-10; rtd 10. *62 Providence Lane, Long Ashton, Bristol BS41 9DN* Tel (01275) 393625 E-mail annandstuart@gmail.com

TAYLOR, Mrs Susan Mary. b 51. Ex Univ LLB73 St Anne's Coll Ox BCL75 Solicitor 78. SEITE 03. **d** 06 **p** 07. NSM Barkingside St Laur *Chelmsf* from 06; Perm to Offic *S'wark* from 10. *Norwood, North End, Buckhurst Hill IG9 5RA* Tel (020) 8504 9867 E-mail suetaylorthorne@aol.com

TAYLOR, Mrs Teresa Mary. b 53. SRN76 SCM78. WEMTC 98. **d** 02 **p** 03. NSM Kingswood *Bris* from 02; Chapl Freeways Trust from 07. *15 Hampton Street, Bristol BS15 1TP* Tel 0117-373 2410 E-mail revtmt@blueyonder.co.uk

TAYLOR, Thomas. b 33. Sarum & Wells Th Coll 77. **d** 80 **p** 81. NSM Heatherlands St Jo *Sarum* 80-82; TV Kinson 82-88; TV Shaston 88-98; Chapl Westmr Memorial Hosp Shaftesbury 88-98; rtd 98; Perm to Offic *Sarum* from 98. *10 Hanover Lane, Gillingham SP8 4TA* Tel (01747) 826569

TAYLOR, Thomas. b 42. St Jo Coll Dur BA64 Leeds Univ MA02. Linc Th Coll 64. **d** 66 **p** 67. C Clitheroe St Mary *Blackb* 66-69; C Skerton St Luke 69-71; C-in-c Penwortham St Leon CD 71-72; V Penwortham St Leon 72-78; R Poulton-le-Sands 78-81; P-in-c Morecambe St Lawr 78-81; R Poulton-le-Sands w Morecambe St Laur 81-85; Chapl Ld Wandsworth Coll Hants 85-92; V Walton-le-Dale *Blackb* 92-94; P-in-c Samlesbury 92-94; V Walton-le-Dale St Leon w Samlesbury St Leon 95-96; RD Leyland 94-96; Hon C Tarleton 03-11; Hon C Rufford and Tarleton from 11. *52 Hesketh Lane, Tarleton, Preston PR4 6AQ* Tel (01772) 813871 E-mail rustichouse@bigfoot.com

TAYLOR, Timothy Robert. b 62. W Midl Coll of Educn BEd87 Cumbria Univ BA10. LCTP 07. **d** 10 **p** 11. NSM Egremont and Haile *Carl* from 10. *42 Abbey Vale, St Bees CA27 0EF* Tel (01946) 822255 E-mail timothy@trtaylor.co.uk

TAYLOR, Willam Goodacre Campbell. See CAMPBELL-TAYLOR, William Goodacre

TAYLOR, William Austin. b 36. Linc Th Coll 65. **d** 67 **p** 68. C Tyldesley w Shakerley *Man* 67-71; R Cheetham St Mark 71-79; TR Peel 79-90; AD Farnworth 83-90; V Pelton *Dur* 90-96; rtd 96; Perm to Offic *Man* 96-08. *36 Tynesbank, Worsley, Manchester M28 8SL* Tel 0161-790 5327

TAYLOR, William Henry. b 56. Kent Univ BA79 Lon Univ MTh81 Lanc Univ MPhil87 FRAS80 SOAS Lon PhD10. Westcott Ho Cam. **d** 83 **p** 84. C Maidstone All SS and St Phil w Tovil *Cant* 83-86; Abp's Adv on Orthodox Affairs 86-88; C St Marylebone All SS *Lon* 86-88; Chapl Guy's Hosp Lon 88; CMS Jordan 88-91; V Ealing St Pet Mt Park *Lon* 91-00; AD Ealing 93-98; Dean Portsm 00-02; P-in-c Notting Hill St Jo and St Pet *Lon* 02-03; V Notting Hill St Jo from 03. *St John's Vicarage, 25 Ladbroke Road, London W11 3PD* Tel (020) 7727 3439 *or* tel and fax 7727 4262 E-mail vicar@stjohnsnottinghill.com

TAYLOR, William Richard de Carteret Martin. b 33. CCC Cam MA57. Westcott Ho Cam 58. **d** 59 **p** 60. C Eastney *Portsm* 59-63; Chapl RN 63-67 and 70-87; V Childe Okeford *Sarum* 67-70; V Manston w Hamoon 67-70; QHC from 83; TR Tisbury *Sarum* 87-89; Chapl Hatf Poly *St Alb* 89-92; Chapl Herts Univ 92-98; rtd 98; Perm to Offic *Ely* from 00. *Lark Rise, 47A New Street, St Neots, Huntingdon PE19 1AJ* Tel (01480) 473598 E-mail bill.taylor2@talktalk.net

TAYLOR, Capt William Thomas. b 61. Rob Coll Cam BA83 BA90. Ridley Hall Cam 88. **d** 91 **p** 92. C Bromley Ch Ch *Roch* 91-95; C St Helen Bishopsgate w St Andr Undershaft etc *Lon* 95-98; R from 98; R St Pet Cornhill from 01. *The Old Rectory, Merrick Square, London SE1 4JB* Tel (020) 7378 8186

TAYLOR-COOK, Andrew. b 62. ERMC. **d** 08 **p** 09. C Wirksworth *Derby* from 08. *57 Yokecliffe Drive, Wirksworth, Matlock DE4 4PF* Tel (01629) 820049 E-mail captainandrewtc@btinternet.com

TAYLOR-KENYON (née THOMPSON), Louise Margaret. b 61. Clare Coll Cam BA83 MA07 Homerton Coll Cam PGCE84 Leeds Univ MA07. NOC 04. **d** 07 **p** 08. C Skipton H Trin *Bradf* 07-10; C Skipton Ch Ch w Carleton 07-10; C Embsay w Eastby from 10; CME Officer from 10. *The Vicarage, 21 Shires Lane, Skipton BD23 6SB* Tel (01756) 798057 Mobile 07545-235362 E-mail louise.taylor-kenyon@bradford.anglican.org

TEAGUE, Gaythorne Derrick. b 24. MBE05. Bris Univ MB, ChB49 MRCGP53. **d** 74 **p** 75. NSM Bris St Andr Hartcliffe 74-86; Perm to Offic *B & W* from 86. *Innisfree, Bell Square, Blagdon, Bristol BS40 7UB* Tel (01761) 462671

TEAL, Andrew Robert. b 64. Birm Univ BA85 PhD06 Ox Brookes Univ PGCE05 Pemb Coll Ox MA08. Ripon Coll Cuddesdon 86. **d** 88 **p** 89. C Wednesbury St Paul Wood Green *Lich* 88-92; TV Sheff Manor 92-97; Asst Dioc Post Ord Tr Officer 93-98; Tutor Ripon Coll Cuddesdon 92-97; V Tickhill w Stainton *Sheff* 97-02; Warden of Readers 98-02; Hd of Th Plater Coll 02-03; Hd of Th and Past Studies 03-05; Chapl Pemb Coll Ox from 05; Fell from 08; Lect Ripon Coll Cuddesdon 05-09; Warden SLG from 09; Lect Th Ox Univ from 07. *Pembroke College, Oxford OX1 1DW* Tel (01865) 286276 Fax 276418 E-mail andrew.teal@theology.ox.ac.uk

TEALE, Adrian. b 53. Univ of Wales (Abth) BA74 CertEd77 MA80 Univ of Wales (Cardiff) MTh89. Wycliffe Hall Ox 78. **d** 80 **p** 81. C Betws w Ammanford *St D* 80-84; V Brynaman w Cwmllynfell from 84; RD Dyffryn Aman 95-01. *Y Dalar Deg, 10 Bryn Road, Upper Brynamman, Ammanford SA18 1AU* Tel (01269) 822275

TEAR, Jeremy Charles. b 67. Westmr Coll Ox BA89 Birm Univ MA99 MCIPD94. Aston Tr Scheme 95 Qu Coll Birm 97. **d** 99 **p** 00. C Timperley *Ches* 99-03; V Macclesfield St Paul 03-10; C Caversham Thameside and Mapledurham *Ox* from 10. *St John's Vicarage, St John's Road, Caversham, Reading RG4 5AN* Tel 0118-946 2884 E-mail revjtear@btinternet.com

TEARE, Mrs Marie. b 46. Open Univ BA81 RSCN67. NOC 95. **d** 98 **p** 99. C Brighouse and Clifton *Wakef* 98-01; V Waggoners *York* 01-08; RD Harthill 02-08; rtd 08; Perm to Offic *York* from 08. *Mayfield Bungalow, Easingwold Road, Huby, York YO61 1HN* Tel (01347) 811565 E-mail marie.teare@btinternet.com

TEARE, Canon Robert John Hugh. b 39. Bris Univ BSc62. Coll of Resurr Mirfield 67. **d** 70 **p** 71. C Fareham SS Pet and Paul *Portsm* 70-73; Chapl K Alfred Coll *Win* 73-78; V Pokesdown St Jas 78-82; R Winnall 82-06; RD Win 89-99; Hon Can Win Cathl 92-06; rtd 06; Chapl CSMV 06-09; Perm to Offic *Ox* 09-11; P-in-c Hanney, Denchworth and E Challow from 11. *29 Elizabeth Drive, Wantage OX12 9YA* Tel (01235) 770966 E-mail robertteare@googlemail.com

TEARNAN, John Herman Janson. b 37. Bris Univ BSc59. Kelham Th Coll 62. **d** 66 **p** 67. C Kettering SS Pet and Paul 66-71; Lic to Offic 71-85; Perm to Offic *St Alb* 82-85 and *Pet* 85-94; Chapl HM YOI Wellingborough 89-90; Chapl HM YOI Glen Parva 90-94; Guyana 94-03; rtd 03; Perm to Offic *Pet* from 05. *14 Rectory Walk, Barton Seagrave, Kettering NN15 6SP* Tel (01536) 510629 E-mail jaytee1937@btinternet.com

TEASDALE, Keith. b 56. Cranmer Hall Dur 86. **d** 88 **p** 89. C Crook *Dur* 88-92; V Dunston 92-10; AD Gateshead W 00-10; V Carl St Cuth w St Mary from 10. *St Cuthbert's Vicarage, 20 St Aidan's Road, Carlisle CA1 1LS* Tel (01228) 810599

TEASDEL, David Charles. b 77. Coll of Resurr Mirfield 05. **d** 08 **p** 09. C Ouzel Valley *St Alb* 08-11; TV Staveley and Barrow Hill *Derby* from 11. *30 Cedar Street, Hollingwood, Chesterfield S43 2LE* E-mail fatherdavidteasdel@gmail.com

TEATHER, Andrew James. b 75. Leeds Univ BA09. Yorks Min Course 07. **d** 09 **p** 10. C Preston St Jo and St Geo *Blackb* from 09. *The Glebe House, 33 Bairstow Street, Preston PR1 3TN* Tel (01772) 200489 E-mail andrewteather@fsmail.net

TEBBS, Richard Henry. b 52. Southn Univ BTh. Sarum & Wells Th Coll 75. **d** 78 **p** 79. C Cinderhill *S'well* 78-82; C Nor St Pet Mancroft w St Jo Maddermarket 82-85; TV Bridport *Sarum* 85-94; TR Yelverton, Meavy, Sheepstor and Walkhampton *Ex* 94-08; P-in-c Frankley *Birm* from 08. *The Rectory, Frankley Green, Birmingham B32 4AS* Tel 0121-475 3724 E-mail tebbsfamily@tiscali.co.uk

TEBBUTT, Christopher Michael. b 55. St Jo Coll Nottm BA94. **d** 96 **p** 97. C Catherington and Clanfield *Portsm* 96-00; P-in-c Southbroom *Sarum* 00-07; V 07-09; TR Canford Magna from 09; RD Wimborne from 11. *The Rectory, Canford Magna, Wimborne BH21 3AF* Tel (01202) 883382 E-mail thetebbutts@southbroom.fslife.co.uk

TEBBUTT, Sandra Eileen. b 56. FBDO78. STETS 96. **d** 99 **p** 00. NSM Blendworth w Chalton w Idsworth *Portsm* 99-00; Chapl Wilts and Swindon Healthcare NHS Trust 00-05; Regional Manager Bible Soc from 05; NSM Southbroom *Sarum* 04-09; NSM Canford Magna from 10. *The Rectory, Canford Magna, Wimborne BH21 3AF* Tel (01202) 883382 E-mail sandratebbutt@biblesociety.org.uk

TEBBY, Ms Janet Elizabeth. b 52. Lady Spencer Chu Coll of Educn CertEd72 Open Univ BA88. ERMC 05. **d** 08 **p** 09. NSM Wootton w Quinton and Preston Deanery *Pet* from 08. *1 New Cottages, Whiston, Northampton NN7 1NN* Tel (01604) 891989 E-mail jtebby@btinternet.com

TEDD, Christopher Jonathan Richard. See HOWITZ, Christopher Jonathan Richard

TEECE, David. b 54. MIET. **d** 06 **p** 07. OLM Normanton *Wakef* 06-07; NSM Stanley 07-10; NSM Ackworth from 10. *61 Hawley, Normanton WF6 1SE* Tel (01924) 891326 Mobile 07757-263627 E-mail david.teece@btconnect.com

TEED, John Michael. b 44. Middx Univ BA04. NTMTC 01. **d** 04 **p** 05. NSM Hanworth All SS *Lon* 04-07; NSM Staines 07-10; Perm to Offic *Ex* from 10. *47 West Cliff Road, Dawlish EX7 9DZ* Tel (01626) 865466 Mobile 07702-244078 E-mail johnteed@sky.com

TEGALLY, Narinder Jit Kaur. b 57. RGN93. SAOMC 99. **d** 02 **p** 03. NSM Welwyn Garden City *St Alb* 02-05; Asst Chapl R Free Hampstead NHS Trust 05-07; Sen Chapl Guy's and St Thos' NHS Foundn Trust from 07; Perm to Offic *St Alb* from 05. *Guy's and St Thomas' NHS Foundation Trust, St Thomas Street, London SE1 9RT* Tel (020) 7188 7188 E-mail narinder@grove-house.org.uk

TEGGARTY, Samuel James Karl. b 53. Dundee Univ BSc77. CITC 98. **d** 01 **p** 02. NSM Newry *D & D* 01-03; NSM Kilkeel from 03. *79 Knockchree Avenue, Kilkeel, Newry BT34 4BP* Tel (028) 4176 9076 E-mail karl@teggarty.fsnet.co.uk

TEGGIN, John. b 26. **d** 83 **p** 84. NSM Dublin Sandford w Milltown *D & G* 84-93; Dir Leprosy Miss 86-96. *Apartment 4, 69 Strand Road, Sandymount, Dublin 4, Republic of Ireland* Tel (00353) (1) 261 1792

TELFER, Andrew Julian. b 68. Essex Univ BA94. Wycliffe Hall Ox BTh97. 87 **p** 98. C Skelmersdale St Paul *Liv* 97-01; C Ashton-in-Makerfield St Thos 01-03; V Whiston from 03. *The Vicarage, 90 Windy Arbor Road, Prescot L35 3SG* Tel 0151-426 6329

TELFER, Canon Frank Somerville. b 30. Trin Hall Cam BA5? MA58. Ely Th Coll 53. **d** 55 **p** 56. C Liv Our Lady and St Nic 55-58; Chapl Down Coll Cam 58-62; Bp's Chapl *Nor* 62-65 Chapl Kent Univ 65-73; Can Res Guildf Cathl 73-95; rtd 96 Perm to Offic *Nor* from 96. *Holbrook, Glandford, Holt NR25 7JI* Tel (01263) 740586

TELFORD, Alan. b 46. St Jo Coll Nottm. **d** 83 **p** 84. C Normanton *Derby* 83-86; TV N Wingfield, Pilsley and Tuptor 86-90; TV N Wingfield, Clay Cross and Pilsley 90-92; P-in-c Oakwood 92-94; V Leic St Chris 94-05; P-in-c Leic St Theodore 05-09; rtd 09. *2 Springfield Cottage, Newmarket Lane, Clay Cross, Chesterfield S45 9AR* Tel (01246) 866988 Mobile 07854-937449 E-mail atelford@talktalk.net

TELFORD, Ms Carolin Judith. b 57. Victoria Univ Wellington BA78. SEITE 02. **d** 05 **p** 06. NSM Lee St Aug *S'wark* 05-07 Chapl St Cuth Coll Epsom New Zealand from 07. *St Cuthbert's College, PO Box 26020, Epsom, Auckland 1344, New Zealand*

TELFORD, Richard Francis. b 46. K Coll Lon 65. **d** 69 **p** 70. C Barkingside H Trin *Chelmsf* 69-72; C Wickford 72-77; P-in-c Romford St Jo 77-80; V 80-82; Perm to Offic 93-96; rtd 08. *Juglans, The Street, Wattisfield, Diss IP22 1NS* E-mail richard telford@hotmail.com

TELLINI, Canon Gianfranco. b 36. Gregorian Univ Rome DTh65. Franciscan Sem Trent 57. **d** 61 **p** 61. In RC Ch 61-66; C Mill Hill Jo Keble Ch *Lon* 66; C Roxbourne St Andr 66-67; Lect Sarum Th Coll 67-69; Sen Tutor 69-74; Vice-Prin Edin Th Coll 74-82; Lect Th Edin Univ 74-95; R Pittenweem *St And* 82-85; R Elie and Earlsferry 82-85; R Dunblane 85-98; Can St Ninian's Cathl Perth from 90; rtd 99. *53 Buchan Drive, Dunblane FK15 9HW* Tel (01786) 823281 E-mail giantellini@mac.com

TEMBEY, David. b 51. **d** 96 **p** 97. NSM Whitehaven *Carl* 96-00; NSM Holme Cultram St Cuth 00-02; NSM Holme Cultram St Mary 00-02; NSM Bromfield w Waverton 00-02; TV Solway Plain from 02. *Holme Cultram Vicarage, Abbeytown, Wigton CA7 4SP* Tel (01697) 361246 Fax 361506 E-mail tembey6@btinternet.com

TEMPERLEY, Robert Noble. b 29. JP. St Jo Coll York CertEd50 ACP52 Dur Univ DAES62. NEOC 85. **d** 88 **p** 88. NSM Ryhope *Dur* 88-97; rtd 98; Perm to Offic *Dur* from 98. *18 Withernsea Grove, Ryhope, Sunderland SR2 0BU* Tel 0191-521 1813

TEMPLE, Mrs Sylvia Mary. b 48. Ex Univ BA70 Univ of Wales (Abth) PGCE71. St D Dioc Tr Course 93. **d** 94 **p** 97. NSM Tenby *St D* 94-99; C 99-00; V Martletwy w Lawrenny and Minwear etc 00-05. *Llwyn Onn, Trafalgar Road, Tenby SA70 7DW*

TEMPLE-WILLIAMS, Alexander. **d** 04 **p** 05. C Pontypool *Mon* 04-09; TV Cyncoed from 09. *40 Felbrigg Crescent, Pontprennau, Cardiff CF23 8SE* Tel (029) 2054 0955

TEMPLEMAN (née WILLIAMS), Mrs Ann Joyce. b 50. St Hugh's Coll Ox BA72 MA75 PGCE73. Cranmer Hall Dur 03. **d** 05 **p** 06. Headmistress Dur High Sch for Girls 98-11; NSM Peterlee *Dur* 05-11; P-in-c Theale and Englefield *Ox* from 11. *The Rectory, Englefield Road, Theale, Reading RG7 5AS* Tel 0118-930 2759 Mobile 07919-620259 E-mail ann@templeman99.freeserve.co.uk

TEMPLEMAN, Peter Morton. b 49. Ch Ch Ox BA71 MA75. Wycliffe Hall Ox MA75. **d** 76 **p** 77. C Cheltenham St Mary, St Matt, St Paul and H Trin *Glouc* 76-79; Chapl St Jo Coll Cam 79-84; P-in-c Finchley St Paul Long Lane 84-85; P-in-c Finchley St Luke 84-85; V Finchley St Paul and St Luke 85-99; V Peterlee *Dur* 99-11; Hon C Theale and Englefield *Ox* from 11. *The Rectory, Englefield Road, Theale, Reading RG7 5AS* Tel 0118-930 2759

TEMPLETON, Iain McAllister. b 57. St Andr Coll Drygrange 80. **d** 85 **p** 86. In RC Ch 85-92; NSM Dornoch *Mor* 95; P-in-c Kirriemuir *St And* 95-99; R Eccleston *Blackb* 99-09; V Walsall St Andr *Lich* from 09. *St Andrew's Vicarage, 119 Hollyhedge Lane, Walsall WS2 8PZ* Tel (01922) 721658 E-mail fatheriain@aol.com

TEN WOLDE, Christine Caroline. b 57. **d** 99 **p** 00. NSM Llanegryn w Aberdyfi w Tywyn *Ban* from 99. *Aber-groes, Abertafol, Aberdovey LL35 0RE* Tel (01654) 767047 Fax 767572 Mobile 07977-108438 E-mail curate@stpeterschurch.org.uk

TENNANT, Cyril Edwin George. b 37. Keble Coll Ox BA59 MA63 Lon Univ BD61 Ex Univ MA03. Clifton Th Coll 59. **d** 62 **p** 63. C Stapleford *S'well* 62-65; C Felixstowe SS Pet and Paul *St E* 65-69; V Gipsy Hill Ch Ch *S'wark* 69-84; V Lee St Mildred 84-90; P-in-c Lundy Is *Ex* 90-92; V Ilfracombe SS Phil and Jas w W Down 90-01; rtd 01; Perm to Offic *Ex* 01-06. *27 Harvest Way, Witney OX28 1BX* Tel (01993) 778977 E-mail cande.tennant@virgin.net

TER BLANCHE, Harold Daniel. b 35. St Paul's Coll Grahamstown LTh85. **d** 63 **p** 64. C Pietermaritzburg St Pet S Africa 63-65; C Durban St Thos 65-72; R Glenloving 73-78; Dioc Missr Zululand 78-82; Chapl Miss to Seamen 82-84; Chapl Grimsby Distr Gen Hosp 84-94; Chapl NE Lincs NHS Trust 94-00; rtd 00; Perm to Offic *Linc* from 00. *25 Collingwood Crescent, Grimsby DN34 5RG* Tel (01472) 276624 E-mail harold.terblanche@virgin.net

'ER HAAR, Roger Edward Lound. b 52. QC92. Magd Coll Ox BA73. **d** 06 **p** 07. OLM Bramley and Grafham *Guildf* from 06. *Howicks, Hurlands Lane, Dunsfold, Godalming GU8 4NT* Tel (020) 7797 8100 E-mail terhaar@crownofficechambers.com

ERESA, Sister. *See* WHITE, Sister Teresa Joan

'TEROM, The Rt Revd Zechariah James. b 41. St Columba's Coll Hazaribagh BA64 Ranchi Univ MA66. Bp's Coll Calcutta BD71. **d** 71 **c** 86. C Hazaribagh India 71-73; Par P Manoharpur 73-76; Bp Chotanagpur 86-09; Moderator Ch of N India 01-09; rtd 09. *Address temp unknown*

'ERRANOVA, Jonathan Rossano (Ross). b 62. Sheff Poly BA85. Oak Hill Th Coll BA88. **d** 88 **p** 89. C Carl St Jo 88-91; C Stoughton *Guildf* 91-94; R Ditton *Roch* from 94; RD Malling 02-07. *The Rectory, 2 The Stream, Ditton, Maidstone ME20 6AG* Tel (01732) 842027

'ERRELL, Richard Charles Patridge. b 43. Wells Th Coll 69. **d** 71 **p** 72. C Shepton Mallet *B & W* 71-76; P-in-c Drayton 76-78; P-in-c Muchelney 76-78; TV Langport Area 78-82; P-in-c Tatworth 82-89; V 89-96; R W Coker w Hardington Mandeville, E Chinnock etc 96-09; rtd 09. *2 Hamdon View, Norton sub Hamdon, Stoke-sub-Hamdon TA14 6SE* Tel (01935) 881330

'ERRETT, Mervyn Douglas. b 43. AKC65. **d** 66 **p** 67. C Par St Mary Boongate 66-69; C Sawbridgeworth *St Alb* 69-74; V Stevenage H Trin 74-85; Perm to Offic from 86; rtd 08. *Red Roofs, 20 Woodfield Road, Stevenage SG1 4BP* Tel (01438) 720152 E-mail a-top@tiscali.co.uk

'ERRY, Christopher Laurence. b 51. Heythrop Coll Lon MA09 FCA80. St Alb Minl Tr Scheme. **d** 83 **p** 84. Hon C Dunstable *St Alb* 83-89; C Abbots Langley 89-92; TV Chambersbury 92-99; Chapl Abbot's Hill Sch *Herts* 96-99; R Southwick St Mich *Chich* 99-03; RD Hove 00-03; Finance and Admin Sec Min Division Abps' Coun 04-09; TR Gt Yarmouth *Nor* from 09; RD Gt Yarmouth from 11. *The Rectory, Town Wall Road, Great Yarmouth NR30 1DJ* Tel (01493) 842915 E-mail gyteamrector@btinternet.com

'ERRY, Colin Alfred. b 49. Trin Coll Bris. **d** 00 **p** 01. C Bexleyheath Ch Ch *Roch* 00-03; V Belvedere All SS 03-10; Chapl Bromley Coll from 10. *The Chaplain's House, Bromley and Sheppard's Colleges, London Road, Bromley BR1 1PE* Tel (020) 8460 4712 *or* tel and fax 8464 3558 E-mail bromcoll@aol.com

'ERRY, Ms Helen Barbara. b 58. Keele Univ BA80 ATCL98. Ripon Coll Cuddesdon 01. **d** 03 **p** 04. C Cainscross w Selsley *Glouc* 03-07; C Minchinhampton 07-08. *48 Cashes Green Road, Stroud GL5 4LN* Tel (01453) 752792

'ERRY, Mrs Hilary June. b 45. SEITE 08. **d** 11. NSM Uckfield *Chich* from 11. *11 St Saviours, Framfield Road, Uckfield TN22 5AS* Tel (01825) 767793 Mobile 07947-923513 E-mail june.terry@tiscali.co.uk

'ERRY, Ian Andrew. b 53. St Jo Coll Dur BA74 St Jo Coll York PGCE75 St Mary's Coll Twickenham MA99 Surrey Univ PhD05. Coll of Resurr Mirfield 78. **d** 80 **p** 81. C Beaconsfield *Ox* 80-83; C N Lynn w St Marg and St Nic *Nor* 83-84; Chapl and Hd RE Eliz Coll Guernsey 84-89; Chapl St Jo Sch Leatherhead 89-92; R Bisley and W End *Guildf* 92-02; Asst Chapl HM Pris Coldingley 99-02; Dioc Dir of Educn *Heref* 02-08; Hon TV W Heref 03-08; Chapl St Edm Sch Cant 08-09; TR Bournemouth Town Cen *Win* from 09. *St Peter's Rectory, 18 Wimborne Road, Bournemouth BH2 6NT* Tel and fax (01202) 554058 E-mail ianterry@live.co.uk

'ERRY, James Richard. b 74. Linc Coll Ox BA95 ACA98. Oak Hill Th Coll BA03. **d** 03 **p** 04. C Harold Wood *Chelmsf* 03-07; C Blackb Ch Ch w St Matt from 07. *9 Mosley Street, Blackburn BB2 3ST* Tel (01254) 670480 E-mail james_terry1@hotmail.com

'ERRY, John Arthur. b 32. S'wark Ord Course. **d** 66 **p** 67. C Plumstead All SS S'wark 66-69; C Peckham St Mary Magd 69-72; V Streatham Vale H Redeemer 72-80; R Sternfield w Benhall and Snape *St E* 80-84; V Stevenage St Mary Shephall *St Alb* 84-86; V Stevenage St Mary Shephall w Aston 86-90; V Cople w Willington 90-97; Chapl Shuttleworth Agric Coll 90-97; rtd 97; Perm to Offic *St E* from 98; *Nor* 98-04; *Ely* from 03. *2 Kestrel Drive, Brandon IP27 0UA* Tel (01842) 812055 E-mail jterry83@hotmail.com

'ERRY, John Michael. b 56. Ex Univ BSc78 Southn Univ MSc88 Anglia Ruskin Univ BA09 CEng93 MIMarEST93. Ridley Hall Cam 06. **d** 09 **p** 10. NSM Fareham St Jo *Portsm* from 09. *112 Abbeyfield Drive, Fareham PO15 5PQ* Tel (01329) 845193 Mobile 07979-815026 E-mail mike@terry-home.co.uk

'ERRY, Justyn Charles. b 65. Keble Coll Ox BA86 St Jo Coll Dur BA95 K Coll Lon PhD03. Cranmer Hall Dur 92. **d** 95 **p** 96. C Paddington St Jo w St Mich *Lon* 95-99; V Kensington St Helen w H Trin 99-05; Assoc Prof Trin Episc Sch for Min USA 05-08; Dean and Pres from 08. *Trinity Episcopal School for Min, 311 Eleventh Street, Ambridge PA 15003-2302, USA* Tel (001) (800) 874 8754 E-mail jterry@tesm.edu

'ERRY, Lydia Patricia Maud. b 44. Open Univ BSc00. **d** 08 **p** 09. OLM Lydd *Cant* from 08. *5 Eastern Road, Lydd, Romney Marsh TN29 9EE* Tel (01797) 320218

TERRY, Marc David. b 78. Trin Coll Bris 08. **d** 10 **p** 11. C Margate H Trin *Cant* from 10. *10 Richmond Avenue, Margate CT9 2NG* Tel (01843) 571033 Mobile 07734-857820 E-mail revmarcterry@gmail.com

TERRY (*née* LEONARD)**, Mrs Nicola Susan.** b 61. Keele Univ BA85. Ridley Hall Cam 07. **d** 09 **p** 10. NSM Alverstoke *Portsm* from 09. *112 Abbeyfield Drive, Fareham PO15 5PQ* Tel (01329) 845193 E-mail revnsterry@googlemail.com

TERRY, Stephen John. b 49. K Coll Lon BD72 AKC74. **d** 75 **p** 76. C Tokyngton St Mich *Lon* 75-78; C Hampstead St Steph w All Hallows 78-81; V Whetstone St Jo 81-89; TR Aldrington *Chich* 89-07; R from 07. *The Rectory, 77 New Church Road, Hove BN3 4BB* Tel (01273) 737915 Fax 206348 E-mail stephenterry@aldrington.wanadoo.co.uk

TESTA, Luigi Richard Frederick. b 30. EMMTC. **d** 85 **p** 86. NSM Castle Donington and Lockington cum Hemington *Leic* 85-95; Perm to Offic from 95. *50 Huntingdon Drive, Castle Donington, Derby DE74 2SR* Tel (01332) 814671

TESTER, Clarence Albert. b 20. Qu Coll Birm 47. **d** 50 **p** 51. C Southmead *Bris* 50-53; C Knowle St Barn 53-55; Chapl Ham Green Hosp Bris 55-70; V Halberton *Ex* 70-85; rtd 85; Perm to Offic *B & W* 86-98. *Elmside, Elmside Walk, Hitchin SG5 1HB*

TETLEY, Brian. b 38. St Jo Coll Dur BA82 ACA62 FCA72. Cranmer Hall Dur 80. **d** 83 **p** 84. C Chipping Sodbury and Old Sodbury *Glouc* 83-86; Chapl and Succ Roch Cath 86-89; R Gravesend H Family w Ifield 89-93; Tutor Westcott Ho Cam 93-94 and 95-96; Tutor Ridley Hall and Prec Ely Cathl 95; C Duxford, Hinxton and Ickleton 97; Perm to Offic 98-99; NSM Worc Cathl 00-03; rtd 03; Perm to Offic *Worc* 03-08 and *Ox* from 08. *21 Cripley Road, Oxford OX2 0AH* Tel (01865) 250209 E-mail briantetley@btinternet.com

TETLEY, Miss Carol Ruth. b 61. Ches Coll of HE BA84. NEOC 06. **d** 09 **p** 10. NSM Anlaby St Pet *York* from 09. *27 Cranberry Way, Hull HU4 7AQ* Tel (01482) 351644 E-mail carol_tetley@lineone.net

TETLEY, The Ven Joy Dawn. b 46. St Mary's Coll Dur BA68 Leeds Univ CertEd69 St Hugh's Coll Ox BA75 MA80 Dur Univ PhD88. NW Ord Course 77. dss 77 **d** 87 **p** 94. Bentley *Sheff* 77-79; Buttershaw St Aid *Bradf* 79-80; Dur Cathl 80-83; Lect Trin Coll Bris 83-86; Chipping Sodbury and Old Sodbury *Glouc* 83-86; Dn Roch Cathl 87-89; Hon Can 90-93; Assoc Dir of Post Ord Tr 87-88; Dir Post Ord Tr 88-93; Hon Par Dn Gravesend H Family w Ifield 89-93; Prin EAMTC *Ely* 93-99; Adn Worc and Can Res Worc Cathl 99-08; rtd 08; Perm to Offic *Ox* from 08. *23 Cripley Road, Oxford OX2 0AH* Tel (01865) 250209 E-mail briantetley@btinternet.com

TETLEY, Matthew David. b 61. Bucks Coll of Educn BSc83. Sarum & Wells Th Coll BTh89. **d** 87 **p** 88. C Kirkby *Liv* 87-90; C Hindley St Pet 90-93; TV Whorlton *Newc* 93-96; V Newbiggin Hall 96-01; P-in-c Longhorsley and Hebron 01-06; Chapl HM Pris Acklington 01-06 and from 08; Chapl HM Pris Frankland 06-08. *HM Prison Acklington, Morpeth NE65 9XF* Tel (01670) 762300 E-mail matthew.tetley@hmps.gsi.gov.uk

TETLOW, John. b 46. St Steph Ho Ox 73. **d** 76 **p** 77. C Stanwell *Lon* 76-77; C Hanworth All SS 77-80; C Somers Town 80-83; TV Wickford and Runwell *Chelmsf* 83-90; P-in-c Walthamstow St Mich 90-96. *6A Bushwood, London E11 3AY* Tel (020) 8989 9076 E-mail johntetlow@tiscali.co.uk

TETLOW, Richard Jeremy. b 42. Trin Coll Cam MA66 Goldsmiths' Coll Lon CQSW74. Qu Coll Birm 81. **d** 83 **p** 84. C Birm St Martin 83-85; C Birm St Martin w Bordesley St Andr 85-88; V Birm St Jo Ladywood 89-01; V Ladywood St Jo and St Pet 01-08; rtd 08; Perm to Offic *Birm* from 08. *26 Sovereign Way, Moseley, Birmingham B13 8AT* Tel 0121-449 4892

TETZLAFF, Silke. b 67. Friedrich Schiller Univ 87 K Coll Lon BA97 AKC97 Anglia Poly Univ MA01. Westcott Ho Cam 99. **d** 01 **p** 02. C Leagrave *St Alb* 01-05; TV Baldock w Bygrave and Weston from 05; C Sandon, Wallington and Rushden w Clothall from 10. *The Vicarage, 14 Munts Meadow, Weston, Hitchin SG4 7AE* Tel (01462) 790330 E-mail silke.tetzlaff@virgin.net

TEVERSON, Ms Nicola Jane. b 65. SEITE. **d** 05 **p** 06. C Bromley St Mark *Roch* 05-09; Perm to Offic from 09. *The Farm House, Blackness Lane, Keston BR2 6HR* Tel (01689) 851174 E-mail nicky.teverson@btinternet.com

TEWKESBURY, Suffragan Bishop of. *See* WENT, The Rt Revd John Stewart

THACKER, Christine Mary. b 44. Simon Fraser Univ BC BA90. Vancouver Sch of Th MDiv93. **d** 92 **p** 93. R Kitimat Ch Ch Canada 89-07; C Boultham *Linc* 00-09; rtd 10; Perm to Offic *Nor* from 10. *2 Church Close, Hunstanton PE36 6BE* Tel (01485) 534860 E-mail christine.thacker@virginmedia.com

THACKER, Ian David. b 59. Oak Hill Th Coll BA91. **d** 91 **p** 92. C Illogan *Truro* 91-94; C Eglwysilan *Llan* 94-96; TV Hornsey Rise Whitehall Park Team *Lon* 96-97; TV Upper Holloway 97-01; Chapl HM YOI Huntercombe and Finnamore from 01. *HM Young Offender Institution, Huntercombe Place, Nuffield, Henley-on-Thames RG9 5SB* Tel (01491) 641711 *or* 641715 Fax 641902 E-mail ithacker@talk21.com

THACKER, Jonathan William. b 53. Lon Univ BA74. Linc Th Coll 76. **d** 79 **p** 80. C Bromyard *Heref* 79-82; C Penkridge w Stretton *Lich* 82-87; V Brothertoft Gp *Linc* 87-96; RD Holland W 92-95; P-in-c Crosby 96-01; V from 01; Chapl Scunthorpe and Goole Hosps NHS Trust 99-01; Chapl N Lincs and Goole Hosps NHS Trust 01. *St George's Vicarage, 87 Ferry Road, Scunthorpe DN15 8LY* Tel and fax (01724) 843328 *or* tel 843336 E-mail jon@han195.freeserve.co.uk

THACKRAY, John Adrian. b 55. Southn Univ BSc76 ACIB84. Coll of Resurr Mirfield 81. **d** 84 **p** 85. C Loughton St Jo *Chelmsf* 84-87; Chapl Bancroft's Sch Woodford Green 87-92; Sen Chapl K Sch Cant 92-01; Chapl Abp's Sch Cant 01-02; Hon Min Can Cant Cathl from 93; Sen Chapl K Sch Roch from 02; Hon PV Roch Cathl from 02. *King's School, Satis House, Boley Hill, Rochester ME1 1TE* Tel (01634) 888555 E-mail thereverendfather@hotmail.com

THACKRAY, William Harry. b 44. Leeds Univ CertEd66. Chich Th Coll 70. **d** 73 **p** 74. C Sheff St Cuth 73-76; C Stocksbridge 76-78; P-in-c Newark St Leon *S'well* 79-80; TV Newark w Hawton, Cotham and Shelton 80-82; V Choral S'well Minster 82-85; V Bawtry w Austerfield 85; P-in-c Misson 85; V Bawtry w Austerfield and Misson 86-93; RD Bawtry 90-93; P-in-c Balderton 93-03; P-in-c Coddington w Barnby in the Willows 98-03; V Biggleswade *St Alb* 03-09; RD Biggleswade 07-09; rtd 09; Hon C Lower Swale *Ripon* from 09. *The Vicarage, 11 Meadow Drive, Scruton, Northallerton DL7 0QW* Tel (01609) 748245 E-mail vicar@the-thackrays.eclipse.co.uk

THAKE (née SEARS), Ms Helen. b 50. Birm Coll of Educn CertEd71. Qu Coll Birm 96. **d** 98 **p** 99. C Hadley *Lich* 98-01; C Cannock 01-06; Chapl HM Pris Swinfen Hall 06-07; Chapl HM Pris Foston Hall from 07. *HM Prison Foston Hall, Foston, Derby DE65 5EN* Tel (01283) 584300

THAKE, Preb Terence. b 41. ALCD65. **d** 66 **p** 67. C Gt Faringdon w Lt Coxwell *Ox* 66-70; C Aldridge *Lich* 70-73; V Werrington 73-82; Chapl HM Det Cen Werrington Ho 73-82; TR Chell *Lich* 82-94; Chapl Westcliffe Hosp 82-94; RD Stoke N 91-94; V Colwich w Gt Haywood 94-00; P-in-c Colton 95-00; R Colton, Colwich and Gt Haywood 00-04; RD Rugeley 98-06; Preb Lich Cathl 94-10; rtd 04. *9 Rowan Court, Belper DE56 1SJ* E-mail tthake@tiscali.co.uk

THAME, Miss Margaret Eve. b 31. SRN54 SCM55. Glouc Sch of Min 85. **d** 88 **p** 94. NSM Pittville All SS *Glouc* 88-94; NSM Cheltenham St Mich 94-02; Perm to Offic from 02. *13 Brighton Road, Cheltenham GL52 6BA* Tel (01242) 241228

THATCHER, Barbara Mary. b 25. Lon Univ BCom. **d** 90 **p** 94. NSM Helensburgh *Glas* 90-01. *228 West Princes Street, Helensburgh G84 8HA* Tel (01436) 672003

THATCHER, Stephen Bert. b 58. Greenwich Univ PGCE03. St Jo Coll Nottm LTh87 ALCD87. **d** 87 **p** 88. C Bargoed and Deri w Brithdir *Llan* 87-89; C Llanishen and Lisvane 89-91; V Llanwnda, Goodwick w Manorowen and Llanstinan *St D* 91-95; P-in-c Coberley, Cowley, Colesbourne and Elkstone *Glouc* 95-96; Dioc Rural Adv 95-96; R New Radnor and Llanfihangel Nantmelan etc *S & B* 96-00; Dioc Tourism Officer 96-99; Dioc Chs and Tourism Rep 97-00; CF from 00. *c/o MOD Chaplains (Army)* Tel (01264) 381140 Fax 381824 E-mail stephen.thatcher2@btopenworld.com

THAWLEY, The Very Revd David Laurie. b 24. St Edm Hall Ox BA47 MA49. Cuddesdon Coll 49. **d** 51 **p** 52. C Bitterne Park *Win* 51-56; C-in-c Andover St Mich CD 56-60; Australia from 60; Can Res Brisbane 64-72; Dean Wangaratta 72-89; rtd 89. *Lavender Cottage, 2 Bond Street, North Caulfield Vic 3161, Australia* Tel (0061) (3) 9571 0513 Mobile 407-811870 E-mail dthawley@bigpond.com

THAYER, Michael David. b 52. Sarum & Wells Th Coll 77. **d** 80 **p** 81. C Minehead *B & W* 80-85; Chapl RN 85-89; TV Lowestoft and Kirkley *Nor* 89-92; Chapl St Helena Hospice Colchester 92-97; Chapl HM Pris Acklington 99-01; Chapl HM Pris Erlestoke 01-03; R S Tawton and Belstone *Ex* 03-07; P-in-c Highweek from 07. *The Rectory, 15 Stoneleigh Close, Newton Abbot TQ12 1QZ* Tel (01626) 201436 E-mail rmhthayer@yahoo.co.uk

THEAKER, David Michael. b 41. **d** 68 **p** 69. C Folkingham w Laughton *Linc* 68-71; C New Cleethorpes 71-74; P-in-c Gt Grimsby St Andr and St Luke 74-77; P-in-c Thurlby 77-79; Perm to Offic *Ely* from 00. *11 Willow Way, Hauxton, Cambridge CB22 5JB* Tel (01223) 873132 E-mail the-theakers@issue-forth.com

THEAKER, John Henry. b 42. MBE01. WEMTC 05. **d** 08 **p** 09. NSM Leominster *Heref* from 08. *Monkland House, Monkland, Leominster HR6 9DE* Tel (01568) 720472 Mobile 07796-595664 E-mail theaker958@btinternet.com

THEAKSTON, Canon Sally Margaret. b 62. UEA BSc84 Ox Univ BA89 K Coll Lon MA94. Ripon Coll Cuddesdon 86. **d** 89 **p** 94. Par Dn Hackney *Lon* 89-93; Par Dn Putney St Mary *S'wark* 93-94; C 94-96; Chapl RN 96-02; TR Gaywood *Nor* 02-09; TR Dereham and Distr from 09; RD Dereham in Mitford from 10; Hon Can Nor Cathl from 10. *The Rectory, 1 Vicarage*

Meadows, Dereham NR19 1TW Tel (01362) 693680 Mobile 07904-070654 E-mail stheakston@aol.com

THELWELL, The Ven John Berry. b 49. Univ of Wales (Ban BD72. Qu Coll Birm 73. **d** 73 **p** 74. C Minera *St As* 73-80; Dio Youth Chapl 78-86; V Gwernaffield and Llanferres 80-93; Chap Clwyd Fire Service 88-94; RD Mold 91-95; TR Hawarden 93-02 Can Cursal St As Cathl 95-02; Prec 98-02; Adn Montgomery from 02; V Berriew from 03. *The Vicarage, Berriew, Welshpoo SY21 8PL* Tel and fax (01686) 640223

THEOBALD, Graham Fitzroy. b 43. ALCD67. **d** 67 **p** 68. C Crookham *Guildf* 67-71; C York Town St Mich 71-74; V Wrecclesham 74-83; Chapl Green Lane Hosp 74-81; R Frimley 83-85; Chapl Frimley Park Hosp 83-85; Perm to Offic *Ox* 90-92 C Easthampstead 92-97; Chapl E Berks NHS Trust 92-03; rtd 03; Perm to Offic *Ox* from 03. *50 Viking, Bracknell RG12 8UI* Tel (01344) 428525 Mobile 07721-408740 E-mail witsend50@waitrose.com

THEOBALD, John Walter. b 33. St Aid Birkenhead 62. **d** 65 **p** 66 C Hindley All SS *Liv* 65-68; C Beverley Minster *York* 68-71; R Loftus 71-86; P-in-c Carlin How w Skinningrove 73-86; Dep Chapl HM Pris Leeds 86-89; Chapl HM Pris Rudgate 89-93 Thorp Arch 89-93; Leeds 93-97; V Leeds St Cypr Harehills *Ripon* 97-01; rtd 01; P-in-c Swillington *Ripon* 01-05. *8 Invernes Road, Garforth, Leeds LS25 2LS*

THEOBALD, Susan Ann. b 61. La Sainte Union Coll BEd83 STETS 07. **d** 10 **p** 11. C Southsea St Jude *Portsm* from 10 *22 Clarence Road, Southsea PO5 2LG* Tel (023) 9235 1096 E-mail s.theobald22@virginmedia.com

THEODOSIUS, Hugh John. b 32. Trin Coll Cam BA56 MA60 Cuddesdon Coll 56. **d** 58 **p** 59. C Milton *Win* 58-62; C Romsey 62-64; C Southampton Maybush St Pet 64-70; V Malden St Jc *S'wark* 70-81; V Billingborough *Linc* 81-94; V Horbling 81-94; V Sempringham w Pointon and Birthorpe 81-94; RD Aveland and Ness w Stamford 87-93; rtd 97; Perm to Offic *Linc* from 00 and *Ely* from 01. *Sempringham House, East Bank, Sutton Bridge Spalding PE12 9YN* Tel (01406) 351977

THEODOSIUS, James William Fletcher. b 73. Univ of Wale (Cardiff) BA94 Selw Coll Cam BA04 MA08 Sussex Uni DPhil09 Cant Ch Ch Univ Coll PGCE96. Westcott Ho Cam 02 **d** 05 **p** 06. C Chich St Paul and Westhampnett 05-09; Dir Reade Tr SWMTC from 09; Chapl Ex Univ from 09. *The Chaplaincy University of Exeter, St Luke's Campus, Heavitree Road, Exeter EX1 2LU* E-mail j.w.f.theodosius@ex.ac.uk

THEODOSIUS, Richard Francis. b 35. Fitzw Coll Cam BA59 Lich Th Coll 69. **d** 71 **p** 72. C Bloxwich *Lich* 71-73; Chapl Blue Coat Comp Sch Walsall 71-73; Chapl Ranby Ho Sch Retforc 73-96; P-in-c Norton Cuckney *S'well* 96-02; rtd 02. *Downlea, 51 Town Street, Lound, Retford DN22 8RT* Tel (01777) 818744

THETFORD, Suffragan Bishop of. *See* WINTON, The Rt Revc Alan Peter

THEWLIS, Andrew James. b 64. Man Univ BSc86. Cranmer Hal Dur 87. **d** 90 **p** 91. C Walshaw Ch Ch *Man* 90-95; P-in-c Jersey St Jo *Win* 95-98; R from 98. *The Rectory, La rue des Landes, St John, Jersey JE3 4AF* Tel (01534) 861677 Mobile 07797- 723828 E-mail athewlis@jerseymail.co.uk

THEWLIS, Brian Jacob. b 24. Melbourne Univ BA49. Coll of Resurr Mirfield 52. **d** 53 **p** 54. C Wednesbury St Jas *Lich* 53-57 Chapl K Coll Auckland New Zealand 57-61; C Sidley *Chich* 59-60; I Reservoir St Geo Australia 61-68; I Malvern St Paul 68-82; I Beaumaris St Mich 82-87; I Frankston St Paul 87-94; rtd 94. *41 Sixth Street, Parkdale Vic 3194, Australia* Tel (0061) (3) 9587 3095

THEWLIS, John Charles. b 49. Van Mildert Coll Dur BA70 PhD75. NOC 78. **d** 81 **p** 82. NSM Hull St Mary Sculcoates *York* 81-83; C Spring Park *Cant* 83-84; C Spring Park All SS *S'wark* 85-86; V Eltham Park St Luke 86-01; R Carshalton from 01. *The Rectory, 2 Talbot Road, Carshalton SM5 3BS* Tel (020) 8647 2366 E-mail rector@jctclerk.demon.co.uk

THEWSEY, Robert Sydney. b 65. Ripon Coll Cuddesdon 99. **d** 01 **p** 02. C Chorlton-cum-Hardy St Clem *Man* 01-04; P-in-c Stretford All SS 04-08; P-in-c Boscastle w Davidstow *Truro* from 08; RD Stratton from 11. *The Rectory, Forrabury, Boscastle PL35 0DJ* Tel (01840) 250359 E-mail robert.thewsey@btinternet.com

THICKE, James Balliston. b 43. Sarum & Wells Th Coll 74. **d** 77 **p** 78. C Wareham *Sarum* 77-80; TV 80-83; Dioc Youth Adv *Dur* 83-87; C Portishead *B & W* 87-90; V Westfield 90-08; RD Midsomer Norton 98-04; Chapl Norton Radstock Coll of FE 00-08; rtd 08. *11 Welton Grove, Midsomer Norton, Radstock BA3 2TS* Tel (01761) 411905 E-mail james@balliston.demon.co.uk

✠**THIRD, The Rt Revd Richard Henry McPhail.** b 27. Em Coll Cam BA50 MA55 Kent Univ Hon DCL90. Linc Th Coll 50. **d** 52 **p** 53 **c** 76. C Mottingham St Andr w St Alban *S'wark* 52-55; C Sanderstead All SS 55-59; V Sheerness H Trin w St Paul *Cant* 59-67; V Orpington All SS *Roch* 67-76; RD Orpington 73-76; Hon Can Roch Cathl 74-76; Suff Bp Maidstone *Cant* 76-80; Suff Bp Dover 80-92; rtd 92; Hon Asst Bp B & W from 92. *25 Church Close, Martock TA12 6DS* Tel (01935) 825519

THIRLWELL, Miss Margaret. b 36. Bris Univ BA59 St Aid Coll Dur DipEd61. d 03 p 04. OLM Binfield *Ox* 03-09; Perm to Offic from 09. *70 Red Rose, Binfield, Bracknell RG42 5LD* Tel (01344) 423920 E-mail margaret@mthirlwell.fsnet.co.uk

THIRTLE, Ms Lucy Rachel. b 62. Ex Univ BA85. Cranmer Hall Dur 97. d 99 p 00. C Basingstoke *Win* 99-04; P-in-c Kingsclere 04-06; P-in-c Ashford Hill w Headley 06; V Kingsclere and Ashford Hill w Headley from 06. *The Vicarage, Fox's Lane, Kingsclere, Newbury RG20 5SL* Tel (01635) 299489 E-mail lucythirtle@btinternet.com

THISELTON, Prof Anthony Charles. b 37. Lon Univ BD59 K Coll Lon MTh64 Sheff Univ PhD77 Dur Univ DD93 Lambeth DD02 FBA10 FKC10. Oak Hill Th Coll 58. d 60 p 61. C Sydenham H Trin *S'wark* 60-63; Tutor Tyndale Hall Bris 63-67; Sen Tutor 67-70; Lect Bibl Studies Sheff Univ 70-79; Sen Lect 79-85; Prof Calvin Coll Grand Rapids 82-83; Special Lect Th Nottm Univ 86-88; Prin St Jo Coll Nottm 86-88; Prin St Jo Coll w Cranmer Hall Dur 88-92; Prof Chr Th Nottm Univ from 92; Can Th Leic Cathl from 94 and S'well Minster from 00. *Department of Theology, Nottingham University, University Park, Nottingham NG7 2RD* Tel 0115-951 5852 Fax 951 5887 E-mail thiselton@ntlworld.com

THISTLETHWAITE, Canon Nicholas John. b 51. Selw Coll Cam BA73 MA77 PhD80. Ripon Coll Cuddesdon BA78 MA83. d 79 p 80. C Newc St Gabr 79-82; Chapl G&C Coll Cam 82-90; Lic to Offic *Ely* 82-90; V Trumpington 90-99; Can Res and Prec Guildf Cathl from 99; Sub-Dean from 06. *3 Cathedral Close, Guildford GU2 7TL* Tel and fax (01483) 569682 *or* tel 547865 E-mail precentor@guildford-cathedral.org

THISTLEWOOD, Michael John. b 31. Ch Coll Cam BA53 MA57. Linc Th Coll 54. d 56 p 57. C N Hull St Mich *York* 56-59; C Scarborough St Mary 59-61; V Kingston upon Hull St Jude w St Steph 61-67; V Newland St Aug 67-72; Asst Master Bemrose Sch Derby 72-80; V Derby St Andr w St Osmund 80-82; Lic to Offic *Ox* 84-95; rtd 88; Perm to Offic *Carl* 88-98; *Derby* 98-05; *Carl* 05-08 and from 09. *44 Blackhall Croft, Blackhall Road, Kendal LA9 4UU*

THODAY, Margaret Frances. b 38. d 03 p 04. OLM Roughton and Felbrigg, Metton, Sustead etc *Nor* 03-08; Perm to Offic from 08. *Flat 3, 4 Norwich Road, Cromer NR27 0AX* Tel (01263) 510945

THODY, Charles Michael Jackson. b 62. Linc Th Coll BTh94. d 94 p 95. C Immingham *Linc* 94-97; P-in-c Leasingham and Cranwell 97-01; P-in-c Bishop Norton, Wadingham and Snitterby 01-03; Chapl Doncaster and S Humber Healthcare NHS Trust 01-03; Chapl Notts Healthcare NHS Trust 03-09; Chapl Rotherham, Doncaster and S Humber NHS Trust from 09. *Chaplaincy, St Catherine's Hospital, Tickhill Road, Doncaster DN4 8QN* Tel (01302) 796000 Fax 796816

THOM, Alastair George. b 60. G&C Coll Cam BA81 MA84 ACA86. Ridley Hall Cam 88. d 91 p 92. C Lindfield *Chich* 91-94; C Finchley St Paul and St Luke *Lon* 94-98; P-in-c Paddington Em Harrow Road from 98; P-in-c W Kilburn St Luke w St Simon and St Jude from 98; AD Westmr Paddington 06-11. *The Vicarage, 19 Macroom Road, London W9 3HY* Tel (020) 8962 0294 E-mail alastairthom@yahoo.co.uk

THOM, Christopher Henry. d 03 p 04. NSM Loose *Cant* from 03. *Old Hill House, Old Loose Hill, Loose, Maidstone ME15 0BN* Tel (01622) 744833 E-mail chthom@ukonline.co.uk

THOM, James. b 31. St Chad's Coll Dur BA53. d 57 p 58. C Middlesbrough St Thos *York* 57-60; C Hornsea and Goxhill 60-62; C S Bank 62-63; V Copmanthorpe 63-75; V Coxwold 75-77; RD Easingwold 77-82; V Coxwold and Husthwaite 77-87; Abp's Adv for Spiritual Direction 86-93; P-in-c Topcliffe 87-93; rtd 93; Perm to Offic *Ripon* and *York* from 93. *34 Hell Wath Grove, Ripon HG4 2JT* Tel (01765) 605083

THOMAS, Adrian Leighton. b 37. Univ of Wales (Lamp) BA62 Univ of Wales (Cardiff) PGCE73. St D Coll Lamp. d 63 p 64. C Port Talbot St Theodore *Llan* 63-70; V Troedrhiwgarth 70-73; C Sandhurst *Ox* 73-77; V Streatley 77-84; P-in-c Moulsford 81-84; V Streatley w Moulsford 84-90; P-in-c Sutton Courtenay w Appleford 90-00; V 00-02; AD Abingdon 96-02; rtd 02; P-in-c Lugano *Eur* 02-06. *13 The Birches, Goring, Reading RG8 9BW* Tel (01491) 872696 E-mail adrianleighton.thomas@gmail.com

THOMAS, Alan. *See* THOMAS, Thomas Alan

THOMAS, Aled Huw. b 59. Univ of Wales (Abth) BD81. St Mich Coll Llan 84. d 85 p 86. C Llandeilo Fawr and Taliaris *St D* 85-86; P-in-c Llangrannog and Llandysiliogogo 86-88; Chapl RAF 88-92; R Ystradgynlais *S & B* 92-97; C 94-10; V St Dogmael's w Moylgrove and Monington *St D* from 10. *The Vicarage, Shingrig, St Dogmael's, Cardigan SA43 3DX* Tel (01239) 613678

THOMAS, The Ven Alfred James Randolph. b 48. St D Coll Lamp. d 71 p 72. C Cydweli and Llandyfaelog *St D* 71-74; C Carmarthen St Dav 74-76; TV Aberystwyth 76-81; V Betws w Ammanford 81-93; RD Dyffryn Aman 90-93; V Carmarthen St Pet and Chapl Carmarthenshire NHS Trust 93-02; Can St D Cathl 96-02; V Bronllys w Llanfilo *S & B* 02-06; P-in-c Llanfrynach and Cantref w Llanhamlach from 06; Adn Brecon

from 03. *The Rectory, Llanfrynach, Brecon LD3 7AJ* Tel (01874) 665667

THOMAS, Andrew Herbert Redding. b 41. Lon Coll of Div 66. d 69 p 70. C Cromer *Nor* 69-72; Holiday Chapl 72-76; R Grimston w Congham 76-83; R Roydon All SS 76-83; C-in-c Ewell St Paul Howell Hill CD *Guildf* 83-89; V Howell Hill 89-95; RD Epsom 93-95; TR Beccles St Mich *St E* 95-04; P-in-c Worlingham w Barnby and N Cove 98-01; rtd 04; Perm to Offic *Nor* and *St E* from 04. *9A Corner Street, Cromer NR27 9HW* Tel (01263) 515091 E-mail ahrthomas@waitrose.com

THOMAS, Andrew John. b 62. Univ of Wales (Abth) BSc84 ACA87. ERMC 04. d 07 p 08. NSM Stevenage H Trin *St Alb* from 07. *1 Ash Drive, St Ippolyts, Hitchin SG4 7SJ* Tel (01462) 421647 E-mail ajt250762@aol.com

THOMAS, Andrew Nigel. b 75. RN99. Westcott Ho Cam 08. d 10 p 11. C The Cookhams *Ox* from 10. *3 The Parish Centre, Sutton Road, Cookham, Maidenhead SL6 9SN* Tel (01628) 521483 Mobile 07793-547628 E-mail and73w@me.com

THOMAS, Andrew Peter. d 08. C Llanishen 08-10. *Address temp unknown*

THOMAS, Andrew Robert. b 80. G&C Coll Cam BA03. Oak Hill Th Coll BA09. d 09 p 10. C Angmering *Chich* from 09. *20 Cumberland Road, Angmering, Littlehampton BN16 4BG* Tel (01903) 786414 Mobile 07786-376615 E-mail andythomas196@yahoo.co.uk

THOMAS, Anne Valerie. *See* NOBLE, Anne Valerie

THOMAS, Arun. *See* THOMAS, John Arun

THOMAS, Austin George. b 23. Open Univ BA75. Wells Th Coll 65. d 67 p 68. C Brislington St Luke 67-73; P-in-c Bris St Geo 73-74; P-in-c Bris St Leon Redfield 74-75; TV E Bris 75-80; R Lyddington w Wanborough 80-88; rtd 88; Perm to Offic *Bris* from 88. *36 Purdy Court, New Station Road, Bristol BS16 3RT* Tel 0117-958 3511

THOMAS, Canon Barry Wilfred. b 41. Univ of Wales (Cardiff) BD75. St Mich Coll Llan 72. d 75 p 76. C Porthmadog *Ban* 75-78; V Llanegryn and Llanfihangel-y-Pennant etc 78-82; TR Llanbeblig w Caernarfon and Betws Garmon etc 82-94; Sec Dioc Coun for Miss and Unity 81-94; Can Ban Cathl 89-94; Chapl Monte Carlo *Eur* 95-00; V Llanfihangel Ystrad and Cilcennin w Trefilan etc *St D* 00-06; rtd 06. *6 Diana Road, Llandeilo SA19 6RR* Tel (01558) 824230

THOMAS, Bernard. *See* THOMAS, The Ven Elwyn Bernard

THOMAS, Bryan. b 36. Univ of Wales (Abth) BA59. St Deiniol's Hawarden 68. d 70 p 71. C Llangynwyd w Maesteg 70-72; V Cwmllynfell *St D* 72-76; V Gors-las 76-82; R Yarnbury *Sarum* 82-97; TR Wylye and Till Valley 97-02; RD Wylye and Wilton 94-98; rtd 02; Perm to Offic *Sarum* from 03 and *B & W* from 05. *11 Ebble Crescent, Warminster BA12 9PF* Tel (01985) 300519

THOMAS, The Ven Charles Edward (Ted). b 27. Univ of Wales (Lamp) BA51. Coll of Resurr Mirfield 51. d 53 p 54. C Ilminster w Whitelackington *B & W* 53-56; Chapl St Mich Coll Tenbury 56-57; C St Alb St Steph *St Alb* 57-58; V Boreham Wood St Mich 58-66; R Monksilver w Brompton Ralph and Nettlecombe *B & W* 66-74; P-in-c Nettlecombe 68-69; R S Petherton w the Seavingtons 74-83; RD Crewkerne 77-83; Adn Wells, Can Res and Preb Wells Cathl 83-93; rtd 93; Perm to Offic *St D* from 93. *Geryfelin, Pentre, Tregaron SY25 6JG* Tel (01974) 298102

THOMAS, Charles Leslie. b 58. Qu Coll Birm 09. d 11. C Sevenhampton w Charlton Abbots, Hawling etc *Glouc* from 11. *The Rectory, Withington, Cheltenham GL54 4BG* Tel (01242) 890650 E-mail coln.river.curate@gmail.com

THOMAS, Charles Moray Stewart Reid. b 53. BNC Ox BA74 MA79. Wycliffe Hall Ox 75. d 78 p 79. C Bradf Cathl 78-81; C Barnsbury St Andr and H Trin w All SS *Lon* 81-90; TV Barnsbury 90-99; Chapl Lon Goodenough Trust 99-08; V Grayshott *Guildf* from 08. *The Vicarage, 10 Vicarage Gardens, Grayshott, Hindhead GU26 6NH* Tel (01428) 606703 E-mail moray@thethomases.org.uk

THOMAS, Cheeramattathu John. b 25. Travancore Univ BA46 BT49 Serampore Coll BD55 United Th Coll Bangalore MA66. Andover Newton Th Coll. d 56 p 57. Singapore 55-60; Sarawak 60-65; C Eastham *Ches* 66-74; V Gt Sutton 75-83; USA from 83; rtd 91. *4622 Pin Oak Lane, Bellaire TX 77401-2504, USA*

THOMAS, Chloe Ann Mary. b 60. GMusRNCM83. Ripon Coll Cuddesdon 07. d 09 p 10. C Knighton St Mary Magd *Leic* from 09. *62 Elms Road, Leicester LE2 3JB* Tel 0116-270 0228 Mobile 07801-886736 E-mail chloe.thomas5@btinternet.com

THOMAS, Clive Alexander. b 49. Open Univ BA77 St Luke's Coll Ex CertEd71. STETS 94. d 97 p 99. NSM Southwick St Mich *Chich* 97-01; C Bridport *Sarum* 01-04; TV Shaston 04-09; TR Shaftesbury from 09. *The Rectory, 10 Heathfields Way, Shaftesbury SP7 9JZ* Tel (01747) 855375 E-mail rev.clive@btinternet.com

✠THOMAS, The Rt Revd David. b 42. Keble Coll Ox BA64 BA66 MA65. St Steph Ho Ox 64. d 67 p 68. c 96. C Hawarden *St As* 67-69; Tutor St Mich Coll Llan 69-70; Chapl 70-75; Sec Ch in Wales Liturg Commn 70-75; Vice-Prin St Steph Ho Ox 75-79; Prin 82-87; V Chepstow *Mon* 79-82; Lic to Offic *Ox* 82-87; V

Newton St Pet *S & B* 87-96; Can Brecon Cathl 94-96; RD Clyne 96; Prov Asst Bp 96-08; rtd 08. *65 Westland Avenue, West Cross, Swansea SA3 5NR*

THOMAS, David. b 49. d 08 p 09. NSM Barnes S'*wark* from 08. *31 Dault Road, London SW18 2NH* Tel (020) 8870 7596 *or* tel and fax 8741 5422 E-mail david@dthomas91.fsnet.co.uk

THOMAS, David Brian. b 45. MIEEE. St D Dioc Tr Course 82. d 85 p 86. NSM Llandysul *St D* 85-87; NSM Lampeter Pont Steffan w Silian 88-92; NSM Lampeter and Ultra-Aeron 92-96; P-in-c Llanfihangel Genau'r-glyn and Llangorwen 96-97; V 97-10; AD Llanbadarn Fawr 00-10; rtd 10. *9 Ty Rhys, The Parade, Carmarthen SA31 1LY*

THOMAS, David Edward. b 60. Univ of Wales (Lamp) BA83. St Mich Coll Llan 85. d 86 p 87. C Killay *S & B* 86-89; P-in-c Newbridge-on-Wye and Llanfihangel Brynpabuan 89-90; V 90-91; V Brecon St David w Llanspyddid and Llanilltyd 91-09; V Glasbury and Llowes w Clyro and Betws from 09. *The Vicarage, 4 The Birches, Glasbury, Hereford HR3 5NW* Tel (01497) 847156

THOMAS, David Geoffrey. b 37. Univ of Wales (Cardiff) BA58. Launde Abbey 70 Qu Coll Birm 71. d 71 p 72. Hon C Fenny Drayton *Leic* 71-75; Chapl Community of the H Family Baldslow Chich 75-77; Perm to Offic *Chich* 77-79; P-in-c Mill End and Heronsgate w W Hyde *St Alb* 79-81; Sen Lect Watford Coll 82-91; R Walgrave w Hannington and Wold and Scaldwell *Pet* 91-01; rtd 01; Perm to Offic *Pet* 01-06. *1 Cypress Close, Desborough, Kettering NN14 2XU* Tel and fax (01536) 763749

THOMAS, The Very Revd David Glynne. b 41. Dur Univ BSc63. Westcott Ho Cam 64. d 67 p 68. C St John's Wood *Lon* 67-70; Min Can St Alb 70-72; Chapl Wadh Coll Ox 72-75; C Ox St Mary V w St Cross and St Pet 72-75; Bp's Dom Chapl 75-78; P-in-c Burnham w Dropmore, Hitcham and Taplow 82-83; R Coolangatta Australia 83-86; R Toowoomba 86-87; Can Res Worc Cathl 87-99; Dean Brisbane 99-03; Chapl to Abp Brisbane 03-06; rtd 06. *173 Edgewater Village, 171 David Low Way, Bli Bli QLD 4560, Australia* Tel (0061) (7) 5450 8224 E-mail davidthomas@westnet.com.au

THOMAS, David Godfrey. b 50. St Chad's Coll Dur BA71 Fitzw Coll Cam BA74 MA78. Westcott Ho Cam 72. d 75 p 76. C Kirkby *Liv* 75-78; TV Cov E 78-88; TR Canvey Is *Chelmsf* 88-92; R Wivenhoe 92-09; R Shenfield from 09. *The Rectory, 41 Worrin Road, Shenfield, Brentwood CM15 8DH* Tel (01277) 220360 E-mail thomas50@tiscali.co.uk

THOMAS, David John. b 34. Univ of Wales (Swansea) St D Coll Lamp. St D Dioc Tr Course 85. d 88 p 89. NSM Cwmaman *St D* 88-96; Public Preacher from 96. *9 New School Road, Garnant, Ammanford SA18 1LL* Tel (01269) 823936

THOMAS, David Richard. b 48. BNC Ox BA71 MA74 Fitzw Coll Cam BA75 MA80 Lanc Univ PhD83. Ridley Hall Cam 73 Qu Coll Birm 79. d 80 p 81. C Anfield St Columba *Liv* 80-83; C Liv Our Lady and St Nic w St Anne 83-85; Chapl CCC Cam 85-90; V Witton *Blackb* 90-93; Bp's Adv on Inter-Faith Relns 90-93; Dir Cen for Study of Islam and Chr-Muslim Relns Selly Oak 93-04; Sen Lect Birm Univ 99-04; Perm to Offic *Derby* from 05. *The Vicarage, Church Square, Melbourne, Derby DE73 8JH* Tel (01332) 864121

THOMAS, David Ronald Holt. b 28. Lich Th Coll 55. d 58 p 59. C Uttoxeter w Bramshall *Lich* 58-61; C Hednesford 61-66; R Armitage from 66; RD Rugeley 88-94. *The Rectory, Hood Lane, Armitage, Rugeley WS15 4AG* Tel (01543) 490278 E-mail davidthomas015@btinternet.com

THOMAS, Canon David Thomas. b 44. St Cath Coll Cam BA66 MA70. Cranmer Hall Dur. d 71 p 72. C Chorlton-cum-Hardy St Clem *Man* 71-74; Chapl Salford Tech Coll 74-79; P-in-c Pendleton St Thos *Man* 75-77; V 77-80; TR Gleadless *Sheff* 80-90; RD Attercliffe 86-90; V Benchill *Man* 90-99; TV Wythenshawe 99-00; AD Withington 99-00; P-in-c Stretford St Matt 00-09; Hon Can Man Cathl 09; rtd 09; Perm to Offic *Man* from 09. *31 Sun Street, Ulverston LA12 7BX* Tel (01229) 585900 E-mail tom-hil@talk21.com

THOMAS, David William Wallace. b 51. St Chad's Coll Dur BA72. St Mich Coll Llan 72. d 75 p 76. C Bargoed and Deri w Brithdir *Llan* 75-79; Hon C 79-81; V Nantymoel w Wyndham 81-84; Chapl RN 84-07. *Address temp unknown*

THOMAS, David Wynford. b 48. Univ of Wales (Abth) LLB70. Qu Coll Birm 76. d 79 p 80. C Swansea St Mary w H Trin and St Mark *S & B* 79-83; P-in-c Swansea St Mark 83-89; Lic to Offic 90. *74 Terrace Road, Swansea SA1 6HU*

THOMAS, Canon Dillwyn Morgan. b 26. Univ of Wales (Lamp) BA50. Qu Coll Birm 50. d 52 p 53. C Dowlais *Llan* 52-59; C Pontypridd St Cath 59-63; V Llanwynno 63-68; V Bargoed w Brithdir 68-74; V Bargoed and Deri w Brithdir 74-75; V Penarth All SS 75-88; Can Llan Cathl 86-88; rtd 88; Perm to Offic *Llan* from 88. *11 Baroness Place, Penarth CF64 3UL* Tel (029) 2025 1698

THOMAS, Dorothy Judith. b 47. Univ of Wales (Cardiff) BA68. Princeton Th Sem MDiv94 MTh96 San Francisco Th Sem DMin01. d 03 p 04. NSM Wargrave w Knowl Hill *Ox* 03-07; Perm to Offic from 09. *7 Cranbourne Hall, Drift Road, Winkfield, Windsor SL4 4FG* Tel (01344) 891699 E-mail djudthomas@hotmail.com

THOMAS (née THOMSON), Mrs Dorothy Lucille. b 39. Univ of Wales (Lamp). d 00 p 10. OLM Pontnewydd *Mon* from 00. *Raldoro, Mount Pleasant Road, Pontnewydd, Cwmbran NP44 1BD* Tel (01633) 771353

THOMAS, Edward. See THOMAS, The Ven Charles Edward

THOMAS, Edward Bernard Meredith. b 21. Leeds Univ BA44 Univ of Qld BEd68 BD72. Coll of Resurr Mirfield 47. d 49 p 50. C St Mary-at-Lambeth S'*wark* 49-54; C Portsea N End St Mark *Portsm* 54-56; V Portsea All SS 56-64; Australia from 64; rtd 92. *33 Highfield Street, Durack Qld 4077, Australia* Tel (0061) (7) 3372 3517

THOMAS, Edward Walter Dennis. b 32. St Mich Coll Llan 61. d 63 p 64. C Loughor *S & B* 63-69; V Ystradfellte 69-74; V Dukinfield St Mark and St Luke *Ches* 74-04; Chapl Gtr Man Police from 77; OCF 88-00; rtd 04; Perm to Offic *Ches* and *Man* from 04. *16 Boyd's Walk, Dukinfield SK16 4TW* Tel 0161-330 1324 E-mail revewdt@aol.com

THOMAS, Canon Eirwyn Wheldon. b 35. St Mich Coll Llan 58. d 61 p 62. C Glanadda *Ban* 61-67; R Llantrisant and Llandeusant 67-75; V Nefyn w Tudweiliog w Llandudwen w Edern 75-01; Can Ban Cathl 97-01; rtd 01. *11 Wenfro Road, Abergele LL22 7LE* Tel (01745) 823587

THOMAS (née REEVES), Mrs Elizabeth Anne. b 45. Sheff Univ BA67 PGCE75. SWMTC 87. d 90 p 94. Par Dn Stoke Damerel *Ex* 90-93; Dioc Children's Adv *Bradf* 93-01; Par Dn Baildon 93-94; C 94-96; P-in-c Denholme Gate 96-01; P-in-c Tuxford w Weston and Markham Clinton S'*well* 01-08; rtd 08. *The Lyrics, 113 The Oval, Retford DN22 7SD* Tel (01777) 700047 E-mail l.a.thomas@btinternet.com

THOMAS, The Ven Elwyn Bernard. b 45. Univ of Wales (Swansea) BSc68. St Mich Coll Llan BD71. d 71 p 72. C Aberdare St Fagan *Llan* 71-74; C Merthyr Dyfan 74-76; R Dowlais 76-86; V Llangynwyd w Maesteg 86-00; Can Llan Cathl 98-00; Adn St As from 00; R Llandyrnog and Llangwyfan from 00. *The Rectory, Ffordd Las, Llandyrnog, Denbigh LL16 4LT* Tel (01824) 790777 Fax 790877 E-mail bernardthomas@bun.com

THOMAS, Canon Ernest Keith. b 49. St Mich Coll Llan 73. d 76 p 77. C Swansea St Gabr *S & B* 76-79; C Killay 79-81; Prec Kimberley Cathl S Africa 81-84; R Kimberley St Aug 84-92; R Kimberley St Alb 89-92; Can Kimberley Cathl 86-92; V Aberdare *Llan* 93-96; Sub-Dean Bloemfontein Cathl S Africa from 96. *PO Box 1523, Bloemfontein, 9300 South Africa* Tel (0027) (51) 447 5951

THOMAS, Canon Euros Lloyd. b 53. Bris Poly LLB75. St Mich Coll Llan 77. d 79 p 80. C Llanelli *St D* 79-84; R Cilgerran w Bridell and Llantwyd 84-07; R Cilgerran w Bridell and Llantwyd and Eglwyswrw from 07; P-in-c Clydau 00-04; AD Cemais and Sub-Aeron 93-08; Can St D Cathl from 03. *The Rectory, Penllyn, Cilgerran, Cardigan SA43 2RZ* Tel (01239) 614500

THOMAS, Frank Lowth. b 22. Lon Coll of Div 64. d 66 p 67. C Walthamstow St Mary *Chelmsf* 66-68; C Bickenhill w Elmdon *Birm* 68-71; R Carlton Colville *Nor* 71-81; R Smallburgh w Dilham w Honing and Crostwight 81-85; rtd 85; Perm to Offic *Nor* from 86. *7 Mill Close, Salhouse, Norwich NR13 6QB* Tel (01603) 720376

THOMAS, Gareth Mark. b 72. Cranmer Hall Dur. d 10 p 11. C Atherton and Hindsford w Howe Bridge *Man* from 10. *St Anne's Vicarage, Powys Street, Atherton, Manchester M46 9AR* Tel (01942) 883902 Mobile 07947-389893 E-mail garethmthomas@hotmail.co.uk

THOMAS, Geoffrey. See THOMAS, David Geoffrey

THOMAS, Geoffrey Brynmor. b 34. K Coll Lon BA56 AKC56. Ridley Hall Cam 58. d 60 p 61. C Harlow New Town w Lt Parndon *Chelmsf* 60-65; V Leyton All SS 65-74; V Haley Hill *Wakef* 74-82; R The Winterbournes and Compton Valence *Sarum* 82-89; TV Cheltenham St Mark *Glouc* 89-92; P-in-c Dowdeswell and Andoversford w the Shiptons etc 92-95; RD Northleach 92-95; rtd 95; Perm to Offic *B & W* from 96. *48 Riverside Walk, Midsomer Norton, Bath BA3 2PD* Tel (01761) 414146 E-mail gbt34@btinternet.com

THOMAS, Geoffrey Charles. b 30. St Jo Coll Nottm LTh ALCD64. d 64 p 65. C York St Paul 64-67; C Cheltenham Ch Ch *Glouc* 67-70; V Whitgift w Adlingfleet *Sheff* 70-74; P-in-c Eastoft 72-74; V Mortomley St Sav 74-88; R Middleton Cheney w Chacombe *Pet* 88-93; rtd 94; Perm to Offic *York* 94-11. *55 Oakland Avenue, York YO31 1DF* Tel (01904) 414082

THOMAS, Canon Geoffrey Heale. b 29. St Mich Coll Llan 58. d 60 p 61. C Llansamlet *S & B* 60-63; Nigeria 63-67; V Swansea St Nic *S & B* 67-80; CF (TA) 72; V Oystermouth *S & B* 80-98; Hon Can Brecon Cathl 92-96; Can 97-98; rtd 98. *19 Ffordd Dryden, Killay, Swansea SA2 7PA* Tel (01792) 206308

THOMAS, George. b 46. Leeds Univ BEd69. Cranmer Hall Dur 75. d 78 p 79. C Highfield *Liv* 78-83; V Chorley St Jas *Blackb* 83-02; P-in-c Blackb St Gabr 02-08; rtd 08; Perm to Offic *Blackb* from 08. *80 Severn Drive, Walton-le-Dale, Preston PR5 4TE* Tel (01772) 330152

THOMAS, Glyn. b 36. Lon Univ BPharm61. St Deiniol's Hawarden 80. d 82 p 83. C Rhyl w St Ann *St As* 83-85; R

Llanycil w Bala and Frongoch and Llangower etc 85-03; RD Penllyn 96-03; rtd 03. *Blaen-y-Coed, 7 Lon Helyg, Abergele LL22 7JQ*
THOMAS, Gordon Herbert. b 43. Guildf Dioc Min Course 00. **d** 00 **p** 01. OLM Cove St Jo *Guildf* from 00. *13 Tay Close, Farnborough GU14 9NB* Tel (01252) 512347 E-mail rev.gordon@tiscali.co.uk
THOMAS, Greville Stephen. b 64. Qu Coll Birm 94. **d** 96 **p** 97. C Hillingdon All SS *Lon* 96-99; C Acton Green 99-04; P-in-c Northolt St Mary 04-06; R from 06. *St Mary's Rectory, Ealing Road, Northolt UB5 6AA* Tel (020) 8841 5691 E-mail greville.thomas@london.anglican.org *or* stmary@northolt.org
THOMAS, Canon Harald Daniel. b 34. FInstTT. **d** 97 **p** 05. Par Dn Pontnewydd *Mon* from 97; Hon Can St Woolos Cathl from 10. *Raldoro, Mount Pleasant Road, Pontnewydd, Cwmbran NP44 1BD* Tel (01633) 771353
THOMAS, Miss Hilary Faith. b 43. Ex Univ BA65 Southn Univ PGCE66. Trin Coll Bris 90. **d** 94 **p** 95. C Yeovil w Kingston Pitney *B & W* 94-98; V Brislington St Luke 98-07; rtd 07. *Brierley, Lower North Street, Cheddar BS27 3HH* Tel (01934) 742207
THOMAS, Hugh. b 25. St D Coll Lamp BA50. **d** 51 **p** 52. C Pen-bre *St D* 51-55; P-in-c Moelgrove and Monington 55-63; V Llanfynydd 63-74; V Pontyates 74-80; V Pontyates and Llangyndeyrn 80-90; rtd 91. *90 Priory Street, Kidwelly SA17 4TY* Tel (01554) 890114
THOMAS, Hugh Vivian. b 57. Kingston Poly LLB80 Barrister-at-Law (Lincoln's Inn) 86. SEITE 02. **d** 05 **p** 06. NSM Knockholt w Halstead *Roch* from 05. *3 The Meadows, Halstead, Sevenoaks TN14 7HD* Tel (01959) 532664 E-mail hughvthomas@btopenworld.com
THOMAS, Canon Huw Glyn. b 42. MBE07. St D Coll Lamp BA62 Linacre Coll Ox BA65 MA69. Wycliffe Hall Ox 62. **d** 65 **p** 66. C Oystermouth *S & B* 65-68; Asst Chapl Solihull Sch 68-69; Chapl and Hd Div 69-73; Selection Sec ACCM 73-78; C Loughton St Jo *Chelmsf* 73-77; V Bury St Jo *Man* 78-83; V Bury St Jo w St Mark 83-86; Dir of Ords 82-87; Can Res and Treas Liv Cathl 87-95; USPG 95-06; Chapl Addis Ababa Ethiopia 95-97; Provost All SS Cathl Cairo 97-01; Can from 01; Prin Edwardes Coll Peshawar Pakistan 01-06; rtd 06; Hon Sen Fell Liv Hope Univ from 07; Perm to Offic *Lon* from 07. *7 Calder Park Court, Calderstones Road, Liverpool L18 3HZ* Tel 0151-724 1581 Mobile 07981-114255 E-mail huwapglyn@yahoo.com
THOMAS, Ian Melville. b 50. Jes Coll Ox BA71 MA75. St Steph Ho Ox 71. **d** 73 **p** 74. PV St D Cathl 73-77; Chapl RAF 77-95; Command Chapl RAF 95-00; V Llanelli *St D* 01-02; TR 02-06; R Eccleston and Pulford *Ches* from 06. *The Rectory, Church Road, Eccleston, Chester CH4 9HT* Tel (01244) 659205 E-mail imt50@hotmail.com
THOMAS, Ian William. b 53. Bedf Coll of Educn CertEd74. Ox Min Course 89. **d** 92 **p** 93. NSM Fenny Stratford *Ox* from 92. *5 Laburnam Grove, Bletchley, Milton Keynes MK2 2JW* Tel (01908) 644457
THOMAS, Canon Idris. b 48. St D Coll Lamp. **d** 71 **p** 72. C Llanbeblig w Caernarfon and Betws Garmon etc *Ban* 71-75; P-in-c Llanaelhaiarn 75-77; R Llanaelhaearn w Clynnog Fawr from 77; RD Arfon 93-00; AD 02-04; Hon Can Ban Cathl from 99. *Y Rheithordy, Trefor, Caernarfon LL54 5HN* Tel (01286) 660547
THOMAS, Irene Jean. b 42. **d** 04 **p** 05. OLM E Wickham *S'wark* from 04. *35 Bowford Avenue, Bexleyheath DA7 4ST* Tel and fax (020) 8303 1855 E-mail irene.thomas@lineone.net
THOMAS, Mrs Iris. b 18. Univ of Wales (Abth) BA39 DipEd40. Llan Ord Course. **d** 80 **p** 97. Hon C Tylorstown *Llan* 80-84; Hon C Ferndale w Maerdy 84-85; rtd 85; Perm to Offic *Llan* from 86. *1 Maerdy Court, Maerdy Road, Ferndale CF3 4BT* Tel (01443) 755235
THOMAS, Jeffrey Malcolm. **d** 10. C Morriston *S & B* from 10. *2 Monmouth Place, Ynysforgan, Swansea SA6 6RF* Tel (01792) 425310 E-mail jeffreymthomas61@yahoo.com
THOMAS, Jennifer Monica. b 58. Wilson Carlile Coll 79 Sarum & Wells Th Coll 91. **d** 93 **p** 94. Par Dn Wandsworth St Paul *S'wark* 93-94; C 94-97; V Forest Hill 97-02; V Mitcham Ascension from 02. *The Vicarage, Sherwood Park Road, Mitcham CR4 1NE* Tel (020) 8764 1258
THOMAS, Jeremy Paul. b 63. Lanc Univ BSc87. Trin Coll Bris 04. **d** 06 **p** 07. C Aughton Ch Ch *Liv* 06-10; P-in-c Ashton-in-Makerfield St Thos from 10. *The Vicarage, 18 Warrington Road, Ashton-in-Makerfield, Wigan WN4 9PF* Tel (01942) 727275
THOMAS, John. *See* THOMAS, Cheeramattathu John
THOMAS, John Arun. b 47. Bombay Univ BA69 MA72 Nottm Univ CertEd80. Oak Hill Th Coll 84. **d** 88 **p** 89. C Liv Ch Ch Norris Green 88-89; C Wavertree St Mary 89-93; V St Mary Cray and St Paul's Cray *Roch* 93-96; India 96-99 and from 04; V Malabar Hill All SS 96-97; Hon Min Scotskirk 97-99; Prin Bombay Scottish Sch 97-99; Australia 99-04. *Address temp unknown* E-mail arunn51@hotmail.com

THOMAS, Canon John Herbert Samuel. b 34. Pemb Coll Cam BA57 MA64. St Mich Coll Llan 57. **d** 58 **p** 59. C Port Talbot St Theodore *Llan* 58-60; C Llantwit Major and St Donat's 60-67; P-in-c Barry All SS 67-74; V Dinas w Penygraig 74-85; V Pontypridd St Cath 85-90; V Pontypridd St Cath w St Matt 90-99; RD Pontypridd 90-99; Can Llan Cathl from 95; rtd 99. *Ty Canon, Salisbury Road, Abercynon, Mountain Ash CF45 4NU* Tel (01443) 742577
THOMAS, John Roger. Trin Coll Carmarthen BA. St Mich Coll Llan. **d** 03 **p** 04. C Cardigan w Mwnt and Y Ferwig w Llangoedmor *St D* 03-06; P-in-c Crymych Gp 06-07; V from 07. *The Vicarage, Newport Road, Crymych SA41 3RJ* Tel (01239) 831811
THOMAS, John Thurston. b 28. Univ of Wales (Swansea) BSc48 DipEd49 Leeds Univ PhD58 CChem FRSC65. Glouc Sch of Min 88. **d** 90 **p** 91. NSM S Cerney w Cerney Wick and Down Ampney *Glouc* 90-96; Perm to Offic *Glouc* 96-01; *S & B* from 01. *4 Nicholl Court, Mumbles, Swansea SA3 4LZ* Tel (01792) 360098
THOMAS, Jonathan Mark Gutteridge. b 66. Southn Univ BSc88. Trin Coll Bris BA10. **d** 10 **p** 11. C Cranleigh *Guildf* from 10. *22 Orchard Gardens, Cranleigh GU6 7LG* Tel 07804-196876 (mobile) E-mail jonathanmgthomas@gmail.com
THOMAS, Judith. *See* THOMAS, Dorothy Judith
THOMAS, Julian Mark. b 48. Ex Univ BA05. SWMTC 00. **d** 03 **p** 04. C Okehampton w Inwardleigh, Bratton Clovelly etc *Ex* 03-07; C Essington *Lich* from 07. *The Vicarage, 21 Wolverhampton Road, Essington, Wolverhampton WV11 2BX* Tel (01922) 478540 E-mail mark.thomas108@o2.co.uk
THOMAS, Mrs June Marion. b 53. Univ of Wales BA53 DipEd54. NEOC 83. dss 86 **d** 87 **p** 94. Stockton St Pet *Dur* 86-87; Hon Par Dn 87-89; NSM Stockton St Mark 89-94; P-in-c 94-01; rtd 01. *50 Brisbane Grove, Stockton-on-Tees TS18 5BP* Tel (01642) 582408
THOMAS, Mrs Karen Rosemary. b 53. Qu Coll Birm 04. **d** 06 **p** 07. C Glenfield *Leic* 06-10; TV Woodfield from 10. *The Rectory, 17 Rectory Lane, Appleby Magna, Swadlincote DE12 7BQ* E-mail karen@fish5.fsnet.co.uk
THOMAS, Keith. b 55. Southlands Coll Lon TCert80. NOC 92. **d** 95 **p** 96. NSM Knuzden *Blackb* 95-98; NSM Darwen St Pet w Hoddlesden 98-04; Tullyallan Sch Darwen 99-04; NSM Turton Moorland Min *Man* from 04. *20 Duxbury Street, Darwen BB3 2LA* Tel (01254) 776484
THOMAS, Kimberley Ann. b 59. Cranmer Hall Dur 02. **d** 04 **p** 05. C Chesterton *Lich* 04-07; V Stretton w Claymills from 07. *The Vicarage, Church Road, Stretton, Burton-on-Trent DE13 0HD* Tel (01283) 565141 E-mail kimberley.thomas@btinternet.com
THOMAS, Leighton. *See* THOMAS, Adrian Leighton
THOMAS, Canon Leslie Richard. b 45. Lon Coll of Div 65. **d** 69 **p** 70. C Knotty Ash St Jo *Liv* 69-72; C Sutton 72-74; TV 74-77; V Banks 77-82; V Gt Crosby All SS 82-92; P-in-c Marthall and Chapl David Lewis Cen for Epilepsy *Ches* 92-02; V Bickerton, Bickley, Harthill and Burwardsley 02-10; RD Malpas 04-10; Hon Can Ches Cathl 07-10; rtd 10. *7 Fairhaven Road, Southport PR9 9UJ* Tel (01704) 227511 E-mail sandstone@tesco.net
THOMAS, Mark. *See* THOMAS, Julian Mark
THOMAS, Preb Mark Wilson. b 51. Dur Univ BA72 Hull Univ MA89. Ripon Coll Cuddesdon 76. **d** 78 **p** 79. C Chapelthorpe *Wakef* 78-81; C Seaford w Sutton *Chich* 81-84; V Gomersal *Wakef* 84-92; TR Almondbury w Farnley Tyas 92-01; RD Almondbury 93-01; Hon Can Wakef Cathl 99-01; P-in-c Shrewsbury St Chad w St Mary *Lich* 01-07; V Shrewsbury St Chad, St Mary and St Alkmund from 07; RD Shrewsbury from 09; Preb Lich Cathl from 11. *25 The Crescent, Town Walls, Shrewsbury SY1 1TH* Tel and fax (01743) 343761 E-mail vicar@stchadschurchshrewsbury.com
THOMAS, Sister Mary Josephine. b 30. Ripon Dioc Tr Coll TCert50 Carl Dioc Tr Course 88. **d** 90 **p** 94. NSM Hawes Side *Blackb* 90-93; NSM St Annes St Marg 93-00; Perm to Offic from 00. *112 St Andrew's Road North, Lytham St Annes FY8 2JQ* Tel (01253) 728016
THOMAS, Michael Longdon Sanby. b 34. Trin Hall Cam BA55 MA60. Wells Th Coll 56. **d** 58 **p** 59. C Sandal St Helen *Wakef* 58-60; Chapl Portsea Cathl 60-63; V Sheffield 64-69; V Portchester 69-98; rtd 98. *188 Castle Street, Portchester, Fareham PO16 9QH* Tel and fax (023) 9242 0416 E-mail thomasfamily73@cwtv.net
THOMAS, Michael Rosser David. b 74. Kent Univ BA96. St Steph Ho Ox BTh02. **d** 02 **p** 03. C Aberavon *Llan* 02-05; Min Can Brecon Cathl 05-08; Succ from 08; P-in-c Brecon St Mary w Llanddew from 08. *The Almonry, Cathedral Close, Brecon LD3 9DP* Tel (01874) 622927 E-mail fr.michael@ntlworld.co.uk
THOMAS, Moray. *See* THOMAS, Charles Moray Stewart Reid
THOMAS, Nigel Bruce. b 63. Univ of Wales BD91. St Jo Coll Nottm MA98. **d** 97 **p** 98. C Millom *Carl* 97-02; R Bentham *Bradf* 02-07; P-in-c St Breoke and Egloshayle *Truro* 07-08; TR Carew *St D* from 08. *The Vicarage, Church Street, Pembroke Dock SA72 6AR* Tel (01646) 682943 E-mail thomas-tribe@hotmail.co.uk

THOMAS, Nigel Clayton. b 52. Leeds Univ BA76 Univ of Wales (Cardiff) PGCE77. ERMC 08. d 11. C Madrid Eur from 11. Rincon de Andalucia 3, Manzanares el Real, 28410 Madrid, Spain Tel (0034) 918 527 276 Mobile 663 665 703 E-mail nigelthomasnta@gmail.com

THOMAS, Ms Pamela Sybil. b 38. Ripon Coll Cuddesdon 88. d 90 p 94. Par Dn Preston w Sutton Poyntz and Osmington w Poxwell Sarum 90-94; C 94-96; P-in-c Weymouth St Edm 96-05; P-in-c Abbotsbury, Portesham and Langton Herring 97-08; Chapl Westhaven Hosp Weymouth 96-08; rtd 08; Hon C Cullompton, Willand, Uffculme, Kentisbeare etc Ex from 08. 5 Cotters Close, Kentesbeare, Cullompton EX15 2DJ Tel (01884) 266741 E-mail rev.thomas@btinternet.com

THOMAS, Canon Patrick Hungerford Bryan. b 52. St Cath Coll Cam BA73 MA77 Leeds Univ BA78 Univ of Wales PhD82. Coll of Resurr Mirfield 76. d 79 p 80. C Aberystwyth St D 79-81; C Carmarthen St Pet 81-82; R Llangeitho and Blaenpennal w Betws Leucu etc 82-84; Warden of Ords 83-86; R Brechfa w Abergorlech etc 84-01; V Carmarthen St Dav from 01; Can St D Cathl from 00. St David's Vicarage, 4 Penllwyn Park, Carmarthen SA31 3BU Tel (01267) 234183 E-mail canon.patrick@yahoo.co.uk

THOMAS, Paul Richard. b 75. Univ of Wales (Cardiff) BA96 MA99 Hon ARAM11. Ripon Coll Cuddesdon BA01 MA06. d 02 p 03. C Wanstead St Mary w Ch Ch Chelmsf 02-06; C St Marylebone w H Trin Lon 06-11; V Paddington St Jas from 11; Chapl St Marylebone C of E Sch 08-11; Chapl R Academy of Music Lon from 08. St James's Vicarage, 6 Gloucester Terrace, London W2 3DD Tel (020) 7262 1265 Mobile 07967-753671 E-mail vicar@stjamespaddington.org.uk

THOMAS, Canon Paul Robert. b 42. OBE02. NOC. d 82 p 83. C Hull St Jo Newland York 82-84; P-in-c Rowley 84-87; Soc Resp Officer Hull 84-87; R Rowley w Skidby 87-88; TR Barking St Marg w St Patr Chelmsf 88-93; Gen Sec and Admin St Luke's Hosp for Clergy 93-03; Can and Preb Chich Cathl from 98; P in O from 99; rtd 03; Perm to Offic Nor from 03. St Anne's Cottage, 37 Scarborough Road, Walsingham NR22 6AB Tel (01328) 820571

THOMAS, The Ven Paul Wyndham. b 55. Oriel Coll Ox BA76 BTh78 MA80. Wycliffe Hall Ox 77. d 79 p 80. C Llangynwyd w Maesteg 79-85; TV Langport Area B & W 85-90; P-in-c Thorp Arch w Walton York 90-93; Clergy Tr Officer 90-04; V Nether w Upper Poppleton 93-04; P-in-c Castle Town Lich 04-11; RD Stafford 05-11; Local Par Development Adv Stafford Area 10-11; Adn Salop from 11. The Vicarage, Tong, Shifnal TF11 8PW Tel (01902) 372622

THOMAS, Peter James. b 53. Lon Univ BSc75. Trin Coll Bris 77. d 80 p 81. C Hucclecote Glouc 80-84; C Loughborough Em Leic 84-85; TV Parr Liv 85-92; V Eckington and Defford w Besford Worc 92-05; RD Pershore 00-05; P-in-c Norton sub Hamdon, W Chinnock, Chiselborough etc B & W from 05; RD Ivelchester from 07. The Rectory, Cat Street, Chiselborough, Stoke-sub-Hamdon TA14 6TT Tel (01935) 881202 E-mail pthomas5@aol.com

THOMAS, Peter Rhys. b 37. TCD BA59 MA72 MInstPkg MCIPD. d 72 p 73. C Cong T, K & A 73-75; I 75-77; C Bingley All SS Bradf 77-79; V Shelf 79-81; Producer Relig Broadcasting Viking Radio 81-84; P-in-c Croxton Linc 81-82; P-in-c Ulceby 81-82; P-in-c Wootton 81-82; P-in-c Ulceby Gp 82; V 82-84; R E and W Tilbury and Linford Chelmsf 84-89; I Celbridge w Straffan and Newcastle-Lyons D & G 89-93; I Youghal Union C, C & R 93-99; Dioc Communications Officer (Cork) 95-99; Can Cork Cathl 97-99; Preb Cloyne Cathl 97-99; rtd 99; Rep Leprosy Miss Munster from 00. Abina Cottage, Ballykenneally, Ballymacoda, Co Cork, Republic of Ireland Tel and fax (00353) (24) 98082 E-mail prthomas@iol.ie

THOMAS, Peter Wilson. b 58. K Coll Lon BD80 AKC80. Ripon Coll Cuddesdon 80. d 82 p 83. C Stockton St Pet Dur 82-85; TV Solihull Birm 85-90; V Rednal 90-05; Chapl MG Rover 95-05; P-in-c Balsall Common 05-10; V from 10. St Peter's House, Holly Lane, Balsall Common, Coventry CV7 7EA Tel and fax (01676) 532721 E-mail frpeter@uwclub.net

THOMAS, Canon Philip Harold Emlyn. b 41. Cant Univ (NZ) BA64 MA77 Dur Univ PhD82. Melbourne Coll of Div BD68. d 68 p 69. C Adelaide H Trin Australia 68-71; Lic to Offic Dio Christchurch New Zealand 71-77; Fell and Chapl Univ Coll Dur 77-83; V Heighington Dur 84-10; AD Darlington 94-00; Hon Can Dur Cathl 07-10; rtd 10. 2 Gloucester Street, Cirencester GL7 2DG E-mail philip.thomas7@btinternet.com

THOMAS, Philip John. b 52. Liv Poly BSc74 Leeds Poly 77. Trin Coll Bris 94. d 96 p 97. C Skelton w Upleatham York 96-97; C Acomb St Steph 97-01; V Woodthorpe S'well from 01; Chapl MU from 03. St Mark's Vicarage, 37A Melbury Road, Nottingham NG5 4PG Tel 0115-926 7859 E-mail stmarks.woodthorpe@ntlworld.com

THOMAS, Ramon Lorenzo. b 44. Victoria Univ Wellington BCA73 Mass Inst of Tech MSc80 CA73. Oak Hill Th Coll 89. d 97 p 98. NSM Yateley Win 97-99; Chairman Judah Trust from

99; Perm to Offic Chich from 10. 58 Rock Gardens, Bognor Regis PO21 2LF Tel (01243) 825523 E-mail judahtrust@aol.com

THOMAS, Rhys. See THOMAS, Peter Rhys

THOMAS, Richard Frederick. b 24. Qu Coll Cam BA45 MA49. Ridley Hall Cam 47. d 49 p 50. C S Croydon Em Cant 49-51; Chapl and Ho Master Haileybury Coll 51-67; Hd Master Angl Ch Sch Jerusalem 67-73; Ho Master Bp Luffa Sch Chich 74-80; Hon C Chich St Pancras and St Jo 78-80; R N Mundham w Hunston and Merston 80-89; Perm to Offic Portsm from 89; C Stansted and Compton, the Mardens, Stoughton and Racton Chich 96-00; rtd 00; Perm to Offic Chich from 00. 16 Brent Court, Emsworth PO10 7JA Tel (01243) 430613 Mobile 07947-518314 E-mail thomasrb@ntlworld.com

THOMAS, Richard Paul. b 50. MIPR. Wycliffe Hall Ox 74. d 76 p 77. C Abingdon w Shippon Ox 76-80; R Win All SS w Chilcomb and Chesil 80-88; Dioc Communications Officer Win 83-89; Ox 89-07. 71B St Thomas Street, Wells BA5 2UY Tel (01749) 671478

THOMAS, Robert Graham. b 53. G&C Coll Cam BA75 MA79 Imp Coll Lon PhD78 CEng82 FIMechE93. SAOMC 04. d 06 p 07. C Bathampton w Claverton B & W 06-10; P-in-c Trowbridge St Jas and Keevil Sarum from 10. The Rectory, Union Street, Trowbridge BA14 8RU Tel (01225) 350647 E-mail rob.thomas@cantab.net

THOMAS, Robin. b 27. St Steph Ho Ox 89. d 89 p 90. NSM Clifton All SS w St Jo Bris 89-94; P-in-c Tintagel Truro 94-97; rtd 97; Perm to Offic Truro from 97. 22 Hendra Vean, Truro TR1 3TU Tel (01872) 271276

THOMAS, Roderick Charles Howell. b 54. LSE BSc75. Wycliffe Hall Ox 91. d 93 p 94. C Plymouth St Andr w St Paul and St Geo Ex 93-95; C Plymouth St Andr and Stonehouse 95-99; P-in-c Elburton 99-05; V from 05. St Matthew's Vicarage, 3 Sherford Road, Plymouth PL9 8DQ Tel (01752) 402771 E-mail roderick.t@virgin.net

THOMAS, Roger. See THOMAS, John Roger

THOMAS, Russen William. b 30. Univ of Wales (Lamp) BA55. St Mich Coll Llan 55. d 57 p 58. C Newport St Jo Bapt Mon 57-59; C Pembroke Dock St D 59-62; R St Florence and Redberth 62-69; V Newport St Julian Mon 69-79; V Stratton Truro 79-88; RD Stratton 83-88; V Lanteglos by Fowey 88-91; Hon Chapl Miss to Seafarers from 88; rtd 92; Chapl Playa de Las Americas Tenerife Eur 93-97; Perm to Offic Cov 97-06 and B & W from 06. St Peter's Cottage, Langford Budville, Wellington TA21 0QZ Tel (01823) 400525 E-mail wen.rus@virgin.net

THOMAS, Mrs Ruth Alison Mary. b 57. York Univ BA79 Dur Univ PGCE80 MA96. NEOC 07. d 09 p 10. NSM Dur St Giles from 09. 68 Gilesgate, Durham DH1 1HY Tel 0191-386 0402 Mobile 07966-387146 E-mail ruththomas@fsmail.net

THOMAS, Mrs Sheila Mary Witton. b 49. STETS 06. d 09 p 10. NSM Marnhull Sarum from 09. 5 Burtonhayes, Burton Street, Marnhull, Sturminster Newton DT10 1PR Tel (01258) 820469 Mobile 07748-974806 E-mail sheila2is@yahoo.co.uk

THOMAS, Simon Jonathan Francklin. b 51. Sheff Univ BA72 Nottm Univ BA78 Open Univ MA02. St Jo Coll Nottm 76. d 80 p 80. SAMS 80-82 and 83-95; Peru 80-82; Bolivia 83-95; C Camberwell All SS S'wark 82; C Ashtead Guildf 96-06; rtd 06. 4 Masefield Road, Harpenden AL5 4JN Tel (01582) 462227 E-mail simonjfthomas@aol.com

THOMAS, Stefan Carl. b 67. Kent Univ BA02 MA04. SEITE 08. d 10. NSM Broadstairs Cant from 10. 195 Bradstow Way, Broadstairs CT10 1AX Tel (01843) 861724 E-mail slazz@btinternet.com

THOMAS, Preb Stephen Blayney. b 35. St D Coll Lamp BA62. Bp Burgess Hall Lamp. d 63 p 64. C Ledbury Heref 63-67; C Bridgnorth w Tasley 67-68; C Clun w Chapel Lawn, Bettws-y-Crwyn and Newcastle 68-73; C Clungunford w Clunbury and Clunton, Bedstone etc 68-73; V Worfield 73-84; RD Bridgnorth 81-83; R Kingsland 84-96; P-in-c Eardisland 84-96; P-in-c Aymestrey and Leinthall Earles w Wigmore etc 84-96; R Kingsland w Eardisland, Aymestrey etc 97-99; Preb Heref Cathl 85-01; rtd 99; Perm to Offic Heref and Worc from 00. 28 Castle Close, Burford, Tenbury Wells WR15 8AY Tel (01584) 819642

THOMAS, Stuart Grahame. b 54. Pemb Coll Cam BA77 MA81 ATCL97. Ridley Hall Cam 85. d 87 p 88. C Guildf H Trin w St Mary 87-91; V Churt 91-94; V Ewell St Fran from 94; Dioc Ecum Officer 99-07; RD Epsom from 07. The Minister's House, 71 Ruxley Lane, Epsom KT19 9FF Tel (020) 8391 1127 E-mail revstuart.thomas@btinternet.com

THOMAS, Susan Linda. b 60. SEITE 08. d 11. NSM Coulsdon St Jo S'wark from 11. 40 West Hill, South Croydon CR2 0SA

THOMAS, Canon Sydney Robert. b 44. Univ of Wales (Swansea) BA65 MA83. St D Coll Lamp LTh67. d 67 p 68. C Llanelli St D 67-77; V Pontyberem 77-01; TR Cwm Gwendraeth 01-08; RD Cydweli 94-05; Can St D Cathl 94-08; Chan 01-03; Treas 03-08; rtd 09. 40 Waungoch, Upper Tumble, Llanelli SA14 6BX Tel (01269) 841677 E-mail sydvic@sydvic.plus.com

THOMAS, Theodore Eilir. b 36. Univ of Wales (Lamp) BA58. Sarum Th Coll 58. d 60 p 61. C Fenton Lich 60-63; C Stourport All SS and St Mich CD Worc 63-67; V Worc H Trin 67-74; P-in-c

Dudley St Fran 74-79; V 79-83; R Plympton St Maurice *Ex* 83-03; rtd 03; P-in-c St John w Millbrook *Truro* from 04. *The Vicarage, Millbrook, Torpoint PL10 1BW* Tel (01752) 822264

THOMAS, Thomas. b 68. Selw Coll Cam BA90. Wycliffe Hall Ox 91. d 93 p 94. C Much Woolton *Liv* 93-97; V Carr Mill 97-10; C Springfield *Birm* 10-11; P-in-c from 11. *172 Woodlands Road, Springfield, Birmingham B11 4ET* Tel 0121-777 1989 Mobile 07980-650801 E-mail revtom@4afairworld.co.uk

THOMAS, Thomas Alan. b 37. K Coll Lon BD60 AKC60. St Boniface Warminster 60. d 61 p 62. C Washington *Dur* 61-65; C Bishopwearmouth St Mary V w St Pet CD 65-70; V Ruishton w Thornfalcon *B & W* 70-82; R Hutton 82-94; V Frome Ch Ch 94-96; Chapl Victoria Hosp Frome 94-96; R Camerton w Dunkerton, Foxcote and Shoscombe *B & W* 96-00; rtd 00; Perm to Offic *B & W* from 00. *12 Farrington Way, Farrington Gurney, Bristol BS39 6US* Tel (01761) 453434

THOMAS, Thomas John Samuel. b 21. St D Coll Lamp BA48. d 49 p 50. C Dafen and Llwynhendy *St D* 49-50; Chapl RAF 52-77; QHC 73-85; V Horsham *Chich* 77-85; rtd 85; Perm to Offic *St D* from 85. *1 Glynhir Road, Llandybie, Ammanford SA18 2TA* Tel (01269) 850726

THOMAS, Virginia Jacqueline. b 48. UEA BA70. Yale Div Sch MDiv97. d 00 p 01. NSM Chelsea St Luke and Ch Ch *Lon* 00-04; NSM W Brompton St Mary w St Pet 04-06; P-in-c 05-06; P-in-c W Brompton St Mary w St Peter and St Jude 06-10; V from 10. *The Vicarage, 24 Fawcett Street, London SW10 9EZ* Tel (020) 7352 5880 *or* 7835 1440 Fax 7370 6562 E-mail ginny@stmarytheboltons.demon.co.uk

THOMAS, Vivian Ivor. b 52. S Bank Univ MSc95 Regent Coll Vancouver MCS97 K Coll Lon PhD02. d 08 p 09. NSM Hammersmith St Paul *Lon* from 08. *76 Rannoch Road, London W6 9SP* Tel (020) 7384 5954 Mobile 07767-777891 E-mail vivian.thomas@btinternet.com

THOMAS, William George. b 29. JP. Birm Univ BA50 CertEd51 FRSA. EAMTC 82. d 85 p 86. NSM Brampton *Ely* 85-87; NSM Bluntisham w Earith 87-89; P-in-c Foxton 89-95; rtd 95; Perm to Offic *Ely* from 95. *3 The Paddock, Bluntisham, Huntingdon PE28 3NR* Tel (01487) 842057 E-mail w.thomas57@btopenworld.com

THOMAS, The Ven William Jordison. b 27. K Coll Cam BA50 MA55. Cuddesdon Coll 51. d 53 p 54. C Byker St Ant *Newc* 53-56; C Berwick H Trin 56-59; V Alwinton w Holystone and Alnham 59-70; V Alston cum Garrigill w Nenthead and Kirkhaugh 70-80; P-in-c Lambley w Knaresdale 72-80; RD Bamburgh and Glendale 81-83; TR Glendale Gp 80-83; Adn Northd and Can Res Newc Cathl 83-92; rtd 92; Perm to Offic *Newc* from 92. *20 Robert Adam Court, Bondgate Without, Alnwick NE66 1PH* Tel (01665) 602644

THOMAS, The Ven William Phillip. b 43. Lich Th Coll 68. d 70 p 71. C Llanilid w Pencoed 70-74; C Pontypridd St Cath 74-76; V Tonyrefail 76-84; Youth Chapl 78-80; RD Rhondda 81-84; R Neath w Llantwit 84-98; Adn Llan 97-08; V Caerau w Ely 98-00; rtd 09. *102 Heol Croesty, Pencoed, Bridgend CF35 5LT*

THOMAS, Wilson Hugo. d 01 p 05. Barbados 01-05; NSM Frimley *Guildf* 05-07. *3B Ansell Road, Frimley GU16 8BS* Tel (01276) 681652 E-mail wilsonthomas56@googlemail.com

THOMAS ANTHONY, Brother. *See* DEHOOP, Brother Thomas Anthony

THOMASSON, Keith Duncan. b 69. St Pet Coll Ox BA91 MA97 Lon Inst of Educn PGCE92. Ripon Coll Cuddesdon BA01 Bossey Ecum Inst Geneva. d 02 p 03. C Lancaster St Mary w St John and St Anne *Blackb* 02-04; C Longridge 04-06; Partnership P E Bris from 06. *11 Vicars Close, Bristol BS16 3TH* Tel 0117-965 7740 E-mail keiththomasson@hotmail.com

THOMPSON (née SMETHAM), Abigail Laura. b 75. K Coll Lon BMus97 Clare Coll Cam BA05. Westcott Ho Cam 03. d 06 p 07. C Sheff Manor 06-10; P-in-c Clifton St Jas from 10. *Clifton Vicarage, 10 Clifton Crescent North, Rotherham S65 2AS* Tel (01709) 363082 Mobile 07947-475073 E-mail rev.abi.thompson@gmail.com

THOMPSON, Adrian David. b 68. Univ of Wales (Abth) BSc93 PhD92 Bris Univ PGCE98. Wycliffe Hall Ox 93. d 05 p 06. C Blackb St Gabr 05-08; Chapl Abp Temple Sch Preston 09-11; TV Cockermouth Area *Carl* from 11. *The Vicarage, 14 Harrot Hill, Cockermouth CA13 0BL* E-mail adrian.cockermouth@gmail.com

THOMPSON, Alan. b 61. Qu Coll Birm 04. d 07 p 08. C Saltley and Washwood Heath *Birm* from 07. *9 Old Oscott Hill, Birmingham B44 9SR* Tel 0121-350 8847 E-mail frathompson@btinternet.com

THOMPSON, Andrew David. b 68. Poly of Wales BSc90 Nottm Univ MA03. Wycliffe Hall Ox 98. d 00 p 01. C Oakwood *Derby* 00-04; Asst Chapl UAE 05-06; Chapl Kuwait from 06. *PO Box 9999, Ahmadi, Kuwait* Tel (00965) 398 5929 E-mail andythompson1968@swissmail.org

THOMPSON, Mrs Angela Lorena Jennifer. b 44. SAOMC 96. d 99 p 00. NSM Chalfont St Giles *Ox* from 99. *3 The Leys, Chesham Bois, Amersham HP6 5NP* Tel (01494) 726654 E-mail angelalj70@hotmail.com

THOMPSON, Canon Anthony Edward. b 38. Bris Univ BA61. Ridley Hall Cam 61. d 63 p 64. C Peckham St Mary Magd *S'wark* 63-66; SAMS Paraguay 67-72; C Otley *Bradf* 72-75; TV Woughton *Ox* 75-82; P-in-c Lower Nutfield *S'wark* 82-02; V S Nutfield w Outwood 02-03; RD Reigate 91-93; Local Min Adv Croydon Episc Area 93-03; Hon Can S'wark Cathl 03; rtd 03; Perm to Offic *Chich* from 04. *3 The Curlews, Shoreham-by-Sea BN43 5UQ* Tel (01273) 440182 E-mail tonythompsonsbs@hotmail.com

THOMPSON, Athol James Patrick. b 34. St Paul's Coll Grahamstown 72. d 74 p 75. S Africa 74-83; P-in-c Dewsbury St Matt and St Jo *Wakef* 84; TV Dewsbury 84-93; Chapl Staincliffe and Dewsbury Gen Hosps Wakef 84-90; Chapl Dewsbury and Distr Hosp 90-93; V Shiregreen St Jas and St Chris *Sheff* 93-99; rtd 99; Perm to Offic *Sheff* from 99. *109 Park Avenue, Chapeltown, Sheffield S35 1WH* Tel 0114-245 1028

THOMPSON, Canon Barry Pearce. b 40. St Andr Univ BSc63 Ball Coll Ox PhD66 Hull Univ MA82. NW Ord Course 76. d 79 p 80. C Cottingham *York* 79-82; V Swine 82-83; Lect Th Hull Univ 83-88; Ind Chapl *York* 83-85; Abp's Adv on Ind Issues 85-88; Can Res Chelmsf Cathl 88-98; Treas and Can Windsor 98-02; rtd 02; Perm to Offic *York* from 03. *44 Topcliffe Road, Sowerby, Thirsk YO7 1RB* Tel (01845) 525170 Mobile 07768-515790 E-mail barry.thompson10@btopenworld.com

THOMPSON, Brian. b 34. MRICS65 FRICS75. St Jo Coll Nottm 81. d 84 p 85. C Bletchley *Ox* 84-87; V Sneyd Green *Lich* 87-99; rtd 99; Perm to Offic *Lich* from 99. *85 Harrington Croft, West Bromwich B71 3RJ* Tel 0121-588 6120 E-mail brian.thompson40@btinternet.com

THOMPSON, Carrie Julia Lucy Jadwiga. b 77. Keble Coll Ox BA99 MA04. St Steph Ho Ox MA06. d 04 p 05. C Camberwell St Giles w St Matt *S'wark* 04-08; V Forton *Portsm* from 08; Chapl St Vincent Sixth Form Coll from 08. *The Vicarage, 10 Spring Garden Lane, Gosport PO12 1HY* Tel (023) 9250 3140 E-mail mother.carrie@btinternet.com

THOMPSON, David. *See* THOMPSON, John David

THOMPSON, David Arthur. b 37. Clifton Th Coll. d 69 p 70. C Finchley Ch Ch *Lon* 69-72; C Barking St Marg w St Patr *Chelmsf* 72-75; TV 75-81; V Toxteth Park St Clem *Liv* 81-91; TR Parr 91-03; rtd 03; Perm to Offic *Sarum* 03-10. *Calm Haven, 21 Arklow Drive, Hale Village, Liverpool L24 5RN* Tel 0151-425 2012

THOMPSON, David John. b 64. Cranmer Hall Dur 92. d 95 p 96. C Poulton-le-Sands w Morecambe St Laur *Blackb* 95-99; V Farington Moss 99-02; V Lea 02-09; Warden Past Assts 06-09; P-in-c Ringley w Prestolee *Man* 09-10; TV Farnworth, Kearsley and Stoneclough from 10. *The Vicarage, 9 Stoneleigh Drive, Radcliffe, Bolton M26 1FZ* Tel (01204) 570992

THOMPSON, David Simon. b 57. Aston Univ BSc82 MRPharmS83. STETS 01. d 04 p 05. NSM Bournemouth H Epiphany *Win* from 04. *15 Cheriton Avenue, Bournemouth BH7 6SD* Tel (01202) 426764 Mobile 07763-052009 E-mail david_iford@hotmail.com

THOMPSON, Canon Donald Frazer. b 20. St Cath Coll Cam BA46 MA49. Coll of Resurr Mirfield 46. d 48 p 49. C Cheshunt *St Alb* 48-52; C Norton 52-56; V Wigan St Anne *Liv* 56-62; V Leeds St Aid *Ripon* 62-73; RD Allerton 70-73; R Adel 73-87; Hon Can Ripon Cathl 75-87; RD Headingley 85-87; rtd 87; Perm to Offic *Cov* from 87. *75 Cubbington Road, Leamington Spa CV32 7AQ* Tel (01926) 773298

THOMPSON, Edward Ronald Charles. b 25. AKC51. d 52 p 53. C Hinckley St Mary *Leic* 52-54; Asst Master St Geo Upper Sch Jerusalem 54-55; Chapl St Boniface Coll Warminster 56-59; R Hawkchurch w Fishpond *Sarum* 59-63; V Camberwell St Mich w All So w Em *S'wark* 63-67; P-in-c St Mary le Strand w St Clem Danes *Lon* 67-74; R 74-93; rtd 93; Perm to Offic *S'wark* from 95. *3 Woodsyre, Sydenham Hill, London SE26 6SS* Tel (020) 8670 8289

THOMPSON, Ms Eileen Carol. b 46. Lon Univ BA69. New Coll Edin MTh92. d 96 p 97. Par Dn Dhaka St Thos Bangladesh 96-97; Presbyter Madras H Cross w St Mich India 97-99; Presbyter in charge Madras St Mary 99-02; V Pallikunu St Geo and Palla Ch Ch 02-04; Min Livingston LEP *Edin* from 04. *53 Garry Walk, Livingston EH54 5AS* Tel (01506) 433451 E-mail eileencthompson@gmail.com

THOMPSON, Elizabeth Gray McManus. d 06 p 07. NSM Garrison w Slavin and Belleek *Clogh* 06-07; NSM Rossorry 07-09; NSM Enniskillen 09-11; Bp's C Aghalurcher w Tattykeeran, Cooneen etc from 11. *En-Rinmon, 6 Tullylammy Road, Irvinestown, Enniskillen BT94 1RN* Tel (028) 6862 8258 E-mail thompson.clogher@ntlworld.com

THOMPSON, Frederick Robert. b 15. Dur Univ LTh40. St Aug Coll Cant 37. d 40 p 41. C Northampton Ch Pet 40-44; C Maidstone All SS Cant 44-46; India 46-57; Area Sec (Dios Birm and Lich) SPG 57-64; V Tutbury *Lich* 64-80; rtd 80; Perm to Offic *Sarum* from 80. *1 Panorama Road, Poole BH13 7RA* Tel (01202) 700735

THOMPSON, Garry John. b 49. Qu Coll Birm. d 96 p 97. C Wilnecote *Lich* 96-99; V Lapley w Wheaton Aston and P-in-c Blymhill w Weston-under-Lizard 99-09; R Watershed 09-11; P-in-c Clifton Campville w Edingale and Harlaston from 11; P-in-c Elford from 11; P-in-c Thorpe Constantine from 11. *The Rectory, 32 Main Street, Clifton Campville, Tamworth B79 0AP* E-mail garry@garrythompson2.wanadoo.co.uk

✠THOMPSON, The Rt Revd Geoffrey Hewlett. b 29. Trin Hall Cam BA52 MA56. Cuddesdon Coll 52. d 54 p 55 c 74. C Northampton St Matt *Pet* 54-59; V Wisbech St Aug *Ely* 59-66; V Folkestone St Sav *Cant* 66-74; Suff Bp Willesden *Lon* 74-79; Area Bp Willesden 79-85; Bp Ex 85-99; rtd 99; Hon Asst Bp Carl from 99. *Low Broomrigg, Warcop, Appleby-in-Westmorland CA16 6PT* Tel (01768) 341281

THOMPSON, Geoffrey Peter. b 58. St Pet Coll Ox BA80 MA82. SEITE 99. d 02 p 03. C Cheam *S'wark* 02-06; C Croydon St Jo 06-11; P-in-c Norbury St Steph and Thornton Heath from 11. *St Stephen's Vicarage, 9 Warwick Road, Thornton Heath CR7 7NH* Tel (020) 8684 3820 E-mail gtchurch@waitrose.com

THOMPSON, Preb Gordon Henry Moorhouse. b 41. Univ of Wales LLM95. K Coll Lon 63 St Boniface Warminster 66. d 67 p 68. C Leominster *Heref* 67-70; C Whitton w Greete and Hope Bagot 70-74; TV 74-89; C Burford III w Lt Heref 70-74; TV 74-89; C Tenbury Wells 70-74; TV 74-89; TV Burford I, Nash and Boraston 74-89; RD Ludlow 83-89; Preb Heref Cathl 85-97; rtd 89; Perm to Offic *Heref* from 89. *The Poplars, Bitterley Village, Ludlow SY8 3HQ* Tel (01584) 891093

THOMPSON, Harold Anthony. b 41. NOC 84. d 87 p 88. C Leeds Belle Is St Jo and St Barn *Ripon* 87-90; V Leeds St Cypr Harehills 90-96; V Shadwell 96-06; rtd 06. *551 Shadwell Lane, Leeds LS17 8AP* Tel 0113-266 5913 E-mail haroldthompson41@hotmail.com

THOMPSON, Hewlett. *See* THOMPSON, The Rt Revd Geoffrey Hewlett

THOMPSON, Ian David. b 51. Hull Univ BSc72. NOC 94. d 97 p 98. C Blackley St Andr *Man* 97-00; P-in-c 00-06; R Burnage St Marg from 06. *St Margaret's Rectory, 250 Burnage Lane, Manchester M19 1FL* Tel 0161-432 1844 E-mail ian@thompsonrev.freeserve.co.uk

THOMPSON, Ian George. b 60. SEITE 99. d 02 p 03. NSM Walworth St Pet *S'wark* 02-05; NSM Dulwich St Clem w St Pet 05-07; Chapl HM Pris Pentonville 07-11; Chapl HM YOI Wetherby from 11. *HM Young Offender Institution, York Road, Wetherby LS22 5ED* Tel (01937) 544200 Mobile 07985-582257 E-mail ian.thompson@hmps.gsi.gov.uk

THOMPSON, James. b 30. Nottm Univ DipEd65. Wycliffe Hall Ox 66. d 66 p 67. C Woodlands *Sheff* 66-69; R Firbeck w Letwell 69-71; V Milnsbridge *Wakef* 71-80; Chapl St Luke's Hosp Huddersfield 71-80; NSM Dewsbury 80-84; Lect Huddersfield Coll FE 80-84; Dioc Chapl Aber Hosps 84-89; Dioc Supernumerary *Ab* 84-89; R Buckie and Portsoy 89-94; rtd 95; Perm to Offic *St As* from 95. *Peace Haven, Fron Park Road, Holywell CH8 7UY* Tel (01352) 712368

THOMPSON, James. b 37. Coll of Resurr Mirfield 64. d 67 p 68. C Shieldfield Ch Ch *Newc* 67-69; C Hendon *Dur* 69-74; V Gateshead St Chad Bensham 74-85; R Easington 85-90; Chapl Thorpe Hosp Easington 85-90; V Cassop cum Quarrington *Dur* 90-06; rtd 06. *43 Heathfield, Sunderland SR2 9EW* Tel 0191-522 9490

THOMPSON, Jeremy James Thomas. b 58. Sunderland Univ BEd92. Cranmer Hall Dur 94. d 96 p 97. C Bedlington *Newc* 96-00; P-in-c Choppington 00-02; V 02-08; R St John Lee from 08; V Warden w Newbrough from 08. *St John Lee Rectory, Acomb, Hexham NE46 4PE* Tel (01434) 600268 E-mail jeremyjtthompson@operamail.com

THOMPSON, John David. b 40. Lon Univ BD65 Ch Ch Ox DPhil69. St Steph Ho Ox 65. d 67 p 68. C Solihull *Birm* 67-71; C Biddestone w Slaughterford *Bris* 71-73; Lect Wells Th Coll 71-72; C Yatton Keynell *Bris* 71-73; C Castle Combe 71-73; V Braughing *St Alb* 74-77; R Digswell 77-82; TR Digswell and Panshanger 82-98; rtd 00. *11 Russell Street, Boddam, Peterhead AB42 3NG* Tel (01779) 472680

THOMPSON, Canon John Michael. b 47. Nottm Univ BTh77. Linc Th Coll 73. d 77 p 78. C Old Brumby *Linc* 77-80; C Grantham 80-81; TV 81-84; V Holton-le-Clay 84-94; V Holton-le-Clay and Tetney 94-97; R Humshaugh w Simonburn and Wark *Newc* from 97; Hon Can Newc Cathl from 11. *The Vicarage, Humshaugh, Hexham NE46 4AA* Tel (01434) 681304

THOMPSON, John Turrell. b 57. Sheff Univ BA(Econ)79 Southn Univ BTh88. Sarum & Wells Th Coll 83. d 86 p 87. C Tavistock and Gulworthy *Ex* 86-90; TV Pinhoe and Broadclyst 90-95; P-in-c Northam w Westward Ho! and Appledore 95-96; TV Bideford, Northam, Westward Ho!, Appledore etc 96-00; rtd 00; Perm to Offic *Ex* from 00. *Brambles Patch, 39 Westermore Drive, Roundswell, Barnstaple EX31 3XU*

THOMPSON, John Wilfred. b 44. CA Tr Coll 66 St Deiniol's Hawarden 84. d 85 p 86. C Rhyl w St Ann *St As* 85-87; R Fritwell w Souldern and Ardley w Fewcott *Ox* 87-97.

19 Tangmere Close, Bicester OX26 4YZ Tel (01869) 601082 Mobile 07813-997491 E-mail thompsonjohnwilfrid@sky.com

THOMPSON (née LILLIE), Mrs Judith Virginia. b 44. LMH Ox BA66 Essex Univ MA73 Univ of E Africa DipEd67. Gilmore Course IDC82. dss 82 d 87 p 94. Lawrence Weston *Bris* 82-85; E Bris 85-95; Hon Par Dn 87-95; Chapl HM Rem Cen Pucklechurch 87-91; Chapl Asst Southmead Hosp Bris 91-95; C Knowle St Barn *Bris* 95-02; Bp's Adv for Past Care for Clergy and Families 97-00; Community Th St Mich Coll Llan 00-05; Dir In-House Tr 02-05; Chapl Worcs Acute Hosps NHS Trust 05-09; rtd 09. *Grove Cottage, Barton Lane, Mere, Warminster BA12 6JA* Tel (01747) 860553 E-mail judithvthompson@aol.com

THOMPSON, Kenneth. b 31. St Deiniol's Hawarden 84. d 87 p 88. Hon Par Dn Upton (Overchurch) *Ches* 87-90; NSM Tranmere St Cath 90-95; rtd 96; Perm to Offic *Ches* from 96. *33 Meadway, Upton, Wirral CH49 6JQ* Tel 0151-677 6433

THOMPSON, Kenneth (Brother Nathanael). b 29. St Deiniol's Hawarden 76. d 78 p 79. SSF from 62; C Llanbeblig w Caernarfon *Ban* 78-80; C Swansea St Gabr *S & B* 84-87; C Dolgellau w Llanfachreth and Brithdir etc *Ban* 95-99. *The Vicarage, 3A High Street, Bentley, Doncaster DN5 0AA* Tel (01302) 876272

THOMPSON, Kevin. b 55. Sheff Univ BEd77. Oak Hill Th Coll. d 89 p 90. C Brinsworth w Catcliffe *Sheff* 89-92; V Kimberworth Park 92-97; V Grenoside 97-98; Perm to Offic from 98. *30 Arnold Avenue, Charnock, Sheffield S12 3JB* Tel 0114-239 6986 E-mail kevin.thompson10@virgin.net

THOMPSON, Livingstone Anthony. b 59. Univ of W Indies BA82 Irish Sch of Ecum MPhil00 TCD PhD03. McCormick Th Sem Chicago MA(TS)89. d 83 p 90. Jamaica 83-05; CITC 05-06. *83 Hermitage Glen, Kells, Co Meath, Republic of Ireland* Tel (00353) (46) 929 3861 Mobile 86-373 7135

THOMPSON, Louise Margaret. *See* TAYLOR-KENYON, Louise Margaret

THOMPSON, Mark William. b 52. St Jo Coll Nottm 77. d 81 p 82. C Barnsbury St Andr and H Trin w All SS *Lon* 81-84; C Addiscombe St Mary *Cant* 84; C Addiscombe St Mary *S'wark* 85-87; V Thorpe Edge *Bradf* 87-94; Chapl Colchester Hosp Univ NHS Foundn Trust from 94. *Colchester General Hospital, Turner Road, Colchester CO4 5JL* Tel (01206) 747474 or 742513 E-mail mark.thompson@essexrivers.nhs.uk

THOMPSON, Martin Eric. b 52. FCCA. Trin Coll Bris 95. d 97 p 98. C Heref St Pet w St Owen and St Jas 97-01; P-in-c Huntley and Longhope *Glouc* 01-02; R Huntley and Longhope, Churcham and Bulley 03-05; P-in-c Worfield *Heref* 05-10; V Twigworth, Down Hatherley, Norton, The Leigh etc *Glouc* from 10. *The Rectory, Tewkesbury Road, Twigworth, Gloucester GL2 9PQ* Tel (01452) 731994 E-mail revmartin@lineone.net

THOMPSON, Matthew. b 68. CCC Cam BA90 MA94 MPhil94. Ridley Hall Cam 91. d 94 p 95. C Hulme Ascension *Man* 94-97; C Langley and Parkfield 97-98; TV 98-00; P-in-c Man Clayton St Cross w St Paul 00-08; AD Ardwick 03-08; P-in-c Bolton St Pet from 08; P-in-c Bolton St Phil from 08; Borough Dean Bolton from 10. *35 Sherbourne Road, Bolton BL1 5NN* Tel (01204) 845332 E-mail vicar@boltonparishchurch.co.uk

THOMPSON, Mervyn Patrick. b 59. Wilson Carlile Coll 84 Coll of Resurr Mirfield 90. d 92 p 93. C Sheff St Cath Richmond Road 92-95; V Thurnscoe St Hilda 95-06; P-in-c Thurnscoe St Helen 99-06; R Thurnscoe 06-11; TR S Shields All SS *Dur* from 11. *The Rectory, Tyne Terrace, South Shields NE34 0NF* Tel 0191-456 1851

THOMPSON, Michael. b 49. NEOC 83. d 86 p 87. C Ashington *Newc* 86-88; C Ponteland 88-91; TV Newc Epiphany 91-98; P-in-c Choppington 98-99; P-in-c Woldingham *S'wark* 99-02; TV Caterham 02-03; TV Saffron Walden w Wendens Ambo, Littlebury etc *Chelmsf* 03-08; R N Hartismere *St E* from 08. *The Rectory, Oakley, Diss IP21 4AN* Tel (01379) 742708 E-mail frmichael.thompson@btinternet.com

THOMPSON, Michael Bruce. b 53. N Carolina Univ BA75 Dallas Th Sem ThM79 Virginia Th Sem 79 Ch Coll Cam PhD88. d 80 p 81. Asst Min New Bern N Carolina 80-83; Chair Youth and Evang and Renewal in E Carolina 81-83; Lect Greek Cam Univ 87-88; Lect St Jo Coll Nottm 88-95; Lect NT and Dir of Studies Ridley Hall Cam from 95; Vice-Prin from 00. *Dashwood House, Sidgwick Avenue, Cambridge CB3 9DA* Tel (01223) 741077 or 741066 Fax 741081 E-mail mbt2@cam.ac.uk

THOMPSON, Michael James. b 55. St Andr Univ MTheol78 Dur Univ MA93. St Mich Coll Llan 78. d 79 p 80. C Aberavon *Llan* 79-81; C Kensington St Mary Abbots w St Geo *Lon* 81-85; Chapl and Sacr Westmr Abbey 85-87; R Lowick w Sudborough and Slipton *Pet* 87-94; P-in-c Islip 87-94; V Sneinton St Steph w St Alb *S'well* 96-98; R Stamford St Mary and St Martin *Linc* 98-04; I Dublin St Bart w Leeson Park *D & G* 04-07; Min Can St Patr Cathl Dublin 04-07; I Youghal Union and Min Can Cork Cathl 08-09; P-in-c Lidgate w Kempston, E and W Lexham, Mileham etc *Nor* 10-11; P-in-c Gt and Lt Dunham w Gt and Lt Fransham and Sporle 10-11. *Address temp unknown* E-mail parson@uppernar.orangehome.co.uk

THOMPSON, Michael John. b 39. Cam Univ MA. d 00 p 01. OLM Badgeworth, Shurdington and Witcombe w Bentham *Glouc* 00-06. *Cornerways, 1 Church Lane, Shurdington, Gloucester GL51 4TJ* Tel (01242) 862467 E-mail mthompson123@aol.com

THOMPSON, Mrs Michelle. b 68. Man Univ BA89. Ripon Coll Cuddesdon 90. d 92 p 94. Par Dn Leigh St Mary *Man* 92-94; Asst Chapl HM Pris Full Sutton 95-97; V York St Hilda 97-00; Dir Reader Tr and Local Min Development *Man* 00-03; Chapl HM Pris Styal from 04. *HM Prison Styal, Styal Road, Styal, Wilmslow SK9 4HR* Tel (01625) 553000

THOMPSON, Canon Neil Hamilton. b 48. SS Hild & Bede Coll Dur BEd72 Leic Univ MA75. S'wark Ord Course 77 Ven English Coll Rome. d 80 p 81. C Merton St Mary *S'wark* 80-82; C Dulwich St Barn 82-84; V Shooters Hill Ch Ch 84-87; V S Dulwich St Steph 87-96; Ldr Post Ord Tr Woolwich Area 94-96; R Limpsfield and Titsey 96-08; Can Res and Prec Roch Cathl from 08. *Easter Garth, The Precinct, Rochester ME1 1SX* Tel (01634) 405265 *or* 810063 Fax 401410 E-mail precentor@rochestercathedral.org

THOMPSON, Patricia. b 60. SRN. NEOC 94. d 97 p 98. NSM Sunderland St Chad *Dur* from 97; Voc Adv from 99. *11 Friarsfield Close, Chapelgarth, Sunderland SR3 2RZ* Tel 0191-522 7911

THOMPSON, Patrick Arthur. b 36. Dur Univ BA59. Qu Coll Birm. d 61 p 62. C W Wickham St Fran *Cant* 61-65; C Portchester *Portsm* 65-68; C Birchington w Acol *Cant* 68-71; V S Norwood St Mark 71-77; P-in-c Norbury St Oswald 77-81; V Norbury St Oswald *S'wark* 81-93; V Sutton New Town St Barn 93-00; rtd 00; Resident P Grantown-on-Spey *Mor* from 04. *Rose Cottage, 2 Market Street, Forres IV36 1EF* Tel (01309) 675917

THOMPSON, Paul. b 58. Ox Univ BA. Ripon Coll Cuddesdon 80. d 83 p 84. Chapl Fazakerley Hosp 83-86; C Kirkby *Liv* 83-86; TV 86-89; Ind Chapl 86-89; Chapl Kirkby Coll of FE 86-89; CF 89-01; Chapl Epsom Coll from 01. *Epsom College, Epsom KT17 4JQ* Tel (01372) 821288 E-mail s-chaplain@epsomcollege.org.uk

THOMPSON, Paul. b 65. TCD BA87. CITC 87. d 89 p 90. C Orangefield w Moneyreagh *D & D* 89-92; I Dromara w Garvaghy 92-97; I Ramoan w Ballycastle and Culfeightrin *Conn* 97-00; Dep Chapl HM Pris Liv 00-01; Chapl HM YOI Portland from 01. *HM Young Offender Institution, The Grove, Portland DT5 1DL* Tel (01305) 820301 Fax 823718

THOMPSON, Paul Noble. b 54. Univ of Wales (Cardiff) BMus77 Univ of Wales (Ban) MPhil04. Coll of Resurr Mirfield. d 80 p 81. C Bargoed and Deri w Brithdir *Llan* 80-83; C Whitchurch 83-84; V Porth w Trealaw 84-90; V Llanharan w Peterston-super-Montem 90-97; Hon C Barry All SS 97-01; Dioc Youth Chapl 90-01; V Lisvane 01-09; Chapl Univ Coll of SS Mark and Jo Plymouth *Ex* from 09. *Staff House 1, The College of St Mark and St John, Derriford Road, Plymouth PL6 8BH* Tel (01752) 636847

THOMPSON, Pauline. See WILLCOX, Mrs Pauline

THOMPSON, Peter Alrick. b 79. QUB BA01 TCD MPhil04 ARIAM99. CITC 01. d 03 p 04. C Clooney w Strathfoyle *D & R* 03-06; I Donaghmore w Upper Donaghmore *Arm* from 06; Hon V Choral Arm Cathl from 06. *St Michael's Rectory, 66 Main Street, Castlecaulfield, Dungannon BT70 3NP* Tel (028) 8776 1214 Mobile 07732-856306 E-mail donaghmore@armagh.anglican.org

THOMPSON, Canon Peter Ross. b 26. St Jo Coll Cam BA47 MB, BChir50. Tyndale Hall Bris. d 60 p 61. C New Malden and Coombe *S'wark* 60-61; BCMS Burma 61-66; R Slaugham *Chich* 66-72; V Polegate 72-92; Can and Preb Chich Cathl 91-92; rtd 92; Perm to Offic *Guildf* from 92. *Tregenna, Barley Mow Lane, Knaphill, Woking GU21 2HX* Tel (01483) 480595

THOMPSON, Mrs Rachel Mary. b 65. Roehampton Inst BA87 Rolle Coll PGCE88 Nottm Univ MA07. EMMTC 04. d 07 p 08. NSM Wilne and Draycott w Breaston *Derby* 07-11; NSM Kirk Hallam from 11. *16 Edge Hill Court, Long Eaton, Nottingham NG10 1PQ* Tel 0115-972 7275 E-mail rev.rach@googlemail.com

THOMPSON, Randolph. b 25. Lich Th Coll 63. d 65 p 66. C Boultham *Linc* 65-68; V Paddock *Wakef* 68-69; P-in-c Cornholme 69-71; V 71-72; Chapl Barnsley Hall and Lea Hosps Bromsgrove 72-84; V Hanley Castle, Hanley Swan and Welland *Worc* 84-89; rtd 89; Perm to Offic *Lich* from 90. *37 Hampton Fields, Oswestry SY11 1TL* Tel (01691) 658484

THOMPSON, Raymond Craigmile. b 42. Man Univ BTh. d 84 p 85. C Clooney *D & R* 84-86; I Urney w Sion Mills 86-92; I Derryvullen N w Castlearchdale *Clogh* 92-05; Chapl to Bp Clogh 02-05; Can Clogh Cathl 03-05; Dean Clogh 05-09; I Clogh w Errigal Portclare 05-09; rtd 09. *En-Rimmon, 6 Tullylammy Road, Irvinestown, Enniskillen BT94 1NN* Tel (028) 6862 8258

THOMPSON, Richard Brian. b 60. Sheff Poly BSc83. Ripon Coll Cuddesdon 86. d 89 p 90. C Thorpe Bay *Chelmsf* 89-92; V Rushmere 92-97; Dep Chapl HM Pris Nor 97-98; Chapl HM Pris Wayland 98-01; Chapl HM Pris Hollesley Bay 01-06; Chapl HM Pris Whitemoor 06-08; Chapl HM Pris and YOI

Warren Hill from 08; Chapl HM Pris Hollesley Bay from 08. *HM Prison, Hollesley Bay Colony, Rectory Road, Hollesley, Woodbridge IP12 3JW* Tel (01394) 412400 E-mail richard.thompson02@hmps.gsi.gov.uk

THOMPSON, Robert Craig. b 72. Univ Coll Dur BA92. Westcott Ho Cam 94. d 96 p 97. C Wigan All SS *Liv* 96-00; P-in-c Ladybrook *S'well* 00-05; P-in-c Bengeo *St Alb* 05-08; TV Hertford from 08. *The Rectory, Byde Street, Hertford SG14 3BS* Tel (01992) 413691 E-mail revrobert@tiscali.co.uk

THOMPSON, Robert George. b 71. K Coll Cam BA93 MA97. Ripon Coll Cuddesdon MTh95. d 97 p 98. C Ruislip St Martin *Lon* 97-01; Chapl Parkside Community NHS Trust Lon 01-09; Chapl R Brompton and Harefield NHS Trust from 09; Hon C Holland Park *Lon* from 09. *Chaplain's Office, Royal Brompton Hospital, Sydney Street, London SW3 6NP* Tel (020) 7352 8121 ext 4740 E-mail r.thompson2@rbht.nhs.uk

THOMPSON, Roger Quintin. b 63. K Coll Lon BA85 AKC85 Nottm Univ PGCE86 MA96. Aston Tr Scheme 92 St Jo Coll Nottm 94. d 96. C Easton H Trin w St Gabr and St Lawr and St Jude *Bris* 96-00; C Lisburn Ch Ch Cathl 00-04; I Kilwaughter w Cairncastle and Craigy Hill from 04. *Cairncastle Rectory, 15 Cairncastle Road, Ballygally, Larne BT40 2RB* Tel (028) 2858 3220 *or* 2826 9552 E-mail rqtfi@btinternet.com

THOMPSON, Ross Keith Arnold. b 53. Sussex Univ BA75 Bris Univ PhD82. Coll of Resurr Mirfield 80. d 82 p 83. C Knowle *Bris* 82-85; TV E Bris 85-94; V Bristol St Aid w St Geo 94-95; V Knowle St Barn and H Cross Inns Court 95-02; Tutor St Mich Coll Llan 02-05; rtd 09. *Grove Cottage, Barton Lane, Mere, Warminster BA12 6JA* Tel (01747) 860553

THOMPSON, Ruth Jean. *See* GOSTELOW, Mrs Ruth Jean

THOMPSON, Mrs Shanthi Hazel Peiris. b 67. Cranmer Hall Dur 07. d 09 p 10. C Kirkby Lonsdale *Carl* from 09. *29 New Road, Kirkby Lonsdale, Carnforth LA6 2AB* Tel 07931-446025 (mobile) E-mail curate@therainbowparish.org

THOMPSON, Stephen Peter. b 45. Lon Univ BSc67 Lon Inst of Educn PGCE71 K Coll Lon BD77 AKC77 SOAS Lon BA82 Poona Univ MPhil85 PhD87 FRAS91. Ripon Coll Cuddesdon. d 00. NSM Bedford Park *Lon* 00-01; NSM Isleworth St Fran 01-08; Perm to Offic from 08. *12 Minsterley Avenue, Shepperton TW17 8QT* Tel (01932) 781805 E-mail revdocstephen@gmail.com

THOMPSON, Thomas Oliver. b 27. TCD 61. d 63 p 64. C Lisburn Ch Ch *Conn* 63-68; Chapl to Ch of Ireland Miss to Deaf and Dumb 68-76; I Glenavy w Tunny and Crumlin 77-92; rtd 92. *34 Strandview Avenue, Portstewart BT55 7LL* Tel (028) 7083 3267

THOMPSON, Canon Timothy. b 34. Fitzw Ho Cam BA59 MA64. Cuddesdon Coll 59. d 61 p 62. C Noel Park St Mark *Lon* 61-64; C Shrub End *Chelmsf* 64-67; New Zealand 67-70; R Tolleshunt Knights w Tiptree *Chelmsf* 70-81; R Colchester St Jas, All SS, St Nic and St Runwald 81-88; RD Colchester 84-88; Hon Can Chelmsf Cathl 85-88; Can Res Chelmsf Cathl 88-01; Vice-Provost 88-00; Vice-Dean 00-01; rtd 01. *44 Sixth Avenue, Chelmsford CM1 4ED* Tel (01245) 260382

THOMPSON, Timothy Charles. b 51. Lon Univ BSc73 AKC. Westcott Ho Cam 75. d 78 p 79. C Ipswich St Mary at Stoke w St Pet etc *St E* 78-81; Ind Chapl *Nor* 81-88; C Lowestoft and Kirkley 81-83; TV 83-88; V Coney Hill *Glouc* 94-98; P-in-c Caister *Nor* 94-00; R from 00. *The Rectory, Rectory Close, Caister-on-Sea, Great Yarmouth NR30 5EG* Tel (01493) 720287 E-mail tim.thompson@ukonline.co.uk

THOMPSON, Canon Timothy William. b 47. Bris Univ CertEd70 Open Univ BA78. EMMTC. d 88 p 89. C Scartho *Linc* 88-91; V Haxey 91-95; P-in-c Surfleet 95-00; Asst Local Min Officer 95-00; RD Elloe W 98-00; P-in-c Linc St Pet-at-Gowts and St Andr 00-09; P-in-c Linc St Botolph 00-09; RD Christianity 02-08; rtd 09; Can and Preb Linc Cathl from 02. *16 Nocton Park Road, Nocton, Lincoln LN4 2BE* Tel (01526) 320171 Mobile 07885-238813 E-mail timwthompson@btinternet.com

THOMPSON, Canon Tom Malcolm. b 38. Dur Univ BA60 Man Univ MPhil93. Bps' Coll Cheshunt 60. d 62 p 63. C Standish *Blackb* 62-65; C Lancaster St Mary 65-67; V Chorley All SS 67-72; V Barrowford 72-78; RD Pendle 75-78; R Northfield *Birm* 78-82; RD Kings Norton 79-82; V Longton *Blackb* 82-94; RD Leyland 89-94; V Nunthorpe *York* 94-03; Can and Preb York Minster 98-03; RD Stokesley 00-03; rtd 03; Perm to Offic *Carl* from 03 and *Blackb* from 08. *Wainstones, 6 Greengate Crescent, Levens, Kendal LA8 8QB* Tel (015395) 61409

THOMPSON-McCAUSLAND, Marcus Perronet. b 31. Trin Coll Cam BA54 MA60. Coll of Resurr Mirfield 57. d 59 p 60. C Perry Barr *Birm* 59-65; V Rubery 65-72; R Cradley *Heref* 72-82; P-in-c Storridge 72-82; P-in-c Mathon 72-82; P-in-c Castle Frome 72-82; Hon C Camberwell St Giles *S'wark* 82-87; Hon C Lydbury N *Heref* 88-89; Hon C Lydbury N w Hopesay and Edgton 89-94; Hon C Wigmore Abbey 95-01; Perm to Offic from 01. *18 Watling Street, Leintwardine, Craven Arms SY7 0LW* Tel (01547) 540228

THOMPSON-VEAR, John Arthur. b 76. Sunderland Univ BA98. St Steph Ho Ox BA02 MA06. **d** 03 **p** 04. C Plymouth Crownhill Ascension *Ex* 03-06; Chapl RN 06-08; TV Harrogate St Wilfrid *Ripon* 08-11; CF(V) from 10. *Address temp unknown* Tel 07799-215148 (mobile) E-mail frjohn@btinternet.com

THOMPSTONE, Canon John Deaville. b 39. BNC Ox BA63 MA67. Ridley Hall Cam 63. **d** 65 **p** 66. C Hoole *Ches* 65-68; C Fulwood *Sheff* 68-71; V Skirbeck H Trin *Linc* 71-77; V Shipley St Pet *Bradf* 77-91; RD Airedale 82-88; V Poynton *Ches* 91-04; Hon Can Ches Cathl 02-04; rtd 04. *Greyfriars, Broadway Road, Childswickham, Broadway WR12 7HP* Tel (01386) 852930 E-mail greyfriars@homecall.co.uk

THOMSETT, Murray Richard. b 32. MBKSTS. Oak Hill Th Coll 91. **d** 92 **p** 93. NSM Whitton SS Phil and Jas *Lon* 92-96; NSM Hampton All SS 96-02; Chapl Terminal 4 Heathrow Airport from 96. *27 Coombe Road, Hampton TW12 3PB* Tel (020) 8979 7549 *or* 8745 2700 E-mail murrayt@nildram.co.uk

THOMSON, Alexander Keith. b 38. Cranmer Hall Dur BA63. **d** 64 **p** 65. C Middleton *Man* 64-68; Chapl Rannock Sch Perthshire 68-72; P-in-c Kinloch Rannoch *St And* 68-72; Asst Chapl Oundle Sch 72-94; Chapl Laxton Sch 88-94; Lic to Offic *Pet* 73-94; Perm to Offic 94-01; rtd 98. *15 Cramond Glebe Gardens, Edinburgh EH4 6NZ* Tel 0131-538 2806

THOMSON, Andrew Maitland. b 43. CA(Z)67. Westcott Ho Cam 78. **d** 80 **p** 81. C Harare Cathl Zimbabwe 80-82; R Kadoma and P-in-c Chegutu 82-87; R Marlborough St Paul Harare 87-92; P-in-c E w N and W Barsham *Nor* 92-95; P-in-c N and S Creake w Waterden 92-94; P-in-c Sculthorpe w Dunton and Doughton 92-94; R N and S Creake w Waterden, Syderstone etc 95-11; rtd 11; C F w W Rudham, Helhoughton etc *Nor* from 11. *3 Charles Road, Fakenham NR21 8JX* Tel (01328) 862557 E-mail pandathomson@btinternet.com

THOMSON, Bruce. *See* THOMSON, Sydney Bruce

THOMSON, Canon Celia Stephana Margaret. b 55. LMH Ox MA83 Birkbeck Coll Lon MA87 K Coll Lon MA94. Sarum & Wells Th Coll 89. **d** 91 **p** 94. Par Dn Southfields St Barn *S'wark* 91-94; C 94-95; V W Wimbledon Ch Ch 95-03; Tutor SEITE 95-00; Voc Adv Lambeth Adnry 96-00; Can Res Glouc Cathl from 03. *3 Miller's Green, Gloucester GL1 2BN* Tel (01452) 415824 E-mail cthomson@gloucestercathedral.org.uk

THOMSON, Christopher Grant. b 71. Cam Univ BTh07. Westcott Ho Cam 05. **d** 07 **p** 08. C Bletchingley and Nutfield *S'wark* 07-11; P-in-c Kenley from 11; P-in-c Purley St Barn from 11. *The Vicarage, 3 Valley Road, Kenley CR8 5DJ* Tel (020) 8660 6981 E-mail revdthomson@btinternet.com

THOMSON, Preb Clarke Edward Leighton. b 19. TD65. Pemb Coll Ox BA41 MA45. Wycliffe Hall Ox 44. **d** 45 **p** 46. C Penge Lane H Trin *Roch* 45-47; Egypt 47-50; C Chelsea All SS *Lon* 50-51; V 51-92; CF (TA) 52-69; Preb St Paul's Cathl 86-92; rtd 92; Perm to Offic *Lon* from 93. *St Wilfrid's, 29 Tite Street, London SW3 4JX* Tel (020) 7565 5829

✠**THOMSON, The Rt Revd David.** b 52. Keble Coll Ox MA78 DPhil78 Selw Coll Cam BA80 MA84 FRSA06 FSA08 FRHistS08. Westcott Ho Cam 78. **d** 81 **p** 82 **c** 08. C Maltby *Sheff* 81-84; TV Banbury *Ox* 84-94; Sec Par and People 84-93; TR Cockermouth w Embleton and Wythop *Carl* 94-02; Adn Carl and Can Res Carl Cathl 02-08; Suff Bp Huntingdon *Ely* from 08. *14 Lynn Road, Ely CB6 1DA* Tel (01353) 662137 Fax 669357 Mobile 07771-864550 E-mail bishop.huntingdon@ely.anglican.org

THOMSON, David Francis. b 54. Salford Univ BA81 CPFA84. NOC 05. **d** 07 **p** 08. NSM New Bury w Gt Lever *Man* 07-10; P-in-c Ainsworth from 10. *The Vicarage, Ainsworth Hall Road, Ainsworth, Bolton BL2 5RY* Tel (01204) 398567 Mobile 07970-461907 E-mail thomsondf@hotmail.com

THOMSON, Elizabeth Jane. b 64. Univ Coll Ox MA85 DPhil89 Trin Coll Cam BA02 Moray Ho Coll of Educn PGCE90. Westcott Ho Cam 00. **d** 03 **p** 04. C Pilton w Croscombe, N Wootton and Dinder *B & W* 03-07; TV Witney *Ox* from 07. *Holy Trinity Vicarage, 4 Maidley Close, Witney OX28 1ER* Tel (01993) 834875 E-mail ejt@jinkaboot.net

THOMSON, Elizabeth Lucy. *See* TALBOT, Mrs Elizabeth Lucy

THOMSON, James. b 39. St Andr Coll Melrose 58 Episc Sem Austin Texas 88. **d** 62 **p** 63. In RC Ch 62-83; C Oklahoma City All So USA 89-90; R Oklahoma St Matt 90-95; Assoc R Oklahoma H Trin 95-05; P-in-c Pittenweem *St And* 06-09; P-in-c Elie and Earlsferry 06-09; rtd 09. *41A South Street, St Andrews KY16 9QR* Tel (01334) 479645 E-mail revjthomson@btinternet.com

THOMSON, James Maclaren. b 69. Grey Coll Dur BA91 Univ Coll Lon MA93. Wycliffe Hall Ox BA99. **d** 00 **p** 01. C Oulton Broad *Nor* 00-04; V Chatteris *Ely* from 04. *The Vicarage, Church Lane, Chatteris PE16 6JA* Tel (01354) 692173 E-mail james@chatteris.org

THOMSON, Canon John Bromilow. b 59. York Univ BA81 Wycliffe Hall Ox BA84 MA91 Nottm Univ PhD01. **d** 85 **p** 86. C Ecclesall *Sheff* 85-89; Tutor St Paul's Coll Grahamstown S Africa 89-92; Asst P Grahamstown St Bart 90-92; Asst Lect Rhodes Univ 91-92; V Doncaster St Mary 93-01; Dir Min from

01; Hon Can Sheff Cathl from 01. *15 Grange View, Balby, Doncaster DN4 0XL* Tel (01302) 570205 *or* (01709) 309143 Fax (01709) 309108 E-mail john.thomson@sheffield.anglican.org

THOMSON, Julian Harley. b 43. AKC70. St Aug Coll Cant 70. **d** 71 **p** 72. C Wellingborough All Hallows *Pet* 71-74; Min Can, Prec and Sacr Ely Cathl 74-80; P-in-c Stuntney 76-80; V Arrington 80-91; R Croydon w Clopton 80-91; R Orwell 80-91; R Wimpole 80-91; V Linton 91-96; R Bartlow 91-96; P-in-c Castle Camps 91-96; TR Linton 96-01; RD Linton 99-01; rtd 01; Perm to Offic *Nor* from 01. *Lavender Cottage, 7 Abbey Road, Great Massingham, King's Lynn PE32 2HN* Tel (01485) 520721 E-mail thomson5816@btinternet.com

THOMSON, Keith. *See* THOMSON, Alexander Keith

THOMSON, Matthew James. b 63. Nottm Univ BA92. St Jo Coll Nottm 92. **d** 95 **p** 96. C Cosham *Portsm* 95-98; C Nailsea Ch Ch w Tickenham *B & W* 98-01; V Congresbury w Puxton and Hewish St Ann from 01; Bp's Healing Adv from 01. *The Vicarage, Station Road, Congresbury, Bristol BS49 5DX* Tel (01934) 833126 E-mail revmatthomson@hotmail.com

THOMSON, Monica Anne. b 38. **d** 06 **p** 07. NSM Stockton Heath *Ches* from 06. *9 Broomfields Road, Appleton, Warrington WA4 3AE* Tel (01925) 604235 E-mail jomo.tomsky@ntlworld.com

THOMSON, Peter Malcolm. b 44. Trin Coll Bris 75. **d** 78 **p** 79. C Tonbridge St Steph *Roch* 78-82; R Cobham w Luddesdowne and Dode 82-90; V Wythall *Birm* 90-02; rtd 02; Perm to Offic *Birm* from 02. *37 Northbrook Road, Shirley, Solihull B90 3NR* Tel 0121-745 9042 E-mail peter@petcar.me.uk

THOMSON, Canon Richard Irving. b 32. Oak Hill Th Coll 57. **d** 60 **p** 61. C Kingston upon Hull H Trin *York* 60-63; C S Croydon Em *Cant* 63-66; V Shoreditch St Leon *Lon* 66-73; Chapl Vevey w Château d'Oex and Villars Eur 73-78; V Reigate St Mary *S'wark* 78-97; Hon Can S'wark Cathl 90-97; rtd 97; Perm to Offic *Win* from 97. *Little Heathfield, Forest Front, Dibden Purlieu, Southampton SO45 3RG* Tel (023) 8084 9613 E-mail richardithomson@compuserve.com

THOMSON, Richard William Byars. b 60. Birm Univ BA86. Ripon Coll Cuddesdon 86. **d** 88 **p** 89. C Moulsecoomb *Chich* 88-90; P-in-c Kirriemuir *St And* 90-94; P-in-c Piddletrenthide w Plush, Alton Pancras etc *Sarum* 94-02; P-in-c Milborne St Andrew w Dewlish 94-02; Chapl Milton Abbey Sch Dorset from 02. *Nether Fen, Milton Abbey, Blandford Forum DT11 0DA* Tel (01258) 881513 E-mail byars22@aol.com

THOMSON, Robert Douglass. b 37. Lon Univ TCert61 Newc Univ DAES70 Dur Univ BEd75. NEOC 76. **d** 79 **p** 80. NSM Shincliffe *Dur* 79-98; Chapl St Aid Coll Dur 93-99. *11 Hill Meadows, High Shincliffe, Durham DH1 2PE* Tel 0191-386 3358

THOMSON, Robin Alexander Stewart. b 43. Ch Coll Cam MA69 K Coll Lon MTh72. SEITE 94. **d** 96 **p** 97. NSM Wimbledon Em Ridgway Prop Chpl *S'wark* 96-02 and from 10; NSM Tooting Graveney St Nic 02-10. *2 Coppice Close, London SW20 9AS* Tel (020) 8540 7748 *or* 8770 9717 Fax 8770 9747

THOMSON, Canon Ronald. b 24. Leeds Univ BA49. Coll of Resurr Mirfield 49. **d** 51 **p** 52. C Sunderland *Dur* 51-54; C Attercliffe w Carbrook *Sheff* 54-57; V Shiregreen St Hilda 57-73; RD Ecclesfield 72-73; V Worsbrough St Mary 73-88; RD Tankersley 75-85; Hon Can Sheff Cathl 77-88; rtd 88; Perm to Offic *Sheff* from 88. *4 St Mary's Garden, Worsbrough, Barnsley S70 5LU* Tel (01226) 203553

THOMSON, Russell. b 39. AKC62. **d** 63 **p** 64. C Hackney *Lon* 63-66; C Plumstead Wm Temple Ch Abbey Wood CD *S'wark* 66-69; TV Strood *Roch* 69-75; V Gillingham St Mary 75-89; V Roch 89-04; Chapl St Bart Hosp Roch 89-94; Chapl Medway NHS Trust 94-04; Chapl Wisdom Hospice 89-04; rtd 04. *Little Heath, Shepherds Way, Fairlight, Hastings TN35 4BD* Tel and fax (01424) 812526

THOMSON, Sydney Bruce. b 49. Fuller Th Sem California MA91 ThM92 Stirling Univ MLitt98. Ox Min Course 05. **d** 07 **p** 08. C Worcs W 07-10; TV Leominster *Heref* from 10. *The New Vicarage, Kimbolton, Leominster HR6 0EJ* Tel (01568) 615295 E-mail beagle6@btinternet.com

THOMSON, Wendy Leigh. b 64. Trin W Univ Vancouver BA87. Wycliffe Hall Ox BTh99. **d** 00 **p** 01. C Oulton Broad *Nor* 00-04; C Chatteris *Ely* from 04. *The Vicarage, Church Lane, Chatteris PE16 6JA* Tel (01354) 692173 E-mail wendy@chatteris.org

THOMSON, Mrs Winifred Mary. b 35. St Mary's Coll Dur BA57 MA58. Qu Coll Birm 79. dss 82 **d** 87 **p** 94. Leic H Spirit 82-86; Oadby 86-92; Par Dn 87-92; rtd 93; Perm to Offic *Leic* from 94. *140 Knighton Church Road, Leicester LE2 3JJ* Tel 0116-270 5863

THOMSON GIBSON, Thomas. *See* GIBSON, Thomas Thomson

THOMSON-GLOVER, Canon William Hugh. b 28. Trin Hall Cam BA52 MA56. Cuddesdon Coll 52. **d** 54 **p** 55. C Stepney St Dunstan and All SS *Lon* 54-58; C Tiverton St Andr *Ex* 58-60; P-in-c 60-63; Chapl Clifton Coll Bris 63-69; V Bris Lockleaze St Mary Magd w St Fran 70-76; P-in-c Sherston Magna w Easton Grey 76-81; P-in-c Luckington w Alderton 76-81; V Sherston Magna, Easton Grey, Luckington etc 81-93; P-in-c

Foxley w Bremilham 84-86; RD Malmesbury 88-93; Hon Can Bris Cathl 91-93; rtd 93; Perm to Offic *Ex* from 93. *Woodgate Farm House, Woodgate, Culmstock, Cullompton EX15 3HW* Tel (01884) 841465

THORBURN, Guy Douglas Anderson. b 50. Trin Coll Ox BA74 MA78. Ridley Hall Cam. **d** 83 **p** 84. C Putney St Marg *S'wark* 83-87; R Moresby *Carl* 87-97; V Gt Clacton *Chelmsf* from 97; RD St Osyth from 07. *St John's Vicarage, Valley Road, Clacton-on-Sea CO15 4AR* Tel (01255) 423435 E-mail revguy.thorburn@virgin.net

THORBURN, Peter Hugh. b 17. Worc Coll Ox BA41 MA43. Wells Th Coll 46. **d** 47 **p** 48. C Mill Hill Jo Keble Ch *Lon* 47-51; Lon Dioc Home Missr Colindale St Matthias 51; V 51-54; V Wigan St Mich *Liv* 54-65; USA 65-68; V Chipping Sodbury and Old Sodbury *Glouc* 68-72; Chapl Withington Hosp Man 72-82; rtd 82; Perm to Offic *B & W* from 83; *Bris* from 85; *Lon* 95-97; Warden Servants of Ch the K from 89. *8 Stoberry Crescent, Wells BA5 2TG* Tel (01749) 672919

THORBURN, Simon Godfrey. b 51. Newc Univ BSc73 Fitzw Coll Cam BA77 MA81 Sheff Univ MMinTheol97. Westcott Ho Cam 75. **d** 78 **p** 79. C Stafford *Lich* 78-82; C Tettenhall Regis 82-83; TV 83-90; Soc Resp Officer *S'wark* 90-97; V Edgbaston St Geo *Birm* 97-09; AD Edgbaston 03-08; Chapl St Geo Sch Edgbaston 99-08; V Oswestry *Lich* from 09; R Rhydycroesau from 09. *The Vicarage, Penylan Lane, Oswestry SY11 2AJ* Tel (01691) 653467 E-mail simon@thorburns.plus.com

THORESEN, Ms Alveen Fern. b 46. Avondale Coll NSW BA(Ed)69 Newc Univ Aus BA76 New England Univ NSW MA82. SAOMC 96. **d** 01 **p** 02. NSM Caversham St Pet and Mapledurham *Ox* 01-10; NSM Boxwell, Leighterton, Didmarton, Oldbury etc *Glouc* from 10. *The Rectory, The Meads, Leighterton, Tetbury GL8 8UW* Tel (01666) 890548 E-mail alveen@waitrose.com

THORIUS, Mrs Lynn Christine. b 51. Newc Univ DAES85. Yorks Min Course 08. **d** 11. NSM E Richmond *Ripon* from 11. *The Retreat, Hornby, Northallerton DL6 2JH* Tel (01609) 881451 Mobile 07788-862397 E-mail rlthorius@tiscali.co.uk

THORLEY, Canon Barry. b 44. Westcott Ho Cam 70. **d** 73 **p** 74. C Camberwell St Giles *S'wark* 73-76; C Moseley St Mary *Birm* 76-78; V Birchfield 78-83; V Brixton St Matt *S'wark* 84-89; C Greenwich St Alfege 96-00; C Thamesmead 00-01; TR 01-06; rtd 06; Hon Can Zanzibar from 04. *St Benet's Chapel, PO Box 104, Nkawie-Toase, Ghana* E-mail thorleybarry@yahoo.co.uk

THORLEY, Mrs Mary Kathleen. b 53. OBE00. Univ of Wales (Swansea) BA74 Glos Coll of Educn PGCE75. St Mich Coll Llan 99. **d** 02 **p** 03. NSM Carmarthen St Pet *St D* 02-05; NSM Carmarthen St Dav from 05. *Bryn Heulog, Heol Penllanffos, Carmarthen SA31 2HL* Tel (01267) 235927

THORN (formerly KINGS), Mrs Jean Alison. b 63. RGN85 Heythrop Coll Lon MTh. Cranmer Hall Dur BA90. **d** 91 **p** 93. Chapl Bris Poly 91-92; Chapl UWE 92-95; Hon C Bris Lockleaze St Mary Magd w St Fran 91-95; C Fishponds All SS 95-96; Hon C 96-97; V Bris Ch the Servant Stockwood 97-01; Hon C Whitchurch 01-04. *The Rectory, Church Street, Burton Bradstock, Bridport DT6 4QS* Tel (01308) 898799

THORN, Kevan. b 67. CBDT1 03. **d** 06 **p** 07. NSM Blackpool H Cross *Blackb* 06-10; NSM Kirkham from 10. *16 Bannistre Close, Lytham St Annes FY8 3HS* Tel (01253) 713088 Fax 08707-621548 E-mail kevanthorn@btopenworld.com

THORN, Mrs Pamela Mary. b 46. Brentwood Coll of Educn BEd78. EAMTC 01. **d** 04 **p** 05. NSM Waterbeach *Ely* from 04. *31 Lode Avenue, Waterbeach, Cambridge CB25 9PX* Tel (01223) 864262 Mobile 07989-491557 E-mail pamandrythorn@btinternet.com

THORN, Peter. b 50. Man Poly BEd79. Ridley Hall Cam 82. **d** 84 **p** 85. C Aughton Ch Ch *Liv* 84-87; C Skelmersdale St Paul 87-90; Dioc Children's Officer 87-92; P-in-c Croft w Southworth 90-92; C Streatley *St Alb* 92-95; R Blofield w Hemblington *Nor* 95-96; P-in-c 96-99; Assoc Dioc Dir of Tr 97-99; V Sheff St Bart 99-01; P-in-c Shotley *St E* 01-07; P-in-c Tweedmouth *Newc* 07-09; P-in-c Claydon and Barham *St E* from 09; C Gt and Lt Blakenham w Baylham and Nettlestead from 09. *The Rectory, 7 Back Lane, Claydon, Ipswich IP6 0EB* Tel (01473) 830362 Mobile 07810-363291 E-mail peterthorn15@hotmail.com

THORN, Robert Anthony D'Venning. b 54. AKC76. Chich Th Coll 75. **d** 77 **p** 78. C Bodmin *Truro* 77-80; TV N Hill w Altarnon, Bolventor and Lewannick 80-83; V Feock and Dioc Ecum Officer 83-90; Broadcasting Officer *Linc* 90-93; V Whitchurch *Bris* 93-04; TR Bride Valley *Sarum* 04-07; R from 07; RD Lyme Bay from 09. *The Rectory, Church Street, Burton Bradstock, Bridport DT6 4QS* Tel (01308) 898799 E-mail jeanandbob@jeanabdbob.demon.co.uk

THORN, Simon Alexander. b 66. Bris Univ BSc89 PhD92 FLS98 FCollP96. Ox Min Course 06. **d** 09 **p** 10. NSM Abingdon *Ox* from 09. *8 Upper Shrubbery, Radley College, Radley, Abingdon OX14 2JG* Tel (01235) 543195 Mobile 07714-194191 E-mail sat@radley.org.uk

THORNALLEY, Graham Paul. b 70. Coll of Resurr Mirfield 05. **d** 07 **p** 08. C Brumby *Linc* 07-09; C Frodingham 09-11; TV

Howden *York* from 11. *The New Vicarage, Portington Road, Eastrington DN14 7QE* E-mail gthornalley@tiscali.co.uk

THORNBOROUGH (née O'MEARA), Ms Colette Margaret Mary. b 63. Univ of Wales (Abth) BA85. Moorlands Bible Coll. **d** 98 **p** 99. C Much Woolton *Liv* 98-02; V Blundellsands St Nic from 02; AD Sefton 08-09; Hon Can Liv Cathl 08-09. *St Nicholas' Vicarage, Nicholas Road, Blundellsands, Liverpool L23 6TS* Tel 0151-924 3551 E-mail revcolette@aol.com

THORNBURGH, Richard Hugh Perceval. b 52. Sarum & Wells Th Coll. **d** 84 **p** 85. C Broadstone *Sarum* 84-87; TV Beaminster Area 87-95; TV Hanley H Ev *Lich* 96-01; R S Elmham and Ilketshall *St E* from 01. *Parsonage House, Low Street, Ilketshall St Margaret, Bungay NR35 1QZ* Tel and fax (01986) 781345 E-mail rhpt@pharisaios.co.uk

THORNBURY, Peter Dawson. b 43. Open Univ BA84 TCD BTh93. CITC 90. **d** 93 **p** 94. C Annagh w Drumgoon, Ashfield etc *K, E & A* 93-96; I Clondehorkey w Cashel *D & R* 96-98; I Mevagh w Glenalla 96-98; Bp's C Kilsaran w Drumcar, Dunleer and Dunany *Arm* 98-06; I Aghaderg w Donaghmore and Scarva *D & D* from 06. *Aghaderg Rectory, 32 Banbridge Road, Loughbrickland, Banbridge BT32 3YB* Tel (028) 4062 4073 E-mail wildthorn@btinternet.com

THORNBY, Mrs Janet. b 40. **d** 06 **p** 07. OLM Cheriton All So w Newington *Cant* 06-10; Perm to Offic from 10. *11 Peene Cottages, Peene, Folkestone CT18 8BB* Tel (01303) 271267 E-mail thornbyrobjan@aol.com

THORNE, Mrs Anita Dawn. b 46. Trin Coll Bris 84. **dss** 86 **d** 87 **p** 94. Asst Chapl Bris Poly 86-88; Par Dn Olveston 88-94; P-in-c 94-96; P-in-c Portland All SS w St Pet *Sarum* 96-05; P-in-c Clutton w Cameley *B & W* 05-10; R Clutton w Cameley, Bishop Sutton and Stowey from 10. *The Rectory, Main Road, Temple Cloud, Bristol BS39 5DA* Tel (01761) 451248 *or* 451315 E-mail anita.thorne@btinternet.com

THORNE, Mrs Anne. b 55. SWMTC 95. **d** 98 **p** 99. C Crediton and Shobrooke *Ex* 98-01; C Beer and Branscombe 01-03; C Seaton and Beer 03-06; P-in-c Braunton from 06. *The Vicarage, Church Street, Braunton EX33 2EL* Tel (01271) 815330 E-mail vicarthorne@aol.com

THORNE, Mrs Margaret. b 58. Kingston Poly BA79 Heythrop Coll Lon MA02 LGSM78. Ox Min Course 05. **d** 08 **p** 09. C Earley St Pet *Ox* from 08. *33 Clevedon Drive, Earley, Reading RG6 5XF* Tel 0118-987 4118 E-mail maggie.thorne@googlemail.com

THORNE, Mrs Marie Elizabeth. b 47. EMMTC 83. **dss** 86 **d** 87 **p** 94. Cleethorpes *Linc* 86-90; C Brigg 90-96; P-in-c New Waltham 96-00; V 00-07; R Gt w Lt Massingham, Harpley, Rougham etc *Nor* from 07. *The Rectory, 68 Station Road, Great Massingham, King's Lynn PE32 2HW* Tel (01485) 520211

THORNETT, Joan. b 38. **d** 07 **p** 09. OLM Stickney Gp *Linc* from 07. *93 Boston Road, Spilsby PE23 5HH* Tel (01790) 754151

THORNEWILL, Canon Mark Lyon. b 25. ALCD56. **d** 56 **p** 58. C-in-c Bradf Cathl 56-59; C-in-c Otley 59-62; R Lifton *Ex* 62-66; R Kelly w Bradstone 62-66; Dir Past Care Norton Hosps Louisville USA 69-84; Hon Can Louisville Cathl from 70; rtd 90. *Soma House, 116 East Campbell Street, Frankfort KY 40601-3508, USA* Tel (001) (502) 696 9274 E-mail mthornewil@aol.com

THORNEYCROFT, Preb Pippa Hazel Jeanetta. b 44. Ex Univ BA65. WMMTC 85. **d** 88 **p** 94. NSM Albrighton *Lich* 88-90; NSM Beckbury, Badger, Kemberton, Ryton, Stockton etc 90-96; P-in-c Shareshill 96-09; P-in-c Essington 07-09; Dioc Adv for Women in Min 93-00; Preb Lich Cathl 99-09; AD Penkridge 01-05; rtd 09; C Tettenhall Wood and Perton *Lich* from 10; Chapl to The Queen from 01. *Poole's Yard, Kemberton, Shifnal TF11 9LL* Tel (01952) 580588 Mobile 07970-869011 E-mail pippa@thorneycroft.plus.com

THORNILEY, Richard James Gordon. b 56. Portsm Poly BA78. St Jo Coll Nottm MTh95. **d** 97 **p** 98. C Bowbrook S *Worc* 97-01; R Church Lench w Rous Lench and Abbots Morton etc from 01. *The Rectory, Station Road, Harvington, Evesham WR11 8NJ* Tel (01386) 870527 E-mail richardgill@rthornley.fsnet.co.uk

THORNLEY, David Howe. b 43. Wycliffe Hall Ox 77. **d** 79 **p** 80. C Burgess Hill St Andr *Chich* 79-83; P-in-c Amberley w N Stoke 83-84; P-in-c Parham and Wiggonholt w Greatham 83-84; V Amberley w N Stoke and Parham, Wiggonholt etc 84-92; P-in-c S w N Bersted 92-99; V 99-08; rtd 08. *Spinnaway Cottage, Church Hill, Slindon, Arundel BN18 0RD* Tel 07941-834920 (mobile)

THORNLEY, Edward Charles. b 84. Ex Univ BA05. Westcott Ho Cam 08 Yale Div Sch 09. **d** 10 **p** 11. C Dereham and Distr *Nor* from 10. *15 George Eliot Way, Dereham NR19 1EX* Tel 07709-674615 (mobile) E-mail edthornley@hotmail.co.uk

THORNLEY, Geoffrey Pearson. b 23. Pemb Coll Cam BA47 MA52. Cuddesdon Coll. **d** 50 **p** 51. C Stepney St Dunstan and All SS *Lon* 50-53; Chapl RN 53-73; Bp's Dom Chapl *Linc* 73-75; P-in-c Riseholme 73-78; P-in-c Scothern w Sudbrooke 77-78; V Dunholme 75-85; Hon PV Linc Cathl 75-85; rtd 85; Chapl Allnutt's Hosp Goring Heath 85-96. *clo E Hylton, Messrs Humphrey & Co, 8-9 The Avenue, Eastbourne BN21 3YA* Tel (01323) 730631 Fax 738355

THORNLEY, Nicholas Andrew. b 56. St Jo Coll Nottm BTh81. **d** 81 **p** 84. C Frodingham *Linc* 81-84; P-in-c Belton 84-85; V 85-90; V Horncastle w Low Toynton 90-98; V High Toynton 98; R Greetham w Ashby Puerorum 98; RD Horncastle 94-98; TR Gainsborough and Morton 98-11; Can and Preb Linc Cathl 98-11; P-in-c Broughton and Duddon *Carl* from 11. *The Vicarage, Broughton-in-Furness LA20 6HS* Tel (01229) 716305 E-mail nick@gains98.fsnet.co.uk

THÖRNQVIST, Miss Karin Elisabet. b 41. Uppsala Univ 64 BD83. **p** 84. Sweden 84-97 and 98-07; C Skegness and Winthorpe *Linc* 97-98; Gen Preacher from 07. *22 Jarvis Gate, Sutton St James, Spalding PE12 0EP*

THORNS, Mrs Joanne. b 64. Sunderland Univ BSc86 MRPharmS. Cranmer Hall Dur 97. **d** 99 **p** 00. C Norton St Mary *Dur* 99-04; C Stockton St Chad 02-04; TV Dur N from 04. *25 Barnard Close, Durham DH1 5XN* Tel 0191-386 8049 E-mail joanne.thorns@durham.anglican.org

THORNTON, Darren Thomas. b 68. Wilson Carlile Coll 90 EAMTC 00. **d** 02 **p** 03. C E Dereham and Scarning *Nor* 02-05; Chapl UEA from 05; P-in-c Nor St Giles from 05. *Vicarage, 44 Heigham Road, Norwich NR2 3AU* Tel (01603) 623724 E-mail d.thornton@uea.ac.uk

THORNTON, David John Dennis. b 32. Kelham Th Coll 52. **d** 56 **p** 57. C New Eltham All SS *S'wark* 56-58; C Stockwell Green St Andr 58-62; V Tollesbury *Chelmsf* 62-74; P-in-c Salcot Virley 72-74; V Kelvedon 74-00; rtd 00; Perm to Offic *Nor* 01-07. *The Old Stable, 24 Pauls Lane, Overstrand, Cromer NR27 0PE* Tel (01263) 579279

THORNTON, Mrs Diana Rachel. b 64. Mert Coll Ox MA86. SEITE 03. **d** 06 **p** 07. C S Wimbledon II Trin and St Pet *S'wark* 06-09; C Cobham and Stoke D'Abernon *Guildf* from 09. *The Rectory, Blundel Lane, Stoke D'Abernon, Cobham KT11 2SE* Tel (01932) 862502 E-mail thethorntons@waitrose.com

THORNTON, Howard Deyes. b 52. Canadian Th Sem MA99. **d** 01 **p** 03. NSM Hanborough and Freeland *Ox* 01-02; C Luton St Mary *St Alb* 02-04; Chapl Luton Univ 02-07; TR Cowley St Jas *Ox* from 07. *Cowley Rectory, 11 Beauchamp Lane, Oxford OX4 3LF* Tel (01865) 747680 E-mail oxfordpilgrims@hotmail.com

THORNTON, John. b 26. St Edm Hall Ox BA53 MA57. Westcott Ho Cam 53. **d** 55 **p** 56. C Woodhall Spa *Linc* 55-58; C Glouc St Steph 58-60; C Wotton St Mary 60-62; P-in-c Gt Witcombe 62-63; R 63-91; Chapl HM Pris Glouc 82-91; rtd 91; Perm to Offic *Glouc* from 91. *24 Spencer Close, Hucclecote, Gloucester GL3 3EA* Tel (01452) 619775

THORNTON, Magdalen Mary. See SMITH, Magdalen Mary

THORNTON, Richard Oliver. b 41. St Paul's Coll Chelt CertEd63. **d** 01. NSM Nettleham *Linc* from 11. *45 High Street, Nettleham, Lincoln LN2 2PL* Tel (01522) 821161 E-mail richard.thornton1@ntlworld.com

THORNTON, Timothy Charles Gordon. b 35. Ch Ch Ox BA58 MA61. Linc Th Coll 60. **d** 62 **p** 63. C Kirkholt CD *Man* 62-64; Tutor Linc Th Coll 64-68; Chapl 66-68; Fiji 69-73; Chapl Brasted Place Coll Westerham 73-74; Can Missr *Guildf* 74-79; P-in-c Hascombe 74-79; V Chobham w Valley End 79-84; V Spelsbury and Chadlington *Ox* 84-87; V Chadlington and Spelsbury, Ascott under Wychwood 87-00; rtd 00; Perm to Offic *Carl* from 01. *The Old Cottage, Warcop, Appleby-in-Westmorland CA16 6NX* Tel (01768) 341239

✠**THORNTON, The Rt Revd Timothy Martin.** b 57. Southn Univ BA78 K Coll Lon MA97. St Steph Ho Ox 78. **d** 80 **p** 81 **c** 01. C Todmorden *Wakef* 80-82; P-in-c Walsden 82-85; Lect Univ of Wales (Cardiff) *Llan* 85-87; Chapl 85-86; Sen Chapl 86-87; Bp's Chapl *Wakef* 87-91; Dir of Ords 88-91; Bp's Chapl *Lon* 91-94; Dep P in O 92-01; Prin NTMTC 94-98; V Kensington St Mary Abbots w St Geo *Lon* 98-01; AD Kensington 00-01; Area Bp Sherborne *Sarum* 01-08; Bp Truro from 08. *Lis Escop, Feock, Truro TR3 6QQ* Tel (01872) 862657 Fax 862037 E-mail bishop@truro.anglican.org

THOROGOOD, Preb John Martin. b 45. Birm Univ BA68 PGCE69. Ox NSM Course 82. **d** 85 **p** 86. NSM Sunningdale *Ox* 85-90; Chapl St Geo Sch Ascot 88-90; TV Camelot Par *B & W* 90-97; V Evercreech w Chesterblade and Milton Clevedon 97-03; RD Cary and Bruton 96-03; R Dulverton and Brushford 03-10; P-in-c Brompton Regis w Upton and Skilgate 08-10; R Dulverton w Brushford, Brompton Regis etc from 10; RD Exmoor 05-09; Preb Wells Cathl from 07. *The Vicarage, High Street, Dulverton TA22 9DW* Tel (01398) 323425 E-mail johnthevicar@toucansurf.com

THOROLD, Alison Susan Joy. See HEALY, Mrs Alison Susan Joy

THOROLD, Jeremy Stephen. b 59. **d** 04 **p** 05. OLM Gainsborough and Morton *Linc* 04-07; NSM Lanteglos by Camelford w Advent and St Teath *Truro* 07-09; P-in-c Menheniot and St Ive and Pensilva w Quethiock 09-11; Bp's Dom Chapl from 11; Minl Development Review Admin from 10. *Lis Escop, Feock, Truro TR3 6QQ* Tel (01872) 862657 Fax 862037 E-mail chaplain@truro.anglican.org

THOROLD, Canon John Stephen. b 35. Bps' Coll Cheshunt 61. **d** 63 **p** 64. C Cleethorpes *Linc* 63-70; V Cherry Willingham w Greetwell 70-77; P-in-c Firsby w Gt Steeping 77-79; R 79-86; R Aswardby w Sausthorpe 77-86; R Halton Holgate 77-86; R Langton w Sutterby 77-86; V Spilsby w Hundleby 77-86; R Lt Steeping 79-86; R Raithby 79-86; V New Sleaford 86-01; RD Lafford 87-96; Can and Preb Linc Cathl 98-01; rtd 01; Perm to Offic *Linc* from 01. *8 Ashwood Close, Horncastle LN9 5HA* Tel (01507) 526562

THOROLD, Trevor Neil. b 63. Hull Univ BA87. Ripon Coll Cuddesdon 87. **d** 89 **p** 90. C W Bromwich St Andr w Ch Ch *Lich* 89-93; Res Min Oswestry 93-97; P-in-c Petton w Cockshutt, Welshampton and Lyneal etc 97-05; Local Min Adv (Shrewsbury) 97-05; RD Ellesmere 98-02. *66B High Street, Wem, Shrewsbury SY4 5DR*

THORP, Adrian. b 55. Clare Coll Cam BA77 MA80 Lon Univ BD80. Trin Coll Bris 77. **d** 80 **p** 81. C Kendal St Thos *Carl* 80-83; C Handforth *Ches* 83-86; V Siddal *Wakef* 86-91; V Bishopwearmouth St Gabr *Dur* 91-05; C Upper Skerne 05-07; R Blaydon and Swalwell from 07. *St Cuthbert's Rectory, Shibdon Road, Blaydon-on-Tyne NE21 5AE* Tel 0191-414 2720 E-mail ahthorp@btinternet.com

THORP, Mrs Alison Claire. b 63. Kingston Poly BSc85. EMMTC 06. **d** 09 **p** 10. NSM Bosworth and Sheepy Gp *Leic* from 09. *Culloden Farm, Gopsall, Atherstone CV9 3QJ* Tel (01530) 270350 E-mail alisonthorp@btconnect.com

THORP, Catherine. b 57. St Luke's Coll Ex BEd79. Oak Hill Th Coll 93. **d** 96 **p** 02. NSM Watford Ch Ch *St Alb* 96-99; NSM Kings Langley 99-05; Perm to Offic from 05. *111 Barton Way, Croxley Green, Rickmansworth WD3 3PB* Tel and fax (01923) 442713 E-mail cthorp57@hotmail.com

THORP, Mrs Helen Mary. b 54. Bris Univ BA75 MA(Theol)77 Dur Univ MA98. Trin Coll Bris 78. **d** 87 **p** 94. NSM Siddal *Wakef* 87-91; NSM Bishopwearmouth St Gabr *Dur* 91-05; NSM Upper Skerne 05-07; NSM Blaydon and Swalwell from 07; Voc Adv 93-05; Tutor Cranmer Hall Dur from 98. *St Cuthbert's Rectory, Shibdon Road, Blaydon-on-Tyne NE21 5AE* Tel 0191-414 2720 E-mail ahthorp@btinternet.com *or* h.m.thorp@durham.ac.uk

THORP, Mrs Maureen Sandra. b 47. Man OLM Scheme 92. **d** 95 **p** 96. OLM Heywood *Man* 95-01; P-in-c Shore and Calderbrook 01-06; V Tonge w Alkrington from 06; Borough Dean Rochdale from 10. *St Michael's Vicarage, 184 Kirkway, Middleton, Manchester M24 1LN* Tel 0161-643 2891 E-mail thorpmaureen@aol.com

THORP, Norman Arthur. b 29. Tyndale Hall Bris 63. **d** 65 **p** 66. C Southsea St Jude *Portsm* 65-68; C Braintree *Chelmsf* 68-73; P-in-c Tolleshunt D'Arcy w Tolleshunt Major 73-75; V 75-83; R N Buckingham *Ox* 83-95; RD Buckingham 90-95; rtd 95; Perm to Offic *Ox* 97-00. *27 Baisley Gardens, Napier Street, Bletchley, Milton Keynes MK2 2NE* Tel (01908) 370221

THORP, Roderick Cheyne. b 44. Ch Ch Ox BA65 MA69. Ridley Hall Cam 66. **d** 69 **p** 70. C Reading Greyfriars *Ox* 69-73; C Kingston upon Hull St Martin *York* 73-76; C Heworth H Trin 76-79; C-in-c N Bletchley CD *Ox* 79-86; TV Washfield, Stoodleigh, Withleigh etc *Ex* 86-96; RD Tiverton 91-96; P-in-c Dolton 96-00; P-in-c Iddesleigh w Dowland 96-00; P-in-c Monkokehampton 96-00; rtd 00; P-in-c Etton w Dalton Holme *York* 00-08; Perm to Offic from 09. *4 Stonegate Court, Stonegate, Hunmanby, Filey YO14 0NZ* Tel (01723) 892628 E-mail aranjay@freeuk.com

THORP, Stephen Linton. b 62. Trin Coll Bris BA92. **d** 92 **p** 93. C Knutsford St Jo and Toft *Ches* 92-96; TV Newton Tracey, Horwood, Alverdiscott etc *Ex* 96-06; R Necton, Holme Hale w N and S Pickenham *Nor* from 06. *The Rectory, School Road, Necton, Swaffham PE37 8HT* Tel (01760) 722021 E-mail slthorp@homecall.co.uk

THORP, Timothy. b 65. St Steph Ho Ox BTh93. **d** 96 **p** 97. C Jarrow *Dur* 96-99; P-in-c N Hylton St Marg Castletown 99-02; C Felpham and Missr Arundel and Bognor *Chich* 02-07; C Arundel w Tortington and S Stoke 07-08; P-in-c Ernesettle *Ex* from 08; P-in-c Whitleigh from 08; C Honicknowle from 08. *St Aidan's Vicarage, 122 Rochford Crescent, Plymouth PL5 2QD* Tel (01752) 350580 E-mail fathertimt@bigfoot.com

THORPE, Preb Christopher David Charles. b 60. Cov Poly BA83. Ripon Coll Cuddesdon 85. **d** 88 **p** 89. C Norton *St Alb* 88-92; TV Blakenall Heath *Lich* 92-99; TR Bilston 99-08; V Shifnal and Sheriffhales from 08; RD Shifnal Cathl from 07. *The Vicarage, Manor Close, Shifnal TF11 9AJ* Tel (01952) 463694 E-mail chris@christhorpe.org

THORPE, Donald Henry. b 34. St Aid Birkenhead 57. **d** 60 **p** 61. C Mexborough *Sheff* 60-64; C Doncaster St Leon and St Jude 64-67; V Doncaster Intake 67-74; V Millhouses H Trin 74-85; Prec Leic Cathl 85-89; TR Melton Gt Framland 89-93; rtd 93; Perm to Offic *Sheff* and *S'well* from 93. *18 All Hallows Drive, Tickhill, Doncaster DN11 9PP* Tel (01302) 743129 E-mail dsthorpe1@tiscali.co.uk

THORPE, Canon Kerry Michael. b 51. Oak Hill Th Coll BD78. **d** 78 **p** 79. C Upton (Overchurch) *Ches* 78-81; C Chester le Street

Dur 81-84; V Fatfield 84-93; V Margate H Trin *Cant* 93-98; C 98-09; Dioc Missr 06-11; Min Harvest New Angl Ch 10-11; Dioc Miss and Growth Adv from 11; Hon Can Cant Cathl from 08. *1 Wealdhurst Park, St Peter's, Broadstairs CT10 2LD* Tel (01843) 871183 E-mail kerrythorpe@harvestnac.freeserve.co.uk

THORPE, Lynne Gail. b 62. Dioc OLM tr scheme 99. **d** 02 **p** 03. OLM Ipswich St Jo *St E* 02-06. *31 King Edward Road, Ipswich IP3 9AN* Tel (01473) 717833

THORPE, Martin Xavier. b 66. Collingwood Coll Dur BSc87 Bris Univ MPhil00 GRSC87. Trin Coll Bris BA94. **d** 94 **p** 95. C Ravenhead *Liv* 94-98; TV Sutton 98-02; V Westbrook St Phil 02-11; P-in-c Westbrook St Jas from 11; Asst Dir CME from 01. *St James's Vicarage, 302 Hood Lane North, Great Sankey, Warrington WA5 1UQ* Tel (01925) 492631 E-mail martinpol.thorpe@talk21.com *or* martin.cme1-4@talk21.com

THORPE, Michael William. b 42. Lich Th Coll 67. **d** 70 **p** 71. C Walthamstow St Mich *Chelmsf* 70-71; C Plaistow St Andr 71; P-in-c Plaistow St Mary 72-74; TV Gt Grimsby St Mary and St Jas *Linc* 74-78; Chapl Grimsby Distr Hosps 78-83; Chapl Roxbourne, Northwick Park and Harrow Hosps 83-87; Chapl St Geo Linc and Linc Co Hosps 87-92; Chapl Ipswich Hosp NHS Trust 92-00. *Moselle Cottage, 68 Lacey Street, Ipswich IP4 2PH* Tel (01473) 421850

THORPE, Richard Charles. b 65. Birm Univ BSc87. Wycliffe Hall Ox 93. **d** 96 **p** 97. C Brompton H Trin w Onslow Square St Paul *Lon* 96-05; P-in-c Shadwell St Paul w Ratcliffe St Jas 05-10; R from 10; P-in-c Bromley by Bow All Hallows from 10. *St Paul's Rectory, 298 The Highway, London E1W 3DH* Tel (020) 7481 2883 *or 7680 2112* E-mail ric.thorpe@stpaulsshadwell.org

THORPE, Trevor Cecil. b 21. Em Coll Cam BA47 MA52. Ridley Hall Cam 48. **d** 50 **p** 51. C Farnborough *Guildf* 50-53; C W Ham All SS *Chelmsf* 53-55; NSM N Weald Bassett from 57. *The Vicarage, Vicarage Lane, North Weald, Epping CM16 6AL* Tel (01992) 522246

THREADGILL, Steven Alan. b 59. Cant Univ (NZ) BA84 MA88 Christchurch Teachers' Coll Dip Teaching88. STETS MA08. **d** 08 **p** 09. C Lee-on-the-Solent *Portsm* from 08. *3 Martlet Close, Lee-on-the-Solent PO13 8FP* E-mail steventhreadgill@yahoo.co.uk

THRELFALL-HOLMES, Miranda. b 73. Ch Coll Cam BA95 MA99 Univ Coll Dur MA97 PhD00 St Jo Coll Dur BA02. Cranmer Hall Dur 00. **d** 03 **p** 04. C Newc St Gabr 03-06; Chapl and Fell Univ Coll Dur from 06. *University College, The Castle, Palace Green, Durham DH1 3RW* Tel 0191-334 4116 E-mail rev.miranda@dsl.pipex.com

THROSSELL, John Julian. b 30. Nottm Univ BSc53 Syracuse Univ PhD56. Oak Hill Th Coll 72. **d** 75 **p** 76. NSM Wheathampstead *St Alb* 75-82; V Codicote 82-88; NSM Halesworth w Linstead, Chediston, Holton etc *St E* 89-95; rtd 91. *1A Sharpe's Hill, Barrow, Bury St Edmunds IP29 5BY* Tel (01284) 810314

THROUP, Ms Caroline Elizabeth. b 64. St Cath Coll Cam BA86 MA90 Man Univ MBA94. St Jo Coll Nottm 08. **d** 10 **p** 11. C Burnage St Marg *Man* from 10. *26 Willow Way, Manchester M20 6JS* Tel 0161-445 8874 E-mail caroline.throup@ntlworld.com

THROWER, Clive Alan. b 41. Sheff Univ BSc62 CEng90. EMMTC 76. **d** 79 **p** 80. C Derby Cathl 79-86; C Spondon 86-91; Soc Resp Officer 86-91; Faith in the City Link Officer 88-91; Dioc Rural Officer 91; P-in-c Ashford w Sheldon 91; V Ashford w Sheldon and Longstone 92-07; Dioc Rural and Tourism Officer 96-07; RD Bakewell and Eyam 04-07; rtd 07; Perm to Offic *Derby* from 07. *Longstone House, 5 Vernon Green, Bakewell DE45 1DT* Tel (01629) 814863 E-mail clive@thrower.org.uk

THROWER, The Very Revd Martin Charles. b 61. EAMTC 95. **d** 98 **p** 99. NSM Ipswich St Bart *St E* 98-01; NSM Bury St Edmunds All SS w St Jo and St Geo 01-03; P-in-c Gt and Lt Whelnetham w Bradfield St George 03-04; P-in-c Lawshall 03-04; P-in-c Hawstead and Nowton w Stanningfield etc 03-04; R St Edm Way 04-09; RD Lavenham 05-09; V Hadleigh, Layham and Shelley from 09; Dean Bocking from 09; RD Hadleigh from 10. *The Deanery, Church Street, Hadleigh, Ipswich IP7 5DT* Tel (01473) 822218 E-mail martin.thrower@btinternet.com

THROWER, Philip Edward. b 41. Kelham Th Coll 61. **d** 66 **p** 67. C Hayes St Mary *Lon* 66-69; C Yeovil *B & W* 69-71; C Shirley St Jo *Cant* 71-77; P-in-c S Norwood St Mark 77-81; V 81-84; V S Norwood St Mark *S'wark* 85-97; V Malden St Jas 97-07; rtd 07; Perm to Offic *S'wark* from 07. *243 Chipstead Way, Banstead SM7 3JN* Tel (01737) 218306

THRUSH, Margaret. b 37. St Mary's Coll Dur BA60. Cranmer Hall Dur BA96. **d** 97 **p** 98. NSM Houghton le Spring *Dur* 97-03; NSM Shadforth and Sherburn from 03. *45 Highgate, Durham DH1 4GA* Tel 0191-386 1958

THUBRON, Thomas William. b 33. Edin Th Coll 62. **d** 65 **p** 66. C Gateshead St Mary *Dur* 65-66; C Shildon 66-67; E Pakistan 68-71; Bangladesh 71-80; V Wheatley Hill *Dur* 80-87; V Dur

St Giles 87-98; rtd 98. *The Old Vicarage, Gable Terrace, Wheatley Hill, Durham DH6 3RA* Tel (01429) 823940

THURBURN-HUELIN, David Richard. b 47. St Chad's Coll Dur BA69 Ex Univ MA98. Westcott Ho Cam 69. **d** 71 **p** 72. C Poplar *Lon* 71-76; Chapl Liddon Ho Lon 76-80; R Harrold and Carlton w Chellington *St Alb* 81-88; V Goldington 88-95; Dir OLM *Truro* 95-00; P-in-c Shipston-on-Stour w Honington and Idlicote *Cov* 01-05; R from 05. *Shipston Rectory, 8 Glen Close, Shipston-on-Stour CV36 4ED* Tel (01608) 661724 E-mail d.r.thurburnhuelin@homecall.co.uk

THURGILL, Sally Elizabeth. b 60. **d** 02 **p** 03. OLM Mattishall and the Tudd Valley *Nor* from 02. *3 Dereham Road, Yaxham, Dereham NR19 1RF* Tel (01362) 692745 E-mail csmsthurgill@ukonline.co.uk

THURLOW, Ms Judith Mary Buller. b 44. Ch Ch Coll Cant CertEd63 Natal Univ DipEd78 BTh94 MTh00. **d** 95 **p** 96. S Africa 95-00; C Port Shepstone St Kath 95-98; C Durban St Paul 99-00; C Orpington All SS *Roch* 00-02; R Kingsdown from 02. *The Rectory, School Lane, West Kingsdown, Sevenoaks TN15 6JL* Tel and fax (01474) 852265 Mobile 07949-272106 E-mail judiththurlow@ukgateway.net

THURMER, Canon John Alfred. b 25. Oriel Coll Ox BA50 MA55 Ex Univ Hon DD91. Linc Th Coll 50. **d** 52 **p** 53. C Lt Ilford St Mich *Chelmsf* 52-55; Chapl and Lect Sarum Th Coll 55-64; Chapl Ex Univ 64-73; Lect 64-85; Can Res and Chan Ex Cathl 73-91; rtd 91; Perm to Offic *Ex* from 91. *38 Velwell Road, Exeter EX4 4LD* Tel (01392) 272277

THURSTON, Ian Charles. b 54. SS Hild & Bede Coll Dur CertEd78. S Dios Minl Tr Scheme 87. **d** 89 **p** 90. C St Chris Cathl Bahrain 89-91; C All Hallows by the Tower etc *Lon* 91-97; V Tottenham H Trin 97-00; R Cheadle w Freehay *Lich* from 00. *The Rectory, Church Street, Cheadle, Stoke-on-Trent ST10 1HU* Tel (01538) 753337

THURSTON-SMITH, Trevor. b 59. Chich Th Coll 83. **d** 86 **p** 87. C Rawmarsh w Parkgate *Sheff* 86-87; C Horninglow *Lich* 87-91; Chapl for People affected by HIV *Leic* 05-11; P-in-c Broughton Astley and Croft w Stoney Stanton from 11. *The Rectory, St Mary's Close, Broughton Astley, Leicester LE9 6ES* Tel (01455) 289636 E-mail trevor@thursmith.co.uk

THURTELL, Victoria Ann. b 59. St Jo Coll Dur BSc82 Univ of Wales (Lamp) BA11 PGCE96. STETS 02. **d** 05 **p** 06. C Chickerell w Fleet *Sarum* 05-08; TV Dorchester from 08. *The Vicarage, 38 Herringston Road, Dorchester DT1 2BS* Tel (01305) 268767 E-mail vickythurtell@gmail.com

TIBBO, George Kenneth. b 29. Reading Univ BA50 MA54. Coll of Resurr Mirfield 55. **d** 57 **p** 58. C W Hartlepool St Aid *Dur* 57-61; V Darlington St Mark 61-74; V Darlington St Mark w St Paul 74-75; R Crook 75-80; V Stanley 76-80; V Oldham St Chad Limeside *Man* 80-87; V Hipswell *Ripon* 87-95; OCF 90-95; rtd 95; P-in-c Nidd *Ripon* 95-01; Perm to Offic 02-04; Hon C Saddleworth *Man* 04-10; Hon C Denshaw from 10. *The Vicarage, Woods Lane, Dobcross, Oldham OL3 5AN* Tel (01457) 829702

TIBBOTT (*née* VINE), **Mrs Carolyn Ann.** b 63. Anglia Poly Univ BSc04. NTMTC BA07. **d** 07 **p** 08. C Gidea Park *Chelmsf* 07-11; V Broomfield from 11. *Broomfield Vicarage, 10 Butlers Close, Chelmsford CM1 7BE* Tel (01245) 440318 E-mail ctibbott@hotmail.com

TIBBS, Canon John Andrew. b 29. AKC53. **d** 54 **p** 55. C Eastbourne St Mary *Chich* 54-57; S Africa 57-62; C Bourne *Guildf* 62-64; Swaziland 64-68; V Sompting *Chich* 69-73; R Ifield 73-78; TR 78-83; V Elstow *St Alb* 83-89; rtd 90; Chapl Bedf Gen Hosp 90-95; Hon Can St Alb 92-95; Perm to Offic from 00. *19 Adelaide Square, Bedford MK40 2RN* Tel (01234) 308737

TIBBS, Simon John. b 71. **d** 08. C Edin Old St Paul from 08. *41 Jeffrey Street, Edinburgh EH1 1DH* E-mail tibbs.simon@googlemail.com

TICE, Richard Ian. b 66. Bris Univ BA88. Wycliffe Hall Ox BTh94. **d** 94 **p** 95. C Langham Place All So *Lon* from 94. *Basement Flat, 141 Cleveland Street, London W1T 6QG* Tel (020) 7388 3280 *or* 7580 3522 E-mail ricospa-grace@allsouls.org

TICKLE, Robert Peter. b 58. St Chad's Coll Dur BA74. St Steph Ho Ox 74. **d** 76 **p** 77. *5 Bramley Court, Orchard Lane, Harrold, Bedford MK43 7BG* Tel (01234) 721417

TICKNER, Canon Colin de Fraine. b 37. Chich Th Coll. **d** 66 **p** 67. C Huddersfield SS Pet and Paul *Wakef* 66-68; C Dorking w Ranmore *Guildf* 68-74; V Shottermill 74-91; RD Godalming 89-91; R Ockley, Okewood and Forest Green 91-97; Hon Can Guildf Cathl 96-97; rtd 97; Adv for Past Care *Guildf* from 97; Chapl St Cath Sch Bramley from 97. *11 Linersh Drive, Bramley, Guildford GU5 0EJ* Tel (01483) 898161 E-mail colin.tickner@sky.com

TICKNER, David Arthur. b 44. MBE89. AKC67. **d** 69 **p** 70. C Thornhill Lees *Wakef* 69-71; C Billingham St Aid *Dur* 71-74; TV 74-78; CF 78-98; Perm to Offic *Guildf* 96-98; R Heysham *Blackb* from 98. *The Rectory, Main Street, Heysham, Morecambe LA3 2RN* Tel and fax (01524) 851422 E-mail david.tickner@tesco.net

TICKNER, Geoffrey John. b 55. Univ of Wales BD82. St Mich Coll Llan 79. **d** 82 **p** 83. C Bourne *Guildf* 82-85; C Grayswood

85-90; V New Haw 90-02; RD Runnymede 98-02; P-in-c Stevenage H Trin *St Alb* from 02; RD Stevenage from 06. *Holy Trinity Vicarage, 18 Letchmore Road, Stevenage SG1 3JD* Tel (01438) 353229 E-mail vicar@holytrinity-stevenage.info

TIDESWELL, Mrs Lynne Maureen Ann. b 49. NOC 02. **d** 05 **p** 06. NSM Stoke-upon-Trent *Lich* 05-10; NSM Knutton from 10. *14 High Lane, Cheddleton Heath Road, Leek ST13 7DY* Tel (01538) 361134 E-mail vicarsrest@talktalk.net

TIDSWELL, David Alan. b 42. CEng73 FIEE84 Univ Coll Chich BA03. St Steph Ho Ox 99. **d** 00 **p** 01. NSM Forest Row *Chich* 00-07; P-in-c Fairwarp 07-10; P-in-c High Hurstwood from 07. *Manapouri, Hammerwood Road, Ashurst Wood, East Grinstead RH19 3SA* Tel (01342) 822808
E-mail datidswell@btinternet.com

TIDY, John Hylton. b 48. AKC72 St Aug Coll Cant 72. **d** 73 **p** 74. C Newton Aycliffe *Dur* 73-78; V Auckland St Pet 78-84; V Burley in Wharfedale *Bradf* 84-92; Dean Jerusalem 92-97; V Surbiton St Andr and St Mark *S'wark* 97-05; RD Kingston 00-05; Israel 05-06; P-in-c Miami Beach All So USA from 06. *4025 Pine Tree Drive, Miami Beach FL 33140-3601, USA* Tel (001) (305) 538 2244
E-mail parishoffice@allsoulsmiamibeach.org

TIERNAN, Paul Wilson. b 54. Man Univ BA76. Coll of Resurr Mirfield 77. **d** 79 **p** 80. C Lewisham St Mary *S'wark* 79-83; V Sydenham St Phil from 83. *St Philip's Vicarage, 122 Wells Park Road, London SE26 6AS* Tel (020) 8699 4930

TIGHE, Derek James. b 58. Ripon Coll Cuddesdon 05. **d** 07 **p** 08. C Wimborne Minster *Sarum* from 07. *29 Venator Place, Wimborne BH21 1DQ* Tel (01202) 849466
E-mail derek.tighe@btinternet.com

TIGWELL, Brian Arthur. b 36. S'wark Ord Course 74. **d** 77 **p** 78. C Purley St Mark *S'wark* 77-80; TV Upper Kennet *Sarum* 80-85; V Devizes St Pet 85-99; Wilts Adnry Ecum Officer 88-99; RD Devizes 92-98; rtd 99; Perm to Offic *Sarum* from 01 and *B & W* from 04. *7 Valentines, Dulverton TA22 9ED* Tel (01398) 324051

TILBY, Miss Angela Clare Wyatt. b 50. Girton Coll Cam BA72 MA76. Cranmer Hall Dur 77. **d** 97 **p** 98. Tutor Westcott Ho Cam 97-11; Vice-Prin 01-06; Hon C Cherry Hinton St Jo *Ely* 97-06; V Cambridge St Benedict from 07. *47 New Square, Cambridge CB1 1EZ* Tel (01223) 355146 Mobile 07966-132045
E-mail angela.tilby@ntlworld.com

TILDESLEY, Edward William David. b 56. SS Hild & Bede Coll Dur BEd79. SAOMC 93. **d** 96 **p** 97. Chapl Shiplake Coll Henley 96-99; NSM Emmer Green *Ox* 96-99; Chapl Oakham Sch 99-00; TV Dorchester *Ox* 00-05; C Aldershot St Mich *Guildf* 05-08; rtd 08. *Address withheld by request* E-mail etildesley@home.gb.com

TILL, Barry Dorn. b 23. Jes Coll Cam BA49 MA49. Westcott Ho Cam 48. **d** 50 **p** 51. C Bury St Mary *Man* 50-53; Fell Jes Coll Cam 53-60; Chapl 53-56; Dean 56-60; Dean Hong Kong 60-64; Attached Ch Assembly 64-65; Prin Morley Coll Lon 66-87; Dir Baring Foundn 87-92; rtd 92. *44 Canonbury Square, London N1 2AW* Tel (020) 7359 0708

TILL, The Very Revd Michael Stanley. b 35. Linc Coll Ox BA60 MA67. Westcott Ho Cam. **d** 64 **p** 65. C St John's Wood *Lon* 64-67; Chapl K Coll Cam 67-70; Dean 70-80; V Fulham All SS and AD Hammersmith *Lon* 81-86; Adn Cant and Can Res Cant Cathl 86-96; Dean Win 96-05; rtd 05; Perm to Offic *Chich* 06-07; P-in-c Petworth and Egdean 07-09. *Ryde House, Angel Street, Petworth GU28 0BG* Tel (01798) 342734

TILLBROOK, Richard Ernest. b 50. St Mark & St Jo Coll Lon CertEd71 ACP76. NTMTC 96. **d** 99 **p** 00. Hd RE Davenant Foundn Sch Loughton 71-03; NSM High Laver w Magdalen Laver and Lt Laver etc *Chelmsf* 99-03; V Colchester St Barn from 03. *St Barnabas' Vicarage, 13 Abbot's Road, Colchester CO2 8BE* Tel (01206) 797481 Mobile 07818-440530
E-mail fathercap@hotmail.com

TILLER, Edgar Henry. b 22. St Francis Bp's Hostel Lincoln. Ex Univ CertEd69 Open Univ BA78 ACP71. Wells Th Coll 57. **d** 59 **p** 60. C Weston-super-Mare St Jo *B & W* 59-62; V Stoke Lane and Leigh upon Mendip 62-67; Asst Master Chaddiford Sch Barnstaple 69-81; Perm to Offic *Ex* 67-05 and *Llan* from 06; rtd 91. *42 Llys Pegasus, Ty Glas Road, Llanishen, Cardiff CF14 5ER*

TILLER, The Ven John. b 38. Ch Ch Ox BA60 MA64 Bris Univ MLitt72. Tyndale Hall Bris 60. **d** 62 **p** 63. C Bedford St Cuth *St Alb* 62-65; C Widcombe *B & W* 65-67; Tutor Tyndale Hall Bris 67-71; Chapl 67-71; Lect Trin Coll Bris 71-73; P-in-c Bedford Ch Ch *St Alb* 73-78; Chief Sec ACCM 78-84; Hon Can St Alb 79-84; Can Res Heref Cathl 84-04; Chan 84-02; Dioc Dir of Tr 91-00; Adn Heref 02-04; rtd 05; Local Miss and Min Adv (Shrewsbury Area) *Lich* 05-09; Hon C Meole Brace 09; Perm to Offic from 10. *2 Pulley Lane, Bayston Hill, Shrewsbury SY3 0JH* Tel (01743) 873595 E-mail canjtiller@aol.com

TILLETT, Leslie Selwyn. b 54. Peterho Cam BA75 MA79 Leeds Univ BA80. Coll of Resurr Mirfield 78. **d** 81 **p** 82. C W Dulwich All SS and Em *S'wark* 81-85; R Purleigh, Cold Norton and Stow Maries *Chelmsf* 85-93; R Beddington *S'wark* 93-05; R Wensum Benefice *Nor* from 05; RD Sparham from 08. *The Rectory, Weston Longville, Norwich NR9 5JU* Tel (01603) 880563
E-mail selwyn@tillett.org.uk

TILLETT, Luke David. b 88. Anglia Ruskin Univ BTh10. Ridley Hall Cam 07. **d** 10 **p** 11. C Guisborough *York* from 10. *16 Lealholm Way, Guisborough TS14 8LN* Tel (01287) 632901 Mobile 07527-077227 E-mail lukedavidtillett@googlemail.com

TILLETT, Michael John Arthur. b 57. Ridley Hall Cam 96. **d** 98 **p** 99. C Framlingham w Saxtead *St E* 98-01; P-in-c Stoke by Nayland w Leavenheath and Polstead 01-03; R 03-10; RD Hadleigh 07-10; R Ipswich St Helen, H Trin, and St Luke from 10. *The Rectory, 42 Clapgate Lane, Ipswich IP3 0RD* Tel (01473) 723467 Mobile 07531-940870 E-mail revtillett@aol.com

TILLETT, Miss Sarah Louise. b 59. Regent Coll Vancouver MCS00. Wycliffe Hall Ox 01. **d** 03 **p** 03. C Knowle *Birm* 03-07; P-in-c Bloxham w Milcombe and S Newington *Ox* from 07. *St Mary's Vicarage, Church Street, Bloxham, Banbury OX15 4ET* Tel (01295) 867508 Mobile 07764-608796
E-mail sarahtillett@tiscali.co.uk

TILLETT, Selwyn. *See* TILLETT, Leslie Selwyn

TILLEY, Canon David Robert. b 38. Kelham Th Coll 58. **d** 63 **p** 64. C Bournemouth St Fran *Win* 63-67; C Moulsecoomb *Chich* 67-70; C Ifield 70-75; TV Warwick *Cov* 76-85; P-in-c Alderminster and Halford 85-96; Dioc Min Tr Adv 85-90; CME Adv 90-04; Assoc Min Willenhall 96-04; Hon Can Cov Cathl 03-04; rtd 04; Perm to Offic *Cov* from 04. *17 Coventry Road, Baginton, Coventry CV8 3AD* Tel and fax (024) 7630 2508
E-mail david.tilley@sagainternet.co.uk

TILLEY, Elizabeth Anne. b 45. Bris Univ BA67 PGCE68. All Nations Chr Coll 72 Lon Bible Coll MA89. **d** 07 **p** 08. OLM Wonersh w Blackheath *Guildf* from 07. *9 Hullmead, Shamley Green, Guildford GU5 0UF* Tel (01483) 891730
E-mail etilley@waitrose.com

TILLEY, James Stephen. b 55. St Jo Coll Nottm BTh84. **d** 84 **p** 85. C Nottingham St Jude *S'well* 84-88; C Chester le Street *Dur* 88-92; Tr and Ed CYFA (CPAS) 92-94; Hd 94-02; Perm to Offic *Cov* 92-06 and *Bris* from 06; C Nailsea H Trin *B & W* from 06. *29 Vynes Way, Nailsea, Bristol BS48 2UG* Tel (01275) 543332 Fax 545803 Mobile 07971-563229
E-mail steve.tilley@htnailsea.org.uk

TILLEY, Peter Robert. b 41. Bris Univ BA62. Sarum & Wells Th Coll 77. **d** 79 **p** 80. C Wandsworth St Paul *S'wark* 79-82; V Mitcham St Mark 82-91; RD Merton 89-91; R Walton St Mary *Liv* 91-92; TR Walton-on-the-Hill 92-98; rtd 98; P-in-c Ghent *Eur* 98-10; P-in-c Knokke 08-10. *15 Edinburgh Close, Uxbridge UB10 8RA* E-mail peter.tilley@telenet.be

TILLIER, Preb Jane Yvonne. b 59. New Hall Cam BA81 PhD85. Ripon Coll Cuddesdon BA90. **d** 91 **p** 94. Par Dn Sheff St Mark Broomhill 91-94; C 94-95; Chapl Glouc Cathl 95-97; P-in-c Madeley *Lich* 97-03; P-in-c Betley 02-03; Perm to Offic 03-04; Chapl and Team Ldr Douglas Macmillan Hospice Blurton 04-08; P-in-c Barlaston *Lich* from 08; Min Development Adv Stafford Area from 10; Preb Lich Cathl from 11. *10 Plantation Park, University of Keele, Keele, Newcastle ST5 5NA* Tel (01782) 639720 E-mail jane@atherton-tillier.co.uk

TILLMAN, Miss Mary Elizabeth. b 43. S Dios Minl Tr Scheme 86. **d** 89 **p** 95. NSM Bridgemary *Portsm* 89-93; NSM Portsea All SS from 93; Adv in Min to People w Disabilities from 93. *3 Fareham Road, Gosport PO13 0XL* Tel (01329) 232589

TILLOTSON, Simon Christopher. b 67. Lon Univ BA90 Trin Coll Cam BA93 MA96. Ridley Hall Cam 91. **d** 94 **p** 95. C Paddock Wood *Roch* 94-98; C Ormskirk *Liv* 98-00; V Aylesford *Roch* 00-07; TV Whitstable *Cant* from 07. *The Vicarage, Church Street, Whitstable CT5 1PG* Tel (01227) 272308 Mobile 07946-527471 E-mail sct@tillotsons.freeserve.co.uk

TILLYER, Preb Desmond Benjamin. b 40. Ch Coll Cam BA63 MA67. Coll of Resurr Mirfield 64. **d** 66 **p** 67. C Hanworth All SS *Lon* 66-70; Chapl Liddon Ho Lon 70-74; V Pimlico St Pet w Westmr Ch Ch *Lon* 74-06; AD Westmr St Marg 85-92; Preb St Paul's Cathl 01-06; rtd 06; Perm to Offic *Nor* from 06. *The Croft House, The Croft, Costessey, Norwich NR8 5DT* Tel (01603) 745654 E-mail thecrofthouse@btinternet.com

TILSON, Canon Alan Ernest. b 46. TCD. **d** 70 **p** 71. C Londonderry Ch Ch *D & R* 70-73; I Inver, Mountcharles and Killaghtee 73-79; I Leckpatrick w Dunnalong 79-89; Bermuda 89-05; Hon Can Bermuda Cathl 96-05; I Tullyaughnish w Kilmacrennan and Killygarvan *D & R* 05-10; rtd 10. *The Brambles, 2 Rinclevan, Dunfanaghy, Co Donegal, Republic of Ireland* Tel (00353) (74) 910 0729
E-mail canonalan@eircom.net

TILSTON, Derek Reginald. b 27. NW Ord Course. **d** 73 **p** 74. NSM Bury St Mark *Man* 73-77; NSM Holcombe 77-82; NSM Bury St Jo 82-83; NSM Bury St Jo w St Mark 83-84; C Bramley *Ripon* 85-87; TV 87-90; R Tendring and Lt Bentley w Beaumont cum Moze *Chelmsf* 90-92; rtd 93; Perm to Offic *St E* from 93. *Cobbler's Cottage, 19 The Street, Wissett, Halesworth IP19 0JE* Tel (01986) 874693

TILT, Dawn Caroline. b 59. Llan Ord Course. **d** 99 **p** 00. NSM Pyle w Kenfig *Llan* 99-00; NSM Ewenny w St Brides Major 00-04; Chapl HM Pris Parc (Bridgend) from 04. *HM Prison Parc, Heol Hopcyn John, Bridgend CF35 6AP* Tel (01656) 300200 E-mail thetilts@hotmail.com

TILTMAN, Alan Michael. b 48. Selw Coll Cam BA70 MA74. Cuddesdon Coll 71. **d** 73 **p** 74. C Chesterton Gd Shep *Ely* 73-77; C Preston St Jo *Blackb* 77-79; Chapl Lancs (Preston) Poly 77-79; TV Man Whitworth 79-86; Chapl Man Univ (UMIST) 79-86; V Urmston 86-99; Dir CME 99-03; C Salford Sacred Trin and St Phil 99-02; V Buckley *St As* from 04. *St Matthew's Vicarage, 114 Church Road, Buckley CH7 3JN* Tel (01244) 550645 E-mail a.tiltman@zoo.co.uk

TILTMAN, Mrs Katherine Joan. b 53. St Hugh's Coll Ox MA74 Man Metrop Univ MSc02. St Mich Coll Llan 09. **d** 11. C Wrexham *St As* from 11. *St Matthew's Vicarage, Church Road, Buckley CH7 3JN* Tel (01244) 550645 Mobile 07753-230644 E-mail katetiltman@hotmail.com

TIMBRELL, Keith Stewart. b 48. Edin Th Coll 72. **d** 74 **p** 75. C Chorley St Pet *Blackb* 74-77; C Altham w Clayton le Moors 77-79; Chapl Whittingham Hosp Preston 79-95; Trust Chapl Dorset Health Care NHS Trust 95-08; rtd 08. *9 Whitecross Close, Poole BH17 9HN* Tel (01202) 604985 Mobile 07788-907965 E-mail clerigo@btinternet.com

TIMBRELL, Maxwell Keith. b 28. St Jo Coll Morpeth ThL51. **d** 51 **p** 52. P-in-c Bourke Australia 52-57; C Sydney Ch Ch St Laur 57-58; C Hanworth All SS *Lon* 59-63; Bush Brothers of St Paul Australia 63-72; R Bourke 68-72; P-in-c Cunnamulla 72-77; P-in-c Weston 77-83; V Ingleby Greenhow w Bilsdale Priory *York* 83-85; P-in-c Kildale etc 85-95; V Ingleby Greenhow w Bilsdale Priory, Kildale etc 85-96; rtd 96; Perm to Offic *York* 96-11. *Jasmine House, Nunnington, York YO62 5US* Tel (01439) 748319

TIMINGS, Mrs Julie Elizabeth. b 54. **d** 10 **p** 11. C New Sleaford *Linc* from 10. *11 Covel Road, Sleaford NG34 8DP* Tel 07931-387186 (mobile)

TIMMINS, Susan Katherine. b 64. Leic Univ BScEng85 MICE91. St Jo Coll Nottm MTh94. **d** 96 **p** 97. C Iver *Ox* 96-00; P-in-c Pendlebury St Jo Man 00-06; V from 06; Hon Assoc Dioc Dir of Ords from 10. *St John's Vicarage, 91 Broomhall Road, Pendlebury, Manchester M27 8XR* Tel 0161-925 0171 E-mail susanktimmins@aol.com

TIMMIS (*née* PITT), Mrs Karen Lesley Finella. b 62. Lon Univ BA84. Chich Th Coll BTh94. **d** 94 **p** 95. C Walton-on-the-Hill *Liv* 94-98; P-in-c Warrington St Barn 98-00; V from 00. *The Vicarage, 73 Lovely Lane, Warrington WA5 1TY* Tel (01925) 633556

TIMOTHY, Miss Bronwen Doris (Bonnie). b 57. Sheff City Poly BSc81 Univ of Wales (Cardiff) PGCE82. St Mich Coll Llan 99. **d** 02 **p** 03. C Tenby *St D* 02-04; C Lampeter and Llanddewibrefi Gp 04-06; V Llanfihangel-ar-arth w Capel Dewi from 06. *Y Ficerdy, Llanfihangel-ar-Arth, Pencader SA39 9HU* Tel (01559) 384858 Mobile 07773-645694

TIMS, Brian Anthony. b 43. Solicitor 64. STETS 95. **d** 98 **p** 99. NSM Whitchurch w Tufton and Litchfield *Win* 98-02; NSM Shipton Bellinger 02-06. *7 Hillside, Whitchurch RG28 7SN* Tel (01256) 895181 E-mail brian@timsfamily.com

TINGAY, Kevin Gilbert Xavier. b 43. Sussex Univ BA79. Chich Th Coll 79. **d** 80 **p** 81. C W Tarring *Chich* 80-83; TV Worth 83-90; R Bradford w Oake, Hillfarrance and Heathfield *B & W* 90-01; RD Tone 96-01; P-in-c Camerton w Dunkerton, Foxcote and Shoscombe 01-10; Bp's Inter Faith Officer 01-10; Bp's Adv for Regional Affairs 01-10; rtd 10. *82B Keyford, Frome BA11 1JJ* Tel (01373) 455778 E-mail kgxt@btinternet.com

TINGLE, Michael Barton. b 31. Bps' Coll Cheshunt 65. **d** 67 **p** 68. C Totteridge *St Alb* 67-70; C Hitchin St Mary 70-73; V Gt Gaddesden 73-78; V Belmont *Lon* 78-86; V Burford w Fulbrook, Taynton, Asthall etc *Ox* 86-97; rtd 97; Perm to Offic *St Alb* 97-05. *The College of St Barnabas, Blackberry Lane, Lingfield RH7 6NJ* Tel (01342) 872836

TINKER, Christopher Graham. b 78. Collingwood Coll Dur BA00. Wycliffe Hall Ox 02. **d** 04 **p** 05. C Houghton *Carl* 04-08; NSM Terrington St Clement *Ely* from 08. *8 Sutton Road, Terrington St Clement, King's Lynn PE34 4PQ* Tel (01553) 827372 E-mail christinker04@aol.com

TINKER, Melvin. b 55. Hull Univ BSc Ox Univ MA. Wycliffe Hall Ox 80. **d** 83 **p** 84. C Wetherby *Ripon* 83-85; Chapl Keele Univ 85-90; V Cheadle All Hallows *Ches* 90-94; V Hull St Jo Newland *York* from 94. *St John's Vicarage, Clough Road, Hull HU6 7PA* Tel (01482) 343658 E-mail melvin@tink.karoo.co.uk

TINNISWOOD, Robin Jeffries. b 41. K Coll Lon BScEng64. Wells Th Coll 67. **d** 70 **p** 71. C Yeovil St Mich *B & W* 70-72; C Gt Marlow *Ox* 72-74; C Christow, Ashton, Trusham and Bridford *Ex* 74-77; P-in-c Ex St Paul 77; TV Heavitree w Ex St Paul 78-79; TV Ifield *Chich* 79-85; Perm to Offic *S'wark* 98-01; P-in-c Cury and Gunwalloe w Mawgan *Truro* 01-03. *Flat 4, 1 Pine Gardens, Horley RH6 7RA*

TINSLEY, Bernard Murray. b 26. Nottm Univ BA51. Westcott Ho Cam 51. **d** 53 **p** 54. C Rotherham *Sheff* 53-56; C Goole 56-58; V Thorpe Hesley 58-61; R Alverdiscott w Huntshaw *Ex* 61-78; R Newton Tracey 61-78; R Beaford and Roborough 67-78; V St Giles in the Wood 67-78; V Yarnscombe 67-78; R Newton Tracey, Alverdiscott, Huntshaw etc 78-88; RD Torrington 81-86;

rtd 88; Perm to Offic *Ex* 88-08. *The Grange, Grange Road, Bideford EX39 4AS* Tel (01237) 471414

TINSLEY, Derek. b 31. ALCM65 BTh93 PhD97. NW Ord Course 73. **d** 76 **p** 77. C Gt Crosby St Faith *Liv* 76-80; V Wigan St Anne 80-85; V Colton w Satterthwaite and Rusland *Carl* 85-93; rtd 93; Perm to Offic *Liv* from 93. *Lyndale, 43 Renacres Lane, Ormskirk L39 8SG*

TINSLEY, Preb Derek Michael. b 35. Lon Coll of Div ALCD66 LTh. **d** 66 **p** 67. C Rainhill *Liv* 66-68; C Chalfont St Peter *Ox* 68-73; P-in-c Maids Moreton w Foxcote 73-74; P-in-c Akeley w Leckhampstead 73-74; P-in-c Lillingstone Dayrell w Lillingstone Lovell 73-74; R N Buckingham 74-82; RD Buckingham 78-82; P-in-c Alstonfield *Lich* 82-84; P-in-c Butterton 82-84; P-in-c Warslow and Elkstones 82-84; P-in-c Wetton 82-84; V Alstonfield, Butterton, Warslow w Elkstone etc 85-95; RD Alstonfield 82-95; Preb Lich Cathl 91-98; V Cheddleton 95-98; Chapl St Edw Hosp Cheddleton 96-98; rtd 98; Perm to Offic *Lich* and *Derby* from 98. *3 Windsor Close, Manor Green, Ashbourne DE6 1RJ* Tel (01335) 346226

TIPLADY, Peter. b 42. Dur Univ MB, BS65 MRCGP72 FFPHM86. Carl Dioc Tr Course 86. **d** 89 **p** 90. NSM Wetheral w Warwick *Carl* 89-05; NSM Holme Eden and Wetheral w Warwick from 05. *Meadow Croft, Wetheral, Carlisle CA4 8JG* Tel (01228) 561611 *or* 603608 E-mail peter.tiplady@mac.com

TIPP (*formerly* NORTHERN), Mrs Elaine Joy. b 54. Leic Univ BSc75. SEITE 00. **d** 03 **p** 04. C Snodland All SS w Ch Ch *Roch* 03-08. *14 Church Road, Murston, Sittingbourne ME10 3RU* Tel (01795) 472574 E-mail 2xp@talktalk.net

TIPP, James Edward. b 45. Heythrop Coll Lon MA93. Oak Hill Th Coll 73. **d** 75 **p** 76. C St Mary Cray and St Paul's Cray *Roch* 75-78; C Southborough St Pet w Ch Ch and St Matt 78-82; R Snodland All SS w Ch Ch 82-08; RD Cobham 96-08; Hon Can Roch Cathl 01-08; rtd 08. *14 Church Road, Murston, Sittingbourne ME10 3RU* Tel (01795) 472574 E-mail 2xp@talktalk.net

TIPPER, Michael William. b 38. Hull Univ BSc59 MSc61. Em Coll Saskatoon 72. **d** 73 **p** 74. Canada 73-77, 79-80, 83-88 and from 91; R Amcotts *Linc* 77-79; V Aycliffe *Dur* 80-83; V Kneesall w Laxton and Wellow *S'well* 88-91; rtd 98. *106 Purdue Court West, Lethbridge AB T1K 4R8, Canada*

TIPPING, Mrs Brenda Margaret. b 44. N Lon Univ CQSW85 Dur Univ MA96. SAOMC 96. **d** 99 **p** 00. NSM Stevenage St Andr and St Geo *St Alb* 99-05; P-in-c S Mymms and Ridge from 05; Chapl among Deaf People from 05; NSM Officer Hertford Adnry from 06. *The Vicarage, 6 Hamilton Close, South Mimms, Potters Bar EN6 3PG* Tel (01707) 643142 E-mail ken@tipping1941.freeserve.co.uk

TIPPING, Canon John Woodman. b 42. AKC65. **d** 66 **p** 67. C Croydon St Sav *Cant* 66-70; C Plaistow St Mary *Roch* 70-72; V Brockley Hill St Sav *S'wark* 72-83; P-in-c Sittingbourne St Mary *Cant* 83-86; V 86-94; P-in-c Mersham w Hinxhill 94-03; P-in-c Mersham w Hinxhill and Sellindge 03-07; P-in-c Sevington 94-07; P-in-c Brabourne w Smeeth 95-00; AD N Lympne 95-02; Hon Can Cant Cathl 03-07; rtd 07; Perm to Offic *St E* from 08. *5 Peace Place, Thorpeness, Leiston IP16 4NA* Tel (01728) 454165 E-mail jwtipping@talk21.com

TIPPLE, Neil. b 58. Loughb Univ BTech81 Aston Univ MSc86. WMMTC 01. **d** 04 **p** 05. C Cov E 04-08; V Haywards Heath Ascension *Chich* from 08. *Ascension Vicarage, 1 Redwood Drive, Haywards Heath RH16 4ER* Tel (01444) 416262 Mobile 07792-198451 E-mail gandawhisky@aol.com

TIRWOMWE, Stephen Warren. b 46. TCert73 Bp Tucker Coll Mukono BD88 Open Univ MA94 Leeds Univ MA01. **d** 81 **p** 82. Uganda 87-97 and from 02; C Osmondthorpe St Phil *Ripon* 97-02; Dioc Miss Co-ord Kigezi from 02. *Abaho Ahurira, PO Box 1091, Kabale, Uganda* Tel (00256) (77) 870467 E-mail swtirwomwe@hotmail.com

TISDALE, Mark-Aaron Buchanan. b 67. Pittsburgh Univ BA94. Westcott Ho Cam 00. **d** 02 **p** 03. C Norton *St Alb* 02-05; P-in-c Clifton and Southill 05-11; Chapl St Edm Sch Cant from 11; CF (ACF) from 10. *3 The Close, St Thomas' Hill, Canterbury CT2 8HS* Tel (01227) 475600

TISSINGTON, Irene Frances. b 50. EMMTC 03. **d** 06 **p** 07. NSM Harworth *S'well* 06-10; Lic to Offic from 10. *14 Station Avenue, Ranskill, Retford DN22 8LF* Tel (01777) 818923 Mobile 07856-892759 E-mail irene@itissington.freeserve.co.uk

TITCOMB, Mrs Claire. b 35. SAOMC 95. **d** 98 **p** 99. OLM Witney *Ox* from 98; Assoc P for Min Development from 01. *30 Beech Road, Witney OX28 6LW* Tel (01993) 771234 E-mail claireroyt@clara.net

TITCOMBE, Peter Charles. See JONES, Peter Charles

TITFORD, Richard Kimber. b 45. UEA BA67. Ripon Coll Cuddesdon 78. **d** 80 **p** 80. C Middleton *Man* 80-83; P-in-c Edwardstone w Groton and Lt Waldingfield *St E* 83-90 and 95-02; R 90-94; P-in-c Boxford 00-02; C Assington w Newton Green and Lt Cornard 00-02; R Boxford, Edwardstone, Groton etc 02-03; rtd 03; Perm to Offic *St E* from 03 and *S'wark* from 10. *2 Chestnut Mews, Friars Street, Sudbury CO10 2AH* Tel and fax (01787) 880303 E-mail titford@keme.co.uk

TITLEY, David Joseph. b 47. Ex Univ BSc Surrey Univ PhD. Wycliffe Hall Ox. d 82 p 83. C Stowmarket *St E* 82-85; C Bloxwich *Lich* 85-90; TV 90-95; V Prees and Fauls 95-00; V Clacton St Paul *Chelmsf* from 00. *The Vicarage, 7 St Alban's Road, Clacton-on-Sea CO15 6BA* Tel (01255) 424760
E-mail titleys@supanet.com

TITLEY, Canon Robert John. b 56. Ch Coll Cam BA78 MA82 K Coll Lon PhD95. Westcott Ho Cam. d 85 p 86. C Lower Sydenham St Mich *S'wark* 85-88; C Sydenham All SS 85-88; Chapl Whitelands Coll of HE 88-94; V W Dulwich All SS 94-06; RD Streatham 04-05; Dioc Dir of Ords and Can Res and Treas S'wark Cathl 06-10; Hon Can from 10; TR Richmond St Mary w St Matthias and St Jo from 10. *The Vicarage, Ormond Road, Richmond TW10 6TH* Tel (020) 8940 0362
E-mail robert.titley@southwark.anglican.org

TIVEY, Nicholas. b 65. Liv Poly BSc89. Ridley Hall Cam 91. d 94 p 95. C Bromborough *Ches* 94-97; TV Walton H Trin *Ox* 97-01; Chapl HM Pris Wayland 01-08; Chapl Nor Sch from 08. *The Chaplain's Office, Norwich School, 70 The Close, Norwich NR1 4DD* Tel (01603) 728450
E-mail ntivey@norwich-school.org.uk

TIZZARD, Peter Francis. b 53. Oak Hill Th Coll 88. d 90 p 91. C Letchworth St Paul w Willian *St Alb* 90-95; I Drumkeeran w Templecarne and Muckross *Clogh* 95-00; P-in-c Ramsgate Ch Ch *Cant* 00-02; V from 02. *24 St Mildred's Avenue, Ramsgate CT11 0HT* Tel (01843) 853732

TOAN, Robert Charles. b 50. Oak Hill Th Coll. d 84 p 85. C Upton (Overchurch) *Ches* 84-87; V Rock Ferry 87-99; RD Birkenhead 97-99; V Plas Newton 99-06; P-in-c Ches Ch Ch 03-06; V Plas Newton w Ches Ch Ch 07-09; RD Ches 02-08; Cambodia from 09. *c/o Ben Toan Esq, 123 Hope Farm Road, Great Sutton, Ellesmere Port CH66 2TJ* Tel 0151-347 9220
E-mail bob.toan@xaltmail.com

TOBIN, Richard Francis. b 44. CertEd. Chich Th Coll 76. d 78 p 79. C W Leigh CD *Portsm* 78-79; C Halstead St Andr w H Trin and Greenstead Green *Chelmsf* 79-87; Youth Chapl 82-87; V S Shields St Simon *Dur* 87-04; V Ipswich All Hallows *St E* 04-09; rtd 09; Perm to Offic *Chelmsf* from 10. *20 Chilton Lodge Road, Sudbury CO10 2HD* Tel (01787) 881319
E-mail ricktobin@btinternet.com

TOBIN, Robert Benjamin. b 70. Harvard Univ AB93 TCD MPhil98 Mert Coll Ox DPhil04 Em Coll Cam BA07 MA11 Ox Univ MA11. Westcott Ho Cam 04. d 07 p 08. C Beaconsfield *Ox* 07-09; Chapl Harvard Univ USA 09-10; Chapl Oriel Coll *Ox* from 10. *Oriel College, Oxford OX1 4EW* Tel (01865) 276580
E-mail robert.tobin@oriel.ox.ac.uk

TODD, Alastair. b 20. CMG71. CCC Ox BA45. Sarum & Wells Th Coll 71. d 73 p 74. C Willingdon *Chich* 73-77; P-in-c Brighton St Aug 77-78; V Brighton St Aug and St Sav 78-86; rtd 86; Perm to Offic *Chich* from 86. *c/o A M F Todd Esq and J H Todd Esq, Ranworth Cottage, Sheath Lane, Oxshott, Leatherhead KT22 0QU*

TODD, Canon Andrew John. b 61. Univ Coll Dur BA84 K Coll Lon MPhil98 Cardiff Univ PhD09. Coll of Resurr Mirfield 85. d 87 p 89. C Thorpe St Andr *Nor* 87-91; Chapl K Alfred Coll Win 91-94; Sen Asst P E Dereham and Scarning *Nor* 94-97; Dir Studies EAMTC *Ely* 94-01; Vice-Prin 97-01; CME Officer *St E* 01-06; Can Res St E Cathl 01-06; Sub Dean 04-06; Dean Chapl Studies St Mich Coll Llan from 06; Hon Research Fell Cardiff Univ from 07. *St Michael and All Angels' College, 54 Cardiff Road, Llandaff, Cardiff CF5 2YJ* Tel (029) 2083 8001 or 2056 3379 Fax 2083 8008 Mobile 07785-560558
E-mail ajt@stmichaels.ac.uk

TODD, Catherine Frances. b 61. Surrey Univ BSc84 Westmr Coll Ox BTh99 RGN84 RM86. EAMTC 96. d 99 p 00. NSM Sutton and Witcham w Mepal *Ely* 99-01; C Horringer *St E* 01-03; R 03-07; Chapl HM Pris Erlestoke 07-10; Chapl HM Pris Glouc 10-11; Chapl HM Pris Leyhill from 11. *HM Prison Leyhill, Wotton-under-Edge, Gloucester GL12 8BT* Tel (01454) 264000
E-mail catherine.todd@hmps.gsi.gov.uk

TODD, Clive. b 57. Linc Th Coll 89. d 91 p 92. C Consett *Dur* 91-93; C Bensham 93-95; P-in-c S Hetton w Haswell 95-98; R Ebchester and V Medomsley 98-04; P-in-c S Lawres Gp *Linc* 04-09; RD Lawres 06-07; P-in-c Thanington *Cant* from 09; Dir of Ords from 09. *The Vicarage, 70 Thanington Road, Canterbury CT1 3XE* Tel (01227) 464516
E-mail clive.todd1@btinternet.com

TODD, Edward Peter. b 44. Cranmer Hall Dur 86. d 88 p 89. C Hindley All SS *Liv* 88-91; P-in-c Wigan St Steph 91-96; V 96-98; P-in-c N Meols 98-03; TR 03-05; rtd 05; P-in-c Scarisbrick *Liv* from 10. *St Mark's Vicarage, 458A Southport Road, Scarisbrick, Ormskirk L40 9RF* Tel (01704) 880363
E-mail revtodd@btopenworld.com

TODD, George Robert. b 21. Sarum & Wells Th Coll 74. d 76 p 77. Hon C Wellington and Distr *B & W* 76-86; Perm to Offic 86-06. *15 John Grinter Way, Wellington TA21 9AR* Tel (01823) 662828

TODD, Ian Campbell. b 56. Westcott Ho Cam. d 04 p 05. C Scotforth *Blackb* 04-08; TV Hitchin *St Alb* from 09. *Holy Saviour Vicarage, St Anne's Road, Hitchin SG5 1QB* Tel (01462) 456140 E-mail iancamtodd@googlemail.com

TODD, Jeremy Stephen Bevan. b 69. Trin Coll Bris BA92. d 97 p 98. C Tufnell Park St Geo and All SS *Lon* 97-99; Perm to Offic *Lon* 03-07 and *S'wark* from 07. *St Augustine's Vicarage, 336 Baring Road, London SE12 0DX* Tel (020) 8857 4941
E-mail jeremytodd@me.com

TODD, Joy Gertrude. b 28. Ox Univ MTh99. d 90 p 94. OLM Guildf H Trin w St Mary 90-99; Perm to Offic from 99. *165 Stoke Road, Guildford GU1 1EY* Tel (01483) 567500

TODD, Michael Edward. b 62. Brighton Poly BA84 Surrey Univ PGCE85. SEITE 96 Ven English Coll Rome 98. d 99 p 05. C Farnham *Guildf* 99-00; Chapl Surrey Inst Art and Design 99-00; Development Officer Surrey Univ 00-02; Progr Manager and Lect Croydon Coll 02-05; Dep Dir City and Islington Coll 05-07; Hon C Camberwell St Giles w St Matt *S'wark* 04-05; Hon C Newington St Mary from 05; Hd of Sch S Thames Coll 07-10; Chapl Trin Sch Lewisham from 11. *1 William Dyce Mews, London SW16 6AW* Tel (020) 8677 7328 Mobile 07946-701279
E-mail mikeytodd@hotmail.com

TODD, Nicholas Stewart. b 61. Open Univ BA03 MA08. Wycliffe Hall Ox 94. d 96 p 97. C Gt Wyrley *Lich* 96-99; V Leaton and Albrighton w Battlefield 99-02; R Holbrook, Stutton, Freston, Woolverstone etc *St E* 02-06; CF from 06. *c/o MOD Chaplains (Army)* Tel (01264) 381140 Fax 381824
E-mail nick@toddsrus.org

TODD, Canon Norman Henry. b 19. PhC Lon Univ BPharm42 Fitzw Ho Cam BA50 MA55 Nottm Univ PhD78. Westcott Ho Cam 50. d 52 p 53. C Aspley *S'well* 52-54; Chapl Westcott Ho Cam 55-58; V Arnold *S'well* 58-65; V Rolleston w Morton 65-69; Can Res S'well Minster 65-69; R Elston w Elston Chapelry 71-76; R E Stoke w Syerston 72-76; V Sibthorpe 72-76; Bp's Adv on Tr 76-83; C Averham w Kelham 76-80; V Rolleston w Morton 80-83; P-in-c Upton 80-83; V Rolleston w Fiskerton, Morton and Upton 83-88; Hon Can S'well Minster 82-88; rtd 88; Perm to Offic *S'well* from 88; Abps' Adv for Bps' Min 88-94. *17 Woodville Drive, Sherwood, Nottingham NG5 2GZ*
E-mail n.todd1@ntlworld.com

TODD, Canon William Moorhouse. b 26. Lich Th Coll 54. d 57 p 58. C W Derby St Mary *Liv* 57-61; V Liv St Chris Norris Green 61-97; Hon Can Liv Cathl 92-97; rtd 97; Perm to Offic *Liv* from 97. *3 Haymans Grove, West Derby, Liverpool L12 7LD* Tel 0151-256 1712

TOFTS, Jack. b 31. Roch Th Coll 66. d 68 p 69. C Richmond *Ripon* 68-71; C Croydon St Jo *Cant* 71-74; P-in-c Welney *Ely* 74-78; P-in-c Upwell Christchurch 74-79; V Gorefield 78-94; R Newton 78-94; R Tydd St Giles 78-94; rtd 96; Perm to Offic *Ely* from 96. *The Birches, Church Road, Walpole St Peter, Wisbech PE14 7NU* Tel (01945) 780455

TOLHURST, David. b 72. Cranmer Hall Dur 07. d 09 p 10. C Middleton St George *Dur* from 09. *8 Westacres, Middleton St George, Darlington DL2 1LJ* Tel (01325) 401850
E-mail david.tolhurst@gmail.com

TOLL, Brian Arthur. b 35. Ely Th Coll 62 Linc Th Coll 64. d 65 p 66. C Cleethorpes *Linc* 65-68; C Hadleigh w Layham and Shelley *St E* 69-72; R Claydon and Barham 72-86; P-in-c Capel w Lt Wenham 86-94; P-in-c Holton St Mary w Gt Wenham 87-91; R Capel St Mary w Lt and Gt Wenham 94-96; P-in-c Ipswich St Mary at the Elms 96-01; Bp's Adv on Deliverance and Exorcism 89-97; rtd 01; Perm to Offic *St E* from 01. *39 Derwent Road, Ipswich IP3 0QR* Tel (01473) 424305
E-mail batoll@ntlworld.com

TOLLER, Elizabeth Margery. b 53. Leeds Univ BA75. Ripon Coll Cuddesdon 84. d 87 p 00. Asst Chapl Leeds Gen Infirmary 87-90; Perm to Offic *Nor* 90-91; Chapl Lt Plumstead Hosp 92-93; Chapl Co-ord HM Pris Nor 93-95; Chapl Gt Yarmouth Coll 96-99; Perm to Offic *S'wark* 99-00; Hon C Wandsworth St Paul from 00; Hon Asst Chapl St Chris Hospice Lon 03-10. *116 Augustus Road, London SW19 6EW* Tel (020) 8788 2024
E-mail mtoller@gmx.de

TOLLER, Heinz Dieter. b 52. NEOC 86. d 87 p 88. C Leeds Gipton Epiphany *Ripon* 87-90; R Coltishall w Gt Hautbois and Horstead *Nor* 90-99; V Wandsworth St Paul *S'wark* from 99; AD Wandsworth from 05. *116 Augustus Road, London SW19 6EW* Tel (020) 8788 2024 Fax 08702-843237 Mobile 07941-291120
E-mail htoller@gmail.com

TOLLEY, Canon George. b 25. Lon Univ BSc45 MSc48 PhD52 Sheff Univ Hon DSc83 Open Univ Hon DUniv84 Hon DSc86 FRSC CBIM. Linc Th Coll 65. d 67 p 68. C Sharrow St Andr *Sheff* 67-90; Hon Can Sheff Cathl 76-98. *74 Furniss Avenue, Sheffield S17 3QP* Tel 0114-236 0538

TOLWORTHY, Canon Colin. b 37. Chich Th Coll 64. d 67 p 68. C Hulme St Phil *Man* 67-70; C Lawton Moor 70-71; C Hangleton *Chich* 72-76; V Eastbourne St Phil 76-87; V Hastings H Trin 87-10; Can and Preb Chich Cathl 03-10; rtd 10. *The Charterhouse, Charterhouse Square, London EC1M 6AN* Tel (020) 7250 0119 E-mail colintolworthy@gmx.com

TOMALIN, Stanley Joseph Edward. b 66. Oak Hill Th Coll BA93. d 96 p 97. C Bitterne *Win* 96-00; C Hailsham *Chich* 00-05; P-in-c Hawkswood CD 01-05; V Hawkswood from 05; RD

Dallington from 07. *Harmers Hay House, 1 Barn Close, Hailsham BN27 1TL* Tel (01323) 846680
E-mail tomalinstan@aol.com

TOMBS, Kenneth Roberts. b 42. Open Univ BA84. S Dios Minl Tr Scheme 92. **d** 95 **p** 96. Dep Hd Twyford C of E High Sch Acton 86-97; Chapl 98-02; rtd 02; NSM Ickenham *Lon* from 95. *91 Burns Avenue, Southall UB1 2LT* Tel (020) 8574 3738
E-mail ken.tombs@btinternet.com

TOME DA SILVA, Carlos Alberto. d 01 p 01. Brazil 01-04; C Risca *Mon* 04-05; C Bassaleg 05-06; CF from 06. *c/o MOD Chaplains (Army)* Tel (01264) 381140 Fax 381824
E-mail betotome@hotmail.com

TOMKINS, Ian James. b 60. Univ of Wales (Cardiff) LLB81 Aston Business Sch MBA90. Ridley Hall Cam. **d** 00 **p** 01. C Bourton-on-the-Water w Clapton *Glouc* 00-04; P-in-c Broxbourne w Wormley *St Alb* 04-07; R 07-10; Adv for Minl Support *Bris* from 10; Hon C Stoke Gifford from 11. *90 Simmonds View, Stoke Gifford, Bristol BS34 8HL* Tel (01454) 774004 E-mail ian-tomkins@lineone.net
or ian.tomkins@bristoldiocese.org

TOMKINS, James Andrew. b 66. R Holloway & Bedf New Coll Lon BA88. SAOMC 01. **d** 04 **p** 06. C Lavendon w Cold Brayfield, Clifton Reynes etc *Ox* 04-05; C Risborough 05-08; TV from 08. *The Rectory, Mill Lane, Monks Risborough, Princes Risborough HP27 9JE* Tel (01844) 275944
E-mail jamestomkins@btinternet.com

TOMKINS, Jocelyn Rachel. *See* WALKER, Jocelyn Rachel

TOMKINS, Justin Mark. b 71. Trin Coll Bris BA10. **d** 11. C Longfleet *Sarum* from 11. *Address temp unknown*
E-mail emall@justintomkins.org

TOMKINSON, Raymond David. b 47. EAMTC 86. **d** 89 **p** 90. NSM Chesterton St Geo *Ely* 89-91; C Sawston 91-93; C Babraham 91-93; P-in-c Wimbotsham w Stow Bardolph and Stow Bridge etc 93-94; R 94-00; RD Fincham 94-97; Dir Old Alresford Place *Win* 00-06; P-in-c Old Alresford and Bighton 00-06; rtd 06; Perm to Offic *Pet* from 07. *8 Uppingham Road, Oakham LE15 6JD* Tel (01572) 756844
E-mail raymondtomkinson@gmail.com

TOMLIN, Graham Stuart. b 58. Linc Coll Ox BA80 MA83 Ex Univ PhD96. Wycliffe Hall Ox BA85. **d** 86 **p** 87. C Ex St Leon w H Trin 86-89; Chapl Jes Coll Ox 89-94; Tutor Wycliffe Hall Ox 89-98; Vice-Prin 98-05; Prin St Paul's Th Cen *Lon* from 05; Dean St Mellitus Coll from 07. *33 Foskett Road, London SW6 3LY* Tel (020) 7731 2732 Mobile 07929-048720
E-mail graham.tomlin@htb.org.uk

TOMLIN, Keith Michael. b 53. Imp Coll Lon BSc75. Ridley Hall Cam 77. **d** 80 **p** 81. C Heywood St Jas *Man* 80-83; C Rochdale 83-84; TV 84-85; Chapl Rochdale Tech Coll 83-85; R Bennington w Leverton *Linc* 85-99; R Leverton 99-01; Chapl HM Pris N Sea Camp 97-01; P-in-c Fotherby *Linc* 01-06; Louthesk Deanery Chapl 06-10. *Address temp unknown*

TOMLINE, Stephen Harrald. b 35. Dur Univ BA57. Cranmer Hall Dur 61. **d** 61 **p** 62. C Blackley St Pet *Man* 61-66; V Audenshaw St Steph 66-90; V Newhey 90-01; rtd 01; Perm to Offic *Carl* from 01. *3 Humphrey Cottages, Stainton, Kendal LA8 0AD* Tel (01539) 560988

TOMLINSON, Anne Lovat. b 56. Edin Univ MA78 PhD85 MTh98. St Jo Coll Nottm 84. **d** 93. Tutor TISEC 93-02; Dir Past Studies 98-00; Perm to Offic *Edin* from 93. *3 Bright's Crescent, Edinburgh EH9 2DB* Tel and fax 0131-668 1322
E-mail anne.tomlinson1@btinternet.com

TOMLINSON, Barry William. b 47. Clifton Th Coll 72. **d** 72 **p** 73. C Pennington *Man* 72-76; SAMS 76-80; Chile 77-80; C-in-c Gorleston St Mary CD *Nor* 80; V Gorleston St Mary 80-88; Chapl Jas Paget Hosp Gorleston 81-87; P-in-c Gt w Lt Plumstead *Nor* 88-89; R Gt w Lt Plumstead and Witton 89-93; R Gt and Lt Plumstead w Thorpe End and Witton 93-98; Chapl Lt Plumstead Hosp 88-94; Chapl Norwich Community Health Partnership NHS Trust 94-95; RD Blofield *Nor* 96-98; R Roughton and Felbrigg, Metton, Sustead etc 99-02; V Margate H Trin *Cant* 98-99; Perm to Offic *Nor* 02-10; P-in-c Brinton, Briningham, Hunworth, Stody etc from 10. *12 Heath Road, Sheringham NR26 8JH* Tel (01263) 820266
E-mail barrywtomlinson@gmail.com

TOMLINSON, David Robert. b 60. Kent Univ BSc82 Chelsea Coll Lon PGCE83 Jes Coll Cam BA92 MA96. Ridley Hall Cam 90. **d** 93 **p** 94. C Godalming *Guildf* 93-98; V Grays North *Chelmsf* 98-08; RD Thurrock 03-08; TR Saffron Walden w Wendens Ambo, Littlebury etc from 09; RD Saffron Walden from 09. *The Rectory, 17 Borough Lane, Saffron Walden CB11 4AG* Tel (01799) 500947
E-mail rector@stmaryssaffronwalden.org

TOMLINSON, David Robert. b 63. Open Univ BA07 St Jo Coll Dur BA09. Cranmer Hall Dur 07. **d** 09 **p** 10. C Shildon *Dur* from 09. *St Francis Vicarage, Burnhope, Newton Aycliffe DL5 7ER* Tel (01325) 310804 Mobile 07546-596079
E-mail smileydavid63@gmail.com

TOMLINSON, David William. b 48. Lon Bible Coll MA95 Westcott Ho Cam 97. **d** 97 **p** 98. NSM W Holloway St Luke *Lon*

97-00; P-in-c 00-01; V from 01. *St Luke's Vicarage, Penn Road, London N7 9RE* Tel and fax (020) 7607 1504
E-mail revdavetomlinson@hotmail.com

TOMLINSON, Eric Joseph. b 45. Lich Th Coll 70 Qu Coll Birm 72. **d** 73 **p** 74. C Cheadle *Lich* 73-76; C Sedgley All SS 77-79; V Ettingshall 79-94; V Horton, Lonsdon and Rushton Spencer from 94. *The Vicarage, Longsdon, Stoke-on-Trent ST9 9QF* Tel (01538) 385318

TOMLINSON, Frederick William. b 58. Glas Univ MA80 Edin Univ BD83. Edin Th Coll 80. **d** 83 **p** 84. C Cumbernauld *Glas* 83-86; C Glas St Mary 86-88; R Edin St Hilda 88-01; R Edin St Fillan 88-01; R Edin St Pet from 01. *3 Bright's Crescent, Edinburgh EH9 2DB* Tel and fax 0131-667 6224
E-mail fred.tomlinson@talk21.com

TOMLINSON, Helen. b 53. **d** 07 **p** 08. OLM Stretford All SS *Man* from 07. *23 Gairloch Avenue, Stretford, Manchester M32 9LL* Tel 0161-865 2723

TOMLINSON, Canon Ian James. b 50. K Coll Lon AKC72 Hull Univ MA90 Ox Univ MTh01. St Aug Coll Cant 72. **d** 73 **p** 74. C Thirsk w S Kilvington and Carlton Miniott etc *York* 73-76; C Harrogate St Wilfrid *Ripon* 76-79; R Appleshaw, Kimpton, Thruxton, Fyfield etc *Win* from 79; Dioc Adv in Past Care and Counselling from 01; Hon Can Win Cathl from 04. *The Rectory, Ragged Appleshaw, Andover SP11 9HX* Tel (01264) 772414 Fax 771302 E-mail ian@raggedappleshaw.freeserve.co.uk

TOMLINSON, Mrs Jean Mary. b 32. K Coll Lon BEd75. S Dios Minl Tr Scheme 84. **d** 87 **p** 94. Hon Par Dn Spring Park All SS *S'wark* 87-92; Chapl HM YOI Hatfield 92-98; Perm to Offic *S'well* from 92. *6 Cheyne Walk, Bawtry, Doncaster DN10 6RS* Tel (01302) 711201

TOMLINSON (née MILLS), Mrs Jennifer Clare. b 61. Trin Hall Cam BA82 MA86. Ridley Hall Cam 88. **d** 91 **p** 94. C Busbridge *Guildf* 91-95; C Godalming 95-98; NSM Grays North *Chelmsf* 98-08; NSM Saffron Walden w Wendens Ambo, Littlebury etc from 08; Par Development Adv (Colchester Area) from 11; Bp's Adv on Women's Min from 11; Chapl Thurrock Primary Care Trust 99-08. *The Rectory, 17 Borough Lane, Saffron Walden CB11 4AG* Tel (01799) 500757 *or* (01708) 740385
E-mail tomlinson.jenny@ntlworld.com

TOMLINSON, John Howard. b 54. Newc Univ BSc76 MICE83. Chich Th Coll 91. **d** 93 **p** 94. C Blewbury, Hagbourne and Upton *Ox* 93-96; C Cowley St Jas 96-97; TV 97-04; TR Upper Wylye Valley *Sarum* from 04; RD Heytesbury from 07. *The Rectory, 1 Bests Lane, Sutton Veny, Warminster BA12 7AU* Tel (01985) 840014 E-mail johnhoward-atuwvt@tiscali.co.uk

TOMLINSON, John William Bruce. b 60. Univ of Wales (Abth) BA82 Man Univ MA90 Birm Univ PhD08. Hartley Victoria Coll 87 Mar Thoma Th Sem Kottayam 90 Linc Th Coll 91. **d** 92 **p** 93. In Methodist Ch 90-91; C Sawley *Derby* 92-95; P-in-c Man Victoria Park 95-98; Dioc CUF Officer 95-98; Chapl St Anselm Hall Man Univ 96-98; V Shelton and Oxon *Lich* 98-04; Ecum Co-ord for Miss and Chief Exec Officer Lincs Chapl Services 04-06; Perm to Offic from 08. *31 Rivehall Avenue, Welton, Lincoln LN2 3LH* Tel (01673) 866159
E-mail dr.pelican@hotmail.com

TOMLINSON, Matthew Robert Edward. b 61. St Chad's Coll Dur BA83 Univ of Wales (Cardiff) BD94. St Mich Coll Llan 92. **d** 94 **p** 95. C Abergavenny St Mary w Llanwenarth Citra *Mon* 94-96; PV Llan Cathl and Chapl Llan Cathl Sch 96-00; V Edgbaston St Aug *Birm* from 00. *St Augustine's Vicarage, 44 Vernon Road, Birmingham B16 9SH* Tel and fax 0121-454 0127 Mobile 07989-915499 E-mail jm.tomlinson@blueyonder.co.uk

TOMPKINS, April. b 51. Man Univ BEd75. EMMTC 05. **d** 07 **p** 08. NSM Belper *Derby* from 07. *8 Derwent Grove, Alfreton DE55 7PB* Tel (01773) 835122
E-mail april_tompkins@hotmail.com

TOMPKINS, David John. b 32. Oak Hill Th Coll 55. **d** 58 **p** 59. C Northampton St Giles *Pet* 58-61; C Heatherlands St Jo *Sarum* 61-63; V Selby St Jas and Wistow *York* 63-73; V Retford St Sav *S'well* 73-87; P-in-c Clarborough w Hayton 84-87; V Kidsgrove *Lich* 87-90; P-in-c Tockwith and Bilton w Bickerton *York* 90-97; rtd 97; Perm to Offic *Pet* 00-03. *49 Wentworth Drive, Oundle, Peterborough PE8 4QF* Tel (01832) 275176

TOMPKINS, Janet. d 11. OLM Mablethorpe w Trusthorpe *Linc* from 11; OLM Sutton, Huttoft and Anderby from 11. *Brigadoon, 51 Rutland Road, Mablethorpe LN12 1EN* Tel (01507) 478078

TOMPKINS, Michael John Gordon. b 35. JP76. Man Univ BSc58 MPS59. NOC 82. **d** 85 **p** 86. C Abington *Pet* 85-87; TV Daventry 87-92; P-in-c Braunston 87-92; TV Daventry, Ashby St Ledgers, Braunston etc 92-93; R Paston 93-98; Perm to Offic *Ches* from 98; rtd 00. *19 Clarendon Close, Chester CH4 7BL* Tel (01244) 659147 E-mail michaeltompkins@onetel.com

TOMPKINS, Peter Michael. b 58. Open Univ BA92 SS Hild & Bede Coll Dur CertEd79. St Jo Coll Nottm MA96. **d** 96 **p** 97. C Bromfield w Waverton *Carl* 96-99; R Woldsburn *York* 99-01; TV E Farnworth and Kearsley *Man* 01-05; P-in-c Laceby and Ravendale Gp *Linc* from 05; P-in-c Brough w Stainmore,

Musgrave and Warcop *Carl* from 11. *The Rectory, Church Brough, Kirkby Stephen CA17 4EJ* Tel (017683) 41238

TOMS, Sheila Patricia. b 33. Cam Univ TCert54 Univ of Wales (Cardiff) BEd77. Llan Ord Course 90. **dss** 91 **d** 94 **p** 97. Canton St Luke *Llan* 91-94; NSM Peterston-super-Ely w St Brides-super-Ely 94-00; P-in-c Newport St Paul *Mon* 00-06; Perm to Offic from 07. *East Wing, Dingestow Court, Dingestow, Monmouth NP25 4DY* Tel (01600) 740262

TONBRIDGE, Archdeacon of. See MANSELL, The Ven Clive Neville Ross

TONBRIDGE, Suffragan Bishop of. See CASTLE, The Rt Revd Brian Colin

TONES, Kevin Edward. b 64. Hertf Coll Ox BA85. Ridley Hall Cam 88. **d** 91 **p** 92. C Warmsworth *Sheff* 91-92; C Thorne 92-96; V Greasbrough 96-11; C Kimberworth, Rawmarsh w Parkgate and Kimberworth Park 10-11; rtd 11. *40A Blakelock Road, Hartlepool TS25 5PG* Tel (01429) 265625 E-mail kevt@worshiptrax.co.uk

TONG, Canon Peter Laurence. b 29. Lon Univ BA50. Oak Hill Th Coll 52. **d** 54 **p** 55. C Everton St Chrys *Liv* 54-56; P-in-c Liv St Sav 56-59; V Blackb Sav 59-65; Chapl Blackb R Infirmary 63-65; V Islington St Andr w St Thos and St Matthias *Lon* 65-75; V Welling *Roch* 75-82; TR Bedworth *Cov* 82-94; Hon Can Cov Cathl 88-94; Hon Can Chile from 89; rtd 94; Perm to Offic *Roch* from 94. *46 Bladindon Drive, Bexley DA5 3BP* Tel (020) 8303 0085

TONGE, Brian. b 36. St Chad's Coll Dur BA58. Ely Th Coll 59. **d** 61 **p** 62. C Fleetwood St Pet *Blackb* 61-65; Chapl Ranby Ho Sch Retford 65-69; Hon C Burnley St Andr w St Marg *Blackb* 69-97; rtd 97; Perm to Offic *Blackb* from 97. *50 Fountains Avenue, Simonstone, Burnley BB12 7PY* Tel (01282) 776518

TONGE, Lister. b 51. K Coll Lon AKC74 Loyola Univ Chicago MPS95. St Aug Coll Cant 74. **d** 75 **p** 76. C Liv Our Lady and St Nic w St Anne 75-78; C Johannesburg Cathl S Africa 78-79; CR 79-91; Lic to Offic *Wakef* 83-91; Perm to Offic *Man* 89-94; USA 93-95; Perm to Offic *Liv* 95-96; Chapl Community of St Jo Bapt from 96; Chapl Ripon Coll Cuddesdon from 05; Lic to Offic Newark USA from 08; Chapl New Coll Ox from 10. *38 Empress Court, Woodin's Way, Oxford OX1 1HF* Tel (01865) 247966 E-mail listertonge@talktalk.net *or* chaplain@new.ox.ac.uk

TONGE, Malcolm. b 53. Lancs Poly BA74 FCA77. NEOC 00. **d** 03 **p** 04. NSM Brookfield *York* 03-07; NSM Ingleby Barwick 07-08; NSM Lower Swale *Ripon* from 08. *8 Meadow Court, Scruton, Northallerton DL7 0QU* E-mail malcolm.tonge@huntsman.com

TONGUE, Charles Garth. b 32. **d** 01 **p** 01. P-in-c Strontian *Arg* from 01; P-in-c Kinlochmoidart from 01. *The Old Smiddy, Anaheilt, Strontian, Acharacle, Argyll PH36 4JA* Tel (01967) 402467 Fax 402269 Mobile 07713-955204

TONGUE, Canon Paul. b 41. St Chad's Coll Dur BA63. **d** 64 **p** 65. C Dudley St Edm *Worc* 64-69; C Sedgley All SS *Lich* 69-70; V Amblecote *Worc* 70-07; Chapl Dudley Gp of Hosps NHS Trust 93-07; Hon Can Worc Cathl 93-07; RD Stourbridge 96-01; rtd 07. *99 Woolhope Road, Worcester WR5 2AP* Tel (01905) 352052 E-mail fatherpaul@freeuk.com

TONKIN, The Ven David Graeme. b 31. Univ of NZ LLB56 LLM57 Barrister-at-Law. Coll of Resurr Mirfield 57. **d** 59 **p** 60. C Hackney Wick St Mary of Eton w St Aug *Lon* 59-62; Chapl Worksop Coll Notts 62-68; Lic to Offic *S'well* 63-68; Jordan 68-74; New Zealand from 74; Can St Pet Cathl Waikato 88-89; Adn Waitomo 89-98; rtd 93. *Box 91, Owhango, New Zealand* Tel and fax (0064) (7) 895 4738

TONKIN, Mrs Jacqueline Anne. b 50. Open Univ BSc02 DipSW02. Yorks Min Course. **d** 11. NSM Langtoft w Foxholes, Butterwick, Cottam etc *York* from 11. *Monument Lodge, Back Street, Langtoft, Driffield YO25 3TD* Tel (01377) 267321 E-mail jacki.tonkin1@btinternet.com

TONKIN, Canon Richard John. b 28. Lon Coll of Div ALCD59 BD60. **d** 60 **p** 61. C Leic Martyrs 60-63; C Keynsham *B & W* 63-66; V Hinckley H Trin *Leic* 66-74; RD Sparkenhoe II 71-74; R Oadby 74-84; V Leic H Apostles 84-93; Hon Can Leic Cathl 83-93; rtd 93; Perm to Offic *Leic* from 93. *39 Shackerdale Road, Wigston, Leicester LE8 1BQ* Tel 0116-281 2517

TONKINSON, Canon David Boyes. b 47. K Coll Lon BD71 AKC78. St Aug Coll Cant 71. **d** 72 **p** 73. C Surbiton St Andr *S'wark* 72-74; C Selsdon St Jo w St Fran *Cant* 75-81; V Croydon St Aug *Cant* 81-84; V Croydon St Aug *S'wark* 85-89; C Easthampstead and Ind Chapl *Ox* 89-96; Chapl Bracknell Coll 93-96; Soc Resp Adv *Portsm* 96-02; Hon Can Portsm Cathl 96-02; Ind Chapl *Win* 02-08; Hon C Heckfield w Mattingley and Rotherwick 06-08; Soc Resp Partnership Development Officer *Guildf* 08-11; rtd 11. *17 Squirrel Close, Sandhurst GU47 9DL* E-mail david.tonkinson@o2.co.uk

TOOBY, Anthony Albert. b 58. Sarum & Wells Th Coll 89. **d** 91 **p** 92. C Warsop *S'well* 91-95; C Ollerton w Boughton 95-98; V Girlington *Bradf* 98-10; P-in-c Mancetter *Cov* from 10. *The Vicarage, Quarry Lane, Mancetter, Atherstone CV9 1NL* Tel (01827) 713266 E-mail tonytooby@virginmedia.com

TOOGOOD, Mrs Gillian Mary. b 58. Ridley Hall Cam 08. **d** 10 **p** 11. C Brentford *Lon* from 10. *5 Fulmer Way, London W13 9XQ* Tel (020) 8567 1299 Mobile 07936-793362 E-mail gill.toogood@tiscali.co.uk

TOOGOOD, John Peter. b 73. Leeds Univ BA95. Ripon Coll Cuddesdon 98. **d** 00 **p** 01. C Sherborne w Castleton and Lillington *Sarum* 00-03; P-in-c Chieveley w Winterbourne and Oare *Ox* 03-10; R E Downland from 10. *The Vicarage, Church Lane, Chieveley, Newbury RG20 8UT* Tel (01635) 247566 E-mail cwando@btinternet.com

TOOGOOD, Ms Melanie Lorraine. b 57. K Coll Lon BD78 AKC78. Ripon Coll Cuddesdon 94. **d** 96 **p** 97. C Shepperton *Lon* 96-99; C Greenford H Cross 99-04; P-in-c Tufnell Park St Geo and All SS 04-06; V from 06. *St George's Vicarage, 72 Crayford Road, London N7 0ND* Tel (020) 7700 0383 E-mail melanietoogood@tesco.net *or* melanie@toogood.info

TOOGOOD, Noel Hare. b 32. Birm Univ BSc54. Wells Th Coll 59. **d** 61 **p** 62. C Rotherham *Sheff* 61-65; C Darlington St Jo *Dur* 65-70; V Burnopfield 70-81; P-in-c Roche *Truro* 81-84; P-in-c Withiel 81-84; R Roche and Withiel 84-91; RD St Austell 88-91; V Madron 91-96; rtd 96; Perm to Offic *Portsm* from 97. *Acorn Cottage, Oakhill Road, Seaview PO34 5AP*

TOOGOOD, Robert Charles. b 45. AKC70. St Aug Coll Cant 70. **d** 71 **p** 72. C Shepperton *Lon* 71-74; C Kirk Ella *York* 74-76; P-in-c Levisham w Lockton 76-81; P-in-c Ebberston w Allerston 76-81; R Kempsey and Severn Stoke w Croome d'Abitot *Worc* 81-92; V Bramley *Win* 92-10; rtd 10. *14 Huntsmead, Alton GU34 2SE*

TOOGOOD, Robert Frederick. b 43. St Paul's Coll Chelt CertEd65 Open Univ BA74. Trin Coll Bris 93. **d** 95 **p** 96. C Southbroom *Sarum* 95-99; TV Langport Area *B & W* 99-04; rtd 04; Perm to Offic *Ox* and *Sarum* from 05. *49 Barrow Close, Marlborough SN8 2BE* Tel (01672) 511468 E-mail bob@toogood12.wanadoo.co.uk

TOOKE, Mrs Sheila. b 44. EAMTC 89. **d** 91 **p** 94. NSM March St Wendreda *Ely* 91-95; P-in-c Upwell Christchurch 95-97; P-in-c Welney 95-97; P-in-c Manea 95-97; R Christchurch and Manea and Welney 97-03; rtd 03; Perm to Offic *Ely* from 03. *The Haven, 21 Wisbech Road, March PE15 8ED* Tel (01354) 652844 E-mail stooke@havenmarch.plus.com

TOOKEY, Preb Christopher Tom. b 41. AKC67. **d** 68 **p** 69. C Stockton St Pet *Dur* 68-71; C Burnham *B & W* 71-77; R Clutton w Cameley 77-81; V Wells St Thos w Horrington 81-06; RD Shepton Mallet 86-95; Chapl Bath and West Community NHS Trust 95-06; Preb Wells Cathl 90-11; rtd 06; Perm to Offic *B & W* from 06. *47 Drake Road, Wells BA5 3LE* Tel (01749) 676006 E-mail christophertookey@hotmail.com

TOOLEY, Geoffrey Arnold. b 27. Lon Coll of Div 55. **d** 58 **p** 59. C Chalk *Roch* 58-60; C Meopham 60-62; P-in-c Snodland and Paddlesworth 62-68; P-in-c Burham 68-76; C Riverhead w Dunton Green 76-79; C S w N Bersted *Chich* 79-83; C-in-c N Bersted CD 83-96; rtd 97. *Hawksworth, Charnwood Road, Bognor Regis PO22 9DN*

TOOLEY, Norman Oliver. b 27. Roch Th Coll. **d** 65 **p** 66. C Gravesend St Mary *Roch* 65-68; C Ormskirk *Liv* 68-73; Chapl Merseyside Cen for the Deaf 73-78; C Bootle Ch Ch 78-80; C W Ham *Chelmsf* 80-86; Chapl RAD 86-92; rtd 92; Perm to Offic *Roch* 92-98. *30 Blackbrook Lane, Bromley BR2 8AY*

TOOMBS, Ian Melvyn. b 39. Hull Univ BA64 MSc90 FCIPD93. Ripon Coll Cuddesdon 07. **d** 07 **p** 08. NSM Alton St Lawr *Win* 07-09; NSM Alton from 10. *31 Princess Drive, Alton GU34 1QE* Tel (01420) 88130

TOON, John Samuel. b 30. Man Univ BA. Bps' Coll Cheshunt 64. **d** 65 **p** 66. C Newark St Mary *S'well* 65-67; C Clewer St Andr *Ox* 67-69; Canada 70, 73-76 and from 78; R Osgathorpe *Leic* 70-72; C Maidstone All SS w St Phil and H Trin *Cant* 76-78; rtd 95; Hon C Portage la Prairie St Mary 95-02; P-in-c N Peace Par 02-05; R Oshawa Gd Shep from 05. *St George's Residence, Unit 104, 505 Simcoe Street South, Oshawa ON L1H 4J9, Canada* Tel (001) (905) 571 5976 E-mail fathertoon@rogers.com

TOOP, Preb Allan Neil. b 49. St Alb Minl Tr Scheme 79 Linc Th Coll 82. **d** 83 **p** 84. C Kempston Transfiguration *St Alb* 83-87; C Ludlow *Heref* 87-92; P-in-c Stokesay and Sibdon Carwood w Halford 92-01; P-in-c Acton Scott 96-01; RD Condover 96-00; V Minsterley from 01; R Habberley from 01; P-in-c Hope w Shelve from 07; Preb Heref Cathl from 06. *The Vicarage, Minsterley, Shrewsbury SY5 0AA* Tel (01743) 791213

TOOP, Mrs Mary-Louise. b 55. Glouc Sch of Min 90. **d** 04 **p** 05. Dir of Ords *Heref* from 00; NSM Minsterley from 04; NSM Habberley from 04; NSM Hope w Shelve from 04. *The Vicarage, Minsterley, Shrewsbury SY5 0AA* Tel (01743) 790399 E-mail maryloutoop@lineone.net

TOOTH, Nigel David. b 47. RMN69. Sarum & Wells Th Coll 71. **d** 74 **p** 75. C S Beddington St Mich *S'wark* 74-77; C Whitchurch *Bris* 77-83; TV Bedminster 83-87; Chapl Dorchester Hosps 87-94; Chapl Herrison Hosp Dorchester 87-94; Chapl W Dorset Gen Hosps NHS Trust 94-11; rtd 11. *5 Hope Terrace, Martinstown, Dorchester DT2 9JN* Tel (01305) 889576 E-mail nigeltooth@hotmail.co.uk

TOOVEY, Preb Kenneth Frank. b 26. K Coll Lon BD51 AKC51. d 52 p 53. C Munster Square St Mary Magd *Lon* 52-60; V Upper Teddington SS Pet and Paul 60-70; V Ruislip St Martin 70-81; RD Hillingdon 75-81; V Greenhill St Jo 81-91; Preb St Paul's Cathl 83-91; rtd 91; Perm to Offic *Lon* 91-10. *30 Wilfred Gardens, Ashby-de-la-Zouch LE65 2GX* Tel (01530) 417937

TOOVEY, Rupert William. b 66. d 10 p 11. NSM Storrington *Chich* from 10. *31 Downsview Avenue, Storrington, Pulborough RH20 4PS*

TOOZE, Margaret Elizabeth. b 27. St Mich Ho Ox 54. dss 83 d 89 p 94. Kenya 61-88; C Bath Walcot *B & W* 89-95; Perm to Offic from 95. *33 Walcot Court, Walcot Gate, Bath BA1 5UB* Tel (01225) 465642

TOPALIAN, Berj. b 51. Sheff Univ BA72 PhD77. Sarum Th Coll 95. d 97 p 98. NSM Clifton Ch Ch w Em *Bris* 97-98; C Bris St Mich and St Paul 98-99; C Cotham St Sav w St Mary and Clifton St Paul 99-01; V Pilning w Compton Greenfield 01-08; Chapl St Monica Home Westbury-on-Trym from 08; Hon Min Can Bris Cathl from 04. *Gate Lodge, St Monica Home, Cote Lane, Bristol BS9 3UN* Tel 0117-949 4020 E-mail berj.topalian@st.monicatrust.org.uk

TOPHAM, Paul Rabey. b 31. Columbia Pacific Univ MA81 DipEd58 MIL66. d 85 p 86. Chapl St Paul's Prep Sch Barnes 85-91; Chapl Toulouse w Biarritz, Cahors and Pau *Eur* 91-94; Perm to Offic *Eur* from 94 and *Lon* 94-97; P-in-c St Margaret's-on-Thames *Lon* 97-00; Hon C Hounslow W Gd Shep 00-05; Hon C Teddington SS Pet and Paul and Fulwell from 00. *5 Marlingdene Close, Hampton TW12 3BJ* Tel (020) 8979 4277 Mobile 07714-650980 E-mail prt418topham@btinternet.com

TOPLEY (née BRANCHE), Caren Teresa. b 59. Avery Hill Coll BEd81. SEITE 94. d 97 p 98. NSM Arlesey w Astwick *St Alb* 97-99; NSM Clifton and Southill from 99. *7 Fairfax Close, Clifton, Shefford SG17 5RH* Tel (01462) 615499 E-mail topley@ntlworld.com

TOPPING, Kenneth Bryan Baldwin. b 27. Bps' Coll Cheshunt 58. d 59 p 60. C Fleetwood St Pet *Blackb* 59-63; V Ringley *Man* 63-70; V Cleator Moor w Cleator *Carl* 70-91; rtd 92; Perm to Offic *Blackb* 92-07. *9 Brunton Park, Bowden, Melrose TD6 0SZ* Tel (01835) 824754

TOPPING, Roy William. b 37. MBE92. S Dios Minl Tr Scheme 91. d 92 p 93. Bahrain 89-94; Chapl Miss to Seamen Milford Haven 94-99; rtd 99; Perm to Offic *Sarum* from 00. *7 Lady Down View, Tisbury, Salisbury SP3 6LL* Tel (01747) 871909

TORDOFF, Donald William. b 45. Nottm Univ BA69. Qu Coll Birm 69. d 71 p 72. C High Harrogate Ch Ch *Ripon* 71-75; C Moor Allerton 75-80; V Bilton 80-92; R Spennithorne w Finghall and Hauxwell 92-01; rtd 01; Perm to Offic *Ripon* from 02 and *York* from 10. *4 Weavers Green, Northallerton DL7 8FJ* Tel (01609) 760155 E-mail don@tordoffs.eclipse.co.uk

TORDOFF (née PARKER), Mrs Margaret Grace. b 40. SRN65 SCM67. Cranmer Hall Dur 81. dss 83 d 87 p 94. Bilton *Ripon* 83-87; C 87-92; Chapl Spennithorne Hall 92; NSM Spennithorne w Finghall and Hauxwell 92-00; rtd 00; Perm to Offic *M & K* and *Ripon* from 00; *York* from 10. *4 Weavers Green, Northallerton DL7 8FJ* Tel (01609) 760155 E-mail margaret@tordoffs.eclipse.co.uk

TORODE, Brian Edward. b 41. St Paul's Coll Chelt TCert63 FCollP93. WEMTC 90. d 93 p 94. Hd Master Elmfield Sch Cheltenham from 82; NSM Up Hatherley *Glouc* 93-94; NSM Cheltenham St Steph 93-95; NSM Cheltenham Em 94-95; NSM Cheltenham Em w St Steph 95-09; NSM S Cheltenham from 10. *23 Arden Road, Leckhampton, Cheltenham GL53 0HG* Tel (01242) 231212 E-mail btsarnia@aol.com

TORRENS, Marianne Rose. See ATKINSON, Marianne Rose

TORRENS, Robert Harrington. b 33. Trin Coll Cam BA56 MA61. Ridley Hall Cam 56. d 58 p 59. C Bromley SS Pet and Paul *Roch* 58-60; C Aylesbury *Ox* 60-63; V Eaton Socon *St Alb* 63-73; Lic to Offic 73-75; V Pittville All SS *Glouc* 75-84; Chapl Frenchay Hosp Bris 84-94; Chapl Manor Park Hosp Bris 84-94; Chapl St Pet Hospice Bris 94-98; P-in-c Chippenham *Ely* 98-01; P-in-c Snailwell 98-01; Perm to Offic *Ely* and *St E* from 01. *68 Barons Road, Bury St Edmunds IP33 2LW* Tel (01284) 752075 E-mail torrensatkinson@aol.com

TORRY, Malcolm Norman Alfred. b 55. St Jo Coll Cam BA76 MA80 K Coll Lon MTh79 LSE MSc96 Lon Univ BD78 PhD90 BA01 BSc10. Cranmer Hall Dur 79. d 80 p 81. C S'wark H Trin w St Matt 80-83; C S'wark Ch Ch 83-88; Ind Chapl 83-88; V Hatcham St Cath 88-96; V E Greenwich Ch Ch w St Andr and St Mich 96-97; TR E Greenwich from 97; RD Greenwich Thameside 98-01. *37 Becquerel Court, West Parkside, London SE10 0QQ* Tel (020) 8858 3006 E-mail malcolm@torry.org.uk

TOSTEVIN, Alan Edwin John. b 41. Trin Coll Bris BA86. d 86 p 87. C Hildenborough *Roch* 86-89; TV Ipsley *Worc* 89-06; rtd 06. *Bowling Green Cottage, Bowling Road, Malvern WR14 4HZ* Tel (01684) 561468 E-mail alan@tostevin41.freeserve.co.uk

TOTNES, Archdeacon of. See RAWLINGS, The Ven John Edmund Frank

TOTNEY (née YATES), Mrs Jennifer Clare. b 83. Dur Univ BA04 MA05 Selw Coll Cam BA08. Westcott Ho Cam 06. d 09

p 10. C White Horse *Sarum* from 09. *124 Fell Road, Westbury BA13 2GP* E-mail jennifer.totney@gmail.com

TOTTEN, Andrew James. b 64. MBE01. QUB BA87 TCD BTh90 Univ of Wales (Cardiff) MTh07. CITC. d 90 p 91. C Newtownards *D & D* 90-94; CF from 94. *c/o MOD Chaplains (Army)* Tel (01264) 381140 Fax 381824 E-mail andrewjtotten@hotmail.com

TOTTERDELL, Mrs Rebecca Helen. b 57. Lon Bible Coll BA80 MA99. Oak Hill Th Coll 88. d 91 p 94. Par Dn Broxbourne w Wormley *St Alb* 91-94; C 94-95; C Stevenage St Nic and Graveley 95-99; P-in-c Benington w Walkern 99-08; Asst Dir of Ords 03-08; Bp's Officer for Women 03-07; Asst Dioc Dir of Ords *Ex* from 09; Hon C Bovey Tracey SS Pet, Paul and Thos w Hennock from 09. *9 Crokers Meadow, Bovey Tracey, Newton Abbot TQ13 9HL* Tel (01626) 833084 E-mail becky.totterdell@mypostoffice.co.uk

TOTTLE, Nicola Rachael. See SKIPWORTH, Nicola Rachael

TOUCHÉ-PORTER, The Most Revd Carlos. Bp Mexico; Presiding Bp Mexico from 04. *San Jeronimo #117, Angel Cp 01000, Del Alvaro Obregón, DF, Mexico* Tel (0052) (55) 5616 3193 Fax 5616 2205 E-mail diomex@avantel.net

TOUCHSTONE, Grady Russell. b 32. Univ of S California 51. Wells Th Coll 63. d 65 p 66. C Maidstone St Mich *Cant* 65-70; USA from 70; rtd 95. *1069 South Gramercy Place, Los Angeles CA 90019-3634, USA* Tel (001) (323) 731 5822 Fax 731 5880 E-mail diomex@avantel.net

TOULMIN, Miles Roger. b 74. BNC Ox BA95. Wycliffe Hall Ox BA06. d 07 p 08. C Brompton H Trin w Onslow Square St Paul *Lon* 07-11; C Onslow Square and S Kensington St Aug from 11. *Holy Trinity Church House, Brompton Road, London SW7 2RW* Tel (020) 7052 0303 E-mail miles.toulmin@htb.org.uk

TOURNAY, Ms Corinne Marie Eliane Ghislaine. b 57. Louvain Univ Belgium Lic82 STB90 MA90. Cuddesdon Coll 92. d 94 p 95. C Redhill St Jo *S'wark* 94-98; V Brockley St Pet from 98. *St Peter's Vicarage, Wickham Way, London SE4 1LT* Tel (020) 8469 0013

TOVAR, Gillian Elaine. See NICHOLLS, Mrs Gillian Elaine

TOVEY, John Hamilton. b 50. Cant Univ (NZ) BA72. St Jo Coll Nottm 78. d 80 p 81. C Hyson Green *S'well* 80-83; C Cashmere New Zealand 83-85; Chapl Christchurch Cathl 85-89; P-in-c Amuri 89-90; V 90-94; C Johnsonville and Churton Park 94-96; P-in-c Churton Park 96-00; V Wainuiomata from 00. *117 Main Road, Wainuiomata, Lower Hutt 5014, New Zealand* Tel (0064) (4) 478 4099 Fax 478 4087 E-mail john.tovey@xtra.co.nz

TOVEY, Phillip Noel. b 56. Lon Univ BA77 Lon Bible Coll BA83 Nottm Univ MPhil88 Lambeth STh95 Ox Brookes Univ PhD06. St Jo Coll Nottm 85. d 87 p 88. C Beaconsfield *Ox* 87-90; C Banbury 90-91; TV 91-95; Chapl Ox Brookes Univ 95-98; P-in-c Holton and Waterperry w Albury and Waterstock 95-97; TV Wheatley 97-98; Dioc Tr Officer from 98; Dir Reader Tr from 04; NSM Wootton and Dry Sandford from 05; Lect Ripon Coll Cuddesdon from 04. *20 Palmer Place, Abingdon OX14 5LZ* Tel (01235) 527077 E-mail phillip.tovey@oxford.anglican.org

TOVEY, Canon Ronald. b 27. AKC51. d 52 p 53. C Glossop *Derby* 52-55; C Chorlton upon Medlock *Man* 55-57; C Hulme St Phil 55-57; C Hulme St Jo 55-57; C Hulme H Trin 55-57; Malawi 57-69; Lesotho 69-85; Adn S Lesotho 77-85; Hon Can Lesotho 85-92; R Reddish *Man* 85-92; rtd 92; Perm to Offic *Pet* 92-07; *Linc* 99-02. *86 Kings Road, Oakham LE15 6PD* Tel (01572) 770628 E-mail ronshir@tovey2.fsnet.co.uk

TOWELL, Alan. b 37. Sarum & Wells Th Coll 86 WMMTC 87. d 89 p 90. C Boultham *Linc* 89-93; P-in-c Scunthorpe Resurr 93-97; rtd 97. *154 Upper Eastern Green Lane, Coventry CV5 7DN* Tel (024) 7646 1881

TOWELL, Geoffrey Leonard. b 37. K Coll Lon BA59. Linc Th Coll 59. d 61 p 62. C Ashbourne w Mapleton *Derby* 61-65; C Claxby w Normanby-le-Wold *Linc* 65-67; V Alkborough w Whitton 67-80; R W Halton 68-80; P-in-c Winteringham 75-80; V Alkborough 81-85; Dioc Ecum Officer 85-91; rtd 91. *40 Lady Frances Drive, Market Rasen, Lincoln LN8 3JJ* Tel (01673) 843983

TOWERS, Canon David Francis. b 32. G&C Coll Cam BA56 MA60. Clifton Th Coll 56. d 58 p 59. C Grassley *Derby* 58-63; V Brixton St Paul *S'wark* 63-75; V Chatteris *Ely* 75-87; RD March 82-87; Hon Can Ely Cathl 85-87; R Burnley St Pet *Blackb* 87-97; rtd 97; Perm to Offic *Bradf* from 99. *9 West View, Langcliffe, Settle BD24 9LZ* Tel (01729) 825803

TOWERS, John Keble. b 19. Keble Coll Ox BA41 MA57. Edin Th Coll 41. d 43 p 44. Chapl Dundee St Paul *Bre* 43-47; India 47-62; R Edin Ch Ch-St Jas 62-71; V Bradf St Oswald Chapel Green 71-78; P-in-c Holme Cultram St Mary *Carl* 78-80; V 80-85; rtd 85; Perm to Offic *Glas* 85-92; Hon C Moffat 92-00. *Lennox House Nursing Home, 22 Lennox Row, Edinburgh EH5 3JW* Tel 0131-552 0581

TOWERS, Patrick Leo. b 43. AKC68 Hull Univ CertEd69. d 74 p 75. Japan 74-81; TV Bourne Valley *Sarum* 81-83; Dioc Youth Officer 81-83; Chapl Oundle Sch 83-86; I Rathkeale w Askeaton and Kilcornan *L & K* 86-89; I Nenagh 89-00; Can Limerick, Killaloe and Clonfert Cathls 97-00; Provost Tuam *T, K & A* 00-09; Can 00-09; I Galway w Kilcummin 00-09; rtd 09. *Doonwood, Mountbellew, Co Galway, Republic of Ireland* Tel (00353) (90) 968 4547 Mobile 86-814 0649 E-mail towers@iol.ie

TOWERS, Terence John. b 33. AKC60. **d** 61 **p** 62. C Bishopwearmouth Gd Shep *Dur* 61-65; V Runham *Nor* 65-67; R Stokesby w Herringby 65-67; V Ushaw Moor *Dur* 67-93; rtd 93. *8 Beech Court, Langley Park, Durham DH7 9XL* Tel 0191-373 0210

TOWLER, Canon David George. b 42. Cranmer Hall Dur 73. **d** 76 **p** 77. C Newbarns w Hawcoat *Carl* 76-80; V Huyton St Geo *Liv* 80-98; V Newburgh w Westhead 98-07; AD Ormskirk 01-06; Hon Can Liv Cathl 03-07; rtd 07. *7 Padstow Close, Southport PR9 9RX* E-mail davidtowler@postmaster.co.uk

TOWLER, John Frederick. b 42. Surrey Univ PhD05. Bps' Coll Cheshunt 62. **d** 66 **p** 67. C Lowestoft St Marg *Nor* 66-71; R Horstead 71-77; Warden Dioc Conf Ho Horstead 71-77; Prec and Min Can Worc Cathl 77-81; rtd 02; Hon C Fordingbridge and Breamore and Hale etc *Win* from 06. *24 Oak Road, Alderholt, Fordingbridge SP6 3BL* Tel (01425) 656595 Mobile 07940-855952 E-mail cjtptners@talktalk.net

TOWLSON, George Eric. b 40. NOC 80. **d** 83 **p** 84. NSM Wakef St Andr and St Mary 83-84; NSM Ox St Mich w St Martin and All SS 84-86; Perm to Offic 86-87; NSM Hoar Cross w Newchurch *Lich* 87-93; C Wednesbury St Paul Wood Green 93-01; rtd 01; Perm to Offic *Lich* from 01. *58 Church Lane, Barton under Needwood, Burton-on-Trent DE13 8HX* Tel (01283) 713673

TOWNEND, John Philip. b 52. Southn Univ BTh95. Sarum & Wells Th Coll 89. **d** 91 **p** 92. C Sherborne w Castleton and Lillington *Sarum* 91-95; P-in-c Wool and E Stoke 95-98; Sacr and Chapl Westmr Abbey 98-01; P-in-c Brightwalton w Catmore, Leckhampstead etc *Ox* 01-10; P-in-c Beedon and Peasemore w W Ilsley and Farnborough 05-10; R W Downland from 10. *The Old Rectory, Church Street, Great Shefford, Hungerford RG17 7DU* Tel (01488) 648164 E-mail john@jptownend.freeserve.co.uk

TOWNEND, Lee Stuart. b 65. St Jo Coll Dur MA08. Cranmer Hall Dur 96. **d** 98 **p** 99. C Buxton w Burbage and King Sterndale *Derby* 98-01; V Loose *Cant* 01-08; P-in-c Ilkley All SS *Bradf* from 08. *The Vicarage, 58 Curly Hill, Ilkley LS29 0BA* Tel (01943) 816035 E-mail leenliz@ukonline.co.uk

TOWNER, Andrew Paul John. b 76. Bris Univ BSc98 Surrey Univ Roehampton PGCE02. Oak Hill Th Coll MTh07. **d** 07. C St Helen Bishopsgate w St Andr Undershaft etc *Lon* 07-10; C Beckenham Ch Ch *Roch* from 10. *5 Thornton Dene, Beckenham BR3 3ND* Tel (020) 8658 9833 Mobile 07956-569983 E-mail andrew.towner@ccb.org.uk

TOWNER, Colin David. b 39. St Pet Coll Ox BA61 MA65 Lon Univ BD63 ARCM72 LRAM73. Tyndale Hall Bris 61. **d** 64 **p** 65. C Southsea St Simon *Portsm* 64-67; C Penge St Jo *Roch* 67-70; V Leic St Chris 70-74; Hon C Southsea St Jude *Portsm* 75-82; Perm to Offic 86-90 and 00-01; C Southsea St Pet 01-03; P-in-c 03-07; P-in-c Portsea St Luke 05-07; rtd 07; Perm to Offic *Ely* from 08. *24 Fenland Road, Wisbech PE13 3QD* Tel (01945) 584556 E-mail sctowner@btinternet.com

TOWNER, Preb Paul. b 51. Bris Univ BSc72 BTh81. Oak Hill Th Coll 78. **d** 81 **p** 82. C Aspley *S'well* 81-84; R Gt Hanwood *Heref* 84-99; RD Pontesbury 93-99; P-in-c Heref St Pet w St Owen and St Jas 99-11; V from 11; RD Heref City 07-10; RD Heref Rural 07-10; RD Heref from 10; Preb Heref Cathl from 96. *The Vicarage, 102 Green Street, Hereford HR1 2QW* Tel (01432) 273676 E-mail preb.paul@btinternet.com

TOWNLEY, The Ven Peter Kenneth. b 55. Sheff Univ BA78. Ridley Hall Cam 78. **d** 80 **p** 81. C Ashton Ch Ch *Man* 80-83; C-in-c Holts CD 83-88; R Stretford All SS 88-96; V Ipswich St Mary-le-Tower *St E* 96-08; RD Ipswich 01-08; Hon Can St E Cathl 03-08; Adn Pontefract *Wakef* from 08. *The Vicarage, Kirkthorpe Lane, Kirkthorpe, Wakefield WF1 5SZ* Tel and fax (01924) 896327 *or* Tel 434459 Fax 364834 E-mail archdeacon.pontefract@wakefield.anglican.org

TOWNLEY, Robert Keith. b 44. TCD MPhil04. St Jo Coll Auckland LTh67. **d** 67 **p** 68. C Devonport H Trin New Zealand 67-70; C Lisburn Ch Ch *Conn* 71-74; C Portman Square St Paul *Lon* 75-80; Dean Ross and I Ross Union *C, C & R* 82-94; Chan Cork Cathl 82-94; Dean Kildare and I Kildare w Kilmeague and Curragh *M & K* 95-06; Chapl Defence Forces 95-06; rtd 06; Lic to Offic *Arm* from 06. *10 Beresford Row, Armagh BT61 9AU* Tel (028) 3752 5667

TOWNLEY, Roger. b 46. Man Univ BSc York Univ MSc. St Deiniol's Hawarden 82. **d** 84 **p** 85. C Longton *Blackb* 84-88; V Penwortham St Leon 88-92; V Wrightington 92-11; Chapl Wrightington Hosp NHS Trust 92-01; Chapl Wrightington Wigan and Leigh NHS Trust 01-11; rtd 11. *10 Hosey Road, Sturminster Newton DT10 1QP* Tel (01258) 471900 E-mail r.townley@talk21.com

TOWNROE, Canon Edward John. b 20. St Jo Coll Ox BA42 MA48 FKC59. Linc Th Coll 42. **d** 43 **p** 44. C Sunderland *Dur*

43-48; Chapl St Boniface Coll Warminster 48-56; Warden 56-69; Lic to Offic *Sarum* 48-93; Perm to Offic from 93; Can and Preb Sarum Cathl 69-93; rtd 85. *St Boniface Lodge, Church Street, Warminster BA12 8PG* Tel (01985) 212355

TOWNS, Ms Claire Louise. b 69. Portsm Poly BA90 Univ of Wales (Cardiff) MSc93 St Jo Coll Nottm MA01. EMMTC 06. **d** 07 **p** 08. C Beeston *S'well* from 07. *3 Muriel Road, Beeston, Nottingham NG9 2HH* Tel 07766-541152 (mobile) E-mail clairetowns@googlemail.com

TOWNSEND, Allan Harvey. b 43. WMMTC 89. **d** 92 **p** 93. NSM Fenton *Lich* 92-96; C Tividale 96-98; P-in-c Saltley and Shaw Hill *Birm* 98-06; P-in-c Washwood Heath 01-06; V Saltley and Washwood Heath 06-09; rtd 09; Perm to Offic *Lich* 09-10 and from 11; C Wolstanton 10. *5 The Croft, Stoke-on-Trent ST4 5HT* Tel (01782) 416333

TOWNSEND, Anne Jennifer. b 38. Lon Univ MB, BS60 MRCS60 LRCP60. S'wark Ord Course 88. **d** 91 **p** 94. NSM Wandsworth St Paul *S'wark* 91-08; Chapl Asst St Geo Hosp Tooting 91-92; Dean MSE 93-99; Perm to Offic from 08. *89E Victoria Drive, London SW19 6PT* Tel (020) 8785 7675 E-mail revdrannetow@yahoo.co.uk

TOWNSEND, Christopher Robin. b 47. St Jo Coll Nottm. **d** 74 **p** 75. C Gt Horton *Bradf* 74-77; C Heaton St Barn 77-78; C Wollaton *S'well* 78-80; V Slaithwaite w E Scammonden *Wakef* from 80. *The Vicarage, Station Road, Slaithwaite, Huddersfield HD7 5AW* Tel and fax (01484) 842748 E-mail robin.townsend@homecall.co.uk

TOWNSEND, Derek William. b 52. Fitzw Coll Cam BA74 Man Univ PhD89. St Jo Coll Nottm 91. **d** 91 **p** 92. C Hazlemere *Ox* 91-95; TV Banbury 95-98; V Banbury St Paul 98-01; Perm to Offic from 11. *24 Lower Lodge Lane, Hazlemere, High Wycombe HP15 7AT* Tel (01494) 715964 Mobile 07855-015519 E-mail bill.townsend@tiscali.co.uk

TOWNSEND, Mrs Diane Rosalind. b 45. Stockwell Coll of Educn CertEd66 K Alfred's Coll Win BEd88. Sarum Th Coll 93. **d** 96 **p** 97. NSM Botley, Durley and Curdridge *Portsm* 96-00; NSM Buriton 00-05; NSM Portsea N End St Mark 05-10; TV 06-10; rtd 10; Perm to Offic *Portsm* from 10. *9 Daisy Lane, Locks Heath, Southampton SO31 6RA* Tel (01489) 574092 E-mail dirobdaisy@aol.com

TOWNSEND, Gary. b 65. Trin Coll Bris. **d** 00 **p** 01. C Minster-in-Sheppey *Cant* 00-04; C Tonbridge SS Pet and Paul *Roch* 04-10; V Henham and Elsenham w Ugley *Chelmsf* from 10. *The Vicarage, Carters Lane, Henham, Bishop's Stortford CM22 6AQ* Tel (01279) 850281 Mobile 07719-876452

TOWNSEND, Canon John Clifford. b 24. St Edm Hall Ox BA48 MA49. Wells Th Coll. **d** 50 **p** 51. C Machen *Mon* 50-51; C Usk and Monkswood w Glascoed Chpl and Gwehelog 51-55; R Melbury Osmond w Melbury Sampford *Sarum* 55-60; Chapl RNVR 57-58; Chapl RNR 58-75; V Branksome St Aldhelm *Sarum* 60-70; R Melksham 70-73; TR 73-80; Can and Preb Sarum Cathl 72-90; RD Bradford 73-80; P-in-c Harnham 80-81; V 81-90; RD Salisbury 80-85; rtd 90; Perm to Offic *Sarum* from 90. *19 Wyke Oliver Close, Preston, Weymouth DT3 6DR* Tel (01305) 833641

TOWNSEND, John Elliott. b 39. ALCD63. **d** 64 **p** 65. C Harold Wood *Chelmsf* 64-68; C Walton *St E* 68-72; V Kensal Rise St Martin *Lon* 72-83; V Hornsey Ch Ch 83-98; V Forty Hill Jes Ch 98-06; rtd 06; Perm to Offic *Chelmsf* from 06. *4 Harper Way, Rayleigh SS6 9NA* Tel (01268) 780938 E-mail johnetbar@internet.com

TOWNSEND, Peter. b 35. AKC63. **d** 64 **p** 65. C Norbury St Oswald *Cant* 64-67; C New Romney w Hope 67-69; C Westborough *Guildf* 69-74; P-in-c Wicken *Pet* 74-87; R Paulerspury 74-84; P-in-c Whittlebury w Silverstone 82-84; V Whittlebury w Paulerspury 84-87; V Greetham and Thistleton w Stretton and Clipsham 87-01; rtd 01; Perm to Offic *Pet* 01-08 and *Leic* from 04. *26 King's Road, Oakham LE15 6PD* Tel (01572) 759286

TOWNSEND, Peter. b 37. Open Univ BA87. Wells Th Coll 67. **d** 69 **p** 70. C Desborough *Pet* 69-72; C Bramley *Ripon* 72-75; C-in-c Newton Hall LEP *Dur* 75-80; P-in-c Newton Hall 80-81; V Hartlepool St Luke 81-03; rtd 03. *348 Stockton Road, Hartlepool TS25 2PW* Tel (01429) 291651 E-mail townsendfamgo@ntlworld.com

TOWNSEND, Philip Roger. b 51. Sheff Univ BA78. Trin Coll Bris 78. **d** 80 **p** 81. C W Streatham St Jas *S'wark* 80-85; C Ardsley *Sheff* 85-88; V Crookes St Tim from 88; AD Hallam from 05. *St Timothy's Vicarage, 152 Slinn Street, Sheffield S10 1NZ* Tel 0114-266 1745 E-mail vicar@sttims.org.uk

TOWNSEND, Robert William. b 68. Univ of Wales (Ban) BA90. St Mich Coll Llan BTh93. **d** 93 **p** 95. C Dolgellau w Llanfachreth and Brithdir etc *Ban* 93-94; Min Can Ban Cathl 94-96; P-in-c Amlwch 96-97; R 97-99; R Llanfair-pwll and Llanddaniel-fab etc 99-03; P-in-c Llanilar w Rhostie and Llangwyryfon etc *St D* 03-06; Dioc Schools Officer 03-06; R Llanberis, Llanrug and Llandinorwig *Ban* 06-11; P-in-c Llandwrog and Llanwnda from 11; Dioc Dir of Educn from 11. *12 Llys y Waun, Waunfawr, Caernarfon LL55 4ZA* Tel (01286) 650262 Mobile 07855-492006 E-mail robert@rectory.net

TOWNSEND, Robin. See TOWNSEND, Christopher Robin

TOWNSEND, William. See TOWNSEND, Derek William

TOWNSHEND, Charles Hume. b 41. St Pet Coll Ox BA64 MA69. Westcott Ho Cam 64. **d** 66 **p** 67. C Warlingham w Chelsham and Farleigh *S'wark* 66-75; R Old Cleeve, Leighland and Treborough *B & W* 75-85; R Bishops Lydeard w Bagborough and Cothelstone 85-95; V N Curry 95-06; rtd 06. *Mutterings, Church Road, Colaton Raleigh, Sidmouth EX10 0LW* Tel (01395) 567460

TOWNSHEND, David William. b 57. Lon Univ PGCE80 Ox Univ MA85. Cranmer Hall Dur 81. **d** 84 **p** 85. C Barking St Marg w St Patr *Chelmsf* 84-87; Canada from 87. *225 Colonel Douglas Crescent, Brockville ON K6V 6W1, Canada*

TOWNSHEND, Edward George Hume. b 43. Pemb Coll Cam BA66 MA70. Westcott Ho Cam 68. **d** 70 **p** 71. C Hellesdon *Nor* 70-74; Ind Chapl 74-81; TV Lowestoft St Marg 74-79; TV Lowestoft and Kirkley 79-81; V Stafford St Jo *Lich* 81-85; P-in-c Tixall w Ingestre 81-85; V Stafford St Jo and Tixall w Ingestre 85-87; R Lich St Chad 87-99; RD Lich 94-99; P-in-c Hammerwich 94-96; C Hamstead St Paul *Birm* 99-02; Chapl Birm Airport 00-05; Sen Ind Chapl 02-05; rtd 05; Perm to Offic *Birm* 05-06. *4 Cathedral Close, Guildford GU2 7TL* Tel (01483) 207831 Mobile 07931-928114 E-mail dryfly57@hotmail.com

TOY, Elizabeth Margaret. b 37. CQSW77. Oak Hill NSM Course 85. **d** 88 **p** 94. NSM Hildenborough *Roch* 88-07. *2 Francis Cottages, London Road, Hildenborough, Tonbridge TN11 8NQ* Tel (01732) 833886 E-mail liz.toy@diocese-rochester.org

TOY, Canon John. b 30. Hatf Coll Dur BA53 MA62 Leeds Univ PhD82. Wells Th Coll 53. **d** 55 **p** 56. C Newington St Paul *S'wark* 55-58; R Soo SCM 58 60; Chapl Fly Th Coll 60-64; Chapl Gothenburg w Halmstad and Jönköping *Eur* 65-69; Asst Chapl St Jo Coll York 69-72; Sen Lect 72-79; Prin Lect 79-83; Can Res and Chan York Minster 83-99; rtd 99; Perm to Offic *Eur* from 99 and *S'well* from 03. *11 Westhorpe, Southwell NG25 0ND* Tel and fax (01636) 812609 E-mail jtoy19@talktalk.net

TOZE, Lissa Melanie. See GIBBONS, Mrs Lissa Melanie

TOZE, Stephen James. b 51. Birm Univ BA79. Qu Coll Birm 76 Westcott Ho Cam 93. **d** 93 **p** 94. C Leominster *Heref* 93-94; R Gt Brickhill w Bow Brickhill and Lt Brickhill *Ox* 94-02; Rural Officer Buckm Adnry 95-02; V Wilshamstead and Houghton Conquest *St Alb* from 02. *The Vicarage, 15 Vicarage Lane, Wilstead, Bedford MK45 3EU* Tel (01234) 740423

TRACEY, Gareth Paul. b 81. K Alfred's Coll Win BA03. St Jo Coll Nottm 06. **d** 09. C Roby *Liv* 09-11; C Eccleston from 11. *St Matthew's Vicarage, 36 St Matthew's Grove, St Helens WA10 3SE* Tel (01744) 612922 Mobile 07880-928644 E-mail gaz@traceytalk.me.uk

TRAFFORD, Mrs Joyce. b 35. NOC 84. **d** 87 **p** 94. Par Dn Chapelthorpe *Wakef* 87-94; C 94-98; rtd 98; Perm to Offic *Wakef* from 98. *1 Gillion Crescent, Durkar, Wakefield WF4 6PP* Tel (01924) 252033

TRAFFORD, Peter. b 39. Chich Th Coll. **d** 83 **p** 84. C Bath Bathwick *B & W* 83-86; Chapl RN 86-90; P-in-c Donnington *Chich* 90-99; V Jarvis Brook 99-04; rtd 04. *26 Bourne Way, Midhurst GU29 9HZ* Tel (01730) 815710

TRAFFORD-ROBERTS, Rosamond Jane. b 40. Qu Coll Birm BA. **d** 95 **p** 96. C Ledbury *Heref* 95-00; Lect St Botolph Aldgate w H Trin Minories *Lon* 00-05; Chapl St Barn-in-Soho 03-05; rtd 05; Perm to Offic *Lon* from 05. *47C St George's Square, London SW1V 3QN* Tel (020) 7828 1122 Mobile 07736-335959 E-mail revdros@hotmail.com

TRAILL, Geoffrey Conway. b 58. Ridley Coll Melbourne BA82 BTh87. **d** 85 **p** 85. Australia 85-87 and from 88; C Shrub End *Chelmsf* 87-88. *1 Albert Street, Point Lonsdale Vic 3225, Australia* Tel (0061) (3) 5258 4624 Mobile 412-381225 Fax 5258 4623 E-mail gtrail@optusnet.com.au

TRAIN, Paul Michael. b 57. Stellenbosch Univ BChD82. SEITE 03. **d** 06 **p** 07. NSM Loughton St Jo *Chelmsf* from 06. *5 Monkchester Close, Loughton IG10 2SN* Tel (020) 8508 2937 E-mail paul@loughtonchurch.org.uk

TRAINOR, Mrs Lynn Joanna. b 65. Bris Univ BSc87 Ex Univ PGCE89. SAOMC 99. **d** 02 **p** 03. C Ascot Heath *Ox* 02-06. *5 Lavender Row, King Edward's Rise, Ascot SL5 8QR* Tel (01344) 890577 E-mail lynn@lynnie.co.uk

TRANTER, John. b 51. St Jo Coll Nottm BA **d** 00 **p** 01. C Gt Wyrley *Lich* 00-04; V Altham w Clayton le Moors *Blackb* from 04. *The Vicarage, Church Street, Clayton le Moors, Accrington BB5 5HT* Tel (01254) 384321 E-mail revjohnt@talktalk.net

TRANTER, Stephen. b 61. Lanc Univ BA81 RGN87 RM89. Trin Coll Bris BA99. **d** 99 **p** 00. C Blackpool St Thos *Blackb* 99-03; P-in-c Blackb St Jas 03-10; P-in-c Blackb St Steph 04-10; Chapl Univ Hosps of Morecambe Bay NHS Trust from 10; P-in-c Ellel w Shireshead *Blackb* from 11. *St John's Vicarage, Chapel Lane, Ellel, Lancaster LA2 0PW* Tel (01524) 65944 E-mail stephentranter@msn.com

TRAPNELL, Miss Sandra. b 51. SEN73 SRN79 RGN87. **d** 08. OLM W Derby Gd Shep *Liv* from 08. *70 Ince Avenue, Anfield, Liverpool L4 7UX* Tel 07999-715201 (mobile)

TRAPNELL, Canon Stephen Hallam. b 30. G&C Coll Cam BA53 MA57 Virginia Th Sem BD56 MDiv70 Hon DD02.

Ridley Hall Cam 53. **d** 56 **p** 57. C Upper Tulse Hill St Matthias *S'wark* 56-59; C Reigate St Mary 59-61; V Richmond Ch Ch 61-72; P-in-c Sydenham H Trin 72-80; R Worting *Win* 80-92; Field Officer Decade of Evang 92-96; Can Shyogwe (Rwanda) from 93; rtd 96; Perm to Offic *Sarum* from 93 and *Win* from 96. *Downs Cottage, Rivar Road, Shalbourne, Marlborough SN8 3QE* Tel and fax (01672) 870514 E-mail stephen.trapnell@tiscali.co.uk

TRASK, Mrs Marion Elizabeth. b 54. Leic Univ BSc75 Brunel Univ PGCE76. Moorlands Bible Coll 82 Oak Hill Th Coll 93. **d** 96 **p** 97. C Bermondsey St Mary w St Olave, St Jo etc *S'wark* 96-00; C Peckham St Mary Magd 00-04; P-in-c Cowden w Hammerwood *Chich* from 10. *The Rectory, Church Street, Cowden, Edenbridge TN8 7JE* Tel (01342) 850221

TRASLER, Canon Graham Charles George. b 44. Ch Ch Ox BA65 MA69. Cuddesdon Coll 66. **d** 68 **p** 69. C Gateshead St Mary *Dur* 68-71; P-in-c Monkwearmouth St Pet 71-79; R Bentley and Binsted *Win* 79-84; R New Alresford w Ovington and Itchen Stoke 84-01; RD Alresford 99-01; P-in-c Stockbridge and Longstock and Leckford 01-03; R 03-09; Hon Can Win Cathl 05-09; rtd 09. *30 Cole Close, Andover SP10 4NL* Tel (01264) 359843 Mobile 07810-693910 E-mail grahamtrasler@tiscali.co.uk

TRATHEN, Paul Kevin. b 69. York Univ BA91 MA93 Jordanhill Coll Glas PGCE94 Middx Univ BA03. NTMTC 00. **d** 03 **p** 04. C Wickford and Runwell *Chelmsf* 03-07; P-in-c Rawreth w Rettendon 07-10; P-in-c Rawreth 10-11; Bp's Chapl 11; Dioc Adv for Faith in the Public Square from 11. *2 James Croft, Galleywood, Chelmsford CM2 8WD* Tel (01245) 260797 Mobile 07871-584997 E-mail ptrathen@chelmsford.anglican.org

TRAVERS, Canon Colin James. b 49. St Pet Coll Ox DA70 MA74. Ridley Hall Cam 70. **d** 72 **p** 73. C Hornchurch St Andr *Chelmsf* 72-75; Youth Chapl 75-77; C Aldersbrook 75-77; V Barkingside St Laur 77-82; V Waltham Abbey 82-88; V S Weald 88-95; Co-ord NTMTC and Hon C Gt Warley and Ingrave St Nic 95-98; P-in-c Gt Canfield w High Roding and Aythorpe Roding 98-02; V Theydon Bois 02-09; Hon Can Chelmsf Cathl 01-09; rtd 09; Perm to Offic *Ely* from 10. *7 Springhead Lane, Ely CB7 4QY* Tel (01353) 659732 E-mail colin@travers.name

TRAVERS, John William. b 48. Open Univ BA84 Hull Univ MA86. Linc Th Coll 75. **d** 78 **p** 79. C Headingley *Ripon* 78-81; TV Louth *Linc* 81-89; P-in-c Shingay Gp *Ely* 89; R 90-95; V Hamble le Rice *Win* from 95. *The Vicarage, High Street, Hamble, Southampton SO31 4JF* Tel and fax (023) 8045 2148 E-mail johntravers@tiscali.co.uk

TRAVIS, Mrs Jean Kathleen. b 42. **d** 03 **p** 04. OLM Benson *Ox* from 03. *25 Old London Road, Benson, Wallingford OX10 6RR* Tel (01491) 838713 E-mail jeantravis@tesco.net

TRAYNOR, Neil Owen. b 70. Worc Coll Ox BA91 MA94 Reading Univ PGCE94 Leeds Univ BA11. Coll of Resurr Mirfield 09. **d** 11. C Barnsley St Mary *Wakef* from 11. *The Vicarage, 186 Racecommon Road, Barnsley S70 6JY* Tel (01226) 247899 Mobile 07887-778757 E-mail neil.traynor@yahoo.com

TRAYNOR, Nigel Martin Arthur. b 58. St Jo Coll Nottm 94. **d** 96 **p** 97. C Wellington All SS w Eyton *Lich* 96-00; P-in-c Pype Hayes *Birm* 00-02; TV Erdington from 02. *St Mary's Vicarage, 1162 Tyburn Road, Birmingham B24 0TB* Tel 0121-373 3534 E-mail nigelt6@msn.com *or* revnigel@yahoo.co.uk

TREACY, Richard James. b 74. Aber Univ BD Univ of Wales (Cardiff) MTh99. **d** 98 **p** 99. C Hillsborough *D & D* 98-02. *14 Downshire Crescent, Hillsborough BT26 6DD* Tel (028) 9268 3098 Mobile 07917-854222 E-mail richard.treacy@btinternet.com

TREADGOLD, The Very Revd John David. b 31. LVO90. Nottm Univ BA58 FRSA91. Wells Th Coll 58. **d** 59 **p** 60. V Choral S'well Minster 59-64; R Wollaton 64-74; V Darlington St Cuth w St Hilda *Dur* 74-81; Can Windsor and Chapl in Windsor Gt Park 81-89; Dean Chich 89-01; CF (TA) 62-67; CF (TAVR) 74-78; Chapl to The Queen 81-89; rtd 01; Perm to Offic *Chich* from 04. *43 Priors Acre, Boxgrove, Chichester PO18 0ER* Tel (01243) 782385 E-mail treadgold@connectfree.co.uk

TREANOR, Canon Desmond Victor. b 28. St Jo Coll Dur BA53 MA59. **d** 54 **p** 55. C Oakwood St Thos *Lon* 54-57; C Sudbury St Andr 57-59; V Lansdown *B & W* 59-66; V Derby St Werburgh 66-68; V Leic St Anne 68-75; V Humberstone 75-86; Hon Can Leic Cathl 78-93; P-in-c Leic St Eliz Nether Hall 81-86; RD Christianity N 82-86; R Gt Bowden w Welham, Glooston and Cranoe 86-93; RD Gartree I 88-93; rtd 93; Perm to Offic *Leic* from 93. *5 Brookfield Way, Kibworth, Leicester LE8 0SA* Tel 0116-279 2750

TREANOR, Terence Gerald. b 29. St Jo Coll Ox BA52 MA56. Wycliffe Hall Ox 52. **d** 54 **p** 55. C Hornsey Ch Ch *Lon* 54-57; C Cambridge H Trin *Ely* 57-60; V Doncaster St Mary *Sheff* 60-66; Chapl Oakham Sch 66-94; rtd 94; Perm to Offic *Leic* and *Pet*

from 94; *Linc* 94-99. *35 Glebe Way, Oakham LE15 6LX* Tel (01572) 757495

TREANOR, Timothy Lyons Victor. b 62. St Jo Coll Cam BA83 MA87 K Coll Lon MA95 Cranfield Univ MSc01. Ripon Coll Cuddesdon BTh08. **d** 08. C Tavistock and Gulworthy *Ex* 08-10; C Ottery St Mary, Alfington, W Hill, Tipton etc from 10. *The Vicarage, Bendarroch Road, West Hill, Ottery St Mary EX11 1UW* Tel (01404) 811499 E-mail tlvtreanor@btinternet.com

TREASURE, Canon Andrew Stephen. b 51. Oriel Coll Ox BA73 MA77. St Jo Coll Nottm BA76. **d** 77 **p** 78. C Beverley Minster *York* 77-81; C Cambridge H Trin *Ely* 81-84; C Cambridge H Trin w St Andr Gt 84-85; V Eccleshill *Bradf* 85-98; P-in-c Bradf St Oswald Chapel Green 98-04; P-in-c Horton 98-04; V Lt Horton from 04; C Bowling St Steph from 05; Hon Can Bradf Cathl from 04. *St Oswald's Vicarage, Christopher Street, Bradford BD5 9DH* Tel (01274) 522717 E-mail stephen.treasure@bradford.anglican.org

TREASURE, Geoffrey. b 39. Hatf Coll Dur BA61 Univ of Wales (Cardiff) DipEd62. Oak Hill NSM Course 90. **d** 93 **p** 94. NSM Forty Hill Jes Ch *Lon* 93-95; Consultant SW England CPAS 95-02; Perm to Offic *B & W* 95-04; P-in-c Stoke St Gregory w Burrowbridge and Lyng 04-07; rtd 07; Perm to Offic *B & W* from 07. *Gable Cottage, West Lyng, Taunton TA3 5AP* Tel (01823) 490458 E-mail gtreasure@onetel.com

TREASURE, Mrs Joy Elvira. b 23. St Anne's Coll Ox MA50 CertEd. S Dios Minl Tr Scheme 80. **dss** 82 **d** 87 **p** 94. Tisbury *Sarum* 82-91; Hon Par Dn 87-91; rtd 92; Perm to Offic *Sarum* 92-06. *Address temp unknown*

TREASURE, Ronald Charles. b 24. Oriel Coll Ox BA48 MA52. Cuddesdon Coll. **d** 50 **p** 51. C Whitby *York* 50-54; C-in-c N Hull St Mich 54-58; V 58-62; V New Malton 62-89; RD Malton 63-75; rtd 89; Perm to Offic *York* from 89. *Castle Walls, Castlegate, Kirkbymoorside, York YO62 6BW* Tel (01751) 432916

TREASURE, Stephen. *See* TREASURE, Canon Andrew Stephen

TREBY, David Alan. b 47. FIBMS72 Bris Poly MSc90. St Jo Coll Nottm MA95. **d** 95 **p** 96. C Camborne *Truro* 95-00; V Stoke Gabriel and Collaton *Ex* from 00. *The Vicarage, Stoke Gabriel, Totnes TQ9 6QX* Tel (01803) 782358 E-mail dave@treby.freeserve.co.uk

TREDENNICK, Canon Angela Nicolette. b 38. SRN62 SCM63. S'wark Ord Course 87. **d** 90 **p** 94. NSM Charlwood *S'wark* 90-92; Par Dn Roehampton H Trin 92-94; C 94-97; RD Wandsworth 95-97; V Redhill St Matt 97-06; RD Reigate 00-03; Hon Can S'wark Cathl 05-06; rtd 06; Hon C Godstone and Blindley Heath *S'wark* 06-09; Perm to Offic from 09. *The Old Curiosity Shop, Chapel Road, Smallfield, Horley RH6 9NW* Tel (01342) 843570 E-mail rev.nicky.hello@amserve.com

TREDWELL, Mrs Samantha Jane. b 69. Nottm Trent Univ BEd92. EMMTC 00. **d** 03 **p** 04. C Skegby w Teversal *S'well* 03-07; TV Newark w Coddington from 07. *Christ Church Vicarage, Boundary Road, Newark NG24 4AJ* Tel (01636) 704969

TREE, Robin Leslie. b 46. Brunel Univ MSc00 Univ of Wales (Lamp) MTh10. S Dios Minl Tr Scheme 89. **d** 92 **p** 93. NSM St Leonards Ch Ch and St Mary *Chich* 92-95; NSM Hastings H Trin 95-98; TV Bexhill St Pet 98-01; V Hampden Park 01-10; P-in-c The Hydneye 08-10; V Hampden Park and The Hydnye from 10. *St Mary's Vicarage, 60 Brassey Avenue, Eastbourne BN22 9QH* Tel (01323) 503166 Mobile 07967-954411 E-mail frrobin.tree@btinternet.com

TREEBY, Stephen Frank. b 46. Man Univ LLB67 Lambeth STh01. Cuddesdon Coll 69. **d** 71 **p** 72. C Ashbourne w Mapleton *Derby* 71-74; C Boulton 74-76; Chapl Trowbridge Coll *Sarum* 76-79; TV Melksham 79-87; V Dilton's-Marsh 87-01; Chapl Westbury Hosp 87-01; R Spetisbury w Charlton Marshall etc *Sarum* 01-11; rtd 11. *5 Walnut Road, Honiton EX14 2UG* Tel (01404) 548715

TREEN, Preb Robert Hayes Mortlock. b 19. New Coll Ox BA46 MA46. Westcott Ho Cam 45. **d** 47 **p** 48. C Bath Abbey w St Jas *B & W* 47-52; PC Pill 52-61; R Bath St Sav 61-76; Preb Wells Cathl from 74; V Bishops Hull 76-84; RD Taunton S 77-81; RD Taunton 81-84; rtd 84; Perm to Offic *B & W* from 84. *20 Dunkirk Memorial House, Bishops Lydeard, Taunton TA4 3BT* Tel (01823) 431220

TREETOPS, Ms Jacqueline. b 47. NEOC 83. **dss** 86 **d** 87 **p** 94. Low Harrogate St Mary *Ripon* 86-87; C Roundhay St Edm 87-95; C Potternewton 95-97; rtd 97; Perm to Offic *Ripon* from 01. *43 Lincombe Bank, Leeds LS8 1QG* Tel 0113-237 0474

TREFUSIS, Charles Rodolph. b 61. Hull Univ BA83. Wycliffe Hall Ox 85. **d** 90 **p** 91. C Blackheath St Jo *S'wark* 90-94; V Purley Ch Ch from 94. *The Vicarage, 38 Woodcote Valley Road, Purley CR8 3AJ* Tel (020) 8660 1790 E-mail ctrefusis@aol.com

TREGALE, Diane Ruth. b 68. Spurgeon's Coll MTh05. St Jo Coll Nottm 07. **d** 08 **p** 09. C Wilford *S'well* 08-11; C Sherborne w Castleton, Lillington and Longburton *Sarum* from 11; Chapl

Gryphon Sch Sherborne from 11. *69 Granville Way, Sherborne DT9 4AT* Tel (01935) 815820 E-mail diane@tregale.co.uk

TREGALE, John Ernest. b 69. Ex Univ BSc90 Sheff Univ MA01. St Jo Coll Nottm 05. **d** 08 **p** 09. C Wilford *S'well* 08-11; C Sherborne w Castleton, Lillington and Longburton *Sarum* from 11. *69 Granville Way, Sherborne DT9 4AT* Tel (01935) 815820 E-mail jono@tregale.co.uk

TREGENZA, Matthew John. b 69. Univ of Wales (Lamp) BA92 BA(Theol)08 SS Coll Cam PGCE93 Lon Univ MA01 FRGS96. Westcott Ho Cam 01. **d** 03 **p** 04. C Marnhull *Sarum* 03-06; TV Mynyddislwyn *Mon* 06-08; P-in-c Blackwood from 08. *The Vicarage, Commercial Street, Pengam, Blackwood NP12 3TX* Tel (01443) 834003 E-mail matthew.tregenza@gmail.com

TREGUNNO, Timothy Frederick. b 79. St Andr Univ MTheol02. St Steph Ho Ox 04. **d** 06 **p** 07. C St Leonards Ch Ch and St Mary *Chich* 06-10; P-in-c Turners Hill from 10. *The Vicarage, Church Road, Turners Hill, Crawley RH10 4PB* Tel (01342) 715278 E-mail frtimt@yahoo.co.uk

TREHARNE, David Owen. b 73. Univ of Wales (Cardiff) BMus94 MPhil06 Bris Univ MEd04 Bris Coll PGCE00. Trin Coll Bris 94. **d** 99 **p** 04. NSM Bassaleg *Mon* 99-00; C Caerphilly *Llan* 04-08; P-in-c Porthkerry and Rhoose from 08; Dioc Voc Adv from 08. *The Vicarage, 6 Milburn Close, Rhoose, Barry CF62 3EJ* Tel (01446) 711713 E-mail dtrevd@aol.com

TREHERNE, Canon Alan Thomas Evans. b 30. Univ of Wales (Lamp) BA53. Wycliffe Hall Ox. **d** 55 **p** 56. C Heref St Pet w St Owen 55-57; India 57-72; C-in-c Netherley Ch Ch CD *Liv* 72-74; R Gateacre 74-75; TR 75-96; RD Farnworth 81-89; Hon Can Liv Cathl 94-96; rtd 96; Perm to Offic *Lich* 96-00 and from 03; RD Oswestry 01-02. *19 Smale Rise, Oswestry SY11 2YL* Tel (01691) 671569 E-mail alan@treherne.co.uk

TRELENBERG, Olaf. b 72. Ridley Hall Cam 06. **d** 08 **p** 09. C Scotforth *Blackb* from 08. *97 Barton Road, Lancaster LA1 4EN* Tel (01524) 844172 Mobile 07877-357332

TRELLIS, The Very Revd Oswald Fitz-Burnell. b 35. Chich Th Coll 73. **d** 74 **p** 75. C Chelmsf All SS 74-79; C-in-c N Springfield CD 79-85; V Heybridge w Langford 85-94; Dean Georgetown Guyana 94-02; P-in-c Doddinghurst and Mountnessing *Chelmsf* 02-04; P-in-c Doddinghurst 04-05; rtd 06; Perm to Offic *Chelmsf* from 06. *31 Douglas Matthew House, White Lyons Road, Brentwood CM14 4YT* Tel (01277) 215954

TREMBATH, Canon Martyn Anthony. b 65. Leeds Univ BA86. Ripon Coll Cuddesdon 88. **d** 90 **p** 91. C Bodmin w Lanhydrock and Lanivet *Truro* 90-91; C St Erth 92-96; C Phillack w Hampstead NHS Trust 96-98; Sen Chapl R Cornwall Hosps Trust 98-10; NSM Godrevy *Truro* 08-10; TR from 10; Hon Can Truro Cathl from 09. *The Rectory, 43 School Lane, St Erth, Hayle TR27 6HN* Tel (01736) 753194 E-mail godrevy-tr@hotmail.co.uk

TREMELLING, Peter Ian. b 53. Ex & Truro NSM Scheme 94. **d** 96 **p** 98. NSM St Illogan *Truro* from 96. *38 Rosewarne Park, Higher Enys Road, Camborne TR14 0AG* Tel (01209) 710518 E-mail reverendpeter@tesco.net

TREMLETT, Canon Andrew. b 64. Pemb Coll Cam BA86 MA90 Qu Coll Ox BA88 MA95 Ex Univ MPhil96 Liv Univ PGCE03. Wycliffe Hall Ox 86. **d** 89 **p** 90. C Torquay St Matthias, St Mark and H Trin *Ex* 89-92; Miss to Seamen 92-94; Asst Chapl Rotterdam *Eur* 92-94; Chapl 94-95; TV Fareham H Trin *Portsm* 95-98; Bp's Dom Chapl 98-03; V Goring-by-Sea *Chich* 03-08; Can Res Bris Cathl 08-10; Can Westmr Abbey and R Westmr St Marg from 10. *5 Little Cloister, Westminster Abbey, London SW1P 3PL* Tel (020) 7654 4806 E-mail andrew.tremlett@blueyonder.co.uk

TREMLETT, The Ven Anthony Frank. b 37. Ex & Truro NSM Scheme 78. **d** 81 **p** 82. C Southway *Ex* 81-82; P-in-c 82-84; V 84-88; RD Plymouth Moorside 86-88; Adn Totnes 88-94; Adn Ex 94-02; rtd 02. *57 Great Berry Road, Crownhill, Plymouth PL6 5AY* Tel (01752) 240052 E-mail tremlettaf@aol.com

TREMTHTHANMOR, Ms Chrys Mymmir Evnath Tristan. b 66. Univ of California BA88. St Mich Coll Llan BA05 MPhil07. **d** 06 **p** 07. C Coity, Nolton and Brackla *Llan* 06-10; TV Daventry, Ashby St Ledgers, Braunston etc *Pet* from 10. *31 Newbury Drive, Daventry NN11 0WQ* Tel (01327) 707925 E-mail vicarwelton@o2.co.uk

TRENCHARD, Hubert John. b 26. S Dios Minl Tr Scheme. **d** 83 **p** 84. NSM Sturminster Marshall *Sarum* 83-87; NSM Blandford Forum and Langton Long 87-96. *20 Chapel Gardens, Blandford Forum DT11 7UY* Tel (01258) 459576

TRENCHARD, Paul Charles Herbert Anstiss. b 53. Liv Univ LLB76. St Steph Ho Ox 77. **d** 80 **p** 81. C Torquay St Martin Barton *Ex* 80-84; R Ashprington, Cornworthy and Dittisham 84-92; R Barnwell w Tichmarsh, Thurning and Clapton *Pet* 92-04. *Place de la Courtille, 71460 Saint-Gengoux-le-National, France* Tel (0033) 3 85 92 64 47 E-mail trenchard@aliceadsl.fr

TRENDALL, Matthew James. b 72. Oriel Coll Ox BA93 MA98. Trin Coll Bris BA10. **d** 10 **p** 11. C Redland *Bris* from 10. *89 Kings Drive, Bishopston, Bristol BS7 8JQ* Tel 0117-329 8663 Mobile 07947-150396 E-mail aliseandmatt@talktalk.net *or* matt@redland.org.uk

TRENDALL, Peter John. b 43. Oak Hill Th Coll 66. **d** 69 **p** 70. C Beckenham Ch Ch *Roch* 69-73; C Bedworth *Cov* 73-76; V Hornsey Rise St Mary *Lon* 76-82; P-in-c Upper Holloway St Steph 80-82; V Hornsey Rise St Mary w St Steph 82-84; V Walthamstow St Mary w St Steph *Chelmsf* 84-85; TR 85-93; P-in-c Chigwell 93-94; TR Chigwell and Chigwell Row 94-08; rtd 08; Perm to Offic *St E* from 08. *11 Harrison Green, Reydon, Southwold IP18 6XA* Tel (01502) 722962

TRENDER, Lawrence. b 37. Bps' Coll Cheshunt 64. **d** 66 **p** 67. C Petersham *S'wark* 66-71; C Malden St Jo 71-73; R Thornham Magna w Thornham Parva *St E* 73-81; R Thornhams Magna and Parva, Gislingham and Mellis 81-87; P-in-c Mellis 73-81; P-in-c Gislingham 73-81; RD Hartismere 85-87; R Skipsea w Ulrome and Barmston w Fraisthorpe *York* 92-01; rtd 01; Perm to Offic *York* from 01. *Stone Cottage, 5 Far Lane, Bewholme, Driffield YO25 8EA* Tel (01964) 533020

TRENHOLME (née ROBERTSON), Jane Lesley. b 54. Man Univ BSc76 Leeds Univ BA06. NOC 03. **d** 06 **p** 07. NSM Northowram *Wakef* 06-08; C Tong *Bradf* from 08; C Laisterdyke 08-10; P-in-c from 10. *Stretchgate, Rookes Lane, Halifax HX3 8PU* Tel (01274) 693392 or 788328 Fax 693356 E-mail jltrenholme@hotmail.co.uk

TRESIDDER, Alistair Charles. b 65. Qu Coll Ox BA88. Cranmer Hall Dur 93. **d** 93 **p** 94. C Limehouse *Lon* 93-98; V W Hampstead St Luke from 98. *St Luke's Vicarage, 12 Kidderpore Avenue, London NW3 7SU* Tel (020) 7794 2634 or 7431 6317 E-mail alistair@alistairtresidder.wanadoo.co.uk

TRETHEWEY, The Ven Frederick Martyn. b 49. Lon Univ BA70 Lambeth STh79. Oak Hill Th Coll 78. **d** 79. C Tollington Park St Mark w St Anne *Lon* 78-82; C Whitehall Park St Andr Hornsey Lane 82-87; TV Hornsey Rise Whitehall Park Team 87-88; V Brockmoor *Lich* 88-93; V Brockmoor *Worc* 93-01; Chapl Russells Hall Hosp Dudley 88-94; Chapl Dudley Gp of Hosps NHS Trust 94-01; RD Himley *Worc* 96-01; Hon Can Worc Cathl 99-01; Adn Dudley from 01. *15 Worcester Road, Droitwich WR9 8AA* Tel and fax (01905) 773301 E-mail fred.trethewey@ntlworld.com

TRETHEWEY, Richard John. b 74. Jes Coll Ox MA02. Wycliffe Hall Ox BA02. **d** 02 **p** 03. C Biddulph *Lich* 02-06; C Knowle *Birm* from 06. *46 Crabmill Close, Knowle, Solihull B93 0NP* Tel (01564) 201010 Mobile 07759-650572 E-mail richard@trethewey.org.uk

TRETT, Peter John. b 44. **d** 97 **p** 98. OLM High Oak, Hingham and Scoulton w Wood Rising *Nor* from 97. *Holly House, 35 Plough Lane, Hardingham, Norwich NR9 4AE* Tel (01953) 850369 E-mail trett@nnbus.co.uk

TREVELYAN, Preb James William Irvine. b 37. Selw Coll Cam BA64 MA67. Cuddesdon Coll 62. **d** 65 **p** 66. C Heston *Lon* 65-68; C Folkestone St Sav *Cant* 68-72; R Lenham w Boughton Malherbe 72-78; P-in-c Honiton, Gittisham, Combe Raleigh, Monkton etc *Ex* 78-79; R 79-83; TR 83-00; Chapl Ex and Distr Community Health Service NHS Trust 78-00; P-in-c Farway w Northleigh and Southleigh *Ex* 84-86; Preb Ex Cathl 95-00; rtd 00; Perm to Offic *Carl* from 02. *Bridge End, Barbon, Carnforth LA6 2LT* Tel (01524) 276530 E-mail jwitrevelyan@onetel.com

TREVELYAN, Mrs Rosemary Elizabeth. b 43. Ex Univ CertEd64 Open Univ BA91. **d** 11. NSM Washingborough w Heighington and Canwick *Linc* from 11. *9 Canterbury Drive, Washingborough, Lincoln LN4 1SJ* Tel (01522) 827874 E-mail rtrev911@hotmail.com

TREVOR, Canon Charles Frederic. b 27. Sarum Th Coll 54. **d** 56 **p** 57. C Sutton in Ashfield St Mich *S'well* 56-58; C Birstall *Leic* 58-61; V Prestwold w Hoton 61-66; V Thornton in Lonsdale w Burton in Lonsdale *Bradf* 66-74; V Kirkby Malham 74-85; P-in-c Coniston Cold 81-85; Hon Can Bradf Cathl 85-92; V Sutton 85-92; RD S Craven 86-91; rtd 92; Perm to Offic *Bradf* from 92. *5 Brooklyn, Threshfield, Skipton BD23 5ER* Tel (01756) 752640

TREVOR-MORGAN, Canon Basil Henry. b 27. Univ of Wales (Lamp) BA51. Wells Th Coll 51. **d** 53 **p** 54. C Chepstow *Mon* 53-56; C Halesowen *Worc* 56-59; CF (TA) 59-92; V Stourbridge St Thos *Worc* 59-76; Chapl Christchurch Hosp 76-92; V Christchurch *Win* 76-92; Hon Can Win Cathl 84-92; rtd 93; Perm to Offic *Sarum* 96-04. *2 Avon House, 112 Graham Road, Malvern WR14 2HX* Tel (01684) 561672

TREW, Mrs Ann Patricia. b 58. Ripon Coll Cuddesdon. **d** 00 **p** 01. C Hambleden Valley *Ox* 00-03; P-in-c Hedsor and Bourne End 03-08; R from 08. *34 Fieldhead Gardens, Bourne End SL8 5RN* Tel (01628) 523046 E-mail ann@aptrew.purplecloud.net

TREW, Jeremy Charles. b 66. Univ of Wales (Abth) BSc89 Leeds Univ MSc92. St Jo Coll Nottm MA94. **d** 97 **p** 98. C Roundhay St Edm *Ripon* 97-01; P-in-c Spofforth w Kirk Deighton 01-07; V Seaton and Beer *Ex* from 07. *The Vicarage, Colyford Road, Seaton EX12 2DF* Tel (01297) 20391 E-mail jeremytrew@hotmail.com

TREW, Robin Nicholas. b 52. UWIST BSc74 Open Univ MA01. St Jo Coll Nottm 87. **d** 89 **p** 90. C Cov H Trin 89-93; V Snitterfield w Bearley 93-02; R Allesley from 02; AD Cov N from

10. The Rectory, Rectory Lane, Allesley, Coventry CV5 9EQ Tel (024) 7640 2006 E-mail robtrew@lineone.net

TREWEEK, Guy Matthew. b 65. LSE BSc(Econ)86 Peterho Cam BA07. Westcott Ho Cam 05. **d** 08 **p** 09. C Hammersmith St Pet *Lon* from 08; P-in-c St Andr-by-the-Wardrobe w St Ann, Blackfriars from 11; P-in-c St Jas Garlickhythe w St Mich Queenhithe etc from 11. *St Andrew's House, St Andrew's Hill, London EC4V 5DE* E-mail guy.treweek@london.anglican.org

TREWEEK (née MONTGOMERY), The Ven Rachel. b 63. Reading Univ BA85. Wycliffe Hall Ox BTh94. **d** 94 **p** 95. C Tufnell Park St Geo and All SS *Lon* 94-99; V Bethnal Green St Jas Less 99-06; CME Officer 99-06; Adn Northolt 06-11; Adn Hackney from 11. *St Andrew's House, St Andrew's Hill, London EC4V 5DE* E-mail archdeacon.hackney@london.anglican.org

TREWEEKS, Mrs Angela Elizabeth. b 35. Gilmore Ho IDC59. dss 59 **d** 87 **p** 94. Chapl Asst St Nic Hosp Newc 85-87; Chapl 87; Hon C Newc St Geo 87-89; Chapl St Mary's Hosp Stannington 92-95; Hon C Rothbury *Newc* 94-96; rtd 95; Perm to Offic *Newc* from 96. *The Nook, Pondicherry, Rothbury, Morpeth NE65 7YS* Tel (01669) 620393

TRICK, Matthew John Harvey. Univ of Wales (Abth) BSc02. St Mich Coll Llan BTh08. **d** 08 **p** 09. C Cowbridge *Llan* 08-10; C Aberavon 10-11; TV from 11. *Holy Trinity Vicarage, Fairway, Port Talbot SA12 7HG* Tel (01639) 689660 Mobile 07793-823406 E-mail matthewtrick@btinternet.com

TRICKETT, Canon Judith. b 50. Open Univ BA00. St Jo Coll Nottm 89. **d** 91 **p** 94. Par Dn Kimberworth *Sheff* 91-93; Dn-in-c Worsbrough Common 93-94; V 94-01; V Herringthorpe 01-10; R Firbeck w Letwell from 10; V Woodsetts from 10; Hon Can Sheff Cathl from 08. *The Rectory, 4A Barker Hades Road, Letwell, Worksop S81 8DF* Tel (01909) 540193 Mobile 07974-404831 E-mail judith.trickett@sheffield.anglican.org

TRICKETT, Stanley Mervyn Wood. b 27. Lich Th Coll 64. **d** 66 **p** 67. C Kington w Huntington *Heref* 66-70; P-in-c Old Radnor 70-81; P-in-c Knill 70-81; V Shrewton *Sarum* 81-97; P-in-c Winterbourne Stoke 81-92; RD Wylye and Wilton 85-89; rtd 97; Perm to Offic *Sarum* from 97. *3 Oakwood Grove, Alderbury, Salisbury SP5 3BN* Tel (01722) 710275

TRICKETT, Preb Susan. b 42. JP89. S Dios Mini Tr Scheme 91. **d** 94 **p** 95. NSM Combe Down w Monkton Combe and S Stoke *B & W* 94-99; Dean Women Clergy and V High Littleton 99-05; Preb Wells Cathl from 00; rtd 05; Perm to Offic *B & W* from 05. *Granville House, Tyning Road, Combe Down, Bath BA2 5ER* Tel (01225) 833007 E-mail susitrickett@mbzonline.com

TRICKEY, Christopher Jolyon. b 57. Jes Coll Cam BA79 MA83 Barrister-at-Law 80. Trin Coll Bris BA90. **d** 90 **p** 91. C Chesham Bois *Ox* 90-94; R Busbridge *Guildf* 94-98; P-in-c Hambledon 97-98; R Busbridge and Hambledon 98-09; Chapl Godalming Coll 01-09; R Nailsea H Trin *B & W* from 09. *The Rectory, 10 Ilminster Close, Nailsea, Bristol BS48 4YU* Tel (01275) 790845 E-mail jolyon.trickey@htnailsea.org.uk

TRICKEY, Mrs Frances Anne. b 59. Keele Univ BA81 Lon Inst of Educn PGCE82 Win Univ BA11. STETS 08. **d** 11. NSM Wraxall *B & W* from 11. *The Rectory, 10 Ilminster Close, Nailsea, Bristol BS48 4YU* Tel (01275) 790845 E-mail francestrickey@btinternet.com

TRICKEY, The Very Revd Frederick Marc. b 35. Dur Univ BA62. Cranmer Hall Dur. **d** 64 **p** 65. C Alton St Lawr *Win* 64-68; V Win St Jo cum Winnall 68-77; Angl Adv Channel TV from 77; R Guernsey St Martin *Win* 77-02; P-in-c Sark 02-03; Dean Guernsey 95-03; Hon Can Win Cathl 95-03; rtd 03. *L'Esperance, La Route des Camps, St Martin, Guernsey GY4 6AD* Tel (01481) 238441

TRICKLEBANK, Steven. b 56. Nottm Univ BTh88. Linc Th Coll 85. **d** 88 **p** 89. C Ditton St Mich *Liv* 88-91; C Wigan All SS 91-93; Chapl Aintree Hosps NHS Trust Liv 93-97; C-in-c St Edm Anchorage Lane CD *Sheff* 97-00; Chapl Doncaster R Infirmary and Montagu Hosp NHS Trust 97-00; V Stocksbridge *Sheff* 00-04; P-in-c Streatham Ch Ch *S'wark* 04-05; P-in-c Streatham Hill St Marg 04-05; V Streatham Ch Ch from 05. *Christ Church Vicarage, 3 Christchurch Road, London SW2 3ET* Tel (020) 8674 5723 E-mail steventricklebank@hotmail.com

TRIFFITT, Jonathan Paul. b 74. St Jo Coll Nottm BA03. **d** 03 **p** 04. C W Kilburn St Luke w St Simon and St Jude *Lon* 03-06; C Paddington Em Harrow Road 03-06; C Sherborne w Castleton etc and Chapl Gryphon Sch Sherborne 06-10; V Southbroom *Sarum* from 10; RD Devizes from 11. *The Vicarage, 31 Fruitfields Close, Devizes SN10 5JY* Tel (01380) 721441 E-mail j.triffitt@btinternet.com

TRIGG, Jeremy Michael. b 51. Open Univ BA88. Ripon Coll Cuddesdon 80. **d** 81 **p** 82. C Roundhay St Edm *Ripon* 81-84; C Harrogate St Wilfrid and St Luke 84-87; TV Pocklington Team *York* 87-90; R Rowley w Skidby 90-97; TV Wolverton *Ox* 97-98; R 98-11; P-in-c Rothwell *Ripon* from 11. *The Vicarage, Beech Grove, Rothwell, Leeds LS26 0EF* Tel 0113-282 2369 E-mail jeremy.trigg@btinternet.com

TRIGG, Preb Jonathan David. b 49. Ex Coll Ox BA71 MA75 Dur Univ PhD92. Cranmer Hall Dur BA82. **d** 83 **p** 84. C Enfield St Andr *Lon* 83-87; V Oakwood St Thos 87-96; AD Enfield

92-96; V Highgate St Mich from 96; P-in-c Highgate All SS from 09; AD W Haringey 00-06; Dir of Ords Edmonton Area from 08; Preb St Paul's Cathl from 10. *The Vicarage, 10 The Grove, London N6 6LB* Tel (020) 8347 5124 *or* 8340 7279 Fax 8348 4635 E-mail jdtrigg@gmail.com

TRILL, Barry. b 42. Chich Th Coll 65. **d** 68 **p** 69. C W Hackney St Barn *Lon* 68-73; TV Is of Dogs Ch Ch and St Jo w St Luke 73-78; P-in-c Hastings All So *Chich* 78-79; V 79-99; rtd 99. *12 Heathlands, Westfield, Hastings TN35 4QZ* Tel (01424) 753595

TRILL, Victor Alfred Mansfield. b 21. St Deiniol's Hawarden. **d** 81 **p** 82. Hon C Prestbury *Ches* 81-83; Hon C Church Hulme 83-85; V Marbury 85-90; rtd 90; Perm to Offic *Ches* from 90. *5 Maisterson Court, Nantwich CW5 5TZ* Tel (01270) 628948

TRIMBLE, Eleanor Louise. b 69. Man Metrop Univ BSc97. Yorks Min Course. **d** 09 **p** 10. C Old Trafford St Jo *Man* from 09. *3 Northleigh Road, Manchester M16 0EG* Tel 0161-900 3103 E-mail eleanor.trimble@btinternet.com

TRIMBLE, Canon John Alexander. b 33. Lon Univ BD65. Edin Th Coll 55. **d** 58 **p** 59. C Glas St Mary 58-60; C Edin St Jo 60-65; R Baillieston *Glas* 65-69; R Falkirk *Edin* 69-86; R Troon *Glas* 86-98; Can St Mary's Cathl 91-98; rtd 98; Perm to Offic *Newc* from 98. *4 Hencotes Mews, Hexham NE46 2DZ* Tel (01434) 603032

TRIMBLE, Thomas Henry. b 36. TCD BTh90. CITC 79. **d** 82 **p** 83. C Seapatrick *D & D* 82-85; I Magheracross *Clogh* 85-90; Bp's Appeal Sec 89-90; I Donegal w Killymard, Lough Eske and Laghey *D & R* 90-01; Can Raphoe Cathl 93-01; rtd 01. *Tyrone House, Tullycullion, Co Donegal, Republic of Ireland* Tel (00353) (74) 974 0706 E-mail harry.trimble@virgin.net

TRIMBY, George Henry. b 44. Trin Coll Bris 84. **d** 86 **p** 87. C Newtown w Llanllwchaiarn w Aberhafesp *St As* 86-88; P-in-c Llanfair DC, Derwen, Llanelidan and Efenechtyd 88-90; V 90-95; V Llanasa 95-09; P-in-c Whitford 98-02; P-in-c Ffynnongroew 99-09; AD Holywell 03-08; rtd 09. *The Rectory, Charlestown Road, Tubbercurry, Co Sligo, Republic of Ireland* Tel (00353) (71) 918 6909

TRIMBY (*née* SOUTHERTON), **Canon Kathryn Ruth.** b 66. Univ of Wales (Lamp) BA88. Sarum & Wells Th Coll 90. **d** 92 **p** 97. C Connah's Quay *St As* 92-97; R Halkyn w Caerfallwch w Rhesycae 97-04; I Tubbercurry w Killoran *T, K & A* from 04; Can Achonry Cathl from 11. *The Rectory, Charlestown Road, Tubbercurry, Co Sligo, Republic of Ireland* Tel (00353) (71) 918 6909 E-mail kathsoutherton@iol.ie

TRIMMER, Penelope Marynice. See DRAPER, Mrs Penelope Marynice

TRINDER, Miss Gillian Joyce. b 68. Birm Univ BA90 Bp Grosseteste Coll PGCE91. Westcott Ho Cam 09. **d** 11. C Whitkirk *Ripon* from 11. *36 Chapel Street, Leeds LS15 7RW*

TRIPLOW, Keith John. b 44. Selw Coll Cam BA66 MA70. Chich Th Coll 70. **d** 72 **p** 73. C Ipswich All Hallows *St E* 72-76; C Dartford H Trin *Roch* 76-78; V Fyfield w Tubney and Kingston Bagpuize *Ox* 78-08; rtd 08. *5 Hyde Road, Denchworth, Wantage OX12 0DR* Tel (01235) 868915

TRIST, Richard McLeod. b 55. Univ of NSW BSEd76. Ridley Coll Melbourne BTh86. **d** 87 **p** 87. C Camberwell St Jo Australia 87-88; P-in-c Cranbourne 88-91; I 91-92; Sen Assoc Min Kew St Hilary 93-96; C Langham Place All So *Lon* 97-01; V Camberwell St Mark Australia from 01; AD Camberwell 03-05. *1 Canterbury Road, Camberwell Vic 3124, Australia* Tel (0061) (3) 9897 1532 *or* 9882 3776 Fax 9882 6514 E-mail richard.trist@bigpond.com *or* stmarksc@bigpond.com

TRISTRAM, Canon Catherine Elizabeth. b 31. Somerville Coll Ox BA53 MA57. dss 83 **d** 87 **p** 94. Holy Is *Newc* 84-87; Hon C 87-01; Hon Can Newc Cathl 94-01; Perm to Offic from 01. *4 Lewins Lane, Holy Island, Berwick-upon-Tweed TD15 2SB* Tel (01289) 389306

TRISTRAM, Geoffrey Robert. b 53. K Coll Lon BA76 Pemb Coll Cam BA78 MA80. Westcott Ho Cam 77. **d** 79 **p** 80. C Weymouth H Trin *Sarum* 79-82; C Gt Berkhamsted *St Alb* 83-85; OSB 85-99; Asst Chapl Oundle Sch 86-88; Sen Chapl 88-91; R Welwyn w Ayot St Peter *St Alb* 91-99; Chapl Qu Victoria Hosp and Danesbury Home 91-99; SSJE USA from 99. *SSJE, 980 Memorial Drive, Cambridge MA 02138, USA* Tel (001) (617) 876 3037

TRISTRAM, Canon Michael Anthony. b 50. Solicitor 76 Ch Ch Coll Cam BA72 MA76. Ripon Coll Cuddesdon 79. **d** 82 **p** 83. C Stanmore *Win* 82-85; R Abbotts Ann and Upper and Goodworth Clatford 85-92; V Pershore w Pinvin, Wick and Birlingham *Worc* 92-03; Hon Can Worc Cathl 00-03; Can Res Portsm Cathl from 03. *51 High Street, Portsmouth PO1 2LU* Tel (023) 9273 1282 *or* 9234 7605 Fax 9229 5480 E-mail michael.tristram@ntlworld.com

TRIVASSE, Keith Malcolm. b 59. Man Univ BA81 CertEd82 MPhil90 Dur Univ MA98. Qu Coll Birm 84. **d** 86 **p** 87. C Prestwich St Marg *Man* 86-88; C Orford St Marg *Liv* 88-90; TV Sunderland *Dur* 90-91; P-in-c N Hylton St Marg Castletown 91-95; R Bothal and Pegswood w Longhirst *Newc* 95-97; P-in-c Bury Ch King *Man* 01-11; P-in-c Bury St Paul 01-03; C Bury,

Roch Valley from 11. *St Paul's Vicarage, Fir Street, Bury BL9 7QG* Tel 0161-761 6991 E-mail keith.trivasse@care4free.net

TRIVASSE, Ms Margaret. b 59. Dur Univ BA80 MA97 New Coll Dur PGCE01 Liv Univ MTh05. NOC 01. **d** 04 **p** 05. NSM Radcliffe *Man* 04-08; NSM Prestwich St Gabr from 08. *St Paul's Vicarage, Fir Street, Bury BL9 7QG* Tel 0161-761 6991 E-mail margtriv@yahoo.co.uk

TRODDEN, Michael John. b 54. K Coll Lon BD77 AKC77 CertEd. Wycliffe Hall Ox 79. **d** 80 **p** 81. C Woodford St Mary w St Phil and St Jas *Chelmsf* 80-87; V Aldborough Hatch 87-96; R Ampthill w Millbrook and Steppingley *St Alb* from 96. *The Rectory, Rectory Lane, Ampthill, Bedford MK45 2EL* Tel (01525) 402320

TROLLOPE, David Harvey. b 41. BSc63. Lon Coll of Div 66. **d** 68 **p** 69. C Bermondsey St Jas w Ch Ch *S'wark* 68-71; CMS Namibia 72-77; Uganda 72-77; Kenya 77-82; V Gt Crosby St Luke *Liv* 82-04; rtd 04; Perm to Offic *Ches* from 04. *26 White House Lane, Heswall, Wirral CH60 1UQ* Tel 0151-342 2648

TROMANS, Kevin Stanley. b 57. St Martin's Coll Lanc BEd79. Aston Tr Scheme 90 Coll of Resurr Mirfield 92. **d** 94 **p** 95. C Rawdon *Bradf* 94-96; C Woodhall 96-98; V Liversedge w Hightown *Wakef* 98-02; V Bierley *Bradf* 02-07; Chapl Co Durham and Darlington NHS Foundn Trust from 07. *University Hospital Durham, North Road, Durham DH1 5TW* Tel 0191-333 2333

TROMBETTI, Lynda Joan. b 52. **d** 03 **p** 04. OLM Dorking w Ranmore *Guildf* from 03. *Mead Cottage, Pilgrims Way, Westhumble, Dorking RH5 6AP* Tel and fax (01306) 884360 Mobile 07968-629364 E-mail theflyingtrombettis@talktalk.net

TROOD, James William. b 68. Cov Poly BSc90 St Jo Coll Dur PGCE91. St Jo Coll Nottm MTh02. **d** 02 **p** 03. C Anchorsholme *Blackb* 02-06; TV Glascote and Stonydelph *Lich* from 06; RD Tamworth from 09. *The Vicarage, 86 Bamford Street, Tamworth B77 2AS* Tel (01827) 305313 Mobile 07713-139571 E-mail jimtrood@btinternet.com

TROTT, Stephen. b 57. Hull Univ BA79 Fitzw Coll Cam BA83 MA87 Univ of Wales (Cardiff) LLM03 FRSA86. Westcott Ho Cam 81. **d** 84 **p** 85. C Hessle *York* 84-87; C Kingston upon Hull St Alb 87-88; R Pitsford w Boughton *Pet* from 88; Sec CME 88-93; Chapl Pitsford Sch from 91. *The Rectory, Humfrey Lane, Boughton, Northampton NN2 8RQ* Tel (01604) 845655 Mobile 07712-863000 Fax 07053-406290 E-mail revstrott@btinternet.com

TROTTER, Harold Barrington (Barry). b 33. Sarum Th Coll 64. **d** 66 **p** 67. C Salisbury St Fran *Sarum* 66-69; Dioc Youth Officer 69-72; V Horton and Chalbury 69-73; R Frenchay *Bris* 73-81; V Henbury 81-99; rtd 99; Perm to Offic *Ex* 00-02; *Glouc* from 02. *14 Butlers Mead, Blakeney GL15 4EH* Tel (01594) 510176

TROUT, Keith. b 49. Trin Coll Bris 90. **d** 92 **p** 93. C Pudsey St Lawr and St Paul *Bradf* 92-97; V Burley *Ripon* from 97. *St Matthias Vicarage, 271 Burley Road, Leeds LS4 2EL* Tel 0113-278 5872 *or* 230 4408 E-mail keithtrout03@stmatthias.co.uk

TRUBY, Canon David Charles. b 57. BA79. Linc Th Coll 79. **d** 82 **p** 83. C Stanley *Liv* 82-85; C Hindley St Pet 85-90; R Brimington *Derby* 90-98; Can Res Derby Cathl 98-03; TR Wirksworth from 03; RD Wirksworth from 08; Hon Can Derby Cathl from 04. *The Rectory, Coldwell Street, Wirksworth, Matlock DE4 4FB* Tel (01629) 824707 E-mail david.truby@btinternet.com

TRUDGETT, Raymond John. b 46. Wilson Carlile Coll 86. **d** 04 **p** 05. Port Chapl and C Aqaba SS Pet and Paul Jordan 04-06; Chapl Medway and Thames Ports *Roch* from 07; Perm to Offic *Cant* and *Chelmsf* from 07. *12 Grizedale Close, Rochester ME1 2UX* Tel (01634) 402720 E-mail trudgett831@btinternet.com

TRUDGILL, Harry Keith. b 25. LCP54 Leeds Univ DipEd49 Lon Univ BD61. St Deiniol's Hawarden 76. **d** 76 **p** 76. In Methodist Ch 58-75; C Glas St Marg 76-78; R Lenzie 78-86; rtd 86; Perm to Offic *Bradf* from 86. *10 Wharfe View, Grassington, Skipton BD23 5NL* Tel (01756) 752114

TRUMAN, Miss Catherine Jane. b 64. Coll of Ripon & York St Jo BEd88. St Jo Coll Nottm 01. **d** 03 **p** 04. C Owlerton *Sheff* 03-06; Hd Academic Progr Wilson Carlile Coll of Evang from 06. *Wilson Carlile College of Evangelism, 50 Cavendish Street, Sheffield S3 7RZ* Tel 0114-278 7020 E-mail j.truman@churcharmy.org.uk

TRUMAN, Miss Charlotte Jane. b 71. Birm Univ BPhil96. Westcott Ho Cam 96. **d** 99 **p** 00. C High Harrogate Ch Ch *Ripon* 99-03; P-in-c Oulton w Woodlesford 03-06; Chapl HM YOI Northallerton 06-09; Chapl HM Pris and YOI New Hall from 09. *HM Prison and Young Offender Institution New Hall, New Hall Way, Flockton, Wakefield WF4 4XX* Tel (01924) 803000 E-mail charlotte.truman@hmps.gsi.gov.uk

TRUMPER, Roger David. b 52. Ex Univ BSc74 K Coll Lon MSc75 Ox Univ BA80 MA85. Wycliffe Hall Ox 78. **d** 81 **p** 82. C Tunbridge Wells St Jo *Roch* 81-84; C Slough *Ox* 84-87; TV Shenley and Loughton 87-88; TV Watling Valley 88-93; R Byfleet *Guildf* 93-05; TV Sidmouth, Woolbrook, Salcombe

Regis, Sidbury etc *Ex* from 05. *All Saints' Vicarage, All Saints' Road, Sidmouth EX10 8ES* Tel (01395) 515963 E-mail roger.thetrumpers@virgin.net

TRUNDLE, Christopher Philip. b 85. Trin Coll Cam BA07 MA10 PGCE08. Coll of Resurr Mirfield 08. **d** 10 **p** 11. C Tottenham St Paul *Lon* from 10. *St Paul's Church, 60 Park Lane, London N17 0JR* E-mail chris.trundle@gmail.com

TRURO, Bishop of. *See* THORNTON, The Rt Revd Timothy Martin

TRURO, Dean of. *See* HARDWICK, The Very Revd Christopher George

TRUSS, Canon Charles Richard. b 42. Reading Univ BA63 Linacre Coll Ox BA66 MA69 K Coll Lon MPhil79. Wycliffe Hall Ox 64. **d** 66 **p** 67. C Leic H Apostles 66-69; C Hampstead St Jo *Lon* 69-72; V Belsize Park 72-79; V Wood Green St Mich 79-82; TR Wood Green St Mich w Bounds Green St Gabr etc 82-85; R Shepperton 85-94; V Waterloo St Jo w St Andr *S'wark* 94-08; RD Lambeth 95-05; Hon Can S'wark Cathl 01-08; Sen Chapl Actors' Ch Union 04-08; rtd 08; Perm to Offic *S'wark* from 08. *12 Camden Cottages, Church Walk, Weybridge KT13 8JT* E-mail richard.truss@btinternet.com

TRUSTRAM, Canon David Geoffrey. b 49. Pemb Coll Ox BA71 MA76 Qu Coll Cam BA73 MA77. Westcott Ho Cam 74. **d** 75 **p** 76. C Surbiton St Mark *S'wark* 75-77; C Surbiton St Andr and St Mark 77-78; C Richmond St Mary w St Matthias and St Jo 78-82; P-in-c Eastry *Cant* 82-88; R Eastry and Northbourne w Tilmanstone etc 88-90; Chapl Eastry Hosp 82-90; V Tenterden St Mildred w Smallhythe *Cant* 90-10; P-in-c Tenterden St Mich 07-10; Hon Can Cant Cathl 96-10; AD Tenterden 99-05; rtd 10; Perm to Offic *Cant* from 11. *Hensmead, New Road, Headcorn, Ashford TN27 9SE* Tel (01622) 892480 Mobile 07811-874806 E-mail trustram@btinternet.com

TSANG, Wing Man. b 52. Lon Univ BSc74 MPhil84 MCB88 MRCPath88 FRCPath96. STETS 99. **d** 02 **p** 03. C Merthyr Tydfil Ch Ch *Llan* 02-05; TV Broadwater *Chich* from 05. *67 Normandy Road, Worthing BN14 7EA* Tel 07961-839018 (mobile) E-mail wing2699@hotmail.com

TSIPOURAS, John George. b 38. Trin Coll Bris 76. **d** 78 **p** 79. C Cheadle Hulme St Andr *Ches* 78-82; V Hurdsfield 82-03; rtd 03; P-in-c W Heath *Birm* from 04; Perm to Offic *Cov* from 04. *5 Ashfurlong Close, Balsall Common, Coventry CV7 7QA* Tel (01676) 534048 E-mail john@tsipouras.org.uk

TUAM, Archdeacon of. *See* HASTINGS, The Ven Gary Lea

TUAM, Dean of. *See* GRIMASON, The Very Revd Alistair John

TUAM, KILLALA AND ACHONRY, Bishop of. *See* ROOKE, The Rt Revd Patrick William

TUAM, Provost of. *See* SANDES, The Very Revd Denis Lindsay

TUBBS, Preb Brian Ralph. b 44. AKC66. **d** 67 **p** 68. C Ex St Thos 67-72; TV Sidmouth, Woolbrook and Salcombe Regis 72-77; R Ex St Jas 77-96; RD Christianity 89-95; V Paignton St Jo and Chapl S Devon Healthcare NHS Foundn Trust 96-09; Preb Ex Cathl 95-09; rtd 09. *58 Dorset Avenue, Exeter EX4 1ND* Tel (01392) 200506 E-mail brtubbs@virginmedia.com

TUBBS, Gary Andrew. b 59. Univ of Wales (Swansea) BA82 Bris Univ MSc84 Bris Poly PGCE84. Oak Hill Th Coll. **d** 00 **p** 01. C Stanwix *Carl* 00-02; C Carl H Trin St Barn 02-08; P-in-c Pennington and Lindal w Marton and Bardsea from 08. *Trinkeld Vicarage, Main Road, Swarthmoor, Ulverston LA12 0RZ* Tel (01229) 583174 E-mail garytubbs@bigfoot.com

TUBBS, Mrs Margaret Amy. b 39. SWMTC. **d** 01. OLM St Martin in Looe *Truro* 01-05; Warden Epiphany Ho 04-08; C Liskeard and St Keyne from 06. *An Gwella House, Brentfields, Looe PL13 2JJ* Tel (01503) 272425 E-mail stablesretreat@onetel.com

TUBBS, Peter Alfred. b 22. G&C Coll Cam BA48 MA53. Linc Th Coll 55. **d** 57 **p** 58. C Tettenhall Regis *Lich* 57-60; C Wellington Ch Ch 60-64; Asst Chapl Keele Univ 65-69; V Cardington *St Alb* 69-85; RD Elstow 77-82; C Sandy 85-89; rtd 89; Perm to Offic *St Alb* from 89. *24 Dulverton Hall, Esplanade, Scarborough YO11 2AR* Tel (01723) 340124

TUCK, Canon Andrew Kenneth. b 42. Kelham Th Coll 63. **d** 68 **p** 69. C Poplar *Lon* 68-74; TV 74-76; V Walsgrave on Sowe *Cov* 76-90; R Farnham *Guildf* from 90; Chapl Surrey Hants Borders NHS Trust 90-95; Chapl Surrey and Borders Partnership NHS Trust from 05; RD Farnham *Guildf* 00-05; Hon Can Guildf Cathl from 09. *The Rectory, Upper Church Lane, Farnham GU9 7PW* Tel (01252) 715412 E-mail office@standrewsfarnham.org

TUCK, David John. b 36. St Cath Coll Cam BA61 MA65. Cuddesdon Coll 61. **d** 63 **p** 64. C Holt and Kelling w Salthouse *Nor* 63-68; Zambia 68-73; V Sprowston *Nor* 73-84; R Beeston St Andr 73-84; RD Nor N 81-84; V Pinner *Lon* 84-01; rtd 01; Perm to Offic *Lon* 02-04 and *St Alb* from 04; Hon C N Harrow St Alb *Lon* from 04. *119 High Street, Northwood HA6 1ED* Tel (01923) 825806 E-mail dandtuck@freeuk.com

TUCK, Gillian. b 40. SRN64 SCM66. Llan Dioc Tr Scheme 93. **d** 97 **p** 98. NSM Pontypridd St Cath w St Matt *Llan* 97-01; P-in-c Pontypridd St Matt and Cilfynydd 01-05; NSM

Pontypridd St Matt and Cilfynydd w Llanwynno 05-08; rtd 08. *4 Maes Glas, Coed y Cwm, Pontypridd CF37 3EJ* Tel (01443) 791049

TUCK, Nigel Graham. b 57. Chich Th Coll 82. **d** 85 **p** 86. C Port Talbot St Theodore *Llan* 85-87; C Llantrisant 87-90; TV Duston *Pet* 90-95; C Aldwick *Chich* 95-98; C-in-c N Bersted CD 98-00; V N Bersted 01-02; rtd 02. *1 Yr Arglawdd, Heathwood Road, Cardiff CF14 4GH*

TUCK, Ralph Thomas. b 42. Worc Coll Ox BA64 Bris Univ CertEd66. NOC 87. **d** 90 **p** 91. NSM S Crosland *Wakef* 90-93; NSM Helme 90-93; Perm to Offic 93-05. *48 Kirkwood Drive, Huddersfield HD3 3WJ*

TUCK, Canon Ronald James. b 47. S'wark Ord Course 75. **d** 78 **p** 79. C Upper Holloway St Pet w St Jo *Lon* 78-81; P-in-c Scottow and Swanton Abbott w Skeyton *Nor* 81-88; R Bradwell from 88; Hon Can Nor Cathl from 10. *The Rectory, Church Walk, Bradwell, Great Yarmouth NR31 8QQ* Tel (01493) 663219 E-mail revtuck@evemail.net

TUCKER, Andrew Michael. b 64. K Coll Lon BD87. Wycliffe Hall Ox 93. **d** 95 **p** 96. C Moreton *Ches* 95-96; C Poynton 96-99; C Polegate *Chich* 99-02; C-in-c Lower Willingdon St Wilfrid CD from 03. *St Wilfrid's House, 90 Broad Road, Lower Willingdon, Eastbourne BN20 9RA* Tel (01323) 482088 E-mail tucker.a@btconnect.com

TUCKER, Canon Anthony Ian. b 50. CA Tr Coll 73 S'wark Ord Course 81. **d** 85 **p** 86. NSM E Ham w Upton Park *Chelmsf* 85-86; NSM S'well Minster 86-90; C Rolleston w Fiskerton, Morton and Upton 90-93; P-in-c Teversal 93-96; Chapl Sutton Cen 93-96; P-in-c Norwell w Ossington, Cromwell and Caunton 96-04; Dioc Tourism Adv 96-04; V Balderton and Barnby-in-the-Willows from 04; AD Newark from 00; Jt AD Newark and S'well from 08; Hon Can S'well Minster from 08. *The Vicarage, Main Street, Balderton, Newark NG24 3NN* Tel (01636) 704811 E-mail tony@cloud9-online.com

TUCKER, Ms Catherine Jane. b 62. Birkbeck Coll Lon BA97. Westcott Ho Cam 09. **d** 11. C Perry Hill St Geo w Ch Ch and St Paul *S'wark* from 11. *20 Gaynesford Road, London SE23 2UQ* Tel (020) 8699 3466 E-mail curateperryhill@hotmail.co.uk

TUCKER, Desmond Robert. b 29. Bris Sch of Min 83. **d** 86 **p** 87. C Bris St Mich 86-88; P-in-c 88-94; rtd 94; Perm to Offic *Bris* from 94. *48 Cranbrook Road, Bristol BS6 7BT* Tel 0117-373 5584

TUCKER, Douglas Greening. b 17. St Aid Birkenhead 49. **d** 52 **p** 53. C Jesmond Clayton Memorial *Newc* 52-56; C Fenham St Jas and St Basil 56-58; V Cowgate 58-62; V Elsham *Linc* 62-85; V Worlaby 62-85; V Bonby 73-85; rtd 85; Perm to Offic *Newc* 85-02. *Balintore, 4 Kilrymont Place, St Andrews KY16 8DH* Tel (01334) 476738

TUCKER, Mrs Gillian Mary. b 57. Bris Poly BEd79. WEMTC 04. **d** 07 **p** 08. NSM Sharpness, Purton, Brookend and Slimbridge *Glouc* from 07. *Hinton Cottage, Hinton, Berkeley GL13 9HZ* Tel (01453) 811105

TUCKER, Harold George. b 21. St Aug Coll Cant 48 Sarum Th Coll 50. **d** 51 **p** 52. C S Molton w Nymet St George *Ex* 51-56; V Mariansleigh and Romansleigh w Meshaw 56-64; R Bratton Fleming 64-73; P-in-c Goodleigh 67-73; P-in-c Stoke Rivers 67-73; P-in-c Parracombe 69-73; P-in-c Martinhoe 69-73; R Whimple 73-86; rtd 86; Perm to Offic *Ex* and *Truro* 86-09. *St Anne's Residential Home, Whitstone, Holsworthy EX22 6UA* Tel (01288) 341800

TUCKER, Ian Malcolm. b 46. S Dios Minl Tr Scheme 86. **d** 89 **p** 90. NSM Pill w Easton in Gordano and Portbury *B & W* 89-95; C Frome St Jo and St Mary 95-99; TV Redruth w Lanner and Treleigh *Truro* 99-04; P-in-c Par from 04; Hon Chapl Miss to Seafarers from 04. *The Vicarage, 42 Vicarage Road, Tywardreath, Par PL24 2PH* Tel (01726) 812775 E-mail iandm@btopenworld.com

TUCKER, Jill. b 47. UMIST BSc68 MSc69 PhD77. Qu Coll Birm 05. **d** 06 **p** 07. NSM Ilmington w Stretton-on-Fosse etc *Cov* 06-09; NSM Shipston-on-Stour w Honington and Idlicote from 09; RD Shipston from 09; Dean of Self-Supporting Min from 11. *The Old House, Back Lane, Oxhill, Warwick CV35 0QN* Tel (01295) 680663 Fax 688103 Mobile 07973-994800 E-mail revjill.tucker@tiscali.co.uk

TUCKER, John Yorke Raffles. b 24. Magd Coll Cam BA49 MA56. Westcott Ho Cam 49. **d** 51 **p** 52. C Shadwell St Paul w Ratcliffe St Jas *Lon* 51-54; C Preston Ascension 54-58; V St Hackney St Mich 58-67; V Belmont 67-78; V Sunbury 78-89; rtd 89; Perm to Offic *Ex* 89-93 and *B & W* from 93. *Tudor Cottage, Fivehead, Taunton TA3 6PJ* Tel (01460) 281330

TUCKER (*née* RAMSAY), Kerry. b 59. Heythrop Coll Lon MA94. Westcott Ho Cam 92. **d** 94 **p** 96. C Westville St Eliz S Africa 95-96; C Charlton St Luke w H Trin *S'wark* 96-99; C Cambridge Gt St Mary w St Mich *Ely* 99-04; V Sunninghill *Ox* 04-08; P-in-c S Ascot 07-08; Perm to Offic from 08; Hon C Byfleet *Guildf* 09-10; Hon C E Horsley and Ockham w Hatchford and Downside from 10. *Diocesan House, Quarry Street, Guildford GU1 3XG* E-mail kerry.ramsay@virgin.net

TUCKER, Michael. b 33. d 84 p 85. NSM Sawston *Ely* 84-87; C Ely 87-90; P-in-c Barton Bendish w Beachamwell and Shingham 90-98; P-in-c Wereham 90-98; rtd 98; Perm to Offic *Nor* 99-04 and *Ely* from 00. *20 Priory Lane, King's Lynn PE30 5DU* Tel (01553) 774707

TUCKER, Canon Michael Owen. b 42. Lon Univ BSc66 Surrey Univ PhD69. Glouc Sch of Min 81. d 84 p 85. NSM Uley w Owlpen and Nympsfield *Glouc* 84-92; P-in-c Amberley 92-09; Dioc NSM Officer 94-09; Hon Can Glouc Cathl 98-09; RD Stonehouse 99-04; rtd 09. *18 Bownham Mead, Rodborough Common, Stroud GL5 5DZ* Tel (01453) 873352
E-mail mike@tuckers.org.uk

TUCKER, Nicholas Harold. b 41. Reading Univ BSc66. NOC 90. d 93 p 94. NSM Ilkley All SS *Bradf* 93-98; P-in-c Uley w Owlpen and Nympsfield *Glouc* 98-06; rtd 06; NSM Nailsworth w Shortwood, Horsley etc *Glouc* 07-08. *29 The Chipping, Tetbury GL8 8EU* Tel (01666) 503188
E-mail nick@tucker141.fsnet.co.uk

TUCKER, Nicholas John Cuthbert. b 74. Birm Univ BSc. Oak Hill Th Coll MTh04. d 04 p 05. C Bebington *Ches* 04-07; Research Fell Oak Hill Th Coll from 07. *Oak Hill Theological College, Chase Side, London N14 4PS* Tel 07957-566714 (mobile) E-mail njctucker@hotmail.com

TUCKER, Richard Parish. b 51. Cam Univ BA72 MA76 Lon Univ BD83. Wycliffe Hall Ox 80. d 83 p 84. C Wellington w Eyton *Lich* 83-84; C Walsall 84-88; TV Dronfield *Derby* 88-90; TV Dronfield w Holmesfield 90-98; V Sutton Coldfield St Columba *Birm* from 98. *St Columba's Vicarage, 280 Chester Road North, Sutton Coldfield B73 6RR* Tel 0121-354 5873
E-mail richardtucker@tiscali.co.uk

TUCKER, Stephen Reid. b 51. New Coll Ox BA72 MA76. Ripon Coll Cuddesdon. d 77 p 78. C Hove All SS *Chich* 77-80; Lect Chich Th Coll 80-86; V Portsea St Alb *Portsm* 86-90; Chapl and Dean of Div New Coll Ox 90-95; P-in-c Ovingdean *Chich* 96-01; Bp's Adv on CME 96-01; V Hampstead St Jo *Lon* from 01. *The Vicarage, 14 Church Row, London NW3 6UU* Tel (020) 7435 0553 *or* 7794 5808 E-mail stucker957@btinternet.com

TUCKER, Mrs Susan. b 53. Stockwell Coll of Educn CertEd74. d 97 p 98. C Taunton St Andr *B & W* 97-01; V Bishops Hull 01-10; RD Taunton 06-10; Chapl St Marg Hospice Taunton 01-07; R Chard St Mary w Combe St Nicholas, Wambrook etc *B & W* from 10. *The Vicarage, Forton Road, Chard TA20 2HJ* Tel (01460) 62320 E-mail suetucker99@btinternet.com

TUCKER, Vivian Clive Temple. b 39. Univ of Wales (Swansea) BSc60 Univ of Wales DipEd61. St As Minl Tr Course 93. d 96 p 97. NSM Gresford w Holt *St As* 96-04; NSM Holt, Rossett and Isycoed 04-09; rtd 09; Perm to Offic *St As* from 09. *8 Snowdon Drive, Ty Gwyn, Wrexham LL11 2UY* Tel (01978) 359226

TUCKETT, Prof Christopher Mark. b 48. Qu Coll Cam MA71 Lanc Univ PhD79. Westcott Ho Cam 71. d 75 p 76. C Lancaster St Mary *Blackb* 75-77; Chapl and Fell Qu Coll Cam 77-79; Lect NT Man Univ 79-89; Sen Lect 89-91; Prof Bibl Studies 91-96; Lect NT Ox Univ 96-06; Prof NT Studies from 06. *Pembroke College, Oxford OX1 1DW* Tel (01865) 276426
E-mail christopher.tuckett@theology.ox.ac.uk

TUCKWELL, Jonathan David. b 77. St Jo Coll Cam MEng00 MA02. Oak Hill Th Coll BA11. d 11. C Cambridge St Andr Less *Ely* from 11. *48 College Fields, Woodhead Drive, Cambridge CB4 1YZ* Tel 07785-576939 (mobile)
E-mail jon@jon-ruth.co.uk

TUCKWELL, Richard Graham. b 46. SS Mark & Jo Univ Coll Plymouth TCert67 Open Univ BA. d 07 p 08. NSM Tarvin *Ches* 07-09; P-in-c Alvanley from 09. *The Vicarage, 47 Arden Lea, Alvanley, Frodsham WA6 9EQ* Tel (01928) 722012 Mobile 07713-485318 E-mail richardtuckwell@tiscali.co.uk

TUDGE, Paul Quartus. b 52. Leeds Univ BEd78. Cranmer Hall Dur 84. d 87 p 88. C Roundhay St Edm *Ripon* 87-90; C Leeds City 91; V Woodside 91-99; Warden of Readers 96-99; V Ilkley All SS *Bradf* 99-08; RD Otley 02-08; P-in-c Farsley from 08; RD Calverley from 10. *The Vicarage, 9 St John's Avenue, Farsley, Pudsey LS28 5DN* Tel 0113-257 0059
E-mail paul.tudge@bradford.anglican.org

TUDGEY, Stephen John. b 51. Nottm Univ BTh81 Westmr Coll Ox MTh00. St Jo Coll Nottm LTh81. d 81 p 82. C Grays Thurrock *Chelmsf* 81-84; C Madeley *Heref* 84-87; R Chilcompton w Downside and Stratton on the Fosse *B & W* 87-03; P-in-c Falmouth K Chas *Truro* from 03; Hon Chapl Miss to Seafarers from 04. *The Rectory, 19 Trescobeas Road, Falmouth TR11 2JB* Tel (01326) 319141
E-mail steve.tudgey@tiscali.co.uk

TUDOR, David Charles Frederick. b 42. Sarum Th Coll 70. d 73 p 74. C Plymouth St Pet *Ex* 73-75; C Reddish *Man* 75-78; P-in-c Hamer 78-80; V Goldenhill *Lich* 80-87; V Meir 87-91; Chapl Asst Nottm City Hosp 91-94; Chapl Cen Sheff Univ Hosps NHS Trust 94-96; V Nottingham St Geo w St Jo *S'well* 96-04; rtd 05; Perm to Offic *Derby* and *S'well* from 05. *102 St Albans Road, Nottingham NG6 9HG* Tel 0115-975 0184 Mobile 07811-866348

TUDOR, David St Clair. b 55. K Coll Lon BD77 AKC77 K Coll Lon MTh89. Ripon Coll Cuddesdon 77. d 78 p 79. C Plumstead St Nic *S'wark* 78-80; C Redhill St Matt 80-83; C-in-c Reigate St Phil CD 83-87; Asst Sec Gen Syn Bd for Miss and Unity 87-88; Perm to Offic *S'wark* 94-97; TV Canvey Is *Chelmsf* 97-00; TR from 00; AD Hadleigh from 08. *St Nicholas House, 210 Long Road, Canvey Island SS8 0JR* Tel (01268) 682586
E-mail dstudor@tiscali.co.uk

TUFFIN, Mrs Gillian Patricia. b 43. S Dios Minl Tr Scheme 91. d 94 p 95. C Gidea Park *Chelmsf* 94-98; TV Stoke-upon-Trent *Lich* 98-01; Admin and Prayer Co-ord Shalom Chr Healing Cen from 02; NSM Northolt Park St Barn *Lon* 02-08; Perm to Offic from 08. *76 Stowe Crescent, Ruislip HA4 7SS* Tel (020) 8864 5394 E-mail g.tuffin@btopenworld.com

TUFFNELL, Nigel Owen. b 65. Teesside Poly BSc90. St Jo Coll Nottm 91. d 94 p 95. C Guisborough *York* 94-97; P-in-c Northwold *Ely* 97-98; P-in-c Stoke Ferry w Wretton 97-98; P-in-c Whittington 97-98; R Northwold and Wretton w Stoke Ferry etc 98-03; Bp's Adv on Environmental Issues 02-03; TR Kegworth, Hathern, Long Whatton, Diseworth etc *Leic* 04-06; Perm to Offic *Nor* 10; Hon C Hopton w Corton from 10. *17 Blyford Road, Lowestoft NR32 4PZ* Tel (01502) 583389

TUFNELL, Edward Nicholas Pember. b 45. Chu Coll Cam MA68. St Jo Coll Nottm BA73. d 73 p 74. C Ealing St Mary *Lon* 73-76; BCMS Tanzania 76-88; P-in-c Lt Thurrock St Jo *Chelmsf* 89-91; V Grays North 91-98; Chapl Thurrock Community Hosp Grays 89-98; P-in-c Bourton-on-the-Water w Clapton *Glouc* 98-05; R Bourton-on-the-Water w Clapton etc 05-11; AD Stow 09-10; rtd 11. *Karibuni, 37 Harrold Priory, Bedford MK41 0SD* Tel (01234) 215440 Mobile 07816-123470
E-mail e.tufnell1979@btinternet.com

TUFNELL, Michael. b 81. Imp Coll Lon BEng05. St Mellitus Coll MA10. d 10 p 11. C Enfield Ch Ch Trent Park *Lon* from 10. *13 Wilton Road, Cockfosters, Barnet EN4 9DX* Tel 07977-139544 (mobile) E-mail michaeltufnell@gmail.com

TUFT, Preb Patrick Anthony. b 31. Selw Coll Cam BA56 MA60. Edin Th Coll 56. d 58 p 59. C Keighley *Bradf* 58-63; PV Chich Cathl 63-68; Min Can St Paul's Cathl 68-74; Hon Min Can St Paul's Cathl 74-94; V Chiswick St Nic w St Mary 74-06; PV Westmr Abbey 74-79; AD Hounslow *Lon* 87-93; P-in-c Chiswick St Paul Grove Park 88-90; Preb St Paul's Cathl 95-06; rtd 07. *68 Worple Road, Isleworth TW7 7HU* Tel (020) 8581 3014 Mobile 07768-892099 E-mail patrick@tuft.tv

TUGWELL, Elizabeth Ann. b 36. SWMTC. d 94 p 95. NSM Ludgvan *Truro* 94-97; NSM St Hilary w Perranuthnoe 94-97; Perm to Offic 99-05; P-in-c Stranraer *Glas* from 05; P-in-c Portpatrick from 05. *Dalry Farmhouse, Kirkcolm, Stranraer DG9 0QD* Tel (01776) 853582

TULK, Giles David. b 65. Leeds Univ BA86. ERMC 06. d 09 p 10. C Stansted Mountfitchet w Birchanger and Farnham *Chelmsf* 09-11; C Bocking St Mary from 11. *3 Hadley Close, Braintree CM7 5LP* E-mail gtulk@waitrose.com

TULL, Preb Christopher Stuart. b 36. Hertf Coll Ox BA60 MA64. Oak Hill Th Coll 60. d 62 p 63. C Stoodleigh *Ex* 62-71; C Washfield 62-71; TV Washfield, Stoodleigh, Withleigh etc 71-74; RD Tiverton 74-75; R Bishops Nympton w Rose Ash 75-77; V Mariansleigh 75-77; TR Bishopsnympton, Rose Ash, Mariansleigh etc 77-99; RD S Molton 80-87 and 95-99; Preb Ex Cathl 84-99; rtd 99; Perm to Offic *B & W* from 04. *The Old Smithy, Challacombe, Barnstaple EX31 4TU* Tel (01598) 763201

TULLETT, Paul Budworth. b 71. Lanc Univ BSc92 Birm Univ MBA00 Anglia Ruskin Univ BA09. Ridley Hall Cam 07. d 09 p 10. C Taunton St Mary *B & W* from 09. *The Glebe House, Whirligig Lane, Taunton TA1 1SQ* Tel (07738-042217 (mobile) E-mail paulof3decades@hotmail.com

TULLETT, Peter Watts. b 46. Qu Coll Birm 92. d 94 p 95. C Worle *B & W* 94-96; Chapl HM YOI Portland 96-01; Perm to Offic *B & W* 02-04; Hon C Uphill 04-06; Perm to Offic from 05. *2 Ferry Lane, Lympsham, Weston-super-Mare BS24 0BT* Tel (01934) 814284 E-mail peter@tullett73.fsnet.co.uk

TULLOCH, Richard James Anthony. b 52. Wadh Coll Ox BA74 Selw Coll Cam BA79. Ridley Hall Cam 76. d 79 p 80. C Morden *S'wark* 79-83; C Jesmond Clayton Memorial *Newc* 83-94; V New Borough and Leigh *Sarum* 94-11; TR Eden, Gelt and Irthing *Carl* from 11. *St Martin's Vicarage, Main Street, Brampton CA8 1SH* Tel (016977) 43104 E-mail rjatulloch@gmail.com

TULLY, David John. b 56. St Jo Coll Dur BA77 Nottm Univ PGCE78. Ridley Hall Cam 81. d 84 p 85. C Gosforth St Nic *Newc* 84-86; C Newburn 86-90; TV Whorlton 90-96; V 96-00; R Gateshead Fell *Dur* 00-09; R Chester le Street from 09. *The Rectory, Lindisfarne Avenue, Chester le Street DH3 3PT* Tel 0191-388 4027 E-mail david.tully@tesco.net

TULLY, Janet Florence. b 43. d 03 p 04. OLM Margate St Jo *Cant* 03-08; Perm to Offic *Nor* from 09. *4 Westgate Court, Wymondham NR18 0PX* Tel 07866-839275 (mobile)

TUNBRIDGE, Genny Louise. b 64. Clare Coll Cam BA85 St Cross Coll Ox DPhil93. Qu Coll Birm BD95. d 96 p 97. C Boston *Linc* 96-00; Lect 00-01; Prec Chelmsf Cathl 01-06; Can

Res 02-06; V Gosforth All SS *Newc* from 06. *All Saints' Vicarage, 33 Brackenfield Road, Newcastle upon Tyne NE3 4DX* Tel 0191-246 1155 *or* 213 0450 E-mail g.tunbridge@allsaints-gosforth.org.uk

TUNGAY, Michael Ian. b 45. Oak Hill Th Coll 70. **d** 73 **p** 74. C Fulham St Mary N End *Lon* 73-75; C Hammersmith St Simon 76-79; P-in-c 79-84; Perm to Offic *S'wark* from 09. *7 Lily Close, London W14 9YA* Tel (020) 8748 3151 E-mail miketungay@uk2.net

TUNLEY, Timothy Mark. b 61. Ridley Hall Cam 89. **d** 92 **p** 93. C Aldborough w Boroughbridge and Roecliffe *Ripon* 92-95; C Knaresborough 95-98; V Swaledale 98-05; TV Seacroft 05-09; Dioc Adv for NSM 03-08; Chapl Miss to Seafarers from 09. *109 Avalon Gardens, Linlithgow Bridge, Linlithgow EH49 7PL* E-mail timtunley@hotmail.com

TUNNICLIFFE, Mrs Jean Sarah. b 36. RGN69. Glouc Sch of Min 89. **d** 92 **p** 94. NSM Dixton *Heref* 92-05; Perm to Offic from 05. *Bryn Awelon, 21 Ridgeway, Wyesham, Monmouth NP25 3JX* Tel (01600) 714115

TUNNICLIFFE, Canon Martin Wyndham. b 31. Keele Univ BA56. Qu Coll Birm 59. **d** 60 **p** 61. C Castle Bromwich SS Mary and Marg *Birm* 60-65; V Shard End 65-73; R Over Whitacre w Shustoke 73-78; V Tanworth 78-88; RD Solihull 89-94; Hon Can Birm Cathl 91-98; rtd 98; Perm to Offic *Birm* from 98. *202 Ralph Road, Shirley, Solihull B90 3LE* Tel and fax 0121-745 6522 E-mail martin@ralph202.wanadoo.co.uk

TUNNICLIFFE, Mrs Siv. b 33. Stockholm Univ MPhil58. SAOMC 94. **d** 97 **p** 98. OLM Wingrave w Rowsham, Aston Abbotts and Cublington *Ox* from 97; OLM Wing w Grove from 04. *Baldway House, Wingrave, Aylesbury HP22 4PA* Tel and fax (01296) 681374

TUNSTALL, Barry Anthony. b 29. Sarum Th Coll 53. **d** 55 **p** 56. C Croxley Green All SS *St Alb* 55-58; C Apsley End 58-63; V N Mymms 63-81; R Kirkby Overblow *Ripon* 81-94; rtd 94; Perm to Offic *B & W* from 01. *23 Mondyes Court, Wells BA5 2QX* Tel (01749) 677004

TUPLING, Mrs Catherine Louise. b 74. Westhill Coll Birm BTh96. Wycliffe Hall Ox 01. **d** 03 **p** 04. C Belper *Derby* 03-07; P-in-c Hathersage w Bamford and Derwent 07-08; P-in-c Hathersage w Bamford and Derwent and Grindleford from 08. *The Vicarage, Church Bank, Hathersage, Hope Valley S32 1AJ* Tel (01433) 650215 E-mail revtup@tup-house.freeserve.co.uk

TUPPER, Michael Heathfield. b 20. St Edm Hall Ox BA41 MA46. Ridley Hall Cam 41. **d** 43 **p** 44. C Win Ch Ch 43-45; Chapl Monkton Combe Sch Bath 45-48; Asst Chapl Shrewsbury Sch 48-59 and 60-79; Kenya 59-60; Hon C Bayston Hill *Lich* 80-98; rtd 98; Perm to Offic *Lich* 99-08. *9 Eric Lock Road, Bayston Hill, Shrewsbury SY3 0HQ* Tel (01743) 722674

✠**TUREI, The Most Revd William Brown.** b 24. BTS76. **d** 49 **p** 50 **c** 92. C Tauranga New Zealand 49-52; V Whangaro Pastorate 52-59; V Te Puke Tauranga Miss Distr 59-64; V Ruatoki Whakatane Pastorate 64-70; V Turanga Pastorate 70-74; V Phillipstown and Maori Missr 74-81; V Waipatu-Moteo Pastorate 81-84; Chapl Napier Pris 84-88; Taonga Whakamana Mahi Minita 89-92; Adn Tairawhiti 82-92; Bp in Tairawhiti 92-05; Bp Aotearoa from 05; Abp New Zealand from 06. *PO Box 568, Gisborne, New Zealand* Tel (0064) (6) 867 8856 Fax 867 8859

TURLEY, Debra. b 67. Oak Hill Th Coll BA91. LCTP 07. **d** 10 **p** 11. C Utley *Bradf* from 10. *10 Railway Street, Utley, Keighley BD20 6AQ* Tel (01535) 500031 E-mail debbi.turley@sky.com

✠**TURNBULL, The Rt Revd Anthony Michael Arnold.** b 35. CBE03 DL05. Keble Coll Ox BA58 MA62 Dur Univ Hon DD03. Cranmer Hall Dur. **d** 60 **p** 61 **c** 88. C Middleton *Man* 60-61; C Luton w E Hyde *St Alb* 61-65; Dir of Ords *York* 65-69; Abp's Dom Chapl 65-69; Chapl York Univ 69-76; V Heslington 69-76; Chief Sec CA 76-84; Can Res Roch Cathl 84-88; Adn Roch 84-88; Bp Roch 88-94; Bp Dur 94-03; rtd 03; Hon Asst Bp *Cant* and *Eur* from 03. *67 Strand Street, Sandwich CT13 9HN* Tel (01304) 611389 E-mail bstmt@btopenworld.com

TURNBULL, Brian Robert. b 43. Chich Th Coll 71. **d** 74 **p** 75. C Norbury St Phil *Cant* 74-76; C Folkestone St Sav 76-77; Hon C Tong *Lich* 83-88; C Jarrow *Dur* 88-89; TV 89-94; P-in-c Hartlepool St Oswald 94-96; V 96-04; rtd 04. *50 The Chare, Leazes Square, Newcastle upon Tyne NE1 4DD* Tel 0191-221 2312 E-mail frbrian@turnbull23.freeserve.co.uk

TURNBULL, James Awty. b 28. Solicitor Bradf Univ HonDLaws97. Cranmer Hall Dur 89. **d** 89 **p** 90. NSM Bolton Abbey *Bradf* 89-98; Perm to Offic from 98. *Deerstones Cottage, Deerstones, Skipton BD23 6JB*

TURNBULL, Michael. See TURNBULL, The Rt Revd Anthony Michael Arnold

TURNBULL, Michael Francis. b 62. Liv Univ BTh99. NOC 95. **d** 98 **p** 99. C Birkenhead Ch Ch *Ches* 98-02; P-in-c Leasowe 02-08; R Wistaston from 08; Asst Warden of Readers from 04. *The Rectory, 44 Church Lane, Wistaston, Crewe CW2 8HA* Tel (01270) 665742 *or* 567119 Mobile 07595-908644 E-mail mfturnbull@gmail.com

TURNBULL, Peter Frederick. b 64. SS Mark & Jo Univ Coll Plymouth BA85. Sarum & Wells Th Coll BTh91. **d** 91 **p** 92. C Upper Norwood All SS *S'wark* 91-95; Chapl HM Pris Dorchester 95-98; C Dorchester *Sarum* 95-98; NSM Melbury 98-99; C Maltby *Sheff* 99-02; TV 02-08; TV Crosslacon *Carl* from 08. *The Vicarage, Trumpet Road, Cleator CA23 3EF* Tel (01946) 810510 E-mail p.turnbull@dogcollar.org.uk

TURNBULL, Richard Duncan. b 60. Reading Univ BA82 St Jo Coll Dur BA92 Dur Univ PhD97 Ox Univ MA05 MICAS85. Cranmer Hall Dur 90. **d** 94 **p** 95. C Portswood Ch Ch *Win* 94-98; V Chineham 98-05; Prin Wycliffe Hall Ox from 05. *Wycliffe Hall, 54 Banbury Road, Oxford OX2 6PW* Tel (01865) 274200 Fax 274215 E-mail richard.turnbull@wycliffe.ox.ac.uk

TURNBULL, Mrs Sally Elizabeth. b 55. Bp Grosseteste Coll BEd78. **d** 11. OLM Owmby Gp *Linc* from 11. *Sunnymede, Faldingworth Road, Spridlington, Market Rasen LN8 2DF* Tel (01673) 862764 E-mail supersonicsal55@gmail.com

TURNBULL, William George. b 25. Lich Th Coll 63. **d** 65 **p** 66. C Nunhead St Silas *S'wark* 65-69; C Portishead *B & W* 69-73; C Holsworthy w Cookbury *Ex* 73-76; P-in-c Bridgerule 76-79; P-in-c Pyworthy w Pancraswyke 77-79; P-in-c Pyworthy, Pancrasweek and Bridgerule 79-80; R 80-81; V Otterton and Colaton Raleigh 81-90; rtd 90; Chapl Convent Companions Jes Gd Shep W Ogwell 90-94; Perm to Offic *Chich* from 94 and *S'wark* 00-07. *The College of St Barnabas, Blackberry Lane, Lingfield RH7 6NJ* Tel (01342) 872871

TURNER, Alan James. b 40. Oak Hill Th Coll BA81. **d** 81 **p** 82. C Bradley *Wakef* 81-84; C Sandal St Helen 84-86; P-in-c Sileby *Leic* 86-87; TR Sileby, Cossington and Seagrave 87-94; R Hollington St Leon *Chich* 94-01; R Frant w Eridge 01-08; rtd 08; Perm to Offic *York* from 10. *Charters Garth, Hutton-le-Hole, York YO62 6UD* Tel (01751) 411949 E-mail alan@ajturner.wanadoo.co.uk

TURNER, Alan Roy. b 51. Sheff Univ BA96 MA99. EMMTC. **d** 00 **p** 01. C Bladon w Woodstock *Ox* 00-03; Chapl Cokethorpe Sch Witney 01-03; TV Brize Norton and Carterton *Ox* 03-09; P-in-c Stonesfield w Combe Longa from 09. *The Rectory, Brook Lane, Stonesfield, Witney OX29 8PR* Tel (01993) 898552 Mobile 07777-670006 E-mail r.turner131@btinternet.com

TURNER, Albert Edward. b 41. Glouc Sch of Min 83. **d** 89 **p** 90. C Woodford St Mary w St Phil and St Jas *Chelmsf* 89-91; R Greatworth and Marston St Lawrence etc *Pet* 91-99; R Somersham w Pidley and Oldhurst *Ely* 99-02; rtd 02; Perm to Offic *St Alb* from 04. *83 Horslow Street, Potton, Sandy SG19 2NX* Tel (01767) 260566 Mobile 07950-097525 E-mail aet546@hotmail.com *or* eddie.turner@bedfordhospital.nhs.uk

TURNER, Alison Joan. b 66. EAMTC. **d** 97 **p** 98. Perm to Offic *Chelmsf* 97-01; PV Ex Cathl from 04. *6 Cathedral Close, Exeter EX1 1EZ* Tel (01392) 272498 Mobile 07958-276651

TURNER, Andrew John. b 52. St Jo Coll Nottm. **d** 83 **p** 84. C Framlingham w Saxtead *St E* 83-86; P-in-c Badingham w Bruisyard and Cransford 86-88; P-in-c Dennington 86-88; R Badingham w Bruisyard, Cransford and Dennington 88-91; Chapl RAF from 91; Perm to Offic *St E* from 10. *9 St Edmunds Square, Honington, Bury St Edmunds IP31 1LT* Tel (01359) 268624 E-mail a.turner682@btinternet.com

TURNER, Ann. See TURNER, Canon Patricia Ann

TURNER, Mrs Ann Elizabeth Hamer. b 38. Ex Univ BA59 PGCE60. Trin Coll Bris 84. **dss** 86 **d** 87 **p** 94. Bath St Luke *B & W* 86-91; Hon C 91-99; Chapl Dorothy Ho Foundn 89-91; C Bath Twerton-on-Avon 91-94; TV 94-96; rtd 98; Perm to Offic *Ex* 00-06; Hon C Ottery St Mary, Alfington, W Hill, Tipton etc from 06. *4 Beech Park, West Hill, Ottery St Mary EX11 1UH* Tel (01404) 813476

TURNER, Anthony John. b 49. St Mich Coll Llan 89. **d** 91 **p** 92. C Coity w Nolton *Llan* 91-95; R Castlemartin w Warren and Angle etc *St D* 95-04; TV Monkton 04-07; TV Cwmbran *Mon* from 07; OCF 95-01. *The Vicarage, Llantarnam, Cwmbran NP44 3BW* Tel (01633) 489280

TURNER, The Ven Antony Hubert Michael. b 30. FCA63. Tyndale Hall Bris 54. **d** 56 **p** 57. C Nottingham St Ann *S'well* 56-58; C Cheadle *Ches* 58-62; PC Macclesfield Ch Ch 62-68; Lic to Offic *S'wark* 68-74; Home Sec BCMS 68-74; V Southsea St Jude *Portsm* 74-86; P-in-c Portsea St Luke 75-80; RD Portsm 79-84; Hon Can Portsm Cathl 85-86; Adn Is of Wight 86-96; rtd 96; Perm to Offic *Portsm* from 96. *15 Avenue Road, Hayling Island PO11 0LX* Tel (023) 9246 5881

TURNER, Benjamin John. b 45. CEng MICE. NOC 82. **d** 85 **p** 86. C Worsley *Man* 85-88; V Elton St Steph 88-95; Asst P Greystoke, Matterdale, Mungrisdale etc *Carl* 95-98; TV Gd Shep TM 98-01; Asst Chapl Leeds Teaching Hosps NHS Trust 01-02; Chapl 02-07; rtd 07. *40 Nightingale Walk, Bingley BD16 3QB* Tel (01274) 568035

TURNER, Canon Carl Francis. b 60. St Chad's Coll Dur BA81. St Steph Ho Ox 83. **d** 85 **p** 86. C Leigh-on-Sea St Marg *Chelmsf* 85-88; C Brentwood St Thos 88-90; TV Plaistow 90-95; P-in-c

95-96; TR Plaistow and N Canning Town 96-01; Prec and Can Res Ex Cathl from 01. *6 Cathedral Close, Exeter EX1 1EZ* Tel (01392) 272498 E-mail precentor@exeter-cathedral.org.uk

TURNER, Carlton John. b 79. Univ of W Indies BA05 Qu Coll Birm MA09. **d** 05 **p** 06. C Bahamas St Greg 05-06; C S Beach All SS and Asst Chapl Main Hosp 06-08; C Nassau Calvery Hill 08-10; TV Bloxwich *Lich* from 10. *6 Cresswell Crescent, Walsall WS3 2UW*

TURNER, Charles Maurice Joseph. b 13. **d** 79 **p** 80. NSM Brislington St Luke 79-83; NSM Bris Ch Ch w St Ewen and All SS 83-84; NSM Bris St Steph w St Nic and St Leon 83-84; NSM City of Bris 84-89; Perm to Offic 89-98. *31 Eagle Road, Bristol BS4 3LQ* Tel 0117-977 6329

TURNER, Christina Caroline. See HODGES, Mrs Christina Caroline

TURNER, Mrs Christine. b 42. EMMTC. **d** 94 **p** 95. Asst Chapl Qu Medical Cen Nottm Univ Hosp NHS Trust 94-97; NSM Hickling w Kinoulton and Broughton Sulney *S'well* 94-97; NSM Cotgrave 97-99; P-in-c Willoughby-on-the-Wolds w Wysall and Widmerpool 99-04; rtd 04. *The Rosarie, Milcombe, Banbury OX15 4RS* Tel (01295) 722330 E-mail revd.christine@care4free.net

TURNER, Christopher Gilbert. b 29. New Coll Ox BA52 MA55. Ox Min Course 91. **d** 92 **p** 93. NSM Hook Norton w Gt Rollright, Swerford etc *Ox* from 92. *Rosemullion, High Street, Great Rollright, Chipping Norton OX7 5RQ* Tel (01608) 737359

TURNER, Christopher James Shepherd. b 48. Ch Ch Ox BA70 MA74. Wycliffe Hall Ox 71. **d** 74 **p** 75. C Rusholme H Trin *Man* 74-78; C Chadderton Ch Ch 78-80; V 80-89; V Selly Park St Steph and St Wulstan *Birm* 89-99; P-in-c Locking *B & W* 99-05; Chapl Weston Hospice 99-05; P-in-c The Quinton *Birm* 05-09; R from 09; AD Edgbaston 08-10. *The Rectory, 773 Hagley Road West, Birmingham B32 1AJ* Tel 0121-422 2031 E-mail chris@quintonchurch.co.uk

TURNER, Christopher Matthew. b 68. Brunel Univ BSc90. Cranmer Hall Dur 01. **d** 03 **p** 04. C Hykeham *Linc* 03-06; P-in-c Mid Marsh Gp from 06; P-in-c Saltfleetby from 06; P-in-c Theddlethorpe from 06. *Mid Marsh Rectory, 37 Tinkle Street, Grimoldby, Louth LN11 8SW* Tel (01507) 327735 E-mail c.turner@which.net

TURNER, Mrs Claire Elizabeth. b 76. Plymouth Univ BA99. Qu Coll Birm 08. **d** 11. C Wednesfield *Lich* from 11. *6 Yale Drive, Wednesfield WV11 3UA* Tel 07748-998227 (mobile) E-mail claireturner29@hotmail.com

TURNER, Colin Peter John. b 42. Clifton Th Coll 63. **d** 66 **p** 67. C Kinson *Sarum* 66-68; C York St Paul 68-72; Org Sec (SE Area) CPAS 73-78; TV Radipole and Melcombe Regis *Sarum* 78-87; R Radstock w Writhlington *B & W* 90-07; R Kilmersdon w Babington 90-07; RD Midsomer Norton 04-07; rtd 07; Perm to Offic *B & W* from 07. *12 Gainsborough Rise, Trowbridge BA14 9HX*

TURNER, Canon David Stanley. b 35. Westmr Coll Ox BA84 MISM69 MISE69. WMMTC 86. **d** 87 **p** 88. NSM Worc St Mich 87-90; Min Shelfield St Mark CD *Lich* 90-95; C Walsall Wood 90-95; Min Can and Chapl St Woolos Cathl 95-97; V Tredegar St Jas 97-05; Hon Can St Bart's Cathl Barrackpore from 96; rtd 05. *30 Wolsey Close, Worcester WR4 9ES* Tel (01905) 350859

TURNER, Derek John. b 54. Univ of Wales (Ban) BSc81 PhD86. St Jo Coll Nottm. **d** 87 **p** 88. C Pelsall *Lich* 87-91; C Stratford-on-Avon w Bishopton *Cov* 91-99; R Leire w Ashby Parva and Dunton Bassett *Leic* 00-06; rtd 06. *The Parsonage, La Rue du Crocquet, St Brelade, Jersey JE3 8BZ* Tel 07713-832676 (mobile) E-mail frderek@cesmail.net

TURNER, Donald. b 29. S'wark Ord Course. **d** 71 **p** 72. C Hounslow St Steph *Lon* 71-76; Hon C Isleworth St Jo 76-78; C Brighton St Pet w Chpl Royal *Chich* 78-80; C Brighton St Pet w Chpl Royal and St Jo 80-85; P-in-c St Leonards SS Pet and Paul 85-87; V 87-91; rtd 91; Hon C Malborough w S Huish, W Alvington and Churchstow *Ex* 93-98; Chapl Las Palmas *Eur* 98-01; Perm to Offic *Ex* from 02. *15 Coombe Meadows, Chillington, Kingsbridge TQ7 2JL* Tel (01548) 531440

TURNER, Dylan Lawrence. b 72. Goldsmiths' Coll Lon BMus96 SS Coll Cam BTh08. Westcott Ho Cam 06. **d** 08 **p** 09. C Strood St Nic w St Mary *Roch* from 08. *12 Cadnam Close, Strood, Rochester ME2 3TS* Tel 07779-225810 (mobile) E-mail dylan.turner@diocese-rochester.org

TURNER, Edgar. See TURNER, Canon Robert Edgar

TURNER, Edward. See TURNER, Albert Edward

TURNER, Edward Nicholas. b 80. Birm Univ BA01 Anglia Ruskin Univ MA08. Westcott Ho Cam 06. **d** 08 **p** 09. C Winchmore Hill St Paul *Lon* 08-11; V Edmonton St Aldhelm from 11. *St Aldhelm's Vicarage, Windmill Road, London N18 1PA* Tel (020) 8807 5336 Mobile 07788-782646 E-mail edd.turner@expertit.net

TURNER, Canon Edward Robert. b 37. Em Coll Cam BA62 BTh66 MA67. Westcott Ho Cam 64. **d** 66 **p** 67. C Salford St Phil w St Steph *Man* 66-69; Chapl Tonbridge Sch 69-81; Adv for In-

Service Tr *Roch* 81-89; Dir of Educn 81-96; Can Res Roch Cathl 81-00; Vice-Dean 88-00; Dioc Adv on Community Affairs 96-00; Consultant Rochester 2000 Trust and Bp's Consultant on Public Affairs 00-02; rtd 02; Perm to Offic *Nor* from 01. *Glebe House, Church Road, Neatishead, Norwich NR12 8BT* Tel (01692) 631295 E-mail aandeturner@broadlandnet.co.uk

TURNER, Mrs Eileen Margaret. b 45. Goldsmiths' Coll Lon TCert66 Ches Coll of HE MTh02. NOC 90. **d** 93 **p** 94. Par Dn Sandal St Cath *Wakef* 93-94; C 94-96; P-in-c Hammerwich *Lich* 96-02; Dir OLM Course 96-02; Dir Ext Studies St Jo Coll Nottm 02-10; rtd 10; Perm to Offic *Sheff* from 11. *1 Holly Court, Endcliffe Vale Road, Sheffield S10 3DS* Tel 0114-268 2282 Mobile 07774-623769 E-mail eileenmturner@gmail.com

TURNER, Mrs Elaine. b 58. Birm Univ BSc79 CEng84 MICE84 MIStructE85. **d** 04 **p** 05. OLM Walesby *Linc* from 04. *Rose Cottage, Normanby-le-Wold, Market Rasen LN7 6SS* Tel (01673) 828142 E-mail elaine-turner58@supanex.com

TURNER, Miss Elizabeth Jane. b 67. Leeds Univ BEng88. Trin Coll Bris 93. **d** 96 **p** 97. C Eccles *Man* 96-00; P-in-c Barrow *Ches* 00-08; Dioc Ecum Officer 00-08; R Thurstaston from 08; Dioc Ecum Officer from 08. *Thurstaston Rectory, 77 Thingwall Road, Wirral CH61 3UB* Tel 0151-648 1816 E-mail jane@turner267.plus.com

TURNER, Canon Francis Edwin. b 29. Sarum Th Coll 54. **d** 57 **p** 58. C Cheriton Street *Cant* 57-61; C Willesborough w Hinxhill 61-64; P-in-c Betteshanger w Ham 64-65; R Northbourne w Betteshanger and Ham 64-70; R Northbourne, Tilmanstone w Betteshanger and Ham 70-74; V Sittingbourne St Mich 74-94; RD Sittingbourne 78-84; Hon Can Cant Cathl 84-94; rtd 94. *6 Cherry Grove, Hungerford RG17 0HP* Tel (01488) 682683

TURNER, Canon Frederick Glynne. b 30. Univ of Wales (Lamp) BA52. St Mich Coll Llan 52. **d** 54 **p** 55. C Aberaman *Llan* 54-60; C Oystermouth *S & B* 60-64; V Abercynon *Llan* 64-71; V Ton Pentre 71-73; TR Ystradyfodwg 73-77; R Caerphilly 77-82; V Whitchurch 82-96; Can Llan Cathl 84-96; Prec 95-96; rtd 96; Perm to Offic *Llan* from 96. *83 Newborough Avenue, Llanishen, Cardiff CF14 5DA* Tel (029) 2075 4443

TURNER, Miss Gaynor. b 44. LNSM course 93. **d** 96 **p** 97. NSM Salford Sacred Trin *Man* 96-99; Asst Chapl among Deaf People from 96. *19 Ellesmere Avenue, Worsley, Manchester M28 0AL*

TURNER, Geoffrey. b 51. Selw Coll Cam BA75 MA78 PGCE75. NOC 90. **d** 93 **p** 94. C E Crompton *Man* 93-96; C Heywood St Luke w All So 96-98; TV Heywood 98-01; TR 01-08; TR Worsley from 08. *8 Landrace Drive, Worsley, Manchester M28 1UY* Tel 0161-799 6082 E-mail gt1951@btinternet.com

TURNER, Geoffrey John. b 45. Aston Univ BSc68 Newc Univ MSc69 PhD72. Cranmer Hall Dur BA74. **d** 75 **p** 76. C Wood End *Cov* 75-79; V Huyton Quarry *Liv* 79-86; Press and Communications Officer *Ely* 86-94; P-in-c Gt w Lt Abington 86-94; P-in-c Hildersham 86-94; V Letchworth St Paul w Willian *St Alb* 94-01; P-in-c Willingham *Ely* 01-02; R 02-08; P-in-c Rampton 01-02; R 02-08; rtd 08; Perm to Offic *Ripon* from 09. *8 Wayside Crescent, Harrogate HG2 8NJ* Tel (01423) 885668 E-mail geoffrey168@btinternet.com

TURNER, Geoffrey James. b 46. St Deiniol's Hawarden 85. **d** 87 **p** 88. C Loughor *S & B* 87-89; C Swansea St Pet 89-90; R New Radnor and Llanfihangel Nantmelan etc 90-96; V Ystalyfera 96-07; RD Cwmtawe 00-06; V Loughor from 07. *The Rectory, 109 Glebe Road, Loughor, Swansea SA4 6SR* Tel (01792) 891958 E-mail geoffrey.turner2@sky.com

✠**TURNER, The Rt Revd Geoffrey Martin.** b 34. Oak Hill Th Coll 60. **d** 63 **p** 64 **c** 94. C Tonbridge St Steph *Roch* 63-66; C Heatherlands St Jo *Sarum* 66-69; V Derby St Pet 69-73; V Chadderton Ch Ch *Man* 73-79; R Bebington *Ches* 79-93; Hon Can Ches Cathl 89-93; RD Wirral N 89-93; Adn Ches 93-94; Suff Bp Stockport 94-00; rtd 00; Perm to Offic *Ches* from 00; Hon Asst Bp Ches from 02. *23 Lang Lane, West Kirby, Wirral CH48 5HG* Tel 0151-625 8504

TURNER, Gerald Garth. b 38. Univ of Wales (Lamp) BA61 St Edm Hall Ox BA63 MA67. St Steph Ho Ox 63. **d** 65 **p** 66. C Drayton in Hales *Lich* 65-68; Chapl Prebendal Sch Chich 68-70; PV Chich Cathl 68-70; C Forest Row 70-72; V Hope *Derby* 72-78; Prec Man Cathl 78-86; Can Res 78-86; R Tattenhall and Handley *Ches* 86-04; rtd 04; Perm to Offic *S'well* from 04. *3 Westgate, Southwell NG25 0JN* Tel (01636) 815233 E-mail ggarthturner@hotmail.com

TURNER, Graham Colin. b 55. Bradf Univ BTech. Oak Hill Th Coll BA81. **d** 81 **p** 82. C Upper Armley *Ripon* 81-86; V Bordesley Green *Birm* 86-05; AD Yardley and Bordesley 00-05; TR Macclesfield Team *Ches* from 05. *The Rectory, 85 Beech Lane, Macclesfield SK10 2DY* Tel (01625) 426110 or 421984 E-mail grahamcturner@hotmail.com

TURNER, Mrs Heather Winifred. b 43. Open Univ BA08 SRN65. Cant Sch of Min 89. **d** 90 **p** 94. Par Dn Orpington All SS *Roch* 90-93; Chapl to the Deaf 93-00; P-in-c Wrotham 95-01; TV E Dereham and Scarning *Nor* 01-02; rtd 02; Perm to Offic *Nor* 02-04; C Darsham *St E* 04-06; C Middleton cum Fordley and Theberton w Eastbridge 04-06; C Westleton w Dunwich 04-06; C Yoxford, Peasenhall and Sibton 04-06; C Blyth Valley 06-07; TV 07; Perm to Offic *St E* from 07 and *Cov* from 08. *Nightingale House, 3 Heathlands, St George's Lane, Reydon, Southwold IP18 6RW* Tel (01502) 723386 E-mail revheatherturner@btinternet.com

TURNER, Henry John Mansfield. b 24. Magd Coll Cam BA45 MA48 Man Univ PhD85. Westcott Ho Cam 48. **d** 50 **p** 51. C Crosby *Linc* 50-52; C Chorlton upon Medlock *Man* 52-55; Inter-Colleg Sec SCM (Man) 52-55; C Leigh St Mary *Man* 55-57; V Rochdale Gd Shep 57-62; India 63-67; V Becontree St Geo *Chelmsf* 67-71; R Weeley 71-79; Chapl St Deiniol's Lib Hawarden 79-80; Sub-Warden 80-86; Perm to Offic *Chelmsf* from 86; Hon C St Botolph without Bishopgate *Lon* from 87. *Merrywood, 25 Fourth Avenue, Frinton-on-Sea CO13 9DU* Tel (01255) 677554

TURNER, James Alfred. b 34. MCIPS76. Ox Min Course 91. **d** 94 **p** 95. NSM Kidlington w Hampton Poyle *Ox* 94-06; Perm to Offic from 06. *11 St Mary's Close, Kidlington, Oxford OX5 2AY* Tel (01865) 375562

TURNER, James Henry. b 51. NOC 99. **d** 02 **p** 03. NSM Middleton St Cross *Ripon* from 02. *38 Acre Crescent, Middleton, Leeds LS10 4DJ* Tel 0113-277 2681 E-mail jameshpturner@aol.com

TURNER, Jane. See TURNER, Miss Elizabeth Jane

TURNER, Jessica Mary. b 60. SS Coll Cam BA81 PGCE82. Trin Coll Bris 88. **d** 91 **p** 94. Par Dn Preston Em *Blackb* 91-94; C Bamber Bridge St Aid 94-95; Chapl Preston Acute Hosps NHS Trust 95-98; Chapl Blackpool Victoria Hosp NHS Trust 98-03; Chapl Blackpool, Fylde and Wyre Hosps NHS Trust 03-05; Hon Can Blackb Cathl 02-05; Chapl Ox Radcliffe Hosps NHS Trust from 06. *Chaplaincy Office, John Radcliffe Hospital, Headley Way, Headington, Oxford OX3 9DU* Tel (01865) 226090 E-mail jessica.turner@orh.nhs.uk

TURNER, John. See TURNER, Henry John Mansfield

TURNER, John. See TURNER, Canon Walter John

TURNER, John David Maurice. b 22. Keble Coll Ox BA45 MA48. Ripon Hall Ox 69. **d** 70 **p** 71. C Crowthorne Ox 70-73; V Cropredy w Gt Bourton 73-79; V Cropredy w Gt Bourton and Wardington 80-83; Perm to Offic *Ox* and *Pet* 83-03; rtd 87. *16 Stuart Court, High Street, Kibworth, Leicester LE8 0LR* Tel (01858) 881378

TURNER, John William. b 43. Sheff Univ BSc73. Wycliffe Hall Ox 86. **d** 88 **p** 89. C Clayton *Bradf* 88-91; C Horton 91-92; V Bankfoot 92-01; V Holland-on-Sea *Chelmsf* 01-05; rtd 05. *20 Grantley Drive, Harrogate HG2 3ST* Tel (01423) 545994 E-mail john.turner15@virgin.net

TURNER, Mrs Karen Lesley. b 48. ERMC. **d** 08 **p** 09. NSM Langelei *St Alb* from 08. *139 Marlins Turn, Hemel Hempstead HP1 3LW* Tel (01442) 250809

TURNER, Canon Keith Howard. b 50. Southn Univ BA71. Wycliffe Hall Ox 72. **d** 75 **p** 76. C Enfield Ch Ch Trent Park *Lon* 75-79; C Chilwell *S'well* 79-83; P-in-c Linby w Papplewick 83-90; R from 90; Hon Can S'well Minster from 02. *The Rectory, Main Street, Linby, Nottingham NG15 8AE* Tel 0115-963 2346 E-mail k.h.turner@btopenworld.com

TURNER, Keith Stanley. b 51. ACIB80. NTMTC 96. **d** 99 **p** 00. C S Hornchurch St Jo and St Matt *Chelmsf* from 99. *16 Wells Gardens, Rainham RM13 7LU* Tel (01708) 554274

TURNER, Kevin Louis Sinclair. b 60. St Jo Coll Nottm BA00. **d** 00 **p** 01. C Mount Pellon *Wakef* 00-05; P-in-c Sowerby 03-05; Evang Adv Croydon Area Miss Team *S'wark* 05-08. *26 Calder, Barkisland Mill, Beestonley Lane, Barkisland, Halifax HX4 0HG* Tel (01422) 377099 Mobile 07702-661527

TURNER, Lawrence John. b 43. Kelham Th Coll 65. **d** 70 **p** 71. C Lower Gornal *Lich* 70-73; C Wednesbury St Paul Wood Green 73-74; C Porthill 75-77; C Wilton *York* 77-80; P-in-c 80-82; R Jersey St Martin *Win* 82-10; rtd 10; Chmn Jersey Miss to Seamen from 82. *10 Gorey Village Main Road, Grouville, Jersey JE3 9EP* Tel (01534) 854294 E-mail ljturner@jerseymail.co.uk

TURNER, Leslie. b 29. NE Lon Poly BSc87. St Jo Coll Dur 50 St Aid Birkenhead 51. **d** 54 **p** 55. C Darwen St Cuth *Blackb* 54-56; C Haslingden w Grane and Stonefold 56-59; V Oswaldtwistle St Paul 59-65; Chapl Belmont and Henderson Hosps Sutton 65-71; St Ebba's Hosp Epsom 65-71; Qu Mary's Carshalton 67-71; Chapl Princess Marina and St Crispin's Hosps 71-87; Chapl Northn Gen Hosp 87-94; Chapl Manfield Hosp Northn 87-94; Chapl St Edm Hosp Northn 87-94; rtd 94; Perm to Offic *Pet* from 94. *20 Banbury Close, Northampton NN4 9UA* Tel (01604) 769233

TURNER, Mrs Lorraine Elizabeth. b 67. Brunel Univ BSc90 Open Univ MA96. Cranmer Hall Dur 01. **d** 03 **p** 04. C Birchwood *Linc* 03-06; TV Louth from 06; C Legbourne and Wold Marsh from 06; Chapl United Lincs Hosps NHS Trust from 07. *Mid Marsh Rectory, 37 Tinkle Street, Grimoldby, Louth LN11 8SW* Tel (01507) 327735 or 327667 E-mail lorraine.t@which.net

TURNER, Mark. b 60. Aston Tr Scheme 87 Sarum & Wells Th Coll BTh92. **d** 92 **p** 93. C New Sleaford *Linc* 92-94; C Bottesford and Muston *Leic* 94-98; C Harby, Long Clawson and Hose 94-98; C Barkestone w Plungar, Redmile and Stathern 94-98; P-in-c Thurnby Lodge 98-00; C Aylestone Park CD 00-03; P-in-c Areley Kings *Worc* 03-05; R from 05; RD Stourport 06-07. *14 Dunley Road, Stourport-on-Severn DY13 0AX* Tel (01299) 829557 E-mail revturner@tinyworld.co.uk

TURNER, Mark Richard Haythornthwaite. b 41. TCD MA67 Linc Coll Ox BA68. Wycliffe Hall Ox 65. **d** 68 **p** 69. C Birtley *Newc* 68-71; C Cambridge Gt St Mary w St Mich *Ely* 71-74; Chapl Loughb Univ 74-79; P-in-c Keele *Lich* 80-85; Chapl Keele Univ 80-85; P-in-c Ashley 85-95; P-in-c Mucklestone 86-95; R Farnborough *Roch* 95-00; P-in-c Upper Tean *Lich* 00-06; Local Min Adv (Stafford) 00-06; rtd 06; Perm to Offic *Lich* from 06; Local Miss and Min Adv (Shrewsbury Area) 09-10. *Craignant Isa, Selattyn, Oswestry SY10 7NS* Tel (01691) 718315 E-mail markrhturner@hotmail.com

TURNER, Martin John. b 34. Trin Hall Cam BA55 MA59. Cuddesdon Coll 58. **d** 60 **p** 61. C Rugby St Andr *Cov* 60-65; C Cov Cathl 65-68; USA 68-70; V Rushmere *St E* 70-82; V Monkwearmouth St Pet *Dur* 82-90; V Bathford *B & W* 90-99; rtd 99; Perm to Offic *B & W* 00-07 and *Truro* from 07. *Hallane End, 4 The Terrace, Lostwithiel PL22 0DT* Tel (01208) 871330 Mobile 07929-231167 E-mail turnerschemanoff@aol.com

TURNER, Mrs Maureen. b 55. Leeds Univ BA78 MA01. St Jo Coll Nottm 84. **d** 87 **p** 94. Par Dn Darlaston St Lawr *Lich* 87-91; C Stratford-on-Avon w Bishopton *Cov* 91-98; Chapl Myton Hamlet Hospice 98-01; NSM Leire w Ashby Parva and Dunton Bassett *Leic* 00-06; Chapl Team Ldr Univ Hosps Leic NHS Trust 01-07; Chapl Team Ldr Jersey Gp of Hosps from 07. *Chaplain's Office, General Hospital, Gloucester Street, St Helier, Jersey JE1 3QS* Tel (01534) 622000

TURNER, Maurice. See TURNER, Charles Maurice Joseph

TURNER, Maurice William. b 27. Sarum Th Coll 53. **d** 56 **p** 57. C Thornhill *Wakef* 56-60; V Gawber 60-71; V Alverthorpe 71-74; V Shelton and Oxon *Lich* 74-81; V Leaton 81-82; P-in-c Battlefield w Albrighton 81-82; V Leaton and Albrighton w Battlefield 82-92; rtd 92; Perm to Offic *Lich* from 93 and *Heref* from 96. *10 Melbourne Rise, Bicton Heath, Shrewsbury SY3 5DA* Tel (01743) 352667

TURNER, Michael Andrew. b 34. K Coll Cam BA59 MA62. Cuddesdon Coll 59. **d** 61 **p** 62. C Luton St Andr *St Alb* 61-64; V 70-77; C-in-c Northolt St Jos *Lon* 64-70; Perm to Offic *St Alb* 77-93; Dep Hd and Chapl Greycoat Hosp Sch 86-93; P-in-c Shilling Okeford *Sarum* 93-99; Chapl Croft Ho Sch Shillingstone 93-99; rtd 99; Perm to Offic *Sarum* from 99; V of Close Sarum Cathl 02-07; Dioc Retirement Officer from 08. *12 Berkshire Road, Harnham, Salisbury SP2 8NY* Tel (01722) 504000 E-mail sarum.turners@ntlworld.com

TURNER, Michael John Royce. b 43. St Jo Coll Dur BA65. Chich Th Coll 65. **d** 67 **p** 68. C Hodge Hill *Birm* 67-71; C Eling, Testwood and Marchwood *Win* 71-72; TV 72-77; R Kirkwall *Ab* 77-85; R Drumlithie *Bre* from 85; R Drumtochty from 85; R Fasque from 85; R Laurencekirk from 85. *Beattie Lodge, Laurencekirk AB30 1HJ* Tel and fax (01561) 377380 E-mail mjrturner@zoo.co.uk

TURNER, Canon Nicholas Anthony. b 51. Clare Coll Cam BA73 MA77 Keble Coll Ox BA77 MA81. Ripon Coll Cuddesdon 76. **d** 78 **p** 79. C Stretford St Matt *Man* 78-80; Tutor St Steph Ho Ox 80-84; V Leeds Richmond Hill *Ripon* 84-91; Offg Chapl RAF and V Ascension St Jo 91-96; Can Th St Helena Cathl from 94; V Raynes Park St Sav *S'wark* 96-01; P-in-c Broughton, Marton and Thornton *Bradf* 01-02; R from 02. *The Rectory, 7 Roundell Drive, West Marton, Skipton BD23 3UL* Tel (01282) 842332 E-mail nicholas.turner@bradford.anglican.org

TURNER (née SYMINGTON), Canon Patricia Ann. b 46. SRN68 RMN71 SCM72. St Steph Ho Ox 82. **dss** 84 **d** 87. Buttershaw St Aid *Bradf* 84-87; TM Manningham 87-91; Ascension Is 91-96; Par Dn Raynes Park St Sav *S'wark* 96-01; Par Dn Broughton, Marton and Thornton *Bradf* from 01; RD Skipton from 05; Assoc Dioc Dir of Ords 04-07; Dir of Ords from 07; Hon Can Bradf Cathl from 09. *The Rectory, 7 Roundell Drive, West Marton, Skipton BD23 3UL* Tel (01282) 842332 E-mail ann.turner@bradford.anglican.org

TURNER, Peter Carpenter. b 39. Oak Hill Th Coll 63. **d** 66 **p** 67. C Chadwell *Chelmsf* 66-69; C Braintree 69-73; R Fyfield 73-87; P-in-c Moreton 77-87; C-in-c Bobbingworth 82-87; P-in-c Willingale w Shellow and Berners Roding 84-87; V E Ham St Geo 87-04; rtd 04; Perm to Offic *Lon* from 05. *9 Llandovery House, Chipka Street, London E14 3LE* Tel (020) 7987 5902 E-mail detox.uk@btinternet.com *or* petercturner@btinternet.com

TURNER, The Ven Peter Robin. b 42. CB98 DL07. St Luke's Coll Ex PGCE70 Open Univ BA79 Westmr Coll Ox MTh96 AKC65. St Boniface Warminster 65. **d** 66 **p** 67. C Crediton *Ex* 66-69; Perm to Offic 69-70; Chapl RAF 70-88; Asst Chapl-in-Chief

RAF 88-95; Chapl-in-Chief RAF 95-98; QHC 92-98; Can and Preb Linc Cathl 95-98; Chapl Dulwich Coll 98-02; Bp's Dom Chapl *S'well* 02-07; Hon Can S'well Minster 02-07; rtd 07; Chapl for Sector Min *S'well* from 07. *12 Chimes Meadow, Southwell NG25 0GB* Tel (01636) 812250 Mobile 07990-633137 E-mail pr.turner@lineone.net

TURNER, Philip. b 54. **d** 11. NSM Gt Sankey *Liv* from 11. *147 Cradley, Widnes WA8 7PN*

TURNER, Ms Philippa Anne. b 64. Trevelyan Coll Dur BA86 Yale Univ MDiv88. **d** 94 **p** 95. Chapl New York Hosp USA 91-95; Assoc P New York Ch of Heavenly Rest 95-08; Chapl R Veterinary Coll *Lon* from 08; Chapl R Free and Univ Coll Medical Sch from 08. *15 Ormonde Mansions, 106A Southampton Row, London WC1B 4PN* Tel (020) 7422 2574 *or* 7468 5145 Mobile 07525-234382 E-mail pturner@rvc.ac.uk

TURNER, Canon Robert Edgar. b 20. TCD BA42 MA51. Linc Th Coll 44. **d** 45 **p** 46. C Kings Heath *Birm* 45-51; Min Can Belf Cathl 51-63; Dean of Res QUB 51-58; Bp's Dom Chapl *D & D* 56-67; I Belfast St Geo *Conn* 58-90; Can Belf Cathl 71-76; Preb Clonmethan St Patr Cathl Dublin 76-90; Dioc Registrar *Conn* 82-06; Prin Registrar from 06; rtd 90. *19 Cricklewood Park, Belfast BT9 5GU* Tel (028) 9066 3214 Fax 9058 6843 E-mail returner@ntlworld.com *or* registrar@connor.anglican.org

TURNER, Robin Edward. b 35. Selw Coll Cam BA57 MA63. Qu Coll Birm 57. **d** 63 **p** 64. C Aveley *Chelmsf* 63-67; C Upminster 67-71; R Goldhanger w Lt Totham 71-80; R Lt Baddow 80-00; Hon Chapl New Hall Sch Essex 80-00; rtd 00; Perm to Offic *Nor* from 00. *29 Swann Grove, Holt NR25 6DP* Tel (01263) 711330

TURNER, Canon Roger Dyke. b 39. Trin Coll Bris 79. **d** 81 **p** 82. C Clevedon St Andr and Ch Ch *B & W* 81-85; R Freshford, Limpley Stoke and Hinton Charterhouse 85-88; V Kenilworth St Jo *Cov* 88-04; RD Kenilworth 90-98; Hon Can Cov Cathl 00-04; rtd 04; Perm to Offic *Birm* 04-05 and *Cov* from 04; P-in-c Barston *Birm* from 05. *8 Priors Close, Balsall Common, Coventry CV7 7FJ* Tel (01676) 533847

TURNER, Roy. *See* TURNER, Alan Roy

TURNER, Ms Ruth Carpenter. b 63. Anglia Ruskin Univ BA09 LLCM83 GLCM84. Ridley Hall Cam 07. **d** 09 **p** 10. C Brampton St Thos *Derby* from 09. *6 Westfield Close, Chesterfield S40 3RS* Tel (01246) 569810 Mobile 07855-714538 E-mail curate@st-thomas-brampton.org

TURNER, St John Alwin. b 31. Dur Univ BA57 MA61. Cranmer Hall Dur. **d** 59 **p** 60. C W Hartlepool St Paul *Dur* 59-62; C S Shore H Trin *Blackb* 62-65; V Huncoat 65-67; Org Sec CMS *Ripon* and *York* 67-72; V Harrogate St Mark *Ripon* 72-94; rtd 96; Perm to Offic *Linc* from 01. *2 The Tilney, Whaplode, Spalding PE12 6UW* Tel (01406) 371390

TURNER, Stewart Gordon. b 54. Ex Univ BTh06. SWMTC 03. **d** 06 **p** 07. NSM Falmouth All SS *Truro* 06-09; C Mawnan from 09; C Budock from 09; P-in-c Constantine from 11. *The Vicarage, Chalbury Heights Brill, Constantine, Falmouth TR11 5UR* Tel (01326) 340259 E-mail stewart.turner@tiscali.co.uk

TURNER, Susan. b 58. Man Univ BA89. NOC 89. **d** 92 **p** 94. NSM Balderstone *Man* 92-93; NSM E Crompton 93-94; Hon C 94-96; Chapl Man Coll of Arts and Tech 92-96; Asst Chapl S Man Univ Hosps NHS Trust 96-97; Chapl Burnley Health Care NHS Trust 97-03; Chapl Cen Man/Man Children's Univ Hosp NHS Trust from 02. *Chaplaincy Office, Manchester Royal Infirmary, Oxford Road, Manchester M13 9WL* Tel 0161-276 45824

TURNER, Sylvia Jean. b 46. Lon Univ 72 Open Univ BA77. Westcott Ho Cam 93. **d** 95 **p** 96. C Whitstable *Cant* 95-99; R Wigmore Abbey *Heref* 99-09; P-in-c Pontesbury I and II 09-11; rtd 11. *Wheelwrights, Witton, Ludlow SY8 3DB* Tel (01584) 890586 E-mail sylvia.turner@virgin.net

TURNER, Tina. b 60. St Jo Coll Nottm BA02. **d** 02 **p** 03. C Halifax All So and St Aug *Wakef* 02-05; C S Beddington and Roundshaw *S'wark* 05-06; TV Warlingham w Chelsham and Farleigh 06-08. *26 Calder, Barkisland Mill, Beestonley Lane, Barkisland, Halifax HX4 0HG* E-mail tina@revturner.fsnet.co.uk

TURNER, Valerie Kay. b 50. SS Paul & Mary Coll Cheltenham BEd72. WMMTC 97 Wycliffe Hall Ox 99. **d** 00 **p** 01. C Cheltenham St Luke and St Jo *Glouc* 04-05; P-in-c Forest of Dean Ch Ch w English Bicknor from 04; P-in-c Lydbrook 04-05. *Christ Church Vicarage, Ross Road, Christchurch, Coleford GL16 7NS* Tel (01594) 836830 E-mail valmark@freenetname.co.uk

TURNER, Canon Walter John. b 29. Bris Univ BA53. Clifton Th Coll 49. **d** 54 **p** 55. C W Bromwich All SS *Lich* 54-58; C-in-c Oxley 58-60; V 60-65; V Wednesfield St Thos 65-74; RD Shifnal 75-83; V Boningale 75-83; V Shifnal 75-83; Preb Lich Cathl 80-83; Can Res and Prec Lich Cathl 83-94; rtd 94; Perm to Offic *Lich* 94-09. *9 Kestrel Close, Newport TF10 8QE* Tel (01952) 820758

TURNER-CALLIS, Mrs Gillian Ruth. b 79. Aber Univ BD03. Wycliffe Hall Ox MTh05. **d** 05 **p** 06. C Shepshed and Oaks in Charnwood *Leic* 05-08; TR Kegworth, Hathern, Long Whatton, Diseworth etc from 08. *The Rectory, 24 Nottingham Road, Kegworth, Derby DE74 2FH* Tel (01509) 673146 Mobile 07974-139881 E-mail gill@thets.demon.co.uk

TURNER-LOISEL, Mrs Elizabeth Anne. b 57. Lanc Univ BA79 MA80 York Univ PGCE81. EMMTC 96. **d** 99 **p** 00. C Eastwood *S'well* and Chapl Nat Sch Hucknall 99-04; P-in-c Annesley w Newstead *S'well* from 04. *The Vicarage, Annesley Cutting, Annesley, Nottingham NG15 0AJ* Tel (01623) 759666 E-mail revd.liz@virgin.net

TURNOCK, Geoffrey. b 38. Leeds Univ BSc61 PhD64 MSOSc. EMMTC 84. **d** 87 **p** 88. NSM Oadby *Leic* 87-00; NSM Okeford *Sarum* 00-04; NSM Dorchester from 05. *10 Billingsmoor Lane, Poundbury, Dorchester DT1 3WT* Tel (01305) 757177 E-mail gt@woodplace.u-net.com

TURP, Paul Robert. b 48. Oak Hill Th Coll BA79. **d** 79 **p** 80. C Southall Green St Jo *Lon* 79-83; V Shoreditch St Leon w St Mich 83-88 and from 00; TR Shoreditch St Leon and Hoxton St Jo 88-00. *The Vicarage, 36 Hoxton Square, London N1 6NN* Tel (020) 7739 2063 E-mail paul@shoreditch0.demon.co.uk

TURPIN, Christine Lesley. b 63. Westcott Ho Cam. **d** 09 **p** 10. C Bredon w Bredon's Norton *Worc* from 09. *20 Cornfield Way, Ashton-under-Hill, Evesham WR11 7TA* Tel (01386) 882263

TURPIN, Canon John Richard. b 41. St D Coll Lamp BA63 Magd Coll Cam BA65 MA70. Cuddesdon Coll 65. **d** 66 **p** 67. C Tadley St Pet *Win* 66-71; V Southampton Thornhill St Chris 71-85; V Ringwood 85-10; Hon Can Win Cathl 99-10; rtd 10. *111 Beaufort Road, Bournemouth BH6 5AU* Tel (01202) 421321 E-mail john.turpin4@btinternet.com

TURPIN, Raymond Gerald. b 35. **d** 97 **p** 98. OLM Brockley Hill St Sav *S'wark* 97-05; Perm to Offic from 05; Retirement Officer Woolwich Area from 08. *60 Bankhurst Road, London SE6 4XN* Tel (020) 8690 6877 *or* 8311 2000

TURRELL, Peter Charles Morphett. b 47. **d** 01 **p** 02. OLM Carshalton Beeches *S'wark* from 01. *62 Stanley Park Road, Carshalton SM5 3HW* Tel (020) 8669 0318

TURRELL, Stephen John. b 35. S'wark Ord Course. **d** 83 **p** 84. NSM W Wickham St Jo *Cant* 83-84; NSM Addington *S'wark* 85-92; NSM Blendworth w Chalton w Idsworth *Portsm* 92-97; Perm to Offic 97-01; NSM Storrington *Chich* 01-06; rtd 06. *29 Timberlands, Storrington, Pulborough RH20 3NF* Tel (01903) 741272

TURTON, Douglas Walter. b 38. Kent Univ BA77 Surrey Univ MSc90 Univ of Wales (Ban) DPhil04. Oak Hill Th Coll 77. **d** 78 **p** 79. C Cant St Mary Bredin 78-80; P-in-c Thornton Heath St Paul 80-81; V 81-84; V Thornton Heath St Paul *S'wark* 85-91; R Eastling w Ospringe and Stalisfield w Otterden *Cant* 91-00; rtd 00. *16 Weatherall Close, Dunkirk, Faversham ME13 9UL* Tel (01227) 752244

TURTON, Neil Christopher. b 45. Wycliffe Hall Ox 77. **d** 79 **p** 80. C Guildf Ch Ch 79-83; C Godalming 83-86; V Wyke 86-92; V Frimley 92-02; RD Surrey Heath 97-02; V Bay Head All SS USA from 02. *All Saints Rectory, 509·Lake Avenue, Bay Head NJ 08742-5367, USA* Tel (001) (732) 892 7478 E-mail neilturton@comcast.net

TURTON, Paul Edward. b 26. St Pet Hall Ox BA50 MA55. Qu Coll Birm 50. **d** 52 **p** 53. C Selly Oak St Mary *Birm* 52-55; C Ward End 55-57; I Netherton CD *Liv* 57-64; V Brockley Hill St Sav *S'wark* 64-68; Perm to Offic 68-70; Dir of Educn *Nor* 70-75; Dep Dir Nat Soc Cen Camberwell 75-77; Dir Nat Soc RE Cen Kensington 78-84; C Eastbourne St Mary *Chich* 84-86; rtd 86; Perm to Offic *Chich* from 87. *32 Churchill Close, Eastbourne BN20 8AJ* Tel (01323) 638089

TUSCHLING, Ruth Mary Magdalen. b 65. Freiburg Univ MA94 CCC Cam PhD04. Westcott Ho Cam BA97. **d** 98 **p** 99. C Hampstead St Jo *Lon* 98-01; Perm to Offic *Ely* 02-04; OSB 04-08; Warden Offa Retreat Ho and Dioc Spirituality Adv *Cov* from 08. *The Vicarage, School Hill, Offchurch, Leamington Spa CV33 9AL* Tel (01926) 334990 E-mail florinequals@googlemail.com

✠**TUSTIN, The Rt Revd David.** b 35. Magd Coll Cam BA57 MA61 Lambeth DD98. Cuddesdon Coll 58. **d** 60 **p** 61 **c** 79. C Stafford St Mary *Lich* 60-63; C St Dunstan in the West *Lon* 63-67; Asst Gen Sec C of E Coun on Foreign Relns 63-67; V Wednesbury St Paul Wood Green *Lich* 67-71; V Tettenhall Regis 71-79; RD Trysull 76-79; Suff Bp Grimsby *Linc* 79-00; Can and Preb Linc Cathl 79-00; rtd 00; Hon Asst Bp Linc from 01. *The Ashes, Tunnel Road, Wrawby, Brigg DN20 8SF* Tel and Fax (01652) 655584 E-mail tustindavid@hotmail.com

TUTTON, Canon John Knight. b 30. Man Univ BSc51. Ripon Hall Ox 53. **d** 55 **p** 56. C Tonge w Alkrington *Man* 55-57; C Bushbury *Lich* 57-59; R Blackley St Andr *Man* 59-67; R Denton Ch Ch 67-95; Hon Can Man Cathl 90-95; rtd 95; Hon C Exminster and Kenn 96-01; Perm to Offic from 01. *2 Hescane Park, Cheriton Bishop, Exeter EX6 6JP* Tel (01647) 24651 E-mail johnktutton@onetel.com

✠**TUTU, The Most Revd Desmond Mpilo.** b 31. UNISA BA K Coll Lon BD MTh FKC78. St Pet Rosettenville LTh. **d** 60 **p** 61 **c** 76. S Africa 60-62; C Golders Green St Alb *Lon* 62-65; C Bletchingley *S'wark* 65-66; S Africa 67-70; Lesotho 70-72; Assoc Dir Th Educn Fund WCC 72-75; C Lee St Aug *S'wark* 72-75; Dean Johannesburg 75-76; Bp Lesotho 76-78; Asst Bp Johannesburg 78-85; Bp Johannesburg 85-86; Abp Cape Town 86-96; rtd 96. *PO Box 1092, Milnerton, 7435 South Africa* Tel (0027) (21) 552 7524 Fax 552 7529 E-mail mpilo@iafrica.com

TWADDELL, William Reginald. b 33. TCD 61. **d** 62 **p** 63. C Belfast Whiterock *Conn* 62-65; I Loughgilly w Clare *Arm* 65-71; I Milltown 71-84; I Portadown St Mark 84-01; Preb Arm Cathl 88-96; Treas 96-98; Prec 98-01; rtd 01. *Tea Cottage, 19 Birches Road, Portadown BT62 1LS* Tel (028) 3885 2520
E-mail reggie.twaddell@hotmail.co.uk

TWEDDELL, Christopher Noel. b 66. Auckland Univ BA93. St Jo Coll Auckland. **d** 92 **p** 93. New Zealand 92-97; C Maindee Newport *Mon* 97-98; P-in-c Discovery Bay Hong Kong 98-00; V New Lynn New Zealand 00-05; Chapl St Pet Sch Cambridge from 06. *St Peter's School, Private Bag 884, Cambridge, New Zealand* Tel (0064) (7) 827 9888 Mobile 27-454 1306
E-mail chaplain@stpeters.school.nz

TWEDDLE, David William Joseph. b 28. Dur Univ BSc50 Open Univ BA97 ATCL56. Wycliffe Hall Ox 54. **d** 56 **p** 57. C Darlington H Trin *Dur* 56-60; P-in-c Prestonpans *Edin* 60-63; PV Linc Cathl 63-65; C Pet St Jo 65-71; Hon Min Can Pet Cathl 68-93; V Southwick w Glapthorn 71-83; P-in-c Benefield 80-83; R Benefield and Southwick w Glapthorn 83-93; RD Oundle 84-89; rtd 94; Perm to Offic *Ely* 94-07. *6 Barton Square, Ely CB7 4DF* Tel (01353) 614393

TWEED, Andrew. b 48. Univ of Wales (Cardiff) BA69 Trin Coll Carmarthen MA97. St Deiniol's Hawarden. **d** 81 **p** 84. NSM Llandrindod w Cefnllys *S & B* 81-87; NSM Llandrindod w Cefnllys and Disserth from 87. *Gwenallt, Wellington Road, Llandrindod Wells LD1 5NB* Tel (01597) 823671
E-mail andrewtweed1@aol.com

TWEEDIE-SMITH, Ian David. b 60. Newc Univ BA83. Wycliffe Hall Ox 83. **d** 85 **p** 86. C Hatcham St Jas *S'wark* 85-89; C Bury St Edmunds St Mary *St E* 89-02; TV Woking St Pet *Guildf* from 02. *The Vicarage, 66 Westfield Road, Woking GU22 9NG* Tel (01483) 770779 Fax 770786
E-mail iantweediesmith@waitrose.com

TWEEDY, Andrew Cyril Mark. b 61. Man Univ BA(Econ)81. SAOMC 98. **d** 01 **p** 02. C Carterton *Ox* 01-03; C Brize Norton and Carterton 03-04; V Bromham w Oakley and Stagsden *St Alb* 04-08; Chapl Barcelona *Eur* from 08. *St George's Church, calle Horacio 38, 08022 Barcelona, Spain* Tel (0034) 934 178 867 Fax 932 128 433 E-mail revdrew81@yahoo.es

TWIDELL, Canon William James. b 30. St Mich Coll Llan 58. **d** 60 **p** 61. C Tonge w Alkrington *Man* 60-63; C High Wycombe All SS *Ox* 63-65; P-in-c Elkesley w Bothamsall *S'well* 65-66; V Bury St Thos *Man* 66-72; V Daisy Hill 72-84; R Flixton St Mich 84-00; AD Stretford 88-98; Hon Can Man Cathl 97-00; rtd 00; Perm to Offic *Man* and *Ches* from 00. *11 Mercer Way, Nantwich CW5 5YD* Tel (01270) 620328

TWINING, Kathryn. b 60. Westcott Ho Cam. **d** 07 **p** 08. C Greenwich St Alfege *S'wark* 07-09; C New Addington from 09. *78 Gascoigne Road, New Addington, Croydon CR0 0NE* Tel (01689) 846156 Mobile 07810-524007
E-mail revdmk.twining@btinternet.com

TWINLEY, David Alan. b 66. Ox Univ BTh00 Heythrop Coll Lon MA10. St Steph Ho Ox 97. **d** 00 **p** 01. C Saffron Walden w Wendens Ambo, Littlebury etc *Chelmsf* 00-03; V Bury w Houghton and Coldwaltham and Hardham *Chich* from 03; RD Petworth from 10. *The Vicarage, Church Lane, Bury, Pulborough RH20 1PB* Tel (01798) 839057 E-mail frdavid@twinley.me.uk

TWISLETON, John Fiennes. b 48. St Jo Coll Ox BA69 MA73 DPhil73. Coll of Resurr Mirfield 73. **d** 76 **p** 77. C New Bentley *Sheff* 76-79; P-in-c Moorends 79-80; V 80-86; USPG 86-90; Prin Alan Knight Tr Cen Guyana 87-90; V Holbrooks *Cov* 90-96; Edmonton Area Missr *Lon* 96-01; Dioc Adv for Miss and Renewal *Chich* 01-09; C Haywards Heath St Rich 01-09; R Horsted Keynes from 09. *The Rectory, Station Road, Horsted Keynes, Haywards Heath RH17 7ED* Tel (01825) 790317
E-mail john@twisleton.co.uk

TWISLETON, Peter. b 50. Linc Th Coll. **d** 84 **p** 85. C Bodmin w Lanhydrock and Lanivet *Truro* 84-87; C Par 87-90; R St Breoke and Egloshayle 90-93; R Bude Haven and Marhamchurch 93-97; V Horbury w Horbury Bridge *Wakef* 98-07; P-in-c Seaham Harbour and Dawdon *Dur* 07; V from 08. *The Vicarage, Maureen Terrace, Seaham SR7 7SN* Tel 0191-581 3385

TWISS, Dorothy Elizabeth. Gilmore Ho 68 Linc Th Coll 70. **d** 87 **p** 94. Chapl Asst RAF 78-91; TV Pewsey *Sarum* 91-95; Chapl HM Pris Drake Hall 95-01; Chapl HM Pris Ford 01-03; rtd 03; Perm to Offic *Portsm* from 05. *41 Rosecott, Havant Road, Horndean, Waterlooville PO8 0XA* Tel 07929-650284 (mobile)
E-mail dorothy.twiss371@btinternet.com

TWITTY, Miss Rosamond Jane. b 54. Univ of Wales (Ban) BSc75 CertEd76. Trin Coll Bris BA89. **d** 90 **p** 94. Par Dn Lt Thurrock

St Jo *Chelmsf* 90-94; C 94-95; C Upper Armley *Ripon* 95-08; TV Langport Area *B & W* from 08. *The Vicarage, 1 New Street, Long Sutton, Langport TA10 9JW* Tel (01458) 241260
E-mail janetwitty@supanet.com

TWOHIG, Brian Robert. b 48. La Trobe Univ Vic BA77 PhD86. St Mich Th Coll Crafers 70. **d** 72 **p** 73. Australia 72-78 and 80-82; C Leatherhead *Guildf* 78-80; TV New Windsor *Ox* 82-92; V Sheff St Cuth 92-97; rtd 97; Perm to Offic *Chich* from 98. *26A Bloomsbury Street, Brighton BN2 1HQ* Tel (01273) 270481

TWOMEY, Jeremiah Francis (Derry). b 50. Man Poly BA83 Univ of Wales (Ban) PGCE85. NEOC 92. **d** 94 **p** 95. C Beverley St Nic *York* 94-96; V Anlaby Common St Mark 96-99; Ind Chapl *Newc* 99-05; V Bedlington from 05. *The Vicarage, 21 Church Lane, Bedlington NE22 5EL* Tel (01670) 829220
E-mail derrytwomey@aol.com

TWOMEY, Jeremiah Thomas Paul. b 46. CITC 87. **d** 87 **p** 88. C Derryloran *Arm* 87-90; I Brackaville w Donaghendry and Ballyclog 90-97; I Mohill w Farnaught, Aughavas, Oughteragh etc *K, E & A* 97-00; Bp's C Belfast Whiterock *Conn* 00-08; C Belfast St Anne from 08. *Address temp unknown*
E-mail ptwomey@esatclear.ie

TWYFORD, Canon Arthur Russell. b 36. ALCD60. **d** 60 **p** 61. C Speke All SS *Liv* 60-64; R Maids Moreton w Foxcote *Ox* 64-72; Asst Dioc Youth Officer 64-70; P-in-c Lillingstone Dayrell w Lillingstone Lovell 70-72; V Desborough *Pet* 72-88; P-in-c Brampton Ash w Dingley 73-77; P-in-c Braybrook 73-77; R Brampton Ash w Dingley and Braybrooke 77-88; RD Kettering 79-87; Can Pet Cathl 81-95; R Stanwick w Hargrave 88-95; rtd 95; Perm to Offic *Pet* 95-07. *chemin des Fées, 46250 Cazals, France* Tel (0033) 5 65 21 66 93 E-mail artwyford@aol.com

TWYNAM, Mrs Susan Elizabeth. b 59. Bath Coll of HE BEd81. SEITE 06. **d** 09 **p** 10. NSM Sidcup St Jo *Roch* from 09. *6 Williams Way, Dartford DA2 7WF* Tel (01322) 559501
E-mail susantwynam@btconnect.com

TYACK, Clare Elizabeth. b 48. **d** 11. NSM Blidworth w Rainworth *S'well* from 11. *The Limes, Main Street, Linby, Nottingham NG15 8AE* Tel 0115-963 2270
E-mail claretyack@yahoo.co.uk

TYDEMAN, Rosemary. *See* WILLIAMS, Mrs Rosemary

TYE, Dominic Geoffrey Bernard. b 43. Lanc Univ BA70 PhD75. Kelham Th Coll 62. **d** 67 **p** 68. SSM 66-78; C Lancaster St Mary *Blackb* 67-70; Lect Kelham Th Coll 70-73; Chapl Woden Hosp Australia 75-76; Teacher Lancaster 78-84; Hd Sixth Form Fleetwood Sch 84-87; Dep Hd Lancaster Girls Gr Sch 87-90; Hd Thorncliffe Sch Barrow-in-Furness 90-97; Co-ord Cen Educn Leadership Man Univ 98-02; rtd 08. *9 Sea View Drive, Hest Bank, Lancaster LA2 6BY* Tel (01524) 823462
E-mail member@dtye.freeserve.co.uk

TYE, Eric John. b 37. St Alb Minl Tr Scheme 78. **d** 81 **p** 82. NSM Rushden St Mary w Newton Bromswold *Pet* 81-07; Perm to Offic from 07. *29 Kingsmead Park, Bedford Road, Rushden NN10 0NF* Tel (01933) 353274
E-mail johnchristye@tiscali.co.uk

TYE, John Raymond. b 31. Lambeth STh64 Linc Th Coll 66. **d** 68 **p** 69. C Crewe St Mich *Ches* 68-71; C Wednesfield St Thos *Lich* 71-76; P-in-c Petton w Cockshutt 76-79; P-in-c Hordley 79; P-in-c Weston Lullingfield 79; R Petton w Cockshutt and Weston Lullingfield etc 79-81; V Hadley 81-84; R Ightfield w Calverhall 84-89; V Ash 84-89; R Calton, Cauldon, Grindon and Waterfall 89-96; RD Alstonfield 95-96; rtd 96; Perm to Offic *Lich* from 05. *38 Aston Street, Wem, Shrewsbury SY4 5AU*

TYERS, Canon John Haydn. b 31. Lon Univ BSc51 Open Univ BA00. Ridley Hall Cam 53. **d** 55 **p** 56. C Nuneaton St Nic *Cov* 55-58; C Rugby St Andr 58-62; V Cov St Anne 62-71; V Keresley and Coundon 71-78; V Atherstone 78-85; P-in-c Pleshey *Chelmsf* 85-91; Warden Pleshey Retreat Ho 85-91; Hon Can Chelmsf Cathl 86-91; P-in-c Ash *Lich* 91-96; P-in-c Ightfield w Calverhall 91-96; rtd 96; Perm to Offic *Heref* 97-08. *30 Stuart Court, High Street, Kibworth, Leicester LE8 0LR* Tel 0116-279 3093

TYERS, Philip Nicolas. b 56. St Jo Coll Nottm BTh84. **d** 84 **p** 85. C Rugby St Matt *Cov* 84-88; TV Cov E 88-95; P-in-c Preston St Matt *Blackb* 95-96; TR Preston Risen Lord 96-06; Co-ord Chapl HM Pris Leeds 06-07; Co-ord Chapl HM Pris Wymott from 07. *HM Prison Wymott, Ulnes Walton Lane, Leyland PR26 8LW* Tel (01772) 442000
E-mail philip.tyers@hmps.gsi.gov.uk

TYLDESLEY, Mrs Vera. b 47. Man Coll of Educn BEd80. **d** 98 **p** 99. OLM Pendlebury St Jo *Man* from 98. *7 Kingsway, Swinton, Manchester M27 4JU* Tel 0161-736 3845

TYLER, Canon Alan William. b 60. Ridley Hall Cam 84. **d** 86 **p** 87. C Bedwellty *Mon* 86-89; C St Mellons and Michaelston-y-Fedw 89-92; V Abersychan and Garndiffaith 92-97; Chapl Glan Hafren NHS Trust 97-99; Sen Chapl Gwent Healthcare NHS Trust from 99; Can St Woolos Cathl from 08. *The Royal Gwent Hospital, Cardiff Road, Newport NP20 2UB* Tel (01633) 234263 *or* 871457 E-mail alan.tyler@gwent.wales.nhs.uk

TYLER, Alison Ruth. b 51. Keele Univ BA74 CQSW78. S'wark Ord Course 93. **d** 95 **p** 96. NSM Hatcham St Cath *S'wark* 95-99; Dep Chapl HM Pris Brixton 99-02; Chapl HM Pris Wormwood

Scrubs 02-07; Learning and Development Manager HM Pris Service Chapl from 07; Hon Chapl S'wark Cathl from 06. *Chaplaincy HQ, Post Point 3.08, 3rd Floor Red Zone, Clive House, 70 Petty France, London SW1H 9HD* Tel 03000-475193 *or* (020) 7207 0756 Fax 03000-476822/3
E-mail alison.tyler01@hmps.gsi.gov.uk
or ar.tyler@ntlworld.com
TYLER, Andrew. b 57. Univ of Wales (Lamp) BA79 Warw Univ MA80 Man Univ BD86. Coll of Resurr Mirfield 83. **d** 87 **p** 88. C Glen Parva and S Wigston *Leic* 87-90; C Didcot All SS *Ox* 90-92; Asst Chapl Chu Hosp Ox 92-93; NSM Caversham St Andr *Ox* 93-97; Co-ord Tr Portfolio (Berks) 96-97; P-in-c Nor St Giles 97-99; P-in-c Norwich St Mary Magd w St Jas 99-00; V 00-08; rtd 08; Hon C Eaton Ch Ch *Nor* from 09. *32 Brian Avenue, Norwich NR1 2PH* Tel (01603) 622158
E-mail xatyler@aol.com
TYLER, Brian Sidney. b 32. MIPI79. Chich Th Coll 62. **d** 64 **p** 65. C Brighton St Mich *Chich* 64-69; C-in-c Southwick St Pet 69-75; Perm to Offic 80; NSM Brighton Resurr 93-94; Chapl St Dunstan's Hosp Brighton 93-95; C Brighton St Matthias *Chich* 95-02; Hon C 02-05; rtd 02; Perm to Offic *Chich* from 05. *318 Ditchling Road, Brighton BN1 6JG* Tel (01273) 559262
TYLER, David Stuart. b 69. Hull Univ BSc91 ACA94. Wycliffe Hall Ox 01. **d** 03 **p** 04. C Ashby-de-la-Zouch St Helen w Coleorton *Leic* 03-05; C Ashby-de-la-Zouch and Breedon on the Hill 05-07; P-in-c Hanborough and Freeland *Ox* from 07. *The Rectory, Swan Lane, Long Hanborough, Witney OX29 8BT* Tel (01993) 881270 E-mail revdavidtyler@googlemail.com
TYLER (née FOSTER), Mrs Frances Elizabeth. b 55. Linc Th Coll 81. **dss** 84 **d** 87 **p** 94. Hampton All SS *Lon* 84-87; Par Dn Brentford 87-91; NSM Walsgrave on Sowe *Cov* from 91; Dioc Adv for Women's Min 97-05; Chapl S Warks Gen Hosps NHS Trust from 08. *The Vicarage, 4 Farber Road, Coventry CV2 2BG* Tel (024) 7661 5152 E-mail revftyler@aol.com
TYLER, Mrs Gaynor. b 46. Univ of Wales (Abth) BA68. S'wark Ord Course 87. **d** 90 **p** 94. NSM Reigate St Luke S Park *S'wark* 90-97; Deanery NSM Maelienydd *S & B* 97-04; NSM Cwmdauddwr w St Harmon and Llanwrthwl 04-05; NSM Llanwrthwl w St Harmon, Rhayader, Nantmel etc 05-06; Perm to Offic from 06. *Dyffryn Farm, Llanwrthwl, Llandrindod Wells LD1 6NU* Tel (01597) 811017
TYLER, John Thorne. b 46. Selw Coll Cam BA68 MA71. Sarum & Wells Th Coll 70. **d** 72 **p** 73. C Frome St Jo *B & W* 72-74; Chapl Huish Coll Taunton 74-93; Hon C Stoke St Gregory w Burrowbridge and Lyng *B & W* 77-93; P-in-c Shepton Beauchamp w Barrington, Stocklinch etc 93-94; TV Ilminster and Distr 94-98; rtd 99; Hon C Quantock Towers *B & W* 99-01; P-in-c Stogursey w Fiddington 01-06; Perm to Offic 06-09; C Chard St Mary w Combe St Nicholas, Wambrook etc 09-10. *24 Ganges Close, Fivehead, Taunton TA3 6PG* Tel (01460) 281574 E-mail tyleruk@hotmail.com
TYLER, Malcolm. b 56. Kent Univ BSc77 Cam Univ BA84. Ridley Hall Cam 82. **d** 85 **p** 86. C Twickenham St Mary *Lon* 85-88; C Acton St Mary 88-91; V Walsgrave on Sowe *Cov* from 91; AD Cov E from 07. *The Vicarage, 4 Farber Road, Coventry CV2 2BG* Tel (024) 7661 5152 *or* 7661 8845
E-mail stmaryssowe@aol.com
TYLER, Paul Graham Edward. b 58. Cranmer Hall Dur. **d** 83 **p** 84. C Stranton *Dur* 83-86; C Collierley w Annfield Plain 86-89; V Esh and Hamsteels 89-92; Chapl HM Pris Frankland from 09. *HM Prison Frankland, Brasside, Durham DH1 5YD* Tel 0191-332 3000
TYLER, Samuel John. b 32. Lon Univ BD57. Oak Hill Th Coll 57. **d** 58 **p** 59. C W Ham All SS *Chelmsf* 58-61; V Berechurch 61-64; R Aythorpe w High and Leaden Roding 64-72; Perm to Offic 73-74; P-in-c Gt Ilford St Jo 74-76; V 76-92; rtd 92. *21 Ash Green, Canewdon, Rochford SS4 3QN* Tel (01702) 258526
TYLER (née WAITE), Mrs Sheila Margaret. b 25. SRN47. Trin Coll Bris 71. **dss** 79 **d** 87 **p** 94. Easton H Trin w St Gabr and St Lawr *Bris* 79-80; Westbury-on-Trym St Alb 81-85; rtd 85; Hon Par Dn Henleaze *Bris* 87-94; Hon C 94-95; Chapl Stoke Park and Purdown Hosps Stapleton 88-90; Perm to Offic *Bris* 95-08; *B & W* 95-00; *Chich* 01-02. *6 Gracey Court, Woodland Road, Broadclyst, Exeter EX5 3GA* Tel (01392) 462872
TYNDALL, Daniel Frank. b 61. Aston Tr Scheme 90 Sarum & Wells Th Coll BTh93. **d** 93 **p** 94. C Wolverhampton *Lich* 93-96; C Bris St Mary Redcliffe w Temple etc 96-01; V Earley St Nic *Ox* 01-08; P-in-c Caversham St Pet and Mapledurham 08-10; P-in-c Caversham St Jo 08-10; R Caversham Thameside and Mapledurham from 10. *20 Church Road, Caversham, Reading RG4 7AD* Tel 0118-947 9505 E-mail dftyndall@gmail.com
TYNDALL, Mrs Elizabeth Mary. b 30. St Andr Univ MA51 Hughes Hall Cam CertEd52. Qu Coll Birm 81. **dss** 83 **d** 87 **p** 94. Rugby *Cov* 83-87; Par Dn Feltham *Lon* 87-91; rtd 92; NSM Vale of White Horse Deanery *Ox* 93-03. *c/o The Revd D F Tyndall, 20 Church Road, Caversham, Reading RG4 7AD*
TYNDALL, Jeremy Hamilton. b 55. Birm Univ MPhil01. St Jo Coll Nottm BTh81 LTh81. **d** 81 **p** 82. C Oakwood St Thos *Lon*

81-84; C Upper Holloway St Pet w St Jo 84-87; TV Halewood *Liv* 87-96; P-in-c Yardley St Edburgha *Birm* 96-99; V 99-01; R Eugene St Thos USA 01-08; Dean Cen Convocation 06-08; TR Cove St Jo *Guildf* from 08. *The Rectory, 55 Cove Road, Farnborough GU14 0EX* Tel (01252) 544544
E-mail rector@parishofcove.org.uk
TYNDALL, Simon James. b 54. LSE BSc(Econ)77 Lon Univ PGCE82 Open Univ MA98. St Jo Coll Nottm 88. **d** 90 **p** 91. C Yeovil w Kingston Pitney *B & W* 90-94; V Rastrick St Jo *Wakef* 94-01; TR Chippenham St Paul w Hardenhuish etc *Bris* from 01; V Kington St Michael from 01; AD Chippenham from 08. *The Rectory, 9 Greenway Park, Chippenham SN15 1QG* Tel (01249) 657216 E-mail simon@tyndall.plus.com
TYNDALL, Canon Timothy Gardner. b 25. Jes Coll Cam BA50. Wells Th Coll 50. **d** 51 **p** 52. C Warsop *S'well* 51-55; R Newark St Leon 55-60; V Sherwood 60-75; P-in-c Bishopwearmouth St Mich w St Hilda *Dur* 75-85; RD Wearmouth 75-85; Hon Can Dur Cathl 83-90; Chief Sec ACCM 85-90; rtd 90; Perm to Offic *Lon* and *S'wark* from 90. *29 Kingswood Road, London W4 5EU* Tel (020) 8994 4516
TYNEY, Canon James Derrick. b 33. TCD. **d** 62 **p** 63. C Ballynafeigh St Jude *D & D* 62-64; C Bangor St Comgall 64-69; I Clonallon w Warrenpoint 69-75; I Groomsport 75-00; Can Belf Cathl 93-00; Dioc Registrar *D & D* 95-00; rtd 00. *27 Sandringham Drive, Bangor BT20 5NA* Tel (028) 9145 5670
TYRER, Ms Jayne Linda. b 59. Goldsmiths' Coll Lon BA81 CertEd82. Sarum & Wells Th Coll 85. **d** 87 **p** 95. C Rochdale *Man* 87-88; Par Dn Heywood St Luke w All So 88-91; Hon Par Dn Burneside *Carl* 91-07; Hon Par Dn Beacon from 07; Chapl Kendal Hosps 91-94; Chapl Westmorland Hosps NHS Trust 94-98; Chapl Univ Hosps of Morecambe Bay NHS Trust from 98. *St Oswald's Vicarage, Burneside, Kendal LA9 6QX* Tel (01539) 722015 E-mail jayne.tyrer@wgh.mbht.nhs.uk
TYRER, Neil. *See* PURVEY-TYRER, Neil
TYREUS, Per Jonas Waldemar (Peter). b 45. Uppsala Univ 66. **p** 71. Sweden 71-00; C Pelton *Dur* 00-03; C Chester le Street 03-11; rtd 11. *27 Castle Riggs, Chester le Street DH2 2DL* E-mail petertyreus@googlemail.com
TYRREL, John Cockett. b 16. Qu Coll Cam BA38 MA42. Ridley Hall Cam 38. **d** 40 **p** 41. C Southall H Trin *Lon* 40-43; Chapl RNVR 43-46; S Africa 46-50; Australia from 50; rtd 81; Perm to Offic Canberra and Goulburn from 81. *20/58 Shackleton Circuit, Mawson ACT 2607, Australia* Tel (0061) (2) 6286 1317
TYRRELL, The Very Revd Charles Robert. b 51. SRN73 Open Univ BA80. Oak Hill Th Coll 74. **d** 77 **p** 78. C Halewood *Liv* 77-80; C St Helens St Helen 80-83; V Banks 83-88; Can Wellington New Zealand 88-94; Dean Nelson from 94. *The Deanery, 365 Trafalgar Street, Nelson 7010, New Zealand* Tel (0064) (3) 548 8574 *or* 548 1008
E-mail charles.tyrell@clear.net.nz
TYRRELL, John Patrick Hammond. b 42. Cranmer Hall Dur 62. **d** 65 **p** 66. C Edin St Jo 65-68; Chapl RN 68-72; Chapl St John's Cathl Hong Kong 72-74 and 78-82; Area Sec SE Asia SOMA UK 78-82; V Westborough *Guildf* 74-78; C Yateley *Win* 82-83; C-in-c Darby Green CD 83-88; V Darby Green 88-96; V Chineham 96-97; rtd 02; Perm to Offic *Linc* from 06. *5 Blacksmith's Court, Metheringham, Lincoln LN4 3YQ* Tel (01526) 322147 E-mail john_tyrrell42@hotmail.com
TYRRELL, Stephen Jonathan. b 39. Sheff Univ BA62. Clifton Th Coll. **d** 65 **p** 66. C Rodbourne Cheney *Bris* 65-68; C Lillington *Cov* 68-72; P-in-c Bishop's Itchington 73-78; V 78-86; V Kington upon Hull St Nic *York* 86-92; TV Cheltenham St Mary, St Matt, St Paul and H Trin *Glouc* 92-04; rtd 04; Perm to Offic *Glouc* from 05. *96 A Fosseway Avenue, Moreton-in-Marsh GL56 0EA* Tel (01608) 812350
TYSOE, James Raymond. b 19. Qu Coll Birm 70. **d** 75 **p** 76. NSM Cov E 75-85; NSM Cov Cathl 85-87; Perm to Offic *Glouc* from 87. *Wisma Mulia, Bridge Road, Frampton on Severn, Gloucester GL2 7HE* Tel (01452) 740890
TYSON, Mrs Frances Mary. b 44. Reading Univ BScAgr68 Wolv Univ PGCE91. St Jo Coll Nottm 01. **d** 02 **p** 03. NSM Walsall *Lich* 02-07; NSM Portswood Ch Ch *Win* from 07. *26 Reynolds Road, Southampton SO15 5GS*
TYSON, Mrs Nigella Jane. b 44. RGN66 Kent Univ BA95. SEITE 96. **d** 97 **p** 98. NSM Aylesham w Adisham, Nonington w Wymynswold and Goodnestone etc *Cant* 97-00; P-in-c Kingsland w Eardisland, Aymestrey etc *Heref* 00-04; R 04-09; rtd 09. *Fairview, Stoke Prior, Leominster HR6 0NE* Tel (01568) 760610 E-mail revnigella@sky.com
TYSON, Canon William Edward Porter. b 25. St Cath Coll Cam BA49 MA52. Ridley Hall Cam 49. **d** 51 **p** 52. C Wilmslow *Ches* 51-54; C Astbury 54-57; V Macclesfield St Pet 57-62; V Over Tabley 62-70; V High Legh 62-70; CF (TA) 64-91; V Church Hulme *Ches* 70-91; Chapl Cranage Hall Hosp 70-91; Hon Can Ches Cathl 82-91; rtd 91; Perm to Offic *Ches* and *Carl* from 91. *59 Kirkhead Road, Allithwaite, Grange-over-Sands LA11 7DD* Tel (01539) 535291
TÄRNEBERG, Helene. *See* STEED, Canon Helene

U

UDAL, Canon Joanna Elizabeth Margaret. b 64. SS Hild & Bede Coll Dur BSc86. Ripon Coll Cuddesdon BTh94. **d** 97 **p** 98. C Whitton St Aug *Lon* 97-00; Asst to Abp Sudan 00-09; Abp's Sec for Angl Communion Affairs *Cant* 09. *Address temp unknown*

UDDIN, Mohan. b 52. Sussex Univ BA74 PGCE75 Lon Bible Coll MA87 PhD98 Anglia Poly Univ MA02. Ridley Hall Cam 99. **d** 03 **p** 04. C Hornchurch St Andr *Chelmsf* 03-07; Perm to Offic *Chelmsf* 08-11 and *Win* 09-12; TV Newbury *Ox* from 10. *St John's Vicarage, 1 Chesterfield Road, Newbury RG14 7QB* Tel (01635) 30900 Mobile 07515-386301 E-mail mohan.uddin@btopenworld.com

UFFINDELL, David Wilfred George. b 37. Qu Coll Birm 72. **d** 75 **p** 76. NSM Harlescott *Lich* 75-07; Perm to Offic from 08. *13 Kenley Avenue, Heath Farm, Shrewsbury SY1 3HA* Tel and fax (01743) 352029 E-mail revuffindell@talktalk.net

UFFINDELL, Harold David. b 61. Down Coll Cam MA87. Wycliffe Hall Ox BA86 MA91 Oak Hill Th Coll 86. **d** 87 **p** 88. C Kingston Hill St Paul *S'wark* 87-91; C Surbiton St Matt 91-98; V Sunningdale *Ox* from 98. *The Vicarage, Sidbury Close, Sunningdale, Ascot SL5 0PD* Tel (01344) 620061 E-mail david@htpcsunn.freeserve.co.uk

UGANDA, Archbishop of. See OROMBI, The Most Revd Henry Luke

UGWUNNA, The Ven Sydney Chukwunma. b 45. Nebraska Wesleyan Univ BSc67 Univ of Nebraska, Linc MEd70 Wayne State Univ PhD79. Virginia Th Sem MDiv96. **d** 96 **p** 97. C Alexandria Resurrection USA 96-97; C Knaresborough *Ripon* 98-02; Dean Trin Th Coll and Adn Umuahia Nigeria 03-06; R Alexandria Meade Memorial USA 06-08; Visiting P Washington Cathl 09-10; R Earleville St Steph 10-11. *The Rectory, 14 Glebe Road, Earleville MD 21919-2144, USA* Tel (001) (410) 275 2863 *or* 275 8785 E-mail revugwunna@gmail.com

ULLMANN, Clair. See FILBERT-ULLMANN, Mrs Clair

ULOGWARA, Canon Obinna Chiadikobi. b 68. Univ of Nigeria BA(Ed)98 Lagos Univ MEd03. Trin Coll Umuahia 87. **d** 90 **p** 91. V Ahiara H Trin Nigeria 90-93; Chapl Secondary Schs Dio Mbaise 90-93; V Irete St Pet 93-95; Chapl Secondary Schs Dio Owerri 94-99; V Egbeada Em 99; V Sari Iganmu St Phil 00-01; V Igbobi St Steph and Hon Chapl to Abp Lagos 01-05; C Dublin Whitechurch *D & G* 05-10; Bp's C Dublin St Geo and St Thos from 10. *St George's Rectory, 96 Lower Drumcondra Road, Dublin 9, Republic of Ireland* Tel (00353) (1) 830 0160 Mobile 87-247 6339 E-mail binagwara@yahoo.com

UMPLEBY, Mark Raymond. b 70. Trin Coll Bris BA99. **d** 99 **p** 00. C Birstall *Wakef* 99-02; TV N Huddersfield 02-06; Dioc Voc Adv 04-06; Chapl David Young Community Academy Leeds from 06. *David Young Community Academy, North Parkway, Leeds LS14 6RF* E-mail markumpleby@hotmail.com

UNDERDOWN, Margaret Jean (Meg). b 49. Univ of Wales (Abth) BSc70. St Mich Coll Llan 06. **d** 08 **p** 09. Chapl HM Pris Cardiff from 03. *HM Prison Cardiff, 1 Knox Road, Cardiff CF24 0UG* Tel (029) 2092 3100

UNDERDOWN, Steven. b 52. Hull Univ BSc75 CertEd76 K Coll Lon PhD02. **d** 88 **p** 04. CSWG 82-02; Chapl Brighton and Sussex Univ Hosps NHS Trust from 03; NSM Hove *Chich* 03-09; P-in-c Hove St Patr from 09. *1 Lyndhurst Corner, Lyndhurst Road, Hove BN3 6FR* Tel (01273) 747889 Mobile 07981-423973 E-mail steven.underdown@hotmail.com *or* steven.underdown@bsuh.nhs.uk

UNDERHILL, Edward Mark Thomas. b 24. Univ Coll Dur BA50. St Aid Birkenhead 50. **d** 52 **p** 53. C Meopham *Roch* 52-54; Prin Kigari Coll Kenya 55-57; PC Gateshead St Geo *Dur* 57-68; V 68-09; rtd 09. *54 Castlehead Close, Keswick CA12 4DJ* Tel (01768) 774271

UNDERHILL, Robin. b 31. Marymount Coll California BA89 Woodbury Univ California BSc90. Claremont Sch of Th MA92. **d** 93 **p** 94. Asst P Beverly Hills All SS USA 93-00; Pastor San Fernando St Simon 00-01; rtd 01; P-in-c Stranraer and Portpatrick *Glas* 01-04; Sec for Scotland Miss to Seafarers from 04. *Tigh Ban, Hightae, Lockerbie DG11 1JN* Tel (01387) 811112 Mobile 07800-798483 E-mail mts_scotland@onetel.com

UNDERHILL, Stanley Robert. b 27. Cant Sch of Min. **d** 82 **p** 83. C New Addington *Cant* 82-84; C Cannock *Lich* 84-86; TV 86-88; R Dymchurch w Burmarsh and Newchurch *Cant* 88-92; rtd 92; Chapl Menorca *Eur* 92-94; Perm to Offic *Cant* 94-04 and *Lon* 05-08. *Charterhouse, Charterhouse Square, London EC1M 6AN* Tel (020) 7490 5059 Mobile 07970-954958 E-mail stanunder@aol.com

UNDERWOOD, Adrian Anthony. b 67. **d** 02 **p** 03. C Sparkhill w Greet and Sparkbrook *Birm* 02-06; C Selly Park St Steph and St Wulstan 06-10; rtd 10. *11 Weoley Park Road, Selly Park, Birmingham B29 6QY* Tel 0121-572 2151 Mobile 07954-140326 E-mail adrianandsarah@blueyonder.co.uk

UNDERWOOD, Brian. b 35. Dur Univ BA57 Keble Coll Ox PGCE76 Dur Univ MA72. Clifton Th Coll 57. **d** 59 **p** 60. C Blackpool Ch Ch *Blackb* 59-61; C New Malden and Coombe *S'wark* 61-64; Travel Sec Pathfinders 64-68; Chapl Chantilly *Eur* 68-69; Home Sec CCCS 69-71; P-in-c Gatten St Paul *Portsm* 71-72; Chapl Lyon w Grenoble and Aix-les-Bains *Eur* 72-75; Asst Chapl Trent Coll Nottm 76-80; Chapl Qu Eliz Gr Sch Blackb 80-85; R Bentham St Jo *Bradf* 85-92; V St Alb Ch Ch *St Alb* 92-00; rtd 00; Perm to Offic *St Alb* from 00. *16 Mitford Close, Bedford MK41 8RF* Tel (01234) 407856

UNDERWOOD, Charles Brian. b 23. Leeds Univ BA48 CertEd. Coll of Resurr Mirfield 48. **d** 50 **p** 51. C Tilehurst St Mich *Ox* 50-53; C Leic St Paul 53-54; Youth Chapl 54-61; V Leic St Geo 57-59; R Harby 59-61; New Zealand 61-62; Dioc Youth Chapl *Bradf* 63-72; R Carleton-in-Craven 63-76; V Twyning *Glouc* 76-88; RD Tewkesbury 81-88; rtd 88; Perm to Offic *Glouc* from 00. *Chavender, 9 Ellendene Drive, Pamington, Tewkesbury GL20 8LU* Tel (01684) 772504 E-mail brian@chavender.fsnet.co.uk

UNDERWOOD, David Richard. b 47. AKC69 St Osyth Coll of Educn PGCE72. St Aug Coll Cant 69. **d** 70 **p** 92. C Witham *Chelmsf* 70-71; Teacher 71-82; Hd Teacher Gt Heath Sch Mildenhall 82-91; NSM Chevington w Hargrave and Whepstead w Brockley *St E* 82-91; Par Dn Haverhill w Withersfield, the Wrattings etc 91-92; TV 92-94; P-in-c Bury St Edmunds St Jo 94-99; RD Thingoe 95-99; P-in-c Bury St Edmunds St Geo 98-99; Dioc Dir of Educn 99-04; Hon Can St E Cathl 03-04; rtd 07. *1 Fishers Way, Godmanchester, Huntingdon PE29 2XE* Tel (01480) 411293 E-mail davidunderwood2@aol.com

UNDERWOOD, John Alan. b 40. Glos Coll of Arts & Tech BSc88 Ox Poly CertEd84 MBCS74. SAOMC 96. **d** 99 **p** 00. OLM Eynsham and Cassington *Ox* 99-10; Perm to Offic from 10. *17 Witney Road, Eynsham, Oxford OX29 4PH* Tel (01865) 881254 *or* 301305 Fax 301301 E-mail junderw549@aol.com

UNDERWOOD, Mrs Susannah Lucy. b 72. Westmr Coll Ox BTh98. ERMC 05. **d** 08 **p** 09. C Stevenage H Trin *St Alb* from 08. *3 Glebe Road, Welwyn AL6 9PB* Tel (01438) 367246 E-mail curate@holytrinity-stevenage.info

UNGOED-THOMAS, Peter. b 27. Pemb Coll Ox BA51 MA67. St Mich Coll Llan. **d** 60 **p** 61. C Llangeinor 60-64; I Dublin Donnybrook *D & G* 64-67; RAChD 67-70; Chapl Leigh C of E Schs 70-74; C Leigh St Mary *Man* 70-74; Lect Warley Coll 74-86; Perm to Offic *Birm* 75-00 and *St D* from 75; Lect Sandwell Coll of F&HE from 86; rtd 94. *93 Heol Felin-Foel, Llanelli SA15 3JQ*

UNITED STATES OF AMERICA, Presiding Bishop of. See JEFFERTS SCHORI, The Most Revd Katharine

UNSWORTH, Philip James. b 41. UEA BEd82 Nottm Coll of Educn CertEd63 Nottm Univ DipEd72. EAMTC 94. **d** 97 **p** 98. NSM Hethersett w Canteloff w Lt and Gt Melton *Nor* 97-00; P-in-c Blofield w Hemblington 00-06; rtd 06; Perm to Offic *Nor* from 06. *55 Campbell Close, Hunstanton PE36 5PJ* Tel (01485) 532436

UNSWORTH, Thomas Foster. b 28. Lon Univ BA56. Lich Th Coll 60. **d** 62 **p** 63. C Northfield *Birm* 62-64; C The Lickey 64-66; V Forcett *Ripon* 66-68; V Bellerby and Leyburn 68-73; Chapl Whittingham Hosp Preston 73-79; V Freckleton *Blackb* 79-83; V S Yardley St Mich *Birm* 83-86; V Sutton w Carlton and Normanton upon Trent etc *S'well* 86-90; rtd 90; Chapl St Raphaël *Eur* 90-97; Perm to Offic *Cant* from 99. *31 Broadlands Avenue, New Romney TN28 8JE* Tel (01797) 361922

UNWIN, Barry. b 70. Sheff Univ BA91. Oak Hill Th Coll BA05. **d** 05 **p** 06. C Hebburn St Jo *Dur* 05-09; C Jarrow Grange 05-09; P-in-c New Barnet St Jas *St Alb* from 09. *St James' Vicarage, 11 Park Road, Barnet EN4 9QA* Tel (020) 8449 4043 E-mail barryunwin@gmail.com

UNWIN, Christopher Michael Fairclough. b 31. Dur Univ BA57. Linc Th Coll 65. **d** 67 **p** 68. C S Shields St Hilda w St Thos *Dur* 67-73; R Tatsfield *S'wark* 73-81; RE Adv to Ch Secondary Schs 73-81; V Newc St Gabr 81-96; RD Newc E 96; rtd 96; Perm to Offic *Dur* and *Newc* from 96. *2 The Cottage, West Row, Greatham, Hartlepool TS25 2HW* Tel (01429) 872781

UNWIN, The Ven Kenneth. b 26. St Edm Hall Ox BA48 MA52. Ely Th Coll 49. **d** 51 **p** 52. C Leeds All SS *Ripon* 51-55; C Dur St Marg 55-59; V Dodworth *Wakef* 59-69; V Royston 69-73; V Wakef St Jo 73-82; Hon Can Wakef Cathl 80-82; RD Wakef 80-81; Adn Pontefract 82-92; rtd 92; Perm to Offic *Bradf* and *Wakef* from 92. *2 Rockwood Close, Skipton BD23 1UG* Tel (01756) 791323

UNWIN, Michael. See UNWIN, Christopher Michael Fairclough

UPCOTT, Derek Jarvis. b 26. CEng FIMechE FBIM. S'wark Ord Course 81. **d** 84 **p** 85. NSM Gt Chesham *Ox* 84-99; Perm to Offic *St Alb* 90-99 and *Ox* from 99. *Bluff Cottage, Blackthorne Lane, Ballinger, Great Missenden HP16 9LN* Tel (01494) 837505 E-mail derek.upcott@activelives.co.uk

UPHILL, Ms Ann Carol. b 54. Westcott Ho Cam 95. **d** 97 **p** 98. C Strood St Nic w St Mary *Roch* 97-01; R Footscray w N Cray

from 01. *The Rectory, Rectory Lane, Sidcup DA14 5BP* Tel and fax (020) 8300 7096 Mobile 07802-883121
E-mail ann.uphill@diocese-rochester.org
or annuphill@lineone.net

UPHILL, Keith Ivan. b 35. Keble Coll Ox BA70 MA74. Wycliffe Hall Ox 67. **d** 70 **p** 71. C Maghull *Liv* 70-73; V Wroxall *Portsm* 73-77; TV Fareham H Trin 77-82; C Havant 82-84; P-in-c Merton St Jo *S'wark* 84-85; V 85-95; rtd 95; Perm to Offic *Portsm* from 95. *20 Wilby Lane, Anchorage Park, Portsmouth PO3 5UF* Tel (023) 9266 6998

UPTON, Anthony Arthur. b 30. Leic Univ MA97 PhD03. Wells Th Coll 61. **d** 63 **p** 64. C Milton *Portsm* 63-67; Chapl RN 67-83; V Foleshill St Laur *Cov* 83-91; rtd 91; Perm to Offic *Cov* from 91. *Redlands Bungalow, Banbury Road, Lighthorne CV35 0AH*

UPTON, Ms Caroline Tracey. b 67. Lon Univ BMus90 Edin Univ BD94. Edin Th Coll 91. **d** 94 **p** 95. C Edin St Martin 94-96; Hon C Edin St Pet 97-99; C 99-01; Chapl Lothian Univ Hosps NHS Trust from 01. *10 (3F1) Montagu Terrace, Edinburgh EH3 5QX* Tel 0131-552 0731 *or* 536 0144
E-mail carrie.upton@luht.scot.nhs.uk

UPTON, Mrs Christina Phoebe. b 61. Man Univ MB, ChB85 Ches Univ MTh04 MRCPsych93. NOC 06. **d** 08 **p** 09. C W Kirby St Bridget *Ches* from 08. *Priory Lodge, Ford Road, Wirral CH49 0TD* Tel 0151-488 5290 E-mail tina.upton@tesco.net

UPTON, Christopher Martin. b 53. Bp Grosseteste Coll CertEd74. EAMTC 94. **d** 97 **p** 98. NSM Gorleston St Andr *Nor* 97-05; NSM Bradwell from 05. *27 Curlew Way, Bradwell, Great Yarmouth NR31 8QX* Tel (01493) 668184
E-mail rev.martin.upton@talk21.com

UPTON, Clement Maurice. b 49. Linc Th Coll 88. **d** 90 **p** 91. C Northampton St Alb *Pet* 90-93; V Laxey and Lonan *S & M* 93-96; V Hipswell *Ripon* 96-01; V Wellingborough St Andr *Pet* 01-10; Chapl Northants Police 05-10; rtd 10. *3 Hewish Court, Landemann Circus, Weston-super-Mare BS22 2NZ* E-mail clem13@talktalk.net

UPTON, Ms Julie. b 61. Ripon Coll Cuddesdon 87. **d** 88 **p** 94. C Kirkstall *Ripon* 88-91; Par Dn E Greenwich Ch Ch w St Andr and St Mich *S'wark* 91-94; C 94; Perm to Offic *S'wark* 01-03 and *St E* 02-03; NSM Manningham *Bradf* 03-04; TV Bramley *Ripon* 04-10; P-in-c Sheff Manor from 10. *St Aidan's Vicarage, 4 Manor Lane, Sheffield S2 1JP* Tel 0114-272 4676
E-mail julie.upton1@googlemail.com

UPTON, Martin. *See* UPTON, Christopher Martin

UPTON, Michael Gawthorne. b 29. AKC53. **d** 54 **p** 55. C Middleton *Man* 54-57; C Plymouth St Andr *Ex* 57-59; Dep Dir of Educn *Cant* 59-63; Hon C Riverhead *Roch* 63-70; Youth Chapl 63-70; Lic to Offic *Ex* 70-94; Chr Aid Area Sec (Devon and Cornwall) 70-94; Chr Aid SW Region Co-ord 73-89; rtd 94; Perm to Offic *Ex* 94-09. *Otter Dell, Harpford, Sidmouth EX10 0NH* Tel (01395) 568448

UPTON, Mrs Susan Dorothy. b 53. Bp Grosseteste Coll CertEd74 Nottm Univ BEd75. EAMTC 99. **d** 02 **p** 03. NSM Bradwell *Nor* from 02. *27 Curlew Way, Bradwell, Great Yarmouth NR31 8QX* Tel (01493) 668184 E-mail sue-upton@talk21.com

UPTON-JONES, Peter John. b 38. Selw Coll Cam BA63 MA67 Liv Univ CertEd64. NOC 90. **d** 92 **p** 93. NSM Formby H Trin *Liv* 92-00; P-in-c Lezayre St Olave Ramsey *S & M* 00-03; V 03-08; P-in-c Kirkbride 00-03; R 03-08; rtd 08; Perm to Offic *S & M* from 09. *Clock Cottage, Glen Road, Colby, Isle of Man IM9 4NT* Tel (01624) 830216 E-mail peteru_j@hotmail.com

UREN, Malcolm Lawrence. b 37. AKC63. **d** 64 **p** 65. C Cant St Martin w St Paul 64-67; C Falmouth K Chas *Truro* 67-71; V St Blazey 71-79; P-in-c Tuckingmill 79-83; V 83-89; V Launceston St Steph w St Thos 89-92; V St Stephen by Launceston 92-96; rtd 00; Perm to Offic *Truro* from 00. *17 Forth An Tewennow, St Mary's Gardens, Phillack, Hayle TR27 4QE* Tel (01736) 756619 E-mail malcolm.uren1@btinternet.com

URMSON-TAYLOR, Ralph. *See* TAYLOR, Ralph Urmson

✠**URQUHART, The Rt Revd David Andrew.** b 52. Ealing Business Sch BA77. Wycliffe Hall Ox 82. **d** 84 **p** 85 **c** 00. C Kingston upon Hull St Nic *York* 84-87; TV Drypool 87-92; V Cov H Trin 92-00; Hon Can Cov Cathl 99-00; Suff Bp Birkenhead *Ches* 00-06; Bp Birm from 06. *Bishop's Croft, Old Church Road, Birmingham B17 0BG* Tel 0121-427 1163 Fax 426 1322 E-mail bishop@birmingham.anglican.org

URQUHART, Canon Edmund Ross. b 39. Univ Coll Ox BA62 MA68. St Steph Ho Ox 62. **d** 64 **p** 65. C Milton *Win* 64-69; C Norton *Derby* 69-73; V Bakewell 73-05; RD Bakewell and Eyam 95-04; Hon Can Derby Cathl 02-05; rtd 05; Perm to Offic *Derby* from 05 and *Lich* from 08. *1 Hambleton Close, Ashbourne DE6 1NG* Tel (01335) 346454

URQUHART, Ian Garnham. b 46. Univ Coll Lon LLB71. Wycliffe Hall Ox 88. **d** 99 **p** 00. C Barnston *Ches* from 99. *8 Antons Road, Wirral CH61 9PT* Tel 0151-648 1512 Fax 648 2402 Mobile 07770-823373 E-mail ian@papintalo.co.uk

URSELL, David John. b 45. MRAC70. SWMTC 92. **d** 95 **p** 96. NSM Dolton *Ex* from 95; Rural Convenor from 95. *Aller Farm, Dolton, Winkleigh EX19 8PP* Tel (01805) 804414 *or* 804737 E-mail ursell@farmersweekly.net

URSELL, Canon Philip Elliott. b 42. Univ of Wales BA66 Ox Univ MA82 Nashotah Ho Wisconsin DD08. St Steph Ho Ox 66. **d** 68 **p** 69. C Newton Nottage *Llan* 68-71; Asst Chapl Univ of Wales (Cardiff) 71-77; Chapl Wales Poly 74-77; Lic to Offic *Llan* 77-07; Chapl Em Coll Cam 77-82; Prin Pusey Ho 82-03; Warden Ascot Priory from 85; Lic to Offic *Ox* from 82; Can Rio Grande from 05. *St Edward's, Ascot Priory, Priory Road, Ascot SL5 8RT* Tel (01344) 885157 E-mail peu@cantab.net

✠**URWIN, The Rt Revd Lindsay Goodall.** b 56. Heythrop Coll Lon MA03 Nashotah Ho Wisconsin Hon DD11. Ripon Coll Cuddesdon 77. **d** 80 **p** 81 **c** 93. C Walworth *S'wark* 80-83; V N Dulwich St Faith 83-88; Dioc Missr *Chich* 88-93; Area Bp Horsham 93-09; Can and Preb Chich Cathl 93-09; P Admin Shrine of Our Lady of Walsingham from 09; Hon Asst Bp Nor from 09; Hon Asst Bp Chich from 09; Hon Asst Bp Pet from 11; Hon Asst Bp Ely from 11; OGS from 91; Provost Woodard Corp (S Division) from 06. *The College, Knight Street, Walsingham NR22 6EF* Tel (01328) 824204
E-mail pr.adm@olw-shrine.org.uk

USHER, George. b 30. Univ of Wales (Swansea) BSc51. St Deiniol's Hawarden 73. **d** 75 **p** 76. NSM Clun w Chapel Lawn *Heref* 75-78; NSM Clun w Chapel Lawn, Bettws-y-Crwyn and Newcastle 79-80; C Shrewsbury St Giles *Lich* 80-83; C Shrewsbury St Giles w Sutton and Atcham 83-84; R Credenhill w Brinsop and Wormsley etc *Heref* 84-98; rtd 98; Perm to Offic *Ex* from 02. *1 Trinity Court, The Esplanade, Sidmouth EX10 8BE* Tel (01395) 513889 E-mail georgeusher@clara.net

USHER, Canon Graham Barham. b 70. Edin Univ BSc93 CCC Cam BA95 MA00. Westcott Ho Cam 93 St Nic Th Coll Ghana 96. **d** 96 **p** 97. C Nunthorpe *York* 96-99; V N Ormesby 99-04; R Hexham *Newc* from 04; AD Hexham from 06; Hon Can Kumasi Ghana from 07. *The Rectory, Eilansgate, Hexham NE46 3EW* Tel (01434) 603121 *or* 602031
E-mail rector@hexhamabbey.org.uk

USHER, Robin Reginald. b 50. AKC74. St Aug Coll Cant 75. **d** 76 **p** 77. C Hulme Ascension *Man* 76-80; P-in-c Newall Green St Fran 80-85; C Atherton 85-87; TV 87-90; V Leigh St Jo 90-99; Chapl Wigan and Leigh Health Services NHS Trust 93-99; V Milnrow *Man* from 99. *The Vicarage, 40 Eafield Avenue, Milnrow, Rochdale OL16 3UN* Tel (01706) 642988
E-mail milnrow.parishchurch@zen.co.uk

USHER-WILSON, Lucian Neville. b 36. Linc Coll Ox MA63 St Andr Univ DipEd64 Open Univ BA75. St Steph Ho Ox 91. **d** 94 **p** 96. NSM Compton and Otterbourne *Win* 94-96; NSM Shill Valley and Broadshire *Ox* from 96. *The Tallat, Westwell, Burford OX18 4JT* Tel (01993) 822464 E-mail neville.uw@virgin.net

UTLEY, Canon Edward Jacob. b 24. AKC52. **d** 53 **p** 54. C Pontefract St Giles *Wakef* 53-56; C Bexhill St Pet *Chich* 56-60; Chapl Asst Bexhill Hosp 56-60; Chapl Dudley Road Hosp Birm 60-89; RD Birm City 75-82; Hon Can Birm Cathl 80-89; rtd 89; Perm to Offic *Birm* from 89. *c/o R H Utley Esq, Loughrigg, 2 Laurel Bank, Tamworth B79 8BA* Tel (01827) 59647

UTTIN, Miss Suzanne. b 72. Trin Coll Bris 09. **d** 11. C Lydney *Glouc* from 11. *12 Almond Walk, Lydney GL15 5LP* Tel (01594) 841494 E-mail revsuttin@hotmail.co.uk

UTTLEY, Mrs Valerie Gail. b 43. Man Univ BA64. NOC 80. **dss** 83 **d** 87 **p** 94. Otley *Bradf* 83-87; Hon Par Dn 87-89; Par Dn Calverley 89-92; Ind Chapl *Ripon* 92-97; C Kirkstall 95-97; V Lofthouse 97-10; rtd 10. *1 Victoria Terrace, Alnwick NE66 1RE* E-mail gailuttley@yahoo.co.uk

V

VACCARO, Mrs Alexandra. b 64. Qu Coll Birm 07. **d** 10 **p** 11. NSM Kidderminster St Mary and All SS w Trimpley etc *Worc* from 10. *18 Batham Road, Kidderminster DY10 2TN* Tel (01562) 515894 E-mail alexvaccaro@fsmail.net

VAIL, David William. b 30. Dur Univ BA56 Sheff Univ DipEd71. Oak Hill Th Coll 56. **d** 58 **p** 59. C Toxteth Park St Bede *Liv* 58-61; Kenya 61-77; Chapl Versailles *Eur* 77-82; Gen Sec Rwanda Miss 82-88; V Virginia Water *Guildf* 88-96; rtd 96; Perm to Offic *Ox* from 98. *36 Silverthorne Drive, Caversham, Reading RG4 7NS* Tel 0118-954 6667

VAIZEY, Martin John. b 37. AKC64. **d** 65 **p** 66. C Bishopwearmouth Gd Shep *Dur* 65-69; C Darlington H Trin 69-72; V Easington Colliery 72-80; C-in-c Bishopwearmouth St Mary V w St Pet CD 80-85; V Sunderland Springwell w Thorney Close 85-88; R Witton Gilbert 88-96; P-in-c Wingate Grange 96-99; V Wheatley Hill and Wingate w Hutton Henry 99-07; rtd 07. *2 Etherley Lane, Bishop Auckland DL14 7QR*

VALE, Thomas Stanley George. b 52. Chich Th Coll 85. **d** 87 **p** 88. C Leic St Phil 87-90; C Knighton St Mary Magd 90-93; P-in-c Leic St Chad 93-97; V 97-01; V Blackfordby and Woodville from 01. *The Vicarage, 11 Vicarage Close, Blackfordby, Swadlincote DE11 8AZ* Tel (01283) 211310 E-mail tvale@webleicester.co.uk

VALENTINE, Derek William. b 24. S'wark Ord Course 65. **d** 68 **p** 69. NSM Battersea St Luke *S'wark* 68-77; NSM Fenstanton *Ely* 77-88; Perm to Offic *Bradf* 88-96. *Address withheld by request*

VALENTINE, Hugh William James. b 56. Bradf Univ BA83 CQSW. S'wark Ord Course 86. **d** 89 **p** 90. NSM Stoke Newington Common St Mich *Lon* 89-92; NSM Westmr St Jas from 92; Bps' Adv in Child Protection Stepney and Two Cities Areas from 96; Bp's Adv in Child Protection *Ox* 96-05. *The Clerk's House, 127 Kennington Road, London SE11 6SF* Tel (020) 7735 3138 Mobile 07760-176704 E-mail mail@hughvalentine.net

VALENTINE, Jeremy Wilfred. b 38. NW Ord Course 76. **d** 79 **p** 80. C Cundall *Ripon* 79-82; TV Huntington *York* 82-87; V Sand Hutton 87-08; P-in-c Whitwell w Crambe, Flaxton and Foston 01-08; RD Buckrose and Bulmer and Malton 98-02; rtd 08; Perm to Offic *York* from 08. *5 Sand Hutton Court, Sand Hutton, York YO41 1LU* Tel (01904) 468443 Fax 468670 E-mail jeremyvalentine@tinyworld.co.uk

VALENTINE, John Harvey. b 63. Ch Ch Ox BA85 MA85. Ridley Hall Cam BA92. **d** 93 **p** 94. C Heigham H Trin *Nor* 93-97; C Ches Square St Mich w St Phil *Lon* 97-00; C Brompton H Trin w Onslow Square St Paul 00-02; P-in-c Holborn St Geo w H Trin and St Bart 02-09; R from 09. *13 Doughty Street, London WC1N 2PL* Tel (020) 7404 9606 *or* 7404 4407 Fax 7831 0588 Mobile 07736-066091 E-mail john.valentine@sgtm.org

VALENTINE, Mrs Katherine Anne. b 58. Newc Poly BA80. ERMC 03. **d** 06 **p** 07. C Haughley w Wetherden and Stowupland *St E* 06-10; P-in-c Pakenham w Norton and Tostock from 10. *The Orwell, Woolpit Road, Norton, Bury St Edmunds IP31 3LU* Tel (01359) 235095 E-mail katherine.valentine@homecall.co.uk

VALIANT, Mrs Lesley Jean. b 51. Whitelands Coll Lon CertEd74 Univ Coll Chich BA99. STETS 99. **d** 01 **p** 02. NSM Bedhampton *Portsm* 01-04; C Southsea St Jude 04-06; Asst to RD Portsm 04-06; TV Pewsey and Swanborough *Sarum* 06-09; TV Modbury, Bigbury, Ringmore w Kingston etc *Ex* from 11. *The Vicarage, 3 Little Gate, Loddiswell, Kingsbridge TQ7 4RB* Tel 07751-168228 (mobile) E-mail ljvaliant@tiscali.co.uk

VALLENTE-KERR, Susan Fiona. b 77. St Martin's Coll Lanc BA98 Ch Ch Coll Cant PGCE00 Moorlands Coll MA08. St Mellitus Coll 08. **d** 11. C Frindsbury w Upnor and Chattenden *Roch* from 11. *85 Rivenhall Way, Hoo, Rochester ME3 9GF* Tel 07875-349029 (mobile) E-mail suziquk@yahoo.co.uk

VALLINS, Canon Christopher. b 43. Hon FRSocMed06. Lich Th Coll 63. **d** 66 **p** 67. C Cuddington *Guildf* 66-70; C Aldershot St Mich 70-73; V W Ewell 73-81; R Worplesdon and Chapl Merrist Wood Coll of Agric and Horticulture 81-89; RD Guildf 86-89; Chapl Epsom Health Care NHS Trust 89-99; Hd Past Care Epsom and St Helier Univ Hosps NHS Trust 99-07; Bp's Adv on Healing *Guildf* 97-07; Bp's Adv for Hosp Chapl from 07; Hon Can Guildf Cathl from 01; Perm to Offic *S'wark* from 07. *Little Watermead, Reigate Road, Hookwood, Horley RH6 0HD* Tel (01293) 824188 Fax 823282 Mobile 07917-337920 E-mail chrisvallins@yahoo.com

VALLIS, Brett Paul Stanley. b 72. G&C Coll Cam BA93 St Jo Coll Dur BA01. Cranmer Hall Dur 99. **d** 02 **p** 03. C Monkseaton St Mary *Newc* 02-05; P-in-c Fatfield *Dur* 05-10; V 10-11; Chapl Dur High Sch for Girls from 11. *26 Kipling Way, Crook DL15 9AJ* E-mail revbrettvallis@yahoo.co.uk

VAN BEVEREN (*née* FORBES), Mrs Susan Margaret. b 64. St Hugh's Coll Ox BA85 MA89. Trin Th Sch Melbourne 95. **d** 96 **p** 96. Ind Chapl Inter-Ch Trade and Ind Miss Australia 96-99; NSM Amsterdam w Den Helder and Heiloo *Eur* 00-03; Officer for Miss in Work and Economic Life *Ox* 03-07; Dioc Adv from 08; NSM S Ascot 07-09; NSM Sunninghill and S Ascot from 09. *5 Vicarage Gardens, Ascot SL5 9DX* Tel (01344) 622045 E-mail svan.beveren@well-centre.org

VAN BLERK, Etienne. b 68. Pretoria Univ BA88 Stellenbosch Univ BTh92 Lebanese American Univ BA96. Ox Min Course 07. **d** 09 **p** 10. C Bicester w Bucknell, Caversfield and Launton *Ox* from 09. *75 Ravencroft, Bicester OX26 6YE* Tel (01869) 369088 Mobile 07795-985942 E-mail etiennevanblerk@btinternet.com

VAN CARRAPIETT, Timothy Michael James. b 39. Chich Th Coll 60. **d** 63 **p** 64. C Sugley *Newc* 63-65; C Newc St Fran 65-69; P-in-c Wrangbrook w N Elmsall CD *Wakef* 69-74; P-in-c Flushing *Truro* 74-75; P-in-c Mylor w Flushing 75-76; P-in-c St Day 76-82; R Aldrington *Chich* 82-87; V Bexhill St Barn 87-01; rtd 01; Perm to Offic *St E* from 01 and *Chelmsf* from 08. *Bear-Wuff Cottage, 9 Tacon Road, Felixstowe IP11 2DT* Tel (01394) 271338

VAN CULIN, Canon Samuel. b 30. OBE. Princeton Univ AB52. Virginia Th Sem DB55 Hon DD77 Gen Th Sem NY Hon DD83. **d** 55 **p** 56. USA 55-83; Sec Gen ACC 83-94; Hon C All Hallows by the Tower etc *Lon* 89-04; Hon Can Cant Cathl 83-94; Hon Can Ibadan from 83; Hon Can Jerusalem from 84; Hon Can S Africa from 89; Hon Can Honolulu from 91; rtd 94; Hon Can Nat Cathl USA from 04. *3900 Watson Place, NW B-5D, Washington DC 20016, USA* Tel (001) (202) 537 6200

VAN D'ARQUE, Christopher Simon Wayne. b 62. St Jo Coll Dur BA99. **d** 99 **p** 00. C Letchworth St Paul w Willian *St Alb* 99-02; C Westminster St Jas the Less *Lon* 02-03; V W Bessacarr *Sheff* 03-10; V Walton St Jo *Derby* from 10. *6 Medlock Road, Walton, Chesterfield S40 3NH* E-mail wordsmith.twentyone@talktalk.net

VAN DE KASTEELE, Peter John. b 39. Magd Coll Cam BA61 MA65. Clifton Th Coll 61. **d** 63 **p** 64. C Eastbourne H Trin *Chich* 63-66; C N Pickenham w S Pickenham etc *Nor* 66-70; R Mursley w Swanbourne and Lt Horwood *Ox* 70-80; Admin Sec Clinical Th Assn from 83; Gen Dir 88-99; Perm to Offic *Glouc* from 83; Hon C Westcote w Icomb and Bledington 88-89; rtd 99. *St Mary's House, Church Westcote, Chipping Norton OX7 6SF* Tel (01993) 830193

van de WEYER, Robert William Bates. b 50. Lanc Univ BA76. S'wark Ord Course 78. **d** 81 **p** 82. Warden Lt Gidding Community 77-98; Hon C Gt w Lt Gidding and Steeple Gidding *Ely* 81-83; P-in-c 83-93; P-in-c Winwick 83-93; P-in-c Hamerton 83-93; P-in-c Upton and Copmanford 83-93; Perm to Offic from 93. *1 Church Cottages, Green Lane, Upton, Huntingdon PE28 5YE* Tel (01480) 890333 E-mail robert@vandeweyer.co.uk

VAN DEN BERG, Jan Jacob. b 56. Sarum & Wells Th Coll 86. **d** 88 **p** 89. C Glouc St Aldate 88-91; C Ollerton w Boughton *S'well* 91-95; P-in-c Scrooby 95-00; P-in-c Blyth 97-00; C Brampton and Farlam and Castle Carrock w Cumrew *Carl* 00-02; TV Eden, Gelt and Irthing 02-05; P-in-c Rockcliffe and Blackford from 05. *The Vicarage, Rockcliffe, Carlisle CA6 4AA* Tel (01228) 674209 E-mail jan@vandenberg.fsnet.co.uk

VAN DEN BERG-OWENS, Jayne. b 65. **d** 11. C Kirkby *Liv* from 11. *6 Brampton Close, Kirkby, Liverpool L32 1BD*

VAN DEN BERGH, Victor Michael Cornelius. b 53. ALBC92. Ridley Hall Cam 02. **d** 03 **p** 04. C Tamworth *Lich* from 03. *St Francis's Vicarage, Masefield Drive, Tamworth B79 8JB* Tel (01827) 65926 Mobile 07770-900712 E-mail vic_vdb@btinternet.com

VAN DEN BOS (*née* MUMFORD), Mrs Clare. b 74. Man Univ BA00. Ripon Coll Cuddesdon 04. **d** 07 **p** 09. C Monkseaton St Mary *Newc* 07-08; C N Shields 08-10. *Address temp unknown* Tel 07780-612760 (mobile) E-mail pestokids@mac.com

van den HOF, Ariadne Rolanda Magdalena. b 71. Univ of Wales (Cardiff) MTh96 Leiden Univ MA05. Old Cath Sem Amersfoort 95 St Mich Coll Llan 98. **d** 99 **p** 00. C Dolgellau w Llanfachreth and Brithdir etc *Ban* 99-01; Min Can Ban Cathl 01-02; P-in-c Trefdraeth w Aberffraw, Llangadwaladr etc 02-03; R 03-06; R Llanffestiniog w Blaenau Ffestiniog etc 06-11; Rural Life Co-ord 04-11; V Shooters Hill Ch Ch *S'wark* from 11. *Christ Church Vicarage, 1 Craigholm, Shooters Hill, London SE18 3RR* Tel (020) 8856 5858 E-mail armvandenhof@gmail.com

VAN DER HART, William Richard. b 76. Homerton Coll Cam BEd99. Wycliffe Hall Ox BTh04. **d** 04 **p** 05. C Bryanston Square St Mary w St Marylebone St Mark *Lon* 04-08; TV Roxeth 08-11; V W Harrow from 11. *65 Butler Road, Harrow HA1 4DS* Tel (020) 8537 7332 Mobile 07968-132129 E-mail william.vanderhart@gmail.com

VAN DER LELY, Janice Kay. b 55. Sheff Univ BA76 Dur Univ PhD79 Webster Univ (USA) MA05 Ox Brookes Univ MA10. Ripon Coll Cuddesdon 08. **d** 09 **p** 10. C Cirencester *Glouc* from 09. *54 Alexander Drive, Cirencester GL7 1UH* Tel (01285) 653144 Mobile 07595-270438 E-mail janvanderlely@googlemail.com

van der LINDE, Herbert John. b 43. Rhodes Univ BA66. Coll of Resurr Mirfield. **d** 68 **p** 69. C Kingston St Luke *S'wark* 68-75; C Chipping Campden w Ebrington *Glouc* 75-78; V Cheltenham St Pet 78-84; V Bussage from 84. *St Michael's Vicarage, Bussage, Stroud GL6 8BB* Tel (01453) 883556

VAN DER PUMP, Charles Lyndon. b 25. FRCM. S'wark Ord Course 86. **d** 88 **p** 89. NSM Primrose Hill St Mary w Avenue Road St Paul *Lon* 88-02; Perm to Offic from 02. *48 Canfield Gardens, London NW6 3JB* Tel and fax (020) 7624 4517 E-mail office@smvph.freeserve.co.uk

VAN DER TOORN, Mrs Stephne. b 53. Natal Univ BA73 Stellenbosch Univ HDipEd75. Th Ext Educn Coll. **d** 93 **p** 95. NSM Pretoria St Mary S Africa 93-01; C Fawley *Win* 01-07; R E Bergholt and Brantham *St E* from 07. *The Rectory, Rectory Lane, Brantham, Manningtree CO11 1PZ* Tel (01206) 392646 E-mail revsteph3@vodafoneemail.co.uk

van der VALK, Jesse. b 59. Nottm Univ BTh84 Birm Univ MPhil88 Avery Hill Coll PGCE85. St Jo Coll Nottm 81. **d** 88 **p** 89. C Droitwich Spa *Worc* 88-92; V Hartshead and Hightown *Wakef* 92-96; R Woolwich St Mary w St Mich *S'wark* from 96; USPG (Lon Volunteers and Co-workers Team) from 97. *The Rectory, 43 Rectory Place, London SE18 5DA* Tel (020) 8465 7307 *or* 8316 4338 E-mail jessevdvalk@aol.com

VAN KOEVERING, Mrs Helen Elizabeth Parsons. b 60. SS Hild & Bede Coll Dur BA82 Trin Coll Bris MPhil99. S Wales Ord Course 01. **d** 02 **p** 03. C Bettws *Mon* 02-03; Bp's Sec Niassa Mozambique from 03. *Diocese do Niassa CP 264, Lichinga, Niassa, Mozambique* Tel and fax (00258) 712 0735 E-mail mark@koev.freeserve.co.uk *or* diocese.niassa@teledata.mz

✠**VAN KOEVERING, The Rt Revd Mark Allan.** b 57. Michigan State Univ BSc79 MSc85. Trin Coll Bris BA99. **d** 99 **p** 00 **c** 03. C Bettws *Mon* 99-01; P-in-c 01-03; Bp Niassa Mozambique from 03. *Diocese do Niassa, CP 264, Lichinga, Niassa, Mozambique* Tel and fax (00258) 712 0735 E-mail mark@koev.freeserve.co.uk *or* diocese.niassa@teledata.mz

VAN KRIEKEN VANNERLEY, David. See VANNERLEY, David van Krieken

VAN LEER, Samuel Wall. b 67. Virginia Univ BA90 California Univ MA91 St Jo Coll Dur BA01. Cranmer Hall Dur 99. **d** 02 **p** 03. C Berne w Neuchâtel *Eur* 02-05; Chapl E Netherlands 05-11; Hon Asst Chapl Utrecht w Zwolle from 11. *Tussenkoelen 16, 9753 KX Haren, The Netherlands* Tel (0031) (50) 785 0703

VAN LEEUWEN, Canon Dirk Willem. b 45. Utrecht Univ LLD71. Th Faculty Brussels 71 S'wark Ord Course 80. **d** 82 **p** 83. Asst Chapl Brussels Cathl 82-84; Chapl Haarlem 84-93; Chapl Antwerp St Boniface 94-06; Assoc Chapl 06-07; Chapl Charleroi 94-00; P-in-c Ypres 97-99; P-in-c Leuven 98-99; Can Brussels Cathl 96-07; Chapl Knokke 01-07; P-in-c Ostend 01-06; P-in-c Bruges 01-03; V Gen to Bp Eur 02-07; Adn NW Eur 05-07; rtd 08. *Koningin Elisabethlei 6, Box 22, 2018 Antwerp, Belgium* Tel (0032) (3) 238 3162 E-mail dirk.vanleeuwen@scarlet.be

VAN STRAATEN, Christopher Jan. b 55. Bris Univ BA77 Natal Univ HDipEd78. Oak Hill Th Coll 90. **d** 92 **p** 93. C Woodley *Ox* 92-96; V Gillingham St Aug *Roch* 96-07; V Aylesford from 07. *The Vicarage, Vicarage Close, Aylesford ME20 7BB* Tel (01622) 717434 E-mail chris.vanstraaten@diocese-rochester.org

van WENGEN, Rosemary Margaret. b 38. Westf Coll Lon BA60 Univ of Leiden MA77 PhD81. SEITE 98. **d** 01 **p** 02. NSM Benenden *Cant* 01-10; NSM Sandhurst w Newenden 04-10; NSM Benenden and Sandhurst from 10. *Beach House, Grange Road, St Michaels, Tenterden TN30 6EF* Tel (01580) 764857 Fax 761405 E-mail r.vanwengen@tiscali.co.uk

VAN ZANDBERGEN, Karen. See BURNETT-HALL, Mrs Karen

VANDYCK, Mrs Salli Diane Seymour. b 39. SEITE 93. **d** 96 **p** 97. NSM Chertsey *Guildf* 96-98; NSM Ross *Heref* 98-03; rtd 03; Perm to Offic *Heref* from 03. *Mickleden, Linton, Ross-on-Wye HR9 7RY* Tel (01989) 720197

VANN, The Ven Cherry Elizabeth. b 58. ARCM78 GRSM80. Westcott Ho Cam 86. **d** 89 **p** 94. Par Dn Flixton St Mich *Man* 89-92; Chapl Bolton Inst of F&HE 92-98; Par Dn Bolton St Pet 92-94; C 94-98; TV E Farnworth and Kearsley 98-04; TR 04-08; Chapl among Deaf People 98-04; AD Farnworth 05-08; Adn Rochdale from 08. *57 Melling Road, Oldham OL4 1PN* Tel 0161-678 1454 Fax 678 1455 E-mail archrochdale@manchester.anglican.org

VANN, Canon Paul. b 41. Univ of Wales (Cardiff) BTh01. St D Coll Lamp 62. **d** 65 **p** 66. C Griffithstown *Mon* 65-67; C Llanfrechfa All SS 67-71; Dioc Youth Chapl 71-72; P-in-c Llanrumney 72-76; V 76-97; Asst Chapl St Woolos Cathl 71-72; P-in-c Llanrumney 72-76; V 76-97; Asst Chapl HM Pris Cardiff 75-78; RD Bassaleg *Mon* 90-99; R Machen 97-07; Can St Woolos Cathl 01-07; rtd 07. *2 Mawdlam Way, North Cornelly, Bridgend CF33 4PJ* Tel (01656) 741543 E-mail vann651@btinternet.com

VANNERLEY, David van Krieken. b 50. Ch Ch Coll Cant CertEd71 Kent Univ BA78 MPhil07 Cant Ch Ch Univ MA11. SEITE 00. **d** 05 **p** 06. NSM St Laur in Thanet *Cant* from 05; Chapl Kent Critical Incident Chapl Service from 10. *34 Cherry Gardens, Herne Bay CT6 5QE* Tel (01227) 369096 E-mail vannerley@aol.com

VANNOZZI, Peter. b 62. Lon Univ BA83 Heythrop Coll Lon MA06. Ripon Coll Cuddesdon BA86 MA91. **d** 87 **p** 88. C Kenton *Lon* 87-90; C Fleet *Guildf* 90-93; V Northwood Hills St Edm *Lon* 93-97; AD Harrow 95-97; V S Dulwich St Steph S'wark 97-05; RD Dulwich 02-05; Can Res Wakef Cathl 05-07; V Hampton Hill *Lon* from 07. *The Vicarage, 46 St James's Road, Hampton TW12 1DQ* Tel and fax (020) 8979 2069 E-mail vicar@stjames-hamptonhill.org.uk

VANSTON, The Ven William Francis Harley. b 24. TCD BA48 MA52. **d** 48 **p** 49. C Belfast St Mary *Conn* 48-51; C Dublin Rathfarnham *D & G* 51-58; I Narraghmore w Fontstown and Timolin 58-65; I Arklow 65-67; I Arklow w Inch 67-73; I Arklow w Inch and Kilbride 73-89; RD Rathdrum 77-89; Adn Glendalough 83-89; rtd 89. *Apartment 9, 65 Strand Road, Sandymount, Dublin 4, Republic of Ireland* Tel (00353) (1) 260 8882

VANSTONE, Preb Walford David Frederick. b 38. Open Univ BA81. AKC69. **d** 70 **p** 71. C Feltham *Lon* 70-75; TV E Runcorn w Halton *Ches* 75-80; V Grange St Andr 80-82; V Hampton All SS *Lon* 82-05; P-in-c Teddington SS Pet and Paul and Fulwell 99-00; AD Hampton 95-03; Preb St Paul's Cathl 99-05; Chapl

Richmond Coll 02-05; rtd 05; Perm to Offic *Lon* from 05. *13 Lammas Close, Staines TW18 4XT* E-mail wvanstone@aol.com

VARAH, Canon Paul Hugh. b 46. St Deiniol's Hawarden 83. **d** 85 **p** 86. C Prestatyn *St As* 85-87; P-in-c Hawarden 87-88; TV 88-89; V Esclusham 89-96; V Connah's Quay from 96; Can Cursal St As Cathl from 08. *The Vicarage, Church Hill, Connah's Quay, Deeside CH5 4AD* Tel and fax (01244) 830224

VARGAS, Eric Arthur Dudley. b 27. BD. S Dios Minl Tr Scheme 81. **d** 83 **p** 84. C Farncombe *Guildf* 83-86; R Ockley, Okewood and Forest Green 86-90; V Kirdford *Chich* 90-93; rtd 93; Perm to Offic *Chich* from 93 and *Portsm* 93-09. *33 Park Crescent, Emsworth PO10 7NT* Tel (01243) 430611

VARGESON, Canon Peter Andrew. b 53. Wycliffe Hall Ox 85. **d** 87 **p** 88. C Yateley *Win* 87-92; V Bursledon from 92; AD Eastleigh 99-06 and from 09; P-in-c Hound from 07; Hon Can Tororo Uganda from 99. *The Vicarage, School Road, Bursledon, Southampton SO31 8BW* Tel (023) 8040 2821 *or* 8040 6021 E-mail peter.vargeson@ukgateway.net

VARLEY (née TRIM), Elizabeth Ann. b 52. Homerton Coll Cam BEd75 Van Mildert Coll Dur PhD85 St Jo Coll Dur BA96. NEOC 94. **d** 96 **p** 97. C Sedgefield *Dur* 96-99; Dir Post-Ord Tr Stepney Area *Lon* 99-02; V Hipswell *Ripon* 02-07; Hon Can Ripon Cathl 05-07; R Bacton w Wyverstone, Cotton and Old Newton etc *St E* from 07. *The Rectory, Church Road, Bacton, Stowmarket IP14 4LJ* Tel (01449) 781245 E-mail liz.varley@csbb.co.uk

VARLEY, Robert. b 36. St Jo Coll Cam BA57 MA64 Man Poly PGCE92. NW Ord Course 71. **d** 74 **p** 75. C Wallasey St Hilary *Ches* 74-77; V Rock Ferry 77-81; Perm to Offic *Man* 82-83; Hon C E Farnworth and Kearsley 83-86; Hon C Walkden Moor 86-87; C 87-89; V Lt Hulton 89-90; Perm to Offic from 97. *66 Normanby Road, Worsley, Manchester M28 7TS* Tel 0161-790 8420

VARNEY, Donald James. b 35. Chich Th Coll 84. **d** 86. NSM Liss *Portsm* 86-05; rtd 05; Perm to Offic *Portsm* 05-10 and *Sarum* from 10. *14 Askwith Close, Sherborne DT9 6DX* Tel (01973) 816684

VARNEY, Peter David. b 38. Univ Coll Dur BA61 MA64. Qu Coll Birm 61. **d** 64 **p** 65. C Newington St Paul *S'wark* 64-66; C Camberwell St Mich w All So w Em 66-67; Perm to Offic Kuching Malaysia 67-68; Hon C Croxley Green All SS *St Alb* 69; Perm to Offic *Roch* 69-72 and 74-84; Asst Chapl CSJB 72-73; Asst Sec Chrs Abroad 74-79; Dir Bloxham Project 84-86; Perm to Offic *Cant* 84-85 and *S'wark* 85-86; P-in-c Thornage w Brinton w Hunworth and Stody *Nor* 87-88; P-in-c Briningham 87-88; P-in-c Melton Constable w Swanton Novers 87-88; Perm to Offic from 88; Chapl Yare and Norvic Clinics and St Andr Hosp *Nor* 90-95; rtd 03. *280 The Pavilion, St Stephens Road, Norwich NR1 3SN* Tel (01603) 760838 E-mail varney@waitrose.com

VARNEY, Stephen Clive. b 59. Qu Mary Coll Lon BSc80 Sussex Univ MSc82 Southn Univ BTh88. Sarum & Wells Th Coll 83. **d** 86 **p** 87. C Riverhead w Dunton Green *Roch* 86-91; V Bostall Heath 91-99; V Bromley St Mark from 99. *St Mark's Vicarage, 51 Hayes Road, Bromley BR2 9AE* Tel (020) 8460 6220 Mobile 07961-117578

VARNHAM, Gerald Stanley. b 29. Sarum & Wells Th Coll 74. **d** 77 **p** 78. Hon C Portchester *Portsm* 77-86; Perm to Offic 88-99. *15 Southampton Road, Fareham PO16 7DZ* Tel (01329) 234182

VARNON, Nicholas Charles Harbord. b 45. St Luke's Coll Ex CertEd71 Open Univ BA83 BPhil91 MA94 Univ of Wales MPhil00. St Mich Coll Llan 91. **d** 93 **p** 94. C Pontypridd St Cath w St Matt *Llan* 93-97; P-in-c Sutton St Nicholas w Sutton St Michael *Heref* 97-04; P-in-c Withington w Westhide 97-04; P-in-c Weybourne Gp *Nor* 04-06; R N Elmham, Billingford, Bintree, Guist etc from 06; CF (ACF) from 00. *The Rectory, 48 Holt Road, North Elmham, Dereham NR20 5JQ* Tel (01362) 668030 E-mail nchv@btinternet.com

VARQUEZ, Leo Bacleon. b 61. St Andr Th Sem Manila 82. **d** 86 **p** 86. P St Andr Philippines 86-91; P St Isidore 92-94; SSF 95-99; NSM Edin St Jo 98-99; NSM Mill End and Heronsgate w W Hyde *St Alb* 99-00; Asst Chapl HM Pris Featherstone 00-02; C Hednesford *Lich* 00-04; C Kingstanding St Luke *Birm* 04-06; Asst Chapl Univ Coll Lon Hosps NHS Foundn Trust 06-08; Chapl N Staffs Hosp NHS Trust from 08. *North Staffordshire Royal Infirmary, Princes Road, Stoke-on-Trent ST4 7LN* Tel (01782) 715444 E-mail leovarquez@yahoo.co.uk

VARTY, John Eric. b 44. Tyndale Hall Bris 68. **d** 71 **p** 72. C Barrow St Mark *Carl* 71-74; C Cheadle *Ches* 74-82; V Cheadle All Hallows 82-89; V Alsager Ch Ch 89-06; rtd 06; Chapl to Bp Stockport *Ches* from 07. *14 Gowy Close, Alsager, Stoke-on-Trent ST7 2HX* Tel (01270) 877360 E-mail vartyj1j2@clara.co.uk

VARTY, Robert. b 46. LRAM. Sarum & Wells Th Coll 84. **d** 86 **p** 87. C Plympton St Mary *Ex* 86-89; TV Northam w Westward Ho! and Appledore 89-95; P-in-c Wigginton *St Alb* 95-00; TV Tring 95-00; rtd 00; Clergy Widow(er)s Officer *Ex* 02-04; Perm to Offic *Ex* 01-04 and *Eur* from 05. *La Butte, 61110 Bellou-sur-Huisne, France* Tel (0033) 2 33 25 55 64 E-mail varty.robert@wanadoo.fr

VASBY-BURNIE, Timothy Roy. b 79. Trin Coll Cam MA00. Wycliffe Hall Ox BTh07. **d** 07 **p** 08. C Stone Ch Ch and Oulton *Lich* 07-10; V Wednesbury St Bart from 10. *The Vicarage, 4 Little Hill, Wednesbury WS10 9DE* Tel 0121-556 0378 E-mail tim@timvb.plus.com

VASEY, Arthur Stuart. b 37. Qu Coll Birm 68. **d** 71 **p** 72. C Shelf *Bradf* 71-73; Australia 74-76; Chapl St Jo Hosp Linc 76-79; P-in-c Tanfield *Dur* 79-84; C Birtley 84-85; C Middlesbrough St Thos *York* 85-86; rtd 02. *Glen Esk, 3 Quarry Bank, Malton YO17 7HA*

VASEY, Mrs Janet Mary. b 41. Margaret McMillan Coll of Educn CertEd62. Local Minl Tr Course 11. **d** 11. NSM Gt Grimsby St Mary and St Jas *Linc* from 11. *34 Western Outway, Grimsby DN34 5EX* Tel (01472) 753145 E-mail jan.vasey@btinternet.com

VASEY-SAUNDERS, Mrs Leah Beverley. b 77. Huddersfield Univ BMus98 St Jo Coll Dur BA03. Cranmer Hall Dur 00. **d** 03 **p** 04. C Whorlton *Newc* 03-04; Hon C Newc St Geo 05-08; TV Cannock *Lich* 08-10; V Heath Hayes from 10; C Hednesford from 08. *St John's Vicarage, 226 Hednesford Road, Heath Hayes, Cannock WS12 3DZ* Tel (01543) 450361 E-mail leah@vasey-saunders.co.uk

VASEY-SAUNDERS, Mark Richard. b 74. Coll of Ripon & York St Jo BA95 St Jo Coll Dur BA00. Cranmer Hall Dur 98. **d** 01 **p** 02. C Ponteland *Newc* 01-04; Chapl Newc Univ 04-08; Perm to Offic *Lich* from 10. *St John's Vicarage, 226 Hednesford Road, Heath Hayes, Cannock WS12 3DZ* Tel (01543) 450361

VASTENHOUT, Jeannetta Hermina. See STOKES, Mrs Jeannetta Hermina

VAUGHAN, Canon Andrew Christopher James. b 61. Univ of Wales (Lamp) BA82. Linc Th Coll 84. **d** 84 **p** 85. C Caerleon *Mon* 84-86; C Magor w Redwick and Undy 86-88; Ind Chapl 84-94; Linc Ind Miss from 94; Can and Preb Linc Cathl from 05. *4 Grange Close, Canwick, Lincoln LN4 2RH* Tel and fax (01522) 528266 Mobile 07702-468549 E-mail vaughanlim@tesco.net

VAUGHAN, Andrew Kenneth. b 64. MCIOB01. Ridley Hall Cam 04. **d** 07 **p** 08. C Chislehurst Ch Ch *Roch* from 07; V Istead Rise from 11. *The Vicarage, Upper Avenue, Istead Rise, Gravesend DA13 9DA* Tel (01474) 832403 Mobile 07977-154809 E-mail andrewvaughan@akv64s.com

VAUGHAN, Brian John. b 38. Lich Th Coll 65. **d** 68 **p** 69. C Fisherton Anger *Sarum* 68-70; C Wareham w Arne 70-73; Asst P Mt Lawley Australia 73; R Dalwallinu 73-76; R Morawa 75-78; Field Officer Bible Soc of W Australia 78-81; Assoc P Mt Lawley 82-86; R Pinjarra 86-96; R Manjimup 96-00; rtd 00. *Milborne, 6 Steeple Retreat, Busselton WA 6280, Australia* Tel (0061) (8) 9751 1225 E-mail sherton38@optusnet.com.au

VAUGHAN, Carole Ann. b 47. Leeds Univ CertEd68. STETS 95. **d** 98 **p** 99. NSM Oakley w Wootton St Lawrence *Win* from 98. *The Rectory, 9 The Drive, Oakley, Basingstoke RG23 7DA* Tel (01256) 780825 E-mail carole@cjvaughan.co.uk

VAUGHAN, Charles Jeremy Marshall. b 52. Man Univ BSc75. St Jo Coll Nottm 83. **d** 85 **p** 86. C Epsom Common Ch Ch *Guildf* 85-88; C Woking Ch Ch 88-93; R Worting *Win* 93-07; R Winklebury and Worting 07-10; R Oakley w Wootton St Lawrence from 10. *The Rectory, 9 The Drive, Oakley, Basingstoke RG23 7DA* Tel (01256) 780825 E-mail jeremy@cjvaughan.co.uk

VAUGHAN, Idris Samuel. b 46. Sarum Th Coll 70. **d** 72 **p** 73. C Workington St Jo *Carl* 72-76; C Foley Park *Worc* 76-79; V Hayton St Mary *Carl* 79-85; Chapl Asst Univ Hosp Nottm 85-90; Chapl Asst Nottm Gen Hosp 85-90; Chapl Stafford Distr Gen Hosp 90-94; Chapl Chase Hosp Cannock 90-94; Chapl Mid Staffs Gen Hosps NHS Trust 94-06; rtd 06; P-in-c Lanzarote *Eur* 06-10. *43 Silkmore Crescent, Stafford ST17 4JL*

VAUGHAN, Jeffrey Charles. b 45. S'wark Ord Course 85. **d** 88 **p** 89. NSM Tottenham St Paul *Lon* 88-91; C Hendon St Alphage 91-95; V Enfield SS Pet and Paul from 95. *The Vicarage, 177 Ordnance Road, Enfield EN3 6AB* Tel (01992) 719770 Fax (020) 8292 8456

VAUGHAN, Jeremy. See VAUGHAN, Charles Jeremy Marshall

VAUGHAN, Patrick Handley. b 38. TCD BA60 BD65 Selw Coll Cam BA62 MA66 Nottm Univ PhD88. Ridley Hall Cam 61. **d** 63 **p** 64. Min Can Bradf Cathl 63-66; Uganda 67-73; P-in-c Slingsby *York* 74-77; Tutor NW Ord Course 74-77; P-in-c Hovingham *York* 74-77; Prin EMMTC S'well 77-90; Hon Can Leic Cathl 87-90; Assoc Lect Open Univ from 94. *113 Upperthorpe Road, Sheffield S6 3EA* Tel 0114-272 2675

✠**VAUGHAN, The Rt Revd Peter St George.** b 30. Selw Coll Cam BA55 MA59 BNC Ox MA63. Ridley Hall Cam. **d** 57 **p** 58 **c** 89. C Birm St Martin 57-63; Chapl Ox Pastorate 63-67; Asst Chapl BNC Ox 63-67; V Galle Face Ch Ch Ceylon 67-72; Prec H Trin Cathl Auckland New Zealand 72-75; Prin Crowther Hall CMS Tr Coll Selly Oak 75-83; Adn Westmorland and Furness *Carl* 83-89; Hon Can Carl Cathl 83-89; Area Bp Ramsbury *Sarum* 89-98; Can and Preb Sarum Cathl 89-98; rtd 98; Hon Asst Bp Bradf 98-01; Hon Can Bradf Cathl from 98; Perm to Offic *Glouc* 01-06; Hon Asst Bp Glouc 06-11; Hon Asst Bp Bris from 02.

Willowbrook, Downington, Lechlade GL7 3DL Tel (01367) 252216

VAUGHAN, Preb Roger Maxwell. b 39. AKC62. **d** 63 **p** 64. C W Bromwich All SS *Lich* 63-65; C Wolverhampton 65-70; V Tunstall Ch Ch 70-79; V Abbots Bromley 79-86; P-in-c Blithfield 85-86; V Abbots Bromley w Blithfield 86-93; V Stafford St Jo and Tixall w Ingestre 93-04; Preb Lich Cathl 99-04; rtd 04; Perm to Offic *Lich* from 04. *51 Crestwood Drive, Stone ST15 0LW* Tel (01785) 812192 E-mail salrog.vaughan@btinternet.com

VAUGHAN, Trevor. b 41. TD91. Cen Lancs Univ BA91. Linc Th Coll 66. **d** 69 **p** 70. C Wyken *Cov* 69-72; C Stratford-on-Avon w Bishopton 72-73; P-in-c Monks Kirby w Withybrook and Copston Magna 73-75; P-in-c Wolvey, Burton Hastings and Stretton Baskerville 73-77; P-in-c Withybrook w Copston Magna 73-77; V Heyhouses *Blackb* 77-80; CF (TA) from 79; V Chorley St Geo *Blackb* 80-83; R Bolton by Bowland w Grindleton *Bradf* 83-89; V Settle 89-91; R Broughton, Marton and Thornton 91-00; V Morecambe St Barn *Blackb* 00-03; P-in-c Sabden and Pendleton 03-06; rtd 06. *3 Westmount Close, Ripon HG4 2HU* Tel (01765) 605591

VAUGHAN-WILSON, Jane Elizabeth. b 61. Magd Coll Ox MA87. Cranmer Hall Dur. **d** 89 **p** 94. Par Dn Ormesby *York* 89-93; Dn-in-c Middlesbrough St Agnes 93-94; P-in-c 94-95; TV Basingstoke *Win* 95-03; Perm to Offic *Truro* from 03. *4 Tolver Road, Penzance TR18 2AG* Tel (01736) 351825

VAYRO, Mark Shaun. b 66. Aston Tr Scheme 88 Linc Th Coll BTh93. **d** 93 **p** 94. C Northampton St Mich w St Edm *Pet* 93-96; TV Duston 96-98; V Elm and Friday Bridge w Coldham *Ely* 98-01. *125 Spalding Road, Pinchbeck, Spalding LN11 3UE*

VAZ, Stanley Hubert. b 62. St Jo Coll Nottm 09. **d** 11. C Stretton w Claymills *Lich* from 11. *23 Lancelot Drive, Stretton, Burton-on-Trent DE13 0GJ* Tel 07803-054057 (mobile) E-mail vaz9301@gmail.com

VEEN, Keith Henry. b 46. **d** 01 **p** 02. OLM Croydon St Pet *S'wark* 01-02; OLM Croydon Ch Ch from 02. *91 The Ridgeway, Croydon CR0 4AH* Tel (020) 8688 3565 E-mail keithveen@veenco.fsnet.co.uk

VELLACOTT, John Patrick Millner. b 29. Ox NSM Course 86. **d** 89 **p** 90. NSM Cholsey *Ox* 89-93; Chapl Nerja *Eur* 93-97; rtd 97; Perm to Offic *Truro* 97-00; Glouc 00-02 and Carl from 03. *5 Stonycroft Drive, Arnside, Carnforth LA5 0EE* Tel (01524) 762800

VELLACOTT, Peter Graham. b 38. EAMTC 90. **d** 93 **p** 94. NSM Framlingham w Saxtead *St E* 93-95; NSM Brandeston w Kettleburgh 95-99; NSM Easton 95-99; P-in-c Brandeston w Kettleburgh and Easton 99-07; rtd 07; Perm to Offic *St E* from 07. *Soham House, Brandeston, Woodbridge IP13 7AX* Tel (01728) 685423

✠**VENABLES, The Most Revd Gregory James.** b 49. Lon Univ CertEd74. **d** 84 **p** 84 **c** 93. SAMS from 77; Paraguay 78-90; C Rainham *Chelmsf* 90-92; C Rainham w Wennington 92-93; Aux Bp Peru and Bolivia 93-95; Bp Bolivia 95-00; Asst Primate of S Cone 95-02; Bp Coadjutor Argentina 00-02; Dioc Bp from 02; Presiding Bp of S Cone from 01. *Rioja 2995, B1636DMG - Olivos, Provincia de Buenos Aires, Argentina* Tel (0054) (11) 4799 7124 E-mail bpgreg@ciudad.com.ar

VENABLES, Canon Margaret Joy. b 37. Bp Otter Coll CertEd57. S Dios Minl Tr Scheme 86. **d** 89 **p** 94. NSM Wilton *B & W* 89-91; C Taunton St Andr 91-97; P-in-c Haynes *St Alb* 97-03; P-in-c Clophill 00-03; R Campton, Clophill and Haynes 03-06; RD Shefford 01-06; Hon Can St Alb 05-06; rtd 06; P-in-c Barnack w Ufford and Bainton *Pet* 06-10; Perm to Offic from 10. *Mulberry Cottage, Witham-on-the-Hill, Bourne PE10 0JH* E-mail margsv@waitrose.com

VENABLES, Philip Richard Meredith. b 58. Magd Coll Ox BA79 CertEd80. Wycliffe Hall Ox 85. **d** 88 **p** 89. C Gillingham St Mark *Roch* 88-93; V Penge St Jo 93-07; R Bebington *Ches* from 07. *The Rectory, Church Road, Bebington, Wirral CH63 3EX* Tel 0151-645 6478 E-mail philip.venables@ntlworld.com

VENESS, Allan Barry. b 39. Lon Inst of Educn TCert60 Sussex Univ BEd81. Bp Otter Coll 94. **d** 97. NSM Felpham *Chich* 97-01; NSM Aldwick 01-06. *1 rue du Tertre Gicquel, 22430 Erquy, France* E-mail veness.allan@orange.fr

VENEZUELA, Bishop of. See GUERRERO, The Rt Revd Orlando

VENN, Richard Frank. b 49. Leeds Univ BSc72 Strathclyde Univ PhD77 CChem FRSC97. Ridley Hall Cam 04. **d** 05 **p** 06. C Margate H Trin *Cant* 05-08; P-in-c Len Valley from 08. *The Vicarage, Old Ashford Road, Lenham, Maidstone ME17 2PX* Tel (01622) 858195 Mobile 07970-288669 E-mail dickvenn@gmail.com

VENNELLS, Ms Paula Anne. b 59. Bradf Univ BA81 FRSA88. SAOMC 02. **d** 05 **p** 06. NSM Bromham w Oakley and Stagsden *St Alb* from 05. *Rushey Ford House, West End Road, Kempston, Bedford MK43 8RU* Tel (01234) 851594 Mobile 07786-174638 E-mail paula@rusheyford.freeserve.co.uk

✠**VENNER, The Rt Revd Stephen Squires.** b 44. DL10. Birm Univ BA65 Linacre Coll Ox BA67 MA71 Lon Univ PGCE72 Birm Univ Hon DD08. St Steph Ho Ox 65. **d** 68 **p** 69 **c** 94. C

Streatham St Pet *S'wark* 68-71; C Streatham Hill St Marg 71-72; C Balham Hill Ascension 72-74; V Clapham St Pet 74-76; Bp's Chapl to Overseas Students 74-76; P-in-c Studley *Sarum* 76; V 76-82; V Weymouth H Trin 82-94; RD Weymouth 88-93; Can and Preb Sarum Cathl 89-94; Suff Bp Middleton *Man* 94-99; Suff Bp Dover *Cant* 99-09; rtd 09; Bp HM Forces from 09; Hon Asst Bp Eur from 11. *83 Hathaway Court, Esplanade, Rochester ME1 1QY* Tel (01634) 838787 *or* (020) 7898 1196 Mobile 07980-743628 E-mail stephen@venner.org.uk

VENNING, Nigel Christopher. b 50. K Coll Lon BD75 AKC75. St Aug Coll Cant 75. d 76 p 77. C Minehead *B & W* 76-80; C Fawley *Win* 80-83; P-in-c Whitestaunton and Combe St Nicholas w Wambrook *B & W* 83-89; R Staplegrove 89-01; P-in-c Norton Fitzwarren 00-01; R Staplegrove w Norton Fitzwarren 01-03; R Blackdown 03-05; RD Taunton 96-01; rtd 05; Perm to Offic *B & W* from 05. *Crispin House, 5 Mendip Edge, Weston-super-Mare BS24 9JF* E-mail nigelvenning@lycos.co.uk

VERE HODGE, Preb Francis. b 19. MC43. Worc Coll Ox BA46 MA46. Cuddesdon Coll 46. d 48 p 49. C Battle *Chich* 48-54; R Iping 54-58; R Linch 54-58; V Kingswood *S'wark* 58-65; V Moorlinch w Stawell and Sutton Mallet *B & W* 65-79; R Greinton 68-79; RD Glastonbury 75-79; P-in-c Lydeard St Lawrence w Combe Florey and Tolland 79-84; Preb Wells Cathl 79-98; rtd 84; Perm to Offic *B & W* 84-99 and *Ex* from 99. *1 Gracey Court, Woodland Road, Broadclyst, Exeter EX5 3GA* Tel (01392) 469005

VERE NICOLL, Charles Fiennes. b 55. Solicitor 79. SAOMC 96. d 99 p 00. NSM Basildon w Aldworth and Ashampstead *Ox* 99-08; Perm to Offic from 08. *Ashvine, Westridge, Highclere, Newbury RG20 9RY* Tel 07768-238128 (mobile) E-mail cvn@cvnsbh.com

VEREKER, Jennifer Lesley. b 45. Totley Hall Coll CertEd66. WMMTC 96. d 99 p 00. NSM Rugby *Cov* 99-03; TV Gt and Lt Coates w Bradley *Linc* 03-08; rtd 08; Perm to Offic *St E* from 08. *Laurelwood, Thurston Road, Great Barton, Bury St Edmunds IP31 2PW* Tel (01359) 234413 E-mail j.vereker@btinternet.com

VEREY, Christopher Douglas. b 46. St Chad's Coll Dur BA68 MA70. Ripon Coll Cuddesdon 02. d 04 p 05. NSM Yate New Town *Bris* 04-09. *2 The Green, Heathend, Wotton-under-Edge GL12 8AR* E-mail chrisverey@tiscali.com.uk

VERHEY, Shawn Gordon. b 59. Ottawa Univ BA88 Liv Univ BTh03. NOC 00. d 04 p 05. NSM Southport SS Simon and Jude w All So *Liv* 04-07; Asst Chapl HM Pris Garth 04-07; Chapl HM YOI Thorn Cross from 07. *HM Young Offender Institution, Arley Road, Appleton, Warrington WA4 4RL* Tel (01925) 605085 E-mail vrhshawn@aol.com

VERNON, Bryan Graham. b 50. Qu Coll Cam BA72 MA76. Qu Coll Birm 73. d 75 p 76. C Newc St Gabr 75-79; Chapl Newc Univ 79-91; Lect Health Care Ethics from 91; Chmn Newc Mental Health Trust 91-94; Perm to Offic from 94. *34 Queens Road, Jesmond, Newcastle upon Tyne NE2 2PQ* Tel 0191-281 3861 E-mail b.g.vernon@ncl.ac.uk

VERNON, John Christie. b 40. Imp Coll Lon BScEng62. Linc Th Coll 63. d 65 p 66. C Barnard Castle *Dur* 65-69; CF 69-90; Asst Chapl Gen 90-92; Chapl Ellesmere Coll 92-99; Perm to Offic *Lich* 99-01; NSM Ellesmere Deanery 01-05 and 06-08; P-in-c Petton w Cockshutt, Welshampton and Lyneal etc 05-06; RD Ellesmere 02-08; Perm to Offic from 08. *The Drift House, Lake House Mews, Grange Road, Ellesmere SY12 9DE* Tel (01691) 623765 Mobile 07778-312226 E-mail john@jvernon.go-plus.net

VERNON, Canon Matthew James. b 71. Collingwood Coll Dur BSc93 Birzac Coll Cam BA96 MA98. Westcott Ho Cam 94. d 97 p 98. C Guildf H Trin w St Mary 97-01; Chapl St Jo Cathl and P-in-c Pokfulam Em Hong Kong 01-09; Can Res St E Cathl from 09. *2 Abbey Precincts, Bury St Edmunds IP33 1RS* Tel (01284) 701472 E-mail canon.pastor@stedscathedral.co.uk

VERNON, Robert Leslie. b 47. Sarum & Wells Th Coll 73. d 76 p 77. C Hartlepool St Luke *Dur* 76-79; C Birm St Geo 79-82; V Bordesley Green 82-86; Dioc Youth Officer *Carl* 86-89; P-in-c Holme 86-89; Dioc Youth Adv *Newc* 89-95; V Ulgham and Widdrington 95-01; P-in-c Pokesdown St Jas *Win* from 01; P-in-c Boscombe St Andr from 09. *St James's Vicarage, 12 Harewood Avenue, Bournemouth BH7 6NQ* Tel (01202) 425918 E-mail revbobvernon@hotmail.com

VERWEY, Mrs Eileen Susan Vivien. b 41. Open Univ BA78 BA93 Goldsmiths' Coll Lon PGCE82. WEMTC 03. d 05 p 06. NSM Burghill *Heref* from 05; NSM Stretton Sugwas from 05; NSM Pipe-cum-Lyde and Moreton-on-Lugg from 05. *Mill Croft House, Staunton-on-Wye, Hereford HR4 7LW* Tel (01981) 500626

VESEY, Nicholas Ivo. b 54. Bris Univ BSc73. Cranmer Hall Dur 95. d 97 p 98. C Tunbridge Wells St Mark *Roch* 97-01; V New Catton St Luke w St Aug *Nor* from 01. *St Luke's Vicarage, 61 Aylsham Road, Norwich NR3 2HF* Tel (01603) 416973 E-mail nicholas.vesey@btopenworld.com

VESSEY, Canon Andrew John. b 45. Bp Otter Coll CertEd67. Sarum & Wells Th Coll 84. d 86 p 87. C Framlingham w Saxtead *St E* 86-89; V Catshill and Dodford *Worc* 89-94; P-in-c Areley Kings 94-95; R 95-02; RD Stourport 00-02; TV Kidderminster St Jo and H Innocents 02-05; TR Cen Swansea *S & B* 05-10; Hon Can Brecon Cathl 10; rtd 10; Perm to Offic *Nor* and *St E* from 10. *3 The Laurels, Fressingfield, Eye IP21 5NZ* Tel (01379) 588389 E-mail andrew.vessey@btinternet.com

VESSEY, Peter Allan Beaumont. b 36. ALCD65. d 64 p 65. C Rayleigh *Chelmsf* 64-67; C Cambridge H Trin *Ely* 67-71; V Kingston upon Hull St Aid Southcoates *York* 71-80; V Swanwick and Pentrich *Derby* 80-94; Perm to Offic from 94; rtd 96. *3 Scarthin Terrace, Scarthin, Cromford, Matlock DE4 3QF* Tel (01629) 825572

VESTERGAARD, David Andrew. b 64. Reading Univ BSc86. Wycliffe Hall Ox 97. d 99 p 00. C Chadderton Ch Ch *Man* 99-02; V Wednesfield Heath *Lich* from 02; AD Wolverhampton from 07. *Holy Trinity Vicarage, Bushbury Road, Wolverhampton WV10 0LY* Tel (01902) 738313 E-mail david@vestergaard.co.uk

VETTERS, Miss Shirley Jacqueline Margaret. b 34. S'wark Ord Course 85. d 88 p 94. NSM E Ham w Upton Park *Chelmsf* 88-91; C Birm St Martin w Bordesley St Andr 91-04; Chapl to the Markets 91-04; rtd 04; Perm to Offic *Chelmsf* from 05. *62 South Street, Manningtree CO11 1BQ* Tel (01206) 393691

VEVERS, Canon Geoffrey Martin. b 51. Oak Hill Th Coll. d 82 p 83. C Wealdstone H Trin *Lon* 82-84; C Harrow Trin St Mich 84-88; V Wandsworth St Steph *S'wark* 88-96; V Battersea Fields from 96; RD Battersea 04-10; Hon Can S'wark Cathl from 06. *St Saviour's Vicarage, 351A Battersea Park Road, London SW11 4LH* Tel (020) 7498 1642

VIBERT (née GREEN), Imogen Elizabeth. b 73. Birm Univ BA96 Cam Univ BTh02. Westcott Ho Cam 99. d 02 p 03. C Poplar *Lon* 02-06; Hon C Upper Clapton St Matt from 06; Hon C Stamford Hill St Thos from 06. *20 Moresby Road, London E5 9LF* Tel (020) 8880 6696 E-mail imogen@vibert.wannadoo.co.uk

VIBERT, Simon David Newman. b 63. Oak Hill Th Coll BA89. d 89 p 90. C Houghton *Carl* 89-92; C-in-c Buxton Trin Prop Chpl *Derby* 92-99; V Wimbledon Park St Luke *S'wark* 99-07; Vice Prin Wycliffe Hall Ox from 07; Dir Sch of Preaching from 08. *Wycliffe Hall, 54 Banbury Road, Oxford OX2 6PW* Tel (01865) 274200 E-mail simon.vibert@wycliffe.ox.ac.uk

VICARS, David. b 22. Leeds Univ BA48. Coll of Resurr Mirfield 48. d 50 p 51. C Newington St Paul *S'wark* 50-54; C Kingston St Luke 54-56; C Cirencester *Glouc* 56-59; Malaysia 59-66; Area Sec USPG *Llan, Mon, St D* and *S & B* 67-77; R Coychurch w Llangan and St Mary Hill 77-90; rtd 90; Perm to Offic *Llan* from 90. *43 Bryn Rhedyn, Pencoed, Bridgend CF35 6TL* Tel (01656) 860920

VICK, Samuel Kenneth Lloyd. b 31. Univ of Wales (Lamp) BA53. Linc Th Coll. d 55 p 56. C Shotton *St As* 55-56; C Wrexham 56-61; C Knowle H Nativity *Bris* 61-67; V Mirfield Eastthorpe St Paul *Wakef* 67-78; V Altofts 78-98; rtd 98; Master Abp Holgate Hosp Hemsworth 98-09. *12 St Peter's Court, Horbury, Wakefield WF4 6AP* Tel (01924) 280136

VICKERMAN, Canon John. b 42. Chich Th Coll 69. d 72 p 73. C Horbury *Wakef* 72-76; C Elland 76-78; V Glass Houghton 78-89; V Bruntcliffe 89-96; V King Cross 96-11; RD Halifax 00-06; Hon Can Wakef Cathl 02-11; rtd 11. *6 St Barnabas, Newland, Malvern WR13 5AX* Tel (01684) 563741

VICKERS (née CONWAY), Mrs Catherine Mary. b 61. Newc Univ BA82 Leeds Univ PGCE83. NEOC 03. d 06 p 07. C Bedale and Leeming *Ripon* 06-08; C Bedale and Leeming and Thornton Watlass 08-10; R Stourdene Gp *Cov* from 10. *The Vicarage, Old Warwick Road, Ettington, Stratford-upon-Avon CV37 7SH* Tel (01789) 748137 E-mail cathvickers@hotmail.com

VICKERS, Dennis William George. b 30. Shrews Ord Course 81. d 86 p 87. NSM Stokesay *Heref* 86-88; NSM Bucknell w Chapel Lawn, Llanfair Waterdine etc 88-92; NSM Wigmore Abbey 93-01; Perm to Offic from 01. *Reeves Holding, Reeves Lane, Stanage, Knighton LD7 1NA* Tel (01547) 530577 Fax 530773

VICKERS, Donald. b 48. Edge Hill Coll of HE DASE80 Univ of Wales (Ban) MEd87. NOC 97. d 00 p 01. NSM Leigh St Mary *Man* 00-05; NSM Westleigh St Pet from 05; Asst Chapl HM Pris Man from 00. *21 Broom Way, Westhoughton, Bolton BL5 3TZ* Tel (01942) 815193 Mobile 07768-492581 E-mail don@dvickers20.freeserve.co.uk

VICKERS, Mrs Janice Audrey Maureen. b 56. d 96 p 97. OLM Woking Ch Ch *Guildf* 96-06; OLM Ottershaw from 06. *7 Langdale Close, Woking GU21 4RS* Tel (01483) 720873 E-mail bobjan@bjvickers.eclipse.co.uk

VICKERS, Mrs Mary Janet. b 57. Westmr Coll Ox MTh97. St Jo Coll Nottm BTh85. dss 85 d 87 p 99. Worc City St Paul and Old St Martin etc 85-89; Par Dn 87-89; World Miss Officer *Worc* 89-92; USPG 92-00; Lic to Offic *Eur* 95-99; Perm to Offic from 99; Perm to Offic Adnry of the Army from 97; NSM Cheswardine, Childs Ercall, Hales, Hinstock etc *Lich* 99-01; NSM Wrecclesham *Guildf* 01-02; NSM Pimperne, Stourpaine,

Durweston and Bryanston *Sarum* 03-05; NSM Hipswell *Ripon* 05-06; NSM W Andover *Win* 07-09; NSM Portway and Danebury 09-10; Ind Chapl *Linc* from 10. *The Rectory, 1A The Avenue, Healing, Grimsby DN41 7NA* Tel (01472) 883481 Mobile 07730-972403 E-mail vickers983@btinternet.com

VICKERS, Michael. b 60. Cranmer Hall Dur BA98. **d** 98 **p** 99. C Monkwearmouth *Dur* 98-00; C Kowloon St Andr Hong Kong 00-07; V Cranham Park *Chelmsf* from 07. *St Luke's Vicarage, 201 Front Lane, Upminster RM14 1LD* Tel (01708) 222562 Fax 223253 E-mail revmichaelvickers@gmail.com

✠**VICKERS, The Rt Revd Michael Edwin.** b 29. Worc Coll Ox BA56 MA56. Cranmer Hall Dur. **d** 59 **p** 60 **c** 88. C Bexleyheath Ch Ch *Roch* 59-62; Chapl Lee Abbey 62-67; V Hull St Jo Newland *York* 67-81; AD Cen and N Hull 72-81; Can and Preb York Minster 81-88; Adn E Riding 81-88; Area Bp Colchester *Chelmsf* 88-94; rtd 94; Hon Asst Bp Blackb from 94. *2 Collingham Park, Lancaster LA1 4PD* Tel (01524) 848492 E-mail micjan@tiscali.co.uk

VICKERS, Peter. b 56. St Jo Coll Nottm LTh85. **d** 85 **p** 86. C Worc St Barn w Ch Ch 85-88; TV Kidderminster St Mary and All SS w Trimpley etc 88-92; Ind Chapl 88-92; CF from 92. *clo MOD Chaplains (Army)* Tel (01264) 381140 Fax 381824

VICKERS, Peter George. b 41. Local Minl Tr Course 90. **d** 93 **p** 94. OLM Cobham *Guildf* 93-04; OLM Cobham and Stoke D'Abernon 04-11; rtd 11. *24 Station Road, Stoke D'Abernon, Cobham KT11 3BN* Tel (01932) 862497 E-mail revpgv@googlemail.com

VICKERS, Randolph. b 36. Newc Univ MA93 FCIM FInstD. St Alb Minl Tr Scheme 77. **d** 80 **p** 82. NSM Hitchin *St Alb* 80-87; NSM Luton Lewsey St Hugh 87-89; NSM Shotley Newc 89-01; rtd 01; Perm to Offic *Newc* from 01. *Beggar's Roost, 26 Painshawfield Road, Stocksfield NE43 7PF* Tel and fax (01661) 842364 E-mail rvickers@christian-healing.com

VICKERSTAFF, John Joseph. b 60. Dur Univ BEd82 Teesside Univ BA84 MA86 MPhil88 ARCO92. Westcott Ho Cam 97. **d** 97 **p** 98. C Halesworth w Linstead, Chediston, Holton etc *St E* 97-99; C Blyth Valley 99-00; TV Ch the King *Newc* 00-05; P-in-c Doveridge, Scropton, Sudbury etc *Derby* 05-10; C Alkmonton, Cubley and Marston Montgomery 07-10; R S Dales from 11. *The Rectory, Main Road, Sudbury, Ashbourne DE6 5HS* Tel (01283) 585098 E-mail grumpy.revs@tiscali.co.uk

VICKERY, Charles William Bryan. b 38. Lich Th Coll 63. **d** 65 **p** 66. C Hove St Barn *Chich* 65-73; Chapl Hostel of God Clapham 73-76; P-in-c Kingston St Luke *S'wark* 76-82; V 82-94; rtd 94. *22 Lord Roseberry Lodge, 6 Elm Grove, Epsom KT18 7LZ* Tel (01372) 749148

VICKERY, Jonathan Laurie. b 58. Bretton Hall Coll BEd80. Wycliffe Hall Ox 81. **d** 84 **p** 85. C Gorseinon *S & B* 84-86; P-in-c Whitton and Pilleth and Cascob etc 86-87; R 87-91; V Crickhowell w Cwmdu and Tretower 91-02; P-in-c Downend *Bris* 02-07; V from 07. *Christ Church Vicarage, Shrubbery Road, Bristol BS16 5TB* Tel 0117-908 9868 E-mail vicar@christchurchdownend.com

VICKERY, Robin Francis. b 48. K Coll Lon BD73 AKC73. **d** 74 **p** 75. C Clapham St Jo *S'wark* 74-77; C Clapham Ch Ch and St Jo 75-77; C Reigate St Luke S Park 77-79; Hon C Clapham H Spirit 80-87 and 02-10; Hon C Clapham Team 87-01; Hon C N Lambeth from 10. *13 Chelsham Road, London SW4 6NR* Tel (020) 7622 4792

VIDAL-HALL, Roderic Mark. b 37. Sheff Univ BSc60. Lich Th Coll 62. **d** 64 **p** 65. C Ilkeston St Mary *Derby* 64-67; C Nether and Over Seale 67-70; V Chellaston 70-84; C Marchington w Marchington Woodlands *Lich* 84-97; C Kingstone w Gratwich 85-97; TV Uttoxeter Area 97-01; rtd 01. *Le Perhou, 22630 Saint-Juvat, France* Tel (0033) 2 96 88 16 34 E-mail mark@vidalhall.co.uk

VIGARS, Anthony Roy. b 54. St Jo Coll Dur BA75. Trin Coll Bris 77. **d** 78 **p** 79. C Barking St Marg w St Patr *Chelmsf* 78-81; C Littleover *Derby* 81-84; C-in-c Stapenhill Immanuel CD 84-90; V Meltham *Wakef* 90-97; V Reading St Jo *Ox* 97-06; rtd 07; Perm to Offic *Ox* 07-08 and *Ex* from 09. *15 Edgcumbe Drive, Tavistock PL19 0ET* Tel (01822) 610539 E-mail vigars@lineone.net

VIGEON, Canon Owen George. b 28. Peterho Cam BA52 MA57. Ely Th Coll 52. **d** 54 **p** 55. C Barrow St Luke *Carl* 54-58; Chapl St Jo Coll York 58-61; V Burnley St Steph *Blackb* 61-69; V Bilsborrow and Asst Dir RE 69-73; V St Annes St Thos 74-85; RD Fylde 80-85; R Halton w Aughton 85-93; Hon Can Blackb Cathl 92-93; rtd 93; Perm to Offic *York* and *Cov* from 04. *10 Hall Lane, Coventry CV2 2AW* Tel (024) 7661 1712 E-mail owenvig@talktalk.net

VIGERS, Neil Simon. b 62. K Coll Lon BD84 MTh87. Linc Th Coll 88. **d** 90 **p** 91. C Chelsea St Luke and Ch Ch *Lon* 90-93; C Staines St Mary and St Pet 93-96; P-in-c Hook *Win* 96-02; R 02-07. *St Andrew's House, 16 Tavistock Crescent, London W11 1AP* Tel (020) 7313 3900 Fax 7313 3999

VIGERS, Patricia Anne. b 31. Lon Inst of Educn TCert53. **d** 99 **p** 00. OLM Betchworth and Buckland *S'wark* 99-06; Perm to Offic from 06. *5 Normanton, Buckland Road, Reigate RH2 9RQ* Tel (01737) 243698

VIGOR, Ms Margaret Ann. b 45. Ripon Coll Cuddesdon 85. **d** 87 **p** 96. Chapl Asst All SS Convent Ox 87-89; Par Dn Basildon St Martin w Nevendon *Chelmsf* 89-91; NSM Billingham St Cuth *Dur* from 96. *15 Mitchell Street, Hartlepool TS26 9EZ* Tel (01429) 867458

VILLAGE, Andrew. b 54. Collingwood Coll Dur BSc75 Edin Univ PhD80 Bris Univ PhD03. Trin Coll Bris BA92. **d** 92 **p** 93. C Northampton St Giles *Pet* 92-95; R Middleton Cheney w Chacombe 95-04; Dir Cen for Min Studies Univ of Wales (Ban) 04-07; Lect York St Jo Univ from 07; Perm to Offic *York* from 08. *York St John University, Lord Mayor's Walk, York YO31 7EX* Tel (01904) 876723 Mobile 07749-484425 E-mail a.village@yorksj.ac.uk

VILLER, Canon Allan George Frederick. b 38. EAMTC 78. **d** 81 **p** 82. NSM Ely 81-85; V Emneth 85-92; V Littleport 92-03; RD Ely 98-03; rtd 03; Hon Can Ely Cathl 01-06; Hon C Barton Bendish w Beachamwell etc 03-06; Perm to Offic *Ely* from 06 and *Nor* from 07. *41 Westfields, Narborough, King's Lynn PE32 1SX* Tel and fax (01760) 337633 E-mail allan@viller.net

VINCE, Mrs Barbara Mary Tudor. b 29. St Alb Minl Tr Scheme 79. **dss** 82 **d** 87 **p** 94. Northwood H Trin *Lon* 82-86; Belmont 86-89; Par Dn 87-89; rtd 90. *10 Risinghill Close, Northwood HA6 3PH*

VINCE, David Eric. b 59. Birm Univ BA81 Nottm Univ BCombStuds85 Goldsmiths' Coll Lon PGCE90. Linc Th Coll 82. **d** 85 **p** 86. C Gt Malvern St Mary *Worc* 85-88; C All Hallows by the Tower etc *Lon* 88-90; Min St Giles Cripplegate w St Bart Moor Lane etc 90-92; R Salwarpe and Hindlip w Martin Hussingtree *Worc* 92-97; R Willersey, Saintbury, Weston-sub-Edge etc *Glouc* 97-03; P-in-c Quinton 02-03; R Mickleton, Willersey, Saintbury etc 03-06; RD Campden 01-06; Perm to Offic *Glouc* and *Worc* 06-07; CF from 07. *clo MOD Chaplains (Army)* Tel (01264) 381140 Fax 381824

VINCENT, Preb Alfred James. b 30. Bris Univ BA54 Lon Univ BD56. Tyndale Hall Bris 50. **d** 54 **p** 55. C Shrewsbury St Julian *Lich* 54-56; C Camborne *Truro* 56-59; V Kenwyn 59-68; Lic to Offic *St Alb* 68; Lect Qu Coll Birm 68-70; Lic to Offic *Birm* 68-70; V Bordesley St Oswald 70-76; V S Shields St Hilda w St Thos *Dur* 76-84; Hon Chapl Miss to Seafarers from 79; V Bude Haven *Truro* 84-89; R Bude Haven and Marhamchurch 89-92; RD Stratton 88-92; Preb St Endellion 90-95; rtd 92; P-in-c Chacewater *Truro* 92-95; Perm to Offic from 95. *5 Raymond Road, Redruth TR15 2HD* Tel (01209) 219263

VINCENT, Bruce Matthews. b 24. Open Univ BA76 Surrey Univ MPhil83. **d** 88 **p** 88. NSM Sidcup St Jo *Roch* 88-94; Perm to Offic from 94. *17 Glenrose Court, 55 Sidcup Hill, Sidcup DA14 6HG* Tel (020) 8302 1869

VINCENT, Christopher Robin. b 30. Sarum Th Coll 57. **d** 60 **p** 61. C Frome St Jo *B & W* 60-64; V Puxton w Hewish St Ann and Wick St Lawrence 64-70; V Buckland Dinham w Elm 70-71; V Buckland Dinham w Elm, Orchardleigh etc 71-77; P-in-c Frome H Trin 77-90; Chapl St Adhelm's Hosp Frome 77-88; RD Frome *B & W* 85-89; V Kewstoke w Wick St Lawrence 90-94; rtd 94; Perm to Offic *B & W* from 94. *Willows Edge, 2 Westwood Close, Weston-super-Mare BS22 6JU* Tel (01934) 517425

VINCENT, David Cyril. b 37. Selw Coll Cam BA60 MA64. Coll of Resurr Mirfield 60. **d** 62 **p** 63. C Cheetwood St Alb *Man* 62-65; C Lawton Moor 65-67; V Wandsworth Common St Mary *S'wark* 67-84; RD Tooting 75-80; R Stoke D'Abernon *Guildf* 84-02; rtd 02; Perm to Offic *B & W* from 04. *29 North Street, Stoke-sub-Hamdon TA14 6QS* Tel (01935) 825438

VINCENT, Henry William Gordon. b 16. Leeds Univ BA42. Coll of Resurr Mirfield 42. **d** 44 **p** 45. C Bridgwater St Jo *B & W* 44-46; C Greenford H Cross *Lon* 46-52; C Teddington St Alb 52-55; V N Hammersmith St Kath 55-64; V Whitton St Aug 64-81; rtd 81; Perm to Offic *Sarum* from 81. *Legh House, 117 Rylands Lane, Weymouth DT4 9QB* Tel (01305) 779509

VINCENT, James. *See* VINCENT, Preb Alfred James

VINCENT, John Leonard. b 61. Univ of Wales (Lamp) BA83 Southn Univ BTh87. Chich Th Coll 84. **d** 87 **p** 88. C Hampton All SS *Lon* 87-90; C Shepperton 90-95; V Whitton SS Phil and Jas 95-03; CF from 03. *clo MOD Chaplains (Army)* Tel (01264) 381140 Fax 381824

VINCENT, Michael Francis. b 48. CertEd70 Open Univ BA83. Sarum & Wells Th Coll 85. **d** 87 **p** 88. C Nuneaton St Mary *Cov* 87-90; C Stockingford 90-91; P-in-c 91-99; V from 99. *Stockingford Vicarage, 90 Church Road, Nuneaton CV10 8LG* Tel and fax (024) 7637 2089 E-mail mick@vincent4850.freeserve.co.uk

VINCENT, Robin. *See* VINCENT, Christopher Robin

VINCENT, Roy David. b 37. Chich Th Coll 81. **d** 83 **p** 84. C Atherton *Man* 83-86; V E Crompton 86-95; P-in-c Burwash *Chich* 95-00; R 00-04; rtd 04. *1 Kelton Croft, Kirkland, Frizington CA26 3YE* Tel (01946) 861300

VINCENT, Stephen Alan. b 74. Dundee Univ BSc98 Cam Univ BTh11. Westcott Ho Cam 08. **d** 11. C Newcastle w Butterton *Lich* from 11. *40 Eleanor Crescent, Newcastle ST5 3SA* Tel (01782) 638054 Mobile 07795-031587 E-mail revstevevincent@gmail.com

VINCER, Ms Louise Claire. b 69. Roehampton Inst BA90 Edin Univ MTh93. Westcott Ho Cam 97. **d** 00 **p** 01. C Waltham H Cross *Chelmsf* 00-04; C Perry Hill St Geo w Ch Ch and St Paul *S'wark* 04-06; C Bermondsey St Anne and St Aug from 06; C Bermondsey St Jas w Ch Ch and St Crispin from 06. *The Rectory, 57 Kennington Park Road, London SE11 4JQ* Tel (020) 7735 2807 E-mail lvincer@btinternet.com

VINCER, Canon Michael. b 41. S Dios Minl Tr Scheme 77. **d** 80 **p** 81. Hon C Littleham w Exmouth 80-92; Miss to Seamen 80-92; Area Sec USPG *Ex* and *Truro* 86-92; Ind Chapl Gtr Man Ind Miss 92-05; Chapl Man Airport 92-05; Hon Can Man Cathl 02-05; rtd 06; Perm to Offic *Man* from 06 and *York* from 08; OCM from 08. *28 Farmanby Close, Thornton Dale, Pickering YO18 7TD* Tel (01751) 467136 E-mail mike.vincer@gmail.com

VINE, Carolyn Ann. *See* TIBBOTT, Mrs Carolyn Ann

VINE, James David. b 67. Brighton Univ BSc95. St Steph Ho Ox. **d** 00 **p** 01. C Eastbourne St Mary *Chich* 00-03; V Stone Cross St Luke w N Langney from 03. *The Vicarage, 8 Culver Close, Eastbourne BN23 8EA* Tel (01323) 764473

VINE, John. b 24. Keble Coll Ox BA45 MA50. St Steph Ho Ox 45. **d** 48 **p** 49. C Hackney Wick St Mary of Eton w St Aug *Lon* 48-50; C Holborn St Alb w Saffron Hill St Pet 50-53; Chapl Ely Th Coll 53-56; Vice-Prin Ely Th Coll 56-60; Hon C St Leonards Ch Ch *Chich* 60-62; Chapl Lich Th Coll 62-67; R Wrington *B & W* 67-69; V Earl's Court St Cuth w St Matthias *Lon* from 69. *St Cuthbert's Clergy House, 50 Philbeach Gardens, London SW5 9EB* Tel (020) 7370 3263

VINE, Michael Charles. b 51. Worc Coll Ox BA73 MA80. Cuddesdon Coll 73. **d** 76 **p** 77. C Wallsend St Luke *Newc* 76-79; C Denton 79-81; V Sugley 81-91; V Shiremoor 91-02; R Wallsend St Pet and St Luke 02-11; rtd 11. *26 Percy Street, North Shields NE30 4HA* E-mail vinemichael@freeuk.co.uk

VINE, Canon Neville Peter. b 54. K Coll Lon BD80 AKC80. Linc Th Coll 80. **d** 81 **p** 82. C Peterlee *Dur* 81-86; Chapl Peterlee Coll 84-86; V Auckland St Pet *Dur* 86-89; Perm to Offic 89-91; R Easington 91-99; R Easington, Easington Colliery and S Hetton 99-03; AD Easington 98-03; V Auckland St Andr and St Anne from 03; AD Auckland from 03; Hon Can Dur Cathl from 03. *4 Conway Grove, Bishop Auckland DL14 6AF* Tel (01388) 604397 E-mail neville.vine@btinternet.com

VINER, Canon Leonard Edwin. b 20. Univ Coll Dur BA43. St Aug Coll Cant 38. **d** 43 **p** 44. C W Molesey *Guildf* 43-45; Miss Likoma Nyasaland 46-52; Warden St Andr Th Coll Likoma 52-56 and 58-60; C Roxbourne St Andr *Lon* 56-58; Chapl St Mich Teacher Tr Coll Malindi Malawi 60-64; Warden St Andr Th Coll Mponda's 64-67; P-in-c Malindi 67-69; R Zomba 69-71; Hon Can S Malawi from 71; R Honing w Crostwight *Nor* 71-75; P-in-c E Ruston 71-73; V 73-75; P-in-c Witton w Ridlington 71-73; V 73-75; C Corby Epiphany w St Jo *Pet* 75-79; V Brigstock w Stanion 79-86; rtd 86; Asst Chapl Lisbon *Eur* 86-87; Chapl Tangier 87-89; Perm to Offic *Pet* from 90. *38 High Street, Brigstock, Kettering NN14 3HA* Tel (01536) 373104

VINEY, Arthur William. b 32. BEd. S Dios Minl Tr Scheme. **d** 82 **p** 83. NSM Clayton w Keymer *Chich* 82-86; NSM Streat w Westmeston 86-94; rtd 94; Perm to Offic *Chich* from 94. *3 The Almshouses of the Holy Name, Brighton Road, Hurstpierpoint, Hassocks BN6 9EF* Tel (01273) 832570 E-mail a.viney@btopenworld.com

VINEY, Peter. b 43. Ox NSM Course. **d** 76 **p** 77. NSM High Wycombe *Ox* from 76. *76 Westmead, Princes Risborough HP27 9HS* Tel (01844) 275461

VIPOND, Canon John. b 17. Lon Univ BD48. ALCD48. **d** 48 **p** 49. C Roxeth Ch Ch *Lon* 48-51; V 51-56; V Pudsey St Lawr *Bradf* 56-73; Hon Can Bradf Cathl 67-73; V St Austell *Truro* 73-83; rtd 83; Perm to Offic *Truro* from 83. *Wisteria, 15 Coffeelake Meadow, Lostwithiel PL22 0LT* Tel (01208) 873141

VIRDEN, Richard. b 40. K Coll Lon BSc61 Univ Coll Lon MSc62 PhD66. **d** 04 **p** 05. OLM N Tyne and Redesdale *Newc* from 04. *Ingram Cottage, West Woodburn, Hexham NE48 2SB* Tel (01434) 270334 E-mail richard.virden@ncl.ac.uk

VIRGO, Canon Leslie Gordon. b 25. Linc Th Coll 56. **d** 58 **p** 59. C Hatcham Park All SS *S'wark* 58-61; C Selsdon *Cant* 61-65; Chapl Warlingham Park Hosp Croydon 65-73; Dioc Adv on Past Care and Counselling 74-11; R Chelsfield *Roch* 74-11; Hon Can Roch Cathl 83-11; rtd 11. *Budloe Cottage, Nupend, Stonehouse GL10 3SP* Tel (01453) 822159 Mobile 07792-085809 E-mail leslie.virgo@tinyworld.co.uk

VIRTUE, Thomas James. b 32. QUB BA56 TCD 58. **d** 58 **p** 59. C Belfast St Mich *Conn* 58-61; C Belfast St Bart 61-63; I Tempo *Clogh* 63-66; P-in-c Glynn w Raloo and Templecorran *Conn* 66-70; TV Ellesmere Port *Ches* 70-74; TV Ches 74-83; V Gt Sutton 83-97; rtd 97; Perm to Offic *Ches* from 97. *48 Saughall Road, Blacon, Chester CH1 5EY* Tel (01244) 399531

VISASH, Peter Henry. b 57. Hockerill Coll of Educn CertEd78 CQSW85. Cranmer Hall Dur 90. **d** 92 **p** 93. C Malpas *Mon* 92-95; R Bettws 95-01; P-in-c Upper Derwent *Carl* from 01; Dioc Rep CMS from 01; Warden of Readers *Carl* from 05.

Thornthwaite Vicarage, Braithwaite, Keswick CA12 5RY Tel (01768) 778243 E-mail peter.vivash@dsl.pipex.com

VIVIAN, Adrian John. b 42. K Coll Lon BD65 AKC66. St Denys Warminster 62. **d** 66 **p** 67. C Bromley St Andr *Roch* 66-69; C Egg Buckland *Ex* 69-73; Perm to Offic 73-84; P-in-c Newton Ferrers w Revelstoke 84-87. *9 Munro Avenue, Yealmpton, Plymouth PL8 2NQ*

VIVIAN, Thomas Keith. b 27. St Jo Coll Cam BA48 MA52. St Deiniol's Hawarden 76. **d** 80 **p** 81. Hd Master Lucton Sch Leominster 62-85; Lic to Offic *Heref* 80-85; P-in-c Chew Stoke w Nempnett Thrubwell *B & W* 85-88; R 88-97; P-in-c Norton Malreward 85-88; R 88-97; RD Chew Magna 92-97; rtd 97; Perm to Offic *B & W* and *Sarum* from 97. *Timberley, Sidmouth Road, Lyme Regis DT7 3ES* Tel (01297) 443547

VIVIAN, Victor Ivan. b 38. Nottm Poly LLB87. EMMTC 91. **d** 94 **p** 95. NSM Basford *S'well* 94-99; Korea 99-03; rtd 03; Perm to Offic *S'well* from 03. *12 Deepdale Road, Wollaton, Nottingham NG8 2FU* Tel 0115-928 3954 E-mail vicvivian@yahoo.com

VLACH, Jane Elizabeth. b 64. Man Univ BA87 BPl88 MRTPI. STETS 07. **d** 11. C Guildf H Trin w St Mary from 11. *27 Pewley Way, Guildford GU1 3PX* Tel (01483) 567716 E-mail office@holytrinityguildford.org.uk

VOAKE, Andrew James Frederick. b 28. Dur Univ BA55. Oak Hill Th Coll 51. **d** 55 **p** 56. C Uxbridge St Marg *Lon* 55; C Fulham St Matt 55-58; C Hove Bp Hannington Memorial Ch *Chich* 58-61; V Kirkdale St Lawr *Liv* 61-63; Chapl Millfield Sch Somerset 63-71; R Bp Latimer Memorial Ch *Birm* 71-73; R Birm Bp Latimer w All SS 73-80; V Crondall and Ewshot *Guildf* 80-90; rtd 90; Perm to Offic *B & W* from 90. *1 St Aubyns Avenue, Weston-super-Mare BS23 4UJ* Tel (01934) 620587

✠**VOBBE, The Rt Revd Joachim Gerhard.** b 47. **p** 72 **c** 95. Chapl Cologne (Old Catholic Ch) 72-74; Chapl Düsseldorf 74-77; R Blumberg 77-82; R Offenbach 82-95; Bp Bonn from 95; Hon Asst Bp Eur from 99. *Gregor-Mendel-Strasse 28, D-53115 Bonn, Germany* Tel (0049) (228) 232285 Fax 238314 E-mail ordinariat@alt-katholisch.de

VOCKINS, Preb Michael David. b 44. OBE96. Univ of Wales (Abth) BSc69. Glouc Sch of Min 85. **d** 88 **p** 89. NSM Cradley w Mathon and Storridge *Heref* from 88; RD Ledbury from 02; Perm to Offic *Worc* from 88; Preb Heref Cathl from 09. *Birchwood Lodge, Birchwood, Storridge, Malvern WR13 5EZ* Tel (01886) 884366 *or* (01905) 748474 E-mail michaelvockins@birchwoodlodge.fsnet.co.uk

VOGT, Charles William Derek. b 36. Ex Univ BA07. EMMTC 83. **d** 86 **p** 87. NSM Ilkeston H Trin *Derby* 86-87; C Derby St Anne and St Jo 87-90; TV Staveley and Barrow Hill 90-95; P-in-c Hasland 95-96; R 97-01; P-in-c Temple Normanton 95-96; V 97-01; rtd 01; Perm to Offic *Ex* from 01. *54 Old Bakery Close, Exeter EX4 2UZ* Tel (01392) 271943

VOGT, Robert Anthony. b 25. Jes Coll Cam BA50 MA54. S'wark Ord Course 60. **d** 63 **p** 64. C Sutton New Town St Barn *S'wark* 63-67; C Kidbrooke St Jas 67-72; V Wood End *Cov* 72-80; RD Cov E 77-80; R Kidbrooke St Jas *S'wark* 80-85; TR 85-90; rtd 90; Perm to Offic *S'wark* from 90. *15 Serica Court, 154 Greenwich High Road, London SE10 8NZ* Tel (020) 8853 3430

VOLLAND, Michael John. b 74. Northumbria Univ BA96 K Coll Lon MA04. Ridley Hall Cam 04. **d** 06 **p** 07. Pioneer Min Glouc City 06-09; C Glouc Cathl 07-09; Dir Miss and Pioneer Min Cranmer Hall Dur from 09. *Cranmer Hall, St John's College, 3 South Bailey, Durham DH1 3RJ* Tel 0191-334 3898 E-mail m.j.volland@durham.ac.uk

VOLTZENLOGEL, Timothy John. b 60. St Jo Coll Dur BA81. Wycliffe Hall Ox BTh00. **d** 00 **p** 01. C Eastbourne All SS *Chich* 00-04; V Church Langley *Chelmsf* 04-11; V Bexhill St Steph *Chich* from 11. *The Vicarage, 67 Woodsgate Park, Bexhill-on-Sea TN39 4DL* Tel (01424) 211186 E-mail tim@timv.freeserve.co.uk

VOOGHT, Canon Michael George Peter. b 38. St Pet Hall Ox BA61 MA65. Chich Th Coll 61. **d** 63 **p** 64. C E Dulwich St Jo *S'wark* 63-66; C Prestbury *Glouc* 66-72; R Minchinhampton 72-85; RD Stonehouse 79-85; V Thornbury 85-02; Hon Can Glouc Cathl 86-02; rtd 02; Perm to Offic *Glouc* from 03. *62 High Street, Thornbury, Bristol BS35 2AN* Tel (01454) 414915

VORLEY, Kenneth Arthur. b 27. Sarum Th Coll 65. **d** 67 **p** 68. C Ashbourne w Mapleton and Clifton *Derby* 67-71; R W Hallam and Mapperley 71-77; V Hemingford Grey *Ely* 78-88; rtd 88; Perm to Offic *Carl* 88-01 and from 03. *Glen Cottage, Braithwaite, Keswick CA12 5SX* Tel (01768) 778535

VOSS, Mrs Philomena Ann. b 35. Edge Hill Coll of HE CertEd55. St Alb Minl Tr Scheme 87 EAMTC 95. **d** 96 **p** 97. NSM Tye Green w Netteswell *Chelmsf* 96-03; NSM Ware St Mary *St Alb* 03-06; Perm to Offic from 06. *21 Queen's Road, Hertford SG13 8AZ* Tel (01992) 554676 E-mail annvoss@tesco.net

VOST, Mrs Jane. b 62. **d** 04 **p** 08. OLM Radcliffe *Man* 04-10; OLM Radcliffe St Andr from 10. *43 Laurel Avenue, Bolton BL3 1AS* Tel (01204) 559161 E-mail jane@standrewsradcliffe.org.uk

VOTH HARMAN, Karin. b 65. Virginia Univ BA87 Sussex Univ MA93 PhD99. Westcott Ho Cam 09. **d** 11. NSM King's Cliffe, Bulwick and Blatherwycke etc *Pet* from 11. *Headmaster's House, Spring Back Way, Uppingham, Oakham LE15 9TT* Tel (01572) 822688 Mobile 07971-936253 E-mail karinvoth@hotmail.com

VOUSDEN, Canon Alan Thomas. b 48. K Coll Lon BSc69. Qu Coll Birm. **d** 72 **p** 73. C Orpington All SS *Roch* 72-76; C Belvedere All SS 76-80; R Cuxton and Halling 80-86; V Bromley St Mark 86-98; Chapl Bromley Hosp 86-94; Chapl Bromley Hosps NHS Trust 94-98; V Rainham *Roch* 98-10; RD Gillingham 00-10; Bp's Dom Chapl from 10; Hon Can Roch Cathl from 99. *Bishopscourt, St Margarets Street, Rochester ME1 1TS* Tel (01634) 814439 Fax 831136 E-mail alan.vousden@rochester.anglican.org

VOWLES, Ms Patricia. b 50. S'wark Ord Course 84. **d** 87 **p** 94. USPG 70-91; NSM Nunhead St Antony w St Silas *S'wark* 87-91; Par Dn Newington St Mary 91-94; Par Dn Camberwell St Mich w All So w Em 91-94; V 94-06; Chapl Cautley Ho Chr Cen 06-10; C Croydon St Jo *S'wark* from 11. *Church House, Barrow Road, Croydon CR0 4EZ* Tel (020) 8688 7006 Mobile 07709-253496 E-mail p.vowles@btinternet.com

VOWLES, Canon Peter John Henry. b 25. Magd Coll Ox BA50 MA55. Westcott Ho Cam 50. **d** 52 **p** 53. C Kings Heath *Birm* 52-56; C Huddersfield St Pet *Wakef* 56-57; PC Perry Beeches *Birm* 57-64; V 64-72; R Cottingham *York* 72-83; R Man St Ann 83-91; Hon Can Man Cathl 83-91; rtd 91; Perm to Offic *Man* from 91. *10 Redshaw Close, Manchester M14 6JB* Tel 0161-257 2065

VROLIJK, Paul Dick. b 64. Delft Univ of Tech MSc88. Trin Coll Bris BA03 PhD08. **d** 04 **p** 05. NSM Gifford Gifford *Bris* 04-08; Chapl Aquitaine *Eur* from 09. *8 chemin du Garonna, 24240 Sigoules, France* Tel (0033) 5 53 23 40 73 E-mail paul.vrolijk@bbox.fr *or* aquitainechaplain@gmail.com

✠VUNAGI, The Most Revd David. b 50. Univ of the S Pacific DipEd76 Univ of Papua New Guinea BEd83. St Jo Coll Auckland BTh91 Vancouver Sch of Th MTh98. **d** 92 **p** 92 **c** 01. Lect Bp Patteson Th Coll Kohimarama Solomon Is 92-93; Prin Selwyn Coll 93-96; Asst P Vancouver St Anselm Canada 96-99; Solomon Is from 98; Prin Selwyn Coll 99; Miss Sec 00; Bp Temotu 01-09; Abp Melanesia and Bp Cen Melanesia from 09. *Selwyn College, PO Box 253, Honiara, Solomon Islands* Tel (00677) 21892 *or* 26101 Fax 21098 E-mail dvunagi@comphq.org.sb

VYE, Mrs Georgina Ann. b 57. SWMTC 06. **d** 09 **p** 10. C Littleham w Exmouth and Lympstone and Woodbury w Exton 09-10; C Ex St Thos and Em from 10. *The Vicarage, Newton St Cyres, Exeter EX5 5BN* Tel (01392) 851556 Mobile 07954-413984 E-mail g.vye@btinternet.com

W

✠WABUKALA, The Most Revd Eliud. b 51. St Paul's Coll Limuru 85 Wycliffe Coll Toronto 91. **d** 88 **c** 96. Canada 91-94; Lect St Paul's Th Coll Limuru 94-96; Bp Bungoma 96-09; Abp Kenya from 09. *PO Box 40502, Nairobi 00100, Kenya* Tel (00254) (2) 714753 Fax 718442 E-mail archoffice@swiftkenya.com

WADDELL, James William Boece. b 74. Trin Coll Bris 06. **d** 08 **p** 09. C Slaugham *Chich* 08-11; C Slaugham and Staplefield Common from 11. *13 Warren Cottages, Horsham Road, Handcross, Haywards Heath RH17 6DJ* Tel (01444) 401934 Mobile 07813-872871 E-mail j.dub.info@gmail.com

WADDELL, Peter Matthew. b 75. Keble Coll Ox BA96 Fitzw Coll Cam MPhil98 PhD02. Westcott Ho Cam 98. **d** 02 **p** 03. C Oxton *Ches* 02-04; Chapl SS Coll Cam 05-10; Past Dean from 10. *Sidney Sussex College, Cambridge CB2 3HU* Tel (01223) 338872 E-mail pastoral.dean@sid.cam.ac.uk *or* peterwad@hotmail.com

WADDINGTON, Gary Richard. b 69. St Chad's Coll Dur BSc91 Heythrop Coll Lon MA05. St Steph Ho Ox BTh96. **d** 96 **p** 97. C Southsea H Spirit *Portsm* 96-00; V Harrogate 00-10; TR Harrogate St Wilfrid *Ripon* from 10. *St Wilfrid's Vicarage, 51B Kent Road, Harrogate HG1 2EU* Tel (01423) 503259 Mobile 07920-464818 E-mail frgaryw@btinternet.com

WADDINGTON-FEATHER, John Joseph. b 33. Leeds Univ BA54 Keele Univ PGCE74 FRSA87. St Deiniol's Hawarden 75. **d** 77 **p** 78. NSM Longden and Annscroft w Pulverbatch *Heref* 77-03; Chapl Asst HM Pris Shrewsbury 77-09; Sudan 84-85; Chapl Prestfelde Sch Shrewsbury 86-96; Ed *The Poetry Church*

95-08; Perm to Offic *Lich* 99-09 and *Heref* from 03. *Fair View, Old Coppice, Lyth Bank, Shrewsbury SY3 0BW* Tel and fax (01743) 872177 E-mail john@feather-books.com

WADDLE, Simon. b 60. Wellington Univ (NZ) BA81. St Jo Coll Auckland 86. **d** 88 **p** 89. New Zealand 88-97; Perm to Offic *Roch* 97-00; Hon C Roch St Marg from 00. *19 Honeypot Close, Rochester ME2 3DU* Tel (020) 7898 1610 Fax 7898 1769

WADE, Canon Andrew John. b 50. Trin Coll Bris. **d** 86 **p** 87. C St Keverne *Truro* 86-89; TV Probus, Ladock and Grampound w Creed and St Erme 89-92; V Constantine 92-00; P-in-c Ludgvan 00-01; P-in-c Marazion 00-01; P-in-c St Hilary w Perranuthnoe 00-01; R Ludgvan, Marazion, St Hilary and Perranuthnoe 01-08; RD Penwith 03-08; TR Probus, Ladock and Grampound w Creed and St Erme from 08; Hon Can Truro Cathl from 08. *The Sanctuary, Wagg Lane, Probus, Truro TR2 4JX* Tel (01726) 882746 E-mail andrewsanctuary@aol.com

WADE, Christopher John. b 54. Trent Poly BSc81 MRICS82 ACIArb88. Aston Tr Scheme 88 Trin Coll Bris. **d** 92 **p** 93. C Barnsley St Geo *Wakef* 92-95; C Whittle-le-Woods *Blackb* 95-99; P-in-c Bulwell St Jo *S'well* 99-03; Dir Heavenfire Min from 03. *46 Hastings Avenue, Whitley Bay NE26 4AG* Tel 084516-65277 E-mail chris@heavenfire.org

WADE, Canon David Peter. b 65. St Jo Coll Nottm LTh92. **d** 92 **p** 93. C Victoria Docks Ascension *Chelmsf* 92-95; P-in-c Victoria Docks St Luke 95-97; V from 97; AD Newham from 07; Hon Can Chelmsf Cathl from 08. *The Vicarage, 16A Ruscoe Road, London E16 1JB* Tel (020) 7476 2076 E-mail davenicky@hotmail.com

WADE, Geoffrey Adrian. b 61. Ripon Coll Cuddesdon. **d** 01 **p** 02. C Worc City St Paul and Old St Martin etc 01-02; C Wordsley 02-04; TV Ilminster and Distr *B & W* 04-10; V Winsmoor from 10. *The Rectory, Shepton Beauchamp, Ilminster TA19 0LP* Tel (01460) 240228 E-mail begw1@greenbee.net

WADE, Walter. b 29. Oak Hill Th Coll 64. **d** 66 **p** 67. C Denton Holme *Carl* 66-69; V Jesmond H Trin *Newc* 69-78; R Moresby *Carl* 78-87; P-in-c Langdale 87-94; Member Rural Life and Agric Team 93-94; rtd 94; Perm to Offic *Carl* from 94. *Manor Cottage, Fellside, Caldbeck, Wigton CA7 8HA* Tel (01697) 478214

WADEY, Ms Rachel Susan. b 71. Lanc Univ BA94 Ox Univ BA98. St Steph Ho Ox 95. **d** 98 **p** 99. C Poulton-le-Fylde *Blackb* 98-01; C Blackpool H Cross 01-03; V Skerton St Chad 03-09; Chapl Prospect Park Hosp Reading from 09. *Prospect Park Hospital, Honey End Lane, Tilehurst, Reading RG30 4EJ* Tel 0118-960 5000 E-mail rachel.wadey@talktalk.net

WADGE, Alan. b 46. Grey Coll Dur BA68 MA72. St Chad's Coll Dur. **d** 70 **p** 71. C Cockerton *Dur* 70-74; C Whitworth w Spennymoor 74-75; P-in-c Shipton Moyne w Westonbirt and Lasborough *Glouc* 75-80; Chapl Westonbirt Sch 75-80; V Dean Forest H Trin *Glouc* 80-83; Chapl Gresham's Sch Holt 83-91; R Ridgeway *Ox* 91-11; RD Wantage 95-01; rtd 11. *8 Underhill, Mere, Warminster BA12 6LU* E-mail alanwadge@hotmail.com

WADHAM, Canon Philip Andrew. b 41. Saltley Tr Coll Birm CertEd70 Bradf Univ MA92. Vancouver Sch of Th BTh80. **d** 79 **p** 80. Canada 80-82; Ecuador 82-85; R Virden Canada 85-88; Area Sec USPG *Wakef* and *Bradf* 88-92; R W Coast Miss Canada 94-97; Regional Miss Co-ord 97-06; rtd 06; P-in-c Sooke from 06. *4544 Rocky Point Road, Victoria BC V9C 4E4, Canada* Tel (001) (250) 391 7436 E-mail pwadham@telus.net

WADLAND, Douglas Bryan. b 33. K Coll Dur BA61 CQSW62. Oak Hill Th Coll 90. **d** 91 **p** 92. NSM Cowley *Lon* 91-93; Asst Chapl Hillingdon Hosp NHS Trust 91-93; P-in-c Wembley St Jo *Lon* 93-00; Chapl Cen Middx Hosp NHS Trust 91-00; rtd 00; Kenya 01-03; Hon C Alperton *Lon* 03-09; Perm to Offic from 09. *55 Copthall Road East, Uxbridge UB10 8SE* Tel (01895) 613904 E-mail wadland@lizbryan.freeserve.co.uk

WADMAN, Vera Margaret. b 51. EAMTC 97. **d** 00 **p** 01. NSM Burnham *Chelmsf* 00-02; NSM Creeksea w Althorne, Latchingdon and N Fambridge 02-09; NSM Creeksea from 09; P-in-c from 10. *Fernlea Cottage, 8 Fernlea Road, Burnham-on-Crouch CM0 8EJ* Tel (01621) 783963 E-mail vera.wadman@allsaintscreeksea.org.uk

WADSWORTH, Mrs Alison Margaret. b 36. Bris Univ CertEd57. **d** 97 **p** 98. OLM Cley Hill Warminster *Sarum* 97-06. *2 Saxon's Acre, Warminster BA12 8HT* Tel (01985) 212510 E-mail awap@blueyonder.co.uk

WADSWORTH, Andrew James. b 56. St Jo Coll Dur BA79 Cam Univ CertEd80 Lambeth STh95 FRSA99. Sarum & Wells Th Coll 84 Chich Th Coll 86. **d** 87 **p** 88. NSM Forest Road and E Grinstead St Swithun *Chich* 87-89; C Shrewsbury St Chad w St Mary *Lich* 89-91; TV Honiton, Gittisham, Combe Raleigh, Monkton etc *Ex* 91-97; V Bulkington w Shilton and Ansty *Cov* 97-06; P-in-c Bognor *Chich* 06-07; V from 07. *St Wilfrid's Vicarage, 17 Victoria Drive, Bognor Regis PO21 2RH* Tel (01243) 821965 E-mail rev.andrew@wadsworths.fsnet.co.uk

WADSWORTH, Andrew John. b 67. Reading Univ BSc88 MRICS90. Wycliffe Hall Ox 99. **d** 01 **p** 02. NSM St Andr and Stonehouse *Ex* 01-05; C Enfield Ch Ch Trent Park *Lon* from 05. *2 Firs Lane, London N21 2HU* Tel (020) 8441 6444 E-mail awadsworth@waddy20.freeserve.co.uk

WADSWORTH, Jean. b 44. St Jo Coll Dur BA71. Cranmer Hall Dur 85. **d** 87 **p** 94. Par Dn Thamesmead *S'wark* 87-92; Par Dn Rotherhithe H Trin 92-94; C 94-98; V New Eltham All SS 98-08; RD Eltham and Mottingham 01-05; rtd 08. *2 Peak Coach House, Cotmaton Road, Sidmouth EX10 8SY*

WADSWORTH, Mrs Mary. b 44. **d** 08 **p** 09. NSM Ashton *Man* from 08. *99 Cranbourne Road, Ashton-under-Lyne OL7 9BW* Tel 0161-330 0713   Mobile 07712-527981
E-mail thewadsat99@aol.com

WADSWORTH, Canon Michael Philip. b 43. Qu Coll Ox BA65 MA68 DPhil75 Cam Univ PhD78. Ripon Hall Ox 67. **d** 70 **p** 71. C Sutton St Mich *York* 70-73; Lect Sussex Univ 73-78; Hon C Hove St Jo 75-78; Fell and Chapl SS Coll Cam 78-81; Dir Th Studies 79-81; CF (TA) from 80; C Ditton St Mich *Liv* 81; V 82-84; Dioc Lay Tr Officer 83-89; V Orford St Marg 84-89; V Haddenham *Ely* 89-98; V Wilburton 89-98; RD Ely 94-98; P-in-c Gt Shelford 98-01; Hon Can Ely Cathl 96-01; rtd 01; Perm to Offic *Ely* and *Linc* from 01. *9 Eastgate, Sleaford NG34 7DL* Tel (01529) 304251

WADSWORTH, Peter Richard. b 52. Qu Coll Ox BA73 MA77. Cuddesdon Coll 74 English Coll Rome 76. **d** 77 **p** 78. C High Wycombe *Ox* 77-81; C Farnham Royal w Hedgerley 81-84; Dioc Ecum Officer *Portsm* 84-90; V E Meon 84-96; V Langrish 84-96; V Elson 96-04; RD Gosport 96-02; V St Alb St Sav *St Alb* from 04. *St Saviour's Vicarage, 25 Sandpit Lane, St Albans AL1 4DF* Tel (01727) 851526 E-mail peter.wadsworth52@ntlworld.com

WADSWORTH, Roy. b 37. NEOC 89. **d** 89 **p** 90. NSM Alne *York* from 89; Ind Chapl 94-03; rtd 02. *The Rosery, Tollerton, York YO61 1PX* Tel (01347) 838212

WAGGETT, Geoffrey James. b 49. Sarum & Wells Th Coll 83. **d** 85 **p** 86. C Newton Nottage *Llan* 85-88; TV Glyncorrwg w Afan Vale and Cymmer Afan 88-89; R 89-99; V Glyncorrwg and Upper Afan Valley 99-00; TR Ebbw Vale *Mon* from 00. *The Rectory, Eureka Place, Ebbw Vale NP23 6PN* Tel (01495) 301723

WAGSTAFF (née JONES), Ms Alison. b 40. K Coll Dur BA63 Man Univ CertEd64. TISEC 95. **d** 98 **p** 99. C Edin St Cuth 98-00; Assoc P Edin St Columba from 00; Chapl St Columba's Hospice 01-05. *27 Cambridge Gardens, Edinburgh EH6 5DH* Tel 0131-554 6702

WAGSTAFF, Andrew Robert. b 56. K Coll Lon BD79 AKC79. Coll of Resurr Mirfield 81. **d** 83 **p** 84. C Newark w Hawton, Cotham and Shelton *S'well* 83-86; C Dublin St Bart w Leeson Park *D & G* 86-89; V Nottingham St Geo w St Jo *S'well* 89-95; V Worksop Priory 95-06; Chapl Antwerp St Boniface *Eur* from 06. *Grétrystraat 39, 2018 Antwerp, Belgium* Tel (0032) (3) 239 3339 E-mail chaplain@boniface.be

WAGSTAFF, The Ven Christopher John Harold. b 36. St D Coll Lamp BA62. **d** 63 **p** 64. C Queensbury All SS *Lon* 63-68; V Tokyngton St Mich 68-73; V Coleford w Staunton *Glouc* 73-83; RD Forest S 76-82; Adn Glouc 83-00; Hon Can Glouc Cathl 83-00; Hon Can St Andr Cathl Njombe (Tanzania) from 93; rtd 00; Perm to Offic *Glouc* from 00. *Karibuni, Collafield, Littledean, Cinderford GL14 3LG* Tel (01594) 825282

WAGSTAFF, Miss Joan. b 33. Gilmore Ho. **dss** 75 **d** 87 **p** 94. Ellesmere Port *Ches* 86-87; Par Dn 87-93; rtd 93; Perm to Offic *Ches* from 93. *41 Heywood Road, Great Sutton, South Wirral CH66 3PS* Tel 0151-348 0884

WAGSTAFF, Michael. b 59. R Holloway Coll Lon BA81. Coll of Resurr Mirfield 86. **d** 89 **p** 90. C Worksop Priory *S'well* 89-92; C Ab Kettleby Gp *Leic* 92-94; TV Leic Resurr 94-00; Dioc Soc Resp Officer *Sheff* 00-08; Chapl RN from 08. *Royal Naval Chaplaincy Service, Mail Point 1-2, Leach Building, Whale Island, Portsmouth PO2 8BY* Tel (023) 9262 5055 Fax 9262 5134

WAGSTAFF, Robert William. b 36. Edin Th Coll 61. **d** 63 **p** 64. C Harringay St Paul *Lon* 63-64; C Mill Hill Jo Keble Ch 64-69; NSM N Lambeth *S'wark* 70-80; NSM Wilden, Hartlebury and Ombersley w Doverdale 80-97; C Shrawley, Witley, Astley and Abberley *Worc* 98-02; rtd 02; Perm to Offic *Worc* from 02. *The Red House, Quarry Bank, Hartlebury, Kidderminster DY11 7TE* Tel (01299) 250883

WAGSTAFFE, Eric Herbert. b 25. St Aid Birkenhead 55. **d** 57 **p** 58. C Harpurhey Ch Ch *Man* 57-60; R 60-69; V Pendlebury St Jo 69-84; V Hoghton *Blackb* 84-91; rtd 91; Perm to Offic *Blackb* 91-02 and *Man* from 95. *3 Chelwood Close, Bolton BL1 7LN* Tel (01204) 596048

WAIN, Phillip. b 54. Aston Tr Scheme 89 Linc Th Coll 93. **d** 93 **p** 94. C Witton *Ches* 93-97; R Lea Gp *Linc* from 97. *The Rectory, 18 Gainsborough Road, Lea, Gainsborough DN21 5HZ* Tel (01427) 613188

WAINAINA, Francis Samson Kamoko. b 51. St Jo Coll Dur MA89. Oak Hill Th Coll BA84. **d** 84 **p** 85. Kenya 84-88; C Upton (Overchurch) *Ches* 89-92; V Ellesmere St Pet *Sheff* 92-95; C York St Mich-le-Belfrey 95-01; V Starbeck *Ripon* from 01. *The Vicarage, 78 High Street, Harrogate HG2 7LW* Tel (01423) 546477 or 889914 E-mail francis.wainaina@talktalk.net

✠**WAINE, The Rt Revd John.** b 30. KCVO96. Man Univ BA51. Ridley Hall Cam 53. **d** 55 **p** 56 **c** 75. C W Derby St Mary *Liv* 55-58; C Sutton 58-60; V Ditton St Mich 60-64; V Southport H Trin 64-69; V Kirkby 69-71; TR 71-75; Suff Bp Stafford *Lich* 75-78; Preb Lich Cathl 75-78; Bp St E 78-86; Bp Chelmsf 86-96; Clerk of the Closet 89-96; rtd 96; Perm to Offic *St E* from 96; Hon Asst Bp St E from 08. *Broadmere, Ipswich Road, Grundisburgh, Woodbridge IP13 6TJ* Tel (01473) 738296 E-mail bpjohn@jwaine.mail1.co.uk

WAINE, The Ven Stephen John. b 59. Westcott Ho Cam 81. **d** 84 **p** 85. C Wolverhampton *Lich* 84-88; Min Can and Succ St Paul's Cathl 88-93; V Romford St Edw *Chelmsf* 93-10; P-in-c Romford Cathl from 10. *28 Merriefield Drive, Broadstone BH18 8BP* Tel (01202) 659427 or 695891 Fax 691418 E-mail addorset@salisbury.anglican.org

WAINWRIGHT, John Pounsberry. b 42. St Steph Ho Ox 64. **d** 66 **p** 67. C Palmers Green St Jo *Lon* 66-70; C Primrose Hill St Mary w Avenue Road St Paul 70-71; P-in-c St John's Wood All SS 71-73; V Hendon All SS Childs Hill from 73. *All Saints' Vicarage, Church Walk, London NW2 2TJ* Tel (020) 7435 3182

WAINWRIGHT, Joseph Allan. b 21. K Coll Lon BD50 AKC50. Columbia Pacific Univ PhD82 Sussex Univ DPhil85. **d** 50 **p** 51. C Boston *Linc* 50-53; Chapl St Paul's Coll Cheltenham 53-62; Educn Sec BCC 62-66; Lect Moray Ho Coll of Educn Edin 66-78; Perm to Offic *Chich* 79-88; rtd 86. *Beggar's Roost, Lewes BN7 1LX* Tel (01273) 477453

WAINWRIGHT, Kevin Frank. b 46. Linc Th Coll 73. **d** 75 **p** 76. C Stand *Man* 75-78; C Radcliffe St Thos and St Jo 78-80; V Kearsley Moor from 80. *St Stephen's Vicarage, Blair Street, Kearsley, Bolton BL4 8QP* Tel (01204) 572535

WAINWRIGHT, Malcolm Hugh. b 47. Man Univ BA68 Nottm Univ MA89. St Jo Coll Nottm MA98. **d** 98 **p** 99. NSM Cotgrave and Owthorpe *S'well* 98-02; P-in-c Plumtree and Tollerton 02-09; Hon C Burton Fleming w Fordon, Grindale etc *York* 09-11; P-in-c Skelton w Shipton and Newton on Ouse from 11. *The Rectory, Church Lane, Skelton, York YO30 1XT* Tel (01904) 471351 E-mail malcolm@mhwainwright.eclipse.co.uk

WAINWRIGHT, Mrs Margaret Gillian. b 45. Qu Mary Coll Lon BA68. EAMTC 00. **d** 03 **p** 04. NSM Combs and Lt Finborough *St E* 03-05; NSM Creeting St Mary, Creeting St Peter etc 05-11; rtd 11. *The Cottage, Elmswell Road, Wetherden, Stowmarket IP14 3LN* Tel (01359) 242653 E-mail margwain@btopenworld.com

WAINWRIGHT, Martin John. b 69. Loughb Univ BEng92. Trin Coll Bris BA98. **d** 98 **p** 99. C Chislehurst Ch Ch *Roch* 98-02; V Camberley St Mary *Guildf* 02-10; V Howell Hill w Burgh Heath from 10. *St Paul's Vicarage, 17 Northey Avenue, Sutton SM2 7HS* Tel (020) 8224 9927 E-mail martin.wainwright@ntlworld.com

WAINWRIGHT, Pauline Barbara. *See* FLORANCE, Mrs Pauline Barbara

WAINWRIGHT, Peter Anthony. b 45. K Coll Lon BD73 MRICS67. Ridley Hall Cam 73. **d** 75 **p** 76. C Ashtead *Guildf* 76-79; V Woking St Paul 79-84; Perm to Offic *Ox* 87-92 and 03-05; P-in-c Harston w Hauxton and Newton *Ely* 05-10; rtd 10; Perm to Offic *Ox* from 10. *9 Wallace End, Aylesbury HP21 7FA* Tel 07814-835528 (mobile) E-mail rev@peterwainwright.plus.com

WAINWRIGHT, Robert Neil. b 52. NEOC 99. **d** 02 **p** 03. NSM Barlby w Riccall *York* 02-05; NSM Selby Abbey from 05. *33 Hillfield, Selby YO8 3ND* Tel (01757) 706216   Mobile 07768-390060 E-mail robbwain@yahoo.com

WAIT, Canon Alan Clifford. b 33. St Cath Soc Ox BA58 MA70. Coll of Resurr Mirfield. **d** 60 **p** 61. C Charlton St Luke w St Paul *S'wark* 60-67; C Caterham 67-72; V N Dulwich St Faith 72-83; RD Dulwich 78-83; V Purley St Barn 83-01; RD Croydon S 93-01; Hon Can S'wark Cathl 01; rtd 01; Perm to Offic *Cant* from 01. *Forgefield Oast, Church Hill, Bethersden, Ashford TN26 3AQ* Tel (01233) 820529

WAITE, Daniel Alfred Norman. b 42. **d** 04 **p** 05. OLM Gorleston St Andr *Nor* from 04. *15 Laburnum Close, Bradwell, Great Yarmouth NR31 8JB* Tel (01493) 664591 E-mail djwaite@btinternet.com

WAITE, John Langton (Tony). b 10. Solicitor 34 ACP37 Man Univ 30. Wycliffe Hall Ox 37. **d** 39 **p** 40. C Hove Bp Hannington Memorial *Ch Chich* 39-41; C Walcot *B & W* 41-42; V Blackheath St Jo *S'wark* 42-48; V Leeds St Geo *Ripon* 48-58; V Woking St Jo *Guildf* 58-76; rtd 76; Perm to Offic *Portsm* from 82. *11 The Crescent, Alverstoke, Gosport PO12 2DH* Tel and fax (023) 9252 1458 E-mail tonywaite@cwcom.net

WAITE, Julian Henry. b 47. Open Univ BA98. Brasted Th Coll 68 Ridley Hall Cam 70. **d** 72 **p** 73. C Wollaton *S'well* 72-76; C Herne Bay Ch Ch *Cant* 76-79; P-in-c Mersham 79-87; Chapl Wm Harvey Hosp Ashford 79-87; V Marden *Cant* 87-93; Chapl HM Pris Blantyre Ho 90-93; Chapl HM Pris Swaleside from 01. *HM Prison Swaleside, Eastchurch, Sheerness ME12 4AX* Tel (01795) 804042 Fax 804200

WAITE, Robin Derek. **d** 05 **p** 06. NSM Derringham Bank *York* 05-06; NSM Woldsburn from 06. *Mulberry Cottage, Parklands Drive, North Ferriby HU14 3EU* Tel (01482) 631162 E-mail rojaw@freezone.co.uk

WAITE, Sheila Margaret. *See* TYLER, Mrs Sheila Margaret

WAIYAKI, Canon Jennie. b 34. MBE88. ALA64. NEOC 89. d 92 p 94. NSM Ulgham and Widdrington *Newc* 92-97; Chapl MU 96-02; Chapl Northumbria Healthcare NHS Trust from 97; NSM Longhorsley and Hebron *Newc* 97-04; Hon Can Newc Cathl from 02. *6 Woodburn Street, Stobswood, Morpeth NE61 5QD* Tel (01670) 791066

WAIZENEKER, Ms Ann Elizabeth. b 56. Southn Univ BSc78. SEITE 05. d 08 p 09. C Chich St Paul and Westhampnett from 08. *The Vicarage, 11 Old Arundel Road, Westhampnett, Chichester PO18 0TH* Tel (01243) 536280

WAKE, Colin Walter. b 50. Oriel Coll Ox BA72 MA. Cuddesdon Coll 74. d 75 p 76. C Sandhurst *Ox* 75-78; C Faversham *Cant* 79-80; TV High Wycombe *Ox* 80-89; R Weston Favell *Pet* 89-06; Chapl St Jo Hosp Weston Favell 89-06; rtd 06. *35 Greenhill, Wootton Bassett, Swindon SN4 8EH*
E-mail c.w.wake@talk21.com

WAKEFIELD, Allan. b 31. Qu Coll Birm 72. d 74 p 75. C Kingsthorpe w Northampton St Dav *Pet* 74-77; TV Clifton *S'well* 77-81; V Bilborough St Jo 81-85; R Bere Ferrers *Ex* 85-91; R Mevagissey and St Ewe *Truro* 91-96; rtd 96; Perm to Offic *Truro* 96-98; Hon C Malborough w S Huish, W Alvington and Churchstow *Ex* 98-02; Perm to Offic from 01. *4 Eden Cottages, Exeter Road, Ivybridge PL21 0BL* Tel (01752) 698724

WAKEFIELD, Andrew Desmond. b 55. K Coll Lon BD77 AKC77. Coll of Resurr Mirfield 77. d 78 p 79. C Mitcham Ascension *S'wark* 78-81; C Putney St Mary 81-86; TV Wimbledon 86-91; Ind Chapl from 90; Dioc Urban Missr 91-97; P-in-c S Wimbledon St Andr 91-97; V from 97. *105 Hartfield Road, London SW19 3TJ* Tel (020) 8542 6566
E-mail andrew.d.wakefield@btopenworld.com

WAKEFIELD, Anne Frances. b 58. St Aid Coll Dur BSc79 Sheff Univ PGCE80. NTMTC 94. d 97 p 98. NSM Danbury *Chelmsf* 97-98; NSM Sherburn w Pittington *Dur* 98-01; Asst Chapl HM Pris Dur 01-03; Chapl HM YOI Northallerton 03-05; Chapl HM Pris Low Newton 05-08; P-in-c Stamford Bridge Gp *York* from 09. *The Rectory, 8 Viking Road, Stamford Bridge, York YO41 1BR* Tel (01759) 371264
E-mail fran.wakefield@btopenworld.com

WAKEFIELD, David Geoffrey. b 43. AMIC90. S'wark Ord Course 84. d 87 p 88. C Addiscombe St Mildred *S'wark* 87-89; C Reigate St Luke S Park 89-93; Chapl HM Pris Bullingdon 93-96; Chapl HM Pris Ranby 96-99; P-in-c Flintham *S'well* 99-08; P-in-c Car Colston w Screveton 99-08; Chapl HM Pris Whatton 99-03; rtd 08; Perm to Offic *York* from 08. *5 Manor Gardens, Hunmanby, Filey YO14 0PT* Tel (01723) 891212 Mobile 07754-219741 E-mail d.g.wakefield@btopenworld.com

WAKEFIELD, David Kenneth. b 64. Ridley Hall Cam 02. d 04 p 05. C Bures w Assington and Lt Cornard *St E* 04-07; P-in-c Burlingham St Edmund w Lingwood, Strumpshaw etc *Nor* 07-09; R from 09. *The Rectory, Barn Close, Lingwood, Norwich NR13 4TS* Tel (01603) 713880
E-mail rev.wake@btinternet.com

WAKEFIELD, Frances. *See* WAKEFIELD, Anne Frances

WAKEFIELD, Gavin Tracy. b 57. Van Mildert Coll Dur BSc78 Sheff Univ CertEd80 Kent Univ PhD98. St Jo Coll Nottm 83. d 86 p 87. C Anston *Sheff* 86-89; C Aston cum Aughton and Ulley 89-91; TV Billericay and Lt Burstead *Chelmsf* 91-98; Dir Miss & Past Studies Cranmer Hall Dur 98-08; Dir Tr, Miss and Min *York* from 09. *The Rectory, 8 Viking Road, Stamford Bridge, York YO41 1BR* Tel (01759) 371264 *or* (01904) 699504
E-mail gavin.wakefield@yorkdiocese.org

WAKEFIELD, Kenneth. b 54. St Jo Coll Dur BA95. d 95 p 96. C E and W Leake, Stanford-on-Soar, Rempstone etc *S'well* 95-98; TV Launceston *Truro* 98-03; P-in-c Boyton, N Tamerton, Werrington etc 03-08; R from 08. *The Rectory, Werrington, Launceston PL15 8TP* Tel (01566) 773932

WAKEFIELD, Mark Jeremy. b 55. York Univ BA77. NTMTC BA07. d 07 p 08. NSM Primrose Hill St Mary w Avenue Road St Paul *Lon* from 07. *15 Evangelist Road, London NW5 1UA* Tel (020) 7267 8202 Mobile 07899-668493
E-mail mark.wakefield@blueyonder.co.uk

WAKEFIELD, Peter. b 48. St Jo Coll Nottm BTh72 ALCD72. d 72 p 73. C Hinckley H Trin *Leic* 72-75; C Kirby Muxloe 75-78; V Barlestone 78-85; TV Padgate *Liv* 85-88; V Quinton w Marston Sicca *Glouc* 91-97; rtd 97. *295 Leach Green Lane, Rednal, Birmingham B45 8EB* Tel 0121-453 6979
E-mail pete.wakefield@orange.fr

WAKEFIELD, Bishop of. *See* PLATTEN, The Rt Revd Stephen George

WAKEFIELD, Dean of. *See* GREENER, The Very Revd Jonathan Desmond Francis

WAKEHAM, Miss Ellen Liesel. b 82. York Univ BA04 CCC Cam BA08. Westcott Ho Cam 06 Yale Div Sch 08. d 09 p 10. C Frodingham *Linc* from 09. *102 Bushfield Road, Scunthorpe DN16 1NA* Tel (01724) 271737 E-mail ellenwakeham@aol.com

WAKEHAM, Geoffrey. d 96 p 97. P-in-c Torrevieja *Eur* 96-00; Asst Chapl 00-01; rtd 01. *6 Juniper Court, Roundswell, Barnstaple EX31 3RL* Tel (01271) 325170

WAKEHAM-DAWSON, Andrew Whistler. b 65. Wye Coll Lon BSc87 Open Univ PhD94. STETS 98. d 01 p 02. NSM Paddington St Sav *Lon* 01-04; Chapl RAF from 04. *Chaplaincy Services, Valiant Block, HQ Air Command, RAF High Wycombe HP14 4UE* Tel (01494) 496800 Fax 496343

WAKELIN, Brian Roy. b 53. Westf Coll Lon BSc74. STETS 96. d 99 p 00. NSM Win Ch Ch from 99. *11 Elm Court, Elm Road, Winchester SO22 5BA* Tel (01962) 868579

WAKELING, Bruce. b 50. Lon Univ BA74. Westcott Ho Cam 74. d 77 p 78. C Weymouth H Trin *Sarum* 77-82; TV Oakdale 82-89; R Clopton w Otley, Swilland and Ashbocking *St E* 89-98; V Rushmere from 98. *The Vicarage, 253 Colchester Road, Rushmere, Ipswich IP4 4SH* Tel (01473) 270976

WAKELING, Miss Faith Georgina. b 65. Anglia Ruskin Univ BA10. Westcott Ho Cam 08. d 10 p 11. C Loughton St Jo *Chelmsf* from 10. *2 Doubleday Road, Loughton IG10 2AT* Tel 07837-968967 (mobile) E-mail faith@loughtonchurch.org.uk

WAKELING, Hugh Michael. b 42. Cape Town Univ BSc63 CEng82 FIChemE94. Wycliffe Hall Ox 71. d 74 p 75. C Kennington St Mark *S'wark* 74-78; C Surbiton Hill Ch Ch 78-80; NSM Richmond H Trin and Ch Ch 80-84; NSM California *Ox* 85-89 and 00-07; NSM Arborfield w Barkham 89-00; Lic to Offic from 07. *61 Roycroft Lane, Finchampstead, Wokingham RG40 4HN* Tel 0118-973 4078

WAKELING, Mrs Joan. b 44. Hockerill Coll Cam CertEd65. S'wark Ord Course 76. dss 79 d 90 p 94. Surbiton Hill Ch Ch *S'wark* 79-80; Richmond H Trin and Ch Ch 80-84; California *Ox* 84-89; Arborfield w Barkham 89-00; NSM 90-00; Chapl Luckley-Oakfield Sch Wokingham 90-05; NSM Finchampstead *Ox* 00-05; P-in-c Raglan w Llandenny and Bryngwyn *Mon* from 05. *The Vicarage, Primrose Green, Raglan, Usk NP15 2DU* Tel (01291) 690330

WAKELING, Rayner Alan. b 58. Portsm Poly BSc79 Bris Univ PGCE80. St Steph Ho Ox. d 01 p 02. C Willesden Green St Andr and St Fran *Lon* 01-05; V Greenhill St Jo 05-11; V Pentonville St Silas w All SS and St James from 11. *St Silas House, 45 Cloudesley Road, London N1 0EL* Tel (020) 7278 1101
E-mail raynerwakeling@hotmail.com

WAKELY, Marcus. b 40. Solicitor 62 FRSA88. EMMTC 84. d 87 p 88. NSM Carrington *S'well* 87-91; C Worksop Priory 91-95; V Sheff St Matt 95-01; rtd 01. *16 Park House Gates, Nottingham NG3 5LX* Tel 0115-960 9038

WAKELY, Roger. b 42. St Paul's Coll Chelt CertEd. S'wark Ord Course 67. d 70 p 71. C Ealing St Mary *Lon* 70-76; Chapl Bp Wand Sch Sunbury-on-Thames 76-82; R Gaulby *Leic* 82-87; V Galleywood Common *Chelmsf* 87-95; Warden of Ords 89-95; rtd 95; Perm to Offic *Chelmsf* 95-99 and *Ex* 99-09. *Linford, Broadway, Sidmouth EX10 8XH*

WAKELY, Simon Nicolas. b 66. K Alfred's Coll Win BA88. St Jo Coll Nottm 89. d 92 p 93. C Wymondham *Nor* 92-95; P-in-c Babbacombe *Ex* 95-08; rtd 08. *29 Studley Road, Torquay TQ1 3JN* Tel (01803) 431016 Mobile 07801-536181
E-mail finbar@tesco.net

WAKEMAN, Canon Hilary Margaret. b 38. EAMTC. dss 85 d 87 p 94. Heigham St Thos *Nor* 85-90; C 87-90; C Nor St Mary Magd w St Jas 90-91; Dn-in-c Norwich-over-the-Water Colegate St Geo 90-91; TD Norwich Over-the-Water 91-94; TV 94-96; Hon Can Nor Cathl 94-96; I Kilmoe Union *C, C & R* 96-01; Dir of Ords 99-01; rtd 01. *Skeagh, Schull, Co Cork, Republic of Ireland* Tel (00353) (28) 28263
E-mail hilary.wakeman@gmail.com

WAKERELL, Richard Hinton. b 55. Qu Coll Birm 81. d 84 p 85. C Gillingham St Mary *Roch* 84-87; C Kingswinford St Mary *Lich* 87-93; V Rickerscote 93. *70 Truro Drive, Plymouth PL5 4PB*

WALDEN, Alan Howard. b 66. Bris Univ BSc86 Lon Business Sch MBA93. Trin Coll Bris BA09. d 09 p 10. C Frimley *Guildf* from 09. *4 Warren Rise, Frimley, Camberley GU16 8SH* Tel 07957-773043 (mobile) E-mail alan.walden@ukgateway.net

✠WALDEN, The Rt Revd Graham Howard. b 31. Univ of Qld BA52 MA54 Ch Ch Ox BLitt60 MLitt80. St Fran Coll Brisbane ThL54. d 54 p 55 c 81. C W Hackney St Barn *Lon* 54-56; C Poplar St Sav w St Gabr and St Steph 57-58; Perm to Offic *Ox* 55-59; Australia from 59; Adn Ballarat 70-89; Bp in Hamilton 81-84; Asst Bp Ballarat 84-89; Bp The Murray 89-01; rtd 01. *13 O'Connor Place, Dubbo NSW 2380, Australia* Tel (0061) (2) 6884 0883

WALDEN, Mrs Jane. b 55. Cartrefle Coll of Educn CertEd76 Chelt & Glouc Coll of HE BA01. WEMTC 02. d 05 p 06. NSM Minchinhampton *Glouc* 05-09; NSM Minchinhampton w Box and Amberley from 09. *Rose Acre, London Road, Brimscombe, Stroud GL5 2TL* Tel (01453) 882314
E-mail jane@minchchurch.org.uk
or jane_walden@hotmail.com

WALDEN, John Edward Frank. b 38. FInstSMM. Oak Hill Th Coll 67. d 69 p 70. C Rainham *Chelmsf* 69-73; P-in-c Elm H Cross Inns Court 73-78; Conf and Publicity Sec SAMS 78-81; Hon C Southborough St Pet w Ch Ch and St Matt *Roch* 78-81; Exec Sec Spanish and Portuguese Ch Aid Soc 80-81; Hon C

Tonbridge St Steph 81-84; R Earsham w Alburgh and Denton *Nor* 84-89; Perm to Offic from 01; rtd 03. *11 Hemmings Close, Norwich NR5 9EH* Tel (01603) 746062
E-mail reverendjohn@fsmail.net
WALDSAX, Mrs Heather. b 58. Bris Univ BA79 PGCE80. STETS 06. **d** 08 **p** 09. NSM Canford Magna *Sarum* from 08. *60 Floral Farm, Canford Magna, Wimborne BH21 3AU* Tel (01202) 889269 E-mail heather@waldsax.net
WALES, David Neville. b 55. Rhodes Univ BA78 Open Univ BSc01. Coll of Resurr Mirfield 80. **d** 82 **p** 83. Zimbabwe 82-88; C Linslade *Ox* 89-91; P-in-c Weston Turville 91-07; R from 07; Voc Adv from 99. *The Rectory, Church Walk, Weston Turville, Aylesbury HP22 5SH* Tel (01296) 613212
E-mail davidnwales@tiscali.co.uk
WALES, Stephen Francis. b 70. Leic Univ BSc93 Leeds Univ BA07. Coll of Resurr Mirfield 05. **d** 07 **p** 08. C Carrington *S'well* 07-10; TV Retford Area from 10. *The Rectory, Rectory Road, Retford DN22 7AY* Tel (01777) 719816
E-mail walesstephen@aol.com
WALES, Archbishop of. *See* MORGAN, The Most Revd Barry Cennydd
WALFORD, Mrs Angela. b 44. Whitelands Coll Lon CertEd76. S Dios Minl Tr Scheme 85. **d** 92 **p** 94. NSM Boyatt Wood *Win* 92-99; Asst Chapl Epsom and St Helier Univ Hosps NHS Trust 99-07; Perm to Offic *S'wark* from 07. *58 Wolseley Road, Mitcham Junction, Mitcham CR4 4JQ* Tel (020) 8646 2841
WALFORD, David. b 46. S'wark Ord Course 75. **d** 78 **p** 79. NSM Hackbridge and N Beddington *S'wark* 78-83; C Fawley *Win* 83-87; C-in-c Boyatt Wood CD 87-90; V Boyatt Wood 90-97; rtd 97; Perm to Offic *S'wark* 98-02; Assoc P S Beddington and Roundshaw 00-07; Hon Chapl Epsom and St Helier NHS Trust 00-03; Asst Chapl Epsom and St Helier Univ Hosps NHS Trust 03-10; Perm to Offic *S'wark* from 10. *58 Wolseley Road, Mitcham Junction, Mitcham CR4 4JQ* Tel (020) 8646 2841
E-mail wols@tinyworld.co.uk
WALFORD, David John. b 47. St Luke's Coll Ex CertEd68 AKC71. St Aug Coll Cant 71. **d** 72 **p** 73. C Oxton *Ches* 72-77; C Neston 77-80; V Backford and Youth Chapl 80-81; C Woodchurch 81; Chapl Fulbourn Hosp 82; Chapl N Man Gen Hosp 82-85; Distr Chapl in Mental Health Ex HA 85-87; Chapl Manager R Devon and Ex Hosp (Wonford) 87-94; Chapl Manager R Devon and Ex NHS Foundn Trust 94-07; rtd 07; Chapl Ex Hospiscare from 08. *Barnhayes Farm, Whimple, Exeter EX5 2UD* Tel (01404) 822863
WALFORD, David Sanderson. b 23. BEM49. Chich Th Coll 78. **d** 79 **p** 80. Hon C Chich St Pet 79-81; C Chich St Paul and St Pet 81-83; P-in-c Wisbech St Aug *Ely* 83-86; rtd 88. *Sibford, Church Hill, Marnhull, Sturminster Newton DT10 1PU* Tel (01258) 820201
WALFORD, Frank Roy. b 35. Birm Univ MB, ChB58. Qu Coll Birm 78. **d** 80 **p** 81. Hon C Walsall Pleck and Bescot *Lich* 80-85; Chr Healing Cen Bordon 85-88; Dep Medical Dir St Wilfrid's Hospice Chich from 88; Perm to Offic *Chich* from 88. *15 Grove Road, Chichester PO19 8AR* Tel (01243) 533947
E-mail ronowal@aol.com
WALFORD, Mrs Marion Gladys. b 54. NTMTC BA08. **d** 08 **p** 09. C Canvey Is *Chelmsf* from 08. *37 Ruskoi Road, Canvey Island SS8 9QN* Tel (01268) 698991
E-mail revmarion@google.com
WALFORD, Robin Peter. b 46. Qu Coll Birm 75. **d** 78 **p** 79. C Radcliffe-on-Trent *S'well* 78-81; TV Newark w Hawton, Cotham and Shelton 81-84; P-in-c Forest Town 84-92; Co-ord Chapl Leeds Community and Mental Health Services 92-97; Perm to Offic *Ripon* from 97. *15 Oaklands Drive, Adel, Leeds LS16 8NZ* Tel 0113-281 7251 E-mail robin.walford@btinternet.com
WALKER, Alan Robert Glaister. b 52. K Coll Cam BA76 MA79 New Coll Ox MA84 Poly Cen Lon LLB91 Heythrop Coll Lon MTh93 Univ of Wales LLM96. St Steph Ho Ox 82. **d** 84 **p** 85. C St John's Wood *Lon* 84-86; Chapl Poly Cen Lon 87-92; Chapl Univ of Westmr 92-94; Chapl Univ Ch Ch the K 87-94; V Hampstead Garden Suburb from 94. *The Vicarage, 1 Central Square, London NW11 7AH* Tel and fax (020) 8455 7206 Mobile 07956-491037 E-mail fatherwalker@aol.com
WALKER, Canon Allen Ross. b 46. Portsm Univ BA94 MA98. Chich Th Coll 86. **d** 88. C Cosham *Portsm* 88-91; Chapl Portsm Mental Health Community 91-97; Dn Portsm Deanery 91-97; Community Chapl Burnham and Slough Deanery *Ox* from 97; AD Burnham and Slough from 05; Hon Can Ch Ch from 06. *The Vicarage, Mill Street, Colnbrook, Slough SL3 0JJ* Tel and fax (01753) 684181 E-mail mrarwalker@aol.com
WALKER, Mrs Amanda Frances. b 62. Cen Sch Speech & Drama BSc85 Univ Coll Lon MSc94 Qu Coll Birm BA09. WMMTC 06. **d** 09 **p** 10. C Stafford *Lich* from 09. *The Vicarage, Victoria Terrace, Stafford ST16 3HA* Tel (01785) 220585 Mobile 07811-326204 E-mail revdmandywalker@btinternet.com
WALKER, Andrew David. b 84. Trin Coll Bris BA10. **d** 11. C S Dales *Derby* from 11. *The Vicarage, Cubley, Ashbourne DE6 2EY* Tel (01335) 330724 Mobile 07763-179203
E-mail adwalker2@googlemail.com

WALKER, Andrew Stephen. b 58. St Chad's Coll Dur BA80 Heythrop Coll Lon MA99. St Steph Ho Ox 83. **d** 85 **p** 86. C Fareham SS Pet and Paul *Portsm* 85-87; C St John's Wood *Lon* 87-93; V Streatham St Pet *S'wark* 93-98; Perm to Offic *Bris* 98-00 and *S'wark* 98-09; R St Edm the King and St Mary Woolnoth etc *Lon* 00-10; P-in-c Lewes St Mich and St Thos at Cliffe w All SS *Chich* from 09. *St Michael's Rectory, St Andrew's Lane, Lewes BN7 1UW* Tel (01273) 474723 Mobile 07931-745853
E-mail andrew.walker@operamail.com
WALKER, Ms Angela Jean. b 55. St Jo Coll Nottm 03. **d** 05 **p** 06. C Kempshott *Win* 05-09; P-in-c Cobham w Luddesdowne and Dode *Roch* from 10. *The Vicarage, Battle Street, Cobham, Gravesend DA12 3DB* Tel (01474) 814332
E-mail ahiangel@aol.com
WALKER, Canon Anthony Charles St John. b 55. Trin Coll Ox MA80. Wycliffe Hall Ox 78. **d** 81 **p** 82. C Bradf Cathl 81-84; C Nottingham St Ann w Em *S'well* 84-88; V Retford St Sav 88-01; TR Retford 02-11; TR Retford Area from 11; AD Retford 00-09; Hon Can S'well Minster 04-11. *St Saviour's Vicarage, 31 Richmond Road, Retford DN22 6SJ* Tel and fax (01777) 703800 E-mail tony@tonywalker.f9.co.uk
WALKER, Arthur Daniel. b 60. Nene Coll Northn BA86 St Martin's Coll Lanc PGCE90 Leeds Univ BA10. Yorks Min Course 07. **d** 10 **p** 11. C Northallerton w Kirby Sigston *York* from 10. *26 Helmsley Way, Northallerton DL7 8SX* Tel (01609) 781029 E-mail arthur.walkerwalker@btinternet.com
WALKER, Canon Arthur Keith. b 33. Dur Univ BSc57 Fitzw Ho Cam BA60 MA64 Leeds Univ PhD68 FRSA94. Lich Th Coll 62. **d** 63 **p** 64. C Slaithwaite w E Scammonden *Wakef* 63-66; V N Wootton *B & W* 66-71; Lect Wells Th Coll 66-71; Can Res and Prec Chich Cathl 71-80; TV Basingstoke *Win* 81-87; Can Res Win Cathl 87-03; rtd 03. *29 Sussex Street, Winchester SO23 8TG* Tel (01962) 864751 E-mail akwalker@prettel.nl
WALKER, Brian Cecil. b 28. FCA62. Cranmer Hall Dur 68. **d** 70 **p** 71. C Heworth w Peasholme St Cuth *York* 70-73; C Attenborough w Chilwell *S'well* 73-75; C Chilwell 75-78; R Trowell 78-89; rtd 89; Perm to Offic *Worc* 89-05 and *Birm* 98-05. *1 Chaucer Road, Bromsgrove B60 2EE* Tel (01527) 579382
WALKER, Cameron. *See* WALKER, Canon John Cameron
WALKER, Mrs Caroline. b 58. **d** 10 **p** 11. NSM Desborough, Brampton Ash, Dingley and Braybrooke *Pet* from 10; Chapl Kettering Gen Hosp NHS Trust from 10. *Nursery Cottage, Butchers Lane, Pytchley, Kettering NN14 1EJ* Tel (01536) 790671 E-mail info@homefarmofpytchley.co.uk
WALKER, Christina. b 08. **d** 08 **p** 09. NSM Birkenshaw w Hunsworth *Wakef* from 08. *Upper Chatts Farm, Cliff Hollins Lane, East Bierley, Bradford BD4 6RH* Tel (01274) 670551
E-mail tinalet@hotmail.com
WALKER, Christopher James Anthony. b 43. Sarum & Wells Th Coll 85. **d** 87 **p** 88. Hon C Durrington *Sarum* 87-89; CF 87-98. *Horseshoe Meadow Farm, Cholderton, Salisbury SP4 0ED* Tel (01980) 629234 E-mail horseshoewalkers@supanet.com
WALKER, Christopher John. b 52. ALA74. Chich Th Coll 75. **d** 78 **p** 79. C Reading All SS *Ox* 78-82; C Stony Stratford 82-84; C Wokingham All SS 84-90; V Headington St Mary 90-98; R S w N Moreton, Aston Tirrold and Aston Upthorpe 98-05; C Abingdon 05-07; rtd 07. *25 Coralberry Drive, Weston-super-Mare BS22 6SQ* E-mail rwalker1202@aol.com
WALKER, Christopher John Deville. b 42. St Jo Coll Dur BA69. Westcott Ho Cam 69. **d** 71 **p** 72. C Portsea St Mary *Portsm* 71-75; C Saffron Walden w Wendens Ambo and Littlebury *Chelmsf* 75-77; C St Martin-in-the-Fields *Lon* 77-80; V Riverhead w Dunton Green *Roch* 80-89; V Chatham St Steph 89-97; R Chislehurst St Nic 97-05; rtd 05; Perm to Offic *Heref* from 05 and *Lich* 06-07; Hon C Shrewsbury St Chad, St Mary and St Alkmund *Lich* from 07. *2 Springbank, Shrewsbury Road, Church Stretton SY6 6HA* Tel (01694) 723444
E-mail chris@riberac.force9.co.uk
WALKER, Daniel. *See* WALKER, Arthur Daniel
WALKER, Canon David. b 48. Linc Th Coll 71. **d** 74 **p** 75. C Arnold *S'well* 74-77; C Crosby *Linc* 77-79; V Scrooby *S'well* 79-86; V Sutton in Ashfield St Mary 86-94; P-in-c Sutton in Ashfield St Mich 89-94; TR Birkenhead Priory *Ches* 94-05; RD Birkenhead 99-05; R Bromborough from 05; Hon Can Ches Cathl from 03. *The Rectory, Mark Rake, Wirral CH62 2DH* Tel 0151-201 5026 E-mail dave.walker48@ntlworld.com
WALKER, Canon David Andrew. b 52. St Andr Univ MTheol75 MA Hull Univ MPhil00. Linc Th Coll 79. **d** 81 **p** 82. C Hessle *York* 81-84; C N Hull St Mich 84-86; V from 86; AD Cen and N Hull 99-10; RD Hull 00-10; Can and Preb York Minster from 01. *St Michael's Vicarage, 214 Orchard Park Road, Hull HU6 9BX* Tel (01482) 803375 E-mail david@stmichaelsnorthhull.org.uk
WALKER, David Andrew. b 76. Van Mildert Coll Dur BSc97. Oak Hill Th Coll MTh07. **d** 07 **p** 08. C Cheadle All Hallows *Ches* 07-11; V Finchley Ch Ch *Lon* from 11. *Christ Church Vicarage, 616 High Road, London N12 0AA* Tel (020) 8445 2532 Mobile 07980-360408 E-mail davasharwhava@yahoo.co.uk
WALKER, David Gilmour. b 73. Plymouth Univ BA96. Wycliffe Hall Ox 07. **d** 09 **p** 10. C Brompton H Trin w Onslow Square

St Paul *Lon* 09-11; C Onslow Square and S Kensington St Aug from 11. *69 Revelstoke Road, London SW18 5NL* Tel 07807-876525 (mobile) E-mail davidgwalker@hotmail.co.uk

WALKER, Canon David Grant. b 23. Bris Univ BA49 Ball Coll Ox DPhil54 FSA60 FRHistS62. **d** 62 **p** 62. NSM Swansea St Mary w H Trin *S & B* 62-86; Chapl and Lect Univ of Wales (Swansea) 62; Sen Lect 63-82; Dir Post-Ord Tr 65-93; Can Brecon Cathl from 72; Prec 79-90; Chan 90-93; Chapl Univ of Wales (Swansea) 75-76; Dir of In-Service Tr from 77; P-in-c Caereithin 86-87. *52 Eaton Crescent, Swansea SA1 4QN* Tel (01792) 472624

WALKER, David Ian. b 41. Bernard Gilpin Soc Dur 64 Bps' Coll Cheshunt 65. **d** 68 **p** 69. C Todmorden *Wakef* 68-72; V Rastrick St Jo 72-77; V Crosland Moor 77-86; R Kirton in Lindsey w Manton *Linc* 86-99; R Grayingham 86-99; V Clee 99-06; OCF 88-06; rtd 07; Perm to Offic *Linc* from 07. *48 Pretymen Crescent, New Waltham, Grimsby DN36 4PB* Tel (01472) 826958 E-mail davidian8@btinternet.com

WALKER, David John. b 47. St Jo Coll Nottm 88. **d** 90 **p** 91. C Strood St Fran *Roch* 90-94; V Larkfield from 94. *The Vicarage, 206 New Hythe Lane, Larkfield, Maidstone ME20 6PT* Tel and fax (01732) 843349 E-mail david.walker@diocese-rochester.org

WALKER, David Meuryn. b 44. Bris Univ BSc66 Nottm Univ PGCE67. NOC 97. **d** 00 **p** 01. NSM Wakef St Jo 00-02; NSM Horbury Junction from 02. *188 Stanley Road, Wakefield WF1 4AE* Tel (01924) 210797 Mobile 07775-583764 E-mail meuryn@blueyonder.co.uk

✠**WALKER, The Rt Revd David Stuart.** b 57. K Coll Cam MA81. Qu Coll Birm. **d** 83 **p** 84 **c** 00. C Handsworth *Sheff* 83-86; TV Maltby 86-91; Ind Chapl 86-91; V Bramley and Ravenfield 91-95; R Bramley and Ravenfield w Hooton Roberts etc 95-00; Hon Can Sheff Cathl 00; Suff Bp Dudley *Worc* from 00. *Bishop's House, Bishop's Walk, Cradley Heath B64 7RH* Tel 0121-550 3407 Fax 550 7340 E-mail bishop.david@cofe-worcester.org.uk

WALKER, Derek Fred. b 46. Trin Coll Bris 71. **d** 74 **p** 75. C St Paul's Cray St Barn *Roch* 74-78; C Rushden w Newton Bromswold *Pet* 78-80; R Kirkby Thore w Temple Sowerby and Newbiggin *Carl* 80-83; V Coppull *Blackb* 83-87; V New Ferry *Ches* 87-96; R Akeman *Ox* from 96. *The Rectory, Alchester Road, Chesterton, Bicester OX26 1UW* Tel and fax (01869) 369815 E-mail akemanbenefice@yahoo.com

WALKER, Duncan Andrew. b 59. **d** 90 **p** 91. C Gorseinon *S & B* 90-91; C Morriston 92-94; V Llanelli Ch Ch *St D* 94-98; V Swansea St Jas *S & B* 98-11; V Pyle w Kenfig *Llan* from 11. *The Vicarage, Pyle Road, Pyle, Bridgend CF33 6PG* Tel (01656) 740500

✠**WALKER, The Rt Revd Edward William Murray (Dominic).** b 48. AKC73 Heythrop Coll Lon MA97 Brighton Univ Hon DLitt98 Univ of Wales LLM05. **d** 72 **p** 72 **c** 97. CGA 67-83; C Wandsworth St Faith *S'wark* 72-73; Bp's Dom Chapl 73-76; R Newington St Mary 76-85; RD S'wark and Newington 80-85; OGS from 83; Superior 90-96; V Brighton St Pet w Chpl Royal and St Jo *Chich* 85-86; P-in-c Brighton St Nic 85-86; TR Brighton St Pet and St Nic w Chpl Royal 86-97; RD Brighton 85-97; Can and Preb Chich Cathl 85-97; Area Bp Reading *Ox* 97-03; Bp Mon from 03. *Bishopstow, Stow Hill, Newport NP20 4EA* Tel (01633) 263510 Fax 259946 E-mail bishop.monmouth@churchinwales.org.uk

WALKER, Mrs Elizabeth. b 42. CQSW85. NEOC 91. **d** 94 **p** 00. NSM Stockton St Chad *Dur* from 94. *29 Bramble Road, Stockton-on-Tees TS19 0NQ* Tel (01642) 615332

WALKER, Canon Elizabeth Margaret Rea. b 49. Ch Ch Coll Cant CertEd70. S'wark Ord Course 89. **d** 92 **p** 94. NSM Ash and Ridley *Roch* 92-97; Chapl St Geo Sch Gravesend 92-97; P-in-c Burham and Wouldham *Roch* 97-05; P-in-c Platt from 05; Assoc Dir of Ords from 97; Hon Can Roch Cathl from 09. *The Vicarage, Comp Lane, Platt, Sevenoaks TN15 8NR* Tel and fax (01732) 885482 Mobile 07931-356502 E-mail liz.walker@diocese-rochester.org

WALKER, Gavin Russell. b 43. FCA78. Coll of Resurr Mirfield 76. **d** 78 **p** 79. C Wakef St Jo 78-81; C Northallerton w Kirby Sigston *York* 81-83; V Whorlton w Carlton and Faceby 83-85; P-in-c Brotherton *Wakef* 85-89; Chapl Pontefract Gen Infirmary 85-89; V Earl's Heaton *Wakef* 89-97; TV Dewsbury 97-99; TV Egremont and Haile *Carl* 99-04; rtd 04. *4 South Parade, Seascale CA20 1PZ* Tel (019467) 29463 Mobile 07986-550886 E-mail staffa@lineone.net

WALKER, Geoffrey. See WALKER, Canon Philip Geoffrey

WALKER, Gerald Roger. b 41. K Coll Lon BD67 AKC67. **d** 68 **p** 69. C High Elswick St Phil *Newc* 68-70; C Goring-by-Sea *Chich* 70-75; R Selsey 75-81; V Hove St Andr Old Ch 81-91; V Copthorne 91-95; rtd 95; NSM Streat w Westmeston *Chich* 95-99; Perm to Offic *S'wark* from 00. *1 Glebe Cottages, Newdigate, Dorking RH5 5AA* Tel (01306) 631587

WALKER, Canon Harvey William. b 26. Edin Univ MA52. St Steph Ho Ox 58. **d** 60 **p** 61. C Newc St Matt w St Mary 60-64; V 64-93; Hon Can Newc Cathl 80-94; rtd 95; Perm to Offic *Newc* from 95. *21 Grosvenor Drive, Whitley Bay NE26 2JP* Tel 0191-252 1858

WALKER, Mrs Hazel. b 47. Coll of Ripon & York St Jo MA01. NOC 97. **d** 00 **p** 01. NSM Crofton *Wakef* from 01; Asst Chapl SW Yorks Mental Health NHS Trust 04-07. *30 Heron Drive, Sandal, Wakefield WF2 6SW* Tel (01924) 259687 *or* 327319 E-mail hazel.walker60@btinternet.com

WALKER, Hugh. See WALKER, John Hugh

WALKER, Ian Richard Stevenson. b 51. Univ of Wales (Lamp) BA73. Qu Coll Birm. **d** 76 **p** 77. C Stainton-in-Cleveland *York* 76-79; C Fulford 79-81; C Kidderminster St Mary *Worc* 81-82; TV Kidderminster St Mary and All SS, Trimpley etc 82-86; R Keyingham w Ottringham, Halsham and Sunk Is from 86-96; RD S Holderness 94-98; V Scartho *Linc* 98-08; P-in-c Epworth Gp from 08. *St Andrew's Rectory, Belton Road, Epworth, Doncaster DN9 1JL* Tel (01427) 873790

WALKER, Mrs Jane Louise. b 63. STETS 03. **d** 06 **p** 07. NSM Alton All SS *Win* 06-09; Chapl Phyllis Tuckwell Hospice Farnham from 10; NSM Rowledge and Frensham *Guildf* from 11. *101 Salisbury Close, Alton GU34 2TP* Tel (01420) 88730 E-mail walker101@btconnect.com

WALKER, Mrs Jillian Francesca. b 41. **d** 99 **p** 00. OLM Blackbourne *St E* from 99. *The Woolpack, Bury Road, Ixworth, Bury St Edmunds IP31 2HX* Tel (01359) 230776 E-mail digger.walker@tiscali.co.uk

WALKER (formerly TOMKINS), Jocelyn Rachel. b 64. Univ of Wales (Ban) BA85 Man Univ PGCE86. NOC 98. **d** 01 **p** 02. C Chadderton St Matt *Man* 01-04; Chapl Asst Salford R Hosps NHS Trust 04-07; P-in-c Maidstone St Martin *Cant* from 07. *St Martin's Vicarage, Northumberland Road, Maidstone ME15 7LP* Tel (01622) 676282 E-mail joss.walker@tiscali.co.uk

WALKER, Canon John. b 51. Aber Univ MA/4 Edin Univ BD78. Edin Th Coll 75. **d** 78 **p** 79. C Broughty Ferry *Bre* 78-81; P-in-c Dundee St Jo 81-85; Ind Chapl 83-88; R Dundee St Luke 85-95; R Alford *Ab* 95-02; R Inverurie from 95; R Auchindoir from 95; P-in-c Kemnay 95-02; Syn Clerk from 08; Can St Andr Cathl from 01. *The Rectory, St Mary's Place, Inverurie AB51 3NW* Tel (01467) 620470 E-mail jwcan@tiscali.co.uk

WALKER, John Anthony Patrick. b 58. Man Metrop Univ PGCE97. Trin Coll Bris BA86. **d** 86 **p** 87. C Canford Magna *Sarum* 86-90; TV Glyncorrwg w Afan Vale and Cymmer Afan *Llan* 90-96; Hd of RE Wentworth High Sch Eccles 97-99; Community Chapl and C Gorton St Phil *Man* 00-03; P-in-c Oldham St Paul 03-04; Perm to Offic *Man* 04-07 and *Cant* from 07. *St Martin's Vicarage, Northumberland Road, Maidstone ME15 7LP* Tel (01622) 676282 E-mail johnwalker-uk@btinternet.com

WALKER, Canon John Cameron. b 31. St Andr Univ MA52. Edin Th Coll 53. **d** 65 **p** 66. C Edin H Cross 65-67; C Perth St Jo *St And* 67-70; Chapl Angl Students Glas 70-74; Youth Chapl Warks Educn Cttee 75-77; Officer Gen Syn Bd of Educn 78-82; C W Hendon St Jo *Lon* 79-82; PV Westmr Abbey 82-84; Chapl Ghent w Ypres *Eur* 84-92; Chapl Ghent 92-98; Miss to Seamen 84-98; Can Brussels Cathl 93-98; rtd 98. *Balhaldie Cottage, 7 King Street, Doune FK16 6DN* Tel (01786) 842250 E-mail jcameronwalker@gmail.com

WALKER, John David. b 44. St Jo Coll Dur BA76. Cranmer Hall Dur 77. **d** 77 **p** 78. C Heworth H Trin *York* 77-81; P-in-c Allerthorpe and Barmby on the Moor w Fangfoss 81-83; TV Pocklington Team 84-89; P-in-c Hovingham 89; TV Street 89-92; R Dunnington 92-99; V Thorne *Sheff* 99-03; rtd 03; Perm to Offic *York* from 03. *9 Bishop Blunt Close, Hessle HU13 9NJ* E-mail john.d.walker@btinternet.com

WALKER, John Frank. b 53. Leeds Univ BEd76 Ripon Coll of Educn CertEd75. NW Ord Course 78. **d** 81 **p** 82. NSM Whitkirk *Ripon* 81-82; C 82-85; V Sutton Courtenay w Appleford *Ox* 85-90; Dioc Children's Adv *S'wark* 90-94; V Walworth St Jo from 94; Youth and Children's Officer Woolwich Episc Area 95-99. *St John's Vicarage, 18 Larcom Street, London SE17 1NQ* Tel (020) 7703 4375

WALKER, John Howard. b 47. Brasted Th Coll 67 Clifton Th Coll 69. **d** 72 **p** 73. C Upton (Overchurch) *Ches* 72-76; Asst Chapl Liv Univ 76-79; V Everton St Chrys 79-82; C Parr Mt 83-86; SAMS 86-94; Area Sec (NE and E Midl) SAMS 86-89; Paraguay 89-94; V Calverley *Bradf* from 95. *Calverley Vicarage, Town Gate, Calverley, Pudsey LS28 5NF* Tel 0113-257 7968 Mobile 07903-836806 E-mail john.walker@bradford.anglican.org

WALKER, John Hugh. b 34. K Coll Lon BD57 AKC57 K Coll Lon MTh75 MA85 Lon Inst of Educn PGCE68. St Boniface Warminster 57. **d** 58 **p** 59. C Southend St Alb *Chelmsf* 58-61; V Gt Ilford St Alb 61-67; Perm to Offic 67-68; Hon C Forest Gate St Edm 68-74; Perm to Offic *Cant* 75-82 and from 87; R Dymchurch w Burmarsh and Newchurch 82-87; rtd 94. *14 Danes Court, Dover CT16 2QE* Tel (01304) 202233

WALKER, Canon John Percival. b 45. CITC 68. **d** 71 **p** 72. C Belfast St Clem *D & D* 71-74; C Magheraculmoney *Clogh* 74-78; C Lisburn St Paul *Conn* 78-81; I Belfast St Ninian 81-88; I Belfast St Mary 88-89; I Belfast St Mary w H Redeemer from 89; Preb Conn Cathl from 98; Treas Conn Cathl from 04. *St Mary's*

Rectory, 558 Crumlin Road, Belfast BT14 7GL Tel and fax (028) 9058 4540 *or* tel 9074 8423
E-mail walkerjohnpercival@googlemail.com
WALKER, Judith Anne. *See* WALKER-HUTCHINSON, Mrs Judith Anne
WALKER, Keith. *See* WALKER, Canon Arthur Keith
WALKER, Keith. b 48. Linc Th Coll 82. **d** 84 **p** 85. C Whickham *Dur* 84-87; C Trimdon Station 87; P-in-c 87-89; V 89-90; R Penshaw 90-98; P-in-c Shiney Row 92-95; P-in-c Herrington 93-95; rtd 98; Hon C Jersey St Brelade *Win* 01-03. *Hallgarth Heights, Kirk Merrington, Spennymoor DL16 7HY* Tel (01388) 827319
WALKER, Mrs Lesley Ann. b 53. Westmr Coll Ox MTh00. S Dios Minl Tr Scheme 85. **d** 88 **p** 94. Par Dn Oakdale *Sarum* 88-92; TD Bridgnorth, Tasley, Astley Abbotts, etc *Heref* 92-94; TV 94-03; Vice-Prin OLM Tr Scheme *Cant* 03-04; Perm to Offic 06-07; R Meneage *Truro* from 07; RD Kerrier from 10. *The Rectory, St Martin, Helston TR12 6BU* Tel (01326) 231971
WALKER, Mrs Linda Joan. b 47. **d** 04 **p** 05. OLM Blurton *Lich* 04-11; OLM Blurton and Dresden from 11. *6 Thackeray Drive, Blurton, Stoke-on-Trent ST3 2HE* Tel (01782) 324895
E-mail linda.walker910@ntlworld.com
WALKER, Marcus Dian Dennison. b 59. WEMTC 04. **d** 07 **p** 08. NSM Churchdown St Jo and Innsworth *Glouc* from 07. *16 Meadowleaze, Gloucester GL2 0PN* Tel (01452) 531621 Mobile 07732-966174
E-mail marcus-walker@blueyonder.co.uk
WALKER, Mrs Margaret Joy. b 44. Westhill Coll Birm TCert66 Newc Univ MA93. CA Tr Coll 80. **dss** 86 **d** 87 **p** 94. Scargill Ho 86-87; Hon Par Dn Monkwearmouth St Andr *Dur* 87; Hon Par Dn Chester le Street 87-93; Hon Chapl Wells Cathl 93-01; Perm to Offic *Cant* 02-05; NSM Stone Street Gp 05-11; AD W Bridge 09-11; Perm to Offic from 11. *1 Ensigne Cottages, Shalmsford Street, Chartham, Canterbury CT4 7RF* Tel (01227) 730805
E-mail margiwalker@uwclub.net
WALKER, Margaret (Mother Lucy Clare). b 37. Guildf Dioc Min Course 99. **d** 01 **p** 02. CSP from 88; Mother Superior from 06; NSM Aldershot St Mich *Guildf* 01-04; NSM Chertsey, Lyne and Longcross 04-07; Lic to Offic from 07. *27 Northcliffe Close, Worcester Park KT4 7DS*
WALKER, Mrs Marion Joyce. b 52. **d** 08 **p** 09. NSM Triangle, St Matt and All SS *St E* from 08. *43 Newbury Road, Ipswich IP4 5EY* Tel (01473) 423753
E-mail mjwalker7653@btinternet.com
WALKER, Mark Alexander (Marcus). b 81. Oriel Coll Ox MA02 MSt04. Ripon Coll Cuddesdon MA10. **d** 11. C Winchmore Hill St Paul *Lon* from 11. *St Paul's Lodge, 58 Church Hill, London N21 1JA* Tel (020) 8886 7288 E-mail curate@spwh.org
WALKER, Lt Col Mark George. b 68. Univ of New England BProfStud00 Canberra Univ MDefStud00 Chas Sturt Univ NSW BTheol07. **d** 06 **p** 07. C Albany St Jo Australia 06-08; Perm to Offic Perth 09; C Balga w Mirrabooka 09-11; NSM Frampton on Severn, Arlingham, Saul etc *Glouc* 11. *Ashleigh House, The Street, Frampton-on-Severn, Gloucester GL2 7ED* Tel 07580-756141 (mobile) E-mail markwalker68@me.com
WALKER, Preb Martin Frank. b 39. St Jo Coll Nottm 71. **d** 73 **p** 74. C Penn *Lich* 73-78; V Bentley 78-82; V Kinver 82-88; R Kinver and Enville 88-91; V Harlescott 91-02; R Broughton w Croxton and Cotes Heath w Standon 02-04; P-in-c 04-07; Preb Lich Cathl 00-09; rtd 04; Hon C Hadley and Wellington Ch Ch *Lich* from 08. *4 Berberis Road, Leegomery, Telford TF1 6XF*
E-mail martin.walker7@btinternet.com
WALKER, Martin John. b 52. Linc Coll Ox BA73 PGCE74 St Jo Coll Dur BA78. Cranmer Hall Dur. **d** 79 **p** 80. C Harlow New Town w Lt Parndon *Chelmsf* 79-81; C Dorchester *Ox* 81-83; Chapl Bath Coll of HE 83-89; TV Southampton (City Cen) *Win* 89-91; Adv in RE and Resources *Sarum* 91-92; Hon C Northolt St Mary *Lon* 92-00; Chapl Bancroft's Sch Woodford Green 92-99; Chapl St Helen's Sch Northwood 99-00; Chapl Wellingborough Sch from 00. *Marsh House, Wellingborough School, Irthlingborough Road, Wellingborough NN8 2BX* Tel (01933) 277271 E-mail revmjwalker@yahoo.com
WALKER, Meuryn. *See* WALKER, David Meuryn
WALKER, Michael John. b 39. St D Coll Lamp BA61. St Aid Birkenhead 61. **d** 63 **p** 64. C Clifton *York* 63-66; C Marfleet 66-69; V Salterhebble St Jude *Wakef* 69-83; V Llangollen w Trevor and Llantysilio *St As* 83-93; RD Llangollen 87-93; V Kerry and Llanmerewig and Dolfor 93-01; RD Cedewain 97-01; rtd 01; Perm to Offic from 01. *Sylfaen-y-Graig, 21 Garth Terrace, Porthmadog LL49 9BE* Tel (01766) 515192
WALKER, Canon Nigel Maynard. b 39. ALCD66. **d** 67 **p** 68. C Southsea St Jude *Portsm* 67-70; C Addington S Africa 70-73; R 73-76; C Abingdon w Shippon *Ox* 76-80; V Upton (Overchurch) *Ches* 80-94; Chapl Brussels and Chan Brussels Cathl 94-04; P-in-c Leuven 02-04; rtd 04; Perm to Offic *Cant* and *Eur* from 05; *Portsm* and *Win* from 10. *12 The Sands, Whitehill, Bordon GU35 9QW* Tel (01420) 477323
E-mail nigelmwalker@gmail.com

WALKER, Mrs Pamela Sarah. b 52. Somerville Coll Ox BA73 MA77 St Jo Coll Dur BA78. Cranmer Hall Dur 76. **dss** 79 **d** 87 **p** 94. Harlow New Town w Lt Parndon *Chelmsf* 79-81; Dorchester *Sarum* 82-83; Bath St Bart *B & W* 85-88; Hon Par Dn 87-88; Par Dn Warmley *Bris* 88-89; Par Dn Bitton 88-89; Par Dn Southampton (City Cen) *Win* 89-92; Par Dn Northolt St Mary *Lon* 92-94; R 94-04; R Corfe Mullen *Sarum* from 04. *The Rectory, 32 Wareham Road, Corfe Mullen, Wimborne BH21 3LE* Tel (01202) 692129 E-mail pswlkr@btinternet.com
WALKER, Paul Gary. b 59. Lon Univ BD. St Jo Coll Nottm 82. **d** 84 **p** 85. C Bowling St Steph *Bradf* 84-87; C Tong 87-90; P-in-c Oakenshaw cum Woodlands 90-97; V Wrose from 97; P-in-c Bolton St Jas w St Chrys from 10; RD Calverley 01-09. *St Cuthbert's Vicarage, 71 Wrose Road, Bradford BD2 1LN* Tel (01274) 611631 E-mail paul.walker@bradford.anglican.org
WALKER, Paul Laurence. b 63. St Chad's Coll Dur BA84. Chich Th Coll BTh90. **d** 88 **p** 89. C Shildon w Eldon *Dur* 88-91; C Barnard Castle w Whorlton 91-93; C Silksworth 93-96; C-in-c Moorside St Wilfrid CD 96-99; V Norton St Mary 99-04; Chapl Manager Tees and NE Yorks NHS Trust from 04. *St Luke's Hospital, Marton Road, Middlesbrough TS4 3AF* Tel (01642) 516068 E-mail paul.walker@tney.northy.nhs.uk
WALKER, Paulette Winifred. b 08 **p** 09. OLM Swinderby *Linc* from 09. *Shepherd's Pasture, 3 Chancery Close, Lincoln LN6 8SD* Tel (01522) 520225 E-mail pwalker03@talktalk.net
WALKER, Pauline Ann. b 51. Open Univ BA87. St As Minl Tr Course 88. **d** 93 **p** 97. NSM Bistre *St As* 93-99; C Bistre 99-04; V Llay from 04. *The Vicarage, First Avenue, Llay, Wrexham LL12 0TN* Tel (01978) 852262
E-mail pawalker200@btinternet.com
WALKER, Pauline Jean. b 49. St Hild Coll Dur BSc72 Homerton Coll Cam PGCE73 Nottm Univ MA96. All Nations Chr Coll 89 St Jo Coll Nottm 94. **d** 96 **p** 97. C Bitterne *Win* 96-01; CMS 01-09; rtd 09. *The Brambles, Packhorse Lane, Kings Norton, Birmingham B38 0DN* Tel (01564) 822396
WALKER, Mrs Pepita. **d** 07 **p** 08. OLM Kemble, Poole Keynes, Somerford Keynes, etc *Glouc* from 07. *Woodstock, Frampton Mansell, Stroud GL6 8JE* Tel (01285) 760211
E-mail pepitawalker1@hotmail.co.uk
WALKER, Percival. *See* WALKER, Canon John Percival
WALKER, Peter Anthony. b 57. Pemb Coll Cam BA79 MA83 St Jo Coll Dur BA86. Cranmer Hall Dur 84. **d** 87 **p** 88. C Chesham Bois *Ox* 87-90; Chapl Bradf Cathl 90-93; TV W Swindon and the Lydiards *Bris* 93-99; V Keresley and Coundon *Cov* 99-10; P-in-c Bidford-on-Avon from 10; P-in-c Exhall w Wixford from 10; P-in-c Salford Priors from 10; P-in-c Temple Grafton w Binton from 10. *The Vicarage, 5 Howard Close, Bidford-on-Avon, Alcester B50 4EL* Tel (01789) 772217
WALKER, Canon Peter Anthony Ashley. b 46. Chich Th Coll 67. **d** 70 **p** 71. C Stamford Hill St Thos *Lon* 70-74; C Bethnal Green St Matt 74-77; V Hackney Wick St Mary of Eton w St Aug 77-84; Warden Rydal Hall *Carl* 84-95; P-in-c Rydal 84-95; P-in-c Porthleven w Sithney *Truro* 95-01; RD Kerrier 96-01; Can Res Truro Cathl from 01; P-in-c Feock 01-10; Chapl Is of Scilly from 10. *The Chaplaincy, Church Road, St Mary's, Isles of Scilly TR21 0NA* Tel (01720) 423911
E-mail scillychaplain@btinternet.com
WALKER, Peter Jeffrey. b 46. Kelham Th Coll 65. **d** 70 **p** 71. C Middlesbrough All SS *York* 70-75 and 77-78; SSF 75-77; C-in-c Wrangbrook w N Elmsall CD *Wakef* 78-82; V Athersley 82-86; SSM 86-88; Perm to Offic *Dur* 88-95; V Hartlepool H Trin 89-95; Dep Chapl HM Pris Birm 95-96; Chapl HM Pris Moorland 96-01; Full Sutton 01-04; Co-ord Chapl HM Pris Ford 04-05 and from 06; P-in-c Ferrybridge and Brotherton *Wakef* 05-06; OGS from 01. *The Chaplains' Office, HM Prison Ford, Arundel BN18 0BX* Tel (01903) 663085 Fax 663001
WALKER, Peter Ronald. b 50. Southn Univ BA72 K Alfred's Coll Win PGCE73. WMMTC 02. **d** 05 **p** 06. NSM Hadley and Wellington Ch Ch *Lich* 05-10; Chapl Shrewsbury and Telford NHS Trust 09-10; TV Rhos-Cystennin *St As* from 10. *The Rectory, Glyn y Marl Road, Llandudno Junction LL31 9NS* Tel (01492) 583579 E-mail peter@walker1592.fsnet.co.uk
WALKER, Peter Sidney Caleb. b 50. St Mich Th Coll Crafers 76. **d** 80 **p** 81. C Devonport Australia 80-81; P-in-c Fingal Valley 81-84; R E Devonport and Spreyton 84-88; R Swallow *Linc* 88-94; R Selworthy, Timberscombe, Wootton Courtenay etc *B & W* 94-01; Chapl Costa del Sol W *Eur* 01-04; R Coxheath, E Farleigh, Hunton, Linton etc *Roch* from 05. *The Rectory, 144 Heath Road, Coxheath, Maidstone ME17 4PL* Tel and fax (01622) 747570 E-mail peterdiana@talktalk.net
WALKER, Canon Peter Stanley. b 56. SRN RMN Nottm Univ BCombStuds. Linc Th Coll 80. **d** 83 **p** 84. C Woodford St Barn *Chelmsf* 83-86; C Brentwood St Thos 86-88; V Colchester St Barn 88-94; P-in-c Colchester St Jas, All SS, St Nic and St Runwald 94-96; V Colchester St Jas and St Paul w All SS etc from 96; Hon Can Chelmsf Cathl from 09. *The Rectory, 76 East Hill, Colchester CO1 2QW* Tel (01206) 866802 Fax 999444
E-mail fatherpeter@walkerssc.freeserve.co.uk

WALKER, Peter William Leyland. b 61. CCC Cam BA82 MA86 PhD87 Ox Univ DPhil96. Wycliffe Hall Ox 87. **d** 89 **p** 90. C Tonbridge SS Pet and Paul *Roch* 89-93; Fell Tyndale Ho Cam 93-96; Tutor Wycliffe Hall Ox from 96; Hon C Abingdon *Ox* 97-06. *Wycliffe Hall, 54 Banbury Road, Oxford OX2 6PW* Tel (01865) 274214 E-mail peter.walker@wycliffe.ox.ac.uk

WALKER, Canon Philip Geoffrey. b 47. St Jo Coll Dur BA70 Oriel Coll Ox BA72 MA76 Newc Univ MA93 Bris Univ PhD01. Ripon Hall Ox 70. **d** 74 **p** 75. C Sheff St Geo 74-77; C Cambridge Gt St Mary w St Mich *Ely* 77-81; V Monkwearmouth St Andr *Dur* 81-87; R Chester le Street 87-93; RD Chester-le-Street 89-93; Dioc Missr *B & W* 93-01; Can Res Wells Cathl 94-01; Prin OLM Tr Scheme *Cant* 02-05; Prin Whitelands Coll Roehampton Inst from 05. *The Principal's Office, Whitelands College, Holybourne Avenue, London SW15 4JD* Tel (020) 8392 3511 Fax 8392 3531 E-mail drgeoffrey.walker@virgin.net

WALKER, Philip Kingsley. b 47. Ox Univ BA70. St Mich Coll Llan. **d** 90 **p** 91. C Maindee Newport *Mon* 90-92; C Llanmartin 92-94; V Bishton 94-98; R Panteg 98-03; R Panteg w Llanfihangel Pontymoile 03-07; rtd 07. *Glan Aber, Lon Isallt, Trearddur Bay, Holyhead LL65 2UP*

WALKER, Raymond. b 28. Carl Dioc Tr Inst 83. **d** 86 **p** 87. NSM Gt Salkeld w Lazonby *Carl* 86-91; C Greystoke, Matterdale, Mungrisdale etc 91-92; TV 92-95; rtd 95. *Brackenrigg, Town Head, Lazonby, Penrith CA10 1AT* Tel (01768) 898314

WALKER, Richard David. b 45. Hull Univ BSc68. S Dios Minl Tr Scheme 92. **d** 95 **p** 96. NSM Horfield St Greg *Bris* 95-98; NSM Lawrence Weston and Avonmouth 98-00; Chapl HM Pris Leic 00-01; Chapl HM Pris Usk and Prescoed 01-03; Hon C Cromhall, Tortworth, Tytherington, Falfield etc *Glouc* 04-07. *Address temp unknown* E-mail j.walker16@btinternet.com

WALKER, Richard John. b 67. Humberside Coll of Educn BSc88 Leeds Univ MSc(Eng)97 St Jo Coll Dur BA04. Cranmer Hall Dur 02. **d** 04 **p** 05. C Scarborough St Mary w Ch Ch and H Apostles *York* 04-08; V Elloughton and Brough w Brantingham from 08. *The Vicarage, Church Lane, Elloughton, Brough HU15 1SP* Tel (01482) 667431

WALKER, Richard Mainprize. b 43. Keele Univ BA DipEd. Wycliffe Hall Ox 84. **d** 86 **p** 87. C Guildf Ch Ch 86-90; V Bradley St Martin *Lich* 90-05; rtd 05. *10 Rockland Park, Largs KA30 8HB* E-mail richardandcelia@btinternet.com

WALKER, Richard Mark. b 63. York Univ BSc84. St Jo Coll Nottm MA00. **d** 00 **p** 01. C Ben Rhydding *Bradf* 00-04; P-in-c Yeadon St Jo 04-08; V Yeadon from 08. *St John's Vicarage, Barcroft Grove, Yeadon, Leeds LS19 7XZ* Tel 0113-250 2272 E-mail richard.walker@bradford.anglican.org

WALKER, Roger. *See* WALKER, Gerald Roger

WALKER, Mrs Ruth. b 51. MAAT95. **d** 03 **p** 04. OLM Camberley St Mary *Guildf* from 03. *73 Verran Road, Camberley GU15 2ND* Tel (01276) 503551 E-mail tandr.walker@ntlworld.com

WALKER (née APPLETON), Mrs Ruth Elizabeth. b 58. St Jo Coll Dur BA79 Hughes Hall Cam PGCE80. St Jo Coll Nottm 86. **d** 88 **p** 94. Par Dn Princes Risborough w Ilmer *Ox* 88-90; C and Congr Chapl Bradf Cathl 90-93; C The Lydiards *Bris* 93-94; NSM W Swindon and the Lydiards 94-96; C Swindon St Jo and St Andr 96-98; Perm to Offic 98-99; C Keresley and Coundon *Cov* 99-10; AD Cov N 04-10; C Bidford-on-Avon from 10; C Exhall w Wixford from 10; C Salford Priors from 10; C Temple Grafton w Binton from 10. *The Vicarage, 5 Howard Close, Bidford-on-Avon, Alcester B50 4EL* Tel (01789) 772217

WALKER, Sharon Anne. b 60. Derby Univ BA99. St Jo Coll Nottm. **d** 02 **p** 03. C Greetham and Thistleton w Stretton and Clipsham *Pet* 02-05; C Cottesmore and Barrow w Ashwell and Burley 02-05; P-in-c Pet St Mary Boongate 05-10; R Street w Walton *B & W* from 10. *The Rectory, Vestry Road, Street BA16 0HZ* E-mail sharonannewalker@hotmail.com

WALKER, Simon Glyn Nicholas. b 82. Trevelyan Coll Dur BA03. Wycliffe Hall Ox BTh11. **d** 11. C Hensingham *Carl* from 11. *11 Park Drive, Whitehaven CA28 7RT* Tel 07713-389980 (mobile) E-mail simongnwalker@hotmail.com

WALKER, Simon Patrick. b 71. Ch Ch Ox BA93. Wycliffe Hall Ox BTh94. **d** 97 **p** 98. C Abingdon *Ox* 97-01; Perm to Offic *Ches* 01-04 and *Ox* from 04. *3 Gladstone Road, Headington, Oxford OX3 8LL* Tel (01865) 766356 *or* 08701-417077 E-mail simon@humanecogroup.com

WALKER, Stanley Frederick. b 48. St Jo Coll Nottm. **d** 84 **p** 85. C Ellesmere Port *Ches* 84-89; V Seacombe 89-97; C Lache cum Saltney 97-03; TV Wrexham *St As* 03-09; C Rhyl w St Ann from 09. *122 Rhuddlan Road, Rhyl LL18 2JD* Tel (01745) 342949 Mobile 07802-960430 E-mail stanwalker@02.co.uk

WALKER, Stephen Michael Maynard. b 62. St Jo Coll Dur BA84. Trin Coll Bris 86. **d** 88 **p** 89. C Eastwood *S'well* 88-92; CF 92-02; C Marple All SS *Ches* 02-06; P-in-c Tewkesbury H Trin *Glouc* 06-10; V from 10. *Holy Trinity Vicarage, 49 Barton Street, Tewkesbury GL20 5PU* Tel (01684) 293233

WALKER, Stephen Patrick. b 62. York Univ BSc83 PGCE84. St Jo Coll Nottm 87. **d** 90 **p** 91. C Hull St Jo Newland *York*

90-94; Min Grove Green LEP *Cant* 94-98; Children's Min Adv 96-98; TV Drypool *York* 98-99; TR 99-04; TR Binsey *Carl* 04-11; RD Derwent 10-11; P-in-c Theydon Bois and Theydon Garnon *Chelmsf* from 11. *The Vicarage, 2 Piercing Hill, Theydon Bois, Epping CM16 7JN* Tel (01992) 814725 E-mail stephenwalker04@gmail.com

WALKER, Mrs Susan Joy. b 52. Univ of Wales (Lamp) BA73 Hull Univ MA91. Qu Coll Birm 75. **dss** 83 **d** 87 **p** 94. Kidderminster St Mary and All SS, Trimpley etc *Worc* 83-86; Keyingham w Ottringham, Halsham and Sunk Is *York* 86-87; Hon Par Dn 87-94; Hon C 94-98; Chapl Hull Coll of FE 89-98; Chapl N Lindsey Coll *Linc* from 98. *St Andrew's Rectory, Belton Road, Epworth, Doncaster DN9 1JL* Tel (01427) 873790 E-mail susanwalker@leggott.ac.uk

WALKER, The Ven Thomas Overington. b 33. Keble Coll Ox BA58 MA61. Oak Hill Th Coll 58. **d** 60 **p** 61. C Woking St Paul *Guildf* 60-62; C St Leonards St Leon *Chich* 62-64; Travelling Sec IVF 64-67; Succ Birm Cathl 67-70; V Harborne Heath 70-91; P-in-c Edgbaston St Germain 83-91; Hon Can Birm Cathl 80-91; RD Edgbaston 89-91; Adn Nottingham *S'well* 91-96; rtd 96; Perm to Offic *Heref* 97-08. *6 Cornbrook, Clee Hill, Ludlow SY8 3QQ* Tel (01584) 890176

WALKER, Trevor John. b 51. Southn Univ BTh80. Sarum & Wells Th Coll 75. **d** 78 **p** 79. C Standish *Blackb* 78-81; P-in-c N Somercotes *Linc* 81-82; P-in-c S Somercotes 81-82; V Somercotes 82-85; R Binbrook Gp from 85. *The Rectory, Louth Road, Binbrook, Lincoln LN8 6BJ* Tel (01472) 398227 Fax 399547 E-mail priest1@compuserve.com

WALKER, Valerie Anne. b 57. Leeds Poly BSc80 Leeds Univ MHSc92 TISEC 07. **d** 10. C Dunfermline *St And* from 10; C Alloa from 10. *Jacaranda, Forgandenny, Perth PH2 9EN* Tel (01738) 813509 Mobile 07720-327766 E-mail revalerian@gmail.com

WALKER, Canon Walter Stanley. b 21. AKC42. Cuddesdon Coll 42. **d** 44 **p** 45. C Southport All SS *Liv* 44-47; Miss to Seamen 47-48; C-in-c Kelsall CD *Ches* 48-53; V Birkenhead St Mary w St Paul 53-61; Chapl Barony Hosp Nantwich 61-66; R Wistaston 61-66; R Bromborough 66-77; R Wallasey St Hilary 77-86; RD Wallasey 77-86; Hon Can Ches Cathl 80-86; rtd 86; Perm to Offic *Ches* from 86. *2 Mill Croft, Neston CH64 3TN* Tel 0151-336 5009

WALKER-HILL, Richard John. b 51. WMMTC 06. **d** 09 **p** 10. C Oakengates and Wrockwardine Wood *Lich* from 09. *65 Trench Road, Trench, Telford TF2 6PF* Tel (01952) 608086 Mobile 07970-379448 E-mail richard@synnexuk.com

WALKER-HUTCHINSON, Mrs Judith Anne. b 58. St Jo Coll Dur BA07 CPFA88. Cranmer Hall Dur 05. **d** 07 **p** 08. C Penhill *Ripon* 07-10; R Haddington *Edin* 10-11. *Westrill, Cotherstone, Barnard Castle DL12 9PF* Tel (01833) 650396 Mobile 07977-507038 E-mail reverendjudith@blackberry.orange.co.uk

WALKEY, Malcolm Gregory Taylor. b 44. Lon Univ. Kelham Th Coll 63. **d** 68 **p** 69. C Oadby *Leic* 68-72; TV Corby SS Pet and Andr w Gt and Lt Oakley 72-79; R Ashton w Hartwell 79-86; TR Halesworth w Linstead, Chediston, Holton etc *St E* 86-91; P-in-c Laxfield 93-01; rtd 01; Perm to Offic *St E* from 02. *4 Church View, Holton, Halesworth IP19 8PB* Tel (01986) 872594

WALL, Colin. b 52. Hull Univ BEd74 Humberside Coll of Educn BA80. NEOC 02. **d** 05 **p** 06. NSM Hedon w Paull *York* 05-08; P-in-c Tuxford w Weston and Markham Clinton *S'well* from 08. *The Vicarage, 30 Lincoln Road, Tuxford, Newark NG22 0HP* Tel (01777) 872917

WALL, Canon David Oliver. b 39. TD JP. Bps' Coll Cheshunt 62. **d** 65 **p** 66. C Lt Ilford St Mich *Chelmsf* 65-68; CF 68-73; R Sudbourne w Orford *St E* 73-76; R Orford w Sudbourne and Chillesford w Butley 76-79; P-in-c Iken 76-79; R Drinkstone 79-82; R Rattlesden 79-82; R Chedburgh w Depden, Rede and Hawkedon 82-99; Sen Chapl ACF from 88; Chapl to Suffolk Fire Service *St E* 91-03; Hon Can *St E* Cathl 96-00; rtd 00; Perm to Offic *Ely* from 01. *Orford House, 43 Corsbie Close, Bury St Edmunds IP33 3ST* Tel (01284) 723232

WALL, Miss Elizabeth Anne. b 51. Birm Univ BDS73. WMMTC 97. **d** 00 **p** 01. NSM Lich St Chad from 00. *Gaia Cottage, 15 Gaia Lane, Lichfield WS13 7LW* Tel (01543) 254891 Mobile 07711-557770 E-mail elizabeth@gaiacottage.wanadoo.co.uk

WALL, John Caswallen. b 60. York Univ BA83 MA85. St Steph Ho Ox BA89. **d** 89 **p** 90. C Ifield *Chich* 89-94; C Brighton St Pet and St Nic w Chpl Royal 94-97; TV Newbury *Ox* 98-05; P-in-c Moulsecoomb *Chich* from 05. *St Andrew's Rectory, Hillside, Brighton BN2 4TA* Tel (01273) 680680 E-mail jocaswall@hotmail.com

WALL, Márcia Zélia. b 59. NOC 04. **d** 07 **p** 08. C Oakenrod and Bamford *Man* 07-10; V Rhodes and Parkfield from 10. *The Vicarage, 5 Wentworth Close, Middleton, Manchester M24 4BD* Tel 0161-643 8701 Mobile 07823-332110 E-mail revdmarciawall@hotmail.co.uk

WALL, Nicholas John. b 46. MBE02 TD01. Brasted Th Coll 69 Trin Coll Bris 71. **d** 73 **p** 74. C Morden *S'wark* 73-78; R Dunkeswell and Dunkeswell Abbey *Ex* 78-83; V Sheldon 78-83;

P-in-c Luppitt 81-83; V Dunkeswell, Sheldon and Luppitt 83-03; V Dunkeswell, Luppitt, Sheldon and Upottery 03-11; rtd 11; CF(V) from 87. *Address temp unknown*

WALL, Mrs Pauline Ann. b 39. Bris Sch of Min 87. **dss 85 d 87 p** 94. Bris Ch the Servant Stockwood 85-99; Hon Par Dn 87-94; Hon C 94-99; Chapl St Brendan's Sixth Form Coll 90-99; rtd 99; Perm to Offic *Bris* from 99. *41 Ladman Road, Bristol BS14 8QD* Tel (01275) 833083

WALL, Richard David. b 78. Ch Ch Ox BA99. St Steph Ho Ox 00. **d** 02 **p** 03. C Bocking St Mary *Chelmsf* 02-05; C Philadelphia St Clem USA from 05. *2013 Appletree Street, Philadelphia PA 19103-1409, USA* Tel (001) (215) 563 1876 Fax 563 7627 E-mail frrichardwall@s-clements.org *or* frrichardwall@yahoo.com

WALL, Robert William. b 52. Ex Coll Ox MA Ex Univ BPhil77. Trin Coll Bris 80. **d** 83 **p** 84. C Blackb Sav 83-86; C Edgware *Lon* 86-89; C Barnsbury 89-90; TV 90-99; V Dalston St Mark w St Bart 99-07; Chapl St Geo Healthcare NHS Trust Lon from 07. *St George's Hospital, Blackshaw Road, London SW17 0QT* Tel (020) 8725 3285 E-mail rob.wall@care4free.net

WALLACE, Preb Alastair Robert. b 50. St Cath Coll Cam BA71 MA75 Lon Univ BD75. Trin Coll Bris 72. **d** 75 **p** 76. C Ex St Leon w H Trin 75-79; Chapl Ridley Hall Cam 79-80; R Bath St Mich w St Paul *B & W* 83-96; RD Bath 90-96; Sub-Dean Wells 96-99; TR Ilminster and Distr 99-10; V Ilminster and Whitelackington from 10; Hon Asst Dioc Missr from 96; Preb Wells Cathl from 96. *The Vicarage, 21 Higher Beacon, Ilminster TA19 9AJ* Tel (01460) 52610 E-mail alastair.wallace@btinternet.com

WALLACE, Mrs Ann. b 29. CITC 92. **d** 95 **p** 96. Aux Min Abbeyleix w Ballyroan etc *C & O* from 95. *Knapton, Abbeyleix, Portlaoise, Co Laois, Republic of Ireland* Tel (00353) (57) 873 1010

WALLACE, Mrs Brenda Claire. b 52. Linc Th Coll 73 S'wark Ord Course 78. **dss** 80 **d** 87 **p** 94. Sutton at Hone *Roch* 80-83; Borstal 83-89; Hon Par Dn 87-89; HM Pris Cookham Wood 83-89; Asst Chapl 87-89; NSM Stansted Mountfitchet *Chelmsf* 89-96; NSM Stansted Mountfitchet w Birchanger and Farnham 97; C Hutton from 97. *The Rectory, 175 Rayleigh Road, Hutton, Brentwood CM13 1LX* Tel (01277) 215115 Fax 263407 E-mail huttonchurch@zetnet.co.uk

WALLACE, David Alexander Rippon. b 39. CEng MIET. Ox Min Course 94. **d** 96 **p** 97. NSM Haddenham w Cuddington, Kingsey etc *Ox* 96-97; NSM Worminghall w Ickford, Oakley and Shabbington 97-02; NSM Aylesbury Deanery from 02. *11 Station Road, Haddenham, Aylesbury HP17 8AN* Tel and fax (01844) 290670 E-mail revd@wallaces.org

WALLACE, Mrs Edwina Margaret. b 49. EMMTC 00. **d** 03 **p** 04. C Broughton Astley and Croft w Stoney Stanton *Leic* 03-07; C Sutton Coldfield St Chad *Birm* from 07. *The Vicarage, 44 Hollyfield Road, Sutton Coldfield B75 7SN* Tel 07766-714261 (mobile) E-mail edwina.wallace@onetel.net

WALLACE, Godfrey Everingham. See EVERINGHAM, Georgina Wendy

WALLACE, Ian Malcolm. b 57. Southn Univ LLB78 Solicitor 79. STETS 06. **d** 09 **p** 10. C Wisley w Pyrford *Guildf* from 09. *Church House, Coldharbour Road, Woking GU22 8SP* Tel (01483) 857592 Mobile 07799-076697 E-mail ian.m.wallace@ntlworld.com

WALLACE, James Stephen. b 60. Plymouth Poly BSc81 St Martin's Coll Lanc 90. Westcott Ho Cam 96. **d** 98 **p** 99. C Newport Pagnell w Lathbury and Moulsoe *Ox* 98-02; USPG Sri Lanka 02-08. *21 Walpole Terrace, Brighton BN2 0ED* Tel (01273) 689289

WALLACE, Julie Michele. b 58. Ox Univ MTh93 Univ Coll Lon MSc02. CA Tr Coll 77. **d** 88 **p** 94. Chapl Middx Poly *Lon* 86-90; Voc Adv CA 90-92; Member CA Counselling Service 92-96; Hon C Bellingham St Dunstan *S'wark* 91-96; TV Kidbrooke St Jas 96-99; Perm to Offic 99-01; Hon C Croydon Woodside 01-03. *6 Pantanas, Treharris CF46 5BN*

WALLACE, Mark David. b 76. Worc Coll Ox BA98 MA01. Oak Hill Th Coll 05. **d** 08 **p** 09. C Trull w Angersleigh *B & W* from 08. *5 Barton Green, Trull, Taunton TA3 7NA* Tel (01823) 350991 Mobile 07772-615378 E-mail markdwallace@btinternet.com

WALLACE, Mark George. b 72. Qu Coll Cam BA94. Oak Hill Th Coll BA08. **d** 08 **p** 09. C Guildf Ch Ch w St Martha-on-the-Hill from 08. *2 Ivor Close, Guildford GU1 2ET* Tel (01483) 567072 E-mail mark@christchurchguildford.com

✠**WALLACE, The Rt Revd Martin William.** b 48. K Coll Lon BD70 AKC70. St Aug Coll Cant 70. **d** 71 **p** 72 **c** 03. C Attercliffe *Sheff* 71-74; C New Malden and Coombe *S'wark* 74-77; V Forest Gate St Mark *Chelmsf* 77-93; RD Newham 82-91; P-in-c Forest Gate Em w Upton Cross 85-89; Hon Can Chelmsf Cathl 89-03; P-in-c Forest Gate All SS 91-93; Dioc ACUPA Link Officer 91-97; P-in-c Bradwell on Sea 93-97; P-in-c St Lawrence 93-97; Ind Chapl Maldon and Dengie Deanery 93-97; Adn Colchester 97-03; Bp's Adv for Hosp Chapl 97-03; Suff Bp Selby *York* from 03. *Bishop's House, Barton-le-Street, Malton YO17 6PL* Tel (01653) 627191 Fax 627193 E-mail bishselby@clara.net

WALLACE, Matt. b 75. Liv Univ BA96. Trin Coll Bris BA11 **d** 11. C Chase Terrace *Lich* from 11. *38 Fair Lady Drive, Burntwood WS7 1ZZ* Tel 07855-960179 (mobile) E-mail matt.wallace@o2.co.uk

WALLACE (née ALEXANDER), Mrs Nancy Joan. b 42. Roehampton Inst TCert64 Ox Brookes Univ BA97 PQCSW97 SAOMC 95. **d** 98 **p** 99. NSM Worminghall w Ickford, Oakley and Shabbington *Ox* 98-02; NSM Aylesbury Deanery from 02. *11 Station Road, Haddenham, Aylesbury HP17 8AN* Tel and fax (01844) 290670 E-mail revn@wallaces.org

WALLACE, Nicholas Robert. b 56. Trin Coll Bris 93. **d** 95 **p** 96. C Fishponds St Jo *Bris* 95-98; P-in-c Barton Hill St Luke w Ch Ch 98-99; P-in-c Barton Hill St Luke w Ch Ch and Moorfields 99-00; R Binstead *Portsm* 00-10; V Havenstreet St Pet 00-10; P Adelaide St Mary Australia from 10. *St Mary's Church, 1167 South Road, St Mary's, Adelaide SA 5042, Australia* E-mail nrwallace@hotmail.com

WALLACE, Raymond Sherwood. b 28. Selw Coll Dunedin (NZ). **d** 52 **p** 54. C Roslyn New Zealand 52-54; C Invercargill 54-55; P-in-c Waitaki 55-58; C St Pancras H Cross w St Jude and St Pet *Lon* 58-64; C N Harrow St Alb 64-67; V Stroud Green H Trin 67-79; V Penwerris *Truro* 79-84; R Wymington w Podington *St Alb* 84-87; rtd 87; Perm to Offic *St Alb* from 87. *141 Dunsmore Road, Luton LU1 5JX* Tel (01582) 455882

WALLACE, Richard Colin. b 39. Mert Coll Ox BA61 MA64. St Chad's Coll Dur 69. **d** 71 **p** 72. Tutor St Chad's Coll Dur 71-72; P-in-c Kimblesworth *Dur* 72-74; Chapl Bradf Univ 74-79; C Bingley All SS 79-80; TV 80-89; V Earby 89-06; P-in-c Kelbrook 01-06; RD Skipton 00-05; rtd 06; Perm to Offic *Bradf* from 08. *15 Holme Park, Bentham, Lancaster LA2 7ND* Tel (015242) 63136 E-mail richard.wallace@bradford.anglican.org

WALLACE, Richard Ernest. b 35. Ridley Coll Melbourne ThL61 ACT61. **d** 61 **p** 62. C Balwyn St Barn Australia 61-62; C S Yarra 62-64; C Bentleigh St Jo 64-65; I Northcote 65-66; C Ipswich St Fran *St E* 67-69; I Belgrave Australia 69-79; Dir Angl Renewal Min 79-82; I Blackburn St Jo 83-92; I Syndal St Jas 92-95; Sen Assoc P Glen Waverley 95-97; I Ringwood E H Trin 97-03; rtd 03. *3 Panorama Road, Kalorama Vic 3766, Australia* Tel (0061) (3) 9728 4595 Mobile 408-596535 E-mail rwallace@melbpc.org.au

WALLACE, Richard John. b 56. Coll of Resurr Mirfield. **d** 82 **p** 83. C Catford St Laur *S'wark* 82-85; C Bellingham St Dunstan 85-87; V 87-95; TR Stanley *Dur* 95-99; V Cockerton from 99. *St Mary's Vicarage, Newton Lane, Cockerton, Darlington DL3 9EX* Tel (01325) 367092

WALLACE, Robert. b 52. Sussex Univ BSc73. Linc Th Coll 73. **d** 76 **p** 77. C Plaistow St Mary *Roch* 76-79; C Dartford H Trin 79-83; V Borstal 83-89; Chapl The Foord Almshouses 83-89; Chapl HM Pris Cookham Wood 83-89; P-in-c Farnham *Chelmsf* 89-96; V Stansted Mountfitchet 89-96; R Stansted Mountfitchet w Birchanger and Farnham 97; R Hutton from 97. *The Rectory, 175 Rayleigh Road, Hutton, Brentwood CM13 1LX* Tel (01277) 215115 Fax 263407 E-mail huttonchurch@zetnet.co.uk

WALLACE, Mrs Susan Marilyn. b 67. Ch Ch Coll Cant BA(Ed)90 Leeds Univ MA06. NOC 03. **d** 06 **p** 07. NSM Acomb St Steph *York* 06-10; NSM York St Mich-le-Belfrey 10; TV Leeds City *Ripon* from 10. *15 Parkside Green, Leeds LS6 4NY* Tel 0113-278 9339 Mobile 07962-071621 E-mail sue.wallace@leedsparishchurch.com

WALLBANK, Alison Patricia. b 59. **d** 09 **p** 10. OLM Whitworth w Facit *Man* from 09. *1 Waingap View, Whitworth, Rochdale OL12 8QD* Tel (01706) 353616 Mobile 07800-955799 E-mail alison@awallbank.fslife.co.uk

WALLER, Annalu. b 63. Cape Town Univ BSc83 MSc88 Dundee Univ PhD92. TISEC 01. **d** 04 **p** 05. Hon C Dundee St Marg *Bre* from 04; Hon Chapl Dundee Univ from 07. *9 Invergowrie Drive, Dundee DD2 1RD* Tel (01382) 644570

WALLER, David James. b 58. Whitelands Coll Lon BA85 K Coll Lon MA95. Ripon Coll Cuddesdon 85. **d** 88 **p** 89. C Tettenhall Regis *Lich* 88-91; Chapl Greenwich Univ 92-97; P-in-c Yiewsley *Lon* 97-01; TR Plymstock and Hooe *Ex* from 01. *The Rectory, 3 Cobb Lane, Plymstock, Plymouth PL9 9BQ* Tel (01752) 403126 E-mail david@waller2000.freeserve.co.uk

WALLER, Derek James Keith. b 54. Em Coll Cam BA75 PGCE76. Trin Coll Bris 88. **d** 91 **p** 92. C Church Stretton *Heref* 91-95; R Appleby Gp *Leic* 95-04; P-in-c Rushden St Pet 04-07; V from 08. *St Peter's Vicarage, 12 Kensington Close, Rushden NN10 6RR* Tel (01933) 356398 E-mail derekwaller@btinternet.com

WALLER, Mrs Elizabeth Alison. b 49. Open Univ BA89 Univ of Cen England in Birm MA99 Wolfs Coll Cam PGCE91. EAMTC 02. **d** 05 **p** 06. NSM Oundle w Ashton and Benefield w Glapthorn *Pet* 05-08; NSM Aldwincle, Clopton, Pilton, Stoke Doyle etc from 08. *Priory Cottage, 40 Church Street, Stilton, Peterborough PE7 3RF* Tel (01733) 242412 E-mail eawaller@btinternet.com

WALLER, Ms Elizabeth Jean. b 58. Keswick Hall Coll BEd BTh. Linc Th Coll 84. **d** 87 **p** 94. Par Dn Mile End Old Town H Trin *Lon* 87-90; Manna Chr Cen 90-91; Chapl LSE *Lon* 91-96; Hon C

Soho St Anne w St Thos and St Pet 91-96; Community Pastor CARA 96-00; NSM Notting Dale St Clem w St Mark and St Jas *Lon* 96-99; Chapl Ealing Hosp NHS Trust from 07. *52 Cromwell Road, Tunbridge Wells TN2 4UD*
E-mail lizawaller@hotmail.com

WALLER, Gordon Robert. b 50. Jes Coll Cam BA72 MA75. **d** 03 **p** 05. OLM Tooting All SS *S'wark* from 03. *131 Ribblesdale Road, London SW16 6JP* Tel (020) 8769 6733
E-mail baldypevsner@yahoo.co.uk

WALLER, John. b 60. Man Univ BA84 Liv Univ MA07. St Jo Coll Nottm 85. **d** 87 **p** 88. C Chorlton-cum-Hardy St Clem *Man* 87-90; R Openshaw 90-95; Chapl Ancoats Hosp Man 93-95; TV Watling Valley *Ox* 95-96; TR 96-03; R Brickhills and Stoke Hammond from 03; AD Mursley 06-11. *The Rectory, 10 Pound Hill, Great Brickhill, Milton Keynes MK17 9AS* Tel (01525) 261062 E-mail john.waller1@virgin.net

WALLER, John Pretyman. b 41. Sarum Th Coll 68. **d** 71 **p** 72. C Ipswich St Jo *St E* 71-74; R Waldringfield w Hemley 74-78; P-in-c Newbourn 74-78; R Waldringfield w Hemley and Newbourn from 78. *The Rectory, Mill Road, Waldringfield, Woodbridge IP12 4PY* Tel (01473) 736247

WALLER, The Rt Revd John Stevens. b 24. Peterho Cam BA48 MA53. Wells Th Coll 48. **d** 50 **p** 51 **c** 79. C Hillingdon St Jo *Lon* 50-52; C Twerton *B & W* 52-55; C-in-c Weston-super-Mare St Andr Bournville CD 55-59; V Weston-super-Mare St Andr Bournville 59-60; R Yarlington 60-63; Youth Chapl 60-63; Tr Officer C of E Youth Coun 63-67; V Frindsbury w Upnor *Roch* 67-72; P-in-c Strood St Fran 67-72; P-in-c Strood St Mary 67-72; P-in-c Strood St Nic 67-72; TR Strood 72-73; RD Strood 67-73; R Harpenden St Nic *St Alb* 73-79; Suff Bp Stafford *Lich* 79-87; Asst Bp B & W 87-04; P-in-c Long Sutton w Long Load 87-88; TV Langport Area 88-89; rtd 89. *The College of St Barnabas, Blackberry Lane, Lingfield RH7 6NJ* Tel (01342) 872818
E-mail jwaller@talk21.com

WALLER, Canon John Watson. b 35. Qu Mary Coll Lon BSc57. Wycliffe Hall Ox 58. **d** 61 **p** 62. C Pudsey St Lawr *Bradf* 61-65; V 74-82; V Mortomley St Sav *Sheff* 65-74; V Pudsey St Lawr and St Paul *Bradf* 82-88; Hon Can Bradf Cathl 84-88; RD Calverley 84-88; V Kingston upon Hull H Trin *York* 88-01; AD Cen and N Hull 94-99; Can and Preb York Minster 95-04; RD Hull 96-00; rtd 01; Perm to Offic *York* from 04. *7 Seven Wells, Amotherby, Malton YO17 6TT* Tel (01653) 691388
E-mail johnandmarywaller@hotmail.com

WALLER, Martha. d 10. NSM Raheny w Coolock *D & G* from 10. *1 The Paddock, Ashdown, Dublin 7, Republic of Ireland* Tel (00353) (1) 868 1655 Mobile 86-349 0571
E-mail martha.waller@ucd.ie

WALLER, Orlando Alfred. b 12. St Aid Birkenhead 39. **d** 41 **p** 42. C Birkenhead St Pet *Ches* 41-42; C Crewe St Barn 42-45; C Gatley 45-49; Min Heald Green St Cath CD 49-51; V Haslington w Crewe Green 51-54; Australia 54-59; V Runcorn St Jo Weston *Ches* 59-63; V Merrington *Dur* 63-70; P-in-c Bearpark 70-71; V 71-76; rtd 77. *22 Thornley Close, Broom Park, Durham DH7 7NN*

WALLER, Philip Thomas. b 56. Ex Coll Ox BA78 MA88 St Jo Coll Dur BA87. Cranmer Hall Dur 85. **d** 88 **p** 89. C Enfield St Andr *Lon* 88-91; C Belper *Derby* 91-95; P-in-c Oakwood 95-05; P-in-c Long Eaton St Jo 05-10; V from 10; Asst Dir of Ords from 09. *St John's Vicarage, 59 Trowell Grove, Long Eaton, Nottingham NG10 4AY* Tel 0115-973 4819
E-mail waller.family59@tiscali.co.uk

WALLES, Bruce Andrew. b 54. Coll of Resurr Mirfield 90. **d** 92 **p** 93. C Maidstone St Martin *Cant* 92-96; TV Banbury *Ox* 96-98; V Banbury St Leon 98-04; V Aintree St Giles w St Pet *Liv* 04. *St Giles's Vicarage, 132 Aintree Lane, Liverpool L10 8LE* Tel 0151-476 5554 E-mail wallba@ntlworld.com

WALLEY, Peter Francis. b 60. Bris Univ BSc82 CEng89 MICE89. Trin Coll Bris 96. **d** 98 **p** 99. C Ex St Jas 98-01; Asst Chapl Brussels *Eur* 01-05; Bp's Dom Chapl *Lich* from 05. *Bishop's House, 22 The Close, Lichfield WS13 7LG* Tel (01543) 306000 Fax 306009 E-mail peter.walley@lichfield.anglican.org

WALLING, Mrs Carolyn. b 47. Rolle Coll CertEd69. Episc Div Sch Cam Mass MDiv87. 86 **p** 87. Saudi Arabia 89; Par Dn Battersea St Mary *S'wark* 91-94; USA 94-96; C Lee Gd Shep w St Pet *S'wark* 96; rtd 07. *PO Box 947, General Post Office, Georgetown, 10820 Penang, Malaysia*

WALLINGTON, Martin John. b 59. SAOMC 95. **d** 98 **p** 99. NSM Chorleywood St Andr *St Alb* 98-03; P-in-c Wooburn *Ox* 03-08; V from 08. *Wooburn Vicarage, Windsor Hill, Wooburn Green, High Wycombe HP10 0EH* Tel (01628) 521209

WALLINGTON, Paul. b 62. Birm Univ BCom83 ACA86. Trin Coll Bris BA94. **d** 94 **p** 95. C Chorley St Laur *Blackb* 94-97; C Darwen St Pet w Hoddlesden 97-98; TV 98-00; rtd 00. *551 Darwen Road, Dunscar, Bolton BL7 9RT* Tel (01204) 308637
E-mail thewallingtons@hotmail.com

WALLIS, Anna Louise. b 73. Leic Univ BSc95 PhD99 Selw Coll Cam BA05 MA09. Westcott Ho Cam 03. **d** 06 **p** 07. C Huddersfield St Pet *Wakef* 06-09; Chapl Sheff Teaching Hosps NHS Foundn Trust 09-11; Perm to Offic *Sheff* from 11. *3 Oak

Apple Walk, Stannington, Sheffield S6 6FA Tel 0114-243 4343
E-mail anna.wallis121@gmail.com

WALLIS, Benjamin John. b 55. Wimbledon Sch of Art BA79. Chich Th Coll 92. **d** 94 **p** 95. C Battersea Ch Ch and St Steph *S'wark* 94-98; C Wood Green St Mich w Bounds Green St Gabr etc *Lon* 98-03; V Barkingside St Geo *Chelmsf* from 03. *St George's Vicarage, Woodford Avenue, Ilford IG2 6XQ* Tel (020) 8550 4149

WALLIS, David Peter. b 72. Ripon Coll Cuddesdon BTh03. **d** 03 **p** 04. C Eastbourne St Mary *Chich* 03-07; P-in-c Ditchling, Streat and Westmeston 07-08; R from 08. *St Margaret's Vicarage, 2 Charlton Gardens, Lewes Road, Ditchling, Hassocks BN6 8WA* Tel (01273) 843165

WALLIS, Ian George. b 57. Sheff Univ BA79 PhD92 St Edm Ho Cam MLitt87. Ridley Hall Cam 88. **d** 90 **p** 91. C Armthorpe *Sheff* 90-92; Chapl and Fell SS Coll Cam 92-95; Hon C Chesterton Gd Shep *Ely* 93-95; R Houghton le Spring *Dur* 95-07; AD Houghton 04-07; Tutor Aston Tr Scheme 93-97; Prin NOC 07-08; V Sheff St Mark Broomhill from 08. *St Mark's Vicarage, 4 St Mark's Crescent, Sheffield S10 2SG* Tel 0114-267 0362 Mobile 07717-417760 E-mail ian.wallis@sero.co.uk

WALLIS, John Anthony. b 36. St Pet Coll Ox BA60 MA65. Clifton Th Coll 60. **d** 62 **p** 63. C Blackpool St Mark *Blackb* 62-65; C Leeds St Geo *Ripon* 65-69; Korea 69-74; Nat Sec (Scotland) OMF 75-78; Home Dir OMF 78-89; Hon C Sevenoaks St Nic *Roch* 78-89; Chapl The Hague *Eur* 89-95; V Northwood *Lon* 89-95; rtd 01; Perm to Offic *Nor* from 03. *Church Cottage, 61 Gayton Road, Grimston, King's Lynn PE32 1BG* Tel (01485) 600336 E-mail johna.wallis@virgin.net

WALLIS, Peter. b 42. K Coll Lon MB, BS68 MRCS AKC68. STETS 98. **d** 01. NSM Clymping and Yapton w Ford *Chich* from 01. *Chanters, 3 Second Avenue, Felpham, Bognor Regis PO22 7LJ* Tel (01243) 584080 Mobile 07885-542651
E-mail revdocpw@gotadsl.co.uk

WALLIS, Raymond Christopher. b 38. Moor Park Coll Farnham 62 Sarum Th Coll 63. **d** 66 **p** 67. C Allerton *Bradf* 66-68; C Langley Marish *Ox* 68-69; C Caister *Nor* 69-73; P-in-c E w W Bradenham 73-80; R Upwell St Pet and Outwell *Ely* 80-84; V Bishopstone *Chich* 84-97; rtd 97; Perm to Offic *Chich* from 97. *15 Llewelyn Lodge, Cooden Drive, Bexhill-on-Sea TN39 3DB* Tel (01424) 220245

WALLMAN-GIRDLESTONE, Jane Elizabeth. b 61. Homerton Coll Cam BEd83. St Steph Ho Ox 89 Sarum & Wells Th Coll BTh92. **d** 93 **p** 94. C Woodbridge St Mary *St E* 93-96; V Ipswich St Thos 96-00; Dir Past Studies and Adv for Women's Min St Mich Coll Llandaff 00-02; Lect TISEC from 03; Lect Qu Foundn Birm 04-05. *Isle View, The Clattach, Alturlie Point, Allanfearn, Inverness IV2 7HZ* Tel (01463) 230708
E-mail wallmanj@isleview.claranet.co.uk

WALLS, Michael Peter. b 38. Cape Town Univ BA57. Wells Th Coll 59. **d** 61 **p** 62. C Morecambe St Barn *Blackb* 61-64; C Birm St Paul 64-66; Ind Chapl 64-74; V Temple Balsall 66-74; Chapl Wroxall Abbey Sch 72-74; V Kings Heath *Birm* 74-76; Hon C Bordesley St Benedict 76-78; Sen Chapl Oakham Sch 78-83; P-in-c Leic St Sav 83-85; P-in-c Knossington and Cold Overton 85-87; P-in-c Owston and Withcote 85-87; V Tilton w Lowesby 85-87; P-in-c 87; V Whatborough Gp 87-90; Bp's Adv Relns w People of Other Faiths 89-93; Hon Can Leic Cathl 89-93; V Leic St Mary 90-93; rtd 93; Perm to Offic *Ban* from 02. *Gwynt y Mor, 1A Bro Cymerau, Pwllheli LL53 5PY* Tel (01758) 613495
E-mail michael.walls@tinyworld.co.uk

WALMISLEY, Andrew John. b 55. Ex Univ BA75 San Francisco State Univ MA90. Ridley Hall Cam 76. **d** 78 **p** 79. C W Brompton St Mary w St Pet *Lon* 78-81; C Portola Valley Ch Ch USA 81-83; C San Francisco St Mary V 83-86; Chapl San Mateo St Matt 86-90; Chapl New York Trin Ch 90-93; R Redwood City St Pet 93-97; R Berkely All So 97-07; Chapl Seabury Hall Coll Prep Sch Makawao from 07. *65 North Holokai Road, Haiku HI 96708, USA* Tel (001) (808) 573 6848
E-mail frandreww@aol.com

WALMSLEY, Derek. b 57. Oak Hill Th Coll 89. **d** 91 **p** 92. C Bletchley *Ox* 91-95; C Utley *Bradf* 95-00; V from 00. *St Mark's Vicarage, Green Head Road, Keighley BD20 6ED* Tel (01535) 607003 E-mail derek.walmsley@bradford.anglican.org *or* dwalmsley9@aol.com

WALMSLEY, Jane. *See* LLOYD, Patricia Jane

WALMSLEY, John William. b 37. Hull Univ BA71 MA73 PhD81. Wycliffe Hall Ox 71. **d** 72 **p** 73. C Clifton *York* 72-74; C Acomb St Steph 74-76; P-in-c Newton upon Ouse 76-81; P-in-c Shipton w Overton 76-81; V York St Thos w St Maurice 81-89; V Barkingside St Laur *Chelmsf* 89-92; Dir Children in Distress 92-01; rtd 01. *966 Lomardy Street, Kingston ON K7M 8M7, Canada* Tel (001) (613) 766 6058

WALMSLEY-McLEOD, Paul Albert. b 56. St Cuth Soc Dur BA82 Cam Univ CertEd83. Westcott Ho Cam 85. **d** 87 **p** 88. C Gt Bookham *Guildf* 87-90; Asst Chapl St Chris Hospice Lon 90-93; Soc Care Team Member Phoenix Ho Fountain Project 93-95; C Catford (Southend) and Downham *S'wark* 95-96; TV 96-99; P-in-c Downham St Barn 00-02; R Friern Barnet St Jas

Lon from 02; AD Cen Barnet from 10. *The Rectory, 147 Friern Barnet Lane, London N20 0NP* Tel (020) 8445 7844 E-mail pawm_friernbarnet@hotmail.com
WALROND-SKINNER, Susan Mary. *See* PARFITT, Susan Mary
WALSALL, Archdeacon of. *See* SIMS, The Ven Christopher Sidney
WALSER (*née* SHIELS), Mrs Rosalinde Cameron. b 47. Edin Univ MA68 Moray Ho Coll of Educn PGCE69. NOC 92. **d** 95 **p** 97. NSM Scarborough St Mary w Ch Ch and H Apostles *York* 95-97; Chapl St Cath Hospice Scarborough 95-97; Chapl Scarborough Coll 95-97; P-in-c E Ayton *York* 97-06; rtd 06; Perm to Offic *York* from 07. *29 Sea Cliff Road, Scarborough YO11 2XU* Tel (01723) 372382
WALSH, Mrs Alexandra (Gussie). b 50. Wycliffe Hall Ox 06. **d** 08 **p** 09. C Penrith w Newton Reigny and Plumpton Wall *Carl* from 08. *18 Skirsgill Close, Penrith CA11 8QF* Tel (01768) 899957
WALSH, David Christopher. b 59. Warwick Univ BA81 St Jo Coll Nottm BA83. Ripon Coll Cuddesdon 00. **d** 02 **p** 03. C Greenwich St Alfege *S'wark* 02-06; C Kensington St Mary Abbots w Ch Ch and St Phil *Lon* from 06; AD Kensington from 11. *2 Pembroke Road, London W8 6NT* Tel (020) 7603 4420 Mobile 07957-656643 E-mail vicar@specr.org
✠**WALSH, The Rt Revd Geoffrey David Jeremy.** b 29. Pemb Coll Cam BA53 MA58. Linc Th Coll 53. **d** 55 **p** 56 **c** 86. C Southgate Ch Ch *Lon* 55-58; SCM Sec Cam 58-61; C Cambridge St St Mary w St Mich *Ely* 58-61; V Moorfields *Bris* 61-66; R Marlborough *Sarum* 66-76; Can and Preb Sarum Cathl 73-76; Adn Ipswich *St E* 76-86; R Elmsett w Aldham 76-80; Suff Bp Tewkesbury *Glouc* 86-95; rtd 95; Perm to Offic *St E* from 95; Hon Asst Bp St E from 08. *6 Warren Lane, Martlesham Heath, Ipswich IP5 3SH* Tel (01473) 620797
WALSH, Geoffrey Malcolm. b 46. Sarum & Wells Th Coll 82. **d** 84 **p** 85. C Wellington and Distr *B & W* 84-87; TV Axminster, Chardstock, Combe Pyne and Rousdon *Ex* 87-90; Chapl RN 90-94; R Huntspill *B & W* from 94. *The Rectory, Church Road, West Huntspill, Highbridge TA9 3RN* Tel and fax (01278) 793950 E-mail g.walsh1@ntlworld.co.uk
WALSH, Gussie. *See* WALSH, Mrs Alexandra
WALSH, John Alan. b 37. Chich Th Coll 63. **d** 66 **p** 67. C Wigan St Anne *Liv* 66-69; C Newport w Longford *Lich* 69-73; V Dunstall 73-83; V Rangemore 73-83; P-in-c Tatenhill 77-83; R Dunstall w Rangemore and Tatenhill 83; V Hartshill 83; rtd 03; Perm to Offic *Ches* from 04. *A9 Plumley Close, Vicars Cross, Chester CH3 5PD* Tel (01244) 310936
WALSH, Neil-Allan. b 72. Cant Ch Ch Univ BA03 Cape Town Univ DipEd97. Westcott Ho Cam 06. **d** 08 **p** 09. C Lt Ilford St Mich *Chelmsf* from 08. *3 Toronto Avenue, London E12 5JF* Tel (020) 8478 8552 Mobile 07903-652874 E-mail neilallanwalsh@yahoo.com
WALSH, Peter. b 64. Liv Univ BA86 Nottm Univ BTh90. Linc Th Coll 87. **d** 90 **p** 91. C Cantley *Sheff* 90-93; C Poulton-le-Fylde *Blackb* 93-95; V Blackpool St Steph 95-03; TR Ches 03-05; V Ches St Oswald and St Thos 05-11; Min Can Ches Cathl 04-05; V W Kirby St Andr from 11; Minl Development Review Officer from 11. *St Andrew's Vicarage, 2 Lingdale Road, Wirral CH48 5DQ* Tel 0151-632 4728 E-mail revpeterwalsh@btconnect.com
WALSH, Sarah Elaine. b 60. LLCM(TD)90 CTABRSM95. NEOC 04. **d** 07 **p** 10. NSM Waggoners *York* 07-08; NSM Crookes St Tim *Sheff* from 09. *211 Heavygate Road, Sheffield S10 1PH* Tel 0114-268 2824 Fax 297 2995 E-mail sarah.e.walsh@btinternet.com
WALSHE, Marie Sylvia. b 54. RGN RCNT. **d** 99 **p** 00. NSM Kilkeel *D & D* 99-00; NSM Down H Trin w Hollymount 00-08; NSM Rathmullan w Tyrella 00-08; NSM Newcastle from 08. *8 Castle View, Dundrum, Newcastle BT33 0SA* Tel (028) 4375 1757 E-mail walshemarie@hotmail.com
WALT, Canon Trevor William. b 52. MBE03. RMN74 RNT79. Ox NSM Course 83. **d** 86 **p** 87. NSM Crowthorne *Ox* 86-89; Chapl Asst Broadmoor Hosp Crowthorne 86-89; Chapl 89-10; Hon Can Ch Ch *Ox* 00-07; Perm to Offic *Chelmsf* from 10; Bp's Adv for Healing and Deliverance Min from 11. *1 Home Bridge Court, Hatfield Road, Witham CM8 1GJ* Tel 07969-109587 (mobile)
WALTER, Donald Alex. b 34. Ripon Hall Ox 57. **d** 60 **p** 61. C Ealing St Steph Castle Hill *Lon* 60-63; Jamaica 63-80; V Twickenham Common H Trin *Lon* 81-00; rtd 00; Perm to Offic *Lon* from 03. *Ebenezer, 23 Hawley Close, Hampton TW12 3XX* Tel (020) 8941 5193 E-mail daw@maperche.co.uk
WALTER, Giles Robert. b 54. Cam Univ MA76. Cranmer Hall Dur 78. **d** 82 **p** 83. C Finchley Ch Ch *Lon* 82-86; C Cambridge H Sepulchre w All SS *Ely* 86-92; C Cambridge H Sepulchre 92-93; P-in-c Tunbridge Wells St Jo *Roch* 93-95; V from 95. *St John's Vicarage, 1 Amherst Road, Tunbridge Wells TN4 9LG* Tel (01892) 521183 *or* 540897
WALTER, Ian Edward. b 47. Edin Univ MA69 Keble Coll Ox BA71 MA78. Cuddesdon Coll 71. **d** 73 **p** 74. C Greenock *Glas* 73-76; C Glas St Mary and Chapl Angl Students Glas 76-79; R

Paisley St Barn 79-84; P-in-c Bolton St Phil *Man* 84-86; V 86-91; Dioc Ecum Officer 88-94; V Elton All SS 91-98; V Stalybridge 98-01; R Hawick *Edin* 01-08; rtd 08. *Balaclava, 56 Dalriac Road, Oban PA34 5JE* Tel (01631) 564855 E-mail ian_walter@btinternet.com
WALTER, Michael. b 36. AKC62. **d** 63 **p** 64. C Middlesbrough St Jo the Ev *York* 63-65; C Sherborne *Win* 65-68; C Bournemouth St Fran 68-69; Prec Newc Cathl 69-71; C Dur St Mar 72-74; P-in-c Deaf Hill cum Langdale 74-77; V Newington w Dairycoates *York* 77-88; Perm to Offic 88-92; C Feltham *Lo* 92-96; Perm to Offic 96-03; rtd 01. *15 Glanville Road, Bromle, BR2 9LN* Tel (020) 8313 3390
WALTER, Noël. b 41. St D Coll Lamp. **d** 66 **p** 67. C Mitcham Ascension *S'wark* 66-71; C Caterham 71-74; OCF 71-74; C Welling *S'wark* 74-82; C Warlingham w Chelsham and Farleigh 82-88; Chapl Warlingham Park Hosp Croydon 82-88; Chapl F Earlswood Hosp Redhill 88-90; Chapl Redhill Gen Hosp 88-91 Chapl E Surrey Hosp Redhill 88-96; Sen Chapl Gt Ormond Street Hosp for Children NHS Trust 96-06; rtd 06; Perm to Offic *Ex* 98-07; C Chagford, Drewsteignton, Hittisleigh etc from 07. *Whiddon View, 13 Bretteville Close, Chagford, Newton Abbo TQ13 8DW* Tel (01647) 432610
WALTER, Peter John. b 44. CEng MIGasE. Chich Th Coll 80. **d** 82 **p** 83. C Leominster *Heref* 82-85; P-in-c Brimfield 85-90; P-in-c Orleton 85-90; R Orleton w Brimfield 91-95; rtd 04. *Mew. Cottage, 39 West Street, Leominster HR6 8EP*
WALTER, Robin. b 37. Univ Coll Dur BA63 MA90 Linacre Coll Ox BA65 MA69. St Steph Ho Ox 63. **d** 66 **p** 68. C Peckham St Jo *S'wark* 66-69; Chapl Lon Univ 69-70; C Dur St Marg 70-74; R Burnmoor 74-79; Asst Master Barnard Castle Sch 79-97; NSM Barnard Castle Deanery 88-97; Hon C Whorlton *Dur* 82-88; P-in-c Redmarshall 97-01; R 01-03; P-in-c Bishopton w G Stainton 97-01; V 01-03; rtd 03; Perm to Offic *York* from 03 and Worc from 04. *The Laurels, Worcester Road, Great Witley, Worcester WR6 6HR* Tel (01299) 890190
WALTERS, Andrew Farrar. b 42. ACP67 St Luke's Coll Ex CertEd71. **d** 81 **p** 82. Hd Master and Warden St Mich Col Tenbury 77-85; Chapl Ex Cathl Sch 85-87; Hd Master Homefield Sch Sutton 87-92; Hd Master Lich Cathl Sch 92-02 Hon C Sutton St Nic *S'wark* 87-92; Chan's V Lich Cathl 93-02 rtd 02. *The Drey, Trallong, Brecon LD3 8HP* Tel and fax (01874 636374 E-mail thedrey@tiscali.co.uk
WALTERS, Christopher Rowland. b 47. Open Univ BA78 Univ of Wales PGCE94. **d** 02 **p** 10. Hd Master Mayflower Chr Sch Pontypool from 90; OLM Abergavenny H Trin *Mon* from 02 *3 Whites Close, Belmont Road, Abergavenny NP7 5HZ* Te (01873) 856109 Mobile 07967-945320 E-mail church@chriswalters.co.uk
WALTERS, David Allan. b 48. Southn Univ MA87 Bath Univ MEd95. **d** 09 **p** 10. OLM Wylye and Till Valley *Sarum* from 09. *Hillside, Chapel Lane, Shrewton, Salisbury SP3 4BX* Tel (01980) 620038 E-mail david.a.walters@hotmail.com
WALTERS, David Michael Trenham. b 46. Open Univ BA86. St D Coll Lamp. **d** 69 **p** 70. C Killay *S & B* 69-72; CF 72-89 and 91-01; Chapl Eagle Ho Prep Sch Crowthorne 89-91; Chapl R Memorial Coll Sandhurst 97-01; P-in-c Llanyrnewydd *S & B* 01-05; V Llanrhidian w Llanyrnewydd from 05. *Westwood Cottage, 65 Pennard Road, Pennard, Swansea SA3 2AD* Tel (01792) 234307
WALTERS, David Trevor. b 37. Ex Coll Ox BA58 MA62. St Steph Ho Ox 62. **d** 64 **p** 65. C Cardiff St Mary *Llan* 64-67; Brecon w Battle *S & B* 69-73; Min Can Brecon Cathl 69-73; V Llanddew and Talachddu 73-78; V Cefncoed and Capel Nantddu 78-80; V Cefn Coed and Capel Nantddu w Vaynor etc 80-87; V Talgarth and Llanelieu 87-04; rtd 04. *16 Dan-y-Bryn, Glasbury, Hereford HR3 5NH* Tel (01497) 842966
WALTERS, Mrs Felicity Ann. b 56. WEMTC. **d** 01 **p** 02. C Glouc St Geo w Whaddon 01-05; C Matson 05-06; P-in-c Huntley and Longhope, Churcham and Bulley 06-11; P-in-c Hadfield *Derby* from 11. *St Andrew's Vicarage, 122 Hadfield Road, Hadfield, Glossop SK13 2DR* Tel (01457) 852431 E-mail walters@revfelicity.plus.com
WALTERS, Canon Francis Raymond. b 24. Ball Coll Ox BA49 MA54. Wycliffe Hall Ox 51. **d** 53 **p** 54. C Boulton *Derby* 53-56; Lect Qu Coll Birm 56-64; Succ Birm Cathl 56-58; C Harborne St Pet 58-64; V Leic St Nic 64-74; Chapl Leic Univ 64-74; R Appleby 74-77; Dioc Dir of Educn 77-89; Hon Can Leic Cathl 77-91; P-in-c Swithland 77-91; rtd 91; Perm to Offic *Nor* from 91. *2 Beeston Common, Sheringham NR26 8ES* Tel (01263) 824414
WALTERS, Ian Robert. b 51. ACA74 FCA81. **d** 85 **p** 86. OLM Ingoldsby *Linc* 85-92; NSM Grantham St Anne New Somerby and Spitalgate 92-94; NSM N Beltisloe Gp 94-06; P-in-c Gosberton, Gosberton Clough and Quadring from 06. *The Vicarage, 6 Wargate Way, Gosberton, Spalding PE11 4NH* Tel and fax (01775) 840694 Mobile 07831-645683 E-mail ian@roberswalters.plus.com
WALTERS, James Arthur. b 78. Selw Coll Cam BA00 PhD07. Westcott Ho Cam 03. **d** 07 **p** 08. C Hampstead St Jo *Lon* 07-10; Chapl LSE from 10; NSM Bloomsbury St Geo w Woburn

Square Ch Ch from 11. *London School of Economics, Houghton Street, London WC2A 2AE* Tel (020) 7955 7965 E-mail j.walters2@lse.ac.uk

WALTERS, Ms Jennifer Betty. b 56. Birm Univ BA77. STETS. **d** 00 **p** 01. NSM Freemantle *Win* 00-07; NSM Southampton Thornhill St Chris from 07. *41A Waterloo Road, Southampton SO15 3BD* Tel (023) 8033 2613

WALTERS, John Philip Hewitt. b 50. Coll of Resurr Mirfield 72. **d** 73 **p** 74. C Llangiwg *S & B* 73-76; Min Can Brecon Cathl 76-79; C Brecon w Battle 76-79; V Merthyr Cynog and Dyffryn Honddu etc 79-83; V Llandeilo Tal-y-bont from 83. *The Vicarage, 28 Bolgoed Road, Pontardulais, Swansea SA4 8JE* Tel (01792) 882468

WALTERS, Leslie Ernest Ward. b 27. Wadh Coll Ox BA51 MA55. Ridley Hall Cam 55. **d** 57 **p** 58. C Heref St Pet w St Owen 57-59; C Morden *S'wark* 59-61; V Felbridge 61-68; V Streatham Immanuel w St Anselm 68-81; V Cotmanhay *Derby* 81-92; Chapl Ilkeston Gen Hosp 81-88; Chapl Ilkeston Community Hosp 88-92; rtd 92; Perm to Offic *Nor* from 93. *Rokeby, 18 Taverham Road, Felthorpe, Norwich NR10 4DR* Tel (01603) 755134

WALTERS, Linda. d 10. NSM Ilfracombe, Lee, Woolacombe, Bittadon etc Ex from 10. *9 South Burrow Road, Ilfracombe EX34 8JE* Tel (01271) 866853

WALTERS, Canon Michael William. b 39. Dur Univ BSc61. Clifton Th Coll 61. **d** 63 **p** 64. C Aldershot H Trin *Guildf* 63-66; C Upper Armley *Ripon* 66-69; NE Area Sec CPAS 69-75; V Hyde St Geo *Ches* 75-82; V Knutsford St Jo and Toft 82-97; P-in-c Congleton St Pet 97-98; TR Congleton 98-05; Hon Can Ches Cathl from 94; rtd 05; Hon C Davenham *Ches* from 05. *27 Alvanley Rise, Northwich CW9 8AY* Tel (01606) 333126 E-mail michael@alvanleyrise.co.uk

WALTERS, Nicholas Humphrey. b 45. K Coll Lon BD67 AKC67. **d** 68 **p** 69. C Weston *Guildf* 68-71; Chapl and Lect NE Surrey Coll of Tech Ewell 71-77; Hon C Ewell 71-77; Warden Moor Park Coll Farnham 77-80; Tutor Surrey Univ from 80; Dir of Studies Guildf Inst from 82; Lic to Offic from 84. *9 Valley View, Godalming GU7 1RD* Tel (01483) 415106 *or* 562142 E-mail n.walters@surrey.ac.uk

WALTERS, Peter. b 27. Leeds Univ BSc48 Univ of Wales (Abth) MSc52. Ripon Coll Cuddesdon 78. **d** 79 **p** 80. C Kingswood *Bris* 79-82; R Stanton St Quintin, Hullavington, Grittleton etc 82-88; rtd 88; Perm to Offic *Glouc* 88-97. *Holly Tree House, 12 Bethany Lane, West Cross, Swansea SA3 5TL* Tel (01792) 405197

WALTERS, Raymond. *See* WALTERS, Canon Francis Raymond

WALTERS, Mrs Sheila Ann Beatrice. b 37. Bris Univ DipEd58. EMMTC 85. **d** 89 **p** 94. NSM Ashby-de-la-Zouch St Helen w Coleorton *Leic* 89-98; Perm to Offic 99-02; NSM Packington w Normanton-le-Heath 02-05; rtd 05; Perm to Offic *Sheff* from 06. *8 Kensington Park, Sheffield S10 4NJ* Tel 0114-229 5497 E-mail churchmatters@sabwalters.co.uk

WALTERS, William Ivan. b 49. CBDTI 04. **d** 07 **p** 08. NSM Lea *Blackb* from 07. *9 Thornpark Drive, Lea, Preston PR2 1RE* Tel (01772) 732573 E-mail ivanwalters@btinternet.com

WALTHEW, Mrs Nancy Jennifer. b 39. Leeds Inst of Educn CertEd59. NOC 92. **d** 95 **p** 96. NSM Wilmslow *Ches* 95-02; Perm to Offic from 04. *44 Upper Culver Lane, St Albans AL1 4EE*

WALTON, Mrs Alison Claire. b 59. Homerton Coll Cam BEd82. Lon Bible Coll Oak Hill Th Coll BA90 MPhil92. **d** 92 **p** 98. C Bedford Ch St *Alb* 92-94; Perm to Offic *St Alb* 94-95 and *S'well* 95-98; NSM Lenton Abbey *S'well* 98-99; Assoc Lect St Jo Coll Nottm 97-99; C Thorley *St Alb* 00-03; V Croxley Green St Oswald 03-07; Dir Ch Study and Practice Ridley Hall Cam from 07. *Ridley Hall, Ridley Hall Road, Cambridge CB3 9HG* Tel (01223) 746580 Fax 746581 E-mail aw438@cam.ac.uk *or* walton.ali@ntlworld.com

WALTON, Ann Beverley. b 56. Huddersfield Poly BSc78 Sheff Poly MPhil84 Coll of Ripon & York St Jo MA97. NOC 00. **d** 03 **p** 04. C Ecclesfield *Sheff* 03-06; R Adwick-le-Street w Skelbrooke from 06. *The Rectory, Village Street, Adwick-le-Street, Doncaster DN6 7AD* Tel (01302) 723224

WALTON, Brian. b 53. Sarum & Wells Th Coll 83. **d** 85 **p** 86. C Silksworth *Dur* 85-86; C Bishopwearmouth St Mich w St Hilda 86-88; Chapl RN 88-92; V Sugley *Newc* 92-95; Chapl Lemington Hosp 92-95; CF from 95. *c/o MOD Chaplains (Army)* Tel (01264) 381140 Fax 381824

WALTON, Mrs Camilla Iris. b 56. STETS 97. **d** 00 **p** 01. C Lyndhurst and Emery Down and Minstead *Win* 00-04; V Boldre w S Baddesley 04-08; TV Beaconsfield *Ox* from 08. *The Parsonage, St Michael's Green, Beaconsfield HP9 2BN* Tel (01494) 673464 Fax 676694 E-mail camillawalton@aol.com

WALTON, David William. b 52. Open Univ BA84 Leeds Univ BA06 Alsager Coll of Educn CertEd74. NOC 03. **d** 06 **p** 07. C Prenton *Ches* 06-08; V Baddiley and Wrenbury w Burleydam from 08. *The Vicarage, The Green, Wrenbury, Nantwich CW5 8EY* Tel (01270) 780398 E-mail rev.david.walton@btinternet.com

WALTON, Frank. b 39. **d** 04 **p** 05. OLM Woodhorn w Newbiggin *Newc* from 04. *6 New Queen Street, Newbiggin-by-the-Sea NE64 6AZ* Tel (01670) 817568 E-mail notlaw@btopenworld.com

WALTON, The Ven Geoffrey Elmer. b 34. Dur Univ BA59. Qu Coll Birm. **d** 61 **p** 62. C Warsop *S'well* 61-65; Dioc Youth Chapl 65-69; V Norwell 65-69; Recruitment Sec ACCM 69-75; V Weymouth H Trin *Sarum* 75-82; RD Weymouth 79-82; Can and Preb Sarum Cathl 81-00; Adn Dorset 82-00; P-in-c Witchampton and Hinton Parva, Long Crichel etc 82-96; V Witchampton, Stanbridge and Long Crichel etc 96-00; rtd 00; Perm to Offic *Sarum* from 01. *Priory Cottage, 6 Hibberds Field, Cranborne, Wimborne BH21 5QL* Tel (01725) 517167

WALTON, John Victor. b 45. Lon Univ BSc67. Linc Th Coll 79. **d** 81 **p** 82. C Stevenage St Mary Shephall *St Alb* 81-85; TV Bourne Valley *Sarum* 85-95; P-in-c Puddletown and Tolpuddle 95-02; R Puddletown, Tolpuddle and Milborne w Dewlish 02-04; rtd 04. *Serenity, Wootton Grove, Sherborne DT9 4DL* Tel (01935) 814435 E-mail life@clara.co.uk

WALTON, Canon Kevin Anthony. b 64. St Chad's Coll Dur BA87 Dur Univ PhD99. Trin Coll Bris BA91. **d** 92 **p** 93. C Stranton *Dur* 92-95; C Hartlepool H Trin 95-96; V Sunderland St Mary and St Pet 96-08; AD Wearmouth 05-08; Can and Chan St Alb from 08. *2 Sumpter Yard, St Albans AL1 1BY* Tel (01272) 890242 E-mail canon@stalbanscathedral.org.uk

WALTON, Luke. b 64. Leeds Univ LLB87. Cranmer Hall Dur BA94. **d** 97 **p** 98. C Didsbury St Jas and Em *Man* 97-02; C Clifton Ch Ch w Em *Bris* 02-06; Arts Development Officer Bible Soc from 06. *Bible Society, Stonehill Green, Westlea, Swindon SN5 7DG* Tel (01793) 418100 Mobile 07799-414199 Fax 418118

WALTON, Mrs Marjorie Sandra. b 46. WMMTC 97. **d** 00 **p** 01. NSM The Whitacres and Shustoke *Birm* 00-04; NSM Water Orton 04-06; NSM Lea Hall from 06. *51 Station Road, Nether Whitacre, Coleshill, Birmingham B46 2JB* Tel (01675) 464641

WALTON, Maurice James. b 31. Liv Univ BArch53 MCD54 RIBA54 MRTPI55. Wycliffe Hall Ox 93. **d** 94 **p** 95. NSM Billing *Pet* 94-97; NSM Brington w Whilton and Norton etc 97-02; rtd 02; Perm to Offic *Pet* from 02. *10A Sutton Street, Flore, Northampton NN7 4LE* Tel (01327) 340254 E-mail maurice.j.walton@googlemail.com

WALTON, Michael Roy. b 74. St Cuth Soc Dur BA95. Oak Hill Th Coll BA09. **d** 09 **p** 10. C W Kilburn St Luke w St Simon and St Jude *Lon* from 09. *2 Church Flats, Fernhead Road, London W9 3EH* Tel 07949-637377 (mobile) E-mail mikewalton@gmail.com

WALTON, Reginald Arthur. b 40. St Jo Coll Nottm 80. **d** 81 **p** 82. C Woodthorpe *S'well* 81-84; P-in-c Nottingham St Andr 84-85; V 85-91; R Moreton *Ches* 91-01; P-in-c Whatton w Aslockton, Hawksworth, Scarrington etc *S'well* 01-05; V 05-07; rtd 07. *19 The Maltsters, Newark NG24 4RU* Tel (01949) 850523 E-mail regwalton@talktalk.net

WALTON, Richard James. b 55. UMIST BSc77 Sheff Univ MEd84 Leeds Univ PhD98 MA10 CPhys MInstP. NOC 07. **d** 09 **p** 10. NSM Warmsworth *Sheff* 09-11; P-in-c Burghwallis and Campsall from 11. *The Rectory, Village Street, Adwick-le-Street, Doncaster DN6 7AD* Tel (01302) 723224 Mobile 07931-526333 E-mail r.j.walton@shu.ac.uk

WALTON, Stephen James. b 71. Mert Coll Ox BA92 MA97. Oak Hill Th Coll BA01. **d** 02 **p** 03. C Thurnby w Stoughton *Leic* 02-07; R Marbury w Tushingham and Whitewell *Ches* from 07. *The Vicarage, Marbury, Whitchurch SY13 4LN* Tel (01948) 663758 E-mail walton_stephen@hotmail.com

WALTON, Stephen John. b 55. Birm Univ BSc76 Fitzw Coll Cam BA79 MA82 Sheff Univ PhD97. Ridley Hall Cam 77. **d** 83 **p** 84. C Bebington *Ches* 83-86; Voc and Min Adv CPAS 86-92; Lic to Offic *St Alb* 86-94; Public Preacher 00-04; Bp's Dom Chapl 94-95; Lect St Jo Coll Nottm 95-99; Lect Lon Bible Coll 99-03; Sen Lect Lon Sch of Th from 03. *London School of Theology, Green Lane, Northwood HA6 2UW* Tel (01923) 456326 Fax 456327 E-mail steve.walton@lst.ac.uk

WAMBUNYA, Timothy Livingstone (Amboko). b 66. Simon of Cyrene Th Inst 93 Oak Hill Th Coll BA94. **d** 97 **p** 98. C Southall Green St Jo *Lon* 97-00; TV Tollington 00-07; Prin Carlile Coll Nairobi from 07. *Carlile College, Jogoo Road, PO Box 72584, Nairobi 00200, Kenya* Tel (00254) (20) 550490 Fax 554970 E-mail t.wamb@virgin.net *or* tim.wambunya@carlilecollege.org

WANDREY, Bryce. b 77. St Olaf Coll Minnesota BA99. Concordia Th Sem Indiana MDiv03 St Steph Ho Ox 07. **d** 08 **p** 09. C Highgate St Mich *Lon* from 08. *All Saints' Vicarage, 1B Church Road, London N6 4QH* E-mail wandreyb@yahoo.com

WANDSWORTH, Archdeacon of. *See* ROBERTS, The Ven Stephen John

WANJIE, Lukas Macharia. b 50. Fitzw Coll Cam BA79 MA83 Birkbeck Coll Lon MSc98. St Paul's Coll Limuru 72 Ridley Hall Cam 76. **d** 75 **p** 76. C Uthiru St Pet Nairobi 75-76; C Mill End and Heronsgate w W Hyde *St Alb* 79; V Westlands St Mark Nairobi 80-84; Prin Trin Bible Coll Nairobi 85-91; C St Alb St Steph 91-94; Perm to Offic 94-95; Race Relations Adv Croydon *S'wark*

95-01; V Bermondsey St Kath w St Bart from 01. *St Katharine's Vicarage, 90 Eugenia Road, London SE16 2RA* Tel (020) 7237 3679 E-mail lukas.wanjie@southwark.anglican.org

WANLISS, Hector. b 62. St Paul's Coll Grahamstown 85. **d** 88 **p** 90. S Africa 88-97; P-in-c Aylesham w Adisham *Cant* 97-99; CF from 99. *c/o MOD Chaplains (Army)* Tel (01264) 381140 Fax 381824

WANN, Canon Denis Francis. b 27. TCD BA55 MA77 Div Test 56. **d** 56 **p** 57. C Belfast St Donard *D & D* 56-58; BCMS Tanzania 58-72; Hon Can Moro from 72; C Lurgan Ch the Redeemer *D & D* 72-73; R Port Kembla Australia 73-78; R Albion Park 78-84; Adn Wollongong and Camden 82-84; R Turramurra 84-91; I Bailieborough w Knockbride, Shercock and Mullagh *K, E & A* 91-95; rtd 95; Hon C Wollongong 96-01. *304 Woodlands, St Luke's Village, 4 Lindsay Evans Place, Dapto NSW 2530, Australia* Tel (0061) (2) 4262 8545 E-mail dwann@telstra.easymail.com.au

WANSTALL, Noelle Margaret. See HALL, Canon Noelle Margaret

WANT, Mrs Angela Patricia. b 47. Kent Univ BA68. EAMTC 02. **d** 05 **p** 06. NSM Newport and Widdington *Chelmsf* 05-10; NSM Saffron Walden w Wendens Ambo, Littlebury etc from 10. *3 Orchard Close, Newport, Saffron Walden CB11 3QT* Tel (01799) 540051 E-mail angelawant@f2s.com

WANYOIKE, Julius Njuguna. b 70. Catholic Univ of E Africa BA99. Bp Kariuki Bible Coll 91. **d** 93 **p** 93. Kenya 93-03; Provost Thika 02-03; Perm to Offic *Birm* 04-05; NSM Erdington from 05. *1 Abbotts Road, Birmingham B24 8HE* Tel 0121-351 1245 E-mail wanyoikejrev@yahoo.com

WARBRICK, Quentin David. b 66. Jes Coll Ox BA88. Cranmer Hall Dur 89. **d** 92 **p** 93. C Birm St Martin w Bordesley St Andr 92-96; C Handsworth St Jas 96-00; V Packwood w Hockley Heath 00-10; AD Shirley 05-10; P-in-c Kings Heath from 10. *The Vicarage, 4 Vicarage Road, Kings Heath, Birmingham B14 7RA* Tel 0121-444 0260 E-mail davidwarbrick@btinternet.com

WARBURTON, Andrew James. b 44. Oak Hill Th Coll 64. **d** 69 **p** 70. C New Milverton *Cov* 69-72; C Fulham St Matt *Lon* 72-76; C Chesham St Mary *Ox* 76-80; TV Gt Chesham 80-94; Chapl Paris St Mich *Eur* 94-97; Asst Chapl Amsterdam w Heiloo 97-99; rtd 99. *Burnbrae, Riccarton, Newcastleton TD9 0SN* Tel (01387) 376293 Mobile 07962-622740 E-mail borderwarburton@yahoo.co.uk

WARBURTON, John Bryce. b 33. St Aid Birkenhead 64. **d** 66 **p** 67. C Padiham *Blackb* 66-69; C Burnley St Pet 69-70; V Tideswell *Derby* 70-81; V Bollington St Jo *Ches* 81-91; V Capesthorne w Siddington and Marton 91-98; rtd 98; Perm to Offic *St E* from 98. *64 Friars Street, Sudbury CO10 2AG* Tel (01787) 371132

WARBURTON, Piers Eliot de Dutton. b 30. Cranmer Hall Dur BA65. **d** 65 **p** 66. C Grassendale *Liv* 65-68; Bermuda 68-71; R Sherborne *Win* 71-76; V Yateley 76-82; R Guernsey St Andr 82-89; V Hartley Wintney, Elvetham, Winchfield etc 89-98; rtd 98; Perm to Offic *Win* from 98; Clergy Widows Officer (Win Adnry) from 04. *Rowan Cottage, Station Road, Chilbolton, Stockbridge SO20 6AL* Tel (01264) 860275 E-mail b.warburton@rowan51.fsnet.co.uk

WARD, Alan William. b 56. Trin Coll Bris 80. **d** 81 **p** 82. C New Ferry *Ches* 81-86; Dioc Youth Officer 86-91; C Charlesworth and Dinting Vale *Derby* 91-96; V Mickleover All SS 96-11; C Mickleover St Jo 06-11; R Wallasey St Hilary *Ches* from 11. *St Hilary's Rectory, Church Hill, Wallasey CH45 3NH* Tel 0151-638 4771 E-mail alancaroline241@btinternet.com

WARD, Alfred John. b 37. Coll of Resurr Mirfield 93. **d** 93 **p** 94. C Hendon St Mary *Lon* 93-00; Chapl Convent of St Mary at the Cross Edgware 00-04; rtd 04; Perm to Offic *Cant* from 05. *60 Valley Road, Dover CT17 0QW* Tel (01304) 824767

WARD, Mrs Alisoun Mary. b 52. Univ of Wales BA74. Ridley Hall Cam 94. **d** 96 **p** 97. C S Woodham Ferrers *Chelmsf* 96-00; TV Southend 00-02. *160 Upper Fant Road, Maidstone ME16 8DJ* Tel (01622) 728202 E-mail rev_soun@hotmail.com

WARD (née WEIGHTMAN), Andrea Frances. b 66. Sheff Univ BA87. Ridley Hall Cam 00. **d** 03 **p** 04. C Handforth *Ches* 03-07; V Blendon *Roch* from 07. *The Vicarage, 37 Bladindon Drive, Bexley DA5 3BS* Tel (020) 8301 5387 Mobile 07983-851105 E-mail andreaward72@gmail.com

WARD, Andrew John. b 65. Cliff Th Coll 85 Trin Coll Bris BA99. **d** 99 **p** 00. C Belper *Derby* 99-03; TV Walbrook Epiphany 03-11; TR from 11. *St Augustine's Rectory, 155 Almond Street, Derby DE23 6LY* Tel (01332) 766603 E-mail andyward.parish@tiscali.co.uk

WARD, Canon Anthony Peter. b 46. Bris Univ BSc67 Ox Univ DipEd68. St Jo Coll Nottm. **d** 82 **p** 83. C Hellesdon *Nor* 82-85; P-in-c Nor St Aug w St Mary 85-91; P-in-c Norwich-over-the-Water Colegate St Geo 85-90; Norfolk Churches' Radio Officer 85-95; TV Norwich Over-the-Water 91-95; V Gorleston St Andr 95-11; RD Gt Yarmouth 98-02; Hon Can Nor Cathl 03-11; rtd 11. *20 The Butts, Belper DE56 1HX* Tel (01773) 821639 E-mail revtw@btinternet.com

WARD, Arthur John. b 32. Lon Univ BD57. St Aid Birkenhead 57. **d** 57 **p** 58. C Ecclesfield *Sheff* 57-60; C Fulwood 60-63; Tutor St Aid Birkenhead 63-66; R Denton St Lawr *Man* 66-74; CMS 74-82; TV Wolverhampton *Lich* 82-90; V Edgbaston SS Mary and Ambrose *Birm* 90-96; rtd 96; Perm to Offic *Heref* from 97. *Bramble Cottage, 6 Lower Forge, Eardington, Bridgnorth WV16 5LQ* Tel (01746) 764758

WARD, Miss Beverley Jayne. b 61. Bolton Inst of Educn CertEd97. St Steph Ho Ox 00. **d** 02 **p** 07. C Standish *Blackb* 02-07; C Thornton-le-Fylde 07-09; P-in-c Eccleston from 09. *30 Lawrence Lane, Eccleston, Chorley PR7 5SJ* Tel 07811-907274 (mobile)

WARD, Brett Ernest. b 62. Univ of Wales MTh06. ACT 86. **d** 89 **p** 89. C E Maitland Australia 89; Asst P 89-91; Asst P Singleton 91-92; P-in-c Weston 92-97; C Forton *Portsm* 97-99; P-in-c 99-05; V 05-07; P-in-c Eltham H Trin *S'wark* 07-10; V from 10. *Holy Trinity Vicarage, 59 Southend Crescent, London SE9 2SD* Tel (020) 8850 1246 *or* 8859 6274 E-mail fr.brett@ht-e.org.uk

WARD, Canon Calvin. b 34. Univ of Wales BA57 DipEd60 Fitzw Ho Cam BA63 MA67. Westcott Ho Cam 61. **d** 64 **p** 65. C Handsworth St Mich *Birm* 64-66; C Shaw Hill 66-69; V Windhill *Bradf* 69-76; V Esholt 76-81; V Oakworth 81-91; V Allerton 91-99; Hon Can Bradf Cathl 94-99; rtd 99; Perm to Offic *Bradf* from 99. *47 Wheatlands Drive, Bradford BD9 5JN* E-mail candmward@blueyonder.co.uk

WARD, Christopher John William. b 36. Bps' Coll Cheshunt 66 Qu Coll Birm 68. **d** 69 **p** 70. C Wednesbury St Bart *Lich* 69-73; CF 73-93; rtd 93; Perm to Offic *Sarum* from 93. *6 Meadow View, Blandford Forum DT11 7JB* Tel (01258) 455140

WARD, Daran. b 65. Brunel Univ BSc88. St Jo Coll Nottm 07. **d** 09 **p** 10. C Hartley Wintney, Elvetham, Winchfield etc from 09. *40 Pool Road, Hartley Wintney, Hook RG27 8RD* Tel (01252) 849572 E-mail daran.ward@gmail.com

WARD, David. b 40. St Jo Coll Nottm 83. **d** 85 **p** 86. C Aspley *S'well* 85-89; V 89-04; rtd 04; Perm to Offic *S'well* from 06. *150 Robins Wood Road, Nottingham NG8 3LD* Tel 0115-929 3231 Mobile 07971-092089

WARD, David Graham. b 51. CBDTI 03. **d** 06 **p** 07. OLM Higher Walton *Blackb* 06-07; NSM 07-10; P-in-c Brindle from 10. *Coppice Farm, Goose Foot Lane, Samlesbury, Preston PR5 0RQ* Tel (01254) 852995 Fax 851101 E-mail david@dbll.co.uk

WARD, Canon David Robert. b 51. Oak Hill Th Coll 74. **d** 77 **p** 78. C Kirkheaton *Wakef* 77-81; V Earl's Heaton 81-88; V Bradley from 88; P-in-c Fixby and Cowcliffe from 09; Hon Can Wakef Cathl from 02. *The Vicarage, 3 St Thomas Gardens, Huddersfield HD2 1SL* Tel (01484) 427838 E-mail davidwardvic@tiscali.co.uk

WARD, Edward. See WARD, Preb William Edward

WARD, Mrs Elizabeth Joyce. b 42. Open Univ BA. WEMTC 04. **d** 06 **p** 07. OLM Painswick, Sheepscombe, Cranham, The Edge etc *Glouc* from 06. *The Gate House, Back Edge Lane, Edge, Stroud GL6 6PE* Tel (01452) 812188

WARD, The Very Revd Frances Elizabeth Fearn. b 59. St Andr Univ MTheol83 Man Univ PhD00 Bradf Univ MA06 RGN87. Westcott Ho Cam 87. **d** 89 **p** 94. Par Dn Westhoughton *Man* 89-93; Tutor Practical Th N Coll Man 93-98; Hon C Bury St Pet 93-98; C Unsworth 98-99; V Bury St Pet 99-05; C Leverhulme 05-06; Bp's Adv on Women in Min 02-04; Hon Can Man Cathl 04-06; Can Res Bradf Cathl 06-10; Dean St E from 10. *The Deanery, The Great Churchyard, Bury St Edmunds IP33 1RS* Tel (01284) 748720 Fax 768655 Mobile 07791-165714 E-mail fefward@gmail.com *or* dean@stedscathedral.org

WARD, Frank Wyatt. b 30. Oak Hill NSM Course 84. **d** 92 **p** 94. NSM Paddington St Pet *Lon* 92-09; NSM Paddington St Mary Magd and St Pet from 09. *82 Hill Rise, Greenford UB6 8PE* Tel (020) 8575 5515

WARD, Garry William. b 67. RGN90 RM92. Qu Coll Birm 01. **d** 03 **p** 04. C Wednesfield *Lich* 03-06; TV Wordsley *Worc* 06-11; V Claverley w Tuckhill *Heref* from 11. *The Vicarage, Lodge Park, Claverley, Wolverhampton WV5 7DP* Tel (01746) 710304 E-mail garry@pundle.co.uk

WARD, Geoffrey Edward. b 30. Linc Th Coll 62. **d** 64 **p** 65. C Oundle *Pet* 64-68; C Weston Favell 68-70; TV 70-72; R Cottingham w E Carlton 72-95; rtd 95; Perm to Offic *Pet* 95-04. *8 Chapman Close, Towcester NN12 7AQ* Tel (01327) 354070

WARD, Prof Graham John. b 55. Fitzw Coll Cam BA80 Selw Coll Cam MA83. Westcott Ho Cam 87. **d** 90 **p** 91. C Bris St Mary Redcliffe w Temple etc 90-92; Chapl Ex Coll Ox 92-94; Dean Peterho Cam 95-99; Prof Contextual Th Man Univ from 99. *Room WG8, University of Manchester, Oxford Road, Manchester M13 9PL* Tel 0161-275 3151 Fax 275 3256 E-mail graham.ward@manchester.ac.uk

WARD, Helen Frances. b 48. EAMTC 02. **d** 04 **p** 05. NSM Gorleston St Andr *Nor* 04-11; rtd 11. *20 The Butts, Belper DE56 1HX* Tel (01773) 821639 E-mail revhw@btinternet.com

WARD, Ian Stanley. b 62. K Coll Lon BD83. Cranmer Hall Dur 84. **d** 86 **p** 87. C Moreton *Ches* 86-89; Chapl RAF from 89. *Chaplaincy Services, Valiant Block, HQ Air Command, RAF High Wycombe HP14 4UE* Tel (01494) 496800 Fax 496343

WARD, Mrs Janice Ann. b 65. Univ of Wales (Lamp) BA86. ERMC 05. **d** 08 **p** 09. C Haverhill w Withersfield *St E* from 08. *St Mary's House, 44 Falklands Road, Haverhill CB9 0EA* Tel (01440) 768916 E-mail jawgransden@aol.com

WARD, Jason David. b 71. Glas Univ BSc93 PhD98. Oak Hill Th Coll BA06. **d** 06 **p** 07. C Cheadle Hulme St Andr *Ches* 06-09; C Harold Wood *Chelmsf* from 09. *8 Archibald Street, Romford RM3 0RH* Tel (01708) 348406 Mobile 07866-361054 E-mail jasethebass@gmail.com

WARD, Jayne. See WARD, Miss Beverley Jayne

WARD, John. See WARD, Arthur John

WARD, John Frederick. b 55. St Mich Coll Llan 81. **d** 84 **p** 85. C Pembroke Dock *St D* 84-86; PV Llan Cathl 86-89; R St Brides Minor w Bettws 89-97; V Shard End *Birm* 97-04; V Twigworth, Down Hatherley, Norton, The Leigh etc *Glouc* 04-10; C Wotton-under-Edge w Ozleworth, N Nibley etc from 10; C Charfield and Kingswood 10-11; C Charfield and Kingswood w Wickwar etc from 11. *20 Haw Street, Wotton-under-Edge GL12 7AQ* Tel (01453) 843409 E-mail john@jward7.orangehome.co.uk

WARD, Prof John Stephen Keith. b 38. Univ of Wales (Cardiff) BA62 Linacre Coll Ox BLitt68 DD97 Trin Hall Cam MA72 DD97. Westcott Ho Cam 72. **d** 72 **p** 73. Lect Philosophy of Relig Lon Univ 71-75; Hon C Hampstead St Jo 72-75; Dean Trin Hall Cam 75-82; Prof Moral and Soc Th K Coll Lon 82-85; Prof Hist and Philosophy of Relig 85-91; Regius Prof Div Ox Univ from 91; Can Res Ch Ch *Ox* from 91. *Christ Church, Oxford OX1 1DP* Tel (01865) 276246 E-mail keith.ward@chch.ox.ac.uk

WARD, Canon John Stewart. b 43. St Jo Coll Dur BA66. Ripon Coll Cuddesdon 77. **d** 79 **p** 80. C High Harrogate Ch Ch *Ripon* 79-82; V Ireland Wood 82-86; Chapl Wells Cathl Sch 86-88; V Menston w Woodhead *Bradf* 88-95; R Bolton Abbey 95-96; RD Skipton 98-00; Hon Can Bradf Cathl 05-06; rtd 06. *41 Lennel Mount, Coldstream TD12 4NS* Tel (01890) 882306

WARD, Jonathan James Hanslip. b 75. Southn Univ LLB98 Anglia Ruskin Univ BA07 Solicitor 02. Ridley Hall Cam 05. **d** 07 **p** 08. C Cheltenham St Mark *Glouc* 07-11; V W Wickham St Jo *S'wark* from 11. *The Rectory, 30 Coney Hill Road, West Wickham BR4 9BX* Tel 07530-546474 (mobile) E-mail jjhward@btinternet.com

WARD, Keith Raymond. b 37. Dur Univ BSc60. Chich Th Coll 63. **d** 65 **p** 66. C Wallsend St Luke *Newc* 65-68; C Wooler 68-74; V Dinnington 74-81; V Bedlington 81-93; V Stannington 93-99; rtd 99; Perm to Offic *Newc* from 00. *2 Ethel's Close, Gloster Meadows, Amble, Morpeth NE65 0GD* Tel (01665) 714357

WARD, Kenneth Arthur. b 22. St D Coll Lamp BA50. Chich Th Coll 50. **d** 52 **p** 53. C Wellingborough St Barn *Pet* 52-55; C Stevenage *St Alb* 55-58; R Daventry *Pet* 58-72; RD Daventry 68-76; R Daventry w Norton 73-79; R Daventry 79-82; V Pattishall w Cold Higham 82-88; rtd 88; Perm to Offic *Pet* from 89. *43 Inlands Rise, Daventry NN11 4DQ*

WARD, Kevin. b 47. Edin Univ MA69 Trin Coll Cam PhD76. **d** 78 **p** 79. CMS 75-92; Uganda 76-90; Qu Coll Birm 91; Perm to Offic *Birm* 91; C Halifax *Wakef* 91-92; P-in-c Charlestown 92-95; NSM Headingley *Ripon* from 95; Lect Leeds Univ from 95. *8 North Grange Mews, Leeds LS6 2EW* Tel 0113-278 7801 E-mail trskw@leeds.ac.uk

WARD, Lionel Owen. b 37. Univ of Wales (Cardiff) BA58 Univ of Wales (Swansea) DipEd59 MA65 Lon Univ PhD70. St Mich Coll Llan 83. **d** 85 **p** 86. NSM Swansea St Mary w H Trin *S & B* 85-89; P-in-c Swansea St Matt w Greenhill 89-00; TV Cen Swansea 00-01; Dioc Dir of Educn 97-01; RD Swansea 98-01; rtd 02; Perm to Offic *S'wark* from 10. *17 Gresham Court, 11 Pampisford Road, Purley CR8 2UU* E-mail lionelward@hotmail.co.uk

WARD, Mrs Marjorie. b 38. Univ of Wales (Abth) BA59 DipEd60. NOC 83. **dss** 86 **d** 87 **p** 94. Keighley St Andr *Bradf* 86-88; Hon Par Dn 87-88; Hon Par Dn Oakworth 88-90; C Allerton 91-99; rtd 99; Perm to Offic *Bradf* from 00. *47 Wheatlands Drive, Bradford BD9 5JN*

WARD, Mark. b 62. Imp Coll Lon BScEng84. Wycliffe Hall Ox BTh93. **d** 93 **p** 94. C Parkham, Alwington, Buckland Brewer etc *Ex* 93-96; C S Molton w Nymet St George, High Bray etc 96-97; TV 97-05; TV Ottery St Mary, Alfington, W Hill, Tipton etc from 05. *The Vicarage, Newton Poppleford, Sidmouth EX10 0HB* Tel (01395) 568390 E-mail revmarkward@btinternet.com

WARD, Matthew Alan James. b 69. Nottm Poly BSc91. Ridley Hall Cam 94. **d** 97 **p** 98. C Birchwood *Linc* 97-00; Chapl Cov Univ 00-05; Chapl Leeds Univ from 05. *96 Becketts Park Drive, Leeds LS6 3PL* Tel 0113-275 5692

WARD, Michael Henry. b 42. St Martin's Coll Lanc BA02. **d** 03 **p** 04. NSM S Shore H Trin *Blackb* 03-06; NSM S Shore St Pet 06-10; Perm to Offic from 10. *509A Lytham Road, Blackpool FY4 1TE* Tel (01253) 404204 E-mail mh.ward@btinternet.com

WARD, Michael Paul. b 68. Regent's Park Coll Ox BA90 MA95 Peterho Cam BA01 MA05 St Andr Univ PhD06. Ridley Hall Cam 99. **d** 04 **p** 05. Chapl Peterho Cam and NSM Gt Shelford *Ely* 04-07; Chapl St Pet Coll Ox from 09. *7A Mortimer Road, Oxford OX4 4UQ* Tel (01865) 771299 Mobile 07941-998072 E-mail mpw27@cam.ac.uk

WARD, Michael Reginald. b 31. BNC Ox BA54 MA58. Tyndale Hall Bris 54. **d** 56 **p** 57. C Ealing St Mary *Lon* 56-59; C Morden *S'wark* 59-61; Area Sec (Midl and E Anglia) CCCS 61-66; V Chelsea St Jo *Lon* 66-73; P-in-c Chelsea St Andr 72-73; V Chelsea St Jo w St Andr 73-76; P-in-c Hawkesbury *Glouc* 76-80; P-in-c Alderley w Hillesley 79-80; P-in-c Bibury w Winson and Barnsley 80-85; V Barkby and Queniborough *Leic* 85-90; R Gunthorpe w Bale w Field Dalling, Saxlingham etc *Nor* 90-98; rtd 98; Perm to Offic *Heref* 98-08 and *Glouc* 00-08. *4 Framland Drive, Melton Mowbray LE13 1HY* Tel (01664) 500039

WARD, Nigel Andrew. b 50. Peterho Cam BA72 MA76. Oak Hill NSM Course 89. **d** 92 **p** 93. NSM Frogmore *St Alb* from 92. *15 Park Street, St Albans AL2 2PE* Tel (01727) 872667

WARD, Patricia. b 43. QUB BA65. St Mich Coll Llan 89. **d** 91 **p** 97. NSM Swansea St Mary w H Trin *S & B* 91-98; C Glantawe 98-99; NSM 99-02; rtd 02. *17 Gresham Court, 11 Pampisford Road, Purley CR8 2UU*

WARD, Peter Macdonald. b 41. **d** 09 **p** 10. NSM Harrow Weald All SS *Lon* from 09. *129 Sylvia Avenue, Pinner HA5 4QL* Tel (020) 8428 7887 Mobile 07733-001777 E-mail wardhatchend@hotmail.com

WARD, Peter Nicholas. b 59. Ban Ord Course 03. **d** 08 **p** 09. NSM Llanwnnog and Caersws w Carno *Ban* 08-11; NSM Bro Ddyfi Uchaf from 11. *Coed Cae, Clatter, Caersws SY17 5NW* Tel (01686) 688034 E-mail peteandsand@btopenworld.com

WARD, Robert. b 60. Em Coll Cam BA81 MA85. Chich Th Coll. **d** 86 **p** 87. C Horfield H Trin *Bris* 86-90; C Stantonbury and Willen *Ox* 90; TV 90-96; V Knowle St Martin *Bris* 96-07; R Cradley w Mathon and Storridge *Heref* from 07. *The Rectory, Cradley, Malvern WR13 5LQ* Tel (01886) 880438 E-mail frrob@wardmail.fslife.co.uk

WARD, Robert Arthur Philip. b 53. Lon Univ BD82 Open Univ BA88. Qu Coll Birm 77. **d** 79 **p** 80. C Balsall Heath St Paul *Birm* 79-82; Chapl RAF 82-98; TR Blakenall Heath *Lich* 98-01; Perm to Offic 05-07; V Ravensthorpe and Thornhill Lees w Savile Town *Wakef* from 07. *The Vicarage, Church Street, Ravensthorpe, Dewsbury WF13 3LA* Tel (01924) 465959 E-mail father.robert@hotmail.co.uk

WARD, Robert Charles Irwin. b 48. Leic Univ LLB70 Madras Bible Sem DD01 Called to the Bar (Inner Temple) 72. St Jo Coll Dur 78. **d** 80 **p** 81. C Byker St Mich w St Lawr *Newc* 80-85; Perm to Offic 86-07; NSM Newc St Andr and St Luke from 07; Dir Clarence Trust and NE Area Revival Min from 86; Asst Chapl HM Pris Frankland 91-95. *1 Hawthorn Villas, The Green, Wallsend NE28 7NT* Tel and fax 0191-234 3969 Mobile 07768-528181 E-mail rwarduk@mac.com

WARD, Canon Robin. b 66. Magd Coll Ox BA87 MA91 K Coll Lon PhD03. St Steph Ho Ox 88. **d** 91 **p** 92. C Romford St Andr *Chelmsf* 91-94; C Willesden Green St Andr and St Fran *Lon* 94-96; V Sevenoaks St Jo *Roch* 96-06; Chapl Invicta Community Care NHS Trust 97-06; Hon Can Roch Cathl 04-06; Prin St Steph Ho Ox from 06. *St Stephen's House, 16 Marston Street, Oxford OX4 1JX* Tel (01865) 247874

WARD, Ronald Albert. b 29. Shoreditch Coll Lon TCert54. Spurgeon's Coll 85. **d** 03 **p** 04. NSM E Blatchington *Chich* 03-06; rtd 07. *Address temp unknown* Tel 07962-120975 (mobile) E-mail revroncurate@aol.com

WARD (née NIXSON), Mrs Rosemary Clare. b 57. Westf Coll Lon BA79 Liv Univ MA80 MPhil82. Aston Tr Scheme 89 Trin Coll Bris BA94. **d** 94 **p** 95. C Bris St Andr Hartcliffe 94-98; C Downend 98-02; P-in-c Broad Blunsdon 02-05; C Highworth w Sevenhampton and Inglesham etc 02-05; Dioc Lay Tr Adv 02-05; Leadership Development Adv CPAS from 05; Perm to Offic *Ox* from 09. *Aldenham, Mount Pleasant, Wardington, Banbury OX17 1SL* Tel (01295) 750045 E-mail rward@cpas.org.uk

WARD, Mrs Sheena Mary. b 55. Newc Univ BA76 PGCE77. **d** 00 **p** 01. OLM Cramlington *Newc* from 00. *17 Yarmouth Drive, Cramlington NE23 1TL* Tel (01670) 732211 E-mail sheena.ward@dsl.pipex.com

WARD, Simon William James. b 71. Dur Univ BA94 Westmr Coll Ox PGCE96. Ripon Coll Cuddesdon 98. **d** 00 **p** 01. C Aldershot St Mich *Guildf* 00-03; TV Sole Bay *St E* 03-09; Bp's Chapl *Nor* from 09. *The Bishop's House, Norwich NR3 1SB* Tel (01603) 614172 Fax 761613 E-mail bishops.chaplain@norwich.anglican.org *or* revdsimon@msn.com

WARD, Stanley. b 34. NEOC. **d** 84 **p** 85. NSM Jarrow *Dur* 84-90; P-in-c Thornley 90-99; rtd 99; Perm to Offic *Ex* from 00. *4 Church Walk, Thornley, Durham DH6 3EN* Tel and fax (01429) 821766

WARD, Stephen Philip. b 49. Sheff Univ BA72. St Steph Ho Ox 77. **d** 79 **p** 80. C Narborough *Leic* 79-80; C Brentwood St Thos *Chelmsf* 81-82; Perm to Offic *Leic* 03-05; NSM Leic St Mary from 05. *56 Moor Lane, Loughborough LE11 1BA* Tel (01509) 216945 E-mail casula@tiscali.co.uk

WARD, Mrs Susan Elizabeth. b 50. NOC 92. **d** 95 **p** 96. NSM Heyside *Man* 95-09; NSM Newhey from 09; NSM Belfield from 09; NSM Milnrow from 09. *45 Fold Green, Chadderton, Oldham OL9 9DX* Tel 0161-620 2839

WARD, Timothy James. b 67. CCC Ox BA90 MA95 Edin Univ PhD99. Oak Hill Th Coll BA95. **d** 99 **p** 00. C Crowborough *Chich* 99-04; TV Hinckley H Trin *Leic* 04-10; R from 10. *Holy Trinity Vicarage, 1 Cleveland Road, Hinckley LE10 0AJ* Tel (01455) 635711 *or* 442750 E-mail vicar@holytrinityhinckley.org.uk

WARD, Timothy John Conisbee. b 62. New Coll Ox BA85 MA02 PGCE86. Wycliffe Hall Ox BA91. **d** 92 **p** 93. C Dorking St Paul *Guildf* 92-96; C Herne Hill *S'wark* 96-02; V Walberton w Binsted *Chich* from 02. *St Mary's Vicarage, The Street, Walberton, Arundel BN18 0PQ* Tel (01243) 551488 E-mail tjcward@uwclub.net

WARD, Timothy William. b 49. Open Univ BA74 Birm Univ BPhil(Ed)93. St Deiniol's Hawarden 78. **d** 79 **p** 80. NSM Handsworth St Mary *Birm* 79-95; Perm to Offic 95-05; NSM Gt Barr *Lich* from 95. *3 Dale Close, Birmingham B43 6AS* Tel 0121-358 1880 *or* 358 2807 E-mail curate.greatbarr@btinternet.com

WARD, Preb William Edward. b 48. TD04. FSAScot71. AKC71. **d** 72 **p** 73. C Heref St Martin 72-77; C Blakenall Heath *Lich* 77-78; TV 78-82; V Astley, Clive, Grinshill and Hadnall 82-91; R Edgmond w Kynnersley and Preston Wealdmoors from 91; P-in-c Tibberton w Bolas Magna and Waters Upton from 02; Chapl Harper Adams Univ Coll from 96; Preb Lich Cathl from 09; CF (TA) 87-05; CF (ACF) 05-10. *The Rectory, 37 High Street, Edgmond, Newport TF10 8JW* Tel (01952) 820217

WARD, William Francis. b 35. Ely Th Coll 61 Coll of Resurr Mirfield 64. **d** 64 **p** 65. C Byker St Ant *Newc* 64-67; C Glas St Marg 67-69; R Glas Ascension 69-74; Chapl RNR 72-74; Chapl RN 74-78; R Arbroath *Bre* 78-99; Hon Chapl Miss to Seafarers from 78; P-in-c Auchmithie *Bre* 79-90; rtd 99. *1 Denholm Gardens, Letham, Angus DD8 2XT* Tel (01307) 818032 Fax 818924 E-mail bykerbill@btinternet.com

WARD-SMITH, Richard. b 46. Ch Ch Coll Cant TCert87 Ex Univ BTh08. SWMTC 05. **d** 08 **p** 09. NSM Week St Mary Circle of Par *Truro* 08-10; NSM Kilkhampton w Morwenstow from 10. *11 Priestacott Park, Kilkhampton EX23 9TH* Tel (01288) 321314 E-mail r.wardsmith@btinternet.com

WARDALE, Harold William. b 40. BSc PhD. Wycliffe Hall Ox 83. **d** 85 **p** 86. C Bedminster St Mich *Bris* 85-89; TV Bishopston 89-96; V Lawrence Weston 96-98; V Lawrence Weston and Avonmouth 99-05; rtd 05. *3 Cleeve Rise, Newent GL18 1BZ* Tel (01531) 822390

WARDALE, Robert Christopher. b 46. Newc Univ BA69. Coll of Resurr Mirfield 77. **d** 79 **p** 80. C Cockerton *Dur* 79-84; P-in-c Hedworth 84-87; V 87-92; V Darlington H Trin 92-06; rtd 06. *24 Beechcroft, Kenton Road, Newcastle upon Tyne NE3 4NB* Tel 0191-285 5284 E-mail wardalerc@aol.com

WARDELL, Gareth Kevin. b 59. York Univ BA81 MA01. Ridley Hall Cam 03. **d** 05 **p** 06. C Selby Abbey *York* 05-08; C Kensington St Mary Abbots w Ch Ch and St Phil *Lon* from 08. *Cottage 1, St Mary Abbot's Vicarage, Vicarage Gate, London W8 4HW* Tel (020) 7937 2364 E-mail wardellgareth@hotmail.com

WARDELL, Stewart Francis. b 68. Chu Coll Cam BA89 Bris Univ MA95. Cuddesdon Coll BA98. **d** 98 **p** 99. C Brentwood St Thos *Chelmsf* 98-02; R Hawkinge w Acrise and Swingfield *Cant* 02-07; C Hound *Win* from 07. *The Vicarage, Grange Road, Netley Abbey, Southampton SO31 5FF* Tel (023) 8045 6866 E-mail sfwardell@onetel.com

WARDEN, John Michael. b 41. Univ Coll Lon BA63 Trin Coll Ox BA65 MA. NEOC 80. **d** 82 **p** 83. NSM Osmotherley w E Harlsey and Ingleby Arncliffe *York* 82-86; V Kirkdale 86-97; V Kirkdale w Harome, Nunnington and Pockley 98-07; rtd 07; Perm to Offic *York* from 07. *Laithwaite Cottage, Appleton Lane, Appleton-le-Street, Malton YO17 6TP* Tel (01653) 699795

WARDEN, Stephen James. b 57. Kent Univ BA79 K Coll Lon MTh86. Wycliffe Hall Ox 81. **d** 83 **p** 84. C Fulham St Mary N End *Lon* 83-85; CF 85-89; Chapl Wycombe Abbey Sch 89-01; Sen Chapl and Hd RS Wellington Coll Berks 01-04; P-in-c Finchampstead *Ox* 04-10; Chapl Mill Hill Sch Lon from 10. *Mill Hill School, The Ridgeway, London NW7 1QS* Tel (020) 8959 1176 E-mail revrjw@hotmail.com

WARDLE, John Argyle. b 47. St Jo Coll Dur BA71 ARCM67 CertEd73. **d** 73 **p** 74. C Mansfield SS Pet and Paul *S'well* 73-77; Chapl St Felix Sch Southwold 77-87; TV Haverhill w Withersfield, the Wrattings etc *St E* 87-90; V Choral S'well Minster 90-99; Bp's Adv on Healing 94-99; R Bridlington Priory *York* 99-08; RD Bridlington 03-08; rtd 08. *27 First Avenue, Bridlington YO15 2JW* Tel (01262) 400127 E-mail g4cva@talktalk.net

WARDLE, Robert. **d** 11. NSM Macclesfield Team *Ches* from 11. *38 Parkgate Road, Macclesfield SK11 7TA*

WARDLE-HARPUR, Canon James. b 31. St Jo Coll Dur BA55. Wells Th Coll 55. **d** 56 **p** 57. C Sheff St Cecilia Parson Cross 56-59; C Maltby 59-61; V Doncaster St Jude 61-64; Pakistan 64-68; R Man Victoria Park 68-75; V Foxton w Gumley and Laughton *Leic* 75-79; V Foxton w Gumley and Laughton and Lubenham 79-82; TR *Leic* Resurr 82-88; V Burrough Hill Pars

88-94; Hon Can *Leic* Cathl 88-94; rtd 96. *Laburnum Cottage, 1 Coates Lane, Starbotton, Skipton BD23 5HZ* Tel (01756) 760401

WARDMAN, Carol Joy. b 56. Lon Univ BA79. NOC 91. **d** 94 **p** 95. NSM Hebden Bridge *Wakef* 94-97; NSM Sowerby 97-10; Dioc Adv for Older People's Issues from 08; NSM Halifax from 10. *25 Scarr Head Road, Sowerby Bridge HX6 3PU* Tel (01422) 316723 E-mail carol.wardman@gmail.com

WARE, Canon John Lawrence. b 37. Nottm Univ BA59. Ridley Hall Cam 59. **d** 62 **p** 63. C Attercliffe *Sheff* 62-66; C Ranmoor 66-68; R Liddington and Soc and Ind Chapl *Bris* 68-74; Bp's Soc and Ind Adv and C-in-c Bris St Thos 74-79; V Kingswood 79-88; RD Bitton 85-87; P-in-c Broad Blunsdon 88-94; P-in-c Blunsdon St Andrew 88-94; R The Blunsdons 94-01; RD Cricklade 88-94; Hon Can Bris Cathl 76-01; rtd 01; Perm to Offic *Bris* from 01; Chapl HM Pris Bris 03-07. *26 Dongola Road, Bishopston, Bristol BS7 9HP* Tel 0117-924 1304 E-mail johnware@blueyonder.co.uk

WARE, Ms Judith Marian. b 52. St Hugh's Coll Ox BA74 MA78 PGCE75. CBDTI 00. **d** 02 **p** 03. NSM Windermere St Mary and Troutbeck *Carl* 02-05; C Thornes and Lupset *Wakef* 05-10; Chapl Wakef Cathl Sch 05-06; R Crumpsall *Man* from 10. *St Matthew's Rectory, 30 Cleveland Road, Manchester M8 4QU* Tel 0161-740 0237 E-mail ware@judithware4.orangehome.co.uk

WARE, Stephen John. b 55. Univ of Wales (Lamp) BA76. Ripon Coll Cuddesdon 77. **d** 79 **p** 80. C Lighthorne *Cov* 79-82; Chapl RAF 82-00; Command Chapl RAF 00-05; Selection Sec Min Division 05; V Bloxham w Milcombe and S Newington *Ox* 05-06; Warden of Readers *Glouc* from 06. *Department of Ministry, 4 College Green, Gloucester GL1 2LR* Tel (01452) 410022 ext 261 E-mail sware@glosdioc.org.uk

WAREHAM, Mrs Caroline. b 32. Lightfoot Ho Dur 55. **dss** 80 **d** 87 **p** 94. Stanwell *Lon* 80-88; Par Dn 87-88; C Epsom St Barn *Guildf* 88-95; C Aldershot St Mich 95-98; rtd 98; Perm to Offic *Sarum* from 00. *17 Homefield, Mere, Warminster BA12 6LT* Tel (01747) 861716

WAREHAM, Mrs Sheila. b 36. CertEd56. NOC 85. **d** 88 **p** 94. NSM Lostock Hall *Blackb* 88-90; NSM Allithwaite *Carl* 90-91; NSM Windermere RD 91-94; P-in-c Colton 94-96; Perm to Offic 97-07. *Lyng Nook, Church Road, Allithwaite, Grange-over-Sands LA11 7RD* Tel (01539) 535237

WARHAM, Mrs Jean. b 55. **d** 00 **p** 01. OLM Newcastle w Butterton *Lich* from 00. *166 High Street, Alsagers Bank, Stoke-on-Trent ST7 8BA* Tel (01782) 721505

WARHURST (née HART), Mrs Jane Elizabeth. b 56. Sheff Univ BA77. NOC 98. **d** 01 **p** 02. C Edge Hill St Cypr w St Mary *Liv* 01-06; V Toxteth St Bede w St Clem from 06. *The Vicarage, 76 Beaumont Street, Liverpool L8 0XA* Tel 0151-709 9880

WARHURST, Richard. b 76. Univ Coll Chich BA99. St Steph Ho Ox 00. **d** 02 **p** 03. C New and Old Shoreham *Chich* 02-06; R Chailey 06-10; Chapl Dorothy House Hospice Winsley from 10. *Dorothy House, Winsley, Bradford-on-Avon BA15 2LE* Tel (01225) 722907

WARING, Graham George Albert. b 37. ACII62. Portsm Dioc Tr Course 86. **d** 87 **p** 02. Chapl Asst Qu Alexandra Hosp Portsm 87-92; NSM Portsea All SS *Portsm* 92-94; NSM Widley w Wymering 94-95; NSM Wisbech St Aug *Ely* 95-98; Chapl King's Lynn and Wisbech Hosps NHS Trust 96-00; NSM Leverington *Ely* 98-00; NSM Southea w Murrow and Parson Drove 98-00; Perm to Offic *York* 00-02; NSM Scarborough St Sav w All SS 02-09; Perm to Offic from 09. *28 Newby Farm Road, Newby, Scarborough YO12 6UN* Tel (01723) 353545 E-mail grachel.waring2@btinternet.com

WARING, Jeffery Edwin. b 53. Trin Coll Bris 80. **d** 83 **p** 84. C Harpurhey Ch Ch *Man* 83-86; TV Eccles 86-92; P-in-c Hamworthy *Sarum* 92-04; P-in-c Red Post from 04. *The Vicarage, East Morden, Wareham BH20 7DW* Tel (01929) 459244

WARING, John Valentine. b 29. St Deiniol's Hawarden 65. **d** 67 **p** 68. C Bistre *St As* 67-71; C Blackpool St Thos *Blackb* 71-72; R Levenshulme St Pet *Man* 72-87; R Caerwys and Bodfari *St As* 87-94; rtd 94. *13 St Mellors Road, Southdown Park, Buckley CH7 2ND* Tel (01244) 547290

WARING, Mrs Margaret Ruth. b 44. Keele Univ CertEd65. SWMTC 86. **d** 90 **p** 94. Par Dn Tavistock and Gulworthy *Ex* 90-94; C 94-96; TV Axminster, Chardstock, All Saints etc 96-04; rtd 04; Perm to Offic *Ex* from 04. *5 The Battens, Stockland, Honiton EX14 9DS* Tel (01404) 881516

WARING, Roger. b 32. CertEd56 Open Univ BA74 ACP66. SWMTC 83. **d** 86 **p** 87. NSM Ex St Sidwell and St Matt 86-90; NSM Tavistock and Gulworthy 90-96; NSM Axminster, Chardstock, All Saints etc 96-99; Perm to Offic from 99. *5 The Battens, Stockland, Honiton EX14 9DS* Tel (01404) 881516

WARING, Mrs Sheila May. b 29. SS Paul & Mary Coll Cheltenham CertEd49. Oak Hill Th Coll 85. **dss** 86 **d** 87 **p** 94. Eastwood *Chelmsf* 86-92; NSM 87-92; Chapl Rochford Hosp 87-92; Chapl Southend Community Care Services NHS Trust 92-99; NSM Prittlewell St Pet *Chelmsf* 92-96; NSM Prittlewell

St Pet w Westcliff St Cedd 96-99; Perm to Offic from 99. *42 Manchester Drive, Leigh-on-Sea SS9 3HR* Tel (01702) 711046

WARKE, Alistair Samuel John. b 66. Ulster Univ BA89. CITC BTh92. **d** 92 **p** 93. C Arm St Mark 92-95; I Killyman 95-04; Hon V Choral Arm Cathl 95-04; Dioc C *Clogh* from 11. *10 Ferndale, Clogher BT76 0AS* Tel (028) 8772 4636 Mobile 07704-809265

✠**WARKE, The Rt Revd Robert Alexander.** b 30. TCD BA52 BD60. **d** 53 **p** 54 **c** 88. C Newtownards *D & D* 53-56; C Dublin St Cath w St Victor *D & G* 56-58; C Dublin Rathfarnham 58-64; Min Can St Patr Cathl Dublin 59-64; I Dunlavin w Ballymore Eustace and Hollywood *D & G* 64-67; I Dublin Drumcondra w N Strand 67-71; I Dublin St Barn 67-71; I Dublin Zion Ch 71-88; Adn Dublin 80-88; Bp C, C & R 88-98; rtd 98. *6 Kerdiff Park, Monread Road, Naas, Co Kildare, Republic of Ireland* Tel (00353) (45) 898144 E-mail rawarke@eircom.net

WARLAND, Peter William. b 35. K Coll Lon 56. **d** 60 **p** 61. C Pemberton St Jo *Liv* 60-64; C Warrington St Elphin 64-66; V Farnworth All SS *Man* 66-71; Chapl RN 71-92; QHC 88-92; Chapl Greenbank and Freedom Fields Hosps Ex 92-00; Chapl St Luke's Hospice Plymouth 94-00; rtd 00; Perm to Offic *Ex* from 00. *122 Wingfield Road, Stoke, Plymouth PL3 4ER* Tel (01752) 561381

WARMAN, Canon John Richard. b 37. Pemb Coll Ox BA61 MA. Ridley Hall Cam 61. **d** 63 **p** 64. C Huyton St Mich *Liv* 63-67; Asst Chapl Liv Univ 67-68; Chapl 68-74; P-in-c Holbrooke *Derby* 74-80; P-in-c Lt Eaton 74-80; R Sawley 80-96; RD Ilkeston 82-92; Hon Can Derby Cathl 91-02; V Allestree 96-02; rtd 02; Perm to Offic *Derby* from 02. *27 Swanmore Road, Littleover, Derby DE23 3SD* Tel (01332) 510089 E-mail jpwarman1@btinternet.com

WARMAN, Miss Marion Alice. b 20. Newnham Coll Cam BA43 MA50. S'wark Ord Course 76. **dss** 79 **d** 87 **p** 94. Spring Grove St Mary *Lon* 79-87; Hon Par Dn 87-94; Hon C from 94; Chapl Asst W Middx Hosp Isleworth 80-93; Chapl Volunteer Hounslow and Spelthorne NHS Trust 93-04; Perm to Offic *Lon* from 93. *43 Thornbury Road, Isleworth TW7 4LE* Tel (020) 8560 5905

WARMAN, Philip Noel. b 64. Roehampton Inst BSc85 PGCE86. Ridley Hall Cam 99. **d** 01 **p** 02. C Burney Lane *Birm* 01-06; C Luton St Mary *St Alb* 06-09; V Brightside w Wincobank *Sheff* from 09. *The Vicarage, 24 Beacon Road, Sheffield S9 1AD* Tel 0114-281 9360

WARNE, Miss Susan Annette. b 39. Man Univ BSc61 Nottm Univ DipEd62. **d** 00 **p** 01. OLM Yoxmere *St E* 00-09; Perm to Offic from 09. *Wynkyns, 22 Oakwood Park, Yoxford, Saxmundham IP17 3JU* Tel (01728) 668410

WARNER, Alan Winston. b 51. Lon Univ BSc73. Coll of Resurr Mirfield 73. **d** 76 **p** 77. C Willenhall St Anne *Lich* 76-78; C Baswich 78-81; V Wednesfield St Greg 81-87; Chapl Frimley Park Hosp 87-94; Chapl Frimley Park Hosp NHS Trust 94-04; Team Ldr Shrewsbury and Telford NHS Trust 04-10; Bp's Adv on Hosp Chapl *Lich* 06-10; rtd 10; Perm to Offic *Nor* from 11. *9 Beachmans Court, Wilson Road, Lowestoft NR33 0HZ* Tel (01502) 218864 E-mail alan.warner@talktalk.net

WARNER, Alison Mary. b 44. Pace Univ USA BA. SAOMC 01. **d** 04 **p** 05. NSM Waterloo St Jo w St Andr *S'wark* from 04. *5 Mace Close, London E1W 2JX* Tel (020) 7481 9197 Mobile 07900-552665 E-mail ali@alwarner.freeserve.co.uk

WARNER, Canon Andrew Compton. b 35. Fitzw Ho Cam BA58 MA62. Westcott Ho Cam 58. **d** 60 **p** 61. C Addlestone *Guildf* 60-64; C-in-c Ash Vale CD 64-71; V Hinchley Wood 71-80; R Gt Bookham 80-00; RD Leatherhead 86-93; Hon Can Guildf Cathl 99-00; rtd 00; Perm to Offic *Win* from 00. *5 Pearman Drive, Andover SP10 2SB* Tel (01264) 391325 E-mail dandawarner@yahoo.co.uk

WARNER, Clifford Chorley. b 38. Hull Univ MA88. EMMTC 76. **d** 79 **p** 80. NSM Swanwick and Pentrich *Derby* 79-88; NSM Allestree 88-98; Perm to Offic from 98. *17 Amber Heights, Ripley DE5 3SP* Tel (01773) 745089

WARNER, David. b 40. AKC63. **d** 64 **p** 65. C Castleford All SS *Wakef* 64-68; Warden Hollowford Tr and Conf Cen Sheff 68-72; R Wombwell *Sheff* 72-83; V Wortley w Thurgoland 83-95; RD Tankersley 88-93; V Worsbrough St Mary 95-00; P-in-c Bildeston w Wattisham *St E* 00-02; P-in-c Whatfield w Semer, Nedging and Naughton 00-02; R Bildeston w Wattisham and Lindsey, Whatfield etc 02-05; rtd 05; Perm to Offic *St E* from 05. *10 Magdalen Street, Eye IP23 7AJ* Tel (01379) 870459 Mobile 07050-111478

WARNER, David Leonard John. b 24. Kelham Th Coll 47. **d** 51 **p** 52. C Mill Hill St Mich *Lon* 51-54; C Pimlico St Sav 54-56; S Africa 56-68; V Bournemouth H Epiphany *Win* 68-78; V Whitchurch w Tufton and Litchfield 78-89; RD Whitchurch 79-89; rtd 89; Perm to Offic *Win* from 89; Hon Chapl Win Cathl from 97. *9 Sparkford Close, Winchester SO22 4NH* Tel (01962) 867343 E-mail david.warner@btinternet.com

WARNER, Dennis Vernon. b 46. Lon Univ BA68 K Coll Lon BD71. **d** 72 **p** 73. C W Bromwich All SS *Lich* 72-75; C Uttoxeter w Bramshall 75-79; NSM Stretton w Claymills from 79. *90 Beech*

Lane, Stretton, Burton-on-Trent DE13 0DU Tel (01283) 548058 *or* (01543) 306080 E-mail dennis.warner@lichfield.anglican.org

WARNER, Canon George Francis. b 36. Trin Coll Ox BA60 MA64 Qu Coll Cam BA63. Westcott Ho Cam 61. **d** 63 **p** 64. C Birm St Geo 63-66; C Maidstone All SS w St Phil and H Trin *Cant* 66-69; Chapl Wellington Coll Berks 69-78; TR Coventry Caludon 78-95; Hon Can Cov Cathl 85-02; RD Cov E 89-95; P-in-c Leamington Priors All SS 95-02; P-in-c Leamington Spa H Trin and Old Milverton 95-02; rtd 02; Perm to Offic *Cov* from 02. *Coll Leys Edge, Fant Hill, Upper Brailes, Banbury OX15 5AY* Tel (01608) 685550

WARNER, James Morley. b 32. S'wark Ord Course 66. **d** 69 **p** 70. C S Mymms K Chas *Lon* 69-72; C Bush Hill Park St Steph 72-75; V W Hendon St Jo 75-98; rtd 98; Perm to Offic *Lon* 98-00; Hon C Wembley Park from 00. *46 Churchill Avenue, Harrow HA3 0AY* Tel (020) 8907 8505 E-mail jim@warner8322.freeserve.co.uk

WARNER, John Philip. b 59. Keble Coll Ox BA80 MA84. St Steph Ho Ox 81. **d** 83 **p** 84. C Brighton Resurr *Chich* 83-87; C Paddington St Mary *Lon* 87-90; V Teddington St Mark and Hampton Wick 90-00; P-in-c Belgrade *Eur* 00-03; P-in-c St Magnus the Martyr w St Marg New Fish Street *Lon* from 03; P-in-c St Mary Abchurch from 04; P-in-c St Clem Eastcheap w St Martin Orgar from 08. *St Magnus the Martyr, Lower Thames Street, London EC3R 6DN* Tel (020) 7626 4481 E-mail saintmagnus@bulldoghome.com

WARNER, Mrs Marjorie Anne. b 53. York Univ BA74 York St Jo Univ MA04. NEOC 06. **d** 09 p 10. NSM Masham and Healey *Ripon* from 09. *26 Larkhill Crescent, Ripon HG4 2HN* Tel (01765) 606961 E-mail marjorie@26lhc.freeserve.co.uk

✠**WARNER, The Rt Revd Martin Clive.** b 58. St Chad's Coll Dur BA80 MA85 PhD03. St Steph Ho Ox 82. **d** 84 **p** 85 **c** 10. C Plymouth St Pet *Ex* 84-88; TV Leic Resurr 88-93; Admin Shrine of Our Lady of Walsingham 93-02; P-in-c Hempton and Pudding Norton 98-00; Hon Can Nor Cathl 00-02; C St Andr Holborn *Lon* 02-03; Can Res St Paul's Cathl 03-10; Suff Bp Whitby *York* from 10. *60 West Green, Stokesley, Middlesbrough TS9 5BD* Tel (01642) 714472 Fax 714475 E-mail bishopofwhitby@yorkdiocese.org

WARNER, Canon Mary. b 52. Univ of Wales (Swansea) BSc73 Aber Univ PhD77. NEOC 90. **d** 93 **p** 94. C Bensham *Dur* 93-96; Asst Chapl Newcastle upon Tyne Hosps NHS Trust 96-98; Chapl Hartlepool and E Durham NHS Trust 98-99; Chapl N Tees and Hartlepool NHS Trust 99-04; Chapl City Hosps Sunderland NHS Trust from 04; Hon Can Dur Cathl from 10. *The Chaplain's Office, Sunderland Royal Hospital, Kayll Road, Sunderland SR4 7TP* Tel 0191-569 9180

WARNER, Canon Michael John William. b 41. Ex Univ MPhil06. Sarum Th Coll 68. **d** 71 **p** 72. C Plympton St Mary *Ex* 71-75; V St Goran w Caerhays *Truro* 75-78; V Bishops Tawton *Ex* 78-79; V Newport 78-79; Perm to Offic *Truro* 79-83; V St Stythians w Perranarworthal and Gwennap 83-93; Sec Dioc Adv Cttee 93-01; P-in-c Budock 93-97; P-in-c Tregony w St Cuby and Cornelly 97-03; C Probus, Ladock and Grampound w Creed and St Erme 02-03; Hon Can Truro Cathl 98-03; rtd 03; Perm to Offic *Truro* from 03. *98 Porthpean Road, St Austell PL25 4PN* Tel (01726) 64130 E-mail m.j.w.w@btinternet.com

WARNER, Nigel Bruce. b 51. St Jo Coll Cam BA72 MA76 ALCM67. Wycliffe Hall Ox 75. **d** 77 **p** 78. C Luton St Mary *St Alb* 77-80; Prec Dur Cathl 80-84; R St John Lee *Newc* 84-91; V Lamesley *Dur* 91-98; V Bishopwearmouth St Nic 98-11; AD Wearmouth 99-05; V Heworth St Mary from 11. *Heworth Vicarage, High Heworth Lane, Gateshead NE10 0PB* Tel 0191-469 2111 E-mail nigel.warner@durham.anglican.org

WARNER, Philip. *See* WARNER, John Philip

WARNER, Canon Robert William. b 32. TCD BA54 MA65 BD65. TCD Div Sch Div Test56. **d** 56 **p** 57. C Wythenshawe St Martin CD *Man* 56-60; R Hulme St Steph w St Mark 60-66; R Droylsden St Mary 66-76; R Stand 76-97; AD Radcliffe and Prestwich 85-96; Hon Can Man Cathl 87-97; rtd 97; Perm to Offic *Man* from 99. *28 Cow Lees, Westhoughton, Bolton BL5 3EG* Tel (01942) 818821

WARNER, Mrs Stephanie Patricia. b 49. Lon Inst BA96. SEITE 05. **d** 07 **p** 08. NSM Mottingham St Andr w St Alban *S'wark* from 07. *54 Stanley Close, London SE9 2BA* Tel (020) 8859 0489

WARNER, Terence. b 36. **d** 92 **p** 93. NSM Leek and Meerbrook *Lich* 92-98; NSM Odd Rode *Ches* 98-03; Perm to Offic *Lich* from 03. *36 Haig Road, Leek ST13 6BZ* Tel (01538) 371988

WARNES, Brian Leslie Stephen. b 40. Natal Univ BSocSc76. Kelham Th Coll 59. **d** 67 **p** 68. C Tonge Moor *Man* 67-71; S Africa 71-87; V Blean *Cant* 87-94; V Te Awamutu St Jo New Zealand 94-98; Chapl to Bp Christchurch 98-04; rtd 05. *57 Killarney Avenue, Torbay, North Shore City 0630, New Zealand* E-mail stephen.warnes@gmail.com

WARNES, David John. b 50. Jes Coll Cam BA72 MA76 PGCE73. EAMTC 01. **d** 04 **p** 05. Chapl Ipswich Sch and NSM Ipswich St Mary-le-Tower *St E* 04-10; NSM Edin St Martin from 10. *2 Upper Gilmore Place, Edinburgh EH3 9NP* Tel 0131-466 6178 Mobile 07732-654603 E-mail warnesdavid@googlemail.com

WARNES, Miss Marjorie. b 32. Leeds Inst of Educn CertEd53. St Jo Coll Nottm 85. **d** 87 **p** 94. C Leamington Priors St Mary *Cov* 87-97; rtd 97; Perm to Offic *Cov* 97-05. *38 Ruston Avenue, Rustington, Littlehampton BN16 2AN* Tel (01903) 778859

WARNES, Warren Hugh. b 23. St Barn Coll Adelaide. **d** 50 **p** 50. C N Adelaide Ch Ch Australia 50-51; Miss Chapl Pinnaroo 51-55; C Narracoorte 55-57; P-in-c Tailem Bend Miss 57-58; C Northolt St Mary *Lon* 58-60 and 62-64; R Tatiara Australia 60-62; V Kings Heath *Pet* 64-71; V Rockingham w Caldecote 71-73; V Gretton w Rockingham and Caldecote 73-83; V Marston St Lawrence w Warkworth and Thenford 83-89; rtd 89; Perm to Offic *Pet* from 89; Officer for Clergy Widows (Northampton) from 90. *17 Thorpe Road, Earls Barton, Northampton NN6 0PJ* Tel (01604) 812935 E-mail warren940@btinternet.com

WARR, Timothy Gerald. b 59. Trin Coll Bris BA86. **d** 88 **p** 89. C Yateley *Win* 88-91; C Chapel Allerton *Ripon* 91-93; V Wortley de Leeds 93-01; TR Borehamwood *St Alb* 01-05; TR Elstree and Borehamwood from 05. *The Rectory, 94 Shenley Road, Borehamwood WD6 1EB* Tel and fax (020) 8207 6603 *or* tel 8905 1365 E-mail tim.warr@btinternet.com

WARREN, The Very Revd Alan Christopher. b 32. CCC Cam BA56 MA60. Ridley Hall Cam 56. **d** 57 **p** 58. C Cliftonville *Cant* 57-59; C Plymouth St Andr *Ex* 59-62; Chapl Kelly Coll Tavistock 62-64; V Leic H Apostles 64-72; Hon Can Cov Cathl 72-78; Dioc Missr 72-78; Provost Leic 78-92; rtd 92; Perm to Offic *Nor* from 92. *9 Queen's Drive, Hunstanton PE36 6EY* Tel (01485) 534533

WARREN, Mrs Barbara. b 46. **d** 08 **p** 09. NSM Uttoxeter Area *Lich* from 08; NSM Rocester and Croxden w Hollington 08-11. *25A Byrds Lane, Uttoxeter ST14 7NE* Tel (01889) 565537 E-mail barbarawarren149@btinternet.com

WARREN, Bunny. *See* WARREN, Gordon Lenham

✠**WARREN, The Rt Revd Cecil Allan.** b 24. Sydney Univ BA51 Qu Coll Ox BA56 MA59. ACT ThL52. **d** 50 **p** 51 **c** 65. Australia 50-83; Can Canberra and Goulburn 63-65; Asst Bp 65-72; Bp 72-83; Asst Bp Derby 83-89; TR Old Brampton and Loundsley Green 83-89; Hon Can Derby Cathl 83-89; rtd 89. *2/19 Sidney Street, Toowoomba Qld 4350, Australia* Tel (0061) (7) 4638 4487

WARREN, Christopher Pelham. b 55. Middx Univ BA05. NTMTC 02. **d** 05 **p** 06. NSM Saffron Walden w Wendens Ambo, Littlebury etc *Chelmsf* 05-08; P-in-c Gt w Lt Chesterford from 08. *The Vicarage, Church Street, Great Chesterford, Saffron Walden CB10 1NP* Tel (01799) 530317 E-mail revchriswarren@googlemail.com

WARREN, David. b 39. S'wark Ord Course. **d** 87 **p** 88. NSM Mottingham St Andr w St Alban *S'wark* 87-05; rtd 05; Perm to Offic *S'wark* from 07. *26 Longcroft, London SE9 3BQ* Tel (020) 8851 4824

WARREN, Eric Anthony. b 28. MBE. Ex & Truro NSM Scheme. **d** 83 **p** 84. NSM Chudleigh *Ex* 83-88; Perm to Offic from 88. *Lower Radway House, Bishopsteignton, Teignmouth TQ14 9SS* Tel (01626) 772135 *or* 779277

WARREN, Frederick Noel. b 30. TCD BA52 MA58 BD66 QUB PhD72. **d** 53 **p** 54. C Belfast St Matt *Conn* 53-56; C Belfast St Geo 56-59; I Castlewellan *D & D* 59-65; I Clonallon w Warrenpoint 65-69; I Newcastle 69-87; Can Belf Cathl 73-76; Preb Wicklow St Patr Cathl Dublin 76-88; I Dunfanaghy, Raymunterdoney and Tullaghbegley *D & R* 87-97; Preb Swords St Patr Cathl Dublin 89-97; rtd 97. *Runclevin, Dufanaghy, Letterkenny, Co Donegal, Republic of Ireland* Tel (00353) (74) 913 6635

WARREN, Geoffrey. *See* WARREN, Robert Geoffrey

WARREN, Geoffrey Richard. b 44. Middx Poly MA91 Middx Univ PhD02. Bps' Coll Cheshunt 66 Qu Coll Birm 68. **d** 69 **p** 70. C Waltham Cross *St Alb* 69-73; C Radlett 73-78; C Tring 78-80; TV Tring 80-95; V Watford St Andr 95-09; RD Watford 05-09; rtd 09. *41 Coombe Valley Road, Preston, Weymouth DT3 6NL* Tel (01305) 832884 E-mail geoffwarren@btinternet.com

WARREN, Mrs Gillian. b 53. Sheff Univ BA74 PGCE75. WMMTC 89. **d** 92 **p** 94. Par Dn Tettenhall Regis *Lich* 92-94; C 94-95; TV Bilston 95-00; R Lich St Chad 00-02; V Wednesbury St Paul Wood Green 02-10; V Albrighton, Boningale and Donington from 10. *The Vicarage, High Street, Albrighton, Wolverhampton WV7 3EQ* Tel (01902) 372701

WARREN, Gordon Lenham (Bunny). b 45. Wycliffe Hall Ox 91. **d** 93 **p** 94. C Sunbury *Lon* 93-96; C Laleham 96-98; R Limehouse from 98; Hon Chapl RN from 08. *Limehouse Rectory, 5 Newell Street, London E14 7HP* Tel (020) 7987 1502 E-mail cpsalm19@aol.com

WARREN, Preb Henry Fiennes. b 21. Keble Coll Ox BA42 MA47. Cuddesdon Coll 42. **d** 48 **p** 49. C Weston-super-Mare St Jo *B & W* 48-53; R Exford 53-75; RD Wiveliscombe 65-73; Preb Wells Cathl from 73; R W Monkton 75-86; rtd 86; Perm to Offic *B & W* from 86. *6 Brookside, Broadway, Ilminster TA19 9RT* Tel (01460) 57922

WARREN, James Randolph. b 54. St Paul's Coll Chelt CertEd75 Bris Univ BEd76 Birm Univ MEd84. Ridley Hall Cam 90. **d** 92 **p** 93. C Boldmere *Birm* 92-95; V Torpoint *Truro* 95-01; Hon

Chapl RN 98-01; V Shottery St Andr *Cov* from 01. *The Vicarage, Church Lane, Shottery, Stratford-upon-Avon CV37 9HQ* Tel (01789) 293381 Fax 296648

WARREN, Malcolm Clive. b 46. St D Coll Lamp. **d** 74 **p** 75. C Newport St Andr *Mon* 74-78; C Risca 78-79; V St Hilary Greenway 79-84; TV Grantham *Linc* 84-90; Ind Chapl *Linc* 87-90 and *Worc* 90-05; P-in-c Dudley St Aug Holly Hall *Worc* 95-96; Perm to Offic 96-97; TV Kidderminster St Mary and All SS w Trimpley etc 97-05; Ind Chapl *Bris* 05-10; TV Pontypool *Mon* from 10. *The Vicarage, Freeholdland Road, Pontnewynydd, Pontypool NP4 8LW* Tel (01495) 741879 Mobile 07971-222739 E-mail malcolm_warren@hotmail.com

WARREN, Martin John. b 59. Ch Coll Cam BA81 MA85. St Jo Coll Nottm LTh85. **d** 86 **p** 87. C Littleover *Derby* 86-90; C Hermitage and Hampstead Norreys, Cold Ash etc *Ox* 90-91; TV 91-97; TV Hermitage 97-02; P-in-c Shebbear, Buckland Filleigh, Sheepwash etc *Ex* from 02. *The Rectory, Shebbear, Beaworthy EX21 5RU* Tel (01409) 281424

WARREN, Michael John. b 40. Kelham Th Coll 59. **d** 64 **p** 65. C Withington St Chris *Man* 64-67; C Worsley 67-69; C Witney *Ox* 69-72; V S Hinksey 72-80; Canada 80-99 and from 02; C Verwood *Sarum* 99-00; rtd 00. *1005-5th Avenue North, Lethbridge AB T1H 0MB, Canada*

WARREN, Michael Philip. b 62. Oak Hill Th Coll BA91 MA04. **d** 94 **p** 95. C Tunbridge Wells St Jo *Roch* 94-98; Assoc Min Heydon, Gt and Lt Chishill, Chrishall etc *Chelmsf* 98-04; V Tunbridge Wells St Pet *Roch* from 04. *St Peter's Vicarage, Bayhall Road, Tunbridge Wells TN2 4TP* Tel (01892) 530384 E-mail elmdonvic@aol.com

WARREN, The Ven Norman Leonard. b 34. CCC Cam BA58 MA62. Ridley Hall Cam 58. **d** 60 **p** 61. C Bedworth *Cov* 60-63; V Leamington Priors St Paul 63-77; R Morden *S'wark* 77-88; TR 88-89; RD Merton 86-89; Adn Roch and Can Res Roch Cathl 89-00; rtd 00; Perm to Offic *Roch* 00-06. *Cornerstone, 6 Hill View, Stratford-upon-Avon CV37 9AY* Tel (01789) 414255

WARREN, Canon Paul Kenneth. b 41. Selw Coll Cam BA63 MA67. Cuddesdon Coll 64. **d** 67 **p** 68. C Lancaster St Mary *Blackb* 67-70; Chapl Lanc Univ 70-78; V Langho Billington 78-83; Bp's Dom Chapl and Chapl Whalley Abbey 83-88; R Standish 88-01; P-in-c Silverdale from 01; Hon Can Blackb Cathl from 91; RD Chorley 92-98; AD Tunstall from 08. *The Vicarage, St John's Grove, Silverdale, Carnforth LA5 0RH* Tel (01524) 701268

WARREN, Peter. b 40. FCA46. Oak Hill Th Coll 77. **d** 79 **p** 80. C Newcastle w Butterton *Lich* 79-82; TV Sutton St Jas and Wawne *York* 82-87; V Ledsham w Fairburn 87-95; R Ainderby Steeple w Yafforth and Kirby Wiske etc *Ripon* 95-03; rtd 03. *5 Bridge Farm, Pollington, Goole DN14 0BF* Tel (01405) 862925 E-mail peter@warren303.orangehome.co.uk

WARREN, Peter John. b 55. Worc Coll of Educn CertEd76. Trin Coll Bris BA86. **d** 86 **p** 87. C W Streatham St Jas *S'wark* 86-91; P-in-c Edin Clermiston Em 91-98; P-in-c Blackpool Ch Ch w All SS *Blackb* 98-03; V 03-09; Co-Pastor Internat Chr Fellowship Phnom Penh from 09. *19 Ash Drive, Poulton-le-Fylde FY6 8DZ* Tel (00855) (12) 235182 E-mail revpwarren@googlemail.com

WARREN, Philip James. b 65. SS Paul & Mary Coll Cheltenham BA87 Hughes Hall Cam PGCE88 Kingston Univ MA93. St Jo Coll Nottm MA99. **d** 00 **p** 01. C Reigate St Mary *S'wark* 00-03; P-in-c Jersey Millbrook St Matt *Win* 03-06; V from 06; P-in-c Jersey St Lawr 03-06; R from 06. *The Rectory, La Route de l'Eglise, St Lawrence, Jersey JE3 1FF* Tel (01534) 869013 E-mail philwarren@jerseymail.co.uk

WARREN, The Ven Robert. b 54. TCD BA78 MA81. CITC 76. **d** 78 **p** 79. C Limerick City *L & K* 78-81; Dioc Youth Adv (Limerick) 79-86; I Adare w Kilpeacon and Croom 81-88; Bp's Dom Chapl 81-95; Dioc Registrar (Limerick etc) from 81; Dioc Registrar (Killaloe etc) from 86; I Tralee w Kilmoyley, Ballymacelligott etc from 88; Can Limerick, Killaloe and Clonfert Cathls 95-96; Chan from 97; Asst Dioc Sec *L & K* from 90; Preb Taney St Patr Cathl Dublin from 04; Adn Limerick, Ardfert and Aghadoe *L & K* from 10. *St John's Rectory, Ashe Street, Tralee, Co Kerry, Republic of Ireland* Tel (00353) (66) 712 2245 *or* 712 4152 Fax 712 9004 Mobile 87-252 1133 E-mail rwarren@indigo.ie

WARREN, Robert Geoffrey. b 51. Trin Coll Bris 79. **d** 82 **p** 83. C Felixstowe SS Pet and Paul *St E* 82-86; V Gazeley w Dalham, Moulton and Kentford 86-90; P-in-c Ipswich St Clem w St Luke and H Trin 90-98; C Gt Finborough w Onehouse and Harleston 98-00; rtd 01; Perm to Offic *B & W* from 02. *5 Clarence House, 17 Clarence Road North, Weston-super-Mare BS23 4AS*

WARREN, Robert Irving. b 38. Univ of BC BA58 Ox Univ MA73. Angl Th Coll (BC). **d** 61 **p** 63. C Lakes Miss Canada 61-66; R Hazelton 69-75; R New Westmr St Barn 75-89; R Northfield *Birm* 89-08; rtd 08; Perm to Offic *Birm* from 08. *300 Lickey Road, Rednal, Birmingham B45 8RY* Tel 0121-453 1572 E-mail riwarren@hotmail.com

WARREN, Robert James. b 58. McGill Univ Montreal BTh82. Montreal Dioc Th Coll. **d** 84 **p** 85. C Victoria St Phil Canada 84-87; R Chibougamau Ch Ch 87-90; R Mascouche and P-in-c

Montreal St Ignatius 90-92; R Westmount Ch of the Advent 92-99; Exec Dir Old Brewery Miss 99-03; Chapl Canadian Grenadier Guards 91-96; Chapl Miss to Seafarers 93-99; R Penicuik *Edin* from 03; P-in-c W Linton from 03. *The Rectory, 23 Broomhill Road, Penicuik EH26 9EE* Tel (01968) 672862 Mobile 07963-914885 E-mail padre@btinternet.com

WARREN, Canon Robert Peter Resker. b 39. Jes Coll Cam BA63 MA. ALCD65. **d** 65 **p** 66. C Rusholme H Trin *Man* 65-68; C Bushbury *Lich* 68-71; V Crookes St Thos *Sheff* 71-90; TR 90-93; RD Hallam 78-83; Hon Can Sheff Cathl 82-93; Can Th Sheff Cathl 93-04; Nat Officer for Evang 93-04; Springboard Missr 98-04; rtd 04; Perm to Offic *Ripon* 03-10. *2 The Fairway, High Hauxley, Morpeth NE65 0JW* Tel (01665) 714697 E-mail robert.warren@ukgateway.net

WARREN, William Frederick. b 55. Sarum & Wells Th Coll 83. **d** 86 **p** 87. C E Greenwich Ch Ch w St Andr and St Mich *S'wark* 86-91; C Richmond St Mary w St Matthias and St Jo 91-95; TV 96-97; V Putney St Marg 97-08; V S Croydon St Pet and St Aug from 08. *St Peter's Vicarage, 20 Haling Park Road, South Croydon CR2 6NE* Tel (020) 8688 4715 E-mail wfwarren2003@yahoo.co.uk

WARRENER, Mrs Kathleen Barbara. b 48. Coll of Resurr Mirfield 09. **d** 11. NSM Pontefract All SS *Wakef* from 11. *45 Northfield Drive, Pontefract WF8 2DJ* Tel (01977) 600232 Mobile 07554-087728 E-mail babs@warrener4389.fsnet.co.uk

WARRICK, Mark. b 54. Aston Univ BSc76 Nottm Univ BCombStuds83. Linc Th Coll 80. **d** 83 **p** 84. C Grantham *Linc* 83-87; C Cirencester *Glouc* 87-91; V Over *Ely* 91-97; V Deeping St James *Linc* 97-09; P-in-c Stamford All SS w St Jo from 09; RD Aveland and Ness w Stamford 06-09 and from 10. *All Saints' Vicarage, Casterton Road, Stamford PE9 2YL* Tel (01780) 756942 E-mail mark.warrick@stamfordallsaints.org.uk

WARRILLOW, Brian Ellis. b 39. Linc Th Coll 81. **d** 83 **p** 84. C Tunstall *Lich* 83-85; C Shrewsbury H Cross 86-87; P-in-c Tilstock 88; P-in-c Whixall 88; V Tilstock and Whixall 89-92; TV Hanley H Ev 92-94; rtd 94; Perm to Offic *Lich* 01-02; P-in-c Menton *Eur* 02-05; Hon C Wolstanton *Lich* 07-10. *43 Charleston Road, Penrhyn Bay, Llandudno LL30 3HB* Tel (01492) 543541 E-mail thewarrillows@netscapeonline.co.uk

WARRILOW, Mrs Christine. b 42. Lanc Univ BA86. NOC 86. **d** 89 **p** 94. C Netherton *Liv* 89-92; C Cantril Farm 92-94; V 94-96; V Hindley Green 96-02; rtd 02; Perm to Offic *Liv* 03-08; Hon C Stanley w Stoneycroft St Paul from 08. *10 Beacon View Drive, Upholland, Skelmersdale WN8 0HL*

WARRINGTON, Katherine Irene (Kay). b 44. Univ of Wales (Swansea) BSc67 DipEd68. St Mich Coll Llan 93. **d** 95. NSM Knighton and Norton *S & B* 95-98; NSM Llywel and Traean-glas w Llanulid 98-00; NSM Trallwng w Bettws Penpont w Aberyskir etc 00-04; Dioc Children's Officer from 96. *17 Ffordd Emlyn, Ystalyfera, Swansea SA9 2EW* Tel (01639) 842874 E-mail kaywarrington@sky.com

WARRINGTON, Archdeacon of. See BRADLEY, The Ven Peter David Douglas

WARRINGTON, Suffragan Bishop of. See BLACKBURN, The Rt Revd Richard Finn

WARWICK, Gordon Melvin. b 31. NOC 79. **d** 80 **p** 81. NSM Darrington *Wakef* 80-87; TV Almondbury w Farnley Tyas 87-95; rtd 95; Perm to Offic *Newc* 95-09. *4 Glencaple Avenue, Dumfries DG1 4SJ* Tel (01387) 257675 E-mail gordonwarwick1931@btinternet.com

WARWICK, Hugh Johnston. b 39. ARCM63. SAOMC 97. **d** 00 **p** 01. NSM Rotherfield Peppard *Ox* 00-02; NSM Rotherfield Peppard and Kidmore End etc 02-08; rtd 08; Perm to Offic *Ox* and *Pet* from 08. *Witan House, 38 Wheeler's Rise, Croughton, Brackley NN13 5ND* Tel (01869) 819577 E-mail hugh@pukekos.co.uk

WARWICK, Canon John Michael. b 37. Fitzw Ho Cam BA58 MA62. Ely Th Coll 58. **d** 60 **p** 61. C Towcester w Easton Neston *Pet* 60-63; C Leighton Buzzard *St Alb* 63-64; C Boston *Linc* 64-66; P-in-c Sutterton 66-72; V 72-74; V Sutton St Mary 74-84; V Bourne 84-02; Can and Preb Linc Cathl 89-02; RD Aveland and Ness w Stamford 93-00; Chapl Bourne Hosps Lincs 84-93; Chapl NW Anglia Healthcare NHS Trust 93-98; rtd 02. *24 Hurst Park Road, Twyford, Reading RG10 0EY* Tel 0118-932 0649

WARWICK, Neil Michael. b 64. Nottm Univ BA86. Ridley Hall Cam 03. **d** 05 **p** 06. C Towcester w Caldecote and Easton Neston etc *Pet* 05-09; V Earley St Nic *Ox* from 09. *St Nicolas' Vicarage, 53 Sutcliffe Avenue, Reading RG6 7JN* Tel 0118-966 5060 E-mail revwarwick@btinternet.com

WARWICK, Archdeacon of. See RODHAM, The Ven Morris

WARWICK, Suffragan Bishop of. See STROYAN, The Rt Revd John Ronald Angus

WASEY, Kim Alexandra Clare. b 77. Man Univ BA99 Birm Univ MPhil03. Qu Coll Birm 00. **d** 02 **p** 03. C Rochdale *Man* 02-04; Chapl Man Univ 04-06; Chapl Man Metrop Univ 04-06; Chapl Salford Univ 06-09; Hon C Man Victoria Park from 09. *St Chrysostom's Rectory, 38 Park Range, Manchester M14 5HQ* Tel 0161-224 6971 Mobile 07944-155772 E-mail kim.wasey@gmail.com

WASH, John Henry. b 46. CEng MIStructE70. **d** 81 **p** 83. OLM Newington St Mary *S'wark* 81-04; Perm to Offic Cyprus and the Gulf from 05. *PO Box 60187, Paphos 8101, Cyprus* Tel (00357) (26) 923860 E-mail wash@emailkissonerga.com

WASHFORD, Mrs Rhonwen Richarde Foster. b 50. RGN99. ERMC 05. **d** 08 **p** 09. NSM Stalham, E Ruston, Brunstead, Sutton and Ingham *Nor* from 08. *Homeleigh, Town Road, Ingham, Norwich NR12 9TA* Tel (01692) 580423 E-mail rhonwenwashford@hotmail.com

WASHINGTON, Linda Jennifer. b 56. BA PGCE. **d** 07 **p** 08. NSM Woburn w Eversholt, Milton Bryan, Battlesden etc *St Alb* from 07. *3 Avenue Mews, Flitwick, Bedford MK45 1BF* Tel (01525) 714442

WASHINGTON, Nigel Leslie. b 50. St Paul's Coll Chelt BEd73 Lon Univ MA83. SAOMC 97. **d** 00 **p** 01. NSM Westoning w Tingrith *St Alb* 00-07; P-in-c from 07. *Bracken, 3 Avenue Mews, Flitwick, Bedford MK45 1BF* Tel (01525) 714442 Mobile 07794-754986 E-mail nigelwash@hotmail.com

WASHINGTON, Canon Patrick Leonard. b 44. Nottm Univ BSc66. St Steph Ho Ox 65. **d** 68 **p** 69. C Fleet *Guildf* 68-71; C Farnham 71-74; TV Staveley and Barrow Hill *Derby* 74-83; V Norbury St Phil *Cant* 83-84; V Norbury St Phil *S'wark* 85-10; RD Croydon N 90-99; Hon Can S'wark Cathl 01-10; rtd 10. *16 Saddington Road, Fleckney, Leicester LE8 8AW* Tel 0116-240 3117

WASSALL, Canon Keith Leonard. b 45. Bede Coll Dur TCert67. Chich Th Coll 68. **d** 71 **p** 72. C Upper Gornal *Lich* 71-74; C Codsall 74-75; TV Hanley All SS 75-79; Asst P Pembroke Bermuda 79-81; V Rickerscote *Lich* 81-92; P-in-c Coven 92-99; Asst Chapl HM Pris Featherstone 92-99; Can Res Bermuda 99-04; C Houghton le Spring *Dur* 04-06; C Eppleton and Hetton le Hole 04-06; C Lyons 04-06; C Millfield St Mark and Pallion St Luke 06-09; rtd 09. *28 Monteigne Drive, Bowburn, Durham DH6 5QB* Tel 0191-377 8709 E-mail klwassall@tiscali.co.uk

WASTELL, Canon Eric Morse. b 33. St Mich Coll Llan. **d** 62 **p** 63. C Oystermouth *S & B* 62-65; C St Jo Cathl Antigua 65-66; R St Mary 66-73; R St Paul 73-74; Dioc Registrar 69-74; Hon Can Antigua 71-74; V Swansea St Gabr *S & B* 74-98; RD Clyne 88-96; Can Brecon Cathl from 90; rtd 98. *18 Belgrave Court, Walter Road, Uplands, Swansea SA1 4PY* Tel (01792) 466709

WASTIE, Canon David Vernon. b 37. Open Univ BA84. Chich Th Coll 79. **d** 81 **p** 82. C Bitterne Park *Win* 81-83; TV Chambersbury *St Alb* 83-87; V Jersey St Luke *Win* 87-95; P-in-c Jersey St Jas 87-93; V 93-95; V Southbourne St Kath 95-99; Hon Can Bukavu from 94; rtd 02; Perm to Offic *Derby* 05-08 and *Win* from 09. *3 Uplands Court, 1 Uplands Road, Bournemouth BH8 9AG* Tel (01202) 514056 Mobile 07816-635202 E-mail canonwastie@hotmail.com

WATCHORN, Canon Brian. b 42. Em Coll Cam BA61 MA65 Ex Coll Ox BA62. Ripon Hall Ox 61. **d** 63 **p** 64. C Bolton St Pet *Man* 63-66; Chapl G&C Coll Cam 66-74; V Chesterton St Geo *Ely* 75-82; Fell Dean and Chapl Pemb Coll Cam 82-06; Hon Can Ely Cathl from 94; Chapter Can 00-10. *34 Petersfield Mansions, Petersfield, Cambridge CB1 1BB* Tel (01223) 322378 E-mail bw214@pem.cam.ac.uk

WATERFIELD, Janet Lyn. b 60. Birm Univ BA06. WMMTC 99. **d** 02 **p** 03. C Bilston *Lich* 02-07; TV from 07. *8 Cumberland Road, Bilston WV14 6LT* Tel (01902) 497794 Mobile 07905-539111 E-mail janwaterfield@blueyonder.co.uk

WATERFORD, Dean of. *Vacant*

WATERHOUSE, Eric Thomas Benjamin. b 24. Lon Univ 60. Kelham Th Coll 47 Qu Coll Birm 50. **d** 51 **p** 52. C Wolverhampton St Pet *Lich* 51-56; C Lower Gornal 56-57; V Walsall St Mark 57-60; R Kings w Dormston *Worc* 60-64; C Worc St Clem 64-77; P-in-c Abberton, Naunton Beauchamp and Bishampton etc 77-80; R 80-92; rtd 92; Perm to Offic *Worc* from 92. *7 Hazel Avenue, Evesham WR11 1XT* Tel (01386) 421312

WATERHOUSE, Canon Peter. b 34. Chich Th Coll 68. **d** 70 **p** 71. C Consett *Dur* 70-73; C Heworth St Mary 73-76; V Stockton St Chad 76-83; V Lanchester 83-11; P-in-c Holmside 03-11; AD Lanchester 90-99; Hon Can Dur Cathl 91-11; rtd 11. *7 Dissington Place, Whickham, Newcastle upon Tyne NE16 5QX*

WATERMAN, Canon Albert Thomas. b 33. Roch Th Coll 61. **d** 64 **p** 65. C Dartford St Alb *Roch* 64-67; V Ilkeston St Jo *Derby* 67-75; V Mackworth St Fran 75-79; V Dartford St Alb *Roch* 79-98; RD Dartford 84-97; Hon Can Roch Cathl 96-98; rtd 98. *19 Beachfield Road, Bembridge PO35 5TN* Tel (01983) 874286

WATERMAN, Mrs Jacqueline Mahalah. b 45. ALCM71. Cant Sch of Min 82. **dss** 85 **d** 87 **p** 94. Wavertree H Trin *Liv* 85-90; Par Dn 87-90; Par Dn Anfield St Columba 90-94; C 94; TV Speke St Aid 94-97; P-in-c Walton St Jo 97-99; V 99-01; C Baildon *Bradf* 01-05; rtd 05; Perm to Offic *Bradf* from 06. *5 Lansdowne Close, Baildon, Shipley BD17 7LA* Tel (01274) 468556

WATERS (née MUNRO-SMITH), Alison Jean. b 73. Regent's Park Coll Ox MA94. Wycliffe Hall Ox 02. **d** 04 **p** 05. C Lostwithiel, St Winnow w St Nectan's Chpl etc *Truro* 04-08; C

Shepperton and Littleton *Lon* from 08. *Littleton Rectory, Squires Bridge Road, Shepperton TW17 0QE* Tel (01932) 562249 E-mail alisonmunrosmith@hotmail.com

WATERS, Arthur Brian. b 34. St Deiniol's Hawarden 71. **d** 73 **p** 74. C Bedwellty *Mon* 73-76; P-in-c Newport All SS 76-81; V Mynyddislwyn 81-91; C-in-c Maesglas Newport CD 91-95; V Maesglas and Duffryn 95-99; rtd 99. *3B Blaen-y-Pant Crescent, Blaen-y-Pant, Newport NP20 5QB* Tel (01633) 855805

WATERS, Brenda Mary. b 51. Bp Otter Coll. **d** 99. NSM Whyke w Rumboldswhyke and Portfield *Chich* 99-04; NSM Chich Cathl from 05; Chapl St Wilfrid's Hospice Chich from 01. *69 Chatsworth Road, Chichester PO19 7YA* Tel (01243) 839415 E-mail brenda.waters@stwh.co.uk

WATERS, Mrs Carolyn Anne. b 52. St Jo Coll Nottm BA02. **d** 00 **p** 01. NSM Frodsham *Ches* 00-02; C Penhill *Bris* 02-06; P-in-c Stopham and Fittleworth *Chich* 06-09; rtd 09. *5 Leybourne Avenue, Newcastle upon Tyne NE12 7AP* Tel 07789-430317 (mobile) E-mail carolyn.anne.waters@googlemail.com

WATERS, Geoffrey. b 64. UMIST BSc85 St Hild Coll Dur PGCE86 Trin Coll Bris BA99. WMMTC 06. **d** 08 **p** 09. NSM Northampton St Giles *Pet* from 08. *26 The Vale, Northampton NN1 4ST* Tel (01604) 792289 E-mail geoff@stgilesnorthampton.org.uk

WATERS, Miss Jill Christine. b 43. CertEd64. Cranmer Hall Dur 82. **dss** 82 **d** 87 **p** 94. New Milverton *Cov* 82-86; Droitwich-le-Moors w Forsbrook *Lich* 86-96; Par Dn 87-94; C 94-96; P-in-c Mow Cop 96-10; rtd 10. *5 Moreland Croft, Minworth, Sutton Coldfield B76 1XZ* Tel 07908-402143 (mobile) E-mail jill.waters@btinternet.com

WATERS, John Michael. b 30. Qu Coll Cam BA53 MA58. Ridley Hall Cam 53. **d** 55 **p** 56. C Southport Ch Ch *Liv* 55-57; C Farnworth 57-62; V Blackb H Trin 63-70; Sec Birm Coun Chr Chs 70-77; Chapl Birm Cathl 70-74; Dioc Ecum Officer 74-77; V Hednesford *Lich* 77-93; RD Rugeley 78-88; rtd 93; P-in-c Etton w Dalton Holme *York* 93-99; Perm to Offic from 00. *Blacksmith's Cottage, Middlewood Lane, Fylingthorpe, Whitby YO22 4UB* Tel (01947) 880422

WATERS, Kenneth Robert. ERMC. **d** 10 **p** 11. NSM Grimshoe *Ely* from 10. *6 The Avenue, Brookville, Thetford IP26 4RF* Tel (01366) 727220 E-mail ken.waters@btinternet.com

WATERS, Mark. b 51. Southn Univ BTh85. Sarum & Wells Th Coll 79. **d** 82 **p** 83. C Clifton All SS w St Jo *Bris* 82-85; P-in-c Brislington St Anne 85-91; Dioc Soc Resp Officer *Sheff* 91-94; Community Org Citizen Organisation Foundn 94-00; NSM Rotherham 94-97; Hon C Gt Crosby St Faith and Waterloo Park St Mary *Liv* 97-00; NSM 05-09; TV Kirkby 00-04; Project Development Manager Ch Action on Poverty 04-05; Progr Manager Participation for Change from 05; NSM Toxteth Park Ch Ch and St Mich w St Andr *Liv* from 09. *30 Victoria Road West, Crosby, Liverpool L23 8UQ* Tel 0151-931 1031 E-mail markwaters@blueyonder.co.uk

WATERS, Stephen. b 49. Chich Th Coll 83. **d** 85 **p** 86. C Baildon *Bradf* 85-87; C Altrincham St Geo *Ches* 87-89; TV Ellesmere Port 89-91; P-in-c Crewe St Jo 91-93; V Mossley 93-98; TV Congleton 98-99; P-in-c Alvanley 99-02; V Penhill *Bris* 02-05; rtd 05. *5 Leybourne Avenue, Newcastle upon Tyne NE12 7AP* Tel 07796-694139 (mobile) E-mail stephen@soulfriend.org.uk

WATERS, William Paul. b 52. Aston Tr Scheme 84 Chich Th Coll 86. **d** 88 **p** 89. C Tottenham St Paul *Lon* 88-91; C Stroud Green H Trin 91-95; TV Wickford and Runwell *Chelmsf* 95-98; Chapl Runwell Hosp Wickford 95-98; Chapl Qu Medical Cen Nottm Univ Hosp NHS Trust 98-10; C Ilkeston H Trin *Derby* from 10. *22 Teesdale Court, Beeston NG9 5PJ* Tel 0115-917 3429 E-mail paulwat04@gmail.com

WATERSON, Graham Peter. b 50. **d** 07 **p** 08. OLM Astley Bridge *Man* 07-10; NSM Thame *Ox* from 10. *The Rectory, 46 High Street, Tetsworth, Thames OX9 7AS* Tel (01844) 281267 Mobile 07747-757657 E-mail peter.waterson@ntlworld.com

WATERSTONE, Albert Thomas. b 23. TCD BA45 BD67. CITC 46. **d** 46 **p** 47. C Kilkenny St Canice Cathl 46-50; P-in-c Borris-in-Ossory w Aghavoe 50-51; I 52-54; I Fiddown w Kilmacow 54-64; I Tullamore w Lynally and Rahan *M & K* 64-73; I Tullamore w Durrow, Newtownfertullagh, Rahan etc 73-90; Can Meath 81-90; rtd 90. *Lynally House, Mocklagh, Blue Ball, Tullamore, Co Offaly, Republic of Ireland* Tel and fax (00353) (57) 932 1367

WATERSTREET, Canon John Donald. b 34. Trin Hall Cam BA58 MA62. Lich Th Coll 58. **d** 60 **p** 61. C Blackheath *Birm* 60-64; C Aston SS Pet and Paul 64-67; R Sheldon 67-77; RD Coleshill 75-77; V Selly Oak St Mary 77-89; RD Edgbaston 84-89; Hon Can Birm Cathl 86-00; R The Whitacres and Shustoke 89-97; C Acocks Green 97-00; rtd 00; Perm to Offic *Birm* from 00. *547 Fox Hollies Road, Hall Green, Birmingham B28 8RL* Tel 0121-702 2080

WATERTON, Dawn. b 46. WMMTC 95. **d** 98 **p** 99. NSM Nuneaton St Nic *Cov* 98-07; NSM Chilvers Coton w Astley from 07. *65 Main Street, Higham on the Hill, Nuneaton CV13 6AH* Tel (01455) 212861

WATES, John Norman. b 43. JP82. BNC Ox MA65 Solicitor 72 FRSA00 Hon FRAM09. **d** 02 **p** 03. OLM Chipstead *S'wark* from 02. *Elmore, High Road, Chipstead, Coulsdon CR5 3SB* Tel (01737) 557550 Fax 552918 E-mail john.wates@btinternet.com

WATHAN, Geraint David. b 75. Univ of Wales (Abth) BTh01. St Mich Coll Llan. **d** 07 **p** 08. C Oystermouth *S & B* 07-09; C Sketty from 09. *St Barnabas' Vicarage, 57 Sketty Road, Swansea SA2 0EN* Tel (01792) 298342 Mobile 07789-254165 E-mail g_wathan@hotmail.com

WATHEN, Mark William Gerard. b 12. TD45. ACIB. K Coll Lon 31. **d** 82 **p** 82. Hon C Broadford *Arg* 82-91; Hon C Fort William 82-91; Hon C Portree 82-96; rtd 96. *Tollgate Cottage, Norwich Road, Marsham, Norwich NR10 5PX* Tel (01263) 732673

WATHERSTON, Peter David. b 42. Lon Univ BSc69 FCA76. Ridley Hall Cam 75. **d** 77 **p** 78. C Barnsbury St Andr *Lon* 77-81; Chapl Mayflower Family Cen Canning Town *Chelmsf* 81-96; Perm to Offic from 96; Dir First Fruit Charity from 97. *264 Plashet Grove, London E6 1DQ* Tel (020) 8548 4676 Fax 8548 4110 Mobile 07913-694678 E-mail pwatherston@aol.com

WATKIN, David Glynne. b 52. Univ of Wales (Lamp) BA74 PhD78 Wolv Univ PGCE87 MTS FRGS. **d** 02 **p** 03. OLM Wolverhampton St Matt *Lich* 02-10; OLM Bilston from 10; Dioc OLM Officer from 06. *3 Alder Dale, Wolverhampton WV3 9JF* Tel (01902) 710842 E-mail d.g.watkin@wlv.ac.uk

WATKIN, David William. b 42. FCA70. Qu Coll Birm 84. **d** 86 **p** 87. C Tunstall *Lich* 86-89; Camberwell Deanery Missr *S'wark* 89-95; V Trent Vale *Lich* 95-01; V Milton 01-10; rtd 10; Perm to Offic *Lich* from 10. *33 Station Grove, Stoke-on-Trent ST2 7EA* Tel (01782) 253237 E-mail davidwwatkin@hotmail.com

WATKIN, Deborah Gail. b 58. Wolv Univ BEd82. **d** 08 **p** 09. OLM Wolverhampton St Matt *Lich* from 08. *3 Alder Dale, Wolverhampton WV3 9JF* Tel (01902) 710842 E-mail debbie_in_the_classroom@hotmail.co.uk

WATKIN, Paul Stephen George. b 75. Anglia Ruskin Univ BA08. Westcott Ho Cam 06. **d** 08 **p** 09. C Harwich Peninsula *Chelmsf* from 08. *19 Beacon Hill Avenue, Harwich CO12 3NR* Tel (01255) 504322 E-mail psgw100@aol.com

WATKIN, Prof Thomas Glyn. b 52. Pemb Coll Ox BA74 MA77 BCL75 Barrister-at-Law (Middle Temple) 76. Llan Dioc Tr Scheme 89. **d** 92 **p** 94. NSM Roath St Martin *Llan* from 92. *49 Cyncoed Road, Penylan, Cardiff CF23 5SB* Tel (029) 2049 5662

WATKINS, Adrian Raymond. b 57. St Andr Univ MA80. Lon Bible Coll 82. **d** 07 **p** 08. Regional Manager (Asia) CMS from 00; Lic to Offic Amritsar India from 07; Perm to Offic *St E* from 08. *13 Churchill Avenue, Ipswich IP4 5DR* Tel (01473) 434024 Mobile 07958-617665 E-mail adrianrwatkins@aol.com

WATKINS, Mrs Andrea. b 71. ERMC. **d** 08 **p** 09. C Heyford w Stowe Nine Churches and Flore etc *Pet* 08-11; P-in-c Blisworth and Stoke Bruerne w Grafton Regis etc from 11. *The Rectory, 37 High Street, Blisworth, Northampton NN7 3BJ* Tel (01604) 879112 E-mail andrealwatkins@hotmail.co.uk

WATKINS, Anthony John. b 42. St D Coll Lamp BA64. St Steph Ho Ox 64. **d** 66 **p** 67. C E Dulwich St Jo *S'wark* 66-71; C Tewkesbury w Walton Cardiff *Glouc* 71-75; Prec and Chapl Choral Ches Cathl 75-81; V Brixworth w Holcot *Pet* from 81. *The Vicarage, Station Road, Brixworth, Northampton NN6 9DF* Tel (01604) 880286

WATKINS, Charles Mark. b 57. Bradf Univ BTech79. Westcott Ho Cam 06. **d** 08 **p** 09. C Almondbury w Farnley Tyas *Wakef* 08-11; TV Castleford from 11; C Smawthorpe from 11. *St Michael's Vicarage, St Michael's Close, Castleford WF10 4ER* Tel (01977) 511659 Mobile 07828-918678 E-mail wattycm@mac.com

WATKINS, Mrs Christine Dorothy (Sue). b 29. **d** 89 **p** 00. Deacon Port Macquarie Australia 89-95; Chapl Port Macquarie Gen Hosp 89-95; Perm to Offic *Chich* 97-00; NSM Crawley 00-05; NSM Edin Gd Shep 05-06; Lic to Offic Grafton Australia 06-11. *22 Stuart Court, High Street, Kibworth, Leicester LE8 0LR* Tel 0116-279 2954

WATKINS, Christopher. b 43. Sarum & Wells Th Coll 88. **d** 90 **p** 91. C Abergavenny St Mary w Llanwenarth Citra *Mon* 90-94; TV Cwmbran 94-96; TV Wordsley *Worc* 00-09; rtd 09. *287 Malpas Road, Newport NP20 6WA* Tel (01633) 661645 E-mail chriswat@blueyonder.co.uk

WATKINS, David James Hier. b 39. Trin Coll Carmarthen CertEd60 Univ of Wales DipEd67 BEd76. St Mich Coll Llan. **d** 90 **p** 91. NSM Oystermouth *S & B* 90-09; Dioc Youth Chapl 91-09; Lect Gorseinon Coll 92-09; rtd 09; Perm to Offic *S & B* from 09. *10 Lambswell Close, Langland, Swansea SA3 4HJ* Tel (01792) 369742

WATKINS (née ROBERTS), Mrs Gwyneth. b 35. Univ of Wales (Swansea) BA MEd. St Mich Coll Llan 90. **d** 91 **p** 97. C Llanbadarn Fawr w Capel Bangor and Goginan *St D* 91-94; P-in-c Maenordeifi and Capel Colman w Llanfihangel etc 94-97; R 97-98; rtd 98. *17 Carlinford, Boscombe Cliff Road, Bournemouth BH5 1JW* Tel (02102) 391076 E-mail gwynethwatkins1@hotmail.com

WATKINS, Mrs Hilary Odette. b 47. New Hall Cam MA73. SAOMC 98. **d** 01 **p** 02. NSM Appleton and Besselsleigh *Ox* 01-04; C Aisholt, Enmore, Goathurst, Nether Stowey etc *B & W* from 04. *The Rectory, Church Road, Spaxton, Bridgwater TA5 1DA* Tel (01278) 671265 E-mail hilary.watkins1@tesco.net

WATKINS, John Graham. b 48. N Lon Poly CQSW74. WEMTC 04. **d** 07 **p** 08. NSM Ledbury *Heref* from 07. *18 Pound Close, Tarrington, Hereford HR1 4AZ* Tel (01432) 890595 E-mail john.watkins@cafcass.gov.uk

WATKINS, Jonathan. b 58. Padgate Coll of Educn BEd79. Trin Coll Bris 90. **d** 92 **p** 93. C Wallington *S'wark* 92-97; C Hartley Wintney, Elvetham, Winchfield etc 97-99; Chapl Win Univ 99-08; P-in-c Stockbridge and Longstock and Leckford *Win* from 10. *The Rectory, 11 Trafalgar Way, Stockbridge SO20 6ET* Tel (01264) 810810

WATKINS, Michael John. b 61. RGN90. Trin Coll Bris 03. **d** 05 **p** 06. C Bath Weston All SS w N Stoke and Langridge *B & W* 05-09; TV Chippenham St Paul w Hardenhuish etc *Bris* 09-10; TV Kington St Michael 09-10. *Address temp unknown* Tel 07814-430782 (mobile) E-mail mic290361@yahoo.co.uk

WATKINS, Michael Morris. b 32. MRCS60 LRCP60. St Jo Coll Nottm 77. **d** 81 **p** 81. C Hornchurch St Andr *Chelmsf* 81-84; P-in-c Snitterfield w Bearley *Cov* 84-90; V 90-92; rtd 93; Perm to Offic *Cov* from 93. *Glaslyn, Riverside, Tiddington Road, Stratford-upon-Avon CV37 7BD* Tel (01789) 298085 E-mail michaelwatkins@talktalk.net

WATKINS, Ms Betty Anne. See MOCKFORD, Mrs Betty Anne

WATKINS, Canon Peter. b 51. Oak Hill Th Coll BA. **d** 82 **p** 83. C Whitnash *Cov* 82-86; V Winnton and Church Lawford 86-99; RD Rugby 94-99; V Finham 99-10; Hon Can Cov Cathl 04-10; rtd 11. *23 St Margaret's Avenue, Wolston, Coventry CV8 3LJ* Tel (024) 7767 5779 E-mail peter.watkins@talktalk.net

WATKINS, Peter Gordon. b 34. St Pet Coll Ox BA57 MA61. Wycliffe Hall Ox 58. **d** 59 **p** 60. C Wolverhampton St Geo *Lich* 59-60; C Burton St Chad 60-61; C Westmr St Jas *Lon* 61-63; USA 63-65; V Ealing Common St Matt *Lon* from 67. *St Matthew's Vicarage, 7 North Common Road, London W5 2QA* Tel (020) 8567 3820 E-mail peterwatkins@amserve.com

WATKINS, Robert Henry. b 30. New Coll Ox BA54 MA60. Westcott Ho Cam 59. **d** 60 **p** 61. C Newc H Cross 60-63; C Morpeth 63-67; V Delaval 67-80; V Lanercost w Kirkcambeck and Walton *Carl* 80-90; rtd 90; Perm to Offic *Carl* from 90. *Lowpark, Loweswater, Cockermouth CA13 0RU* Tel (01900) 85242

WATKINS, Sue. See WATKINS, Mrs Christine Dorothy

WATKINS, Susan Jane. See HEIGHT, Susan Jane

WATKINS, Canon William Hywel. b 36. St D Coll Lamp BA58. Wycliffe Hall Ox 58. **d** 61 **p** 62. C Llanelli *St D* 61-68; V Llwynhendy 68-72; V Slebech and Uzmaston w Boulston 78-01; RD Daugleddau 87-01; Hon Can St D Cathl 91-93; Can St D Cathl 93-01; rtd 01. *Nant-yr-Arian, Llanbadarn Fawr, Aberystwyth SY23 3SZ* Tel and fax (01970) 623359

WATKINS-JONES, Arthur Basil. b 24. Sarum Th Coll 67. **d** 69 **p** 70. C Broadstone *Sarum* 69-73; P-in-c Winterbourne Stickland and Turnworth etc 73-76; R 76-78; P-in-c Lilliput 78-82; V 82-89; rtd 89; Perm to Offic *Sarum* from 89. *Oak Cottage, 31 Danecourt Road, Poole BH14 0PG* Tel (01202) 746074

WATKINSON, Adam John McNicol. b 68. Keble Coll Ox BA89 MA93 St Martin's Coll Lanc PGCE90. NOC 01. **d** 03 **p** 04. NSM Croston and Bretherton *Blackb* 03-05; Chapl Ormskirk Sch 02-03; Chapl Liv Coll 03-06; Chapl Repton Sch Derby from 06. *4 Boot Hill, Repton, Derby DE65 6FT* Tel (01283) 559284 E-mail ajw@repton.org.uk

WATKINSON, Neil. b 64. Univ Coll Lon BSc86. Oak Hill Th Coll BA04. **d** 04 **p** 05. C Maidenhead St Andr and St Mary *Ox* 04-08; C Singapore St Geo from 08. *St George's Church, Minden Road, Singapore 248816, Republic of Singapore* Tel (0065) 6473 2877 E-mail info@stgeorges.org.sg

WATKINSON, Ronald Frank. b 48. BA. EAMTC. **d** 04 **p** 05. NSM Paston *Pet* 04-10; P-in-c Pet St Paul from 10. *St Paul's Vicarage, 414 Lincoln Road, Peterborough PE1 2PA* Tel (01733) 314117 E-mail revronkingdomyouth@btinternet.com

WATKINSON, Stephen Philip. b 75. York Univ BSc96 DPhil03 Edin Univ MSc97. Oak Hill Th Coll BTh09. **d** 09 **p** 10. C Blackb Redeemer from 09. *17 Douglas Close, Blackburn BB2 4FF* Tel 07793-143393 (mobile) E-mail spwatkinson@talktalk.net

WATLING, His Honour Brian. b 35. QC79. K Coll Lon LLB56 Barrister 57. **d** 87 **p** 88. NSM Lavenham *St E* 87-90; NSM Nayland w Wiston 90-03; NSM Boxford, Edwardstone, Groton etc 03-07; Perm to Offic from 07. *5 High Street, Nayland, Colchester CO6 4JE*

WATLING, Sister Rosemary Dawn. b 32. Newnham Coll Cam BA70 MA73. Gilmore Course 70. **dss** 85 **d** 87 **p** 94. CSA 79-90; Paddington St Mary *Lon* 85-86; E Bris 86-87; Hon Par Dn 87; Par Dn Clifton H Trin, St Andr and St Pet 87-94; C 94-95; rtd 95; NSM Wraxall *B & W* 96-02; Perm to Offic 02-08. *20 Gracey Court, Woodland Road, Broadclyst, Exeter EX5 3GA* Tel (01392) 460319

WATSON, Adam Stewart. b 75. Southn Univ BA99 Chich Univ QTS05. St Jo Coll Nottm 08. **d** 10 **p** 11. C Alton *Win* from 10. *13 Walnut Close, Alton GU34 2BA* Tel (01420) 362054 E-mail watson_adam3@sky.com

WATSON, Canon Alan. b 34. Lon Univ LLB58. Linc Th Coll 58. **d** 60 **p** 61. C Spring Park *Cant* 60-63; C Sheerness H Trin w St Paul 63-68; R Allington 68-73; P-in-c Maidstone St Pet 73; R Allington and Maidstone St Pet 73-99; Hon Can Cant Cathl 85-99; RD Sutton 86-92; rtd 99; Perm to Offic *B & W* and *Sarum* from 00. *68 Southgate Drive, Wincanton BA9 9ET* Tel (01963) 34368 E-mail are48@mypostoffice.co.uk

WATSON, Alan. b 41. AKC64. St Boniface Warminster. **d** 65 **p** 66. C Hendon St Ignatius *Dur* 65-68; C Sheff St Cecilia Parson Cross 68-70; C Harton Colliery *Dur* 70-72; TV 72-74; R Gorton Our Lady and St Thos *Man* 74-82; TR Swinton St Pet 82-87; TR Swinton and Pendlebury 87-89; R Rawmarsh w Parkgate *Sheff* 89-94; P-in-c Dunscroft St Edwin 96-99; V 99-09; rtd 10; Perm to Offic *Sheff* from 10; CMP from 98. *27 Gleadless Drive, Sheffield S12 2QL* Tel 0114-265 5407 E-mail alan@alanwatsonb.wanadoo.co.uk

WATSON, Albert Victor. b 44. Ridley Hall Cam 85. **d** 87 **p** 88. C Hornchurch St Andr *Chelmsf* 87-94; P-in-c Tye Green w Netteswell 94-95; R from 95; RD Harlow 99-04. *The Rectory, Tawneys Road, Harlow CM18 6QR* Tel (01279) 425138 E-mail albert@watson2119.fsworld.co.uk

WATSON, Alfred Keith. b 39. Birm Univ BSc61. Ox Min Course 93. **d** 96 **p** 97. NSM Aylesbury w Bierton and Hulcott *Ox* 96-01; NSM Ludgvan, Marazion, St Hilary and Perranuthnoe *Truro* 01-06; rtd 06. *Studio Cottage, Wesley Square, Mousehole, Penzance TR19 6RU* Tel (01736) 732906 Mobile 07963-434697

✠**WATSON, The Rt Revd Andrew John.** b 61. CCC Cam BA82 MA90. Ridley Hall Cam 84. **d** 87 **p** 88 **c** 08. C Ipsley *Worc* 87-91; C Notting Hill St Jo and St Pet *Lon* 91-96; V E Twickenham St Steph 96-08; AD Hampton 03-08; Suff Bp Aston *Birm* from 08. *Bishop's Lodge, 16 Coleshill Street, Sutton Coldfield B72 1SH* Tel 0121-427 5141 *or* 354 6632 Fax 428 1114 E-mail bishopofaston@birmingham.anglican.org

WATSON, Andrew Murray. b 57. St Jo Coll Nottm BA07. **d** 07 **p** 09. C Kennington St Jo w St Jas *S'wark* 07-09; C Sanderstead from 09. *285 Limpsfield Road, South Croydon CR2 9DG* Tel (020) 3252 2045 Mobile 07970-677241 E-mail andrew.email@btopenworld.com

WATSON, Anne-Marie Louise. See RENSHAW, Mrs Anne-Marie Louise

WATSON, Beverly Anne. b 64. K Coll Cam BA86 MA90 Surrey Univ MA08 ALCM83. STETS 05. **d** 08 **p** 09. C Spring Grove St Mary *Lon* 08; C Aston and Nechells *Birm* from 08. *Bishop's Lodge, 16 Coleshill Street, Sutton Coldfield B72 1SH* Tel 0121-355 3365 Mobile 07895-197940 E-mail beverly@watsons.myzen.co.uk

WATSON, Craig. b 60. Bath Univ BSc82 CertEd82 York St Jo Coll MA04. NOC 00. **d** 03 **p** 04. NSM Thorpe Edge *Bradf* 03-04; NSM Halliwell St Pet *Man* from 04. *39 New Church Road, Bolton BL1 5QQ* Tel (01204) 457559 E-mail craig@stpetersparish.info

WATSON, David. See WATSON, Canon Leonard Alexander David

WATSON, The Very Revd Derek Richard. b 38. Selw Coll Cam BA61 MA65. Cuddesdon Coll 62. **d** 64 **p** 65. C New Eltham All SS *S'wark* 64-66; Chapl Ch Coll Cam 66-70; Bp's Dom Chapl *S'wark* 70-73; V Surbiton St Mark 73-77; V Surbiton St Andr and St Mark 77-78; Can Res and Treas S'wark Cathl 78-82; Dioc Dir of Ords 78-82; P-in-c Chelsea St Luke *Lon* 82-85; R 85-87; P-in-c Chelsea Ch Ch 86-87; R Chelsea St Luke and Ch Ch 87-96; AD Chelsea 90-96; Dean Sarum 96-02; rtd 02. *29 The Precincts, Canterbury CT1 2EP* Tel (01227) 865238

WATSON, Derek Stanley. b 54. NEOC 92. **d** 95 **p** 96. C W Acklam *York* 95-98; C-in-c Ingleby Barwick CD 98-00; V Ingleby Barwick 00-06; V Middlesbrough St Martin w St Cuth from 06. *St Chad's Vicarage, Emerson Avenue, Linthorpe, Middlesbrough TS5 7QW* Tel (01642) 814999 E-mail derek@watson1954.freeserve.co.uk

WATSON, Mrs Diane Elsie. b 44. NOC 92. **d** 95 **p** 96. C Grange St Andr *Ches* 95-00; C Runcorn H Trin 96-00; R Thurstaston 00-07; rtd 07. C Oxton *Ches* from 08. *32 School Lane, Prenton CH43 7RQ* Tel 0151-652 4288 E-mail de.watson@btinternet.com

WATSON, Mrs Elsada Beatrice (Elsie). b 30. WMMTC. **d** 89 **p** 94. NSM Birm St Pet 89-90; NSM Lozells St Paul and St Silas 90-93; Par Dn 93-94; C 94-96; Perm to Offic from 96; rtd 96. *4 Maidstone Road, Birmingham B20 3EH* Tel 0121-356 0626

WATSON, Emma Louise. b 69. Birm Univ BA91 Leeds Metrop Univ BSc97. St Jo Coll Nottm. **d** 10 **p** 11. NSM Birkenhead Priory *Ches* from 10. *3 Beech Road, Bebington, Wirral CH63 8PE* Tel 0151-200 0644 E-mail emlowat@tiscali.co.uk

WATSON, Geoffrey. b 48. Liv Univ BEd71. Linc Th Coll 81. **d** 83 **p** 84. C Hartlepool St Luke *Dur* 83-87; P-in-c Shadforth 87-94; Soc Resp Officer 87-94; Dioc Rural Development Adv 90-94; V Staveley, Ings and Kentmere *Carl* from 94. *The Vicarage,*

Kentmere Road, Staveley, Kendal LA8 9PA Tel (01539) 821267 E-mail geof_watson@talktalk.net

WATSON, Mrs Gillian Edith. b 49. Cov Coll of Educn CertEd70. LCTP 06. d 09 p 10. NSM Standish *Blackb* from 09; Chapl Wrightington Wigan and Leigh NHS Trust from 09. *89 Whitehall Avenue, Appley Bridge, Wigan WN6 9JY* Tel (01257) 251326 *or* (01942) 822324 E-mail gillian.e.watson@gmail.com

WATSON, Gordon Mark Stewart. b 67. Wolv Poly BA90 DipEd. CITC BTh95. d 95 p 96. C Ballymoney w Finvoy and Rasharkin *Conn* 95-98; I Brackaville w Donaghendry and Ballyclog *Arm* 98-01; I Killesher K, E & A 01-06; I Trory w Killadeas *Clogh* from 06. *Trory Rectory, Rossfad, Ballinamallard, Enniskillen BT94 2LS* Tel and fax (028) 6638 8477 Mobile 07710-924660 E-mail trory@clogher.anglican.org

WATSON, Graeme Campbell Hubert. b 35. Ch Ch Ox BA58 BA59 MA61. Coll of Resurr Mirfield 59. d 61 p 62. C Edin St Mary 61-63; C Carrington *S'well* 63-67; Tanzania 67-77; Tutor St Cyprian's Coll Ngala 67-69; Vice-Prin St Mark's Th Coll Dar es Salaam 69-73; P-in-c Dar es Salaam St Alb 74-77; P-in-c Kingston St Mary w Broomfield *B & W* 77-80; V 80-81; R Kingston St Mary w Broomfield etc 81-95; P-in-c Feock *Truro* 95-00; Tutor SWMTC 95-00; rtd 00; Perm to Offic *Truro* 00-02 and *Lon* from 02. *75 Winston Road, London N16 9LN* Tel (020) 7249 8701 E-mail gchwatson@blueyonder.co.uk

WATSON, Hartley Roger. b 40. Lon Univ BD91 MTh94. K Coll Lon. d 64 p 65. C Noel Park St Mark *Lon* 64-67; C Munster Square St Mary Magd 67-68; C Stamford Hill St Jo 68-70; Chapl RAF 70-76; R St Breoke *Truro* 76-84; P-in-c Egloshayle 82-84; R Wittering w Thornhaugh and Wansford *Pet* 84-00; RD Barnack 98-00; R Brigstock w Stanion and Lowick and Sudborough 00-07; rtd 07; Chapl Beauchamp Community from 07. *The Chaplain's House, Newland, Malvern WR13 5AX* Tel (01684) 891529 *or* 562100

WATSON, Henry Stanley. b 36. d 72 p 74. NSM Bethnal Green St Jas Less *Lon* 72-83 and 89-93; NSM Old Ford St Paul w St Steph and St Mark 83-88; NSM Scarborough St Mary w Ch Ch and H Apostles *York* 93-97; P-in-c Seamer 97-03; rtd 03; Hon C Fauls *Lich* 03-08. *14 Oakfield Park, Much Wenlock TF13 6HJ* Tel (01952) 728794

WATSON, The Ven Ian Leslie Stewart. b 50. Wycliffe Hall Ox 79. d 81 p 82. C Plymouth St Andr w St Paul and St Geo *Ex* 81-85; TV Ilsley *Wore* 85-90; V Woodley St Jo the Ev *Ox* 90-92; TR Woodley 92-95; Chapl Amsterdam w Den Helder and Heiloo *Eur* 95-01; Chief Exec ICS 01-07; Can Gib Cathl 02-07; Adn Cov from 07. *9 Armorial Road, Coventry CV3 6GH* Tel (024) 7641 7750 *or* 7652 1337 Mobile 07714-214790 E-mail ian.watson@covcofe.org *or* bootsandden@hotmail.com

WATSON, James Valentine John Giles. b 65. Newc Univ BA87 Ox Univ BA91 MA97. Ripon Coll Cuddesdon 89. d 92 p 93. C Newc St Geo 92-95; TV Daventry, Ashby St Ledgers, Braunston etc *Pet* 95-00; V Woodplumpton *Blackb* 00-03; TR Wheatley *Ox* 03-10; Chapl Old Buckenham Hall Sch from 10. *Old Buckenham Hall School, Brettenham, Ipswich IP7 7PH* Tel (01449) 740252 E-mail jvjgwatson1@gmail.com

WATSON, The Ven Jeffrey John Seagrief. b 39. Em Coll Cam BA61 MA65. Clifton Th Coll 62. d 65 p 66. C Beckenham Ch Ch *Roch* 65-69; C Southsea St Jude *Portsm* 69-71; V Win Ch Ch 71-81; V Bitterne 81-93; RD Southampton 83-93; Hon Can Win Cathl 91-93; Adn Win 93-04; Hon Can Ely Cathl 93-04; rtd 04; Perm to Offic *Win* from 04. *7 Ferry Road, Hythe, Southampton SO45 5GB* Tel (023) 8084 1189

WATSON, John. b 34. AKC59. d 60 p 61. C Stockton St Pet *Dur* 60-64; C Darlington H Trin 64-66; V Swalwell 66-68; Perm to Offic *Dur* 68-69; *Leic* 69-74; *Man* 74-76; rtd 76. *The Flat, 194 Abington Avenue, Northampton NN1 4QA* Tel (01604) 624300 E-mail john.moirawatson@virginmedia.com

WATSON, John Calum. b 69. Spurgeon's Coll BD96. Trin Coll Bris MA03. d 03 p 04. C Richmond H Trin and Ch Ch *S'wark* 03-06; TV Deptford St Jo w H Trin and Ascension 06-08; V Tupsley w Hampton Bishop *Heref* from 08. *The Vicarage, 107 Church Road, Hereford HR1 1RT* Tel (01432) 379110 E-mail john@allyu.org.uk

WATSON, Preb John Francis Wentworth. b 28. St Jo Coll Nottm LTh59. d 59 p 60. C Egham *Guildf* 59-62; C-in-c Ewell St Paul Howell Hill CD 62-66; R Ashtead 66-72; V Plymouth St Andr w St Paul and St Geo *Ex* 72-96; Angl Adv TV SW 83-93; Westcountry TV 93-94; Preb Ex Cathl 84-94; rtd 94; Perm to Offic *Ex* from 97. *Woodland House, Western Road, Ivybridge PL21 9AL* Tel (01752) 893735

WATSON, John Lionel. b 39. G&C Coll Cam BA61 MA65. Ridley Hall Cam 62. d 64 p 65. C Toxteth Park St Philemon w St Silas *Liv* 64-69; C Morden *S'wark* 69-73; C Cambridge St Phil *Ely* 73-74; Chapl Elstree Sch Woolhampton 74-77; R Woolhampton w Midgham *Ox* 77-81; R Woolhampton w Midgham and Beenham Valance 81-95; Perm to Offic *Win* from 97; rtd 00. *Westfield House, Littleton Road, Crawley, Winchester SO21 2QD* Tel (01962) 776892

WATSON, Jonathan Ramsay George. b 38. Oriel Coll Ox BA61 MA65 DipEd62. Ridley Hall Cam 88. d 90 p 91. C Locks Heath *Portsm* 90-94; V Erith St Paul *Roch* 94-01; rtd 01; Perm to Offic Chich from 01. *14 Park Crescent, Midhurst GU29 9ED* Tel (01730) 816145 E-mail jrgwatson@netscapeonline.co.uk

WATSON, Julie Ann. b 61. Westcott Ho Cam. d 11. C Malvern Link w Cowleigh *Worc* from 11. *4 Malus Close, Malvern WR14 2WD* Tel (01684) 564848

WATSON, Julie Sandra. b 59. Liv Poly BSc81 Teesside Poly PhD86. NEOC 99. d 02 p 03. NSM Redcar *York* from 02; Dean Self-Supporting Min from 09. *20 Talisker Gardens, Redcar TS10 2TG* Tel (01642) 478147 E-mail j.s.watson@tees.ac.uk

WATSON, Keith. See WATSON, Alfred Keith

WATSON, Kenneth Roy. b 27. CEng68 MIMechE68. EMMTC 83. d 86 p 87. NSM Ashby-de-la-Zouch St Helen w Coleorton 90-93; rtd 93; Perm to Offic *Leic* and *Derby* from 93. *36 Chatsworth Court, Park View, Ashbourne DE6 1PF* Tel (01335) 343929

WATSON, Laurence Leslie. b 31. Keble Coll Ox BA55 MA59. Ely Th Coll. d 57 p 58. C Solihull *Birm* 57-60; C Digswell *St Alb* 60-62; V Smethwick St Steph *Birm* 62-67; V Billesley Common 67-95; rtd 95; Perm to Offic *Cov* and *Birm* from 95. *10 Redwing Close, Bishopton, Stratford-upon-Avon CV37 9EX* Tel (01789) 294569

WATSON, Canon Leonard Alexander David. b 37. Man Univ BSc59. Coll of Resurr Mirfield 62. d 64 p 65. C Rawmarsh w Parkgate *Sheff* 64-68; C Empangeni S Africa 69-74; TV E Runcorn w Halton *Ches* 74-79; TV Sanderstead All SS *S'wark* 79-86; TR Selsdon St Jo w St Fran 86-98; RD Croydon Addington 90-95; P-in-c Horne and Outwood 98-02; Hon Can S'wark Cathl 02-03; rtd 02; Perm to Offic *Win* from 03. *White Gables, Station Road, East Tisted, Alton GU34 3QX* Tel (01420) 588317 E-mail dadiwatson@hotmail.com

WATSON, Mark. See WATSON, Gordon Mark Stewart

WATSON, Mark Edward. b 68. Birm Univ BEng91. St Jo Coll Nottm 07. d 09 p 10. C Higher Bebington *Ches* from 09. *3 Beech Road, Bebington, Wirral CH63 8PE* Tel 0151-200 0644 Mobile 07838-441568 E-mail mewatson@tiscali.co.uk

WATSON, Michael Paul. b 58. Trin Coll Bris 91. d 93 p 94. C Derby St Alkmund and St Werburgh 93-99; Lt Rock St Andr USA 00-01; R Bridge Community Austin from 01. *10636 Floral Park Drive, Austin TX 78759-5104, USA* Tel (001) (512) 527 8823 E-mail mike.bridgepoint@worldnet.att.net

WATSON, Nicholas Edgar. b 67. St Cath Coll Cam BA88 MA92. Wycliffe Hall Ox BA91. d 92 p 93. C Benfieldside *Dur* 92-95; C-in-c Stockton Green Vale H Trin CD 95-96; P-in-c Stockton H Trin 96-00; Chapl Ian Ramsey Sch Stockton 95-00; P-in-c Breadsall and Warden of Readers *Derby* 00-09; TR Wednesfield *Lich* from 09. *The Rectory, 9 Vicarage Road, Wednesfield, Wolverhampton WV11 1SB* Tel (01902) 731462 E-mail newatson@btopenworld.com

WATSON, Prof Paul Frederick. b 44. MRCVS69 RVC(Lon) BSc66 BVetMed69 Sydney Univ PhD73 Lon Univ DSc95. Oak Hill NSM Course 86. d 88 p 89. NSM Muswell Hill St Jas w St Matt *Lon* 88-96; NSM Edmonton St Aldhelm 96-01; Perm to Offic *Lon* and *St Alb* from 01. *50 New Road, Ware SG12 7BY* Tel (01920) 466941 E-mail pwatson@rvc.ac.uk

WATSON, Paul Robert. b 66. St Andr Univ MA89 Glas Univ BD95 MTh00. d 00 p 01. C Glas St Ninian 00-04; R Bieldside *Ab* from 09. *The Rectory, Baillieswells Road, Bieldside, Aberdeen AB15 9AP* Tel (01224) 861552 E-mail paul@stdevenicks.org.uk

WATSON, Paul William. b 55. Huddersfield Poly BA. St Jo Coll Nottm. d 86 p 87. C Meltham Mills *Wakef* 86-89; C Meltham 89-90; TV Borehamwood *St Alb* 90-96; V Oswaldtwistle Immanuel and All SS *Blackb* 96-08; rtd 08. *214 Union Road, Oswaldtwistle, Accrington BB5 3EG* Tel (01254) 381441

WATSON, Peter David. b 69. St Andr Univ MA92 Westmr Coll Ox PGCE93. Cranmer Hall Dur 04. d 06 p 07. C Boston Spa and Thorp Arch w Walton *York* 06-10; R Brayton from 10. *The Rectory, Doncaster Road, Brayton, Selby YO8 9HE* Tel (01757) 704707 E-mail petercharlotte@pwatson14.freeserve.co.uk

WATSON, Philip. b 60. RGN83. Qu Coll Birm 86. d 89 p 90. C Ordsall *S'well* 89-93; TV Benwell *Newc* 93-99; V Stocking Farm *Leic* 99-10; R Barwell w Potters Marston and Stapleton from 10. *The Rectory, 14 Church Lane, Barwell, Leicester LE9 8DG* Tel (01455) 446993 E-mail frpwatson@aol.com

WATSON, Richard Francis. b 40. Yorks Min Course 08. d 09 p 10. NSM Ilkley All SS *Bradf* from 09. *23 St Helen's Way, Ilkley LS29 8NP* Tel (01943) 430108

WATSON, Canon Richard Frederick. b 66. Avery Hill Coll BA87. Trin Coll Bris 91. d 93 p 94. C Kempston Transfiguration *St Alb* 93-97; TV Dunstable 97-03; R E Barnet from 03; RD Barnet 05-11; Can Res and Sub-Dean St Alb from 11. *Deanery Barn, Sumpter Yard, Holywell Hill, St Albans AL1 1BY* Tel (01727) 890201 E-mail rf.watson@btopenworld.com *or* subdean@stalbanscathedral.org

WATSON, Richard Rydill. b 47. Sarum & Wells Th Coll 74. **d** 77 **p** 78. C Cayton w Eastfield *York* 77-80; C Howden 80-82; P-in-c Burton Pidsea and Humbleton w Elsternwick 82-83; V Dormanstown 83-87; V Cotehill and Cumwhinton *Carl* 87-89; Chapl Harrogate Distr and Gen Hosp 89-94; Chapl Harrogate Health Care NHS Trust 94-99; Asst Chapl Oldham NHS Trust 99-02; Asst Chapl Pennine Acute Hosps NHS Trust 02-07; Chapl from 07; P-in-c Shaw *Man* 99-07. *North Manchester General Hospital, Delaunays Road, Manchester M8 6RB* Tel 0161-795 4567

WATSON, Robert Bewley. b 34. Bris Univ BA59. Clifton Th Coll 56. **d** 61 **p** 62. C Bebington *Ches* 61-65; C Woking St Jo *Guildf* 65-68; V Knaphill 68-98; rtd 98; Perm to Offic *Guildf* from 98. *Endrise, 1 Wychelm Road, Lightwater GU18 5RT* Tel (01276) 453822

WATSON, Roger. See WATSON, Hartley Roger

WATSON, The Ven Sheila Anne. b 53. St Andr Univ MA75 MPhil80. Edin Th Coll 79. **dss** 79 **d** 87 **p** 94. Bridge of Allan *St And* 79-80; Alloa 79-80; Monkseaton St Mary *Newc* 80-84; Adult Educn Officer *Lon* 84-87; Hon C Chelsea St Luke and Ch 87-96; Selection Sec ABM 92-93; Sen Selection Sec 93-96; Adv on CME *Sarum* 97-02; Dir of Min 98-02; Can and Preb Sarum Cathl 00-02; Adn Buckingham *Ox* 02-07; Adn Cant and Can Res Cant Cathl from 07. *29 The Precincts, Canterbury CT1 2EP* Tel (01227) 865238 E-mail archdeacon@canterbury-cathedral.org

WATSON, Stephanie Abigail. See MOYES, Mrs Stephanie Abigail

WATSON, Timothy Daniel. b 71. ERMC. **d** 11. C Liv Cathl from 11. *20 Lady Chapel Close, Liverpool L1 7BZ*

WATSON, Canon Timothy Patrick. b 38. ALCD66. **d** 66 **p** 67. C Northwood Em *Lon* 66-70; TV High Wycombe *Ox* 70-76; Gen Sec ICS 76-82; R Bath Weston All SS w N Stoke *B & W* 82-93; R Bath Weston All SS w N Stoke and Langridge 93-94; TR Cheltenham St Mary, St Matt, St Paul and H Trin *Glouc* 94-03; rtd 03; Perm to Offic *Glouc* from 04; Can Kitgum from 05. *The Gateways, Farm Lane, Leckhampton, Cheltenham GL53 0NN* Tel (01242) 514298 E-mail tigertimwatson@yahoo.co.uk

WATSON, William. b 36. Ripon Hall Ox 64. **d** 66 **p** 67. C Leamington Priors H Trin *Cov* 66-69; V Salford Priors 69-74; V Malin Bridge *Sheff* 74-79; Chapl Shrewsbury R Hosps 79-89; Chapl R Hallamshire Hosp Sheff 89-92; Chapl Cen Sheff Univ Hosps NHS Trust 92-93; P-in-c Alveley and Quatt *Heref* 93-96; Chapl N Gen Hosp NHS Trust Sheff 96-01; Chapl Weston Park Hosp Sheff 96-99; Chapl Cen Sheff Univ Hosps NHS Trust 99-01; rtd 96; Perm to Offic *Sheff* 01-07. *101 Larkfield Lane, Southport PR9 8NP* Tel (01704) 226055

WATSON, William Henry Dunbar. b 31. Univ of W Ontario BA60. **d** 58 **p** 60. C Westmr St Jas *Lon* 58-60; Canada 60-04; Asst Chapl and Prec Gibraltar Cathl 04-10. *1803-30 Hillsboro Avenue, Toronto ON M5R 1S7, Canada*

WATSON, William Lysander Rowan. b 26. TCD BA47 MA50 Clare Coll Cam MA52 St Pet Hall Ox MA57. **d** 49 **p** 50. C Chapelizod and Kilmainham *D & G* 49-51; Tutor Ridley Hall Cam 51-55; Chapl 55-57; Chapl St Pet Coll Ox 57-93; Fell and Tutor 59-93; Sen Tutor 77-81; Vice Master 83-85; Lect Th Ox Univ 60-93; rtd 93. *Llandaff Barn, 11 Thames Street, Eynsham, Witney OX29 4HF* Tel (01865) 464198 E-mail lysander.watson@ntlworld.com

WATSON WILLIAMS, Richard Hamilton Patrick. b 31. SS Coll Cam BA57 MA62. St Aug Coll Cant. **d** 59 **p** 60. C Dorking St Paul *Guildf* 59-63; C Portsea St Mary *Portsm* 63-66; V Culgaith *Carl* 66-71; V Kirkland 66-71; V Wigton 72-79; Warden Dioc Conf Ho Crawshawbooth *Man* 79-82; P-in-c Crawshawbooth 79-82; Master Lady Kath Leveson Hosp 82-98; P-in-c Temple Balsall *Birm* 82-84; V 84-98; rtd 98; Perm to Offic *Glouc* from 98. *16 Barton Mews, Barton Road, Tewkesbury GL20 5RP* Tel (01684) 290509

WATT, The Very Revd Alfred Ian. b 34. FRSA95. Edin Th Coll 57. **d** 60 **p** 61. Chapl St Paul's Cathl Dundee 60-63; Prec 63-66; P-in-c Dundee H Cross 64-66; R Arbroath 66-69; R Perth St Ninian *St And* 69-82; Provost St Ninian's Cathl Perth 69-82; Can St Ninian's Cathl Perth 82-98; R Kinross 82-95; Dean St Andr 89-98; rtd 98. *33 Stirling Road, Milnathort, Kinross KY13 9XS* Tel and fax (01577) 865711 E-mail alfred@alfredwatt4.orangehome.co.uk

WATT-WYNESS, Gordon. b 25. St Jo Coll Dur 70. **d** 72 **p** 73. C Scarborough St Mary w Ch Ch, St Paul and St Thos *York* 72-76; R Rossington *Sheff* 76-90; rtd 90; Perm to Offic *York* 90-11. *15 Newton Court, Crescent Road, Filey YO14 9LL* Tel (01723) 516608

WATTERS, Mrs Kay. b 44. SAOMC 98. **d** 01 **p** 02. OLM Prestwood and Gt Hampden *Ox* 01-07; Chapl to Bp Buckingham 04-07; rtd 07; Perm to Offic *Ox* and Cyprus and the Gulf from 07. *44 Akamantos, 8700 Drouseia, Paphos, Cyprus* Tel (00357) (26) 332128 E-mail kay watters@hotmail.com

WATTERSON, Canon Susan Mary. b 50. S & M Dioc Inst 84. **d** 87 **p** 94. NSM Rushen *S & M* 87-89; Hon Par Dn Castletown

89-94; C 94-96; Dioc Youth Officer 87-91; Bp's Adv for Healing Min 91-94; Asst Chapl Bris Univ 96-99; Hon C Bris St Mich and St Paul 96-99; Project Leader Galway Chr Tr Inst 99-00; I Youghal Union *C, C & R* 00-03; Dir Ch's Min of Healing 03-07; P-in-c Killarney w Aghadoe and Muckross *L & K* from 07; Can Limerick, Killaloe and Clonfert Cathls from 10. *The Rectory, Rookery Road, Ballycasheen, Killarney, Co Kerry, Republic of Ireland* Tel (00353) (64) 31832

WATTLEY, Jeffery Richard. b 57. Univ of Wales (Abth) BSc(Econ)79. Trin Coll Bris BA92. **d** 92 **p** 93. C Reading Greyfriars *Ox* 92-96; V Wonersh *Guildf* 96-98; V Wonersh w Blackheath 98-06; V Egham from 06. *Mauley Cottage, 13 Manorcrofts Road, Egham TW20 9LU* Tel (01784) 432066 E-mail jeff@stjohnsegham.com

WATTS, Mrs Aline Patricia. b 57. St Jo Coll Nottm 02. **d** 04 **p** 05. C Lache cum Saltney *Ches* 04-08; P-in-c Leasowe from 08. *St Chad's Vicarage, 70 Castleway North, Wirral CH46 1RW* Tel 0151-677 6889 E-mail alinewatts@tiscali.co.uk

WATTS, Canon Anthony George. b 46. K Coll Lon BD69 AKC69 Lon Univ CertEd70. Sarum & Wells Th Coll 82. **d** 84 **p** 85. C Wimborne Minster and Holt *Sarum* 84-87; P-in-c Shilling Okeford 87-92; Chapl Croft Ho Sch Shillingstone 87-92; R W Parley *Sarum* 92-00; RD Wimborne 98-00; TR Cley Hill Warminster 00-06; Can and Preb Sarum Cathl 00-06; rtd 06; Chapl Warminster Sch from 07. *2 Freesia Close, Warminster BA12 7RL* Tel (01985) 847302 E-mail tandgwatts@aol.com

WATTS, Anthony John. b 30. AKC59. **d** 60 **p** 61. C Whitburn *Dur* 60-63; C Croxdale 63-65; V Warrington St Pet *Liv* 65-70; V Peel *Man* 70-78; P-in-c Bury St Mark 78-81; V Davyhulme Ch Ch 81-99; Chapl Trafford Gen Hosp 89-94; Chapl Trafford Healthcare NHS Trust 94-98; rtd 99; Perm to Offic *Ches* from 00. *11 Brackenfield Way, Winsford CW7 2UX* Tel (01606) 590803

WATTS, Daniel John. b 70. Wycliffe Hall Ox 04. **d** 06 **p** 07. C Paddock Wood *Roch* 06-09; C Harrogate St Mark *Ripon* from 09. *20 Stone Rings Lane, Harrogate HG2 9HY* Tel 07977-126438 (mobile) E-mail daniel.watts11@btinternet.com

WATTS, David Henry. b 27. Ex Coll Ox BA50 MA55. Wells Th Coll 51. **d** 53 **p** 54. C Haslemere *Guildf* 53-55; C Chelmsf Cathl 55-58; Succ Chelmsf Cathl 55-58; V Chessington *Guildf* 58-62; Educn Officer Essex Educn Cttee 62-70; HMI of Schs 70-87; Hon C Wetherby *Ripon* 79-87; P-in-c Healaugh w Wighill, Bilbrough and Askham Richard *York* 87-89; Chapl HM Pris Askham Grange 87-96; rtd 89; Perm to Offic *York* from 98. *24 Grove Road, Boston Spa, Wetherby LS23 6AP* Tel (01937) 842317

WATTS, Canon Frank Walter. b 30. St Boniface Warminster 53 K Coll Lon AKC54. **d** 54 **p** 55. C Llandough w Leckwith 54-56; C Llanishen and Lisvane 56-59; C Gt Marlow *Ox* 59-60; R Black Bourton 60-63; V Carterton 60-63; C-in-c Brize Norton 61-63; V Brize Norton and Carterton 63-69; Australia from 69; Hon Can Perth from 78; rtd 95. *Villa 5, 178-180 Fern Road, Wilson WA 6107, Australia* Tel and fax (0061) (8) 9258 4532 Mobile 408-094991 E-mail frawawa@southwest.com.au

WATTS, Canon Fraser Norman. b 46. Magd Coll Ox BA68 MA74 K Coll Lon MSc70 PhD75 CPsychol89 FBPsS80. Westcott Ho Cam 88. **d** 90 **p** 91. NSM Harston w Hauxton *Ely* 90-95; P-in-c 91-95; Fell Qu Coll Cam from 94; Lect Cam Univ from 94; Chapl Cam St Edw *Ely* from 95; Hon Can Ely Cathl from 08. *19 Grantchester Road, Cambridge CB3 9ED* Tel (01223) 359253 Fax 763003 E-mail fnw1001@hermes.cam.ac.uk

WATTS, Gordon Sidney Stewart. b 40. CITC 63. **d** 66 **p** 67. C Belfast St Steph *Conn* 66-69; CF 69-94; V Boldre w S Baddesley *Win* 94-96; P-in-c Warmfield *Wakef* 96-02; Sub Chapl HM Pris Wakef 97-02; Chapl Huggens Coll Northfleet 02-07; rtd 07. *8 Bramwell Avenue, Prenton CH43 0RH* Tel 0151-200 0861 Mobile 07967-134101 E-mail gss.watts@ntlworld.com

WATTS, Graham Hadley Lundie. b 74. Man Metrop Univ BA95. Ridley Hall Cam 98. **d** 02 **p** 03. C Camberley St Paul *Guildf* 02-06; C Northwood Em *Lon* from 06. *10 Northwood Way, Northwood HA6 1AT* Tel (01923) 823718 E-mail graham.watts7@ntlworld.com

WATTS, Ian Charles. b 63. Hull Univ BA85. Linc Th Coll 86. **d** 88 **p** 89. C W Kirby St Bridget *Ches* 88-93; V High Lane 93-00; P-in-c Newton in Mottram 00-04; P-in-c Burnley St Cuth *Blackb* from 04. *St James's Vicarage, Church Street, Briercliffe, Burnley BB10 2HU* Tel (01282) 423700 *or* 424978 E-mail rev.ian.watts@ntlworld.com

WATTS, John Michael. **d** 04 **p** 10. OLM Ashtead *Guildf* from 04; Asst Chapl Guy's and St Thos' NHS Foundn Trust from 04. *31 Broadhurst, Ashtead KT21 1QB* Tel (01372) 275134 E-mail jmwatts@waitrose.com

WATTS, John Robert. b 39. Leeds Univ BSc60 MSc63 DipEd63. Oak Hill Th Coll 88. **d** 90 **p** 91. C Partington and Carrington *Ches* 90-93; P-in-c Tintwistle 93-98; V Hollingworth w Tintwistle 98-04; RD Mottram 99-03; rtd 04; Perm to Offic *Ches* from 04. *16 Norley Drive, Vicars Cross, Chester CH3 5PG* Tel (01244) 350439 E-mail revrobwatts@hotmail.com

WATTS, John Stanley. b 28. LCP62 Birm Univ DipEd65 MEd72 Nottm Univ MPhil83. Qu Coll Birm 83. **d** 86 **p** 87. Lect Wolverhampton Poly 77-90; Hon C Dudley St Fran *Worc* 86-91; Lect Wolverhampton Univ 90-93; Hon C Sedgley St Mary 91-98; Perm to Offic from 98. *5 Warren Drive, Sedgley, Dudley DY3 3RQ* Tel (01902) 661265

WATTS, Jonathan Peter (Jonah). b 52. Lon Univ BA74. Ripon Coll Cuddesdon 07. **d** 08 **p** 09. C Crayford *Roch* from 08; V Twyford and Owslebury and Morestead etc *Win* from 11. *The Vicarage, 157 Main Road, Colden Common, Winchester SO21 1TL* Tel (01962) 712136
E-mail jonah.watts1@btinternet.com

WATTS, Mrs Mary Kathleen. b 31. Lon Univ BA86. Gilmore Ho 73. **dss** 77 **d** 87 **p** 94. Lower Streatham St Andr *S'wark* 77-88; C 87-88; C Streatham Immanuel w St Anselm 87-88; C Streatham Immanuel and St Andr 90-91; rtd 91; Perm to Offic *S'wark* 91-94 and from 05; Hon C Norbury St Oswald 94-05. *15 Bromley College, London Road, Bromley BR1 1PE* Tel (020) 8290 6615

WATTS, Matthew David. b 79. Clare Coll Cam BA01 MA04 MSci01 St Jo Coll Dur BA05. Cranmer Hall Dur 03. **d** 06 **p** 07. C Comberton and Toft w Caldecote and Childerley *Ely* 06-09; V Burnside-Harewood New Zealand from 09. *40 Kendal Avenue, Burnside, Christchurch 8053, New Zealand* Tel (0064) (3) 358 8174 E-mail vicar@burnside.org.nz

WATTS, Paul George. b 43. Nottm Univ BA67. Wells Th Coll 67. **d** 69 **p** 70. C Sherwood *S'well* 69-74; Chapl Trent (Nottm) Poly 74-80; V Nottingham All SS 80-84; Public Preacher 84-06; rtd 06. *14 Chestnut Grove, Nottingham NG3 5AD* Tel 0115-960 9964 Mobile 07952-369066 E-mail wattses@yahoo.co.uk

WATTS, Sir Philip Beverley. b 45. KCMG02. Leeds Univ BSc66 MSc69 Ox Brookes Univ BA11 FInstP80 FEI90 FGS98 FRGS98. Ox Min Course 09. **d** 11. NSM Binfield *Ox* from 11. *Sunnyridge, Hill Farm Lane, Binfield, Bracknell RG42 5NR* Tel (01344) 305965 E-mail philbwatts@gmail.com

WATTS (née SIMPER), Rachel Dawn. b 67. K Coll Lon BD89. Westcott Ho Cam 90. **d** 92 **p** 94. Par Dn Clitheroe St Mary *Blackb* 92-94; C 94-95; C Nor St Pet Mancroft w St Jo Maddermarket 95-97; V Slyne w Hest *Blackb* 97-04; V Briercliffe from 04; Women's Min Adv 00-11; Hon Can Blackb Cathl 10-11; R Uppingham w Ayston and Wardley w Belton *Pet* from 11. *The Rectory, London Road, Uppingham, Oakham LE15 9TJ* E-mail rachel.watts1@ntlworld.com

WATTS, Ms Rebecca Harriet. b 61. St Cath Coll Cam BA83 MA Welsh Coll of Music & Drama 84. Wycliffe Hall Ox 87. **d** 90 **p** 94. C Goldsworth Park *Guildf* 90-94; Chapl Wadh Coll Ox 94-97; C Ox St Mary V w St Cross and St Pet 94-97; Chapl Somerville Coll Ox 97-98; Perm to Offic *Newc* 98-99 and from 02. *15 Woodbine Avenue, Gosforth, Newcastle upon Tyne NE3 4EU* Tel 0191-285 9840

WATTS, Robert. See WATTS, John Robert

WATTS, Roger Edward. b 39. S'wark Ord Course 85. **d** 88 **p** 89. C Belmont *S'wark* 88-92; R Godstone 92-97; R Godstone and Blindley Heath 97-09; rtd 09; Perm to Offic *S'wark* from 09. *9 Longland Avenue, Storrington, Pulborough RH20 4HY* Tel (01903) 740205

WATTS, Roger Mansfield. b 41. Univ of Wales (Cardiff) BSc63 CEng76 MIET76. Chich Th Coll 89. **d** 91 **p** 92. C Chippenham St Andr w Tytherton Lucas *Bris* 91-93; C Henfield w Shermanbury and Woodmancote *Chich* 93-96; R Jedburgh *Edin* 96-99; R Wingerworth *Derby* 99-06; rtd 06. *Chez Watts, Vedelle, 24610 Villefranche-de-Lonchat, France* Tel (0033) 5 53 81 82 16

WATTS, Ms Samantha Alison Lundie. b 70. Birm Univ BA92 Cam Univ BA01. Ridley Hall Cam 99. **d** 02 **p** 03. C Camberley St Paul *Guildf* 02-06; NSM Northwood HA *Lon* from 06. *10 Northwood Way, Northwood HA6 1AT* Tel (01923) 823718 E-mail sami.watts@ntlworld.com

WATTS, Scott Antony. b 67. JP08. FRMetS99 MCMI00. EAMTC 00. **d** 03 **p** 04. NSM Brampton *Ely* 03-07; Chapl St Jo Hospice Moggerhanger 07-09; Lead Chapl Hinchingbrooke Health Care NHS Trust from 09. *Hinchingbrooke Health Care NHS Trust, Hinchingbrooke Hospital, Huntingdon PE29 6NT* Tel (01480) 847474 Mobile 07590-840401 E-mail scott.watts@hinchingbrooke.nhs.uk

WATTS, Thomas Annesley. b 79. K Coll Cam BA01 MA05. Oak Hill Th Coll MTh08. **d** 08. C Wharton *Ches* from 08. *27 Leven Avenue, Winsford CW7 3TA* Tel (01606) 593555 Mobile 07764-679210 E-mail tom@tomandsue.net

WATTS, Mrs Valerie Anne. b 44. UEA BEd79. EAMTC 90. **d** 93 **p** 94. NSM N Walsham and Edingthorpe *Nor* from 93. *15 Millfield Road, North Walsham NR28 0EB* Tel (01692) 405119 E-mail topcatjohn@talktalk.net

WATTS, William Henry Norbury. b 51. CertEd. St Jo Coll Nottm 87. **d** 89 **p** 90. C S Molton w Nymet St George, High Bray etc *Ex* 89-93; TV Swanage and Studland *Sarum* 93-10; P-in-c Basildon w Aldworth and Ashampstead *Ox* from 10. *The Vicarage, Pangbourne Road, Upper Basildon, Reading RG8 8LS* Tel (01491) 671714 E-mail willwatts@f2s.com

WAUD, John David. b 31. NOC 82. **d** 85 **p** 86. C Cayton w Eastfield *York* 85-88; R Brandesburton 88-93; R Beeford w

Frodingham and Foston 93-99; rtd 99; Perm to Offic *York* from 00. *21 Lowfield Road, Beverley HU17 9RF* Tel (01482) 864726 E-mail jdw2@jdw2.karoo.co.uk

WAUDBY, Miss Christine. b 45. TCert66. Trin Coll Bris. **d** 90 **p** 94. C Weston-super-Mare Ch Ch *B & W* 90-94; C Blackheath *Birm* 94-99; Perm to Offic 99-03; NSM Ipsley *Worc* 03-10; rtd 10. *Address temp unkown*

WAUDE, Andrew Leslie. b 74. Leeds Univ BA02. Coll of Resurr Mirfield 99. **d** 02 **p** 03. C Swinton and Pendlebury *Man* 02-05; C Lower Broughton Ascension 05-07; P-in-c Nottingham St Geo w St Jo *S'well* from 07; P-in-c Sneinton St Cypr from 07. *The Vicarage, 19 Marston Road, Nottingham NG3 7AN* Tel 0115-940 2868 Mobile 07708-004478 E-mail father.waude@googlemail.com

WAUGH, Ian William. b 52. Bede Coll Dur DipEd74 BEd75. NEOC 99. **d** 02 **p** 03. NSM Benfieldside *Dur* from 02. *36 Muirfield Close, Shotley Bridge, Consett DH8 5XE* Tel (01207) 591923 Mobile 07808-412953 E-mail ian-barbara-waugh@lineone.net

WAUGH, Mrs Jane Leitch. b 38. CertEd61 Toronto Univ MDiv83. Trin Coll Toronto 80. **d** 84 **p** 94. Canada 84-87; Par Dn Dunnington *York* 88-90; Perm to Offic 90-93 and from 96; NSM York St Olave w St Giles 93-96; rtd 98. *c/o Messrs Langleys, Queens House, Micklegate, York YO1 6WG* Tel (01904) 610886

WAUGH, Nigel John William. b 56. TCD BA78 MA81. CITC 76. **d** 79 **p** 80. C Ballymena *Conn* 79-82; C Ballyholme *D & D* 82-84; I Bunclody w Kildavin *C & O* 84-86; I Bunclody w Kildavin and Clonegal 86-91; I Bunclody w Kildavin, Clonegal and Kilrush 91-98; Preb Ferns Cathl 88-91; Treas 91-96; Radio Officer (Cashel) 90-91; (Ferns) 92-98; Dioc Info Officer (Ferns) 91-98; Prec Ferns Cathl 96-98; I Delgany *D & G* from 98. *The Rectory, 8 Elsinore, Delgany, Greystones, Co Wicklow, Republic of Ireland* Tel (00353) (1) 287 4515 Fax 287 7578 Mobile 86-102 8888 E-mail delgany@glendalough.anglican.org

WAXHAM, Derek Frank. b 33. Oak Hill Th Coll 76. **d** 79 **p** 80. NSM Old Ford St Paul w St Steph and St Mark *Lon* 79-89; NSM Bow w Bromley St Leon from 89. *39 Hewlett Road, London E3 5NA* Tel (020) 8980 1748

WAY, Miss Alison Janet. b 61. York Univ BSc83 FIBMS86. St Mich Coll Llan 02. **d** 04 **p** 05. C Basingstoke *Win* 04-08; P-in-c Woodhill *Sarum* 08-10; R from 10. *The Vicarage, Clyffe Pypard, Swindon SN4 7PY* Tel (01793) 739044 E-mail alisonway@tiscali.co.uk

WAY, Andrew Lindsay. b 43. Linc Th Coll 76. **d** 78 **p** 79. C Shenfield *Chelmsf* 78-82; C Waltham *Linc* 82-84; V New Waltham 84-89; R Duxford *Ely* 89-94; V Hinxton 89-94; V Ickleton 89-94; P-in-c Doddington w Benwick 94-97; P-in-c Wimblington 94-97; R Doddington w Benwick and Wimblington 97-98; R Eythorne and Elvington w Waldershare etc *Cant* 98-09; AD Dover 00-03; rtd 09; Perm to Offic *Cant* from 09. *4 Lion Walk, The Street, Ash, Canterbury CT3 2AW* Tel (01304) 814349 E-mail albeway@clara.net

WAY, Mrs Barbara Elizabeth. b 47. Open Univ BA82 Hull Univ PGCE86. Linc Th Coll IDC78. **dss** 78 **d** 87 **p** 94. Shenfield *Chelmsf* 78-82; Adult Educn Adv *Linc* 82-85; Dioc Lay Min Adv 85; New Waltham 82-89; Min 87-89; Tetney 86-89; Min 87-89; NSM Duxford, Ickleton and Hinxton *Ely* 89-94; Dir Past Studies EAMTC 91-94; Min Pampisford 92-94; P-in-c Coates 94-95; TV Whittlesey, Pondersbridge and Coates 95-98; Local Min Adv *Cant* 98-02; Dioc Dir of Reader Selection and Tr 00-02; Dioc Adv in Women's Min 02-04; P-in-c Whitfield w Guston 02-10; Chapl E Kent Hosps NHS Trust 06-08; rtd 10; Perm to Offic *Cant* from 10. *4 Lion Walk, The Street, Ash, Canterbury CT3 2AW* Tel (01304) 814349 E-mail belway@clara.co.uk

WAY, Colin George. b 31. St Cath Coll Cam BA55 MA59 Lon Inst of Educn PGCE58. EAMTC. **d** 84 **p** 85. NSM Hempnall *Nor* 84-87; C Gaywood, Bawsey and Mintlyn 87-90; R Acle w Fishley and N Burlingham 90-96; RD Blofield 95-96; rtd 96; Perm to Offic *Nor* 96-97 and from 02; P-in-c Pulham Market, Pulham St Mary and Starston 97-99; Hon C Eaton 99-02. *347 Unthank Road, Norwich NR4 7QG* Tel (01603) 458363 E-mail cw@eatonparish.com

WAY, David. b 54. Pemb Coll Ox MA DPhil St Jo Coll Dur BA. Cuddesdon Coll 83. **d** 85 **p** 86. C Chenies and Lt Chalfont *Ox* 85-87; C Chenies and Lt Chalfont, Latimer and Flaunden 87-88; Tutor and Dir Studies Sarum & Wells Th Coll 88-93; Selection Sec Min Division from 94; Sec Minl Educn Cttee from 94; Th Educn Sec Min Division from 99. *Ministry Division, Church House, Great Smith Street, London SW1P 3AZ* Tel (020) 7898 1405 Fax 7898 1421 E-mail david.way@churchofengland.org

WAY, David Charles. b 61. St Mich Coll Llan BTh94. **d** 97 **p** 98. C Cardiff St Mary and St Steph w St Dyfrig etc *Llan* 97-02; V Aberaman and Abercwmboi w Cwmaman from 02. *St Margaret's Vicarage, Gladstone Street, Aberaman, Aberdare CF44 6SA* Tel (01685) 872871 E-mail david.way@dtn.ntl.com

WAY, Lawrence William. b 32. St Mich Coll Llan 77. **d** 79 **p** 80. C Merthyr Dyfan *Llan* 79-82; V Abercynon 82-84; TV Cwmbran *Mon* 84-86; V Caerwent w Dinham and Llanfair Discoed etc

86-90; V Pontnewydd 90-93; rtd 93. *8 Ceredig Court, Llanyravon, Cwmbran NP44 8SA* Tel (01633) 865309 Fax 876830 E-mail frway.angelus@virgin.net

WAY, Michael David. b 57. K Coll Lon BD78 AKC78. St Steph Ho Ox 79. **d** 80 **p** 83. C Bideford *Ex* 80-81; Hon C Wembley Park St Aug *Lon* 81-84; C Kilburn St Aug w St Jo 84-89; V Earlsfield St Jo *S'wark* 89-92; Project Co-ord CARA 92-99; Consultant Cen Sch for Counselling and Therapy 99-00; Dir RADICLE *Lon* from 00. *14 St Peter's Gardens, London SE27 0PN* Tel (020) 8670 3439 *or* 7932 1129

WAYNE, Kenneth Hammond. b 31. Bps' Coll Cheshunt 58. **d** 61 **p** 62. C Eyres Monsell CD *Leic* 61-62; C Loughborough Em 62-65; C-in-c Staunton Harold 65-73; V Breedon w Isley Walton 65-73; V Leic St Phil 73-85; V Ault Hucknall *Derby* 85-95; rtd 95; Perm to Offic *S'well* from 96. *The Haven, 3 Burton Walk, East Leake, Loughborough LE12 6LB* Tel (01509) 852848

WAYTE, Christopher John. b 28. Lon Univ BSc54. Wells Th Coll 54. **d** 56 **p** 57. C Maidstone St Martin *Cant* 56-60; C W Wickham St Jo 60-61; C Birchington w Acol 61-64; C-in-c Buckland Valley CD 64-68; R Biddenden 68-80; Chapl ATC 71-86; P-in-c Boughton Monchelsea *Cant* 80-85; V St Margarets-at-Cliffe w Westcliffe etc 85-91; rtd 92; Perm to Offic *Cant* from 92. *9 St John's Road, Hythe CT21 4BE* Tel (01303) 263060 E-mail audrey@wayte93.freeserve.co.uk

WEAKLEY, Susan Margaret. b 52. SEITE 05. **d** 08 **p** 09. NSM Merstham and Gatton *S'wark* 08-10; NSM Merstham, S Merstham and Gatton from 10. *81 Parkhurst Road, Horley RH6 8EX* Tel (01293) 786693 Mobile 07834-368509

WEARMOUTH, Alan Wilfred. b 54. Bris Univ BEd76. Glouc Sch of Min 83. **d** 88 **p** 89. NSM Coleford w Staunton *Glouc* 88-06; C Coleford, Staunton, Newland, Redbrook etc from 06. *Windhover, 2 Broadwell Bridge, Broadwell, Coleford GL16 7GA* Tel (01594) 832660 Mobile 07811-118736 E-mail alanw22uk@yahoo.co.uk

WEARN, Simon Joseph. b 76. Pemb Coll Cam BA00 MEng00. Oak Hill Th Coll BA09. **d** 09 **p** 10. C Gt Faringdon w Lt Coxwell *Ox* from 09. *42 Tuckers Road, Faringdon SN7 7YG* Tel (01367) 243553 Mobile 07980-910104 E-mail simon@wearn.org.uk

WEATHERILL, Stephen Robert. b 70. Roehampton Inst BA98 Nottm Univ MA00. St Jo Coll Nottm 98. **d** 00 **p** 02. C Bridlington Priory *York* 00-01; NSM Kendal St Thos *Carl* from 02. *31 Hallgarth Circle, Kendal LA9 5NW* E-mail stephen@stkmail.org.uk

WEATHERLEY, Miss Mary Kathleen. b 36. SRN57 SCM59. SWMTC 78. **dss** 82 **d** 87 **p** 94. Littleham w Exmouth 82-84; Heavitree w Ex St Paul 85-87; Hon Par Dn 87-88; Chapl Asst R Devon and Ex Hosp 85-93; Lic to Offic *Ex* 88-94; NSM Littleham w Exmouth 94-98; Perm to Offic from 98. *11 The Hollows, Exmouth EX8 1QT* Tel (01395) 265528

WEATHERSTONE, Timothy Andrew Patrick. b 59. Bedf Coll Lon BSc81 UEA MSc82. ERMC 05. **d** 08 **p** 09. C Bowthorpe *Nor* 08-11; TV Barnham Broom and Upper Yare from 11; C Shipdham w E and W Bradenham from 11. *The Rectory, The Street, Reymerston, Norwich NR9 4AG* Tel (01362) 858748 Mobile 07967-190976 E-mail timweatherstone@mac.com

WEATHRALL, Ian Charles. b 22. OBE75. AKC47. **d** 47 **p** 48. C Southampton St Mary w H Trin *Win* 47-51; India from 51; Brotherhood of Ascension from 51; Hd 70-88; rtd 92. *7 Court Lane, Delhi 110 054, India* Tel (0091) (11) 396 8515

WEAVER, Alan William. b 63. Linc Th Coll 95. **d** 95 **p** 96. C Seaford w Sutton *Chich* 95-98; C Langney 98-01; P-in-c The Haven CD 02-05; P-in-c Jarvis Brook 05-07; V from 07. *St Michael's Vicarage, Crowborough Hill, Crowborough TN6 2HJ* Tel (01892) 661565 E-mail angyalanweaver@waitrose.com

WEAVER, Canon Angela Mary. b 48. WMMTC 92. **d** 95 **p** 96. C Hill *Birm* 95-99; V Hamstead St Paul 99-06; AD Handsworth 05-06; Hon Can Birm Cathl 05-06; Can Res Guildf Cathl from 06. *4 Cathedral Close, Guildford GU2 7TL* Tel (01483) 547863 Mobile 07813-807853 E-mail angela@guildford-cathedral.org

WEAVER, Brian John. b 34. Oak Hill Th Coll 82. **d** 84 **p** 85. C Nailsea H Trin *B & W* 84-88; R Nettlebed w Bix and Highmore *Ox* 88-98; rtd 98; Hon C Warfield *Ox* 99-05; Perm to Offic *Lich* from 06. *11A Leslie Road, Sutton Coldfield B74 3BS* Tel 0121-580 8086 E-mail bri_jac@onetel.com

WEAVER, David Anthony. b 43. Hatf Coll Dur BSc65. Lich Th Coll 68. **d** 71 **p** 72. C Walsall Wood *Lich* 71-75; C Much Wenlock w Bourton *Heref* 75-76; Canada 76-79 and 82; V Mow Cop *Lich* 79-82; P-in-c Burntwood 82-00; V 00-08; Chapl St Matt Hosp Burntwood 83-95; rtd 08. *Stone Gables, Ampney Crucis, Cirencester GL7 5RS* Tel (01285) 851674

WEAVER, David Sidney George. b 46. Univ of Wales (Cardiff) BA67 MA71 Goldsmiths' Coll Lon MA01 Lon Univ CertEd76. SEITE 07. **d** 09 **p** 10. NSM Hove All SS *Chich* from 09. *31 Coombe Lea, Grand Avenue, Hove BN3 2ND* Tel (01273) 566551 Mobile 07811-145656 E-mail david@synapticslearning.co.uk

WEAVER, Mrs Diane Beverley. b 57. LCTP 06. **d** 09 **p** 10. C Steeton *Bradf* from 09. *1 Westview Way, Keighley BD20 6JD* Tel (01535) 664566

WEAVER, Duncan Charles. b 60. Open Univ BA99. St Jo Coll Nottm 92. **d** 94 **p** 95. C Watford *St Alb* 94-98; TV Bourne Valley *Sarum* 98-01; CF from 01. *c/o MOD Chaplains (Army)* Tel (01264) 381140 Fax 381824

WEAVER, Fiona Margaret. b 61. Westcott Ho Cam 99. **d** 00 **p** 01. C Islington St Jas w St Pet *Lon* 00-03; Asst Chapl Univ of N Lon 00-02; Asst Chapl Lon Metrop Univ 01-03; Chapl 03-05; Lead Chapl from 05. *123 Calabria Road, London N5 1HS* Tel (020) 7359 5808 *or* 7133 2030 Fax 7133 2813 E-mail f.weaver@londonmet.ac.uk

WEAVER, Ian Douglas. b 65. Ridley Coll Melbourne BMin96. **d** 96 **p** 96. C Essendon St Thos Australia 96; C E Frankston 97-98; TV Rushden St Mary w Newton Bromswold *Pet* 98-02; Dioc Youth Min Facilitator Melbourne Australia 03-05; P-in-c E Geelong from 05. *230 McKillop Street, East Geelong Vic 3219, Australia* Tel (0061) (3) 5241 6895 *or* 5221 5353 Fax 5222 5400 Mobile 409-604006 E-mail ianweaver@optusnet.com.au

WEAVER, Canon John. b 28. Ex Coll Ox BA51 MA55. St Steph Ho Ox 52. **d** 55 **p** 56. C Ex St Dav 55-58; S Africa from 58; Hon Can Mthatha from 61; Adn Midl 84-95; Hon Can Pietermaritzburg from 95. *PO Box 56, Underberg, 3257 South Africa* Tel (0027) (33) 701 1124

WEAVER, Mrs Joyce Margaret. b 43. **d** 00 **p** 01. OLM Warrington St Ann *Liv* from 00. *71 Orford Avenue, Warrington WA2 8PQ* Tel (01925) 634993 E-mail joycearniew@aol.com

WEAVER, Canon Michael Howard. b 39. Southn Univ MPhil95. Chich Th Coll 63. **d** 66 **p** 67. C Kidderminster St Jo *Worc* 66-69; Br Honduras 69-71; TV Droitwich *Worc* 71-76; V Arundel w Tortington and S Stoke *Chich* 76-96; P-in-c Clymping 84-87; RD Arundel and Bognor 88-93; Sub Chapl HM Pris Ford 77-96; V Lymington *Win* 96-04; Chapl Southn Community Services NHS Trust 96-04; rtd 04; Hon Can Enugu from 94; Perm to Offic *Win* from 04 and *Portsm* from 05; AD W Wight *Portsm* from 10. *Dolphin Cottage, High Street, Freshwater PO40 9JU* Tel and fax (01983) 753786 E-mail junovicarage@hotmail.com

WEAVER, Canon William. b 40. Man Univ BA63 BD65. **d** 74 **p** 75. Lect Th Leeds Univ 67-91; Hon C Clifford *York* 82-86; Chapl K Edw Sch Birm 91-94; Provost Woodard Schs (Midl Division) 94-03; Hon Can Derby Cathl from 96; Perm to Offic from 96. *20 St Peter's Garth, Thorner, Leeds LS14 3EE* Tel 0113-289 3689

WEBB, Anthony John. b 24. Sarum & Wells Th Coll 79. **d** 81 **p** 82. C Yeovil *B & W* 81-84; P-in-c Cossington 84-87; P-in-c Woolavington 84-87; P-in-c Bawdrip 87; V Woolavington w Cossington and Bawdrip 87-91; rtd 91; Perm to Offic *B & W* from 91. *18 Channel Court, Burnham-on-Sea TA8 1NE* Tel (01278) 787483

WEBB, Arthur Robert. b 33. Lanc Univ MA82 FRSA LCP67. Wells Th Coll 69. **d** 70 **p** 70. C W Drayton *Lon* 70-72; Hd Master St Jas Cathl Sch Bury St Edmunds 72-86; Min Can St E Cathl 72-87; Succ St E Cathl 81-87; P-in-c Seend and Bulkington *Sarum* 87-88; V 88-91; R Heytesbury and Sutton Veny 91-96; rtd 96; Perm to Offic *B & W* from 96; *Sarum* from 98; *Bris* from 00; P-in-c Las Palmas *Eur* 04-08. *27 Marlborough Buildings, Bath BA1 2LY* Tel (01225) 484042

WEBB, Mrs Barbara Mary. b 39. Bedf Coll Lon BA60 Cam Univ PGCE61. Wycliffe Hall Ox 00. **d** 02 **p** 03. NSM Cumnor *Ox* 02-05; NSM Stanford in the Vale w Goosey and Hatford 05-09; P-in-c Shippon 09-10; rtd 10; Perm to Offic *Ox* from 10. *50 West St Helen Street, Abingdon OX14 5BP* Tel (01235) 202873 E-mail derry_barbara@msn.com

WEBB, Mrs Brenda Lynn. b 45. Stockwell Coll of Educn CertEd66. EAMTC 97. **d** 00 **p** 01. NSM Saxmundham w Kelsale cum Carlton *St E* 00-10; Teacher Beacon Hill Sch 00-10. *48 Pightle Close, Elmswell, Bury St Edmunds IP30 9EL* Tel (01359) 242925

WEBB, Catharine Rosemary Wheatley. b 39. **d** 05 **p** 06. OLM Redhill St Matt *S'wark* from 05. *6 Hurstleigh Drive, Redhill RH1 2AA* Tel and fax (01737) 769763 Mobile 07709-700602 E-mail webbcrw@aol.com

WEBB, Christopher Scott. b 70. Univ of Wales (Abth) BSc. Trin Coll Bris BA96. **d** 96 **p** 97. C Dafen *St D* 96-98; C Cowbridge *Llan* 98-01; Officer for Renewal, Par Development and Local Ecum 01-04; V Llanfair Caereinion, Llanllugan and Manafon *St As* 04-07; President of Renovaré USA from 07. *8 Inverness Drive East, Suite 102, Englewood CO 80112-5609, USA*

WEBB, Cyril George. b 19. Roch Th Coll 64. **d** 66 **p** 67. C Bournemouth St Andr *Win* 66-71; V Micheldever 71-72; V Micheldever and E Stratton, Woodmancote etc 72-79; V Bubwith w Ellerton and Aughton *York* 79-83; I Tomregan w Drumlane *K, E & A* 83-86; rtd 86; Perm to Offic *Cant* 90-98. *62 Columbia Avenue, Whitstable CT5 4EH* Tel (01227) 264687

WEBB, David William. b 30. MRINA. Cant Sch of Min 86. **d** 89 **p** 90. NSM Sittingbourne St Mary *Cant* 89-95; Hon C Iwade 95-02; Perm to Offic from 02. *16 School Lane, Iwade, Sittingbourne ME9 8SE* Tel (01795) 424502

WEBB, Mrs Diane. b 45. **d** 93 **p** 94. OLM Stowmarket *St E* 93-05; OLM Haughley w Wetherden and Stowupland 05-10; Chapl W

Suffolk Hosps NHS Trust from 10. *36 Wordsworth Road, Stowmarket IP14 1TT* Tel (01449) 677880 E-mail revdiane.webb@btinternet.com
WEBB, Diane Silvia. Birm Univ BA66 Dur Univ MA93. NOC 82. **dss** 85 **d** 03 **p** 04. Wyther *Ripon* 85-86; Perm to Offic *York* 95-99; rtd 03; NSM Bow Common *Lon* 03-08; Perm to Offic *Cant* 08-09; NSM Selling w Throwley, Sheldwich w Badlesmere etc from 09. *The Rectory, Vicarage Lane, Selling, Faversham ME13 9RD* Tel (01227) 750144 E-mail diane@webb.lcbroadband.co.uk
WEBB, Dominic Mark. b 68. Oriel Coll Ox BA91. Wycliffe Hall Ox BA93. **d** 96 **p** 97. C Cradley *Worc* 96-99; C Leyton Ch Ch *Chelmsf* 99-02; P-in-c St Helier *S'wark* 02-06; Hon C Stratford New Town St Paul *Chelmsf* from 07. *32A Lister Road, London E11 3DS* Tel (020) 8558 6354 E-mail webbdom@googlemail.com
WEBB, Mrs Eileen Marion. b 46. Bingley Coll of Educn CertEd. **d** 08 **p** 09. OLM Cheriton St Martin *Cant* from 08; OLM Cheriton All So w Newington from 08. *4 Westfield Lane, Etchinghill, Folkestone CT18 8BZ* Tel (01303) 864272 Fax 864272 Mobile 07867-546929 E-mail bryleen@aol.com
WEBB, Frances Mary. *See* BATTIN, Mrs Frances Mary
WEBB, Mrs Gillian Anne. b 49. Whitelands Coll Lon CertEd71 Heythrop Coll Lon MA04. St Alb Minl Tr Scheme 83. **dss** 86 **d** 87 **p** 94. Kempston Transfiguration *St Alb* 86-96; NSM 87-96; NSM Kempston All SS 96-08; P-in-c Marston Morteyne w Lidlington from 08. *2 Hillson Close, Marston Moretaine, Bedford MK43 0QN* Tel (01234) 767256 E-mail webbg@marston2.freeserve.co.uk
WEBB, Canon Gregory John. b 55. Man Univ LLB77. Oak Hill Th Coll 89. **d** 91 **p** 92. C Bury St Edmunds St Geo *St E* 91-94; P-in-c Bury St Edmunds All SS 94-02; TR Bury St Edmunds All SS w St Jo and St Geo 02-08; RD Thingoe 01-08; P-in-c Sudbury and Chilton from 08; Hon Can St E Cathl from 07. *The Rectory, Christopher Lane, Sudbury CO10 2AS* Tel (01787) 372611 E-mail gregorywebb@btinternet.com
WEBB, Harold William. b 37. St Chad's Coll Dur BA59. St Steph Ho Ox 59. **d** 61 **p** 62. C Plumstead St Nic *S'wark* 61-65; C De Aar S Africa 65; R Prieska 65-68; R Vryburg 68-70; Sacr Wakef Cathl 71-72; P-in-c Lane End *Ox* 72-76; V Lane End w Cadmore End 76-84; Chapl to the Deaf *Guildf* 84-96; V Roade and Ashton w Hartwell *Pet* 96-02; rtd 02; Perm to Offic *Chich* from 02. *16 Harrow Drive, West Wittering, Chichester PO20 8EJ* Tel (01243) 673460
WEBB (née EDWARDS), Mrs Helen Glynne. b 57. SRN79 RMN81 Birkbeck Coll Lon MSc94. Wycliffe Hall Ox 88. **d** 90 **p** 94. Par Dn Clapham St Jas *S'wark* 90-94; Chapl Asst Southmead Health Services NHS Trust 94-97; Perm to Offic *Bris* from 97. *13 The Green, Olveston, Bristol BS35 4DN* Tel and fax (01454) 615827
WEBB, Mrs Janice Beryl. b 49. Dioc OLM tr scheme 05. **d** 08 **p** 09. NSM Stour Vale *Sarum* 08-11; NSM Barbourne *Worc* from 11. *5 Victoria Street, Worcester WR3 7BE* Tel (01905) 28682
WEBB, Jennifer Rose. b 48. Leeds Univ BA70 Bedf Coll Lon CQSW72. **d** 96 **p** 97. OLM Ham St Rich *S'wark* 96-05; NSM March St Mary *Ely* from 05; NSM March St Pet from 05. *3 Wherry Close, March PE15 9BX* Tel (01354) 650855 E-mail revdjennywebb@btinternet.com
WEBB, John. *See* WEBB, William John
WEBB, John Christopher Richard. b 38. ACA63 FCA74. Wycliffe Hall Ox 64. **d** 67 **p** 68. C Hendon St Paul Mill Hill *Lon* 67-71; CF 71-93; R Bentworth and Shalden and Lasham *Win* 93-03; RD Alton 98-02; rtd 03; Perm to Offic *B & W* from 04. *Lower Farm Cottage, Church Street, Podimore, Yeovil BA22 8JE* Tel (01935) 841465 E-mail john.c.r.webb@ukgateway.net
WEBB, Jonathan Paul. b 62. Bapt Th Coll Johannesburg BTh98. **d** 02 **p** 03. NSM Linden S Africa 02-04; Asst P Bryanston 04-06; TV Bury St Edmunds All SS w St Jo and St Geo *St E* 07-10; V E Molesey *Guildf* from 10. *St Paul's Vicarage, 101 Palace Road, East Molesey KT8 9DU* Tel (020) 8979 1580 E-mail jp.webb@btinternet.com
WEBB, Kenneth Gordon. b 47. Lon Univ MB, BS71. Trin Coll Bris BA92. **d** 93 **p** 94. C Cheltenham St Mark *Glouc* 93-97; Banchang Ch Ch Thailand 97-02; P-in-c Duns *Edin* from 02. *The Rectory, Wellfield, Duns TD11 3EH* Tel (01361) 884658 *or* 882209 Mobile 07990-866918 E-mail ken.webb@homecall.co.uk
WEBB, Marjorie Valentine (Sister Elizabeth). b 31. Bedf Coll Lon Westmr Coll Ox MTh98. **d** 88 **p** 94. CSF from 55; Revd Mother 71-86; Lic to Bp Heref 86-90; Perm to Offic *Lon* 88-90; Lic to Offic *Lich* 90-91; *B & W* from 95; *Cant* 95-00; *Birm* 97-00; *Lich* from 00; *Lon* from 02; Green Chapl from 09. *The Vicarage, 11 St Mary's Road, London E13 9AE* Tel (020) 8852 4019 E-mail elizabethcsf@franciscans.org.uk
WEBB, Martin George. b 46. SS Mark & Jo Coll Chelsea CertEd68 Leeds Univ MEd95. NOC 82. **d** 85 **p** 86. NSM Brotherton *Wakef* 85-87; Perm to Offic *York* 95-98; NSM Bethnal Green St Barn *Lon* 98-03; NSM Bromley by Bow All

Hallows 03-08; P-in-c Selling w Throwley, Sheldwich w Badlesmere etc *Cant* from 08. *The Rectory, Vicarage Lane, Selling, Faversham ME13 9RD* Tel (01227) 750144 E-mail martin@webb.lcbroadband.co.uk
WEBB, Michael David. b 59. K Coll Lon BD82 PGCE83. Ripon Coll Cuddesdon 88. **d** 90 **p** 91. C Broughton Astley *Leic* 90-93; C Hugglescote w Donington, Ellistown and Snibston 93-94; TV 94-98; R Castleford All SS and Whitwood *Wakef* 98-01; P-in-c Glass Houghton 98-01; TR Castleford 02; rtd 02; Perm to Offic *S'well* from 06. *7 St Peter's Close, Farndon, Newark NG24 3SN* Tel (01636) 702548 E-mail michael@webbs-web.co.uk
WEBB, Canon Michael John. b 49. Linc Coll Ox BA70 MA74. Linc Th Coll 70. **d** 72 **p** 73. C Tring *St Alb* 72-75; C Chipping Barnet 75-78; C Chipping Barnet w Arkley 78-82; TV Cullercoats St Geo *Newc* 82-89; V Newc H Cross 89-97; Chapl MU 96-02; V Newc St Gabr 97-06; AD Newc E 97-04; V Alnwick 06-11; Hon Can Newc Cathl 02-11; rtd 11. *Underne, 24 Wordsworth Street, Keswick CA12 4BZ* Tel (01768) 771180 E-mail michaeljwebb1@btinternet.com
WEBB, Nikola. *See* MARSHALL, Pauline Nikola
WEBB, Norma Fay. b 39. K Coll Dur BDS62. **d** 04 **p** 05. OLM Thornhill and Whitley Lower *Wakef* 04-09; Perm to Offic from 10. *24 High Street, Thornhill, Dewsbury WF12 0PS* Tel (01924) 463574 E-mail normafwebb@aol.com
WEBB, Paul. *See* WEBB, Jonathan Paul
WEBB, Peter Henry. b 55. Nottm Univ BA77. St Steph Ho Ox 77. **d** 79 **p** 80. C Lancing w Coombes *Chich* 79-82; C The Hydneye CD 82-84; C-in-c 84-86; Chapl Sunderland Distr Gen Hosp 86-94; Chapl City Hosps Sunderland NHS Trust from 94. *The Chaplain's Office, Sunderland Royal General Hospital, Kayll Road, Sunderland SR4 7TP* Tel 0191-565 6256 *or* 569 9180
WEBB, Rex Alexander Francis. b 32. Ely Th Coll 56. **d** 58 **p** 59. C Millbrook *Win* 58-60; Australia from 60; rtd 97. *54 Annaburoo Crescent, Tiwi, Darwin NT 0810, Australia* Tel (0061) (8) 8927 6084
WEBB, Richard. b 38. Oak Hill NSM Course 91. **d** 94 **p** 95. NSM Hanwell St Mary w St Chris *Lon* 94-04; rtd 04; Perm to Offic *Cant* from 05. *1 Haffenden Meadow, Charing, Ashford TN27 0JR* Tel (01233) 714663
WEBB, Canon Richard Frederick. b 42. Cant Sch of Min. **d** 84 **p** 85. C Ipswich St Clem w H Trin *St E* 84-87; R Rougham and Beyton w Hessett 87-91; R Rougham, Beyton w Hessett and Rushbrooke 91-92; P-in-c Woodbridge St Jo 92-98; P-in-c Saxmundham 98-04; P-in-c Kelsale-cum-Carlton, Middleton, Theberton etc 02-04; R Saxmundham w Kelsale cum Carlton 04-10; RD Saxmundham 03-05; Hon Can St E Cathl 06-10; rtd 10; Perm to Offic *St E* from 10. *48 Pightle Close, Elmswell, Bury St Edmunds IP30 9EL* Tel (01359) 242925 E-mail richard.webb380@btinternet.com
WEBB, Robert. *See* WEBB, Arthur Robert
WEBB, Rosemary. *See* WEBB, Catharine Rosemary Wheatley
WEBB, Rosemary. b 59. **d** 10 **p** 11. NSM Ascot Heath *Ox* from 10. *The Parsonage, King Edward's Road, Ascot SL5 8PD* Tel (01344) 890198 E-mail rosiewebb@btinternet.com
WEBB, Rowland James. b 33. Roch Th Coll 64. **d** 67 **p** 68. C Tavistock and Gulworthy *Ex* 67-70; Chapl RN 70-86; R Mundford w Lynford *Nor* 86-90; V Burnham *Chelmsf* 90-98; rtd 98; Perm to Offic *Chelmsf* from 98. *4 Pine Drive, Ingatestone CM4 9EF*
WEBB, Timothy Robert. b 57. Univ of Wales (Abth) BA79 Univ of Wales (Ban) BTh03 CQSW89. **d** 03 **p** 04. C Machynlleth w Llanwrin and Penegoes *Ban* 03-06; C Llyn and Eifionydd Deanery from 07. *Ty'n yr Ardd, Lon Gerddi, Edern, Pwllheli LL53 8YS* Tel (01758) 720416 Mobile 07765-298575 E-mail tim-webb@tiscali.co.uk
WEBB, William John. b 43. Cuddesdon Coll 68. **d** 71 **p** 72. C Weston Favell *Pet* 71-73; C Newport w Longford *Lich* 74-77; C Baswich 77-79; P-in-c Stonnall and Wall 79-83; V Prees and Fauls 83-95; V St Martin's 95-06; rtd 06; Perm to Offic *Lich* from 09. *29 Newington Way, Craven Arms SY7 9PS* Tel (01588) 673442
WEBBER, Adam Andrew. b 79. St Chad's Coll Dur BA00 St Mary's Coll Dur MA01. Ridley Hall Cam 08. **d** 10 **p** 11. C Cowplain *Portsm* from 10. *24 Wincanton Way, Waterlooville PO7 8NW* Tel (02392) 232313 E-mail adamwebber@live.co.uk
WEBBER, David Price. b 39. Chich Th Coll 90. **d** 91 **p** 92. NSM Shoreham Beach *Chich* 91-93; NSM Hove St Patr 93-96; Turks and Caicos Is from 96. *PO Box 24, Grand Turk, Turks and Caicos Islands*
WEBBER, The Very Revd Eric Michael. b 16. Lon Univ BD54 Univ of Tasmania MEd77 MHums85. AKC43. **d** 43 **p** 44. C Clapham H Spirit *S'wark* 43-47; C Wimbledon 47-50; R Eshowe S Africa 56-58; R Lapworth and Baddesley-Clinton 56-58; Dean Hobart Australia 59-71; Sen Lect RS Tasmanian Coll Adv Educn 71-81; rtd 94. *5B Kendrick Court, Dynnyrne Tas 7005, Australia* Tel (0061) (3) 6223 6413
WEBBER, John Arthur. b 45. Keble Coll Ox BA67 MA71 Gen Th Sem NY STM85. Cuddesdon Coll 70. **d** 71 **p** 72. C Penarth All SS *Llan* 71-74; USPG Bangladesh 75-84 and 85-91; USA 84-85;

Asst P Stepney St Dunstan and All SS *Lon* 91-97; Bp's Adv on Inter-Faith Relns 91-04; P-in-c Bethnal Green St Barn 97-00; Dir of Ords 00-04; TR Llantwit Major 04-10; rtd 10. *2 Arundel Place, Cardiff CF11 8DP* Tel (029) 2039 6400 Mobile 07745-874839 E-mail johnwebber342@btinternet.com

WEBBER, Lionel Frank. b 35. Kelham Th Coll St Mich Coll Llan. **d** 60 **p** 61. C Bolton Sav *Man* 60-63; C Aberavon *Llan* 63-65; R Salford Stowell Memorial *Man* 65-69; V Aberavon H Trin *Llan* 69-74; TV Stantonbury *Ox* 74-76; TR Basildon St Martin w H Cross and Laindon *Chelmsf* 76-79; P-in-c Nevendon 77-79; RD Basildon 79-89; R Basildon St Martin w Nevendon 79-95; R Basildon St Martin 95-01; Hon Can Chelmsf Cathl 84-01; Chapl to The Queen 94-01; rtd 01. *12 Ramblers Way, Burnham-on-Crouch CM0 8LR* Tel (01621) 785152

WEBBER, Lorna Violet. b 40. **d** 06 **p** 07. OLM Woodbridge St Jo and Bredfield *St E* 06-10; rtd 10; Perm to Offic *St E* from 10. *Deo Gratias, 43 Through Duncans, Woodbridge IP12 4EA* Tel (01394) 384634 E-mail lorna@stjohnswoodbridge.org.uk

WEBBER, Canon Michael Champneys Wilfred. b 48. Man Univ BA71 MA(Theol)78. Cuddesdon Coll 73. **d** 75 **p** 76. C Caterham *S'wark* 75-79; P-in-c Kidbrooke St Jas 79-84; TV 84-85; V Earls Barton *Pet* 87-09; RD Wellingborough 00-06; P-in-c Daventry, Ashby St Ledgers, Braunston etc from 09; Can Pet Cathl from 04. *The Rectory, Glebe Close, Daventry NN11 4FB* Tel (01327) 876893 E-mail michaelc.webber@btinternet.com

WEBBER, Raymond John. b 40. Linc Th Coll 84. **d** 85 **p** 86. C Helston *Truro* 85; C Helston and Wendron 85-90; TV 90-93; R Kenton, Mamhead, Powderham, Cofton and Starcross *Ex* 93-03; rtd 03; Perm to Offic *Truro* from 03. *1 Seton Gardens, Camborne TR14 7JS* Tel (01209) 711360

WEBBER, Thomas George Edward. b 63. LSE BSc84. Trin Coll Bris. **d** 98 **p** 99. C Churchdown *Glouc* 98-02; TV Stoke Gifford *Bris* from 02. *The Vicarage, Mautravers Close, Bradley Stoke, Bristol BS32 8ED* Tel 0117-931 2222 E-mail tomandchriswebber@tiscali.co.uk

WEBBER, Toby Roderic. b 75. St Jo Coll Dur BA96. Wycliffe Hall Ox BA01. **d** 02 **p** 03. C Chorley St Laur *Blackb* 02-06; P-in-c Bamber Bridge St Aid from 06; P-in-c Walton-le-Dale St Leon w Samlesbury St Leon from 11. *St Aidan's Vicarage, Longworth Street, Bamber Bridge, Preston PR5 6GN* Tel (01772) 335310 E-mail tobywebber@dsl.pipex.com

WEBBLEY, Ms Rachel Catharine. b 75. Hatf Coll Dur BA98. Qu Coll Birm BA03. **d** 04 **p** 05. C Bicester w Bucknell, Caversfield and Launton *Ox* 04-07; TV Whitstable *Cant* from 07. *28A West Cliff, Whitstable CT5 1DN* Tel (01227) 273329 E-mail rcwebbley@hotmail.com

WEBLEY, Robin Bowen. b 32. St Mich Coll Llan 87. **d** 89 **p** 90. C St D Cathl 89-91; Min Can St D Cathl 89-91; R Castlemartin w Warren and Angle etc 91-94; Succ St D Cathl 94-00; rtd 00. *Whiteleys, Stepaside, Narberth SA67 8NS* Tel (01834) 813603

WEBSTER, David Leslie Holbarow. b 37. SAOMC 00. **d** 02 **p** 03. NSM Hurst *Ox* 02-04; NSM Earley St Nic 04-07; Perm to Offic from 07. *515 Reading Road, Winnersh, Wokingham RG41 5HL* Tel 0118-979 4568 Fax 961 9575 E-mail dlhwebster@supanet.com

WEBSTER, David Robert. b 32. Selw Coll Cam BA56 MA60. Linc Th Coll 56. **d** 58 **p** 59. C Billingham St Cuth *Dur* 58-61; C Doncaster St Geo *Sheff* 61-64; Chapl Doncaster R Infirmary 61-64; V Lumley *Dur* 64-76; V Belmont 76-93; rtd 93. *25 Eldon Grove, Hartlepool TS26 9LY* Tel (01429) 425915 E-mail david.webster50@ntlworld.com

WEBSTER, Dennis Eric. b 39. Fitzw Ho Cam BA60 MA64. Linacre Coll Ox MA70 Lon Univ CertEd61. Wycliffe Hall Ox 62. **d** 65 **p** 66. C Herne Bay Ch Ch *Cant* 65-68; C Tulse Hill H Trin *S'wark* 68-69; Missr Kenya 70-75; Chapl Pierrepont Sch Frensham 75-91; R Chiddingfold *Guildf* 91-02; rtd 02; Perm to Offic *Guildf* from 02. *Sylvan Cottage, 24 Longdown Road, Lower Bourne, Farnham GU10 3JL* Tel (01252) 713919

WEBSTER, Derek Herbert. b 34. FRSA82 Hull Univ BA55 Lon Univ BD55 Leic Univ MEd68 PhD73. Lambeth STh67 Linc Th Coll 76. **d** 76 **p** 77. Lect Hull Univ from 72; Reader from 97; NSM Cleethorpes *Linc* from 76. *60 Queen's Parade, Cleethorpes DN35 0DG* Tel (01472) 693786 E-mail dwebster@edrev.demon.co.uk

WEBSTER, Canon Diane Margaret. b 43. Oak Hill NSM Course 91. **d** 94 **p** 95. NSM Welwyn Garden City *St Alb* 94-99; P-in-c Burley Ville *Win* 99-10; RD Christchurch 03-10; Hon Can Win Cathl 08-10; rtd 10. *Burwood, The Rise, Brockenhurst SO42 7SJ* Tel (01590) 624927 E-mail diane.mwebster@tiscali.co.uk

WEBSTER, Geoffrey William. b 36. St Alb Mini Tr Scheme 77. **d** 80 **p** 81. NSM Harlington *St Alb* 80-82; C Belmont *Dur* 82-86; R Gateshead Fell 86-94; P-in-c Hamsterley 94-95; V Hamsterley and Witton-le-Wear 95-02; rtd 02. *38A Owton Manor Lane, Hartlepool TS25 3AE* Tel (01429) 265798

WEBSTER, Canon Glyn Hamilton. b 51. SRN73. Cranmer Hall Dur 74. **d** 77 **p** 78. C Huntington *York* 77-81; V York St Luke 81-92; Chapl York Distr Hosp 81-92; Sen Chapl York Health Services NHS Trust 92-99; Can and Preb York Minster 94-99;

Can Res York Minster from 99; RD City of York 97-04; Assoc Dioc Dir of Ords 05-10. *4 Minster Yard, York YO1 7JD* Tel (01904) 620877 Fax 557201 E-mail chancellor@yorkminster.org

WEBSTER, Prof John Bainbridge. b 55. Clare Coll Cam MA81 PhD82. **d** 83 **p** 84. Chapl and Dep Sen Tutor St Jo Coll Dur 83-86; Hon C Bearpark *Dur* 83-86; Assoc Prof Systematic Th Wycliffe Coll Toronto 86-93; Prof Systematic Th 93-95; Ramsay Armitage Prof Systematic Th 95-96; Lady Marg Prof Div and Can Res Ch Ch *Ox* 96-03; Prof Systematic Th Aber Univ from 03. *King's College, University of Aberdeen, Aberdeen AB24 3FX* Tel (01224) 272890

WEBSTER, John Kelsey. b 62. SAOMC 00. **d** 03 **p** 04. NSM Woolhampton w Midgham and Beenham Valance *Ox* 03-06; P-in-c Tallangatta Australia from 06. *61 Queen Elizabeth Drive, Tallangatta Vic 3700, Australia* Tel and fax (0061) (2) 6071 2545 Mobile 44-849 9093 E-mail frjohnw@bigpond.com

WEBSTER, The Ven Martin Duncan. b 52. Nottm Univ BSc74. Linc Th Coll 75. **d** 78 **p** 79. C Thundersley *Chelmsf* 78-81; C Canvey Is 81-82; TV 82-86; V Nazeing 86-99; RD Harlow 88-99; TR Waltham H Cross 99-09; Hon Can Chelmsf Cathl 00-09; Adn Harlow from 09. *Glebe House, Church Lane, Sheering, Bishop's Stortford CM22 7NR* Tel (01279) 734524 Fax 734426 E-mail a.harlow@chelmsford.anglican.org

WEBSTER, Mrs Monica. b 39. DipCOT60. WMMTC 94. **d** 97 **p** 98. NSM Wolverton w Norton Lindsey and Langley *Cov* 97-01; Asst Chapl to the Deaf 97-01; NSM Stoneleigh w Ashow and Baginton 98-01; Chapl to the Deaf and Hard of Hearing *Carl* from 01; NSM Aldingham, Dendron, Rampside and Urswick 02-06; NSM Pennington and Lindal w Marton and Bardsea 02-06; rtd 06. *4 Chelsea Court, Milnthorpe LA7 7DJ* Tel (01539) 564731

WEBSTER, Mrs Patricia Eileen. b 34. St Gabr Coll Lon TCert54. Gilmore Ho 56. **d** 87 **p** 94. Par Dn Belmont *Dur* 87-93; rtd 93. *25 Eldon Grove, Hartlepool TS26 9LY* Tel (01429) 425915 E-mail david.webster50@ntlworld.com

WEBSTER, Rosamond Mary. *See* LATHAM, Mrs Rosamond Mary

WEBSTER, Sarah Vernoy. b 38. Univ of Georgia BSc61. S'wark Ord Course 87. **d** 90 **p** 94. NSM Primrose Hill St Mary w Avenue Road St Paul *Lon* 90-01; Hon C Ann Arbor St Andr USA from 02. *4179 Eastgate Drive, Ann Arbor MI 48103, USA* Tel (001) (734) 424 2750 E-mail revsallyweb@comcast.net

WEBSTER, Stephen Jeremy. b 71. Leic Univ BA92 PGCE93. Wycliffe Hall Ox 05. **d** 07 **p** 08. C Oundle w Ashton and Benefield w Glapthorn *Pet* from 07. *41 Hillfield Road, Oundle, Peterborough PE8 4QR* Tel (01832) 275631 E-mail stephen.webster@yahoo.co.uk

WEDDERSPOON, The Very Revd Alexander Gillan. b 31. Jes Coll Ox BA54 MA61 Lon Univ BD62. Cuddesdon Coll. **d** 61 **p** 62. C Kingston All SS *S'wark* 61-63; Lect RE Lon Univ 63-66; Educn Adv C of E Sch Coun 66-70; Can Res Win Cathl 72-80; Treas 80-85; Vice-Dean 80-87; Dean Guildf 87-01; rtd 01; Perm to Offic *Guildf* from 01. *1 Ellery Close, Cranleigh GU6 8DF* Tel (01483) 548586 E-mail alex@wedderspoon.fsnet.co.uk

WEDGBURY, John William. b 53. RMCS BSc78. St Jo Coll Nottm 84. **d** 87 **p** 88. C Foord St Jo *Cant* 87-91; V Mangotsfield *Bris* 91-92; NSM Manselton *S & B* 00-02; P-in-c Caereithin 02-05; NSM Swansea St Thos and Kilvey from 05. *4 Ffynone Drive, Swansea SA1 6DD* Tel (01792) 464194

WEDGE, Christopher Graham. b 67. LSE BSc(Econ)89 Huddersfield Univ PGCE94. NOC 00. **d** 06 **p** 07. C Castleford Wakef 06-09; Dep Chapl Manager United Lincs Hosps NHS Trust 09-11; C Boston *Linc* from 11. *St Thomas's Vicarage, 2 Linley Drive, Boston PE21 7EJ* Tel (01205) 352381 E-mail chrisshef@hotmail.com

WEDGEWORTH, Canon Michael John. b 40. MBE10. Nottm Univ BSc62. Wesley Ho Cam MA66. **d** 93 **p** 94. In Methodist Ch 66-93; NSM Feniscowles *Blackb* 93-96; Sec DBF 95-05; Hon P Blackb Cathl from 95; Lic to Offic from 96; Hon Can Blackb Cathl from 03. *Abbott House, 74 King Street, Whalley, Clitheroe BB7 9SN* Tel (01254) 825694 E-mail mike.wedgeworth@blackburn.anglican.org.uk

WEDGWOOD, George Peter. b 26. St Jo Coll Dur BA51 MA56. **d** 52 **p** 53. C Barrow St Mark *Carl* 52-54; Chapl Sedbergh Sch 54-57; P-in-c Dur St Cuth 57-63; Chapl Dur High Sch 58-63; Chapl, Hd of Div and Sen Lect St Kath Coll *Liv* 63-69; Prin Lect 69-83; Hd of Div Liv Coll of HE 84-86; P-in-c Kirkoswald, Renwick and Ainstable *Carl* 86-88; rtd 88; Perm to Offic *Carl* 88-92 and *Liv* 92-97; Hon C Hawick *Edin* 02-05. *Lakeside View, Auchry, Turriff AB53 5TP* Tel (01888) 544619

WEDGWOOD GREENHOW, Stephen John Francis. b 57. Man Univ BA82. Edin Th Coll MTh84. **d** 84 **p** 85. C Wythenshawe Wm Temple Ch *Man* 84-87; USA from 87. *556 North George Washington Boulevard, Yuba City CA 95993, USA* Tel (001) (530) 822 0691

WEEDEN, Simon Andrew. b 55. York Univ BA79. Wycliffe Hall Ox 88. **d** 90 **p** 91. C Gt Chesham *Ox* 90-94; P-in-c Haversham w Lt Linford, Tyringham w Filgrave 94-97; R Lamp 97-99; P-in-c Bramshott and Liphook *Portsm* 99-00; R 00-10; RD Petersfield

04-09; TR Whitton *Sarum* from 10. *The Rectory, Back Lane, Ramsbury, Marlborough SN8 2QH* E-mail simon@weeden.plus.com

WEEDING, Paul Stephen. b 62. Leic Poly BSc. Ripon Coll Cuddesdon 88. **d** 90 **p** 91. C Llanishen and Lisvane 90-93; C Merthyr Tydfil Ch Ch 93-97; V Abercynon 97-03; Asst Chapl Qu Medical Cen Nottm Univ Hosp NHS Trust from 03. *Trust Headquarters, Derby Road, Nottingham NG7 2UH* Tel 0115-924 9924

✠**WEEKES, The Rt Revd Ambrose Walter Marcus.** b 19. CB70. AKC41 Linc Th Coll 41. **d** 42 **p** 43 **c** 77. C New Brompton St Luke *Roch* 42-44; Chapl RNVR 44-46; Chapl RN 46-69; Chapl of the Fleet and Adn for the RN 69-72; QHC from 69; Can Gib Cathl 71-73; Chapl Tangier 72-73; Dean Gib 73-77; Aux Bp Eur 77-80; Suff Bp Eur 80-86; Dean Brussels 81-86; rtd 86; Hon Asst Bp Roch 86-88; Hon Asst Bp Eur from 89; Chapl Montreux w Gstaad 89-92; Perm to Offic *Lon* from 03. *Charterhouse, Charterhouse Square, London EC1M 6AN* Tel (020) 7251 4201

WEEKES, Cecil William. b 31. CITC. **d** 78 **p** 79. NSM Glenageary *D & G* 78-80; Bp's V Kilkenny Cathl 80-83; I Carlow w Urglin and Staplestown 83-90; Can Leighlin Cathl 88-96; Can Ossory Cathl 88-96; I Lismore w Cappoquin, Kilwatermoy, Dungarvan etc 90-96; Dean Lismore 90-96; Chan Cashel Cathl 90-96; Prec Waterford Cathl 90-96; rtd 96. *The Cottage, Danesfort Road, Bennettsbridge, Co Kilkenny, Republic of Ireland* Tel and fax (00353) (56) 772 7711 E-mail cwweekes@eircom.net

WEEKES, David John. b 34. Magd Coll Cam BA59 MA68 Lon Univ PGCE68 Aber Univ MTh79. Clifton Th Coll 62. **d** 64 **p** 65. C Cheadle *Ches* 64-68; Uganda 69-73; Perm to Offic *St And* 73-74, Chapl and Hd of RE Fettes Coll Edin 74-94; Warden and Chapl Lee Abbey Internat Students' Club Kensington 94-01; rtd 01; Perm to Offic *Lon* 94-03. *Loaning Hill, Kilmany, Cupar KY15 4PT* Tel (01382) 330137 Mobile 07855-761970 E-mail davidweekes@hotmail.com

WEEKS, Ms Jane Anne. b 61. UEA BA00. Aston Tr Scheme 95 EAMTC 97. **d** 00 **p** 01. C Hadleigh *St E* 00-02; C Hadleigh, Layham and Shelley 02-03; Chapl HM Pris Bullwood Hall 03-06; Chapl HM Pris Cookham Wood 06-08; Perm to Offic *Cant* 09-10; R Hever, Four Elms and Mark Beech *Roch* from 10. *The Rectory, Rectory Lane, Hever, Edenbridge TN8 7LH* Tel (01732) 862249 E-mail revweeks@hotmail.com

WEEKS, Timothy Robert. b 47. SAOMC 03. **d** 08 **p** 09. NSM Royston *St Alb* from 08; Chapl Princess Alexandra Hosp NHS Trust from 08. *6 Chantry Road, Bishop's Stortford CM23 2SF* Tel (01279) 831404 *or* (01763) 243265 Mobile 07974-866016 E-mail angela.mweeks@ntlworld.com

WEETMAN, Mrs Dorothy. b 41. **d** 03 **p** 04. OLM Prudhoe *Newc* 03-09; rtd 09. *Station Gate East, Eltringham Road, Prudhoe NE42 6LA* Tel (01661) 834538

WEETMAN, Canon John Charles. b 66. Qu Coll Ox BA87 MA92. Trin Coll Bris BA91. **d** 91 **p** 92. C Hull St Jo Newland *York* 91-95; V Boosbeck w Moorsholm 95-02; V Redcar 02-11; RD Guisborough 99-11; V Selby Abbey from 11; Can and Preb York Minster from 05. *The Abbey Vicarage, 32A Leeds Road, Selby YO8 4HX* Tel (01757) 705130 E-mail weetman217@btinternet.com

WEIGHTMAN, Andrea Frances. See WARD, Mrs Andrea Frances

WEIGHTMAN, David Courtenay. b 47. FRICS88. **d** 04 **p** 05. OLM Oxted and Tandridge *S'wark* from 04. *13 Silkham Road, Oxted RH8 0NP* Tel (01883) 715420 Fax 717336 Mobile 07739-456947 E-mail david@survez.co.uk

WEIL, Thomas James. b 53. K Coll Lon BSc74 PhD79 AKC74. S Tr Scheme 95. **d** 97 **p** 99. NSM Stoughton *Guildf* 97-03; Perm to Offic *Lon* from 03. *17 Lyons Drive, Guildford GU2 9YP* Tel (01483) 234535

WEIR, David Alexander. b 69. City Univ BSc91 Fitzw Coll Cam BA94 MA99 Chich Univ BA08. Westcott Ho Cam 92. **d** 95 **p** 97. C Locks Heath *Portsm* 95-96; C W Leigh 96-00; C Leigh Park and Warren Park 00-01; Perm to Offic 03-05; NSM Portsea St Mary 05-08; Perm to Offic *Truro* 08-09; P-in-c Exford, Exmoor, Hawkridge and Withypool *B & W* from 09; P-in-c Exton and Winsford and Cutcombe w Luxborough from 11. *The Rectory, Exford, Minehead TA24 7LX* Tel (01643) 831330 E-mail david.weir122@btinternet.com

WEIR, Graham Francis. b 52. GSM LASI. NOC 88. **d** 91 **p** 92. NSM High Crompton *Man* 91-92; NSM Heyside 92-94; Asst Chapl Bolton Hosps NHS Trust 94-96; Chapl from 96; Dep Hd of Chapl from 04. *The Chaplain's Office, Royal Bolton Hospital, Minerva Road, Farnworth, Bolton BL4 0JR* Tel (01204) 390770 *or* 390390 E-mail graham.weir@boltonh-tr.nwest.nhs.uk

WEIR, John Michael Vavasour. b 48. K Coll Lon BD72 AKC72 MA00. **d** 73 **p** 74. C Hatfield Hyde *St Alb* 73-76; C St Mich 76-79; Asst Chapl Oslo St Edm *Eur* 80-81; V Bethnal Green St Pet w St Thos *Lon* 81-04; Chapl Qu Eliz Hosp for Children Lon 81-98; Chapl Team Ldr Toc H 01-10; Sen Chapl Dubai and Sharjah w N Emirates 04-10; rtd 10. *38 Belgrave Road, London E1 0NQ* Tel (020) 7791 7957 E-mail arabnyte2003@yahoo.co.uk

WEIR, John William Moon. b 36. St Luke's Coll Ex CertEd69 Ex Univ BEd76. SWMTC 82. **d** 85 **p** 86. NSM Meavy, Sheepstor and Walkhampton *Ex* 85-87; NSM Yelverton, Meavy, Sheepstor and Walkhampton 87-05; Hd Master Princetown Primary Sch 86-94; Sub-Chapl HM Pris Dartmoor 86-94; Perm to Offic from 05. *Goblin's Green, Dousland, Yelverton PL20 6ND* Tel (01822) 852671

WEIR, Nicholas James. b 77. Pemb Coll Cam BA98 MA02 Green Coll Ox BM, BCh01 MRCPsych05. Oak Hill Th Coll MTh11. **d** 11. C Eastrop *Win* from 11. *15 Camwood Close, Basingstoke RG21 3BL* Tel (01256) 830028 E-mail nick.weir@stmarys-basingstoke.org.uk

WEIR, Ms Rachel Sian Shapland. b 66. Newnham Coll Cam BA88 MA91 Barrister 91. Ripon Coll Cuddesdon 04. **d** 07 **p** 08. Asst Nat Adv for Inter Faith Relns 07-08; NSM Wolvercote *Ox* 07-09; NSM Headington Quarry 09-11; Chapl Helen and Douglas Ho Ox from 11. *Blackhall Farm, Garford Road, Oxford OX2 6UY* Tel 07815-729565 (mobile) E-mail rachelssweir@yahoo.co.uk

WEIR, William Daniel Niall. b 57. UEA BA79. Ripon Coll Cuddesdon 80. **d** 83 **p** 84. C Chelsea St Luke *Lon* 83-87; PV Westmr Abbey 85-89; C Poplar *Lon* 87-88; TV 88-93; P-in-c Forest Gate Em w Upton Cross *Chelmsf* 93-97; V 97-99; Asst Chapl Southn Univ Hosps NHS Trust 99-00; Trust Chapl 00-03; R W Hackney St Barn *Lon* from 03. *The Rectory, 306 Amhurst Road, London N16 7UE* Tel (020) 7254 3235 E-mail niall.weir@mac.com

WEISSERHORN, Julian Timothy David Moritz. See GADSBY, Julian Timothy David Moritz

WELANDER, Canon David Charles St Vincent. b 25. FSA. Lon Coll of Div BD47 ALCD47. **d** 48 **p** 49. C Heigham H Trin *Nor* 48-51; Tutor Oak Hill Th Coll 51-52; Chapl and Tutor Lon Coll of Div 52-56; V Iver *Ox* 56-63; V Cheltenham Ch Ch *Glouc* 63-75; RD Cheltenham 73-75; Can Res Glouc Cathl 75-91; rtd 91; Perm to Offic *Glouc* 91-98 and *Bris* from 91. *Willow Cottage, 1 Sandpits Lane, Sherston Magna, Malmesbury SN16 0NN* Tel (01666) 840180

WELBOURN, David Anthony. b 41. K Coll Lon BD63 AKC63. St Boniface Warminster 63. **d** 64 **p** 65. C Stockton St Chad *Dur* 64-67; C S Westoe 69-74; Ind Chapl 69-80; Ind Chapl *Nor* 80-90; Ind and Commerce Officer *Guildf* 90-06; rtd 06. *3 Windgates, Guildford GU4 7DJ* Tel and fax (01483) 825541 E-mail david@dwelbourn.freeserve.co.uk

WELBY, Alexander. See WELBY, Richard Alexander Lyon

✠**WELBY, The Rt Revd Justin Portal.** b 56. Trin Coll Cam BA78 MA90 St Jo Coll Dur BA91 Hon FCT. Cranmer Hall Dur 89. **d** 92 **p** 93 **c** 11. C Chilvers Coton w Astley *Cov* 92-95; R Southam 95-02; V Ufton 96-02; Can Res Cov Cathl 02-07; Co-Dir Internat Min 02-05; Sub-Dean 05-07; P-in-c Cov H Trin 07; Dean Liv 07-11; Bp Dur from 11. *The Bishop's Office, Auckland Castle, Bishop Auckland DL14 7NR* Tel (01388) 602576 E-mail bishop.of.durham@ldurham.anglican.org

WELBY, Peter Edlin Brown. b 34. Open Univ BA75. St Jo Coll Dur 75. **d** 77 **p** 78. C Auckland St Andr and St Anne *Dur* 77-79; C S Westoe 79-81; V Tudhoe 81-93; R Croxdale and Tudhoe 93-99; rtd 99. *Blyth House, 9 Rhodes Terrace, Nevilles Cross, Durham DH1 4JW* Tel 0191-384 8295

WELBY, Richard Alexander Lyon. b 58. St Jo Coll Nottm BTh81 Leeds Univ MA93. Ridley Hall Cam 83. **d** 84 **p** 85. C Stoke Bishop *Bris* 84-88; V Bowling St Steph *Bradf* 88-95; P-in-c Hatherleigh, Meeth, Exbourne and Jacobstowe 95-05. *2 Fernleigh Court, Fore Street, North Tawton EX20 2ED* Tel (01837) 89055 Mobile 07935-232058 E-mail alex.welby@virgin.net

WELCH, Amanda Jane. b 58. **d** 04 **p** 05. OLM Worplesdon *Guildf* from 04. *Glenlea, Liddington New Road, Guildford GU3 3AH* Tel (01483) 233091 E-mail curate@worplesdonparish.com *or* welchfam@tiscali.co.uk

WELCH, David John. b 52. NTMTC 98. **d** 01 **p** 02. C Walthamstow *Chelmsf* 01-05; V Harlow St Mary and St Hugh w St Jo the Bapt from 05. *St Mary's Vicarage, 5 Staffords, Harlow CM17 0JR* Tel and fax (01279) 450633 E-mail davewelch@talktalkbusiness.net

WELCH, Derek. b 27. Keble Coll Ox BA51 MA57. Coll of Resurr Mirfield 51. **d** 53 **p** 54. C Middlesbrough St Jo the Ev *York* 53-58; C Oswaldtwistle Immanuel *Blackb* 58-59; V Accrington St Andr 59-65; V Salesbury 66-72; V Heyhouses on Sea 73-92; rtd 92; Perm to Offic *Blackb* from 92. *76 St Thomas's Road, Lytham St Annes FY8 1JR* Tel (01253) 781449

WELCH, Gordon Joseph. b 47. Man Univ BSc68 MSc69 PhD72. NOC 84. **d** 87 **p** 88. NSM Upton Ascension *Ches* 87-98; Lic to Offic 99-00; NSM Backford and Capenhurst 00-02; NSM Ellesmere Port from 02; RD Wirral S from 06. *6 St James's Avenue, Upton, Chester CH2 1NA* Tel (01244) 382196 Mobile 07890-993948

WELCH, Canon Grant Keith. b 40. AKC63. **d** 64 **p** 65. C Nottingham St Mary *S'well* 64-68; V Cinderhill 68-73; R Weston Favell *Pet* 73-88; Master St Jo Hosp Weston Favell 73-88; Can Pet Cathl 83-88; P-in-c Gt Houghton 84-85; C Loughton St Jo *Chelmsf* 89-92; TR 92-05; AD Epping Forest 00-04; rtd 05; Perm to Offic *B & W* from 05. *7 Hayes Lane, Compton Dundon, Somerton TA11 6PB* Tel (01458) 272526 E-mail juliawelch@waitrose.com

WELCH, Ian Michael. b 59. Warwick Univ BA81 Connecticut Univ MA84. Ripon Coll Cuddesdon 00. **d** 02 **p** 03. C Lee St Aug *S'wark* 02-05; P-in-c Mottingham St Andr w St Alban 05-11; R from 11. *The Rectory, 233 Court Road, London SE9 4TQ* Tel (020) 8851 1909 E-mail office@standrewschurch.freeserve.co.uk

WELCH, John Harry. b 52. Oak Hill Th Coll 85. **d** 87 **p** 88. C Parr *Liv* 87-90; V W Derby St Luke 90-00; V Eccleston Park 00-07; P-in-c St Helens St Matt Thatto Heath 06-07; TR Eccleston from 07. *St James's Vicarage, 159A St Helen's Road, Prescot L34 2QB* Tel 0151-426 6421

WELCH, Canon Michael Robin. b 33. MBE81. St Chad's Coll Dur BSc55. Wells Th Coll 57. **d** 59 **p** 60. C S Shields St Hilda *Dur* 59-63; CF (R of O) 61-88; Warden and Tr Officer Dioc Youth Cen *Newc* 63-68; Soc and Ind Adv *Portsm* 68-96; V Portsea All SS 72-85; V Swanmore St Barn 85-96; RD Bishop's Waltham 88-93; Hon Can Portsm Cathl 92-96; rtd 96; Perm to Offic *Sarum* from 96. *Southwell, Church Street, Mere, Warminster BA12 6LS* Tel (01747) 860047

WELCH, Pamela Jean. b 47. Girton Coll Cam MA76 K Coll Lon BD79 AKC79 PhD05. Qu Coll Birm 79. **dss** 80 **d** 87. Tottenham H Trin *Lon* 80-84; Asst Chapl Bryanston Sch 84-87; Perm to Offic *Chich* 87-94; C Mornington St Mary New Zealand from 02; rtd 07. *23 Byron Street, Mornington, Dunedin 9011, New Zealand* Tel and fax (0064) (3) 453 0052 E-mail welchfam@byronhurst.com

WELCH, Paul Baxter. b 47. Lanc Univ BEd74 MA75. St Alb Minl Tr Scheme 80. **d** 83 **p** 84. NSM Heath and Reach *St Alb* 83-84; Bp's Sch Adv *Win* 84-89; P-in-c Clungunford w Clunbury and Clunton, Bedstone etc *Heref* 89-93; V Wellingborough All SS *Pet* 93-01; R Pulborough *Chich* from 01; RD Storrington from 04. *The Rectory, 2 London Road, Pulborough RH20 1AP* Tel (01798) 875773 E-mail paul.welch@virgin.net

WELCH, Rebecca Anne. b 79. Leic Univ BSc00. Wycliffe Hall Ox 06. **d** 09 **p** 10. C Cov Cathl from 09. *65 Cotswold Drive, Coventry CV3 6EZ* Tel (024) 7652 1200 E-mail becky.welch@coventrycathedral.org.uk

WELCH, Mrs Sally Ann. b 62. Pemb Coll Ox MA88. SAOMC 96. **d** 99 **p** 00. NSM Abingdon *Ox* 99-01; P-in-c Kintbury w Avington 01-05; R Cherbury w Gainfield 05-09; C Ox St Giles and SS Phil and Jas w St Marg from 09. *St Margaret's Vicarage, St Margaret's Road, Oxford OX2 6RX* Tel (01865) 512319 Mobile 07974-439630 E-mail sally.welch@19a.org.uk

WELCH, The Ven Stephan John. b 50. Hull Univ BA74 Lon Univ MTh98. Qu Coll Birm 74. **d** 77 **p** 78. C Waltham Cross *St Alb* 77-80; P-in-c Reculver *Cant* 80-86; P-in-c Herne Bay St Bart 82-86; V Reculver and Herne Bay St Bart 86-92; V Hurley and Stubbings *Ox* 92-00; P-in-c Hammersmith St Pet *Lon* 00-06; AD Hammersmith and Fulham 01-06; Adn Middx from 06. *98 Dukes Avenue, London W4 2AF* Tel (020) 8742 8308 E-mail archdeacon.middlesex@london.anglican.org

WELDON, Nicholas Patrick. b 77. UWE BSc99. Oak Hill Th Coll BA07. **d** 07 **p** 08. C Moreton-in-Marsh w Batsford, Todenham etc *Glouc* 07-11; P-in-c N Tawton, Bondleigh, Sampford Courtenay etc *Ex* from 11. *The Rectory, Essington Close, North Tawton EX20 2EX* Tel (01837) 880183 Mobile 07970-984190 E-mail npweldon@gmail.com

WELDON, Robert Price. b 57. SEITE 06. **d** 09 **p** 10. NSM Caterham *S'wark* from 09. *Arran Lodge, 45 Boxwood Way, Warlingham CR6 9SB* Tel (01883) 625448 Mobile 07929-866879 E-mail bob.weldon@tiscali.co.uk

WELDON, William Ernest. b 41. TCD BA62 MA66. **d** 64 **p** 65. C Belfast Trin Coll Miss *Conn* 64-67; C Carnmoney 67-71; Chapl RN 71-96; QHC 93-96; Hon C Holbeton *Ex* 96-01; Perm to Offic from 01. *3 Garden Close, Holbeton, Plymouth PL8 1NQ* Tel (01752) 830139 E-mail billanddinahweldon@btopenworld.com

WELFORD, Gillian Margaret. Westf Coll Lon BA65. **d** 04 **p** 05. OLM Chiddingfold *Guildf* from 04. *15 Woodberry Close, Chiddingfold, Godalming GU8 4SF* Tel (01428) 683620

WELHAM, Clive Richard. b 54. **d** 80 **p** 81. C Bellingham St Dunstan *S'wark* 80-84; Chapl Goldsmiths' Coll Lon 84-95; V Plumstead Ascension 95-10; P-in-c Plumstead St Mark and St Marg 07-10; V Plumstead Common from 10. *The Vicarage, 42 Jago Close, London SE18 2TY* Tel (020) 8854 3395

WELLER, David Christopher. b 60. UWIST BSc83. St Jo Coll Nottm MA96. **d** 96 **p** 97. C Wednesfield Heath *Lich* 96-99; TV Glascote and Stonydelph 99-05; Chapl Rio de Janeiro Ch Ch Brazil 05-11; P-in-c Pheasey *Lich* from 11. *88 Hillingford Avenue, Birmingham B43 7HN* Tel 0121-603 9802 Mobile 07890-691228 E-mail pheaseyvicar@gmail.com

WELLER, Richard Morton. b 33. Selw Coll Cam BA57 MA61. Wells Th Coll 61. **d** 63 **p** 64. C Stockingford *Cov* 63-66; C Pontefract St Giles *Wakef* 66-68; C-in-c Stockton St Jas CD *Dur* 68-74; V E Ardsley *Wakef* 74-83; V Heckmondwike 83-91; V Birstall 91-96; RD Birstall 92-96; V Gawber 96-01; rtd 01; Perm

to Offic *Wakef* from 02. *14 Callis Way, Penistone, Sheffield S36 6UH* Tel (01226) 379760

WELLER (née SPENCE), Susan Karen. b 65. Leeds Univ BSc86 Liv Univ PhD89. Wycliffe Hall Ox BA95. **d** 96 **p** 97. C Caverswall and Weston Coyney w Dilhorne *Lich* 96-00; C Wilnecote 00-05; Dioc Adv for Women in Min 00-04; Brazil 05-11; Perm to Offic *Lich* from 11. *88 Hillingford Avenue, Birmingham B43 7HN* Tel 0121-603 9802

WELLINGTON, Bishop of. See BROWN, The Rt Revd Thomas John

WELLINGTON, James Frederick. b 51. Leic Univ LLB72 Fitzw Coll Cam BA76. Ridley Hall Cam 74. **d** 77 **p** 78. C Mill Hill Jo Keble Ch *Lon* 77-80; C Wood Green St Mich w Bounds Green St Gabr etc 80-83; V Stocking Farm *Leic* 83-90; V Gt Glen, Stretton Magna and Wistow etc 90-98; Warden of Readers 91-97; RD Gartree II 96-98; TR Syston 98-07; RD Goscote 00-06; Hon Can Leic Cathl 94-07; R Keyworth and Stanton-on-the-Wolds and Bunny etc *S'well* from 07; AD E Bingham from 08. *The Rectory, Nottingham Road, Keyworth, Nottingham NG12 5FD* Tel 0115-937 2017 E-mail jhcwelli@btinternet.com

WELLS, Adrian Mosedale. b 61. SWMTC 96. **d** 99 **p** 00. NSM Kingskerswell w Coffinswell *Ex* 99-02; NSM Wolborough and Ogwell 02-07; C from 07. *St Bartholomew's House, 1 St Bartholomew Way, Ogwell, Newton Abbot TQ12 6YW* Tel (01626) 331147 E-mail amwells@talktalk.net

WELLS, Andrew Stuart. b 48. St Jo Coll Dur BA71 Man Metrop Univ PGCE04. Cranmer Hall Dur. **d** 74 **p** 75. C Walmsley *Man* 74-77; C Failsworth H Family 77-79; R Openshaw 79-90; V Hindsford 90-98. *1 Henry Street, Haslington, Crewe CW1 5PS* Tel (01270) 585303 E-mail andrewwells@hotmail.com

WELLS, Canon Anthony Martin Giffard. b 42. Open Univ BA02. St Jo Coll Nottm 72. **d** 74 **p** 75. C Orpington Ch Ch *Roch* 74-78; P-in-c Odell *St Alb* 78-82; R 82-86; P-in-c Pavenham 78-82; V 82-86; RD Sharnbrook 81-86; R Angmering *Chich* 86-98; RD Arundel and Bognor 93-98; Chapl Paris St Mich *Eur* 98-06; Adn France 02-06; Can Gib Cathl 02-06; rtd 06; Perm to Offic *Eur* from 06. *Shaunbrook House, Clark's Lane, Long Compton, Shipston-on-Stour CV36 5LB* Tel (01608) 684337 E-mail anthonymgwells@btinternet.com

WELLS, Antony Ernest. b 36. Oak Hill Th Coll 58. **d** 61 **p** 62. C Bethnal Green St Jas Less *Lon* 61-64; SAMS Paraguay 64-69; V Kirkdale St Athanasius *Liv* 69-73; SAMS Argentina 73-75; V Warfield *Ox* 75-81; V Fairfield *Liv* 81-83; C Rainhill 83-85; TV Cheltenham St Mark *Glouc* 85-89; P-in-c Forest of Dean Ch Ch w English Bicknor 89-95; rtd 97; C Pinhoe and Broadclyst *Ex* 02-04. *4 Case Gardens, Seaton EX12 2AP* Tel (01297) 20482

WELLS, Miss Cecilia Isabel. b 24. Bedf Coll Lon BA45. St Mich Ho *Ox* 56. **dss** 62 **d** 87. Chester le Street *Dur* 74-84; rtd 84; Perm to Offic *Ches* from 84. *Elm House, 76 Pillory Street, Nantwich CW5 5SS* Tel (01270) 627258

WELLS, Charles Francis. b 39. Oak Hill Th Coll. **d** 85 **p** 86. C Southend St Sav Westcliff *Chelmsf* 85-89; P-in-c E and W Horndon w Lt Warley 89-96; V E and W Horndon w Lt Warley and Childerditch 96-97; P-in-c Tillingham 97-04; rtd 04; Perm to Offic *Chelmsf* from 04. *14 Irvington Close, Leigh-on-Sea SS9 4NJ* Tel (01702) 512041

WELLS, Daniel Michael. b 74. Trin Coll Cam MA95 Cam Inst of Educn PGCE97. Wycliffe Hall Ox BTh05. **d** 06 **p** 07. C Plymouth St Andr and Stonehouse *Ex* 06-09; C W Hampstead St Luke *Lon* from 09. *40 Ingham Road, London NW6 1DE* Tel (020) 7443 9704 E-mail dan@wellsweb.org.uk

WELLS, David. See WELLS, Canon William David Sandford

WELLS, David. b 63. Imp Coll Lon BSc85 ARCS85. EAMTC 97. **d** 00 **p** 01. C Sprowston w Beeston *Nor* 00-03; P-in-c Drayton w Felthorpe 03-05; R Drayton from 05. *The Rectory, 46 School Road, Drayton, Norwich NR8 6EF* Tel (01603) 864749 E-mail david.wells@btinternet.com

WELLS, Mrs Gillian Lesley. b 50. Nor Ord Course 07. **d** 10 **p** 11. OLM Reepham, Hackford w Whitwell, Kerdiston etc *Nor* from 10. *4 Moorhouse Close, Reepham, Norwich NR10 4EG* Tel (01603) 872788 E-mail gilliewells1@btinternet.com

WELLS, Isabel. See WELLS, Miss Cecilia Isabel

WELLS, Jeremy Stephen. b 47. Nottm Univ BA69 UWE MSc97. Chich Th Coll 72. **d** 73 **p** 74. C S Yardley St Mich *Birm* 73-76; C St Marychurch *Ex* 76-78; P-in-c Bridgwater H Trin *B & W* 78-82; P-in-c Brent Knoll 82-84; P-in-c E Brent w Lympsham 82-84; R Brent Knoll, E Brent and Lympsham 84-99; Perm to Offic *Chich* 99-07; rtd 07. *15A Victoria Close, Burgess Hill RH15 9QS* Tel (01444) 244275

WELLS, Jo Bailey. b 65. CCC Cam BA87 MA90 Minnesota Univ MA90 St Jo Coll Dur BA92 PhD97. Cranmer Hall Dur. **d** 95 **p** 96. Chapl Clare Coll Cam 95-98; Dean 98-01; Perm to Offic *Nor* 99-04; Tutor Ridley Hall Cam 01-05; Dir Angl Studies Duke Div Sch N Carolina USA from 05. *Duke University Divinity School, Durham NC 27708-0967, USA* Tel (001) (919) 660 3576 Fax 660 3473 E-mail jwells@div.duke.edu

WELLS, John Michael. b 35. Mert Coll Ox BA58 MA61. Westcott Ho Cam 60. **d** 62 **p** 63. C Hornchurch St Andr *Chelmsf* 62-64; C Barking St Marg 64-66; C Wanstead H Trin Hermon

Hill 66-69; V Elm Park St Nic Hornchurch 69-76; Offg Chapl RAF 69-76; R Wakes Colne w Chappel *Chelmsf* 76-79; Project Officer Cathl Cen for Research and Tr 79-81; Hon Chapl Chelmsf Cathl 79-81; Area Sec CMS *Chelmsf* and *Ely* 81-88; E Cen Co-ord 85-91; Area Sec *Chelmsf* and *St E* 88-91; Public Preacher *Chelmsf* 82-91; V Hanging Heaton *Wakef* 92-96; rtd 00; Perm to Offic *Chelmsf* from 00. *2 Clarkesmead, Tiptree, Colchester CO5 0BX* Tel (01621) 819899

WELLS, John Rowse David. b 27. Kelham Th Coll 53. **d** 57 **p** 58. SSM from 57; Lic to Offic *S'well* 57-59; Lic to Offic Adelaide Australia 59-65; Tutor St Mich Th Coll Crafers 61-65; C Teyateyaneng Lesotho 65-67; R Mantsonyane St Jas 67-77; Can SS Mary and Jas Cathl Maseru 77-96; Adn Cen Lesotho 85-95; Perm to Offic Melbourne Australia from 97. *St Michael's Priory, 75 Watsons Road, Diggers Rest Vic 3427, Australia* Tel (0061) (3) 9740 1618 Fax 9740 0007 E-mail ssm.melbourne@bigpond.com

WELLS, Judith Margaret. b 48. Whitelands Coll Lon CertEd71. Trin Coll Bris 09. **d** 11. OLM Purton *Bris* from 11. *The Live and Let Live, 7 Upper Pavenhill, Purton, Swindon SN5 4DQ* Tel (01793) 770627 Mobile 07760-400257 E-mail judith@judithwells.wanadoo.co.uk

WELLS, Leslie John. b 61. Univ of Wales (Ban) BTh06. **d** 04 **p** 05. OLM St Helier *S'wark* 04-08; C Morden 08-10; TV from 10. *5 Willows Avenue, Morden SM4 5SG* E-mail leswells80@hotmail.com

WELLS, Lydia Margaret. b 50. St Aid Coll Dur BA72 Sheff Univ MPhil92 Leeds Univ MA00. NOC 97. **d** 00 **p** 01. C Adwick-le-Street w Skelbrooke *Sheff* 00-03; V Doncaster Intake 03-09; V Sheff St Pet and St Oswald from 09. *St Peter's Vicarage, 17 Ashland Road, Sheffield S7 1RH* Tel 0114-250 9716 Mobile 07977-740813 E-mail lydwells@tesco.net *or* lydia.wells@sheffield.anglican.org

WELLS, Mark Wynne-Eyton. b 20. Peterho Cam BA48 MA54. Westcott Ho Cam 48. **d** 50 **p** 51. C Heene *Chich* 50-53; C Sullington 53-57; R Slinfold 57-59; S Rhodesia 59-62; V Stoke by Nayland w Leavenheath *St E* 62-88; RD Hadleigh 71-76 and 85-86; rtd 88; Perm to Offic *Nor* from 88. *Stable Cottage, Church Lane, South Raynham, Fakenham NR21 7HE* Tel (01328) 838386

WELLS, Michael John. b 46. Univ Coll Ox BA68 MA73 Solicitor 74. S Dios Minl Tr Scheme 92. **d** 95 **p** 96. NSM Brighton St Pet w Chpl Royal *Chich* 95-98; Sen C 99-04; NSM Brighton St Bart 98-99; rtd 04; Perm to Offic *Chich* 04-10; P-in-c Brighton Annunciation from 10. *35 Park Crescent, Brighton BN2 3HB* Tel (01273) 600735

WELLS, Canon Nicholas Anthony. b 60. Cranmer Hall Dur 88. **d** 91 **p** 92. C Accrington St Jo w Huncoat *Blackb* 91-94; C Douglas St Geo and St Barn *S & M* 94-95; C Douglas All SS and St Thos 95-97; V Onchan 97-03; V Netherton *Liv* 03-07; AD Bootle 05-07; P-in-c Maghull 07-09; TR Maghull and Melling from 09; AD Ormskirk from 10; Hon Can Liv Cathl from 05. *The Rectory, 20 Damfield Lane, Liverpool L31 6DD* Tel 0151-286 2310 E-mail nick.the-vic@blueyonder.co.uk

WELLS, Canon Peter Robert. b 59. Wilson Carlile Coll 78 Sarum & Wells Th Coll 87. **d** 89 **p** 90. CA from 81; C Mortlake w E Sheen *S'wark* 89-93; Dir St Marylebone Healing and Counselling Cen 93-97; TV N Lambeth *S'wark* 97-00; Chapl Trin Hospice Lon 97-03; Chapl Brighton and Sussex Univ Hosps NHS Trust from 03; Can and Preb Chich Cathl from 10. *Royal Sussex County Hospital, Eastern Road, Brighton BN2 5BE* Tel (01273) 696955 ext 7495 E-mail peter.wells@bsuh.nhs.uk

WELLS, Philip Anthony. b 57. BA MPhil. Coll of Resurr Mirfield. **d** 84 **p** 85. C Wylde Green *Birm* 84-87; Chapl and Succ Birm Cathl 87-91; Bp's Dom Chapl 91-97; V Polesworth from 97. *The Vicarage, High Street, Polesworth, Tamworth B78 1DU* Tel (01827) 892340 E-mail polesworthabbey@aol.com

WELLS, Philip Anthony. b 83. UEA BA04 Leeds Univ BA07 MA08. Coll of Resurr Mirfield 05. **d** 08 **p** 09. C Holt w High Kelling *Nor* 08-11; Bp's Dom Chapl *Wakef* from 11. *Bishop's Lodge, Woodthorpe Lane, Wakefield WF2 6JL* Tel (01924) 255349 Fax 250202 Mobile 07813-929549 E-mail pwells@bishopofwakefield.org.uk

WELLS, Richard John. b 46. St Mich Coll Llan 68 Cuddesdon Coll 70. **d** 71 **p** 72. C Kingston upon Hull St Alb *York* 71-75; C Addlestone *Guildf* 75-80; V Westborough w Milford and Chapl Milford Hosp Godalming 88-96; R Westbourne *Chich* 96-08; rtd 08. *39 Merryfield Crescent, Angmering, Littlehampton BN16 4DA* Tel (01903) 776607

WELLS, Robert Crosby. b 28. St Jo Coll Dur BA52. **d** 54 **p** 55. C S Shore H Trin *Blackb* 54-59; C-in-c Lea CD 59-69; V Ribby w Wrea 69-93; rtd 93; Perm to Offic *Blackb* from 93. *4 Myra Road, Fairhaven, Lytham St Annes FY8 1EB* Tel (01253) 739851

WELLS, The Ven Roderick John. b 36. Dur Univ BA63 Hull Univ MA85. Cuddesdon Coll 63. **d** 65 **p** 66. C Lambeth St Mary the Less *S'wark* 65-68; P-in-c 68-71; R Skegness *Linc* 71-77; P-in-c Winthorpe 77; R Skegness and Winthorpe 77-78; TR St and Cathl 86-01; Adn Stow 89-01; V Hackthorn w Cold Hanworth 89-93; P-in-c N w S Carlton 89-93; rtd 01;

Perm to Offic *Linc* and *Pet* from 01. *17 Ruddle Way, Langham, Oakham LE15 7NZ* Tel (01572) 756532 E-mail venrjw@googlemail.com

WELLS, Mrs Sally Ursula. b 40. St Mark's Coll Canberra BTh93 Ripon Coll Cuddesdon 96. **d** 97 **p** 98. Asst Chapl Vienna *Eur* 97-02; Perm to Offic 02-06; rtd 06. *10 Park Street, Salisbury SP1 3AU* Tel (01722) 322954 E-mail wellsfrance@gmail.com

WELLS, Canon Samuel Martin Bailey. b 65. Mert Coll Ox BA87 MA95 Edin Univ BD91 Dur Univ PhD96. Edin Th Coll 88. **d** 91 **p** 92. C Wallsend St Luke *Newc* 91-95; C Cherry Hinton St Andr *Ely* 95-97; C Teversham 95-97; P-in-c Earlham St Eliz *Nor* 97-03; RD Nor S 99-03; P-in-c Cambridge St Mark *Ely* 03-05; Can Th and Wiccamical Preb Chich Cathl from 04; Dean Duke Chpl Duke Univ N Carolina USA from 05. *Duke University, Durham NC 27708-0967, USA* Tel (001) (919) 684 2177 Fax 681 8660 E-mail samwells@bigfoot.com

WELLS, Terry Roy John. b 45. EAMTC 89. **d** 92 **p** 93. C Martlesham w Brightwell *St E* 92-95; R Higham, Holton St Mary, Raydon and Stratford 95-00; TV Walton and Trimley 00-07; rtd 07; Perm to Offic *Chelmsf* from 07. *Apartment 2, 1 The Maltings, The Quayside Maltings, High Street, Mistley, Manningtree CO11 1AL* Tel (01206) 392957 E-mail terry.wells@tesco.net

WELLS, Canon William David Sandford. b 41. JP. Oriel Coll Ox BA64 MA66. Ridley Hall Cam 63. **d** 65 **p** 66. C Gt Malvern St Mary *Worc* 65-70; V Crowle 70-84; P-in-c Himbleton w Huddington 78-84; V E Bowbrook 84-89; Hon Can Worc Cathl 84-07; RD Droitwich 84-96; R Bowbrook S 89-07; rtd 07. *25 Greenmead Avenue, Everton, Lymington SO41 0UF* Tel (01590) 642499 E-mail david.wells25@tiscali.co.uk

WELLS, Archdeacon of. *See* SULLIVAN, The Ven Nicola Ann

WELLS, Dean of. *See* CLARKE, The Very Revd John Martin

WELSBY, George Andrew. b 61. St Martin's Coll Lanc BA82 Leeds Univ BA98. Coll of Resurr Mirfield 96. **d** 98 **p** 99. C W Derby St Jo *Liv* 98-02; V Nuneaton St Mary *Cov* 02-07; Perm to Offic *Lich* 08-10; V Willenhall St Giles from 10; V Willenhall St Anne from 10; CMP from 06. *St Giles's Vicarage, Walsall Street, Willenhall WV13 2ER* Tel (01902) 605722

WELSH, Angus Alexander. b 30. Trin Coll Cam BA54 MA59. St Jo Coll Dur. **d** 56 **p** 57. C Jesmond Clayton Memorial *Newc* 56-60; C Fenham St Jas and St Basil 60-62; V Bacup St Jo *Man* 62-68; Tristan da Cunha 68-71; St Vincent 72-78; R Heysham *Blackb* 78-88; V Blackb St Steph 88-96; rtd 96; Perm to Offic *Newc* from 96. *23 Low Stobhill, Morpeth NE61 2SF* Tel (01670) 513261

WELSH, Colin. CITC. **d** 09 **p** 10. C Jordanstown *Conn* from 09. *5 Lenamore Park, Newtownabbey BT37 0PD* Tel (028) 9086 3310 E-mail colin.welsh@talktalk.net

WELSH, Jennifer Ann. b 48. Univ Coll Lon BA. **d** 81 **p** 98. NSM Newport St Matt *Mon* 81-85; NSM Risca 85-04; NSM Maindee Newport 04-09. *470 Caerleon Road, Newport NP19 7LW* Tel (01633) 258287

WELSH, Mrs Jennifer Lee. b 59. Calgary Univ BSc81. Cam Episc Div Sch (USA) MDiv87. **d** 87 **p** 88. C Calgary H Nativity Canada 87-89; Asst Chapl HM Pris Linc 89-94; Asst Chapl HM Pris Win 95-02; Chapl to Lutheran Students 03-08; Perm to Offic *Win* 95-02 and *Lon* 03-08; Chapl Univ Coll *Lon* from 08; C St Pancras w St Jas and Ch from 08. *21 Vincent Square, London SW1P 2NA* Tel (020) 7834 1300 E-mail jenniferwelsh@yahoo.co.uk

WELSH, Maxwell Wilfred. b 29. Bp's Coll Calcutta 55. **d** 58 **p** 59. India 58-72; C Cannock *Lich* 73-76; C Wednesfield 76-79; V Milton 79-86; V Croxton w Broughton and Adbaston 86-00; rtd 00; Perm to Offic *Lich* from 01. *24 Churchfield Road, Eccleshall, Stafford ST21 6AG* Tel (01785) 850530

WELSH, Philip Peter. b 48. Keble Coll Ox BA69 MA73 Selw Coll Cam BA72 MA76. Westcott Ho Cam 71. **d** 73 **p** 74. C W Dulwich All SS and Em *S'wark* 73-76; C Surbiton St Andr and St Mark 76-79; Lect St Steph Coll Delhi India 79-81; V Malden St Jo *S'wark* 81-87; Min Officer *Linc* 87-94; Tr Basingstoke *Win* 94-02; V Westmr St Steph w St Jo *Lon* from 02. *21 Vincent Square, London SW1P 2NA* Tel (020) 7834 1300 E-mail parishoffice@sswsj.org

WELSH, Robert Leslie. b 32. Sheff Univ BA54. St Jo Coll Dur. **d** 58 **p** 59. C S Westoe *Dur* 58-62; C Darlington St Cuth 62-66; CF (TA) 64-67; V E Rainton *Dur* 66-85; R W Rainton 66-85; R Wolsingham and Thornley 85-97; rtd 97. *12 Lea Green, Wolsingham, Bishop Auckland DL13 3DU* Tel (01388) 528529

WELSMAN, Derek Brian. b 65. Trin Coll Bris. **d** 99 **p** 00. C Ash *Guildf* 99-02; V Easebourne *Chich* 02-10; P-in-c Lurgashall, Lodsworth and Selham 08-10; V Easebourne, Lodsworth and Selham from 10; RD Midhurst from 10; Chapl K Edw VII Hosp Midhurst from 02. *The Priory, Easebourne, Midhurst GU29 0AJ* Tel (01730) 812655 *or* 813341 E-mail derekwelsman@btinternet.com

WELTERS, Mrs Elizabeth Ann. b 49. Bris Univ BSc70 Reading Univ PGCE71. SAOMC 94. **d** 97 **p** 98. NSM Aylesbury w Bierton and Hulcott *Ox* 97-03; NSM Schorne 03-10; rtd 10; Perm to Offic *Ox* from 11. *19 Scampton Close, Bicester*

OX26 4FF Tel (01869) 249481 E-mail lizwelters@yahoo.co.uk
WEMYSS, Canon Gary. b 52. Cranmer Hall Dur 79. **d** 80 **p** 81. C
Blackb St Jas 80-83; C Padiham 83-86; V Stalmine 86-90; P-in-c
Egton-cum-Newland and Lowick *Carl* 90-03; V Egton-cum-
Newland and Lowick and Colton from 03; RD Furness 04-10;
Hon Can Carl Cathl from 08. *The Vicarage, Penny Bridge,
Ulverston LA12 7RQ* Tel (01229) 861285
E-mail gwemyss@clara.co.uk
WENHAM, David. b 45. Pemb Coll Cam BA67 MA Man Univ
PhD70. Ridley Hall Cam 81. **d** 84 **p** 85. Tutor Wycliffe Hall Ox
84-07; Dean 02-05; Vice-Prin 05-96; NSM Shelswell *Ox* 96-02;
NSM Cumnor 03-07; Sen Tutor Trin Coll Bris from 07. *Trinity
College, Stoke Hill, Bristol BS9 1JP* Tel 0117-968 0244 Fax 968
7470
WENHAM, Michael Timothy. b 49. Pemb Coll Cam MA75.
Wycliffe Hall Ox. **d** 86 **p** 87. C Norbury *Ches* 86-89; V Stanford
in the Vale w Goosey and Hatford *Ox* 89-09; rtd 09; Perm to
Offic *Ox* from 09. *19 Churchward Close, Grove, Wantage
OX12 0QZ* Tel (01235) 760094 Mobile 07719-715640
E-mail michaeltwenham@googlemail.com
WENHAM, Peter William. b 47. Pemb Coll Cam MA73 MD85
FRCS76. St Jo Coll Nottm 98. **d** 01 **p** 02. NSM Wollaton Park
S'well 01-06; NSM Nottingham W Deanery 06-07; P-in-c
Edwalton from 07. *The Vicarage, Village Street, Edwalton,
Nottingham NG12 4AB* Tel 0115-923 2034
✠WENT, The Rt Revd John Stewart. b 44. CCC Cam BA66
MA70. Oak Hill Th Coll 67. **d** 69 **p** 70. C 96. C Northwood Em
Lon 69-75; V Margate H Trin *Cant* 75-83; Vice-Prin Wycliffe
Hall Ox 83-89; Adn Surrey *Guildf* 89-96; Chmn Dioc Coun for
Unity and Miss 90-96; Suff Bp Tewkesbury *Glouc* from 96; Hon
Can Glouc Cathl from 96. *Bishop's House, Church Road,
Staverton, Cheltenham GL51 0TW* Tel (01242) 680188 Fax
680233 E-mail bishop@star.co.uk
WENZEL, Peggy Sylvia. STh. Gilmore Ho. **d** 88 **p** 94. Perm to
Offic *Sarum* 88-08. *Church Cottage, Church Street, Pewsey
SN9 5DL* Tel (01672) 563834
WERNER, Canon Donald Kilgour. b 39. Univ of Wales BA61
Linacre Coll Ox BA64 MA67. Wycliffe Hall Ox 61. **d** 64 **p** 65. C
Wrexham *St As* 64-69; Chapl Brasted Place Coll Westerham
69-73; Chapl Bris Univ 73-76; Hon C Clifton St Paul 73-76;
Chapl Keele Univ 77-79; P-in-c Keele 77-79; C York St Mich-le-
Belfrey 79-83; Dir of Evang 79-83; R Holborn St Geo w H Trin
and St Bart *Lon* 83-02; Hon Can Bujumbura from 99; Prof and
Dean Th Light Univ Burundi from 03; Lic Preacher *Lon* 02-04;
rtd 05. *7 Minstrel Close, Hucknall NG15 7NZ* Tel 0115-963 1504
Mobile 07837-181565 E-mail donaldinburundi@hotmail.com
WERRELL, Ralph Sidney. b 29. Hull Univ PhD02. Tyndale Hall
Bris 54. **d** 56 **p** 57. C Penn Fields *Lich* 56-60; C Champion Hill
St Sav *S'wark* 60-61; R Danby Wiske w Yafforth *Ripon* 61-65;
P-in-c Hutton Bonville *York* 61-65; R Combs *St E* 65-75; V
Bootle Ch Ch *Liv* 75-80; R Scole, Brockdish, Billingford, Thorpe
Abbots etc *Nor* 80-83; R Southam w Stockton *Cov* 83-89; R
Southam 89-94; rtd 95; Perm to Offic *Birm* and *Cov* from 95;
Lich from 01. *Sameach, 2A Queens Road, Kenilworth CV8 1JQ*
Tel and fax (01926) 858677
WERRETT, Olivia Margaret. b 50. Bp Otter Coll 00. **d** 03. NSM
Bexhill St Pet *Chich* from 03. *127 Pebsham Lane, Bexhill-on-Sea
TN40 2RP* Tel (01424) 214144
E-mail olivia@1950werrett.freeserve.co.uk
WERWATH, Wolfgang Albert Richard Kurt. b 22. Ripon Hall Ox
54. **d** 56 **p** 57. C Hamer *Man* 56-58; C N Reddish 58-59; V
Chadderton St Luke 59-67; V Whitfield *Derby* 67-75; V Bretby w
Newton Solney 75-88; rtd 88; Perm to Offic *Derby* from 88 and
S'well from 90. *28 D'Ayncourt Walk, Farnsfield, Newark
NG22 8DP* Tel (01623) 882635
WESSON, Preb John Graham. b 38. St Pet Coll Ox BA62 MA68.
Clifton Th Coll 63. **d** 65 **p** 66. C Southport Ch Ch w St Andr *Liv*
65-68; C Ox St Ebbe w St Pet 68-71; Chapl Poly Cen Lon 71-76;
C-in-c Edin St Thos 76-82; Dir Past Studies Trin Coll Bris 82-86;
R Birm St Martin w Bordesley St Andr 86-96; RD Birm City
88-95; Hon Can Birm Cathl 91-96; Dir Local Min Development
Lich 96-98; Team Ldr Min Division 99-03; Team Ldr Bd of Min
99-03; C Lich St Mich w St Mary and Wall 96-03; Preb Lich
Cathl 97-03; rtd 03. *11 Gordon Drive, Abingdon OX14 3SW* Tel
(01235) 526088
WESSON, William James. b 60. Lon Univ BA82 Leeds Univ
BA07. Coll of Resurr Mirfield 05. **d** 07 **p** 08. C Moulsecoomb
Chich from 07. *St Andrew's Rectory, Hillside, Brighton BN2 4TA*
WEST, Alan David. b 61. Southn Univ BTh92 Thames Valley
Univ MA97. Aston Tr Scheme 87 Sarum & Wells Th Coll 89.
d 92 **p** 93. C S'wark St Geo the Martyr w St Jude 92-94; C
S'wark St Geo w St Alphege and St Jude 95-96; V Boscoppa
Truro 96-02; Chapl Mt Edgcumbe Hospice 02-05; Chapl R
Cornwall Hosps Trust from 05. *Royal Cornwall Hospital,
Treliske, Truro TR1 3LJ* Tel (01872) 252883
E-mail alan.west@rcht.cornwall.nhs.uk
WEST, Andrew Victor. b 59. Wycliffe Hall Ox 87. **d** 90 **p** 91. C
Leyland St Andr *Blackb* 90-94; C Blackpool St Jo 94-96; TV
Bedworth *Cov* 96-98; Chapl Cheltenham and Glouc Coll of HE
98-01; Chapl Glos Univ 01-03; Chapl St Martin's Coll *Carl*

03-07; Chapl Cumbria Univ 07-10; C Carl St Jo 03-10; R
Gateshead Fell *Dur* from 10. *The Rectory, 45 Shotley Gardens,
Low Fell, Gateshead NE9 5DP* Tel 0191-442 2463
WEST, Bernard Kenneth. b 31. Linc Th Coll. **d** 67 **p** 68. C E Ham
St Geo *Chelmsf* 67-71; C Gt Bookham *Guildf* 71-73; R
Esperance Australia 73-76; C Dalkeith 76-79; P-in-c Carine
80-82; R Carine w Duncraig 82-84; C Ravensthorpe 85-87; rtd
87. *9 Beaufort Street, Katanning WA 6317, Australia* Tel (0061)
(8) 9821 4571
WEST, Bryan Edward. b 39. Avery Hill Coll CertEd69 BEd80
Kent Univ MA86. Cant Sch of Min 85. **d** 88 **p** 89. NSM
Gravesend H Family w Ifield *Roch* 88-92; C Gravesend St Geo
92-95; NSM Hatcham Park All SS *S'wark* 95-98; NSM
Stambridge and Ashingdon w S Fambridge *Chelmsf* 98-01;
NSM Canvey Is 01-06; Chapl Southend Health Care NHS Trust
99-06; Perm to Offic *Chelmsf* from 06. *The Rectory, 7 Merlin End,
Colchester CO4 3FW* Tel (01206) 866145
E-mail bryanwest@tiscali.co.uk
WEST, Miss Caroline Elisabeth. b 61. RGN84. Wycliffe Hall Ox
93. **d** 95. NSM Eastrop *Win* from 95. *19 Beaulieu Court,
Riverdene, Basingstoke RG21 4DQ* Tel (01256) 350389 *or* 464249
E-mail caroline.west@stmarys-basingstoke.org.uk
WEST, Mrs Christine Cecily. TCD BA60 MA63 HDipEd61.
CITC 91. **d** 94 **p** 95. NSM Bray *D & G* 94-96; NSM Kilternan
96-99; Lic to Offic from 99. *55 Beech Park Road, Foxrock, Dublin
18, Republic of Ireland* Tel (00353) (1) 289 6374
WEST, Clive. b 35. QUB BD75 Stranmillis Coll TCert57. CITC
62. **d** 64 **p** 65. C Lisburn Ch Ch Cathl 64-68; Asst Master
Lisnagarvey Sec Sch Lisburn 68-70; C Belfast All SS 70-75; I
84-00; Can Belf Cathl 95-00; I Mullabrack w Kilcluney *Arm*
76-84; rtd 00. *16 Stormont Park, Belfast BT4 3GX* Tel (028) 9041
9317 E-mail clivewest@tiscali.co.uk
WEST, David Marshall. b 48. St Jo Coll Dur BA70. **d** 73 **p** 74. C
Wylde Green *Birm* 73-76; C Wokingham St Paul *Ox* 76-79; V
Hurst 79-88; V Maidenhead St Luke 88-95; C Whitley Ch Ch
95-99; P-in-c Reading Ch Ch 99-05; V from 05. *Christ Church
Vicarage, 4 Vicarage Road, Reading RG2 7AJ* Tel 0118-987 1250
E-mail revdmwest@hotmail.com
WEST, Mrs Deirdre Ann. b 47. **d** 10 **p** 11. OLM Campsea Ashe w
Marlesford, Parham and Hacheston *St E* from 10; OLM
Brandeston w Kettleburgh and Easton from 10. *Smokey House,
The Common, Turnstall, Woodbridge IP12 2JR* Tel (01728)
688340 E-mail deirdre.west@btinternet.com
WEST, Derek Elvin. b 47. Hull Univ BA69. Westcott Ho Cam 71.
d 73 **p** 74. C Walthamstow St Pet *Chelmsf* 73-77; C Chingford SS
Pet and Paul 77-80; TV W Slough *Ox* 80-88; Slough Community
Chapl 88-95; TV Upton cum Chalvey from 95. *St Peter's
Vicarage, 52 Montem Lane, Slough SL1 2QJ* Tel (01753) 520725
WEST, Mrs Elizabeth Maxine. b 47. Liv Univ BA69 Lon Inst of
Educn PGCE70 K Coll Lon BA95 AKC. NTMTC. **d** 99 **p** 00.
NSM Hornsey H Innocents *Lon* 99-00; NSM Highgate St Mich
00-03; C from 03. *West Villa, Inderwick Road, London N8 9JU*
Tel (020) 8348 3042
WEST, Canon Eric Robert Glenn. b 55. QUB BA79 Man Univ
DipEd80. CITC BTh92. **d** 92 **p** 93. C Enniskillen *Clogh* 92-95; I
Lisbellaw 95-00; CF 00-03; I Annagh w Drumgoon, Ashfield etc
K, E & A 03-06; I Derryvullen N w Castlearchdale *Clogh* from
06; Can St Patr Cathl Dublin from 11. *6 The Everglades,
Enniskillen BT74 6FE* Tel (028) 6634 6870 Mobile
07969-332530 E-mail glenn.west55@hotmail.com
WEST, Henry Cyrano. b 28. K Coll Lon. **d** 51 **p** 52. C Braunstone
Leic 51-53; C Wandsworth St Anne *S'wark* 53-55; C Raynes
Park w St Sav 55-58; CF 58-63; V Sculcoates *York* 63-71; P-in-c
Kingston upon Hull St Jude w St Steph 71-75; Lic to Offic *Cov*
71-75 and *Man* 75-87; Hon C Hulme Ascension *Man* 87-94; rtd
91; Perm to Offic *Man* 91-08. *6 King's Drive, Middleton,
Manchester M24 4FB* Tel 0161-643 4410
WEST, Jeffrey James. b 50. OBE06. Worc Coll Ox BA72 BPhil74
MA76 FSA11 FRSA01. Ripon Coll Cuddesdon 05. **d** 07 **p** 08.
NSM Banbury *Ox* from 07. *St Mary's Centre, Horse Fair,
Banbury OX16 0AA* Tel 07766-198484 (mobile)
E-mail curate@stmaryschurch-banbury.org.uk
WEST, Keith. See RYDER-WEST, Keith
WEST (formerly WINDIATE), Mrs Mary Elizabeth. b 49. Linc
Th Coll 94. **d** 94 **p** 95. C Loughton St Jo *Chelmsf* 94-98; P-in-c
Ashingdon w S Fambridge 98-01; P-in-c Stambridge 98-01; TV
Canvey Is 01-07; P-in-c Greenstead w Colchester St Anne 07-08;
TR from 08. *The Rectory, 7 Merlin End, Colchester CO4 3FW*
Tel (01206) 866145 E-mail mothermary2@tiscali.co.uk
WEST, Maxine. See WEST, Mrs Elizabeth Maxine
WEST, Canon Michael Brian. b 39. Bris Univ BSc60. Linc Th
Coll 64. **d** 66 **p** 67. C Bp's Hatfield *St Alb* 66-69; Ind Chapl 69-81;
Sen Ind Chapl 71-81; Hon Can St Alb 78-81; Sen Ind Chapl and
Hon Can Sheff Cathl 81-01; Dir Open Forum for Economic
Regeneration 02-04; rtd 04; Perm to Offic *Sheff* from 02.
23 Walton Road, Sheffield S11 8RE Tel 0114-266 2188
E-mail mike.west23@tiscali.co.uk
WEST, Canon Michael Frederick. b 50. Trin Coll Ox BA72 MA76
UEA PhD96. Westcott Ho Cam 72. **d** 74 **p** 75. C

Wolverhampton *Lich* 74-78; C Hanley H Ev 78-79; TV 79-82; Dioc Youth Officer *St E* 83-88; V Ipswich St Thos 88-95; Prin OLM Scheme 96-03; Hon Can St E Cathl 96-03; Can Res and Chan Linc Cathl 03-08; Dioc Dir Formation in Discipleship and Min 03-06; TR Wrexham *St As* from 08; AD Wrexham from 08; Chan St As Cathl from 11. *Llwyn Endaf, 3 Craigmillar Road, Wrexham LL12 7AR* Tel (01978) 355808
E-mail rector@wrexhamparish.org.uk

WEST, Michael John. b 33. Imp Coll Lon BScEng54 ARSM54 CEng60 FIMMM68 FREng89 Hon FIMMM96. S'wark Ord Course 85. **d** 88 **p** 89. NSM Caterham *S'wark* 88-98; Perm to Offic *Chich* from 97. *Minstrels, The Causeway, Horsham RH12 1HE* Tel (01403) 263437 Fax 249604
E-mail mwest.viabt@btinternet.com

WEST, Michael Oakley. b 31. Open Univ BA97. Bris Bapt Coll 53 Wells Th Coll 62. **d** 63 **p** 64. C Swindon Ch Ch *Bris* 63-66; Libya 66-68; R Lydiard Millicent w Lydiard Tregoz *Bris* 68-75; V Breage w Germoe *Truro* 75-82; CMS 82-91; Chapl Tel Aviv 82-89; Chapl Shiplake Coll Henley 91-94; Asst Chapl Bryanston Sch 94-95; rtd 96; Perm to Offic *Eur* 95-97 and Lon 96-97; Lic to Offic Spokane USA from 97. *1932 East 25th Avenue, Spokane WA 99203, USA*

WEST, Paul. b 66. Newc Univ Aus BA87 DipEd94. Westcott Ho Cam 04. **d** 06 **p** 07. C Albury Australia 06-08; C Dee Why 08-09; Asst P King Street 09-10; P-in-c Wisbech SS Pet and Paul *Ely* from 10. *The Vicarage, Love Lane, Wisbech PE13 1HP* Tel (01945) 580375 Mobile 07584-897143
E-mail ppaulwest@hotmail.com

WEST, Paul Leslie. b 57. OLM course 96. **d** 99 **p** 00. OLM Kinnerley w Melverley and Knockin w Maesbrook *Lich* from 99. *Braddan, Farm Hall, Kinnerley, Oswestry SY10 8EG* Tel (01691) 682600

WEST, Penelope Ann. Chelt & Glouc Coll of HE MA98 Univ of Wales (Lamp) MPhil08 FIBMS72. **d** 00 **p** 01. NSM Hartpury w Corse and Staunton *Glouc* 00-09; NSM Ashleworth, Corse, Hartpury, Hasfield etc from 09. *Catsbury Cottage, Corsend Road, Hartpury GL19 3BP* Tel (01425) 700314
E-mail revpennyahamer@aol.com

WEST, Peter Harcourt. b 29. **d** 59 **p** 60. C Histon *Ely* 59-60; C Hampreston *Sarum* 60-61; C Braintree *Chelmsf* 61-63; Perm to Offic from 72; rtd 94. *Westgates, 139 Witham Road, Black Notley, Braintree CM77 8LR* Tel (01376) 323048

WEST, Canon Philip William. b 48. Magd Coll Ox BA70 MA78. St Jo Coll Nottm BA74. **d** 75 **p** 76. C Rushden w Newton Bromswold Pet 75-79; C Pitsmoor w Ellesmere *Sheff* 79-83; V Attercliffe 83-89; Ind Chapl 85-90; P-in-c Darnall 86-89; V Stannington from 89; P-in-c Sheff St Bart 02-07; AD Hallam 96-02; Hon Can Sheff Cathl from 01. *The Vicarage, 214 Oldfield Road, Stannington, Sheffield S6 6DY* Tel 0114-232 4490 or 234 5586

WEST, Reginald Roy. b 28. St Deiniol's Hawarden 74. **d** 74 **p** 75. C Abergavenny St Mary w Llanwenarth Citra *Mon* 74-77; V Tredegar St Jas 77-96; rtd 96; Lic to Offic *Mon* from 96. *2 Croesonen Park, Abergavenny NP7 6PD* Tel (01873) 857043

WEST, Ruth. b 09 **p** 10. C Waterford w Killea, Drumcannon and Dunhill *C & O* from 09. *The Rectory, Church Road, Tramore, Co Waterford, Republic of Ireland* E-mail ruthjwest@hotmail.com

WEST, Stephen Peter. b 52. Liv Univ CertEd74. Oak Hill Th Coll 87. **d** 89 **p** 90. C Gateacre *Liv* 89-92; V Liv All So Springwood 92-02; TV Teignmouth, Ideford w Luton, Ashcombe etc *Ex* from 02. *The Vicarage, 3 Moors Park, Bishopsteignton, Teignmouth TQ14 9RH* Tel and fax (01626) 775247
E-mail spmwest@btinternet.com

WEST, Mrs Suzanne Elizabeth. b 46. STETS 04. **d** 07 **p** 08. NSM Portsea St Geo *Portsm* from 07. *64 Melville Road, Gosport PO12 4QX* Tel (023) 9278 8782
E-mail melville64@ntlworld.com

WEST, Canon Thomas Roderic. b 55. BTh90. TCD Div Sch. **d** 86 **p** 87. C Dromore Cathl 86-89; I Carrowdore w Millisle 89-95; I Moira from 95; Can Dromore Cathl from 05; Chan from 08. *The Rectory, 1 Main Street, Moira, Craigavon BT67 0LE* Tel (028) 9261 1268 *or* 9261 7333 E-mail roderic@moiraparish.org.uk

WEST, Timothy Ralph. b 53. Bath Univ BSc75. Ridley Hall Cam 82. **d** 85 **p** 86. C Mildenhall *St E* 85-88; TV Melbury *Sarum* 88-92; TR 92-98; TR Preston w Sutton Poyntz and Osmington w Poxwell from 98. *The Rectory, Sutton Road, Preston, Weymouth DT3 6BX* Tel (01305) 833142 Mobile 07000-785720
E-mail t.r.west@psion.net

WEST AFRICA, Archbishop of. *See* AKROFI, The Most Revd Justice Ofei

WEST CUMBERLAND, Archdeacon of. *See* PRATT, The Ven Richard David

WEST HAM, Archdeacon of. *See* COCKETT, The Ven Elwin Wesley

WEST-LINDELL, Stein Erling. b 54. BA. Linc Th Coll 82. **d** 84 **p** 85. C Allington and Maidstone St Pet *Cant* 84-87; R Orlestone w Snave and Ruckinge w Warehorne 87-93; R Byfield w Boddington and Aston le Walls *Pet* 93-99; V Nor Lakenham

St Alb and St Mark from 99. *St Alban's Vicarage, Eleanor Road, Norwich NR1 2RE* Tel (01603) 621843

WESTALL, Jonathan Mark. b 67. Nottm Univ BSc88 K Coll Lon PGCE93 St Jo Coll Dur BA98. Cranmer Hall Dur 96. **d** 99 **p** 00. C St Helier *S'wark* 99-02; C Reading Greyfriars *Ox* 02-06; V E Acton St Dunstan w St Thos *Lon* from 06. *The Vicarage, 54 Perryn Road, London W3 7NA* Tel (020) 8743 4117
E-mail jonwestall@btinternet.com

✠**WESTALL, The Rt Revd Michael Robert.** b 39. Qu Coll Cam BA62 MA66. Cuddesdon Coll 63 Harvard Div Sch 65. **d** 66 **p** 67 **c** 01. C Heref St Martin 66-70; India 70-83; Vice Prin Bp's Coll Calcutta 76-79; Prin 79-83; Prin St Mark's Th Coll Dar-es-Salaam Tanzania 84-92; R Alfrick, Lulsley, Suckley, Leigh and Bransford *Worc* 93-00; Bp SW Tanganyika 01-06; rtd 06; P-in-c Torquay St Luke *Ex* from 07; Hon Asst Bp Ex from 07. *St Luke's Vicarage, 1 Mead Road, Torquay TQ2 6TE* Tel (01803) 605437

WESTBROOK, Canon Colin David. b 36. Oriel Coll Ox BA59. St Steph Ho Ox MA63. **d** 61 **p** 62. C Roath St Martin *Llan* 61-66; C Roath 66-74; V Llantarnam *Mon* 74-79; V Newport St Jo Bapt 79-07; P-in-c from 07; Hon Can St Woolos Cathl 88-91; Can from 91; Warden of Ords 91-99. *St John's Vicarage, 62 Oakfield Road, Newport NP20 4LP* Tel (01633) 265581

WESTBROOK (née REED), Mrs Ethel Patricia Ivy. b 42. Bris Univ CertEd63. Cant Sch of Min 82. **dss** 84 **d** 87 **p** 94. Fawkham and Hartley *Roch* 84-85; Asst Dir of Educn 84-86; Chapl at Hoo w Cooling 85-86; Corby SS Pet and Andr w Gt and Lt Oakley 86-90; Par Dn 87-90; Par Dn Roch 90-94; C Rainham 94-99; V Joydens Wood St Barn 99-05; Dioc Chapl MU 01-05; rtd 05; Hon C Banstead *Guildf* 05-11; Perm to Offic *Roch* from 05. *5 Victoria Mews, Station Road, Westgate-on-Sea CT8 8RQ*
E-mail patriciawipe@yahoo.co.uk

WESTBY, Martyn John. b 61. Leeds Univ BA83. Trin Coll Bris 96. **d** 98 **p** 99. C Drypool *York* 98-01; P-in-c Cherry Burton from 01; Chapl Bp Burton Coll York from 01; Assoc Dioc Dir of Ords York 05-10; C Etton w Dalton Holme from 11. *The Rectory, Main Street, Cherry Burton, Beverley HU17 7RF* Tel (01964) 503036

WESTCOTT, James John. b 55. St Jo RC Sem Surrey 76. **d** 81 **p** 82. In RC Ch 81-93; C Westmr St Steph w St Jo *Lon* 93-96; P-in-c Haggerston St Chad 96-01; V from 01. *St Chad's Vicarage, Dunloe Street, London E2 8JR* Tel (020) 7613 2229
E-mail chad@jameswestcott.co.uk

WESTERMANN-CHILDS, Miss Emma Jane. b 71. Univ of Wales (Ban) BA93 Ox Univ MTh99. Ripon Coll Cuddesdon 96. **d** 98 **p** 99. C Launceston *Truro* 98-01; P-in-c St Stephen in Brannel from 01. *The Rectory, 70 Rectory Road, St Stephen, St Austell PL26 7RL* Tel (01726) 822236
E-mail emma.childs@btinternet.com

WESTERN, Canon Robert Geoffrey. b 37. Man Univ BSc60. Qu Coll Birm. **d** 62 **p** 63. C Sedbergh *Bradf* 62-65; PV Linc Cathl 65-73; Hd Master Linc Cathl Sch 74-96; Can and Preb Linc Cathl 74-96; rtd 97. *2 Guldrey House, Guldrey Lane, Sedbergh LA10 5DS* Tel (01539) 621426

WESTHAVER, George Derrick. b 68. St Mary's Univ Halifax NS BA92. Wycliffe Coll Toronto MDiv98. **d** 97 **p** 98. C Teversham and Cherry Hinton St Andr *Ely* 97-00; TV The Ramseys and Upwood 00-03; Chapl Linc Coll Ox 03-06; C Ox St Mich w St Martin and All SS 03-06; R Halifax St Geo Canada from 07. *2222 Brunswick Avenue, Halifax NS B3K 2Z3, Canada* Tel (001) (902) 423 1059 Fax 423 0897 E-mail gwesthaver@gmail.com

WESTLAKE, Michael Paul. b 34. Ex Coll Ox BA56 MA64. Wells Th Coll 59. **d** 61 **p** 62. C Southmead *Bris* 61-67; V Eastville St Thos 67-74; V Eastville St Thos w St Anne 74-83; P-in-c Easton St Mark 79-83; V Marshfield w Cold Ashton and Tormarton etc 83-01; rtd 01; Perm to Offic *Birm* from 01. *65 Duxford Road, Great Barr, Birmingham B42 2JD* Tel 0121-358 7030

WESTLAND, Richard Theodore. b 27. **d** 87 **p** 88. OLM Freiston w Butterwick *Linc* 87-97; rtd 97; Perm to Offic *Linc* from 97. *76 Brand End Road, Butterwick, Boston PE22 0JD* Tel (01205) 760572

WESTLEY, Stuart. b 24. Em Coll Cam BA48 MA52 Man Univ DASE84. Wells Th Coll 49. **d** 50 **p** 51. C Prestwich St Marg *Man* 50-53; C Tonge w Alkrington 53-55; C-in-c Oldham St Ambrose 55-58; Lic to Offic *Blackb* 58-70; Chapl Arnold Sch Blackpool 58-66; Asst Chapl Denstone Coll Uttoxeter 70-73; Chapl Ermysted's Gr Sch Skipton 73-85; Hon C Blackpool St Mich *Blackb* 75-77; Perm to Offic *Bradf* 77-78; Lic to Offic 78-85; C Padiham *Blackb* 85-89; rtd 89; Perm to Offic *Blackb* from 89. *17 Fosbrooke House, Clifton Drive, Lytham St Annes FY8 5RQ* E-mail s.westley@amserve.net

WESTMINSTER, Archdeacon of. *Vacant*

WESTMINSTER, Dean of. *See* HALL, The Very Revd John Robert

WESTMORELAND, Mrs Diane Ruth. b 57. Man Univ BA78. NEOC 95. **d** 98 **p** 99. NSM Tadcaster w Newton Kyme *York* 98-99; C 99-02; P-in-c Stamford Bridge Gp 02-08; P-in-c Amble

Newc from 08. *The Vicarage, Straffen Court, Amble, Morpeth NE65 0HA* Tel (01665) 714560 E-mail diane@dianewestmoreland.com

WESTMORLAND AND FURNESS, Archdeacon of. *Vacant*

WESTNEY, Michael Edward William. b 29. Lich Th Coll 64. **d** 65 **p** 66. C Hughenden *Ox* 65-68; C Banbury 68-71; TV Trunch *Nor* 71-78; V Reading St Matt *Ox* 78-83; TV W Slough 83-88; TR 88-94; rtd 94; Perm to Offic *Ox* 97-00. *59 Portland Close, Burnham, Slough SL2 2LT* Tel (01628) 660052

WESTON, Canon David Wilfrid Valentine. b 37. Lanc Univ PhD93. **d** 67 **p** 68. OSB 60-84; Lic to Offic *Ox* 67-84; Prior Nashdom Abbey 71-74; Abbot 74-84; C Chorley St Pet *Blackb* 84-85; V Pilling 85-89; Bp's Dom Chapl *Carl* 89-94; Can Res Carl Cathl 94-05; Lib 95-05; Vice-Dean 00; rtd 05. *40 St James Road, Carlisle CA2 5PD* Tel (01228) 550331

WESTON, Gary James. b 72. Westmr Coll Ox BTh95. Wycliffe Hall Ox 02. **d** 04 **p** 05. C Barrow St Paul *Carl* 04-08; C S Barrow 08-09; P-in-c Hinckley H Trin *Leic* 09-10; V Hinckley St Jo from 10. *The Vicarage, 7 Rosemary Way, Hinckley LE10 0LN* Tel (01455) 233552 E-mail gary.weston@ukonline.co.uk

WESTON, Ivan John. b 45. MBE88. Chich Th Coll 71. **d** 74 **p** 75. C Harlow St Mary Magd *Chelmsf* 74-77; Chapl RAF 77-00; Perm to Offic *Nor* 93-94 and *Ely* from 00. *2 The Furlongs, Needingworth, St Ives PE27 4TX* Tel (01480) 462107

WESTON, John Oglivy. b 30. St Pet Coll Ox BA66 MA70. Linc Th Coll 71. **d** 71 **p** 72. Lect Trent (Nottm) Poly 66-82; Hon C Long Clawson and Hose *Leic* 71-82; Hon C Bingham *S'well* 82-85; Lic to Offic 85-91; rtd 91; Perm to Offic *Heref* from 91. *Mowbray Lodge, Marshbrook, Church Stretton SY6 6QE* Tel (01694) 781288

WESTON, Mrs Judith. b 36. Open Univ BA75 MSR56. St Jo Coll Nottm 84. **dss** 85 **d** 87 **p** 94. Huddersfield H Trin *Wakef* 85-87; Par Dn 87-91; Par Dn Wakef St Andr and St Mary 91-94; C 94-95; Chapl Huddersfield NHS Trust 95-98; rtd 96; Perm to Offic *Wakef* from 98. *Overcroft, 8A Newland Road, Huddersfield HD5 0QT* Tel (01484) 453591

WESTON, Canon Keith Aitken Astley. b 26. Trin Hall Cam BA51 MA55. Ridley Hall Cam 51. **d** 53 **p** 54. C Weston-super-Mare Ch Ch *B & W* 53-56; C Cheltenham St Mark *Glouc* 56-59; PC Clevedon Ch Ch *B & W* 59-64; R Ox St Ebbe w H Trin and St Pet 64-85; RD Ox 71-76; Hon Can Ch Ch 81-85; Dir Post-Ord Tr *Nor* 85-90; Dioc Dir of Ords 85-91; P-in-c Nor St Steph 85-91; Hon Brigade Chapl Norfolk Co Fire Service 90-91; rtd 91; Hon C Thame *Ox* from 91. *18 Moor End Lane, Thame OX9 3BQ* Tel (01844) 215441

WESTON, Neil. b 51. Jes Coll Ox BA73 MA78. Ridley Hall Cam 74. **d** 76 **p** 77. C Ealing St Mary *Lon* 76-80; P-in-c Pertenhall w Swineshead *St Alb* 80-89; P-in-c Dean w Yelden, Melchbourne and Shelton 80-89; R The Stodden Churches 89-91; R Newhaven *Chich* 91-98; P-in-c Radcliffe-on-Trent and Shelford etc *S'well* 98-04; R 04-05; V Radcliffe-on-Trent and Shelford 06-09; R Kington w Huntington, Old Radnor, Kinnerton etc *Heref* from 09. *The Vicarage, Church Road, Kington HR5 3AG* Tel (01544) 230525 E-mail kington.vicar@ymail.com

WESTON, Paul David Astley. b 57. Trin Hall Cam BA80 MA83 Westmr Coll Ox MPhil92 K Coll Lon PhD02. Wycliffe Hall Ox 83. **d** 85 **p** 86. C New Malden and Coombe *S'wark* 85-89; Lect Oak Hill Th Coll 89-97; Vice-Prin 97-00; Gen Sec UCCF 00-01; Assoc Lect Ridley Hall Cam 02-03; Tutor from 03; Perm to Offic *Ely* from 03. *Ridley Hall, Ridley Hall Road, Cambridge CB3 9HG* Tel (01223) 746580 Fax 746581 E-mail pdaw2@cam.ac.uk

WESTON, Phillip Richard. b 76. Bath Univ BSc99 York Univ MSc02. Wycliffe Hall Ox BA09. **d** 10 **p** 11. C Aughton Ch Ch *Liv* from 10. *25 Peet Avenue, Ormskirk L39 4SH* Tel (01695) 577958 Mobile 07939-129631 E-mail home@phweston.com

WESTON, Ralph Edward Norman. b 30. Worc Ord Coll 67. **d** 69 **p** 70. C Harborne St Pet *Birm* 69-71; CF 71-75; Chapl Oswestry Sch 75-85; Chapl Rotherham Distr Gen Hosp 85-95; CF (ACF) 87-95; TV Thorverton, Cadbury, Upton Pyne etc *Ex* 95-99; rtd 95; Perm to Offic *Ex* from 99. *10 Rogers Close, Tiverton EX16 6UW* Tel and fax (01884) 259622

WESTON, Canon Stephen John Astley. b 55. Aston Univ BSc77. Ridley Hall Cam 78. **d** 81 **p** 82. C Gt Chesham *Ox* 81-85; C Southport Ch Ch *Liv* 85-87; P-in-c Gayhurst w Ravenstone, Stoke Goldington etc *Ox* 87-91; R 91-96; RD Newport 92-95; V Chipping Norton 96-01; TR from 01; AD Chipping Norton 02-07; Hon Can Ch Ch from 06. *The Vicarage, Church Street, Chipping Norton OX7 5NT* Tel (01608) 642688 E-mail revsweston@lineone.net

WESTON, Timothy Bernard Charles. b 48. **d** 03 **p** 04. OLM Watton w Carbrooke and Ovington *Nor* 03-07; OLM Ashill, Carbrooke, Ovington and Saham Toney from 07. *Sunset Barn, Morton Lane, Weston Longville, Norwich NR9 5JL* Tel (01603) 879115 E-mail rev.weston@btinternet.com

WESTON, Mrs Virginia Anne. b 58. UEA BSc79. Wycliffe Hall Ox 84. **d** 87 **p** 02. Par Dn New Malden and Coombe *S'wark* 87-89; Lic to Offic *Lon* 89-01; Chapl to People at Work in Cam

Ely 02-06. *65 Manor Place, Cambridge CB1 1LJ* Tel (01223) 462279 E-mail virginiaweston@yahoo.co.uk

WESTWOOD, Canon John Richard. b 55. Clare Coll Cam BA77 MA81 Lambeth MA98. Ripon Coll Cuddesdon 77. **d** 79 **p** 80. C Oakham w Hambleton and Egleton *Pet* 79-81; C Oakham, Hambleton, Egleton, Braunston and Brooke 81-83; V Gt w Lt Harrowden and Orlingbury 83-90; V Wellingborough St Andr 90-99; RD Wellingborough 92-97; R Irthlingborough 99-10; P-in-c Rothwell w Orton, Rushton w Glendon and Pipewell from 10; C Broughton w Loddington and Cransley etc from 10; Warden of Readers 95-05; Can Pet Cathl from 97. *The Vicarage, High Street, Rothwell, Kettering NN14 6BQ* Tel (01536) 710268 E-mail revdjohn.westwood@tesco.net

WESTWOOD, Peter. b 38. Open Univ BA76. AKC65. **d** 65 **p** 66. C Acomb St Steph *York* 65-68; Chapl HM Youth Cust Cen Onley 69-73; Chapl HM Pris Leic 73-77; Maidstone 77-81; Dur 81-87; Brixton 87-93; Wormwood Scrubs 93-98; Perm to Offic *S'wark* from 98; rtd 99. *St Stephen's Church, College Road, London SE21 7HN* Tel (020) 8693 0082

WESTWOOD, Richard Andrew. b 64. Nottm Univ BSc85 PGCE86. St Jo Coll Nottm 02. **d** 04 **p** 05. C Gt Wyrley *Lich* from 04. *46 Gorsey Lane, Great Wyrley, Walsall WS6 6EX* Tel (01922) 419161 E-mail rrejas@ic24.net

WESTWOOD, Timothy. b 61. Wolv Poly MBA91. WMMTC 95. **d** 98 **p** 99. NSM Sedgley St Mary *Worc* from 98. *5 Deborah Close, Wolverhampton WV2 3HS* Tel (01902) 831078 E-mail twestwood@blueyonder.co.uk

WETHERALL, Canon Cecil Edward (Ted). b 29. St Jo Coll Dur 49. **d** 56 **p** 57. C Ipswich St Aug *St E* 56-59; R Hitcham 59-79; P-in-c Brettenham 61-63; P-in-c Kettlebaston 71-91; R Hitcham w Lt Finborough 79-91; P-in-c Preston 83-91, Hon Can St E Cathl 83-91; rtd 92; Perm to Offic *St E* 92-97; Asst Chapl Athens w Kifissia, Patras, Thessaloniki etc *Eur* 92-96. *Kastraki, Tolo, Nafplio, 210 56 Argolis, Greece*

WETHERALL, Mrs Joanne Elizabeth Julia. b 62. STETS 02. **d** 05 **p** 06. NSM Godalming *Guildf* 05-09; TV Tring St Alb from 09. *The Vicarage, Station Road, Aldbury, Tring HP23 5RS* Tel (01442) 851200 E-mail joanne.wetherall@btinternet.com

WETHERALL, Canon Nicholas Guy. b 52. Lon Univ BMus73 Ox Univ CertEd75. Chich Th Coll 82. **d** 84 **p** 85. C Cleobury Mortimer w Hopton Wafers *Heref* 84-87; TV Leominster 87-92; V Cuckfield *Chich* from 92; RD Cuckfield 99-03; Can and Preb Chich Cathl from 08. *The Vicarage, Broad Street, Cuckfield, Haywards Heath RH17 5LL* Tel (01444) 454007

WETHERELL, Ms Eileen Joyce. b 44. Westf Coll Lon BSc66. S Dios Minl Tr Scheme 89. **d** 92 **p** 94. Par Dn Southampton Maybush St Pet *Win* 92-94; C 94-96; TV Totton 96-04; V Hythe from 04; Dioc Adv for Women's Min from 02. *The Vicarage, 14 Atheling Road, Hythe, Southampton SO45 6BR* Tel (023) 8084 2461 E-mail eileenwetherell@btinternet.com

WETHERELL, Philippa Clare. b 80. Univ of Wales (Cardiff) BSc02. Trin Coll Bris BA08. **d** 09. C W Derby St Mary and St Jas *Liv* from 09. *4 The Armoury, West Derby, Liverpool L12 5EL* Tel 07770-892639 (mobile) E-mail phillyfrog@yahoo.com

WEYMAN, Canon Richard Darrell George. b 46. Lon Univ BA Bris Univ PhD. Sarum & Wells Th Coll. **d** 84 **p** 85. C Sherborne w Castleton and Lillington *Sarum* 84-88; V Malden St Jo *S'wark* 88-92; P-in-c Marnhull *Sarum* 92-11; Dir Post Ord Tr 92-11; Can and Preb Sarum Cathl 99-11; Dioc Adv in Spiritual Direction 06-11; C Okeford and Hazelbury Bryan and the Hillside Par 08-11; rtd 11. *Millers Cottage, Angel Lane, Shaftesbury SP7 8DF* E-mail dweyman@btinternet.com

WEYMAN PACK-BERESFORD, John Derek Henry. b 31. Wells Th Coll 69. **d** 70 **p** 71. C Headley All SS *Guildf* 70-76; V Westcott 76-97; RD Dorking 84-89; rtd 97; Perm to Offic *Truro* from 99. *Kittiwake, Polurrian Cliff, Mullion, Helston TR12 7EW* Tel (01326) 240457

WEYMONT, Martin Eric. b 48. St Jo Coll Dur BA69 MA74 Fitzw Coll Cam PGCE73 Lon Inst of Educn PhD89 Open Univ BSc96. Westcott Ho Cam 71. **d** 73 **p** 74. C Blackheath *Birm* 73-76; Hon C Willesden St Matt *Lon* 76-77; Hon C Belmont 77-79; P-in-c W Twyford 79-85; NSM Cricklewood St Mich 85-88; Chapl St Pet Coll Sch *Wolv* 88-91; Hon C Wolverhampton *Lich* 88-91; NSM Bickershaw *Liv* 91-97; P-in-c Mells w Buckland Dinham, Elm, Whatley etc *B & W* from 97. *The Rectory, Gay Street, Mells, Frome BA11 3PT* Tel (01373) 812320 Fax 813778

WHALE, Desmond Victor. b 35. Bris Sch of Min 81. **d** 84 **p** 85. Lic to Offic *Bris* 84-88; C Parr *Liv* 88-91; R Winfarthing w Shelfanger w Burston w Gissing etc *Nor* 91-00; RD Redenhall 97-99; rtd 00; Perm to Offic *Nor* from 00 and *Sarum* from 01. *47 Cornbrash Rise, Hilperton, Trowbridge BA14 7TS* Tel (01225) 768537 Mobile 07887-717052 E-mail deswhale@talktalk.net

WHALE, Noel Raymond. b 41. Ox Univ. **d** 70 **p** 71. C Amersham *Ox* 70-73; C Geelong Australia 73-76; Perm to Offic Australia 76-79; I Altona 76-79; I 79-85; I Ivanhoe 86-97; Prec and Min Can St Paul's Cathl 97-01; I Bundoora St Pet 01-11. *PO Box 443, Bulleen VIC 3105, Australia* Tel (0061) 41-219 6127 (mobile) E-mail jonahnoel@hotmail.com

WHALE, Peter Richard. b 49. Auckland Univ MA72 BSc73 Down Coll Cam BA74 MA79 Otago Univ BD78 Ex Univ PhD90. St Jo Coll Auckland 75. **d** 77 **p** 78. C Takapuna New Zealand 77-80; Chapl K Coll Auckland 81-85; TV Saltash *Truro* 85-90; Jt Dir SW Minl Tr Course 86-90; Preb St Endellion 89-90; Prin WMMTC 90-92; rtd 04. *6 Bluebell Walk, Coventry CV4 9XR* Tel (024) 7646 4894 E-mail petegray@btinternet.com

WHALES, Jeremy Michael. b 31. Bris Univ MA82. Lambeth STh72 Wycliffe Hall Ox 59. **d** 61 **p** 62. C W Wimbledon Ch Ch *S'wark* 61-64; Lect St Paul's Coll Cheltenham 64-67; Asst Chapl and Sen Lect 67-74; Chapl 74-78; Assoc Chapl and Sen Lect Coll of SS Paul and Mary Cheltenham 78-84; V Cheltenham St Luke and St Jo *Glouc* 85-92; rtd 92; Perm to Offic *Glouc* from 92; Clergy Widows Officer (Cheltenham Adnry) 96-99. *5 Robert Burns Avenue, Cheltenham GL51 6NU* Tel (01242) 527583

WHALEY, Stephen John. b 57. York Univ BA79. Cranmer Hall Dur BA85. **d** 86 **p** 87. C Selby Abbey *York* 86-90; V Derringham Bank from 90; AD W Hull 98-00. *110 Calvert Road, Hull HU5 5DH* Tel (01482) 352175

WHALLEY, Anthony Allen. b 41. Linc Th Coll 77. **d** 79 **p** 80. C Upton cum Chalvey *Ox* 79-83; R Newton Longville w Stoke Hammond and Whaddon 83-96; R Winslow w Gt Horwood and Addington 99-06; rtd 06. *2 Charlock Road, Malvern WR14 3SR* Tel (01684) 562897 E-mail tony.rosemary@btinternet.com

WHALLEY, Mrs Constance Mary. b 55. CBDTI 99. **d** 02 **p** 03. NSM Garstang St Helen and St Michaels-on-Wyre *Blackb* from 02. *Brierfield, Stoney Lane, Goosnargh, Preston PR3 2WH* Tel (01995) 640652

WHALLEY, Edward Ryder Watson. b 31. G&C Coll Cam BA54 MA59. Westcott Ho Cam 55. **d** 57 **p** 58. C Ashton-on-Ribble St Andr *Blackb* 57-60; Chapl Magd Coll Cam 60-63; C Arnold *S'well* 63-67; rtd 96; Perm to Offic *Lon* from 03. *6 Cranleigh, 137-139 Ladbroke Road, London W11 3PX* Tel (020) 7727 1985

WHALLEY, George Peter. b 40. **d** 86 **p** 86. NSM Ellon *Ab* from 86; NSM Cruden Bay from 86. *128 Braehead Drive, Cruden Bay, Peterhead AB42 0NW* Tel (01779) 812511 E-mail peter_whalley@btinternet.com

WHALLEY, Jonathan Peter Lambert. b 60. Wm Booth Memorial Coll 87. St Jo Coll Nottm BA97. **d** 97 **p** 98. C Hattersley *Ches* 97-01; V The Marshland *Sheff* 01-09; P-in-c Wolsingham and Thornley *Dur* from 09; P-in-c Satley, Stanley and Tow Law from 09; CF(V) from 02. *The Rectory, 14 Rectory Lane, Wolsingham, Bishop Auckland DL13 3AJ* Tel (01388) 527340

WHALLEY, Michael Thomas. b 30. AKC55. **d** 56 **p** 57. C Nottingham All SS *S'well* 56-58; C Clifton St Fran 58-60; C Mansfield SS Pet and Paul 60; V N Wilford St Faith 60-66; Asst Chapl HM Pris Man 66-67; Chapl HM Youth Cust Cen Dover 67-69; Lic to Offic *Linc* 70-75; Chapl HM Pris Aylesbury 75-79; C Aylesbury *Ox* 79-83; P-in-c Bierton w Hulcott 83-89; TV Aylesbury w Bierton and Hulcott 89-95; rtd 95; Perm to Offic *Linc* from 97. *17 Willowfield Avenue, Nettleham, Lincoln LN2 2TH* Tel (01522) 595372

WHALLEY, Peter. *See* WHALLEY, George Peter

✠WHALON, The Rt Revd Pierre Welté. b 52. Boston Univ BMus74 Duquesne Univ MMus81. Virginia Th Sem MDiv85. **d** 85 **p** 85 **c** 01. R N Versailles All So USA 85-91; R Philadelphia St Paul 91-93; R Fort Pierce St Andr 93-01; Bp in Charge Convocation of American Chs in Eur from 01; Hon Asst Bp Eur from 02. *23 avenue George V, 75008 Paris, France* Tel (0033) 1 53 23 84 04 *or* tel and fax 1 47 20 02 23 E-mail bppwhalon@aol.com *or* cathedral@american.cathedral.com

WHARTON, Christopher Joseph. b 33. Keble Coll Ox BA57 MA61. **d** 79 **p** 80. NSM Harpenden St Nic *St Alb* 79-93; R Kimpton w Ayot St Lawrence 93-00; Perm to Offic from 00. *97 Overstone Road, Harpenden AL5 5PL* Tel (01582) 761164

WHARTON, Ms Gillian Vera. b 66. TCD BTh93 MPhil99 HDipEd02. CITC 90. **d** 93 **p** 94. C Glenageary *D & G* 93-96; PV Ch Ch Cathl Dublin from 96; Dioc Youth Officer 96-02; I Lucan w Leixlip 96-00; Chapl Rathdown Sch 00-04; I Dublin Booterstown *D & G* from 04; I Dublin Mt Merrion from 04. *The Rectory, 10 Cross Avenue, Blackrock, Co Dublin, Republic of Ireland* Tel (00353) (1) 288 7118 *or* 283 5873 Mobile 87-230 0767 E-mail gillwharton@hotmail.com *or* booterstown@dublin.anglican.org

✠WHARTON, The Rt Revd John Martin. b 44. Van Mildert Coll Dur BA69 Linacre Coll Ox BTh71 MA76. Ripon Hall Ox 69. **d** 72 **p** 73 **c** 92. C Birm St Pet 72-75; C Croydon St Jo *Cant* 76-77; Dir Past Studies Ripon Coll Cuddesdon 77-83; C Cuddesdon *Ox* 79-83; Sec to Bd of Min and Tr *Bradf* 83-92; Dir Post-Ord Tr 84-92; Hon Can Bradf Cathl 84-92; Can Res Bradf Cathl 92; Bp's Officer for Min and Tr 92; Area Bp Kingston *S'wark* 92-97; Bp Newc from 97. *The Bishop's House, 29 Moor Road South, Newcastle upon Tyne NE3 1PA* Tel 0191-285 2220 Fax 284 6933 E-mail bishop@newcastle.anglican.org

WHARTON, Miss Kate Elizabeth. b 78. Leeds Metrop Univ BSc00. Wycliffe Hall Ox BTh05. **d** 05 **p** 06. C W Derby St Luke *Liv* 05-09; P-in-c Everton St Geo from 09. *St George's Vicarage,*

40 Northumberland Terrace, Liverpool L5 3QG Tel 0151-263 6005

WHARTON, Richard Malcolm. b 69. Univ of Cen England in Birm BA91 PGCE92. Ripon Coll Cuddesdon BTh98. **d** 98 **p** 99. C Weoley Castle *Birm* 98-01; C Hall Green Ascension 01-04; P-in-c Hall Green St Mich 03-08; Chapl Univ Hosp Birm NHS Foundn Trust from 08. *15 Raglan Road, Birmingham B5 7RA* Tel 0121-440 2196

WHARTON, Susan Jane. b 58. Leeds Univ BSc79 Coll of Ripon & York St Jo MA00. NOC 96. **d** 99 **p** 00. C Bingley All SS *Bradf* 99-03; P-in-c Weston w Denton 03-08; P-in-c Leathley w Farnley, Fewston and Blubberhouses 03-08; C Washburn and Mid-Wharfe 08-09; P-in-c from 09. *The Vicarage, Askwith, Otley LS21 2HX* Tel (01943) 461139 E-mail sue.wharton@bradford.anglican.org *or* sue@whartons.org.uk

WHARTON, Thomas Geoffrey. b 72. Glas Univ BA93. Westcott Ho Cam 03. **d** 05 **p** 06. C Linton in Craven and Burnsall w Rylstone *Bradf* 05-09; TV Knight's Enham and Smannell w Enham Alamein *Win* from 09. *The Rectory, Dunhills Lane, Enham Alamein, Andover SP11 6HU* Tel (01264) 352827 E-mail thomas@wharton15.plus.com

WHATELEY, Stuart David. b 44. Ripon Hall Ox 71. **d** 73 **p** 74. C Chilvers Coton w Astley *Cov* 73-76; Chapl Miss to Seafarers 76-10; rtd 10. *10 Merryman Garth, Hedon, Hull HU12 8NJ* Tel (01482) 899166 E-mail humber@mtsmail.org

WHATELEY, Thomas Roderick (Rod). b 52. St Jo Coll Nottm 94. **d** 96 **p** 97. C Willesborough *Cant* 96-99; P-in-c Cliftonville 99-03; R Orlestone w Snave and Ruckinge w Warehorne etc from 03. *The Rectory, Cock Lane, Ham Street, Ashford TN26 2HU* Tel (01233) 732274 E-mail rod.whateley@tiscali.co.uk

WHATLEY, Lionel Frederick. b 50. St Paul's Coll Grahamstown 77. **d** 79 **p** 80. C Uitenhage S Africa 79-80; R Newton Park 80-83; R Alexandria Plurality 83-84; R Waterberg 84-90; R Letaba 90-99; Adn NE 95-99; V Gen 97-99; R Ashington, Washington and Wiston w Buncton *Chich* 99-05; TV Langport Area *B & W* 05-07; P-in-c Worthing Ch the King *Chich* 07-08; V Worthing H Trin w Ch Ch 08-11; P-in-c Highbrook and W Hoathly from 11. *The Vicarage, West Hoathly, East Grinstead RH19 4QF* Tel (01342) 810494 E-mail lionel.whatley@virginmedia.com

WHATLEY, Roger James. b 49. Chich Th Coll 94. **d** 96 **p** 04. NSM Newport St Jo *Portsm* from 96. *Beechcroft, 46 Trafalgar Road, Newport PO30 1QG* Tel (01983) 825938 E-mail whatleys138@btinternet.com

WHATMORE, Michael John. b 30. Bris Univ BA51 St Cath Soc Ox BA53 MA54. Wycliffe Hall Ox 56. **d** 56 **p** 58. C Bexley St Mary *Roch* 56-57; C Keston 57-59; C Bromley St Mark 59-61; Distr Sec (GB) Bible Soc 61-64; R Stanningley St Thos *Ripon* 64-67; V Speke All SS *Liv* 67-70; Teacher & Sen Tutor Barton Peveril Coll 70-92; rtd 92; Perm to Offic *Win* from 92. *26 Grebe Close, Milford on Sea, Lymington SO41 0XA* Tel (01590) 644892

WHATMOUGH, Michael Anthony. b 50. ARCO71 Ex Univ BA72. Edin Th Coll BD81. **d** 81 **p** 82. C Edin St Hilda and Edin St Fillan 81-84; C Salisbury St Thos and St Edm *Sarum* 84-86; R Salisbury 90-93; V Bris St Mary Redcliffe w Temple etc 93-04; Perm to Offic *Lich* 08-10; C Cannock and Huntington from 10; C Hatherton from 10. *St Luke's Vicarage, 18 Queen Street, Cannock WS11 1AE* Tel (01543) 509091 Mobile 07711-335050 E-mail tony@whatmough.org.uk

WHATSON, Mark Edwin Chadwick. b 57. Southn Univ BSc79 CEng83 MIMechE83. NOC 86. **d** 88 **p** 91. NSM Church Hulme *Ches* 88-91; NSM Goostrey 91-95; NSM Hardwicke, Quedgeley and Elmore w Longney *Glouc* 95-98; C Thornbury 98-01; Ind Chapl 99-01; R Freshwater *Portsm* from 01; R Yarmouth from 01. *1 The Nurseries, Freshwater PO40 9FG* Tel and fax (01983) 752010 E-mail mark.whatson@bigfoot.com

WHATTON, Joanna Nicola. *See* PAYNE, Mrs Joanna Nicola

WHAWELL, Arthur Michael. b 38. SRN59. Sarum & Wells Th Coll 74. **d** 76 **p** 77. C Cottingham *York* 76-79; P-in-c Bessingby and Carnaby 79-84; V Birchencliffe *Wakef* 84-87; Chapl Huddersfield R Infirmary 84-87; V St Bart Less and Chapl St Barts Hosp Lon 87-95; P-in-c Wormingford, Mt Bures and Lt Horkesley *Chelmsf* 95-00; V 00-03; rtd 03; Perm to Offic *Pet* from 05. *Cherry Trees, Benefield Road, Upper Glapthorn, Peterborough PE8 5BQ* Tel (01832) 272500 E-mail mwhawell@tiscali.co.uk

WHEALE, Alan Leon. b 43. Hull Univ MA92 AKC69. St Aug Coll Cant 69. **d** 70 **p** 71. C Tamworth *Lich* 70-73; C Cheddleton 73-75; V Garretts Green *Birm* 75-78; V Perry Beeches 78-83; V Winshill *Derby* 83-84; Deputation Appeals Org (E Midl) CECS 84-86; C Arnold *S'well* 86-88; V Daybrook 88-96; R Clifton Campville w Edingale and Harlaston *Lich* 96-06; P-in-c Thorpe Constantine 96-06; P-in-c Elford 97-06; rtd 06; Perm to Offic *Lich* 06-08; Hon C Tamworth from 08. *22 Marlborough Crescent, Burton-on-Trent DE15 9DF* E-mail alan-wheale@supanet.com

WHEALE, Sarah Ruth. *See* BULLOCK, Canon Sarah Ruth

WHEAT, Charles Donald Edmund. b 37. Nottm Univ BA70 Sheff Univ MA76. Kelham Th Coll 57. **d** 62 **p** 63. C Sheff Arbourthorne 62-67; Lic to Offic *S'well* 67-70; SSM from 69;

Chapl St Martin's Coll Lanc 70-73; Prior SSM Priory Sheff 73-75; Lic to Offic *Sheff* 73-97; C Ranmoor 75-77; Asst Chapl Sheff Univ 75-77; Chapl 77-80; Prov SSM in England 81-91; Dir 82-89; Lic to Offic *Blackb* 81-88; V Middlesbrough All SS *York* 88-95; Roehampton Inst *S'wark* 96-97; Chapl OHP 97-98; Prior St Antony's Priory Dur 98-01; V Middlesbrough St Thos *York* 01-03; rtd 03; Hon C S Bank *York* 03-07; Perm to Offic *York* 07-11 and *Ox* from 11. *SSM Priory, 1 Linford Lane, Willen, Milton Keynes MK15 9DL* E-mail ssmmbro@aol.com

WHEATLEY, David. b 44. d 02 p 03. OLM Castleford *Wakef* 02-09; Master Abp Holgate Hosp Hemsworth from 09. *The Master's Lodge, Robin Lane, Hemsworth, Pontefract WF9 4PP* Tel (01977) 610434

WHEATLEY, David Maurice. b 69. Man Poly BA91. Wycliffe Hall Ox 02. d 05 p 06. C Cheltenham St Mary, St Matt, St Paul and H Trin *Glouc* 05-07; C Cheltenham H Trin and St Paul 07-08; Chapl Headington Sch from 10. *Headington School, Headington Road, Headington, Oxford OX3 7TD* Tel (01865) 759100

WHEATLEY (née GRAHAM), Mrs Fiona Karen. b 57. Hull Univ BA84 De Montfort Univ PGCE94. SAOMC 03. d 06 p 07. C Stevenage St Hugh and St Jo *St Alb* 06-10; TV Bp's Hatfield, Lemsford and N Mymms from 10. *St John's Vicarage, Bishops Rise, Hatfield AL10 9BZ* Tel (01707) 271559 E-mail fkwheatley@googlemail.com

WHEATLEY, Gordon Howard. b 29. Trin Coll Cam MA52. Lon Bible Coll. d 90 p 91. C Cockley Cley w Gooderstone *Nor* 90-94; C Didlington 90-94; C Gt and Lt Cressingham w Threxton 90-94; C Hilborough w Bodney 90-94; C Oxborough w Foulden and Caldecote 90-94; P-in-c Mundford w Lynford 94-98, P-in-c Ickburgh w Langford 94-98; P-in-c Cranwich 94-98; rtd 98; Perm to Offic *Nor* 98-10. *204 Baxter Village, 8 Robinsons Road, Frankston Vic 3199, Australia* Tel (0061) (3) 5971 2569 E-mail revgordon@tiscali.co.uk

WHEATLEY, Ian James. b 62. Chich Th Coll BTh94. d 94 p 95. C Braunton *Ex* 94-97; Chapl RN from 97. *Royal Naval Chaplaincy Service, Mail Point 1-2, Leach Building, Whale Island, Portsmouth PO2 8BY* Tel (023) 9262 5055 Fax 9262 5134

WHEATLEY, Jane. See WHEATLEY, Miss Sarah Jane

WHEATLEY, John. b 14. d 77 p 78. NSM Cambois *Newc* 77-87; rtd 87; Perm to Offic *Newc* from 87. *20 Cypress Gardens, Blyth NE24 2LP* Tel (01670) 353353

WHEATLEY, Michael Robert Pierce. d 10 p 11. NSM Burry Port and Pwll *St D* from 10. *Maes-y-Fedwen, Manordeilo, Llandeilo SA19 7BW* Tel (01550) 777796

WHEATLEY, The Ven Paul Charles. b 38. St Jo Coll Dur BA61. Linc Th Coll 61. d 63 p 64. C Bishopston *Bris* 63-68; Youth Chapl 68-73; V Swindon St Paul 73-77; TR Swindon Dorcan 77-79; R Ross *Heref* 79-81; P-in-c Brampton Abbotts 79-81; RD Ross and Archenfield 79-91; Preb Heref Cathl 87-91; Adn Sherborne *Sarum* 91-03; P-in-c W Stafford w Frome Billet 91-03; rtd 03; Perm to Offic *Heref* from 04. *The Farthings, Bridstow, Ross-on-Wye HR9 6QF* Tel (01989) 566965 E-mail paulwheatley@buckcastle.plus.com

✠**WHEATLEY, The Rt Revd Peter William.** b 47. Qu Coll Ox BA69 MA73 Pemb Coll Cam BA71 MA75. Ripon Hall Ox 72. d 73 p 74 c 99. C Fulham All SS *Lon* 73-78; V St Pancras H Cross w St Jude and St Pet 78-82; P-in-c Hampstead All So 82-90; P-in-c Kilburn St Mary 82-90; P-in-c Kilburn St Mary w All So 90-95; V W Hampstead St Jas 82-95; Dir Post-Ord Tr 85-95; AD N Camden 88-93; Adn Hampstead 95-99; Area Bp Edmonton from 99. *27 Thurlow Road, London NW3 5PP* Tel (020) 7435 5890 Fax 7435 6049 E-mail bishop.edmonton@london.anglican.org

WHEATLEY, Miss Sarah Jane. b 45. St Gabr Coll Lon Dip Teaching67. St Alb Minl Tr Scheme 77. d 96 p 97. NSM Meppershall w Campton and Stondon *St Alb* 96-99; P-in-c Shillington 99-03; V Gravenhurst, Shillington and Stondon from 03. *All Saints' Vicarage, Vicarage Close, Shillington, Hitchin SG5 3LS* Tel (01462) 713797 or 731170 E-mail jane.wheatley5@btinternet.com

WHEATLEY PRICE, Canon John. b 31. Em Coll Cam BA54 MA58. Ridley Hall Cam 54. d 56 p 57. C Drypool St Andr and St Pet *York* 56-59; CMS 59-76; Uganda 60-74; Adn Soroti 72-74; Hon Can Soroti 78-97; Adn N Maseno *Kenya* 74-76; V Clevedon St Andr *B & W* 76-82; V Clevedon St Andr and Ch Ch 82-87; Chapl Amsterdam *Eur* 87-92; P-in-c Cromford *Derby* 92-95; P-in-c Matlock Bath 92-95; V Matlock Bath and Cromford 95-96; rtd 96; Perm to Offic *Sarum* 96-01 and *Birm* from 01. *2 Beausale Drive, Knowle, Solihull B93 0NS* Tel (01564) 730067 E-mail john@wheatleyprice.co.uk

WHEATON, Canon Christopher. b 49. St Jo Coll Nottm BTh80. d 80 p 81. C Hatcham St Jas *S'wark* 80-83; C Warlingham w Chelsham and Farleigh 83-87; V Carshalton Beeches from 87; RD Sutton from 03; Hon Can S'wark Cathl from 07. *The Vicarage, 38 Beeches Avenue, Carshalton SM5 3LW* Tel (020) 8647 6056 E-mail good.shepherd@btinternet.com

WHEATON, Canon David Harry. b 30. St Jo Coll Ox BA53 MA56 Lon Univ BD55. Oak Hill Th Coll 58. d 59 p 60. Tutor Oak Hill Th Coll 59-62; Prin 71-86; C Enfield Ch Ch Trent Park *Lon* 59-62; R Ludgershall *Ox* 62-66; V Onslow Square St Paul *Lon* 66-71; Chapl Brompton Hosp 69-71; Hon Can St Alb 76-96; V Ware Ch Ch 86-96; RD Hertford 88-91; rtd 96; Chapl to The Queen 90-00; Perm to Offic *Ox* 96-08; *St Alb* 96-10; *Sarum* from 09. *17 Riverside Road, Blandford Forum DT11 7ES* Tel (01258) 489996

WHEATON, Patrick Edward. b 78. Ex Coll Ox BA00. Trin Coll Bris BA08. d 09 p 10. C Shill Valley and Broadshire *Ox* from 09. *The Vicarage, Filkins, Lechlade GL7 3JQ* Tel 07974-986608 (mobile) E-mail paddywheaton@gmx.net

WHEATON, Canon Ralph Ernest. b 32. St Jo Coll Dur BA54. Cranmer Hall Dur. d 58 p 59. C Evington *Leic* 58-63; V Bardon Hill 63-71; V Whitwick St Jo the Bapt 71-81; RD Akeley S 79-81; V Blyth *S'well* 81-96; P-in-c Scofton w Osberton 83-96; RD Worksop 83-93; Hon Can S'well Minster 86-96; P-in-c Langold 86-91; rtd 96; Perm to Offic *Linc* 99-02 and *S'well* from 02. *Petriburg, Main Street, Hayton, Retford DN22 9LL* Tel (01777) 705910

WHEBLE, Eric Clement. b 23. S'wark Ord Course 68. d 71 p 72. C Croydon H Trin *Cant* 71-78; Hon C Croydon St Sav 78-80; Hon C Norbury St Oswald 80-81; TV Selsdon St Jo w St Fran 81-84; TV Selsdon St Jo w St Fran *S'wark* 85-88; rtd 88; Perm to Offic *Portsm* and *Win* from 88. *23 Holmesland Drive, Botley, Southampton SO30 2SH* Tel (01489) 798050

WHEELDON, William Dennis. b 25. Leeds Univ BA51. Coll of Resurr Mirfield 52. d 54 p 56. CR 55-76; Tutor Codrington Coll Barbados 59-63; Vice-Prin 63-66; Prin Coll of Resurr Mirfield 66-75; P-in-c New Whittington *Derby* 83-87; P-in-c Belper Ch Ch and Milford 87-90; rtd 90; Perm to Offic *Bradf* 90-04. *3 The Lodge, Newfield Drive, Menston, Ilkley LS29 6JQ*

WHEELER, Preb Alexander Quintin Henry (Alastair). b 51. Lon Univ BA73 MBACP07. St Jo Coll Nottm 74. d 77 p 78. C Kenilworth St Jo *Cov* 77-80; C Madeley *Heref* 80-83; P-in-c Draycott-le-Moors *Lich* 83-84; P-in-c Forsbrook 83-84; R Draycott-le-Moors w Forsbrook 84-91; V Nailsea Ch Ch *B & W* 91-96; R Nailsea Ch Ch w Tickenham 96-10; RD Portishead 95-01; V Wells St Cuth w Wookey Hole from 10; RD Shepton Mallet from 11; Preb Wells Cathl from 03. *3 Orchard Lea, Wells BA5 2LZ* Tel (01749) 672193 E-mail aqhw@aol.com

WHEELER, Canon Andrew Charles. b 48. CCC Cam BA69 MA72 Makerere Univ Kampala MA72 Leeds Univ PGCE72. Trin Coll Bris BA88. d 88 p 88. CMS from 76; C Whitton *Sarum* 88-89; C All SS Cathl Cairo Egypt 89-92; Co-ord for Th Educn Sudan 92-00; C All SS Cathl Nairobi Kenya 92-00; Abp's Sec for Angl Communion Affairs *Cant* 00-01; C Guildf St Sav from 02; Dioc World Miss Adv from 06. *8 Selbourne Road, Guildford GU4 7JP* Tel (01483) 455333 E-mail andrew.wheeler@st-saviours.org.uk

WHEELER, Anthony. See WHEELER, Richard Anthony

WHEELER (née MILLAR), Mrs Christine. b 55. City of Lon Poly BSc76 DipCOT81. S Dios Minl Tr Scheme 84. d 87 p 94. NSM Kingston Buci *Chich* 87-89; Par Dn Merstham and Gatton *S'wark* 89-94; C 94-96; R Rockland St Mary w Hellington, Bramerton etc *Nor* 96-04; Perm to Offic from 04. *Mayland, Low Road, Strumpshaw, Norwich NR13 4HU* Tel (01603) 713583 E-mail emailcw@btinternet.com

WHEELER, David Ian. b 49. Southn Univ BSc70 PhD78. NOC 87. d 90 p 91. C Blackpool St Jo *Blackb* 90-94; R Old Trafford St Jo *Man* 94-05; P-in-c Irlam 05-08; V from 08. *The Vicarage, Vicarage Road, Irlam, Manchester M44 6WA* Tel 0161-775 2461

WHEELER, David James. b 49. Leeds Univ MA95 CQSW74. S Dios Minl Tr Scheme 87. d 90 p 91. C Hythe *Cant* 90-92; C Knaresborough *Ripon* 92-97; Asst Sec Resp Officer 94-97; P-in-c Gt and Lt Ouseburn w Marton cum Grafton etc 97-01; V 01-05; Jt AD Ripon 01-05; V Cobbold Road St Sav w St Mary *Lon* from 05. *St Saviour's Vicarage, Cobbold Road, London W12 9LN* Tel (020) 8743 4769 E-mail sacerdote@btopenworld.com

WHEELER, Sister Eileen Violet. b 28. TCert48 Newnham Coll Cam MA52. Chich Th Coll 85. dss 86 d 87 p 95. Bexhill St Pet *Chich* 86-95; Hon Par Dn 87-90; Par Dn 90-94; Hon C 94-95; rtd 94; Hon C Bexhill St Mark *Chich* 95-00; Perm to Offic 00-02; Hon C Newhaven 02-08; Hon C St Leonards St Ethelburga and St Leon from 08. *17 Glebe Close, Bexhill-on-Sea TN39 3UY* Tel (01424) 848150

WHEELER, Graham John. b 39. St Mich Coll Llan BD78. d 66 p 67. C Roath St Martin *Llan* 66-71; C Cadoxton-juxta-Barry 71-75; Perm to Offic 75-79; C Highcliffe w Hinton Admiral *Win* 79-83; C Milton 83-90; P-in-c Bournemouth St Ambrose 90-06; rtd 06. *10 Durley Chine Court, 36 West Cliff Road, Bournemouth BH2 5HJ* Tel (01202) 764957

WHEELER, Mrs Helen Mary. b 38. Qu Coll Birm 04. d 06 p 07. NSM Smethwick Resurr *Birm* from 06. *99 Brookfield Road, Birmingham B18 7JA* Tel 0121-554 4721 Mobile 07804-450099 E-mail helen.wheeler@mail.com

WHEELER, James Albert. b 49. Sarum & Wells Th Coll 74. d 76 p 77. C Orpington All SS *Roch* 76-79; C Roch 79-81; C Bexley

St Jo 81-84; V Penge Lane H Trin 84-93; P-in-c Tunbridge Wells St Luke 93-99; V 99-09; P-in-c Southborough St Thos from 09. *The Vicarage, 28 Pennington Road, Southborough, Tunbridge Wells TN4 0SL* Tel (01892) 529624
E-mail james.wheeler@diocese-rochester.org

WHEELER, John David. b 31. Selw Coll Cam BA54 MA58. Ely Th Coll 54. **d** 56 **p** 57. C Charlton St Luke w St Paul *S'wark* 56-60; C Northolt St Mary *Lon* 61-63; V Bush Hill Park St Mark 64-71; V Ealing St Pet Mt Park 71-74; V Truro St Paul 74-79; V Truro St Paul and St Clem 79-80; P-in-c Hammersmith St Sav *Lon* 80-83; V Cobbold Road St Sav w St Mary 83-96; rtd 96; Perm to Offic *Heref* 96-01 and *Chich* 01-09. *63 Nelson Road, Twickenham TW2 7AR* Tel (020) 8755 2018

WHEELER, Julian Aldous. b 48. Nottm Univ BTh74. Kelham Th Coll 70. **d** 75 **p** 76. C Bideford *Ex* 75-79; Lic to Offic 79-86; Hon C Parkham, Alwington, Buckland Brewer etc 86-03. *Manorfield, Mount Raleigh Avenue, Bideford EX39 3NR* Tel (01237) 477271 E-mail wheelerb58@btinternet.com

WHEELER, Leonie Marjorie. b 50. Univ of W Aus BA75 St Ant Coll Ox DPhil81. Qu Coll Birm 04. **d** 06 **p** 07. C Hadley and Wellington Ch Ch *Lich* 06-09; P-in-c Church Aston from 09; Chapl to the Deaf from 09. *St Andrew's Rectory, 7 Wallshead Way, Church Aston, Newport TF10 9JG* Tel (01952) 810942

WHEELER, Preb Madeleine. b 42. Gilmore Course 76. **dss** 78 **d** 87 **p** 94. Ruislip Manor St Paul *Lon* 78-92; Par Dn 87-91; TD 91-92; Chapl for Women's Min (Willesden Episc Area) 86-95; P-in-c N Greenford All Hallows 94-00; Preb St Paul's Cathl 95-00; rtd 00; Perm to Offic *St Alb* from 00 and *Lon* from 02. *178A Harefield Road, Uxbridge UB8 1PP* Tel (01895) 257274

WHEELER, Nicholas Charles. b 50. LVO09. Leic Univ BA72. SEITE 00. **d** 03 **p** 04. NSM Blackheath St Jo *S'wark* 03-08; Perm to Offic 08-11; NSM Eltham H Trin from 11. *52 Oakways, London SE9 2PD* Tel (020) 8859 7819

WHEELER, Nicholas Gordon Timothy. b 59. BCombStuds84. Linc Th Coll. **d** 84 **p** 85. C Hendon St Alphage *Lon* 84-87; C Wood Green St Mich w Bounds Green St Gabr etc 87-89; TV 89-93; R Cranford 93-02; V Ruislip St Mary from 02. *St Mary's Vicarage, 9 The Fairway, Ruislip HA4 0SP* Tel (020) 8845 3485 Mobile 07946-111968 E-mail nicholasgwheeler@aol.com

WHEELER, Nicholas Paul. b 60. Ox Univ BA86 MA91. Wycliffe Hall Ox 83. **d** 87 **p** 88. C Wood Green St Mich w Bounds Green St Gabr etc *Lon* 87-91; Chapl to Bp Edmonton 91-96; P-in-c Somers Town 96-03; P-in-c Old St Pancras w Bedford New Town St Matt 96-03; P-in-c Camden Town St Mich w All SS and St Thos 96-03; P-in-c Camden Square St Paul 96-03; TR Old St Pancras 03-08; Brazil from 08. *Address temp unknown*

WHEELER, Richard Anthony (Tony). b 23. St Chad's Coll Dur BA46 MA48. **d** 48 **p** 49. C Kingswinford St Mary *Lich* 48-52; C Toxteth Park St Agnes *Liv* 52-54; V Upholland 54-64; R Dorchester H Trin w Frome Whitfield *Sarum* 64-73; TV Dorchester 73-87; rtd 87; Perm to Offic *Sarum* from 87. *30 Mountain Ash Road, Dorchester DT1 2PB* Tel (01305) 264811 E-mail peewheet@cix.compulink.co.uk

WHEELER, Canon Richard Roy. b 44. K Coll Lon BD72. St Aug Coll Cant. **d** 74 **p** 74. C Brixton St Matt *S'wark* 74-78; Dir St Matt Meeting Place Brixton 78-79; Sec BCC Community Work Resource Unit 79-82; TV Southampton (City Cen) *Win* 83-88; TR 88-98; Hon Can Win Cathl 94-98; Soc Resp Adv *St Alb* 98-09; Can Res St Alb 01-09; rtd 09. *182 Moordown, London SE18 3NF* Tel (020) 8856 1075

WHEELER, Mrs Sally Ann Violet. b 59. Westmr Coll Ox BEd81. SAOMC 94. **d** 97 **p** 98. NSM Chippenham St Paul w Hardenhuish etc *Bris* 97-01; C Gtr Corsham and Lacock 01-04; TV from 04. *The Vicarage, Folly Lane, Lacock, Chippenham SN15 2LL* Tel (01249) 730272
E-mail wheelers.7@btinternet.com

WHEELER-KILEY, Mrs Susan Elizabeth. b 47. **d** 06 **p** 07. NSM S Norwood St Mark *S'wark* from 06. *35 St Luke's Close, London SE25 4SX* Tel (020) 8656 9923 Mobile 07890-780572
E-mail fs.kiley@btinternet.com

WHEELHOUSE, Brian Clifford Dunstan. b 69. St Steph Ho Ox BTh93. **d** 96 **p** 97. C Brighton Resurr *Chich* 96-99; C Hangleton 99-00; Perm to Offic 00-01; C Kingstanding St Luke *Birm* 01-03; V Houghton Regis *St Alb* from 03. *The Vicarage, Bedford Road, Houghton Regis, Dunstable LU5 5DJ* Tel and fax (01582) 867593

WHEELWRIGHT, Michael Harvey. b 39. Bps' Coll Cheshunt 64. **d** 67 **p** 68. C Glen Parva and S Wigston *Leic* 67-70; C Evington 70-74; V Leic St Eliz Nether Hall 74-79; Chapl Prudhoe Hosp Northd 79-99; Perm to Offic *Dur* from 95 and *Newc* from 99; rtd 04. *6 Nunnykirk Close, Ovingham, Prudhoe NE42 6BP* Tel (01661) 835749

WHELAN, Miss Patricia Jean. b 33. ACA55 FCA82. Dalton Ho Bris 58. **dss** 64 **d** 87 **p** 94. Stapleford *S'well* 62-69; Aylesbury *Ox* 69-75; Bushbury *Lich* 75-77; Patchway *Bris* 77-81; Trin Coll Bris 81-82; W Swindon LEP 82-86; High Wycombe *Ox* 86-87; Par Dn 87-91; Par Dn Ox St Ebbe w St Pet 91-93; rtd 93. *81 Cogges Hill Road, Witney OX28 3XU* Tel (01993) 779099

WHELAN, Peter Warwick Armstrong. b 34. Southn Univ BTh80 Open Univ BA80. Sarum Th Coll 69. **d** 71 **p** 72. C Salisbury

WHELAN, Raymond Keith. b 40. Cant Sch of Min 85. **d** 88 **p** 91. C Eastbourne St Andr *Chich* 88-93; C-in-c Parklands St Wilfrid CD 93-95; TV Chich 95-01; V Chich St Wilfrid 00-01; rtd 04; Perm to Offic *Chich* from 04. *9 Ruislip Gardens, Aldwick, Bognor Regis PO21 4LB* Tel (01243) 264865 E-mail wdiosc@aol.com

WHERLOCK, Mrs Evalene Prudence. b 50. WEMTC 98. **d** 01 **p** 02. NSM Bishopsworth and Bedminster Down *Bris* from 01. *63 Bridgwater Road, Bedminster Down, Bristol BS13 7AX* Tel 0117-964 1035 Mobile 07899-932763
E-mail evawherlock@ukonline.co.uk

WHERRY, Anthony Michael. b 44. Nottm Univ BA65. WMMTC 88. **d** 91 **p** 92. NSM Worc City St Paul and Old St Martin etc 91-95; NSM Worc E Deanery 95-02; NSM Worc SE from 02. *2 Redfern Avenue, Worcester WR5 1PZ* Tel (01905) 358532 Mobile 07780-677942 E-mail tony@wherry222.fsnet.co.uk

WHETTEM, Canon John Curtiss. b 27. Peterho Cam BA50 MA55. Wycliffe Hall Ox 50. **d** 52 **p** 53. C Clifton Ch Ch *Bris* 52-55; C Wandsworth All SS *S'wark* 55-58; V Soundwell *Bris* 58-63; Youth Chapl 63-68; Chapl Bris Cathl 64-68; R N Mundham w Hunston *Chich* 68-80; P-in-c Oving w Merston 75-80; TR Swanborough *Sarum* 80-92; RD Pewsey 84-89; rtd 92; Perm to Offic *Sarum* from 92. *32 Hogshill Street, Beaminster DT8 3AA* Tel (01308) 863050

WHETTER, Michael Arnold. b 30. Bris Univ BA51. Wells Th Coll 53. **d** 55 **p** 56. C Dursley *Glouc* 55-58; C Coppenhall *Ches* 58-61; R Ches H Trin 61-71; V Stockport St Alb Hall Street 72-90; V Offerton 90-91; Chapl Cherry Tree Hosp Stockport 72-91; Chapl Offerton Hosp Stockport 72-91; V Bollington St Jo *Ches* 91-00; rtd 00; Perm to Offic *Glouc* from 00. *Knapp Cottage, Selsley West, Stroud GL5 5LJ* Tel (01453) 822920

WHETTINGSTEEL, Raymond Edward. b 44. S Dios Minl Tr Scheme 79. **d** 82 **p** 83. NSM Sholing *Win* 82-84; C Southampton Maybush St Pet 84-89; R Hatherden w Tangley, Weyhill and Penton Mewsey 89-09; rtd 09. *20 Clover Way, Hedge End, Southampton SO30 4RP* Tel (01489) 787033
E-mail ray_whettingsteel@hotmail.com

WHETTLETON, Timothy John. b 53. Univ of Wales (Swansea) BA74. St Mich Coll Llan 97. **d** 99 **p** 00. C Llansamlet *S & B* 99-01; P-in-c Gowerton 01-05. *Address temp unknown*

WHETTON, Nicholas John. b 56. Open Univ BA94. St Jo Coll Nottm 83. **d** 86 **p** 87. C Hatfield *Sheff* 86-90; V Cornholme *Wakef* 90-96; P-in-c Livesey *Blackb* 96-99; V 99-03; P-in-c Ewood 96-97; Chapl HM Pris Hull from 03. *The Chaplain's Office, HM Prison, Hedon Road, Hull HU9 5LS* Tel (01482) 282200

✠**WHINNEY, The Rt Revd Michael Humphrey Dickens.** b 30. Pemb Coll Cam BA55 MA59. Gen Th Sem (NY) STM90 Ridley Hall Cam 55. **d** 57 **p** 58 **c** 82. C Rainham *Chelmsf* 57-60; Hd Cam Univ Miss Bermondsey 60-67; Chapl 67-73; V Bermondsey St Jas w Ch Ch *S'wark* 67-73; Adn S'wark 73-82; Suff Bp Aston *Birm* 82-85; Bp S'well 85-88; Asst Bp Birm 88-95; Can Res Birm Cathl 92-95; rtd 96; Hon Asst Bp Birm from 96. *3 Moor Green Lane, Moseley, Birmingham B13 8NE* Tel and fax 0121-249 2856 E-mail michael.whinney@btinternet.com

WHINNEY, Nigel Patrick Maurice. b 43. Open Univ BA91. SWMTC 95. **d** 97 **p** 98. NSM Ilminster and Distr *B & W* 97-08; Bp's Officer for Ord NSM (Taunton Adnry) 99-06; RD Crewkerne and Ilminster 01-07; rtd 08. *The Monks Dairy, Isle Brewers, Taunton TA3 6QL* Tel (01460) 281975
E-mail n.whinney@virgin.net

WHINTON, William Francis Ivan. b 35. NOC 77. **d** 80 **p** 81. NSM Stockport St Mary *Ches* 80-82; NSM Disley 82-87; V Birtles 87-00; Dioc Officer for Disabled 89-00; rtd 00; Chapl for Deaf People *Ches* 00-04; Perm to Offic *Ches* from 05 and *Lich* from 09. *Allmeadows Cottage, Wincle, Macclesfield SK11 0QJ* Tel (01260) 227278

WHIPP, Antony Douglas. b 46. Leeds Univ BSc68 Lanc Univ PhD04. Ripon Coll Cuddesdon 84. **d** 86 **p** 87. C Dalston *Carl* 86-89; V Holme Cultram St Mary 89-96; V Holme Cultram St Cuth 89-96; V Kells 96-00; V Hartlepool St Aid *Dur* 00-05; R Ebchester from 05; V Medomsley from 05. *The Rectory, Shaw Lane, Consett DH8 0PY* Tel (01207) 563348
E-mail tony.whipp@durham.anglican.org

WHIPP, Margaret Jane. b 55. LMH Ox BA76 Sheff Univ MB, ChB79 MRCP82 FRCR86 Hull Univ MA99 Glas Univ PhD08. NOC 87. **d** 90 **p** 94. NSM Wickersley *Sheff* 90-98; Tutor Cranmer Hall Dur 98-99; Dir Practical Th NEOC 00-04; Ecum Chapl Ox Brookes Univ 04-08; Lect Past Studies Ox Min Course 06-08; Dean of Studies Ripon Coll Cuddesdon from 08. *The Mullings, 71 Sandfield Road, Headington, Oxford OX3 6RW* Tel (01865) 765409
E-mail margaret.whipp@ripon-cuddesdon.ac.uk

WHITAKER, Anthony. b 50. SS Mark & Jo Coll Chelsea CertEd72 Middx Univ BA02. NTMTC 99. **d** 02 **p** 03. C

Blackmore and Stondon Massey *Chelmsf* 02-06; P-in-c St Keverne *Truro* 06-11; C Churt and Hindhead *Guildf* from 11. *The Vicarage, Old Kiln Lane, Churt, Farnham GU10 2HX* Tel (01428) 713368 Mobile 07905-013017 E-mail tony_whitaker@btinternet.com

WHITAKER, Benjamin. See WHITAKER, Michael Benjamin

WHITAKER, David Arthur Edward. b 27. New Coll Ox BA50 MA55. Wells Th Coll 51. **d** 53 **p** 54. C W Bridgford *S'well* 53-56; CF 56-58; V Clifton St Fran *S'well* 58-63; Basutoland 63-66; Lesotho 66-69; R Buckerell *Ex* 69-76; R Feniton 69-76; P-in-c Tiverton St Pet 76-79; R 79-92; rtd 92; Perm to Offic *Heref* from 92. *Wits End, Hereford Road, Weobley, Hereford HR4 8SW* Tel (01544) 318669

WHITAKER, Irene Anne. b 57. **d** 01 **p** 02. OLM Parr *Liv* 01-06; TV Bootle from 06. *The Vicarage, Elm Road, Seaforth, Liverpool L21 1BH* Tel 0151-920 2205 Mobile 07771-581886 E-mail irene369@blueyonder.co.uk

WHITAKER, Margaret Scott. b 45. Dioc OLM tr scheme 00 EAMTC 04. **d** 03 **p** 04. OLM Eaton *Nor* 03-05; C Sprowston w Beeston 05-07; C New Catton Ch Ch 07-11; R Horsford, Felthorpe and Hevingham from 11. *The Rectory, 1B Gordon Godfrey Way, Horsford, Norwich NR10 3SG* Tel (01603) 710357 Mobile 07717-317900 E-mail mwhitaker1@btinternet.com

WHITAKER, Michael Benjamin. b 60. Nottm Univ BA83. Sarum & Wells Th Coll 85. **d** 87 **p** 88. C Gt Grimsby St Mary and St Jas *Linc* 87-91; C Abingdon *Ox* 91-95; Chapl to the Deaf *Sarum* 95-00; Perm to Offic *Win* 97-00; Asst Chapl to the Deaf *Ox* from 00; Chapl HM Pris Grendon and Spring Hill from 07. *HM Prison Grendon, Grendon Underwood, Aylesbury HP18 0TL* Tel (01865) 736100 E-mail whitaker@tribeandclan.freeserve.co.uk

WHITBY, Suffragan Bishop of. See WARNER, The Rt Revd Martin Clive

WHITCOMBE, William Ashley. b 78. UEA BA01. St Steph Ho Ox BTh04. **d** 04 **p** 05. C W Hendon St Jo *Lon* 04-08; Chapl HM Pris Wormwood Scrubs from 08. *HM Prison Wormwood Scrubs, Du Cane Road, London W12 0TU* Tel (020) 8588 3227 E-mail williama.whitcombe@hmps.gsi.gov.uk

WHITCROFT, Graham Frederick. b 42. Oak Hill Th Coll 64. **d** 66 **p** 67. C Cromer *Nor* 66-69; C Attercliffe *Sheff* 69-72; V Kimberworth Park 72-85; V Lepton *Wakef* 85-07; RD Kirkburton 98-05; rtd 07; Perm to Offic *Wakef* from 07. *18 Far Croft, Lepton, Huddersfield HD8 0LS* Tel (01484) 609868 E-mail whitcroft@btopenworld.com

WHITE, Alan. b 18. Man Univ BSc39 MSc40 St Cath Soc Ox BA42 MA46 Leeds Univ MEd52. Ripon Hall Ox 40. **d** 42 **p** 43. C Leic St Marg 42-45; Chapl and Asst Master Leeds Gr Sch 45-56; Lic to Offic *Worc* 56-89; Asst Master Bromsgrove Sch 56-72; Chapl 72-83; rtd 83; P-in-c Tardebigge *Worc* 89-00; Perm to Offic from 00. *25 Leadbetter Drive, Bromsgrove B61 7JG* Tel (01527) 877955

WHITE, Preb Alan. b 43. Ex Univ BA65. Chich Th Coll 65. **d** 68 **p** 69. C Upper Clapton St Matt *Lon* 68-72; C Southgate Ch Ch 72-76; P-in-c Friern Barnet St Pet le Poer 76-79; V 79-85; TR Ex St Thos and Em 85-08; RD Christianity 99-03; Preb Ex Cathl 03-08; rtd 08. *Flat 3, 7 Courtenay Road, Newton Abbot TQ12 1HP* Tel (01626) 332451 E-mail revalan.white@btopenworld.com

WHITE, Canon Alison Mary. b 56. St Aid Coll Dur BA78 Leeds Univ MA94. Cranmer Hall Dur 83. **dss** 86 **d** 87 **p** 94. NSM Chester le Street *Dur* 86-89; Dioc Adv in Local Miss 89-93; Hon Par Dn Birtley 89-93; Dir Past Studies Cranmer Hall Dur 93-98; Dir of Ords *Dur* 98-00; Springboard Missr 00-04; Adult Educn Officer *Pet* 05-10; Can Pet Cathl 09-10; Hon Can Th Sheff Cathl from 10; P-in-c Riding Mill *Newc* from 11; Adv for Spirituality and Spiritual Direction from 11. *The Vicarage, Riding Mill NE44 6AT* Tel (01434) 682120 E-mail alisonmarywhite@btinternet.com

WHITE, Canon Andrew Paul Bartholomew. b 64. MIOT85 ABIST85. Ridley Hall Cam 86. **d** 90 **p** 91. C Battersea Rise St Mark *S'wark* 90-93; P-in-c Balham Hill Ascension 93-97; V 97-98; Dir Internat Min and Can Res Cov Cathl 98-05; Chapl Iraq from 05; President Foundn for Relief and Reconciliation in the Middle E from 05. *The Croft, 106 Shepherds Way, Liphook GU30 7HH* Tel (01428) 723939 *or* (00964) (7901) 265723 E-mail apbw2@cam.ac.uk

WHITE, Andrew Peter. b 65. Lon Univ BA87. Sarum & Wells Th Coll BTh94. **d** 94 **p** 95. C Croydon St Matt *S'wark* 94-96; C S Wimbledon H Trin and St Pet 96-98; TV Droitwich Spa *Worc* 98-05; RD Droitwich 02-04; P-in-c Hartlebury 05-07; Bps' Chapl 05-10; R Kirkley St Pet and St Jo *Nor* from 10. *Kirkley Rectory, Rectory Road, Lowestoft NR33 0ED* Tel (01502) 502155

WHITE, Anne Margaret. b 55. Nottm Univ BEd78. STETS 07. **d** 10 **p** 11. NSM Guernsey St Andr *Win* from 10. *Kings Lea, Skins Lane, St Peter Port, Guernsey GY1 1SB* Tel (01481) 716277 Mobile 07911-712274 E-mail white.anne19@gmail.com

WHITE, Antony. See FELTHAM-WHITE, Antony James

WHITE, Camilla Elizabeth Zoë. b 56. Somerville Coll Ox BA78 MA83 Heythrop Coll Lon MA06. Ripon Coll Cuddesdon 05. **d** 07 **p** 08. NSM Bramley and Grafham *Guildf* from 07. *Bramley Mill, Mill Lane, Bramley, Guildford GU5 0HW* Tel (01483) 892645 E-mail camillawhite@waitrose.com

WHITE, Mrs Christine Margaret. b 46. Cov Coll of Educn CertEd68 Kingston Univ BA96. **d** 07 **p** 08. OLM Cuddington *Guildf* from 07. *5 Lady Hay, Worcester Park KT4 7LT* Tel (020) 8337 1665

WHITE, Canon Christopher Norman Hessler. b 32. TD76. St Cath Coll Cam BA56 MA60. Cuddesdon Coll 57. **d** 59 **p** 60. C Solihull *Birm* 59-62; C Leeds St Aid *Ripon* 62-65; CF (TA) 64-85; V Aysgarth *Ripon* 65-74; R Richmond 74-76; P-in-c Hudswell w Downholme and Marske 75-76; R Richmond w Hudswell 76-97; RD Richmond 75-80 and 93-97; Hon Can Ripon Cathl 89-97; Chapl St Fran Xavier Sch Richmond 89-97; rtd 97; Perm to Offic *Ripon* from 97. *Orchard House, Aske, Richmond DL10 5HN* Tel (01748) 850968

WHITE, Colin Davidson. b 44. St And Dioc Tr Course 86. **d** 88 **p** 89. NSM Glenrothes *St And* 88-89; P-in-c 89-90; P-in-c Leven 90-92; R 92-95; V Grimethorpe *Wakef* 95-01; P-in-c Kellington w Whitley 01-02; TV Knottingley and Kellington w Whitley 02-10; rtd 10. *42 Glendale Avenue North, Belfast BT8 6LB* Tel (028) 9029 6037 Mobile 07973-795560 E-mail col_the_rev@hotmail.co.uk

WHITE, Crispin Michael. b 42. Southn Univ MA98 PhD06 FRSA94. Bps' Coll Cheshunt 62. **d** 65 **p** 66. C S Harrow St Paul *Lon* 65-67; C Mill Hill St Mich 67-68; I Labrador St Clem Canada 68-71; Toc H Padre (W Region) 71-75; (E Midl Region) 75-82; Ind Chapl *Portsm* 82-98; P-in-c Hatfield Broad Oak and Bush End *Chelmsf* 98-04; Ind Chapl 98-07; Harlow 98-04; Lon Thames Gateway 04-07; rtd 07. *6 Downlands, Firsdown Close, Worthing BN13 3BQ* Tel and fax (01903) 830785 Mobile 07962-057436 E-mail postmaster@crispinwhite.plus.com

WHITE, Canon David Christopher. b 51. Lon Univ LLB73. St Jo Coll Nottm 86. **d** 88 **p** 89. C Bulwell St Mary *S'well* 88-92; V Nottingham All SS 92-98; TR Clarendon Park St Jo w Knighton St Mich *Leic* 98-05; R Emmaus Par Team 05-07; TR Fosse from 07; Bp's NSM Officer 02-08; Hon Can Leic Cathl from 08. *The Rectory, Upper Church Street, Syston, Leicester LE7 1HR* Tel 0116-260 8276 E-mail davidwhite264@btinternet.com

WHITE, David John. b 26. Leeds Univ BA53. Coll of Resurr Mirfield 53. **d** 55 **p** 56. C Brighton St Pet *Chich* 55-58; C Wednesbury St Jas *Lich* 58-60; C Bishops Hull St Jo *B & W* 60-61; R Morton *Derby* 61-62; In RC Ch 62-73; Lect Whitelands Coll Lon 73-75; R Tregony w St Cuby and Cornelly *Truro* 75-79; R Castle Bromwich SS Mary and Marg *Birm* 79-83; V Plymouth St Simon *Ex* 83-88; R Lapford, Nymet Rowland and Coldridge 88-93; RD Chulmleigh 93; rtd 93; Perm to Offic *Ex* 94-99. *The Belvedere, Peak Hill Road, Sidmouth EX10 0NW* Tel (01395) 513365

WHITE, Canon David Paul. b 58. Oak Hill Th Coll. **d** 84 **p** 85. C Toxteth Park St Clem *Liv* 84-87; C Woodford Wells *Chelmsf* 87-89; C Woodside Park St Barn *Lon* 89-90; TV Canford Magna *Sarum* 90-93; V York St Mich-le-Belfrey 93-99; V St Austell *Truro* 99-10; Dioc Dir Miss 05-10; Hon Can Truro Cathl 05-10; V Chorleywood St Andr *St Alb* from 10. *St Andrew's Vicarage, 37 Quickley Lane, Chorleywood, Rickmansworth WD3 5AE* Tel (01923) 332102 E-mail davidwhite305@yahoo.com

WHITE, Derek. b 35. MBE97. **d** 84 **p** 85. C St Marylebone St Cypr *Lon* 84-96; Bp's Chapl for the Homeless 87-01; P-in-c St Mary le Strand w St Clem Danes 96-01; rtd 01; Perm to Offic *S'wark* from 04. *80 Coleraine Road, London SE3 7PE* Tel (020) 8858 3622

WHITE, Mrs Doreen. b 51. RCN BSc95. **d** 05 **p** 06. OLM Shelswell *Ox* 05-07; NSM Fawley *Win* from 07. *86 Rollestone Road, Holbury, Southampton SO45 2GZ* Tel (023) 8089 7062 E-mail revdoreen@yahoo.co.uk

WHITE, Douglas Richard Leon. b 49. Linc Th Coll 81. **d** 83 **p** 84. C Warsop *S'well* 83-88; V Kirkby in Ashfield St Thos 88-93; Asst Chapl Qu Medical Cen Nottm Univ Hosp NHS Trust 93-98; Chapl Cen Notts Healthcare NHS Trust 98-01; Chapl Mansfield Distr Primary Care Trust 01-02; Chapl Geo Eliot Hosp NHS Trust Nuneaton 02-06; Chapl Mary Ann Evans Hospice 02-06; Chapl Compton Hospice 06-08; Chapl Marie Curie Hospice Solihull from 08; Chapl Primrose Hospice Bromsgrove from 08. *1 Glebe Avenue, Bedworth CV12 0DP* Tel (024) 7636 0417 *or* 0121-254 7800 E-mail rickwhite29@btinternet.com

WHITE, Eric James. b 46. **d** 01 **p** 02. OLM Pennington *Man* 01-11; C from 11. *18 Clifton Road, Leigh WN7 3LS* Tel (01942) 678758 E-mail jackieanderic@penningtonchurch.com

✠**WHITE, The Rt Revd Francis.** b 49. Univ of Wales (Cardiff) BSc(Econ)70. St Jo Coll Nottm. **d** 80 **p** 81 **c** 02. C Dur St Nic 80-84; C Chester le Street 84-87; Chapl Dur and Chester le Street Hosps 87-89; V Birtley *Dur* 89-97; RD Chester-le-Street 93-97; Adn Sunderland and Hon Can Dur Cathl 97-02; Can Pet Cathl from 02; Suff Bp Brixworth 02-10; Asst Bp Newc from 10. *Bishop's House, 29 Moor Road South, Newcastle-upon-Tyne NE3 1PA* Tel 0191-285 2220 E-mail bishopfrank@newcastle.anglican.org

WHITE, Canon Gavin Donald. b 27. Toronto Univ BA49 Trin Coll Toronto BD61 Gen Th Sem NY STM68 Lon Univ PhD70. St Steph Ho Ox 51. **d** 53 **p** 54. C Quebec St Matt 53-55; Chapl Dew Line 56-57; Miss Knob Lake 57-58; Miss Kideleko Zanzibar 59-62; Lect St Paul's Th Coll Limuru Kenya 62-66; C Hampstead St Steph *Lon* 68-70; Lect Glas Univ 71-92; Lic to Offic *Glas* 71-90; rtd 92; Hon Can St Mary's Cathl from 92; Hon C St Andrews All SS *St And* from 94. *85D Market Street, St Andrews KY16 9NX* Tel (01334) 477338 E-mail gavin.d.white@ukgateway.net

WHITE, Geoffrey Brian. b 54. Jes Coll Ox BA76 MA80. St Steph Ho Ox 76. **d** 79 **p** 80. C Huddersfield St Pet *Wakef* 79-82; C Flixton St Mich *Man* 82-84; TV Westhoughton 84-91; V Stevenage St Mary Shephall w Aston *St Alb* 91-06; RD Stevenage 01-06; R Norton *Sheff* from 06. *Norton Rectory, Norton Church Road, Norton, Sheffield S8 8JQ* Tel 0114-274 5066 E-mail geoffreywhite333@hotmail.com

WHITE, Canon Geoffrey Gordon. b 28. Selw Coll Cam BA50 MA54. Cuddesdon Coll 51. **d** 53 **p** 54. C Bradford-on-Avon H Trin *Sarum* 53-56; C Kennington St Jo *S'wark* 56-61; V Leeds St Wilfrid *Ripon* 61-63; Chapl K Coll Hosp Lon 63-66; V Aldwick *Chich* 66-76; V Brighton Gd Shep Preston 76-93; Can and Preb Chich Cathl 90-93; rtd 93; Hon C Stepney St Dunstan and All SS *Lon* 94-10. *Flat 65, Telfords Yard, London E1W 2BQ* Tel (020) 7480 6585 E-mail jwhite.telford@virgin.net

WHITE, Gillian Margaret. b 57. Qu Eliz Coll Lon BSc79 Sheff Univ MEd96 PhD02 Nottm Univ MA07. EMMTC 05. **d** 07 **p** 08. NSM Derby St Paul from 07. *The Rectory, The Village, West Hallam, Ilkeston DE7 6GR* Tel 0115-932 4695 Mobile 07973-866848 E-mail g.m.white@tesco.net

WHITE, Miss Hazel Susan. b 65. Nottm Univ BA88. Qu Coll Birm 05. **d** 07 **p** 08. C Woodfield *Leic* from 07. *The Vicarage, Mill Street, Packington, Ashby-de-la-Zouch LE65 1WL* Tel (01530) 564333

WHITE, Hugh Richard Bevis. b 55. New Coll Ox BA78 Ox Univ DPhil85. S'wark Ord Course 93. **d** 96 **p** 97. NSM Westcote Barton w Steeple Barton, Duns Tew etc *Ox* 96-99; NSM Ox St Mary V w St Cross and St Pet 99-01; V Deddington w Barford, Clifton and Hempton from 01. *28 Duns Tew, Bicester OX25 6JR* Tel (01869) 347889

WHITE, Ian Jeffrey. b 57. Leeds Univ BSc80 PhD86 BA05 CChem83 MRSC83. Coll of Resurr Mirfield 03. **d** 05 **p** 06. C Stanningley St Thos *Ripon* 05-09; P-in-c Adel from 09; Dioc Environment Officer from 06. *The Rectory, 25 Church Lane, Adel, Leeds LS16 8DQ* Tel 0113-267 3676 E-mail rev.ianwhite@tesco.net

WHITE, Ian Terence. b 56. CertEd. Ripon Coll Cuddesdon 83. **d** 86 **p** 87. C Maidstone St Martin *Cant* 86-89; C Earley St Pet *Ox* 89-91; TV Schorne 91-96; V St Osyth *Chelmsf* 96-00; V The Suttons w Tydd *Linc* 00-04; rtd 04; Perm to Offic *Nor* from 06 and *St E* from 10. *9 Haling Way, Thetford IP24 1EY* Tel (01842) 820180 E-mail reviawnhite@aol.com

WHITE, Miss Janice. b 49. Trin Coll Bris IDC76. **d** 91 **p** 94. C Claygate *Guildf* 91-98; Assoc Min Stanford-le-Hope w Mucking *Chelmsf* from 98. *Glebe House, Wharf Road, Stanford-le-Hope SS17 0BY* Tel (01375) 645542 E-mail wheeze4god@aol.com

WHITE, Jeremy Spencer. b 54. St Luke's Coll Ex BEd78. Wycliffe Hall Ox 81. **d** 84 **p** 85. C S Molton w Nymet St George, High Bray etc *Ex* 84-87; TV 87-95; V Sway *Win* 95-00; P-in-c Uplyme w Axmouth *Ex* 00-03; R 03-09; RD Honiton 06-07; rtd 09. *Oakleigh, Woodbury Lane, Axminster EX13 5TL* Tel (01297) 32299 E-mail jeremy.white@onetel.net

WHITE, Jo. See WHITE, Julia Mary

WHITE, Canon John Austin. b 42. LVO04. Hull Univ BA64. Coll of Resurr Mirfield 64. **d** 66 **p** 67. C Leeds St Aid *Ripon* 66-69; Asst Chapl Leeds Univ 69-73; Chapl NOC 73-82; Can and Prec Windsor from 82. *4 The Cloisters, Windsor Castle, Windsor SL4 1NJ* Tel (01753) 848787 E-mail john.white@stgeorges-windsor.org

WHITE, John Christopher. b 62. Keble Coll Ox BA84. Wycliffe Hall Ox 86. **d** 89 **p** 90. C Southway *Ex* 89-93; TV Plymouth Em, St Paul Efford and St Aug 93-99; Hon C Abbotskerswell 99-05; Perm to Offic *Birm* 05-10; TV Kings Norton from 10. *The Vicarage, 115 Balden Road, Harborne, Birmingham B32 2EL* Tel 0121-427 2410 or 458 3289 E-mail jwhite.harborne@btinternet.com

WHITE, John Cooper. b 58. LTCL79 K Alfred's Coll Win BEd82 Lon Univ MA92 FRSA94. St Steph Ho Ox 86. **d** 89 **p** 90. C Christchurch *Win* 89-93; P-in-c Bournemouth St Alb 93-94; V 94-00; P-in-c Southbourne St Kath 00-04; V from 04. *St Katharine's Vicarage, 7 Wollaston Road, Bournemouth BH6 4AR* Tel (01202) 423986 E-mail jcoopw@btconnect.com

WHITE, Canon John Francis. b 47. Qu Coll Cam BA69 MA73. Cuddesdon Coll 72. **d** 72 **p** 73. Sacr Wakef Cathl 72-73; Prec 73-76; V Thurlstone 76-82; P-in-c Hoyland Swaine 81-82; V Chapelthorpe 82-06; RD Chevet 96-05; V Lindley 06-10; Hon Can Wakef Cathl 00-10; rtd 10. *16 Thorne End Road, Staincross, Barnsley S75 6NR* E-mail john.white80@virgin.net

WHITE, John Malcolm. b 54. Aston Univ BSc77. Trin Coll Bris BA87. **d** 87 **p** 88. C Harborne Heath *Birm* 87-91; C S Harrow St Paul *Lon* 91-93; TV Roxeth 93-96; V Derby St Alkmund and St Werburgh from 96. *The Vicarage, 200 Duffield Road, Derby DE22 1BL* Tel and fax (01332) 348339

WHITE, John McKelvey. b 57. QUB BA. **d** 82 **p** 83. C Clooney *D & R* 82-84; C Belfast H Trin *Conn* 84-86; I Kilcronaghan w Draperstown, Ballynascreen *D & R* 86-94; I Ballybeen *D & D* 94-04; I Lurgan St Jo from 04. *St John's Rectory, Sloan Street, Lurgan, Craigavon BT66 8NT* Tel (028) 3832 2770

WHITE, Canon John Neville. b 41. Edin Univ MA63. Cranmer Hall Dur. **d** 65 **p** 66. C Sedgefield *Dur* 65-68; C Stoke *Cov* 68-72; V Wrose *Bradf* 72-90; V Farsley 90-06; RD Calverley 93-98; Hon Can Bradf Cathl 96-06; rtd 06; Perm to Offic *Bradf* from 08. *34 Fourlands Drive, Bradford BD10 9SJ* Tel (01274) 415875

WHITE, John William. b 37. CEng71 MIMechE71. SAOMC 98. **d** 01 **p** 02. NSM Sandhurst *Ox* 01-10; Perm to Offic from 10. *21 Broom Acres, Sandhurst GU47 8PN* Tel (01344) 774349

WHITE (née REDMAN), Mrs Julia Elizabeth Hithersay. b 43. St Alb Minl Tr Scheme 87 SAOMC 99. **d** 99 **p** 00. NSM Harpenden St Jo *St Alb* from 99. *The Folly, 71 Station Road, Harpenden AL5 4RL* Tel (01582) 763869

WHITE, Julia Mary (Jo). b 52. Harris Coll CertEd73 Man Univ BEd85 MEd87 PhD92. NOC 00. **d** 03 **p** 04. C Ashbourne w Mapleton *Derby* 03-07; R Wingerworth from 07. *The Rectory, Longedge Lane, Wingerworth, Chesterfield S42 6PU* Tel (01246) 234242 E-mail jo@whiteshouse.plus.net

WHITE, Julian Edward Llewellyn. b 53. St D Coll Lamp BA79 Bp Burgess Hall Lamp 73 Chich Th Coll 79. **d** 79 **p** 80. C Newport St Mark *Mon* 79-83; TV Llanmartin 83-86; R Llandogo and Tintern 86-90 and 91-98; P-in-c St Paul and St Thos St Kitts-Nevis 90-91; V Mathern and Mounton w St Pierre from 98; AD Netherwent from 05. *St Tewdric's Vicarage, Mathern, Chepstow NP16 6JA* Tel (01291) 622317

WHITE, Justin Michael. b 70. Keble Coll Ox MEng93 Warwick Univ MA94 Trin Coll Cam BA00. Westcott Ho Cam 98. **d** 01 **p** 02. C Chippenham St Andr w Tytherton Lucas *Bris* 01-04; Chapl SS Helen and Kath Sch Abingdon 04-06; Jun Chapl Win Coll from 06. *Winchester College, Winchester SO2 9NA* Tel (01962) 621100 Mobile 07866-073023 E-mail justin_white@mac.com

WHITE, Kenneth Charles. b 26. Tyndale Hall Bris 48. **d** 54 **p** 56. Chapl Lotome Sch Karamoja Uganda 54-55; Lic to Offic Mombasa Kenya 55-57; C Morden *S'wark* 57-60; V Ramsey St Mary's w Ponds Bridge *Ely* 60-66; V Leyton Ch Ch *Chelmsf* 66-81; V Totland Bay *Portsm* 81-91; rtd 91; Perm to Offic *Llan* 91-07 and *Lon* from 08. *286A Torbay Road, Harrow HA2 9QW*

WHITE, Malcolm Robert. b 46. Man Univ BSc68. Cranmer Hall Dur 74. **d** 77 **p** 78. C Linthorpe *York* 77-81; C Sutton St Jas and Wawne 81-83; V Upper Holloway St Pet w St Jo *Lon* 83-95; TV Burnham w Dropmore, Hitcham and Taplow *Ox* 95-00; CMS Jordan 00-07; rtd 07; Perm to Offic *Ox* from 08. *Cherry Cottage, 1 Wymers Wood Road, Burnham, Slough SL1 8JQ* Tel (01628) 669085 E-mail whitesmv@gmail.com

WHITE, Marilyn Jeanne. b 32. Avery Hill Coll CertEd69. WMMTC 85. **d** 88 **p** 94. NSM Westbury-on-Severn w Flaxley and Blaisdon *Glouc* 88-98; Perm to Offic *B & W* from 98. *7 Harbutts, Bathampton, Bath BA2 6TA* Tel (01225) 464450

WHITE (née DUNCOMBE), Mrs Maureen Barbara. b 42. Bris Univ BA63 Ox Univ DipEd64. Oak Hill Th Coll 87. **d** 89 **p** 00. NSM Wallington *S'wark* 89-91; Perm to Offic *Win* 99-00; NSM Totton 00-07; rtd 07. *Address temp unknown* Tel 07712-418224 (mobile) E-mail derek@dhandmbwhite.plus.com

WHITE, Michael Godfrey. b 46. SAOMC 98. **d** 02 **p** 03. OLM Shelswell *Ox* 02-07; NSM Fawley *Win* from 07. *86 Rollestone Road, Holbury, Southampton SO45 2GZ* Tel (023) 8089 7062 E-mail revmikewhite@yahoo.co.uk

WHITE, Nancy Kathleen. b 71. Roehampton Inst BA96 PGCE97 Leeds Univ MA07. NOC 05. **d** 07 **p** 08. NSM Erringden *Wakef* 07-10; NSM Todmorden from 10. *774 Rochdale Road, Todmorden OL14 7UA* Tel (01706) 812007 E-mail nancy.white@3-c.coop

✠WHITE, The Rt Revd Patrick George Hilliard. Toronto Univ BA67 DMin93. Wycliffe Coll Toronto MDiv77. **d** 77 **p** 78 **c** 09. Canada 77-97; Bermuda from 97; Bp Bermuda from 09. *Diocesan Office, PO Box HM 769, Hamilton HM CX, Bermuda* Tel (001) (441) 292 6987 Fax 292 5421

WHITE, Paul John. b 68. Middx Univ LLB90 Bris Univ LLM92. NTMTC BA08. **d** 08 **p** 09. C Appledore w Brookland, Fairfield, Brenzett etc *Cant* from 08; C Woodchurch from 08. *The Rectory, 6 Rectory Close, Woodchurch, Ashford TN26 3QJ* Tel (01233) 860686 Mobile 07970-072757 E-mail pauljohnwhite@gmail.com

WHITE, Paul Matthew. b 73. Univ Coll Lon BSc94 K Coll Lon PGCE95. Oak Hill Th Coll BA07. **d** 07 **p** 08. C Southborough St Pet w Ch Ch and St Matt etc *Roch* from 07; C Ox St Andr from 11. *20 Haynes Road, Marston, Oxford OX3 0SF* Tel 07790-697354 (mobile) E-mail ppwhites@hotmail.com

✠**WHITE, The Rt Revd Paul Raymond.** b 49. St Mark's Coll Canberra BTh86 Heythrop Coll Lon MTh89. **d** 85 **p** 86 **c** 02. C N Goulburn Australia 85-87; P-in-c Reigate St Phil *S'wark* 87-89; R Queanbeyan Australia 89-92; V Redhill St Matt *S'wark* 92-97; V E Ivanhoe Australia 97-00; Dir Th Educn 00-07; Melbourne (W Region) 02-07; (S Region) from 07. *Anglican Centre, 209 Flinders Lane, Melbourne Vic 3000, Australia* Tel (0061) (3) 9653 4214 Fax 9653 4266 E-mail sthregbish@melbourne.anglican.com.au

WHITE, Peter Francis. b 27. St Edm Hall Ox BA51 MA55. Ridley Hall Cam 51. **d** 53 **p** 54. C Drypool St Columba *York* 53-56; V Dartford St Edm *Roch* 56-62; CF 62-78; R Barming *Roch* 78-89; rtd 89; Perm to Offic *Wakef* 89-98. *Middleton House Cottage, Middleton on the Hill, Ludlow SY8 4BE* Tel (01568) 750454

WHITE, Peter John. b 26. St Aid Birkenhead 57. **d** 60 **p** 61. C Toxteth Park St Gabr *Liv* 60-62; C Huyton St Mich 62-63; V Thornham w Gravel Hole *Man* 63-68; C Keighley *Bradf* 68-71; C Newington w Dairycoates *York* 71-75; C Frodingham *Linc* 75-80; R Mareham-le-Fen and Revesby 80-86; V Wrawby 86-91; V Melton Ross w New Barnetby 86-91; rtd 91; Perm to Offic *Linc* 91-95 and *Wakef* from 96. *3 Park Avenue, Wakefield WF2 8DS* Tel (01924) 201438

WHITE, Philip Craston. b 59. York Univ BA81 Nottm Univ PGCE84. Trin Coll Bris. **d** 99 **p** 00. C Countesthorpe w Foston *Leic* 99-03; C-in-c Hamilton CD 03-09; C Leic H Trin w St Jo from 09. *56 Vicarage Lane, Humberstone, Leicester LE5 1EE* Tel 0116-210 4967

WHITE, Philip William. b 53. Bede Coll Dur CertEd75 Coll of Ripon & York St Jo MA01. St Jo Coll Nottm 89. **d** 91 **p** 92. C Clifton *York* 91-95; TV Heworth H Trin 95-01; P-in-c Scarborough St Jas w H Trin from 01; Tr Officer E Riding from 01. *St James's Vicarage, 24 Seamer Road, Scarborough YO12 4DT* Tel (01723) 361469 Mobile 07720-010066 E-mail phil@vicarage.netkonect.co.uk

WHITE, Canon Phillip George. b 33. Univ of Wales (Lamp) BA54. St Mich Coll Llan 54. **d** 56 **p** 57. C Tongwynlais *Llan* 56-58; C Mountain Ash 58-60; C Aberavon 60-62; Area Sec (Middx) CMS 62-64; V Treherbert *Llan* 64-76; P-in-c Treorchy 75-76; V Treherbert w Treorchy 76-77; V Pyle w Kenfig 77-99; RD Margam 86-99; Can Llan Cathl from 91; rtd 99. *8 Heol Fair, Porthcawl CF36 5LA* Tel (01656) 786297

WHITE, Mrs Priscilla Audrey. b 62. St Hugh's Coll Ox BA84 MA88. Wycliffe Hall Ox 87. **d** 89 **p** 94. Par Dn Southway *Ex* 89-93; NSM Plymouth Em, St Paul Efford and St Aug 93-99; P-in-c Abbotskerswell 99-05; P-in-c Harborne St Faith and St Laur *Birm* from 05; AD Edgbaston from 10. *The Vicarage, 115 Balden Road, Harborne, Birmingham B32 2EL* Tel 0121-427 2410 E-mail priscillawhite.harborne@btinternet.com

WHITE, Richard. See WHITE, Douglas Richard Leon

WHITE, Richard Alfred. b 49. CQSW. St Jo Coll Nottm. **d** 90 **p** 91. C Leic St Phil 90-95; C Old Dalby and Nether Broughton 95-98; R Ibstock w Heather 98-10; rtd 10. *3 Marston Way, Heather, Coalfield LE67 2RR* Tel (01530) 260676 E-mail richard49white@googlemail.com

WHITE, Richard Allen. b 25. Open Univ BA78 Southn Univ MPhil88 MTh95. Sarum & Wells Th Coll 78. **d** 81 **p** 82. NSM Bursledon *Win* 81-85; C W End 85-90; C Fareham SS Pet and Paul *Portsm* 90-95; Chapl St Chris Hosp Fareham 92-98; rtd 96; Perm to Offic *Portsm* and *Win* from 96. *11 Quay Haven, Swanwick, Southampton SO31 7DE* Tel (01489) 576529

WHITE, Canon Richard Stanley. b 70. Trin Coll Bris BA02. **d** 03 **p** 04. C Haydock St Mark *Liv* 03-06; Pioneer Min Dream Network 06-09; Can for Miss and Evang from 09. *3 Cathedral Close, Liverpool L1 7BR* Tel 0151-702 7243 E-mail richard.white@liverpoolcathedral.org.uk

WHITE, Canon Robert Charles. b 61. Mansf Coll Ox BA83. St Steph Ho Ox 83. **d** 85 **p** 86. C Forton *Portsm* 85-88; C Portsea N End St Mark 88-92; V Warren Park 92-00; P-in-c Leigh Park 94-96; V 96-00; RD Havant 98-00; V Portsea St Mary from 00; AD Portsm from 11; Hon Can Portsm Cathl from 97. *St Mary's Vicarage, Fratton Road, Portsmouth PO1 5PA* Tel (023) 9282 2687 *or* 9282 2990 Fax 9235 9320 E-mail revrcwhite@aol.com

WHITE, The Ven Robin Edward Bantry. b 47. TCD BA70 BD79. CITC 72. **d** 72 **p** 73. C Dublin Zion Ch *D & G* 72-76; Min Can St Patr Cathl Dublin 76-79; C Taney Ch Ch *D & G* 76-79; I Abbeystrewry Union *C, C & R* 79-89; I Douglas Union w Frankfield 89-02; I Moviddy Union from 02; Can Cork Cathl from 89; Can Ross Cathl 89-93; Adn Cork, Cloyne and Ross from 93; Preb Castleknock St Patr Cathl Dublin from 09. *Moviddy Rectory, Aherla, Co Cork, Republic of Ireland* Tel (00353) (21) 733 1511 Mobile 87-286 2178 E-mail archdeacon@cork.anglican.org *or* robinbw@ccrd.ie

WHITE, Roderick Harry. b 55. Trin Coll Bris BA86. **d** 86 **p** 87. C Northampton St Giles *Pet* 86-89; C Godley cum Newton Green *Ches* 89-93; P-in-c 93-99; R Northiam *Chich* from 99. *The Rectory, 24 High Meadow, Northiam, Rye TN31 6GA* Tel (01797) 253118 E-mail rod@rodwhite.freeuk.com

WHITE, Roger David. b 37. Univ of Wales (Cardiff) BTh91. St Mich Coll Llan. **d** 66 **p** 67. C Mountain Ash *Llan* 66-71; C Port Talbot St Theodore 71-74; V Caerhun w Llangelynin *Ban* 74-85; R Llanbedrog w Llannor w Llanfihangel etc 85-88; V Llangeinor 88-90; V Spittal w Trefgarn and Ambleston w St Dogwells *St D* 90-98; V Abergwili w Llanfihangel-uwch-Gwili etc 98-00; rtd 00. *Tir Na Nog, 18 Bryn Cir, Llanerchymedd LL71 8EG* Tel (01248) 470159

WHITE, Roger Ian Scott. b 41. Leeds Univ BA62 Culham Coll Ox PGCE70. Coll of Resurr Mirfield 62. **d** 64 **p** 65. C Wotton-under-Edge *Glouc* 64-69; NSM Rugby St Andr *Cov* 71-80; W Germany 80-82; P-in-c Brinklow *Cov* 82-86; R 86-90; P-in-c Harborough Magna 82-86; R 86-90; P-in-c Monks Kirby w Pailton and Stretton-under-Fosse 82-86; V 86-90; Germany 90-92; V Lydgate w Friezland *Man* 92-01; Chapl Hamburg *Eur* 01-11; rtd 11. *Spannwisch 7, 22159 Hamburg, Germany* Tel (0049) (40) 664316 E-mail roger.white@gmx.de

✠**WHITE, The Rt Revd Roger John.** b 41. Eden Th Sem (USA) BA65 Seabury-Western Th Sem Hon DCL86 Kelham Th Coll. **d** 66 **p** 67 **c** 84. C Manston *Ripon* 66-69; V Olney St Alb USA 69-81; R Alton St Paul 71-80; R Indianapolis Trin Ch 80-84; Bp Milwaukee 84-03; rtd 03. *700 Waters Edge Road, #25, Racine WI 53402-1557, USA* Tel (001) (262) 752 1415 Fax 752 1514 Mobile 414-630 2883 E-mail rjwhite787@aol.com

WHITE, Ronald Henry. b 36. Bris Univ BSc58. SWMTC 82. **d** 85 **p** 86. C Ivybridge *Ex* 85-87; C Ivybridge w Harford 87-88; V Blackawton and Stoke Fleming 88-95; V Stoke Fleming, Blackawton and Strete 95-00; RD Woodleigh 95-99; rtd 00; Perm to Offic *Ex* from 02. *10 Hollingarth Way, Hemyock, Cullompton EX15 3YR* Tel (01823) 681020

WHITE, Canon Roy Sidney. b 34. Sarum Th Coll 62. **d** 65 **p** 66. C Selsdon *Cant* 65-68; C Ranmoor *Sheff* 68-72; V Croydon St Andr *Cant* 72-78; Dir Abp Coggan Tr Cen 78-85; Dir of Chr Stewardship *S'wark* 85-91; Hon Can S'wark Cathl 85-91; Can Res S'wark Cathl 91-99; Vice Provost S'wark 91-99; rtd 99; Perm to Offic *Cant* 00-09. *52 Manton Court, Kings Road, Horsham RH13 5AE* Tel (01403) 248036

WHITE, Mrs Ruth Anna. b 45. Aoyama Gakuin Tokyo BA68 Grenoble Univ. Westmr Coll Cam 83 EAMTC 98. **d** 99 **p** 00. NSM Leyton St Mary w St Edw and St Luke *Chelmsf* 99-03; NSM Leytonstone St Jo from 03; Asst Chapl among deaf and deaf-blind people from 99. *18A Barclay Road, London E11 3DG* Tel and fax (020) 8558 5692 Mobile 07960-580837 E-mail revrwhite@btinternet.com

WHITE, Mrs Sally Margaret. b 59. Univ of Wales (Cardiff) BTh01. St Mich Coll Llan 99. **d** 01 **p** 02. C Berkeley w Wick, Breadstone, Newport, Stone etc *Glouc* 01-05; Co-ord Chapl HM Pris Bedf 05-09; Chapl HM Pris Jersey 09; Chapl Jersey Gp of Hosps from 09. *HM Prison Jersey, La Rue Baal, St Brelade, Jersey JE3 8HQ* Tel (01534) 497200

WHITE, Sandy Dulcie. b 44. **d** 98 **p** 99. OLM W Streatham St Jas *S'wark* 98-05; Perm to Offic *Wakef* 05-07; NSM Cornholme and Walsden from 07. *774 Rochdale Road, Todmorden OL14 7UA* Tel (01706) 812007

WHITE, Mrs Sheelagh Mary. NEOC 02. **d** 05 **p** 06. C Windy Nook St Alb *Dur* 05-10; P-in-c Oxclose from 10; Dioc Ecum Officer from 10. *37 Brancepeth Road, Washington NE38 0LA* Tel 0191-415 9468

WHITE, Simon Inigo Dexter. b 58. York Univ BA80 Nottm Univ PGCE81. St Jo Coll Nottm 87. **d** 90 **p** 91. C Chadkirk *Ches* 90-94; C Stockport St Geo 94; TV Stockport SW 94-99; Chapl Stockport Gr Sch 94-99; P-in-c W Hallam and Mapperley *Derby* 99-02; P-in-c Stanley 99-02; R W Hallam and Mapperley w Stanley from 02. *The Rectory, The Village, West Hallam, Ilkeston DE7 6GR* Tel 0115-932 4695 E-mail s.i.d.white@tesco.net

WHITE, Simon James Hithersay. b 65. St Jo Coll Nottm 01. **d** 03 **p** 04. C Alnwick *Newc* 03-06; P-in-c Felton from 06; P-in-c Longframlington w Brinkburn from 06. *The Vicarage, 1 Benlaw Grove, Felton, Morpeth NE65 9NG* Tel (01670) 787263 E-mail simonjhwhite@breathemail.net

WHITE, The Very Revd Stephen Ross. b 58. Hull Univ BA79 QUB DPhil93. Ripon Coll Cuddesdon BA84. **d** 85 **p** 86. C Redcar *York* 85-88; P-in-c Gweedore, Carrickfin and Templecrone *D & R* 88-92; Bp's Dom Chapl 91-92; Dean Raphoe 92-02; I Raphoe w Raymochy and Clonleigh 93-01; Dean Killaloe and Clonfert *L & K* from 02. *The Deanery, Killaloe, Co Clare, Republic of Ireland* Tel (00353) (61) 376687 E-mail dean@killaloe.anglican.org

WHITE, Mrs Susan Margaret. b 48. Univ of E Lon BA84 Brunel Univ MBA94 Anglia Poly Univ MA04. EAMTC 01. **d** 04 **p** 05. C Harwich Peninsula *Chelmsf* 04-08; P-in-c Alkham w Capel le Ferne and Hougham *Cant* from 08; AD Dover from 11. *The Vicarage, 20 Alexandra Road, Capel le Ferne, Folkestone CT18 7LD* Tel (01303) 240539 E-mail suewhite712@hotmail.com

WHITE, Sister Victoria Joan. b 36. Wellesley Coll (USA) BA58 Harvard Univ STB61 Lon Univ CertEd74 Hon DD86. **dss** 75 **d** 87 **p** 94. CSA from 72; Teacher Burlington-Danes Sch 74-76; Lect Inst of Chr Studies *Lon* 76-78; Gen Sec World Congress of

Faiths 77-81; Lect Dioc Readers' Course *S'wark* 81-89; Asst Abp's Sec for Ecum Affairs 81-82; Ed *Distinctive Diaconate News* from 81; Ed *DIAKONIA News* 87-03; Ed *Distinctive News of Women in Ministry* from 94; Lic to Offic *Lon* 94-06; Perm to Offic from 06; Chapl Angl Communion Office from 04. *St Andrew's House, 16 Tavistock Crescent, London W11 1AP* Tel (020) 7221 4604 E-mail teresajoan@btinternet.com

WHITE (*née* BUTLER)**, Mrs Valerie Joyce.** b 58. EAMTC 99. **d** 02 **p** 03. NSM Southminster *Chelmsf* 02-06; Hon Chapl Miss to Seafarers Tilbury 05-06; C Bury St Edmunds All SS w St Jo and St Geo *St E* 06-08; TV Walton and Trimley from 08. *The Vicarage, Church Lane, Trimley St Martin, Felixstowe IP11 0SW* Tel (01394) 286388 E-mail valthevic@talktalk.net

WHITE, Canon Vernon Philip. b 53. Clare Coll Cam BA75 MA79 Oriel Coll Ox MLitt80. Wycliffe Hall Ox. **d** 77 **p** 78. Tutor Wycliffe Hall Ox 77-83; Chapl and Lect Ex Univ 83-87; R Wotton and Holmbury St Mary *Guildf* 87-93; Dir of Ords 87-93; Can Res and Chan Linc Cathl 93-01; Prin STETS 01-11; Can Westmr Abbey from 11; Visiting Prof K Coll Lon from 11; Can Th Win Cathl from 06. *3 Little Cloisters, London SW1P 3PL* Tel (020) 7654 4808 E-mail vernon.white@westminster-abbey.org

WHITE, William Frederick. b 30. St Jo Coll Nottm. **d** 02. NSM Hillingdon St Jo *Lon* 02-06; NSM Cowley 06-08; Asst Chapl Hillingdon Hosp NHS Trust 02-08; Perm to Offic *Lon* from 08. *31A Copperfield Avenue, Hillingdon, Uxbridge UB8 3NU* Tel (01895) 236746 Mobile 07754-234233 E-mail billwhite2001@hotmail.com

WHITE, William John. b 54. BSc. Wycliffe Hall Ox. **d** 84 **p** 85. C Bowdon *Ches* 84-87; C Chadkirk 87-90; R Wistaston 90-07; RD Nantwich 98-01; TR Gd Shep TM *Carl* from 07. *The Rectory, Greystoke, Penrith CA11 0TJ* Tel (01768) 483293

WHITE SPUNNER, Mrs Jessie Janet. b 37. SRN59 SCM61. CITC 91. **d** 94 **p** 95. NSM Shinrone w Aghancon etc *L & K* 94-10; rtd 10. *St Albans, Church Street, Birr, Co Offaly, Republic of Ireland* Tel (00353) (57) 912 5637 Mobile 86-814 0213 E-mail janwspun@iol.ie

WHITEHALL, Adrian Leslie. b 53. Leeds Univ MB, ChB76 Sheff Univ MMedSc93 MRCGP80. Ridley Hall Cam 04. **d** 06 **p** 07. C Todwick *Sheff* 06-09; Tanzania from 10. *St Margaret's Church, PO Box 306, Pare Avenue, Moshi, Tanzania* Tel (00255) (76) 829 2937 E-mail adrian@awhitehall.freeserve.co.uk

WHITEHEAD, Alexander. *See* WHITEHEAD, Canon Matthew Alexander

WHITEHEAD, Barry. b 30. Oriel Coll Ox BA53 MA62. St Steph Ho Ox 53. **d** 55 **p** 56. C Edgehill St Dunstan *Liv* 55-58; C Upholland 58-61; Ind Chapl 61-90; CF (TA) 64-78; V Aspull *Liv* 77-96; rtd 96; Perm to Offic *Blackb* and *Liv* from 96; *Nor* from 01. *5 Sedgely, Standish, Wigan WN6 0BZ* Tel (01257) 427160

WHITEHEAD, Brian. b 36. SRN58. S'wark Ord Course 72. **d** 75 **p** 77. C Croydon St Aug *Cant* 75-78; C St Marychurch *Ex* 78-80; V Devonport St Mark Ford 80-87; V Castle Donington and Lockington cum Hemington *Leic* 87-98; Chapl Asmara St Geo Eritrea 98-99; Vice Provost All SS Cathl Cairo 99-00; Assoc P Abu Dhabi 00-01; rtd 01; Perm to Offic *Nor* 01-07. *1 Sarisbury Close, Bognor Regis PO22 8JN* Tel (01243) 866549 E-mail britone@uk.packardbell.org

WHITEHEAD, Christopher Martin Field. b 36. ALCD62. **d** 62 **p** 63. C Higher Openshaw *Man* 62-63; C Halliwell St Pet 64-66; V Owlerton *Sheff* 66-75; V Hunmanby w Muston *York* 75-95; RD Scarborough 91-94; R Lockington and Lund and Scarborough w Leconfield 95-01; rtd 01; Perm to Offic *York* from 01. *59 Cornelian Drive, Scarborough YO11 3AL* Tel (01723) 377837

WHITEHEAD, David. b 62. Newc Univ BSc83 MSc85 PhD89. St Jo Coll Nottm BA09. **d** 07 **p** 08. C Ambleside w Brathay *Carl* 07-10; TV Kirkby Lonsdale from 10. *The Vicarage, Vicarage Lane, Kirkby Lonsdale, Carnforth LA6 2BA* Tel (015242) 72078 E-mail vicar@therainbowparish.org

WHITEHEAD, Canon Derek. b 27. St Jo Coll Cam BA50 MA55 Lon Univ BD60 Lanc Univ PhD73. Wells Th Coll 55. **d** 56 **p** 57. C Lower Broughton Ascension *Man* 56-59; Chapl Highgate Sch Lon 63-65; Lect Div Lancs (Preston) Poly *Blackb* 65-79; Dir of Educn *Chich* 79-94; rtd 94; P-in-c Fletching *Chich* 93-03; Can and Preb Chich Cathl 82-98; Perm to Offic from 05. *2 Sheffield Park House, Uckfield TN22 3QY* Tel (01825) 790734

WHITEHEAD, Frederick Keith. b 35. K Coll Lon BD58 AKC58. St Boniface Warminster 58. **d** 59 **p** 60. C S Shore H Trin *Blackb* 59-63; C Whitfield *Derby* 63-66; Lic to Offic 66-93; V Glossop 93-98; Chapl Shire Hill Hosp Glossop 93-99; rtd 99; Perm to Offic *Derby* from 98. *7 Badgers Way, Glossop SK13 6PP* Tel (01457) 852717

WHITEHEAD, Gordon James. b 42. Culham Coll of Educn DipEd64. Clifton Th Coll 66. **d** 72 **p** 74. C Romford Gd Shep *Chelmsf* 73; SAMS Santiago Chile 74-87; C Coleraine *Conn* 87-94; I Errigle Keerogue w Ballygawley and Killeshil *Arm* 94-02; I Bright w Ballee and Killough *D & D* 02-07; rtd 07. *75 Kensington Manor, Dollingstown, Craigavon BT66 7HR* Tel (028) 3831 7989 E-mail whitehead105@btinternet.com

WHITEHEAD, Canon Hazel. b 54. K Coll Lon BD76 AKC76 Lambeth MA97. Oak Hill Th Coll 93. **d** 94 **p** 95. Tutor Dioc Min Course *Guildf* 94-96; Prin 96-05; C Oatlands 95-04; Dioc Dir Minl Tr from 05; Hon Can Guildf Cathl from 03. *The Rectory, The Spinning Walk, Shere, Guildford GU5 9HN* Tel (01483) 202394 E-mail hazel.whitehead@cofeguildford.org.uk

WHITEHEAD, Ian Richard. b 63. St Jo Coll Nottm BA95. **d** 95 **p** 96. C Hillmorton *Cov* 95-97; C Whitnash 97-99; R Rolleston *Lich* from 99; V Anslow from 99. *The Rectory, Church Road, Rolleston-on-Dove, Burton-on-Trent DE13 9BE* Tel (01283) 810132 *or* 810151 E-mail revirwhite@aol.com

WHITEHEAD, Mrs Jennifer Jane. b 45. St Jo Coll York CertEd67. **d** 98 **p** 99. OLM Winterton Gp *Linc* from 98. *11 Queen Street, Winterton, Scunthorpe DN15 9TR* Tel (01724) 734027

WHITEHEAD, Mrs Joanne Louise. b 71. Hull Univ BA92 PGCE93 Nottm Univ MA08. EMMTC 05. **d** 08 **p** 09. C Oakwood *Derby* from 08. *4 Baverstock Close, Chellaston, Derby DE73 6ST* Tel (01332) 703464 E-mail jo.whitehead@tiscali.co.uk

WHITEHEAD, John Stanley. b 38. Jes Coll Cam BA63 MA67 MPhil. Westcott Ho Cam 63. **d** 64 **p** 65. C Batley All SS *Wakef* 64-67; C Mitcham St Mark *S'wark* 67-70; C Frinsbury w Upnor *Roch* 70-72; TV Strood 72-75; R Halstead 75-82; V Betley *Lich* 82-85; V Betley and Keele 85-01; Asst Chapl Keele Univ 82-01; Perm to Offic *Ches* 02-09; C Acton and Worleston, Church Minshull etc 10. *Paddock House, Longhill Lane, Hankelow, Crewe CW3 0JG* Tel (01270) 812607 E-mail john@whitehead400.freeserve.co.uk

WHITEHEAD, Canon Matthew Alexander. b 44. Leeds Univ BA65 Birm Univ MA75 St Chad's Coll Dur DipEd66 Newc Univ MPhil03. Qu Coll Birm. **d** 69 **p** 70. C Bingley All SS *Bradf* 69-72; C Keele and Asst Chapl Keele Univ 72-74; Bp's Dom Chapl *Dur* 74-80; V Escomb and Witton Park 74-80; V Birtley 80-89; RD Chester-le-Street 84-89; V Stockton St Pet 89-00; V The Trimdons 00-03; Dioc Warden of Readers 94-03; Hon Can Dur Cathl 96-03; P-in-c Stow Gp *Linc* 03-09; rtd 09; Dioc Warden of Readers *Linc* from 03; Can and Preb Linc Cathl from 04. *77 Yarborough Crescent, Lincoln LN1 3NE* Tel 07518-746643 (mobile) E-mail alex.whitehead@lincoln.anglican.org

WHITEHEAD, Canon Michael Hutton. b 33. St Chad's Coll Dur 54. **d** 58 **p** 59. CMP from 59; C Southwick St Columba *Dur* 58-64; V Hendon St Ignatius 64-70; P-in-c Sunderland 67-80; V Hendon 70-80; V Hendon and Sunderland 80-87; Hon Can Dur Cathl from 84; V Hartlepool St Aid 87-98; RD Hartlepool 91-95; rtd 98. *4 West Row, Greatham, Hartlepool TS25 2HW* Tel (01429) 872922

WHITEHEAD, Nicholas James. b 53. Univ of Wales (Ban) BTh07 ACIB. Ridley Hall Cam 86. **d** 88 **p** 89. C Bourne *Guildf* 88-92; V Hersham 92-10; RD Emly 06-10; R Shere, Albury and Chilworth from 10. *The Rectory, The Spinning Walk, Shere, Guildford GU5 9HN* Tel (01483) 202394 Mobile 07946-389583 E-mail nick@nickhaze.demon.co.uk

WHITEHEAD, Paul Conrad. b 60. St Jo Coll Nottm LTh92. **d** 92 **p** 93. C Mansfield Woodhouse *S'well* 92-96; C Carlton-in-the-Willows 96-02; C Colwick 96-02; CF (TA) from 96; NSM Trowell, Awsworth and Cossall *S'well* from 04. *84 Hillside Road, Beeston, Nottingham NG9 3AT* Tel 0115-919 7030 Mobile 07973-727221 E-mail paulkirsten@ntlworld.com

WHITEHEAD, Philip. b 34. Kelham Th Coll 55. **d** 59 **p** 60. C Sugley *Newc* 59-62; C Alnwick St Paul 62-63; C Newc St Gabr 63-66; C Gosforth All SS 66-67; V Kenton Ascension 67-75; V Spittal 75-88; P-in-c Scremerston 81-88; V Cresswell and Lynemouth 88-96; Perm to Offic from 96; rtd 96. *13 Abbey Gate, Morpeth NE61 2XL* Tel (01670) 514953

WHITEHEAD, Canon Robin Lawson. b 53. Bris Univ BA76 Lon Univ MA96. St Steph Ho Ox 77. **d** 80 **p** 81. C Cheshunt *St Alb* 80-83; C E Grinstead St Swithun *Chich* 83-85; V Friern Barnet St Pet le Poer *Lon* 85-92; R Friern Barnet St Jas 92-95; C Wood Green St Mich w Bounds Green St Gabr etc 96-97; TR Leic Resurr 97-04; V Boston *Linc* 04-05; TR from 05; RD Holland E 09-10; RD Holland W 09-10; RD Holland from 10; Can and Preb Linc Cathl from 09. *The Vicarage, Wormgate, Boston PE21 6NP* Tel (01205) 362992 E-mail robin.whitehead@virgin.net

WHITEHOUSE, Alan Edward. b 35. CEng66. Glouc Sch of Min 89. **d** 92 **p** 93. NSM Evesham *Worc* 92-96; NSM Evesham w Norton and Lenchwick 96-02; rtd 02; Perm to Offic *Worc* from 03. *The Coppice, 56 Elm Road, Evesham WR11 3DW* Tel (01386) 442427 E-mail alan.coppice@btopenworld.com

WHITEHOUSE, David Garner. b 70. Sheff Univ BEng91. EAMTC 03. **d** 05 **p** 06. C Cheadle *Ches* 05-10; P-in-c Southport SS Simon and Jude w All So *Liv* from 10. *The Vicarage, 72 Roe Lane, Southport PR9 7HT* E-mail davidgwhitehouse@googlemail.com

WHITEHOUSE, Nigel Andrew. b 57. St Mary's RC Sem Birm 75 Westcott Ho Cam 91. **d** 80 **p** 81. In RC Ch 81-87; C Whittlesey and Pondersbridge *Ely* 92-94; P-in-c Newton 94-98; R 98-03;

P-in-c Gorefield 94-98; V 98-03; P-in-c Tydd St Giles 94-98; R 98-03; TR Whittlesey, Pondersbridge and Coates from 03; Hon Asst Dir of Ords from 09; RD March from 09. *The Rectory, 9A St Mary's Street, Whittlesey, Peterborough PE7 1BG* Tel (01733) 203676 E-mail nigel.whitehouse@talktalk.net

WHITEHOUSE, Canon Susan Clara. b 48. R Holloway Coll Lon BA70. Westcott Ho Cam 87. d 89 p 94. Par Dn Farnley *Ripon* 89-93; Dioc Development Rep 92-03; C Bedale and Thornton Watlass w Thornton Steward 93-96; V Aysgarth and Bolton cum Redmire 96-06; R Penhill from 06; Hon Can Ripon Cathl from 02; AD Wensley 03-05. *The Vicarage, Carperby, Leyburn DL8 4DQ* Tel (01969) 663235
E-mail suewhitehouse@carperby.fsnet.co.uk

WHITELEY, Canon Robert Louis. b 28. Leeds Univ BA48. Coll of Resurr Mirfield 50. d 52 p 53. C Hollinwood *Man* 52-55; Br Honduras 56-61; V Illingworth *Wakef* 61-68; V Westgate Common 68-75; Can Res Wakef Cathl 75-80; Hon Can Wakef Cathl 80-93; V Almondbury 80-82; TR Almondbury w Farnley Tyas 82-92; RD Almondbury 81-93; rtd 93; Perm to Offic Wakef from 93 and Ox 98-10. *The Bungalow, Manormead, Tilford Road, Hindhead GU26 6RA* Tel (01428) 607157

WHITELOCK, Mrs Susan Karen. b 62. STETS 98. d 01 p 06. NSM Portsea N End St Mark *Portsm* 01-06; NSM Portsea St Mary from 06. *404 Copnor Road, Portsmouth PO3 5EW* Tel 07903-414029 (mobile) E-mail sue.whitelock@ntlworld.com

WHITEMAN, Canon Cedric Henry. b 28. Lich Th Coll 59. d 61 p 62. C Abington *Pet* 61-64; V Kettering St Andr 64-79; RD Kettering 73-79; Can Pet Cathl 77-79; V Rotherham *Sheff* 79-87; RD Rotherham 79-86; Hon Can Sheff Cathl 85-98; Bp's Dom Chapl 86-99; V Wentworth 87-91, rtd 91; Perm to Offic Sheff from 99. *11 Thornbrook Close, Chapeltown, Sheffield S35 2BB* Tel 0114-245 7479 E-mail cedric.whiteman@btinternet.com

WHITEMAN, Christopher Henry Raymond. b 51. Portsm Poly BA73 Worc Coll of Educn PGCE74 Open Univ BSc97. St Jo Coll Nottm MA99. d 90 p 91. C Rockland St Mary w Hellington, Bramerton etc *Nor* 90-93; P-in-c Gillingham w Geldeston, Stockton, Ellingham etc 93-94; R 94-04; R Culworth w Sulgrave and Thorpe Mandeville etc *Pet* 04-11; rtd 11. *28 Penterry Park, Chepstow NP16 5AZ*
E-mail chrwhiteman@aol.com

WHITEMAN, The Ven Rodney David Carter. b 40. Ely Th Coll 61. d 64 p 65. C Kings Heath *Birm* 64-70; V Rednal 70-79; V Erdington St Barn 79-89; RD Aston 81-86 and 88-89; Hon Can Birm Cathl 85-89; Adn Bodmin *Truro* 89-00; Adn Cornwall 00-05; P-in-c Cardynham and Helland 89-94; Hon Can Truro Cathl 89-05; rtd 06. *22 Treverbyn Gardens, Sandy Hill, St Austell PL25 3AW* Tel (01726) 879043

WHITESIDE, Canon Peter George. b 30. St Cath Coll Cam BA55 MA61. Cuddesdon Coll 55. d 57 p 58. C Westmr St Steph w St Jo *Lon* 57-61; Chapl Clifton Coll Bris 61-70; Hd Master Linc Cathl Sch 71-73; Can and Preb Linc Cathl 72-73; Australia 74-92; Prin and Chapl Wadhurst C of E Gr Sch 74-89; TV Brentford *Lon* 92-97; C Ashington w E St Luke Australia 98-00; C Ormond 00-05; rtd 05. *52 Cove Road, Rustington, Littlehampton BN16 2QN* Tel (01903) 786566
E-mail linda655@btinternet.com

WHITFIELD, Charles. b 25. St Pet Hall Ox BA49 MA53. Ridley Hall Cam 49. d 51 p 52. C Ecclesfield *Sheff* 51-54; C Grassendale *Liv* 54-56; C Neasden cum Kingsbury St Cath *Lon* 56-58; C St Martin-in-the-Fields 58-59; V Bromley H Trin *Roch* 59-68; V Egg Buckland *Ex* 68-90; rtd 90; Perm to Offic *Ex* from 99. *23 Chapel Meadow, Buckland Monachorum, Yelverton PL20 7LR*

WHITFIELD, Joy Verity. *See* CHAPMAN, Mrs Joy Verity

WHITFIELD, Leslie Turnbull. b 43. Cardiff Univ LLM10 CEng72 MIET72 MCMI74. St Jo Coll Nottm MA00. d 00 p 01. C Bottesford w Ashby *Linc* 00-03; P-in-c Mablethorpe w Trusthorpe 03-07; Ind Chapl 07-08; rtd 08. *3 Burland Court, Washingborough, Lincoln LN4 1HL* Tel (01522) 791195 Mobile 07913-247783 E-mail rev.les@tiscali.co.uk

WHITFIELD, Canon Trevor. b 48. Bedf Coll Lon BSc71 Bris Univ PGCE73 Fitzw Coll Cam BA78 MA88. Ridley Hall Cam 76. d 79 p 80. C Battersea St Pet and St Paul *S'wark* 79-82; Chapl Stockholm w Uppsala *Eur* 82-83; C-in-c Roundshaw St Paul CD *S'wark* 83-89; Asst Chapl R Victoria Infirmary Newc 89-92; Asst Chapl Berne w Neuchâtel *Eur* 92-95; Chapl Utrecht w Amersfoort, Harderwijk and Zwolle 95-02; Chapl Maisons-Laffitte from 02; Can Gib Cathl from 10. *15 avenue Carnot, 78600 Maisons-Laffitte, France* Tel (0033) 1 39 62 34 97
E-mail htcml@aol.com

WHITFIELD, William. b 47. Open Univ BA80 Univ of Wales (Cardiff) LLM95 FRSH81. STETS 01. d 04 p 05. NSM Marchwood *Win* 04-08; NSM Millbrook from 08. *35 The Rowans, Marchwood, Southampton SO40 4YW* Tel (023) 8086 0399 E-mail william.whitfield@btinternet.com

WHITFORD, Judith. *See* POLLINGER, Canon Judith

WHITFORD (née FAULKNER), Mrs Margaret Evelyn. b 54. Goldsmiths' Coll Lon BEd77. EAMTC 98. d 01 p 02. C Grays Thurrock *Chelmsf* 01-05; C Bradwell on Sea 05-08; C Bradwell

on Sea and St Lawrence from 08; C Brandon and Santon Downham w Elveden etc *St E* from 11. *The Rectory, 7 Walton Way, Brandon IP27 0HP* E-mail mandlz@btinternet.com

WHITFORD, William Laurence. b 56. Open Univ BA92. NOC 92. d 95 p 96. C Hindley All SS *Liv* 95-99; P-in-c E and W Tilbury and Linford *Chelmsf* 99-04; R 04-05; P-in-c Bradwell on Sea 05-08; R Bradwell on Sea and St Lawrence from 08; R Brandon and Santon Downham w Elveden etc *St E* from 11. *The Rectory, 7 Walton Way, Brandon IP27 0HP*
E-mail mandlz@btinternet.com

WHITHAM, Ian Scott. b 66. Oak Hill Th Coll. d 01 p 02. C Yateley *Win* 01-03; C Yateley and Eversley 03-05; V W Ewell *Guildf* from 05. *All Saints' Vicarage, 7 Church Road, West Ewell, Epsom KT19 9QY* Tel (020) 8393 4357 Mobile 07946-394467
E-mail ian.witham@ntlworld.com

WHITING, Graham James. b 58. Bris Univ BSc81. Chich Th Coll 83. d 86 p 88. C Portslade St Nic and St Andr *Chich* 86-87; C W Tarring 87-91; C Seaford w Sutton 91-94; P-in-c Bournemouth St Clem *Win* 94-02; V Findon Valley *Chich* from 02. *The Vicarage, 2 Central Avenue, Worthing BN14 0DS* Tel (01903) 872900 E-mail graham.whiting@lineone.net

WHITING, Joseph Alfred. b 41. Oak Hill Th Coll 82. d 85 p 86. Hon C Sidcup St Andr *Roch* 85-88; C Southborough St Pet w Ch Ch and St Matt 88-92; C Aldridge *Lich* 92-97; TV Rye *Chich* 97-02; rtd 02; Perm to Offic *Roch* from 02. *71 Ash Tree Drive, West Kingsdown, Sevenoaks TN15 6LW* Tel (01474) 853202
E-mail whitings71@tiscali.co.uk

WHITING, Mark Justin Robert. b 70. St Steph Ho Ox 99. d 01 p 02. C Sevenoaks St Jo *Roch* 01-04; P-in-c Derby St Bart 04-07; Chapl RN 07-08; Perm to Offic *Portsm* 09; NSM Paulsgrove 09-10; P-in-c Portsea Ascension from 10. *The Vicarage, 98 Kirby Road, Portsmouth PO2 0PW* Tel 07876-032709 (mobile)
E-mail frmarkwhiting@aol.com

WHITING, Stephen. b 60. Cranmer Hall Dur 06. d 08 p 09. C Scarborough St Mary w Ch Ch and H Apostles *York* from 08. *13 Woodall Avenue, Scarborough YO12 7TH* Tel (01723) 350016 Mobile 07789-950881 E-mail stevewhiting.1@btinternet.com

WHITLEY, Brian. b 58. Dundee Univ BA97 Portsm Univ MA(Ed)00 RMN84 RGN84. STETS BA07. d 07 p 08. C Easthampstead *Ox* 07-10; P-in-c Woodplumpton *Blackb* from 10. *Woodplumpton Vicarage, Sandy Lane, Lower Bartle, Preston PR4 0RX* Tel (01772) 690355 Mobile 07851-859296
E-mail bwhitley2@ntlworld.com

WHITLEY, Eric Keir. b 47. Salford Univ BSc68. Trin Coll Bris 77. d 79 p 80. C Nottingham St Ann w Em *S'well* 79-83; V Donisthorpe and Moira w Stretton-en-le-Field *Leic* 83-91; V Thorpe Acre w Dishley 91-00; V Loughb Gd Shep from 00. *21 Parklands Drive, Loughborough LE11 2SZ* Tel (01509) 211005

WHITLEY, John Duncan Rooke. b 29. Trin Coll Cam BA51 MA55 Jordan Hill Coll Glas CertEd82. Coll of Resurr Mirfield 52. d 54 p 55. C Ashington *Newc* 54-59; C Chiswick St Nic w St Mary *Lon* 59-61; V Ware St Mary *St Alb* 61-71; Can Missr Edin 71-74; Chapl R Edin Hosp 71-74; Dioc Educn Officer *Edin* 71-74; Hon Asst Dioc Supernumerary from 74; Asst Chapl Lothian Primary Healthcare NHS Trust 95-04; TV Edin St Columba from 99. *114 Viewforth, Edinburgh EH10 4LN* Tel and fax 0131-229 0130 Mobile 07774-402551
E-mail john.whitley@blueyonder.co.uk

WHITLEY, John William. b 46. TCD BA68. Cranmer Hall Dur BA71. d 71 p 72. C Belfast St Mary Magd *Conn* 71-73; C Toxteth St Philemon w St Gabr *Liv* 73-78; P-in-c Toxteth Park St Cleopas 78-88; TV Toxteth St Philemon w St Gabr and St Cleopas 89-95; P-in-c Litherland St Paul Hatton Hill 95-02; V from 02. *St Paul's Vicarage, Watling Avenue, Liverpool L21 9NU* Tel 0151-928 2705 E-mail anthea.whitley@virgin.net

WHITLEY (née ALLISON), Rosemary Jean. b 45. LTCL67. Trin Coll Bris 75 St Jo Coll Nottm 94. d 95 p 99. NSM Loughb Gd Shep *Leic* 95-98 and from 00; NSM Thorpe Acre w Dishley 98-00. *21 Parklands Drive, Loughborough LE11 2SZ* Tel (01501) 211005

WHITLOCK, Canon James Frederick. b 44. Ch Coll Cam BA75 MA78. Westcott Ho Cam 73. d 76 p 77. C Newquay *Truro* 76-79; P-in-c St Mawgan w St Ervan and St Eval 79-81; R 81; Bp's Dom Chapl 82-85; Dioc Dir of Ords 82-85; V Leagrave *St Alb* 85-89; TR Probus, Ladock and Grampound w Creed and St Erme *Truro* 89-95; V Penzance St Mary w St Paul 95-00; P-in-c Penzance St Jo 97-00; Hon Can Truro Cathl 98-00; rtd 00; Perm to Offic *Truro* from 00. *10 Barlandhu, Newlyn, Penzance TR18 5QT* Tel (01736) 330474

WHITMARSH, Mrs Pauline. d 04 p 05. OLM Bramshaw and Landford w Plaitford *Sarum* 04-06; OLM Forest and Avon from 06. *Dovera, North Lane, Nomansland, Salisbury SP5 2BU* Tel (01794) 390534 E-mail plwhitmarsh@tiscali.co.uk

WHITMORE, Benjamin Nicholas. b 66. Imp Coll Lon BEng88. Cranmer Hall Dur 89. d 92 p 93. C Gt Wyrley *Lich* 92-95; C Hednesford 95-00; V Walsall Pleck and Bescot 00-07; Hon C Wallsall and Walsall St Paul 05-07; V Penn from 07.

St Bartholomew's Vicarage, 68 Church Hill, Penn, Wolverhampton WV4 5JD Tel (01902) 341399 E-mail bennyjo@vicres.fsnet.co.uk

WHITMORE, Edward James. b 36. Lon Univ BD66. Tyndale Hall Bris. d 68 p 69. Tanzania 68-76; Lic to Offic Blackb 77-09. 74 Greencroft,' Penwortham, Preston PR1 9LB Tel (01772) 746522

WHITMORE, Miss Jane Frances. b 30. dss 79 d 87 p 94. Elloughton and Brough w Brantingham York 79-83; Foley Park Worc 83-87; C Frimley Guildf 87-96; rtd 96; Perm to Offic Worc from 96. The Grange, 26 Middleton Road, Marlpool, Kidderminster DY11 5EY

WHITMORE, Stephen Andrew. b 53. Sheff Univ BSc74. St Jo Coll Nottm 89. d 91 p 92. C Newbury Ox 91-95; TV High Wycombe from 95. 70 Marlow Road, High Wycombe HP11 1TH Tel (01494) 438722 E-mail steve@stjohnschurch.freeserve.co.uk

WHITNALL, Robert Edward (Dominic). b 14. Magd Coll Ox BA37. Cuddesdon Coll 37. d 38 p 39. C Staveley Derby 38-44; CR from 47; S Africa 47-66; Hon C Battyeford Wakef from 68; rtd 84. House of the Resurrection, Stocks Bank Road, Mirfield WF14 0BN Tel (01924) 483335

WHITNEY, Charles Edward. b 46. Goldsmiths' Coll Lon BA71 TCert72 ACP75. WEMTC 01. d 04 p 05. NSM Tewkesbury w Walton Cardiff and Twyning Glouc from 04; NSM Deerhurst and Apperley w Forthampton etc from 10. Sarn Hill Lodge, Bushley Green, Bushley, Tewkesbury GL20 6AD Tel (01684) 296764

WHITNEY, John Charles. b 59. St Jo Coll Dur BATM11. Cranmer Hall Dur 09. d 11. C Kirkheaton Wakef from 11. 12 Greenfield Crescent, Grange Moor, Wakefield WF4 4WA Tel (01924) 849437

WHITTAKER, Mrs Angela. b 68. Birm Univ BA89 St Martin's Coll Lanc PGCE91. NEOC 98. d 00 p 01. C Houghton le Spring Dur 00-04; TV Kirkby Lonsdale Carl 04-09; P-in-c Natland from 09; P-in-c Old Hutton and New Hutton from 09. The Vicarage, Natland, Kendal LA9 7QQ Tel (01539) 560355 E-mail a-awhittaker@tiscali.co.uk

WHITTAKER, Brian Lawrence. b 39. Univ of Wales MTh06. Clifton Th Coll 63. d 66 p 67. C Whitton and Thurleston w Akenham St E 66-69; C Normanton Wakef 69-74; P-in-c Castle Hall, Stalybridge and Dukinfield Ch Ch Ches 74-77; V Stalybridge H Trin and Ch Ch 77-83; TR Bucknall and Bagnall Lich 83-91; R Draycott-le-Moors w Forsbrook 91-05; rtd 05; Perm to Offic Lich from 05. 6 Rubens Way, Stoke-on-Trent ST3 7GQ Tel (01782) 397765 E-mail brianlesley.whittaker@tesco.net

WHITTAKER, Bryan. b 58. Southn Univ BTh82. Chich Th Coll 82. d 84 p 85. C Whitleigh Ex 84-88; C Corringham Chelmsf 88-92; V Rush Green 92-94. 361 Dagenham Road, Romford RM7 0XX

WHITTAKER, Derek. b 30. OBE85. Liv Univ BEng51 PhD58 CEng65. d 93 p 95. Zambia 93-96; NSM Broom Leys Leic 97-00; rtd 00; Perm to Offic Leic from 00. 44 St David's Crescent, Coalville LE67 4ST Tel (01530) 831071

WHITTAKER, Mrs Diane Claire. b 57. Newc Poly BA79 Thames Poly BSc87 Univ of Wales (Abth) MA92. ERMC 06. d 08. C Welwyn St Alb from 08. St Michael's House, 3 London Road, Woolmer Green, Knebworth SG3 6JU Tel (01438) 811815

WHITTAKER, Edward Geoffrey. b 59. Birm Univ BSc82 Avery Hill Coll PGCE85 Dur Univ MA95. Westcott Ho Cam 97. d 99 p 00. C Neston Ches 99-02; V Rocester and Croxden w Hollington Lich 02-10; P-in-c Uttoxeter Area 07-11; TR from 11; RD Uttoxeter 04-11. The Vicarage, 12 Orchard Close, Uttoxeter ST14 7DZ Tel (01889) 563644

WHITTAKER, Garry. b 59. St Jo Coll Nottm 89. d 91 p 92. C Denton Ch Ch Man 91-95; P-in-c Waterhead 95-05; TR Bacup and Stacksteads from 05. 10 Park Crescent, Bacup OL13 9RL Tel (01706) 873362

WHITTAKER, Mrs Jennifer Margaret. b 43. Glas Univ MA64. SAOMC 00. d 03 p 04. NSM Martley and Wichenford, Knightwick etc Worc 03-08; NSM Worcs W from 09. The Key Barn, Half Key, Malvern WR14 1UP Tel (01886) 833897 E-mail jen.whittaker@tiscali.co.uk

WHITTAKER, Jeremy Paul. b 59. Ox Univ MA. Ripon Coll Cuddesdon 82. d 84 p 85. C Crowthorne Ox 84-87; C Westborough Guildf 87-88; TV 88-91; Chapl Pierrepont Sch Frensham 91-95; Perm to Offic Guildf from 95. 6 Springhaven Close, Guildford GU1 2JP

WHITTAKER, John. b 69. Leic Univ BA90 ACA93. Ripon Coll Cuddesdon BTh00. d 00 p 01. C Melton Mowbray Leic 00-03; P-in-c Barrow upon Soar w Walton le Wolds 03-11; P-in-c Wymeswold and Prestwold w Hoton 05-11; V Hinckley St Mary from 11. 2 The Rills, Hinckley LE10 1NA Tel (01455) 698732 E-mail johnhelena@tiscali.co.uk

WHITTAKER, Karl Paul. b 55. ATL. CITC BTh95. d 95 p 96. C Killowen D & R 95-99; I Annaghmore Arm 99-04; P-in-c Sunbury St Mary Australia 04-05; I Errigal w Garvagh D & R from 05. St Paul's Rectory, 58 Station Road, Garvagh, Coleraine BT51 5LA Tel (028) 2955 8226

WHITTAKER, Canon Peter Harold. b 39. AKC62. d 63 p 64. C Walton St Mary Liv 63-67; C Ross Heref 67-70; R Bridgnorth St Mary 70-78; P-in-c Oldbury 70-78; TR Bridgnorth, Tasley, Astley Abbotts and Oldbury 78-81; RD Bridgnorth 78-81; Preb Heref Cathl 80-81; V Leighton Buzzard w Eggington, Hockliffe etc St Alb 81-92; RD Dunstable 84-85; R Barton-le-Cley w Higham Gobion and Hexton 92-04; Hon Can St Alb 92-04; rtd 04; Perm to Offic Lich from 06. 12 Aldersley Way, Ruyton XI Towns, Shrewsbury SY4 1NE Tel (01939) 260059

WHITTAKER, William Paul. See STAFFORD-WHITTAKER, William Paul

WHITTALL, The Very Revd Christopher Gordon. b 50. OAM07. Macquarie Univ (NSW) BA77 Sydney Univ MA87 Gen Th Sem NY STM88. St Jo Coll Morpeth BD80. d 79 p 80. C Orange E Australia 79-80; C Blayney 80-83; R Bourke 83-87; Vice Prin St Jo Coll Morpeth 87-90; Dean Rockhampton 90-10; Chapl to Abp Wales Llan from 10. Llys Esgob, The Cathedral Green, Llandaff, Cardiff CF5 2EB Tel (029) 2056 2400 E-mail chaplain.archbishop@churchinwales.org.uk

WHITTAM, Canon Kenneth Michael. b 26. Ball Coll Ox BA50 MA54. Cuddesdon Coll 50. d 52 p 53. C Adlington Blackb 52-55; C St Annes St Thos 55-58; R Halton w Aughton 58-62; R Colne St Bart 62-66; Chapl Highgate Sch Lon 66-75; V Shotwick Ches 75-89; Can Res Ches Cathl and Dioc Missr 75-85; Hon Can Ches Cathl 85-90; Clergy Study Officer 85-91; rtd 91; Perm to Offic Ches from 91. 22 Warwick Close, Little Neston, Neston CH64 0SR Tel 0151-336 8541

WHITTING, Dominic Peter. b 85. Cant Ch Ch Univ BA07. Ripon Coll Cuddesdon 07. d 10 p 11. C St Breoke and Egloshayle Truro from 10. Boscarne, 2 Trenant Vale, Wadebridge PL27 6AJ Tel (01208) 816562 E-mail domwhitting@hotmail.com

WHITTINGHAM, Mrs Janet Irene. b 49. d 03 p 04. OLM Pendleton Man 03-09; OLM Salford All SS from 09. 24 Aylesbury Close, Salford M5 4FQ Tel 0161-736 5878

WHITTINGHAM, Peter. b 58. Sheff Univ BA79 PGCE. St Jo Coll Nottm 88. d 90 p 91. C Northowram Wakef 90-93; C Airedale w Fryston 93-96; V Wrenthorpe 96-06; P-in-c Alverthorpe 02-06; V Attercliffe and Darnall Sheff from 06; Chapl Shrewsbury Hosp from 11. The Chaplain's House, Shrewsbury Hospital, Norfolk Road, Sheffield S2 2SU Tel 0114-275 9997 E-mail peter.whittingham@sheffield.anglican.org

WHITTINGHAM, Ronald Norman. b 43. Linc Coll Ox BA65 MA68. Coll of Resurr Mirfield 65. d 67 p 68. C Horninglow Lich 67-69; C Drayton in Hales 69-70; C Uttoxeter w Bramshall 71-75; P-in-c Burton St Paul 75-80; V Shareshill 80-83; V Silverdale and Knutton Heath 83-89; P-in-c Alsagers Bank 83-89; V Silverdale and Alsagers Bank 89-92; V Honley Wakef 92-99; TV Hugglescote w Donington, Ellistown and Snibston Leic 99-02; TV Leic Presentation 02-07; C Leic St Chad 03-07; rtd 07; Perm to Offic Lich from 08. 848 High Lane, Stoke-on-Trent ST6 6HG

WHITTINGTON, David John. b 45. OBE01. Qu Coll Ox BA67 MA71. Coll of Resurr Mirfield 69. d 71 p 72. Chapl St Woolos Cathl 71-72; Chapl Qu Coll and C Ox St Mary V w St Cross and St Pet 72-76; V Stockton Dur 77-98; Hon Can Dur Cathl 93-98; Can Res and Dioc Dir Educn 98-03; Nat Sch Development Officer Abps' Coun 03-08; rtd 08. The Gatehouse Flat, Brancepeth Castle, Brancepeth, Durham DH7 8DE Tel 07702-036344 (mobile) E-mail dj.whittington@btinternet.com

WHITTINGTON, Peter Graham. b 68. Ox Poly BA90. Trin Coll Bris BA95. d 95 p 96. C Gateacre Liv 95-99; V Huyton St Geo 99-05; V Orrell from 05. St Luke's Vicarage, 10 Lodge Road, Orrell, Wigan WN5 7AT Tel (01695) 623410 E-mail whitts01@surfaid.org

WHITTINGTON, Richard Hugh. b 47. MBE74. Sarum & Wells Th Coll. d 93 p 94. C Enfield St Jas Lon 93-96; P-in-c Ightham Roch 96-97; R 97-01; Chapl R Hosp Chelsea from 01. The Chaplaincy, The Royal Hospital Chelsea, Royal Hospital Road, London SW3 4SL Tel (020) 7881 5234 or 7881 5260 Fax 7881 5463 Mobile 07979-360025 E-mail chaplain@chelsea-pensioners.org.uk

WHITTINGTON, Mrs Sharon Ann. b 56. Leeds Univ BA79 PGCE80. NEOC. d 00 p 01. NSM The Street Par York 00-03; P-in-c York St Thos w St Maurice 03-05; NSM York St Olave w St Giles 03-09; NSM York St Helen w St Martin 04-09; Perm to Offic from 09. 30 Marygate, York YO30 7BH Tel (01904) 627401

WHITTLE, Alan. b 29. K Coll Lon BD52 AKC52. d 53 p 54. C Combe Down B & W 53-55; C Bath Twerton-on-Avon 55-57; Australia 57-66; R Aston Rowant w Crowell Ox 66-68; Lic to Offic S'wark 69-72; V Mitcham Ch Ch 72-92; rtd 92; Perm to Offic S'wark 92-07. 117 May Cross Avenue, Morden SM4 4DF Tel (020) 8540 0201

WHITTLE, Ian Christopher. b 60. Univ Coll Dur BA81 Fitzw Coll Cam BA88 MA91. Ridley Hall Cam 85. d 88 p 89. C S Petherton w the Seavingtons B & W 88-91; Asst Chapl The Hague Eur 91-97; P-in-c Gayton Gp of Par Nor 97-99; R Gayton, Gayton Thorpe, E Walton, E Winch etc 99-10; RD

Lynn 02-08; R Stiffkey and Bale from 10. *The Vicarage, 2 Holt Road, Langham, Holt NR25 7BX* Tel (01328) 830246

WHITTLE, John William. b 46. Qu Mary Coll Lon BA68. Sarum & Wells Th Coll 84. d 86 p 87. C Blandford Forum and Langton Long etc *Sarum* 86-88; NSM Pimperne, Stourpaine, Durweston and Bryanston from 02. *The Cottage, Queens Road, Blandford Forum DT11 7JZ* Tel (01258) 454789 E-mail johnwhittle@hotmail.com

WHITTLE, Naomi Clare. b 54. Colchester Inst of Educn BA75 Lon Univ PGCE76 Middx Univ MA(Theol)99 LGSM77. SEITE 95. d 98 p 99. C Catford (Southend) and Downham *S'wark* 98-02; P-in-c Shooters Hill Ch Ch 02; V 02-10; Chapl Oxleas NHS Foundn Trust 06-10; V Stockwell St Andr and St Mich *S'wark* from 10. *St Michael's Vicarage, 78 Stockwell Park Road, London SW9 0DA* Tel (020) 7274 6357 E-mail naomiwhittle@tiscali.co.uk

WHITTLE, Robin Jeffrey. b 51. Bris Univ BA72 Leic Univ CQSW75. Sarum & Wells Th Coll 85. d 87 p 88. C Henbury *Bris* 87-91; V Capel *Guildf* 91-96; Chapl among Deaf People 96-09; Perm to Offic *Roch* and *S'wark* 97-99; P-in-c Walton-on-the-Hill 99-04; V Tattenham Corner 04-09; V Findon w Clapham and Patching *Chich* from 09. *The Rectory, School Hill, Findon, Worthing BN14 0TR* Tel (01903) 873601 E-mail bobwhittle@btinternet.com

WHITTLE, Mrs Sheila Margaret. b 36. Glouc Th Course 83 NY Th Sem MA88 Vancouver Sch of Th. d 90 p 90. R Bulkley Valley Canada 90-93; C Dunbar St Phil 93; P-in-c Maple Ridge St Jo the Divine 93-95; Lethbridge St Mary the Virgin 95-97; NSM Portsea N End St Mark *Portsm* 97-98; P-in-c Lezant w Lawhitton and S Petherwin w Trewen *Truro* 98-02; rtd 02; Perm to Offic *Glouc* from 03. *71 Graylag Crescent, Walton Cardiff, Tewkesbury GL20 7RR* Tel (01684) 299981 E-mail sheila_whittle@onetel.com

WHITTLESEA, Grahame Stanley Jack Hammond. b 37. Kent Univ LLM95. d 05 p 06. OLM Blean *Cant* 05-09; rtd 09; Perm to Offic *Cant* from 09; Retirement Officer (Cant Adnry) from 10. *4 Eastbridge Hospital, High Street, Canterbury CT1 2BD* Tel (01227) 472536 Mobile 07866-037774 E-mail gandawhittlesea@tiscali.co.uk

WHITTOCK (née MARBUS), Alida Janny. b 52. RGN78. STETS 00. d 03 p 07. NSM Weymouth H Trin *Sarum* 03-09; NSM Abbotsbury, Portesham and Langton Herring from 09. *The Rectory, Church Lane, Portesham, Weymouth DT3 4HB* Tel (01305) 871217 E-mail adamarbus@aol.com

WHITTOCK, Carol Jean. b 51. Goldsmiths' Coll Lon BA74 Univ of Wales (Abth) PGCE76. WEMTC d 10. NSM Longden and Annscroft w Pulverbatch *Heref* from 10; NSM Gt Hanwood from 10. *The Rectory, Plealey Lane, Longden, Shrewsbury SY5 8ET* Tel (01743) 861237 E-mail carol@germandirect.co.uk

WHITTOCK, Preb Michael Graham. b 47. Hull Univ BA69 Fitzw Coll Cam BA71 MA76. Westcott Ho Cam 69 Union Th Sem Virginia 71. d 72 p 73. C Kirkby *Liv* 72-76; C Prescot 76-79; R Methley w Mickletown *Ripon* 79-92; RD Whitkirk 88-92; V Morley St Pet w Churwell *Wakef* 92-01; R Longden and Annscroft w Pulverbatch *Heref* from 01; R Gt Hanwood from 01; RD Pontesbury from 08; Preb Heref Cathl from 10. *The Rectory, Plealey Lane, Longden, Shrewsbury SY5 8ET* Tel (01743) 861003 Fax 861237 E-mail mwhittock@germandirect.co.uk

WHITTOME, Donald Marshall. b 26. Cam Univ BA50 MA53. S Dios Minl Tr Scheme. d 84 p 85. NSM Henfield w Shermanbury and Woodmancote *Chich* 84-93; P-in-c Poynings w Edburton, Newtimber and Pyecombe 93-97; rtd 97; Perm to Offic *Chich* from 97. *Quaker's Rest, 7 Dean Court Road, Rottingdean, Brighton BN2 7DE* Tel (01273) 705508 Fax 271475 E-mail donaldwhitome@hotmail.com

WHITTON, Alysoun. St Steph Ho Ox. d 10 p 11. NSM Hampstead Em W End Lon from 10. *35 Uplands Road, London N8 9NN* Tel (020) 8348 8709 Mobile 07985-020203 E-mail alysoun.whitton@gmail.com

WHITTY, Gordon William. b 35. WMMTC. d 82 p 83. NSM Willenhall St Giles *Lich* 82-84; NSM Coseley Ch 84-85; C 85-87; TV Hanley H Ev 87-91; P-in-c Meir 91-98; P-in-c Hanbury w Newborough and Rangemore 98-99; V 99-03; rtd 03; Perm to Offic *Derby* from 04. *14 Cardrona Close, Oakwood, Derby DE21 2JN* Tel (01332) 726320 E-mail gordonwhitty@vinweb.co.uk

WHITTY, Harold George. b 41. TCD BA64 MA67. CITC Div Test65. d 65 p 66. C Willowfield *D & D* 65-68; C Lisburn Ch Ch *Conn* 68-71; Bp's Dom Chapl 70-71; Asst Dir Exhibitions CMJ 71-72; C Enfield Ch Ch Trent Park *Lon* 72-75; TV Washfield, Stoodleigh, Withleigh etc *Ex* 75-83; R 83-84; TR 84-93; P-in-c Aylesbeare, Rockbeare, Farringdon etc 02-04; RD Tiverton 82-84; P-in-c Allithwaite *Carl* 93-97; TV Cartmel Peninsula 97-02; Local Min Officer 99-02; rtd 04. *Wagon Works, Jericho Street, Thorverton, Exeter EX5 5PA* Tel (01392) 860397 E-mail harold.whitty@btinternet.com

WHITWAM, Miss Diana Morgan. b 28. MCSP54. d 93 p 94. OLM Stoke-next-Guildf 93-01; Perm to Offic from 02. *13 Abbots Hospital, High Street, Guildford GU1 3AJ* Tel (01483) 565977 E-mail dwhitwam@onetel.com

WHITWELL, Canon John Peter. b 36. Open Univ BA07. Qu Coll Birm 62. d 65 p 66. C Stepney St Dunstan and All SS *Lon* 65-68; C Chingford SS Pet and Paul *Chelmsf* 68-71; V Walthamstow St Sav 71-78; P-in-c Lt Ilford St Mich 78-88; R 88-98; RD Newham 91-97; Hon Can Chelmsf Cathl 96-98; rtd 98; Perm to Offic *Ox* from 99. *152 Bath Road, Banbury OX16 0TT* Tel (01295) 266243 E-mail jandawhitwell@aol.com

WHITWELL, Timothy John. b 72. Westmr Coll Ox BTh97 Leeds Univ MA00. Coll of Resurr Mirfield 97. d 99 p 00. C Middlesbrough Ascension *York* 99-02; R Loftus and Carlin How w Skinningrove 02-08; Chapl Lich Cathl Sch and Prec's V Lich Cathl 08-10; Chapl The Peterborough Sch from 10. *The Peterborough School, Thorpe Road, Peterborough PE3 6JF* Tel (01733) 343357 E-mail timothy.whitwell@talk21.com

WHITWORTH, Benjamin Charles Battams. b 49. CCC Ox BA71 MA85. Linc Th Coll 83. d 85 p 86. C Swanborough *Sarum* 85-88; C Sherborne w Castleton and Lillington 88-91; V Milborne Port w Goathill *B & W* 91-98; rtd 98; Perm to Offic *B & W* from 00. *13 The Avenue, Taunton TA1 1EA* Tel (01823) 272442

WHITWORTH, Canon Duncan. b 47. K Coll Lon BD69 AKC69. St Aug Coll Cant 69. d 70 p 71. C Tonge Moor *Man* 70-73; C Upper Norwood St Jo *Cant* 73-78; Asst Chapl Madrid *Eur* 78-82; Chapl Br Embassy Ankara 82-83; V Douglas St Matt *S & M* from 84; RD Douglas from 91; Can St German's Cathl from 96. *St Matthew's Vicarage, Alexander Drive, Douglas, Isle of Man IM2 3QN* Tel (01624) 676310

WHITWORTH, Canon Patrick John. b 51. Ch Ch Ox BA72 MA76 St Jo Coll Dur MA78. d 76 p 77. C York St Mich-le-Belfrey 76-79; C Brompton H Trin w Onslow Square St Paul *Lon* 79-84; V Gipsy Hill Ch Ch *S'wark* 84-95; R Bath Weston All SS w N Stoke and Langridge *B & W* from 95; RD Bath 03-10; Hon Can Bauchi from 95. *The Vicarage, Weston, Bath BA1 4BU* Tel (01225) 421159 E-mail pwhitworth@metronet.co.uk

WHITWORTH, Vincent Craig. b 80. Nottm Univ BA01. St Jo Coll Nottm MTh06. d 07 p 08. C Parr *Liv* from 07. *80 Waterdale Crescent, St Helens WA9 3PD* Tel (01744) 832793 Mobile 07759-920922 E-mail vincentwhitworth@hotmail.com

WHYBORN, Robert. b 42. NOC 87. d 90 p 91. NSM Milnrow *Man* 90-97; NSM Greenfield 97-03; NSM Saddleworth 03-05; rtd 05; Perm to Offic *Man* from 05. *4 Jackman Avenue, Heywood OL10 2NS* E-mail revrob8@aol.com

WHYBROW, Paul Andrew. b 59. St Paul's Coll Chelt BEd80 Oak Hill Th Coll BA90. Wycliffe Hall Ox 95. d 97 p 98. C Magor *Mon* 97-00; V Poughill *Truro* from 00. *The Vicarage, Poughill, Bude EX23 9ER* Tel (01288) 355183 E-mail pa.whybrow@btinternet.com

WHYSALL, Canon Joan. b 42. Lady Mabel Coll CertEd64 Nottm Univ MA01. EMMTC 98. d 01 p 02. NSM Trowell, Awsworth and Cossall *S'well* 01-06; P-in-c Cinderhill from 06; Hon Can S'well Minster from 10. *The Vicarage, 587 Nuthall Road, Nottingham NG8 6AD* Tel 0115-970 8151 Fax 08701-371114 E-mail joan.whysall@btinternet.com

WHYTE, Alastair John. b 61. Coll of Ripon & York St Jo BA83 Lanc Univ MA95. Sarum & Wells Th Coll 83. d 85 p 86. C Chorley St Geo *Blackb* 85-88; C Poulton-le-Fylde 88-91; V Wesham 91-00; Chapl Wesham Park Hosp Preston 91-94; Chapl Blackpool, Wyre and Fylde Community NHS Trust 94-02; P-in-c Treales *Blackb* 98-00; V Garstang St Thos 00-02; AD Garstang 02; Perm to Offic *Man* from 10. *14 Waterbarn Lane, Bacup OL13 0NR*

WHYTE, Duncan Macmillan. b 25. St Jo Coll Dur BA49 St Cath Soc Ox BA51 MA57. Wycliffe Hall Ox 49. d 51 p 53. C Garston *Liv* 51-56; C St Leonards St Leon *Chich* 56-59; V Southsea St Simon *Portsm* 59-66; Gen Sec Lon City Miss 66-92; Hon C Blackheath St Jo *S'wark* 66-92; rtd 92; Perm to Offic *Sarum* from 92. *1 The Meadows, Salisbury SP1 2SS* Tel (01722) 330528

WHYTE, Mrs Elizabeth. b 48. SWMTC 04. d 07 p 08. NSM Ludgvan, Marazion, St Hilary and Perranuthnoe *Truro* from 07. *1 Cranfield, Alexandra Road, Penzance TR18 4LZ* Tel (01736) 362595 E-mail whytes8@aol.com

WHYTE, Henry Lewis. b 38. ALCD70 LTh74. d 70 p 71. C Crawley *Chich* 70-74; V Bermondsey St Jas w Ch Ch *S'wark* 74-82; V Kingston Hill St Paul 82-94; V Blackheath Park St Mich 94-02; rtd 02; Perm to Offic *S'wark* from 03. *6 Horn Park Lane, London SE12 8UU* Tel (020) 8318 9837

WHYTE, Canon Robert Euan. b 44. St Pet Coll Ox BA67. Cuddesdon Coll 67. d 69 p 70. C Blackheath Ascension *S'wark* 69-73; SSC 73-87; NSM Lewisham St Swithun *S'wark* 73-76; NSM Heston *Lon* 76-77; C Rusthall *Roch* 77-88; V 88-08; RD Tunbridge Wells 91-96; Hon Can Roch Cathl 00-08; rtd 08. *9 Thornhill Avenue, Belper DE56 1SH* Tel (01773) 880531 E-mail whyterobert@hotmail.com

WHYTE, William Hadden. b 75. Wadh Coll Ox BA97 MA03 MSt98 DPhil02. SAOMC 03. d 06 p 07. NSM Kidlington w

Hampton Poyle *Ox* from 06. *St John's College, Oxford OX1 3JP* Tel (01865) 277338 Fax 277435
E-mail william.whyte@sjc.ox.ac.uk

WIBBERLEY, Anthony Norman. b 36. K Coll Lon BSc58 AKC58. Sarum & Wells Th Coll 76. **d** 79 **p** 80. Hon C Tavistock and Gulworthy *Ex* 79-86; R Hoby cum Rotherby w Brooksby, Ragdale & Thru'ton *Leic* 86-90; V Ingol *Blackb* 90-96; Perm to Offic *Ely* 97-05; rtd 00. *13 Missleton Court, Cherry Hinton Road, Cambridge CB1 8BL*

WIBROE, Andrew Peter. b 56. K Coll Lon BD83 AKC83 Thames Poly PGCE91. Ripon Coll Cuddesdon 83. **d** 86 **p** 87. C Purley St Mark *S'wark* 86-88; C Boyne Hill *Ox* 89-90; Hon C Milton next Gravesend Ch Ch *Roch* from 90. *32 Ayelands, New Ash Green, Longfield DA3 8JN* Tel (01474) 879014
E-mail peter.wibroe@diocese-rochester.org
or peterwibroe@aol.com

WICK, Canon Patricia Anne. b 54. Lon Bible Coll BA80. Oak Hill Th Coll 84. **dss** 86 **d** 87 **p** 94. Halliwell St Luke *Man* 86-87; Par Dn 87-91; Par Dn Drypool *York* 91-94; C 94-95; TV 95-97; Perm to Offic 98-99; CMS Sudan from 98; Can Maridi from 09. *PO Box 845, Arua, Uganda* E-mail t.wick@bushnet.net
or patricia@rcs-communication.com

WICKENS, Andrew Peter. b 63. St Jo Coll Dur BA85 Magd Coll Cam MEd97 PGCE95 ARCM84. Westcott Ho Cam 98. **d** 00 **p** 01. C Louth *Linc* 00-03; TV 03-07; Lect Boston 07-10; PV Linc Cathl 01-11; R Newton Heath *Man* from 11. *All Saints' Rectory, 2 Culcheth Lane, Manchester M40 1LR* Tel 0161-219 1807
E-mail andrew.wickens08@btinternet.com

WICKENS, Andrew St Lawrence John. b 63. Mert Coll Ox BA85 Birm Univ MPhil94 Dur Univ PGCE86. Qu Coll Birm 89. **d** 92 **p** 93. C Birchfield *Birm* 92-96; Perm to Offic 96-97 and 00-01; Zambia 97-00; P-in-c St Mich Cathl Kitwe 99-00; Lect St Paul's United Th Coll Limuru Kenya 01-05; P-in-c Dudley St Jas *Worc* 05-09; TV Dudley from 09; Educn Chapl from 09. *St James's Vicarage, The Parade, Dudley DY1 3JA* Tel (01384) 214487
E-mail awickens@cofe-worcester.org.uk

WICKENS, John Philip. b 33. Open Univ BA76. K Coll Lon 57. **d** 61 **p** 62. C Hatcham Park All SS *S'wark* 61-64; USA 64-66; Tutor Richmond Fellowship Coll 66-95; Hon C Sutton Ch Ch *S'wark* 68-83; Hon C Benhilton 83-95; rtd 95; Perm to Offic *Worc* from 95. *West Villa, 196 West Malvern Road, Malvern WR14 4AZ* Tel (01684) 574043

WICKENS, Laurence Paul. b 52. Selw Coll Cam BA74 MA78 Leeds Univ PhD90 CEng80 MIET80 MIMechE81 EurIng90. EAMTC 02. **d** 06 **p** 07. NSM Cambridge St Barn *Ely* 06-08; NSM Meole Brace *Lich* 08-11. *2 Perivale Close, Shrewsbury SY3 6DH* Tel (01743) 367707 Mobile 07811-551583
E-mail laurence.wickens@gmail.com

WICKENS, Mrs Moira. b 56. S Dios Minl Tr Scheme 91. **d** 94 **p** 08. NSM Ifield *Chich* 94-96; C Saltdean 96-03; C Ovingdean and Schs Liaison Officer 03-06; C Kingston Buci 06-08; P-in-c 08-10; Dioc Voc Adv 06-10; R New Fishbourne from 10; P-in-c Appledram from 10. *The Rectory, 31 Caspian Close, Fishbourne, Chichester PO18 8AY* Tel (01273) 783364

WICKHAM, Mrs Jennifer Ruth. b 68. Univ of W Ontario BA91. Cranmer Hall Dur BA98. **d** 98 **p** 99. C Ponteland *Newc* 98-00; Assoc P Ottawa St Geo Canada from 01. *57A Tauvette Street, Ottawa ON K1B 3A2, Canada* Tel (001) (613) 590 7921 *or* 235 1636 E-mail ajwickham@yahoo.com *or*
revjw.stgeorge@cyberus.ca

WICKHAM, Lionel Ralph. b 32. St Cath Coll Cam BA57 MA61 PhD LRAM. Westcott Ho Cam 57. **d** 59 **p** 60. C Boston *Linc* 59-61; Tutor Cuddesdon Coll 61-63; V Cross Stone *Wakef* 63-67; Lect Th Southn Univ 67-78; Sen Lect 78-81; V Honley 81-87; Lect Cam Univ 87-00; NSM W Wratting *Ely* 89-00; NSM Weston Colville 89-00; rtd 00; Perm to Offic *Wakef* from 99. *19 Barrowstead, Skelmanthorpe, Huddersfield HD8 9UW* Tel (01484) 864185 E-mail lpatristic@aol.com

WICKHAM, Robert James. b 72. Grey Coll Dur BA94. Ridley Hall Cam 95. **d** 98 **p** 99. C Willesden St Mary *Lon* 98-01; C Somers Town 01-03; TV Old St Pancras 03-07; R St John-at-Hackney from 07. *The Rectory, 11 Clapton Square, London E5 8HP* Tel (020) 8985 5374 E-mail rectorofhackney@aol.com

WICKINGS, Luke Iden. b 59. Sheff Poly BA81. Oak Hill Th Coll BA90. **d** 90 **p** 91. C Fulham St Mary N End *Lon* 90-94; C Bletchley *Ox* 94-00; V W Norwood St Luke *S'wark* 00-07. *12 Osborne Gardens, Thornton Heath CR7 8PA* Tel (020) 8653 7767

WICKRAMASINGHE, Rosemary Ethel. b 32. Reading Univ ATD52 K Coll Lon BD85 AKC85. SAOMC 93. **d** 96 **p** 97. NSM Godrevy *Truro* 96-05; rtd 05; Perm to Offic *Truro* from 05. *10 Glebe Row, Phillack, Hayle TR27 5AJ* Tel (01736) 757850

WICKS, Christopher Blair. b 59. Oak Hill Th Coll BA88. **d** 88 **p** 89. C Edmonton All SS w St Mich *Lon* 88-92; C Southborough St Pet w Ch Ch and St Matt etc *Roch* 92-96; TV from 96. *72 Powder Mill Lane, Southborough, Tunbridge Wells TN4 9EJ* Tel (01892) 529098
E-mail chris.wicks@diocese-rochester.org

WICKS, Susan Lynn. b 66. Trin Coll Bris 96. **d** 98 **p** 99. C Whitburn *Dur* 98-03; TV S Carl from 03. *St Elisabeth's Vicarage, Arnside Road, Carlisle CA1 3QA* Tel (01228) 596427

WICKSTEAD, Canon Gavin John. b 46. St Chad's Coll *Dur* BA67. Linc Th Coll 82. **d** 84 **p** 85. C Louth *Linc* 84-87; P-in-c E Markham and Askham *S'well* 87-89; P-in-c Headon w Upton 87-89; P-in-c Grove 87-89; R E Markham w Askham, Headon w Upton and Grove 90-92; P-in-c Skegness and Winthorpe *Linc* 92-97; R 97-01; V Holbeach 01-11; RD Elloe E 05-07; Can and Preb Linc Cathl from 05; rtd 11. *1 Aspen Drive, Sleaford NG34 7GN* Tel (01529) 410231
E-mail wickstead@btinternet.com

WIDDECOMBE, Roger James. b 70. Wycliffe Hall Ox. **d** 03 **p** 04. C Downend *Bris* 03-06; C Cheltenham St Mary, St Matt, St Paul and H Trin *Glouc* 06-07; TV Cheltenham H Trin and St Paul from 07. *85 Brunswick Street, Cheltenham GL50 4HA* Tel and fax (01242) 519520 E-mail roger@widde.com

WIDDESS, Jonathan Mark. b 73. Univ of Wales (Abth) BScEcon95. Wycliffe Hall Ox 07. **d** 09 **p** 10. C Gabalfa *Llan* from 09. *27 Pen-y-Bryn Road, Gabalfa, Cardiff CF14 3LG* Tel 07595-996534 (mobile) E-mail jwiddess@gmail.com

WIDDESS, Mrs Margaret Jennifer. b 48. Bedf Coll Lon BA70 Clare Hall Cam PGCE75 Lambeth MA03. EAMTC 94. **d** 97 **p** 98. NSM Cambridge St Botolph *Ely* from 97. *69 Gwydir Street, Cambridge CB1 2LG* Tel (01223) 313908
E-mail mjwiddess@btinternet.com

WIDDICOMBE, Peter John. b 52. Univ of Manitoba BA74 St Cath Coll Ox MPhil77 St Cross Coll Ox DPhil90. Wycliffe Coll Toronto MDiv81. **d** 81 **p** 82. Canada 81-84 and from 93; C Ox St Andr 84-86; Acting Chapl Trin Coll Ox 88; Linc Coll Ox 89; P-in-c Penn 90-93. *1204-36 James Street South, Hamilton ON L8P 4W4, Canada*

WIDDOWS, David Charles Roland. b 52. Hertf Coll Ox BA75 MA79. St Jo Coll Nottm BA77. **d** 79 **p** 80. C Blackley St Andr *Man* 79-83; P-in-c Rochdale Deeplish St Luke 83-84; V 84-92; TR Stoke Gifford *Bris* 92-96; Chapl Lee Abbey 96-10; P-in-c Wiveliscombe and the Hills *B & W* 10-11; R from 11. *The Rectory, South Street, Wiveliscombe, Taunton TA4 2LZ* Tel 07890-758751 (mobile)

WIDDOWS, Edward John. b 45. Lon Coll of Div 66. **d** 70 **p** 71. C Formby St Pet *Liv* 70-72; C Uckfield, Isfield and Lt Horsted *Chich* 72-73; C Babbacombe *Ex* 73-76; V Sithney *Truro* 76-78; RD Kerrier 77-78; V Bude Haven 78-84; P-in-c Laneast w St Clether and Tresmere 84-85; P-in-c N Hill w Altarnon, Bolventor and Lewannick 84-85; P-in-c Boyton w N Tamerton 84-85; P-in-c N Petherwin 84-85; R Collingham w S Scarle and Besthorpe and Girton *S'well* 85-92; R Guernsey St Michel du Valle *Win* 92-99; R Compton and Otterbourne 99-02; rtd 02; Perm to Offic *Pet* from 02 and *Leic* from 08. *Glebe Cottage, 4 Spring Back Way, Uppingham, Oakham LE15 9TT* Tel (01572) 821980 E-mail ewiddows01@aol.com

WIDDOWS, Heather Susan. b 65. Open Univ BA76. Moray Ord Course 91. **d** 96 **p** 97. NSM Kishorn *Mor* from 96; NSM Poolewe from 96. *2 Fasaich, Strath, Gairloch IV21 2DB* Tel (01445) 712176 E-mail heather_widdows@yahoo.co.uk

WIDDOWSON, Charles Leonard. b 28. ALCD62. **d** 62 **p** 63. C Radcliffe-on-Trent *S'well* 62-66; R Newark Ch Ch 66-69; Australia from 69; rtd 93. *5 Sharrock Avenue, Cheltenham Vic 3192, Australia* Tel (0061) (3) 9584 9004

WIDDOWSON, Robert William. b 47. Linc Th Coll 83. **d** 85 **p** 86. C Syston *Leic* 85-88; R Husbands Bosworth w Mowsley and Knaptoft etc 88-93; R Asfordby 93-98; P-in-c Ab Kettleby Gp 93-98; P-in-c Old Dalby and Nether Broughton 95-98; P-in-c Charlton Musgrove, Cucklington and Stoke Trister *B & W* 98-03; P-in-c Ashwick w Oakhill and Binegar from 03; Adv in Rural Affairs from 98. *The Rectory, Fosse Road, Oakhill, Bath BA3 5HU* Tel and fax (01749) 841688
E-mail ruralrobert@fsmail.net

WIECK, Malcolm Rayment. b 44. Solicitor 70. **d** 08 **p** 09. OLM Bratton, Edington and Imber, Erlestoke etc *Sarum* from 08. *Sandy Lane Cottage, 12 Westbury Road, Edington, Westbury BA13 4QD* Tel (01380) 830256 Mobile 07623-483986
E-mail malcolm.wieck@btinternet.com

WIFFEN, Richard Austin. b 58. St Pet Coll Ox BA80. Trin Coll Bris BA90. **d** 90 **p** 91. C Bowdon *Ches* 90-93; C Ellesmere Port 93-94; TV 94-02; Hon C 02-07. *Lime Tree Farm, Stanney Lane, Little Stanney, Chester CH2 4HT* Tel 0151-355 1654

WIFFEN, Ronald. b 38. Open Th Coll BA99. SEITE 99. **d** 01 **p** 02. NSM Canvey Is *Chelmsf* 01-04; P-in-c Bowers Gifford w N Benfleet 06-09; NSM SW Gower *S & B* 06-08; P-in-c Southport St Luke *Liv* 08-09; rtd 09; Perm to Offic *Chelmsf* from 09. *40 Gladwyns, Basildon SS15 5JA* Tel (01268) 410682

WIFFIN, Susan Elizabeth. *See* MACDONALD, Susan Elizabeth

WIGFIELD, Thomas Henry Paul. b 26. Edin Th Coll 46. **d** 49 **p** 50. C Seaham w Seaham Harbour *Dur* 49-52; C Dur St Marg 52-54; V Fatfield 54-63; Asst Dir Chs' TV Cen 63-79; Perm to Offic *Lon* 63-91; Perm to Offic *St Alb* 66-91; Hd of Services Foundn for Chr Communication 79-84; Chs' Liaison Officer 84-91; rtd 91; Perm to Offic *Ox* from 91. *16 Fishers Field, Buckingham MK18 1SF* Tel (01280) 817893

WIGGEN, Richard Martin. b 42. Open Univ BA78 Hull Univ MA86. Qu Coll Birm 64. **d** 67 **p** 68. C Penistone w Midhope *Wakef* 67-70; C Leeds St Pet *Ripon* 70-73; Asst Youth Chapl *Glouc* 73-76; Youth Officer *Liv* 76-80; V Kirkstall *Ripon* 80-90; V Meanwood 90-07; rtd 07. *19 Shadwell Lane, Leeds LS17 6DP* Tel 0113-266 5241 E-mail wiggen@btopenworld.com

WIGGINS, Gillian Holt. b 33. Birm Univ MB, ChB56. **d** 03 **p** 04. NSM Ascot Heath *Ox* 03-08; Perm to Offic from 09. *Keren, 2 Kiln Lane, Winkfield, Windsor SL4 2DU* Tel (01344) 884008 E-mail gilliwig@aol.com

WIGGINS, Karl Patrick. b 38. MRICS64 FRICS87. Trin Coll Bris BD72. **d** 72 **p** 73. C Hildenborough *Roch* 72-76; Hon C Reading St Barn *Ox* 76-78; Hon C Chieveley w Winterbourne and Oare 78-80; Hon C Earley St Nic 80-83; Hon C Reading St Jo 83-88; Hon C Beech Hill, Grazeley and Spencers Wood 88-98; rtd 98; Perm to Offic *Ox* 99. *Willow Cottage, 37 New Road, Bradford-on-Avon BA15 1AP* Tel (01225) 867007 E-mail kk-wiggins@msn.com

WIGGINTON, Canon Peter Walpole. b 20. Edin Th Coll 40. **d** 43 **p** 44. C Derby St Jas 43-46; C Brimington 46; C Gedling *S'well* 46-49; PV S'well Minster 49-52; V Rolleston w Morton 52-56; R W Keal *Linc* 56-83; R E Keal 57-83; R E and W Keal 83-88; RD Bolingbroke 66-88; Can and Preb Linc Cathl 77-88; R Bolingbroke 83-88; R Toynton All Saints w Toynton St Peter 83-88; rtd 88; Chapl Trin Hosp Retford 88-05; Perm to Offic *S'well* from 91. *Trinity Cottage, River Lane, Retford DN22 7DZ* Tel (01777) 860352

WIGGLESWORTH, Canon Mark. b 60. Clare Coll Cam BA82. St Jo Coll Nottm 89. **d** 92 **p** 93. C Brinsworth w Catcliffe *Sheff* 92-93; C Brinsworth w Catcliffe and Treeton 93-95; C Goole 95-96; V Askern 96-11; AD Adwick 05-11; Dir Miss and Pioneer Min from 11; Hon Can Sheff Cathl from 10. *The New Rectory, Grange Lane, Burghwallis, Doncaster DN6 9JL* Tel (01302) 707815 Mobile 07818-416424 E-mail mark.dmpm@gmail.com

WIGGS, Robert James. b 50. Pemb Coll Cam BA72 MA CertEd. Qu Coll Birm 78. **d** 80 **p** 81. C Stratford St Jo and Ch Ch w Forest Gate St Jas *Chelmsf* 80-83; C E Ham w Upton Park 83-86; TV 86-91; TR Grays Thurrock 91-99; Perm to Offic from 99. *113 Moulsham Street, Chelmsford CM2 0JN* Tel (01245) 359138 E-mail robwiggs@live.com

WIGHT, Canon Dennis Marley. b 53. Southn Univ BTh87. Sarum & Wells Th Coll 82. **d** 85 **p** 86. C Gillingham *Sarum* 85-87; Appeals Org CECS from 87; Perm to Offic *Birm* 89-90; V Coseley Ch Ch *Lich* 90-93; V Coseley Ch Ch *Worc* 93-94; R Stoke Prior, Wychbold and Upton Warren 94-02; RD Droitwich 96-99; V Dale and St Brides w Marloes *St D* 02-10; AD Roose 05-10; Dioc Warden Ords 09-11; Bp's Chapl from 10; Dir of Min from 10; Hon Can St D Cathl from 09. *The Vicarage, Water Street, Ferryside SA17 5RT* Tel (01267) 267192 E-mail denniswight@churchinwales.org.uk

WIGHT (*née* JONES), **Mrs Sian Hilary.** b 54. CertEd75 Birm Univ BEd76 Southn Univ BTh87. Sarum & Wells Th Coll 82. **dss** 85 **d** 87 **p** 94. Ex St Sidwell and St Matt 85-88; Par Dn 87-88; Perm to Offic *Lich* 89-90 and 93-96; Hon Par Dn Coseley Ch Ch 90-93; Hon Par Dn Coseley Ch Ch *Worc* 93-94; NSM Stoke Prior, Wychbold and Upton Warren 94-02; NSM Dale and St Brides w Marloes *St D* 02-05; P-in-c Herbrandston and Hasguard w St Ishmael's 05-10; P-in-c St Ishmael's w Llan-saint and Ferryside from 10. *The Vicarage, Water Street, Ferryside SA17 5RT* Tel (01267) 267192

WIGHTMAN, David William Lyle. b 44. SNWTP. **d** 08 **p** 09. NSM Macclesfield Team *Ches* from 08. *The Old Vicarage, 12 Ryles Park Road, Macclesfield SK11 8AH* Tel (01625) 266283 *or* 428443 E-mail david.wightman1@ntlworld.com

WIGHTMAN, William David. b 39. Birm Univ BA61. Wells Th Coll 61. **d** 63 **p** 64. C Rotherham *Sheff* 63-67; C Castle Church *Lich* 67-70; V Buttershaw St Aid *Bradf* 70-76; V Cullingworth 76-83; R Peterhead *Ab* 83-91; R Strichen, Old Deer and Longside 90-91; Provost St Andr Cathl 91-02; R Aberdeen St Andr 91-02; P-in-c Aberdeen St Ninian 91-02; Hon Can Ch Ch Cathl Connecticut from 91; rtd 02; Perm to Offic *York* from 04. *66 Wold Road, Pocklington, York YO42 2QG* Tel (01759) 301369 E-mail davidwightman@ntlworld.com

WIGLEY, Brian Arthur. b 31. Qu Coll Birm. **d** 82 **p** 83. C Houghton le Spring *Dur* 82-85; C Louth *Linc* 85-86; TV 86-89; Chapl City Hosp NHS Trust Birm 89-95; rtd 95; Perm to Offic *Ex* 95-09. *3 Willows Close, Frogmore, Kingsbridge TQ7 2NY* Tel (01548) 531374

WIGLEY, Canon Harry Maxwell (Max). b 38. Oak Hill Th Coll 61. **d** 64 **p** 65. C Upton (Overchurch) *Ches* 64-67; C Gateacre *Liv* 67-69; C Chadderton Ch Ch *Man* 67; V Gt Horton *Bradf* 69-88; Hon Can Bradf Cathl 85-03; V Pudsey St Lawr and St Paul 88-96; V Yeadon St Jo 96-03; rtd 03; Hon Dioc Ev *Bradf* from 04. *20 Collier Lane, Baildon, Shipley BD17 5LN* Tel (01274) 581988 E-mail max.wigley@bradford.anglican.org *or* maxwigley@aol.com

WIGLEY, Canon Jennifer. b 53. Bris Univ BA74 Birm Univ MA75 Ox Univ CertEd76. Qu Coll Birm 86. **d** 87 **p** 97. C

Llangollen w Trevor and Llantysilio *St As* 87-89; C Swansea St Jas *S & B* 89-94; NSM Aberystwyth *St D* 95-98; Tutor St Mich Coll Llan 98-00; C Sketty *S & B* 98-00; Chapl Univ of Wales (Swansea) 00-02; Dep Dir S Wales Ord Course from 02; TV Cen Cardiff *Llan* 03-06; R Radyr from 06; AD Llan from 10; Can Llan Cathl from 11. *The Rectory, 52 Heol Isaf, Radyr, Cardiff CF15 8DY* Tel (029) 2084 2417 E-mail jennifer.wigley@ntlworld.com

WIGLEY, Mrs Trudie Anne. b 69. Somerville Coll Ox BA91 ACIB94. Ripon Coll Cuddesdon 09. **d** 11. NSM Swindon Ch Ch *Bris* from 11. *11 Merlin Way, Swindon SN3 5AN* Tel 07711-919781 (mobile) E-mail trudie@wigley.org.uk

WIGMORE, John Anthony Kingsland. b 62. Oak Hill Th Coll 05. **d** 07 **p** 08. C Braintree *Chelmsf* from 07; R Winklebury and Worting from 11. *The Rectory, Glebe Lane, Worting, Basingstoke RG23 8QA* Tel (01256) 331531 E-mail jakwigmore@googlemail.com

WIGMORE, Mrs Lisa Jayn. b 66. Trin Coll Bris 09. **d** 11. C Horfield H Trin *Bris* from 11. *52 Gladstone Street, Staple Hill, Bristol BS16 4RF* Tel 0117-957 4297 Mobile 07799-883790 E-mail lisawigmore@blueyonder.co.uk

WIGNALL, Daniel Robert Phillip. b 65. Ox Poly BEd88. St Jo Coll Nottm MA98. **d** 98 **p** 99. C Fletchamstead *Cov* 98-01; C Abingdon *Ox* 01-07; V Shottermill *Guildf* from 07. *The Vicarage, Vicarage Lane, Haslemere GU27 1LQ* Tel (01428) 645878 E-mail vicar@shottermillparish.org.uk

WIGNALL, Canon Paul Graham. b 49. Lanc Univ BA72 Qu Coll Cam BA74 MA78. Westcott Ho Cam 72. **d** 74 **p** 75. C Chesterton Gd Shep *Ely* 74-76; Min Can Dur Cathl 76-79; Tutor Ripon Coll Cuddesdon 80-84; P-in-c Aston Rowant w Crowell *Ox* 81-83; C Shepherd's Bush St Steph w St Thos *Lon* 84-85; P-in-c St Just-in-Roseland and St Mawes *Truro* 99-01; C St Agnes and Mithian w Mount Hawke 01-06; Dir Tr and Development 01-05; Dir Min and Miss Resources 05-06; Hon Can Truro Cathl 05-06; rtd 06; IME Adv *Cov* from 08; Hon C Aston Cantlow and Wilmcote w Billesley 08-11. *Wilmcote Vicarage, Church Road, Wilmcote, Stratford-upon-Avon CV37 9XD* Tel (01789) 262825 E-mail paul@paulwignall.wanadoo.co.uk

WIGRAM, Andrew Oswald. b 39. Lon Univ BD64. Bps' Coll Cheshunt 61. **d** 64 **p** 65. C Marton-in-Cleveland *York* 64-69; Kenya 69-82; Warden Trin Coll Nairobi 77-82; V Westcliff St Mich *Chelmsf* 82-95; RD Southend 89-94; R Cropwell Bishop w Colston Bassett, Granby etc *S'well* 95-05; rtd 05. *38 Pierremont Crescent, Darlington DL3 9PB* Tel (01325) 371473 E-mail andrew.wigram@ntlworld.com

WIGRAM, John Michael. b 67. Ex Univ BSc88. St Jo Coll Nottm MTh04. **d** 05 **p** 06. C Hazlemere *Ox* 05-08; R Hambleden Valley from 08. *The Rectory, Hambledon, Henley-on-Thames RG9 6RP* Tel (01491) 571231 Mobile 07986-732452 E-mail wigram@ntlworld.com

WIGRAM (*née* CHAPMAN), **Mrs Rachel Grace.** b 67. Ex Univ BA88. St Jo Coll Nottm 03. **d** 05 **p** 06. C Hazlemere *Ox* 05-08; Perm to Offic from 08. *The Rectory, Hambledon, Henley-on-Thames RG9 6RP* Tel (01494) 571231 Mobile 07986-732452 E-mail wigram@ntlworld.com

WIGRAM, Miss Ruth Margaret. b 41. CertEd63. Cranmer Hall Dur 83. **dss** 84 **d** 87 **p** 94. Shipley St Paul and Frizinghall *Bradf* 84-90; Par Dn 87-90; Asst Dioc Dir of Ords 90-96; C Skipton H Trin 90-96; V Easby w Skeeby and Brompton on Swale etc *Ripon* 96-06; rtd 07; Perm to Offic *York* from 07. *Maythorn, 30 Ainderby Road, Northallerton DL7 8HD* Tel (01609) 761852 E-mail ruthwigram@hotmail.co.uk

WIKELEY, Canon John Roger Ian. b 41. AKC64. **d** 65 **p** 66. C Southport H Trin *Liv* 65-69; C Padgate Ch Ch 69-71; TV Padgate 71-73; R 73-74; TR 74-85; TR W Derby St Mary 85-98; V 98-06; P-in-c W Derby St Jas 04-06; AD W Derby 04-06; Hon Can Liv Cathl 94-06; rtd 06. *72 Carisbrooke Drive, Southport PR9 7JD* Tel (01704) 225412 E-mail jviw@blueyonder.co.uk

WIKNER, Richard Hugh. b 46. MSI. St Alb Minl Tr Scheme 79. **d** 94 **p** 95. NSM Lt Heath *St Alb* from 94. *Koinonia, 5 The Avenue, Potters Bar EN6 1EG* Tel (01707) 650437 E-mail hughwikner@lineone.net

✠**WILBOURNE, The Rt Revd David Jeffrey.** b 55. Jes Coll Cam BA78 MA82. Westcott Ho Cam 79. **d** 81 **p** 82 **c** 09. C Stainton-in-Cleveland *York* 81-85; Chapl Asst Hemlington Hosp 81-85; P Monk Fryston and S Milford *York* 85-91; Abp's Dom Chapl 91-97; Dir of Ords 91-97; V Helmsley 97-09; P-in-c Upper Ryedale 09; Can and Preb York Minster 08-09; Asst Bp Llan from 09; Dir of Min from 10. *6 Llandaff Chase, Llandaff, Cardiff CF5 2NA* Tel (029) 2056 2400 Fax 2057 7129 E-mail asstbishop@churchinwales.org.uk

WILBRAHAM, Canon David Anthony. b 59. Oak Hill Th Coll BA88. **d** 88 **p** 89. C Ince Ch Ch *Liv* 88-91; Min St Helens St Helen 91-93; Perm to Offic *Guildf* 96-99; NSM Hindhead 99-00; V 00-03; V Churt and Hindhead 03-07; Chapl Thames Valley Police Force *Ox* from 07; Hon Can Ch Ch from 11. *292 Thorney Leys, Witney OX28 5PB* Tel (01993) 706656 Mobile 07779-262302 E-mail davidwilbraham@lineone.net

WILBY, Mrs Jean (Sister Davina). b 38. Open Univ BA82. Wycliffe Hall Ox 83. **dss** 85 **d** 87 **p** 94. Maidenhead St Andr and St Mary *Ox* 85-87; C 87; TD Hermitage and Hampstead Norreys, Cold Ash etc 87-91; Lic to Offic 92-95; All SS Convent Ox 91-95; NSM Iffley *Ox* 94-95; C Denham 95-98; rtd 98; P-in-c Woolstone w Gotherington and Oxenton etc *Glouc* 98-06. *2 Somerset House, Knapp Road, Cheltenham GL50 3QQ* Tel (01242) 584096

WILBY, Timothy David. b 59. Univ Coll Dur BA80 MA87 Open Univ BA09 ALCM11. Ripon Coll Cuddesdon 81. **d** 83 **p** 84. C Standish *Blackb* 83-86; CF 86-89; V Chorley All SS *Blackb* 89-95; V Penwortham St Leon 95-00; TR Fellside Team 00-07; P-in-c Chorley St Geo 07-11; V from 11; P-in-c Charnock Richard from 11. *St George's Vicarage, Letchworth Place, Chorley PR7 2HJ* Tel (01772) 263064 E-mail stgeorgeschorley@aol.com

WILBY, Canon Wendy Ann. b 49. St Hugh's Coll Ox BA71 MA93 Leeds Univ MA01 ARCM69 LRAM72. NEOC. **d** 90 **p** 94. Par Dn Barwick in Elmet *Ripon* 90-93; C High Harrogate St Pet 93-94; P-in-c Birstwith 94-01; AD Harrogate 00-01; Chapl St Aid Sch Harrogate 94-01; V Halifax *Wakef* 01-07; RD Halifax 06-07; Can Res Bris Cathl from 07; Dean Women's Min from 11. *55 Salisbury Road, Redland, Bristol BS6 7AS* Tel 0117-904 6903 *or* 926 4879 E-mail wwilby@blueyonder.co.uk

WILCOCK, Mrs Linda Jane. b 46. Nottm Univ TDip67. **d** 09 **p** 10. OLM Melbury *Sarum* from 09. *6 Mulberry Orchard, West End, Cattistock, Dorchester DT2 0JA* Tel (01300) 321112 Mobile 07788-618412 E-mail p.wilcock@virgin.net

WILCOCK, Michael Jarvis. b 32. Dur Univ BA54. Tyndale Hall Bris 60. **d** 62 **p** 63. C Southport Ch Ch *Liv* 62-65; C St Marylebone All So w SS Pet and Jo *Lon* 65-69; V Maidstone St Faith *Cant* 69-77; Dir Past Studies Trin Coll Bris 77-82; V Dur St Nic 82-98; rtd 98; Perm to Offic *Chich* from 98. *1 Tudor Court, 51 Carlisle Road, Eastbourne BN21 4JR* Tel (01323) 417170

WILCOCK, Paul Trevor. b 59. Bris Univ BA Leeds Univ MA93. Trin Coll Bris 83. **d** 87 **p** 88. C Kirkheaton *Wakef* 87-90; Chapl Huddersfield Poly 90-92; Chapl Huddersfield Univ 92-93; Dir Student Services from 93; Chapl W Yorkshire Police from 02; NSM Huddersfield H Trin 92-09; NSM Bradley from 09. *25 Mendip Avenue, Huddersfield HD3 3QG* Tel (01484) 325232 E-mail paulwilcock@aol.com

WILCOCK, Terence Granville. b 50. Open Univ BA82. EAMTC 99. **d** 02 **p** 03. NSM Oundle w Ashton and Benefield w Glapthorn *Pet* 02-04; NSM Crosscrake *Carl* 04-11; P-in-c 06-11; NSM Old Hutton and New Hutton 06-09; Asst Chapl Gtr Athens *Eur* from 11. *Church House, Gavalomori, Chania 73008, Crete, Greece* Tel (0030) (2825) 023270 E-mail creteanglicans@yahoo.co.uk

WILCOCKSON, Stephen Anthony. b 51. Nottm Univ BA73 Ox Univ BA75 MA81. Wycliffe Hall Ox 73. **d** 76 **p** 77. C Pudsey St Lawr *Bradf* 76-78; C Wandsworth All SS *S'wark* 78-81; V Rock Ferry *Ches* 81-86; V Lache cum Saltney 86-95; V Howell Hill w Burgh Heath *Guildf* 95-09; RD Epsom 00-07; Par Miss Development Officer *Ches* from 09. *11 Lytham Drive, Winsford CW7 2GH* Tel (01606) 860322 E-mail stevewilcockson@yahoo.com

WILCOX, Anthony Gordon. b 41. ALCD67. **d** 67 **p** 68. C Cheltenham Ch Ch *Glouc* 67-72; C Beccles St Mich *St E* 72-74; TV 74-81; V Ipswich All SS 81-06; rtd 06; Perm to Offic *St E* from 06. *58 Sproughton Court Mews, Sproughton, Ipswich IP8 3AJ* Tel (01473) 461561

WILCOX, Brian Howard. b 46. Westcott Ho Cam 71. **d** 73 **p** 74. C Kettering SS Pet and Paul 73-78; V Eye 78-82; R Clipston w Naseby and Haselbech w Kelmarsh 82-90; V Hornsea w Atwick *York* 90-97; RD N Holderness 95-97; R Uckfield *Chich* from 97; R Isfield from 97; R Lt Horsted from 97. *The Rectory, Belmont Road, Uckfield TN22 1BP* Tel (01825) 762251 E-mail howab@aol.com

WILCOX, Canon Colin John. b 43. St Mich Coll Llan 84. **d** 86 **p** 87. C Newport St Andr *Mon* 86-88; C Llanmartin 88-90; TV 90-92; V Griffithstown 92-08; Hon Can St Woolos Cathl 07-08; rtd 08; Perm to Offic *Mon* from 08 and *Llan* from 09. *2 Davies Place, Cardiff CF5 3AQ, or The Bungalow, Dingestow, Monmouth NP25 4DZ* Tel (029) 2025 4294 *or* (01600) 740680

✠**WILCOX, The Rt Revd David Peter.** b 30. St Jo Coll Ox BA52 MA56. Linc Th Coll 52. **d** 54 **p** 55 **c** 86. C St Helier *S'wark* 54-56; C Ox St Mary V 56-59; Tutor Linc Th Coll 59-60; Chapl 60-61; Sub-Warden 61-63; India 64-70; R Gt w Lt Gransden *Ely* 70-72; Can Res Derby Cathl 72-77; Warden EMMTC 73-77; Prin Ripon Coll Cuddesdon 77-85; V Cuddesdon *Ox* 77-85; Suff Bp Dorking *Guildf* 86-95; rtd 95; Hon Asst Bp Chich from 95. *4 The Court, Hoo Gardens, Willingdon, Eastbourne BN20 9AX* Tel (01323) 506108

WILCOX, David Thomas Richard. b 42. Down Coll Cam BA63 Regent's Park Coll Ox BA66. **d** 95 **p** 96. C Bris St Mary Redcliffe w Temple etc 95-97; TV Yate New Town 97-02; Hon C 02-06; rtd 02; Perm to Offic *B & W* from 06. *26 Lethbridge Road, Wells BA5 2FN* Tel (01749) 673689

WILCOX, Graham James. b 43. Qu Coll Ox BA64 MA75 Lon Univ BD97 MTh02. Ridley Hall Cam 64. **d** 66 **p** 67. C Edgbaston St Aug *Birm* 66-69; C Sheldon 69-72; Asst Chapl Wrekin Coll Telford 72-74; C Asterby w Goulceby *Linc* 74-77; R 77-81; R Benniworth w Market Stainton and Ranby 77-81; R Donington on Bain 77-81; R Stenigot 77-81; R Gayton le Wold w Biscathorpe 77-81; V Scamblesby w Cawkwell 77-81; R Asterby Gp 81-88; V Sutton le Marsh 88-90; R Sutton, Huttoft and Anderby 90-98; R Fyfield, Moreton w Bobbingworth etc *Chelmsf* 98-07; rtd 07; Perm to Offic *Cov* from 07. *7 Swallow Close, Stratford-upon-Avon CV37 6TT* Tel (01789) 551759 E-mail g.wilcox4@ntlworld.com

WILCOX, Haydon Howard. b 56. Sarum & Wells Th Coll. **d** 82 **p** 83. C Fishponds St Jo *Bris* 82-85; TV Hucknall Torkard *S'well* 85-91; R Bilsthorpe 91-99; R Eakring 91-99; P-in-c Maplebeck 91-99; P-in-c Winkburn 91-99; P-in-c Aldershot St Mich *Guildf* 99-03; V 03; Perm to Offic 03-09; Chapl CSP from 07. *46 Barn Meadow Close, Church Crookham, Aldershot GU52 0YB* Tel and fax (01252) 621639 E-mail haydonwilcox@mac.com

WILCOX, Heather Yvonne. b 72. ERMC 05. **d** 08 **p** 09. C Pakefield *Nor* from 08; R Stratton St Mary w Stratton St Michael etc from 11. *The Rectory, 8 Flowerpot Lane, Long Stratton, Norwich NR15 2TS* Tel 07932-416233 (mobile) E-mail hwackywilcox@uwclub.net

WILCOX, Canon Hugh Edwin. b 37. St Edm Hall Ox BA62 MA66. St Steph Ho Ox 62. **d** 64 **p** 65. C Colchester St Jas, All SS, St Nic and St Runwald *Chelmsf* 64-66; Hon C Clifton St Paul *Bris* 66-68; SCM 66-68; Sec Internat Dept BCC 68-76; Asst Gen Sec 74-76; V Ware St Mary *St Alb* 76-03; Hon Can St Alb 96-03; rtd 03; Perm to Offic *St Alb* from 03. *The Briars, 1 Briary Lane, Royston SG8 9BX* Tel (01763) 244212 E-mail hugh.wilcox@btinternet.com

WILCOX, Canon Jeffry Reed. b 40. MBE05. K Coll Lon AKC65 BA78 Westmr Coll Ox MTh97. **d** 66 **p** 67. C Ryhope *Dur* 66-69; C Cockerton 69-71; P-in-c Pallion 71-82; R Streatham St Leon *S'wark* 82-06; RD Streatham 92-00; Hon Can S'wark Cathl 05-06; rtd 06. *4 Lower Broad Street, Ludlow SY8 1PQ* Tel (01584) 877199 E-mail jeffrywilcox@yahoo.co.uk

WILCOX, John Bower. b 28. AKC55. **d** 58 **p** 59. C Orford St Marg *Liv* 58-60; C W Derby St Mary 60-63; Ind Chapl *Linc* 63-74; R Aisthorpe w W Thorpe and Scampton 63-74; R Brattleby 64-74; Ind Chapl *York* 74-89; P-in-c Middlesbrough St Cuth 89-93; Urban Development Officer 89-93; rtd 93; Perm to Offic *York* from 93. *5 Duncan Avenue, Redcar TS10 5BX* Tel (01642) 489683

WILCOX, Canon Peter Jonathan. b 61. St Jo Coll Dur BA84 MA91 St Jo Coll Ox DPhil93. Ridley Hall Cam BA86. **d** 87 **p** 88. C Preston on Tees *Dur* 87-90; NSM Ox St Giles and SS Phil and Jas w St Marg 90-93; TV Gateshead *Dur* 93-98; Dir Urban Miss Cen Cranmer Hall 93-98; P-in-c Walsall St Paul *Lich* 98-06; Hon C Walsall and Walsall Pleck and Bescot 05-06; Can Res Lich Cathl from 06. *13 The Close, Lichfield WS13 7LD* Tel (01543) 306241 *or* 306240 E-mail pete.wilcox@lichfield-cathedral.org

WILCOX, Stephen Charles Frederick. b 75. Qu Coll Ox BA97 ACA00. Oak Hill Th Coll 04. **d** 07 **p** 08. C Kirk Ella and Willerby *York* 07-11; V Anlaby St Pet from 11; V Anlaby Common St Mark from 11. *The Vicarage, Church Street, Anlaby, Hull HU10 7DG* Tel 07905-122239 (mobile) E-mail scfwilcox@yahoo.co.uk

WILD, Alan James. b 46. **d** 97 **p** 98. OLM Walworth St Pet *S'wark* from 97. *67 Liverpool Grove, London SE17 2HP* Tel (020) 7708 1216

WILD, Hilda Jean. b 48. Linc Th Coll 95. **d** 95 **p** 96. C Newark *S'well* 95-99; V Earlsdon *Cov* from 99. *St Barbara's Vicarage, 24 Rochester Road, Coventry CV5 6AG* Tel (024) 7667 4057

WILD, Roger Bedingham Barratt. b 40. Hull Univ MA93. ALCD64. **d** 65 **p** 65. C Shipley St Pet *Bradf* 65-68; C Pudsey St Lawr 68-71; P-in-c Rawthorpe *Wakef* 71-73; V 73-78; V Ripon H Trin 78-93; RD Ripon 86-93; OCF 80-91; R Barwick in Elmet *Ripon* 93-01; Asst Chapl Trin Th Coll Singapore 02-05; rtd 05; Perm to Offic *York* from 06. *Saddlers Cottage, 15 Chapel Street, Thirsk YO7 1LU* Tel (01845) 524985 E-mail rbbwild@hotmail.com

WILDE, David Wilson. b 37. Lon Coll of Div ALCD61 BD62. **d** 62 **p** 63. C Kirkheaton *Wakef* 62-66; C Attenborough w Chilwell *S'well* 66-72; P-in-c Bestwood Park 72-83; R Kimberley 83-07; rtd 07. *2 Main Street, Kimberley, Nottingham NG16 2LL* Tel 0115-938 5315 E-mail christwl@aol.co.uk

WILDEY, Canon Ian Edward. b 51. St Chad's Coll Dur BA72. Coll of Resurr Mirfield 72. **d** 74 **p** 75. C Westgate Common *Wakef* 74-77; C Barnsley St Mary 77-81; V Ravensthorpe 81-95; R Barnsley St Mary 95-07; Dir Educn 96-98 and from 07; Hon Can Wakef Cathl from 00. *29 Intake Lane, Barnsley S75 2HX* Tel (01226) 291779 E-mail ian.wildey@sky.com

WILDING, Canon Anita Pamela. b 38. MBE01. Blackpool and Fylde Coll of Further Tech TCert61. CMS Tr Coll Chislehurst 65. **dss** 89 **d** 92 **p** 93. CMS Kenya 87-04; Chapl Kabare Girls' High Sch 92-04; Chapl St Andr Primary Boarding Sch Kabare 92-04; rtd 04; Perm to Offic *Blackb* from 04. *5 The Fairways, 35*

The Esplanade, Knott End-on-Sea, Poulton-le-Fylde FY6 0AD
Tel (01253) 810642 E-mail pamwilding@gofast.co.uk
WILDING, David. b 43. K Coll Lon BD67 AKC67. **d** 68 **p** 69. C
Thornhill *Wakef* 68-70; C Halifax St Jo Bapt 70-72; V Scholes
72-79; V Lightcliffe 79-97; rtd 97; Perm to Offic *Wakef* from 97.
10 Stratton Park, Rastrick, Brighouse HD6 3SN Tel (01484)
387651
WILDING, Michael Paul. b 57. Chich Th Coll 82. **d** 85 **p** 86. C
Treboeth *S & B* 85-87; C Llangiwg 87-88; V Defynnog w
Rhydybriw and Llandeilo'r-fan 88-00; V Defynnog, Llandilo'r
Fan, Llanulid, Llywel etc from 00. *The Vicarage, Sennybank,
Sennybridge, Brecon LD3 8PP* Tel (01874) 638927
WILDING, Pamela. See WILDING, Canon Anita Pamela
WILDS, The Ven Anthony Ronald. b 43. Hatf Coll Dur BA64.
Bps' Coll Cheshunt 64. **d** 66 **p** 67. C Newport Pagnell *Ox* 66-72;
P-in-c Chipili Zambia 72-75; V Chandler's Ford *Win* 75-85; V
Andover w Foxcott 85-97; RD Andover 89-94; Hon Can Win
Cathl 91-97; TR Solihull *Birm* 97-01; Hon Can Birm Cathl
00-01; Adn Plymouth *Ex* 01-10; rtd 10. *9 rue du Commerce,
49490 Meigne-le-Vicomte, France* Tel (0033) 2 41 82 24 52
E-mail tonywilds@gmail.com
WILES, Mrs Cathryn. b 51. BEd. **d** 04 **p** 05. NSM Wandsworth
Common St Mary *S'wark* 04-11; Chapl SW Lon and St George's
Mental Health NHS Trust from 06. *10 Waldeck Grove, London
SE27 0BE* Tel (020) 8761 4017 *or* 8682 6265
E-mail cathryn.wiles@ntlworld.com
WILES, Roger Kenneth. b 58. Witwatersrand Univ BA80.
St Paul's Coll Grahamstown 81. **d** 83 **p** 84. C Johannesburg
St Gabr S Africa 83-84; C Belgravia St Jo 84-85; Chapl Jeppe
Boys' High Sch 85-86; Chapl Witwatersrand Univ 86-93, R
Edenvale Em 94-99; P-in-c Edin Clermiston Em 99-05; V
Poulton Lancelyn H Trin *Ches* from 05. *6 Chorley Way, Wirral
CH63 9LS* Tel 0151-334 6780
WILFORD (formerly GIBSON), Laura Mary. b 50. NOC 85.
d 88 **p** 94. Par Dn Foley Park *Worc* 88-90; Par Dn Kidderminster
St Jo and H Innocents 90-94; TV 94-96; P-in-c Mamble w
Bayton, Rock w Heightington etc 96-99; TV Cartmel Peninsula
Carl 99-01; Jt Dir of Ords 00-01; P-in-c Worminghall w Ickford,
Oakley and Shabbington *Ox* 01-06; rtd 06. *5 Cookson Way,
Brough with St Giles, Catterick Garrison DL9 4XG* Tel (01748)
830017 E-mail lauramwilford@hotmail.co.uk
WILKERSON, Ms Valerie Anne. b 40. Leeds Univ BA62 RGN77
RM78. St Jo Coll Nottm 03. **d** 04 **p** 05. NSM Alrewas and
Wychnor *Lich* 04-10; Perm to Offic from 11. *22 Chaseview Road,
Alrewas, Burton-on-Trent DE13 7EL* Tel (01283) 790612
E-mail valwilkerson@aol.com
WILKES, Andrew Edward. b 63. **d** 10 **p** 11. NSM Whyke w
Rumboldswhyke and Portfield *Chich* 10-11; NSM Chich
St Wilfrid from 11. *17 Duncan Road, Chichester PO19 3NQ* Tel
(01243) 839990
WILKES, Jonathan Peter. b 66. Leic Poly BA88 K Coll Lon
MA00. Ripon Coll Cuddesdon BTh96. **d** 96 **p** 97. C Hackney
Lon 96-00; P-in-c Paddington St Pet 00-06; P-in-c Paddington
St Mary Magd 04-06; P-in-c Paddington All SS w St Jo *S'wark*
06-07; TR from 07. *All Saints' Vicarage, 15 Woodbines Avenue,
Kingston upon Thames KT1 2AZ* Tel (020) 3132 8717
WILKES, Robert Anthony. b 48. Trin Coll Ox BA70 MA73.
Wycliffe Hall Ox 71. **d** 74 **p** 75. C Netherton *Liv* 74-77; V 77-81;
Bp's Dom Chapl 81-85; CMS Pakistan 85-86; Regional Sec
Middle E and Pakistan 87-98; P-in-c Mossley Hill St Matt and
St Jas *Liv* 98-05; TR Mossley Hill 05-06; Hon Can Liv Cathl
03-06; Dean Birm 06-09; P-in-c Ox St Mich w St Martin and All
SS from 09. *St Frideswide's Vicarage, 23 Botley Road, Oxford
OX2 0BL* Tel (01865) 722724 E-mail revwilkes@btinternet.com
WILKIE, Michael John David. b 65. Oak Hill Th Coll BA90 Ex
Univ PGCE94. SWMTC 98. **d** 00 **p** 01. NSM Combe Martin,
Berrynarbor, Lynton, Brendon etc *Ex* 00-05. *Address temp
unknown*
WILKIN, Kenneth. b 54. Open Univ BA97. S'wark Ord Course 86
Wilson Carlile Coll. **d** 88 **p** 89. C Wolverhampton *Lich* 88-92; V
W Bromwich St Andr w Ch 92-98; Dep Chapl HM Pris
Pentonville 98-00; Chapl HM Pris Holloway from 00. *HM
Prison Holloway, 1 Parkhurst Road, London N7 0NU* Tel (020)
7979 4561 E-mail kenneth.wilkin@hmps.gsi.gov.uk
or kwilkin@aol.com
WILKIN, Paul John. b 56. Linc Th Coll 88. **d** 90 **p** 91. C
Leavesden *St Alb* 90-93; C Jersey St Brelade *Win* 93-97; V
Squirrels Heath *Chelmsf* 97-07; R Stansted Mountfitchet w
Birchanger and Farnham from 07. *The Rectory, 5 St John's
Road, Stansted CM24 8JP* Tel (01279) 812203
E-mail paulwilkin@iname.com
WILKIN, Rose Josephine. See HUDSON-WILKIN, Mrs Rose
Josephine
WILKINS, Mrs Janice Joy. b 49. St D Coll Lamp 90. **d** 93 **p** 97.
NSM Tredegar St Jas *Mon* 93-96; NSM Newbridge 96-01; C
Mynyddislwyn 97-01; V Abercarn and Cwmcarn 01-06; AD
Bedwellty 05-06; rtd 06. *10 Overdene, Pontllanfraith, Blackwood
NP12 2JS* Tel (01495) 225720

WILKINS, Michael Richard. b 71. W Sussex Inst of HE BA92.
Trin Coll Bris 07. **d** 09 **p** 10. C Bath Walcot *B & W* from 09.
5 The Linleys, Bath BA1 2XE Tel (01225) 317114 Mobile
07825-789168 E-mail mike@walcotchurch.org.uk
WILKINS, Nicki Anne. b 68. Indiana Univ BA91 Yale Univ
MDiv03. **d** 05 **p** 07. NSM St Andrews St Andr *St And* from 05.
Address temp unknown E-mail nwilkins@btinternet.com
WILKINS, Ralph Herbert. b 29. Lon Univ BD61. St Aug Coll
Cant 72. **d** 73 **p** 74. C Epsom Common Ch Ch *Guildf* 73-76; C
Haslemere 77-79; P-in-c Market Lavington and Easterton *Sarum*
79-82; V 82-90; P-in-c Puddletown and Tolpuddle 90-94; P-in-c
Milborne St Andrew w Dewlish 92-94; P-in-c Piddletrenthide w
Plush, Alton Pancras etc 92-94; rtd 94; Perm to Offic *Ab*
and *Heref* from 02. *The Mill, Marton, Welshpool SY21 8JY* Tel
(01938) 580566
WILKINS, Miss Susan Stafford. b 47. Dur Univ BA. Sarum Th
Coll. **dss** 82 **d** 87 **p** 94. Redlynch and Morgan's Vale *Sarum*
82-88; Hon Par Dn 87-88; Hon Par Dn Bemerton 88-90; Par Dn
Hilperton w Whaddon and Staverton etc 90-94; TV Worle
B & W 94-99; P-in-c Hallwood *Ches* 99-04; V Hallwood Ecum
Par from 04; RD Frodsham from 06. *The Vicarage, 6 Kirkstone
Crescent, Runcorn WA7 3JQ* Tel (01928) 713101
E-mail suewilkins@hallwoodlep.fsnet.co.uk
WILKINS, Vernon Gregory. b 53. Trin Coll Cam MA74 Ox Univ
BA88. Wycliffe Hall Ox 86. **d** 89 **p** 90. C Boscombe St Jo *Win*
89-91; C Bursledon 91-94; V Ramsgate St Luke *Cant* 94-03; Dir
Tr Bromley Chr Tr Cen Trust from 03; Hon C Bromley Ch Ch
Roch from 03. *29 Heathfield Road, Bromley BR1 3RN* Tel (020)
8464 5135 E-mail vernon@vgwilkins.freeserve.co.uk
WILKINSON, Adrian Mark. b 68. TCD BA90 MA94 BTh94
NUI MA00 HDipEd91. CITC 91. **d** 94 **p** 95. C Douglas Union
w Frankfield *C, C & R* 94-97; I Dunboyne Union *M & K* 97-02;
Chapl NUI 97-02; Min Can St Patr Cathl Dublin 97-02; I
Rathmolyon w Castlerickard, Rathcore and Agher *M & K*
01-02; I Douglas Union w Frankfield *C, C & R* from 02. *The
Rectory, Carrigaline Road, Douglas, Cork, Republic of Ireland*
Tel (00353) (21) 489 1539 E-mail amwilkinson@eircom.net
WILKINSON, Canon Alan Bassindale. b 31. St Cath Coll Cam
BA54 MA58 PhD59 DD97. Coll of Resurr Mirfield 57. **d** 59
p 60. C Kilburn St Aug *Lon* 59-61; Chapl St Cath Coll Cam
61-67; V Barrow Gurney *B & W* 67-70; Asst Chapl and Lect
St Matthias's Coll Bris 67-70; Prin Chich Th Coll 70-74; Can and
Preb Chich Cathl 70-74; Warden Verulam Ho 74-75; Dir of Aux
Min Tr *St Alb* 74-75; Sen Lect Crewe and Alsager Coll of HE
75-78; Hon C Alsager St Mary *Ches* 76-78; Dioc Dir of Tr *Ripon*
78-84; P-in-c Thornthwaite w Thruscross and Darley 84-88; Hon
Can Ripon Cathl 84-88; Perm to Offic *Portsm* from 88; Hon P
Portsm Cathl from 88; Hon Dioc Th 93-01; Hon Chapl Portsm
Cathl 94-01; rtd 96; Visiting Lect Portsm Univ 98-05. *17A High
Street, Portsmouth PO1 2LP* Tel (023) 9273 6270
WILKINSON, Alice Margaret Marion. See BISHOP, Mrs Alice
Margaret Marion
WILKINSON, Andrew Wilfrid. b 66. Nottm Univ BTh96 Lanc
Univ MA99. Linc Th Coll 93. **d** 96 **p** 97. C Longridge *Blackb*
96-99; V Garstang St Helen and St Michaels-on-Wyre from 99;
AD Garstang from 02; CF (TA) from 02. *The Vicarage, 6
Vicarage Lane, Churchtown, Preston PR3 0HW* Tel and fax
(01995) 602294 E-mail awilkinson703@btinternet.com
WILKINSON (née PHILPOTT), Canon Barbara May. b 48.
Leeds Univ BA69 CertEd70 MA90. NOC 90. **d** 93 **p** 94. NSM
Carleton and Lothersdale *Bradf* 93-96; C Steeton 96-00; Asst
Chapl Airedale NHS Trust 96-01; Hd Chapl Services 01-07; Hon
Can Bradf Cathl from 04; RD S Craven 04-07. *37 Aire Valley
Drive, Bradley, Keighley BD20 9HY* Tel (01535) 636339
E-mail barbara.wilkinson@bradford.anglican.org
WILKINSON, Carol Ann. b 54. Lon Univ BD88 Man Univ
PhD95. CBDTI 04. **d** 06 **p** 07. NSM Poulton Carleton and
Singleton *Blackb* 06-09; Lic to Offic from 09. *52 Lowick Drive,
Poulton-le-Fylde FY6 8HB* Tel (01253) 350700 Mobile
07894-830305
WILKINSON, Mrs Christine Margaret. b 52. Man Univ BA74
Neville's Cross Coll of Educn Dur PGCE75 Birm Univ MEd78.
d 04 **p** 05. OLM Eythorne and Elvington w Waldershare etc
Cant 04-11; NSM Littlebourne and Ickham w Wickhambreaux
etc from 11. *The Vicarage, Church Road, Littlebourne,
Canterbury CT3 1UA* Tel (01227) 721233
E-mail chriswilk.shep@virgin.net
WILKINSON, David Andrew. b 62. BA83. Oak Hill Th Coll
BA85. **d** 88 **p** 89. C Upton (Overchurch) *Ches* 88-91; C Fulham
St Matt *Lon* 91-94; V Duffield *Derby* 94-99; V Finchley St Paul
and St Luke *Lon* 99-03. *Honeysuckle Cottage, 19 Church Street,
Windermere LA23 1AQ* Tel (015394) 43069
WILKINSON, David Edward Paul. b 36. Univ of Wales
(Swansea) BSc57. St Mich Coll Llan 57. **d** 59 **p** 60. C Brecon w
Battle *S & B* 59-60; Min Can Brecon Cathl 60-66; R Llanelwedd
w Llanfaredd, Cwmbach Llechryd etc 66-72; V Seacroft 72-74;
Asst Master Churchmead Sch Datchet 75-82; TV Seacroft *Ripon*
82-01; rtd 01; Hon Min Can Ripon Cathl 01-07; Hon C Bishop
Monkton and Burton Leonard 01-07; Perm to Offic *St As* from

07. *Lyngrove, New High Street, Ruabon, Wrexham LL14 6PW* Tel (01978) 822725 Mobile 07909-961197 E-mail paulwilkinson36@googlemail.com

WILKINSON, Edward. b 55. Cranmer Hall Dur 86. **d** 88 **p** 89. C Bishopwearmouth St Nic *Dur* 88-92; P-in-c Newbottle 92-96; V from 96. *The Vicarage, Newbottle, Houghton le Spring DH4 4EP* Tel 0191-584 3244

WILKINSON, Edwin. b 29. Oak Hill Th Coll 53. **d** 56 **p** 57. C Blackb Ch Ch 56-58; C Cheltenham St Mark *Glouc* 58-61; V Tiverton St Geo *Ex* 61-66; V Rye Harbour *Chich* 66-73; V Camber and E Guldeford 73-79; V Westfield 79-87; V Bexhill St Steph 87-93; rtd 93; Perm to Offic *Chich* from 93. *51 Anderida Road, Eastbourne BN22 0PZ* Tel (01323) 503083

WILKINSON, Mrs Elizabeth Mary. b 65. St Edm Hall Ox MA91. NEOC 02. **d** 05 **p** 06. C Harlow Green and Lamesley *Dur* 05-09; P-in-c Burnmoor from 09. *The Rectory, 91 Old Durham Road, Gateshead NE8 4BS* Tel 0191-477 3990

WILKINSON, Geoffrey. *See* WILKINSON, Roy Geoffrey

WILKINSON, Canon Guy Alexander. b 48. Magd Coll Cam BA69. Ripon Coll Cuddesdon 85. **d** 87 **p** 88. C Coventry Caludon 87-90; P-in-c Ockham w Hatchford *Guildf* 90-91; R 91-94; Bp's Dom Chapl 90-94; V Small Heath *Birm* 94-99; Adn Bradf 99-04; Abp's Sec for Inter Faith Relns from 05; Nat Adv for Inter Faith Relns from 05. *Lambeth Palace, London SE1 7JU,* or *Church House, Great Smith Street, London SW1P 3AZ* Tel (020) 7898 1477 *or* 7898 1247 Mobile 07932-652315 E-mail guy.wilkinson@churchofengland.org

WILKINSON, Miss Helen Mary. b 53. Homerton Coll Cam BEd76. Trin Coll Bris 02. **d** 04 **p** 05. C Newbury *Ox* 04-08; C Northwood Em from 08. *54 Rofant Road, Northwood HA6 3BE* Tel (01923) 829163 Mobile 07790-262631

WILKINSON, James Daniel. b 73. Westmr Coll Ox BTh95 Reading Univ MA07 MBACP04. St Steph Ho Ox 97. **d** 99 **p** 00. C Wantage 99-02; P-in-c S Hinksey from 02; Sec to Bp Ebbsfleet 02-04. *The Vicarage, 33 Vicarage Road, Oxford OX1 4RD* Tel (01865) 245879 E-mail frjwilkinson@gmail.com

WILKINSON, John Andrew. b 59. Pemb Coll Ox BA83 MA87 St Jo Coll Dur BA86. Cranmer Hall Dur 84. **d** 87 **p** 88. C Broadheath *Ches* 87-91; TV Worthing Ch the King *Chich* 91-97; Chapl Chantilly *Eur* 97-06; Asst Chapl Fontainebleau 06-11; Chapl from 11; Can Malta Cathl from 10. *9 rue des Provenceaux, 77300 Fontainebleau, France* Tel (0033) 1 60 71 86 55 E-mail chaplain@fontainebleauchurch.org

WILKINSON, John David. b 36. AKC59. **d** 60 **p** 61. C Wythenshawe Wm Temple Ch CD *Man* 60-63; C Morley St Pet w Churwell *Wakef* 63-65; V Robert Town 65-75; V Battyeford 75-88; V Airedale w Fryston 88-98; P-in-c Cawthorne 98-04; rtd 04; Perm to Offic *Wakef* from 05; Retirement Officer (Pontefract Adnry) from 06. *29 Pontefract Road, Ferry Bridge, Knottingley WF11 8PN* Tel (01977) 607250

WILKINSON, Canon John Donald. b 29. Mert Coll Ox BA54 MA56 Louvain Univ Belgium LTh59 Lon Univ PhD82 FSA80. Gen Th Sem (NY) Hon STD63 Cuddesdon Coll 54. **d** 56 **p** 57. C Stepney St Dunstan and All SS *Lon* 56-59; Jerusalem 61-63; Gen Ed USPG 63-69; Dean St Geo Coll Jerusalem 69-75; Can Jerusalem 73-75; P-in-c S Kensington H Trin w All SS *Lon* 75-78; Bp's Dir of Clergy Tr 75-79; Dir Br Sch of Archaeology Jerusalem 79-83; USA 83-91; NSM Kensington St Mary Abbots w St Geo *Lon* 91-94; rtd 94; Hon C St Marylebone St Cypr *Lon* 94-98; Perm to Offic 98-08. *7 Tenniel Close, London W2 3LE* Tel and fax (020) 7229 9205

WILKINSON, John Lawrence. b 43. Ch Coll Cam BA65 MA69 Birm Univ MLitt91. Qu Coll Birm 67 Gen Th Sem (NY) STB69. **d** 69 **p** 70. C Braunstone *Leic* 69-71; C Hodge Hill *Birm* 71-74; P-in-c Aston St Jas 75-84; Tutor Qu Coll Birm 85-95; Hon C Birm St Geo 86-95; V Kings Heath 95-08; Hon Can Birm Cathl 99-08; rtd 09; Perm to Offic *Birm* from 09. *203 Barclay Road, Smethwick B67 5LA* Tel 0121-434 3526 E-mail jrwilkinson@dsl.pipex.com

WILKINSON, John Stoddart. b 47. CQSW83. St D Coll Lamp. **d** 70 **p** 71. C Kells *Carl* 70-72; C Barrow St Geo w St Luke 72-74; Perm to Offic *Mon* 74-89; Sub-Chapl HM YOI Hewell Grange 89-90; Sub-Chapl HM Rem Cen Brockhill 89-90; rtd 02. *10 Fern Drive, Neyland, Milford Haven SA73 1RA*

WILKINSON, Jonathan Charles. b 61. Leeds Univ BA83. Wycliffe Hall Ox 85. **d** 87 **p** 88. C Plymouth St Andr w St Paul and St Geo *Ex* 87-90; C Oulton Broad *Nor* 90-93; V Hallwood *Ches* 93-99; TR Gateshead *Dur* from 99. *The Rectory, 91 Old Durham Road, Gateshead NE8 4BS* Tel 0191-477 3990 E-mail wilkinson@clara.net

WILKINSON, Mrs Joyce Aileen. b 29. BSc(Econ) MA. **d** 99 **p** 00. NSM Bredon w Bredon's Norton *Worc* 99-04; rtd 04; Perm to Offic *Worc* from 04. *Foxgloves, Back Lane, Bredon, Tewkesbury GL20 7LH* Tel (01684) 773389

WILKINSON, Canon Julia Mary. b 52. Cam Inst of Educn CertEd73 Open Univ BA85 Univ of Wales (Ban) BD89. Trin Th Coll 92. **d** 92 **p** 94. Par Dn High Wycombe *Ox* 92-94; C 94-96; TV 96-01; Bp's Adv for Women in Ord Min 97-01; P-in-c St Merryn *Truro* 01-05; P-in-c St Issey w St Petroc Minor 01-05;

R St Merryn and St Issey w St Petroc Minor from 06; Co Dioc Dir of Ords from 01; Hon Can Truro Cathl from 06. *The Rectory, Glebe Crescent, St Issey, Wadebridge PL27 7HJ* Tel and fax (01841) 540314 E-mail revjulia@stpetroc.fsnet.co.uk

WILKINSON, Canon Keith Howard. b 48. Hull Univ BA70 FRSA94 MCT99. Westcott Ho Cam 74. **d** 76 **p** 77. C Pet St Jude 76-79; Chapl Eton Coll 79-84; Perm to Offic *Pet* 82-94; Chapl Malvern Coll 84-89; Hd Master Berkhamsted Sch Herts 89-96; Lic to Offic *St Alb* 89-96; Hd Master K Sch Cant 96-07; Hon Can Cant Cathl 96-07; Sen Chapl Eton Coll from 08. *3 Savile House, Eton College, Windsor SL4 0TD*

WILKINSON, The Ven Kenneth Samuel. b 31. TCD BA60 MA69. CITC 60. **d** 60 **p** 61. C Dublin St Michan w St Paul *D & G* 60-63; Min Can St Patr Cathl Dublin 62-67; C Dublin Ch Ch Leeson Park *D & G* 63-67; I Killegney *C & O* 67-70; I Enniscorthy w Clone, Clonmore, Monart etc 70-02; Preb Ferns Cathl 83-88; Adn Ferns 88-02; Dioc Dir of Ords 94-02; rtd 02. *149 Hazelwood, Old Coach Road, Gorey, Co Wexford, Republic of Ireland* Tel (00353) (53) 942 0784

WILKINSON, Margaret Anne. b 46. Lon Univ MB, BS70 MSc74 MRCPsych77. SAOMC 95. **d** 98 **p** 99. NSM Heston *Lon* 98-06; Chapl HM YOI Feltham 01-06; NSM Penge Lane H Trin *Roch* from 07. *27 River Grove Park, Beckenham BR3 1HX* Tel (020) 8650 2312 E-mail revdrwilkinson@doctors.org.uk

WILKINSON, Miss Marlene Sandra. b 45. SRN71. Trin Coll Bris IDC78. **dss** 78 **d** 93 **p** 94. Wrose *Bradf* 78-82; Chapl St Luke's Hosp Bradf 78-82; Past Tutor Aston Tr Scheme 79-81; W Yorkshire CECS 82-84; Westgate Common *Wakef* 84-86; E Ardsley 86-92; Wakef St Jo 92-94; NSM 93-94; TV Barrow St Geo w St Luke *Carl* 94-00; TV Darwen St Pet w Hoddlesden *Blackb* 00-02; rtd 03; Perm to Offic *Wakef* from 10. *4 Hopefield Court, East Ardsley, Wakefield WF3 2LL* Tel (01924) 872825

WILKINSON, Mrs Mary Frances. b 52. St As Minl Tr Course 99. **d** 03 **p** 04. NSM Shotton *St As* 03-05; NSM Llandrillo and Llandderfel from 05. *8 Felin Goed, Llandrillo, Corwen LL21 0SJ* Tel (01490) 440522

WILKINSON, Matthew John George. b 81. St Cuth Soc Dur BSc02. St Mich Coll Llan BA06. **d** 06 **p** 07. C Wrexham *St As* 06-11. *Address temp unknown* E-mail mjgwilkinson@hotmail.com

WILKINSON, Michael Alan. b 27. Selw Coll Cam BA51. Westcott Ho Cam 52. **d** 53 **p** 54. C Swindon Ch Ch *Bris* 53-57; C Knowle St Barn 57-59; C Eltham St Jo *S'wark* 59-65; C Sydenham St Barn 65-77; Perm to Offic *Ex* 77-84; P-in-c Yealmpton 84-91; P-in-c Brixton 87-91; V Yealmpton and Brixton 91-97; RD Ivybridge 91-93; rtd 97; Perm to Offic *Ex* from 97. *The Old Forge, Kingston, Kingsbridge TQ7 4PT* Tel (01548) 810424

WILKINSON, Paul. *See* WILKINSON, David Edward Paul

WILKINSON, Paul. b 51. Sarum & Wells Th Coll 75. **d** 78 **p** 79. C Allerton *Bradf* 78-80; C Baildon 80-83; V Hengoed w Gobowen *Lich* 83-90; V Potterne w Worton and Marston *Sarum* 90-03; Chapl Roundway Hosp Devizes 92-03; P-in-c Leckhampton St Pet *Glouc* 03-09; P-in-c Cheltenham Em w St Steph 08-09; TR S Cheltenham from 10. *The Rectory, Church Road, Leckhampton, Cheltenham GL53 0QJ* Tel (01242) 513647 E-mail pwilkinson@vicarage79.fsnet.co.uk

WILKINSON, Paul Martin. b 56. Brunel Univ BSc. Wycliffe Hall Ox 83. **d** 86 **p** 87. C Hinckley H Trin *Leic* 86-90; V Newbold on Avon *Cov* from 90. *The Vicarage, Main Street, Newbold, Rugby CV21 1HH* Tel (01788) 543055 Fax 542458 E-mail paulwilkinson54@btinternet.com

WILKINSON, Peter David Lloyd. b 67. Trin Coll Ox BA89 MA93. Ridley Hall Cam BA94. **d** 95 **p** 96. C Brampton St Thos *Derby* 95-98; C Tunbridge Wells St Jo *Roch* 98-02; C Ox St Ebbe w H Trin and St Pet from 02. *10 Lincoln Road, Oxford OX1 4TB* Tel (01865) 728885 E-mail pete@peteandjules.freeserve.co.uk

WILKINSON, Robert. *See* WILKINSON, Walter Edward Robert

WILKINSON, Robert Ian. b 43. MIMunE73 MICE84 CEng73. Oak Hill NSM Course. **d** 88 **p** 89. NSM Hawkwell *Chelmsf* 88-89; NSM Thundersley 89-91; C New Thundersley 91-94; V Berechurch St Marg w St Mich 94-06; rtd 06; Perm to Offic *Bradf* from 07. *140 Keighley Road, Skipton BD23 2QT* Tel (01756) 799748

WILKINSON, Robert John. b 66. Birkbeck Coll Lon BA98 Fitzw Coll Cam BA00 ACIB90. Westcott Ho Cam 98. **d** 01 **p** 02. C Southgate Ch Ch *Lon* 01-04; TV Wood Green St Mich w Bounds Green St Gabr etc from 04. *27 Collings Close, London N22 8RL* Tel (020) 8881 9836 E-mail robert.wilkinson@london.anglican.org

WILKINSON, Robert Matthew. b 21. TCD BA46. TCD Div Sch 47. **d** 47 **p** 48. C Limerick St Lawr w H Trin and St Jo *L & K* 47-49; C Arm St Mark 49-51; I Mullavilly 51-55; I Derryloran 55-73; Can Arm Cathl 67-73; I Ballymore 73-87; Treas Arm Cathl 73-75; Chan 75-83; Prec 83-87; rtd 87. *60 Coleraine Road, Portrush BT56 8HN* Tel (028) 7082 2758

WILKINSON, Robert Samuel. b 52. Wycliffe Hall Ox 92. **d** 94 **p** 95. C Boughton Monchelsea *Cant* 94-96; C Parkwood CD

95-96; C Plymouth St Andr and Stonehouse *Ex* 96-01; P-in-c Whimple, Talaton and Clyst St Lawr 01-11; TV Cullompton, Willand, Uffculme, Kentisbeare etc from 11. *The Rectory, Old Village, Willand, Cullompton EX15 2RH* Tel (01884) 32509

WILKINSON, Roger. b 46. K Coll Lon BA68 AKC68 AKC72. St Aug Coll Cant 72. d 73 p 74. C Lt Stanmore St Lawr *Lon* 73-76; Asst Chapl St Geo Hosp Lon 76-78; Chapl Hounslow and Spelthorne HA 78-88; TV Langley and Parkfield *Man* 88-89; C Shelf and Buttershaw St Aid *Bradf* 89-90; Chapl Asst Ipswich Hosp NHS Trust 90-94; C Fingringhoe w E Donyland and Abberton etc *Chelmsf* 94-01; P-in-c Greensted-juxta-Ongar w Stanford Rivers 01-04; P-in-c Stapleford Tawney w Theydon Mt 01-04; R Greensted-juxta-Ongar w Stanford Rivers etc 04-07; rtd 07; Perm to Offic *Chelmsf* from 07. *9 Iona Walk, Rowhedge, Colchester CO5 7JD* Tel (01206) 728882
E-mail roger606wilkinson@btinternet.com

WILKINSON, Roy Geoffrey. b 42. Open Univ BSc93 Linc Univ MSc99. Sarum Th Coll 67. d 70 p 71. C Belsize Park *Lon* 70-73; C Heston 73-75; C Hythe *Cant* 75-79; V Croydon Woodside 79-86; NSM Skegness and Winthorpe *Linc* 96-97; Asst Mental Health Chapl Linc Distr Healthcare NHS Trust 96-97; Chapl Lincs Partnership NHS Trust 97-05; rtd 05; Hon C Linc All SS from 06. *287 Monks Road, Lincoln LN2 5JZ* Tel (01522) 522671 Mobile 07745-755614
E-mail sarah@comfort123.freeserve.co.uk

WILKINSON, Canon Simon Evelyn. b 49. Nottm Univ BA74. Cuddesdon Coll 74. d 76 p 77. C Cheam *S'wark* 76-78; P-in-c Warlingham w Chelsham and Farleigh 78-83; Hd RS Radley Coll 83-89; R Bishop's Waltham and Upham *Portsm* 89-97; TR Shaston *Sarum* 97-03; P-in-c Amesbury from 03; RD Stonehenge 03-10; Can and Preb Sarum Cathl from 05. *The Vicarage, Church Street, Amesbury, Salisbury SP4 7EU* Tel (01980) 623145 E-mail s-wilkinson@ylol.com

WILKINSON, Stephen. b 69. Brighton Poly BEng91. Ridley Hall Cam 08. d 10 p 11. C Gtr Corsham and Lacock *Bris* from 10. *The Vicarage, Wadswick Lane, Neston, Corsham SN13 9TA* Tel (01225) 810743 Mobile 07786-228436
E-mail vicarofdidley@hotmail.com

WILKINSON, Stephen Graham. b 64. Leeds Univ BA08. NOC 05. d 08 p 09. Chapl to Police and NSM Pennington *Man* 08-11; TV Cramlington *Newc* from 11. *St Nicholas' Vicarage, 1 Cateran Way, Cramlington NE23 6EX* Tel (01670) 714271
E-mail revd.steve.wilkinson@googlemail.com

WILKINSON, Walter Edward Robert. b 38. St Andr Univ MA60. Lon Coll of Div BD63 ALCD63. d 63 p 64. C High Wycombe *Ox* 63-70; PV, Succ and Sacr Roch Cathl 70-73; P-in-c Asby w Ormside *Carl* 73-80; R Cherry Burton *York* 80-95; RD Beverley 88-94; P-in-c Grasmere *Carl* 95-03; rtd 03; Perm to Offic *Carl* from 03. *4 Heversham Gardens, Heversham, Milnthorpe LA7 7RA* Tel (01539) 564044 E-mail bob@carliol.clara.co.uk

WILKS, Eric Percival. b 32. Wells Th Coll 67. d 68 p 69. C Fladbury w Throckmorton, Wyre Piddle and Moor *Worc* 68-70; Perm to Offic from 70. *4 Catherine Cottages, Droitwich Road, Hartlebury, Kidderminster DY10 4EL* Tel (01299) 251580

WILKS, Ernest Howard. b 26. Oak Hill Th Coll 64. d 66 p 67. C Slough *Ox* 66-69; R Gressenhall w Longham and Bittering Parva *Nor* 69-77; Area Sec CMS *St E* and *Nor* 77-83; P-in-c Deopham w Hackford *Nor* 83-84; P-in-c Morley 83-84; P-in-c Wicklewood and Crownthorpe 83-84; R Morley w Deopham, Hackford, Wicklewood etc 84-88; CMS Nigeria 89-91; rtd 91; Perm to Offic *Nor* from 91. *23 Eckling Grange, Dereham NR20 3BB* Tel (01362) 690485

WILL, Nicholas James. b 53. Birm Univ LLB75. Qu Coll Birm 93. d 95 p 96. C Bridgnorth, Tasley, Astley Abbotts, etc *Heref* 95-00; R Raveningham Gp *Nor* from 00. *The Rectory, Church Road, Thurlton, Norwich NR14 6RN* Tel (01508) 548648

WILLANS, Jonathan Michael Arthur. b 60. QUB BD. CITC 83. d 85 p 86. C Larne and Inver *Conn* 85-88; R Hawick *Edin* 88-91; P-in-c Brockham Green *S'wark* from 91; P-in-c Leigh from 91. *The Vicarage, Clayhill Road, Leigh, Reigate RH2 8PD* Tel and fax (01306) 611224

WILLANS, William Richard Gore. b 48. Qu Coll Ox BA70 MA74 Ox Univ PGCE71. CITC 77. d 79 p 80. C Bonne Bay Canada 79-80; P-in-c Bonne Bay N 80-82; R 82-87; R Thunder Bay St Thos 87-98; I Craigs w Dunaghy and Killagan *Conn* from 98. *Craigs Rectory, 95 Hillmount Road, Cullybackey, Ballymena BT42 1NZ* Tel (028) 2588 0248 *or* 2588 2225
E-mail willans@btinternet.com

WILLARD, John Fordham. b 38. K Coll Lon BD62 AKC62. d 63 p 64. C Balham Hill Ascension *S'wark* 63-67; C Leigh Park *Portsm* 67-73; P-in-c Leigh Park St Clare *Portsm* 73-75; R Bishop's Waltham 75-87; P-in-c Upham 78-79; R 79-87; V Dalston H Trin w St Phil *Lon* 87-97; P-in-c Haggerston All SS 90-97; P-in-c Fairford *Glouc* 97-98; V Fairford and Kempsford w Whelford 98-04; rtd 04; Perm to Offic *Glouc* from 05. *15 Highwood Avenue, Cheltenham GL53 0JJ* Tel (01242) 530051

WILLCOCK, Canon Richard William. b 39. Hertf Coll Ox BA62 MA66. Ripon Hall Ox 62. d 64 p 65. C Ashton St Mich *Man* 64-68; Bp's Dom Chapl 68-72; V Charlestown 72-75; Chapl

Casterton Sch Lancs 75-80; V Bamford *Man* 80-92; R Framlingham w Saxtead *St E* 92-04; RD Loes 95-97; Warden of Readers 98-03; Hon Can St E Cathl 00-04; rtd 04. *High Green Cottage, Sandford, Appleby-in-Westmorland CA16 6NR* Tel (017683) 51021

WILLCOX, Canon Frederick John. b 29. Kelham Th Coll 49. d 54 p 55. C Tranmere St Paul *Ches* 54-56; Lic to Offic *S'well* 57-61; Miss P St Patr Miss Bloemfontein S Africa 62-65; Dir 65-70; P-in-c Derby St Andr w St Osmund 70-74; V 74-80; V Netherton St Andr *Worc* 80-94; Hon Can Worc Cathl 91-94; rtd 94; Perm to Offic *Worc* 94-10. *1 Capel Court, The Burgage, Prestbury, Cheltenham GL52 3EL* Tel (01242) 256373

WILLCOX (née THOMPSON), Mrs Pauline. b 44. EMMTC 81. dss 84 d 87 p 94. Derby St Aug 84-88; Par Dn 87-88; Par Dn Boulton 88-90; Par Dn Allestree 91-94; C 94-97; Sub-Chapl HM Pris Sudbury 92-94; P-in-c Hartington, Biggin and Earl Sterndale *Derby* 97-01; rtd 01; Perm to Offic *Derby* 01-06; Chapl HM Pris Jersey 06-09. *9 Clos du Roncherez, Le Pont du Val, St Brelade, Jersey JE3 8FG* Tel (01534) 745160
E-mail paulinewillcox@jerseymail.co.uk

WILLCOX, Ralph Arthur. b 32. Cranfield Inst of Tech MSc80. St Alb Minl Tr Scheme 86. d 89 p 90. NSM Aspley Guise w Husborne Crawley and Ridgmont *St Alb* 89-92; Chapl HM Pris Bedf 92-99; Asst Chapl 99-02; Lic to Offic *St Alb* 92-03; rtd 02; Perm to Offic *St Alb* from 03. *5 Church Road, Woburn Sands, Milton Keynes MK17 8TE* Tel (01908) 582510

WILLCOX, Richard John Michael. b 39. Birm Univ BSc62 PhD67. Qu Coll Birm 78. d 80 p 81. C Boldmere *Birm* 80-83; V Edgbaston SS Mary and Ambrose 83-89; V Evercreech w Chesterblade and Milton Clevedon *B & W* 89-97; Dioc Development Rep 90-01; V Bridgwater H Trin 97-01; rtd 01; Perm to Offic *Heref* from 05. *The Briars, Ledbury Road, Wellington Heath, Ledbury HR8 1NB* Tel (01531) 636191
E-mail rswillcox@aol.com

WILLESDEN, Area Bishop of. See BROADBENT, The Rt Revd Peter Alan

WILLETT, Canon Allen Gardiner. b 20. Bris Univ BA51 Lon Univ BD54. Clifton Th Coll 47. d 54 p 55. C Rawtenstall St Mary *Man* 54-57; Nigeria 57-58; Tutor Clifton Th Coll 58-60; C Wallington *S'wark* 60-62; Tutor All Nations Miss Coll Taplow 62-63; V Bedminster St Luke w St Silas *Bris* 63-68; V Galleywood Common *Chelmsf* 68-87; RD Chelmsf 81-86; Hon Can Chelmsf Cathl 85-87; rtd 87; Perm to Offic *Pet* 87-00; Ely 90-97; *Linc* 90-99; *Chelmsf* and *St E* from 01. *61 Ashdown Way, Ipswich IP3 8RL* Tel (01473) 423751
E-mail allenmary@willett61.freeserve.co.uk

WILLETT, Frank Edwin. b 45. Kelham Th Coll 64. d 68 p 69. C Oswestry H Trin *Lich* 68-71; C Bilston St Leon 71-74; USPG Zambia 75-80; V Curbar and Stoney Middleton *Derby* 80-88; Area Sec USPG *Derby* and *Leic* 88-91; V Chesterfield St Aug *Derby* 91-98; Chapl Walton Hosp 91-98; Ind Chapl *Derby* 98-03; P-in-c Brampton St Mark 03-09; P-in-c Loundsley Green 03-09; rtd 10; Hon C Boldre w S Baddesley *Win* from 09. *The Vicarage, Pilley Hill, Pilley, Lymington SO41 5QF* Tel (01590) 677528
E-mail ff_willett@yahoo.co.uk

WILLETT, Canon Geoffrey Thomas. b 38. Dur Univ BA59 MA82. Cranmer Hall Dur. d 62 p 63. C Widnes St Paul *Liv* 62-65; C Harborne Heath *Birm* 65-68; V Wakef St Andr and St Mary 68-75; V Hinckley H Trin *Leic* 75-89; TR 89; RD Sparkenhoe II 84-87; RD Sparkenhoe W 87-89; P-in-c Markfield 89-90; R 90-99; P-in-c Thornton, Bagworth and Stanton 96-99; R Markfield, Thornton, Bagworth and Stanton etc 99-04; RD Sparkenhoe E 91-99; Hon Can Leic Cathl 87-04; rtd 04; Perm to Offic *Derby* and *Leic* from 04; Lich from 10. *22 Clifton Way, Burton-on-Trent DE15 9DW* Tel (01283) 548868

WILLETT, Canon John Ivon. b 40. Ch Ch Ox BA63 MA65. Chich Th Coll 61. d 63 p 64. C Leic St Andr 63-66; C Bordesley St Alb *Birm* 66-72; Min Can, Prec and Sacr Pet Cathl 72-82; R Uppingham w Ayston and Wardley w Belton 82-99; Can Pet Cathl 97-99; V Cantley *Sheff* from 99; AD Doncaster 04-10. *St Wilfrid's Vicarage, 200 Cantley Lane, Doncaster DN4 6PA* Tel (01302) 535133

WILLETT, Stephen John. b 54. Ridley Hall Cam 88. d 90 p 91. C Chapeltown *Sheff* 90-94; V Hackenthorpe from 94; AD Attercliffe from 07. *The Vicarage, 63 Sheffield Road, Sheffield S12 4LR* Tel 0114-248 4486 E-mail stephen.willet@tesco.net

WILLETTS, Ms Mary Elizabeth Willetts. b 33. St Hild Coll Dur BA54 Hughes Hall Cam CertEd55. Cranmer Hall Dur 02. d 02 p 03. NSM Stockton-on-the-Forest w Holtby and Warthill *York* from 02. *Walnut Cottage, Warthill, York YO19 5XL* Tel (01904) 489874

WILLETTS, Simon Peter. b 75. St Jo Coll Nottm. d 10 p 11. C Leamington Priors St Paul *Cov* from 10. *3 Sheepcote Close, Leamington Spa CV32 5YD*

WILLETTS, Mrs Susan. b 60. EMMTC 05. d 08 p 09. C Burton All SS w Ch Ch *Lich* 08-11; TV Uttoxeter Area from 11. *1A Moor Street, Burton-on-Trent DE14 3SU*

WILLEY, David Geoffrey. b 53. Imp Coll Lon BSc74. Oak Hill Th Coll BA86. d 86 p 87. C Cromer *Nor* 86-90; R High Halstow

w All Hallows and Hoo St Mary *Roch* 90-94; R Gravesend St Geo 94-02; TR N Farnborough *Guildf* from 02; RD Aldershot from 06. *The Rectory, 66 Church Avenue, Farnborough GU14 7AP* Tel (01252) 544754
E-mail rector@stpetersfarnborough.org.uk

WILLEY, Graham John. b 38. Moray Ord Course 91. **d** 93 **p** 94. NSM W Coast Jt Congregations *Mor* 93-99; NSM Stirling *St And* 99-03; rtd 03; Perm to Offic *St And* from 03. *The Cedars, Main Street, Killin FK21 8TN* Tel (01567) 820366

WILLIAMS, Alan Ronald Norman. b 60. RMN85. Linc Th Coll 95. **d** 95 **p** 96. C Malvern Link w Cowleigh *Worc* 95-99; TV 03-08; V Risca *Mon* 99-03; P-in-c Amblecote *Worc* from 08. *The Vicarage, 4 The Holloway, Amblecote, Stourbridge DY8 4DL* E-mail alan.r.williams@btinternet.com

WILLIAMS, Aled Jones. b 56. Univ of Wales (Ban) BA77. St Mich Coll Llan 77. **d** 79 **p** 80. C Conwy w Gyffin *Ban* 79-82; R Llanrug 82-86; R Machynlleth and Llanwrin 86-87; Member L'Arche Community 88-95; V Ynyscynhaearn w Penmorfa and Porthmadog 95-01; V Porthmadog and Ynyscynhaearn and Dolbenmaen 01-09; rtd 10. *Cwm, Llwyn Brith, Criccieth LL52 0TA* Tel (01766) 522176

WILLIAMS, Canon Aled Wyn. b 47. Univ of Wales (Abth) BA69. St Mich Coll Llan 69. **d** 71 **p** 72. C Llanelli *St D* 71-73; P-in-c Capel Colman w Llanfihangel Penbedw etc 73-74; V 74-81; V Llanddewi Brefi w Llanbadarn Odwyn 81-84; V Llanddewi Brefi w Llanbadarn Odwyn, Cellan etc 84-01; V Lampeter and Llanddewibrefi Gp 01-06; TR Bro Teifi Sarn Helen 06-11; AD Lampeter and Ultra-Aeron 96-11; Can St D Cathl 97-11; rtd 11. *Cwmawel, Llanllwni, Pencader SA39 9DR*

WILLIAMS, Alfred Donald. b 26. St Aid Birkenhead 57. **d** 59 **p** 60. C Ordsall *S'well* 59-62; V Ladybrook 62-70; P-in-c Newark Ch Ch 70-71; R Gotham 72-88; P-in-c W Leake w Kingston-on-Soar and Ratcliffe-on-Soar 72-81; rtd 88; Perm to Offic *Bradf* from 88. *20 Grassington Road, Skipton BD23 1LL* Tel (01756) 794496

WILLIAMS, Miss Alison Lindsay. b 47. Univ of Wales (Abth) BA69 PGCE70. Wycliffe Hall Ox 00. **d** 00 **p** 01. C Stratton St Margaret w S Marston etc *Bris* 00-04; TV Chalke Valley *Sarum* from 04. *The Vicarage, Nunton, Salisbury SP5 4HP* Tel (01722) 330628 E-mail alisonlwilliams@fish.co.uk

WILLIAMS, Amanda Clare. See WILLIAMS-POTTER, Mrs Amanda Clare

WILLIAMS, Mrs Amanda Joy. b 61. Glos Univ BA10. WEMTC 08. **d** 10. C Tupsley w Hampton Bishop *Heref* from 10. *Canal Cottage, Monkhide, Ledbury HR8 2TX* Tel (01531) 670753 E-mail monkhide@btinternet.com

WILLIAMS, Mrs Andrea Caroll. b 46. Brighton Univ BA05. Trin Coll Bris 06. **d** 07 **p** 08. NSM Ore St Helen and St Barn *Chich* from 07. *34 Fellows Road, Hastings TN34 3TY* Tel 07806-463558 (mobile) E-mail hastingsgang@onetel.com

WILLIAMS, Andrew Barrington. b 62. Ripon Coll Cuddesdon 96. **d** 98 **p** 99. C Oswaldtwistle Immanuel and All SS *Blackb* 98-01; C Whittle-le-Woods 01-02; P-in-c Hillock *Man* 02-08; P-in-c Unsworth 07-08; P-in-c Radcliffe St Andr from 08. *St Andrew's Vicarage, St Andrew's View, Radcliffe, Manchester M26 4HE* Tel 0161-723 2427
E-mail revandywilliams@yahoo.co.uk

WILLIAMS, Andrew David. b 67. Univ of Wales (Lamp) BA91. Linc Th Coll 93. **d** 93 **p** 94. C Perry Street *Roch* 93-96; C Ealing St Pet Mt Park *Lon* 96-00; R Finchley St Mary 00-08; Warden of Readers Edmonton Area 05-08; R Applecross Australia from 08. *2 Mitchell Street, Ardross WA 6153, Australia* Tel (0061) (8) 9417 4330 or 9364 1718 E-mail perth08@googlemail.com

WILLIAMS, Andrew Gibson. b 31. Edin Univ MA57. Edin Th Coll 56. **d** 59 **p** 60. C Todmorden *Wakef* 59-61; C Clitheroe St Mary *Blackb* 61-63; V Burnley St Jas 63-65; CF (TA) 64-65; CF 65-71; R Winterslow *Sarum* 71-84; P-in-c Condover *Heref* 84-88; P-in-c Acton Burnell w Pitchford 84-88; P-in-c Frodesley 84-88; R Condover w Frodesley, Acton Burnell etc 88-90; R Whimple, Talaton and Clyst St Lawr *Ex* 90-94; rtd 94; Perm to Offic *Ex* 94-08. *5 St Barnabas, Beauchamp Community, Newland, Malvern WR13 5AX* Tel (01684) 568061

WILLIAMS, Andrew John. b 64. Univ Coll Lon BSc85 Keele Univ PGCE87 Lon Univ MSc91. STETS 08. **d** 11. NSM Twickenham All Hallows *Lon* from 11. *51 Moor Mead Road, Twickenham TW1 1JS* Tel 07824-310311 (mobile)
E-mail andrew.williams.london@gmail.com

WILLIAMS, Canon Andrew Joseph. b 55. St Jo Coll Nottm BTh81. **d** 81 **p** 82. C Hollington St Leon *Chich* 81-84; C Sutton Coldfield H Trin *Birm* 84-87; Perm to Offic 87-01; Chapl Blue Coat Comp Sch Walsall 91-01; Chapl St Elphin's Sch Matlock 01-04; Lic to Offic *Derby* 01-06; Can Res Bradf Cathl from 06. *2 Cathedral Close, Bradford BD1 4EG* Tel (01274) 777728 E-mail andy.williams@bradfordcathedral.org

WILLIAMS, Andrew Thomas. b 66. Ex Univ LLB88 Solicitor 90. Trin Coll Bris BA00. **d** 00 **p** 01. C Whitchurch *Ex* 00-03; C Chorleywood St Andr *St Alb* 03-09; Pastor Greenwich Trin Ch USA from 09. *Trinity Church, 15 Sherwood Place, Greenwich CT 06830, USA* Tel (001) (203) 618 0808 Fax 618 0888 E-mail elena.w@virgin.net

WILLIAMS, Mrs Angela. b 50. Univ of Wales (Ban) BTh05. **d** 05 **p** 06. Min Can Ban Cathl 05-09; V Llandegfan w Llandysilio from 09; Dioc Children's Officer 05-11; Warden of Readers from 11. *The Vicarage, Mona Road, Menai Bridge LL59 5EA* Tel (01248) 717265

WILLIAMS, Anthea Elizabeth. b 50. Trevelyan Coll Dur BA71 Kent Univ MA97 Middx Univ MSc00 Univ of E Lon PhD10. Linc Th Coll 72. **dss** 79 **d** 87 **p** 94. St Marylebone Ch Ch *Lon* 79-84; Maidstone St Martin *Cant* 84-91; Par Dn 87-91; Dn-in-c Rolvenden 91-94; P-in-c 94-04; P-in-c Newenden 01-04; Chapl E Kent NHS and Soc Care Partnership Trust 91-04; Hon Chapl Kent Police from 95; Perm to Offic *Cant* and *Roch* from 04. *2 Redwater Cottages, Cranbrook TN17 2LX* Tel (01580) 892191 E-mail chaplain2sk@btinternet.com

WILLIAMS, Anthony. b 39. **d** 03 **p** 04. NSM Iver *Ox* 03-10; Perm to Offic from 10. *4 Syke Ings, Iver SL0 9ET* Tel (01753) 653849

WILLIAMS, Anthony David. b 38. LRCP62 MRCS62 MRCGP68. S Dios Minl Tr Scheme 87. **d** 90 **p** 91. NSM Jersey St Pet *Win* 90-92; NSM Jersey St Helier from 92. *Beau Vallon Ouest, Mont de la Rosier, St Saviour, Jersey JE2 7HF* Tel (01534) 863859 E-mail tonyw@jerseymail.co.uk

WILLIAMS, Anthony James. b 57. **d** 08 **p** 09. NSM Bream *Glouc* from 08. *Sunnyside, Bailey Hill, Yorkley, Lydney GL15 4RT* Tel (01594) 516162 E-mail info@vineyhilladventure.org

WILLIAMS, The Very Revd Arfon. b 58. Univ of Wales (Abth) BD83 Univ of Wales (Ban) MA84. Wycliffe Hall Ox 83. **d** 84 **p** 85. C Carmarthen St Dav *St D* 84-86; TV Aberystwyth 86-88; V Glanogwen *Ban* 88-94; C Ewhurst and Dir Oast Ho Retreat Cen *Chich* 95-98; Asst to RD Rye 95-98; Co-ord for Adult Educn (E Sussex Area) 97-98; I Jordanstown *Conn* 98-02; Adn Meirionnydd *Ban* 02-04; R Dolgellau w Llanfachreth and Brithdir etc 02-04; Dean Elphin and Ardagh *K, E & A* from 04; I Sligo w Knocknarea and Rosses Pt from 04. *The Deanery, Strandhill Road, Sligo, Republic of Ireland* Tel (00353) (71) 915 7993 E-mail arvonwilliams@eircom.net

WILLIAMS, Preb Arthur Edwin. b 33. Leeds Univ BA57. Coll of Resurr Mirfield 57. **d** 59 **p** 60. C Wednesfield St Thos *Lich* 59-62; C Codsall 62-65; V 83-98; V Coseley St Chad 65-73; R Kingswinford H Trin 73-81; TR Wordsley 81-83; RD Himley 77-83; Preb Lich Cathl 82-98; RD Penkridge 89-94; rtd 98; Perm to Offic *Heref* from 99 and *Lich* 01-09. *2 Campbell Close, Bridgnorth WV16 5PD* Tel (01746) 761344

WILLIAMS, Barrie. b 33. Em Coll Cam BA54 MA58 Bris Univ MLitt71. Lambeth STh75 Ripon Hall Ox 62. **d** 63 **p** 64. C Penwortham St Mary *Blackb* 63-65; Hon C Salisbury St Martin *Sarum* 65-77; Chapl St Edw K and Martyr Cam *Ely* 77-84; Asst Chapl Trin Hall Cam 77-84; R Ashley w Weston by Welland and Sutton Bassett *Pet* 84-85; Asst Chapl St Hilda's Priory and Sch Whitby 85-97; rtd 98; Perm to Offic *York* from 98. *Flat 5, Grinkle Court, 9 Chubb Hill Road, Whitby YO21 1JU* Tel (01947) 600766

WILLIAMS, Benjamin James. b 85. Pemb Coll Ox BA06 Wolfs Coll Ox MSt07. Ox Min Course 07. **d** 10 **p** 11. NSM Cowley St Jo *Ox* from 10. *30 Stockmore Street, Oxford OX4 1JT* Tel 07540-784156 (mobile) E-mail hishtafel@hotmail.com

WILLIAMS, Brian. See WILLIAMS, Herbert Brian

WILLIAMS, Brian. b 48. WMMTC. **d** 83 **p** 84. NSM Lich St Chad 83-03; Asst Chapl Sandwell Health Care NHS Trust 98; Angl Chapl 98-99; Chapl Burton Hosps NHS Trust 99-03; Chapl R Bournemouth and Christchurch Hosps NHS Trust from 03. *Royal Bournemouth Hospital, Castle Lane East, Bournemouth BH7 7DW* Tel (01202) 704221 or 303626

WILLIAMS, Brian Frederick. b 55. Philippa Fawcett Coll CertEd77 BEd78. SEITE 98. **d** 01 **p** 02. NSM Folkestone St Mary and St Eanswythe *Cant* 01-10; NSM Folkestone St Mary, St Eanswythe and St Saviour 09-11; Perm to Offic from 11. *79 Surrenden Road, Folkestone CT19 4EB* Tel (01303) 276242 E-mail brianwilliams@cheritonfolk.fsnet.co.uk

WILLIAMS, Brian Luke. b 54. AKC75. St Steph Ho Ox 76. **d** 77 **p** 78. C Kettering St Mary *Pet* 77-80; C Walsall St Gabr Fulbrook *Lich* 80-83; P-in-c Sneyd 83-85; V from 85; RD Stoke N 94-99. *Sneyd Vicarage, Hamil Road, Stoke-on-Trent ST6 1AP* Tel and fax (01782) 825841

WILLIAMS, Brian Thomas. b 48. Linc Th Coll 89. **d** 91 **p** 92. C Liss *Portsm* 91-95; C Portsea N End St Mark 95-98; Perm to Offic 98; NSM Wymering 05-07; NSM Lee-on-the-Solent from 07. *56 Old Road, Gosport PO12 1RE*

WILLIAMS, Bryan George. b 37. **d** 01 **p** 02. OLM Fazeley *Lich* 01-05; rtd 05. *Address temp unknown*

WILLIAMS, Ms Carol Jean Picknell. b 45. FCIPD89. Ox NSM Course 86. **d** 89 **p** 94. NSM High Wycombe *Ox* 89-97; P-in-c Penn 97-01; rtd 01; Perm to Offic *Heref* from 02. *Châtelaine House, Kinsham, Presteigne LD8 2HP* Tel (01544) 267067 E-mail caroljpwilliams@compuserve.com

WILLIAMS, Mrs Carole. b 61. LCTP 05. **d** 08 **p** 09. NSM Oswaldtwistle St Paul *Blackb* from 08. *20 Abbot Clough Avenue, Blackburn BB1 3LP* Tel (01254) 677708 E-mail carole.williams@blackburn.anglican.org

WILLIAMS, Mrs Catherine Anne. b 65. Selw Coll Cam BA87 MA91. SEITE 98. **d** 00 **p** 01. C Chatham St Steph *Roch* 00-02; C Bishop's Cleeve *Glouc* 03-06; Dioc Voc Officer 06-10; Asst Dioc Dir of Ords 08-10; Selection Sec Min Division from 10; Public Preacher *Glouc* from 11. *Ministry Division, Church House, Great Smith Street, London SW1P 3AZ* Tel (020) 7898 1000 Mobile 07966-709577 E-mail catherine.williams@churchofengland.org

WILLIAMS, Ms Catherine Lois. b 51. Swansea Coll of Educn CertEd74 Univ of Wales (Swansea) BEd80. St Mich Coll Llan. **d** 00 **p** 01. C Gorseinon *S & B* 00-02; C Cen Swansea 03; TV from 03. *Christ Church Vicarage, 226 Oystermouth Road, Swansea SA1 3UH* Tel (01792) 652606

WILLIAMS (née BRERETON), Mrs Catherine Louise. b 69. St Aid Coll Dur BSc90 Cranfield Univ MSc92 Fitzw Coll Cam BTh00. Ridley Hall Cam 97. **d** 00 **p** 01. C S Bank *York* 00-03; V Middlesbrough St Chad 03-09; TV Woughton *Ox* from 09. *10 Forest Rise, Eaglestone, Milton Keynes MK6 5EU* Tel (01908) 674742 E-mail cathi@woughton.org

✠**WILLIAMS, The Rt Revd Cecil Javed.** b 42. Punjab Univ MA(Ed)67 Peshawar Univ MA72. **d** 87 **p** 88 c 01. C Tarnab and St Jo Cathl Peshawar Pakistan 87-90; V St Jo Cathl Peshawar 90-01; Asst Bp Peshawar 01-02; C Potternewton *Ripon* 02-06; rtd 07; Perm to Offic *Bradf* from 07. *48 Button Hill, Leeds LS7 3DA* Tel 0113-262 1408 Mobile 07882-171040 E-mail cecilwilliams42@hotmail.com

WILLIAMS, Canon Cecil Peter. b 41. TCD BA63 MA67 Lon Univ BD67 PhD86 Bris Univ MLitt77. Clifton Th Coll 64. **d** 67 **p** 68. C Maghull *Liv* 67-70; Lic to Offic *Bris* 70-91; Tutor Clifton Th Coll 70-72; Tutor Trin Coll Bris 72-91; Lib 73-81; Course Ldr 81-85; Vice-Prin 85-91, V Ecclesall *Sheff* 91 06; Hon Can Sheff Cathl 01-06; rtd 06; Hon C Jersey Gouray St Martin *Win* from 06. *Gouray Vicarage, Le Grande Route de Faldouet, St Martin, Jersey JE3 6UA* Tel (01534) 853255 Mobile 07801-353786 E-mail peter.williams@gouraychurch.co.uk

WILLIAMS, Mrs Christine Mary. b 51. City Univ BSc72 Middx Univ BA05. NTMTC 02. **d** 05 **p** 06. NSM Pitsea w Nevendon *Chelmsf* 05-08; TV Grays Thurrock from 08. *2 Foxleigh, Billericay CM12 9NS* Tel (01277) 654370 E-mail christine.mwilliams@btopenworld.com

WILLIAMS, Christopher David. b 62. Spurgeon's Coll BD99. St Jo Coll Nottm MA06. **d** 06 **p** 07. C Haslemere and Grayswood *Guildf* 06-08; C Godalming 08-09; R Liss *Portsm* from 09. *The Rectory, 111 Station Road, Liss GU33 7AQ* Tel 07803-135739 (mobile) E-mail revchris@talktalk.net

WILLIAMS, Preb Clive Gregory. b 45. Trin Coll Bris 83. **d** 85 **p** 86. C Bedhampton *Portsm* 85-88; V Highley w Billingsley, Glazeley etc *Heref* 88-98; P-in-c Stottesdon w Farlow, Cleeton St Mary etc 08-10; RD Bridgnorth 96-05; Preb Heref Cathl from 99. *The Vicarage, Church Street, Highley, Bridgnorth WV16 6NA* Tel (01746) 861612 E-mail highleyrectory@aol.com

WILLIAMS, The Ven Colin Henry. b 52. Pemb Coll Ox BA73 MA78. St Steph Ho Ox BA80. **d** 81 **p** 82. C Liv St Paul Stoneycroft 81-84; TV Walton St Mary 84-89; Chapl Walton Hosp Liv 86-89; Bp's Dom Chapl *Blackb* 89-94; Chapl Whalley Abbey 89-94; V Poulton-le-Fylde 94-99; Adn Lancaster 99-05; Gen Sec Conf of Eur Chs 05-10; Can Gib Cathl 07-10; TR Ludlow *Heref* from 10. *6 Summerfields, Ludlow SY8 2QA* Tel (01584) 872143 E-mail colin_w@bluewin.ch

WILLIAMS, David. b 43. ACA65 FCA. K Coll Lon AKC69 BD69. **d** 70 **p** 71. C Walkden Moor *Man* 70-72; C Deane 72-75; V Horwich St Cath 75-81; Hon C Chorley All SS *Blackb* 84-86; P-in-c Weeton 86-87; V Singleton w Weeton 87-97; C Lancaster St Mary w St John and St Anne 98-00; Chapl HM Pris Lanc Castle 98-00; rtd 00; Perm to Offic *Man* 02-08 and from 10. *153 Crompton Way, Bolton BL2 2SQ* Tel (01524) 382362 E-mail goodfornowt@aol.com

WILLIAMS, Canon David. b 49. BTh. **d** 88 **p** 89. C Lurgan etc w Ballymachugh, Kildrumferton etc *K, E & A* 88-91; I Kinsale Union *C, C & R* from 91; Miss to Seafarers from 91; Can Cork and Cloyne Cathls 95-97; Treas Cork Cathl from 97; Preb Tymothan St Patr Cathl Dublin from 97. *St Multose Rectory, 3 Abbey Court, Kinsale, Co Cork, Republic of Ireland* Tel (00353) (21) 477 2220 E-mail dhw@gofree.indigo.ie

WILLIAMS, David Alun. b 65. St Thos Hosp Lon MB, BS88 All Nations Chr Coll MA98. Wycliffe Hall Ox BTh94. **d** 94 **p** 95. C Ware Ch Ch *St Alb* 94-97; Crosslinks Kenya from 98; Perm to Offic *St Alb* 98-00. *PO Box 72584, Carlile College, Nairobi, Kenya* Tel (00254) (2) 715561

WILLIAMS, David Frank. b 48. S Dios Minl Tr Scheme 91. **d** 94 **p** 95. NSM Romsey *Win* from 94. *24 Feltham Close, Romsey SO51 8PB* Tel (01794) 524050 E-mail revdfw@talk21.com

WILLIAMS, David Gareth. b 58. Lon Univ BD81. Ripon Coll Cuddesdon 82. **d** 84 **p** 85. C Chandler's Ford *Win* 84-88; C Alton St Lawr 88-90; R Crawley and Littleton and Sparsholt w Lainston 90-97; P-in-c Andover 97-09; TR Risborough *Ox* from 09. *The Rectory, Church Lane, Princes Risborough HP27 9AW* Tel (01844) 344784 E-mail rector@stmarysrisborough.org.uk

WILLIAMS, David Gerald Powell. b 35. St Mich Coll Llan. **d** 62 **p** 63. C Canton St Jo *Llan* 62-64; Field Tr Officer Ch in Wales

Prov Youth Coun 63-70; Prov Youth Chapl 65-70; V Treharris *Llan* 70-75; R Flemingston w Gileston and St Hilary 75-78; Warden of Ords 77-80; Dir Past Studies and Chapl St Mich Coll Llan 78-80; Sub-Warden 79-80; Dir Ch in Wales Publications and Communications 80-85; Prov Dir of Educn Ch in Wales 80-85; Dir of Miss Ch in Wales 85-87; Hon Can Llan Cathl 84-93; V Pendoylan w Welsh St Donats 87-93; R Llandudno *Ban* 93-95; Press Officer to Abp of Wales 93-00; rtd 00. *7 The Manor House, St Hilary, Cowbridge CF71 7DP*

WILLIAMS, Canon David Gordon. b 43. Selw Coll Cam BA65 MA69. Oak Hill Th Coll 66. **d** 68 **p** 69. C Maidstone St Luke *Cant* 68-71; C Rugby St Matt *Cov* 71-73; P-in-c Budbrooke 73-74; V 74-81; V Lenton *S'well* 81-87; TR Cheltenham St Mark *Glouc* 87-03; Hon Can Glouc Cathl 96-03; R Toodyay w Goomalling Australia 03-08; rtd 08; Miss Development P Avon Deanery 08-09; Perm to Offic Perth from 08 and *Derby* from 09. *83 Chellaston Lane, Aston-on-Trent, Derby DE72 2AX* E-mail revdwilliams@westnet.com.au

WILLIAMS, David Grant. b 61. Bris Univ BSocSc83. Wycliffe Hall Ox 86. **d** 89 **p** 90. C Ecclesall *Sheff* 89-92; V Dore 92-02; RD Ecclesall 97-02; V Win Ch Ch from 02. *Christ Church Vicarage, Sleepers Hill, Winchester SO22 4ND* Tel (01962) 862414 Mobile 07889-547095 E-mail vicarccwinch@aol.com

WILLIAMS, David Henry. b 33. Trin Coll Cam BA56 MA60 PhD77. St D Coll Lamp 67. **d** 69 **p** 70. C Monmouth 69-70; Chapl St Woolos Cathl 70-71; P-in-c Six Bells 71-76; Libya 76-79; P-in-c Crumlin *Mon* 79-80; R Llanddewi Skirrid w Llanvetherine etc 80-83; Perm to Offic 83-87; Guest Master Caldey Abbey 83-87; V Buttington and Pool Quay *St As* 87-95; Chapl Warsaw *Eur* 95 97; rtd 97. *4 Clos-y-Drindod, Buarth Road, Aberystwyth SY23 1LR* Tel (01970) 612736 E-mail dhw.1933@ukonline.co.uk

WILLIAMS, Canon David Humphrey. b 23. Em Coll Cam BA49 MA54. St Steph Ho Ox 49. **d** 51 **p** 52. C Daybrook *S'well* 51-55; C-in-c Bilborough St Jo Bapt CD 55-62; V Bilborough St Jo 62-63; RD Bulwell 70-88; P-in-c Bestwood Park 71-78; R Hucknall Torkard 63-71; TR 71-88; Hon Can S'well Minster 75-88; rtd 88; Perm to Offic *S'well* from 88. *12 Wollaton Paddocks, Nottingham NG8 2ED* Tel 0115-928 0639

WILLIAMS, David Ivan Ross. b 47. Imp Coll Lon BSc70 Leic Univ MSc72 ARCS70 FBIS. STETS 00. **d** 03 **p** 04. NSM Havant *Portsm* 03-10; Perm to Offic *Ex* from 10. *11 Manor Gardens, Exbourne, Okehampton EX20 3RW* Tel (01837) 851710 Mobile 07866-772025 E-mail david@dirw.demon.co.uk

WILLIAMS, David James. b 42. Chich Th Coll 67. **d** 70 **p** 71. C Charlton-by-Dover St Bart *Cant* 70-74; C Dorking w Ranmore *Guildf* 74-77; C Guildf H Trin w St Mary 77-78; P-in-c E Molesey St Paul 78-88; V Burpham 88-94; rtd 95. *1 Taleworth Close, Ashtead KT21 2PU* Tel (01372) 278056

WILLIAMS, David John. b 30. Open Univ BA79. St D Coll Lamp 64. **d** 66 **p** 67. C Mold *St As* 66-69; C Llanrhos 69-71; R Llangynhafal and Llanbedr Dyffryn Clwyd 71-86; P-in-c Llanychan 77-86; RD Dyffryn Clwyd 86-95; R Ruthin w Llanrhydd 86-95; rtd 95. *16 The Park, Ruthin LL15 1PW* Tel (01824) 705746

WILLIAMS, Canon David John. b 38. AKC62. **d** 63 **p** 64. C Benchill *Man* 63-66; C Heywood St Jas 66-69; V Leesfield 69-73; Chapl TS Arethusa 73-74; TV Southend St Jo w St Mark, All SS w St Fran etc *Chelmsf* 74-80; V Horndon on the Hill 80-93; RD Thurrock 83-92; P-in-c Rochford 93-02; RD Rochford 96-02; P-in-c Sutton w Shopland 98-02; Hon Can Chelmsf Cathl 99-02; rtd 02; Perm to Offic *Ripon* from 02. *29 Stonebeck Avenue, Harrogate HG1 2BN* Tel (01423) 522828

WILLIAMS, David John. b 43. Wadh Coll Ox BA64. St Jo Coll Nottm 73. **d** 75 **p** 76. C Newcastle w Butterton *Lich* 75-79; P-in-c Oulton 79-89; P-in-c Stone Ch Ch 84-89; V Stone Ch Ch and Oulton 89-96; P-in-c Ashley 96-04; P-in-c Mucklestone 96-04; R Ashley and Mucklestone 04-07; rtd 07. *23 Gravel Hill, Ludlow SY8 1QR* Tel (01630) 672210 E-mail williamsjandm@btinternet.com

WILLIAMS, David John. b 52. NOC 92. **d** 95 **p** 96. C Gt Crosby St Luke *Liv* 95-99; V W Derby St Jas 99-04; Chapl R Liverpool Children's NHS Trust from 99. *Alder Hey Children's Hospital, Eaton Road, Liverpool L12 2AP* Tel 0151-228 4811 E-mail revdw1999@hotmail.com

WILLIAMS, Canon David Leslie. b 35. ALCD63. **d** 63 **p** 64. C Bexleyheath Ch Ch *Roch* 63-64; C Gt Faringdon w Lt Coxwell *Ox* 64-66; CMS Uganda 67-73; C Shortlands *Roch* 73-74; Fiji 74-77; V Bromley H Trin *Roch* 77-86; R Meopham w Nurstead 86-96; RD Cobham 86-96; Chapl Thames Gateway NHS Trust 96-01; Hon Can Roch Cathl 98-01; Perm to Offic from 02. *107 Ploughmans Way, Gillingham ME8 8LT* Tel (01634) 372545

WILLIAMS, David Michael. b 50. JP86. Ex Univ BA71 Lon Univ MA77 FSA81 FRSA82. SEITE 05. **d** 08 **p** 09. NSM Redhill St Jo *S'wark* 08-10; NSM Redhill St Matt 10-11; P-in-c Gt Coxwell w Buscot, Coleshill etc *Ox* from 11. *The Vicarage, Great Coxwell, Faringdon SN7 7NG* Tel (01367) 240665 E-mail davidwilliams24@btinternet.com

WILLIAMS, David Michael Rochfort. b 40. St Mich Coll Llan 62. **d** 65 **p** 66. C Pembroke Dock *St D* 65-68; Chapl Miss to Seamen and Ind Chapl 68-71; P-in-c Walwyn's Castle w Robeston W 68-70; R 70-71; Ind Chapl *Mon* 71-74; Hon Chapl St Woolos Cathl 71-74; V Blaenavon w Capel Newydd 74-77; Ind Chapl *St As* 77-88; V Whitford 81-87; V Ruabon 87-92; TR Cen Telford *Lich* 92-00; R Burton and Rosemarket *St D* 00-02; Chapl Miss to Seafarers Milford Haven 00-02; Southampton 02-05; rtd 05; Perm to Offic *Ox* from 05. *13 Sturt Road, Charlbury, Chipping Norton OX7 3SX* Tel (01608) 811284

WILLIAMS, David Norman. b 54. Lanc Univ BSc76 Leeds Univ BA83. Coll of Resurr Mirfield 81. **d** 84 **p** 85. C Ireland Wood *Ripon* 84-87; C Beeston 87-91; V Cross Roads cum Lees *Bradf* 91-99; V Skipton Ch Ch 99-07; P-in-c Carleton and Lothersdale 03-07; V Skipton Ch Ch w Carleton from 07. *Christ Church Vicarage, Carleton Road, Skipton BD23 2BE* Tel (01756) 793612 E-mail dngc@hotmail.co.uk

WILLIAMS, David Paul. *See* HOWELL, David Paul

WILLIAMS, Canon David Roger. b 49. Open Univ BA. St D Coll Lamp. **d** 73 **p** 74. C Llansamlet *S & B* 73-76; C Oystermouth 76-79; V Aberedw w Llandeilo Graban and Llanbadarn etc 79-81; V Brynmawr 81-89; V Newport St Julian *Mon* 89-09; R Penarth and Llandough from 09; Hon Can St Woolos Cathl from 09. *The Rectory, 13 Hickman Road, Penarth CF64 2AJ* Tel (029) 2070 9897 E-mail fr.rogerwilliams@uwclub.net

WILLIAMS (formerly WRIGHT), Denise Ann. b 42. **d** 98. Par Dn Machen *Mon* 98-07; Par Dn Bedwas w Machen w Rudry from 07. *16 Tollgate Close, Caerphilly CF83 3AY* Tel (029) 2086 9792

WILLIAMS, Denise Laraine. b 50. Liv Univ TCert71. NOC 00. **d** 03 **p** 04. C Padgate *Liv* 03-08; P-in-c Cinnamon Brow from 08. *The Rectory, 35 Station Road South, Padgate, Warrington WA2 0PD* Tel (01925) 831297

WILLIAMS, Derek. b 27. Man Univ BSc49. St Deiniol's Hawarden 76. **d** 78 **p** 79. NSM Abergele *St As* 78-97; rtd 97; Perm to Offic *St As* from 97. *48 Eldon Drive, Abergele LL22 7DA* Tel (01745) 833479

WILLIAMS, Derek Ivor. b 37. ACA61 FCA71. **d** 05 **p** 06. OLM Chollerton w Birtley and Thockrington *Newc* from 05. *Buteland House, Bellingham, Hexham NE48 2EX* Tel (01434) 220389

WILLIAMS, Derek Lawrence. b 45. Tyndale Hall Bris 65. **d** 69 **p** 70. C Cant St Mary Bredin 69-71; Gen Sec Inter-Coll Chr Fellowship 71-75; Lic to Offic *St Alb* 78-84 and *Bris* 85-92; Par and Miss Co-ord Northampton St Giles *Pet* 93-97; Dioc Millennium Officer 98-00; Communications Officer *Pet* 00-05 and *Eur* 02-05; Bp's Admin and Press Officer 05-10; Hon C Brington w Whilton and Norton etc 02-08; rtd 11; Dioc Media Adv *Pet* from 11. *7 Montrose Close, Market Harborough LE16 9LJ* Tel (01858) 432709 Mobile 07770-981172 E-mail derek.williams@peterborough-diocese.org.uk

WILLIAMS, Derwyn Gavin. b 69. Trin Coll Cam BA89 MA93. Ripon Coll Cuddesdon. **d** 94 **p** 95. C Harpenden St Nic *St Alb* 94-97; Bp's Dom Chapl 97-00; R Sandy from 00; RD Biggleswade from 09. *The Rectory, High Street, Sandy SG19 1AQ* Tel (01767) 680512 E-mail rector@sandyparishchurch.org.uk

WILLIAMS, Diana Mary. b 36. Bris Univ CertEd56 Leeds Univ BSc57. Oak Hill Th Coll 86. **d** 87 **p** 94. C S Mymms K Chas *St Alb* 87-95; V 95-98; R Sandon, Wallington and Rushden w Clothall 98-04; RD Buntingford 01-06; rtd 04; Perm to Offic *Ely* from 05. *7 Cockhall Close, Litlington, Royston SG8 0RB* Tel (01763) 853079 E-mail di.williams@btinternet.com

WILLIAMS, Ms Diane Patricia. b 53. Dur Univ CertEd74 Lanc Univ MA84. Cranmer Hall Dur 84. **dss** 86 **d** 87 **p** 94. Clubmoor *Liv* 86-90; Par Dn 87-90; Dioc Lay Tr Officer 90-96; Par Dn Everton St Geo 90-94; Assoc P 94-96; Chapl Lanc Univ 96-00; Chapl Edin Univ from 00. *Chaplaincy Centre, The University of Edinburgh, 1 Bristo Square, Edinburgh EH8 9AL* Tel 0131-650 2596 Fax 650 9111 E-mail chaplain@ed.ac.uk

WILLIAMS, Diane Ruth. b 52. Hull Univ BA80 Nottm Univ MA94. Linc Th Coll 92. **d** 94 **p** 95. C Stokesley *York* 94-98; TV Louth *Linc* 98-06; Chapl Linc and Louth NHS Trust 98-01; Chapl United Lincs Hosps NHS Trust 01-06; P-in-c Needham Market w Badley *St E* from 06; RD Bosmere from 09. *10 Meadow View, Needham Market, Ipswich IP6 8RH* Tel (01449) 720316 E-mail dnwil2@aol.com

WILLIAMS, Donald. *See* WILLIAMS, Alfred Donald

WILLIAMS, Mrs Donna Ann. b 64. St Jo Coll Nottm BA00. **d** 00 **p** 01. C Denton St Lawr *Man* 00-03; C Ashton Ch Ch 02-03; P-in-c Droylsden St Martin 03-10; P-in-c Unsworth from 10; P-in-c Hillock from 10. *St George's Vicarage, Hollins Lane, Bury BL9 8JJ* Tel 0161-796 8007 E-mail sweetpea@dwilliams11.freeserve.co.uk

WILLIAMS, Dorian George. b 26. Barrister-at-Law (Gray's Inn) 52. WMMTC 91. **d** 93 **p** 94. NSM Edvin Loach w Tedstone Delamere etc *Heref* 93-98; Perm to Offic from 98. *Howberry, Whitbourne, Worcester WR6 5RZ* Tel (01886) 821189

WILLIAMS, Dylan John. b 72. Univ of Wales (Ban) BTh97. Ripon Coll Cuddesdon 97. **d** 99 **p** 00. C Holyhead *Ban* 99-01; C

Dolgellau w Llanfachreth and Brithdir etc 01-02; P-in-c Amlwch 02-03; R 03-10; P-in-c Porthmadoc and Ynyscynhaearn and Dolbenmaen from 10; AD Llyn and Eifionydd from 10; Asst Dir of Ords from 11. *The Vicarage, Porthmadog LL49 9PA* Tel (01766) 514951 E-mail dylwilliams@lineone.net

WILLIAMS, Edward Ffoulkes (Peter). b 34. ALA65. Chich Th Coll 71. **d** 73 **p** 74. C Kidderminster St Geo *Worc* 73-78; TV Worc St Barn w Ch Ch 78-82; R Exhall w Wixford and V Temple Grafton w Binton *Cov* 82-00; rtd 00; Perm to Offic *Truro* from 00. *Penpons Cottage, Treviskey, Lanner, Redruth TR16 6AU* Tel (01209) 820230

WILLIAMS, Edward Heaton. b 18. St Aid Birkenhead 56. **d** 58 **p** 59. C Timperley *Ches* 58-62; V Macclesfield St Pet 62-66; Sec Dioc Miss Bd 63-67; R Wistaston 66-81; Dioc Bd for Miss and Unity 67-69; V Burton 81-85; rtd 85; Perm to Offic *Ox* 85-94 and *Pet* from 85. *4 Bowmens Lea, Aynho, Banbury OX17 3AG* Tel (01869) 810533

WILLIAMS, Prof Edward Sydney. b 23. FRCP FRCR K Coll Lon BSc PhD MB, BS MD AKC. Sarum & Wells Th Coll 84. **d** 87 **p** 88. NSM Bramley and Grafham *Guildf* 87-89; Hon C Shamley Green 89-94; Perm to Offic 94-05. *Little Hollies, The Close, Wonersh, Guildford GU5 0PA* Tel (01483) 892591

WILLIAMS (née WITHERS), Mrs Eleanor Jane. b 61. Univ of Wales Coll of Medicine MB, BCh85 Anglia Ruskin Univ MA07 MRCGP07. ERMC 04. **d** 07 **p** 08. NSM Milton *Ely* 07-11; V Burwell w Reach from 11. *The Vicarage, 22 Isaacson Road, Burwell, Cambridge CB25 0AF* Tel (01638) 741262 E-mail eleanorjw99@hotmail.com *or* vicar@stmarysburwell.org.uk

WILLIAMS, Elfed Owain. b 24. Newc Univ DipAdEd74. St Deiniol's Hawarden 79. **d** 81 **p** 82. Hon C Whorlton *Newc* 81-82; Hon C Elham w Denton and Wootton *Cant* 82-86; R Barham w Bishopsbourne and Kingston 86-91; rtd 91; Perm to Offic *Newc* from 91. *Chusan, 31 Ryecroft Way, Wooler NE71 6DY* Tel (01668) 281253

WILLIAMS, Emlyn Cadwaladr. b 64. St Jo Coll Nottm 02. **d** 04 **p** 05. C Glanogwen w St Ann's w Llanllechid *Ban* 04-07; R Llanfihangel Ysgeifiog w Llangristiolus etc from 07. *The Rectory, Holyhead Road, Gaerwen LL60 6HP* Tel (01248) 421275 E-mail ecsaer@aol.com

WILLIAMS (née CALDERWOOD), Emma Louise. b 74. Derby Univ BSc96 Univ of Wales (Cardiff) MTh07. St Mich Coll Llan BTh05. **d** 06 **p** 07. C Stanley w Stoneycroft St Paul *Liv* from 06. *28 Brooklands Road West, Liverpool L13 3BQ* Tel 0151-228 2426 E-mail revdem1411@btinternet.com

WILLIAMS, Eric Rees. b 30. Roch Th Coll 60 St Deiniol's Hawarden 71. **d** 72 **p** 73. C Llanelli *St D* 72-75; P-in-c Tregaron 75-76; V 76-82; RD Lampeter and Ultra-Aeron 82-87; V Tregaron w Ystrad Meurig and Strata Florida 82-87; V St Dogmael's w Moylgrove and Monington 87-98; rtd 98. *Ty Elli, 1 Heol Derw, Cardigan SA43 1NH* Tel (01239) 612296

WILLIAMS, Evelyn Joyce. b 37. Cant Sch of Min 86. **d** 89 **p** 94. NSM Sittingbourne H Trin w Bobbing *Cant* 89-09; rtd 09; Perm to Offic *Cant* from 09. *32 Rock Road, Sittingbourne ME10 1JF* Tel (01795) 470372

WILLIAMS, Frederick Errol. b 41. MBIM80. Sarum & Wells Th Coll 86. **d** 88 **p** 89. C Milton *Win* 88-91; P-in-c Chilbolton cum Wherwell 91-94; R 94-06; RD Andover 99-06; rtd 06; TV Fairford Deanery *Glouc* from 10. *The Vicarage, Bibury, Cirencester GL7 5NT* Tel (01285) 740128 E-mail errolsue69@btinternet.com

WILLIAMS, Gareth Wynn. b 67. St D Coll Lamp BA88 Hull Univ MA89 Trin Coll Carmarthen PGCE06. Westcott Ho Cam 89. **d** 91 **p** 92. C Mold *St As* 91-93; TV Hawarden 93-95; Ecum Chapl Glam Univ 95-99; Lect Cardiff Univ from 99; Dir Academic Studies St Mich Coll Llan 99-04; Vice-Prin 02-04; V Roath *Llan* 04-05; Perm to Offic from 05; Hd RS Hawthorn Comp Sch Pontypridd 06-08; Chapl Bp of Llan High Sch from 08. *12 Fairwater Grove West, Llandaff, Cardiff CF5 2JQ* Tel (029) 2056 9581 E-mail fmailk@gwwilliams.net

WILLIAMS, Gavin John. b 61. Down Coll Cam BA84 Wycliffe Hall Ox BA88 Barrister-at-Law 85. **d** 89 **p** 90. C Muswell Hill St Jas w St Matt *Lon* 89-92; Asst Chapl Shrewsbury Sch 92-95; Chapl 95-02; Chapl Westmr Sch from 02; PV Westmr Abbey from 05. *Westminster School, Little Dean's Yard, London SW1P 3PF* Tel (020) 7963 1128 E-mail gavin.williams@westminster.org.uk

WILLIAMS, Geoffrey Thomas. b 35. Ox NSM Course 77. **d** 80 **p** 81. NSM Earley St Bart *Ox* 80-82; NSM Reading St Luke 82-85; V Wembley Park St Aug *Lon* 85-86; C-in-c S Kenton Annunciation CD 86-90; V Streatham Hill St Marg *S'wark* 90-03; rtd 03; Perm to Offic *S'wark* from 04. *78 Park Court, Battersea Park Road, London SW11 4LE* Tel (020) 7498 8272

WILLIAMS, Preb George Maxwell Frazer. b 42. TCD BA65 MA69. Cuddesdon Coll 65. **d** 67 **p** 68. C Bolton St Jas w St Chrys *Bradf* 67-70; C Lich St Chad 70-73; V Shawbury 73-79; P-in-c Moreton Corbet 73-79; V Withnell H Trin 79-86; TR 86-88; V Penn 88-07; Preb Lich Cathl 96-07; RD Trysull 02-06; rtd 07. *2 Highbury Close, Shrewsbury SY2 6SN* Tel (01743) 362315

WILLIAMS, George Ola. b 55. Bradf Univ PhD90 Waterloo Lutheran Univ MA83. St Jo Coll Nottm MTh95. **d** 96 **p** 97. C Enfield St Jas *Lon* 96-00; V Allerton *Bradf* from 00. *The Vicarage, Ley Top Lane, Allerton, Bradford BD15 7LT* Tel (01274) 541948 E-mail george.williams@bradford.anglican.org

WILLIAMS, Canon Giles Peter. b 54. Lon Univ BA77 MA78. Trin Coll Bris 80. **d** 82 **p** 83. C Reading Greyfriars *Ox* 82-85; Rwanda Miss 85-90; Mid-Africa Min (CMS) 90-94; Can Kigali Cathl Rwanda from 90; V Woking St Jo *Guildf* 95-10; RD Woking 08-10; Chapl Cannes *Eur* from 10. *Résidence Kent, 4 avenue Général Ferrié, 06400 Cannes, France* Tel (0033) (4) 93 94 54 61 Fax 93 94 04 43 E-mail mail@holytrinitycannes.org

WILLIAMS, Glyn. b 54. K Coll Lon BD77 AKC77. Ripon Coll Cuddesdon 77. **d** 78 **p** 79. C Coppenhall *Ches* 78-81; C Northampton St Alb *Pet* 81-82; TV Birkenhead Priory *Ches* 82-85; Chapl RAF 85-90 and from 96; Dep Chapl HM Pris Wandsworth 90-91; Chapl HM Pris Elmley 91-95. *Chaplaincy Services, Valiant Block, HQ Air Command, RAF High Wycombe HP14 4UE* Tel (01494) 496800 Fax 496343

WILLIAMS, Graham Parry. b 46. Bp Burgess Hall Lamp 67. **d** 70 **p** 71. C Ebbw Vale *Mon* 70-73; C Trevethin 73-74; V Nantyglo 74-76; Chapl RN 76-85; R Northlew w Ashbury *Ex* 85-87; R Bratton Clovelly w Germansweek 85-87; TV Pontypool *Mon* 88-90; C Skegness and Winthorpe *Linc* 90-91; V Sutton Bridge 91-94; P-in-c Witham Gp 94-97; P-in-c Ruskington 97-01; R 01-03; RD Lafford 02-03; P-in-c Ringstone in Aveland Gp 03-10; rtd 10. *7 Wilkie Drive, Folkingham, Sleaford NG34 0UE* Tel (01529) 497632 E-mail frgraham@btinternet.com

WILLIAMS, Gwenllian. *See* GILES, Mrs Gwenllian

WILLIAMS, Gwilym Elfed. b 33. Univ of Wales (Lamp) BA53. St Mich Coll Llan 53. **d** 56 **p** 57. C Llandudno *Ban* 56-59; C Aberdare *Llan* 59-63; C Penarth All SS 63-65; R Eglwysilan 65-70; V Mountain Ash 70-81; V Llanblethian w Cowbridge and Llandough etc 81-93; P-in-c St Hilary 87-91; V Lisvane 93-00; rtd 00; Perm to Offic *Glouc* 01-07. *55 Heol Llanishen Fach, Cardiff CF14 6LB* Tel (029) 2062 3855

WILLIAMS, Gwyneth. b 47. **d** 10 **p** 11. NSM Gravesend St Geo *Roch* from 10. *8 Christchurch Road, Gravesend DA12 1JL* Tel (01474) 351052 E-mail gwyneth.williams@btinternet.com

WILLIAMS, Harri Alan McClelland. b 85. Ball Coll Ox BA07. St Mich Coll Llan BA10. **d** 10 **p** 11. C Haverfordwest *St D* from 10. *St Thomas House, 3 Scarrowscant Lane, Haverfordwest SA61 1EP* Tel (01437) 768593 Mobile 07891-473144 E-mail harri1985@gmail.com

WILLIAMS, Preb Heather Marilyn. b 42. Oak Hill Th Coll 82. **dss** 85 **d** 87 **p** 94. Taunton Lyngford *B & W* 85-89; Hon C 87-89; C Worle 89-94; V Weston-super-Mare St Andr Bournville 94-03; Preb Wells Cathl 02-03; rtd 04; Perm to Offic *B & W* from 04. *2 Cliff Road, Worlebury, Weston-super-Mare BS22 9SF* Tel (01934) 420711 E-mail williams.heather@btinternet.com

WILLIAMS, Helena Maria Alija. *See* CERMAKOVA, Ms Helena Maria Alija

WILLIAMS, Henry Gordon. b 33. JP83. St Aid Birkenhead 57. **d** 60 **p** 61. C Radcliffe St Mary *Man* 60-63; Australia from 63; rtd 99. *36 Onslow Street, PO Box 259, Northampton WA 6535, Australia* Tel (0061) (8) 9934 1259 Fax 9934 1507 E-mail hgw@wn.com.au

WILLIAMS, The Ven Henry Leslie. b 19. Univ of Wales (Lamp) BA41. St Mich Coll Llan 41. **d** 43 **p** 44. C Aberdovey *Ban* 43-45; C Ban Cathl 45-48; Chapl RN 48-49; C Ches St Mary 49-53; V Barnston 53-84; CF (TA) 54-62; RD Wirral N *Ches* 67-75; Hon Can Ches Cathl 72-75; Adn Ches 75-88; rtd 88; Perm to Offic *Ches* from 88. *1 Bartholomew Way, Chester CH4 7RJ* Tel (01244) 675296

WILLIAMS, Herbert Brian. b 18. BNC Ox BA39 MA48. Linc Th Coll 80. **d** 81 **p** 82. NSM Asterby Gp *Linc* 81-94; rtd 88; Perm to Offic *Linc* 94-97. *55 Upgate, Louth LN11 9HD* Tel (01507) 608093

WILLIAMS, Hilary Susan. *See* PETTMAN, Mrs Hilary Susan

WILLIAMS, Howell Mark. b 56. Univ of Wales (Cardiff) BD87. St Mich Coll Llan 84. **d** 87 **p** 88. C Swansea St Thos and Kilvey *S & B* 87-89; TV Aberystwyth *St D* 89-93; V Hirwaun *Llan* 93-99; V Swansea St Pet *S & B* from 99; AD Penderi from 05. *St Peter's Vicarage, 59 Station Road, Fforestfach, Swansea SA5 5AU* Tel (01792) 581514 E-mail stpeters2@googlemail.com

WILLIAMS, Hugh Marshall. b 38. Lon Univ MB, BS62 Liv Univ MChOrth71 K Coll Lon MA10 FRCS70. SAOMC 95. **d** 97 **p** 98. NSM Lt Compton w Chastleton, Cornwell etc *Ox* 97-01; NSM Chipping Norton 01-08; rtd 08; Perm to Offic *Ox* from 08; *Cov* and *Glouc* from 09. *Wayside, Worcester Road, Salford, Chipping Norton OX7 5YJ* Tel (01608) 646933 Mobile 07889-343456 E-mail hmmwayside@yahoo.co.uk

WILLIAMS, Canon Hugh Martin. b 45. AKC73. St Aug Coll Cant 73. **d** 74 **p** 75. C Heston *Lon* 74-78; Chapl City Univ 78-84; PV Westmr Abbey 82-84; V Newquay *Truro* 84-93; V Christchurch *Win* 93-10; Hon Can Win Cathl 04-10; Preacher Charterhouse and Dep Master from 10. *Preacher's Residence,*

3 Stable Court, Charterhouse, Charterhouse Square, London EC1M 6AU Tel (020) 7490 0498 Mobile 07904-186414 E-mail hugh.m.williams@ukgateway.net

WILLIAMS, Ian Withers. b 43. Linc Th Coll 68. **d** 69 **p** 70. C Burney Lane *Birm* 69-72; C Cleobury Mortimer w Hopton Wafers *Heref* 72-75; V Knowbury 75-79; P-in-c Coreley w Doddington 75-79; V Lich Ch Ch 79-06; rtd 06; Perm to Offic *Heref* from 07. *23 The Oaklands, Tenbury Wells WR15 8FB* Tel (01584) 810528 Mobile 07711-260521

WILLIAMS, Ifan. b 24. St D Coll Lamp 54. **d** 56 **p** 57. C Llangefni w Tregaean *Ban* 56-60; R Llanfachreth 60-67; Dioc Youth Officer 62-65; Area Sec (Merioneth) USPG 63-89; P-in-c Brithdir and Bryncoedifor *Ban* 65-67; R Ffestiniog w Blaenau Ffestiniog 67-89; RD Ardudwy 80-89; rtd 89; Perm to Offic *Ban* from 89. *Cil-y-Coed, 6 Stad Penrallt, Llanystumdwy, Criccieth LL52 0SR* Tel (01766) 522978

WILLIAMS, Mrs Ikuko. b 58. Internat Chr Univ Tokyo BA82 W Michigan Univ MA83 Leeds Univ BA07. NOC 04. **d** 07 **p** 08. NSM Burmantofts St Steph and St Agnes *Ripon* 07-10; NSM Leeds St Cypr Harehills 07-10; Chapl Leeds Teaching Hosps NHS Trust from 10. *97 Gledhow Lane, Leeds LS8 1NE* Tel 0113-266 2385 E-mail ikuko.williams@ntlworld.com

WILLIAMS, James Llanfair Warren. b 48. St Mich Coll Llan 92. **d** 92 **p** 93. C Pembroke Dock *St D* 92-93; C Pembroke Dock w Cosheston w Nash and Upton 93-95; V Cwmaman 95-98; Chapl Costa Blanca *Eur* 98-00; V Meifod w Llangynyw w Pont Robert w Pont Dolanog *St As* from 01. *The Vicarage, Meifod SY22 6DH* Tel (01938) 500231

WILLIAMS, James Nicholas Owen. b 39. MBE. CEng. S'wark Ord Course. **d** 82 **p** 83. C Petersfield w Sheet *Portsm* 82-86; TV Droitwich Spa *Worc* 86-88; R Church Lench w Rous Lench and Abbots Morton 88-94; V Milton *B & W* 94-04; RD Locking 99-04; rtd 04; Dioc Ecum Officer *B & W* 04-08; Hon C Pill, Portbury and Easton-in-Gordano from 04. *151 Charlton Mead Drive, Brentry, Bristol BS10 6LP* Tel 0117-950 4152 E-mail nick.williams@bathwells.anglican.org

WILLIAMS, Janet Patricia. *See* FFRENCH, Mrs Janet Patricia

WILLIAMS, Janet Patricia. b 61. Univ Coll Ox BA83 MSt85 K Alfred's Coll Win PhD98. WEMTC 06. **d** 09 **p** 10. NSM Cirencester *Glouc* from 09. *April Cottage, Elkstone, Gloucester GL53 9PB* Tel (01242) 870148 Mobile 07989-707257 E-mail jpw@cirencester.ac.uk

WILLIAMS, Jeff. b 62. Southn Univ BA MA MPhil Univ of Wales PGCE Surrey Univ BA. STETS 04. **d** 07 **p** 08. NSM Hedge End St Luke *Win* from 07. *32 Goodlands Vale, Hedge End, Southampton SO30 4SL* Tel (01489) 781448 E-mail jeff.w@ntlworld.com

WILLIAMS, Jeffrey. *See* WILLIAMS, Robert Jeffrey Hopkin

WILLIAMS, Jeffrey. b 52. Llan Ord Course. **d** 03 **p** 04. NSM Cardiff St Mary and St Steph w St Dyfrig etc *Llan* 03-07; Chapl Malta and Gozo *Eur* from 07. *Bishop's House, 75 Rudolphe Street, Sliema SLM14, Malta GC* Tel (00356) 2133 0575 Fax 2133 3677 E-mail jeffreywilliams@ntlworld.com

WILLIAMS, Ms Jennifer Ruth. b 66. St Hugh's Coll Ox BA88 PGCE89 Man Univ MA00. Wycliffe Hall Ox 98 NOC 00. **d** 00 **p** 01. C Heatons *Man* 00-04; Hon C Burnage St Marg 04-05; Lect Wycliffe Hall Ox from 05; C Wootton and Dry Sandford *Ox* from 11. *The Vicarage, Wootton Village, Boars Hill, Oxford OX1 5JL* Tel (01865) 735661 Mobile 07784-304985 E-mail jenniwilliams@wycliffe.ox.ac.uk

WILLIAMS, John. *See* WILLIAMS, David John

WILLIAMS, Canon John. b 31. AKC56. **d** 57 **p** 58. C Cockerton *Dur* 57-60; C Camberwell St Geo *S'wark* 60-62; C Stockton St Chad *Dur* 62-65; V 65-68; R Longnewton 65-75; Soc Resp Officer 68-83; Hon Can Dur Cathl 80-83; Bp's Officer for Min *Lich* 83-96; Preb Lich Cathl 83-96; C Lich St Mary w St Mich 95-96; rtd 96; NSM Edin Ch Ch from 97. *2 Fox Spring Rise, Edinburgh EH10 6NE* Tel and fax 0131-445 2983 E-mail jwilliams@foxsprings.plus.com

WILLIAMS, John. b 33. St Chad's Coll Dur BA04. Coll of Resurr Mirfield 05. **d** 07 **p** 08. C Upper Skerne *Dur* 07-10; C Liv Our Lady and St Nic from 10. *Pepys Flat, Liverpool Parish Church, Old Churchyard, Liverpool L2 8TZ*

WILLIAMS, John Anthony. b 53. G&C Coll Cam BA75 MA79 St Jo Coll Dur BA83 PhD86. Cranmer Hall Dur 81. **d** 86 **p** 87. C Beverley Minster *York* 86-89; C Cloughton 89-90; P-in-c 90-93; Clergy Tr Officer E Riding 89-93; P-in-c Emley and Dioc Minl Tr Officer *Wakef* 93-98; Min Scheme Officer 98-06; Co-ord for Local Min 02-06; Dean Wakef Min Scheme 06-08; Hon Can Wakef Cathl 08; Sen Lect York St Jo Univ from 08. *13 Marston Crescent, Acomb, York YO25 5DQ* Tel (01904) 784476 E-mail j.a.williams23@btinternet.com

WILLIAMS, John Barrie. b 38. Univ of Wales (Cardiff) MSc77 DipEd80 PhD91. St Mich Coll Llan 89. **d** 87 **p** 88. NSM Newcastle *Llan* 87-89; C Port Talbot St Theodore 89; Perm to Offic from 89. *Shorncliffe, 11 Priory Oak, Bridgend CF31 2HY* Tel (01656) 660369

WILLIAMS, John Beattie. b 42. Univ of Wales BA66. Cuddesdon Coll 67. **d** 69 **p** 69. C St Helier *S'wark* 69-70; C

Yeovil H Trin *B & W* 70-76; Chapl to the Deaf *Sarum* 76-78; P-in-c Ebbesbourne Wake w Fifield Bavant and Alvediston 76-78; Chapl to the Deaf *B & W* 78-83; TV Fareham H Trin *Portsm* 83-94; R W Wittering and Birdham w Itchenor *Chich* from 94. *The Rectory, Pound Road, West Wittering, Chichester PO20 8AJ* Tel (01243) 514057
E-mail info@stpeterandstpaul.plus.com

WILLIAMS, John David Anthony. b 55. Open Univ BA98. St Steph Ho Ox 85. **d** 87 **p** 88. C Paignton St Jo *Ex* 87-90; C Heavitree w Ex St Paul 90-91; TV 91-01; P-in-c Exminster and Kenn from 01. *The Rectory, Milbury Lane, Exminster, Exeter EX6 8AD* Tel (01392) 824283
E-mail john_williams55@btinternet.com

WILLIAMS, John Francis Meyler. b 34. St Jo Coll Cam BA56 MA60. Sarum & Wells Th Coll 79. **d** 81 **p** 82. C Hadleigh w Layham and Shelley *St E* 81-84; P-in-c Parham w Hacheston 84-87; P-in-c Campsey Ashe and Marlesford 84-87; R Campsea Ashe w Marlesford, Parham and Hacheston 87-95; P-in-c Kedington 95-97; rtd 97; Chapl St Kath Convent Parmoor 97-98; Perm to Offic *Ox* 01-05. *7 Capel Court, The Burgage, Prestbury, Cheltenham GL52 3EL* Tel (01242) 577764
E-mail john.williams34@btinternet.com

WILLIAMS, John Frederick Arthur. b 26. Lon Univ BSc50 Southn Univ PhD53. Ridley Hall Cam 63. **d** 65 **p** 66. C Cambridge H Sepulchre w All SS *Ely* 65-66; P-in-c Cambridge St Mark 66-67; V Portswood Ch Ch *Win* 67-90; Assoc V 90-93; C Win Ch Ch 93-96; rtd 96; Perm to Offic *Win* from 96. *120 Bellemoor Road, Southampton SO5 7QY* Tel (023) 8077 1482

WILLIAMS, John Gilbert. b 36. St Aid Birkenhead 64. **d** 67 **p** 68. C Bollington St Jo *Ches* 67-69; C Oxton 69-72; P-in-c Acton Beauchamp and Evesbatch 72-76; P-in-c Castle Frome *Heref* 72-76; P-in-c Bishop's Frome 72-76; R Kingsland 76-83; P-in-c Eardisland 77-83; P-in-c Aymestry and Leinthall Earles 82-83; R Cradley w Mathon and Storridge 83-94; R Norton St Philip w Hemington, Hardington etc *B & W* 94-01; rtd 01; Perm to Offic *St D* from 02. *Bronydd, Parc y Plas, Aberporth, Cardigan SA43 2BJ* Tel (01239) 810268 E-mail cynwyl@tiscali.co.uk

WILLIAMS, Canon John Heard. b 35. Bris Univ BA58. Clifton Th Coll 59. **d** 59 **p** 60. C Tunbridge Wells Ch Ch *Roch* 59-65; V Forest Gate St Sav *Chelmsf* 65-75; P-in-c W Ham St Matt 72-75; TR Forest Gate St Sav w W Ham St Matt from 75; Hon Can Chelmsf Cathl 82-05. *St Saviour's Rectory, Sidney Road, London E7 0EF* Tel (020) 8534 6109
E-mail jheardwilliams@yahoo.co.uk

WILLIAMS, John Keith. b 63. Ridley Hall Cam 95. **d** 97 **p** 98. C Potters Bar *St Alb* 97-99; C Bishop's Stortford St Mich 99-01; P-in-c Bishop's Stortford 01-08; TR Cheshunt from 08. *The Vicarage, Churchgate, Cheshunt, Waltham Cross EN8 9DY* Tel (01992) 623121

WILLIAMS, Prof John Mark Gruffydd. b 52. St Pet Coll Ox BA73 MSc76 MA77 DPhil79 Ox Univ DSc FBPsS84. EAMTC 86. **d** 89 **p** 90. NSM Girton *Ely* 89-91; Perm to Offic *Ban* 91-03; NSM Wheatley *Ox* 03-09; Perm to Offic from 09. *Hollyfield Cottage, 17 Bell Lane, Wheatley, Oxford OX33 1XY* Tel (01865) 422037 E-mail mark.williams@psychiatry.oxford.ac.uk

WILLIAMS, John Michael. b 44. CQSW74 MBASW. St Deiniol's Hawarden 80. **d** 83 **p** 84. NSM Llanrhos *St As* 83-94; P-in-c Brynymaen w Trofarth 94-95; V 95-99; V Llanrhaeadr-yng-Nghinmeirch and Prion w Nantglyn from 99. *The Vicarage, Llanrhaeadr, Denbigh LL16 4NN* Tel (01745) 890250 E-mail vicar@stdyfnog.org.uk

WILLIAMS, Canon John Peter Philip. b 49. Open Univ BA84. Chich Th Coll 71. **d** 72 **p** 73. C Abergele *St As* 72-77; R Henllan and Llannefydd 77-82; R Henllan and Llannefydd and Bylchau from 82; AD Denbigh 98-09; Hon Can St As Cathl from 01. *The Rectory, Henllan, Denbigh LL16 5BB* Tel (01745) 812628

WILLIAMS, John Roger. b 31. Bris Univ BA55 Lon Univ BD57. Tyndale Hall Bris 57. **d** 57 **p** 58. C Islington H Trin Cloudesley Square *Lon* 57-60; Travelling Sec IVF 60-64; V Selly Hill St Steph *Birm* 64-74; P-in-c Chilwell *S'well* 74-75; V 75-90; Dioc Tourism Officer 90-95; P-in-c Perlethorpe 90-95; P-in-c Norton Cuckney 90-95; rtd 95; Perm to Offic *Derby* from 95. *Derwent Lights, 4 Wyntor Avenue, Winster, Matlock DE4 2DU* Tel (01629) 650142

WILLIAMS, Canon John Roger. b 37. Westmr Coll Ox MTh97. Lich Th Coll 60. **d** 63 **p** 64. C Wem *Lich* 63-66; C Wolverhampton St Pet 66-69; R Pudleston w Hatf *Heref* 69-74; P-in-c Stoke Prior and Ford w Humber 69-74; P-in-c Docklow 69-74; V Fenton *Lich* 74-81; R Shipston-on-Stour w Honington and Idlicote *Cov* 81-92; RD Shipston 83-90; Hon Can Cov Cathl 90-00; R Lighthorne 92-00; V Chesterton 92-00; V Newbold Pacey w Moreton Morrell 92-00; P-in-c Denstone w Ellastone and Stanton *Lich* 00-05; Master St Jo Hosp Lich 05-11; rtd 11; Perm to Offic *Lich* from 11. *3 Curborough Road, Lichfield WS13 7NG* Tel (01543) 419339

WILLIAMS, John Strettle. b 44. MBE00. DipEd73 BA84. NOC 77. **d** 80 **p** 81. Chapl Cen Liv Coll of FE 80-85; Chapl City Coll Liv 85-09; NSM Liv St Paul Stoneycroft 80-83; NSM Liv Our

Lady and St Nic 83-09; Chapl RNR 84-90; CF (TA) from 95; rtd 09. *28 Brook Street, Whiston, Prescot L35 5AP* Tel 0151-426 9598

WILLIAMS, John Trefor. b 23. Worc Ord Coll 65. **d** 67 **p** 68. C Paignton St Jo *Ex* 67-72; V Winkleigh 72-80; P-in-c Ashreigney 73-79; R 79-80; P-in-c Brushford 75-79; V 79-80; R Broadwoodkelly 79-80; P-in-c Berrynarbor 80-81; P-in-c Combe Martin 80-81; R Combe Martin and Berrynarbor 81-92; rtd 92; Perm to Offic *Ex* from 92. *7 Gracey Court, Woodland Road, Broadclyst, Exeter EX5 3GA* Tel (01392) 461130

WILLIAMS, Jonathan Anthony. b 65. Wycliffe Hall Ox BTh95. **d** 98 **p** 99. C Denton Ch Ch *Man* 98-02; R Burnage St Marg 02-05; Hon C Ox St Matt 09-11; P-in-c Wootton and Dry Sandford from 11. *The Vicarage, Wootton Village, Boars Hill, Oxford OX1 5JL* Tel (01865) 735661
E-mail jon.williams@oxford.anglican.org

WILLIAMS, Jonathan Lane. b 59. Dorset Inst of HE 85. STETS 96. **d** 99 **p** 00. NSM Moordown *Win* from 99. *28 Queen Mary Avenue, Moordown, Bournemouth BH9 1TS* Tel and fax (01202) 531630 Mobile 07977-444186
E-mail jonathan.williams7@ntlworld.com

WILLIAMS, Canon Jonathan Simon. b 60. Univ of Wales (Cardiff) BSc81. Coll of Resurr Mirfield 83. **d** 86 **p** 87. C Gelligaer *Llan* 86-89; C Cwmbran *Mon* 89-90; TV 90-97; V Marshfield and Peterstone Wentloog etc 97-00; TR Bassaleg from 00; AD Bassaleg from 99; Can St Woolos Cathl from 07. *The Vicarage, 1 Church View, Bassaleg, Newport NP10 8ND* Tel (01633) 893258 E-mail jonathanwilliams770@btinternet.com

WILLIAMS, Mrs Josephine. b 42. NOC 05. **d** 07 **p** 08. NSM Bootle Ch Ch *Liv* from 07. *179 Worcester Road, Bootle L20 9AE* Tel 0151-933 7729 Fax 525 1995
E-mail josiewilliams1@aol.com

WILLIAMS, Ms Josephine Mary. b 47. Reading Univ BEd78 Hatf Poly MEd87. SAOMC 96. **d** 99 **p** 00. NSM Terriers Ox 99-02; Chapl HM YOI Aylesbury 02-09; rtd 09; Perm to Offic *Ox* from 09. *5 Abbotts Vale, Chesham HP5 3HN* Tel (01494) 791089

WILLIAMS, Joyce. See WILLIAMS, Mrs Kathleen Joyce

WILLIAMS, Julian Thomas. b 65. Clare Coll Cam BA87. Wycliffe Hall Ox BA90. **d** 91 **p** 92. Min Can St D Cathl 91-94; C St D Cathl 91-94; V Cil-y-Cwm and Ystrad-ffin w Rhandirmwyn etc 94-00; R Nursling and Rownhams *Win* from 00. *The Vicarage, 27 Horns Drove, Rownhams, Southampton SO16 8AH* Tel (023) 8073 8293

WILLIAMS, Miss Juliet Susan Joyce. b 83. K Coll Lon BA04. Ridley Hall Cam 09. **d** 11. C St Agnes and Mount Hawke w Mithian *Truro* from 11. *The Vicarage, Church Road, Mount Hawke, Truro TR4 8ED* Tel (01209) 891172 Mobile 07813-660961 E-mail emailjubean@gmail.com

WILLIAMS, Mrs Kathleen Joyce. b 47. Dur Univ TCert71. St Jo Coll Nottm 03. **d** 05 **p** 06. C Exning St Martin w Landwade *St E* 05-08; V from 08. *The Vicarage, 1 New River Green, Exning, Newmarket CB8 7HS* Tel (01638) 577825
E-mail joyfulwilliams2004@yahoo.co.uk

WILLIAMS, Keith. b 37. St Jo Coll Nottm 83. **d** 85 **p** 86. C Holbeck *Ripon* 85-88; R Swillington 88-95; V Batley All SS *Wakef* 95-01; P-in-c Purlwell 95-00; rtd 01; Perm to Offic *Ripon* from 01. *17 Kirkfield Drive, Colton, Leeds LS15 9DR* Tel 0113-260 5852 Mobile 07709-027328
E-mail kwilliams000@btclick.com

WILLIAMS, Keith Douglas. b 41. EMMTC 86. **d** 89 **p** 90. NSM Netherfield w Colwick *S'well* 89-07; NSM Gedling 95-07; Chapl Notts Healthcare NHS Trust 95-03; rtd 07; Perm to Offic *S'well* from 07. *36 Bramble Court, Carnarvon Grove, Gedling, Nottingham NG4 3HX* Tel 0115-961 4850
E-mail keiwil@ntlworld.com

WILLIAMS, Keith Graham. b 38. Reading Univ MSc70 MRICS62. Cranmer Hall Dur. **d** 77 **p** 78. C Almondbury *Wakef* 77-81; C Chapelthorpe 81-82; V Ryhill 82-88; V E Ardsley 88-99; RD Wakef 96-99; rtd 03; Perm to Offic *Chich* from 03. *The Granary, 52-54 Belle Hill, Bexhill-on-Sea TN40 2AP* Tel (01424) 734093

WILLIAMS, Kelvin George John. b 36. ALCD62. **d** 62 **p** 63. C Bath Abbey w St Jas *B & W* 62-65; CF (TA) 64-65 and 70-79; Chapl R Nat Hosp for Rheumatic Diseases Bath 64-65; CF 65-68; C Clevedon St Andr *B & W* 68-70; V Ston Easton w Farrington Gurney 70-74; P-in-c Bradford 74-75; R Bradford w Oake, Hillfarrance and Heathfield 75-76; NSM Puriton and Pawlett 89-91; V 92-02; NSM Bridgwater Deanery 91-92; rtd 02; Perm to Offic *B & W* 03-04 and from 07; P-in-c Weston Zoyland w Chedzoy 04-07. *Highlands, Knowleyards Road, Middlezoy, Bridgwater TA7 0NY* Tel (01823) 698415
E-mail kelvin@revwilliams.freeserve.co.uk

WILLIAMS, (née HANNAH), Mrs Kimberley Victoria. b 75. Bp Grosseteste Coll BSc98. Ripon Coll Cuddesdon BTh01. **d** 01 **p** 02. C Machynlleth w Llanwrin and Penegoes *Ban* 01-02; C Twrcelyn Deanery 02-10; P-in-c Porthmadoc and Ynyscynhaearn and Dolbenmaen from 10. *The Vicarage, Porthmadog LL49 9PA* Tel (01766) 514951
E-mail kimwilliams@lineone.net

WILLIAMS, Lee Lawrence. b 75. St Steph Ho Ox 98. **d** 01 **p** 02. C Cowbridge *Llan* 01-04. *34 Queens Drive, Llantwit Fadre, Pontypridd CF83 2NT*

WILLIAMS, Mrs Linda Leonie Paula. b 56. UEA BA79. SEITE 04. **d** 07 **p** 08. NSM Kenley *S'wark* 07-10; C Harpenden St Nic *St Alb* from 10. *10 Cross Way, Harpenden AL5 4RA* Tel (01582) 713007 E-mail lindalpwilliams@hotmail.co.uk

WILLIAMS, Lloyd. b 43. Oak Hill Th Coll 71. **d** 74 **p** 75. C Laisterdyke *Bradf* 74-77; C Hoole *Ches* 77-80; V Rawthorpe *Wakef* 80-84; HM Pris Leeds 84-85; Chapl HM Pris Cardiff 85-88; Chapl HM Pris Aldington 88-95; R Aldington w Bonnington and Bilsington *Cant* 88-95; RD N Lympne 94-95; P-in-c Tuen Mun Hong Kong 95-99; V Clayton *Bradf* 99-03; rtd 03; Perm to Offic *York* 04-07 and *Wakef* from 08. *46 Royd Court, Mirfield WF14 9DJ* Tel (01924) 480898 Mobile 07866-604345

WILLIAMS, Lois. *See* WILLIAMS, Ms Catherine Lois

WILLIAMS, Mrs Louise Margaret. b 66. Lanc Univ BA87. St Jo Coll Nottm 88. **d** 91 **p** 94. Par Dn W Ham *Chelmsf* 91-94; C Harold Hill St Geo 94-95; Perm to Offic 95-96; C Southend St Sav Westcliff 95-10; Chapl Asst Southend Health Care NHS Trust 97-10; R S Shoebury *Chelmsf* from 10. *The Rectory, 42 Church Road, Shoeburyness, Southend-on-Sea SS3 9EU* E-mail revlwilliams@aol.com

WILLIAMS, Marion. d 08 **p** 09. NSM Glouc St Cath from 08. *6 Kingsholm Square, Gloucester GL1 2QJ* Tel (01452) 538440 E-mail marion-williams@hotmail.co.uk

WILLIAMS, Mark. b 64. St Mich Coll Llan BTh94. **d** 97 **p** 98. C Mountain Ash *Llan* 97; C Mountain Ash and Miskin 97-99; C Neath w Llantwit 99-01; V Skewen from 02. *New Skewen Vicarage, 39 Hill Road, Neath Abbey, Neath SA10 7NT* Tel (01792) 814116

WILLIAMS, Mark. b 73. Pemb Coll Cam BA94 MA98 Ox Univ BA98 MA02. Ripon Coll Cuddesdon 95 Ven English Coll Rome 97. **d** 98 **p** 99. C Caerphilly *Llan* 98-00; V Walworth St Chris *S'wark* 00-10; P-in-c Kennington St Jo w St Jas 10; V from 10; Warden Pemb Coll (Cam) Miss from 00; Dioc Voc Adv from 02. *The Vicarage, 92 Vassall Road, London SW9 6JA* Tel (020) 7735 9340 E-mail fr_mark@yahoo.com

WILLIAMS, Mark John. b 66. St Martin's Coll Lanc BA88 PGCE92 Heythrop Coll Lon MA07. Cranmer Hall Dur 98. **d** 00 **p** 01. C Hockerill *St Alb* 00-03; TV Chipping Barnet 03-09; V Burnley St Matt w H Trin *Blackb* from 09. *St Matthew's Vicarage, Harriet Street, Burnley BB11 4JH* Tel (01282) 424849 E-mail mark.john.williams@lineone.net

WILLIAMS, Mark Robert. b 62. Spurgeon's Coll Lon BA83 Univ Coll of Swansea PGCE84. Ripon Coll Cuddesdon 99. **d** 01 **p** 02. C Wellington and Distr *B & W* 01-05; V Belmont *S'wark* from 05. *St John's Vicarage, Belmont Rise, Sutton SM2 6EA* Tel (020) 8642 2363 E-mail blots@lineone.net

WILLIAMS, The Ven Martin Inffeld. b 37. SS Coll Cam BA62 MA92. Chich Th Coll 62. **d** 64 **p** 65. C Greenford H Cross *Lon* 64-70; Tutor Chich Th Coll 70-75; Vice-Prin 75-77; V Roath St German *Llan* 77-92; Adn Margam 92-01; Adn Morgannwg 02-04; Treas Llan Cathl 92-04; V Penydarren 92-04; rtd 04. *29 Blackfriars Court, Brecon LD3 8LJ* Tel (01874) 622351

WILLIAMS, Martin Jonathan. b 63. Birm Univ BA84. Trin Coll Bris 96. **d** 98 **p** 99. C Bisley and W End *Guildf* 98-01; C Gerrards Cross and Fulmer *Ox* 01-09; R from 09. *The Rectory, Oxford Road, Gerrards Cross SL9 7DJ* Tel (01753) 892571 Mobile 07974-010703 E-mail williamsmartinj@cs.com

WILLIAMS, Mary Edith. b 50. Darlington Tr Coll BEd73. Cranmer Hall Dur 00. **d** 02 **p** 03. C Filey *York* 02-06; V from 06. *The Vicarage, 5 Belle Vue Crescent, Filey YO14 9AD* Tel (01723) 512745 E-mail brmewilliams@supanet.com

WILLIAMS, Mary Elizabeth. b 72. Huddersfield Univ BMus96. Qu Coll Birm BA06. **d** 06 **p** 07. C Birstall and Wanlip *Leic* 06-09. *Address temp unknown* E-mail mary@eclectic.myzen.co.uk

WILLIAMS, Mervyn Gwynne. b 66. WEMTC 97. **d** 06 **p** 07. NSM Stokesay *Heref* from 06; NSM Halford w Sibdon Carwood from 06; NSM Acton Scott from 06; Perm to Offic *Lich* from 08; Chapl Shrewsbury and Telford NHS Trust from 10. *Synolds Farm, All Stretton, Church Stretton SY6 6JP* Tel (01694) 722093

WILLIAMS, Mervyn Rees. b 28. Univ of Wales (Swansea) BA49 Lon Univ PGCE54. St Deiniol's Hawarden 68. **d** 72 **p** 73. NSM Llangollen w Trevor and Llantysilio *St As* 72-94; rtd 94. *12 Wern Road, Llangollen LL20 8DU* Tel (01978) 860369

WILLIAMS, Canon Meurig Llwyd. b 61. Univ of Wales (Abth) BA83 PGCE84 Univ of Wales (Cardiff) BD90. Westcott Ho Cam 90. **d** 92 **p** 93. C Holyhead w Rhoscolyn w Llanfair-yn-Neubwll *Ban* 92-95; P-in-c Denio w Abererch 95-96; V 96-99; V Cardiff Dewi Sant *Llan* 99-05; Adn Ban 05-11; TR Bangor 06-11; TV 11; Bp's Commissary and Chapl *Eur* from 11; Can Malta Cathl from 11. *Bishop's Lodge, Church Lane, Worth, Crawley RH10 7RT* Tel (01293) 883051 Fax 884479 E-mail meurig.williams@churchofengland.org

WILLIAMS, Michael. *See* WILLIAMS, David Michael Rochfort

WILLIAMS, Michael. b 70. St Jo Coll Nottm BA98. **d** 98 **p** 99. C Shifnal *Lich* 98-01; TV Stafford 01-06; TR Penkridge 06-09; Asst Chapl Staffs Univ from 09. *42 Longhurst Drive, Stafford ST16 3RG* Tel (01785) 223823 E-mail revmickwilliams@btinternet.com

WILLIAMS, Michael Dermot Andrew. b 57. Ex Univ BA86 Lon Univ MA02. Ripon Coll Cuddesdon 90. **d** 92 **p** 93. NSM Christow, Ashton, Trusham and Bridford *Ex* 92-97; NSM Marston w Elsfield *Ox* 97-99; Chief Exec Radcliffe Infirmary NHS Trust 97-99; V Shipton-under-Wychwood w Milton, Fifield etc *Ox* 99-02; RD Chipping Norton 01-02; Exec Dir Thames Valley HA 02-05; NSM Kennington 04-05; Chief Exec Taunton and Somerset NHS Trust from 05; Hon C Topsham *Ex* from 07; Hon C Countess Wear from 09. *3 Perriams, Old Ebford Lane, Ebford, Exeter EX3 0QB* Tel (01392) 874087 E-mail williamsmda@btinternet.com

WILLIAMS, Michael John. b 31. St Edm Hall Ox BA53 MA57. Wells Th Coll 53. **d** 55 **p** 56. C Wood Green St Mich *Lon* 55-59; C Bedminster St Aldhelm *Bris* 59-62; C Witney *Ox* 62-65; C Thatcham 66-70; Perm to Offic *Ex* 70-81; C Rainhill *Liv* 81-86; Chapl Whiston Hosp 83-86; rtd 86; Perm to Offic *Ex* from 86. *1 Bramble Lane, Crediton EX17 1DA* Tel (01363) 774005

WILLIAMS, Canon Michael Joseph. b 42. St Jo Coll Dur BA68. Bernard Gilpin Soc Dur 63 Cranmer Hall Dur 64. **d** 70 **p** 71. C Toxteth Park St Philemon *Liv* 70-75; TV Toxteth St Philemon w St Gabr 75-78; Dir Past Studies St Jo Coll Dur 78-88; Prin NOC 89-99; Hon Can Liv Cathl 92-99; P-in-c Bolton St Pet *Man* 99-04; V 04-07; P-in-c Bolton St Phil 04-07; Hon Can Man Cathl 00-07; AD Bolton 02-05; rtd 07; Perm to Offic *Man* from 08. *51 Cotswold Drive, Horwich, Bolton BL6 7DE* Tel (01204) 667162

WILLIAMS, Michael Robert John. b 41. Cranmer Hall Dur 67. **d** 70 **p** 71. C Middleton *Man* 70-73; C-in-c Blackley White Moss St Mark CD 73-79; R Blackley St Mark White Moss 79-86; R Gorton Em 86-96; R Gorton Em w St Jas 96-06; rtd 06; Perm to Offic *Man* from 06. *26 Hawthorn Avenue, Bury BL8 1DU* Tel 0161-761 4712

WILLIAMS, Mrs Nia Catrin. b 69. Univ of Wales (Cardiff) BTh96. St As Minl Tr Course 97. **d** 98 **p** 99. C Llanrhos *St As* 98-02; C Colwyn Bay 02-06; P-in-c Towyn and St George 06-08; V Glanogwen and Llanllechid w St Ann's and Pentir *Ban* 08; AD Ogwen from 10. *Y Ficardy, 5 Rhos y Nant, Bethesda, Bangor LL57 3PP* Tel (01248) 605149 E-mail niacatrinwilliams@btopenworld.com

WILLIAMS, Nicholas Jolyon. b 68. Univ of Wales (Swansea) BA89. Wycliffe Hall Ox BTh96. **d** 96 **p** 97. C Ditton *Roch* 96-99; C N Farnborough *Guildf* 99-05; P-in-c Tongham from 05. *The Vicarage, Poyle Road, Tongham, Farnham GU10 1DU* Tel (01252) 782224 E-mail nickthevic@stpaulstongham.org.uk

WILLIAMS, Nicholas Lindsey. b 62. Birkbeck Coll Lon BA02 Kent Univ BA09. SEITE 06. **d** 09 **p** 10. NSM Dartford H Trin *Roch* 09-11; P-in-c Darenth from 11. *Darenth Vicarage, Lane End, Dartford DA2 7JR* Tel (01322) 227153 Mobile 07747-617262 E-mail nick.williams@rochester-diocese.org

WILLIAMS, Nick. *See* WILLIAMS, James Nicholas Owen

WILLIAMS, Nigel Howard. b 63. St Mich Coll Llan 93. **d** 95 **p** 96. C Denbigh and Nantglyn *St As* 95-97; P-in-c Llanrwst and Llanddoget and Capel Garmon 97-98; R 98-04; V Colwyn Bay 04-08; V Colwyn Bay w Brynymaen from 08; AD Rhos 04-09. *The Vicarage, 27 Walshaw Avenue, Colwyn Bay LL29 7UY* Tel (01492) 539522

WILLIAMS, Norman Ernest. b 23. IEng FIEEE MIET. Llan Dioc Tr Scheme 78. **d** 82 **p** 83. NSM Llanblethian w Cowbridge and Llandough etc 82-93; rtd 93; Perm to Offic *Llan* from 93. *The Poplars, Southgate, Cowbridge CF71 7BD* Tel (01446) 772107 E-mail normanewilliams@compuserve.com

WILLIAMS, Norman Leigh. b 26. Open Univ BA86 Trin Coll Carmarthen 83. **d** 85 **p** 86. NSM Loughor *S & B* 85-96; NSM Adnry Gower 87-96; rtd 96. *Gorwydd Villa, 13 The Woodlands, Gowerton, Swansea SA4 3DP* Tel (01792) 874853

WILLIAMS, Olivia Hazel. b 55. Dun Laoghaire Inst CertEd98 TCD BTh01. CITC 98. **d** 01 **p** 02. C Greystones *D & G* 01-05; Abp's Dom Chapl 03-05; I Carlow w Urglin and Stapleston *C & O* from 05. *The Rectory, Green Road, Carlow, Republic of Ireland* Tel (00353) (59) 913 2565 E-mail williams.olivia2@gmail.com *or* carlow@leighlin.anglican.org

WILLIAMS, Owen David. b 38. S'wark Ord Course 72. **d** 75 **p** 76. NSM Tatsfield *S'wark* 75-80; C Maidstone All SS w St Phil and H Trin *Cant* 80-81; C Maidstone All SS and St Phil w Tovil 81-82; V St Nicholas at Wade w Sarre and Chislet w Hoath 82-92; TV Bruton and Distr *B & W* 92-98; R Kirkby Fleetham w Langton on Swale and Scruton *Ripon* 98-03; rtd 03; P-in-c Walford and St John, Howle Hill etc *Heref* 03-08; Hon C Ross w Walford 08-10. *The Vicarage, Walford, Ross-on-Wye HR9 5QP* Tel (01989) 562703

WILLIAMS, Canon Paul Andrew. b 62. Oak Hill Th Coll BA91. **d** 91 **p** 92. C Ware Ch Ch *St Alb* 91-94; C Harold Wood *Chelmsf* 94-99; C Langham Place All So from 99; V Fulwood *Sheff* from 06; Hon Can Sheff Cathl from 11. *The Vicarage, 2 Chorley Drive, Sheffield S10 3RR* Tel 0114-230 1911 E-mail paulwilliams@fulwoodchurch.co.uk

✠**WILLIAMS, The Rt Revd Paul Gavin.** b 68. Grey Coll Dur BA89. Wycliffe Hall Ox 90. **d** 92 **p** 93 **c** 09. C Muswell Hill St Jas w St Matt *Lon* 92-96; C Clifton Ch Ch w Em *Bris* 96-99; R Gerrards Cross and Fulmer *Ox* 99-09; Hon Can Ch Ch 07-09; Area Bp Kensington *Lon* from 09. *Dial House, Riverside, Twickenham TW1 3DT* Tel 020-8892 7781 Fax 8891 3969 E-mail bishop.kensington@dlondon.org.uk

WILLIAMS, Canon Paul Rhys. b 58. St Andr Univ MTheol82. Westcott Ho Cam 83. **d** 86 **p** 87. Asst Chapl Selw Coll Cam 86-87; C Chatham St Steph *Roch* 87-90; V Gillingham St Aug 90-95; Bp's Dom Chapl 95-03; Hon Can Roch Cathl 01-03; V Tewkesbury w Walton Cardiff and Twyning *Glouc* from 03; AD Tewkesbury and Winchcombe from 09; Hon Can Glouc Cathl from 06. *Abbey House, Church Street, Tewkesbury GL20 5SR* Tel (01684) 293333 *or* 850959 Fax 273113 E-mail vicar@tewkesburyabbey.org.uk

WILLIAMS, Paul Robert. b 66. Huddersfield Poly BA88. Wycliffe Hall Ox. **d** 99 **p** 00. C Roxeth *Lon* 99-03; C Harlow St Mary and St Hugh w St Jo the Bapt *Chelmsf* 03-08; Eurasia Network Developer Radstock Min Mongolia from 09. *Address temp unknown* E-mail paul@radstock.org

WILLIAMS, Mrs Pauline Mary. b 52. Univ of Wales (Cardiff) BD96 Trin Coll Carmarthen PGCE97. St Mich Coll Llan 00. **d** 02 **p** 03. C Coity w Nolton *Llan* 02-06; P-in-c Abercynon 06-11; V Baglan from 11; Dioc Children's Officer from 06. *44 Ynys y Gored, Port Talbot SA13 2EB* Tel (01639) 698878 Mobile 07974-652211 E-mail williamspm89@hotmail.com

WILLIAMS, Penny. See ANDREWS, Ms Penny

WILLIAMS, Canon Peris Llewelyn. b 39. Univ of Wales (Lamp) BA59. Qu Coll Birm 59. **d** 62 **p** 63. C Upton Ascension *Ches* 62-65; C Davenham 65-68; C Grange St Andr 68-73; TV E Runcorn w Halton 73-74; V Backford 74-80; Youth Chapl 74-80; V Witton 80-88; V Hoylake 86-93; R Ches H Trin 93-02; Hon Can Ches Cathl 98-02; rtd 02; Perm to Offic *Ches* and *Lon* 02. *Padarn, 65 Long Lane, Chester CH2 2PG* Tel (01244) 341305

WILLIAMS, Peter. See WILLIAMS, Canon Cecil Peter

WILLIAMS, Peter. See WILLIAMS, Edward Ffoulkes

WILLIAMS, Peter Charles. b 50. SWMTC 98. **d** 01 **p** 02. OLM Landrake w St Erney and Botus Fleming *Truro* from 01. *5 North Road, Landrake, Saltash PL12 5EL* Tel (01752) 851260 E-mail peterfreda@5northroad.fsnet.co.uk

WILLIAMS, Peter Hurrell. b 34. Keble Coll Ox BA58 MA61. Tyndale Hall Bris 62. **d** 64 **p** 65. C Sparkbrook Ch Ch *Birm* 64-67; C Rushden St Pet 67-70; P-in-c Clapham Park All SS *S'wark* 70-78; R Stanford-le-Hope w Mucking *Chelmsf* 78-92; P-in-c Gt Oakley w Wix 92-96; R Gt Oakley w Wix and Wrabness 96-97; rtd 97; Perm to Offic *Chelmsf* from 01. *3 Hillcrest Close, Horndon-on-the-Hill, Stanford-le-Hope SS17 8LS* Tel (01375) 643697

WILLIAMS, Canon Peter John. b 55. Southn Univ BTh80. Chich Th Coll 76. **d** 80 **p** 81. C Chepstow *Mon* 80-84; C Morriston *S & B* 84-85; V Glantawe 85-88; R Reynoldston w Penrice and Llangennith 88-05; R Llangennith w Llanmadoc and Cheriton from 05; Dioc Soc Resp Officer from 88; Hon Can Brecon Cathl from 04. *The Vicarage, Llangennith, Swansea SA3 1HU* Tel (01792) 386391 E-mail peterwilliams.bsr@swanseabrecon.org.uk

WILLIAMS, Philip Allan. b 48. Bris Univ BSc69 CertEd74. Trin Coll Bris 86. **d** 88 **p** 89. C Heref St Pet w St Owen and St Jas 88-93; R Peterchurch w Vowchurch, Turnastone and Dorstone 93-96; P-in-c Holmer w Huntington 96-01; V from 01. *The Vicarage, Holmer, Hereford HR4 9RG* Tel (01432) 273200 E-mail revphil@holmer.supanet.com

WILLIAMS, Canon Philip Andrew. b 64. Sheff Univ BA86. St Jo Coll Dur 88. **d** 90 **p** 91. C Hillsborough and Wadsley Bridge *Sheff* 90-94; C Lenton Abbey *S'well* 94-96; P-in-c 96-02; C Wollaton Park 94-96; V Porchester from 02; AD Gedling from 05; Hon Can S'well Minster from 11. *St James's Vicarage, Marshall Hill Drive, Nottingham NG3 6FY* Tel 0115-960 6185 E-mail phil.stjames@virgin.net

WILLIAMS, Philip James. b 52. St Chad's Coll Dur BA73. Coll of Resurr Mirfield 74. **d** 76 **p** 77. C Stoke upon Trent *Lich* 76-80; TV 80; Chapl N Staffs Poly 80-84; TV Stoke-upon-Trent 80-84; R Shrewsbury St Giles w Sutton and Atcham from 84. *St Giles's Rectory, 127 Abbey Foregate, Shrewsbury SY2 6LY* Tel (01743) 356426 E-mail flyingvic@btinternet.com

WILLIAMS, Ray. b 23. Lon Univ DipEd46. St Aid Birkenhead 56. **d** 58 **p** 59. C Sparkhill St Jo *Birm* 58-60; Area Sec CMS *Chelmsf* and *St Alb* 60-65; V Shenstone *Lich* 65-73; Asst P Blenheim New Zealand 73-78; V Wakefield and Tapawera 78-83; P-in-c Murchison 79-82; Asst P Nelson All SS 83-85; Asst P Havelock and the Sounds 92-96. *8 Kivell Street, Ranui Heights, Porirua 6006, New Zealand* Tel (0064) (4) 238 8911

WILLIAMS, Raymond Howel. b 27. St Jo Coll Cam BA49 MA51 Ball Coll Ox BLitt63. St Jo Coll Nottm 72 NW Ord Course 73. **d** 73 **p** 74. C Derby St Pet 73-76; C Enfield Ch Ch Trent Park *Lon* 75-81; V S Mymms K Chas *St Alb* 81-94; NSM 94-95; rtd 94; Perm to Offic *St Alb* from 95 and *Ely* from 05. *7 Cockhall Close, Litlington, Royston SG8 0RB* Tel (01763) 853079

WILLIAMS, Rhys. See WILLIAMS, Thomas Rhys

WILLIAMS, Richard Dennis. b 57. LTCL79. Coll of Resurr Mirfield 79. **d** 82 **p** 83. C Roath *Llan* 82-85; C Penarth w Lavernock 85-88; V Abertillery *Mon* 88-95; V Tredunnoc and Llantrisant w Llanhennock etc 95-01; V Hay w Llanigon and Capel-y-Ffin *S & B* from 01. *19 Gypsy Castle Lane, Hay-on-Wye, Hereford HR3 1XX* Tel (01497) 820448

WILLIAMS, Canon Richard Elwyn. b 57. Hull Univ BA79. Coll of Resurr Mirfield 79. **d** 81 **p** 82. C Altrincham St Geo *Ches* 81-84; C Stockport St Thos 84-85; C Stockport St Thos w St Pet 86; R Withington St Crispin *Man* 86-95; V Alveston *Cov* from 95; RD Fosse 99-07; Hon Can Cov Cathl from 06. *The Vicarage, Wellesbourne Road, Alveston, Stratford-upon-Avon CV37 7QB* Tel (01789) 292777 E-mail rickvic@fsmail.net

WILLIAMS, Canon Richard Henry Lowe. b 31. Liv Univ BA52. K Coll (NS) BD64 Ridley Hall Cam 54. **d** 56 **p** 57. C Drypool St Andr and St Pet *York* 56-59; Canada 59-64; V Kirkdale St Athanasius *Liv* 64-68; R Much Woolton 68-79; R Croft w Southworth 79-89; Dioc Communications Officer 79-97; Hon Can Liv Cathl 88-97; R Wavertree St Mary 89-97; rtd 97; Perm to Offic *Liv* from 97. *16 Childwall Crescent, Liverpool L16 7PQ* Tel 0151-722 7962

WILLIAMS, Richard Huw. b 63. Bradf and Ilkley Coll BA85. St Jo Coll Nottm 86. **d** 89 **p** 90. C Forest Gate St Edm *Chelmsf* 89-90; C Plaistow 90-92; C Canning Town St Matthias 92-96; V Southend St Sav Westcliff 96-10; RD Southend 05-10; Perm to Offic from 10. *The Rectory, 42 Church Road, Shoeburyness, Southend-on-Sea SS3 9EU*

WILLIAMS, Richard Lawrence. b 62. Warw Univ BSc83 ACA87. Wycliffe Hall Ox 95. **d** 97 **p** 98. C Wallington *S'wark* 97-00; V Addiscombe St Mary Magd w St Martin 00-09; P-in-c Cranbrook *Cant* from 09. *The Vicarage, Waterloo Road, Cranbrook TN17 3JQ* Tel (01580) 712150 E-mail revrwilliams@talktalk.net

WILLIAMS, Robert. b 49. **d** 97 **p** 98. C W Derby St Mary *Liv* 97-01; R Golborne 01-07; V Childwall St Dav from 07; V Stoneycroft All SS from 07. *St David's Vicarage, Rocky Lane, Childwall, Liverpool L16 1JA* Tel 0151-722 4549

WILLIAMS, Robert Edward. b 42. Ex Univ BA63. Lich Th Coll. **d** 65 **p** 66. C Wednesbury St Paul Wood Green *Lich* 65-67; C Whitchurch 67-69; P-in-c Whixall 69-72; P-in-c Edstaston 69-72; CF 72-91; R Cheriton w Tichborne and Beauworth *Win* 91-01; R Upper Itchen 01-02; rtd 02. *84 Portway, Warminster BA12 8QE*

WILLIAMS, Robert Edward. b 50. St Mich Coll Llan BD74 CertEd79. **d** 74 **p** 75. C Flint *St As* 74-77; Asst Chapl Sandbach Sch 79-80; Chapl and Hd RE 80-88; CF 88-05; Chapl Ellesmere Coll 05-08. *Address temp unknown*

WILLIAMS, Robert Jeffrey Hopkin. b 62. Univ of Wales (Abth) BA84 ALAM. Chich Th Coll BTh90. **d** 90 **p** 91. C Eastbourne St Mary *Chich* 90-94; R Upper St Leonards St Jo 94-02; V Twickenham St Mary *Lon* from 02. *37 Arragon Road, Twickenham TW1 3NG* Tel (020) 8892 2318

WILLIAMS, The Ven Robert John. b 51. Cartrefle Coll of Educn CertEd72 Univ of Wales (Ban) BEd73 MA92. St Mich Coll Llan BD76. **d** 76 **p** 77. C Swansea St Mary and H Trin *S & B* 76-78; Chapl Univ of Wales (Swansea) 78-84; Children's Adv 81-88; Asst Dir of Educn 81-88; Bp's Chapl for Th Educn 83-88; R Reynoldston w Penrice and Llangennith 84-88; R Denbigh and Nantglyn *St As* 88-94; V Sketty *S & B* 94-99; Dir of Ords 94-99; P-in-c Port Eynon w Rhosili and Llanddewi and Knelston 99-03; Can Brecon Cathl 95-00; Adn Gower from 00. *56 Pinewood Road, Uplands, Swansea SA2 0LT* Tel (01792) 297817

WILLIAMS, Roger. See WILLIAMS, Canon David Roger

WILLIAMS, Roger. See WILLIAMS, Canon John Roger

WILLIAMS, Roger Anthony. b 54. Univ of Wales (Lamp) BA76. Bp Burgess Hall Lamp 72 Qu Coll Birm 76. **d** 78 **p** 79. C Llanelli *St D* 78-82; V Monkton 82-86; Chapl to the Deaf *B & W* 86-90; Chapl to the Deaf *Ox* from 90. *Denchworth House, Denchworth, Wantage OX12 0DX* Tel and Minicom (01235) 868442 Fax 867402 E-mail roger@williams24.freeserve.co.uk

WILLIAMS, Roger Stewart. b 54. Qu Coll Cam BA75 MA79. Wycliffe Hall Ox BA78 MA82. **d** 79 **p** 80. C Hamstead St Paul *Birm* 79-82; C Barking St Marg w St Patr *Chelmsf* 82-85; V Mildmay Grove St Jude and St Paul *Lon* 85-95; P-in-c Charles w Plymouth St Matthias *Ex* 95-09; Chapl Plymouth Univ 95-09; TR Bloxwich *Lich* from 09. *Bloxwich Rectory, 3 Elmore Row, Walsall WS3 2HR* E-mail rswilliams@supanet.com

WILLIAMS, Roger Thomas. b 54. Man Univ BSc76 Birm Univ MSc78 PhD83 Pemb Coll Cam PGCE92. Ridley Hall Cam 00. **d** 02 **p** 03. C Cambridge St Martin *Ely* 02-05; V Cambridge H Cross from 05. *Holy Cross Vicarage, 192 Peverel Road, Cambridge CB5 8RL* Tel (01223) 413343 Mobile 07751-601066 E-mail rogertw11@hotmail.com

WILLIAMS, Ronald Ernest Nathan. b 66. Univ of Sierra Leone BSc95. St Jo Coll Nottm MPhil05. **d** 05 **p** 06. C Cowplain *Portsm* 05-09; V Rusthall *Roch* from 09. *The Vicarage, Bretland Road, Rusthall, Tunbridge Wells TN4 8PB* Tel (01892) 521357 Mobile 07796-655225 E-mail ronnierenw@hotmail.com

WILLIAMS, Ronald Hywel. b 35. St D Coll Lamp BA62. **d** 63 **p** 64. C Machynlleth and Llanwrin *Ban* 63-66; C Llanaber 66-69; C Hawarden *St As* 69-73; R Llansantffraid Glan Conwy and Eglwysbach 73-77; V Rhosllannerchrugog 77-88; R Cilcain and Nannerch and Rhydymwyn 88-92; V Llanbadarn Fawr w Capel Bangor and Goginan *St D* 92-95; V Llanbadarn Fawr 95-00; RD Llanbadarn Fawr 94-00; rtd 00. *15 Maes y Garn, Bow Street SY24 5DS* Tel (01970) 820247

WILLIAMS (*née* **TYDEMAN**), **Mrs Rosemary (Rose).** b 47. Roehampton Inst TCert69. SAOMC 97. **d** 00 **p** 01. NSM Walton H Trin *Ox* 00-03; NSM E and W Horndon w Lt Warley and Childerditch *Chelmsf* from 03. *The Rectory, 147 Thorndon Avenue, West Horndon, Brentwood CM13 3TR* Tel (01277) 811223 E-mail stevecgs@ukonline.co.uk

WILLIAMS, Ms Rowan Clare. b 67. K Coll Cam BA90 MA93 Jes Coll Cam BA05. Westcott Ho Cam 02. **d** 05 **p** 06. C Leic Resurr 05-08; Chapl Univ Hosps Leic NHS Trust 08-10; Chapl York Univ from 10. *St Lawrence's Vicarage, 11 Newland Park Close, York YO10 3HW* Tel (01904) 415460 Mobile 07919-861912 E-mail rcw514@york.ac.uk

✠**WILLIAMS, The Most Revd and Rt Hon Rowan Douglas.** b 50. PC02. Ch Coll Cam BA71 MA75 Wadh Coll Ox DPhil75 DD89 Erlangen Hon DrTheol99 FBA90 Hon FGCM00. Coll of Resurr Mirfield 75. **d** 77 **p** 78 **c** 92. Tutor Westcott Ho Cam 77-80; Hon C Chesterton St Geo *Ely* 80-83; Lect Div Cam Univ 80-86; Dean Clare Coll Cam 84-86; Can Th Leic Cathl 81-92; Lady Marg Prof Div Ox Univ 86-92; Can Res Ch Ch *Ox* 86-92; Bp Mon 92-02; Abp Wales 99-02; Abp Cant from 02. *Lambeth Palace, London SE1 7JU,* or *The Old Palace, Canterbury CT1 2EE* Tel (020) 7898 1200 *or* (01227) 459401 Fax (020) 7401 9886

WILLIAMS, Canon Roy. b 28. Ely Th Coll 58. **d** 60 **p** 61. C Daybrook *S'well* 60-63; V Bilborough St Jo 63-73; V Arnold 73-92; Hon Can S'well Minster 85-92; rtd 92; Perm to Offic *S'well* from 92. *10 Maris Drive, Burton Joyce, Nottingham NG14 5AJ* Tel 0115-931 2030

WILLIAMS, Mrs Sandra Elizabeth. b 60. STETS 06. **d** 09 **p** 10. C Wrockwardine Deanery *Lich* from 09. *The Parsonage, Upton Magna, Shrewsbury SY4 4TZ* E-mail sandra.williams3@btinternet.com

WILLIAMS (*née* **CROSLAND), Mrs Sarah Rosita.** b 50. St Mary's Coll Chelt CertEd71 BEd72. EAMTC 01. **d** 03 **p** 04. C Warmley, Syston and Bitton *Bris* 03-06; Asst Chapl Tervuren Eur 06-09; P-in-c Lydd *Cant* from 09. *All Saints' Rectory, Park Street, Lydd, Romney Marsh TN29 9AY* Tel (01797) 320345 E-mail revsarahwilliams@porfalas.plus.com

WILLIAMS, Canon Shamus Frank Charles. b 57. St Cath Coll Cam BA79 MA83. Ripon Coll Cuddesdon 81. **d** 84 **p** 85. C Swanage and Studland *Sarum* 84-87; C St Alb St Pet *St Alb* 87-90; TV Saffron Walden w Wendens Ambo and Littlebury *Chelmsf* 90-95; R Shingay Gp *Ely* from 95; RD Shingay from 97; Hon Can Ely Cathl from 05. *The Vicarage, Church Street, Guilden Morden, Royston SG8 0JD* Tel (01763) 853067 E-mail shamuswilliams@waitrose.com

WILLIAMS, Mrs Sheena Jane. b 72. Aber Univ LLB95. STETS 07. **d** 10 **p** 11. C Swaythling *Win* from 10. *14 Underwood Road, Southampton SO16 7BZ* Tel (023) 8070 1527 Mobile 07787-155321 E-mail rev@williamspost.me.uk

WILLIAMS, Stephen Clark. b 47. Univ of Wales (Cardiff) BSc(Econ)69 Warw Univ MSc70. Wycliffe Hall Ox 91. **d** 93 **p** 94. C High Wycombe *Ox* 93-96; C Walton H Trin 96-97; TV 97-03; Acting TR 01-03; P-in-c E and W Horndon w Lt Warley and Childerditch *Chelmsf* from 03; Ind Chapl from 05. *The Rectory, 147 Thorndon Avenue, West Horndon, Brentwood CM13 3TR* Tel (01277) 811223 E-mail stevecgs@ukonline.co.uk

WILLIAMS, Stephen Grant. b 51. K Coll Lon BD73 AKC73. **d** 75 **p** 76. C Paddington Ch Ch *Lon* 75-78; C Paddington St Jas 78-80; Chapl LSE 80-91; Chapl (Sen) Lon Univs from 91. *15 Wilmington Square, London WC1X 0ER* Tel (020) 7837 1782 *or* 7580 9812 Fax 7631 3210 E-mail chaplaincy@lon.ac.uk

WILLIAMS, Stephen James. b 52. Lon Univ BSc73. Ridley Hall Cam 73. **d** 78 **p** 79. C Waltham Abbey *Chelmsf* 78-82; C Bedford St Paul *St Alb* 82-86; P-in-c Chalgrave 86-88; V Harlington from 86. *The Vicarage, Church Road, Harlington, Dunstable LU5 6LE* Tel (01525) 872413 E-mail sjw@harlingtonchurch.org.uk *or* sjw@lutonsfc.ac.uk

WILLIAMS, The Very Revd Stephen John. b 49. Univ of NSW BA73 DipEd73 Cam Univ BA77 MA81 Macquarie Univ (NSW) MA92. Ridley Hall Cam 75. **d** 78 **p** 79. Lect Th Bp Tucker Coll Uganda 78; C Brompton H Trin w Onslow Square St Paul *Lon* 79-82; C Shenton Park Australia 82-83; Chapl Blue Mountains Gr Sch 84-90; R W Lindfield 91-01; Dean Armidale from 02. *PO Box 749, Armidale NSW 2350, Australia* Tel (0061) (2) 6772 2269 Fax 6772 0188 E-mail dean@northnet.com.au

WILLIAMS, Stephen Lionel. b 48. St Kath Coll Liv CertEd73 Open Univ BA77. NOC 93. **d** 96 **p** 97. NSM Hough Green St Basil and All SS *Liv* 96-99; C Padgate 99-02; V Walton St Jo *L9 8HF* Tel and fax 0151-525 3458 E-mail frstephen320@hotmail.com

WILLIAMS, Canon Stephen Stuart. b 60. Magd Coll Ox BA82 Dur Univ BA88. Cranmer Hall Dur 86. **d** 89 **p** 90. C W Derby Gd Shep *Liv* 89-93; Relig Affairs Producer BBC Radio Merseyside 92-00; TV Liv Our Lady and St Nic w St Anne 93-01; P-in-c Prestwich St Gabr *Man* from 01; C Prestwich St Mary from 10; C Prestwich St Marg from 10; Bp's Dom Chapl 01-05; Interfaith Adv from 05; Hon Can Man Cathl from 10. *St Gabriel's Vicarage, 8 Bishops Road, Prestwich, Manchester M25 0HT* Tel 0161-773 8839 *or* 792 2096 Mobile 07813-436170 E-mail saintgabriel@talktalk.net

WILLIAMS, Susan. b 50. Swansea Coll of Educn CertEd72. Ban Ord Course 94. **d** 97 **p** 98. NSM Criccieth w Treflys *Ban* 97-00; P-in-c 00-01; P-in-c Criccieth and Treflys w Llanystumdwy etc 01-02; R 02-10; rtd 11. *Taleifion, High Street, Criccieth LL52 0RN* Tel (01766) 523222 *or* (01248) 354999 Fax 523183 E-mail rev.sue-williams@btopenworld.com

WILLIAMS, Mrs Susan Glynnis. b 41. Nottm Univ MA00. EMMTC 05. **d** 06 **p** 07. NSM Graffoe Gp *Linc* from 06. *69 High Street, Navenby, Lincoln LN5 0ET* Tel (01522) 810445

WILLIAMS, Ms Susan Jean. b 54. Ches Coll of HE MTh00 Lanc Univ MA02 PhD09. NOC 95. **d** 98 **p** 99. C Prescot *Liv* 98-01; Perm to Offic *Blackb* 01-02; C Scotforth 02-05; P-in-c Chipping and Whitewell 05-09; Warden of Readers and Past Assts from 09; Vice-Prin LCTP from 05. *St Leonard's House, Potter Lane, Samlesbury, Preston PR5 0UE* Tel (01772) 877930 Mobile 07904-076864 E-mail williams.ammasue@googlemail.com

WILLIAMS, Mrs Susan Merrilyn Marsh. b 62. Univ of Wales (Ban) BTh05. Ban Ord Course 00. **d** 03 **p** 04. C Botwnnog w Bryncroes *Ban* 03-08; P-in-c Nefyn w Tudweiliog w Llandudwen w Edern 08-11; V from 11. *The Vicarage, Lon Isaf, Morfa Nefyn, Pwllheli LL53 6BS* Tel (01758) 720494 E-mail susannefyn@aol.com

WILLIAMS, Suzan. b 71. WEMTC. **d** 11. C Church Stretton *Heref* from 11. *26 Churchill Road, Church Stretton SY6 6AE* Tel (01694) 722588 Mobile 07921-825532 E-mail suzan.williams@strettonparish.org.uk

WILLIAMS, Terence. b 36. Univ of Wales (Abth) BSc57 Univ of Wales (Cardiff) MA67 Aston Univ PhD71. Glouc Sch of Min 78. **d** 81 **p** 81. NSM Deerhurst, Apperley w Forthampton and Chaceley *Glouc* 81-87; NSM Tarrington w Stoke Edith, Aylton, Pixley etc *Heref* 87-88; P-in-c Upper and Lower Slaughter w Eyford and Naunton *Glouc* 88-91; P-in-c Redmarley D'Abitot, Bromesberrow w Pauntley etc 91-95; R 95-99; RD Forest N 95-99; rtd 99; Perm to Offic *Glouc* 99-02; P-in-c Hasfield w Tirley and Ashleworth 02-05. *Meadowside, Gloucester Road, Hartpury, Gloucester GL19 3BT* Tel (01452) 700644

WILLIAMS, Terence James. b 76. St Jo Coll Dur BA05. Cranmer Hall Dur 02. **d** 05 **p** 06. C Bolsover *Derby* 05-09; P-in-c Codnor from 09; P-in-c Horsley and Denby from 11; C Morley w Smalley and Horsley Woodhouse from 11; RD Heanor from 11. *The Vicarage, 20 Codnor Denby Lane, Codnor, Ripley DE5 9SN* Tel (01773) 742516 E-mail wterry774@aol.com

WILLIAMS, Terence John. b 36. Univ of Wales BSc62. St Deiniol's Hawarden 85. **d** 86 **p** 87. C Llangyfelach *S & B* 86-88; C Morriston 88-89; V Llanwrtyd w Llanddulas in Tir Abad etc 89-91; V Llanedi w Tycroes and Saron *St D* 91-00; rtd 01. *Coedmawr, 50 Swansea Road, Penllergaer, Swansea SA4 9AQ* Tel (01792) 892110

WILLIAMS, Thomas Bruce. b 41. Oak Hill Th Coll 74. **d** 76 **p** 77. C Liskeard w St Keyne and St Pinnock *Truro* 76-79; Min Bush Ch Aid Soc Paraburdoo Australia 79-80; C W Pilbara 79-81; R Wyndham and Kununurra 81-83; R Wyalkatchem w Dowerin and Koorda 83-87; R Tennan Creek 93-99; rtd 99; Perm to Offic Bendigo from 99. *1 Thomas Street, Bendigo Vic 3550, Australia* Tel (0061) (3) 5444 0485

WILLIAMS, Thomas Rhys. b 40 **p** 05. NSM Llandygai and Maes y Groes *Ban* 04-05; NSM Bangor 05-07; Perm to Offic from 07. *Groeslon, Talybont, Bangor LL57 3YG* Tel (01248) 372934

WILLIAMS, Timothy John. b 54. BEd83. Trin Coll Carmarthen. **d** 89 **p** 90. NSM Llansamlet *S & B* 89-97; P-in-c Bryngwyn and Newchurch and Llanbedr etc 97-01; V Aberedw w Llandeilo Graban and Llanbadarn etc 01-10; V Brecon St David w Llanspyddid and Llanilltyd from 10. *Maes y Haf, Llanspyddid, Brecon LD3 8PB* Tel (01874) 624774

WILLIAMS, Timothy John. b 64. Kent Univ BA86. St Mich Coll Llan BD89. **d** 89 **p** 90. C Killay *S & B* 89-91; C Llwynderw 91-94; V Knighton and Norton 94-00; P-in-c Whitton w Pilleth w Cascob 99-00; V Killay from 00; Dioc Communications Officer from 10. *The Vicarage, 30 Goetre Fach Road, Killay, Swansea SA2 7SG* Tel (01792) 204233 E-mail fr_tim_williams@ntlworld.com

WILLIAMS, Tracey. b 62. **d** 11. NSM Sunninghill and S Ascot *Ox* from 11. *14 Devon Chase, Warfield, Bracknell RG42 3JN* Tel (01344) 412159

✠**WILLIAMS, The Rt Revd Trevor Russell.** b 48. TCD BA71. St Jo Coll Nottm BA73. **d** 74 **p** 75 **c** 08. C Maidenhead St Andr and St Mary *Ox* 74-77; Asst Chapl QUB 78-80; Relig Broadcasting Producer BBC 81-88; I Newcastle *D & D* 88-93; Ldr Corrymeela Community 93-03; I Belfast H Trin and St Silas

Conn 03-08; Preb Rathmichael St Patr Cathl Dublin 02-08; Bp L & K from 08. *Rien Roe, Adare, Co Limerick, Republic of Ireland* Tel (00353) (61) 396244
E-mail bishop@limerick.anglican.org

WILLIAMS, Canon Trevor Stanley Morlais. b 38. Jes Coll Ox BA63 Univ of E Africa MA67. Westcott Ho Cam BA67. **d** 67 **p** 68. C Clifton St Paul *Bris* 67-70; Asst Chapl Bris Univ 67-70; Chapl and Fell Trin Coll Ox 70-05; Hon Can Ch Ch *Ox* 93-05; rtd 05. *13 Southmoore End, Oxford OX2 6RF* Tel (01865) 553975 E-mail trevor.williams@trinity.ox.ac.uk

WILLIAMS, Valerie Jane. b 53. **d** 03 **p** 04. OLM Merstham and Gatton *S'wark* 03-10; OLM Merstham, S Merstham and Gatton from 10. *Merstham Lodge, Harps Oak Lane, Merstham, Redhill RH1 3AN* Tel (01737) 644850
E-mail valwilliams@vwilliams99.freeserve.co.uk

WILLIAMS, Walter Haydn. b 31. Univ of Wales (Lamp) BA53 Selw Coll Cam BA55 MA60. St Mich Coll Llan 55. **d** 56 **p** 57. C Denbigh *St As* 56-58; V Choral St As Cathl 58-61; C St As 58-61; R Llanfyllin 61-68; V Northop 68-73; V Mold 73-86; RD Mold 79-86; Can St As Cathl 77-82; Prec 81-82; Preb and Chan 82-86; R Overton and Erbistock and Penley 86-94; Chmn Ch of Wales Liturg Cttee 86-94; rtd 94. *2 Park Lane, Craig y Don, Llandudno LL30 1PQ* Tel (01492) 877294

WILLIAMS, William David Brynmor. b 48. Open Univ BA89. St D Coll Lamp 71. **d** 72 **p** 73. C Killay *S & B* 72-74; C Wokingham All SS *Ox* 74-75; CF 75-77; C Spilsby w Hundleby *Linc* 83-87; R Meppershall w Campton and Stondon *St Alb* 87-90; V Hemsby *Nor* 90-96; P-in-c Winterton w E and W Somerton and Horsey 94-96; rtd 96. *The Old School, 14 Weekley, Kettering NN16 9UW* Tel (01536) 417612

WILLIAMS, William Garmon. b 42. Univ of Wales (Abth) BA64. Linc Univ Sch of Th & Min Studies 04. **d** 09 **p** 10. OLM Spring Line Gp *Linc* from 09; Chapl Linc Distr Health Services and Hosps NHS Trust from 10. *16 The Green, Ingham, Lincoln LN1 2XT* Tel and fax (01522) 730365 Mobile 07811-347579
E-mail jennywilliams.bees@virgin.net

WILLIAMS-HUNTER, Ian Roy. b 44. Trin Coll Bris 71. **d** 73 **p** 74. C Redhill H Trin *S'wark* 73-75; C Deane *Man* 76-80; R Hartshorne *Derby* 80-02; P-in-c Bretby w Newton Solney 01-02; R Hartshorne and Bretby from 02. *The Rectory, 74 Woodville Road, Hartshorne, Swadlincote DE11 7ET* Tel (01283) 217866
E-mail ianrwhunter@aol.com

WILLIAMS-POTTER, Mrs Amanda Clare. b 69. Univ of Wales (Ban) BD90. Westcott Ho Cam 90. **d** 92 **p** 97. C Carmarthen St Dav *St D* 92-94; Chapl Trin Coll Carmarthen 94-99; V Llannon *St D* 99-01; TV Cwm Gwendraeth 01-05; C Cynwil Elfed and Newchurch 05-07; Bp's Chapl and Communications Officer 05-08. *3 Blende Road, Llandeilo SA19 6NE*

WILLIAMSON, Alfred Michael. b 28. Kelham Th Coll 53. **d** 58 **p** 59. C Nottingham St Geo w St Jo *S'well* 58-64; SSM 60-64; V Kenwyn St Geo *Truro* 64-73; V St Agnes 73-87; R Beverley w Brookton Australia 87-93; rtd 93. *19 Lakeview Crescent, Forster NSW 2428, Australia* Tel (0061) (2) 6554 8702
E-mail coomba@tsn.cc

WILLIAMSON, Alister. See WILLIAMSON, Ivan Alister

WILLIAMSON, Andrew John. b 39. MRPharmS62. St Alb Minl Tr Scheme 82. **d** 85 **p** 86. NSM Oxhey All SS *St Alb* 85-88; NSM Bricket Wood 88-97; NSM Campbeltown *Arg* 97-08; Lic to Offic from 08. *Pier View, Low Askomil, Campbeltown PA28 6EP* Tel (01586) 551478 Mobile 07970-708191
E-mail aj.gsw@tiscali.co.uk

WILLIAMSON, Mrs Anne. b 57. **d** 04 **p** 05. NSM Blackheath St Jo *S'wark* 04-08; Co-ord Chapl Greenwich and Bexley Cottage Hospice from 08. *160 Langton Way, London SE3 7JR* Tel (020) 8853 5309 E-mail annecwilliamson@aol.com

WILLIAMSON, Canon Anthony William. b 33. OBE77 DL98. Trin Coll Ox BA56 MA60. Cuddesdon Coll 56. **d** 60 **p** 61. Hon C Cowley St Jas *Ox* 60-79; TV 79-89; Dir of Educn (Schs) 89-00; Hon Can Ch Ch 94-00; rtd 00. *9 The Goggs, Watlington OX49 5JX* Tel (01491) 612143
E-mail tony_williamson@lineone.net

WILLIAMSON, Brian. See WILLIAMSON, John Brian Peter

WILLIAMSON, David Barry. b 56. St Jo Coll Nottm 80. **d** 83 **p** 84. C N Mymms *St Alb* 83-86; C Burley *Ripon* 86-92; Project Worker CECS 92-96; Youth and Children's Adv *B & W* 96-04; Dir Time For God from 04. *Time For God, 2 Chester House, Pages Lane, London N10 1PR* Tel (020) 8883 1504 Fax 8365 2471

WILLIAMSON, Desmond Carl. b 63. QUB BSc84 Westmr Coll Ox MTh03. Trin Coll Bris 03. **d** 05 **p** 06. C Portishead *B & W* 05-10; V Tattenham Corner *Guildf* from 10. *St Mark's Vicarage, St Mark's Road, Epsom KT18 5JH* Tel (01737) 353011
E-mail deswilliams@tiscali.co.uk

WILLIAMSON, Edward MacDonald. b 42. CITC 67. **d** 69 **p** 70. C Limerick St Mary *L & K* 69-70; CF 70-73; C Penzance St Mary w St Paul *Truro* 73-76; V Mullion 76-81; rtd 81; Perm to Offic *Truro* from 81. *Hazelmere, The Commons, Mullion, Helston TR12 7HZ* Tel (01326) 240865

WILLIAMSON, Henry Lyttle (Ray). b 47. Lon Bible Coll BA02. **d** 95 **p** 96. P-in-c Edin St Marg 96-02; P-in-c Edin St Salvador 02-04; NSM Edin St Ninian 04-07. *6/5 St Triduana's Rest, Edinburgh EH7 6LN* Tel 0131-652 0111 Mobile 07718-971914

WILLIAMSON, Ivan Alister. b 63. TCD BTh90. CITC 87. **d** 90 **p** 91. C Lisburn St Paul *Conn* 90-95; C Roxbourne St Andr *Lon* 95-99; Lect QUB from 95; Bp's C Ematris w Rockcorry, Aghabog and Aughnamullan *Clogh* 99-01; I Errigle Keerogue w Ballygawley and Killeshil *Arm* 05-10. *Richmond Rectory, 24 Old Omagh Road, Ballygawley, Dungannon BT70 2AA* Tel (028) 8556 7857 Mobile 07814-983746
E-mail revdalisterwilliamson@yahoo.co.uk

WILLIAMSON, Mrs Jennifer Irene. b 44. Glas Univ MA66 Sunderland Poly Dip Teaching79. NEOC 89. **d** 92 **p** 94. NSM Easby w Brompton on Swale and Bolton on Swale *Ripon* 92-95; P-in-c Gilling and Kirkby Ravensworth 95-05; rtd 05. *65 Whitefields Drive, Richmond DL10 7DL* Tel (01748) 824365

WILLIAMSON, John Brian Peter. b 30. Selw Coll Cam PhD55 CEng EurIng FIMechE FIEE FInstP FWeldI. WMMTC. **d** 84 **p** 87. NSM Malvern H Trin and St Jas *Worc* 84-94; Perm to Offic from 94. *Monkfield House, Newland, Malvern WR13 5BB* Tel (01905) 830522

WILLIAMSON, Kathleen Lindsay. b 50. Leeds Univ Medical Sch MB, ChB74 Liv Univ BSc87. NOC 00. **d** 03 **p** 04. NSM Stretton and Appleton Thorn *Ches* 03-06; NSM Frodsham from 06. *37 Waterside Drive, Frodsham WA6 7NF* Tel 07899-664068 (mobile)

WILLIAMSON, Mrs Mary Christine. b 46. Bulmershe Coll of HE BEd79. SWMTC 05. **d** 09 **p** 10. NSM Launceston *Truro* from 09. *73 St John's Road, Launceston PL15 7DE* Tel (01566) 778902 Mobile 07900-477181
E-mail marywilliamson73@tiscali.co.uk

WILLIAMSON, Michael. See WILLIAMSON, Alfred Michael

WILLIAMSON, Canon Michael John. b 39. ALCD63. **d** 64 **p** 65. C Pennington *Man* 64-67; C Higher Openshaw 67-69; P-in-c Man St Jerome w Ardwick St Silas 69-72; C-in-c Holts CD 72-77; R Droylsden St Mary 77-04; Hon Can Man Cathl 97-04; rtd 04; Perm to Offic *Man* from 04. *49 Ennerdale Road, Astley, Tyldesley, Manchester M29 7AR* Tel (01942) 870274

WILLIAMSON, Olwen Joan. b 43. **d** 03 **p** 04. OLM Mortlake w E Sheen *S'wark* from 03. *25 Christchurch Road, London SW14 7AB* Tel and fax (020) 8876 7183
E-mail olwenontour@hotmail.com

WILLIAMSON, Paul Nicholas. b 55. Univ of Otago BTh79 Nottm Univ MPhil93. St Jo Coll Auckland 80. **d** 80 **p** 81. C Andersons Bay New Zealand 80-82; V Winton-Otautau 82-86; C Selston *S'well* 86-88; V St Kilda New Zealand 88-92; Min Educator 88-92; V Milton-Tuapeka and Taieri 92-96; V Hataitai-Kilbirnie from 96; Nat Co-ord Angl Renewal Min 99-03; Ldr New Wine from 03. *94 Hamilton Road, Hataitai, Wellington 6021, New Zealand* Tel (0064) (4) 971 2140 or 386 3041 Fax 386 3041 E-mail leader@new-wine.net.nz

WILLIAMSON, Paul Stewart. b 48. K Coll Lon BD71 AKC71. **d** 72 **p** 73. C Deptford St Paul *S'wark* 72-75; Hon C Kennington St Jo 76-77; C Hoxton H Trin w St Mary *Lon* 78-83; C St Marylebone All SS 83-84; C Willesden St Mary 84-85; Perm to Offic 86-89; C Hanworth St Geo 89-92; P-in-c from 92. *The Rectory, 7 Blakewood Close, Feltham TW13 7NL* Tel (020) 8844 0457

WILLIAMSON, Ralph James. b 62. LSE BSc(Econ)84. Ripon Coll Cuddesdon BA89 MA97. **d** 90 **p** 91. C Southgate St Andr *Lon* 90-93; TV Ross w Brampton Abbotts, Bridstow, Peterstow etc *Heref* 93-97; Chapl Ch Ch Ox from 97. *Christ Church, Oxford OX1 1DP* Tel (01865) 276236

WILLIAMSON, Ray. See WILLIAMSON, Henry Lyttle

WILLIAMSON, Robert Harvey (Robin). b 45. **d** 02 **p** 03. OLM Maidstone St Luke *Cant* from 02. *Holly Bank, Bower Mount Road, Maidstone ME16 8AU* Tel (01622) 682959
E-mail robin.helen@tesco.net

WILLIAMSON, Robert John. b 55. K Coll Lon BA77. Coll of Resurr Mirfield 78. **d** 79 **p** 80. C Kirkby *Liv* 79-82; C Warrington St Elphin 82-84; P-in-c Burneside *Carl* 84-90; V Walney Is 90-00; V Darlington St Cuth *Dur* from 00. *The Vicarage, 26 Upsall Drive, Darlington DL3 8RB* Tel (01325) 358911

✠**WILLIAMSON, The Rt Revd Robert Kerr (Roy).** b 32. Kingston Univ DEd98. Oak Hill Th Coll 61. **d** 63 **p** 64 **c** 84. C Crowborough *Chich* 63-66; V Hyson Green *S'well* 66-72; V Nottingham St Ann w Em 72-76; V Bramcote 76-79; Adn Nottingham 78-84; Bp Bradf 84-91; Bp S'wark 91-98; rtd 98; Hon Asst Bp S'well and Nottm from 98. *30 Sidney Road, Beeston, Nottingham NG9 1AN* Tel and fax 0115-925 4901
E-mail roywilliamson@waitrose.com

WILLIAMSON, Robin. See WILLIAMSON, Robert Harvey

WILLIAMSON, Roger Brian. b 38. Imp Coll Lon BSc59 MIET61. St Steph Ho Ox 01. **d** 02 **p** 03. NSM Harting w Elsted and Treyford cum Didling *Chich* 02-05; P-in-c Stedham w Iping from 05. *The Rectory, The Street, Stedham, Midhurst GU29 0NQ* Tel (01730) 817570 Mobile 07767-266031
E-mail rogerwilliamson1@btinternet.com

WILLIAMSON, Mrs Sheilagh Catherine. b 54. Dur Inst of Educn CertEd76 St Martin's Coll Lanc MA00. CBDTI 97. **d** 00 **p** 01. C Darlington St Hilda and St Columba *Dur* 00-03; P-in-c from 03. *The Vicarage, 26 Upsall Drive, Darlington DL3 8RB* Tel (01325) 358911

WILLIAMSON, Canon Thomas George. b 33. AKC57. **d** 58 **p** 59. C Winshill *Derby* 58-61; C Hykeham *Linc* 61-64; V Brauncewell w Dunsby 64-78; R S w N Leasingham 64-78; RD Lafford 78-87; V Cranwell 78-80; R Leasingham 78-80; V Billinghay 80-87; V Gosberton 87-97; V Gosberton, Gosberton Clough and Quadring 97-98; Can and Preb Linc Cathl 94-98; rtd 98; Perm to Offic *Linc* 98-01. *10 Newton Way, Woolsthorpe, Grantham NG33 5NR* Tel (01476) 861749
E-mail thomas.williamson1@btinternet.com

WILLIE, Canon Andrew Robert. b 43. Bris Univ BA65 Fitzw Coll Cam BA73 MA77. Ridley Hall Cam 71. **d** 74 **p** 75. Chapl St Woolos Cathl 74-79; Chapl St Woolos Hosp Newport 75-79; V Newbridge *Mon* 79-85; V Mathern and Mounton w St Pierre 85-98; Post-Ord Tr Officer 85-98; Warden of Readers from 91; V Newport St Mark from 98; Can St Woolos Cathl from 02. *The Vicarage, 7 Gold Tops, Newport NP20 4PH* Tel (01633) 263321

WILLINK, Simon Wakefield. b 29. Magd Coll Cam BA52 MA55. Cuddesdon Coll 52. **d** 54 **p** 55. C Thornbury *Glouc* 54-57; C Tetbury w Beverston 57-60; R Siddington w Preston 60-64; New Zealand 65-71; C Kelburn St Mich 65; V Takapau 65-70; Lic to Offic Waiapu 70-80; Perm to Offic *Ex* 90-92; Hon C Sidmouth, Woolbrook, Salcombe Regis, Sidbury etc 92-01; rtd 01; Perm to Offic *Ex* 01-08. *55B North End, Ditchling, Hassocks BN6 8TE*

WILLIS, Andrew Lyn. b 48. Univ of Wales (Lamp) BA73. **d** 74 **p** 75. C Swansea St Mary w H Trin and St Mark *S & B* 74-81; V Glasbury and Llowes 81-83; Chapl RAF 83-03; Chapl Moray Hosps from 04. *Deanshaugh Croft, Mulben, Keith AB55 6YJ* Tel (01542) 860240

WILLIS, Anthony Charles Sabine. b 53. Ex Coll Ox MA82. ERMC 05. **d** 07 **p** 08. NSM Hatfield Hyde *St Alb* 07-10; Perm to Offic *Newc* 08-10. *Leazes House, Alston CA9 3NH* Tel (01434) 382682 E-mail acswillis@gmail.com

WILLIS, Anthony David. b 40. Sarum & Wells Th Coll 87. **d** 89 **p** 90. C Ivybridge w Harford *Ex* 89-92; C Catherington and Clanfield *Portsm* 92-94; R Ellesborough, The Kimbles and Stoke Mandeville *Ox* 94-08; rtd 08; Perm to Offic *Ox* from 09. *12 Fairford Leys Way, Aylesbury HP19 7FQ* Tel (01296) 431934 E-mail revwillis@btinternet.com

WILLIS, Canon Anthony John. b 38. MBE00. Univ of Wales (Lamp) BA62. Qu Coll Birm. **d** 64 **p** 65. C Kidderminster St Jo *Worc* 64-68; C Dunstable *St Alb* 68-72; V Rubery *Birm* 72-80; R Salwarpe and Hindlip w Martin Hussingtree *Worc* 80-92; Chapl to Agric and Rural Life 85-03; Hon Can Worc Cathl 99-03; rtd 03; Perm to Offic *Worc* from 04. *1 Snowberry Avenue, Home Meadow, Worcester WR4 0JA* Tel (01905) 723509
E-mail jwillis@cofe-worcester.org.uk

WILLIS, Christopher Charles Billopp. b 32. MCIPD. Bps' Coll Cheshunt 57. **d** 59 **p** 60. C Golders Green St Alb *Lon* 59-61; C N Harrow St Alb 61-64; V Shaw and Whitley *Sarum* 64-69; Ind Chapl *Ex* 69-77; C Swimbridge 70-77; Lic to Offic 77-92; Chapl W Buckland Sch Barnstaple 77-92; rtd 92; Perm to Offic *Ex* from 97. *Rose Cottage, Chittlehampton, Umberleigh EX37 9PU* Tel (01769) 540289

WILLIS, David Anthony. b 81. Ripon Coll Cuddesdon BA10. **d** 10 **p** 11. C Ifield *Chich* from 10. *1 Francis Edwards Way, Crawley RH11 8GG* Tel (01293) 851027 E-mail curate@ifieldparish.org

WILLIS, David George. b 45. Oak Hill Th Coll BA79. **d** 79 **p** 80. C Wallington *S'wark* 79-84; V Ramsgate St Mark *Cant* 84-89; Hon C Woodnesborough w Worth and Staple 94-02; Hon C Eastry and Northbourne w Tilmanstone etc 02-06; Perm to Offic from 06. *33 Boystown Place, Eastry, Sandwich CT13 0DS* Tel (01304) 611959 E-mail davidandjane@f2s.com

WILLIS, Hugh. b 39. Bris Univ BDS63 MGDSRCSEng82 FRSH87. **d** 98 **p** 99. OLM Charminster and Stinsford *Sarum* 98-08; Perm to Offic from 09. *Glebe Farmhouse, West Hill, Charminster, Dorchester DT2 9RD* Tel and fax (01305) 262940 E-mail tournai@aol.com

WILLIS, Mrs Jane Elizabeth. b 59. Wycliffe Hall Ox 06. **d** 08 **p** 09. C Shrewsbury H Cross *Lich* from 08. *14 Langholm Drive, Shrewsbury SY2 5UN* Tel (01743) 353021
E-mail revjanewillis@btinternet.com

WILLIS, Mrs Jennifer Anne. b 41. Bp Otter Coll TCert63. Local Minl Tr Course 10. **d** 11. NSM Wingerworth *Derby* from 11. *9 Pond Lane, Wingerworth, Chesterfield S42 6TW* Tel (01246) 554430 E-mail jean.willis@uwclub.net

WILLIS, John. *See* WILLIS, Canon Anthony John

WILLIS, Joyce Muriel. b 42. Open Univ BA86 CQSW73. EAMTC 86. **d** 89 **p** 94. NSM Hadleigh *St E* 89-02; NSM Hadleigh, Layham and Shelley 02-07; rtd 07; Perm to Offic *St E* from 07. *26 Ramsey Road, Hadleigh, Ipswich IP7 6AN* Tel (01473) 823165 E-mail willisjm@lineone.net

WILLIS, Mrs Patricia. b 50. RGN85 Brunel Univ BSc95 Ox Brookes Univ PGDE98. SAOMC 96. **d** 99 **p** 00. C Warmley,

Syston and Bitton *Bris* 99-03; V Hanham 03-10; rtd 10; Perm to Offic *Ox* from 10. *30 Tallis Lane, Reading RG30 3EB* Tel 07731-331154 (mobile) E-mail rev.pat.willis@blueyonder.co.uk

WILLIS, Paul. b 54. SAOMC. **d** 06 **p** 07. C High Wycombe *Ox* 06-10; TV from 10. *The Vicarage, Micklefield Road, High Wycombe HP13 7HU* Tel (01494) 520323 Mobile 07857-309018 E-mail paulwillis54@btinternet.com

WILLIS, Peter Ambrose Duncan. b 34. Kelham Th Coll 55 Lich Th Coll 58. **d** 59 **p** 60. C Sevenoaks St Jo *Roch* 59-63; Trinidad and Tobago 63-68; P-in-c Diptford *Ex* 68-69; R 69-85; P-in-c N Huish 68-69; R 69-85; R Diptford, N Huish, Harberton and Harbertonford 85-96; rtd 99. *Sun Cottage, Church Street, Modbury, Ivybridge PL21 0QR* Tel (01548) 830541

WILLIS, The Very Revd Robert Andrew. b 47. Warw Univ BA68. Cuddesdon Coll 70. **d** 72 **p** 73. C Shrewsbury St Chad *Lich* 72-75; V Choral Sarum Cathl 75-78; TR Tisbury 78-87; RD Chalke 82-87; V Sherborne w Castleton and Lillington 87-92; Can and Preb Sarum Cathl 88-92; RD Sherborne 91-92; Chapl Cranborne Chase Sch 78-92; Dean Heref 92-01; P-in-c Heref St Jo 92-01; Dean Cant from 01. *The Deanery, The Precincts, Canterbury CT1 2EP* Tel (01227) 865264 or 762862
E-mail dean@canterbury-cathedral.org

WILLIS, Mrs Rosemary Ann. b 39. **d** 93 **p** 96. OLM Fressingfield, Mendham etc *St E* 93-09; Perm to Offic from 09. *Priory House, Fressingfield, Eye IP21 5PH* Tel (01379) 586254

WILLIS, Thomas Charles. b 30. Bps' Coll Cheshunt 55. **d** 58 **p** 59. C Anlaby Common St Mark *York* 58-61; C Middlesbrough St Martin 61-63; V Kingston upon Hull St Paul w Sculcoates Ch Ch 63-69; P-in-c Sculcoates St Silas 67-69; V Sculcoates St Paul w Ch Ch and St Silas 69-80; V Bridlington H Trin and Sewerby w Marton 80-96; rtd 96; Perm to Offic *York* from 96. *23 Hillcrest Drive, Beverley HU17 7JL* Tel (01482) 888511

WILLMINGTON, John Martin Vanderlure. b 45. St D Coll Lamp BA69. St Steph Ho 69. **d** 71 **p** 72. C Upper Teddington SS Pet and Paul *Lon* 71-75; C Kensington St Mary Abbots w St Geo 75-83; R Perivale 83-91; V Acton Green from 91. *206 St Alban's Avenue, London W4 5JU* Tel (020) 8994 5735 E-mail willmington@actongreen.demon.co.uk

WILLMONT, Anthony Vernon. b 35. Lich Th Coll 62. **d** 63 **p** 64. C Yardley St Edburgha *Birm* 63-65; C Smethwick H Trin w St Alb 65-68; V Ropley w W Tisted *Win* 68-77; V Ipswich St Aug *St E* 77-84; R King's Worthy *Win* 84-90; R Headbourne Worthy 84-90; R Lapworth *Birm* 90-99; R Baddesley Clinton 90-99; P-in-c Thornton in Lonsdale w Burton in Lonsdale *Bradf* 99-02; rtd 02; Perm to Offic *Bradf* from 02. *9 Lowcroft, Butts Lane, Bentham, Lancaster LA2 2FD* Tel (01524) 261655

WILLMOTT, Robert Owen Noel. b 41. Lich Th Coll 65. **d** 68 **p** 69. C Perry Hill St Geo *S'wark* 68-71; C Denham *Ox* 71-76; P-in-c Tingewick w Water Stratford 76-77; P-in-c Radclive 76-77; R Tingewick w Water Stratford, Radclive etc 77-89; R Wingrave w Rowsham, Aston Abbotts and Cublington 89-06; P-in-c Wing w Grove 04-06; rtd 06. *34 Portfield Way, Buckingham MK18 1BB* Tel (01280) 813057

✠**WILLMOTT, The Rt Revd Trevor.** b 50. St Pet Coll Ox BA71 MA74. Westcott Ho Cam. **d** 74 **p** 75 **c** 02. C Norton *St Alb* 74-77; Asst Chapl Oslo w Bergen, Trondheim and Stavanger *Eur* 78-79; Chapl Naples w Sorrento, Capri and Bari 79-83; R Ecton *Pet* 83-89; Warden Ecton Ho 83-89; Dioc Dir of Ords and Dir Post-Ord Tr *Pet* 86-97; Can Res, Prec and Sacr Pet Cathl 89-97; Adn Dur and Can Res Dur Cathl 97-02; Suff Bp Basingstoke *Win* 02-09; Suff Bp Dover *Cant* from 10. *The Bishop's Office, Old Palace, Canterbury CT1 2EE* Tel (01227) 459382
E-mail bishop@bishcant.org

WILLOUGHBY, Diane Joyce. b 56. SWMTC. **d** 10 **p** 11. NSM St Agnes and Mount Hawke w Mithian *Truro* from 10. *Laurel Cottage, 1 Churchtown, Illogan TR16 4SW* Tel (01209) 843891 E-mail illogan@hotmail.co.uk

WILLOUGHBY, Francis Edward John. b 38. St Jo Coll Nottm. **d** 83 **p** 84. C Tonbridge SS Pet and Paul *Roch* 83-87; V Sutton at Hone 87-02; P-in-c Horton Kirby 00-02; rtd 03; Perm to Offic *Chich* from 03. *23 Mountjoy, Battle TN33 0EQ* Tel (01424) 775234

WILLOUGHBY, Canon Paul Moore. b 60. BA. **d** 86 **p** 87. C Dublin St Patr Cathl Gp 86-90; C Glenageary 90-92; I Dublin Booterstown 92-94; I Kilmocomogue C, C & R from 94; Can Cork and Ross Cathls from 00. *The Rectory, Durrus, Bantry, Co Cork, Republic of Ireland* Tel (00353) (27) 61011 Fax 61608 E-mail paul@durrusfete.ie

WILLOUGHBY, Mrs Serena Louise. b 72. Oak Hill Th Coll BA96. **d** 96 **p** 97. C St Paul's Cray St Barn *Roch* 96-99; C Hildenborough 99-00; Perm to Offic 03-06; P-in-c Sevenoaks Weald from 06. *The Vicarage, Church Road, Weald, Sevenoaks TN14 6LT* Tel (01732) 463291 Mobile 07786-076382 E-mail johnser@20judd.fsnet.co.uk

WILLOWS, David Keith. b 70. St Jo Coll Dur BA90 K Coll Lon MA94 PhD99. Wycliffe Hall Ox. **d** 95 **p** 96. C Ox St Mary V w St Cross and St Pet 95-97; Asst Chapl Oxon Mental Healthcare NHS Trust 97-00; P-in-c St Martin Ludgate *Lon* 00-01; Research

Dir Paternoster Cen from 00. *104C Camden Street, London NW1 0HY* Tel (020) 7248 6233
E-mail david.willows@paternostercentre.com
WILLOWS, Michael John. b 35. Sarum & Wells Th Coll 70. **d** 72 **p** 73. C Pershore w Wick *Worc* 72-75; Ind Chapl 75-88; P-in-c Astley 75-81; P-in-c Hallow 81-85; V 85-88; V Wollaston 88-05; rtd 05. *39 Hyperion Road, Stourton, Stourbridge DY7 6SD* Tel (01384) 379794
WILLOX, Peter. b 63. Sunderland Poly BSc85. Cranmer Hall Dur 86. **d** 89 **p** 90. C Bradley *Wakef* 89-92; C Utley *Bradf* 92-95; TV Bingley All SS 95-02; Chapl St Martin's Coll and C Ambleside w Brathay *Carl* 02-07; P-in-c Ben Rhydding *Bradf* from 07. *St John's Vicarage, 28 Wheatley Avenue, Ben Rhydding, Ilkley LS29 8PT* Tel (01943) 607363 *or* 601430
E-mail peterwillox@yahoo.co.uk
WILLS, Andrea. CITC. **d** 09 **p** 10. NSM Killala w Dunfeeny, Crossmolina, Kilmoremoy etc *T, K & A* from 09. *Address temp unknown*
WILLS, David. b 58. Oak Hill Th Coll 92. **d** 94 **p** 95. C Chadwell *Chelmsf* 94-99; P-in-c Darlaston St Lawr *Lich* 99-09; R 09-10; C Darlaston All SS 99-10; TR Bilston from 10. *The Vicarage, Dover Street, Bilston WV14 6AW* Tel (01902) 491560
WILLS, Preb David Stuart Ralph. b 36. Chich Th Coll 64. **d** 66 **p** 67. C Bodmin *Truro* 66-70; V Bude Haven 70-78; TV Banbury *Ox* 78-83; Accredited Cllr from 81; V Launceston St Steph w St Thos *Truro* 83-88; P-in-c Kenwyn St Geo 88-93; V Truro St Geo and St Jo 93-96; Preb St Endellion 95-01; rtd 96. *Garden Cottage, Penwinnick Road, St Agnes TR5 0LA* Tel (01872) 553020 Fax 553121 Mobile 07773-402109
E-mail david.wills@cpt.cornwall.nhs.uk
WILLS, Edward Richard. b 64. STETS 07. **d** 10 **p** 11. NSM Wedmore w Theale and Blackford *B & W* from 10. *Beonna House, St Mary's Road, Meare, Glastonbury BA6 9SR* Tel (01458) 860212 Mobile 07971-511564
E-mail eddie@beonna.co.uk
WILLS, Canon Ian Leslie. b 49. Wycliffe Hall Ox 77. **d** 80 **p** 81. C Henbury *Bris* 80; C Gtr Corsham 80-83; C Whitchurch 83-86; Chapl HM Rem Cen Pucklechurch 86-96; P-in-c Pucklechurch and Abson w Dyrham *Bris* 86-87; V Pucklechurch and Abson 87-99; V Soundwell from 99; Hon Can Bris Cathl from 06. *Soundwell Vicarage, 46 Sweets Road, Bristol BS15 1XQ* Tel 0117-967 1511 E-mail ian.wills@bristoldiocese.org
WILLS, Morley. b 35. Ex & Truro NSM Scheme. **d** 80 **p** 81. NSM St Enoder *Truro* 80-82; NSM Kenwyn St Geo 82-85; NSM Truro St Paul and St Clem 85-88; P-in-c Crantock 89-05; rtd 05. *81 Vyvyan Drive, Quintrell Downs, Newquay TR8 4NF* Tel (01637) 872648
WILLS, Nicholas Richard. b 71. Birm Univ BA93. Cranmer Hall Dur. **d** 99 **p** 00. C Boldmere *Birm* 99-03; P-in-c Kettering St Andr *Pet* 03-11; V from 11. *St Andrew's Vicarage, Lindsay Street, Kettering NN16 8RG* Tel and fax (01536) 513858
E-mail nickandbecky@ntlworld.com
WILLSON, Andrew William. b 64. Oriel Coll Ox BA85 Nottm Univ BTh90 MA98. Linc Th Coll 87. **d** 90 **p** 91. C Northampton St Mary *Pet* 90-93; C Cov E 93-96; Perm to Offic 96-01; Chapl Solihull Sixth Form Coll 98-01; Assoc Chapl Imp Coll *Lon* 01-03; Co-ord Chapl from 03; Assoc Chapl R Coll of Art 01-03; Co-ord Chapl from 03. *1 Porchester Gardens, London W2 3LA* Tel (020) 7229 6359
E-mail mary-andrew@clarkewillson.fsnet.co.uk
WILLSON, Stephen Geoffrey. b 63. St Jo Coll Nottm BTh90. **d** 90 **p** 91. C Newport St Andr *Mon* 90-92; C Risca 92-94; TV Cyncoed 94-96; Dioc Youth Chapl 94-99; Lay Past Asst 96-98; TV Cyncoed 98-01; TR from 01. *The Rectory, 256 Cyncoed Road, Cardiff CF23 6RU* Tel (029) 2075 2138
E-mail swillson@talktalk.net
WILLSON, Stuart Leslie. b 61. Nottm Univ BA83. Sarum & Wells Th Coll 83. **d** 84 **p** 85. C Llandrindod w Cefnllys *S & B* 84-85; Chapl Angl Students Univ of Wales (Swansea) 85-88; C Llwynderw 85-88; Ind Chapl Gatwick Airport *Chich* 88-95; Nene Coll of HE Northn 95-98; Dir Fundraising and Communication CUF from 98. *1D Northstead Cottage, Northstead Road, London SW2 3JN* Tel (020) 8674 3146
E-mail stuart@willson.freeserve.co.uk
WILLSON-THOMAS, Chloe Ann Mary. See THOMAS, Chloe Ann Mary
WILMAN, Arthur Garth. b 37. EAMTC 84. **d** 87 **p** 88. NSM Swavesey *Ely* 87-90; NSM Fen Drayton w Conington 87-90; NSM Hardwick 90-98; NSM Toft w Caldecote and Childerley 90-98; Perm to Offic from 98. *37 Prentice Close, Longstanton, Cambridge CB24 3DY* Tel (01954) 781400
E-mail wilman@ukonline.co.uk
WILMAN, Mrs Dorothy Ann Jane. b 38. Reading Univ BSc60. Westcott Ho Cam 89. **d** 90 **p** 94. NSM Toft w Caldecote and Childerley *Ely* 90-93; Dean's Asst Trin Hall Cam 92-98; Asst Chapl Cam St Edw *Ely* 93-98; P-in-c Hemingford Abbots 98-02; P-in-c Houghton w Wyton 98-02; rtd 02; Perm to Offic *Ely* from

02. *37 Prentice Close, Longstanton, Cambridge CB24 3DY* Tel (01954) 781400 E-mail dorothywilman@ukonline.co.uk
WILMAN, Leslie Alan. b 37. Selw Coll Cam BA61 MA65. Ridley Hall Cam 61. **d** 63 **p** 64. C Skipton H Trin *Bradf* 63-67; C Guiseley 67-69; V Morton St Luke 69-79; R Swanton Morley w Worthing *Nor* 79-82; P-in-c E Bilney w Beetley 79-82; P-in-c Hoe 80-82; R Swanton Morley w Worthing, E Bilney, Beetley etc 82-89; R Swanton Morley w Beetley w E Bilney and Hoe 89-00; RD Brisley and Elmham 87-93; rtd 00; Perm to Offic *Nor* from 00. *7 Wallers Lane, Foulsham, Dereham NR20 5TN* Tel (01328) 684109 E-mail lesliewilman@btinternet.com
WILMER, John Watts. b 26. Lich Th Coll 56. **d** 58 **p** 59. C Wolverhampton Ch Ch *Lich* 58-60; C Fenton 60-63; V Dresden 63-76; TV Sutton St Jas and Wawne *York* 76-80; R Bishop Wilton w Full Sutton 80; P-in-c Kirby Underdale w Bugthorpe 80; R Bishop Wilton w Full Sutton, Kirby Underdale etc 80-87; V York St Hilda 87-91; rtd 92; Perm to Offic *York* from 92. *27 Hunters Way, Dringhouses, York YO24 1JL* Tel (01904) 709591
WILMOT, David Mark Baty. b 60. Liv Univ BA82. Sarum & Wells Th Coll 84. **d** 87 **p** 88. C Penrith w Newton Reigny and Plumpton Wall *Carl* 87-91; C St Alb St Pet *St Alb* 91-93; Chapl City Coll St Alb 92-93; V Milton *Lich* 93-01; RD Leek 96-01; V Windermere St Mary and Troutbeck *Carl* from 01. *St Mary's Vicarage, Ambleside Road, Windermere LA23 1BA* Tel (01539) 443032
WILMOT, Canon Jonathan Anthony de Burgh. b 48. St Jo Coll Nottm BTh74. **d** 74 **p** 75. C Cambridge St Martin *Ely* 74-77; Chapl Chantilly *Eur* 77-82; Asst Chapl Paris St Mich 80-82; Chapl Versailles 82-87; V Blackheath St Jo *S'wark* 88-95; V Reading Greyfriars *Ox* from 95; Hon Can Ch Ch from 08. *Greyfriars Vicarage, 28 Westcote Road, Reading RG30 2DE* Tel 0118-959 6015 *or* 956 9688
E-mail jonathan.wilmot@greyfriars.org.uk
WILMOT, Stuart Leslie. b 42. Oak Hill Th Coll 64. **d** 68 **p** 69. C Spitalfields Ch Ch w All SS *Lon* 68-71; C Islington St Mary 71-74; P-in-c Brixton St Paul *S'wark* 75-81; R Mursley w Swanbourne and Lt Horwood *Ox* 81-91; P-in-c Bermondsey St Jas w Ch Ch *S'wark* 91-96; V 96-99; V Bermondsey St Jas w Ch Ch and St Crispin 99-02; P-in-c Bermondsey St Anne 91-93; P-in-c Bermondsey St Anne and St Aug 93-96; V 96-02; RD Bermondsey 96-00; rtd 02. *Amberlea, College, East Chinnock, Yeovil BA22 9DY*
WILSHERE, Daile Marie. b 70. STETS 06. **d** 09 **p** 10. C Preston w Sutton Poyntz and Osmington w Poxwell *Sarum* from 09. *8 Buddleia Close, Weymouth DT3 6SG* Tel (01305) 835096
E-mail team.curate@live.co.uk
✠**WILSON, The Rt Revd Alan Thomas Lawrence.** b 55. St Jo Coll Cam BA77 MA81 Ball Coll Ox DPhil89. Wycliffe Hall Ox 77. **d** 79 **p** 80 **c** 03. Hon C Eynsham *Ox* 79-81; C 81-82; C Caversham St Pet and Mapledurham etc 82-89; V Caversham St Jo 89-92; R Sandhurst 92-03; RD Sonning 98-03; Hon Can Ch Ch from 02; Area Bp Buckm from 03. *Sheridan, Grimms Hill, Great Missenden HP16 9BG* Tel (01494) 862173 Fax 890508
E-mail atwilson@macline.co.uk
or bishopbucks@oxford.anglican.org
WILSON, Canon Alfred Michael Sykes. b 32. Jes Coll Cam BA56 MA61. Ridley Hall Cam 56. **d** 58 **p** 59. C Fulwood *Sheff* 58-63; V Gt Horton *Bradf* 63-69; R Rushden w Newton Bromswold *Pet* 69-76; RD Higham 75-83; P-in-c Rushden St Pet 75-77; R Rushden w Newton Bromswold 77-83; Can Pet Cathl 77-97; R Preston and Ridlington w Wing and Pilton 83-97; RD Rutland 85-95; rtd 97; Perm to Offic *Nor* from 98. *Swallow Cottage, 2 Little Lane, Blakeney, Holt NR25 7NH* Tel (01263) 740975
WILSON, Andrew. See WILSON, Canon James Andrew Christopher
WILSON, Canon Andrew Alan. b 47. Nottm Univ BA68. St Steph Ho Ox 68. **d** 71 **p** 72. C Streatham St Paul *S'wark* 71-75; TV Catford (Southend) and Downham 75-80; V Malden St Jas 80-89; Chapl Croydon Community Mental Health Unit 89-94; Chapl Bethlem and Maudsley NHS Trust Lon 94-99; Chapl S Lon and Maudsley NHS Foundn Trust 99-11; Mental Health Chapl (Croydon) 00-11; Hon Can S'wark Cathl 05-11; rtd 11; Perm to Offic *S'wark* from 11. *Flat 2, 308 Croydon Road, Wallington SM6 7LQ*
WILSON, Andrew Kenneth. b 62. Oak Hill Th Coll BA91. **d** 91 **p** 92. C Springfield H Trin *Chelmsf* 91-96; V Sidcup Ch Ch *Roch* 96-10. *Release International, PO Box 54, Orpington BR5 9RT* Tel (01689) 823491 Fax 834647
WILSON, Andrew Marcus William. b 69. Ex Coll Ox BA91 CCC Cam BA93 K Coll Lon MA99. Westcott Ho Cam 91. **d** 94 **p** 95. C Forest Gate Em w Upton Cross *Chelmsf* 94-99; TV Poplar *Lon* 99-09; R S Hackney St Jo w Ch Ch from 09. *The Rectory, 19 Church Crescent, London E9 7DH* Tel (020) 8985 5145
E-mail andrewwilson@bigfoot.com
WILSON, Andrew Martin. b 60. Bris Univ BSc82 Univ Coll Chich BA04. Trin Coll Bris 97. **d** 99 **p** 00. C Broadwater *Chich* 99-07; V Portsdown *Portsm* from 07. *Portsdown Vicarage, 1A*

London Road, Widley, Waterlooville PO7 5AT Tel (023) 9237 5360 E-mail wilson@ntlworld.com *or* vicar@christchurchportsdown.org

WILSON, Antony Charles. b 69. Em Coll Cam MA92 PGCE92. Wycliffe Hall Ox 01. **d** 03 **p** 04. C Bath Walcot *B & W* 03-08; V Ipswich St Jo *St E* from 08. *St John's Vicarage, Cauldwell Hall Road, Ipswich IP4 4QE* Tel (01473) 721070 E-mail antony@stjohnsipswich.org

WILSON, Arthur Guy Ross. b 28. St Aid Birkenhead 58. **d** 59 **p** 60. C Bexley St Mary *Roch* 59-63; C Gravesend St Geo 63-66; C Belvedere All SS 66-70; V Brighton St Matthias *Chich* 70-77; V Bradf St Clem 77-84; Lic to Offic 84-87; C Baildon 87-88; V Skirwith, Ousby and Melmerby w Kirkland *Carl* 88-93; C Menston w Woodhead *Bradf* 93-96; Chapl High Royds Hosp Menston 93-96; rtd 96; Perm to Offic *Derby* 96-98; Hon C Tamworth *Lich* 98-03; Perm to Offic from 04. *43 Borough Road, Tamworth B79 8AW* Tel (01827) 310224

WILSON, Ashley Peter. b 58. Edin Univ BSc81 BVM&S83 St Jo Coll Dur BA99. Cranmer Hall Dur 97. **p** 01. C Nunthorpe *York* 00-03; P-in-c Rounton w Welbury 03-08; Chapl St Chad's Coll *Dur* from 08. *St Chad's College, 18 North Bailey, Durham DH1 3RH* Tel 0191-334 3362 *or* 334 3358 E-mail ashley.wilson@dur.ac.uk

WILSON, Mrs Barbara Anne. b 38. Brighton Poly BEd79. **d** 04. NSM Southwick *Chich* 04-11; NSM Kingston Buci from 11. *10 Phoenix Crescent, Southwick, Brighton BN42 4HR* Tel (01273) 269771 Mobile 07814-655121 E-mail barbara.a.wilson@btinternet.com

WILSON, Mrs Barbara Joyce. b 51. CBDTI 98. **d** 01 **p** 02. OLM Leyland St Jo *Blackb* 01-07; NSM from 07. *43 Hall Lane, Leyland PR25 3YD* Tel (01772) 435340 E-mail barbara.j.wilson@btinternet.com

WILSON, Barry Frank. b 58. Man Metrop Univ BA89 MPhil94 MTh99 Keele Univ PGCE90. NOC 94. **d** 97 **p** 98. C Stone St Mich w Aston St Sav *Lich* 97-99; Chapl St Mary and St Anne's Sch Abbots Bromley 00-04; V Betley *Lich* from 04; V Madeley from 04. *The Vicarage, Vicarage Lane, Madeley, Crewe CW3 9PQ* Tel (01782) 750205

WILSON, Barry Richard. b 46. WMMTC 88. **d** 91 **p** 92. NSM Leek and Meerbrook *Lich* 91-93; C Styvechale *Cov* 93-98; V Chesterton *Lich* from 98. *The Vicarage, Church Street, Chesterton, Newcastle ST5 7HJ* Tel (01782) 562479 E-mail barry-hazel@breathemail.net

WILSON, Bernard Martin. b 40. St Jo Coll Cam BA63 MA68 Lon Univ CertEd67. Ripon Hall Ox 72. **d** 73 **p** 74. C Bilton *Cov* 73-77; Dioc Development Officer *Birm* 78-83; Soc Resp Officer *Derby* 83-90; V Darley Abbey 83-90; Chapl Derbyshire R Infirmary 88-90; Educn Unit Dir Traidcraft Exchange 91; V Mickleover St Jo *Derby* 92-98; Adv to Bd of Miss and Soc Resp *Leic* 98-03; rtd 03; Perm to Offic *Leic* 03-06 and *Lich* from 06. *2 Dargate Close, Shrewsbury SY3 9QE* Tel (01743) 236300

WILSON (née HESLOP), Mrs Caroline Susan. b 62. St Cath Coll Cam BA83 MA87 ALCM79. Ox Min Course 06. **d** 09 **p** 10. NSM Caversham St Andr *Ox* 09-11; Perm to Offic from 11. *Chilterns, 9 Beech Road, Purley on Thames, Reading RG8 8DR* Tel 0118-984 1523 E-mail caroline.s.wilson@btinternet.com

WILSON, Cecil Henry. b 40. CITC 67. **d** 69 **p** 70. C Lurgan St Jo *D & D* 69-72; Min Can Dromore Cathl 72-75; Youth Sec CMS Ireland 75-80; N Regional Sec 80-87; Gen Sec 87-07; Can Belf Cathl 00-07; rtd 07. *42A Magheraknock Road, Ballynahinch BT24 8TJ* Tel (028) 9756 4300

WILSON, Charles Roy. b 30. Brasted Th Coll 56 St Aid Birkenhead 57. **d** 59 **p** 60. C Kirkdale St Paul N Shore *Liv* 59-62; C St Helens St Mark 62-66; V Wolverhampton St Matt *Lich* 66-74; V Ripley *Derby* 74-88; V Willington 88-95; V Findern 88-95; rtd 95; Perm to Offic *Derby* from 95. *Jubilate, 12 Oak Tree Close, Swanwick, Alfreton DE55 1FG* Tel (01773) 541822

WILSON, Christella Helen. b 62. Yorks Min Course 08. **d** 11. C Pannal w Beckwithshaw *Ripon* from 11. *80 Beckwith Crescent, Harrogate HG2 0BH* Tel (01423) 705580 E-mail christella.wilson@yahoo.co.uk

WILSON (née BRAVERY), The Ven Christine Louise. b 58. STETS 94. **d** 97 **p** 98. C Henfield w Shermanbury and Woodmancote *Chich* 97-02; TV Hove 02-08; P-in-c Goring-by-Sea 08-10; Adn Chesterfield *Derby* from 10. *The Old Vicarage, Church Street, Baslow, Bakewell DE45 1RY* Tel (01246) 583023 E-mail archchesterfield@derby.anglican.org

WILSON, Christopher Harry. b 59. Man Univ MusB80 Ox Univ MTh01. Wycliffe Hall Ox 88. **d** 91 **p** 92. C S Lafford *Linc* 91-95; P-in-c Billingborough 95-96; P-in-c Sempringham w Pointon and Birthorpe 95-96; P-in-c Horbling 95-96; P-in-c Aslackby and Dowsby 95-96; V Billingborough Gp 96-03; P-in-c Leamington Priors All SS *Cov* from 03; Jt P-in-c Leamington Spa H Trin from 03. *Clive House, Kenilworth Road, Leamington Spa CV32 5TL* Tel (01926) 424016 E-mail holy.trinity@btopenworld.com

WILSON, Mrs Claire Frances. b 43. Hull Univ BA65. SWMTC 85. **d** 87 **p** 94. Par Dn Belsize Park *Lon* 87-94; C 94-97; C Chingford SS Pet and Paul *Chelmsf* 97-09; rtd 09. *Ground Floor*

Flat, 26 Frognal Lane, London NW3 7DT Tel (020) 7794 3801 E-mail revclairewilson@btinternet.com

WILSON, Colin Edward. b 63. Ripon Coll Cuddesdon BTh94. **d** 94 **p** 95. C High Wycombe *Ox* 94-98; P-in-c Broadwell, Evenlode, Oddington and Adlestrop *Glouc* 98-00; P-in-c Westcote w Icomb and Bledington 98-00; R Broadwell, Evenlode, Oddington, Adlestrop etc 00-03; Perm to Offic *Eur* 03-05; P-in-c Finchingfield and Cornish Hall End etc *Chelmsf* from 05. *The Vicarage, Bardfield Road, Finchingfield, Braintree CM7 4JR* Tel (01371) 810309

WILSON, David. b 67. BSc94 St Jo Coll Dur BA00. Cranmer Hall Dur 97. **d** 00 **p** 01. C Nantwich *Ches* 00-03; P-in-c Waverton 03-05; R Waverton w Aldford and Bruera 05-08; R St Andrews St Andr *St And* from 08. *The Rectory, Queen's Terrace, St Andrews KY16 9QF* Tel 07760-378085 (mobile)

WILSON, David Brian. b 47. QUB BA68. CITC 71. **d** 71 **p** 72. C Ballyholme *D & D* 71-74; C Guildf Ch Ch 74-78; I Arvagh w Carrigallen, Gowna and Columbkille *K, E & A* 78-81; R Clogherny w Seskinore and Drumnakilly *Arm* 81-95; I Caledon w Brantry 95-11; rtd 11. *Address temp unknown*

WILSON, Preb David Gordon. b 40. Man Univ BSc61 Clare Coll Cam BA63 MA68. Ridley Hall Cam 63. **d** 65 **p** 66. C Clapham Common St Barn *S'wark* 65-69; C Onslow Square St Paul *Lon* 69-73; V Leic H Apostles 73-84; V Spring Grove St Mary *Lon* 84-05; P-in-c Isleworth St Fran 00-05; Chapl Brunel Univ 90-02; AD Hounslow 97-02; Preb St Paul's Cathl 02-05; rtd 05; Perm to Offic *Portsm* from 05. *8 Clover Close, Locks Heath, Southampton SO31 6SQ* Tel and fax (01489) 571426 E-mail david.gwilson20@ntlworld.com

WILSON, David Mark. b 53. Lon Univ BSc75 Wycliffe Hall Ox BA77 MA82. **d** 78 **p** 79. C Romford Gd Shep *Chelmsf* 78-81; C Cheadle Hulme St Andr *Ches* 81-85; V Huntington and Chapl Bp's Blue Coat C of E High Sch 85-95; V Birkenhead Ch Ch *Ches* 95-04; V Over St Jo 04-10; P-in-c W Coker w Hardington Mandeville, E Chinnock etc *B & W* from 10; P-in-c E Coker w Sutton Bingham and Closworth from 10. *The Rectory, 7 Cedar Fields, West Coker, Yeovil BA22 9DB* Tel (01935) 862328 E-mail thevicar@fastmail.co.uk

WILSON, Deborah May. b 61. Man Univ BA84 PhD95 Lanc Univ PGCE88. Cranmer Hall Dur 03. **d** 06 **p** 07. NSM Hartlepool St Luke *Dur* from 06. *10 Lindisfarne Close, Hartlepool TS27 3JN* Tel (01429) 265938 E-mail deborah.wilson3@ntlworld.com

WILSON, Derrick. b 33. Oak Hill Th Coll 69. **d** 71 **p** 72. C Lurgan Ch the Redeemer *D & D* 71-74; C Willowfield 74-75; I 83-88; I Knocknamuckley 75-83; I Tullylish 88-98; rtd 98. *Hollycroft, 6 Thornhill Crescent, Tandragee, Craigavon BT62 2NZ* Tel (028) 3884 9900

WILSON, Mrs Dorothy Jean. b 35. St Mary's Coll Dur BA57 DipEd58 Newc Poly LLB78. NEOC 86. **d** 88 **p** 96. NSM Dur St Giles 88-03; Perm to Offic *Newc* 88-96; Chapl Northumbria Univ 94-96; Chapl N Dur Healthcare NHS Trust 97-02; NSM Shadforth and Sherburn *Dur* from 03. *86 Gilesgate, Durham DH1 1HY* Tel 0191-386 5016

WILSON, Edith Yvonne. b 43. St Martin's Coll Lanc MA98. CBDTI 97. **d** 97 **p** 98. NSM Skerton St Chad *Blackb* 97-05; Perm to Offic from 05. *28 Roedean Avenue, Morecambe LA4 6SB* Tel (01524) 417097 E-mail yvonne@wilson7.freeserve.co.uk

WILSON, Canon Erik. b 51. Lanc Univ BA72. Trin Coll Bris 83. **d** 85 **p** 86. C Linthorpe *York* 85-89; V Hull St Martin w Transfiguration 89-98; AD W Hull 96-98; V Linthorpe from 98; RD Middlesbrough 05-11; Can and Preb York Minster from 05. *St Barnabas' Vicarage, 8 The Crescent, Middlesbrough TS5 6SQ* Tel (01642) 817306 E-mail erik.wilson@ntlworld.com

WILSON, Frances Mary. b 61. Leeds Univ BA98 MPhil06. Westcott Ho Cam. **d** 00 **p** 01. C Rothwell *Ripon* 00-04; V Catterick from 04; Initial Reader Tr Officer 04-11; P-in-c Balkwell *Newc* from 11. *St Peter's Vicarage, The Quadrant, North Shields NE29 7JA* E-mail mo.frances@tiscali.co.uk

WILSON, Francis. b 34. ACP67. Cuddesdon Coll 71. **d** 73 **p** 74. C Newc St Fran 73-79; V Wallsend St Jo 79-99; rtd 99; Perm to Offic *Newc* from 99. *65 Bede Close, Holystone, Newcastle upon Tyne NE12 9SP* Tel 0191-270 0848

WILSON, Frederick John. b 25. Lon Univ BScEng45. Oak Hill Th Coll 68. **d** 70 **p** 71. C Wandsworth All SS *S'wark* 70-75; P-in-c Garsdon w Lea and Cleverton *Bris* 75-84; P-in-c Charlton w Brokenborough and Hankerton 80-84; Chapl Barn Fellowship Whatcombe Ho 84-87; C Corby Epiphany w St Jo *Pet* 87-92; rtd 92; Perm to Offic *Linc* 93-02; *Pet* from 93; *Ely* from 05. *2 Thorseby Close, Peterborough PE3 9QS* Tel (01733) 263386

WILSON, Geoffrey. See WILSON, Samuel Geoffrey

WILSON, Geoffrey. b 42. **d** 97 **p** 98. OLM Gunton St Pet *Nor* 97-08; NSM Lowestoft St Marg from 08. *7 Monet Square, Gunton, Lowestoft NR32 4LZ* Tel (01502) 564064

WILSON, Geoffrey Samuel Alan. b 46. TCD BA69 QUB DipEd70 TCD MA72. CITC BTh93. **d** 96 **p** 97. C Glendermott *D & R* 96-99; I Camus-juxta-Mourne from 99. *The Rectory, Newtown Street, Strabane BT82 8DW* Tel (028) 7188 2314 Mobile 07889-877790 E-mail recwil27@yahoo.co.uk

WILSON, George Thomas. b 47. CBDTI 97. **d** 00 **p** 01. NSM Barrow St Paul *Carl* 00-06; P-in-c Bootle, Corney, Whicham and Whitbeck 06-10; NSM Cartmel Peninsula from 10. *Address temp unknown* E-mail george860@btinternet.com

WILSON, Graham Whitelaw. b 46. Leeds Univ CertEd77 Birm Univ MPhil00 Derby Univ DMin03. EMMTC. **d** 95 **p** 96. NSM Burbage w Aston Flamville *Leic* 95-97; C 97-01; C Fenn Lanes Gp 01-04; Perm to Offic from 04. *10 The Courtyard, Higham Lane, Stoke Golding, Nuneaton CV13 6EX* Tel (01455) 213598 E-mail gwwilson@btinternet.com

WILSON, Canon Harold. b 29. St Jo Coll Ox BA53 MA57. Ridley Hall Cam 57. **d** 59 **p** 60. C Leamington Priors St Mary *Cov* 59-61; C Walsgrave on Sowe 61-64; V Potters Green 64-67; Chapl Barcelona *Eur* 67-73; V Bursledon *Win* 73-83; RD Eastleigh 75-83; V Yateley 83-94; RD Odiham 85-88; Hon Can Win Cathl 87-94; rtd 94; Perm to Offic *Win* from 94. *11 Hill Meadow, Overton, Basingstoke RG25 3JD* Tel (01256) 771825

WILSON, Mrs Heather Clarissa. b 49. Hull Univ BA71 Leic Univ PGCE72 Anglia Poly Univ MA05. EAMTC 01. **d** 03 **p** 04. NSM Duston *Pet* from 03; TV from 06. *St Francis House, Eastfield Road, Duston, Northampton NN5 6TQ* Tel (01604) 753679 Mobile 07702-033727 E-mail heather@wilson1214.freeserve.co.uk

WILSON, Mrs Hilary Anne. b 47. **d** 05 **p** 06. OLM Gt Chesham *Ox* 05-09; NSM from 09. *6 Greenway, Chesham HP5 2BL* Tel and fax (01494) 775564 E-mail hilaryaw6@aol.com

WILSON, Ian Andrew. b 57. Nottm Univ BTh89. Linc Th Coll 86. **d** 89 **p** 90. C Whitton and Thurleston w Akenham *St E* 89-93; P-in-c Elmsett w Aldham 93-02; R Elmsett w Aldham, Hintlesham, Chattisham etc 02; Chapl Woodbridge Sch from 03. *12 Moorfield Road, Woodbridge IP12 4JN* Tel (01394) 384573

WILSON, Mrs Irene Margaret. b 49. Leeds Univ BA83 ALCM69. Yorks Min Course 09. **d** 11. NSM Kingston upon Hull H Trin *York* from 11. *10 Westgate, North Cave, Brough HU15 2NJ* Tel (01430) 470719 Mobile 07711-996519 E-mail irene@mulberryhouse.karoo.co.uk

WILSON, James. b 65. St Steph Ho Ox. **d** 01 **p** 02. C Whitchurch *Bris* 01-03; C Horfield St Greg 03-05; P-in-c from 05. *St Gregory's Vicarage, Filton Road, Horfield, Bristol BS7 0PD* Tel 0117-969 2839 E-mail revjameswilson@aol.com

WILSON, Canon James Andrew Christopher. b 48. Ex & Truro NSM Scheme. **d** 82 **p** 83. NSM Plymouth Crownhill Ascension *Ex* 82-83; NSM Yelverton 83-85; C Plymstock 85-87; R Lifton 87-92; R Kelly w Bradstone 87-92; V Broadwoodwidger 87-92; R Calstock *Truro* from 92; RD E Wivelshire 00-11; Hon Can Truro Cathl from 04. *The Rectory, Sand Lane, Calstock PL18 9QX* Tel (01822) 832518 E-mail andrew.wilson@virgin.net

WILSON, James Kenneth. b 47. **d** 88 **p** 89. C Holyhead w Rhoscolyn w Llanfair-yn-Neubwll *Ban* 88-91; Chapl RAF 91-07; Mental Health Chapl Lincs Partnership NHS Foundn Trust from 07. *Lincolnshire Partnership NHS Trust, Cross O'Cliff, Bracebridge Heath, Lincoln LN4 2HN* Tel (01522) 513355 E-mail ken.wilson@lpt.nhs.uk

WILSON, James Lewis. b 39. TCD BA62 HDipEd63 MA65 BD71. TCD Div Sch Div Test74. **d** 74 **p** 75. C Enniskillen *Clogh* 74-76; C Belfast St Matt *Conn* 76-79; I Killeshandra w Killegar K, E & A 79-81; I Derrylane 79-81; I Loughgilly w Clare *Arm* 81-10; rtd 10. *2 Tramway Drive, Bushmills BT57 8YS* Tel (028) 2073 1353

WILSON, James Robert. b 36. CITC. **d** 66 **p** 67. C Ballywillan *Conn* 67-73; I Drummaul 73-79; I Drummaul w Duneane and Ballyscullion 79-01; Preb Conn Cathl 96; Treas 96-98; Chan 98-01; rtd 01. *90 Killycowan Road, Glarryford, Ballymena BT44 9HJ* Tel (028) 2568 5737

WILSON, Jane Jennifer. b 43. Ch Ch Coll Cant TCert65 Open Univ BA84. Wycliffe Hall Ox 89. **d** 91 **p** 94. Par Dn Northwood Em *Lon* 91-94; C 94-98; TV Blythburgh w Reydon *St E* 98; TV Sole Bay 98-02; TR 02-07; RD Halesworth 01-07; Hon Can St E Cathl 05-07; P-in-c Offwell, Northleigh, Farway, Cotleigh etc *Ex* 07-11. *The Rectory, Offwell, Honiton EX14 9SB* Tel (01404) 831636 E-mail janeoffwell@aol.com

WILSON, Mrs Janet Mary. b 44. Bedf Coll of Educn TCert66 SRN74. **d** 03 **p** 04. OLM S Croydon Em *S'wark* 03-10; Perm to Offic from 11. *Elmwood, 2 Weybourne Place, Sanderstead CR2 0RZ* Tel (020) 8657 2105 E-mail revjanwilson@blueyonder.co.uk

WILSON, Janet Mary. b 54. SAOMC 02. **d** 05 **p** 06. C Oxhey All SS *St Alb* 05-09; TV Cheshunt from 09. *St Clement's House, 4 Haddestoke Gate, Cheshunt EN8 0XJ* Tel (01992) 479882 E-mail janwilson@waitrose.com

WILSON, Jayaker. b 92 **p** 93. India 92-05; Perm to Offic *Chelmsf* from 05. *153 Northbrooks, Harlow CM19 4DQ* Tel (01279) 412240

WILSON, Jeffery. **d** 06 **p** 07. OLM Kirton in Lindsey w Manton *Linc* from 06; OLM Grayingham from 06. *34 Richdale Avenue, Kirton Lindsey, Gainsborough DN21 4BL* Tel (01652) 648687 E-mail jeff-wilson13@yahoo.co.uk

WILSON, John Anthony. b 34. Linc Th Coll. **d** 83 **p** 84. C Nunthorpe *York* 83-85; V Whorlton w Carlton and Faceby

85-94; V E Coatham 94-99; rtd 99; Perm to Offic *York* 00-08 and Ripon 00-03; P-in-c Lower Swale *Ripon* 03-08; Perm to Offic *York* from 10. *29 Letch Hill Drive, Bourton-on-the-Water, Cheltenham GL54 2DQ* Tel (01451) 820571 E-mail johnjean.wilson@virgin.net

WILSON, John Clifford. b 32. AKC56. **d** 57 **p** 58. C Bordesley St Andr *Birm* 57-59; C Kings Norton 59-61; Somalia and Aden 61-63; V Lydbrook *Glouc* 64-67; TV Bow w Bromley St Leon *Lon* 69-73; P-in-c Stepney St Pet w St Benet 73-80; P-in-c Long Marton w Dufton and w Milburn *Carl* 80-81; R 81-87; V Annesley Our Lady and All SS *S'well* 87-95; V Annesley w Newstead 95-97; rtd 97; Perm to Offic *Heref* from 98. *Cwm Well Cottage, Upper Cwm, Little Dewchurch, Hereford HR2 6PS* Tel (01432) 840559

WILSON, John Frederick. b 33. Qu Coll Birm 58. **d** 61 **p** 62. C Jarrow St Paul *Dur* 61-65; C Monkwearmouth All SS 65-68; Br Honduras 68-71; V Scunthorpe Resurr *Linc* 71-90; Chapl Divine Healing Miss Crowhurst 90-91; V Terrington St Clement *Ely* 91-99; rtd 99; Perm to Offic *Ely* from 99. *7 Oakleigh Crescent, Godmanchester, Huntingdon PE29 2JJ* Tel (01480) 392791 E-mail john@jaywil.freeserve.co.uk

WILSON, Canon John Hamilton. b 29. St Chad's Coll Dur BA53. Sarum Th Coll 53. **d** 55 **p** 56. C W End *Win* 55-59; C Fishponds St Mary *Bris* 59-64; V Bedminster St Fran 64-73; RD Bedminster 68-73; R Horfield H Trin 73-96; Hon Can Bris Cathl 77-96; rtd 96; Perm to Offic *Bris* from 96. *2 West Croft, Bristol BS9 4PQ* Tel and fax 0117-962 9204

WILSON, John Lake. b 34. Linc Th Coll 74. **d** 76 **p** 77. C N Lynn w St Marg and St Nic *Nor* 76-80; V Narborough w Narford 80-85; R Pentney St Mary Magd w W Bilney 80-85; V Lakenham St Mark 85-93; P-in-c Trowse 92-93; V Lakenham St Mark w Trowse 93-98; Chapl Whitlingham Hosp 93-98; rtd 98; Perm to Offic *Nor* from 98. *Slinmoor, Warham Road, Wells-next-the-Sea NR23 1NE* Tel (01328) 711035

WILSON, Canon Judith Anne. b 48. Keele Univ BA71 Leic Univ PGCE72. S Dios Minl Tr Scheme 92. **d** 95 **p** 96. NSM Slaugham *Chich* 95-96; Sub Chapl HM Pris Wandsworth 95-96; Chapl HM Pris and YOI Hollesley Bay 96-01; Chapl HM Pris Nor 01-09; Chapl Gt Hosp Nor from 09; P-in-c Nor St Helen from 09; Bp's Adv for Women's Min 04-10; Hon Asst Dioc Dir of Ords from 09; Hon Can Nor Cathl from 07. *Calthorpe Lodge, Bishopgate, Norwich NR1 4EJ* Tel (01603) 622022 E-mail revjudithwilson@tiscali.co.uk

WILSON, Julian John. b 64. Collingwood Coll Dur BSc85 Liv Univ BTh. NOC 01. **d** 04 **p** 05. C Uttoxeter Area *Lich* 04-07; Chapl Denstone Coll Uttoxeter 07-09; R Baschurch and Weston Lullingfield w Hordley *Lich* from 09; World Development Officer (Salop) from 11. *The Rectory, Baschurch, Shrewsbury SY4 2EB* Tel (01939) 260305

WILSON, Mrs Kathleen. b 47. Bucks Coll of Educn BSc90 Ox Brookes Univ MBA93 RGN69. **d** 03 **p** 04. OLM Iver *Ox* 03-10; P-in-c Colbury *Win* from 10. *The Vicarage, Deerleap Lane, Totton, Southampton SO40 7EH* Tel (023) 8029 2132 Mobile 07770-944054

WILSON, Kenneth. b 59. Selw Coll Cam BA82 MA82 Birm Univ MPhil95 MRICS84. S'wark Ord Course 86. **d** 89 **p** 90. C Walthamstow St Pet *Chelmsf* 89-92; TV Wolverhampton *Lich* 92-97; Perm to Offic 00-08. *6 Westland Road, Wolverhampton WV3 9NY* Tel and fax (01902) 561485 E-mail kw@soulofindia.com

WILSON, Ms Lauretta Joy. b 64. Bath Univ BSc87 CertEd87. SAOMC 02. **d** 05 **p** 06. C Boxmoor St Jo *St Alb* 05-08; TV Langelei from 08. *St Benedict's Vicarage, Peascroft Road, Hemel Hempstead HP3 8EP* Tel (01442) 243934 E-mail ljwilson33@btinternet.com

WILSON, Louis. b 68. Bris Univ LLB91. Oak Hill Th Coll BA09. **d** 09 **p** 10. NSM Broadwell, Evenlode, Oddington, Adlestrop etc *Glouc* from 09. *The Vicarage, Chapel Lane, Bledington, Chipping Norton OX7 6UZ* E-mail louisandjennywilson@hotmail.com

WILSON, Mrs Maree Elizabeth. b 49. **d** 06 **p** 07. C Geneva *Eur* 06-11; TV Ludlow *Heref* from 11. *The Vicarage, Bromfield, Ludlow SY8 2JP* Tel (01584) 856731

WILSON, Marjorie Jayne. See SHIPTON, Mrs Marjorie Jayne

WILSON, Mark Anthony John. b 56. TCD BA80. CITC 75. **d** 80 **p** 81. C Dublin Rathfarnham *D & G* 80-83; Bp's C Dublin Finglas 83-85; I Celbridge w Straffan and Newcastle-Lyons 85-88; CF 88-93; I Dundalk w Heynestown *Arm* 93-03; Chapl Adelaide and Meath Hosp Dublin from 04. *7 Newlands Park, Clondalkin, Dublin 22, Republic of Ireland* Tel (00353) 87-669 3215 (mobile)

WILSON, The Ven Mark John Crichton. b 46. Clare Coll Cam BA67 MA70. Ridley Hall Cam 67. **d** 69 **p** 70. C Luton w E Hyde *St Alb* 69-72; C Ashtead *Guildf* 72-77; Chapl and Hd RE Epsom Coll 77-81; V Epsom Common Ch Ch *Guildf* 81-96; RD Epsom 87-92; Adn Dorking 96-05; Hon Can Guildf Cathl 96-09; Warden Community of St Pet Woking 03-07; Public Preacher *Guildf* 05-09; rtd 09; Perm to Offic *Guildf* from 09. *The Rectory, Parsonage Way, Frimley, Camberley GU16 8HZ* Tel (01276) 62820 E-mail mjcw.personal@ntlworld.com

WILSON, Martin. *See* WILSON, Bernard Martin

WILSON, Canon Mavis Kirby. b 42. Ex Univ BA64 Cam Univ CertEd71. S Dios Minl Tr Scheme 82. **dss** 84 **d** 87 **p** 94. Chessington *Guildf* 84-85; Epsom St Martin 85-86; Epsom Common Ch Ch 86-87; C 87-96; Dioc Adv in Miss, Evang, and Par Development 90-02; R Frimley from 02; Hon Can Guildf Cathl from 94. *The Rectory, 3 Parsonage Way, Frimley, Camberley GU16 8HZ* Tel (01276) 23309
E-mail mwilson2@toucansurf.com

WILSON, Mervyn Raynold Alwyn. b 33. Qu Coll Cam BA57 MA61. Ripon Hall Ox 57. **d** 59 **p** 60. C Rubery *Birm* 59-62; C Kings Norton 62-63; V Hamstead St Bernard 63-69; R Bermondsey St Mary w St Olave, St Jo etc *S'wark* 69-78; R Bulwick, Blatherwycke w Harringworth and Laxton *Pet* 78-03; rtd 03; Perm to Offic *B & W* from 04. *The Red Post House, Fivehead, Taunton TA3 6PX* Tel (01460) 281555
E-mail mervyn@ratilova.freeserve.co.uk

WILSON, The Very Revd Mervyn Robert. b 22. Bris Univ BA51 Lon Univ BD58. Tyndale Hall Bris 52. **d** 52 **p** 53. C Ballymacarrett St Patr *D & D* 52-56; C Donaghcloney 56-59; C Newtownards 59-61; I Ballyphilip w Ardquin 61-70; I Newry St Patr 70-92; Preb Dromore Cathl 83-85; Can Belf Cathl 85-89; Dean Dromore *D & D* 90-92; rtd 92. *31 Manor Drive, Lisburn BT28 1JH* Tel (028) 9266 6361

WILSON, Michael. *See* WILSON, Canon Alfred Michael Sykes

WILSON, Canon Michael. b 44. Liv Univ BA66 Fitzw Coll Cam BA68 MA73 De Montfort Univ MBA94. Westcott Ho Cam. **d** 69 **p** 70. C Worksop Priory *S'well* 69-71; C Gt Malvern St Mary *Worc* 71-75; V Leic St Anne 75-85; TR Leic Ascension 85-88; Hon Can Leic Cathl 85-88; Can Res and Treas 88-09, rtd 09; Perm to Offic *Pet* from 09. *8 Wensum Close, Oakham LE15 6FU* Tel (01572) 720853 E-mail mwilson@keme.co.uk

WILSON, Neil. b 61. Newc Univ BA83. Ripon Coll Cuddesdon 85. **d** 88 **p** 89. C Wallsend St Luke *Newc* 88-91; C Monkseaton St Pet 91-93; V Earsdon and Backworth 93-04; P-in-c Newc St Jo from 04. *3 Crossway, Jesmond, Newcastle upon Tyne NE2 3QH* Tel 0191-212 0181 E-mail frneilwilson@aol.com

WILSON, Paul David. b 64. Cranmer Hall Dur 96. **d** 98 **p** 99. C Bramley and Ravenfield w Hooton Roberts etc *Sheff* 98-01; V Hatfield from 01; AD Snaith and Hatfield from 11. *The Vicarage, 2 Vicarage Close, Hatfield, Doncaster DN7 6HN* Tel (01302) 840280 E-mail paul.wilson@sheffield.anglican.org

WILSON, Paul Edward. b 43. Ridley Hall Cam 81. **d** 83 **p** 84. C Brighstone and Brooke w Mottistone *Portsm* 83-86; C Shorwell w Kingston 83-86; TV Tring *St Alb* 86-90; P-in-c Renhold 90-91; Chapl HM Pris Bedf 90-91; V Buckfastleigh w Dean Prior *Ex* 91-96; P-in-c Stockland, Dalwood, Kilmington and Shute 96-00; TR Melbury *Sarum* 00-03; rtd 03; Perm to Offic *Portsm* from 05. *Palm Trees, 42 Whitecross Avenue, Shanklin PO37 7ER* Tel (01983) 864654
E-mail paul.elizabeth@btinternet.com

WILSON, Paul Thomas Wardley. b 43. AKC67. St Aug Coll Cant. **d** 70 **p** 71. C Tokyngton St Mich *Lon* 70-74; Soc Community Worker *Roch* 74-81; Perm to Offic 81-90; Lic to Offic *Cant* 83-88; Sen Adv Coun for Soc Resp from 83; Chief Exec Carr Gomm Soc from 88. *Carr Gomm Society, 6-12 Tabard Street, London SE1 4JU* Tel (020) 7397 5300

WILSON, Peter Dennis. b 51. **d** 03 **p** 04. OLM Benwell *Newc* from 03. *34 Benwell Lane, Benwell, Newcastle upon Tyne NE15 6RR* Tel 0191-273 2856

WILSON, Peter John. b 43. CertEd76 BEd84. Linc Th Coll. **d** 71 **p** 72. C Stretford St Matt *Man* 71-73; C Rugby St Andr *Cov* 73-76; TV Rugby 86-92; Hon C Bilton 76-79; Asst Dir of Educn Stewardship *Carl* 92-02; P-in-c Dacre 95-02; Hon Can Carl Cathl 98-02; R Stone St Mich and St Wulfad w Aston St Sav *Lich* 02-05; rtd 05. *83 Salisbury Road, Stafford ST16 3SE*
E-mail ptr@wln1.fsnet.co.uk

WILSON, Peter Sheppard. b 39. TCD BA61. CITC Div Test 62. **d** 62 **p** 63. C Killowen *D & R* 62-68; C Portadown St Columba *Arm* 68-70; I Convoy w Monellan and Donaghmore *D & R* 70-78; V Castletown *S & M* 78-83; R Kilmacolm and Bridge of Weir *Glas* 83-85; I Camus-juxta-Bann *D & R* 85-92; Bp's Dom Chapl 90-92; I Maguiresbridge w Derrybrusk *Clogh* 92-05; Chapl to Bp Clogh 98-00; Can Clogh Cathl 03-05; rtd 05. *25 Grogey Road, Fivemiletown BT75 0SQ* Tel (028) 8952 1883

WILSON, Peter Stuart. b 45. Yorks Min Course 08. **d** 09 **p** 10. NSM Haworth *Bradf* from 09; NSM Cross Roads cum Lees from 09. *25 Branshaw Grove, Keighley BD22 6NH* Tel (01535) 674972 Mobile 07870-134272
E-mail peter@peterwilson25.wanadoo.co.uk

WILSON, Quentin Harcourt. b 45. K Coll Lon AKC68 BD76 Cen Lancs Univ MA97 York Univ PhD07 FTCL75. St Aug Coll Cant 69. **d** 70 **p** 71. C Is of Dogs Ch Ch and St Jo w St Luke *Lon* 70-72; C Muswell Hill St Jas 72-77; Succ and Sacr Ex Cathl 77-81; Min Can Windsor 81-84; V Langho Billington *Blackb* 84-89; P-in-c Burnley St Pet 97-98; R 98-02; rtd 02; Chapl Castle Howard 03-05; RD S Ryedale *York* 06-11; P-in-c Old Malton

from 10; C New Malton from 10; C Weaverthorpe w Helperthorpe, Luttons Ambo etc from 11. *The Coach House, East Heslerton, Malton YO17 8RN* Tel (01944) 728060 Mobile 07970-878013 E-mail qhwilson@btinternet.com

WILSON, Mrs Rachel Elizabeth. b 56. Keswick Hall Coll BEd79. NOC 00. **d** 03 **p** 04. NSM Slaidburn and Long Preston w Tosside *Bradf* 03-10; NSM Lower Wharfedale *Ripon* from 10; Min in Deaf Community *Bradf* and *Ripon* from 09. *The Vicarage, Old Pool Bank, Pool in Wharfedale, Otley LS21 1EJ* Tel 0113-284 3706 E-mail revrachel.wilson@dsl.pipex.com

WILSON, Richard Graham. b 67. Bris Univ BSc91 DipSW93. Trin Coll Bris BA01. **d** 01 **p** 02. C Wandsworth St Mich *S'wark* 01-05; TR Bath Twerton-on-Avon *B & W* from 05. *The Rectory, Watery Lane, Bath BA2 1RL* Tel (01225) 421438
E-mail richard@stmichaelstwerton.com

WILSON, Canon Robert Malcolm (Robin). b 35. St Andr Univ MA59. ALCD62. **d** 62 **p** 63. C Wallington *S'wark* 62-66; C Dur St Nic 66-70; V Colchester St Pet *Chelmsf* 70-01; RD Colchester 93-98; Hon Can Chelmsf Cathl 94-01; rtd 01; Perm to Offic *St E* and *Chelmsf* from 01. *Hawthorns, Melton Road, Melton, Woodbridge IP12 1NH* Tel (01394) 383514

WILSON, Robert Stoker. b 39. Dur Univ BSc62. Oak Hill Th Coll 62. **d** 64 **p** 65. C High Elswick St Paul *Newc* 64-68; C Kirkheaton 68-70; Youth Chapl *Liv* 70-73; P-in-c S Shields St Steph *Dur* 73-78; R 78-83; Youth Chapl 73-77; P-in-c S Shields St Aid 81-83; V Greenside 83-94; P-in-c Fatfield 94-98; P-in-c Coniscliffe 98-04; Dioc Adv for IT 98-04; rtd 04. *9 Augusta Close, Darlington DL1 3HT* Tel 07808-911928 (mobile) E-mail stoker.wilson@durham.anglican.org

WILSON, Mrs Rosamund Cynthia. b 54. Univ of Wales MSc94 MCSP75. Trin Coll Bris. **d** 01 **p** 02. NSM Stoke Bishop *Bris* 01-05; C Frenchay and Winterbourne Down 05-06; NSM Abbots Leigh w Leigh Woods from 07. *10 Druid Stoke Avenue, Bristol BS9 1DD* Tel 0117-968 7554 E-mail rosw@another.com

WILSON, Roy. *See* WILSON, Charles Roy

WILSON, Samuel Geoffrey. b 62. CITC BTh04. **d** 04 **p** 05. C Swanlinbar w Tomregan, Kinawley, Drumlane etc *K, E & A* 04-07; I Kildallon and Swanlinbar 07-09; I Lurgan Ch the Redeemer *D & D* from 09. *Shankill Rectory, 62 Bainbridge Road, Lurgan, Craigavon BT6 7HG* Tel (028) 3832 3341 Mobile 07540-898841 E-mail geoffwilson@utvinternet.com

WILSON, Simon Anthony. b 67. Portsm Poly BA88. Cranmer Hall Dur 96. **d** 99 **p** 00. NSM Barnham Broom *Nor* 99-00; NSM Barnham Broom and Upper Yare 00-02; NSM Hellesdon 02-03; Public Preacher from 03; Chapl Norfolk Constabulary (Cen Area) from 05; Chapl Norfolk Fire Service from 05; Co-ord Dioc Forum for Soc and Community Concerns from 06; Co Ecum Officer from 10. *The Rectory, 1 Guist Road, Foulsham, Dereham NR20 5RZ* Tel (01362) 683275
E-mail simon.wilson@norwich.anglican.org

WILSON, Stephen Charles. b 51. Newc Univ BA73 Cam Univ MA82. Westcott Ho Cam BA78. **d** 79 **p** 80. C Fulham All SS *Lon* 79-82; C W Hampstead St Jas 82-85; P-in-c Alexandra Park St Sav 85-93; V Preston next Faversham, Goodnestone and Graveney *Cant* from 93; Hon Min Can Cant Cathl from 98; Asst Dir of Ords 07-10. *The Vicarage, Preston Lane, Faversham ME13 8LG* Tel (01795) 536801
E-mail scwilson@coolblue.eclipse.co.uk

WILSON, Stephen Graham. b 70. Ridley Hall Cam 09. **d** 11. C Overton w Laverstoke and Freefolk *Win* from 11. *21 Lordsfield Gardens, Overton, Basingstoke RG25 3EW* Tel (01256) 771402 Mobile 07968-272116
E-mail revstephenwilson@btinternet.com

WILSON, Canon Stephen John. b 45. Bradf Univ BTech69. Trin Coll Bris 90. **d** 92 **p** 93. C Marple All SS *Ches* 92-96; P-in-c Moulton 96-01; Chapl Mid Cheshire Hosps Trust 96-99; V Hyde St Geo *Ches* 01-10; RD Mottram 03-08; Hon Can Ches Cathl 06-10; rtd 10. *18 Green Park, Weaverham, Northwich CW8 3EH* Tel (01606) 851294 E-mail stephenjwilson@talktalk.net

WILSON, Stoker. *See* WILSON, Robert Stoker

WILSON, Stuart Arnold. b 47. SWMTC 94. **d** 97 **p** 98. NSM Okehampton w Inwardleigh, Bratton Clovelly etc *Ex* 97-02; TV 02-09; rtd 10. *Red Spider Cottage, Bratton Clovelly, Okehampton EX20 4JD* Tel (01837) 871248
E-mail s.wilson45@btinternet.com

WILSON, Susan Annette. b 60. Bath Univ BPharm81 PhD86 MRPharmS82. Westcott Ho Cam 98. **d** 00 **p** 01. C Newc St Geo 00-03; Chapl Dame Allan's Schs Newc 02-03; TV Willington *Newc* 03-07; V Newc St Gabr from 07. *St Gabriel's Vicarage, 9 Holderness Road, Newcastle upon Tyne NE6 5RH* Tel 0191-276 3957 E-mail susan.wilson@tinyworld.co.uk

WILSON, Miss Susan Elizabeth. b 52. Lady Spencer Chu Coll of Educn BEd75. WEMTC 96. **d** 99 **p** 00. NSM Saltford w Corston and Newton St Loe *B & W* 99-06; P-in-c Heversham and Milnthorpe *Carl* from 06. *The Vicarage, Woodhouse Lane, Heversham, Milnthorpe LA7 7EW* Tel (01539) 563125
E-mail revsuewilson@tiscali.co.uk

WILSON, Mrs Sylvia. b 57. Teesside Univ BA96 Newc Univ MA99. **d** 08 **p** 09. OLM Preston-on-Tees and Longnewton *Dur*

from 08. *7 Daltry Close, Yarm TS15 9XQ* Tel (01642) 892254 Mobile 07886-852154
E-mail sylviawilson@allsaints-church.co.uk
WILSON, Thomas Irven. b 30. TCD BA51 Div Test 52 MA58. **d** 53 **p** 54. C Ballymena *Conn* 53-56; Chapl RAF 56-85; Asst Chapl-in-Chief 73-85; QHC from 80; rtd 85. *Rathclaren House, Kilbrittain, Co Cork, Republic of Ireland* Tel (00353) (23) 49689
WILSON, Canon Thomas Roderick. b 26. St Pet Hall Ox BA50 MA55. Sarum Th Coll 50. **d** 52 **p** 53. C Poulton-le-Sands *Blackb* 52-56; C Altham w Clayton le Moors 56-58; V Habergham Eaves H Trin 58-78; RD Burnley 70-78; Hon Can Blackb Cathl 75-89; V Bare 78-81; P-in-c Accrington St Jas 81-82; P-in-c Accrington St Paul 81-82; V Accrington St Jas w St Paul 82-89; rtd 89; Perm to Offic *Blackb* from 89. *Fosbrooke House, 8 Clifton Drive, Lytham St Annes FY8 5RQ*
WILSON, Canon Timothy Charles. b 62. Oak Hill Th Coll BA90. **d** 90 **p** 91. C Highley *Heref* 90-94; C Margate H Trin *Cant* 94-98; P-in-c Margate St Phil 98-02; V 02-03; V Gt Chart from 03; AD Ashford from 11; Hon Can Cant Cathl from 11. *The Rectory, The Street, Great Chart, Ashford TN23 3AY* Tel (01233) 620371
E-mail tandcwilson@lineone.net
WILSON, Timothy John. b 58. St Pet Coll Ox MA80. Trin Coll Bris 81. **d** 83 **p** 84. C Gt Horton *Bradf* 83-86; C Handforth *Ches* 86-90; V Halifax All SS *Wakef* 90-07; TR Southgate *Chich* from 07. *The Rectory, Forester Road, Crawley RH10 6EH* Tel (01293) 523463 E-mail wilsons@domini.org
WILSON, Tom. b 78. Ox Univ BA01. Wycliffe Hall Ox BA07. **d** 07 **p** 08. C Toxteth St Philemon w St Gabr and St Cleopas *Liv* from 07. *4 Caryl Grove, Liverpool L8 6RN* Tel 0151-708 4115 Mobile 07759-823104 E-mail tom@toxethteam.org.uk
WILSON (née NICHOLSON), Mrs Veronica Mary. b 66. Nene Coll Northn BSc88 Ches Coll of HE PGCE90. Cranmer Hall Dur 96. **d** 99 **p** 00. C Barnham Broom *Nor* 99-00; C Barnham Broom and Upper Yare 00-02; C Hellesdon 02-06; V Foulsham, Guestwick, Stibbard, Themelthorpe etc from 06. *The Rectory, Guist Road, Foulsham, Dereham NR20 5RZ* Tel (01362) 683275
WILSON, Walter. b 33. Wm Temple Coll Rugby 55. **d** 59 **p** 60. C Sheff St Swithun 59-63; Ind Chapl 63-66; C Attercliffe 63-66; R Swallow w Cabourn *Linc* 66-72; Dioc Youth Officer *Heref* 72-77; Chapl Ipswich Sch 77-94; rtd 94; Perm to Offic *St E* 94-02. *Riverside Cottage, Mendlesham Green, Stowmarket IP14 5RF* Tel (01449) 766198
WILSON, William Adam. b 53. Sheff Univ BA74 St Jo Coll Dur BA84. Cranmer Hall Dur 82. **d** 85 **p** 86. C S Croydon Em *S'wark* 85-89; C Wandsworth All SS 89-93; Chapl Fontainebleau *Eur* 93-00; V S Lambeth St Steph *S'wark* from 00. *The Vicarage, St Stephen's Terrace, London SW8 1DH* Tel (020) 7564 1930 *or* 7735 8461 Fax 7735 7171
E-mail vicar@ststephenssouthlambeth.org.uk
WILSON, William Gerard. b 42. St Chad's Coll Dur BA65. **d** 67 **p** 68. C Hollinwood *Man* 67-71; V Oldham St Jas 71-79; R Birch w Fallowfield 79-93; V Paddington St Jas *Lon* 93-10; AD Westmr Paddington 97-06; rtd 10. *20 Portland Street, Brighton BN1 1RN* Tel 07976-363480 (mobile) E-mail synaxis52@hotmail.com
WILSON, William John. b 25. CEng MIET MRTvS. S Dios Minl Tr Scheme 79. **d** 82 **p** 83. NSM Weeke *Win* 82-88; NSM Win St Barn 89-95; Hon Chapl R Hants Co Hosp Win 89-95; rtd 95; Perm to Offic *Win* 95-04. *23 Buriton Road, Winchester SO22 6JE* Tel (01962) 881904
WILSON, Yvonne. *See* WILSON, Edith Yvonne
WILSON-BARKER, Mrs Carol Amanda. b 64. Ex Univ BA08. SWMTC 00. **d** 03 **p** 05. C Godrevy *Truro* 03-07; TV Hale w Badshot Lea *Guildf* from 07. *The Vicarage, 12 Badshot Lea Road, Badshot Lea, Farnham GU9 9LD* Tel (01252) 327044
E-mail carolw953@aol.com
WILSON-BROWN, Nigel Hugh. b 65. Goldsmiths' Coll Lon BSc87. Wycliffe Hall Ox 95. **d** 97 **p** 98. C Wimbledon Em Ridgway Prop Chpl *S'wark* 97-00; Chapl K Sch Bruton from 00. *King's School, Plox, Bruton BA10 0ED* Tel (01749) 814200 *or* 813326 E-mail chaplain@kingsbruton.somerset.sch.uk
WILTON, Mrs Carlyn Zena. b 54. R Holloway Coll Lon BA75 Southn Univ PGCE76. SWMTC 99. **d** 02 **p** 03. NSM Carbis Bay w Lelant *Truro* from 02. *Venton Elwyn, 61 Queensway, Hayle TR27 4NL* Tel (01736) 752863 E-mail ventonelwyn@aol.com
WILTON, Christopher. b 52. Lon Univ LLB75 Solicitor 79. NEOC 97. **d** 00 **p** 01. NSM Sherburn in Elmet w Saxton *York* from 00; P-in-c 03-09; V from 09; RD Selby from 06. *The Vicarage, 2 Sir John's Lane, Sherburn in Elmet, Leeds LS25 6BJ* Tel (01977) 682122 Mobile 07968-268622
E-mail frwilton@aol.com
WILTON, Canon Gary Ian. b 60. Bath Univ BSc83 Trin Coll Bris MA93 Nottm Univ EdD05. Wycliffe Hall Ox 85. **d** 88 **p** 89. C Clevedon St Andr and Ch Ch *B & W* 88-92; Lect UWE Bris 92-93; TV Bath Twerton-on-Avon *B & W* 93-97; Dir Studies and Lect Wilson Carlile Coll of Evang 98-04; Assoc Prin 04-05; Sen Lect York St Jo Univ 05-08; Hd Postgraduate Progr 06-08; C of E Rep Eur Union and Can Brussels Cathl from 08. *Pro-Cathedral of the Holy Trinity, 29 rue Capitaine Crespel, B-1050 Brussels, Belgium* Tel (0032) (2) 511 7183
E-mail gary.wilton@htbrussels.com

WILTON (née ADAMS), Mrs Gillian Linda. b 57. SRN79 SCM81. Trin Coll Bris 82. **dss** 85 **d** 87 **p** 94. Easton H Trin w St Gabr and St Lawr and St Jude *Bris* 85-91; Par Dn 87-91; Regional Adv (SW) CMJ 91-97; Perm to Offic *B & W* 92-93; NSM Bath Twerton-on-Avon 93-97; Chapl Sheff Children's Hosp NHS Trust 98-06; Chapl Team Ldr Sheff Children's NHS Foundn Trust 06-10; Perm to Offic *Eur* 08-10; Asst Chapl Tervuren from 10; P-in-c Leuven 10-11. *St Paul's Church Centre, Hoornzeelstraat 24, 3080 Tervuren, Belgium* Fax (0032) (2) 767 3435
WILTON, Glenn Warner Paul. b 33. Miami Univ Ohio BSc55 Catholic Univ of America 69 Univ of Washington Seattle MSW76. Pontifical Beda Coll Rome 66 Ch Div Sch of the Pacific (USA) 77. **d** 65 **p** 66. In RC Ch 65-72; NSM Seattle USA 77-81; Chapl Pastures Hosp Derby 82-88; Chapl St Martin's Hosp Cant 89-93; Chapl St Aug Hosp Cant 89-93; Chapl E Kent NHS and Soc Care Partnership Trust 93-03; rtd 03; Perm to Offic *Cant* from 03. *10 Lichfield Avenue, Canterbury CT1 3YA* Tel (01227) 454230 E-mail gwpaulwilton@yahoo.co.uk
WILTS, Archdeacon of. *Vacant*
WILTSE, Joseph August Jean Paul. b 41. Leeds Univ BA64. Coll of Resurr Mirfield 64. **d** 66 **p** 67. C Airedale w Fryston *Wakef* 66-70; Canada from 70. *6983 Richmond Street, Powell River BC V8A 1H7, Canada*
WILTSHIRE, Mrs Jennifer Mary. b 42. Trin Coll Bris 09. **d** 11. OLM Southwell *Bris* from 11. *19 Yew Tree Drive, Bristol BS15 4UA* Tel 0117-957 0435
E-mail jenny.wiltshire410@btinternet.com
WILTSHIRE, John Herbert Arthur. b 27. S'wark Ord Course 63. **d** 66 **p** 67. C Lee Gd Shep w St Pet *S'wark* 66-69; Min W Dulwich Em CD 69-79; R Coulsdon St Jo 79-93; rtd 93; Perm to Offic *Ches* from 93. *66 Meadow Lane, Willaston, Neston CH64 2TZ* Tel 0151-327 6668
WILTSHIRE, Robert Michael. b 50. WMMTC. **d** 89 **p** 90. NSM Droitwich Spa *Worc* 89-93; Asst Chapl HM Pris Wormwood Scrubs 93-94; Chapl HM Pris Standford Hill 94-97; Chapl HM Pris Whitemoor 97-99; Asst Chapl Gen of Pris 99-06; Chapl HM Pris Shrewsbury from 06. *HM Prison, The Dana, Shrewsbury SY1 2HR* Tel (01743) 273000 Fax 273001
E-mail robert.wiltshire@hmps.gsi.gov.uk
WIMBUSH, Canon Timothy. b 44. JP. St Steph Ho Ox. **d** 68 **p** 69. C Hobs Moat *Birm* 68-71; C W Wycombe *Ox* 71-76; R Wykeham from 76; RD Deddington 86-00; Hon Can Ch Ch from 95. *The Rectory, Sibford Gower, Banbury OX15 5RW* Tel (01295) 780555
WIMSETT, Paul. b 58. Univ of Wales (Abth) BSc(Econ)79 Hull Univ MA86. St Jo Coll Nottm 82. **d** 85 **p** 86. C Nuneaton St Nic *Cov* 85-89; C Loughborough Em *Leic* 89-92; TV Totnes, Bridgetown and Berry Pomeroy etc *Ex* 92-99; V Chudleigh w Chudleigh Knighton and Trusham from 99; RD Moreton from 05. *The Vicarage, Parade, Chudleigh, Newton Abbot TQ13 0JF* Tel (01626) 853241 E-mail wimsett@tesco.net
WIMSHURST, Michael Alexander. b 33. St Jo Coll Ox BA58. Westcott Ho Cam 59. **d** 60 **p** 61. C Lewisham St Mary *S'wark* 60-65; India 66-70; V Battersea St Pet *S'wark* 71-73; V Battersea St Pet and St Paul 73-97; rtd 97; Perm to Offic *Cant* from 98. *50 Broad Street, Canterbury CT1 2LS* Tel (01227) 457889
WINBOLT-LEWIS, Martin John. b 46. Fitzw Coll Cam BA69 MA72. St Jo Coll Nottm. **d** 75 **p** 76. C Highbury Ch Ch *Lon* 75-78; C Nottingham St Nic *S'well* 79-82; R Carlton Colville *Nor* 82-83; R Carlton Colville w Mutford and Rushmere 83-88; V Burley *Ripon* 88-96; Asst Chapl Pinderfields and Pontefract Hosps NHS Trust 96-99; Chapl 00-02; Lead Chapl 00-02; Lead Chapl Mid Yorks Hosps NHS Trust 02-05; Hd Chapl Services 05-10; rtd 11. *Owl Pen, 2 Old Manor Farm, Bramhope, Leeds LS16 9BA* Tel 0113-284 2274
E-mail winboltlewis@btinternet.com
WINCHESTER, Gordon Law. b 50. Trin Coll Bris. **d** 82 **p** 83. C Cheadle *Ches* 82-84; Asst Chapl Amsterdam *Eur* 84-88; C Hove Bp Hannington Memorial Ch *Chich* 88-96; V Wandsworth All SS *S'wark* 96-04; P-in-c Ewhurst *Chich* 04-05; R from 05; P-in-c Bodiam 04-05; V from 05. *The Rectory, Ewhurst Green, Robertsbridge TN32 5TB* Tel (01580) 830268
E-mail gordon.winchester@btinternet.com
WINCHESTER, Paul. b 44. St Pet Coll Ox BA66 MA70 Weymouth Coll of Educn PGCE73. Ridley Hall Cam 67. **d** 69 **p** 70. C Wednesfield Heath *Lich* 69-72; Perm to Offic *Sarum* 73-84; R Tushingham and Whitewell *Ches* 84-02; Perm to Offic *Ox* from 02. *12 The Pines, Faringdon SN7 8AU* Tel (01367) 240725 E-mail paulwinchester@tiscali.co.uk
WINCHESTER, Paul Marc. b 53. Univ of Wales (Lamp) BA80. St Mich Coll Llan 82. **d** 84 **p** 85. C Bedwellty *Mon* 84-86; C Chepstow 86-89; V Cwmcarn 89-93; V Fleur-de-Lis 93-98; R Bedwas and Rudry 98-05; P-in-c Llantilio Pertholey w Bettws Chpl etc 05-10; V Brynmawr *S & B* from 10. *14 Valley View, Brynmawr, Ebbw Vale NP23 4SN* Tel (01495) 315324
WINCHESTER, Archdeacon of. *See* HARLEY, The Ven Michael
WINCHESTER, Bishop of. *Vacant*

WINCHESTER, Dean of. *See* ATWELL, The Very Revd James Edgar

WINDEBANK, Clive Leonard. b 41. New Coll Ox BA62 MA85. Ox NSM Course 75. **d** 78 **p** 79. Asst Chapl Ahmadi Kuwait 78-83; NSM Brompton H Trin w Onslow Square St Paul *Lon* 83-84; NSM Basildon w Aldworth and Ashampstead *Ox* 85-88; NSM Streatley w Moulsford 88-00; NSM Wallingford 00-03; Chapl Abu Dhabi St Andr UAE from 03. *The Coombe House, The Coombe, Streatley, Reading RG8 9QL* Tel (01491) 872174

WINDIATE, Mary Elizabeth. *See* WEST, Mrs Mary Elizabeth

WINDLE, Mrs Catharine Elizabeth. b 72. Hatf Coll Dur BA95 Homerton Coll Cam PGCE96. St Jo Coll Nottm MTh02. **d** 03 **p** 04. C Hucknall Torkard *S'well* 03-05; Hon C Hullavington, Norton and Stanton St Quintin *Bris* 05-06; P-in-c Bath Widcombe *B & W* 06-08; Hon C Malmesbury w Westport and Brokenborough *Bris* from 09. *Selwyn House, Pool Gastons Road, Malmesbury SN16 0DE* Tel (01666) 826369
E-mail royandkatie@googlemail.com

WINDLE, Christopher Rodney. b 45. Univ of Wales (Lamp) BA66. Qu Coll Birm. **d** 70 **p** 71. C Lache cum Saltney *Ches* 70-73; C Stockton Heath 73-76; P-in-c Bredbury St Barn 76-83; V 83-07; rtd 07; Perm to Offic *Ches* from 07. *6 Norbury Avenue, Marple, Stockport SK6 6NB* Tel 0161-427 0375

WINDLEY, Caroline Judith. b 62. Trent Poly BA84 Nottm Univ MA97 CQSW84. St Jo Coll Nottm MA96. **d** 97 **p** 98. C Kidderminster St Geo *Worc* 97-01; P-in-c Quarry Bank 01-07; TV Brierley Hill 07-08; RD Kingswinford 04-08; Area Dir of Ord and Adv in Voc Development *Ox* from 08. *1 Cavalry Path, Aylesbury HP19 9RP* Tel (01296) 432921 *or* (01865) 208283
E-mail caroline.windley@oxford.anglican.org

WINDMILL, Roy Stanley. b 17. Sarum Th Coll. **d** 54 **p** 55. C Wells St Cuth w Coxley and Wookey Hole *B & W* 54-58; R Honiley *Cov* 58-64; PC Wroxall 58-64; V Meriden 64-66; C Cov H Trin 66-70; P-in-c Kineton 70-75; P-in-c Combroke w Compton Verney 70-75; C Wraxall *B & W* 76-78; P-in-c Holton 78-82; rtd 82; Perm to Offic *B & W* 82-97; Perm to Offic *Ex* 82-98. *21 Rectory Drive, Burnham-on-Sea TA8 2DT* Tel (01278) 782715

WINDON, Gary. b 62. N Staffs Poly BSc85. Qu Coll Birm 98. **d** 00 **p** 01. C Penn *Lich* 00-04; TV Radcliffe *Man* 04-08; P-in-c Wrexham *St As* from 08; Chapl Nightingale Ho Hospice from 08. *The Vicarage, Vicarage Hill, Rhostyllen, Wrexham LL14 4AR* Tel (01978) 311179 E-mail gary@windon.org.uk
or minister@rhostyllenchurches.org.uk

WINDRIDGE, Michael Harry. b 47. Sarum & Wells Th Coll 91. **d** 93 **p** 94. C Hempnall *Nor* 93-96; NSM Twickenham St Mary *Lon* 96-97; Perm to Offic *Nor* from 98. *Fritton Cottage, The Common, Fritton, Norwich NR15 2QS* Tel (01508) 498577

WINDRIDGE, Peter William Roland. b 23. BScEng MIMechE. Sarum & Wells Th Coll 82. **d** 84 **p** 85. NSM Shirley St Jo *Cant* 84; NSM Shirley St Jo *S'wark* 85-86; NSM New Addington 86-95; rtd 95; Perm to Offic *S'wark* from 95. *16 Mill Court, 44 Brighton Road, South Croydon CR2 6AS* Tel (020) 8681 8739

WINDROSS, Preb Andrew. b 49. Univ of Wales (Ban) BA71. Cuddesdon Coll 71. **d** 74 **p** 75. C Wakef St Jo 74-78; C Bromley All Hallows *Lon* 78-83; V De Beauvoir Town St Pet 83-02; AD Hackney 89-94; Bp's Officer for Ordained Min Stepney Area 02-11; Hon C S Hackney St Mich w Haggerston St Paul 02-11; Preb St Paul's Cathl 02-11; rtd 11. *31 Lavender Grove, London E8 3LU* Tel and fax (020) 7254 7440

WINDROSS, Anthony Michael. b 50. CCC Cam BA72 MA75 Birm Univ PGCE73. S Dios Minl Tr Scheme 90. **d** 93 **p** 94. NSM Eastbourne St Mary *Chich* 93-97; C E Grinstead St Swithun 97-99; V Sheringham *Nor* 99-08; V Hythe *Cant* from 08. *St Leonard's Vicarage, Oak Walk, Hythe CT21 5DN* Tel (01303) 266217 E-mail amw@windross.fsnet.co.uk

WINDSLOW, Canon Kathryn Alison. b 62. Southn Univ BTh83 K Coll Lon MPhil01. Linc Th Coll 84. **dss** 86 **d** 87 **p** 94. Littlehampton and Wick *Chich* 86-89; Par Dn 87-89; Dn-in-c Scotton w Northorpe *Linc* 89-94; P-in-c 94-97; Asst Local Min Officer 89-97; Local Min Officer and Prin OLM Course 97-02; R Graffoe Gp from 02; Can and Preb Linc Cathl from 09; Bp's Adv in Women's Min from 08. *The Rectory, Vicarage Lane, Wellingore, Lincoln LN5 0JF* Tel (01522) 810246
E-mail kathryn.windslow@btinternet.com

WINDSOR, Graham. b 35. G&C Coll Cam BA57 MA64 PhD67 Lon Univ BD60. Clifton Th Coll 58 Trin Coll Bris 79. **d** 79 **p** 80. C Rainham *Chelmsf* 79-82; rtd 00. *Yanbian University, College of Science and Technology, Yanji, Jilin, China 133000* Tel (0086) (43) 3291 2500 Fax 3291 2510
E-mail graham_windsor@hotmail.com

WINDSOR, Julie Fiona. b 59. Ridley Hall Cam 98. **d** 00 **p** 01. C Chertsey *Guildf* 00-04; TV Papworth *Ely* 04-08; TR from 08. *Elsworth Rectory, The Drift, Elsworth, Cambridge CB23 8JN* Tel (01954) 267535 E-mail fiona.windsor@ely.anglican.org

WINDSOR, Mark James. b 75. Bath Univ BSc98. Wycliffe Hall Ox BTh08. **d** 08 **p** 09. C Felsted and Lt Dunmow *Chelmsf* from 08. *7 Tanton Road, Little Dunmow, Dunmow CM6 3GS* Tel (01371) 821996 E-mail markwindsor923@btinternet.com

WINDSOR, Dean of. *See* CONNER, The Rt Revd David John

WINFIELD, Canon Flora Jane Louise. b 64. Univ of Wales (Lamp) BA85 Virginia Th Sem DD10 FRSA98. Ripon Coll Cuddesdon 87. **d** 89 **p** 94. Par Dn Stantonbury and Willen *Ox* 89-92; Co Ecum Officer *Glouc* 92-94; Chapl Mansf Coll Ox 94-97; Local Unity Sec Coun for Chr Unity 97-02; CF (TA) from 97; Can Res Win Cathl 02-05; Asst Sec Gen World Conf of Relig for Peace 05-06; Special Adv from 06; Sec Internat Affairs CTBI 06-09; Abp's Sec for Angl Relns *Cant* from 07; P-in-c St Mary at Hill w St Andr Hubbard etc *Lon* from 08. *Lambeth Palace, London SE1 7JU* E-mail flora.winfield@lambethpalace.org.uk

WINFIELD, Miss June Mary. b 29. Gilmore Ho 57. **dss** 66 **d** 87 **p** 94. Is of Dogs Ch Ch and St Jo w St Luke *Lon* 66-68; Bracknell *Ox* 68-74; Dean of Women's Min 74-80; St Marylebone w H Trin *Lon* 80-82; Ind Chapl 82-89; rtd 89; NSM Ealing St Steph Castle Hill *Lon* 89-97; Asst Dioc Dir Ords Willesden Area 94-97; Perm to Offic 97-02. *25 Trinity Road, Marlow SL7 3AN* Tel (01628) 484317

WING, Mrs Julie. b 62. Teesside Univ BSc99. NEOC 02. **d** 05 **p** 06. C Sunderland St Chad *Dur* 05-09; TV Gt Aycliffe from 09. *20 Haslewood Road, Newton Aycliffe DL5 4XF* Tel (01325) 320278 Mobile 07910-293936
E-mail julie_wing_1@hotmail.com

WING, Miss Myra Susan. b 45. Cranmer Hall Dur 92. **d** 94 **p** 95. C Appledore w Brookland, Fairfield, Brenzett etc *Cant* 94-98; Hon C Wittersham w Stone and Ebony 95-98; V Grayshott *Guildf* 98-08; rtd 08; Perm to Offic *Cant* from 09. *142 Minster Road, Westgate-on-Sea CT8 8DQ* Tel (01843) 836430
E-mail susan@wing63.fsnet.co.uk

WINGATE, Canon Andrew David Carlile. b 44. Worc Coll Ox BA66 MA71 MPhil68 Birm Univ PhD95. Linc Th Coll 70. **d** 72 **p** 73. C Halesowen *Worc* 72-75; Lect Tamilnadu Th Sem India 76-82; Prin WMMTC 82-90; Prin United Coll of Ascension Selly Oak 90-00; Hon Can Birm Cathl 97-00; Dir Min and Tr Leic 00-03; Dir Interfaith Relns and Co-ord Lay Tr 03-10; rtd 10; Can Th Leic Cathl from 00; Chapl to The Queen from 07. *23 Roundhill Road, Leicester LE5 5RJ* Tel 0116-221 6146 Mobile 07808-586259 E-mail andangwingate@ntlworld.com

WINGATE, Canon David Hugh. b 22. Qu Coll Cam BA48 MA53. Qu Coll Birm 47. **d** 49 **p** 50. C Cov St Mary 49-52; V Wolston 52-56; V Cov All SS 56-60; R Patterdale *Carl* 60-66; Chapl United Leeds Hosp 66-71; Chapl Garlands Cumberland and Westmoreland Hosps 71-86; V Cotehill and Cumwhinton *Carl* 72-86; Hon Can-Carl Cathl 85-86; rtd 87; Perm to Offic *Carl* from 87-01 and *Bradf* from 02. *c/o Mrs T Grisdale, 3 Northolme Crescent, Leeds LS16 5HU*

WINGFIELD, Christopher Laurence. b 57. Westmr Coll Ox BTh99. Ripon Coll Cuddesdon 93. **d** 95 **p** 96. C Hadleigh *St E* 95-99; P-in-c Melton 99-00; R 00-01; R Sproughton w Burstall, Copdock w Washbrook etc 01-09; RD Samford 06-09; P-in-c Bromsgrove St Jo *Worc* from 09. *The Vicarage, 12 Kidderminster Road, Bromsgrove B61 7JW* Tel (01527) 876517 Mobile 07703-814022 E-mail chris.wingfield@btinternet.com

WINGFIELD DIGBY, Andrew Richard. b 50. Keble Coll Ox BA72. Wycliffe Hall Ox 74. **d** 77 **p** 78. C Cockfosters Ch Ch CD *Lon* 77-80; C Hadley Wood St Paul Prop Chpl 80-84; Dir Chrs in Sport 84-02; V Ox St Andr from 02; Six Preacher Cant Cathl from 97. *St Andrew's Vicarage, 46 Charlbury Road, Oxford OX2 6UX* Tel (01865) 310370 *or* tel and fax 311212 Mobile 07768-611232
E-mail andrew.wingfield.digby@standrewsoxford.org

WINKETT, Miss Lucy Clare. b 68. Selw Coll Cam BA90 MA94 ARCM92. Qu Coll Birm BD94. **d** 95 **p** 96. C Lt Ilford St Mich *Chelmsf* 95-97; Min Can and Chapl St Paul's Cathl 97-03; Can Res and Prec 03-10; R Westmr St Jas from 10. *St James's Rectory, 197 Piccadilly, London W1J 9LL* Tel (020) 7248 1817 E-mail rector@st-james-piccadilly.org

WINKS, Paul David. b 45. Ex Univ BA67. Cuddesdon Coll 68. **d** 70 **p** 71. C Rickerscote *Lich* 70-73; Chapl RAF 73-75; C Yate *Bris* 76-77; TV Yate New Town 77-83; P-in-c Leigh upon Mendip w Stoke St Michael *B & W* 83-84; V 84-10; rtd 10. *21 Alfords Ridge, Coleford, Radstock BA3 5YJ*

WINN, Alan John. b 42. FRSA73. **d** 01 **p** 02. OLM Ringwould w Kingsdown *Cant* 01-04; OLM Ringwould w Kingsdown and Ripple etc from 05. *Chilterns, Back Street, Ringwould, Deal CT14 8HL* Tel (01304) 361030 E-mail revjohnwinn@aol.com

WINN, Mrs Jean Elizabeth. b 58. Man Univ BSc80. Wycliffe Hall Ox 85. **d** 88 **p** 98. C W Derby St Luke *Liv* 88-89; Perm to Offic 89-98; NSM Seaforth 98-02; NSM Anfield St Marg from 02. *St Margaret's Vicarage, Rocky Lane, Liverpool L6 4BA* Tel 0151-263 3118

WINN, Paul William James. b 44. Liv Univ BSc66. EMMTC 86. **d** 89 **p** 90. NSM Spalding St Paul *Linc* 89-98; Perm to Offic 98-00; P-in-c Cowbit 00-01; V 01-07; rtd 07. *6 Hawthorn Chase, Moulton, Spalding PE12 6GA* Tel (01406) 373662
E-mail paulwinn80@hotmail.com

WINN, Peter Anthony. b 60. Worc Coll Ox BA82 MA86. Wycliffe Hall Ox 83. **d** 86 **p** 87. C W Derby Gd Shep *Liv* 86-89; V Seaforth 89-02; P-in-c Anfield St Marg 02-09; V from 09. *St Margaret's Vicarage, Rocky Lane, Liverpool L6 4BA* Tel 0151-263 3118

WINN, Simon Reynolds. b 66. Bris Univ BA88. Trin Coll Bris 96. **d** 98 **p** 99. C Portswood Ch Ch *Win* 98-02; V Northolt St Jos *Lon* 02-10; Dir of Ords Willesden Area 07-10; V Hataitai-Kilbirnie New Zealand from 10. *94 Hamilton Road, Hataitai, Wellington 6021, New Zealand* Tel (0064) (4) 971 2140 *or* 971 2142 E-mail simonwinn66@yahoo.co.uk *or* vicar@allsaints.org.nz

WINNARD, Jack. b 30. Oak Hill Th Coll 79. **d** 81 **p** 82. C Skelmersdale St Paul *Liv* 81-84; C Goose Green 84-85; V Wigan St Barn Marsh Green 85-98; rtd 99; Perm to Offic *Liv* from 00. *Maranatha, 11 Beech Walk, Winstanley, Wigan WN3 6DH* Tel (01942) 222339

WINNEY, Mrs Samantha Jane. b 71. St Mellitus Coll BA10. **d** 10 **p** 11. NSM Harwich Peninsula *Chelmsf* from 10. *Wisteria, Mill Lane, Bradfield, Manningtree CO11 2UT* Tel (01255) 870618 Mobile 07903-522955 E-mail rev.samantha@googlemail.com

WINNINGTON-INGRAM, David Robert. b 59. Hertf Coll Ox BA82 MA85 K Coll Cam BA89. Westcott Ho Cam 87. **d** 90 **p** 91. C Bishop's Cleeve *Glouc* 90-94; TV Colyton, Southleigh, Offwell, Widworthy etc *Ex* 94-00; V S Brent and Rattery from 00. *The Vicarage, Firswood, South Brent TQ10 9AN* Tel (01364) 649070 *or* 72774 E-mail wis100acre.wood@virgin.net

WINSLADE, Richard Clive. b 69. Aston Tr Scheme 91 Linc Th Coll BTh93. **d** 96 **p** 97. C Waltham Cross *St Alb* 96-99; C Leavesden 99-03; R Maulden from 03. *The Rectory, Clophill Road, Maulden, Bedford MK45 2AA* Tel and fax (01525) 403139 E-mail member@rwinslade.fsnet.co.uk

WINSPER, Arthur William (Brother Benedict). b 46. Ox Brookes Univ BA10. Glas NSM Course 89. **d** 91 **p** 92. SSF from 70; NSM Barrowfield *Glas* 91-96; P-in-c St Aug Miss Penhalonga Zimbabwe 96-98; Perm to Offic *Worc* 98-09 and *Sheff* 09-11. *St Peter's Vicarage, Druridge Drive, Newcastle upon Tyne NE5 3LP* Tel 0191-286 9913

✠**WINSTANLEY, The Rt Revd Alan Leslie.** b 49. Nottm Univ BTh72. St Jo Coll Nottm 68 ALCD72. **d** 72 **p** 73 **c** 88. C Livesey *Blackb* 72-75; C Gt Sankey *Liv* 75-77; P-in-c Penketh 75-77; V 78-81; SAMS 81-93; Bp Bolivia and Peru 88-93; V Eastham *Ches* 94-03; Hon Asst Bp Ches 94-03; V Whittle-le-Woods *Blackb* from 03; Hon Asst Bp Blackb from 03. *The Vicarage, Preston Road, Whittle-le-Woods, Chorley PR6 7PS* Tel (01257) 241291 E-mail alan.winstanley@talktalk.net

WINSTANLEY, John Graham. b 47. K Coll Lon 67. **d** 71 **p** 72. C Wandsworth St Paul *S'wark* 71-74; Chapl Salford Univ 75-79; R Kersal Moor 79-87. *14 Lyndhurst Avenue, Prestwich, Manchester M25 0GF* Tel 0161-740 2715 Fax 720 6916 E-mail john@blots.co.uk

WINSTON, Canon Jeremy Hugh. b 54. Trin Coll Carmarthen BEd76 BA CertEd. St Steph Ho Ox 78. **d** 79 **p** 80. C Bassaleg *Mon* 79-83; Dioc Children's Adv 79-89; V Itton and St Arvans w Penterry and Kilgwrrwg etc 83-93; V Abergavenny St Mary w Llanwenarth Citra from 93; RD Abergavenny from 02; P-in-c Govilon w Llanfoist w Llanelen from 09; Can St Woolos Cathl from 02. *St Mary's Vicarage, Monk Street, Abergavenny NP7 5ND* Tel (01873) 853168 E-mail jeremy.winston@virgin.net

WINSTONE, Canon Peter John. b 30. Jes Coll Ox BA52 MA56. Ridley Hall Cam 53. **d** 55 **p** 56. C Bitterne *Win* 55-58; C Keighley *Bradf* 58-60; PC Fairweather Green 60-67; V Clapham 67-84; R Leathley w Farnley, Fewston and Blubberhouses 84-95; Hon Can Bradf Cathl 89-95; rtd 95; Perm to Offic *Worc* from 95. *7 Kingfisher Close, Worcester WR5 3RY* Tel (01905) 763114

WINTER, Andrew Christopher. b 73. Dur Univ BSc95 PGCE96. **d** 03 **p** 04. C Mosman St Clem Australia 03-05; NSM Hinckley H Trin *Leic* 06-10; Chapl Ipswich Sch from 10. *Ipswich School, Henley Road, Ipswich IP1 3SG* Tel (01473) 408300

WINTER, Anthony Cathcart. b 28. FCA. Ridley Hall Cam 54. **d** 56 **p** 57. C Childwall St Dav *Liv* 56-58; C Hackney St Jo *Lon* 58-63; V Newmarket All SS *St E* 63-73; Lic to Offic 74-81; Perm to Offic *Lon* 78-81 and 97-99; Hon C St Andr-by-the-Wardrobe w St Ann, Blackfriars 81-86; Hon C Smithfield St Bart Gt 86-95; Chapl S'wark Cathl from 99. *25 Bowater House, Golden Lane Estate, London EC1Y 0RJ* Tel (020) 7490 5765 Fax 7490 1064

WINTER, Dagmar. b 63. Heidelberg Univ DrTheol96. Herborn Th Sem 93. **d** 96 **p** 97. C Bromley St Mark *Roch* 96-99; C Hexham *Newc* 99-06; P-in-c Kirkwhelpington, Kirkharle, Kirkheaton and Cambo from 06; Dioc Officer for Rural Affairs from 06. *The Vicarage, Kirkwhelpington, Newcastle upon Tyne NE19 2RT* Tel (01830) 540260 E-mail dagmar@winternet.freeserve.co.uk

WINTER, Canon David Brian. b 29. K Coll Lon BA53 CertEd54. Oak Hill NSM Course. **d** 87 **p** 88. NSM Finchley St Paul and St Luke *Lon* 87-89; Hd Relig Broadcasting BBC 87-89; Bp's Officer for Evang *Ox* 89-95; P-in-c Ducklington 89-95; Hon Can Ch Ch 95; rtd 95; Hon C Hermitage *Ox* 95-00; Hon C Dorchester 02-05; Perm to Offic 00-02 and from 06. *51 Nideggen Close, Thatcham RG19 4HS* Tel (01635) 873639 E-mail david_winter1@btinternet.com

WINTER, Canon Dennis Graham St Leger. b 33. K Coll Lon BSc54 AKC54. Tyndale Hall Bris BD62. **d** 61 **p** 62. C Pennycross *Ex* 61-64; C Maidstone St Faith *Cant* 64-66; V Paddock Wood *Roch* 66-99; RD Tonbridge 89-95; RD Paddock Wood 95-99; Hon Can Roch Cathl 90-99; rtd 99; Perm to Offic *Newc* from 00. *4 Oaky Balks, Alnwick NE66 2QE* Tel (01665) 602658

WINTER, Mrs Fiona Helen. b 64. Sheff Univ BSc87. NEOC 97. **d** 00. NSM Gt Ayton w Easby and Newton-in-Cleveland *York* 00-02. *9 The Acres, Stokesley, Middlesbrough TS9 5QA* Tel (01642) 713146

WINTER, Jonathan Gay. b 37. Lon Inst of Educn DipEd84. AKC64. **d** 65 **p** 66. C W Dulwich All SS and Em *S'wark* 65-69; Asst Master Kidbrooke Sch 69-77; Norwood Sch 77-80; Dep Hd Lewisham Sch 80-89; Hon C Dulwich St Barn 90-98; Chapl Dulwich Coll 95-98; Cllr from 98; Dean of MSE (Woolwich) 00-04; Perm to Offic *S'wark* from 08. *160 Turney Road, London SE21 7JJ* Tel and fax (020) 7274 3060 Mobile 07811-529503 E-mail jonathanwinter@btinternet.com

WINTER, Mrs Mary Elizabeth. b 56. Man Univ BEd78 Leeds Univ AdDipEd85. Yorks Min Course 08. **d** 11. C Skipton Ch Ch w Carleton *Bradf* from 11; C Skipton H Trin from 11. *10 Carleton Avenue, Skipton BD23 2TE* Tel (01756) 792547 Mobile 07813-687680 E-mail mary.winter@hotmail.co.uk

WINTER, Nichola Jane. b 58. Trevelyan Coll Dur BA79. Dioc OLM tr scheme 99. **d** 02 **p** 03. OLM Aldeburgh w Hazlewood *St E* from 02; Chapl Suffolk Coastal Primary Care Trust from 06. *Threeways, Donkey Lane, Friston, Saxmundham IP17 1PL* Tel (01728) 688979 E-mail njwinter@clara.co.uk

WINTER, Rebecca Anne. See BEVAN, Mrs Rebecca Anne

WINTER, Stephen Christopher. b 55. Southn Univ BA76. Trin Coll Bris 85. **d** 88 **p** 89. C Birm St Luke 88-92; TV Kings Norton 92-98; Ind Chapl *Worc* 98-04; Asst Dir Development (Discipleship) from 04; C Finstall from 04. *1 Marlbrough Avenue, Bromsgrove B60 2PG* Tel (01527) 575737 *or* (01905) 732813 E-mail swinter@cofe-worcester.co.uk

WINTER, Thomas Andrew. b 24. Wadh Coll Ox BA51 MA63. Ely Th Coll 51. **d** 53 **p** 54. C Horninglow *Lich* 53-56; S Africa 56-83; R Woodston *Ely* 83-90; rtd 90; Perm to Offic *Ely* 90-97 and *Chich* from 90. *6 The Close, Shoreham-by-Sea BN43 5AH* Tel (01273) 452606

WINTERBOTTOM, Canon Ian Edmund. b 42. St Andr Univ MA66. Linc Th Coll 66. **d** 68 **p** 69. C Blackb St Steph 68-71; C Wingerworth *Derby* 71-73; P-in-c Brimington 73-77; R 77-89; RD Bolsover and Staveley 86-93; R Pleasley 89-94; P-in-c Shirebrook 92-94; TR E Scarsdale 94-00; Hon Can Derby Cathl 95-08; Prin Ind Chapl 00-08; rtd 08. *17 Coach Way, Willington, Derby DE65 6ES* Tel (01283) 704322 E-mail ianwinterbottom@aol.com

WINTERBURN, Derek Neil. b 60. Bris Univ BSc82 Ox Univ BA85. Wycliffe Hall Ox 83. **d** 86 **p** 87. C Mildmay Grove St Jude and St Paul *Lon* 86-89; C Hackney Marsh 89-91; TV 91-96; V Hampton St Mary from 96; AD Hampton from 08. *St Mary's Vicarage, Church Street, Hampton TW12 2EB* Tel (020) 8979 3071 Fax 8941 7221 E-mail stmary@bigfoot.com *or* vicar@winterburn.me.uk

WINTGENS, Peter Brendon. b 47. Surrey Univ BSc70. SEITE 06. **d** 09 **p** 10. NSM Battersea St Mary *S'wark* from 09. *5 Beechmore Road, London SW11 4ET* Tel (020) 7720 9708 E-mail wintgens@btinternet.com

WINTLE, Anthony Robert. b 44. K Coll Lon 64. St Mich Coll Llan. **d** 68 **p** 69. C Llandaff N 68-70; C Baglan 70-75; V Treharris 75-86; V Treharris w Bedlinog 86-90; R St Fagans w Michaelston-super-Ely from 90. *The Rectory, Greenwood Lane, St Fagans, Cardiff CF5 6EL* Tel (029) 2056 5869

WINTLE, David Robert. b 56. Open Univ BA84. Qu Coll Birm 93. **d** 95 **p** 96. C Cov St Mary 95-00; P-in-c Ryton-on-Dunsmore w Bubbenhall 00-05; P-in-c Baginton 02-05; V Baginton w Bubbenhall and Ryton-on-Dunsmore from 05. *The Vicarage, Church Road, Ryton on Dunsmore, Coventry CV8 3ET* Tel (024) 7630 1283 E-mail david@wintled.fsnet.co.uk

WINTLE, Graham. b 52. Bris Univ BSc73. Oak Hill Th Coll BA86. **d** 86 **p** 87. C Southgate *Chich* 86-89; C New Malden and Coombe *S'wark* 89-92; V Surbiton Hill Ch Ch 92-06; R Willoughby Australia from 06. *211 Mowbray Road, Willoughby NSW 2068, Australia* Tel (0061) (2) 9411 2172 E-mail graham.wintle@gmail.com

WINTLE, Canon Ruth Elizabeth. b 31. Westf Coll Lon BA53 St Hugh's Coll Ox BA67 MA74. St Mich Ho Ox 63. **dss** 72 **d** 87 **p** 94. Tutor St Jo Coll Dur 72-74; Selection Sec ACCM 74-83; St Jo in Bedwardine *Worc* 83-87; Par Dn 87-94; Dir of Ords 84-92; Hon Can Worc Cathl 87-97; rtd 95; Bp's Adv on Women's Min *Worc* 95-97; Perm to Offic from 98. *6 Kenswick Manor, Lower Broadheath, Worcester WR2 6QB* Tel (01905) 641470

✠**WINTON, The Rt Revd Alan Peter.** b 58. Sheff Univ BA83 PhD87. Linc Th Coll 91. **d** 91 **p** 92 **c** 09. C Southgate Ch Ch *Lon* 91-95; P-in-c St Paul's Walden and Dioc CME Officer *St Alb* 95-99; R Welwyn w Ayot St Peter 99-05; TR Welwyn 05-09; Hon Can St Alb 07-09; Suff Bp Thetford *Nor* from 09. *The Red House, 53 Norwich Road, Stoke Holy Cross, Norwich NR14 8AB* Tel (01508) 491014 Fax 538371 E-mail bishop.thetford@norwich.anglican.org

WINTON, Ms Philippa Mary. b 56. Nottm Univ BA78. Trin Coll Bris 79. **dss** 83 **d** 87 **p** 94. Sheff St Jo 83-86; Sheff Gillcar St Silas 86-87; Chapl Asst R Hallamshire Hosp Sheff 87; Hon Par Dn Linc St Faith and St Martin w St Pet 90-92; Chapl Asst W Middx Univ Hosp Isleworth 92-93; Perm to Offic *Lon* 93-95 and *St Alb* 95-09. *The Red House, 53 Norwich Road, Stoke Holy Cross, Norwich NR14 8AB*

WINTON, Stanley Wootton. b 30. Sarum & Wells Th Coll 70. **d** 72 **p** 73. C Birkenhead St Jas w St Bede *Ches* 72-75; V 75-79; TR Ellesmere Port 79-88; Chapl Ellesmere Port and Manor Hosps 79-95; R Delamere *Ches* 88-95; rtd 95; Perm to Offic *Ches* from 95. *26 Wimborne Avenue, Thingwall, Wirral CH61 7UL* Tel 0151-648 0176

WINTOUR, Mrs Anne Elizabeth. b 52. **d** 03 **p** 04. OLM Melksham *Sarum* from 03; OLM Atworth w Shaw and Whitley from 07; OLM Broughton Gifford, Gt Chalfield and Holt from 07. *Weavers House, 264 Sandridge Lane, Bromham, Chippenham SN15 2JW* Tel (01380) 850880
E-mail anniewintour@btinternet.com

WINWARD, Stuart James. b 36. Open Univ BA85. Lich Th Coll 65. **d** 68 **p** 69. C Lytham St Cuth *Blackb* 68-71; C Padiham 71-73; V Musbury 73-84; R Old Trafford St Hilda *Man* 84-89; V Davyhulme St Mary 89-98; rtd 98; Perm to Offic *Ches* from 99. *1 Walnut Grove, Sale M33 6AJ* Tel 0161-905 1039

WIPPELL, David Stanley. b 46. Univ of Qld BSc67 Selw Coll Cam BA77 MA. Westcott Ho Cam 76. **d** 78 **p** 79. C Wolvercote w Summertown *Ox* 78-80; Asst Chapl St Edw Sch Ox 78-00; Chapl 00-06; Housemaster 85-97; Chapl St Hugh's Coll Ox 80-85; NSM Ray Valley *Ox* from 06. *3 The Rise, Islip, Kidlington OX5 2TG* Tel (01865) 849497
E-mail davidwippell@hotmail.com

WISE, David Reginald. b 46. Glas Univ BSc68 QUB PhD74 LRAM67. Edin Th Coll 72. **d** 74 **p** 75. Chapl St Andr Cathl 74-75; C Ayr *Glas* 75-78; R Airdrie 78-81; P-in-c Gartcosh 78-81; P-in-c Leic St Nic 81-82; Chapl Leic Univ 81-89; TV Leic H Spirit 82-89; Chapl St Hilda's Priory and Sch Whitby 89-96; TV Louth *Linc* 96-98; V Mexborough *Sheff* from 98. *The Vicarage, Church Street, Mexborough S64 0ER* Tel (01709) 582321

WISE, Jacqueline Joy. b 65. Yorks Min Course. **d** 09 **p** 10. C Crewe All SS and St Paul w St Pet *Ches* from 09. *41 South Crofts, Nantwich CW5 5SG*

WISE, Canon Pamela Margaret. b 51. CertEd73 BA79. Ripon Coll Cuddesdon 89. **d** 91 **p** 94. Par Dn Tokyngton St Mich *Lon* 91-94; C N Greenford All Hallows 94; C Bedford All SS *St Alb* 94-97; TV Hitchin 97-03; V Oxhey All SS from 03; Hon Can St Alb from 09. *All Saints' Vicarage, Gosforth Lane, Watford WD19 7AX* Tel (020) 8421 5949
E-mail pamela.wise@gmail.com

WISE, Richard Edmund. b 67. Clare Coll Cam BA88 MusB89 LRAM91. Cranmer Hall Dur 01. **d** 03 **p** 04. C Stanmore *Win* 03-07; P-in-c Bishopstoke 07-09; R from 09. *The Rectory, 14 Stoke Park Road, Eastleigh SO50 6DA* Tel (023) 8061 2192
E-mail rwise@talktalk.net

WISEMAN, Canon David John. b 51. Lon Univ BD80 Derby Univ MA99. Cranmer Hall Dur 77. **d** 80 **p** 81. C Bilston *Lich* 80-84; P-in-c W Bromwich St Phil 84-86; V 86-89; P-in-c Cheetham St Mark *Man* 89-94; Dioc Community Relns Officer 89-96; P-in-c Ashton H Trin 94-99; TR Ashton 00-03; Chapl Tameside Coll 94-03; Soc Resp Adv *Pet* 03-07; P-in-c Northampton Ch Ch from 07; AD Gtr Northn from 07; Can Pet Cathl from 09. *Christ Church Vicarage, 3 Christ Church Road, Northampton NN1 5LL* Tel (01604) 633254
E-mail david@wiseman50.freeserve.co.uk

WISEMAN, John. b 56. Sarum & Wells Th Coll 80. **d** 83 **p** 84. C Swinton St Pet *Man* 83-87; C Swinton and Pendlebury 87-88; TV Atherton 88-93; V Bedford Leigh 93-02; V Lt Lever from 02. *The Vicarage, Market Street, Little Lever, Bolton BL3 1HH* Tel (01204) 700936

WISEMAN, Sister Julie. b 53. ERMC 05. **d** 08 **p** 09. NSM Roughton and Felbrigg, Metton, Sustead etc *Nor* 08-10; Public Preacher from 10. *32B Beeston Common, Sheringham NR26 8ES* Tel (01263) 825623 E-mail juliessl@btinternet.com

WISHART, Michael Leslie. b 48. St Mich Coll Llan 70. **d** 73 **p** 74. C Llangyfelach *S & B* 73-76; Chapl RN 76-80 and 85-96; V Beguildy and Heyope *S & B* 80-84; V Gowerton 84-85; Chapl RNR 80-85; R Dowlais *Llan* 97-04; R Bishops Lydeard w Bagborough and Cothelstone *B & W* 04-11; rtd 11. *Address temp unknown* E-mail michael.wishart@btinternet.com

WISKEN, Canon Brian Leonard. b 34. Dur Univ BA58. Linc Th Coll 58. **d** 60 **p** 61. C Lobley Hill *Dur* 60-63; C Ipswich All Hallows *St E* 63-65; P-in-c Scunthorpe All SS *Linc* 65-69; 69-71; Dioc Stewardship Adv 70-75; R Panton w Wragby 71-75; V Langton by Wragby 71-75; R Cleethorpes 75-77; TR 77-89; V Linc St Nic w St Jo Newport 89-99; Can and Preb Linc Cathl 88-00; rtd 99; Perm to Offic *Nor* and *St E* from 99. *49 Gainsborough Drive, Lowestoft NR32 4NJ* Tel (01502) 512378 E-mail b.wisken@btinternet.com

WISKEN, Robert Daniel. b 30. ACT. **d** 60 **p** 60. C N Rockhampton St Barn Australia 60; V N Rockhampton St Matt

WINTON, Ms Philippa Mary. 61-63; V Winton *Man* 63-65; R Luddington w Hemington and Thurning *Pet* 65-69; P-in-c Clopton *St E* 66-69; V Ipswich All SS 69-73; V Sompting *Chich* 74-78; Org Sec (SW England) CECS 78-80; R Edmundbyers w Muggleswick *Dur* 80-83; R Wexham *Ox* 83-86; Australia from 86; rtd 95. *1 Elizabeth Lodge, 12 Elizabeth Avenue, Broadbeach, QLD 4218, Australia* E-mail randjwisken@bigpond.com

WITCHELL, David William. b 47. St Jo Coll Nottm BTh75. **d** 75 **p** 76. C Northampton St Mary *Pet* 75-78; C Oakham w Hambleton and Egleton 78-81; C Oakham, Hambleton, Egleton, Braunston and Brooke 81-82; V Weedon Bec w Everdon 82-90; V Wellingborough St Barn 90-00; RD Wellingborough 98-00; P-in-c Paignton St Paul Preston *Ex* 00-02; V Paignton Ch Ch and Preston St Paul from 03; RD Torbay 03-09. *St Paul's Vicarage, Locarno Avenue, Paignton TQ3 2DH* Tel (01803) 522872

WITCHELL, Derek William Frederick. b 49. SAOMC 00. **d** 03 **p** 04. C Bloxham w Milcombe and S Newington *Ox* 03-06; P-in-c Wing w Grove from 06; P-in-c Wingrave w Rowsham, Aston Abbotts and Cublington from 06; P-in-c Cheddington w Mentmore from 08. *The Vicarage, 27B Aylesbury Road, Wing, Leighton Buzzard LU7 0PD* Tel (01296) 682320 Mobile 07847-167507 E-mail witchell@psaconnect.net

WITCHER, Ian. b 49. CertEd93 Lon Inst of Educn Lic97. **d** 97 **p** 98. OLM Shaston *Sarum* 97-08. *7 Old Boundary Road, Shaftesbury SP7 8ND* Tel (01747) 854878

WITCOMBE, Canon John Julian. b 59. Cam Univ MA84 Nottm Univ MPhil91. St Jo Coll Nottm BA83. **d** 84 **p** 85. C Birtley *Dur* 84-87; C Chilwell S'well 87-91; V Lodge Moor St Luke *Sheff* 91-95; TR Uxbridge *Lon* 95-98; Dean St Jo Coll Nottm 98-05; Officer for Min *Glouc* 05-10; Hon Can Glouc Cathl 09-10; Can Res Glouc Cathl from 10; Dir Discipleship and Min from 10. *St Paul's Vicarage, 2 King Edward's Avenue, Gloucester GL1 5DA* Tel (01452) 500443 E-mail jwitcombe@glosdioc.org.uk

WITCOMBE, Michael David. b 53. Univ of Wales (Lamp) BA76. Qu Coll Birm 76. **d** 78 **p** 79. C Neath w Llantwit 78-80; C Whitchurch 80-83; V Newcastle 83-02; P-in-c Ewenny 84-86; V Llanishen from 02. *The Vicarage, 2 The Rise, Llanishen, Cardiff CF14 0RA* Tel (029) 2075 2545

WITCOMBE, Ricarda Jane. b 64. Ch Coll Cam BA86 MA90. St Jo Coll Nottm MA(TS)99. **d** 01 **p** 02. C Wilford S'well 01-05; P-in-c Glouc St Paul 05-09; V Glouc St Paul and St Steph from 09. *St Paul's Vicarage, 2 King Edward's Avenue, Gloucester GL1 5DA* Tel (01452) 500443
E-mail ricarda@ricarda.fsnet.co.uk

WITCOMBE, Simon Christopher. b 61. Dundee Univ MA83 PGCE84 Dur Univ BA90. St Jo Coll Dur 88. **d** 91 **p** 92. C Earlham St Anne *Nor* 91-95; Assoc P Skegness and Winthorpe *Linc* 95-98; Gen Preacher 95-98; R Woodhall Spa Gp 98-07; V Codsall *Lich* from 07. *The Vicarage, 52 Church Road, Codsall, Wolverhampton WV8 1EH* Tel (01902) 842168
E-mail witcombe@tinyonline.co.uk

WITHERIDGE, John Stephen. b 53. Kent Univ BA76 Ch Coll Cam BA78 MA82 FRSA98. Ridley Hall Cam 78. **d** 79 **p** 80. C Luton St Mary *St Alb* 79-82; Asst Chapl Marlborough Coll 82-84; Abp's Chapl *Cant* 84-87; Conduct Eton Coll 87-96; Hd Charterhouse Sch Godalming from 96; Perm to Offic *Guildf* 96-09. *Charterhouse, Godalming GU7 2DJ* Tel (01483) 291600 Fax 291647

WITHERS, Mrs Christine Mary. b 37. ALA60. Gilmore Ho. **dss** 81 **d** 87 **p** 94. Chorleywood Ch Ch *St Alb* 81-86; Darley *Derby* 86-92; C 87-92; Chapl HM Pris Drake Hall 92-95; P-in-c Standon and Cotes Heath *Lich* 96-98; Perm to Offic *Heref* from 98. *St Mary's Close, Westbury, Shrewsbury SY5 9QX* Tel (01743) 885038

WITHERS, Eleanor. See WILLIAMS, Mrs Eleanor Jane

WITHERS, Geoffrey Edward. b 68. QUB BSc90 TCD BTh93. CITC 90. **d** 93 **p** 94. C Ballymena w Ballyclug *Conn* 93-97; I Monkstown 97-01; Chapl RAF from 01. *Chaplaincy Services, Valiant Block, HQ Air Command, RAF High Wycombe HP14 4UE* Tel (01494) 496800 Fax 496343
E-mail stchap.dgcs@ptc.raf.mod.uk *or* gwithers@vodafone.net

WITHERS, Miss Gillian. b 58. Stranmillis Coll BEd80. St Jo Coll Nottm 94. **d** 97 **p** 98. NSM Mossley *Conn* 97-03; C Bangor St Comgall *D & D* 03-05; V Knock 05-08; I Grey Abbey w Kircubbin from 08. *4 Rectory Wood, Portaferry, Newtownards BT22 1LJ* Tel (028) 4272 9307
E-mail vicarofdibley@hotmail.com

WITHERS, John Geoffrey. b 39. St Jo Coll Dur BA61 Birm Univ CertEd63 CQSW72. SWMTC 84. **d** 87 **p** 88. NSM Drewsteignton *Ex* 87-01; P-in-c 99-01; P-in-c Hittisleigh and Spreyton 99-01; P-in-c Chagford, Drewsteignton, Hittisleigh etc 01; C 01-07; Sub Chapl HM Pris Ex 96-07; Perm to Offic *Ex* from 07. *Lane's End, Broadwoodwidger, Lifton PL16 0JH* Tel (01566) 780544

WITHERS, Michael. b 41. TCD BA66 Edin Univ BD70 QUB MTh83 Birm Univ PGCE67. Union Th Sem (NY) STM71. **d** 71 **p** 73. C Seagoe *D & D* 71-77; C Seapatrick 77-80; I Belfast St

Chris 80-89; I Movilla 89-96; rtd 96. *11 Earlswood Road, Belfast BT4 3DY* Tel (028) 9047 1037

WITHERS, Michael Selby. b 36. Sheff Univ BA61 PGCE62. SAOMC 93. **d** 96 **p** 97. NSM Bletchley *Ox* 96-97; NSM Ellesborough, The Kimbles and Stoke Mandeville 97-01; NSM Risborough 01-05; Perm to Offic from 05. *The Welcome (rear house), Town Lane, Wooburn Green, High Wycombe HP10 0PL* Tel (01628) 526304 E-mail mandhwithers@waitrose.com

WITHEY, Michael John. b 45. Open Univ BA80 Ox Univ MTh98. Oak Hill Th Coll 71. **d** 74 **p** 75. C St Alb St Paul *St Alb* 74-76; C Luton St Mary 77; C Luton St Fran 77-80; V Woodside w E Hyde 80-87; CF (TA) 83-87; Dioc Stewardship Adv *Ox* 87-89; Chapl HM YOI Onley 89-91; V Hengoed w Gobowen *Lich* 91-95; Chapl Robert Jones and Agnes Hunt Orthopaedic Hosp 91-95; P-in-c Chasetown *Lich* 95-00; V 00-02; V Stroud H Trin *Glouc* from 02; Chapl Cotswold and Vale Primary Care Trust 02-06; Chapl Glos Primary Care Trust from 06; Chapl Glos Partnership Trust from 02. *Holy Trinity Vicarage, 10 Bowbridge Lane, Stroud GL5 2JW* Tel (01453) 764551

WITHINGTON, Brian James. b 54. Leic Univ MSc01 CQSW76. EAMTC 94. **d** 97 **p** 98. NSM Pet St Jo 97-04; P-in-c Broughton w Loddington and Cransley etc 04-10; C from 10; RD Kettering from 07; Bp's Adv for Pioneer Min from 10. *The Rectory, Gate Lane, Broughton, Kettering NN14 1ND* Tel and fax (01536) 791373 E-mail brian.andco@virgin.net

WITHINGTON, George Kenneth. b 37. Birm Univ BA59. Wells Th Coll 59. **d** 61 **p** 62. C Hartcliffe St Andr CD *Bris* 61-65; V Swindon St Jo 65-73; V Cricklade w Latton 73-97; RD Cricklade 94-97; rtd 97; Perm to Offic *Heref* and *Worc* from 97. *19 Oak Drive, Colwall, Malvern WR13 6RA* Tel (01684) 540590

WITHINGTON, Canon Keith. b 32. Univ of Wales (Lamp) BA55. Qu Coll Birm 55. **d** 57 **p** 58. C Bournville *Birm* 57-61; V 61-00; RD Moseley 81-91; Hon Can Birm Cathl 83-00; rtd 00; Perm to Offic *Birm* and *Worc* from 00. *44 Dugard Way, Droitwich WR9 8UX* Tel (01905) 795847 E-mail kw1000@bushinternet.com

WITHINGTON, Paul Martin. b 60. Kent Univ BSc86. Trin Coll Bris 01. **d** 03 **p** 04. C Elworth and Warmingham *Ches* 03-06; TV Congleton from 06. *The Vicarage, 14 Chapel Street, Congleton CW12 4AB* Tel (01260) 278288

WITHNELL, Roderick David. b 55. EMMTC 86 Ridley Hall Cam 89. **d** 90 **p** 91. C Shenfield *Chelmsf* 90-94; C Woodleigh and Loddiswell *Ex* 94-95; TV Modbury, Bigbury, Ringmore w Kingston etc 95-00; Canada 00-01; TR Burrington, Chawleigh, Cheldon, Chulmleigh etc *Ex* from 01. *The Rectory, Church Lane, Chulmleigh EX18 7BY* Tel (01769) 580537

WITHY, John Daniel Forster. b 38. ALCD64. **d** 64 **p** 65. C Belfast St Aid *Conn* 64-68; Dir Chr Conf Cen Sion Mills from 68. *2 Zion House, 120 Melmont Road, Strabane BT82 9ET* Tel (028) 8165 8672

WITT, Canon Bryan Douglas. b 52. St Mich Coll Llan BD84. **d** 84 **p** 85. C Betws w Ammanford *St D* 84-87; V Llanllwni 87-91; V Llangennech and Hendy 91-04; V St Clears w Llangynin and Llanddowror etc from 04; Hon Can St D Cathl from 11. *The Vicarage, Bridge Street, St Clears, Carmarthen SA33 4EE* Tel (01994) 230266

WITTER, Mrs Tania Judy Ingram. b 37. Girton Coll Cam BA58 MA63. Oak Hill Th Coll 94. **d** 95 **p** 96. NSM Highbury Ch Ch w St Jo and St Sav *Lon* 95-03; Perm to Offic *Lon* and *Eur* from 03. *26 Viewpoint Apartments, 30-32 Highbury Grove, London N5 2DL* Tel (020) 7226 6908 E-mail tania.witter@btinternet.com

WITTS, Donald Roger. b 47. Cranmer Hall Dur 86. **d** 88 **p** 89. C Leyland St Ambrose *Blackb* 88-90; C Staines St Mary and St Pet *Lon* 90-93; Ind Missr *Man* 93-95; Dioc Communications Officer *Cant* 95-00; P-in-c Blean 95-01; P-in-c Birchington w Acol and Minnis Bay 01-03; V from 03. *All Saints' Vicarage, 15 Minnis Road, Birchington CT7 9SE* Tel (01843) 841117 E-mail don.witts@btopenworld.com

WITTS, Graham Robert. b 53. Newc Univ BEd Bris Univ MA01. Linc Th Coll 79. **d** 82 **p** 83. C Horncastle w Low Toynton *Linc* 82-85; TV Gt Grimsby St Mary and St Jas 85-89; TR Yelverton, Meavy, Sheepstor and Walkhampton *Ex* 89-93; C Glastonbury w Meare *B & W* 93-03; RD Glastonbury 00-03; V Burnham from 03; Warden of Readers Wells Adnry from 10. *The Vicarage, Rectory Road, Burnham-on-Sea TA8 2BZ* Tel (01278) 782991 E-mail thewittsonweb@hotmail.com

WOADDEN, Christopher Martyn. b 56. St Jo Coll Nottm LTh. **d** 87 **p** 88. C Mickleover All SS *Derby* 87-90; C Wirksworth w Alderwasley, Carsington etc 90-92; C Wirksworth 92; TV Gt and Lt Coates w Bradley *Linc* 92-98; V Holton-le-Clay and Tetney 98-07; V Holton-le-Clay, Tetney and N Cotes from 07. *The Vicarage, Church Walk, Holton-le-Clay, Grimsby DN36 5AN* Tel (01472) 824082

WOAN, Miss Susan Ann. b 52. Univ of Wales (Abth) BSc72 Lon Univ PGCE73 Ch Ch Coll Cant MA91 Rob Coll Cam BA95. Ridley Hall Cam 93. **d** 96 **p** 97. C Histon *Ely* 96-97; C Radipole and Melcombe Regis *Sarum* 97-00; Chapl Bournemouth and

Poole Coll of FE *Win* 00-04; Hon C Bournemouth St Jo w St Mich 00-04; Vice-Prin Dioc Min Course *Nor* 04-06; Prin Dioc Min Course from 07; Vice-Prin ERMC from 07. *2 Conesfora Drive, Norwich NR1 2BB* Tel (01603) 622579 *or* 729812 E-mail sue.woan@dial.pipex.com *or* suewoan@norwich.anglican.org

WODEHOUSE, Armine Boyle. b 24. Oak Hill Th Coll 83. **d** 86 **p** 86. NSM Gt Parndon *Chelmsf* 86-92; Perm to Offic *Eur* 89-92; Chapl Menton 92-99; rtd 99; Perm to Offic *Lon* from 02. *Flat 12, 105 Onslow Square, London SW7 3LU* Tel (020) 7584 4845

WODEHOUSE, Carol Lylie. *See* KIMBERLEY, Countess of

WODEMAN, Cyril Peter Guy. b 28. Qu Coll Cam BA50 MA55 ARCO54 LRAM58 ARCM58. Cranmer Hall Dur 72. **d** 73 **p** 74. C Penwortham St Mary *Blackb* 73-77; V Burnley St Steph 77-85; V Hornby w Claughton 85-93; rtd 93; Perm to Offic *Blackb* and *Carl* from 93. *5 Harling Bank, Kirkby Lonsdale, Carnforth LA6 2DJ* Tel (01524) 272474

WOFFENDEN (née HANCOCK), Mrs Dorothy Myfanwy. b 41. NOC 01. **d** 03 **p** 04. NSM Brinnington w Portwood *Ches* 03-05; C Waverton w Aldford and Bruera 05-09. *8 Churchill Crescent, Marple, Stockport SK6 6HJ* Tel 0161-427 6839 E-mail dwoffenden@smartone.co.uk

WOLFE, Canon Michael Matheson. b 29. Pemb Coll Ox BA49 MA53. Cuddesdon Coll 51. **d** 53 **p** 54. C Moorfields *Bris* 53-57; P-in-c Fochabers *Mor* 57-58; Sub-Warden Aberlour Orphanage 58-59; V Southport St Paul *Liv* 59-65; V Upholland 65-73; TR 73-82; RD Ormskirk 78-82; RD Ormskirk and Hon Can Liv Cathl 78-82; Can Res Liv Cathl 82-96; Merseyside Ecum Officer 82-89; AD Toxteth and Wavertree 89-96; rtd 96; Perm to Offic *Liv* from 97; Hon Chapl Liv Cathl from 97. *23 Hunters Lane, Liverpool L15 8HL* Tel 0151-733 1541

WOLFENDEN, Peter Graham. b 40. St Pet Coll Ox BA63 MA66. Linc Th Coll 62. **d** 64 **p** 65. C Adlington *Blackb* 64-66; Asst Master Barton Peveril Gr Sch 66-69; Chapl Bp Wordsworth Sch Salisbury 69-72; Hon C Bishopstoke *Win* 66-72; Hon C Ponteland *Newc* 72-02; Hd Master Richard Coates Middle Sch Ponteland 78-01; Chapl Malta and Gozo *Eur* 02-07; Chapl Málaga 07-10; P-in-c Ovingdean *Chich* from 10. *St Wulfran's Rectory, 21 Ainsworth Avenue, Ovingdean, Brighton BN2 7BG* E-mail anglican@onel.net

WOLLASTON, Canon Barbara Kathleen. b 30. LSE BSc(Soc)64. Gilmore Ho 51. **d** 87 **p** 94. Dir Past Studies Qu Coll Birm 80-89; Dioc Dir of Ords *S'wark* 89-94; rtd 94; Perm to Offic *Lich* from 94. *21 Chapel Street, Wem, Shrewsbury SY4 5ER* Tel (01939) 232229

WOLLEY, John. BSc. **d** 85 **p** 86. Hon C Croydon St Aug *S'wark* 85-89; Perm to Offic *Linc* 89-01. *7 Royal Oak Court, Upgate, Louth LN11 9JA* Tel (01507) 601614

WOLLEY, Richard. b 33. CCC Ox BA56 MA58. S Dios Minl Tr Scheme 82. **d** 85 **p** 86. NSM Brighton Resurr *Chich* 85-88; C 88-89; C Brighton St Geo w St Anne and St Mark 89-91; R Buxted and Hadlow Down 91-98; rtd 98; Perm to Offic *Chich* from 98; RD Uckfield 04-06. *18 Millington Court, Mill Lane, Uckfield TN22 5AZ* Tel (01825) 761042 E-mail elwandrw@tiscali.co.uk

WOLSTENCROFT, The Ven Alan. b 37. Cuddesdon Coll. **d** 69 **p** 70. C Halliwell St Thos *Man* 69-71; C Stand 71-73; V Wythenshawe St Martin 73-80; AD Withington 78-91; Chapl Wythenshawe Hosp Man 80-89; V Baguley *Man* 80-91; V Bolton St Pet 91-98; Hon Can Man Cathl 86-98; Can Res 98-04; Adn Man 98-04; rtd 04; Perm to Offic *Man* from 04; Rtd Clergy and Widows Officer from 04. *The Bakehouse, 1 Latham Row, Horwich, Bolton BL6 6QZ* Tel (01204) 469985 E-mail alanchrisw@tiscali.co.uk

WOLTON, Andrew John. b 54. Cranfield Univ MDA00. St Jo Coll Nottm BA08. **d** 08 **p** 09. C Bures w Assington and Lt Cornard *St E* 08-11; R Saxmundham w Kelsale cum Carlton from 11. *The Rectory, Manor Gardens, Saxmundham IP17 1ET* Tel (01728) 602687 Mobile 07769-946364 E-mail andywolton@btinternet.com

WOLVERHAMPTON, Area Bishop of. *See* GREGORY, The Rt Revd Clive Malcolm

WOLVERSON, Marc Ali Morad. b 68. Univ of Kansas BA91. Ripon Coll Cuddesdon 93. **d** 96 **p** 97. C Nantwich *Ches* 96-99; C Baton Rouge St Luke USA 99-00; C Bramhall *Ches* 00-04; V High Lane 04-09; P-in-c Douglas All SS *S & M* from 09. *All Saints' Vicarage, 62 Ballabrooie Way, Douglas, Isle of Man IM1 4HB* Tel (01624) 621547 E-mail frmarcw@yahoo.co.uk

WOMACK, Michael John. b 62. Anglia Ruskin Univ MA07. Westcott Ho Cam 08. **d** 10 **p** 11. C Framlingham w Saxtead *St E* from 10. *17 Fulchers Field, Framlingham, Woodbridge IP13 9HT* Tel (01728) 621362 Mobile 07500-925490 E-mail framcurate@btinternet.com

WOMERSLEY, Sally Ann. b 61. Westcott Ho Cam 06. **d** 08 **p** 09. C Charing w Charing Heath and Lt Chart *Cant* 08-11; Chapl Cant Ch Ch Univ from 11. *27 Monastery Street, Canterbury CT1 1NJ* Tel (01227) 459758 E-mail sallywomersley@yahoo.co.uk

WONG (née RUNDLE), Hilary. b 65. St Hugh's Coll Ox BA88 Cheltenham & Glouc Coll of HE PGCE90. Trin Coll Bris 01. **d** 03 **p** 04. C Chipping Sodbury and Old Sodbury *Glouc* 03-07; P-in-c St Helier *S'wark* 07-11; V from 11. *St Peter's Vicarage, 193 Bishopsford Road, Morden SM4 6BH* Tel (020) 8685 9878 E-mail hilary1593wong@hotmail.co.uk

WOO, Arthur Cheumin. b 66. Qu Univ Kingston Ontario BSc89 MEng91. St Jo Coll Nottm MTh08. **d** 08 **p** 09. C Highworth w Sevenhampton and Inglesham etc *Bris* from 08. *14 Brookfield, Highworth, Swindon SN6 7HY* Tel (01793) 763197

WOOD, Alastair Paul. b 59. Ox Min Course 06. **d** 09 **p** 10. C Headington Quarry *Ox* from 09. *35 Stapleton Road, Headington, Oxford OX3 7LX* Tel (01865) 751815 Mobile 07948-989153 E-mail narniacurate09@btinternet.com

WOOD, Mrs Ann Rene. b 49. St Deiniol's Hawarden 87. **d** 90 **p** 94. Par Dn Bamber Bridge St Aid *Blackb* 90-93; C W Burnley All SS 93-95; V Marton Moss 95-00; Hon Can Blackb Cathl 98-00; R Whiston *Sheff* 00-07; V Kimberworth 07-11; AD Rotherham 04-08; P-in-c Kimberworth Park 10-11; C Rawmarsh w Parkgate 10-11; C Greasbrough 10-11; rtd 11. *3 Winston Avenue, Lytham St Annes FY8 3NS* Tel (01253) 788199 E-mail ann.wood6@btopenworld.com

WOOD (née BLACKBURN), Mrs Anne Dorothy. b 54. Keele Univ BA76 Bradf Univ MSc90. NOC 95. **d** 98 **p** 99. NSM Batley St Thos *Wakef* 98-00; Jt P-in-c Morley St Paul 01-02; C Bruntcliffe 01-02; C Morley 02-03; TV 03-07; TV Oakenshaw, Wyke and Low Moor *Bradf* 07-10; Chapl Wakefield Hospice from 11. *24 Heaton Avenue, Dewsbury WF12 8AQ* Tel (01924) 456282 Mobile 07929-452439 E-mail anne.d.wood@talk21.com

WOOD, Preb Anthony James. b 38. Kelham Th Coll 58. **d** 63 **p** 64. C Shrewsbury St Alkmund *Lich* 63; C Harlescott 63-66; C Porthill 66-70; P-in-c Priorslee 70-76; Chapl Telford Town Cen 73-76; V Barton-under-Needwood 76-77; V Barton under Needwood w Dunstall 77-09; V Barton under Needwood w Dunstall and Tatenhill 09-10; RD Tutbury 02-10; Preb Lich Cathl 08-09; rtd 10; Perm to Offic *Lich* from 11. *2 Shipley Close, Branston, Burton-on-Trent DE14 3HB* Tel (01283) 516772 E-mail tonywood@preb.co.uk

WOOD, Barbara Ann. b 49. St Mich Coll Llan 00. **d** 02 **p** 03. C Glan Ely *Llan* 02-05; P-in-c Llanharan w Peterston-super-Montem from 05. *The Vicarage, Brynna Road, Brynna, Pontyclun CF72 9QE* Tel (01443) 226307 E-mail babswood01@hotmail.com

WOOD, Barry. b 56. Open Univ BA87 Sheff Univ MMin01 CQSW81. St Steph Ho Ox 87. **d** 89 **p** 90. C Tranmere St Paul w St Luke *Ches* 89-92; TV Ches 92-94; P-in-c S Tawton and Belstone *Ex* 94-00; R 00-02; RD Okehampton 98-02; TR Wylye and Till Valley *Sarum* 02-03; rtd 03; Perm to Offic *Ex* 03-05 and Truro 05-07; Hon C Chaffcombe, Cricket Malherbie etc *B & W* 07-09; Hon C Blackdown 09-11. *5 Case Gardens, Seaton EX12 2AP*

WOOD, Beresford Donald Richard. b 32. Leeds Univ BA58. Cant Sch of Min 91. **d** 94 **p** 95. Chapl St Mary's Sch Westbrook from 94; NSM Folkestone St Mary and St Eanswythe *Cant* 94-02; Perm to Offic from 02. *St Katherine's Cottage, Pound Lane, Elham, Canterbury CT4 6TS* Tel (01303) 840817

WOOD, Canon Beryl Jean. b 54. Linc Th Coll 85. **d** 87 **p** 94. C Gaywood, Bawsey and Mintlyn *Nor* 87-93; Asst Chapl Univ Hosp Nottm 93-95; R Shipdham w E and W Bradenham *Nor* 95-06; RD Dereham in Mitford 00-04; Hon Can Nor Cathl 05-06; Dep Warden Launde Abbey *Leic* 06-09; TR Gaywood *Nor* from 10. *St Faith's Rectory, Gayton Road, King's Lynn PE30 4DZ* Tel (01553) 774582 E-mail beryljwood@yahoo.com

WOOD, Mrs Brenda. b 46. Eliz Gaskell Coll Man TCert67 Leeds Metrop Univ BEd94 Leeds Univ MA04. NOC 00. **d** 03 **p** 04. NSM Kirkstall *Ripon* 03-11; rtd 11. *18 Wentworth Crescent, Leeds LS17 7TW* Tel 0113-226 7991 E-mail bwood@ntlworld.com

WOOD, Canon Brian Frederick. b 31. Leeds Univ BA52. Coll of Resurr Mirfield 55. **d** 57 **p** 58. C Wigan St Anne *Liv* 57-60; C Elland *Wakef* 60-63; V Carlinghow 63-73; V Drighlington 73-94; RD Birstall 83-92; Hon Can Wakef Cathl 89-94; rtd 94; Perm to Offic *Bradf* and *Wakef* from 94. *10 Grove Road, Menston, Ilkley LS29 6JD* Tel (01943) 872820

WOOD, Brian Richard. b 49. Sheff Univ BA70 MCMI78 RIBA85 MRICS00 FCIOB00. Ox Min Course 04. **d** 07 **p** 08. NSM Blenheim *Ox* from 07. *Glebe Cottage, Shipton Bottom, Shipton-on-Cherwell, Kidlington OX5 1JJ* Tel (01865) 379203 E-mail bwood@brookes.ac.uk

WOOD, Mrs Bryony Ann. b 59. St Jo Coll Nottm BA10. **d** 10 **p** 11. C Derby St Pet and Ch Ch w H Trin 10-11; C Ashbourne w Mapleton from 11. *The New Vicarage, Chapel Lane, Clifton, Ashbourne DE6 2GL* Tel (01335) 344585 Mobile 07967-113028 E-mail bryony.wood@yahoo.co.uk

WOOD, Ms Carolyn Marie Therese. b 57. Sussex Univ BA91. St Mich Coll Llan 02. **d** 04 **p** 05. C Monkton *St D* 04-07; Perm to Offic 08-10; NSM Cydweli Deanery from 10. *38 Trem y Mynydd, Burry Port SA16 0UY* Tel (01554) 830947 E-mail vicartubbs@gmail.com

WOOD, Catherine Rosemary. b 54. Melbourne Coll of Div 82 St Jo Coll Auckland 83. **d** 83 **p** 84. C Howick New Zealand 83-87; C Auckland St Paul 88; P-in-c Mangere E 89-90; Co-ord Environmental Educn 90-95; N Fieldworker Chr World Service 96-01; Hon C Glen Eden 90-97; NSM Auckland Cathl 98-01; Perm to Offic *S'wark* 01-02; P-in-c Tatsfield 02-08; C Limpsfield and Titsey 02-03; Min Limpsfield Chart St Andr CD 03-08; Perm to Offic from 08; Chapl HM Pris Latchmere Ho from 09. *St Michael's Convent, 56 Ham Common, Richmond TW10 7JH* Tel (020) 8940 8711 Mobile 07960-088873 E-mail catswhiskers@ukonline.co.uk

WOOD, Christine Denise. b 48. EMMTC. **d** 05 **p** 06. NSM Clifton *S'well* 05-07; Asst Chapl Notts Healthcare NHS Trust 07-10; Lead Chapl St Andr Healthcare from 10; NSM Morton and Stonebroom w Shirland *Derby* from 09. *St Andrew's Healthcare, Sherwood Avenue, Sherwood Oaks Business Park, Mansfield NG18 4GW* Tel (01623) 665280

WOOD, Christopher David. b 60. Worc Coll Ox BA83 Leeds Univ MA06. Coll of Resurr Mirfield 04. **d** 06 **p** 07. C King's Lynn St Marg w St Nic *Nor* 06-09; R Hunstanton St Mary w Ringstead Parva etc from 09. *The Rectory, Broad Lane, Brancaster, King's Lynn PE31 8AU* Tel (01485) 211180 E-mail shepherd1760@hotmail.co.uk

WOOD, Christopher William. b 44. Rhodes Univ BA66 UNISA BTh82. St Bede's Coll Umtata 79. **d** 80 **p** 82. S Africa 80-87; C Houghton Regis *St Alb* 87-00; C Milton *Portsm* 00-03; Perm to Offic *Lich* from 04. *27 Penton Walk, Stoke-on-Trent ST3 3DG* Tel (01782) 311779

WOOD, Mrs Claire. b 63. SAOMC 03. **d** 06 **p** 07. C Buckingham *Ox* 06-09; R Olney from 09. *Olney Rectory, 9 Orchard Rise, Olney MK46 5HB* Tel (01234) 713308 Mobile 07896-696842 E-mail revclairewood@gmail.com

WOOD, Canon Colin Arthur. b 41. S'wark Ord Course 86. **d** 89 **p** 90. C Tadworth *S'wark* 89-93; TV Morden 93-06; Hon Can S'wark Cathl 05-06; rtd 06. *4 Palm Close, 130 Barrack Lane, Bognor Regis PO21 4EF* Tel (01243) 264192

WOOD, David Arthur. b 30. Man Univ BA51. Lich Th Coll 59. **d** 61 **p** 62. C Ashton Ch Ch *Man* 61-64; C Elton All SS 64-68; Dioc Youth Adv *Newc* 68-72; R Cramlington 72-73; TR 73-83; V Wylam 83-86; TV Egremont and Haile *Carl* 86-94; rtd 94; Perm to Offic *Carl* from 94. *6 John Street, Maryport CA15 6JT* Tel (01900) 816706

WOOD, David Christopher. b 52. Oak Hill Th Coll 89. **d** 91 **p** 92. C Kendal St Thos *Carl* 91-95; P-in-c Asby, Bolton and Crosby Ravensworth 95-05; P-in-c Barton, Pooley Bridge and Martindale from 05. *The Vicarage, Pooley Bridge, Penrith CA10 2LT* Tel (01768) 486220 E-mail revdavidcwood@hotmail.com

WOOD, David John. b 48. Newc Univ BSc70 PGCE71 Open Univ MA91. **d** 01 **p** 02. OLM Bedlington *Newc* 01-07; NSM Shotley from 07. *St John's Vicarage, Snod's Edge, Shotley Bridge, Consett DH8 9TL* Tel (01207) 255665 E-mail davwd50@hotmail.com

WOOD, David Michael. b 39. Chich Th Coll. **d** 82 **p** 83. C Epping St Jo *Chelmsf* 82-85; C Totton *Win* 85-88; V Southway *Ex* 88-97; P-in-c Black Torrington, Bradford w Cookbury etc 97-01; R 01-04; rtd 04; Perm to Offic *Portsm* from 04. *47 Queens Crescent, Stubbington, Fareham PO14 2QG*

WOOD, Dennis William. b 28. Qu Mary Coll Lon BSc53 Glas Univ PhD57. NEOC 82. **d** 85 **p** 85. NSM Stanhope *Dur* 85-86; NSM Stanhope w Frosterley 86-94; NSM Eastgate w Rookhope 86-94; NSM Melrose *Edin* from 94. *Gordonlee, Ormiston Terrace, Melrose TD6 9SP* Tel (01896) 823835

WOOD, Donald. b 40. **d** 95 **p** 96. NSM Caldicot *Mon* 95-99; P-in-c Llangwm Uchaf and Llangwm Isaf w Gwernesney etc 99-06; Lic to Offic from 06. *13 Deepweir, Caldicot NP26 5JG* Tel (01291) 425214

WOOD, Edward Berryman. b 33. Ely Th Coll 54. **d** 57 **p** 58. C Aldershot St Mich *Guildf* 57-60; C Worplesdon 60-62; V Littleport St Matt *Ely* 62-64; V Balham St Jo Bedf Hill *S'wark* 64-71; V New Eltham All SS 71-84; RD Eltham (Sub-Deanery) 79-82; P-in-c Woldingham 84-98; rtd 98; Perm to Offic *Chich* 99-07. *The College of St Barnabas, Blackberry Lane, Lingfield RH7 6NJ* Tel (01342) 872844 E-mail tandem@collegeofstbarnabas.com

WOOD, Edward Francis. b 28. Chich Th Coll 56. **d** 58 **p** 59. C Newc St Fran 58-62; C High Elswick St Phil 62-64; C Delaval 64-67; C-in-c Shiremoor CD 67-68; V Shiremoor and Dioc Broadcasting Adv 68-78; C Newc St Geo 78-82; C Newc Epiphany 82-93; rtd 93; Perm to Offic *Newc* from 93. *52 Albemarle Avenue, Newcastle upon Tyne NE2 3NQ* Tel 0191-284 5338 E-mail franciswood@waitrose.com

WOOD, Elaine Mary. See RICHARDSON, Elaine Mary

WOOD, Mrs Elizabeth Jane. b 51. Ch Ch Coll Cant DipEd73. NEOC 88. **d** 01 **p** 02. C Denton *Newc* 01-04; V N Sunderland from 04; V Beadnell from 04. *The Vicarage, South Lane, North Sunderland, Seahouses NE68 7TU* Tel (01665) 720202 E-mail jane.wood3@btopenworld.com

WOOD, Elizabeth Lucy. b 35. WMMTC 89. **d** 92 **p** 94. NSM Wellingborough St Mark *Pet* 92-95; P-in-c Stanwick w Hargrave 95-00; Perm to Offic from 00; Chapl to Retired Clergy and Clergy Widows' Officer from 08. *21 Meadow Way, Irthlingborough, Wellingborough NN9 5RS* Tel (01933) 652319 E-mail elizwood@tiscali.co.uk

WOOD, Francis. See WOOD, Edward Francis

WOOD, Geoffrey. b 33. Tyndale Hall Bris 56. **d** 61 **p** 62. C Tranmere St Cath *Ches* 61-64; C Newburn *Newc* 64-68; R Gt Smeaton w Appleton upon Wiske *Ripon* 69-79; P-in-c Cowton w Birkby 73-79; P-in-c Danby Wiske w Yafforth and Hutton Bonville 76-79; R Gt Smeaton w Appleton Wiske and Birkby etc 79-89; R Fressingfield, Mendham etc *St E* 92-98; rtd 98; Perm to Offic *Dur* 98-04; Lic to Offic *Edin* 08-10. *15 Greencroft Close, Darlington DL3 8HW* Tel (01325) 380309

WOOD, Geoffrey James. b 47. NOC 88. **d** 91 **p** 92. C Stainton-in-Cleveland *York* 91-94; V Middlesbrough St Oswald 94-99; V Eskdaleside w Ugglebarnby and Sneaton 99-06; rtd 06; Perm to Offic *York* from 06. *22 Hedley Street, Guisborough TS14 6EG* Tel (01287) 619286 E-mail frgeoff@btinternet.com

WOOD, George Albert. b 22. St Paul's Coll Grahamstown. **d** 54 **p** 55. C Hillcrest S Africa 54-57; C W Suburbs Pretoria 57-60; C Cheam *S'wark* 60-63; R Eshowe S Africa 63-69; Can Zululand 68-73; Dean Eshowe 70-73; R Port Elizabeth Ch the K 74-77; Area Sec USPG *Chich* from 78; TV Littlehampton and Wick *Chich* 86-88; rtd 88; Perm to Offic *Chich* from 88. *3 Orchard Gardens, Rustington, Littlehampton BN16 3HN* Tel (01903) 787746

WOOD, Heather Dawn. See ATKINSON, Mrs Heather Dawn

WOOD, Miss Helen Ruth. b 54. Bedf Coll Lon BA75. Glouc Sch of Min 87. **d** 91 **p** 94. NSM Up Hatherley *Glouc* 91-94; NSM Cheltenham Em w St Steph 94-09; NSM S Cheltenham from 10; Asst Chapl Cheltenham Ladies' Coll from 91. *9 Southfield Manor Park, Sandy Lane, Charlton Kings, Cheltenham GL53 9DJ* Tel (01242) 242793 E-mail woodh@cheltladiescollege.org

WOOD, Jane. See WOOD, Mrs Elizabeth Jane

WOOD, Jane. b 52. Ripon Coll Cuddesdon. **d** 08 **p** 09. C Kirby Muxloe *Leic* from 08. *106 Hinckley Road, Leicester Forest East, Leicester LE3 3JS* Tel 0116-238 6344

WOOD, Mrs Jennifer Sarah. b 40. Sarum Dioc Tr Coll CertEd60. Oak Hill Th Coll 92. **d** 94 **p** 95. C St Illogan *Truro* 94-98; R Heanton Punchardon w Marwood *Ex* 98-10; C Ilfracombe SS Phil and Jas w W Down 09-10; rtd 10. *32 Stallards, Braunton EX33 1BP*

WOOD, John. b 37. LNSM course 75. **d** 77 **p** 79. NSM Haddington *Edin* from 77. *7 Herdmanflatt, Haddington EH41 3LN* Tel (01620) 822838

WOOD, John Anthony Scriven. b 48. Leeds Univ BSc70. St Jo Coll Nottm 76. **d** 79 **p** 80. C Colwich *Lich* 79-82; C W Bridgford *S'well* 82-90; V Gamston and Bridgford 90-95; Chapl Kings Mill Cen NHS Trust 95-01; Chapl Sherwood Forest Hosps NHS Trust from 01; NSM Morton and Stonebroom w Shirland *Derby* from 08. *The King's Mill Centre, Mansfield Road, Sutton in Ashfield NG17 4JL* Tel (01623) 622515 ext 4137 *or* 0115-982 0969

WOOD, John Arthur. b 23. Roch Th Coll 68. **d** 70 **p** 71. C Wetherby *Ripon* 70-71; P-in-c Sheff Arbourthorne 71-75; TV Sheff Manor 75-81; R Rodney Stoke w Draycott *B & W* 81-88; rtd 88; Perm to Offic *Sheff* from 88. *36 The Glen, Sheffield S10 3FN* Tel 0114-266 5173

WOOD, John Maurice. b 58. Qu Coll Cam BA80 MA83. Wycliffe Hall Ox BA87. **d** 87 **p** 88. C Northwood Em *Lon* 87-91; C Muswell Hill St Jas w St Matt 91-94; P-in-c S Tottenham St Ann 94-01; V from 01. *St Ann's Vicarage, South Grove, London N15 5QG* Tel and fax (020) 8800 3506 Mobile 07771-867359 E-mail johnwood@st-anns.fsnet.co.uk

WOOD, John Samuel. b 47. Lanchester Poly Cov BSc69 Sheff Univ CChell. Westcott Ho Cam 72. **d** 81 **p** 82. NSM Haverhill *St E* 81-83; C Whitton and Thurleston w Akenham 83-86; P-in-c Walsham le Willows 86-88; P-in-c Finningham w Westhorpe 86-88; R Walsham le Willows and Finningham w Westhorpe 88-94; Min Can St E Cathl 89-94; TR Whitstable *Cant* 94-02; Chapl E Kent Community NHS Trust 94-02; Hon Min Can Cant Cathl 96-02; TR Swanage and Studland *Sarum* from 02; RD Purbeck from 07. *The Rectory, 12 Church Hill, Swanage BH19 1HU* Tel (01929) 422916 Fax 422291 E-mail john.s.wood@btinternet.com

WOOD, Kathleen. b 46. EMMTC 04. **d** 06 **p** 07. NSM Newhall *Derby* 06-09; NSM Etwall w Egginton 09-10; P-in-c Stapenhill Immanuel from 10. *28 Eastfield Road, Midway, Swadlincote DE11 0DG* Tel (01283) 212490 E-mail rkw28@tiscali.co.uk

WOOD, Keith. b 49. St Steph Ho Ox 76. **d** 78 **p** 79. C Bognor *Chich* 78-81; C Hangleton 81-83; R W Blatchington 83-87; V W Worthing St Jo 87-96; R Winchelsea and Icklesham 96-00; rtd 00. *The Bungalow, Lower Locrenton, St Keyne, Liskeard PL14 4RN*

WOOD, Canon Keith Ernest. b 33. Qu Coll Ox BA55 BCL56 MA70. Wycliffe Hall Ox 56. **d** 58 **p** 59. C Barking St Marg

Chelmsf 58-61; Min Basildon St Andr ED 61-70; V Brampton Bierlow *Sheff* 70-82; R Grasmere *Carl* 82-94; RD Windermere 89-94; Hon Can Carl Cathl 91-94 and 98-01; Bp's Dom Chapl 94-01; rtd 01; Perm to Offic *Carl* from 01. *The Old Tower, Brackenburgh, Calthwaite CA11 9PW* Tel (01768) 894273 Fax 894019

WOOD, Laurence Henry. b 27. Kelham Th Coll 47. **d** 52 **p** 53. C Ravensthorpe *Wakef* 52-55; C Almondbury 55-58; V Linthwaite 58-64; R Bonsall and V Cromford *Derby* 64-70; V Longwood *Wakef* 70-76; V Liversedge 76-92; rtd 92; Perm to Offic *Wakef* from 92. *203 The Rock, Gillroyd Lane, Linthwaite, Huddersfield HD7 5SR* Tel (01484) 843499

WOOD, Mrs Lorna. b 43. EAMTC 85. **d** 88 **p** 94. NSM Sprowston *Nor* 88-90; NSM Sprowston w Beeston 90-95; P-in-c Nor St Helen 95-01; Chapl Gt Hosp Nor 95-99; NSM Coltishall w Gt Hautbois and Horstead *Nor* 01-04; Perm to Offic 04-07 and from 10; NSM Thorpe St Andr 07-10. *39 Inman Road, Sprowston, Norwich NR7 8JT* Tel (01603) 400150 E-mail robert.wood68@btinternet.com

WOOD (née DROBIG), Mrs Marion. b 76. Hannover Univ MA01 Pemb Coll Ox DPhil05. ERMC 04. **d** 06 **p** 07. C Newmarket All SS *St E* 06-09; R Shaw cum Donnington *Ox* from 09. *The Rectory, Well Meadow, Shaw, Newbury RG14 2DS* Tel (01635) 600532 Mobile 07979-534948 E-mail mariondrobig@hotmail.com

WOOD, Mark. See WOOD, The Rt Revd Stanley Mark

WOOD, Mark Robert. b 68. Trin Coll Ox BA89 ALCM83 ARCO89. STETS 02. **d** 05 **p** 06. C Mere w W Knoyle and Maiden Bradley *Sarum* 05-08; P-in-c Wilton w Netherhampton and Fugglestone from 08. *The Rectory, 27A West Street, Wilton, Salisbury SP2 0DL* Tel (01722) 742393 Mobile 07770-305990 E-mail mands@thewoods2006.orangehome.co.uk

WOOD, Martin. See WOOD, Canon Nicholas Martin

WOOD, Martin Robert. b 65. Birm Univ BSc86. Trin Coll Bris 98. **d** 00 **p** 01. C Wells St Cuth w Wookey Hole *B & W* 00-03; C Shepton Mallet w Doulting 03-07; P-in-c Tedburn St Mary, Whitestone, Oldridge etc *Ex* 07-10; V Tedburn St Mary, Cheriton Bishop, Whitestone etc from 10. *The Rectory, Church Lane, Cheriton Bishop, Exeter EX6 6HY* Tel (01647) 24119 E-mail revwood@btinternet.com

WOOD, Michael Edmund. b 46. Dur Univ BA67 PGCE68. Coll of Resurr Mirfield 94. **d** 96 **p** 97. NSM Battyeford *Wakef* from 96; Asst Chapl Kirkwood Hospice Huddersfield 96-97; Chapl from 97. *9 Dorchester Road, Huddersfield HD2 2JZ* Tel (01484) 536496 E-mail revmike@kirkwoodhospice.co.uk

WOOD, Michael Paul. b 55. Nottm Univ BCombStuds. Linc Th Coll. **d** 84 **p** 85. C Marton *Blackb* 84-88; TV Ribbleton 88-93; V Blackpool St Mary 93-00; P-in-c S Shore St Pet 98-00; RD Blackpool 96-00; TR Brighouse and Clifton *Wakef* 00-08; RD Brighouse and Elland 06-08; TR Castleford from 08; P-in-c Smawthorpe from 11. *The Rectory, 15 Barnes Road, Castleford WF10 5AA* Tel (01977) 518127 E-mail frmw@hotmail.co.uk

WOOD, Mrs Michaela. b 67. **d** 01 **p** 02. NSM Sunbury *Lon* 01-04; NSM Whitton St Aug 04-06; NSM Aylesbury w Bierton and Hulcott *Ox* from 06. *The Rectory, 1 Parson's Fee, Aylesbury HP20 2QZ* Tel (01296) 424276 E-mail michaelawood@aol.com

WOOD, Canon Nicholas Martin. b 51. AKC74 Univ of Wales (Lamp) MTh09. **d** 75 **p** 76. C E Ham w Upton Park *Chelmsf* 75-78; C Leyton St Luke 78-81; V Rush Green 81-91; Chapl Barking Tech Coll 81-91; TR Elland *Wakef* 91-05; RD Brighouse and Elland 96-05; Hon Can Wakef Cathl 00-05; Par Development Adv (Bradwell Area) *Chelmsf* from 05; Chapl to Bp Bradwell from 11; Hon C Basildon St Martin from 11; Hon Can Chelmsf Cathl from 08. *101 London Road, Bowers Gifford, Basildon SS13 2DU* Tel (01268) 552219 E-mail mwood@chelmsford.anglican.org

WOOD, Paul Dominic. b 52. Tas Coll of Ad Educn DipEd80. Ridley Coll Melbourne BTh87. **d** 87 **p** 88. C Newtown St Jas Australia 87-89; C Launceston St Jo 89-91; TV Ifield *Chich* 92-95; P-in-c Lancefield w Romsey Australia 96-97; I 97-00; R Mansfield 01-05. *38 Pine Street, Reservoir Vic 3073, Australia* Tel and fax (0061) (3) 9478 0841 E-mail qwoodies@bigpond.com

WOOD, Philip James. b 48. Bris Univ BSc69 Westmr Coll Ox MTh93. Oak Hill Th Coll 71. **d** 74 **p** 75. C Islington St Mary *Lon* 74-77; C Stapenhill w Cauldwell *Derby* 77-80; V Walthamstow St Luke *Chelmsf* 80-94; AD Waltham Forest 89-94; Can Chelmsf Cathl 93-94; NSM Hackney Wick St Mary of Eton w St Aug *Lon* 01-02; TV Becontree W *Chelmsf* 02-07; V Becontree St Thos from 07. *St Thomas's Vicarage, 187 Burnside Road, Dagenham RM8 2JN* Tel (020) 8590 6190 E-mail phillip.wood@tiscali.co.uk

WOOD, Philip Norman. b 52. EMMTC 97. **d** 00 **p** 01. NSM Pleasley Hill *S'well* 00-04; NSM Mansfield St Aug 00-04; NSM Ladybrook 00-04; TV Newton Flotman, Swainsthorpe, Tasburgh, etc *Nor* 04-08; R Bacton, Happisburgh, Hempstead w

Eccles etc from 08. *The Rectory, The Hill, Happisburgh, Norwich NR12 0PW* Tel (01692) 650313 Mobile 07961-524495 E-mail philyvonne@hotmail.com

WOOD, Ms Rachel Astrid. b 71. Birm Univ BA92 MA99. Qu Coll Birm BD98. **d** 99 **p** 00. C Attercliffe, Darnall and Tinsley *Sheff* 99-01; C Roundhay St Edm *Ripon* 01-04. *The Vicarage, Dunblane Crescent, Newcastle upon Tyne NE5 2BE* Tel 0191-267 2058

WOOD, Raymond John Lee. b 28. ACII55 ACIArb. Linc Th Coll 66. **d** 68 **p** 69. C Beaconsfield *Ox* 68-72; CF 70-72; V Wath-upon-Dearne w Adwick-upon-Dearne *Sheff* 72-77; R St Tudy w Michaelstow *Truro* 77-86; P-in-c St Mabyn 82-86; R St Tudy w St Mabyn and Michaelstow 86-95; Chapl Bodmin Fire Brigade from 91; rtd 95; Perm to Offic *Truro* from 96. *1 Wesley Chapel, Harewood Road, Calstock PL18 9QN* Tel (01822) 835918 E-mail rlwood@tesco.net

WOOD, Richard. *See* WOOD, Beresford Donald Richard

WOOD, Richard James. b 71. Oak Hill Th Coll BA07. **d** 08 **p** 09. C Dagenham *Chelmsf* 08-09; C Leyton Ch Ch from 09. *57 Lindley Road, London E10 6QT* Tel (020) 8558 5781 E-mail woodyis@mac.com

WOOD, Richard Stanton. b 79. Univ of Wales (Abth) BSc02 Univ of Wales (Cardiff) BA08. **d** 08 **p** 09. C Henfynyw w Aberaeron and Llanddewi Aberarth etc *St D* 08-11; TV Llanelli from 11. *Christ Church Vicarage, New Dock Road, Llanelli SA15 2HE* Tel (01554) 770599 Mobile 07855-817740 E-mail revdrich@gmail.com

WOOD, Roger Graham. b 49. K Coll Lon BD. Chich Th Coll 74. **d** 76 **p** 77. C Skipton H Trin *Bradf* 76-79; Dioc Youth Chapl 79-87; V Queensbury 87-96, P-in-c Langcliffe w Stainforth and Horton 96-01; V from 01; RD Bowland from 08. *The Vicarage, Stainforth, Settle BD24 9PG* Tel (01729) 823010 E-mail roger.wood@bradford.anglican.org *or* rgwood@lineone.net

WOOD, Roger William. b 43. Leeds Univ BA65 MA67 Fitzw Coll Cam BA69 MA75. Westcott Ho Cam 67. **d** 70 **p** 71. C Bishop's Stortford St Mich *St Alb* 70-74; C Sundon w Streatley 75-79; V Streatley 80-09; rtd 09. *8 Ramsey Road, Barton-le-Clay, Bedford MK45 4PE* Tel (01582) 883277

WOOD, Ronald Ernest. b 49. Sarum & Wells Th Coll 79. **d** 81 **p** 82. C Weston-super-Mare Cen Par *B & W* 81-84; C Forest of Dean Ch Ch w English Bicknor *Glouc* 84-88; R Sixpenny Handley w Gussage St Andrew etc *Sarum* 88-05; P-in-c Seale, Puttenham and Wanborough *Guildf* 05-10; rtd 10; Hon C Camelot Par *B & W* from 10. *Fourposts, Long Street, Galhampton, Yeovil BA22 7AZ* Tel (01963) 441192

WOOD, Sarah. *See* WOOD, Mrs Jennifer Sarah

WOOD, Shane Grant Lindsay. b 60. Southn Univ BTh91. St Steph Ho Ox 95. **d** 97 **p** 98. C Parkstone St Pet w Branksea and St Osmund *Sarum* 97-00; V Teddington SS Pet and Paul and Fulwell *Lon* 00-06; TR Aylesbury w Bierton and Hulcott *Ox* from 06. *The Rectory, Parson's Fee, Aylesbury HP20 2QZ* Tel (01296) 424276 E-mail shaneglwood@aol.com

WOOD, Stanley Charles. b 26. Glouc Th Course 80. **d** 83 **p** 84. NSM Lower Cam w Coaley *Glouc* 83-87; P-in-c Shipton Moyne w Westonbirt and Lasborough 87-91; rtd 92; Perm to Offic *Glouc* 92-05. *Henlow Court, Henlow Drive, Dursley GL11 4BE* Tel (01453) 542850

✠**WOOD, The Rt Revd Stanley Mark.** b 19. Univ of Wales (Cardiff) BA40. Coll of Resurr Mirfield 40. **d** 42 **p** 43 **c** 71. C Cardiff St Mary *Llan* 42-45; C Sophiatown Miss S Africa 45-47; R Bloemhof 47-50; P-in-c St Cypr Miss Johannesburg 50-55; R Marandellas S Rhodesia 55-65; Can Mashonaland 61-65; Dean Salisbury 65-70; Bp Matabeleland 71-77; Asst Bp Heref 77-81; Suff Bp Ludlow 81-87; Adn Ludlow 82-83; Preb Heref Cathl 77-87; rtd 87. *The College of St Barnabas, Blackberry Lane, Lingfield RH7 6NJ* Tel (01342) 872857 E-mail markwood@collegeofstbarnabas.com

WOOD, Stella Margaret. b 70. Trin Coll Ox BA91 MA DPhil95. STETS 95. **d** 97 **p** 98. NSM Mere w Knoyle and Maiden Bradley *Sarum* 97-08; Chapl Sherborne Sch for Girls 00-08; Teacher from 08; Lic to Rd Sarum 08-11; Co-ord for Learning and Discipleship *Sarum* from 11. *The Rectory, 27A West Street, Wilton, Salisbury SP2 0DL* Tel (01722) 744575 E-mail mands@thewoods2006.orangehome.co.uk

WOOD, Steven Paul. b 54. Fitzw Coll Cam MA75. ERMC. **d** 07 **p** 08. NSM Hitchin *St Alb* 07-10; P-in-c Streatley from 10. *Tythe Farm House, Streatley Road, Sundon, Luton LU3 3PH* Tel (01525) 876197 Mobile 07704-922984 E-mail steve.wood@stmargaret-streatley.org.uk

WOOD, Stuart Hughes. b 32. ACIB64. Guildf Dioc Min Course 93. **d** 95 **p** 96. OLM Camberley St Martin Old Dean *Guildf* 95-02; OLM Camberley St Paul 99-02; OLM Camberley St Mich Yorktown 99-02; rtd 02; Perm to Offic *Guildf* 02-05. *42 Roundway, Camberley GU15 1NS* Tel (01276) 22115 E-mail stuart.wood1@tesco.net

WOOD, Susan Joyce. b 52. Sheff City Coll of Educn CertEd74. **d** 09 **p** 10. OLM Ramsbottom and Edenfield *Man* from 09. *243 Whittingham Drive, Ramsbottom, Bury BL0 9NY* Tel (01706) 825464 E-mail woodsuej@btinternet.com

WOOD, Susan Pauline. b 47. Maria Grey Coll Lon TCert68. STETS 07. **d** 10 **p** 11. NSM Staines *Lon* from 10. *60 St Nicholas Drive, Shepperton TW17 9LD* Tel (01932) 228712 E-mail sue_p.wood@yahoo.co.uk

WOOD, Sylvia Marian. *See* CHAPMAN, Canon Sylvia Marian

WOOD, Timothy Robert. b 55. **d** 02 **p** 03. OLM Maidstone St Paul *Cant* 02-06; NSM Hayling Is St Andr *Portsm* from 08; NSM N Hayling St Pet from 08. *9 Ward Court, 65 Seafront, Hayling Island PO11 0AL* Tel (023) 9246 1575 E-mail jane_wood@lineone.net

✠**WOOD, The Rt Revd Wilfred Denniston.** b 36. KA00. Gen Th Sem NY Hon DD86 Open Univ Hon DUniv00 Univ of W Indies Hon LLD02 FRSA93. Codrington Coll Barbados 57. **d** 61 **p** 62 **c** 85. C Hammersmith St Steph *Lon* 62-63; C Shepherd's Bush St Steph w St Thos 63-74; Bp's Chapl for Community Relns 67-74; V Catford St Laur *S'wark* 74-82; Hon Can S'wark Cathl 77-82; RD E Lewisham 77-82; Borough Dean S'wark 82-85; Adn S'wark 82-85; Suff Bp Croydon 85-91; Area Bp Croydon 91-02; rtd 02. *69 Pegwell Gardens, Christ Church, Barbados* Tel (001) (246) 420 1822 Fax 420 3426 E-mail wilfredwoodbarbados@caribsurf.com

WOOD-ROBINSON, David Michael. b 28. Glas Univ BSc50 Lon Univ BD54. **d** 57 **p** 57. C Erith St Jo *Roch* 57-58; CMS Japan 58-71; R Holton and Waterperry *Ox* 71-88; RD Aston and Cuddesdon 88-92; R Holton and Waterperry w Albury and Waterstock 88-94; Chapl Ox Brookes Univ 90-94; rtd 94. *16 Pound Meadow, Ledbury HR8 2EU* Tel (01531) 632347

WOODALL, David Paul. b 59. Ches Coll of HE BTh03. NOC 00. **d** 03 **p** 04. C Darwen St Pet w Hoddlesden *Blackb* 03-06; TV Bacup and Stacksteads *Man* from 06. *Christ Church Vicarage, Greensnook Lane, Bacup OL13 9DQ* Tel and fax (01706) 878293

WOODALL, Johanna Karin (Hanna). b 62. Leic Univ BA84 PGCE86. Trin Coll Bris BA06. **d** 06 **p** 07. C Winchcombe *Glouc* 06-09; Hon C Churchdown St Jo and Innsworth 10; NSM Badgeworth, Shurdington and Witcombe w Bentham from 10. *12 Priory Street, Cheltenham GL52 6DG* Tel (01242) 250012 E-mail hanna woodall@yahoo.co.uk

WOODALL, Mrs Lynda Edith Maria. b 53. Leeds Univ BA07. NOC 04. **d** 07 **p** 08. C Goodshaw and Crawshawbooth *Man* 07-10; V Whitworth w Facit from 10. *St John's Vicarage, Stud Brow, Facit, Rochdale OL12 8LU* Tel (01706) 878293 E-mail lyn.woodall@googlemail.com

WOODALL, Reginald Homer. b 38. St Mich Coll Llan 59. **d** 61 **p** 62. C Newtown w Llanllwchaiarn w Aberhafesp *St As* 61-65; C Rhosddu 65-66; C Hawarden 66-70; CF 70-74; C Thornton Heath St Jude *Cant* 74-77; TV Cannock *Lich* 77-79; TV Basildon St Martin w H Cross and Laindon etc *Chelmsf* 79-84; P-in-c Canning Town St Cedd 84-93; rtd 93. *64 Stephens Road, London E15 3JL*

WOODALL, Ms Rosemary Helen. b 80. Newc Univ BSc01. Ripon Coll Cuddesdon BA09. **d** 10 **p** 11. C Glouc City and Hempsted from 10. *38 St Mary's Square, Gloucester GL1 2QT* Tel (01452) 422829 Mobile 07816-420788 E-mail rosiewoodall@hotmail.co.uk

WOODASON, Antony Norman. b 37. MCIPD96. SWMTC 02. **d** 04 **p** 05. NSM Bovey Tracey St Jo w Heathfield *Ex* 04-06; C Shaldon, Stokeinteignhead, Combeinteignhead etc from 06. *The Rectory, Stokeinteignhead, Newton Abbot TQ12 4QB* Tel (01626) 871013 E-mail madwoodason@nosadoow.fsnet.co.uk

WOODBRIDGE, Trevor Geoffrey. b 31. Lon Univ BSc52. ALCD57. **d** 58 **p** 59. C Bitterne *Win* 58-61; C Ilkeston St Mary *Derby* 61-65; Area Sec CMS *Ex* and *Truro* 65-81; SW Regional Sec 70-81; TV Clyst St George, Aylesbeare, Clyst Honiton etc *Ex* 82-84; V Aylesbeare, Rockbeare, Farringdon etc 85-95; rtd 95; Perm to Offic *Ex* 95-09. *17 Lowfield Crescent, Silsden, Keighley BD20 0QE* Tel (01535) 658216

WOODCOCK, Anne Caroline. b 63. Man Metrop Univ BA97 Man Univ MA07 RGN. SNWTP 08. **d** 10 **p** 11. C Newton in Mottram *Ches* 10-11; C Newton in Mottram w Flowery Field from 11. *St Stephen's Vicarage, 154 Bennett Street, Hyde SK14 4SS* Tel 0161-351 1535 Mobile 07960-114969 E-mail annie.woodcock@virginmedia.com

WOODCOCK, Canon Carolyn. b 47. NOC BTh98. **d** 98 **p** 99. NSM Laneside *Blackb* 98-00; Chapl HM Pris Lanc Castle 00-10; Hon Can Blackb Cathl 08-10; rtd 10; Perm to Offic *Blackb* from 10. *Address temp unknown*

WOODCOCK, Edward Marsden. b 47. Hull Univ MSc01 Leeds Univ MA03. Coll of Resurr Mirfield 01. **d** 03 **p** 04. C Wrenthorpe *Wakef* 03-06; C Alverthorpe 03-06; P-in-c Ferrybridge from 06; P-in-c Brotherton from 06. *St Andrew's Vicarage, 5 Pontefract Road, Ferrybridge, Knottingley WF11 8PN* Tel (01977) 672772 E-mail edward@thewoodcocks.plus.com

WOODCOCK, John Charles Gerard. b 31. Kelham Th Coll 52. **d** 56 **p** 57. Min S Africa 56-62 and 76-83; Lesotho 62-76; Chapl Bede Ho Staplehurst 83-87; C Auckland St Andr and St Anne *Dur* 87-88. *3 Helena Terrace, Cockton Hill, Bishop Auckland DL14 6BP* Tel (01388) 604956

WOODCOCK, Matthew Ross. b 75. Portsm Univ BA97. Cranmer Hall Dur 09. **d** 11. C Kingston upon Hull H Trin *York*

from 11. *1 Ha'penny Bridge Way, Hull HU9 1HD* Tel (01482) 214192 Mobile 07852-340616 E-mail mattwoodcock630@gmail.com

WOODCOCK, Michael David. b 67. Avery Hill Coll BEd91. Wycliffe Hall Ox BTh96. **d** 96 **p** 97. C Orpington Ch Ch *Roch* 96-99; R Knockholt w Halstead 99-06; P-in-c Crosthwaite Kendal *Carl* from 06; P-in-c Cartmel Fell from 06; P-in-c Winster from 06; P-in-c Witherslack from 06. *The Vicarage, Crosthwaite, Kendal LA8 8HT* Tel (015395) 68276

WOODCOCK, Michael Paul. b 71. Univ of Greenwich BA93. St Jo Coll Nottm MA98. **d** 99 **p** 00. C Brinsley w Underwood *S'well* 99-02; C New Malden and Coombe *S'wark* 02-07; C Ambleside w Brathay *Carl* 07-10; TV Loughrigg 10; Chapl Cumbria Univ 07-10; P-in-c Dromana Australia from 10. *Address temp unknown* E-mail paul-woodcock@sky.com

WOODCOCK, Mrs Michelle Lisa. b 74. Dartington Coll of Art BA96 Cant Ch Ch Univ PGCE98. LCTP 08. **d** 10 **p** 11. NSM Kendal St Thos *Carl* from 10; NSM Crook from 10; NSM Crosthwaite Kendal from 10; NSM Cartmel Fell from 10; NSM Winster from 10; NSM Witherslack from 10; NSM Helsington from 10; NSM Underbarrow from 10. *The Vicarage, Crosthwaite, Kendal LA8 8HX* Tel (015395) 68276 E-mail michellewoodcock74@hotmail.com

WOODCOCK, Nicholas Ethelbert. b 46. ACertCM74 FRSA90. Cant Sch of Min 80. **d** 90 **p** 91. Chief Exec and Co Sec Keston Coll Kent 89-92; NSM Clerkenwell H Redeemer w St Phil *Lon* 90-92; NSM Clerkenwell H Redeemer and St Mark 92-93; Chapl RN 93-01; Min Can, Prec and Sacr Ely Cathl 01-03; R Lavenham w Preston *St E* 03-09; Min Can *St E* Cathl 03-09; Chapl Morden Coll Blackheath from 09. *Morden College, 19 St Germans Place, London SE3 0PW* Tel (020) 8858 3365 E-mail chaplain@mordencollege.org

WOODE, Mrs Elizabeth. b 43. **d** 06 **p** 07. NSM Middlewich w Byley *Ches* from 06. *6 The Grange, Hartford, Northwich CW8 1QH* Tel (01606) 75030 E-mail tonylizwoode@hotmail.com

WOODERSON, Mrs Marguerite Ann. b 44. RGN SCM. Qu Coll Birm 86. **d** 89 **p** 94. Par Dn Stoneydelph St Martin CD *Lich* 89-90; Par Dn Glascote and Stonydelph 90-91; Par Dn Chasetown 91-94; C 94; C-in-c Chase Terrace St Jo Distr Ch 92-94; Chapl Naas Gen Hosp 94-98; I Celbridge w Straffan and Newcastle-Lyons *D & G* 98-06. *15 rue des Ecoles, Trélissac, 24750 Périgueux, France* Tel (0033) 5 53 06 39 76 Mobile 8 68 51 25 57 E-mail annwooderson@mac.com

WOODERSON, Michael George. b 39. Southn Univ BA61. Lon Coll of Div BD69. **d** 69 **p** 70. C Morden *S'wark* 69-73; C Aldridge *Lich* 73-81; V Chasetown and P-in-c Hammerwich 91-94; RD Lich 86-94; Preb Lich Cathl 89-94; I Naas w Kill and Rathmore *M & K* 94-06; rtd 06. *15 rue des Ecoles, Trélissac, 24750 Périgueux, France* Tel (0033) 5 53 06 39 76 E-mail mgwooderson@eircom.net

WOODGATE, Mrs Elizabeth Mary. b 66. W Sussex Inst of HE BEd87. St Jo Coll Nottm MTh02. **d** 02 **p** 04. C Crofton *Portsm* 02-03; C Lee-on-the-Solent 03-05; C Rowner and Bridgemary 05-07; Kuwait from 07. *PO Box 9999, Ahmadi 61010, Kuwait* Tel (00965) 9746 2804 (mobile) E-mail bethpoppy@hotmail.com

WOODGATES, Mrs Margaret. b 47. St D Coll Lamp BA67. WMMTC 00. **d** 03 **p** 04. NSM Redditch, The Ridge *Worc* 03-05; NSM Redditch Ch the K 05-06; NSM Finstall from 06. *18 Warwick Hall Gardens, Bromsgrove B60 2AU* Tel (01527) 577785 E-mail margaret.wood@tesco.net

WOODGER, John McRae. b 36. Univ of Wales MTh08. Tyndale Hall Bris 60. **d** 63 **p** 64. C Heref St Pet w St Owen 63-66; C Macclesfield St Mich *Ches* 66-69; V Llangarron w Llangrove *Heref* 69-74; P-in-c Garway 70-74; R Church Stretton 74-84; Preb Heref Cathl 82-84; V Watford *St Alb* 84-01; rtd 01; Perm to Offic *Heref* from 01. *39 Bronte Drive, Ledbury HR8 2FZ* Tel (01531) 636745 E-mail woodger@talktalk.net

WOODGER, John Page. b 30. Master Mariner 56. St Aid Birkenhead 56. **d** 59 **p** 60. C Kimberworth *Sheff* 59-62; Chapl HM Borstal Pollington 62-70; C Goole *Sheff* 62-63; V Balne 63-70; C Halesowen *Worc* 70-74; V Cookley 74-81; TV Droitwich 81-85; TV Bedminster *Bris* 85-93; rtd 93; Perm to Offic *Bris* 93-97 and *Worc* from 98. *1 Barbel Crescent, Worcester WR5 3QU* Tel (01905) 769065

WOODGER, Richard William. b 50. Sarum & Wells Th Coll 76. **d** 79 **p** 80. C Chessington *Guildf* 79-82; C Frimley and Frimley Green 82-85; V N Holmwood 85-90; TR Headley All SS 90-98; TR Penrith w Newton Reigny and Plumpton Wall *Carl* 98-05; P-in-c Northleach w Hampnett and Farmington etc *Glouc* from 05; C Sherborne, Windrush, the Barringtons etc from 08; AD Northleach 09-10. *The Vicarage, Mill End, Northleach, Cheltenham GL54 3HL* Tel (01451) 860293 E-mail dickwoodger@yahoo.co.uk

WOODHALL, Peter. b 32. Edin Th Coll 57. **d** 60 **p** 61. C Carl St Barn 60-63; Hon Chapl Estoril *Eur* 63-65; Chapl RN 66-82; TR Is of Scilly *Truro* 82-90; V Mithian w Mount Hawke 90-95; rtd 97. *17 Emu Close, Heath and Reach, Leighton Buzzard LU7 0AT*

WOODHAM, Richard Medley Swift. b 43. Master Mariner 70. S'wark Ord Course 71. **d** 73 **p** 74. C Gravesend St Aid *Roch* 73-75; C Chessington *Guildf* 75-78; R Horstead and Warden Dioc Conf Ho *Nor* 78-87; Youth Chapl *Nor* 78-88; V Nor St Mary Magd w St Jas 87-91; TR Norwich Over-the-Water 91-98; P-in-c Lakenham St Jo 98-99; V Nor Lakenham St Jo and All SS and Tuckswood 99-06; RD Nor E 02-06; rtd 06; Perm to Offic *Nor* from 06. *40 Anchor Street, Coltishall, Norwich NR12 7AQ* Tel (01603) 736411 E-mail richard.woodham@virgin.net

WOODHAMS, Raymond John. b 40. Garnett Coll Lon CertEd68 IEng. STETS 98. **d** 01 **p** 02. NSM E Blatchington *Chich* 01-08; NSM E Blatchington and Bishopstone from 08. *The Long House, West Dean, Seaford BN25 4AL* Tel and fax (01323) 870432 E-mail raymondj.woodhams@virgin.net

WOODHAMS, Roy Owen. b 57. ARCM76 GRSM78 Lon Inst of Educn TCert79. Ripon Coll Cuddesdon 91. **d** 93 **p** 94. C Deal St Leon and St Rich and Sholden *Cant* 93-97; P-in-c Cherbury *Ox* 97-02; P-in-c Gainfield 99-02; R Cherbury w Gainfield 02-04; AD Vale of White Horse 01-04; V Fleet *Guildf* from 04. *The Vicarage, Branksomewood Road, Fleet GU51 4JU* Tel (01252) 616361 E-mail vicar@parishoffleet.org.uk

WOODHAMS, Mrs Sophie Harriet. b 27. Cranmer Hall Dur 66. dss 80 **d** 87. Raveningham *Nor* 80-81; Henleaze *Bris* 81-87; rtd 87. *22 Manormead, Tilford, Hindhead GU26 6RA* Tel (01428) 602500

WOODHEAD, Mrs Bernice. b 45. **d** 01 **p** 02. OLM Shore *Man* from 01; OLM Calderbrook from 01. *2 Mount Avenue, Littleborough OL15 9JP* Tel (01706) 379517

WOODHEAD, Christopher Godfrey. b 26. Pemb Coll Cam BA50 MA55. Ely Th Coll 50. **d** 52 **p** 53. C Barnsley St Edw *Wakef* 52-54; C Mill Hill St Mich *Lon* 54-58; C Sandridge *St Alb* 58-66; R Earl Stonham *St E* 66-72; V Hoo St Werburgh *Roch* 72-88; C Cheam *S'wark* 88-91; rtd 91; Perm to Offic *Cant* from 91. *43 Clare Drive, Herne Bay CT6 7QU* Tel (01227) 374137

WOODHEAD, Miss Helen Mary. b 35. Bedf Coll Lon BA57. Westcott Ho Cam 86. **d** 87 **p** 94. Par Dn Daventry *Pet* 87-90; Asst Dioc Dir of Ords *Guildf* 90-00; C Godalming 90-95; C Worplesdon 95-00; rtd 00; Perm to Offic *Lich* from 00. *12 Barley Croft, Whittington, Lichfield WS14 9LY* Tel (01543) 432345

WOODHEAD, Canon Michael. b 51. St Jo Coll Nottm 88. **d** 90 **p** 91. C Stannington *Sheff* 90-93; V Deepcar 93-01; TV Crookes St Thos 01-05; TR from 05; Hon Can Sheff Cathl from 11. *St Thomas Church, Nairn Street, Sheffield S10 1UL* Tel 0114-267 1090 E-mail mick.woodhead@sheffield.anglican.org

WOODHEAD, Mrs Sandra Buchanan. b 42. Man Poly BA82 Man Univ BD85. St Deiniol's Hawarden. dss 86 **d** 87 **p** 94. High Lane *Ches* 86-90; Hon Par Dn 87-90; C Brinnington w Portwood 91-94; V 94-00; R Withington St Paul *Man* 00-09; rtd 09. *Woodbank, Light Alders Lane, Disley, Stockport SK12 2LW* Tel (01663) 765708 E-mail deniswoodhead@btinternet.com

WOODHEAD-KEITH-DIXON, James Addison. b 25. St Aid Birkenhead 44. **d** 48 **p** 49. C Upperby St Jo *Carl* 48-50; C Dalton-in-Furness 50-52; V Blawith w Lowick 52-59; V Lorton 59-80; Chapl Puerto de la Cruz Tenerife *Eur* 80-82; TV Bellingham/Otterburn Gp *Newc* 82-83; TR 83-91; TR N Tyne and Redesdale 91-92; rtd 92. *Culpee House, Creebridge, Newton Stewart DG8 6NR*

WOODHOUSE, Canon Alison Ruth. b 43. Bedf Coll of Educn CertEd64. Dalton Ho Bris 68. dss 79 **d** 87 **p** 94. Bayston Hill *Lich* 79-81; W Derby St Luke *Liv* 81-86; Burscough Bridge 86-95; Par Dn 87-94; C 94-95; V Formby St Luke 95-07; AD Sefton 00-05; Hon Can Liv Cathl 02-07; rtd 07; Chapl to The Queen from 06. *16 Fountains Way, Liverpool L37 4HE* Tel (01704) 877423

WOODHOUSE, The Ven Andrew Henry. b 23. DSC45. Qu Coll Ox BA48 MA49. Linc Th Coll 48. **d** 50 **p** 51. C Poplar All SS w St Frideswide *Lon* 50-56; V W Drayton 56-70; RD Hillingdon 67-70; Adn Ludlow *Heref* 70-82; R Wistanstow 70-82; P-in-c Acton Scott 70-73; Can Res Heref Cathl 82-91; Treas 82-85; Adn Heref 82-91; rtd 91; Perm to Offic *Guildf* from 91. *Orchard Cottage, Bracken Close, Woking GU22 7HD* Tel (01483) 760671

WOODHOUSE, The Ven Charles David Stewart. b 34. Kelham Th Coll 55. **d** 59 **p** 60. C Leeds Halton St Wilfrid *Ripon* 59-63; Youth Chapl *Liv* 63-66; Bermuda 66-69; Asst Gen Sec CEMS 69-70; Gen Sec 70-76; Bp's Dom Chapl *Ex* 76-81; R Ideford, Luton and Ashcombe 76-81; V Hindley St Pet *Liv* 81-92; Adn Warrington 81-01; Hon Can Liv Cathl 83-01; rtd 01; Perm to Offic *Liv* from 03. *9 Rob Lane, Newton-le-Willows WA12 0DR*

WOODHOUSE, David Edwin. b 45. Lon Univ BSc68. Cuddesdon Coll 68. **d** 71 **p** 72. C E Dulwich St Jo *S'wark* 71-74; Lic to Offic 74-77; Perm to Offic *Bris* 77-79; Lic to Offic *Carl* rtd 10. *Kingsbury Hall, The Green, Calne SN11 8DG* Tel (01249) 821521 Fax 817246 E-mail kingsburyhallcd@aol.com

WOODHOUSE, David Maurice. b 40. Lon Univ BA62. Clifton Th Coll 63. **d** 65 **p** 66. C Wellington w Eyton *Lich* 65-68; C Meole Brace 68-71; V Crunch 71-82; P-in-c Gt Haywood 78-82; R Clitheroe St Jas *Blackb* 82-88; Ellel Grange Chr Healing Cen 88-91; V The Lye and Stambermill *Worc* 91-99; Chapl Acorn Chr Foundn 99-02; Dioc Healing Adv *Guildf* 00-02; rtd 02; Perm to Offic *Blackb* from 04. *1 Lilac Avenue, Penwortham, Preston PR1 9PB* Tel (01772) 742088 E-mail david.woodhouse@classicfm.net

WOODHOUSE, Canon Keith Ian. b 33. K Coll Lon 54. **d** 58 **p** 59. C Stockton St Chad CD *Dur* 58-61; C Man St Aid 61-64; V Peterlee *Dur* 64-99; AD Easington 72-98; Hon Can Dur Cathl 79-99; rtd 99; Dioc Pensions and Widows Officer *Dur* from 00. *85 Baulkham Hills, Penshaw, Houghton le Spring DH4 7RZ* Tel and fax 0191-584 3977 E-mail keithianwoodhouse@excite.com

WOODHOUSE, Canon Patrick Henry Forbes. b 47. Ch Ch Ox BA69 MA81. St Jo Coll Nottm 69 Lon Coll of Div ALCD71 LTh71. **d** 72 **p** 73. C Birm St Martin 72-74; C Whitchurch *Bris* 75-76; C Harpenden St Nic *St Alb* 76-80; Tanzania 80-81; Soc Resp Officer *Ely* 81-85; P-in-c Dean 81-85; Dir Soc Resp *Win* 85-90; V Chippenham St Andr w Tytherton Lucas *Bris* 90-00; Can Res and Prec Wells Cathl from 00. *4 The Liberty, Wells BA5 2SU* Tel and fax (01749) 673188 E-mail pwoodhouse@liberty4.fsnet.co.uk

WOODHOUSE, Canon Thomas Mark Bews. b 66. Cheltenham & Glouc Coll of HE BA98 Glos Univ MA05 FRSA05. Aston Tr Scheme 90 Westcott Ho Cam 92. **d** 95 **p** 96. C Cainscross w Selsley *Glouc* 95-98; V Hardwicke and Elmore w Longney 98-05; P-in-c Wootton Bassett *Sarum* 05-10; V from 10; RD Calne from 06; Can and Preb Sarum Cathl from 09. *The Vicarage, Glebe Road, Wootton Bassett, Swindon SN4 7DU* Tel (01793) 854302

WOODING, Alison. b 67. Yorks Min Course 05. **d** 10 **p** 11. C Ranmoor *Sheff* from 10. *Flat 1, 5 Ranmoor Park Road, Sheffield S10 3GX* Tel 0114-230 8417 Mobile 07891-064370 E-mail alisonwooding@hotmail.com

WOODING JONES, Andrew David. b 61. Oak Hill Th Coll BA91. **d** 91 **p** 92. C Welling *Roch* 91-95; TV Crookes St Thos *Sheff* 95-00; Resident Dir Ashburnham Trust from 00; NSM Ashburnham w Penhurst *Chich* from 01. *Ashburnham Christian Trust, Ashburnham Place, Battle TN33 9NF* Tel (01424) 892244 Fax 892243 E-mail andrewwj@ashburnham.org.uk

WOODLEY, David James. b 38. K Coll Lon BD61 AKC61 Open Univ BA98. **d** 62 **p** 63. C Lancing St Jas *Chich* 62-64; C St Alb St Pet *St Alb* 64-67; Malaysia 67-70; Lic to Offic *Linc* 71-72; V Westoning w Tingrith *St Alb* 72-77; Asst Chapl HM Pris Wormwood Scrubs 77-78; Chapl HM Pris Cardiff 78-84; Chapl HM Rem Cen Risley 84-92; Chapl HM Pris Styal 92-98; rtd 98; Perm to Offic *Ches* 98-07. *18 Longcroft Road, Yeovil BA21 4RR*

WOODLEY, Canon John Francis Chapman. b 33. Univ of Wales (Lamp) BA58. Edin Th Coll 58. **d** 60 **p** 61. C Edin All SS 60-65; Chapl St Andr Cathl 65-67; Prec 67-71; R Glas St Oswald 71-77; P-in-c Cumbernauld 77-93; Can St Mary's Cathl 82-99; CSG from 82; R Dalbeattie *Glas* 93-99; rtd 99; Hon Can St Mary's Cathl from 99; Dioc Supernumerary 99-03; Lic to Offic from 03. *3 Highbraigh Drive, Rutherglen, Glasgow G73 3RR* Tel 0141-647 3118 E-mail jfcwoodley@talk21.com

WOODLEY, The Ven Ronald John. b 25. Bps' Coll Cheshunt 50. **d** 53 **p** 54. C Middlesbrough St Martin *York* 53-58; C Whitby 58-61; C-in-c Middlesbrough Berwick Hills CD 61-66; V Middlesbrough Ascension 66-71; R Stokesley 71-85; RD Stokesley 77-85; Can and Preb York Minster 82-00; Adn Cleveland 85-91; rtd 91; Perm to Offic *Ripon* from 91 and *York* from 00. *2A Minster Court, York YO1 7JJ* Tel (01904) 679675

WOODLEY, Simon Andrew. b 66. Liv Univ BA88 Univ of Cen England in Birm 96. Ridley Hall Cam BTh00. **d** 00 **p** 01. C Birm St Martin w Bordesley St Andr 00-04; TR Bemerton *Sarum* from 04. *St Michael's Rectory, St Michael's Road, Salisbury SP2 9EQ* Tel (01722) 333750

WOODMAN, Brian Baldwin. b 35. Leeds Univ BA57 PhD73. NOC 84. **d** 87 **p** 88. C Guiseley w Esholt *Bradf* 87-90; TV Bingley All SS 90-94; P-in-c St Merryn *Truro* 94-00; rtd 00; Perm to Offic *Truro* from 00. *Penty an Garth, Trevance, St Issey, Wadebridge PL27 7QF* Tel (01841) 541387

WOODMAN, Christopher James. b 65. Chich Th Coll BTh93. **d** 93 **p** 94. C Leigh-on-Sea St Marg *Chelmsf* 93-97; TV Canvey Is 97-00; TV Moulsecoomb *Chich* 00-03; C Brighton St Matthias 03-06; TV Brighton Resurr 06-09; V Brighton St Luke Queen's Park 09-10; P-in-c Fareham SS Pet and Paul *Portsm* from 10. *St Peter and St Paul's Vicarage, 22 Harrison Road, Fareham PO16 7EJ* E-mail cjw@btinternet.com

WOODMAN, Oliver Nigel. b 47. FCIPD. Sarum Th Coll 67. **d** 70 **p** 82. C Stepney St Dunstan and All SS *Lon* 70-71; NSM Ovingdean w Rottingdean and Woodingdean *Chich* 81-87; NSM Eastbourne St Sav and St Pet 88-93; Asst to RD Eastbourne 93-98; NSM Eastbourne St Sav and St Pet 98-01; Perm to Offic *Win* 02-10; Hon Chapl Win and Eastleigh Healthcare NHS Trust 09-10; Perm to Offic *Lich* from 10. *25A Wissage Lane, Lichfield WS13 6DF* Tel (01543) 256655 E-mail ojwoodman56@googlemail.com

WOODMAN, The Ven Peter Wilfred. b 36. Univ of Wales (Lamp) BA58. Wycliffe Hall Ox 58. **d** 60 **p** 61. C New Tredegar *Mon* 60-61; C Newport St Paul 61-64; C Llanfrechfa All SS 64-67; V Llantilio Pertholey w Bettws Chpl etc *Mon* 67-74; V Bassaleg 74-90; Can St Woolos Cathl 84-01; V Caerwent w Dinham and Llanfair Discoed etc

90-96; Adn Mon 93-01; R Mamhilad and Llanfihangel Pontymoile 96-01; rtd 01. *Glaslyn, 40 Longhouse Barn, Penperlleni, Pontypool NP4 0BD* Tel (01873) 881322

WOODMANSEY, Michael Balfour. b 55. Leic Univ BSc. Ridley Hall Cam. **d** 83 **p** 84. C St Paul's Cray St Barn *Roch* 83-89; C S Shoebury *Chelmsf* 89-93; R Stifford 93-01; TR Heworth H Trin *York* 01-07; R Heworth H Trin and St Wulstan from 07. *Heworth Rectory, Melrosegate, York YO31 0RP* Tel (01904) 422958 E-mail michael@mwoodmansey.freeserve.co.uk

WOODMORE, Mrs Dilys Mary. b 44. SAOMC 98. **d** 01 **p** 02. NSM Dedworth *Ox* 01-04; NSM Burchetts Green from 04. *59 Terrington Hill, Marlow SL7 2RE* Tel (01628) 486274

WOODROFFE, Ian Gordon. b 46. Edin Th Coll 69. **d** 72 **p** 73. C Soham *Ely* 72-75; P-in-c Swaffham Bulbeck 75-80; Youth Chapl 75-80; V Cambridge St Jas 80-87; Chapl Mayday Univ Hosp Thornton Heath 87-94; Chapl Mayday Healthcare NHS Trust Thornton Heath 94-97; Staff Cllr Epsom and St Helier NHS Trust 97-02. *4 Station Road, Swaffham Bulbeck, Cambridge CB25 0NW* Tel (01223) 813122

WOODROW, Miss Alinda Victoria. b 60. Newnham Coll Cam BA82 MA86. Ripon Coll Cuddesdon 04. **d** 06 **p** 07. C Attleborough w Besthorpe *Nor* 06-08; C Sprowston w Beeston from 08. *6 Wroxham Road, Norwich NR7 8TZ* Tel (01603) 418296 E-mail alinda@sprowston.org.uk

WOODS, The Very Revd Alan Geoffrey. b 42. TD93. ACCA65 FCCA80. Sarum Th Coll 67. **d** 70 **p** 71. C Bedminster St Fran *Bris* 70-73; Youth Chapl 73-76; Warden Legge Ho Res Youth Cen 73-76; P-in-c Neston 76-79; TV Gtr Corsham 79-81; CF (TA) 80-94; P-in-c Charminster *Sarum* 81-83; V Charminster and Stinsford 83-90; RD Dorchester 85-90; Chapl Dorchester Hosps 86-87; V Calne and Blackland *Sarum* 90-96; RD Calne 90-96; Chapl St Mary's Sch Calne 90-96; Can and Preb Sarum Cathl 92-96; Sen Chapl Malta and Gozo *Eur* 96-03; Chan Malta Cathl 96-03; Dean Gib 03-08; V Gen to Bp Eur 03-05; Adn Gib 05-08; P-in-c Málaga 06-07; rtd 08; Perm to Offic *Sarum* and *Eur* from 08. *6 Maumbury Square, Weymouth Avenue, Dorchester DT1 1TY* Tel (01305) 264877 E-mail abwoods@tiscali.co.uk

WOODS, Charles William. b 31. Lich Th Coll 55. **d** 58 **p** 59. C Hednesford *Lich* 58-62; V Wilnecote 62-67; V Basford 67-76; V Chasetown 76-81; P-in-c Donington 81-83; V 83-96; V Boningale 83-96; RD Shifnal 84-89; rtd 96; Perm to Offic *Lich* from 96. *17 Campion Drive, Telford TF2 7RH* Tel (01952) 677134

WOODS, Christopher Guy Alistair. b 35. Dur Univ BA60. Clifton Th Coll 60. **d** 62 **p** 63. C Rainham *Chelmsf* 62-65; C Edin St Thos 65-69; Sec Spanish and Portuguese Ch Aid Soc 69-79; C Willesborough w Hinxhill *Cant* 74-80; P-in-c Murston w Bapchild and Tonge 80-87; R 87-90; R Gt Horkesley *Chelmsf* 90-98; RD Dedham and Tey 91-98; rtd 98; P-in-c Tenerife Sur *Eur* 99-00; Perm to Offic *Chelmsf* from 00. *Bluebonnet, Mill Lane, Bradfield, Manningtree CO11 2UT* Tel (01255) 870411

WOODS, Christopher Morrison. b 77. St Andr Univ MA00 TCD BTh04. CITC 01. **d** 04 **p** 05. C Dundela St Mark *D & D* 04-07; Chapl Ch Coll Cam 07-10; Sec C of E Liturg Commn and Nat Worship Development Officer Abps' Coun from 11. *Church House, Great Smith Street, London SW1P 3AZ* Tel (020) 7898 1365 E-mail christopher.woods@churchofengland.org

WOODS, David Arthur. b 28. Bris Univ BA52. Tyndale Hall Bris 48. **d** 53 **p** 54. C Camborne *Truro* 53-56; C Bromley Ch Ch *Roch* 56-58; V Tewkesbury H Trin *Glouc* 58-66; V Stapleford *S'well* 66-70; Miss to Seamen 70-93; Hon Chapl Miss to Seamen 70-93; V Fowey *Truro* 70-93; RD St Austell 80-88; rtd 93; Perm to Offic *Truro* from 93. *Linden, 7 Richmond Road, Pelynt, Looe PL13 2NH* Tel (01503) 220374

WOODS, David Benjamin. b 42. Linc Th Coll 88. **d** 90 **p** 91. C Louth *Linc* 90-93; P-in-c Ingoldmells w Addlethorpe 93-97; R 97-01; P-in-c Sutton Bridge 01-08; rtd 08; Hon C Digby Gp *Linc* from 08. *The Rectory, 1 Thomas à Becket Close, Digby, Lincoln LN4 3GA* Tel (01526) 323794 E-mail revwoods@ukonline.co.uk

WOODS, David Edward. b 36. City Univ FBCO61 FSMC61. SWMTC 83 S Dios Minl Tr Scheme 94. **d** 95 **p** 96. NSM Bemerton *Sarum* 95-98; NSM Salisbury St Martin 98-00; NSM Laverstock 98-00; NSM Salisbury St Martin and Laverstock 00-05; Perm to Offic *Truro* from 05. *8 Tower Meadows, St Buryan, Penzance TR19 6AJ* Tel (01736) 811253

WOODS, Edward Christopher John. b 44. NUI BA67. CITC 66. **d** 67 **p** 68. C Drumglass *Arm* 67-70; C Belfast St Mark *Conn* 70-73; I Kilcolman *L & K* 73-78; I Portarlington w Cloneyhurke and Lea *M & K* 78-84; Chan Kildare Cathl 81-84; I Killiney Ballybrack *D & G* 85-92; I Dublin Rathfarnham from 93; Dir of Ords (Dub) from 98; Internship Co-ord CITC from 10. *Rathfarnham Rectory, Rathfarnham, Terenure, Dublin 6W, Republic of Ireland* Tel and fax (00353) (1) 490 5543 E-mail anneted@gofree.indigo.ie

WOODS, Canon Eric John. b 51. Magd Coll Ox BA72 MA77 Trin Coll Cam BA77 MA83 FRSA94. Westcott Ho Cam 75. **d** 78 **p** 79. C Bris St Mary Redcliffe w Temple etc 78-81; Hon C Clifton St Paul 81-83; Asst Chapl Bris Univ 81-83; V Wroughton

83-93; RD Wroughton 88-93; V Sherborne w Castleton, Lillington and Longburton *Sarum* from 93; Chapl Sherborne Sch for Girls 93-99; RD Sherborne *Sarum* 96-04; Can and Preb Sarum Cathl from 98; Chapl Dorset Community NHS Trust 93-00; Chapl SW Dorset Primary Care Trust from 01; Chapl St Antony's Leweston Sch Sherborne from 03. *The Vicarage, Abbey Close, Sherborne DT9 3LQ* Tel (01935) 812452 Fax 812206 E-mail vicar@sherborneabbey.com

WOODS, Frederick James. b 45. Southn Univ BA66 MPhil74 Fitzw Coll Cam BA76 MA79. Ridley Hall Cam 74. **d** 77 **p** 78. C Stratford-on-Avon w Bishopton *Cov* 77-81; V Warminster Ch Ch *Sarum* 81-96; RD Heytesbury 95-96; TR Woodley *Ox* 96-01; V Colchester St Pet and St Botolph *Chelmsf* 01-11; rtd 11. *36 Church Road, Otley, Ipswich IP6 9NP* Tel (01473) 890786 E-mail fredjwoods@hotmail.com

WOODS, Geoffrey Edward. b 49. Lon Univ BD70 K Coll Lon MA94. Tyndale Hall Bris 67. **d** 73 **p** 74. C Gipsy Hill Ch Ch *S'wark* 73-76; C Uphill *B & W* 76-79; R Swainswick w Langridge and Woolley 79-84; Perm to Offic *Bris* 84-96; NSM Colerne w N Wraxall from 96; NSM By Brook from 06. *22 Watergates, Colerne, Chippenham SN14 8DR* Tel (01225) 743675

WOODS, John William Ashburnham. b 22. Reading Univ BSc50. NW Ord Course 73 St Jo Coll Lusaka 69. **d** 71 **p** 74. C Kitwe Zambia 71-72; C Goole *Sheff* 73-75; P-in-c Firbeck w Letwell 75-76; R 76-82; P-in-c Woodsetts 75-76; V 76-82; Bp's Rural Adv 80-92; R Barnburgh w Melton on the Hill 82-92; RD Wath 86-92; rtd 92; NSM Birdsall w Langton *York* 93-96; P-in-c Settrington w N Grimston, Birdsall w Langton 96-98; Perm to Offic from 00. *15 Deansfield Court, Furlongs Avenue, Norton, Malton YO17 9DJ* Tel (01653) 604455 E-mail revjwoods@btinternet.com

WOODS, Joseph Richard Vernon. b 31. Solicitor 57. Cuddesdon Coll 58. **d** 60 **p** 61. C Newc St Gabr 60-63; Trinidad and Tobago 63-67; Chapl Long Grove Hosp Epsom 67-76; P-in-c Ewell St Fran *Guildf* 76-79; V 79-87; V Englefield Green 87-96; rtd 96; Perm to Offic *Win* from 97. *8 Wren Close, Christchurch BH23 4BD* Tel (01425) 270799 E-mail trendi2@btinternet.com

WOODS, Michael. b 57. Ripon Coll Cuddesdon 99. **d** 01 **p** 02. C Bamber Bridge St Aid *Blackb* 01-06; P-in-c Rishton 06-11; V from 11. *The Vicarage, Somerset Road, Rishton, Blackburn BB1 4BP* Tel (01254) 886191 E-mail mwoods4@supanet.com

WOODS, Canon Michael Spencer. b 44. K Coll Lon BD66 AKC66 Sheff Univ MMinTheol99. **d** 67 **p** 68. C Sprowston *Nor* 67-70; Malaysia 70-74; TV Hempnall *Nor* 74-79; TV Halesworth w Linstead, Chediston, Holton etc *St E* 79-85; TR Braunstone *Leic* 85-92; RD Sparkenhoe E 89-91; TR Gt Yarmouth *Nor* 92-09; Hon Can Nor Cathl 96-09; rtd 09. *4 Old Church Close, Caistor St Edmund, Norwich NR14 8QX* Tel (01508) 493650 E-mail michael.woods@rjt.co.uk

WOODS, Canon Norman Harman. b 35. K Coll Lon BD62 AKC62. **d** 63 **p** 64. C Poplar All SS w St Frideswide *Lon* 63-68; C-in-c W Leigh CD *Portsm* 68-76; V Hythe *Cant* 76-01; RD Elham 83-89; Hon Can Cant Cathl 90-01; rtd 01; Perm to Offic *Cant* from 01. *36 Abbey Gardens, Canterbury CT2 7EU* Tel (01227) 470957 E-mail normanwoods@v21.me.net

WOODS, Richard. See WOODS, Joseph Richard Vernon

WOODS, Richard Thomas Evelyn Brownrigg. b 51. St Steph Ho Ox 83. **d** 85 **p** 86. C Southgate Ch Ch *Lon* 85-88; C Northampton All SS w St Kath *Pet* 88-89; V Maybridge *Chich* 89-99; V E Dean 99-05; R Singleton 99-05; V W Dean 99-05; R E Dean, Singleton, and W Dean from 05. *The Rectory, Singleton, Chichester PO18 0EZ* Tel and fax (01243) 811213 E-mail rector_singleton@hotmail.com

WOODS, Roger Andrew. b 60. Southn Univ BSc81. Oak Hill Th Coll BA01. **d** 98 **p** 99. C Audley *Lich* 98-02; TV Leek and Meerbrook from 02. *St Luke's Vicarage, Novi Lane, Leek ST13 6NR* Tel (01538) 386109

WOODS, Tanya Joy. b 73. CITC 99. **d** 02 **p** 03. NSM Killesher *K, E & A* 02-11; NSM Annagh w Drumaloor, Cloverhill and Drumlane from 11. *Cornacrea, Cavan Town, Republic of Ireland* Tel (00353) (49) 433 2188 *or* (42) 966 9229 Mobile 86-060 2450 Fax (42) 966 9119 E-mail revtanyawoods@hotmail.com

WOODS, Theodore Frank Spreull. b 37. Cam Univ BA58 DipEd80. Wells Th Coll 60. **d** 62 **p** 63. C Stocking Farm CD *Leic* 62-67; Papua New Guinea 67-77; V Knighton St Jo *Leic* 77-80; Chapl Angl Ch Gr Sch Brisbane Australia 80-88; Chapl Hillbrook Angl Sch 89-06; rtd 06. *44 Merle Street, Carina Qld 4152, Australia* Tel (0061) (7) 3398 4437 Mobile 40-961 6150 E-mail tandlwoods@bigpond.com

WOODS, Timothy James. b 52. Poly Cen Lon BA78 MSc79 Ex Univ MA96 ACIB75. Qu Coll Birm 81. **d** 83 **p** 84. C Brierley Hill *Lich* 83-86; C Stoneydelph St Martin CD 86-88; World Development Officer 86-88; Chr Aid Area Sec (SE Lon) 88-91; V Estover *Ex* 91-97; TR Brixham w Churston Ferrers and Kingswear 97-00; Dir Bd of Ch and Soc *Sarum* 00-05; RD Salisbury 05-07; Advocacy and Middle E Desk Officer USPG 05-08; Regional Co-ord Wales and W of England 10; In Methodist Ch 08-09; C Kingsteignton and Teigngrace *Ex* from

10. *The Manse, Berry Lane, Kingsteignton, Newton Abbot TQ12 3AT* Tel (01626) 356581 E-mail timbar.woods@tiscali.co.uk

WOODS, Mrs Valerie Irene. b 44. Trin Coll Bris 82. **dss** 84 **d** 87 **p** 94. Coleford w Staunton *Glouc* 84-88; C 87-88; TD Bedminster *Bris* 88-94; TV 94-95; Chapl HM Rem Cen Pucklechurch 95-96; Chapl HM Pris Eastwood Park 96-00; V Wood End *Cov* 01-10; P-in-c Potters Green 08-10; rtd 11. *1 Beechrome Drive, Earl Shilton, Leicester LE9 7DW*

WOODS, William. See WOODS, Charles William

WOODSFORD, Canon Andrew Norman. b 43. Nottm Univ BA65. Ridley Hall Cam 65. **d** 67 **p** 68. C Radcliffe-on-Trent *S'well* 67-70; P-in-c Ladybrook 70-73; P-in-c Barton in Fabis 73-81; P-in-c Thrumpton 73-81; R Gamston w Eaton and W Drayton 81-88; Chapl Bramcote Sch Notts 81-93; Warden of Readers *S'well* 88-08; Hon Can S'well Minster 93-08; RD Retford 93-00; rtd 08. *3 Clinton Rise, Gamston, Retford DN22 0QJ* Tel (01777) 838706 E-mail woodsford@.msn.com

WOODSFORD, Martyn Paul. b 64. Oak Hill Th Coll 01. **d** 03 **p** 04. C Southover *Chich* 03-07; P-in-c S Malling 07-09; R Adelaide St Luke Australia from 09. *17 Whitmore Square, Adelaide SA 5000, Australia* E-mail revwoody@macdream.net

WOODWARD, Andrew John. b 59. ACIB85. SEITE 96. **d** 99 **p** 00. NSM Weybridge *Guildf* 99-03; NSM St Botolph Aldgate w H Trin Minories *Lon* 03-07; Perm to Offic *Guildf* 03-07; P-in-c Kemp Town St Mary *Chich* from 07. *11 West Drive, Brighton BN2 0GD* Tel (01273) 698601 E-mail thewoodys1@tiscali.co.uk

WOODWARD, Anthony John. b 50. Salford Univ BSc78. St Jo Coll Nottm 79. **d** 81 **p** 82. C Deane *Man* 81-84; CF 84-87; R Norris Bank *Man* 87-90; V Lostock St Thos and St Jo 92-96; Perm to Offic 96-01; C Halliwell 01-02; TV 02-04; P-in-c Chard and Distr *B & W* 04-06; V Chard St Mary 06-09; P-in-c Combe St Nicholas w Wambrook and Whitestaunton 08-09; rtd 09. *Sloe Cottages, 194 Thurlbear Road, Thurlbear, Taunton TA3 5DQ* E-mail revtonywoodward@btinternet.com

WOODWARD, Arthur Robert Harry (Bob). b 28. **d** 76 **p** 77. Rhodesia 76-80; Zimbabwe 80-87; Adn E Harare 82-87; R Wymington w Podington *St Alb* 87-97; RD Sharnbrook 89-97; rtd 97; Perm to Offic *Portsm* from 97. *9 Briarfield Gardens, Horndean, Waterlooville PO8 9HX* Tel (023) 9259 6983 E-mail woodward@bushinternet.com

WOODWARD, Clive Ian. b 49. City of Lon Poly BSc84. STETS 01. **d** 04 **p** 05. NSM Willingdon *Chich* 04-06; Chapl E Sussex Hosps NHS Trust from 06. *The Chaplaincy Office, The Conquest Hospital, The Ridge, St Leonards-on-Sea TN37 7RD* Tel (01424) 757088 E-mail clive.woodward@tiscali.co.uk *or* chaplain@esht.nhs.uk

WOODWARD, Canon Ian. b 44. OLM course 96. **d** 97 **p** 98. OLM Queen Thorne *Sarum* 97-99; Adv to Bd of Ch and Soc 97-00; NSM Wilton w Netherhampton and Fugglestone 00-02; R Bere Regis and Affpuddle w Turnerspuddle from 02; Can Res and Prec Sarum Cathl from 07. *The Vicarage, West Street, Bere Regis, Wareham BH20 7HQ* Tel (01929) 471262 Mobile 07973-318866 E-mail revianw@btinternet.com

WOODWARD, Canon James Welford. b 61. K Coll Lon BD82 AKC82 Lambeth STh85 Birm Univ MPhil91 Open Univ PhD99 FRSA07. Westcott Ho Cam 83. **d** 85 **p** 86. C Consett *Dur* 85-87; Bp's Dom Chapl *Ox* 87-90; Chapl Qu Eliz Hosp Birm 90-96; Distr Chapl Co-ord S Birm HA 90-96; Chapl Manager Univ Hosp Birm NHS Trust 92-96; P-in-c Middleton *Birm* 96-98; P-in-c Wishaw 96-98; Bp's Adv on Health and Soc Care 96-09; V Temple Balsall 98-09; Master Foundn and Hosp of Lady Katherine Leveson 98-09; Dir Leveson Cen for the Study of Ageing, Spirituality and Soc Policy 00-09; Can Windsor from 09. *6 The Cloisters, Windsor Castle, Windsor SL4 1NJ* Tel (01753) 848709 E-mail james.woodward@stgeorges-windsor.org

WOODWARD, Canon John Clive. b 35. Univ of Wales (Lamp) BA56. St Jo Coll Dur 56. **d** 58 **p** 59. C Risca *Mon* 58-63; C Chepstow 63-66; V Ynysddu 66-74; V Newport Ch Ch 74-84; Can St Woolos Cathl 82-00; TR Cyncoed 84-00; rtd 00. *17 Carisbrooke Way, Cyncoed, Cardiff CF23 9HS* Tel (029) 2048 4448

WOODWARD, Mrs Margaret Ruth. b 59. EMMTC 04. **d** 08 **p** 09. NSM E Bridgford and Kneeton *S'well* from 08; NSM Flintham from 08; NSM Car Colston w Screveton from 08. *The Vicarage, Woods Lane, Flintham, Newark NG23 5LR* Tel (01636) 525567 E-mail maggie.woodward@ntlworld.com

WOODWARD, Mark Christian. b 73. Univ of Wales (Lamp) BA95 Trin Coll Carmarthen PGCE97. Trin Coll Bris MA02. **d** 02 **p** 03. C Egham *Guildf* 02-06; R Stoke-next-Guildf from 06; Chapl Guildf Coll of FE and HE from 06. *8 Brockway Close, Guildford GU1 2LW* Tel (01483) 301393 Mobile 07949-630031 E-mail mark@stjohnstoke.com

WOODWARD, Matthew Thomas. b 75. Brunel Univ BA97 K Coll Lon MA99 Anglia Poly Univ MA05. Westcott Ho Cam 99. **d** 01 **p** 02. C Hampstead St Jo *Lon* 01-05; P-in-c Pimlico St Mary 05-10; R San Mateo Transfiguration USA from 10.

3900 Alameda de las Pulgas, San Mateo CA 94403-4110, USA Tel (001) (650) 341 8206 E-mail matthewwoodward@mac.com

WOODWARD, Merriel Frances. b 55. **d** 11. NSM Langney *Chich* from 11. *61 Rowan Avenue, Eastbourne BN22 0RX* Tel (01323) 509891

WOODWARD (née HIGGINS), Mrs Natasha Caroline. b 76. Clare Coll Cam BA98 MA02. Westcott Ho Cam 03. **d** 06 **p** 07. C Crayford *Roch* 06-07; C Orpington All SS 08-10; C Chingford SS Pet and Paul *Chelmsf* from 10. *Old Church House, 1A Priory Avenue, London E4 8AA* Tel (020) 8529 3738 Mobile 07758-579369 E-mail natasha.c.woodward@gmail.com

WOODWARD, Canon Peter Cavell. b 36. St Cath Coll Cam BA58 MA62. Bps' Coll Cheshunt 58. **d** 60 **p** 61. C Chingford St Anne *Chelmsf* 60-63; Madagascar 63-75; V Weedon Bec Pet 75-76; P-in-c Everdon 75-76; V Weedon Bec w Everdon 76-81; RD Daventry 79-81; Can Pet Cathl 81-02; V Brackley St Pet w St Jas 81-02; Chapl Brackley Cottage Hosp 81-02; RD Brackley 82-88; rtd 02; Perm to Offic *Pet* from 02; Chapl to Retired Clergy and Clergy Widows' Officer from 08. *7 Glastonbury Road, Northampton NN4 8BB* Tel (01604) 660679 E-mail peterandmary@oddbod.org.uk

WOODWARD, Robert. *See* WOODWARD, Arthur Robert Harry

WOODWARD, Roger David. b 38. WMMTC 87. **d** 90 **p** 91. C Castle Bromwich SS Mary and Marg *Birm* 90-93; C Kingstanding St Luke 93-04; C Kingstanding St Mark 93-04; rtd 04; Hon C Kingstanding St Mark *Birm* 04-07. *10 Baldwin Road, Bewdley DY12 2BP* Tel (01299) 401119

WOODWARDS, David George. b 36. K Coll Lon BD62 MTh73. Oak Hill Th Coll 62. **d** 64 **p** 65. C Heworth H Trin *York* 64 66; Chapl St Pet Coll Kaduna Nigeria 67-71; V Edwardstone w Groton *St E* 72-82; RD Sudbury 81-88; R Glemsford 82-88; P-in-c Hartest w Boxted, Somerton and Stanstead 85-88; Hon Can St E Cathl 87-94; R Thorndon w Rishangles, Stoke Ash, Thwaite etc 88-94; RD Hartismere 88-93; rtd 98; Perm to Offic *St E* from 99 and *Chelmsf* from 03. *4 Cricketers Close, Sudbury CO10 2AL* Tel (01787) 374160 Fax 883312 E-mail tradrev@aol.com

WOODWELL, Sister Anita Marie. b 42. Nottm Univ BA74 CertEd80. St Deiniol's Hawarden 85. **dss** 87 **d** 87 **p** 05. Mottram in Longdendale w Woodhead *Ches* 86-89; Par Dn 87-89; TD Birkenhead Priory 89; Perm to Offic *Ban* from 01 and *St D* from 04; P-in-c Llanfrechfa and Llanddewi Fach w Llandegfeth *Mon* 05-09; Dioc Adv on Spirituality from 09. *1 White Houses, Pentwyn, Abersychan, Pontypool NP4 7SY* Tel (01495) 753195 E-mail awoodwell@yahoo.com

WOOFF, Ms Erica Mielle. b 67. City Univ BSc90 Lon Inst of Educn MA95. SEITE 02. **d** 05 **p** 06. C Sydenham St Bart *S'wark* 05-08; P-in-c Charlton 08-09; R from 09. *St Thomas House, Maryon Road, London SE7 8DJ* Tel (020) 8855 1718 E-mail ericauk@aol.com

WOOKEY, Canon Frances Anne. b 52. ACII73. WEMTC 94. **d** 97 **p** 98. C Glouc St Jas and All SS 97-01; V Hanley Castle, Hanley Swan and Welland *Worc* from 01; P-in-c Upton-on-Severn, Ripple, Earls Croome etc from 11; RD Upton from 05; Hon Can Worc Cathl from 07. *Thistledown, Pendock, Gloucester GL19 3PW* Tel (01531) 650146 E-mail fwookey@fides.demon.co.uk

WOOKEY, Stephen Mark. b 54. Em Coll Cam BA76 MA80. Wycliffe Hall Ox 77. **d** 80 **p** 81. C Enfield Ch Ch Trent Park *Lon* 80-84; Asst Chapl Paris St Mich *Eur* 84-87; C Langham Place All So *Lon* 87-96; R Moreton-in-Marsh w Batsford, Todenham etc *Glouc* from 96; RD Stow 99-04. *The Rectory, Bourton Road, Moreton-in-Marsh GL56 0BG* Tel (01608) 652680 E-mail stevewookey@mac.com

WOOLCOCK, Christine Ann. *See* FROUDE, The Ven Christine Ann

WOOLCOCK, John. b 47. Open Univ BA82 BA86. Wm Temple Coll Rugby 69 Sarum & Wells Th Coll 70. **d** 72 **p** 73. C Kells *Carl* 72-76; C Barrow St Matt 76-78; R Distington 78-86; V Staveley w Kentmere 86-93; Soc Resp Officer 89-93; Hon Can Carl Cathl 91-93; TR Egremont and Haile 93-08; P-in-c Seascale and Drigg from 08; RD Calder from 07. *The Vicarage, The Banks, Seascale CA20 1QT* Tel (01946) 728217

WOOLCOCK, Mrs Olwen Sylvia. b 57. Birm Univ BA78. WEMTC 02. **d** 05 **p** 06. C Claines St Jo *Worc* 05-08; TR Hugglescote w Donington, Ellistown and Snibston *Leic* from 08. *The Rectory, 12 Grange Road, Hugglescote, Coalville LE67 2BQ* Tel (01530) 832557 Mobile 07913-977579 E-mail olwen@woolcock.org

WOOLDRIDGE, Derek Robert. b 33. Nottm Univ BA57. Oak Hill Th Coll. **d** 59 **p** 60. C Chesterfield H Trin *Derby* 59-63; C Heworth w Peasholme St Cuth *York* 63-70; R York St Paul 70-00; rtd 01; Perm to Offic *York* from 01. *80 Grantham Drive, York YO26 4TZ* Tel (01904) 798393 E-mail drw@100york.freeserve.co.uk

WOOLDRIDGE, John Bellamy. b 27. Tyndale Hall Bris 54. **d** 56 **p** 57. C Norbury *Ches* 56-58; C Bramcote *S'well* 58-60; R Eccleston *Ches* 60-66; NW Area Sec CPAS 66-68; P-in-c Knutsford St Jo *Ches* 68-71; V Knutsford St Jo and Toft 71-79; V

Gt Clacton *Chelmsf* 79-82; V Disley *Ches* 82-88; Min Buxton Trin Prop Chpl *Derby* 88-92; rtd 92; Perm to Offic *Derby* and *S'well* from 92. *227 Bramcote Lane, Nottingham NG8 2QL* Tel 0115-928 8332

WOOLF, Ms Elizabeth Louise. b 73. Qu Coll Cam BA95 MA99. Wycliffe Hall Ox BA05. **d** 06 **p** 07. C Holborn St Geo w H Trin and St Bart *Lon* 06-08; C Hammersmith St Paul 08-09; C Leamington Priors St Paul *Cov* from 09. *40 Leicester Street, Leamington Spa CV32 4TE* E-mail lizzy@stpl.org.uk

WOOLHOUSE, Kenneth. b 38. BNC Ox BA61 MA65. Cuddesdon Coll. **d** 64 **p** 65. C Old Brumby *Linc* 64-67; Pastor Michaelshoven Soc Work Village W Germany 67-68; Chapl Cov Cathl 68-75; C-in-c Hammersmith SS Mich and Geo White City Estate CD *Lon* 75-81; Dir Past Studies Chich Th Coll 81-86; P-in-c Birdham w W Itchenor *Chich* 81-86; Chapl W Sussex Inst of HE 86-95; TV N Lambeth *S'wark* 95-01; rtd 01; Perm to Offic *S'wark* from 01. *15 Tavistock Tower, Russell Place, London SE16 7PQ* Tel (020) 7237 8147

WOOLLARD, David John. b 39. Leic Univ BSc62. Trin Coll Bris 86. **d** 88 **p** 89. C Clifton *York* 88-91; C York St Luke 91-94; V Selby St Jas 94-07; V Wistow 94-96; rtd 07; Perm to Offic *York* from 07. *6 Town Street, Settrington, Malton YO17 8NR* Tel (01944) 768665 E-mail d.wool@virgin.net

WOOLLASTON, Brian. b 53. CertEd76. St Paul's Coll Grahamstown 81. **d** 83 **p** 84. C Kington w Huntington, Old Radnor, Kinnerton etc *Heref* 88-89; C Tupsley 89-91; V Newbridge-on-Wye and Llanfihangel Brynpabuan etc *S & B* 91-98; CF 98-03; V Whiteshill and Randwick *Glouc* from 03. *The Vicarage, 98 Farmhill Lane, Stroud GL5 4DD* Tel (01453) 764757

WOOLLCOMBE (née DEARMER), Mrs Juliet. b 38. St Mary's Coll Dur BA60 Hughes Hall Cam DipEd61. Gilmore Course 74. **dss** 77 **d** 87 **p** 94. St Marylebone Ch Ch *Lon* 77-80; Dean of Women's Min (Lon Area) 87-89; Dn-in-c Upton Snodsbury and Broughton Hackett etc *Worc* 89-94; NSM Pershore w Pinvin, Wick and Birlingham 94-98; rtd 98; Perm to Offic *Worc* 98-10 and *Cant* from 11. *36 Sturry Court Mews, Sturry Hill, Sturry, Canterbury CT2 0ND* Tel (01227) 710346 E-mail julietatashdale@talk21.com

WOOLLEY, Canon Francis Bertram Hopkinson. b 43. Sarum & Wells Th Coll 75. **d** 78 **p** 79. C Halesowen *Worc* 78-81; TV Droitwich 81-86; TV Cambridge Ascension *Ely* 86-92; R Leverington 92-01; P-in-c Wisbech St Mary 92-98; P-in-c Southea w Murrow and Parson Drove 98-01; P-in-c Balsham 01-02; P-in-c W Wickham 01-02; P-in-c Weston Colville 01-02; P-in-c W Wratting 01-02; R Balsham, Weston Colville, W Wickham etc 02-08; P-in-c 08-09; Hon Can Ely Cathl 05-08; rtd 08; Perm to Offic *Ox* from 09. *66 Cranham Street, Oxford OX2 6DD* E-mail francis.woolley@tesco.net

WOOLMER, Preb John Shirley Thursby. b 42. Wadh Coll Ox BA63 MA69. St Jo Coll Nottm 70. **d** 71 **p** 72. Asst Chapl Win Coll 72-75; C Ox St Aldate w H Trin 75-82; R Shepton Mallet w Doulting *B & W* 82-02; Chapl Bath and West Community NHS Trust 97-01; Preb Wells Cathl 00-02; NSM Leic H Trin w St Jo 02-07; Par Evang 02-07; Springboard Missr 02-04; rtd 07. *Fig Tree Cottage, Roecliffe Road, Cropston, Leicester LE7 7HQ* Tel 0116-235 5237

WOOLMER, Kelvin Frederick. b 55. EAMTC 98. **d** 01 **p** 02. NSM Squirrels Heath *Chelmsf* 01-05; NSM Harold Hill St Paul 05-06; P-in-c Stratford New Town St Paul from 06; Ind Chapl from 06. *St Paul's Vicarage, 65 Maryland Road, London E15 1JL* Tel (020) 8534 4243 E-mail kelvin.woolmer@ntlworld.com

WOOLNOUGH, Murray Robert. Wycliffe Hall Ox 07. **d** 09 **p** 10. C Newbury *Ox* 09-11; P-in-c Woy Woy Australia from 11. *151 Blackwell Road, Woy Woy NSW 2256, Australia* E-mail mrwoolnough@gmail.com

WOOLSTENHOLMES, Cyril Esmond. b 16. Bede Coll Dur BA37 MA41. **d** 39 **p** 40. C Leadgate *Dur* 39-44; C Darlington St Cuth 44-46; C W Hartlepool St Paul 46-50; V Tudhoe Grange 50-67; R Shadforth 67-82; rtd 82. *12 Wearside Drive, The Sands, Durham DH1 1LE* Tel 0191-384 3763

WOOLVEN, Mrs Catherine Merris. b 60. Trin Coll Bris 07. **d** 09 **p** 10. Chapl Lee Abbey 09-10; C Kilmington, Stockland, Dalwood, Yarcombe etc *Ex* from 10. *The Vicarage, Yarcombe, Honiton EX14 9BD* Tel (01404) 861763 Mobile 07754-582395 E-mail katewoolven@hotmail.co.uk

WOOLVEN, Ronald. b 36. Oak Hill Th Coll 60. **d** 63 **p** 64. C Romford Gd Shep *Chelmsf* 63-68; C Widford 68-73; P-in-c Barling w Lt Wakering 73-84; V 84-05; rtd 05; Perm to Offic *Chelmsf* from 05. *119 Ness Road, Shoeburyness, Southend-on-Sea SS3 9BS* Tel (01702) 294826 E-mail r.woolven@btopenworld.com

WOOLVERIDGE, Gordon Hubert. b 27. CCC Cam BA51 MA55 Barrister-at-Law 52. S Dios Minl Tr Scheme 81. **d** 84 **p** 85. NSM St Edm the King w St Nic Acons etc *Lon* 84-85; NSM Chich St Paul and St Pet 85-88; P-in-c Greatham w Empshott and Hawkley w Prior's Dean *Portsm* 88-92; rtd 92; Perm to Offic *Sarum* from 93. *21 Back Lane, Cerne Abbas, Dorchester DT2 7JW* Tel (01300) 341020

WOOLWAY, Joanne. *See* GRENFELL, Canon Joanne Woolway

WOOLWICH, Area Bishop of. *Vacant*

WOON, Canon Edward Charles. b 43. SWMTC 94. **d** 96 **p** 97. OLM Tuckingmill *Truro* 96-02; P-in-c from 02; TV Redruth w Lanner and Treleigh from 04; Hon Can Truro Cathl from 09. *All Saints' Vicarage, 35 Roskear, Camborne TR14 8DG* Tel (01209) 715910   Mobile 07974-431863
E-mail eddie.woon@btopenworld.com

WOOSTER, Patrick Charles Francis. b 38. Qu Coll Birm 63. **d** 65 **p** 66. C Chippenham St Andr w Tytherton Lucas *Bris* 65-70; C Cockington *Ex* 70-72; V Stone w Woodford *Glouc* 72-73; P-in-c Hill 72-73; V Stone w Woodford and Hill 73-99; rtd 99; Perm to Offic *Worc* from 99. *20 Hylton Road, Hampton, Evesham WR11 2QB* Tel (01386) 45907

WOOSTER, Mrs Ruth Mary. b 45. SAOMC 95. **d** 98 **p** 99. OLM High Wycombe *Ox* from 98. *2 Beechwood View, Wycombe Road, Saunderton, High Wycombe HP14 4HR*
E-mail ruth@woosies.freeserve.co.uk

WOOTTON, Philip Charles. b 63. Hatf Coll Dur BA85 Dur Inst of Educn PGCE86. Cranmer Hall Dur 98. **d** 00 **p** 01. C Meopham w Nurstead *Roch* 00-04; TV S Chatham H Trin from 04. *29 Keefe Close, Chatham ME5 9AG* Tel (01634) 660087
E-mail philip.wootton@diocese-rochester.org

WORCESTER, Archdeacon of. *See* MORRIS, The Ven Roger Anthony Brett

WORCESTER, Bishop of. *See* INGE, The Rt Revd John Geoffrey

WORCESTER, Dean of. *See* ATKINSON, The Very Revd Peter Gordon

WORDSWORTH, Jeremy Nathaniel. b 30. Clare Coll Cam BA54 MA58. Ridley Hall Cam 54. **d** 56 **p** 57. C Gt Baddow *Chelmsf* 56-59; Chapl Felsted Sch 59-63; Chapl Sherborne Sch 63-71; PV and Succ S'wark Cathl 71-73; P-in-c Stone *Worc* 73-77; V Malvern St Andr 77-82; V Combe Down w Monkton Combe and S Stoke *B & W* 82-95; rtd 95; Perm to Offic *B & W* from 05. *4 The Glebe, Hinton Charterhouse, Bath BA2 7SB* Tel (01225) 722520 E-mail hintonwordys@ukonline.co.uk

WORDSWORTH, Paul. b 42. Birm Univ BA64. Wells Th Coll 64. **d** 66 **p** 67. C Anlaby St Pet *York* 66-71; C Marfleet 71-72; TV 72-77; V Sowerby 77-90; P-in-c Sessay 77-90; V York St Thos w St Maurice 90-01; Local Community Miss Project Ldr 90-96; Abp's Miss Adv 96-00; Miss Strategy Development Officer 01-07; Abp's Officer for Miss and Evang 01-07; rtd 07; Perm to Offic *York* from 07. *10 Burniston Grove, York YO10 3RP* Tel (01904) 426891   Mobile 07711-371046
E-mail paul.wordsworth@homecall.co.uk

WORGAN, Maurice William. b 40. Ely Th Coll 62 Sarum Th Coll 64. **d** 65 **p** 66. C Cranbrook *Cant* 65-69; C Maidstone St Martin 69-72; R Lyminge w Paddlesworth 72-73; P-in-c Stanford w Postling and Radegund 72-73; R Lyminge w Paddlesworth, Stanford w Postling etc 73-88; V Cant St Dunstan w H Cross 88-09; rtd 09; Perm to Offic *Cant* from 09. *22 Holmscroft Road, Herne Bay CT6 6PE* Tel (01227) 363339
E-mail maurice@maurice-worgan.co.uk

WORKMAN, John Lewis. b 26. St Deiniol's Hawarden 82. **d** 83 **p** 84. C Brecon St Mary and Battle w Llanddew *S & B* 83-86; Min Can Brecon Cathl 83-86; P-in-c Swansea St Luke 86-87; V 87-95; rtd 95. *12 Grove House, Clyne Close, Mayals, Swansea SA3 5HL* Tel (01792) 405674

WORKMAN, Michael. b 49. Univ Coll Lon BSc70 Reading Univ PhD75. WEMTC 03. **d** 06 **p** 07. NSM Cheltenham St Mary w St Matt *Glouc* from 06. *Owls Barn, Badgeworth Lane, Badgeworth, Cheltenham GL51 4UH* Tel (01242) 863360 Mobile 07762-545098 E-mail curate@stmattscheltl.org.uk

WORLEDGE, Paul Robert. b 70. Hertf Coll Ox BA91 Lon Inst of Educn PGCE92. Oak Hill Th Coll BA00. **d** 00 **p** 01. C Boscombe St Jo *Win* 00-04; V Ramsgate St Luke *Cant* from 04; AD Thanet from 09. *St Luke's Vicarage, St Luke's Avenue, Ramsgate CT11 7JX* Tel (01843) 592562
E-mail worledge@bigfoot.com

WORLEY, William. b 37. TD89. Cranmer Hall Dur 69. **d** 72 **p** 73. C Consett *Dur* 72-76; V Seaton Carew 76-03; CF (TA) from 77; rtd 03; Perm to Offic *Dur* from 03. *5 Peakston Close, Hartlepool TS26 0PN*

WORMALD, Roy Henry. b 42. Chich Th Coll 64. **d** 67 **p** 68. C Walthamstow St Mich *Chelmsf* 67-69; C Cov St Thos 69-72; C Cov St Jo 69-72; C Wood Green St Mich *Lon* 72-77; P-in-c Hanwell St Mellitus 77-80; V Hanwell St Mellitus w St Mark 80-95; C Hillingdon St Jo 95-99; R Kirkley St Pet and St Jo *Nor* 99-09; rtd 09; Perm to Offic *Nor* from 09 and *St E* from 11. *12 Coppleston Close, Worlingham, Beccles NR34 7SF* Tel (01502) 713331

WORN, Nigel John. b 56. Sarum & Wells Th Coll. **d** 84 **p** 85. C Walworth St Jo *S'wark* 84-88; Succ S'wark Cathl 88-92; V Mitcham Ascension 92-01; RD Merton 97; V Kew from 01. *The Vicarage, 278 Kew Road, Kew, Richmond TW9 3EE* Tel (020) 8940 4616 E-mail nigel.worn@which.net

WORRALL, Frederick Rowland. b 27. **d** 86 **p** 87. NSM Chellaston *Derby* 86-93; NSM Barrow-on-Trent w Twyford and Swarkestone 94-97; Perm to Offic from 97. *37 St Peter's Road, Chellaston, Derby DE73 6UU* Tel (01332) 701890

WORRALL, Peter Henry. b 62. CA Tr Coll 85 WMMTC 93. **d** 9 **p** 96. C Bromsgrove St Jo *Worc* 95-99; P-in-c Hartlebury 99-04 Par Support Officer CA 06-07; TV Redditch H Trin *Worc* from 07. *1 Hennals Avenue, Redditch B97 5RX* Tel (01527) 879500

WORRALL, Suzanne. *See* SHERIFF, Canon Suzanne

WORSDALE, Barry. **d** 10 **p** 11. NSM Elloughton and Brough w Brantingham *York* from 10. *45 Augustus Drive, Brough HU15 1DH* Tel (01482) 669189

WORSDALL, John Robin. b 33. Dur Univ BA57. Linc Th Co' 62. **d** 63 **p** 64. C Manthorpe w Londonthorpe *Linc* 63-66; C Folkingham w Laughton 66-68; V New Bolingbroke w Carrington 68-74; P-in-c S Somercotes 74-80; V N Somercote 74-80; P-in-c Stickney 80-82; P-in-c E Ville w Mid Ville 80-82; P-in-c Stickford 80-82; R Stickney Gp 82-98; rtd 98. *2 Streather Court, Raunds, Wellingborough NN9 6DR* Tel (01933) 460078

WORSFOLD, Ms Caroline Jayne. b 61. St Steph Ho Ox. **d** 8 **p** 94. Chapl Asst Leic R Infirmary 88-90; C Sunderlan Pennywell St Thos *Dur* 90-91; Sunderland HA Chapl 90-94 Chapl Priority Healthcare Wearside NHS Trust 94-06; Chap Northumberland, Tyne and Wear NHS Foundn Trust from 06 *The Barton Centre, Cherry Knowle Hospital, Ryhope, Sunderlan SR2 0NB* Tel 0191-565 6256 ext 43370 *or* 522 7347
E-mail caroline.worsfold@stw.nhs.uk

WORSFOLD, John. b 24. Keble Coll Ox BA50 MA50 Cuddesdon Coll 50. **d** 51 **p** 52. C Clapham H Spirit *S'wark* 51-62 C Richmond St Mary w St Matthias and St Jo 62-63; C Shirley St Geo *Cant* 63-80; C Croydon H Sav 80-84; C Croydon H Sav S'wark 85-89; rtd 90; Perm to Offic *S'wark* from 90 and *Roch* from 03. *clo Pumfrey & Lythaby Solicitors, 155-159 High Street Orpington BR6 0LN* Tel (01689) 833657 Fax 825906

WORSFOLD, Richard Vernon. b 64. Ex Univ LLB86. Cranmer Hall Dur BA94. **d** 95 **p** 96. C Countesthorpe w Foston *Leic* 95-99; TV Bradgate Team 99-01; TR 01-09; V Leic Martyrs from 09. *49 Westcotes Drive, Leicester LE3 0QT* Tel 0116-223 2632
E-mail rworsfold@btconnect.com

WORSLEY, Mrs Christine Anne. b 52. Hull Univ BA73 Bris Univ CertEd74 Birm Univ MPhil94. WMMTC 82. **dss** 84 **d** 87 **p** 94. Smethwick St Mary *Birm* 84-87; Par Dn Smethwick H Trin w St Alb 87-89; Par Dn Coventry Caludon 89-91; Chapl Mytor Hamlet Hospice 91-95; Tutor WMMTC 95-04; Minl and Adul Learning Officer *Ely* from 05. *8 Hertford Close, Ely CB6 3QS* Tel (01353) 666628 *or* 652733
E-mail christine.worsley@ely.anglican.org

WORSLEY, Howard John. b 61. Man Univ BA83 Leeds Univ PGCE85 Birm Univ PhD00. St Jo Coll Nottm MTh93. **d** 93 **p** 94. C Huthwaite *S'well* 93-96; V Radford St Pet 96-01; Dir Studies St Jo Coll Nottm 02-04; Dir of Educn *S'well* 04-10; Hon of Educn *Lon* 10-11; Chapl S Bank Univ from 11. *483C Southwark Park Road, London SE16 2JP* Tel (020) 7237 6324 Mobile 07528-565600 E-mail h.j.worsley@aol.com

WORSLEY, Malcolm. b 37. Carl Dioc Tr Inst 94. **d** 96 **p** 97. NSM Hawes Side *Blackb* 96-98 and 01-04; NSM Lt Thornton 98-01; rtd 04; Perm to Offic *Blackb* from 04. *14 Winslow Avenue, Carleton, Poulton-le-Fylde FY6 7PQ* Tel (01253) 882208 *or* 621859 Fax 751156 E-mail m_worsley@dial.pipex.com

WORSLEY, Richard John. b 52. Qu Coll Cam BA74 MA78 Univ of Wales CertEd76 Birm Univ MPhil91 Warwick Univ MA96. Qu Coll Birm. **d** 80 **p** 81. C Styvechale *Cov* 80-84; V Smethwick H Trin w St Alb *Birm* 84-89; TV Coventry Caludon 89-96; Hon C Binley 97-05; Perm to Offic *Ely* from 05. *8 Hertford Close, Ely CB6 3QS* Tel (01353) 666628
E-mail richardjworsley@btinternet.com

WORSLEY, Ruth Elizabeth. b 62. **d** 96 **p** 97. C Basford w Hyson Green *S'well* 96-99; C Hyson Green and Forest Fields 99-01; P-in-c 01-08; AD Nottingham N 06-08; P-in-c Sneinton St Chris w St Phil 08-10; Dean of Women's Min 07-10; Hon Can S'well Minster 07-10; Par Development Officer Woolwich Area *S'wark* from 10; Chapl to The Queen from 09. *483C Southwark Park Road, London SE16 2JP* Tel 07917-693285 (mobile)
E-mail ruthworsley@aol.com

WORSNIP, Harry. b 29. St Alb Minl Tr Scheme 89. **d** 92 **p** 93. NSM Arlesey w Astwick *St Alb* 92-96; NSM Goldington 96-99; Perm to Offic from 00. *28 Milburn Road, Bedford MK41 0NZ* Tel (01234) 266422

WORSSAM, Brother Nicholas Alan. b 65. Selw Coll Cam BA87 MA91. Qu Coll Birm MA04. **d** 06 **p** 07. SSF from 99. *Glasshampton Monastery, Shrawley, Worcester WR6 6TQ* Tel (01299) 896345   Fax 896083
E-mail nicholasalanssf@franciscans.org.uk

WORSSAM, Richard Mark. b 61. St Jo Coll Dur BA83 Selw Coll Cam BA92 Heythrop Coll Lon MA06 K Coll Lon MSc09. Ridley Hall Cam 90. **d** 93 **p** 94. C Green Street Green and Pratts Bottom *Roch* 93-97; R Fawkham and Hartley 97-08; V Otford from 08. *The Vicarage, The Green, Otford, Sevenoaks TN14 5PD* Tel (01959) 525417 *or* 523185
E-mail richard.worssam@tiscali.co.uk

WORT, Gavin. b 78. K Alfred's Coll Win BTh99 St Jo Coll Dur MA10. Westcott Ho Cam 00. d 02 p 03. C Eastleigh *Win* 02-06; Chapl Northumbria Univ 06-11; V Newc H Cross from 11. *Holy Cross Vicarage, 16 Whittington Grove, Newcastle upon Tyne NE5 2QP* Tel 0191-274 5580 E-mail g.wort@btopenworld.com

WORTHEN, Canon Jeremy Frederick. b 65. Rob Coll Cam BA86 MPhil88 Toronto Univ PhD92. Ripon Coll Cuddesdon 92. d 94 p 95. C Bromley SS Pet and Paul *Roch* 94-97; Tutor SEITE 97-05; Prin from 05; Wiccamical Preb Chich Cathl from 09; Hon Can Cant Cathl from 11. *SEITE, Ground Floor Offices, Sun Pier House, Medway Street, Chatham ME4 4HF* Tel (01634) 832299 E-mail j.f.worthen@kent.ac.uk

WORTHINGTON, George. b 35. AKC60. d 61 p 62. C Stockton St Pet *Dur* 61-65; C Poulton-le-Fylde *Blackb* 65-67; V Trawden 67-76; P-in-c Gressingham 76-78; P-in-c Arkholme 76-78; P-in-c Whittington 77-78; V Whittington w Arkholme and Gressingham 78-91; V Warton St Paul 91-00; rtd 00; Perm to Offic *Blackb* from 00 and *Carl* from 02. *4 Cavendish Gardens, Kirby Lonsdale, Carnforth LA6 3BW* Tel (01524) 271699

WORTHINGTON, Mark. b 55. Solicitor 80 Leeds Poly BA77. Cranmer Hall Dur 93. d 93 p 94. C Monkwearmouth St Andr *Dur* 93-96; C Chester le Street 96-00; V Harlow Green and Lamesley from 00. *The Vicarage, Lamesley, Gateshead NE11 0EU* Tel 0191-487 6490 E-mail mark.worthington@durham.anglican.org

WORTLEY, Prof John Trevor. b 34. Dur Univ BA57 MA60 DD86 Lon Univ PhD69 FRHistS. Edin Th Coll 57. d 59 p 60. C Huddersfield St Jo *Wakef* 59-64; Canada from 64; Prof Medieval Hist Manitoba Univ 69-02; Visiting Prof Sorbonne Univ 99; rtd 02. *298 Yale Avenue, Winnipeg MB R3M 0M1, Canada or Manitoba University, Winnipeg MB R3T 2N2, Canada* Tel (001) (204) 284 7554 E-mail wortley@cc.umanitoba.ca

WORTLEY, Mrs Lyn Sharon. b 59. Open Univ BA94 Coll of Ripon & York St Jo MA98. NOC 95. d 98 p 99. C Greasbrough *Sheff* 98-01; P-in-c Bramley and Ravenfield w Hooton Roberts etc 01-04; V Bramley from 04. *The Vicarage, 88 Main Street, Bramley, Rotherham S66 2SQ* Tel (01709) 702828 E-mail lyn.wortley@btinternet.com

WOSTENHOLM, David Kenneth. b 56. Edin Univ BSc77 MB, ChB80 Southn Univ BTh88. Chich Th Coll 82. d 85 p 86. C Leytonstone St Marg w St Columba *Chelmsf* 85-90; V Brighton Annunciation *Chich* 90-01; TR Hove 01-07; RD Hove 03-05; P-in-c Glas St Matt from 07. *104 Erradale Street, Glasgow G22 6PT* Tel 0141-336 7480 *or* 347 1726 Mobile 07908-537085 E-mail stmatthews@btclick.com *or* david.wostenholm@hotmail.co.uk

WOTHERSPOON, David Colin. b 36. Portsm Coll of Tech CEng65 MIMechE65. St Jo Coll Dur 76. d 78 p 79. C Blackb St Gabr 78-81; V Witton 81-90; Chapl Berne w Neuchâtel *Eur* 90-01; rtd 01; Perm to Offic *Blackb* from 01. *300 Pleckgate Road, Blackburn BB1 8QU* Tel (01254) 249743

WOTTON, David Ashley. b 44. Chich Th Coll 71. d 74 p 75. C Allington and Maidstone St Pet *Cant* 74-77; C Ham St Andr *S'wark* 78-79; Chapl HM Rem Cen Latchmere Ho 78-79; C Tattenham Corner and Burgh Heath *Guildf* 85-88; P-in-c E Molesey St Mary 88-93; R Headley w Box Hill 93-06; Offg Chapl RAF 93-06; rtd 06. *Lion House, 6 Copper Beeches, St Leonards-on-Sea TN37 7RR* Tel (01424) 757122

WRAGG, Christopher William. b 60. SEITE 97. d 00 p 01. C Gt Warley Ch Ch *Chelmsf* 00-01; V Warley Ch Ch and Gt Warley St Mary 01-04; TV Buckhurst Hill 04-08; V Squirrels Heath from 08. *30 Wakefield Close, Hornchurch RM11 2TH* Tel (020) 8504 6698 Mobile 07014-507147 E-mail vicarchris@btinternet.com

WRAGG, Peter Robert. b 46. Lon Univ BSc68. Sarum & Wells Th Coll 71. d 74 p 75. C Feltham *Lon* 74-79; TV Hackney 79-85; P-in-c Isleworth St Mary 85-94; V Feltham from 94. *The Vicarage, Cardinal Road, Feltham TW13 5AL* Tel (020) 8890 6681 *or* 8890 2011 E-mail peter.wragg@tesco.net

WRAIGHT, John Radford. b 38. St Chad's Coll Dur BA62. d 64 p 65. C Shildon *Dur* 64-67; C Newton Aycliffe 67-70; C Darlington St Jo 70-75; P-in-c Livingston LEP *Edin* 75-80; TV Carl H Trin and St Barn 80-85; P-in-c Lindale w Field Broughton 85-95; R Middleton Tyas w Croft and Eryholme *Ripon* 95-03; rtd 03. *14 Colorado Grove, Darlington DL1 2YW* Tel (01325) 354613 E-mail j.r.wraight@amserve.net

WRAKE, John. b 28. RMA. Clifton Th Coll 56. d 59 p 60. C Gt Baddow *Chelmsf* 59-62; CF 62-66; V Tilton w Lowesby *Leic* 66-73; R Maresfield *Chich* 73-79; rtd 93. *Parkfield, Batts Ridge Road, Maresfield, Uckfield TN22 2HJ* Tel (01825) 762727

WRAPSON, Donald. b 36. St Aid Birkenhead 60. d 65 p 66. C Bacup St Sav *Man* 65-68; C Wolverhampton St Matt *Lich* 68-72; C Normanton *Derby* 72-78; V Dordon *Birm* 78-82; Chapl Birm Accident Hosp and Selly Oak Hosp 82-92; Chapl Trauma Unit Birm Gen Hosp 92-95; Chapl S Birm Community Health NHS Trust 95-01; rtd 01; Perm to Offic *Worc* from 03. *7 Glebe Road, Avelchurch, Birmingham B48 7PS* Tel 0121-445 6568 E-mail donaldwrapson@tiscali.co.uk

WRATTEN, Martyn Stephen. b 34. AKC58 St Boniface Warminster 58. d 59 p 60. C Wandsworth Common St Mary *S'wark* 59-62; C Putney St Mary 62-65; C Pembury *Roch* 65-70; R Stone 70-76; Chapl Joyce Green Hosp Dartford 70-73; Stone Ho Hosp Kent 73-76; Hillcrest Hosp and Netherne Hosp Coulsdon 76-87; Hon C Netherne St Luke CD *S'wark* 76-87; V Gt Doddington *Pet* 87-88; V Gt Doddington and Wilby 88-95; Hon C N Petherton w Northmoor Green *B & W* 95-96; rtd 95; Perm to Offic *B & W* from 96. *1 Baymead Close, North Petherton, Bridgwater TA6 6QZ* Tel (01278) 662873

✠WRAW, The Rt Revd John Michael. b 59. Linc Coll Ox BA81 Fitzw Ho Cam BA84. Ridley Hall Cam 82. d 85 p 86 c 11. C Bromyard *Heref* 85-88; TV Sheff Manor 88-92; V Clifton St Jas 92-01; P-in-c Wickersley 01-04; AD Rotherham 98-04; Hon Can Sheff Cathl 01-04; Adn Wilts *Sarum* 04-11; Area Bp Bradwell *Chelmsf* from 11. *Bishop's House, Orsett Road, Horndon-on-the-Hill, Stanford-le-Hope SS17 8NS* Tel (01375) 673806 Fax 674222

WRAY, Christopher. b 48. Hull Univ BA70. Cuddesdon Coll 70. d 73 p 74. C Brighouse *Wakef* 73-76; C Almondbury 76-78; C Tong *Bradf* 78-80; V Ingleton w Chapel le Dale 80-86; R Brompton Regis w Upton and Skilgate *B & W* 86-91; V Yoxford and Peasenhall w Sibton *St E* 91-94; Perm to Offic *Carl* 94-97; R Brough w Stainmore, Musgrave and Warcop 97-02; R Walkingham Hill *Ripon* 02-07; V Ripponden *Wakef* from 07; V Barkisland w W Scammonden from 07. *St Bartholomew's Vicarage, Ripponden, Sowerby Bridge HX6 4DF* Tel (01422) 822239

WRAY, Christopher Brownlow. b 46. Open Univ BA91. Oak Hill Th Coll 86. d 88 p 89. C Quidenham *Nor* 88 91; TV Chippenham St Paul w Hardenhuish etc *Bris* 91-97; P-in-c Chipping Sodbury and Old Sodbury *Glouc* 97-09; P-in-c Horton and Lt Sodbury 04-09; rtd 09; Hon C Hardington Vale *B & W* from 11. *52 Linden Park, Shaftesbury SP7 8RN* Tel (01747) 851961 E-mail wrays1@directsave.net

WRAY, Kenneth Martin. b 43. Linc Th Coll 72. d 75 p 76. C Shipley St Paul *Bradf* 75-79; V Edlington *Sheff* 79-85; V Nether Hoyland St Pet 85-97; V Up Hatherley *Glouc* 97-04; rtd 07. *5 Benall Avenue, Cheltenham GL51 6AF* Tel (01242) 236966 E-mail kmartinw026@btinternet.com

WRAY, Martin John. b 51. St Steph Ho Ox 86. d 88 p 89. C E Boldon *Dur* 88-90; C Seaham w Seaham Harbour 90-92; P-in-c Chopwell 92-95; V 95-97; C Shildon 98-00; C Croxdale and Tudhoe 00-04; P-in-c 04-06; C Spennymoor, Whitworth and Merrington 04-06; V Horsley Hill St Lawr 06-11; rtd 11. *18 Greenside Drift, South Shields NE33 3ND* E-mail m.wray@sky.com

WRAY, Michael. b 49. Univ of Wales (Cardiff) BSc(Econ)77 Keele Univ PGCE78 RGN87. Ripon Coll Cuddesdon 80. d 82 p 83. C Blackpool St Steph *Blackb* 82-83; C Torrisholme 83-84; NSM Headington Quarry *Ox* 93-95; C Kennington *Cant* 95-99; CF (TA) 95-99; P-in-c Isham w Pytchley *Pet* 99-04; Chapl Rockingham Forest NHS Trust 99-01; Chapl Northants Healthcare NHS Trust 01-04; R Potterspury w Furtho and Yardley Gobion etc *Pet* 04-11; rtd 11. *The Vicarage, 11 Church Lane, Potterspury, Towcester NN12 7PU* Tel (01908) 542428 E-mail revwray@btinternet.com

WRAYFORD, Geoffrey John. b 38. Ex Coll Ox BA61 MA65. Linc Th Coll 61. d 63 p 64. C Cirencester *Glouc* 63-69; Chapl Chelmsf Cathl 69-74; V 70-74; V Canvey Is 74-76; TR 76-80; P-in-c Woodlands *B & W* 80-88; V 89-92; P-in-c Frome St Jo 80-88; P-in-c Frome Ch Ch 80-85; P-in-c Frome St Mary 85-88; V Frome St Jo and St Mary 89-92; V Minehead 92-03; Chapl Taunton and Somerset NHS Trust 92-03; rtd 03; Perm to Offic *B & W* from 07. *Little Garth, Longmeadow Road, Lympstone, Exmouth EX8 5LF* Tel (01395) 267838 E-mail geoffjanw@gail.wanadoo.co.uk

WREN, Ann. *See* WREN, Mrs Kathleen Ann

WREN, Christopher John. b 54. Dur Univ BEd76 MA85. St Steph Ho Ox 77. d 79 p 80. C Stockton St Pet *Dur* 79-82; C Newton Aycliffe 82-85; V Gateshead St Chad Bensham 85-91; TR Bensham 91-98; V Marton *Blackb* from 98. *St Paul's Vicarage, 55 Vicarage Lane, Marton, Blackpool FY4 4EF* Tel (01253) 762679 *or* 692047 Mobile 07957-323184 E-mail wthenest@aol.com *or* wrenpaul1@aol.com

WREN, Douglas Peter. b 59. Lanc Univ BA82. Trin Coll Bris BA88. d 88 p 89. C Nantwich *Ches* 88-91; C Chatham St Phil and St Jas *Roch* 91-94; R Kingsdown 94-02; R Speldhurst w Groombridge and Ashurst from 02. *The Rectory, Southfields, Speldhurst, Tunbridge Wells TN3 0PD* Tel (01892) 862821 E-mail douglas.wren@diocese-rochester.org

WREN, John Aubrey. b 46. St Chad's Coll Dur BA69 Sussex Univ MA92. Cuddesdon Coll 72. d 74 p 75. C Fenny Stratford and Water Eaton *Ox* 74-77; TV Brighton Resurr *Chich* 77-84; V Eastbourne St Andr 84-92; V Hove St Barn and St Agnes 92-96. *24 Marlborough Road, Lowestoft NR32 3BU* Tel (01502) 530243

WREN, Mrs Kathleen Ann. b 59. Dur Univ BA83. dss 85 d 87. Gateshead St Cuth w St Paul *Dur* 85-86; Gateshead St Chad Bensham 86-91; Par Dn 87-91; Adv for Women's Min 90-98; Par

Dn Bensham 91-94; C 94-98; Hon Can Dur Cathl 93-98; C Marton *Blackb* from 98. *St Paul's Vicarage, 55 Vicarage Lane, Marton, Blackpool FY4 4EF* Tel (01253) 762679 Fax 318791 E-mail wthenest@aol.com

WREN, Comdr Richard. b 35. S Dios Minl Tr Scheme 88. **d** 90 **p** 91. NSM Tisbury *Sarum* 90-01; TV 95-01; TV Nadder Valley 01-05; rtd 05; Perm to Offic *Sarum* from 06. *Gaston House, Tisbury, Salisbury SP3 6LG* Tel (01747) 870674 E-mail twowrens@cuffslane.plus.com

WRENBURY, The Revd and Rt Hon Lord (John Burton Buckley). b 27. K Coll Cam BA48 MA48 Solicitor 52. S'wark Ord Course 87. **d** 90 **p** 91. NSM Brightling, Dallington, Mountfield etc *Chich* from 90. *Oldcastle, Dallington, Heathfield TN21 9JP* Tel (01435) 830400 E-mail john.wrenbury@btinternet.com

WRENN, Peter Henry. b 34. Lon Univ BA56. Qu Coll Birm 58. **d** 60 **p** 61. C Dronfield *Derby* 60-64; C Hessle *York* 64-65; V Loscoe *Derby* 65-70; Asst Chapl Solihull Sch 71-77; Chapl 77-97; rtd 97; Perm to Offic *Birm* from 97. *63 Shakespeare Drive, Shirley, Solihull B90 2AN* Tel 0121-744 3941

WREXHAM, Archdeacon of. See GRIFFITHS, The Ven Shirley Thelma

WRIGHT, Alan James. b 38. Chich Th Coll 63. **d** 66 **p** 67. C Edgehill St Dunstan *Liv* 66-69; Swaziland 69-71; P-in-c Seaforth *Liv* 71-76; V Taunton All SS *B & W* 76-95; rtd 99. *Bethel, Langford Lane, Norton Fitzwarren, Taunton TA2 6NZ* Tel (01823) 326558

WRIGHT, Alan Richard. b 31. **d** 96 **p** 97. OLM Quidenham Gp *Nor* 96-04; Perm to Offic from 04. *Upgate Farm, Carleton Rode, Norwich NR16 1NJ* Tel (01953) 860300

WRIGHT, Alan William. b 44. Hull Univ BA66 Bris Univ PGCE67 AMusTCL71. **d** 95 **p** 96. OLM Barton upon Humber *Linc* from 95. *1 Birchdale, Barton-upon-Humber DN18 5ED* Tel (01652) 632364 E-mail wrighttherewrightnow@hotmail.com

WRIGHT, Alfred John. b 22. Wycliffe Hall Ox 66. **d** 66 **p** 67. C Newbury St Jo *Ox* 66-71; V E Challow 71-91; Chapl Community of St Mary V Wantage 75-89; rtd 91; Perm to Offic *Ox* 92-09. *Polperro, Hampstead Norreys Road, Hermitage, Thatcham RG18 9RS* Tel (01635) 202889 E-mail sheba@eggconnect.net

WRIGHT, Andrew David Gibson. b 58. St Andr Univ MTheol81. Ridley Hall Cam. **d** 83 **p** 84. C W Derby Gd Shep *Liv* 83-86; C Carl H Trin and St Barn 86-88; V Wigan St Jas w St Thos *Liv* 88-91; Chapl St Edw Sch Ox 91-97 and 06-07; Ho Master 97-07; Miss Chapl R Nat Miss to Deep Sea Fishermen from 07. *46 Yarborough Road, East Cowes PO32 6SH* Tel (01983) 291855 *or* (01489) 566910 E-mail andrew@rnmdsf.org.uk

WRIGHT, Anna Chang. b 55. Univ of San Carlos Cebu City BA74 Univ of Philippines MA78 Ban Univ BTh07. **d** 02 **p** 03. OLM Blyth Valley *St E* from 02. *Rose End, Back Road, Wenhaston, Halesworth IP19 9DY* Tel (01502) 478411 E-mail awright@dircon.co.uk

WRIGHT, Anne. See WRIGHT, Miss Jacqueline Anne

WRIGHT, Anthony. See WRIGHT, Derek Anthony

WRIGHT, Canon Anthony John. b 47. Ex Univ MA98 ACA70 FCA77. Ripon Coll Cuddesdon 86. **d** 88 **p** 89. C Kidderminster St Mary and All SS w Trimpley etc *Worc* 88-91; P-in-c Offenham and Bretforton 91-96; R Backwell w Chelvey and Brockley *B & W* 96-02; RD Portishead 01-02; P-in-c Tetbury w Beverston *Glouc* 02-03; R 03-06; R Tetbury, Beverston, Long Newnton etc from 07; Hon Can Glouc Cathl from 11. *The Vicarage, 6 The Green, Tetbury GL8 8DN* Tel (01666) 502333 Fax 500893 E-mail sheba.wright@virgin.net

WRIGHT, Canon Anthony Robert. b 49. Lanchester Poly Cov BA70. St Steph Ho Ox 70. **d** 73 **p** 74. C Amersham on the Hill *Ox* 73-76; C Reading St Giles 76-78; P-in-c Prestwood 78-84; P-in-c Wantage 84-87; V 87-92; RD Wantage 84-92; P-in-c W w E Hanney 88-91; V Portsea St Mary *Portsm* 92-98; Hon Can Portsm Cathl 96-98; R Westmr St Marg 98-10; Chapl to Speaker of Ho of Commons 98-10; Can Westmr Abbey 98-10; rtd 10. *52 West End, Witney OX28 1NF* Tel (01993) 774160 E-mail priestpainter@googlemail.com

WRIGHT, Canon Barry Owen. b 38. S'wark Ord Course 66. **d** 69 **p** 70. C Plumstead Ascension *S'wark* 69-74; Hon C Welling 74-89; Hon Can S'wark Cathl 79-89; Sen Chapl W Midl Police *Birm* 89-93; Sen Chapl Metrop Police *Lon* 93-09; V Mill Hill St Mich 02-10; rtd 10. *54 Elmbourne Drive, Belvedere DA17 6JF* Tel (01322) 463564 E-mail bwrg8@aol.com

WRIGHT, Caroline. b 09 **p** 10. NSM Pontesbury I and II *Heref* from 09. *1 Higher Netley, Netley, Dorrington, Shrewsbury SY5 7SY* Tel (01743) 718790 E-mail info@carosbandb.co.uk

WRIGHT, Preb Catherine Jane. b 62. Bris Univ BA84 MA92 PhD00 Selw Coll Cam BA96. Ridley Hall Cam 94. **d** 97 **p** 98. C Highworth w Sevenhampton and Inglesham etc *Bris* 97-00; Perm to Offic *Ex* 00-01; NSM Stoke St Gregory w Burrowbridge and Lyng *B & W* 01-05; Dioc Voc Adv from 02; Assoc Dir of Ords from 02; Dean of Women Clergy and Preb Wells Cathl from 05; Dir IME 4-7 from 10. *The Rectory, West Monkton, Taunton TA2 8QT* Tel (01823) 413380 E-mail catherine.wright@bathwells.anglican.org

WRIGHT, Charles Kenneth. b 38. CEng73 MIMechE73 MBIM91. Sarum & Wells Th Coll 91. **d** 93 **p** 94. C Bridgwater St Mary, Chilton Trinity and Durleigh *B & W* 93-96; Chapl Workington *Carl* 96-03; C Camerton, Seaton and W Seaton 96-03; Chapl W Cumbria Health Care NHS Trust 96-01; Chapl N Cumbria Acute Hosps NHS Trust 01-03; rtd 03; Perm to Offic *Carl* from 03. *Naemair, 72 Ruskin Close, High Harrington, Workington CA14 4LS* Tel (01946) 833536

WRIGHT, Christopher Joseph Herbert. b 47. St Cath Coll Cam BA69 MA73 PhD77. Ridley Hall Cam 75. **d** 77 **p** 78. C Tonbridge SS Pet and Paul *Roch* 77-81; Perm to Offic *St Alb* 82-01; BCMS India 83-88; Tutor and Dir Studies All Nations Chr Coll Ware 88-93; Prin 93-04. *Address temp unknown*

WRIGHT, Christopher Nigel. b 39. Kelham Th Coll 60. **d** 65 **p** 66. C Ellesmere Port *Ches* 65-69; C Latchford Ch 69-72; C Gt Budworth 72-75; C Wigan St Andr *Liv* 75-76; V New Springs 77-82; C Dovecot 82-85; C Rainford 85-89; rtd 89; Perm to Offic *Liv* 89-01. *105 Ilfracombe Road, Sutton Leach, St Helens WA9 4NN* Tel (01744) 821199

WRIGHT, Clifford. See WRIGHT, The Rt Revd Royston Clifford

WRIGHT, Canon Clifford Nelson. b 35. K Coll Lon BD59 AKC59. **d** 60 **p** 61. C Stevenage *St Alb* 60-67; V Camberwell St Luke *S'wark* 67-81; RD Camberwell 75-80; Hon Can S'wark Cathl 79-80; TR Basingstoke *Win* 81-93; RD Basingstoke 84-93; Hon Can Win Cathl 89-00; R Win St Matt 93-00; rtd 00; Perm to Offic *Win* from 01. *1 Valley Dene, Dibden Purlieu, Southampton SO45 4NG* Tel (023) 8084 5898 E-mail cliffwright@waitrose.com

WRIGHT, David Evan Cross. b 35. K Coll Lon BD64 AKC64. **d** 65 **p** 66. C Morpeth *Newc* 65-69; C Benwell St Jas 69-70; C Bushey *St Alb* 70-74; V High Wych 74-77; R High Wych and Gilston w Eastwick 77-80; V St Alb St Mary Marshalswick 80-89; P-in-c Sandridge 87-89; R Lenham w Boughton Malherbe *Cant* 89-00; P-in-c Fuengirola St Andr *Eur* 01-06; Perm to Offic *Chich* 01-06. *536 Urban, Cerros del Aguila, 29649 Mijas (Málaga), Spain*

WRIGHT, David Henry. b 23. Keble Coll Ox BA48. St Steph Ho Ox 52. **d** 54 **p** 55. C Penton Street St Silas w All SS *Lon* 54-57; V Barnsbury St Clem 57-66; V Wandsworth St Anne *S'wark* 66-73; P-in-c Stanley *St And* 73-75; R Dunkeld 73-92; R Strathtay 75-92; rtd 92; Hon C Aberdeen St Marg from 00. *28 Midstocket Mews, Aberdeen AB15 5FG* Tel (01224) 636554

WRIGHT, David William. b 63. Liv Univ LLB85 Fitzw Coll Cam BA92 Cam Univ MA96 Univ of Wales (Cardiff) LLM99 Barrister 86. Westcott Ho Cam 90. **d** 93 **p** 94. C Chorlton-cum-Hardy St Clem *Man* 93-97; P-in-c Donnington Wood *Lich* 97-99; V 99-09; TR Cen Wolverhampton from 09; AD Wolverhampton from 11. *The Rectory, 42 Park Road East, Wolverhampton WV1 4QA* Tel (01902) 423388 Mobile 07977-543735 E-mail david.wright@lichfield.anglican.org

WRIGHT, Denise Ann. See WILLIAMS, Denise Ann

WRIGHT, Derek Anthony. b 35. ACP66 Lon Univ CertEd57. Cranmer Hall Dur 80. **d** 81 **p** 82. C Auckland St Andr and St Anne *Dur* 81-83; V Cornforth 83-87; P-in-c Thornley 87-88; R Gt and Lt Glemham, Blaxhall etc *St E* 88-90; V Evenwood *Dur* 90-93; P-in-c Satley and Tow Law 93-95; V 95-99; rtd 99. *39 Hilltop Road, Bearpark, Durham DH7 7TA*

WRIGHT, Edward Maurice Alexanderson. b 54. Wycliffe Hall Ox. **d** 88 **p** 91. C Maidstone St Luke *Cant* 88-93; R Cliffe at Hoo w Cooling *Roch* from 93. *St Helen's Rectory, Church Street, Cliffe, Rochester ME3 7PY* Tel (01634) 220220 E-mail edward.wright@diocese-rochester.org

WRIGHT, Edward Michael. b 37. St Cath Soc Ox BA61 MA65. Cuddesdon Coll. **d** 64 **p** 65. C Willesden St Andr *Lon* 64-68; Bahamas 68-71; V Lewisham St Steph and St Mark *S'wark* 72-80; V Ox St Barn and St Paul 80-07; rtd 07; Perm to Offic *Ox* from 08. *9 Binswood Avenue, Headington, Oxford OX3 8NY* E-mail emichaelwright@ntlworld.com

WRIGHT, Frank Albert. b 51. Portsm Univ MA02. Sarum & Wells Th Coll 80. **d** 83 **p** 84. C Buckingham *Ox* 83-86; C Newport Pagnell w Lathbury and Moulsoe 86-89; TV W Slough 89-95; TR 95-99; TR Fareham H Trin *Portsm* 99-09; Dioc Interfaith Adv 01-06; R Westbourne *Chich* from 09. *The Rectory, Westbourne Road, Westbourne, Emsworth PO10 8UL* Tel (01243) 372867 E-mail westrecwbourne@tiscali.co.uk

WRIGHT, Frederic Ian. b 46. City Univ BSc85. Wycliffe Hall Ox BTh94. **d** 94 **p** 95. C Carl St Jo 94-98; C Bassenthwaite, Isel and Setmurthy 98-02; TV Binsey 02-07. *Aden House, The Square, Allonby, Maryport CA15 6QA* Tel (01900) 881095

WRIGHT, Frederick John. b 15. AKC42. **d** 42 **p** 43. C Brierley Hill *Lich* 42-45; C Walsall Pleck and Bescot 45-49; V W Bromwich Gd Shep 49-54; R Headless Cross *Worc* 54-67; R Romsley 67-80; rtd 80; Perm to Offic *Ely* from 97. *Rosevear, 3 Drury Lane, Colne, Huntingdon PE28 3NB* Tel (01487) 840518

WRIGHT, Graham. b 50. Oak Hill Th Coll 73. **d** 76 **p** 77. C Northampton St Giles *Pet* 76-79; C Man Resurr 79-82; V Barkingside St Laur *Chelmsf* 82-88; Chapl K Geo V Hosp Ilford 82-88; P-in-c Yoxford and Chapl Suffolk Constabulary *St E* 88-90; Perm to Offic *Linc* 03-05; Lic Preacher 05-07; R

Rockingham w Safety Bay Australia from 07. *PO Box 799, Rockingham WA 6968, Australia* Tel (0061) (8) 9523 1430 *or* 9527 1417 Fax 9527 1483 Mobile 48-892 7141
E-mail therockingrev@bigpond.com
WRIGHT, Graham John Aston. b 57. Moorlands Th Coll 77 Wycliffe Hall Ox 05. **d** 06 **p** 07. NSM Marston w Elsfield *Ox* 06-08; Asst Chapl St Edw Sch Ox 06-08; Chapl Queenswood Sch Herts from 09. *Queenswood School, Shepherds Way, Brookmans Park, Hatfield AL9 6NX* Tel (01707) 602500
E-mail graham.wright@queenswood.org
WRIGHT, Mrs Heather Margaret. b 47. EAMTC 93. **d** 96 **p** 97. NSM Heigham St Thos *Nor* 96-99; Hon Asst Dioc Chapl among deaf and deaf-blind people from 99; NSM Sprowston w Beeston from 03. *133 Moore Avenue, Norwich NR6 7LQ* Tel (01603) 301329 Fax and minicom as telephone
E-mail rev@wrighth.freeserve.co.uk
WRIGHT, Mrs Hilary. d 08. OLM Parkstone St Pet and St Osmund w Branksea *Sarum* from 08. *18 Springfield Crescent, Poole BH14 0LL* Tel (01202) 747369
WRIGHT, Howard John Douglas. b 64. BA85. Trin Coll Bris BA94. **d** 96 **p** 97. C Ipswich St Matt *St E* 96-00; V Four Marks *Win* from 00; RD Alton from 09. *The Vicarage, 22 Lymington Bottom, Four Marks, Alton GU34 5AA* Tel (01420) 563344
E-mail howardwright@xalt.co.uk
WRIGHT, Hugh Edward. b 57. BNC Ox BA79 MA87 Ex Univ CertEd81. Sarum & Wells Th Coll 85. **d** 87 **p** 88. C Hobs Moat *Birm* 87-90; C W Drayton *Lon* 90-92; V Oakfield St Jo *Portsm* from 92; RD E Wight 00-05. *St John's Vicarage, Victoria Crescent, Ryde PO33 1DQ* Tel (01983) 562863
E-mail hewright@stjohnsryde.freeserve.co.uk
WRIGHT, Ian. *See* WRIGHT, Frederic Ian
WRIGHT, Ian. b 65. Coll of Resurr Mirfield 97. **d** 99 **p** 00. C S Lafford *Linc* 99-01; C Hawley H Trin *Guildf* 01-03; Chapl Bonn w Cologne *Eur* 03-06; P-in-c Armley w New Wortley *Ripon* from 06. *19 St Mary's Park Green, Armley, Leeds LS12 3UY* Tel 0113-263 8620
WRIGHT, Miss Jacqueline Anne. b 39. Dalton Ho Bris 67. **dss** 76 **d** 87 **p** 94. BCMS Uganda 71-77; N Area Sec BCMS 78-88; Pudsey St Lawr and St Paul *Bradf* 82-88; Hon Par Dn 87-88; Par Dn Kingston upon Hull H Trin *York* 88-93; Hd of Min amongst Women CPAS 93-02; CPAS Consultant (W Midl) 96-02; Regional Consultant (Midl) 99-02; Perm to Offic *Cov* 93-04 and *York* from 04; rtd 02. *Oxenby, Whitby Road, Pickering YO18 7HL* Tel (01751) 472689
E-mail jacquelinewright@btopenworld.com
WRIGHT, Mrs Jean. b 41. Man Univ BA63 CertEd64. Carl Dioc Tr Inst 88. **d** 91 **p** 94. NSM Kirkby Stephen w Mallerstang etc *Carl* from 91. *Mains View, Crosby Garrett, Kirkby Stephen CA17 4PR* Tel (01768) 371457
WRIGHT, Jill Estella. b 51. **d** 10 **p** 11. NSM Cliffe at Hoo w Cooling *Roch* from 10. *Buckland Farm, Buckland Road, Cliffe, Rochester ME3 7RT* Tel (01634) 220184
E-mail wrights.buckland@virgin.net
WRIGHT, John. *See* WRIGHT, Nicholas John
WRIGHT, John. *See* WRIGHT, Alfred John
WRIGHT, John. *See* WRIGHT, Canon Anthony John
WRIGHT, John Alastair. b 30. FRSA72. Cranmer Hall Dur 62. **d** 64 **p** 65. C Thornton-le-Fylde *Blackb* 64-67; Miss to Seamen 67-72; V Darlington St Luke *Dur* 72-78; Community Chapl Darlington 78-89; rtd 89. *4 Grasmere, Agar Nook, Coalville LE67 4SH* Tel (01530) 837390
WRIGHT, John Douglas. b 42. Birm Univ BSc64 CertEd66. St Steph Ho Ox 69. **d** 69 **p** 70. C Swanley St Mary *Roch* 69-74; C Stockwell Green St Andr *S'wark* 74-79; V Leigh St Jo *Man* 79-82; P-in-c Whitehawk *Chich* 82-11; V from 11. *St Cuthman's Vicarage, 1 St Cuthman's Close, Whitehawk, Brighton BN2 5HW* Tel (01273) 699424 Mobile 07944-419007
E-mail jonda9@gmail.com
WRIGHT, Canon John Harold. b 36. Dur Univ BA58 Ch Ch Coll Cant MA96 ATCL. Ely Th Coll 58. **d** 61 **p** 62. C Boston *Linc* 61-64; C Willesborough w Hinxhill *Cant* 64-68; V Westwell 68-75; R Eastwell w Boughton Aluph 68-75; V Rolvenden 75-84; R Cheriton St Martin 84-01; Hon Can Cant Cathl 97-01; rtd 01; Perm to Offic *Cant* from 01. *1 Cliff Road, Hythe CT21 5XA* Tel (01303) 265303
WRIGHT, Jonathan James Gerald. b 67. Oak Hill Th Coll. **d** 10 **p** 11. C Horncastle Gp *Linc* from 10. *9 Langton Drive, Horncastle LN9 5AJ*
WRIGHT, Judith Mary. b 44. Ex Univ MSc98 BA10 SRN10 SCM10. SWMTC 04. **d** 07 **p** 08. NSM Silverton, Butterleigh, Bickleigh and Cadeleigh *Ex* 07-11; C Bradninch and Clyst Hydon from 11; C Broadhembury, Payhembury and Plymtree from 11. *4 Hele Square, Hele, Exeter EX5 4PN* Tel (01392) 882019 E-mail j.j.wright@btinternet.com
WRIGHT, Miss Julia Mary. b 64. Reading Univ BA88. Trin Coll Bris 96. **d** 98 **p** 99. C Woodley *Ox* 98-03; TV Aylesbury w Bierton and Hulcott 03-05; C Bernwode 05-07; Chapl Burrswood Chr Hosp from 08. *The Chaplaincy, Burrswood, Groombridge, Tunbridge Wells TN3 9PY* Tel (01892) 863637 Fax 863623

WRIGHT, Ken. *See* WRIGHT, Charles Kenneth
WRIGHT, Canon Kenyon Edward. b 32. CBE99. Glas Univ MA53 Fitzw Coll Cam BA55 Serampore Coll MTh61 Edin Univ DLitt00. Wesley Ho Cam 53. **d** 71 **p** 71. In Meth Ch India 57-71; Dir Urban Min Cov Cathl 71-81; Dir of Internat Min and Can Res 72-81; Public Preacher 72-74; Gen Sec Scottish Chs Coun 81-90; Dir Scottish Chs Ho Dunblane 81-90; Dir Kairos Trust 90-92; Hon C Glas H Cross 91-92; rtd 92; P-in-c Glencarse Bre 94-00. *1 Churchill Close, Ettington, Stratford-upon-Avon CV37 7SP* Tel and fax (01789) 740356 Mobile 07801-849941
E-mail kenyonwright@aol.com
WRIGHT, Kevin John. b 54. Southn Univ BSc75 PGCE76. Ox Min Course 06. **d** 10 **p** 11. C Radley and Sunningwell *Ox* from 10; C Kennington from 10. *10 Culham Close, Abingdon OX14 2AS* Tel (01235) 799676 Mobile 07808-171884
E-mail kjwright2010@talktalk.net
WRIGHT, Mrs Kim Beatrice Elizabeth. b 66. STETS 07. **d** 10 **p** 11. NSM Walton-on-Thames *Guildf* from 10. *Address withheld by request* Tel 07941-947866 (mobile)
E-mail kdomwright@virginmedia.com
WRIGHT, Lawrence Charles. b 57. Hull Univ MA94. EMMTC 93. **d** 96 **p** 96. C Heathridge and Joondalup Australia 96-98; C Penzance St Jo *Truro* 98-02; TV Penzance St Mary w St Paul and St Jo 02-04; Manager Relig Affairs Yarlswood Immigration and Detention Cen 04-06; Chapl W Lon YMCA 06-07; SSF from 07; R Birm St Geo from 09. *St George's Rectory, 100 Bridge Street West, Birmingham B19 2YX* Tel 07964-452417 (mobile)
E-mail larryssf@googlemail.com
WRIGHT, Leslie Vandernoll. b 24. Trin Hall Cam MA50. Ridley Hall Cam 49. **d** 51 **p** 52. C Aldershot H Trin *Guildf* 51-53; C Cambridge H Trin *Ely* 53-57; V Marston *Ox* 57-59; Asst Master Castle Ct Sch Parkstone 59-61; Asst Chapl Stowe Sch 61-64; Hd Master St Mich Prep Sch Five Oaks Jersey 64-66; Chapl Windlesham Ho Sch Sussex 66-68; Chapl Vevey *Eur* 68-73; Hd St Geo Sch Clarens 73-89; rtd 89; Chapl Lugano *Eur* 89-92. *18 avenue Schubert, Domaine Château Tournon, 83440 Montauroux, France* Tel (0033) 4 94 47 62 43
E-mail leslie.wright@orange.fr
WRIGHT, Mrs Louisa Mary (Lisa). b 33. S'wark Ord Course. **d** 87 **p** 94. NSM Streatham Hill St Marg *S'wark* 87-95; Hon C Streatham St Leon 95-02; rtd 02; Perm to Offic *S'wark* from 02. *19 Hillside Road, London SW2 3HL* Tel (020) 8671 8037
WRIGHT, Mrs Marion Jane. b 47. Whitelands Coll Lon CertEd69. Cranmer Hall Dur 73. **d** 00 **p** 02. NSM Scalby *York* from 00. *3 East Park Road, Scalby, Scarborough YO13 0PZ* Tel (01723) 350208
WRIGHT, Martin. b 48. Avery Hill Coll BEd81 K Alfred's Coll Win CertEd69 LRAM76. SAOMC 95. **d** 98 **p** 99. NSM St Alb St Mary Marshalswick *St Alb* 98-01; C Gt Berkhamsted 02-05; V Reigate St Mark *S'wark* from 05. *St Mark's Vicarage, 8 Alma Road, Reigate RH2 0DA* Tel (01737) 241161 Mobile 07774-923550 E-mail mwright@stmarksreigate.co.uk
WRIGHT, Canon Martin Neave. b 37. AKC61. St Boniface Warminster. **d** 62 **p** 63. C Corby St Columba *Pet* 62-65; Ind Chapl 65-71; Nigeria 71-75; P-in-c Honiley *Cov* 75-84; P-in-c Wroxall 75-84; Ind Chapl 75-84; Soc Resp Officer 84-96; Hon Can Cov Cathl 95-96; Bp's Chapl and Past Asst *B & W* 96-02; Preb Wells Cathl 96-02; Sub-Dean Wells 00-02; rtd 02; Perm to Offic *Cov* from 02. *2 Honiwell Close, Harbury, Leamington Spa CV33 9LY* Tel (01926) 613699
WRIGHT, Michael. *See* WRIGHT, Edward Michael
WRIGHT, Canon Michael. b 30. St Chad's Coll Dur BA55 De Montfort Univ MPhil04. **d** 56 **p** 57. C New Cleethorpes *Linc* 56-59; C Skegness 59-62; V Louth St Mich 62-73; R Stewton 62-73; R Warmsworth *Sheff* 73-86; Warden Dioc Readers' Assn 81-86; Hon Can Sheff Cathl 82-95; V Wath-upon-Dearne w Adwick-upon-Dearne 86-94; V Wath-upon-Dearne 94-95; RD Wath 92-95; rtd 95; Perm to Offic *Linc* from 95. *17 Ashfield Road, Sleaford NG34 7DZ* Tel (01529) 415698
WRIGHT, Michael Christopher. b 44. Leeds Univ BA65 CertEd67 MSc75 Sheff Univ PhD02 FRSA95. Wells Th Coll 65. **d** 67 **p** 68. C Dormanstown *York* 67-69; Perm to Offic *Linc* 69-88 and *Sheff* 71-95; Hd Master Eastmoor High Sch Wakef 84-87; Hd Master Carleton High Sch Pontefract 87-95; C-in-c St Edm Anchorage Lane CD *Sheff* 95-96; Chapl Doncaster R Infirmary and Montagu Hosp NHS Trust 95-01; Research Fell Sheff Univ 01-03; Sen Research Fell Lanc Univ from 03; Hon C Gt Snaith *Sheff* 01-07; Perm to Offic *Wakef* from 01; *Eur* from 06; *Sheff* from 07. *Orchard End, Finkle Street, Hensall, Goole DN14 0QY* Tel (01977) 661900 *or* (01524) 593152
E-mail mc.wright@btinternet.com
or m.c.wright@lancaster.ac.uk
WRIGHT, Michael George. b 52. WEMTC 01. **d** 04 **p** 05. NSM Woodchester and Brimscombe *Glouc* from 04. *The Trumpet, West End, Minchinhampton, Stroud GL6 9JA* Tel (01453) 883027 Mobile 07974-303527
E-mail thetrumpet.antiques@virgin.net
WRIGHT, Michael John. b 38. Dur Univ MA91. Chich Th Coll 59. **d** 62 **p** 63. C Yate *Glouc* 62-65; C Kirby Moorside w

Gillamoor *York* 65-68; V 68-72; V Bransdale cum Farndale 68-72; V Kirkbymoorside w Gillamoor, Farndale etc 72-73; Dioc Communications Officer 72-74; V Ormesby 74-80; P-in-c Middlesbrough St Cuth 81-88; Perm to Offic 88-99; NSM W Acklam 91-97; Chapl Butterwick Hospice Stockton-on-Tees 97-99; Chapl S Dur Hospice Bp Auckland 97-99; rtd 03. *25 Thornfield Road, Middlesbrough TS5 5DD* Tel (01642) 816247 E-mail mjw@careatwork.fsnet.co.uk

WRIGHT, Nicholas John. b 65. Liv Univ BA87. Wycliffe Hall Ox 89. d 92 p 93. C Burley *Ripon* 92-95; C Brightside w Wincobank *Sheff* 95-97; TV Sheff Manor 97-03; Perm to Offic from 03. *22 Norfolk Road, Sheffield S2 2SX*

WRIGHT, Canon Nicholas Mark. b 59. Loughb Univ BSc80. Qu Coll Birm 82. d 85 p 86. C Coney Hill *Glouc* 85-89; C Rotherham *Sheff* 89-91; TV Worc SE 91-98; R Inkberrow w Cookhill and Kington w Dormston from 98; Hon Can Worc Cathl from 11. *The Vicarage, High Street, Inkberrow, Worcester WR7 4DU* Tel (01386) 792222 E-mail ncbjmswright@btinternet.com

✠**WRIGHT, The Rt Revd Prof Nicholas Thomas.** b 48. Ex Coll Ox BA71 MA75 DPhil81 DD00. Wycliffe Hall Ox BA73. d 75 p 76 c 03. Fell Mert Coll Ox 75-78; Chapl 76-78; Chapl and Fell Down Coll Cam 78-81; Asst Prof NT Studies McGill Univ Montreal 81-86; Chapl and Fell Worc Coll Ox and Univ Lect Th 86-93; Dean Lich 93-99; Can Th Cov Cathl 92-99; Lector Theologiae and Can Westmr Abbey 00-03; Bp Dur 03-10; Chair NT and Early Christianity St Andr Univ from 10. *St Mary's College, South Street, St Andrews KY16 9JU* E-mail ntw2@st-andrews.ac.uk

WRIGHT, Nigel Christopher James. b 67. Leeds Univ BA07 FCCA99. NOC 04. d 07 p 08. NSM Utley *Bradf* 07-10; NSM Oxenhope from 10. *High Hob Cote Farm, Hob Cote Lane, Oakworth, Keighley BD22 0RW* Tel (01535) 644855 Fax 613396 Mobile 07970-751670 E-mail nigel@nwaccounting.co.uk

WRIGHT, Ms Pamela Anne. b 45. Open Univ BSc00. St As Minl Tr Course 01. d 03 p 10. NSM Llanrhos *St As* 03-09; NSM Rhos-Cystennin from 09. *Brackenrigg, Bryn Pydew Road, Bryn Pydew, Llandudno Junction LL31 9JH* Tel (01492) 541552 Fax 541652 Mobile 07850-180420 E-mail pamscot45@aol.com

WRIGHT, Miss Pamela Jean. b 38. ALA63. NTMTC 02. d 03 p 04. NSM Harrow Trin St Mich *Lon* 03-05; NSM Harrow Weald St Mich 05-08. *Address temp unknown* E-mail pamelajwright@btinternet.com

WRIGHT, Ms Patricia. b 46. MBE02. SRN68. S'wark Ord Course 80. dss 85 d 89. Asst Chapl R Lon Hosp (Mile End) 83-85; Bethnal Green St Matt w St Jas the Gt *Lon* 85-88; Hon C St Botolph Aldgate w H Trin Minories 89-05; Cathl Dn and Dioc HIV/AIDS Co-ord Swaziland 00-04; Hon C St Geo-in-the-East St Mary from 06. *8 Royal Mint Street, London E1 8LG* Tel (020) 7265 1814 E-mail patw@patthedeacon.com

WRIGHT, Mrs Patricia Yvonne. b 51. d 10 p 11. OLM Bramford *St E* from 10; OLM Gt and Lt Blakenham w Baylham and Nettlestead from 10. *Hildern, Whitton Leyer, Bramford IP8 4BD* Tel (01473) 464748

WRIGHT, The Ven Paul. b 54. K Coll Lon BD78 AKC78 Heythrop Coll Lon MTh90 Univ of Wales (Lamp) DMin09. Ripon Coll Cuddesdon 78. d 79 p 80. C Beckenham St Geo *Roch* 79-83; Chapl Ch Sch Richmond 83-85; C Richmond St Mary w St Matthias and St Jo *S'wark* 83-85; V Gillingham St Aug *Roch* 85-90; R Crayford 90-99; RD Erith 93-97; V Sidcup St Jo 99-03; Adn Bromley and Bexley from 03; Hon Can Roch Cathl from 98. *The Archdeaconry, The Glebe, Chislehurst BR7 5PX* Tel and fax (020) 8467 8743 Mobile 07985-902601 E-mail archdeacon.bromley@rochester.anglican.org

WRIGHT, Paul Stephen. b 66. Cen Lancs Univ BA88 Liv Univ MA96. Westcott Ho Cam 90. d 93 p 94. C Upholland *Liv* 93-96; CF 96-08; Sen CF from 08. *c/o MOD Chaplains (Army)* Tel (01980) 615804 Fax 615800

WRIGHT, Canon Peter. b 35. K Coll Lon AKC61 Hull Univ MA86. St Boniface Warminster 61. d 62 p 63. C Goole *Sheff* 62-67; V Norton Woodseats St Chad 67-80; R Aston cum Aughton 80-84; P-in-c Ulley 80-84; Chapl Rotherham Priority Health Services NHS Trust 80-84; R Aston cum Aughton and Ulley *Sheff* 84-93; TR Aston cum Aughton w Swallownest, Todwick etc 93-00; RD Laughton 85-93; Chapter Clerk and Hon Can Sheff Cathl 92-00; rtd 00; Perm to Offic *Sheff* from 01; Chapl to Rtd Clergy and Clergy Widows Officer from 09. *40 Chancet Wood Drive, Sheffield S8 7TR* Tel and fax 0114-274 7218 E-mail allsaints.pw@talk21.com

WRIGHT, Peter Reginald. b 34. St Chad's Coll Dur BA60. Linc Th Coll 60. d 62 p 63. C Lt Ilford St Mich *Chelmsf* 62-65; C Billingham St Aid *Dur* 65-68; TV 68-71; TR 71-76; Chapl Portsm Poly 76-87; Sec Chapls in HE Gen Syn Bd of Educn 88-95; rtd 95; Perm to Offic *Portsm* 95-10. *6 Garden Lane, Southsea PO5 3DP* Tel (023) 9273 6651

WRIGHT, Peter Westrope. b 24. Kelham Th Coll 43. d 48 p 49. C Pimlico St Barn *Lon* 48-50; C Sidley *Chich* 50-59; R E Blatchington 59-73; P-in-c Lewes St Mich 73-75; TV Lewes All SS, St Anne, St Mich and St Thos 75-84; TR 84-87; rtd 89; Perm

to Offic *Chich* from 89. *17 South Street, Lewes BN7 2BT* Tel (01273) 473332

WRIGHT, Philip. b 32. G&C Coll Cam BA53 MA57. Wells Th Coll 56. d 57 p 58. C Barnard Castle *Dur* 57-60; C Heworth St Mary 60-64; V Tow Law 64-70; V Tanfield 70-78; V Gateshead Ch Ch 78-02; rtd 02. *Meldon, High Heworth Lane, Gateshead NE10 0PB* Tel 0191-469 2161

WRIGHT, Phillip. b 35. Kelham Th Coll 57 St Aid Birkenhead 59. d 61 p 62. C Goldthorpe *Sheff* 61-65; V Doncaster St Jude 65-71; V Kettering All SS *Pet* 71-82; V S Kirkby *Wakef* 82-94; rtd 98. *2 The Grove, Wickersley, Rotherham S66 2BP* Tel (01709) 543922 E-mail thegrove@onetel.com

WRIGHT, Robert. See WRIGHT, Canon Anthony Robert

WRIGHT, Robert Charles. b 31. Roch Th Coll 65. d 67 p 68. C Manston *Ripon* 67-70; C Moor Allerton 70-74; P-in-c Terrington St John *Ely* 74-79; P-in-c Walpole St Andrew 74-75; V Terrington St John 80-91; V Tilney St Lawrence 80-91; V Tilney All Saints 80-91; R Stiffkey and Cockthorpe w Morston, Langham etc *Nor* 91-96; rtd 96; Perm to Offic *Nor* from 96. *Glenfinnan, 83 Childs Way, Sheringham NR26 8TX* Tel (01263) 822535

WRIGHT, Canon Robert Doogan. b 24. TCD BA46 MA. TCD Div Sch Div Test 47. d 47 p 48. C Carnmoney *Conn* 47-49; C Belfast St Jas 49-51; C Belfast St Matt 51-53; P-in-c Belfast Whiterock 53-57; I Magheragall 57-64; I Belfast St Mark 64-70; I Carrickfergus 70-82; Can Conn Cathl 79-86; I Killead w Gartree 82-86; Chan Conn Cathl 83-86; rtd 86. *15 Mount Pleasant Road, Newtownabbey BT37 0NQ* Tel (028) 9086 2179

WRIGHT, Robert John. b 47. St Jo Coll Dur BA70. SEITE 00. d 03 p 04. NSM Notting Hill St Jo *Lon* 03-06; NSM Notting Hill St Pet 03-06; NSM N Hammersmith St Kath 06-08; NSM Cheddington w Mentmore *Ox* from 08. *The Rectory, 29 Mentmore Road, Cheddington, Leighton Buzzard LU7 0SD* Tel (01296) 661358 Mobile 07988-978419 E-mail robert@robert-wright.com

✠**WRIGHT, The Rt Revd Royston Clifford.** b 22. Univ of Wales BA42. St Steph Ho Ox 43. d 45 p 46 c 86. C Bedwas *Mon* 45-47; C Newport St Jo Bapt 47-49; C Walton St Mary *Liv* 49-51; Chapl RNVR 50-51; Chapl RN 51-68; V Blaenavon w Capel Newydd *Mon* 68-74; RD Pontypool 73-74; TR Ebbw Vale 74-77; Can St Woolos Cathl 74-77; Adn Mon 77-88; Adn Newport 77-86; Bp Mon 86-91; rtd 91; Lic to Offic *Mon* from 91. *23 Rupert Brooke Drive, Newport NP20 3HP* Tel (01633) 250770

WRIGHT (née PRECIOUS), Sally Joanne. b 75. Hatf Coll Dur BA97 Anglia Poly Univ MA03. Westcott Ho Cam 00. d 02 p 03. C Chich St Paul and Westhampnett 02-05; Perm to Offic *S'wark* 05-06; Hon C Peckham St Jo w St Andr 06-09; Chapl Guildhall Sch of Music and Drama *Lon* 06-09; Hon C Witney *Ox* from 09. *The Rectory, 13 Station Lane, Witney OX28 4BB* Tel (01993) 704441 E-mail sallywright29@yahoo.co.uk

WRIGHT, Samuel. See WRIGHT, Canon William Samuel

WRIGHT, Simon Christopher. b 44. AKC67. d 68 p 69. C Bitterne Park *Win* 68-72; C Kirkby *Liv* 72-74; V Wigan St Anne 74-79; Abp's Dom Chapl and Dioc Dir of Ords *York* 79-84; V W Acklam 84-00; RD Middlesbrough 87-98; Can and Preb York Minster 94-00; V Dartmouth and Dittisham *Ex* 00-10; rtd 10; Perm to Offic *York* from 10. *48 Langton Road, Norton, Malton YO17 9AD* Tel (01653) 698106 E-mail simon@simonwright.fsnet.co.uk

WRIGHT, Stephen Irwin. b 58. Ex Coll Ox BA80 MA84 Selw Coll Cam BA85 MA90 Lanc Univ MA92 St Jo Coll Dur PhD97. Ridley Hall Cam 83. d 86 p 87. C Newbarns w Hawcoat *Carl* 86-90; C Burton and Holme 90-94; NSM Esh *Dur* 94-97; NSM Hamsteels 94-97; C Consett 97-98; Dir Coll of Preachers 98-06; Tutor Spurgeon's Coll from 06; Perm to Offic *S'wark* from 09. *Spurgeon's College, 189 South Norwood Hill, London SE25 6DJ* Tel (020) 8653 0850 or 8768 0378 ext 233 Fax 8711 0959 E-mail s.wright@spurgeons.ac.uk

WRIGHT, Canon Stephen Mark. b 60. Keele Univ BA83. Trin Coll Bris 86. d 89 p 90. C Thorne *Sheff* 89-92; CMS 92-05; Nigeria 93-98; Hon Can Asaba from 98; Chapl Ahmadi St Paul Kuwait 99-03; Chapl Dubai and Sharjah w N Emirates from 03. *PO Box 7415, Dubai, United Arab Emirates* Tel (00971) (4) 884 4904 E-mail stephenw@emirates.net.ae

WRIGHT, Stewart. See WRIGHT, Canon William Charles Stewart

WRIGHT, Stuart Kendle. b 73. d 08 p 09. C Tollington *Lon* from 08. *Emmanuel Vicarage, 145 Hornsey Road, London N7 6DU* Tel (020) 7607 1737 Mobile 07867-888999 E-mail vegetablestu@blueyonder.co.uk

WRIGHT, Thomas. See WRIGHT, The Rt Revd Prof Nicholas Thomas

WRIGHT, Tim Stanley. b 63. Derby Coll of Educn BEd86. St Jo Coll Dur 89. d 92 p 93. C Eccleshill *Bradf* 92-96; TV Southend *Chelmsf* 96-00; V Boulton *Derby* from 00. *The Vicarage, 1 St Mary's Close, Alvaston, Derby DE24 0GF* Tel (01332) 572308 E-mail revboulton@tiscali.co.uk

WRIGHT, Timothy. b 63. NUU BSc85. Cranmer Hall Dur 86. d 89 p 90. C Bramcote *S'well* 89-93; I Glenavy w Tunny and

Crumlin *Conn* 93-98; Chapl RAF from 98; Perm to Offic *Lich* 01-08. *Chaplaincy Services, Valiant Block, HQ Air Command, RAF High Wycombe HP14 4UE* Tel (01494) 496800 Fax 496343

WRIGHT, Timothy John. b 41. K Coll Lon BD63 AKC63. **d** 64 **p** 65. C Highfield *Ox* 64-68; Asst Chapl Worksop Coll Notts 68-71; Chapl Malvern Coll 71-77; Ho Master 77-86; Hd Master Jo Lyon Sch Harrow 86-01; rtd 01. *Beech House, Colwall Green, Malvern WR13 6DX* Tel (01684) 541102

WRIGHT, Timothy John. b 54. Nottm Univ BA76. Ripon Coll Cuddesdon 90. **d** 92 **p** 93. C Dawlish *Ex* 92-95; TV Teignmouth, Ideford w Luton, Ashcombe etc 95-01; Chapl Wycombe Abbey Sch 01-08; NSM Wycombe Deanery 08-09; P-in-c Petworth *Chich* from 09; P-in-c Egdean from 09. *The Rectory, Rectory Lane, Petworth GU28 0DB* Tel (01798) 342505

WRIGHT, Toby Christopher. b 75. New Coll Ox BA98 MA01 Leeds Univ MA01. Coll of Resurr Mirfield 99. **d** 01 **p** 02. C Petersfield *Portsm* 01-04; P-in-c Peckham St Jo w St Andr *S'wark* 04-06; V 06-09; AD Camberwell 06-09; TR Witney *Ox* from 09. *The Rectory, 13 Station Lane, Witney OX28 4BB* Tel (01993) 704441 E-mail toby.wright@btinternet.com

WRIGHT, Mrs Vyvienne Mary. b 35. S Dios Minl Tr Scheme 80. **dss** 83 **d** 87 **p** 94. Martock w Ash *B & W* 83-00; Hon C 87-00; Perm to Offic from 00. *36 Church Close, Martock TA12 6DS* Tel (01935) 823292

WRIGHT, Canon William Charles Stewart. b 53. Ulster Poly BSc81. CITC BTh95. **d** 95 **p** 96. C Ballyholme *D & D* 95-98; I Conwal Union w Gartan *D & R* from 98; Can Raphoe Cathl from 10. *Conwal Rectory, New Line Road, Letterkenny, Co Donegal, Republic of Ireland* Tel (00353) (74) 912 2573 E-mail stewartwright@live.ie

WRIGHT, Canon William Samuel. b 59. TCD BTh89 MA90. **d** 87 **p** 88. C Belfast St Aid *Conn* 87-91; Sec Dioc Bd of Miss 90-91; I Cleenish w Mullaghdun *Clogh* 91-99; I Lisburn Ch Ch Cathl from 99; Can and Preb Conn Cathl from 01. *Cathedral Rectory, 11D Magheralave, Lisburn BT28 3BE* Tel (028) 9209 0260 E-mail sam.wright@lisburncathedral.org

WRIGHTSON, Bernard. b 25. CertEd50 ACP65. Linc Th Coll 83. **d** 83 **p** 84. NSM Alford w Rigsby *Linc* 83-86; Perm to Offic 86-89; NSM Mablethorpe w Trusthorpe 89-94; Perm to Offic 94-04. *Pipits Acre, 64 Church Lane, Mablethorpe LN12 2NU* Tel (01507) 472394

WRIGLEY, George Garnett. b 50. St Cath Coll Cam BA71 Loughb Coll of Educn PGCE72. NTMTC 02. **d** 04 **p** 05. NSM Hounslow H Trin w St Paul *Lon* 04-08; P-in-c Langdale *Carl* 08-10; TV Loughrigg from 10. *The Vicarage, Chapel Stile, Ambleside LA22 9JG* Tel (015394) 37267 E-mail georgewrig@hotmail.com

WRISDALE, Jean May. b 40. **d** 90 **p** 94. OLM Fotherby *Linc* from 90. *The Meadows, Livesey Road, Ludborough, Grimsby DN36 5SQ* Tel (01472) 840474

WROE, Mark. b 69. Surrey Univ BA92. Ridley Hall Cam 94. **d** 96 **p** 97. C Chilvers Coton w Astley *Cov* 96-00; P-in-c Heworth St Alb *Dur* 00-03; V Windy Nook St Alb 03-07; V Jesmond H Trin *Newc* from 07; P-in-c Newc St Barn and St Jude from 07. *13 Glastonbury Grove, Newcastle upon Tyne NE2 2HA* Tel 0191-240 1017 E-mail mark.wroe@htjesmond.org.uk

WROE, Martin Daniel Edward. b 61. NTMTC. **d** 04 **p** 05. NSM Covent Garden St Paul *Lon* 04-07; NSM W Holloway St Luke from 07. *45 Penn Road, London N7 9RE* Tel (020) 7607 6086 E-mail martinwroe@blueyonder.co.uk

WYARD, Peter Joseph. b 54. Pemb Coll Cam MA76 Sussex Univ MSc80 Brunel Univ MSc88 Anglia Ruskin Univ MA07. EAMTC 99. **d** 02 **p** 03. C Framlingham w Saxtead *St E* 02-05; P-in-c Riverside *Ox* 05-08; V Colnbrook and Datchet from 08. *St Mary's Vicarage, London Road, Datchet, Slough SL3 9JW* Tel (01753) 580467 E-mail peter.wyard@btinternet.com

WYATT, Colin. b 27. Ex Coll Ox BA54 MA55 Lon Univ BD62. Tyndale Hall Bris 60. **d** 63 **p** 64. C Radipole *Sarum* 63-66; C Southborough St Pet *Roch* 66-67; V Tetsworth *Ox* 67-72; Lect Bible Tr Inst Glas 72-74; R Hurworth *Dur* 74-79; P-in-c Dinsdale w Sockburn 74-76; R 76-79; R Sadberge 79-84; R Bacton w Wyverstone and Cotton *St E* 84-92; rtd 92; Perm to Offic *Ripon* from 92. *20 Harrogate Road, Ripon HG4 1SR* Tel (01765) 606810

WYATT, Canon David Stanley Chadwick. b 36. Fitzw Ho Cam BA59 MA71. Ely Th Coll 59. **d** 61 **p** 62. C Rochdale *Man* 61-63; Bp's Dom Chapl 63-68; R Salford St Paul w Ch Ch from 68; P-in-c Salford Ordsall St Clem 91-96; P-in-c Lower Broughton Ascension from 05; AD Salford 97; Hon Can Man Cathl from 82. *St Paul's Church House, Broadwalk, Salford M6 5FX* Tel 0161-736 8868

WYATT, Peter Charles. b 62. Bris Univ BSc85 CEng MIEE92. St Jo Coll Nottm 05. **d** 07 **p** 08. C Becontree St Thos *Chelmsf* 07-11; Min Selsdon St Fran CD *S'wark* from 11. *St Francis' Vicarage, 146 Tedder Road, Croydon CR2 8AH* Tel (020) 8657 7864 E-mail peter.michelle@gmail.com

WYATT, Peter John. b 38. Kelham Th Coll 58. **d** 64 **p** 65. C N Stoneham *Win* 64-68; C Brixham *Ex* 68-69; Dominica 69-75; Zambia 76-78; P-in-c Ettington *Cov* 78-79; V Butlers Marston

and the Pillertons w Ettington 79-86; V Codnor and Loscoe *Derby* 86-91; Chapl for Deaf People 91-03; rtd 03; Perm to Offic *Heref* from 04. *16 Cae Melyn, Tregynon, Newtown SY16 3EF* Tel (01686) 650368

WYATT, Richard Norman. b 21. LVCM. **d** 84 **p** 85. C Puttenham and Wanborough *Guildf* 84-90; Perm to Offic *Chich* 91-93 and from 97; P-in-c Stedham w Iping 93-97; rtd 97; RD Midhurst *Chich* 98-99. *Trenethick, June Lane, Midhurst GU29 9EL* Tel (01730) 813447 E-mail norman.wyatt@homecall.co.uk

WYATT, Royston Dennis. b 36. FRICS67. Sarum & Wells Th Coll 74. **d** 77 **p** 78. NSM Canford Magna *Sarum* 77-82; V Abbotsbury, Portesham and Langton Herring 82-88; Dioc Missr *Linc* 88-95; R Welford w Weston *Glouc* 95-05; RD Campden 96-01; rtd 05; Perm to Offic *B & W* from 06. *78 Lower Meadow, Ilminster TA19 9DP* Tel (01460) 53996 E-mail revrdw@talktalk.net

WYATT (*née* OWEN), **Canon Susan Elizabeth.** b 53. Bris Univ BSc75 Bath Univ PGCE78. EAMTC 97. **d** 00 **p** 01. Asst Dioc Adv in Miss and Evang *Ely* from 00; C Over 00-06; C Long Stanton w St Mich 02-06; V Cherry Hinton St Jo from 06; Hon Can Ely Cathl from 10. *St John's Vicarage, 9 Luard Road, Cambridge CB2 8PJ* Tel (01223) 247451 *or* 241316 Mobile 07713-241261 E-mail sue.wyatt1@ntlworld.com *or* sue.wyatt@ely.anglican.org

WYATT, Trevor. b 60. Keele Univ BSc81. SEITE 97. **d** 00 **p** 01. NSM Wilmington *Roch* from 00. *216 Birchwood Road, Wilmington, Dartford DA2 7HA* Tel (01322) 666521 Mobile 07860-306746 E-mail trevor.wyatt@diocese-rochester.org *or* trevor.wyatt@bt.com

WYBER, Richard John. b 47. G&C Coll Cam BA69 MA72 FCA73. SEITE 03. **d** 06 **p** 07. NSM Wanstead St Mary w Ch Ch *Chelmsf* from 06. *7 Mornington Close, Woodford Green IG8 0TT* Tel (020) 8504 2447

WYBREW, Canon Hugh Malcolm. b 34. Qu Coll Ox BA58 MA. Linc Th Coll 59. **d** 60 **p** 61. C E Dulwich St Jo *S'wark* 60-64; Tutor St Steph Ho Ox 65-71; Chapl Bucharest *Eur* 71-73; V Pinner *Lon* 73-83; Chapl RNR 73-92; C Walsall *Lich* 76-77; Dean Jerusalem 86-89; Hon Can Gib Cathl 89-04; V Ox St Mary Magd 89-04; Hon Can Ch Ch 01-04; rtd 04. *96 Warwick Street, Oxford OX4 1SY* Tel (01865) 241355 E-mail hugh.wybrew@queens.ox.ac.uk

WYER, Mrs Janet Beatrice. b 58. UEA BA00. ERMC 04. **d** 07 **p** 08. C Loddon, Sisland, Chedgrave, Hardley and Langley *Nor* 07-10; C Nor St Pet Mancroft w St Jo Maddermarket from 10. *63 Recreation Road, Norwich NR2 3PA* Tel 07990-576118 (mobile) E-mail wyer@supanet.com

WYER, Keith George. b 45. St Paul's Coll Chelt CertEd66 K Coll Lon BD71 AKC71. St Aug Coll Cant 71. **d** 72 **p** 73. C Moseley St Mary *Birm* 72-76; Chapl RNR 73-92; C Walsall *Lich* 76-77; Min Walsall St Martin 77-79; Chapl Colston's Sch Bris 79-86; Chapl Kelly Coll Tavistock 86-92; R Combe Martin and Berrynarbor *Ex* 92-95; TR Combe Martin, Berrynarbor, Lynton, Brendon etc 96-10; RD Shirwell 95-01; rtd 10. *Highlands, 6 Holland Park Avenue, Combe Martin, Ilfracombe EX34 0HL* E-mail keith@wyer.org

WYKES, Peter. b 44. Lon Univ MB, BS68. Ban & St As Minl Tr Course 97. **d** 00 **p** 01. NSM Trefnant w Tremeirchion *St As* 00-01; NSM Cefn w Trefnant w Tremeirchion from 01. *Clattwm, 1 Plas Chambres Road, Denbigh LL16 5UP* Tel (01745) 730263

WYLAM, John. b 43. AKC66 FE TCert75. **d** 67 **p** 68. C Derby St Bart 67-70; SSF 70-73; C Seaton Hirst *Newc* 74-77; V Byker St Silas 77-83; V Alwinton w Holystone and Alnham 83-98; R Chollerton w Birtley and Thockrington 98-09; rtd 09. *Nether House, Garleigh Road, Rothbury, Morpeth NE65 7RG* Tel (01669) 622805 E-mail johnwylam@btopenworld.com

WYLD, Kevin Andrew. b 58. St Cath Coll Ox BA79 MA85 Univ Coll Dur MSc83 Edin Univ BD85. Edin Th Coll 82. **d** 85 **p** 86. C Winlaton *Dur* 85-87; C Houghton le Spring 87-90; V Medomsley 90-95; V High Spen and Rowlands Gill 95-00; R Winter Park St Rich USA 00-04. *15 Hullock Road, Newton Aycliffe DL5 4LT* Tel (01325) 312286 E-mail kevinwyld@gmail.com

WYLES, Mrs Kate. b 66. STETS. **d** 11. C Godalming *Guildf* from 11. *43 Wolseley Road, Godalming GU7 3EA* Tel (01483) 421287 E-mail jkwyles@hotmail.co.uk

WYLIE, Alan. b 47. Is of Man Tr Inst 88. **d** 92 **p** 93. NSM Douglas St Geo *S & M* 92-97; NSM Challoch *Glas* 97-00; P-in-c Motherwell from 00; P-in-c Wishaw from 00. *The Rectory, 14 Crawford Street, Motherwell ML1 3AD* Tel (01698) 249441 E-mail alan.rev@hotmail.com

WYLIE, Clive George. b 64. QUB BSc86 TCD BTh90 MA93. CITC 87. **d** 90 **p** 91. C Drumglass w Moygashel *Arm* 90-93; I Tynan, Aghavilly and Middletown 93-98; Hon V Choral Arm Cathl 93-98; Team P Glas E End 98-03; TR 03-08; Miss 21 Co-ord 98-03; Perm to Offic *Nor* from 09. *14 Bridewell Street, Walsingham NR22 6BJ* Tel (01328) 820291 Mobile 07970-875052 E-mail columba.osb@gmail.com

WYLIE, David Victor. b 61. ACA86 LSE BSc(Econ)82 Leeds Univ BA91. Coll of Resurr Mirfield 89. **d** 92 **p** 93. C Kilburn

St Aug w St Jo *Lon* 92-95; C Heston 95-98; Chapl RN from 98. *Royal Naval Chaplaincy Service, Mail Point 1-2, Leach Building, Whale Island, Portsmouth PO2 8BY* Tel (023) 9262 5055 Fax 9262 5134

WYLIE-SMITH, Ms Megan Judith. b 52. S'wark Ord Course 88. **d** 91 **p** 94. C Greenstead *Chelmsf* 91-94; C W Ham 94-97; TV Becontree S 97-01; rtd 01; Perm to Offic *Chelmsf* from 01. *67 Gordon Road, London E11 2RA* Tel (020) 8530 6434 E-mail megan@wylie-smith.freeserve.co.uk

WYNBURNE, Canon John Paterson Barry. b 48. St Jo Coll Dur BA70. Wycliffe Coll Toronto MDiv72 Ridley Hall Cam 72. **d** 73 **p** 74. C Gt Stanmore *Lon* 73-76; Chapl Bucharest w Sofia *Eur* 76-77; C Dorking w Ranmore *Guildf* 77-80; V Send 80-88; V York Town St Mich 88-93; V Camberley St Mich Yorktown 93-95; TR Beaconsfield *Ox* 95-09; AD Amersham 04-09; V Long Crendon w Chearsley and Nether Winchendon from 09; Hon Can Ch Ch from 11. *The Vicarage, 84A High Street, Long Crendon, Aylesbury HP18 9AL* Tel (01844) 201424 E-mail revwynburne@btinternet.com

WYNES, Michael John. b 33. AKC57. **d** 58 **p** 59. C Gt Berkhamsted *St Alb* 58-62; C Silverhill St Matt *Chich* 62-65; C Wilton *B & W* 65-68; R Berkley w Rodden 68-77; V Priddy 77-86; V Westbury sub Mendip w Easton 77-86; C Milton 86-93; rtd 93; Perm to Offic *B & W* from 95. *23A Fairways, Wells BA5 2DF* Tel (01749) 673778

WYNFORD-HARRIS, Robert William. b 61. Anglia Ruskin Univ BA. Ridley Hall Cam 06. **d** 08 **p** 09. C Sawbridgeworth *St Alb* from 08. *St Mary's Lodge, Knight Street, Sawbridgeworth CM21 9AX* Tel (01279) 723398 E-mail wynhar@hotmail.com

WYNN, Edward Laurence. b 65. Leeds Metrop Univ BSc96 Leeds Univ MA02 RGN88. NOC 98. **d** 01 **p** 02. C Emley *Wakef* 01-04; C Flockton cum Denby Grange 01-04; Chapl RAF from 04. *Chaplaincy Services, Valiant Block, HQ Air Command, RAF High Wycombe HP14 4UE* Tel (01494) 496800 Fax 496343 Mobile 07714-062869 E-mail eddie@wynn11.freeserve.co.uk

WYNN, Richard David. b 44. Univ Coll of Rhodesia & Nyasaland Inst of Educn TCert65. St Paul's Coll Grahamstown 86. **d** 88 **p** 89. C Kirby-Hilton Ascension S Africa 88-91; R Ixopo St Jo 91-99; R Richmond-cum-Byrne St Mary 99-02; P-in-c Cinderford St Steph w Littledean *Glouc* 02-10; P-in-c Cinderford St Jo 06-10; P-in-c Stopham and Fittleworth *Chich* from 10. *The Rectory, Church Lane, Fittleworth, Pulborough RH20 1HL* Tel (01798) 865455

WYNN (née ARMSTRONG), Rosemary. b 40. **d** 06. OLM Sturminster Newton, Hinton St Mary and Lydlinch *Sarum* from 06. *2 Alder Close, Sturminster Newton DT10 1AJ* Tel (01258) 472656 E-mail rwsturminster@orangehome.co.uk

WYNNE, Preb Alan John. b 46. St Luke's Coll Ex CertEd71. St Steph Ho Ox BA71 MA75. **d** 71 **p** 72. C Watford St Pet *St Alb* 71-74; Chapl Liddon Ho Lon 74-75; Chapl Abp Tenison's Sch Kennington 75-86; Hon C St Marylebone Annunciation Bryanston Street *Lon* 81-86; V Hoxton St Anne w St Columba 86-94; TR Poplar from 94; Preb St Paul's Cathl from 01; AD Tower Hamlets 01-06. *Poplar Rectory, Newby Place, London E14 0EY* Tel and fax (020) 7987 3133 *or* tel 7538 9198 E-mail alan@poplar22.fsnet.co.uk

WYNNE (née GORTON), Mrs Angela Deborah. b 60. Leeds Univ BSc82 CSci04. CBDTI 04. **d** 07 **p** 08. NSM Penwortham St Mary *Blackb* 07-11; NSM Chorley St Geo from 11; NSM Charnock Richard from 11. *11 Freeman's Lane, Charnock Richard, Chorley PR7 5ER* Tel (01257) 791760 E-mail adwynne@yahoo.co.uk

WYNNE, The Very Revd Frederick John Gordon. b 44. Chu Coll Cam BA66 MA70. CITC 81. **d** 84 **p** 85. C Dublin St Patr Cathl Gp 84-86; C Romsey *Win* 86-89; R Broughton, Bossington, Houghton and Mottisfont 89-97; I Dunleckney w Nurney, Lorum and Kiltennel *C & O* 97-08; I Leighlin w Grange Sylvae, Shankill etc 08-10; Chan Ossory Cathl 00-10; Chan Leighlin Cathl 00-04; Dean Leighlin 04-10; rtd 10. *12 Avenue Road, Lymington SO41 9GJ* Tel (01590) 672082

WYNNE, Preb Geoffrey. b 41. K Coll Lon BD64 AKC64 Lon Univ BSc(Soc)75 Heythrop Coll Lon MTh86. **d** 66 **p** 67. C Wolverhampton St Pet *Lich* 66-70; Chapl Wolv Poly 66-79; Sen Chapl 79-92; Sen Chapl Wolv Univ 92-10; Dir of Ords 76-83; Preb Lich Cathl 83-10; AD Wolverhampton 03-10; Bp's Adv for Univ and HE Chapl 04-10; rtd 10. *West House, Haywood Drive, Wolverhampton WV6 8RF* Tel (01902) 219196 E-mail g.wynne@wlv.ac.uk

WYNNE, Ian Charles. b 53. Bris Univ MB, ChB76 FRCGP06. SNWTP 09. **d** 11. NSM Haydock St Jas *Liv* from 11. *123 Ashton Road, Newton-le-Willows WA12 0AH* Tel 07885-823786 (mobile) E-mail ian_cw@hotmail.com

WYNNE, Jago Robert Owen. b 76. Magd Coll Cam BA98 MA01. Wycliffe Hall Ox 08. **d** 10 **p** 11. C Onslow Square and S Kensington St Aug *Lon* from 10. *30 Almeric Road, London SW11 1HL* Tel (020) 7738 2304 Mobile 07979-606720 E-mail jago.wynne@gmail.com *or* jago.wynne@htb.org.uk

WYNNE, Jean. **d** 02 **p** 03. NSM Mullingar, Portnashangan, Moyliscar, Kilbixy etc *M & K* 02-10; Lic to Offic from 10.

3 Doctor's Court, Rathangan, Co Kildare, Republic of Ireland Tel (00353) (45) 524057 Mobile 86-356 4590

WYNNE, Mrs Teresa Anne Jane. b 58. Anglia Poly Univ BEd94 Middx Univ BA07. NTMTC 04. **d** 07 **p** 08. C Takeley w Lt Canfield *Chelmsf* 07-10; P-in-c Lexden from 10. *The Rectory, 2 Wroxham Close, Colchester CO3 3RQ* Tel (01206) 575966 E-mail teresa.wynne@btinternet.com

WYNNE-GREEN, Roy Rowland. b 36. Chich Th Coll 67. **d** 70 **p** 71. C Fleetwood St Pet *Blackb* 70-73; C Cen Torquay *Ex* 73-75; Chapl SW Hosp and Chapl Asst St Thos Hosp Lon 75-85; Chapl R Surrey Co Hosp Guildf 85-94; Chapl R Surrey Co Hosp NHS Trust 94-01; Chapl Heathlands Mental Health Trust Surrey 94-98; Chapl Surrey Hants Borders NHS Trust 98-01; rtd 01; Perm to Offic *Guildf* from 02. *St Benedict's House, 6 Lawn Road, Guildford GU2 5DE* Tel (01483) 574582

WYNNE-JONES, Nicholas Winder. b 45. Jes Coll Ox BA67 MA72 Selw Coll Cam 71. Oak Hill Th Coll 69. **d** 72 **p** 73. C St Marylebone All So w SS Pet and Jo *Lon* 72-75; Chapl Stowe Sch 75-83; V Gt Clacton *Chelmsf* 83-95; V Beckenham Ch Ch *Roch* from 95; RD Beckenham 00-05. *Christ Church Vicarage, 18 Court Downs Road, Beckenham BR3 6LR* Tel (020) 8650 3847 Fax 8658 9532 E-mail nick.wynnejones@diocese-rochester.org *or* vicar@ccb.org.uk

WYNTER, Michael Pallant. b 48. Ripon Coll Cuddesdon 93. **d** 95 **p** 96. C Hughenden *Ox* 95-98; P-in-c Norton sub Hamdon, W Chinnock, Chiselborough etc *B & W* 98-01; R 01-05; RD Ivelchester 01-04; Perm to Offic *Ox* 05-08; C Hazlemere from 08; rtd 11. *Minster Cottage, Manaccan, Helston TR12 6HR* Tel (01326) 231639

Y

YABBACOME, David Wallace. b 55. Bp Otter Coll BEd. Linc Th Coll. **d** 83 **p** 84. C Egham Hythe *Guildf* 83-86; C Cen Telford *Lich* 86-87; TV 87-92; R Cheadle w Freehay 92-00; V Linc St Nic w St Jo Newport from 00. *St Nicholas' Vicarage, 103 Newport, Lincoln LN1 3EE* Tel (01522) 525653 Mobile 07779-557541 E-mail revyabb@ntlworld.com

YABSLEY, Mrs Janet. b 42. St Alb Minl Tr Scheme 81. **dss** 84 **d** 87 **p** 94. Luton St Andr *St Alb* 84-87; NSM Luton St Aug Limbury 87-00; NSM Luton All SS w St Pet 00-06; Perm to Offic from 06. *11 Dale Road, Dunstable LU5 4PY* Tel (01582) 661480 E-mail ian@yabsley1.fsnet.co.uk

YACOMENI, Peter Frederick. b 34. Worc Coll Ox BA58 MA61. Wycliffe Hall Ox 58. **d** 60 **p** 61. C New Malden and Coombe S'wark 60-64; C Bethnal Green St Jas Less *Lon* 64-68; V Barton Hill St Luke w Ch Ch *Bris* 68-75; V Bishopsworth 75-86; RD Bedminster 84-86; P-in-c Wick w Doynton 86-87; V Wick w Doynton and Dyrham 87-98; RD Bitton 95-98; Chapl Wilts and Swindon Healthcare NHS Trust from 98; rtd 98; Perm to Offic *Bris* from 98. *15 Orwell Close, Malmesbury SN16 9UB* Tel (01666) 826628

YACOMENI, Thomas Peter Bruce. b 71. Ex Univ BEng94. Trin Coll Bris BA09. **d** 09 **p** 10. C Weston-super-Mare St Paul *B & W* from 09. *15 Clarence Road North, Weston-super-Mare BS23 4AT* Tel (01934) 643851 Mobile 07786-806640 E-mail tom.yacomeni@googlemail.com

YALLOP, John. b 47. BA79. Oak Hill Th Coll 79. **d** 79 **p** 80. C Brinsworth w Catcliffe *Sheff* 79-81; C Heeley 81-83; C Pitsmoor Ch Ch 83-86; V Ellesmere St Pet 86-88; C Worksop St Jo *S'well* 90-94; P-in-c Cliftonville *Cant* 94-99. *Address temp unknown*

YAM, David Tong Kho. See HAOKIP, Canon David Tongkhoyam

YANDELL, Caroline Jane. b 63. St Hugh's Coll Ox BA85 MA92 Bris Univ MB, ChB97 LSHTM MSc05 Bris Univ PhD07 Wolfs Coll Cam BTh08 St Jo Coll Cam MPhil09 MRCGP01. Ridley Hall Cam 06. **d** 09 **p** 10. C Henleaze *Bris* from 09. *87 Sea Mills Lane, Stoke Bishop, Bristol BS9 1DX* E-mail cy236@cam.ac.uk

YANGON, Bishop of. See SAN SI HTAY, The Most Revd Samuel

YAP, Thomas Fook Piau. b 75. Leeds Univ BA89 MA99. St Jo Coll Nottm MTh02. **d** 03 **p** 04. C Starbeck *Ripon* 03-07; Chapl Essex Univ from 07. *Mariners, Rectory Hill, Wivenhoe, Colchester CO7 9LB* Tel (01206) 823430 E-mail revthomas@hotmail.co.uk

YATES, Alan John Richard. b 38. Lon Univ LDS62. **d** 99 **p** 00. OLM Cley Hill Warminster *Sarum* 99-07; OLM Cley Hill Villages 07-08. *212 Pottle Street, Horningsham, Warminster BA12 7LX* Tel and fax (01985) 844374 Mobile 07970-864714 E-mail revajry@googlemail.com

YATES, Andrew Martin. b 55. St Chad's Coll Dur BA77. Linc Th Coll 78. **d** 80 **p** 81. C Brightside St Thos and St Marg *Sheff*

p80-83; TV Haverhill w Withersfield, the Wrattings etc *St E* 84-90; Ind Chapl 84-90; R Aylesham w Adisham *Cant* 90-96; P-in-c Dudley St Aug Holly Hall *Worc* 96-03; Chapl Merry Hill Shopping Cen 96-03; P-in-c Tresillian and Lamorran w Merther *Truro* from 03; P-in-c St Michael Penkevil from 03; Dioc Soc Resp Officer from 03. *The Rectory, 18 Fore Street, Tregony, Truro TR2 5RN* Tel (01872) 530507 E-mail yatesasb@aol.com

YATES, Canon Anthony Hugh. b 39. Univ of Wales BA62. Wycliffe Hall Ox 62. **d** 65 **p** 66. C Withington St Crispin *Man* 65-68; C Sheff St Cecilia Parson Cross 68-73; V Middlesbrough St Thos *York* 73-82; V Fenton *Lich* 82-95; V Kilburn St Aug w St Jo *Lon* 95-11; rtd 11; CMP from 69; Hon Can Koforidua from 07. *8 Bishop Street, London N1 8PH* Tel (020) 7704 6275 Mobile 07947-646377 E-mail fatheryates@btinternet.com

YATES, Mrs Esther Christine. b 46. Moray Ho Coll of Educn DipEd67 Cartrefle Coll of Educn BEd80. St As Minl Tr Course 02. **d** 05 **p** 06. NSM Newtown w Llanllwchaiarn w Aberhafesp *St As* 05-07; NSM Llanllwchaiarn and Newtown w Aberhafesp from 07. *Gwawr-y-Grug, 7 Mill Fields, Milford, Newtown SY16 3JP* Tel (01686) 625559

YATES, Francis Edmund. b 49. Ox Univ BEd72 Sheff Univ MEd88. Linc Th Coll 95. **d** 95 **p** 96. C Chesterfield St Mary and All SS *Derby* 95-98; P-in-c Newlyn St Newlyn *Truro* 98-03; Dioc Adv for Schs and RE 98-03; P-in-c Tideswell *Derby* 03-11; V from 11; C Wormhill, Peak Forest w Peak Dale and Dove Holes 07-11. *The Vicarage, 6 Pursglove Drive, Tideswell, Buxton SK17 8PA* Tel (01298) 871317 E-mail fryates@msn.com

YATES, Miss Joanna Mary. b 49. St Anne's Coll Ox BA71 MA74 K Coll Lon PGCE72. S'wark Ord Course 89. **d** 91 **p** 94. Promotions and Publications Officer Nat Soc 85-95; Chapl Ch Ho Westmr 91-95; C Regent's Park St Mark *Lon* 91-95; C Finchley St Mary 95-01; TV Leeds City *Ripon* 01-09; rtd 09. *8 Frith Court, London NW7 1JP* Tel (020) 8349 1076 Mobile 07961-654430

YATES, Keith Leonard. b 36. K Coll Lon BD AKC61 Nottm Univ MPhil79. Wells Th Coll. **d** 69 **p** 70. C Luton Ch Ch *St Alb* 69-73; Hon C Luton St Andr 73-76; R Grimoldby w Manby *Linc* 76-80; P-in-c Yarburgh 76-78; R 78-80; P-in-c Alvingham w N and S Cockerington 76-78; V 78-80; P-in-c Gt w Lt Carlton 77-78; R 78-80; C Lect Sarum & Wells Th Coll 80-87; R Upper Chelsea H Trin *Lon* 87-96; rtd 96; Perm to Offic *Sarum* from 97. *50 Culverhayes, Beaminster DT8 3DG* Tel (01308) 863409

YATES, Lindsay Anne. b 69. Selw Coll Cam BA91 MA95 Univ of Wales (Lamp) MTh10 Barrister 92. Ripon Coll Cuddesdon BTh99. **d** 99 **p** 00. C Bampton w Clanfield *Ox* 99-02; Chapl Pemb Coll Cam 02-06; Chapl Westcott Ho Cam from 07. *Westcott House, Jesus Lane, Cambridge CB5 8BP,* or *The Vicarage, Church Hill, London N21 1JA* Tel (01223) 741014 *or* (020) 8886 3545 E-mail laa26@cam.ac.uk

YATES, Margaret. b 51. **d** 10 **p** 11. NSM W Woodhay w Enborne, Hampstead Marshall etc *Ox* 10-11; NSM Kintbury w Avington 10-11; NSM Walbury Beacon from 11. *5 Halfway Cottages, Bath Road, Newbury RG20 8NG* Tel (01488) 658092 E-mail m.h.yates@reading.ac.uk

YATES, Michael Anthony. b 48. Oak Hill Th Coll. **d** 82 **p** 83. C Hebburn St Jo *Dur* 82-85; C Sheldon *Birm* 85-87; V Lea Hall 87-92; TV Old Brampton and Loundsley Green *Derby* 92-98; V Loundsley Green 98-01; V Riddings and Ironville 01-07; P-in-c Seale and Lullington w Coton in the Elms 07-11; R from 11. *The Rectory, 24 Church Street, Netherseal, Swadlincote DE12 9AF* Tel (01283) 761179 E-mail mikeanbike@tiscali.co.uk

YATES, Michael Peter. b 47. JP91. Leeds Univ BA69 MA70 MPhil85 Potchefstroom Univ PhD03. Coll of Resurr Mirfield 69. **d** 71 **p** 72. C Crewe St Andr *Ches* 71-76; V Wheelock 76-79; Chapl Rainhill Hosp Liv 79-89; Chapl Barnsley Distr Gen Hosp 89-94; Chapl Barnsley Distr Gen Hosp NHS Trust 94-11; Chapl Barnsley Hosp NHS Foundn Trust 05-11; rtd 11. *40 Rainton Grove, Barnsley S75 2QZ* E-mail mpyates@hotmail.com

YATES, Paul David. b 47. Sussex Univ BA73 DPhil80. Sarum & Wells Th Coll 88. **d** 91 **p** 92. NSM Lewes All SS, St Anne, St Mich and St Thos *Chich* 91-00; NSM Lewes St Mich and St Thos at Cliffe w All SS 00-10; NSM Lewes St Anne and St Mich and St Thos etc from 10. *17 St Swithun's Terrace, Lewes BN7 1UJ* Tel (01273) 473463

YATES, Peter Francis. b 47. Sheff Univ BA69. Kelham Th Coll 69. **d** 74 **p** 75. C Mexborough *Sheff* 74-78; C Sevenoaks St Jo *Roch* 78-81; CSWG from 81; Lic to Offic Chich from 85. *The Monastery, Crawley Down, Crawley RH10 4LH* Tel (01342) 712074

YATES, Raymond Paul. b 55. Oak Hill Th Coll BA88. **d** 88 **p** 89. C Bootle St Mary w St Paul *Liv* 88-91; C Drypool *York* 91-92; TV 92-97; C Orpington All SS *Roch* 97-00; R Beeford w Frodingham and Foston *York* 00-06; RD N Holderness 02-06; Chapl HM Pris Hull 01-02; P-in-c Quinton Road W St Boniface *Birm* 06-09; V from 09. *The Vicarage, Quinton Road West, Birmingham B32 2QD* Tel 0121-427 8551 *or* 426 3166 E-mail raymondyates@btinternet.com

YATES, Richard. See YATES, Alan John Richard

YATES, Ricky. See YATES, Warwick John

YATES, Canon Roger Alan. b 47. Trin Coll Cam BA68 MA72 MB, BChir71 Bris Univ PhD75 MRCP77 FFPM93. NOC 84. **d** 87 **p** 88. NSM Wilmslow *Ches* from 87; Bp's Officer for NSM from 93; Hon Can Ches Cathl from 99; RD Knutsford from 06. *3 Racecourse Park, Wilmslow SK9 5LU* Tel (01625) 520246 E-mail raycandoc@yahoo.co.uk

YATES, Mrs Rosamund. b 63. Rob Coll Cam BA84 MA88. Oak Hill Th Coll BA93. **d** 93. C Holloway St Mary Magd *Lon* 93-95; NSM Tervuren w Liège *Eur* 95-97; NSM W Ealing St Jo w St Jas *Lon* 01-05; Perm to Offic *Eur* 05-08; NSM E Acton St Dunstan w St Thos *Lon* from 08. *14 Rosemount Road, London W3 9LR* Tel (020) 8993 6614 E-mail rosyates@tiscali.co.uk

YATES, Mrs Siân. b 57. Univ of Wales (Ban) Westmr Coll Ox MTh91. Linc Th Coll 78. **d** 80 **p** 94. C Risca *Mon* 80-83; Chapl Ch Hosp Horsham 83-85; TD Haverhill w Withersfield, the Wrattings etc *St E* 85-90; Dioc Youth Chapl *Cant* 90-93; Assoc Min Cant St Martin and St Paul 93-96; Educn Chapl *Worc* 96-03; P-in-c Dudley St Jas 96-03; P-in-c Dudley St Barn 01-02; P-in-c Tregony w St Cuby and Cornelly *Truro* from 03; Dioc Adv in RE from 03. *The Rectory, 18 Fore Street, Tregony, Truro TR2 5RN* Tel (01872) 530507 E-mail yatesasb@aol.com

YATES, Timothy Edward. b 35. Magd Coll Cam BA59 MA62 Uppsala Univ DTh78. Ridley Hall Cam 58. **d** 60 **p** 61. C Tonbridge SS Pet and Paul *Roch* 60-63; Tutor St Jo Coll Dur 63-71; Warden Cranmer Hall Dur 71-79; P-in-c Darley w S Darley *Derby* 79-82; R Darley 82-90; Dioc Dir of Ords 85-95; Hon Can Derby Cathl 89-00; C Ashford w Sheldon and Longstone 90-00; rtd 00; Perm to Offic *Derby* from 01; Hon Fell St Jo Coll Dur from 04. *Holly House, South Church Street, Bakewell DE45 1FD* Tel (01629) 812686

YATES, Timothy John Sturgis. b 56. Bradf Univ BTech83 Univ Coll Lon PhD86. ERMC 05. **d** 07 **p** 08. NSM Gt Chesham *Ox* from 07. *16 Chapmans Crescent, Chesham HP5 2QU* Tel (01494) 772914 Mobile 07802-155072 E-mail timyates3@btinternet.com

YATES, Warwick John (Ricky). b 52. Univ of Wales (Lamp) BA78. Wycliffe Hall Ox 87. **d** 89 **p** 90. C Hoddesdon *St Alb* 89-93; R Finmere w Mixbury, Cottisford, Hardwick etc *Ox* 93-95; R Shelswell 95-08; P-in-c Prague *Eur* from 08. *Pat'anka 2614/11B, Flat 7, 160 00 Praha 6 - Dejvice, Czech Republic* Tel (00420) (2) 3331 0266 E-mail chaplain@anglican.cz

YATES, William Herbert. b 35. Man Univ BA59. Chich Th Coll 60. **d** 61 **p** 62. C Blackpool St Steph *Blackb* 61-65; C Wednesbury St Jo *Lich* 65-69; V Porthill 69-78; R Norton in the Moors 78-84; R Church Aston 84-00; rtd 00; Perm to Offic *Lich* from 01. *83 Stallington Road, Blythe Bridge, Stoke-on-Trent ST11 9PD* Tel (01782) 397182

YATES, Mrs Yvonne Louise. b 52. NEOC 01. **d** 04 **p** 05. NSM Kirkbymoorside w Gillamoor, Farndale etc *York* 04-07; Chapl Oakhill Secure Tr Cen 07-08; Co-ord Chapl HM Pris Kirklevington Grange 08-11; TV Combe Martin, Berrynarbor, Lynton, Brendon etc *Ex* from 11. *The Rectory, Lee Road, Lynton EX35 6BP* Tel (01598) 753251 E-mail ylyates@btinternet.com

YAU, Timothy Sang. b 71. Ridley Hall Cam 06. **d** 08 **p** 09. C Farcet Hampton *Ely* from 08. *Church House, 40 Hargate Way, Hampton Hargate, Peterborough PE7 8DW* Tel (01733) 277863 *or* 567414 Mobile 07974-587841 E-mail tim.yau@ely.anglican.org

YEADON, Mrs Penelope Susan. b 60. NEOC 03. **d** 06 **p** 07. NSM Penhill *Ripon* from 06. *Dale Cottage, Aysgarth, Leyburn DL8 3AB* Tel (01969) 663505

YEADON, Ms Victoria Jane. b 69. Univ Coll Lon BSc91 MSc92 Anglia Ruskin Univ BA09. Ridley Hall Cam 07. **d** 09 **p** 10. C Deptford St Nic and St Luke *S'wark* from 09. *41 Creek Road, London SE8 3BU* Tel 07952-292113 (mobile) E-mail jane@deptfordchurch.org

YEARWOOD, Jean Cornilia. b 43. Heythrop Coll Lon MA05 RGN74 RM76. **d** 07 **p** 08. NSM Croydon Woodside *S'wark* from 07. *59 Bradley Road, London SE19 3NT* Tel (020) 8771 7743 E-mail j.yearwood@btopenworld.com

YEATS, Charles. b 56. Natal Univ BCom77 University of Natal MBA79 Ball Coll Ox MA85 K Coll Lon MTh90 Dur Univ PhD99. Wycliffe Hall Ox 85. **d** 87 **p** 88. C Islington St Mary *Lon* 87-90; Research Fell Whitefield Inst Ox 90-92; Chapl and Fell Univ Coll Dur 92-00; Perm to Offic *Dur* 00-08. *328 Archery Rise, Durham DH1 4LA* Tel 0191-384 0606

YELDHAM, Anthony Paul Richard. See KYRIAKIDES-YELDHAM, Anthony Paul Richard

YELDHAM, Denise. b 51. Leeds Univ BSc72 MB, ChB75 Univ of Wales (Lamp) MA08 MRCPsych80. Westcott Ho Cam 06. **d** 08. C Plymstock and Hooe *Ex* 08-11. *14 Neville House, 19 Page Street, London SW1P 4JX* Tel 07980-689851 (mobile) E-mail denise.yeldham@btinternet.com

YELLAND, Jeffrey Charles. b 46. CEng MIStructE72. STETS 98. **d** 01 **p** 02. NSM Effingham w Lt Bookham *Guildf* 01-04; NSM Dorking St Paul from 04. *32 Hookfield, Epsom KT19 8JG* Tel and fax (01372) 807096 Mobile 07918-030513 E-mail jeff@stpaulsdorking.org.uk

YENDALL, John Edward Thomas. b 52. St Jo Coll Dur BA88. Cranmer Hall Dur 84. d 88 p 89. C Bangor 88-90; C Botwnnog 90-91; R Trefdraeth w Aberffraw etc 91-01; RD Malltraeth 97-01; V Llanwddyn and Llanfihangel-yng-Nghwynfa etc *St As* 01-07; V Llanrhaeadr ym Mochnant etc 07-11; P-in-c Llansantffraid Glyn Ceirog and Llanarmon etc from 11. *The Vicarage, High Street, Glyn Ceiriog, Llangollen LL20 7EH* Tel (01691) 718425

✠YEOMAN, The Rt Revd David. b 44. St Mich Coll Llan 66. d 70 p 71 c 04. C Cardiff St Jo *Llan* 70-72; C Caerphilly 72-76; V Ystrad Rhondda w Ynyscynon 76-81; V Mountain Ash 81-96; Br Coity w Nolton 96-04; Can Llan Cathl 00-09; Asst Bp Llan 04-09; Adn Morgannwg 04-06; rtd 09. *4 Llety Gwyn, Bridgend CF31 1RG* Tel (01656) 649919 Mobile 07971-926631

YEOMAN, Douglas. b 35. ACII63. d 77 p 78. NSM Edin St Martin 77-96; NSM Edin St Luke 79-90; Chapl Edinburgh Healthcare NHS Trust 95-99; Chapl Lothian Primary Healthcare NHS Trust 98-06; NSM Edin St Cuth 96-06; Lic to Offic from 06. *6 Craiglockhart Crescent, Edinburgh EH14 1EY* Tel 0131-443 5449 E-mail d.yeoman@tiscali.co.uk

YEOMAN, Miss Ruth Jane. b 60. Sheff Univ BSc82 MSc85 Dur Univ PGCE83. Ripon Coll Cuddesdon BA90 MA94. d 91 p 94. C Coleshill *Birm* 91-95; C Hodge Hill 95-01; Bp's Adv for Children's Work 95-01; L'Arche Lambeth Community 01-03; Perm to Offic *S'wark* 01-03 and *Birm* 03; V Menston w Woodhead *Bradf* from 03. *The Vicarage, 12 Fairfax Gardens, Menston, Ilkley LS29 6ET* Tel (01943) 877739 *or* 872433 Mobile 07752-912646 E-mail vicar@stjohnmenston.org.uk *or* ruthjyeoman@hotmail.com

YEOMANS, Robert John. b 44. AKC66. d 67 p 68. C Pontesbury I and II *Heref* 67-70; Asst Youth Officer *St Alb* 70-72; Project Officer (Dio St Alb) Gen Syn Bd of Educn 73-77; V Is of Dogs Ch Ch and St Jo w St Luke *Lon* 77-87; V Waterloo St Jo w St Andr *S'wark* 87-93; Chapl United Bris Healthcare NHS Trust 93-02; Chapl Ex Hospiscare 02-06; rtd 06; Perm to Offic *Truro* from 02. *The White Barn, Maxworthy, Launceston PL15 8LY* Tel (01566) 781570 E-mail r.yeomans@virgin.net

YERBURGH, Canon David Savile. b 34. Magd Coll Cam BA57 MA61. Wells Th Coll 57. d 59 p 60. C Cirencester *Glouc* 59-63; C Bitterne Park *Win* 63-67; V Churchdown St Jo *Glouc* 67-74; RD Glouc N 73-74; V Charlton Kings St Mary 74-85; R Minchinhampton 85-95; Hon Can Glouc Cathl 86-95; rtd 95; Perm to Offic *Sarum* from 95. *2 Mill Race Close, Mill Road, Salisbury SP2 7RX* Tel (01722) 320064

YERBURGH, Peter Charles. b 31. Magd Coll Cam BA53 MA57. Wells Th Coll 53. d 55 p 56. C Southbroom *Sarum* 55-58; Chapl Wells Cathl Sch 58-71; Chapl Durlston Court Sch 71-91; rtd 91. *2 Mill Race Close, Mill Road, Salisbury SP2 7RX* Tel (01722) 327796

YERBURY, Gregory Howard. b 67. Trin Coll Bris BA93. St Jo Coll Nottm 94. d 96 p 97. C Crofton *Portsm* 96-00; P-in-c Bolton St Jo *Man* 00-06; P-in-c Bolton Breightmet St Jas 05-06; TR Leverhulme 06-11; TR Penkridge *Lich* from 11. *The Rectory, New Road, Penkridge, Stafford ST19 5DN* Tel (01785) 714344

YEWDALL, Mrs Mary Doreen. b 23. Nottm Univ DipEd71 BTh85. EMMTC 76. dss 79 d 87 p 94. Kirkby in Ashfield St Thos *S'well* 79-81; Daybrook 81-87; Par Dn 87-89; rtd 89; Hon Par Dn Bilsthorpe *S'well* 89-91; Hon Par Dn Eakring 89-91; Hon Par Dn Winkburn 89-91; Hon Par Dn Maplebeck 89-91; NSM Norton juxta Malton *York* 92-95; NSM Whitwell w Crambe, Flaxton, Foston etc 95-98; Perm to Offic from 98. *4 Dulverton Hall, Esplanade, Scarborough YO11 2AR* Tel (01723) 340130

YIEND, Paul Martin. b 57. UEA BA80. St Jo Coll Nottm MA96. d 92 p 94. C Bushbury *Lich* 92-95; Asst Chapl Brussels *Eur* 99-00; P-in-c Charleroi 00-03; P-in-c Liège from 00. *rue Basse des Canes 11, 5300 Andenne, Belgium* Tel and fax (0032) (85) 844482 E-mail paul.yiend@skynet.be

YILDIRIM, Engin. d 07 p 08. C Istanbul *Eur* from 07. *Swedish Chapel of Istanbul, Seraskerci Çikmazi, No 9, Beyoglu, Istanbul, Turkey* E-mail beyogluanglican@yahoo.com

YONG, Sok Han. b 61. Malaysia Th Sem BTheol86. d 10 p 11. NSM Ox St Aldate 10-11; NSM Abingdon from 11. *Address temp unknown*

YONGE, James Mohun (Brother Amos). b 47. Keele Univ BA71. WMMTC 91. d 94 p 95. SSF from 76. *The Friary, Hilfield, Dorchester DT2 7BE* Tel (01300) 341345 Fax 341293

✠YOON, The Rt Revd Paul Hwan. b 38. d 67 c 82. Bp Taejon 87-02; Presiding Bp Korea 00-02; rtd 02. *PO Box 22, Taejon 300-600, Republic of Korea* Tel (0082) (42) 256 9987 Fax 255 8918

YORK, Canon Humphrey Bowmar. b 28. St Chad's Coll Dur BA54 Univ of Wales (Lamp) MA04. d 55 p 56. C Beamish *Dur* 55-57; C Tettenhall Regis *Lich* 57-62; P-in-c Lansallos w Pelynt *Truro* 62-63; R Lanreath 62-67; V Pelynt 63-67; P-in-c Lanlivery 67-74; P-in-c Luxulyan 67-74; P-in-c Lanlivery w Luxulyan 74-83; RD Bodmin 76-82; R Antony w Sheviock 83-93; Hon

Can Truro Cathl 90-93; rtd 93; Perm to Offic *Truro* and *Sarum* from 93. *8 Huntingdon Street, Bradford-on-Avon BA15 1RF* E-mail canonhumphrey@tinyworld.co.uk

YORK, Archbishop of. See SENTAMU, The Most Revd and Rt Hon John Tucker Mugabi

YORK, Archdeacon of. See SEED, The Ven Richard Murray Crosland

YORK, Dean of. See JONES, The Very Revd Keith Brynmor

YORKE, John Andrew. b 47. Cranmer Hall Dur 70. d 73 p 74. C Spitalfields Ch Ch w All SS *Lon* 73-78; R Tuktoyaktuk Canada 78-88; R Fort Mcpherson 89-92; V Totland Bay *Portsm* from 92; V Thorley from 95. *The Vicarage, Alum Bay New Road, Totland Bay PO39 0ES* Tel (01983) 752031 E-mail andy.yorke@lineone.net

YORKE, The Very Revd Michael Leslie. b 39. Magd Coll Cam BA62 MA66. Cuddesdon Coll 62. d 64 p 65. C Croydon St Jo *Cant* 64-68; Succ Chelmsf Cathl 68-69; Prec and Chapl 69-73; Dep Dir Cathl Cen for Research and Tr 72-74; P-in-c Ashdon w Hadstock 74-76; R 76-78; Can Res Chelmsf Cathl 78-88; Vice-Provost 84-88; P-in-c N Lynn w St Marg and St Nic *Nor* 88-92; P-in-c King's Lynn St Marg w St Nic 92-94; Chmn Dioc Adv Bd for Min 90-94; Hon Can Nor Cathl 93-94; Provost Portsm 94-99; Dean Lich 99-04; rtd 04; Perm to Offic *Nor* from 04. *Westgate House, The Green, Burnham Market, King's Lynn PE31 8HD* Tel (01328) 738833

YORKSTONE, Peter. b 48. Loughb Univ BTech72. Oak Hill Th Coll 79. d 81 p 82. C Blackpool St Thos *Blackb* 81-85; V Copp 85-00; P-in-c Giggleswick and Rathmell w Wigglesworth *Bradf* 00-07; V Kettlewell w Conistone, Hubberholme etc from 07. *The Vicarage, Westgate, Kettlewell, Skipton BD23 5QU* Tel (01756) 760237 E-mail peter.yorkstone@bradford.anglican.org

YOUATT, Jennifer Alison. See MONTGOMERY, Canon Jennifer Alison

YOUDE, Paul Crosland. b 47. Birm Univ LLB68. WEMTC 93. d 96 p 97. NSM Cheltenham St Luke and St Jo *Glouc* 96-99; C Cirencester 99-03; P-in-c Lydney 03-09; P-in-c Woolaston w Alvington and Aylburton 07-09; rtd 09; Hon C Kemble, Poole Keynes, Somerford Keynes etc *Glouc* from 09. *The Vicarage, Church Road, Kemble, Cirencester GL7 6AG* Tel (01285) 770049 E-mail paul.youde@btinternet.com

YOUELL, Mrs Deborah Mary. b 57. STETS 01. d 04. NSM Cowplain *Portsm* 04-08; NSM Crookhorn from 08. *42 The Yews, Horndean, Waterlooville PO8 0BH* Tel (023) 9279 9946 E-mail deborah.youell@ntlworld.com

YOUENS, Edward. See MONTAGUE-YOUENS, Canon Hubert Edward

YOUINGS, Adrian. b 65. Ex Univ BSc86 Bath Univ PhD90. Wycliffe Hall Ox 93. d 96 p 97. C Dorking St Paul *Guildf* 96-99; C S Croydon Em *S'wark* 99-03; R Trull w Angersleigh *B & W* from 03. *The Rectory, Wild Oak Lane, Trull, Taunton TA3 7JT* Tel (01823) 253518

YOULD, Guy Martin. b 37. Keble Coll Ox BA61 MA65 Magd Coll Ox BD68 Hull Univ PhD80 Lambeth STh75 FSAScot75. St Steph Ho Ox 61. d 63 p 64. C Middlesbrough St Jo the Ev *York* 63-65; Chapl Magd Coll and C Cowley St Jo *Ox* 65-68; Asst Chapl Radley Coll 68-71; C W Kirby St Bridget *Ches* 71-74; Chapl Loretto Sch Musselburgh 74; V Liscard St Mary w St Columba *Ches* 74-78; St Barn Coll Belair Australia 78-80; C Doncaster St Leon and St Jude *Sheff* 80-81; V Brodsworth w Hooton Pagnell, Frickley etc 81-87; Chapl St Mary's Sch Wantage 87-93; R Chapel Chorlton, Maer and Whitmore *Lich* 93-98; P-in-c Altarnon w Bolventor, Laneast and St Clether *Truro* 98-02; P-in-c Lezant 98-02; rtd 03; C Gt and Lt Torrington and Frithelstock *Ex* 03-05; P-in-c Bishopstone *Chich* from 05. *The Vicarage, Bishopstone, Seaford BN25 2UD* Tel (01323) 892972

YOUNG, Andrew Charles. b 54. FIBMS83. NOC 98. d 01 p 02. C Heywood *Man* 01-05; TV Eccles from 05. *St Paul's Vicarage, Egerton Road, Eccles, Manchester M30 9LR* Tel 0161-789 2420 E-mail andrew.young66@ntlworld.com

YOUNG, Andrew John. b 50. St Jo Coll Dur BA73. Westcott Ho Cam 73. d 75 p 89. C Nailsworth *Glouc* 75-76; NSM Yeovil w Kingston Pitney *B & W* 89-93; NSM Tintinhull w Chilthorne Domer, Yeovil Marsh etc from 93. *15 Cook Avenue, Chard TA20 2JR* Tel (01460) 62182

YOUNG, Miss Anne Patricia. b 44. Cov Coll of Educn CertEd66 Leeds Univ BEd76 Sheff Univ MEd82 Liv Univ BTh05. NOC 01. d 05 p 06. NSM Middlestown *Wakef* 05-10; NSM Emley from 11; NSM Flockton cum Denby Grange from 11. *58 The Crofts, Emley, Huddersfield HD8 9RU* Tel and fax (01924) 840738 Mobile 07906-835309 E-mail anne@ayoung94.fsbusiness.co.uk

YOUNG, Arthur. b 65. Belf Bible Coll BTh92. CITC 99. d 01 p 02. C Donaghadee *D & D* 01-04; I Tullylish from 04. *Tullylish Rectory, 100 Banbridge Road, Gilford, Craigavon BT63 6DL* Tel and fax (028) 3883 1298

YOUNG, Canon Brian Thomas. b 42. Linc Th Coll 67. d 70 p 71. C Monkseaton St Mary *Newc* 70-73; C Berwick H Trin 73-77; P-in-c Gt Broughton *Carl* 77-80; V Gt Broughton and

Broughton Moor 80-83; V Chorley *Ches* 83-90; V Alderley Edge 90-07; RD Knutsford 96-06; Hon Can Ches Cathl 97-07; rtd 07. *6 St Denys Avenue, Sleaford NG34 8AR* Tel (01529) 306332 E-mail byoung@alderley.fsworld.co.uk

YOUNG, Canon Charles John. b 24. Open Univ BA98. Qu Coll Birm 52. **d** 55 **p** 56. C Dudley St Thos *Worc* 55-58; C Beeston *S'well* 58-61; V Lady Bay 61-66; R Kirkby in Ashfield 66-75; V Balderton 75-92; RD Newark 82-90; Hon Can S'well Minster 84-92; rtd 92; Bp's Chapl for Rtd Clergy *S'well* 92-04; Perm to Offic from 04. *9 The Paddocks, Newark NG24 1SS* Tel (01636) 613445

YOUNG, Christopher Terence. b 53. Cape Town Univ BA76 UNISA BTh80. St Bede's Coll Umtata 79. **d** 80 **p** 81. S Africa 80-86 and from 88; C Rainham *Chelmsf* 86-88. *Riversong Cottage, 11 Church Street, Villiersdorp, 6848 South Africa* Tel and fax (0027) (28) 840 0841 Mobile 82-377 8401

✠**YOUNG, The Rt Revd Clive.** b 48. St Jo Coll Dur BA70. Ridley Hall Cam 70. **d** 72 **p** 73 **c** 99. C Neasden cum Kingsbury St Cath *Lon* 72-75; C Hammersmith St Paul 75-79; P-in-c Old Ford St Paul w St Steph 79-82; V Old Ford St Paul w St Steph and St Mark 82-92; AD Tower Hamlets 88-92; Adn Hackney 92-99; V St Andr Holborn 92-99; Suff Bp Dunwich *St E* from 99. *28 Westerfield Road, Ipswich IP4 2UJ* Tel (01473) 222276 Fax 210303 E-mail bishop.clive@stedmundsbury.anglican.org

YOUNG, Daniel George Harding. b 52. New Coll Ox BA73 MA83 Westmr Coll Ox PGCE74. Cranmer Hall Dur 77. **d** 80 **p** 81. C Bushbury *Lich* 80-83; Chapl Dean Close Sch Cheltenham 83-99; Titus Trust 99-10; Perm to Offic *Win* 01-10; C Knutsford St Jo and Toft *Ches* from 10. *35 Beggarmans Lane, Knutsford WA16 9BA* Tel (01565) 228216 Mobile 0/9/4-945651 E-mail dan-young@tiscali.co.uk

YOUNG, David. b 37. STh79 Open Univ PhD89. Ely Th Coll 61 Linc Th Coll 64. **d** 67 **p** 68. C Crofton *Wakef* 67-68; C Heckmondwike 68-71; V Stainland 71-76; R Patrington w Winestead *York* 76-80; Chapl Winestead Hosp 76-80; Gen Preacher *Linc* from 80; Chapl St Jo Hosp Linc 80-90; Chapl N Lincs Mental Health Unit 90-93; Chapl Linc Distr Healthcare NHS Trust 93-97; Dep Chapl 98-04; rtd 04. *Westview, Aisthorpe, Lincoln LN1 2SG* Tel (01522) 730912

YOUNG, David Charles. b 54. Open Univ BA95 PGCE97 CQSW82. SEITE 03. **d** 06 **p** 07. NSM Haywards Heath St Wilfrid *Chich* from 06. *4 Ashurst Place, Heath Road, Haywards Heath RH16 3EJ* Tel (01444) 416074 Mobile 07921-144480 E-mail youngshouse1@yahoo.co.uk

YOUNG, David John. b 43. Nottm Univ BA64 MPhil89 Lambeth STh87. Coll of Resurr Mirfield 64. **d** 66 **p** 67. C Warsop *S'well* 66-68; C Harworth 68-71; P-in-c Hackenthorpe Ch Ch *Derby* 71-73; TV Frecheville and Hackenthorpe 73-75; V Chaddesden St Phil 75-83; R Narborough and Huncote *Leic* 83-89; RD Guthlaxton I 87-90; Chapl Leic Univ 90-95; V Eyres Monsell 95-98; Perm to Offic 98-99; rtd 03. *57 Castle Fields, Leicester LE4 1AN* Tel 0116-236 5634

YOUNG, David Lun Ming. b 81. Leeds Univ BA02 St Jo Coll Dur BA09. Cranmer Hall Dur 07. **d** 10 **p** 11. C Upper Armley *Ripon* from 10. *50 Lane End, Pudsey, Leeds LS28 9AD* Tel 07736-678558 (mobile) E-mail revdaveyoung@gmail.com

YOUNG, Derek John. b 42. St D Coll Lamp. **d** 73 **p** 74. C Griffithstown *Mon* 73-76; C Ebbw Vale 76-77; V Penmaen 77-81; V Penmaen and Crumlin 81-87; Chapl Oakdale Hosp Gwent 83-87; V New Tredegar *Mon* 87-99; V Llanfihangel Crucorney w Oldcastle etc from 99. *The Vicarage, Llanfihangel Crucorney, Abergavenny NP7 8DH* Tel (01873) 890349

YOUNG, George William. b 31. Lon Coll of Div ALCD55. **d** 56 **p** 57. C Everton Em *Liv* 56-58; C Halliwell St Pet *Man* 58-61; V Newburn *Newc* 61-67; P-in-c Tyler's Green *Ox* 67-69; V 69-80; Lic to Offic 80-84; Area Sec (W England) SAMS 80-84; Hon C Purley Ch Ch *S'wark* 84-87; V Beckenham St Jo *Roch* 87-92; rtd 92; Perm to Offic *S'wark* from 92. *9 Shortacres, High Street, Nutfield, Redhill RH1 4HJ* Tel (01737) 822363

YOUNG, Mrs Hilary Antoinette Francesca. b 57. **d** 01 **p** 02. NSM Thorne *Sheff* 01-03; C 03-05; V Wigan St Jas w St Thos *Liv* from 05. *97 Melrose Drive, Wigan WN3 6EG* Tel (01942) 225311 E-mail hyoung.youngvic@virgin.net

YOUNG, Hyacinth Loretta. b 49. NTMTC 95. **d** 98 **p** 99. NSM Harlesden All So *Lon* 98-00; TV Wembley Park from 00. *The Vicarage, 194 Windermere Avenue, Wembley HA9 8QT* Tel (020) 8908 2252 E-mail hyacinth512@aol.com

YOUNG, Iain Clavering. b 56. Newc Poly BA79. Coll of Resurr Mirfield 80. **d** 83 **p** 84. C Wallsend St Luke *Newc* 83-86; C Horton 86-87; V 87-92; V Friern Barnet St Pet le Poer *Lon* 92-95; C Holborn St Alb w Saffron Hill St Pet 96-97; P-in-c Hoxton H Trin w St Mary 97-02; V 02-09; Chapl Moorfields Eye Hosp NHS Trust 97-03; P-in-c Lavender Hill Ascension etc *S'wark* from 09. *The Clergy House, Pountney Road, London SW11 5TU* Tel (020) 7228 5340 E-mail iain.young@ifightpoverty.com

YOUNG, Jeremy Michael. b 54. Ch Coll Cam BA76 MA80 Lon Univ MTh94. Coll of Resurr Mirfield 78. **d** 80 **p** 81. C Whitworth w Spennymoor *Dur* 80-83; C Boxmoor St Jo *St Alb* 83-86; V Croxley Green St Oswald 86-94; Dir Past Studies CITC

94-99; Lic to Offic *D & G* 99-03; Perm to Offic *B & W* from 06. *Westerley House, Tellisford, Bath BA2 7RL* Tel (01373) 830920 E-mail jeremy_young@mac.com

YOUNG, John. *See* YOUNG, David John

YOUNG, Canon John David. b 37. Lon Univ BD65 Sussex Univ MA77. Clifton Th Coll 62. **d** 65 **p** 66. C Plymouth St Jude *Ex* 65-68; Hd of RE Northgate Sch Ipswich 68-71; Chapl and Sen Lect Bp Otter Coll Chich 71-81; Chapl and Sen Lect W Sussex Inst of HE 77-81; Chapl and Sen Lect York St Jo Coll 81-87; C York St Paul 87-88; Dioc Ev 88-02; Can and Preb York Minster 92-03; Miss Strategy Development Officer 00-02; rtd 02; Lic to Offic *York* 02-10; Perm to Offic from 10. *72 Middlethorpe Grove, York YO24 1JY* Tel (01904) 704195 E-mail john.young@yorkcourses.co.uk

YOUNG, John Kenneth. Edin Th Coll 62. **d** 64 **p** 65. C Gosforth All SS *Newc* 64-67; C Newc St Gabr 67-69; R Bowers Gifford *Chelmsf* 69-72; R Bowers Gifford w N Benfleet 72-75; P-in-c Kirkwhelpington *Newc* 75-79; P-in-c Kirkharle 77-79; P-in-c Kirkheaton 75-79; P-in-c Cambo 77-79; V Kirkwhelpington, Kirkharle, Kirkheaton and Cambo 79-82; V Gosforth St Nic 82-92; V Healey and Slaley 92-97; rtd 97; Perm to Offic *Newc* from 97. *1 Raynes Close, Morpeth NE61 2XX* Tel (01670) 515191

YOUNG, John Robert. b 43. SSM 63. **d** 68 **p** 69. C Ch Ch Cathl Darwin Australia 68-70; C Murrumbeena 70-72; C Stocking Farm *Leic* 72-74; P-in-c W Reservoir Australia 75-78; I Montmorency 78-85; I E Burwood 85-96; R Warracknabeal 96-00; R Port Fairy 00-05; R Yea from 05. *St Luke's Rectory, Pellisier Street, PO Box 60, Yea Vic 3717, Australia* Tel (0061) (3) 5797 2281 Fax 5797 2082

YOUNG, Canon Jonathan Frederick. b 25. Univ of Wales (Lamp) BA51 Birm Univ MA81. St Mich Coll Llan 51. **d** 53 **p** 54. C Roath St Martin *Llan* 53-59; Lic to Offic *Ox* 59-74; SSJE 62-71; Bp's Chapl for Community Relns *Birm* 71-74; Chapl Coun for Soc Resp 74-85; Hon Can Birm Cathl 84-85; USA from 85; rtd 90. *1573 Cambridge Street, Apt 606, Cambridge MA 02138-4377, USA* Tel (001) (617) 945 1072 E-mail youngmj@aol.com

YOUNG, Canon Jonathan Priestland. b 44. AKC68. **d** 69 **p** 70. C Clapham H Trin *S'wark* 69-73; C Mitcham St Mark 73-74; V Godmanchester *Ely* 74-82; P-in-c Cambridge St Giles w St Pet 82; P-in-c Chesterton St Luke 82; TR Cambridge Ascension 82-01; Chapl St Jo Coll Sch Cam 88-93; P-in-c Ellington *Ely* 01-02; P-in-c Grafham 01-02; P-in-c Easton 01-02; P-in-c Spaldwick w Barham and Woolley 01-02; R E Leightonstone from 02; P-in-c Alconbury cum Weston 04-11; P-in-c Buckworth 04-11; P-in-c Hamerton 09-11; P-in-c Winwick 09-11; P-in-c Gt w Lt Gidding and Steeple Gidding 09-11; RD Leightonstone 02-04; Hon Can Ely Cathl from 01. *The Rectory, Parson's Drive, Ellington, Huntingdon PE28 0AU,* or *15 Causeway, Godmanchester, Huntingdon PE29 2HA* Tel and fax (01480) 891695 *or* tel 453350 E-mail jonathan.young@ely.anglican.org

YOUNG, Karen Heather. *See* ROSS, Mrs Karen Heather

YOUNG, Kathleen Margaret. *See* BROWN, Mrs Kathleen Margaret

YOUNG, Kenneth. *See* YOUNG, John Kenneth

YOUNG, Leonard Thomas. b 55. Ches Coll of HE BTh04 Leeds Univ MA06. Coll of Resurr Mirfield 04. **d** 06 **p** 07. C Failsworth H Family *Man* 06-09; P-in-c Man Clayton St Cross w St Paul from 09. *St Cross Rectory, 54 Clayton Hall Road, Manchester M11 4WH* Tel 0161-223 0766 E-mail frleonardyoung@aol.com

YOUNG, Mrs Margaret Elizabeth. b 66. Open Univ BSc00. SNWTP 07. **d** 10 **p** 11. NSM Wythenshawe *Man* from 10. *8 Bronington Close, Manchester M22 4ZQ* Tel 0161-945 9864 E-mail margareteyoung@btopenworld.com

YOUNG, Martin Edward. b 20. Oriel Coll Ox BA41 MA45. Cuddesdon Coll 41. **d** 43 **p** 44. C Newbury *Ox* 43-45; C Wymondham *Nor* 45-49; C Gt Berkhamsted *St Alb* 49-51; V Littlemore *Ox* 51-64; R Wootton w Quinton *Pet* 64-72; R Wootton w Quinton and Preston Deanery 72-78; V Welford w Sibbertoft 78-82; V Welford w Sibbertoft and Marston Trussell 82-88; rtd 88; Perm to Offic *Pet* 88-98. *2 Knutsford Lane, Long Buckby, Northampton NN6 7RL* Tel (01327) 843929

YOUNG, Martin John. b 72. Univ Coll Lon BSc93. Oak Hill Th Coll BA01. **d** 01 **p** 02. C Heigham H Trin *Nor* 01-05; P-in-c Nor St Andr from 05. *24 Carnoustie, Norwich NR4 6AY* Tel (01603) 498821 E-mail martin@standrewsnorwich.org *or* mjy@ntlworld.com

YOUNG, Mrs Maureen. b 47. SEITE 02. **d** 04. NSM Roughey *Chich* 04-11; NSM Rusper w Colgate from 11. *29 Badgers Close, Horsham RH12 5RU* Tel (01403) 263119 E-mail deaconmaureen@googlemail.com

YOUNG, Maurice. *See* YOUNG, William Maurice

YOUNG, Max Jonathan. b 49. **d** 07 **p** 07. NSM Filey *York* 06-10; Perm to Offic *Ox* from 10. *8 Eastfield Court, Church Street, Faringdon SN7 8SL* Tel (01367) 243120 E-mail max1234@btinternet.com

YOUNG, Norman Keith. b 35. EAMTC 85. **d** 87 **p** 88. C Burwell *Ely* 87-91; V Swaffham Bulbeck and Swaffham Prior w Reach

91-92; V Barnby Dun *Sheff* 92-05; Ind Chapl 92-05; AD Doncaster 98-04; rtd 05; P-in-c Aspull St Eliz *Liv* 05-06; Hon C Haigh and Aspull from 06. *97 Melrose Drive, Wigan WN3 6EG* Tel (01942) 225311 E-mail norman@youngvic.u-net.com

YOUNG, Peter John. b 26. Pemb Coll Cam BA49 MA54. Ridley Hall Cam 49. **d** 51 **p** 52. C Cheadle *Ches* 51-54; Malaya 54-63; Malaya from 63; rtd 92. *247 Jalan 5l48, 46000 Petaling Jaya, Selangor, Malaysia* Tel (0060) (3) 7782 9269 Fax 7783 0849

YOUNG, Philip Anderson. b 53. St Jo Coll Dur BA75 Fitzw Coll Cam BA78 MA89. Ridley Hall Cam 75. **d** 78 **p** 79. C Surbiton St Andr and St Mark *S'wark* 78-80; NSM Aylsham *Nor* 04-05; C Bressingham w N and S Lopham and Fersfield 05-07; C Roydon St Remigius 05-07; V Heigham St Thos from 07. *St Thomas's Vicarage, 77 Edinburgh Road, Norwich NR2 3RL* Tel (01603) 624390 E-mail philipyoung@btinternet.com

YOUNG, Rachel Elizabeth. b 61. Man Univ MusB82 Leeds Univ MA09 Lon Inst of Educn PGCE84. NOC 06. **d** 09 **p** 10. NSM Beverley Minster *York* from 09. *Monument House, 4 King Street, Woodmansey, Beverley HU17 0TE* Tel (01482) 861883 E-mail rachel.e.young@tesco.net

YOUNG, Richard Christian. b 65. Southn Univ LLB87 Solicitor 91. St Jo Coll Nottm 02. **d** 04 **p** 05. C Alperton *Lon* 04-07; V Yiewsley from 07. *St Matthew's Vicarage, 93 High Street, Yiewsley, West Drayton UB7 7QH* Tel (01895) 442093 Mobile 07886-782473 E-mail richard@theyoungones.org.uk

YOUNG, Richard Michael. b 63. **d** 96 **p** 97. NSM Brunswick *Man* from 96. *2 Birch Grove, Rusholme, Manchester M14 5JY* Tel 0161-225 0884 Mobile 07778-817784 E-mail richard_young@3igroup.com

YOUNG, Robert William. b 47. MRTPI73. Cranmer Hall Dur 10. **d** 11. NSM Owlerton *Sheff* from 11. *101 Carr Road, Sheffield S6 2WY* Tel 0114-231 3036 E-mail robwyoung101@gmail.com

YOUNG, Stephen. b 33. St Edm Hall Ox MA61. St Jo Coll Nottm 75 ALCD77. **d** 77 **p** 78. C Crofton *Portsm* 77-81; C Rainham *Chelmsf* 81-87; V Ramsgate Ch Ch *Cant* 87-98; rtd 98; Perm to Offic *Cant* from 98. *9 Egerton Drive, Cliftonville, Margate CT9 9YE* Tel (01843) 223071

YOUNG, Stephen Edward. b 52. K Coll Lon BD73 AKC73 Ch Ch Coll Cant CertEd74 Open Univ PhD04. **d** 75 **p** 76. C Walton St Mary *Liv* 75-79; C St Marylebone All SS *Lon* 83; C Pimlico St Gabr 83-85; Chapl Whitelands Coll of HE *S'wark* 85-88; Asst Chapl St Paul's Sch Barnes 88-91; Chapl 91-02; Chapl Dulwich Coll 02-11; Hon C Pimlico St Mary Bourne Street *Lon* 94-11; C Wilton Place St Paul from 11; P in from 91. *Flat 7, 32-33 Wilton Place, London SW1X 8SH* Tel (020) 7201 9996 E-mail stephen@spkb.org

YOUNG, Steven Peter. b 81. Lon Inst BA02 Leeds Univ BA07 MA08. Coll of Resurr Mirfield 05. **d** 08 **p** 09. C W Hendon St Jo *Lon* 08-11; P-in-c Mill Hill St Mich from 11; C Mill Hill Jo Keble Ch from 11. *St Michael's Vicarage, 9 Flower Lane, London NW7 2JA* Tel (020) 8959 1857 Mobile 07590-636912 E-mail steven_young81@hotmail.com

YOUNG, Stuart Kincaid. b 59. **d** 95 **p** 96. C Letchworth St Paul w Willian *St Alb* 95-00; V Pucklechurch and Abson *Bris* from 00. *The Vicarage, Westerleigh Road, Pucklechurch, Bristol BS16 9RD* Tel 0117-937 2260 E-mail vicar@pucklechurchandabson.org.uk

YOUNG, William Maurice. b 32. St Jo Coll Nottm 80. **d** 81 **p** 82. C Harlescott *Lich* 81-84; V Hadley 84-94; rtd 94; Perm to Offic *Heref* from 94. *Old Chapel School, Newport Street, Clun, Craven Arms SY7 8JZ* Tel (01588) 640846

YOUNGER, Jeremy Andrew. b 46. Nottm Univ BA68 Bris Univ MA71. Wells Th Coll 68. **d** 70 **p** 71. C Basingstoke *Win* 70-74; C Harpenden St Nic *St Alb* 74-76; Dir Communications 77-81; Chapl Sarum & Wells Th Coll 77-81; V Clifton All SS w St Jo *Bris* 81-84; Relig Affairs Producer BBC Radio Nottm *S'well* 84-86; C Bow w Bromley St Leon *Lon* 86-88; Projects and Min Manager Westmr St Jas 89-93; Hon C St Marylebone All SS 89-93; New Zealand from 93. *1l102 Valley Road, Mount Eden, Auckland 1024, New Zealand* Tel (0064) (9) 630 7867 E-mail jeremyyounger@clear.net.nz

YOUNGS, Denise. WMMTC. **d** 09 **p** 10. NSM Lich St Mich w St Mary and Wall from 09. *10 Tame Avenue, Burntwood WS7 9JQ* Tel (01543) 672646

YOUNGS-DUNNETT, Elizabeth Nigella. b 43. **d** 05 **p** 06. OLM Alde River *St E* from 05. *The Cottage, Ship Corner, Blaxhall, Woodbridge IP12 2DY* Tel (01728) 688248

YOUNGSON, David Thoms. b 38. Cuddesdon Coll 71. **d** 73 **p** 74. C Norton St Mary *Dur* 73-76; C Hartlepool St Paul 76-79; P-in-c Stockton St Jo CD 79-84; V Stockton St Jo 84-86; V Owton Manor 86-90; rtd 90; Perm to Offic *Dur* 90-99. *35 Buxton Gardens, Billingham TS22 5AJ*

YULE, John David. b 49. G&C Coll Cam BA70 MA74 PhD76. Westcott Ho Cam 79. **d** 81 **p** 82. C Cherry Hinton St Andr *Ely* 81-84; C Almondbury w Farnley Tyas *Wakef* 84-87; V Swavesey *Ely* 87-95; V Fen Drayton w Conington 87-95; R Fen Drayton w Conington and Lolworth etc from 95. *The Vicarage, Honey Hill,*

Fen Drayton, Cambridge CB24 4SF Tel (01954) 231903 Fax 202816 E-mail vicar@honeyhill.org

YULE, Robert White. b 49. FCMA81. St Jo Coll Nottm. **d** 88 **p** 89. C Wilford *S'well* 88-91; TV Bestwood 91-96; P-in-c Selston 96-98; V 98-00; C Watford St Pet *St Alb* from 00. *68 Tudor Avenue, Watford WD24 7NX* Tel (01923) 223510, 337002 *or* 337000 E-mail bob.yule@soulsurvivor.com

Z

ZAIDI-CROSSE, Philip Kenneth. b 63. **d** 05 **p** 06. NSM Erdington *Birm* from 05. *34 Watt Road, Birmingham B23 6ET* Tel 0121-624 4752

ZAIR, Richard George. b 52. Newc Univ BSc74. Trin Coll Bris 75 St Jo Coll Dur 79. **d** 80 **p** 81. C Bishopsworth *Bris* 80-83; C New Malden and Coombe *S'wark* 83-91; Dir of Evang CPAS 91-99; Regional Dir 99-09; P-in-c Marcham w Garford *Ox* from 09. *1 All Saints Close, Marcham, Abingdon OX13 6PE* Tel (01865) 391319 E-mail r_zair@yahoo.co.uk

ZAMMIT, Mark Timothy Paul. b 60. Ox Brookes Univ MA07. Aston Tr Scheme 90 Sarum & Wells Th Coll 94. **d** 94 **p** 95. C Bitterne Park *Win* 94-98; TV Shaston *Sarum* 98-03; TR 03-08; RD Blackmore Vale 01-08; Chapl Port Regis Prep Sch 99-08; P-in-c Durrington *Sarum* from 08; C Avon Valley from 08; RD Stonehenge from 10. *The Rectory, Church Street, Durrington, Salisbury SP4 8AL* Tel and fax (01980) 653953 E-mail zammitparish@yahoo.co.uk

ZANDSTRA-HOUGH, Wendy Lorraine. See HOUGH, Wendy Lorraine

ZANKER, Mrs Diana. b 39. Leeds Univ BA01 Edge Hill Coll of HE TCert59. NOC 04. **d** 05 **p** 06. NSM Leeds St Aid *Ripon* from 05. *10 Mount Gardens, Leeds LS17 7QN* Tel 0113-267 5893 E-mail diana@zanker.org

ZAPHIRIOU, Paul Victor. b 49. Hamilton Coll (NY) BA73 INSEAD MBA74. Wycliffe Hall Ox 00. **d** 02 **p** 03. C Holborn St Geo w H Trin and St Bart *Lon* 02-06; V Holloway St Mary Magd from 06; Bp's Adv for Corporate Soc Resp from 05. *108 Liverpool Road, London N1 0RE* Tel (020) 7226 0854 Mobile 07899-796409 E-mail paul.zaphiriou@n7parish.net

ZAREK, Jennifer Hilary. b 51. Newnham Coll Cam BA72 MA76 Southn Univ MSc73 PhD78 Ox Univ BTh98 Garnett Coll Lon CertEd83. St Steph Ho Ox 95. **d** 97 **p** 98. C Caterham *S'wark* 97-00; V Hutton Cranswick w Skerne, Watton and Beswick *York* 00-05; rtd 05. *Horsedale House, Silver Street, Huggate, York YO42 1YB* Tel (01377) 288525

ZASS-OGILVIE, Ian David. b 38. MRICS72 FRICS80. AKC65 St Boniface Warminster 65. **d** 66 **p** 67. C Washington *Dur* 66-70; Bp's Soc and Ind Adv for N Dur 70-73; Hon C Newc St Jo 73-75; V Tynemouth St Jo 75-78; Hon C St Marylebone St Mary *Lon* 78-81; V Bromley St Jo *Roch* 81-84; R Keith, Huntly and Aberchirder *Mor* 84-88; R Edin St Pet 88-00; Dir Churches' Regional Commn in the NE *Newc* and *Dur* 00-05; rtd 05. *12 St Giles Close, Gilesgate, Durham DH1 1XH* Tel 0191-383 0887 E-mail ianzassogilvie@tiscali.co.uk

ZEAL, Stanley Allan. b 33. Leeds Univ BA55. Coll of Resurr Mirfield. **d** 57 **p** 58. C Perry Hill St Geo *S'wark* 57-61; C Cobham *Guildf* 61-64; R Ash and V Ash Vale 64-69; V Aldershot St Mich 69-98; Chapl Northfield Hosp Aldershot 69-98; rtd 98. *4 Spencers Row, Cardiff CF5 2EP* Tel (029) 2056 0778

ZIETSMAN, Sheila. **d** 90 **p** 91. C Geashill w Killeigh and Ballycommon *M & K* 90-91; C Mullingar, Portnashangan, Moyliscar, Kilbixy etc 91-96; Chapl Wilson's Hosp Sch Multyfarnham 91-96; Chapl E Glendalough Sch from 96. *East Glendalough School, Station Road, Wicklow, Republic of Ireland* Tel (00353) (404) 69608 Fax 68180

ZIHNI, Andrew Stephen. b 77. Mert Coll Ox BA99 MA06. St Steph Ho Ox BA01. **d** 02 **p** 03. C Goldthorpe w Hickleton *Sheff* 02-06; Min Can Windsor from 06; Chapl St Geo Sch Windsor from 06. *24 The Cloisters, Windsor Castle, Windsor SL4 1NJ* Tel (01753) 848781 *or* 848710 Fax 620165 E-mail frazihni4277@aol.com

ZIPFEL, Marilyn Ellen. b 48. Open Univ BA94 MA98 Goldsmiths' Coll Lon TCert70 LTCL97. Dioc OLM tr scheme 01. **d** 03 **p** 04. OLM Oulton Broad *Nor* from 03. *Rozel, Station Road, Lowestoft NR32 4QF* Tel (01502) 583825 Mobile 07818-093133 E-mail marilynzipfel@talktalk.net

ZORAB, Mark Elston. b 53. FRICS77. Mon Dioc Tr Scheme 92. **d** 94. NSM St Arvans w Penterry, Itton, Devauden etc *Mon* from 94. *Oak Cottage, Itton Road, Chepstow NP16 6BQ* Tel (01291) 626222 *or* 672138 E-mail fr.mark@elstons.co.uk

ZOTOV, Mrs Carolyn Ann. b 47. Lady Mabel Coll CertEd68 Open Univ BA78. EMMTC 91. **d** 92 **p** 94. NSM Hykeham *Linc* 92-94; NSM Aisthorpe w Scampton w Thorpe le Fallows etc 94; C Ingham w Cammeringham w Fillingham 94-97; C Linc Minster Gp 97-01; rtd 01; Assoc P Nettleham *Linc* from 01. *Greenleaves, 1 The Drive, Church Lane, Lincoln LN2 1QR* Tel (01522) 525435 E-mail caz@greenleaves.fsnet.co.uk

ZUCCA, Peter Rennie. b 43. **d** 96 **p** 97. NSM Spotland *Man* 96-99; NSM Bamford 99-05; NSM Rochdale St Geo w St Alb 99-05; NSM Oakenrod and Bamford from 05. *19 Judith Street, Rochdale OL12 7HS* Tel (01706) 675830 *or* 346003

ZVIMBA, Josephat. b 60. SEITE. **d** 04 **p** 05. C W Norwood St Luke *S'wark* 04-07; V Dalston St Mark w St Bart *Lon* from 07. *St Mark's Vicarage, Sandringham Road, London E8 2LL* Tel (020) 7241 1771 E-mail janjosh@talktalk.net

ZWALF, Canon Willem Anthony Louis (Wim). b 46. AKC68. **d** 71 **p** 72. C Fulham St Etheldreda w St Clem *Lon* 71-74; Chapl City Univ 74-78; R Coalbrookdale, Iron-Bridge and Lt Wenlock *Heref* 78-90; V Wisbech SS Pet and Paul *Ely* 90-08; P-in-c Wisbech St Aug 03-04; C 04-08; RD Wisbech Lynn Marshland 02-08; Hon Can Ely Cathl 07-08; rtd 09. *1 The Dell, Oakham LE15 6JG* Tel (01572) 770082 E-mail wimzwalf@aol.com

THE
CLERGY CHARITIES
making grant applications simpler

THE TWO LEADING CLERGY CHARITIES now work together with a unified grant-making system. Applications are considered by a common body of trustees who are responsible for the affairs of both organisations, making the process simpler for anyone wishing to apply.

IN 2010 AROUND £1.8M WAS AWARDED in grants for a wide range of purposes including:
Assistance for special needs education
School clothing and school trips
Clerical clothing, holidays and resettlement
Heating and home maintenance for the retired
Bereavement expenses and some of the expenses arising from separation and divorce, as well as
Cases of emergency, illness and misfortune

DONATIONS AND LEGACIES are always welcome to help us maintain this level of support.

FOR MORE INFORMATION
please contact us at:
1 Dean Trench Street, London SW1P 3HB
Tel: 020 7799 3696
Email: enquiries@clergycharities.org.uk
www.clergycharities.org.uk

Corporation of the Sons of the Clergy Charity No. 207736
Friends of the Clergy Corporation Charity No. 264724
Both registered in England and Wales

DEACONESSES

BENNETT, Miss Doreen. b 29. St Mich Ho Ox 60. **dss** 79. Moreton *Ches* 79-80; Dewsbury Moor *Wakef* 80-86; Germany 86-91; rtd 89; Perm to Offic *Blackb* 95-02 and from 04. *27 Stuart Court, High Street, Kibworth, Leicester LE8 0LR* Tel 0116-279 3812

BRIERLY, Margaret Ann. b 32. Dalton Ho Bris 54. **dss** 85. Wreningham *Nor* 85-86; Tetsworth, Adwell w S Weston, Lewknor etc *Ox* 86-95; rtd 95; Perm to Offic *Blackb* from 03. *13 Pinewood Avenue, Brookhouse, Lancaster LA2 9NU*

BUTLER, Miss Ann. b 41. St Mich Ho Ox 67 Dalton Ho Bris IDC69. **dss** 82. Bucknall and Bagnall *Lich* 82-87; Leyton St Mary w St Edw *Chelmsf* 89-97; Leyton St Mary w St Edw and St Luke 97-02; rtd 02; Perm to Offic *Lich* from 10. *40 Lichfield Street, Stone ST15 8NB* Tel (01785) 818160

CARTER, Miss Crystal Dawn. b 49. SRN77 RSCN77. Trin Coll Bris 79. **dss** 82. Hengrove *Bris* 82-86; Dagenham *Chelmsf* 86-88; Perm to Offic from 88; rtd 08. *41 Rusholme Avenue, Dagenham RM10 7ND* Tel (020) 8596 0451 Mobile 07762-849403

COOPER, Janet Pamela. b 46. Glos Coll of Educn TCert67 Ox Poly CETD79. Trin Coll Bris. **dss** 83. Patchway *Bris* 83-88; Perm to Offic *Glouc* 90-96. *Ephraim Cottage, Kington Mead Farm, Kington Road, Thornbury, Bristol BS35 1PQ* Tel (01454) 415280 E-mail jan.ephraimcottage@uhu.co.uk

DEE, Mary. b 21. St Chris Coll Blackheath 55. **dss** 64. Shottermill Guildf 63-66; Bishop's Waltham *Portsm* 66-72; Cumnor *Ox* 75-81; rtd 81. *Flat 4, 45 Oxford Avenue, Bournemouth BH6 5HT* Tel (01202) 424240

ESSAM, Susan Catherine. b 46. Southn Univ BA67 CertEd68. Linc Th Coll. **dss** 80. Pershore w Pinvin, Wick and Birlingham *Worc* 78-82; CMS Nigeria from 83. *Bishopscourt, PO Box 6283, Jos, Plateau State, Nigeria* Tel (00234) (806) 876 9443 E-mail susanessam@aol.com

EVANS (*née* CHERRETT), **Mrs Diana.** b 59. Somerville Coll Ox BA81 MA85 Warwick Univ CertEd96. St Steph Ho Ox 81. **dss** 84. Sherborne w Castleton and Lillington *Sarum* 84-88; Northampton St Paul *Pet* 93-98; Sec Dioc Adv Cttee 94-08; Hd Places of Worship Policy English Heritage from 08; Lic to Offic *Pet* 98-10. *21 Beaumont Street, London W1G 6DQ* Tel (020) 7935 8965

GOUGH, Janet Ainley. b 46. SRN67 RSCN68 SCM70. Dalton Ho Bris 70. **dss** 76. Leic H Apostles 73-80; Kansas City All SS USA 80-81; Perm to Offic *Leic* 81-96 and from 05. *410 Hinckley Road, Leicester LE3 0WA* Tel 0116-285 4284 E-mail jangough@hotmail.co.uk

GRIERSON, Miss Janet. b 13. Westf Coll Lon BA34. Lambeth STh37 MA82 Greyladies Coll 34 K Coll Lon 34. **dss** 48. Vice-Prin Gilmore Ho 48-55; Prin 55-60; Lect Div St Mary's Coll Ban 62-63; Prin Lect RE Summerfield Coll Kidderminster 63-75; rtd 75; Perm to Offic *Worc* from 75. *Davenham, 148 Graham Road, Malvern WR14 2HY* Tel (01684) 569341

HAMILTON, Miss Pamela Moorhead. b 43. SRN64 SCM66. Trin Coll Bris 75. **dss** 77. Derby St Pet and Ch Ch w H Trin 77-84; Bedworth *Cov* from 85; rtd 03. *10 William Street, Bedworth, Nuneaton CV12 9DS* Tel (024) 7649 1608

HARRIS, Audrey Margaret. See STOKES, Audrey Margaret

HARRISON, Mrs Ann. b 55. Ex Univ BSc77. Linc Th Coll 79. **dss** 82. Acomb H Redeemer *York* 82-83; Lic to Offic *Wakef* 83-91. *The Vicarage, Church Hill, Easingwold, York YO61 3JT* Tel (01347) 821394

HEWITT, Miss Joyce Evelyn. b 30. SRN51 SCM55. St Mich Ho Ox IDC61. **dss** 67. Spitalfields Ch Ch w All SS *Lon* 67-70; CMJ 71-73; Canonbury St Steph *Lon* 73-75; Chorleywood RNIB Coll for Blind Girls 75-88. *16 Ashridge Court, Station Road, Newbury RG14 7LL* Tel (01635) 47829

HIDER, Ms Margaret Joyce Barbara. b 25. St Mich Ho Ox 52. **dss** 77. Bris H Cross Inns Court 77-84; Uphill *B & W* 84-89; rtd 89; Perm to Offic *B & W* 89-05. *15 Stuart Court, High Street, Kibworth, Leicester LE8 0LR* Tel 0116-279 6885

HINDE, Miss Mavis Mary. b 29. Lightfoot Ho Dur. **dss** 65. Hitchin St Mary *St Alb* 65-68; Ensbury *Sarum* 69-70; Portsea St Alb *Portsm* 70-76; Houghton Regis *St Alb* 77-85; Eaton Socon 85-94; rtd 94; Perm to Offic *Ely* from 94. *8 Burnt Close, Eynesbury, St Neots PE19 2LZ* Tel (01480) 218219

HORNBY-NORTHCOTE, Mrs Vivien Sheena. b 42. Birkbeck Coll Lon BA91 Warwick Univ MA96. Gilmore Course 74. **dss** 79. Mitcham St Olave *S'wark* 79-81; St Dunstan in the West 86; rtd 98. *3 Priory Mews, Sidney Street, Cheltenham GL52 6DJ* Tel (01242) 525659

MacCORMACK, Mrs June Elizabeth. b 45. Ab Dioc Tr Course 82 St Jo Coll Nottm 85. **dss** 86. Bieldside *Ab* from 86. *5 Overton Park, Dyce, Aberdeen AB21 7FT* Tel (01224) 722691 E-mail june@maccormack.co.uk

MOORHOUSE, Olga Marian. b 28. Dalton Ho Bris 54. **dss** 63. Wolverhampton St Matt *Lich* 62-68; Fazakerley Em *Liv* 68-70; Huyton St Geo 70-76; Blurton *Lich* 76-88; rtd 88. *37 Rosalind Grove, Wednesfield, Wolverhampton WV11 3RZ* Tel (01902) 630128

MORGAN, Beryl. b 19. Dalton Ho Bris 47. **dss** 77. Princess Marg Hosp Swindon 69-79; rtd 79. *Ty Clyd, 120 Beacons Park, Brecon LD3 9BP* Tel (01874) 622398

NORTHCOTE, Vivien. See HORNBY-NORTHCOTE, Mrs Vivien Sheena

OBEE, Sister Monica May. b 37. **dss** 82. Radford *Cov* 82-97; rtd 97. *14 The Hill, Walsingham NR22 6DF* Tel (01328) 821033

OLIVER, Miss Kathleen Joyce. b 44. Man Univ BA65. NOC 80. **dss** 83. Littleborough *Man* from 83. *Littleborough Christian Centre, 43 Todmorden Road, Littleborough OL15 9EA* Tel (01706) 376477 Fax 375520

OLPHIN, Miss Maureen Rose. b 30. Lon Univ BSc Sheff Univ DipEd. **dss** 84. Sheff St Barn and St Mary 84-90; rtd 90. *clo G Johnson Esq, Mayfields, 1A Bishopton Lane, Ripon HG4 2QN* Tel (01765) 607956

PIERSON, Mrs Valerie Susan (Sue). b 44. TCert65. Trin Coll Bris 76. **dss** 79. Fulham St Matt *Lon* from 79. *48 Peterborough Road, London SW6 3EB* Tel (020) 7731 6544 Fax 7731 1858 E-mail sue@lancepierson.org

PRICE, Mrs Patricia Kate Lunn. See SCHMIEGELOW, Patricia Kate Lunn

RAINEY, Miss Irene May. b 14. RSCN36 SCM38. Gilmore Ho 69. **dss** 72. Filton *Bris* 70-74; Crowthorne *Ox* 74-79; rtd 79; Perm to Offic *Ely* 80-03. *12 Stevens Close, Cottenham, Cambridge CB24 8TT* Tel (01954) 251634

SAMPSON, Miss Hazel. b 35. Lightfoot Ho Dur 58. **dss** 64. Fenton *Lich* 64-67; Gt Wyrley 67-69; Chapl Asst Manor Hosp Walsall 69-76; Lich St Mary w St Mich 76-95; rtd 95; Perm to Offic *Lich* 95-03. *107 Walsall Road, Lichfield WS13 8DD* Tel (01543) 419664

SCHMIEGELOW, Patricia Kate Lunn. b 37. St Mich Ho Ox IDC65. **dss** 86. The Hague *Eur* 86-89; Perm to Offic *Glouc* from 90; Gen Sec ICS 92-97; rtd 97. *Waterside, Coln St Aldwyns, Cirencester GL7 5AJ* Tel and fax (01285) 750218

SELWOOD, Miss Eveline Mary. b 34. **dss** 76. Huddersfield St Jo *Wakef* 76-79; King Cross 79-85; rtd 94; Perm to Offic *Wakef* from 94. *clo Ms A 1 Ledger, Brookfield House, 2 Doctor Lane, Flockton, Wakefield WF4 4UZ* Tel (01924) 848448

SPROSON, Doreen. b 31. St Mich Ho Ox IDC58. **dss** 70. Wandsworth St Mich *S'wark* 68-71; Women's Sec CMS 71-74; Goole *Sheff* 74-76; Kirby Muxloe *Leic* 76-77; Perm to Offic *S'wark* 85-97; rtd 91. *20 Huggens' College, College Road, Northfleet, Gravesend DA11 9LL* Tel (01474) 325262

STOKES, Audrey Margaret. b 39. Dalton Ho Bris 68. **dss** 82. Collier Row St Jas *Chelmsf* 82-85; Woking St Mary *Guildf* 85-95; rtd 95. *1 Greet Park Close, Southwell NG25 0EE*

SYMES, Miss Annabel. b 41. AIMLS68. S Dios Minl Tr Scheme 79. **dss** 85. Chapl Asst Salisbury NHS Foundn Trust from 85; Barford St Martin, Dinton, Baverstock etc *Sarum* 89-01; Nadder Valley from 01. *7 Shaftesbury Road, Barford St Martin, Salisbury SP3 4BL* Tel (01722) 744110

TAYLOR, Muriel. b 28. CA Tr Coll 48. **dss** 76. Gateshead Fell *Dur* 76-86; Gateshead Harlow Green 86-88; rtd 88. *18 Beechwood Avenue, Gateshead NE9 6PP* Tel 0191-487 6902

THUMWOOD, Janet Elizabeth. b 30. STh60. Trin Coll Toronto 58. **dss** 62. Canada 62-63; Mile End Old Town H Trin *Lon* 63-65; CSF 66-77; rtd 90. *24 Ramsay Hall, 11-13 Byron Road, Worthing BN11 3HN* Tel (01903) 203586

WEBB, Sybil Janet. b 20. SRN42 SCM43. Gilmore Course 69. **dss** 77. Worthing St Geo *Chich* 77-80; rtd 80; Perm to Offic *Chich* from 80. *42 Ham Road, Worthing BN11 2QX* Tel (01903) 202997

WRIGHT, Edith Mary. b 22. St Hugh's Coll Ox MA46 DipEd46. Gilmore Ho STh58. **dss** 61. St Marylebone St Mary *Lon* 58-71; Lect Linc Th Coll 71-73; Oatlands *Guildf* 73-76; Roehampton H Trin *S'wark* 76-82; rtd 82. *26 Hazelwood Close, Harrow HA2 6HD* Tel 0181-863 7320

WRIGHT, Gloria Mary. b 40. **dss** 83. Smethwick St Matt w St Chad *Birm* 83-84; Tottenham H Trin *Lon* 84-86; rtd 00. *5 The Pastures, Anstey, Leicester LE7 7QR*

DIOCESAN, AREA, SUFFRAGAN AND ASSISTANT BISHOPS AND PROVINCIAL EPISCOPAL VISITORS IN ENGLAND, WALES, SCOTLAND AND IRELAND

BATH AND WELLS
Bishop of Bath and Wells — P B PRICE
Honorary Assistant Bishops — P E BARBER
G H CASSIDY
J F PERRY
W M D PERSSON
B ROGERSON
R F SAINSBURY
R H M THIRD
Suffragan Bishop of Taunton — P D MAURICE

BIRMINGHAM
Bishop of Birmingham — D A URQUHART
Honorary Assistant Bishops — A P HALL
A C DUMPER
I K MOTTAHEDEH
M W SINCLAIR
M H D WHINNEY
Suffragan Bishop of Aston — A J WATSON

BLACKBURN
Bishop of Blackburn — N S READE
Honorary Assistant Bishops — LORD HOPE OF THORNES
M E VICKERS
A L WINSTANLEY
Suffragan Bishop of Burnley — J W GODDARD
Suffragan Bishop of Lancaster — G S PEARSON

BRADFORD
Bishop of Bradford — N BAINES
Honorary Assistant Bishops — C O BUCHANAN
LORD HOPE OF THORNES
M W JARRETT

BRISTOL
Bishop of Bristol — M A HILL
Honorary Assistant Bishops — P J FIRTH
J R G NEALE
P ST G VAUGHAN
Suffragan Bishop of Swindon — L S RAYFIELD

CANTERBURY
Archbishop of Canterbury, Primate — R D WILLIAMS
of All England and Metropolitan
Honorary Assistant Bishops — G A CRAY
M F GEAR
J R A LLEWELLIN
Suffragan Bishop of Dover — T WILLMOTT
Suffragan Bishop of Maidstone — Vacant
Suffragan Bishop of Ebbsfleet — J M R BAKER
(Provincial Episcopal Visitor)
Suffragan Bishop of Richborough — N BANKS
(Provincial Episcopal Visitor)

CARLISLE
Bishop of Carlisle — J W S NEWCOME
Honorary Assistant Bishops — A A K GRAHAM
I M GRIGGS
G L HACKER
R M HARDY
R C A HENDERSON
J H RICHARDSON
J R SATTERTHWAITE
G H THOMPSON
Suffragan Bishop of Penrith — R J FREEMAN

CHELMSFORD
Bishop of Chelmsford — S G COTTRELL
Honorary Assistant Bishops — J M BALL
C D BOND
Area Bishop of Barking — D J L HAWKINS
Area Bishop of Bradwell — J M WRAW
Area Bishop of Colchester — C H MORGAN

CHESTER
Bishop of Chester — P R FORSTER
Honorary Assistant Bishops — C F BAZLEY
G G DOW
J D HAYDEN
W A PWAISIHO
G M TURNER
Suffragan Bishop of Birkenhead — G K SINCLAIR
Suffragan Bishop of Stockport — R R ATWELL

CHICHESTER
Bishop of Chichester — J W HIND
Honorary Assistant Bishops — M E ADIE
K L BARHAM
R D FARRER
R A JUPP
C C LUXMOORE
M R J MANKTELOW
M E MARSHALL
L G URWIN
D P WILCOX
Area Bishop of Horsham — M C R SOWERBY
Area Bishop of Lewes — W P BENN

COVENTRY
Bishop of Coventry — C J COCKSWORTH
Honorary Assistant Bishop — D R J EVANS
Suffragan Bishop of Warwick — J R A STROYAN

DERBY
Bishop of Derby — A L J REDFERN
Honorary Assistant Bishops — R M C BEAK
J NICHOLLS
Suffragan Bishop of Repton — H I J SOUTHERN

DURHAM
Bishop of Durham
Honorary Assistant Bishops — M W JARRETT
S W SYKES
Suffragan Bishop of Jarrow — M W BRYANT

ELY
Bishop of Ely — S D CONWAY
Honorary Assistant Bishops — S BARRINGTON-WARD
P S DAWES
J B TAYLOR
L G URWIN
Suffragan Bishop of Huntingdon — D THOMSON

EXETER
Bishop of Exeter — M L LANGRISH
Honorary Assistant Bishops — I C DOCKER
R S HAWKINS
J P MASON
A M SHAW
M R WESTALL
Suffragan Bishop of Crediton — R J S EVENS
Suffragan Bishop of Plymouth — J F FORD

GLOUCESTER
Bishop of Gloucester — M F PERHAM
Honorary Assistant Bishops — P J FIRTH
P B HARRIS
D W M JENNINGS
J R G NEALE
Suffragan Bishop of Tewkesbury — J S WENT

GUILDFORD
Bishop of Guildford — C J HILL
Honorary Assistant Bishops — M A BAUGHEN
C J BENNETTS
C W HERBERT
Suffragan Bishop of Dorking — I J BRACKLEY

HEREFORD
Bishop of Hereford — A M PRIDDIS
Suffragan Bishop of Ludlow — A J MAGOWAN

LEICESTER
Bishop of Leicester — T J STEVENS
Assistant Bishop — C J BOYLE
Honorary Assistant Bishop — C J F SCOTT

LICHFIELD
Bishop of Lichfield — J M GLEDHILL
Honorary Assistant Bishops — D E BENTLEY
I K MOTTAHEDEH
Area Bishop of Shrewsbury — M J RYLANDS
Area Bishop of Stafford — G P ANNAS
Area Bishop of Wolverhampton — C M GREGORY

LINCOLN
Bishop of Lincoln — C LOWSON
Honorary Assistant Bishops — J E BROWN
D G SNELGROVE
D TUSTIN
Suffragan Bishop of Grantham — T W ELLIS
Suffragan Bishop of Grimsby — D D J ROSSDALE

DIOCESAN, AREA, SUFFRAGAN AND ASSISTANT BISHOPS

LIVERPOOL
Bishop of Liverpool — J S JONES
Honorary Assistant Bishops — M W JARRETT
I C STUART
Suffragan Bishop of Warrington — R F BLACKBURN

LONDON
Bishop of London — R J C CHARTRES
Honorary Assistant Bishop — E HOLLAND
Area Bishop of Edmonton — P W WHEATLEY
Suffragan Bishop of Fulham — *Vacant*
Area Bishop of Kensington — P G WILLIAMS
Area Bishop of Stepney — A NEWMAN
Area Bishop of Willesden — P A BROADBENT

MANCHESTER
Bishop of Manchester — N S MCCULLOCH
Honorary Assistant Bishops — R W N HOARE
M W JARRETT
Suffragan Bishop of Hulme — *Vacant*
Suffragan Bishop of Middleton — M DAVIES
Suffragan Bishop of Bolton — C P EDMONDSON

NEWCASTLE
Bishop of Newcastle — J M WHARTON
Assistant Bishops — F WHITE
K E GILL
M W JARRETT
J H RICHARDSON

NORWICH
Bishop of Norwich — G R JAMES
Honorary Assistant Bishops — E N DEVENPORT
A C FOOTTIT
P J FOX
R GARRARD
D K GILLETT
D LEAKE
M J MENIN
L G URWIN
Suffragan Bishop of Lynn — C J MEYRICK
Suffragan Bishop of Thetford — A P WINTON

OXFORD
Bishop of Oxford — J L PRITCHARD
Honorary Assistant Bishops — K A ARNOLD
J F E BONE
A K CRAGG
W J D DOWN
J H GARTON
A R M GORDON
J N JOHNSON
P J NOTT
F H A RICHMOND
H W SCRIVEN
Area Bishop of Buckingham — A T L WILSON
Area Bishop of Dorchester — C W FLETCHER
Area Bishop of Reading — A J PROUD

PETERBOROUGH
Bishop of Peterborough — D S ALLISTER
Honorary Assistant Bishops — L G URWIN
J R FLACK
Suffragan Bishop of Brixworth — J E HOLBROOK

PORTSMOUTH
Bishop of Portsmouth — C R J FOSTER
Honorary Assistant Bishops — M E ADIE
G W E C ASHBY

RIPON AND LEEDS
Bishop of Ripon and Leeds — J R PACKER
Honorary Assistant Bishops — C O BUCHANAN
G C HANDFORD
M W JARRETT
D E JENKINS
Suffragan Bishop of Knaresborough — J H BELL

ROCHESTER
Bishop of Rochester — J H LANGSTAFF
Honorary Assistant Bishops — M F GEAR
D HAMID
Suffragan Bishop of Tonbridge — B C CASTLE

ST ALBANS
Bishop of St Albans — A G C SMITH
Honorary Assistant Bishops — D J FARMBROUGH
R J N SMITH
Suffragan Bishop of Bedford — R N INWOOD
Suffragan Bishop of Hertford — P BAYES

ST EDMUNDSBURY AND IPSWICH
Bishop of St Edmundsbury and Ipswich — W N STOCK
Honorary Assistant Bishops — G H REID
J WAINE
G D J WALSH
Suffragan Bishop of Dunwich — C YOUNG

SALISBURY
Bishop of Salisbury — N R HOLTAM
Honorary Assistant Bishops — J K CAVELL
D M HALLATT
J D G KIRKHAM
Area Bishop of Ramsbury — *Vacant*
Area Bishop of Sherborne — G R KINGS

SHEFFIELD
Bishop of Sheffield — S J L CROFT
Honorary Assistant Bishops — D C HAWTIN
M W JARRETT
Suffragan Bishop of Doncaster — *Vacant*

SODOR AND MAN
Bishop of Sodor and Man — R M E PATERSON

SOUTHWARK
Bishop of Southwark — C T J CHESSUN
Honorary Assistant Bishops — D J ATKINSON
LORD HARRIES OF PENTREGARTH
A D CHESTERS
M D DOE
P S M SELBY
Area Bishop of Kingston-upon-Thames — R I CHEETHAM
Area Bishop of Woolwich — *Vacant*
Area Bishop of Croydon — *Vacant*

SOUTHWELL AND NOTTINGHAM
Bishop of Southwell and Nottingham — P R BUTLER
Honorary Assistant Bishops — J T FINNEY
M W JARRETT
R J MILNER
R K WILLIAMSON
Suffragan Bishop of Sherwood — A PORTER

TRURO
Bishop of Truro — T M THORNTON
Honorary Assistant Bishop — J F FORD
Suffragan Bishop of St Germans — R SCREECH

WAKEFIELD
Bishop of Wakefield — S G PLATTEN
Honorary Assistant Bishops — T F BUTLER
M W JARRETT
Suffragan Bishop of Pontefract — A W ROBINSON

WINCHESTER
Bishop of Winchester — *Vacant*
Honorary Assistant Bishops — J A BAKER
S H BURROWS
J DENNIS
J A ELLISON
C W HERBERT
Suffragan Bishop of Basingstoke — P HANCOCK
Suffragan Bishop of Southampton — J H FROST

WORCESTER
Bishop of Worcester — J G INGE
Honorary Assistant Bishops — C J MAYFIELD
J RUHUMULIZA
Suffragan Bishop of Dudley — D S WALKER

YORK
Archbishop of York, Primate of England and Metropolitan — J T M SENTAMU
Honorary Assistant Bishops — C C BARKER
R G G FOLEY
D G GALLIFORD
M HENSHALL
D R LUNN
D J SMITH
Suffragan Bishop of Hull — R M C FRITH
Suffragan Bishop of Selby — M W WALLACE
Suffragan Bishop of Whitby — M C WARNER
Suffragan Bishop of Beverley — M W JARRETT
(Provincial Episcopal Visitor)

GIBRALTAR IN EUROPE
Bishop of Gibraltar in Europe — D G ROWELL
Suffragan Bishop in Europe — D HAMID
Honorary Assistant Bishops — R GARRARD
E HOLLAND
LORD HOPE OF THORNES
M R J MANKTELOW
D J SMITH
F L SOARES
D S STANCLIFFE
J B TAYLOR
S S VENNER
J G VOBBE
A W M WEEKES
P W WHALON
J R FLACK

CHURCH IN WALES

ST ASAPH
Bishop of St Asaph — G K CAMERON

BANGOR
Bishop of Bangor — A T G JOHN

ST DAVIDS
Bishop of St Davids — J W EVANS

LLANDAFF
Bishop of Llandaff — B C MORGAN
Assistant Bishop — D J WILBOURNE

MONMOUTH
Bishop of Monmouth — E W M WALKER

SWANSEA AND BRECON
Bishop of Swansea and Brecon — J D E DAVIES
Honorary Assistant Bishop — J K OLIVER

SCOTTISH EPISCOPAL CHURCH

ABERDEEN AND ORKNEY
Bishop of Aberdeen and Orkney — R A GILLIES

ARGYLL AND THE ISLES
Bishop of Argyll and the Isles — K PEARSON

BRECHIN
Bishop of Brechin — N PEYTON

EDINBURGH
Bishop of Edinburgh — B A SMITH

GLASGOW AND GALLOWAY
Bishop of Glasgow and Galloway — G D DUNCAN
Honorary Assistant Bishop — J M TAYLOR

MORAY, ROSS AND CAITHNESS
Bishop of Moray, Ross and Caithness — M J STRANGE

ST ANDREWS, DUNKELD AND DUNBLANE
Bishop of St Andrews, Dunkeld and — D R CHILLINGWORTH
Dunblane

CHURCH OF IRELAND

ARMAGH
Archbishop of Armagh and Primate — A E T HARPER
of All Ireland and Metropolitan

CASHEL AND OSSORY
Bishop of Cashel and Ossory — M A J BURROWS

CLOGHER
Bishop of Clogher — F J MCDOWELL

CONNOR
Bishop of Connor — A F ABERNETHY

CORK, CLOYNE AND ROSS
Bishop of Cork, Cloyne and Ross — W P COLTON

DERRY AND RAPHOE
Bishop of Derry and Raphoe — K R GOOD

DOWN AND DROMORE
Bishop of Down and Dromore — H C MILLER

DUBLIN AND GLENDALOUGH
Archbishop of Dublin, Bishop of — M G ST A JACKSON
Glendalough, Primate of Ireland
and Metropolitan

KILMORE, ELPHIN AND ARDAGH
Bishop of Kilmore, Elphin and Ardagh — K H CLARKE

LIMERICK AND KILLALOE
Bishop of Limerick and Killaloe — T R WILLIAMS

MEATH AND KILDARE
Bishop of Meath and Kildare — R L CLARKE

TUAM, KILLALA AND ACHONRY
Bishop of Tuam, Killala and Achonry — P W ROOKE

BISHOPS IN THE HOUSE OF LORDS

The Archbishops of Canterbury and York, and the Bishops of London, Durham and Winchester always have seats in the House of Lords. Twenty-one of the remaining Diocesan Bishops also sit in the Upper House, and they do so according to their dates of seniority. When a vacancy arises, it is filled by the senior Diocesan Bishop without a seat, and the vacated See is placed at the foot of the list of those awaiting seats. Translation of a Bishop from one See to another does not affect his right to sit in the House of Lords.

The Bishop of Sodor and Man and the Bishop of Gibraltar in Europe are not eligible to sit in the House of Lords, but the former has a seat in the Upper House of the Tynwald, Isle of Man.

ARCHBISHOPS

	Enthroned	Entered House of Lords
CANTERBURY	2003	2003
YORK	2005	2006

BISHOPS SITTING IN THE HOUSE OF LORDS
(as at 1 December 2011)

	Became Diocesan Bishop	Entered House of Lords
LONDON	1995	1996
DURHAM	2011	awaiting introduction
WINCHESTER	vacant	
MANCHESTER	1992	1997
CHESTER	1996	2001
NEWCASTLE	1997	2003
LIVERPOOL	1998	2003
LEICESTER	1999	2003
NORWICH	1999	2004
EXETER	2000	2005
RIPON AND LEEDS	2000	2006
CHICHESTER	2001	2008
BATH AND WELLS	2002	2008
WAKEFIELD	2003	2009
BRISTOL	2003	2009
LICHFIELD	2003	2009
BLACKBURN	2004	2009
HEREFORD	2004	2009
GLOUCESTER	2004	2009
GUILDFORD	2004	2010
DERBY	2005	2010
BIRMINGHAM	2006	2010
OXFORD	2007	2011
ST EDMUNDSBURY AND IPSWICH	2007	2011

BISHOPS AWAITING SEATS IN THE HOUSE OF LORDS
(in order of seniority)

	Became Diocesan Bishop
WORCESTER	2007
COVENTRY	2008
TRURO	2008
SHEFFIELD	2009
ST ALBANS	2009
CARLISLE	2009
SOUTHWELL AND NOTTINGHAM	2009
PETERBOROUGH	2010
PORTSMOUTH	2010
CHELMSFORD	2010
ROCHESTER	2010
ELY	2010
SOUTHWARK	2011
BRADFORD	2011
SALISBURY	2011
LINCOLN	2011

HISTORICAL SUCCESSION OF ARCHBISHOPS AND BISHOPS

In a number of dioceses, especially for the mediaeval period, the dating of some episcopal appointments is not known for certain. For ease of reference, the date of consecration is given when known, or, in the case of more modern appointments, the date of confirmation of election. More information on the dates of individual bishops can be found in the Royal Historical Society's *Handbook of British Chronology*.

ENGLAND

PROVINCE OF CANTERBURY

Canterbury

Description of arms. Azure, an archiepiscopal cross in pale or surmounted by a pall proper charged with four crosses patée fitchée sable.

597	Augustine
604	Laurentius
619	Mellitus
624	Justus
627	Honorius
655	Deusdedit
668	Theodorus
693	Berhtwald
731	Tatwine
735	Nothelm
740	Cuthbert
761	Bregowine
765	Jaenberht
793	Æthelheard
805	Wulfred
832	Feologild
833	Ceolnoth
870	Æthelred
890	Plegmund
914	Æthelhelm
923	Wulfhelm
942	Oda
959	Ælfsige
959	Byrhthelm
960	Dunstan
c.988	Athelgar
990	Sigeric Serio
995	Ælfric
1005	Ælfheah
1013	Lyfing [Ælfstan]
1020	Æthelnoth
1038	Eadsige
1051	Robert of Jumièges
1052	Stigand
1070	Lanfranc
1093	Anselm
1114	Ralph d'Escures
1123	William de Corbeil
1139	Theobald of Bec
1162	Thomas Becket
1174	Richard [of Dover]
1184	Baldwin
1193	Hubert Walter
1207	Stephen Langton

1229	Richard le Grant
1234	Edmund Rich
1245	Boniface of Savoy
1273	Robert Kilwardby
1279	John Pecham
1294	Robert Winchelsey
1313	Walter Reynolds
1328	Simon Mepham
1333	John Stratford
1349	Thomas Bradwardine
1349	Simon Islip
1366	Simon Langham
1368	William Whittlesey
1375	Simon Sudbury
1381	William Courtenay
1396	Thomas Arundel[1]
1398	Roger Walden
1414	Henry Chichele
1443	John Stafford
1452	John Kempe
1454	Thomas Bourgchier
1486	John Morton
1501	Henry Deane
1503	William Warham
1533	Thomas Cranmer
1556	Reginald Pole
1559	Matthew Parker
1576	Edmund Grindal
1583	John Whitgift
1604	Richard Bancroft
1611	George Abbot
1633	William Laud
1660	William Juxon
1663	Gilbert Sheldon
1678	William Sancroft
1691	John Tillotson
1695	Thomas Tenison
1716	William Wake
1737	John Potter
1747	Thomas Herring
1757	Matthew Hutton
1758	Thomas Secker
1768	Frederick Cornwallis
1783	John Moore
1805	Charles Manners Sutton
1828	William Howley
1848	John Bird Sumner
1862	Charles Thomas Longley
1868	Archibald Campbell Tait
1883	Edward White Benson
1896	Frederick Temple
1903	Randall Thomas Davidson
1928	Cosmo Gordon Lang
1942	William Temple
1945	Geoffrey Francis Fisher
1961	Arthur Michael Ramsey
1974	Frederick Donald Coggan
1980	Robert Alexander Kennedy Runcie
1991	George Leonard Carey
2002	Rowan Douglas Williams

London

Description of arms. Gules, two swords in saltire argent hilts and pommels or.

	Theanus
	Eluanus
	Cadar
	Obinus
	Conanus
	Palladius
	Stephanus
	Iltutus
	Theodwinus
	Theodredus
	Hilarius
314	Restitutus
	Guitelinus
	Fastidius
	Vodinus
	Theonus
c.604	Mellitus
664	Cedd[2]
666	Wini
675	Eorcenwald
693	Waldhere
716	Ingwald
745	Ecgwulf
772	Wigheah
782	Eadbeorht
789	Eadgar
793	Coenwalh
796	Eadbald
798	Heathoberht
803	Osmund
c.811	Æthelnoth
824	Ceolberht
862	Deorwulf
898	Swithwulf
898	Heahstan
900	Wulfsige
c.926	Æthelweard
926	Leofstan
926	Theodred
—	Wulfstan I
953	Brihthelm
959	Dunstan
964	Ælfstan
996	Wulfstan II
1004	Ælfhun
1014	Ælfwig

---

[1] On 19 October 1399 Boniface IX annulled Arundel's translation to St Andrews and confirmed him in the See of Canterbury.
[2] See vacant for a term of years.

1035 Ælfweard
1044 Robert of Jumièges
1051 William
1075 Hugh of Orival
1086 Maurice
1108 Richard de Belmeis
1128 Gilbert [the Universal]
1141 Robert de Sigillo
1152 Richard de Belmeis II
1163 Gilbert Foliot
1189 Richard Fitz Neal
1199 William of Ste-Mere-Eglise
1221 Eustace de Fauconberg
1229 Roger Niger
1244 Fulk Basset
1260 Henry Wingham
1263 Henry of Sandwich
1274 John Chishull
1280 Richard Gravesend
1306 Ralph Baldock
1313 Gilbert Segrave
1317 Richard Newport
1319 Stephen Gravesend
1338 Richard Bintworth
1340 Ralph Stratford
1355 Michael Northburgh
1362 Simon Sudbury
1375 William Courtenay
1382 Robert Braybrooke
1404 Roger Walden
1406 Nicholas Bubwith
1407 Richard Clifford
1421 John Kempe
1426 William Gray
1431 Robert Fitz-Hugh
1436 Robert Gilbert
1450 Thomas Kempe
1489 Richard Hill
1496 Thomas Savage
1502 William Warham
1504 William Barons [Barnes]
1506 Richard Fitz-James
1522 Cuthbert Tunstall [Tonstall]
1530 John Stokesley
1540 Edmund Bonner
1550 Nicholas Ridley
1553 Edmund Bonner (restored)
1559 Edmund Grindal
1570 Edwin Sandys
1577 John Aylmer
1595 Richard Fletcher
1597 Richard Bancroft
1604 Richard Vaughan
1607 Thomas Ravis
1610 George Abbot
1611 John King
1621 George Monteigne
    [Mountain]
1628 William Laud
1633 William Juxon
1660 Gilbert Sheldon
1663 Humfrey Henchman
1676 Henry Compton
1714 John Robinson
1723 Edmund Gibson
1748 Thomas Sherlock
1761 Thomas Hayter
1762 Richard Osbaldeston
1764 Richard Terrick
1778 Robert Lowth
1787 Beilby Porteus
1809 John Randolph
1813 William Howley
1828 Charles James Blomfield
1856 Archibald Campbell Tait

1869 John Jackson
1885 Frederick Temple
1897 Mandell Creighton
1901 Arthur Foley Winnington-
    Ingram
1939 Geoffrey Francis Fisher
1945 John William Charles Wand
1956 Henry Colville Montgomery
    Campbell
1961 Robert Wright Stopford
1973 Gerald Alexander Ellison
1981 Graham Douglas Leonard
1991 David Michael Hope
1995 Richard John Carew Chartres

Westminster[1]

1540 Thomas Thirlby

Winchester

Description of arms. Gules, two keys
endorsed and conjoined at the bows in
bend, the upper or, the lower argent,
between which a sword in bend sinister
of the third, hilt and pommel gold.

BISHOPS OF THE WEST SAXONS
634 Birinus
650 Ægilberht

BISHOPS OF WINCHESTER
660 Wine
670 Leutherius
676 Haedde
705 Daniel
744 Hunfrith
756 Cyneheard
778 Æthelheard
778 Ecbald
785 Dudd
c.785 Cyneberht
803 Eahlmund
814 Wigthegn
825 Herefrith[2]
838 Eadmund
c.838 Eadhun
839 Helmstan
852 Swithhun
867 Ealhferth
877 Tunberht
879 Denewulf
909 Frithestan
931 Byrnstan
934 Ælfheah I
951 Ælfsige I
960 Brihthelm
963 Æthelwold I
984 Ælfheah II
1006 Cenwulf
1006 Æthelwold II
c.1014 Ælfsige II
1032 Ælfwine

1043 Stigand
    Ælfsige III?
1070 Walkelin
1107 William Giffard
1129 Henry of Blois
1174 Richard of Ilchester (Toclyve)
1189 Godfrey de Lucy
1205 Peter des Roches
1244 Will. de Raleigh
1260 Aymer de Valance [of
    Lusignan]
1262 John Gervaise
1268 Nicholas of Ely
1282 John of Pontoise
1305 Henry Merewell [or
    Woodlock]
1316 John Sandale
1320 Rigaud of Assier
1323 John Stratford
1333 Adam Orleton
1346 William Edendon [Edington]
1367 William of Wykeham
1404 Henry Beaufort
1447 William of Waynflete
1487 Peter Courtenay
1493 Thomas Langton
1501 Richard Fox
1529 Thomas Wolsey
1531 Stephen Gardiner (deposed)
1551 John Ponet [Poynet]
1553 Stephen Gardiner (restored)
1556 John White (deposed)
1561 Robert Horne
1580 John Watson
1584 Thomas Cowper [Cooper]
1595 William Wickham
    [Wykeham]
1596 William Day
1597 Thomas Bilson
1616 James Montague
1619 Lancelot Andrewes
1628 Richard Neile
1632 Walter Curll
1660 Brian Duppa
1662 George Morley
1684 Peter Mews
1707 Jonathan Trelawney
1721 Charles Trimnell
1723 Richard Willis
1734 Benjamin Hoadly
1761 John Thomas
1781 Brownlow North
1820 George Pretyman Tomline
1827 Charles Richard Sumner
1869 Samuel Wilberforce
1873 Edward Harold Browne
1891 Anthony Wilson Thorold
1895 Randall Thomas Davidson
1903 Herbert Edward Ryle
1911 Edward Stuart Talbot
1923 Frank Theodore Woods
1932 Cyril Forster Garbett
1942 Mervyn George Haigh
1952 Alwyn Terrell Petre Williams
1961 Sherard Falkner Allison
1975 John Vernon Taylor
1985 Colin Clement Walter James
1995 Michael Charles Scott-Joynt

Bath and Wells

Description of arms. Azure, a saltire per saltire quarterly counterchanged or and argent.

BISHOPS OF WELLS

909 Athelm
925 Wulfhelm I
928 Ælfheah
938 Wulfhelm II
956 Byrhthelm
974 Cyneweard
979 Sigegar
997 Ælfwine
999 Lyfing
1013 Æthelwine (ejected)
1013 Beorhtwine (deposed)
    Æthelwine (restored)
    Beorhtwine (restored)
1024 Brihtwig [also Merehwit]
1033 Duduc
1061 Gisa
1088 John of Tours [de Villula]

BISHOPS OF BATH

1090 John of Tours [de Villula]
1123 Godfrey
1136 Robert
1174 Reg. Fitz Jocelin
1192 Savaric FitzGeldewin

BATH AND GLASTONBURY

1206 Jocelin of Wells

BATH AND WELLS

1244 Roger of Salisbury
1248 William Bitton I
1265 Walter Giffard
1267 William Bitton II
1275 Robert Burnell
1293 William of March
1302 Walter Hasleshaw
1309 John Droxford
1329 Ralph of Shrewsbury
1364 John Barnet
1367 John Harewell
1386 Walter Skirlaw
1388 Ralph Erghum
1401 Henry Bowet
1407 Nicholas Bubwith
1425 John Stafford
1443 Thomas Beckington
1466 Robert Stillington
1492 Richard Fox
1495 Oliver King
1504 Adriano de Castello [di Corneto]
1518 Thomas Wolsey
1523 John Clerk
1541 William Knight
1548 William Barlow
1554 Gilbert Bourne
1560 Gilbert Berkeley
1584 Thomas Godwin
1593 John Still
1608 James Montague
1616 Arthur Lake
1626 William Laud

1628 Leonard Mawe
1629 Walter Curll
1632 William Piers
1670 Robert Creighton
1673 Peter Mews
1685 Thomas Ken (deposed)
1691 Richard Kidder
1704 George Hooper
1727 John Wynne
1743 Edward Willes
1774 Charles Moss
1802 Richard Beadon
1824 George Henry Law
1845 Richard Bagot
1854 Robert John Eden, Lord Auckland
1869 Arthur Charles Hervey
1894 George Wyndham Kennion
1921 St John Basil Wynne Wilson
1937 Francis Underhill
1943 John William Charles Wand
1946 Harold William Bradfield
1960 Edward Barry Henderson
1975 John Monier Bickersteth
1987 George Leonard Carey
1991 James Lawton Thompson
2002 Peter Bryan Price

Birmingham

Description of arms. Per pale indented or and gules, five roundels, two, two, and one, and in chief two crosses patée all counterchanged.

1905 Charles Gore
1911 Henry Russell Wakefield
1924 Ernest William Barnes
1953 John Leonard Wilson
1969 Laurence Ambrose Brown
1978 Hugh William Montefiore
1987 Mark Santer
2002 John Mugabi Sentamu
2006 David Andrew Urquhart

Bristol

Description of arms. Sable, three ducal coronets in pale or.

1542 Paul Bush
1554 John Holyman
1562 Richard Cheyney
1581 John Bullingham (held Gloucester and Bristol 1586–9)
1589 Richard Fletcher
    [See vacant for ten years]
1603 John Thornborough
1617 Nicholas Felton

1619 Rowland Searchfield
1623 Robert Wright
1633 George Coke
1637 Robert Skinner
1642 Thomas Westfield
1644 Thomas Howell
1661 Gilbert Ironside
1672 Guy Carleton
1679 William Gulston
1684 John Lake
1685 Jonathan Trelawney
1689 Gilbert Ironside
1691 John Hall
1710 John Robinson
1714 George Smalridge
1719 Hugh Boulter
1724 William Bradshaw
1733 Charles Cecil
1735 Thomas Secker
1737 Thomas Gooch
1738 Joseph Butler
1750 John Conybeare
1756 John Hume
1758 Philip Yonge
1761 Thomas Newton
1782 Lewis Bagot
1783 Christopher Wilson
1792 Spencer Madan
1794 Henry Reginald Courtenay
1797 Ffolliott Herbert Walker Cornewall
1803 George Pelham
1807 John Luxmoore
1808 William Lort Mansel
1820 John Kaye
1827 Robert Gray
1834 Joseph Allen
[1836 to 1897 united with Gloucester]
1897 George Forrest Browne
1914 George Nickson
1933 Clifford Salisbury Woodward
1946 Frederick Arthur Cockin
1959 Oliver Stratford Tomkins
1976 Ernest John Tinsley
1985 Barry Rogerson
2003 Michael Arthur Hill

Chelmsford

Description of arms. Or, on a saltire gules a pastoral staff of the first and a sword argent, hilt and pommel gold.

1914 John Edwin Watts-Ditchfield
1923 Frederic Sumpter Guy Warman
1929 Henry Albert Wilson
1951 Sherard Falkner Allison
1962 John Gerhard Tiarks
1971 Albert John Trillo
1986 John Waine
1996 John Freeman Perry
2003 John Warren Gladwin
2010 Stephen Geoffrey Cottrell

Chichester

Description of arms. Azure, our blessed Lord in judgement seated in His throne, His dexter hand upraised or, His sinister hand holding an open book proper, and issuant from His mouth a two-edged sword point to the sinister gules.

BISHOPS OF SELSEY

681	Wilfrid
716	Eadberht
731	Eolla
733	Sigga [Sigeferth]
765	Aaluberht
c.765	Öswald [Ösa]
780	Gislhere
786	Tota
c.789	Wihthun
c.811	Æthelwulf
824	Cynered
845	Guthheard
900	Wighelm
909	Beornheah
931	Wulfhun
943	Ælfred
955	Daniel
956	Brihthelm
963	Eadhelm
980	Æthelgar
990	Ordbriht
1009	Ælfmaer
1032	Æthelric I
1039	Grimketel
1047	Heca
1058	Æthelric II
1070	Stigand

BISHOPS OF CHICHESTER

1075	Stigand
1088	Godfrey
1091	Ralph Luffa
1125	Seffrid I [d'Escures Pelochin]
1147	Hilary
1174	John Greenford
1180	Seffrid II
1204	Simon FitzRobert
1215	Richard Poore
1218	Ranulf of Wareham
1224	Ralph Nevill
1245	Richard Wich
1254	John Climping
1262	Stephen Bersted [or Pagham]
1288	Gilbert de St Leofard
1305	John Langton
1337	Robert Stratford
1362	William Lenn
1369	William Reade
1386	Thomas Rushock
1390	Richard Mitford
1396	Robert Waldby
1397	Robert Reade
1417	Stephen Patrington
1418	Henry de la Ware

1421	John Kempe
1421	Thomas Polton
1426	John Rickingale
1431	Simon Sydenham
1438	Richard Praty
1446	Adam de Moleyns
1450	Reginald Pecock
1459	John Arundel
1478	Edward Story
1504	Richard Fitz-James
1508	Robert Sherburne
1536	Richard Sampson
1543	George Day (deposed)
1552	John Scory
1553	George Day (restored)
1557	John Christopherson
1559	William Barlow
1570	Richard Curtis
1586	Thomas Bickley
1596	Anthony Watson
1605	Lancelot Andrewes
1609	Samuel Harsnett
1619	George Carleton
1628	Richard Montague
1638	Brian Duppa
1642	Henry King
1670	Peter Gunning
1675	Ralph Brideoake
1679	Guy Carleton
1685	John Lake
1689	Simon Patrick
1691	Robert Grove
1696	John Williams
1709	Thomas Manningham
1722	Thomas Bowers
1724	Edward Waddington
1731	Francis Hare
1740	Matthias Mawson
1754	William Ashburnham
1798	John Buckner
1824	Robert James Carr
1831	Edward Maltby
1836	William Otter
1840	Philip Nicholas Shuttleworth
1842	Ashurst Turner Gilbert
1870	Richard Durnford
1896	Ernest Roland Wilberforce
1908	Charles John Ridgeway
1919	Winfrid Oldfield Burrows
1929	George Kennedy Allen Bell
1958	Roger Plumpton Wilson
1974	Eric Waldram Kemp
2001	John William Hind

Coventry

Description of arms. Gules, within a bordure argent charged with eight torteaux, a cross potent quadrate of the second.

1918	Huyshe Wolcott Yeatman-Biggs
1922	Charles Lisle Carr
1931	Mervyn George Haigh
1943	Neville Vincent Gorton

1956	Cuthbert Killick Norman Bardsley
1976	John Gibbs
1985	Simon Barrington-Ward
1998	Colin James Bennetts
2008	Christopher John Cocksworth

Derby

Description of arms. Purpure, a cross of St Chad argent beneath three fountains in chief.

1927	Edmund Courtenay Pearce
1936	Alfred Edward John Rawlinson
1939	Geoffrey Francis Allen
1969	Cyril William Johnston Bowles
1988	Peter Spencer Dawes
1995	Jonathan Sansbury Bailey
2005	Alastair Llewellyn John Redfern

Dorchester[1]

634	Birinus
650	Agilbert
c.660	Ætla
c.888	Ahlheard

Ely

Description of arms. Gules, three ducal coronets or.

1109	Hervey
1133	Nigel
1174	Geoffrey Ridel
1189	William Longchamp
1198	Eustace
1220	John of Fountains
1225	Geoffrey de Burgo
1229	Hugh of Northwold
1255	William of Kilkenny
1258	Hugh of Balsham
1286	John of Kirkby
1290	William of Louth
1299	Ralph Walpole
1303	Robert Orford
1310	John Ketton
1316	John Hotham
1337	Simon Montacute
1345	Thomas de Lisle
1362	Simon Langham
1367	John Barnet
1374	Thomas Arundel
1388	John Fordham

[1] Originally a West Saxon, after Ahlheard's time a Mercian, bishopric. See transferred to Lincoln 1077.

1426 Philip Morgan
1438 Lewis of Luxembourg
1444 Thomas Bourgchier
1454 William Grey
1479 John Morton
1486 John Alcock
1501 Richard Redman
1506 James Stanley
1515 Nicholas West
1534 Thomas Goodrich
1555 Thomas Thirlby
1559 Richard Cox
1600 Martin Heton
1609 Lancelot Andrewes
1619 Nicolas Felton
1628 John Buckeridge
1631 Francis White
1638 Matthew Wren
1667 Benjamin Laney
1675 Peter Gunning
1684 Francis Turner
1691 Simon Patrick
1707 John Moore
1714 William Fleetwood
1723 Thomas Greene
1738 Robert Butts
1748 Thomas Gooch
1754 Matthias Mawson
1771 Edmund Keene
1781 James Yorke
1808 Thomas Dampier
1812 Bowyer Edward Sparke
1836 Joseph Allen
1845 Thomas Turton
1864 Edward Harold Browne
1873 James Russell Woodford
1886 Alwyne Frederick Compton
1905 Frederick Henry Chase
1924 Leonard Jauncey White-
      Thomson
1934 Bernard Oliver Francis
      Heywood
1941 Harold Edward Wynn
1957 Noel Baring Hudson
1964 Edward James Keymer
      Roberts
1977 Peter Knight Walker
1990 Stephen Whitefield Sykes
2000 Anthony John Russell
2010 Stephen David Conway

Exeter

Description of arms. Gules, a sword
erect in pale argent hilt or surmounted
by two keys addorsed in saltire gold.

BISHOPS OF CORNWALL

870 Kenstec
893 Asser
931 Conan
950 Æthelge[ard]
c.955 Daniel
963 Wulfsige Comoere
990 Ealdred

1009 Æthelsige
1018 Buruhwold
1027 Lyfing, Bishop of
      Crediton, Cornwall
      and Worcester
1046 Leofric, Bishop of
      Crediton and
      Cornwall
[See transferred to Exeter 1050]

BISHOPS OF CREDITON

909 Eadwulf
934 Æthelgar
953 Ælfwold I
973 Sideman
979 Ælfric
987 Ælfwold II
1008 Ælfwold III
1015 Eadnoth
1027 Lyfing
1046 Leofric[1]

BISHOPS OF EXETER

1050 Leofric
1072 Osbern Fitz-Osbern
1107 Will. Warelwast
1138 Robert Warelwast
1155 Robert II of Chichester
1161 Bartholomew
1186 John the Chanter
1194 Henry Marshall
1214 Simon of Apulia
1224 William Brewer
1245 Richard Blund
1258 Walter Bronescombe
1280 Peter Quinel [Wyvill]
1292 Thomas Bitton
1308 Walter Stapeldon
1327 James Berkeley
1328 John Grandisson
1370 Thomas Brantingham
1395 Edmund Stafford
1419 John Catterick
1420 Edmund Lacy
1458 George Nevill
1465 John Booth
1478 Peter Courtenay
1487 Richard Fox
1493 Oliver King
1496 Richard Redman
1502 John Arundel
1505 Hugh Oldham
1519 John Veysey (resigned)
1551 Miles Coverdale
1553 John Veysey (restored)
1555 James Turberville
1560 William Alley [or Allei]
1571 William Bradbridge
1579 John Woolton
1595 Gervase Babington
1598 William Cotton
1621 Valentine Carey
1627 Joseph Hall
1642 Ralph Brownrigg
1660 John Gauden
1662 Seth Ward
1667 Anthony Sparrow
1676 Thomas Lamplugh
1689 Jonathan Trelawney
1708 Offspring Blackall
1717 Lancelot Blackburn
1724 Stephen Weston
1742 Nicholas Claget
1747 George Lavington
1762 Frederick Keppel

1778 John Ross
1792 William Buller
1797 Henry Reginald
      Courtenay
1803 John Fisher
1807 George Pelham
1820 William Carey
1830 Christopher Bethell
1831 Henry Phillpotts
1869 Frederick Temple
1885 Edward Henry
      Bickersteth
1901 Herbert Edward Ryle
1903 Archibald Robertson
1916 Rupert Ernest William
      Gascoyne Cecil
1936 Charles Edward Curzon
1949 Robert Cecil Mortimer
1973 Eric Arthur John Mercer
1985 Geoffrey Hewlett
      Thompson
1999 Michael Laurence
      Langrish

Gibraltar in Europe

Description of arms. Argent, in base
rising out of the waves of the sea a
rock proper, thereon a lion guardant
or supporting a passion cross erect
gules, on a chief engrailed of the last a
crosier in bend dexter and a key in
bend sinister or surmounted by a
Maltese cross argent fimbriated gold.

BISHOPS OF GIBRALTAR

1842 George Tomlinson
1863 Walter John Trower
1868 Charles Amyand Harris
1874 Charles Waldegrave Sandford
1904 William Edward Collins
1911 Henry Joseph Corbett Knight
1921 John Harold Greig
1927 Frederick Cyril Nugent
      Hicks
1933 Harold Jocelyn Buxton
1947 Cecil Douglas Horsley
1953 Frederick William Thomas
      Craske
1960 Stanley Albert Hallam Eley
1970 John Richard Satterthwaite[2]

BISHOPS OF GIBRALTAR IN
EUROPE

1980 John Richard
      Satterthwaite
1993 John William Hind
2001 Douglas Geoffrey Rowell

---

[1] Removed See from Crediton.   [2] Bishop of Fulham and Gibraltar from 1970 to 1980.

Gloucester

Description of arms. Azure, two keys addorsed in saltire the wards upwards or.

1541 John Wakeman *alias*
      Wiche
1551 John Hooper
1554 James Brooks
1562 Richard Cheyney[1]
1581 John Bullingham[2]
1598 Godfrey Goldsborough
1605 Thomas Ravis
1607 Henry Parry
1611 Giles Thompson
1612 Miles Smith
1625 Godfrey Goodman
1661 William Nicolson
1672 John Pritchett
1681 Robert Frampton
1691 Edward Fowler
1715 Richard Willis
1721 Joseph Wilcocks
1731 Elias Sydall
1735 Martin Benson
1752 James Johnson
1760 William Warburton
1779 James Yorke
1781 Samuel Hallifax
1789 Richard Beadon
1802 George Isaac
      Huntingford
1815 Henry Ryder
1824 Christopher Bethell
1830 James Henry Monk
[1836 to 1897, united with
      Bristol]

BISHOPS OF GLOUCESTER AND
BRISTOL

1836 James Henry Monk
1856 Charles Baring
1861 William Thomson
1863 Charles John Ellicott[3]

BISHOPS OF GLOUCESTER

1897 Charles John Ellicott
1905 Edgar Charles Sumner
      Gibson
1923 Arthur Cayley Headlam
1946 Clifford Salisbury
      Woodward
1954 Wilfred Marcus Askwith
1962 Basil Tudor Guy
1975 John Yates
1992 Peter John Ball
1993 David Edward Bentley
2004 Michael Francis Perham

Guildford

Description of arms. Gules, two keys conjoined wards outwards in bend, the uppermost or, the other argent, interposed between them in bend sinister a sword of the third, hilt and pommel gold, all within a bordure azure charged with ten wool-packs argent.

1927 John Harold Greig
1934 John Victor Macmillan
1949 Henry Colville Montgomery
      Campbell
1956 Ivor Stanley Watkins
1961 George Edmund Reindorp
1973 David Alan Brown
1983 Michael Edgar Adie
1994 John Warren Gladwin
2004 Christopher John Hill

Hereford

Description of arms. Gules, three leopards' faces jessant-de-lis reversed or.

676 Putta
688 Tyrhtel
710 Torhthere
c.731 Wahistod
736 Cuthberht
741 Podda
c.758 Acca
c.770 Headda
777 Aldberht
786 Esne
c.788 Ceolmund
c.798 Utel
801 Wulfheard
824 Beonna
c.832 Eadwulf
c.839 Cuthwulf
866 Mucel
c.866 Deorlaf
888 Cynemund
890 EadBar
c.931 Tidhelm
940 Wulfhelm
c.940 Ælfric
971 Æthelwulf
1016 Æthelstan
1056 Leofgar
1056 Ealdred, Bishop of Hereford
      and Worcester

1060 Walter
1079 Robert Losinga
1096 Gerard
1107 Reinhelm
1115 Geoffrey de Clive
1121 Richard de Capella
1131 Robert de Bethune
1148 Gilbert Foliot
1163 Robert of Melun
1174 Robert Foliot
1186 William de Vere
1200 Giles de Braose
1216 Hugh of Mapenore
1219 Hugh Foliot
1234 Ralph Maidstone
1240 Peter d'Aigueblanche
1269 John Breton
1275 Thomas Cantilupe
1283 Richard Swinfeld
1317 Adam Orleton
1327 Thomas Chariton
1344 John Trilleck
1361 Lewis Charleton
1370 William Courtenay
1375 John Gilbert
1389 John Trefnant
1404 Robert Mascall
1417 Edmund Lacy
1420 Thomas Polton
1422 Thomas Spofford
1449 Richard Beauchamp
1451 Reginald Boulers
1453 John Stanbury
1474 Thomas Milling
1492 Edmund Audley
1502 Adriano de Castello [di
      Corneto]
1504 Richard Mayeu
1516 Charles Booth
1535 Edward Fox
1539 John Skip
1553 John Harley
1554 Robert Parfew or Wharton
1559 John Scory
1586 Herbert Westfaling
1603 Robert Bennett
1617 Francis Godwin
1634 Augustine Lindsell
1635 Matthew Wren
1635 Theophilus Field
1636 George Coke
1661 Nicolas Monk
1662 Herbert Croft
1691 Gilbert Ironside
1701 Humphrey Humphries
1713 Philip Bisse
1721 Benjamin Hoadly
1724 Henry Egerton
1746 James Beauclerk
1787 John Harley
1788 John Butler
1803 Ffolliott Herbert Walker
      Cornewall
1808 John Luxmoore
1815 George Isaac
      Huntingford
1832 Edward Grey
1837 Thomas Musgrave
1848 Renn Dickson Hampden
1868 James Atlay
1895 John Percival
1918 Herbert Hensley Henson
1920 Martin Linton Smith
1931 Charles Lisle Carr
1941 Richard Godfrey Parsons
1949 Tom Longworth

---

[1] Also Bishop of Bristol.   [2] Held Gloucester and Bristol 1581-9.   [3] Gloucester only from 1897.

1961 Mark Allin Hodson
1974 John Richard Gordon
     Eastaugh
1990 John Keith Oliver
2004 Anthony Martin Priddis

Leicester

see also under Lincoln
Description of arms. Gules, a pierced
cinquefoil ermine, in chief a lion
passant guardant grasping in the dexter
forepaw a cross crosslet fitchée or.

NEW FOUNDATION

1927 Cyril Charles Bowman
     Bardsley
1940 Guy Vernon Smith
1953 Ronald Ralph Williams
1979 Cecil Richard Rutt
1991 Thomas Frederick Butler
1999 Timothy John Stevens

Lichfield

Description of arms. Per pale gules and
argent, a cross potent quadrate in the
centre per pale argent and or between
four crosses patée those to the dexter
argent and those to the sinister gold.

BISHOPS OF MERCIA

656 Diuma[1]
658 Ceollach
659 Trumhere
662 Jaruman

BISHOPS OF LICHFIELD

669 Chad[2]
672 Winfrith
676 Seaxwulf
691 Headda[3]
731 Aldwine
737 Hwita

757 Hemele
765 Cuthfrith
769 Berhthun
779 Hygeberht[4]
801 Aldwulf
816 Herewine
818 Æthelwald
830 Hunberht
836 Cyneferth
845 Tunberht
869 Eadberht
883 Wulfred
900 Wigmund or Wilferth
915 Ælfwine
941 Wulfgar
949 Cynesige
964 Wynsige
975 Ælfheah
1004 Godwine
1020 Leofgar
1026 Brihtmaer
1039 Wulfsige
1053 Leofwine
1072 Peter

BISHOPS OF LICHFIELD,
CHESTER, AND
COVENTRY[5]

1075 Peter
1086 Robert de Limesey[5]
1121 Robert Peche
1129 Roger de Clinton
1149 Walter Durdent
1161 Richard Peche
1183 Gerard La Pucelle
1188 Hugh Nonant
1198 Geoffrey Muschamp
1215 William Cornhill
1224 Alex. Stavensby
1240 Hugh Pattishall
1246 Roger Weseham
1258 Roger Longespee
1296 Walter Langton
1322 Roger Northburgh
1360 Robert Stretton
1386 Walter Skirlaw
1386 Richard le Scrope
1398 John Burghill
1415 John Catterick
1420 William Heyworth
1447 William Booth
1452 Nicholas Close
1453 Reginald Boulers
1459 John Hales
1493 William Smith
1496 John Arundel
1503 Geoffrey Blyth
1534 Rowland Lee
1541 [Chester formed as a
     bishopric]
1543 Richard Sampson
1554 Ralph Baynes
1560 Thomas Bentham
1580 William Overton
1609 George Abbot
1610 Richard Neile
1614 John Overall
1619 Thomas Morton
1632 Robert Wright

1644 Accepted Frewen
1661 John Hackett
1671 Thomas Wood
1692 William Lloyd
1699 John Hough
1717 Edward Chandler
1731 Richard Smalbroke
1750 Fred. Cornwallis
1768 John Egerton
1771 Brownlow North
1775 Richard Hurd
1781 James Cornwallis [4th Earl
     Cornwallis]
1824 Henry Ryder
1836 [Coventry transferred to
     Worcester diocese]
1836 Samuel Butler
1840 James Bowstead
1843 John Lonsdale
1868 George Augustus Selwyn
1878 William Dalrymple
     Maclagan
1891 Augustus Legge
1913 John Augustine
     Kempthorne
1937 Edward Sydney Woods
1953 Arthur Stretton Reeve
1975 Kenneth John Fraser
     Skelton
1984 Keith Norman Sutton
2003 Jonathan Michael
     Gledhill

Lincoln

Description of arms. Gules, two lions
passant guardant or, on a chief azure,
the Virgin ducally crowned sitting on a
throne issuant from the chief, on her
dexter arm the infant Jesus, and in her
sinister hand a sceptre all gold.

BISHOPS OF LINDSEY

634 Birinus
650 Agilbert
660 Aetlai
678 Eadhaed
680 Æthelwine
693 (?)Edgar
731 (?)Cyneberht
733 Alwig
750 Aldwulf
767 Ceolwulf
796 Eadwulf
839 Beorhtred
869 Burgheard
933 Ælfred
953 Leofwine
996 Sigefrith

---

[1] Archbishop of the Mercians, the Lindisfari, and the Middle Angles.
[2] Bishop of the Mercians and the Lindisfari.
[3] Bishop of Lichfield and Leicester.
[4] Archbishop of Lichfield after 787.
[5] 1102 Robert de Limesey, Bishop of Lichfield, moved the See to Coventry. Succeeding bishops are usually termed *of Coventry* until 1228. Then
Coventry and Lichfield was the habitual title until the Reformation. *Chester* was used by some 12th-century bishops, and popularly afterwards.
After the Reformation *Lichfield and Coventry* was used until 1846.

BISHOPS OF LEICESTER

- 664 Wilfrid, translated from York
- 679 Cuthwine
- 691 Headda[1] (founder of Lichfield Cathedral 705–37)
- 727 Aldwine
- 737 Torhthelm
- 764 Eadberht
- 785 Unwona
- 803 Wernberht
- 816 Raethhun
- 840 Ealdred
- 844 Ceolred
- 874 [See of Leicester removed to Dorchester]

BISHOPS OF DORCHESTER

(after it became a Mercian See)
- c.888 Ahlheard
- 900 Wigmund or Wilferth
- 909 Cenwulf
- 925 Wynsige
- c.951 Osketel
- 953 Leofwine
- 975 Ælfnoth
- 979 Æscwig
- 1002 Ælfheln
- 1006 Eadnoth I
- 1016 Æthelric
- 1034 Eadnoth II
- 1049 Ulf
- 1053 Wulfwig
- 1067 Remigius

BISHOPS OF LINCOLN

- 1072 Remigius
- 1094 Robert Bloett
- 1123 Alexander
- 1148 Robert de Chesney
- 1183 Walter de Coutances
- 1186 Hugh of Avalon
- 1203 William of Blois
- 1209 Hugh of Wells
- 1235 Robert Grosseteste
- 1254 Henry Lexington [Sutton]
- 1258 Richard Gravesend
- 1280 Oliver Sutton [Lexington]
- 1300 John Dalderby
- 1320 Henry Burghersh
- 1342 Thomas Bek
- 1347 John Gynewell
- 1363 John Bokyngham [Buckingham]
- 1398 Henry Beaufort
- 1405 Philip Repingdon
- 1420 Richard Fleming
- 1431 William Gray
- 1436 William Alnwick
- 1450 Marmaduke Lumley
- 1452 John Chedworth
- 1472 Thomas Rotherham [Scott]
- 1480 John Russell
- 1495 William Smith
- 1514 Thomas Wolsey
- 1514 William Atwater
- 1521 John Longland
- 1547 Henry Holbeach [Rands]
- 1552 John Taylor
- 1554 John White
- 1557 Thomas Watson
- 1560 Nicholas Bullingham
- 1571 Thomas Cooper
- 1584 William Wickham
- 1595 William Chaderton
- 1608 William Barlow

- 1614 Richard Neile
- 1617 George Monteigne [Mountain]
- 1621 John Williams
- 1642 Thomas Winniffe
- 1660 Robt. Sanderson
- 1663 Benjamin Laney
- 1667 William Fuller
- 1675 Thomas Barlow
- 1692 Thomas Tenison
- 1695 James Gardiner
- 1705 William Wake
- 1716 Edmund Gibson
- 1723 Richard Reynolds
- 1744 John Thomas
- 1761 John Green
- 1779 Thomas Thurlow
- 1787 George Pretyman [Pretyman Tomline after June 1803]
- 1820 George Pelham
- 1827 John Kaye
- 1853 John Jackson
- 1869 Christopher Wordsworth
- 1885 Edward King
- 1910 Edward Lee Hicks
- 1920 William Shuckburgh Swayne
- 1933 Frederick Cyril Nugent Hicks
- 1942 Henry Aylmer Skelton
- 1946 Leslie Owen
- 1947 Maurice Henry Harland
- 1956 Kenneth Riches
- 1975 Simon Wilton Phipps
- 1987 Robert Maynard Hardy
- 2001 John Charles Saxbee
- 2011 Christopher Lowson

Norwich

Description of arms. Azure, three labelled mitres or.

BISHOPS OF DUNWICH

- 631 Felix
- 648 Thomas
- c.653 Berhtgils [Boniface]
- c.670 Bisi
- c.673 Æcce
- 693 Alric (?)
- 716 Eardred
- 731 Aldbeorht I
- 747 Æscwulf
- 747 Eardwulf
- 775 Cuthwine
- 775 Aldbeorht II
- 781 Ecglaf
- 781 Heardred
- 793 Ælfhun
- 798 Tidferth
- 824 Waermund[2]
- 825 Wilred
- 836 Husa
- 870 Æthelwold

BISHOPS OF ELMHAM

- 673 Beaduwine
- 706 Nothberht
- c.731 Heathulac

- 736 Æthelfrith
- 758 Eanfrith
- c.781 Æthelwulf
- c.785 Alhheard
- 814 Sibba
- 824 Hunferth
- 824 Hunbeorht
- 836 Cunda[3]
- c.933 Ælfred[4]
- c.945 Æthelweald
- 956 Eadwulf
- 970 Ælfric I
- 974 Theodred I
- 982 Theodred II
- 997 Æthelstan
- 1001 Ælfgar
- 1021 Ælfwine
- 1038 Ælfric II
- 1039 Ælfric III
- 1043 Stigand[5]
- 1043 Grimketel[6]
- 1044 Stigand (restored)
- 1047 Æthelmaer

BISHOPS OF THETFORD

- 1070 Herfast
- 1086 William de Beaufai
- 1091 Herbert Losinga

BISHOPS OF NORWICH

- 1091 Herbert Losinga
- 1121 Everard of Montgomery
- 1146 William de Turbe
- 1175 John of Oxford
- 1200 John de Gray
- 1222 Pandulf Masca
- 1226 Thomas Blundeville
- 1239 William Raleigh
- 1245 Walter Suffield or Calthorp
- 1258 Simon Walton
- 1266 Roger Skerning
- 1278 William Middleton
- 1289 Ralph Walpole
- 1299 John Salmon
- 1325 [Robert de Baldock]
- 1325 William Ayermine
- 1337 Anthony Bek
- 1344 William of Norwich [Bateman]
- 1356 Thomas Percy
- 1370 Henry Spencer [Dispenser]
- 1407 Alexander Tottington
- 1413 Richard Courtenay
- 1416 John Wakeryng
- 1426 William Ainwick
- 1436 Thomas Brown
- 1446 Walter Lyhert [le Hart]
- 1472 James Goldwell
- 1499 Thomas Jane
- 1501 Richard Nykke
- 1536 William Reppes [Rugge]
- 1550 Thomas Thirlby
- 1554 John Hopton
- 1560 John Parkhurst
- 1575 Edmund Freke
- 1585 Edmund Scambler
- 1595 William Redman
- 1603 John Jegon
- 1618 John Overall
- 1619 Samuel Harsnett
- 1629 Francis White

---

[1] Bishop of Leicester and Lichfield.
[2] Bishop of Dunwich or Elmham.
[3] Bishop of Elmham or Dunwich.
[4] Bishop of Elmham or Lindsey.
[5] Deposed before consecration.
[6] Bishop of Selsey and Elmham.

1632 Richard Corbet	1737 Thomas Secker
1635 Matthew Wren	1758 John Hume
1638 Richard Montagu	1766 Robert Lowth
1641 Joseph Hall	1777 John Butler
1661 Edward Reynolds	1788 Edward Smallwell
1676 Antony Sparrow	1799 John Randolph
1685 William Lloyd	1807 Charles Moss
1691 John Moore	1812 William Jackson
1708 Charles Trimnell	1816 Edward Legge
1721 Thomas Green	1827 Charles Lloyd
1723 John Leng	1829 Richard Bagot
1727 William Baker	1845 Samuel Wilberforce
1733 Robert Butts	1870 John Fielder Mackarness
1738 Thomas Gooch	1889 William Stubbs
1748 Samuel Lisle	1901 Francis Paget
1749 Thomas Hayter	1911 Charles Gore
1761 Philip Yonge	1919 Hubert Murray Burge
1783 Lewis Bagot	1925 Thomas Banks Strong
1790 George Horne	1937 Kenneth Escott Kirk
1792 Charles Manners	1955 Harry James Carpenter
Sutton	1971 Kenneth John Woollcombe
1805 Henry Bathurst	1978 Patrick Campbell Rodger
1837 Edward Stanley	1987 Richard Douglas Harries
1849 Samuel Hinds	2007 John Lawrence Pritchard
1857 John Thomas Pelham	
1893 John Sheepshanks	
1910 Bertram Pollock	

Peterborough

Description of arms. Gules, two keys in saltire the wards upwards between four cross crosslets fitchée or.

1942 Percy Mark Herbert	1541 John Chamber
1959 William Launcelot Scott	1557 David Pole
Fleming	1561 Edmund Scambler
1971 Maurice Arthur Ponsonby	1585 Richard Howland
Wood	1601 Thomas Dove
1985 Peter John Nott	1630 William Piers
1999 Graham Richard James	1633 Augustine Lindsell
	1634 Francis Dee
	1639 John Towers
	1660 Benjamin Laney

Oxford

Description of arms. Sable, a fess argent, in chief three demi-ladies couped at the waist heads affrontée proper crowned or arrayed and veiled of the second, in base an ox of the last, horned and hoofed gold, passing a ford barry wavy of six azure and argent.

1542 Robert King[1]	1663 Joseph Henshaw
1558 [Thomas Goldwell]	1679 William Lloyd
1567 Hugh Curen [Curwen]	1685 Thomas White
1589 John Underhill	1691 Richard Cumberland
1604 John Bridges	1718 White Kennett
1619 John Howson	1729 Robert Clavering
1628 Richard Corbet	1747 John Thomas
1632 John Bancroft	1757 Richard Terrick
1641 Robert Skinner	1764 Robert Lambe
1663 William Paul	1769 John Hinchliffe
1665 Walter Blandford	1794 Spencer Madan
1671 Nathaniel Crewe	1813 John Parsons
[Lord Crewe]	1819 Herbert Marsh
1674 Henry Compton	1839 George Davys
1676 John Fell	1864 Francis Jeune
1686 Samuel Parker	1868 William Connor Magee
1688 Timothy Hall	1891 Mandell Creighton
1690 John Hough	1897 Edward Carr Glyn
1699 William Talbot	1916 Frank Theodore Woods
1715 John Potter	1924 Cyril Charles Bowman
	Bardsley
	1927 Claude Martin Blagden
	1949 Spencer Stottisbury Gwatkin
	Leeson
	1956 Robert Wright Stopford
	1961 Cyril Eastaugh

Portsmouth

Description of arms. Per fess or and gules, in chief upon waves of the sea proper a lymphad sable, and in base two keys conjoined wards outwards in bend, the uppermost or, the other argent, interposed between them in bend sinister a sword also argent, hilt and pommel gold.

1927 Ernest Neville Lovett
1936 Frank Partridge
1942 William Louis Anderson
1949 William Launcelot Scott
     Fleming
1960 John Henry Lawrence Phillips
1975 Archibald Ronald McDonald
     Gordon
1985 Timothy John Bavin
1995 Kenneth William Stevenson
2010 Christopher Richard James
     Foster

1972 Douglas Russell Feaver
1984 William John Westwood
1996 Ian Patrick Martyn Cundy
2010 Donald Spargo Allister

Rochester

Description of arms. Argent, on a saltire gules an escallop or.

604 Justus
624 Romanus
633 Paulinus
644 Ithamar
664 Damianus
669 Putta
676 Cwichelm
678 Gebmund
716 Tobias
727 Aldwulf
741 Dunn
747 Eardwulf
772 Diora
785 Waermund I
805 Beornmod
844 Tatnoth
868 Badenoth
868 Waermund II
868 Cuthwulf
880 Swithwulf
900 Ceolmund
c.926 Cyneferth
c.934 Burhric

---

[1] Bishop Rheon. *in partibus.* Of Oseney 1542-5. See transferred to Oxford 1545.

949	Beorhtsige
955	[Daniel?] Rochester or Selsey
964	Ælfstan
995	Godwine I
1046	Godwine II
1058	Siward
1076	Arnost
1077	Gundulf
1108	Ralph d'Escures
1115	Ernulf
1125	John
1137	John II
1142	Ascelin
1148	Walter
1182	Waleran
1185	Gilbert Glanvill
1215	Benedict of Sausetun [Sawston]
1227	Henry Sandford
1238	Richard Wendene
1251	Lawrence of St Martin
1274	Walter Merton
1278	John Bradfield
1283	Thomas Ingoldsthorpe
1292	Thomas of Wouldham
1319	Hamo Hethe
1353	John Sheppey
1362	William of Whittlesey
1364	Thomas Trilleck
1373	Thomas Brinton
1389	William Bottlesham [Bottisham]
1400	John Bottlesham
1404	Richard Young
1419	John Kempe
1422	John Langdon
1435	Thomas Brouns
1437	William Wells
1444	John Low
1468	Thomas Rotherham [otherwise Scott]
1472	John Alcock
1476	John Russell
1480	Edmund Audley
1493	Thomas Savage
1497	Richard Fitz-James
1504	John Fisher
1535	John Hilsey [Hildesleigh]
1540	Nicolas Heath
1544	Henry Holbeach
1547	Nicholas Ridley
1550	John Ponet [Poynet]
1551	John Scory
1554	Maurice Griffith
1560	Edmund Gheast [Guest]
1572	Edmund Freke
1576	John Piers
1578	John Young
1605	William Barlow
1608	Richard Neile
1611	John Buckeridge
1628	Walter Curil
1630	John Bowle
1638	John Warner
1666	John Dolben
1683	Francis Turner
1684	Thomas Sprat
1713	Francis Atterbury
1723	Samuel Bradford
1731	Joseph Wilcocks
1756	Zachary Pearce
1774	John Thomas
1793	Samuel Horsley
1802	Thomas Dampier
1809	Walker King
1827	Hugh Percy
1827	George Murray

1860	Joseph Cotton Wigram
1867	Thomas Legh Claughton
1877	Anthony Wilson Thorold
1891	Randall Thomas Davidson
1895	Edward Stuart Talbot
1905	John Reginald Harmer
1930	Martin Linton Smith
1940	Christopher Maude Chavasse
1961	Richard David Say
1988	Anthony Michael Arnold Turnbull
1994	Michael James Nazir-Ali
2010	James Henry Langstaff

St Albans

Description of arms. Azure, a saltire or, overall a sword erect in pale proper, hilt and pommel gold, in chief a celestial crown of the same.

1877	Thomas Legh Claughton
1890	John Wogan Festing
1903	Edgar Jacob
1920	Michael Bolton Furse
1944	Philip Henry Loyd
1950	Edward Michael Gresford Jones
1970	Robert Alexander Kennedy Runcie
1980	John Bernard Taylor
1995	Christopher William Herbert
2009	Alan Gregory Clayton Smith

St Edmundsbury and Ipswich

Description of arms. Per pale gules and azure, between three ducal coronets a demi-lion passant guardant conjoined to the demi-hulk of an ancient ship or.

1914	Henry Bernard Hodgson
1921	Albert Augustus David
1923	Walter Godfrey Whittingham
1940	Richard Brook
1954	Arthur Harold Morris
1966	Leslie Wilfrid Brown
1978	John Waine
1986	John Dennis
1997	John Hubert Richard Lewis
2007	William Nigel Stock

Salisbury

Description of arms. Azure, our Lady crowned, holding in her dexter arm the infant Jesus, and in her sinister arm a sceptre all or, round both the heads circles of glory gold.

BISHOPS OF SHERBORNE

705	Ealdhelm
709	Forthhere
736	Hereweald
774	Æthelmod
793	Denefrith
801	Wigberht
825	Ealhstan
868	Heahmund
877	Æthelheah
889	Wulfsige I
900	Asser
c.909	Æthelweard
c.909	Waerstan
925	Æthelbald
925	Sigehelm
934	Ælfred
943	Wulfsige II
958	Ælfwold I
979	Æthelsige I
992	Wulfsige III
1002	Æthelric
1012	Æthelsige II
1017	Brihtwine I
1017	Ælfmaer
1023	Brihtwine II
1045	Ælfwold II
1058	Hereman, Bishop of Ramsbury

BISHOPS OF RAMSBURY

909	Æthelstan
927	Oda
949	Ælfric I
951	Osulf
970	Ælfstan
981	Wulfgar
986	Sigeric
993	Ælfric II
1005	Brihtwold
1045	Hereman[1]

BISHOPS OF SALISBURY

1078	Osmund Osmer
1107	Roger
1142	Jocelin de Bohun
1189	Hubert Walter
1194	Herbert Poore
1217	Richard Poore
1229	Robert Bingham
1247	William of York
1257	Giles of Bridport
1263	Walter de la Wyle
1274	Robert Wickhampton
1284	Walter Scammel
1287	Henry Brandeston

---

[1] Ramsbury was added to Sherbourne in 1058 when Hereman became Bishop of Sherbourne. The See was moved to Salisbury in 1078.

1289 William de la Corner
1292 Nicholas Longespee
1297 Simon of Ghent
1315 Roger de Mortival
1330 Robert Wyville
1375 Ralph Erghum
1388 John Waltham
1395 Richard Mitford
1407 Nicholas Bubwith
1407 Robert Hallum
1417 John Chaundler
1427 Robert Nevill
1438 William Aiscough
1450 Richard Beauchamp
1482 Lionel Woodville
1485 Thomas Langton
1494 John Blythe
1500 Henry Deane
1502 Edmund Audley
1525 Lorenzo Campeggio
1535 Nicholas Shaxton
1539 John Salcot [Capon]
1560 John Jewell
1571 Edmund Gheast [Guest]
1577 John Piers
1591 John Coldwell
1598 Henry Cotton
1615 Robert Abbot
1618 Martin Fotherby
1620 Robert Townson [Toulson]
1621 John Davenant
1641 Brian Duppa
1660 Humfrey Henchman
1663 John Earle
1665 Alexander Hyde
1667 Seth Ward
1689 Gilbert Burnet
1715 William Talbot
1721 Richard Wilis
1723 Benjamin Hoadly
1734 Thomas Sherlock
1748 John Gilbert
1757 John Thomas
1761 Robert Hay Drummond
1761 John Thomas
1766 John Hume
1782 Shute Barrington
1791 John Douglas
1807 John Fisher
1825 Thomas Burgess
1837 Edward Denison
1854 Walter Kerr Hamilton
1869 George Moberly
1885 John Wordsworth
1911 Frederic Edward Ridgeway
1921 St Clair George Alfred
        Donaldson
1936 Ernest Neville Lovett
1946 Geoffrey Charles Lester
        Lunt
1949 William Louis Anderson
1963 Joseph Edward Fison
1973 George Edmund Reindorp
1982 John Austin Baker
1993 David Staffurth Stancliffe
2011 Nicholas Roderick Holtam

Southwark

Description of arms. Argent, eleven
fusils in cross conjoined, seven in pale
fesswise, four in fess palewise, in the
dexter chief a mitre all gules.

1905 Edward Stuart Talbot
1911 Hubert Murray Burge
1919 Cyril Forster Garbett
1932 Richard Godfrey Parsons
1942 Bertram Fitzgerald Simpson
1959 Arthur Mervyn Stockwood
1980 Ronald Oliver Bowlby
1991 Robert Kerr Williamson
1998 Thomas Frederick Butler
2011 Christopher Thomas James
        Chessun

Truro

Description of arms. Argent, on a
saltire gules a sword and key or and in
base a fleur-de-lis sable all within a
bordure of the last charged with fifteen
besants.

1877 Edward White Benson
1883 George Howard Wilkinson
1891 John Gott
1906 Charles William Stubbs
1912 Winfrid Oldfield Burrows
1919 Frederic Sumpter Guy Warman
1923 Walter Howard Frere
1935 Joseph Wellington Hunkin
1951 Edmund Robert Morgan
1960 John Maurice Key
1973 Graham Douglas Leonard
1981 Peter Mumford
1990 Michael Thomas Ball
1997 William Ind
2008 Timothy Martin Thornton

Worcester

Description of arms. Argent, ten
torteaux, four, three, two, and one.

680 Bosel
691 Oftfor

693 Ecgwine
718 Wilfrid I
745 Milred
775 Waermund
777 Tilhere
781 Heathured
798 Deneberht
822 Heahberht
845 Alhhun
873 Waerferth
915 Æthelhun
922 Wilferth II
929 Cenwald
957 Dunstan
961 Oswald
992 Ealdwulf
1002 Wulfstan I
1016 Leofsige
1027 Lyfing
1033 Brihtheah
1040 Ælfric Puttoc, Bishop of York
        and Worcester
1041 Lyfing (restored)
1046 Ealdred Bishop of Hereford
        and Worcester 1056–60
1062 Wulfstan II
1096 Samson
1115 Theulf
1125 Simon
1151 John of Pagham
1158 Aldred
1164 Roger of Gloucester
1180 Baldwin
1186 William of Northolt
1191 Robert Fitz Ralph
1193 Henry de Sully
1196 John of Coutances
1200 Mauger
1214 Walter de Gray
1216 Silvester of Evesham
1218 William of Blois
1237 Walter Cantilupe
1266 Nicolas of Ely
1268 Godfrey Giffard
1302 William Gainsborough
1308 Walter Reynolds
1313 Walter Maidstone
1317 Thomas Cobham
1327 Adam Orleton
1334 Simon Montacute
1337 Thomas Hempnall
1339 Wulstan Bransford
1350 John Thoresby
1353 Reginald Brian
1362 John Barnet
1364 William of Whittlesey
1369 William Lenn
1375 Henry Wakefield
1396 Robert Tideman of
        Winchcomb
1401 Richard Clifford
1407 Thomas Peverel
1419 Philip Morgan
1426 Thomas Polton
1435 Thomas Bourgchier
1444 John Carpenter
1476 John Alcock
1487 Robert Morton
1497 Giovanni de' Gigli
1499 Silvestro de' Gigli
1521 Julius de Medici Guilio de
        Medici (administrator)
1523 Geronimo Ghinucci
1535 Hugh Latimer
1539 John Bell
1544 Nicholas Heath (deposed)
1552 John Hooper
1554 Nicholas Heath (restored)
1555 Richard Pates
1559 Edwin Sandys

1571 Nicholas Bullingham	1683 William Thomas	1905 Huyshe Wolcott Yeatman-
1577 John Whitgift	1689 Edward Stillingfleet	Biggs
1584 Edmund Freke	1699 William Lloyd	1919 Ernest Harold Pearce
1593 Richard Fletcher	1717 John Hough	1931 Arthur William Thomson
1596 Thomas Bilson	1743 Isaac Maddox	Perowne
1597 Gervase Babington	1759 James Johnson	1941 William Wilson Cash
1610 Henry Parry	1774 Brownlow North	1956 Lewis Mervyn Charles-
1617 John Thornborough	1781 Richard Hurd	Edwards
1641 John Prideaux	1808 Ffolliott Herbert Walker	1971 Robert Wylmer Woods
1660 George Morley	Cornewall	1982 Philip Harold Ernest
1662 John Gauden	1831 Robert James Carr	Goodrich
1662 John Earle	1841 Henry Pepys	1997 Peter Stephen Maurice
1663 Robert Skinner	1861 Henry Philpott	Selby
1671 Walter Blandford	1891 John James Stewart Perowne	2007 John Geoffrey Inge
1675 James Fleetwood	1902 Charles Gore	

PROVINCE OF YORK

York

Description of arms. Gules, two keys in saltire argent, in chief a regal crown proper.

BISHOPS

314 Eborius
625 Paulinus
    [Vacancy 633–64]
664 Cedda
664 Wilfrid I
678 Bosa (retired)
686 Bosa (restored)
691 Wilfrith (restored)
706 John of Beverley
718 Wilfrid II

ARCHBISHOPS

734 Egberht
767 Æthelberht
780 Eanbald I
796 Eanbald II
808 Wulfsige
837 Wigmund
854 Wulfhere
900 Æthelbald
c.928 Hrothweard
931 Wulfstan I
956 Osketel
971 Oswald
971 Edwald
992 Ealdwulf[1]
1003 Wulfstan II
1023 Ælfric Puttoc
1041 Æthelric
1051 Cynesige
1061 Ealdred
1070 Thomas I of Bayeux
1100 Gerard
1109 Thomas II
1119 Thurstan
1143 William Fitzherbert
1147 Henry Murdac

1153 William Fitzherbert
    (restored)
1154 Roger of Pont l'Eveque
1191 Geoffrey Plantagenet
1215 Walter de Gray
1256 Sewal de Bovill
1258 Godfrey Ludham
    [Kineton]
1266 Walter Giffard
1279 William Wickwane
1286 John Romanus [le
    Romeyn]
1298 Henry Newark
1300 Thomas Corbridge
1306 William Greenfield
1317 William Melton
1342 William de la Zouche
1352 John Thoresby
1374 Alexander Neville
1388 Thomas Arundel
1396 Robert Waldby
1398 Richard le Scrope
1407 Henry Bowet
1426 John Kempe
1452 William Booth
1464 George Nevill
1476 Lawrence Booth
1480 Thomas Rotherham
    [Scott]
1501 Thomas Savage
1508 Christopher Bainbridge
1514 Thomas Wolsey
1531 Edward Lee
1545 Robert Holgate
1555 Nicholas Heath
1561 Thomas Young
1570 Edmund Grindal
1577 Edwin Sandys
1589 John Piers
1595 Matthew Hutton
1606 Tobias Matthew
1628 George Monteigne
    [Mountain]
1629 Samuel Harsnett
1632 Richard Neile
1641 John Williams
1660 Accepted Frewen
1664 Richard Sterne
1683 John Dolben
1688 Thomas Lamplugh
1691 John Sharp
1714 William Dawes
1724 Lancelot Blackburn
1743 Thomas Herring
1747 Matthew Hutton

1757 John Gilben
1761 Roben Hay Drummond
1777 William Markham
1808 Edward Venables Vernon
    Harcourt
1847 Thomas Musgrave
1860 Charles Thomas Longley
1863 William Thomson
1891 William Connor Magee
1891 William Dalrymple
    Maclagan
1909 Cosmo Gordon Lang
1929 William Temple
1942 Cyril Forster Garbett
1956 Arthur Michael Ramsey
1961 Frederick Donald Coggan
1975 Stuart Yarworth Blanch
1983 John Stapylton Habgood
1995 David Michael Hope
2005 John Tucker Mugabi Sentamu

Durham

Description of arms. Azure, a cross or between four lions rampant argent.

BISHOPS OF LINDISFARNE[2]

635 Aidan
651 Finan
661 Colman
664 Tuda
    [Complications involving
    Wilfrid and Chad]
681 Eata
685 Cuthberht
    [Vacancy during which
    Wilfrid administered the
    See]
688 Eadberht
698 Eadfenh
731 Æthelweald
740 Cynewulf
781 Higbald
803 Ecgberht

---

[1] Ealdwulf and Wulfstan II held the Sees of York and Worcester together, Ælfric Puttoc held both 1040-41 and Ealdred 1060-61.
[2] See transferred to Chester-le-Street 883.

821 Heathwred
830 Ecgred
845 Eanberht
854 Eardwulf

BISHOPS OF HEXHAM

664 Wilfrith
678 Eata
681 Tunberht
684 Cuthbert
685 Eata (restored)
687 John of Beverley
709 Acca
734 Frithoberht
767 Ahimund
781 Tilberht
789 Æthelberht
797 Heardred
800 Eanberht
813 Tidferth

BISHOPS OF CHESTER-LE-STREET[1]

899 Eardwulf
899 Cutheard
915 Tilred
925 Wigred
944 Uhtred
944 Seaxhelm
944 Ealdred
968 Ælfsige
990 Aldhun

BISHOPS OF DURHAM

990 Aldhun d. 1018
     [See vacant 1018–1020]
1020 Edmund
c.1040 Eadred
1041 Æthelric
1056 Æthelwine
1071 Walcher
1081 William of Saint Calais
1099 Ralph [Ranulf] Flambard
1133 Geoffrey Rufus
1143 William of Sainte-Barbe
1153 Hugh of le Puiset
1197 Philip of Poitiers
1217 Richard Marsh
1228 Richard Poore
1241 Nicholas Farnham
1249 Walter Kirkham
1261 Robert Stichill
1274 Robert of Holy Island
1284 Anthony Bek
1311 Richard Kellaw
1318 Lewis de Beaumont
1333 Richard of Bury
1345 Thomas Hatfield
1382 John Fordham
1388 Walter Skirlaw
1406 Thomas Langley
1438 Robert Nevill
1457 Lawrence Booth
1476 William Dudley
1485 John Shirwood
1494 Richard Fox
1502 William Senhouse
     [Sever]
1507 Christopher
     Bainbridge
1509 Thomas Ruthall
1523 Thomas Wolsey
1530 Cuthbert Tunstall
1561 James Pilkington
1577 Richard Barnes
1589 Matthew Hutton

1595 Tobias Matthew
1606 William James
1617 Richard Neile
1628 George Monteigne
     [Mountain]
1628 John Howson
1632 Thomas Morton
1660 John Cosin
1674 Nathaniel Crew
     [Lord Crew]
1721 William Talbot
1730 Edward Chandler
1750 Joseph Butler
1752 Richard Trevor
1771 John Egerton
1787 Thomas Thurlow
1791 Shute Barrington
1826 William Van Mildert
1836 Edward Maltby
1856 Charles Thomas Longley
1860 Henry Montagu Villiers
1861 Charles Baring
1879 Joseph Barber Lightfoot
1890 Brooke Foss Westcott
1901 Handley Carr Glyn
     Moule
1920 Herbert Hensley Henson
1939 Alwyn Terrell Petre
     Williams
1952 Arthur Michael Ramsey
1956 Maurice Henry Harland
1966 Ian Thomas Ramsey
1973 John Stapylton Habgood
1984 David Edward Jenkins
1994 Anthony Michael Arnold
     Turnbull
2003 Nicholas Thomas Wright
2011 Justin Portal Welby

Blackburn

Description of arms. Per fess gules and or, in chief two keys in saltire wards downwards argent, in base a rose of the first barbed and seeded proper.

1926 Percy Mark Herbert
1942 Wilfred Marcus Askwith
1954 Walter Hubert Baddeley
1960 Charles Robert Claxton
1972 Robert Arnold Schürhoff
     Martineau
1982 David Stewart Cross
1989 Alan David Chesters
2004 Nicholas Stewart Reade

Bradford

Description of arms. Azure, two keys in saltire or, in chief a woolpack proper corded gold.

1920 Arthur William Thomson
     Perowne
1931 Alfred Walter Frank Blunt
1956 Frederick Donald Coggan
1961 Clement George St Michael
     Parker
1972 Ross Sydney Hook
1981 Geoffrey John Paul
1984 Robert Kerr Williamson
1992 David James Smith
2002 David Charles James
2011 Nicholas Baines

Carlisle

Description of arms. Argent, on a cross sable a labelled mitre or.

1133 Æthelwulf
1203 Bernard
1219 Hugh of Beaulieu
1224 Walter Mauclerc
1247 Silvester Everdon
1255 Thomas Vipont
1258 Robert de Chause
1280 Ralph Ireton
1292 John of Halton
1325 John Ross
1332 John Kirkby
1353 Gilbert Welton
1363 Thomas Appleby
1396 Robert Reade
1397 Thomas Merks
1400 William Strickland
1420 Roger Whelpdale
1424 William Barrow
1430 Marmaduke Lumley
1450 Nicholas Close
1452 William Percy
1462 John Kingscote
1464 Richard le Scrope
1468 Edward Story
1478 Richard Bell
1496 William Senhouse
     [Sever]
1504 Roger Layburne
1508 John Penny
1521 John Kite
1537 Robert Aldrich

---

[1] See transferred to Durham 995.

1556 Owen Oglethorpe
1561 John Best
1570 Richard Barnes
1577 John May
1598 Henry Robinson
1616 Robert Snowden
1621 Richard Milbourne
1624 Richard Senhouse
1626 Francis White
1629 Barnabas Potter
1642 James Ussher
1660 Richard Sterne
1664 Edward Rainbowe
1684 Thomas Smith
1702 William Nicolson
1718 Samuel Bradford
1723 John Waugh
1735 George Fleming
1747 Richard Osbaldeston
1762 Charles Lyttleton
1769 Edmund Law
1787 John Douglas
1791 Edward Venables Vernon
    [Harcourt]
1808 Samuel Goodenough
1827 Hugh Percy
1856 Henry Montagu Villiers
1860 Samuel Waldegrave
1869 Harvey Goodwin
1892 John Wareing Bardsley
1905 John William Diggle
1920 Henry Herbert Williams
1946 Thomas Bloomer
1966 Sydney Cyril Bulley
1972 Henry David Halsey
1989 Ian Harland
2000 Geoffrey Graham Dow
2009 James William Scobie
    Newcome

Chester

Description of arms. Gules, three labelled mitres or.

1541 John Bird
1554 George Cotes
1556 Cuthbert Scott
1561 William Downham
1579 William Chaderton
1595 Hugh Bellott
1597 Richard Vaughan
1604 George Lloyd
1616 Thomas Morton
1619 John Bridgeman
1660 Brian Walton
1662 Henry Ferne
1662 George Hall
1668 John Wilkins
1673 John Pearson
1686 Thomas Cartwright
1689 Nicolas Stratford
1708 William Dawes
1714 Francis Gastrell
1726 Samuel Peploe
1752 Edmund Keene
1771 William Markham
1777 Beilby Porteus

1788 William Cleaver
1800 Henry William Majendie
1810 Bowyer Edward Sparke
1812 George Henry Law
1824 Charles James Blomfield
1828 John Bird Sumner
1848 John Graham
1865 William Jacobson
1884 William Stubbs
1889 Francis John Jayne
1919 Henry Luke Paget
1932 Geoffrey Francis Fisher
1939 Douglas Henry Crick
1955 Gerald Alexander Ellison
1974 Hubert Victor Whitsey
1982 Michael Alfred Baughen
1996 Peter Robert Forster

Liverpool

Description of arms. Argent, an eagle with wings expanded sable, holding in its dexter claw an ancient inkhorn proper, around its head a nimbus or, a chief paly azure and gules, the dexter charged with an open book or, inscribed with the words 'Thy Word is Truth', the sinister charged with a lymphad gold.

1880 John Charles Ryle
1900 Francis James Chavasse
1923 Albert Augustus David
1944 Clifford Arthur Martin
1966 Stuart Yarworth Blanch
1975 David Stuart Sheppard
1998 James Stuart Jones

Manchester

Description of arms. Or, on a pale engrailed gules three mitres of the first, on a canton of the second three bendlets enhanced gold.

1848 James Prince Lee
1870 James Fraser
1886 James Moorhouse
1903 Edmund Arbuthnott Knox
1921 William Temple
1929 Frederic Sumpter Guy
    Warman
1947 William Derrick Lindsay
    Greer
1970 Patrick Campbell Rodger
1979 Stanley Eric Francis Booth-
    Clibborn

1993 Christopher John
    Mayfield
2002 Nigel Simeon McCulloch

Newcastle

Description of arms. Gules, a cross between four lions rampant or, on a chief gold three triple-towered castles of the first.

1882 Ernest Roland Wilberforce
1896 Edgar Jacob
1903 Arthur Thomas Lloyd
1907 Norman Dumenil John
    Straton
1915 Herbert Louis Wild
1927 Harold Ernest Bilbrough
1941 Noel Baring Hudson
1957 Hugh Edward Ashdown
1973 Ronald Oliver Bowlby
1981 Andrew Alexander Kenny
    Graham
1997 John Martin Wharton

Ripon and Leeds
(Ripon until 1999)

Description of arms. Argent, on a saltire gules two keys wards upwards or, on a chief of the second a Holy Lamb proper.

*c.*678 Eadheath

NEW FOUNDATION

1836 Charles Thomas Longley
1857 Robert Bickersteth
1884 William Boyd Carpenter
1912 Thomas Wortley Drury
1920 Thomas Banks Strong
1926 Edward Arthur Burroughs
1935 Geoffrey Charles Lester
    Lunt
1946 George Armitage Chase
1959 John Richard Humpidge
    Moorman
1975 Stuart Hetley Price
1977 David Nigel de Lorentz
    Young
2000 John Richard Packer

Sheffield

Description of arms. Azure, a crosier in pale ensigned by a fleur-de-lis vert, between in fess a key surmounted by a sword in saltire to the dexter, and to the sinister eight arrows interlaced and banded saltirewise, all or.

1914 Leonard Hedley Burrows
1939 Leslie Stannard Hunter
1962 Francis John Taylor
1971 William Gordon Fallows
1980 David Ramsay Lunn
1997 John Nicholls
2009 Steven John Lindsey Croft

Sodor and Man[1]

Description of arms. Argent, upon a pedestal between two coronetted pillars the Virgin Mary with arms extended, in her dexter hand a church proper and in base upon an escutcheon, surmounted by a mitre, the arms of Man – viz. gules, three legs in armour conjoined at the thigh and flexed at the knee.

447 Germanus
    Conindrius
    Romulus
    Machutus
    Conanus
    Contentus
    Baldus
    Malchus
    Torkinus
    Brendanus
[Before 1080 Roolwer]
    William
    Hamond
1113 Wimund
1151 John
1160 Gamaliel
    Ragnald
    Christian of Argyle
    Michael

1203 Nicholas de Meaux
    Nicholas II
1217 Reginald
1226 John
1229 Simon of Argyle
1252 Richard
1275 Mark of Galloway
1305 Alan
1321 Gilbert Maclelan
1329 Bernard de Linton
1334 Thomas
1348 William Russell
1387 John Donegan
1387 Michael
1392 John Sproten
1402 Conrad
1402 Theodore Bloc
1429 Richard Messing Andrew
1435 John Seyre
1455 Thomas Burton
1458 Thomas Kirklam
1472 Angus
1478 Richard Oldham
1487 Hugh Blackleach
1513 Hugh Hesketh
1523 John Howden
1546 Henry Man
1556 Thomas Stanley
1570 John Salisbury
1576 John Meyrick
1600 George Lloyd
1605 John Philips
1634 William Forster
1635 Richard Parr
1661 Samuel Rutter
1663 Isaac Barrow
1671 Henry Bridgman
1683 John Lake
1685 Baptist Levinz
1698 Thomas Wilson
1755 Mark Hildesley
1773 Richard Richmond
1780 George Mason
1784 Claudius Crigan
1814 George Murray
1828 William Ward
1838 James Bowstead
1840 Henry Pepys
1841 Thomas Vowler Short
1847 Walter Augustus Shirley
1847 Robert John Eden
1854 Horatio Powys
1877 Rowley Hill
1887 John Wareing Bardsley
1892 Norman Dumenil John
    Straton
1907 Thomas Wortley Drury
1912 James Denton Thompson
1925 Charles Leonard Thornton-
    Duesbury
1928 William Stanton Jones
1943 John Ralph Strickland
    Taylor
1954 Benjamin Pollard
1966 George Eric Gordon
1974 Vernon Sampson Nicholls
1983 Arthur Henry Attwell
1989 Noël Debroy Jones
2003 Graeme Paul Knowles
2008 Robert Mar Erskine Paterson

Southwell and Nottingham (Southwell until 2005)

Description of arms. Sable, three fountains proper, on a chief or a pale azure, charged with a representation of the Virgin Mary seated bearing the Infant Christ or between a stag lodged proper and two staves raguly crossed vert.

1884 George Ridding
1904 Edwyn Hoskyns
1926 Bernard Oliver Francis
    Heywood
1928 Henry Mosley
1941 Frank Russell Barry
1964 Gordon David Savage
1970 John Denis Wakeling
1985 Michael Humphrey Dickens
    Whinney
1988 Patrick Burnet Harris
1999 George Henry Cassidy
2009 Paul Roger Butler

Wakefield

Description of arms. Or, a fleur-de-lis azure, on a chief of the last three celestial crowns gold.

1888 William Walsham How
1897 George Rodney Eden
1928 James Buchanan Seaton
1938 Campbell Richard Hone
1946 Henry McGowan
1949 Roger Plumpton Wilson
1958 John Alexander Ramsbotham
1968 Eric Treacy
1977 Colin Clement Walter James
1985 David Michael Hope
1992 Nigel Simeon McCulloch
2003 Stephen George Platten

---

[1] Included in the province of York by Act of Parliament 1542. Prior to Richard Oldham there is some uncertainty as to several names and dates. From 1425 to 1553 there was an English and Scottish succession. It is not easy to say which claimant was Bishop either *de jure* or *de facto.*

BISHOPS SUFFRAGAN IN ENGLAND

Aston (Birmingham)

1954 Clement George St Michael Parker
1962 David Brownfield Porter
1972 Mark Green
1982 Michael Humphrey Dickens Whinney
1985 Colin Ogilvie Buchanan
1989–92 *no appointment*
1992 John Michael Austin
2005–2008 *no appointment*
2008 Andrew John Watson

Barking (Chelmsford)

[in St Albans diocese to 1914]
1901 Thomas Stevens
1919 James Theodore Inskip
1948 Hugh Rowlands Gough
1959 William Frank Percival Chadwick
1975 Albert James Adams
1983 James William Roxburgh
1991 Roger Frederick Sainsbury
2002 David John Leader Hawkins

Barrow-in-Furness (Carlisle)

1889 Henry Ware
1909 Campbell West-Watson
1926 Henry Sidney Pelham
1944 *in abeyance*

Basingstoke (Winchester)

1973 Colin Clement Walter James
1977 Michael Richard John Manktelow
1994 Douglas Geoffrey Rowell
2002 Trevor Willmott
2010 Peter Hancock

Bedford (St Albans)

1537 John Hodgkins[1]
1560–1879 *in abeyance*
1879 William Walsham How[2]
1888 Robert Claudius Billing[3]
1898–1935 *in abeyance*
1935 James Lumsden Barkway
1939 Aylmer Skelton
1948 Claude Thomas Thellusson Wood
1953 Angus Campbell MacInnes
1957 Basil Tudor Guy
1963 Albert John Trillo
1968 John Tyrrell Holmes Hare
1977 Andrew Alexander Kenny Graham
1981 David John Farmbrough
1994 John Henry Richardson
2003 Richard Neil Inwood

Berwick (Durham)

1536 Thomas Sparke
1572 *in abeyance*

Beverley (York)

1889 Robert Jarratt Crosthwaite
1923–94 *in abeyance*
1994 John Scott Gaisford
2000 Martyn William Jarrett

Birkenhead (Chester)

1965 Eric Arthur John Mercer
1974 Ronald Brown
1993 Michael Laurence Langrish
2000 David Andrew Urquhart
2007 Gordon Keith Sinclair

Bolton (Manchester)

1984 David George Galliford
1991 David Bonser
1999 David Keith Gillett
2008 Christopher Paul Edmondson

Bradwell (Chelmsford)

1968 William Neville Welch
1973 John Gibbs
1976 Charles Derek Bond
1993 Laurence Alexander Green
2011 John Michael Wraw

Bristol (Worcester)

1538 Henry Holbeach [Rands]
1542 *became diocesan see*

Brixworth (Peterborough)

1989 Paul Everard Barber
2002 Francis White
2011 John Edward Holbrook

Buckingham (Oxford)

1914 Edward Domett Shaw
1921 Philip Herbert Eliot
1944 Robert Milton Hay
1960 Gordon David Savage
1964 George Christopher Cutts Pepys
1974 Simon Hedley Burrows
1994 Colin James Bennetts
1998 Michael Arthur Hill
2003 Alan Thomas Lawrence Wilson

Burnley (Blackburn)

[in Manchester diocese to 1926]
1901 Edwyn Hoskyns
1905 Alfred Pearson
1909 Henry Henn
1931 Edgar Priestley Swain
1950 Charles Keith Kipling Prosser
1955 George Edward Holderness
1970 Richard Charles Challinor Watson
1988 Ronald James Milner
1994 Martyn William Jarrett
2000 John William Goddard

Colchester (Chelmsford)

[in London diocese to 1845
in Rochester diocese to 1877
in St Albans diocese 1877–1914]
1536 William More
1541–91 *in abeyance*
1592 John Sterne
1608–1882 *in abeyance*
1882 Alfred Blomfield
1894 Henry Frank Johnson
1909 Robert Henry Whitcombe

[Chapman column]

1922 Thomas Alfred Chapman
1933 Charles Henry Ridsdale
1946 Frederick Dudley Vaughan Narborough
1966 Roderic Norman Coote
1988 Michael Edwin Vickers
1995 Edward Holland
2001 Christopher Heudebourck Morgan

Coventry (Worcester)

see also under Lichfield
1891 Henry Bond Bowlby
1894 Edmund Arbuthnott Knox
1903–18 *no appointment*
1918 *became diocesan see*

Crediton (Exeter)

1897 Robert Edward Trefusis
1930 William Frederick Surtees
1954 Wilfred Arthur Edmund Westall
1974 Philip John Pasterfield
1984 Peter Everard Coleman
1996 Richard Stephen Hawkins
2004 Robert John Scott Evens

Croydon (Southwark)

(in Canterbury diocese to 1985)
1904 Henry Horace Pereira
1924–30 *no appointment*
1930 Edward Sydney Woods
1937 William Louis Anderson
1942 Maurice Henry Harland
1947 Cuthbert Killick Norman Bardsley
1957 John Taylor Hughes
1977 Geoffrey Stuart Snell
1985 Wilfred Denniston Wood
2003 Nicholas Baines

Derby (Southwell)

1889 Edward Ash Were
1909 Charles Thomas Abraham
1927 *became diocesan see*

Doncaster (Sheffield)

1972 Stuart Hetley Price
1976 David Stewart Cross
1982 William Michael Dermot Persson
1993 Michael Frederick Gear
2000 Cyril Guy Ashton

Dorchester (Oxford)

see also under Dorchester (diocesan see) and Lincoln
1939 Gerald Burton Allen
1952 Kenneth Riches
1957 David Goodwin Loveday
1972 Peter Knight Walker
1979 Conrad John Eustace Meyer
1988 Anthony John Russell
2000 Colin William Fletcher

Dorking (Guildford)

[in Winchester diocese to 1927]
1905 Cecil Henry Boutflower
1909–68 *in abeyance*
1968 Kenneth Dawson Evans

---

[1] Appointed for the diocese of London.   [2] Appointed for the diocese of London.
[3] Appointed for the diocese of London, and retained title after resigning his suffragan duties in 1895.

1986 David Peter Wilcox
1996 Ian James Brackley

Dover (Canterbury)

1537 Richard Yngworth
1545 Richard Thornden
1557–69 *no appointment*
1569 Richard Rogers
1597–1870 *in abeyance*
1870 Edward Parry
1890 George Rodney Eden
1898 William Walsh
1916 Harold Ernest Bilbrough
1927 John Victor Macmillan
1935 Alfred Careywollaston Rose
1957 Lewis Evan Meredith
1964 Anthony Paul Tremlett
1980 Richard Henry McPhail
      Third
1992 John Richard Allan Llewellin
1999 Stephen Squires Venner
2010 Trevor Willmott

Dudley (Worcester)

1974 Michael Ashley Mann
1977 Anthony Charles Dumper
1993 Rupert William Noel Hoare
2000 David Stuart Walker

Dunwich (St Edmundsbury and Ipswich)

see also under Norwich

1934 Maxwell Homfray Maxwell-
      Gumbleton
1945 Clement Mallory Ricketts
1955 Thomas Herbert Cashmore
1967 David Rokeby Maddock
1977 William Johnston
1980 Eric Nash Devenport
1992 Jonathan Sansbury Bailey
1995 Timothy John Stevens
1999 Clive Young

Ebbsfleet (Canterbury)

1994 John Richards
1998 Michael Alan Houghton
2000 Andrew Burnham
2011 Jonathan Mark Richard Baker

Edmonton (London)

1970 Alan Francis Bright Rogers
1975 William John Westwood
1985 Brian John Masters
1999 Peter William Wheatley

Europe (Europe)

1980 Ambrose Walter Marcus
      Weekes
1986 Edward Holland
1995 Henry William Scriven
2002 David Hamid

Fulham (London)[1]

1926 Basil Staunton Batty
1947 William Marshall Selwyn
1949 George Ernest Ingle
1955 Robert Wright Stopford
1957 Roderic Norman Coote

1966 Alan Francis Bright Rogers
1970 John Richard Satterthwaite[2]
1980–1982 *no appointment*
1982 Brian John Masters
1985 Charles John Klyberg
1996 John Charles Broadhurst

Grantham (Lincoln)

1905 Welbore MacCarthy
1920 John Edward Hine
1930 Ernest Morell Blackie
1935 Arthur Ivan Greaves
1937 Algernon Augustus Markham
1949 Anthony Otter
1965 Ross Sydney Hook
1972 Dennis Gascoyne Hawker
1987 William Ind
1997 Alastair Lewellyn John Redfern
2006 Timothy William Ellis

Grimsby (Lincoln)

1935 Ernest Morell Blackie
1937 Anhur Ivan Greaves
1958 Kenneth Healey
1966 Gerald Fitzmaurice Colin
1979 David Tustin
2000 David Douglas James Rossdale

Guildford (Winchester)

1874 John Sutton Utterton
1888 George Henry Sumner
1909 John Hugh Granville
      Randolph
1927 *became diocesan see*

Hertford (St Albans)

1968 Albert John Trillo
1971 Hubert Victor Whitsey
1974 Peter Mumford
1982 Kenneth Harold Pillar
1990 Robin Jonathan Norman
      Smith
2001 Christopher Richard James
      Foster
2010 Paul Bayes

Horsham (Chichester)

1968 Simon Wilton Phipps
1975 Ivor Colin Docker
1991 John William Hind
1993 Lindsay Goodall Urwin
2009 Mark Crispin Rake Sowerby

Hull (York)

1538 Robert Sylvester (Pursglove)
1579–1891 *in abeyance*
1891 Richard Frederick Lefevre
      Blunt
1910 John Augustus Kempthome
1913 Francis Gurdon
1929–31 *no appointment*
1931 Bemard Oliver Francis
      Heywood
1934 Henry Townsend Vodden
1957 George Fredenck Townley
1965 Hubert Laurence Higgs
1977 Geoffrey John Paul
1981 Donald George Snelgrove

1994 James Stuart Jones
1998 Richard Michael Cockayne
      Frith

Hulme (Manchester)

1924 John Charles Hill
1930 Thomas Sherwood Jones
1945 Hugh Leycester Homby
1953 Kenneth Venner Ramsey
1975 David George Galliford
1984 Colin John Fraser Scott
1999 Stephen Richard Lowe

Huntingdon (Ely)

1966 Robert Arnold Schürhoff
      Martineau
1972 Eric St Quintin Wall
1980 William Gordon Roe
1997 John Robert Flack
2003 John Geoffrey Inge
2008 David Thomson

Ipswich (Norwich)

1536 Thomas Manning[3]
?–1899 *in abeyance*[4]
1899 George Carnac Fisher
1906 Henry Luke Paget
1909 *no appointment*
1914 *became diocesan see with
      St Edmundsbury*

Islington (London)

1898 Charles Henry Turner
1923 *in abeyance*

Jarrow (Durham)

1906 George Nickson
1914 John Nathaniel Quirk
1924 Samuel Kirshbaum Knight
1932 James Geoffrey Gordon
1939 Leslie Owen
1944 David Colin Dunlop
1950 John Alexander Ramsbotham
1958 Mervyn Armstrong
1965 Alexander Kenneth
      Hamilton
1980 Michael Thomas Ball
1990 Alan Smithson
2002 John Lawrence Pritchard
2007 Mark Watts Bryant

Kensington (London)

1901 Frederic Edward Ridgeway
1911 John Primatt Maud
1932 Bertram Fitzgerald Simpson
1942 Henry Colville Montgomery
      Campbell
1949 Cyril Eastaugh
1962 Edward James Keymer
      Roberts
1964 Ronald Cedric Osbourne
      Goodchild
1981 Mark Santer
1987 John George Hughes
1994–96 *no appointment*
1996 Michael John Colclough
2009 Paul Gavin Williams

[1] From 1926 to 1980 exercised the Bishop of London's extra-diocesan jurisdiction over chaplaincies in Northern and Central Europe. Since 1996 has assisted the Diocesan Bishop in all matters not delegated to the Areas, and in pastoral care of parishes operating under the London Plan.
[2] Bishop of Fulham and Gibraltar.
[3] Manning does not appear to have acted as a suffragan bishop in the diocese of Norwich.
[4] The date of Manning's death is not known.

Kingston-upon-Thames (Southwark)

1905 Cecil Hook
1915 Samuel Mumford Taylor
1922 Percy Mark Herbert
1927 Frederick Ochterlony Taylor Hawkes
1952 William Percy Gilpin
1970 Hugh William Montefiore
1978 Keith Norman Sutton
1984 Peter Stephen Maurice Selby
1992 John Martin Wharton
1997 Peter Bryan Price
2002 Richard Ian Cheetham

Knaresborough (Ripon)

1905 Lucius Frederick Moses Bottomley Smith
1934 Paul Fulcrand Dalacour de Labilliere
1938 John Norman Bateman-Champain
1948 Henry Handley Vully de Candole
1965 John Howard Cruse
1972 Ralph Emmerson
1979 John Dennis
1986 Malcolm James Menin
1997 Frank Valentine Weston
2004 James Harold Bell

Lancaster (Blackburn)

1936 Benjamin Pollard
1955 Anthony Leigh Egerton Hoskyns-Abrahall
1975 Dennis Fountain Page
1985 Ian Harland
1990 John Nicholls
1998 Geoffrey Stephen Pedley
2006 Geoffrey Seagrave Pearson

Leicester (Peterborough)

see also under Lichfield and Lincoln

1888 Francis Henry Thicknesse
1903 Lewis Clayton
1913 Norman MacLeod Lang
1927 became diocesan see

Lewes (Chichester)

1909 Leonard Hedley Burrows
1914 Herbert Edward Jones
1920 Henry Kemble Southwell
1926 Thomas William Cook
1929 William Champion Streatfield
1929 Hugh Maudsley Hordern
1946 Geoffrey Hodgson Warde
1959 James Herbert Lloyd Morrell
1977 Peter John Ball
1992 Ian Patrick Martyn Cundy
1997 Wallace Parke Benn

Ludlow (Hereford)

1981 Stanley Mark Wood
1987 Ian Macdonald Griggs
1994 John Charles Saxbee
2002 Michael Wrenford Hooper
2009 Alistair James Magowan

Lynn (Norwich)

1963 William Somers Llewellyn

1972 William Aubrey Aitken
1986 David Edward Bentley
1994 David John Conner
1999 Anthony Charles Foottit
2004 James Henry Langstaff
2011 Cyril Jonathan Meyrick

Maidstone (Canterbury)

1944 Leslie Owen
1946–56 no appointment
1956 Stanley Woodley Betts
1966–69 no appointment
1969 Geoffrey Lewis Tiarks
1976 Richard Henry McPhail Third
1980 Robert Maynard Hardy
1987 David James Smith
1992 Gavin Hunter Reid
2001 Graham Alan Cray

Malmesbury (Bristol)

1927 Ronald Erskine Ramsay
1946 Ivor Stanley Watkins
1956 Edward James Keymer Roberts
1962 Clifford Leofric Purdy Bishop
1973 Frederick Stephen Temple
1983 Peter James Firth
1994 renamed Swindon

Marlborough

1537 Thomas Morley (Bickley)[1]
c1561–1888 in abeyance
1888 Alfred Earle[2]
1919 in abeyance

Middleton (Manchester)

1927 Richard Godfrey Parsons
1932 Cecil Wilfred Wilson
1938 Arthur Fawssett Alston
1943 Edward Worsfold Mowll
1952 Frank Woods
1958 Robert Nelson
1959 Edward Ralph Wickham
1982 Donald Alexander Tytler
1994 Stephen Squires Venner
1999 Michael Augustine Owen Lewis
2008 Mark Davies

Nottingham (Lincoln)

[in York diocese to 1837]

1567 Richard Barnes
1570–1870 in abeyance
1870 Henry Mackenzie
1877 Edward Trollope
1893 in abeyance

Penrith (Carlisle)

see also under Richmond

1537 John Bird[3]
1539–1888 in abeyance
1888 John James Pulleine[4]
1939 Grandage Edwards Powell
1944 Herbert Victor Turner
1959 Sydney Cyril Bulley
1967 Reginald Foskett
1970 William Edward Augustus Pugh
1979 George Lanyon Hacker

1994 Richard Garrard
2002 James William Scobie Newcome
2011 Robert John Freeman

Plymouth (Exeter)

1923 John Howard Bertram Masterman
1934 Francis Whitfield Daukes
1950 Norman Harry Clarke
1962 Wilfred Guy Sanderson
1972 Richard Fox Cartwright
1982 Kenneth Albert Newing
1988 Richard Stephen Hawkins
1996 John Henry Garton
2005 John Frank Ford

Pontefract (Wakefield)

1931 Campbell Richard Hone
1939 Tom Longworth
1949 Arthur Harold Morris
1954 George William Clarkson
1961 Eric Treacy
1968 William Gordon Fallows
1971 Thomas Richard Hare
1993 John Thornley Finney
1998 David Charles James
2002 Anthony William Robinson

Ramsbury (Salisbury)

see also under Salisbury

1974 John Robert Geoffrey Neale
1989 Peter St George Vaughan
1999 Peter Fearnley Hullah
2006 Stephen David Conway

Reading (Oxford)

1889 James Leslie Randall
1909–42 in abeyance
1942 Arthur Groom Parham
1954 Eric Henry Knell
1972 Eric Wild
1982 Ronald Graham Gregory Foley
1989 John Frank Ewan Bone
1997 Edward William Murray Walker
2004 Stephen Geoffrey Cottrell
2011 Andrew John Proud

Repton (Derby)

1965 William Warren Hunt
1977 Stephen Edmund Verney
1986 Francis Henry Arthur Richmond
1999 David Christopher Hawtin
2007 Humphrey Ivo John Southern

Richborough (Canterbury)

1995 Edwin Ronald Barnes
2002 Keith Newton
2011 Norman Banks

Richmond (Ripon)

1889 John James Pulleine[5]
1913 Francis Charles Kilner
1921 in abeyance

---

[1] Appointed for the diocese of London.   [2] Appointed for the diocese of London, but retained the title while Dean of Exeter 1900-18.
[3] Appointed for the diocese of Lichfield.   [4] Appointed for the diocese of Ripon.
[5] His suffragan title was changed from Penrith to Richmond by Royal Warrant.

St Germans (Truro)

1905 John Rundle Cornish
1918–74 *in abeyance*
1974 Cecil Richard Rutt
1979 Reginald Lindsay Fisher
1985 John Richard Allan Llewellin
1993 Graham Richard James
2000 Royden Screech

Selby (York)

1939 Henry St John Stirling
      Woollcombe
1941 Carey Frederick Knyvett
1962 Douglas Noel Sargent
1972 Morris Henry St John
      Maddocks
1983 Clifford Conder Barker
1991 Humphrey Vincent Taylor
2003 Martin William Wallace

Shaftesbury (Salisbury)

[in Bristol diocese 1542–1836]
1539 John Bradley
? *in abeyance*[1]

Sheffield (York)

1901 John Nathaniel Quirk
1914 *became diocesan see*

Sherborne (Salisbury)

1925 Robert Crowther Abbott
1928 Gerald Burton Allen
1936 Harold Nickinson Rodgers
1947 John Maurice Key
1960 Victor Joseph Pike
1976 John Dudley Galtrey Kirkham
2001 Timothy Martin Thornton
2009 Graham Ralph Kings

Sherwood (Southwell)

1965 Kenneth George Thompson
1975 Harold Richard Darby
1989 Alan Wyndham Morgan
2006 Anthony Porter

Shrewsbury (Lichfield)

1537 Lewis Thomas[2]
1561–1888 *in abeyance*
1888 Sir Lovelace Tomlinson
      Stamer
1905–40 *in abeyance*
1940 Eric Knightley Chetwode
      Hamilton
1944 Robert Leighton Hodson
1959 William Alonzo Parker
1970 Francis William Cocks
1980 Leslie Lloyd Rees
1987 John Dudley Davies
1994 David Marrison Hallatt
2001 Alan Gregory Clayton Smith
2009 Mark James Rylands

Southampton (Winchester)

1895 William Awdry
1896 George Carnac Fisher
1898 The Hon Arthur Temple
      Lyttelton
1903 James Macarthur
1921 Cecil Henry Boutflower
1933 Arthur Baillie Lumsdaine
      Karney
1943 Edmund Robert Morgan

1951 Kenneth Edward Norman
      Lamplugh
1972 John Kingsmill Cavell
1984 Edward David Cartwright
1989 John Freeman Perry
1996 Jonathan Michael Gledhill
2004 Paul Roger Butler
2010 Jonathan Hugh Frost

Southwark (Rochester)

1891 Huyshe Wolcott Yeatman-
      Biggs
1905 *became diocesan see*

Stafford (Lichfield)

1909 Edward Ash Were
1915 Lionel Payne Crawfurd
1934 Douglas Henry Crick
1938 Lemprière Durell Hammond
1958 Richard George Clitherow
1975 John Waine
1979 John Stevens Waller
1987 Michael Charles Scott-Joynt
1996 Christopher John Hill
2005 Alfred Gordon Mursell
2010 Geoffrey Peter Annas

Stepney (London)

1895 George Forrest Browne
1897 Arthur Foley Winnington-
      Ingram
1901 Cosmo Gordon Lang
1909 Henry Luke Paget
1919 Henry Mosley
1928 Charles Edward Curzon
1936 Robert Hamilton Moberly
1952 Joost de Blank
1957 Francis Evered Lunt
1968 Ernest Urban Trevor
      Huddleston
1978 James Lawton Thompson
1992 Richard John Carew Chartres
1996 John Mugabi Sentamu
2003 Stephen John Oliver
2011 Adrian Newman

Stockport (Chester)

1949 Frank Jackson Okell
1951 David Henry Saunders
      Saunders-Davies
1965 Rupert Gordon Strutt
1984 Frank Pilkington Sargeant
1994 Geoffrey Martin Turner
2000 William Nigel Stock
2008 Robert Ronald Atwell

Swindon (Bristol)

1994 Michael David Doe
2005 Lee Stephen Rayfield

Taunton (Bath and Wells)

1538 William Finch
1559–1911 *in abeyance*
1911 Charles Fane de Salis
1931 George Arthur Hollis
1945 Harry Thomas
1955 Mark Allin Hodson
1962 Francis Horner West
1977 Peter John Nott
1986 Nigel Simeon McCulloch
1992 John Hubert Richard Lewis
1997 William Allen Stewart
1998 Andrew John Radford
2006 Peter David Maurice

Tewkesbury (Gloucester)

1938 Augustine John Hodson
1955 Edward Barry Henderson
1960 Forbes Trevor Horan
1973 Thomas Carlyle Joseph
      Robert Hamish Deakin
1986 Geoffrey David Jeremy
      Walsh
1996 John Stewart Went

Thetford (Norwich)

see also under Norwich
1536 John Salisbury
1570–1894 *in abeyance*
1894 Arthur Thomas Lloyd
1903 John Philips Alcott Bowers
1926–45 *no appointment*
1945 John Walker Woodhouse
1953 Manin Patrick Grainge
      Leonard
1963 Eric William Bradley
      Cordingly
1977 Hugh Charles Blackburne
1981 Timothy Dudley-Smith
1992 Hugo Ferdinand de Waal
2001 David John Atkinson
2009 Alan Peter Winton

Tonbridge (Rochester)

1959 Russell Berridge White
1968 Henry David Halsey
1973 Philip Harold Ernest
      Goodrich
1982 David Henry Bartleet
1993 Brian Arthur Smith
2002 Brian Colin Castle

Warrington (Liverpool)

1918 Martin Linton Smith
1920 Edwin Hone Kempson
1927 Herbert Gresford Jones
1946 Charles Robert Claxton
1960 Laurence Ambrose Brown
1970 John Monier Bickersteth
1976 Michael Henshall
1996 John Richard Packer
2000 David Wilfred Michael
      Jennings
2009 Richard Finn Blackburn

Warwick (Coventry)

1980 Keith Appleby Arnold
1990 Clive Handford
1996 Anthony Martin Priddis
2005 John Ronald Angus Stroyan

Whalley (Blackburn)

[in Manchester diocese to 1926]
1909 Atherton Gwillym Rawstorne
1936 *in abeyance*

Whitby (York)

1923 Harry St John Stirling
      Woollcombe
1939 Harold Evelyn Hubbard
1947 Walter Hubert Baddeley
1954 Philip William Wheeldon
1961 George D'Oyly Snow
1972 John Yates
1976 Clifford Conder Barker
1983 Gordon Bates
1999 Robert Sidney Ladds
2010 Martin Clive Warner

---

[1] The date of Bradley's death is not known.   [2] Not appointed for Lichfield, but probably for Llandaff.

Willesden (London)

1911 William Willcox Perrin
1929 Guy Vernon Smith
1940 Henry Colville Montgomery
      Campbell
1942 Edward Michael Gresford
      Jones
1950 Gerald Alexander Ellison
1955 George Ernest Ingle
1964 Graham Douglas Leonard
1974 Geoffrey Hewlett Thompson
1985 Thomas Frederick Butler

1992 Geoffrey Graham Dow
2001 Peter Alan Broadbent

Wolverhampton (Lichfield)

1979 Barry Rogerson
1985 Christopher John Mayfield
1994 Michael Gay Bourke
2007 Clive Malcolm Gregory

Woolwich (Southwark)

1905 John Cox Leeke

1918 William Woodcock
      Hough
1932 Arthur Llewellyn Preston
1936 Leslie Hamilton Lang
1947 Robert William Stannard
1959 John Arthur Thomas
      Robinson
1969 David Stuart Sheppard
1975 Michael Eric Marshall
1984 Albert Peter Hall
1996 Colin Ogilvie Buchanan
2005 Christopher Thomas James
      Chessun

WALES

Archbishops of Wales

1920 Alfred George Edwards
      (St Asaph 1889–1934)
1934 Charles Alfred Howell Green
      (Bangor 1928–44)
1944 David Lewis Prosser
      (St Davids 1927 50)
1949 John Morgan (Llandaff
      1939–57)
1957 Alfred Edwin Morris
      (Monmouth 1945–67)
1968 William Glyn Hughes Simon
      (Llandaff 1957–71)
1971 Gwilym Owen Williams
      (Bangor 1957–82)
1983 Derrick Greenslade
      Childs (Monmouth
      1972–87)
1987 George Noakes (St Davids
      1982–91)
1991 Alwyn Rice Jones (St Asaph
      1982–99)
1999 Rowan Douglas Williams
      (Monmouth 1992–2002)
2003 Barry Cennydd Morgan
      (Llandaff 1999–)

Bangor[1]

Description of arms. Gules, a bend or guttée de poix between two mullets pierced argent.

c.550 Deiniol [Daniel]
c.775 Elfod [Elbodugen]
1092 Herve
[*Vacancy* 1109–20]
1120 David the Scot
1140 Maurice (Meurig)
[*Vacancy* 1161–77]
1177 Guy Rufus [Gwion Goch]
[*Vacancy* c1190–95]

1195 Alan [Alban]
1197 Robert of Shrewsbury
[*Vacancy* 1212–15]
1215 Cadwgan
1237 Richard
1267 Anian [or Einion]
1307 Gruflydd ab Iowerth
1309 Anian [Einion] Sais
1328 Matthew de Englefield
1357 Thomas de Ringstead
1366 Gervase de Castro
1371 Hywel ap Gronwy
1372 John Gilbert
1376 John Swaffham
1400 Richard Young
[*Vacancy* c1404–8]
1408 Benedict Nicolls
1418 William Barrow
1425 John Cliderow
1436 Thomas Cheriton
1448 John Stanbury
1453 James Blakedon
1465 Richard Edenham
1495 Henry Dean
1500 Thomas Pigot
1505 Thomas Penny
1509 Thomas Skevington
1534 John Salcot [or Capon]
1539 John Bird
1542 Arthur Bulkeley
1555 William Glynn
1559 Rowland Meyrick
1566 Nicholas Robinson
1586 Hugh Bellot
1596 Richard Vaughan
1598 Henry Rowlands
1616 Lewis Bayly
1632 David Dolben
1634 Edmund Griffith
1637 William Roberts
1666 Robert Morgan
1673 Humphrey Lloyd
1689 Humphrey Humphreys
1702 John Evans
1716 Benjamin Hoadley
1721 Richard Reynolds
1723 William Baker
1728 Thomas Sherlock
1734 Charles Cecil
1738 Thomas Herring
1743 Matthew Hutton
1748 Zachary Pearce
1756 John Egerton
1769 John Ewer
1775 John Moore

1783 John Warren
1800 William Cleaver
1807 John Randolph
1809 Henry William Majendie
1830 Christopher Bethell
1859 James Colquhoun Campbell
1890 Daniel Lewis Lloyd
1899 Watkin Herbert Williams
1925 Daniel Davies
1928 Charles Alfred Howell Green
      (Archbishop of Wales 1934)
1944 David Edwardes Davies
1949 John Charles Jones
1957 Gwilym Owen Williams
      (Archbishop of Wales 1971)
1982 John Cledan Mears
1993 Barry Cennydd Morgan
1999 Francis James Saunders Davies
2004 Phillip Anthony Crockett
2008 Andrew Thomas Griffith John

Llandaff[2]

Description of arms. Sable, two pastoral staves endorsed in saltire, the dexter or, the sinister argent. On a chief azure three labelled mitres or.

c.550 Teiliau
c.872 Cyfeiliag
c.880 Libiau
c.940 Marchlwys
  982 Gwyzan
c.995 Bledri
1027 Joseph
1056 Herewald
1107 Urban
[*Vacancy of six years*]
1140 Uchtryd
1148 Nicolas ap Gwrgant
[*Vacancy of two years*]
1186 William Saltmarsh
1193 Henry of Abergavenny

---

[1] Very few of the names of the Celtic bishops have been preserved.
[2] The traditional list of bishops of the Celtic Church has little historical foundation. But the names of the following, prior to Urban, may be regarded as fairly trustworthy, though the dates are very uncertain.

1219   William of Goldcliff
1230   Elias of Radnor
1245   William de Burgh
1254   John de Ware
1257   William of Radnor
1266   Willam de Breuse [or Brus]
1297   John of Monmouth
1323   John of Eaglescliffe
1344   John Paschal
1361   Roger Cradock
1383   Thomas Rushook
1386   William Bottesham
1389   Edmund Bromfield
1393   Tideman de Winchcomb
1395   Andrew Barret
1396   John Burghill
1398   Thomas Peverel
1408   John de la Zouch [Fulford]
1425   John Wells
1441   Nicholas Ashby
1458   John Hunden
1476   John Smith
1478   John Marshall
1496   John Ingleby
1500   Miles Salley
1517   George de Athequa
1537   Robert Holdgate
       [or Holgate]
1545   Anthony Kitchin
1567   Hugh Jones
1575   William Blethin
1591   Gervase Babington
1595   William Morgan
1601   Francis Godwin
1618   George Carleton
1619   Theophilus Field
1627   William Murray
1640   Morgan Owen
1660   Hugh Lloyd
1667   Francis Davies
1675   William Lloyd
1679   William Beaw
1706   John Tyler
1725   Robert Clavering
1729   John Harris
1739   Matthias Mawson
1740   John Gilbert
1749   Edward Cressett
1755   Richard Newcome
1761   John Ewer
1769   Jonathan Shipley
1769   Shute Barrington
1782   Richard Watson
1816   Herbert Marsh
1819   William Van Mildert
1826   Charles Richard Sumner
1828   Edward Copleston
1849   Alfred Ollivant
1883   Richard Lewis
1905   Joshua Pritchard Hughes
1931   Timothy Rees
1939   John Morgan (Archbishop of
       Wales 1949)
1957   William Glyn Hughes Simon
       (Archbishop of Wales 1968)
1971   Eryl Stephen Thomas
1975   John Richard Worthington
       Poole-Hughes
1985   Roy Thomas Davies
1999   Barry Cennydd Morgan
       (Archbishop of Wales 2003)

Monmouth

Description of arms. Per pale azure
and sable, two crosiers in satire or
between in chief a besant charged with
a lion passant guardant gules, in fess
two fleurs-de-lis and in base a fleur-de-
lis all of the third.

1921   Charles Alfred Howell Green
1928   Gilbert Cunningham Joyce
1940   Alfred Edwin Monahan
1945   Alfred Edwin Morris
       (Archbishop of Wales 1957)
1968   Eryl Stephen Thomas
1972   Derrick Greenslade Childs
       (Archbishop of Wales 1983)
1986   Royston Clifford Wright
1992   Rowan Douglas Williams
       (Archbishop of Wales 1999)
2003   Edward William Murray
       Walker

St Asaph[1]

Description of arms. Sable, two keys
endorsed in saltire the wards upwards
argent.

*c.*560   Kentigern
*c.*573   Asaph
1143   Gilbert
1152   Geoffrey of Monmouth
1154   Richard
1160   Godfrey
1175   Adam
1183   John I
1186   Reiner
1225   Abraham
1235   Hugh
1242   Hywel Ab Ednyfed
1249   Anian I [or Einion]
1267   John II
1268   Anian II
1293   Llywelyn de Bromfield
1315   Dafydd ap Bleddyn
1346   John Trevor I
1357   Llywelyn ap Madoc ab Ellis
1377   William de Spridlington
1382   Lawrence Child
1390   Alexander Bache
1395   John Trevor II
1411   Robert de Lancaster
1433   John Lowe

1444   Reginald Pecock
1451   Thomas Bird *alias* Knight
1471   Richard Redman
1496   Michael Deacon
1500   Dafydd ab Iorwerth
1504   Dafydd ab Owain
1513   Edmund Birkhead
1518   Henry Standish
1536   Robert Warton [or Parfew]
1555   Thomas Goldwell
1560   Richard Davies
1561   Thomas Davies
1573   William Hughes
1601   William Morgan
1604   Richard Parry
1624   John Hanmer
1629   John Owen
1660   George Griffith
1667   Henry Glemham
1670   Isaac Barrow
1680   William Lloyd
1692   Edward Jones
1703   George Hooper
1704   William Beveridge
1708   Will. Fleetwood
1715   John Wynne
1727   Francis Hare
1732   Thomas Tanner
1736   Isaac Maddox
1744   Samuel Lisle
1748   Robert Hay Drummond
1761   Richard Newcome
1769   Jonathan Shipley
1789   Samuel Hallifax
1790   Lewis Bagot
1802   Samuel Horsley
1806   William Cleaver
1815   John Luxmore
1830   William Carey
1846   Thomas Vowler Short
1870   Joshua Hughes
1889   Alfred George Edwards
       (Archbishop of Wales 1920)
1934   William Thomas Havard
1950   David Daniel Bartlett
1971   Harold John Charles
1982   Alwyn Rice Jones (Archbishop
       of Wales 1991)
1999   John Stewart Davies
2009   Gregory Kenneth Cameron

St Davids[2]

Description of arms. Sable, on a cross
or five cinquefoils of the first.

*c.*601   David
*c.*606   Cynog
831   Sadyrnfyw
       Meurig
*c.*840   Novis
       ?Idwal
*c.*906   Asser
       Llunwerth
944   Eneuris

---

[1] Prior to the Norman period there is considerable uncertainty as to names and dates.
[2] The following names occur in early records though the dates given cannot always be reconciled.

c.961 Rhydderch
c.999 Morgeneu
1023 Morgeneu
1023 Erwyn
1039 Tramerin
1061 Joseph
1061 Bleddud
1072 Sulien
1078 Abraham
1080 Sulien
1085 Wilfrid
1115 Bernard
1148 David Fitz-Gerald
1176 Peter de Leia
1203 Geoffrey de Henlaw
1215 Gervase [Iorwerth]
1231 Anselm le Gras
1248 Thomas le Waleys
1256 Richard de Carew
1280 Thomas Bek
1296 David Martin
1328 Henry Gower
1347 John Thoresby
1350 Reginald Brian
1352 Thomas Fastolf
1362 Adam Houghton
1389 John Gilbert
1397 Guy de Mohne
1408 Henry Chichele
1414 John Catterick
1415 Stephen Patrington
1418 Benedict Nichols
1434 Thomas Rodburn
        [Rudborne]
1442 William Lindwood
1447 John Langton
1447 John de la Bere
1460 Robert Tully
1482 Richard Martin
1483 Thomas Langton
1485 Hugh Pavy
1496 John Morgan [Young]
1505 Robert Sherborn
1509 Edward Vaughan
1523 Richard Rawlins

1536 William Barlow
1548 Robert Ferrar
1554 Henry Morgan
1560 Thomas Young
1561 Richard Davies
1582 Marmaduke Middleton
1594 Anthony Rudd
1615 Richard Milbourne
1621 William Laud
1627 Theophilus Field
1636 Roger Mainwaring
1660 William Lucy
1678 William Thomas
1683 Laurence Womock
1686 John Lloyd
1687 Thomas Watson
[Vacancy 1699–1705]
1705 George Bull
1710 Philip Bisse
1713 Adam Ottley
1724 Richard Smallbrooke
1731 Elias Sydall
1732 Nicholas Claggett
1743 Edward Willes
1744 Richard Trevor
1753 Anthony Ellis
1761 Samuel Squire
1766 Robert Lowth
1766 Charles Moss
1774 James Yorke
1779 John Warren
1783 Edward Smallwell
1788 Samuel Horsley
1794 William Stewart
1801 George Murray
1803 Thomas Burgess
1825 John Banks Jenkinson
1840 Connop Thirlwall
1874 William Basil Tickell Jones
1897 John Owen
1927 David Lewis Prosser
        (Archbishop of Wales 1944)
1950 William Thomas Havard
1956 John Richards Richards

1971 Eric Matthias Roberts
1982 George Noakes (Archbishop
        of Wales 1987)
1991 John Ivor Rees
1996 David Huw Jones
2002 Carl Norman Cooper
2008 John Wyn Evans

Swansea and Brecon

Description of arms. Per fess azure and
or, in chief surmounting a catherine
wheel issuant an eagle rising regardant
of the second and in base a fleur-de-lis
of the first.

1923 Edward Latham Bevan
1934 John Morgan
1939 Edward William Williamson
1953 William Glyn Hughes Simon
1958 John James Absalom Thomas
1976 Benjamin Noel Young
        Vaughan
1988 Dewi Morris Bridges
1999 Anthony Edward Pierce
2008 John David Edward Davies

Provincial Assistant Bishop

1996–2008 David Thomas

SCOTLAND

Sources: Bp Dowden's *The Bishops of Scotland* (Glasgow 1912), for all the sees up to the Reformation, and for Aberdeen and Moray to the present time.

For bishops after the Reformation (and for a few of the earliest ones before Queen Margaret) – Grub, *Ecclesiastical History of Scotland* (Edinburgh 1861, 4 Vols.) and Bp Keith and Bp Russel, *Scottish Bishops* (2nd ed. Edinburgh 1824).

Scottish episcopal elections became subject immediately to Roman confirmation in 1192. The subordination of the Scottish Church to York became less direct in 1165, and its independence was recognized in a bill of Celestine III in 1192. St Andrews was raised to metropolitan rank on 17 August 1472 and the Archbishop became primate of all Scotland with the same legative rights as the Archbishop of Canterbury on 27 March 1487.

The dates in the margin are those of the consecration or translation to the particular see of the bishops named; or in the case of bishops elect, who are not known to have been consecrated, they are those of the election; or in the case of titular bishops, of the date of their appointment.

The date of the death has been given where there was a long interregnum, or where there is dislocation (as at the Reformation and at the Revolution), or for some special reason to make the history intelligible.

The extra information in the list of College Bishops is given for the reason just stated.

St Andrews

St Andrews, Dunkeld and Dunblane

Description of arms. Quarterly, 1st azure, a saltire argent (for the See of St Andrews); 2nd per fess sable and vert, an open book proper in base, fore-edges and binding or, a dove argent, her wings displayed in chief perching thereon and holding in her beak a spray of olive of the second (for the See of Dunkeld); 3rd chevronny or and gules, a saltire engrailed azure, charged at the fess point with a crescent inverted argent (for the See of Dunblane); 4th azure, a saltire argent supported in front of and by St Andrew enhaloed or and vested pupure with mantle vert, and in base a crescent inverted of the second (for the See of St Andrews).

906 Cellach I
915(?) Fothad I
955 Malisius I
963 Maelbridge
970 Cellach II
996(?) Malasius II
(?) Malmore
1025 Alwyn
1028 Maelduin
1055 Tuthald or Tuadal
1059 Fothad II
1077 ⎫ Gregory (elect)
to ⎬ Catharas (elect)
1107 ⎭ Edmarus (elect)
         Godricus (elect)
1109 Turgot
1120 Eadmer (elect)
1127 Robert
1159 Waldeve (elect)
1160 Ernald
1165 Richard
1178 Hugh
1180 John the Scot
1198 Roger de Beaumon
1202 William Malveisin
1238 Geoffrey (elect)
1240 David de Bernham
1253 Robert de Stuteville (elect)
1254 Abel de Golin

1255 Gamelin
1273 William Wischard
1280 William Fraser
1298 William de Lamberton
1328 James Bennet
1342 William de Laundels
1385 Stephen de Pay (elect)
1386(?) Walter Trayl
1388 Alexander de Neville
1398 Thomas de Arundel
1401 Thomas Stewart (elect)
1402 Walter de Danielston
         (elect)
1403(?) Gilbert Greenlaw
1403 Henry Wardlaw
1408 John Trevor
1440 James Kennedy

ARCHBISHOPS

1465 Patrick Graham
1478 William Scheves
1497 James Stewart (elect)
1504 Alexander Stewart (elect)
1513 John Hepburn (elect)
1513 Innocenzo Cibo (elect)
1514 Andrew Forman
1522 James Betoun
1538 David Betoun [coadjutor]
1547 John Hamilton
1551 Gavin Hamilton [coadjutor]
         died 1571
1572 John Douglas (titular)
1576 Patrick Adamson (titular) died
         1592
1611 George Gladstanes
1615 John Spottiswoode, died 1639
1661 James Sharp
1679 Alexander Burnet
1684 Arthur Rose, died 1704

BISHOPS OF FIFE

[1704–26 See vacant]
1726 James Rose
1733 Robert Keith
1743 Robert White
1761 Henry Edgar

BISHOPS OF ST ANDREWS

1842 Patrick Torry
1853 Charles Wordsworth
1893 George Howard Wilkinson
1908 Charles Edward Plumb
1931 Edward Thomas Scott Reid
1938 James Lumsden Barkway
1949 Arnold Brian Burrowes
1955 John William Alexander Howe
1969 Michael Geoffrey Hare Duke
1995 Michael Harry George Henley
2005 David Robert Chillingworth

†Dunkeld

849(?) Tuathal
865(?) Flaithbertach
1114 Cormac
1147 Gregory
1170 Richard I
1178 Walter de Bidun (elect)
1183(?) John I, the Scot
1203 Richard II, de Prebenda
1212(?) John II, de Leycester
1214(?) Hugh de Sigillo
1229 Matthew Scot (elect)
1229 Gilbert
1236(?) Geoffrey de Liberatione
1252 Richard III, of Inverkeithing
1273(?) Robert de Stuteville
1283(?) Hugh de Strivelin [Stirling]
         (elect)
1283 William
1288 Matthew de Crambeth
1309 John de Leek (elect)
1312 William Sinclair
1337 Malcolm de Innerpeffray
         (elect)
1344 Richard de Pilmor
1347 Robert de Den (elect)
1347(?) Duncan de Strathearn
1355 John Luce
1370 John de Carrick (elect)
1371(?) Michael de Monymusk
1377(?) Andrew Umfray (elect)
1379 John de Peblys [? of Peebles]
1379 Robert de Derling
1390(?) Nicholas Duffield
1391 Robert Sinclair
1398(?) Robert de Cardeny
1430 William Gunwardby
1437 Donald MacNaughton (elect)
1438 James Kennedy
1440(?) Thomas Livingston
1440 Alexander de Lawedre
         [Lauder] (elect)
1442 James de Brois [Brewhous]
1447 William Turnbull (elect)
1448 John Ralston
1452(?) Thomas Lauder
1476 James Livingston
1483 Alexander Inglis (elect)
1484 George Brown
1515 Andrew Stewart (elect)
1516 Gavin Douglas
1524 Robert Cockburn
1526(?) George Crichton
1546 John Hamilton
1552 Robert Crichton
1572 James Paton (titular)
1585 Peter Rollock (titular)
1607 James Nicolson (titular)
1611(?) Alexander Lindsay (deposed
         1638)
1662 George Haliburton

† Indicates a diocese no longer extant, or united with another diocese.

1665 Henry Guthrie
1677 William Lindsay
1679 Andrew Bruce
1686 John Hamilton
1717 Thomas Rattray
1743 John Alexander
1776(?) Charles Rose
1792 Jonathan Watson
1808 Patrick Torry
1842 Held with St Andrews

†Dunblane

1162 Laurence
c.1180 Symon
1196 W[illelmus]
1198 Jonathan
1215 Abraham
1225 Ralph (elect)
1227 Osbert
1233 Clement
1259 Robert de Prebenda
1284 William I
1296 Alpin
1301 Nicholas
1307 Nicholas de Balmyle
1318(?) Roger de Balnebrich (elect)
1322 Maurice
c.1347 William II
c.1361 Walter de Coventre
c.1372 Andrew
c.1380 Dougal
1403(?) Finlay or Dermoch
1419 William Stephen
1430 Michael Ochiltree
1447(?) Robert Lauder
1468 John Hepburn
1487 James Chisolm
1527 William Chisolm I
1561 William Chisolm II
      [coadjutor]
1575 Andrew Graham (titular)
1611 George Graham
1616 Adam Bellenden
1636 James Wedderburn
1661 Robert Leighton
1673 James Ramsay
1684 Robert Douglas
[1716–31 See vacant]
1731 John Gillan
1735 Robert White
1744 Thomas Ogilvie (elect)
1774 Charles Rose, died 1791
1776 Held with Dunkeld

Edinburgh

Description of arms. Azure, a saltire and, in chief, a labelled mitre argent.

1634 William Forbes
1634 David Lindsay
1662 George Wishart
1672 Alexander Young
1679 John Paterson
1687 Alexander Rose
1720 John Fullarton
1727 Arthur Millar
1727 Andrew Lumsden
1733 David Freebairn

[1739–76 See vacant]
1776 William Falconer
1787 William Abernethy
      Drummond
1806 Daniel Sandford
1830 James Walker
1841 Charles Hughes Terrot
1872 Henry Cotterill
1886 John Dowden
1910 George Henry Somerset
      Walpole
1929 Harry Seymour Reid
1939 Ernest Denny Logie Danson
1947 Kenneth Charles Harman
      Warner
1961 Kenneth Moir Carey
1975 Alastair Iain Macdonald
      Haggart
1986 Richard Frederick Holloway
2001 Brian Arthur Smith

Aberdeen
Aberdeen and Orkney

Description of arms. Azure, parted per pale: dexter, a chevron round embattled on its upper edge between a fleur-de-lis argent ensigned of an open crown or in dexter chief, and in base a bishop proper, attired of the second, mitred and holding in his sinister hand a pastoral staff of the third, his dexter hand raised in benediction over three children gules issuant from a cauldron of the third; sinister, an open boat or, an anchor argent pendant from its prow, issuant therefrom a saint proper, attired of the third, enhaloed and holding in his sinister hand a pastoral staff of the second; over all and issuant from the chief a sunburst or, the central ray projected along the palar line to the base.

BISHOPS AT MURTHLAC

(?) Beyn [Beanus]
(?) Donort
(?) Cormac

BISHOPS AT ABERDEEN

1132 Nechtan
c.1150 Edward
c.1172 Matthew
c.1201 John
c.1208 Adam de Kalder
1228 Matthew Scot (elect)
1230 Gilbert de Strivelyn
1240 Radulf de Lamley
1247 Peter de Ramsey
1258 Richard de Pottun
1272 Hugh de Bennum
1282 Henry le Chene
1329 Walter Herok (elect)
1329 Alexander I, de Kyninmund
1344 William de Deyn
1351 John de Rate
1356 Alexander II, de Kyninmund

1380 Adam de Tynyngham
1391 Gilbert de Grenlaw
1422 Henry de Lychton [Leighton]
c.1441 Ingram de Lindsay
1458 Thomas Spens
1480 Robert Blackadder (elect)
1488 William Elphinstone
1515 Robert Forman (elect)
1516 Alexander Gordon
1519 Gavin Dunbar
1529 George Learmonth [coadjutor]
1533 William Stewart
1547 William Gordon
1577 David Cunningham (elect)
1611 Peter Blackburn
1616 Alexander Forbes
1618 Patrick Forbes of Corse
1635 Adam Bellenden [Bannatyne]
1662 David Mitchell
1663 Alexander Burnet
1664 Patrick Scougal
1682 George Halyburton
[1715–21 See vacant]
1721 Archibald Campbell
1724 James Gadderar
1733 William Dunbar
1746 Andrew Gerard
1768 Robert Kilgour
1786 John Skinner
1816 William Skinner
1857 Thomas George Spink
      Suther
1883 Arthur Gascoigne Douglas
1906 Rowland Ellis
1912 Anthony Mitchell
1917 Frederic Llewellyn Deane
1943 Herbert William Hall
1956 Edward Frederick Easson
1973 Ian Forbes Begg
1978 Frederick Charles Darwent
1992 Andrew Bruce Cameron
2007 Robert Arthur Gillies

†Orkney

1035 Henry
1050 Turolf
1072 John I
1072 Adalbert
1073 Radulf
1102 William I, 'the Old'
1108 Roger
1114 Radulf Novell
1168(?) William II
1188(?) Bjarni
1224 Jofreyrr
1248 Henry I
1270 Peter
1286 Dolgfinn
1310 William III
c.1369 William IV
c.1384 Robert Sinclair
1384(?) John
1394 Henry II
1396(?) John Pak
1407 Alexander Vaus (elect)
1415 William Stephenson
1420 Thomas Tulloch
1461 William Tulloch
1477 Andrew Painter
1500 Edward Stewart
1524 John Benston [coadjutor]
1526(?) Robert Maxwell
1541 Robert Reid
1559 Adam Bothwell
1611 James Law
1615 George Graham
1639 Robert Barron (elect)
1661 Thomas Sydserf
1664 Andrew Honeyman

1677 Murdo Mackenzie
1688 Andrew Bruce, See afterwards
      administered with Caithness
1857 Held with Aberdeen

Brechin

Description of arms. Or, three piles in point purpure.

1153(?) Samson
1178 Turpin
1202 Radulf
1215 Hugh
1218 Gregory
1246 Albin
1269(?) William de Crachin
      (elect)
1275 William Comyn
1296 Nicholas
1298 John de Kyninmund
1328 Adam de Moravia
1350 Philip Wilde
1351 Patrick de Locrys
      [Leuchars]
1383 Stephen de Cellario
1411 Walter Forrester
1426 John de Crannach
1455 George Schoriswood
1464 Patrick Graham
1465 John Balfour
1489 William Meldrum
1523 John Hepburn
1557 Donald Campbell (elect)
1565(?) John Sinclair (elect)
1566 Alexander Campbell
      (titular)
1610 Andrew Lamb
1619 David Lindsay
1634 Thomas Sydserf
1635 Walter Whitford
1662 David Strachan
1672 Robert Laurie
1678 George Haliburton
1682 Robert Douglas
1684 Alexander Cairncross
1684 James Drummond
1695–1709 Held with Edinburgh
1709 John Falconar
1724 Robert Norrie
1726 John Ochterlonie
1742 James Rait
1778 George Innes
1787 William Abernethy
      Drummond
1788 John Strachan
1810 George Gleig
1840 David Moir
1847 Alexander Penrose Forbes
1876 Hugh Willoughby Jermyn
1904 Walter John Forbes Robberds
1935 Kenneth Donald Mackenzie
1944 Eric Graham
1959 John Chappell Sprott
1975 Lawrence Edward Luscombe
1990 Robert Taylor Halliday
1997 Neville Chamberlain
2005 John Ambrose Cyril Mantle
2011 Nigel Peyton

Moray

Moray, Ross and Caithness

Description of arms. Party per fess and in chief per pale: 1 or, two lions combatant gules, pulling at a cushion of the last issuant from a crescent azure, on a chief wavy of the third three mullets argent (for the See of Moray); 2 argent, a bishop standing in the sinister vested purpure, mitred and holding in his sinister hand a crosier or and pointing with the dexter hand to a saint affontée, his hands clasped on this breast proper, habited gules, above his head a halo of the third (for the See of Ross); 3 azure, issuant from an antique boat or, a demi-bishop proper vested argent, his mitre and pastoral staff in hand sinister of the second, accompanied by two demi-angels, one in the dexter and the other in the sinister chief holding open books proper, their wings addorsed, also of the second (for the See of Caithness).

1114 Gregory
1153(?) William
1164 Felix
1172 Simon de Tonei
1187 Richard de Lincoln
1203 Brice de Douglas
1224(?) Andrew de Moravia
1244(?) Simon
1251 Radulf de Leycester (elect)
1253 Archibald
1299 David de Moravia
1326 John de Pilmor
1363 Alexander Bur
1397 William de Spyny
1407 John de Innes
1415 Henry Leighton
1422 Columba de Dunbar
1437 John de Winchester
1460(?) James Stewart
1463 David Stewart
1477 William de Tulloch
1487 Andrew Stewart
1501(?) Andrew Forman
1516(?) James Hepburn
1525 Robert Shaw
1532(?) Alexander Stewart
1538(?) Patrick Hepburn
1574 George Douglas
1611 Alexander Douglas
1623 John Guthrie
1662 Murdo Mackenzie
1677 James Aitken
1680 Colin Falconer
1687 Alexander Rose
1688 William Hay
1707 Held with Edinburgh
1725 Held with Aberdeen
1727 William Dunbar
1737 George Hay (elect)
1742 William Falconar
1777 Arthur Petrie
1787 Andrew Macfarlane

1798 Alexander Jolly
1838 Held with Ross
1851 Robert Eden
1886 James Butler Knill Kelly
1904 Arthur John Maclean
1943 Piers Holt Wilson
1953 Duncan Macinnes
1970 George Minshull Sessford
1994 Gregor Macgregor
1999 John Michael Crook
2007 Mark Jeremy Strange

†Ross

1131(?) Macbeth
1150(?) Simon
1161 Gregory
1195 Reginald
1213 Andrew de Moravia (elect)
1215(?) Robert I
1250 Robert II
1272 Matthew
1275(?) Robert II de Fyvin
1295(?) Adam de Derlingtun (elect)
1297(?) Thomas de Dundee
1325 Roger
1351 Alexander Stewart
1372 Alexander de Kylwos
1398(?) Alexander de Waghorn
1418 Thomas Lyell (elect)
      Griffin Yonge (elect)
1420 John Bulloch
1441(?) Andrew de Munro (elect)
1441(?) Thomas Tulloch
1464(?) Henry Cockburn
1478 John Wodman
1481 William Elphinstone (elect)
1483 Thomas Hay
1492 John Guthrie
1498 John Frisel [Fraser]
c.1507 Robert Cockburn
1525 James Hay
c.1539 Robert Cairncross
1552 David Painter
1561(?) Henry Sinclair
1566 John Lesley
1575 Alexander Hepburn
1611 David Lindsay
1613 Patrick Lindsay
1633 John Maxwell
1662 John Paterson
1679 Alexander Young
1684 James Ramsay
1696 See vacant or held with
      Caithness until 1727
1727 Held with Moray
1742 Held with Caithness
1762 Robert Forbes
1777 Held with Moray
1819 David Low
1851 Held with Moray

†Caithness

c.1146 Andrew
c.1187 John
1214 Adam
1223(?) Gilbert de Moravia
1250(?) William
1263 Walter de Baltrodin
1273(?) Nicholas (elect)
1275 Archibald Herok
1278 Richard (elect)
1279(?) Hervey de Dundee (elect)
1282 Alan de St Edmund
1295 John or James (elect)
1296 Adam de Derlingtun
1297 Andrew
1306 Fercard Belegaumbe
1328(?) David
1341 Alan de Moravia

1343 Thomas de Fingask	1339 William Rae	1235 Odo Ydonc (elect)
1370 Malcolm de Dumbrek	1367 Walter Wardlaw	1235 Gilbert
1381 Alexander Man	1388 Matthew de Glendonwyn	1255 Henry
1414 Alexander Vaus	1391 John Framisden (titular)	1294 Thomas de Kircudbright [de
1425 John de Crannach	1408 William Lauder	Daltoun]
1428 Robert Strabrok	1427 John Cameron	1327 Simon de Wedale
1446 John Innes	1447 James de Brois [Brewhouse]	1355 Michael Malconhalgh
1448 William Mudy	1448 William Turnbull	1359(?) Thomas Macdowell (elect)
1478(?) Prospero Camogli de Medici	1456 Andrew de Durrisdeer	1359 Thomas
1484(?) John Sinclair (elect)	1475 John Laing	1364 Adam de Lanark
1502 Andrew Stewart I	1483 George Carmichael (elect)	(?) David Douglas, died 1373
1517(?) Andrew Stewart II		(?) James Carron (resigned 1373)
1542 Robert Stewart (elect)	ARCHBISHOPS	1378 Ingram de Kethnis (elect)
1600 George Gledstanes (elect)	1483 Robert Blackadder	1379 Oswald
1611 Alexander Forbes	(Archbishop 9 Jan 1492)	1380 Thomas de Rossy
1616 John Abernethy	1509 James Betoun I	(?) Francis Ramsay, died 1402
1662 Patrick Forbes	1525 Gavin Dunbar	1406 Elisaeus Adougan
1680 Andrew Wood	1551 Alexander Gordon	1414(?) Gilbert Cavan (elect)
[1695 See vacant]	1552 James Betoun II (restored	1415 Thomas de Butil
1731 Robert Keith	1587)	1422 Alexander Vaus
1741 Wm. Falconas	1571 John Porterfield (titular)	1451 Thomas Spens
1762 Held with Ross	1573 James Boyd (titular)	1457(?) Thomas Vaus (elect)
[1742 See Vacant]	1581 Robert Montgomery (titular)	1459 Ninian Spot
1777 Held with Moray	1585 William Erskine (titular)	1482(?) George Vaus
	1610 John Spottiswoode	1508(?) James Betoun (elect)
	1615 James Law	1509(?) David Arnot
Glasgow	1633 Patrick Lindsay	1526 Henry Wemyss
	1661 Andrew Fairfoul	1541(?) Andrew Dury
Glasgow and Galloway	1664 Alexander Burnet (restored	1559(?) Alexander Gordon
	1674)	1610 Gavin Hamilton
	1671 Robert Leighton, died 1684	1612(?) William Couper
	(resigned 1674)	1619 Andrew Lamb
	1679 Arthur Rose	1635 Thomas Sydserf
	1684 Alexander Cairncross, died	1661 James Hamilton
	1701	1675 John Paterson
	1687 John Paterson,[1] died 1708	1679 Arthur Rose
	[1708 Vacant]	1680 James Aitken
		1688 John Gordon, died 1726
	BISHOPS	1697 Held with Edinburgh
	1731 Alexander Duncan, died 1733	1837 Held with Glasgow

Description of arms. Party per pale:
dexter, vert, a fess wavy argent charged
with a bar wavy azure between a
representation of St Mungo issuant
from the fess proper, habited or, his
dexter hand raised in benediction and
in his sinister hand a Celtic cross of
the same in chief, in nombril point a
salmon proper and in base an annulet
of the fourth; sinister, argent a
representation of St Ninian standing
full-faced proper, clothed in a
pontifical robe purpure, on his head
a mitre and in his dexter hand a crosier
or.

550(?) Kentigern or Mungo (no
    record of his successors)
1114(?) (Michael)
1118(?) John
1147 Herbert
1164 Ingram
1175 Jocelin
1199 Hugh de Roxburgh (elect)
1200 William Malveisin
1202 Florence (elect)
1208 Walter de St Albans
1233 William de Bondington
1259 Nicholas de Moffat (elect)
1259 John de Cheam
1268 Nicholas de Moffat (elect)
1271 William Wischard (elect)
1273 Robert Wischard
1317 Stephen de Donydouer (elect)
1318 John de Eglescliffe
1323 John de Lindsay
1337 John Wischard

[1733 Vacant]
1787 Held with Edinburgh
1805 William Abernethy
    Drummond
1809–37 Held with Edinburgh
1837 Michael Russell
1848 Walter John Trower
1859 William Scott Wilson
1888 William Thomas Harrison
1904 Archibald Ean Campbell
1921 Edward Thomas Scott Reid
1931 John Russell Darbyshire
1938 John Charles Halland How
1952 Francis Hamilton Moncreiff
1974 Frederick Goldie
1981 Derek Alec Rawcliffe
1991 John Mitchell Taylor
1998 Idris Jones
2010 Gregor Duthrie Duncan

†Galloway or Candida Casa or Whithorn[2]

Ninian, died 432(?)
(?) Octa
681 Trumwine
731 Penthelm, died 735(?)
735 Frithowald, died 764
763 Pehtwine, died 776
777 Ethelbert
791 Beadwulf
1140 Gilla-Aldan
1154 Christian
1189 John
1214 Walter

Argyll or Lismore

Argyll and The Isles

Description of arms. Azure, two
crosiers in saltire and in chief a mitre
or.

1193 Harald
1240 William
1253 Alan
1268 Laurence de Erganis
1300 Andrew
1342 Angusde Ergadia (elect)
1344 Martinde Ergaill
1387 John Dugaldi
1397(?) Bean Johannis
1420(?) Finlay de Albany
1428 George Lauder
1476 Robert Colquhoun
1504 David Hamilton
1532 Robert Montgomery
1539(?) William Cunningham (elect)
1553(?) James Hamilton (elect)

---

[1] After the deposition of John Paterson at the Revolution the See ceased to be Archiepiscopal.
[2] The traditional founder of the See is St Ninian, but nothing authentic is known of the bishops prior to the accession of Gilla-Aldan
between 1133 and 1140.

1580 Neil Campbell (titular)
1611 John Campbell (titular)
1613 Andrew Boyd
1637 James Fairlie
1662 David Fletcher
1665 John Young (elect)
1666 William Scroggie
1675 Arthur Rose
1679 Colin Falconer
1680 Hector Maclean
1688 Alexander Monro (elect)
Held with Ross
1847 Alexander Ewing
1874 George Mackarness
1883 James Robert Alexander
    Chinnery-Haldane
1907 Kenneth Mackenzie
1942 Thomas Hannay
1963 Richard Knyvet Wimbush
1977 George Kennedy Buchanan
    Henderson
1993 Douglas MacLean
    Cameron
2004 Alexander Martin Shaw
2011 Kevin Pearson

†The Isles

900 Patrick
1080 Roolwer
1080 William
1095 Hamundr
1138 Wimund
1152 John I
1152(?) Ragnald
1154 Gamaliel
1170 Christian
1194 Michael
1210 Nicholas I
1219 Nicholas II of Meaux
1226(?) Reginald
1226 Simon
1249 Laurence (elect)
1253 Richard
1275 Gilbert (elect)
1275 Mark
1305 Alan
1324 Gilbert Maclelan
1328 Bernard de Linton
1331 Thomas de Rossy
1349 William Russell
1374 John Donkan
1387 Michael
1392 John Sproten (Man)
    (titular)
1402(?) Conrad (Man) (titular)
1402(?) Theodore Bloc (Man)
    (titular)
1410 Richard Messing (Man)
1422 Michael Anchire
1425(?) John Burgherlinus (Man)
1428 Angus I
1441(?) John Hectoris [McCachane]
    Macgilleon

1472 Angus II
1487 John Campbell
1511 George Hepburn
1514 John Campbell (elect)
1530(?) Ferchar MacEachan
    (elect)
1550(?) Roderick Maclean
1553(?) Alexander Gordon
1567 John Carswell (titular)
1573 John Campbell
1605 Andrew Knox
1619 Thomas Knox
1628 John Leslie
1634 Neil Campbell
1662 Robert Wallace
1677 Andrew Wood
1680 Archibald Graham [or
    McIlvernock]
    Held with Orkney and
    Caithness
1819 Held with Argyll

College Bishops, Consecrated without Sees

1705 John Sage, died 1711
1705 John Fullarton (Edinburgh
    1720), died 1727
1709 Henry Christie, died 1718
1709 John Falconar (Fife 1720),
    died 1723
1711 Archibald Campbell
    (Aberdeen 1721), died 1744
1712 James Gadderar (Aberdeen
    1725, Moray 1725), died
    1733
1718 Arthur Millar (Edinburgh
    1727), died 1727
1718 William Irvine, died 1725
1722 Andrew Cant, died 1730
1722 David Freebairn (Edinburgh
    1733)
1726 John Ochterlonie (Brechin
    1731), died 1742
1726 James Ross (Fife 1731), died
    1733
1727 John Gillan (Dunblane 1731),
    died 1735
1727 David Ranken, died 1728

Bishops who have held the Office of Primus

1704 Alexander Rose (Edinburgh
    1704–20)
1720 John Fullarton (Edinburgh
    1720–27)
1727 Arthur Millar (Edinburgh
    1727)
1727 Andrew Lumsden (Edinburgh
    1727–33)
1731 David Freebairn (Edinburgh
    1733–39)

1738 Thomas Rattray (Dunkeld
    1727–43)
1743 Robert Keith (Caithness
    1731–41)
1757 Robert White (Dunblane
    1735–43, St Andrews
    1743–61)
1762 William Falconar (Orkney and
    Caithness 1741–62)
1782 Robert Kilgour (Aberdeen
    1768–86)
1788 John Skinner (Aberdeen
    1786–1816)
1816 George Gleig (Brechin
    1810–40)
1837 James Walker (Edinburgh
    1880–41)
1841 William Skinner (Aberdeen
    1816–57)
1857 Charles Hughes Terrot
    (Edinburgh 1841–72)
1862 Robert Eden (Moray, Ross,
    and Caithness 1851–86)
1886 Hugh Willoughby Jermyn
    (Brechin 1875–1903)
1901 James Butler Knill Kelly
    (Moray, Ross, and Caithness
    1886–1904)
1904 George Howard Wilkinson (St
    Andrews, Dunkeld, and
    Dunblane 1893–1907)
1908 Walter John Forbes Robberds
    (Brechin 1904–34)
1935 Arthur John Maclean (Moray,
    Ross, and Caithness
    1904–43)
1943 Ernest Denny Logie Danson
    (Edinburgh 1939–46)
1946 John Charles Halland How
    (Glasgow and Galloway
    1938–52)
1952 Thomas Hannay (Argyll and
    The Isles 1942–62)
1962 Francis Hamilton Moncreiff
    (Glasgow and Galloway
    1952–74)
1974 Richard Knyvet Wimbush
    (Argyll and The Isles
    1963–77)
1977 Alastair Iain Macdonald
    Haggart (Edinburgh
    1975–85)
1985 Lawrence Edward Luscombe
    (Brechin 1975–90)
1990 George Kennedy Buchanan
    Henderson (Argyll and The
    Isles 1977–92)
1992 Richard Frederick Holloway
    (Edinburgh 1986–2000)
2000 Andrew Bruce Cameron
    (Aberdeen 1992–2006)
2006 Idris Jones (Glasgow and
    Galloway 1998–2009)
2009 David Robert Chillingworth
    (St Andrews, Dunkeld, and
    Dunblane 2005–)

IRELAND

PROVINCE OF ARMAGH

†Achonry

BISHOPS

c.558 Cathfuidh
1152 Mael Ruanaid ua Ruadain
1159 Gille na Naehm O Ruadain
 [Gelasius]
1208 Clemens O Sniadaig
1220 Connmach O Torpaig [Carus]
1226 Gilla Isu O Cleirig [Gelasius]
1237 Tomas O Ruadhan
1238 Oengus O Clumain [Elias]
1251 Tomas O Maicin
1266 Tomas O Miadachain
 [Dionysus]
1286 Benedict O Bracain
1312 David of Kilheny
1348 David II
1348 Nicol Alias Muircheartach O
 hEadhra
1374 William Andrew
1385 Simon
c.1390 Tomas mac Muirgheasa
 MacDonn-chadha
1401 Brian mac Seaain O hEadhra
1410 Maghnus O h Eadhra
1424 Donatus
1424 Richard Belmer
1436 Tadhg O Dalaigh
1442 James Blakedon
1449 Cornelius O Mochain
1463 Brian O hEasdhra [Benedictus]
1470 Nicholas Forden
1475 Robert Wellys
1484 Thomas fitzRichard
1484 Tomas O Conghalain
1489 John Bustamente
1492 Thomas Ford
1508 Eugenius O Flannagain
1522 Cormac O Snighe
1547 Thomas O Fihilly
1562 Eugene O'Harte
1613 Miler Magrath (with Cashel)
 United to Killala 1622

†Annadown

BISHOPS

1189 Conn ua Mellaig [Concors]
1202 Murchad ua Flaithbertaig
1242 Tomas O Mellaig
1251 Conchobar [Concors]
1283 John de Ufford
1308 Gilbert O Tigernaig
1323 Jacobus O Cethernaig
1326 Robert Petit
1328 Albertus
1329 Tomas O Mellaig
1359 Dionysius
1393 Johannes
1394 Henry Trillow
1402 John Bryt
1408 John Wynn
1421 John Boner [Camere]
1425 Seean Mac Braddaigh
1428 Seamus O Lonnghargain
1431 Donatus O Madagain
1446 Thomas Salscot
1450 Redmund Bermingham
1458 Thomas Barrett

1496 Francis Brunand
1540 John Moore
United to Tuam c.1555

†Ardagh

454 Mel
c.670 Erard
874 Faelghus
 Cele 1048
1152 Mac Raith ua Morain
1172 Gilla Crist O hEothaig
 [Christianus]
 O'Tirlenain 1187
 ua hEislinnen
 Annud O Muiredaig 1216
1217 Robert
1224 M.
1228 Loseph mac Teichthechain
1229 Mac Raith Mac Serraig
1232 Gilla Isu mac in Scelaige O
 Tormaid [Gelasius]
1232 Iocelinus
1238 Brendan Mac Teichthechain
1256 Milo of Dunstable
1290 Matha O'h-Eothaig
 [Mattheus]
1323 Robert Wirsop (did not get
 possession)
1324 Mac Eoaighseoan
1347 Eoghan O Ferghail
 [Audovenus]
1368 William Mac Carmaic
1373 Cairbre O'Ferghail
 [Charles]
1373 John Aubrey
1392 Henry Nony (did not get
 possession)
1396 Comedinus Mac Bradaigh
 [Gilbert]
1400 Adam Leyns
1419 Conchobar O'Ferghail
 [Cornelius]
1425 Risdeard O'Ferghail
[1444 O'Murtry, not consecrated
 resigned]
1445 Cormac Mac
 Shamhradhain
1462 Seaan O'Ferghail
1467 Donatus O'Ferghail
1482 William O'Ferghail
1517 Ruaidri O'Maoileoin
1517 Rory O'Mallone [Roger O
 Melleine]
1541 Richard O'Ferrall
1553 Patrick MacMahon
[1572 John Garvey, not
 consecrated]
1583 Lysach O'Ferrall
1604 Robert Draper
1613 Thomas Moigne
1679 William Bedell
1633 John Richardson
1661 Robert Maxwell
1673 Francis Marsh
1682 William Sheridan
1692 Ulysses Burgh
1604–33, 1661–92 and 1692–1751
 Held by the Bishops of
 Kilmore

1751–1839 Held by the Archbishops
 of Tuam
United to Kilmore 1839

Armagh

Description of arms. Azure, an archiepiscopal staff in pale argent ensigned with a cross pattée or, surmounted by a pall argent fimbriated and fringed or, charged with four crosses pattées-fitchées sable.

BISHOPS

444 Patrick
 Benignus 467
 Jarlath 481
 Cormac 497
 Dubthach 513
 Ailill I 526
 Ailill II 536
 David O'Faranan 551
 Carlaen 588
 MacLaisre 623
–640 Thomian MacRonan
 Segeni 688
 Suibhne 730
–732 Congusa
 Affinth 794
–811 Nundha
–818 Artri
 835 Forannan
 Mael Patraic I 862
 Fethgna 875
 Cathasach MacRobartach 883
 Mochta 893
900 Maelaithghin
 Cellach
 Mael Ciarain 915
 Joseph 936
 Mael Patraic II 936
 Cathasach MacDolgen 966
 Maelmiure 994
 Airindach 1000
 Maeltuile 1032
1032 Hugh O'Ferris
 Mael Patraic III 1096
1099 Caincomrac O'Boyle

ARCHBISHOPS

1105 Cellach mac Aeda meic Mael
 Isu [Celsus]
1132 Mael maedoc Ua Morgair
 [Malachais]
1137 Gilla Meic Liac mac
 Diarmata meic Ruaidri
 [Gelasius]
1174 Conchobar O Conchaille
 [Concors]

† Indicates a diocese no longer extant, or united with another diocese.

1175 Gille in Coimhedh O Caran
    [Gilbertus]
1180 Tomaltach O Conchobair
    [Thomas]
1184 Mael Isu Ua Cerbaill
    [Malachias]
1202 Echdonn mac Gilla Uidir
    [Eugenius]
1217 Lucas Neterville
1227 Donatus O Fidabra
1240 Albert Suebeer of Cologne
1247 Reginald
1258 Abraham O'Conallain
1261 Mael Patraic O Scannail
1270 Nicol Mac Mael Isu
1303 Michael MacLochlainn (not
    confirmed)
1304 Dionysius (not confirmed)
1306 John Taaffe
1307 Walter Jorz
1311 Roland Jorz
1324 Stephen Segrave
1334 David Mag Oireachtaigh
1347 Richard FitzRalph
1362 Milo Sweetman
1383 John Colton
1404 Nicholas Fleming
1418 John Swayne
1439 John Prene
1444 John Mey
1457 John Bole [Bull]
1471 John Foxhalls or
    Foxholes
1475 Edmund Connesburgh
1480 Ottaviano Spinelli [de
    Palatio]
1513 John Kite
1521 George Cromer
1543 George Dowdall
1552 Hugh Goodacre
1553 George Dowdall (again)
[1560 Donat MacTeague, not
    recognized by the Crown,
    1562]
1563 Adam Loftus
1568 Thomas Lancaster
1584 John Long
1589 John Garvey
1595 Henry Ussher
1613 Christopher Hampton
1625 James Ussher
[Interregnum 1656–61]
1661 John Bramhall
1663 James Margetson
1679 Michael Boyle
1703 Narcissus Marsh
1714 Thomas Lindsay
1724 Hugh Boulter
1742 John Hoadly
1747 George Stone
1765 Richard Robinson
    [afterwards Baron
    Rokeby]
1795 William Newcome
1800 William Stuart
1822 John George Beresford
United to Clogher 1850–86
1862 Marcus Gervais Beresford
1886 Robert Bentknox
1893 Robert Samuel Gregg
1896 William Alexander
1911 John Baptist Crozier
1920 Charles Frederick D'Arcy
1938 John Godfrey FitzMaurice
    Day
1939 John Allen Fitzgerald
    Gregg
1959 James McCann
1969 George Otto Simms
1980 John Ward Armstrong

1986 Robert Henry Alexander
    Eames
2007 Alan Edwin Thomas Harper

Clogher

Description of arms. Azure, a bishop seated in full pontificals proper, in the act of benediction, and holding his pastoral staff in the left hand.

*c.*493 MacCarthinn or
    Ferdachrioch
    Ailill 869
1135 Cinaeth O Baigill
1135 Gilla Crist O Morgair
    [Christianus] (moved his see
    to Louth)

BISHOPS OF LOUTH

1135 Gilla Crist O Morgair
    [Christianus]
1138 Aed O Ceallaide [Edanus]
1178 Mael Isu O Cerbaill
    [Malachias]
1187 Gilla Crist O Mucaran
    [Christinus]
1194 Mael Isu Ua Mael
    Chiarain
1197 Gilla Tigernaig Mac Gilla
    Ronain [Thomas]

BISHOPS OF CLOGHER

1218 Donatus O Fidabra
1228 Nehemias
1245 David O Bracain
1268 Michael Mac an tSair
1287 Matthew Mac Cathasaigh I
–1310 Henricus
1316 Gelasius O Banain
1320 Nicholas Mac Cathasaigh
1356 Brian Mac Cathmaoil
    [Bernard]
1362 Matthew Mac Cathasaigh II
 — Aodh O hEothaigh [*alias* O
    Neill]
1373 John O Corcrain
    [Wurzburg]
1390 Art Mac Cathmhail
1433 Piaras Mag Uidhir [Petrus]
1450 Rossa mac Tomais Oig Mag
    Uidhir [Rogerius]
1475 Florence Woolley
[1484 Niall mac Seamuis Mac
    Mathghamna]
1484 John Edmund de Courci
1494 Seamus Mac Pilip Mac
    Mathghamna
1500 Andreas
1502 Nehemias O Cluainin
1504 Giolla Padraig O Conalaigh
    [Patrick]
1505 Eoghan Mac Cathmhail
    [Eugenius]
1517 Padraig O Cuilin
1535 Aodh O Cearbhalain [Odo]
1517 Patrick O'Cullen
1535 Hugh O'Carolan
1570 Miler Magrath
1605 George Montgomery

1621 James Spottiswood
1645 Henry Jones
1661 John Leslie
1671 Robert Leslie
1672 Roger Boyle
1691 Richard Tennison
1697 St George Ashe
1717 John Stearne
1745 Robert Clayton
1758 John Garnett
1782 John Hotham
1796 William Foster
1797 John Porter
1819 John George Beresford
1820 Percy Jocelyn
1822 Robert Ponsonby Tottenham
    Luftus
United to Armagh 1850–86
1886 Charles Maurice Stack
1903 Charles Frederick D'Arcy
1908 Maurice Day
1923 James MacManaway
1944 Richard Tyner
1958 Alan Alexander Buchanan
1970 Richard Patrick Crosland
    Hanson
1973 Robert William Heavener
1980 Gordon McMullan
1986 Brian Desmond Anthony
    Hannon
2002 Michael Geoffrey St Aubyn
    Jackson
2011 Francis John McDowell

Connor

Description of arms. Azure, a lamb passant supporting with the dexter foreleg a staff proper flying therefrom a pennant argent charged with a saltire gules between three cross crosslets or; on a chief of the last two crosiers in saltire of the first.

506 Oengus MacNessa 514
    Lughadh 543
640 Dimma Dubh [the Black]
    Duchonna the Pious 725
    Cunnen or Cuinden 1038
    Flann O'Sculu 1117
1124 Mael Maedoc Ua Morgair
    [Malachias]
–1152 MaelPatraic O'Banain
1172 Nehemias
1178 Reginaldus
1226 Eustacius
1242 Adam
1245 Isaac de Newcastle-on-Tyne
1258 William de Portroyal
1261 William de Hay [or la Haye]
1263 Robert de Flanders
1275 Peter de Dunach
1293 Johannes
1320 Richard
1321 James de Couplith
1323 John de Eglecliff
1323 Robert Wirsop
1324 Jacabus O Cethernaig
1353 William Mercier
1374 Paulus
1389 Johannes

[1420 Seaan O Luachrain, not
    consecrated]
1423 Eoghan O'Domhnaill
1429 Domhnall O'Meraich
1431 John Fossade [Festade]
1459 Patricius
1459 Simon Elvington
United to Down 1441
1945 Charles King Irwin
1956 Robert Cyril Hamilton Glover
    Elliott
1969 Arthur Hamilton Butler
1981 William John McCappin
1987 Samuel Greenfield Poyntz
1995 James Edward Moore
2002 Alan Edwin Thomas
    Harper
2007 Alan Francis Abernethy

Derry

Derry and Raphoe

Description of arms. Party per pale:
dexter gules, two swords in saltire
proper, the hilts in base or, and on a
chief azure a harp or stringed argent
(for the See of Derry); sinister ermine,
a chief per pale azure and or, the first
charged with a sun in splendour of the
last, the second with a cross pattée
gules (for the See of Raphoe).

    Caencomhrac 927
–937 Finachta MacKellach
–949 Mael Finnen

BISHOPS OF MAGHERA
(Where the See was in the twelfth
and the thirteenth centuries)
1107 Mael Coluim O Brolchain
 — Mael Brigte O Brolchain
1152 O Gormgaile Muiredach O
    Cobthaigh [Mauricius]
1173 Amhlaim O Muirethaig
1185 Fogartach O Cerballain
    [Florentius]
c.1230 Gilla in Coimhded O
    Cerballain [Germanus]
c.1280 Fogartach O
    Cerballain II
    [Florentius]

BISHOPS OF DERRY
(Where the See was resettled)
1295 Enri Mac Airechtaig
    [O'Reghly] [of Ardagh]
1297 Gofraid MacLochlainn
    [Godfrey]
1316 Aed O Neill [Odo]
1319 Michael Mac Lochlainn
    [Maurice]
1349 Simon
1391 Johannes
1391 John Dongan
1394 Seoan O Mochain
1398 Aodh [Hugo]
1401 Seoan O Flannabhra
1415 Domhnall Mac Cathmhail
1419 Domhnall O Mearaich
1429 Eoghan O Domhnaill
    [Eugenius]

1433 John Oguguin
[1456 John Bole, appointment not
    completed, translated to
    Armagh]
1458 Bartholomew O Flannagain
c.1464 Johannes
1467 Nicholas Weston
1485 Domhnall O Fallamhain
1501 Seamus mac Pilip Mac
    Mathghamna [MacMahon]
1520 Ruaidhri O Domhnaill
1520 Rory O'Donnell
1554 Eugene O'Doherty
1568 F. [doubtful authority]
1569 Redmond O'Gallagher
[1603 Denis Campbell, not
    consecrated]
1605 George Montgomery
1610 Brutus Babington
[1611 Christopher Hampton,
    consecrated]
1613 John Tanner
1617 George Downham
1634 John Bramhall
1661 George Wild
1666 Robert Mossom
1680 Michael Ward
1681 Ezekiel Hopkins
1691 William King
1703 Charles Hickman
1714 John Hartstonge
1717 St George Ashe
1718 William Nicolson
1727 Henry Downes
1735 Thomas Rundle
1743 Carew Reynell
1745 George Stone
1747 William Barnard
1768 Frederick Augustus Hervey
    [afterwards Earl of
    Bristol]
1803 William Knox
1831 Richard Ponsonby
Raphoe united to Derry from 1834
1853 William Higgin
1867 William Alexander
1896 George Alexander Chadwick
    (resigned)
1916 Joseph Irvine Peacocke
1945 Robert M'Neil Boyd
1958 Charles John Tyndall
1970 Cuthbert Irvine Peacocke
1975 Robert Henry Alexander
    Eames
1980 James Mehaffey
2002 Kenneth Raymond Good

Down

Down and Dromore

Description of arms. Quarterly, 1 and 4
azure, two keys endorsed in saltire the
wards in chief or, surmounted in the
fess point by a lamb passant proper
(for the See of Down); 2 and 3 Argent,
two keys endorsed in saltire the wards
in chief gules, surmounted by an open
book in fess proper between two
crosses pattées-fitchées in pale sable
(for the See of Dromore).

Fergus 584
Suibhne 825
Graithene 956
Finghin 964
Flaithbertach 1043
MaelKevin 1086
— Mael Muire 1117
Oengus Ua Gormain 1123
— [Anonymous]
c.1124 Mael Maedoc O Morgair
    [Malachias]
1152 Mael Isu mac in Chleirig
    Chuirr [Malachias]
1175 Gilla Domangairt Mac
    Cormaic
c.1176 Echmilid [Malachias]
c.1202 Radulfus
1224 Thomas
1251 Randulphus
1258 Reginaldus
1265 Thomas Lydel
1277 Nicholas le Blund
1305 Thomas Ketel
1314 Thomas Bright
1328 John of Baliconingham
1329 Ralph of Kilmessan
1353 Richard Calf I
1365 Robert of Aketon
1367 William White
1369 Richard Calf [II]
1386 John Ross
1394 John Dongan
1413 John Cely [or Sely]
1445 Ralph Alderle

BISHOPS OF DOWN AND CONNOR

1441 John Fossard
1447 Thomas Pollard
1451 Richard Wolsey
1456 Thomas Knight
1469 Tadhg O Muirgheasa
    [Thaddaeus]
1489 Tiberio Ugolino
1520 Robert Blyth
1542 Eugene Magennis
1565 James MacCawell
1569 John Merriman
1572 Hugh Allen
1593 Edward Edgeworth
1596 John Charden
1602 Roben Humpston
1607 John Todd (resigned)
1612 James Dundas
1613 Robert Echlin
1635 Henry Leslie
1661 Jeremy Taylor
1667 Roger Boyle
1672 Thomas Hacket
1694 Samuel Foley
1695 Edward Walkington
1699 Edward Smyth
1721 Francis Hutchinson
1739 Carew Reynell
1743 John Ryder
1752 John Whitcombe
1752 Robert Downes
1753 Arthur Smyth
1765 James Traill
1784 William Dickson
1804 Nathaniel Alexander
1823 Richard Mant

BISHOPS OF DOWN, CONNOR AND
DROMORE

1849 Robert Bent Knox
1886 William Reeves
1892 Thomas James Welland
1907 John Baptist Crozier
1911 Charles Frederick D'Arcy

1919 Charles Thornton Primrose
      Grierson
1934 John Frederick McNeice
1942 Charles King Irwin

**BISHOPS OF DOWN AND
DROMORE**

1945 William Shaw Kerr
1955 Frederick Julian Mitchell
1970 George Alderson Quin
1980 Robert Henry Alexander
      Eames
1986 Gordon McMullan
1997 Harold Creeth Miller

†Dromore

Mael Brighde 974
Riagan 1101
1197 Ua Ruanada
1227 Geraldus
1245 Andreas
1284 Tigernach I
1290 Gervasius
—   Tigernach II
1309 Florentius Mac Donnocain
1351 Anonymous
1366 Milo
1369 Christophorus Cornelius 1382
1382 John O'Lannoy
1398 Thomas Orwell
1400 John Waltham
1402 Roger Appleby
1408 Richard Payl
1410 Marcus
1411 John Chourles
1414 Seaan O Ruanadha
1419 Nicholas Wartre
1429 Thomas Rackelf
1431 William
1431 David Chirbury
1450 Thomas Scrope [Bradley]
1450 Thomas Radcliff
1456 Donatus O h-Anluain
      [Ohendua]
1457 Richard Messing
1463 William Egremond
—   Aonghus [Aeneas] 1476
1476 Robert Kirke
1480 Yvo Guillen
1483 George Braua
1511 Tadhg O Raghallaigh
      [Thaddeus]
1536 Quintin O Quigley [Cogley]
1539 Roger McHugh
1540 Arthur Magennis
1607 John Todd
[1613 John Tanner, not
      consecrated]
1613 Theophilus Buckworth
1661 Robert Leslie
1661 Jeremy Taylor (administered
      the diocese)
1667 George Rust
1671 Essex Digby
1683 Capel Wiseman
1695 Tobias Pullein
1713 John Stearne
1717 Ralph Lambert
1727 Charles Cobbe
1732 Henry Maule
1744 Thomas Fletcher
1745 Jemmett Browne
1745 George Marlay
1763 John Oswald
1763 Edward Young
1765 Henry Maxwell
1766 William Newcome
1775 James Hawkins
1780 William de la Poer Beresford

1782 Thomas Percy
1811 George Hall
1812 John Leslie
1819 James Saurin
United to Down since 1842

†Elphin

Domnall mac Flannacain Ua
      Dubhthaig 1136
Muiredach O Dubhthaig 1150
1152 Mael Isu O Connachtain
      Flannacan O Dubhthaig 1168
c.1177 Tomaltach mac Aeda
      Ua Conchobhair [Thomas]
c.1180 Florint Ua Riacain Ui
      Maelrvanaid
1206 Ardgar O Conchobhair
1226 Dionysius O Mordha
c.1230 Alanus
1231 Donnchad mac Fingein O
      Conchobhair [Dionysius
      Donatus]
1245 Eoin O Mugroin
1247 Tomaltach macToirrdelbaig O
      Conchobhair [Thomas]
1260 Mael Sechlainn O
      Conchobhair [Milo]
1262 Tomas mac Fergail mac
      Diarmata
1266 Muiris O Conchobhair
[1285 Amiaim O Tommaltaig, not
      consecrated]
1285 Gilla Isu mac in Liathana O
      Conchobhair
1297 Maelsechlainn mac Briain
      [Malachias]
1303 Donnchad O Flannacain,
      [Donatus]
1307 Cathal O Conchobhair
1310 Mael Sechlainn Mac Aedha
1313 Lurint O Lachtnain [Laurence]
1326 Sean O Finnachta
1355 Carolus
1357 Gregory O Mochain
1372 Thomas Barrett
1383 Seoan O Mochain
1407 Seaan O Grada
1405 Gerald Caneton
1412 Thomas Colby
1418 Robert Fosten
1421 Edmund Barrett
1427 Johannes
1429 Laurence O Beolain
1429 William O hEidighean
1448 Conchobhar O Maolalaidh
1458 Nicholas O Flanagan
1487 Hugo Arward
1492 Rlocard mac Briain O
      gCuanach
1499 George Brana
1501 Cornelius O Flannagain
1508 Christopher Fisher
1525 John Maxey
1539 William Maginn 1541(?)
1539 Gabriel de Sancto Serio
1541 Conach or Con O'Negall or
      O'Shyagall
1552 Roland Burke [de Burgo]
1582 Thomas Chester
1583 John Lynch
1611 Edward King
1639 Henry Tilson
1661 John Parker
1667 John Hodson
1691 Simon Digby
1720 Henry Downes
1724 Theophilus Bolton
1730 Robert Howard
1740 Edward Synge

1762 William Gore
1772 Jemmett Browne
1775 Charles Dodgson
1795 John Law
1810 Power le Poer Trench
1819 John Leslie 1854
United to Kilmore and Ardagh on
the death of Bishop Beresford in
1841, when Bishop Leslie became
Bishop of the united dioceses.

†Killala

Muiredach
Kellach
O Maolfogmair I 1137
O Maolfogmair II 1151
Imar O Ruaidhin 1176
1179 O Maolfogmair III
1199 Domnall Ua Becdha
1207 Cormac O'Tarpy
      O'Kelly 1214
1226 Aengus O Maolfogmair [Elias]
      Gille Cellaig O Ruaidhin
1253 Seoan O Laidlg
1281 Donnchad O Flaithbertaig
      [Donatus]
1307 John Tankard
      Sean O Flaithim 1343
1344 James Bermingham
1347 William O DusucBhda
1351 Robert Elyot
1381 Thomas Lodowys
1383 Conchobar O Coineoil
      [Cornelius]
1390 Thomas Horwell [Orwell]
1400 Thomas Barrett
1403 Muircheartach Cleirach mac
      Donnchadha O DusucBhda
      Connor O'Connell 1423
1427 Fergal Mac Martain
1431 Thaddaeus Mac Creagh
1432 Brian O Coneoil
1447 Robert Barrett
1452 Ruaidhri Bairead [Barrett]
1453 Thomas
1459 Richard Viel
      Miler O'Connell
1461 Donatus O Conchobhair
1470 Tomas Bairead [Barrett]
1487 John de Tuderto [Seaan O
      Caissin]
1500 Thomas Clerke
1508 Malachias O Clumhain
1513 Risdeard Bairead
1545 Redmond O'Gallagher
1570 Donat O'Gallagher
1580 John O'Casey
1592 Owen O'Conor
1613 Miler Magrath
Achonry united to Killala 1622
1623 Archibald Hamilton
1630 Archibald Adair (deposed, but
      subsequently restored)
164? John Maxwell
1661 Henry Hall
1664 Thomas Bayly
1671 Thomas Otway
1680 John Smith
1681 William Smyth
1682 Richard Tennison
1691 William Lloyd
1717 Henry Downes
1720 Charles Cobbe
1727 Robert Howard
1730 Robert Clayton
173? Mordecai Cary
175? Richard Robinson
      [afterwards Baron Rokeby]
1759 Samuel Hutchinson

1781 William Cecil Pery
1784 William Preston
1787 John Law
1795 John Porter
1798 Joseph Stock
1810 James Verschoyle
United to Tuam since 1834

Kilmore

Kilmore, Elphin and Ardagh

Description of arms. Argent, on a cross azure a pastoral staff enfiling a mitre, all or (for the See of Kilmore). Sable, two pastoral staves in saltire or, in base a lamb couchant, argent (for the See of Elphin). Or, a cross gules between four trefoils slipped vert, on a chief sable, a key erect of the first (for the See of Ardagh).

— Aed Ua Finn 1136
— Muirchenach Ua
    Maelmoeherge 1149
1152 Tuathal Ua Connachtaig
    [Thadeus]
1202 Mi Ua Dobailen
— Flann O Connachtaig
    [Florentius] 1231
1237 Congalach Mac Idneoil
1251 Simon O Ruairc
1286 Mauricius
— Matha Mac Duibne 1314
1320 Padraig O Cridecain
— Conchobhar Mac
    Conshnamha [Ford] 1355
1356 Richard O Raghilligh
1373 Johannes
1388 Thomas Rushook
1392 Sean O Raghilligh I [John]
1398 Nicol Mac Bradaigh
1401 Sean O'Raghilligh II
1407 John Stokes
1409 David O'Fairchellaigh
1422 Domhnall O Gabhann
1445 Aindrias Mac Bradaigh
1455 Fear Sithe Mag Dhuibhne
1465 Sean O Raghilligh II
1476 Cormac Mag Shamhradhain
1480 Tomas MacBradaigh
1512 Diarmaid O Raghilligh
1530 Edmund Nugent
1540 Sean Mac Bradaigh
1585 John Garvey
1604 Robert Draper
1613 Thomas Moigne
1629 William Bedell
1643 Robert Maxwell
1673 Francis Marsh
1682 William Sheridan
1693 William Smyth
1699 Robert Wetenhall
1715 Timothy Godwin
1727 Josiah Hott
1742 Joseph Story
1757 John Cradock
1772 Denison Cumberland
1775 George Lewis Jones
1790 William Foster

1796 Charles Broderick
1802 George de la Poer Beresford
Ardagh united to Kilmore 1839
Elphin united to Kilmore 1841
1841 John Leslie
1854 Marcus Gervais Beresford
1862 Hamilton Verschoyle
1870 Charles Leslie
1870 Thomas Carson
1874 John Richard Darley
1884 Samuel Shone
1897 Alfred George Elliott
1915 William Richard Moore
1930 Arthur William Barton
1939 Albert Edward Hughes
1950 Frederick Julian Mitchell
1956 Charles John Tyndall
1959 Edward Francis Butler Moore
1981 William Gilbert Wilson
1993 Michael Hugh Gunton Mayes
2001 Kenneth Harbert Clarke

†Mayo

Gerald 732
Muiredach [or Murray]
Moinraoht 732
Aidan 773
1172 Gilla Isu Ua Mailin
    Cele O Dubhthaig 1210
1210 ?Patricius
1428 William Prendergast
1430 Nicholas 'Wogmay'
1439 Odo O h-Uiginn
1432 Martin Campania
1457 Simon de Duren
1493 John Bel
1541 Eugenius Macan Brehon
United to Tuam 1559

†Raphoe

Sean O Gairedain
Donell O Garvan
Felemy O Syda
Oengus O'Lappin 959
1150 Muiredhach O'Cofley
1156 Gille in Coimhded Ua Carain
    [Gilbertus]
— Anonymous
1204 Mael Isu Ua Doirig
— Anonymous
1253 Mael Padraig O Scannail
    [Patricius]
1263 John de Alneto
1265 Cairpre O Scuapa
1275 Fergal O Firghil [Florentius]
1306 Enri Mac-in-Chrossain
    [Henricus]
1319 Tomas Mac Carmaic Ui
    Domhnaill
1363 Padraig Mac Maonghail
1367 Conchobar Mac Carmaic Ui
    Domhnaill [Cornelius]
1397 Seoan MacMenmain
1400 Eoin MacCarmaic [Johannes]
–1413 Anthony
–1414 Robert Rubire
1416 John McCormic
1420 Lochlainn O Gallchobhair I
    [Laurentius]
1440 Cornelius Mac Giolla Brighde
1443 Lochlainn O Gallchobhair II
    [Laurentius]
1479 John de Rogeriis
1482 Meanma Mac Carmail
    [Menclaus Mac Carmacain]
1514 Conn O Cathain [Cornelius]
1534 Eamonn O Gallchobhair
1547 Arthur o'Gallagher

1563 Donnell Magonigle [or
    McCongail]
[1603 Denis Campbell, not
    consecrated]
1605 George Montgomery
1611 Andrew Knox
1633 John Leslie
1661 Robert Leslie
1671 Ezekiel Hopkins
1682 William Smyth
1693 Alexander Cairncross
1701 Robert Huntington
1702 John Pooley
1713 Thomas Lindsay
1714 Edward Synge
1716 Nicholas Forster
1744 William Barnard
1747 Philip Twysden
1753 Robert Downes
1763 John Oswald
1780 James Hawkins
1807 John George Beresford
1819 William Magee
1822 William Bissett
United to Derry since 1834

Tuam

Tuam, Killala and Achonry

Description of arms. Azure beneath a triple architectural canopy three figures, in the centre the Blessed Virgin Mary holding in her arms the Holy Child, between, on the dexter the figure of a bishop (St Jarlath) in pontificalibus and in the act of benediction, and, on the sinister St John supporting with his left arm a lamb argent, each in proper vestments or, the hands, feet, and faces proper.

BISHOPS

Murrough O'Nioc 1032
Hugh O'Hessian 1085
Cathusach Ua Conaill 1117
O Clerig 1137
Muiredach Ua Dubhthaig
    1150

ARCHBISHOPS

1152 Aed Ua h-Oisin [Edanus]
1167 Cadhla Ua Dubhthaig
    [Catholicus]
1202 Felix Ua Ruanada
1236 Mael Muire O Lachtain
    [Marianus]
1250 Flann Mac Flainn [Florentius]
[1256 James O'Laghtnan, not
    confirmed or consecrated]
1257 Walter de Salerno
1258 Tomaltach O Conchobair
    [Thomas]
1286 Stephen de Fulbourn
1289 William de Bermingham
1312 Mael Sechlainn Mac Aeda
1348 Tomas MacCerbhaill
    [MacCarwill]
1364 Eoin O Grada
1372 Gregory O Mochain I

1384 Gregory O Mochain II
1387 William O Cormacain
1393 Muirchertach mac Pilb O
     Cellaigh
1410 John Babingle
1411 Cornelius
1430 John Bermingham
     [Winfield]
1438 Tomas mac Muirchearthaigh
     O Cellaigh
1441 John de Burgo
1452 Donatus O Muiredaigh
1485 William Seoighe [Joyce]
1503 Philip Pinson
1506 Muiris O Fithcheallaigh
1514 Tomas O Maolalaidh
1537 Christopher Bodkin
1573 William O'Mullally [or Lealy]
Annadown united to Tuam c.1555
Mayo united to Tuam 1559
1595 Nehemiah Donnellan

1609 William O'Donnell [or
     Daniel]
1629 Randolph or Ralph
     Barlow
1638 Richard Boyle
1645 John Maxwell
1661 Samuel Pullen
1667 John Parker
1679 John Vesey
1716 Edward Synge
1742 Josiah Hort
1752 John Ryder
1775 Jemmett Browne
1782 Joseph Dean Bourke
     [afterwards Earl of
     Mayo]
1794 William Beresford [afterwards
     Baron Decies]
1819 Power le Poer Trench
Killala united to Tuam from
     1834

BISHOPS

1839 Thomas Plunket [afterwards
     Baron Plunket]
1867 Charles Brodrick Bernard
1890 James O'Sullivan
1913 Benjamin John Plunket
1920 Arthur Edwin Ross
1923 John Ort
1928 John Mason Harden
1932 William Hardy Holmes
1939 John Winthrop Crozier
1958 Arthur Hamilton Butler
1970 John Coote Duggan
1986 John Robert Winder Neill
1998 Richard Crosbie Aitken
     Henderson
2011 Patrick William Rooke

PROVINCE OF DUBLIN

†Ardfert

BISHOPS

Anmchad O h-Anmchada
1117
1152 Mael Brenain Ua Ronain
     Gilla Mac Aiblen
     O'Anmehadha 1166
     Domnall O Connairche
     1193
1200 David Ua Duibdithrib
     Anonymous 1217
1218 John
1218 Gilbertus
1237 Brendan
1253 Christianus
1257 Philippus
1265 Johannes
1286 Nicolaus
1288 Nicol O Samradain
1336 Ailin O hEichthighirn
1331 Edmund of Caermaerthen
1348 John de Valle
1372 Cornelius O Tigernach
1380 William Bull
1411 Nicholas FitzMaurice
1404 Nicholas Ball
1405 Tomas O Ceallaigh
1409 John Attilburgh
     [Artilburch]
1450 Maurice Stack
1452 Maurice O Conchobhair
1461 John Stack
1461 John Pigge
1473 Philip Stack
1495 John FitzGerald
[See vacant in 1534]
1536 James FitzMaurice
1588 Nicholas Kenan
1600 John Crosbie
1622 John Steere
1628 William Steere
1641 Thomas Fulwar
United to Limerick 1661

†Ardmore

1153 Eugenius
Incorporated with Lismore
     1192

Cashel

Cashel, Waterford, Lismore, Ossory,
Ferns and Leighlin

Description of arms. Gules, two keys
addorsed in saltire the wards in
chief, or.

BISHOPS

Cormac MacCuillenan 908
Donnell O'Heney 1096 *or* 1098

ARCHBISHOPS

c.1111 Mael Ios Ua h-Ainmire
       Mael Iosa Ua Fogludha
       [Mauricius] 1131
       Domnall Ua Conaing 1137
       Gilla Naomh O'Marty 1149
–1152 Donat O'Lonergan I
–c.1160 M.
1172 Domnall O h-Ualla-chain
       [Donatus]
1186 Muirghes O h-Enna [Matheus]
c.1208 Donnchad Ua
       Longargain I [Donatus]
1216 Donnchad Ua Longargain II
       [Donatus]
1224 Mairin O Briain [Marianus]
1238 David mac Ceallaig [O'Kelly]
1254 David Mac Cearbaill [Mac
       Carwill]
1290 Stiamna O Bracain
1303 Maurice Mac Cearbaill
1317 William FitzJohn
1327 Seoan Mac Cearbaill
1329 Walter le Rede
1332 Eoin O Grada
1346 Radulphus O Cellaigh [Kelly]
1362 George Roche [de Rupe]

1365 Tomas Mac Cearbhaill
1374 Philip of Torrington
1382 Michael
1384 Peter Hackett
1406 Richard O Hedian
1442 John Cantwell I
1452 John Cantwell II
1484 David Creagh
1504 Maurice FitzGerald
1525 Edmund Butler
1553 Roland Baron or FitzGerald
1567 James MacCawell
Emly united to Cashel 1569
1571 Miler Magrath (Bishop of
     Cashel and Waterford from
     1582)
1623 Malcolm Hamilton
1630 Archibald Hamilton
1661 Thomas Fulwar
1667 Thomas Price
[See vacant 1685–91]
1691 Narcissus Marsh
1694 William Palliser
[1727 William Nicolson, not
     enthroned]
1727 Timothy Goodwin
1730 Theophilus Bolton
1744 Arthur Price
1752 John Whitcombe
1754 Michael Cox
1779 Charles Agar
1801 Charles Brodrick
1822 Richard Laurence
Waterford and Lismore united to
Cashel from 1833; on the death of
Abp Laurence in 1838 the province
was united to Dublin and the see
ceased to be an Archbishopric

BISHOPS

1839 Stephen Creagh Sandes
1843 Robert Daly
1872 Maurice FitzGerald
     Day
1900 Henry Stewart O'Hara
1919 Robert Miller
1931 John Frederick McNeice
1935 Thomas Arnold Harvey
1958 William Cecil De Pauley

1968 John Ward Armstrong
Ossory united to Cashel 1977
1980 Noel Vincent Willoughby
1997 John Robert Winder
         Neill
2003 Peter Francis Barrett
2006 Michael Andrew James
         Burrows

†Clonfert

Moena, or Moynean, or
   Moeinend 572
Cummin the Tall 662
Ceannfaeladh 807
Laithbheartach 822
Ruthnel or Ruthme 826
Cormac MacEdain 922
Ciaran O'Gabbla 953
Cathal 963
Eochu 1031
O'Corcoran 1095
Muiredach Ua h-Enlainge 1117
Gille Patraic Ua Ailcinned
   1149
c.1152 Petrus Ua Mordha
11/2 Mall Isu mac in Baird
1179 Celechair Ua h-Armedaig
Muirchertach Ua'Maeluidir
   1187
Domnall Ua Finn 1195
Muirchertach Ua Carmacain
   1204
1205 Mael Brigte Ua hErurain
1224 Cormac O Luimlin [Carus]
1248 Thomas
1259 Tomas mac Domnaill Moire O
         Cellaig
1266 Johannes de Alatre
1296 Robert
c.1302 John
1308 Gregorius O Brocaig
1320 Robert Le Petit
1322 Seoan O Leaain
1347 Tomas mac Gilbert O Cellaigh I
1378 Muircheartach mac Pilib O
         Cellaigh [Maurice]
1393 William O Cormacain
1398 David Corre
1398 Enri O Conmaigh
1405 Tomasi O Cellaigh II
1410 Cobhthach O Madagain
1438 Seaan O hEidin
1441 John White
1447 Conchobhar O Maolalaidh
1448 Cornelius O Cuinnlis
1463 Matthaeus Mag Raith
1508 David de Burgo
1509 Dionysius O'Mordha
1534 Roland de Burgo
1536 Richard Nangle
1580 Hugh
1582 Stephen Kirwan
1602 Roland Lynch
1627 Robert Dawson
1644 William Baily
1665 Edward Wolley
1691 William FitzGerald
1722 Theophilus Bolton
1724 Arthur Price
1730 Edward Synye
1732 Mordecai Cary
1716 John Whitcombe
1752 Arthur Smyth
1753 William Carmichael
1758 William Gote
1762 John Oswald
1763 Denison Cumberland
1772 Walter Cope
1782 John Law

1787 Richard Marlay
1795 Charles Broderick
1796 Hugh Hamilton
1798 Matthew Young
1801 George de la l'oer Beresford
1802 Nathaniel Alexander
1804 Christopher Butson
United to Killaloe since 1834

†Clonmacnoise

-663 Baitan O'Cormac
-839 Joseph [of Rossmore]
         Maclodhar 890
         Cairbre Crom 904
         Loingsech 919
-940 Donough I
-953 Donough II
-966 Cormae O Cillin
         Maenach 971
         Conaing O'Cosgraigh 998
         Male Poil 1001
         Flaithbertach 1038
         Celechar 1067
         O'Mallaen 1093
         Christian Aherne 1104
?1111 Domnall mac Flannacain Ua
         Dubthaig
1152 Muirchertach Ua Maeluidir
         Cathal Ua Maeileoin 1207
c.1207 Muirchertach Ua Muiricen
1214 Aed O Maeileoin I
1227 Aed O Maeileoin II [Elias]
1236 Thomas Fitzpatrick
1252 Tomas O Cuinn
1280 Anonymous
1282 Gilbert (not consecrated)
1290 William O Dubhthaig
1298 William O Finnein
1303 Domnall O Braein
1324 Lughaid O Dalaigh
1337 Henricus
1349 Simon
1369 Richard [Braybroke]
1371 Hugo
1388 Philippus O Maoil
1389 Milo Corr
1397 O'Gallagher
1397 Philip Nangle
1423 David Prendergast
1426 Cormac Mac Cochlain
         [Cornelius]
1444 Sean O Dalaigh
1449 Thomas
1458 Robertus
1458 William
1459 John
1487 Walter Blake
1509 Tomas O Maolalaidh
1516 Quintin O h-Uiginn
1539 Richard O'Hogan
1539 Florence Kirwan
1556 Peter Wall [Wale]
United to Meath 1569

†Cloyne

Reachtaidh 887
1148 Gilla na Naem O Muirchertaig
         [Nehemias]
         Ua Dubcroin 1159
         Ua Flannacain 1167
1177 Matthaeus Ua Mongaig
1201 Laurence Ua Suilleabain
1205 C.
1281 Luke
c.1224 Florence
1226 Daniel
1237 David mac Cellaig [O'Kelly]
1240 Ailinn O Suilleabain

1247 Daniel
1265 Reginaldus
1275 Alan O Longain
1284 Nicholas of Effingham
1323 Maurice O Solchain
1333 John Brid
1351 John Whitekot
1363 John Swaffham
1376 Richard Wye
1394 Gerard Caneton
1413 Adam Payn
United to Cork 1418–1638
1638 George Synge
1661–78 Held by the Bishops of Cork
1679 Patrick Sheridan
1683 Edward Jones
1693 William Palliser
1694 Tobias Pullein
1695 St George Ashe
1697 John Pooley
1702 Charles Crow
1726 Henry Maule
1732 Edward Synge
1734 George Berkeley
1753 James Stopford
1759 Robert Johnson
1767 Frederick Augustus Hervery
1768 Charles Agar
1780 George Chinnery
1781 Richard Woodward
1794 William Bennett
1820 Charles Mongan Warhurton
1826 John Brinkley
United to Cork on the death of Bp
Brinkley in 1835

Cork

Cork, Cloyne and Ross

Description of arms. Argent, on a plain
cross, the ends pattée, gules, a pastoral
staff, surmounted on a mitre, or (for
the See of Cork). Azure, a mitre proper
labelled or, between three crosses
pattées-fitchées argent (for the See of
Cloyne). No arms are borne for the See
of Ross.

Donnell 876
Soer Bhreatach 892
DusucBhdhurn O'Stefam 959
Cathmogh 969
Mugron O'Mutan 1057
1138 Gregory
? Ua Menngorain 1147
1148 Gilla Aedha Ua Maigin
1174 [Gregorius] O h-Aedha
         [O Hea]
c.1182 Reginaldus I
1187 Aicher
1192 Murchad Ua h-Aedha
         Anonymous 1214
1215 Mairin Ua Briain [Marianus]
1225 Gilbertus
1248 Laurentius
1265 William of Jerpoint
1267 Reginaldus
1277 Robert Mac Donnchada

1302 Seoan Mac Cearbaill [Mac Carwill]
1321 Philip of Slane
1327 Walter le Rede
1330 John of Ballyconingham
1347 John Roche
1359 Gerald de Barri
1396 Roger Ellesmere
1406 Richard Kynmoure
1409 Patrick Fox
1409 Milo fitzJohn
1425 John Paston
1418 Adam Payn
1429 Jordan Purcell
1463 Gerald FitzGerald
1472 William Roche (Coadjutor)
1490 Tadhg Mac Carthaigh
1499 John FitzEdmund FitzGerald
1499 Patrick Cant
1523 John Benet
1536 Dominic Tyrre [Tirrey]
1562 Roger Skiddy
1570 Richard Dyxon
1572 Matthew Sheyn
Ross united to Cork 1583
1583 William Lyon
1618 John Boyle
1620 Richard Boyle
1638 William Chappell
1661 Michael Boyle
1663 Edward Synge
1679 Edward Wetenhall
1699 Dive Downes
1710 Peter Browne
1735 Robert Clayton
1745 Jemmett Browne
1772 Isaac Mann
1789 Euseby Cleaver
1789 William Foster
1790 William Bennet
1794 Thomas Stopford
1805 John George Beresford
1807 Thomas St Laurence
1831 Samuel Kyle
Cloyne united to Cork from 1835
1848 James Wilson
1857 William FitzGerald
1862 John Gregg
1878 Robert Samuel Gregg
1894 William Edward Meade
1912 Charles Benjamin Dowse
1933 William Edward Flewett
1938 Robert Thomas Hearn
1952 George Otto Sims
1957 Richard Gordon Perdue
1978 Samuel Greenfield Poyntz
1988 Robert Alexander Warke
1999 William Paul Colton

Dublin

Dublin and Glendalough

Description of arms. Azure, an episcopal staff argent, ensigned with a cross pattée or, surmounted by a pallium of the second edged and fringed or, charged with five crosses formée fitchée, sable.

BISHOPS

Sinhail 790
c.1028 Dunan [Donatus]
1074 Gilla Patraic
1085 Donngus
1096 Samuel Ua'h-Aingliu

ARCHBISHOPS

1121 Grene [Gregorius]
1162 Lorcan Ua'Tuathail [Laurentius]
1182 John Cumin
1213 Henry de Loundres
Glendalough united to Dublin
1230 Luke
125? Fulk de Sandford
1279 John de Derlington
1286 John de Sandford
1295 Thomas de Chadworth
1296 William de Hotham
1299 Richard de Ferings
[1307 Richard de Havering, not consecrated]
1311 John de Leche
1317 Alexander de Bicknor
1349 John de St Paul
1363 Thomas Minot
1376 Robert de Wikeford
1391 Robert Waldeby
1396 Richard Northalis
1397 Thomas Cranley
1418 Richard Talbot
1451 Michael Tregury
1472 John Walton
1484 Walter Fitzsimons
1512 William Rokeby
1521 Hugh Inge
1529 John Alan
1535 George Browne
1555 Hugh Curwin
1567 Adam Loftus
1605 Thomas Jones
1619 Lancelot Bulkeley
1661 James Margetson
1663 Michael Boyle
1679 John Parker
1682 Francis Marsh
1694 Narcissus Marsh
1703 William King
1730 John Hoadly
1743 Charles Cobbe
1765 William Carmichael
1766 Arthur Smyth
1772 John Cradock
1779 Robert Fowler
1801 Charles Agar [Earl of Normanton]
1809 Euseby Cleaver
1820 John George Beresford
1822 William Magee
1831 Richard Whately
Kildare united to Dublin 1846
1864 Richard Chenevix Trench (resigned)
1885 William Conyngham [Lord Plunket]
1897 Joseph Ferguson Peacocke
1915 John Henry Bernard
1919 Charles Frederick D'Arcy
1920 John Allen Fitzgerald Gregg
1939 Arthur William Barton
1956 George Otto Simms
1969 Alan Alexander Buchanan
1977 Henry Robert McAdoo
1985 Donald Arthur Richard Caird
1996 Walton Newcome Francis
2002 John Robert Winder Neill
2011 Michael Geoffrey St Aubyn Jackson

†Emly

Raidghil 881
Ua Ruaich 953
Faelan 980
MaelFinan 1030
Diarmait Ua Flainnchua 1114
1152 Gilla in Choimhded Ua h-Ardmhail Mael Isu Ua Laigenain 1163
1172 Ua Meic Stia
1177 Charles O'Buacalla
1177 Isaac O'Hamery
1192 Ragnall Ua Flainnchua
1205 M.
1209 William
1212 Henry
1227 John Collingham
1238 Daniel
1238 Christianus
1251 Gilbert O'Doverty
1266 Florence or Laurence O'hAirt
1272 Matthew MacGormain
1275 David O Cossaig
1286 William de Clifford
1306 Thomas Cantock [Quantock]
1309 William Roughead
1335 Richard le Walleys
1353 John Esmond
1363 David Penlyn [Foynlyn]
1363 William
1405 Nicholas Ball
1421 John Rishberry
1422 Robert Windell
1428 Thomas de Burgo
1428 Robert Portland
1445 Cornelius O Cuinnlis
1444 Robert
1448 Cornelius O Maolalaidh
1449 William O Hetigan
1476 Pilib O Cathail
1494 Donatus Mac Briain
1498 Cinneidigh Mac Briain
1507 Tomas O hUrthaille
1543 Angus O'Hernan
1551 Raymond de Burgo
United to Cashel 1569
Transferred to Limerick 1976

†Ferns

−598 Edan [or Maedoc or Hugh]
Maeldogair 676
Coman 678
Diratus 693
Cillenius 715
Cairbre O'Kearney 1095
Ceallach Ua Colmain 1117
Mael Eoin Ua Dunacain 1125
Ua Cattain 1135
1178 Loseph Ua h-Aeda
1186 Ailbe Ua Maelmuaid [Albinus]
1224 John of St John
1254 Geoffrey of St John
1258 Hugh of Lamport
1283 Richard of Northampton
1304 Simon of Evesham
1305 Robert Walrand
1312 Adam of Northampton
1347 Hugh de Saltu [of Leixlip]
1347 Geoffrey Grandfeld
1349 John Esmond
1350 William Charnells
1363 Thomas Dene
1400 Patrick Barret
1418 Robert Whittey
1453 Tadhg O Beirn
1457 John Purcell I
1479 Laurence Nevill
1505 Edmund Comerford

1510 Nicholas Comyn
1519 John Purcell II
1539 Alexander Devereux
1566 John Devereux
1582 Hugh Allen
Leighlin united to Ferns 1597
1600 Robert Grave
1601 Nicholas Statford
1605 Thomas Ram
1635 George Andrews
1661 Robert Price
1667 Richard Boyle
1683 Narcissus Marsh
1691 Bartholomew Vigors
1722 Josiah Hort
1727 John Hoadly
1730 Arthur Price
1734 Edward Synge
1740 George Stone
1743 William Cottrell
1744 Robert Downes
1752 John Garnet
1758 William Carmichael
1758 Thomas Salmon
1759 Richard Robinson
1761 Charles Jackson
1765 Edward Young
1772 Joseph Deane Bourke
1782 Walter Cope
1787 William Preston
1789 Euseby Cleaver
1809 Percy Jocelyn
1820 Robert Ponsonby Tottenham
       Loftus
1822 Thomas Elrington
United to Ossory 1835

†Glendalough

Dairchell 678
Eterscel 814
Dungal 904
Cormac 927
Nuadha 920 [or Neva]
Gilda Na Naomh
       c.1080
Cormac O'Mail 1101
Aed Ua Modain 1126
1140 Anonymous
1152 Gilla na Naem
1157 Cinaed O Ronain [Celestinus]
1176 Maelcallann Ua Cleirchen
       [Malchus]
1186 Macrobius
1192 William Piro
1214 Robert de Bedford
United to Dublin
After the union with Dublin some
rival bishops appear
c.1216 Bricheus
1468 John
1475 Michael
1481 Denis White John 1494
1494 Ivo Ruffi
1495 John
1500 Francis Fitzjohn of Corduba

†Iniscattery (Scattery Island)

861 Aidan
959 Cinaeda O'Chommind
973 Scandlam O'Lenz
       O'Bruil 1069
       O'Bruil II 1081
       Dermot O Lennain 1119
       Aed Ua Bechain I 1188
       Cearbhal Ua'h-Enna
       [Carolus] 1193
1360 Tomas Mac Mathghamhna
1392 John Donkan

1414 Richard Belmer
       Dionysius 1447
1447 John Grene
Incorporated with Limerick

†Kells

Mael Finnen 968
c.1152 Tuathal Ua Connachtarg
1185 Anonymous
1202 M. Ua Dobailen
Incorporated with Meath

†Kildare

Conlaedh 520
Hugh [or Hed] the Black 639
Maeldoborcon 709
Eutigern 762
Lomthiull 787
Snedbran 787
Tuatchar 834
Orthanach 840
Aedgene Britt 864
Macnghal 870
Lachtnan 875
Suibhne 881
Scannal 885
Lergus 888
Mael Findan 950
Annchadh 981
Murrough McFlan 986
1030 MaelMartain
       MaelBrighde 1042
       Finn 1085
       MaelBrighde O Brolchan
       1097
       Hugh [Heremon] 1100
       Ferdomnach 1101
       Cormac O Cathassaig 1146
       Ua Duibhin 1148
1152 Finn mac Mael Muire Mac
       Cianain
       Fin mac Gussain Ua
       Gormain
1161 Malachias Ua Brain
1177 Nehemias
1206 Cornelius Mac Fealain
1223 Ralph of Bristol
1233 John of Taunton
1258 Simon of Kilkenny
1280 Nicholas Cusack
1300 Walter Calf [de Veel]
1333 Richard Houlot
1352 Thomas Giffard
1366 Robert of Aketon
       [Acton]
1404 John Madock
1431 William fitzEdward
1449 Geoffrey Hereford
1456 John Bole [Bull]
1464 Richard Lang
1474 David Cone
1475 James Wall
       William Barret
1480 Edward Lane
1526 Thomas Dillon
1529 Walter Wellesley
1540 William Miagh
1550 Thomas Lancaster
1555 Thomas Leverous
1560 Alexander Craik
1564 Robert Daly
1583 Daniel Neylan
1604 William Pilsworth
1636 Robert Ussher
1644 William Golborne
1661 Thomas Price
1667 Ambrose Jones
1679 Anthony Dopping

1682 William Moreton
1705 Welbore Ellis
1731 Charles Cobbe
1743 George Stone
1745 Thomas Fletcher
1761 Richard Robinson
1765 Charles Jackson
1790 George Lewis Jones
1804 Charles Lindsay
United to Dublin after the death of
       Bp Lindsay in 1846
1976 Separated from Dublin and
       united to Meath

†Kilfenora

1172 Anonymous
1205 F.
1224 Johannes
1254 Christianus
       Anonymous 1264
1266 Mauricius
1273 Florentius O Tigernaig
1281 Congalach [O Lochlainn]
1291 G.
1299 Simon O Cuirrin
1303 Maurice O Briain
1323 Risdeard O Lochlainn
c.1355 Dionysius
1372 Henricus
       Cornelius
1390 Patricius
1421 Feidhlimidh mac
       Mathghamhna O Lochlainn
       [Florentius]
1433 Fearghal
1434 Dionysius O Connmhaigh
1447 John Greni
1476 [? Denis] O Tombaigh
1491 Muircheartach mac
       Murchadha O Briain
       [Mauricius]
1514 Maurice O'Kelly
1541 John O'Neylan
-1585 Daniel, bishop-elect
1606 Bernard Adams [with
       Limerick q.v.]
1617 John Steere
1622 William Murray
[1628 Richard Betts, not
       consecrated]
1630 James Heygate
1638 Robert Sibthorp
1661-1741 Held by the Archbishops
       of Tuam
1742-52 Held by the Bishop of
       Clonfert
United to Killaloe 1752

†Killaloe

BISHOPS

       O'Gerruidher 1054
       Domnall Ua hEnna 1098
       Mael Muire O Dunain 1117
       Domnall Ua Conaing 1131
       Domnall Ua Longargain 1137
       Tadg Ua Longargain 1161
       Donnchad mac Diarmata Ua
       Briain 1164
1179 Constantin mac Toirrdelbaig
       Ua Briain
1194 Diarmait Ua Conaing
1201 Conchobhar Ua h-Enna
       [Cornelius]
1217 Robert Travers
1221 Domnall Ua h-Enna
       [Donatus]
1231 Domnall O Cenneitig
       [Donatus]

1253 Isoc O Cormacain [Isaac]
1268 Mathgamain O h-Ocain [O
    Hogan]
1281 Maurice O h-Ocain
1299 David Mac Mathghamna
    [Mac Mahon]
1317 Tomas O Cormacain I
1323 Brian O Cosgraig
1326 David Mac Briain [David of
    Emly]
?1326 Natus O Heime
1343 Tomas O h-Ogain
1355 Tomas O Cormacain II
1389 Mathghamain Mag Raith
1400 Donatus Mag Raith
1409 Robert Mulfield
1418 Eugenius O Faolain
1423 Thadeus Mag Raith I
1429 Seamus O Lonnghargain
1443 Donnchadh mac
    Toirdhealbhaigh O Briain
1460 Thadeus Mag Raith II
1463 Matthaeus O Griobhtha
1483 Toirdhealbhach mac
    Mathghamhna O Briain
    [Theodoricus]
1523 Thadeus
1526 Seamus O Cuirrin
1546 Cornelius O Dea
1554 Turlough [or Terence]
    O'Brien II
1570 Maurice [or Murtagh]
    O'Brien-Arra
1613 John Rider
1633 Lewis Jones
1647 Edward Parry
1661 Edward Worth
1669 Daniel Wytter
1675 John Roan
1693 Henry Ryder
1696 Thomas Lindsay
1713 Thomas Vesey
1714 Nicholas Forster
1716 Charles Carr
1740 Joseph Story
1742 John Ryder
1743 Jemmet Browne
1745 Richard Chenevix
1746 Nicholas Synge
Kilfenora united to Killaloe 1752
1771 Robert Fowler
1779 George Chinnery
1780 Thomas Barnard
1794 William Knox
1803 Charles Dalrymple Lindsay
1804 Nathaniel Alexander
1804 Robert Ponsonby Tottenham
    Loftus
1820 Richard Mant
1823 Alexander Arbuthnot
1828 Richard Ponsonby
1831 Edmund Knox [with Clonfert]
Clonfert united to Killaloe 1834
Kilmacduagh united to Killaloe
    1834
1834 Christopher Butson
1836 Stephen Crengh Sandes
1839 Ludlow Tonson [afterwards
    Baron Riversdale]
1862 William FitzGerald
1884 William Bennet Chester
1893 Frederick Richards Wynne
1897 Mervyn Archdall
1912 Charles Benjamin Dowse
1913 Thomas Sterling Berry
    (resigned)
1924 Henry Edmund Patton
1943 Robert M'Neil Boyd
1945 Hedley Webster
1953 Richard Gordon Perdue

1957 Henry Arthur Stanistreet
1972 Edwin Owen
1976 United to Limerick

†Kilmacduagh

? Ua Cleirig 1137
    Imar Ua Ruaidin 1176
    Rugnad O'Rowan 1178
1179 Mac Gilla Cellaig Ua Ruaidin
1206 Ua Cellaig
    Mael Muire O Connmaig
    1224
1227 Aed [Odo]
    Conchobhar O Muiredaig 1247
1248 Gilla Cellaig O Ruaidin
    [Gilbertus]
1249 David yFredrakern
1254 Mauricius O Leaain
1284 David O Setachain
1290 Luirint O Lachtnain
    [Laurentius]
1307 Lucas
1326 Johannes
1360 Nicol O Leaain
1394 Gregory O Leaain
1405 Enri O Connmhaigh
1409 Dionysius
1409 Eugene O Faolain
1418 Diarmaid O Donnchadha
1419 Nicol O Duibhghiolla
1419 Seaan O Connmhaigh
1441 Dionysius O Donnchadha
1479 Cornelius O Mullony
1503 Matthaeus O Briain
1533 Christopher Bodkin
1573 Stephen O'Kirwan
[1584 Thomas Burke, not
    consecrated]
1587 Roland Lynch
1627–1836 Held in commendam by
    the Bishops of Clonfert
United to Killaloe since 1834

†Leighlin

–633 Laserian or Molaise
–865 Mainchin
–940 Conella McDonegan Daniel
    969
    Cleitic O'Muinic 1050
c.1096 Ferdomnac
    Mael Eoin Ua Dunacain 1125
    Sluaigedach Ua Cathain 1145
1152 Dungal O Caellaide
1192 Johannes
1197 Johannes
1202 Herlewin
1217 Richard [Fleming]
1228 William le Chauniver
1252 Thomas
1275 Nicholas Chever
1309 Maurice de Blanchville
1321 Meiler le Poer
1344 Radulphus O Ceallaigh
1349 Thomas of Brakenberg
1360 Johannes
1362 William (not consecrated)
1363 John Young
1371 Philip FitzPeter
1385 John Griffin
1398 Thomas Peverell
1400 Richard Bocomb
1419 John Mulgan
1432 Thomas Fleming
— Diarmaid 1464
1464 Milo Roche
1490 Nicholas Magwyr
1513 Thomas Halsey
1524 Mauricius O Deoradhain

1527 Matthew Sanders
1550 Robert Travers
1555 Thomas O'Fihelly
1567 Donnell or Daniel Cavanagh
1589 Richard Meredith
United to Ferns since 1597 on the
    death of Bp Meredith

Limerick

*Limerick, Ardfert, Aghadoe, Killaloe,
Kilfenora, Clonfert, Kilmacduagh and
Emly*

Description of arms. Azure two keys
addorsed in saltire the wards upwards;
in the dexter chief a crosier paleways,
in the sinister a mitre, all or.

–1106 Gilli alias Gilla Espaic
1140 Patricius
1150 Erolb [? = Harold]
1152 Torgesius
1179 Brictius
1203 Donnchad Ua'Briain
    [Donatus]
1207 Geoffrey
–1215 Edmund
1223 Hubert de Burgo
1252 Robert de Emly or Neil
1273 Gerald [or Miles] de Mareshall
1302 Robert de Dundonald
1312 Eustace de Aqua or de l'Eau
1336 Maurice de Rochfort
1354 Stephen Lawless
1360 Stephen Wall [de Valle]
1369 Peter Curragh
1399 Bernardus O Conchobhair
1400 Conchobhar O Deadhaidh
1426 John Mothel (resigned)
Iniscattery incorporated with
    Limerick
1456 Thomas Leger
1458 William Russel, *alias* Creagh
1463 Thomas Arthur
[1486 Richard Stakpoll, not
    consecrated]
1486 John Dunowe
1489 John O'Phelan [Folan]
1524 Sean O Cuinn
1551 William Casey
1557 Hugh de Lacey or Lees
    (deposed)
1571 William Casey
1594 John Thornburgh
1604 Bernard Adams
1626 Francis Gough
1634 George Webb
1643 Robert Sibthorp
Ardfert united to Limerick 1661
1661 Edward Synge
1664 William Fuller
1667 Francis Marsh
1673 John Vesey
1679 Simon Digby
1692 Nathaniel Wilson
1695 Thomas Smyth
1725 William Burscough
1755 James Leslie
1771 James Averill

1772 William Gore
1784 William Cecil Pery
1794 Thomas Barnard
1806 Charles Morgan Warburton
1820 Thomas Elrington
1823 John Jebb
1834 Edmund Knox
1849 William Higgin
1854 Henry Griffin
1866 Charles Graves
1899 Thomas Bunbury
1907 Raymond D'Audemra Orpen
1921 Harry Vere White
1934 Charles King Irwin
1942 Evelyn Charles Hodges
1961 Robert Wyse Jackson
1970 Donald Arthur Richard Caird
Killaloe united to Limerick 1976
Emly transferred to Limerick 1976
1976 Edwin Owen
1981 Walton Newcome Francis
    Empey
1985 Edward Flewett Darling
2000 Michael Hugh Gunton Mayes
2008 Trevor Russell Williams

†Lismore

Ronan 764
Cormac MacCuillenan 918
–999 Cinneda O'Chonmind
    Niall mac Meic Aedacain
    1113
    Ua Daightig 1119
1121 Mael Isu Ua h-Ainmere
    Mael Muire Ua Loingsig 1150
1151 Gilla Crist Ua Connairche
    [Christianus]
1179 Felix
Ardmore incorporated with Lismore
    1192
1203 Malachias, O'Heda or
    O'Danus
1216 Thomas
1219 Robert of Bedford
1228 Griffin Christopher
1248 Ailinn O Suilleabain
1253 Thomas
1270 John Roche
1280 Richard Corre
1309 William Fleming
1310 R.
1322 John Leynagh
1356 Roger Cradock, provision
    annulled
1358 Thomas le Reve
United to Waterford 1363

Meath

Meath and Kildare

Description of arms. Sable three mitres
argent, two, and one.

BISHOPS OF THE SEE OF CLONARD

Senach 588
–640 Colman 654
    DusucBhduin O'Phelan 718
    Tole 738

–778 Fulartach 779
    Clothcu 796
    Clemens 826
    Cormac MacSuibhne
    Cumsuth 858
    Suarlech 870
    Ruman MacCathasaid 922
    Colman MacAilild 926
    Tuathal O'Dubhamaigh 1028

BISHOPS OF MEATH

1096 Mael Muire Ua Dunain
1128 Eochaid O Cellaig
1151 Etru Ua Miadacain
    [Eleuzerius]
1177 Echtigern mac Mael Chiarain
    [Eugenius]
1192 Simon Rochfort
(The See was transferred from
    Clonard to Newtown near
    Trim, 1202)
Kells incorporated with Meath
1224 Donan De [Deodatus] (not
    consecrated)
1227 Ralph Petit
1231 Richard de la Corner
1253 Geoffrey Cusack
1255 Hugo de Taghmon
1283 Walter de Fulburn
1287 Thomas St Leger
1322 Seoan Mac Cerbaill [John
    MacCarwill]
1327 William de Paul
1350 William St Leger
1353 Nicholas [Allen]
1369 Stephen de Valle [Wall]
1380 William Andrew
1385 Alexander Petit [or de Balscot]
1401 Robert Montayne
1412 Edward Dantesey
[1430 Thomas Scurlog, apparently
    not consecrated]
1430 William Hadsor
1435 William Silk
1450 Edmund Ouldhall
1460 William Shirwood
1483 John Payne
1507 William Rokeby
1512 Hugh Inge
1523 Richard Wilson
1529 Edward Staples
1554 William Walsh
1563 Hugh Brady
Clonmacnoise united to Meath
    1569
1584 Thomas Jones
1605 Roger Dod
1612 George Montgomery
1621 James Usher
1625 Anthony Martin
[Interregnum 1650–61]
1661 Henry Leslie
1661 Henry Jones
1682 Anthony Dopping
1697 Richard Tennison
1705 William Moreton
1716 John Evans
1724 Henry Downes
1727 Ralph Lambert
1732 Welbore Ellis
1734 Arthur Price
1744 Henry Maule
1758 William Carmichael
1765 Richard Pococke
1765 Arthur Smyth
1766 Henry Maxwell
1798 Thomas Lewis O'Beirne
1823 Nathaniel Alexander

1840 Charles Dickinson
1842 Edward Stopford
1850 Thomas Stewart Townsend
1852 James Henderson Singer
1866 Samuel Butcher
1876 William Conyngham [Lord
    Plunket]
1885 Charles Parsons Reichel
1894 Joseph Ferguson Peacocke
1897 James Bennett Keene
1919 Benjamin John Plunket
1926 Thomas Gibson George
    Collins
1927 John Orr
1938 William Hardy Holmes
1945 James McCann
1959 Robert Bonsall Pike
Kildare united to Meath 1976
1976 Donald Arthur Richard Caird
1985 Walton Newcome Francis
    Empey
1996 Richard Lionel Clarke

†Ossory

Dermot 973
1152 Domnall Ua Fogartaig
1180 Felix Ua Duib Slaine
1202 Hugo de Rous [Hugo Rufus]
1220 Peter Mauveisin
1231 William of Kilkenny
1233 Walter de Brackley
1245 Geoffrey de Turville
1251 Hugh de Mapilton
1260 Geoffrey St Leger
1287 Roger of Wexford
1289 Michael d'Exeter
1303 William FitzJohn
1317 Richard Ledred
1361 John de Tatenhale
1366 William
— John of Oxford
1371 Alexander Petit [de Balscot]
1387 Richard Northalis
1396 Thomas Peverell
1399 John Waltham
1400 John Griffin
1400 John
1401 Roger Appleby
1402 John Waltham
1407 Thomas Snell
1417 Patrick Foxe
1421 Dionysius O Deadhaidh
1427 Thomas Barry
1460 David Hacket
1479 Seaan O hEidigheain
1487 Oliver Cantwell
1528 Milo Baron [or FitzGerald]
1553 John Bale
1554 John Tonory
1567 Christopher Gaffney
1577 Nicholas Walsh
1586 John Horsfall
1610 Richard Deane
1613 Jonas Wheeler
1641 Griffith Williams
1672 John Parry
1678 Benjamin Parry
1678 Michael Ward
1680 Thomas Otway
1693 John Hartstonge
1714 Thomas Vesey
1731 Edward Tennison
1736 Charles Este
1741 Anthony Dopping
1743 Michael Cox
1754 Edward Maurice
1755 Richard Pococke
1765 Charles Dodgson
1775 William Newcome

1779 John Hotham
1782 William Heresford
1795 Thomas Lewis O'Beirne
1799 Hugh Hamilton
1806 John Kearney
1813 Robert Fowler
Ferns united to Ossory 1835
1842 James Thomas O'Brien
1874 Robert Samuel Gregg
1878 William Pakenham Walsh
1897 John Baptist Crozier
1907 Charles Frederick D'Arcy
1911 John Henry Bernard
1915 John Allen Fitzgerald Gregg
1920 John Godfrey FitzMaurice
      Day
1938 Ford Tichbourne
1940 John Percy Phair
1962 Henry Robert McAdoo
United to Cashel 1977

†Ross

Nechtan MacNechtain 1160
Isaac O'Cowen 1161
O'Carroll 1168
1177 Benedictus
1192 Mauricius
1198 Daniel
1224 Fineen O Clothna [Florentius]
c.1250 Malachy
1254 Mauricius
1269 Walter O Mithigein
1275 Peter O h-Uallachain
      [? Patrick]
1291 Laurentius
1310 Matthaeus O Finn
1331 Laurentius O h-Uallachain
1336 Dionysius
1379 Bernard O Conchobhair
1399 Peter Curragh
1400 Thadeus O Ceallaigh
1401 Mac Raith O hEidirsgeoil
      [Macrobius]
1402 Stephen Brown
1403 Matthew
1418 Walter Formay

1424 John Bloxworth
1426 Conchobhar Mac
      Fhaolchadha [Cornelius]
      Maurice Brown 1431
1431 Walter of Leicester
1434 Richard Clerk
1448 Domhnall O Donnobhain
      John 1460
1460 Robert Colynson
−1464 Thomas
1464 John Hornse alias Skipton
1473 Aodh O hEidirsgeoil [Odo]
1482 Tadhg Mac Carthaigh
1494 John Edmund Courci
1517 Seaan O Muirthile
1519 Tadgh O Raghallaigh
      [Thaddeus]
1523 Bonaventura
1526 Diarmaid Mac Carthaigh
1544 Dermot McDonnell
1551 John
1554 Maurice O'Fihelly
1559 Maurice O'Hea
1561 Thomas O'Herlihy
1582 William Lyon [with Cork and
      Cloyne after 1581]
United to Cork 1583

†Waterford

1096 Mael lus Ua h-Ainmere
1152 Toistius
1175 Augustinus Ua Selbaig
      Anonymous 1199
1200 Robert I
1204 David the Welshman
1210 Robert II [Breathnach]
1223 William Wace
1227 Walter
1232 Stephen
1250 Henry
1252 Philip
1255 Walter de Southwell
1274 Stephen de Fulbourn
1286 Walter de Fulbourn
1308 Matthew
1323 Nicholas Welifed

1338 Richard Francis
1349 Robert Elyot
1350 Roger Cradock
Lismore united to Waterford
      1363
1363 Thomas le Reve
1394 Robert Read
1396 Thomas Sparklord
1397 John Deping
1400 Thomas Snell
1407 Roger of Appleby (see under
      Ossory)
1409 John Geese
1414 Thomas Colby
1421 John Geese
1426 Richard Cantwell
1446 Robert Poer
1473 Richard Martin
1475 John Bulcomb
1480 Nicol O hAonghusa
1483 Thomas Purcell
1519 Nicholas Comyn
1551 Patrick Walsh
1579 Marmaduke Middleton
1582 Miler Magrath (Bishop
      of Cashel and
      Waterford)
1589 Thomas Wetherhead [or
      Walley]
1592 Miler Magrath
1608 John Lancaster
1619 Michael Boyle
1636 John Atherton
1641 Archibald Adair
1661 George Baker
1666 Hugh Gore
1691 Nathaniel Foy
1708 Thomas Mills
1740 Charles Este
1746 Richard Chenevix
1779 William Newcome
1795 Richard Marlay
1802 Power le Poer Trench
1810 Joseph Stock
1813 Richard Bourke
United to Cashel under Church
      Temporalities Act 1833

CATHEDRALS

CHURCH OF ENGLAND

(BATH AND) WELLS (St Andrew) Dean J M CLARKE,
Can Res P H F WOODHOUSE, A FEATHERSTONE,
THE VEN N A SULLIVAN, G M DODDS,
Sub-Dean D R OSBORNE,

BIRMINGHAM (St Philip) Dean C OGLE,
Can Res P HOWELL-JONES, N A HAND, J E CHAPMAN,
Y L RICHMOND

BLACKBURN (St Mary) Dean C J ARMSTRONG,
Can Res A D HINDLEY, S I PENFOLD, I G STOCKTON

BRADFORD (St Peter) Dean D J ISON,
Can Res A J WILLIAMS, S J C CORLEY,
Can Th K N MEDHURST

BRISTOL (Holy Trinity) Dean D M HOYLE,
Can Res T J HIGGINS, W A WILBY, R D BULL

CANTERBURY (Christ) Dean R A WILLIS,
Can Res E F CONDRY, D C EDWARDS, C P IRVINE,
Prec D G MACKENZIE MILLS

CARLISLE (Holy Trinity) Dean M C BOYLING,
Can Res B R McCONNELL, M A MANLEY,
THE VEN K I ROBERTS

CHELMSFORD (St Mary, St Peter and St Cedd)
Dean P S M JUDD, Can Res A W A KNOWLES, S J POTHEN,
I R MOODY

CHESTER (Christ and Blessed Virgin Mary) Dean
G F McPHATE, Vice-Dean C W HUMPHRIES,
Can Res R J BROOKE, Can Th L C A ALEXANDER,
P Pastor C BULL

CHICHESTER (Holy Trinity) Dean N A FRAYLING,
Can Res N T SCHOFIELD, A W N S CANE, I GIBSON,
PV D NASON

COVENTRY (St Michael) Dean J D IRVINE,
Sub-Dean T J PULLEN, Can Res D A STONE,
C R A WELCH, G J BARTLEM

DERBY (All Saints) Dean J H DAVIES, Can Res E J JONES,
D PERKINS, Can Th A BROWN, Chapl R M C LEIGH

DURHAM (Christ and Blessed Virgin Mary)
Dean M SADGROVE, Can Res D J KENNEDY, R BROWN,
S A CHERRY, THE VEN I JAGGER, Min Can D J SUDRON

ELY (Holy Trinity) Dean M J CHANDLER,
Can Res A L HARGRAVE, C P PRITCHARD, J R GARRARD,
Min Can T P HUMPHRY

EXETER (St Peter) Dean vacant, Can Res C F TURNER,
A P GODSALL, I C MORTIMER, A E NORMAN-WALKER

GLOUCESTER (St Peter and Holy Trinity) Dean S D LAKE,
Can Res N C HEAVISIDES, C S M THOMSON,
THE VEN N H SIDAWAY, N M ARTHY, J J WITCOMBE

GUILDFORD (Holy Spirit) Dean V A STOCK,
Sub-Dean N J THISTLETHWAITE,
Can Res A M TOWNSHEND, S A BEAKE

HEREFORD (Blessed Virgin Mary and St Ethelbert)
Dean M E TAVINOR, Can Res A PIPER, C PULLIN,
Min Can P A ROW

LEICESTER (St Martin) Dean V F FAULL,
Can Res J B NAYLOR, P C HACKWOOD, D R M MONTEITH,
J ARENS

LICHFIELD (Blessed Virgin Mary and St Chad)
Dean A J DORBER, Can Res C F LILEY, P J WILCOX,
W W BELL, Dean's V P LOCKETT, Chan's V P L HOLLIDAY,
Prec's V J M McHALE

LINCOLN (Blessed Virgin Mary) Dean P J W BUCKLER,
Can Res A H NUGENT, G J KIRK, M D HOCKNULL

LIVERPOOL (Christ) Dean J P WELBY,
Can Res M C DAVIES, C DOWDLE, E J P GOMES,
Can for Miss and Evang R S WHITE, C T D WATSON

LONDON (St Paul) Dean G P KNOWLES,
Can Res THE RT REVD M J COLCLOUGH, G A FRASER,
M D OAKLEY, M H J HAMPEL, Min Can J RENDELL,
A C R HAMMOND, S F L EYNSTONE

MANCHESTER (St Mary, St Denys and St George)
Dean R M GOVENDER, Can Res R A G SHANKS, G M MYERS,
A W HARDY, C R E JONES

NEWCASTLE (St Nicholas) Dean C C DALLISTON,
Can Res P R STRANGE, THE VEN G V MILLER, S J BAMBER

NORWICH (Holy Trinity) Dean G C M SMITH,
Can Res J M HASELOCK, R CAPPER, P M DOLL

OXFORD (Christ Church) Dean C A LEWIS,
Can Res J S K WARD, G L PATTISON, THE VEN J R H HUBBARD,
N J BIGGAR, J J NEWELL

PETERBOROUGH (St Peter, St Paul and St Andrew)
Dean C W TAYLOR, Can Res J W BAKER, R B RUDDOCK,
D S PAINTER

PORTSMOUTH (St Thomas of Canterbury)
Dean D C BRINDLEY, Can Res D T ISAAC,
M A TRISTRAM, N R RALPH, N L BIDDLE

RIPON (AND LEEDS) (St Peter and St Wilfrid)
Dean K M JUKES, Can Res K PUNSHON, P GREENWELL,
C P J CLEMENT, N A BUXTON

ROCHESTER (Christ and Blessed Virgin Mary)
Dean vacant, Can Res P J HESKETH, N H THOMPSON,
THE VEN S D BURTON-JONES, C R L RYAN

ST ALBANS (St Alban) Dean J P H JOHN,
Sub-Dean R F WATSON, Can Res D L STAMPS, K A WALTON,
J KIDDLE, Min Can A R MATTHEWS, A S JANES

ST EDMUNDSBURY (St James) Dean F E F WARD,
Can Res C J BURDON, M J VERNON, M R EASTWOOD

SALISBURY (Blessed Virgin Mary) Dean J OSBORNE,
Can Res D J C DAVIES, E C PROBERT, M P J BONNEY,
I WOODWARD

SHEFFIELD (St Peter and St Paul) Dean P E BRADLEY,
Can Res J W GRENFELL, S C COWLING, C M BURKE

SODOR AND MAN (St German) Dean THE BISHOP,
Vic-Dean N P GODFREY, C J McGOWAN

SOUTHWARK (St Saviour and St Mary Overie)
Dean vacant, Can Res B A SAUNDERS, A P NUNN, J E STEEN,
L K ROBERTS, Succ A J M MACHAM

SOUTHWELL (Blessed Virgin Mary) Dean J A GUILLE,
Can Res J D JONES, N J COATES, E B PRUEN

TRURO (St Mary) Dean C G HARDWICK,
Can Res P R GAY, P A A WALKER, R C BUSH, P C LAMBERT

WAKEFIELD (All Saints) Dean J D F GREENER,
Can Res A W ROBINSON, J A LAWSON, M G RAWSON,
A S MACPHERSON, A M HOFBAUER

**WINCHESTER (Holy Trinity, St Peter, St Paul and
St Swithun)** Dean J E ATWELL, Can Res R G A RIEM,
M A M ST JOHN-CHANNELL, S C PITTIS

WORCESTER (Christ and Blessed Virgin Mary)
Dean P G ATKINSON, Can Res A L PETTERSEN,
D J STANTON, THE VEN R A B MORRIS, G A BYRNE,
Min Can M R DORSETT, C M MANSHIP

YORK (St Peter) Dean K B JONES, Can Res G H WEBSTER,
J L DRAPER, P J MOGER, THE VEN R M C SEED

Collegiate Churches

WESTMINSTER ABBEY
ST GEORGE'S CHAPEL, WINDSOR
See Royal Peculiars, p. 1003.

Diocese in Europe

GIBRALTAR (Holy Trinity) Dean J A B PADDOCK
MALTA Valletta (St Paul) Pro-Cathedral S H GODFREY
BRUSSELS (Holy Trinity) Pro-Cathedral Chan R N INNES

CHURCH IN WALES

BANGOR (St Deiniol) Dean S H JONES
LLANDAFF (St Peter and St Paul) Dean J T LEWIS,
  PV J A L BAKER
MONMOUTH Newport (St Woolos) Dean *vacant*,
  Min Can R W HAYTER

ST ASAPH (St Asaph) Dean C N L POTTER,
  Can Res M K R STALLARD, M R BALKWILL,
  Chapl V C ROWLANDS, V R HANCOCK
ST DAVIDS (St David and St Andrew) Dean D J R LEAN,
  Min Can J S BENNETT, R J PATTINSON
(SWANSEA AND) BRECON (St John the Evangelist)
  Dean G O MARSHALL, Min Can D M JONES

SCOTTISH EPISCOPAL CHURCH

For the members of the chapter the *Scottish Episcopal Church Directory* should be consulted.

Aberdeen and Orkney
ABERDEEN (St Andrew) Provost R E KILGOUR,
  C M PATERSON

Argyll and The Isles
OBAN (St John) Provost N D MACCALLUM
CUMBRAE (Holy Spirit) Cathedral of The Isles
Provost A M SHAW *Bishop of Argyll and The Isles*

Brechin
DUNDEE (St Paul) Provost J R AULD

Edinburgh
EDINBURGH (St Mary) Provost G J T FORBES,
  Vice Provost M J HARRIS

Glasgow and Galloway
GLASGOW (St Mary) Provost K HOLDSWORTH,
  Vice Provost C L BLAKEY

Moray, Ross and Caithness
INVERNESS (St Andrew) Provost A R GORDON

St Andrews, Dunkeld and Dunblane
PERTH (St Ninian) Provost H B FARQUHARSON

CHURCH OF IRELAND

Most cathedrals are parish churches, and the dean is usually, but not always, the incumbent. For the members of the chapter the *Church of Ireland Directory* should be consulted. The name of the dean is given, together with those of other clergy holding full-time appointments.

NATIONAL CATHEDRAL OF ST PATRICK, Dublin Dean R B MacCARTHY, **Dean's V** C W MULLEN

CATHEDRAL OF ST ANNE, Belfast Dean J O MANN
(St Anne's is a cathedral of the dioceses of Down and Dromore and of Connor)

Province of Armagh

Armagh
ARMAGH (St Patrick) *vacant*

Clogher
CLOGHER (St Macartan) K R J HALL
ENNISKILLEN (St Macartin) *vacant*

Derry and Raphoe
DERRY (St Columb) W W MORTON
RAPHOE (St Eunan) J HAY

Down and Dromore
DOWN (Holy and Undivided Trinity) T H HULL
DROMORE (Christ the Redeemer) S H LOWRY

Connor
LISBURN (Christ) J F A BOND *Dean of Connor*
  I W S WRIGHT

Kilmore, Elphin and Ardagh
KILMORE (St Fethlimidh) W R FERGUSON
SLIGO (St Mary and St John the Baptist) A WILLIAMS

Tuam, Killala and Achonry
TUAM (St Mary) A J GRIMASON
KILLALA (St Patrick) *vacant*

Province of Dublin

Dublin and Glendalough
DUBLIN (Holy Trinity) Christ Church D P M DUNN

Meath and Kildare
TRIM (St Patrick) R W JONES *Dean of Clonmacnoise*
KILDARE (St Brigid) J J MARSDEN

Cashel and Ossory
CASHEL (St John the Baptist) P J KNOWLES
WATERFORD (Blessed Trinity) Christ Church *vacant*
LISMORE (St Carthage) P R DRAPER
KILKENNY (St Canice) K M POULTON *Dean of Ossory*
LEIGHLIN (St Laserian) T W GORDON
FERNS (St Edan) P G MOONEY

Cork, Cloyne and Ross
CORK (St Fin Barre) N K DUNNE
CLOYNE (St Colman) A G MARLEY
ROSS (St Fachtna) C L PETERS

Limerick and Killaloe
LIMERICK (St Mary) *vacant*
KILLALOE (St Flannan) S R WHITE

ROYAL PECULIARS, CLERGY OF THE QUEEN'S HOUSEHOLD, ETC.

Royal Peculiars

Description of arms. Azure the reputed arms of Edward the Confessor, viz. a cross patonce between five martlets or, on a chief of the same, between two double roses of Lancaster and York, barbed and seeded proper, a pale charged with the Royal arms (viz. Quarterly of France and England).

Collegiate Church of St Peter Westminster (Westminster Abbey) **Dean** J R HALL,
Cans R P REISS, J B HEDGES, A TREMLETT, V P WHITE,
Min Cans G G P C NAPIER, M D MACEY,
PVs P A BAGOTT, A R BODDY, P F BRADSHAW,
L J BURGESS, P A E CHESTER, A C COLES, J W CROSSLEY,
B D FENTON, R C GODSALL, J M GOODALL, A G GYLE,
S E HARTLEY, R J HUDSON-WILKIN, E J LEWIS, P MCGEARY,
D A PETERS, G D SWINTON, G J WILLIAMS

Description of arms. The arms of the Order of the Garter, viz. Argent, a St George's Cross gules. The shield is encircled by the blue Garter with its motto.

Queen's Free Chapel of St George Windsor Castle (St George's Chapel) **Dean** THE RT REVD
D J CONNER, **Cans** J A WHITE, J A OVENDEN,
H E FINLAY, J W WOODWARD, **Min Cans** M J BOAG,
A S ZIHNI

The Queen's Household

Royal Almonry

High Almoner THE RT REVD N S MCCULLOCH (Bishop of Manchester)
Sub-Almoner W S SCOTT

The College of Chaplains

Clerk of the Closet THE RT REVD C J HILL (Bishop of Guildford)
Deputy Clerk of the Closet W S SCOTT

Chaplains to The Queen

C P ANDREWS	K B GARLICK	J A OVENDEN
G R P ASHENDEN	R A J HILL	S C PALMER
P D L AVIS	R J HUDSON-WILKIN	J B V RIVIERE
H W BEARN	G I KOVOOR	R B RUDDOCK
J V BYRNE	J LEE	C W J SAMUELS
G M CALVER	E J LEWIS	A M SHEPHERD
P N CALVERT	W A MATTHEWS	C M SMITH
A CLITHEROW	P MILLER	P H J THORNEYCROFT
R T COOPER	G MOFFAT	A D C WINGATE
A R EASTER	J W R MOWLL	A R WOODHOUSE
C M FARRINGTON	W A NOBLETT	R E WORSLEY

Extra Chaplains to The Queen

A D CAESAR	J G M W MURPHY	E A JAMES
J P ROBSON		

Chapels Royal

Dean of the Chapels Royal THE BISHOP OF LONDON
Sub-Dean of the Chapels Royal W S SCOTT
Priests in Ordinary R D E BOLTON, P R THOMAS, S E YOUNG
Deputy Priests in Ordinary R J HALL, D R MULLINER,
M D OAKLEY
Domestic Chaplain, Buckingham Palace W S SCOTT
Domestic Chaplain, Windsor Castle THE DEAN OF WINDSOR
Domestic Chaplain, Sandringham J B V RIVIERE
Chaplain, Royal Chapel, Windsor Great Park
J A OVENDEN
Chaplain, Hampton Court Palace D R MULLINER
Chaplain, HM Tower of London R J HALL

The Queen's Chapel of the Savoy

Chaplain P J GALLOWAY

Royal Memorial Chapel, Sandhurst

Chaplain J R B GOUGH

Royal Foundation of St Katharine in Ratcliffe

Master J D M PATON

DIOCESAN OFFICES

CHURCH OF ENGLAND

BATH AND WELLS
Diocesan Office, The Old Deanery, Wells BA5 2UG
Tel (01749) 670777 Fax 674240 E-mail general@bathwells.anglican.org
Web www.bathwells.anglican.org

BIRMINGHAM
Diocesan Office, 175 Harborne Park Road, Birmingham B17 0BH
Tel 0121–426 0400 Fax 428 1114 E-mail reception@birmingham.anglican.org
Web www.birmingham.anglican.org

BLACKBURN
Church House, Cathedral Close, Blackburn BB1 5AA
Tel (01254) 503070 Fax 667309 E-mail diocese@blackburn.anglican.org
Web www.blackburn.anglican.org

BRADFORD
Kadugli House, Elmsley Street, Steeton, Keighley BD20 6SE
Tel (01535) 650555 Fax 650550 E-mail office@kadugli.org.uk
Web www.bradford.anglican.org

BRISTOL
Diocesan Church House, 23 Great George Street, Bristol BS1 5QZ
Tel 0117–906 0100 Fax 925 0460
Web www.bristol.anglican.org

CANTERBURY
Diocesan House, Lady Wootton's Green, Canterbury CT1 1NQ
Tel (01227) 459401 Fax 450964 E-mail reception@diocant.org
Web www.canterbury.anglican.org

CARLISLE
Church House, West Walls, Carlisle CA3 8UE
Tel (01228) 522573 Fax 815400 E-mail enquiries@carlislediocese.org.uk
Web www.carlisle.anglican.org.uk

CHELMSFORD
Diocesan Office, 53 New Street, Chelmsford CM1 1AT
Tel (01245) 294400 Fax 294477 E-mail mail@chelmsford.anglican.org
Web www.chelmsford.anglican.org

CHESTER
Church House, Lower Lane, Aldford, Chester CH3 6HP
Tel (01244) 681973 Fax 620456 E-mail churchhouse@chester.anglican.org
Web www.chester.anglican.org

CHICHESTER
Diocesan Church House, 211 New Church Road, Hove BN3 4ED
Tel (01273) 421021 Fax 421041 E-mail admin@diochi.org.uk
Web www.diochi.org.uk

COVENTRY
1 Hill Top, Coventry CV1 5AB
Tel (024) 7652 1200 Fax 7652 1330 E-mail simon.lloyd@covcofe.org
Web www.coventry.anglican.org

DERBY
Derby Church House, Full Street, Derby DE1 3DR
Tel (01332) 388650 Fax 292969 E-mail finance@derby.anglican.org
Web www.derby.anglican.org

DURHAM
Diocesan Office, Auckland Castle, Market Place, Bishop Auckland DL14 7QJ
Tel (01388) 604515 Fax 603695 E-mail diocesan.office@durham.anglican.org
Web www.durham.anglican.org

ELY
Diocesan Office, Bishop Woodford House, Barton Road, Ely CB7 4DX
Tel (01353) 652701 Fax 652745 E-mail office@ely.anglican.org
Web www.ely.anglican.org

EUROPE
Diocesan Office, 14 Tufton Street, London SW1P 3QZ
Tel (020) 7898 1155 Fax 7898 1166 E-mail diocesan.office@churchofengland.org
Web www.europe.anglican.org

EXETER
The Old Deanery, The Cloisters, Cathedral Close, Exeter EX1 1HS
Tel (01392) 272686 Fax 499594 E-mail admin@exeter.anglican.org
Web www.exeter.anglican.org

GLOUCESTER
Church House, College Green, Gloucester GL1 2LY
Tel (01452) 410022 Fax 308324 E-mail church.house@glosdioc.org.uk
Web www.glosdioc.org.uk

GUILDFORD	Diocesan House, Quarry Street, Guildford GU1 3XG Tel (01483) 571826 Fax 790333 Web www.guildford.anglican.org
HEREFORD	Diocesan Office, The Palace, Hereford HR4 9BL Tel (01432) 373300 Fax 352952 E-mail diooffice@hereford.anglican.org Web www.hereford.anglican.org
LEICESTER	St Martin's House, 7 Peacock Lane Leicester LE1 5PZ Tel 0116–261 5200 Fax 261 5220 E-mail jonathan.kerry@leccofe.org Web www.leicester.anglican.org
LICHFIELD	St Mary's House, The Close, Lichfield WS13 7LD Tel (01543) 306030 Fax 306039 E-mail info@lichfield.anglican.org Web www.lichfield.anglican.org
LINCOLN	Diocesan Office, The Old Palace, Lincoln LN2 1PU Tel (01522) 504050 E-mail administrator@lincoln.anglican.org Web www.lincoln.anglican.org
LIVERPOOL	St James's House, 20 St James Road, Liverpool L1 7BY Tel 0151–709 9722 Fax 709 2885 Web www.liverpool.anglican.org
LONDON	Diocesan House, 36 Causton Street, London SW1P 4AU Tel (020) 7932 1100 Fax 7932 1112 E-mail keith.robinson@london.anglican.org Web www.london.anglican.org
MANCHESTER	Diocesan Church House, 90 Deansgate, Manchester M3 2GH Tel 0161–828 1400 Fax 828 1480 E-mail manchesterdbf@manchester.anglican.org Web www.manchester.anglican.org
NEWCASTLE	Church House, St John's Terrace, North Shields NE29 6HS Tel 0191–270 4100 Fax 270 4101 E-mail info@newcastle.anglican.org Web www.newcastle.anglican.org
NORWICH	Diocesan House, 109 Dereham Road, Easton, Norwich NR9 5ES Tel (01603) 880853 Fax 881083 E-mail janet.guy@norwich.anglican.org Web www.norwich.anglican.org
OXFORD	Diocesan Church House, North Hinksey Lane, Botley, Oxford OX2 0NB Tel (01865) 208200 Fax 790470 E-mail diosec@oxford.anglican.org Web www.oxford.anglican.org
PETERBOROUGH	The Palace, Peterborough PE1 1YB Tel (01733) 887000 Fax 555271 E-mail office@peterborough-diocese.org.uk Web www.peterborough-diocese.org.uk
PORTSMOUTH	First Floor, Peninsular House, Wharf Road, Portsmouth PO2 8HB Tel (023) 9289 9650 Fax 9289 9651 Web www.portsmouth.anglican.org
RIPON AND LEEDS	Ripon and Leeds Diocesan Office, St Mary's Street, Leeds LS9 7DP Tel 0113–200 0540 Fax 249 1129 E-mail reception@riponleeds-diocese.org.uk Web www.ripon.anglican.org
ROCHESTER	St Nicholas Church, Boley Hill, Rochester ME1 1SL Tel (01634) 560000 Fax 408942 E-mail enquiries@rochester.anglican.org Web www.rochester.anglican.org
ST ALBANS	Holywell Lodge, 41 Holywell Hill, St Albans AL1 1HE Tel (01727) 854532 Fax 844469 E-mail mail@stalbans.anglican.org Web www.stalbans.anglican.org
ST EDMUNDSBURY AND IPSWICH	St Nicholas Centre, 4 Cutler Street, Ipswich IP1 1UQ Tel (01473) 298500 Fax 298501 E-mail dbf@stedmundsbury.anglican.org Web www.stedmundsbury.anglican.org
SALISBURY	Church House, Crane Street, Salisbury SP1 2QB Tel (01722) 411922 Fax 411990 E-mail enquiries@salisbury.anglican.org Web www.salisbury.anglican.org
SHEFFIELD	Diocesan Church House, 95/99 Effingham Street, Rotherham S65 1BL Tel (01709) 309100 Fax 512550 E-mail reception@sheffield.anglican.org Web www.sheffield.anglican.org

SODOR AND MAN   Thie yn Aspick, 4 The Falls, Tromode Road, Douglas, Isle of Man
IM4 4PZ
Tel (01624) 622108 E-mail secretary@sodorandman.im
Web www.sodorandman.im

SOUTHWARK   Trinity House, 4 Chapel Court, Borough High Street, London SE1 1HW
Tel (020) 7939 9400 Fax 7939 9468 E-mail trinity@southwark.anglican.org
Web www.southwark.anglican.org

SOUTHWELL AND   Dunham House, 8 Westgate, Southwell NG25 0JL
NOTTINGHAM   Tel (01636) 814331 Fax 815084 E-mail mail@southwell.anglican.org
Web www.southwell.anglican.org

TRURO   Diocesan House, Kenwyn, Truro TR1 1JQ
Tel (01872) 274351 Fax 222510 E-mail info@truro.anglican.org
Web www.truro.anglican.org

WAKEFIELD   Church House, 1 South Parade, Wakefield WF1 1LP
Tel (01924) 371802 Fax 364834 E-mail reception@wakefield.anglican.org

WINCHESTER   The Diocesan Office, Old Alresford Place, Old Alresford, Alresford SO24 9DH
Tel (01962) 737300 Fax 7373585 E-mail reception@winchester.anglican.org
Web www.winchester.anglican.org

WORCESTER   The Old Palace, Deansway, Worcester WR1 2JE
Tel (01905) 20537 Fax 612302 E-mail generalinfo@cofe-worcester.org.uk
Web www.cofe-worcester.org.uk

YORK   Diocesan House, Aviator Court, Clifton Moor, York YO30 4WJ
Tel (01904) 699500 Fax 699501 E-mail office@yorkdiocese.org
Web www.dioceseofyork.org.uk

CHURCH IN WALES

BANGOR   Diocesan Office, Cathedral Close, Bangor LL57 1RL
Tel (01248) 354999 Fax 353882 Web www. churchinwales.org.uk/bangor

LLANDAFF   Diocesan Office, The Court, Coychurch, Bridgend CF35 5EH
Tel (01656) 868868 Fax 868869 Web www.churchinwales.org.uk/llandaff

MONMOUTH   Diocesan Office, 64 Caerau Road, Newport NP20 4HJ
Tel (01633) 267490 Fax 265586 Web www.churchinwales.org.uk/monmouth

ST ASAPH   St Asaph Diocesan Board of Finance, High Street, St Asaph LL17 0RD
Tel (01745) 532591 Fax 530078 Web www. churchinwales.org.uk/asaph

ST DAVIDS   Diocesan Office, Abergwili, Carmarthen SA31 2JG
Tel (01267) 236145 Fax 223046 Web www.churchinwales.org.uk/david

SWANSEA AND   Swansea and Brecon Diocesan Centre, Cathedral Close, Brecon
BRECON   LD3 9DP
Tel (01874) 623716 Fax 623716 Web www.churchinwales.org.uk/swanbrec

SCOTTISH EPISCOPAL CHURCH

ABERDEEN AND   St Clement's Church House, Mastrick Drive, Aberdeen AB16 6UF
ORKNEY   Tel (01224) 662247 Fax 662168 E-mail office@aberdeen.anglican.org
Web www.aberdeen.anglican.org

ARGYLL AND THE   St Moluag's Diocesan Centre, Croft Avenue, Oban PA34 5JJ
ISLES   Tel (01631) 570870 Fax 570411 E-mail office@argyll.anglican.org
Web www.argyll.anglican.org

BRECHIN   Diocesan Office, Unit 14 Prospect III, Technology Park, Gemini Crescent, Dundee
DD2 1SW
Tel (01382) 562244 E-mail office@brechin.anglican.org
Web www.thedioceseofbrechin.org

EDINBURGH   Diocesan Centre, 21A Grosvenor Crescent, Edinburgh EH12 5EL
Tel 0131–538 7033 Fax 538 7088 E-mail office@edinburgh.anglican.org
Web www.edinburgh.anglican.org

GLASGOW AND   Diocesan Office, 5 St Vincent Place, Glasgow G1 2DH
GALLOWAY   Tel 0141–221 6911 Fax 221 7014 E-mail office@glasgow.anglican.org
Web www.glasgow.anglican.org

MORAY, ROSS
AND CAITHNESS

Fairview, 48 Saltburn, Invergordon IV18 0JY
Tel (01349) 854984 (mornings only) E-mail office@moray.anglican.org
Web www.moray.anglican.org

ST ANDREWS,
DUNKELD AND
DUNBLANE

Perth Diocesan Centre, 28A Balhousie Street, Perth PH1 5HJ
Tel (01738) 443173 Fax 443174 E-mail office@standrews.anglican.org
Web www.standrews.anglican.org

CHURCH OF IRELAND

PROVINCE OF ARMAGH

ARMAGH

Church House, 46 Abbey Street, Armagh BT61 7DZ
Tel (028) 3752 2858 Fax 3751 0596 E-mail office@armagh.anglican.org
Web armagh.anglican.org

CLOGHER

Diocesan Office, St Macartin's Cathedral Hall, Hall's Lane, Enniskillen BT74 7DR
Tel and fax (028) 6634 7879 E-mail secretary@clogher.anglican.org
Web clogher.anglican.org

CONNOR

Diocesan Office, Church of Ireland House, 61/67 Donegall Street, Belfast
BT1 2QH
Tel (028) 9082 8830 Fax 9032 1635 E-mail office@diocoff-belfast.org
Web www.connor.anglican.org

DERRY AND
RAPHOE

Diocesan Office, 24 London Street, Londonderry BT48 6RQ
Tel (028) 7126 2440 Fax 7137 2100 E-mail office@derry.anglican.org
Web www.derry.anglican.org

DOWN AND
DROMORE

Diocesan Office, Church of Ireland House, 61/67 Donegall Street, Belfast
BT1 2QH
Tel (028) 9032 2268 or 9032 3188 Fax 9032 1635 E-mail office@diocoff-belfast.org
Web www.down.anglican.org

KILMORE

Kilmore Diocesan Office, The Rectory, Cootehill, Co Cavan, Republic of Ireland
Tel (00353) (49) 555 9954 Fax 555 9957 E-mail office@kilmore.anglican.org
Web www.kilmore.anglican.org

ELPHIN AND
ARDAGH

The Market House, Blacklion, Co Cavan, Republic of Ireland
Tel (00353) (71) 985 3792 E-mail diosecea@eirom.net

TUAM, KILLALA
AND ACHONRY

Stonehall House, Ballisodare, Co Sligo, Republic of Ireland
Tel (00353) (71) 916 7280 Fax 913 0264 E-mail hsherlock@iolfree.ie
Web www.tuam.anglican.org

PROVINCE OF DUBLIN

CASHEL AND
OSSORY

Diocesan Office, St Canice's Library, Kilkenny, Republic of Ireland
Tel (00353) (56) 776 1910 or 772 27248 Fax 51813
E-mail office@cashel.anglican.org Web www.cashel.anglican.org

CORK, CLOYNE
AND ROSS

St Nicholas' House, 14 Cove Street, Cork, Republic of Ireland
Tel (00353) (21) 500 5080 Fax 432 0960
E-mail secretary@cork.anglican.org Web www.cork.anglican.org

DUBLIN AND
GLENDALOUGH

Diocesan Office, Church of Ireland House, Church Avenue,
Rathmines, Dublin 6, Republic of Ireland
Tel (00353) (1) 496 6981 Fax 497 2865
E-mail office@dublin.anglican.org Web www.dublin.anglican.org

LIMERICK,
KILLALOE AND
ARDFERT

St John's Rectory, Ashe Street, Tralee, Co Kerry, Republic of Ireland
Tel (00353) (66) 712 2245 Fax 712 9004
E-mail secretary@limerick.anglican.org Web www.limerick.anglican.org

MEATH AND
KILDARE

Meath and Kildare Diocesan Centre, Moyglare, Maynooth,
Co Kildare, Republic of Ireland
Tel (00353) (1) 629 2163 E-mail diomeath@iol.ie or office@meath.anglican.org
Web www.meath.anglican.org

ARCHDEACONRIES, DEANERIES AND RURAL/AREA DEANS OF THE CHURCH OF ENGLAND AND THE CHURCH IN WALES

The numbers given to the deaneries below correspond to those given in the benefice entries in the combined benefice and church index for England (p. 1016) and for Wales (p. 1194). Where an archdeaconry comes within the jurisdiction of a suffragan or area bishop under an established scheme, the respective bishop is indicated.

CHURCH OF ENGLAND

BATH AND WELLS

ARCHDEACONRY OF WELLS

1. AXBRIDGE   T D HAWKINGS
2. BRUTON AND CARY   R A HOSKINS
3. FROME   C ALSBURY
4. GLASTONBURY JURISDICTION   R J RAY
5. IVELCHESTER   P J THOMAS
6. YEOVIL   A PERRIS
7. SHEPTON MALLET   A Q H WHEELER

ARCHDEACONRY OF BATH

8. BATH   M C LLOYD WILLIAMS
9. CHEW MAGNA   J P KNOTT
10. LOCKING   R J TAYLOR
11. MIDSOMER NORTON   C S HARE
12. PORTISHEAD   N A HECTOR

ARCHDEACONRY OF TAUNTON

13. SEDGEMOOR *Vacant*
14. CREWKERNE AND ILMINSTER   A F TATHAM
15. EXMOOR   S STUCKES
16. QUANTOCK   S L CAMPBELL
17. TAUNTON   G J BOUCHER
18. TONE   C F E ROWLEY

BIRMINGHAM

ARCHDEACONRY OF BIRMINGHAM

1. BIRMINGHAM CITY CENTRE
   A G LENOX-CONYNGHAM
2. EDGBASTON   P A WHITE
3. HANDSWORTH   H HINGLEY
4. KINGS NORTON   C J CORKE
5. MOSELEY   P G BABINGTON
6. SHIRLEY   D J SENIOR
7. WARLEY   A H PERRY

ARCHDEACONRY OF ASTON

8. ASTON   A J JOLLEY
9. COLESHILL   B S CASTLE
10. POLESWORTH   M A HARRIS
11. SOLIHULL   M J PARKER
12. SUTTON COLDFIELD   M I RHODES
13. YARDLEY AND BORDESLEY   P H SMITH

BLACKBURN

ARCHDEACONRY OF BLACKBURN

1. ACCRINGTON   T R SMITH
2. BLACKBURN AND DARWEN   A RAYNES
3. BURNLEY   M A JONES
4. CHORLEY *Vacant*
5. LEYLAND *Vacant*
6. PENDLE   A W RINDL
7. WHALLEY   M WOODS

ARCHDEACONRY OF LANCASTER

8. BLACKPOOL   S J COX
9. GARSTANG   A W WILKINSON
10. KIRKHAM   P D LAW-JONES
11. LANCASTER AND MORECAMBE   M R PEATMAN
12. POULTON   M P KEIGHLEY
13. PRESTON   T W LIPSCOMB
14. TUNSTALL   P K WARREN

BRADFORD

ARCHDEACONRY OF BRADFORD

1. AIREDALE   G S HODGSON
2. BOWLING AND HORTON   P M BILTON
3. CALVERLEY   P Q TUDGE
4. OTLEY   C NORMAN

ARCHDEACONRY OF CRAVEN

5. BOWLAND   R G WOOD
6. EWECROSS   I F GREENHALGH
7. SKIPTON   P A TURNER
8. SOUTH CRAVEN   S A GRIFFITHS

BRISTOL

ARCHDEACONRY OF BRISTOL

1. BRISTOL SOUTH   D G OWEN
2. BRISTOL WEST   C M PILGRIM
3. CITY DEANERY   M D INESON

ARCHDEACONRY OF MALMESBURY

4. CHIPPENHAM   S J TYNDALL
5. KINGSWOOD AND SOUTH GLOUCESTERSHIRE
   S JONES
6. NORTH WILTSHIRE   N J ARCHER
7. SWINDON   S M STEVENETTE

CANTERBURY

ARCHDEACONRY OF CANTERBURY

1. EAST BRIDGE   S J A HARDY
2. WEST BRIDGE   S J A HARDY
3. CANTERBURY   M F BALL
4. RECULVER   R L HAWKES
5. THANET   P R WORLEDGE

ARCHDEACONRY OF ASHFORD

6. ASHFORD   T C WILSON
7. DOVER   S M WHITE
8. ELHAM *Vacant*
9. SANDWICH   S W COOPER

ARCHDEACONRY OF MAIDSTONE

10. WEALD   W J HORNSBY
11. ROMNEY *Vacant*
12. MAIDSTONE   A W SEWELL
13. NORTH DOWNS   P S HOLLINS
14. OSPRINGE   A C OEHRING
15. SITTINGBOURNE   J H G LEWIS
16. TENTERDEN   J T M DESROSIERS

CARLISLE

ARCHDEACONRY OF CARLISLE

1. APPLEBY *Vacant*
2. BRAMPTON   G M CREGEEN
3. CARLISLE   M A MANLEY
4. PENRITH   R A MOATT

ARCHDEACONRY OF WEST CUMBERLAND

5. CALDER   J WOOLCOCK
6. DERWENT   W E SANDERS
7. SOLWAY   M E DAY

ARCHDEACONRY OF WESTMORLAND AND FURNESS

8. BARROW   I K HOOK
9. FURNESS   A C BING
10. KENDAL   T J HARMER
11. WINDERMERE   J J RICHARDS

CHELMSFORD

ARCHDEACONRY OF WEST HAM

(BISHOP OF BARKING)

1. BARKING AND DAGENHAM   R K GAYLER
2. HAVERING   D C MARSHALL
3. NEWHAM   D P WADE
4. REDBRIDGE   P G HARCOURT
5. WALTHAM FOREST   S M P SAXBY

ARCHDEACONRY OF SOUTHEND

(BISHOP OF BRADWELL)

6. BASILDON   M A SHAW
7. BRENTWOOD   I H JORYSZ
8. CHELMSFORD NORTH   C I HAMPTON
9. CHELMSFORD SOUTH   A T GRIFFITHS
10. HADLEIGH   D ST C TUDOR
11. MALDON AND DENGIE   S E MANLEY
12. ROCHFORD   M J LODGE
13. SOUTHEND-ON-SEA   S M BURDETT
14. THURROCK   D BARLOW

ARCHDEACONRY OF COLCHESTER

(BISHOP OF COLCHESTER)

15. BRAINTREE   P A NEED
16. COLCHESTER   I A HILTON
17. DEDHAM AND TEY   P C BANKS
18. DUNMOW AND STANSTED   C M HAWKES
19. HINCKFORD   L BOND
20. HARWICH   P E MANN
21. SAFFRON WALDEN   D R TOMLINSON
22. ST OSYTH   G D A THORBURN
23. WITHAM   G B T BAYLISS

ARCHDEACONRY OF HARLOW

(BISHOP OF BARKING)

24. EPPING FOREST   J M SMITH
25. HARLOW   M J HARRIS
26. ONGAR   A SMITH

CHESTER

ARCHDEACONRY OF CHESTER

1. BIRKENHEAD   P M FROGGATT
2. CHESTER   M HART
3. FRODSHAM   S S WILKINS
4. GREAT BUDWORTH   A G BROWN
5. MALPAS   K E HINE
6. MIDDLEWICH   L P EDEN
7. WALLASEY   G J COUSINS
8. WIRRAL NORTH   G A ROSSITER
9. WIRRAL SOUTH   D S FISHER

ARCHDEACONRY OF MACCLESFIELD

10. BOWDON   J SUTTON
11. CONGLETON   D TAYLOR
12. KNUTSFORD   R A YATES
13. MACCLESFIELD   E W L DAVIES
14. MOTTRAM   R J LAMEY
15. NANTWICH   W J BAKER
16. CHADKIRK   P J JENNER
17. CHEADLE   R I MCLAREN
18. STOCKPORT   A J BELL

CHICHESTER

ARCHDEACONRY OF CHICHESTER

1. ARUNDEL AND BOGNOR   M J STANDEN
2. BRIGHTON   A H MANSON-BRAILSFORD
3. CHICHESTER   R W HUNT
4. HOVE   K D RICHARDS
5. WORTHING *Vacant*

ARCHDEACONRY OF HORSHAM

6. CUCKFIELD   C R BREEDS
7. EAST GRINSTEAD   J K PEATY
8. HORSHAM   G S BRIDGEWATER
9. HURST   K M O'BRIEN
10. MIDHURST   D B WELSMAN
11. PETWORTH   D A TWINLEY
12. STORRINGTON   P B WELCH
13. WESTBOURNE   C R JENKINS

ARCHDEACONRY OF LEWES AND HASTINGS

14. BATTLE AND BEXHILL   E F P BRYANT
15. DALLINGTON   S J E TOMALIN
16. EASTBOURNE   J T GUNN
17. HASTINGS   C H KEY
18. LEWES AND SEAFORD   G M DAW
19. ROTHERFIELD   J R JAMES
20. RYE *Vacant*
21. UCKFIELD   D M HALL

COVENTRY

ARCHDEACONRY OF COVENTRY

1. COVENTRY EAST   M TYLER
2. COVENTRY NORTH   R N TREW
3. COVENTRY SOUTH   S R BURCH
4. KENILWORTH   S R BURCH
5. NUNEATON   P B ALLAN
6. RUGBY   M P SAXBY

ARCHDEACONRY OF WARWICK

7. ALCESTER *Vacant*
8. FOSSE   C E MIER
9. SHIPSTON   J TUCKER
10. SOUTHAM   J E ARMSTRONG
11. WARWICK AND LEAMINGTON   P MANUEL

DERBY

ARCHDEACONRY OF CHESTERFIELD

1. ALFRETON   P D BROOKS
2. BAKEWELL AND EYAM   A S MONTGOMERIE
3. BOLSOVER AND STAVELEY   H GUEST
4. BUXTON   J O GOLDSMITH
5. CHESTERFIELD   N V JOHNSON
6. GLOSSOP   J C BAINES
7. WIRKSWORTH   D C TRUBY

ARCHDEACONRY OF DERBY

8. ASHBOURNE   C A MITCHELL
9. DERBY NORTH   J F HOLLYWELL
10. DERBY SOUTH   J A SEARLE
11. DUFFIELD   J M PAGE
12. HEANOR   T J WILLIAMS
13. EREWASH   I E GOODING
14. LONGFORD   A G MURPHIE
15. MELBOURNE   A LUKE
16. REPTON   L A DE POMERAI

DURHAM

ARCHDEACONRY OF DURHAM

1. DURHAM   R W LAWRANCE
2. EASINGTON   A MILNE
3. HARTLEPOOL   C J COLLISON
4. LANCHESTER   R G BIRCHALL
5. SEDGEFIELD   K LUMSDON

ARCHDEACONRY OF AUCKLAND

6. AUCKLAND   N P VINE
7. BARNARD CASTLE   A J HARDING
8. DARLINGTON   J R DOBSON
9. STANHOPE   V T FENTON
10. STOCKTON   D M BROOKE

ARCHDEACONRY OF SUNDERLAND

11. CHESTER-LE-STREET   D C GLOVER
12. GATESHEAD *Vacant*
13. GATESHEAD WEST *Vacant*
14. HOUGHTON LE SPRING *Vacant*
15. JARROW   W E BRAVINER
16. WEARMOUTH   R G E BRADSHAW

ELY

ARCHDEACONRY OF CAMBRIDGE

1. BOURN   M R MATTHEWS
2. CAMBRIDGE NORTH   N I MOIR
3. CAMBRIDGE SOUTH   D H JONES
4. FORDHAM AND QUY   T M ALBAN JONES
5. GRANTA *Vacant*
6. NORTH STOWE   N J BLANDFORD-BAKER
7. SHINGAY   S F C WILLIAMS

ARCHDEACONRY OF HUNTINGDON AND WISBECH

8. ELY   P TAYLOR
9. FINCHAM AND FELTWELL   D J EVANS
10. HUNTINGDON   E B ATLING
11. MARCH   N A WHITEHOUSE
12. ST IVES   F J KILNER
13. ST NEOTS   A S REED
14. WISBECH LYNN MARSHLAND   E J PENNY
15. YAXLEY   P M GRIFFITH

EXETER

ARCHDEACONRY OF EXETER

1. AYLESBEARE   D R PRICE
2. CADBURY   S G C SMITH
3. CHRISTIANITY *Vacant*
4. CULLOMPTON *Vacant*
5. HONITON   S E ROBERTS
6. KENN   G K MAYER
7. OTTERY   D H JAMES
8. TIVERTON *Vacant*

ARCHDEACONRY OF TOTNES

9. MORETON   P WIMSETT
10. NEWTON ABBOT AND IPPLEPEN   I C EGLIN
11. OKEHAMPTON   S W COOK
12. TORBAY   G H MAUDE
13. TOTNES *Vacant*
14. WOODLEIGH   N A BARKER

ARCHDEACONRY OF BARNSTAPLE

15. BARNSTAPLE   P H HOCKEY
16. HARTLAND   S C HENDERSON
17. HOLSWORTHY   K M ROBERTS
18. SHIRWELL *Vacant*
19. SOUTH MOLTON   P J ATTWOOD
20. TORRINGTON   K D MATHERS

ARCHDEACONRY OF PLYMOUTH

21. IVYBRIDGE   D ARNOTT
22. PLYMOUTH DEVONPORT   D J NIXON
23. PLYMOUTH MOORSIDE   D B M GILL
24. PLYMOUTH SUTTON   N H P MCKINNEL
25. TAVISTOCK *Vacant*

GLOUCESTER

ARCHDEACONRY OF GLOUCESTER

1. FOREST SOUTH   P A BRUNT
2. GLOUCESTER CITY   R C SIMPSON
3. SEVERN VALE   R J A MITCHELL
4. STROUD   S A BOWEN
5. WOTTON   R H AXFORD

ARCHDEACONRY OF CHELTENHAM

6. CHELTENHAM   T F L GRIFFITHS
7. CIRENCESTER   J E JESSOP
8. FAIRFORD   B C ATKINSON
9. NORTH COTSWOLD   V N JAMES
10. TEWKESBURY AND WINCHCOMBE   P R WILLIAMS

GUILDFORD

ARCHDEACONRY OF SURREY

1. ALDERSHOT   D G WILLEY
2. CRANLEIGH   J N E BUNDOCK
3. FARNHAM   A E GELL
4. GODALMING   J M FELLOWS
5. GUILDFORD   F SCAMMELL
6. SURREY HEATH   A BODY

ARCHDEACONRY OF DORKING

7. DORKING   P D BRYER
8. EMLY   C S BOURNE
9. EPSOM   S G THOMAS
10. LEATHERHEAD   E R JENKINS
11. RUNNYMEDE   T J HILLIER
12. WOKING   C J BLAIR

HEREFORD

ARCHDEACONRY OF HEREFORD

1. ABBEYDORE   A F EVANS
2. BROMYARD   C M SYKES
3. HEREFORD   P TOWNER
4. KINGTON AND WEOBLEY   S HOLLINGHURST
5. LEDBURY   M D VOCKINS
6. LEOMINSTER   M C CLUETT
7. ROSS AND ARCHENFIELD   E C GODDARD

ARCHDEACONRY OF LUDLOW

8. BRIDGNORTH   S H CAWDELL
9. CLUN FOREST   R T SHAW
10. CONDOVER   S A LOWE
11. LUDLOW   C A LORDING
12. PONTESBURY   M G WHITTOCK
13. TELFORD SEVERN GORGE   M W LEFROY

LEICESTER

ARCHDEACONRY OF LEICESTER

1. CITY OF LEICESTER   A K FORD
2. FRAMLAND (Melton) *Vacant*
3. GARTREE FIRST DEANERY (Harborough)   M F RUSK
4. GARTREE SECOND DEANERY (Wigston)   M F RUSK
5. GOSCOTE   R M GLADSTONE

ARCHDEACONRY OF LOUGHBOROUGH

6. AKELEY EAST (Loughborough) *Vacant*
7. GUTHLAXTON *Vacant*
8. NORTH WEST LEICESTERSHIRE   B A ROBERTSON
9. SPARKENHOE EAST   P G HOOPER
10. SPARKENHOE WEST (Hinckley and Bosworth)
    T H C MEYRICK

LICHFIELD

ARCHDEACONRY OF LICHFIELD

1. LICHFIELD   J W ALLAN
2. PENKRIDGE   S C WITCOMBE
3. RUGELEY   M J NEWMAN
4. TAMWORTH   J W TROOD

ARCHDEACONRY OF STOKE-ON-TRENT

5. ALSTONFIELD   M P SKILLINGS
6. CHEADLE   S J OSBOURNE
7. ECCLESHALL   N A CLEMAS
8. LEEK   M J PARKER
9. NEWCASTLE   T B BLOOR
10. STAFFORD   J J DAVIS
11. STOKE NORTH   P R CLARK
12. STOKE   D P LINGWOOD
13. STONE   P D DAKIN
14. TUTBURY   M R FREEMAN
15. UTTOXETER   B S P LEATHERS

ARCHDEACONRY OF SALOP

16. EDGMOND AND SHIFNAL   K HODSON
17. ELLESMERE   P J EDGE
18. HODNET   C P BEECH
19. OSWESTRY   A R BAILEY
20. SHREWSBURY   M W THOMAS
21. TELFORD   V C SWEET
22. WEM AND WHITCHURCH   R R HAARHOFF
23. WROCKWARDINE   D F CHANTREY

ARCHDEACONRY OF WALSALL

24. TRYSULL   M P HOBBS
25. WALSALL   M C RUTTER
26. WEDNESBURY   R E INGLESBY
27. WEST BROMWICH   A J SMITH
28. WOLVERHAMPTON   A J JONES

LINCOLN

ARCHDEACONRY OF STOW

1. AXHOLME, ISLE OF   M E BURSON-THOMAS
2. CORRINGHAM   R PROSSER
3. LAWRES   P D GODDEN
4. MANLAKE   M E BURSON-THOMAS
5. WEST WOLD   I ROBINSON
6. YARBOROUGH   D P ROWETT

ARCHDEACONRY OF LINDSEY

7. BOLINGBROKE   P F COATES
8. CALCEWAITHE AND CANDLESHOE   T STEELE
9. GRIMSBY AND CLEETHORPES *Vacant*
10. HAVERSTOE *Vacant*
11. HORNCASTLE   A J BOYD
12. LOUTHESK   S A ALLISON

ARCHDEACONRY OF LINCOLN

13. AVELAND AND NESS WITH STAMFORD   M WARRICK
14. BELTISLOE   A T HAWES
15. CHRISTIANITY   D J OSBOURNE
16. ELLOE EAST   R J SEAL
17. ELLOE WEST   R J SEAL
18. GRAFFOE   N J BUCK
19. GRANTHAM   C P ANDREWS
20. HOLLAND   R L WHITEHEAD
21. LAFFORD   J A PATRICK
22. LOVEDEN   A J MEGAHEY

LIVERPOOL

ARCHDEACONRY OF LIVERPOOL

1. BOOTLE   R J DRIVER
2. HUYTON   J A TAYLOR
3. LIVERPOOL NORTH   H CORBETT
4. LIVERPOOL SOUTH   C J CROOKS
5. SEFTON *Vacant*
6. TOXTETH AND WAVERTREE   M R STANFORD
7. WALTON   R S BRIDSON
8. WEST DERBY   S MCGANITY

ARCHDEACONRY OF WARRINGTON

9. NORTH MEOLS   P C GREEN
10. ST HELENS   M G COCKAYNE
11. ORMSKIRK   N A WELLS
12. WARRINGTON   S P ATTWATER
13. WIDNES   D J GAIT
14. WIGAN   M J SHERWIN
15. WINWICK   J M MATTHEWS

LONDON

ARCHDEACONRY OF LONDON

1. THE CITY   O C M ROSS

ARCHDEACONRY OF CHARING CROSS

2. WESTMINSTER PADDINGTON   J R ALLCOCK
3. WESTMINSTER ST MARGARET   P A E CHESTER
4. WESTMINSTER ST MARYLEBONE   L A MOSES

ARCHDEACONRY OF HACKNEY

(BISHOP OF STEPNEY)

5. HACKNEY   J F PORTER-PRYCE
6. ISLINGTON   M W LEARMOUTH
7. TOWER HAMLETS   A J E GREEN

ARCHDEACONRY OF MIDDLESEX

(BISHOP OF KENSINGTON)

8. CHELSEA   D P E REINDORP
9. HAMMERSMITH AND FULHAM   G Q D PIPER

10. HAMPTON   D N WINTERBURN
11. HOUNSLOW   D J SIMPSON
12. KENSINGTON   D C WALSH
13. SPELTHORNE   D R MCDOUGALL

ARCHDEACONRY OF HAMPSTEAD

(BISHOP OF EDMONTON)

14. BARNET, CENTRAL   P A WALMSLEY-MCLEOD
15. BARNET, WEST   T G CLEMENT
16. CAMDEN, NORTH (Hampstead)   A D CAIN
17. CAMDEN, SOUTH (Holborn and St Pancras)
   A J B MELDRUM
18. ENFIELD   R D JAMES
19. HARINGEY, EAST   O A FAGBEMI
20. HARINGEY, WEST   P F M GOFF

ARCHDEACONRY OF NORTHOLT

(BISHOP OF WILLESDEN)

21. BRENT   F M-L SCROGGIE
22. EALING   C RAMSAY
23. HARROW   R C BARTLETT
24. HILLINGDON   S EVANS

MANCHESTER

ARCHDEACONRY OF MANCHESTER

1. ARDWICK   I D GOMERSALL
2. HEATON   L S IRELAND
3. HULME   S D A KILLWICK
4. MANCHESTER, NORTH   D J A BURTON
5. STRETFORD   J D HUGHES
6. WITHINGTON   I MCVEETY

ARCHDEACONRY OF BOLTON

7. BOLTON   D R PETCH
8. BURY   G F JOYCE
9. DEANE   R C COOPER
10. RADCLIFFE AND PRESTWICH   D A PLUMMER
11. ROSSENDALE *Vacant*
12. WALMSLEY   W L OLIVER

ARCHDEACONRY OF ROCHDALE

13. ASHTON-UNDER-LYNE   R FARNWORTH
14. HEYWOOD AND MIDDLETON   P H MILLER
15. OLDHAM EAST   A BUTLER
16. OLDHAM WEST   D R PENNY
17. ROCHDALE *Vacant*

ARCHDEACONRY OF SALFORD

18. ECCLES   J P SHEEHY
19. LEIGH   R W BUCKLEY
20. SALFORD   A I SALMON

NEWCASTLE

ARCHDEACONRY OF NORTHUMBERLAND

1. BEDLINGTON   P J BRYARS
2. NEWCASTLE CENTRAL   P J CUNNINGHAM
3. NEWCASTLE EAST   K HUNT
4. NEWCASTLE WEST   J R SINCLAIR
5. TYNEMOUTH   A J HUGHES

ARCHDEACONRY OF LINDISFARNE

6. ALNWICK   J A ROBERTSON
7. BAMBURGH AND GLENDALE   B C HURST
8. BELLINGHAM   S M RAMSARAN
9. CORBRIDGE   D B HEWLETT
10. HEXHAM   G B USHER
11. MORPETH *Vacant*
12. NORHAM   G R KELSEY

NORWICH

ARCHDEACONRY OF NORWICH

1. NORWICH EAST   P L HOWARD
2. NORWICH NORTH   P D MACKAY
3. NORWICH SOUTH   A M STRANGE

ARCHDEACONRIES, DEANERIES AND RURAL/AREA DEANS

ARCHDEACONRY OF NORFOLK

4. BLOFIELD   P CUBITT
5. DEPWADE   D L P SOCHON
6. GREAT YARMOUTH   C L TERRY
7. HUMBLEYARD   C J DAVIES
8. LODDON   R H PARSONAGE
9. LOTHINGLAND   I R BENTLEY
10. REDENHALL   A C BILLETT
11. THETFORD AND ROCKLAND   M C JACKSON
12. ST BENET AT WAXHAM AND TUNSTEAD   W HILL

ARCHDEACONRY OF LYNN

13. BRECKLAND   S R NAIRN
14. BRISLEY AND ELMHAM *Vacant*
15. BURNHAM AND WALSINGHAM   P McCRORY
16. HEACHAM AND RISING   S DAVIES
17. DEREHAM IN MITFORD   S M THEAKSTON
18. HOLT   H C STOKER
19. INGWORTH   B T FAULKNER
20. LYNN   C J IVORY
21. REPPS   D E COURT
22. SPARHAM   L S TILLETT

OXFORD

ARCHDEACONRY OF OXFORD

(BISHOP OF DORCHESTER)
1. ASTON AND CUDDESDON   S E BOOYS
2. BICESTER AND ISLIP   P T C MASHEDER
3. CHIPPING NORTON   J K FRENCH
4. COWLEY   J B GILLINGHAM
5. DEDDINGTON   P FREETH
6. HENLEY   G D FOULIS BROWN
7. OXFORD   J A ELLIS
8. WITNEY   W G BLAKEY
9. WOODSTOCK   E E S JONES

ARCHDEACONRY OF BERKSHIRE

(BISHOP OF READING)
10. ABINGDON   P J MCKELLEN
11. BRACKNELL   N A PARISH
12. BRADFIELD   P L DEWEY
13. MAIDENHEAD AND WINDSOR   J R G HYDE
14. NEWBURY   R E BALL
15. READING   B SHENTON
16. SONNING   D P HODGSON
17. VALE OF WHITE HORSE   R M A HANCOCK
18. WALLINGFORD   E J CARTER
19. WANTAGE   J C ROBERTSON

ARCHDEACONRY OF BUCKINGHAM

20. AMERSHAM   D C CARR
21. AYLESBURY   A K E BLYTH
22. BUCKINGHAM   R M BUNDOCK
23. BURNHAM AND SLOUGH   A R WALKER
24. CLAYDON *Vacant*
25. MILTON KEYNES   T NORWOOD
26. MURSLEY   L P R MEERING
27. NEWPORT   C E PUMFREY
28. WENDOVER   M C DEARNLEY
29. WYCOMBE   D A PICKEN

PETERBOROUGH

ARCHDEACONRY OF NORTHAMPTON

1. BRACKLEY   M R H BELLAMY
2. BRIXWORTH   M Y GARBUTT
3. DAVENTRY   A SLATER
4. NORTHAMPTON, GREATER   D J WISEMAN
5. TOWCESTER   P D MCLEOD
6. WELLINGBOROUGH   A M LYNETT

ARCHDEACONRY OF OAKHAM

7. CORBY   R J LEE
8. HIGHAM   G L BROCKHOUSE
9. KETTERING   B J WITHINGTON
10. OUNDLE   R J ORMSTON
11. PETERBOROUGH   G M JESSOP
12. RUTLAND   L T FRANCIS-DEHQANI

PORTSMOUTH

ARCHDEACONRY OF THE MEON

1. BISHOP'S WALTHAM   S H HOLT
2. FAREHAM   S P GIRLING
3. GOSPORT   J W DRAPER
4. PETERSFIELD   W P M HUGHES

ARCHDEACONRY OF PORTSDOWN

5. HAVANT   J G P JEFFERY
6. PORTSMOUTH   R C WHITE

ARCHDEACONRY OF ISLE OF WIGHT

7. WIGHT, EAST   G E MORRIS
8. WIGHT, WEST   M H WEAVER

RIPON AND LEEDS

ARCHDEACONRY OF RICHMOND

1. HARROGATE   N C SINCLAIR
2. RICHMOND   S R HAWORTH
3. RIPON   M S EVANS
4. WENSLEY   B S DIXON

ARCHDEACONRY OF LEEDS

5. ALLERTON   A L TAYLOR
6. ARMLEY   K A P DOWLING
7. HEADINGLEY   S SMITH
8. WHITKIRK   M P BENWELL

ROCHESTER

ARCHDEACONRY OF ROCHESTER

1. COBHAM *Vacant*
2. DARTFORD   R ARDING
3. GILLINGHAM   J P JENNINGS
4. GRAVESEND   R OATES
5. ROCHESTER   P T KERR
6. STROOD   J F SOUTHWARD

ARCHDEACONRY OF TONBRIDGE

7. MALLING   J D BROWN
8. PADDOCK WOOD   G A SMITH
9. SEVENOAKS *Vacant*
10. SHOREHAM   S R JONES
11. TONBRIDGE   M E BROWN
12. TUNBRIDGE WELLS   B S SENIOR

ARCHDEACONRY OF BROMLEY AND BEXLEY

13. BECKENHAM   P MILLER
14. BROMLEY   M M CAMP
15. ERITH   A K LANE
16. ORPINGTON   J P COLWILL
17. SIDCUP   S SEALY

ST ALBANS

ARCHDEACONRY OF ST ALBANS

1. BERKHAMSTED   M N R BOWIE
2. HEMEL HEMPSTEAD   D M LAWSON
3. HITCHIN   M A H RODEN
4. RICKMANSWORTH   D J SNOWBALL
5. ST ALBANS   D RIDGEWAY
6. WATFORD   D J MIDDLEBROOK
7. WHEATHAMPSTEAD   W J M GIBBS

ARCHDEACONRY OF BEDFORD

8. AMPTHILL AND SHEFFORD   M F J BRADLEY
9. BEDFORD   R C HIBBERT
10. BIGGLESWADE   D G WILLIAMS
11. DUNSTABLE   R J ANDREWS
12. LUTON   S PURVIS
13. SHARNBROOK   D G MASON

ARCHDEACONRY OF HERTFORD

14. BARNET   M J BURNS
15. BISHOP'S STORTFORD   C D BOULTON
16. BUNTINGFORD   R M MORGAN

17. CHESHUNT   C J SELBY
18. WELWYN HATFIELD   C GARNER
19. HERTFORD AND WARE   P M HIGHAM
20. STEVENAGE   G J TICKNER

ST EDMUNDSBURY AND IPSWICH
ARCHDEACONRY OF IPSWICH

1. BOSMERE   D R WILLIAMS
2. COLNEYS   R C HINSLEY
3. HADLEIGH   M C THROWER
4. IPSWICH   I D J MORGAN
5. SAMFORD   D B SINGLETON
6. STOWMARKET   B B BILSTON
7. WOODBRIDGE   H C SANDERS

ARCHDEACONRY OF SUDBURY

8. CLARE   I M FINN
9. IXWORTH   J W FULTON
10. LAVENHAM   M I MCNAMARA
11. MILDENHALL   S J MITCHELL
12. SUDBURY   R L C KING
13. THINGOE   A R GATES

ARCHDEACONRY OF SUFFOLK

14. BECCLES AND SOUTH ELMHAM   S J PITCHER
15. HALESWORTH   S J PITCHER
16. HARTISMERE   A M MITCHAM
17. HOXNE   F O NEWTON
18. LOES   G W OWEN
19. SAXMUNDHAM   N J HARTLEY

SALISBURY
ARCHDEACONRY OF SHERBORNE

1. DORCHESTER   P J SMITH
2. LYME BAY   R A D'V THORN
3. SHERBORNE   H G PEARSON
4. WEYMOUTH AND PORTLAND   K I HOBBS

ARCHDEACONRY OF DORSET

5. BLACKMORE VALE   D R R SEYMOUR
6. MILTON AND BLANDFORD   S F EVERETT
7. POOLE   J H T DE GARIS
8. PURBECK   J S WOOD
9. WIMBORNE   C M TEBBUTT

ARCHDEACONRY OF SARUM

10. ALDERBURY   V S PERRETT
11. CHALKE   D E HENLEY
12. SALISBURY   D J J R LINAKER
13. STONEHENGE   M T P ZAMMIT

ARCHDEACONRY OF WILTS

14. BRADFORD   A E EVANS
15. CALNE   T M B WOODHOUSE
16. DEVIZES   J P TRIFFITT
17. HEYTESBURY   J H TOMLINSON
18. MARLBOROUGH   A G STUDDERT-KENNEDY
19. PEWSEY   M EDWARDS

SHEFFIELD
ARCHDEACONRY OF SHEFFIELD AND ROTHERHAM

1. ATTERCLIFFE   S J WILLETT
2. ECCLESALL   P A INGRAM
3. ECCLESFIELD   R A STORDY
4. HALLAM   P R TOWNSEND
5. LAUGHTON   G SCHOFIELD
6. ROTHERHAM   D C BLISS

ARCHDEACONRY OF DONCASTER

7. ADWICK-LE-STREET   S J GARDNER
8. DONCASTER   J M FODEN
9. DONCASTER, WEST   N M REDEYOFF
10. SNAITH AND HATFIELD   P D WILSON
11. TANKERSLEY   K J E HALE
12. WATH   N H ELLIOTT

SODOR AND MAN
ARCHDEACONRY OF SODOR AND MAN

1. CASTLETOWN AND PEEL   P C ROBINSON
2. DOUGLAS   D WHITWORTH
3. RAMSEY   N D GREENWOOD

SOUTHWARK
ARCHDEACONRY OF LEWISHAM AND GREENWICH
(BISHOP OF WOOLWICH)

1. CHARLTON   K W HITCH
2. DEPTFORD   N D R NICHOLLS
3. ELTHAM AND MOTTINGHAM   E CRANMER
4. LEWISHAM, EAST   R D BAINBRIDGE
5. LEWISHAM, WEST   M J KINGSTON
6. PLUMSTEAD   H D OWEN

ARCHDEACONRY OF SOUTHWARK
(BISHOP OF WOOLWICH)

7. BERMONDSEY *Vacant*
8. CAMBERWELL *Vacant*
9. DULWICH   D L GWILLIAMS
10. SOUTHWARK AND NEWINGTON   A P DODD

ARCHDEACONRY OF LAMBETH
(BISHOP OF KINGSTON)

11. LAMBETH NORTH   S M SICHEL
12. LAMBETH SOUTH   S P GATES
13. MERTON   S H COULSON

ARCHDEACONRY OF WANDSWORTH
(BISHOP OF KINGSTON)

14. BATTERSEA   G N OWEN
15. KINGSTON   D J HOUGHTON
16. RICHMOND AND BARNES   T J E MARWOOD
17. TOOTING   W ROEST
18. WANDSWORTH   H D TOLLER

ARCHDEACONRY OF CROYDON

19. CROYDON ADDINGTON   M R MCKINNEY
20. CROYDON CENTRAL   T A MAPSTONE
21. CROYDON NORTH   B A MASON
22. CROYDON SOUTH   C F SPURWAY
23. SUTTON   C WHEATON

ARCHDEACONRY OF REIGATE
(BISHOP OF CROYDON)

24. CATERHAM   D J SWAN
25. GODSTONE   G PADDICK
26. REIGATE   G A BARBER

SOUTHWELL AND NOTTINGHAM
ARCHDEACONRY OF NEWARK

1. BASSETLAW AND BAWTRY   J P SMITHURST
2. MANSFIELD   J M A ADAMS
3. NEWARK   A I TUCKER
4. NEWSTEAD   R KELLETT
5. RETFORD *Vacant*
6. WORKSOP *Vacant*

ARCHDEACONRY OF NOTTINGHAM

7. BEESTON *Vacant*
8. EAST BINGHAM   J F WELLINGTON
9. WEST BINGHAM   J W BENTHAM
10. GEDLING   P A WILLIAMS
12. NOTTINGHAM NORTH   J J LEPINE
13. NOTTINGHAM CENTRAL   R M CLARK
14. NOTTINGHAM WEST *Vacant*
15. SOUTHWELL   A I TUCKER

TRURO
ARCHDEACONRY OF CORNWALL

1. ST AUSTELL   M L BARRETT
2. CARNMARTH NORTH   O STEVENS
3. CARNMARTH SOUTH   J HARRIS
4. KERRIER   L A WALKER

5. PENWITH R H PESKETT
6. POWDER A G BASHFORTH
7. PYDAR C M MALKINSON

ARCHDEACONRY OF BODMIN

8. STRATTON R S THEWSEY
9. TRIGG MAJOR *Vacant*
10. TRIGG MINOR AND BODMIN S L BRYAN
11. WIVELSHIRE, EAST P R SHARPE
12. WIVELSHIRE, WEST A R INGLEBY

WAKEFIELD

ARCHDEACONRY OF HALIFAX

1. ALMONDBURY R J STEEL
2. BRIGHOUSE AND ELLAND D BURROWS
3. CALDER VALLEY J T ALLISON
4. HALIFAX J S BRADBERRY
5. HUDDERSFIELD M RAILTON-CROWDER
6. KIRKBURTON J R JONES

ARCHDEACONRY OF PONTEFRACT

7. BARNSLEY S P RACE
8. BIRSTALL A F LAWSON
9. DEWSBURY P D MAYBURY
10. PONTEFRACT R G COOPER
11. WAKEFIELD S P KELLY

WINCHESTER

ARCHDEACONRY OF WINCHESTER

1. ALRESFORD P H N COLLINS
2. ALTON H J D WRIGHT
3. ANDOVER J P HARKIN
4. BASINGSTOKE A BOTHAM
5. ODIHAM P W DYSON
6. WHITCHURCH C DALE
7. WINCHESTER A W GORDON

ARCHDEACONRY OF BOURNEMOUTH

8. BOURNEMOUTH A L MCPHERSON
9. CHRISTCHURCH M R GODSON
10. EASTLEIGH P A VARGESON
11. LYNDHURST D J FURNESS
12. ROMSEY R A CORNE
13. SOUTHAMPTON G J PHILBRICK

THE CHANNEL ISLANDS

14. GUERNSEY K P MELLOR
15. JERSEY R F KEY

WORCESTER

ARCHDEACONRY OF WORCESTER

1. EVESHAM R L COURT
2. MALVERN W D NICHOL
3. MARTLEY AND WORCESTER WEST *Vacant*
4. PERSHORE S K RENSHAW
5. UPTON C A MOSS
6. WORCESTER EAST K A BOYCE

ARCHDEACONRY OF DUDLEY

7. BROMSGROVE *Vacant*
8. DROITWICH S P KERR
9. DUDLEY S H CARTER
10. KINGSWINFORD *Vacant*
11. KIDDERMINSTER K N JAMES
12. STOURBRIDGE A L HAZLEWOOD
13. STOURPORT L S GRACE

YORK

ARCHDEACONRY OF YORK

(BISHOP OF SELBY)
1. AINSTY, NEW P E BRISTOW
2. DERWENT A CLEMENTS
3. EASINGWOLD J HARRISON
4. SELBY C WILTON
5. SOUTH WOLD J C FINNEMORE
6. SOUTHERN RYEDALE P H BOWES
7. YORK, CITY OF C W M BALDOCK

ARCHDEACONRY OF EAST RIDING

(BISHOP OF HULL)
8. BEVERLEY A BAILEY
9. BRIDLINGTON P J PIKE
10. HARTHILL *Vacant*
11. HOLDERNESS, NORTH C J SIMMONS
12. HOLDERNESS, SOUTH S V COPE
13. HOWDEN J H LITTLE
14. HULL T M H BOYNS
15. SCARBOROUGH M P DUNNING

ARCHDEACONRY OF CLEVELAND

(BISHOP OF WHITBY)
16. GUISBOROUGH G J PACEY
17. MIDDLESBROUGH D P BLACK
18. MOWBRAY R F ROWLING
19. NORTHERN RYEDALE P J MOTHERSDALE
20. STOKESLEY W J FORD
21. WHITBY D S COOK

CHURCH IN WALES

ST ASAPH

ARCHDEACONRY OF ST ASAPH

1. ST ASAPH   D Q BELLAMY
2. DENBIGH   J P SMITH
3. DYFFRYN CLWYD   P V F CHEW
4. HOLYWELL   J D P LOMAS
5. LLANRWST   C R OWEN
6. RHOS   J P ATACK

ARCHDEACONRY OF MONTGOMERY

7. CEDEWAIN   A S GRIMWOOD
8. CAEREINION   D E B FRANCIS
9. LLANFYLLIN   P POWELL
10. POOL   T E BENNETT

ARCHDEACONRY OF WREXHAM

11. BANGOR ISYCOED   D T B LEWIS
12. GRESFORD   S M HUYTON
13. HAWARDEN   M J BATCHELOR
14. LLANGOLLEN   A C SULLY
15. MINERA   N W CARTER
16. MOLD   A W A COPPING
17. PENLLYN AND EDEIRNION   H PENTON
18. WREXHAM   M F WEST

BANGOR

ARCHDEACONRY OF BANGOR

1. ARFON   J L JONES
2. ARLLECHWEDD   J E NICE
3. LLIFON AND TALYBOLION   M M BRADY
4. MALLTRAETH   P MCLEAN
5. OGWEN   N C WILLIAMS
6. TINDAETHWY AND MENAI   R G R SMITH
7. TWRCELYN   G W EDWARDS

ARCHDEACONRY OF MEIRIONNYDD

8. ARDUDWY   R A BEACON
9. ARWYSTLI   H A CHIPLIN
10. CYFEILIOG AND MAWDDWY   J M RILEY
11. LLYN AND EIFIONYDD   D J WILLIAMS
12. YSTUMANER   R B D REES

ST DAVIDS

ARCHDEACONRY OF ST DAVIDS

1. DAUGLEDDAU   G D GWYTHER
3. DEWISLAND AND FISHGUARD   R GRIFFITHS
3. PEMBROKE   M BUTLER
4. ROOSE   A M CHADWICK

ARCHDEACONRY OF CARDIGAN

5. CEMAIS AND SUB-AERON *Vacant*
6. EMLYN *Vacant*
7. GLYN AERON   C L BOLTON
8. LAMPETER AND ULTRA-AERON   P W DAVIES
9. LLANBADARN FAWR   J P LIVINGSTONE

ARCHDEACONRY OF CARMARTHEN

10. CARMARTHEN   L L RICHARDSON
11. CYDWELI   P C JONES
12. DYFFRYN AMAN   M L REES
13. LLANGADOG AND LLANDEILO   W R HUGHES
14. ST CLEARS   J GAINER

LLANDAFF

ARCHDEACONRY OF LLANDAFF

1. CARDIFF   M R PREECE
2. LLANDAFF   J WIGLEY
3. PENARTH AND BARRY   J M HUGHES

ARCHDEACONRY OF MARGAM

4. BRIDGEND   S J BEVERLY
5. MARGAM   C J AMOS
6. NEATH   P A LEWIS
7. VALE OF GLAMORGAN   P M LEONARD

ARCHDEACONRY OF MORGANNWG

8. CAERPHILLY   R DONKIN
9. CYNON VALLEY   R I JONES
10. MERTHYR TYDFIL   M J DAVIES
11. PONTYPRIDD   M D GABLE
12. RHONDDA   C R LEWIS-JENKINS

MONMOUTH

ARCHDEACONRY OF MONMOUTH

1. ABERGAVENNY   J H WINSTON
2. MONMOUTH   S L GUEST
3. NETHERWENT   J E L WHITE
4. RAGLAN-USK   T G CLEMENT

ARCHDEACONRY OF NEWPORT

5. BASSALEG   J S WILLIAMS
6. BEDWELLTY   T MORGAN
7. BLAENAU GWENT *Vacant*
8. NEWPORT   D NEALE
9. PONTYPOOL   J V MOLE

SWANSEA AND BRECON

ARCHDEACONRY OF BRECON

1. BRECON   B H JOHN
2. BUILTH *Vacant*
3. CRICKHOWELL   K RICHARDS
4. HAY   R T EDWARDS
5. MAELIENYDD   A G LOAT

ARCHDEACONRY OF GOWER

6. CLYNE   G E BENNETT
7. CWMTAWE   D I DAVIES
8. GOWER   J W GRIFFIN
9. LLWCHWR   D ROBERTS
10. PENDERI   H M WILLIAMS
11. SWANSEA   H V PARSELL

ENGLISH BENEFICES AND CHURCHES

An index of benefices, conventional districts, local ecumenical projects, and proprietary chapels (shown in bold type), together with entries for churches and other licensed places of worship listed on the Parish Index of the Central Board of Finance. Where the church name is the same as that of the benefice (or as that of the place whose name forms the beginning of the benefice name), the church entry is omitted. Church dedications are indicated in brackets.

The benefice entry gives the full legal name, followed by the diocese, its deanery number (p. 1008), the patron(s), and the name(s) and appointment(s) of clergy serving there (if there are none, the telephone number of the parsonage house is given). The following are the main abbreviations used; for others see the full list of abbreviations.

C	Curate	P	Patron(s)
C-in-c	Curate-in-charge	P-in-c	Priest-in-charge
Dn-in-c	Deacon-in-charge	Par Dn	Parish Deacon
Dss	Deaconess	R	Rector
Hon C	Honorary Curate	TM	Team Minister
Hon Par Dn	Honorary Parish Deacon	TR	Team Rector
Min	Minister	TV	Team Vicar
NSM	Non-stipendiary Minister	V	Vicar

Listed below are the elements in place names which are not normally treated as substantive in the index:

CENTRAL	HIGHER	MUCH	OVER
EAST	LITTLE	NETHER	SOUTH
GREAT	LOW	NEW	THE
GREATER	LOWER	NORTH	UPPER
HIGH	MIDDLE	OLD	WEST

Thus WEST WIMBLEDON (Christ Church) appears as **WIMBLEDON, WEST (Christ Church)** and CENTRAL TELFORD as **TELFORD, CENTRAL**. The only exception occurs where the second element of the place name is a common noun thus, NEW LANE remains as **NEW LANE**, and WEST TOWN as **WEST TOWN**.

AB KETTLEBY (St James) and Holwell w Asfordby *Leic 2*
P *DBP, MMCET and V Rothley (jt)* **P-in-c** S A PATERSON
ABBAS and Templecombe, Henstridge and Horsington *B & W 2*
P *Bp and Ch Trust Fund Trust* R P HALLETT
ABBERLEY (St Mary) *see* Shrawley, Witley, Astley and Abberley *Worc*
ABBERLEY (St Michael) *as above*
ABBERTON (St Andrew) *see* Fingringhoe w E Donyland and Abberton etc *Chelmsf*
ABBERTON (St Edburga), The Flyfords, Naunton Beauchamp and Bishampton w Throckmorton *Worc 4* P *Bp and Croome Estate Trustees (1 turn), and Ld Chan (1 turn)*
R C A FAIRCLOUGH, C L M BUSFIELD, NSM J M JAMES
ABBESS RODING (St Edmund King and Martyr)
see S Rodings *Chelmsf*
ABBEY CHAPEL (St Mary) *see* Annesley w Newstead *S'well*
ABBEY HULTON (St John) *see* Bucknall *Lich*
ABBEY WOOD (St Michael and All Angels) *S'wark 6* P *Bp*
V D A SHERRATT, NSM D C ROBINSON
ABBEY WOOD (William Temple) *see* Thamesmead *S'wark*
ABBEYDALE *see* Sheff St Pet and St Oswald *Sheff*
ABBEYDALE (St John the Evangelist) *Sheff 2*
P *Mrs C Longworth, Sir Samuel Roberts Bt, K B Jones, and J A Goodwin Esq* V *vacant* 0114-236 0786
ABBEYDORE (St Mary) *see* Ewyas Harold w Dulas, Kenderchurch etc *Heref*
ABBEYLANDS Team Ministry *Ripon 7* P *Patr Bd*
TR R E HAYES, TV L J ASHTON, NSM B M HAWKINS
ABBEYSTEAD (Christ Church) *see* Dolphinholme w Quernmore and Over Wyresdale *Blackb*
ABBOTS BICKINGTON (St James) *see* Bradworthy, Sutcombe, Putford etc *Ex*
ABBOTS BROMLEY (St Nicholas), Blithfield, Colton, Colwich and Great Haywood *Lich 3* P *Bp and D&C (jt)* R S C DAVIS, C J LEONARDI, G STATON, NSM M A DAVYS, L J FARRINGTON
ABBOTS LANGLEY (St Lawrence) *St Alb 6* P *Bp*
V J M M SPREADBURY, C M A DAVIS
ABBOTS LEIGH (Holy Trinity) w Leigh Woods *Bris 2* P *Bp*
P-in-c D J SMITH, NSM R C WILSON
ABBOTS MORTON (St Peter) *see* Church Lench w Rous Lench and Abbots Morton etc *Worc*
ABBOTS RIPTON (St Andrew) w Wood Walton *Ely 10* P *Lord de Ramsey (2 turns), D&C (1 turn)* **P-in-c** E B ATLING, C B A STEWART
ABBOTSBURY (St Mary) *see* Highweek *Ex*
ABBOTSBURY (St Nicholas), Portesham and Langton Herring *Sarum 4* P *The Hon C A Townshend and Bp (alt)*
P-in-c A J WHITTOCK
ABBOTSHAM (St Helen) *Ex 16* P *PCC* V *vacant*
ABBOTSKERSWELL (Blessed Virgin Mary) *Ex 10*
P *Ld Chan* **P-in-c** J F LEONARD, C G STILL

ABBOTSLEY (St Margaret) *see* Gt Gransden and Abbotsley and Lt Gransden etc *Ely*
ABBOTSWOOD (St Nicholas Family Centre) *see* Yate New Town *Bris*
ABBOTTS ANN (St Mary) and Upper Clatford and Goodworth Clatford *Win 3* P *Exors T P de Paravicini Esq and Bp (jt)*
R D N A BROAD
ABDON (St Margaret) *Heref 11* P *Bp* R I E GIBBS
ABENHALL (St Michael) w Mitcheldean *Glouc 3* P *DBP*
P-in-c D A GILL
ABERFORD (St Ricarius) w Micklefield *York 4* P *Abp and Oriel Coll Ox (jt)* V *vacant* 0113-232 0975
ABINGDON (Christ Church) (St Helen) (St Michael and All Angels) (St Nicolas) *Ox 10* P *Patr Bd* TR E C MILLER,
TV P A SMITH, T C DAVIS, C J K PATEL, K O DUNNETT,
NSM T W HEWES, L HODGES, J A TAFT, S A THORN, P S SHIRRAS,
J R BAUN, S H YONG
ABINGER (St James) cum Coldharbour *Guildf 7* P *Ch Patr Trust and J P M H Evelyn Esq (alt)* R A N BERRY
ABINGTON (St Peter and St Paul) *Pet 4* P *Bp* R P J BALL,
C C W PECK
ABINGTON, GREAT (St Mary the Virgin) w LITTLE (St Mary) *Ely 5* P *MMCET* **P-in-c** J M NORRIS
ABINGTON PIGOTTS (St Michael and All Angels)
see Shingay Gp *Ely*
ABNEY (Mission Room) *see* Hope, Castleton and Bradwell *Derby*
ABRAM (St John) *Liv 14* P *R Wigan* **P-in-c** A E STEIN
ABRIDGE (Holy Trinity) *see* Lambourne w Abridge and Stapleford Abbotts *Chelmsf*
ABSON (St James the Great) *see* Pucklechurch and Abson *Bris*
ABTHORPE (St John the Baptist) *see* Silverstone and Abthorpe w Slapton etc *Pet*
ACASTER MALBIS (Holy Trinity) *York 1*
P *R A G Raimes Esq* V C I COATES,
NSM P J MACNAUGHTON
ACASTER SELBY (St John) *see* Appleton Roebuck w Acaster Selby *York*
ACCRINGTON Christ Church *Blackb 1* P *Bp and V S Shore H Trin (jt)* V *vacant* (01254) 235089
ACCRINGTON Christ the King (St James) (St Paul) (St Andrew) (St Peter) (St Clement) (St Mary Magdalen) *Blackb 1* P *Patr Bd* TV L W CARSON-FEATHAM
ACCRINGTON (St John) w Huncoat St Augustine *Blackb 1*
P *Bp and V Accrington St Jas w St Paul (jt)* NSM A J BINKS
ACKLAM (St John the Baptist) *see* W Buckrose *York*
ACKLAM, WEST (St Mary) *York 17* P *Trustees*
V J H HEARN
ACKLETON (Mission Room) *see* Worfield *Heref*
ACKLINGTON (St John the Divine) *see* Warkworth and Acklington *Newc*

ACKWORTH (All Saints) (St Cuthbert) *Wakef 10*   **P** *Duchy of Lanc*   **R** P HARTLEY,   **NSM** D TEECE

ACLE (St Edmund) w Fishley; North Burlingham; Beighton w Moulton *Nor 4*   **P** *Bp and Ch Soc Trust (jt)*   **R** M GREENLAND

ACOCKS GREEN (St Mary) *Birm 13*   **P** *Trustees*   **V** A T BULLOCK,   **NSM** R ANETTS

ACOL (St Mildred) *see* Birchington w Acol and Minnis Bay *Cant*

ACOMB (Holy Redeemer) *York 7*   **P** *The Crown*   **V** M A HAND,   **NSM** J O G HARDING

ACOMB (St Stephen) *York 7*   **P** *Trustees*   **V** P A HORSLEY

ACOMB MOOR (James the Deacon) *York 7*   **P** *Abp*   **V** A A HORSMAN

ACRISE (St Martin) *see* Hawkinge w Acrise and Swingfield *Cant*

ACTON (All Saints) w Great Waldingfield *St E 12*   **P** *Bp*   **P-in-c** C M HALLETT

ACTON (St Mary) *Lon 22*   **P** *Bp*   **R** D J BRAMMER,   **NSM** M J SPREDBURY

ACTON (St Mary) and Worleston, Church Minshull and Wettenhall *Ches 15*   **P** *Bp, V Over St Chad, and R C Roundell Esq (jt)*   **V** P A LILLICRAP,   **C** K E HINE, A J SANDERS

ACTON, EAST (St Dunstan w St Thomas) *Lon 22*   **P** *Bp*   **V** J M WESTALL,   **NSM** R YATES

ACTON, NORTH (St Gabriel) *Lon 22*   **P** *Bp*   **V** T J N L'ESTRANGE

ACTON, WEST (St Martin) *Lon 22*   **P** *Bp*   **V** N P HENDERSON,   **NSM** B E BARNETT-COWAN

ACTON BEAUCHAMP (St Giles) *see* Frome Valley *Heref*

ACTON BURNELL (St Mary) *see* Condover w Frodesley, Acton Burnell etc *Heref*

ACTON GREEN (St Peter) (All Saints) *Lon 22*   **P** *Bp*   **V** J M V WILLMINGTON,   **C** B E F PEARSON

ACTON ROUND (St Mary) *Heref 8*   **P** *DBP*   **Hon C** H J PATTERSON

ACTON SCOTT (St Margaret) *Heref 10*   **P** *DBP*   **P-in-c** M L COPE,   **NSM** M G WILLIAMS

ACTON TRUSSELL (St James) *see* Penkridge *Lich*

ACTON TURVILLE (St Mary) *see* Boxwell, Leighterton, Didmarton, Oldbury etc *Glouc*

ADBASTON (St Michael and All Angels), High Offley, Knightley, Norbury, Woodseaves, Gnosall and Moreton *Lich 7*   **P** *Bp*   **R** M S BRIDGEN,   **NSM** K M HAMMOND,   **OLM** E HAYCOCK

ADDERBURY (St Mary) w Milton *Ox 5*   **P** *New Coll Ox*   **V** S W FLETCHER

ADDERLEY (St Peter), Ash, Calverhall, Ightfield and Moreton Say *Lich 18*   **P** *C C Corbet Esq, A E H Heber-Percy Esq, T C Heywood-Lonsdale Esq, and R Whitchurch (jt)*   **R** M L E LAST

ADDINGHAM (St Michael) *see* Cross Fell Gp *Carl*

ADDINGHAM (St Peter) *Bradf 4*   **P** *J R Thompson-Ashby Esq*   **R** A R TAWN,   **NSM** B CLARKE

ADDINGTON (St Margaret) *see* Birling, Addington, Ryarsh and Trottiscliffe *Roch*

ADDINGTON (St Mary) *see* Winslow w Gt Horwood and Addington *Ox*

ADDINGTON (St Mary) *S'wark 19*   **P** *Abp*   **V** J M MALES,   **C** C L DOWLAND-PILLINGER

ADDINGTON, GREAT (All Saints) w LITTLE (St Mary the Virgin) and Woodford *Pet 8*   **P** *Bp and DBP (alt)*   **P-in-c** J T P HALL,   **NSM** P M TATE

ADDINGTON, NEW (St Edward) *S'wark 19*   **P** *Bp*   **V** M POWELL,   **C** M K TWINING,   **NSM** E ILORI

ADDISCOMBE (St Mary Magdalene) *S'wark 20*   **P** *Trustees*   **V** A S JOHNSON

ADDISCOMBE (St Mildred) *S'wark 20*   **P** *Bp*   **V** R C HAGON,   **Hon C** B F J GOODWIN

ADDLESTONE (St Augustine) (St Paul) *Guildf 11*   **P** *Bp*   **V** B H BEECROFT,   **C** C M BEECROFT

ADDLETHORPE (St Nicholas) *see* Skegness Gp *Linc*

ADEL (St John the Baptist) *Ripon 7*   **P** *Brig R G Lewthwaite, D R Lewthwaite Esq, and J V Lewthwaite Esq (jt)*   **P-in-c** I J WHITE

ADEYFIELD (St Barnabas) *see* Hemel Hempstead *St Alb*

ADFORTON (St Andrew) *see* Wigmore Abbey *Heref*

ADISHAM (Holy Innocents) *see* Aylesham w Adisham *Cant*

ADLESTROP (St Mary Magdalene) *see* Broadwell, Evenlode, Oddington, Adlestrop etc *Glouc*

ADLINGFLEET (All Saints) *see* The Marshland *Sheff*

ADLINGTON (St John's Mission Church) *see* Prestbury *Ches*

ADLINGTON (St Paul) *Blackb 4*   **P** *Bp*   **V** vacant (01257) 480253

ADSTOCK (St Cecilia) *see* Lenborough *Ox*

ADSTONE (All Saints) *see* Lambfold *Pet*

ADSWOOD (St Gabriel's Mission Church) *see* Stockport St Geo *Ches*

ADVENT (St Adwena) *see* Lanteglos by Camelford w Advent *Truro*

ADWELL (St Mary) *see* Thame *Ox*

ADWICK-LE-STREET (St Laurence) w Skelbrooke *Sheff 7*   **P** *Mrs P N Fullerton and Bp (alt)*   **R** A B WALTON

ADWICK-UPON-DEARNE (St John the Baptist) *see* Barnburgh w Melton on the Hill etc *Sheff*

AFFPUDDLE (St Lawrence) *see* Bere Regis and Affpuddle w Turnerspuddle *Sarum*

AIGBURTH (St Anne) *Liv 4*   **P** *Trustees*   **V** G G AMEY

AIKTON (St Andrew) *see* Barony of Burgh *Carl*

AINDERBY STEEPLE (St Helen) *see* Lower Swale *Ripon*

AINSDALE (St John) *Liv 9*   **P** *R Walton, Bp, and Adn (jt)*   **V** G J BIRCH

AINSTABLE (St Michael and All Angels) *see* Inglewood Gp *Carl*

AINSWORTH (Christ Church) *Man 10*   **P** *Bp*   **P-in-c** D F THOMSON

AINTREE (St Giles) w St Peter *Liv 7*   **P** *Bp*   **V** B A WALLES

AIREDALE (Holy Cross) w Fryston *Wakef 10*   **P** *Bp*   **V** T A IBBOTSON

AIRMYN (St David), Hook and Rawcliffe *Sheff 10*   **P** *Bp and Ch Soc Trust (jt)*   **V** P J BALL

AISHOLT (All Saints), Enmore, Goathurst, Nether Stowey, Over Stowey and Spaxton w Charlynch *B & W 16*   **P** *Bp, D&C Windsor, MMCET, and Ch Trust Fund Trust (jt)*   **R** C L MARSHALL,   **C** S R MORLEY, H O WATKINS,   **NSM** J W GUTTRIDGE

AISLABY (St Margaret) *see* Lower Esk *York*

AISTHORPE (St Peter) *see* Spring Line Gp *Linc*

AKELEY (St James) *see* N Buckingham *Ox*

AKEMAN *Ox 2*   **P** *New Coll and Ch Ch (1 turn), Qu Coll, St Jo Coll, and Period and Country Houses Ltd (1 turn)*   **R** D F WALKER,   **NSM** J M HEMMINGS

ALBERBURY (St Michael and All Angels) w Cardeston *Heref 12*   **P** *Bp and Sir Michael Leighton Bt (alt)*   **P-in-c** V J TAIT,   **OLM** M E NEAL

ALBOURNE (St Bartholomew) w Sayers Common and Twineham *Chich 9*   **P** *Bp (2 turns), Ex Coll Ox (1 turn)*   **R** D M SWYER

ALBRIGHTON (St John the Baptist) *see* Leaton and Albrighton w Battlefield *Lich*

ALBRIGHTON (St Mary Magdalene), Boningale and Donington *Lich 16*   **P** *Haberdashers' Co and MMCET (jt)*   **V** G WARREN

ALBURGH (All Saints) *see* Ditchingham, Hedenham, Broome, Earsham etc *Nor*

ALBURY (St Helen) Tiddington *see* Wheatley *Ox*

ALBURY (St Mary), Braughing, Furneux Pelham, Lt Hadham, Much Hadham and Stocking Pelham *St Alb 15*   **P** *Patr Bd*   **TR** C D BOULTON

ALBURY (St Peter and St Paul) *see* Shere, Albury and Chilworth *Guildf*

ALBY (St Ethelbert) *see* Erpingham w Calthorpe, Ingworth, Aldborough etc *Nor*

ALCESTER (St Nicholas) and Arrow w Oversley and Weethley *Cov 7*   **P** *Marquess of Hertf*   **R** D C CAPRON,   **Hon C** M L EAMAN

ALCISTON (not known) *see* Arlington, Berwick, Selmeston w Alciston etc *Chich*

ALCOMBE (St Michael the Archangel) *B & W 15*   **P** *Bp*   **V** S STUCKES,   **C** K J CROSS

ALCONBURY (St Peter and St Paul) cum Weston *Ely 10*   **P** *D&C Westmr*   **P-in-c** M P JEPP,   **NSM** M C FLAHERTY

ALDBOROUGH (St Andrew) w Boroughbridge and Roecliffe *Ripon 3*   **P** *D&C York and Bp (alt)*   **V** P J SMITH

ALDBOROUGH (St Mary) *see* Erpingham w Calthorpe, Ingworth, Aldborough etc *Nor*

ALDBOROUGH HATCH (St Peter) *Chelmsf 4*   **P** *The Crown*   **V** C NICHOLSON

ALDBOURNE (St Michael) *see* Whitton *Sarum*

ALDBROUGH (St Bartholomew) and Mappleton w Goxhill and Withernwick *York 11*   **P** *Ld Chan, Abp, and Adn E Riding (by turn)*   **P-in-c** S J K RICE-OXLEY

ALDBROUGH (St Paul) *see* Forcett and Aldbrough and Melsonby *Ripon*

ALDBURY (St John the Baptist) *see* Tring *St Alb*

ALDE, UPPER *St E 18*   **P** *R C Rous Esq, DBP, and CPAS (jt)*   **R** J P T OLANCZUK

ALDE RIVER Benefice, The *St E 19*   **P** *Earl of Guilford, Major P W Hope-Cobbold, DBP, CPAS, Miss S F R Heycock-Hollond, and Exors Mrs A C V Wentworth (jt)*   **R** B J SLATTER,   **OLM** E N YOUNGS-DUNNETT

ALDEBURGH (St Peter and St Paul) w Hazlewood *St E 19*
   P *Mrs A C V Wentworth* **V** N J HARTLEY, **C** C J COOK,
   OLM N J WINTER
ALDEBY (St Mary) *see* Raveningham Gp *Nor*
ALDENHAM (St John the Baptist), Radlett and Shenley *St Alb 5*
   P *Patr Bd* **TR** W J HOGG, **TV** R A FLETCHER, V C ORAM,
   NSM A G HOGG, D D PRICE
ALDERBROOK (St Richard) *see* Crowborough *Chich*
ALDERBURY (St Mary the Virgin) *see* Clarendon *Sarum*
ALDERCAR (St John) *see* Langley Mill *Derby*
ALDERFORD (St John the Baptist) *see* Wensum Benefice *Nor*
ALDERHOLT (St James) *Sarum 9* **P** *DBP* **V** P J MARTIN,
   OLM D A DENNIS
ALDERLEY (St Kenelm) *see* Wotton-under-Edge w
   Ozleworth, N Nibley etc *Glouc*
ALDERLEY (St Mary) w Birtles *Ches 12* **P** *Trustees and Bp*
   (alt) **R** J C MILNES
ALDERLEY EDGE (St Philip) *Ches 12* **P** *Trustees*
   V P J PARRY, **NSM** L C A ALEXANDER, L LONSDALE
ALDERMASTON (St Mary the Virgin) and Woolhampton
   Ox 12 **P** *Bp, Keble Coll Ox, CPAS, Lady Dugdale, Worc Coll*
   Ox, and DBP (jt) **R** R A BEVAN, **NSM** D FOOTE, E M OKE
ALDERMINSTER (St Mary and Holy Cross) *see* Stourdene
   Gp *Cov*
ALDERNEY (St Anne) *Win 14* **P** *The Crown* **V** S M MASTERS
ALDERSBROOK (St Gabriel) *Chelmsf 4* **P** *DBP*
   V M J HAWKES
ALDERSHOT (Holy Trinity) *Guildf 1* **P** *CPAS*
   V G P H NEWTON, **C** G R MANSFIELD,
   NSM C J B KELLAGHER
ALDERSHOT (St Augustine) *Guildf 1* **P** *Bp* **V** K M HODGES,
   OLM J W A HARVEY
ALDERSHOT (St Michael the Archangel) (Ascension) *Guildf 1*
   P *Bp* **V** J A MARTIN, **C** T S MOORE
ALDERSLEY (Christ the King) *see* Tettenhall Regis *Lich*
ALDERTON (St Andrew) *see* Wilford Peninsula *St E*
ALDERTON (St Giles) *see* Sherston Magna, Easton Grey,
   Luckington etc *Bris*
ALDERTON (St Margaret) *see* Blisworth and Stoke Bruerne w
   Grafton Regis etc *Pet*
ALDERTON (St Margaret of Antioch) *see* Winchcombe *Glouc*
ALDERWASLEY (All Saints) *see* Wirksworth *Derby*
ALDFIELD (St Lawrence) *see* Fountains Gp *Ripon*
ALDFORD (St John the Baptist) *see* Waverton w Aldford and
   Bruera *Ches*
ALDHAM (St Margaret and St Catherine) *see* Marks Tey and
   Aldham *Chelmsf*
ALDHAM (St Mary) *see* Elmsett w Aldham, Hintlesham,
   Chattisham etc *St E*
ALDINGBOURNE (St Mary the Virgin), Barnham and
   Eastergate *Chich 1* **P** *Bp and D&C (jt)* **R** S P HOLLAND,
   NSM C R S HARDING, A R BRANT, S M HIGGINS
ALDINGHAM (St Cuthbert) and Dendron and Rampside and
   Urswick *Carl 9* **P** *Prime Min (1 turn), V Dalton-in-Furness*
   and Resident Landowners of Urswick (1 turn)
   P-in-c A M ARMSTRONG
ALDINGTON (St Martin) w Bonnington and Bilsington and
   Lympne w West Hythe *Cant 11* **P** *Abp* **C** N COOPER,
   Hon C R I MARTIN, **NSM** P F HILL, M P JONES
ALDRIDGE (St Mary the Virgin) (St Thomas) *Lich 25*
   P *MMCET* **C** E D COCKSHAW, J FISHER,
   NSM A G BURNAGE, **OLM** S E QUIBELL
ALDRINGHAM (St Andrew) *see* Whinlands *St E*
ALDRINGTON (St Leonard) *Chich 4* **P** *Bp* **R** S J TERRY
ALDSWORTH (St Bartholomew) *see* Sherborne, Windrush,
   Barringtons etc *Glouc*
ALDWARK (St Stephen) *see* Alne *York*
ALDWICK (St Richard) *Chich 1* **P** *Bp* **V** L C J NAGEL
ALDWINCLE (St Peter), Clopton, Pilton, Stoke Doyle, Thorpe
   Achurch, Titchmarsh and Wadenhoe *Pet 10*
   P *G C Capron Esq, Wadenhoe Trust, Soc Merchant Venturers*
   Bris, and DBP (jt) **R** J B MYNORS, **NSM** E A WALLER
ALDWORTH (St Mary the Virgin) *see* Basildon w Aldworth
   and Ashampstead *Ox*
ALEXANDRA PARK (St Andrew) *Lon 20* **P** *Bp* **V** A F PYBUS
ALFINGTON (St James and St Anne) *see* Ottery St Mary,
   Alfington, W Hill, Tipton etc *Ex*
ALFOLD (St Nicholas) and Loxwood *Guildf 2* **P** *Bp and*
   CPAS (jt) **R** *vacant* (01403) 752320
ALFORD (All Saints) *see* Six Pilgrims *B & W*
ALFORD (St Wilfrid) w Rigsby *Linc 8* **P** *Bp*
   OLM W A HORTON, K A GOODING, R D BARRETT
ALFRED JEWEL *B & W 13* **P** *D&C Windsor (4 turns), Bp*
   (2 turns), Sir Benjamin Slade Bt (1 turn) **R** J HASLAM,
   C P DENISON, **NSM** M H HASLAM

ALFRETON (St Martin) *Derby 1* **P** *Bp*
   P-in-c F J C MERCURIO, **NSM** S L MASON
ALFRICK (St Mary Magdalene) *see* Worcs W *Worc*
ALFRISTON (St Andrew) w Lullington, Litlington and West
   Dean *Chich 18* **P** *Ld Chan (3 turns), R A Brown Esq (1 turn),*
   and Duke of Devonshire (1 turn) **R** J E HOWSON
ALGARKIRK (St Peter and St Paul) and Fosdyke *Linc 20*
   P *Prime Min and Bp (alt)* **P-in-c** G MORGAN
ALHAMPTON (Mission Church) *see* Fosse Trinity *B & W*
ALKBOROUGH (St John the Baptist) *Linc 4* **P** *Bp*
   V A F PLEDGER
ALKERTON (St Michael and All Angels) *see* Ironstone *Ox*
ALKHAM (St Anthony) w Capel le Ferne and Hougham *Cant 7*
   P *Abp* **P-in-c** S M WHITE
ALKMONTON (St John) *see* S Dales *Derby*
ALL CANNINGS (All Saints) *see* Bishop's Cannings, All
   Cannings etc *Sarum*
ALL SAINTS *see* Hightertown and Baldhu *Truro*
ALL SAINTS (All Saints) *see* Axminster, Chardstock, All
   Saints etc *Ex*
ALL STRETTON (St Michael and All Angels) *see* Church
   Stretton *Heref*
ALLENDALE (St Cuthbert) w Whitfield *Newc 10* **P** *Viscount*
   Allendale and J C Blackett-Ord Esq (alt) **R** J W RUSSELL
ALLENS CROSS (St Bartholomew) *Birm 4* **P** *Bp*
   P-in-c P A FLEMING
ALLENS GREEN (Mission Church) *see* High Wych and
   Gilston w Eastwick *St Alb*
ALLEN'S ROUGH (Worship Centre) *see* Bentley Em and
   Willenhall H Trin *Lich*
ALLENSMORE (St Andrew) *see* Cagebrook *Heref*
ALLENTON (St Edmund) and Shelton Lock *Derby 15* **P** *Bp*
   P-in-c G MARTIN
ALLER (St Andrew) *see* Langport Area *B & W*
ALLERSTON (St John) *see* Thornton Dale w Allerston,
   Ebberston etc *York*
ALLERTHORPE (St Botolph) *see* Barmby Moor Gp *York*
ALLERTON (All Hallows) *see* Mossley Hill *Liv*
ALLERTON (not known) *see* Mark w Allerton *B & W*
ALLERTON (St Peter) (St Francis of Assisi) *Bradf 1* **P** *Bp*
   V G O WILLIAMS
ALLERTON BYWATER (St Mary) *see* Kippax w Allerton
   Bywater *Ripon*
ALLESLEY (All Saints) *Cov 2* **P** *J R W Thomson-Bree Esq*
   R R N TREW, **NSM** L J EDWARDS
ALLESLEY PARK (St Christopher) and Whoberley *Cov 3*
   P *Bp* **V** G L PRINGLE, **OLM** L J CLARKE
ALLESTREE (St Edmund King and Martyr) and Darley Abbey
   Derby 11 **P** *Bp and DBP (jt)* **V** C A DYER, **C** C L RHODES,
   NSM P A MALLINSON, J CALDWELL
ALLESTREE (St Nicholas) *Derby 11* **P** *Bp* **V** W F BATES,
   NSM J M NEEDLE
ALLHALLOWS (All Saints) *see* Binsey *Carl*
ALLINGTON (St John the Baptist) *see* Bourne Valley *Sarum*
ALLINGTON (St Nicholas) and Maidstone St Peter *Cant 12*
   P *Abp* **P-in-c** M L BORLEY
ALLINGTON (St Swithin) *see* Bridport *Sarum*
ALLINGTON, EAST (St Andrew) *see* Modbury, Bigbury,
   Ringmore w Kingston etc *Ex*
ALLINGTON, WEST (Holy Trinity) *see* Saxonwell *Linc*
ALLITHWAITE (St Mary) *see* Cartmel Peninsula *Carl*
ALLONBY (Christ Church), Cross Canonby and Dearham *Carl 7*
   P *TR Solway Plain, D&C, and Bp (jt)* **V** M E DAY,
   NSM M FOGG
ALMELEY (St Mary) *see* Eardisley w Bollingham, Willersley,
   Brilley etc *Heref*
ALMER (St Mary) *see* Red Post *Sarum*
ALMONDBURY (St Michael and St Helen) (St Mary)
   (All Hallows) w Farnley Tyas *Wakef 1* **P** *DBP*
   TR D F HANDLEY, **TV** M L BROWELL
ALMONDSBURY (St Mary the Virgin) and Olveston *Bris 2*
   P *Bp and D&C (jt)* **V** P W ROWE, **C** R J CREW,
   Hon C D R F BAIN, **OLM** D H BONE
ALNE (St Mary) *York 3* **P** *CPAS and MMCET (alt)*
   P-in-c C J PARK, **NSM** R WADSWORTH
ALNE, GREAT (St Mary Magdalene) *see* Kinwarton w Gt
   Alne and Haselor *Cov*
ALNHAM (St Michael and All Angels) *see* Upper Coquetdale
   Newc
ALNMOUTH (St John the Baptist) *see* Lesbury w Alnmouth
   Newc
ALNWICK (St Michael and St Paul) *Newc 6* **P** *Duke of Northd*
   C R L SQUIRES
ALPERTON (St James) *Lon 21* **P** *CPAS* **C** T N CROWE,
   NSM A S JACOB

ALPHAMSTONE (not known) *see* N Hinckford *Chelmsf*

ALPHETON (St Peter and St Paul) *see* Chadbrook *St E*

ALPHINGTON (St Michael and All Angels), Shillingford St George and Ide *Ex 3* **P** *DBP, D&C, and Mrs J M Michelmore (jt)* **P-in-c** S L BESSENT, **C** C M MASON, J J CLARK

ALRESFORD (St Andrew) and Frating w Thorrington *Chelmsf 22* **P** *Bp* **V** P C M SCOTT

ALRESFORD, NEW (St John the Baptist) *see* Arle Valley *Win*

ALRESFORD, OLD (St Mary) *as above*

ALREWAS (All Saints) *Lich 1* **P** *Bp* **V** J W ALLAN, **NSM** P A L MADDOCK, A A LOW

ALSAGER (Christ Church) *Ches 11* **P** *Bp* **V** T S MAY

ALSAGER (St Mary Magdalene) (St Patrick's Mission Church) *Ches 11* **P** *Bp* **V** R J ISHERWOOD

ALSAGERS BANK (St John) *Lich 9* **P** *Bp* **P-in-c** P T W DAVIES

ALSOP-EN-LE-DALE (St Michael and All Angels) *see* Fenny Bentley, Thorpe, Tissington, Parwich etc *Derby*

ALSTON MOOR (St Augustine) *Newc 10* **P** *Bp* **R** J R GLOVER

ALSTONE (St Margaret) *see* Overbury w Teddington, Alstone etc *Worc*

ALSTONFIELD (St Peter), Butterton, Ilam, Warslow w Elkstone and Wetton *Lich 5* **P** *Bp, DBP, V Mayfield, and Sir Peter Walker-Okeover Bt (jt)* **V** A C BALLARD, **NSM** A J HACK

ALSWEAR (not known) *see* Bishopsnympton, Rose Ash, Mariansleigh etc *Ex*

ALTARNON (St Nonna) w Bolventor, Laneast and St Clether *Truro 9* **P** *Bp, D&C, and SMF (jt)* **P-in-c** A C R BALFOUR, **C** R E B MAYNARD

ALTCAR (St Michael and All Angels) and Hightown *Liv 5* **P** *Bp* **P-in-c** S J SMITH, **NSM** D C M TAYLOR

ALTHAM (St James) w Clayton le Moors *Blackb 1* **P** *DBP and Trustees (alt)* **V** J TRANTER, **NSM** D J BACON

ALTHORNE (St Andrew) and Latchingdon w North Fambridge *Chelmsf 11* **P** *Abp and Ld Chan (alt)* **V** S E MANLEY

ALTHORPE (St Oswald) *see* Belton Gp *Linc*

ALTOFTS (St Mary Magdalene) *Wakef 11* **P** *Meynall Ingram Trustees* **P-in-c** S J HOTCHEN

ALTON Resurrection (All Saints) (St Lawrence) *Win 2* **P** *Bp and D&C (jt)* **V** P G H DOORES, **C** P A BARLOW, A S WATSON, **NSM** T C L HELLINGS, I M TOOMBS

ALTON (St Peter) w Bradley-le-Moors and Denstone w Ellastone and Stanton and Mayfield *Lich 15* **P** *Earl of Shrewsbury, DBP, Personal Reps Col Sir Walter Bromley-Davenport, Bp, and Ch School Trust (jt)* **V** B S P LEATHERS, **C** J RICHARDSON, R P OWEN

ALTON BARNES (St Mary the Virgin) *see* Vale of Pewsey *Sarum*

ALTON COMMON (Mission Room) *see* Alton w Bradley-le-Moors and Denstone etc *Lich*

ALTON PANCRAS (St Pancras) *see* Piddle Valley, Hilton, Cheselbourne etc *Sarum*

ALTRINCHAM (St George) *Ches 10* **P** *V Bowdon* **V** E J BETTS, **C** M A JONES

ALTRINCHAM (St John the Evangelist) *Ches 10* **P** *Bp* **P-in-c** E J BETTS, **C** M A JONES

ALVANLEY (St John the Evangelist) *Ches 3* **P** *Bp* **P-in-c** R G TUCKWELL

ALVASTON (St Michael and All Angels) *Derby 15* **P** *PCC* **P-in-c** C G PEARSON, **NSM** I P MUNRO, J H HENDERSON SMITH

ALVECHURCH (St Lawrence) *Worc 7* **P** *Bp* **R** D H MARTIN

ALVEDISTON (St Mary) *see* Chalke Valley *Sarum*

ALVELEY (St Mary the Virgin) and Quatt *Heref 8* **P** *J W H Thompson Esq and Lady Labouchere (jt)* **R** N P ARMSTRONG, **NSM** R M SIMS

ALVERDISCOTT (All Saints) *see* Newton Tracey, Horwood, Alverdiscott etc *Ex*

ALVERSTOKE (St Faith) (St Francis) (St Mary) *Portsm 3* **P** *Bp* **R** E A GOODYER, **C** P G HISCOCK, **NSM** R A FORSE, N S TERRY

ALVERSTONE (Church Hall) *see* Brading w Yaverland *Portsm*

ALVERTHORPE (St Paul) *Wakef 11* **P** *Bp* **P-in-c** G A SYKES, **NSM** K KIDD

ALVESCOT (St Peter) *see* Shill Valley and Broadshire *Ox*

ALVESTON (St Helen) and Littleton-on-Severn w Elberton *Bris 2* **P** *Bp and D&C (jt)* **V** D J POLE

ALVESTON (St James) *Cov 8* **P** *R Hampton Lucy w Charlecote and Loxley* **V** R E WILLIAMS, **NSM** M KENT

ALVINGHAM (St Adelwold) *see* Mid Marsh Gp *Linc*

ALVINGTON (St Andrew) *see* Woolaston w Alvington and Aylburton *Glouc*

ALVINGTON, WEST (All Saints) *see* Thurlestone, S Milton, W Alvington etc *Ex*

ALWALTON (St Andrew) and Chesterton *Ely 15* **P** *Bp and Sir Philip Naylor-Leyland Bt (jt)* **V** M J INGHAM

ALWINGTON (St Andrew) *see* Parkham, Alwington, Buckland Brewer etc *Ex*

ALWINTON (St Michael and All Angels) *see* Upper Coquetdale *Newc*

ALWOODLEY (St Barnabas) *see* Moor Allerton and Shadwell *Ripon*

AMBERGATE (St Anne) and Heage *Derby 11* **P** *V Duffield and Exors M A T Johnson Esq* **C** J M PAGE, **NSM** D C BEECH

AMBERLEY (Holy Trinity) *see* Minchinhampton w Box and Amberley *Glouc*

AMBERLEY (no dedication) *see* Marden w Amberley and Wisteston *Heref*

AMBERLEY (St Michael) w North Stoke and Parham, Wiggonholt and Greatham *Chich 12* **P** *Bp and Parham Estate Trustees (jt)* **P-in-c** A M PATTENDEN

AMBLE (St Cuthbert) *Newc 6* **P** *Bp* **P-in-c** D R WESTMORELAND, **NSM** C C ASKEW

AMBLECOTE (Holy Trinity) *Worc 12* **P** *Bp* **P-in-c** A R N WILLIAMS

AMBLESIDE (St Mary) *see* Loughrigg *Carl*

AMBROSDEN (St Mary the Virgin) *see* Ray Valley *Ox*

AMCOTTS (St Mark) *see* Belton Gp *Linc*

AMERSHAM (St Leonard) *see* Chesham Bois *Ox*

AMERSHAM (St Mary the Virgin) *Ox 20* **P** *Capt F Tyrwhitt Drake* **R** T J L HARPER, **C** C J SYMCOX, **NSM** D C CARR, D A MOORE BROOKS

AMERSHAM ON THE HILL (St Michael and All Angels) *Ox 20* **P** *Bp* **V** D M GLOVER, **C** A J CRAWLEY, **NSM** P R BINNS, P C SOUNDY, **OLM** S ROBERTS

AMESBURY (St Mary and St Melor) *Sarum 13* **P** *D&C Windsor* **P-in-c** S E WILKINSON

AMINGTON (St Editha) *Birm 10* **P** *Bp* **V** M A HARRIS

AMOTHERBY (St Helen) *see* The Street Par *York*

AMPFIELD (St Mark), Chilworth and N Baddesley *Win 12* **P** *Mrs P M A T Chamberlayne-Madonald* **V** P M GILKS, **C** C M A MAXIM, **NSM** V J LAWRENCE, C G STRIDE

AMPLEFORTH (St Hilda) w Oswaldkirk, Gilling East and Stonegrave *York 19* **P** *Abp and Trin Coll Cam (jt) and Prime Min (by turn)* **V** S F BOND

AMPNEY (St Mary) *see* Fairford Deanery *Glouc*

AMPNEY (St Peter) *as above*

AMPNEY CRUCIS (Holy Rood) *as above*

AMPORT (St Mary) *see* Portway and Danebury *Win*

AMPTHILL (St Andrew) w Millbrook and Steppingley *St Alb 8* **P** *Ld Chan* **R** M J TRODDEN

AMPTON (St Peter) *see* Blackbourne *St E*

AMWELL, GREAT (St John the Baptist) w St Margaret's and Stanstead Abbots *St Alb 19* **P** *Bp, Peache Trustees, and Haileybury Coll (jt)* **V** E A DONALDSON

AMWELL, LITTLE (Holy Trinity) *see* Hertford *St Alb*

ANCASTER (St Martin) *see* Ancaster Wilsford Gp *Linc*

ANCASTER WILSFORD Group, The *Linc 22* **P** *Bp (2 turns), DBP (1 turn), and Mrs G V Hoare (1 turn)* **P-in-c** A J LITTLEWOOD

ANCHORSHOLME (All Saints) *Blackb 8* **P** *Bp, V Bispham, and Ch Soc Trust (jt)* **P-in-c** S M DNISTRIANSKYJ

ANCOATS (All Souls) *see* Manchester Gd Shep and St Barn *Man*

ANCROFT (St Anne) *see* Lowick and Kyloe w Ancroft *Newc*

ANDERBY (St Andrew) *see* Sutton, Huttoft and Anderby *Linc*

ANDOVER (St Mary) *Win 3* **P** *St Mary's Coll Win* **P-in-c** J P HARKIN

ANDOVER (St Thomas) *see* Pastrow *Win*

ANDOVER, WEST (St Michael and All Angels) *see* Portway and Danebury *Win*

ANDREAS (St Andrew) (St Jude Chapelry) *S & M 3* **P** *The Crown* **R** *vacant*

ANERLEY (Christ Church) (St Paul) *Roch 13* **P** *Patr Bd* **TR** M D FITTER, **TV** C L GARDINER

ANFIELD (St Columba) *Liv 7* **P** *Bp* **V** R S BRIDSON, **NSM** K L MILLER

ANFIELD (St Margaret) *Liv 3* **P** *Bp* **V** P A WINN, **NSM** J E WINN, S J LUCAS

ANGELL TOWN (St John the Evangelist) *S'wark 11* **P** *Bp* **P-in-c** M R MALLETT, **NSM** P J MILLIGAN

ANGERSLEIGH (St Michael) *see* Trull w Angersleigh *B & W*

ANGLESEY Group, The *Ely 4* **P** *Trin Coll Cam, D&C, and Bp (jt)* **V** D H LEWIS

ANGMERING (St Margaret) *Chich 1* **P** *J F P Somerset Esq and Ch Patr Trust (jt)* **R** M J STANDEN, **C** B J REDDING, A R THOMAS, **NSM** P S GILES

ANKER PARISHES *see* Wolvey w Burton Hastings, Copston Magna etc *Cov*

ANLABY (St Peter) *York 14* **P** *Trustees* **V** S C F WILCOX, **NSM** C R TETLEY

ANLABY COMMON (St Mark) Hull *York 14* **P** *Abp* **V** S C F WILCOX

ANMER (St Mary) *see* Dersingham w Anmer and Shernborne *Nor*

ANNESLEY (Our Lady and All Saints) w Newstead *S'well 4* **P** *Exors Major R P Chaworth-Musters* **P-in-c** E A TURNER-LOISEL, **NSM** K CHARLES

ANNFIELD PLAIN (St Aidan) *see* Collierley w Annfield Plain *Dur*

ANNSCROFT (Christ Church) *see* Longden and Annscroft w Pulverbatch *Heref*

ANSFORD (St Andrew) *see* Castle Cary w Ansford *B & W*

ANSLEY (St Lawrence) and Arley *Cov 5* **P** *Ch Patr Trust, N W H Sylvester Esq, and A C D'O Ransom Esq (jt)* **R** P B ALLAN

ANSLOW (Holy Trinity) *Lich 14* **P** *MMCET* **V** I R WHITEHEAD

ANSTEY (St George) *see* Hormead, Wyddial, Anstey, Brent Pelham etc *St Alb*

ANSTEY (St Mary) and Thurcaston w Cropston *Leic 9* **P** *Bp and Em Coll Cam (jt)* **R** D S MCDONOUGH

ANSTEY, EAST (St Michael) *see* Bishopsnympton, Rose Ash, Mariansleigh etc *Ex*

ANSTEY, WEST (St Petrock) *as above*

ANSTON (St James) *Sheff 5* **P** *Bp* **V** M CAUNT, **C** C J BETSON

ANSTY (St James) *see* Nadder Valley *Sarum*

ANSTY (St James) and Shilton *Cov 2* **P** *Ld Chan* **NSM** N W STEVENS

ANSTY (St John) *see* Cuckfield *Chich*

ANTINGHAM (St Mary) *see* Trunch *Nor*

ANTONY (St James the Great) w Sheviock *Truro 11* **P** *Bp and Col Sir John Carew-Pole Bt (alt)* **P-in-c** L PARKER

ANTROBUS (St Mark), Aston by Sutton, Little Leigh and Lower Whitley *Ches 4* **P** *Bp, V Gt Budworth, Lord Daresbury, and B H Talbot Esq (jt)* **V** R J DIGGLE

ANWICK (St Edith) *see* Ruskington Gp *Linc*

APETHORPE (St Leonard) *see* Nassington w Yarwell and Woodnewton w Apethorpe *Pet*

APLEY (St Andrew) *see* Bardney *Linc*

APPERLEY (Holy Trinity) *see* Deerhurst and Apperley w Forthampton etc *Glouc*

APPLEBY (St Bartholomew) *see* Winterton Gp *Linc*

APPLEBY (St Lawrence) *see* Heart of Eden *Carl*

APPLEBY MAGNA (St Michael and All Angels) *see* Woodfield *Leic*

APPLEDORE (St Mary) *see* Bideford, Northam, Westward Ho!, Appledore etc *Ex*

APPLEDORE (St Peter and St Paul) w Brookland and Fairfield and Brenzett w Snargate *Cant 11* **P** *Abp* **C** P J WHITE, **NSM** S J BODY, K FAZZANI, P L M FOGDEN

APPLEDRAM (St Mary the Virgin) *Chich 3* **P** *D&C* **P-in-c** M WICKENS

APPLEFORD (St Peter and St Paul) *see* Sutton Courtenay w Appleford *Ox*

APPLESHAW (St Peter) Kimpton, Thruxton, Fyfield and Shipton Bellinger *Win 3* **P** *Bp (1 turn), and Bp, D&C, and M H Routh Esq (1 turn)* **R** I J TOMLINSON, **Hon C** S C KERSLEY, **NSM** A E MCKENZIE

APPLETHWAITE (St Mary) *see* Windermere St Mary and Troutbeck *Carl*

APPLETON (All Saints) *see* The Street Par *York*

APPLETON (St Lawrence) *Ox 10* **P** *Magd Coll Ox* **P-in-c** L L SAPWELL

APPLETON (St Mary Magdalene) *see* Stockton Heath *Ches*

APPLETON-LE-MOORS (Christ Church) *see* Lastingham w Appleton-le-Moors, Rosedale etc *York*

APPLETON ROEBUCK (All Saints) w Acaster Selby *York 1* **P** *Abp* **P-in-c** C I COATES, **NSM** P J MACNAUGHTON

APPLETON THORN (St Cross) *see* Stretton and Appleton Thorn *Ches*

APPLETON WISKE (St Mary) *see* E Richmond *Ripon*

APPLETREEWICK (St John the Baptist) *see* Burnsall w Rylstone *Bradf*

APPLEY BRIDGE (All Saints) *Blackb 4* **P** *Bp* **C** S A GLYNN

APSLEY END (St Mary) *see* Langelei *St Alb*

APULDRAM (St Mary the Virgin) *see* Appledram *Chich*

ARBORFIELD (St Bartholomew) w Barkham *Ox 16* **P** *DBP* **R** E P BICKERSTETH, **C** J P BIDGOOD, L J O PARKER

ARBORY (St Columba) *S & M 1* **P** *The Crown* **V** P C ROBINSON, **NSM** C L BARRY

ARBOURTHORNE (St Paul) and Norfolk Park *Sheff 1* **P** *Bp and V Sheffield (jt)* **V** J T HODGES, **NSM** C C HODGES

ARBURY (Good Shepherd) *see* Chesterton Gd Shep *Ely*

ARDELEY (St Lawrence) *St Alb 16* **P** *D&C St Paul's* **P-in-c** M J LEVERTON

ARDINGLY (St Peter) *Chich 6* **P** *MMCET* **R** J H CRUTCHLEY

ARDINGTON (Holy Trinity) *see* Wantage Downs *Ox*

ARDLEIGH (St Mary the Virgin) and Bromleys, The *Chelmsf 20* **P** *Ld Chan (2 turns), CR (1 turn), Wadh Coll Ox (1 turn)* **R** R E FARRELL

ARDLEIGH GREEN (All Saints) *see* Squirrels Heath *Chelmsf*

ARDLEY (St Mary) *see* Cherwell Valley *Ox*

ARDSLEY (Christ Church) *Sheff 12* **P** *R Darfield* **V** D W FRY

ARDSLEY, EAST (St Gabriel) (St Michael) *Wakef 11* **P** E C S J G *Brudenell Esq* **V** G COGGINS

ARDSLEY, WEST (St Mary) *Wakef 8* **P** E C S J G *Brudenell Esq* **V** B A J BARRACLOUGH

ARDWICK (St Benedict) *see* Longsight St Luke *Man*

ARDWICK (St Jerome and St Silas) *see* Manchester Gd Shep and St Barn *Man*

ARELEY KINGS (St Bartholomew) *Worc 13* **P** *R Martley* **R** M TURNER

ARICONIUM: Aston Ingham, Hope Mansel, Linton, The Lea, Upton Bishop and Weston-under-Penyard *Heref 7* **P** *Bp (3 turns), St Jo Coll Ox (2 turns), Exors Preb H L Whatley (1 turn)* **R** N S PATTERSON

ARKENDALE (St Bartholomew) *see* Walkingham Hill *Ripon*

ARKENGARTHDALE (St Mary) *see* Swaledale *Ripon*

ARKESDEN (St Mary the Virgin) *see* Clavering and Langley w Arkesden etc *Chelmsf*

ARKHOLME (St John the Baptist) *see* Hornby w Claughton and Whittington etc *Blackb*

ARKLEY (St Peter) *see* Chipping Barnet *St Alb*

ARKSEY (All Saints) *see* New Bentley w Arksey *Sheff*

ARLE VALLEY Benefice, The *Win 1* **P** *Bp* **R** P H N COLLINS, **NSM** B C FLETCHER

ARLECDON (St Michael) *see* Crosslacon *Carl*

ARLESEY (St Andrew) (St Peter) w Astwick *St Alb 8* **P** *DBP* **V** S D EDWARDS

ARLEY (St Michael) *see* Ansley and Arley *Cov*

ARLEY (St Wilfrid) *as above*

ARLEY, UPPER (St Peter) *see* Kidderminster St Mary and All SS w Trimpley etc *Worc*

ARLINGHAM (St Mary the Virgin) *see* Frampton on Severn, Arlingham, Saul etc *Glouc*

ARLINGTON (St James) *see* Shirwell, Loxhore, Kentisbury, Arlington, etc *Ex*

ARLINGTON (St Pancras), Berwick, Selmeston w Alciston and Wilmington *Chich 18* **P** *Bp Lon, D&C, Miss I M Newson, and Mrs R Fitzherbert (jt)* **R** P M BLEE, **Hon C** A N STAMP

ARMATHWAITE (Christ and St Mary) *see* Inglewood Gp *Carl*

ARMINGHALL (St Mary) *see* Stoke H Cross w Dunston, Arminghall etc *Nor*

ARMITAGE (Holy Trinity) (St John the Baptist) *Lich 3* **P** *Bp* **R** D R H THOMAS

ARMITAGE BRIDGE (St Paul) *see* Em TM *Wakef*

ARMLEY (St Bartholomew) w New Wortley *Ripon 6* **P** *Bp, DBP, and Hyndman Trustees (jt)* **P-in-c** I WRIGHT, **C** G NEWTON

ARMLEY, UPPER (Christ Church) *Ripon 6* **P** *Ch Patr Trust* **V** A SEN, **C** D L M YOUNG

ARMLEY HEIGHTS (Church of the Ascension) *see* Upper Armley *Ripon*

ARMTHORPE (St Leonard and St Mary) *Sheff 8* **P** *Bp* **R** R LANDALL

ARNCLIFFE (St Oswald) *see* Kettlewell w Conistone, Hubberholme etc *Bradf*

ARNE (St Nicholas) *see* Wareham *Sarum*

ARNESBY (St Peter) *see* Hexagon *Leic*

ARNOLD (Emmanuel) *see* Bestwood Em w St Mark *S'well*

ARNOLD (St Mary) *S'well 10* **P** *Bp* **V** K L SHILL, **C** L V NICOLLS

ARNSIDE (St James) *Carl 10* **P** *Bp* **P-in-c** D P COOPER

ARRETON (St George) *Portsm 7* **P** *Bp* **V** J F O'SHAUGHNESSY

ARRINGTON (St Nicholas) *see* Orwell Gp *Ely*

ARROW (Holy Trinity) *see* Alcester and Arrow w Oversley and Weethley *Cov*

ARTHINGTON (St Peter) *see* Lower Wharfedale *Ripon*

ARTHINGWORTH (St Andrew) and Harrington w Oxendon and East Farndon *Pet 2* **P** *St Jo Coll Ox (2 turns), Nugee Foundn (2 turns), and Bp (1 turn)* **R** M Y GARBUTT, **NSM** D SPENCELEY

ARTHURET (St Michael and All Angels) w Kirkandrews-on-Esk and Nicholforest *Carl 2* **P** *Sir James Graham Bt (2 turns), Bp (1 turn)* **R** R TAGUE

ARUNDEL (St Nicholas) w Tortington and South Stoke *Chich 1* **P** *Bp (2 turns), Duke of Norfolk (1 turn)* **V** R D FARRER

ASBY (St Peter) *see* Heart of Eden *Carl*
ASCENSION Team Ministry, The *Leic 1* **P** *Patr Bd*
 TV L B PADMORE
ASCOT, NORTH (St Mary and St John) *see* Ascot Heath *Ox*
ASCOT, SOUTH (All Souls) *see* Sunninghill and S Ascot *Ox*
ASCOT HEATH (All Saints) *Ox 11* **P** *Bp* **R** D D HANNAH,
 NSM R WEBB
ASCOTT UNDER WYCHWOOD (Holy Trinity) *see* Chase *Ox*
ASFORDBY (All Saints) *see* Ab Kettleby and Holwell w
 Asfordby *Leic*
ASGARBY (St Andrew) *see* Heckington Gp *Linc*
ASH (Christ Church) *see* Adderley, Ash, Calverhall, Ightfield etc
 Lich
ASH (Holy Trinity) *see* Martock w Ash *B & W*
ASH (St Nicholas) w Westmarsh *Cant 1* **P** *Abp*
 V J SWEATMAN
ASH (St Peter) *Guildf 1* **P** *Win Coll* **R** K R M BRISTOW,
 NSM C L MONK
ASH (St Peter and St Paul) *Roch 1* **P** J R A B *Scott Esq*
 R *Vacant*
ASH (Thomas Chapel) *see* Sampford Peverell, Uplowman,
 Holcombe Rogus etc *Ex*
ASH PRIORS (Holy Trinity) *see* Milverton w Halse, Fitzhead
 and Ash Priors *B & W*
ASH VALE (St Mary) *Guildf 1* **P** *Bp* **V** N J LAMBERT
ASHAMPSTEAD (St Clement) *see* Basildon w Aldworth and
 Ashampstead *Ox*
ASHBOCKING (All Saints) *see* Clopton w Otley, Swilland and
 Ashbocking *St E*
ASHBOURNE (St John the Baptist) *Derby 8* **P** *Wright Trustees*
 NSM P A SHORT
ASHBOURNE (St Oswald) w Mapleton *Derby 8* **P** *Bp*
 P-in-c G P POND, **C** M C DOYLE, B A WOOD,
 NSM P A SHORT
ASHBRITTLE (St John the Baptist) *see* Wellington and Distr
 B & W
ASHBURNHAM (St Peter) w Penhurst *Chich 14*
 P *Ashburnham Chr Trust* **P-in-c** F R CUMBERLEGE,
 NSM A D WOODING JONES, J H SYKES
ASHBURTON (St Andrew), Bickington, Buckland in the Moor,
 Holne, Huccaby, Leusdon, Princetown, Postbridge, and
 Widecombe-in-the-Moor *Ex 9* **P** *Duchy of Cornwall (1 turn),
 Patr Bd (1 turn)* **TV** C E COOPER, **P-in-c** D C SHERWOOD
ASHBURY (St Mary the Virgin) *see* Shrivenham and Ashbury
 Ox
ASHBY (St Catherine) *see* Bottesford w Ashby *Linc*
ASHBY (St Mary) *see* Somerleyton, Ashby, Fritton,
 Herringfleet etc *Nor*
ASHBY (St Mary) *see* Thurton *Nor*
ASHBY (St Paul) *see* Bottesford w Ashby *Linc*
ASHBY, WEST (All Saints) *see* Hemingby Gp *Linc*
ASHBY-BY-PARTNEY (St Helen) *see* Partney Gp *Linc*
ASHBY-CUM-FENBY (St Peter) *see* Laceby and Ravendale
 Gp *Linc*
ASHBY DE LA LAUNDE (St Hibald) *see* Digby Gp *Linc*
ASHBY-DE-LA-ZOUCH (Holy Trinity) (St Helen) and Breedon
 on the Hill *Leic 8* **P** *Patr Bd* **TR** B A ROBERTSON,
 TV T L PHILLIPS, **C** N P GURNEY, NSM J W A DAWSON,
 T R PARKERSON
ASHBY FOLVILLE (St Mary) *see* S Croxton Gp *Leic*
ASHBY MAGNA (St Mary) *see* Willoughby Waterleys,
 Peatling Magna etc *Leic*
ASHBY PARVA (St Peter) *see* Upper Soar *Leic*
ASHBY PUERORUM (St Andrew) *see* Horncastle Gp *Linc*
ASHBY ST LEDGERS (St Mary) *see* Daventry, Ashby
 St Ledgers, Braunston etc *Pet*
ASHCHURCH (St Nicholas) and Kemerton *Glouc 10* **P** *DBP
 and K Storey Esq (jt)* **R** R E ROBERTS
ASHCOMBE (St Nectan) *see* Teignmouth, Ideford w Luton,
 Ashcombe etc *Ex*
ASHCOTT (All Saints) *see* Shapwick w Ashcott and Burtle
 B & W
ASHDON (All Saints) *see* Saffron Walden w Wendens Ambo,
 Littlebury etc *Chelmsf*
ASHE (Holy Trinity and St Andrew) *see* N Waltham and
 Steventon, Ashe and Deane *Win*
ASHEN (St Augustine) *see* Ridgewell w Ashen, Birdbrook and
 Sturmer *Chelmsf*
ASHENDON (St Mary) *see* Bernwode *Ox*
ASHFIELD, GREAT (All Saints) *see* Badwell and Walsham
 St E
ASHFIELD CUM THORPE (St Mary) *see* Mid Loes *St E*
ASHFORD (St Hilda) *Lon 13* **P** *Bp* **V** C A ROGERS
ASHFORD (St Mary the Virgin) *Cant 6* **P** *Abp*
 P-in-c C G PREECE, **C** J KHOVACS

ASHFORD (St Matthew) *Lon 13* **P** *Ld Chan* **V** R E HORTON
ASHFORD (St Peter) *see* Barnstaple *Ex*
ASHFORD, SOUTH (Christ Church) *Cant 6* **P** *Abp*
 P-in-c A M HIRST
ASHFORD, SOUTH (St Francis of Assisi) *Cant 6* **P** *Abp*
 P-in-c A M HIRST
ASHFORD BOWDLER (St Andrew) *see* Ludlow *Heref*
ASHFORD CARBONEL (St Mary) *as above*
ASHFORD COMMON (St Benedict) *see* Upper Sunbury St
 Sav *Lon*
ASHFORD HILL (St Paul) *see* Kingsclere and Ashford Hill w
 Headley *Win*
ASHFORD IN THE WATER (Holy Trinity) *see* Bakewell,
 Ashford w Sheldon and Rowsley *Derby*
ASHILL (Blessed Virgin Mary) *see* Isle Valley *B & W*
ASHILL (St Nicholas), Carbrooke, Ovington and Saham Toney
 Nor 13 **P** *Bp, New Coll Ox, Cam Univ, and SMF (jt)*
 V J E ATKINS, **OLM** T B C WESTON
ASHILL (St Stephen) *see* Cullompton, Willand, Uffculme,
 Kentisbeare etc *Ex*
ASHINGDON (St Andrew) w South Fambridge, Canewdon and
 Paglesham *Chelmsf 12* **P** *D&C Westmr, Hyndman Trustees,
 and CCC Cam (jt)* **R** T F CLAY
ASHINGTON (Holy Sepulchre) *Newc 11* **P** *Bp* **V** E A BLAND,
 NSM L BEADLE
ASHINGTON (St Matthew) *see* Canford Magna *Sarum*
ASHINGTON (St Peter and St Paul), Washington and Wiston w
 Buncton *Chich 12* **P** *Bp and R H Goring Esq (alt)*
 R C W MACLAY, **C** J A C SEAR
ASHINGTON (St Vincent) *see* Chilton Cantelo, Ashington,
 Mudford, Rimpton etc *B & W*
ASHLEWORTH (St Bartholomew), Corse, Hartpury, Hasfield,
 Maisemore, Staunton and Tirley *Glouc 3* **P** *Bp and
 W G F Meath-Baker Esq (1 turn), Ld Chan (1 turn), Bp
 (1 turn), and Bp and DBP (1 turn)* **R** R I MERCHANT,
 NSM P A WEST
ASHLEY (St Elizabeth) *see* Hale and Ashley *Ches*
ASHLEY (St James), Crudwell, Hankerton and Oaksey *Bris 6*
 P *Bp and Personal Reps W A Sole (3 turns), Duchy of
 Lancaster(1 turn)* **R** B RAVEN
ASHLEY (St John the Baptist) and Mucklestone and Broughton
 and Croxton *Lich 7* **P** *Bp, Meynell Ch Trustees,
 Mrs F F Friend, and T A J Hall Esq (jt)* **R** J P EADES
ASHLEY (St Mary the Virgin) *see* Stoke Albany w Wilbarston
 and Ashley etc *Pet*
ASHLEY (St Mary) w Silverley *Ely 4* **P** *Bp and DBP (alt)*
 P-in-c M A GURNER
ASHLEY (St Peter) *see* Milton *Win*
ASHLEY (St Peter and St Paul) *see* Somborne w Ashley *Win*
ASHLEY GREEN (St John the Evangelist) *see* Gt Chesham *Ox*
ASHMANHAUGH (St Swithin), Barton Turf, Beeston
 St Laurence, Horning, Irstead and Neatishead *Nor 12* **P** *Bp
 and Sir Ronald Preston Bt (jt)* **R** S A ELLISON,
 OLM R R HUME
ASHMANSWORTH (St James) *see* NW Hants *Win*
ASHMORE (St Nicholas) *see* Iwerne Valley *Sarum*
ASHMORE PARK (St Alban) *see* Wednesfield *Lich*
ASHOVER (All Saints) and Brackenfield w Wessington *Derby 5*
 P *Exors Revd J J C Nodder, Duke of Devonshire, V Crich and
 S Wingfield, and DBF (jt)* **R** R G LAWRENCE
ASHOW (Assumption of Our Lady) *see* Stoneleigh w Ashow
 Cov
ASHPERTON (St Bartholomew) *see* Ledbury *Heref*
ASHPRINGTON (St David) *see* Totnes w Bridgetown, Berry
 Pomeroy etc *Ex*
ASHREIGNEY (St James) *Ex 20* **P** *DBP* **R** P J NORMAN
ASHTEAD (St George) (St Giles) *Guildf 10* **P** *Bp*
 R R J KITELEY, **C** S R BUTLER, J A LEVASIER, J M LEVASIER,
 OLM J M WATTS
ASHTON (Annunciation) *see* Breage w Godolphin and Germoe
 Truro
ASHTON (St John the Baptist) *see* Christow, Ashton, Bridford,
 Dunchideock etc *Ex*
ASHTON (St Michael and All Angels) *see* Roade and Ashton w
 Hartwell *Pet*
ASHTON, WEST (St John) *see* Trowbridge St Thos and W
 Ashton *Sarum*
ASHTON GATE (St Francis) *see* Bedminster *Bris*
ASHTON HAYES (St John the Evangelist) *Ches 2*
 P *Keble Coll Ox* **P-in-c** B R K PERKES
ASHTON-IN-MAKERFIELD (Holy Trinity) *Liv 14* **P** *Bp*
 R D R ABBOTT
ASHTON-IN-MAKERFIELD (St Thomas) *Liv 14*
 P *R Ashton-in-Makerfield H Trin* **P-in-c** J P THOMAS
ASHTON KEYNES (Holy Cross), Leigh and Minety *Bris 6*
 P *Bp* **P-in-c** B RAVEN, **C** J A S ASHBY, NSM S E DANBY

ASHTON-ON-RIBBLE (St Andrew)   see W Preston *Blackb*
ASHTON-ON-RIBBLE (St Michael and All Angels)   *as above*
ASHTON UNDER HILL (St Barbara)   see Overbury w
Teddington, Alstone etc *Worc*
ASHTON-UNDER-LYNE (Christ Church) *Man 13*   **P** *Bp*
V L P LONGDEN,   **OLM** A A HILLS
ASHTON-UNDER-LYNE Good Shepherd (Holy Trinity)
(St James) (St Michael and All Angels) (St Gabriel) (St Peter)
Man 13   **P** *Patr Bd*   **TR** R FARNWORTH,
TV J M A PARTRIDGE,   **C** R W A REECE,   **NSM** R FOX,
M WADSWORTH,   **OLM** P E LODGE
ASHTON-UPON-MERSEY (St Martin) *Ches 10*   **P** *SMF*
R R J E CLACK
ASHTON-UPON-MERSEY (St Mary Magdalene) *Ches 10*
P *Trustees*   **V** S B RANKIN,   **C** C G FOSTER,
NSM J BEAUMONT
ASHURST (St James) *Chich 12*   **P** *MMCET*   **R** P M RAMPTON
ASHURST (St Martin of Tours)   see Speldhurst w Groombridge
and Ashurst *Roch*
ASHURST WOOD (St Dunstan)   see Forest Row *Chich*
ASHWATER (St Peter ad Vincula), Halwill, Beaworthy, Clawton
and Tetcott w Luffincott *Ex 17*   **P** *Ld Chan (1 turn),*
Ms C A Friswell, Lt-Col Sir John Molesworth-St Aubyn Bt, and
Bp (jt) (2 turns).   **P-in-c** J E LUCAS
ASHWELL (St Mary)   see Oakham, Ashwell, Braunston,
Brooke, Egleton etc *Pet*
ASHWELL (St Mary the Virgin) w Hinxworth and Newnham
St Alb 16   **P** *Bp, N J A Farr Esq, and T D Smyth Esq (jt)*
(1 turn), Bp (3 turns).   **P-in-c** C J BALL
ASHWELLTHORPE (All Saints), Forncett, Fundenhall,
Hapton, Tacolneston and Wreningham *Nor 7*   **P** *Bp, Keble Coll*
Ox, Ch Coll Cam, and MMCET (by turn)   **P-in-c** A R GOOD,
OLM J A L COOPER
ASHWICK (St James) w Oakhill and Binegar *B & W 7*   **P** *Bp*
P-in-c R W WIDDOWSON
ASHWICKEN (All Saints)   see Gayton, Gayton Thorpe, E
Walton, E Winch etc *Nor*
ASHWORTH (St James)   see Norden w Ashworth *Man*
ASKAM (Church Centre)   see Dalton-in-Furness and
Ireleth-with-Askam *Carl*
ASKAM (St Peter)   *as above*
ASKERN (St Peter) *Sheff 7*   **P** *Bp*   **V** *vacant* (01302) 700404
ASKERSWELL (St Michael), Loders, Powerstock and
Symondsbury *Sarum 2*   **P** *Bp, D&C, and Lady Laskey*
(3 turns), Ld Chan (1 turn)   **R** J DELANEY,   **OLM** E D MARSH
ASKHAM (St Nicholas)   see Retford Area *S'well*
ASKHAM (St Peter)   see Lowther and Askham and Clifton and
Brougham *Carl*
ASKHAM BRYAN (St Nicholas) *York 1*   **P** *Abp*
P-in-c G R MUMFORD
ASKHAM RICHARD (St Mary)   see Healaugh w Wighill,
Bilbrough and Askham Richard *York*
ASKRIGG (St Oswald) w Stallingbusk *Ripon 4*   **P** *V Aysgarth*
P-in-c A B CHAPMAN,   **NSM** I M ROBINSON, M D BLANCH
ASLACKBY (St James)   see Billingborough Gp *Linc*
ASLACTON (St Michael)   see Bunwell, Carleton Rode,
Tibenham, Gt Moulton etc *Nor*
ASLOCKTON (St Thomas)   see Whatton w Aslockton,
Hawksworth, Scarrington etc *S'well*
ASPALL (St Mary of Grace)   see Debenham and Helmingham
St E
ASPATRIA (St Kentigern) w Hayton and Gilcrux *Carl 7*   **P** *Bp*
V C R SHAW,   **Hon C** D R KING
ASPENDEN (St Mary), Buntingford and Westmill *St Alb 16*
P *CPAS, MCET, and K Coll Lon (jt)*   **P-in-c** I R HILL,
NSM G HOWDLE
ASPLEY (St Margaret) *S'well 14*   **P** *Trustees*
P-in-c J G HUTCHINSON
ASPLEY GUISE (St Botolph) w Husborne Crawley and
Ridgmont *St Alb 8*   **P** *Ld Chan (1 turn), Trustees Bedf Estates*
(1 turn), and Bp (2 turns).   **R** G BRADSHAW
ASPULL (St Elizabeth)   see Haigh and Aspull *Liv*
ASSINGTON (St Edmund)   see Bures w Assington and Lt
Cornard *St E*
ASTBURY (St Mary) and Smallwood *Ches 11*   **P** *Sir Richard*
Baker Wilbraham Bt   **R** J D SHARPLES
ASTERBY Group, The *Linc 11*   **P** *Bp, DBP, Exors*
J N Heneage Esq, and F Smith Esq (jt)   **R** A C BUXTON
ASTHALL (St Nicholas)   see Burford w Fulbrook, Taynton,
Asthall etc *Ox*
ASTLEY (St Mary the Virgin)   see Chilvers Coton w Astley *Cov*
ASTLEY (St Mary), Clive, Grinshill and Hadnall *Lich 22*
P *D R B Thompson Esq*   **P-in-c** R R HAARHOFF
ASTLEY (St Peter)   see Shrawley, Witley, Astley and Abberley
Worc

ASTLEY (St Stephen), Tyldesley and Mosley Common *Man 19*
P *DBP and V Leigh*   **TR** R J CARMYLLIE,   **TV** J J HARTLEY,
C J STRATON,   **NSM** J HARNEY,   **OLM** A J DAND
ASTLEY ABBOTTS (St Calixtus)   see Bridgnorth, Tasley,
Astley Abbotts, etc *Heref*
ASTLEY BRIDGE (St Paul) *Man 12*   **P** *The Crown*
V N J MCKEE
ASTON (St Giles)   see Wigmore Abbey *Heref*
ASTON (St James) (St Peter and St Paul) and Nechells *Birm 8*
P *Patr Bd*   **V** A J JOLLEY,   **C** J A ARNOLD, B A WATSON
ASTON (St Mary)   see Woore and Norton in Hales *Lich*
ASTON (St Mary)   see Stevenage St Mary Shephall w Aston
St Alb
ASTON (St Peter)   see Antrobus, Aston by Sutton, Lt Leigh etc
Ches
ASTON (St Saviour)   see Stone St Mich and St Wulfad w Aston
St Sav Lich
ASTON, LITTLE (St Peter) *Lich 1*   **P** *Patr Bd*   **V** P MOON,
OLM D T BROOK
ASTON, NORTH (St Mary the Virgin)   see Steeple Aston w N
Aston and Tackley *Ox*
ASTON ABBOTS (St James the Great)   see Wingrave w
Rowsham, Aston Abbotts and Cublington *Ox*
ASTON BOTTERELL (St Michael and All Angels)   see Ditton
Priors w Neenton, Burwarton etc *Heref*
ASTON CANTLOW (St John the Baptist) and Wilmcote w
Billesley *Cov 7*   **P** *SMF*   **P-in-c** R LIVINGSTON,
Hon C P R BROWN
ASTON CLINTON (St Michael and All Angels) w Buckland and
Drayton Beauchamp *Ox 28*   **P** *Bp, A R Pegg Esq, and Jes Coll*
Ox (jt)   **R** E J MOXLEY,   **C** A M ALLEN
ASTON CUM AUGHTON (All Saints) w Swallownest and Ulley
Sheff 5   **P** *Bp*   **TR** I JENNINGS,   **C** L C BETSON
ASTON EYRE (not known)   see Morville w Aston Eyre *Heref*
ASTON FLAMVILLE (St Peter)   see Burbage w Aston
Flamville *Leic*
ASTON INGHAM (St John the Baptist)   see Ariconium *Heref*
ASTON-LE-WALLS (St Leonard), Byfield, Boddington, Eydon
and Woodford Halse *Pet 1*   **P** *Bp, CCC Ox, and Em Coll Cam*
(2 turns), Ld Chan (1 turn)   **R** S CROSS,   **NSM** G D MOORE
ASTON ON TRENT (All Saints), Elvaston, Weston on Trent and
Shardlow, Barrow upon Trent with Twyford and Swarkestone
Derby 15   **P** *Bp, Earl of Harrington, and Repton Sch (jt)*
R A LUKE,   **NSM** J M INGRAM, P HYGATE
ASTON ROWANT (St Peter and St Paul)   see Chinnor,
Sydenham, Aston Rowant and Crowell *Ox*
ASTON SANDFORD (St Michael and All Angels)
see Haddenham w Cuddington, Kingsey etc *Ox*
ASTON SOMERVILLE (St Mary)   see Winchcombe *Glouc*
ASTON-SUB-EDGE (St Andrew)   see Mickleton, Willersey w
Saintbury etc *Glouc*
ASTON TIRROLD (St Michael)   see The Churn *Ox*
ASTON UPTHORPE (All Saints)   *as above*
ASTWELL Group of Parishes, The *Pet 1*   **P** *Bp, Worc Coll Ox,*
Ox Univ, Mert Coll Ox, DBP, and Jes Coll Ox (jt)
R W T ADAMS,   **NSM** D E MICKLETHWAITE
ASTWICK (St Guthlac)   see Arlesey w Astwick *St Alb*
ASTWOOD (St Peter)   see Sherington w Chicheley, N Crawley,
Astwood etc *Ox*
ASTWOOD BANK (St Matthias and St George)   see Redditch
Ch the K *Worc*
ASWARBY (St Denys)   see S Lafford *Linc*
ASWARDBY (St Helen)   see Partney Gp *Linc*
ATCHAM (St Eata)   see Shrewsbury St Giles w Sutton and
Atcham *Lich*
ATHELINGTON (St Peter)   see Stradbroke, Horham,
Athelington and Redlingfield *St E*
ATHELNEY Benefice, The *B & W 13*   **P** *D&C*   **V** P A STAPLE
ATHERINGTON (St Mary)   see Newton Tracey, Horwood,
Alverdiscott etc *Ex*
ATHERSLEY (St Helen) *Wakef 7*   **P** *Bp*   **V** R H MARSHALL,
C P CARTWRIGHT
ATHERSTONE (St Mary) *Cov 5*   **P** *V Mancetter*
V P I HARRIS
ATHERTON (St John the Baptist) (St George) (St Philip) and
Hindsford w Howe Bridge *Man 19*   **P** *DBP*
TR R W BUCKLEY,   **TV** R W SINCLAIR, K BAINES,
C G M THOMAS
ATLOW (St Philip and St James)   see Hulland, Atlow, Kniveton,
Bradley and Hognaston *Derby*
ATTENBOROUGH (St Mary the Virgin) *S'well 7*   **P** *CPAS*
P-in-c S M HEMSLEY HALLS,   **C** J L STEPHENS
ATTERCLIFFE (St Alban) and Darnall *Sheff 1*   **P** *Bp, Dean*
Sheff, and Sheff Ch Burgesses Trust (jt)   **V** P WHITTINGHAM
ATTLEBOROUGH (Assumption of the Blessed Virgin Mary) w
Besthorpe *Nor 11*   **P** *CR and Mrs S P J Scully (jt)*
R M C JACKSON,   **C** T R LILLEY

ATTLEBOROUGH (Holy Trinity) *Cov 5* **P** *V Nuneaton* **V** C JONES

ATTLEBRIDGE (St Andrew) *see* Wensum Benefice *Nor*

ATWICK (St Lawrence) *see* Hornsea w Atwick *York*

ATWORTH (St Michael and All Angels) w Shaw and Whitley *Sarum 14* **P** *D&C Bris and R Melksham (alt)* **V** J PERRETT, **C** A E EVANS, **NSM** J DARLING, **OLM** E A FIELDEN, A E WINTOUR

AUBOURN (St Peter) *see* Bassingham Gp *Linc*

AUCKLAND (St Andrew) (St Anne) *Dur 6* **P** *Bp* **V** N P VINE

AUCKLAND (St Helen) *Dur 6* **P** *Bp* **V** R I MCTEER, **C** G L NAYLOR

AUCKLAND (St Peter) *Dur 6* **P** *The Crown* **V** vacant (01388) 661856

AUCKLEY (St Saviour) *see* Finningley w Auckley *Sheff*

AUDENSHAW (St Hilda) *Man 13* **P** *Bp* **V** J H KERSHAW

AUDENSHAW (St Stephen) *Man 13* **P** *Bp* **V** P R DIXON

AUDLEM (St James) *see* Wybunbury and Audlem w Doddington *Ches*

AUDLEY (St James the Great) *Lich 9* **P** *Ch Soc Trust* **V** P W DAVIES, **C** G K CHELASHAW

AUGHTON (All Saints) *see* Bubwith w Skipwith *York*

AUGHTON (Christ Church) *Liv 11* **P** *R Aughton St Mich* **V** R MOUGHTIN, **C** P R WESTON

AUGHTON (St Michael) and Bickerstaffe *Liv 11* **P** *Bp and Earl of Derby (jt)* **R** A A HOUSLEY

AUGHTON (St Saviour) *see* Slyne w Hest and Halton w Aughton *Blackb*

AUKBOROUGH (St John the Baptist) *see* Alkborough *Linc*

AULT HUCKNALL (St John the Baptist) and Scarcliffe *Derby 3* **P** *Bp and Duke of Devonshire (alt)* **V** A L BELL

AUNSBY (St Thomas of Canterbury) *see* S Lafford *Linc*

AUST (not known) *see* Almondsbury and Olveston *Bris*

AUSTERFIELD (St Helen) *see* Bawtry w Austerfield and Misson *S'well*

AUSTREY (St Nicholas) *see* N Warks *Birm*

AUSTWICK (Epiphany) *see* Clapham-with-Keasden and Austwick *Bradf*

AVEBURY (St James) *see* Upper Kennet *Sarum*

AVELEY (St Michael) and Purfleet *Chelmsf 14* **P** *Bp* **P-in-c** A T FRANKLAND, **C** A J HUDSON

AVENING (Holy Cross) w Cherington *Glouc 7* **P** E A Tarlton Esq (1 turn), D&C (2 turns) **NSM** C CARTER

AVERHAM (St Michael and All Angels) w Kelham *S'well 3* **P** *DBP* **R** vacant

AVETON GIFFORD (St Andrew) *see* Modbury, Bigbury, Ringmore w Kingston etc *Ex*

AVINGTON (St Mary) *see* Itchen Valley *Win*

AVON DASSETT w Farnborough and Fenny Compton *Cov 8* **P** G V L Holbech Esq and Mrs A D Seyfried (jt), CCC Ox, and Bp(alt) **P-in-c** M G CADWALLADER

AVON-SWIFT Group *see* Gilmorton, Peatling Parva, Kimcote etc *Leic*

AVON VALLEY *Sarum 13* **P** *Bp (3 turns), MOD (2 turns), and Ch Hosp (1 turn)* **C** M T P ZAMMIT, **NSM** R A BUSSEY, T DRAYCOTT

AVON VALLEY PARTNERSHIP *see* Fordingbridge and Breamore and Hale etc *Win*

AVONMOUTH (St Andrew) *see* Lawrence Weston w Avonmouth *Bris*

AWBRIDGE (All Saints) *see* Michelmersh and Awbridge and Braishfield etc *Win*

AWLISCOMBE (St Michael and All Angels) *see* Honiton, Gittisham, Combe Raleigh, Monkton etc *Ex*

AWRE (St Andrew) *see* Newnham w Awre and Blakeney *Glouc*

AWSWORTH (St Peter) *see* Trowell, Awsworth and Cossall *S'well*

AXBRIDGE (St John the Baptist) w Shipham and Rowberrow *B & W 1* **P** *Bp and D&C (alt)* **R** T D HAWKINGS, **NSM** A M HEMMING

AXFORD (St Michael) *see* Whitton *Sarum*

AXMINSTER (St Mary), Chardstock, All Saints, Combpyne w Rousdon and Membury *Ex 5* **P** *Bp* **P-in-c** J W STREETING, **C** J ABBOTT

AXMOUTH (St Michael) *see* Uplyme w Axmouth *Ex*

AYCLIFFE (Church Centre) *see* Dover St Mary *Cant*

AYCLIFFE, GREAT (St Andrew) (St Clare) *Dur 5* **P** *Patr Bd* **TR** L POTTER, **TV** J WING

AYLBURTON (St Mary) *see* Woolaston w Alvington and Aylburton *Glouc*

AYLBURTON COMMON (Mission Church) *see* Lydney *Glouc*

AYLESBEARE (Blessed Virgin Mary), Rockbeare, Farringdon, Clyst Honiton and Sowton *Ex 1* **P** *Bp and D&C (jt)* **P-in-c** M J PARTRIDGE, **C** S J DYSON, K P SPRAY, C S T CANT

AYLESBURY (Holy Trinity) *see* Walton H Trin *Ox*

AYLESBURY (St Mary the Virgin) w Bierton and Hulcott *Ox 21* **P** *Bp and Patr Bd (jt)* **TR** S G L WOOD, **TV** C M ACKFORD, **C** D M CLOAKE, A D WILLIS, **NSM** M WOOD

AYLESBY (St Lawrence) *see* Keelby Gp *Linc*

AYLESFORD (St Peter and St Paul) *Roch 7* **P** *D&C* **V** C J VAN STRAATEN

AYLESHAM (St Peter) w Adisham *Cant 1* **P** *Abp* **P-in-c** J M B HONNOR, **C** J V COLEMAN, **NSM** D N J HALE

AYLESTONE (St Andrew) w St James *Leic 1* **P** *Bp* **R** D APPLEBY

AYLESTONE PARK (Church of the Nativity) *see* Emmaus Par Team *Leic*

AYLMERTON (St John the Baptist), Runton, Beeston Regis, Gresham *Nor 21* **P** *Bp and Guild of All So (2 turns), Duchy of Lanc (1 turn)* **P-in-c** A B BARTON

AYLSHAM (St Michael) *Nor 19* **P** *D&C Cant* **V** R D BRANSON

AYLTON (not known) *see* Ledbury *Heref*

AYMESTREY (St John the Baptist and St Alkmund) *see* Kingsland w Eardisland, Aymestrey etc *Heref*

AYNHO (St Michael) and Croughton w Evenley and Farthinghoe and Hinton-in-the-Hedges w Steane *Pet 1* **P** *Bp (2 turns), Mrs E A J Cartwright-Hignett (1 turn), Magd Coll Ox (1 turn), and Ld Chan (1 turn)* **R** G A BARKER, **NSM** E G SMITH

AYOT ST LAWRENCE (St Lawrence) *see* Kimpton w Ayot St Lawrence *St Alb*

AYOT ST PETER (St Peter) *see* Welwyn *St Alb*

AYSGARTH (St Andrew) *see* Penhill *Ripon*

AYSTON (St Mary the Virgin) *see* Uppingham w Ayston and Wardley w Belton *Pet*

AYTHORPE RODING (St Mary) *see* Gt Canfield w High Roding and Aythorpe Roding *Chelmsf*

AYTON, EAST (St John the Baptist) *see* Seamer w East Ayton *York*

AYTON, GREAT (All Saints) (Christ Church) w Easby and Newton under Roseberry *York 20* **P** *Abp* **V** P H PEVERELL, **NSM** G S JAQUES, J C DEAN

BABBACOMBE (All Saints) *Ex 12* **P** *V St Marychurch* **P-in-c** P E JONES

BABCARY (Holy Cross) *see* Six Pilgrims *B & W*

BABRAHAM (St Peter) *Ely 5* **P** *H R T Adeane Esq* **P-in-c** A C PARTRIDGE

BABWORTH (All Saints) *see* Retford Area *S'well*

BACKFORD (St Oswald) and Capenhurst *Ches 9* **P** *Bp* **R** S M SOUTHGATE

BACKWELL (St Andrew) w Chelvey and Brockley *B & W 12* **P** *DBP* **R** M R CAMPBELL

BACKWORTH (St John) *see* Earsdon and Backworth *Newc*

BACONSTHORPE (St Mary) *see* Barningham w Matlaske w Baconsthorpe etc *Nor*

BACTON (St Andrew), Happisburgh, Hempstead w Eccles and Lessingham, Ridlington, Sea Palling w Waxham, Walcott, and Witton *Nor 12* **P** *Bp, Earl of Kimberley, K Coll Cam, and Sir Edward Evans-Lombe (jt)* **R** P N WOOD

BACTON (St Faith) *see* Ewyas Harold w Dulas, Kenderchurch etc *Heref*

BACTON (St Mary the Virgin) w Wyverstone, Cotton and Old Newton, and Wickham Skeith *St E 6* **P** *Patr Bd (2 turns), Ld Chan (1 turn)* **R** E A VARLEY, **C** J C LALL

BACUP (Christ Church) and Stacksteads *Man 11* **P** *Patr Bd* **TR** G WHITTAKER, **TV** D P WOODALL, **OLM** D ALLEN

BADBY (St Mary) w Newnham and Charwelton w Fawsley and Preston Capes *Pet 3* **P** *Bp* **P-in-c** S A FAULKNER

BADDESLEY, NORTH (All Saints' Mission Church) *see* Ampfield, Chilworth and N Baddesley *Win*

BADDESLEY, NORTH (St John the Baptist) *as above*

BADDESLEY, SOUTH (St Mary the Virgin) *see* Boldre w S Baddesley *Win*

BADDESLEY CLINTON (St Michael) *Birm 6* **P** T W Ferrers-Walker Esq **R** P H GERARD

BADDESLEY ENSOR (St Nicholas) w Grendon *Birm 10* **P** *Bp, V Polesworth, and PCC (jt)* **P-in-c** R E CHAMBERLAIN

BADDILEY (St Michael) and Wrenbury w Burleydam *Ches 15* **P** V Acton and Bp (alt) **V** D W WALTON, **NSM** R M HARRISON

BADDOW, GREAT (Meadgate Church Centre) (St Mary the Virgin) (St Paul) *Chelmsf 9* **P** *Patr Bd* **TR** D P RITCHIE, **TV** M A FARAH, A S M COPELAND, **C** G R HAMBORG, **Hon C** R C MATTHEWS, **NSM** S M SOUTHEE

BADDOW, LITTLE (St Mary the Virgin) *Chelmsf 9* **P** *Bp* **P-in-c** C A ASHLEY, **C** G R HAMBORG

BADGER (St Giles) *see* Beckbury, Badger, Kemberton, Ryton, Stockton etc *Lich*

BADGEWORTH (Holy Trinity), Shurdington and Witcombe w Bentham *Glouc 3* **P** *Bp and F D Hicks Beach Esq (jt)*

R R J A MITCHELL, C S A DANGERFIELD,
NSM A CHAMPION, J K WOODALL
BADGWORTH (St Congar) *see* Crook Peak *B & W*
BADLESMERE (St Leonard) *see* Selling w Throwley,
Sheldwich w Badlesmere etc *Cant*
BADMINTON (St Michael and All Angels) *see* Boxwell,
Leighterton, Didmarton, Oldbury etc *Glouc*
BADMINTON, LITTLE (St Michael and All Angels) *as above*
BADSEY (St James) w Aldington and Offenham and Bretforton
Worc 1 P *Bp and Ch Ch Ox (jt)* V R L COURT,
NSM A M POTTER
BADSHOT LEA (St George) *see* Hale w Badshot Lea *Guildf*
BADSWORTH (St Mary the Virgin) *Wakef 10* P *DBP*
R D MATHERS
BADWELL (St Mary) and Walsham *St E 9* P *Bp, DBP,*
R M Martineau Esq, and Soc of the Faith (jt) P-in-c S A LONG
BAG ENDERBY (St Margaret) *see* S Ormsby Gp *Linc*
BAGBOROUGH (St Pancras) *see* Bishops Lydeard w
Bagborough and Cothelstone *B & W*
BAGBY (St Mary) *see* Thirkleby w Kilburn and Bagby *York*
BAGENDON (St Margaret) *see* Stratton, N Cerney, Baunton
and Bagendon *Glouc*
BAGINTON (St John the Baptist) w Bubbenhall and
Ryton-on-Dunsmore *Cov 6* P *D&C (2 turns), Bp (1 turn),*
Lord Leigh and Bp (1 turn) V D R WINTLE
BAGNALL (St Chad) w Endon *Lich 8* P *R Leek and Meerbrook*
and A D Owen Esq (jt) V A J BETTS
BAGSHOT (Good Shepherd) *see* Savernake *Sarum*
BAGSHOT (St Anne) *Guildf 6* P *Ld Chan* V D J CHILLMAN
BAGULEY (St John the Divine) Brooklands *Man 6* P *Bp and*
A W Hargreaves Esq (jt) V I MCVEETY
BAGWORTH (The Holy Rood) *see* Markfield, Thornton,
Bagworth and Stanton etc *Leic*
BAILDON (St John the Evangelist) (St Hugh Mission Church)
(St James) *Bradf 1* P *J P Baxter Esq* V J D NOWELL,
C P DEO, NSM S KENNEDY, C SKELTON
BAIN VALLEY Group, The *Linc 11* P *Baroness*
Willoughby de Eresby, R H Spurrier Esq, and DBP (1 turn),
Ld Chan (1 turn) NSM R E DONE, OLM M DONE
BAINTON (St Andrew) *see* Woldsburn *York*
BAINTON (St Mary) *see* Barnack w Ufford and Bainton *Pet*
BAKEWELL (All Saints), Ashford in the Water w Sheldon and
Rowsley *Derby 2* P *Bp, D&C, and Duke of Rutland (jt)*
V A P KAUNHOVEN
BALBY (St John the Evangelist) *Sheff 9* P *Bp* V B J INSTON
BALCOMBE (St Mary) *Chich 6* P *P A D Secretan Esq*
P-in-c D J BURTON
BALDERSBY (St James) *see* Topcliffe, Baldersby w Dishforth,
Dalton etc *York*
BALDERSTONE (St Leonard) *Blackb 7* P *V Blackb*
P-in-c P D ROLFE
BALDERSTONE (St Mary) *Man 17* P *Trustees*
P-in-c A FORD
BALDERTON (St Giles) and Barnby-in-the-Willows *S'well 3*
P *Bp and Ld Chan (alt)* V A I TUCKER
BALDOCK (St Mary the Virgin) w Bygrave and Weston
St Alb 16 P *Patr Bd* TR A P HOLFORD, TV S TETZLAFF
BALDWIN (St Luke) *see* Marown *S & M*
BALE (All Saints) *see* Stiffkey and Bale *Nor*
BALHAM (St Mary and St John the Divine) *S'wark 17* P *Bp*
and Keble Coll Ox (jt) V W ROEST, OLM R E SERBUTT
BALHAM HILL (Ascension) *S'wark 17* P *Bp* V S J HANCE,
C K V SEAGRAVE, NSM D V PENNIECOOKE, P J HOUGHTON
BALKWELL (St Peter) *Newc 5* P *Bp* P-in-c F M WILSON
BALLAM (St Matthew) *see* Ribby cum Wrea and Weeton
Blackb
BALLAUGH (St Mary) (St Mary Old Church) *S & M 3*
P *The Crown* R C D ROGERS
BALLIDON (All Saints) *see* Wirksworth *Derby*
BALLINGER (St Mary Mission Hall) *see* Gt Missenden w
Ballinger and Lt Hampden *Ox*
BALLINGHAM (St Dubricius) *see* Heref S Wye *Heref*
BALSALL COMMON (St Peter) *Birm 11* P *Bp*
V P W THOMAS
BALSALL HEATH (St Barnabas) *see* Sparkbrook St Agatha w
Balsall Heath St Barn *Birm*
BALSALL HEATH (St Paul) and Edgbaston *Birm 5* P *Bp and*
Sir Euan Anstruther-Gough-Calthorpe Bt (jt) V C A GRYLLS,
C D BUCKLEY, NSM U H K LANDMANN
BALSCOTE (St Mary Magdalene) *see* Ironstone *Ox*
BALSHAM (Holy Trinity), Weston Colville, West Wickham and
West Wratting *Ely 5* P *Bp, D&C, and Charterhouse (jt)*
P-in-c J M NORRIS
BALTERLEY (All Saints' Memorial Church) *see* Barthomley
Ches

BALTONSBOROUGH (St Dunstan) w Butleigh, West Bradley
and West Pennard *B & W 4* P *Bp* P-in-c J A JACK
BAMBER BRIDGE (St Aidan) *Blackb 5* P *Bp*
P-in-c T R WEBBER
BAMBER BRIDGE (St Saviour) *Blackb 5* P *V Blackb*
P-in-c G HALSALL
BAMBURGH (St Aidan) *Newc 7* P *Exors Lady Armstrong*
V B C HURST
BAMFORD (St John the Baptist) *see* Hathersage w Bamford
and Derwent and Grindleford *Derby*
BAMFORD (St Michael) *see* Oakenrod and Bamford *Man*
BAMFURLONG (Good Shepherd) *see* Abram *Liv*
BAMPTON (Holy Trinity) (St James) (St Mary) w Clanfield
Ox 8 P *Bp, DBP, St Jo Coll Ox, D&C Ex, and*
B Babington-Smith Esq (jt) V D J LLOYD
BAMPTON (St Michael and All Angels), Morebath, Clayhanger,
Petton and Huntsham *Ex 8* P *Bp, DBP, and D&C (jt)*
V L BURGON
BAMPTON (St Patrick) *see* Shap w Swindale and Bampton w
Mardale *Carl*
BAMPTON ASTON (St James) *see* Bampton w Clanfield *Ox*
BAMPTON LEW (Holy Trinity) *as above*
BAMPTON PROPER (St Mary) *as above*
BANBURY (St Francis) *Ox 5* P *Bp* V D JACKSON,
C C T GAYNOR
BANBURY (St Hugh) *Ox 5* P *Bp* P-in-c P S DAVIES
BANBURY (St Leonard) *Ox 5* P *Bp* P-in-c E S BURCHELL
BANBURY (St Mary) *Ox 5* P *Bp* P-in-c L J GREEN,
C B J SHIN, NSM J J WEST, S NEWBY
BANBURY (St Paul) *Ox 5* P *Bp* P-in-c E N COOMBS,
C L R FOSTER
BANHAM (St Mary) *see* Quidenham Gp *Nor*
BANKFOOT (St Matthew) *Bradf 2* P *Bp* P-in-c J W HINTON
BANKS (St Stephen's Church within the School) Conventional
District *Liv 9* Min R J GIBBS
BANNINGHAM (St Botolph) *see* King's Beck *Nor*
BANSFIELD *St E 8* P *DBP, Mrs G S M Slater, and Ld Chan*
(by turn) R S J ABBOTT
BANSTEAD (All Saints) *Guildf 9* P *Bp* V M PALLIS
BANWELL (St Andrew) *B & W 10* P *D&C Bris*
P-in-c J W FRANKS
BAPCHILD (St Lawrence) *see* Murston w Bapchild and Tonge
Cant
BAR HILL (not known) *Ely 6* P *Bp* P-in-c R H ADAMS
BARBON (St Bartholomew) *see* Kirkby Lonsdale *Carl*
BARBOURNE (St Stephen) *Worc 6* P *Bp* V S W CURRIE,
NSM G D MORPHY, J B WEBB
BARBROOK (St Bartholomew) *see* Combe Martin,
Berrynarbor, Lynton, Brendon etc *Ex*
BARBY (St Mary) w Kilsby *Pet 3* P *Bp*
R P M DE LA P BERESFORD
BARCHESTON (St Martin) *see* S Warks Seven Gp *Cov*
BARCOMBE (St Francis) (St Mary the Virgin) *Chich 18*
P *Ld Chan* R J W HOLLINGSWORTH
BARDFIELD, GREAT (St Mary the Virgin) and LITTLE
(St Katherine) *Chelmsf 18* P *Ch Union Trust*
P-in-c R W F BEAKEN
BARDFIELD SALING (St Peter and St Paul) *see* Stebbing and
Lindsell w Gt and Lt Saling *Chelmsf*
BARDNEY (St Laurence) *Linc 11* P *DBP (1 turn), Bp*
(2 turns), and St Jo Coll Cam (1 turn) NSM H E JEFFERY
BARDON HILL (St Peter) *see* Coalville w Bardon Hill and
Ravenstone *Leic*
BARDSEA (Holy Trinity) *see* Pennington and Lindal w Marton
and Bardsea *Carl*
BARDSEY (All Hallows) *Ripon 5* P *G L Fox Esq*
V C PUCKRIN
BARDSLEY (Holy Trinity) *Man 16* P *Wm Hulme Trustees*
V A D GRANT, OLM E M LOWE
BARDWELL (St Peter and St Paul) *see* Blackbourne *St E*
BARE (St Christopher) *Blackb 11* P *Bp* V D L HEAP
BARFORD (St Botolph) *see* Barnham Broom and Upper Yare
Nor
BARFORD (St John) *see* Deddington w Barford, Clifton and
Hempton *Ox*
BARFORD (St Martin) *see* Nadder Valley *Sarum*
BARFORD (St Michael) *see* Deddington w Barford, Clifton
and Hempton *Ox*
BARFORD (St Peter) w Wasperton and Sherbourne *Cov 8*
P *Major J M Mills, R Hampton Lucy, and Lady Jeryl*
Smith-Ryland (jt) P-in-c D C JESSETT, NSM C O S S DAVIES
BARFORD, GREAT (All Saints) *see* Riversmeet *St Alb*
BARFREYSTONE (St Nicholas) *see* Eythorne and Elvington
w Waldershare etc *Cant*
BARHAM (St Giles) *see* E Leightonstone *Ely*

BARHAM (St John the Baptist) w Bishopsbourne and Kingston
Cant 1 **P** *Abp* **P-in-c** S J A HARDY,
NSM E R G HOPTHROW, L A HARDY
BARHAM (St Mary) *see* Claydon and Barham *St E*
BARHAM DOWNS *see* Barham w Bishopsbourne and
Kingston *Cant*
BARHOLME (St Martin) *see* Uffington Gp *Linc*
BARKBY (St Mary) *see* Fosse *Leic*
BARKESTONE (St Peter and St Paul) *see* Vale of Belvoir *Leic*
BARKHAM (St James) *see* Arborfield w Barkham *Ox*
BARKING (St Erkenwald) *Chelmsf 1* **P** *Bp* **V** C N POOLEY
BARKING (St Margaret) (St Patrick) *Chelmsf 1* **P** *Patr Bd*
TR G M TARRY, **TV** W T SMALLMAN, G M BARLEY
BARKING (St Mary) *see* Ringshall w Battisford, Barking w
Darmsden etc *St E*
BARKINGSIDE (Holy Trinity) *Chelmsf 4* **P** *V* Gt Ilford
V E A J CARGILL THOMPSON
BARKINGSIDE (St Cedd) *Chelmsf 4* **P** *Bp*
V S G O O OLUKANMI, **NSM** M FLINTOFT-CHAPMAN
BARKINGSIDE (St Francis of Assisi) *Chelmsf 4* **P** *Bp*
V A R FENBY
BARKINGSIDE (St George) *Chelmsf 4* **P** *Bp* **V** B J WALLIS
BARKINGSIDE (St Laurence) *Chelmsf 4* **P** *Bp* **V** E A GUEST,
NSM S M TAYLOR
BARKISLAND (Christ Church) w West Scammonden *Wakef 4*
P *V Halifax* **V** C WRAY, **NSM** C A HIRST
BARKSTON (St Nicholas) and Hough Group, The *Linc 22*
P *Sir Oliver Thorold Bt; the Revd J R H Thorold and
J R Thorold Esq; Lord Brownlow; and Sir Lyonel Tollemache Bt
(by turn)* **C** L E M HALL, **NSM** S J HADLEY
BARKSTON ASH (Holy Trinity) *see* Sherburn in Elmet w
Saxton *York*
BARKWAY (St Mary Magdalene), Reed and Buckland w Barley
St Alb 16 **P** *The Crown and DBP (alt)* **P-in-c** S C HILLMAN,
NSM S O FALASCHI-RAY
BARKWITH Group, The *Linc 5* **P** *D&C, J N Heneage Esq,
K Coll Lon, and DBP (by turn)* **P-in-c** P C PATRICK
BARKWITH, EAST (St Mary) *see* Barkwith Gp *Linc*
BARLASTON (St John the Baptist) *Lich 13* **P** *Countess of
Sutherland* **P-in-c** J Y TILLIER
BARLAVINGTON (St Mary), Burton w Coates and Sutton w
Bignor *Chich 11* **P** *Lord Egremont and Miss J B Courtauld (jt)*
P-in-c D C G BROWN
BARLBOROUGH (St James) and Renishaw *Derby 3*
P *Prime Min and Sir Reresby Sitwell Bt (alt)* **C** H GUEST,
S T SHORT, **NSM** M GUEST
BARLBY (All Saints) w Riccall *York 2* **P** *Abp and
V Hemingbrough (jt)* **P-in-c** F LOFTUS
BARLESTONE (St Giles) *see* Newbold de Verdun, Barlestone
and Kirkby Mallory *Leic*
BARLEY (St Margaret of Antioch) *see* Barkway, Reed and
Buckland w Barley *St Alb*
BARLING (All Saints) w Little Wakering *Chelmsf 12* **P** *D&C
St Paul's and Bp (alt)* **P-in-c** A J HURD, **NSM** T G A BROWN
BARLING MAGNA (All Saints) *see* Barling w Lt Wakering
Chelmsf
BARLINGS (St Edward) *Linc 3* **P** *DBP* **V** R G SPAIGHT
BARLOW (not known) *see* Brayton *York*
BARLOW, GREAT (St Lawrence) *see* Old Brampton and Great
Barlow *Derby*
BARLOW MOOR (Emmanuel) *see* Didsbury St Jas and Em
Man
BARMBY MOOR Group, The (St Catherine) *York 5* **P** *Abp
(1 turn), Abp and Trustees Duke of Norfolk's Settlement
Everingham Fund (2 turns)* **V** G M DALLEY,
NSM J H DAWKINS
BARMING (St Margaret of Antioch) w West Barming *Roch 7*
P *Ld Chan* **R** N S MCGREGOR
BARMING HEATH (St Andrew) *Cant 12* **P** *Abp* **V** B REED
BARMSTON (All Saints) *see* Skipsea and Barmston w
Fraisthorpe *York*
BARNACK (St John the Baptist) w Ufford and Bainton *Pet 11*
P *Bp and St Jo Coll Cam (alt)* **R** *vacant* (01780) 740234
BARNACRE (All Saints) *see* Scorton and Barnacre and Calder
Vale *Blackb*
BARNARD CASTLE (St Mary) w Whorlton *Dur 7* **P** *Trin Coll
Cam* **V** A J HARDING, **C** A P MILLER
BARNARDISTON (All Saints) *see* Stourhead *St E*
BARNBURGH (St Peter) w Melton on the Hill and
Aldwick-upon-Dearne *Sheff 12* **P** *Ld Chan (2 turns), Bp
(1 turn)* **R** *vacant* (01709) 892598
BARNBY (St John the Baptist) *see* Worlingham w Barnby and
N Cove *St E*
BARNBY, EAST (Mission Chapel) *see* Hinderwell, Roxby and
Staithes etc *York*

BARNBY DUN (St Peter and St Paul) *Sheff 8* **P** *Bp*
P-in-c J M FODEN, **NSM** J BARKER
BARNBY IN THE WILLOWS (All Saints) *see* Balderton and
Barnby-in-the-Willows *S'well*
BARNEHURST (St Martin) *Roch 15* **P** *Bp* **V** G J BOWEN
BARNES Team Ministry, The (St Mary) (Holy Trinity)
(St Michael and All Angels) *S'wark 16* **P** *Patr Bd*
TR R M SEWELL, **TV** P W HOLLAND, J BOULTON-REYNOLDS,
NSM A J ROBERTS, D A THOMAS
BARNET (Christ Church) *see* S Mimms Ch Ch *Lon*
BARNET (St John the Baptist) *see* Chipping Barnet *St Alb*
BARNET (St Stephen) *as above*
BARNET, EAST (St Mary the Virgin) *St Alb 14* **P** *The Crown*
R R F WATSON
BARNET, NEW (St James) *St Alb 14* **P** *Ch Patr Trust*
P-in-c B UNWIN
BARNET VALE (St Mark) *see* Chipping Barnet *St Alb*
BARNETBY LE WOLD (St Barnabas) *see* N Wolds Gp *Linc*
BARNEY (St Mary), Fulmodeston w Croxton, Hindringham,
Thursford, Great and Little Snoring w Kettlestone and
Pensthorpe *Nor 15* **P** *Lord Hastings, St Jo Coll Cam, D&C,
DBP, and CCC Cam (by turn)* **R** J MUGGLETON
BARNHAM (St Gregory) *see* Blackbourne *St E*
BARNHAM (St Mary) *see* Aldingbourne, Barnham and
Eastergate *Chich*
BARNHAM BROOM (St Peter and St Paul) and Upper Yare
Nor 17 **P** *Patr Bd* **TV** T A P WEATHERSTONE,
P-in-c A-L ALDER, **OLM** R A JACKSON
BARKNINGHAM (St Andrew) *see* Stanton, Hopton, Market
Weston, Barningham etc *St E*
BARNINGHAM (St Mary the Virgin) w Matlaske w
Baconsthorpe w Plumstead w Hempstead *Nor 18* **P** *Duchy of
Lanc (1 turn), Lady Mott-Radclyffe, CPAS, and D&C (jt)
(1 turn)* **P-in-c** W M CARTWRIGHT
BARNINGHAM (St Michael and All Angels) w Hutton Magna
and Wycliffe *Ripon 2* **P** *Bp and V Gilling and Kirkby
Ravensworth (jt)* **P-in-c** J M RICHARDS
BARNINGHAM, LITTLE (St Andrew), Blickling, Edgefield,
Itteringham w Mannington, Oulton w Irmingland, Saxthorpe w
Corpusty and Wickmere w Wolterton *Nor 19* **P** *Bp, Lord
Walpole, SMF, MMCET (2 turns), and Pemb Coll Cam (1 turn)*
P-in-c M J HARRISON
BARNINGHAM WINTER (St Mary the Virgin)
see Barningham w Matlaske w Baconsthorpe etc *Nor*
BARNOLDBY LE BECK (St Helen) *Linc 10* **P** *Ld Chan*
NSM A HUNDLEBY
BARNOLDSWICK (Holy Trinity) (St Mary le Gill) w Bracewell
Bradf 7 **P** *Bp* **V** J R LANCASTER
BARNSBURY (St Andrew) *Lon 6* **P** *Patr Bd*
TR M W LEARMOUTH, **TV** D E FELL, **C** M FLETCHER,
J S SWIFT
BARNSLEY (St Edward the Confessor) *Wakef 7* **P** *Bp*
P-in-c M S POSKITT
BARNSLEY (St George's Parish Church Centre) *Wakef 7* **P** *Bp*
V D P J MUNBY
BARNSLEY (St Mary) *see* Fairford Deanery *Glouc*
BARNSLEY (St Mary) *Wakef 7* **P** *Bp*
P-in-c P R S DUCKWORTH, **C** N O TRAYNOR, **NSM** A J EARL
BARNSLEY (St Paul) Old Town *see* Barnsley St Mary *Wakef*
BARNSLEY (St Peter and St John the Baptist) *Wakef 7* **P** *Bp*
V *vacant* (01226) 282220
BARNSTAPLE (St Peter and St Mary Magdalene) (Holy
Trinity) *Ex 15* **P** *Patr Bd (4 turns), Ld Chan (1 turn)*
TV S G MAY, G CHAVE-COX, P K NIEMIEC, D M FLETCHER,
N B DILKES, **C** A DODWELL
BARNSTON (Christ Church) *Ches 8* **P** *Bp* **C** I G URQUHART
BARNSTON (St Andrew) *see* Gt Dunmow and Barnston
Chelmsf
BARNSTONE (St Mary Mission Room) *see* Cropwell Bishop w
Colston Bassett, Granby etc *S'well*
BARNT GREEN (St Andrew) *see* Cofton Hackett w Barnt
Green *Birm*
BARNTON (Christ Church) *Ches 4* **P** *Bp* **V** P NEWMAN
BARNWELL (All Saints) (St Andrew), Hemington, Luddington
in the Brook, Lutton, Polebrook and Thurning *Pet 10* **P** *Bp,
MMCET, Em Coll Cam, DBP, and Sir Philip
Naylor-Leyland Bt (jt)* **R** C R IEVINS
BARNWOOD (St Lawrence) *Glouc 2* **P** *D&C*
P-in-c A MORRIS, **NSM** A D HAYMAN, L SPARKES
BARONY OF BURGH, The (St Michael) *Carl 3* **P** *Patr Bd*
R *vacant* (01228) 576324
BARR, GREAT (St Margaret) *Lich 25* **P** *M D S Farnham*
V M C RUTTER, **NSM** T W WARD
BARRINGTON (All Saints) *see* Orwell Gp *Ely*
BARRINGTON (Blessed Virgin Mary) *see* Winsmoor *B & W*

BARRINGTON, GREAT (St Mary) *see* Sherborne, Windrush, the Barringtons etc *Glouc*
BARRINGTON, LITTLE (St Peter) *as above*
BARROW (All Saints) *St E 13* **P** *Ld Chan (1 turn), Mrs E C Gordon-Lennox, the Russell-Cooke Trust Co and Bp (1 turn), and St Jo Coll Cam (1 turn)* **V** B L K SHERLOCK
BARROW and Goxhill *Linc 6* **P** *Ld Chan* **V** J C GIRTCHEN
BARROW (St Bartholomew) *Ches 2* **P** *D Okell Esq* **R** C A RANDALL
BARROW (St Giles) *see* Broseley w Benthall, Jackfield, Linley etc *Heref*
BARROW, NORTH (St Matthew) (St James the Great) *Carl 8* **P** *Patr Bd* **TR** M PEAT, **C** R M JOHN
BARROW, NORTH (St Nicholas) *see* Six Pilgrims *B & W*
BARROW, SOUTH (St Peter) *as above*
BARROW GURNEY (The Blessed Virgin Mary and St Edward King and Martyr) *see* Long Ashton w Barrow Gurney and Flax Bourton *B & W*
BARROW HILL (St Andrew) *see* Staveley and Barrow Hill *Derby*
BARROW-IN-FURNESS (St Aidan) *see* S Barrow *Carl*
BARROW-IN-FURNESS (St George) *as above*
BARROW-IN-FURNESS (St John the Evangelist) *Carl 8* **P** *DBP* **P-in-c** S HUGHES
BARROW-IN-FURNESS (St Luke) *see* S Barrow *Carl*
BARROW-IN-FURNESS (St Mark) *Carl 8* **P** *Bp* **V** I K HOOK, **C** E A A NORTHEY, J E NORTHEY
BARROW-IN-FURNESS (St Mary the Virgin) *see* Walney Is *Carl*
BARROW IN FURNESS (St Paul) *Carl 8* **P** *Simeon's Trustees* **R** D H PRICE, **NSM** E A BATES
BARROW-ON-HUMBER (Holy Trinity) *see* Barrow and Goxhill *Linc*
BARROW-ON-TRENT (St Wilfrid) *see* Aston on Trent, Elvaston, Weston on Trent etc *Derby*
BARROW UPON SOAR (Holy Trinity) w Walton le Wolds *Leic 6* **P** *St Jo Coll Cam and DBP (jt)* **P-in-c** R M PADDISON, **Hon C** M R SAMUEL, **NSM** N J MCGINTY
BARROWBY (All Saints) and Gonerby, Great *Linc 19* **P** *R Grantham, and Duke of Devonshire (by turn)* **R** P HOPKINS
BARROWDEN (St Peter) and Wakerley w South Luffenham and Morcott w Duddington and Tixover *Pet 12* **P** *Burghley Ho Preservation Trust, P W Rowley Esq, and Bp (3 turns), Ball Coll Ox (1 turn)* **P-in-c** G ANGELL
BARROWFORD (St Thomas) and Newchurch-in-Pendle *Blackb 6* **P** *Ld Chan and trustees (alt)* **V** J M HALLOWS
BARSHAM (Holy Trinity) *see* Wainford *St E*
BARSHAM, EAST (All Saints) *see* Walsingham, Houghton and Barsham *Nor*
BARSHAM, NORTH (All Saints) *as above*
BARSHAM, WEST (The Assumption of the Blessed Virgin Mary) *as above*
BARSTON (St Swithin) *Birm 11* **P** *MMCET* **P-in-c** R D TURNER
BARTHOMLEY (St Bertoline) *Ches 11* **P** *Lord O'Neill* **P-in-c** D C SPEEDY, **Hon C** C A M SPEEDY
BARTLEY (Mission Church) *see* Copythorne *Win*
BARTLEY GREEN (St Michael and All Angels) *Birm 2* **P** *Bp* **V** K S ELLIS, **C** E J SPARROW, **NSM** B M A ROBERTS
BARTLOW (St Mary) *see* Linton *Ely*
BARTON (St Cuthbert w St Mary) *see* E Richmond *Ripon*
BARTON (St Lawrence) *see* Fellside Team *Blackb*
BARTON (St Mark's Chapel) w Peel Green (St Michael and All Angels) (St Catherine) *Man 18* **P** *Bp and TR Eccles* **P-in-c** B LAMB
BARTON (St Martin) *see* Torquay St Martin Barton *Ex*
BARTON (St Michael), Pooley Bridge and Martindale *Carl 4* **P** *Bp and Earl of Lonsdale (jt)* **P-in-c** D C WOOD
BARTON (St Paul) *Portsm 8* **P** *R Whippingham* **V** P E PIMENTEL
BARTON (St Peter) *see* Lordsbridge *Ely*
BARTON, GREAT (Holy Innocents) *St E 13* **P** *Sir Michael Bunbury Bt* **P-in-c** A R GATES
BARTON BENDISH (St Andrew) w Beachamwell and Shingham *Ely 9* **P** *Bp and DBP (alt)* **P-in-c** B L BURTON
BARTON HARTSHORN (St James) *see* The Claydons and Swan *Ox*
BARTON HILL (St Luke w Ch Ch) and Moorfields St Matthew *Bris 3* **P** *Bp, CPAS, and V Bris St Phil and St Jacob w Em (jt)* **P-in-c** D FRAZER, **NSM** J M GAINSBOROUGH
BARTON IN FABIS (St George) *S'well 9* **P** *Ld Chan* **P-in-c** R I COLEMAN
BARTON-LE-CLEY (St Nicholas) w Higham Gobion and Hexton *St Alb 8* **P** *The Crown (3 turns), Mrs F A A Cooper (1 turn)* **R** G H NEWTON

BARTON-LE-STREET (St Michael) *see* The Street Par *York*
BARTON MILLS (St Mary) *see* Mildenhall *St E*
BARTON-ON-THE-HEATH (St Lawrence) *see* S Warks Seven Gp *Cov*
BARTON SEAGRAVE (St Botolph) w Warkton *Pet 9* **P** *Ch Soc Trust (2 turns), Duke of Buccleuch (1 turn)* **R** M W LUCAS
BARTON ST DAVID (St David) *see* Wheathill Priory Gp *B & W*
BARTON STACEY (All Saints) *see* Lower Dever *Win*
BARTON TURF (St Michael) *see* Ashmanhaugh, Barton Turf etc *Nor*
BARTON UNDER NEEDWOOD (St James) w Dunstall and Tatenhill *Lich 14* **P** *Bp and Sir Rupert Hardy Bt (jt)* **V** A R RIDLEY
BARTON UPON HUMBER (St Mary) *Linc 6* **P** *Bp* **V** D P ROWETT, **C** K E COLWELL, **NSM** A E BROWN, **OLM** A W WRIGHT
BARTON UPON IRWELL (St Catherine) *see* Barton w Peel Green *Man*
BARWELL (St Mary) w Potters Marston and Stapleton *Leic 10* **P** *R J W Titley Esq* **R** P WATSON
BARWICK (St Mary Magdalene) *see* Yeovil H Trin w Barwick *B & W*
BARWICK IN ELMET (All Saints) *Ripon 8* **P** *Duchy of Lanc* **P-in-c** A J NICHOLSON
BASCHURCH (All Saints) and Weston Lullingfield w Hordley *Lich 17* **P** *Ch Patr Trust and Bp (jt)* **R** J J WILSON
BASCOTE HEATH (Chapel) *see* Radford Semele *Cov*
BASEGREEN (St Peter) *see* Gleadless *Sheff*
BASFORD (St Leodegarius) (St Aidan) *S'well 12* **P** *Bp* **V** R SHAW
BASFORD (St Mark) *Lich 9* **P** *Bp* **P-in-c** T B BLOOR, **NSM** F P DUNN
BASFORD, NEW (St Augustine) *see* Basford St Leodegarius and St Aid *S'well*
BASHLEY (St John) *see* Milton *Win*
BASILDON (St Andrew) (Holy Cross) *Chelmsf 6* **P** *Bp* **TV** M A SHAW, **C** R P BINKS
BASILDON (St Martin of Tours) *Chelmsf 6* **P** *Bp* **R** E E MCCAFFERTY, **Hon C** N M WOOD
BASILDON (St Stephen) w Aldworth and Ashampstead *Ox 12* **P** *St Jo Coll Cam, Simeon's Trustees, and DBF (by turn)* **P-in-c** W H N WATTS, **OLM** A KIGGELL
BASING, OLD (St Mary) and Lychpit *Win 4* **P** *Magd Coll Ox* **V** A S BISHOP, **C** M JONES
BASINGSTOKE (All Saints) (St Michael) *Win 4* **P** *Patr Bd* **TR** J M STOKER, **TV** R E RUTHERFORD, S P HEATHER, M A PHILLIPS, A BOTHAM, **NSM** P PALMER
BASINGSTOKE Brighton Hill (Christ the King) *see* Basingstoke *Win*
BASINGSTOKE Popley (Bethlehem Chapel) *as above*
BASINGSTOKE South Ham (St Peter) *as above*
BASLOW (St Anne) and Eyam *Derby 2* **P** *Duke of Devonshire and Earl Temple (jt)* **R** A S MONTGOMERIE
BASSENTHWAITE (St Bega) *see* Binsey *Carl*
BASSENTHWAITE (St John) *as above*
BASSETT (St Michael and All Angels) *see* N Stoneham and Bassett *Win*
BASSETT GREEN (St Christopher) *as above*
BASSINGBOURN (St Peter and St Paul) *Ely 7* **P** *D&C Westmr* **P-in-c** D C R MCFADYEN
BASSINGHAM Group, The (St Michael and All Angels) *Linc 18* **P** *Lady Jean Nevile, CCC Ox, Lord Middleton, Bp, and W R S Brown Esq (jt)* **R** N J BUCK
BASSINGTHORPE (St Thomas à Becket) *see* N Beltisloe Gp *Linc*
BASTON (St John the Baptist) *see* Ness Gp *Linc*
BASWICH or Berkswich (Holy Trinity) *Lich 10* **P** *Bp* **V** P A GRAYSMITH, **NSM** E J BISHOP, J G COTTERILL, K A SHAW
BATCOMBE (Blessed Virgin Mary) *see* Bruton and Distr *B & W*
BATCOMBE (St Mary) *see* Wriggle Valley *Sarum*
BATH Bathwick (St John the Baptist) (Blessed Virgin Mary) *B & W 8* **P** *Bp* **R** D J PROTHERO
BATH (Christ Church) Proprietary Chapel *B & W 10* **P** *R Walcot* *vacant*
BATH (Holy Trinity) *B & W 8* **P** *SMF* **P-in-c** M S HART
BATH Odd Down (St Philip and St James) w Combe Hay *B & W 8* **P** *Simeon's Trustees* **V** A BAIN, **NSM** M JOYCE
BATH (St Barnabas) w Englishcombe *B & W 8* **P** *Bp* **P-in-c** C A SOURBUT
BATH (St Bartholomew) *B & W 8* **P** *Simeon's Trustees* **V** I R LEWIS, **C** J D MILLER

BATH (St Luke) *B & W 8*   **P** *Simeon's Trustees*
P-in-c M D H FRANKUM
BATH (St Mary Magdalene) Holloway, Extra-parochial
Chapelry *B & W 10*   **P** *Bath Municipal Charities for Ld Chan*
Min W G BURMAN
BATH (St Michael) w St Paul *B & W 8*   **P** *CPAS*
R M C LLOYD WILLIAMS, **C** S P FAUX
BATH (St Saviour) w Swainswick and Woolley *B & W 8*
P *Ch Patr Trust and Or Coll Ox (jt)*   **R** M J NORMAN,
NSM K V HOWES
BATH (St Stephen)   *see Charlcombe w Bath St Steph B & W*
BATH Twerton-on-Avon (Ascension) (St Michael) *B & W 8*
P *Patr Bd*   **TR** R G WILSON, **TV** R J PIMM
BATH Walcot (St Andrew) (St Swithin) *B & W 8*   **P** *Simeon's*
Trustees   **P-in-c** S G HOLLAND, **C** M R WILKINS
BATH Weston (All Saints) w North Stoke and Langridge *B & W 8*
P *Ld Chan*   **R** P J WHITWORTH, **C** M A JONES,
NSM J N RAWLINSON, P J NORMAN, C A R BURGESS
BATH Weston (St John the Evangelist) (Emmanuel) w Kelston
B & W 8   **P** *Ld Chan*   **R** C R GARRETT
BATH Widcombe (St Matthew) (St Thomas à Becket) *B & W 8*
P *Simeon's Trustees*   **C** T S BUCKLEY, **NSM** D D SIRCAR
BATH ABBEY (St Peter and St Paul) w St James *B & W 8*
P *Simeon's Trustees*   **R** T E MASON, **C** A J P GARROW,
C E ROBSON, A W MCCONNAUGHIE, **NSM** S E HARTLEY
BATHAMPTON (St Nicholas) w Claverton *B & W 8*
P *D&C Bris and Personal Reps R L D Skrine Esq (jt)*
R P BURDEN
BATHEALTON (St Bartholomew)   *see Wellington and Distr*
B & W
BATHEASTON (St John the Baptist) (St Catherine) *B & W 8*
P *Ch Ch Ox*   **V** A J FRY
BATHFORD (St Swithun) *B & W 8*   **P** *D&C Bris*
P-in-c J E BURGESS
BATHWICK (Blessed Virgin Mary)   *see Bath Bathwick B & W*
BATHWICK (St John the Baptist)   *as above*
BATLEY (All Saints) and Purlwell *Wakef 9*
P E C S J G *Brudenell Esq, Trustees D Stubley Esq, and Bp (jt)*
V A P JOHNSON, **OLM** B R ASQUITH
BATLEY (St Thomas) *Wakef 9*   **P** *V Batley*   **P-in-c** P A CRABB,
C M J A CARPENTER
BATLEY CARR (Holy Trinity)   *see Dewsbury Wakef*
BATSFORD (St Mary)   *see Moreton-in-Marsh w Batsford,*
Todenham etc Glouc
BATTERSEA (Christ Church and St Stephen) *S'wark 14*   **P** *Bp*
and V Battersea St Mary (alt)   **V** G N OWEN
BATTERSEA (St George)   *see Battersea Fields S'wark*
BATTERSEA (St Luke) *S'wark 14*   **P** *Bp*   **V** E A MORSE,
NSM K J SMITH
BATTERSEA (St Mary) *S'wark 14*   **P** *Earl Spencer*
V S BUTLER, **C** A C BOULTER, **NSM** P B WINTGENS
BATTERSEA (St Michael) Wandsworth Common *S'wark 14*
P *V Battersea St Mary*   **V** A H STEVENS, **NSM** S Z BRECH
BATTERSEA (St Peter) (St Paul) *S'wark 14*   **P** *V Battersea*
St Mary   **P-in-c** P J S PERKIN, **C** R P MALONE
BATTERSEA FIELDS (St Saviour) (All Saints) (St George)
S'wark 14   **P** *Bp, CPAS, and Ch Patr Trust (jt)*
V G M VEVERS, **C** S A A ANAND
BATTERSEA PARK (All Saints)   *see Battersea Fields S'wark*
BATTERSEA PARK (St Saviour)   *as above*
BATTERSEA RISE (St Mark) *S'wark 14*   **P** *V Battersea*
St Mary   **V** P J S PERKIN, **NSM** D A LARLEE, V STOTT
BATTISFORD (St Mary)   *see Ringshall w Battisford, Barking w*
Darmsden etc St E
BATTLE (Church of the Ascension) (St Mary the Virgin)
Chich 14   **P** *The Crown*   **V** J J W EDMONDSON
BATTLE HILL (Good Shepherd)   *see Willington Newc*
BATTLESDEN (St Peter and All Saints)   *see Woburn w*
Eversholt, Milton Bryan, Battlesden etc St Alb
BATTYEFORD (Christ the King) *Wakef 9*   **P** *V Mirfield*
P-in-c M A MCLEAN, **Hon C** R F WHITNALL,
NSM M E WOOD
BAUGHURST (St Stephen) and Ramsdell and Wolverton w
Ewhurst and Hannington *Win 4*   **P** *Ld Chan, Duke of*
Wellington, and Bp (by turn)   **P-in-c** D BARLOW
BAULKING (St Nicholas)   *see Uffington, Shellingford,*
Woolstone and Baulking Ox
BAUMBER (St Swithin)   *see Hemingby Gp Linc*
BAUNTON (St Mary Magdalene)   *see Stratton, N Cerney,*
Baunton and Bagendon Glouc
BAVERSTOCK (St Editha)   *see Nadder Valley Sarum*
BAWBURGH (St Mary and St Walstan)   *see Easton, Colton,*
Marlingford and Bawburgh Nor
BAWDESWELL (All Saints)   *see Lyng, Sparham, Elsing,*
Bylaugh, Bawdeswell etc Nor

BAWDRIP (St Michael and All Angels)   *see Woolavington w*
Cossington and Bawdrip B & W
BAWDSEY (St Mary)   *see Wilford Peninsula St E*
BAWTRY (St Nicholas) w Austerfield and Misson *S'well 1*   **P** *Bp*
P-in-c J E T STRICKLAND
BAXENDEN (St John) *Blackb 1*   **P** *Bp*   **P-in-c** J N FIELDER
BAXTERGATE (St Ninian)   *see Whitby w Ruswarp York*
BAXTERLEY (not known) w Hurley and Wood End and
Merevale w Bentley *Birm 10*   **P** *Ld Chan (1 turn), Bp and*
Sir William Dugdale Bt (1 turn)   **R** J E GASPER
BAYDON (St Nicholas)   *see Whitton Sarum*
BAYFORD (Mission Room)   *see Charlton Musgrove,*
Cucklington and Stoke Trister B & W
BAYFORD (St Mary)   *see Lt Berkhamsted and Bayford,*
Essendon etc St Alb
BAYLHAM (St Peter)   *see Gt and Lt Blakenham w Baylham*
and Nettlestead St E
BAYSTON HILL (Christ Church) *Lich 20*   **P** *V Shrewsbury*
H Trin w St Julian   **V** T M LOMAX, **NSM** K J LOMAX
BAYSWATER (St Matthew) *Lon 2*   **P** *Exors Dame Jewell*
Magnus-Allcroft   **V** *vacant* (020) 7229 2192
BAYTON (St Bartholomew)   *see Mamble w Bayton, Rock w*
Heightington etc Worc
BEACHAMPTON (Assumption of the Blessed Virgin Mary)
see Buckingham Ox
BEACHAMWELL (St Mary)   *see Barton Bendish w*
Beachamwell and Shingham Ely
BEACON Parishes   *see Painswick, Sheepscombe, Cranham, The*
Edge etc Glouc
BEACON Team Ministry, The *Carl 10*   **P** *Patr Bd*
V N L DAVIES, **TV** M J SHEPHERD, **C** R A LATHAM, **Hon**
C C V TAYLOR, **NSM** M MASHITER, **OLM** J F RADLEY,
Hon Par Dn J L TYRER
BEACON, The *York 10*   **P** *Ld Chan (2 turns), Sir Charles*
Legard Bt (1 turn)   **P-in-c** J H ANDERSON
BEACONSFIELD (St Mary and All Saints) (St Michael and All
Angels) *Ox 20*   **P** *Patr Bd*   **TR** J P BROOKS,
TV C I WALTON, **C** C M MESSERVY, **NSM** C T T ROGERS,
C E CROISDALE-APPLEBY
BEADLAM (St Hilda)   *see Kirkdale w Harome, Nunnington*
and Pockley York
BEADNELL (St Ebba) *Newc 7*   **P** *Newc Dioc Soc*   **V** E J WOOD
BEAFORD (All Saints)   *see Newton Tracey, Horwood,*
Alverdiscott etc Ex
BEALINGS, GREAT (St Mary) and LITTLE (All Saints) w
Playford and Culpho *St E 7*   **P** *Lord Cranworth (1 turn), Bp*
(3 turns)   **P-in-c** P C E STENTIFORD
BEAMINSTER AREA (St Mary of the Annunciation) *Sarum 2*
P *Patr Bd*   **TR** D F B BALDWIN, **TV** S M SYMONS
BEAMISH (St Andrew)   *see Ch the K Dur*
BEARD (St George)   *see New Mills Derby*
BEARLEY (St Mary the Virgin)   *see Snitterfield w Bearley Cov*
BEARPARK (St Edmund)   *see Dur N Dur*
BEARSTED (Holy Cross) w Thurnham *Cant 13*   **P** *Abp*
V J CORBYN, **C** S J BRADFORD, **NSM** L E LUDLOW,
OLM J H E MANNERS
BEARWOOD (St Catherine) *Ox 16*   **P** *Bp*   **NSM** S J KING
BEARWOOD (St Mary the Virgin) *Birm 7*   **P** *V Smethwick*
V A H PERRY
BEAUCHAMP RODING (St Botolph)   *see S Rodings Chelmsf*
BEAUDESERT (St Nicholas) and Henley-in-Arden w Ullenhall
Cov 7   **P** *MMCET, Bp, and High Bailiff of*
Henley-in-Arden (jt)   **R** J F GANJAVI
BEAULIEU (Blessed Virgin and Holy Child) and Exbury and
East Boldre *Win 11*   **P** *Bp and Lord Montagu of Beaulieu (jt)*
P-in-c C R SMITH
BEAUMONT CUM MOZE (St Leonard and St Mary)
see Tendring and Lt Bentley w Beaumont cum Moze Chelmsf
BEAUMONT LEYS (Christ the King) *Leic 1*   **P** *Bp*
V A K FORD, **NSM** S R DELAFORCE
BEAUWORTH (St James)   *see Upper Itchen Win*
BEAUXFIELD (St Peter)   *see Whitfield w Guston Cant*
BEAWORTHY (St Alban)   *see Ashwater, Halwill, Beaworthy,*
Clawton etc Ex
BEBINGTON (St Andrew) *Ches 8*
P M C *Saunders-Griffiths Esq*   **R** P R M VENABLES,
C D G B NEWSTEAD, D W LABDON
BEBINGTON, HIGHER (Christ Church) *Ches 8*
P C J C *Saunders-Griffiths Esq*   **V** A E SAMUELS,
C M E WATSON
BECCLES (St Michael the Archangel) (St Luke's Church Centre)
St E 14   **P** *Simeon's Trustees*   **R** J N BEAUCHAMP,
C M PHILLIPS-LAST
BECK ROW (St John)   *see Mildenhall St E*
BECKBURY (St Milburga), Badger, Kemberton, Ryton,
Stockton and Sutton Maddock *Lich 16*   **P** *Lord Hamilton of*

Dalzell, Or Coll Ox, and MMCET (2 turns), Ld Chan (1 turn)
R K HODSON
BECKENHAM (Christ Church) Roch 13   P Ch Trust Fund
Trust   V N W WYNNE-JONES,   C A P J TOWNER,
Hon C J T ANSCOMBE
BECKENHAM (Holy Trinity)   see Penge Lane H Trin Roch
BECKENHAM (St Barnabas) Roch 13   P Keble Coll Ox
V vacant (020) 8650 3332
BECKENHAM (St George) Roch 13   P Bp   R P E FRANCIS
BECKENHAM (St James) Elmers End Roch 13   P Bp
V L C CARBERRY
BECKENHAM (St John the Baptist) Eden Park Roch 13
P Ch Trust Fund Trust, Bp and Adn Bromley (jt)   V N LANG,
C E A LANDER
BECKENHAM (St Michael and All Angels) w St Augustine
Roch 13   P SMF and Bp (jt)   V vacant (020) 8778 6569
BECKENHAM, NEW (St Paul) Roch 13   P Bp   V v c SHORT,
Hon C N E BAINES
BECKERMET (St Bridget) (St Bridget Old Church) (St John) w
Ponsonby Carl 5   P Bp, Adn W Cumberland, P Stanley Esq,
and PCCs of Beckermet St Jo and St Bridget (jt)   V vacant
(01946) 841327
BECKFORD (St John the Baptist)   see Overbury w Teddington,
Alstone etc Worc
BECKHAM, WEST (St Helen and All Saints)   see Weybourne
Gp Nor
BECKINGHAM (All Saints)   see Brant Broughton and
Beckingham Linc
BECKINGHAM (All Saints) and Walkeringham and Misterton w
West Stockwith S'well 1   P Bp, Ld Chan, and D&C (by turn)
P-in-c J D HENSON
BECKINGTON (St George) w Standerwick, Berkley, Rodden,
Lullington and Orchardleigh B & W 3   P Bp (3 turns), Ch Soc
Trust (1 turn), and Exors A Duckworth Esq
R A W G CHALKLEY
BECKLEY (All Saints) and Peasmarsh Chich 20   P Univ Coll
Ox and SS Coll Cam (alt)   R C F HOPKINS,
NSM W F G DOLMAN
BECKLEY (Assumption of the Blessed Virgin Mary)
see Wheatley Ox
BECKTON (St Mark) Chelmsf 3   P Bp   V O J BALOGUN
BECKWITHSHAW (St Michael and All Angels)   see Pannal w
Beckwithshaw Ripon
BECONTREE (St Cedd) Chelmsf 1   P Bp   V vacant (020) 8592
5900
BECONTREE (St Elisabeth) Chelmsf 1   P Bp   V S J HANNA
BECONTREE (St George) Chelmsf 1   P Bp
V S L SMALLWOOD
BECONTREE (St Mary) Chelmsf 1   P CPAS   V E J FLEMING,
NSM C C ASINUGO
BECONTREE (St Thomas) Chelmsf 1   P Bp   V P J WOOD,
NSM J PALMER
BECONTREE SOUTH (St Alban) (St John the Divine)
(St Martin) Chelmsf 1   P Patr Bd   TR P J SAYER
BEDALE (St Gregory) and Leeming and Thornton Watlass
Ripon 4   P Bp, Sir Henry Beresford-Peirse Bt, R Kirklington w
Burnestonand Wath and Pickhill, and D S Dodsworth Esq (jt)
R vacant (01677) 422103
BEDDINGHAM (St Andrew)   see Glynde, W Firle and
Beddingham Chich
BEDDINGTON (St Francis' Church Hall)   see S Beddington
and Roundshaw S'wark
BEDDINGTON (St Mary) S'wark 23   P D&C
R J MIDDLEMISS
BEDDINGTON, SOUTH (St Michael and All Angels) and
Roundshaw S'wark 23   P Bp   V A M A GBEBIKAN,
NSM S L BILLIN, E J GOODRIDGE
BEDFIELD (St Nicholas)   see Worlingworth, Southolt,
Tannington, Bedfield etc St E
BEDFONT, EAST (St Mary the Virgin) Lon 11   P Ld Chan
V G D G PRICE
BEDFORD (All Saints) St Alb 9   P Bp   P-in-c J M MACLEOD,
C M NAYLOR
BEDFORD (Christ Church) St Alb 9   P Bp   V R C HIBBERT,
C F R GIBSON
BEDFORD (St Andrew) St Alb 9   P Ld Chan   V C M DENT,
Hon C J A ROWLANDS
BEDFORD (St John the Baptist) (St Leonard) St Alb 9
P MMCET   R N COOPER
BEDFORD (St Mark) St Alb 9   P Bp   V C ROYDEN,
NSM G R CAPPLEMAN
BEDFORD (St Martin) St Alb 9   P Bp   P-in-c R S STOKES
BEDFORD (St Michael and All Angels)   see Elstow St Alb
BEDFORD (St Paul) St Alb 9   P Bp   V J G PEDLAR
BEDFORD (St Peter de Merton) w St Cuthbert St Alb 9
P Ld Chan   R M L FUDGER

BEDFORD LEIGH (St Thomas) (All Saints' Mission) Man 19
P V Leigh St Mary   V R DIXON
BEDFORD PARK (St Michael and All Angels) Lon 11   P Bp
V K J MORRIS,   C S F STAVROU,   NSM G MORGAN
BEDGROVE (Holy Spirit) Ox 21   P DBP   V M G KUHRT,
C G E LANE
BEDHAMPTON (St Nicholas's Mission Church) (St Thomas)
Portsm 5   P Bp   R D J PROUD
BEDINGFIELD (St Mary)   see Eye St E
BEDINGHAM (St Andrew)   see Hempnall Nor
BEDLINGTON (St Cuthbert) Newc 1   P D&C Dur
V J F TWOMEY,   NSM I J HENNEBRY
BEDMINSTER (St Aldhelm) (St Paul) Bris 1   P Bp
C C L GARDINER, M F JEFFERY, N J HAY
BEDMINSTER (St Michael and All Angels) Bris 1   P Bp
V D S MOSS
BEDMINSTER DOWN (St Oswald)   see Bishopsworth and
Bedminster Down Bris
BEDMONT (Ascension)   see Abbots Langley St Alb
BEDNALL (All Saints)   see Penkridge Lich
BEDSTONE (St Mary)   see Clungunford w Clunbury and
Clunton, Bedstone etc Heref
BEDWORTH (All Saints) Cov 5   P Patr Bd   TR R W HARE,
TV M J HAMMOND,   C P A P DEN HAAN,   Dss P M HAMILTON
BEDWYN, GREAT (St Mary)   see Savernake Sarum
BEDWYN, LITTLE (St Michael)   as above
BEECH (St Peter)   see Alton Win
BEECH, HIGH (Holy Innocents)   see Waltham H Cross
Chelmsf
BEECH HILL (St Anne)   see Wigan St Anne Liv
BEECH HILL (St Mary the Virgin)   see Loddon Reach Ox
BEECHDALE ESTATE (St Chad)   see Blakenall Heath Lich
BEECHINGSTOKE (St Stephen)   see Vale of Pewsey Sarum
BEEDING (St Peter) and Bramber w Botolphs Chich 12   P Bp
R J W A CHALLIS
BEEDING, LOWER (Holy Trinity) (St John the Evangelist)
Chich 8   P Bp   P-in-c M J BENSON
BEEDON (St Nicholas)   see E Downland Ox
BEEFORD (St Leonard) w Frodingham and Foston York 11
P Abp and Ch Soc Trust (jt)   R J E GRAINGER-SMITH
BEELEY (St Anne) and Edensor Derby 2   P Duke of Devonshire
V vacant (01246) 582130
BEELSBY (St Andrew)   see Laceby and Ravendale Gp Linc
BEENHAM VALENCE (St Mary)   see Aldermaston and
Woolhampton Ox
BEER (St Michael)   see Seaton and Beer Ex
BEER HACKETT (St Michael)   see Gifle Valley Sarum
BEERCROCOMBE (St James)   see Beercrocombe w Curry
Mallet, Hatch Beauchamp etc B & W
BEERCROCOMBE (St James) w Curry Mallet, Hatch
Beauchamp, Orchard Portman, Staple Fitzpaine, Stoke
St Mary w Thurlbear and West Hatch B & W 14   P Bp,
Ch Trust Fund Trust, and D&C (4 turns), Duchy of Cornwall
(1 turn)   R P A REYNOLDS,   NSM C R AGER, M L GODIN
BEESANDS (St Andrew)   see Stokenham, Slapton, Charleton w
Buckland etc Ex
BEESBY (St Andrew)   see Saleby w Beesby and Maltby Linc
BEESTON (St Andrew)   see Sprowston w Beeston Nor
BEESTON (St John the Baptist) S'well 7   P Duke of Devonshire
V W R PLIMMER,   C C L TOWNS
BEESTON (St Mary the Virgin) Ripon 6   P Patr Bd
P-in-c W A D BERRYMAN,   C J SMITH
BEESTON HILL (Holy Spirit) and Hunslet Moor St Peter w
St Cuthbert Ripon 6   P Bp and TR Leeds City (jt)
V R W SHAW
BEESTON NEXT MILEHAM (St Mary the Virgin)
see Litcham w Kempston, E and W Lexham, Mileham etc Nor
BEESTON REGIS (All Saints)   see Aylmerton, Runton, Beeston
Regis and Gresham Nor
BEESTON RYLANDS (St Mary)   see Beeston S'well
BEESTON ST LAURENCE (St Laurence)   see Ashmanhaugh,
Barton Turf etc Nor
BEETHAM (St Michael and All Angels) Carl 10   P Bp
P-in-c A T SCHOFIELD,   NSM G M BERESFORD JONES
BEETLEY (St Mary)   see Dereham and Distr Nor
BEGBROKE (St Michael)   see Blenheim Ox
BEIGHTON (All Saints)   see Acle w Fishley, N Burlingham,
Beighton w Moulton Nor
BEIGHTON (St Mary the Virgin) Sheff 1   P Bp
P-in-c M H E HEALEY
BEKESBOURNE (St Peter)   see Bridge Cant
BELAUGH (St Peter)   see Wroxham w Hoveton and Belaugh
Nor
BELBROUGHTON (Holy Trinity) w Fairfield and Clent
Worc 12   P Ld Chan and St Jo Coll Ox (alt)   R B J MAPLEY

BELCHALWELL (St Aldheim) *see* Hazelbury Bryan and the Hillside Par *Sarum*
BELCHAMP (St Paul and St Andrew) *see* N Hinckford *Chelmsf*
BELCHAMP OTTEN (St Ethelbert and All Saints) *as above*
BELCHAMP WALTER (St Mary the Virgin) *as above*
BELCHFORD (St Peter and St Paul) *see* Hemingby Gp *Linc*
BELFIELD (St Ann) *Man 17* P *Bp* P-in-c G W LINDLEY, NSM S E WARD
BELFORD (St Mary) and Lucker *Newc 7* P *V Bamburgh and Beadnell and Bp (alt)* V J J BECKWITH
BELGRAVE (St Michael and All Angels) *see* Leic Resurr *Leic*
BELGRAVE (St Paul) *see* Wilnecote *Lich*
BELHUS PARK (All Saints) *see* S Ockendon and Belhus Park *Chelmsf*
BELLE GREEN (Mission) *see* Ince Ch Ch w Wigan St Cath *Liv*
BELLE ISLE (St John and St Barnabas) *see* Leeds Belle Is St Jo and St Barn *Ripon*
BELLEAU (St John the Baptist) *see* Legbourne and Wold Marsh *Linc*
BELLERBY (St John) *see* Leyburn w Bellerby *Ripon*
BELLFIELD (St Mark) *see* Sutton St Jas and Wawne *York*
BELLINGDON (St John the Evangelist) *see* Gt Chesham *Ox*
BELLINGHAM (St Cuthbert) *see* N Tyne and Redesdale *Newc*
BELLINGHAM (St Dunstan) *S'wark 4* P *Bp* NSM D L RILEY
BELMONT (St Anselm) *Lon 23* P *Bp* V C M A ROBINSON
BELMONT (St John) *S'wark 23* P *R Cheam* V M R WILLIAMS, NSM A E DOERR
BELMONT (St Mary Magdalene) and Pittington *Dur 1* P *Prime Min and D&C (alt)* V D M JOHNSON, C J A ASHURST
BELMONT (St Peter) *see* Turton Moorland Min *Man*
BELPER (Christ Church) (St Faith's Mission Church) w Turnditch *Derby 11* P *Bp* P-in-c J M PAGE, C I N L BLACK, NSM A M V ROOME
BELPER (St Peter) *Derby 11* P *V Duffield* P-in-c A M STRATTON, C R E MARSZALEK, NSM A TOMPKINS
BELSIZE PARK (St Peter) *Lon 16* P *D&C Westmr* P-in-c P S NICHOLSON, NSM M W SPEEKS
BELSTEAD (St Mary the Virgin) *see* Sproughton w Burstall, Copdock w Washbrook etc *St E*
BELSTONE (St Mary) *see* S Tawton and Belstone *Ex*
BELTINGHAM (St Cuthbert) *see* Haydon Bridge and Beltingham w Henshaw *Newc*
BELTISLOE, NORTH Group *Linc 14* P *Ch Coll Cam, Sir Lyonel Tollemache Bt, D&C, Bp, DBP, Sir Richard Welby Bt, and Baroness Willoughby de Eresby (jt)* R vacant (01476) 585237
BELTON (All Saints) and Burgh Castle *Nor 6* P *Bp and Ld Chan (alt)* R R J BUNN
BELTON Group, The (All Saints) *Linc 1* P *Bp and Prime Min (alt)* V T D BUCKLEY
BELTON (St John the Baptist) *see* Kegworth, Hathern, Long Whatton, Diseworth etc *Leic*
BELTON (St Peter) *see* Uppingham w Ayston and Wardley w Belton *Pet*
BELTON (St Peter and St Paul) *see* Barkston and Hough Gp *Linc*
BELVEDERE (All Saints) *Roch 15* P *DBP* P-in-c W J EDWARDS
BELVEDERE (St Augustine) *Roch 15* P *Bp* V C W JONES
BEMBRIDGE (Holy Trinity) (St Luke's Mission Church) *Portsm 7* P *V Brading* V A P MENNISS, NSM L M BUSHELL
BEMERTON (St Andrew) (St John the Evangelist) (St Michael and All Angels) *Sarum 12* P *Prime Min (2 turns) and Bp (1 turn)* TR S A WOODLEY, Hon C B H MEARDON, NSM S J DREWETT
BEMPTON (St Michael) w Flamborough, Reighton w Speeton *York 9* P *Patr Bd* V P J PIKE, C E C HASSALL, NSM S J SMALE
BEN RHYDDING (St John the Evangelist) *Bradf 4* P *V Ilkey* P-in-c P WILLOX, NSM J H COPSEY
BENCHILL (St Luke the Physician) *see* Wythenshawe *Man*
BENEFIELD (St Mary the Virgin) *see* Oundle w Ashton and Benefield w Glapthorn *Pet*
BENENDEN (St George and St Margaret) and Sandhurst *Cant 16* P *Abp* P-in-c C B HILL, NSM R M VAN WENGEN
BENFIELDSIDE (St Cuthbert) *Dur 4* P *Bp* V M JACKSON, NSM I W WAUGH
BENFLEET, SOUTH (St Mary the Virgin) *Chelmsf 10* P *D&C Westmr* V vacant (01268) 792294
BENGEO (Holy Trinity) *see* Hertford *St Alb*
BENGEO (St Leonard) *as above*
BENGEWORTH (St Peter) *Worc 1* P *Bp* V B D COLLINS
BENHALL (St Mary) *see* Alde River *St E*

BENHILTON (All Saints) *S'wark 23* P *Bp* P-in-c P J HARNDEN
BENINGTON (All Saints) *see* Freiston, Butterwick w Bennington, and Leverton *Linc*
BENINGTON (St Peter) w Walkern *St Alb 20* P *Trustees Ripon Coll Ox and K Coll Cam (alt), and Bp* P-in-c M J LEVERTON
BENNETTS END (St Benedict) *see* Langelei *St Alb*
BENNIWORTH (St Julian) *see* Asterby Gp *Linc*
BENSHAM AND TEAMS (St Chad) *Dur 12* P *Bp* V M M GILLEY
BENSINGTON (St Helen) *see* Benson *Ox*
BENSON (St Helen) *Ox 1* P *Ch Ch Ox* V G J BURRELL, NSM D C GIFFORD, OLM J K TRAVIS
BENTHAM (St John the Baptist) (St Margaret) *Bradf 6* P *Bp* NSM S C DAWSON
BENTILEE (St Stephen) *see* Bucknall *Lich*
BENTLEY (Emmanuel) and Willenhall Holy Trinity *Lich 28* P *Patr Bd* TR M S HATHORNE, TV J D DEAKIN, S L HOUGH, NSM C A HATHORNE
BENTLEY (St Mary) *see* Sproughton w Burstall, Copdock w Washbrook etc *St E*
BENTLEY (St Mary), Binsted and Froyle *Win 2* P *D&C, Adn Surrey, and Guild of All So (jt)* R Y DUBREUIL
BENTLEY (St Peter) *Sheff 7* P *Bp* V D R FOUNTAIN
BENTLEY (St Peter) *see* Rowley w Skidby *York*
BENTLEY, GREAT (St Mary the Virgin) *Chelmsf 22* P *Bp* V W B METCALFE
BENTLEY, LITTLE (St Mary) *see* Tendring and Lt Bentley w Beaumont cum Moze *Chelmsf*
BENTLEY, LOWER (St Mary) *see* Redditch H Trin *Worc*
BENTLEY, NEW (St Philip and St James) w Arksey *Sheff 7* P *Bp and DBP (jt)* V S P DICKINSON
BENTLEY COMMON (St Paul), Kelvedon Hatch and Navestock *Chelmsf 7* P *Bp* R M N JAMES
BENTLEY HEATH (St James) *see* Dorridge *Birm*
BENTWORTH (St Mary), Lasham, Medstead and Shalden *Win 2* P *J L Jervoise Esq and Ld Chan (alt)* R B R G FLENLEY
BENWELL Team, The (St James) (St John) (Venerable Bede) *Newc 4* P *Bp* TR C R PICKFORD, TV T M FERGUSON, C R B CROSS, OLM P D WILSON
BEOLEY Church Hill (St Andrew's Church Centre) *see* Redditch H Trin *Worc*
BEOLEY (St Leonard) *as above*
BEPTON (St Mary) *see* Cocking, Bepton and W Lavington *Chich*
BERDEN (St Nicholas) *see* Manuden w Berden and Quendon w Rickling *Chelmsf*
BERE ALSTON (Holy Trinity) *see* Bere Ferrers *Ex*
BERE FERRERS (St Andrew) *Ex 25* P *DBP* R N C LAW
BERE REGIS (St John the Baptist) and Affpuddle w Turnerspuddle *Sarum 8* P *Ball Coll Ox (2 turns), Bp (1 turn)* R I WOODWARD
BERECHURCH (St Margaret w St Michael) *Chelmsf 16* P *Bp* V A I FORDYCE, C P E DAVIES
BERGH APTON (St Peter and St Paul) *see* Thurton *Nor*
BERGHOLT, EAST (St Mary the Virgin) and Brantham *St E 5* P *Em Coll Cam* R S VAN DER TOORN, NSM A J MORTIMER, R J NEEDLE
BERGHOLT, WEST (St Mary the Virgin) and Great Horkesley *Chelmsf 17* P *Bp and Ball Coll Ox (alt)* R C HORSEMAN
BERINSFIELD (St Mary and St Berin) *see* Dorchester *Ox*
BERKELEY (St Mary the Virgin) w Wick, Breadstone, Newport, Stone, Woodford and Hill *Glouc 5* P *Bp, Berkeley Will Trustees, and Mrs J D Jenner-Fust (jt)* V R J AVERY, NSM R P CHIDLAW
BERKHAMSTED, GREAT (All Saints) (St Peter), Great Gaddesden, Little Gaddesden, Nettleden and Potten End *St Alb 1* P *Patr Bd* TR M R BOWIE, TV P J NASH, J B RUSSELL, NSM L GEOGHEGAN
BERKHAMSTED, LITTLE (St Andrew) and Bayford, Essendon and Ponsbourne *St Alb 19* P *Marquess of Salisbury (2 turns), CPAS (1 turn), and Bp (1 turn)* R P M HIGHAM, NSM J D COPE
BERKHAMSYTCH (St Mary and St John) *see* Ipstones w Berkhamsytch and Onecote w Bradnop *Lich*
BERKLEY (Blessed Virgin Mary) *see* Beckington w Standerwick, Berkley, Rodden etc *B & W*
BERKSWELL (St John the Baptist) *Cov 4* P *Trustees Col C J H Wheatley* P-in-c M Q BRATTON
BERKSWICH (Holy Trinity) *see* Baswich *Lich*
BERMONDSEY (St Anne) and St Augustine *S'wark 7* P *Bp and F W Smith Esq (alt)* V S J R HARTLEY, C L C VINCER
BERMONDSEY (St Hugh) Charterhouse Mission Conventional District *S'wark 10* C-in-c B A SAUNDERS, NSM L SCOTT-GARNETT

BERMONDSEY (St James w Christ Church) and St Crispin
S'wark 7   **P** *The Crown, Bp, and R Bermondsey St Mary*
(by turn)   **V** S J R HARTLEY,   **C** L C VINCER,
OLM S C CATTON
BERMONDSEY (St Katharine) w St Bartholomew *S'wark 7*
P *Bp and R Rotherhithe St Mary w All SS (jt)*   **V** L M WANJIE
BERMONDSEY (St Mary Magdalen w St Olave, St John and
St Luke) *S'wark 7*   **P** *Ch Patr Soc (2 turns), Ld Chan (1 turn),*
and Bp (1 turn)   **R** C D MOORE
BERNEY, GREAT (St John)   *see* Langdon Hills *Chelmsf*
BERNWODE *Ox 21*   **P** *Bp, CPAS, Earl Temple of Stowe, and*
Sir Henry Aubrey-Fletcher Bt (jt)   **R** C D STIRLING,
C L J CRAWLEY, J EDMANS
BERRICK SALOME (St Helen)   *see* Chalgrove w Berrick
Salome *Ox*
BERRINGTON (All Saints)   *see* Wenlock *Heref*
BERROW (Blessed Virgin Mary) and Breane *B & W 1*   **P** *Adn*
Wells   **R** S F LACY
BERROW (St Faith) w Pendock, Eldersfield, Hollybush and
Birtsmorton *Worc 5*   **P** *Bp, D&C, and Exors Sir Berwick*
Lechmere Bt (jt)   **R** M A ROGERS,   **NSM** A E L ELSTON
BERRY POMEROY (St Mary)   *see* Totnes w Bridgetown, Berry
Pomeroy etc *Ex*
BERRYNARBOR (St Peter)   *see* Combe Martin, Berrynarbor,
Lynton, Brendon etc *Ex*
BERSTED, NORTH (Holy Cross) *Chich 1*   **P** *Abp*
P-in-c G A CLARKE
BERSTED, SOUTH (St Mary Magdalene) w NORTH *Chich 1*
P *Abp*   **V** T M CROOK
BERWICK (Holy Trinity) (St Mary) *Newc 12*   **P** *Bp (2 turns),*
D&C Dur (1 turn)   **V** A HUGHES
BERWICK (St John)   *see* Chalke Valley *Sarum*
BERWICK (St Michael and All Angels)   *see* Arlington, Berwick,
Selmeston w Alciston etc *Chich*
BERWICK PARK (Good Shepherd)   *see* Wood Green St Mich
w Bounds Green St Gabr etc *Lon*
BERWICK ST JAMES (St James)   *see* Wylye and Till Valley
Sarum
BESFORD (St Peter's Chapelry)   *see* Defford w Besford *Worc*
BESSACARR, WEST (St Francis of Assisi) *Sheff 8*   **P** *Bp*
V R A HEARD
BESSELSLEIGH (St Lawrence) *Ox 10*   **P** *Ox Ch Trust*
P-in-c L L SAPWELL
BESSINGBY (St Magnus) (St Mark) *York 9*   **P** *Patr Bd*
P-in-c J G COUPER,   **C** D N H CHISLETT
BESSINGHAM (St Mary)   *see* Roughton and Felbrigg, Metton,
Sustead etc *Nor*
BESTHORPE (All Saints)   *see* Attleborough w Besthorpe *Nor*
BESTHORPE (Holy Trinity)   *see* E Trent *S'well*
BESTWOOD (Emmanuel) (St Mark) *S'well 12*   **P** *Bp and Ch*
Patr Trust (jt)   **P-in-c** E SNOWDEN
BESTWOOD (St Matthew on the Hill) (St Philip) *S'well 12*
P *Bp and Ch Patr Trust (jt)*   **V** E A MORRIS
BESTWOOD/RISE PARK Local Ecumenical Partnership
S'well 9 vacant
BESTWOOD PARK (no dedication) w Rise Park *S'well 12*
P *Bp and Ch Patr Trust (jt)*   **V** C N J ROOMS
BESWICK (St Margaret)   *see* Hutton Cranswick w Skerne,
Watton and Beswick *York*
BETCHWORTH (St Michael and All Angels) and Buckland
S'wark 26   **P** *D&C Windsor and All So Coll Ox (jt)*
R C A COSLETT
BETHERSDEN (St Margaret) w High Halden *Cant 16*   **P** *Abp*
V *vacant* (01233) 820266
BETHESDA (Shared Church)   *see* Hallwood Ecum Par *Ches*
BETHNAL GREEN (St Barnabas) *Lon 7*   **P** *D&C Cant*
V B C RALPH
BETHNAL GREEN (St James the Less) *Lon 7*   **P** *CPAS*
V A J LOGAN
BETHNAL GREEN (St John)   *see* St Jo on Bethnal
Green *Lon*
BETHNAL GREEN (St Matthew w St James the Great) *Lon 7*
P *Bp*   **R** K J SCULLY,   **NSM** J E BLACKBURN
BETHNAL GREEN (St Peter) (St Thomas) *Lon 7*   **P** *City Corp*
V A ATKINSON
BETHUNE ROAD (St Andrew)   *see* Stoke Newington St Andr
Lon
BETLEY (St Margaret) *Lich 9*   **P** *DBP*   **V** B F WILSON,
NSM G A BAILEY,   **OLM** P LANE
BETTISCOMBE (St Stephen)   *see* Golden Cap Team *Sarum*
BETTON STRANGE (St Margaret)   *see* Wenlock *Heref*
BETTWS-Y-CRWYN (St Mary)   *see* Clun w Bettws-y-Crwyn
and Newcastle *Heref*
BEVENDEN (Holy Nativity)   *see* Moulsecoomb *Chich*
BEVERLEY (St Mary) *York 8*   **P** *Abp*   **V** *vacant* (01482)
881437

BEVERLEY (St Nicholas) *York 8*   **P** *Abp*   **V** J A EVANS,
C M MARTINSON,   **NSM** R MERRYWEATHER
BEVERLEY MINSTER (St John and St Martin) *York 8*
P *Simeon's Trustees*   **V** J J FLETCHER,   **C** F R MAYER-JONES,
NSM R E YOUNG
BEVERSTON (St Mary the Virgin)   *see* Tetbury, Beverston,
Long Newnton etc *Glouc*
BEWBUSH (Community Centre)   *see* Ifield *Chich*
BEWCASTLE (St Cuthbert), Stapleton and Kirklinton w
Hethersgill *Carl 2*   **P** *Bp, D&C, and DBP (jt)*
R P A GREENHALGH
BEWDLEY (St Anne)   *see* Ribbesford w Bewdley and Dowles
Worc
BEWERLEY GRANGE (Chapel)   *see* Upper Nidderdale *Ripon*
BEWHOLME (St John the Baptist)   *see* Sigglesthorne w
Nunkeeling and Bewholme *York*
BEWICK, OLD (Holy Trinity)   *see* Glendale Gp *Newc*
BEXHILL (All Saints)   *see* Sidley *Chich*
BEXHILL (St Augustine) *Chich 14*   **P** *Bp*   **V** R COATES,
Hon C P A FROSTICK
BEXHILL (St Barnabas) *Chich 14*   **P** *Bp*
P-in-c G R CROSTHWAITE
BEXHILL (St Mark) *Chich 14*   **P** *Bp*   **R** J J FRAIS
BEXHILL (St Peter) (St Michael) (Good Shepherd) (St Andrew)
Chich 14   **P** *Bp*   **TR** E F P BRYANT,   **TV** S D HUGGINS,
Hon C G R CROSTHWAITE,   **NSM** O M WERRETT
BEXHILL (St Stephen) *Chich 14*   **P** *Bp*   **V** T J VOLTZENLOGEL,
C N G BURTON
BEXLEY (St John the Evangelist) *Roch 17*   **P** *The Crown*
V S I LAMB
BEXLEY (St Mary) *Roch 17*   **P** *Bp*   **V** P A SPREADBURY
BEXLEYHEATH (Christ Church) *Roch 15*   **P** *Bp*
V F D JAKEMAN,   **C** C F MORRISON
BEXLEYHEATH (St Peter) *Roch 15*   **P** *Bp*
P-in-c J R CHARLES
BEXWELL (St Mary)   *see* Denver and Ryston w Roxham and
W Dereham etc *Ely*
BEYTON (All Saints)   *see* Rougham, Beyton w Hessett and
Rushbrooke *St E*
BIBURY (St Mary)   *see* Fairford Deanery *Glouc*
BICESTER (St Edburg) w Bucknell, Caversfield and Launton
Ox 2   **P** *Patr Bd*   **TR** T A SCOTT,   **TV** C A BOYCE,
R C MATHEW,   **C** E VAN BLERK,   **NSM** R B ATKINS
BICKENHILL (St Peter) *Birm 11*   **P** *Birm Dioc Trustees*
P-in-c D C J BALLARD
BICKER (St Swithin) *Linc 20*   **P** *D&C*   **P-in-c** D D S DE VERNY
BICKERSHAW (St James and St Elizabeth) *Liv 14*   **P** *Bp*
P-in-c A E STEIN
BICKERSTAFFE Four Lane Ends (not known)   *see* Aughton
St Mich and Bickerstaffe *Liv*
BICKERSTAFFE (Holy Trinity)   *as above*
BICKERTON (Holy Trinity)   *see* Malpas and Threapwood and
Bickerton *Ches*
BICKINGTON (St Andrew)   *see* Fremington, Instow and
Westleigh *Ex*
BICKINGTON (St Mary the Virgin)   *see* Ashburton,
Bickington, Buckland in the Moor etc *Ex*
BICKINGTON, HIGH (St Mary)   *see* Newton Tracey,
Horwood, Alverdiscott etc *Ex*
BICKLEIGH Roborough (St Mary the Virgin) and Shaugh Prior
Ex 23   **P** *Patr Bd*   **C** M B BROWN,   **NSM** M J FAIRALL,
D K COLEMAN
BICKLEIGH (St Mary)   *see* Silverton, Butterleigh, Bickleigh
and Cadeleigh *Ex*
BICKLEIGH DOWN (School)   *see* Bickleigh and Shaugh Prior
Ex
BICKLEY (St George) *Roch 14*   **P** *SMF*   **V** O C G HIGGS
BICKLEY (St Wenefrede) *Ches 5*   **P** *Marquess of Cholmondeley*
V *vacant*
BICKNACRE (St Andrew)   *see* Woodham Ferrers and
Bicknacre *Chelmsf*
BICKNOLLER (St George)   *see* Quantock Towers *B & W*
BICKNOR (St James)   *see* Tunstall and Bredgar *Cant*
BICTON (Holy Trinity), Montford w Shrawardine and Fitz
Lich 20   **P** *Earl of Powis, N E E Stephens Esq, and*
J G O Wingfield Esq (jt)   **P-in-c** C H DEAKIN,
Hon C R M PARSONS
BICTON (St Mary)   *see* E Budleigh w Bicton and Otterton *Ex*
BIDBOROUGH (St Lawrence)   *see* Southborough St Pet w Ch
Ch and St Matt etc *Roch*
BIDDENDEN (All Saints) and Smarden *Cant 16*   **P** *Abp*
P-in-c A BIENFAIT,   **OLM** J R DARKINS
BIDDENHAM (St James) *St Alb 9*   **P** *Bp*   **P-in-c** S L HUCKLE,
C J NASH
BIDDESTONE (St Nicholas)   *see* By Brook *Bris*

BIDDISHAM (St John the Baptist)   *see* Crook Peak *B & W*
BIDDLESDEN (St Margaret)   *see* W Buckingham *Ox*
BIDDULPH (St Lawrence) *Lich 8*   **P** *MMCET*
  V M S J CANNAM
BIDDULPH MOOR (Christ Church) and Knypersley *Lich 8*
  P *Ch Patr Trust and MMCET (jt)*   **R** J A DAWSWELL
BIDEFORD (St Mary) (St Peter East the Water), Northam,
  Westward Ho!, Appledore, Weare Giffard, Littleham,
  Landcross and Monkleigh *Ex 16*   **P** *Patr Bd*   **TV** P J DOBBIN,
  I J LOVETT, J EWINGTON,   **P-in-c** C P ROSE-CASEMORE,
  C T H F BENSON,   **NSM** A GLOVER
BIDFORD-ON-AVON (St Laurence) *Cov 7*   **P** *Bp*
  P-in-c P A WALKER,   **C** R E WALKER,   **NSM** S M HENWOOD
BIDSTON (St Oswald) *Ches 1*   **P** *Bp*   **V** R E IVESON,
  C J S GILLIES
BIELBY (St Giles)   *see* Holme and Seaton Ross Gp *York*
BIERLEY (St John the Evangelist) *Bradf 2*   **P** *DBP*
  P-in-c D G KENNEDY
BIERLEY, EAST (St Luke)   *see* Birkenshaw w Hunsworth
  Wakef
BIERTON (St James the Great)   *see* Aylesbury w Bierton and
  Hulcott *Ox*
BIGBURY (St Lawrence)   *see* Modbury, Bigbury, Ringmore w
  Kingston etc *Ex*
BIGBY (All Saints)   *see* N Wolds Gp *Linc*
BIGGIN (St Thomas)   *see* Taddington, Chelmorton and
  Monyash etc *Derby*
BIGGIN HILL (St Mark) *Roch 14*   **P** *Bp*   **V** J M MCLAREN
BIGGLESWADE (St Andrew) *St Alb 10*   **P** *Bp*
  P-in-c G C SCOTT
BIGHTON (All Saints)   *see* Arle Valley *Win*
BIGNOR (Holy Cross)   *see* Barlavington, Burton w Coates,
  Sutton and Bignor *Chich*
BIGRIGG (St John)   *see* Egremont and Haile *Carl*
BILBOROUGH (St John the Baptist) *S'well 14*   **P** *Bp*
  P-in-c A J CARTWRIGHT
BILBOROUGH (St Martin) w Strelley *S'well 14*   **P** *SMF*
  P-in-c A J CARTWRIGHT,   **C** D C CORCORAN
BILBROOK (Holy Cross) and Coven *Lich 2*   **P** *Bp*
  V D C BAKER
BILBROUGH (St James)   *see* Healaugh w Wighill, Bilbrough
  and Askham Richard *York*
BILDESTON (St Mary Magdalene) w Wattisham and Lindsey,
  Whatfield w Semer, Nedging and Naughton *St E 3*   **P** *Abp, Bp,*
  CPAS, Jes Coll Cam, and Reformation Ch Trust (jt)
  R B STANTON
BILHAM *Sheff 12*   **P** *Bp, Major W Warde-Aldam,*
  W G A Warde-Norbury Esq, and Mrs S Grant-Dalton (jt)
  P-in-c C D LETHBRIDGE
BILLERICAY (Christ Church) (Emmanuel) (St John the Divine)
  (St Mary Magdalen) and Little Burstead *Chelmsf 6*   **P** *Bp*
  TR P A CARR,   **TV** W M PIDGEON, P A GAMBLING,   **C** T LOH
BILLESDON (St John the Baptist)   *see* Church Langton cum
  Tur Langton etc *Leic*
BILLESLEY COMMON (Holy Cross) *Birm 5*   **P** *Bp*
  V P OGILVIE
BILLING, GREAT (St Andrew) w LITTLE (All Saints) *Pet 4*
  P *BNC Ox and Bp (alt)*   **R** S R PALMER,   **C** R MULFORD
BILLINGBOROUGH Group, The (St Andrew) *Linc 13*
  P *Prime Min (2 turns), Bp and St Jo Coll Dur (1 turn)*
  P-in-c A K E SORENSEN,   **OLM** J G SPREADBURY, A L STEELE
BILLINGE (St Aidan) *Liv 14*   **P** *R Wigan*   **V** A OVEREND
BILLINGFORD (St Leonard)   *see* Scole, Brockdish, Billingford,
  Thorpe Abbots etc *Nor*
BILLINGFORD (St Peter)   *see* N Elmham, Billingford, Bintree,
  Guist etc *Nor*
BILLINGHAM (St Aidan) *Dur 10*   **P** *D&C*   **V** vacant (01642)
  557010
BILLINGHAM (St Cuthbert) *Dur 10*   **P** *D&C*
  NSM M A VIGOR
BILLINGHAM (St Luke) *Dur 10*   **P** *D&C*   **V** T P PARKER
BILLINGHAM (St Mary Magdalene) *Dur 10*   **P** *D&C*
  P-in-c D M BROOKE,   **NSM** P CLAYTON
BILLINGHAM (St Mary Magdalene)   *see* Grindon, Stillington
  and Wolviston *Dur*
BILLINGHAY (St Michael)   *see* Carr Dyke Gp *Linc*
BILLINGSHURST (St Mary the Virgin) *Chich 8*   **P** *Bp*
  V B J PRITCHARD
BILLINGSLEY (St Mary)   *see* Highley w Billingsley, Glazeley
  etc *Heref*
BILLINGTON (St Michael and All Angels)   *see* Ouzel Valley
  St Alb
BILLOCKBY (All Saints)   *see* S Trin Broads *Nor*
BILLY MILL (St Aidan) *Newc 5*   **P** *Bp*   **V** H C GREENWOOD
BILNEY, EAST (St Mary)   *see* Dereham and Distr *Nor*

BILSBORROW (St Hilda)   *see* Fellside Team *Blackb*
BILSBY (Holy Trinity) w Farlesthorpe *Linc 8*   **P** *Bp*   **V** vacant
BILSDALE MIDCABLE (St John)   *see* Upper Ryedale *York*
BILSDALE PRIORY (St Hilda)   *see* Ingleby Greenhow, Bilsdale
  Priory etc *York*
BILSINGTON (St Peter and St Paul)   *see* Aldington w
  Bonnington and Bilsington etc *Cant*
BILSON (Mission Church)   *see* Cinderford w Littledean *Glouc*
BILSTHORPE (St Margaret) *S'well 15*   **P** *DBP*
  P-in-c R D SEYMOUR-WHITELEY,   **NSM** M A GROVES
BILSTON (St Leonard) (St Chad) (St Mary the Virgin) *Lich 28*
  P *Patr Bd*   **TR** D WILLS,   **TV** J L WATERFIELD,
  OLM C E DAVIES, D G WATKIN
BILTON (St John the Evangelist) and St Luke *Ripon 1*   **P** *Bp*
  TR A MORT,   **TV** D J MCCLINTOCK,   **C** C J FALKINGHAM
BILTON (St Mark) *Cov 6*   **P** *N M Assheton Esq*
  R T D COCKELL,   **C** R A BURLEY,   **NSM** G HEIGHTON,
  OLM M J SHARPE
BILTON, NEW (St Oswald)   *see* Rugby W *Cov*
BILTON-IN-AINSTY (St Helen)   *see* Tockwith and Bilton w
  Bickerton *York*
BILTON IN HOLDERNESS (St Peter) *York 12*   **P** *Abp*
  V R J E MAJOR
BINBROOK Group, The (St Mary) *Linc 10*   **P** *Ld Chan, DBP*
  and G F Sleight Esq (alt)   **R** T J WALKER
BINCOMBE (Holy Trinity) w Broadwey, Upwey and Buckland
  Ripers *Sarum 4*   **P** *G&C Coll Cam (2 turns),*
  Miss M B F Frampton (1 turn), and Bp (1 turn)
  R R A C SIMMONS
BINEGAR (Holy Trinity)   *see* Ashwick w Oakhill and Binegar
  B & W
BINFIELD (All Saints) (St Mark) *Ox 11*   **P** *Ld Chan*
  NSM P B WATTS
BINGFIELD (St Mary)   *see* St Oswald in Lee w Bingfield *Newc*
BINGHAM (St Mary and All Saints) *S'well 8*   **P** *The Crown*
  R D L HARPER
BINGLEY (All Saints) *Bradf 1*   **P** *Bp*   **NSM** C M LOW
BINGLEY (Holy Trinity) *Bradf 1*   **P** *Bp*   **V** A J CLARKE,
  NSM C M LOW
BINHAM (St Mary)   *see* Stiffkey and Bale *Nor*
BINLEY (St Bartholomew) *Cov 1*   **P** *Bp*   **V** E E JONES,
  NSM R W BROMLEY
BINLEY WOODS Local Ecumenical Partnership *Cov 1*
  Min J CHEVERTON
BINSEY (St Margaret)   *see* Osney *Ox*
BINSEY Team Ministry *Carl 6*   **P** *Patr Bd*
  TV P M F STREATFEILD,   **NSM** C C FRYER-SPEDDING
BINSTEAD (Holy Cross) *Portsm 7*   **P** *Bp*
  P-in-c C C ETHERTON
BINSTED (Holy Cross)   *see* Bentley, Binsted and Froyle *Win*
BINSTED (St Mary)   *see* Walberton w Binsted *Chich*
BINTON (St Peter)   *see* Temple Grafton w Binton *Cov*
BINTREE (St Swithin)   *see* N Elmham, Billingford, Bintree,
  Guist etc *Nor*
BIRCH (St James) w Fallowfield *Man 3*   **P** *Bp*   **R** W G RAINES
BIRCH (St Mary)   *see* Rhodes *Man*
BIRCH-IN-RUSHOLME (St Agnes) w Longsight St John w
  St Cyprian *Man 1*   **P** *Prime Min and Bp (alt)*
  P-in-c S M EDWARDS,   **C** L E DOSE
BIRCHAM, GREAT (St Mary the Virgin)   *see* Docking, the
  Birchams, Stanhoe and Sedgeford *Nor*
BIRCHAM NEWTON (All Saints)   *as above*
BIRCHANGER (St Mary the Virgin)   *see* Stansted Mountfitchet
  w Birchanger and Farnham *Chelmsf*
BIRCHENCLIFFE (St Philip the Apostle)   *see* Birkby and
  Birchencliffe *Wakef*
BIRCHES HEAD (St Matthew)   *see* Hanley H Ev *Lich*
BIRCHFIELD (Holy Trinity) *Birm 3*   **P** *Bp*   **P-in-c** E I PITTS,
  NSM L M ARLIDGE
BIRCHILLS, THE (St Andrew)   *see* Walsall St Andr *Lich*
BIRCHIN COPPICE (St Peter)   *see* Kidderminster St Jo and H
  Innocents *Worc*
BIRCHINGTON (All Saints) w Acol and Minnis Bay *Cant 5*
  P *Abp*   **V** D R WITTS
BIRCHMOOR (St John)   *see* Polesworth *Birm*
BIRCHOVER (St Michael)   *see* Youlgreave, Middleton,
  Stanton-in-Peak etc *Derby*
BIRCHWOOD (Mission Church)   *see* Blackdown *B & W*
BIRCHWOOD (St Luke) *Linc 15*   **P** *Bp*   **V** J B PAVEY
BIRCHWOOD (Transfiguration) *Liv 12*   **P** *Bp, Adn, and*
  R Warrington (jt)   **P-in-c** D J PRESCOTT
BIRCLE (St John the Baptist) *Man 8*   **P** *R Middleton St Leon*
  V A R BROCKBANK,   **NSM** D ALTHAM
BIRDBROOK (St Augustine)   *see* Ridgewell w Ashen,
  Birdbrook and Sturmer *Chelmsf*

BIRDHAM (St James)   *see* W Wittering and Birdham w Itchenor *Chich*

BIRDINGBURY (St Leonards)   *see* Leam Valley *Cov*

BIRDLIP (St Mary in Hamlet)   *see* Brimpsfield w Birdlip, Syde, Daglingworth etc *Glouc*

BIRDSALL (St Mary)   *see* W Buckrose *York*

BIRKBY (St Cuthbert) Huddersfield and Birchencliffe *Wakef 5* **P** *V Lindley and Bp (jt)*   **V** M RAILTON-CROWDER, **NSM** M FOSSEY,   **OLM** J SARGENT

BIRKBY (St John the Evangelist) Huddersfield and Woodhouse *Wakef 5*   **P** *Bp and DBP (jt)*   **P-in-c** D J CARPENTER

BIRKBY (St Peter)   *see* E Richmond *Ripon*

BIRKDALE (St James) *Liv 9*   **P** *Trustees*   **P-in-c** I G MAINEY, **C** A C DOWSETT

BIRKDALE (St John) *Liv 9*   **P** *Trustees*   **V** P C CATON

BIRKDALE (St Peter) *Liv 9*   **P** *Trustees*   **P-in-c** I G MAINEY, **C** A C DOWSETT,   **OLM** E LOXHAM

BIRKENHEAD (Christ Church) *Ches 1*   **P** *Bp*   **V** A J HASLAM

BIRKENHEAD (St James) w St Bede *Ches 1*   **P** *Trustees* **V** S M MANSFIELD,   **NSM** S M LANGERHUIZEN

BIRKENHEAD PRIORY (Christ the King) *Ches 1*   **P** *Patr Bd* **R** D J AYLING,   **NSM** E L WATSON

BIRKENSHAW (St Paul) w Hunsworth *Wakef 8*   **P** *V Birstall* **V** M J LOWLES,   **NSM** D S ANDREW, C WALKER, **OLM** R DAVIDSON

BIRKIN (St Mary)   *see* Haddlesey w Hambleton and Birkin *York*

BIRLEY (St Peter)   *see* Canon Pyon w King's Pyon, Birley and Wellington *Heref*

BIRLING (All Saints), Addington, Ryarsh and Trottiscliffe *Roch 7*   **P** *Bp*   **R** L K SHUKER

BIRLING, LOWER (Christ Church)   *see* Snodland All SS w Ch Ch *Roch*

BIRLINGHAM (St James the Great)   *see* Pershore w Pinvin, Wick and Birlingham *Worc*

BIRMINGHAM (Bishop Latimer w All Saints) *Birm 3* **P** *St Martin's Trustees*   **R** G F KIMBER

BIRMINGHAM (St George) *Birm 8*   **P** *St Martin's Trustees* **R** L C WRIGHT,   **NSM** C A B GEORGE, M A HINKS

BIRMINGHAM (St George w St Michael)   *see* Edgbaston St Geo *Birm*

BIRMINGHAM (St John the Evangelist)   *see* Ladywood St Jo and St Pet *Birm*

BIRMINGHAM (St Luke) *Birm 1*   **P** *Trustees* **V** A G LENOX-CONYNGHAM

BIRMINGHAM (St Martin-in-the-Bull-Ring) w Bordesley St Andrew *Birm 1*   **P** *St Martin's Trustees*   **R** S W JONES, **C** E C M SYKES,   **NSM** E BLAIR-CHAPPELL

BIRMINGHAM (St Paul) *Birm 1*   **P** *St Martin's Trustees* **V** M R GILBERT

BIRSTALL (St James the Great) and Wanlip *Leic 5*   **P** *Bp and C A Palmer-Tomkinson Esq (jt)*   **V** V J JUPP,   **C** S A CROFTS

BIRSTALL (St Peter) *Wakef 8*   **P** *Bp*   **V** P J KNIGHT

BIRSTWITH (St James)   *see* Hampsthwaite and Killinghall and Birstwith *Ripon*

BIRTLES (St Catherine)   *see* Alderley w Birtles *Ches*

BIRTLEY (St Giles)   *see* Chollerton w Birtley and Thockrington *Newc*

BIRTLEY (St John the Evangelist) *Dur 11*   **P** *R Chester le Street* **V** E G LLOYD,   **Hon C** B M C BROGGIO

BIRTSMORTON (St Peter and St Paul)   *see* Berrow w Pendock, Eldersfield, Hollybush etc *Worc*

BISBROOKE (St John the Baptist)   *see* Lyddington, Bisbrooke, Caldecott, Glaston etc *Pet*

BISCATHORPE (St Helen)   *see* Asterby Gp *Linc*

BISCOT (Holy Trinity) *St Alb 12*   **P** *Bp*   **V** T B SINGH

BISHAM (All Saints)   *see* Gt Marlow w Marlow Bottom, Lt Marlow and Bisham *Ox*

BISHAMPTON (St James)   *see* Abberton, The Flyfords, Naunton Beauchamp etc *Worc*

BISHOP AUCKLAND (St Andrew) (St Anne)   *see* Auckland St Andr and St Anne *Dur*

BISHOP AUCKLAND (St Peter)   *see* Auckland St Pet *Dur*

BISHOP AUCKLAND Woodhouse Close Area of Ecumenical Experiment (Conventional District) *Dur 10*   **C-in-c** B JONES, **OLM** L DODDS

BISHOP BURTON (All Saints) *York 8*   **P** *Abp* **P-in-c** A BAILEY

BISHOP CAUNDLE (not known)   *see* Vale of White Hart *Sarum*

BISHOP MIDDLEHAM (St Michael)   *see* Upper Skerne *Dur*

BISHOP MONKTON (St John the Baptist)   *see* Ripon Cathl *Ripon*

BISHOP NORTON (St Peter), Waddingham and Snitterby *Linc 6*   **P** *Bp and The Crown (alt)*   **R** *vacant* (01673) 818551

BISHOP SUTTON (Holy Trinity)   *see* Clutton w Cameley, Bishop Sutton and Stowey *B & W*

BISHOP THORNTON (St John the Evangelist)   *see* Markington w S Stainley and Bishop Thornton *Ripon*

BISHOP WILTON (St Edith)   *see* Garrowby Hill *York*

BISHOPDALE (Mission Room)   *see* Penhill *Ripon*

BISHOPHILL JUNIOR (St Mary)   *see* York St Clem w St Mary Bishophill *York*

BISHOPHILL SENIOR (St Clement w St Mary)   *as above*

BISHOP'S CANNINGS (St Mary the Virgin), All Cannings and Etchilhampton *Sarum 16*   **P** *DBP*   **P-in-c** W D LANG, **C** P A STROWGER,   **NSM** S G ASCOUGH

BISHOP'S CASTLE (St John the Baptist) w Mainstone, Lydbury North and Edgton *Heref 9*   **P** *Earl of Powis (3 turns), Ld Chan (1 turn), and Mrs R E Bell (1 turn)* **P-in-c** S A C FOUNTAIN

BISHOP'S CLEEVE (St Michael and All Angels) and Woolstone w Gotherington and Oxenton *Glouc 10*   **P** *Patr Bd* **TR** M ALLEN,   **TV** M S HOLLOWAY,   **C** D BRAE, **NSM** J PHILLIPS

BISHOP'S FROME (St Mary the Virgin)   *see* Frome Valley *Heref*

BISHOPS GREEN (Community Church)   *see* Burghclere w Newtown and Ecchinswell w Sydmonton *Win*

BISHOP'S HATFIELD (St Etheldreda) (St Luke) (St John) (St Michael and All Angels), Lemsford and North Mymms *St Alb 18*   **P** *Patr Bd*   **TR** R E PYKE,   **TV** E C CARDALE, J BOOTHBY, F K WHEATLEY,   **C** M K BROWN, **NSM** S E MARSH, S M STILWELL

BISHOP'S HULL (St John the Evangelist)   *see* Taunton St Jo *B & W*

BISHOPS HULL (St Peter and St Paul) *B & W 17* **P** *Adn Taunton*   **V** P J HUGHES

BISHOP'S ITCHINGTON (St Michael) *Cov 10*   **P** *Bp* **P-in-c** M C GREEN

BISHOP'S LAVINGTON (All Saints)   *see* The Lavingtons, Cheverells, and Easterton *Sarum*

BISHOPS LYDEARD (Blessed Virgin Mary) w Bagborough and Cothelstone *B & W 18*   **P** *D&C (3 turns), Ms P M G Mitford (1 turn)*   **R** *vacant*

BISHOPS NORTON (St John the Evangelist)   *see* Twigworth, Down Hatherley, Norton, The Leigh etc *Glouc*

BISHOP'S STORTFORD (Holy Trinity) *St Alb 15*   **P** *Bp* **P-in-c** S MARTIN,   **NSM** S A TARRAN

BISHOP'S STORTFORD (St Michael) *St Alb 15*   **P** *Bp* **V** R A V MARCHAND,   **C** A M SEARLE,   **NSM** D C HINGE, J E KNIGHT

BISHOP'S SUTTON (St Nicholas) and Ropley and West Tisted *Win 1*   **P** *Peache Trustees*   **R** R J SUCH

BISHOP'S TACHBROOK (St Chad) *Cov 11*   **P** *Bp* **P-in-c** E SCRIVENS

BISHOPS TAWTON (St John the Baptist)   *see* Barnstaple *Ex*

BISHOP'S WALTHAM (St Peter) *Portsm 1*   **P** *Bp* **R** J C HUNT,   **NSM** J BELOE

BISHOP'S WOOD (St Mary)   *see* Hartlebury *Worc*

BISHOPSBOURNE (St Mary)   *see* Barham w Bishopsbourne and Kingston *Cant*

BISHOPSNYMPTON (St Mary the Virgin), Rose Ash, Mariansleigh, Molland, Knowstone, East Anstey and West Anstey *Ex 19*   **P** *DBP*   **P-in-c** A C JONES

BISHOPSTEIGNTON (St John the Baptist)   *see* Teignmouth, Ideford w Luton, Ashcombe etc *Ex*

BISHOPSTOKE (St Mary) (St Paul) *Win 10*   **P** *Bp* **R** R E WISE

BISHOPSTON (Church of the Good Shepherd)   *see* Bishopston and St Andrews *Bris*

BISHOPSTON (St Michael and All Angels)   *as above*

BISHOPSTON (St Michael and All Angels) (Church of the Good Shepherd) and St Andrews *Bris 3*   **P** *Patr Bd* **TV** R J BURBRIDGE,   **P-in-c** J C W STEVENSON, **NSM** B J PULLAN, V LEE,   **OLM** S A TRUSCOTT

BISHOPSTONE (St Andrew)   *see* E Blatchington and Bishopstone *Chich*

BISHOPSTONE (St John the Baptist)   *see* Chalke Valley *Sarum*

BISHOPSTONE (St Lawrence)   *see* Credenhill w Brinsop and Wormsley etc *Heref*

BISHOPSTONE (St Mary the Virgin)   *see* Lyddington and Wanborough and Bishopstone etc *Bris*

BISHOPSTROW (St Aldhelm) and Boreham *Sarum 17*   **P** *DBP* **R** D R A BRETT

BISHOPSWOOD (All Saints)   *see* Dixton, Wyesham, Bishopswood, Whitchurch etc *Heref*

BISHOPSWOOD (St John the Evangelist) *Lich 2*   **P** *V Brewood* **V** C A HOST,   **NSM** M J COULTER

BISHOPSWORTH (St Peter) and Bedminster Down *Bris 1* **P** *Bp*   **TR** T R J GODDEN,   **TV** I L GARRETT, **NSM** E P WHERLOCK, R A LANE

BISHOPTHORPE (St Andrew) *York 1* P *Abp* V C I COATES,
NSM P J MACNAUGHTON

BISHOPTON (St Peter) w Great Stainton *Dur 10* P *Ld Chan*
V D M BROOKE, NSM P CLAYTON

BISHOPWEARMOUTH (Good Shepherd) *Dur 16* P *Bp*
P-in-c B SKELTON, NSM D RAINE

BISHOPWEARMOUTH (St Gabriel) *Dur 16* P *V Sunderland*
P-in-c J R MCMANNERS, NSM J P TALBOT

BISHOPWEARMOUTH (St Luke Pallion) *see* Millfield St
Mark and Pallion St Luke *Dur*

BISHOPWEARMOUTH (St Mary) *see* Millfield St Mary *Dur*

BISHOPWEARMOUTH (St Nicholas) (Christ Church) *Dur 16*
P *Bp* V *vacant* 0191-522 6444 *or* 520 2127

BISLEY (All Saints), Chalford, France Lynch, and Oakridge
Glouc 4 P *Bp and Adn Glouc (1 turn), and Ld Chan (1 turn)*
V S G RICHARDS, NSM S J JARVIS, R M BRYANT

BISLEY (St John the Baptist) and West End (Holy Trinity)
Guildf 6 P *Bp* R A J ARMITT, NSM D H ROBINSON,
OLM R ABBOTT

BISPHAM (All Hallows) *Blackb 8* P *Ch Soc Trust* R S J COX,
C A C HOWARD

BISTERNE (St Paul) *see* Ringwood *Win*

BITCHFIELD (St Mary Magdalene) *see* N Beltisloe Gp *Linc*

BITTADON (St Peter) *see* Ilfracombe, Lee, Woolacombe,
Bittadon etc *Ex*

BITTERING PARVA (St Peter and St Paul) *see* Gressenhall w
Longham w Wendling etc *Nor*

BITTERLEY (St Mary) *see* Ludlow *Heref*

BITTERNE (Holy Saviour) *Win 13* P *Bp*
P-in-c A M M PARKER

BITTERNE PARK (All Hallows) (Ascension) *Win 13* P *Bp*
V S J CHAPMAN, C G I COLLINGRIDGE

BITTESWELL (St Mary) *see* Lutterworth w Cotesbach and
Bitteswell *Leic*

BITTON (St Mary) *see* Warmley, Syston and Bitton *Bris*

BIX (St James) *see* Nettlebed w Bix, Highmoor, Pishill
etc *Ox*

BIXLEY (St Wandregesilus) *see* Poringland *Nor*

BLABY (All Saints) *Leic 7* P *Bp* P-in-c J G GIBBINS

BLACK BOURTON (St Mary the Virgin) *see* Shill Valley and
Broadshire *Ox*

BLACK NOTLEY (St Peter and St Paul) *Chelmsf 15*
P *St Jo Coll Cam* P-in-c E J BENDREY, C R J KEAN

BLACK TORRINGTON (St Mary), Bradford w Cookbury,
Thornbury and Highampton *Ex 17* P *DBP*
P-in-c K M ROBERTS

BLACKAWTON (St Michael) *see* Stoke Fleming, Blackawton
and Strete *Ex*

BLACKBIRD LEYS (Holy Family) *Ox 4* P *Bp*
NSM S R BURNE, P D BAKER

BLACKBOURNE *St E 9* P *Patr Bd* TR P R GARBETT,
TV E A JUMP, NSM A J REDMAN, OLM D A NEUPERT,
J F WALKER, S M NUTT

BLACKBROOK (St Paul) *see* Parr *Liv*

BLACKBURN (Christ Church w St Matthew) *Blackb 2* P *Bp*
V A RAYNES, NSM J R TERRY

BLACKBURN Christ the King (St Luke) (St Mark) *Blackb 2*
P *Bp and V Blackb (jt)* V F E GREEN

BLACKBURN (St Barnabas) *Blackb 2* P *Bp*
P-in-c J P MILTON-THOMPSON

BLACKBURN (St Francis) (St Aidan) *Blackb 2* P *Bp*
V *vacant* (01254) 610570

BLACKBURN (St Gabriel) *Blackb 2* P *Bp* V S P CORBETT

BLACKBURN (St James) *Blackb 2* P *Bp* C C E BROOKS

BLACKBURN (St Luke) *see* Blackb Christ the King *Blackb*

BLACKBURN (St Michael and All Angels) (Holy Trinity
Worship Centre) w St John the Evangelist *Blackb 2*
P *V Blackb* P-in-c L M DANIELS

BLACKBURN (St Silas) *Blackb 2* P *Trustees*
P-in-c A F RANSON

BLACKBURN (St Stephen) *Blackb 2* P *Trustees* V *vacant*
(01254) 255546

BLACKBURN St Thomas (St Jude) *Blackb 2* P *Bp and
Trustees (alt)* P-in-c L M DANIELS

BLACKBURN The Redeemer (St Bartholomew) (The Saviour)
Blackb 2 P *Bp and CPAS (jt)* V R A H MARSHALL,
C S P WATKINSON

BLACKDOWN Benefice, The *B & W 14* P *DBP (4 turns),
Pitminster PCC and Corfe PCC (1 turn)* R S M GREEN

BLACKDOWN (Holy Trinity) *see* Beaminster Area *Sarum*

BLACKFEN (Good Shepherd) *see* Lamorbey H Redeemer
Roch

BLACKFORD (Holy Trinity) *see* Wedmore w Theale and
Blackford *B & W*

BLACKFORD (St John the Baptist) *see* Rockcliffe and
Blackford *Carl*

BLACKFORD (St Michael) *see* Camelot Par *B & W*

BLACKFORDBY (St Margaret) and Woodville *Leic 8* P *Bp*
V T S G VALE

BLACKHALL (St Andrew), Castle Eden and Monkhesleden
Dur 2 P *Bp* R G LIDDLE

BLACKHAM (All Saints) *see* Withyham St Mich *Chich*

BLACKHEATH (All Saints) *S'wark 4* P *V Lewisham St Mary*
V N W S CRANFIELD, Hon C R C PEERS,
OLM T W CHATTERTON

BLACKHEATH (Ascension) *see* Deptford St Jo w H Trin and
Ascension *S'wark*

BLACKHEATH (St John the Evangelist) *S'wark 1* P *CPAS*
V P J FARLEY-MOORE, NSM A M BESWETHERICK

BLACKHEATH (St Martin) *see* Wonersh w Blackheath *Guildf*

BLACKHEATH (St Paul) *Birm 7* P *Bp* V M J SERMON,
NSM C G CHRISTENSEN

BLACKHEATH PARK (St Michael and All Angels) *S'wark 1*
P *Bp* V A R CHRISTIE, C J E CROUCHER, NSM A SCOTT

BLACKLAND (St Peter) *see* Marden Vale *Sarum*

BLACKLANDS Hastings (Christchurch and St Andrew) *Chich 17*
P *Ch Patr Trust* V *vacant* (01424) 422551

BLACKLEY (Holy Trinity) *Man 4* P *Bp* R P A STAMP

BLACKLEY (St Andrew) *Man 4* P *Bp* P-in-c I C FELLOWS

BLACKLEY (St Mark) White Moss *Man 4* P *D&C* R *vacant*
0161-740 7558

BLACKLEY (St Paul) *Man 4* P *Bp* P-in-c E M ROBERTS

BLACKLEY (St Peter) *Man 4* P *D&C* P-in-c E M ROBERTS

BLACKMOOR (St Matthew) and Whitehill *Portsm 4* P *Earl of
Selborne* NSM W N MALLAS, L C PAGE

BLACKMORE (St Laurence) and Stondon Massey *Chelmsf 26*
P *Bp* V A SMITH

BLACKPOOL (Christ Church w All Saints) (St Andrew)
Blackb 8 P *Bp and Trustees (jt)* P-in-c A BYROM

BLACKPOOL (Holy Cross) South Shore *Blackb 8* P *Bp*
V S EDWARDS

BLACKPOOL (Holy Trinity) *see* S Shore H Trin *Blackb*

BLACKPOOL (St John) *Blackb 8* P *Trustees*
P-in-c D CONNOLLY

BLACKPOOL (St Mark) *Blackb 8* P *CPAS* V S E BROOK,
C H HORNBY

BLACKPOOL (St Mary) South Shore *Blackb 8* P *Bp*
V *vacant* (01253) 342713

BLACKPOOL (St Michael and All Angels) *Blackb 8* P *Bp*
P-in-c S E BROOK, C H HORNBY

BLACKPOOL (St Paul) Marton *see* Marton *Blackb*

BLACKPOOL (St Paul's Worship Centre) *Blackb 8* P *Trustees*
V J E SHAW

BLACKPOOL (St Peter) *see* S Shore St Pet *Blackb*

BLACKPOOL (St Stephen on the Cliffs) *Blackb 8* P *Bp,
R Bispham All Hallows, and Ch Wardens (jt)* V A G SAGE

BLACKPOOL (St Thomas) *Blackb 8* P *CPAS*
P-in-c R F T MURPHY

BLACKPOOL (St Wilfrid) Mereside *Blackb 8* P *Bp*
V P H HUDSON

BLACKROD (St Catherine) (Scot Lane School) *Man 9*
P *V Bolton-le-Moors St Pet* V R C COOPER, C S FLETCHER,
M C BEHREND, P DEVER, M J DAY, OLM C MCCABE,
P D HARLEY, T LITHERLAND

BLACKTOFT (Holy Trinity) *see* Howden *York*

BLACKWATER (St Barnabas) *see* Arreton *Portsm*

BLACKWELL (All Saints) and Salutation *Dur 8* P *Bp*
V J R DOBSON

BLACKWELL (St Catherine) *see* The Lickey *Birm*

BLACKWELL (St Werburgh) w Tibshelf *Derby 1* P *Bp and
MMCET (jt)* V G MANLEY

BLACON (Holy Trinity) *see* Ches H Trin *Ches*

BLADON (St Martin) *see* Blenheim *Ox*

BLAGDON (St Andrew) w Compton Martin and Ubley *B & W 9*
P *Bp and Sir John Wills Bt (jt)* R J L CHAMBERLAIN

BLAGREAVES (St Andrew) *Derby 10* P *Bp, Churchwardens,
and CPAS (jt)* V P G BYSOUTH

BLAISDON (St Michael and All Angels)
see Westbury-on-Severn w Flaxley, Blaisdon etc *Glouc*

BLAKEDOWN (St James the Great) *see* Churchill-in-Halfshire
w Blakedown and Broome *Worc*

BLAKEMERE (St Leonard) *see* Cusop w Blakemere,
Bredwardine w Brobury etc *Heref*

BLAKENALL HEATH (Christ Church) *Lich 25* P *Patr Bd*
TR P H MYERS

BLAKENEY (All Saints) *see* Newnham w Awre and Blakeney
Glouc

BLAKENEY (St Nicholas w St Mary and St Thomas) w Cley,
Wiveton, Glandford and Letheringsett *Nor 18* P *Bp and Keble
Coll Ox (jt)* R N G BATCOCK, NSM J M FAWCETT

BLAKENHALL (St Luke) *see* Wolverhampton St Luke *Lich*

BLAKENHAM, GREAT (St Mary) and LITTLE (St Mary) w
Baylham and Nettlestead *St E 1* **P** *Bp and MMCET (jt)*
C P THORN, **OLM** P Y WRIGHT
BLAKESLEY (St Mary) *see Lambfold Pet*
BLANCHLAND (St Mary's Abbey) w Hunstanworth and
Edmundbyers and Muggleswick *Newc 9*
P *D E Scott-Harden Esq, Lord Crewe's Trustees and D&C (alt)*
P-in-c D J IRVINE, **NSM** J LYNCH
BLANDFORD FORUM (St Peter and St Paul) and Langton
Long *Sarum 6* **P** *Bp* **R** T STOREY, **NSM** R A COLDWELL
BLANDFORD ST MARY (St Mary) *see Spetisbury w*
Charlton Marshall etc *Sarum*
BLANKNEY (St Oswald) *see Metheringham w Blankney and*
Dunston *Linc*
BLASTON (St Giles) *see Six Saints circa Holt Leic*
BLATCHINGTON, EAST (St John the Evangelist) (St Peter)
and Bishopstone *Chich 18* **P** *Bp and Bp Lon (alt)*
NSM R J WOODHAMS
BLATCHINGTON, WEST (St Peter) *Chich 4* **P** *Bp*
R D B SMITH
BLAXHALL (St Peter) *see Alde River St E*
BLAYDON (St Cuthbert) and Swalwell *Dur 13* **P** *Bp*
R A THORP, **C** M P TARLING, **NSM** H M THORP, B HOWELL
BLEADON (St Peter and St Paul) *B & W 10* **P** *Guild of All So*
P-in-c P T STEVENS
BLEAN (St Cosmus and St Damian) *Cant 3* **P** *Master of*
Eastbridge Hosp **P-in-c** S C E LAIRD
BLEASBY (St Mary) *see Thurgarton w Hoveringham and*
Bleasby etc *S'well*
BLEASDALE (St Eadmor) *see Fellside Team Blackb*
BLEATARN (Chapel of Ease) *see Brough w Stainmore,*
Musgrave and Warcop *Carl*
BLEDINGTON (St Leonard) *see Broadwell, Evenlode,*
Oddington, Adlestrop etc *Glouc*
BLEDLOW (Holy Trinity) *see Risborough Ox*
BLEDLOW RIDGE (St Paul) *see W Wycombe w Bledlow*
Ridge, Bradenham and Radnage *Ox*
BLENDON (St James the Great) *Roch 17* **P** *The Crown*
V A F WARD, **NSM** P A PERCIVAL
BLENDWORTH (Holy Trinity) w Chalton w Idsworth *Portsm 5*
P *Bp* **P-in-c** R A DONALD
BLENHEIM *Ox 9* **P** *Patr Bd* **TR** A M DAFFERN,
TV A PARKINSON, **NSM** S C HENSON, C A W SANDERS,
B R WOOD, A PROUDLEY, C J Y HAYNS
BLETCHINGDON (St Giles) *see Akeman Ox*
BLETCHINGLEY (St Mary) and Nutfield *S'wark 25*
P *Em Coll Cam and Jes Coll Ox (jt)* **R** P MOSELING,
NSM N C ROBERTS
BLETCHLEY (St Mary) (St John's District Church) *Ox 25*
P *DBP* **R** M J ARCHER, **C** C BUTT
BLETCHLEY, NORTH (Whaddon Way Church) Conventional
District *Ox 25 vacant (01908) 751370*
BLETSOE (St Mary) *see Riseley w Bletsoe St Alb*
BLEWBURY (St Michael and All Angels) *see The Churn Ox*
BLICKLING (St Andrew) *see Lt Barningham, Blickling,*
Edgefield etc *Nor*
BLIDWORTH (St Mary of the Purification) w Rainworth
S'well 2 **P** *DBP and Ld Chan (alt)* **P-in-c** H ROBINSON,
NSM C E TYACK
BLIDWORTH, NEW (St Andrew) *see Blidworth w Rainworth*
S'well
BLINDLEY HEATH (St John the Evangelist) *see Godstone*
and Blindley Heath *S'wark*
BLISLAND (St Protus and St Hyacinth) w St Breward *Truro 10*
P *SMF and D&C (alt)* **P-in-c** S L BRYAN
BLISWORTH (St John the Baptist) and Stoke Bruerne w Grafton
Regis and Alderton *Pet 5* **P** *BNC Ox and MMCET (2 turns),*
Ld Chan (1 turn) **P-in-c** A L WATKINS
BLITHFIELD (St Leonard) *see Abbots Bromley, Blithfield,*
Colton, Colwich etc *Lich*
BLO' NORTON (St Andrew) *see Guiltcross Nor*
BLOCKLEY (St Peter and St Paul) w Aston Magna and Bourton
on the Hill *Glouc 9* **P** *Lord Dulverton and DBP (jt)*
P-in-c G L HUMPHRIES
BLOFIELD (St Andrew) w Hemblington *Nor 4* **P** *G&C Coll*
Cam **R** P CUBITT
BLOOMSBURY (St George) w Woburn Square (Christ Church)
Lon 17 **P** *Ld Chan* **R** D T PEEBLES, **NSM** J A WALTERS
BLORE RAY (St Bartholomew) *see Calton, Cauldon, Grindon,*
Waterfall etc *Lich*
BLOXHAM (Our Lady of Bloxham) w Milcombe and South
Newington *Ox 5* **P** *Ex Coll Ox and Eton Coll (jt)*
P-in-c S L TILLETT
BLOXHOLME (St Mary) *see Digby Gp Linc*
BLOXWICH (All Saints) (Holy Ascension) *Lich 25* **P** *Patr Bd*
TR R S WILLIAMS, **TV** C J TURNER, K A LOWTHER,
NSM M ARNOLD

BLOXWORTH (St Andrew) *see Red Post Sarum*
BLUBBERHOUSES (St Andrew) *see Washburn and*
Mid-Wharfe *Bradf*
BLUCHER (St Cuthbert) *see Newburn Newc*
BLUE BELL HILL (St Alban) *see S Chatham H Trin Roch*
BLUNDELLSANDS (St Michael) *Liv 5* **P** *Trustees*
P-in-c M C FREEMAN
BLUNDELLSANDS (St Nicholas) *Liv 5* **P** *Trustees*
V C M M THORNBOROUGH
BLUNDESTON (St Mary) *see Somerleyton, Ashby, Fritton,*
Herringfleet etc *Nor*
BLUNHAM (St Edmund King and Martyr and St James)
see Riversmeet St Alb
BLUNSDON (St Andrew) *see N Swindon St Andr Bris*
BLUNTISHAM (St Mary) cum Earith w Colne and Holywell
cum Needingworth *Ely 12* **P** *Ch Ch Ox and Bp (jt)*
V S M ANTHONY, **C** S M BOWDEN-PICKSTOCK
BLURTON (St Alban) *see Blurton and Dresden Lich*
BLURTON (St Bartholomew) (St Alban) and Dresden *Lich 12*
P *Bp* **OLM** H T ADAMS, L J WALKER
BLYBOROUGH (St Alkmund) *see Glentworth Gp Linc*
BLYFORD (All Saints) *see Blyth Valley St E*
BLYMHILL (St Mary) *see Watershed Lich*
BLYTH (St Cuthbert) *Newc 1* **P** *Bp* **V** *vacant (01670) 352410*
BLYTH (St Mary) *Newc 1* **P** *Bp* **V** A J ELDER
BLYTH (St Mary and St Martin) and Scrooby w Ranskill *S'well 1*
P *Bp and Trin Coll Cam (jt)* **V** *vacant (01909) 591229*
BLYTH VALLEY Team Ministry, The *St E 15* **P** *Patr Bd*
TR E L RENNARD, **TV** E M CANNON, **OLM** A C WRIGHT
BLYTHBURGH (Holy Trinity) *see Sole Bay St E*
BLYTON (St Martin) *see Corringham and Blyton Gp Linc*
BOARHUNT (St Nicholas) *see Southwick w Boarhunt Portsm*
BOARSTALL (St James) *see Bernwode Ox*
BOBBING (St Bartholomew) *see Sittingbourne H Trin w*
Bobbing *Cant*
BOBBINGTON (Holy Cross) *see Smestow Vale Lich*
BOBBINGWORTH (St Germain) *see Fyfield, Moreton w*
Bobbingworth etc *Chelmsf*
BOCKING (St Mary) *Chelmsf 15* **P** *Abp Cant* **R** P A NEED,
C G D TULK
BOCKING (St Peter) *Chelmsf 15* **P** *Abp Cant*
P-in-c T BARNES
BOCKLETON (St Michael) *see Leominster Heref*
BOCONNOC (not known) *see Lostwithiel, St Winnow w*
St Nectan's Chpl etc *Truro*
BODDINGTON (St John the Baptist) *see Aston-le-Walls,*
Byfield, Boddington, Eydon etc *Pet*
BODDINGTON (St Mary Magdalene) *see Twigworth, Down*
Hatherley, Norton, The Leigh etc *Glouc*
BODENHAM (St Michael and All Angels), Felton and Preston
Wynne *Heref 3* **P** *Bp* **P-in-c** H M SHORT
BODHAM (All Saints) *see Weybourne Gp Nor*
BODIAM (St Giles) *Chich 20* **P** *All So Coll Ox*
V G L WINCHESTER
BODICOTE (St John the Baptist) *Ox 5* **P** *New Coll Ox*
V B L M PHILLIPS, **OLM** B C GARDNER
BODINNICK (St John) *see Lanteglos by Fowey Truro*
BODLE STREET GREEN (St John the Evangelist)
see Warbleton and Bodle Street Green Chich
BODMIN (St Petroc) (St Lawrence w St Leonard) w Lanhydrock
and Lanivet *Truro 10* **P** *DBP* **TR** G G C MINORS,
NSM C F CLEMOW, E J MUNDAY, R A MAY, S I BAWDEN
BODNEY (St Mary) *see Hilborough w Bodney Nor*
BOGNOR (St Wilfrid) *Chich 1* **P** *Abp* **V** A J WADSWORTH,
NSM T MARSHALL
BOLAM (St Andrew) *see Heighington Dur*
BOLAM (St Andrew) w Whalton and Hartburn w Meldon
Newc 11 **P** *Ld Chan (2 turns), J I K Walker Esq (1 turn), and*
D&C Dur (1 turn) **R** M A G BRYCE, **OLM** F J SAMPLE
BOLAS MAGNA (St John the Baptist) *see Tibberton w Bolas*
Magna and Waters Upton *Lich*
BOLDMERE (St Michael) *Birm 12* **P** *Birm Dioc Trustees*
V P D RATTIGAN, **C** A J HOWETT
BOLDON (St Nicholas) *Dur 15* **P** *Bp* **P-in-c** J S BAIN
BOLDON, EAST (St George) *Dur 15* **P** *Bp* **P-in-c** J S BAIN,
NSM M R DEVINE
BOLDRE (St John the Baptist) w South Baddesley *Win 11*
P *Bp and Lord Teynham (jt)* **P-in-c** N R SMART,
Hon C F E WILLETT
BOLDRE, EAST (St Paul) *see Beaulieu and Exbury and E*
Boldre *Win*
BOLDRON (Mission Room) *see Startforth and Bowes and*
Rokeby w Brignall *Ripon*
BOLE (St Martin) *see Retford Area S'well*
BOLINGBROKE (St Peter and St Paul) *see Marden Hill Gp*
Linc

BOLINGBROKE, NEW (St Peter) *see* Sibsey w Frithville *Linc*

BOLLINGHAM (St Silas) *see* Eardisley w Bollingham, Willersley, Brilley etc *Heref*

BOLLINGTON (Holy Trinity) *see* Rostherne w Bollington *Ches*

BOLLINGTON (St Oswald) (Holy Trinity) *Ches 13*
P *V Prestbury* **V** V W HYDON

BOLNEY (St Mary Magdalene) *Chich 6* **P** *K Coll Lon*
P-in-c K D LITTLEJOHN

BOLNHURST (St Dunstan) *see* Keysoe w Bolnhurst and Lt Staughton *St Alb*

BOLSOVER (St Mary and St Laurence) *Derby 3* **P** *Bp*
V *vacant* (01246) 824888

BOLSTERSTONE (St Mary) *Sheff 3*
P *R B Rimington-Wilson Esq* **V** K J BARNARD

BOLTBY (Holy Trinity) *see* Felixkirk w Boltby *York*

BOLTON (All Saints) *see* Binsey *Carl*

BOLTON (All Saints) *Carl 1* **P** *V Morland w Thrimby etc*
P-in-c S J FYFE

BOLTON Breightmet (St James) *see* Leverhulme *Man*

BOLTON Chapel (unknown) *see* Whittingham and Edlingham w Bolton Chapel *Newc*

BOLTON (Christ Church) *see* Heaton Ch Ch w Halliwell St Marg *Man*

BOLTON (St Chad) *see* Leverhulme *Man*

BOLTON (St James w St Chrysostom) *Bradf 3* **P** *Bp*
P-in-c P G WALKER

BOLTON (St Mary the Virgin) *see* Deane *Man*

BOLTON Top o' th' Moss (St John the Evangelist)
see Leverhulme *Man*

BOLTON, WEST (Emmanuel) (St Luke) (St Matthew w St Barnabas) (St Paul) (St Thomas the Apostle) *Man 7*
P *Patr Bd* **TR** A S CORNES, **TV** D R PETCH, F ADMAN,
C G F PAGE, **NSM** M A J TAYLOR, **OLM** S FOSTER

BOLTON ABBEY (St Mary and St Cuthbert) *Bradf 7* **P** *Duke of Devonshire* **R** G MOFFAT, **NSM** J D BENNETT

BOLTON BY BOWLAND (St Peter and St Paul) w Grindleton *Bradf 5* **P** *Bp and V Hurst Green and Mitton (jt)*
R D W MEWIS, **Hon C** J R BROCKLEHURST

BOLTON LE MOORS (St Bede) *Man 9* **P** *Bp*
P-in-c V ASHWORTH, **NSM** T ASHWORTH,
OLM D J BARRETT

BOLTON LE MOORS (St Peter) *Man 7* **P** *Bp*
P-in-c M THOMPSON, **Hon C** J A HORROCKS,
NSM K G C NEWPORT, B S GASKELL

BOLTON LE MOORS (St Philip) *Man 7* **P** *Bp and Hulme Trustees (alt)* **P-in-c** M THOMPSON

BOLTON LE MOORS (St Simon and St Jude) *Man 7*
P *Trustees* **P-in-c** G KENNEDY

BOLTON-LE-SANDS (Holy Trinity) *Blackb 14* **P** *Bp*
P-in-c G H CAPON

BOLTON ON SWALE (St Mary) *see* Easby w Skeeby and Brompton on Swale etc *Ripon*

BOLTON PERCY (All Saints) *York 1* **P** *Abp*
P-in-c G R MUMFORD

BOLTON-UPON-DEARNE (St Andrew the Apostle) *Sheff 12*
P *Meynall Ch Trust* **V** *vacant* (01709) 893163

BOLTONS, THE *see* W Brompton St Mary w St Peter and St Jude *Lon*

BOLVENTOR (Holy Trinity) *see* Altarnon w Bolventor, Laneast and St Clether *Truro*

BOMERE HEATH (Mission Room) *see* Leaton and Albrighton w Battlefield *Lich*

BONBY (St Andrew) *Linc 6* **P** *DBP* **V** G O MITCHELL

BONCHURCH (St Boniface) (St Boniface Old Church) *Portsm 7*
P *Ch Patr Trust* **R** G E MORRIS, **NSM** V M HEENAN

BONDLEIGH (St James the Apostle) *see* N Tawton, Bondleigh, Sampford Courtenay etc *Ex*

BONEY HAY *see* Chase Terrace *Lich*

BONINGALE (St Chad) *see* Albrighton, Boningale and Donington *Lich*

BONNINGTON (St Rumwold) *see* Aldington w Bonnington and Bilsington etc *Cant*

BONSALL (St James the Apostle) *see* Wirksworth *Derby*

BOOKER (St Birinus' Mission Church) *see* High Wycombe *Ox*

BOOKHAM, GREAT (St Nicolas) *Guildf 10* **P** *Bp*
R A D JENKINS, **C** C D BESSANT

BOOKHAM, LITTLE (not known) *see* Effingham w Lt Bookham *Guildf*

BOONGATE (St Mary) *see* Pet St Mary Boongate *Pet*

BOOSBECK (St Aidan) and Lingdale *York 16* **P** *Abp*
P-in-c V E M-B HAYNES

BOOTHBY GRAFFOE (St Andrew) *see* Graffoe Gp *Linc*

BOOTHBY PAGNELL (St Andrew) *see* N Beltisloe Gp *Linc*

BOOTHSTOWN (St Andrew's Church Institute) *see* Worsley *Man*

BOOTLE (Christ Church) *Liv 1* **P** *Bp* **V** T RICH,
NSM J WILLIAMS

BOOTLE (St Andrew) (St Leonard) (St Mary w St Paul) (St Matthew) (St Thomas) *Liv 1* **P** *Patr Bd* **TR** R J DRIVER,
TV J C M BISSEX, I A WHITAKER

BOOTLE (St Michael and All Angels), Corney, Whicham and Whitbeck *Carl 5* **P** *Earl of Lonsdale* **P-in-c** I N JAMES

BORASTON (not known) *see* Tenbury *Heref*

BORDEN (St Peter and St Paul) *Cant 15* **P** *SMF*
V J H G LEWIS

BORDER Group of Parishes *see* Llanyblodwel, Llanymynech, Morton and Trefonen *Lich*

BORDERLINK PARISHES *see* Cusop w Blakemere, Bredwardine w Brobury etc *Heref*

BORDESLEY (St Alban and St Patrick) *see* Highgate *Birm*

BORDESLEY (St Benedict) *Birm 13* **P** *Keble Coll Ox*
NSM P L CADOGAN

BORDESLEY GREEN (St Paul) *see* Ward End w Bordesley Green *Birm*

BORDON (St Mark) *Guildf 3* **P** *Bp* **V** D J SCOTT-BROMLEY,
NSM W N MALLAS

BOREHAM (St Andrew) *Chelmsf 9* **P** *Bp* **P-in-c** L P BATSON,
NSM A L KOSLA

BOREHAM (St John the Evangelist) *see* Bishopstrow and Boreham *Sarum*

BOREHAMWOOD (All Saints) *see* Elstree and Borehamwood *St Alb*

BOREHAMWOOD (Holy Cross) *as above*

BOREHAMWOOD (St Michael and All Angels) *as above*

BORLEY (not known) *see* N Hinckford *Chelmsf*

BOROUGH GREEN (Good Shepherd) *Roch 10* **P** *Bp*
V A J POWELL

BOROUGHBRIDGE (St James) *see* Aldborough w Boroughbridge and Roecliffe *Ripon*

BORROWASH (St Stephen's Chapel) *see* Ockbrook *Derby*

BORROWDALE (St Andrew) *see* Upper Derwent *Carl*

BORSTAL (St Matthew) *Roch 5* **P** *V Rochester St Marg*
V *vacant* (01634) 845948

BORWICK (St Mary) *see* Warton St Oswald w Yealand Conyers *Blackb*

BOSBURY (Holy Trinity) *see* Ledbury *Heref*

BOSCASTLE w Davidstow *Truro 10* **P** *Duchy of Cornwall (1 turn), DBP (2 turns)* **P-in-c** R S THEWSEY,
NSM M PARSONS

BOSCOMBE (St Andrew) *see* Bourne Valley *Sarum*

BOSCOMBE (St Andrew) *Win 8* **P** *Bp* **P-in-c** R L VERNON,
NSM N J HOULTON

BOSCOMBE (St John the Evangelist) *Win 8* **P** *Peache Trustees*
V R P KHAKHRIA

BOSCOPPA *Truro 1* **P** *Prime Min* **P-in-c** S D MICHAEL

BOSHAM (Holy Trinity) *Chich 13* **P** *Bp* **V** M J LANE

BOSLEY (St Mary the Virgin) and North Rode (St Michael) w Wincle (St Michael) and Wildboarclough (St Saviour) *Ches 13*
P *Bp, V Prestbury, and Earl of Derby (jt)* **V** S BREED

BOSSALL (St Botolph) *see* Sand Hutton *York*

BOSSINGTON (St James) *see* Broughton, Bossington, Houghton and Mottisfont *Win*

BOSTALL HEATH (St Andrew) *Roch 15* **P** *DBP*
V S SHAHZAD

BOSTON (Holy Trinity) *see* Skirbeck H Trin *Linc*

BOSTON (St Botolph) (St Christopher) *Linc 20* **P** *Bp*
TR R L WHITEHEAD, **C** C G WEDGE, H W F JONES

BOSTON (St Nicholas) *see* Skirbeck St Nic *Linc*

BOSTON (St Thomas) *see* Boston *Linc*

BOSTON SPA (St Mary) *see* Bramham *York*

BOSWORTH (St Peter) and Sheepy Group *Leic 10* **P** *Patr Bd (2 turns), Ld Chan (1 turn)* **TR** J F PLANT,
TV J G HARGREAVES, **C** A P CAIN, **NSM** A C HOLDSTOCK,
G R JACKSON, A C THORP

BOTCHERBY (St Andrew) *see* Carl St Aid and Ch Ch *Carl*

BOTESDALE (St Botolph) *see* Redgrave cum Botesdale w Rickinghall *St E*

BOTHAL (St Andrew) and Pegswood w Longhirst *Newc 11*
P *Bp* **R** J C PARK

BOTHAMSALL (Our Lady and St Peter) *see* Retford Area *S'well*

BOTHENHAMPTON (Holy Trinity) *see* Bridport *Sarum*

BOTLEY (All Saints) *Portsm 1* **P** *Bp* **NSM** R E SCHOFIELD

BOTLEY (St Peter and St Paul) *see* Osney *Ox*

BOTLEYS AND LYNE (Holy Trinity) *see* Chertsey, Lyne and Longcross *Guildf*

BOTOLPHS (St Botolph) *see* Beeding and Bramber w Botolphs *Chich*

BOTTESFORD (St Mary the Virgin)   see Vale of Belvoir *Leic*
BOTTESFORD (St Peter) w Ashby *Linc 4*   P *Patr Bd*
TR P J LILEY,   TV G M LINES
BOTTISHAM (Holy Trinity)   see Anglesey Gp *Ely*
BOTUS FLEMING (St Mary)   see Landrake w St Erney and
Botus Fleming *Truro*
BOUGHTON (All Saints) *Ely 3*   P *Bp*   P-in-c B L BURTON
BOUGHTON (St John the Baptist)   see Pitsford w Boughton *Pet*
BOUGHTON (St Matthew)   see Ollerton w Boughton *S'well*
BOUGHTON ALUPH (All Saints)   see Wye w Brook and
Hastingleigh etc *Cant*
BOUGHTON ALUPH (St Christopher)   as above
BOUGHTON MALHERBE (St Nicholas)   see Len Valley *Cant*
BOUGHTON MONCHELSEA (St Augustine) (St Peter)
Cant 13   P *Abp*   V R G DAVIS
BOUGHTON UNDER BLEAN (St Barnabas) (St Peter and
St Paul) w Dunkirk and Hernhill *Cant 14*   P *Abp*
P-in-c J BURROWS
BOULGE (St Michael) w Burgh, Grundisburgh and Hasketon
St E 7   P *Bp and DBP (jt)*   P-in-c H C SANDERS,
NSM W E GOURLAY
BOULMER (St Andrew)   see Longhoughton w Howick *Newc*
BOULTHAM (Holy Cross) (St Helen) *Linc 15*   P *DBP*
R D J OSBOURNE,   C M M ROSE
BOULTON (St Mary the Virgin) *Derby 15*   P *Bp*
V T S WRIGHT
BOUNDSTONE (Mission Church)   see Wrecclesham *Guildf*
BOURN (St Helena and St Mary)   see Papworth *Ely*
BOURNE (St Peter and St Paul) *Linc 13*   P *DBP*
V C J ATKINSON,   C S F CLEATON,   OLM P W R LISTER
BOURNE, The (St Thomas) and Tilford *Guildf 3*   P *Bp and Adn*
Surrey (alt)   Hon C J W BELL,   OLM E M POWELL
BOURNE, LOWER (St Martin)   see The Bourne and Tilford
Guildf
BOURNE END (St John)   see Sunnyside w Bourne End *St Alb*
BOURNE END (St Mark)   see Hedsor and Bourne End *Ox*
BOURNE STREET (St Mary)   see Pimlico St Mary Bourne
Street *Lon*
BOURNE VALLEY *Sarum 10*   P *Patr Bd*   TR V S PERRETT,
TV P A OSTLI-EAST,   C P F D TAYLOR, G A HUNT,
Hon C P A JOYCE,   NSM T G MANN, D M COATES
BOURNEMOUTH (All Saints)   see Pokesdown All SS *Win*
BOURNEMOUTH (Christ Church)   see Westbourne Ch Ch
Chpl *Win*
BOURNEMOUTH (Holy Epiphany) *Win 8*   P *Bp*
NSM D S THOMPSON
BOURNEMOUTH (St Alban) *Win 8*   P *Bp*   V R L NASH
BOURNEMOUTH (St Ambrose) *Win 8*   P *Bp*   V *vacant*
(01202) 764957
BOURNEMOUTH (St Andrew) Bennett Road *Win 8*
P *Trustees*   V G M ROBERTS,   Hon C J W DAVIES
BOURNEMOUTH (St Barnabas) Queen's Park
see Holdenhurst and Iford *Win*
BOURNEMOUTH (St Christopher)   see Southbourne St Chris
Win
BOURNEMOUTH (St Clement) *Win 8*   P *DBP*
C J W E RODLEY
BOURNEMOUTH (St Francis) *Win 8*   P *CR*   V *vacant*
(01202) 529336 *or* tel and fax 511845
BOURNEMOUTH (St James)   see Pokesdown St Jas *Win*
BOURNEMOUTH (St John) (St Michael and All Angels) *Win 8*
P *Bp and S R Willcox Esq (jt)*   P-in-c R D BALDOCK
BOURNEMOUTH (St John the Baptist)   see Moordown *Win*
BOURNEMOUTH (St John the Evangelist)   see Boscombe St
Jo *Win*
BOURNEMOUTH (St Katharine)   see Southbourne St Kath
Win
BOURNEMOUTH (St Luke) *Win 8*   P *Bp*   V R L NASH
BOURNEMOUTH (St Nicholas)   see Southbourne St Kath
Win
BOURNEMOUTH Town Centre (St Augustin) (St Peter)
(St Stephen) w St Swithun and Holy Trinity *Win 8*   P *Patr Bd*
TR I A TERRY,   TV R C N HARGER,   Hon C B G APPS
BOURNVILLE (St Andrew)   see Weston-super-Mare St Andr
Bournville *B & W*
BOURNVILLE (St Francis) *Birm 5*   P *Bp*   V P G BABINGTON,
C S M RUDGE,   NSM J M ADAMS
BOURTON (Holy Trinity)   see Wenlock *Heref*
BOURTON (St George)   see Upper Stour *Sarum*
BOURTON (St James)   see Shrivenham and Ashbury *Ox*
BOURTON (St Peter) w Frankton and Stretton on Dunsmore w
Princethorpe *Cov 6*   P *Bp (2 turns), Simeon's Trustees*
(1 turn), and Mrs J H Shaw-Fox (1 turn)   P-in-c B C CLUTTON
BOURTON, GREAT (All Saints)   see Shires' Edge *Ox*
BOURTON ON THE HILL (St Lawrence)   see Blockley w
Aston Magna and Bourton on the Hill *Glouc*

BOURTON-ON-THE-WATER (St Lawrence) w Clapton and
The Rissingtons *Glouc 9*   P *Wadh Coll Ox, DBP and*
C T R Wingfield Esq, and Ld Chan (by turn)
R R C ROSBOROUGH,   NSM J Y CARMAN, S M COX
BOVEY, NORTH (St John the Baptist)   see Moretonhampstead,
Manaton, N Bovey and Lustleigh *Ex*
BOVEY TRACEY (St John the Evangelist) w Heathfield *Ex 9*
P *Guild of All So*   V *vacant* (01626) 833451
BOVEY TRACEY (St Peter and St Paul and St Thomas of
Canterbury) w Hennock *Ex 9*   P *Prime Min (2 turns),*
MMCET (1 turn)   V W G HAMILTON,   C D J CARRINGTON,
Hon C J E SPENCER, R H TOTTERDELL
BOVINGDON (St Lawrence) *St Alb 4*   P *Ch Soc Trust*
V *vacant* (01442) 833298
BOW (All Hallows)   see Bromley by Bow All Hallows *Lon*
BOW (St Bartholomew) w Broad Nymet *Ex 2*   P *DBP*
R *vacant* (01363) 82566
BOW (St Mary) and Holy Trinity w Bromley St Leonard *Lon 7*
P *Bp and Grocers' Co (jt)*   NSM D F WAXHAM
BOW BRICKHILL (All Saints)   see Brickhills and Stoke
Hammond *Ox*
BOW COMMON (St Paul) *Lon 7*   P *Bp*   V D G ROSS
BOWBROOK NORTH: Feckenham and Hanbury and Stock and
Bradley *Worc 8*   P *Bp and D&C (jt)*   P-in-c J H GREEN,
NSM F B KINGS
BOWBROOK SOUTH: Crowle w Bredicot and Hadzor w
Oddingley and Tibberton and Himbleton and Huddington
Worc 8   P *Bp, D&C, R J G Berkeley Esq. and*
J F Bennett Esq (jt)   P-in-c J H GREEN,   NSM F B KINGS,
S J MORRIS
BOWBURN (Christ the King)   see Cassop cum Quarrington
Dur
BOWDEN, GREAT (St Peter and St Paul)   see Market
Harborough and The Transfiguration etc *Leic*
BOWDEN, LITTLE (St Hugh)   as above
BOWDEN, LITTLE (St Nicholas)   as above
BOWDEN HILL (St Anne)   see Gtr Corsham and Lacock *Bris*
BOWDON (St Luke) (St Mary the Virgin) *Ches 10*   P *Bp*
V R M H PREECE,   NSM S G TALBOT
BOWERCHALKE (Holy Trinity)   see Chalke Valley *Sarum*
BOWERS GIFFORD (St John) (St Margaret) w North Benfleet
Chelmsf 6   P *Em Coll Cam and Brig R H C Bryhers CBE (alt)*
P-in-c D A O IBIAYO
BOWES (St Giles)   see Startforth and Bowes and Rokeby w
Brignall *Ripon*
BOWES PARK (St Michael-at-Bowes)   see Wood Green St Mich
w Bounds Green St Gabr etc *Lon*
BOWLEE (St Thomas)   see Rhodes *Man*
BOWLING (St John) *Bradf 2*   P *V Bradford*   V H K ASTIN,
NSM C BARNES
BOWLING (St Stephen) *Bradf 2*   P *CPAS*
P-in-c J W HINTON,   C A S TREASURE
BOWNESS-ON-SOLWAY (St Michael), Kirkbride and Newton
Arlosh *Carl 3*   P *Earl of Lonsdale (2 turns), V Holme Cultram*
(1 turn)   R R P BLACKETT
BOWTHORPE (St Michael) *Nor 3*   P *Bp and CPAS (jt)*
P-in-c S C STOKES
BOX (St Barnabas)   see Minchinhampton w Box and Amberley
Glouc
BOX (St Thomas à Becket) w Hazlebury and Ditteridge *Bris 4*
P *Bp*   P-in-c J M ANDERSON-MACKENZIE,   NSM A M E KEMP,
OLM C SOUTHGATE
BOX HILL (St Andrew)   see Headley w Box Hill *Guildf*
BOX RIVER   see Boxford, Edwardstone, Groton etc *St E*
BOXFORD (St Andrew)   see E Downland *Ox*
BOXFORD (St Mary), Edwardstone, Groton, Little Waldingfield
and Newton *St E 12*   P *DBP and The Hon Thomas Lindsay*
(1 turn), Ld Chan (2 turns), Peterho Cam (1 turn)
P-in-c J SWEETMAN
BOXGROVE (St Mary and St Blaise) *Chich 3*   P *Duke of*
Richmond and Gordon   P-in-c I M FORRESTER
BOXLEY (St Mary the Virgin and All Saints) w Detling *Cant 13*
P *Abp*   P-in-c P S HOLLINS,   NSM E A ATTAWAY
BOXMOOR (St John the Evangelist) *St Alb 2*   P *Bp*
V J S REVELEY,   C E M HOOD,   NSM R C GOATLY
BOXTED (Holy Trinity)   see Glemsford, Hartest w Boxted,
Somerton etc *St E*
BOXTED (St Peter)   see Langham w Boxted *Chelmsf*
BOXWELL (St Mary the Virgin), Leighterton, Didmarton,
Oldbury-on-the-Hill, Sopworth, Badminton w Little
Badminton, Acton Turville, Hawkesbury, Westonbirt and
Lasborough *Glouc 5*   P *Duke of Beaufort, J A Hutley Esq, and*
Westonbirt Sch (jt)   R N C J MULHOLLAND,
NSM H K NICHOLS, E M NICHOLS, A F THORESEN
BOXWORTH (St Peter)   see Papworth *Ely*

BOYATT WOOD (St Peter) *Win 10* **P** *Bp* **V** B ROSTILL
BOYLESTONE (St John the Baptist), Church Broughton,
Dalbury, Longford, Long Lane, Radbourne, Sutton on the Hill
and Trusley *Derby 14* **P** *Patr Bd* **R** P M BISHOP,
NSM J M LEGH
BOYNE HILL (All Saints) *Ox 13* **P** *Bp* **V** J M HARRIS,
C D K M DAVISON
BOYNTON (St Andrew) *see* Rudston w Boynton, Carnaby and
Kilham *York*
BOYTHORPE (St Francis) *see* Chesterfield St Aug *Derby*
BOYTON (Holy Name), North Tamerton, Werrington,
St Giles-in-the-Heath and Virginstow *Truro 9* **P** *Duke
of Cornwall, MMCET, Ld Chan, and R Williams Esq (by turn)*
R K WAKEFIELD
BOYTON (St Andrew) *see* Wilford Peninsula *St E*
BOYTON (St Mary the Virgin) *see* Upper Wylye Valley *Sarum*
BOZEAT (St Mary) *see* Wollaston w Strixton and Bozeat etc *Pet*
BRABOURNE (St Mary the Blessed Virgin) *see* Smeeth w
Monks Horton and Stowting and Brabourne *Cant*
BRACEBOROUGH (St Margaret) *see* Uffington Gp *Linc*
BRACEBRIDGE (All Saints) *Linc 15*
P *Mrs B M Ellison-Lendrum* **P-in-c** H C MIDDLETON
BRACEBRIDGE HEATH (St John the Evangelist) *Linc 15*
P *Bp* **V** H C MIDDLETON
BRACEBY (St Margaret) *see* N Beltisloe Gp *Linc*
BRACEWELL (St Michael) *see* Barnoldswick w Bracewell
Bradf
BRACKENFIELD (Holy Trinity) *see* Ashover and
Brackenfield w Wessington *Derby*
BRACKLEY (St Peter w St James) *Pet 1* **P** *Bp* **V** N J GANDY,
C A R SHORTER
BRACKNELL (Holy Trinity) *Ox 11* **P** *Bp*
TV L P P JESUDASON, **P-in-c** N A PARISH, C J E MANLEY,
Hon C M G CLARKE
BRACON ASH (St Nicholas) *see* Mulbarton w Bracon Ash,
Hethel and Flordon *Nor*
BRADBOURNE (All Saints) *see* Wirksworth *Derby*
BRADDAN (St Brendan) *S & M 2* **P** *Bp* **V** P S FREAR
BRADDEN (St Michael) *see* Towcester w Caldecote and Easton
Neston etc *Pet*
BRADELEY (St Mary and All Saints), Church Eaton,
Derrington and Haughton *Lich 10* **P** *Bp and
Mrs M N Nutt (jt)* **R** *vacant* (01785) 780201
BRADENHAM (St Botolph) *see* W Wycombe w Bledlow
Ridge, Bradenham and Radnage *Ox*
BRADENHAM, WEST (St Andrew) *see* Shipdham w E and W
Bradenham *Nor*
BRADENSTOKE (St Mary) *see* Lyneham w Bradenstoke
Sarum
BRADFIELD (St Andrew) and Stanford Dingley *Ox 12*
P *Ch Soc Trust* NSM R C OBIN, L E BLISS, OLM R S GREEN
BRADFIELD (St Giles) *see* Trunch *Nor*
BRADFIELD (St Lawrence) *see* Mistley w Manningtree and
Bradfield *Chelmsf*
BRADFIELD (St Nicholas) *Sheff 3* **P** *V Ecclesfield*
R A T ISAACSON
BRADFIELD COMBUST (All Saints) *see* St Edm Way *St E*
BRADFIELD ST CLARE (St Clare), Bradfield St George w
Little Whelnetham, Cockfield, Felsham and Gedding *St E 10*
P *St Jo Coll Cam (1 turn), Bp and Lt-Col J G Aldous (1 turn)*
R *vacant* (01284) 828385
BRADFIELD ST GEORGE (St George) *see* Bradfield St Clare,
Bradfield St George etc *St E*
BRADFORD (All Saints) *see* Black Torrington, Bradford w
Cookbury etc *Ex*
BRADFORD (St Augustine) Undercliffe *Bradf 3* **P** *V Bradf*
P-in-c D BARTON, C D J MUGHAL, T A MILNE,
NSM A CHALLENGER
BRADFORD (St Clement) *Bradf 3* **P** *Bp (2 turns) and Trustees
(1 turn)* **P-in-c** D BARTON, C D J MUGHAL, T A MILNE,
NSM A CHALLENGER
BRADFORD (St Martin) *see* Heaton St Martin *Bradf*
BRADFORD (St Oswald) *see* Lt Horton *Bradf*
BRADFORD (St Saviour) *see* Fairweather Green *Bradf*
BRADFORD (St Stephen) *see* Bowling St Steph *Bradf*
BRADFORD (St Wilfrid) (St Columba w St Andrew) *Bradf 2*
P *Bp* **V** P M BILTON, NSM G A BRIGHOUSE
BRADFORD, SOUTH *see* Oakenshaw, Wyke and Low Moor
Bradf
BRADFORD, WEST (St Catherine) *see* Waddington *Bradf*
BRADFORD ABBAS (St Mary the Virgin) *see* Gifle Valley
Sarum
BRADFORD ON AVON (Christ Church) and Villages, North
Sarum 14 **P** *D&C Bris (2 turns), Bp (1 turn), V Bradf H Trin
(1 turn)* **R** H K JAMESON, NSM B F CHAPMAN

BRADFORD-ON-AVON (Holy Trinity) *Sarum 14* **P** *D&C*
P-in-c J M ABECASSIS, C P ELLIOTT
BRADFORD ON TONE (St Giles) *see* Deane Vale *B & W*
BRADFORD PEVERELL (Church of the Assumption),
Stratton, Frampton and Sydling St Nicholas *Sarum 1* **P** *Win
Coll and Bp (alt)* **P-in-c** P J SMITH, Hon C G M BOULT
BRADGATE TEAM, The - Ratby cum Groby w Newton Linford
Leic 9 **P** *Patr Bd* **TR** P G HOOPER, **TV** L D CORKE,
NSM H HAYES
BRADING (St Mary the Virgin) w Yaverland *Portsm 7*
P *Hon Mrs I S T Monck and Trin Coll Cam (jt)* **R** *vacant*
(01983) 407262
BRADLEY (All Saints) *see* Hulland, Atlow, Kniveton, Bradley
and Hognaston *Derby*
BRADLEY (All Saints) *see* Farleigh, Candover and Wield *Win*
BRADLEY (St George) *see* Gt and Lt Coates w Bradley *Linc*
BRADLEY (St John the Baptist) *see* Bowbrook N *Worc*
BRADLEY (St Martin) *Lich 28* **P** *Baldwin Pugh Trustees*
V R T M J DUCKETT
BRADLEY (St Mary) *see* Cononley w Bradley *Bradf*
BRADLEY (St Thomas) *Wakef 5* **P** *Bp* **V** D R WARD,
C C B REARDON, NSM P T WILCOCK
BRADLEY, GREAT (St Mary the Virgin) *see* Stourhead *St E*
BRADLEY, LITTLE (All Saints) *as above*
BRADLEY, NORTH (St Nicholas), Southwick, Heywood and
Steeple Ashton *Sarum 14* **P** *Win Coll and Magd Coll Cam (jt)*
V J R PARKER, OLM L J DOVE, A R J LONGDON
BRADLEY, WEST (not known) *see* Baltonsborough w
Butleigh, W Bradley etc *B & W*
BRADLEY-LE-MOORS (St Leonard) *see* Alton w
Bradley-le-Moors and Denstone etc *Lich*
BRADLEY STOKE (Christ the King) *see* Stoke Gifford *Bris*
BRADLEY STOKE NORTH (Holy Trinity) Conventional
District *Bris 5 vacant* (01454) 617569
BRADMORE (Mission Room) *see* Keyworth and
Stanton-on-the-Wolds and Bunny etc *S'well*
BRADNINCH (St Disen) and Clyst Hydon *Ex 4* **P** *D&C and
D&C Windsor (jt)* C J M WRIGHT
BRADNOP (Mission Church) *see* Ipstones w Berkhamsytch
and Onecote w Bradnop *Lich*
BRADOC (Blessed Virgin Mary) *see* Lanreath, Pelynt and
Bradoc *Truro*
BRADPOLE (Holy Trinity) *see* Bridport *Sarum*
BRADSHAW (St John the Evangelist) and Holmfield *Wakef 4*
P *Bp* **V** K A SHOESMITH
BRADSHAW (St Maxentius) *see* Turton Moorland Min *Man*
BRADWELL (Holy Trinity) *see* Cressing w Stisted and
Bradwell etc *Chelmsf*
BRADWELL (St Barnabas) *see* Hope, Castleton and Bradwell
Derby
BRADWELL (St Barnabas) *see* Wolstanton *Lich*
BRADWELL (St Lawrence and Methodist United)
see Stantonbury and Willen *Ox*
BRADWELL (St Nicholas) *Nor 6* **P** *Bp* **R** R J TUCK,
NSM S D UPTON, C M UPTON
BRADWELL, NEW (St James) *see* Stantonbury and Willen *Ox*
BRADWELL ON SEA (St Thomas) (St Peter-on-the-Wall) and
St Lawrence *Chelmsf 11* **P** *Bp* **R** W L WHITFORD,
C M E WHITFORD
BRADWORTHY (St John the Baptist), Sutcombe, Putford,
Abbots Bickington and Bulkworthy *Ex 17* **P** *Prime Min and
Bp (alt)* **R** R B DORRINGTON
BRAFFERTON (St Peter) w Pilmoor, Myton-on-Swale and
Thormanby *York 3* **P** *Abp and Prof Sir Anthony Milnes
Coates Bt (jt)* **P-in-c** C J PARK
BRAFIELD ON THE GREEN (St Laurence) *see* Cogenhoe
and Gt and Lt Houghton w Brafield *Pet*
BRAILES (St George) *Cov 9* **P** *D&C* **V** N J MORGAN,
NSM J W ROLFE
BRAILSFORD (All Saints) w Shirley, Osmaston w Edlaston and
Yeaveley *Derby 8* **P** *Bp, Earl Ferrers, and Sir Peter
Walker-Okeover Bt (by turn)* **R** P M TAYLOR,
C P L MICHELL
BRAINTREE (St Michael) *Chelmsf 15* **P** *Ch Trust Fund Trust*
V C O MASON, C J A K WIGMORE
BRAINTREE (St Paul) *Chelmsf 15* **P** *Ch Trust Fund Trust*
V R W SEWELL
BRAISHFIELD (All Saints) *see* Michelmersh and Awbridge
and Braishfield etc *Win*
BRAITHWAITE (St Herbert) *see* Upper Derwent *Carl*
BRAITHWELL (St James) *see* Ravenfield, Hooton Roberts and
Braithwell *Sheff*
BRAMBER (St Nicholas) *see* Beeding and Bramber w Botolphs
Chich
BRAMBLETON (not known) *see* The Bourne and Tilford
Guildf

BRAMCOTE (St Michael and All Angels) S'well 7   P CPAS
P-in-c P F REYNOLDS
BRAMDEAN (St Simon and St Jude)   see Upper Itchen Win
BRAMDEAN COMMON (Church in the Wood)   as above
BRAMERTON (St Peter)   see Rockland St Mary w Hellington,
Bramerton etc Nor
BRAMFIELD (St Andrew)   see Blyth Valley St E
BRAMFIELD (St Andrew), Stapleford, Waterford and
Watton-at-Stone St Alb 19   P R M A Smith Esq (3 turns),
Grocers' Co (1 turn)   R B D S FAIRBANK
BRAMFORD (St Mary the Virgin) St E 1   P D&C Cant
P-in-c J M SEGGAR,   OLM P Y WRIGHT
BRAMHALL (St Michael and All Angels) (Hall Chapel) Ches 17
P Trustees   V S R MARSH,   NSM A HYDE
BRAMHAM (All Saints) York 1   P Ch Ch Ox, G F Lane
Fox Esq, and Lady Elizabeth Hastings Estate Charity (jt)
V P E BRISTOW,   C A J GRANT,   NSM P M ANSLOW
BRAMHOPE (St Giles) Ripon 7   P Trustees   P-in-c J L SMITH
BRAMLEY (Holy Trinity) and Grafham Guildf 2   P Ld Chan
V J N E BUNDOCK,   NSM C E Z WHITE,
OLM R E L TER HAAR
BRAMLEY (St Francis) Sheff 6   P Bp and Sir Philip
Naylor-Leyland Bt (jt)   V L S WORTLEY,
Hon C D J FRANKLIN
BRAMLEY (St James) Win 4   P Qu Coll Ox
P-in-c R W POLITT,   NSM J R LENTON
BRAMLEY (St Peter) Ripon 6   P DBP   TR I T RODLEY,
TV M R COUTTS
BRAMPFORD SPEKE (St Peter), Cadbury, Newton St Cyres,
Poltimore, Rewe, Stoke Canon, Thorverton and Upton Pyne
Ex 2   P Bp, Earl of Iddlesleigh, DBP, D&C (1 turn), Ld Chan
(1 turn)   R D J DETTMER,   NSM S SHEPPARD, J A DALLEN
BRAMPTON (St Mark) Derby 5   P Bp   V vacant (01246)
234015
BRAMPTON (St Martin)   see Eden, Gelt and Irthing Carl
BRAMPTON (St Mary Magdalene) Ely 10   P Bp
R M R GREENFIELD
BRAMPTON (St Michael) Heref 7   P Bp (7 turns), D&C
(2 turns), Exors Brig A F L Clive (1 turn)   V A KNIGHT
BRAMPTON (St Peter)   see Bure Valley Nor
BRAMPTON (St Peter)   see Hundred River St E
BRAMPTON (St Thomas the Martyr) Derby 5   P Bp
R M J BARNES,   C R C TURNER, M R BROOMHEAD,
NSM J M LIDGATE
BRAMPTON, OLD (St Peter and St Paul) (Cutthorpe Institute)
and Great Barlow Derby 5   P Bp and TR Staveley and Barrow
Hill (jt)   R vacant
BRAMPTON ABBOTTS (St Michael)   see Brampton Heref
BRAMPTON ASH (St Mary)   see Desborough, Brampton Ash,
Dingley and Braybrooke Pet
BRAMPTON BIERLOW (Christ Church) Sheff 12
P V Wath-upon-Dearne   V P E BOLD
BRAMPTON BRYAN (St Barnabas)   see Wigmore Abbey
Heref
BRAMSHALL (St Laurence)   see Uttoxeter Area Lich
BRAMSHAW (St Peter)   see Forest and Avon Sarum
BRAMSHILL (Mission Church)   see Darby Green and Eversley
Win
BRAMSHOTT (St Mary the Virgin) and Liphook Portsm 4
P Qu Coll Ox   P-in-c V W INGLIS-JONES,   C A BENNETT
BRANCASTER (St Mary the Virgin)   see Hunstanton St Mary
w Ringstead Parva etc Nor
BRANCEPETH (St Brandon) Dur 1   P Bp
P-in-c R L SIMPSON
BRANCEPETH, NEW (St Catherine)   see Brandon and Ushaw
Moor Dur
BRANDESBURTON (St Mary) and Leven w Catwick York 11
P St Jo Coll Cam, Exors Sir Henry Strickland-Constable Bt, and
Simeon's Trustees (jt)   P-in-c J E GRAINGER-SMITH,
C C J SIMMONS
BRANDESTON (All Saints) w Kettleburgh and Easton St E 18
P J Austin Esq, Capt J L Round-Turner, and MMCET (jt)
P-in-c H V EDWARDS,   NSM R E R ALDERSON,
OLM D A WEST
BRANDLESHOLME (St Francis House Chapel)   see Kirklees
Valley Man
BRANDON (Chapel)   see Barkston and Hough Gp Linc
BRANDON (St John the Evangelist) and Ushaw Moor Dur 1
P R Brancepeth   V P BROWN,   Hon C D B GODSELL
BRANDON (St Peter) and Santon Downham w Elveden and
Lakenheath St E 11   P Ld Chan (1 turn), Bp, M F Carter Esq,
Earl of Iveagh, and D&C Ely (2 turns)   R W L WHITFORD,
C M E WHITFORD,   NSM P W TAMS
BRANDON PARVA (All Saints)   see Barnham Broom and
Upper Yare Nor

BRANDSBY (All Saints)   see Crayke w Brandsby and Yearsley
York
BRANDWOOD (St Bede) Birm 5   P Bp   V A M DELMEGE,
NSM R J REYNOLDS
BRANKSEA ISLAND (St Mary)   see Parkstone St Pet and St
Osmund w Branksea Sarum
BRANKSOME (St Aldhelm) (St Francis) Sarum 7   P Bp
V S R BATTY,   NSM J P T G SMITH
BRANKSOME (St Clement) (St Barnabas) Sarum 8
P MMCET   V J G V FOSTER
BRANKSOME PARK (All Saints) Sarum 7   P MMCET
V J V BERRY,   C N D JACKSON
BRANSCOMBE (St Winifred)   see Colyton, Musbury,
Southleigh and Branscombe Ex
BRANSDALE (St Nicholas)   see Kirkbymoorside w Gillamoor,
Farndale etc York
BRANSFORD (St John the Baptist)   see Worcs W Worc
BRANSGORE (St Mary the Virgin) and Hinton Admiral Win 9
P Sir George Meyrick Bt and Exors P W Jesson (jt)
P-in-c P A RICKMAN
BRANSHOLME (St John)   see Sutton St Jas and Wawne York
BRANSTON (All Saints) w Nocton and Potterhanworth Linc 18
P Stowe Sch (2 turns), Ld Chan (1 turn), and Nocton Ltd
(1 turn)   C J S PARKIN
BRANSTON (St Saviour) Lich 14   P Simeon's Trustees
V M K ELLOR
BRANSTON BY BELVOIR (St Guthlac)   see High Framland
Par Leic
BRANT BROUGHTON (St Helen) and Beckingham Linc 22
P Bp and Sir Richard Sutton Bt (alt)   R A J MEGAHEY
BRANT ROAD (Church Centre)   see Bracebridge Linc
BRANTHAM (St Michael and All Angels)   see E Bergholt and
Brantham St E
BRANTINGHAM (All Saints)   see Elloughton and Brough w
Brantingham York
BRANXTON (St Paul) Newc 12   P Abp   P-in-c G R KELSEY,
NSM L E GARDHAM
BRASSINGTON (St James)   see Wirksworth Derby
BRASTED (St Martin) Roch 9   P Abp   P-in-c L A GREEN
BRATHAY (Holy Trinity)   see Loughrigg Carl
BRATOFT (St Peter and St Paul)   see Burgh Gp Linc
BRATTLEBY (St Cuthbert)   see Spring Line Gp Linc
BRATTON (St James the Great) (Oratory), Edington and Imber,
Erlestoke and Coulston Sarum 16   P Bp and V Westbury (jt)
R G SOUTHGATE,   OLM M R WIECK
BRATTON CLOVELLY (St Mary the Virgin)   see Okehampton
w Inwardleigh, Bratton Clovelly etc Ex
BRATTON FLEMING (St Peter)   see Shirwell, Loxhore,
Kentisbury, Arlington, etc Ex
BRATTON ST MAUR (St Nicholas)   see Bruton and Distr
B & W
BRAUGHING (St Mary the Virgin)   see Albury, Braughing,
Furneux Pelham, Lt Hadham etc St Alb
BRAUNSTON (All Saints)   see Daventry, Ashby St Ledgers,
Braunston etc Pet
BRAUNSTON (All Saints)   see Oakham, Ashwell, Braunston,
Brooke, Egleton etc Pet
BRAUNSTONE PARK (St Peter) Leic 1   P Bp   V J C BURCH
BRAUNSTONE TOWN (St Crispin) Leic 9   P Bp
P-in-c A C DEEGAN
BRAUNTON (St Brannock) Ex 15   P Bp   P-in-c A THORNE,
Hon C L A BUTTLE,   NSM J S LOVEDAY
BRAXTED, GREAT (All Saints)   see Tolleshunt Knights w
Tiptree and Gt Braxted Chelmsf
BRAXTED, LITTLE (St Nicholas)   see Wickham Bishops w Lt
Braxted Chelmsf
BRAY (St Michael) and Braywood Ox 13   P Bp
V R M COWLES
BRAY, HIGH (All Saints)   see S Molton w Nymet St George,
High Bray etc Ex
BRAYBROOKE (All Saints)   see Desborough, Brampton Ash,
Dingley and Braybrooke Pet
BRAYDESTON (St Michael)   see Brundall w Braydeston and
Postwick Nor
BRAYTON (St Wilfrid) York 4   P Abp   R P D WATSON
BREADSALL (All Saints) Derby 9   P Miss
A I M Harpur-Crewe   P-in-c A J MADDOCKS,
NSM D M MORRISON
BREADSTONE (St Michael and All Angels)   see Berkeley w
Wick, Breadstone, Newport, Stone etc Glouc
BREAGE (St Breaca) w Godolphin and Germoe Truro 4   P Bp
and Ld Chan (alt)   P-in-c P A PRINCE,
NSM S A CHALCRAFT
BREAM (St James) Glouc 1   P Bp   P-in-c G C A STOREY,
NSM A J WILLIAMS

BREAMORE (St Mary)   see Fordingbridge and Breamore and Hale etc *Win*

BREAN (St Bridget)   see Berrow and Breane *B & W*

BREARTON (St John the Baptist)   see Knaresborough *Ripon*

BREASTON (St Michael)   see Wilne and Draycott w Breaston *Derby*

BRECKLES (St Margaret)   see Caston, Griston, Merton, Thompson etc *Nor*

BREDBURY (St Barnabas) *Ches 16*   **P** *V Bredbury St Mark* **P-in-c** B J SWORD

BREDBURY (St Mark) *Ches 16*   **P** *Bp*   **P-in-c** A D BULL

BREDE (St George) w Udimore *Chich 20*   **P** *Bp and Mrs M E Crook (alt)*   **R** M N HARPER

BREDENBURY (St Andrew) *Heref 2*   **P** *DBP, V Bromyard, and Lt-Col H H Barneby (jt)*   **R** L A MONEY

BREDFIELD (St Andrew)   see Woodbridge St Jo and Bredfield *St E*

BREDGAR (St John the Baptist)   see Tunstall and Bredgar *Cant*

BREDHURST (St Peter)   see S Gillingham *Roch*

BREDICOT (St James the Less)   see Bowbrook S *Worc*

BREDON (St Giles) w Bredon's Norton *Worc 4*   **P** *Bp* **R** M T C BAYNES,   **C** C L TURPIN

BREDON'S NORTON (not known)   see Bredon w Bredon's Norton *Worc*

BREDWARDINE (St Andrew)   see Cusop w Blakemere, Bredwardine w Brobury etc *Heref*

BREDY, LITTLE (St Michael and All Angels)   see Bride Valley *Sarum*

BREEDON-ON-THE-HILL (St Mary and St Hardulph) see Ashby-de-la-Zouch and Breedon on the Hill *Leic*

BREIGHTMET (St James)   see Leverhulme *Man*

BREIGHTMET Top o' th' Moss (St John the Evangelist) as above

BREINTON   (Common Mission Hall)   see W Heref *Heref*

BREINTON   (St Michael)   as above

BREMHILL (St Martin)   see Marden Vale *Sarum*

BRENCHLEY (All Saints) *Roch 8*   **P** *D&C Cant*   **V** R C PAGET

BRENDON (St Brendon)   see Combe Martin, Berrynarbor, Lynton, Brendon etc *Ex*

BRENT, EAST (The Blessed Virgin Mary)   see Brent Knoll, E Brent and Lympsham *B & W*

BRENT, SOUTH (St Petroc) and Rattery *Ex 13*   **P** *Bp and Sir Rivers Carew Bt (jt)*   **V** D R WINNINGTON-INGRAM

BRENT ELEIGH (St Mary)   see Monks Eleigh w Chelsworth and Brent Eleigh etc *St E*

BRENT KNOLL (St Michael) and East Brent and Lympsham *B & W 1*   **P** *Adn Wells (1 turn), Bp (2 turns)* **P-in-c** S W LEWIS

BRENT PELHAM (St Mary the Virgin)   see Hormead, Wyddial, Anstey, Brent Pelham etc *St Alb*

BRENT TOR (Christ Church)   see Peter Tavy, Mary Tavy, Lydford and Brent Tor *Ex*

BRENT TOR (St Michael)   as above

BRENTFORD (St Paul w St Lawrence and St George) (St Faith) *Lon 11*   **P** *Bp*   **TR** D J SIMPSON,   **TV** D M DURKIN, **C** G M TOOGOOD

BRENTRY (St Mark)   see Henbury *Bris*

BRENTS and Davington w Oare and Luddenham, The *Cant 14* **P** *Abp and Ld Chan (alt)*   **P-in-c** A A DUGUID

BRENTWOOD (St George the Martyr) *Chelmsf 7*   **P** *DBP* **V** G F JENKINS

BRENTWOOD (St Thomas) *Chelmsf 7*   **P** *DBP* **V** C E HEWITT,   **C** G SUMPTER

BRENZETT (St Eanswith)   see Appledore w Brookland, Fairfield, Brenzett etc *Cant*

BRERETON (St Michael) and Rugeley *Lich 3*   **P** *Patr Bd* **TR** M J NEWMAN,   **TV** W H HEATH, L M DOWNS, **C** K M BILLSON,   **OLM** J L BRITTLE, B D TABERNOR

BRERETON (St Oswald) *Ches 11*   **P** *DBP*   **V** *vacant (01477) 533263*

BRESSINGHAM (St John the Baptist)   see Upper Waveney *Nor*

BRETBY (St Wystan)   see Hartshorne and Bretby *Derby*

BRETFORTON (St Leonard)   see Badsey w Aldington and Offenham and Bretforton *Worc*

BRETHERTON (St John the Baptist)   see Croston and Bretherton *Blackb*

BRETTENHAM (St Andrew)   see E w W Harling, Bridgham w Roudham, Larling etc *Nor*

BRETTENHAM (St Mary)   see Rattlesden w Thorpe Morieux, Brettenham etc *St E*

BRETTON (Holy Spirit)   see Pet H Spirit Bretton *Pet*

BRETTON PARK (St Bartholomew)   see Woolley *Wakef*

BREWHAM, SOUTH (St John the Baptist)   see Bruton and Distr *B & W*

BREWOOD (St Mary and St Chad) *Lich 2*   **P** *Bp*   **V** C A HOST, **NSM** M J COULTER

BRICETT, GREAT (St Mary and St Lawrence)   see Ringshall w Battisford, Barking w Darmsden etc *St E*

BRICKENDON (Holy Cross and St Alban)   see Lt Berkhamsted and Bayford, Essendon etc *St Alb*

BRICKET WOOD (St Luke) *St Alb 5*   **P** *CPAS* **V** M RAJKOVIC

BRICKHILL, GREAT (St Mary)   see Brickhills and Stoke Hammond *Ox*

BRICKHILL, LITTLE (St Mary Magdalene)   as above

BRICKHILL, NORTH (St Mark)   see Bedf St Mark *St Alb*

BRICKHILLS and Stoke Hammond, The *Ox 26*   **P** *Bp, Major Sir Philip Pauncefort-Duncombe Bt, St Edw Sch Ox, and Cam Univ (jt)*   **R** J WALLER

BRICKLEHAMPTON (St Michael)   see Elmley Castle w Bricklehampton and Combertons *Worc*

BRIDE (St Bridget)   see Kirkbride *S & M*

BRIDE VALLEY *Sarum 2*   **P** *Sir Robert Williams Bt and G A L-F Pitt-Rivers Esq (jt)*   **R** R A D'V THORN, **NSM** R R ROGERS

BRIDEKIRK (St Bridget)   see Cockermouth Area *Carl*

BRIDESTOWE (St Bridget)   see Okehampton w Inwardleigh, Bratton Clovelly etc *Ex*

BRIDFORD (St Thomas à Becket)   see Christow, Ashton, Bridford, Dunchideock etc *Ex*

BRIDGE Parishes, The *Sarum 9*   **P** *Eton Coll and Nat Trust (alt)*   **P-in-c** A J H EDWARDS

BRIDGE (St Peter) *Cant 1*   **P** *Abp and St Jo Coll Ox (jt)* **V** S D ROWLANDS,   **C** J C BALDWIN

BRIDGE SOLLARS (St Andrew)   see Credenhill w Brinsop and Wormsley etc *Heref*

BRIDGEMARY (St Matthew) *Portsm 3*   **P** *Bp* **P-in-c** R J PRESTON

BRIDGERULE (St Bridget)   see Pyworthy, Pancrasweek and Bridgerule *Ex*

BRIDGETOWN (St John the Evangelist)   see Totnes w Bridgetown, Berry Pomeroy etc *Ex*

BRIDGFORD, EAST (St Peter) and Kneeton *S'well 8*   **P** *Magd Coll Ox (2 turns), C G Neale Esq (1 turn)* **NSM** M R WOODWARD

BRIDGFORD, WEST (St Giles) (St Luke) *S'well 9* **P** *Waddington Trustees*   **P-in-c** L J PROUDLOVE, **C** I M HAMLEY

BRIDGHAM (St Mary)   see E w W Harling, Bridgham w Roudham, Larling etc *Nor*

BRIDGNORTH (St Mary Magdalene) (St Leonard) (St James), Tasley, Astley Abbotts, Oldbury and Quatford *Heref 8*   **P** *DBP (3 turns) and Ld Chan (1 turn)*   **TR** S H CAWDELL, **C** H T GREENHAM,   **NSM** A ROGERS

BRIDGWATER (Holy Trinity) and Durleigh St Hugh *B & W 13* **P** *Bp (2 turns) and Ld Chan (1 turn)*   **V** W H H LANE

BRIDGWATER (St Francis of Assisi) *B & W 13*   **P** *Bp* **V** B D JOY,   **C** R B HICKS

BRIDGWATER (St John the Baptist) *B & W 13*   **P** *Bp* **P-in-c** G M KIRK

BRIDGWATER (St Mary) and Chilton Trinity *B & W 13* **P** *Ld Chan*   **V** C J P CHADWICK,   **C** J R HICKS

BRIDLINGTON (Emmanuel) *York 9*   **P** *Trustees* **V** C J MCCARTHY,   **C** B J NORTON

BRIDLINGTON (Holy Trinity) and Sewerby w Marton *York 9* **P** *Abp*   **V** D J MATHER

BRIDLINGTON (St Mary's Priory Church) *York 9*   **P** *Simeon's Trustees*   **R** E W A CRAGG,   **C** A J MORELAND, **NSM** J L OATES

BRIDLINGTON QUAY (Christ Church) *York 9* **P** *R Bridlington Priory*   **V** J G COUPER,   **C** D N H CHISLETT

BRIDPORT (St Mary) *Sarum 2*   **P** *Patr Bd (2 turns) and Ld Chan (1 turn)*   **TR** A EVANS,   **TV** P R H EDWARDS, **NSM** M PREUSS-HIGHAM, A M AYLING, S GEORGE, **OLM** J E MOORE

BRIDSTOW (St Bridget)   see Brampton *Heref*

BRIERCLIFFE (St James) *Blackb 3*   **P** *Hulme Trustees* **V** R D WATTS

BRIERFIELD (St Luke) *Blackb 6*   **P** *Bp*   **P-in-c** A W RINDL, **Hon C** E A SAVILLE

BRIERLEY (St Paul)   see Grimethorpe w Brierley *Wakef*

BRIERLEY HILL (St Michael) (St Paul) *Worc 10*   **P** *Ld Chan (2 turns), Patr Bd (1 turn)*   **TV** D J HOSKIN, **NSM** B I PRITCHETT

BRIGG (St John the Evangelist), Wrawby and Cadney cum Howsham *Linc 6*   **P** *Bp*   **V** G O MITCHELL,   **C** D J EAMES

BRIGHAM (St Bridget), Great Broughton and Broughton Moor *Carl 7*   **P** *Bp and Earl of Lonsdale (jt)*   **NSM** F A KEEGAN, A-M L STUART

BRIGHOUSE (St Chad)   see Lightcliffe and Hove Edge *Wakef*

BRIGHOUSE (St Martin) and Clifton *Wakef 2*   **P** *Bp* **V** S C SPENCER

BRIGHSTONE (St Mary the Virgin) and Brooke w Mottistone
Portsm 8   P *Bp (2 turns), D&C St Paul's (1 turn)*
Hon C D L DENNIS

BRIGHTLING (St Thomas of Canterbury), Dallington,
Mountfield and Netherfield *Chich 15*   P *Bp, Adn Lewes and
Hastings, H C Grissell Esq, Mrs A Egerton, and
Mrs L A Fraser (jt)*   NSM J B B WRENBURY

BRIGHTLINGSEA (All Saints) (St James) *Chelmsf 22*
P *Ld Chan*   P-in-c P A BALDWIN

BRIGHTON (Annunciation) *Chich 2*   P *Wagner Trustees*
P-in-c M J WELLS,   Hon C R L CLARKE

BRIGHTON (Chapel Royal) *Chich 2*   P *Bp*   P-in-c D J BIGGS

BRIGHTON (Good Shepherd) Preston *Chich 2*   P *Bp*
P-in-c F P A MASCARENHAS,   Hon C C E JAMES

BRIGHTON (St Bartholomew) *Chich 2*   P *Wagner Trustees*
V *vacant* (01273) 685142 *or* 620491

BRIGHTON (St Cuthman)   *see* Whitehawk *Chich*

BRIGHTON (St George w St Anne and St Mark) *Chich 2*   P *Bp*
and V Brighton (jt)   V A H MANSON-BRAILSFORD,
NSM P G PANNETT

BRIGHTON (St John)   *see* Preston St Jo w Brighton St Aug and
St Sav *Chich*

BRIGHTON (St Luke) Queen's Park *Chich 2*   P *Bp*
C J NEWSON

BRIGHTON (St Martin) w St Wilfrid and St Alban *Chich 2*
P *SMF*   V *vacant* (01273) 604687

BRIGHTON (St Mary the Virgin)   *see* Kemp Town St Mary
Chich

BRIGHTON (St Matthias) *Chich 2*   P *V Preston*
P-in-c E J POLLARD

BRIGHTON (St Michael and All Angels) *Chich 2*   P *SMF*
V R S FAYERS,   C B A NORTH, M J LYON

BRIGHTON (St Nicholas) *Chich 2*   P *Bp*   V R CHAVNER,
C B GRAY-HAMMOND,   NSM J-J S AIDLEY

BRIGHTON (St Paul) *Chich 2*   P *Wagner Trustees*
P-in-c R S FAYERS,   NSM J N BALDRY

BRIGHTON (St Peter) *Chich 2*   P *Bp and V Brompton
H Trin (jt)*   V R M COATES,   C J P GUMBEL

BRIGHTON, NEW (St James) (Emmanuel) *Ches 7*   P *Bp*
V F R CAIN,   C K L FREEMAN

BRIGHTSIDE (St Thomas and St Margaret) w Wincobank
Sheff 3   P *The Crown and Sheff Ch Burgesses (alt)*
V P N WARMAN,   C P J GOODACRE,   NSM B M KIMARU

BRIGHTWALTON (All Saints)   *see* W Downland *Ox*

BRIGHTWELL (St Agatha)   *see* Wallingford *Ox*

BRIGHTWELL (St John the Baptist)   *see* Martlesham w
Brightwell *St E*

BRIGHTWELL BALDWIN (St Bartholomew)   *see* Ewelme,
Brightwell Baldwin, Cuxham w Easington *Ox*

BRIGNALL (St Mary)   *see* Startforth and Bowes and Rokeby w
Brignall *Ripon*

BRIGSLEY (St Helen)   *see* Laceby and Ravendale Gp *Linc*

BRIGSTOCK (St Andrew) w Stanion and Lowick and
Sudborough *Pet 7*   P *Bp (2 turns), L G Stopford Sackville Esq
(1 turn)*   P-in-c C G SIMPSON

BRILL (All Saints)   *see* Bernwode *Ox*

BRILLEY (St Mary)   *see* Eardisley w Bollingham, Willersley,
Brilley etc *Heref*

BRIMFIELD (St Michael)   *see* Leominster *Heref*

BRIMINGTON (St Michael) *Derby 3*   P *V Chesterfield*
R D B COOKE

BRIMPSFIELD (St Michael) w Birdlip, Syde, Daglingworth,
The Duntisbournes, Winstone, Miserden and Edgeworth *Glouc 7*
P *Ld Chan (1 turn), Bp, DBP, Major M N T H Wills and
CCC Ox (1 turn)*   R J E JESSOP,   NSM R H GEORGE

BRIMPTON (St Peter)   *see* Aldermaston and Woolhampton *Ox*

BRIMSCOMBE (Holy Trinity)   *see* Woodchester and
Brimscombe *Glouc*

BRINDLE (St James) *Blackb 4*   P *Trustees*   P-in-c D G WARD

BRINGHURST (St Nicholas)   *see* Six Saints circa Holt *Leic*

BRINGTON (All Saints) w Molesworth and Old Weston *Ely 10*
P *Bp*   R *vacant* (01832) 710207

BRINGTON (St Mary w St John) w Whilton and Norton and
Church Brampton w Chapel Brampton and Harlestone and East
Haddon and Holdenby *Pet 2*   P *Patr Bd (5 turns), Prime Min
(1 turn)*   R S J KIPLING,   Hon C A D RICHARDS

BRININGHAM (St Maurice)   *see* Brinton, Briningham,
Hunworth, Stody etc *Nor*

BRINKBURN (St Peter and St Paul)   *see* Longframlington w
Brinkburn *Newc*

BRINKHILL (St Philip)   *see* S Ormsby Gp *Linc*

BRINKLEY (St Mary)   *see* Raddesley Gp *Ely*

BRINKLOW (St John the Baptist)   *see* Revel Gp *Cov*

BRINKWORTH (St Michael and All Angels) w Dauntsey *Bris 6*
P *Bp*   R D ORMSTON,   C R K EAST

BRINNINGTON (St Luke) w Portwood St Paul *Ches 18*   P *Bp*
V C A FURNESS,   C L J HITCHEN

BRINSCALL (St Luke)   *see* Heapey and Withnell *Blackb*

BRINSLEY (St James the Great) w Underwood *S'well 4*   P *Bp*
P-in-c D A STEVENSON,   NSM E MURRAY

BRINSOP (St George)   *see* Credenhill w Brinsop and Wormsley
etc *Heref*

BRINSWORTH (St Andrew)   *see* Rivers Team *Sheff*

BRINTON (St Andrew), Briningham, Hunworth, Stody, Swanton
Novers and Thornage *Nor 18*   P *J S Howlett Esq, Lord
Hastings, and DBP (by turn)*   P-in-c B W TOMLINSON

BRISLEY (St Bartholomew)   *see* Upper Wensum Village Gp
Nor

BRISLINGTON (St Anne) *Bris 1*   P *Bp*   V *vacant* 0117-983
0283

BRISLINGTON (St Christopher) *Bris 1*   P *Simeon's Trustees*
V N HAWKINS,   OLM P A HUNTER

BRISLINGTON (St Cuthbert) *Bris 1*   P *Bp*
P-in-c I L GARRETT

BRISLINGTON (St Luke) *Bris 1*   P *Bp*   P-in-c D M DEWES,
C A J DOARKS

BRISTOL (Christ Church) w St Ewen, All SS and St George
Bris 3   P *J E Heal Esq*   P-in-c R D HOYAL

BRISTOL (Christ the Servant) Stockwood *Bris 1*   P *Bp*
V D G OWEN,   C A W E SCHUMAN

BRISTOL Lockleaze (St Mary Magdalene w St Francis) *Bris 3*
P *Bp*   V J J HASLER,   NSM J MARKER,   OLM E R MILLS

BRISTOL St Aidan w St George *Bris 3*   P *Bp and SMF*
NSM J F J GOODRIDGE,   OLM T M DENLEY

BRISTOL (St Andrew) Hartcliffe *Bris 1*   P *Bp*   V R H MARTIN

BRISTOL (St Andrew w St Bartholomew)   *see* Bishopston and
St Andrews *Bris*

BRISTOL (St Anne w St Mark and St Thomas)   *see* Eastville St
Anne w St Mark and St Thos *Bris*

BRISTOL (St Leonard) Redfield   *see* E Bris St Ambrose and St
Leon *Bris*

BRISTOL (St Mary the Virgin) Redcliffe w Temple and
Bedminster St John the Baptist *Bris 1*   P *Bp*
P-in-c S J TAYLOR,   C W L HOUGH,   NSM S H E JONES

BRISTOL (St Matthew and St Nathanael) (St Katharine) *Bris 3*
P *Bp and CPAS (jt)*   P-in-c M D INESON,   C T M LORD,
NSM E G INESON,   OLM J M CAITHNESS

BRISTOL St Paul's (St Agnes) *Bris 3*   P *Ld Chan and Patr Bd
(alt)*   P-in-c B GREEN

BRISTOL (St Philip and St Jacob w Emmanuel) *Bris 3*
P *Trustees*   P-in-c T J SILK

BRISTOL (St Stephen) w St James and St John the Baptist w
St Michael and St George *Bris 3*   P *Ld Chan (1 turn), Bp, Bris
Ch Trustees, and D&C (2 turns)*   P-in-c T J HIGGINS,
C E A KESTEVEN, N S ADAMS

BRISTOL, EAST (St Aidan)   *see* Bristol St Aid w St Geo *Bris*

BRISTOL, EAST (St Ambrose) (St Leonard) *Bris 3*   P *Bp*
V R D JAMES,   NSM J F J GOODRIDGE

BRISTOL, EAST (St George)   *see* Bristol St Aid w St Geo *Bris*

BRISTON (All Saints), Burgh Parva, Hindolveston and Melton
Constable *Nor 18*   P *Bp, Lord Hastings, and D&C (jt)*
P-in-c J G SYKES

BRITFORD (St Peter)   *see* Chalke Valley *Sarum*

BRITWELL St George *Ox 23*   P *Eton Coll*
V J S W CHORLTON,   C C A M STYLES

BRITWELL SALOME (St Nicholas)   *see* Icknield *Ox*

BRIXHAM (St Mary) (All Saints) w Churston Ferrers and
Kingswear *Ex 12*   P *The Crown*   TR T R DEACON,
TV I H BLYDE

BRIXTON (St Mary)   *see* Yealmpton and Brixton *Ex*

BRIXTON (St Matthew) (St Jude) *S'wark 11*   P *Abp and Ch Soc
Trust (jt)*   V S M SICHEL

BRIXTON (St Paul) (St Saviour) *S'wark 11*   P *Ch Soc Trust*
P-in-c B GOODYEAR

BRIXTON, NORTH (Christ Church)   *see* Brixton Road Ch Ch
S'wark

BRIXTON DEVERILL (St Michael)   *see* Cley Hill Villages
Sarum

BRIXTON ROAD (Christ Church) *S'wark 11*   P *CPAS*
V T J JEFFREYS,   NSM J CONNELL

BRIXWORTH (All Saints) w Holcot *Pet 2*   P *Bp*
V A J WATKINS

BRIZE NORTON (St Britius) and Carterton *Ox 8*   P *Patr Bd*
TR W G BLAKEY,   TV J T MADDERN,   C J REID

BROAD BLUNSDON (St Leonard)   *see* Broad Blunsdon *Bris*

BROAD BLUNSDON (St Leonard) *Bris 7*   P *Bp*
P-in-c G D SOWDEN

BROAD CAMPDEN (St Michael and All Angels)   *see* Chipping
Campden w Ebrington *Glouc*

BROAD HINTON (St Peter ad Vincula)   *see* Upper Kennet
Sarum

BROAD LANE (Licensed Room) *see* Wybunbury and Audlem w Doddington *Ches*
BROAD OAK (St George) *see* Heathfield *Chich*
BROAD TOWN (Christ Church) *see* Woodhill *Sarum*
BROADBOTTOM (St Mary Magdalene) *see* Mottram in Longdendale *Ches*
BROADBRIDGE HEATH (St John) *see* Horsham *Chich*
BROADCHALKE (All Saints) *see* Chalke Valley *Sarum*
BROADCLYST (St John the Baptist) *see* Pinhoe and Broadclyst *Ex*
BROADFIELD (Christ the Lord) *see* Southgate *Chich*
BROADHEATH (Christ Church) *see* Worc St Clem and Lower Broadheath *Worc*
BROADHEATH (St Alban) *Ches 10* **P** *Bp* **V** H SCARISBRICK, **NSM** T HODSON
BROADHEMBURY (St Andrew the Apostle and Martyr), Payhembury and Plymtree *Ex 7* **P** *W Drewe Esq, Ex Coll Ox, and Or Coll Ox (by turn)* **P-in-c** R S CRITTALL, **C** C E EDMONDS, J M WRIGHT
BROADHEMPSTON (St Peter and St Paul), Woodland, Staverton w Landscove and Littlehempston *Ex 13* **P** *Prime Min (1 turn), D&C and Bp (1 turn)* **R** N R C PEARKES
BROADMAYNE (St Martin) *see* Watercombe *Sarum*
BROADOAK (St Paul) *see* Askerswell, Loders, Powerstock and Symondsbury *Sarum*
BROADSTAIRS (Holy Trinity) *Cant 5* **P** *V St Peter-in-Thanet* **P-in-c** D J ROPER, **NSM** S C THOMAS
BROADSTAIRS (St Andrew) *see* Thanet St Andr CD *Cant*
BROADSTONE (not known) *see* Diddlebury w Munslow, Holdgate and Tugford *Heref*
BROADSTONE (St John the Baptist) *Sarum 7* **P** *Bp* **V** M FREDRIKSEN
BROADWAS (St Mary Magdalene) *see* Worcs W *Worc*
BROADWATER (St Mary) (St Stephen) (Queen Street Church Centre) *Chich 5* **P** *Patr Bd* **TR** P E IRWIN-CLARK, **TV** W M TSANG, G R NEAL, E V QUIBELL, **C** M J LUFF
BROADWATER DOWN *see* Tunbridge Wells St Mark *Roch*
BROADWATERS (St Oswald) *see* Kidderminster St Mary and All SS w Trimpley etc *Worc*
BROADWAY (St Aldhem and St Eadburga) *see* Isle Valley *B & W*
BROADWAY (St Eadburgha) (St Michael and All Angels) w Wickhamford *Worc 1* **P** *Peache Trustees and Ch Ch Ox (jt)* **V** *vacant* (01386) 852352
BROADWELL (Good Shepherd) *see* Coleford, Staunton, Newland, Redbrook etc *Glouc*
BROADWELL (St Paul), Evenlode, Oddington, Adlestrop and Westcote w Icomb and Bledington *Glouc 9* **P** *Bp, Ch Soc Trust, Lord Leigh and DBP (1 turn), and Ch Ch Ox and D&C Worc (1 turn)* **R** R J RENDALL, **NSM** L WILSON
BROADWELL (St Peter and St Paul) *see* Shill Valley and Broadshire *Ox*
BROADWEY (St Nicholas) *see* Bincombe w Broadwey, Upwey and Buckland Ripers *Sarum*
BROADWINDSOR (St John the Baptist) *see* Beaminster Area *Sarum*
BROADWOODKELLY (All Saints) *Ex 20* **P** *DBP* **R** P J NORMAN
BROADWOODWIDGER (St Nicholas) *see* Lifton, Broadwoodwidger, Stowford etc *Ex*
BROCKDISH (St Peter and St Paul) *see* Scole, Brockdish, Billingford, Thorpe Abbots etc *Nor*
BROCKENHURST (St Nicholas) (St Saviour) *Win 11* **P** E J F Morant Esq **P-in-c** N R SMART, **Hon C** R DROWN
BROCKHALL (St Peter and St Paul) *see* Heyford w Stowe Nine Churches and Flore etc *Pet*
BROCKHAM GREEN (Christ Church) *S'wark 26* **P** *Hon R P Hamilton* **P-in-c** J M A WILLANS, **NSM** F G LEHANEY
BROCKHAMPTON (All Saints) *see* Fownhope w Mordiford, Brockhampton etc *Heref*
BROCKHAMPTON (Chapel) *see* Bromyard and Stoke Lacy *Heref*
BROCKHOLES (St George) *see* Honley *Wakef*
BROCKLESBY PARK (All Saints) *Linc 6* **P** *Earl of Yarborough* **V** *vacant* (01469) 560641
BROCKLEY (St Andrew) *see* Horringer *St E*
BROCKLEY (St Peter) *S'wark 2* **P** *Bp* **V** C M E G TOURNAY
BROCKLEY HILL (St Saviour) *S'wark 5* **P** V Forest Hill Ch Ch **V** A S PEBERDY, **NSM** M ONUIGBO
BROCKMOOR (St John) *see* Brierley Hill *Worc*
BROCKWORTH (St George) *Glouc 3* **P** *DBP* **V** D A GILL
BROCTON (All Saints) *see* Baswich *Lich*
BRODSWORTH (St Michael and All Angels) *see* Bilham *Sheff*
BROKENBOROUGH (St John the Baptist) *see* Malmesbury w Westport and Brokenborough *Bris*

BROKERS WOOD (All Saints) *see* White Horse *Sarum*
BROMBOROUGH (St Barnabas) *Ches 9* **P** *D&C* **R** D WALKER
BROME (St Mary) *see* N Hartismere *St E*
BROMESWELL (St Edmund) *see* Wilford Peninsula *St E*
BROMFIELD (St Mary the Virgin) *see* Ludlow *Heref*
BROMFIELD (St Mungo) *see* Solway Plain *Carl*
BROMFORD FIRS (not known) *see* Hodge Hill *Birm*
BROMHAM (St Nicholas) *see* Rowde and Bromham *Sarum*
BROMHAM (St Owen) w Oakley and Stagsden *St Alb 13* **P** *Bp* **P-in-c** L BOND, **NSM** D J HARPHAM, P A VENNELLS
BROMLEY (Christ Church) *Roch 14* **P** *CPAS* **V** I J BROOMFIELD, **C** N R T HISCOCKS, **Hon C** V G WILKINS
BROMLEY (Holy Trinity Mission Church) *see* Pensnett *Worc*
BROMLEY (St Andrew) *Roch 14* **P** *Bp* **P-in-c** A M KING, **NSM** E J DAVIS
BROMLEY (St John the Evangelist) *Roch 14* **P** *Bp* **P-in-c** A D MCCLELLAN
BROMLEY (St Mark) *Roch 14* **P** *V Bromley SS Pet & Paul* **V** S C VARNEY, **C** A RICHARDSON
BROMLEY (St Mary) *see* Plaistow St Mary *Roch*
BROMLEY (St Peter and St Paul) *Roch 14* **P** *Bp* **V** M M CAMP
BROMLEY, GREAT (St George) *see* Ardleigh and The Bromleys *Chelmsf*
BROMLEY BY BOW (All Hallows) *Lon 7* **P** *Bp and Grocers' Co (jt)* **P-in-c** R C THORPE, **C** C I ROGERS, **NSM** R M ROGERS
BROMLEY COMMON (Holy Trinity) *Roch 14* **P** *The Crown* **V** R BRISTOW, **NSM** G E COLLETT
BROMLEY COMMON (St Augustine) *Roch 14* **P** *Bp* **V** K C BARNES
BROMLEY COMMON (St Luke) *Roch 14* **P** *Bp* **V** M G P INSLEY
BROMLEY CROSS (St Andrew's Mission Church) *see* Turton Moorland Min *Man*
BROMPTON (Holy Trinity) *see* Onslow Square and S Kensington St Aug *Lon*
BROMPTON (St Thomas) w Deighton *York 18* **P** *D&C Dur* **V** J M E COOPER
BROMPTON, NEW (St Luke) *Roch 3* **P** *Bp* **P-in-c** P MATTHIAS
BROMPTON, WEST (St Jude) (St Mary) St Peter *Lon 8* **P** *Bp and Sir Laurence Magnus Bt (jt)* **V** V J THOMAS, **C** R M LAMPARD
BROMPTON-BY-SAWDON (All Saints) *see* Upper Derwent *York*
BROMPTON ON SWALE (St Paul) *see* Easby w Skeeby and Brompton on Swale etc *Ripon*
BROMPTON RALPH (The Blessed Virgin Mary) *see* Wiveliscombe and the Hills *B & W*
BROMPTON REGIS (Blessed Virgin Mary) *see* Dulverton w Brushford, Brompton Regis etc *B & W*
BROMSBERROW (St Mary the Virgin) *see* Redmarley D'Abitot, Bromesberrow, Pauntley etc *Glouc*
BROMSGROVE (All Saints) *Worc 7* **P** *V Bromsgrove St Jo* **P-in-c** B A ROBERTSON
BROMSGROVE (St John the Baptist) *Worc 7* **P** *D&C* **P-in-c** C L WINGFIELD, **C** T D ATFIELD, **NSM** M C T B JONES
BROMWICH, WEST (All Saints) (St Mary Magdalene) *Lich 27* **P** *Bp* **C** A J SMITH, **C** G S DAVIS, P J SELLICK, **OLM** A M BIRD
BROMWICH, WEST (Good Shepherd w St John) *Lich 27* **P** *Bp* **V** K S NJENGA, **NSM** M BEDEAU
BROMWICH, WEST (Holy Trinity) *Lich 27* **P** *Peache Trustees* **V** J N ROBBIE
BROMWICH, WEST (St Andrew) (Christ Church) *Lich 27* **P** *Bp and V W Bromwich All SS (jt)* **V** M J CLARIDGE
BROMWICH, WEST (St Francis of Assisi) *Lich 27* **P** *Bp* **V** R A FARRELL, **C** A K W HUGHES
BROMWICH, WEST (St James) (St Paul) *Lich 27* **P** *Bp and V Tipton St Martin and St Paul* **V** D HART
BROMWICH, WEST (St Peter) *Lich 27* **P** *Bp* **NSM** R C GILBERT
BROMWICH, WEST (St Philip) *Lich 27* **P** *Bp* **P-in-c** P O DANIEL
BROMYARD (St Peter) and Stoke Lacy *Heref 2* **P** *Bp (4 turns), Exors P H G Morgan Esq (1 turn)* **V** G T G SYKES, **C** J T KINSELLA, **NSM** C A STOKES, C M SYKES, D B HYETT
BROMYARD DOWNS (Mission Church) *see* Bromyard and Stoke Lacy *Heref*
BRONDESBURY (Christ Church) (St Laurence) *Lon 21* **P** *Ld Chan* **R** D E NENO, **C** N CRITCHLOW
BRONDESBURY St Anne w Kilburn (Holy Trinity) *Lon 21* **P** *Bp and Ch Patr Soc (alt)* **V** F B CAPIE, **NSM** L C F HILLEL

BROOK (St Mary)   *see* Wye w Brook and Hastingleigh etc *Cant*

BROOKE (St Mary the Virgin)   *see* Brighstone and Brooke w Mottistone *Portsm*

BROOKE (St Peter)   *see* Oakham, Ashwell, Braunston, Brooke, Egleton etc *Pet*

BROOKE (St Peter), Kirstead, Mundham w Seething and Thwaite *Nor 5*   **P** *G&C Coll Cam, Gt Hosp and Countess Ferrers, and Ld Chan (by turn)*   **R** J H ROBSON

BROOKE STREET (St Alban the Martyr)   *see* Holborn St Alb w Saffron Hill St Pet *Lon*

BROOKEND (Mission Room)   *see* Sharpness, Purton, Brookend and Slimbridge *Glouc*

BROOKFIELD (St Anne), Highgate Rise *Lon 17*   **P** *Bp*   **V** A J B MELDRUM

BROOKFIELD (St Margaret) *York 20*   **P** *Abp*   **P-in-c** W J FORD,   **C** N GREEN

BROOKFIELD (St Mary) *Lon 17*   **P** *Bp*   **V** C G POPE

BROOKHOUSE (St Paul)   *see* Caton w Littledale *Blackb*

BROOKHURST (St Peter's Chapel)   *see* Eastham *Ches*

BROOKING (St Barnabas)   *see* Totnes w Bridgetown, Berry Pomeroy etc *Ex*

BROOKLAND (St Augustine)   *see* Appledore w Brookland, Fairfield, Brenzett etc *Cant*

BROOKLANDS   *see* Baguley *Man*

BROOKSBY (St Michael and All Angels)   *see* Upper Wreake *Leic*

BROOKSIDE (Pastoral Centre)   *see* Cen Telford *Lich*

BROOKWOOD (St Saviour)   *see* Knaphill w Brookwood *Guildf*

BROOM (St Matthew)   *see* Bidford-on-Avon *Cov*

BROOM LEYS (St David) *Leic 8*   **P** *Bp*   **V** J W STEVENSON

BROOM VALLEY (St Barnabas)   *see* Rotherham *Sheff*

BROOME (St Michael)   *see* Ditchingham, Hedenham, Broome, Earsham etc *Nor*

BROOME (St Peter)   *see* Churchill-in-Halfshire w Blakedown and Broome *Worc*

BROOMFIELD (St Margaret)   *see* Hollingbourne and Hucking w Leeds and Broomfield *Cant*

BROOMFIELD (St Mary and All Saints)   *see* W Monkton w Kingston St Mary, Broomfield etc *B & W*

BROOMFIELD (St Mary w St Leonard) *Chelmsf 8*   **P** *Bp*   **V** C A TIBBOTT

BROOMFLEET (St Mary)   *see* S Cave and Ellerker w Broomfleet *York*

BROOMHILL (St Mark)   *see* Sheff St Mark Broomhill *Sheff*

BROSELEY (All Saints) w Benthall, Jackfield, Linley, Willey and Barrow *Heref 13*   **P** *Patr Bd*   **R** M A KINNA,   **NSM** B D SHINTON

BROTHERTOFT Group, The (Christ Church) (St Gilbert of Sempringham) *Linc 20*   **P** *Bp (2 turns), V Algarkirk (1 turn)*   **P-in-c** R E TAYLOR

BROTHERTON (St Edward the Confessor) *Wakef 10*   **P** *D&C York*   **P-in-c** E M WOODCOCK

BROTTON PARVA (St Margaret) *York 16*   **P** *Abp*   **R** *vacant* (01287) 676275

BROUGH (All Saints)   *see* Elloughton and Brough w Brantingham *York*

BROUGH (St Michael) w Stainmore, Musgrave and Warcop *Carl 1*   **P** *Bp (2 turns) and Lord Hothfield (1 turn)*   **P-in-c** P M TOMPKINS

BROUGHAM (St Wilfrid Chapel)   *see* Lowther and Askham and Clifton and Brougham *Carl*

BROUGHTON (All Saints)   *see* Warboys w Broughton and Bury w Wistow *Ely*

BROUGHTON (All Saints), Marton and Thornton *Bradf 7*   **P** *Ch Ch Ox and Exors Dame Harriet Nelson (jt)*   **R** N A TURNER,   **C** P A TURNER

BROUGHTON (no church) *Ox 21*   **P** *Ch Patr Trust*   **V** *vacant*

BROUGHTON (St Andrew) w Loddington and Cransley and Thorpe Malsor *Pet 9*   **P** *Ld Chan (1 turn), Bp (2 turns), and Keble Coll Ox (1 turn)*   **C** B J WITHINGTON, C H DOBSON, R A PRIESTLEY, J R WESTWOOD, M L PRIESTLEY,   **NSM** M L PRIESTLEY

BROUGHTON (St James) (St Clement and St Matthias) St John the Baptist *Man 20*   **P** *Patr Bd*   **OLM** J S CORRIE

BROUGHTON (St John the Baptist) *Blackb 13*   **P** *Trustees*   **V** S FOX

BROUGHTON (St Mary) *Lich 22*   **P** *D R B Thompson Esq*   **P-in-c** P F BARNES,   **OLM** A EVANS

BROUGHTON (St Mary) *Linc 6*   **P** *MMCET*   **R** *vacant* (01652) 652506

BROUGHTON (St Mary Magdalene) (Holy Innocents) and Duddon *Carl 9*   **P** *V Millom, Lt-Col D A S Pennefather, and Ch Patr Trust (by turn)*   **P-in-c** N A THORNLEY

BROUGHTON (St Mary the Virgin)   *see* Wykeham *Ox*

BROUGHTON (St Mary) w Bossington and Houghton and Mottisfont *Win 12*   **P** *Ld Chan (1 turn), Mr and Mrs*

R G L Pugh, A Humbert Esq and Miss R A Humbert (jt) (2 turns)   **R** R A CORNE

BROUGHTON (St Peter)   *see* Ashley and Mucklestone and Broughton and Croxton *Lich*

BROUGHTON, GREAT (Christ Church)   *see* Brigham, Gt Broughton and Broughton Moor *Carl*

BROUGHTON, LOWER (Ascension) *Man 20*   **P** *Trustees*   **P-in-c** D S C WYATT

BROUGHTON, NETHER (St Mary the Virgin)   *see* Old Dalby, Nether Broughton, Saxelbye etc *Leic*

BROUGHTON, UPPER (St Luke)   *see* Hickling w Kinoulton and Broughton Sulney *S'well*

BROUGHTON ASTLEY (St Mary) and Croft w Stoney Stanton *Leic 7*   **P** *Patr Bd*   **P-in-c** T THURSTON-SMITH

BROUGHTON GIFFORD (St Mary the Virgin), Great Chalfield and Holt St Katharine *Sarum 14*   **P** *D&C Bris (3 turns), Ld Chan (2 turns), and R C Floyd Esq (1 turn)*   **P-in-c** A E EVANS,   **C** C E PARR, J PERRETT,   **NSM** J DARLING, E M BENNETT,   **OLM** E A FIELDEN, A E WINTOUR

BROUGHTON HACKETT (St Leonard)   *see* Peopleton and White Ladies Aston w Churchill etc *Worc*

BROUGHTON IN FURNESS (St Mary Magdalene)   *see* Broughton and Duddon *Carl*

BROUGHTON MILLS (Holy Innocents)   *as above*

BROUGHTON MOOR (St Columba)   *see* Brigham, Gt Broughton and Broughton Moor *Carl*

BROUGHTON POGGS (St Peter)   *see* Shill Valley and Broadshire *Ox*

BROWN CANDOVER (St Peter)   *see* Farleigh, Candover and Wield *Win*

BROWN CLEE   *see* Ditton Priors w Neenton, Burwarton etc *Heref*

BROWN EDGE (St Anne) *Lich 8*   **P** *Bp*   **P-in-c** R J S GRIGSON

BROWNHILL (St Saviour) *Wakef 8*   **P** *V Batley*   **V** P N A SENIOR

BROWNHILLS (St James)   *see* Ogley Hay *Lich*

BROWNSOVER (Christ Church)   *see* Clifton w Newton and Brownsover *Cov*

BROWNSWOOD PARK (St John the Evangelist) *Lon 5*   **P** *City Corp*   **P-in-c** J D CLARK

BROXBOURNE (St Augustine) w Wormley *St Alb 17*   **P** *Bp and Peache Trustees (jt)*   **R** *vacant* (01992) 462382

BROXHOLME (All Saints)   *see* Saxilby Gp *Linc*

BROXTED (St Mary the Virgin) w Chickney and Tilty and Great and Little Easton *Chelmsf 18*   **P** *Mrs F Spurrier (2 turns), DBP (1 turn), and MMCET (1 turn)*   **P-in-c** I E CRAWFORD

BROXTOWE (St Martha) *S'well 14*   **P** *Bp*   **P-in-c** J M KIRKHAM

BRUERA (St Mary)   *see* Waverton w Aldford and Bruera *Ches*

BRUISYARD (St Peter)   *see* Upper Alde *St E*

BRUMBY (St Hugh) (All Saints) *Linc 4*   **P** *Bp*   **TR** C A B MARTIN,   **OLM** A K PEAT

BRUNDALL (St Lawrence) w Braydeston and Postwick *Nor 4*   **P** *Bp and MMCET (jt)*   **R** D L SMITH

BRUNDISH (St Lawrence)   *see* Laxfield, Cratfield, Wilby and Brundish *St E*

BRUNSTEAD (St Peter)   *see* Stalham, E Ruston, Brunstead, Sutton and Ingham *Nor*

BRUNSWICK (Christ Church) *Man 3*   **P** *Ch Soc Trust*   **R** S J T GATENBY,   **NSM** R M YOUNG

BRUNSWICK (St Cuthbert)   *see* Ch the King *Newc*

BRUNTCLIFFE (St Andrew)   *see* Morley *Wakef*

BRUNTINGTHORPE (St Mary)   *see* Hexagon *Leic*

BRUNTON PARK (St Aidan)   *see* Ch the King *Newc*

BRUSHFORD (St Mary the Virgin) *Ex 20*   **P** *D&C*   **V** P J NORMAN

BRUSHFORD (St Nicholas)   *see* Dulverton w Brushford, Brompton Regis etc *B & W*

BRUTON (St Mary the Virgin) and District *B & W 2*   **P** *Patr Bd*   **P-in-c** J M BAILEY,   **C** T G RAE SMITH,   **Hon C** M D ELLIS

BRYANSTON SQUARE (St Mary) w St Marylebone (St Mark) *Lon 4*   **P** *The Crown*   **R** J P T PETERS,   **C** E B W FLINT,   **NSM** B J KISSELL

BRYANSTON STREET (Annunciation)   *see* St Marylebone Annunciation Bryanston Street *Lon*

BRYHER (All Saints)   *see* Is of Scilly *Truro*

BRYMPTON (St Andrew)   *see* Odcombe, Brympton, Lufton and Montacute *B & W*

BRYN (St Chad)   *see* Clun w Bettws-y-Crwyn and Newcastle *Heref*

BRYN (St Peter) *Liv 14*   **P** *Bp*   **V** D J HOOTON

BUBBENHALL (St Giles)   *see* Baginton w Bubbenhall and Ryton-on-Dunsmore *Cov*

BUBWITH (All Saints) w Skipwith *York 2*   **P** *Abp and D&C, Ld Chan (alt)*   **P-in-c** R M KIRKMAN

BUCKDEN (St Mary) w the Offords *Ely 13* **P** *Bp and Ld Chan (alt)* **R** A M BARRETT, **C** T D M HAYWARD

BUCKENHAM, NEW (St Martin) *see* Quidenham Gp *Nor*

BUCKENHAM, OLD (All Saints) *as above*

BUCKERELL (St Mary and St Giles) *see* Honiton, Gittisham, Combe Raleigh, Monkton etc *Ex*

BUCKFAST SANCTUARY (not known) *see* Buckfastleigh w Dean Prior *Ex*

BUCKFASTLEIGH (Holy Trinity) (St Luke's Mission) w Dean Prior *Ex 13* **P** *D&C (2 turns), DBP (1 turn)* **V** D J ROWLAND

BUCKHORN WESTON (St John the Baptist) *see* Stour Vale *Sarum*

BUCKHURST HILL (St Elisabeth) (St John the Baptist) (St Stephen) *Chelmsf 24* **P** *Patr Bd* **TR** I D FARLEY, **C** C J BRIXTON

BUCKINGHAM (St Peter and St Paul) *Ox 22* **P** *Bp, Adn Buckm, Mrs S A J Doulton, G&C Coll Cam, New Coll Ox, and Exors R J Dalziel Smith Esq (jt)* **R** W O C PEARSON-GEE, **NSM** J F KING

BUCKINGHAM, NORTH *Ox 22* **P** *Ch Soc Trust, Mrs J M Williams, and D J Robarts Esq (by turn)* **R** J A TALING

BUCKINGHAM, WEST *Ox 22* **P** *Bp, D&C Westmr, G Purefoy Esq, and R L Randall Esq (1 turn), New Coll Ox (1 turn), and DBP (1 turn)* **P-in-c** E A SIMPSON, **NSM** C P CARTER

BUCKLAND (All Saints) *see* Aston Clinton w Buckland and Drayton Beauchamp *Ox*

BUCKLAND (St Mary the Virgin) *see* Cherbury w Gainfield *Ox*

BUCKLAND (St Mary the Virgin) *see* Betchworth and Buckland *S'wark*

BUCKLAND (St Michael) *see* Winchcombe *Glouc*

BUCKLAND, EAST (St Michael) *see* S Molton w Nymet St George, High Bray etc *Ex*

BUCKLAND, WEST (Blessed Virgin Mary) *see* Wellington and Distr *B & W*

BUCKLAND, WEST (St Peter) *see* Swimbridge w W Buckland and Landkey *Ex*

BUCKLAND BREWER (St Mary and St Benedict) *see* Parkham, Alwington, Buckland Brewer etc *Ex*

BUCKLAND DINHAM (St Michael and All Angels) *see* Mells w Buckland Dinham, Elm, Whatley etc *B & W*

BUCKLAND FILLEIGH (St Mary and Holy Trinity) *see* Shebbear, Buckland Filleigh, Sheepwash etc *Ex*

BUCKLAND-IN-DOVER (St Andrew) (St Nicholas) *Cant 7* **P** *Abp* **R** T FOREMAN

BUCKLAND IN THE MOOR (St Peter) *see* Ashburton, Bickington, Buckland in the Moor etc *Ex*

BUCKLAND MONACHORUM (St Andrew) *Ex 25* **P** *Bp* **V** G M COTTER

BUCKLAND NEWTON (Holy Rood), Cerne Abbas, Godmanstone and Minterne Magna *Sarum 1* **P** *Adn Sherborne, Lord Digby, D H C Batten Esq, G E H Gallia Esq, and Col J L Yeatman (jt)* **V** J T L STILL, **NSM** P A C KENNEDY

BUCKLAND RIPERS (St Nicholas) *see* Bincombe w Broadwey, Upwey and Buckland Ripers *Sarum*

BUCKLAND ST MARY (Blessed Virgin Mary) *see* Blackdown *B & W*

BUCKLAND TOUT SAINTS (St Peter) *see* Stokenham, Slapton, Charleton w Buckland etc *Ex*

BUCKLAND VALLEY (St Nicholas) *see* Buckland-in-Dover *Cant*

BUCKLEBURY (St Mary) w Marlston *Ox 12* **P** *C J Pratt Esq* **P-in-c** J T D M GADSBY, **NSM** R C OBIN, L E BLISS

BUCKLEBURY, UPPER (All Saints) *see* Bucklebury w Marlston *Ox*

BUCKLERS HARD (St Mary) *see* Beaulieu and Exbury and E Boldre *Win*

BUCKLESHAM (St Mary) *see* Nacton and Levington w Bucklesham etc *St E*

BUCKMINSTER (St John the Baptist) *see* S Framland *Leic*

BUCKNALL (St Margaret) *see* Woodhall Spa Gp *Linc*

BUCKNALL Team Ministry, The (St Mary the Virgin) *Lich 12* **P** *Patr Bd* **TR** N W R EVANS, **TV** M N STEPHENS, **C** D A FRASER, D STREET, **OLM** J MARSHALL

BUCKNELL (St Mary) w Chapel Lawn, Llanfair Waterdine and Stowe *Heref 9* **P** *Earl of Powis, Grocers' Co, and J Coltman Rogers Esq (jt)* **P-in-c** D C HOARE

BUCKNELL (St Peter) *see* Bicester w Bucknell, Caversfield and Launton *Ox*

BUCKROSE, WEST *York 6* **P** *Ld Chan (1 turn), Lord Middleton and Abp (3 turns)* **R** J S HILL

BUCKROSE CARRS *York 6* **P** *Prime Min, H J N Cholmley Esq, Sir Philip Naylor-Leyland Bt, and D&C (by turn)* **R** J M DUKE

BUCKS MILLS (St Anne) *see* Parkham, Alwington, Buckland Brewer etc *Ex*

BUCKWORTH (All Saints) *Ely 10* **P** *Bp* **P-in-c** M P JEPP

BUDBROOKE (St Michael) *Cov 11* **P** *MMCET* **P-in-c** D A BROWN, **C** C A HICKS, **OLM** M LODGE

BUDE HAVEN (St Michael and All Angels) and Marhamchurch *Truro 8* **P** *Bp and PCC (jt)* **R** *vacant* (01288) 352318

BUDLEIGH, EAST (All Saints) w Bicton and Otterton *Ex 1* **P** *Lord Clinton* **C** E A CHARLTON

BUDLEIGH SALTERTON (St Peter) *Ex 1* **P** *Lord Clinton* **C** E A CHARLTON

BUDOCK (St Budock) *Truro 3* **P** *Bp* **V** G K BENNETT, **C** S G TURNER

BUDWORTH, GREAT (St Mary and All Saints) *Ches 4* **P** *Ch Ch Ox* **V** A G BROWN

BUDWORTH, LITTLE (St Peter) *see* Whitegate w Lt Budworth *Ches*

BUGBROOKE (St Michael and All Angels), Harpole, Kislingbury and Rothersthorpe *Pet 3* **P** *Bp, Exors E W Harrison, DBP, and Sir Philip Naylor-Leyland Bt (jt)* **R** S R J FRENCH

BUGLAWTON (St John the Evangelist) *see* Congleton *Ches*

BUGTHORPE (St Andrew) *see* Garrowby Hill *York*

BUILDWAS (Holy Trinity) *see* Wrockwardine Deanery *Lich*

BULCOTE (Holy Trinity) *see* Burton Joyce w Bulcote and Stoke Bardolph *S'well*

BULFORD (St Leonard) *see* Avon Valley *Sarum*

BULKELEY (All Saints) *see* Tattenhall w Burwardsley and Handley *Ches*

BULKINGTON (Christ Church) *see* Seend, Bulkington and Poulshot *Sarum*

BULKINGTON (St James) *Cov 5* **P** *Ld Chan* **P-in-c** P J MESSAM

BULKWORTHY (St Michael) *see* Bradworthy, Sutcombe, Putford etc *Ex*

BULLEY (St Michael and All Angels) *see* Huntley and Longhope, Churcham and Bulley *Glouc*

BULLINGHOPE, UPPER (St Peter) *see* Heref S Wye *Heref*

BULLINGTON (St Michael and All Angels) *see* Lower Dever *Win*

BULMER (St Andrew) *see* N Hinckford *Chelmsf*

BULMER (St Martin) *see* Howardian Gp *York*

BULPHAN (St Mary the Virgin) *see* Orsett and Bulphan and Horndon on the Hill *Chelmsf*

BULWELL (St John the Divine) *S'well 12* **P** *Bp* **V** D GRAY

BULWELL (St Mary the Virgin and All Souls) *S'well 12* **P** *Bp* **P-in-c** A J NICOLLS

BULWICK (St Nicholas) *see* King's Cliffe, Bulwick and Blatherwycke etc *Pet*

BUNBURY (St Boniface) and Tilstone Fearnall *Ches 5* **P** *Haberdashers' Co* **V** R J GATES

BUNCTON (All Saints) *see* Ashington, Washington and Wiston w Buncton *Chich*

BUNGAY (Holy Trinity) w St Mary *St E 14* **P** *DBP* **P-in-c** I B BYRNE, **NSM** L JACQUET, **OLM** R C B ALLEN, J E A MILLER

BUNNY (St Mary the Virgin) *see* Keyworth and Stanton-on-the-Wolds and Bunny etc *S'well*

BUNTINGFORD (St Peter) *see* Aspenden, Buntingford and Westmill *St Alb*

BUNWELL (St Michael and All Angels), Carleton Rode, Tibenham, Great Moulton and Aslacton *Nor 5* **P** *Bp and DBP (alt)* **R** M I KNOWLES

BURBAGE (All Saints) *see* Savernake *Sarum*

BURBAGE (Christ Church) *see* Buxton w Burbage and King Sterndale *Derby*

BURBAGE (St Catherine) w Aston Flamville *Leic 10* **P** *Ball Coll Ox* **R** F D JENNINGS, **NSM** R STEPHEN, D J J A F MCCLEAN

BURCHETTS GREEN *Ox 13* **P** *DBP and Bp (jt)* **V** K B NICHOLLS, **NSM** D M WOODMORE, T M MOLYNEUX

BURE VALLEY Benefice, The *Nor 19* **P** *Bp, Mercers' Co, and J M Roberts Esq (jt)* **R** P M HANSELL, **C** A KAMBLE-HANSELL, **OLM** J GOODMAN, G G GOODMAN

BURES (St Mary the Virgin) w Assington and Lt Cornard *St E 12* **P** *DBP and Bp (jt)* **V** R L C KING, **NSM** K M KING, M J CANTACUZENE, **OLM** J L GOYMOUR

BURFORD (St John the Baptist) w Fulbrook, Taynton, Asthall, Swinbrook and Widford *Ox 8* **P** *Bp and Capt D Mackinnon (jt)* **V** R M COOMBS, **C** J HUNTER DUNN, **NSM** S BLAKE, **OLM** C REAVLEY

BURFORD (St Mary) *see* Tenbury *Heref*

BURGATE (St Mary)   *see* N Hartismere *St E*
BURGESS HILL (St Andrew) *Chich 9*   **P** *Bp*   **V** S R JELLEY
BURGESS HILL (St Edward) *Chich 9*   **P** *Bp Chich, Bp*
Horsham, and R Clayton w Keymer (jt)   **V** D M BRADSHAW,
NSM S S MACCARTHY
BURGESS HILL (St John the Evangelist) *Chich 9*   **P** *Bp Chich,*
Bp Horsham, and R Clayton w Keymer (jt)   **V** K M O´BRIEN
BURGH Group, The *Linc 8*   **P** *Bp (2 turns),*
H J Montgomery-Massingberd Esq (1 turn), SMF (1 turn)
R T STEELE
BURGH (St Botolph)   *see* Boulge w Burgh, Grundisburgh and
Hasketon *St E*
BURGH (St Margaret and St Mary)   *see* S Trin Broads *Nor*
BURGH (St Peter)   *see* Raveningham Gp *Nor*
BURGH-BY-SANDS (St Michael)   *see* Barony of Burgh *Carl*
BURGH CASTLE (St Peter and St Paul)   *see* Belton and Burgh
Castle *Nor*
BURGH HEATH (St Mary the Virgin)   *see* Howell Hill w Burgh
Heath *Guildf*
BURGH LE MARSH (St Peter and St Paul)   *see* Burgh Gp *Linc*
BURGH-NEXT-AYLSHAM (St Mary)   *see* Bure Valley *Nor*
BURGH-ON-BAIN (St Helen)   *see* Asterby Gp *Linc*
BURGH PARVA (St Mary)   *see* Briston, Burgh Parva,
Hindolveston etc *Nor*
BURGHCLERE (Ascension) (All Saints) w Newtown and
Ecchinswell w Sydmonton *Win 6*   **P** *Earl of Carnarvon*
R D G BARTHOLOMEW
BURGHFIELD (St Mary the Virgin) *Ox 12*   **P** *Earl of*
Shrewsbury   **R** G J LOVELL
BURGHILL (St Mary the Virgin) *Heref 3*   **P** *DBP*
NSM E S V VERWEY, P A LITTLEWOOD
BURGHWALLIS (St Helen) and Campsall *Sheff 7*   **P** *Bp*
(2 turns), Mrs E H I Ellison-Anne (1 turn)
P-in-c R J WALTON
BURHAM (Methodist Church) and Wouldham *Roch 5*   **P** *Bp*
and Ld Chan (alt)   **P-in-c** J M BRADSHAW
BURITON (St Mary the Virgin) *Portsm 4*   **P** *Bp*
R W P M HUGHES,   **NSM** J M BEE
BURLESCOMBE (St Mary)   *see* Sampford Peverell,
Uplowman, Holcombe Rogus etc *Ex*
BURLEY (St Matthias) *Ripon 7*   **P** *G M Bedford Esq,*
J C Yeadon Esq, E Beety Esq, Mrs M E Dunham, and
Mrs L M Rawse (jt)   **V** K TROUT,   **NSM** H BURLEY
BURLEY IN WHARFEDALE (St Mary the Virgin) *Bradf 4*
P *Bp*   **V** M BURLEY
BURLEY VILLE (St John the Baptist) *Win 9*   **P** *V Ringwood*
V *vacant (01425)* 402303
BURLEYDAM (St Mary and St Michael)   *see* Baddiley and
Wrenbury w Burleydam *Ches*
BURLINGHAM (St Andrew)   *see* Acle w Fishley, N
Burlingham, Beighton w Moulton *Nor*
BURLINGHAM (St Edmund King and Martyr) w Lingwood,
Strumpshaw w Hassingham and Buckenham *Nor 4*   **P** *Ch Soc*
Trust, MMCET, and Bp (jt)   **R** D K WAKEFIELD
BURLTON (St Anne)   *see* Loppington w Newtown *Lich*
BURMANTOFTS (St Stephen and St Agnes) *Ripon 5*
P *Ch Trust Fund Trust*   **P-in-c** A S KASIBANTE
BURMARSH (All Saints)   *see* Dymchurch w Burmarsh and
Newchurch *Cant*
BURMINGTON (St Nicholas and St Barnabas)   *see* S Warks
Seven Gp *Cov*
BURNAGE (St Margaret) *Man 2*   **P** *Bp*   **R** I D THOMPSON,
C C E THROUP
BURNAGE (St Nicholas) *Man 6*   **P** *Trustees*   **P-in-c** R MANN
BURNBY (St Giles)   *see* Londesborough Wold *York*
BURNESIDE (St Oswald)   *see* Beacon *Carl*
BURNESTON (St Lambert)   *see* Kirklington w Burneston and
Wath and Pickhill *Ripon*
BURNETT (St Michael)   *see* Keynsham *B & W*
BURNEY LANE (Christ Church)   *see* Ward End w Bordesley
Green *Birm*
BURNHAM (St Andrew) *B & W 1*   **P** *D&C*   **V** G R WITTS,
NSM P A KINGDOM
BURNHAM (St Mary the Virgin) *Chelmsf 11*
P *N D Beckett Esq and Walsingham Coll Trust (jt)*
V M R NORTH
BURNHAM (St Peter) *Ox 23*   **P** *Eton Coll*   **V** W S JACKSON,
C J D BARLOW
BURNHAM DEEPDALE (St Mary)   *see* Hunstanton St Mary
w Ringstead Parva etc *Nor*
BURNHAM NORTON (St Margaret)   *see* Burnham Gp of Par
Nor
BURNHAM-ON-CROUCH (St Mary the Virgin)   *see* Burnham
Chelmsf
BURNHAM-ON-SEA (St Andrew)   *as above*

BURNHAM OVERY (St Clement)   *see* Burnham Gp of Par *Nor*
BURNHAM THORPE (All Saints)   *as above*
BURNHAM ULPH (All Saints)   *as above*
BURNHAM WESTGATE (St Mary), Burnham Norton,
Burnham Overy, Burnham Thorpe, and Burnham Sutton w Ulph
(The Burnham Group of Parishes) *Nor 15*   **P** *Ch Coll Cam*
(1 turn), Ld Chan (2 turns), and DBP (1 turn)
R G E D HITCHINS
BURNLEY (St Andrew) w St Margaret and Burnley St James
Blackb 3   **P** *Prime Min and R Burnley St Pet (alt)*
V P R HAPGOOD-STRICKLAND
BURNLEY (St Catherine) (St Alban) and St Paul *Blackb 3*
P *R Burnley*   **V** R T D PARKER
BURNLEY (St Cuthbert) *Blackb 3*   **P** *R Burnley*
P-in-c I C WATTS
BURNLEY (St Mark) *Blackb 3*   **P** *Bp*   **V** *vacant (01282)*
428178
BURNLEY (St Matthew the Apostle) Habergham Eaves w Holy
Trinity *Blackb 3*   **P** *R Burnley*   **V** M J WILLIAMS
BURNLEY (St Peter) (St Stephen) *Blackb 3*   **P** *Bp and DBP (jt)*
R T A G BILL,   **Hon C** L LAYCOCK
BURNLEY, WEST (All Saints) *Blackb 3*   **P** *Bp and*
R Burnley (jt)   **C** C W HILL
BURNMOOR (St Barnabas) *Dur 14*   **P** *Lord Lambton*
P-in-c E M WILKINSON
BURNOPFIELD (St James) *Dur 4*   **P** *Bp*   **V** R G BIRCHALL,
NSM H MURRAY
BURNSALL (St Wilfrid) w Rylstone *Bradf 7*   **P** *Exors Earl of*
Craven and CPAS (jt)   **P-in-c** D MACHA,   **C** F JENKINS
BURNT OAK (St Alphage)   *see* Hendon St Alphage *Lon*
BURNT YATES (St Andrew)   *see* Ripley w Burnt Yates *Ripon*
BURNTWOOD (Christ Church) *Lich 1*   **P** *D&C*
V M M MATTOCKS,   **NSM** R L C BULL
BURPHAM (Holy Spirit) (St Luke) Guildford *Guildf 5*   **P** *Bp*
V C J MATTHEWS,   **NSM** J C L RUNNACLES
BURPHAM (St Mary the Virgin) *Chich 1*   **P** *D&C*
P-in-c W R KILFORD
BURRADON (Good Shepherd)   *see* Weetslade *Newc*
BURRILL (Mission Church)   *see* Bedale and Leeming and
Thornton Watlass *Ripon*
BURRINGTON (Holy Trinity)   *see* Wrington w Butcombe and
Burrington *B & W*
BURRINGTON (Holy Trinity), Chawleigh, Cheldon,
Chulmleigh, Meshaw, Thelbridge, Wembworthy, Witheridge and
the Worlingtons *Ex 19*   **P** *Patr Bd*   **TR** R D WITHNELL,
TV D A PRESCOTT
BURRINGTON (St George)   *see* Wigmore Abbey *Heref*
BURROUGH GREEN (St Augustine of Canterbury)
see Raddesley Gp *Ely*
BURROUGH HILL Parishes, The: Burrough on the Hill, Great
Dalby, Little Dalby, Pickwell and Somerby *Leic 2*   **P** *Bp, DBP,*
and Mrs M Burdett Fisher (jt)   **P-in-c** S LEIGHTON
BURROUGH ON THE HILL (St Mary the Virgin)
see Burrough Hill Pars *Leic*
BURROWBRIDGE (St Michael)   *see* Athelney *B & W*
BURROWSVILLE (St Mark)   *see* Gt Clacton *Chelmsf*
BURSCOUGH BRIDGE (St John) (St Andrew) (St Cyprian)
Liv 11   **P** *V Ormskirk*   **P-in-c** J R JONES,
C I R GREENWOOD,   **NSM** E HEANEY,   **OLM** B ABRAHAM
BURSDON MOOR (St Martin)   *see* Parkham, Alwington,
Buckland Brewer etc *Ex*
BURSEA (Chapel)   *see* Holme and Seaton Ross Gp *York*
BURSLEDON Pilands Wood (St Paul)   *see* Bursledon *Win*
BURSLEDON (St Leonard) *Win 10*   **P** *Bp*   **V** P A VARGESON,
C J E OGLEY,   **NSM** C A PARKES
BURSLEM (St John the Baptist) (St Paul) *Lich 11*   **P** *Bp and*
MMCET (jt)   **R** D L MCINDOE
BURSLEM (St Werburgh) *Lich 11*   **P** *Bp*   **V** K L ROUND
BURSTALL (St Mary the Virgin)   *see* Sproughton w Burstall,
Copdock w Washbrook etc *St E*
BURSTEAD, GREAT (St Mary Magdalene) *Chelmsf 6*   **P** *Bp*
V S SWIFT
BURSTEAD, LITTLE (St Mary)   *see* Billericay and Lt Burstead
Chelmsf
BURSTOCK (St Andrew)   *see* Beaminster Area *Sarum*
BURSTON (St Mary)   *see* Winfarthing w Shelfanger w Burston
w Gissing etc *Nor*
BURSTON (St Rufin)   *see* Mid Trent *Lich*
BURSTOW (St Bartholomew) w Horne *S'wark 25*   **P** *Ld Chan*
and Bp (alt)   **R** C E GALE
BURSTWICK (All Saints) w Thorngumbald *York 12*   **P** *Abp*
V A J BURDON,   **Hon C** I J BLYTH
BURTLE (St Philip and St James)   *see* Shapwick w Ashcott and
Burtle *B & W*
BURTON (All Saints) w Christ Church *Lich 14*   **P** *CPAS and*
Ch Soc Trust (jt)   **V** N R IRONS

BURTON (St Aidan) (St Paul) *Lich 14* P *Bp and Lord Burton (jt)* V P A FARTHING, NSM P J ORTON
BURTON (St James) and Holme *Carl 10* P *Simeon's Trustees* P-in-c P G BAXENDALE
BURTON (St Luke) and Sopley *Win 9* P *Bp and D&C Cant (alt)* P-in-c M C SURMAN
BURTON (St Nicholas) and Shotwick *Ches 9* P *D&C (1 turn) and St Jo Hosp Lich (2 turns)* V C M HELM
BURTON w COATES (St Agatha) *see* Barlavington, Burton w Coates, Sutton and Bignor *Chich*
BURTON AGNES (St Martin) *see* The Beacon *York*
BURTON BRADSTOCK (St Mary) *see* Bride Valley *Sarum*
BURTON BY LINCOLN (St Vincent) *see* Spring Line Gp *Linc*
BURTON COGGLES (St Thomas à Becket) *see* N Beltisloe Gp *Linc*
BURTON DASSETT (All Saints) *Cov 8* P *Bp* P-in-c M G CADWALLADER
BURTON FLEMING (St Cuthbert) w Fordon, Grindale and Wold Newton *York 9* P *Abp and MMCET (jt)* P-in-c G J OWEN, NSM B E HODGSON
BURTON GREEN (Chapel of Ease) *see* Kenilworth St Nic *Cov*
BURTON HASTINGS (St Botolph) *see* Wolvey w Burton Hastings, Copston Magna etc *Cov*
BURTON IN LONSDALE (All Saints) *see* Thornton in Lonsdale w Burton in Lonsdale *Bradf*
BURTON JOYCE (St Helen) w Bulcote and Stoke Bardolph *S'well 10* P *MMCET* P-in-c G R HARPER
BURTON LATIMER (St Mary the Virgin) *Pet 9* P *Bp* R *vacant* (01536) 722959
BURTON LAZARS (St James) *see* Melton Mowbray *Leic*
BURTON LEONARD (St Leonard) *see* Ripon Cathl *Ripon*
BURTON-ON-TRENT (All Saints) *see* Burton All SS w Ch Ch *Lich*
BURTON-ON-TRENT (St Aidan) *see* Burton St Aid and St Paul *Lich*
BURTON-ON-TRENT (St Chad) *Lich 14* P *Bp* P-in-c G J CROSSLEY
BURTON-ON-TRENT (St Modwen) *see* Burton St Modwen *Lich*
BURTON-ON-TRENT (St Paul) *see* Burton St Aid and St Paul *Lich*
BURTON OVERY (St Andrew) *see* Glen Magna cum Stretton Magna etc *Leic*
BURTON PEDWARDINE (St Andrew and the Blessed Virgin Mary and St Nicholas) *see* Helpringham w Hale *Linc*
BURTON PIDSEA (St Peter) and Humbleton w Elsternwick *York 12* P *Ld Chan and D&C (alt)* V J L CAMPBELL
BURTON UPON STATHER (St Andrew) *see* Flixborough w Burton upon Stather *Linc*
BURTON-UPON-TRENT (St Modwen) *Lich 14* P *Bp* V *vacant* (01283) 544054
BURTONWOOD (St Michael) *Liv 15* P *R Warrington* Hon C A LITTON
BURWARDSLEY (St John) *see* Tattenhall w Burwardsley and Handley *Ches*
BURWASH (St Bartholomew) *Chich 14* P *BNC Ox* R S M FRANCE, NSM P A SHAW
BURWASH WEALD (St Philip) *Chich 15* P *Bp* V *vacant* (01435) 883287
BURWELL (St Andrew) (St Mary) w Reach *Ely 4* P *DBP* V E J WILLIAMS
BURY (All Saints) *see* Kirklees Valley *Man*
BURY (Christ Church) *see* Walmersley Road, Bury *Man*
BURY (Holy Cross) *see* Warboys w Broughton and Bury w Wistow *Ely*
BURY (St John the Evangelist) w Houghton and Coldwaltham and Hardham *Chich 11* P *Pemb Coll Ox, D&C, and Col Sir Brian Barttelot Bt (jt)* V D A TWINLEY, C D C BERESFORD
BURY (St John w St Mark) *see* Walmersley Road, Bury *Man*
BURY (St Mary the Virgin) *Man 8* P *Earl of Derby* R J C FINDON, C G F JOYCE
BURY St Paul *Man 8* P *Trustees* V *vacant* 0161-761 6991
BURY (St Stephen) *see* Elton St Steph *Man*
BURY, NEW (St Catherine) (St George) (St James) w Great Lever *Man 7* P *Bp* TR R J HORROCKS, TV J A PENN, C G DAVID, OLM N A COWELL, E V LARKIN, J GREENHALGH
BURY, NORTH *see* Bury St Edmunds All SS w St Jo and St Geo *St E*
BURY, ROCH VALLEY (Christ the King) (St Peter) *Man 8* P *Patr Bd* C K M TRIVASSE, NSM J M SMITH
BURY ST EDMUNDS (All Saints) (St John the Evangelist) (St George) *St E 13* P *Patr Bd* TR J PARR, C P J PAYNE, NSM E KIRBY, OLM J C MANN
BURY ST EDMUNDS (Cathedral of St James) District *St E 13* V *vacant*

BURY ST EDMUNDS (Christ Church) Moreton Hall *St E 13* P *Bp, V Bury St Edm St Jas, and V Bury St Edm St Mary (jt)* V J L ALDERTON-FORD, NSM N T CORWIN
BURY ST EDMUNDS (St Mary) (St Peter's District Church) *St E 13* P *Hyndman Trustees* V M D ROGERS, C M C O LAWSON, OLM D T CROFTS
BURYTHORPE (All Saints) *see* W Buckrose *York*
BUSBRIDGE (St John the Baptist) and Hambledon *Guildf 4* P *Patr Bd* R S D K TAYLOR, NSM M P W SPENCER, OLM A SPENCER
BUSCOT (St Mary) *see* Gt Coxwell w Buscot, Coleshill etc *Ox*
BUSH END (St John the Evangelist) *see* Hatfield Broad Oak and Bush End *Chelmsf*
BUSH HILL PARK (St Mark) *Lon 18* P *Bp* V P C ATHERTON, NSM S E HEARD
BUSH HILL PARK (St Stephen) *Lon 18* P *V Edmonton All SS* V R J ANNIS
BUSHBURY (St Mary) *Lich 28* P *Patr Bd* TR P A DOBSON, TV I R M POOLE, G R SMITH, C R C MERRICK
BUSHEY (Holy Trinity) (St James) (St Paul) *St Alb 6* P *Bp* R G E W BUCKLER, C C N DRURY, NSM B R ADAMS
BUSHEY HEATH (St Peter) *St Alb 6* P *Bp* V A J BURTON
BUSHLEY (St Peter) *see* Longdon, Castlemorton, Bushley, Queenhill etc *Worc*
BUSHMEAD (Christ Church) *St Alb 12* P *Bp* P-in-c M J BURRELL
BUSSAGE (St Michael and All Angels) *Glouc 4* P *Bp* V H J VAN DER LINDE
BUTCOMBE (St Michael and All Angels) *see* Wrington w Butcombe and Burrington *B & W*
BUTLEIGH (St Leonard) *see* Baltonsborough w Butleigh, W Bradley etc *B & W*
BUTLERS MARSTON (St Peter and St Paul) *see* Stourdene Gp *Cov*
BUTLEY (St John the Baptist) *see* Wilford Peninsula *St E*
BUTTERCRAMBE (St John the Evangelist) *see* Sand Hutton *York*
BUTTERLEIGH (St Matthew) *see* Silverton, Butterleigh, Bickleigh and Cadeleigh *Ex*
BUTTERMERE (St James) *see* Lorton and Loweswater w Buttermere *Carl*
BUTTERMERE (St James the Great) *see* Savernake *Sarum*
BUTTERSHAW (St Aidan) *see* Shelf w Buttershaw St Aid *Bradf*
BUTTERSHAW (St Paul) *Bradf 2* P *Bp* P-in-c T J-L GUILLEMIN, C R I TAYLOR
BUTTERTON (St Bartholomew) *see* Alstonfield, Butterton, Ilam etc *Lich*
BUTTERTON (St Thomas) *see* Newcastle w Butterton *Lich*
BUTTERWICK (Mission Chapel) *see* The Street Par *York*
BUTTERWICK (St Andrew) *see* Freiston, Butterwick w Bennington, and Leverton *Linc*
BUTTERWICK (St Nicholas) *see* Langtoft w Foxholes, Butterwick, Cottam etc *York*
BUTTERWICK, EAST (St Andrew) *see* Messingham *Linc*
BUTTERWICK, WEST (St Mary the Virgin) *see* Epworth Gp *Linc*
BUTTSBURY (St Mary) *see* Margaretting w Mountnessing and Buttsbury *Chelmsf*
BUXHALL (St Mary) *see* Gt Finborough w Onehouse, Harleston, Buxhall etc *St E*
BUXTED (St Margaret the Queen) (St Mary) and Hadlow Down *Chich 21* P *Abp, Bp, and Wagner Trustees (jt)* R E N L FRANCE, NSM D J BLACKDEN
BUXTON (St Andrew) *see* Bure Valley *Nor*
BUXTON (St Anne) (St John the Baptist) (St Mary the Virgin) w Burbage and King Sterndale *Derby 4* P *Patr Bd* TR J F HUDGHTON, TV C I LOWDON, C C F EDWARDS
BUXTON (Trinity Chapel) Proprietary Chapel *Derby 4* C-in-c R MARSDEN, C P D HANCOCK
BUXWORTH (St James) *see* Hayfield and Chinley w Buxworth *Derby*
BY BROOK *Bris 4* P *Patr Bd* P-in-c J M PHILPOTT, NSM G E WOODS
BYERS GREEN (St Peter) *Dur 6* P *Bp* R *vacant* (01388) 606659
BYFIELD (Holy Cross) *see* Aston-le-Walls, Byfield, Boddington, Eydon etc *Pet*
BYFLEET (St Mary) *Guildf 12* P *Ld Chan* R J H MCCABE, Hon C P M S ROSS-MCCABE
BYFLEET, WEST (St John) *Guildf 12* P *Bp* P-in-c A B ELKINS, C J K ELKINS
BYFORD (St John the Baptist) *see* Letton w Staunton, Byford, Mansel Gamage etc *Heref*
BYGRAVE (St Margaret of Antioch) *see* Baldock w Bygrave and Weston *St Alb*

BYKER (St Anthony) *Newc 3*   **P** *Bp*   **P-in-c** D M MADZIMURE
BYKER St Mark and Walkergate (St Oswald) *Newc 3*   **P** *Bp and*
Ch Trust Fund Trust (jt)   **V** K MOULDER
BYKER (St Martin) Newcastle upon Tyne *Newc 3*   **P** *Bp*
P-in-c S E HERBERT
BYKER (St Michael w St Lawrence) *Newc 3*   **P** *Bp*
P-in-c S E HERBERT
BYKER (St Silas) *Newc 3*   **P** *Bp*   **NSM** A F TAYLOR
BYLAND, OLD (All Saints)   *see* Upper Ryedale *York*
BYLAUGH (St Mary)   *see* Lyng, Sparham, Elsing, Bylaugh,
Bawdeswell etc *Nor*
BYLEY CUM LEES (St John the Evangelist)   *see* Middlewich w
Byley *Ches*
BYRNESS (St Francis)   *see* N Tyne and Redesdale *Newc*
BYTHAM, LITTLE (St Medardus)   *see* Castle Bytham w
Creeton *Linc*
BYTHORN (St Lawrence)   *see* Keyston and Bythorn *Ely*
BYTON (St Mary)   *see* Pembridge w Moor Court, Shobdon,
Staunton etc *Heref*
BYWELL (St Peter) and Mickley *Newc 9*   **P** *Bp and Adn*
Lindisfarne (jt)   **V** W RIGBY
BYWORTH (St Francis)   *see* Farnham *Guildf*
CABLE STREET (St Mary)   *see* St Geo-in-the-East St Mary
Lon
CABOURN (St Nicholas)   *see* Swallow *Linc*
CADBURY (St Michael and All Angels)   *see* Brampford Speke,
Cadbury, Newton St Cyres etc *Ex*
CADBURY, NORTH (St Michael the Archangel)   *see* Camelot
Par *B & W*
CADBURY, SOUTH (St Thomas à Becket)   *as above*
CADDINGTON (All Saints) *St Alb 12*   **P** *D&C St Paul's*
P-in-c R C PYKE
CADEBY (All Saints)   *see* Bosworth and Sheepy Gp *Leic*
CADELEIGH (St Bartholomew)   *see* Silverton, Butterleigh,
Bickleigh and Cadeleigh *Ex*
CADGWITH (St Mary)   *see* St Ruan w St Grade and
Landewednack *Truro*
CADISHEAD (St Mary the Virgin) *Man 18*   **P** *Bp*   **V** A E KAY,
OLM J DODD, J STEPHENS
CADMORE END (St Mary le Moor)   *see* Lane End w Cadmore
End *Ox*
CADNEY (All Saints)   *see* Brigg, Wrawby and Cadney cum
Howsham *Linc*
CADOGAN SQUARE (St Simon Zelotes)   *see* Upper Chelsea
St Sav and St Simon *Lon*
CAERHAYS (St Michael)   *see* St Goran w Caerhays *Truro*
CAGE GREEN (St Philip)   *see* Tonbridge SS Pet and Paul *Roch*
CAGEBROOK Parishes *Heref 1*   **P** *Bp (2 turns), Prime Min*
(1 turn)   **R** C L DYSON,   **NSM** E A HITCHINER
CAINSCROSS (St Matthew) w Selsley *Glouc 4*   **P** *Bp and*
Sir Charles Marling Bt (alt)   **P-in-c** K C FLEMING,
NSM M J PAGE, C J BIRKETT
CAISTER NEXT YARMOUTH (Holy Trinity) (St Edmund)
Nor 6   **P** *SMF*   **R** T C THOMPSON
CAISTOR Group, The (St Peter and St Paul) *Linc 5*   **P** *Bp and*
D&C (jt)   **V** I ROBINSON,   **Hon C** S W ANDREW,
NSM J MCMANN
CAISTOR ST EDMUNDS (St Edmund)   *see* Stoke H Cross w
Dunston, Arminghall etc *Nor*
CALBOURNE (All Saints) w Newtown *Portsm 8*   **P** *Bp*
V D J BEVINGTON,   **NSM** J C LEACH
CALCOT (St Birinus)   *see* Tilehurst St Cath and Calcot *Ox*
CALDBECK (St Mungo) (Fellside), Castle Sowerby and
Sebergham *Carl 3*   **P** *Bp and D&C (alt)*
P-in-c N L ROBINSON,   **Hon C** M L RICHES,
NSM K M ASHBRIDGE
CALDECOTE (All Saints), Northill and Old Warden *St Alb 10*
P *Grocers' Co (2 turns), R O Shuttleworth Remembrance Trust*
(1 turn)   **V** F COLEMAN,   **NSM** J S HUMPHRIES
CALDECOTE (St Michael and All Angels)   *see* Lordsbridge *Ely*
CALDECOTE (St Theobald and St Chad)   *see* Weddington and
Caldecote *Cov*
CALDECOTT (St John the Evangelist)   *see* Lyddington,
Bisbrooke, Caldecott, Glaston etc *Pet*
CALDER GROVE (St John the Divine)   *see* Chapelthorpe
Wakef
CALDER VALE (Mission)   *see* Scorton and Barnacre and
Calder Vale *Blackb*
CALDER VALE (St John the Evangelist)   *as above*
CALDERBROOK (St James the Great) *Man 17*   **P** *Bp*
P-in-c J MCGRATH,   **OLM** B WOODHEAD
CALDMORE (St Michael and All Angels) w All Saints Palfrey
Lich 25   **P** *Bp*   **V** F R MILLER
CALDWELL (Chapel)   *see* Forcett and Aldbrough and
Melsonby *Ripon*

CALDWELL (St Giles)   *see* Stapenhill w Cauldwell *Derby*
CALDY (Church of the Resurrection and All Saints)   *see* W
Kirby St Bridget *Ches*
CALEDONIAN ROAD (All Saints Hall)   *see* Barnsbury *Lon*
CALIFORNIA (St Mary and St John) *Ox 16*   **P** *DBP*
V *vacant* 0118-973 0030
CALLINGTON (St Mary)   *see* S Hill w Callington *Truro*
CALLOW END (St James)   *see* Powick and Guarlford and
Madresfield w Newland *Worc*
CALMORE (St Anne)   *see* Totton *Win*
CALNE (Holy Trinity)   *see* Marden Vale *Sarum*
CALNE (St Mary the Virgin)   *as above*
CALOW (St Peter) and Sutton cum Duckmanton *Derby 3*   **P** *Bp*
and V Chesterfield (jt)   **R** *vacant* (01246) 273486
CALSHOT (St George)   *see* Fawley *Win*
CALSTOCK (St Andrew) *Truro 11*   **P** *Duchy of Cornwall*
R J A C WILSON,   **C** R OAKES,   **NSM** L S SCOTT
CALSTONE WELLINGTON (St Mary the Virgin)
see Oldbury *Sarum*
CALTHORPE (Our Lady w St Margaret)   *see* Erpingham w
Calthorpe, Ingworth, Aldborough etc *Nor*
CALTHWAITE (All Saints)   *see* Inglewood Gp *Carl*
CALTON (St Mary the Virgin), Cauldon, Grindon, Waterfall and
Blore Ray w Okeover *Lich 5*   **P** *Bp and Sir Peter*
Walker-Okeover Bt (jt)   **R** M P SKILLINGS
CALUDON   *see* Coventry Caludon *Cov*
CALVELEY CHURCH (not known)   *see* Bunbury and Tilstone
Fearnall *Ches*
CALVERHALL or CORRA (Holy Trinity)   *see* Adderley, Ash,
Calverhall, Ightfield etc *Lich*
CALVERLEIGH (St Mary the Virgin)   *see* Washfield,
Stoodleigh, Withleigh etc *Ex*
CALVERLEY (St Wilfrid) *Bradf 3*   **P** *Bp*   **V** J H WALKER,
C S M KAYE
CALVERTON (All Saints) *Ox 25*   **P** *DBP*   **R** R NORTHING
CALVERTON (St Wilfrid) *S'well 15*   **P** *Bp*   **V** P HEMSTOCK,
NSM M N TAYLOR
CAM (St George) w Stinchcombe *Glouc 5*   **P** *Bp*
V J M MCKENZIE,   **NSM** S J FISHER, S C A ACLAND
CAM, LOWER (St Bartholomew) w Coaley *Glouc 5*   **P** *Bp*
V I A ROBB
CAM VALE *B & W 2*   **P** *Bp and DBP (2 turns), CPAS,*
MMCET and Revd G Bennett (1 turn)   **R** M J M PERRY,
NSM R A HOSKINS
CAMBER (St Thomas)   *see* Rye *Chich*
CAMBERLEY (St Martin) Old Dean *Guildf 6*   **P** *Bp*
V R J PECK
CAMBERLEY (St Mary) *Guildf 6*   **P** *Bp*   **V** A J KNOWLES,
OLM R WALKER
CAMBERLEY (St Michael) Yorktown *Guildf 6*   **P** *Bp*
V B NICOLE,   **OLM** K M MURRAY
CAMBERLEY (St Paul) (St Mary) *Guildf 6*   **P** *Bp*
V M CHESTER,   **C** G L SHAW,   **OLM** C V ISHERWOOD,
S H STEPHENS
CAMBERLEY HEATHERSIDE (Community Centre) *Guildf 6*
P *Bp*   **P-in-c** L J W BAIN
CAMBERWELL (All Saints) Blenheim Grove *S'wark 8*
P *Ch Trust Fund Trust*   **V** J M MORTIMER
CAMBERWELL (Christ Church) *S'wark 8*   **P** *Trustees*
V H R BALFOUR,   **Hon C** J A NICKOLS
CAMBERWELL (St George) *S'wark 8*   **P** *Bp and Trin Coll*
Cam (jt)   **V** N J ELDER,   **C** J SAXTON,   **OLM** M JOHN
CAMBERWELL (St Giles) (St Matthew) *S'wark 8*   **P** *Bp*
V N P GEORGE,   **NSM** S NJOKA,   **OLM** I L RUSSELL
CAMBERWELL (St Luke) *S'wark 8*   **P** *Bp*   **V** J D JELLEY
CAMBERWELL (St Michael and All Angels w All Souls w
Emmanuel) *S'wark 10*   **P** *DBP*   **V** E J OGLESBY,
NSM D SWABY
CAMBERWELL (St Philip) and St Mark *S'wark 7*
P *The Crown*   **NSM** P A ALDEN
CAMBO (Holy Trinity)   *see* Kirkwhelpington, Kirkharle,
Kirkheaton and Cambo *Newc*
CAMBOIS St Peter (St Andrew's Mission Church) and
Sleekbur n *Newc 1*   **P** *D&C*   **V** J BLAKESLEY
CAMBORNE (St Martin and St Meriadoc) *Truro 2*   **P** *Ch Soc*
Trust   **P-in-c** M J FIRBANK,   **C** O STEVENS,
NSM D E HARVEY, M CARVETH
CAMBOURNE *Ely 1*   **P** *Bp*   **V** *vacant*
CAMBRIDGE Ascension (St Giles) (St Luke the Evangelist)
(St Augustine of Canterbury) (All Souls Chapel) *Ely 2*   **P** *Bp*
TR P A KING,   **TV** J C BUNKER,   **NSM** A C RIGELSFORD
CAMBRIDGE (Good Shepherd)   *see* Chesterton Gd Shep *Ely*
CAMBRIDGE (Holy Cross) *Ely 2*   **P** *Bp*   **V** R T WILLIAMS
CAMBRIDGE (Holy Sepulchre) (St Andrew the Great) *Ely 2*
P *PCC*   **V** A D M PAINE,   **C** B R ELFICK, J C POOLE,
N J BUTTERY

CAMBRIDGE (Holy Trinity) *Ely 3* **P** *D&C and Peache Trustees (jt)* **V** R A CHARKHAM, **NSM** C M MEAKIN
CAMBRIDGE (St Andrew the Less) (Christ Church) *Ely 2* **P** *Ch Trust Fund Trust* **V** S N MIDGLEY, **C** C A LOWE, J D TUCKWELL
CAMBRIDGE (St Barnabas) *Ely 3* **P** *V Cam St Paul* **V** A F MACLAURIN, **C** T J FINNEMORE
CAMBRIDGE (St Benedict) *Ely 3* **P** *CCC Cam* **V** A C W TILBY, **NSM** D P FORD, R M NICHOLLS
CAMBRIDGE (St Botolph) *Ely 3* **P** *Qu Coll Cam* **P-in-c** W HORBURY, **NSM** M J WIDDESS
CAMBRIDGE (St Clement) *Ely 2* **P** *Jes Coll Cam* **V** *vacant*
CAMBRIDGE (St Edward King and Martyr) Proprietary Chapel *Ely 3*, F N WATTS **NSM** M J RAMSHAW
CAMBRIDGE (St James) *Ely 3* **P** *Bp* **P-in-c** J BRUECK, **NSM** S J PLANT
CAMBRIDGE (St John the Evangelist) *see* Cherry Hinton St Jo *Ely*
CAMBRIDGE (St Mark) *Ely 3* **P** *DBP* **P-in-c** M A GUITE, **Hon C** M M G ROBERTS
CAMBRIDGE (St Martin) (St Thomas) *Ely 3* **P** *V Cam St Paul* **V** S O LEEKE, **NSM** J D A PARSONS
CAMBRIDGE (St Mary the Great) w St Michael *Ely 2* **P** *Trin Coll Cam* **V** J R E BINNS, **C** P J HAYLER, A M SHILSON-THOMAS
CAMBRIDGE (St Mary the Less) *Ely 3* **P** *Peterho Cam* **NSM** M A BISHOP
CAMBRIDGE (St Matthew) *Ely 2* **P** *V Cam St Andr the Less* **P-in-c** F L PRICE
CAMBRIDGE (St Paul) *Ely 3* **P** *Ch Trust Fund Trust* **V** M S BECKETT
CAMBRIDGE (St Philip) (St Stephen) *Ely 3* **P** *Ch Trust Fund Trust* **V** S TAYLOR, **NSM** R A HIGGINSON, S J BUTLER
CAMDEN SQUARE (St Paul) *see* Old St Pancras *Lon*
CAMDEN TOWN (St Michael) *as above*
CAMEL, WEST (All Saints) *see* Cam Vale *B & W*
CAMELFORD (St Julitta) *see* Lanteglos by Camelford w Advent *Truro*
CAMELFORD (St Thomas of Canterbury) *as above*
CAMELOT Parishes, The *B & W 2* **P** *Patr Bd* **R** T G RAE SMITH, **Hon C** R E WOOD
CAMELSDALE (St Paul) *see* Lynchmere and Camelsdale *Chich*
CAMERTON (St Peter) *see* Timsbury w Priston, Camerton and Dunkerton *B & W*
CAMERTON (St Peter), Seaton and West Seaton *Carl 7* **P** *D&C and Ch Trust Fund Trust (jt)* **V** I GRAINGER, **NSM** I FEARON
CAMMERINGHAM (St Michael) *see* Spring Line Gp *Linc*
CAMP HILL (St Mary and St John) *Cov 5* **P** *Bp* **V** S D SNEATH
CAMPBELL ROOMS (not known) *see* Parr *Liv*
CAMPDEN HILL (St George) *see* Holland Park *Lon*
CAMPSALL (St Mary Magdalene) *see* Burghwallis and Campsall *Sheff*
CAMPSEA ASHE (St John the Baptist) w Marlesford, Parham and Hacheston *St E 18* **P** *Prime Min, Ch Soc Trust, and J S Schreiber Esq (by turn)* **R** H V EDWARDS, **OLM** D A WEST
CAMPTON (All Saints), Clophill and Haynes *St Alb 8* **P** *Bp and Ball Coll Ox (alt)* **R** D HENLEY
CANALSIDE Benefice, The *Sarum 14* **P** *Viscount Long, Magd Coll Cam, and R Trowbridge St Jas and Keevil (by turn)* **P-in-c** S A BALL, **OLM** J M CLARK
CANDLESBY (St Benedict) *see* Partney Gp *Linc*
CANEWDON (St Nicholas) *see* Ashingdon w S Fambridge, Canewdon and Paglesham *Chelmsf*
CANFIELD, GREAT (St Mary) w High Roding and Aythorpe Roding *Chelmsf 18* **P** *A Sainthill Esq, Ch Soc Trust, and Bp (by turn)* **P-in-c** E C GARRETT
CANFIELD, LITTLE (All Saints) *see* Takeley w Lt Canfield *Chelmsf*
CANFORD CLIFFS (Transfiguration) and Sandbanks *Sarum 7* **P** *Bp* **V** J C OAKES
CANFORD HEATH (St Paul) *see* N Poole Ecum Team *Sarum*
CANFORD MAGNA (no dedication) (Bearwood) (The Lantern) *Sarum 9* **P** *Patr Bd* **TR** C M TEBBUTT, **TV** A M RIMMER, G BOLAND, **NSM** A SIMPSON, A P HANSON, H WALDSAX, S E TEBBUTT, **OLM** C CLARK, B S PROBERT
CANLEY (St Stephen) *Cov 3* **P** *Bp* **P-in-c** P FINDLEY, **NSM** A M HOWARTH, C R HOWARTH
CANNING TOWN (St Luke) *see* Victoria Docks St Luke *Chelmsf*
CANNING TOWN (St Matthias) *see* Plaistow and N Canning Town *Chelmsf*

CANNINGTON (Blessed Virgin Mary), Otterhampton, Combwich and Stockland *B & W 16* **P** *Bp* **R** P MARTIN
CANNOCK (St Luke) and Huntington *Lich 3* **P** *Bp and D&C (jt)* **V** P O HART, **C** M A WHATMOUGH, **OLM** D J SUNLEY, M E FRONDIGOUN
CANON FROME (St James) *see* Ledbury *Heref*
CANON PYON (St Lawrence) w King's Pyon, Birley and Wellington *Heref 6* **P** *Bp, Ch Union, and D&C (jt)* **V** M C CLUETT
CANONBURY (St Stephen) *Lon 6* **P** *V Islington St Mary* **V** N J GROARKE, **C** C D NEWMAN, **NSM** M E EVANS
CANTERBURY (All Saints) *Cant 3* **P** *Abp* **P-in-c** M J STACE, **OLM** N L BRACEWELL
CANTERBURY City Centre *see* Cant St Pet w St Alphege and St Marg etc *Cant*
CANTERBURY (St Dunstan w Holy Cross) *Cant 3* **P** *Abp* **P-in-c** M F BALL, **NSM** K C GOODMAN
CANTERBURY (St Martin) (St Paul) *Cant 3* **P** *Abp* **R** N M HALL, **C** P R RATCLIFF
CANTERBURY (St Mary Bredin) *Cant 3* **P** *Simeon's Trustees* **V** B J DE LA T DE BERRY
CANTERBURY (St Peter w St Alphege) (St Mildred) and St Margaret w St Mary de Castro *Cant 3* **P** *The Crown* **P-in-c** M F BALL, **NSM** E A CHAPMAN, **OLM** I W J TAYLOR
CANTERBURY (St Stephen) *see* Hackington *Cant*
CANTLEY (St Margaret) *see* Freethorpe, Wickhampton, Halvergate etc *Nor*
CANTLEY (St Wilfrid) *Sheff 8* **P** *Guild of All So* **V** J I WILLETT
CANTLEY, NEW (St Hugh of Lincoln) (Holy Trinity) *Sheff 8* **P** *Guild of All So and SMF (jt)* **V** W J STOKOE
CANTRIL FARM (St Jude) *see* Stockbridge Village *Liv*
CANVEY ISLAND (St Anne) (St Katherine's Worship Centre) (St Nicholas) *Chelmsf 10* **P** *Bp and Patr Bd (jt)* **TR** D ST C TUDOR, **TV** T J HIDE, **C** M G WALFORD, **NSM** J M BARHAM
CANWELL (St Mary, St Giles and All Saints) *Lich 4* **P** *Bp* **V** H J BAKER, **Hon C** M R F MACLACHLAN, **NSM** R G DAVIES
CANWICK (All Saints) *see* Washingborough w Heighington and Canwick *Linc*
CAPEL (St John the Baptist) *see* Surrey Weald *Guildf*
CAPEL (St Thomas à Becket) *see* Tudeley cum Capel w Five Oak Green *Roch*
CAPEL LE FERNE (St Radigund) *see* Alkham w Capel le Ferne and Hougham *Cant*
CAPEL ST MARY (St Mary) w Little Wenham and Great Wenham *St E 5* **P** *Bp and SMF (jt)* **R** D B SINGLETON
CAPENHURST (Holy Trinity) *see* Backford and Capenhurst *Ches*
CAPESTHORNE (Holy Trinity) *see* Marton, Siddington w Capesthorne, and Eaton etc *Ches*
CAR COLSTON (St Mary) w Screveton *S'well 8* **P** *H S Blagg Esq* **NSM** M R WOODWARD
CARBIS BAY (St Anta and All Saints) w Lelant (St Uny) *Truro 5* **P** *Bp* **P-in-c** J A SEYMOUR, **NSM** C Z WILTON
CARBROOKE (St Peter and St Paul) *see* Ashill, Carbrooke, Ovington and Saham Toney *Nor*
CARBURTON (St Giles) *see* Worksop Priory *S'well*
CARDESTON (St Michael) *see* Alberbury w Cardeston *Heref*
CARDINGTON (St James) *Heref 10* **P** *Rt Hon Sir Frederick Corfield* **P-in-c** J GROVES
CARDINGTON (St Mary) *see* Elstow *St Alb*
CARDYNHAM (St Mewbud) *see* St Neot and Warleggan w Cardynham *Truro*
CAREBY (St Stephen) *see* Castle Bytham w Creeton *Linc*
CARHAM (St Cuthbert) *see* Cornhill w Carham *Newc*
CARHAMPTON (St John the Baptist) *see* Dunster, Carhampton, Withycombe w Rodhuish etc *B & W*
CARHARRACK (St Piran's Mission Church) *see* Chacewater w St Day and Carharrack *Truro*
CARISBROOKE (St John the Baptist) *see* Newport St Jo *Portsm*
CARISBROOKE (St Mary the Virgin) *Portsm 8* **P** *Qu Coll Ox* **P-in-c** M C BAGG
CARISBROOKE St Nicholas in the Castle *Portsm 8* **P** *Qu Coll Ox* **P-in-c** M C BAGG
CARLBY (St Stephen) *see* Ryhall w Essendine and Carlby *Pet*
CARLECOATES (St Anne) *see* Penistone and Thurlstone *Wakef*
CARLETON (St Chad) *see* Poulton Carleton and Singleton *Blackb*
CARLETON (St Mary the Virgin) *see* Skipton Ch Ch w Carleton *Bradf*
CARLETON (St Michael) and E Hardwick *Wakef 10* **P** *V Pontefract and Cawood Trustees (jt)* **V** S A STACEY

CARLETON (St Peter) *see* Rockland St Mary w Hellington, Bramerton etc *Nor*

CARLETON, EAST (St Mary) *see* Swardeston w E Carleton, Intwood, Keswick etc *Nor*

CARLETON IN CRAVEN *see* Skipton Ch Ch w Carleton *Bradf*

CARLETON RODE (All Saints) *see* Bunwell, Carleton Rode, Tibenham, Gt Moulton etc *Nor*

CARLIN HOW (St Helen) *see* Loftus and Carlin How w Skinningrove *York*

CARLINGHOW (St John the Evangelist) *see* Staincliffe and Carlinghow *Wakef*

CARLISLE Belah (St Mark) *see* Stanwix *Carl*

CARLISLE (Holy Trinity) (St Barnabas) *Carl 3* **P** *Patr Bd* **P-in-c** E M C HANCOCK, **C** J H POWLEY

CARLISLE (St Aidan) and Christ Church *Carl 3* **P** *Bp* **V** R J OAKLEY

CARLISLE (St Cuthbert) *Carl 3* **P** *D&C* **V** K TEASDALE

CARLISLE (St Herbert) w St Stephen *Carl 3* **P** *Bp* **V** A JONES

CARLISLE (St James) *see* Denton Holme *Carl*

CARLISLE (St John the Evangelist) *Carl 3* **P** *CPAS* **V** S DONALD

CARLISLE (St Luke) Morton *Carl 3* **P** *Bp* **V** *vacant* (01228) 515693

CARLISLE (St Michael) *see* Stanwix *Carl*

CARLISLE, SOUTH Team Ministry (St John the Baptist) (St Elisabeth) *Carl 3* **P** *Patr Bd* **TR** T J HYSLOP, **TV** S L WICKS, **C** C G Y HYSLOP

CARLTON (St Aidan) *see* Helmsley *York*

CARLTON (St Andrew) *see* Nailstone and Carlton w Shackerstone *Leic*

CARLTON (St Bartholomew) *see* Guiseley w Esholt *Bradf*

CARLTON (St Botolph) *see* Whorlton w Carlton and Faceby *York*

CARLTON (St John the Baptist) *S'well 10* **P** *Bp* **V** A M LUCKCUCK

CARLTON (St John the Evangelist) *Wakef 7* **P** *DBP* **P-in-c** R H MARSHALL, **C** P CARTWRIGHT

CARLTON (St Mary) *see* Harrold and Carlton w Chellington *St Alb*

CARLTON (St Peter) *see* Raddesley Gp *Ely*

CARLTON (St Peter) *see* Saxmundham w Kelsale cum Carlton *St E*

CARLTON, EAST (St Peter) *see* Gretton w Rockingham and Cottingham w E Carlton *Pet*

CARLTON, GREAT (St John the Baptist) *see* Mid Marsh Gp *Linc*

CARLTON, NORTH (St Luke) *see* Spring Line Gp *Linc*

CARLTON, SOUTH (St John the Baptist) *as above*

CARLTON BY SNAITH (St Mary) and Drax *York 4* **P** *Abp and Ch Trust Fund Trust (jt)* **P-in-c** J H MDUMULLA

CARLTON COLVILLE (St Peter) and Mutford *Nor 9* **P** *Simeon's Trustees and G&C Coll Cam (jt)* **V** J S BISHOP

CARLTON CURLIEU (St Mary the Virgin) *see* Glen Magna cum Stretton Magna etc *Leic*

CARLTON FOREHOE (St Mary) *see* Barnham Broom and Upper Yare *Nor*

CARLTON HUSTHWAITE (St Mary) *see* Coxwold and Husthwaite *York*

CARLTON-IN-LINDRICK (St John the Evangelist) and Langold w Oldcotes *S'well 6* **P** *Bp and Ld Chan (alt)* **P-in-c** J L BLATHERWICK

CARLTON-IN-THE-WILLOWS (St Paul) *S'well 10* **P** *MMCET* **R** B HALL

CARLTON-LE-MOORLAND (St Mary) *see* Bassingham Gp *Linc*

CARLTON MINIOTT (St Lawrence) *see* Thirsk *York*

CARLTON-ON-TRENT (St Mary) *see* Sutton w Carlton and Normanton upon Trent etc *S'well*

CARLTON SCROOP (St Nicholas) *see* Caythorpe *Linc*

CARNABY (St John the Baptist) *see* Rudston w Boynton, Carnaby and Kilham *York*

CARNFORTH (Christ Church) *Blackb 14* **P** *Bp* **V** S L JONES, **C** C G HOLDEN

CARNFORTH (Holy Trinity) *see* Bolton-le-Sands *Blackb*

CARPENTER'S ARMS, The *see* Deal, The Carpenter's Arms *Cant*

CARR CLOUGH (St Andrew) *see* Kersal Moor *Man*

CARR DYKE GROUP, The *Linc 21* **P** *Sir Philip Naylor-Leyland Bt and Ld Chan (alt)* **V** *vacant* (01526) 861746

CARR MILL (St David) *Liv 10* **P** *V St Helens St Mark and Bp (jt)* **V** S L DAVIES

CARRINGTON (St John the Evangelist) *S'well 12* **P** *Bp* **V** J M MACGILLIVRAY, **C** M GALLAGHER

CARRINGTON (St Paul) *see* Sibsey w Frithville *Linc*

CARSHALTON (All Saints) *S'wark 23* **P** *Bp* **R** J C THEWLIS, **NSM** D R BILLIN

CARSHALTON BEECHES (Good Shepherd) *S'wark 23* **P** *Bp* **V** C WHEATON, **OLM** P C M TURRELL

CARSINGTON (St Margaret) *see* Wirksworth *Derby*

CARTERTON (St John the Evangelist) *see* Brize Norton and Carterton *Ox*

CARTMEL FELL (St Anthony) *Carl 10* **P** *Bp* **P-in-c** M D WOODCOCK, **C** M F J ALLEN, **NSM** M L WOODCOCK, B J CROWE

CARTMEL PENINSULA Team Ministry, The (St Mary and St Michael) *Carl 11* **P** *Patr Bd* **TR** N J ASH, **TV** R JACKSON, **NSM** D S SIMON, F M G ETHERINGTON, G T WILSON

CASSINGTON (St Peter) *see* Eynsham and Cassington *Ox*

CASSOP CUM QUARRINTON *Dur 5* **P** *Bp* **P-in-c** J LIVESLEY

CASTERTON (Holy Trinity) *see* Kirkby Lonsdale *Carl*

CASTERTON, GREAT (St Peter and St Paul) and LITTLE (All Saints) w Pickworth and Tickencote *Pet 12* **P** *Burghley Ho Preservation Trust (2 turns), Lord Chesham (1 turn), and Bp (1 turn)* **P-in-c** J M SAUNDERS

CASTLE ACRE (St James) *see* Nar Valley *Nor*

CASTLE ASHBY (St Mary Magdalene) *see* Yardley Hastings, Denton and Grendon etc *Pet*

CASTLE BOLTON (St Oswald) *see* Penhill *Ripon*

CASTLE BROMWICH (St Clement) *Birm 9* **P** *Bp* **V** S C CARTER

CASTLE BROMWICH (St Mary and St Margaret) *Birm 9* **P** *Earl of Bradf* **R** G A DOUGLAS, **C** A J BROWN

CASTLE BYTHAM (St James) w Creeton *Linc 14* **P** *D&C, Bp, Ld Chan, and DBP (by turn)* **R** *vacant* (01780) 410166

CASTLE CAMPS (All Saints) *see* Linton *Ely*

CASTLE CARROCK (St Peter) *see* Eden, Gelt and Irthing *Carl*

CASTLE CARY (All Saints) w Ansford *B & W 2* **P** *Bp* **P-in-c** E A MORTIMER

CASTLE CHURCH (St Mary) *Lich 10* **P** *Bp* **V** P J SOWERBUTTS, **NSM** C V SYKES

CASTLE COMBE (St Andrew) *see* By Brook *Bris*

CASTLE DONINGTON (St Edward the King and Martyr) and Lockington cum Hemington *Leic 6* **P** *Lady Gretton and C H C Coaker Esq (jt)* **V** A Q MICKLETHWAITE

CASTLE EATON (St Mary the Virgin) *see* Fairford Deanery *Glouc*

CASTLE EDEN (St James) *see* Blackhall, Castle Eden and Monkhesleden *Dur*

CASTLE FROME (St Michael) *see* Frome Valley *Heref*

CASTLE HEDINGHAM (St Nicholas) *see* Sible Hedingham w Castle Hedingham *Chelmsf*

CASTLE HILL (St Philip) *see* Hindley All SS *Liv*

CASTLE RISING (St Lawrence) *Nor 16* **P** *G Howard Esq* **R** J B V RIVIERE

CASTLE SOWERBY (St Kentigern) *see* Caldbeck, Castle Sowerby and Sebergham *Carl*

CASTLE TOWN (St Thomas and St Andrew) *Lich 10* **P** *Hyndman Trustees* **V** *vacant* (01785) 258796

CASTLE VALE (St Cuthbert of Lindisfarne) w Minworth *Birm 12* **P** *Bp* **V** J B A COPE

CASTLE VIEW ESTATE (St Francis) *see* Langley Marish *Ox*

CASTLECROFT (The Good Shepherd) *see* Tettenhall Wood and Perton *Lich*

CASTLEFIELDS (All Saints and St Michael) *see* Shrewsbury All SS w St Mich *Lich*

CASTLEFORD (St Michael and All Angels) *see* Smawthorpe *Wakef*

CASTLEFORD Team Parish (All Saints) *Wakef 10* **P** *Duchy of Lanc and Bp (alt)* **TR** M F WOOD, **TV** C M WATKINS, **C** P W ATKINSON

CASTLEMORTON (St Gregory) *see* Longdon, Castlemorton, Bushley, Queenhill etc *Worc*

CASTLESIDE (St John the Evangelist) *Dur 4* **P** *Bp* **V** *vacant* (01207) 590086

CASTLETHORPE (St Simon and St Jude) *see* Hanslope w Castlethorpe *Ox*

CASTLETON (St Edmund) *see* Hope, Castleton and Bradwell *Derby*

CASTLETON (St Mary Magdalene) *see* Sherborne w Castleton, Lillington and Longburton *Sarum*

CASTLETON (St Michael and St George) *see* Danby w Castleton and Commondale *York*

CASTLETON MOOR (St Martin) *Man 14* **P** *Bp* **P-in-c** F C GUITE

CASTLETOWN (St Mary) *S & M 1* **P** *Bp* **V** P C ROBINSON

CASTON (St Cross), Griston, Merton, Thompson, Stow Bedon, Breckles and Great Hockham *Nor 13* **P** *Bp and DBP (jt)* **R** R W NICHOLS

CASTOR (St Kyneburgha) w Sutton and Upton w Marholm
  Pet 11 **P** *Sir Philip Naylor-Leyland Bt (2 turns),*
  Mrs V S V Gunnery (1 turn) **R** W S D BURKE,
  NSM R HEMINGRAY
CATCLIFFE (St Mary) *see Rivers Team Sheff*
CATCOTT (St Peter) *see W Poldens B & W*
CATERHAM (St Mary the Virgin) (St Laurence) (St Paul)
  (St John the Evangelist) *S'wark 24* **P** *Bp* **TR** D J SWAN,
  TV G P REEVES, J GARTON, C A BRADSHAW, **C** S A NADARAJAH,
  NSM R P WELDON
CATESBY (St Mary) *see Daventry, Ashby St Ledgers,*
  Braunston etc Pet
CATFIELD (All Saints) *see Ludham, Potter Heigham, Hickling*
  and Catfield Nor
CATFORD (St Andrew) *S'wark 4* **P** *Bp* **P-in-c** L T MCKENNA
CATFORD (St John) and Downham *S'wark 4* **P** *Bp*
  TR M A HART, **TV** P G JORDAN, **C** S J DENNIS
CATFORD (St Laurence) *S'wark 4* **P** *Bp* **V** C F PICKSTONE,
  OLM I J FARQUHAR
CATHERINGTON (All Saints) and Clanfield *Portsm 5* **P** *Bp*
  V G B HILL, **C** A COLLINSON, **NSM** A M GOTHARD
CATHERSTON LEWESTON (St Mary) *see Golden Cap Team*
  Sarum
CATON (St Paul) w Littledale *Blackb 14* **P** *V Lanc*
  P-in-c G A POLLITT
CATSFIELD (St Laurence) and Crowhurst *Chich 14* **P** *Bp and*
  J P Papillon (alt) **R** M A BRYDON
CATSHILL (Christ Church) and Dodford *Worc 7* **P** *Bp*
  C B A ROBERTSON, C A HOLZAPFEL
CATTERICK (St Anne) *Ripon 2* **P** *Bp* **V** F M WILSON,
  C P J MATTHEWS
CATTHORPE (St Thomas) *see Gilmorton, Peatling Parva,*
  Kimcote etc Leic
CATTISTOCK (St Peter and St Paul) *see Melbury Sarum*
CATTON (All Saints) *see Stamford Bridge Gp York*
CATTON (St Nicholas and the Blessed Virgin Mary)
  see Walton-on-Trent w Croxall, Rosliston etc Derby
CATTON, NEW (Christ Church) *Nor 2* **P** *Bp*
  V K G CROCKER
CATTON, NEW (St Luke) w St Augustine *Nor 2* **P** *Bp, D&C,*
  and CPAS (jt) **V** N I VESEY
CATTON, OLD (St Margaret) *Nor 2* **P** *D&C* **V** A D PARSONS
CATWICK (St Michael) *see Brandesburton and Leven w*
  Catwick York
CATWORTH, GREAT *see Catworth Magna Ely*
CATWORTH MAGNA (St Leonard) *Ely 10* **P** *BNC Ox*
  R *vacant*
CAULDON (St Mary and St Laurence) *see Calton, Cauldon,*
  Grindon, Waterfall etc Lich
CAUNDLE MARSH (St Peter and St Paul) *see Vale of White*
  Hart Sarum
CAUNTON (St Andrew) *see Norwell w Ossington, Cromwell*
  and Caunton S'well
CAUSEWAY HEAD (St Paul) *see Solway Plain Carl*
CAUTLEY (St Mark) *see Sedbergh, Cautley and Garsdale*
  Bradf
CAVENDISH (St Mary) *see Stour Valley St E*
CAVENHAM (St Andrew) *see Mildenhall St E*
CAVERSFIELD (St Laurence) *see Bicester w Bucknell,*
  Caversfield and Launton Ox
CAVERSHAM (Park Church) *see Emmer Green w Caversham*
  Park Ox
CAVERSHAM (St Andrew) *Ox 15* **P** *Bp* **V** N D JONES
CAVERSHAM (St John the Baptist) *see Caversham Thameside*
  and Mapledurham Ox
CAVERSHAM (St Peter) *as above*
CAVERSHAM HEIGHTS (St Andrew) *see Caversham St Andr*
  Ox
CAVERSHAM PARK Local Ecumenical Partnership
  Ox 15 vacant
CAVERSHAM THAMESIDE (St Peter) (St John the Baptist)
  and Mapledurham *Ox 15* **P** *Ch Ch Ox, Eton Coll, and Bp (jt)*
  R D F TYNDALL, **C** G FANCOURT, J C TEAR,
  OLM S K F KNEE-ROBINSON, M PYKE
CAVERSWALL (St Peter) and Weston Coyney w Dilhorne *Lich 6*
  P *D&C* **V** S J OSBOURNE, **NSM** L P LUCKING
CAWOOD (All Saints) w Ryther and Wistow *York 4* **P** *Abp and*
  Ld Chan (alt) **R** I M W ELLERY
CAWSAND (St Andrew's Mission Church) *see Maker w Rame*
  Truro
CAWSTON (St Agnes) w Booton and Brandiston, Haveringland
  and Heydon *Nor 19* **P** *Pemb Coll Cam (3 turns), DBP (1 turn)*
  P-in-c T W HARRIS
CAWTHORNE (All Saints) *Wakef 7* **P** *S W Fraser Esq*
  P-in-c S A REYNOLDS, **NSM** J E DAYKIN

CAXTON (St Andrew) *see Papworth Ely*
CAYNHAM (St Mary) *see Ludlow Heref*
CAYTHORPE (St Aidan) *see Lowdham w Caythorpe, and*
  Gunthorpe S'well
CAYTHORPE (St Vincent) *Linc 22* **P** *Bp, J F Fane Esq, and*
  S J Packe-Drury-Lowe Esq (by turn) **P-in-c** J FRESHNEY
CAYTON (St John the Baptist) w Eastfield *York 15* **P** *Abp*
  V A CAMPBELL-WILSON
CENTRAL *see under substantive place names*
CERNE ABBAS (St Mary) *see Buckland Newton, Cerne*
  Abbas, Godmanstone etc Sarum
CERNEY, NORTH (All Saints) *see Stratton, N Cerney,*
  Baunton and Bagendon Glouc
CERNEY, SOUTH (All Hallows) w Cerney Wick, Siddington
  and Preston *Glouc 7* **P** *Bp and Mrs P Chester-Master (1 turn),*
  Ld Chan (1 turn) **V** D BOWERS
CERNEY WICK (Holy Trinity) *see S Cerney w Cerney Wick,*
  Siddington and Preston Glouc
CHACELEY (St John the Baptist) *see Deerhurst and Apperley*
  w Forthampton etc Glouc
CHACEWATER (St Paul) w St Day and Carharrack *Truro 2*
  P *D&C and R Kenwyn w St Allen (jt)* **P-in-c** P J KNIBBS,
  C A T NEAL, **Hon C** D R CARRIVICK, **NSM** N J POTTER
CHACOMBE (St Peter and St Paul) *see Chenderit Pet*
CHADBROOK *St E 12* **P** *Bp and DBP (jt)* **R** I M G FRIARS
CHADDERTON (Christ Church) (St Saviour) *Man 16*
  P *Trustees* **V** J G SIMMONS, **C** J C EVANS
CHADDERTON (Emmanuel) (St George) *Man 16* **P** *Trustees*
  V E D H LEAF
CHADDERTON (St Mark) *Man 16* **P** *The Crown*
  V A COOKE
CHADDERTON (St Matthew) St Luke *Man 16* **P** *Bp and*
  Prime Min (alt) **V** D R PENNY, **NSM** D E LUKE
CHADDESDEN (St Mary) *Derby 9* **P** *MMCET*
  V W A STILLWELL
CHADDESDEN (St Philip) w Derby St Mark *Derby 9* **P** *Bp*
  V R J SHRISUNDER, **Hon C** M R FUTERS
CHADDESLEY CORBETT (St Cassian) and Stone *Worc 11*
  P *Ld Chan* *vacant (01562) 69438*
CHADDLEWORTH (St Andrew) *see W Downland Ox*
CHADLINGTON (St Nicholas) *see Chase Ox*
CHADSMOOR (St Aidan) (St Chad) *Lich 3* **P** *Bp and*
  D&C (jt) **V** *vacant*
CHADWELL (Emmanuel) (St Mary) *Chelmsf 14*
  P *Ch Soc Trust* *vacant (01375) 842176*
CHADWELL HEATH (St Chad) *Chelmsf 1* **P** *Vs Dagenham*
  and Ilford (alt) **V** M J COURT, **NSM** C J HARDING
CHAFFCOMBE (St Michael and All Angels), Cricket Malherbie
  w Knowle St Giles, Tatworth, Thorncombe and Winsham
  B & W 14 **P** *Bp and C G S Eyre Esq (jt)* **V** T F PRICE,
  Hon C J EVANS
CHAGFORD (St Michael), Drewsteignton, Hittisleigh, Spreyton,
  Gidleigh, and Throwleigh *Ex 11* **P** *Bp, Guild of All So, Trustees*
  Lady Hayter-Hames Discretionary Settlement, and Exors
  B Drew Esq (jt) **C** N WALTER
CHAILEY (St Peter) *Chich 21* **P** *J P B Tillard Esq*
  P-in-c J M MASKELL
CHALBURY (All Saints) *see Horton, Chalbury, Hinton Martel*
  and Holt St Jas Sarum
CHALDON (St Peter and St Paul) *see Caterham S'wark*
CHALDON HERRING (St Nicholas) *see The Lulworths,*
  Winfrith Newburgh and Chaldon Sarum
CHALE (St Andrew) *Portsm 8* **P** *Keble Coll Ox*
  Hon C D L DENNIS
CHALFIELD, GREAT (All Saints) *see Broughton Gifford, Gt*
  Chalfield and Holt Sarum
CHALFONT, LITTLE (St George) *see Chenies and Lt*
  Chalfont, Latimer and Flaunden Ox
CHALFONT ST GILES (St Giles) *Ox 20* **P** *Bp*
  R T A STACEY, **NSM** A L J THOMPSON, M T BLEAKLEY
CHALFONT ST PETER (St Peter) *Ox 20* **P** *St Jo Coll Ox*
  R C H OVERTON, **NSM** N RODE, J A KING,
  OLM W GRAHAM
CHALFORD (Christ Church) *see Bisley, Chalford, France*
  Lynch, and Oakridge Glouc
CHALGRAVE (All Saints) *see Toddington and Chalgrave*
  St Alb
CHALGROVE (St Mary) w Berrick Salome *Ox 1* **P** *Ch Ch Ox*
  V I G H COHEN
CHALK (St Mary) *Roch 4* **P** *R Milton* **V** N I BOURNE,
  C A L HAMMILL
CHALKE VALLEY (Team Ministry) *Sarum 11* **P** *Bp, DBP, and*
  K Coll Cam (by turn) **TR** D E HENLEY, **TV** R C REDDING,
  A L WILLIAMS, **NSM J A TAYLOR
CHALLACOMBE (Holy Trinity) *see Shirwell, Loxhore,*
  Kentisbury, Arlington, etc Ex

CHALLOCK (St Cosmas and St Damian)   *see* Chilham w
Challock and Molash *Cant*
CHALLOW, EAST (St Nicolas)   *see* Hanney, Denchworth and E
Challow *Ox*
CHALLOW, WEST (St Laurence)   *see* Ridgeway *Ox*
CHALTON (St Michael and All Angels)   *see* Blendworth w
Chalton w Idsworth *Portsm*
CHALVEY (St Peter)   *see* Upton cum Chalvey *Ox*
CHALVINGTON (St Bartholomew)   *see* Laughton w Ripe and
Chalvington *Chich*
CHANDLER'S FORD (St Boniface) (St Martin in the Wood)
Win 10   **P** *Bp*   **V** I N BIRD,   **C** M E SMITH, F C GIBBS,
NSM L BUNTING
CHANTRY (Holy Trinity)   *see* Mells w Buckland Dinham, Elm,
Whatley etc *B & W*
CHAPEL ALLERTON (St Matthew) *Ripon* 5   **P** *V Leeds*
St Pet   **V** D M ROBINSON,   **NSM** S RUSHOLME
CHAPEL CHORLTON (St Laurence), Maer and Whitmore
Lich 7   **P** *Bp and G Cavenagh-Mainwaring Esq (jt)*
R N A CLEMAS
CHAPEL-EN-LE-FRITH (St Thomas à Becket) *Derby* 4
P *PCC*   **V** N R BRALESFORD
CHAPEL GREEN (St Oswald)   *see* Lt Horton *Bradf*
CHAPEL HOUSE (Holy Nativity) *Newc* 4   **P** *Bp*
P-in-c P KENNEY,   **NSM** A E MARR,   **OLM** D P MARR,
R AYRE
CHAPEL LAWN (St Mary)   *see* Bucknell w Chapel Lawn,
Llanfair Waterdine etc *Heref*
CHAPEL LE DALE (St Leonard)   *see* Ingleton w Chapel le Dale
Bradf
CHAPEL PLAISTER (not known)   *see* Box w Hazlebury and
Ditteridge *Bris*
CHAPEL ST LEONARDS (St Leonard) w Hogsthorpe *Linc* 8
P *V Willoughby St Helen*   **P-in-c** T R BARDELL
CHAPELTHORPE (St James) *Wakef* 11   **P** *V Sandal*
V I M GASKELL
CHAPELTOWN (St John the Baptist) *Sheff* 3   **P** *Bp*
V R A STORDY,   **C** A P OATRIDGE
CHAPMANSLADE (St Philip and St James)   *see* Cley Hill
Villages *Sarum*
CHAPPEL (St Barnabas)   *see* Gt and Lt Tey w Wakes Colne and
Chappel *Chelmsf*
CHARBOROUGH (St Mary)   *see* Red Post *Sarum*
CHARD (Blessed Virgin Mary) w Combe St Nicholas,
Wambrook and Whitestaunton *B & W* 14   **P** *Bp and*
T V D Eames Esq (jt)   **R** S TUCKER,   **C** J A FALLON,
V M HOARE
CHARD (Good Shepherd) and Cricket St Thomas *B & W* 14
P *Bp*   **V** vacant (01460) 61012
CHARDSTOCK (All Saints)   *see* Axminster, Chardstock, All
Saints etc *Ex*
CHARDSTOCK (St Andrew)   *as above*
CHARFIELD (St John) and Kingswood w Wickwar,
Rangeworthy and Hillesley *Glouc* 5   **P** *Bp, DBP,*
R W Neeld Esq, and Earl of Ducie (jt)   **R** D J RUSSELL,
C J F WARD,   **NSM** V J KERNER
CHARFORD (St Andrew)   *see* Bromsgrove St Jo *Worc*
CHARING (St Peter and St Paul)   *see* G7 Benefice *Cant*
CHARING HEATH (Holy Trinity)   *as above*
CHARLBURY (St Mary the Virgin) w Shorthampton *Ox* 3
P *St Jo Coll Ox*   **V** J K FRENCH,   **NSM** J W FIELDEN
CHARLCOMBE (Blessed Virgin Mary) w Bath (St Stephen)
B & W 8   **P** *DBP and Simeon's Trustees (jt)*
P-in-c P A HAWTHORN
CHARLECOTE (St Leonard)   *see* Hampton Lucy w Charlecote
and Loxley *Cov*
CHARLES (St John the Baptist)   *see* S Molton w Nymet
St George, High Bray etc *Ex*
CHARLES w Plymouth St Matthias *Ex* 24   **P** *Ch Patr Trust*
P-in-c P R BRYCE
CHARLESTOWN (St George)   *see* Salford All SS *Man*
CHARLESTOWN (St Paul) *Truro* 1   **P** *The Crown*   **V** vacant
(01726) 75688
CHARLESTOWN (St Thomas the Apostle)   *see* Southowram
and Claremount *Wakef*
CHARLESWORTH (St John the Evangelist) and Dinting Vale
Derby 6   **P** *The Crown (2 turns), Bp (1 turn)*   **C** I K STUBBS,
NSM R G ALLARD
CHARLETON (St Mary)   *see* Stokenham, Slapton, Charleton w
Buckland etc *Ex*
CHARLTON (All Saints)   *see* Chalke Valley *Sarum*
CHARLTON (Holy Trinity)   *see* Wantage *Ox*
CHARLTON (St John)   *see* Fladbury, Hill and Moor, Wyre
Piddle etc *Worc*
CHARLTON (St John the Baptist)   *see* Garsdon, Lea and
Cleverton and Charlton *Bris*

CHARLTON (St John the Baptist)   *see* St Bartholomew *Sarum*
CHARLTON (St Luke w Holy Trinity) (St Richard) (St Thomas)
S'wark 1   **P** *Bp and Viscount Gough (jt)*   **R** E M WOOFF,
NSM M R HOUSE,   **OLM** B J SPONG, E A NEWMAN
CHARLTON (St Peter)   *see* Vale of Pewsey *Sarum*
CHARLTON (St Thomas the Apostle)   *see* Pastrow *Win*
CHARLTON, SOUTH (St James)   *see* Glendale Gp *Newc*
CHARLTON ABBOTS (St Martin)   *see* Sevenhampton w
Charlton Abbots, Hawling etc *Glouc*
CHARLTON ADAM (St Peter and St Paul)   *see* Somerton w
Compton Dundon, the Charltons etc *B & W*
CHARLTON HORETHORNE (St Peter and St Paul)
see Milborne Port w Goathill etc *B & W*
CHARLTON-IN-DOVER (St Peter and St Paul) *Cant* 7
P *Keble Coll Ox*   **P-in-c** C S JOHNSON
CHARLTON KINGS (Holy Apostles) *Glouc* 6   **P** *R Cheltenham*
P-in-c R J PATERSON,   **C** R C ROSBOROUGH
CHARLTON KINGS (St Mary) *Glouc* 6   **P** *Bp*
V M GARLAND,   **C** L A HILL
CHARLTON MACKRELL (Blessed Virgin Mary)
see Somerton w Compton Dundon, the Charltons etc *B & W*
CHARLTON MARSHALL (St Mary the Virgin)
see Spetisbury w Charlton Marshall etc *Sarum*
CHARLTON MUSGROVE (St Stephen), Cucklington
and Stoke Trister *B & W* 2   **P** *Bp*   **P-in-c** J S PENBERTHY
CHARLTON ON OTMOOR (St Mary)   *see* Ray Valley *Ox*
CHARLWOOD (St Nicholas) *S'wark* 26   **P** *DBP*
R W G CAMPEN
CHARMINSTER (St Mary the Virgin) and Stinsford *Sarum* 1
P *The Hon C A Townshend and Bp (alt)*   **V** P J SMITH,
C P J M STONE,   **NSM** R P VAN DER HART, W I FOBISTER
CHARMOUTH (St Andrew)   *see* Golden Cap Team *Sarum*
CHARNEY BASSETT (St Peter)   *see* Cherbury w Gainfield *Ox*
CHARNOCK RICHARD (Christ Church) *Blackb* 4   **P** *DBF*
P-in-c T D WILBY,   **NSM** A D WYNNE
CHARSFIELD W DEBACH (St Peter)   *see* Mid Loes *St E*
CHART, GREAT (St Mary) *Cant* 6   **P** *Abp*
P-in-c T C WILSON
CHART, LITTLE (St Mary)   *see* G7 Benefice *Cant*
CHART SUTTON (St Michael)   *see* Headcorn and The Suttons
Cant
CHARTERHOUSE-ON-MENDIP (St Hugh)   *see* Blagdon w
Compton Martin and Ubley *B & W*
CHARTHAM (St Mary) *Cant* 2   **P** *Abp*   **P-in-c** P A BROWN,
C P GREIG
CHARWELTON (Holy Trinity)   *see* Badby w Newham and
Charwelton w Fawsley etc *Pet*
CHASE *Ox* 3   **P** *Bp and D&C Ch Ch (jt)*   **R** M E J ABREY
CHASE *Sarum* 6   **P** *Bp, Adn Dorset, Ch Soc Trust, Pemb Coll*
Cam, Univ Coll Ox, J P C Bourke Esq (4 turns), Ld Chan
(1 turn)   **R** M J FOSTER,   **C** M R B DURRANT,
Hon C W H G JOHNSTONE
CHASE TERRACE (St John) *Lich* 1   **P** *Bp*   **V** D B LEAKE,
C M WALLACE,   **NSM** L HOOD,   **OLM** D POOLE
CHASETOWN (St Anne) *Lich* 1   **P** *V Burntwood*
V V G HATTON
CHASETOWN (St John)   *see* Chase Terrace *Lich*
CHASTLETON (St Mary the Virgin)   *see* Chipping Norton *Ox*
CHATBURN (Christ Church) and Downham *Blackb* 7   **P** *Hulme*
Trustees and Lord Clitheroe (jt)   **P-in-c** R NICHOLSON
CHATHAM (Christ the King)   *see* Prince's Park *Roch*
CHATHAM (St Mary and St John) *Roch* 5   **P** *D&C*
P-in-c B P ADAMS
CHATHAM (St Paul w All Saints) *Roch* 5   **P** *Bp*
V K M JOHNSON
CHATHAM (St Philip and St James) *Roch* 5   **P** *Ch Soc Trust*
V M L J SAUNDERS,   **C** D R J GREEN,   **NSM** S C SPENCER
CHATHAM (St Stephen) *Roch* 5   **P** *Bp*   **V** A L SMITH
CHATHAM, SOUTH Holy Trinity (St William) (St Alban)
(St David) *Roch* 5   **P** *Bp*   **TR** M ILYAS,   **TV** J S CURRIE,
P C WOOTTON
CHATTENDEN (Bishop Gundulph)   *see* Frindsbury w Upnor
and Chattenden *Roch*
CHATTERIS (St Peter and St Paul) *Ely* 11   **P** *G&C Coll Cam*
V J M THOMSON,   **C** W L THOMSON
CHATTISHAM (All Saints and St Margaret)   *see* Elmsett w
Aldham, Hintlesham, Chattisham etc *St E*
CHATTON (Holy Cross)   *see* Glendale Gp *Newc*
CHAULDEN (St Stephen)   *see* Hemel Hempstead *St Alb*
CHAVEY DOWN (St Martin)   *see* Winkfield and Cranbourne
Ox
CHAWLEIGH (St James)   *see* Burrington, Chawleigh, Cheldon,
Chulmleigh etc *Ex*
CHAWTON (St Nicholas)   *see* Northanger *Win*
CHEADLE (All Hallows) (St Philip's Mission Church) *Ches* 17
P *R Cheadle*   **V** P W HIGHTON

CHEADLE (St Cuthbert) (St Mary) *Ches 17*   **P** *Ch Soc Trust*
R R S MUNRO,   **C** J E M NEWMAN, E F A L SCRASE-FIELD,
G A LUCAS,   **Hon C** M A LOWE,   **NSM** N C HALL
CHEADLE (St Giles) w Freehay *Lich 6*   **P** *DBP*
R I C THURSTON
CHEADLE HULME (All Saints) *Ches 17*   **P** *Bp*   **V** H B EALES,
C D A PARKER
CHEADLE HULME (Emmanuel) Conventional District *Ches 17*
C-in-c R G IVESON
CHEADLE HULME (St Andrew) *Ches 17*   **P** *R Cheadle*
V D W GUEST
CHEAM (St Dunstan) (St Alban the Martyr) (St Oswald)
S'wark 23   **P** *Patr Bd*   **TR** D N MILLER,   **OLM** D W F BRICE
CHEAM COMMON (St Philip)   *see Worcester Park Ch Ch w St
Phil S'wark*
CHEARSLEY (St Nicholas)   *see Long Crendon w Chearsley
and Nether Winchendon Ox*
CHEBSEY (All Saints), Creswell, Ellenhall, Ranton and
Seighford *Lich 7*   **P** *D&C, Qu Eliz Grant Trustees, Trustees Earl
of Lich, and J Eld Esq (jt)*   **V** A HETHERINGTON
CHECKENDON (St Peter and St Paul)   *see Langtree Ox*
CHECKLEY (Mission Room)   *see Fownhope w Mordiford,
Brockhampton etc Heref*
CHECKLEY (St Mary and All Saints)   *see Uttoxeter Area Lich*
CHEDBURGH (All Saints)   *see Chevington w Hargrave,
Chedburgh w Depden etc St E*
CHEDDAR (St Andrew) *B & W 1*   **P** *D&C*   **P-in-c** S M ROSE,
C C J BUTLER
CHEDDINGTON (St Giles) w Mentmore *Ox 26*   **P** *Earl of
Rosebery*   **P-in-c** D W F WITCHELL,   **NSM** R J WRIGHT
CHEDDLETON (St Edward the Confessor) *Lich 8*   **P** *Bp*
P-in-c L R PRICE
CHEDDON FITZPAINE (The Blessed Virgin Mary)   *see W
Monkton w Kingston St Mary, Broomfield etc B & W*
CHEDGRAVE (All Saints)   *see Loddon, Sisland, Chedgrave,
Hardley and Langley Nor*
CHEDISTON (St Mary)   *see Blyth Valley St E*
CHEDWORTH (St Andrew), Yanworth and Stowell, Coln Rogers
and Coln St Denys *Glouc 9*   **P** *Ld Chan (2 turns), Qu Coll Ox
(1 turn)*   **P-in-c** S J GOUNDREY-SMITH
CHEDZOY (The Blessed Virgin Mary)   *see Weston Zoyland w
Chedzoy B & W*
CHEETHAM (St John the Evangelist) *Man 4*   **P** *Patr Bd*
P-in-c D J A BURTON
CHEETHAM (St Mark)   *see Lower Crumpsall w Cheetham St
Mark Man*
CHELBOROUGH, EAST (St James)   *see Melbury Sarum*
CHELBOROUGH, WEST (St Andrew)   *as above*
CHELDON (St Mary)   *see Burrington, Chawleigh, Cheldon,
Chulmleigh etc Ex*
CHELFORD (St John the Evangelist) w Lower Withington
Ches 12   **P** J M Dixon Esq   **P-in-c** M SHAW
CHELL (St Michael) *Lich 11*   **P** *Ch Patr Trust and V Newchapel
St Jas (jt)*   **V** S S PRATT
CHELL HEATH (Saviour)   *see Chell Lich*
CHELLASTON (St Peter) *Derby 15*   **P** *Bp*   **V** vacant (01332)
704835
CHELLS (St Hugh)   *see Stevenage St Hugh and St Jo St Alb*
CHELLS (St John)   *as above*
CHELMARSH (St Peter)   *see Highley w Billingsley, Glazeley etc
Heref*
CHELMONDISTON (St Andrew)   *see Shoreline St E*
CHELMORTON AND FLAGG (St John the Baptist)
see Taddington, Chelmorton and Monyash etc Derby
CHELMSFORD (All Saints) (St Michael's Church Centre)
Chelmsf 8   **P** *Bp*   **V** M A HALL
CHELMSFORD (Ascension) *Chelmsf 8*   **P** *Bp*   **V** vacant
(01245) 353914
CHELMSFORD (St Andrew) *Chelmsf 8*   **P** *Bp*
V P H GREENLAND,   **NSM** S E IVES
CHELMSLEY WOOD (St Andrew) *Birm 9*   **P** *Bp*
R J M FATHERS,   **NSM** C A CAMP
CHELSEA (All Saints) (Old Church) *Lon 8*   **P** *R Chelsea
St Luke and Earl Cadogan (jt)*   **V** D P E REINDORP
CHELSEA (St John w St Andrew) (St John) *Lon 8*   **P** *CPAS and
Lon Coll of Div (jt)*   **V** P R DAWSON,   **NSM** A MASON
CHELSEA (St Luke) (Christ Church) *Lon 8*   **P** *Earl Cadogan*
R B LEATHARD,   **C** J B HEARD, N R DUNN
CHELSEA, UPPER (Holy Trinity) *Lon 8*   **P** *Earl Cadogan*
R A R GILLION,   **Hon C** N NASSAR,   **NSM** R G RAINFORD
CHELSEA, UPPER (St Saviour) (St Simon Zelotes) *Lon 8*
P *R Upper Chelsea H Trin w St Jude and Hyndman's
Trustees (jt)*   **P-in-c** M R J NEVILLE
CHELSFIELD (St Martin of Tours) *Roch 16*   **P** *All So Coll Ox*
R P A SPREADBRIDGE

CHELSHAM (St Christopher)   *see Warlingham w Chelsham
and Farleigh S'wark*
CHELSHAM (St Leonard)   *as above*
CHELSTON (St Peter)   *see Cockington Ex*
CHELSWORTH (All Saints)   *see Monks Eleigh w Chelsworth
and Brent Eleigh etc St E*
CHELTENHAM (All Saints)   *see N Cheltenham Glouc*
CHELTENHAM Benefice, The NORTH *Glouc 6*   **P** *Patr Bd*
TR M G COZENS,   **TV** S W ELDRIDGE, D J PAPWORTH,
C D A GARDINER,   **Hon C** P R ILES,   **NSM** P T BROWN,
M J FRENCH, A J SWINBANK, E PALIN
CHELTENHAM (Christ Church) *Glouc 6*   **P** *Simeon's Trustees*
V T J E MAYFIELD,   **C** J FAULL
CHELTENHAM (Emmanuel)   *see S Cheltenham Glouc*
CHELTENHAM (Holy Trinity) (St Paul) *Glouc 6*   **P** *Patr Bd*
TR M R BAILEY,   **TV** T R GREW, R J WIDDECOMBE,
Hon C A S COLLISHAW,   **NSM** G L DICKINSON
CHELTENHAM (St Luke and St John) *Glouc 6*
P *R Cheltenham and Simeon's Trustees (alt)*
P-in-c R C PESTELL,   **NSM** Y R BRAE
CHELTENHAM (St Mark) (St Barnabas) (St Aidan)
(Emmanuel) *Glouc 6*   **P** *Patr Bd*   **TR** R J PATERSON,
TV R E CROFTON, P D SMITH,   **NSM** A M OSMOND,
OLM B E HORNE, M L D HORNE
CHELTENHAM (St Mary) (St Matthew) *Glouc 6*   **P** *Simeon's
Trustees*   **R** T F L GRIFFITHS,   **C** M C BAKER,
NSM M WORKMAN, T CURTIS
CHELTENHAM (St Michael) *Glouc 6*   **P** *Bp*
P-in-c R C PESTELL,   **NSM** Y R BRAE
CHELTENHAM (St Stephen)   *see S Cheltenham Glouc*
CHELTENHAM, SOUTH *Glouc 6*   **P** *Patr Bd*
TR P WILKINSON,   **C** R P FITTER,   **NSM** H R WOOD,
J D HYDE, J M RODWELL, B E TORODE, B K C DUNLOP
CHELTENHAM, WEST Team Ministry   *see Cheltenham St
Mark Glouc*
CHELVESTON (St John the Baptist)   *see Higham Ferrers w
Chelveston Pet*
CHELVEY (St Bridget)   *see Backwell w Chelvey and Brockley
B & W*
CHELWOOD (St Leonard)   *see Publow w Pensford, Compton
Dando and Chelwood B & W*
CHELWOOD GATE (not known)   *see Danehill Chich*
CHENDERIT *Pet 1*   **P** *Bp and BNC Ox (2 turns), Ld Chan
(1 turn)*   **R** D P RANDELL,   **NSM** T D RICHARDS
CHENIES (St Michael) and Little Chalfont, Latimer and
Flaunden *Ox 20*   **P** *Bedford Estates Trustees and Lord
Chesham (jt)*   **R** D G ALLSOP,   **NSM** R F BOUGHTON,
J-S S GALLANT
CHEQUERBENT (St Thomas)   *see Westhoughton and
Wingates Man*
CHEQUERFIELD (St Mary)   *see Pontefract St Giles Wakef*
CHERBURY w Gainfield *Ox 17*   **P** *Bp, DBP, Jes Coll, Oriel Coll,
and Worc Coll Ox (jt)*   **R** N D S PHAIR,   **NSM** J HANCE
CHERHILL (St James the Great)   *see Oldbury Sarum*
CHERINGTON (St John the Baptist)   *see S Warks Seven Gp
Cov*
CHERINGTON (St Nicholas)   *see Avening w Cherington Glouc*
CHERITON (All Souls) w Newington *Cant 8*   **P** *Abp*
P-in-c H C JONES,   **OLM** E M WEBB
CHERITON (St Martin) *Cant 8*   **P** *Abp*   **R** H C JONES,
NSM R W BELLAMY,   **OLM** E M WEBB
CHERITON (St Michael and All Angels)   *see Upper Itchen Win*
CHERITON, NORTH (St John the Baptist)   *see Camelot Par
B & W*
CHERITON BISHOP (St Mary)   *see Tedburn St Mary,
Cheriton Bishop, Whitestone etc Ex*
CHERITON FITZPAINE (St Matthew)   *see N Creedy Ex*
CHERITON STREET   *see Cheriton All So w Newington Cant*
CHERRY BURTON (St Michael) *York 8*   **P** *Mrs P J Burton*
P-in-c M J WESTBY
CHERRY HINTON (St Andrew) *Ely 3*   **P** *Peterho Cam*
V B J LINNEY
CHERRY HINTON (St John the Evangelist) *Ely 3*   **P** *Bp*
V S E WYATT,   **C** J A GAWTHROPE,   **Hon C** P S HESLAM,
NSM C I A FRASER
CHERRY WILLINGHAM (St Peter and St Paul)   *see S Lawres
Gp Linc*
CHERTSEY (St Peter w All Saints), Lyne and Longcross
Guildf 11   **P** *Bp and Haberdashers' Co (jt)*   **V** T J HILLIER,
C C BEAZLEY-LONG,   **Hon C** W K PUGH,
NSM L W GAMLEN,   **OLM** C B PATTINSON
CHERWELL VALLEY *Ox 2*   **P** *Patr Bd*   **TR** P E HUNT,
TV E B GREEN,   **C** I R BISCOE
CHESELBORNE (St Martin)   *see Piddle Valley, Hilton,
Cheselbourne etc Sarum*

CHESHAM, GREAT (Christ Church) (Emmanuel) (St Mary the Virgin) *Ox 20* **P** *Patr Bd* **TR** S J L CANSDALE, **TV** J M SHEPHERD, **C** M S R COLES, **NSM** T J S YATES, H A WILSON

CHESHAM BOIS (St Leonard) *Ox 20* **P** *Peache Trustees* **R** P H DAVIES, **C** J B MURRAY, R J BAKER, **NSM** C C CLARE

CHESHUNT (St Mary the Virgin) *St Alb 17* **P** *Patr Bd* **TR** J K WILLIAMS, **TV** J M WILSON, J E DICKER, C J SELBY, **C** K I MITCHELL, D J BAVERSTOCK

CHESSINGTON (St Mary the Virgin) *Guildf 9* **P** *Mert Coll Ox* **V** *vacant* (020) 8391 4855

CHESTER (Christ Church) *see* Plas Newton w Ches Ch Ch *Ches*

CHESTER (Holy Trinity without the Walls) *Ches 2* **P** *Bp* **C** C P BURKETT, **NSM** M R NEEDHAM

CHESTER (St Barnabas) *see* Ches St Pet w St Jo *Ches*

CHESTER (St Mary on the Hill) *Ches 2* **P** *Duke of Westmr* **R** P C O DAWSON, **C** R P BURTON, **NSM** M A PICKERING, R H MOSLEY

CHESTER St Oswald (St Thomas of Canterbury) *Ches 2* **P** *D&C* **V** *vacant* (01244) 399990

CHESTER (St Paul) *Ches 2* **P** *R Ches* **V** S T PENDLEBURY, **NSM** S M HILDRETH

CHESTER (St Peter) (St John the Baptist) *Ches 2* **P** *Bp and Duke of Westminster (jt)* **V** D N CHESTERS

CHESTER GREEN (St Paul) *see* Derby St Paul *Derby*

CHESTER LE STREET (St Mary and St Cuthbert) *Dur 11* **P** *St Jo Coll Dur* **R** D J TULLY, **C** J ANDERSON

CHESTER SQUARE (St Michael) (St Philip) *Lon 3* **P** *Duke of Westmr* **V** C C MARNHAM, **C** W P H COLERIDGE

CHESTERBLADE (The Blessed Virgin Mary) *see* Evercreech w Chesterblade and Milton Clevedon *B & W*

CHESTERFIELD (Holy Trinity) (Christ Church) *Derby 5* **P** *CPAS* **R** D J HORSFALL

CHESTERFIELD (St Augustine) *Derby 5* **P** *Bp* **P-in-c** J S CROFT

CHESTERFIELD (St Mary and All Saints) *Derby 5* **P** *Bp* **V** M R KNIGHT

CHESTERFORD, GREAT (All Saints) w LITTLE (St Mary the Virgin) *Chelmsf 21* **P** *Bp* **P-in-c** C P WARREN

CHESTERTON (Good Shepherd) *Ely 2* **P** *Bp* **V** D J MAHER, **C** A J LEES-SMITH

CHESTERTON (Holy Trinity) (St Chad) *Lich 9* **P** *Prime Min* **V** B R WILSON, **C** K A RODDY, **NSM** S SIDEBOTTOM

CHESTERTON (St Andrew) *Ely 2* **P** *Trin Coll Cam* **V** N I MOIR, **NSM** D H PEYTON JONES, A J COLES

CHESTERTON (St George) *Ely 2* **P** *Bp* **Hon C** H E HOBDAY, **NSM** L B TAYLOR

CHESTERTON (St Giles) *Cov 8* **P** *Lady Willoughby de Broke* **C** N S DUNLOP

CHESTERTON (St Lawrence) *see* Cirencester *Glouc*

CHESTERTON (St Michael) *see* Alwalton and Chesterton *Ely*

CHESTERTON, GREAT (St Mary) *see* Akeman *Ox*

CHESWARDINE (St Swithun), Childs Ercall, Hales, Hinstock, Sambrook and Stoke on Tern *Lich 18* **P** *Patr Bd* **TR** D A ACKROYD, **NSM** L CHAPMAN

CHET VALLEY, The *see* Loddon, Sisland, Chedgrave, Hardley and Langley *Nor*

CHETNOLE (St Peter) *see* Wriggle Valley *Sarum*

CHETTISHAM (St Michael and All Angels) *see* Ely *Ely*

CHETTLE (St Mary) *see* Chase *Sarum*

CHETTON (St Giles) *see* Ditton Priors w Neenton, Burwarton etc *Heref*

CHETWODE (St Mary and St Nicholas) *see* The Claydons and Swan *Ox*

CHETWYND (St Michael and All Angels) *see* Newport w Longford, and Chetwynd *Lich*

CHEVELEY (St Mary) *Ely 4* **P** *DBP and Mrs D A Bowlby (alt)* **P-in-c** M A GURNER

CHEVENING (St Botolph) *Roch 9* **P** *Abp* **R** C J SMITH

CHEVERELL, GREAT (St Peter) *see* The Lavingtons, Cheverells, and Easterton *Sarum*

CHEVERELL, LITTLE (St Peter) *as above*

CHEVINGTON (All Saints) w Hargrave, Chedburgh w Depden, Rede and Hawkedon *St E 8* **P** *Guild of All So (1 turn), Ld Chan (2 turns), Bp and DBP (1 turn)* **R** *vacant* (01284) 850512

CHEVINGTON (St John the Divine) *Newc 6* **P** *Bp* **Hon C** F L BROOKS

CHEVITHORNE (St Thomas) *see* Tiverton St Pet and Chevithorne w Cove *Ex*

CHEW MAGNA (St Andrew) w Dundry, Norton Malreward and Stanton Drew *B & W 9* **P** *Bp and Adn (jt)* **R** C R M ROBERTS, **NSM** S E LOVERN

CHEW STOKE (St Andrew) w Nempnett Thrubwell *B & W 9* **P** *Bp and SMF (jt)* **P-in-c** C R M ROBERTS, **NSM** V L BARLEY

CHEWTON (Mission Church) *see* Keynsham *B & W*

CHEWTON MENDIP (St Mary Magdalene) w Ston Easton, Litton and Emborough *B & W 7* **P** *Earl Waldegrave (2 turns), Bp (1 turn)* **P-in-c** T C OSMOND, **NSM** H J LATTY

CHEYLESMORE (Christ Church) *Cov 3* **P** *Ch Trust Fund Trust* **V** F P SELDON

CHICHELEY (St Laurence) *see* Sherington w Chicheley, N Crawley, Astwood etc *Ox*

CHICHESTER (St Pancras and St John) *Chich 3* **P** *Simeon's Trustees (2 turns), St Jo Chpl Trustees (1 turn)* **R** M J T PAYNE

CHICHESTER (St Paul) and Westhampnett St Peter *Chich 3* **P** *Bp and D&C (jt)* **R** R W HUNT, **C** P D C KANE, A E WAIZENEKER, **NSM** S T FLASHMAN

CHICHESTER (St Wilfrid) *Chich 3* **P** *Bp* **V** P M GILBERT, **NSM** A E WILKES

CHICKERELL (St Mary) w Fleet *Sarum 4* **P** *Bp* **R** R J PRESS, **OLM** M LEE

CHICKLADE (All Saints) *see* Nadder Valley *Sarum*

CHIDDINGFOLD (St Mary) *Guildf 4* **P** *Ld Chan* **R** S A BROUGH, **OLM** G M WELFORD

CHIDDINGLY (not known) w East Hoathly *Chich 21* **P** *Bp* **R** P A HODGINS

CHIDDINGSTONE (St Mary) w Chiddingstone Causeway *Roch 11* **P** *Abp and Bp (jt)* **P-in-c** S M BEAUMONT

CHIDDINGSTONE CAUSEWAY (St Luke) *see* Chiddingstone w Chiddingstone Causeway *Roch*

CHIDEOCK (St Giles) *see* Golden Cap Team *Sarum*

CHIDHAM (St Mary) *Chich 13* **P** *Bp* **P-in-c** D C PAIN

CHIEVELEY (St Mary the Virgin) *see* E Downland *Ox*

CHIGNAL SMEALEY (St Nicholas) *see* The Chignals w Mashbury *Chelmsf*

CHIGNALS w Mashbury, The *Chelmsf 8* **P** *CPAS (2 turns), Bp (1 turn)* **R** *vacant*

CHIGWELL (St Mary) (St Winifred) and Chigwell Row *Chelmsf 24* **P** *The Crown and Patr Bd (alt)* **TR** M E LAMBERT, **TV** B W KING

CHIGWELL ROW (All Saints) *see* Chigwell and Chigwell Row *Chelmsf*

CHILBOLTON (St Mary) *see* Downs Benefice *Win*

CHILCOMB (St Andrew) *see* E Win *Win*

CHILCOMBE (not known) *see* Bride Valley *Sarum*

CHILCOMPTON (St John the Baptist) w Downside and Stratton on the Fosse *B & W 11* **P** *Bp, MMCET, and V Midsomer Norton (jt)* **P-in-c** C D NORTH, **C** S P BURROW

CHILCOTE (St Matthew's Chapel) *see* Clifton Campville w Edingale and Harlaston *Lich*

CHILDE OKEFORD (St Nicholas) *see* Okeford *Sarum*

CHILDERDITCH (All Saints and St Faith) *see* E and W Horndon w Lt Warley and Childerditch *Chelmsf*

CHILDREY (St Mary the Virgin) *see* Ridgeway *Ox*

CHILDS ERCALL (St Michael and All Angels) *see* Cheswardine, Childs Ercall, Hales, Hinstock etc *Lich*

CHILDS HILL (All Saints) *see* Hendon All SS Childs Hill *Lon*

CHILDSWYCKHAM (St Mary the Virgin) *see* Winchcombe *Glouc*

CHILDWALL (All Saints) *Liv 4* **P** *Bp* **V** G J RENISON, **C** R J PHILLIPS, **OLM** S J GILLIES

CHILDWALL (St David) *Liv 4* **P** *Bp* **V** R WILLIAMS, **NSM** S-A MASON

CHILDWALL VALLEY (St Mark) *see* Gateacre *Liv*

CHILDWICK (St Mary) *see* St Alb St Mich *St Alb*

CHILFROME (Holy Trinity) *see* Melbury *Sarum*

CHILHAM (St Mary) w Challock and Molash *Cant 2* **P** *Abp and Viscount Massereene and Ferrard (jt)* **V** C R DUNCAN

CHILLENDEN (All Saints) *see* Nonington w Wymynswold and Goodnestone etc *Cant*

CHILLESFORD (St Peter) *see* Wilford Peninsula *St E*

CHILLINGHAM (St Peter) *see* Glendale Gp *Newc*

CHILLINGTON (St James) *see* Winsmoor *B & W*

CHILMARK (St Margaret of Antioch) *see* Nadder Valley *Sarum*

CHILTHORNE DOMER (Blessed Virgin Mary) *see* Tintinhull w Chilthorne Domer, Yeovil Marsh etc *B & W*

CHILTINGTON, EAST (not known) *see* Plumpton w E Chiltington cum Novington *Chich*

CHILTINGTON, WEST (St Mary) *Chich 12* **P** *Bp* **R** D M BEAL

CHILTON (All Saints) *see* Harwell w Chilton *Ox*

CHILTON (St Aidan) *Dur 5* **P** *Bp* **V** *vacant* (01388) 720243

CHILTON (St Mary) *see* Bernwode *Ox*

CHILTON CANTELO (St James) *see* Ashington, Mudford, Rimpton and Marston Magna *B & W 6* **P** *DBP and D&C, D&C Bris, and Bp Lon (by turn)* **P-in-c** M G W HAYES

CHILTON FOLIAT (St Mary)　*see* Whitton *Sarum*
CHILTON MOOR (St Andrew) *Dur 14*　**P** *Bp*
P-in-c D NEWTON
CHILTON POLDEN (St Edward)　*see* W Poldens *B & W*
CHILTON TRINITY (Holy Trinity)　*see* Bridgwater St Mary
　and Chilton Trinity *B & W*
CHILVERS COTON (All Saints) w Astley *Cov 5*　**P** *Viscount*
Daventry　**NSM** D WATERTON
CHILWELL (Christ Church) *S'well 7*　**P** *CPAS*　**V** A R HOWE,
　C S P BARRON, L P B O'BOYLE,　**NSM** L HEPTINSTALL,
　J M CORCORAN
CHILWORTH (St Denys)　*see* Ampfield, Chilworth and N
　Baddesley *Win*
CHILWORTH (St Thomas)　*see* Shere, Albury and Chilworth
　Guildf
CHINEHAM (Christ Church) *Win 4*　**P** *Bp*　**V** I R BENTLEY,
　NSM G C RANDALL
CHINESE CONGREGATION　*see* St Martin-in-the-Fields
　Lon
CHINGFORD (All Saints) (St Peter and St Paul) *Chelmsf 5*
　P *Bp*　**R** T W PAGE,　**C** N C WOODWARD, A M SUMMERS
CHINGFORD (St Anne) *Chelmsf 5*　**P** *Bp*　**V** J R BULLOCK
CHINGFORD (St Edmund) *Chelmsf 5*　**P** *Bp*
　V L A GOLDSMITH,　**NSM** P J MONGER
CHINLEY (St Mary)　*see* Hayfield and Chinley w Buxworth
　Derby
CHINNOCK, EAST (Blessed Virgin Mary)　*see* W Coker w
　Hardington Mandeville, E Chinnock etc *B & W*
CHINNOCK, MIDDLE (St Margaret)　*see* Norton sub
　Hamdon, W Chinnock, Chiselborough etc *B & W*
CHINNOCK, WEST (Blessed Virgin Mary)　*as above*
CHINNOR (St Andrew), Sydenham, Aston Rowant and Crowell
　Ox 1　**P** *Bp, DBP, and Peache Trustees (jt)*
　R J M KINCHIN-SMITH,　**C** H L O'SULLIVAN,
　OLM S Q HUTTON
CHIPPENHAM (St Andrew) w Tytherton Lucas *Bris 4*
　P *Ch Ch Ox*　**V** S C TATTON-BROWN
CHIPPENHAM (St Margaret)　*see* Three Rivers Gp *Ely*
CHIPPENHAM (St Paul) w Hardenhuish and Langley Burrell
　Bris 4　**P** *Patr Bd*　**TR** S J TYNDALL,　**C** S J RUSHTON,
　OLM D J KILMISTER
CHIPPENHAM (St Peter) *Bris 4*　**P** *Bp*　**P-in-c** A M GUBBINS,
　NSM A J LOVE
CHIPPERFIELD (St Paul)　*see* Sarratt and Chipperfield *St Alb*
CHIPPING (St Bartholomew) and Whitewell (St Michael)
　Blackb 7　**P** *Bp and Hulme Trustees (jt)*　**P-in-c** J V SCOTT
CHIPPING BARNET (St John the Baptist) (St Mark)
　(St Stephen) *St Alb 14*　**P** *Prime Min (2 turns) and Bp (1 turn)*
　TR S H SPEERS,　**TV** T D CHAPMAN,　**C** C E BALLINGER,
　NSM J KRAFT
CHIPPING CAMPDEN (St James) w Ebrington *Glouc 9*
　P *Peache Trustees (1 turn), Earl of Harrowby (2 turns)*
　P-in-c D C M COOK,　**C** S E HAYES
CHIPPING NORTON (St Mary the Virgin) *Ox 3*　**P** *Patr Bd*
　TR S J A WESTON,　**NSM** A J B KEITH, J P JONES
CHIPPING ONGAR (St Martin) w Shelley *Chelmsf 26*
　P *Guild of All So and Keble Coll Ox*　**R** S M COOPER,
　NSM B L SURTEES
CHIPPING SODBURY (St John the Baptist)　*see* Sodbury Vale
　Glouc
CHIPPING WARDEN (St Peter and St Paul)　*see* Culworth w
　Sulgrave and Thorpe Mandeville etc *Pet*
CHIPSTABLE (All Saints)　*see* Wiveliscombe and the Hills
　B & W
CHIPSTEAD (Good Shepherd)　*see* Chevening *Roch*
CHIPSTEAD (St Margaret of Antioch) *S'wark 26*　**P** *Abp*
　R P J BATEMAN,　**C** H J FRASER,　**OLM** J N WATES
CHIRBURY (St Michael) *Heref 12*　**P** *Sir David Wakeman Bt*
　and Bp (alt)　**P-in-c** R N LEACH
CHIRTON (St John the Baptist)　*see* Redhorn *Sarum*
CHISELBOROUGH (St Peter and St Paul)　*see* Norton sub
　Hamdon, W Chinnock, Chiselborough etc *B & W*
CHISHILL, GREAT (St Swithun)　*see* Icknield Way Villages
　Chelmsf
CHISHILL, LITTLE (St Nicholas)　*as above*
CHISLEDON (Holy Cross)　*see* Ridgeway *Sarum*
CHISLEHURST (Annunciation) *Roch 14*　**P** *Keble Coll*
　V W B BEAR
CHISLEHURST (Christ Church) *Roch 14*　**P** *CPAS*
　V J M ADAMS,　**C** D G S JOHNSTON, A K VAUGHAN
CHISLEHURST (St Nicholas) *Roch 14*　**P** *Bp*　**R** A A MUSTOE,
　C J DURRANS,　**NSM** J B HURN
CHISLET (St Mary the Virgin)　*see* St Nicholas at Wade w Sarre
　and Chislet w Hoath *Cant*
CHISWICK (St Michael) *Lon 11*　**P** *V St Martin-in-the-Fields*
　V *vacant* (020) 8994 3173

CHISWICK (St Michael and All Angels)　*see* Bedford Park *Lon*
CHISWICK (St Nicholas w St Mary Magdalene) *Lon 11*
　P *D&C St Paul's*　**V** S F BRANDES,　**C** A M ALEXANDER
CHISWICK (St Paul) Grove Park *Lon 11*　**P** *V Chiswick*
　V M C RILEY
CHITHURST (St Mary)　*see* Rogate w Terwick and Trotton w
　Chithurst *Chich*
CHITTERNE (All Saints and St Mary)　*see* Wylye and Till
　Valley *Sarum*
CHITTERNE (St Mary)　*as above*
CHITTLEHAMHOLT (St John)　*see* S Molton w Nymet
　St George, High Bray etc *Ex*
CHITTLEHAMPTON (St Hieritha)　*as above*
CHITTS HILL (St Cuthbert) *Lon 19*　**P** *CPAS*　**V** D M DALEY
CHIVELSTONE (St Sylvester)　*see* Stokenham, Slapton,
　Charleton w Buckland etc *Ex*
CHOBHAM (St Lawrence) w Valley End *Guildf 6*　**P** *Bp and*
　Brig R W Acworth (alt)　**V** A BODY,　**OLM** C J BEDFORD
CHOLDERTON (St Nicholas)　*see* Bourne Valley *Sarum*
CHOLESBURY (St Lawrence)　*see* Hawridge w Cholesbury and
　St Leonard *Ox*
CHOLLERTON w Birtley and Thockrington *Newc 8*
　P *Mrs P I Enderby (2 turns), Newc Dioc Soc (1 turn)*
　R M J SLADE,　**OLM** D I WILLIAMS
CHOLSEY (St Mary) and Moulsford *Ox 18*　**P** *Ld Chan and Bp*
　(alt)　**V** A M PETIT,　**NSM** D A LEE-PHILPOT,
　OLM V M L GIBBONS
CHOPPARDS (Mission Room)　*see* Upper Holme Valley *Wakef*
CHOPPINGTON (St Paul the Apostle) *Newc 1*　**P** *D&C*
　V T MOAT
CHOPWELL (St John the Evangelist) *Dur 13*　**P** *Bp*
　P-in-c P R MURRAY
CHORLEY (All Saints) *Blackb 4*　**P** *Bp*　**V** E N STRASZAK
CHORLEY (St George) *Blackb 4*　**P** *R Chorley*　**V** T D WILBY,
　NSM P MASON, A D WYNNE
CHORLEY (St James) *Blackb 4*　**P** *R Chorley*　**V** D K PHILLIPS
CHORLEY (St Laurence) *Blackb 4*　**P** *Bp*　**R** M B COX,
　NSM J H TAYLOR
CHORLEY (St Peter) *Blackb 4*　**P** *R Chorley*　**V** *vacant* (01257)
　263423
CHORLEY (St Philip)　*see* Alderley Edge *Ches*
CHORLEYWOOD (Christ Church) *St Alb 4*　**P** *CPAS*
　V G A COLLINS,　**C** R E JENKINSON
CHORLEYWOOD (St Andrew) *St Alb 4*　**P** *Bp*　**V** D P WHITE,
　C A J REID
CHORLTON-CUM-HARDY (St Clement) (St Barnabas)
　Man 3　**P** *D&C*　**R** K FLOOD,　**C** J N GRANT,　**OLM** J KING
CHORLTON-CUM-HARDY (St Werburgh) *Man 3*　**P** *Bp*
　R A F DAWTRY,　**OLM** M J CLEALL-HILL
CHRISHALL (Holy Trinity)　*see* Icknield Way Villages *Chelmsf*
CHRIST THE KING comprising the parishes of Tanfield,
Stanley and South Moor *Dur 4*　**P** *Bp (4 turns), Prime Min*
　(1 turn)　**TR** A JOHNSTON
CHRIST THE KING in the Diocese of Newcastle *Newc 2*
　P *Patr Bd*　**TR** A J SHIPTON,　**TV** M A EDWARDS
CHRISTCHURCH (Christ Church) and Manea and Welney
　Ely 11　**P** *Bp and R T Townley Esq (jt)*
　P-in-c K P FITZGIBBON
CHRISTCHURCH (Holy Trinity) *Win 9*　**P** *Bp*
　P-in-c C J MANN,　**C** D M JORDAN, A HAWTHORNE,
　NSM A M SMITH
CHRISTCHURCH Stourvale (St George)　*see* Christchurch
　Win
CHRISTIAN MALFORD (All Saints)　*see* Draycot *Bris*
CHRISTLETON (St James) *Ches 2*　**P** *Bp*　**R** M COWAN
CHRISTON (Blessed Virgin Mary)　*see* Crook Peak *B & W*
CHRISTOW (St James), Ashton, Bridford, Dunchideock,
　Dunsford and Doddiscombsleigh *Ex 6*　**P** *Bp, MMCET, SMF,*
　Mrs J M Michelmore, Viscount Exmouth, and
　F C Fulford Esq (jt)　**V** G K MAYER
CHUDLEIGH (St Mary and St Martin) w Chudleigh Knighton
　and Trusham *Ex 9*　**P** *Patr Bd*　**V** P WIMSETT,
　NSM M J FLETCHER
CHUDLEIGH KNIGHTON (St Paul)　*see* Chudleigh w
　Chudleigh Knighton and Trusham *Ex*
CHULMLEIGH (St Mary Magdalene)　*see* Burrington,
　Chawleigh, Cheldon, Chulmleigh etc *Ex*
CHURCH ASTON (St Andrew) *Lich 16*　**P** *R Edgmond*
　P-in-c L M WHEELER
CHURCH BRAMPTON (St Botolph)　*see* Brington w Whilton
　and Norton etc *Pet*
CHURCH BROUGHTON (St Michael)　*see* Boylestone,
　Church Broughton, Dalbury, etc *Derby*
CHURCH CONISTON (St Andrew) *Carl 9*　**P** *Peache Trustees*
　P-in-c M R EAST

CHURCH EATON (St Editha)   *see* Bradeley, Church Eaton, Derrington and Haughton *Lich*

CHURCH HONEYBOURNE (St Ecgwyn)   *see* Pebworth, Dorsington, Honeybourne etc *Glouc*

CHURCH HULME (St Luke) *Ches 11*   **P** *V Sandbach* **V** P MASON

CHURCH IN THE WOOD   *see* Hollington St Leon *Chich*

CHURCH KIRK (St James) *Blackb 1*   **P** Hulme Trustees **R** N A ASHTON

CHURCH KNOWLE (St Peter)   *see* Corfe Castle, Church Knowle, Kimmeridge etc *Sarum*

CHURCH LANGLEY (Church and Community Centre) *Chelmsf 25*   **P** *V Harlow*   **Hon C** S E BRAZIER-GIBBS

CHURCH LANGTON (St Peter) cum Tur Langton, Thorpe Langton and Shangton, Billesdon cum Goadby and Rolleston and Skeffington *Leic 3*   **P** *Bp, E Brudenell Esq, and MMCET (jt)*   **P-in-c** M B W COOK

CHURCH LAWFORD (St Peter)   *see* Wolston and Church Lawford *Cov*

CHURCH LAWTON (All Saints) *Ches 11*   **P** *J Lawton Esq* **R** G L JOYCE

CHURCH LENCH (All Saints) w Rous Lench and Abbots Morton and Harvington *Worc 1*   **P** *Bp and D&C (jt)* **R** R J G THORNILEY,   **NSM** F M BATTIN

CHURCH MINSHULL (St Bartholomew)   *see* Acton and Worleston, Church Minshull etc *Ches*

CHURCH OAKLEY (St Leonard)   *see* Oakley w Wootton St Lawrence *Win*

CHURCH PREEN (St John the Baptist)   *see* Wenlock *Heref*

CHURCH STRETTON (St Laurence) *Heref 10*   **P** *Ch Patr Trust*   **R** R H O HILL,   **C** S WILLIAMS,   **Hon C** V R MORRIS,   **NSM** A J HUGHES, N CLEATON

CHURCHAM (St Andrew)   *see* Huntley and Longhope, Churcham and Bulley *Glouc*

CHURCHDOWN (St Andrew) (St Bartholomew) *Glouc 3* **P** *D&C*   **V** J G PERKIN,   **C** J M HILLS

CHURCHDOWN (St John the Evangelist) and Innsworth *Glouc 3*   **P** *Bp*   **V** K I MORGAN,   **C** D J FORMAN, **NSM** M D D WALKER, P J DONALD

CHURCHILL (All Saints)   *see* Chipping Norton *Ox*

CHURCHILL (St John the Baptist) and Langford *B & W 10* **P** *D&C Bris*   **P-in-c** K M SAX

CHURCHILL-IN-HALFSHIRE (St James) w Blakedown and Broome *Worc 12*   **P** *Exors Viscount Cobham and N A Bourne Esq (alt)*   **P-in-c** P G HARRISON,   **C** D M COOKSEY

CHURCHOVER (Holy Trinity)   *see* Revel Gp *Cov*

CHURCHSTANTON (St Peter and St Paul)   *see* Blackdown *B & W*

CHURCHSTOKE (St Nicholas) w Hyssington and Sarn *Heref 9* **P** *The Crown (1 turn), Earl of Powis (2 turns)*   **NSM** I R BALL

CHURCHSTOW (St Mary)   *see* Thurlestone, S Milton, W Alvington etc *Ex*

CHURCHTOWN (St Helen)   *see* Garstang St Helen and St Michaels-on-Wyre *Blackb*

CHURN, The (Aston Tirrold w Aston Upthorpe, Blewbury, Hagbourne, North Moreton, South Moreton, and Upton) *Ox 18* **P** *Bp and Magd Coll Ox (1 turn), Adn Berks and Hertf Coll Ox (1 turn)*   **R** J P ST JOHN NICOLLE,   **C** G N BORROWDALE, **OLM** L G N BUTLER

CHURSTON FERRERS (St Mary the Vigin)   *see* Brixham w Churston Ferrers and Kingswear *Ex*

CHURT (St John the Evangelist) and Hindhead *Guildf 3* **P** *Adn Surrey*   **V** R T BODLE,   **C** A WHITAKER, **NSM** M E JACKSON

CHURWELL (All Saints)   *see* Morley *Wakef*

CHUTE (St Nicholas)   *see* Savernake *Sarum*

CHYNGTON (St Luke)   *see* Seaford w Sutton *Chich*

CINDERFORD (St John the Evangelist) (St Stephen) w Littledean *Glouc 1*   **P** *Prime Min and Ch Patr Trust (alt)* **V** M J BARNSLEY,   **Hon C** G L BURN

CINDERHILL (Christ Church) *S'well 14*   **P** *Bp* **P-in-c** J WHYSALL

CINNAMON BROW (Resurrection) *Liv 12*   **P** *Bp, Adn, and R Warrington (jt)*   **P-in-c** D L WILLIAMS

CIPPENHAM (St Andrew) *Ox 23*   **P** *Eton Coll*   **V** S SMITH

CIRENCESTER (St John the Baptist) *Glouc 7*   **P** *Bp* **V** L W DOOLAN,   **C** J K VAN DER LELY, H N GILBERT, **Hon C** M J BETTIS,   **NSM** R M FRANKLIN, J P WILLIAMS, P A LIGHT

CLACTON, GREAT (St John the Baptist) *Chelmsf 22* **P** *Ch Patr Trust*   **V** G D A THORBURN,   **C** T M MULRYNE

CLACTON, LITTLE (St James)   *see* Weeley and Lt Clacton *Chelmsf*

CLACTON-ON-SEA (St Christopher) (St James) *Chelmsf 22* **P** *Bp*   **V** A P D SPOONER

CLACTON-ON-SEA (St Paul) *Chelmsf 22*   **P** *Ch Patr Trust* **V** D J TITLEY

CLAINES (St George w St Mary Magdalene)   *see* Worc City *Worc*

CLAINES (St John the Baptist) *Worc 6*   **P** *Bp*   **V** S M AGNEW, **C** N G KALENIUK

CLANDON, EAST (St Thomas of Canterbury) and WEST (St Peter and St Paul) *Guildf 5*   **P** *Earl of Onslow and Bp (alt)* **R** B L PREECE,   **NSM** D M MACMILLAN

CLANFIELD (St James)   *see* Catherington and Clanfield *Portsm*

CLANFIELD (St Stephen)   *see* Bampton w Clanfield *Ox*

CLANNABOROUGH (St Petrock)   *see* N Creedy *Ex*

CLAPHAM (Christ Church) (St John the Evangelist) *S'wark 11* **P** *Bp*   **V** P J ROSE-CASEMORE,   **C** A J SWEENEY, **NSM** S PEAKE

CLAPHAM (Holy Spirit) *S'wark 11*   **P** *Bp*   **V** J A BLUNDEN, **NSM** R A BURGE-THOMAS

CLAPHAM (Holy Trinity) (St Peter) *S'wark 11*   **P** *DBP* **V** D O ISHERWOOD,   **NSM** C A CLARKE, R C B JONES

CLAPHAM (St James) *S'wark 12*   **P** *CPAS* **P-in-c** N K GUNASEKERA,   **Hon C** J MARSHALL, **NSM** J OHEN

CLAPHAM (St Mary the Virgin)   *see* Findon w Clapham and Patching *Chich*

CLAPHAM (St Paul) *S'wark 11*   **P** *Bp*   **V** D L MATTHEWS, **NSM** R A MCELWEE

CLAPHAM (St Thomas of Canterbury) *St Alb 13*   **P** *MMCET* **V** S J LILEY

CLAPHAM COMMON (St Barnabas) *S'wark 14*   **P** *Ch Trust Fund Trust*   **V** R G TAYLOR,   **NSM** K W BISHOP

CLAPHAM PARK (All Saints) *S'wark 12*   **P** *CPAS* **P-in-c** G W BRIGGS,   **C** J O ANI

CLAPHAM PARK (St Stephen)   *see* Telford Park *S'wark*

CLAPHAM-WITH-KEASDEN (St James) and Austwick *Bradf 6*   **P** *Bp*   **V** I F GREENHALGH

CLAPTON (St James)   *see* Bourton-on-the-Water w Clapton etc *Glouc*

CLAPTON (St James) *Lon 5*   **P** *Bp*   **V** R BROWN, **NSM** H R GEORGE

CLAPTON (St Peter)   *see* Aldwincle, Clopton, Pilton, Stoke Doyle etc *Pet*

CLAPTON, UPPER (St Matthew) *Lon 5*   **P** *D&C Cant* **P-in-c** V A ROBERTS,   **Hon C** I E VIBERT

CLAPTON COMMON (St Thomas)   *see* Stamford Hill St Thos *Lon*

CLARBOROUGH (St John the Baptist)   *see* Retford Area *S'well*

CLARE (St Peter and St Paul)   *see* Stour Valley *St E*

CLAREMOUNT (St Thomas the Apostle)   *see* Southowram and Claremount *Wakef*

CLARENCE GATE GARDENS (St Cyprian)   *see* St Marylebone St Cypr *Lon*

CLARENDON (Team Ministry) *Sarum 11*   **P** *Team Coun* **TR** N H S BERSWEDEN,   **TV** E M MOORE-BICK,   **C** A N POPPE, **NSM** F J DUNLOP,   **OLM** C M BUTTIMER

CLARENDON PARK (St John the Baptist)   *see* Emmaus Par Team *Leic*

CLATFORD, UPPER (All Saints)   *see* Abbotts Ann and Upper and Goodworth Clatford *Win*

CLATWORTHY (St Mary Magdalene)   *see* Wiveliscombe and the Hills *B & W*

CLAUGHTON VILLAGE (St Bede)   *see* Birkenhead St Jas w St Bede *Ches*

CLAVERDON (St Michael and All Angels) w Preston Bagot *Cov 7*   **P** *Bp*   **P-in-c** T M MASON

CLAVERHAM (St Barnabas)   *see* Yatton Moor *B & W*

CLAVERING (St Mary and St Clement) and Langley w Arkesden and Wicken Bonhunt *Chelmsf 21*   **P** *Ch Hosp and Keble Coll Ox (jt)*   **P-in-c** M A DAVIS

CLAVERLEY (All Saints) w Tuckhill *Heref 8*   **P** *Bp and E M A Thompson Esq (jt)*   **V** G W WARD

CLAVERTON (Blessed Virgin Mary)   *see* Bathampton w Claverton *B & W*

CLAVERTON DOWN (St Hugh)   *as above*

CLAWTON (St Leonard)   *see* Ashwater, Halwill, Beaworthy, Clawton etc *Ex*

CLAXBY (St Mary)   *see* Walesby *Linc*

CLAXTON (St Andrew)   *see* Rockland St Mary w Hellington, Bramerton etc *Nor*

CLAY CROSS (St Bartholomew)   *see* N Wingfield, Clay Cross and Pilsley *Derby*

CLAY HILL (St John the Baptist) (St Luke) *Lon 18*   **P** *V Enfield St Andr and Bp (jt)*   **V** R E M DOWLER

CLAYBROOKE (St Peter)   *see* Upper Soar *Leic*

CLAYDON and Barham *St E 1*   **P** *G R Drury Esq* **P-in-c** P THORN,   **OLM** C B AUSTIN, J V ABLETT

CLAYDON (St James the Great)   *see* Shires' Edge *Ox*
CLAYDONS, The (St Mary) (All Saints) and Swan *Ox 24*
   P *Patr Bd*   **TR** D A HISCOCK,   **TV** P M KNIGHT,
   NSM A MANN
CLAYGATE (Holy Trinity) *Guildf 8*   **P** *Ch Patr Trust*
   V P J J PLYMING,   **C** A C COWIE, R G LLOYD,
   NSM L M MORGAN, M R HARLE
CLAYHANGER (Holy Trinity Worship Centre)   *see* Ogley Hay
   Lich
CLAYHANGER (St Peter)   *see* Bampton, Morebath,
   Clayhanger, Petton etc *Ex*
CLAYHIDON (St Andrew)   *see* Hemyock w Culm Davy,
   Clayhidon and Culmstock *Ex*
CLAYPOLE (St Peter) *Linc 22*   **P** *DBP (2 turns), The Revd*
   J R H Thorold and J R Thorold Esq (1 turn)   **R** vacant (01636)
   626224
CLAYTON (St Cross w St Paul)   *see* Man Clayton St Cross w St
   Paul *Man*
CLAYTON (St James the Great) *Lich 9*   **P** *Bp*
   V N M EDWARDS
CLAYTON (St John the Baptist) *Bradf 2*   **P** *V Bradf*
   C S M STOBART
CLAYTON (St John the Baptist) w Keymer *Chich 9*   **P** *BNC Ox*
   P-in-c C J POWELL
CLAYTON BROOK (Community Church)
   see Whittle-le-Woods *Blackb*
CLAYTON LE MOORS (All Saints)   *see* Altham w Clayton le
   Moors *Blackb*
CLAYTON LE MOORS (St James)   *as above*
CLAYTON WEST w HIGH HOYLAND (All Saints)   *see* High
   Hoyland, Scissett and Clayton W *Wakef*
CLAYWORTH (St Peter)   *see* Everton, Mattersey, Clayworth
   and Gringley *S'well*
CLEADON (All Saints) *Dur 15*   **P** *R Whitburn*
   P-in-c V J CUTHBERT
CLEADON PARK (St Mark and St Cuthbert) *Dur 15*   **P** *Bp*
   P-in-c R O DICK,   **C** A Y BENNETT
CLEARWELL (St Peter)   *see* Coleford, Staunton, Newland,
   Redbrook etc *Glouc*
CLEASBY (St Peter)   *see* E Richmond *Ripon*
CLEATOR (St Leonard)   *see* Crosslacon *Carl*
CLEATOR MOOR (St John)   *as above*
CLECKHEATON (St John the Evangelist) *Wakef 8*
   P *V Birstall*   **P-in-c** B H G JAMES
CLECKHEATON (St Luke) (Whitechapel) *Wakef 8*   **P** *Bp and*
   Sir Martin Wilson (jt)   **P-in-c** B H G JAMES,   **NSM** R M CAVE
CLEDFORD (Mission Room)   *see* Middlewich w Byley *Ches*
CLEE, NEW (St John the Evangelist) (St Stephen) *Linc 9*   **P** *Bp*
   V J W ELLIS
CLEE, OLD (Holy Trinity and St Mary the Virgin) *Linc 9*   **P** *Bp*
   P-in-c R G HOLDEN
CLEE HILL (St Peter)   *see* Tenbury *Heref*
CLEE ST MARGARET (St Margaret)   *see* Ludlow *Heref*
CLEETHORPE (Christ Church)   *see* Clee *Linc*
CLEETHORPES St Aidan *Linc 9*   **P** *Bp*   **P-in-c** R G HOLDEN
CLEETHORPES (St Francis) Conventional District
   Linc 9 vacant (01472) 691215
CLEETHORPES (St Peter) *Linc 9*   **P** *Bp*   **R** P HUNTER,
   NSM D H WEBSTER
CLEETON (St Mary)   *see* Stottesdon w Farlow, Cleeton
   St Mary etc *Heref*
CLEEVE (Holy Trinity)   *see* Yatton Moor *B & W*
CLEEVE, OLD (St Andrew), Leighland and Treborough
   B & W 15   **P** *Selw Coll Cam (2 turns), Personal Reps*
   G R Wolseley Esq (1 turn)   **R** vacant (01984) 640576
CLEEVE HILL (St Peter)   *see* Bishop's Cleeve and Woolstone w
   Gotherington etc *Glouc*
CLEEVE PRIOR (St Andrew) and The Littletons *Worc 1*
   P *D&C and Ch Ch Ox (alt)*   **V** D R EVANS
CLEHONGER (All Saints)   *see* Cagebrook *Heref*
CLENCHWARTON (St Margaret) and West Lynn *Ely 14*
   P *DBP*   **R** A J DAVEY
CLENT (St Leonard)   *see* Belbroughton w Fairfield and Clent
   Worc
CLEOBURY MORTIMER (St Mary the Virgin) w Hopton
   Wafers, Neen Sollars and Milson, Neen Savage w Kinlet and
   Doddington *Heref 11*   **P** *Patr Bd (2 turns), Ld Chan (1 turn)*
   R W A BUCK,   **C** K I PRICE,   **Hon C** R G SMITH,
   NSM M H DABORN
CLEOBURY NORTH (St Peter and St Paul)   *see* Ditton Priors
   w Neenton, Burwarton etc *Heref*
CLERKENWELL (Our Most Holy Redeemer) *Lon 6*
   P *Trustees*   **V** P A BAGOTT,   **C** M BRANDON,
   NSM J S STOKES
CLERKENWELL (St James and St John) (St Peter) *Lon 6*
   P *Ch Patr Trust and PCC (jt)*   **V** A J BAUGHEN

CLERKENWELL (St Mark) *Lon 6*   **P** *City Corp*
   V P A BAGOTT,   **C** J K BUCHANAN
CLEVEDON (St Andrew) (Christ Church) (St Peter) *B & W 12*
   P *Simeon's Trustees (1 turn), Ld Chan (2 turns)*
   V T J BAILLIE,   **C** C J JENNINGS, S A SMITH
CLEVEDON (St John the Evangelist) *B & W 12*   **P** *SMF*
   V R JACKSON
CLEVEDON, EAST (All Saints) w Clapton in Gordano, Walton
   Clevedon, Walton in Gordano and Weston in Gordano *B & W 12*
   P *Bp and SMF (jt)*   **R** N A HECTOR,   **Hon C** I D CORBETT,
   A I COOK,   **NSM** B L GUZEK
CLEVELEYS (St Andrew) *Blackb 12*   **P** *Trustees*
   V D E REEVES
CLEWER (St Andrew) *Ox 13*   **P** *Eton Coll*   **P-in-c** L M BROWN,
   C L A J TAYLOR
CLEWER (St Stephen)   *see* New Windsor *Ox*
CLEY (St Margaret)   *see* Blakeney w Cley, Wiveton, Glandford
   etc *Nor*
CLEY HILL Villages, The *Sarum 17*   **P** *Bp and DBP (jt)*
   R N PAYNE,   **OLM** D J BRITTEN
CLIBURN (St Cuthbert)   *see* Morland, Thrimby, Gt Strickland
   and Cliburn *Carl*
CLIDDESDEN (St Leonard)   *see* Farleigh, Candover and Wield
   Win
CLIFFE (St Andrew)   *see* Hemingbrough *York*
CLIFFE, SOUTH (St John)   *see* N Cave w Cliffe *York*
CLIFFE AT HOO (St Helen) w Cooling *Roch 6*   **P** *D&C*
   R E M A WRIGHT,   **NSM** J E WRIGHT
CLIFFORD (St Luke) *York 1*   **P** *G Lane-Fox Esq*
   P-in-c K F A GABBADON
CLIFFORD (St Mary the Virgin)   *see* Cusop w Blakemere,
   Bredwardine w Brobury etc *Heref*
CLIFFORD CHAMBERS (St Helen)
   see Stratford-upon-Avon, Luddington etc *Cov*
CLIFFORDS MESNE (St Peter)   *see* Newent and Gorsley w
   Cliffords Mesne *Glouc*
CLIFFSEND (St Mary the Virgin)   *see* St Laur in Thanet *Cant*
CLIFTON (All Saints) and Southill *St Alb 8*   **P** *Bp and*
   C E S Whitbread Esq (jt)   **NSM** C T TOPLEY
CLIFTON (All Saints w St John) *Bris 2*   **P** *Bp*
   P-in-c R D HOYAL,   **NSM** R DURBIN
CLIFTON (Christ Church w Emmanuel) *Bris 2*   **P** *Simeon's*
   Trustees   **P-in-c** P J LANGHAM,   **C** W P MASSEY, D A CLARK
CLIFTON (Holy Trinity) *Derby 8*   **P** *Mrs M F Stanton,*
   T W Clowes Esq, and V Ashbourne (by turn)
   P-in-c G P POND,   **NSM** P A SHORT
CLIFTON (Holy Trinity) (St Francis) (St Mary the Virgin)
   S'well 9   **P** *DBP*   **TR** S E CLARK,   **TV** A V NOBLE,
   C R H DAVEY, B SELBY
CLIFTON (Holy Trinity, St Andrew the Less and St Peter) *Bris 2*
   P *Simeon's Trustees*   **P-in-c** N S CRAWLEY,
   OLM F M HOUGHTON
CLIFTON (Mission Church)   *see* Conisbrough *Sheff*
CLIFTON (St Anne) (St Thomas) *Man 18*   **P** *Bp*
   V J R BAXENDALE,   **OLM** A P GORDON
CLIFTON (St Cuthbert)   *see* Lowther and Askham and Clifton
   and Brougham *Carl*
CLIFTON (St James) *Sheff 6*   **P** *Bp*   **P-in-c** A L THOMPSON
CLIFTON (St John the Evangelist)   *see* Lund *Blackb*
CLIFTON (St John the Evangelist)   *see* Brighouse and Clifton
   Wakef
CLIFTON (St Luke), Dean and Mosser *Carl 6*   **P** *Patr Bd*
   R vacant (01900) 603886
CLIFTON (St Paul)   *see* Cotham St Sav w St Mary and Clifton
   St Paul *Bris*
CLIFTON (St Philip and St James) *York 7*   **P** *Trustees*
   V D O CASSWELL,   **C** D C ROE,   **NSM** L I CHESTER
CLIFTON, NORTH (St George)   *see* E Trent *S'well*
CLIFTON CAMPVILLE (St Andrew) w Edingale and Harlaston
   Lich 4   **P** *Bp and Major F C Pipe-Wolferstan (jt)*
   R G J THOMPSON
CLIFTON HAMPDEN (St Michael and All Angels)
   see Dorchester *Ox*
CLIFTON-ON-TEME (St Kenelm)   *see* Worcs W *Worc*
CLIFTON REYNES (St Mary the Virgin)   *see* Lavendon w Cold
   Brayfield, Clifton Reynes etc *Ox*
CLIFTON UPON DUNSMORE (St Mary) w Newton and
   Brownsover *Cov 6*   **P** *Bp and H A F W*
   Boughton-Leigh Esq (jt)   **V** T A DAVIS,   **OLM** D J BUSSEY
CLIFTONVILLE (St Paul) *Cant 5*   **P** *Ch Patr Trust*
   P-in-c P L S ELLISDON
CLIPPESBY (St Peter)   *see* Martham and Repps with Bastwick,
   Thurne etc *Nor*
CLIPSHAM (St Mary)   *see* Cottesmore and Burley, Clipsham,
   Exton etc *Pet*

CLIPSTON (All Saints) w Naseby and Haselbech w Kelmarsh
Pet 2 **P** *Ch Coll Cam, DBP, Mrs M F Harris, Exors
Miss C V Lancaster (by turn)* **R** D W FAULKS
CLIPSTONE (All Saints) *S'well 2* **P** *Bp* **V** *vacant* (01623)
623916
CLITHEROE (St James) *Blackb 7* **P** *Trustees*
R M W L PICKETT, **C** A S GRAY
CLITHEROE (St Mary Magdalene) *Blackb 7* **P** *J R Peel Esq*
P-in-c A W FROUD, **NSM** P W SHEPHERD
CLITHEROE (St Paul) Low Moor *Blackb 7* **P** *Bp*
V R NICHOLSON
CLIVE (All Saints) *see* Astley, Clive, Grinshill and Hadnall *Lich*
**CLODOCK (St Clydog) and Longtown w Craswall, Llanveynoe,
St Margaret's, Michaelchurch Escley and Newton** *Heref 1*
P *DBP (2 turns), MMCET (1 turn)* **V** N G LOWTON
CLOFORD (St Mary) *see* Nunney and Witham Friary,
Marston Bigot etc *B & W*
CLOPHILL (St Mary the Virgin) *see* Campton, Clophill and
Haynes *St Alb*
CLOPTON (St Mary) w Otley, Swilland and Ashbocking *St E 7*
P *Ld Chan and Bp (alt)* **P-in-c** G HEDGER, **NSM** J D HALL,
OLM C G LA T BEAUMONT
CLOSWORTH (All Saints) *see* E Coker w Sutton Bingham and
Closworth *B & W*
CLOTHALL (St Mary Virgin) *see* Sandon, Wallington and
Rushden w Clothall *St Alb*
**CLOUGHTON (St Mary) and Burniston w Ravenscar and
Staintondale** *York 15* **P** *Abp* **P-in-c** E KITCHING
CLOVELLY (All Saints) *see* Parkham, Alwington, Buckland
Brewer etc *Ex*
CLOVELLY (St Peter) *as above*
CLOWNE (St John the Baptist) *Derby 3* **P** *Ld Chan*
P-in-c S T SHORT
CLOWS TOP (Mission Room) *see* Mamble w Bayton, Rock w
Heightington etc *Worc*
CLUBMOOR (St Andrew) *Liv 8* **P** *Bp* **V** S MCGANITY,
OLM S J JAMIESON
CLUMBER PARK (St Mary the Virgin) *see* Worksop Priory
S'well
CLUN (St George) w Bettws-y-Crwyn and Newcastle *Heref 9*
P *Earl of Powis* **NSM** A OGRAM
CLUNBURY (St Swithin) *see* Clungunford w Clunbury and
Clunton, Bedstone etc *Heref*
**CLUNGUNFORD (St Cuthbert) w Clunbury and Clunton,
Bedstone and Hopton Castle** *Heref 9* **P** *Earl of Powis,
Mrs S B Rocke, M S C Brown Esq, and Sir Hugh Ripley Bt (jt)*
R S B BELL
CLUNTON (St Mary) *see* Clungunford w Clunbury and
Clunton, Bedstone etc *Heref*
**CLUTTON (St Augustine of Hippo) w Cameley, Bishop Sutton
and Stowey** *B & W 9* **P** *Bp, DBP, and Exors
J P Hippisley Esq (jt)* **R** A D THORNE
CLYFFE PYPARD (St Peter) *see* Woodhill *Sarum*
CLYMPING (St Mary the Virgin) and Yapton w Ford *Chich 1*
P *Bp (2 turns), Ld Chan (1 turn)* **R** R H HAYES,
NSM P WALLIS
CLYST HEATH *see* Ex Trin CD *Ex*
CLYST HONITON (St Michael and All Angels) *see* Aylesbeare,
Rockbeare, Farringdon etc *Ex*
CLYST HYDON (St Andrew) *see* Bradninch and Clyst Hydon
Ex
CLYST ST GEORGE (St George) *see* Clyst St Mary, Clyst
St George etc *Ex*
CLYST ST LAWRENCE (St Lawrence) *see* Whimple, Talaton
and Clyst St Lawr *Ex*
**CLYST ST MARY (St Mary), Clyst St George and Woodbury
Salterton** *Ex 1* **P** *Lord Wraxall, D&C, and S Radcliffe (jt)*
P-in-c K P SPRAY, **C** C S T CANT
**COALBROOKDALE (Holy Trinity), Iron-Bridge and Little
Wenlock** *Heref 13* **P** *Bp, Lord Forester, V Madeley, and
V Much Wenlock (jt)* **P-in-c** I S NAYLOR,
NSM J M EDWARDS, P M JORDAN
COALEY (St Bartholomew) *see* Lower Cam w Coaley *Glouc*
COALPIT HEATH (St Saviour) *Bris 5* **P** *Bp* **V** C P LUNT
COALVILLE (Christ Church) w Bardon Hill and Ravenstone
Leic 8 **P** *Simeon's Trustees and R Hugglescote (2 turns),
Ld Chan (1 turn)* **V** M J T JOSS
COASTAL Group, The *see* Bacton, Happisburgh, Hempstead w
Eccles etc *Nor*
COATES (Holy Trinity) *see* Whittlesey, Pondersbridge and
Coates *Ely*
COATES (St Edith) *see* Stow Gp *Linc*
COATES (St Matthew) *see* Kemble, Poole Keynes, Somerford
Keynes etc *Glouc*
**COATES, GREAT (St Nicholas) and LITTLE (Bishop Edward
King Church) (St Michael) w Bradley** *Linc 9* **P** *Patr Bd*

TR P M MULLINS, **TV** T STOTT, **C** G L HUYSSE-SMITH,
Hon C A I MCCORMICK
COATES, NORTH (St Nicholas) *see* Holton-le-Clay, Tetney
and N Cotes *Linc*
COATHAM (Christ Church) and Dormanstown *York 16*
P *Trustees* **V** A PHILLIPSON
COBBOLD ROAD St Saviour w St Mary *Lon 9* **P** *Bp*
V D J WHEELER, **NSM** P P Y MULLINGS
COBERLEY (St Giles), Cowley, Colesbourne and Elkstone
Glouc 7 **P** *H W G Elwes Esq (2 turns), Ld Chan (1 turn), and
W\Cdr H T Price (1 turn)* **P-in-c** J W HOLDER,
NSM C R POOLEY
COBHAM Sole Street (St Mary's Church Room) *see* Cobham w
Luddesdowne and Dode *Roch*
**COBHAM (St Andrew) (St John the Divine) and Stoke
D'Abernon** *Guildf 10* **P** *D C H Combe Esq and K Coll
Cam (jt)* **R** E R JENKINS, **C** D R THORNTON,
OLM R PITTARIDES
COBHAM (St Mary Magdalene) w Luddesdowne and Dode
Roch 1 **P** *Earl of Darnley and CPAS (alt)*
P-in-c A J WALKER, **NSM** A E BEETY
COBO (St Matthew) *see* Guernsey St Matt *Win*
COBRIDGE (Christ Church) *see* Hanley H Ev *Lich*
COCKAYNE HATLEY (St John the Baptist) *see* Potton w
Sutton and Cockayne Hatley *St Alb*
**COCKERHAM (St Michael) w Winmarleigh St Luke and
Glasson Christ Church** *Blackb 11* **P** *Bp (2 turns), Trustees
(1 turn)* **V** M B ROBERTS
COCKERINGTON, SOUTH (St Leonard) *see* Mid Marsh Gp
Linc
**COCKERMOUTH AREA Team, The (All Saints) (Christ
Church)** *Carl 6* **P** *Patr Bd* **TR** W E SANDERS,
TV A D THOMPSON, **C** P J PYE, **NSM** I J HALSALL
COCKERNHOE (St Hugh) *see* Luton St Fran *St Alb*
COCKERTON (St Mary) *Dur 8* **P** *Bp* **V** R J WALLACE
COCKFIELD (St Mary) *Dur 7* **P** *Bp* **P-in-c** F J GRIEVE,
C E L JOHNSON
COCKFIELD (St Peter) *see* Bradfield St Clare, Bradfield St
George etc *St E*
COCKFOSTERS (Christ Church) Trent Park *see* Enfield Ch Ch
Trent Park *Lon*
COCKING (not known), Bepton and West Lavington *Chich 10*
P *Ld Chan, and Bp, Rathbone Trust Co and Cowdray Trust (alt)*
P-in-c C J BRADLEY
COCKINGTON (St George and St Mary) (St Matthew) *Ex 12*
P *Bp* **V** A K F MACEY
COCKLEY CLEY (All Saints) w Gooderstone *Nor 13* **P** *Bp*
P-in-c D J HANWELL, **C** G D GARRETT
COCKSHUTT (St Simon and St Jude) *see* Petton w Cockshutt,
Welshampton and Lyneal etc *Lich*
COCKYARD (Church Hall) *see* Chapel-en-le-Frith *Derby*
**CODDENHAM (St Mary) w Gosbeck and Hemingstone w
Henley** *St E 1* **P** *Pemb Coll Cam (2 turns), Lord de Saumarez
(1 turn)* **P-in-c** T P HALL, **OLM** H NORRIS
CODDINGTON (All Saints) *see* Colwall w Upper Colwall and
Coddington *Heref*
CODDINGTON (All Saints) *see* Newark w Coddington *S'well*
CODDINGTON (St Mary) *see* Farndon and Coddington *Ches*
CODFORD (St Mary) *see* Upper Wylye Valley *Sarum*
CODFORD (St Peter) *as above*
CODICOTE (St Giles) *St Alb 18* **P** *Abp* **V** L J BIGGS
CODNOR (St James) *Derby 12* **P** *The Crown*
V M M MOOKERJI, **P-in-c** T J WILLIAMS, **NSM** C C HOLDEN
CODSALL (St Nicholas) *Lich 2* **P** *Bp and Lady Wrottesley (jt)*
V S C WITCOMBE, **C** P E SLUSAR, **NSM** M A O FOX,
OLM R G LINTERN
CODSALL WOOD (St Peter) *see* Codsall *Lich*
COFFEEHALL (Community Church) *see* Woughton *Ox*
COFFINSWELL (St Bartholomew) *see* Kingskerswell w
Coffinswell *Ex*
COFTON (St Mary) *see* Kenton, Mamhead, Powderham,
Cofton and Starcross *Ex*
COFTON HACKETT (St Michael) w Barnt Green *Birm 4*
P *Bp* **V** R S HELDOM, **NSM** D M COLLINS
**COGENHOE (St Peter) and Great Houghton and Little
Houghton w Brafield on the Green** *Pet 6*
P *C G V Davidge Esq, Mrs A C Usher, Magd Coll Ox, and
DBP (jt)* **R** R B STAINER
COGGES (St Mary) and South Leigh *Ox 8* **P** *Bp and Payne
Trustees (jt)* **V** A J SWEENEY, **C** A J D PRITCHARD, M F KEEN,
NSM T P EDGE
COGGESHALL (St Peter ad Vincula) w Markshall *Chelmsf 17*
P *Bp (2 turns), SMF (1 turn)* **V** P C BANKS, **C** R J MORTON,
NSM J L HOWES
COGGESHALL, LITTLE (St Nicholas) *see* Coggeshall w
Markshall *Chelmsf*

COKER, EAST (St Michael and All Angels) w Sutton Bingham and Closworth *B & W 6* P *D&C Ex* P-in-c D M WILSON, Hon C J C HATTON

COKER, WEST (St Martin of Tours) w Hardington Mandeville, East Chinnock and Pendomer *B & W 6* P *MMCET and Ox Chs Trust, and DBP (alt)* P-in-c D M WILSON, Hon C J C HATTON

COLATON RALEIGH (St John the Baptist) *see* Ottery St Mary, Alfington, W Hill, Tipton etc *Ex*

COLBURN (St Cuthbert) *see* Hipswell *Ripon*

COLBURY (Christ Church) *Win 11* P *Bp* P-in-c K WILSON

COLBY (Belle Abbey Church) *see* Arbory *S & M*

COLBY (St Giles) *see* King's Beck *Nor*

COLCHESTER (Christ Church w St Mary at the Walls) *Chelmsf 16* P *Bp* R P R NORRINGTON, NSM J SAMS

COLCHESTER (St Anne) *see* Greenstead w Colchester St Anne *Chelmsf*

COLCHESTER (St Barnabas) Old Heath *Chelmsf 16* P *Bp* V R E TILLBROOK

COLCHESTER (St James) and St Paul w All Saints, St Nicholas and St Runwald *Chelmsf 16* P *Bp* R P S WALKER, NSM A T OH

COLCHESTER (St John the Evangelist) *Chelmsf 16* P *Adn Colchester* C J A NOLES, Hon C P H ADAMS, NSM G NOLES

COLCHESTER (St Michael) Myland *Chelmsf 16* P *Ball Coll Ox* P-in-c R G GIBBS, NSM J CHANDLER, R TALLOWIN

COLCHESTER (St Peter) (St Botolph) *Chelmsf 16* P *Bp and Simeon's Trustees (jt)* C A FINCH

COLCHESTER (St Stephen) *see* Colchester, New Town and The Hythe *Chelmsf*

COLCHESTER, New Town and The Hythe (St Stephen, St Mary Magdalene and St Leonard) *Chelmsf 16* P *Ball Coll Ox (2 turns), Ld Chan (1 turn)* R I A HILTON

COLD ASH (St Mark) *see* Hermitage *Ox*

COLD ASHBY (St Denys) *see* Guilsborough and Hollowell and Cold Ashby etc *Pet*

COLD ASHTON (Holy Trinity) *see* Marshfield w Cold Ashton and Tormarton etc *Bris*

COLD ASTON (St Andrew) *see* Northleach w Hampnett and Farmington etc *Glouc*

COLD BRAYFIELD (St Mary) *see* Lavendon w Cold Brayfield, Clifton Reynes etc *Ox*

COLD HIGHAM (St Luke) *see* Pattishall w Cold Higham and Gayton w Tiffield *Pet*

COLD KIRBY (St Michael) *see* Upper Ryedale *York*

COLD NORTON (St Stephen) w Stow Maries *Chelmsf 11* P *Bp and Charterhouse (jt)* V S E MANLEY

COLD OVERTON (St John the Baptist) *see* Whatborough Gp *Leic*

COLD SALPERTON (All Saints) *see* Sevenhampton w Charlton Abbots, Hawling etc *Glouc*

COLDEAN (St Mary Magdalene) *see* Moulsecoomb *Chich*

COLDEN COMMON (Holy Trinity) *see* Twyford and Owslebury and Morestead etc *Win*

COLDHAM (St Etheldreda) *see* Fen Orchards *Ely*

COLDHARBOUR (Christ Church) *see* Abinger cum Coldharbour *Guildf*

COLDHARBOUR (St Alban Mission Church) *see* Mottingham St Andr w St Alban *S'wark*

COLDHURST (Holy Trinity) and Oldham St Stephen and All Martyrs *Man 16* P *Patr Bd* V N G SMEETON, C R D BATTERSHELL

COLDRED (St Pancras) *see* Eythorne and Elvington w Waldershare etc *Cant*

COLDRIDGE (St Matthew) *see* N Creedy *Ex*

COLDWALTHAM (St Giles) *see* Bury w Houghton and Coldwaltham and Hardham *Chich*

COLEBROOKE (St Andrew) *Ex 2* P *D&C* V *vacant*

COLEBY (All Saints) *see* Graffoe Gp *Linc*

COLEFORD (Holy Trinity) w Holcombe *B & W 11* P *Bp and V Kilmersdon (jt)* P-in-c V BONHAM, NSM C R D CRIDLAND

COLEFORD (St John the Evangelist), Staunton, Newland, Redbrook and Clearwell *Glouc 1* P *Bp* V D I LAWRENCE, C S BICK, A W WEARMOUTH, NSM M M HALE

COLEGATE (St George) *see* Nor St Geo Colegate *Nor*

COLEHILL (St Michael and All Angels) *Sarum 9* P *Governors of Wimborne Minster* V J W GOODALL, OLM L L MCGREGOR

COLEMAN'S HATCH (Holy Trinity) *see* Hartfield w Coleman's Hatch *Chich*

COLEORTON (St Mary the Virgin) *see* Ashby-de-la-Zouch and Breedon on the Hill *Leic*

COLERNE (St John the Baptist) w North Wraxall *Bris 4* P *New Coll and Oriel Coll Ox (alt)* P-in-c J M PHILPOTT, NSM G E WOODS

COLESBOURNE (St James) *see* Coberley, Cowley, Colesbourne and Elkstone *Glouc*

COLESHILL (All Saints) *see* Amersham *Ox*

COLESHILL (All Saints) *see* Gt Coxwell w Buscot, Coleshill etc *Ox*

COLESHILL (St Peter and St Paul) *Birm 9* P *J K Wingfield Digby Esq* V R N PARKER, C K M LARKIN

COLEY Norwood Green (St George) *see* Coley *Wakef*

COLEY (St John the Baptist) *Wakef 2* P *V Halifax* V M K MADELEY

COLGATE (St Saviour) *see* Rusper w Colgate *Chich*

COLINDALE (St Matthias) *Lon 15* P *Bp* P-in-c J E I HAWKINS

COLKIRK (St Mary) *see* Upper Wensum Village Gp *Nor*

COLLATON (St Mary the Virgin) *see* Stoke Gabriel and Collaton *Ex*

COLLIER ROW (Ascension) *see* Romford Ascension Collier Row *Chelmsf*

COLLIER ROW (Good Shepherd) *see* Romford Gd Shep *Chelmsf*

COLLIER ROW (St James) and Havering-atte-Bower *Chelmsf 2* P *CPAS and Bp (jt)* P-in-c D C MARSHALL, C A T POULTNEY, Hon C A MARSHALL, NSM D J STAINER

COLLIER STREET (St Margaret) *see* Yalding w Collier Street *Roch*

COLLIERLEY (St Thomas) w Annfield Plain *Dur 4* P *Bp and The Crown (alt)* V *vacant* (01207) 236254

COLLIERS END (St Mary) *see* High Cross *St Alb*

COLLIERS WOOD (Christ Church) *see* Merton Priory *S'wark*

COLLINGBOURNE DUCIS (St Andrew) *see* Savernake *Sarum*

COLLINGBOURNE KINGSTON (St Mary) *as above*

COLLINGHAM (All Saints) *see* E Trent *S'well*

COLLINGHAM (St John the Baptist) *as above*

COLLINGHAM (St Oswald) w Harewood *Ripon 1* P *Earl of Harewood and G H H Wheler Esq (jt)* V *vacant* (01937) 573975

COLLINGTON (St Mary) *see* Bredenbury *Heref*

COLLINGTREE (St Columba) w Courteenhall and Milton Malsor *Pet 5* P H C Wake Esq, G Phipps-Walker Esq, and Hyndman Trustees (by turn)* C J SAFFORD, M J BURTON

COLLYHURST (The Saviour) *Man 4* P *Bp and Trustees (jt)* P-in-c C FALLONE, OLM M B ROGERS

COLLYWESTON (St Andrew) *see* Ketton, Collyweston, Easton-on-the-Hill etc *Pet*

COLMWORTH (St Denys) *see* Wilden w Colmworth and Ravensden *St Alb*

COLN ROGERS (St Andrew) *see* Chedworth, Yanworth and Stowell, Coln Rogers etc *Glouc*

COLN ST ALDWYN (St John the Baptist) *see* Fairford Deanery *Glouc*

COLN ST DENYS (St James the Great) *see* Chedworth, Yanworth and Stowell, Coln Rogers etc *Glouc*

COLNBROOK (St Thomas) and Datchet *Ox 23* P *Bp and D&C Windsor (jt)* V P J WYARD, C M J DAVIS

COLNE (Christ Church) (Holy Trinity) (St Bartholomew) and Villages *Blackb 6* P *Patr Bd* TR A W RINDL, C C STERRY, J R H CRAWFORD, NSM P BROOK, N J C KROUKAMP

COLNE (St Helen) *see* Bluntisham cum Earith w Colne and Holywell etc *Ely*

COLNE, THE UPPER, Parishes of Great Yeldham, Little Yeldham, Stambourne, Tilbury-juxta-Clare and Toppesfield *Chelmsf 19* P *Prime Min, Ld Chan, Bp, Duchy of Lancaster, and Trustees of the late Miss W M N Brett (by turn)* P-in-c B C DENNIS

COLNE ENGAINE (St Andrew) *see* Halstead Area *Chelmsf*

COLNEY (St Andrew) *see* Cringleford and Colney *Nor*

COLNEY (St Peter) *see* London Colney St Pet *St Alb*

COLNEY HEATH (St Mark) *St Alb 5* P *Trustees* V H J SPANNER, NSM J SUTTIE

COLSTERWORTH Group, The (St John the Baptist) *Linc 14* P *Bp (2 turns), Mrs R S McCorquodale, The Revd J R H Thorold and J R Thorold Esq (1 turn)* P-in-c E J LOMAX

COLSTON BASSETT (St John the Divine) *see* Cropwell Bishop w Colston Bassett, Granby etc *S'well*

COLTISHALL (St John the Baptist) w Great Hautbois, Frettenham, Hainford, Horstead and Stratton Strawless *Nor 19* P *D&C, Bp, K Coll Cam, and Ch Soc Trust (jt)* R C J ENGELSEN, OLM K A DIGNUM

COLTON (Holy Trinity) *see* Egton-cum-Newland and Lowick and Colton *Carl*

COLTON (St Andrew) *see* Easton, Colton, Marlingford and Bawburgh *Nor*

COLTON (St Mary the Virgin) *see* Abbots Bromley, Blithfield, Colton, Colwich etc *Lich*

COLTON (St Paul) *see* Bolton Percy *York*

COLWALL (St Crispin's Chapel) (St James the Great) w Upper Colwall (Good Shepherd) and Coddington *Heref 5*   P *Bp* R M J HORTON, NSM A C LANYON-HOGG

COLWALL, UPPER (Good Shepherd) *see* Colwall w Upper Colwall and Coddington *Heref*

COLWICH (St Michael and All Angels) *see* Abbots Bromley, Blithfield, Colton, Colwich etc *Lich*

COLWICK (St John the Baptist) *S'well 10*   P *DBP* P-in-c R B CHAPMAN, C J E LAMB

COLYFORD (St Michael) *see* Colyton, Musbury, Southleigh and Branscombe *Ex*

COLYTON (St Andrew), Musbury, Southleigh and Branscombe *Ex 5*   P *D&C* P-in-c H DAWSON

COMBE (St Swithin) *see* Walbury Beacon *Ox*

COMBE DOWN (Holy Trinity) (St Andrew) w Monkton Combe and South Stoke *B & W 8*   P *R Bath, Ox Chs Trust, and Comdr H R Salmer (jt)*   P-in-c P H KENCHINGTON, C T S BUCKLEY

COMBE FLOREY (St Peter and St Paul) *see* Lydeard St Lawrence and Combe Florey *B & W*

COMBE HAY (not known) *see* Bath Odd Down w Combe Hay *B & W*

COMBE LONGA (St Laurence) *see* Stonesfield w Combe Longa *Ox*

COMBE MARTIN (St Peter ad Vincula), Berrynarbor, Lynton, Brendon, Countisbury, Parracombe, Martinhoe and Trentishoe *Ex 18*   P *Patr Bd* TV Y L YATES, P-in-c C D STEED, NSM S L GRAHAM

COMBE PYNE (St Mary the Virgin) *see* Axminster, Chardstock, All Saints etc *Ex*

COMBE RALEIGH (St Nicholas) *see* Honiton, Gittisham, Combe Raleigh, Monkton etc *Ex*

COMBE ST NICHOLAS (St Nicholas) *see* Chard St Mary w Combe St Nicholas, Wambrook etc *B & W*

COMBEINTEIGNHEAD (All Saints) *see* Shaldon, Stokeinteignhead, Combeinteignhead etc *Ex*

COMBERFORD (St Mary and St George) *see* Wigginton *Lich*

COMBERTON (St Mary) *see* Lordsbridge *Ely*

COMBERTON, GREAT (St Michael) *see* Elmley Castle w Bricklehampton and Combertons *Worc*

COMBERTON, LITTLE (St Peter) *as above*

COMBROKE (St Mary and St Margaret) w Compton Verney *Cov 8*   P *Bp* P-in-c B J JACKSON, C R J COOKE

COMBS (St Mary) and Little Finborough *St E 6*   P *Bp and Pemb Coll Ox (jt)* P-in-c J C ROSS, OLM A M LAY

COMBWICH (St Peter) *see* Cannington, Otterhampton, Combwich and Stockland *B & W*

COMER GARDENS (St David) *see* Worc St Clem and Lower Broadheath *Worc*

COMMONDALE (St Peter) *see* Danby w Castleton and Commondale *York*

COMPSTALL (St Paul) *see* Werneth *Ches*

COMPTON (All Saints), Hursley, and Otterbourne *Win 7* P *Bp, Mrs P M A T Chamberlayne-Macdonald, and Lord Lifford (jt)* R W A PRESCOTT

COMPTON (St Mary) *see* Farnham *Guildf*

COMPTON (St Mary and St Nicholas) *see* Hermitage *Ox*

COMPTON (St Mary), the Mardens, Stoughton and Racton *Chich 13*   P *Bp Lon (1 turn), Bp (2 turns)* P-in-c J D STRAIN

COMPTON (St Nicholas) w Shackleford and Peper Harow *Guildf 4*   P *Bp and Major J R More-Molyneux (jt)* R J M FELLOWS, NSM J LEE

COMPTON, LITTLE (St Denys) *see* Chipping Norton *Ox*

COMPTON, NETHER (St Nicholas) *see* Queen Thorne *Sarum*

COMPTON, OVER (St Michael) *as above*

COMPTON ABBAS (St Mary the Virgin) *see* Shaftesbury *Sarum*

COMPTON ABDALE (St Oswald) *see* Northleach w Hampnett and Farmington etc *Glouc*

COMPTON BASSETT (St Swithin) *see* Oldbury *Sarum*

COMPTON BEAUCHAMP (St Swithun) *see* Shrivenham and Ashbury *Ox*

COMPTON BISHOP (St Andrew) *see* Crook Peak *B & W*

COMPTON CHAMBERLAYNE (St Michael) *see* Fovant, Sutton Mandeville and Teffont Evias etc *Sarum*

COMPTON DANDO (Blessed Virgin Mary) *see* Publow w Pensford, Compton Dando and Chelwood *B & W*

COMPTON DUNDON (St Andrew) *see* Somerton w Compton Dundon, the Charltons etc *B & W*

COMPTON GREENFIELD (All Saints) *see* Pilning w Compton Greenfield *Bris*

COMPTON MARTIN (St Michael) *see* Blagdon w Compton Martin and Ubley *B & W*

COMPTON PAUNCEFOOT (Blessed Virgin Mary) *see* Camelot Par *B & W*

COMPTON VALENCE (St Thomas à Beckett) *see* The Winterbournes and Compton Valence *Sarum*

CONDICOTE (St Nicholas) *see* Stow on the Wold, Condicote and The Swells *Glouc*

CONDOVER (St Andrew and St Mary) w Frodesley, Acton Burnell and Pitchford *Heref 10*   P *Bp, Revd E W Serjeantson, and Mrs C R Colthurst (jt)* R J C W ROSE, NSM M G GILLIONS

CONEY HILL (St Oswald) *Glouc 2*   P *The Crown* V *vacant* (01452) 523618

CONEY WESTON (St Mary) *see* Stanton, Hopton, Market Weston, Barningham etc *St E*

CONEYSTHORPE (Chapel) *see* The Street Par *York*

CONGERSTONE (St Mary the Virgin) *see* Bosworth and Sheepy Gp *Leic*

CONGHAM (St Andrew) *see* Grimston, Congham and Roydon *Nor*

CONGLETON (St James) *Ches 11*   P *Bp* V C J SANDERSON

CONGLETON (St John the Evangelist) (St Peter) (St Stephen) *Ches 11*   P *Patr Bd* TR D TAYLOR, TV P M WITHINGTON

CONGRESBURY (St Andrew) w Puxton and Hewish St Ann *B & W 10*   P *MMCET* V M J THOMSON, C T J ERRIDGE

CONINGSBY (St Michael) *see* Bain Valley Gp *Linc*

CONINGTON (St Mary) *see* Fen Drayton w Conington and Lolworth etc *Ely*

CONISBROUGH (St Peter) *Sheff 9*   P *Bp* V A C GRIFFITHS

CONISCLIFFE (St Edwin) *Dur 8*   P *Bp* P-in-c J R DOBSON

CONISHOLME (St Peter) *see* Somercotes and Grainthorpe w Conisholme *Linc*

CONISTON (St Andrew) *see* Church Coniston *Carl*

CONISTON COLD (St Peter) *see* Gargrave w Coniston Cold *Bradf*

CONISTONE (St Mary) *see* Kettlewell w Conistone, Hubberholme etc *Bradf*

CONONLEY (St John the Evangelist) w Bradley *Bradf 8*   P *Bp* V J C PEET

CONSETT (Christ Church) *Dur 4*   P *Bp* P-in-c V SHEDDEN

CONSTABLE LEE (St Paul) *Man 11*   P *CPAS* P-in-c M R SHORT

CONSTANTINE (St Constantine) *Truro 4*   P *D&C* P-in-c S G TURNER

COOKBURY (St John the Baptist and the Seven Maccabes) *see* Black Torrington, Bradford w Cookbury etc *Ex*

COOKHAMS, The (Holy Trinity) (St John the Baptist) *Ox 13* P *Mrs E U Rogers* V M D SMITH, C A N THOMAS, N PLANT

COOKHILL (St Paul) *see* Inkberrow w Cookhill and Kington w Dormston *Worc*

COOKLEY (St Michael and All Angels) *see* Heveningham *St E*

COOKLEY (St Peter) *see* Wolverley and Cookley *Worc*

COOKRIDGE (Holy Trinity) *Ripon 7*   P *R Adel* V J F HAMILTON

COOMBE (Christ Church) *see* New Malden and Coombe *S'wark*

COOMBE BISSET (St Michael and All Angels) *see* Chalke Valley *Sarum*

COOMBES (not known) *see* Lancing w Coombes *Chich*

COOMBS WOOD (St Ambrose) *see* Blackheath *Birm*

COOPERSALE (St Alban) *see* Epping Distr *Chelmsf*

COPDOCK (St Peter) *see* Sproughton w Burstall, Copdock w Washbrook etc *St E*

COPFORD (St Michael and All Angels) w Easthorpe and Messing w Inworth *Chelmsf 23*   P *Ld Chan, Duchy of Lanc, and DBP (by turn)* R C J GARLAND

COPGROVE (St Michael) *see* Walkingham Hill *Ripon*

COPLE (All Saints), Moggerhanger and Willington *St Alb 10* P *Bp (2 turns), Ch Ch Ox (1 turn)* V L KLIMAS, NSM J R BUCK

COPLESTON CENTRE *see* Peckham St Sav *S'wark*

COPLEY (Wakef 4)   P *V Halifax* V *vacant* (01422) 652964

COPMANTHORPE (St Giles) *York 1*   P *R York St Clement w St Mary Bishophill* P-in-c G R MUMFORD

COPNOR (St Alban) *see* Portsea St Alb *Portsm*

COPNOR (St Cuthbert) *see* Portsea St Cuth *Portsm*

COPP (St Anne) w Inskip *Blackb 9*   P *V Garstang St Helen and St Michaels-on-Wyre* V D GASKELL

COPPENHALL (All Saints and St Paul) *see* Crewe All SS and St Paul w St Pet *Ches*

COPPENHALL (St Laurence) *see* Penkridge *Lich*

COPPENHALL (St Michael) *Ches 15*   P *Bp* R C H RAZZALL

COPPULL (not known) *Blackb 4*   P *R Standish* V J HUDSON, Hon C P M SHOOTER

COPPULL (St John) *Blackb 4* **P** *R Standish*
P-in-c J HUDSON, **Hon C** P M SHOOTER
COPSTON MAGNA (St John) *see* Wolvey w Burton Hastings, Copston Magna etc *Cov*
COPT HEWICK (Holy Innocents) *see* Ripon Cathl *Ripon*
COPT OAK (St Peter) *see* Markfield, Thornton, Bagworth and Stanton etc *Leic*
COPTHORNE (St John the Evangelist) *Chich 7* **P** *Bp*
V S G HILL, **NSM** P SMITH, E J LOGAN
COPYTHORNE (St Mary) *Win 11* **P** *Bp Liv*
P-in-c J R REEVE, **C** A K NUTT
COQUETDALE, UPPER *Newc 6* **P** *Duchy of Lanc (2 turns), Ld Chan (1 turn), and Duke of Northumberland (1 turn)*
NSM S D JOYNER, T A J GRAY, **OLM** C R STACY
CORBRIDGE (St Andrew) w Halton and Newton Hall *Newc 9*
P *D&C Carl* V D B HEWLETT
CORBY (Epiphany) (St John the Baptist) *Pet 7*
P *E Brudenell Esq* **R** *vacant* (01536) 402837
CORBY (St Columba and the Northern Saints) *Pet 7* **P** *Bp*
P-in-c R J LEE
CORBY (St Peter and St Andrew) (Kingswood Church) *Pet 7*
P *Bp* **P-in-c** J M COLLINS
CORBY GLEN (St John the Evangelist) *Linc 14* **P** *Ld Chan (2 turns), Sir Simon Benton Jones Bt (1 turn)*
P-in-c M A E BARTON
CORELEY (St Peter) *see* Tenbury *Heref*
CORFE (St Nicholas) *see* Blackdown *B & W*
CORFE CASTLE (St Edward the Martyr), Church Knowle, Kimmeridge Steeple w Tyneham *Sarum 8* **P** *Major M J A Bond, Nat Trust, and Bp (jt)* **P-in-c** I JACKSON, C A HAGENBUCH
CORFE MULLEN (St Hubert) *Sarum 9* **P** *Bp*
R P S WALKER, **NSM** S RICHARDS
CORHAMPTON (not known) *see* Meon Bridge *Portsm*
CORLEY (not known) *see* Fillongley and Corley *Cov*
CORNARD, GREAT (St Andrew) *St E 12* **P** *Bp*
V C J RAMSEY, C J G BLEAZARD
CORNARD, LITTLE (All Saints) *see* Bures w Assington and Lt Cornard *St E*
CORNELLY (St Cornelius) *see* Tregony w St Cuby and Cornelly *Truro*
CORNEY (St John the Baptist) *see* Bootle, Corney, Whicham and Whitbeck *Carl*
CORNFORTH (Holy Trinity) and Ferryhill *Dur 5* **P** *D&C (2 turns), Bp (1 turn)* V K LUMSDON
CORNHILL (St Helen) w Carham *Newc 12* **P** *Abp (2 turns), E M Straker-Smith Esq (1 turn)* **P-in-c** G R KELSEY, **NSM** L E GARDHAM
CORNHOLME (St Michael and All Saints) and Walsden *Wakef 3* **P** *Bp and DBP (jt)* V C SMITH, **NSM** S D WHITE, **OLM** I M GREENMAN
CORNISH HALL END (St John the Evangelist) *see* Finchingfield and Cornish Hall End etc *Chelmsf*
CORNWELL (St Peter) *see* Chipping Norton *Ox*
CORNWOOD (St Michael and All Angels) *Ex 21* **P** *Bp*
P-in-c F G DENMAN
CORNWORTHY (St Peter) *see* Totnes w Bridgetown, Berry Pomeroy etc *Ex*
CORONATION SQUARE (St Aidan) *see* Cheltenham St Mark *Glouc*
CORRA (Holy Trinity) *see* Adderley, Ash, Calverhall, Ightfield etc *Lich*
CORRINGHAM (St John the Evangelist) (St Mary the Virgin) and Fobbing *Chelmsf 14* **P** *Bp and SMF (jt)* **R** D ROLLINS
CORRINGHAM (St Lawrence) and Blyton Group, The *Linc 2* **P** *Ld Chan (2 turns), Bp (1 turn), Meynell Ch Trustees (1 turn)* **P-in-c** M BRISCOE, **NSM** C A SULLY
CORSCOMBE (St Mary the Virgin) *see* Melbury *Sarum*
CORSE (St Margaret) *see* Ashleworth, Corse, Hartpury, Hasfield etc *Glouc*
CORSENSIDE (All Saints) *see* N Tyne and Redesdale *Newc*
CORSENSIDE (St Cuthbert) *as above*
CORSHAM, GREATER (St Bartholomew) and Lacock *Bris 4* **P** *Patr Bd* **TV** S A V WHEELER, **P-in-c** A R JOHNSON, C S WILKINSON
CORSLEY (St Margaret of Antioch) *see* Cley Hill Villages *Sarum*
CORSLEY (St Mary the Virgin) *as above*
CORSTON (All Saints) *see* Saltford w Corston and Newton St Loe *B & W*
CORSTON (All Saints) *see* Gt Somerford, Lt Somerford, Seagry, Corston etc *Bris*
CORTON (St Bartholomew) *see* Hopton w Corton *Nor*
CORTON (St Bartholomew) *see* Abbotsbury, Portesham and Langton Herring *Sarum*

CORTON DENHAM (St Andrew) *see* Cam Vale *B & W*
CORYTON (St Andrew) *see* Milton Abbot, Dunterton, Lamerton etc *Ex*
COSBY (St Michael and All Angels) and Whetstone *Leic 7*
P *Bp* V C D ALLEN, C P L BAILEY
COSELEY (Christ Church) (St Cuthbert) *Worc 10* **P** *Bp*
V H M HUMPHREY, **NSM** R L ROWSON
COSELEY (St Chad) *Worc 10* **P** *Bp* V A HOWES
COSGROVE (St Peter and St Paul) *see* Potterspury w Furtho and Yardley Gobion etc *Pet*
COSHAM (St Philip) *Portsm 6* **P** *Bp* **P-in-c** J L STRAW, **Hon C** B R COOK
COSSALL (St Catherine) *see* Trowell, Awsworth and Cossall *S'well*
COSSINGTON (All Saints) *see* Sileby, Cossington and Seagrave *Leic*
COSSINGTON (Blessed Virgin Mary) *see* Woolavington w Cossington and Bawdrip *B & W*
COSTESSEY (St Edmund) *Nor 3* **P** *Gt Hosp Nor*
V N J S PARRY
COSTESSEY, NEW (St Helen) *see* Costessey *Nor*
COSTOCK (St Giles) *see* E and W Leake, Stanford-on-Soar, Rempstone etc *S'well*
COSTON (St Andrew) *see* S Framland *Leic*
COTEBROOKE (St John and Holy Cross) *see* Tarporley *Ches*
COTEHELE HOUSE (Chapel) *see* Calstock *Truro*
COTEHILL (St John the Evangelist) *see* Scotby and Cotehill w Cumwhinton *Carl*
COTES HEATH (St James) and Standon and Swynnerton and Tittensor *Lich 13* **P** *Bp, V Eccleshall, and Simeon's Trustees (jt)* **R** S G MCKENZIE
COTESBACH (St Mary) *see* Lutterworth w Cotesbach and Bitteswell *Leic*
COTGRAVE (All Saints) *S'well 8* **P** *DBP* **R** P D S MASSEY
COTHAM (St Saviour w St Mary) and Clifton St Paul *Bris 3*
P *Bp* **P-in-c** J R HOLROYD
COTHELSTONE (St Thomas of Canterbury) *see* Bishops Lydeard w Bagborough and Cothelstone *B & W*
COTHERIDGE (St Leonard) *see* Worcs W *Worc*
COTHERSTONE (St Cuthbert) *see* Romaldkirk w Laithkirk *Ripon*
COTLEIGH (St Michael and All Angels) *see* Offwell, Northleigh, Farway, Cotleigh etc *Ex*
COTMANHAY (Christ Church) *Derby 13* **P** *Bp* V P J DAVEY
COTON (St Peter) *see* Lordsbridge *Ely*
COTON-IN-THE-ELMS (St Mary) *see* Seale and Lullington w Coton in the Elms *Derby*
COTTENHAM (All Saints) *Ely 6* **P** *Bp* **P-in-c** K A HODGINS
COTTERED (St John the Baptist) w Broadfield and Throcking *St Alb 16* **P** *Bp* **P-in-c** M J LEVERTON
COTTERIDGE (St Agnes) *Birm 4* **P** *R Kings Norton*
NSM R R COLLINS
COTTERSTOCK (St Andrew) *see* Warmington, Tansor and Cotterstock etc *Pet*
COTTESBROOKE (All Saints) *see* Guilsborough and Hollowell and Cold Ashby etc *Pet*
COTTESMORE (St Nicholas) and Burley, Clipsham, Exton, Greetham, Stretton and Thistleton *Pet 12* **P** *Bp, DBP, E R Hanbury Esq, and Sir David Davenport-Handley (jt)*
V R J LUBKOWSKI
COTTIMORE (St John) *see* Walton-on-Thames *Guildf*
COTTINGHAM (St Mary) *York 14* **P** *Abp* **R** P A SMITH, C A J BIGG
COTTINGHAM (St Mary Magdalene) *see* Gretton w Rockingham and Cottingham w E Carlton *Pet*
COTTINGLEY (St Michael and All Angels) *Bradf 1* **P** *Bp*
P-in-c G S HODGSON, C T P LEWIS
COTTINGWITH, EAST (St Mary) *see* Derwent Ings *York*
COTTISFORD (St Mary the Virgin) *see* Shelswell *Ox*
COTTON (St Andrew) *see* Bacton w Wyverstone, Cotton and Old Newton etc *St E*
COTTON (St John the Baptist) *see* Kingsley and Foxt-w-Whiston and Oakamoor etc *Lich*
COTTON MILL (St Julian) *see* St Alb St Steph *St Alb*
COTTONSTONES (St Mary) *see* Sowerby *Wakef*
COUGHTON (St Peter) *Cov 7* **P** *Bp* **P-in-c** C CAPRON
COULSDON (St Andrew) *S'wark 22* **P** *Bp* V L SIMS, **NSM** T F MUNRO
COULSDON (St John) *S'wark 22* **P** *Abp* **R** P C ROBERTS, C L FLETCHER, **NSM** S P STOCKS, S L THOMAS
COULSTON, EAST (St Thomas of Canterbury) *see* Bratton, Edington and Imber, Erlestoke etc *Sarum*
COUND (St Peter) *see* Wenlock *Heref*
COUNDON (St James) and Eldon *Dur 6* **P** *Bp and Prime Min (alt)* **P-in-c** G NICHOLSON

COUNTESS WEAR (St Luke) *Ex 3*   **P** *V Topsham*
P-in-c R W C JEFFERY,   **Hon C** M D A WILLIAMS,
NSM J J HORWOOD
COUNTESTHORPE (St Andrew) w Foston *Leic 7*   **P** *DBP and*
Bp (alt)   **P-in-c** D E HEBBLEWHITE,   **C** A S W BOOKER,
NSM M D GILLESPIE
COUNTISBURY (St John the Evangelist)   *see* Combe Martin,
Berrynarbor, Lynton, Brendon etc *Ex*
COURTEENHALL (St Peter and St Paul)   *see* Collingtree w
Courteenhall and Milton Malsor *Pet*
COVE (St John the Baptist) (St Christopher) *Guildf 1*   **P** *Bp*
TR J H TYNDALL,   **TV** E T PRIOR, S J STEWART,
OLM G H THOMAS
COVEHITHE (St Andrew)   *see* Wrentham, Covehithe w
Benacre etc *St E*
COVEN (St Paul)   *see* Bilbrook and Coven *Lich*
COVEN HEATH (Mission Church)   *see* Bushbury *Lich*
COVENEY (St Peter ad Vincula) *Ely 8*   **P** *Bp*   **P-in-c** P TAYLOR
COVENHAM (Annunciation of the Blessed Virgin Mary)
see Fotherby *Linc*
COVENT GARDEN (St Paul) *Lon 3*   **P** *Bp*   **R** S J GRIGG
COVENTRY Caludon *Cov 1*   **P** *Bp and Ld Chan (alt)*
TR W M SMITH,   **TV** K S REEVES, L A MUDD,   **C** J P TAYLOR
COVENTRY Holbrooks (St Luke)   *see* Holbrooks *Cov*
COVENTRY (Holy Trinity) *Cov 2*   **P** *Ld Chan*
V D F MAYHEW,   **C** J A S HILL
COVENTRY (St Francis of Assisi) North Radford *Cov 2*   **P** *Bp*
P-in-c J D IRVINE,   **NSM** M W HAYWARD
COVENTRY (St George) *Cov 2*   **P** *Bp*   **V** A J EVANS
COVENTRY (St John the Baptist) *Cov 2*   **P** *Trustees*
R P N SUCH
COVENTRY (St Mary Magdalen) *Cov 3*   **P** *Bp*   **V** *vacant* (024)
7667 5838
COVENTRY (St Nicholas)   *see* Radford *Cov*
COVENTRY EAST (St Anne and All Saints) (St Margaret)
(St Peter) (St Alban) *Cov 1*   **P** *Patr Bd*   **TR** S W M HARTLEY,
TV P M BULLOCK
COVERACK (St Peter)   *see* St Keverne *Truro*
COVERDALE (St Botolph)   *see* Middleham w Coverdale and E
Witton etc *Ripon*
COVINGHAM (St Paul)   *see* Swindon Dorcan *Bris*
COVINGTON (All Saints)   *see* Kym Valley *Ely*
COWARNE, LITTLE (not known)   *see* Bredenbury *Heref*
COWARNE, MUCH (St Mary the Virgin)   *see* Frome Valley
Heref
COWBIT (St Mary) *Linc 17*   **P** *Ld Chan and DBP (alt)*
V *vacant* (01406) 373630
COWCLIFFE (St Hilda)   *see* Fixby and Cowcliffe *Wakef*
COWDEN (St Mary Magdalene) w Hammerwood *Chich 7*
P *Ch Soc Trust*   **P-in-c** M E TRASK
COWES (Holy Trinity) (St Mary the Virgin) *Portsm 8*
P *Trustees and V Carisbrooke St Mary (jt)*   **V** R J EMBLIN,
C D J HINKS,   **NSM** K H G MORRIS
COWES (St Faith) *Portsm 8*   **P** *Bp*   **V** L MCROSTIE
COWES, EAST (St James)   *see* Whippingham w E Cowes *Portsm*
COWESBY (St Michael) *York 18*   **P** *Abp*   **R** I D HOUGHTON,
NSM T A LEWIS
COWFOLD (St Peter) *Chich 9*   **P** *Bp Lon*
P-in-c K D LITTLEJOHN
COWGATE (St Peter) *Newc 4*   **P** *Bp*   **V** A PATERSON
COWGILL (St John the Evangelist)   *see* Dent w Cowgill *Bradf*
COWICK (Holy Trinity)   *see* Gt Snaith *Sheff*
COWLAM (St Mary)   *see* Waggoners *York*
COWLEIGH (St Peter)   *see* Malvern Link w Cowleigh *Worc*
COWLEY (Holy Trinity)   *see* Headington Quarry *Ox*
COWLEY (St James) (St Francis) *Ox 4*   **P** *Patr Bd*
TR H D THORNTON,   **NSM** R W CHAND
**COWLEY (St John) (St Alban) (St Bartholomew) (St Mary and
St John)** *Ox 4*   **P** *St Steph Ho Ox*   **V** J A ROMANIS,
NSM S M ALKIRE, B J WILLIAMS, M H B REES
COWLEY (St Laurence) *Lon 24*   **P** *Bp*   **R** S M HARDWICKE
COWLEY (St Mary)   *see* Coberley, Cowley, Colesbourne and
Elkstone *Glouc*
COWLEY CHAPEL (St Antony)   *see* Brampford Speke,
Cadbury, Newton St Cyres etc *Ex*
COWLING (Holy Trinity)   *see* Sutton w Cowling and
Lothersdale *Bradf*
COWLINGE (St Margaret)   *see* Bansfield *St E*
COWPEN (St Benedict)   *see* Horton *Newc*
COWPLAIN (St Wilfrid) *Portsm 5*   **P** *Bp*   **V** P H MOORE,
C A A WEBBER,   **NSM** R LOVEMAN
COWTON, EAST (All Saints)   *see* E Richmond *Ripon*
COWTON, SOUTH (St Luke's Pastoral Centre)   *as above*
COX GREEN (Good Shepherd) *Ox 13*   **P** *Bp*   **P-in-c** J R HICKS
COXFORD Group, The   *see* E w W Rudham, Helhoughton etc
Nor

**COXHEATH (Holy Trinity), East Farleigh, Hunton, Linton and
West Farleigh** *Roch 7*   **P** *Ld Chan (1 turn), Abp, Lord
Cornwallis, and D&C (1 turn)*   **R** P S C WALKER,
NSM D W JONES, E A DOYLE
COXHOE (St Mary)   *see* Kelloe and Coxhoe *Dur*
COXLEY (Christ Church) w Godney, Henton and Wookey
B & W 7   **P** *Bp*   **P-in-c** A SYER
**COXWELL, GREAT (St Giles) w Buscot, Coleshill and Eaton
Hastings** *Ox 17*   **P** *Bp and Lord Faringdon (jt)*
P-in-c D M WILLIAMS
COXWELL, LITTLE (St Mary)   *see* Gt Faringdon w Lt Coxwell
Ox
COXWOLD (St Michael) and Husthwaite *York 3*   **P** *Abp*
V I B KITCHEN,   **NSM** N L CHAPMAN
CRABBS CROSS (St Peter)   *see* Redditch Ch the K *Worc*
CRADLEY (St James) w Mathon and Storridge *Heref 5*   **P** *Bp*
and *D&C Westmr (jt)*   **R** R WARD,   **NSM** M D VOCKINS
CRADLEY (St Katherine's Mission Church)   *see* Halas *Worc*
CRADLEY (St Peter)   *as above*
CRADLEY HEATH (St Luke)   *see* Reddal Hill St Luke *Worc*
CRAGG VALE (St John the Baptist in the Wilderness)
see Erringden *Wakef*
CRAKEHALL (St Gregory) *Ripon 4*   **P** *Sir Henry
Beresford-Peirse Bt*   **P-in-c** B S DIXON,   **NSM** J T OLDFIELD
CRAMBE (St Michael)   *see* Whitwell w Crambe and Foston
York
CRAMLINGTON (St Nicholas) *Newc 1*   **P** *Bp*
TR S W HEWITT,   **TV** S G WILKINSON,   **C** T J HARVEY,
OLM S M WARD
CRAMPMOOR (St Swithun)   *see* Romsey *Win*
**CRANBORNE (St Mary and St Bartholomew) w Boveridge,
Edmondsham, Wimborne St Giles and Woodlands** *Sarum 9*
P *Viscount Cranborne, Earl of Shaftesbury, and
Mrs J E Smith (jt)*   **R** D J PASKINS
CRANBOURNE (St Peter)   *see* Winkfield and Cranbourne *Ox*
CRANBROOK (St Dunstan) *Cant 10*   **P** *Abp*
P-in-c R L WILLIAMS,   **Hon C** J A TAPPER
CRANFIELD (St Peter and St Paul) and Hulcote w Salford
St Alb 9   **P** *MMCET*   **R** H K SYMES-THOMPSON
CRANFORD (Holy Angels) *Lon 11*   **P** *Dunstan) Lon 11*
P *R J G Berkeley Esq and Sir Hugo Huntington-Whiteley Bt (jt)*
R M J GILL
**CRANFORD (St John the Baptist) w Grafton Underwood and
Twywell** *Pet 9*   **P** *Boughton Estates, DBP, and Sir John
Robinson Bt (by turn)*   **R** D H P FOOT
CRANHAM (All Saints) *Chelmsf 2*   **P** *St Jo Coll Ox*
P-in-c S J BREWSTER,   **NSM** G K W ARBER
CRANHAM (St James the Great)   *see* Painswick, Sheepscombe,
Cranham, The Edge etc *Glouc*
CRANHAM PARK Moor Lane (not known)   *see* Cranham
Park *Chelmsf*
CRANHAM PARK (St Luke) *Chelmsf 2*   **P** *Bp*   **V** M VICKERS,
C K J BROWNING
CRANLEIGH (St Nicolas) *Guildf 2*   **P** *Bp*   **R** N P NICHOLSON,
C J M G THOMAS,   **NSM** D C FRETT
CRANMER Group   *see* Whatton w Aslockton, Hawksworth,
Scarrington etc *S'well*
CRANMORE, WEST (St Bartholomew)   *see* Shepton Mallet w
Doulting *B & W*
CRANOE (St Michael)   *see* Welham, Glooston and Cranoe and
Stonton Wyville *Leic*
CRANSFORD (St Peter)   *see* Upper Alde *St E*
CRANSLEY (St Andrew)   *see* Broughton w Loddington and
Cransley etc *Pet*
CRANTOCK (St Carantoc)   *see* Perranzabuloe and Crantock w
Cubert *Truro*
CRANWELL (St Andrew) *Linc 21*   **P** *DBP*
P-in-c C PENNOCK
CRANWICH (St Mary) *Nor 13*   **P** *CPAS*   **R** *vacant*
CRANWORTH (St Mary the Virgin)   *see* Barnham Broom and
Upper Yare *Nor*
CRASSWALL (St Mary)   *see* Clodock and Longtown w
Craswall, Llanveynoe etc *Heref*
CRASTER (Mission Church)   *see* Embleton w Rennington and
Rock *Newc*
CRATFIELD (St Mary)   *see* Laxfield, Cratfield, Wilby and
Brundish *St E*
CRATHORNE (All Saints) *York 20*   **P** *Lord Crathorne*
R P J SANDERS,   **Hon C** A J HUTCHINSON
CRAWCROOK (Church of the Holy Spirit)   *see* Greenside *Dur*
CRAWFORD (District Church)   *see* Upholland *Liv*
CRAWLEY (St John the Baptist) *Chich 7*   **P** *Bp*
TR M D LILES,   **TV** F J M POLE, S J MURRAY,   **C** J M BALDWIN,
NSM F A HENDRY
CRAWLEY (St Mary)   *see* Downs Benefice *Win*

CRAWLEY, NORTH (St Firmin) *see* Sherington w Chicheley, N Crawley, Astwood etc *Ox*

CRAWLEY DOWN (All Saints) *Chich 7* **P** *R Worth*
V A J HALE

CRAWSHAWBOOTH (St John) *see* Goodshaw and Crawshawbooth *Man*

CRAY (St Barnabas) *see* St Paul's Cray St Barn *Roch*

CRAY (St Mary and St Paulinus) *see* St Mary Cray and St Paul's Cray *Roch*

CRAY, NORTH (St James) *see* Footscray w N Cray *Roch*

CRAYFORD (St Paulinus) *Roch 15* **P** *Bp* **R** A K LANE, **C** J P WATTS, **NSM** S CORRY

CRAYKE (St Cuthbert) w Brandsby and Yearsley *York 3* **P** *The Crown and Abp (alt)* **R** I B KITCHEN

CRAZIES HILL (Mission Room) *see* Wargrave w Knowl Hill *Ox*

CREAKE, NORTH (St Mary) and SOUTH (St Mary) w Waterden, Syderstone w Barmer and Sculthorpe *Nor 15* **P** *Bp, Earl Spencer, Earl of Leicester, Guild of All So, J Labouchere Esq, Mrs M E Russell, and DBP (jt)* **R** *vacant (01328) 823433*

CREATON, GREAT (St Michael and All Angels) *see* Guilsborough and Hollowell and Cold Ashby etc *Pet*

CREDENHILL (St Mary) Brinsop and Wormsley, Mansel Lacy and Yazor, Kenchester, Bridge Sollers and Bishopstone *Heref 3* **P** *R M Ecroyd Esq, Major D J C Davenport and Bp (3 turns), Ld Chan (1 turn)* **NSM** A C DEANE

CREDITON (Holy Cross) (St Lawrence) Shobrooke and Sandford w Upton Hellions *Ex 2* **P** *12 Govs of Crediton Ch* **R** N GUTHRIE, **C** C R CARLYON, D J A DOBLE

CREECH ST MICHAEL (St Michael) and Ruishton w Thornfalcon *B & W 17* **P** *Bp, MMCET, and Dr W R C Batten (jt)* **V** R S HARRIS

CREED (St Crida) *see* Probus, Ladock and Grampound w Creed and St Erme *Truro*

CREEDY, NORTH: Cheriton Fitzpaine, Woolfardisworthy, Kennerley, Washford Pyne, Puddington, Poughill, Stockleigh English, Morchard Bishop, Stockleigh Pomeroy, Down St Mary, Clannaborough, Lapford, Nymet Rowland, and Coldridge *Ex 2* **P** *Ld Chan (1 turn), Patr Bd (5 turns)* **TR** S G C SMITH, **TV** L C STARRS, **NSM** K J CROSS

CREEKMOOR (Christ Church) *see* N Poole Ecum Team *Sarum*

CREEKSEA (All Saints) *Chelmsf 11* **P** *Bp* **P-in-c** V M WADMAN

CREETING (St Peter) *see* Creeting St Mary, Creeting St Peter etc *St E*

CREETING ST MARY (St Mary), Creeting St Peter and Earl Stonham w Stonham Parva *St E 1* **P** *DBP (2 turns), Pemb Coll Cam (1 turn)* **P-in-c** C M EVERETT, **OLM** B J GALLAGHER

CREETON (St Peter) *see* Castle Bytham w Creeton *Linc*

CREGNEISH (St Peter) *see* Rushen *S & M*

CRESSAGE (Christ Church) *see* Wenlock *Heref*

CRESSBROOK (St John the Evangelist) *see* Tideswell *Derby*

CRESSING (All Saints) w Stisted and Bradwell-juxt-Coggeshall and Pattiswick *Chelmsf 15* **P** *Bp, Exors Mrs D E G Keen, and Abp (by turn)* **P-in-c** R V SAMS

CRESSINGHAM, GREAT (St Michael) and LITTLE (St Andrew), w Threxton *Nor 13* **P** *Bp and Sec of State for Defence* **C** D J HANWELL

CRESSWELL (St Bartholomew) and Lynemouth *Newc 11* **P** *Bp* **V** A E SIMPSON

CRESWELL (St Mary Magdalene) *see* Elmton *Derby*

CRETINGHAM (St Peter) *see* Mid Loes *St E*

CREWE (All Saints and St Paul) (St Peter) *Ches 15* **P** *Bp* **V** S J CLAPHAM, **C** J J WISE

CREWE (Christ Church) *Ches 15* **P** *Bp* **P-in-c** W J BAKER, **NSM** H RUGMAN

CREWE (St Andrew w St John the Baptist) *Ches 15* **P** *Bp* **V** W J BAKER, **NSM** H RUGMAN

CREWE (St Barnabas) *Ches 15* **P** *Bp* **V** R D POWELL

CREWE GREEN (St Michael and All Angels) *see* Haslington w Crewe Green *Ches*

CREWKERNE (St Bartholomew) *see* Wulfric Benefice *B & W*

CREWTON (St Peter) *see* Boulton *Derby*

CRICH (St Mary) and South Wingfield *Derby 1* **P** *Ch Trust Fund Trust and Duke of Devonshire (jt)* **V** P D BROOKS, **NSM** J W GRAY, A J REDSHAW, D HIGGON

CRICK (St Margaret) and Yelvertoft w Clay Coton and Lilbourne *Pet 2* **P** *MMCET and St Jo Coll Ox (jt)* **R** D M LAKE

CRICKET MALHERBIE (St Mary Magdalene) *see* Chaffcombe, Cricket Malherbie etc *B & W*

CRICKET ST THOMAS (St Thomas) *see* Chard Gd Shep and Cricket St Thomas *B & W*

CRICKLADE (St Sampson) w Latton *Bris 6* **P** *D&C, Bp, and Hon P N Eliot (by turn)* **P-in-c** J A S ASHBY, **NSM** S E DANBY

CRICKLEWOOD (St Gabriel) and St Michael *Lon 21* **P** *Bp* **V** J E MORRIS

CRICKLEWOOD (St Peter) *Lon 15* **P** *Bp* **P-in-c** K G M HILTON-TURVEY

CRIFTINS (St Matthew) w Dudleston and Welsh Frankton *Lich 17* **P** *Bp and V Ellesmere (jt)* **P-in-c** S C AIREY, **OLM** K E DAVIES

CRIMPLESHAM (St Mary) *see* Downham Market and Crimplesham w Stradsett *Ely*

CRINGLEFORD (St Peter) and Colney *Nor 7* **P** *Exors E H Barclay Esq and Gt Hosp Nor (alt)* **R** H D BUTCHER, **C** H L CRACKNELL

CROCKENHILL (All Souls) *Roch 2* **P** *Bp* **P-in-c** N J BUNKER

CROCKERNWELL (Holy Trinity) *see* Tedburn St Mary, Cheriton Bishop, Whitestone etc *Ex*

CROCKHAM HILL (Holy Trinity) *Roch 11* **P** *J St A Warde Esq* **P-in-c** S A J MITCHELL, **C** R JONES

CROFT (All Saints) *see* The Wainfleet Gp *Linc*

CROFT (Christ Church) *see* Newchurch w Croft *Liv*

CROFT (St Michael and All Angels) *see* Leominster *Heref*

CROFT (St Michael and All Angels) *see* Broughton Astley and Croft w Stoney Stanton *Leic*

CROFT (St Peter) *see* E Richmond *Ripon*

CROFTON (All Saints) *Wakef 11* **P** *Duchy of Lanc* **NSM** H WALKER, **OLM** A JORDAN

CROFTON (Holy Rood) (St Edmund) *Portsm 2* **P** *Bp* **V** S P GIRLING, **NSM** C R PRESTIDGE, K A MACFARLANE

CROFTON (St Paul) *Roch 16* **P** *V Orpington* **V** B A ABAYOMI-COLE, **C** C A BREWER

CROFTON PARK (St Hilda w St Cyprian) *S'wark 5* **P** *V Lewisham St Mary* **V** S G BATES

CROGLIN (St John the Baptist) *Carl 2* **P** *D&C* **P-in-c** D A CRAVEN, **NSM** A MAGUIRE

CROMER (St Peter and St Paul) *Nor 21* **P** *CPAS* **V** D E COURT, **C** D G FREDERICK, **OLM** P E NEALE

CROMFORD (St Mary) *see* Matlock Bath and Cromford *Derby*

CROMHALL (St Andrew), Tortworth, Tytherington, Falfield and Rockhampton *Glouc 5* **P** *Bp, R Thornbury and Oldbury etc, Adn, and J Leigh Esq (1 turn), Earl of Ducie, Oriel Coll Ox, and MMCET (1 turn)* **C** J A D'ESTERRE

CROMPTON (Holy Trinity) *see* Royton St Paul and Shaw *Man*

CROMPTON, EAST (St James) *Man 15* **P** *Bp* **P-in-c** L CONNOLLY, **OLM** W H MOSTON

CROMPTON, HIGH (St Mary) *Man 15* **P** *Bp* **P-in-c** A BUTLER, **C** C L ROTERS

CROMPTON FOLD (St Saviour) *see* E Crompton *Man*

CROMWELL (St Giles) *see* Norwell w Ossington, Cromwell and Caunton *S'well*

CRONDALL (All Saints) and Ewshot *Guildf 3* **P** *Bp* **V** K E HUTCHINSON, **NSM** B D BURBIDGE, S M R CUMMING-LATTEY

CROOK (St Catherine) *Carl 10* **P** *CPAS* **C** M F J ALLEN, **NSM** M L WOODCOCK, B J CROWE

CROOK (St Catherine) *Dur 9* **P** *R Brancepeth* **P-in-c** V T FENTON

CROOK PEAK *B & W 1* **P** *Ld Chan, Bp, Bp Lon, and R M Dod Esq (by turn)* **R** K R BROWN

CROOKES (St Thomas) *Sheff 4* **P** *Patr Bd* **TR** M WOODHEAD, **C** N J HAIGH

CROOKES (St Timothy) *Sheff 4* **P** *Sheff Ch Burgesses* **V** P R TOWNSEND, **NSM** S E WALSH

CROOKHAM (Christ Church) *Guildf 1* **P** *V Crondall and Ewshot* **V** M S NICHOLLS, **NSM** D J MISTLIN

CROOKHORN (Good Shepherd) *Portsm 5* **P** *Simeon's Trustees* **V** J D NAUDE, **NSM** D M YOUELL

CROPREDY (St Mary the Virgin) *see* Shires' Edge *Ox*

CROPTHORNE (St Michael) *see* Fladbury, Hill and Moor, Wyre Piddle etc *Worc*

CROPTON (St Gregory) *see* Lastingham w Appleton-le-Moors, Rosedale etc *York*

CROPWELL BISHOP (St Giles) w Colston Bassett, Granby w Elton, Langar cum Barnstone and Tythby w Cropwell Butler *S'well 8* **P** *CPAS and Bp, Ld Chan (alt)* **R** E B GAMBLE

CROSBY (St George) (St Michael) *Linc 4* **P** *Sir Reginald Sheffield Bt* **V** J W THACKER

CROSBY, GREAT (All Saints) *Liv 5* **P** *R Sefton, Bp, V St Luke, and CPAS (jt)* **P-in-c** M C FREEMAN

CROSBY, GREAT (St Faith) and Waterloo Park St Mary the Virgin *Liv 1* **P** *St Chad's Coll Dur and Trustees (jt)* **V** N G KELLEY, **Hon C** D A SMITH, **NSM** D A MCDOUGALL

CROSBY, GREAT (St Luke) *Liv 5*   **P** *R Sefton*
P-in-c P H SPIERS,   **C** S M ELLIOTT,   **OLM** B A CHAMBERS
CROSBY GARRETT (St Andrew) *see Kirkby Stephen w Mallerstang etc Carl*
CROSBY-ON-EDEN (St John the Evangelist) *see Eden, Gelt and Irthing Carl*
CROSBY RAVENSWORTH (St Lawrence) *Carl 1*   **P** *DBP*
P-in-c S J FYFE
CROSCOMBE (Blessed Virgin Mary) *see Pilton w Croscombe, N Wootton and Dinder B & W*
CROSLAND, SOUTH (Holy Trinity) *see Em TM Wakef*
CROSLAND MOOR (St Barnabas) and Linthwaite *Wakef 5*
  P *Bp and R Almondbury (jt)*   **C** J M HONEYMAN
CROSS CANONBY (St John the Evangelist) *see Allonby, Cross Canonby and Dearham Carl*
CROSS FELL Group, The *Carl 4*   **P** *D&C (2 turns) and DBP (1 turn)*   **V** R A MOATT,   **NSM** S J BAMPING
CROSS GREEN (St Hilda) *see Hunslet w Cross Green Ripon*
CROSS GREEN (St Saviour) *see Leeds Richmond Hill Ripon*
CROSS HEATH (St Michael and All Angels) *Lich 9*   **P** *Bp*
  V D J LLOYD
CROSS IN HAND (St Bartholomew) *see Waldron Chich*
CROSS ROADS cum Lees (St James) *Bradf 8*   **P** *Bp*
P-in-c P MAYO-SMITH,   **NSM** P S WILSON
CROSS STONE (St Paul) *see Todmorden Wakef*
CROSS TOWN (St Cross) *see Knutsford St Cross Ches*
CROSSCRAKE (St Thomas) *Carl 10*   **P** *V Heversham and Milnthorpe*   **P-in-c** I J E SWIFT,   **NSM** D A PRESTON
CROSSENS (St John) *see N Meols Liv*
CROSSFLATTS (St Aidan) *see Bingley All SS Bradf*
CROSSLACON Team Ministry *Carl 5*   **P** *Patr Bd*
  TR J E CURTIS,   **TV** P F TURNBULL
CROSSPOOL (St Columba) *Sheff 4*   **P** *Bp*
P-in-c F M ECCLESTON,   **NSM** L A FURBEY
CROSTHWAITE (St Kentigern) Keswick *Carl 6*   **P** *Bp*
  V A S E PENNY,   **C** M F J ALLEN
CROSTHWAITE (St Mary) Kendal *Carl 10*   **P** *DBP*
P-in-c M D WOODCOCK,   **NSM** M L WOODCOCK, B J CROWE
CROSTON (St Michael and All Angels) and Bretherton *Blackb 4*
  P *M G Rawstorne Esq*   **P-in-c** D J REYNOLDS
CROSTWICK (St Peter) *see Horsham St Faith, Spixworth and Crostwick Nor*
CROSTWIGHT (All Saints) *see Smallburgh w Dilham w Honing and Crostwight Nor*
CROUCH END HILL (Christ Church) *see Hornsey Ch Ch Lon*
CROUGHTON (All Saints) *see Aynho and Croughton w Evenley etc Pet*
CROWAN (St Crewenna) and Treslothan *Truro 2*
  P *D L C Roberts Esq and Mrs W A Pendarves (jt)*
  V P DOUGLASS,   **C** M L PASCOE
CROWBOROUGH (All Saints) *Chich 19*   **P** *Ld Chan*
  V A C J CORNES,   **C** J P FRITH, R A EVANS,   **NSM** J A HOBBS
CROWBOROUGH (St John the Evangelist) *Chich 19*   **P** *Guild of All So*   **P-in-c** R J NORBURY
CROWCOMBE (Holy Ghost) *see Quantock Towers B & W*
CROWELL (Nativity of the Blessed Virgin Mary) *see Chinnor, Sydenham, Aston Rowant and Crowell Ox*
CROWFIELD (All Saints) w Stonham Aspal and Mickfield *St E 1*   **P** *DBP, Bp, and Lord de Saumarez (alt)*
P-in-c T P HALL,   **OLM** H NORRIS
CROWHURST (St George) *see Catsfield and Crowhurst Chich*
CROWHURST (St George) *see Lingfield and Crowhurst S'wark*
CROWLAND (St Mary and St Bartholomew and St Guthlac) *Linc 17*   **P** *Earl of Normanton*   **P-in-c** C H BROWN
CROWLE Group, The (St Oswald) *Linc 1*   **P** *Bp (2 turns), Prime Min (1 turn)*   **P-in-c** T D BUCKLEY,   **OLM** M STONIER
CROWLE (St John the Baptist) *see Bowbrook S Worc*
CROWMARSH GIFFORD (St Mary Magdalene) *see Wallingford Ox*
CROWN EAST AND RUSHWICK (St Thomas) *see Worc Dines Green St Mich and Crown E, Rushwick Worc*
CROWNHILL (Ascension) *see Plymouth Crownhill Ascension Ex*
CROWTHORNE (St John the Baptist) *Ox 16*   **P** *Bp*
  V L M CORNWELL
CROWTON (Christ Church) *see Norley, Crowton and Kingsley Ches*
CROXALL-CUM-OAKLEY (St John the Baptist) *see Walton-on-Trent w Croxall, Rosliston etc Derby*
CROXBY (All Saints) *see Swallow Linc*
CROXDALE (St Bartholomew) and Tudhoe *Dur 6*   **P** *D&C*
P-in-c G NORMAN
CROXDEN (St Giles) *see Rocester and Croxden w Hollington Lich*
CROXLEY GREEN (All Saints) *St Alb 4*   **P** *V Rickmansworth*
P-in-c M R MUGAN,   **NSM** M P L KINGSLEY

CROXLEY GREEN (St Oswald) *St Alb 4*   **P** *Bp*
P-in-c R J RILEY-BRALEY
CROXTETH (St Paul) *Liv 8*   **P** *R W Derby and Bp (jt)*
  V I G BROOKS
CROXTETH PARK (St Cuthbert) *Liv 8*   **P** *Bp*   **V** A PRINCE
CROXTON (All Saints) *see Thetford Nor*
CROXTON Group, The SOUTH (St John the Baptist) *Leic 2*
  P *DBP, Ch Soc Trust, and MMCET (jt)*   **P-in-c** S LEIGHTON,
  NSM A R LEIGHTON
CROXTON (St James) *see Papworth Ely*
CROXTON (St John the Evangelist) *Linc 6*   **P** *Ld Chan*
  R *vacant*
CROXTON (St Paul) *see Ashley and Mucklestone and Broughton and Croxton Lich*
CROXTON KERRIAL (St Botolph and St John the Baptist) *see High Framland Par Leic*
CROYDE (St Mary Magdalene) *see Georgeham Ex*
CROYDON (All Saints) *see Orwell Gp Ely*
CROYDON (Christ Church) Broad Green *S'wark 20*
  P *Simeon's Trustees*   **V** W MUNCEY,   **OLM** K H VEEN
CROYDON (Holy Saviour) *S'wark 21*   **P** *Bp*
  V X SOOSAINAYAGAM
CROYDON (St Andrew) *S'wark 20*   **P** *Trustees*
P-in-c K L W SYLVIA
CROYDON (St John the Baptist) *S'wark 20*   **P** *Abp*
  V C J L BOSWELL,   **C** K L A FARRELL, T GOODE, P VOWLES,
  S J H GOATCHER
CROYDON (St Mary Magdalene) *see Addiscombe St Mary Magd w St Martin S'wark*
CROYDON (St Matthew) *S'wark 20*   **P** *V Croydon*
  V S J D FOSTER,   **NSM** R A HINDER
CROYDON (St Michael and All Angels w St James) *S'wark 20*
  P *Trustees*   **V** D P MINCHEW
CROYDON Woodside (St Luke) *S'wark 21*   **P** *Bp*
  V N C GOLDING,   **NSM** J C YEARWOOD
CROYDON, SOUTH (Emmanuel) *S'wark 20*   **P** *Ch Trust Fund Trust*   **V** T A MAPSTONE,   **C** B C SHEPHERD
CROYDON, SOUTH (St Peter) (St Augustine) *S'wark 20*
  P *V Croydon and Bp (jt)*   **V** W F WARREN,   **NSM** L M FOX
CROYLAND (St Mary and St Bartholomew and St Guthlac) *see Crowland Linc*
CRUDGINGTON (St Mary Mission Church) *see Wrockwardine Deanery Lich*
CRUDWELL (All Saints) *see Ashley, Crudwell, Hankerton and Oaksey Bris*
CRUMPSALL (St Matthew w St Mary) *Man 4*   **P** *Bp*
  R J M WARE
CRUMPSALL, LOWER (St Thomas) w Cheetham St Mark *Man 4*   **P** *Bp*   **V** *vacant* 0161-792 3123
CRUNDALE (St Mary the Blessed Virgin) w Godmersham *Cant 2*   **P** *Abp*   **P-in-c** I G CAMPBELL
CRUWYS MORCHARD (Holy Cross) *see Washfield, Stoodleigh, Withleigh etc Ex*
CRUX EASTON (St Michael and All Angels) *see NW Hants Win*
CUBBINGTON (St Mary) *Cov 11*   **P** *Bp*   **V** *vacant* (01926) 423056
CUBERT (St Cubert) *see Perranzabuloe and Crantock w Cubert Truro*
CUBLEY (St Andrew) *see S Dales Derby*
CUBLINGTON (St Nicholas) *see Wingrave w Rowsham, Aston Abbotts and Cublington Ox*
CUCKFIELD (Holy Trinity) *Chich 6*   **P** *Bp*
  V N G WETHERALL,   **C** S J HALL
CUCKLINGTON (St Lawrence) *see Charlton Musgrove, Cucklington and Stoke Trister B & W*
CUDDESDON (All Saints) *see Wheatley Ox*
CUDDINGTON (St Mary) *Guildf 9*   **P** *Bp*   **V** A K SILLIS,
  OLM C M WHITE
CUDDINGTON (St Nicholas) *see Haddenham w Cuddington, Kingsey etc Ox*
CUDHAM (St Peter and St Paul) and Downe *Roch 16*
  P *Ch Soc Trust and Bp (jt)*   **V** W J MUSSON,
P-in-c E H HESELWOOD
CUDWORTH (St John) *Wakef 7*   **P** *Bp*   **V** D NICHOLSON
CUDWORTH (St Michael) *see Winsmoor B & W*
CUFFLEY (St Andrew) *see Northaw and Cuffley St Alb*
CULBONE (St Beuno) *see Oare w Culbone B & W*
CULFORD (St Mary) *see Lark Valley St E*
CULGAITH (All Saints) *see Cross Fell Gp Carl*
CULHAM (St Paul) *see Dorchester Ox*
CULLERCOATS (St George) *Newc 5*   **P** *Duke of Northumberland*   **V** A J HUGHES,   **C** G M SHORT,
  NSM J R A SERGEANT
CULLERCOATS (St Paul) *see Tynemouth Cullercoats St Paul Newc*

CULLINGWORTH (St John the Evangelist) *Bradf 8*   **P** *Bp*
  P-in-c S R EVANS,   **C** S MCCARTER,   **NSM** E MOY
CULLOMPTON (St Andrew) (Langford Chapel), Willand,
  Uffculme, Kentisbeare, and Blackborough *Ex 4*   **P** *Patr Bd*
  TV R S WILKINSON,   **P-in-c** E Q HOBBS,   **C** B L HARDING,
  S C GARNER,   **Hon C** P S THOMAS,   **NSM** L M BARLEY
CULM DAVY (St Mary's Chapel)   *see* Hemyock w Culm Davy,
  Clayhidon and Culmstock *Ex*
CULM VALLEY   *see* Cullompton, Willand, Uffculme,
  Kentisbeare etc *Ex*
CULMINGTON (All Saints)   *see* Ludlow *Heref*
CULMSTOCK (All Saints)   *see* Hemyock w Culm Davy,
  Clayhidon and Culmstock *Ex*
CULPHO (St Botolph)   *see* Gt and Lt Bealings w Playford and
  Culpho *St E*
CULWORTH (St Mary the Virgin) w Sulgrave and Thorpe
  Mandeville and Chipping Warden w Edgcote and Moreton
  Pinkney *Pet 1*   **P** T M Sergison-Brooke Esq, DBP,
  D L P Humfrey Esq, Ch Patr Trust, and Oriel Coll Ox (jt)
  R *vacant* (01295) 760383
CUMBERWORTH (St Helen)   *see* Sutton, Huttoft and Anderby
  Linc
CUMBERWORTH (St Nicholas), Denby and Denby Dale
  Wakef 6   **P** *Bp and V Penistone (jt)*   **P-in-c** G CLAY
CUMDIVOCK (St John)   *see* Dalston w Cumdivock, Raughton
  Head and Wreay *Carl*
CUMMERSDALE (St James)   *see* Denton Holme *Carl*
CUMNOR (St Michael) *Ox 10*   **P** St Pet Coll *Ox*
  V G N MAUGHAN,   **NSM** H A AZER, J PRYCE-WILLIAMS,
  P F M BHUTTA
CUMREW (St Mary the Virgin)   *see* Eden, Gelt and Irthing *Carl*
CUMWHINTON (St John's Hall)   *see* Scotby and Cotehill w
  Cumwhinton *Carl*
CUMWHITTON (St Mary the Virgin)   *see* Eden, Gelt and
  Irthing *Carl*
CUNDALL (St Mary and All Saints)   *see* Kirby-on-the-Moor,
  Cundall w Norton-le-Clay etc *Ripon*
CURBAR (All Saints)   *see* Longstone, Curbar and Stony
  Middleton *Derby*
CURBRIDGE (St Barnabas)   *see* Sarisbury *Portsm*
CURBRIDGE (St John the Baptist)   *see* Witney *Ox*
CURDRIDGE (St Peter) *Portsm 1*   **P** *D&C Win*
  NSM R E SCHOFIELD
CURDWORTH (St Nicholas and St Peter ad Vincula)
  (St George), Middleton and Wishaw *Birm 12*   **P** *Bp*   **R** *vacant*
  (01675) 470384
CURRY, NORTH (St Peter and St Paul)   *see* Athelney *B & W*
CURRY MALLET (All Saints)   *see* Beercrocombe w Curry
  Mallet, Hatch Beauchamp etc *B & W*
CURRY RIVEL (St Andrew) w Fivehead and Swell *B & W 14*
  P *D&C Bris (1 turn), P G H Speke Esq (2 turns)*
  R J M LANGDOWN
CURY (St Corentine) and Gunwalloe *Truro 4*   **P** *Bp*
  P-in-c S O GRIFFITHS
CUSOP (St Mary) w Blakemere, Bredwardine w Brobury,
  Clifford, Dorstone, Hardwicke, Moccas and Preston-on-Wye
  Heref 1   **P** *Bp, D&C, CPAS, MMCET, P M I S Trumper Esq,*
  S Penoyre Esq, and Mrs P Chester-Master (jt)
  R D A R SODADASI,   **Hon C** S F BARNES,
  OLM R R D DAVIES-JAMES
CUSTOM HOUSE (Ascension)   *see* Victoria Docks Ascension
  Chelmsf
CUTCOMBE (St John the Evangelist)   *see* Exton and Winsford
  and Cutcombe w Luxborough *B & W*
CUTSDEAN (St James)   *see* The Guitings, Cutsdean, Farmcote
  etc *Glouc*
CUXHAM (Holy Rood)   *see* Ewelme, Brightwell Baldwin,
  Cuxham w Easington *Ox*
CUXTON (St Michael and All Angels) and Halling *Roch 6*
  P *Bp and D&C (jt)*   **R** R I KNIGHT
CUXWOLD (St Nicholas)   *see* Swallow *Linc*
CWM HEAD (St Michael)   *see* Wistanstow *Heref*
DACRE (Holy Trinity) w Hartwith and Darley w Thornthwaite
  Ripon 3   **P** *Bp, D&C, V Masham and Healey, and*
  Mrs K A Chapman (jt)   **P-in-c** M S EVANS,   **NSM** A J COLLINS
DACRE (St Andrew) *Carl 4*   **P** *Trustees*   **P-in-c** R C PATTISON
DADLINGTON (St James)   *see* Fenn Lanes Gp *Leic*
DAGENHAM (St Martin)   *see* Becontree S *Chelmsf*
DAGENHAM (St Peter and St Paul) *Chelmsf 1*   **P** *Ch Soc Trust*
  V R M REITH,   **C** K J C BUSH
DAGLINGWORTH (Holy Rood)   *see* Brimpsfield w Birdlip,
  Syde, Daglingworth etc *Glouc*
DAGNALL (All Saints)   *see* Kensworth, Studham and
  Whipsnade *St Alb*
DAISY HILL (St James) *Man 9*   **P** *Bp*   **P-in-c** J C BRADING,
  C G A LAWSON

DALBURY (All Saints)   *see* Boylestone, Church Broughton,
  Dalbury, etc *Derby*
DALBY (St James)   *see* Patrick *S & M*
DALBY (St Lawrence and Blessed Edward King)   *see* Partney
  Gp *Linc*
DALBY (St Peter)   *see* Howardian Gp *York*
DALBY, GREAT (St Swithun)   *see* Burrough Hill Pars *Leic*
DALBY, LITTLE (St James)   *as above*
DALBY, OLD (St John the Baptist), Nether Broughton, Saxelbye
  w Shoby, Grimston and Wartnaby *Leic 2*   **P** *Bp, MMCET,*
  V Rothley, and Personal Reps K J M Madocks-Wright Esq (jt)
  V J S HOPEWELL
DALE ABBEY (All Saints)   *see* Stanton-by-Dale w Dale Abbey
  and Risley *Derby*
DALE HEAD (St James)   *see* Long Preston w Tosside *Bradf*
DALHAM (St Mary), Gazeley, Higham, Kentford and Moulton
  St E 11   **P** *Bp (2 turns), Ch Coll Cam (1 turn),*
  C E L Philipps Esq (1 turn), and D W Barclay Esq (1 turn)
  V S J MITCHELL
DALLAM (St Mark) *Liv 12*   **P** *R Warrington and Bp (jt)*
  V P J MARSHALL
DALLINGHOO (St Mary)   *see* Mid Loes *St E*
DALLINGTON (St Giles)   *see* Brightling, Dallington,
  Mountfield etc *Chich*
DALLINGTON (St Mary) *Pet 4*   **P** *Earl Spencer*
  P-in-c S N MOUSIR-HARRISON
DALLOWGILL (St James)   *see* Fountains Gp *Ripon*
DALSTON (Holy Trinity) w St Philip and Haggerston All Saints
  Lon 5   **P** *Ld Chan and Bp (alt)*   **V** R J HUDSON-WILKIN
DALSTON (St Mark w St Bartholomew) *Lon 5*   **P** *Ch Patr*
  Trust   **V** J ZVIMBA
DALSTON (St Michael) w Cumdivock, Raughton Head and
  Wreay *Carl 3*   **P** *Bp, DBP, and D&C (jt)*   **V** S P CARTER,
  NSM H R CARTER
DALTON (Holy Trinity)   *see* Newburn *Newc*
DALTON (Holy Trinity) *Sheff 6*   **P** *Bp*   **V** M INESON
DALTON (St James)   *see* Gilling and Kirkby Ravensworth *Ripon*
DALTON (St John the Evangelist)   *see* Topcliffe, Baldersby w
  Dishforth, Dalton etc *York*
DALTON (St Michael and All Angels) *Liv 11*   **P** *Bp*
  V T C BARTON
DALTON, NORTH (All Saints)   *see* Woldsburn *York*
DALTON, SOUTH   *see* Dalton le Dale and New Seaham *Dur*
DALTON HOLME (St Mary)   *see* Etton w Dalton Holme *York*
DALTON-IN-FURNESS (St Mary) and Ireleth-with-Askam
  Carl 9   **P** *Bp*   **V** A MITCHELL,   **M** COWAN
DALTON LE DALE (St Andrew) and New Seaham *Dur 2*   **P** *Bp*
  and D&C (alt)   **V** P T HARRISON
DALWOOD (St Peter)   *see* Kilmington, Stockland, Dalwood,
  Yarcombe etc *Ex*
DAMERHAM (St George)   *see* W Downland *Sarum*
DANBURY (St John the Baptist) *Chelmsf 9*   **P** *Lord Fitzwalter*
  R M G BLYTH,   **C** C M BALL
DANBY (St Hilda) w Castleton and Commondale *York 21*
  P *Viscountess Downe*   **V** M J HAZELTON
DANBY WISKE (not known)   *see* E Richmond *Ripon*
DANEHILL (All Saints) *Chich 21*   **P** *Ch Soc Trust*
  V D M HALL,   **C** S G RAE
DANESMOOR (St Barnabas)   *see* N Wingfield, Clay Cross and
  Pilsley *Derby*
DARBY END (St Peter) *Worc 9*   **P** *Bp*   **V** S H CARTER
DARBY GREEN (St Barnabas) and Eversley *Win 5*   **P** *Bp*
  V M W SAUNDERS
DARENTH (St Margaret) *Roch 2*   **P** *D&C*
  P-in-c N L WILLIAMS
DARESBURY (All Saints) *Ches 4*   **P** *D G Greenhall Esq*
  V D R FELIX
DARFIELD (All Saints) *Sheff 12*   **P** *MMCET*   **R** D HILDRED
DARLASTON (All Saints) *Lich 26*   **P** *Simeon's Trustees*
  P-in-c J R BARNETT,   **C** R E INGLESBY
DARLASTON (St Lawrence) *Lich 26*   **P** *Bp and Simeon's*
  Trustees (jt)   **R** E J FAIRLESS,   **C** R E INGLESBY
DARLEY (Christ Church)   *see* Dacre w Hartwith and Darley w
  Thornthwaite *Ripon*
DARLEY (St Helen) *Derby 7*   **P** *Bp*   **R** *vacant* (01629) 734257
DARLEY, SOUTH (St Mary the Virgin), Elton and Winster
  Derby 7   **P** *Bp and DBF (jt)*   **Hon C** J MARSHALL
DARLEY ABBEY (St Matthew)   *see* Allestree St Edm and
  Darley Abbey *Derby*
DARLINGSCOTT (St George)   *see* Tredington and
  Darlingscott *Cov*
DARLINGTON (All Saints)   *see* Blackwell All SS and
  Salutation *Dur*
DARLINGTON (Holy Trinity) *Dur 8*   **P** *Adn Dur*
  P-in-c N J W BARKER

DARLINGTON (St Cuthbert) *Dur 8* **P** *Lord Barnard*
V R J WILLIAMSON
DARLINGTON St Hilda and (St Columba) *Dur 8* **P** *Bp*
P-in-c S C WILLIAMSON, **NSM** D V ROBINSON
DARLINGTON (St James) *Dur 8* **P** *The Crown*
V I L GRIEVES
DARLINGTON (St Mark) w St Paul *Dur 8* **P** *Bp and St Jo Coll*
Dur **V** P A BAKER, **C** P J SMITH
DARLINGTON (St Matthew) and St Luke *Dur 8* **P** *Bp*
P-in-c L M GIBBONS
DARLINGTON, EAST (St John) (St Herbert) *Dur 8*
P *The Crown* **TR** M L DENT, **TV** C M BLAKESLEY,
C L J ROGERS
DARNALL (Church of Christ) *see* Attercliffe and Darnall *Sheff*
DARRINGTON (St Luke and All Saints) *see* Went Valley
Wakef
DARSHAM (All Saints) *see* Yoxmere *St E*
DARTFORD (Christ Church) *Roch 2* **P** *V Dartford H Trin*
V R J MORTIMER
DARTFORD (Holy Trinity) *Roch 2* **P** *Bp* **V** M J HENWOOD
DARTFORD (St Alban) *Roch 2* **P** *V Dartford H Trin*
V C F GILBERT
DARTFORD (St Edmund the King and Martyr) *Roch 2* **P** *Bp*
V *vacant* (01322) 225335 *or* 228984
DARTINGTON (Old St Mary's Church Tower) *see* Totnes w
Bridgetown, Berry Pomeroy etc *Ex*
DARTINGTON (St Mary) *as above*
DARTMOUTH (St Petrox) (St Saviour) and Dittisham *Ex 13*
P *Sir John Seale Bt, DBP, and Bp (jt)*
P-in-c W P G HAZLEWOOD
DARTMOUTH PARK (St Mary) *see* Brookfield St Mary *Lon*
DARTON (All Saints) *Wakef 7* **P** *Bp* **P-in-c** S A REYNOLDS
DARWEN (St Barnabas) *Blackb 2* **P** *Bp* **V** L R COLLINSON
DARWEN (St Cuthbert) w Tockholes St Stephen *Blackb 2* **P** *Bp*
P-in-c D G MOORE
DARWEN (St Peter) *Blackb 2* **P** *Bp and V Blackburn (jt)*
V A HOLLIDAY, **NSM** C GOULD, P A BELSHAW
DARWEN, LOWER (St James) *Blackb 2* **P** *V Blackb*
P-in-c T J HOROBIN
DARWEN, OVER (St James) *Blackb 2* **P** *V Blackb*
P-in-c T N DYER, **NSM** M E CROOK
DASSETT MAGNA (All Saints) *see* Burton Dassett *Cov*
DATCHET (St Mary the Virgin) *see* Colnbrook and Datchet *Ox*
DATCHWORTH (All Saints) *see* Welwyn *St Alb*
DAUBHILL (St George the Martyr) *see* W Bolton *Man*
DAUNTSEY (St James Great) *see* Brinkworth w Dauntsey *Bris*
DAVENHAM (St Wilfrid) *Ches 6* **P** *Bp* **R** M C R CRIPPS,
Hon C M W WALTERS
DAVENTRY (Holy Cross), Ashby St Ledgers, Braunston,
Catesby, Hellidon, Staverton and Welton *Pet 3* **P** *Patr Bd*
TV S R D BROWN, C M E T TREMHTHANMOR, E M COWLEY,
P-in-c M C W WEBBER
DAVIDSTOW (St David) *see* Boscastle w Davidstow *Truro*
DAVINGTON (St Mary Magdalene) *see* The Brents and
Davington w Oare and Luddenham *Cant*
DAVYHULME (Christ Church) *Man 5* **P** *Bp* **P-in-c** R J HILL
DAVYHULME (St Mary) *Man 5* **P** *Bp* **V** C S FORD,
OLM A S JONES
DAWLEY (Holy Trinity) *see* Cen Telford *Lich*
DAWLEY (St Jerome) *see* W Hayes *Lon*
DAWLISH (St Gregory) *Ex 6* **P** *D&C* **P-in-c** S E O CROFT,
C D A BURTON, **NSM** H M BAYS, E P PARKES
DAWLISH WARREN (Church Hall) *see* Kenton, Mamhead,
Powderham, Cofton and Starcross *Ex*
DAYBROOK (St Paul) *S'well 12* **P** *Bp* **P-in-c** S A BAYLIS,
NSM R C STEPHENS
DAYLESFORD (St Peter) *see* Chipping Norton *Ox*
DE BEAUVOIR TOWN (St Peter) *Lon 5* **P** *Bp*
V J F PORTER-PRYCE, **C** F C DYER
DEAL (St Andrew) *Cant 9* **P** *Abp* **V** *vacant* (01304) 374354
DEAL (St George the Martyr) *Cant 9* **P** *Abp* **V** C G SPENCER,
C S PORTER, **OLM** L G APPS-HUGGINS
DEAL (St Leonard) (St Richard) and Sholden w Great
Mongeham *Cant 9* **P** *Abp* **P-in-c** D W FLEWKER,
NSM P T KAVANAGH
DEAL The Carpenter's Arms (extra-parochial place)
Cant 9 vacant
DEAN (All Hallows) *see* The Stodden Churches *St Alb*
DEAN (St Oswald) *see* Clifton, Dean and Mosser *Carl*
DEAN COURT (St Andrew) *see* Cumnor *Ox*
DEAN FOREST (Christ Church) *see* Forest of Dean Ch Ch w
English Bicknor *Glouc*
DEAN FOREST (St Paul) *see* Parkend and Viney Hill *Glouc*
DEAN PRIOR (St George the Martyr) *see* Buckfastleigh w
Dean Prior *Ex*

DEANE (All Saints) *see* N Waltham and Steventon, Ashe and
Deane *Win*
DEANE (St Mary the Virgin) *Man 9* **P** *Patr Bd*
TR T P CLARK, **TV** J G ARMSTRONG, **C** S W BAZELY,
OLM J M DAVIES, E B PLANT
DEANE VALE Benefice, The *B & W 18* **P** *Bp and PCCs*
Heathfield, Hillfarrance, and Oake (jt) **R** A NORRIS
DEANSHANGER (Holy Trinity) *see* Passenham *Pet*
DEARHAM (St Mungo) *see* Allonby, Cross Canonby and
Dearham *Carl*
DEARNLEY (St Andrew) *Man 17* **P** *Bp* **P-in-c** S A JONES,
NSM G D MANCO
DEBDEN (St Mary the Virgin) and Wimbish w Thunderley
Chelmsf 21 **P** *Bp* **P-in-c** H M DAVEY
DEBENHAM (St Mary Magdalene) and Helmingham *St E 18*
P *Ld Chan, Lord Henniker, MMCET, Bp, and Lord Tollemache
(by turn)* **P-in-c** P A W COTTON, **NSM** R J BARNES,
OLM P A R WILKES
DEDDINGTON (St Peter and St Paul) Barford, Clifton and
Hempton *Ox 5* **P** *D&C Windsor and Bp (jt)*
V H R B WHITE, **C** D D INMAN
DEDHAM (St Mary the Virgin) *Chelmsf 17* **P** *Duchy of Lanc
and Lectureship Trustees (alt)* **V** G G MOATE
DEDWORTH (All Saints) *Ox 13* **P** *Bp* **P-in-c** L M BROWN,
C L A J TAYLOR
DEEPCAR (St John the Evangelist) *Sheff 3* **P** *Bp*
P-in-c D B JEANS, **C** H R ISAACSON
DEEPING, WEST (St Andrew) *see* Uffington Gp *Linc*
DEEPING ST JAMES (St James) *Linc 13* **P** *Burghley Ho
Preservation Trust* **P-in-c** J E DONALDSON,
NSM S M C MARSHALL
DEEPING ST NICHOLAS (St Nicholas) *see* Spalding St Jo w
Deeping St Nicholas *Linc*
DEEPLISH (St Luke) and Newbold *Man 17* **P** *Bp*
V P J MAGUMBA
DEERHURST (St Mary) and Apperley w Forthampton,
Chaceley, Tredington, Stoke Orchard and Hardwicke *Glouc 10*
P *Bp, V Longdon, and J S Yorke Esq (jt)* **P-in-c** T E CLAMMER,
NSM C E WHITNEY
DEFFORD (St James) w Besford *Worc 4* **P** *D&C Westmr*
V S K RENSHAW
DEIGHTON (All Saints) *see* Brompton w Deighton *York*
DELABOLE (St John the Evangelist) *see* St Teath *Truro*
DELAMERE (St Peter) *Ches 6* **P** *The Crown*
P-in-c B R K PERKES
DELAVAL (Our Lady) *Newc 1* **P** *Lord Hastings*
V P J BRYARS, **OLM** D R ORMESHER
DEMBLEBY (St Lucia) *see* S Lafford *Linc*
DENABY, OLD (Mission Church) *see* Mexborough *Sheff*
DENABY MAIN (All Saints) *Sheff 7* **P** *Bp* **V** R C DAVIES
DENBURY (St Mary the Virgin) *see* Ipplepen, Torbryan and
Denbury *Ex*
DENBY (St John the Evangelist) *see* Cumberworth, Denby and
Denby Dale *Wakef*
DENBY (St Mary the Virgin) *see* Horsley and Denby *Derby*
DENBY DALE (Holy Trinity) *see* Cumberworth, Denby and
Denby Dale *Wakef*
DENCHWORTH (St James) *see* Hanney, Denchworth and E
Challow *Ox*
DENDRON (St Matthew) *see* Aldingham, Dendron, Rampside
and Urswick *Carl*
DENESIDE (All Saints) *see* Seaham *Dur*
DENFORD (Holy Trinity) *see* Thrapston, Denford and Islip
Pet
DENGIE (St James) w Asheldham *Chelmsf 11* **P** *Bp* **R** *vacant*
DENHAM (St John the Baptist) *see* Hoxne w Denham,
Syleham and Wingfield *St E*
DENHAM (St Mark) (St Mary the Virgin) *Ox 20*
P *L J Way Esq* **R** J A HIRST
DENHAM (St Mary) *see* Barrow *St E*
DENHAM, NEW (St Francis) *see* Denham *Ox*
DENHOLME *Bradf 8* **P** *Bp* **P-in-c** S R EVANS, **NSM** E MOY
DENMARK PARK (St Saviour) *see* Peckham St Sav *S'wark*
DENMEAD (All Saints) *Portsm 5* **P** *Ld Chan*
V S M EDWARDS, **NSM** A C L JOHNSON, S A OSBORNE
DENNINGTON (St Mary) *see* Upper Alde *St E*
DENSHAW (Christ Church) *Man 15* **P** *Bp* **Hon C** G K TIBBO
DENSTON (St Nicholas) *see* Bansfield *St E*
DENSTONE (All Saints) *see* Alton w Bradley-le-Moors and
Denstone etc *Lich*
DENT (St Andrew) w Cowgill *Bradf 6* **P** *Bp and Sidesmen of
Dent (alt)* **V** P J BOYLES, **NSM** C A BROWN
DENTON (Christ Church) *Man 13* **P** *Bp*
P-in-c S A HARRISON
DENTON Dane Bank (St George) *see* Denton Ch Ch *Man*

DENTON (Holy Spirit) *Newc 4* **P** *Bp* **V** J GOODE
DENTON (St Andrew) *see* Harlaxton Gp *Linc*
DENTON (St Helen) *see* Washburn and Mid-Wharfe *Bradf*
DENTON (St Lawrence) *Man 13* **P** *Earl of Wilton*
P-in-c E M POPE
DENTON (St Leonard) w South Heighton and Tarring Neville
Chich 18 **P** *MMCET and Bp (alt)* **R** P J OWEN
DENTON (St Margaret) *see* Yardley Hastings, Denton and
Grendon etc *Pet*
DENTON (St Mary) *see* Ditchingham, Hedenham, Broome,
Earsham etc *Nor*
DENTON (St Mary Magdalene) *see* Elham w Denton and
Wootton *Cant*
DENTON, NETHER (St Cuthbert) *see* Lanercost, Walton,
Gilsland and Nether Denton *Carl*
DENTON HOLME (St James) *Carl 3* **P** *Trustees*
V J R LIBBY
DENVER (St Mary) and Ryston w Roxham and West Dereham
and Bexwell *Ely 9* **P** *G&C Coll Cam and Bp (jt)*
R J M T M GRUNDY
DENVILLE (Christchurch Centre) *see* Havant *Portsm*
DEOPHAM (St Andrew) *see* High Oak, Hingham and Scoulton
w Wood Rising *Nor*
DEPDEN (St Mary the Virgin) *see* Chevington w Hargrave,
Chedburgh w Depden etc *St E*
DEPTFORD Brockley (St Peter) *see* Brockley St Pet *S'wark*
DEPTFORD (St John) (Holy Trinity) (Ascension) *S'wark 2*
P *Patr Bd* **TR** C S BAINBRIDGE, **TV** T A DONNELLY,
NSM E R NEWNHAM
DEPTFORD (St Nicholas) (St Luke) *S'wark 2* **P** *MMCET,
Peache Trustees, and CPAS (jt)*
P-in-c L A J CODRINGTON-MARSHALL, **C** V J YEADON
DEPTFORD (St Paul) *S'wark 2* **P** *Bp* **R** P D BUTLER
DERBY (St Alkmund and St Werburgh) *Derby 9* **P** *Simeon's
Trustees* **V** J M WHITE, **C** J A BURGESS
DERBY (St Andrew w St Osmund) *Derby 10* **P** *Bp*
P-in-c G MARTIN, **NSM** V M HART, J M LYON
DERBY (St Anne) (St John the Evangelist) *Derby 9* **P** *Bp*
V *vacant* (01332) 32681
DERBY (St Augustine) *see* Walbrook Epiphany *Derby*
DERBY (St Barnabas) *Derby 9* **P** *Bp* P-in-c D G HONOUR
DERBY (St Bartholomew) *Derby 10* **P** *Bp* **V** *vacant* (01332)
347709
DERBY (St Luke) *Derby 9* **P** *Bp* **V** G W SILLIS
DERBY (St Mark) *see* Chaddesden St Phil w Derby St Mark
Derby
DERBY (St Paul) *Derby 9* **P** *Bp* P-in-c M S MITTON,
NSM G M WHITE
DERBY (St Peter and Christ Church w Holy Trinity) *Derby 10*
P *CPAS* P-in-c P D MORRIS
DERBY (St Thomas) *see* Walbrook Epiphany *Derby*
DERBY, WEST (Good Shepherd) *Liv 8* **P** *Bp and
R W Derby (jt)* **OLM** S TRAPNELL
DERBY, WEST (St James) (St Mary) *Liv 8* **P** *Bp and
Adn Liv (jt)* **V** J M COLEMAN, **C** P C WETHERELL,
NSM S C LEDBETTER, M A MONTROSE
DERBY, WEST (St John) *Liv 8* **P** *Trustees*
P-in-c S J P FISHER
DERBY, WEST (St Luke) *Liv 2* **P** *Bp* P-in-c A D STOTT
DERBYHAVEN (Chapel) *see* Malew *S & M*
DERBYSHIRE HILL (St Philip) *see* Parr *Liv*
DEREHAM (St Nicholas) and District *Nor 17* **P** *Ld Chan
(2 turns), Patr Bd (1 turn)* **TR** S M THEAKSTON,
TV A F AUBREY-JONES, **C** E C THORNLEY,
NSM K G PILGRIM, **OLM** J L NURSEY
DEREHAM, WEST (St Andrew) *see* Denver and Ryston w
Roxham and W Dereham etc *Ely*
DERRINGHAM BANK (Ascension) (St Thomas) *York 14*
P *Abp* **V** S J WHALEY
DERRINGTON (St Matthew) *see* Bradeley, Church Eaton,
Derrington and Haughton *Lich*
DERRY HILL (Christ Church) *see* Marden Vale *Sarum*
DERSINGHAM (St Nicholas) w Anmer and Shernborne *Nor 16*
P *Ld Chan* **R** M J BROCK
DERWENT, UPPER *Carl 6* **P** *V Keswick St Jo (1 turn),
V Crosthwaite (2 turns)* P-in-c P H VIVASH, **NSM** G E PYE
DERWENT, UPPER *York 19* **P** *Viscountess Downe (1 turn),
Sir Philip Naylor-Leyland (Bt) (1 turn), Abp (2 turns)*
V S G HILL
DERWENT INGS *York 2* **P** *Abp, Lt Col J Darlington, and
Sir Mervyn Dunnington-Jefferson Bt (jt)* **C** C N B MORGAN,
NSM P A BURGESS
DESBOROUGH (St Giles), Brampton Ash, Dingley and
Braybrooke *Pet 9* **P** *Bp, Earl Spencer, and DBP (by turn)*
P-in-c P S SEATON-BURN, **NSM** N M CLARKE, C H WALKER

DESFORD (St Martin) and Peckleton w Tooley *Leic 9*
P *Ld Chan* **R** R G SHARPE
DETHICK (St John the Baptist), Lea and Holloway *Derby 7*
P *Bp, V Crich, and DBF (jt)* **NSM** J D POSTON
DETLING (St Martin) *see* Boxley w Detling *Cant*
DEVER, LOWER *Win 7* **P** *Bp and D&C (jt)* **R** M D BAILEY,
NSM K P KOUSSEFF
DEVER, UPPER *Win 7* **P** *Lord Northbrook (3 turns), Bp
(2 turns)* **V** S A FOSTER
DEVIZES (St John) (St Mary) *Sarum 16* **P** *Ld Chan*
R P RICHARDSON
DEVIZES (St Peter) *Sarum 16* **P** *Bp* P-in-c P J MOSS
DEVONPORT (St Bartholomew) and Ford St Mark *Ex 22*
P *Bp and Trustees (jt)* **V** *vacant* (01752) 562623
DEVONPORT (St Boniface) *see* Devonport St Boniface and
St Phil *Ex*
DEVONPORT (St Boniface) (St Philip) *Ex 22* **P** *Bp*
P-in-c A B SHAW
DEVONPORT (St Budeaux) *Ex 22* **P** *V Plymouth St Andr w
St Paul and St Geo* **V** S J BEACH, **C** G R SHIRLEY
DEVONPORT St Michael (St Barnabas) *Ex 22* **P** *Bp and
Trustees Lord St Levan (jt)* P-in-c T J BUCKLEY
DEVONPORT (St Thomas) *see* Plymouth St Pet and H
Apostles *Ex*
DEVONPORT, NORTH *see* Devonport St Boniface and St Phil
Ex
DEVORAN (St John the Evangelist and St Petroc) *Truro 6*
P *Bp* P-in-c P J KNIBBS, **C** A T NEAL, **Hon
C** D R CARRIVICK, **NSM** H V SPONG, N J POTTER
DEWCHURCH, LITTLE (St David) *see* Heref S Wye *Heref*
DEWCHURCH, MUCH (St David) *see* Wormelow Hundred
Heref
DEWLISH (All Saints) *see* Puddletown, Tolpuddle and
Milborne w Dewlish *Sarum*
DEWSALL (St Michael) *see* Heref S Wye *Heref*
DEWSBURY (All Saints) (St Mark) (St Matthew and St John the
Baptist) *Wakef 10* **P** *Bp, Adn Pontefract, RD Dewsbury, and
Lay Chmn Dewsbury Deanery Syn (jt)* **TR** K PARTINGTON,
TV K ROBERTSON, **C** T R C HINEY, L E SENIOR,
NSM A B POLLARD
DEWSBURY (St Matthew and St John the Baptist)
see Dewsbury *Wakef*
DEWSBURY (All Saints) *as above*
DEWSBURY (St Mark) *as above*
DEWSBURY MOOR (St John the Evangelist) *as above*
DHOON (Christ Church) *see* Maughold *S & M*
DIBDEN (All Saints) *Win 11* **P** *MMCET* **R** J CURRIN,
C S HAYWARD
DIBDEN PURLIEU (St Andrew) *see* Dibden *Win*
DICKER, UPPER (Holy Trinity) *see* Hellingly and Upper
Dicker *Chich*
DICKLEBURGH (All Saints) and The Pulhams *Nor 10*
P *Ld Chan (1 turn), Patr Bd (2 turns), Prime Min (1 turn)*
R J H E ROSKELLY, **NSM** N W STEER, **OLM** P D SCHWIER,
D J ADLAM
DIDBROOK (St George) *see* Winchcombe *Glouc*
DIDCOT (All Saints) *Ox 18* **P** *BNC Ox* P-in-c K M BECK,
C H R BOORMAN, **NSM** A J EDWARDS
DIDCOT (St Peter) *Ox 18* **P** *Bp* P-in-c E J CARTER,
OLM J CARTER
DIDDINGTON (St Laurence) *see* The Paxtons w Diddington
Ely
DIDDLEBURY (St Peter) w Munslow, Holdgate and Tugford
Heref 11 **P** *Bp (3 turns), D&C (1 turn)* **R** I E GIBBS
DIDLINGTON (St Michael) *Nor 13* **P** *CPAS* **V** *vacant*
DIDMARTON (St Lawrence) *see* Boxwell, Leighterton,
Didmarton, Oldbury etc *Glouc*
DIDSBURY (St James) (Emmanuel) *Man 6* **P** *Patr Bd*
TR N J BUNDOCK, **TV** J B EDSON, **C** A L OXBORROW
DIDSBURY, WEST (Christ Church) and Withington
St Christopher *Man 6* **P** *Trustees and Prime Min (alt)*
R A PILKINGTON, **C** A J J DEVADASON
DIGBY GROUP, The (St Thomas of Canterbury) *Linc 21*
P *Mrs H E Gillatt, Ld Chan, and DBP (by turn)*
Hon C D B WOODS
DIGMOOR (Christ the Servant) *see* Upholland *Liv*
DIGSWELL (St John the Evangelist) (Christ the King) and
Panshanger *St Alb 18* **P** *Patr Bd* **TR** C GARNER,
TV D J CATTLE, **NSM** K E SUCKLING, A E COUPER
DILHAM (St Nicholas) *see* Smallburgh w Dilham w Honing
and Crostwight *Nor*
DILHORNE (All Saints) *see* Caverswall and Weston Coyney w
Dilhorne *Lich*
DILSTON (St Mary Magdalene) *see* Corbridge w Halton and
Newton Hall *Newc*

DILTON or LEIGH (Holy Saviour)   *see* White Horse *Sarum*
DILTON MARSH (Holy Trinity)   *as above*
DILWYN AND STRETFORD (St Mary the Virgin)
   see Leominster *Heref*
DINDER (St Michael and All Angels)   *see* Pilton w Croscombe,
   N Wootton and Dinder *B & W*
DINEDOR (St Andrew)   *see* Heref S Wye *Heref*
DINES GREEN (St Michael)   *see* Worc Dines Green St Mich
   and Crown E, Rushwick *Worc*
DINGLEY (All Saints)   *see* Desborough, Brampton Ash,
   Dingley and Braybrooke *Pet*
**DINNINGTON (St Leonard) w Laughton-en-le-Morthen and
   Throapham** *Sheff 5*   **P** *Bp and J C Athorpe Esq (jt)*   **R** *vacant*
   (01909) 562335
DINNINGTON (St Matthew)   *see* Ch the King *Newc*
DINNINGTON (St Nicholas)   *see* Merriott w Hinton,
   Dinnington and Lopen *B & W*
DINSDALE (St John the Baptist) w Sockburn *Dur 8*   **P** *D&C*
   and Sherburn Hosp (alt)   **P-in-c** A J MARTIN
DINTING VALE (Holy Trinity)   *see* Charlesworth and Dinting
   Vale *Derby*
DINTON (St Mary)   *see* Nadder Valley *Sarum*
DINTON (St Peter and St Paul)   *see* Stone w Dinton and
   Hartwell *Ox*
**DIPTFORD (St Mary the Virgin), North Huish, Harberton,
   Harbertonford, Halwell and Moreleigh** *Ex 13*   **P** *Bp and
   D&C (jt)*   **R** J C OUGH,   **C** C M S LUFF, H C JEVONS,
   Hon C B PETTY
DIPTON (St John the Evangelist) and Leadgate *Dur 4*   **P** *Bp*
   V D G HERON
DISCOED (St Michael)   *see* Presteigne w Discoed, Kinsham,
   Lingen and Knill *Heref*
DISEWORTH (St Michael and All Angels)   *see* Kegworth,
   Hathern, Long Whatton, Diseworth etc *Leic*
DISHLEY (All Saints)   *see* Thorpe Acre w Dishley *Leic*
DISLEY (St Mary the Virgin) *Ches 16*   **P** Lord Newton
   V M J OWENS
DISS Heywood (St James the Great)   *see* Diss *Nor*
DISS (St Mary) *Nor 10*   **P** *Bp*   **R** A C BILLETT,   **C** J PARES
DISTINGTON (Holy Spirit) *Carl 7*   **P** *Earl of Lonsdale*
   R *vacant* (01946) 833737
**DITCHINGHAM (St Mary), Hedenham, Broome, Earsham,
   Alburgh and Denton** *Nor 10*   **P** *Abp, Bp, Countess Ferrers,
   J M Meade Esq, and St Jo Coll Cam (jt)*   **R** L BUTLER,
   OLM B L CRAMP, S L CRAMP, R A KIRKPATRICK
DITCHLING (St Margaret), Streat and Westmeston *Chich 9*
   P *Bp*   **R** D P WALLIS
DITTERIDGE (St Christopher)   *see* Box w Hazlebury and
   Ditteridge *Bris*
DITTISHAM (St George)   *see* Dartmouth and Dittisham *Ex*
DITTON (St Basil and All Saints)   *see* Hough Green St Basil and
   All SS *Liv*
DITTON (St Michael) (St Thomas) *Liv 13*   **P** *Bp*
   V L RILEY-DAWKIN,   **OLM** L MOSS
DITTON (St Peter ad Vincula) *Roch 7*   **P** *Ch Trust Fund Trust*
   R J R TERRANOVA,   **NSM** P M PAYNE
**DITTON PRIORS (St John the Baptist) w Neenton, Burwarton,
   Cleobury North, Aston Botterell, Wheathill and Loughton and
   Chetton** *Heref 8*   **P** *Bp, Princess Josephine zu Loewenstein, and
   Exors Viscount Boyne (jt)*   **P-in-c** J N ROWLAND
**DIXTON (St Peter), Wyesham, Bishopswood, Whitchurch and
   Ganarew** *Heref 7*   **P** *Bp (5 turns), Ld Chan (1 turn)*
   V K V CECIL,   **NSM** R J STEPHENS,   **OLM** P A POWDRILL
DOBCROSS (Holy Trinity)   *see* Saddleworth *Man*
DOBWALLS (St Peter)   *see* Liskeard and St Keyne *Truro*
DOCCOMBE (Chapel)   *see* Moretonhampstead, Manaton, N
   Bovey and Lustleigh *Ex*
DOCK (Mission Church)   *see* Immingham *Linc*
DOCKENFIELD (Church of the Good Shepherd)
   see Rowledge and Frensham *Guildf*
DOCKING (St Mary), the Birchams, Stanhoe and Sedgeford
   Nor 16   **P** *Bp, D&C, and Mrs A J Ralli (3 turns), The Crown
   (1 turn)*   **V** P R COOKE
DOCKLOW (St Bartholomew)   *see* Leominster *Heref*
DODBROOKE (St Thomas à Beckett)   *see* Kingsbridge and
   Dodbrooke *Ex*
DODDERHILL (St Augustine)   *see* Droitwich Spa *Worc*
DODDINGHURST (All Saints) *Chelmsf 7*   **P** *Bp*
   P-in-c G FRITH
DODDINGTON (All Saints)   *see* Quantock Coast *B & W*
DODDINGTON (St John)   *see* Wybunbury and Audlem w
   Doddington *Ches*
DODDINGTON (St John the Baptist)   *see* Cleobury Mortimer
   w Hopton Wafers etc *Heref*
DODDINGTON (St John the Baptist), Newnham and Wychling
   Cant 14   **P** *Abp, Adn, and Exors Sir John Croft Bt (jt)*
   NSM R A BIRCH

DODDINGTON (St Mary and St Michael)   *see* Glendale Gp
   Newc
DODDINGTON (St Mary) w Benwick and Wimblington *Ely 11*
   P *Bp, St Jo Coll Dur, and R Raynar Esq (jt)*   **R** *vacant* (01354)
   740692
DODDINGTON (St Peter)   *see* Skellingthorpe w Doddington
   Linc
DODDINGTON, GREAT (St Nicholas) and Wilby *Pet 6*
   P *Exors Lt-Col H C M Stockdale and Ld Chan (alt)*
   P-in-c C J PEARSON
DODDISCOMBSLEIGH (St Michael)   *see* Christow, Ashton,
   Bridford, Dunchideock etc *Ex*
DODFORD (Holy Trinity and St Mary)   *see* Catshill and
   Dodford *Worc*
DODFORD (St Mary the Virgin)   *see* Weedon Bec w Everdon
   and Dodford *Pet*
DODLESTON (St Mary) *Ches 2*   **P** *D&C*   **P-in-c** E H CLARKE
DODWORTH (St John the Baptist) *Wakef 7*   **P** *V Silkston*
   V S P RACE
DOGMERSFIELD (All Saints)   *see* Hartley Wintney,
   Elvetham, Winchfield etc *Win*
DOGSTHORPE (Christ the Carpenter)   *see* Pet Ch Carpenter
   Pet
**DOLPHINHOLME (St Mark) w Quernmore and Over
   Wyresdale** *Blackb 11*   **P** *Bp and V Lanc (jt)*
   P-in-c C J RIGNEY
DOLTON (St Edmund King and Martyr) *Ex 20*   **P** *Ch Soc Trust*
   P-in-c C A BRODRIBB,   **NSM** D J URSELL
DONCASTER (Holy Trinity)   *see* New Cantley *Sheff*
DONCASTER Intake (All Saints) *Sheff 8*   **P** *Bp*   **V** *vacant*
   (01302) 343119
DONCASTER (St George) (St Edmund's Church Centre) *Sheff 8*
   P *Bp*   **V** A P SHACKERLEY,   **C** M J ROWBERRY, J A DAVIS
DONCASTER (St Hugh of Lincoln)   *see* New Cantley *Sheff*
DONCASTER (St James) *Sheff 9*   **P** *Hyndman's Trustees*
   V A MURRAY
DONCASTER (St Jude)   *see* Edlington and Hexthorpe *Sheff*
DONCASTER (St Leonard and St Jude) *Sheff 7*   **P** *The Crown*
   V N J PAY
DONCASTER (St Paul) *Sheff 8*   **P** *Hyndman's
   Trustees and Bp (jt)*   **V** R B RADLEY
DONHEAD ST ANDREW (St Andrew)   *see* St Bartholomew
   Sarum
DONHEAD ST MARY (St Mary the Virgin)   *as above*
DONINGTON (St Cuthbert)   *see* Albrighton, Boningale and
   Donington *Lich*
DONINGTON (St Mary and the Holy Rood) *Linc 20*
   P *Simeon's Trustees*   **P-in-c** D D S DE VERNY
DONINGTON-ON-BAIN (St Andrew)   *see* Asterby Gp *Linc*
DONISTHORPE (St John)   *see* Woodfield *Leic*
DONNINGTON (St George) *Chich 3*   **P** *Bp*   **P-in-c** C R BEARD
DONNINGTON WOOD (St Matthew) *Lich 21*   **P** *Bp*
   P-in-c P M SMITH
DONYATT (Blessed Virgin Mary)   *see* Isle Valley *B & W*
DONYLAND, EAST (St Lawrence)   *see* Fingringhoe w E
   Donyland and Abberton etc *Chelmsf*
**DORCHESTER (St George) (St Mary the Virgin) (St Peter,
   Holy Trinity and All Saints)** *Sarum 1*   **P** *Patr Bd (3 turns),
   Ld Chan (1 turn)*   **TR** H W B STEPHENS,   **TV** V A THURTELL,
   R A BETTS,   **C** P S KING,   **Hon C** J H GOOD,
   NSM G TURNOCK, J M CULLIFORD, R L BASSETT,
   OLM J LACY-SMITH
DORCHESTER (St Peter and St Paul) *Ox 1*   **P** *Patr Bd*
   TR S E BOOYS,   **TV** N A R HAWKES, R M LATHAM,
   C D R CLEUGH, H F CLEUGH,   **NSM** A F ILSLEY,
   OLM D W HAYLETT
DORDON (St Leonard) *Birm 10*   **P** *V Polesworth*
   V A SIMMONS
DORE (Christ Church) *Sheff 2*   **P** *Sir Philip Naylor-Leyland Bt*
   V M J HUNTER
DORKING (St Martin) w Ranmore *Guildf 7*   **P** *Bp*
   NSM D J COWAN,   **OLM** L J TROMBETTI, S V PEACE
DORKING (St Paul) *Guildf 7*   **P** *Ch Patr Trust*   **V** P D BRYER,
   C S M HOAD,   **NSM** J C YELLAND,   **OLM** J A FIRTH
DORMANSLAND (St John) *S'wark 25*   **P** *Bp*   **V** G PADDICK,
   NSM E RANDALL
DORMANSTOWN (All Saints)   *see* Coatham and
   Dormanstown *York*
DORMINGTON (St Peter)   *see* Fownhope w Mordiford,
   Brockhampton etc *Heref*
DORMSTON (St Nicholas)   *see* Inkberrow w Cookhill and
   Kington w Dormston *Worc*
DORNEY (St James the Less)   *see* Eton w Eton Wick, Boveney
   and Dorney *Ox*

DORRIDGE (St Philip) *Birm 6* **P** *Bp* **V** T D HILL-BROWN,
Hon **C** R J HILL-BROWN
DORRINGTON (St Edward) w Leebotwood, Longnor,
Stapleton, Smethcote and Woolstaston *Heref 10* **P** *DBP and*
J J C Coldwell Esq (jt) **R** *vacant* (01743) 718578
DORRINGTON (St James) *see* Digby Gp *Linc*
DORSINGTON (St Peter) *see* Pebworth, Dorsington,
Honeybourne etc *Glouc*
DORSTONE (St Faith) *see* Cusop w Blakemere, Bredwardine w
Brobury etc *Heref*
DORTON (St John the Baptist) *see* Bernwode *Ox*
DOSTHILL (St Paul) *Birm 10* **P** *Bp* **V** J L C SHAW
DOTTERY (St Saviour) *see* Askerswell, Loders, Powerstock and
Symondsbury *Sarum*
DOUGLAS (All Saints) *S & M 2* **P** *Bp*
P-in-c M A M WOLVERSON
DOUGLAS (Christ Church) *Blackb 4* **P** *Bp* **P-in-c** S A GLYNN
DOUGLAS (St George) *S & M 2* **P** *Bp* **V** B SMITH
DOUGLAS (St Matthew the Apostle) *S & M 2* **P** *Bp*
V D WHITWORTH
DOUGLAS (St Ninian) *S & M 2* **P** *CPAS*
P-in-c J P COLDWELL, **NSM** E D MARCHMENT
DOUGLAS (St Thomas the Apostle) *S & M 2* **P** *Bp*
P-in-c I BRADY, **NSM** L BRADY
DOUGLAS-IN-PARBOLD (Christ Church) *see* Douglas
Blackb
DOULTING (St Aldhelm) *see* Shepton Mallet w Doulting
B & W
DOVE HOLES (St Paul) *see* Peak Forest and Dove Holes *Derby*
DOVECOT (Holy Spirit) *Liv 2* **P** *Bp* **P-in-c** J R STOTT
DOVER Buckland Valley (St Nicholas) *see* Buckland-in-Dover
Cant
DOVER (St Martin) *Cant 7* **P** *CPAS* **V** K G GARRETT,
OLM P M DAY
DOVER (St Mary the Virgin) *Cant 7* **P** *Abp, Ld Warden of*
Cinque Ports, and Ld Lt of Kent (jt) **V** D G RIDLEY,
NSM P A GODFREY, S J CAROLAN-EVANS
DOVER (St Peter and St Paul) *see* Charlton-in-Dover *Cant*
DOVERCOURT (All Saints) *see* Harwich Peninsula *Chelmsf*
DOVERDALE (St Mary) *see* Ombersley w Doverdale *Worc*
DOVERIDGE (St Cuthbert) *see* S Dales *Derby*
DOVERSGREEN (St Peter) *see* Reigate St Luke w Doversgreen
S'wark
DOWDESWELL (St Michael) *see* Sevenhampton w Charlton
Abbots, Hawling etc *Glouc*
DOWLAND (St Peter) *see* Iddesleigh w Dowland *Ex*
DOWLES Button Oak (St Andrew) *see* Ribbesford w Bewdley
and Dowles *Worc*
DOWLISHWAKE (St Andrew) *see* Winsmoor *B & W*
DOWN, East (St John the Baptist) *see* Shirwell, Loxhore,
Kentisbury, Arlington, etc *Ex*
DOWN AMPNEY (All Saints) *see* Fairford Deanery *Glouc*
DOWN HATHERLEY (St Mary and Corpus Christi)
see Twigworth, Down Hatherley, Norton, The Leigh etc *Glouc*
DOWN ST MARY (St Mary the Virgin) *see* N Creedy *Ex*
DOWNDERRY (St Nicholas) *see* St Germans *Truro*
DOWNE (St Mary Magdalene) *see* Cudham and Downe *Roch*
DOWNEND (Christ Church) (Church Centre) *Bris 5* **P** *Peache*
Trustees **V** J L VICKERY, **C** P J PETERSON,
Hon **C** J DOBSON
DOWNHAM (St Barnabas) *S'wark 4* **P** *Bp* **V** *vacant*
(020) 8698 4851
DOWNHAM (St Leonard) *see* Chatburn and Downham *Blackb*
DOWNHAM (St Leonard) *see* Ely *Ely*
DOWNHAM (St Luke) *see* Catford (Southend) and Downham
S'wark
DOWNHAM (St Margaret) w South Hanningfield *Chelmsf 9*
P *Bp* **R** S A ROBERTSON, **NSM** M K SEAMAN, J ANDREWS
DOWNHAM, NORTH (St Mark) *see* Catford (Southend) and
Downham *S'wark*
DOWNHAM MARKET (St Edmund) and Crimplesham w
Stradsett *Ely 9* **P** *Bp* **R** J W MATHER, **NSM** A D DAVIES
DOWNHEAD (All Saints) *see* Leigh upon Mendip w Stoke
St Michael *B & W*
DOWNHOLME (St Michael and All Angels) *see* Richmond w
Hudswell and Downholme and Marske *Ripon*
DOWNLEY (St James the Great) *see* High Wycombe *Ox*
DOWNS Benefice, The *Win 3* **P** *Ld Chan (1 turn), Bp and*
Marquess Camden (1 turn) **R** J MONTAGUE, **C** S P RASON,
NSM J A AUSSANT, J BROWN
DOWNS BARN and NEAT HILL (Community Church)
see Stantonbury and Willen *Ox*
DOWNSFOOT *see* Selling w Throwley, Sheldwich w
Badlesmere etc *Cant*
DOWNSHIRE HILL (St John) *see* Hampstead St Jo Downshire
Hill Prop Chpl *Lon*

DOWNSIDE (St Michael's Chapel) *see* E Horsley and Ockham
w Hatchford and Downside *Guildf*
DOWNSWAY (All Souls Worship Centre) *see* Southwick *Chich*
DOWNTON (St Giles) *see* Wigmore Abbey *Heref*
DOWNTON (St Lawrence) *see* Forest and Avon *Sarum*
DOWSBY (St Andrew) *see* Billingborough Gp *Linc*
DOXEY (St Thomas and St Andrew) *see* Castle Town *Lich*
DOXFORD (St Wilfrid) *Dur 16* **P** *Bp* **P-in-c** J MORGAN
DOYNTON (Holy Trinity) *see* Wick w Doynton and Dyrham
Bris
DRAKES BROUGHTON (St Barnabas) *see* Stoulton w
Drake's Broughton and Pirton etc *Worc*
DRAUGHTON (St Augustine) *see* Skipton H Trin *Bradf*
DRAUGHTON (St Catherine) *see* Maidwell w Draughton,
Lamport w Faxton *Pet*
DRAX (St Peter and St Paul) *see* Carlton and Drax *York*
DRAYCOT *Bris 6* **P** *Bp, D&C Sarum, and R W Neeld Esq (jt)*
P-in-c G W HEWITT, **NSM** E M BONE
DRAYCOTT (St Mary) *see* Wilne and Draycott w Breaston
Derby
DRAYCOTT (St Peter) *see* Rodney Stoke w Draycott *B & W*
DRAYCOTT IN THE CLAY (St Augustine) *see* Hanbury,
Newborough, Rangemore and Tutbury *Lich*
DRAYCOTT-LE-MOORS (St Margaret) w Forsbrook *Lich 6*
P *Bp* **R** D C BICKERSTETH, **OLM** J L PRETTY
DRAYTON (Iron Mission Room) *see* Chaddesley Corbett and
Stone *Worc*
DRAYTON (St Catherine) *see* Langport Area *B & W*
DRAYTON (St Leonard and St Catherine) *see* Dorchester *Ox*
DRAYTON (St Margaret) *Nor 2* **P** *Bp* **R** D WELLS,
C D A MCCLEAN
DRAYTON (St Peter) *see* Ironstone *Ox*
DRAYTON (St Peter) Berks *Ox 10* **P** *Bp* **NSM** R BRUCE
DRAYTON, EAST (St Peter) *see* Retford Area *S'well*
DRAYTON, LITTLE (Christ Church) *Lich 18* **P** *V Drayton in*
Hales **P-in-c** H G SNOOK
DRAYTON, WEST (St Martin) *Lon 24* **P** *Bp* **V** O J FIELD
DRAYTON, WEST (St Paul) *see* Retford Area *S'well*
DRAYTON BASSETT (St Peter) *Lich 4* **P** *Bp* **R** H J BAKER,
Hon **C** M R F MACLACHLAN, **NSM** R G DAVIES
DRAYTON-BEAUCHAMP (St Mary the Virgin) *see* Aston
Clinton w Buckland and Drayton Beauchamp *Ox*
DRAYTON IN HALES (St Mary) *Lich 18* **P** *C C Corbet Esq*
P-in-c M P TANNER, **OLM** C SIMPSON
DRAYTON PARSLOW (Holy Trinity) *see* Newton Longville,
Mursley, Swanbourne etc *Ox*
DRESDEN (Resurrection) *see* Blurton and Dresden *Lich*
DREWSTEIGNTON (Holy Trinity) *see* Chagford,
Drewsteignton, Hittisleigh etc *Ex*
DRIFFIELD (St Mary) *see* Fairford Deanery *Glouc*
DRIFFIELD, GREAT (All Saints) and LITTLE (St Peter)
York 10 **P** *Abp* **V** *vacant* (01377) 253394
DRIGG (St Peter) *see* Seascale and Drigg *Carl*
DRIGHLINGTON (St Paul) *Wakef 8* **P** *Bp* **P-in-c** S M ASKEY
DRIMPTON (St Mary) *see* Beaminster Area *Sarum*
DRINGHOUSES (St Edward the Confessor) *York 7* **P** *Abp*
V C W M BALDOCK, **NSM** S M COLLIER
DRINKSTONE (All Saints) *see* Woolpit w Drinkstone *St E*
DROITWICH SPA (St Andrew w St Mary de Witton)
(St Nicholas) (St Peter) (St Richard) *Worc 8* **P** *Bp*
TV D C OWEN, D A CHAPLIN, **NSM** R HOLDEN, A D MORRIS
DRONFIELD (St John the Baptist) w Holmesfield *Derby 5*
P *Ld Chan* **TV** C D I REES, W R EARDLEY, **NSM** R DOVE
DROPMORE (St Anne) *see* Taplow and Dropmore *Ox*
DROXFORD (St Mary and All Saints) *see* Meon Bridge *Portsm*
DROYLSDEN (St Andrew) *Man 13* **P** *Bp*
P-in-c J A HEMSWORTH
DROYLSDEN (St Martin) *Man 13* **P** *Bp*
P-in-c J H FARNWORTH
DROYLSDEN (St Mary) (St John) *Man 13* **P** *Bp*
R A M BAILIE
DRY DODDINGTON (St James) *see* Claypole *Linc*
DRY DRAYTON (St Peter and St Paul) *see* Lordsbridge *Ely*
DRY SANDFORD (St Helen) *see* Wootton and Dry Sandford
Ox
DRYBROOK (Holy Trinity), Lydbrook and Ruardean *Glouc 1*
P *Prime Min and Bp (alt)* **R** N R BROMFIELD,
Hon **C** F H LONG, **OLM** W J CAMMELL
DRYPOOL (St Columba) (St John) *York 14* **P** *Patr Bd*
TR P J F GOODEY, **TV** C J GRUNDY, J V TAYLOR
DUCKLINGTON (St Bartholomew) *Ox 8* **P** *DBP*
P-in-c R J EDY
DUCKMANTON (St Peter and St Paul) *see* Calow and Sutton
cum Duckmanton *Derby*
DUDDENHOE END (The Hamlet Church) *see* Icknield Way
Villages *Chelmsf*

DUDDESTON (St Matthew) *see* Aston and Nechells *Birm*
DUDDINGTON (St Mary) *see* Barrowden and Wakerley w S Luffenham etc *Pet*
DUDDON (St Peter) *see* Tarvin *Ches*
DUDLESTON (St Mary) *see* Criftins w Dudleston and Welsh Frankton *Lich*
DUDLEY (St Andrew) *see* Netherton St Andr *Worc*
DUDLEY (St Augustine) (St Barnabas) (St Francis) (St James) (St Thomas and St Luke) *Worc 9* **P** *Patr Bd* **TV** C M BROWNE, A ST L J WICKENS, J A OLIVER
DUDLEY (St Edmund King and Martyr) *Worc 9* **P** *Bp* **V** *vacant* (01384) 252532
DUDLEY (St John) Kate's Hill *Worc 9* **P** *Bp* **V** *vacant* (01384) 253807
DUDLEY (St Paul) *see* Weetslade *Newc*
DUDLEY WOOD (St John) *Worc 9* **P** *V Netherton* **V** *vacant* (01384) 832164
DUFFIELD (St Alkmund) and Little Eaton *Derby 11* **P** *Patr Bd* **V** M A PICKLES, **C** D E BARNSLEY
DUFTON (St Cuthbert) *see* Heart of Eden *Carl*
DUKINFIELD (St John) (St Alban Mission Church) *Ches 14* **P** *R Stockport St Mary* **V** T J HAYES
DUKINFIELD (St Luke) *Ches 14* **P** *Bp* **P-in-c** D L SCHOFIELD
DUKINFIELD (St Mark) *Ches 14* **P** *Bp* **P-in-c** A C COX
DULCOTE (All Saints) *see* Wells St Cuth w Wookey Hole *B & W*
DULLINGHAM (St Mary) *see* Raddesley Gp *Ely*
DULOE (St Cuby), Herodsfoot, Morval and St Pinnock *Truro 12* **P** *Ld Chan, Ch Soc Trust, and Ball Coll Ox (by turn)* **P-in-c** A C HODGE, **C** A R INGLEBY
DULVERTON (All Saints) w Brushford, Brompton Regis, Upton and Skilgate *B & W 15* **P** *Bp, D&C, Em Coll Cam, and Keble Coll Ox (jt)* **R** J M THOROGOOD, **Hon C** J H GRAY
DULWICH (St Barnabas) *S'wark 9* **P** *Bp* **V** D L GWILLIAMS, **Hon C** A G BUCKLEY
DULWICH (St Clement) St Peter *S'wark 9* **P** *Bp* **V** M E A COULTER, **C** V J HUGHES
DULWICH, EAST (St John the Evangelist) *S'wark 9* **P** *Ripon Coll Cuddesdon* **V** C L J RICHARDSON, **C** H P EGGLESTON, **Hon C** R A SHAW, A MUSODZA, **OLM** A CLARKE
DULWICH, NORTH (St Faith) *S'wark 9* **P** *Bp* **NSM** G T ARNOLD
DULWICH, SOUTH (St Stephen) *S'wark 9* **P** *Dulwich Coll* **V** B G SCHUNEMANN, **C** N D DAVIES
DULWICH, WEST (All Saints) *S'wark 12* **P** *Bp* **V** D J STEPHENSON, **C** M E BOWDEN
DULWICH, WEST (Emmanuel) *S'wark 12* **P** *Bp* **V** K G A ANSAH, **OLM** H O KIMBER
DUMBLETON (St Peter) *see* Winchcombe *Glouc*
DUMMER (All Saints) *see* Farleigh, Candover and Wield *Win*
DUNCHIDEOCK (St Michael and All Angels) *see* Christow, Ashton, Bridford, Dunchideock etc *Ex*
DUNCHURCH (St Peter) *Cov 6* **P** *Bp* **P-in-c** M J GARRATT
DUNCTON (Holy Trinity) *Chich 11* **P** *Lord Egremont* **R** *vacant*
DUNDRY (St Michael) *see* Chew Magna w Dundry, Norton Malreward etc *B & W*
DUNHAM, GREAT (St Andrew) and LITTLE (St Margaret), w Great and Little Fransham and Sporle *Nor 14* **P** *Hertf Coll Ox, Ch Soc Trust, Magd Coll Cam, and DBP (by turn)* **R** *vacant* (01328) 701466
DUNHAM MASSEY (St Margaret) (St Mark) (All Saints) *Ches 10* **P** *J G Turnbull Esq* **V** J J E SUTTON
DUNHAM-ON-THE-HILL (St Luke) *see* Helsby and Dunham-on-the-Hill *Ches*
DUNHAM-ON-TRENT (St Oswald) *see* Retford Area *S'well*
DUNHOLME (St Chad) *see* Welton and Dunholme w Scothern *Linc*
DUNKERTON (All Saints) *see* Timsbury w Priston, Camerton and Dunkerton *B & W*
DUNKESWELL (Holy Trinity) (St Nicholas), Luppitt, Sheldon and Upottery *Ex 5* **P** *MMCET, Bp, and D&C (jt)* **V** *vacant* (01404) 891243
DUNMOW, GREAT (St Mary the Virgin) and Barnston *Chelmsf 18* **P** *Ld Chan (2 turns), CPAS (1 turn)* **R** D S AINGE, **NSM** R DREW, P G TARRIS
DUNMOW, LITTLE (St Mary the Virgin) *see* Felsted and Lt Dunmow *Chelmsf*
DUNNINGTON (not known) *see* Salford Priors *Cov*
DUNNINGTON (St Nicholas) *see* Beeford w Frodingham and Foston *York*
DUNNINGTON (St Nicholas) *York 2* **P** *Abp* **P-in-c** N W R BIRD, **NSM** A C BORTHWICK
DUNS TEW (St Mary Magdalene) *see* Westcote Barton w Steeple Barton, Duns Tew etc *Ox*

DUNSBY (All Saints) *see* Ringstone in Aveland Gp *Linc*
DUNSCROFT (St Edwin) *Sheff 10* **P** *Bp* **P-in-c** J TALLANT
DUNSDEN (All Saints) *see* Shiplake w Dunsden and Harpsden *Ox*
DUNSFOLD (St Mary and All Saints) and Hascombe *Guildf 2* **P** *Bp and SMF (jt)* **P-in-c** P M JENKINS
DUNSFORD (St Mary) *see* Christow, Ashton, Bridford, Dunchideock etc *Ex*
DUNSFORTH (St Mary) *see* Aldborough w Boroughbridge and Roecliffe *Ripon*
DUNSLAND (Mission Church) *see* Ashwater, Halwill, Beaworthy, Clawton etc *Ex*
DUNSLEY (Mission Room) *see* Whitby w Ruswarp *York*
DUNSMORE (Chapel of the Ressurection) *see* Ellesborough, The Kimbles and Stoke Mandeville *Ox*
DUNSOP BRIDGE (St George) *see* Slaidburn *Bradf*
DUNSTABLE (St Augustine of Canterbury) (St Fremund the Martyr) (St Peter) *St Alb 11* **P** *Bp* **TR** R J ANDREWS, **TV** M C HATHAWAY, P M DRAPER, **C** V M GOODMAN
DUNSTALL (St Mary) *see* Barton under Needwood w Dunstall and Tatenhill *Lich*
DUNSTAN (St Leonard) *see* Penkridge *Lich*
DUNSTAN (St Peter) *see* Metheringham w Blankney and Dunston *Linc*
DUNSTER (St George), Carhampton, Withycombe w Rodhuish, Timberscombe and Wootton Courtenay *B & W 15* **P** *Bp* **R** K L BRANT, **NSM** M N ALLSO
DUNSTON (Church House) *see* Newbold w Dunston *Derby*
DUNSTON (St Nicholas) w (Christ Church) *Dur 13* **P** *Bp* **V** D ATKINSON
DUNSTON (St Remigius) *see* Stoke H Cross w Dunston, Arminghall etc *Nor*
DUNSWELL (St Faith's Mission Church) *see* Hull St Jo Newland *York*
DUNTERTON (All Saints) *see* Milton Abbot, Dunterton, Lamerton etc *Ex*
DUNTISBOURNE ABBOTS (St Peter) *see* Brimpsfield w Birdlip, Syde, Daglingworth etc *Glouc*
DUNTISBOURNE ROUS (St Michael and All Angels) *as above*
DUNTON (St Martin) *see* Schorne *Ox*
DUNTON (St Mary Magdalene) w Wrestlingworth and Eyeworth *St Alb 10* **P** *Ld Chan and DBP (alt)* **P-in-c** L C DEW
DUNTON BASSETT (All Saints) *see* Upper Soar *Leic*
DUNWICH (St James) *see* Yoxmere *St E*
DURHAM (St Giles) *Dur 1* **P** *D&C* **V** A B BARTLETT, **C** J E CANDY, **NSM** R A M THOMAS
DURHAM (St Margaret of Antioch) and Neville's Cross St John *Dur 1* **P** *D&C* **R** B T HUISH, **NSM** N C CHATER
DURHAM (St Nicholas) *Dur 1* **P** *CPAS* **V** J S BELLAMY, **C** S V MELLOR, **NSM** D V DAY, P S JOHNSON, C H PATTERSON
DURHAM (St Oswald King and Martyr) and Shincliffe *Dur 1* **P** *D&C* **P-in-c** P Z KASHOURIS, **C** P J REGAN
DURHAM NORTH (St Cuthbert) *Dur 1* **P** *Patr Bd* **TR** R W LAWRANCE, **TV** J THORNS, C A DICK, **C** T E GLOVER, **NSM** O R OMOLE, E STRAFFORD
DURLEIGH (St Hugh) *see* Bridgwater H Trin and Durleigh *B & W*
DURLEY (Holy Cross) *Portsm 1* **P** *Ld Chan* **NSM** R E SCHOFIELD
DURNFORD (St Andrew) *see* Woodford Valley w Archers Gate *Sarum*
DURRINGTON (All Saints) *Sarum 13* **P** *D&C Win* **P-in-c** M T P ZAMMIT, **NSM** R A BUSSEY, T DRAYCOTT
DURRINGTON (St Symphorian) *Chich 5* **P** *Bp* **V** N A TAYLOR
DURSLEY (St James the Great) *Glouc 5* **P** *Bp* **R** J C G BROMLEY, **C** E DENNO, **NSM** I N GARDNER
DURSTON (St John the Baptist) *see* Alfred Jewel *B & W*
DURWESTON (St Nicholas) *see* Pimperne, Stourpaine, Durweston and Bryanston *Sarum*
DUSTON Team, The (St Francis) (St Luke) *Pet 4* **P** *Bp* **TV** A W BAINES, **NSM** H C WILSON, S M COLES
DUSTON, NEW (Mission Church) *see* Duston *Pet*
DUTTON (Licensed Room) *see* Antrobus, Aston by Sutton, Lt Leigh etc *Ches*
DUXFORD (St Peter) w St John *Ely 5* **P** *Bp* **P-in-c** J H MARTIN
DYMCHURCH (St Peter and St Paul) w Burmarsh and Newchurch *Cant 11* **P** *Abp* **R** *vacant* (01303) 872150
DYMOCK (St Mary the Virgin) *see* Redmarley D'Abitot, Bromesberrow, Pauntley etc *Glouc*
DYRHAM (St Peter) *see* Wick w Doynton and Dyrham *Bris*
EAGLE (All Saints) *see* Swinderby *Linc*
EAKRING (St Andrew) *S'well 15* **P** *DBP* **P-in-c** R D SEYMOUR-WHITELEY

EALING (All Saints) *Lon 22* **P** *Bp* **V** N P HENDERSON,
C J D C DODD, **NSM** B E BARNETT-COWAN
EALING (Ascension) *see* Hanger Hill Ascension and W
Twyford St Mary *Lon*
EALING (Christ the Saviour) *Lon 22* **P** *Bp* **V** A F DAVIS
EALING (St Barnabas) *Lon 22* **P** *Bp* **V** D G DEBOYS
EALING (St Mary) *Lon 22* **P** *Bp* **V** S D PAYNTER
EALING (St Paul) *Lon 22* **P** *Bp* **V** M P MELLUISH,
C B D HINGSTON, C FOX
EALING (St Peter) Mount Park *Lon 22* **P** *Bp* **V** M POWELL,
NSM M J JOACHIM, J O A CHOUFAR, N K STEPHENSON
EALING (St Stephen) Castle Hill *Lon 22* **P** *D&C St Paul's*
V S M NEWBOLD, **C** S R MORRIS
EALING, WEST (St John) w St James *Lon 22* **P** *Bp*
V P S MACKENZIE, **C** C M DUNK, S F METRY, S A HITCHINER,
NSM A T RUST
EALING COMMON (St Matthew) *Lon 22* **P** *Bp*
V P G WATKINS
EARBY (All Saints) w Kelbrook *Bradf 7* **P** *Bp* **V** H FIELDEN
EARDISLAND (St Mary the Virgin) *see* Kingsland w
Eardisland, Aymestrey etc *Heref*
**EARDISLEY (St Mary Magdalene) w Bollingham, Willersley,
Brilley, Michaelchurch, Whitney, Winforton, Almeley and
Kinnersley** *Heref 4* **P** *Patr Bd* **R** M J SMALL
EARL SHILTON (St Simon and St Jude) w Elmesthorpe *Leic 10*
P *Bp* **V** G GITTINGS
EARL SOHAM (St Mary) *see* Mid Loes *St E*
EARL STERNDALE (St Michael and All Angels)
see Taddington, Chelmorton and Monyash etc *Derby*
EARL STONHAM (St Mary) *see* Creeting St Mary, Creeting
St Peter etc *St E*
EARLESFIELD (The Epiphany) *see* Grantham, Earlesfield
Linc
EARLESTOWN (St John the Baptist) *see* Newton *Liv*
EARLEY (St Nicolas) *Ox 15* **P** *DBP* **V** N M WARWICK
EARLEY (St Peter) *Ox 15* **P** *DBP* **V** R R D SPEARS,
C M R C THORNE
EARLEY Trinity *Ox 15* **P** *DBP* **P-in-c** J SALMON,
NSM C A MACKRELL
**EARLEY, LOWER Trinity Church Local Ecumenical
Partnership** *Ox 15 vacant*
EARLHAM (St Anne) (St Elizabeth) (St Mary) *Nor 3* **P** *Bp and
Trustees (jt)* **C** D A COUSINS, **OLM** R M A HOUGHTON,
K M BROWN
EARLS BARTON (All Saints) *Pet 6* **P** *DBP* **P-in-c** M J HAYES
EARLS COLNE (St Andrew) *see* Halstead Area *Chelmsf*
EARL'S COURT (St Cuthbert) (St Matthias) *Lon 12*
P *Trustees* **V** J VINE
EARL'S COURT (St Philip) *see* Kensington St Mary Abbots w
Ch Ch and St Phil *Lon*
EARLS CROOME (St Nicholas) *see* Upton-on-Severn, Ripple,
Earls Croome etc *Worc*
EARL'S HEATON *see* Dewsbury *Wakef*
EARL'S HEATON (St Peter) *as above*
EARLSDON (St Barbara) *Cov 3* **P** *Bp* **V** H J WILD
EARLSFIELD (St Andrew) *S'wark 18* **P** *Bp* **V** J BROWN,
NSM V A HACKETT
EARLSFIELD (St John the Divine) *S'wark 18* **P** *Bp*
V C E ROBERTS
EARLY (St Bartholomew) *see* Reading St Luke w St Bart *Ox*
EARNLEY (not known) and East Wittering *Chich 3* **P** *Bp*
(2 turns), Bp Lon (1 turn) **R** S J DAVIES
EARNSHAW BRIDGE (St John) *see* Leyland St Jo *Blackb*
EARSDON (St Alban) and Backworth *Newc 5* **P** *Bp*
V J A FRANCE, **NSM** A B BEESTON
EARSHAM (All Saints) *see* Ditchingham, Hedenham, Broome,
Earsham etc *Nor*
EARSWICK, NEW (St Andrew) *see* Huntington *York*
EARTHAM (St Margaret) *see* Slindon, Eartham and
Madehurst *Chich*
EASBY (Chapel) *see* Gt Ayton w Easby and Newton under
Roseberry *York*
**EASBY (St Agatha) w Skeeby and Brompton on Swale and Bolton
on Swale** *Ripon 2* **P** *Bp* **V** L A CHEETHAM
EASEBOURNE (St Mary), Lodsworth and Selham *Chich 10*
P *Cowdray Trust and Rathbone Trust (jt)* **V** D B WELSMAN,
NSM A M HALLIWELL
EASINGTON (All Saints) *see* Withernsea w Owthorne and
Easington etc *York*
EASINGTON (All Saints) w Liverton *York 16* **P** *Ld Chan*
P-in-c M E GARDNER
EASINGTON (St Hugh) *see* Banbury St Hugh *Ox*
EASINGTON (St Mary) and Easington Colliery *Dur 2* **P** *Bp*
P-in-c C W PEARSON
EASINGTON (St Peter) *see* Ewelme, Brightwell Baldwin,
Cuxham w Easington *Ox*

EASINGTON COLLIERY (The Ascension) *see* Easington and
Easington Colliery *Dur*
EASINGWOLD (St John the Baptist and All Saints) w Raskelf
York 3 **P** *Abp* **V** J HARRISON
EAST *see also under substantive place name*
EAST DEAN (All Saints), Singleton, and West Dean *Chich 13*
P *Bp (2 turns), D&C (1 turn)* **R** R T E B WOODS
EAST DEAN (St Simon and St Jude) w Friston and Jevington
Chich 16 **P** *Duke of Devonshire (1 turn), D&C (2 turns)*
R D A BAKER, **C** A L SMITH
EAST DEAN (St Winifred) *see* Lockerley and E Dean w E and
W Tytherley *Win*
EAST DOWNLAND *Ox 14* **P** *Bp and Adn (jt)*
R J P TOOGOOD, **C** K E STACEY, **NSM** D F BROWN
EAST FERRY (St Mary the Virgin) *see* Scotter w E Ferry *Linc*
**EAST HAM (St Bartholomew) (St Mary Magdalene) w Upton
Park** *Chelmsf 3* **P** *Patr Bd* **TV** Q B D PEPPIATT,
C F B QUIST, **NSM** A R EASTER
EAST HAM (St George and St Ethelbert) *Chelmsf 3* **P** *Bp*
V D T HAOKIP, **NSM** G J ANAN
EAST HAM (St Paul) *Chelmsf 3* **P** *Ch Patr Trust*
V M L PLAYLE, **C** C CHAMBERS
EAST LANE (St Mary) *see* W Horsley *Guildf*
EAST MARSHLAND *Ely 14* **P** *Bp and MMCET (1 turn),
Pemb Coll Cam (2 turns), Prime Min (1 turn), and Ld Chan
(1 turn)* **V** M N DALE, **NSM** B E A PEARMAN
EAST ORCHARD (St Thomas) *see* Shaftesbury *Sarum*
EAST WINCH (All Saints) *see* Gayton, Gayton Thorpe, E
Walton, E Winch etc *Nor*
EASTBOURNE (All Saints) *Chich 16* **P** *Trustees*
V W R LOVATT, **C** N S CORNELL
EASTBOURNE (All Souls) *Chich 16* **P** *Ch Soc Trust*
V M D REDHOUSE
EASTBOURNE (Christ Church) (St Philip) *Chich 16* **P** *Bp and
V Eastbourne (jt)* **C** C R GORING
EASTBOURNE (Holy Trinity) *Chich 16* **P** *V Eastbourne*
V P J COEKIN
EASTBOURNE (St Andrew) *Chich 16* **P** *Bp* **V** D J KING
EASTBOURNE (St Elisabeth) *Chich 16* **P** *Bp*
V D J GILLARD, **NSM** J A PREECE
EASTBOURNE (St John) Meads *Chich 16* **P** *Trustees*
V A M LAMB
EASTBOURNE (St Mary) *Chich 16* **P** *Bp* **V** T O MENDEL,
C N P HAIGH, **NSM** H F POWNALL
EASTBOURNE (St Michael and All Angels) Ocklynge *Chich 16*
P *V Eastbourne* **V** S T MATTAPALLY
EASTBOURNE (St Richard of Chichester) *see* Langney *Chich*
EASTBOURNE (St Saviour and St Peter) *Chich 16* **P** *Keble
Coll Ox* **V** J T GUNN
EASTBOURNE The Haven *see* The Haven CD *Chich*
EASTBURY (St James the Great) and East Garston *Ox 14*
P *Bp and Ch Ch Ox (alt)* **P-in-c** A W CUMBERLIDGE
EASTCHURCH (All Saints) w Leysdown and Harty *Cant 15*
P *Abp and Keble Coll Ox (jt)* **NSM** B BIRCH
EASTCOMBE (St Augustine) *see* Bussage *Glouc*
EASTCOTE (St Lawrence) *Lon 24* **P** *Bp* **V** S DANDO
**EASTER, HIGH (St Mary the Virgin) and Good Easter w
Margaret Roding** *Chelmsf 18* **P** *Bp Lon, Trustees
R K Shepherd Esq, and D&C St Paul's (by turn)* **R** *vacant*
(01245) 231429
EASTERGATE (St George) *see* Aldingbourne, Barnham and
Eastergate *Chich*
EASTERN GREEN (St Andrew) *Cov 3* **P** *R Allesley*
P-in-c G P SMITH
EASTERTON (St Barnabas) *see* The Lavingtons, Cheverells,
and Easterton *Sarum*
EASTFIELD (Holy Nativity) *see* Cayton w Eastfield *York*
EASTGATE (All Saints) *see* Upper Weardale *Dur*
**EASTHAM (St Mary the Blessed Virgin) (St Peter's Chapel)
(Chapel of the Holy Spirit)** *Ches 9* **P** *D&C* **V** E A GLOVER,
C S E BURTON, **NSM** M Q COATS
EASTHAM (St Peter and St Paul) *see* Teme Valley S *Worc*
EASTHAMPSTEAD (St Michael and St Mary Magdalene)
Ox 11 **P** *Ch Ch Ox* **R** G S COLE, **C** K A SLADEN,
R R STACEY, P M BESTLEY
EASTHOPE (St Peter) *see* Wenlock *Heref*
EASTHORPE (St Mary the Virgin) *see* Copford w Easthorpe
and Messing w Inworth *Chelmsf*
**EASTINGTON (St Michael and All Angels), Frocester,
Haresfield, Moreton Valence, Standish and Whitminster**
Glouc 4 **P** *Bp and J F Bengough Esq (1 turn), DBP and Exors
Lady Mary Cooper (1 turn)* **R** R J R AMYS
EASTLEACH (St Andrew) *see* Fairford Deanery *Glouc*
EASTLEIGH (All Saints) *Win 10* **P** *Bp* **V** R P DAVIES,
NSM K ROWBERRY

EASTLEIGH Nightingale Avenue (St Francis)   *see* Eastleigh *Win*

EASTLING (St Mary) w Ospringe and Stalisfield w Otterden *Cant 14*   **P** *The Crown*   **R** *vacant* (01795) 890487

EASTMOORS (St Mary Magdalene)   *see* Helmsley *York*

EASTNEY (St Margaret) *Portsm 6*   **P** *Bp*   **V** R M SMITH

EASTNOR (St John the Baptist)   *see* Ledbury *Heref*

EASTOFT (St Bartholomew)   *see* The Marshland *Sheff*

EASTOKE (St Andrew)   *see* Hayling Is St Andr *Portsm*

EASTON (All Hallows) *Bris 3*   **P** *R Bris St Steph*   **P-in-c** R D HOYAL

EASTON (All Saints)   *see* Brandeston w Kettleburgh and Easton *St E*

EASTON (Holy Trinity w St Gabriel and St Lawrence and St Jude) *Bris 3*   **P** *Trustees*   **P-in-c** P J NOTT, **NSM** D J P MOORE

EASTON (St Mary)   *see* Itchen Valley *Win*

EASTON (St Paul)   *see* Westbury sub Mendip w Easton *B & W*

EASTON (St Peter)   *see* E Leightonstone *Ely*

EASTON (St Peter), Colton, Marlingford and Bawburgh *Nor 17*   **P** *Bp, D&C, Adn, and Sir Edward Evans-Lombe (jt)*   **P-in-c** D J PLATTIN

EASTON, GREAT (St Andrew)   *see* Six Saints circa Holt *Leic*

EASTON, GREAT (St John and St Giles)   *see* Broxted w Chickney and Tilty etc *Chelmsf*

EASTON, LITTLE (not known)   *as above*

EASTON GREY (not known)   *see* Sherston Magna, Easton Grey, Luckington etc *Bris*

EASTON IN GORDANO (St George)   *see* Pill, Portbury and Easton-in-Gordano *B & W*

EASTON MAUDIT (St Peter and St Paul)   *see* Wollaston w Strixton and Bozeat etc *Pet*

EASTON NESTON (St Mary)   *see* Towcester w Caldecote and Easton Neston etc *Pet*

EASTON ON THE HILL (All Saints)   *see* Ketton, Collyweston, Easton-on-the-Hill etc *Pet*

EASTON ROYAL (Holy Trinity)   *see* Vale of Pewsey *Sarum*

EASTOVER (St John the Baptist)   *see* Bridgwater St Jo *B & W*

EASTRINGTON (St Michael)   *see* Howden *York*

EASTROP (St Mary) *Win 4*   **P** *CPAS*   **R** C L HAWKINS, **C** N J WEIR, **NSM** C E WEST

EASTRY (St Mary Blessed Virgin) and Northbourne w Tilmanstone and Betteshanger w Ham *Cant 9*   **P** *Abp and Lord Northbourne (jt)*   **P-in-c** J M A ROBERTS,   **OLM** J A PILCHER

EASTTHORPE (St Paul)   *see* Mirfield *Wakef*

EASTVILLE (St Anne w St Mark and St Thomas) *Bris 3*   **P** *Bp*   **V** P J HAYWARD

EASTVILLE (St Paul)   *see* Stickney Gp *Linc*

EASTWELL (St Michael)   *see* Ironstone Villages *Leic*

EASTWICK (St Botolph)   *see* High Wych and Gilston w Eastwick *St Alb*

EASTWOOD (St David) *Chelmsf 10*   **P** *Bp*   **V** P D JOYCE

EASTWOOD (St Laurence and All Saints) *Chelmsf 10*   **P** *Ld Chan*   **V** S R SPENCER

EASTWOOD (St Mary) *S'well 4*   **P** *J N Plumptre Esq*   **P-in-c** D A STEVENSON,   **NSM** E MURRAY

EATON (All Saints)   *see* Retford Area *S'well*

EATON (Christ Church)   *see* Marton, Siddington w Capesthorne, and Eaton etc *Ches*

EATON (Christ Church) *Nor 3*   **P** *D&C*   **V** P H RICHMOND, **Hon C** A TYLER

EATON (St Andrew) *Nor 3*   **P** *D&C*   **V** P R RODD

EATON (St Denys)   *see* Ironstone Villages *Leic*

EATON (St Thomas)   *see* Tarporley *Ches*

EATON, LITTLE (St Paul)   *see* Duffield and Lt Eaton *Derby*

EATON BISHOP (St Michael and All Angels)   *see* Cagebrook *Heref*

EATON BRAY (St Mary the Virgin) w Edlesborough *St Alb 11*   **P** *DBP*   **P-in-c** C C MCCLUSKEY

EATON HASTINGS (St Michael and All Angels)   *see* Gt Coxwell w Buscot, Coleshill etc *Ox*

EATON SOCON (St Mary) *St Alb 10*   **P** *E W Harper Esq*   **V** T S ROBB,   **C** D R MILLER

EATON SQUARE (St Peter)   *see* Pimlico St Pet w Westmr Ch Ch *Lon*

EATON-UNDER-HEYWOOD (St Edith)   *see* Hope Bowdler w Eaton-under-Heywood *Heref*

EBBERSTON (St Mary)   *see* Thornton Dale w Allerston, Ebberston etc *York*

EBBESBOURNE WAKE (St John the Baptist)   *see* Chalke Valley *Sarum*

EBCHESTER (St Ebba) *Dur 4*   **P** *Bp*   **R** A D WHIPP

EBERNOE (Holy Trinity)   *see* N Chapel w Ebernoe *Chich*

EBONY (St Mary the Virgin)   *see* Wittersham w Stone and Ebony *Cant*

EBREY WOOD (Mission Chapel)   *see* Wrockwardine Deanery *Lich*

EBRINGTON (St Eadburgha)   *see* Chipping Campden w Ebrington *Glouc*

ECCHINSWELL (St Lawrence)   *see* Burghclere w Newtown and Ecchinswell w Sydmonton *Win*

ECCLES (St Mary the Virgin)   *see* Quidenham Gp *Nor*

ECCLES (St Mary the Virgin) (St Andrew) *Man 18*   **P** *Patr Bd and Ld Chan (alt)*   **TR** E A CROFTON,   **TV** A-L CRITCHLOW, A C YOUNG,   **NSM** M S MASEMOLA

ECCLESALL (St Gabriel)   *see* Greystones *Sheff*

ECCLESALL BIERLOW (All Saints) *Sheff 2*   **P** *Dean*   **V** S D BESSANT,   **NSM** S A P HUNTER

ECCLESFIELD (St Mary the Virgin) *Sheff 3*   **P** *DBF*   **V** D G HARTLEY

ECCLESFIELD (St Paul)   *see* Sheff St Paul *Sheff*

ECCLESHALL (Holy Trinity) *Lich 7*   **P** *Bp*   **V** J H GRAHAM

ECCLESHILL (St Luke) *Bradf 3*   **P** *V Bradf*   **V** J P HARTLEY

ECCLESTON (Christ Church)   *see* Eccleston *Liv*

ECCLESTON (St Luke)   *as above*

ECCLESTON (St Mary the Virgin) *Blackb 4*   **P** *DBP*   **P-in-c** B J WARD

ECCLESTON (St Mary the Virgin) and Pulford *Ches 2*   **P** *Duke of Westmr*   **R** I M THOMAS

ECCLESTON (St Thomas)   *see* St Helens Town Cen *Liv*

ECCLESTON Team, The *Liv 10*   **P** *Patr Bd*   **TR** J H WELCH, **TV** P G DAY, W FORSTER,   **C** G P TRACEY

ECCLESTON, GREAT   *see* Copp w Inskip *Blackb*

ECCLESTON PARK (St James)   *see* Eccleston *Liv*

ECKINGTON (Holy Trinity) *Worc 4*   **P** *D&C Westmr*   **V** S K RENSHAW

ECKINGTON (St Peter and St Paul) and Ridgeway *Derby 3*   **P** *The Crown and Patr Bd (alt)*   **R** H L SAVAGE, **NSM** I A PRICE

ECKINGTON, UPPER (St Luke)   *see* Eckington and Ridgeway *Derby*

ECTON (St Mary Magdalene) *Pet 6*   **P** *The Crown*   **P-in-c** C J PEARSON

EDALE (Holy and Undivided Trinity) *Derby 2*   **P** *Rep Landowners*   **NSM** S H COCKSEDGE

EDBURTON (St Andrew)   *see* Poynings w Edburton, Newtimber and Pyecombe *Chich*

EDEN, Gelt and Irthing Team Ministry, The *Carl 2*   **P** *Patr Bd*   **TR** R J A TULLOCH,   **TV** E GOUGH, E A JOHNSEN

EDEN PARK (St John the Baptist)   *see* Beckenham St Jo *Roch*

EDENBRIDGE (St Peter and St Paul) *Roch 11*   **P** *Bp*   **V** S A J MITCHELL,   **C** R JONES

EDENFIELD (not known)   *see* Ramsbottom and Edenfield *Man*

EDENHALL (St Cuthbert)   *see* Cross Fell Gp *Carl*

EDENHAM (St Michael) w Witham on the Hill and Swinstead *Linc 14*   **P** *Baroness Willoughby de Eresby, Ld Chan, and Bp (by turn)*   **V** A T HAWES,   **C** D PICKETT, **NSM** I K WILLIAMS

EDENSOR (St Paul)   *see* Longton Hall *Lich*

EDENSOR (St Peter)   *see* Beeley and Edensor *Derby*

EDGBASTON (St Augustine) *Birm 2*   **P** *Bp*   **V** M R E TOMLINSON

EDGBASTON (St Bartholomew) *Birm 2*   **P** *Sir Euan Anstruther-Gough-Calthorpe Bt*   **V** A J JOYCE

EDGBASTON (St George w St Michael) (St Michael's Hall) *Birm 2*   **P** *Sir Euan Anstruther-Gough-Calthorpe Bt*   **V** J M FRANCIS

EDGBASTON (St Germain) *Birm 2*   **P** *Trustees*   **V** H A SCRIVEN,   **C** W A BROWN

EDGBASTON (St Mary and St Ambrose)   *see* Balsall Heath and Edgbaston SS Mary and Ambrose *Birm*

EDGCOTE (St James)   *see* Culworth w Sulgrave and Thorpe Mandeville etc *Pet*

EDGCOTT (St Michael)   *see* The Claydons and Swan *Ox*

EDGE, THE (St John the Baptist)   *see* Painswick, Sheepscombe, Cranham, The Edge etc *Glouc*

EDGE HILL (St Dunstan)   *see* St Luke in the City *Liv*

EDGE HILL (St Mary)   *see* Liv All SS *Liv*

EDGEFIELD (School Room)   *see* Worsley *Man*

EDGEFIELD (St Peter and St Paul)   *see* Lt Barningham, Blickling, Edgefield etc *Nor*

EDGELEY (St Mark) (St Matthew) and Cheadle Heath *Ches 18*   **P** *Bp*   **V** D T BREWSTER,   **NSM** J M JOHNSON, S MAYO

EDGESIDE (St Anne)   *see* Rossendale Middle Valley *Man*

EDGWORTH (St Mary)   *see* Brimpsfield w Birdlip, Syde, Daglingworth etc *Glouc*

EDGMOND (St Peter) w Kynnersley and Preston Wealdmoors *Lich 16*   **P** *Bp, Adn Salop, Ld Chan, MMCET, and Preston Trust Homes Trustees (jt)*   **R** W E WARD, **NSM** D N H STOKES-HARRISON

EDGTON (St Michael the Archangel) see Bishop's Castle w Mainstone, Lydbury N etc *Heref*

EDGWARE (St Alphage) see Hendon St Alphage *Lon*

EDGWARE (St Andrew) (St Margaret) (St Peter) *Lon 15* **P** *MMCET* **TR** M D CLARK, **TV** P E BERRY, **C** S W J REA, **NSM** K CHRISTODOULOU

EDINGALE (Holy Trinity) see Clifton Campville w Edingale and Harlaston *Lich*

EDINGLEY (St Giles) w Halam *S'well 14* **P** *Bp* **P-in-c** D MCCOULOUGH

EDINGTHORPE (All Saints) see N Walsham and Edingthorpe *Nor*

EDINGTON (St George) see W Poldens *B & W*

EDINGTON (St Mary, St Katharine and All Saints) see Bratton, Edington and Imber, Erlestoke etc *Sarum*

EDITHMEAD (Mission) see Burnham *B & W*

EDLASTON (St James) see Brailsford w Shirley, Osmaston w Edlaston etc *Derby*

EDLINGHAM (St John the Baptist w Bolton Chapel) see Whittingham and Edlingham w Bolton Chapel *Newc*

EDLINGTON (St Helen) see Hemingby Gp *Linc*

EDLINGTON (St John the Baptist) and Hexthorpe *Sheff 9* **P** *Bp* **V** *vacant* (01709) 858358

EDMONDSHAM (St Nicholas) see Cranborne w Boveridge, Edmondsham etc *Sarum*

EDMONTON (All Saints) (St Michael) *Lon 18* **P** *D&C St Paul's* **V** S J OWEN, **C** K M SALA

EDMONTON (St Aldhelm) *Lon 18* **P** *V Edmonton All SS* **V** E N TURNER

EDMONTON (St Alphege) *Lon 18* **P** *Bp* **V** R C KNOWLING, **C** A C NEWCOMBE

EDMONTON (St Mary w St John) (St Mary's Centre) *Lon 18* **P** *D&C St Paul's* **P-in-c** N H ASBRIDGE, **NSM** J A NOWAK

EDMONTON (St Matthew) see Ponders End St Matt *Lon*

EDMONTON (St Peter w St Martin) *Lon 18* **P** *Bp* **V** C D MITCHELL

EDMUNDBYERS (St Edmund) see Blanchland w Hunstanworth and Edmundbyers etc *Newc*

EDSTASTON (St Mary the Virgin), Fauls, Prees, Tilstock and Whixall *Lich 22* **P** *R Wem, R Whitchurch, and Bp (jt)* **V** D J POMERY, **NSM** D HOLLINGS, **OLM** S E ARMSTRONG

EDSTON (St Michael) see Kirby Misperton w Normanby, Edston and Salton *York*

EDVIN LOACH (St Mary) w Tedstone Delamere, Tedstone Wafer, Upper Sapey, Wolferlow and Whitbourne *Heref 2* **P** *Bp, BNC Ox, Sir Francis Winnington Bt, and D P Barneby Esq (jt)* **P-in-c** D P HOWELL

EDWALTON (Holy Rood) *S'well 8* **P** *Exors Major R P Chaworth-Musters* **P-in-c** P W WENHAM, **NSM** P A EDWARDS

EDWARDSTONE (St Mary the Virgin) see Boxford, Edwardstone, Groton etc *St E*

EDWINSTOWE (St Mary) *S'well 2* **P** *Earl Manvers' Trustees* **V** *vacant* (01623) 822430

EDWYN RALPH (St Michael) see Bredenbury *Heref*

EFFINGHAM (St Lawrence) w Little Bookham *Guildf 10* **P** *Keble Coll Ox* **V** A J K MACKENZIE, **NSM** I M MCKILLOP

EFFORD (St Paul) see Plymouth Em, St Paul Efford and St Aug *Ex*

EGDEAN (St Bartholomew) *Chich 11* **P** *Bp* **P-in-c** T J WRIGHT

EGERTON (St James) see G7 Benefice *Cant*

EGG BUCKLAND (St Edward) *Ex 23* **P** *Ld Chan* **V** *vacant* (01752) 701399

EGGESFORD (All Saints) see Burrington, Chawleigh, Cheldon, Chulmleigh etc *Ex*

EGGINTON (St Michael) see Ouzel Valley *St Alb*

EGGINTON (St Wilfrid) see Etwall w Egginton *Derby*

EGGLESCLIFFE (St John the Baptist) *Dur 10* **P** *Bp* **R** T J D OLLIER

EGGLESTON (Holy Trinity) *Dur 7* **P** *The Crown* **V** *vacant*

EGHAM (St John the Baptist) *Guildf 11* **P** *Ch Soc Trust* **V** J R WATTLEY, **C** M S FRANCIS, **NSM** T M SUDWORTH

EGHAM HYTHE (St Paul) *Guildf 11* **P** *Bp* **P-in-c** M D A ROPER, **NSM** S M LOVEDAY

EGLETON (St Edmund) see Oakham, Ashwell, Braunston, Brooke, Egleton etc *Pet*

EGLINGHAM (St Maurice) see Glendale Gp *Newc*

EGLOSHAYLE (St Petroc) see St Breoke and Egloshayle *Truro*

EGLOSKERRY (St Petrock and St Keri), North Petherwin, Tremaine, Tresmere and Trewen *Truro 9* **P** *Duchy of Cornwall and Bp (alt)* **V** G PENGELLY, **NSM** G DARBY

EGMANTON (Our Lady of Egmanton) *S'well 3* **P** *SMF* **V** C C LEVY

EGREMONT (St Mary and St Michael) and Haile *Carl 5* **P** *Patr Bd* **TR** T R LEE, **TV** L D GRAY, **NSM** B J JEAPES, L V FULKER, T R TAYLOR, M C DANKS-FLOWER

EGTON (St Hilda) see Middle Esk Moor *York*

EGTON-CUM-NEWLAND (St Mary the Virgin) and Lowick and Colton *Carl 9* **P** *Patr Bd* **V** G WEMYSS, **NSM** J HENSON

EIGHT ASH GREEN (All Saints) see Fordham *Chelmsf*

EIGHTON BANKS (St Thomas) *Dur 12* **P** *Bp* **P-in-c** D M SNOWBALL

ELBERTON (St John) see Alveston and Littleton-on-Severn w Elberton *Bris*

ELBURTON (St Matthew) *Ex 24* **P** *CPAS* **V** R C H THOMAS, **C** R A HUDSON

ELDENE (not known) see Swindon Dorcan *Bris*

ELDERSFIELD (St John the Baptist) see Berrow w Pendock, Eldersfield, Hollybush etc *Worc*

ELDON (St Mark) see Coundon and Eldon *Dur*

ELDWICK (St Lawrence) see Bingley All SS *Bradf*

ELFORD (St Peter) *Lich 4* **P** *Bp* **P-in-c** G J THOMPSON, **NSM** D BURGESS

ELHAM (St Mary the Virgin) w Denton and Wootton *Cant 8* **P** *Abp and Mert Coll Ox (jt)* **P-in-c** D J ADLINGTON

ELING (St Mary) see Totton *Win*

ELING, NORTH (St Mary) see Copythorne *Win*

ELKESLEY (St Giles) see Retford Area *S'well*

ELKINGTON, SOUTH (All Saints) see Louth *Linc*

ELKSTONE (St John the Baptist) see Alstonfield, Butterton, Ilam etc *Lich*

ELKSTONE (St John the Evangelist) see Coberley, Cowley, Colesbourne and Elkstone *Glouc*

ELLACOMBE (Christ Church) *Ex 12* **P** *Ch Patr Trust* **V** *vacant*

ELLAND (All Saints) (St Mary the Virgin) *Wakef 2* **P** *Bp, Adn Halifax, and V Halifax (jt)* **TR** D BURROWS, **C** R A CHAPMAN, M ASKEY, **OLM** P E CHADWICK

ELLASTONE (St Peter) see Alton w Bradley-le-Moors and Denstone etc *Lich*

ELLEL (St John the Evangelist) w Shireshead *Blackb 11* **P** *V Cockerham w Winmarleigh and Glasson* **P-in-c** S TRANTER, **C** G S PEARSON, **NSM** D S TATE

ELLENBROOK (St Mary's Chapel) see Worsley *Man*

ELLENHALL (St Mary) see Chebsey, Creswell, Ellenhall, Ranton etc *Lich*

ELLERBURN (St Hilda) see Thornton Dale w Allerston, Ebberston etc *York*

ELLERBY (St James) see Skirlaugh w Long Riston, Rise and Swine *York*

ELLERKER (not known) see S Cave and Ellerker w Broomfleet *York*

ELLESBOROUGH (St Peter and St Paul), The Kimbles and Stoke Mandeville *Ox 28* **P** *Chequers Trustees, The Hon I Hope-Morley, and D&C Linc (by turn)* **R** J E HENDERSON, **NSM** M I G DIXON

ELLESMERE (St Mary) *Lich 17* **P** *Bp* **V** P J EDGE

ELLESMERE (St Peter) *Sheff 3* **P** *Bp* **V** *vacant* 0114-276 2555

ELLESMERE PORT *Ches 9* **P** *Bp* **R** G B MCGUINNESS, **NSM** G J WELCH

ELLINGHAM (St Mary) see Gillingham w Geldeston, Stockton, Ellingham etc *Nor*

ELLINGHAM (St Mary and All Saints) and Harbridge and Hyde w Ibsley *Win 9* **P** *Earl of Normanton and Keble Coll Ox (jt)* **V** *vacant* (01425) 650853

ELLINGHAM (St Maurice) *Newc 7* **P** *D&C Dur* **V** B C HURST

ELLINGHAM, GREAT (St James), LITTLE (St Peter), Rockland All Saints, Rockland St Peter and Shropham w Snetterton *Nor 11* **P** *Bp, Major E H C Garnier, and CCC Cam (jt)* **R** *vacant* (01953) 457644

ELLINGTON (All Saints) see E Leightonstone *Ely*

ELLISFIELD (St Martin) see Farleigh, Candover and Wield *Win*

ELLISTOWN (St Christopher) see Hugglescote w Donington, Ellistown and Snibston *Leic*

ELLOUGHTON (St Mary) and Brough w Brantingham *York 13* **P** *Abp and D&C Dur (jt)* **V** R J WALKER, **Hon C** C R DUXBURY, **NSM** B WORSDALE

ELM (All Saints) see Fen Orchards *Ely*

ELM (St Mary Magdalene) see Mells w Buckland Dinham, Elm, Whatley etc *B & W*

ELM PARK (St Nicholas) Hornchurch *Chelmsf 2* **P** *Bp* **NSM** R MORTON

ELMBRIDGE (St Mary) see Elmley Lovett w Hampton Lovett and Elmbridge etc *Worc*

ELMDON (St Nicholas)   see Icknield Way Villages *Chelmsf*
ELMDON (St Nicholas) (St Stephen's Church Centre) (Valley
  Church Centre) *Birm 11*   **P** *Ch Trust Fund Trust*   **R** *vacant*
  0121-743 6336
ELMDON HEATH (St Francis of Assisi)   see Solihull *Birm*
ELMERS END (St James)   see Beckenham St Jas *Roch*
ELMESTHORPE (St Mary)   see Earl Shilton w Elmesthorpe
  Leic
ELMHAM, NORTH (St Mary), Billingford, Bintree, Guist,
  Twyford and Worthing *Nor 22*   **P** *Bp, Earl of Leicester, G & C
  Coll Cam, and DBP (jt)*   **R** N C H VARNON
ELMHAM, SOUTH (St Cross) (St James) (St Margaret)
  (St Peter) (St Michael and All Angels) and Ilketshall *St E 14*
  P *Bp (3 turns), Ld Chan (1 turn), and Duke of Norfolk (1 turn)*
  R R H P THORNBURGH
ELMHURST (Mission Room)   see Lich St Chad *Lich*
ELMLEY   see Emley *Wakef*
ELMLEY CASTLE (St Mary) w Bricklehampton and the
  Combertons *Worc 4*   **P** *Bp*   **R** T J HENDERSON
ELMLEY LOVETT (St Michael) w Hampton Lovett and
  Elmbridge w Rushdock *Worc 8*   **P** *Bp and Ch Coll Cam (alt)*
  P-in-c S P KERR,   **NSM** S L BARRETT
ELMORE (St John the Baptist)   see Hardwicke and Elmore w
  Longney *Glouc*
ELMSALL, NORTH (St Margaret)   see Badsworth *Wakef*
ELMSALL, SOUTH (St Mary the Virgin) *Wakef 10*   **P** *Bp*
  V P M WITTS
ELMSETT (St Peter) w Aldham, Hintlesham, Chattisham and
  Kersey *St E 3*   **P** *Bp, MMCET, and St Chad's Coll Dur (jt)*
  R T E FFRENCH,   **C** J P FFRENCH
ELMSTEAD (St Anne and St Laurence) *Chelmsf 20*   **J** *Jes Coll
  Cam*   **P-in-c** T C PLATTS
ELMSTED (St James the Great)   see Stone Street Gp *Cant*
ELMSTONE (not known)   see Wingham w Elmstone and
  Preston w Stourmouth *Cant*
ELMSTONE HARDWICKE (St Mary Magdalene)   see N
  Cheltenham *Glouc*
ELMSWELL (St John) *St E 10*   **P** *MMCET*
  R M I MCNAMARA,   **C** D M RUDDICK
ELMTON (St Peter) *Derby 3*   **P** *Bp*   **P-in-c** A S G PIKE,
  NSM J A PALMER
ELSDON (St Cuthbert)   see N Tyne and Redesdale *Newc*
ELSECAR (Holy Trinity)   see Worsbrough w Elsecar *Sheff*
ELSENHAM (St Mary the Virgin)   see Henham and Elsenham
  w Ugley *Chelmsf*
ELSFIELD (St Thomas of Canterbury)   see Marston w Elsfield
  Ox
ELSHAM (All Saints)   see N Wolds Gp *Linc*
ELSING (St Mary)   see Lyng, Sparham, Elsing, Bylaugh,
  Bawdeswell etc *Nor*
ELSON (St Thomas) *Portsm 3*   **P** *DBP*   **V** S P RUNDELL,
  NSM M A HAY
ELSTEAD (St James) *Guildf 4*   **P** *Adn Surrey*   **R** J J PAGE,
  OLM P R J MUIR
ELSTED (St Paul)   see Harting w Elsted and Treyford cum
  Didling *Chich*
ELSTERNWICK (St Laurence)   see Burton Pidsea and
  Humbleton w Elsternwick *York*
ELSTON (All Saints) w Elston Chapelry *S'well 3*
  P J C S *Darwin Esq*   **P-in-c** D HOLLIS
ELSTOW (St Mary and St Helena) *St Alb 9*   **P** *Patr Bd*
  TR J R CROCKER,   **TV** S T SMITH
ELSTREE (St Nicholas) and Borehamwood *St Alb 14*
  P *Patr Bd (3 turns), Ld Chan (1 turn)*   **TR** T G WARR,
  TV R C A LESLIE, A-M L RENSHAW, K J GARDINER
ELSWICK (St Stephen) (St Paul) *Newc 4*   **P** *Ch Soc Trust and
  Trustees (jt)*   **V** G R CURRY
ELSWICK, HIGH (St Philip)   see Newc St Phil and St Aug and
  St Matt w St Mary *Newc*
ELSWORTH (Holy Trinity)   see Papworth *Ely*
ELTHAM (Holy Trinity) *S'wark 3*   **P** *Bp*   **V** B E WARD,
  C J C BLACKSTONE,   **NSM** S J CHARLES, N C WHEELER
ELTHAM (St Barnabas) *S'wark 3*   **P** *Bp*   **V** S COOK,   **Hon**
  C G E STEVENSON,   **NSM** S E BLACKALL, W J DAVID
ELTHAM (St John the Baptist) *S'wark 3*   **P** *DBP*
  P-in-c J F BRYSON
ELTHAM (St Saviour) *S'wark 3*   **P** *Bp*   **P-in-c** W J SAUNDERS
ELTHAM, NEW (All Saints) *S'wark 3*   **P** *Bp*   **V** A S ROSE
ELTHAM PARK (St Luke) *S'wark 3*   **P** *Bp*   **V** E CRANMER
ELTISLEY (St Pandionia and St John the Baptist)   see Papworth
  Ely
ELTON (All Saints)   see S Darley, Elton and Winster *Derby*
ELTON (All Saints)   see Kirklees Valley *Man*
ELTON (All Saints) w Stibbington and Water Newton *Ely 15*
  P *Sir Peter Proby Bt, Sir Philip Naylor-Leyland Bt, and Keble
  Coll Ox (jt)*   **P-in-c** D W SPENCER

ELTON (St John) *Dur 10*   **P** *St Chad Coll Dur*
  P-in-c P D ASHDOWN
ELTON (St Mary the Virgin)   see Wigmore Abbey *Heref*
ELTON (St Stephen) *Man 8*   **P** *V Elton All SS*   **V** D J FRENCH
ELTON-ON-THE-HILL (St Michael)   see Cropwell Bishop w
  Colston Bassett, Granby etc *S'well*
ELVASTON (St Bartholomew)   see Aston on Trent, Elvaston,
  Weston on Trent etc *Derby*
ELVEDEN (St Andrew and St Patrick)   see Brandon and Santon
  Downham w Elveden etc *St E*
ELVETHAM HEATH Local Ecumenical Partnership *Guildf 1*
  Min D G M PRICE
ELVINGTON (Holy Trinity)   see Derwent Ings *York*
ELWICK HALL (St Peter)   see Hart w Elwick Hall *Dur*
ELWORTH (St Peter) and Warmingham *Ches 11*
  P V *Sandbach, Q H Crewe Esq and J C Crewe Esq (alt)*
  R D J PAGE,   **C** J R L PRIOR
ELY (Holy Trinity w St Mary) (St Peter) *Ely 8*   **P** *Patr Bd*
  TR A J HULME,   **TV** M HARPER, M E C TALBOT,   **C** R GILBERT,
  Hon C M J M HUGHES,   **NSM** J I HULME
EMBERTON (All Saints)   see Lamp *Ox*
EMBLETON (Holy Trinity) w Rennington and Rock *Newc 6*
  P *Mert Coll Ox*   **V** P D HARRATT
EMBLETON (St Cuthbert)   see Cockermouth Area *Carl*
EMBROOK (Community of St Nicholas)   see Wokingham St
  Paul *Ox*
EMBSAY (St Mary the Virgin) w Eastby *Bradf 7*   **P** R *Skipton
  H Trin*   **P-in-c** A P BOTWRIGHT,   **C** L M TAYLOR-KENYON,
  NSM A L SPRAGGETT
EMERY DOWN (Christ Church)   see Lyndhurst and Emery
  Down and Minstead *Win*
EMLEY (St Michael the Archangel) *Wakef 6*   **P** *Lord Savile*
  P-in-c F J MARSH,   **NSM** A P YOUNG
EMMANUEL Team Ministry, The *Wakef 1*   **P** *Patr Bd*
  TR S GOTT,   **TV** S J BUCHANAN,   **NSM** D KENT,
  OLM C A SYKES
EMMAUS Parish Team, The *Leic 1*   **P** *Bp*   **R** J APPLEBY,
  TV S KUMAR
EMMER GREEN (St Barnabas) w Caversham Park *Ox 15*
  P *Bp and Ch Ch Ox (jt)*   **R** D E CHANDLER,
  OLM M L DIMMICK
EMNETH (St Edmund)   see Fen Orchards *Ely*
EMPINGHAM (St Peter), Edith Weston, Lyndon, Manton,
  North Luffenham, Pilton, Preston, Ridlington, Whitwell and
  Wing *Pet 12*   **P** *Bp, Baroness Willoughby de Eresby, Sir John
  Conant Bt, Em Coll Cam, and DBP (jt)*   **Hon C** R A MASON
EMPSHOTT (Holy Rood)   see Greatham w Empshott and
  Hawkley w Prior's Dean *Portsm*
EMSCOTE (All Saints)   see Warwick *Cov*
EMSWORTH (St James)   see Warblington w Emsworth *Portsm*
ENBORNE (St Michael and All Angels)   see Walbury Beacon
  Ox
ENDCLIFFE (St Augustine) *Sheff 2*   **P** *Ch Burgesses*
  P-in-c P W BECKLEY
ENDERBY (St John the Baptist) w Lubbesthorpe and Thurlaston
  Leic 7   **P** *Bp and F B Drummond Esq*   **P-in-c** J C TAYLOR
ENDON (St Luke)   see Bagnall w Endon *Lich*
ENFIELD (Christ Church) Trent Park *Lon 18*   **P** *Ch Trust Fund
  Trust*   **V** R D JAMES,   **C** M TUFNELL, A J WADSWORTH,
  T W C LAKE
ENFIELD (St Andrew) *Lon 18*   **P** *Trin Coll Cam*   **V** M M EDGE,
  C L P BEADLE
ENFIELD (St George) *Lon 18*   **P** *Bp*   **V** C J FULLER
ENFIELD (St James) (St Barnabas) *Lon 18*   **P** *V Enfield*
  V S LEADER,   **NSM** J M FOOT
ENFIELD (St John the Baptist)   see Clay Hill St Jo and St Luke
  Lon
ENFIELD (St Luke)   as above
ENFIELD (St Mark)   see Bush Hill Park St Mark *Lon*
ENFIELD (St Matthew)   see Ponders End St Matt *Lon*
ENFIELD (St Michael and All Angels) *Lon 18*   **P** *V Enfield*
  P-in-c S TAYLOR
ENFIELD (St Peter and St Paul) *Lon 18*   **P** *Bp*
  V J C VAUGHAN
ENFIELD (St Stephen)   see Bush Hill Park St Steph *Lon*
ENFIELD CHASE (St Mary Magdalene) *Lon 18*   **P** *Bp*
  V G J GILES,   **NSM** J W FISH, M S LUNN
ENFORD (All Saints)   see Avon Valley *Sarum*
ENGLEFIELD (St Mark)   see Theale and Englefield *Ox*
ENGLEFIELD GREEN (St Jude) *Guildf 11*   **P** *Bp*
  V M R EWBANK
ENGLISH BICKNOR (St Mary)   see Forest of Dean Ch Ch w
  English Bicknor *Glouc*
ENGLISHCOMBE (St Peter)   see Bath St Barn w Englishcombe
  B & W

ENHAM ALAMEIN (St George) *see* Knight's Enham and Smannell w Enham Alamein *Win*

ENMORE (St Michael) *see* Aisholt, Enmore, Goathurst, Nether Stowey etc *B & W*

ENMORE GREEN (St John the Evangelist) *see* Shaftesbury *Sarum*

ENNERDALE (St Mary) *see* Lamplugh w Ennerdale *Carl*

ENSBURY PARK (St Thomas) *Sarum 7* P *Bp* V S A EVANS

ENSTONE (St Kenelm) *see* Chase *Ox*

ENVILLE (St Mary the Virgin) *see* Kinver and Enville *Lich*

EPPERSTONE (Holy Cross), Gonalston, Oxton and Woodborough *S'well 15* P *Bp, Ld Chan, and C P L Francklin Esq (by turn)* **P-in-c** A R GILES, **NSM** M N TAYLOR

EPPING District (All Saints) (St John the Baptist) *Chelmsf 24* P *Patr Bd* **TR** G CONNOR, **TV** B C MORRISON, C H E-A GHEORGHIU GOULD

EPSOM (St Barnabas) *Guildf 9* P *Bp* V M C PRESTON

EPSOM (St Martin) (St Stephen on the Downs) *Guildf 9* P *Bp* V S J TALBOTT, **NSM** B ALSOP

EPSOM COMMON (Christ Church) *Guildf 9* P *Bp* V R A DONOVAN, **OLM** S A CURTIS

EPWELL (St Anne) *see* Wykeham *Ox*

EPWORTH Group, The (St Andrew) *Linc 1* P *Prime Min (2 turns), Ld Chan (1 turn)* **P-in-c** I R S WALKER

ERCALL, HIGH (St Michael and All Angels) *see* Wrockwardine Deanery *Lich*

ERDINGTON Christ the King *Birm 8* P *Bp* V R R SOUTER, C L M GASTON, **NSM** M A ROBINSON

ERDINGTON Team Ministry, The (St Barnabas) (St Chad) *Birm 8* P *Patr Bd* **TR** F C EVANS, **TV** N M A TRAYNOR, C A D RAMBLE, **NSM** E BLAIR-CHAPPELL, J N WANYOIKE, P K ZAIDI-CROSSE

ERIDGE GREEN (Holy Trinity) *see* Frant w Eridge *Chich*

ERISWELL (St Laurence and St Peter) *see* Mildenhall *St E*

ERITH (Christ Church) *Roch 15* P *Bp* V J DRAYCOTT

ERITH (St John the Baptist) *Roch 15* P *Bp* V *vacant* (01322) 332555

ERITH (St Paul) Northumberland Heath *Roch 15* P *CPAS* V G CLARKE, **NSM** M A NORMAN

ERLESTOKE (Holy Saviour) *see* Bratton, Edington and Imber, Erlestoke etc *Sarum*

ERMINE (St John) *see* Linc St Jo *Linc*

ERMINGTON (St Peter and St Paul) and Ugborough *Ex 21* P *Prime Min (1 turn), Bp and Grocers' Co (3 turns)* C J C OUGH, H C JEVONS, C M S LUFF

ERNESETTLE (St Aidan) *Ex 23* P *Bp* **P-in-c** T THORP, C D R BAILEY

ERPINGHAM (St Mary) w Calthorpe, Ingworth, Aldborough, Thurgarton and Alby w Thwaite *Nor 19* P *Bp, Lord Walpole, Gt Hosp Nor, Mrs S M Lilly, and DBP (by turn)* R B T FAULKNER

ERRINGDEN *Wakef 3* P *Bp and V Halifax (jt)* V J T ALLISON, **NSM** A MAUDE

ERWARTON (St Mary the Virgin) *see* Shoreline *St E*

ERYHOLME (St Mary) *see* E Richmond *Ripon*

ESCOMB (no dedication) *Dur 6* P *Bp* **P-in-c** R W DEIMEL, **NSM** M M DEIMEL

ESCOT (St Philip and St James) *see* Feniton and Escot *Ex*

ESCRICK (St Helen) and Stillingfleet w Naburn *York 2* P *Abp, D&C, and C D Forbes Adam Esq (jt)* R R M KIRKMAN

ESH (St Michael and All Angels) and Hamsteels *Dur 1* P *Prime Min* V M J PEERS

ESHER (Christ Church) (St George) *Guildf 8* P *Wadh Coll Ox* R W A J ALLBERRY, **OLM** H E KEMPSTER

ESHOLT (St Paul) *see* Guiseley w Esholt *Bradf*

ESK, LOWER *York 21* P *Abp* V D S COOK

ESK MOOR, MIDDLE *York 21* P *Abp* V C M HADDON-REECE

ESKDALE (St Catherine) (St Bega's Mission), Irton, Muncaster and Waberthwaite *Carl 5* P *Bp, Adn W Cumberland, Mrs P Gordon-Duff-Pennington, and P Stanley Esq (jt)* V A C BAKER

ESSENDINE (St Mary the Virgin) *see* Ryhall w Essendine and Carlby *Pet*

ESSENDON (St Mary the Virgin) *see* Lt Berkhamsted and Bayford, Essendon etc *St Alb*

ESSINGTON (St John the Evangelist) *Lich 2* P *Bp, R Bushbury, R Wednesfield, and Simeon's Trustees (jt)* **P-in-c** S BOWIE, C J M THOMAS

ESTON (Christ Church) w Normanby *York 17* P *Abp* **TR** J G BLAKELEY

ESTOVER (Christ Church) *Ex 23* P *Bp* V *vacant* (01752) 703713

ETAL (St Mary the Virgin) *see* Ford and Etal *Newc*

ETCHILHAMPTON (St Andrew) *see* Bishop's Cannings, All Cannings etc *Sarum*

ETCHING HILL (The Holy Spirit) *see* Brereton and Rugeley *Lich*

ETCHINGHAM (Assumption and St Nicholas) *Chich 15* P *Bp* **P-in-c** E C FRANCE

ETHERLEY (St Cuthbert) *Dur 6* P *Bp* **P-in-c** R W DEIMEL, **NSM** M M DEIMEL

ETON (St John the Evangelist) w Eton Wick, Boveney and Dorney *Ox 23* P *Eton Coll and Mrs J M Palmer (jt)* V L J HOLT, C J V BINNS

ETON WICK (St John the Baptist) *see* Eton w Eton Wick, Boveney and Dorney *Ox*

ETTINGSHALL (Holy Trinity) *Lich 28* P *Bp* V A J JONES

ETTINGTON (Holy Trinity and St Thomas of Canterbury) *see* Stourdene Gp *Cov*

ETTON (St Mary) w Dalton Holme *York 8* P *Lord Hotham* C M J WESTBY

ETTON (St Stephen) w Helpston and Maxey *Pet 11* P *Sir Philip Naylor-Leyland Bt (2 turns), D&C (1 turn)* **P-in-c** H P GEISOW

ETWALL (St Helen) w Egginton *Derby 14* P *Bp, Sir Henry Every Bt, Major J W Chandos-Pole, and DBP (by turn)* R F B SOLMAN

EUSTON (St Genevieve) *see* Blackbourne *St E*

EUXTON (not known) *Blackb 4* P *Bp* V J G RILEY, **NSM** P H SMITH

EVE HILL (St James the Great) *see* Dudley *Worc*

EVEDON (St Mary) *see* Ruskington Gp *Linc*

EVENLEY (St George) *see* Aynho and Croughton w Evenley etc *Pet*

EVENLODE (St Edward King and Martyr) *see* Broadwell, Evenlode, Oddington, Adlestrop etc *Glouc*

EVENWOOD (St Paul) *Dur 7* P *Bp* **P-in-c** F J GRIEVE

EVERCREECH (St Peter) w Chesterblade and Milton Clevedon *B & W 2* P *DBP* **NSM** R F REAKES

EVERDON (St Mary) *see* Weedon Bec w Everdon and Dodford *Pet*

EVERINGHAM (St Everilda) *see* Holme and Seaton Ross Gp *York*

EVERSDEN, GREAT (St Mary) *see* Lordsbridge *Ely*

EVERSDEN, LITTLE (St Helen) *as above*

EVERSHOLT (St John the Baptist) *see* Woburn w Eversholt, Milton Bryan, Battlesden etc *St Alb*

EVERSHOT (St Osmund) *see* Melbury *Sarum*

EVERSLEY (St Mary) *see* Darby Green and Eversley *Win*

EVERTON (Holy Trinity), Mattersey, Clayworth and Gringley-on-the-Hill *S'well 1* P *Bp and Ld Chan (alt)* **P-in-c** J P SMITHURST

EVERTON (St George) *Liv 3* P *Bp* **P-in-c** K E WHARTON

EVERTON (St Mary) *see* Gamlingay and Everton *Ely*

EVERTON (St Mary) *see* Milford *Win*

EVERTON (St Peter) (St John Chrysostom) (Emmanuel) *Liv 3* P *Patr Bd* R H CORBETT, C E F LOUDON

EVESBATCH (St Andrew) *see* Frome Valley *Heref*

EVESHAM (All Saints w St Lawrence) w Norton and Lenchwick *Worc 1* P *Bp and D&C (jt)* V A SPURR

EVINGTON (St Denys) *Leic 1* P *Bp* V S B HEYGATE

EVINGTON (St Stephen) *see* Twigworth, Down Hatherley, Norton, The Leigh etc *Glouc*

EVINGTON, NORTH (St Stephen) *Leic 1* P *Bp* **NSM** L M HUGHES

EWELL (St Francis of Assisi) Ruxley Lane *Guildf 9* P *Bp* V S G THOMAS, **NSM** E R RICHARDSON

EWELL (St Mary the Virgin) *Guildf 9* P *Bp* V R J E DEWHURST

EWELL, WEST (All Saints) *Guildf 9* P *Bp* V I S WHITHAM

EWELME (St Mary the Virgin), Brightwell Baldwin, Cuxham w Easington *Ox 1* P *F D Wright Esq and Mert Coll Ox, Prime Min (alt)* **P-in-c** J P MEYER

EWERBY (St Andrew) *see* Kirkby Laythorpe *Linc*

EWHURST (St James the Great) *Chich 20* P *K Coll Cam* R G L WINCHESTER

EWHURST (St Peter and St Paul) *Guildf 2* P *Ld Chan* R D A MINNS, **OLM** P E HISLOP, T J SELLER

EWOOD (St Bartholomew) *see* Blackb Redeemer *Blackb*

EWSHOT (St Mary the Virgin) *see* Crondall and Ewshot *Guildf*

EWYAS HAROLD (St Michael and All Angels) w Dulas, Kenderchurch, Abbeydore, Bacton, Kentchurch, Llangua, Rowlestone, Llancillo, Walterstone, Kilpeck, St Devereux and Wormbridge *Heref 1* P *Bp, E Harley Esq, Mrs B Sexton, J Lucas-Scudamore Esq, Mrs M Barneby, G Clive Esq, and D&C (2 turns), Ld Chan (1 turn)* R A F EVANS

EXBOURNE (St Mary the Virgin) *see* Hatherleigh, Meeth, Exbourne and Jacobstowe *Ex*

FARLEIGH, WEST (All Saints) *as above*
FARLEIGH HUNGERFORD (St Leonard) *see* Hardington Vale *B & W*
FARLEIGH WALLOP (St Andrew) *see* Farleigh, Candover and Wield *Win*
FARLESTHORPE (St Andrew) *see* Bilsby w Farlesthorpe *Linc*
FARLEY (All Saints) *see* Clarendon *Sarum*
FARLEY CHAMBERLAYNE (St John) *see* Michelmersh and Awbridge and Braishfield etc *Win*
FARLEY GREEN (St Michael) *see* Shere, Albury and Chilworth *Guildf*
FARLEY HILL (St John the Baptist) *St Alb 12* **P** *Bp*
P-in-c D F SANDERS
FARLEY HILL (St John the Evangelist) *see* Loddon Reach *Ox*
FARLINGTON (St Andrew) (Church of the Resurrection) *Portsm 6* **P** *Mrs S J Wynter-Bee and Nugee Foundn (jt)*
R P D GULLY
FARLINGTON (St Leonard) *see* Forest of Galtres *York*
FARLOW (St Giles) *see* Stottesdon w Farlow, Cleeton St Mary etc *Heref*
FARMBOROUGH (All Saints) and Marksbury and Stanton Prior *B & W 9* **P** *MMCET (3 turns), Duchy of Cornwall (1 turn), and DBF (1 turn)* **R** J P KNOTT, **C** T NIXON
FARMCOTE (St Faith) *see* The Guitings, Cutsdean, Farmcote etc *Glouc*
FARMINGTON (St Peter) *see* Northleach w Hampnett and Farmington etc *Glouc*
FARMOOR (St Mary) *see* Cumnor *Ox*
FARNBOROUGH (All Saints) *see* E Downland *Ox*
FARNBOROUGH (St Botolph) *see* Avon Dassett w Farnborough and Fenny Compton *Cov*
FARNBOROUGH (St Giles) (St Nicholas) *Roch 16* **P** *Em Coll Cam* **R** M J HUGHES, **C** A M NEWMAN, **NSM** J DRIVER
FARNBOROUGH, NORTH (St Peter) (Good Shepherd) *Guildf 1* **P** *Patr Bd* **TR** D G WILLEY, **TV** R M BENNETTS, **C** W W NORTH, C F HOLT, **NSM** R N COBBOLD
FARNBOROUGH, SOUTH (St Mark) *Guildf 1* **P** *Bp* **V** I C HEDGES
FARNCOMBE (St John the Evangelist) *Guildf 4* **P** *Bp* **R** J RATTUE
FARNDALE (St Mary) *see* Kirkbymoorside w Gillamoor, Farndale etc *York*
FARNDON (St Chad) and Coddington *Ches 5* **P** *Duke of Westmr and D&C (jt)* **P-in-c** D SCURR
FARNDON (St Peter) w Thorpe, Hawton and Cotham *S'well 3* **P** *Ld Chan* **P-in-c** W D MILNER, **NSM** P R SMITH
FARNDON, EAST (St John the Baptist) *see* Arthingworth, Harrington w Oxendon and E Farndon *Pet*
FARNHAM (St Andrew) (St Francis) (St Mary) *Guildf 3* **P** *Bp* **R** A K TUCK, **NSM** J M LIEVESLEY
FARNHAM (St Laurence) *see* Chase *Sarum*
FARNHAM (St Mary) *see* Alde River *St E*
FARNHAM (St Mary the Virgin) *see* Stansted Mountfitchet w Birchanger and Farnham *Chelmsf*
FARNHAM (St Oswald) *see* Walkingham Hill *Ripon*
FARNHAM COMMON (St John the Evangelist) *see* Farnham Royal w Hedgerley *Ox*
FARNHAM ROYAL (St Mary the Virgin) w Hedgerley *Ox 23* **P** *Bp and Eton Coll (jt)* **R** G H SAUNDERS, **NSM** H CHAMBERLAIN
FARNHAM ROYAL SOUTH (St Michael) *see* Manor Park and Whitby Road *Ox*
FARNINGHAM (St Peter and St Paul) *see* Eynsford w Farningham and Lullingstone *Roch*
FARNLEY (All Saints) *see* Washburn and Mid-Wharfe *Bradf*
FARNLEY (St Michael) *Ripon 6* **P** *Bp* **P-in-c** K A P DOWLING
FARNLEY, NEW (St James) *see* Farnley *Ripon*
FARNLEY TYAS (St Lucias) *see* Almondbury w Farnley Tyas *Wakef*
FARNSFIELD (St Michael) *S'well 15* **P** *Bp* **P-in-c** R D SEYMOUR-WHITELEY, **NSM** M A GROVES
FARNWORTH (All Saints) *see* Farnworth, Kearsley and Stoneclough *Man*
FARNWORTH (All Saints) (St John), Kearsley and Stoneclough *Man 7* **P** *Ld Chan and Patr Bd (alt)* **TR** C H PHARAOH, **TV** D J THOMPSON, **OLM** P S CASTLE
FARNWORTH (St George) *see* New Bury w Gt Lever *Man*
FARNWORTH (St James) *as above*
FARNWORTH (St John) *see* Farnworth, Kearsley and Stoneclough *Man*
FARNWORTH (St Luke) (Bold Mission) (Cronton Mission) *Liv 13* **P** *V Prescot St Mary* **V** H M MORBY, **Hon C** R JONES
FARRINGDON (All Saints) *see* Northanger *Win*

FARRINGDON (St Petrock and St Barnabas) *see* Aylesbeare, Rockbeare, Farringdon etc *Ex*
FARRINGTON GURNEY (St John the Baptist) *see* Paulton w Farrington Gurney and High Littleton *B & W*
FARSLEY (St John the Evangelist) *Bradf 3* **P** *V Calverley* **P-in-c** P Q TUDGE, **C** P R ARNOLD
FARTHINGHOE (St Michael and All Angels) *see* Aynho and Croughton w Evenley etc *Pet*
FARTHINGSTONE (St Mary the Virgin) *see* Lambfold *Pet*
FARWAY (St Michael and All Angels) *see* Offwell, Northleigh, Farway, Cotleigh etc *Ex*
FATFIELD (St George) *Dur 11* **P** *Lord Lambton* **C** J A MIDDLETON
FAULKBOURNE (St Germanus) *see* Fairstead w Terling and White Notley etc *Chelmsf*
FAULS (Holy Emmanuel) *see* Edstaston, Fauls, Prees, Tilstock and Whixall *Lich*
FAVELL, WEST (Emmanuel) *see* Northampton Em *Pet*
FAVERSHAM (St Mary of Charity) *Cant 14* **P** *D&C* **P-in-c** A C OEHRING, **C** J L PETTIT, **NSM** N M ASH, G Y REED
FAWDON (St Mary the Virgin) *Newc 2* **P** *Bp* **P-in-c** S MCCORMACK, **OLM** M A ATKINSON
FAWKENHURST *Cant 6* **P** *DBP* **R** *vacant*
FAWKHAM (St Mary) and Hartley *Roch 1* **P** *Bp and D&C (jt)* **R** J A FLETCHER, **NSM** E M ROBERTSON
FAWLEY (All Saints) *Win 11* **P** *Bp* **R** B P JAMES, **NSM** M G WHITE, D WHITE
FAWLEY (St Mary) *see* W Downland *Ox*
FAWLEY (St Mary the Virgin) *see* Hambleden Valley *Ox*
FAWSLEY (St Mary the Virgin) *see* Badby w Newham and Charwelton w Fawsley etc *Pet*
FAZAKERLEY (Emmanuel) (St Paul) *Liv 7* **P** *Patr Bd* **TR** M SIMMONS, **TV** M A HINDLEY
FAZAKERLEY (St Nathanael) *see* Walton-on-the-Hill *Liv*
FAZELEY (St Paul) (St Barnabas) *Lich 4* **P** *Bp* **V** H J BAKER, **NSM** R G DAVIES
FEATHERSTONE (All Saints) (St Thomas) *Wakef 10* **P** *Ch Ch Ox and Bp (jt)* **V** I GROSU
FEATHERSTONE (School Chapel) *see* Haltwhistle and Greenhead *Newc*
FECKENHAM (St John the Baptist) *see* Bowbrook N *Worc*
FEERING (All Saints) *see* Kelvedon and Feering *Chelmsf*
FELBRIDGE (St John) *S'wark 25* **P** *DBP* **V** S G BOWEN
FELBRIGG (St Margaret) *see* Roughton and Felbrigg, Metton, Sustead etc *Nor*
FELIXKIRK (St Felix) w Boltby *York 18* **P** *Abp* **V** I D HOUGHTON, **NSM** T A LEWIS
FELIXSTOWE (St John the Baptist) (St Edmund) *St E 2* **P** *Bp* **P-in-c** R C HINSLEY, **OLM** E J CORKER
FELIXSTOWE (St Peter and St Paul) (St Andrew) (St Nicholas) *St E 2* **P** *Ch Trust Fund Trust* **V** J L ASTON, **OLM** H STALKER
FELKIRK (St Peter) *Wakef 10* **P** *Bp* **P-in-c** J HADJIOANNOU
FELLING (Christ Church) *Dur 12* **P** *CPAS* **V** T J DAVIDSON
FELLISCLIFFE (Mission Church) *see* Hampsthwaite and Killinghall and Birstwith *Ripon*
FELLSIDE TEAM, The *Blackb 9* **P** *Patr Bd* **TR** J W FINCH, **TV** S P C COOPER, **NSM** M A SHERDLEY
FELMERSHAM (St Mary) *see* Sharnbrook, Felmersham and Knotting w Souldrop *St Alb*
FELMINGHAM (St Andrew) *see* King's Beck *Nor*
FELPHAM (St Mary the Virgin) *Chich 1* **P** *D&C* **R** T L PESKETT
FELSHAM (St Peter) *see* Bradfield St Clare, Bradfield St George etc *St E*
FELSTED (Holy Cross) and Little Dunmow *Chelmsf 18* **P** *CPAS* **V** C J TAYLOR, **C** M J WINDSOR
FELTHAM (Christ Church) (St Dunstan) *Lon 11* **P** *Bp* **V** P R WRAGG
FELTHORPE (St Margaret) *see* Horsford, Felthorpe and Hevingham *Nor*
FELTON (St Katharine and the Noble Army of Martyrs) *see* Winford w Felton Common Hill *B & W*
FELTON (St Michael and All Angels) *Newc 6* **P** *Bp* **P-in-c** S J H WHITE, **NSM** P T ASKEW
FELTON (St Michael the Archangel) *see* Bodenham, Felton and Preston Wynne *Heref*
FELTWELL (St Mary) *see* Grimshoe *Ely*
FEN AND HILL Group, The *Linc 11* **P** *Bp, DBP, G J R Wiggins-Davies Esq, and Lt Col J L M Dymoke (jt)* **R** A J BOYD, **OLM** K A BUSH
FEN DITTON (St Mary the Virgin) *Ely 4* **P** *Bp* **P-in-c** M C BOWERS
FEN DRAYTON (St Mary the Virgin) w Conington and Lolworth and Swavesey *Ely 6* **P** *The Crown, Jes Coll Cam, SMF, and Ch Coll Cam (by turn)* **R** J D YULE

FEN ORCHARDS, The *Ely 14* **P** *Bp* **V** D L MASON
FENCE-IN-PENDLE (St Anne) and Higham *Blackb 6* **P** *Bp and Ld Chan (alt)* **V** *vacant* (01282) 617316
FENCOTE (St Andrew) *see* Lower Swale *Ripon*
FENHAM (Holy Cross) *see* Newc H Cross *Newc*
FENHAM (St James and St Basil) *Newc 4* **P** *Bp*
V N P DARBY, **C** H E ARNOLD, D L DELAP
FENISCLIFFE (St Francis) *see* Blackb St Fran and St Aid *Blackb*
FENISCOWLES (Immanuel) *Blackb 2* **P** *V Blackb*
P-in-c D J ROSCOE
FENITON (St Andrew) and Escot *Ex 7* **P** *DBP and J M Kennaway Esq (jt)* **P-in-c** S G FRANKLIN
FENN LANES Group, The *Leic 10* **P** *Bp, D&C, and Lord O'Neill (jt)* **R** L J BLAY
FENNY BENTLEY (St Edmund King and Martyr), Thorpe, Tissington, Parwich and Alsop-en-le-Dale *Derby 8* **P** *Bp, D A G Shields Esq, and Sir Richard FitzHerbert Bt (jt)*
R A B LARKIN
FENNY COMPTON (St Peter and St Clare) *see* Avon Dassett w Farnborough and Fenny Compton *Cov*
FENNY DRAYTON (St Michael and All Angels) *see* Fenn Lanes Gp *Leic*
FENNY STRATFORD (St Martin) *Ox 25* **P** *Bp*
V V J A BULLOCK, **NSM** I W THOMAS
FENSTANTON (St Peter and St Paul) *Ely 10* **P** *Bp*
P-in-c R P MCKENZIE
FENTON (All Saints) *see* Claypole *Linc*
FENTON (Christ Church) *Lich 12* **P** *R Stoke-on-Trent*
V D A CAMERON
FENWICK and MOSS (St John) *see* Fishlake w Sykehouse and Kirk Bramwith etc *Sheff*
FEOCK (St Feock) *Truro 6* **P** *Bp* **P-in-c** P J KNIBBS,
C A T NEAL, **Hon C** D R CARRIVICK, **NSM** B J HESELTINE,
H V SPONG, N J POTTER
FERHAM PARK (St Paul) *see* Masbrough *Sheff*
FERNDOWN (St Mary) *see* Hampreston *Sarum*
FERNHAM (St John the Evangelist) *see* Shrivenham and Ashbury *Ox*
FERNHURST (St Margaret) *Chich 10* **P** *Rathbone Trust Co and Cowdray Trust (jt)* **P-in-c** A N ROCKEY
FERNILEE (Holy Trinity) *see* Whaley Bridge *Ches*
FERRIBY, NORTH (All Saints) *York 14* **P** *H Trin Hull and Distr Ch Patr Soc Ltd* **P-in-c** M C BRAILSFORD,
NSM G K PAULUS
FERRIBY, SOUTH (St Nicholas) *Linc 6* **P** *Bp*
R D P ROWETT
FERRING (St Andrew) *Chich 5* **P** *D&C* **P-in-c** G S INGRAM
FERRYBRIDGE (St Andrew) *Wakef 10* **P** *D&C York*
P-in-c E M WOODCOCK
FERRYHILL (St Luke) *see* Cornforth and Ferryhill *Dur*
FERRYHILL (St Martha and St Mary) *as above*
FERSFIELD (St Andrew) *see* Upper Waveney *Nor*
FETCHAM (St Mary) *Guildf 10* **P** *Bp* **R** P H BOUGHTON,
C M E DE QUIDT, **NSM** E M V BOUGHTON
FEWSTON (St Michael and St Lawrence) *see* Washburn and Mid-Wharfe *Bradf*
FIDDINGTON (St Martin) *see* Quantock Coast *B & W*
FIELD BROUGHTON (St Peter) *see* Cartmel Peninsula *Carl*
FIELD DALLING (St Andrew) *see* Stiffkey and Bale *Nor*
FIFEHEAD MAGDALEN (St Mary Magdalene) *see* Stour Vale *Sarum*
FIFEHEAD NEVILLE (All Saints) *see* Hazelbury Bryan and the Hillside Par *Sarum*
FIFIELD (St John the Baptist) *see* Shipton-under-Wychwood w Milton, Fifield etc *Ox*
FIFIELD BAVANT (St Martin) *see* Chalke Valley *Sarum*
FIGHELDEAN (St Michael and All Angels) *see* Avon Valley *Sarum*
FILBY (All Saints) *see* S Trin Broads *Nor*
FILEY (St John) (St Oswald) *York 15* **P** *PCC*
V M E WILLIAMS
FILKINS (St Peter) *see* Shill Valley and Broadshire *Ox*
FILLEIGH (St Paul) *see* S Molton w Nymet St George, High Bray etc *Ex*
FILLINGHAM (St Andrew) *see* Spring Line Gp *Linc*
FILLONGLEY (St Mary and All Saints) and Corley *Cov 5*
P *Bp and Ch Soc Trust (jt)* **P-in-c** I D KENNEDY
FILTON (St Gregory) *see* Horfield St Greg *Bris*
FILTON (St Peter) *Bris 5* **P** *Bp* **R** B R ARMAN,
NSM M E DESMOND
FILWOOD PARK (St Paul) *Bris 1* **P** *Bp and Bris Ch Trustees (jt)*
V A G PALMER
FIMBER (St Mary) *see* Waggoners *York*

FINBOROUGH, GREAT (St Andrew) w Onehouse, Harleston, Buxhall and Shelland *St E 6* **P** *Bp* **P-in-c** C CHILDS,
OLM A E H CRUICKSHANKS
FINBOROUGH, LITTLE (St Mary) *see* Combs and Lt Finborough *St E*
FINCHAM (St Martin) *Ely 9* **P** *Bp* **P-in-c** B L BURTON
FINCHAMPSTEAD (St James) *Ox 16* **P** *DBP*
NSM J R EDWARDS, **OLM** B A BAYMAN
FINCHFIELD (St Thomas) *see* Tettenhall Wood and Perton *Lich*
FINCHINGFIELD (St John the Baptist) and Cornish Hall End and Wethersfield w Shalford *Chelmsf 15* **P** *Mrs E M Bishop and Bp (alt)* **P-in-c** C E WILSON
FINCHLEY (Christ Church) *Lon 14* **P** *Ch Patr Trust*
V D A WALKER
FINCHLEY (Holy Trinity) *Lon 16* **P** *Bp* **V** *vacant* (020) 8883 8720
FINCHLEY (St Barnabas) *see* Woodside Park St Barn *Lon*
FINCHLEY (St Mary) *Lon 14* **P** *Bp* **R** P A DAVISON
FINCHLEY (St Paul) (St Luke) *Lon 14* **P** *Simeon Trustees and Ch Patr Trust (jt)* **V** N R PYE
FINCHLEY, EAST (All Saints) *Lon 14* **P** *Bp* **V** C R HARDY
FINDERN (All Saints) *Derby 16* **P** *Bp* **V** S A STARKEY
FINDON (St John the Baptist) w Clapham and Patching *Chich 5*
P *Abp, Bp, and J E P Somerset Esq (jt)* **V** R J WHITTLE
FINDON VALLEY (All Saints) *Chich 5* **P** *Bp*
V G J WHITING, **NSM** B A MILES
FINEDON (St Mary the Virgin) *Pet 8* **P** *Bp*
P-in-c R K R COLES
FINGEST (St Bartholomew) *see* Hambleden Valley *Ox*
FINGHALL (St Andrew) *see* Spennithorne w Finghall and Hauxwell *Ripon*
FINGRINGHOE (St Andrew) w East Donyland and Abberton w Langenhoe *Chelmsf 16* **P** *Bp (3 turns), Ld Chan (1 turn)*
R R J MARTIN
FINHAM (St Martin in the Fields) *Cov 3* **P** *Bp* **V** *vacant* (024) 7641 8330
FINMERE (St Michael) *see* Shelswell *Ox*
FINNINGHAM (St Bartholomew) *see* Badwell and Walsham *St E*
FINNINGLEY (Holy Trinity and St Oswald) w Auckley *Sheff 9*
P *Bp* **R** N M REDEYOFF
FINSBURY (St Clement) (St Barnabas) (St Matthew) *Lon 5*
P *D&C St Paul's* **V** D E ALLEN
FINSBURY PARK (St Thomas) *Lon 6* **P** *Abp* **V** S R COLES,
NSM V R ATTA-BAFFOE, P NASHASHIBI
FINSTALL (St Godwald) *Worc 7* **P** *V Stoke Prior*
P-in-c C A HOLZAPFEL, **C** S C WINTER,
NSM M WOODGATES
FINSTHWAITE (St Peter) *see* Leven Valley *Carl*
FINSTOCK (Holy Trinity) *see* Forest Edge *Ox*
FIR VALE (St Cuthbert) *see* Sheff St Cuth *Sheff*
FIRBANK (St John the Evangelist), Howgill and Killington *Bradf 6* **P** *Ld Chan and V Sedbergh (alt)* **P-in-c** A W FELL
FIRBECK (St Martin) w Letwell *Sheff 5* **P** *Bp* **R** J TRICKETT
FIRLE, WEST (St Peter) *see* Glynde, W Firle and Beddingham *Chich*
FIRSBY (St Andrew) *see* Spilsby Gp *Linc*
FIRSWOOD (St Hilda) and Gorse Hill *Man 5* **P** *Prime Min*
R T R MALKIN
FISHBOURNE, NEW (St Peter and St Mary) *Chich 3*
P *Ld Chan* **R** M WICKENS
FISHBURN (St Catherine) *see* Upper Skerne *Dur*
FISHERMEAD (Trinity Church) *see* Woughton *Ox*
FISHERTON ANGER (St Paul) *Sarum 12* **P** *Ch Patr Trust*
R A S W CULLIS, **C** R T MORGAN, **NSM** A B KEATING
FISHLAKE (St Cuthbert) w Sykehouse and Kirk Bramwith w Fenwick and Moss *Sheff 10* **P** *Duchy of Lanc (1 turn), D&C Dur (2 turns), and Bp (1 turn)* **R** E S ATHERFOLD
FISHLEY (St Mary) *see* Acle w Fishley, N Burlingham, Beighton w Moulton *Nor*
FISHPOND (St John the Baptist) *see* Golden Cap Team *Sarum*
FISHPONDS (All Saints) *Bris 3* **P** *Bp*
NSM J F J GOODRIDGE
FISHPONDS (St John) *Bris 3* **P** *Bp* **NSM** J F J GOODRIDGE,
OLM N G CALLEN
FISHPONDS (St Mary) *Bris 3* **P** *Bp* **NSM** J F J GOODRIDGE
FISHTOFT (St Guthlac) *Linc 20* **P** *DBP* **R** M A R COOPER
FISKERTON (St Clement) *see* S Lawres Gp *Linc*
FITTLETON (All Saints) *see* Avon Valley *Sarum*
FITTLEWORTH (St Mary the Virgin) *see* Stopham and Fittleworth *Chich*
FITTON HILL (St Cuthbert) *see* Bardsley *Man*
FITZ (St Peter and St Paul) *see* Bicton, Montford w Shrawardine and Fitz *Lich*

FITZHEAD (St James) *see* Milverton w Halse, Fitzhead and Ash Priors *B & W*

FITZWILLIAM (St Maurice) *see* Kinsley w Wragby *Wakef*

FIVE ASHES (Church of the Good Shepherd) *see* Mayfield *Chich*

FIVE OAK GREEN (St Luke) *see* Tudeley cum Capel w Five Oak Green *Roch*

FIVE SAINTS *see* New Bury w Gt Lever *Man*

FIVEHEAD (St Martin) *see* Curry Rivel w Fivehead and Swell *B & W*

FIXBY (St Francis) and Cowcliffe, Huddersfield *Wakef 5*
P *DBP* P-in-c D R WARD, C C B REARDON

FLACKWELL HEATH (Christ Church) *Ox 29* P *DBP*
V C D BULL, NSM G P HARTNELL, J M ROTH,
OLM M H COURTNEY

FLADBURY (St John the Baptist), Hill and Moor, Wyre Piddle, Cropthorne and Charlton *Worc 4* P *Bp and D&C (jt)*
P-in-c L M BUSFIELD, C A FAIRCLOUGH, C L M BUSFIELD

FLAMBOROUGH (St Oswald) *see* Bempton w Flamborough, Reighton w Speeton *York*

FLAMSTEAD (St Leonard) *St Alb 7* P *Univ Coll Ox*
P-in-c J F H GREEN

FLAUNDEN (St Mary Magdalene) *see* Chenies and Lt Chalfont, Latimer and Flaunden *Ox*

FLAX BOURTON (St Michael and All Angels) *see* Long Ashton w Barrow Gurney and Flax Bourton *B & W*

FLAXLEY (St Mary the Virgin) *see* Westbury-on-Severn w Flaxley, Blaisdon etc *Glouc*

FLAXTON (St Lawrence) *see* Sand Hutton *York*

FLECKNEY (St Nicholas) *see* Wistow *Leic*

FLECKNOE (St Mark) *see* Leam Valley *Cov*

FLEET (All Saints) (St Philip and St James) *Guildf 1* P *Bp*
V R O WOODHAMS, C A SISTIG, NSM J J SISTIG

FLEET (Holy Trinity) *see* Chickerell w Fleet *Sarum*

FLEET (Old Church) *as above*

FLEET (St Mary Magdalene) w Gedney *Linc 16* P *The Crown and DBP (alt)* P-in-c R J GODDARD

FLEETWOOD (St David) *Blackb 12* P *Bp and Meynell Trustees (jt)* P-in-c J M HALL, NSM A J SHAW

FLEETWOOD (St Nicholas) *Blackb 12* P *Bp and Meynell Trustees (jt)* V P J BENFIELD

FLEETWOOD (St Peter) *Blackb 12* P *Meynell Trustees*
V J M HALL, NSM A J SHAW

FLEGG COASTAL Benefice, The: Hemsby, Winterton, East and West Somerton and Horsey *Nor 6* P *Bp, D&C, SMF, and Major R A Ferrier (jt)* P A R LING, NSM A T CADMORE

FLEGG GROUP (Martham) *see* Martham and Repps with Bastwick, Thurne etc *Nor*

FLEGG GROUP (Ormesby) *see* Ormesby St Marg w Scratby, Ormesby St Mich etc *Nor*

FLEGG GROUP (South Trinity Broads) *see* S Trin Broads *Nor*

FLEMPTON (St Catherine of Alexandria) *see* Lark Valley *St E*

FLETCHAMSTEAD (St James) *Cov 3* P *Bp* V S R BURCH,
C C D HOGGER, OLM A M RICHARDS

FLETCHING (St Mary and St Andrew) *Chich 21* P *Abp*
V *vacant* (01825) 722498

FLETTON (St Margaret) *Ely 15* P *Sir Philip Naylor-Leyland Bt* P-in-c W P L GAMMON

FLIMBY (St Nicholas) *see* Maryport, Netherton and Flimby *Carl*

FLIMWELL (St Augustine of Canterbury) *see* Ticehurst and Flimwell *Chich*

FLINTHAM (St Augustine of Canterbury) *S'well 8*
P R H T Hildyard Esq NSM M R WOODWARD

FLITCHAM (St Mary the Virgin) *see* Sandringham w W Newton and Appleton etc *Nor*

FLITTON (St John the Baptist) *see* Silsoe, Pulloxhill and Flitton *St Alb*

FLITWICK (St Andrew) (St Peter and St Paul) *St Alb 8* P *DBP*
V M F J BRADLEY

FLIXBOROUGH (All Saints) w Burton upon Stather *Linc 4*
P *Sir Reginald Sheffield Bt* P-in-c A F PLEDGER

FLIXTON (St John) *Man 5* P *Bp* V K J MASSEY,
OLM R W GREEN, B R CORKE, J N EDGE, M SURREY

FLIXTON (St Mary) *see* S Elmham and Ilketshall *St E*

FLIXTON (St Michael) *Man 5* P *Bp* P-in-c V L JOHNSON,
NSM A CLEPHANE

FLOCKTON (St James the Great) cum Denby Grange *Wakef 6*
P R Carter's Trustees P-in-c F J MARSH, NSM A P YOUNG

FLOOKBURGH (St John the Baptist) *see* Cartmel Peninsula *Carl*

FLORDON (St Michael) *see* Mulbarton w Bracon Ash, Hethel and Flordon *Nor*

FLORE (All Saints) *see* Heyford w Stowe Nine Churches and Flore etc *Pet*

FLOWTON (St Mary) *see* Somersham w Flowton and Offton w Willisham *St E*

FLUSHING (St Peter) *see* Mylor w Flushing *Truro*

FLYFORD FLAVELL (St Peter) *see* Abberton, The Flyfords, Naunton Beauchamp etc *Worc*

FOBBING (St Michael) *see* Corringham and Fobbing *Chelmsf*

FOLESHILL (St Laurence) *Cov 2* P *Ld Chan*
V M R CLEVELAND

FOLESHILL (St Paul) *Cov 2* P *Ld Chan* V A J CANNING

FOLEY PARK (Holy Innocents) *see* Kidderminster St Jo and H Innocents *Worc*

FOLKE (St Lawrence) *see* Vale of White Hart *Sarum*

FOLKESTONE (St Augustine) (St Mary and St Eanswythe) (St Saviour) *Cant 8* P *Abp* V B C R JOHNSON,
NSM R C SIEBERT

FOLKESTONE (St John the Baptist) *see* Foord St Jo *Cant*

FOLKESTONE (St Peter) *Cant 8* P *Trustees* V *vacant* (01303) 254472

FOLKESTONE Trinity Benefice, The (Holy Trinity w Christ Church) (St George) *Cant 8* P *Abp and Ld Chan (alt)*
P-in-c M W HAYTON, C S FITZGERALD, NSM R O SMITH,
K M MCNEICE

FOLKESWORTH (St Helen) *see* Stilton w Denton and Caldecote etc *Ely*

FOLKINGHAM (St Andrew) *see* S Lafford *Linc*

FOLKINGTON (St Peter ad Vincula) *Chich 18*
P *Mrs S J Harcourt-Smith* V *vacant*

FOLKTON (St John) *see* Willerby w Ganton and Folkton *York*

FOLLIFOOT (St Joseph and St James) *see* Spofforth w Kirk Deighton *Ripon*

FONTHILL BISHOP (All Saints) *see* Nadder Valley *Sarum*

FONTHILL GIFFORD (Holy Trinity) *as above*

FONTMELL MAGNA (St Andrew) *see* Iwerne Valley *Sarum*

FOOLOW (St Hugh) *see* Baslow and Eyam *Derby*

FOORD (St John the Baptist) *Cant 8* P *CPAS* V J LEACH,
C K HARLOW

FOOTSCRAY (All Saints) w North Cray *Roch 17* P *Bp and Ld Chan (alt)* R A C UPHILL

FORCETT (St Cuthbert) and Aldbrough and Melsonby *Ripon 2*
P *DBP and Univ Coll Ox (alt)* P-in-c S R HAWORTH

FORD (St Andrew) *see* Clymping and Yapton w Ford *Chich*

FORD (St John of Jerusalem) *see* Leominster *Heref*

FORD (St John the Evangelist) *see* Colerne w N Wraxall *Bris*

FORD (St Mark) *see* Devonport St Bart and Ford St Mark *Ex*

FORD (St Michael) *Heref 12* P *Bp* P-in-c V J TAIT,
OLM M E NEAL

FORD (St Michael and All Angels) and Etal *Newc 12* P *Lord Joicey* R V T DICKINSON

FORD END (St John the Evangelist) *see* Gt Waltham w Ford End *Chelmsf*

FORDCOMBE (St Peter) *see* Penshurst and Fordcombe *Roch*

FORDHAM (All Saints) *Chelmsf 17* P *Reformation Ch Trust, Ball Coll Ox (alt)* C A R F B GAGE

FORDHAM (St Peter and St Mary Magdalene) *see* Three Rivers Gp *Ely*

FORDHOUSES (St James) *see* Bushbury *Lich*

FORDINGBRIDGE (St Mary) and Breamore and Hale with the Charfords *Win 9* P *K Coll Cam, Sir Edward Hulse Bt, and P N Hickman Esq (jt)* R M R GODSON, C T ROBINSON,
Hon C P D ASHTON, P F MURPHY, J F TOWLER,
NSM S T HORNE

FORDON (St James) *see* Burton Fleming w Fordon, Grindale etc *York*

FOREBRIDGE (St Paul) *see* Stafford St Paul Forebridge *Lich*

FOREMARK (St Saviour) and Repton w Newton Solney *Derby 16* P *Bp and DBP (jt)* V P S PAINE,
NSM J C SCOTT

FOREST (St Stephen) *see* Rainow w Saltersford and Forest *Ches*

FOREST AND AVON *Sarum 10* P *Patr Bd* TR F H GIMSON,
TV D G BACON, NSM V BATCHELOR,
OLM P J WHITMARSH

FOREST EDGE *Ox 3* P *Bp, V Charlbury, and Sir Mark Norman Bt (jt)* V P J MANSELL, NSM B FORD, S C JONES

FOREST GATE (All Saints) (St Edmund) *Chelmsf 3* P *Bp*
P-in-c B K SHIPSIDES, C L H K DAVIES

FOREST GATE (Emmanuel w St Peter) Upton Cross *Chelmsf 3*
P *Bp* V C CHIKE

FOREST GATE (St James) *see* Stratford St Jo w Ch Ch and St Jas *Chelmsf*

FOREST GATE (St Mark) *Chelmsf 3* P *Ch Patr Trust*
V P J STOW

FOREST GATE (St Saviour) w West Ham St Matthew *Chelmsf 3*
P *Patr Bd* TR J H WILLIAMS, TV J M MURPHY

FOREST GREEN (Holy Trinity) *see* Ockley, Okewood and Forest Green *Guildf*

FOREST HILL (Christ Church) *see* Perry Hill St Geo w Ch Ch and St Paul *S'wark*

FOREST HILL (St Augustine) *see* Sydenham H Trin and St Aug *S'wark*

FOREST HILL (St Nicholas) *see* Wheatley *Ox*

FOREST HILL (St Paul) *see* Perry Hill St Geo w Ch Ch and St Paul *S'wark*

FOREST-IN-TEESDALE (St Mary the Virgin) *see* Middleton-in-Teesdale w Forest and Frith *Dur*

FOREST OF DEAN (Christ Church) w English Bicknor *Glouc 1* **P** *The Crown (3 turns), SMF (1 turn)* **P-in-c** V K TURNER, **NSM** H RODWELL

FOREST OF DEAN (Holy Trinity) *see* Drybrook, Lydbrook and Ruardean *Glouc*

FOREST OF GALTRES (Farlington, Marton w Moxby, Sheriff Hutton, and Sutton-on-the-Forest) *York 3* **P** *Abp (2 turns), Ld Chan (1 turn)* **V** C C ELLIS

FOREST ROW (Holy Trinity) *Chich 7* **P** *V E Grinstead* **V** N H LAMB, **C** P J STEPHENS

FOREST TOWN (St Alban) *S'well 2* **P** *Bp* **P-in-c** P J STEAD

FORESTSIDE (Christ Church) *see* Stansted *Chich*

FORMBY (Holy Trinity) *Liv 5* **P** *Trustees* **C** K ROGERS

FORMBY (St Luke) *Liv 5* **P** *Bp* **V** H T NICOL, **C** M A RIDGE

FORMBY (St Peter) *Liv 5* **P** *R Walton* **V** P W ORMROD

FORNCETT (St Peter) *see* Ashwellthorpe, Forncett, Fundenhall, Hapton etc *Nor*

FORNCETT END (St Edmund) *as above*

FORNHAM ALL SAINTS (All Saints) *see* Lark Valley *St E*

FORNHAM ST MARTIN (St Martin) *as above*

FORRABURY (St Symphorian) *see* Boscastle w Davidstow *Truro*

FORSBROOK (St Peter) *see* Draycott-le-Moors w Forsbrook *Lich*

FORTHAMPTON (St Mary) *see* Deerhurst and Apperley w Forthampton etc *Glouc*

FORTON (All Saints) *Lich 16* **P** *Bp* **V** *vacant*

FORTON (St James) *see* Ellel w Shireshead *Blackb*

FORTON (St John the Evangelist) *Portsm 3* **P** *DBP* **V** C J L J THOMPSON

FORTY HILL (Jesus Church) *Lon 18* **P** *V Enfield* **V** I H CROFTS

FOSDYKE (All Saints) *see* Algarkirk and Fosdyke *Linc*

FOSSE Team, The *Leic 5* **P** *Patr Bd* **TR** D C WHITE, **TV** L D BRABIN-SMITH, J IQBAL, **C** E P ANGELL, **NSM** I M HILL, C M COLDICOTT

FOSSE TRINITY *B & W 7* **P** *Bp and Canon D S Salter (jt)* **P-in-c** C M DONKERSLEY

FOSTON (All Saints) *see* Whitwell w Crambe and Foston *York*

FOSTON (St Bartholomew) *see* Countesthorpe w Foston *Leic*

FOSTON (St Peter) *see* Saxonwell *Linc*

FOSTON-ON-THE-WOLDS (St Andrew) *see* Beeford w Frodingham and Foston *York*

FOTHERBY (St Mary) *Linc 12* **P** *Ld Chan (1 turn), DBP, MMCET and G F Sleight Esq (1 turn), and Bp (1 turn)* **P-in-c** S A ALLISON, **OLM** J M WRISDALE

FOTHERINGHAY (St Mary and All Saints) *see* Warmington, Tansor and Cotterstock etc *Pet*

FOULDEN (All Saints) *see* Oxborough w Foulden and Caldecote *Nor*

FOULRIDGE (St Michael and All Angels) *see* Colne and Villages *Blackb*

FOULSHAM (Holy Innocents), Guestwick, Stibbard, Themelthorpe and Wood Norton *Nor 22* **P** *Bp, DBP, Mrs H M Cook, Lord Hastings, and B E Bulwer-Long Esq (jt)* **V** V M WILSON, **C** D W A RIDER

FOUNTAINS Group, The *Ripon 3* **P** *D&C* **R** *vacant* (01765) 658260

FOUR ELMS (St Paul) *see* Hever, Four Elms and Mark Beech *Roch*

FOUR MARKS (Good Shepherd) *Win 2* **P** *Bp* **V** H J D WRIGHT

FOUR OAKS (All Saints) *Birm 12* **P** *Bp* **V** D A LEAHY, **C** J J BRIDGE, **NSM** R M SHEPPARD

FOURSTONES (St Aidan) *see* Warden w Newbrough *Newc*

FOVANT (St George), Sutton Mandeville and Teffont Evias w Teffont Magna and Compton Chamberlayne *Sarum 11* **P** *Reformation Ch Trust, Bp, and Ch Soc Trust (jt)* **R** *vacant* (01722) 714826

FOWEY (St Fimbarrus) *Truro 1* **P** *Ch Soc Trust* **P-in-c** P DE GREY-WARTER

FOWLMERE (St Mary), Foxton, Shepreth and Thriplow *Ely 7* **P** *Bp* **R** L A CHURCH

FOWNHOPE (St Mary) w Mordiford, Brockhampton and Fawley and Woolhope *Heref 3* **P** *D&C (4 turns), and Major R J Hereford (1 turn)* **NSM** M M DEES

FOXCOTE (St James the Less) *see* Peasedown St John w Wellow and Foxcote etc *B & W*

FOXDALE (St Paul) *S & M 1* **P** *The Crown and Bp (alt)* **V** *vacant*

FOXEARTH (St Peter and St Paul) *see* N Hinckford *Chelmsf*

FOXHAM (St John the Baptist) *see* Marden Vale *Sarum*

FOXHILL (Chapel) *see* Frodsham *Ches*

FOXHOLE (St Boniface) *see* Paignton St Jo *Ex*

FOXHOLES (St Mary) *see* Langtoft w Foxholes, Butterwick, Cottam etc *York*

FOXLEY (not known) *see* Sherston Magna, Easton Grey, Luckington etc *Bris*

FOXLEY (St Thomas) *see* Lyng, Sparham, Elsing, Bylaugh, Bawdeswell etc *Nor*

FOXT (St Mark the Evangelist) *see* Kingsley and Foxt-w-Whiston and Oakamoor etc *Lich*

FOXTON (St Andrew) w Gumley and Laughton *Leic 3* **P** *Bp Leic and D&C Linc (alt)* **P-in-c** I L JOHNSON

FOXTON (St Laurence) *see* Fowlmere, Foxton, Shepreth and Thriplow *Ely*

FOY (St Mary) *see* Brampton *Heref*

FRADLEY (St Stephen) *see* Alrewas *Lich*

FRADSWELL (St James the Less) *see* Mid Trent *Lich*

FRAISTHORPE (St Edmund King and Martyr) *see* Skipsea and Barmston w Fraisthorpe *York*

FRAMFIELD (St Thomas à Becket) *Chich 21* **P** *Mrs E R Wix* **V** C D LAWRENCE

FRAMILODE (St Peter) *see* Frampton on Severn, Arlingham, Saul etc *Glouc*

FRAMINGHAM EARL (St Andrew) *see* Poringland *Nor*

FRAMINGHAM PIGOT (St Andrew) *see* Thurton *Nor*

FRAMLAND Parishes, The HIGH *Leic 2* **P** *Duke of Rutland and Sir Lyonel Tollemache Bt (jt)* **R** *vacant* (01476) 870188

FRAMLAND, SOUTH *Leic 2* **P** *Ld Chan, Duke of Rutland, Lady Gretton, and Sir Lyonel Tollemache Bt (by turn)* **P-in-c** R A KING

FRAMLINGHAM (St Michael) w Saxtead *St E 18* **P** *Pemb Coll Cam* **P-in-c** G W OWEN, **C** M J WOMACK, **OLM** M LAMB

FRAMPTON (St Mary) *see* Bradford Peverell, Stratton, Frampton etc *Sarum*

FRAMPTON (St Mary) (St Michael) *Linc 20* **P** *Trustees* **P-in-c** C W B SOWDEN

FRAMPTON COTTERELL (St Peter) and Iron Acton *Bris 5* **P** *SMF and Ch Ch Ox (jt)* **C** D B HARREX, M A CLACKER

FRAMPTON MANSELL (St Luke) *see* Kemble, Poole Keynes, Somerford Keynes etc *Glouc*

FRAMPTON ON SEVERN (St Mary), Arlingham, Saul, Fretherne and Framilode *Glouc 4* **P** *DBP, V Standish w Haresfield etc, Brig Sir Jeffrey Darell Bt, and Bp (jt)* **P-in-c** A E SPARGO, **NSM** M J NOAH

FRAMSDEN (St Mary) *see* Debenham and Helmingham *St E*

FRAMWELLGATE MOOR (St Aidan) *see* Dur N *Dur*

FRANCE LYNCH (St John the Baptist) *see* Bisley, Chalford, France Lynch, and Oakridge *Glouc*

FRANCHE (St Barnabas) *see* Kidderminster St Mary and All SS w Trimpley etc *Worc*

FRANKBY (St John the Divine) w Greasby St Nicholas *Ches 8* **P** *D&C* **V** K P OWEN, **C** G S FOSTER, **NSM** E M OLLMAN

FRANKLEY (St Leonard) *Birm 4* **P** *Bp* **P-in-c** R H TEBBS

FRANKTON (St Nicholas) *see* Bourton w Frankton and Stretton on Dunsmore etc *Cov*

FRANSHAM, GREAT (All Saints) *see* Gt and Lt Dunham w Gt and Lt Fransham and Sporle *Nor*

FRANSHAM, LITTLE (St Mary) *as above*

FRANT (St Alban) w Eridge *Chich 19* **P** *Bp and Marquess of Abergavenny (jt)* **R** J M PACKMAN

FREASLEY (St Mary) *see* Dordon *Birm*

FRECHEVILLE (St Cyprian) *Sheff 2* **P** *Bp* **R** M J GILLINGHAM

FRECKENHAM (St Andrew) *see* Mildenhall *St E*

FRECKLETON (Holy Trinity) *Blackb 10* **P** *Bp* **P-in-c** J E C PERCIVAL, **NSM** T B SCHOLZ

FREEBY (St Mary) *see* Melton Mowbray *Leic*

FREEHAY (St Chad) *see* Cheadle w Freehay *Lich*

FREELAND (St Mary the Virgin) *see* Hanborough and Freeland *Ox*

FREEMANTLE (Christ Church) *Win 13* **P** *Bp* **P-in-c** B L COX

FREETHORPE (All Saints), Wickhampton, Halvergate w Tunstall, Reedham, Cantley and Limpenhoe w Southwood *Nor 4* **P** *Patr Bd* **R** D ROGERS

FREEZYWATER (St George) *see* Enfield St Geo *Lon*

FREISTON (St James), Butterwick w Bennington, and Leverton *Linc 20* **P** *Ld Chan and Bp (alt)* **P-in-c** A J HIGGINSON, **C** N J BATES

FREMINGTON (St Peter), Instow and Westleigh *Ex 15*
 P *D&C, Christie Trustees, and MMCET (jt)* **R** P H HOCKEY,
 C R E AUSTIN, G CALWAY
FRENCHAY (St John the Baptist) and Winterbourne Down
 Bris 5 **P** *St Jo Coll Ox and SMF (jt)* **C** S J PULLIN,
 M A CLACKER, **OLM** J M LEE
FRENSHAM (St Mary the Virgin) *see* Rowledge and Frensham
 Guildf
**FRESHFORD (St Peter) w Limpley Stoke and Hinton
 Charterhouse** *B & W 8* **P** *Simeon's Trustees and V Norton
 St Phil (jt)* **P-in-c** J M HOFFMANN
FRESHWATER (All Saints) (St Agnes) *Portsm 8* **P** *St Jo Coll
 Cam* **R** M E C WHATSON, **C** R STUART-BOURNE
**FRESSINGFIELD (St Peter and St Paul), Mendham, Metfield,
 Weybread and Withersdale** *St E 17* **P** *Bp, Em Coll Cam,
 Ch Soc Trust, and SMF (jt)* **P-in-c** S A LOXTON,
 NSM P A SCHWIER
FRESTON (St Peter) *see* Holbrook, Stutton, Freston,
 Woolverstone etc *St E*
FRETHERNE (St Mary the Virgin) *see* Frampton on Severn,
 Arlingham, Saul etc *Glouc*
FRETTENHAM (St Swithin) *see* Coltishall w Gt Hautbois,
 Frettenham etc *Nor*
FRIAR PARK (St Francis of Assisi) *see* W Bromwich St Fran
 Lich
FRIARMERE (St Thomas) *see* Saddleworth *Man*
FRICKLEY (All Saints) *see* Bilham *Sheff*
FRIDAY BRIDGE (St Mark) *see* Fen Orchards *Ely*
FRIDAYTHORPE (St Mary) *see* Waggoners *York*
FRIERN BARNET (All Saints) *Lon 14* **P** *Bp* **V** A V BENJAMIN
FRIERN BARNET (St James the Great) (St John the Evangelist)
 Lon 14 **P** *D&C St Paul's* **R** P A WALMSLEY-MCLEOD
FRIERN BARNET (St Peter le Poer) *Lon 14* **P** *D&C St Paul's*
 P-in-c B W BRIDGEWOOD
FRIESTHORPE (St Peter) *see* Middle Rasen Gp *Linc*
FRIETH (St John the Baptist) *see* Hambleden Valley *Ox*
FRIEZLAND (Christ Church) *see* Saddleworth *Man*
FRILSHAM (St Frideswide) *see* Hermitage *Ox*
FRIMLEY (St Francis) (St Peter) *Guildf 6* **P** *R Ash*
 R M K WILSON, **C** A H WALDEN, **OLM** M MASSEY
FRIMLEY GREEN (St Andrew) and Mytchett *Guildf 6* **P** *Bp*
 V S EDWARDS, **OLM** C D COWELL
FRINDSBURY (All Saints) w Upnor and Chattenden *Roch 6*
 P *Bp* **V** I D BROWN, **C** S F VALLENTE-KERR
FRING (All Saints) *see* Snettisham w Ingoldisthorpe and Fring
 Nor
FRINGFORD (St Michael) *see* Shelswell *Ox*
FRINSTED (St Dunstan) *see* Tunstall and Bredgar *Cant*
**FRINTON (St Mary Magdalene) (St Mary the Virgin Old
 Church)** *Chelmsf 22* **P** *CPAS* **R** D E SMITH
FRISBY-ON-THE-WREAKE (St Thomas of Canterbury)
 see Upper Wreake *Leic*
FRISKNEY (All Saints) *Linc 20* **P** *Bp*
 P-in-c F J M COTTON-BETTERIDGE, **C** N J BATES
FRISTON (St Mary Magdalene) *see* Whinlands *St E*
FRISTON (St Mary the Virgin) *see* E Dean w Friston and
 Jevington *Chich*
FRITCHLEY (Mission Room) *see* Crich and S Wingfield *Derby*
FRITHELSTOCK (St Mary and St Gregory) *see* Gt and Lt
 Torrington and Frithelstock *Ex*
FRITHVILLE (St Peter) *see* Sibsey w Frithville *Linc*
FRITTENDEN (St Mary) *see* Sissinghurst w Frittenden *Cant*
FRITTON (St Catherine) *see* Hempnall *Nor*
FRITTON (St Edmund) *see* Somerleyton, Ashby, Fritton,
 Herringfleet etc *Nor*
FRITWELL (St Olave) *see* Cherwell Valley *Ox*
FRIZINGHALL (St Margaret) *Bradf 1* **P** *Bp*
 P-in-c S P HACKING, **C** S D LEES
FRIZINGTON (St Paul) *see* Crosslacon *Carl*
FROCESTER (St Andrew) *see* Eastington, Frocester, Haresfield
 etc *Glouc*
FRODESLEY (St Mark) *see* Condover w Frodesley, Acton
 Burnell etc *Heref*
FRODINGHAM (St Lawrence) *Linc 4* **P** *Lord St Oswald*
 P-in-c M A E ASTIN, **C** E L WAKEHAM, D J SWANNACK,
 NSM M DUNFORD, T R ASTIN
FRODINGHAM, NORTH (St Elgin) *see* Beeford w
 Frodingham and Foston *York*
FRODSHAM (St Lawrence) *Ches 3* **P** *Ch Ch Ox*
 V M H MILLS, **NSM** K L WILLIAMSON
FROGMORE (Holy Trinity) *St Alb 5* **P** *CPAS*
 V D R HEATH-WHYTE, **NSM** N A WARD
FROLESWORTH (St Nicholas) *see* Upper Soar *Leic*
FROME (Christ Church) *B & W 3* **P** *Bp* **P-in-c** N A MAXTED
FROME (Holy Trinity) *B & W 3* **P** *Bp* **V** G A OWEN,
 C N P GRIFFIN

FROME (St John the Baptist) *B & W 3* **P** *DBP* **V** C ALSBURY
FROME (St Mary the Virgin) *B & W 3* **P** *Bp* **V** N A MAXTED
FROME ST QUINTON (St Mary) *see* Melbury *Sarum*
FROME VALLEY Group of Parishes, The *Heref 2* **P** *Bp
 (6 turns), MMCET (2 turns), D&C (1 turn)* **V** J A DAVIES,
 NSM C M SYKES, R P PRIEST
FROME VAUCHURCH (St Mary) *see* Melbury *Sarum*
FROMES HILL (St Matthew) *see* Frome Valley *Heref*
FROSTENDEN (All Saints) *see* Wrentham, Covehithe w
 Benacre etc *St E*
FROSTERLEY (St Michael and All Angels) *see* Upper
 Weardale *Dur*
FROXFIELD (All Saints) *see* Whitton *Sarum*
FROXFIELD (St Peter) *see* Steep and Froxfield w Privett
 Portsm
FROXFIELD (St Peter on the Green) *as above*
FROYLE (Assumption of the Blessed Virgin Mary) *see* Bentley,
 Binsted and Froyle *Win*
FRYERNING (St Mary the Virgin) *see* Ingatestone w Fryerning
 Chelmsf
FRYSTON (St Peter) *see* Airedale w Fryston *Wakef*
FUGGLESTONE (St Peter) *see* Wilton w Netherhampton and
 Fugglestone *Sarum*
FULBECK (St Nicholas) *see* Caythorpe *Linc*
FULBOURN (St Vigor w All Saints) *Ely 4* **P** *St Jo Coll Cam*
 R A A GOODMAN
FULBROOK (St Gabriel) *see* Walsall St Gabr Fulbrook *Lich*
FULBROOK (St James the Great) *see* Burford w Fulbrook,
 Taynton, Asthall etc *Ox*
FULFORD (St Oswald) *York 7* **P** *Abp* **V** *vacant* (01904)
 633261
FULFORD-IN-STONE (St Nicholas) w Hilderstone *Lich 13*
 P *D&C* **P-in-c** P D DAKIN, **NSM** C E DAKIN
FULHAM (All Saints) *Lon 9* **P** *Bp* **V** J P HAWES,
 C P A SEABROOK, **NSM** E MCGREGOR
FULHAM (Christ Church) *Lon 9* **P** *CPAS* **V** S C R LEES,
 C J A HARDING
FULHAM (St Alban) (St Augustine) *Lon 9* **P** *Bp and City
 Corp (jt)* **V** *vacant* (020) 7381 1500 *or* 7385 0724
FULHAM (St Andrew) Fulham Fields *Lon 9* **P** *Bp* **V** *vacant*
 (020) 7385 5023
FULHAM (St Dionis) Parson's Green *Lon 9* **P** *Bp*
 V T J STILWELL, **C** W P G LEAF
FULHAM (St Etheldreda) (St Clement) *Lon 9* **P** *Bp*
 P-in-c J F H HENLEY
FULHAM (St Mary) North End *Lon 9* **P** *Ch Soc Trust*
 V R W CURL
FULHAM (St Matthew) *Lon 9* **P** *Ch Patr Trust*
 V G Q D PIPER, **Dss** V S PIERSON
FULHAM (St Peter) *Lon 9* **P** *Bp* **P-in-c** R B C STANDRING,
 C E J KENDALL
FULKING (Good Shepherd) *see* Poynings w Edburton,
 Newtimber and Pyecombe *Chich*
FULL SUTTON (St Mary) *see* Garrowby Hill *York*
FULLETBY (St Andrew) *see* Hemingby Gp *Linc*
FULMER (St James) *see* Gerrards Cross and Fulmer *Ox*
FULMODESTON (Christ Church) *see* Barney, Fulmodeston w
 Croxton, Hindringham etc *Nor*
FULSHAW (St Anne) *see* Wilmslow *Ches*
FULSTOW (St Laurence) *see* Fotherby *Linc*
FULWOOD (Christ Church) *Blackb 13* **P** *V Lanc*
 V B R MCCONKEY, **C** P G HAMBORG
FULWOOD (Christ Church) *Sheff 4* **P** *CPAS*
 V P A WILLIAMS, **C** A R A REES, E F Q PENNINGTON,
 B C COOPER
FULWOOD Lodge Moor (St Luke) *see* Lodge Moor St Luke
 Sheff
FULWOOD (St Cuthbert) *see* Preston St Cuth *Blackb*
FUNDENHALL (St Nicholas) *see* Ashwellthorpe, Forncett,
 Fundenhall, Hapton etc *Nor*
FUNTINGTON (St Mary) and Sennicotts *Chich 13* **P** *Bp*
 V C W W HOWARD
FUNTLEY (St Francis) *see* Fareham SS Pet and Paul *Portsm*
FURNACE GREEN (St Andrew) *see* Southgate *Chich*
FURNESS VALE (St John) *see* Disley *Ches*
FURNEUX PELHAM (St Mary the Virgin) *see* Albury,
 Braughing, Furneux Pelham, Lt Hadham etc *St Alb*
FURNHAM (Good Shepherd) *see* Chard Gd Shep and Cricket
 St Thomas *B & W*
FURTHO (St Bartholomew) *see* Potterspury w Furtho and
 Yardley Gobion etc *Pet*
FURZE PLATT (St Peter) *Ox 13* **P** *Bp* **V** M A BALFOUR,
 C E K HONEY, **NSM** J R G HYDE
FURZEBANK (Worship Centre) *see* Bentley Em and
 Willenhall H Trin *Lich*

FURZEDOWN (St Paul)   *see* Streatham St Paul *S'wark*
FURZTON (not known)   *see* Watling Valley *Ox*
FYFIELD (St Nicholas)   *see* Upper Kennet *Sarum*
FYFIELD (St Nicholas)   *see* Appleshaw, Kimpton, Thruxton, Fyfield etc *Win*
FYFIELD (St Nicholas) w Tubney and Kingston Bagpuize *Ox 10*   **P** *St Jo Coll Ox*   **P-in-c** D A A PICKERING
FYFIELD (St Nicholas), Moreton w Bobbingworth and Willingale w Shellow and Berners Roding *Chelmsf 26*   **P** *Ld Chan, St Jo Coll Cam, MMCET, and Major G N Capel-Cure (by turn)*   **P-in-c** V ROSS
FYLINGDALES (St Stephen) and Hawsker cum Stainsacre *York 21*   **P** *Abp*   **P-in-c** J D PURDY
G7 Benefice *Cant 6*   **P** *Abp, D&C, and Lord Hothfield (jt)*   **NSM** S A STARKINGS
GADDESBY (St Luke)   *see* S Croxton Gp *Leic*
GADDESDEN, GREAT (St John the Baptist)   *see* Gt Berkhamsted, Gt and Lt Gaddesden etc *St Alb*
GADDESDEN, LITTLE (St Peter and St Paul)   *as above*
GADEBRIDGE (St Peter)   *see* Hemel Hempstead *St Alb*
GAINFORD (St Mary) *Dur 7*   **P** *Trin Coll Cam*   **P-in-c** M JACQUES
GAINSBOROUGH (All Saints) (St George) and Morton *Linc 2*   **P** *Bp*   **C** G S BARROW
GALLEY COMMON (St Peter)   *see* Hartshill and Galley Common *Cov*
GALLEYWOOD (Junior School Worship Centre)   *see* Galleywood Common *Chelmsf*
GALLEYWOOD COMMON (St Michael and All Angels) *Chelmsf 9*   **P** *CPAS*   **V** A T GRIFFITHS,   **C** S R GILLINGHAM
GALMINGTON (St Michael) *B & W 17*   **P** *Bp*   **V** C SNELL,   **C** P J IRVING
GALMPTON (Chapel of The Good Shepherd)   *see* Brixham w Churston Ferrers and Kingswear *Ex*
GAMESLEY (Bishop Geoffrey Allen Church and County Centre)   *see* Charlesworth and Dinting Vale *Derby*
GAMLINGAY (St Mary the Virgin) and Everton *Ely 13*   **P** *Bp, Clare Coll Cam, and Down Coll Cam (by turn)*   **R** S ROTHWELL
GAMLINGAY HEATH (St Sylvester)   *see* Gamlingay and Everton *Ely*
GAMSTON and Bridgford *S'well 5*   **P** *DBP*   **P-in-c** M A FRASER,   **C** T J PARKER
GAMSTON (St Peter)   *see* Retford Area *S'well*
GANAREW (St Swithin)   *see* Dixton, Wyesham, Bishopswood, Whitchurch etc *Heref*
GANTON (St Nicholas)   *see* Willerby w Ganton and Folkton *York*
GARBOLDISHAM (St John the Baptist)   *see* Guiltcross *Nor*
GARFORD (St Luke)   *see* Marcham w Garford *Ox*
GARFORTH (St Mary the Virgin) *Ripon 8*   **P** *DBP*   **P-in-c** G W COOPER,   **NSM** H BANKS
GARGRAVE (St Andrew) w Coniston Cold *Bradf 5*   **P** *Bp*   **P-in-c** R C GEDDES
GARRETTS GREEN (St Thomas) and Tile Cross *Birm 9*   **P** *Bp*   **V** B S CASTLE,   **NSM** M MACLACHLAN
GARRIGILL (St John)   *see* Alston Moor *Newc*
GARROWBY HILL *York 5*   **P** *Ld Chan (1 turn), Abp, D&C, and Earl of Halifax (3 turns)*   **R** J C FINNEMORE
GARSDALE (St John the Baptist)   *see* Sedbergh, Cautley and Garsdale *Bradf*
GARSDON (All Saints), Lea and Cleverton and Charlton *Bris 6*   **P** *Ch Soc Trust and Bp (jt)*   **R** R K EAST,   **NSM** P C ASHBY
GARSINGTON (St Mary)   *see* Wheatley *Ox*
GARSTANG (St Helen) Churchtown and St Michaels-on-Wyre *Blackb 9*   **P** *Dr I R H Jackson and R P Hornby Esq (jt)*   **V** A W WILKINSON,   **NSM** C M WHALLEY
GARSTANG (St Thomas) *Blackb 9*   **P** *V Churchtown St Helen*   **P-in-c** S B GREY,   **NSM** A J ROBERTS
GARSTON (St Michael) *Liv 4*   **P** *Trustees*   **P-in-c** R L METCALF
GARSTON, EAST (All Saints)   *see* Eastbury and E Garston *Ox*
GARSWOOD (St Andrew)   *see* Ashton-in-Makerfield H Trin *Liv*
GARTHORPE (St Mary)   *see* Crowle Gp *Linc*
GARTON IN HOLDERNESS (St Michael)   *see* Roos and Garton w Tunstall, Grimston and Hilston *York*
GARTON-ON-THE-WOLDS (St Michael and All Angels)   *see* Woldsburn *York*
GARVESTON (St Margaret)   *see* Barnham Broom and Upper Yare *Nor*
GARWAY (St Michael)   *see* St Weonards *Heref*
GASTARD (St John the Baptist)   *see* Gtr Corsham and Lacock *Bris*
GATCOMBE (St Olave) *Portsm 8*   **P** *Qu Coll Ox*   **P-in-c** M C BAGG
GATE BURTON (St Helen)   *see* Lea Gp *Linc*

GATE HELMSLEY (St Mary)   *see* Sand Hutton *York*
GATEACRE (St Stephen) *Liv 4*   **P** *Bp*   **TR** P H JANVIER,   **TV** J L MCKELVEY,   **C** N H LEA-WILSON,   **NSM** K A CANTY
GATEFORTH (St Mary's Mission Room)   *see* Haddlesey w Hambleton and Birkin *York*
GATELEY (St Helen)   *see* Upper Wensum Village Gp *Nor*
GATESHEAD Lobley Hill (All Saints)   *see* Hillside *Dur*
GATESHEAD (St Chad)   *see* Bensham and Teams *Dur*
GATESHEAD (St Edmund's Chapel w Holy Trinity) (Venerable Bede) *Dur 12*   **P** *Bp and The Crown (alt)*   **TR** J C WILKINSON,   **TV** J O M CRAIG,   **NSM** E CARR, A PHILLIPS
GATESHEAD (St George) *Dur 12*   **P** *Trustees*   **V** vacant 0191-487 5587
GATESHEAD (St Helen) *Dur 12*   **P** *Bp*   **V** B M HARRISON,   **NSM** D BROWN
GATESHEAD (St Ninian) Harlow Green   *see* Harlow Green and Lamesley *Dur*
GATESHEAD FELL (St John) *Dur 12*   **P** *Bp*   **R** A V WEST
GATLEY (St James) *Ches 17*   **P** *R Stockport St Thos*   **V** R E READ
GATTEN (St Paul) *Portsm 7*   **P** *Ch Patr Trust*   **V** P G ALLEN
GATTON (St Andrew)   *see* Merstham, S Merstham and Gatton *S'wark*
GAULBY (St Peter) *Leic 4*   **P** *Ch Soc Trust*   **P-in-c** J MORLEY
GAUTBY (All Saints)   *see* Bardney *Linc*
GAWBER (St Thomas) *Wakef 7*   **P** *V Darton*   **P-in-c** M S POSKITT
GAWCOTT (Holy Trinity)   *see* Lenborough *Ox*
GAWSWORTH (St James) *Ches 13*   **P** *T R R Richards Esq*   **R** W A PWAISIHO
GAYDON (St Giles) w Chadshunt *Cov 8*   **P** *Bp*   **P-in-c** M G CADWALLADER
GAYHURST (St Peter) w Ravenstone, Stoke Goldington and Weston Underwood *Ox 27*   **P** *Bp and Lord Hesketh (jt)*   **R** C E PUMFREY,   **Hon C** J M LAWRENCE
GAYTON (St Mary)   *see* Pattishall w Cold Higham and Gayton w Tiffield *Pet*
GAYTON (St Nicholas), Gayton Thorpe, East Walton, East Winch w West Bilney, Ashwicken w Leziate and Bawsey *Nor 20*   **P** *Bp, Capt H Birkbeck, and W O Lancaster Esq (jt)*   **P-in-c** J M HOLMES,   **NSM** S M MARTIN
GAYTON (St Peter)   *see* Mid Trent *Lich*
GAYTON LE WOLD (St Peter)   *see* Asterby Gp *Linc*
GAYTON THORPE (St Mary)   *see* Gayton, Gayton Thorpe, E Walton, E Winch etc *Nor*
GAYWOOD (St Faith) King's Lynn *Nor 20*   **P** *Patr Bd*   **TR** B J WOOD,   **TV** D R GINGRICH,   **C** L A HUMPHREYS,   **E A MARTIN,   **OLM** H E BERRY
GAZELEY (All Saints)   *see* Dalham, Gazeley, Higham, Kentford and Moulton *St E*
GEDDING (St Mary the Virgin)   *see* Bradfield St Clare, Bradfield St George etc *St E*
GEDDINGTON (St Mary Magdalene) w Weekley *Pet 9*   **P** *Boughton Estates*   **P-in-c** F G GODBER
GEDLING (All Hallows) *S'well 10*   **P** *DBP*   **R** M J TAYLOR,   **NSM** E C KIRK
GEDNEY (St Mary Magdalene)   *see* Fleet w Gedney *Linc*
GEDNEY DROVE END (Christ Church)   *see* Lutton w Gedney Drove End, Dawsmere *Linc*
GEDNEY HILL (Holy Trinity) (St Polycarp) *Linc 16*   **P** *Bp*   **V** R J MORRISON
GEE CROSS (Holy Trinity) (St Philip's Mission Room) *Ches 14*   **P** *V Werneth*   **V** M I BENNETT,   **C** J HALSTEAD
GELDESTON (St Michael)   *see* Gillingham w Geldeston, Stockton, Ellingham etc *Nor*
GENTLESHAW (Christ Church) *Lich 1*   **P** *MMCET*   **P-in-c** M J BUTT,   **OLM** L MCKEON
GEORGEHAM (St George) *Ex 15*   **P** *MMCET*   **P-in-c** M C NEWBON,   **NSM** S OLDHAM
GERMAN (St German) *S & M 1*   **P** *Bp*   **V** N P GODFREY
GERMAN (St John the Baptist) *S & M 1*   **P** *Bp*   **P-in-c** A M CONVERY
GERMANSWEEK (St German)   *see* Okehampton w Inwardleigh, Bratton Clovelly etc *Ex*
GERMOE (St Germoe)   *see* Breage w Godolphin and Germoe *Truro*
GERRANS (St Gerran) w St Anthony-in-Roseland and Philleigh *Truro 6*   **P** *Bp and MMCET (jt)*   **P-in-c** J K EDWARDS
GERRARDS CROSS (St James) and Fulmer *Ox 20*   **P** *Bp and Simeon's Trustees (jt)*   **R** M J WILLIAMS,   **C** P D MANN,   **T J HOLBIRD, J R LEACH,   **NSM** M R L BEEBEE, S D SWINNEY
GESTINGTHORPE (St Mary)   *see* Knights and Hospitallers Par *Chelmsf*
GIDDING, GREAT (St Michael) w LITTLE (St John) and Steeple Gidding *Ely 10*   **P** *Sir Philip Naylor-Leyland Bt and Bp (alt)*   **P-in-c** M P JEPP

GIDEA PARK (St Michael) *Chelmsf 2* **P** *Bp* **V** M A H FINCH, **OLM** R W FINCH

GIDLEIGH (Holy Trinity) *see* Chagford, Drewsteignton, Hittisleigh etc *Ex*

GIFLE VALLEY *Sarum 3* **P** *J K Wingfield Digby Esq and Win Coll (alt)* **P-in-c** H G PEARSON, **NSM** M ANDERSON

GIGGETTY LANE (The Venerable Bede) *see* Smestow Vale *Lich*

GIGGLESWICK (St Alkelda) and Rathmell w Wigglesworth *Bradf 5* **P** *Bp and Ch Trust Fund Trust (jt)* **NSM** A T HELM

GILCRUX (St Mary) *see* Aspatria w Hayton and Gilcrux *Carl*

GILDERSOME (St Peter) *Wakef 8* **P** *V Batley* **V** A F LAWSON

GILLAMOOR (St Aidan) *see* Kirkbymoorside w Gillamoor, Farndale etc *York*

GILLING (St Agatha) and Kirkby Ravensworth *Ripon 2* **P** *Bp and A C P Wharton Esq (jt)* **P-in-c** J M RICHARDS, **Hon C** A GLEDHILL

GILLING EAST (Holy Cross) *see* Ampleforth w Oswaldkirk, Gilling E etc *York*

GILLINGHAM (Holy Trinity) *Roch 3* **P** *Bp* **P-in-c** A M SPREADBRIDGE

GILLINGHAM (St Augustine) *Roch 3* **P** *Bp* **P-in-c** J P JENNINGS

GILLINGHAM (St Barnabas) *Roch 3* **P** *Bp* **V** *vacant*

GILLINGHAM (St Luke) *see* New Brompton St Luke *Roch*

GILLINGHAM (St Mark) *Roch 3* **P** *Hyndman Trustees* **P** in c P G GUINNEE, **C** C E MCWATT

GILLINGHAM (St Mary Magdalene) *Roch 3* **P** *DBP* **P-in-c** S M PATTLE

GILLINGHAM (St Mary the Virgin) and Milton-on-Stour *Sarum 5* **P** *Bp* **P-in-c** J P GREENWOOD, **C** N J MERCER, **NSM** T F HEATON

GILLINGHAM (St Mary) w Geldeston w Stockton w Ellingham St Mary and Kirby Cane *Nor 8* **P** *Ld Chan (1 turn), Bp, MMCET and Ch Trust Fund Trust (1 turn)* **P-in-c** J L ODDY-BATES

GILLINGHAM, SOUTH (St Matthew) *Roch 3* **P** *Patr Bd* **TR** B APPLETON, **TV** S C FERRIS, P J BARNES, **NSM** G R LEWIS, E HURST

GILLOW HEATH (Mission Room) *see* Biddulph *Lich*

GILMORTON (All Saints), Peatling Parva, Kimcote cum Walton, North Kilworth, South Kilworth, Misterton, Swinford, Catthorpe, Shawell and Stanford *Leic 7* **P** *Patr Bd (5 turns), Ld Chan (1 turn)* **TV** E L DAVIES, **NSM** J R KENNEDY

GILSLAND (St Mary Magdalene) *see* Lanercost, Walton, Gilsland and Nether Denton *Carl*

GILSTEAD (St Wilfrid) *see* Bingley H Trin *Bradf*

GILSTON (St Mary) *see* High Wych and Gilston w Eastwick *St Alb*

GIMINGHAM (All Saints) *see* Trunch *Nor*

GIPPING (Chapel of St Nicholas) *see* Haughley w Wetherden and Stowupland *St E*

GIPSY HILL (Christ Church) *S'wark 12* **P** *CPAS* **V** *vacant*

GIPTON (Church of the Epiphany) *see* Leeds Gipton Epiphany *Ripon*

GIRLINGTON (St Philip) *Bradf 1* **P** *Simeon's Trustees* **P-in-c** F J ROBERTSON

GIRTON (St Andrew) *Ely 6* **P** *Ld Chan* **R** M J MAXWELL, **NSM** M C BARROW

GIRTON (St Cecilia) *see* E Trent *S'well*

GISBURN (St Mary the Virgin) *Bradf 5* **P** *Bp* **V** *vacant* (01200) 415935

GISLEHAM (Holy Trinity) *see* Kessingland, Gisleham and Rushmere *Nor*

GISLINGHAM (St Mary) *see* S Hartismere *St E*

GISSING (St Mary the Virgin) *see* Winfarthing w Shelfanger w Burston w Gissing etc *Nor*

GITTISHAM (St Michael) *see* Honiton, Gittisham, Combe Raleigh, Monkton etc *Ex*

GIVENDALE, GREAT (St Ethelberga) *see* Pocklington Wold *York*

GLAISDALE (St Thomas) *see* Middle Esk Moor *York*

GLANDFORD (St Martin) *see* Blakeney w Cley, Wiveton, Glandford etc *Nor*

GLANTON (St Peter) *see* Whittingham and Edlingham w Bolton Chapel *Newc*

GLANVILLES WOOTTON (St Mary the Virgin) *see* Vale of White Hart *Sarum*

GLAPTHORN (St Leonard) *see* Oundle w Ashton and Benefield w Glapthorn *Pet*

GLAPWELL (St Andrew) *see* Ault Hucknall and Scarcliffe *Derby*

GLASCOTE (St George) and Stonydelph *Lich 4* **P** *Patr Bd* **TR** I H MURRAY, **TV** J W TROOD, **C** J R IDDON,

OLM M R LE-WORTHY, R J LOCKWOOD, P D FAULTLESS, K R LINDSAY-SMITH

GLASCOTE HEATH (St Peter) *see* Glascote and Stonydelph *Lich*

GLASSHOUGHTON (St Paul) *see* Castleford *Wakef*

GLASSON (Christ Church) *see* Cockerham w Winmarleigh and Glasson *Blackb*

GLASTON (St Andrew) *see* Lyddington, Bisbrooke, Caldecott, Glaston etc *Pet*

GLASTONBURY (St John the Baptist) (St Benedict) w Meare *B & W 4* **P** *Bp* **P-in-c** D J L MACGEOCH, **C** D M GREENFIELD

GLATTON (St Nicholas) *see* Sawtry and Glatton *Ely*

GLAZEBURY (All Saints) w Hollinfare *Liv 15* **P** *Bp and R Warrington (jt)* **C** P L GRAY

GLAZELEY (St Bartholomew) *see* Highley w Billingsley, Glazeley etc *Heref*

GLEADLESS (Christ Church) *Sheff 1* **P** *DBP* **TR** H A JOWETT

GLEADLESS VALLEY (Holy Cross) *see* Heeley and Gleadless Valley *Sheff*

GLEM VALLEY United Benefice, The *see* Glemsford, Hartest w Boxted, Somerton etc *St E*

GLEMHAM, GREAT (All Saints) *see* Alde River *St E*

GLEMHAM, LITTLE (St Andrew) *as above*

GLEMSFORD (St Mary the Virgin), Hartest w Boxted, Somerton and Stanstead (Glem Valley United Benefice) *St E 12* **P** *Bp, Prime Min and Ch Soc Trust (by turn)* **TR** P J PRIGG

GLEN AULDYN (Mission Church) *see* Lezayre *S & M*

GLEN GROUP, The *Linc 17* **P** *Bp* **C** L PUGH, **OLM** P E HARDINGHAM

GLEN MAGNA (St Cuthbert) cum Stretton Magna w Carlton Curlieu and Burton Overy *Leic 4* **P** *Bp, Dr A Llewellyn, and Sir Geoffrey Palmer Bt (jt)* **P-in-c** M J IRELAND

GLEN PARVA and South Wigston *Leic 4* **P** *Bp* **V** P DAY

GLENDALE Group, The *Newc 7* **P** *Patr Bd (4 turns), Ld Chan (1 turn)* **TR** R B S BURSTON, **TV** J B SMITH, M J PENFOLD

GLENEAGLES Conventional District *Pet 6* **Min** M C PEREIRA

GLENFIELD (St Peter) *Leic 9* **P** *Bp* **R** J E SHARPE, **C** S F BRADLEY

GLENHOLT (St Anne) *see* Bickleigh and Shaugh Prior *Ex*

GLENTHAM (St Peter) *see* Owmby Gp *Linc*

GLENTWORTH Group, The (St Michael) *Linc 2* **P** *Bp, MMCET, and Ch Soc Trust (jt)* **P-in-c** M BRISCOE, **NSM** C A SULLY

GLINTON (St Benedict) *see* Peakirk w Glinton and Northborough *Pet*

GLODWICK (St Mark w Christ Church) *Man 15* **P** *Bp* **V** G HOLLOWOOD

GLOOSTON (St John the Baptist) *see* Welham, Glooston and Cranoe and Stonton Wyville *Leic*

GLOSSOP (All Saints) *Derby 6* **P** *Patr Bd* **P-in-c** I K STUBBS

GLOUCESTER (St Aldate) Finlay Road *Glouc 2* **P** *Bp* **V** *vacant* (01452) 523906

GLOUCESTER (St Barnabas) *see* Tuffley *Glouc*

GLOUCESTER (St Catharine) *Glouc 2* **P** *Bp* **P-in-c** J M ITUMU, **NSM** M WILLIAMS, B D CLIFFORD

GLOUCESTER (St George) w Whaddon *Glouc 2* **P** *Bp* **P-in-c** D R SMITH, **NSM** A E SMITH

GLOUCESTER (St James and All Saints) (Christ Church) *Glouc 2* **P** *Bp* **V** R C SIMPSON, **NSM** J M HOWARD, P R GIFFORD

GLOUCESTER (St Michael) *see* Tuffley *Glouc*

GLOUCESTER (St Oswald) *see* Coney Hill *Glouc*

GLOUCESTER (St Paul) and St Stephen *Glouc 2* **P** *Bp* **V** R J WITCOMBE, **NSM** G HUBBARD, J R MURPHY

GLOUCESTER CITY St Mark (St Mary de Crypt) (St John the Baptist) (St Mary de Lode) (St Nicholas) and Hempsted *Glouc 2* **P** *D&C (1 turn), Bp (3 turns), Ld Chan (1 turn)* **R** N M ARTHY, **C** R H WOODALL

GLOUCESTER DOCKS Mariners' Church Proprietary Chapel *Glouc 2* **P** *Ch Soc Trust vacant*

GLOUCESTER ROAD (St Stephen) *see* S Kensington St Steph *Lon*

GLUSBURN (All Saints) *see* Sutton w Cowling and Lothersdale *Bradf*

GLYMPTON (St Mary) *see* Wootton w Glympton and Kiddington *Ox*

GLYNDE (St Mary), West Firle and Beddingham *Chich 18* **P** *Bp and D&C Windsor (alt)* **P-in-c** P C OWEN-JONES

GNOSALL (St Lawrence) *see* Adbaston, High Offley, Knightley, Norbury etc *Lich*

GOADBY (St John the Baptist) *see* Church Langton cum Tur Langton etc *Leic*

GOADBY MARWOOD (St Denys) *see* Ironstone Villages *Leic*

GOATHILL (St Peter) *see* Milborne Port w Goathill etc *B & W*
GOATHLAND (St Mary) *see* Middle Esk Moor *York*
GOATHURST (St Edward the King and Martyr) *see* Aisholt, Enmore, Goathurst, Nether Stowey etc *B & W*
GOBOWEN (All Saints) *see* Selattyn and Hengoed w Gobowen *Lich*
GOBOWEN ROAD (Mission Room) *see* Oswestry *Lich*
GODALMING (St Peter and St Paul) *Guildf 4* **P** *Bp*
TR K M ROBERTS, C K E WYLES, **OLM** R HARVIE
GODINGTON (Holy Trinity) *see* Shelswell *Ox*
GODLEY cum Newton Green (St John the Baptist) *Ches 14* **P** *R Cheadle* **P-in-c** M D HARRIES
GODMANCHESTER (St Mary) *Ely 10* **P** *D&C Westmr* **P-in-c** D W BUSK
GODMANSTONE (Holy Trinity) *see* Buckland Newton, Cerne Abbas, Godmanstone etc *Sarum*
GODMERSHAM (St Lawrence the Martyr) *see* Crundale w Godmersham *Cant*
GODREVY *Truro 5* **P** *Patr Bd* **TR** M A TREMBATH, **NSM** P C JOHNSON, P M MURLEY
GODSHILL (All Saints) *Portsm 7* **P** *Guild of All So* **V** J M RYDER
GODSHILL (St Giles) *see* Fordingbridge and Breamore and Hale etc *Win*
GODSTONE (St Nicholas) and Blindley Heath *S'wark 25* **P** *Bp and T Goad Esq (jt)* **R** P C GOODRIDGE
GOFF'S OAK (St James) *see* Cheshunt *St Alb*
GOLBORNE (St Thomas) *Liv 15* **P** *Bp* **P-in-c** J W REED
GOLCAR (St John the Evangelist) *Wakef 5* **P** *V Huddersfield* V R M F CROMPTON, C C H GWINNETT
GOLDEN CAP TEAM (Team Ministry) *Sarum 2* **P** *Patr Bd* **TR** S J SKINNER, **TV** J M SKINNER
GOLDEN GREEN (Mission) *see* Hadlow *Roch*
GOLDEN VALLEY (St Matthias) *see* Riddings and Ironville *Derby*
GOLDENHILL (St John the Evangelist) and Tunstall *Lich 11* **P** *Bp* **V** T W J STATHER
GOLDERS GREEN (St Alban the Martyr and St Michael) *Lon 15* **P** *Bp* **V** R G MORTON
GOLDHANGER (St Peter) *see* Gt Totham and Lt Totham w Goldhanger *Chelmsf*
GOLDINGTON (St Mary the Virgin) *St Alb 9* **P** *Bp* **V** R L HOWLETT, **C** C N NJOKU
GOLDS HILL (St Paul) *see* W Bromwich St Jas w St Paul *Lich*
GOLDSBOROUGH (St Mary) *see* Knaresborough *Ripon*
GOLDSWORTH PARK (St Andrew) *Guildf 12* **P** *Bp* **V** R J N COOK, **NSM** C A HARRISON, **OLM** P R B DONAGHY
GOLDTHORPE (St John the Evangelist and St Mary Magdalene) w Hickleton *Sheff 12* **P** *CR (2 turns), Earl of Halifax (1 turn)* **V** C R SCHAEFER, **Hon C** A BRISCOE
GOMERSAL (St Mary) *Wakef 8* **P** *Bp* **P-in-c** K NICHOLL, **NSM** S FISHER
GONALSTON (St Laurence) *see* Epperstone, Gonalston, Oxton and Woodborough *S'well*
GONERBY, GREAT (St Sebastian) *see* Barrowby and Gt Gonerby *Linc*
GOOD EASTER (St Andrew) *see* High and Gd Easter w Margaret Roding *Chelmsf*
GOOD SHEPHERD TEAM MINISTRY, The *Carl 4* **P** *Patr Bd* **TR** W J WHITE, **TV** R C PATTINSON, H M K BRETT YOUNG
GOODERSTONE (St George) *see* Cockley Cley w Gooderstone *Nor*
GOODLEIGH (St Gregory) *see* Barnstaple *Ex*
GOODMANHAM (All Saints) *York 5* **P** *Abp* **R** D J EVERETT
GOODMAYES (All Saints) *Chelmsf 4* **P** *Hyndman Trustees* **V** P H NYATSANZA
GOODMAYES (St Paul) *Chelmsf 4* **P** *Bp* **V** B J RUTT-FIELD
GOODNESTONE (Holy Cross) *see* Nonington w Wymynswold and Goodnestone etc *Cant*
GOODRICH (St Giles), Marstow, Welsh Bicknor, Llangarron, Llangrove and Welsh Newton w Llanrothal *Heref 7* **P** *Bp (2 turns), D&C and DBP (2 turns)* **V** S C MONDON, **NSM** R J STEPHENS, **OLM** P A POWDRILL
GOODRINGTON (St George) *Ex 12* **P** *Bp* **V** G H MAUDE
GOODSHAW (St Mary and All Saints) and Crawshawbooth *Man 11* **P** *Bp and Wm Hulme Trustees (jt)* **P-in-c** J S MONTGOMERY, **OLM** D SMITH
GOODWORTH CLATFORD (St Peter) *see* Abbotts Ann and Upper and Goodworth Clatford *Win*
GOOLE (St John the Evangelist) (St Mary) (Mariners' Club and Chapel) *Sheff 10* **P** *Bp* **V** vacant (01405) 765582
GOOSE GREEN (St Paul) *Liv 14* **P** *Bp* **P-in-c** N J COOK
GOOSEY (All Saints) *see* Stanford in the Vale w Goosey and Hatford *Ox*

GOOSNARGH (St Mary the Virgin) *see* Fellside Team *Blackb*
GOOSTREY (St Luke) w Swettenham *Ches 11* **P** *V Sandbach and MMCET (jt)* **V** I GODFREY, **NSM** P E SOULT
GORAN HAVEN (St Just) *see* St Goran w Caerhays *Truro*
GORDON HILL (St Michael and All Angels) *see* Enfield St Mich *Lon*
GOREFIELD (St Paul) *see* Wisbech St Mary and Guyhirn w Ring's End etc *Ely*
GORING (St Thomas of Canterbury) and Streatley with South Stoke *Ox 6* **P** *Ch Ch Ox and Bp (jt)* **V** M K BLAMEY, C L J HEYN, **NSM** E J DOWDING
GORING-BY-SEA (St Mary) (St Laurence) *Chich 4* **P** *Bp* **V** G J BUTLER, **NSM** P MATTHEWS
GORLESTON (St Andrew) *Nor 6* **P** *Ch Trust Fund Trust* C M K SIMM, D R CURRIE, **OLM** D A N WAITE
GORLESTON (St Mary Magdalene) *Nor 6* **P** *Bp and Ch Trust Fund Trust (jt)* **V** L E RICKETTS
GORNAL (St Peter) and Sedgley *Worc 10* **P** *Patr Bd* **TR** S R BUCKLEY, **TV** A G STAND, **C** R T PARKER-MCGEE
GORNAL, LOWER (St James the Great) *Worc 10* **P** *Bp* **V** J W MOTT
GORSLEY (Christ Church) *see* Newent and Gorsley w Cliffords Mesne *Glouc*
GORTON (Emmanuel) (St James) (St Philip) and Abbey Hey *Man 1* **P** *Patr Bd and Prime-Min (alt)* **TR** J FARADAY, **TV** F SHER
GOSBECK (St Mary) *see* Coddenham w Gosbeck and Hemingstone w Henley *St E*
GOSBERTON (St Peter and St Paul), Gosberton Clough and Quadring *Linc 17* **P** *Bp and D&C (jt)* **P-in-c** I R WALTERS, **OLM** P E HARDINGHAM
GOSBERTON CLOUGH (St Gilbert and St Hugh) *see* Gosberton, Gosberton Clough and Quadring *Linc*
GOSCOTE, EAST (St Hilda) *see* Fosse *Leic*
GOSFIELD (St Katherine) *see* Halstead Area *Chelmsf*
GOSFORTH (All Saints) *Newc 2* **P** *Bp* **V** G L TUNBRIDGE, C A MAXWELL, **NSM** R B BIRNIE
GOSFORTH (St Hugh) *Newc 2* **P** *Bp* **P-in-c** A J CAVANAGH
GOSFORTH (St Mary) w Nether Wasdale and Wasdale Head *Carl 5* **P** *Bp, Earl of Lonsdale, V St Bees, and PCCs (jt)* **P-in-c** J M S FALKNER
GOSFORTH (St Nicholas) *Newc 2* **P** *Bp* **V** P J CUNNINGHAM, **C** M A C DALLISTON, **NSM** M C DOUGLASS
GOSFORTH, NORTH (St Columba) *see* Ch the King *Newc*
GOSFORTH VALLEY (St Andrew) *see* Dronfield w Holmesfield *Derby*
GOSPEL END (St Barnabas) *see* Gornal and Sedgley *Worc*
GOSPEL LANE (St Michael) *see* Hall Green St Mich *Birm*
GOSPEL OAK (All Hallows) *see* Hampstead St Steph w All Hallows *Lon*
GOSPEL OAK (St Martin) *see* Kentish Town St Martin w St Andr *Lon*
GOSPORT (Christ Church) *Portsm 3* **P** *Bp* **V** A G DAVIS
GOSPORT (Holy Trinity) *Portsm 3* **P** *Abp* **V** A G DAVIS
GOSSOPS GREEN (St Alban) *see* Ifield *Chich*
GOTHAM (St Lawrence) *S'well 9* **P** *Bp* **P-in-c** R I COLEMAN
GOUDHURST (St Mary the Virgin) w Kilndown *Cant 10* **P** *Abp and Prime Min (alt)* **V** W J HORNSBY, **NSM** T K ELSWORTH
GOULCEBY (All Saints) *see* Asterby Gp *Linc*
GOXHILL (All Saints) *see* Barrow and Goxhill *Linc*
GOXHILL (St Giles) *see* Aldbrough, Mappleton w Goxhill and Withernwick *York*
GRADE (St Grada and the Holy Cross) *see* St Ruan w St Grade and Landewednack *Truro*
GRAFFHAM (St Giles) w Woolavington *Chich 11* **P** *Bp* **P-in-c** S J N GRAY
GRAFFOE Group *Linc 18* **P** *Ch Coll Cam, D&C and DBP, Viscountess Chaplin, Oriel Coll Ox, and Mrs P N Fullerton (by turn)* **R** K A WINDSLOW, **NSM** S G WILLIAMS
GRAFHAM (All Saints) *see* E Leightonstone *Ely*
GRAFHAM (St Andrew) *see* Bramley and Grafham *Guildf*
GRAFTON, EAST (St Nicholas) *see* Savernake *Sarum*
GRAFTON FLYFORD (St John the Baptist) *see* Abberton, The Flyfords, Naunton Beauchamp etc *Worc*
GRAFTON REGIS (St Mary) *see* Blisworth and Stoke Bruerne w Grafton Regis etc *Pet*
GRAFTON UNDERWOOD (St James the Apostle) *see* Cranford w Grafton Underwood and Twywell *Pet*
GRAHAME PARK (St Augustine) Conventional District *Lon 15* **C-in-c** D C BATLEY-GLADDEN
GRAIN (St James) w Stoke *Roch 6* **P** *DBP* **V** vacant (01634) 270263
GRAINSBY (St Nicholas) *see* The North-Chapel Parishes *Linc*

GRAINTHORPE (St Clement)　*see* Somercotes and
　Grainthorpe w Conisholme *Linc*
GRAMPOUND (St Nun)　*see* Probus, Ladock and Grampound
　w Creed and St Erme *Truro*
GRAMPOUND ROAD Mission Church　*as above*
GRANBOROUGH (St John the Baptist)　*see* Schorne *Ox*
GRANBY (All Saints)　*see* Cropwell Bishop w Colston Bassett,
　Granby etc *S'well*
GRANDBOROUGH (St Peter)　*see* Leam Valley *Cov*
GRANGE (Holy Trinity)　*see* Upper Derwent *Carl*
GRANGE (St Andrew) *Ches 3*　P *Bp*　V　W S H DOCHERTY
GRANGE FELL (not known)　*see* Cartmel Peninsula *Carl*
GRANGE MOOR (St Bartholomew)　*see* Kirkheaton *Wakef*
GRANGE-OVER-SANDS (St Paul)　*see* Cartmel Peninsula
　Carl
GRANGE PARK Local Ecumenical Partnership *Pet 4*
　Min　C H FF NOBBS
GRANGE PARK (St Peter) *Lon 18*　P *Bp*　V　E G GREER
GRANGE VILLA (St Columba)　*see* Pelton and W Pelton *Dur*
GRANGETOWN (St Aidan) *Dur 16*　P *V Ryhope*
　V　C COLLINS
GRANGETOWN (St Hilda of Whitby) *York 17*　P *Abp*
　V　I M GRAHAM
GRANSDEN, GREAT (St Bartholomew) and Abbotsley and Lt
　Gransden and Waresley *Ely 13*　P *Pemb Coll Cam (1 turn),
　Clare Coll Cam (2 turns), and Ball Coll Ox (1 turn)*
　P-in-c　C M FURLONG
GRANSDEN, LITTLE (St Peter and St Paul)　*see* Gt Gransden
　and Abbotsley and Lt Gransden etc *Ely*
GRANTCHESTER (St Andrew and St Mary) *Ely 3*　P *CCC
　Cam*　P-in-c　S P MEWS
GRANTHAM Earlesfield *Linc 19*　P *Bp*　V　S G ROWLAND
GRANTHAM Harrowby w Londonthorpe *Linc 19*　P *Bp*
　P-in-c　C P BOLAND,　NSM　A P JABLONSKI
GRANTHAM Manthorpe *Linc 19*　P *Bp*
　P-in-c　C P ANDREWS,　NSM　J POTTS
GRANTHAM (St Anne) New Somerby and St John Spitalgate
　Linc 19　P *Bp and R Grantham (jt)*　P-in-c　S G ROWLAND
GRANTHAM (St John the Evangelist)　*see* Grantham,
　Manthorpe *Linc*
GRANTHAM (St Wulfram) *Linc 19*　P *Bp*　R　C P ANDREWS,
　C　A J JABLONSKI,　NSM　J T FARLEY, J M ROWLAND
GRANTHAM (The Ascension)　*see* Grantham, Harrowby w
　Londonthorpe *Linc*
GRANTHAM (The Epiphany)　*see* Grantham, Earlesfield *Linc*
GRAPPENHALL (St Wilfrid) *Ches 4*　P *P G Greenall Esq*
　R　M B KELLY
GRASBY (All Saints)　*see* Caistor Gp *Linc*
GRASMERE (St Oswald) *Carl 11*　P *Qu Coll Ox*
　R　C J BUTLAND
GRASSENDALE (St Mary) *Liv 4*　P *Trustees*　P-in-c　P ELLIS,
　NSM　P SALTMARSH, N ARNOLD
GRATELEY (St Leonard)　*see* Portway and Danebury *Win*
GRATWICH (St Mary the Virgin)　*see* Uttoxeter Area *Lich*
GRAVELEY (St Botolph)　*see* Papworth *Ely*
GRAVELEY (St Mary)　*see* Stevenage St Nic and Graveley
　St Alb
GRAVELLY HILL (All Saints) *Birm 8*　P *Bp*
　V　G R MENSINGH,　NSM　A R FRASER
GRAVENEY (All Saints)　*see* Preston next Faversham,
　Goodnestone and Graveney *Cant*
GRAVENHURST, Shillington and Stondon *St Alb 8*　P *Bp*
　V　S J WHEATLEY
GRAVESEND (Holy Family) w Ifield *Roch 4*　P *Bp and Lt-Col
　F B Edmeades (jt)*　R　vacant (01474) 356221 or 363038
GRAVESEND (St Aidan) *Roch 4*　P *Bp*　C　R A MARTIN,
　NSM　J P LITTLEWOOD
GRAVESEND (St George) *Roch 4*　P *Bp*　R　J C STONE,
　NSM　G WILLIAMS, L M LAWRENCE
GRAVESEND (St Mary) *Roch 4*　P *R Gravesend*　V　R OATES
GRAYINGHAM (St Radegunda) *Linc 6*　P *Bp*
　OLM　J WILSON
GRAYRIGG (St John)　*see* Beacon *Carl*
GRAYS NORTH (St John the Evangelist) *Chelmsf 14*　P *Bp*
　V　C P RUSSELL
GRAYS THURROCK (St Peter and St Paul) *Chelmsf 14*
　P *DBP*　TR　D BARLOW,　TV　A J GOWING-CUMBER,
　M A REYNOLDS,　C　D P REDFIELD,　NSM　C M WILLIAMS,
　J G CHEGE
GRAYSHOTT (St Luke) *Guildf 3*　P *Bp*　V　C M S R THOMAS,
　Hon C　G E KNIFTON,　NSM　H J BENNET
GRAYSWOOD (All Saints)　*see* Haslemere and Grayswood
　Guildf
GRAYTHWAITE (Mission Room)　*see* Hawkshead and Low
　Wray w Sawrey and Rusland etc *Carl*

GREASBROUGH (St Mary) *Sheff 6*　P *Sir Philip
　Naylor-Leyland Bt*　C　J T BIRBECK
GREASBY (St Nicholas)　*see* Frankby w Greasby *Ches*
GREASLEY (St Mary) *S'well 4*　P *Bp*　P-in-c　D A MARVIN
GREAT　*see also under substantive place name*
GREAT CAMBRIDGE ROAD (St John the Baptist and
　St James) *Lon 19*　P *D&C St Paul's*　V　P B LYONS
GREAT GLEN (St Cuthbert)　*see* Glen Magna cum Stretton
　Magna etc *Leic*
GREAT MOOR (St Saviour)　*see* Stockport St Sav *Ches*
GREATER　*see under substantive place name*
GREATFORD (St Thomas à Becket)　*see* Uffington Gp *Linc*
GREATHAM (not known)　*see* Amberley w N Stoke and
　Parham, Wiggonholt etc *Chich*
GREATHAM (St John the Baptist) *Dur 3*　P *Trustees*
　P-in-c　P T ALLINSON
GREATHAM (St John the Baptist) w Empshott and Hawkley w
　Prior's Dean *Portsm 4*　P *DBP*　R　D H HEATLEY
GREATSTONE (St Peter)　*see* Lydd *Cant*
GREATWORTH (St Peter)　*see* Chenderit *Pet*
GREAVE FOLD (Holy Innocents)　*see* Romiley *Ches*
GREEN HAMMERTON (St Thomas)　*see* Gt and Lt Ouseburn
　w Marton cum Grafton etc *Ripon*
GREEN HAWORTH (St Clement)　*see* Accrington Ch the King
　Blackb
GREEN HEATH (St Saviour)　*see* Hednesford *Lich*
GREEN STREET GREEN (St Mary) and Pratts Bottom
　Roch 16　P *Bp*　V　K A CARPANI,　C　P J AVANN
GREEN VALE (Holy Trinity)　*see* Stockton H Trin w St Mark
　Dur
GREENFIELD　*see* Bridgwater H Trin and Durleigh *B & W*
GREENFIELD (St Mary)　*see* Saddleworth *Man*
GREENFIELDS (United Church)　*see* Shrewsbury St Geo w
　Greenfields *Lich*
GREENFORD (Holy Cross) (St Edward the Confessor) *Lon 22*
　P *K Coll Cam*　R　N RICHARDSON
GREENFORD, NORTH (All Hallows) *Lon 22*　P *Bp*
　V　P F HEAZELL,　Hon C　S J COLLIER,　NSM　D C DAVIS,
　M W J DEAN
GREENGATES (St John the Evangelist) *Bradf 3*　P *D&C*
　P-in-c　G S DARLISON
GREENHAM (St Mary the Virgin) *Ox 14*　P *Bp*
　V　J P H CLARKE,　NSM　B R JONES, J BRAMHALL
GREENHAM (St Peter)　*see* Wellington and Distr *B & W*
GREENHEAD (St Cuthbert)　*see* Haltwhistle and Greenhead
　Newc
GREENHILL (St John the Baptist) *Lon 23*　P *Bp, Adn, and
　V Harrow St Mary (jt)*　Hon C　D P BYRNE
GREENHILL (St Peter) *Sheff 2*　P *Bp*　P-in-c　E H STEELE
GREENHITHE (St Mary) *Roch 2*　P *Ch Soc Trust and Personal
　Reps Canon T L Livermore (jt)*　R　R D BARRON
GREENHOW HILL (St Mary)　*see* Upper Nidderdale *Ripon*
GREENLANDS (St Anne) *Blackb 8*　P *Bp and V Blackpool
　St Steph (jt)*　V　A M BARTLETT
GREENLANDS (St John the Evangelist)　*see* Ipsley *Worc*
GREEN'S NORTON (St Bartholomew)　*see* Towcester w
　Caldecote and Easton Neston etc *Pet*
GREENSIDE (St John) *Dur 13*　P *R Ryton w Hedgefield*
　V　C W DEVONISH,　NSM　C A FRISWELL
GREENSTEAD (St Andrew) (St Edmund's Church Hall)
　(St Matthew) w Colchester St Anne *Chelmsf 16*　P *Patr Bd and
　Ld Chan (alt)*　TR　M E WEST,　TV　J H LE SEVE,
　C　T MCFADDEN,　NSM　A C BUSHELL
GREENSTEAD GREEN (St James Apostle)　*see* Halstead Area
　Chelmsf
GREENSTED-JUXTA-ONGAR (St Andrew) w Stanford Rivers
　and Stapleford Tawney w Theydon Mount *Chelmsf 26*
　P *Bp Lon and DBP (1 turn), and Duchy of Lanc (1 turn)*
　P-in-c　A A PETRINE
GREENWICH (St Alfege) *S'wark 1*　P *The Crown*
　V　C J E MOODY,　C　Y GOOLJARY
GREENWICH, EAST (Christ Church) (St Andrew w
　St Michael) (St George) *S'wark 1*　P *Patr Bd*
　TR　M N A TORRY,　TV　D P CLACEY,　C　J S FRASER,　Hon
　C　J P LEE,　OLM　C A FINNERTY
GREETE (St James)　*see* Tenbury *Heref*
GREETHAM (All Saints)　*see* Horncastle Gp *Linc*
GREETHAM (St Mary the Virgin)　*see* Cottesmore and Burley,
　Clipsham, Exton etc *Pet*
GREETLAND (St Thomas) and West Vale *Wakef 2*
　P *V Halifax*　P-in-c　T L SWINHOE,　C　D BURROWS
GREETWELL (All Saints)　*see* S Lawres Gp *Linc*
GREINTON (St Michael and All Angels) *B & W 4*　P *Bp*
　P-in-c　J K L POWELL
GRENDON (All Saints)　*see* Baddesley Ensor w Grendon *Birm*

GRENDON (St Mary)   see Yardley Hastings, Denton and Grendon etc *Pet*

GRENDON BISHOP (St John the Baptist)   see Bredenbury *Heref*

GRENDON UNDERWOOD (St Leonard)   see The Claydons and Swan *Ox*

GRENOSIDE (St Mark) *Sheff 3*   **P** *Bp and V Ecclesfield (jt)*   **V** J M KILNER

GRESHAM (All Saints)   see Aylmerton, Runton, Beeston Regis and Gresham *Nor*

GRESLEY (St George and St Mary) *Derby 16*   **P** *Simeon's Trustees*   **V** D T PERRETT

GRESSENHALL (Assumption of the Blessed Virgin Mary) w Longham w Wendling and Bittering Parva *Nor 14*   **P** *Ld Chan (1 turn), CPAS (2 turns)*   **P-in-c** R J MARSDEN, **NSM** K D BLOGG

GRESSINGHAM (St John the Evangelist)   see Hornby w Claughton and Whittington etc *Blackb*

GRETTON (Christ Church)   see Winchcombe *Glouc*

GRETTON (St James the Great) w Rockingham and Cottingham w East Carlton *Pet 7*   **P** *Bp, Comdr L M M Saunders Watson, Sir Geoffrey Palmer Bt, and BNC Ox (jt)*   **P-in-c** S J M READING

GREWELTHORPE (St James)   see Fountains Gp *Ripon*

GREYSTOKE (St Andrew)   see Gd Shep TM *Carl*

GREYSTONES (St Gabriel) *Sheff 2*   **P** *Dean*   **V** P W BECKLEY

GREYWELL (St Mary)   see N Hants Downs *Win*

GRIMEHILLS (St Mary)   see Darwen St Barn *Blackb*

GRIMETHORPE (St Luke) w Brierley *Wakef 7*   **P** *Bp*   **V** P D NEEDHAM

GRIMLEY (St Bartholomew)   see Hallow and Grimley w Holt *Worc*

GRIMOLDBY (St Edith)   see Mid Marsh Gp *Linc*

GRIMSARGH (St Michael) *Blackb 13*   **P** *R Preston*   **V** *vacant* (01772) 653283

GRIMSBURY (St Leonard)   see Banbury St Leon *Ox*

GRIMSBY (St Augustine of Hippo) *Linc 9*   **P** *TR Gt Grimsby SS Mary and Jas*   **V** S W JONES

GRIMSBY, GREAT (St Andrew w St Luke and All Saints) *Linc 9*   **P** *Bp*   **P-in-c** T H ATKINSON

GRIMSBY, GREAT (St Mary and St James) (St Hugh) (St Mark) (St Martin) *Linc 9*   **P** *Bp*   **TV** D SHENTON, **C** S R HOLT, **NSM** J M VASEY

GRIMSBY, LITTLE (St Edith)   see Fotherby *Linc*

GRIMSBY, WEST   see Gt and Lt Coates w Bradley *Linc*

GRIMSHOE *Ely 9*   **P** *Bp, G&C Coll Cam, and Ld Chan (by turn)*   **R** J A HORAN, **NSM** K R WATERS

GRIMSTEAD, EAST (Holy Trinity)   see Clarendon *Sarum*

GRIMSTEAD, WEST (St John)   *as above*

GRIMSTON (St Botolph), Congham and Roydon *Nor 20*   **P** *Qu Coll Cam, Bp, and G Howard Esq (jt)*   **R** W A HOWARD

GRIMSTON (St John the Baptist)   see Old Dalby, Nether Broughton, Saxelbye etc *Leic*

GRIMSTON, NORTH (St Nicholas)   see W Buckrose *York*

GRINDALE (St Nicholas)   see Burton Fleming w Fordon, Grindale etc *York*

GRINDLEFORD (St Helen)   see Hathersage w Bamford and Derwent and Grindleford *Derby*

GRINDLETON (St Ambrose)   see Bolton by Bowland w Grindleton *Bradf*

GRINDON (All Saints)   see Calton, Cauldon, Grindon, Waterfall etc *Lich*

GRINDON (St James), Stillington and Wolviston *Dur 10*   **P** *Bp (2 turns), D&C (1 turn)*   **R** D M BROOKE, **NSM** P CLAYTON

GRINDON (St Oswald)   see Sunderland St Thos and St Oswald *Dur*

GRINGLEY-ON-THE-HILL (St Peter and St Paul)   see Everton, Mattersey, Clayworth and Gringley *S'well*

GRINSDALE (St Kentigern)   see Barony of Burgh *Carl*

GRINSHILL (All Saints)   see Astley, Clive, Grinshill and Hadnall *Lich*

GRINSTEAD, EAST (St Mary the Virgin) *Chich 7*   **P** *Bp*   **V** P R SEAMAN, **NSM** J GAYFORD

GRINSTEAD, EAST (St Swithun) *Chich 7*   **P** *Bp*   **V** C EVERETT-ALLEN, **C** M F EMINSON, **NSM** J K PEATY, G M W PARRY, D IVORSON

GRINSTEAD, WEST (St George) *Chich 8*   **P** *Bp*   **R** W E M HARRIS

GRINTON (St Andrew)   see Swaledale *Ripon*

GRISTHORPE (St Thomas)   see Filey *York*

GRISTON (St Peter and St Paul)   see Caston, Griston, Merton, Thompson etc *Nor*

GRITTLETON (St Mary the Virgin)   see By Brook *Bris*

GRIZEBECK (The Good Shepherd)   see Kirkby Ireleth *Carl*

GROBY (St Philip and St James)   see Bradgate Team *Leic*

GROOMBRIDGE (St John the Evangelist)   see Speldhurst w Groombridge and Ashurst *Roch*

GROOMBRIDGE, NEW (St Thomas) *Chich 19*   **P** *R Withyham*   **V** *vacant* (01892) 864265

GROSMONT (St Matthew)   see Middle Esk Moor *York*

GROSVENOR CHAPEL (no dedication) Chapel of Ease in the parish of Hanover Square St George w St Mark *Lon 3*   **P-in-c** B D FENTON,   **Hon C** S D DEWEY

GROTON (St Bartholomew)   see Boxford, Edwardstone, Groton etc *St E*

GROVE (St Helen)   see Retford Area *S'well*

GROVE (St John the Baptist) *Ox 19*   **P** *D&C Windsor*   **V** J C ROBERTSON,   **C** P A EDDY,   **NSM** P D B GOODING

GROVE GREEN (St John) Local Ecumenical Partnership *Cant 15 vacant* (01622) 739294

GROVE PARK (St Augustine)   see Lee St Aug *S'wark*

GROVEHILL (Resurrection)   see Hemel Hempstead *St Alb*

GRUNDISBURGH (St Mary the Virgin)   see Boulge w Burgh, Grundisburgh and Hasketon *St E*

GUARLFORD (St Mary)   see Powick and Guarlford and Madresfield w Newland *Worc*

GUERNSEY (Holy Trinity) *Win 14*   **P** *Trustees*   **V** J P HONOUR

GUERNSEY L'Islet (St Mary)   see Guernsey St Sampson *Win*

GUERNSEY (St Andrew de la Pommeraye) *Win 14*   **P** *The Crown*   **P-in-c** D R I DEKKER,   **NSM** A M WHITE

GUERNSEY (St John the Evangelist) *Win 14*   **P** *Trustees*   **V** A T SHARP

GUERNSEY (St Marguerite de la Foret) *Win 14*   **P** *The Crown*   **P-in-c** M R CHARMLEY,   **NSM** L S LE VASSEUR

GUERNSEY (St Martin) *Win 14*   **P** *The Crown*   **R** M R KEIRLE,   **NSM** R G BELLINGER, T B CHARMLEY

GUERNSEY (St Matthew) *Win 14*   **P** *R Ste Marie du Castel*   **V** C E SELIM,   **NSM** J LE BILLON

GUERNSEY (St Michel du Valle) *Win 14*   **P** *The Crown*   **R** K C NORTHOVER

GUERNSEY (St Peter Port) *Win 14*   **P** *The Crown*   **R** K P MELLOR,   **NSM** J E D LUFF

GUERNSEY (St Philippe de Torteval) *Win 14*   **P** *The Crown*   **R** M A STRIKE

GUERNSEY (St Pierre du Bois) *Win 14*   **P** *The Crown*   **R** M A STRIKE

GUERNSEY (St Sampson) *Win 14*   **P** *The Crown*   **P-in-c** P D BASKERVILLE

GUERNSEY (St Saviour) (Chapel of St Apolline) *Win 14*   **P** *The Crown*   **P-in-c** M R CHARMLEY,   **NSM** L S LE VASSEUR

GUERNSEY (St Stephen) *Win 14*   **P** *R St Peter Port*   **V** P J CARRINGTON

GUERNSEY (Ste Marie du Castel) *Win 14*   **P** *The Crown*   **R** C E SELIM,   **NSM** J LE BILLON

GUESTLING (St Lawrence)   see Fairlight, Guestling and Pett *Chich*

GUESTWICK (St Peter)   see Foulsham, Guestwick, Stibbard, Themelthorpe etc *Nor*

GUILDEN MORDEN (St Mary)   see Shingay Gp *Ely*

GUILDEN SUTTON (St John the Baptist)   see Plemstall w Guilden Sutton *Ches*

GUILDFORD (All Saints) *Guildf 5*   **P** *Bp*   **V** B L MESSHAM

GUILDFORD (Christ Church) (St Martha-on-the-Hill) *Guildf 5*   **P** *Simeon's Trustees and Duke Northd (jt)*   **C** M G WALLACE, **NSM** B B MIRZANIA, B G MCNAIR SCOTT

GUILDFORD (Holy Spirit)   see Burpham *Guildf*

GUILDFORD (Holy Trinity) (St Mary the Virgin) (St Michael) *Guildf 5*   **P** *Bp*   **R** R L COTTON,   **C** J E VLACH,   **OLM** B D ROBERTS, R M PIERCE, J J HEDGECOCK

GUILDFORD (St Clare)   see Westborough *Guildf*

GUILDFORD (St Francis)   *as above*

GUILDFORD (St Luke)   see Burpham *Guildf*

GUILDFORD (St Nicolas) *Guildf 5*   **P** *Bp*   **R** A H NORMAN, **C** B C R PERKINS

GUILDFORD (St Saviour) *Guildf 5*   **P** *Simeon's Trustees*   **R** M C LAWSON,   **C** T J DARWENT, A C WHEELER

GUILSBOROUGH (St Ethelreda) and Hollowell and Cold Ashby and Cottesbrooke w Great Creaton and Thornby and Ravensthorpe and Spratton *Pet 2*   **P** *Bp, DBP, A R MacDonald-Buchanan Esq, and J S McCall Esq (jt)*   **R** M R BATTISON,   **NSM** C MOSS

GUILTCROSS *Nor 11*   **P** *Bp, Mrs C Noel, Exors C P B Goldson, and DBP (jt)*   **P-in-c** M J BULL, **OLM** D R A SHEPPARD

GUISBOROUGH (St Nicholas) *York 16*   **P** *Abp*   **R** G J PACEY, **C** L D TILLETT

GUISELEY (St Oswald King and Martyr) w Esholt *Bradf 4*   **P** *Patr Bd*   **TR** G B ATHERTON,   **NSM** I RATHBONE

GUIST (St Andrew)   see N Elmham, Billingford, Bintree, Guist etc *Nor*

GUITING POWER (St Michael) *see* The Guitings, Cutsdean, Farmcote etc *Glouc*

GUITINGS, Cutsdean, Farmcote, Upper and Lower Slaughter w Eyford and Naunton, The *Glouc 9* **P** *Bp, Ch Ch Ox, Guiting Manor Amenity Trust, and F E B Witts Esq (jt)* **R** V N JAMES

GULDEFORD, EAST (St Mary) *see* Rye *Chich*

GULVAL (St Gulval) and Madron *Truro 5* **P** *Ld Chan and Bp (jt)* **P-in-c** T ST J HAWKINS, **OLM** P A T HORDER

GULWORTHY (St Paul) *see* Tavistock and Gulworthy *Ex*

GUMLEY (St Helen) *see* Foxton w Gumley and Laughton *Leic*

GUNBY (St Nicholas) *see* Witham Gp *Linc*

GUNBY (St Peter) *see* Burgh Gp *Linc*

GUNHOUSE (St Barnabas) *see* Trentside E *Linc*

GUNN CHAPEL (Holy Name) *see* Swimbridge w W Buckland and Landkey *Ex*

GUNNERTON (St Christopher) *see* Chollerton w Birtley and Thockrington *Newc*

GUNNESS (St Barnabas) *see* Trentside E *Linc*

GUNNISLAKE (St Anne) *see* Calstock *Truro*

GUNTHORPE (St John the Baptist) *see* Lowdham w Caythorpe, and Gunthorpe *S'well*

GUNTHORPE (St Mary) *see* Stiffkey and Bale *Nor*

GUNTON St Peter (St Benedict) *Nor 9* **P** *CPAS* **R** *vacant* (01502) 580707

GUNWALLOE (St Winwalloe) *see* Cury and Gunwwalloe *Truro*

GURNARD (All Saints) *Portsm 8* **P** *Bp* **V** L MCROSTIE, **NSM** D M NETHERWAY

GUSSAGE (St Andrew) *see* Sixpenny Handley w Gussage St Andrew etc *Sarum*

GUSSAGE ALL SAINTS (All Saints) *see* Chase *Sarum*

GUSSAGE ST MICHAEL (St Michael) *as above*

GUSTARD WOOD (St Peter) *see* Wheathampstead *St Alb*

GUSTON (St Martin of Tours) *see* Whitfield w Guston *Cant*

GWEEK (Mission Church) *see* Constantine *Truro*

GWENNAP (St Weneppa) *see* St Stythians w Perranarworthal and Gwennap *Truro*

GWINEAR (St Winnear) *see* Godrevy *Truro*

GWITHIAN (St Gwithian) *as above*

HABBERLEY (St Mary) *Heref 12* **P** *Bp* **R** A N TOOP, **NSM** M-L TOOP

HABERGHAM (All Saints) *see* W Burnley All SS *Blackb*

HABERGHAM EAVES (St Matthew the Apostle) *see* Burnley St Matt w H Trin *Blackb*

HABROUGH Group, The (St Margaret) *Linc 10* **P** *DBP* **P-in-c** M W PAGE-CHESTNEY, **NSM** V N PAGE-CHESTNEY

HABTON, GREAT (St Chad) *see* Kirby Misperton w Normanby, Edston and Salton *York*

HACCOMBE (St Blaise) *see* Shaldon, Stokeinteignhead, Combeinteignhead etc *Ex*

HACCONBY (St Andrew) *see* Ringstone in Aveland Gp *Linc*

HACHESTON (St Andrew) *see* Campsea Ashe w Marlesford, Parham and Hacheston *St E*

HACKBRIDGE and Beddington Corner (All Saints) *S'wark 23* **P** *Bp* **V** A O ROLAND

HACKENTHORPE (Christ Church) *Sheff 2* **P** *Bp* **V** S J WILLETT, **C** R A HEARD

HACKFORD (St Mary the Virgin) *see* High Oak, Hingham and Scoulton w Wood Rising *Nor*

HACKINGTON (St Stephen) *Cant 3* **P** *Adn Cant* **R** J G LEWIS-ANTHONY, **Hon C** S C E LAIRD

HACKNESS (St Peter) w Harwood Dale *York 15* **P** *Lord Derwent* **V** *vacant* (01723) 882224

HACKNEY Mount Pleasant Lane (St Matthew) *see* Upper Clapton St Matt *Lon*

HACKNEY (St James) *see* Clapton St Jas *Lon*

HACKNEY (St John) *see* St John-at-Hackney *Lon*

HACKNEY (St Luke) Homerton Terrace *see* Homerton St Luke *Lon*

HACKNEY (St Thomas) *see* Stamford Hill St Thos *Lon*

HACKNEY, OVER (Mission Room) *see* Darley *Derby*

HACKNEY, SOUTH (St John of Jerusalem) (Christ Church) *Lon 5* **P** *Lord Amherst* **R** A M W WILSON, **NSM** J GAU

HACKNEY, SOUTH (St Michael and All Angels) London Fields w Haggerston (St Paul) *Lon 5* **P** R S Hackney St Jo w Ch Ch **V** D GERRANS

HACKNEY, WEST St Barnabas (St Paul) *Lon 5* **P** *Bp* **R** W D N WEIR, **C** J E F BUCHAN

HACKNEY MARSH (All Souls) *Lon 5* **P** *Patr Bd* **TR** D SILVESTER, **TV** A E MELANIPHY, **C** N NGURURI, **NSM** T A HALEY

HACKNEY WICK (St Mary of Eton) (St Augustine) *Lon 5* **P** *Eton Coll* **V** *vacant* (020) 8986 8159

HACKTHORN (St Michael and All Angels) *see* Owmby Gp *Linc*

HADDENHAM (Holy Trinity) *Ely 8* **P** *Adn Ely* **V** F E G BRAMPTON

HADDENHAM (St Mary the Virgin) w Cuddington, Kingsey and Aston Sandford *Ox 21* **P** *D&C Roch* **P-in-c** M R HODSON, **NSM** H C BARNES, J D HAWKINS

HADDESLEY (St John the Baptist) *see* Haddlesey w Hambleton and Birkin *York*

HADDISCOE (St Mary) *see* Raveningham Gp *Nor*

HADDLESEY w Hambleton and Birkin *York 4* **P** *Abp and Simeon's Trustees (jt)* **P-in-c** A V BURR

HADDON (St Mary) *see* Stilton w Denton and Caldecote etc *Ely*

HADDON, EAST (St Mary the Virgin) *see* Brington w Whilton and Norton etc *Pet*

HADDON, OVER (St Anne) *see* Bakewell, Ashford w Sheldon and Rowsley *Derby*

HADDON, WEST (All Saints) *see* Long Buckby w Watford and W Haddon w Winwick *Pet*

HADFIELD (St Andrew) *Derby 6* **P** *Bp* **P-in-c** F A WALTERS, **C** I K STUBBS, **NSM** R F HEELEY

HADHAM, LITTLE (St Cecilia) *see* Albury, Braughing, Furneux Pelham, Lt Hadham etc *St Alb*

HADHAM, MUCH (St Andrew) *as above*

HADLEIGH (St Barnabas) *Chelmsf 10* **P** *Bp* **P-in-c** M BROSNAN

HADLEIGH (St James the Less) *Chelmsf 10* **P** *Dr P W M Copeman* **P-in-c** D R CHILDS, **C** C J BROWN

HADLEIGH (St Mary), Layham and Shelley *St E 3* **P** *St Jo Coll Cam and Abp (alt)* **V** M C THROWER

HADLEY (Holy Trinity) and Wellington Christ Church *Lich 21* **P** *Bp, Adn Salop, and V Wellington All SS w Eyton* **V** V C SWEET, **C** J E HOLMES, **Hon C** M F WALKER

HADLEY WOOD (St Paul) Proprietary Chapel *Lon 18* **Min** R MACKAY

HADLOW (St Mary) *Roch 8* **P** *Exors Miss I N King* **V** G A SMITH, **C** C B STOCKING

HADLOW DOWN (St Mark) *see* Buxted and Hadlow Down *Chich*

HADNALL (St Mary Magdalene) *see* Astley, Clive, Grinshill and Hadnall *Lich*

HADSTOCK (St Botolph) *see* Saffron Walden w Wendens Ambo, Littlebury etc *Chelmsf*

HADZOR w Oddingley (St James) *see* Bowbrook S *Worc*

HAGBOURNE (St Andrew) *see* The Churn *Ox*

HAGGERSTON (St Chad) *Lon 5* **P** *The Crown* **V** J J WESTCOTT, **C** R J STAGG

HAGLEY (St John the Baptist) *Worc 12* **P** *Exors Viscount Cobham* **R** R J C NEWTON

HAGLEY, WEST (St Saviour) *see* Hagley *Worc*

HAGNABY (St Andrew) *see* Marden Hill Gp *Linc*

HAGWORTHINGHAM (Holy Trinity) *as above*

HAIGH (St David) w Aspull *Liv 14* **P** R Wigan **V** S G PRITCHARD, **Hon C** N K YOUNG, **OLM** M L PERRIN

HAIL WESTON (St Nicholas) *see* Gt Staughton w Hail Weston w Southoe *Ely*

HAILE (not known) *see* Egremont and Haile *Carl*

HAILES (Chapel) *see* Winchcombe *Glouc*

HAILEY (St John the Evangelist) *see* Witney *Ox*

HAILSHAM (St Mary) *Chich 15* **P** *Ch Soc Trust* **V** D J BOURNE, **C** D T HENDERSON

HAINAULT (St Paul) *Chelmsf 4* **P** *Bp* **P-in-c** K ASHTON, **NSM** S M HARTLEY

HAINFORD (All Saints) *see* Coltishall w Gt Hautbois, Frettenham etc *Nor*

HAINTON (St Mary) *see* Barkwith Gp *Linc*

HALA (St Paul's Centre) *see* Scotforth *Blackb*

HALAM (St Michael) *see* Edingley w Halam *S'well*

HALAS *Worc 9* **P** *Patr Bd* **TV** D MELVILLE, M RUTTER, **P-in-c** R S HALL, **C** M K LECLEZIO

HALBERTON (St Andrew) *see* Sampford Peverell, Uplowman, Holcombe Rogus etc *Ex*

HALCON *see* Taunton All SS *B & W*

HALDEN, HIGH (St Mary the Virgin) *see* Bethersden w High Halden *Cant*

HALDENS (Christ the King) *see* Digswell and Panshanger *St Alb*

HALDON *see* Teignmouth, Ideford w Luton, Ashcombe etc *Ex*

HALE (St David) *see* Timperley *Ches*

HALE (St John the Evangelist) w Badshot Lea *Guildf 3* **P** *Patr Bd* **TV** C A WILSON-BARKER

HALE (St Mary) *see* S Widnes *Liv*

HALE (St Mary) *see* Fordingbridge and Breamore and Hale etc *Win*

HALE (St Peter) and Ashley *Ches 10* **P** *V Bowdon* **V** E J H LANE, **C** A D H DAWSON, **NSM** C E HOLMES

HALE, GREAT (St John the Baptist) *see* Helpringham w Hale *Linc*
HALE, UPPER (St Mark) *see* Hale w Badshot Lea *Guildf*
HALE BARNS (All Saints) w Ringway *Ches 10* **P** *Bp*
V R D CLARKE, **NSM** G C JAQUISS
HALEBANK (St Mary Mission) *see* S Widnes *Liv*
HALES (St Mary) *see* Cheswardine, Childs Ercall, Hales, Hinstock etc *Lich*
HALESOWEN (St John the Baptist) *see* Halas *Worc*
HALESWORTH (St Mary) *see* Blyth Valley *St E*
HALEWOOD (St Nicholas) (St Mary) *Liv 4* **P** *Bp*
TR A D J JEWELL
HALEY HILL (All Souls) *see* Halifax *Wakef*
HALFORD (Our Blessed Lady) *see* Stourdene Gp *Cov*
HALFORD (St Thomas) w Sibdon Carwood *Heref 10* **P** *Bp and R Holden (alt)* **P-in-c** M L COPE, **NSM** M G WILLIAMS
HALFWAY (St Peter) *see* Minster-in-Sheppey *Cant*
HALIFAX (All Saints) *Wakef 4* **P** *Ch Trust Fund Trust*
P-in-c S LEES, **NSM** J C K FREEBORN
HALIFAX (Holy Trinity) (St Jude) *Wakef 4* **P** *Bp, V Halifax, and trustees (jt)* **V** M C RUSSELL, **NSM** M RUSSELL
HALIFAX (St Anne-in-the-Grove) *see* Southowram and Claremount *Wakef*
HALIFAX St Augustine (School Hall) and Mount Pellon *Wakef 4* **P** *Bp, Simeon's Trustees, and local trustees (jt)*
V J HELLEWELL, **NSM** S M HEPTINSTALL
HALIFAX (St Hilda) *Wakef 4* **P** *Bp* **P-in-c** A J STREET
HALIFAX MINSTER (St John the Baptist) (All Souls) *Wakef 4*
P *The Crown* **V** H J BARBER, **C** R N FIRTH, **Hon C** P A BALDWIN, **NSM** C J WARDMAN
HALL GREEN (Church of the Ascension) *Birm 6* **P** *Bp, V Yardley, and Vice-Chmn of PCC (jt)* **V** D J SENIOR
HALL GREEN (St Michael) *Birm 6* **P** *Bp* **P-in-c** M OKELLO
HALL GREEN (St Peter) *Birm 6* **P** *Bp* **V** M W STEPHENSON, **C** J LEWIS-GREGORY, **NSM** S C HAYES
HALL STREET (St Andrew) *see* Stockport St Mary *Ches*
HALLAM, WEST (St Wilfred) and Mapperley w Stanley *Derby 13* **P** *Bp* **R** S I D WHITE, **NSM** P J OWEN-JONES, J FACEY, I OWEN-JONES
HALLATON (St Michael and All Angels) and Allexton, w Horninghold, Tugby, and East Norton, and Slawston *Leic 3* **P** *Bp, DBP, and E Brudenell Esq (jt)* **P-in-c** N MORGAN
HALLING (St John the Baptist) *see* Cuxton and Halling *Roch*
HALLINGBURY, GREAT (St Giles) (St Andrew) and LITTLE (St Mary the Virgin) *Chelmsf 25* **P** *Bp and Charterhouse (jt)*
P-in-c J A GREEN
HALLIWELL (St Luke) *see* W Bolton *Man*
HALLIWELL (St Margaret) *see* Heaton Ch Ch w Halliwell St Marg *Man*
HALLIWELL (St Peter) (Barrow Bridge Mission) (St Andrew's Mission Church) *Man 7* **P** *Trustees* **V** P D HARDINGHAM, **C** M A COWLING, **NSM** C WATSON
HALLOUGHTON (St James) *see* Thurgarton w Hoveringham and Bleasby etc *S'well*
HALLOW (St Philip and St James) and Grimley w Holt *Worc 3*
P *Bp* **R** R N LATHAM
HALLWOOD Ecumenical Parish (St Mark) *Ches 3* **P** *DBP*
V S S WILKINS
HALSALL (St Cuthbert), Lydiate and Downholland *Liv 11*
P *Bp and Brig D H Blundell-Hollinshead-Blundell (jt)*
R P L ROBINSON, **NSM** B C KEAL
HALSE (Mission Church) *see* Brackley St Pet w St Jas *Pet*
HALSE (St James) *see* Milverton w Halse, Fitzhead and Ash Priors *B & W*
HALSETOWN (St John's in the Fields) *Truro 5* **P** *D&C*
V E V A FOOT, **C** D GALANZINO
HALSHAM (All Saints) *see* Keyingham w Ottringham, Halsham and Sunk Is *York*
HALSTEAD (St Margaret) *see* Knockholt w Halstead *Roch*
HALSTEAD AREA Team Ministry, The (St Andrew) *Chelmsf 19*
P *Patr Bd* **TR** J F BLORE, **TV** V J BROOKS, S E CRUSE, **C** S N LODGE, **NSM** M H M BURSELL, **OLM** H R MOTHERSOLE
HALSTOCK (St Mary) *see* Melbury *Sarum*
HALSTOW, HIGH (St Margaret) (All Hallows) and Hoo St Mary *Roch 6* **P** *MMCET and Ch Soc Trust (jt)*
R S G GWILT
HALSTOW, LOWER (St Margaret) *see* Upchurch w Lower Halstow *Cant*
HALTER DEVIL (Mission Room) *see* Mugginton and Kedleston *Derby*
HALTON (St Mary) *Ches 3* **P** *Bp* **P-in-c** A MITCHELL
HALTON (St Michael and All Angels) *see* Wendover and Halton *Ox*
HALTON (St Oswald and St Cuthbert and King Alfwald) *see* Corbridge w Halton and Newton Hall *Newc*

HALTON (St Wilfred) *see* Slyne w Hest and Halton w Aughton *Blackb*
HALTON (St Wilfrid) *see* Leeds Halton St Wilfrid *Ripon*
HALTON, EAST (St Peter) *see* Habrough Gp *Linc*
HALTON, WEST (St Etheldreda) *see* Alkborough *Linc*
HALTON HOLGATE (St Andrew) *see* Spilsby Gp *Linc*
HALTON QUAY (St Indract's Chapel) *see* St Dominic, Landulph and St Mellion w Pillaton *Truro*
HALTON WEST (Mission Church) *see* Hellifield *Bradf*
HALTWHISTLE (Holy Cross) and Greenhead *Newc 10* **P** *Bp*
V vacant (01434) 320215
HALVERGATE (St Peter and St Paul) *see* Freethorpe, Wickhampton, Halvergate etc *Nor*
HALWELL (St Leonard) *see* Diptford, N Huish, Harberton, Harbertonford etc *Ex*
HALWILL (St Peter and St James) *see* Ashwater, Halwill, Beaworthy, Clawton etc *Ex*
HAM (All Saints) *see* Savernake *Sarum*
HAM (St Andrew) *S'wark 15* **P** *K Coll Cam*
V S BROCKLEHURST
HAM (St Barnabas Mission Church) *see* Chard St Mary w Combe St Nicholas, Wambrook etc *B & W*
HAM (St James the Less) *see* Plymouth St Pet and H Apostles *Ex*
HAM (St Richard) *S'wark 16* **P** *Bp* **V** P J H DUNN, **NSM** F M FORWARD
HAMBLE LE RICE (St Andrew) *Win 10* **P** *St Mary's Coll Win*
V J W TRAVERS
HAMBLEDEN VALLEY (St Mary the Virgin) *Ox 29* **P** *Bp, Viscount Hambleden, and Miss M Mackenzie (jt)*
R J M WIGRAM, **NSM** J H MAIS
HAMBLEDON (St Peter) *see* Busbridge and Hambledon *Guildf*
HAMBLEDON (St Peter and St Paul) *Portsm 1* **P** *Ld Chan*
P-in-c R I P COUTTS, **NSM** J E PRICE
HAMBLETON (St Andrew) *see* Oakham, Ashwell, Braunston, Brooke, Egleton etc *Pet*
HAMBLETON (St Mary) *see* Haddlesey w Hambleton and Birkin *York*
HAMBLETON (The Blessed Virgin Mary) *see* Waterside Par *Blackb*
HAMBRIDGE (St James the Less) *see* Kingsbury Episcopi w E Lambrook, Hambridge etc *B & W*
HAMER (All Saints) *Man 17* **P** *Bp* **V** vacant (01706) 355591
HAMERINGHAM (All Saints) *see* Fen and Hill Gp *Linc*
HAMERTON (All Saints) *Ely 10* **P** *G R Petherick Esq*
P-in-c M P JEPP
HAMILTON Conventional District *Leic 1* **Min** E RAWLINGS
HAMILTON TERRACE (St Mark) *see* St Marylebone St Mark Hamilton Terrace *Lon*
HAMMER (St Michael) *see* Lynchmere and Camelsdale *Chich*
HAMMERFIELD (St Francis of Assisi) *see* Boxmoor St Jo *St Alb*
HAMMERSMITH (Holy Innocents) (St John the Evangelist) *Lon 9* **P** *Bp* **P-in-c** D W G MATTHEWS, **NSM** A H MEAD, S R G MCDOWELL
HAMMERSMITH (St Luke) *Lon 9* **P** *Bp* **V** R D E JONES
HAMMERSMITH (St Matthew) *Lon 9* **P** *Trustees*
V G H CHIPLIN
HAMMERSMITH (St Michael and St George) *see* Shepherd's Bush St Steph w St Thos *Lon*
HAMMERSMITH St Paul *Lon 9* **P** *Bp* **V** S G DOWNHAM, **C** A J MEANEY, M HOGG, **Hon C** R Q EDWARDS, **NSM** V I THOMAS
HAMMERSMITH (St Peter) *Lon 9* **P** *Bp* **V** J RECORD, **C** G M TREWEEK
HAMMERSMITH (St Simon) *Lon 9* **P** *Simeon's Trustees*
V C J COLLINGTON
HAMMERSMITH, NORTH (St Katherine) *Lon 9* **P** *Bp*
P-in-c J TATE
HAMMERWICH (St John the Baptist) *Lich 1* **P** *Hammerwich Ch Lands Trustees* **P-in-c** M J BUTT
HAMMERWOOD (St Stephen) *see* Cowden w Hammerwood *Chich*
HAMMOON (St Paul) *see* Okeford *Sarum*
HAMNISH (St Dubricius and All Saints) *see* Leominster *Heref*
HAMPDEN, GREAT (St Mary Magdalene) *see* Prestwood and Gt Hampden *Ox*
HAMPDEN, LITTLE (not known) *see* Gt Missenden w Ballinger and Lt Hampden *Ox*
HAMPDEN PARK (St Mary) and The Hydnye *Chich 16* **P** *Bp*
V R L TREE, **Hon C** J HAY, **NSM** J MANN
HAMPNETT (St George) *see* Northleach w Hampnett and Farmington etc *Glouc*
HAMPRESTON (All Saints) *Sarum 9* **P** *Patr Bd*
TR M J A HOWARD, **TV** L S CLOW, S A L PIX, **NSM** L F HORLOCK

HAMPSTEAD Belsize Park (St Peter) *see* Belsize Park *Lon*
HAMPSTEAD (Christ Church) *Lon 16*   **P** *Trustees*
  V P D CONRAD,   **Hon C** P J W BLACKBURN
HAMPSTEAD (Emmanuel) West End *Lon 16*   **P** *Trustees*
  P-in-c J G F KESTER,   **NSM** A WHITTON
HAMPSTEAD (St James) *see* Kilburn St Mary w All So and W
  Hampstead St Jas *Lon*
HAMPSTEAD (St John) *Lon 16*   **P** *DBP*   **V** S R TUCKER,
  C E R DINWIDDY SMITH
HAMPSTEAD (St John) Downshire Hill Proprietary Chapel
  Lon 16   **Min** J G L GOULD
HAMPSTEAD St Stephen w (All Hallows) *Lon 16*   **P** *DBP and*
  D&C Cant (jt)   **V** D N C HOULDING
HAMPSTEAD, SOUTH (St Saviour) *Lon 16*   **P** *V Hampstead*
  St Jo   **P-in-c** P S NICHOLSON,   **NSM** M W SPEEKS
HAMPSTEAD, WEST (Holy Trinity) *Lon 16*   **P** *MMCET*
  V A K KEIGHLEY,   **C** C M BURROWS
HAMPSTEAD, WEST (St Cuthbert) *Lon 16*   **P** *Ch Trust Fund*
  Trust   **NSM** D W JOHN
HAMPSTEAD, WEST (St Luke) *Lon 16*   **P** *CPAS*
  V A C TRESIDDER,   **C** D M WELLS
HAMPSTEAD GARDEN SUBURB (St Jude on the Hill)
  Lon 15   **P** *Bp*   **V** A R G WALKER
HAMPSTEAD NORREYS (St Mary) *see* Hermitage *Ox*
HAMPSTHWAITE (St Thomas à Becket) and Killinghall and
  Birstwith *Ripon 1*   **P** *Mrs S J Finn, Sir James Aykroyd Bt,*
  Sir Thomas Ingilby Bt, and Bp (jt)   **V** G A F HINCHCLIFFE
HAMPTON (All Saints) *Lon 10*   **P** *Ld Chan*   **V** J A GITTOES
HAMPTON (St Andrew) *see* Herne Bay Ch Ch *Cant*
HAMPTON (St Andrew) w Sedgeberrow and
  Hinton-on-the-Green *Worc 1*   **P** *Ch Ch Ox, D&C Worc, and*
  Laslett's Charity (jt)   **P-in-c** M J G BINNEY,   **NSM** C W PARR
HAMPTON (St Mary the Virgin) *Lon 10*   **P** *Ld Chan*
  V D N WINTERBURN,   **C** D Z LLOYD
HAMPTON, GREAT AND LITTLE (St Andrew)
  see Hampton w Sedgeberrow and Hinton-on-the-Green *Worc*
HAMPTON BISHOP (St Andrew) *see* Tupsley w Hampton
  Bishop *Heref*
HAMPTON GAY (St Giles) *see* Akeman *Ox*
HAMPTON HILL (St James) *Lon 10*   **P** *V Hampton St Mary*
  V P VANNOZZI
HAMPTON IN ARDEN (St Mary and St Bartholomew) *Birm 11*
  P *Guild of All So*   **P-in-c** D C J BALLARD
HAMPTON LOVETT (St Mary and All Saints) *see* Elmley
  Lovett w Hampton Lovett and Elmbridge etc *Worc*
HAMPTON LUCY (St Peter ad Vincula) w Charlecote and
  Loxley *Cov 8*   **P** *Sir Edmund Fairfax-Lucy Bt (3 turns),*
  Col A M H Gregory-Hood (1 turn)   **P-in-c** D C JESSETT,
  NSM C O S S DAVIES
HAMPTON POYLE (St Mary the Virgin) *see* Kidlington w
  Hampton Poyle *Ox*
HAMPTON WICK (St John the Baptist) *see* Teddington St
  Mark and Hampton Wick *Lon*
HAMSEY (St Peter) *Chich 18*   **P** *Bp*   **P-in-c** D BASTIDE
HAMSTALL RIDWARE (St Michael and All Angels) *see* The
  Ridwares and Kings Bromley *Lich*
HAMSTEAD (St Bernard) *Birm 3*   **P** *Bp*   **P-in-c** H HINGLEY,
  Hon C R C HINGLEY
HAMSTEAD (St Paul) *Birm 3*   **P** *Bp*   **V** M S PRASADAM,
  C P A HARRISON
HAMSTEAD MARSHALL (St Mary) *see* Walbury Beacon *Ox*
HAMSTERLEY (St James) and Witton-le-Wear *Dur 6*   **P** *Bp*
  and The Crown (alt)   **P-in-c** R W DEIMEL,   **NSM** M M DEIMEL
HAMWORTHY (St Gabriel) (St Michael) *Sarum 7*
  P *MMCET*   **R** S D GODDARD,   **C** P G GODDARD
HANBOROUGH (St Peter and St Paul) and Freeland *Ox 9*
  P *St Jo Coll Ox*   **P-in-c** D S TYLER,   **NSM** M S BRITT,
  J A GARDNER,   **OLM** P T BALL
HANBURY (St Mary the Virgin) *see* Bowbrook N *Worc*
HANBURY (St Werburgh), Newborough, Rangemore and
  Tutbury *Lich 14*   **P** *Duchy of Lancaster (1 turn), DBP and*
  Lord Burton (1 turn)   **V** A E MANN,   **NSM** L REES,
  OLM E A F SHEPPARD
HANCHURCH (Chapel of Ease) *see* Trentham *Lich*
HANDBRIDGE (St Mary without the Walls) *see* Ches St Mary
  Ches
HANDCROSS (All Saints) *see* Slaugham and Staplefield
  Common *Chich*
HANDFORTH (St Chad) *Ches 17*   **P** *R Cheadle*
  V S J BURMESTER
HANDLEY (All Saints) *see* Tattenhall w Burwardsley and
  Handley *Ches*
HANDLEY (St John the Baptist) *see* Eckington and Ridgeway
  Derby
HANDLEY (St Mark) *see* N Wingfield, Clay Cross and Pilsley
  Derby

HANDSACRE (St Luke) *see* Armitage *Lich*
HANDSWORTH (St Andrew) *Birm 3*   **P** *Bp*   **V** E J NEWEY,
  C J E M HOUGHTON
HANDSWORTH (St James) *Birm 3*   **P** *Bp*   **V** D J P ISIORHO,
  NSM M FARR
HANDSWORTH (St Mary) *Sheff 1*   **P** *DBP*   **R** K H JOHNSON
HANDSWORTH (St Mary) (Epiphany) *Birm 3*   **P** *Bp*
  R B A HALL
HANDSWORTH (St Michael) (St Peter) *Birm 3*   **P** *Bp*
  P-in-c R F PAILING,   **NSM** J M CHAUDHARY
HANDSWORTH WOODHOUSE (St James) *see* Woodhouse
  St Jas *Sheff*
HANFORD (St Matthias) *Lich 13*   **P** *Bp*   **V** E W MCLEOD,
  C S A MORRIS
HANGER HILL (Ascension) and West Twyford *Lon 22*   **P** *Bp*
  and DBP (jt)   **V** S J REED
HANGER LANE (St Ann) *see* S Tottenham St Ann *Lon*
HANGING HEATON (St Paul) *Wakef 9*   **P** *R Dewsbury*
  P-in-c P A CRABB,   **C** M J A CARPENTER
HANGLETON (St Helen) (St Richard) *Chich 4*   **P** *Bp*
  V K G PERKINTON,   **C** M C C BARTER
HANHAM (Christ Church) (St George) *Bris 5*   **P** *Bp*   **V** *vacant*
  0117-967 3580
HANKERTON (Holy Cross) *see* Ashley, Crudwell, Hankerton
  and Oaksey *Bris*
HANLEY (All Saints) *see* Stoke-upon-Trent *Lich*
HANLEY Holy Evangelists (St Luke) *Lich 11*   **P** *Bp*
  TR K R HAYWOOD,   **TV** P R CLARK, C J BROAD,
  C I S CARTER
HANLEY (St Chad) *see* Hanley H Ev *Lich*
HANLEY CASTLE (St Mary), Hanley Swan and Welland
  Worc 5   **P** *Ld Chan and Exors Sir Berwick Lechmere Bt (alt)*
  V F A WOOKEY,   **NSM** L D BEDFORD, G S CROSS
HANLEY CHILD (St Michael and All Angels) *see* Teme Valley
  S *Worc*
HANLEY SWAN (St Gabriel) *see* Hanley Castle, Hanley Swan
  and Welland *Worc*
HANLEY WILLIAM (All Saints) *see* Teme Valley S *Worc*
HANNAH (St Andrew) cum Hagnaby w Markby *Linc 8*   **P** *Bp*
  and Mrs A M Johnson (alt)   **R** *vacant*
HANNEY (St James the Great), Denchworth and East Challow
  Ox 19   **P** *Bp (2 turns), Worc Coll Ox (1 turn)*
  P-in-c R J H TEARE
HANNINGFIELD, EAST (All Saints) *Chelmsf 9*   **P** *CPAS*
  P-in-c P PENNELL
HANNINGFIELD, WEST (St Mary and St Edward) *Chelmsf 9*
  P *DBP*   **P-in-c** S W NEED
HANNINGTON (All Saints) *see* Baughurst, Ramsdell,
  Wolverton w Ewhurst etc *Win*
HANNINGTON (St John the Baptist) *see* Highworth w
  Sevenhampton and Inglesham etc *Bris*
HANNINGTON (St Peter and St Paul) *see* Walgrave w
  Hannington and Wold and Scaldwell *Pet*
HANOVER SQUARE (St George) *Lon 3*   **P** *Bp*
  R R N S LEECE
HANSLOPE (St James the Great) w Castlethorpe *Ox 27*   **P** *Bp*
  V G E ECCLESTONE
HANWELL (St Mary) (St Christopher) *Lon 22*   **P** *Bp*
  R M R GRAYSHON,   **C** E J MOODY,   **NSM** H M V COSSTICK
HANWELL (St Mellitus w St Mark) *Lon 22*   **P** *Bp*
  V J O HEREWARD,   **NSM** M MASIH
HANWELL (St Peter) *see* Ironstone *Ox*
HANWELL (St Thomas) *Lon 22*   **P** *The Crown*   **V** *vacant* (020)
  8567 5280
HANWOOD, GREAT (St Thomas) *Heref 12*   **P** *Lt-Col*
  H de Grey-Warter   **R** M G WHITTOCK,   **NSM** C J WHITTOCK,
  L R BURNS
HANWORTH (All Saints) *Lon 11*   **P** *Bp*
  P-in-c H C REYNOLDS
HANWORTH (St Bartholomew) *see* Roughton and Felbrigg,
  Metton, Sustead etc *Nor*
HANWORTH (St George) *Lon 11*   **P** *Lee Abbey Movement*
  P-in-c P S WILLIAMSON
HANWORTH (St Richard of Chichester) *Lon 11*   **P** *Bp*
  V C W HOLMES
HAPPISBURGH (St Mary) *see* Bacton, Happisburgh,
  Hempstead w Eccles etc *Nor*
HAPTON (St Margaret) *see* Padiham w Hapton and Padiham
  Green *Blackb*
HAPTON (St Margaret) *see* Ashwellthorpe, Forncett,
  Fundenhall, Hapton etc *Nor*
HARBERTON (St Andrew) *see* Diptford, N Huish, Harberton,
  Harbertonford etc *Ex*
HARBERTONFORD (St Peter) *as above*
HARBLEDOWN (St Michael and All Angels) *Cant 3*   **P** *Abp*
  R M A MORRIS

HARBORNE (St Faith and St Laurence) *Birm 2*   **P** *Bp*
P-in-c P A WHITE
HARBORNE (St Peter) *Birm 2*   **P** *Bp*   **V** C S RALPH
HARBORNE HEATH (St John the Baptist) *Birm 2*   **P** *Ch Soc*
Trust   **V** N A DI CASTIGLIONE,   **C** T J MEATHREL,
A W SPENCER
HARBOROUGH MAGNA (All Saints) *see* Revel Gp *Cov*
HARBRIDGE (All Saints) *see* Ellingham and Harbridge and
Hyde w Ibsley *Win*
HARBURY (All Saints) and Ladbroke *Cov 10*   **P** *Bp*
P-in-c C R GROOCOCK,   **C** A L GOLDTHORP
HARBY (All Saints) *see* E Trent S'well
HARBY (St Mary the Virgin) *see* Vale of Belvoir *Leic*
HARDEN (St Saviour) and Wilsden *Bradf 8*   **P** *Bp, Adn,*
V Bradf, and R Bingley Esq (jt)   **P-in-c** S R EVANS,
NSM E MOY
HARDENHUISH (St Nicholas) *see* Chippenham St Paul w
Hardenhuish etc *Bris*
HARDHAM (St Botolph) *see* Bury w Houghton and
Coldwaltham and Hardham *Chich*
HARDINGHAM (St George) *see* Barnham Broom and Upper
Yare *Nor*
HARDINGSTONE (St Edmund) and Horton and Piddington
Pet 4   **P** *Bp*   **V** *vacant* (01604) 760110
HARDINGTON MANDEVILLE (Blessed Virgin Mary)
see W Coker w Hardington Mandeville, E Chinnock etc *B & W*
HARDINGTON VALE *B & W 3*   **P** *Bp and*
J B Owen-Jones Esq (jt)   **R** N A DONE,   **Hon C** C B WRAY
HARDLEY (St Margaret) *see* Loddon, Sisland, Chedgrave,
Hardley and Langley *Nor*
HARDMEAD (St Mary) *see* Sherington w Chicheley, N
Crawley, Astwood etc *Ox*
HARDRAW (St Mary and St John) *see* Hawes and Hardraw
Ripon
HARDRES, LOWER (St Mary) *see* Bridge *Cant*
HARDRES, UPPER (St Peter and St Paul) *see* Stone Street Gp
Cant
HARDSTOFT (St Peter) *see* Ault Hucknall and Scarcliffe *Derby*
HARDWICK (St James) *see* Stockton St Jas *Dur*
HARDWICK (St Leonard) *see* Mears Ashby and Hardwick
and Sywell etc *Pet*
HARDWICK (St Margaret) *see* Hempnall *Nor*
HARDWICK (St Mary) *see* Lordsbridge *Ely*
HARDWICK, EAST (St Stephen) *see* Carleton and E
Hardwick *Wakef*
HARDWICK-CUM-TUSMORE (St Mary) *see* Shelswell *Ox*
HARDWICKE (Holy Trinity) *see* Cusop w Blakemere,
Bredwardine w Brobury etc *Heref*
HARDWICKE (St Mary the Virgin) *see* Schorne *Ox*
HARDWICKE (St Nicholas) and Elmore w Longney *Glouc 4*
P *Adn Glouc and Ld Chan (alt)*   **V** A N JAMES,
NSM G R W PARFITT
HAREBY (St Peter and St Paul) *see* Marden Hill Gp *Linc*
HAREFIELD (St Mary the Virgin) *Lon 24*   **P** *The Hon*
J E F Newdegate   **V** W M DAVIES
HAREHILLS (St Aidan) *see* Leeds St Aid *Ripon*
HAREHILLS (St Cyprian and St James) *see* Leeds St Cypr
Harehills *Ripon*
HARESCOMBE (St John the Baptist) *see* Painswick,
Sheepscombe, Cranham, The Edge etc *Glouc*
HARESFIELD (St Peter) *see* Eastington, Frocester, Haresfield
etc *Glouc*
HAREWOOD (Methodist Chapel) *see* Collingham w
Harewood *Ripon*
HARFORD (St Petroc) *see* Ivybridge w Harford *Ex*
HARGRAVE (All Saints) *see* Raunds, Hargrave, Ringstead and
Stanwick *Pet*
HARGRAVE (St Edmund King and Martyr) *see* Chevington w
Hargrave, Chedburgh w Depden etc *St E*
HARGRAVE (St Peter) *Ches 5*   **P** *Bp*   **V** P B BARROW
HARKSTEAD (St Mary) *see* Shoreline *St E*
HARLASTON (St Matthew) *see* Clifton Campville w Edingale
and Harlaston *Lich*
HARLAXTON Group, The (St Mary and St Peter) *Linc 19*
P *Bp, DBP, Sir Richard Welby Bt, D&C, and Duke of*
Rutland (jt)   **P-in-c** K HANSON
HARLESCOTT (Holy Spirit) (Emmanuel) *Lich 20*   **P** *Bp*
V M H SALMON
HARLESDEN (All Souls) *Lon 21*   **P** *The Crown*
V M D MOORHEAD,   **NSM** M D ENGLER
HARLESDEN (St Mark) *see* Kensal Rise St Mark *Lon*
HARLESTON (St Augustine) *see* Gt Finborough w Onehouse,
Harleston, Buxhall etc *St E*
HARLESTON (St John the Baptist) *see* Redenhall, Harleston,
Wortwell and Needham *Nor*

HARLESTONE (St Andrew) *see* Brington w Whilton and
Norton etc *Pet*
HARLEY (St Mary) *see* Wenlock *Heref*
**HARLING, EAST (St Peter and St Paul) w West, Bridgham w
Roudham, Larling, Brettenham and Rushford** *Nor 11*
P *Ld Chan (1 turn), DBP, Sir Robin Nugent Bt,*
C D F Musker Esq, Major E H C Garnier, and Exors Sir John
Musker (3 turns)   **R** S M OAKLAND,   **OLM** L J FRY
HARLINGTON (Christ Church) *see* W Hayes *Lon*
HARLINGTON (St Mary the Virgin) *St Alb 8*   **P** *Bp*
V S J WILLIAMS
HARLINGTON (St Peter and St Paul) *Lon 24*   **P** *Bp*
R M E SMITH
HARLOW (St Mary and St Hugh w St John the Baptist)
Chelmsf 25   **P** *Simeon's Trustees and Bp (alt)*   **V** D J WELCH,
C O FRANKLIN,   **Hon C** S E BRAZIER-GIBBS
HARLOW (St Mary Magdalene) *Chelmsf 25*   **P** *V Harlow*
St Mary and St Hugh etc   **V** J R CORBYN,   **NSM** G R NEAVE,
P A CRACKNELL
HARLOW Town Centre (St Paul) w Little Parndon *Chelmsf 25*
P *Patr Bd*   **TR** M J HARRIS,   **C** S J KNIGHT
HARLOW GREEN (St Ninian) and Lamesley *Dur 12*   **P** *Bp*
V M WORTHINGTON
HARLSEY, EAST (St Oswald) *see* Osmotherley w Harlsey and
Ingleby Arncliffe *York*
HARLTON (Assumption of the Blessed Virgin Mary)
see Lordsbridge *Ely*
HARMANSWATER (St Paul) *see* Bracknell *Ox*
HARMER HILL (St Andrew) *see* Myddle *Lich*
HARMONDSWORTH (St Mary the Virgin) *Lon 24*   **P** *DBP*
NSM A O CHRISTIAN-IWUAGWU
HARMSTON (All Saints) *see* Graffoe Gp *Linc*
HARNHAM (St George) (All Saints) *Sarum 12*   **P** *Bp (1 turn),*
V Britford (2 turns)   **V** D P SCRACE,   **NSM** J G POPPLETON
HARNHILL (St Michael and All Angels) *see* Fairford Deanery
Glouc
HAROLD HILL (St George) *Chelmsf 2*   **P** *Bp*   **V** E POW
HAROLD HILL (St Paul) *Chelmsf 2*   **P** *Bp*   **V** R D MOUL
HAROLD WOOD (St Peter) *Chelmsf 2*   **P** *New Coll Ox*
V D P BANTING,   **C** A J GREY, J D WARD
HAROME (St Saviour) *see* Kirkdale w Harome, Nunnington
and Pockley *York*
HARPENDEN (St John the Baptist) *St Alb 7*   **P** *DBP*
P-in-c P L SEGRAVE-PRIDE,   **C** A J DUNCAN,
NSM J E H WHITE, C E BURCH
HARPENDEN (St Nicholas) (All Saints) *St Alb 7*   **P** *Ld Chan*
R C D FUTCHER,   **C** L L P WILLIAMS, R M LEACH
HARPFORD (St Gregory the Great) *see* Ottery St Mary,
Alfington, W Hill, Tipton etc *Ex*
HARPHAM (St John of Beverley) *see* The Beacon *York*
HARPLEY (St Lawrence) *see* Gt w Lt Massingham, Harpley,
Rougham etc *Nor*
HARPOLE (All Saints) *see* Bugbrooke, Harpole, Kislingbury
etc *Pet*
HARPSDEN (St Margaret) *see* Shiplake w Dunsden and
Harpsden *Ox*
HARPSWELL (St Chad) *see* Glentworth Gp *Linc*
**HARPTREE, EAST (St Laurence) w WEST (Blessed Virgin
Mary) and Hinton Blewett** *B & W 9*   **P** *Duchy of Cornwall*
R *vacant* (01761) 221239
HARPUR HILL (St James) *see* Buxton w Burbage and King
Sterndale *Derby*
HARPURHEY (Christ Church) *Man 4*   **P** *Bp and Trustees (jt)*
R M J P MCGURK
HARPURHEY (St Stephen) *see* Harpurhey *Man*
HARRABY (St Elisabeth) *see* S Carl *Carl*
HARRIETSHAM (St John the Baptist) *see* Len Valley *Cant*
HARRINGAY (St Paul) *Lon 19*   **P** *Bp*   **P-in-c** T D PIKE,
C P J HENDERSON,   **NSM** P G ATHERTON
HARRINGTON (St Mary) *Carl 7*   **P** *Mrs E H S Thornely*
R *vacant* (01946) 830215
HARRINGTON (St Mary) *see* S Ormsby Gp *Linc*
HARRINGTON (St Peter and St Paul) *see* Arthingworth,
Harrington w Oxendon and E Farndon *Pet*
HARRINGWORTH (St John the Baptist) *see* Lyddington,
Bisbrooke, Caldecott, Glaston etc *Pet*
HARROGATE (St Luke's Church Centre) *see* Bilton *Ripon*
HARROGATE (St Mark) *Ripon 1*   **P** *Peache Trustees*
V G W DONEGAN-CROSS,   **C** D J WATTS
HARROGATE (St Wilfrid) *Ripon 1*   **P** *Bp*
TR G R WADDINGTON,   **NSM** T G BURRELL
HARROGATE, HIGH (Christ Church) *Ripon 1*   **P** *Bp*
V J J HENSHALL,   **C** H M BAILEY,   **NSM** C M SEDGEWICK
HARROGATE, HIGH (St Peter) *Ripon 1*   **P** *Ch Patr Trust*
V A M SHEPHERD,   **C** B G HEGARTY, T J HURREN,
NSM S E PEARCE

HARROGATE, LOW (St Mary) *Ripon 4*   **P** *Peace Trustees*
P-in-c M J CAREY
HARROLD (St Peter and All Saints) and Carlton w Chellington
St Alb 13   **P** *Bp*   **P-in-c** J FOX
HARROW (Church of the Holy Spirit)   *see* Kenton *Lon*
HARROW (Holy Trinity)   *see* Wealdstone H Trin *Lon*
HARROW (St John the Baptist)   *see* Greenhill St Jo *Lon*
HARROW (St Peter)   *see* W Harrow *Lon*
HARROW, NORTH (St Alban) *Lon 23*   **P** *Bp*   **V** J A FOSTER,
Hon **C** D J TUCK,   **NSM** P BAGULEY
HARROW, SOUTH (St Paul) *Lon 23*   **P** *R St Bride Fleet Street*
w Bridewell and Trin Gough Square   **V** I P DOWSETT,
C A R J COOPER
HARROW, WEST (St Peter) *Lon 23*   **P** *Bp and Ch Patr*
Trust (jt)   **V** W R VAN DER HART
HARROW GREEN (Holy Trinity and St Augustine of Hippo)
see Leytonstone H Trin and St Aug Harrow Green *Chelmsf*
HARROW ON THE HILL (St Mary) *Lon 23*   **P** *Bp, Adn, and*
Hd Master Harrow Sch (jt)   **V** T J GOSDEN
HARROW WEALD (All Saints) *Lon 23*   **P** *Bp, Adn, V Harrow*
St Mary, and R Bushey (jt)   **V** J J MERCER,   **C** J STOWELL,
NSM P M WARD
HARROW WEALD (St Michael and All Angels) *Lon 23*   **P** *Bp*
V G E HEWLETT
HARROWBARROW (All Saints)   *see* Calstock *Truro*
HARROWBY (The Ascension)   *see* Grantham, Harrowby w
Londonthorpe *Linc*
HARROWDEN, GREAT (All Saints) w LITTLE (St Mary the
Virgin) and Orlingbury and Isham w Pytchley *Pet 6*   **P** *Bp and*
Sir Philip Naylor-Leyland Bt (jt)   **R** S P DOMMETT,
NSM C A OSTLER
HARSTON (All Saints) w Hauxton and Newton *Ely 5*   **P** *Bp*
(2 turns), D&C (1 turn)   **NSM** R G HOWELLS, B HADFIELD
HARSTON (St Michael and All Angels)   *see* High Framland Par
Leic
HARSWELL (St Peter)   *see* Holme and Seaton Ross Gp *York*
HART (St Mary Magdalene) w Elwick Hall *Dur 3*   **P** *Bp and*
DBP (alt)   **P-in-c** J BURBURY
HART COMMON (not known)   *see* Westhoughton and
Wingates *Man*
HARTBURN (All Saints)   *see* Stockton St Pet *Dur*
HARTBURN (St Andrew)   *see* Bolam w Whalton and Hartburn
w Meldon *Newc*
HARTCLIFFE (St Andrew)   *see* Bris St Andr Hartcliffe *Bris*
HARTEST (All Saints)   *see* Glemsford, Hartest w Boxted,
Somerton etc *St E*
HARTFIELD (St Mary) w Coleman's Hatch *Chich 19*   **P** *Bp and*
Earl De la Warr (jt)   **R** P E P BRICE,   **NSM** N T LEVISEUR
HARTFORD (All Saints)   *see* Huntingdon w the Stukeleys *Ely*
HARTFORD (St John the Baptist) *Ches 6*   **P** *Ch Soc Trust*
V M I A SMITH,   **C** J T HUGHES,   **NSM** G AGAR
HARTFORD HUNDRED (WEST) Group   *see* Lt
Berkhamstead and Bayford, Essendon etc *St Alb*
HARTHILL (All Hallows) and Thorpe Salvin *Sheff 5*   **P** *Bp*
P-in-c G SCHOFIELD
HARTING (St Mary and St Gabriel) w Elsted and Treyford cum
Didling *Chich 10*   **P** *Bp*   **R** *vacant* (01730) 825234
HARTINGTON (St Giles)   *see* Taddington, Chelmorton and
Monyash etc *Derby*
HARTISMERE, NORTH *St E 16*   **P** *MMCET, K Coll Cam,*
Bp, and DBP (jt)   **R** M THOMPSON,   **OLM** V A MANNING
HARTISMERE, SOUTH *St E 16*   **P** *Bp, Comdr*
F P Brooke-Popham, MMCET, Ch Soc Trust, SMF, and Lord
Henniker (jt)   **C** C M S ROBINSON,   **NSM** A HARDING
HARTLAND (St Nectan)   *see* Parkham, Alwington, Buckland
Brewer etc *Ex*
HARTLAND COAST   *as above*
HARTLEBURY (St James) *Worc 8*   **P** *Bp*   **P-in-c** S P KERR,
NSM S L BARRETT
HARTLEPOOL (Holy Trinity) (St Mark's Centre) *Dur 3*   **P** *Bp*
V R HALL
HARTLEPOOL (St Aidan) (St Columba) *Dur 3*   **P** *Bp*
P-in-c J P RHODES
HARTLEPOOL (St Hilda) *Dur 3*   **P** *Bp*   **P-in-c** C J COLLISON
HARTLEPOOL (St Luke) *Dur 3*   **P** *Bp*   **V** M R JUDSON,
C P W JUDSON,   **NSM** D M WILSON
HARTLEPOOL (St Oswald) *Dur 3*   **P** *Bp*   **V** G BUTTERY
HARTLEPOOL (St Paul) *Dur 3*   **P** *Bp*   **V** R E MASSHEDAR
HARTLEY (All Saints)   *see* Fawkham and Hartley *Roch*
HARTLEY, NEW (St Michael and All Angels)   *see* Delaval
Newc
HARTLEY BROOK (Mission Hall)   *see* Becontree St Mary
Chelmsf
HARTLEY MAUDITT (St Leonard)   *see* Northanger *Win*
HARTLEY WESPALL (St Mary)   *see* Sherfield-on-Loddon and
Stratfield Saye etc *Win*

HARTLEY WINTNEY (St John the Evangelist), Elvetham,
Winchfield and Dogmersfield *Win 5*   **P** *Bp and Sir Euan*
Anstruther-Gough-Calthorpe Bt (jt)   **V** R A EWBANK,
C D WARD
HARTLIP (St Michael and All Angels)   *see* Newington w
Hartlip and Stockbury *Cant*
HARTOFT (Mission Room)   *see* Lastingham w
Appleton-le-Moors, Rosedale etc *York*
HARTON (St Peter) (St Lawrence) *Dur 15*   **P** *D&C*
V R O DICK,   **C** A Y BENNETT
HARTPLAIN (not known) *Portsm 5*   **P** *DBP*   **V** T E JESSIMAN
HARTPURY (St Mary the Virgin)   *see* Ashleworth, Corse,
Hartpury, Hasfield etc *Glouc*
HARTSHEAD (St Peter)   *see* Roberttown w Hartshead *Wakef*
HARTSHILL (Holy Trinity) and Galley Common *Cov 5*
P *Ch Patr Trust and Bp (jt)*   **P-in-c** H D BARNES
HARTSHILL (Holy Trinity), Penkhull and Trent Vale *Lich 12*
P *Patr Bd*   **TV** S R DUTTON,   **OLM** C J RUSHTON
HARTSHORNE (St Peter) and Bretby *Derby 16*   **P** *Bp and*
MMCET (jt)   **R** I R WILLIAMS-HUNTER
HARTWELL (St John the Baptist)   *see* Roade and Ashton w
Hartwell *Pet*
HARTWITH (St Jude)   *see* Dacre w Hartwith and Darley w
Thornthwaite *Ripon*
HARTY (St Thomas Apostle)   *see* Eastchurch w Leysdown and
Harty *Cant*
HARVINGTON (St James)   *see* Church Lench w Rous Lench
and Abbots Morton etc *Worc*
HARWELL (St Matthew) w Chilton *Ox 18*   **P** *DBP and*
CPAS (jt)   **OLM** P M ROLLS
HARWICH PENINSULA, The (St Nicholas) *Chelmsf 20*
P *Patr Bd*   **TR** P E MANN,   **TV** E O ADOYO,
C P S G WATKIN,   **NSM** G M MOORE, S J WINNEY
HARWOOD (Christ Church) *Man 12*   **P** *DBP*   **V** W L OLIVER,
OLM H MOLLOY, M J FROST
HARWOOD, GREAT (St Bartholomew) St John *Blackb 7*
P *Patr Bd*   **P-in-c** C R PENFOLD
HARWOOD DALE (St Margaret)   *see* Hackness w Harwood
Dale *York*
HARWORTH (All Saints) *S'well 1*   **P** *Sir John Whitaker Bt*
P-in-c J JOHNSON
HASBURY (St Margaret)   *see* Halas *Worc*
HASCOMBE (St Peter)   *see* Dunsfold and Hascombe *Guildf*
HASELBECH (St Michael)   *see* Clipston w Naseby and
Haselbech w Kelmarsh *Pet*
HASELBURY PLUCKNETT (St Michael and All Angels)
see Wulfric Benefice *B & W*
HASELEY (St Mary)   *see* Hatton w Haseley, Rowington w
Lowsonford etc *Cov*
HASELEY, GREAT (St Peter)   *see* Gt w Lt Milton and Gt
Haseley *Ox*
HASELOR (St Mary and All Saints)   *see* Kinwarton w Gt Alne
and Haselor *Cov*
HASELTON (St Andrew)   *see* Northleach w Hampnett and
Farmington etc *Glouc*
HASFIELD (St Mary)   *see* Ashleworth, Corse, Hartpury,
Hasfield etc *Glouc*
HASKETON (St Andrew)   *see* Boulge w Burgh, Grundisburgh
and Hasketon *St E*
HASLAND (St Paul) *Derby 5*   **P** *V Chesterfield*
R M R AINSCOUGH
HASLEMERE (St Bartholomew) (St Christopher) and
Grayswood *Guildf 4*   **P** *Ld Chan*   **P-in-c** M E BOWDEN,
NSM B A STEELE-PERKINS, D J ORME
HASLINGDEN (St James) w Grane and Stonefold *Blackb 1*
P *Bp and Hulme Trustees (jt)*   **V** T R SMITH,
NSM R L MULLIGAN, D ALLSOP
HASLINGDEN (St Peter)   *see* Laneside *Blackb*
HASLINGDEN (St Thomas)   *see* Musbury *Blackb*
HASLINGFIELD (All Saints)   *see* Lordsbridge *Ely*
HASLINGTON (St Matthew) w Crewe Green St Michael
Ches 15   **P** *Bp*   **V** S A LAWSON
HASSALL GREEN (St Philip)   *see* Sandbach Heath w
Wheelock *Ches*
HASSINGHAM (St Mary)   *see* Burlingham St Edmund w
Lingwood, Strumpshaw etc *Nor*
HASTINGLEIGH (St Mary the Virgin)   *see* Wye w Brook and
Hastingleigh etc *Cant*
HASTINGS (Christ Church and St Andrew)   *see* Blacklands
Hastings Ch Ch and St Andr *Chich*
HASTINGS (Emmanuel and St Mary in the Castle) *Chich 17*
P *MMCET and Hyndman Trustees (alt)*   **NSM** R BROWNING
HASTINGS (Holy Trinity) *Chich 17*   **P** *Bp*   **V** *vacant* (01424)
441766
HASTINGS (St Clement) (All Saints) *Chich 17*   **P** *Bp*
P-in-c R L FEATHERSTONE

HASTINGS (St Peter and St Paul)   *see* Hollington St Jo *Chich*
HASWELL (St Paul), Shotton and Thornley *Dur 2*   P *Bp*
V D BODDY,   NSM A STAINSBY
HATCH, WEST (St Andrew)   *see* Beercrocombe w Curry
Mallet, Hatch Beauchamp etc *B & W*
HATCH BEAUCHAMP (St John the Baptist)   *as above*
HATCH END (St Anselm) *Lon 23*   P *Bp*   V C PEARCE
HATCH WARREN AND BEGGARWOOD (Immanuel) *Win 4*
P *Bp*   P-in-c L M HARRIS
HATCHAM (St Catherine) *S'wark 2*   P *Haberdashers' Co*
V S A JAMES,   NSM J ELLIOTT,   OLM A C OBIORA
HATCHAM (St James) (St George) (St Michael) *S'wark 2*
P *Ch Patr Soc*   V N D R NICHOLLS,   C A C REES
HATCHAM PARK (All Saints) *S'wark 2*   P *Hyndman Trustees*
(2 turns), Haberdashers' Co (1 turn)   V O J BEAMENT,
OLM J FRANCIS
HATCLIFFE (St Mary)   *see* Laceby and Ravendale Gp *Linc*
HATFIELD   *see* Bp's Hatfield, Lemsford and N Mymms *St Alb*
HATFIELD (St Lawrence) *Sheff 10*   P *Bp*   V P D WILSON,
NSM G BECKETT
HATFIELD (St Leonard)   *see* Leominster *Heref*
HATFIELD BROAD OAK (St Mary the Virgin) and Bush End
Chelmsf 25   P *Bp*   P-in-c N A WORMELL
HATFIELD HEATH (Holy Trinity) and Sheering *Chelmsf 25*
P *Ch Ch Ox and V Hatfield Broad Oak (alt)*   R S H GIBBS
HATFIELD HYDE (St Mary Magdalene) *St Alb 18*
P *Marquess of Salisbury*   P-in-c A A LAUCKNER
HATFIELD PEVEREL (St Andrew) w Ulting *Chelmsf 23*   P *Bp*
V S R NORTHFIELD
HATFIELD REGIS   *see* Hatfield Broad Oak and Bush End
Chelmsf
HATHERDEN (Christ Church)   *see* Pastrow *Win*
HATHERLEIGH (St John the Baptist) Meeth, Exbourne and
Jacobstowe *Ex 11*   P *CPAS, Lord Clinton, DBP, and Keble Coll
Ox (jt)*   P-in-c R P HANSFORD
HATHERN (St Peter and St Paul)   *see* Kegworth, Hathern,
Long Whatton, Diseworth etc *Leic*
HATHEROP (St Nicholas)   *see* Fairford Deanery *Glouc*
HATHERSAGE (St Michael and All Angels) w Bamford and
Derwent, and Grindleford *Derby 2*   P *Duke of Devonshire,
Earl Temple, and A C H Barnes Esq (jt)*   P-in-c C L TUPLING
HATHERTON (St Saviour) *Lich 3*   P *A R W Littleton Esq*
V P O HART,   C M A WHATMOUGH, W E HASSALL
HATLEY ST GEORGE (St George)   *see* Gamlingay and
Everton *Ely*
HATTERS LANE (St Andrew)   *see* High Wycombe *Ox*
HATTERSLEY (St Barnabas) *Ches 14*   P *Bp*
P-in-c L A HARDING
HATTON (All Saints) *Derby 14*   P *Bp and
N J M Spurrier Esq (jt)*   P-in-c A L MARTIN
HATTON (Holy Trinity) w Haseley, Rowington w Lowsonford
and Honiley and Wroxall *Cov 4*   P *Bp*   R K J MOBBERLEY,
NSM S MOBBERLEY
HATTON (St Stephen)   *see* Hemingby Gp *Linc*
HAUGH (St Leonard)   *see* S Ormsby Gp *Linc*
HAUGHLEY (St Mary the Virgin) w Wetherden and Stowupland
St E 6   P *Ld Chan, Bp, and DBP (by turn)*   V D J SWALES,
C P I CLARKE
HAUGHTON (Mission Room)   *see* Bunbury and Tilstone
Fearnall *Ches*
HAUGHTON (St Anne) *Man 13*   P *DBP*
P-in-c A S MITCHELL
HAUGHTON (St Chad)   *see* Whittington and W Felton w
Haughton *Lich*
HAUGHTON (St Giles)   *see* Bradeley, Church Eaton,
Derrington and Haughton *Lich*
HAUGHTON (St Mary the Virgin) *Man 13*   P *Bp*
R M J DOWLAND
HAUGHTON LE SKERNE (St Andrew) *Dur 8*   P *Bp*
OLM S E BRUCE, S CHEW
HAUTBOIS, GREAT (Holy Trinity)   *see* Coltishall w Gt
Hautbois, Frettenham etc *Nor*
HAUXTON (St Edmund)   *see* Harston w Hauxton and Newton
Ely
HAUXWELL (St Oswald)   *see* Spennithorne w Finghall and
Hauxwell *Ripon*
HAVANT (St Faith) *Portsm 5*   P *Bp*   R P A W JONES,
C P A MANN
HAVEN, THE Conventional District *Chich 16*
Min J B P BROOK
HAVENSTREET (St Peter) *Portsm 7*   P *SMF*
P-in-c C C ETHERTON
HAVERHILL (St Mary the Virgin) w Withersfield *St E 8*   P *Bp*
V I M FINN,   C J A WARD
HAVERIGG (St Luke)   *see* Millom *Carl*

HAVERING-ATTE-BOWER (St John)   *see* Collier Row St Jas
and Havering-atte-Bower *Chelmsf*
HAVERINGLAND (St Peter)   *see* Cawston w Booton and
Brandiston etc *Nor*
HAVERSHAM (St Mary)   *see* Lamp *Ox*
HAVERSTOCK HILL (Holy Trinity)   *see* Kentish Town St Silas
and H Trin w St Barn *Lon*
HAVERTHWAITE (St Anne)   *see* Leven Valley *Carl*
HAWBUSH (St Paul)   *see* Brierley Hill *Worc*
HAWES (St Margaret) and Hardraw *Ripon 4*   P *Bp, V Aysgarth
and Bolton cum Redmire, Mrs R Metcalfe, and
W H Willan Esq (jt)*   P-in-c A B CHAPMAN,
NSM I M ROBINSON, M D BLANCH
HAWES SIDE (St Christopher) and Marton Moss St Nicholas
Blackb 8   P *Bp*   V G PIPER,   C M P MCMURRAY,
NSM S BALDWIN
HAWKCHURCH (St John the Baptist)   *see* Golden Cap Team
Sarum
HAWKEDON (St Mary)   *see* Chevington w Hargrave,
Chedburgh w Depden etc *St E*
HAWKESBURY (St Mary)   *see* Boxwell, Leighterton,
Didmarton, Oldbury etc *Glouc*
HAWKHURST (St Laurance) *Cant 10*   P *Ch Ch Ox*
V R G DREYER
HAWKINGE (St Luke) w Acrise and Swingfield *Cant 8*   P *Abp*
P-in-c R P GRINSELL
HAWKLEY (St Peter and St Paul)   *see* Greatham w Empshott
and Hawkley w Prior's Dean *Portsm*
HAWKRIDGE (St Giles)   *see* Exford, Exmoor, Hawkridge and
Withypool *B & W*
HAWKSHAW (St Mary)   *see* Holcombe and Hawkshaw *Man*
HAWKSHEAD (St Michael and All Angels) and Low Wray w
Sawrey and Rusland and Satterthwaite *Carl 11*   P *Bp*
V J S DIXON,   NSM N F HALLAM
HAWKSWOOD (Emmanuel) *Chich 15*   P *Ch Soc Trust*
V S J E TOMALIN
HAWKSWORTH (St Mary and All Saints)   *see* Whatton w
Aslockton, Hawksworth, Scarrington etc *S'well*
HAWKSWORTH WOOD (St Mary)   *see* Abbeylands *Ripon*
HAWKWELL (Emmanuel) (St Mary the Virgin) *Chelmsf 12*
P *CPAS*   R P H SMITH
HAWKWOOD (St Francis)   *see* Chingford SS Pet and Paul
Chelmsf
HAWLEY (Holy Trinity) *Guildf 1*   P *Keble Coll Ox*
V M W NEALE
HAWLEY, SOUTH (All Saints)   *see* Hawley H Trin *Guildf*
HAWLING (St Edward)   *see* Sevenhampton w Charlton Abbots,
Hawling etc *Glouc*
HAWNBY (All Saints)   *see* Upper Ryedale *York*
HAWORTH (St Michael and All Angels) *Bradf 8*   P *V Bradf
and Haworth Ch Lands Trust (jt)*   P-in-c P MAYO-SMITH,
NSM P S WILSON
HAWRIDGE (St Mary) w Cholesbury and St Leonard *Ox 28*
P *Bp, Chpl Trust, and Neale's Charity (jt)*   R D J BURGESS
HAWSKER (All Saints)   *see* Fylingdales and Hawsker cum
Stainsacre *York*
HAWSTEAD (All Saints)   *see* St Edm Way *St E*
HAWTHORN (St Michael and All Angels) and Murton *Dur 2*
P *D&C and I Pemberton Esq (alt)*   R A MILNE
HAWTON (All Saints)   *see* Farndon w Thorpe, Hawton and
Cotham *S'well*
HAXBY (St Mary) and Wigginton *York 7*   P *Abp and
Ld Chan (alt)*   R S JARRATT,   C F M GRANDEY,
NSM P A JACKSON
HAXEY (St Nicholas) *Linc 1*   P *Ld Chan*   P-in-c J N GREEN
HAY MILL (St Cyprian)   *see* Yardley St Cypr Hay Mill *Birm*
HAYDOCK (St James) *Liv 15*   P *R Ashton-in-Makerfield*
V R MIDDLETON,   NSM G J HARDMAN, I C WYNNE
HAYDOCK (St Mark) *Liv 10*   P *MMCET*   V M G COCKAYNE,
C A J BRUCE, F HINDS
HAYDON BRIDGE (St Cuthbert) and Beltingham w Henshaw
Newc 10   P *Bp and V Haltwhistle and Greenhead (jt)*
V J E HAMPSON
HAYDON WICK (St John) *Bris 7*   P *CPAS*   V R W ADAMS,
NSM R E COOK
HAYES (St Anselm) *Lon 24*   P *Bp*   V *vacant* (020) 8573 0958
HAYES (St Edmund of Canterbury) *Lon 24*   P *Bp*
V S M MORING,   NSM S J LAFFORD
HAYES (St Mary) *Lon 24*   P *Keble Coll Ox*
R P L DE S HOMEWOOD
HAYES (St Mary the Virgin) *Roch 14*   P *D&C*
R G D GRAHAM,   NSM M HALLAM
HAYES, NORTH (St Nicholas) *Lon 24*   P *Bp and Keble Coll
Ox (jt)*   V J A EVANS
HAYES, WEST (Christ Church) (St Jerome) *Lon 24*   P *Bp and
Hyndman Trustees (jt)*   V I W JONES

HAYFIELD (St Matthew) and Chinley w Buxworth *Derby 6*
  P *Bp and Resident Freeholders (jt)* V H A EDGERTON
HAYLE (St Elwyn) *see Godrevy Truro*
HAYLING, NORTH (St Peter) *Portsm 5* P *DBP*
  V A C LEONARD, NSM T R WOOD
HAYLING, SOUTH (St Mary) *Portsm 5* P *DBP*
  V P M J GINEVER, NSM P K PAYNE
HAYLING ISLAND (St Andrew) Eastoke *Portsm 5* P *DBP*
  V A C LEONARD, NSM T R WOOD
HAYNES (Mission Room) *see Campton, Clophill and Haynes
  St Alb*
HAYNES (St Mary) *as above*
HAYTON (St James) *see Aspatria w Hayton and Gilcrux Carl*
HAYTON (St Martin) *see Londesborough Wold York*
HAYTON (St Mary Magdalene) *see Eden, Gelt and Irthing Carl*
HAYTON (St Peter) *see Retford Area S'well*
HAYWARDS HEATH (Church of the Ascension) *Chich 6* P *Bp*
  V N TIPPLE, C S A SAMPSON
HAYWARDS HEATH (Church of the Presentation)
  see Haywards Heath St Wilfrid Chich
HAYWARDS HEATH (St Richard) *Chich 6* P *Bp* Hon
  C L D POODHUN
HAYWARDS HEATH (St Wilfrid) (Church of the Presentation)
  Chich 6 P *Bp* V R C W SMITH, C A C LETSCHKA,
  NSM J M ELLIOTT, D C YOUNG
HAYWOOD, GREAT (St Stephen) *see Abbots Bromley,
  Blithfield, Colton, Colwich etc Lich*
HAZELBURY BRYAN (St Mary and St James) and the Hillside
  Parishes *Sarum 5* P *Duke of Northd (2 turns),*
  *M J Scott-Williams Esq, G A L-F Pitt-Rivers Esq, Exors
  F N Kent Esq, and Bp (1 turn each)* C W T RIDDING,
  D R R SEYMOUR
HAZELWELL (St Mary Magdalen) *Birm 5* P *Bp*
  V A C PRIESTLEY
HAZELWOOD (St John the Evangelist), Holbrook and Milford
  Derby 11 P *Bp and DBP (jt)* V *vacant* (01332) 840161
HAZLEMERE (Holy Trinity) *Ox 21* P *Peache Trustees*
  V P C COLLIER, C M J MEARDON, M P WYNTER
HEACHAM (St Mary) *Nor 16* P *Bp* V S DAVIES
HEADBOURNE WORTHY (St Swithun) *Win 7* P *Univ Coll
  Ox and Lord Northbrook (alt)* R A W GORDON,
  NSM E CHASE
HEADCORN (St Peter and St Paul) and The Suttons *Cant 10*
  P *Abp* V B L CURNEW, C C P LAVENDER
HEADINGLEY (St Chad) *see Far Headingley St Chad Ripon*
HEADINGLEY (St Michael and All Angels) *Ripon 7*
  P *V Leeds St Pet* Hon C C BARRETT, NSM D W PEAT,
  K WARD
HEADINGLEY (St Oswald) *see Far Headingley St Chad Ripon*
HEADINGTON (St Andrew) *Ox 4* P *Keble Coll Ox*
  V D W MCFARLAND
HEADINGTON (St Mary) *Ox 4* P *Bp* V *vacant* (01865)
  761886
HEADINGTON QUARRY (Holy Trinity) *Ox 4* P *Bp*
  V T J STEAD, C A P WOOD
HEADLESS CROSS (St Luke) *see Redditch Ch the K Worc*
HEADLEY (All Saints) *Guildf 3* P *Qu Coll Ox* R *vacant*
  (01428) 717321
HEADLEY (St Mary the Virgin) w Box Hill (St Andrew) *Guildf 9*
  P *Bp* P-in-c L HARKNETT, NSM I A JACOBSON
HEADLEY (St Peter) *see Kingsclere and Ashford Hill w
  Headley Win*
HEADON (St Peter) *see Retford Area S'well*
HEADSTONE (St George) *Lon 23* P *Bp* V S R KEEBLE
HEAGE (St Luke) *see Ambergate and Heage Derby*
HEALAUGH (St John the Baptist) w Wighill, Bilbrough and
  Askham Richard *York 1* P *Abp (3 turns),*
  A G Wailes-Fairbairn Esq (1 turn) P-in-c P P ROBINSON,
  NSM M R SHAW
HEALD GREEN (St Catherine) *Ches 17* P *Bp*
  V J F AMBROSE
HEALEY (Christ Church) *Man 17* P *Bp* P-in-c L O RUDEN
HEALEY (St John) *Newc 9* P *V Bywell St Pet*
  P-in-c D J IRVINE, NSM J LYNCH
HEALEY (St Paul) *see Masham and Healey Ripon*
HEALEY (War Memorial Mission) *see S Ossett Wakef*
HEALING (St Peter and St Paul) *see Keelby Gp Linc*
HEAMOOR (St Thomas) *see Gulval and Madron Truro*
HEANOR (St Laurence) *Derby 12* P *Wright Trustees*
  P-in-c D J PATTIMORE, NSM K PATTIMORE
HEANTON PUNCHARDON (St Augustine) w Marwood *Ex 15*
  P *CPAS (3 turns), St Jo Coll Cam (1 turn)*
  P-in-c I M ROBERTSON, NSM M E CRANSTON
HEAP BRIDGE (St Thomas and St George) *see Heywood St
  Marg and Heap Bridge Man*

HEAPEY (St Barnabas) and Withnell *Blackb 4* P *V Leyland*
  P-in-c A F HOGARTH
HEAPHAM (All Saints) *see Lea Gp Linc*
HEART OF EDEN *Carl 1* P *Patr Bd* TR S A LUNN,
  TV R C A HENDERSON, C S SARVANANTHAN, NSM J COX
HEATH (All Saints) *Derby 5* P *Duke of Devonshire and
  Simeon's Trustees (jt)* V A LOVE
HEATH (Mission Church) *see Uttoxeter Area Lich*
HEATH, LITTLE (Christ Church) *St Alb 14* P *Ch Patr Trust*
  P-in-c S P REES, C W D MARTIN, NSM R H WIKNER
HEATH, THE (not known) *see Ludlow Heref*
HEATH AND REACH (St Leonard) *see Ouzel Valley St Alb*
HEATH HAYES (St John) *Lich 3* P *Bp and D&C (jt)*
  V L B VASEY-SAUNDERS, NSM S P REYNOLDS,
  OLM E J STEWARDSON
HEATH TOWN (Holy Trinity) *see Wednesfield Heath Lich*
HEATHER (St John the Baptist) *see Ibstock w Heather Leic*
HEATHERLANDS (St John) *Sarum 7* P *MMCET*
  V P J TAYLOR, C P D HOMDEN
HEATHERYCLEUGH (St Thomas) *see Upper Weardale Dur*
HEATHFIELD (All Saints) *Chich 15* P *Bp* P-in-c D A GUEST
HEATHFIELD (St Catherine) *see Bovey Tracey St Jo w
  Heathfield Ex*
HEATHFIELD (St John the Baptist) *see Deane Vale B & W*
HEATHFIELD (St Richard) *Chich 15* P *Bp* P-in-c P M JONES
HEATON (Christ Church) w Halliwell St Margaret *Man 7*
  P *Patr Bd* V J FRENCH, C H T SCANLAN,
  NSM J W DAVIES
HEATON (St Barnabas) *Bradf 1* P *Trustees*
  P-in-c C MACLAREN, NSM M C FISHER
HEATON (St Gabriel) *see Newc St Gabr Newc*
HEATON (St Martin) *Bradf 1* P *Bp* P-in-c C MACLAREN
HEATON, HIGH (St Francis) *see Newc St Fran Newc*
HEATON CHAPEL (St Thomas) *see Heatons Man*
HEATON MERSEY (St John the Baptist) *as above*
HEATON MOOR (St Paul) *as above*
HEATON NORRIS (Christ w All Saints) *as above*
HEATON REDDISH (St Mary) *Man 2* P *Trustees*
  P-in-c S O'ROURKE
HEATONS *Man 2* P *Patr Bd (4 turns), Prime Min (1 turn)*
  TR M H MAXWELL, TV D BROWNHILL,
  OLM G H RICHARDS, D MACIVER
HEAVITREE (St Michael and All Angels) (St Lawrence)
  (St Loye) and St Mary Steps *Ex 3* P *Patr Bd*
  TV J F SEWARD, P R MORRELL, P-in-c R H S EASTOE,
  C A S M SHOKRALLA
HEBBURN (St Cuthbert) (St Oswald) *Dur 15* P *Prime Min and
  TR Jarrow (alt)* V *vacant* 0191-422 1145
HEBBURN (St John) *Dur 15* P *Bp* P-in-c D T OSMAN,
  C S C E CAKE
HEBDEN (St Peter) *see Linton in Craven Bradf*
HEBDEN BRIDGE (St James) and Heptonstall *Wakef 3*
  P *V Halifax* V H PASK
HEBRON (St Cuthbert) *see Mitford and Hebron Newc*
HECK (St John the Baptist) *see Gt Snaith Sheff*
HECKFIELD (St Michael) *see Whitewater Win*
HECKINGTON Group, The (St Andrew) *Linc 21* P *Bp*
  V *vacant* (01529) 460302
HECKMONDWIKE (All Souls) (St James) *Wakef 8*
  P *V Birstall* P-in-c J BULLOCK, NSM P J DAWSON,
  OLM J C LEE
HEDDINGTON (St Andrew) *see Oldbury Sarum*
HEDDON-ON-THE-WALL (St Andrew) *Newc 9* P *Ld Chan*
  P-in-c A D MCCARTAN
HEDENHAM (St Peter) *see Ditchingham, Hedenham,
  Broome, Earsham etc Nor*
HEDGE END (St John the Evangelist) *Win 10* P *Bp*
  V C M ROWBERRY, NSM S E LITJENS
HEDGE END (St Luke) *Win 10* P *Bp* V A G H GAY,
  NSM J WILLIAMS
HEDGERLEY (St Mary the Virgin) *see Farnham Royal w
  Hedgerley Ox*
HEDNESFORD (St Peter) *Lich 3* P *Bp*
  C L B VASEY-SAUNDERS
HEDON (St Augustine) w Paull *York 12* P *Abp*
  P-in-c K M LAWRIE
HEDSOR (St Nicholas) and Bourne End *Ox 29* P *Bp*
  R A P TREW, NSM R A PAYNE, M RODE
HEDWORTH (St Nicholas) *Dur 15* P *The Crown*
  P-in-c J S BAIN, C J A SKELLEY, Hon C D M DUKE
HEELEY (Christ Church) and Gleadless Valley *Sheff 1* P *DBP
  and Prime Min (alt)* C D J MIDDLETON
HEENE (St Botolph) *Chich 5* P *D&C* R P R ROBERTS
HEIGHAM (Holy Trinity) *Nor 3* P *Ch Trust Fund Trust*
  R A M STRANGE, C M G HUDDLESTON

HEIGHAM (St Barnabas) (St Bartholomew) *Nor 3* **P** *Bp*
P-in-c E HUTCHEON
HEIGHAM (St Thomas) *Nor 3* **P** *Bp* **V** P A YOUNG
HEIGHINGTON (not known) *see* Washingborough w
Heighington and Canwick *Linc*
HEIGHINGTON (St Michael) *Dur 8* **P** *D&C*
P-in-c L M GIBBONS
HEIGHTINGTON (St Giles) *see* Mamble w Bayton, Rock w
Heightington etc *Worc*
HELFORD (St Paul's Mission Church) *see* Meneage *Truro*
HELHOUGHTON (All Saints) *see* E w W Rudham,
Helhoughton etc *Nor*
HELIDON (St John the Baptist) *see* Daventry, Ashby
St Ledgers, Braunston etc *Pet*
HELIONS BUMPSTEAD (St Andrew) *see* Steeple Bumpstead
and Helions Bumpstead *Chelmsf*
HELLAND (St Helena) *Truro 10* **P** *MMCET*
P-in-c S L BRYAN
HELLESDON (St Mary) (St Paul and St Michael) *Nor 2* **P** *Bp*
V P E GRIFFITHS
HELLIFIELD (St Aidan) *Bradf 5* **P** *Ch Ch Ox* **V** *vacant*
(01729) 850243
HELLINGLY (St Peter and St Paul) and Upper Dicker *Chich 15*
P *Abp and Bp (jt)* **V** C M HILL
HELMDON (St Mary Magdalene) *see* Astwell Gp *Pet*
HELME (Christ Church) *see* Meltham *Wakef*
HELMINGHAM (St Mary) *see* Debenham and Helmingham
St E
HELMSHORE (St Thomas) *see* Musbury *Blackb*
HELMSLEY (All Saints) *York 19* **P** *The Hon Jake Duncombe*
P-in-c T J ROBINSON, **NSM** J B NICHOLSON, M D B SINCLAIR
HELMSLEY, UPPER (St Peter) *see* Sand Hutton *York*
HELPERTHORPE (St Peter) *see* Weaverthorpe w
Helperthorpe, Luttons Ambo etc *York*
HELPRINGHAM (St Andrew) w Hale *Linc 21* **P** *Ld Chan*
(2 turns), D&C (1 turn), DBP (1 turn), and the Rt Revd A C
Foottit (1 turn) **R** *vacant* (01529) 421435
HELPSTON (St Botolph) *see* Etton w Helpston and Maxey *Pet*
HELSBY (St Paul) and Dunham-on-the-Hill *Ches 3* **P** *Bp*
P-in-c M SAVILLE
HELSINGTON (St John the Baptist) *Carl 10* **P** *V Kendal*
H Trin **P-in-c** T J HARMER, **NSM** M L WOODCOCK,
B J CROWE
HELSTON (St Michael) and Wendron *Truro 4* **P** *Patr Bd*
TR D G MILLER, **OLM** D NOAKES
HEMBLINGTON (All Saints) *see* Blofield w Hemblington *Nor*
HEMEL HEMPSTEAD (Holy Trinity) Leverstock Green
see Langelei *St Alb*
HEMEL HEMPSTEAD (St Benedict) Bennetts End *as above*
HEMEL HEMPSTEAD (St Mary) *St Alb 2* **P** *Ld Chan*
TR S R ALLEN, **TV** C K PERERA, P J STEVENSON, J C HILL,
R W GRAHAM, **NSM** T J BARTON
HEMEL HEMPSTEAD (St Mary) Apsley End *see* Langelei
St Alb
HEMINGBROUGH (St Mary the Virgin) *York 2* **P** *Abp*
P-in-c F LOFTUS
HEMINGBY Group, The (St Margaret) *Linc 11* **P** *Bp, DBP,*
Keble Coll Ox (2 turns), and Ld Chan (1 turn) **R** A C BUXTON
HEMINGFORD ABBOTS (St Margaret of Antioch) *Ely 10*
P *Lord Hemingford* **P-in-c** P H CUNLIFFE
HEMINGFORD GREY (St James) *Ely 10* **P** *CPAS*
V P H CUNLIFFE
HEMINGSTONE (St Gregory) *see* Coddenham w Gosbeck
and Hemingstone w Henley *St E*
HEMINGTON (Blessed Virgin Mary) *see* Hardington Vale
B & W
HEMINGTON (St Peter and St Paul) *see* Barnwell, Hemington,
Luddington in the Brook etc *Pet*
HEMLEY (All Saints) *see* Waldringfield w Hemley and
Newbourn *St E*
HEMLINGTON (St Timothy) *York 20* **P** *Abp* **V** R A DESICS
HEMPNALL (St Margaret) *Nor 5* **P** *Ld Chan (1 turn),*
Patr Bd (5 turns) **TR** M M KINGSTON, **TV** E N BILLETT
HEMPSTEAD (All Saints) *see* Barningham w Matlaske w
Baconsthorpe etc *Nor*
HEMPSTEAD (All Saints) *see* S Gillingham *Roch*
HEMPSTEAD (St Andrew) *see* The Sampfords and Radwinter
w Hempstead *Chelmsf*
HEMPSTEAD (St Andrew) *see* Bacton, Happisburgh,
Hempstead w Eccles etc *Nor*
HEMPSTED (St Swithun) *see* Glouc City and Hempsted *Glouc*
HEMPTON (Holy Trinity) and Pudding Norton *Nor 15*
P *The Crown* **P-in-c** A D BUIK
HEMPTON (St John the Evangelist) *see* Deddington w Barford,
Clifton and Hempton *Ox*

HEMSBY (St Mary) *see* Flegg Coastal Benefice *Nor*
HEMSWELL (All Saints) *see* Glentworth Gp *Linc*
HEMSWORTH (St Helen) *Wakef 10* **P** *Bp* **R** R W HART
HEMYOCK (St Mary) w Culm Davy, Clayhidon and Culmstock
Ex 4 **P** *DBP, SMF, and D&C (jt)* **R** *vacant* (01823) 681589
HENBURY (St Mary the Virgin) *Bris 2* **P** *Lord Middleton*
(1 turn), Bp (3 turns) **V** D P LLOYD
HENBURY (St Thomas) *Ches 13* **P** *Bp* **P-in-c** W G BOWNESS
HENDFORD (Holy Trinity) *see* Yeovil H Trin w Barwick
B & W
HENDFORD (St Mary the Virgin and All Saints) *as above*
HENDON (All Saints) Childs Hill *Lon 15* **P** *Bp*
V J P WAINWRIGHT
HENDON (St Alphage) *Lon 15* **P** *Bp* **V** H D MOORE,
C C H KIM
HENDON (St Ignatius) *Dur 16* **P** *Bp* **R** A C JONES,
C S H J EDMONDS
HENDON (St Mary) (Christ Church) *Lon 15* **P** *Bp*
V T G CLEMENT, **C** D P SANDHAM, **Hon C** R S LADDS
HENDON (St Paul) Mill Hill *Lon 15* **P** *Bp* **V** A J SHAW,
C J E LOWE
HENDON, WEST (St John) *Lon 15* **P** *Bp* **V** J E I HAWKINS,
NSM T J HALTON
HENDRED, EAST (St Augustine of Canterbury) *see* Wantage
Downs *Ox*
HENDRED, WEST (Holy Trinity) *as above*
HENFIELD (St Peter) w Shermanbury and Woodmancote
Chich 9 **P** *Bp* **R** A M CUTTING, **C** A F MARTIN,
NSM C M BENNETT
HENGROVE (Christ Church) *Bris 1* **P** *Bp and Simeon's*
Trustees (alt) **P-in-c** N HAWKINS
HENHAM (St Mary the Virgin) and Elsenham w Ugley
Chelmsf 21 **P** *Ch Hosp, Ch Soc Trust, and Bp (jt)*
V G TOWNSEND, **C** J P RICHARDSON, **NSM** J D GANNON
HENLEAZE (St Peter) *Bris 2* **P** *Bp* **V** C M PILGRIM,
C C J YANDELL, **NSM** I A BAILEY
HENLEY (St Peter) *see* Coddenham w Gosbeck and
Hemingstone w Henley *St E*
HENLEY IN ARDEN (St John the Baptist) *see* Beaudesert and
Henley-in-Arden w Ullenhall *Cov*
HENLEY-ON-THAMES (Holy Trinity) *Ox 6* **P** *R Rotherfield*
Greys St Nich **V** D R B CARTER
HENLEY-ON-THAMES (St Mary the Virgin) w Remenham
Ox 6 **P** *Bp and Jes Coll Ox (jt)* **R** M R GRIFFITHS
HENLOW (St Mary the Virgin) and Langford *St Alb 8*
P *Ld Chan* **P-in-c** S A GROOM, **NSM** P E CRITCHLEY
HENNOCK (St Mary) *see* Bovey Tracey SS Pet, Paul and Thos
w Hennock *Ex*
HENNY, GREAT (St Mary) *see* N Hinckford *Chelmsf*
HENSALL (St Paul) *see* Gt Snaith *Sheff*
HENSHAW (All Hallows) *see* Haydon Bridge and Beltingham
w Henshaw *Newc*
HENSINGHAM (St John) (Keekle Mission) *Carl 5* **P** *Trustees*
V F T PEARSON, **C** S G N WALKER
HENSTEAD (St Mary) *see* Wrentham, Covehithe w Benacre
etc *St E*
HENSTRIDGE (St Nicholas) *see* Abbas and Templecombe,
Henstridge and Horsington *B & W*
HENTLAND (St Dubricius) *see* St Weonards *Heref*
HENTON (Christ Church) *see* Coxley w Godney, Henton and
Wookey *B & W*
HEPPLE (Christ Church) *see* Upper Coquetdale *Newc*
HEPTONSTALL (St Thomas à Becket and St Thomas the
Apostle) *see* Hebden Bridge and Heptonstall *Wakef*
HEPWORTH (Holy Trinity) *see* Upper Holme Valley *Wakef*
HEPWORTH (St Peter) w Hinderclay, Wattisfield and
Thelnetham *St E 9* **P** *Bp, K Coll Cam, MMCET, and*
P J Holt-Wilson Esq (jt) **R** J W FULTON
HEREFORD (St Francis) *see* Heref S Wye *Heref*
HEREFORD (St John the Baptist) *Heref 3* **P** *D&C* **V** *vacant*
HEREFORD (St Martin) *see* Heref S Wye *Heref*
HEREFORD (St Paul) *see* Tupsley w Hampton Bishop *Heref*
HEREFORD (St Peter w St Owen) (St James) *Heref 3*
P *Simeon's Trustees* **V** P TOWNER, **C** J COORE, A J CLARK,
NSM P W MASSEY, **OLM** S A LITTLE
HEREFORD, LITTLE (St Mary Magdalene) *see* Tenbury
Heref
HEREFORD, WEST Team Ministry (All Saints) (Holy Trinity)
(St Barnabas Church Centre) (St Nicholas) *Heref 3* **P** *Patr Bd*
(3 turns) Ld Chan (1 turn) **TR** R NORTH, **TV** B P CHAVE,
C B M JACOBS
HEREFORD SOUTH WYE (St Francis) (St Martin) *Heref 3*
P *Patr Bd* **TR** J D REESE, **C** A M HODDER, P J BROWN,
R C GREEN, **Hon C** P J GILL, **OLM** C R EVANS
HERMITAGE (Holy Trinity) *Ox 14* **P** *Patr Bd* **TR** R E BALL,
TV A H LYNN, **NSM** M C CAWTE

HERMITAGE (St Mary)   *see* Wriggle Valley *Sarum*

HERNE (St Martin) *Cant 4*   **P** *Abp*   **V** E M RICHARDSON, C J M STANIFORTH,   **OLM** J L HADLOW

HERNE BAY (Christ Church) (St Andrew's Church and Centre) *Cant 4*   **P** *Simeon's Trustees*   **V** A W EVERETT,   **C** M G LANE, **OLM** S PARRETT

HERNE BAY (St Bartholomew)   *see* Reculver and Herne Bay St Bart *Cant*

HERNE HILL (St Paul) (St Saviour) *S'wark 9*   **P** *Bp and Simeon's Trustees (jt)*   **V** C T BARKER,   **NSM** G S TAYLEUR

HERNER (Chapel)   *see* Barnstaple *Ex*

HERNHILL (St Michael)   *see* Boughton under Blean w Dunkirk and Hernhill *Cant*

HERODSFOOT (All Saints)   *see* Duloe, Herodsfoot, Morval and St Pinnock *Truro*

HERONSGATE (St John the Evangelist)   *see* Mill End and Heronsgate w W Hyde *St Alb*

HERRIARD (St Mary)   *see* N Hants Downs *Win*

HERRINGFLEET (St Margaret)   *see* Somerleyton, Ashby, Fritton, Herringfleet etc *Nor*

HERRINGSWELL (St Ethelbert)   *see* Mildenhall *St E*

HERRINGTHORPE (St Cuthbert) *Sheff 6*   **P** *Bp* **P-in-c** K R SKIDMORE

HERRINGTON (St Aidan), Penshaw and Shiney Row *Dur 14* **P** *Bp and Prime Min (alt)*   **P-in-c** S W OSMAN, **NSM** M S GOURLEY

HERSHAM (St Peter) *Guildf 8*   **P** *Bp*   **V** M FLETCHER, **NSM** J W ANDREW,   **OLM** S H GRAY

HERSTMONCEUX (All Saints) and Wartling *Chich 15*   **P** *Bp* **NSM** J M MANNING

HERSTON (St Mark)   *see* Swanage and Studland *Sarum*

HERTFORD (All Saints) (St Andrew) *St Alb 19*   **P** *Ld Chan (1 turn), Duchy of Lanc (2 turns), Patr Bd (1 turn)* **TR** J M H LOVERIDGE,   **TV** R C THOMPSON, N L SHARP, H A STEWART,   **C** E P JAMES,   **NSM** W J CHURCH, D R PEPPER

HERTFORD HEATH (Holy Trinity)   *see* Hertford *St Alb*

HERTINGFORDBURY (St Mary)   *as above*

HESKET-IN-THE-FOREST (St Mary the Virgin) *see* Inglewood Gp *Carl*

HESKETH (All Saints) w Becconsall *Blackb 5*   **P** *Trustees* **P-in-c** N E DAVIS,   **C** A P ARNOLD

HESLERTON, EAST (St Andrew)   *see* Buckrose Carrs *York*

HESLERTON, WEST (All Saints)   *as above*

HESLINGTON (St Paul) *York 2*   **P** *Abp*   **V** *vacant* (01904) 410389

HESSAY (St John the Baptist)   *see* Rufforth w Moor Monkton and Hessay *York*

HESSENFORD (St Anne)   *see* St Germans *Truro*

HESSETT (St Ethelbert)   *see* Rougham, Beyton w Hessett and Rushbrooke *St E*

HESSLE (All Saints) *York 14*   **P** *Ld Chan*   **V** T M H BOYNS, **C** A C SIMPSON

HESTER WAY LANE (St Silas)   *see* Cheltenham St Mark *Glouc*

HESTON (All Saints) (St Leonard) *Lon 11*   **P** *Bp* **V** D COLEMAN

HESWALL (Church of the Good Shepherd) (St Peter) *Ches 8* **P** W A B Davenport Esq   **R** J R GIBBS,   **C** J W BRIDGMAN, J C BRIDGMAN,   **NSM** A C G LEACH

HETHE (St Edmund King and Martyr and St George) *see* Shelswell *Ox*

HETHEL (All Saints)   *see* Mulbarton w Bracon Ash, Hethel and Flordon *Nor*

HETHERSETT (St Remigius) w Canteloff w Little Melton and Great Melton *Nor 7*   **P** *G&C Coll Cam, E C Evans-Lombe Esq, and Em Coll Cam (by turn)*   **R** D B LAMMAS

HETHERSGILL (St Mary)   *see* Bewcastle, Stapleton and Kirklinton etc *Carl*

HETTON, SOUTH (Holy Trinity) *Dur 2*   **P** *Bp*   **V** *vacant*

HETTON-LYONS w Eppleton *Dur 14*   **P** *Bp (1 turn), Prime Min (2 turns)*   **R** A ANDERSON,   **C** J K MENZIES

HEVENINGHAM (St Margaret) w Ubbeston, Huntingfield and Cookley *St E 15*   **P** *Capt the Revd J S Peel* **P-in-c** A B NORTON

HEVER (St Peter), Four Elms and Mark Beech *Roch 11*   **P** *Bp and C Talbot Esq (jt)*   **R** J A WEEKS,   **NSM** V J IZOD

HEVERSHAM (St Peter) and Milnthorpe *Carl 10* **P** *Trin Coll Cam*   **P-in-c** S E WILSON,   **NSM** R RUTTER

HEVINGHAM (St Mary the Virgin and St Botolph) *see* Horsford, Felthorpe and Hevingham *Nor*

HEWELSFIELD (St Mary Magdalene)   *see* St Briavels w Hewelsfield *Glouc*

HEWISH (Good Shepherd)   *see* Wulfric Benefice *B & W*

HEWORTH (Christ Church) *York 7*   **P** *Ch Trust Fund Trust* **V** T MCDONOUGH

HEWORTH (Holy Trinity) (St Wulstan) *York 7*   **P** *Ch Trust Fund Trust*   **R** M B WOODMANSEY

HEWORTH (St Alban)   *see* Windy Nook St Alb *Dur*

HEWORTH (St Mary) *Dur 12*   **P** *Bp*   **V** N B WARNER

HEXAGON, THE: Arnesby w Shearsby, Bruntingthorpe, Husbands Bosworth, Mowsley and Knaptoft, and Theddingworth *Leic 7*   **P** *Bp and DBP (jt)*   **C** A C RHOADES

HEXHAM (St Andrew) *Newc 10*   **P** *Mercers' Co and Viscount Allendale (alt)*   **R** G B USHER,   **C** J E ANDERSON, **NSM** A R CURRIE

HEXTABLE (St Peter)   *see* Swanley St Paul *Roch*

HEXTHORPE (St Jude)   *see* Edlington and Hexthorpe *Sheff*

HEXTON (St Faith)   *see* Barton-le-Cley w Higham Gobion and Hexton *St Alb*

HEY (St John the Baptist)   *see* Medlock Head *Man*

HEYBRIDGE (St Andrew) (St George) w Langford *Chelmsf 11* **P** *D&C Ch St Paul's and Lord Byron (alt)*   **V** J LOW

HEYBROOK BAY (Holy Nativity)   *see* Wembury *Ex*

HEYDON (Holy Trinity)   *see* Icknield Way Villages *Chelmsf*

HEYDON (St Peter and St Paul)   *see* Cawston w Booton and Brandiston etc *Nor*

HEYDOUR (St Michael and All Angels)   *see* Ancaster Wilsford Gp *Linc*

HEYFORD (St Peter and St Paul) w Stowe Nine Churches and Flore w Brockhall *Pet 3*   **P** *The Revd S Hope, Ch Ch Ox, DPB and Bp (by turn)*   **R** A SLATER

HEYFORD, LOWER (St Mary)   *see* Cherwell Valley *Ox*

HEYFORD, UPPER (St Mary)   *as above*

HEYHOUSES (St Nicholas)   *see* Sabden and Pendleton *Blackb*

HEYHOUSES ON SEA (St Anne)   *see* St Annes St Anne *Blackb*

HEYSHAM (St Peter) (St Andrew) (St James) *Blackb 11* **P** C E C Royds Esq   **R** D A TICKNER

HEYSHOTT (St James) *Chich 10*   **P** *Bp*   **P-in-c** C BOXLEY

HEYSIDE (St Mark) *Man 16*   **P** *Trustees*   **V** R MORRIS

HEYTESBURY (St Peter and St Paul)   *see* Upper Wylye Valley *Sarum*

HEYTHROP (St Nicholas)   *see* Chase *Ox*

HEYWOOD (All Souls)   *see* Sudden and Heywood All So *Man*

HEYWOOD (St James) *Man 14*   **P** *Bp*   **V** *vacant* (01706) 369754

HEYWOOD (St John) (St Luke) *Man 14*   **P** *Patr Bd* **V** M D CARLISLE

HEYWOOD (St Margaret) and Heap Bridge *Man 14* **P** *Patr Bd*   **P-in-c** S J BANKS,   **OLM** I WARRINGTON, J M GEARY

HIBALDSTOW (St Hybald)   *see* Scawby, Redbourne and Hibaldstow *Linc*

HICKLETON (St Wilfrid)   *see* Goldthorpe w Hickleton *Sheff*

HICKLING (St Luke) w Kinoulton and Broughton Sulney (Upper Broughton) *S'well 8*   **P** *Prime Min, Qu Coll Cam, and Bp (by turn)*   **R** *vacant* (01949) 81657

HICKLING (St Mary)   *see* Ludham, Potter Heigham, Hickling and Catfield *Nor*

HIGH   *see also under substantive place name*

HIGH CROSS (St John the Evangelist) *St Alb 19*   **P** *DBP* **V** B EBELING

HIGH GREEN (St Saviour)   *see* Mortomley St Sav High Green *Sheff*

HIGH HAM (St Andrew)   *see* Langport Area *B & W*

HIGH LANE (St Thomas) *Ches 16*   **P** *R Stockport* **V** J E PARKER

HIGH LEGH (St John)   *see* High Legh *Ches*

HIGH OAK, Hingham and Scoulton w Wood Rising *Nor 7* **P** *Patr Bd*   **TR** C B REED,   **OLM** P J TRETT, S A HOLT

HIGHAM (St John the Evangelist)   *see* Fence-in-Pendle and Higham *Blackb*

HIGHAM (St John the Evangelist) and Merston *Roch 6*   **P** *St Jo Coll Cam*   **V** J F SOUTHWARD

HIGHAM (St Mary), Holton St Mary, Raydon and Stratford St Mary *St E 3*   **P** *Duchy of Lanc, Reformation Ch Trust, and Mrs S E F Holden*   **R** R M PAUL

HIGHAM FERRERS (St Mary the Virgin) w Chelveston *Pet 8* **P** *Bp*   **V** G L BROCKHOUSE

HIGHAM GOBION (St Margaret)   *see* Barton-le-Cley w Higham Gobion and Hexton *St Alb*

HIGHAM GREEN (St Stephen)   *see* Dalham, Gazeley, Higham, Kentford and Moulton *St E*

HIGHAM HILL (St Andrew)   *see* Walthamstow St Andr *Chelmsf*

HIGHAM-ON-THE-HILL (St Peter)   *see* Fenn Lanes Gp *Leic*

HIGHAMPTON (Holy Cross)   *see* Black Torrington, Bradford w Cookbury etc *Ex*

HIGHAMS PARK (All Saints) Hale End *Chelmsf 5*   **P** *Bp* **V** C A MCGHIE

HIGHBRIDGE (St John the Evangelist) *B & W 1*   **P** *Bp* **V** S M J CROSSMAN

HIGHBROOK (All Saints) and West Hoathly *Chich 6* **P** *Ld Chan*   **P-in-c** L F WHATLEY

HIGHBURY (Christ Church) (St John) (St Saviour) *Lon 6*
  P *Ch Trust Fund Trust and Islington Ch Trust (jt)*
  V J D BREWSTER,   **C** T GOLDING
HIGHBURY NEW PARK (St Augustine) *Lon 6*   **P** *Trustees*
  V C T MAIN
HIGHCLERE (St Michael and All Angels) *see* NW Hants *Win*
HIGHCLIFFE (St Mark) *Win 9*   **P** *Bp*   **V** G K TAYLOR
HIGHER *see also under substantive place name*
HIGHER FOLD Leigh (St Matthew) *see* Bedford Leigh *Man*
HIGHERTOWN (All Saints) and Baldhu *Truro 6*   **P** *Bp and*
  Viscount Falmouth (alt)   **V** G W SMYTH
HIGHFIELD (All Saints) *Ox 4*   **P** *Bp*   **V** J E COCKE
HIGHFIELD (Christ Church) *see* Portswood Ch Ch *Win*
HIGHFIELD (St Catherine) *see* New Bury w Gt Lever *Man*
HIGHFIELD (St Mary) *see* Sheff St Mary Bramall Lane *Sheff*
HIGHFIELD (St Matthew) *Liv 14*   **P** *Trustees*
  V R L PEARSON
HIGHFIELD (St Paul) *see* Hemel Hempstead *St Alb*
HIGHGATE (All Saints) *Lon 20*   **P** *Bp*   **P-in-c** J D TRIGG
HIGHGATE (St Alban and St Patrick) *Birm 13*   **P** *Keble Coll*
  Ox   **P-in-c** P SULTAN
HIGHGATE (St Augustine) *Lon 20*   **P** *Bp*   **P-in-c** P F M GOFF
HIGHGATE (St Michael) *Lon 20*   **P** *Bp*   **V** J D TRIGG,
  C B WANDREY, T RENZ, E M WEST
HIGHGATE CENTRE *see* Bredbury St Barn *Ches*
HIGHGATE RISE (St Anne) *see* Brookfield St Anne, Highgate
  Rise *Lon*
HIGHLEY (St Mary) w Billingsley, Glazeley and Deuxhill and
  Chelmarsh *Heref 8*   **P** *MMCET*   **V** C G WILLIAMS,
  NSM V R SMITH
HIGHMORE (St Paul) *see* Nettlebed w Bix, Highmoor, Pishill
  etc *Ox*
HIGHNAM (Holy Innocents), Lassington, Rudford, Tibberton
  and Taynton *Glouc 3*   **P** *D&C, T J Fenton Esq, and*
  A E Woolley (jt)   **NSM** S TAYLOR
HIGHTERS HEATH (Immanuel) *Birm 5*   **P** *Bp*
  V K J R CLARKE
HIGHTOWN (All Saints) *see* Castleford *Wakef*
HIGHTOWN (St Barnabas) *see* Liversedge w Hightown *Wakef*
HIGHTOWN (St Stephen) *see* Altcar and Hightown *Liv*
HIGHWEEK (All Saints) (St Mary) *Ex 10*   **P** *Bp*
  P-in-c M D THAYER
HIGHWORTH (St Michael) w Sevenhampton and Inglesham and
  Hannington *Bris 7*   **P** *Bp (4 turns), Mrs M G Hussey-Freke*
  (1 turn)   **V** G D SOWDEN,   **C** A C WOO
HILBOROUGH (All Saints) w Bodney *Nor 13*   **P** *DBP*
  C D J HANWELL
HILDENBOROUGH (St John the Evangelist) *Roch 11*
  P *V Tonbridge*   **V** J C CHANDLER,   **NSM** S BRAID
HILDERSHAM (Holy Trinity) *Ely 5*   **P** *Trustees*
  P-in-c J M NORRIS
HILDERSTONE (Christ Church) *see* Fulford w Hilderstone
  Lich
HILFIELD (St Nicholas) *see* Wriggle Valley *Sarum*
HILGAY (All Saints) *Ely 9*   **P** *Hertf Coll Ox*   **R** D J EVANS
HILL (St James) *Birm 12*   **P** *Bp*   **V** A W MOORE,
  C A J BOWNASS,   **NSM** A R PLATTS
HILL (St Michael) *see* Berkeley w Wick, Breadstone, Newport,
  Stone etc *Glouc*
HILL CROOME (St Mary) *see* Upton-on-Severn, Ripple, Earls
  Croome etc *Worc*
HILL TOP (Mission Room) *see* Greasley *S'well*
HILL TOP (St James) *see* W Bromwich St Jas w St Paul *Lich*
HILLESDEN (All Saints) *see* Lenborough *Ox*
HILLESLEY (St Giles) *see* Charfield and Kingswood w
  Wickwar etc *Glouc*
HILLFARRANCE (Holy Cross) *see* Deane Vale *B & W*
HILLINGDON (All Saints) *Lon 24*   **P** *Bp*   **V** D P BANISTER
HILLINGDON (St John the Baptist) *Lon 24*   **P** *Bp*
  V R W HARRISON,   **NSM** G PINNELL
HILLINGTON (St Mary the Virgin) *Nor 16*
  P E W Dawnay Esq   **R** J B V RIVIERE
HILLMORTON (St John the Baptist) *Cov 6*   **P** *Bp and*
  TR Rugby   **V** A P HAINES,   **NSM** M I SIMMONS
HILLOCK (St Andrew) *Man 10*   **P** *Bp and R Stand All SS*
  P-in-c D A WILLIAMS
HILLSBOROUGH and Wadsley Bridge (Christ Church) *Sheff 4*
  P *Ch Patr Trust*   **P-in-c** K FARROW,   **C** F M KOUBLE
HILLSIDE Lobley Hill and Marley Hill *Dur 13*   **P** *Bp and*
  Prime Min (alt)   **V** R K HOPPER
HILLTOP (Mission Room) *see* Bagnall w Endon *Lich*
HILMARTON (St Lawrence) *see* Woodhill *Sarum*
HILPERTON MARSH (St Mary Magdalen) *see* Canalside
  Benefice *Sarum*
HILSTON (St Margaret) *see* Roos and Garton w Tunstall,
  Grimston and Hilston *York*

HILTON (All Saints) *see* Piddle Valley, Hilton, Cheselbourne etc
  Sarum
HILTON (St Mary Magdalene) *Ely 10*   **P** *Bp*
  P-in-c D W BUSK
HILTON (St Peter) *see* Stainton w Hilton *York*
HILTON w Marston-on-Dove *Derby 14*   **P** *N J M Spurrier Esq*
  V A G MURPHIE,   **C** J C CANT,
  NSM S K MATSON DE LAURIER
HIMBLETON (St Mary Magdalen) *see* Bowbrook S *Worc*
HIMLEY (St Michael and All Angels) *see* Smestow Vale *Lich*
HINCASTER (Mission Room) *see* Heversham and Milnthorpe
  Carl
HINCHLEY WOOD (St Christopher) *Guildf 8*   **P** *Bp*
  V J S KRONENBERG,   **NSM** L K KAYE-BESLEY, C A MULLINS
HINCKFORD, NORTH *Chelmsf 19*   **P** *Patr Bd (4 turns),*
  Ld Chan (1 turn)   **TR** E G BUCHANAN,   **TV** M H KING,
  NSM V E GAGEN
HINCKLEY (Assumption of St Mary the Virgin) (St Francis)
  (St Paul) *Leic 10*   **P** *Bp*   **V** J WHITTAKER,   **NSM** J A GIBBS
HINCKLEY (Holy Trinity) *Leic 10*   **P** *DBP*   **R** T J WARD
HINCKLEY (St John the Evangelist) *Leic 10*   **P** *DBP*
  V G J WESTON
HINDERCLAY (St Mary) *see* Hepworth, Hinderclay,
  Wattisfield and Thelnetham *St E*
HINDERWELL (St Hilda), Roxby and Staithes w Lythe,
  Ugthorpe and Sandsend *York 21*   **P** *Abp*   **R** B J PYKE,
  NSM J EVETTS-SECKER
HINDHEAD (St Alban) *see* Churt and Hindhead *Guildf*
HINDLEY (All Saints) *Liv 14*   **P** *R Wigan*   **P-in-c** A BEAHAN
HINDLEY (St Peter) *Liv 14*   **P** *St Pet Coll Ox*   **V** S A MATHER
HINDLEY GREEN (St John) *Liv 14*   **P** *Bp*   **V** M J SHERWIN,
  NSM C A CLOSE
HINDOLVESTON (St George) *see* Briston, Burgh Parva,
  Hindolveston etc *Nor*
HINDON (St John the Baptist) *see* Nadder Valley *Sarum*
HINDRINGHAM (St Martin) *see* Barney, Fulmodeston w
  Croxton, Hindringham etc *Nor*
HINGHAM (St Andrew) *see* High Oak, Hingham and Scoulton
  w Wood Rising *Nor*
HINKSEY, NEW (St John the Evangelist) *see* S Hinksey *Ox*
HINKSEY, NORTH (St Lawrence) *see* Osney *Ox*
HINKSEY, SOUTH (St Laurence) *Ox 7*   **P** *Bp*
  P-in-c J D WILKINSON
HINSTOCK (St Oswald) *see* Cheswardine, Childs Ercall, Hales,
  Hinstock etc *Lich*
HINTLESHAM (St Nicholas) *see* Elmsett w Aldham,
  Hintlesham, Chattisham etc *St E*
HINTON ADMIRAL (St Michael and All Angels)
  see Bransgore and Hinton Admiral *Win*
HINTON AMPNER (All Saints) *see* Upper Itchen *Win*
HINTON BLEWETT (St Margaret) *see* E w W Harptree and
  Hinton Blewett *B & W*
HINTON CHARTERHOUSE (St John the Baptist)
  see Freshford, Limpley Stoke and Hinton Charterhouse *B & W*
HINTON-IN-THE-HEDGES (Holy Trinity) *see* Aynho and
  Croughton w Evenley etc *Pet*
HINTON MARTEL (St John the Evangelist) *see* Horton,
  Chalbury, Hinton Martel and Holt St Jas *Sarum*
HINTON-ON-THE-GREEN (St Peter) *see* Hampton w
  Sedgeberrow and Hinton-on-the-Green *Worc*
HINTON PARVA (St Swithun) *see* Lyddington and
  Wanborough and Bishopstone etc *Bris*
HINTON ST GEORGE (St George) *see* Merriott w Hinton,
  Dinnington and Lopen *B & W*
HINTON ST MARY (St Mary) *see* Sturminster Newton,
  Hinton St Mary and Lydlinch *Sarum*
HINTON WALDRIST (St Margaret) *see* Cherbury w Gainfield
  Ox
HINTS (St Bartholomew) *Lich 1*   **P** *Personal Reps A E Jones Esq*
  V F A HASKETT
HINXHILL (St Mary) *see* Mersham w Hinxhill and Sellindge
  Cant
HINXTON (St Mary and St John) *Ely 5*   **P** *Jes Coll Cam*
  P-in-c J H MARTIN
HINXWORTH (St Nicholas) *see* Ashwell w Hinxworth and
  Newnham *St Alb*
HIPSWELL (St John the Evangelist) *Ripon 2*   **P** *Bp*
  V J E KEARTON,   **C** T STEPHENS
HISTON (St Andrew) *Ely 6*   **P** *MMCET*
  V N J BLANDFORD-BAKER,   **C** P H BUTLER,
  NSM J M GLOVER
HITCHAM (All Saints) *see* Rattlesden w Thorpe Morieux,
  Brettenham etc *St E*
HITCHAM (St Mary) *Ox 23*   **P** *Eton Coll*   **V** *vacant* (01628)
  602881

HITCHIN (Holy Saviour) (St Faith) (St Mark) (St Mary)
St Alb 3 **P** *Patr Bd* **TR** M A H RODEN, **TV** I C TODD,
J F MAINWARING, C C M SABEY-CORKINDALE, **C** O J LEARMONT,
NSM F S E GIBBS

HITHER GREEN (St Swithun) *see* Lewisham St Swithun
S'wark

HITTISLEIGH (St Andrew) *see* Chagford, Drewsteignton,
Hittisleigh etc *Ex*

HIXON (St Peter) *see* Mid Trent *Lich*

HOAR CROSS (Holy Angels) w Newchurch *Lich 14* **P** *Bp and
Meynell Ch Trustees* **P-in-c** P G GREEN

HOARWITHY (St Catherine) *see* St Weonards *Heref*

HOATH (Holy Cross) *see* St Nicholas at Wade w Sarre and
Chislet w Hoath *Cant*

HOATHLY, EAST (not known) *see* Chiddingly w E Hoathly
Chich

HOATHLY, WEST (St Margaret) *see* Highbrook and W
Hoathly *Chich*

HOBS MOAT (St Mary) *Birm 11* **P** *Bp* **P-in-c** L GRANNER

HOBY (All Saints) *see* Upper Wreake *Leic*

HOCKERILL (All Saints) *St Alb 15* **P** *Bp Lon*
P-in-c K I GOSS

HOCKERING (St Michael) *see* Mattishall and the Tudd Valley
Nor

HOCKERTON (St Nicholas) *see* Kirklington w Hockerton
S'well

HOCKHAM, GREAT (Holy Trinity) *see* Caston, Griston,
Merton, Thompson etc *Nor*

HOCKLEY (St Matthew) *see* Wilnecote *Lich*

HOCKLEY (St Paul) *see* Birm St Paul *Birm*

HOCKLEY (St Peter and St Paul) *Chelmsf 12* **P** *Wadh Coll Ox*
V *vacant* (01702) 203668

HOCKLIFFE (St Nicholas) *see* Ouzel Valley *St Alb*

HOCKWOLD w WILTON (St James) *see* Grimshoe *Ely*

HOCKWORTHY (St Simon and St Jude) *see* Sampford
Peverell, Uplowman, Holcombe Rogus etc *Ex*

HODDESDON (St Catherine and St Paul) *St Alb 17* **P** *Peache
Trustees* **V** P PARKS

HODDESDON (St Cuthbert) *see* Rye Park St Cuth *St Alb*

HODDLESDEN (St Paul) *Blackb 2* **P** *Bp* **C** T N DYER

HODGE HILL (St Philip and St James) *Birm 9* **P** *Bp*
P-in-c A D BARRETT

HODNET (St Luke) w Weston under Redcastle *Lich 18*
P *A E H Heber-Percy Esq* **P-in-c** C P BEECH

HODTHORPE (St Martin) *see* Whitwell *Derby*

HOE (St Andrew) *see* Dereham and Distr *Nor*

HOE, WEST (St Michael) *see* Plymouth St Andr and
Stonehouse *Ex*

HOGGESTON (Holy Cross) *see* Schorne *Ox*

HOGHTON (Holy Trinity) *Blackb 5* **P** *V Leyland*
P-in-c D C DICKINSON

HOGNASTON (St Bartholomew) *see* Hulland, Atlow,
Kniveton, Bradley and Hognaston *Derby*

HOGSTHORPE (St Mary) *see* Chapel St Leonards w
Hogsthorpe *Linc*

HOLBEACH (All Saints) *Linc 16* **P** *Bp* **C** D C SWEETING

HOLBEACH FEN (St John) *Linc 16* **P** *Bp*
P-in-c R J MORRISON, **OLM** B A HUTCHINSON

HOLBEACH MARSH (St Luke) (St Mark) (St Martin) *Linc 16*
P *V Holbeach* **P-in-c** R J GODDARD

HOLBECK (St Luke the Evangelist) *Ripon 6* **P** *Bp, V Leeds
St Pet, and Meynell Ch Trust (jt)* **P-in-c** C BUTLER

HOLBETON (All Saints) *Ex 21* **P** *The Crown* **V** *vacant*

HOLBORN (St Alban the Martyr) w Saffron Hill St Peter
Lon 17 **P** *D&C St Paul's* **V** C M SMITH, **NSM** R G CORP

**HOLBORN (St George the Martyr) Queen Square (Holy
Trinity) (St Bartholomew) Grays Inn Road** *Lon 17*
P *Ch Soc Trust* **R** J H VALENTINE, **C** D L INGALL

HOLBORN (St Giles-in-the-Fields) *see* St Giles-in-the-Fields
Lon

**HOLBROOK (All Saints), Stutton, Freston, Woolverstone and
Wherstead** *St E 5* **P** *Patr Bd* **R** G P CLEMENT,
NSM J G PENDORF

HOLBROOK (St Michael) *see* Hazelwood, Holbrook and
Milford *Derby*

HOLBROOK ROAD (St Swithin) *see* Belper *Derby*

HOLBROOKS (St Luke) *Cov 2* **P** *Bp* **V** C DUNKLEY,
C M J BAILEY

HOLBURY (Good Shepherd) *see* Fawley *Win*

HOLCOMBE (Emmanuel) (Canon Lewis Hall) and Hawkshaw
Man 8 **P** *R Bury St Mary and F Whowell Esq (jt)*
R P H SUMSION, **OLM** R W AIREY

HOLCOMBE (St Andrew) *see* Coleford w Holcombe *B & W*

HOLCOMBE (St George) *see* Dawlish *Ex*

HOLCOMBE BURNELL (St John the Baptist) *see* Tedburn St
Mary, Cheriton Bishop, Whitestone etc *Ex*

HOLCOMBE ROGUS (All Saints) *see* Sampford Peverell,
Uplowman, Holcombe Rogus etc *Ex*

HOLCOT (St Mary and All Saints) *see* Brixworth w Holcot *Pet*

HOLDENHURST (St John the Evangelist) and Iford *Win 8*
P *Bp* **V** A L MCPHERSON, **C** I P FLETCHER, **Hon
C** J NIGHTINGALE, **NSM** N M BENCE, J M SEARE, N S LEGRAND

HOLDGATE (Holy Trinity) *see* Diddlebury w Munslow,
Holdgate and Tugford *Heref*

HOLFORD (St Mary the Virgin) *see* Quantock Coast *B & W*

HOLGATE (St Paul) *see* York St Paul *York*

**HOLKHAM (St Withiburga) w Egmere w Warham,
Wells-next-the-Sea and Wighton** *Nor 15* **P** *Viscount Coke
(2 turns), M J Beddard Esq (2 turns), and D&C(1 turn)*
R A V DOUGLAS

HOLLACOMBE (St Petroc) *see* Holsworthy w Hollacombe and
Milton Damerel *Ex*

HOLLAND, GREAT (All Saints) *see* Kirby-le-Soken w Gt
Holland *Chelmsf*

HOLLAND, NEW (Christ Church) *see* Barrow and Goxhill
Linc

HOLLAND FEN (All Saints) *see* Brothertoft Gp *Linc*

HOLLAND-ON-SEA (St Bartholomew) *Chelmsf 22* **P** *Ch Patr
Trust* **P-in-c** P A JOHNSON

HOLLAND PARK (St George the Martyr) (St John the Baptist)
Lon 12 **P** *Trustees and Bp (jt)* **V** M G FULLER, **Hon
C** R G THOMPSON

HOLLESLEY (All Saints) *see* Wilford Peninsula *St E*

HOLLINFARE (St Helen) *see* Glazebury w Hollinfare *Liv*

**HOLLINGBOURNE (All Saints) and Hucking w Leeds and
Broomfield** *Cant 13* **P** *Abp* **P-in-c** N FRY, **Hon C** R M GILL

HOLLINGDEAN (St Richard) *see* Brighton St Matthias *Chich*

HOLLINGTON (St John the Evangelist) *see* Rocester and
Croxden w Hollington *Lich*

HOLLINGTON (St John the Evangelist) (St Peter and St Paul)
Chich 17 **P** *Ch Patr Trust* **C** C RUDGE, **NSM** M HINKLEY

HOLLINGTON (St Leonard) (St Anne) *Chich 17*
P *E G Brabazon Esq* **R** D I CHARNOCK, **C** V G DOIDGE

HOLLINGWORTH (St Hilda) *see* Milnrow *Man*

HOLLINGWORTH (St Mary) w Tintwistle *Ches 14* **P** *Patr Bd*
V R A K LAW

HOLLINSWOOD (not known) *see* Cen Telford *Lich*

HOLLINWOOD (St Margaret) and Limeside *Man 16* **P** *Bp
and V Prestwich (jt)* **V** D HAWTHORN, **C** S B SAYER

HOLLOWAY (Emmanuel) *see* Tollington *Lon*

HOLLOWAY Hanley Road (St Saviour) *as above*

HOLLOWAY (St Francis of Assisi) *see* W Holloway St Luke
Lon

HOLLOWAY (St Mary Magdalene) (St David) *Lon 6* **P** *Bp and
V Islington St Mary (jt)* **V** P V ZAPHIRIOU, **C** J K RUST

HOLLOWAY, UPPER (All Saints) *see* Tufnell Park St Geo and
All SS *Lon*

**HOLLOWAY, UPPER (St Andrew) (St John) (St Mary)
(St Peter)** *Lon 6* **P** *Patr Bd* **TV** R J POWELL, W K DORGU,
C B T ASMELASH, **NSM** S PADDOCK, P M TAYLOR

HOLLOWAY, WEST (St Luke) *Lon 6* **P** *Lon Coll Div Trustees*
V D W TOMLINSON, **NSM** M D E WROE

HOLLOWELL (St James) *see* Guilsborough and Hollowell and
Cold Ashby etc *Pet*

HOLLY HALL (St Augustine) *see* Dudley *Worc*

HOLLY HILL (Church Centre) *see* Frankley *Birm*

HOLLYBUSH (All Saints) *see* Berrow w Pendock, Eldersfield,
Hollybush etc *Worc*

HOLLYM (St Nicholas) *see* Patrington w Hollym, Welwick and
Winestead *York*

HOLMBRIDGE (St David) *see* Upper Holme Valley *Wakef*

HOLMBURY ST MARY (St Mary the Virgin) *see* Wotton and
Holmbury St Mary *Guildf*

HOLMCROFT (St Bertelin) *see* Stafford *Lich*

HOLME (All Saints) and Seaton Ross Group, The *York 5*
P *St Jo Coll Cam and Ld Chan (alt)* **R** N T B STRAFFORD

HOLME (Holy Trinity) *see* Burton and Holme *Carl*

HOLME (St Giles) *see* Yaxley and Holme w Conington *Ely*

HOLME (St Giles) *see* E Trent *S'well*

HOLME, EAST (St John the Evangelist) *see* Wareham *Sarum*

HOLME CULTRAM (St Cuthbert) *see* Solway Plain *Carl*

HOLME CULTRAM (St Mary) *as above*

HOLME EDEN (St Paul) and Wetheral w Warwick *Carl 2*
P *D&C and DBP (jt)* **R** D A CRAVEN, **NSM** P TIPLADY,
A MAGUIRE

HOLME HALE (St Andrew) *see* Necton, Holme Hale w N and
S Pickenham *Nor*

HOLME-IN-CLIVIGER (St John) w Worsthorne *Blackb 3*
P *Patr Bd* **V** R K HENSHALL

HOLME-NEXT-THE-SEA (St Mary) *see* Hunstanton St Mary
w Ringstead Parva etc *Nor*

HOLME-ON-SPALDING-MOOR (All Saints)   *see* Holme and
Seaton Ross Gp *York*
HOLME-ON-SPALDING-MOOR (Old School Mission Room)
as above
HOLME PIERREPONT (St Edmund King and Martyr)
see Lady Bay w Holme Pierrepont and Adbolton *S'well*
HOLME RUNCTON (St James) w South Runcton and
Wallington *Ely 9*   P *Bp*   R J C W NOLAN
HOLME VALLEY, The UPPER *Wakef 6*   P *Patr Bd*
TR J S ROBERTSHAW,   TV M D ELLERTON, K GRIFFIN,
N M HEATON,   NSM S W DIXON,   OLM G B BAMFORD
HOLME WOOD (St Christopher)   *see* Tong *Bradf*
HOLMER (St Bartholomew) (St Mary) w Huntington *Heref 3*
P *D&C*   V P A WILLIAMS
HOLMER GREEN (Christ Church)   *see* Penn Street *Ox*
HOLMES CHAPEL (St Luke)   *see* Church Hulme *Ches*
HOLMESDALE (St Philip)   *see* Dronfield w Holmesfield *Derby*
HOLMESFIELD (St Swithin)   *as above*
HOLMEWOOD (St Alban Mission)   *see* Heath *Derby*
HOLMFIELD (St Andrew)   *see* Bradshaw and Holmfield *Wakef*
HOLMFIRTH (Holy Trinity)   *see* Upper Holme Valley *Wakef*
HOLMPTON (St Nicholas)   *see* Withernsea w Owthorne and
Easington etc *York*
HOLMSIDE (St John the Evangelist) *Dur 4*   P *The Crown*
V *vacant* (01207) 529274
HOLMWOOD (St Mary Magdalene)   *see* Surrey Weald *Guildf*
HOLMWOOD, NORTH (St John the Evangelist) *Guildf 7*
P *Bp*   V S K TANSWELL
HOLNE (St Mary the Virgin)   *see* Ashburton, Bickington,
Buckland in the Moor etc *Ex*
HOLNEST (Church of the Assumption)   *see* Vale of White Hart
Sarum
HOLSWORTHY (St Peter and St Paul) w Hollacombe and
Milton Damerel *Ex 17*   P *DBP and Mrs F M Palmer (jt)*
R R M REYNOLDS
HOLT (St Andrew) w High Kelling *Nor 18*   P *St Jo Coll Cam*
R H C STOKER
HOLT (St James)   *see* Horton, Chalbury, Hinton Martell and
Holt St Jas *Sarum*
HOLT (St Katharine)   *see* Broughton Gifford, Gt Chalfield and
Holt *Sarum*
HOLT (St Martin)   *see* Hallow and Grimley w Holt *Worc*
HOLTBY (Holy Trinity)   *see* Stockton-on-the-Forest w Holtby
and Warthill *York*
HOLTON (St Bartholomew)   *see* Wheatley *Ox*
HOLTON (St Nicholas)   *see* Camelot Par *B & W*
HOLTON (St Peter)   *see* Blyth Valley *St E*
HOLTON-CUM-BECKERING (All Saints)   *see* Wragby Gp
Linc
HOLTON-LE-CLAY (St Peter), Tetney and North Cotes *Linc 10*
P *Ld Chan, Bp, and Duchy of Lancaster (by turn)*
V C M WOADDEN
HOLTON-LE-MOOR (St Luke)   *see* Kelsey Gp *Linc*
HOLTON ST MARY (St Mary)   *see* Higham, Holton St Mary,
Raydon and Stratford *St E*
HOLTS (St Hugh) Conventional District *Man 14* *vacant* 0161-620
1646
HOLTSPUR (St Thomas)   *see* Beaconsfield *Ox*
HOLWELL (St Laurence)   *see* Vale of White Hart *Sarum*
HOLWELL (St Leonard)   *see* Ab Kettleby and Holwell w
Asfordby *Leic*
HOLWELL (St Mary the Virgin)   *see* Shill Valley and Broadshire
Ox
HOLWELL (St Peter), Ickleford and Pirton *St Alb 3*   P *DBP
and D&C Ely (jt)*   R J M ROBERTSON,   NSM M S HOLFORD
HOLWORTH (St Catherine by the Sea)   *see* Watercombe *Sarum*
HOLY ISLAND (St Mary the Virgin) *Newc 12*   P *Bp*
V P M COLLINS
HOLYBOURNE (Holy Rood)   *see* Alton *Win*
HOLYMOORSIDE (St Peter)   *see* Brampton St Thos *Derby*
HOLYSTONE (St Mary the Virgin)   *see* Upper Coquetdale
Newc
HOLYWELL (St Cross)   *see* Ox St Mary V w St Cross and St
Pet *Ox*
HOLYWELL (St John the Baptist)   *see* Bluntisham cum Earith
w Colne and Holywell etc *Ely*
HOLYWELL (St Mary)   *see* Seghill *Newc*
HOMERSFIELD (St Mary)   *see* S Elmham and Ilketshall *St E*
HOMERTON (Christ Church on the Mead)   *see* Hackney
Marsh *Lon*
HOMERTON (St Barnabas w St Paul)   *as above*
HOMERTON (St Luke) *Lon 5*   P *St Olave Hart Street Trustees*
V E BLATCHLEY
HOMINGTON (St Mary the Virgin)   *see* Chalke Valley *Sarum*
HONEYCHURCH (St Mary)   *see* N Tawton, Bondleigh,
Sampford Courtenay etc *Ex*

HONICKNOWLE (St Francis) *Ex 23*   P *Ld Chan*
P-in-c D R BAILEY,   C T THORP
HONILEY (St John the Baptist)   *see* Hatton w Haseley,
Rowington w Lowsonford etc *Cov*
HONING (St Peter and St Paul)   *see* Smallburgh w Dilham w
Honing and Crostwight *Nor*
HONINGHAM (St Andrew) *Nor 17*   P *DBP*   V *vacant*
HONINGTON (All Saints)   *see* Shipston-on-Stour w
Honington and Idlicote *Cov*
HONINGTON (All Saints)   *see* Blackbourne *St E*
HONINGTON (St Wilfred)   *see* Barkston and Hough Gp *Linc*
HONITON (St Michael) (St Paul), Gittisham, Combe Raleigh,
Monkton, Awliscombe and Buckerell *Ex 5*   P *DBP*
TR S E ROBERTS,   Hon C R C H SAUNDERS
HONLEY (St Mary) *Wakef 1*   P *R Almondbury*
V D K BARNES
HONOR OAK PARK (St Augustine)   *see* Sydenham H Trin and
St Aug *S'wark*
HOO (All Hallows)   *see* High Halstow w All Hallows and Hoo
St Mary *Roch*
HOO (St Andrew and St Eustachius)   *see* Mid Loes *St E*
HOO (St Werburgh) *Roch 6*   P *D&C*   V *vacant* (01634) 250291
HOOBROOK (St Cecilia)   *see* Kidderminster St Geo *Worc*
HOOE (St John the Evangelist)   *see* Plymstock and Hooe *Ex*
HOOE (St Oswald) *Chich 14*   P *Bp*   V S R EARL
HOOK (St John the Evangelist)   *see* Whitewater *Win*
HOOK (St Mary the Virgin)   *see* Airmyn, Hook and Rawcliffe
Sheff
HOOK (St Mary) w Warsash *Portsm 2*   P *Bp*   V A P NORRIS,
NSM P J MILLS
HOOK (St Paul) *S'wark 15*   P *The Crown*
V C P HOLLINGSHURST,   NSM P J KELLEY,
OLM D E HEATHER
HOOK COMMON (Good Shepherd)   *see* Upton-on-Severn,
Ripple, Earls Croome etc *Worc*
HOOK NORTON (St Peter) w Great Rollright, Swerford and
Wigginton *Ox 3*   P *Bp, DBP, BNC Ox, and Jes Coll Ox (jt)*
R J ACREMAN,   NSM C G TURNER, W CUNNINGHAM
HOOKE (St Giles)   *see* Beaminster Area *Sarum*
HOOLE (All Saints) *Ches 2*   P *Simeon's Trustees*
V R J KIRKLAND,   NSM R ACKROYD
HOOLE (St Michael) *Blackb 5*   P *Reps of Mrs E A Dunne and
Mrs D Downes (jt)*   P-in-c D A BAINES
HOOLEY (Mission Hall)   *see* Redhill St Jo *S'wark*
HOOTON (St Paul) *Ches 9*   P *Trustees*   V K HOWARD
HOOTON PAGNELL (All Saints)   *see* Bilham *Sheff*
HOOTON ROBERTS (St John)   *see* Ravenfield, Hooton
Roberts and Braithwell *Sheff*
HOPE (Holy Trinity) w Shelve *Heref 12*   P *New Coll Ox
(3 turns), J J C Coldwell Esq (1 turn)*   P-in-c A N TOOP,
NSM M-L TOOP
HOPE (St James)   *see* Eccles *Man*
HOPE (St Peter), Castleton and Bradwell *Derby 2*   P *Bp and
D&C Lich (jt)*   P-in-c I A DAVIS
HOPE BAGOT (St John the Baptist)   *see* Tenbury *Heref*
HOPE BOWDLER (St Andrew) w Eaton-under-Heywood
Heref 10   P *DBP, Bp Birm, and Mrs R Bell (jt)*
P-in-c J GROVES,   NSM J M BELLAMY
HOPE COVE (St Clements)   *see* Salcombe and Malborough w S
Huish *Ex*
HOPE MANSEL (St Michael)   *see* Ariconium *Heref*
HOPE-UNDER-DINMORE (St Mary the Virgin)
see Leominster *Heref*
HOPESAY (St Mary the Virgin)   *see* Hopesay *Heref*
HOPESAY (St Mary the Virgin) *Heref 9*   P *Earl of Powis
(3 turns), Mrs R E Bell (1 turn)*   R *vacant* (01588) 680609
HOPTON (All Saints)   *see* Stanton, Hopton, Market Weston,
Barningham etc *St E*
HOPTON (St Peter)   *see* Mid Trent *Lich*
HOPTON w Corton *Nor 9*   P *Ld Chan and D&C (alt)*
V R A KEY,   Hon C N O TUFFNELL
HOPTON, UPPER (St John the Evangelist)   *see* Mirfield *Wakef*
HOPTON CASTLE (St Edward)   *see* Clungunford w Clunbury
and Clunton, Bedstone etc *Heref*
HOPTON WAFERS (St Michael and All Angels)   *see* Cleobury
Mortimer w Hopton Wafers etc *Heref*
HOPWAS (St Chad)   *see* Tamworth *Lich*
HOPWOOD (St John)   *see* Heywood St Jo and St Luke *Man*
HORAM (Christ Church) (St James) *Chich 15*   P *Bp*
V P-J GUY
HORBLING (St Andrew)   *see* Billingborough Gp *Linc*
HORBURY (St Peter and St Leonard) w Horbury Bridge
(St John) *Wakef 11*   P *Dean*   V B T B BELL,
C I D MCCORMACK
HORBURY JUNCTION (St Mary) *Wakef 11*   P *DBP*
P-in-c K R M CAMPBELL,   NSM D M WALKER

HORDEN (St Mary) *Dur 2* **P** *Bp* **V** K SMITH, **NSM** D S CARR

HORDLE (All Saints) *Win 11* **P** *Bp* **V** P J TAYLOR, **NSM** B J KENT

HORDLEY (St Mary the Virgin) *see* Baschurch and Weston Lullingfield w Hordley *Lich*

HORFIELD (Holy Trinity) *Bris 3* **P** *Bp* **P-in-c** J S F HADLEY, **C** L J WIGMORE, **NSM** H M BLANCHARDE, **OLM** P L HINE

HORFIELD (St Gregory) *Bris 3* **P** *Bp* **P-in-c** J WILSON

HORHAM (St Mary) *see* Stradbroke, Horham, Athelington and Redlingfield *St E*

HORKESLEY, GREAT (All Saints) *see* W Bergholt and Gt Horkesley *Chelmsf*

HORKESLEY, GREAT (St John) *as above*

HORKESLEY, LITTLE (St Peter and St Paul) *see* Wormingford, Mt Bures and Lt Horkesley *Chelmsf*

HORKSTOW (St Maurice) *Linc 6* **P** *DBP* **V** D P ROWETT

HORLEY (St Bartholomew) (St Francis) (St Wilfrid) *S'wark 26* **P** *Patr Bd* **TR** S P DAVIE, **C** D J L MCHARDIE, **NSM** K F CAPPER

HORLEY (St Etheldreda) *see* Ironstone *Ox*

HORLEY ROW (St Wilfrid) *see* Horley *S'wark*

HORMEAD (St Nicholas), Wyddial, Anstey, Brent Pelham and Meesden *St Alb 16* **P** *St Jo Coll Cam, Ch Coll Cam, and Bp (by turn)* **P-in-c** C KIMBERLEY

HORN HILL (St Paul) *see* Chalfont St Peter *Ox*

HORN PARK (St Francis) *see* Eltham St Jo *S'wark*

HORNBLOTTON (St Peter) *see* Six Pilgrims *B & W*

HORNBY (St Margaret) w Claughton and Whittington w Arkholme and Gressingham *Blackb 14* **P** *Patr Bd* **V** vacant (015242) 21238

HORNBY (St Mary) *Ripon 4* **P** *D&C York* **P-in-c** B S DIXON, **NSM** J T OLDFIELD

HORNCASTLE Group, The (St Mary the Virgin) *Linc 11* **P** *Bp, Baroness Willoughby de Eresby and D&C (jt)* **R** A C BUXTON, **C** J J G WRIGHT, **NSM** J F PARKIN, A C FORD

HORNCHURCH Elm Park (St Nicholas) *see* Elm Park St Nic Hornchurch *Chelmsf*

HORNCHURCH (Holy Cross) *Chelmsf 2* **P** *Bp and New Coll Ox (alt)* **P-in-c** J D PEARSON

HORNCHURCH (St Andrew) (St George) (St Matthew and St John) *Chelmsf 2* **P** *New Coll Ox* **V** B R HOBSON, **C** J W SUTTON, C A HENRY

HORNCHURCH, SOUTH (St John and St Matthew) *Chelmsf 2* **P** *MMCET* **V** A F BURFORD, **C** K S TURNER

HORNDALE (St Francis) *see* Gt Aycliffe *Dur*

HORNDON EAST (St Francis) and West Horndon w Little Warley and Childerditch *Chelmsf 7* **P** *Sir Antony Browne's Sch and Bp (by turn)* **P-in-c** S C WILLIAMS, **NSM** R WILLIAMS

HORNDON ON THE HILL (St Peter and St Paul) *see* Orsett and Bulphan and Horndon on the Hill *Chelmsf*

HORNE (St Mary) *see* Burstow w Horne *S'wark*

HORNING (St Benedict) *see* Ashmanhaugh, Barton Turf etc *Nor*

HORNINGHOLD (St Peter) *see* Hallaton and Allexton, w Horninghold, Tugby etc *Leic*

HORNINGLOW (St John the Divine) *Lich 14* **P** *Trustees* **V** M R FREEMAN, **C** G T READING

HORNINGSEA (St Peter) *Ely 4* **P** *St Jo Coll Cam* **P-in-c** M C BOWERS

HORNINGSHAM (St John the Baptist) *see* Cley Hill Villages *Sarum*

HORNINGTOFT (St Edmund) *see* Upper Wensum Village Gp *Nor*

HORNSEA (St Nicholas) w Atwick *York 11* **P** *Ld Chan* **V** P LAMB

HORNSEY (Christ Church) *Lon 20* **P** *Bp* **V** D O AGBELUSI

HORNSEY (Holy Innocents) *Lon 20* **P** *Bp* **V** T D PIKE, **C** P J HENDERSON, **NSM** P G ATHERTON

HORNSEY (St Mary) (St George) *Lon 20* **P** *Bp* **R** vacant (020) 8883 6846

HORNSEY RISE (St Mary) *see* Upper Holloway *Lon*

HORNTON (St John the Baptist) *see* Ironstone *Ox*

HORRABRIDGE (St John the Baptist) *see* Sampford Spiney w Horrabridge *Ex*

HORRINGER (St Leonard) *St E 13* **P** *Bp and DBP (jt)* **R** R J GRIFFITHS

HORSEHEATH (All Saints) *see* Linton *Ely*

HORSELL (St Mary the Virgin) *Guildf 12* **P** *Bp* **V** R JONES, **C** A L BROWN

HORSENDON (St Michael and All Angels) *see* Risborough *Ox*

HORSEY (All Saints) *see* Flegg Coastal Benefice *Nor*

HORSFORD (All Saints), Felthorpe and Hevingham *Nor 2* **P** *Sir Thomas Agnew Beevor Bt and Bp (jt)* **R** M S WHITAKER

HORSFORTH (St Margaret) *see* Abbeylands *Ripon*

HORSHAM (Holy Trinity) (St Leonard) (St Mary the Virgin) (St Mark) *Chich 8* **P** *Patr Bd* **TR** G S BRIDGEWATER, **TV** W E L SOUTER, H J HUGHES, D W BOUSKILL, R S COLDICOTT, **C** P A FRANCIS, **NSM** J ELVIDGE, N LOVELESS, B SINTON

HORSHAM ST FAITH (St Andrew and St Mary), Spixworth and Crostwick *Nor 2* **P** *Bp and DBP (jt)* **R** A M BEANE

HORSINGTON (All Saints) *see* Woodhall Spa Gp *Linc*

HORSINGTON (St John the Baptist) *see* Abbas and Templecombe, Henstridge and Horsington *B & W*

HORSLEY (Holy Trinity) *see* N Tyne and Redesdale *Newc*

HORSLEY (St Clement) and Denby *Derby 12* **P** *Bp and Mrs L B Palmer (jt)* **P-in-c** T J WILLIAMS, **NSM** C C HOLDEN

HORSLEY (St Martin) *see* Nailsworth w Shortwood, Horsley etc *Glouc*

HORSLEY, EAST (St Martin) and Ockham w Hatchford and Downside *Guildf 10* **P** *D&C Cant and Bp (jt)* **R** M E BUSSMANN, **Hon C** K TUCKER, **NSM** S C CONWAY, **OLM** E A BURKE

HORSLEY, WEST (St Mary) *Guildf 10* **P** *Col A R N Weston* **R** J R PORTER

HORSLEY HILL (St Lawrence the Martyr) South Shields *Dur 15* **P** *D&C* **V** vacant 0191-456 1747

HORSLEY WOODHOUSE (St Susanna) *see* Morley w Smalley and Horsley Woodhouse *Derby*

HORSMONDEN (St Margaret) *Roch 8* **P** *Bp* **P-in-c** P MEIER

HORSPATH (St Giles) *see* Wheatley *Ox*

HORSTEAD (All Saints) *see* Coltishall w Gt Hautbois, Frettenham etc *Nor*

HORSTED, LITTLE (St Michael and All Angels) *Chich 21* **P** *Rt Revd P J Ball* **R** B H WILCOX, **NSM** C HOWARTH

HORSTED KEYNES (St Giles) *Chich 6* **P** *Bp* **R** J F TWISLETON

HORSTED PARVA (St Michael and All Angels) *see* Lt Horsted *Chich*

HORTON (St James the Elder) *see* Sodbury Vale *Glouc*

HORTON (St Mary Magdalene) *see* Hardingstone and Horton and Piddington *Pet*

HORTON (St Mary the Virgin) *Newc 1* **P** *V Woodhorn w Newbiggin* **P-in-c** D W CARBERRY, **NSM** J R SWINHOE

HORTON (St Michael and All Angels) and Wraysbury *Ox 23* **P** *Major J M Halford and D&C Windsor (jt)* **V** C S P DOUGLAS LANE, **NSM** A M PARRY

HORTON (St Michael), Lonsdon and Rushton Spencer *Lich 8* **P** *Bp and R Leek and Meerbrook (jt)* **V** E J TOMLINSON, **OLM** J A R LOVATT

HORTON (St Peter) *see* Isle Valley *B & W*

HORTON (St Wolfrida), Chalbury, Hinton Martel and Holt St James *Sarum 9* **P** *DBP and Governors of Wimborne Minster (jt)* **P-in-c** A A GEE, **NSM** L MORRIS

HORTON, GREAT (St John the Evangelist) *Bradf 2* **P** *V Bradf* **P-in-c** I S SLATER

HORTON, LITTLE (All Saints) (St Oswald) *Bradf 2* **P** *Bp and J F Bardsley Esq (jt)* **V** A S TREASURE, **C** J W HINTON, J NICHOLAS, **NSM** M M MALEK

HORTON-CUM-STUDLEY (St Barnabas) *see* Wheatley *Ox*

HORTON-IN-RIBBLESDALE (St Oswald) *see* Langcliffe w Stainforth and Horton *Bradf*

HORTON KIRBY (St Mary) and Sutton-at-Hone *Roch 2* **P** *Bp and D&C (jt)* **V** F C PAPANTONIOU

HORWICH (Holy Trinity) (St Catherine) (St Elizabeth) and Rivington *Man 9* **P** *Patr Bd* **TR** S FLETCHER, **TV** M C BEHREND, P DEVER, **C** M J DAY, R C COOPER, **OLM** T LITHERLAND, P D HARLEY, C MCCABE

HORWOOD (St Michael) *see* Newton Tracey, Horwood, Alverdiscott etc *Ex*

HORWOOD, GREAT (St James) *see* Winslow w Gt Horwood and Addington *Ox*

HORWOOD, LITTLE (St Nicholas) *see* Newton Longville, Mursley, Swanbourne etc *Ox*

HOSE (St Michael) *see* Vale of Belvoir *Leic*

HOTHAM (St Oswald) *York 13* **P** *Ld Chan* **P-in-c** P G FAULKNER, **NSM** S J HUMPHRIES

HOTHFIELD (St Margaret) *see* G7 Benefice *Cant*

HOUGH GREEN (St Basil and All Saints) *Liv 13* **P** *Bp* **V** P W DAWKIN

HOUGH-ON-THE-HILL (All Saints) *see* Barkston and Hough Gp *Linc*

HOUGHAM (All Saints) *as above*

HOUGHAM (St Laurence) *see* Alkham w Capel le Ferne and Hougham *Cant*

HOUGHTON (All Saints) *see* Broughton, Bossington, Houghton and Mottisfont *Win*

HOUGHTON (St Giles) *see* Walsingham, Houghton and Barsham *Nor*

HOUGHTON (St John the Evangelist) (St Peter) *Carl 3*
P *Trustees* V S N AUSTEN, C T A BODDAM-WHETHAM
HOUGHTON (St Martin) *see* E w W Rudham, Helhoughton etc *Nor*
HOUGHTON (St Mary) w Wyton *Ely 10* P *Bp*
P-in-c E B ATLING, C B A STEWART
HOUGHTON (St Nicholas) *see* Bury w Houghton and Coldwaltham and Hardham *Chich*
HOUGHTON, GREAT (St Mary) *see* Cogenhoe and Gt and Lt Houghton w Brafield *Pet*
HOUGHTON, GREAT (St Michael and All Angels) Conventional District *Sheff 12 vacant*
HOUGHTON, LITTLE (St Mary the Blessed Virgin) *see* Cogenhoe and Gt and Lt Houghton w Brafield *Pet*
HOUGHTON, NEW (Christ Church) *see* E Scarsdale *Derby*
HOUGHTON CONQUEST (All Saints) *see* Wilshamstead and Houghton Conquest *St Alb*
HOUGHTON LE SPRING (St Michael and All Angels) *Dur 14*
P *Bp* R S J PINNINGTON, C D G HUNTLEY, NSM M LEE
HOUGHTON-ON-THE-HILL (St Catharine) Keyham and Hungarton *Leic 4* P *Bp* R *vacant* 0116-241 5828
HOUGHTON REGIS (All Saints) (St Thomas) *St Alb 11*
P *DBP* V B C D WHEELHOUSE
HOUND (St Edward the Confessor) (St Mary the Virgin) *Win 10*
P *St Mary's Coll Win* P-in-c P A VARGESON,
C S F WARDELL
HOUNSLOW (Holy Trinity) (St Paul) *Lon 11* P *Bp*
V M F HERBERT, NSM N LAWRENCE
HOUNSLOW (St Stephen) *Lon 11* P *Bp* V R L RAMSDEN
HOUNSLOW WEST (Good Shepherd) *Lon 11* P *Bp*
V K A BUCKLER
HOVE (All Saints) *Chich 4* P *Bp* V P S J RITCHIE,
C T I MACLEOD, NSM D S G WEAVER
HOVE (Bishop Hannington Memorial Church) (Holy Cross)
Chich 4 P *Trustees* V P R MOON, C J J MILSON,
J S RADCLIFFE
HOVE (St Andrew Old Church) *Chich 4* P *Bp*
V J R SWINDELLS
HOVE (St Barnabas) and St Agnes *Chich 4* P *Bp and V Hove*
(alt) P-in-c K D RICHARDS
HOVE (St John the Baptist) *Chich 4* P *Bp* V P S J DOICK,
NSM J F GREENFIELD
HOVE St Patrick *Chich 4* P *Bp, V Hove, and V Brighton (jt)*
P-in-c S UNDERDOWN
HOVE (St Philip) *see* Aldrington *Chich*
HOVE EDGE (St Chad) *see* Lightcliffe and Hove Edge *Wakef*
HOVERINGHAM (St Michael) *see* Thurgarton w Hoveringham and Bleasby etc *S'well*
HOVETON (St John) *see* Wroxham w Hoveton and Belaugh *Nor*
HOVETON (St Peter) *as above*
HOVINGHAM (All Saints) *see* The Street Par *York*
HOW CAPLE (St Andrew and St Mary) *see* Brampton *Heref*
HOWARDIAN GROUP, The *York 6* P *Abp and Hon*
S B G Howard (jt) R M C PARKIN
HOWDEN Team Ministry, The (St Peter) *York 13* P *Abp*
(4 turns), Ld Chan (1 turn) TR J H LITTLE,
TV G P THORNALLEY
HOWDEN-LE-WEAR St Mary the Virgin and Hunwick *Dur 9*
P *Bp and V Auckland St Andr (alt)* V S IRWIN,
NSM S L NICHOLSON
HOWE (St Mary the Virgin) *see* Poringland *Nor*
HOWE BRIDGE (St Michael and All Angels) *see* Atherton and Hindsford w Howe Bridge *Man*
HOWELL (St Oswald) *see* Heckington Gp *Linc*
HOWELL HILL (St Paul) w Burgh Heath *Guildf 9* P *Bp*
V M J WAINWRIGHT, C I P HUGHES, NSM B W RICHARDS
HOWGILL (Holy Trinity) *see* Firbank, Howgill and Killington *Bradf*
HOWICK (St Michael and All Angels) *see* Longhoughton w Howick *Newc*
HOWSHAM (St John) *see* Sand Hutton *York*
HOXNE (St Peter and St Paul) w Denham, Syleham and Wingfield *St E 17* P *Bp and DBP (jt)* C F O NEWTON,
S A LOXTON
HOXTON (Holy Trinity) (St Mary) *Lon 5* P *Bp* V *vacant*
(020) 7253 4796
HOXTON (St Anne) (St Columba) *Lon 5* P *The Crown*
P-in-c I C CZERNIAWSKA EDGCUMBE
HOXTON (St John the Baptist) w Ch Ch *Lon 5*
P *Haberdashers' Co and Adn (jt)* V G HUNTER
HOYLAKE (Holy Trinity and St Hildeburgh) *Ches 8* P *Bp*
V M J FLOWERDEW, NSM J C HARRISON
HOYLAND (St Peter) (St Andrew) *Sheff 11* P *Bp and Sir Philip Naylor-Leyland Bt (jt)* V R B PARKER

HOYLAND, HIGH (All Saints), Scissett and Clayton West
Wakef 6 P *Bp* P-in-c J E COUSANS
HOYLANDSWAINE (St John the Evangelist) and Silkstone w Stainborough *Wakef 7* P *Bp* NSM M E REED
HUBBERHOLME (St Michael and All Angels) *see* Kettlewell w Conistone, Hubberholme etc *Bradf*
HUCCABY (St Raphael) *see* Ashburton, Bickington, Buckland in the Moor etc *Ex*
HUCCLECOTE (St Philip and St James) *Glouc 2* P *Bp*
P-in-c A J AXON, C J E ROSS-MCNAIRN
HUCKING (St Margaret) *see* Hollingbourne and Hucking w Leeds and Broomfield *Cant*
HUCKLOW, GREAT (Mission Room) *see* Hope, Castleton and Bradwell *Derby*
HUCKNALL TORKARD (St Mary Magdalene) (St Peter and St Paul) (St John's Mission Church) *S'well 4* P *Bp*
TR K HERROD, C S DIDUK, NSM P H JONES
HUDDERSFIELD All Saints (St Thomas) *Wakef 5* P *DBP*
P-in-c L A PINFIELD
HUDDERSFIELD (Holy Trinity) *Wakef 5* P *Simeon's Trustees*
V C C PRENTIS, NSM R C SWINDELL
HUDDERSFIELD (St Francis) Fixby *see* Fixby and Cowcliffe *Wakef*
HUDDERSFIELD (St Hilda) Cowcliffe *as above*
HUDDERSFIELD (St John the Evangelist) *see* Birkby and Woodhouse *Wakef*
HUDDERSFIELD (St Peter) *Wakef 5* P *DBP* V S A MOOR
HUDDERSFIELD, NORTH (St Cuthbert) *see* Birkby and Birchencliffe *Wakef*
HUDDINGTON (St James) *see* Bowbrook S *Worc*
HUDSWELL (St Michael and All Angels) *see* Richmond w Hudswell and Downholme and Marske *Ripon*
HUGGATE (St Mary) *see* Pocklington Wold *York*
HUGGLESCOTE (St John the Baptist) w Donington, Ellistown and Snibston *Leic 8* P *Bp* TR O S WOOLCOCK,
NSM R M PASSEY
HUGHENDEN (St Michael) *Ox 29* P *DBP* V S N CRONK,
NSM H E PETERS
HUGHLEY (St John the Baptist) *see* Wenlock *Heref*
HUISH (St James the Less) *see* Shebbear, Buckland Filleigh, Sheepwash etc *Ex*
HUISH (St Nicholas) *see* Vale of Pewsey *Sarum*
HUISH, SOUTH (Holy Trinity) *see* Salcombe and Malborough w S Huish *Ex*
HUISH CHAMPFLOWER (St Peter) *see* Wiveliscombe and the Hills *B & W*
HUISH EPISCOPI (Blessed Virgin Mary) *see* Langport Area *B & W*
HULCOTE (St Nicholas) *see* Cranfield and Hulcote w Salford *St Alb*
HULCOTT (All Saints) *see* Aylesbury w Bierton and Hulcott *Ox*
HULL (Ascension) *see* Derringham Bank *York*
HULL (Holy Apostles) *see* Kingston upon Hull H Trin *York*
HULL (Most Holy and Undivided Trinity) *as above*
HULL (St Aidan) Southcoates *see* Kingston upon Hull St Aid Southcoates *York*
HULL (St Alban) *see* Kingston upon Hull St Alb *York*
HULL (St Cuthbert) *York 14* P *Abp* V J C COWAN
HULL (St George) *see* Marfleet *York*
HULL (St Giles) *as above*
HULL (St Hilda) *as above*
HULL (St John) Newland *York 14* P *Abp* V M TINKER,
C L J MCMUNN
HULL (St John the Baptist) *see* Newington w Dairycoates *York*
HULL (St Martin) w The Transfiguration *York 14* P *Abp*
V S R J ELLIOTT
HULL (St Mary) Sculcoates *York 14* P *V Sculcoates*
P-in-c J G LEEMAN
HULL (St Mary the Virgin) Lowgate *see* Kingston upon Hull St Mary *York*
HULL (St Matthew w St Barnabas) *see* Kingston upon Hull St Matt w St Barn *York*
HULL (St Nicholas) *see* Kingston upon Hull St Nic *York*
HULL (St Paul) *see* Sculcoates *York*
HULL (St Philip) *see* Marfleet *York*
HULL (St Stephen) *see* Sculcoates *York*
HULL (St Thomas) *see* Derringham Bank *York*
HULL, NORTH (St Michael and All Angels) *York 14* P *Abp*
V D A WALKER, NSM A RICHARDS
HULLAND (Christ Church), Atlow, Kniveton, Bradley and Hognaston *Derby 8* P *Patr Bd* R C A MITCHELL
HULLAVINGTON (St Mary Magdalene), Norton and Stanton St Quintin *Bris 6* P *Bp, Eton Coll, and R W Neeld Esq (jt)*
P-in-c C P BRYAN, Hon C M M MASLEN, NSM S R EVANS

HULLBRIDGE (St Thomas of Canterbury) *see* Rettendon and Hullbridge *Chelmsf*

HULME (Ascension) *Man 3* P *Trustees* R A J SERVANT, NSM H E EVANS

HULME WALFIELD (St Michael) *see* Marton, Siddington w Capesthorne, and Eaton etc *Ches*

HULTON, LITTLE (St John the Baptist) *see* Walkden and Lt Hulton *Man*

HULTON, OVER (St Andrew) *see* Deane *Man*

HUMBER (St Mary the Virgin) *see* Leominster *Heref*

HUMBERSTON (St Peter) *Linc 10* P *Bp* V B V EAST, OLM P R SALMON

HUMBERSTONE (St Mary) *see* Ascension TM *Leic*

HUMBERSTONE, NEW (St Barnabas) *see* Leic St Barn CD *Leic*

HUMBLE, WEST (St Michael) *see* Leatherhead and Mickleham *Guildf*

HUMBLETON (St Peter) *see* Burton Pidsea and Humbleton w Elsternwick *York*

HUMPHREY PARK (St Clement) *see* Urmston *Man*

HUMSHAUGH (St Peter) w Simonburn and Wark *Newc 8* P *Bp* R J M THOMPSON

HUNCOAT (St Augustine) *see* Accrington St Jo w Huncoat *Blackb*

HUNCOTE (St James the Greater) *see* Narborough and Huncote *Leic*

HUNDLEBY (St Mary) *see* Spilsby Gp *Linc*

HUNDON (All Saints) *see* Stour Valley *St E*

HUNDRED RIVER Benefice, The *St E 14* P *DBP, Shadingfield Properties Ltd, Bp, Miss to Seamen, and F D L Barnes Esq (by turn)* R P J NELSON, C M E ALLWOOD, OLM J M LOFTUS

HUNGARTON (St John the Baptist) *see* Houghton-on-the-Hill, Keyham and Hungarton *Leic*

HUNGERFORD (St Lawrence) and Denford *Ox 14* P *D&C Windsor* V A W SAWYER

HUNMANBY (All Saints) w Muston *York 15* P *MMCET* V J W R HATTAN

HUNNINGHAM (St Margaret) *Cov 10* P *Ld Chan* P-in-c J T H BRITTON, C D R PATTERSON

HUNSDON (St Dunstan) (St Francis) w Widford and Wareside *St Alb 19* P *DBP* P-in-c M P DUNSTAN

HUNSINGORE (St John the Baptist) *see* Lower Nidderdale *Ripon*

HUNSLET (St Mary the Virgin) w Cross Green *Ripon 6* P *Keble Coll Ox, Bp and TR Leeds City (jt)* V A J LANE

HUNSLET MOOR (St Peter's Christian Community Centre) *see* Beeston Hill and Hunslet Moor *Ripon*

HUNSLEY (St Peter) *see* Rowley w Skidby *York*

HUNSTANTON (St Edmund) w Ringstead *Nor 16* P *H Le Strange Esq* V J S BLOOMFIELD

HUNSTANTON (St Mary) w Ringstead Parva, Holme-next-the-Sea, Thornham, Brancaster, Burnham Deepdale and Titchwell *Nor 16* P *Bp, Exors of the late H le Strange Esq, and Exors of the late H S N Simms-Adams Esq (jt)* R C D WOOD

HUNSTANWORTH (St James) *see* Blanchland w Hunstanworth and Edmundbyers etc *Newc*

HUNSTON (St Leodegar) *see* N Mundham w Hunston and Merston *Chich*

HUNSTON (St Michael) *see* Badwell and Walsham *St E*

HUNTINGDON (All Saints w St John the Baptist) (St Barnabas) (St Mary) w the Stukeleys *Ely 10* P *Ld Chan (1 turn), Patr Bd (2 turns)* TR A J MILTON, TV J M SAVAGE, NSM J J MARTIN

HUNTINGFIELD (St Mary) *see* Heveningham *St E*

HUNTINGTON (All Saints) *York 7* P *D&C* R I G BIRKINSHAW, C P G CARMAN

HUNTINGTON (St Luke) *Ches 2* P *Bp* V I J HUTCHINGS

HUNTINGTON (St Mary Magdalene) *see* Holmer w Huntington *Heref*

HUNTINGTON (St Thomas) *see* Cannock and Huntington *Lich*

HUNTINGTON (St Thomas à Becket) *see* Kington w Huntington, Old Radnor, Kinnerton etc *Heref*

HUNTLEY (St John the Baptist) and Longhope, Churcham and Bulley *Glouc 3* P *Bp and D&C (jt)* R *vacant* (01452) 831735

HUNTON (St James) *see* Upper Dever *Win*

HUNTON (St Mary) *see* Coxheath, E Farleigh, Hunton, Linton etc *Roch*

HUNTS CROSS (St Hilda) *Liv 4* P *Bp* P-in-c E J DURHAM

HUNTSHAM (All Saints) *see* Bampton, Morebath, Clayhanger, Petton etc *Ex*

HUNTSHAW (St Mary Magdalene) *see* Newton Tracey, Horwood, Alverdiscott etc *Ex*

HUNTSPILL (St Peter and All Hallows) *B & W 1* P *Ball Coll Ox* R G M WALSH

HUNWICK (St Paul) *see* Howden-le-Wear and Hunwick *Dur*

HUNWORTH (St Lawrence) *see* Brinton, Briningham, Hunworth, Stody etc *Nor*

HURDSFIELD (Holy Trinity) *Ches 13* P *Hyndman Trustees* V I M RUMSEY, C J C ALLISTER

HURLEY (Resurrection) *see* Baxterley w Hurley and Wood End and Merevale etc *Birm*

HURLEY (St Mary the Virgin) *see* Burchetts Green *Ox*

HURSLEY (All Saints) *see* Compton, Hursley, and Otterbourne *Win*

HURST *see* Fawkenhurst *Cant*

HURST (St John the Evangelist) *Man 13* P *The Crown* V A L OWENS, OLM P C CARLIN

HURST (St Nicholas) *Ox 16* P *Bp* Hon C C SMITH, NSM J H A HATTAWAY

HURST GREEN (Holy Trinity) *Chich 15* P *Bp* V *vacant*

HURST GREEN (St John the Evangelist) *S'wark 25* P *Bp* V D F G BUTLIN, NSM W M HARVEY

HURST GREEN (St John the Evangelist) and Mitton *Bradf 5* P *Bp and J E R Aspinall Esq (jt)* P-in-c G F MACK, C D W MEWIS, Hon C J R BROCKLEHURST, NSM G DEARDEN, J R GOODALL, A B JEPSON

HURSTBOURNE PRIORS (St Andrew), Longparish, St Mary Bourne and Woodcott *Win 6* P *Bp and J C Woodcock Esq (jt)* V M A COPPEN, NSM D M MARSDEN, T E HEMMING

HURSTBOURNE TARRANT (St Peter) and Faccombe and Vernham Dean and Linkenholt *Win 5* P *Bp* P-in-c D J KEIGHLEY

HURSTPIERPOINT (Holy Trinity) (St George) *Chich 9* P *Hurstpierpoint Coll* R J B A JOYCE, C W KEMP

HURSTWOOD, HIGH (Holy Trinity) *Chich 21* P *Abp* P-in-c D A TIDSWELL

HURWORTH (All Saints) *Dur 8* P *Ch Soc Trust* P-in-c A J MARTIN

HUSBANDS BOSWORTH (All Saints) *see* Hexagon *Leic*

HUSBORNE CRAWLEY (St Mary Magdalene or St James) *see* Aspley Guise w Husborne Crawley and Ridgmont *St Alb*

HUSTHWAITE (St Nicholas) *see* Coxwold and Husthwaite *York*

HUTHWAITE (All Saints) *S'well 4* P *V Sutton-in-Ashfield* P-in-c C A K MAIDEN, C A H DIGMAN

HUTTOFT (St Margaret) *see* Sutton, Huttoft and Anderby *Linc*

HUTTON (All Saints) (St Peter) *Chelmsf 7* P *D&C St Paul's* R R WALLACE, C B C WALLACE, NSM A BAXTER

HUTTON (Blessed Virgin Mary) and Locking *B & W 10* P *DBP and MMCET (jt)* C R A LEE, A L LEE, NSM J A BIRKETT

HUTTON, OLD (St John the Baptist) and New Hutton (St Stephen) *Carl 10* P *V Kendal* P-in-c A WHITTAKER, NSM D A PRESTON

HUTTON BUSCEL (St Matthew) *see* Upper Derwent *York*

HUTTON CRANSWICK (St Peter) w Skerne, Watton and Beswick *York 10* P *Abp* NSM B J LEES, H J BOON

HUTTON HENRY (St Francis) *see* Wheatley Hill and Wingate w Hutton Henry *Dur*

HUTTON-IN-THE-FOREST (St James) *see* Inglewood Gp *Carl*

HUTTON-LE-HOLE (St Chad) *see* Lastingham w Appleton-le-Moors, Rosedale etc *York*

HUTTON MAGNA (St Mary) *see* Barningham w Hutton Magna and Wycliffe *Ripon*

HUTTON ROOF (St John the Divine) *see* Kirkby Lonsdale *Carl*

HUTTON RUDBY (All Saints) *see* Rudby in Cleveland w Middleton *York*

HUTTONS AMBO (St Margaret) *see* Howardian Gp *York*

HUXHAM (St Mary the Virgin) *see* Brampford Speke, Cadbury, Newton St Cyres etc *Ex*

HUXLEY (St Andrew) *see* Hargrave *Ches*

HUYTON (St George) *Liv 2* P *Bp* V C DORAN

HUYTON (St Michael) *Liv 2* P *Earl of Derby* V J A STANLEY

HUYTON QUARRY (St Gabriel) *Liv 2* P *V Huyton St Mich* V M K ROGERS

HYDE (Holy Ascension) *see* Ellingham and Harbridge and Hyde w Ibsley *Win*

HYDE (Holy Trinity) Gee Cross *see* Gee Cross *Ches*

HYDE (St George) *Ches 14* P *R Stockport St Mary* V J C PARKER

HYDE (St John the Baptist) Godley cum Newton Green *see* Godley cum Newton Green *Ches*

HYDE (St Mary) Newton in Mottram *see* Newton in Mottram w Flowery Field *Ches*

HYDE (St Thomas) *Ches 14* **P** *Bp* **P-in-c** P J HIBBERT

HYDE, WEST (St Thomas of Canterbury) *see* Mill End and Heronsgate w W Hyde *St Alb*

HYDE HEATH (Mission Church) *see* Lt Missenden *Ox*

HYDE PARK CRESCENT (St John) *see* Paddington St Jo w St Mich *Lon*

HYDNEYE (St Peter) *see* Hampden Park and The Hydnye *Chich*

HYKEHAM (All Saints) (St Hugh) (St Michael and All Angels) *Linc 18* **P** *Ld Chan and Bp (alt)* **TR** R S EYRE, **C** A J CHAPMAN, **NSM** G F REID

HYLTON, SOUTH (St Mary) *Dur 16* **P** *Bp* **V** *vacant* 0191-534 2325

HYSON GREEN (St Stephen) and Forest Fields *S'well 12* **P** *CPAS* **P-in-c** C R BURROWS

HYSSINGTON (St Etheldreda) *see* Churchstoke w Hyssington and Sarn *Heref*

HYTHE Butts Ash (St Anne) *see* Hythe *Win*

HYTHE (St John the Baptist) *Win 11* **P** *Bp* **V** E J WETHERELL

HYTHE (St Leonard) (St Michael and All Angels) *Cant 8* **P** R Saltwood **V** A M WINDROSS, **C** C N DATCHLER

HYTHE, WEST (St Mary) *see* Aldington w Bonnington and Bilsington etc *Cant*

IBBERTON (St Eustace) *see* Hazelbury Bryan and the Hillside Par *Sarum*

IBSTOCK (St Denys) w Heather *Leic 8* **P** *Bp and MMCET (jt)* **R** *vacant* (01530) 260246

IBSTONE (St Nicholas) *see* Stokenchurch and Ibstone *Ox*

ICKBURGH (St Peter) w Langford *Nor 13* **P** *Bp* **R** *vacant*

ICKENHAM (St Giles) *Lon 24* **P** *Eton Coll* **R** A M GUTHRIE, **NSM** K R TOMBS

ICKFORD (St Nicholas) *see* Worminghall w Ickford, Oakley and Shabbington *Ox*

ICKHAM (St John the Evangelist) *see* Littlebourne and Ickham w Wickhambreaux etc *Cant*

ICKLEFORD (St Katherine) *see* Holwell, Ickleford and Pirton *St Alb*

ICKLESHAM (St Nicolas) *see* Winchelsea and Icklesham *Chich*

ICKLETON (St Mary Magdalene) *Ely 5* **P** *Ld Chan* **P-in-c** J H MARTIN

ICKLINGHAM (All Saints w St James) *see* Mildenhall *St E*

ICKNIELD *Ox 1* **P** *Ld Chan (1 turn), Ch Ch Ox (1 turn), Bp and Earl of Macclesfield (1 turn)* **R** C I EVANS, **NSM** A M PATERSON, **OLM** A J B CLAYTON

ICKNIELD WAY VILLAGES *Chelmsf 21* **P** *Patr Bd* **R** A COLEBROOKE, **C** J D LOWE

ICOMB (St Mary) *see* Broadwell, Evenlode, Oddington, Adlestrop etc *Glouc*

IDBURY (St Nicholas) *see* Shipton-under-Wychwood w Milton, Fifield etc *Ox*

IDDESLEIGH (St James) w Dowland *Ex 20* **P** *Bp* **P-in-c** C A BRODRIBB

IDE (St Ida) *see* Alphington, Shillingford St George and Ide *Ex*

IDE HILL (St Mary the Virgin) *see* Sundridge w Ide Hill and Toys Hill *Roch*

IDEFORD (St Mary the Virgin) *see* Teignmouth, Ideford w Luton, Ashcombe etc *Ex*

IDEN (All Saints) *see* Rye *Chich*

IDLE (Holy Trinity) *Bradf 3* **P** *V Calverley* **P-in-c** R P GAMBLE, **C** J SMITH

IDLICOTE (St James the Great) *see* Shipston-on-Stour w Honington and Idlicote *Cov*

IDRIDGEHAY (St James) *see* Wirksworth *Derby*

IDSWORTH (St Hubert) *see* Blendworth w Chalton w Idsworth *Portsm*

IFFLEY (St Mary the Virgin) *Ox 4* **P** *Ch Ch Ox* **V** A R MCKEARNEY

IFIELD (St Margaret) *Chich 7* **P** *Bp* **TR** S F E NEWHAM, **TV** D G STANIFORD, **C** D A WILLIS, **NSM** D M GOODWIN, M P HANSON

IFIELD (St Margaret) *see* Gravesend H Family w Ifield *Roch*

IFORD (St Nicholas) w Kingston and Rodmell *Chich 18* **P** *Bp* **V** G M DAW, **NSM** M C BROWN

IFORD (St Saviour) *see* Holdenhurst and Iford *Win*

IGHTFIELD (St John the Baptist) *see* Adderley, Ash, Calverhall, Ightfield etc *Lich*

IGHTHAM (St Peter) *Roch 10* **P** *C B Winnifrith Esq* **R** S R JONES

IKEN (St Botolph) *see* Wilford Peninsula *St E*

ILAM (Holy Cross) *see* Alstonfield, Butterton, Ilam etc *Lich*

ILCHESTER (St Mary Major) w Northover, Limington, Yeovilton and Podimore *B & W 5* **P** *Bp Lon (7 turns), Bp (1 turn), and Wadh Coll Ox (1 turn)* **R** *vacant* (01935) 840296

ILDERTON (St Michael) *see* Glendale Gp *Newc*

ILFORD, GREAT (St Alban) *Chelmsf 4* **P** *Bp* **V** S HALSTEAD

ILFORD, GREAT (St Andrew) *Chelmsf 4* **P** *Bp* **P-in-c** M SEGAL

ILFORD, GREAT (St John the Evangelist) *Chelmsf 4* **P** *Bp* **V** J A H EVENS, **C** G E EZE

ILFORD, GREAT (St Luke) *Chelmsf 4* **P** *Bp* **P-in-c** J BROWN, **Hon C** A W M RITCHIE, **NSM** B D DEUCHAR DE MELLO

ILFORD, GREAT (St Margaret of Antioch) (St Clement) *Chelmsf 4* **P** *Patr Bd* **V** S G PUGH

ILFORD, GREAT (St Mary) *Chelmsf 4* **P** *V Gt Ilford* **P-in-c** G E J P JONES

ILFORD, LITTLE (St Barnabas) *Chelmsf 3* **P** *Bp* **V** J A RAMSAY

ILFORD, LITTLE (St Michael and All Angels) *Chelmsf 3* **P** *Hertf Coll Ox* **R** B J LEWIS, **C** N-A WALSH

ILFRACOMBE (Holy Trinity) (St Peter), Lee, Woolacombe, Bittadon and Mortehoe *Ex 15* **P** *Patr Bd* **TV** G A B KING-SMITH, **P-in-c** R D HARRIS, **C** I SNARES, **NSM** L WALTERS

ILFRACOMBE (St Philip and St James) w West Down *Ex 15* **P** *Bp and Ch Trust Fund Trust (jt)* **P-in-c** M H W ROGERS, **C** I SNARES

ILKESTON (Holy Trinity) *Derby 13* **P** *Bp* **C** W P WATERS

ILKESTON (St John the Evangelist) *Derby 13* **P** *V Ilkeston St Mary* **NSM** C J GRAHAM

ILKESTON (St Mary the Virgin) *Derby 13* **P** *Bp* **V** M D PETITT

ILKETSHALL ST ANDREW (St Andrew) *see* Wainford *St E*

ILKETSHALL ST JOHN (St John the Baptist) *see* S Elmham and Ilketshall *St E*

ILKETSHALL ST LAWRENCE (St Lawrence) *as above*

ILKETSHALL ST MARGARET (St Margaret) *as above*

ILKLEY (All Saints) *Bradf 4* **P** *Hyndman Trustees* **P-in-c** L S TOWNEND, **C** R F PARKINSON, **NSM** R F WATSON, M P REID

ILKLEY (St Margaret) *Bradf 4* **P** *CR* **P-in-c** P C GRAY, **NSM** A G BROWN, R G KELLETT

ILLOGAN (St Illogan) *see* St Illogan *Truro*

ILLSTON (St Michael and All Angels) *see* Gaulby *Leic*

ILMER (St Peter) *see* Risborough *Ox*

ILMINGTON (St Mary) and Stretton-on-Fosse and Ditchford w Preston-on-Stour w Whitchurch and Atherstone-on-Stour *Cov 9* **P** *Bp, MMCET, and Ms C A Alston-Roberts-West (jt)* **P-in-c** C GOBLE, **Hon C** G W KUHRT

ILMINSTER (Blessed Virgin Mary) and Whitelackington *B & W 14* **P** *Bp* **V** A R WALLACE

ILSINGTON (St Michael) *Ex 9* **P** *D&C Windsor* **V** *vacant* (01364) 661193

ILSLEY, EAST (St Mary) *see* Hermitage *Ox*

ILSLEY, WEST (All Saints) *see* E Downland *Ox*

ILTON (St Peter) *see* Isle Valley *B & W*

IMMINGHAM (St Andrew) *Linc 10* **P** *DBP* **P-in-c** M W PAGE-CHESTNEY, **NSM** S V PAGE-CHESTNEY

IMPINGTON (St Andrew) *Ely 6* **P** *Adn Ely* **P-in-c** N J BLANDFORD-BAKER, **C** P H BUTLER, **NSM** J M GLOVER

INCE (St James) *see* Thornton-le-Moors w Ince and Elton *Ches*

INCE IN MAKERFIELD (Christ Church) w Wigan St Catharine *Liv 14* **P** *Bp, R Wigan and Simeon's Trustees (jt)* **V** S NICHOLSON

INCE IN MAKERFIELD (St Mary) *Liv 14* **P** *Simeon's Trustees* **V** D W LONG

INDIAN QUEEN (St Francis) *see* St Enoder *Truro*

INGATESTONE (St Edmund and St Mary) w Fryerning *Chelmsf 7* **P** *Bp and Wadh Coll Ox (jt)* **V** P SHERRING, **NSM** J W SALT

INGESTRE (St Mary the Virgin) *see* Stafford St Jo and Tixall w Ingestre *Lich*

INGHAM (All Saints) *see* Spring Line Gp *Linc*

INGHAM (Holy Trinity) *see* Stalham, E Ruston, Brunstead, Sutton and Ingham *Nor*

INGHAM (St Bartholomew) *see* Blackbourne *St E*

INGLEBY ARNCLIFFE (All Saints) *see* Osmotherley w Harlsey and Ingleby Arncliffe *York*

INGLEBY BARWICK (St Francis) *York 20* **P** *Abp* **V** J C ROUNDTREE

INGLEBY GREENHOW (St Andrew), Bilsdale Priory and Kildale w Kirkby-in-Cleveland *York 20* **P** *Abp, Adn Cleveland, Bp Whitby, Viscount De L'Isle, R G Beckett Esq, and A H W Sutcliffe Esq (jt)* **V** M A HEADING

INGLETON (St John the Evangelist) *Dur 8* **P** *Lord Barnard* **P-in-c** K STEVENTON

INGLETON (St Mary the Virgin) w Chapel le Dale *Bradf 6* **P** *Bp* **V** C H ELLIS

INGLEWOOD Group, The *Carl 4* **P** *Bp, D&C, CCC Ox, and E P Ecroyd Esq (jt)* **R** E M SMITH, **C** J H DAVIS, **NSM** J J H SMITH

INGOL (St Margaret) *Blackb 13* **P** *Bp* **V** *vacant* (01772) 727280

INGOLDISTHORPE (St Michael) *see* Snettisham w Ingoldisthorpe and Fring *Nor*

INGOLDMELLS (St Peter and St Paul) *see* Skegness Gp *Linc*

INGOLDSBY (St Bartholomew) *see* N Beltisloe Gp *Linc*

INGRAM (St Michael) *see* Glendale Gp *Newc*

INGRAVE (St Nicholas) (St Stephen) *Chelmsf 7* **P** *Bp and Ch Patr Trust (jt)* **V** P S HAMILTON

INGRAVE (St Stephen) Conventional District *Chelmsf 7* **NSM** J A SEDANO

INGROW (St John the Evangelist) with Hainworth *Bradf 8* **P** *Bp* **V** C H KIRKE

INGS (St Anne) *see* Staveley, Ings and Kentmere *Carl*

INGWORTH (St Lawrence) *see* Erpingham w Calthorpe, Ingworth, Aldborough etc *Nor*

INHAM NOOK (St Barnabas) *see* Chilwell *S'well*

INKBERROW (St Peter) w Cookhill and Kington w Dormston *Worc 1* **P** *Bp* **R** N M WRIGHT, **NSM** D HAYWARD-WRIGHT

INKERSALL (St Columba) *see* Staveley and Barrow Hill *Derby*

INKPEN (St Michael) *see* Walbury Beacon *Ox*

INNS COURT (Holy Cross) *see* Filwood Park *Bris*

INSKIP (St Peter) *see* Copp w Inskip *Blackb*

INSTOW (All Saints Chapel) *see* Fremington, Instow and Westleigh *Ex*

INSTOW (St John the Baptist) *as above*

INTAKE (All Saints) *see* Doncaster Intake *Sheff*

INTWOOD (All Saints) *see* Swardeston w E Carleton, Intwood, Keswick etc *Nor*

INWARDLEIGH (St Petroc) *see* Okehampton w Inwardleigh, Bratton Clovelly etc *Ex*

INWORTH (All Saints) *see* Copford w Easthorpe and Messing w Inworth *Chelmsf*

IPING (St Mary) *see* Stedham w Iping *Chich*

IPPLEPEN (St Andrew), Torbryan and Denbury *Ex 10* **P** *D&C Windsor and SMF (jt)* **V** I C EGLIN

IPSDEN (St Mary the Virgin) *see* Langtree *Ox*

IPSLEY (St Peter) *Worc 7* **P** *Patr Bd* **TR** G E P NATHANIEL, **TV** R W HARDING

IPSTONES (St Leonard) w Berkhamsytch and Onecote w Bradnop *Lich 6* **P** *Bp and R Leek and Meerbrook (jt)* **P-in-c** M J EVANS

IPSWICH (All Hallows) *St E 4* **P** *Bp* **P-in-c** A J OAKEY-JONES

IPSWICH (All Saints) *see* Triangle, St Matt and All SS *St E*

IPSWICH (St Andrew) *St E 4* **P** *Bp* **V** S R LLOYD

IPSWICH (St Augustine of Hippo) *St E 4* **P** *Bp* **V** L F SIMPKINS

IPSWICH (St Bartholomew) *St E 4* **P** *Bp* **V** P J CARTER

IPSWICH (St Helen) (Holy Trinity) (St Clement w St Luke) *St E 4* **P** *Ch Patr Trust* **R** M J A TILLETT, **OLM** S J POTTER

IPSWICH (St John the Baptist) *St E 4* **P** *Simeon's Trustees* **V** A C WILSON, **C** B E MECHANIC

IPSWICH (St Margaret) *St E 4* **P** *Simeon's Trustees* **V** D CUTTS

IPSWICH (St Mary at Stoke) (St Peter) (St Francis) (St Clare's Church Centre) *St E 4* **P** *Bp* **TR** I D J MORGAN, **TV** A L CHESWORTH, M S G MORGAN, **NSM** J FENNELL

IPSWICH (St Mary at the Elms) *St E 4* **P** *Guild of All So* **P-in-c** S J RAINE

IPSWICH (St Mary-le-Tower) (St Nicholas) *St E 4* **P** *Bp (3 turns), Ch Patr Trust (1 turn)* **V** C A G JENKIN

IPSWICH (St Matthew) *see* Triangle, St Matt and All SS *St E*

IPSWICH (St Thomas) *St E 4* **P** *Bp* **V** P BOURNER

IPSWICH Triangle (Community Centre) *see* Triangle, St Matt and All SS *St E*

IPSWICH Waterfront Churches *see* Ipswich St Helen, H Trin, and St Luke *St E*

IPSWICH, SOUTH WEST *see* Ipswich St Mary at Stoke w St Pet and St Fran *St E*

IRBY (St Chad's Mission Church) *see* Thurstaston *Ches*

IRBY-IN-THE-MARSH (All Saints) *see* Burgh Gp *Linc*

IRBY ON HUMBER (St Andrew) *see* Laceby and Ravendale Gp *Linc*

IRCHESTER (St Katharine) *Pet 8* **P** *Bp* **V** J SIMMONS

IRCHESTER, LITTLE (St John) *see* Irchester *Pet*

IREBY (St James) *see* Binsey *Carl*

IRELAND WOOD (St Paul) *Ripon 7* **P** *R Adel* **P-in-c** J L SMITH, **NSM** L E LUDKIN

IRLAM (St John the Baptist) *Man 18* **P** *Trustees* **V** D I WHEELER, **OLM** J DODD, J STEPHENS

IRNHAM (St Andrew) *see* Corby Glen *Linc*

IRON ACTON (St James the Less) *see* Frampton Cotterell and Iron Acton *Bris*

IRON-BRIDGE (St Luke) *see* Coalbrookdale, Iron-Bridge and Lt Wenlock *Heref*

IRONSTONE: Drayton, Hanwell, Horley, Hornton, Shenington w Alkerton, and Wroxton w Balscote *Ox 5* **P** *Ld Chan (1 turn), Bp, Earl De la Warr, and DBP (1 turn)* **R** J READER, **Hon C** B J HYDER-SMITH

IRONSTONE VILLAGES Family of Churches, The *Leic 2* **P** *Lady Gretton, Ld Chan, Duke of Rutland, Bp, and Sir Lyonel Tollemache Bt (by turn)* **R** B A STARK, **C** H G ORRIDGE, **NSM** P C CONNELL

IRONVILLE (Christ Church) *see* Riddings and Ironville *Derby*

IRSTEAD (St Michael) *see* Ashmanhaugh, Barton Turf etc *Nor*

IRTHINGTON (St Kentigern) *see* Eden, Gelt and Irthing *Carl*

IRTHLINGBOROUGH (St Peter) *Pet 8* **P** *Sir Philip Naylor-Leyland Bt* **P-in-c** J T P HALL, **NSM** P M TATE

IRTON (St Paul) *see* Eskdale, Irton, Muncaster and Waberthwaite *Carl*

ISEL (St Michael) *see* Binsey *Carl*

ISFIELD (St Margaret) *Chich 21* **P** *Abp* **R** B H WILCOX, **Hon C** F J FOX-WILSON, **NSM** C HOWARTH

ISHAM (St Peter) *see* Gt w Lt Harrowden and Orlingbury and Isham etc *Pet*

ISLE ABBOTTS (Blessed Virgin Mary) *see* Isle Valley *B & W*

ISLE BREWERS (All Saints) *as above*

ISLE OF DOGS (Christ Church and St John) (St Luke) *Lon 7* **P** *Bp* **V** T F PYKE, **NSM** A J KEIGHLEY, T C KEIGHLEY

ISLE VALLEY *B & W 14* **P** *Bp, D&C Bris, and Dr W P Palmer (jt)* **V** A F TATHAM

ISLEHAM (St Andrew) *see* Three Rivers Gp *Ely*

ISLES OF SCILLY: St Mary's, St Agnes, St Martin's, Bryher and Tresco *Truro 5* **P** *Duchy of Cornwall*, **Chapl** P A A WALKER

ISLEWORTH (All Saints) *Lon 11* **P** *D&C Windsor* **P-in-c** A L BROOKER, **NSM** V LUCKETT

ISLEWORTH (St Francis of Assisi) *Lon 11* **P** *Bp* **NSM** A BURGESS

ISLEWORTH (St John the Baptist) *Lon 11* **P** *V Isleworth All SS* **P-in-c** T A GILLUM

ISLEWORTH (St Luke) *see* Spring Grove St Mary *Lon*

ISLEWORTH (St Mary) Osterley Road *as above*

ISLEWORTH (St Mary the Virgin) *see* Hounslow H Trin w St Paul *Lon*

ISLEY WALTON (All Saints) *see* Ashby-de-la-Zouch and Breedon on the Hill *Leic*

ISLINGTON (St James the Apostle) (St Peter) *Lon 6* **P** *Bp* **V** A J BURNISTON

ISLINGTON (St Jude and St Paul) *see* Mildmay Grove St Jude and St Paul *Lon*

ISLINGTON (St Mary) *Lon 6* **P** *CPAS* **V** S J HARVEY, **C** M A OBORNE

ISLINGTON (St Mary Magdalene) *see* Holloway St Mary Magd *Lon*

ISLIP (St Nicholas) *see* Ray Valley *Ox*

ISLIP (St Nicholas) *see* Thrapston, Denford and Islip *Pet*

ISTEAD RISE (St Barnabas) *Roch 4* **P** *Bp* **V** A K VAUGHAN

ITCHEN, UPPER *Win 1* **P** *Prime Min (2 turns), D&C (1 turn)* **R** A N M CLARKE

ITCHEN ABBAS (St John the Baptist) *see* Itchen Valley *Win*

ITCHEN VALLEY, The *Win 1* **P** *Ld Chan* **P-in-c** A M MICKLEFIELD

ITCHENOR, WEST (St Nicholas) *see* W Wittering and Birdham w Itchenor *Chich*

ITCHINGFIELD (St Nicholas) w Slinfold *Chich 7* **P** *Bp* **R** J C N GAY

ITTERINGHAM *see* Lt Barningham, Blickling, Edgefield etc *Nor*

IVEGILL (Christ Church) *see* Inglewood Gp *Carl*

IVER (St Peter) *Ox 23* **P** *Trustees* **V** T W EADY, **C** G V R HOWARD, **OLM** B J GRIFFITHS

IVER HEATH (St Margaret) *Ox 23* **P** *Trustees* **R** *vacant* (01753) 654470

IVINGHOE (St Mary the Virgin) w Pitstone and Slapton and Marsworth *Ox 26* **P** *Bp and Ch Ch Ox (jt)* **V** T E DOYLE, **C** C J PETERS

IVINGTON (St John) *see* Leominster *Heref*

IVY HATCH (not known) *see* Ightham *Roch*

IVY ROW (Mission Room) *see* Roos and Garton w Tunstall, Grimston and Hilston *York*

IVYBRIDGE (St John the Evangelist) w Harford *Ex 21* **P** *Bp* **V** C H OSBORNE

IVYCHURCH (St George) *see* St Mary's Bay w St Mary-in-the-Marsh etc *Cant*

IWADE (All Saints) *Cant 15* **P** *Adn Maidstone* **P-in-c** A J AMOS, **C** H E NELSON

IWERNE COURTNEY (St Mary) *see* Iwerne Valley *Sarum*

IWERNE MINSTER (St Mary)   *as above*
IWERNE VALLEY *Sarum 7*   **P** *D&C Windsor, DBP,*
G A L F Pitt-Rivers Esq, and A C L Sturge Esq (jt)
V S F EVERETT,   **C** M PERRY,   **NSM** J H SIMMONS,
OLM M A O MULLEY
IXWORTH (St Mary)   *see Blackbourne St E*
IXWORTH THORPE (All Saints)   *as above*
JACKFIELD (St Mary)   *see Broseley w Benthall, Jackfield,*
Linley etc Heref
JACOBSTOW (St James)   *see Week St Mary Circle of Par Truro*
JACOBSTOWE (St James)   *see Hatherleigh, Meeth, Exbourne*
and Jacobstowe Ex
JARROW (St John the Baptist) (St Mark) (St Paul) (St Peter)
Dur 15   **P** *Bp*   **TR** W E BRAVINER,   **TV** J LANCASTER
JARROW GRANGE (Christ Church) *Dur 15*   **P** *Lord*
Northbourne   **P-in-c** D T OSMAN
JARVIS BROOK (St Michael and All Angels) *Chich 19*   **P** *Bp*
V A W WEAVER
JERSEY (All Saints) *Win 15*   **P** *R St Helier, Bp, and The Crown*
(by turn)   **V** D G GRANTHAM,   **NSM** G L BAUDAINS
JERSEY Gouray (St Martin) *Win 15*   **P** *Bp and The Crown (alt)*
Hon C C P WILLIAMS
JERSEY Greve d'Azette (St Nicholas)   *see Jersey St Clem Win*
JERSEY (Holy Trinity) *Win 15*   **P** *The Crown*
R G J HOUGHTON
JERSEY Millbrook (St Matthew) *Win 15*   **P** *The Crown*
V P J WARREN
JERSEY (St Andrew) *Win 15*   **P** *Dean of Jersey*   **V** M S TAYLOR
JERSEY (St Brelade) (Communicare Chapel) (St Aubin) *Win 15*
P *The Crown*   **R** M F W BOND,   **NSM** J A DAVY
JERSEY (St Clement) *Win 15*   **P** *The Crown*   **R** D M SHAW,
NSM M J DRYDEN, T LE COUTEUR
JERSEY (St Helier) *Win 15*   **P** *The Crown*   **P-in-c** R F KEY,
NSM A D WILLIAMS
JERSEY (St James) *Win 15*   **P** *Bp*   **V** D R D JONES,
NSM A F PEARCE
JERSEY (St John) *Win 15*   **P** *The Crown*   **R** A J THEWLIS
JERSEY (St Lawrence) *Win 15*   **P** *The Crown*   **R** P J WARREN,
C S M HUNTLEY
JERSEY (St Luke) *Win 15*   **P** *Bp and The Crown (alt)*
V D R D JONES,   **NSM** A F PEARCE
JERSEY (St Mark) *Win 15*   **P** *Bp*   **V** M P L SHEA
JERSEY (St Martin) *Win 15*   **P** *The Crown*   **R** *vacant* (01534)
854294
JERSEY (St Mary) *Win 15*   **P** *The Crown*   **R** J NAYLOR,
NSM A F PEARCE
JERSEY (St Ouen) (St George) *Win 15*   **P** *The Crown*
R I PALLENT
JERSEY (St Paul) Proprietary Chapel *Win 15*   **Min** P J BROOKS
JERSEY (St Peter) *Win 15*   **P** *The Crown*   **R** M R POOLTON,
NSM N J M FREELAND
JERSEY (St Saviour) *Win 15*   **P** *The Crown*   **R** A C SWINDELL,
NSM J J ILTON, C PRICE
JERSEY (St Simon) *Win 15*   **P** *R St Helier, Bp, and The Crown*
(by turn)   **V** D G GRANTHAM,   **NSM** G L BAUDAINS
JERSEY DE GROUVILLE (St Martin) (St Peter la Roque)
Win 15   **P** *The Crown*   **R** M L LANGE-SMITH,
NSM R C DUPRÉ
JESMOND (Clayton Memorial Church) *Newc 2*   **P** *Trustees*
V D R J HOLLOWAY,   **C** J J S PRYKE,   **Hon C** A F MUNDEN
JESMOND (Holy Trinity) *Newc 2*   **P** *Trustees*   **V** M WROE,
C T SANDERSON
JESMOND (St George)   *see Newc St Geo and St Hilda Newc*
JESMOND (St Hilda)   *as above*
JEVINGTON (St Andrew)   *see E Dean w Friston and Jevington*
Chich
JOYDENS WOOD (St Barnabas) *Roch 17*   **P** *Bp*
V R E L HARDING
JURBY (St Patrick) *S & M 3*   **P** *Bp*   **V** *vacant*
KATE'S HILL (St John)   *see Dudley St Jo Worc*
KEA (All Hallows) (Old Church) *Truro 6*   **P** *V St Clement*
P-in-c C S PEER,   **C** C R BOYLE
KEAL, EAST (St Helen)   *see Marden Hill Gp Linc*
KEAL, WEST (St Helen)   *as above*
KEARSLEY MOOR (St Stephen) *Man 20*   **P** *R E Farnworth*
and Kearsley   **V** K F WAINWRIGHT
KEASDEN (St Matthew)   *see Clapham-with-Keasden and*
Austwick Bradf
KEDINGTON (St Peter and St Paul)   *see Stourhead St E*
KEEDWELL HILL (Ascension)   *see Long Ashton w Barrow*
Gurney and Flax Bourton B & W
KEELBY Group, The (St Bartholomew) *Linc 10*
P *J E Spilman Esq and DBP (1 turn), Bp (1 turn)*
P-in-c M W PAGE-CHESTNEY
KEELE (St John the Baptist) *Lich 9*
P *T H G Howard-Sneyd Esq*   **V** *vacant*

KEEVIL (St Leonard)   *see Trowbridge St Jas and Keevil Sarum*
KEGWORTH (St Andrew), Hathern, Long Whatton, Diseworth,
Belton and Osgathorpe *Leic 6*   **P** *Patr Bd*
TR G R TURNER-CALLIS,   **TV** T E EDMONDS,
NSM L A BUTLER
KEIGHLEY (All Saints) *Bradf 8*   **P** *Bp and R Keighley St Andr*
P-in-c J L PRITCHARD,   **Hon C** M S FOY
KEIGHLEY (St Andrew) *Bradf 8*   **P** *Bp*   **P-in-c** P J MOTT,
NSM E A CAISSIE
KEINTON MANDEVILLE (St Mary Magdalene)
see Wheathill Priory Gp B & W
KELBROOK (St Mary)   *see Earby w Kelbrook Bradf*
KELBY (St Andrew)   *see Ancaster Wilsford Gp Linc*
KELHAM (St Wilfrid)   *see Averham w Kelham S'well*
KELLAWAYS (St Giles)   *see Draycot Bris*
KELLET, NETHER (St Mark)   *see Bolton-le-Sands Blackb*
KELLET, OVER (St Cuthbert) *Blackb 14*   **P** *Reformation Ch*
Trust   **V** K CLAPHAM
KELLING (St Mary)   *see Weybourne Gp Nor*
KELLINGTON (St Edmund)   *see Knottingley and Kellington*
w Whitley Wakef
KELLOE (St Helen) and Coxhoe *Dur 5*   **P** *Bp*   **V** *vacant*
0191-377 3722
KELLS (St Peter) *Carl 5*   **P** *Bp*   **P-in-c** J A EVANS,
OLM A J BANKS
KELLY (St Mary the Virgin)   *see Lifton, Broadwoodwidger,*
Stowford etc Ex
KELMARSH (St Denys)   *see Clipston w Naseby and Haselbech*
w Kelmarsh Pet
KELMSCOTT (St George)   *see Shill Valley and Broadshire Ox*
KELSALE (St Peter)   *see Saxmundham w Kelsale cum Carlton*
St E
KELSALL (St Philip) *Ches 2*   **P** *V Tarvin*   **V** P J MACKRIELL
KELSEY Group, The *Linc 5*   **P** *Bp (3 turns), J M B Young Esq*
and S B Young Esq (1 turn)   **R** *vacant* (01652) 678924
KELSEY, NORTH (All Hallows)   *see Kelsey Gp Linc*
KELSEY, SOUTH (St Mary)   *as above*
KELSHALL (St Faith)   *see Therfield w Kelshall St Alb*
KELSTERN (St Faith)   *see Binbrook Gp Linc*
KELSTON (St Nicholas)   *see Bath Weston St Jo w Kelston*
B & W
KELVEDON (St Mary the Virgin) and Feering *Chelmsf 23*
P *Bp*   **V** D S REYNISH
KELVEDON HATCH (St Nicholas)   *see Bentley Common,*
Kelvedon Hatch and Navestock Chelmsf
KEMBERTON (St Andrew)   *see Beckbury, Badger, Kemberton,*
Ryton, Stockton etc Lich
KEMBLE (All Saints), Poole Keynes, Somerford Keynes w
Sharncote, Coates, Rodmarton and Sapperton w Frampton
Mansell *Glouc 7*   **P** *Bp, Lord Bathurst, Mrs L R Rank, Guild of*
All So, and DBP (2 turns), Duchy of Lanc (1 turn)
P-in-c M B SANDERS,   **Hon C** P C YOUDE,
NSM G A GIBBENS,   **OLM** P WALKER
KEMERTON (St Nicholas)   *see Ashchurch and Kemerton*
Glouc
KEMP TOWN (St Mary) *Chich 2*   **P** *Bp, Mrs R A Hinton,*
A C R Elliott Esq, T J Elliott Esq, and the Revd Canon
D H McKittrick (jt)   **P-in-c** A J WOODWARD
KEMPSEY (St Mary the Virgin) and Severn Stoke w Croome
d'Abitot *Worc 5*   **P** *D&C and Croome Estate Trustees (alt)*
R P R HOLZAPFEL
KEMPSFORD (St Mary)   *see Fairford Deanery Glouc*
KEMPSHOTT (St Mark) *Win 4*   **P** *Bp*   **V** K J TAYLOR,
C C A GILLHAM,   **NSM** R P BOWSKILL, A BOWSKILL
KEMPSTON (All Saints) *St Alb 9*   **P** *Bp*   **P-in-c** S L HUCKLE,
C J NASH
KEMPSTON (Transfiguration) *St Alb 9*   **P** *Bp*
P-in-c L A HUMPHREYS,   **C** W T BRITT
KEMSING (St Mary the Virgin) w Woodlands *Roch 10*   **P** *DBP*
P-in-c J R OAKLEY
KENARDINGTON (St Mary)   *see Orlestone w Snave and*
Ruckinge w Warehorne etc Cant
KENCHESTER (St Michael)   *see Credenhill w Brinsop and*
Wormsley etc Heref
KENCOT (St George)   *see Shill Valley and Broadshire Ox*
KENDAL (Holy Trinity) (All Hallows Chapel) *Carl 10*   **P** *Trin*
Coll Cam   **P-in-c** R J SANER-HAIGH,   **C** A RUSSELL,
NSM P SMITH, P A HENDERSON
KENDAL (St Thomas) *Carl 10*   **P** *CPAS*   **V** T R MONTGOMERY,
C M F J ALLEN,   **NSM** S R WEATHERILL, W J HOLLIDAY,
M L WOODCOCK, B J CROWE
KENDAL (St George)   *see Beacon Carl*
KENDERCHURCH (St Mary)   *see Ewyas Harold w Dulas,*
Kenderchurch etc Heref
KENDRAY (St Andrew) *Sheff 12*   **P** *V Ardsley*
V P C W JACKSON

KENILWORTH (St John) *Cov 4* **P** *Simeon's Trustees*
V A M ATTWOOD, **OLM** J M MULLANEY
KENILWORTH (St Nicholas) (St Barnabas) *Cov 4* **P** *Ld Chan*
V R W E AWRE, **C** K I MASSEY
KENLEY (All Saints) *S'wark 22* **P** *Abp* **P-in-c** C G THOMSON,
NSM D C HADLEY
KENLEY (St John the Baptist) *see* Wenlock *Heref*
KENN (St Andrew) *see* Exminster and Kenn *Ex*
KENN (St John the Evangelist) *see* Yatton Moor *B & W*
KENNERLEIGH (St John the Baptist) *see* N Creedy *Ex*
KENNET, EAST (Christ Church) *see* Upper Kennet *Sarum*
KENNET, UPPER *Sarum 18* **P** *Bp* **P-in-c** M T SHEPHERDSON
KENNETT (St Nicholas) *see* Three Rivers Gp *Ely*
KENNINGHALL (St Mary) *see* Guiltcross *Nor*
KENNINGTON (St John the Divine w St James the Apostle)
S'wark 11 **P** *Ripon Coll Cuddesdon and Bp (jt)*
V M WILLIAMS, **C** D M B PENNELLS
KENNINGTON (St Mark) *S'wark 11* **P** *Abp* **V** *vacant* (020)
7793 7050
KENNINGTON (St Mary) *Cant 6* **P** *Abp* **P-in-c** R D KING
P-in-c P J MCKELLEN, **C** E L COLEY, K J WRIGHT
KENNINGTON (St Swithun) *Ox 10* **P** *Bp*
KENNINGTON CROSS (St Anselm) *see* N Lambeth *S'wark*
KENNINGTON PARK (St Agnes) *S'wark 10* **P** *Trustees*
vacant (020) 7735 3860
KENNY HILL (St James) *see* Mildenhall *St E*
KENSAL GREEN (St John) *Lon 2* **P** *Bp* **V** A K DANGERFIELD
KENSAL RISE (St Mark) *Lon 21* **P** *Bp and Trustees (it)*
V O H D RYDER, **Hon C** R L SMITH, **NSM** T P GODDARD
KENSAL RISE (St Martin) *Lon 21* **P** *Bp and Trustees (jt)*
V G P NOYCE, **Hon C** E J BARRATT
KENSAL TOWN (St Thomas) (St Andrew) (St Philip) *Lon 12*
P *Hyndman Trustees* **P-in-c** M A MILLER
KENSINGTON (St Barnabas) *Lon 12* **P** *V Kensington St Mary
Abbots w St Geo and Ch Ch* **V** T M HUMPHREY,
C S G D LARKIN
KENSINGTON (St Clement) *see* Notting Dale St Clem w St
Mark and St Jas *Lon*
KENSINGTON (St George) *see* Holland Park *Lon*
KENSINGTON (St Helen) (Holy Trinity) *Lon 12* **P** *Bp*
V S R DIVALL
KENSINGTON (St James) *see* Notting Dale St Clem w St
Mark and St Jas *Lon*
KENSINGTON (St Luke) *see* S Kensington St Luke *Lon*
KENSINGTON (St Mary Abbots) (Christ Church) (St Philip)
Lon 12 **P** *Bp* **V** G W CRAIG, **C** G K WARDELL, D C WALSH,
Hon C R P MARSHALL, **NSM** L A PERRY, I AJIBADE
KENSINGTON, NORTH (St Michael and All Angels)
see Notting Hill St Mich and Ch Ch *Lon*
KENSINGTON, SOUTH (Holy Trinity w All Saints) *Lon 3*
P *D&C Westmr* **P-in-c** E M V RUSSELL
KENSINGTON, SOUTH (St Jude) Courtfield Gardens *see* W
Brompton St Mary w St Peter and St Jude *Lon*
KENSINGTON, SOUTH St Luke *Lon 8* **P** *Ch Patr Trust*
V A N BEAVIS
KENSINGTON, SOUTH (St Stephen) *Lon 12* **P** *Guild of
All So* **V** R F BUSHAU
KENSINGTON, WEST (St Andrew) *see* Fulham St Andr *Lon*
KENSINGTON, WEST (St Mary) *see* Fulham St Mary N End
Lon
KENSINGTON, WEST (St Mary) The Boltons *see* W
Brompton St Mary w St Peter and St Jude *Lon*
KENSWORTH (St Mary the Virgin), Studham and Whipsnade
St Alb 11 **P** *Ld Chan and D&C St Paul's (alt)*
V N Y LENTHALL
KENT TOWN *see* E Molesey *Guildf*
KENTCHURCH (St Mary) *see* Ewyas Harold w Dulas,
Kenderchurch etc *Heref*
KENTFORD (St Mary) *see* Dalham, Gazeley, Higham,
Kentford and Moulton *St E*
KENTISBEARE (St Mary) *see* Cullompton, Willand,
Uffculme, Kentisbeare etc *Ex*
KENTISBURY (St Thomas) *see* Shirwell, Loxhore, Kentisbury,
Arlington, etc *Ex*
KENTISH TOWN (St Benet and All Saints) *Lon 17*
P *Prime Min and D&C St Paul's (alt)* **V** R N ARNOLD
KENTISH TOWN (St Luke) *see* Oseney Crescent St Luke *Lon*
KENTISH TOWN (St Martin) (St Andrew) *Lon 17* **P** *Exors
Dame Jewell Magnus-Allcroft* **P-in-c** C J BRICE
KENTISH TOWN (St Silas) and (Holy Trinity) w St Barnabas
Lon 17 **P** *Bp and D&C St Paul's (jt)* **V** G C ROWLANDS,
NSM M G BURRIDGE
KENTMERE (St Cuthbert) *see* Staveley, Ings and Kentmere
Carl
KENTON (All Saints) *see* Debenham and Helmingham *St E*

**KENTON (All Saints), Mamhead, Powderham, Cofton and
Starcross** *Ex 6* **P** *Earl of Devon, D&C Ex, D&C Sarum, and
SMF (jt)* **C** O IBE-ENWO, D A BURTON, **Hon C** P DAWKES
KENTON (Ascension) *Newc 2* **P** *Bp* **P-in-c** L CHAPMAN
KENTON (St Mary the Virgin) *Lon 23* **P** *Bp* **V** E J LEWIS
KENTON, SOUTH (Annunciation) *see* Wembley Park *Lon*
KENWYN (St Keyne) w St Allen *Truro 6* **P** *Bp*
P-in-c C P PARSONS, **OLM** R W HUMPHRIES
KERESLEY (St Thomas) and Coundon *Cov 2* **P** *Bp* **V** *vacant*
(024) 7633 2717
KERESLEY END (Church of the Ascension) *see* Keresley and
Coundon *Cov*
KERRIDGE (Holy Trinity) *see* Bollington *Ches*
KERSAL, LOWER (St Aidan) *see* Salford All SS *Man*
KERSAL MOOR (St Paul) *Man 20* **P** *Trustees*
R L K BATTYE, **C** C J SHELLEY
KERSEY (St Mary) *see* Elmsett w Aldham, Hintlesham,
Chattisham etc *St E*
KERSWELL GREEN (St John the Baptist) *see* Kempsey and
Severn Stoke w Croome d'Abitot *Worc*
KESGRAVE (All Saints) *St E 4* **P** *Bp* **V** R SPITTLE,
C C A ALLEN, **NSM** C J NUNN
KESSINGLAND (St Edmund), Gisleham and Rushmere *Nor 9*
P *Ld Chan (1 turns) and Bp (2 turns)* **R** L M DOMONEY
KESTON (not known) (St Audrey) *Roch 14* **P** *D&C*
R D F SPRINGTHORPE
KESWICK (All Saints) *see* Swardeston w E Carleton, Intwood,
Keswick etc *Nor*
KESWICK (St John) *Carl 6* **P** *Trustees* **V** A E PYE
KESWICK, EAST (St Mary Magdalene) *see* Bardsey *Ripon*
KETLEY (St Mary the Virgin) *see* Cen Telford *Lich*
KETTERING (All Saints) *Pet 9* **P** *SMF*
P-in-c A R G DUTTON
KETTERING (Christ the King) *Pet 9* **P** *R Barton Seagrave w
Warkton* **V** R J BEWLEY, **C** P W FROST,
NSM P M SIMMONS
KETTERING (St Andrew) *Pet 9* **P** *Bp* **V** N R WILLS,
C K M TAYLOR, **NSM** H M GOMPERTZ
KETTERING (St Mary the Virgin) (St John the Evangelist) *Pet 9*
P *SMF* **V** *vacant* (01536) 512736
KETTERING (St Peter and St Paul) (St Michael and All Angels)
Pet 9 **P** *Comdr L M M Saunders Watson*
R D M J BARRINGTON, **C** G S ROBERTS, **NSM** J S SMITH,
L S MCCORMACK
KETTERINGHAM (St Peter) *see* Swardeston w E Carleton,
Intwood, Keswick etc *Nor*
KETTLEBASTON (St Mary) *see* Monks Eleigh w Chelsworth
and Brent Eleigh etc *St E*
KETTLEBROOK (St Andrew) *see* Tamworth *Lich*
KETTLEBURGH (St Andrew) *see* Brandeston w Kettleburgh
and Easton *St E*
KETTLENESS (St John the Baptist) *see* Hinderwell, Roxby and
Staithes etc *York*
KETTLESTONE (All Saints) *see* Barney, Fulmodeston w
Croxton, Hindringham etc *Nor*
KETTLETHORPE (St Peter and St Paul) *see* Saxilby Gp *Linc*
**KETTLEWELL (St Mary) w Conistone, Hubberholme and
Arncliff w Halton Gill** *Bradf 7* **P** *Bp, Mrs J E Wright, and
W R G Bell Esq (jt)* **V** P YORKSTONE, **C** F JENKINS
**KETTON (St Mary the Virgin), Collyweston, Easton-on-the-Hill,
Tinwell and Wittering** *Pet 12* **P** *Burghley Ho Preservation
Trust, Bp, and Ld Chan (by turn)* **P-in-c** A D RAYMENT, **Hon
C** J M SAUNDERS
KEW (St Anne) *S'wark 16* **P** *The Crown* **V** J WORN
KEW (St Francis of Assisi) *Liv 9* **P** *Bp, Adn Warrington, and
V Southport All SS and All So (jt)* **V** A P J GALBRAITH
KEW St Philip and All Saints) (St Luke) *S'wark 16* **P** *Bp*
V P W HART
KEWSTOKE (St Paul) *see* Milton and Kewstoke *B & W*
KEYHAM (All Saints) *see* Houghton-on-the-Hill, Keyham and
Hungarton *Leic*
KEYHAM, NORTH (St Thomas) *see* Plymouth St Pet and H
Apostles *Ex*
**KEYINGHAM (St Nicholas) w Ottringham, Halsham and Sunk
Island** *York 12* **P** *Abp (3 turns), DBP (1 turn)* **R** *vacant*
(01964) 622171
KEYMER (St Cosmas and St Damian) *see* Clayton w Keymer
Chich
KEYMER (St Francis of Assisi) *as above*
KEYNSHAM (St Francis) (St John the Baptist) *B & W 9*
P *Patr Bd* **TR** S A M'CAW, **TV** A D JUDGE, S G HOWELL
KEYSOE (St Mary the Virgin) w Bolnhurst and Little Staughton
St Alb 13 **P** *CCC Ox (1 turn), Bp (2 turns)* **V** *vacant*
(01234) 708251
KEYSTON (St John the Baptist) and Bythorn *Ely 10*
P *Sir Philip Naylor-Leyland Bt (2 turns), Bp (1 turn)*
R *vacant*

KEYWORTH (St Mary Magdalene) and Stanton-on-the-Wolds and Bunny w Bradmore *S'well 8* **P** *Bp and Ld Chan (alt)* **R** J F WELLINGTON, **C** C FRENCH

KIBWORTH (St Wilfrid) and Smeeton Westerby and Saddington *Leic 4* **P** *Mert Coll Ox and Bp (jt)* **P-in-c** L FREMMER

KIDBROOKE (St James) (Holy Spirit) *S'wark 1* **P** *Patr Bd* **R** K W HITCH, **NSM** M CAVE

KIDBROOKE (St Nicholas) *S'wark 1* **P** *Bp and Simeon's Trustees (jt)* **V** T M LINKENS

KIDDERMINSTER (St George) (St Chad) (St John the Baptist Church Hall) *Worc 11* **P** *Patr Bd* **TV** J AYOK-LOEWENBERG, **P-in-c** H A BURTON, **C** O A DOUGLAS-PENNANT

KIDDERMINSTER (St John the Baptist) (Holy Innocents) *Worc 11* **P** *Patr Bd* **TR** D J ARNOLD, **TV** D GEORGE

KIDDERMINSTER (St Mary and All Saints) w Trimpley, Franche, Broadwaters and Upper Arley *Worc 11* **P** *Bp* **TR** D O BELL, **TV** J H H ASHTON, R A LAWLEY, **C** K M GREEN, **NSM** A VACCARO

KIDDERMINSTER WEST *see* Kidderminster St Jo and H Innocents *Worc*

KIDDINGTON (St Nicholas) *see* Wootton w Glympton and Kiddington *Ox*

KIDLINGTON (St Mary the Virgin) w Hampton Poyle *Ox 7* **P** *Patr Bd* **TR** J A ELLIS, **TV** H A CAMPBELL, **C** G K STRAINE, **NSM** W H WHYTE

KIDLINGTON, SOUTH (St John the Baptist) *see* Kidlington w Hampton Poyle *Ox*

KIDMORE END (St John the Baptist) *see* Rotherfield Peppard and Kidmore End etc *Ox*

KIDSGROVE (St Thomas) *Lich 9* **P** *MMCET* **V** I BAKER

KILBURN (Mission Room) *see* Horsley and Denby *Derby*

KILBURN (St Augustine) (St John) *Lon 2* **P** *SMF* **V** *vacant* (020) 7624 1637

KILBURN (St Mary) *see* Thirkleby w Kilburn and Bagby *York*

KILBURN (St Mary w All Souls) Priory Road and W Hampstead St James *Lon 16* **P** *Bp, Ch Patr Trust, and trustees (jt)* **V** A D CAIN, **C** C E CARGILL, **NSM** M-E B R BRAGG, **R** HUTCHISON

KILBURN, WEST (St Luke) (St Simon) (St Jude) *Lon 2* **P** *CPAS* **P-in-c** A G THOM, **C** M R WALTON, J F BARRY, **NSM** B A ENWUCHOLA

KILBY (St Mary Magdalene) *see* Wistow *Leic*

KILDALE (St Cuthbert) *see* Ingleby Greenhow, Bilsdale Priory etc *York*

KILDWICK (St Andrew) *Bradf 8* **P** *Ch Ch Ox* **V** R A R FIGG

KILHAM (All Saints) *see* Rudston w Boynton, Carnaby and Kilham *York*

KILKHAMPTON (St James the Great) w Morwenstow *Truro 8* **P** *DBP and Bp (jt)* **NSM** R WARD-SMITH

KILLAMARSH (St Giles) *Derby 3* **P** *The Crown* **P-in-c** H GUEST, **NSM** M GUEST

KILLERTON (Holy Evangelist) *see* Pinhoe and Broadclyst *Ex*

KILLINGHALL (St Thomas the Apostle) *see* Hampsthwaite and Killinghall and Birstwith *Ripon*

KILLINGHOLME, NORTH AND SOUTH (St Denys) *see* Habrough Gp *Linc*

KILLINGTON (All Saints) *see* Firbank, Howgill and Killington *Bradf*

KILLINGWORTH (St John) *Newc 1* **P** *V Longbenton St Bart* **V** D M GRAY

KILMERSDON (St Peter and St Paul) w Babington *B & W 11* **P** *Lord Hylton* **R** S K GREATOREX, **NSM** J A COLE

KILMESTON (St Andrew) *see* Upper Itchen *Win*

KILMINGTON (St Giles) *see* Kilmington, Stockland, Dalwood, Yarcombe etc *Ex*

KILMINGTON (St Giles), Stockland, Dalwood, Yarcombe and Shute *Ex 5* **P** *Bp and D&C (2 turns), Prime Min (1 turn)* **V** A C MCCOLLUM, **C** C M WOOLVEN, **NSM** L A MILLS

KILMINGTON (St Mary the Virgin) *see* Upper Stour *Sarum*

KILNDOWN (Christ Church) *see* Goudhurst w Kilndown *Cant*

KILNGREEN (Diggle Mission Church) *see* Saddleworth *Man*

KILNHURST (St Thomas) *Sheff 12* **P** *Ld Chan* **V** A R BREWERTON

KILNWICK (All Saints) *see* Woldsburn *York*

KILPECK (St Mary and St David) *see* Ewyas Harold w Dulas, Kenderchurch etc *Heref*

KILSBY (St Faith) *see* Barby w Kilsby *Pet*

KILVERSTONE (St Andrew) *see* Thetford *Nor*

KILVINGTON (St Mary) *S'well 3* **P** *E G Staunton Esq* **P-in-c** D HOLLIS

KILVINGTON, SOUTH (St Wilfrid) *see* Thirsk *York*

KILWORTH, NORTH (St Andrew) *see* Gilmorton, Peatling Parva, Kimcote etc *Leic*

KILWORTH, SOUTH (St Nicholas) *as above*

KIMBERLEY (Holy Trinity) *S'well 7* **P** *Bp* **P-in-c** B M HOLBROOK

KIMBERLEY (St Peter) *see* Barnham Broom and Upper Yare *Nor*

KIMBERWORTH (St Thomas) (St Mark) *Sheff 6* **P** *Bp* **C** J T BIRBECK

KIMBERWORTH PARK (St John) *Sheff 6* **P** *Bp* **C** J T BIRBECK

KIMBLE, GREAT (St Nicholas) *see* Ellesborough, The Kimbles and Stoke Mandeville *Ox*

KIMBLE, LITTLE (All Saints) *as above*

KIMBLESWORTH (St Philip and St James) *see* Dur N *Dur*

KIMBOLTON (St Andrew) *see* Kym Valley *Ely*

KIMBOLTON (St James the Great) *see* Leominster *Heref*

KIMCOTE (All Saints) *see* Gilmorton, Peatling Parva, Kimcote etc *Leic*

KIMMERIDGE (St Nicholas of Myra) *see* Corfe Castle, Church Knowle, Kimmeridge etc *Sarum*

KIMPTON (St Peter and St Paul) *see* Appleshaw, Kimpton, Thruxton, Fyfield etc *Win*

KIMPTON (St Peter and St Paul) w Ayot St Lawrence *St Alb 7* **P** *Bp* **P-in-c** L E SUMMERS

KINETON (St Peter) *Cov 8* **P** *Lady Willoughby de Broke* **P-in-c** B J JACKSON, **C** R J COOKE

KING CROSS (St Paul) *Wakef 4* **P** *Bp* **V** *vacant* (01422) 352933

KING STERNDALE (Christ Church) *see* Buxton w Burbage and King Sterndale *Derby*

KINGHAM (St Andrew) *see* Chipping Norton *Ox*

KINGMOOR (St Peter) *see* Houghton *Carl*

KING'S BECK *Nor 12* **P** *Bp, D&C, P H C Barber Esq, and J T D Shaw Esq (jt)* **R** S A SMITH

KINGS BROMLEY (All Saints) *see* The Ridwares and Kings Bromley *Lich*

KING'S CAPLE (St John the Baptist) *see* Wormelow Hundred *Heref*

KING'S CLIFFE (All Saints), Bulwick and Blatherwycke and Laxton *Pet 10* **P** *Bp, G T G Conant Esq, and F and A George Ltd (jt)* **R** P J DAVIES, **NSM** K VOTH HARMAN

KINGS HEATH (All Saints) *Birm 5* **P** *V Moseley St Mary* **P-in-c** Q D WARBRICK

KINGS HEATH (St Augustine) *Pet 4* **P** *Bp* **P-in-c** A J B SYMES

KING'S HILL (St Andrew) *see* Wednesbury St Bart *Lich*

KINGS LANGLEY (All Saints) *see* Langelei *St Alb*

KING'S LYNN (All Saints) *see* S Lynn *Nor*

KING'S LYNN (St John the Evangelist) *Nor 20* **P** *Bp* **V** C J CHILD

KING'S LYNN (St Margaret) (St Edmund) w St Nicholas *Nor 20* **P** *D&C* **R** C J IVORY, **C** S E KIMMIS

KING'S LYNN (St Peter) *see* Clenchwarton and W Lynn *Ely*

KING'S NORTON (St John the Baptist) *see* Gaulby *Leic*

KINGS NORTON (St Nicolas) *Birm 4* **P** *Patr Bd* **TR** R J MORRIS, **TV** J C WHITE, **C** J B CROOKS

KING'S PYON (St Mary the Virgin) *see* Canon Pyon w King's Pyon, Birley and Wellington *Heref*

KINGS RIPTON (St Peter) *Ely 10* **P** *Lord de Ramsey* **P-in-c** E B ATLING, **C** B A STEWART

KING'S SOMBORNE *see* Somborne w Ashley *Win*

KING'S STANLEY (St George) *see* The Stanleys *Glouc*

KING'S SUTTON (St Peter and St Paul) and Newbottle and Charlton *Pet 1* **P** *SMF and Lady Townsend (jt)* **V** M R H BELLAMY

KING'S WALDEN (St Mary) and Offley w Lilley *St Alb 3* **P** *Sir Thomas Pilkington Bt (2 turns), St Jo Coll Cam (1 turn), D K C Salusbury-Hughes Esq and Mrs P A L McGrath (2 turns)* **P-in-c** T J BELL, **NSM** A J T HINKSMAN

KING'S WORTHY (St Mary) (St Mary's Chapel) *Win 7* **P** *Univ Coll Ox and Lord Northbrook (alt)* **R** A W GORDON, **NSM** E CHASE

KINGSBRIDGE (St Edmund the King and Martyr) and Dodbrooke *Ex 14* **P** *Bp* **R** *vacant* (01548) 856231

KINGSBURY (Holy Innocents) *Lon 21* **P** *D&C St Paul's* **V** C F MORTON, **NSM** A J HOPKINS

KINGSBURY (St Andrew) *Lon 21* **P** *The Crown* **V** J T SMITH

KINGSBURY (St Peter and St Paul) *Birm 10* **P** *Bp* **P-in-c** J E GASPER

KINGSBURY EPISCOPI (St Martin) w East Lambrook, Hambridge and Earnshill *B & W 14* **P** *Bp (2 turns), D&C (1 turn)* **V** A R ELWOOD

KINGSCLERE (St Mary) and Ashford Hill w Headley *Win 6* **P** *Bp* **V** L R THIRTLE, **C** P A BANCROFT

KINGSCLERE WOODLANDS (St Paul) *see* Kingsclere and Ashford Hill w Headley *Win*

KINGSCOTE (St John the Baptist) *see* Nailsworth w Shortwood, Horsley etc *Glouc*

KINGSDON (All Saints) *see* Somerton w Compton Dundon, the Charltons etc *B & W*
KINGSDOWN (St Edmund the King and Martyr) *Roch 10* **P** *D&C* **R** J M B THURLOW
KINGSDOWN (St John the Evangelist) *see* Ringwould w Kingsdown and Ripple etc *Cant*
KINGSEY (St Nicholas) *see* Haddenham w Cuddington, Kingsey etc *Ox*
KINGSHURST (St Barnabas) *Birm 9* **P** *Bp* **V** F J JOHNSON
KINGSKERSWELL (St Mary) w Coffinswell *Ex 10* **P** *V St Marychurch* **V** J F LEONARD
KINGSLAND (St Michael and All Angels) w Eardisland, Aymestrey and Leinthall Earles *Heref 6* **P** *DBP (2 turns), Ld Chan (1 turn)* **R** R S TAYLOR
KINGSLEY (All Saints) *see* Northanger *Win*
KINGSLEY (St John the Evangelist) *see* Norley, Crowton and Kingsley *Ches*
KINGSLEY (St Werburgh) and Foxt-w-Whiston and Oakamoor w Cotton *Lich 6* **P** R Cheadle w Freehay and Mrs N A Faulkner (jt) **R** A M HINDLE, **NSM** C M RICHARDSON
KINGSLEY MOOR (St John the Baptist) *see* Kingsley and Foxt-w-Whiston and Oakamoor etc *Lich*
KINGSNORTH (St Michael and All Angels) and Shadoxhurst *Cant 6* **P** *Abp* **P-in-c** S E MCLACHLAN
KINGSNYMPTON (St James) *see* S Molton w Nymet St George, High Bray etc *Ex*
KINGSTAG (not known) *see* Sturminster Newton, Hinton St Mary and Lydlinch *Sarum*
KINGSTANDING (St Luke) *Birm 3* **P** *Bp* **V** N J JARVIS, **C** L A COX
KINGSTANDING (St Mark) *Birm 3* **P** *Bp* **V** P CALVERT, **NSM** P GILLON
KINGSTEIGNTON (St Michael) and Teigngrace *Ex 10* **P** *Bp* **P-in-c** M P SMITH, **C** T J WOODS, **NSM** S J GILL
KINGSTHORPE (St John the Baptist) w Northampton St David *Pet 4* **P** *Patr Bd* **TV** E M REW, **P-in-c** L J BUTLER
KINGSTON (All Saints and St Andrew) *see* Papworth *Ely*
KINGSTON (St Giles) *see* Barham w Bishopsbourne and Kingston *Cant*
KINGSTON (St James) *see* Modbury, Bigbury, Ringmore w Kingston etc *Ex*
KINGSTON (St James) *see* Shorwell w Kingston *Portsm*
KINGSTON (St James), Langton Matravers and Worth Matravers *Sarum 8* **P** *Bp, D E Scott Esq, and R Swanage and Studland (jt)* **P-in-c** G E BURRETT
KINGSTON (St Pancras) *see* Iford w Kingston and Rodmell *Chich*
KINGSTON (St Winifred) and Ratcliffe-on-Soar *S'well 9* **P** *D&C* **P-in-c** R I COLEMAN
KINGSTON BAGPUIZE (St John the Baptist) *see* Fyfield w Tubney and Kingston Bagpuize *Ox*
KINGSTON BUCI (St Julian) *Chich 4* **P** *Lord Egremont* **P-in-c** T S STRATFORD, **NSM** B A WILSON
KINGSTON DEVERILL (St Mary) *see* Cley Hill Villages *Sarum*
KINGSTON HILL (St Paul) *S'wark 15* **P** *DBP* **V** S C COUPLAND, **C** S I A LIYANAGE, **NSM** F M M DE QUIDT
KINGSTON LACY (St Stephen) *see* Bridge Par *Sarum*
KINGSTON LISLE (St John the Baptist) *see* Ridgeway *Ox*
KINGSTON PARK (not known) *Newc 2* **P** *Bp* **V** R C MILLS
KINGSTON SEYMOUR (All Saints) *see* Yatton Moor *B & W*
KINGSTON ST MARY (The Blessed Virgin Mary) *see* W Monkton w Kingston St Mary, Broomfield etc *B & W*
KINGSTON UPON HULL (Ascension) *see* Derringham Bank *York*
KINGSTON UPON HULL (Most Holy and Undivided Trinity) *York 14* **P** *H Trin Hull & Distr Ch Patr Soc Ltd* **P-in-c** N D BARNES, **C** M R WOODCOCK, M E BALL, **NSM** I M WILSON
KINGSTON UPON HULL (St Aidan) Southcoates *York 14* **P** *Simeon's Trustees* **V** M A FRYER, **C** R P PHILLIPS
KINGSTON UPON HULL (St Alban) *York 14* **P** *Abp* **V** D JAGO, **C** J R ROSIE
KINGSTON UPON HULL (St Cuthbert) *see* Hull St Cuth *York*
KINGSTON UPON HULL (St John the Baptist) *see* Newington w Dairycoates *York*
KINGSTON UPON HULL (St Martin) *see* Hull St Martin w Transfiguration *York*
KINGSTON UPON HULL (St Mary) Sculcoates *see* Hull St Mary Sculcoates *York*
KINGSTON UPON HULL (St Mary the Virgin) *York 14* **P** *Abp* **P-in-c** M R B HILLS
KINGSTON UPON HULL (St Matthew w St Barnabas) *York 14* **P** V Hull H Trin **P-in-c** T A COTSON

KINGSTON UPON HULL (St Nicholas) *York 14* **P** *Abp* **P-in-c** P COPLEY
KINGSTON UPON HULL (St Paul) *see* Sculcoates *York*
KINGSTON UPON HULL (St Stephen) *as above*
KINGSTON UPON HULL (St Thomas) *see* Derringham Bank *York*
KINGSTON UPON THAMES (All Saints) (St John the Evangelist) *S'wark 15* **P** *Patr Bd* **TR** J P WILKES, **TV** V A MAUNDER, **NSM** S A CRAGG
KINGSTON UPON THAMES (St Luke) *S'wark 15* **P** *Bp* **V** M G HISLOP
KINGSTON VALE (St John the Baptist) *S'wark 15* **P** *Bp* **P-in-c** A R BECK
KINGSTONE (St John and All Saints) *see* Winsmoor *B & W*
KINGSTONE (St John the Baptist) *see* Uttoxeter Area *Lich*
KINGSTONE (St Michael and All Angels) *see* Cagebrook *Heref*
KINGSWEAR (St Thomas of Canterbury) *see* Brixham w Churston Ferrers and Kingswear *Ex*
KINGSWINFORD (St Mary) *Worc 10* **P** *Patr Bd* **P-in-c** G KENDALL, **NSM** J E ARNOLD
KINGSWOOD (Church of the Ascension) (Holy Trinity) *Bris 5* **P** *Patr Bd* **TR** P G HUZZEY, **TV** A J MASON, **NSM** T M TAYLOR, L W CARR
KINGSWOOD (St Andrew) *S'wark 26* **P** *Bp and R&S Ch Trust (jt)* **V** G A BARBER, **NSM** A G F BOWYER
KINGSWOOD (St Mary the Virgin) *see* Charfield and Kingswood w Wickwar etc *Glouc*
KINGSWOOD, LOWER (Wisdom of God) *see* Kingswood *S'wark*
KINGTON (St James) *see* Inkberrow w Cookhill and Kington w Dormston *Worc*
KINGTON (St Mary) w Huntington, Old Radnor, Kinnerton and Titley *Heref 4* **P** *Patr Bd* **R** N WESTON, **NSM** P J BUCKINGHAM
KINGTON, WEST (St Mary the Virgin) *see* By Brook *Bris*
KINGTON LANGLEY (St Peter) *see* Draycot *Bris*
KINGTON MAGNA (All Saints) *see* Stour Vale *Sarum*
KINGTON ST MICHAEL (St Michael) *Bris 4* **P** *Patr Bd* **V** S J TYNDALL, **C** S J RUSHTON, **OLM** D J KILMISTER
KINGWESTON (All Saints) *see* Wheathill Priory Gp *B & W*
KINLET (St John the Baptist) *see* Cleobury Mortimer w Hopton Wafers etc *Heref*
KINNERLEY (St Mary) w Melverley and Knockin w Maesbrook *Lich 19* **P** W H C Montgomery Esq, Sir Brooke Boothby Bt, and Viscount Boyne (jt) **P-in-c** R C BOWERS, **OLM** P L WEST, D K GOUGH
KINNERSLEY (St James) *see* Eardisley w Bollingham, Willersley, Brilley etc *Heref*
KINNERTON (St Mary the Virgin) *see* Kington w Huntington, Old Radnor, Kinnerton etc *Heref*
KINNERTON, HIGHER (All Saints) *see* Dodleston *Ches*
KINNINVIE (Mission Room) *see* Barnard Castle w Whorlton *Dur*
KINOULTON (St Luke) *see* Hickling w Kinoulton and Broughton Sulney *S'well*
KINSBOURNE GREEN (St Mary) *see* Harpenden St Nic *St Alb*
KINSHAM (All Saints) *see* Presteigne w Discoed, Kinsham, Lingen and Knill *Heref*
KINSLEY (Resurrection) w Wragby *Wakef 10* **P** *Bp and Lord St Oswald (jt)* **V** J HADJIOANNOU, **NSM** R H BAILEY, **S** HULME
KINSON (St Andrew) (St Philip) and West Howe *Sarum 7* **P** *Patr Bd* **TR** R G SAUNDERS, **TV** P J NESBITT, **NSM** D ROBERTS
KINTBURY (St Mary the Virgin) *see* Walbury Beacon *Ox*
KINVER (St Peter) and Enville *Lich 24* **P** *Bp, Mrs A D Williams, and DBP (jt)* **R** D J BLACKBURN, **C** M W SOAR, **Hon C** M MORRIS
KINWARTON (St Mary the Virgin) w Great Alne and Haselor *Cov 7* **P** *Bp* **P-in-c** D C CAPRON, **Hon C** M L EAMAN
KIPPAX (St Mary the Virgin) w Allerton Bywater *Ripon 8* **P** *Bp* **TR** W P B CARLIN, **TV** J SYKES
KIPPINGTON (St Mary) *Roch 9* **P** *DBP* **V** D B KITLEY, **NSM** L LEITHEAD
KIRBY, WEST (St Andrew) *Ches 8* **P** *D&C* **V** P WALSH
KIRBY, WEST (St Bridget) *Ches 8* **P** *D&C* **C** C P UPTON, **NSM** D K CHESTER
KIRBY, WEST (St Michael and All Angels) *see* Newton *Ches*
KIRBY BEDON (St Andrew) *see* Rockland St Mary w Hellington, Bramerton etc *Nor*
KIRBY BELLARS (St Peter) *see* Upper Wreake *Leic*
KIRBY CANE (All Saints) *see* Gillingham w Geldeston, Stockton, Ellingham etc *Nor*

KIRBY GRINDALYTHE (St Andrew) *see* Weaverthorpe w Helperthorpe, Luttons Ambo etc *York*

KIRBY KNOWLE (St Wilfrid) *see* Kirkby Knowle *York*

KIRBY-LE-SOKEN (St Michael) w Great Holland *Chelmsf 22* **P** *Bp and CPAS (jt)* **R** M D J HOLDAWAY

KIRBY MISPERTON (St Laurence) w Normanby, Edston and Salton *York 19* **P** *Lady Clarissa Collin, Abp, and St Jo Coll Cam (by turn)* **R** *vacant* (01751) 431288

KIRBY MUXLOE (St Bartholomew) *Leic 9* **P** *Bp* **TR** T L RINGLAND, **C** J WOOD, **NSM** A HUMPHREY

KIRBY-ON-THE-MOOR (All Saints), Cundall w Norton-le-Clay and Skelton-cum-Newby *Ripon 3* **P** *Bp, Sir Arthur Collins, and R E J Compton Esq (jt)* **P-in-c** A J ASKEW

KIRBY SIGSTON (St Lawrence) *see* Northallerton w Kirby Sigston *York*

KIRBY UNDERDALE (All Saints) *see* Garrowby Hill *York*

KIRBY WISKE (St John the Baptist) *see* Lower Swale *Ripon*

KIRDFORD (St John the Baptist) *Chich 11* **P** *Lord Egremont* **P-in-c** P R REDPARTH

KIRK ARBORY (St Columba) *see* Arbory *S & M*

KIRK BRAMWITH (St Mary) *see* Fishlake w Sykehouse and Kirk Bramwith etc *Sheff*

KIRK DEIGHTON (All Saints) *see* Spofforth w Kirk Deighton *Ripon*

KIRK ELLA (St Andrew) and Willerby *York 14* **P** *Patr Bd* **TR** J S JUCKES, **TV** N J LITTLE, **C** T D PUTT

KIRK FENTON (St Mary) w Kirkby Wharfe and Ulleskelfe *York 1* **P** *Abp, J Fielden Esq, and A A Warburton Esq (jt)* **P-in-c** S SHERIFF

KIRK HALLAM (All Saints) *Derby 13* **P** *Bp* **P-in-c** D FERGUS, **NSM** R M THOMPSON

KIRK HAMMERTON (St John the Baptist) *see* Lower Nidderdale *Ripon*

KIRK IRETON (Holy Trinity) *see* Wirksworth *Derby*

KIRK LANGLEY (St Michael) *Derby 11* **P** *G Meynell Esq and J M Clark-Maxwell Esq (alt)* **P-in-c** A P HARPER, **C** D A GLEN

KIRK MAUGHOLD (St Maughold) *see* Maughold *S & M*

KIRK ONCHAN (St Peter) *see* Onchan *S & M*

KIRK PATRICK (Holy Trinity) *see* Patrick *S & M*

KIRK SANDALL and Edenthorpe (Good Shepherd) *Sheff 8* **P** *Ld Chan* **R** M E GREGORY, **C** S A HANCOX

KIRK SANTON (St Sanctain) *see* Santan *S & M*

KIRK SMEATON (St Peter) *see* Went Valley *Wakef*

KIRKANDREWS ON EDEN (St Mary) *see* Barony of Burgh *Carl*

KIRKANDREWS ON ESK (St Andrew) *see* Arthuret w Kirkandrews-on-Esk and Nicholforest *Carl*

KIRKBAMPTON (St Peter) *see* Barony of Burgh *Carl*

KIRKBRIDE (St Bride) *see* Bowness-on-Solway, Kirkbride and Newton Arlosh *Carl*

KIRKBRIDE (St Bridget) *S & M 3* **P** *The Crown* **R** *vacant*

KIRKBURN (St Mary) *see* Woldsburn *York*

KIRKBURTON (All Hallows) *Wakef 6* **P** *Bp* **P-in-c** G CLAY, **OLM** R A CHAMBERS

KIRKBY (St Andrew) *see* Kelsey Gp *Linc*

KIRKBY (St Chad) (St Mark) (St Martin) (St Andrew) *Liv 7* **P** *Patr Bd* **TR** T R STRATFORD, **TV** A J HEBER, J D FAGAN, **C** J VAN DEN BERG-OWENS

KIRKBY, SOUTH (All Saints) *Wakef 10* **P** *Guild of All So* **V** T H KAYE

KIRKBY FLEETHAM (St Mary) *see* Lower Swale *Ripon*

KIRKBY GREEN (Holy Cross) *see* Digby Gp *Linc*

KIRKBY IN ASHFIELD (St Thomas) *S'well 4* **P** *Bp* **P-in-c** N A POPHAM

KIRKBY IN ASHFIELD (St Wilfrid) *S'well 4* **P** *Bp* **P-in-c** G R PATCHELL, **NSM** A DEMPSTER

KIRKBY-IN-CLEVELAND (St Augustine) *see* Ingleby Greenhow, Bilsdale Priory etc *York*

KIRKBY-IN-MALHAMDALE (St Michael the Archangel) *Bradf 5* **P** *D&C* **P-in-c** H M BAKER

KIRKBY IRELETH (St Cuthbert) *Carl 9* **P** *D&C York* **P-in-c** M COWAN

KIRKBY KNOWLE (St Wilfrid) *York 18* **P** *Abp* **V** I D HOUGHTON, **NSM** T A LEWIS

KIRKBY LAYTHORPE (St Denys) *Linc 21* **P** *Bp and DBP (alt)* **P-in-c** J A PATRICK, **OLM** V GREENE

KIRKBY LONSDALE (St Mary the Virgin) Team Ministry *Carl 10* **P** *Patr Bd* **TR** R J SNOW, **TV** D WHITEHEAD, **C** S H P THOMPSON

KIRKBY MALHAM (St Michael the Archangel) *see* Kirkby-in-Malhamdale *Bradf*

KIRKBY MALLORY (All Saints) *see* Newbold de Verdun, Barlestone and Kirkby Mallory *Leic*

KIRKBY MALZEARD (St Andrew) *see* Fountains Gp *Ripon*

KIRKBY-ON-BAIN (St Mary) *see* Bain Valley Gp *Linc*

KIRKBY OVERBLOW (All Saints) *see* Lower Wharfedale *Ripon*

KIRKBY RAVENSWORTH (St Peter and St Felix) *see* Gilling and Kirkby Ravensworth *Ripon*

KIRKBY STEPHEN (not known) w Mallerstang and Crosby Garrett w Soulby *Carl 1* **P** *Bp, Earl of Lonsdale, and Lord Hothfield (jt)* **NSM** J WRIGHT

KIRKBY THORE (St Michael) w Temple Sowerby and Newbiggin *Carl 1* **P** *Lord Hothfield (3 turns), Major and Mrs Sawrey-Cookson (1 turn)* **P-in-c** S A LUNN

KIRKBY UNDERWOOD (St Mary and All Saints) *see* Ringstone in Aveland Gp *Linc*

KIRKBY WHARFE (St John the Baptist) *see* Kirk Fenton w Kirkby Wharfe and Ulleskelfe *York*

KIRKBY WOODHOUSE (St John the Evangelist) *S'well 4* **P** *Bp* **P-in-c** M R ESSEX

KIRKBYMOORSIDE (All Saints) w Gillamoor, Farndale and Bransdale *York 19* **P** *Lady Clarissa Collin* **V** *vacant* (01751) 431452

KIRKDALE (St Athanaseus with St Mary) *Liv 3* **P** *Simeon's Trustees* **V** *vacant* 0151-933 6860

KIRKDALE (St Gregory) w Harome, Nunnington and Pockley *York 19* **P** *Abp, Adn Cleveland, and Lady Clarissa Collin (2 turns), Ox Univ (1 turn)* **P-in-c** A C DE SMET

KIRKDALE (St Lawrence) *Liv 3* **P** *CPAS* **V** M GRIFFIN, **OLM** J D GARNER

KIRKDALE (St Paul) *see* Bootle *Liv*

KIRKHAM (St Michael) *Blackb 10* **P** *Ch Ch Ox* **V** R W BUNDAY, **NSM** K THORN

KIRKHAUGH (Holy Paraclete) *see* Alston Moor *Newc*

KIRKHEATON (St Bartholomew) *see* Kirkwhelpington, Kirkharle, Kirkheaton and Cambo *Newc*

KIRKHEATON (St John the Baptist) *Wakef 1* **P** *Ch Trust Fund Trust* **R** R J STEEL, **C** J C WHITNEY

KIRKHOLT (St Thomas) *Man 17* **P** *Bp* **P-in-c** S D MORGAN

KIRKLAND (Mission Church) *see* Lamplugh w Ennerdale *Carl*

KIRKLAND (St Lawrence) *see* Cross Fell Gp *Carl*

KIRKLEATHAM (St Cuthbert) (St Hilda) *York 16* **P** *Abp* **V** M JACKSON

KIRKLEES VALLEY *Man 8* **P** *R Bury St Mary* **V** S D J COOK, **Hon C** P J BEDDINGTON

KIRKLEVINGTON (St Martin) w Picton, and High and Low Worsall *York 20* **P** *Abp (3 turns), V Northallerton w Kirby Sigston (1 turn)* **V** P J SANDERS, **Hon C** A J HUTCHINSON

KIRKLEY (St Peter and St John) *Nor 9* **P** *Bp and DBP (jt)* **R** A P WHITE

KIRKLINGTON (St Michael) w Burneston and Wath and Pickhill *Ripon 4* **P** *Ch Soc Trust, Mrs M St B Anderson, G W Prior-Wandesforde Esq, and DBP (jt)* **P-in-c** R E HIND, **C** L M SOUTHERN

KIRKLINGTON (St Swithin) w Hockerton *S'well 15* **P** *Bp* **P-in-c** R D SEYMOUR-WHITELEY

KIRKLINTON (St Cuthbert) *see* Bewcastle, Stapleton and Kirklinton etc *Carl*

KIRKNEWTON (St Gregory) *see* Glendale Gp *Newc*

KIRKOSWALD (St Oswald), Renwick, Great Salkeld and Lazonby *Carl 4* **P** *Bp* **R** D M FOWLER

KIRKSTALL (St Stephen) *see* Abbeylands *Ripon*

KIRKSTEAD (St Leonard) *see* Woodhall Spa Gp *Linc*

KIRKTHORPE (St Peter) *see* Warmfield *Wakef*

KIRKWHELPINGTON (St Bartholomew) w Kirkharle and Kirkheaton, and Cambo *Newc 11* **P** *Ld Chan (2 turns), J P P Anderson Esq (1 turn), and Bp (1 turn)* **P-in-c** D WINTER, **OLM** F H DOWER

KIRMINGTON (St Helen) *see* Brocklesby Park *Linc*

KIRMOND-LE-MIRE (St Martin) *see* Walesby *Linc*

KIRSTEAD (St Margaret) *see* Brooke, Kirstead, Mundham w Seething and Thwaite *Nor*

KIRTLING (All Saints) *Ely 4* **P** *Mrs D A Bowlby and Countess Ellesmere (alt)* **P-in-c** M A GURNER

KIRTLINGTON (St Mary the Virgin) *see* Akeman *Ox*

KIRTON (Holy Trinity) *S'well 3* **P** *SMF* **R** C C LEVY

KIRTON (St Mary and St Martin) *see* Nacton and Levington w Bucklesham etc *St E*

KIRTON HOLME (Christ Church) *see* Brothertoft Gp *Linc*

KIRTON IN HOLLAND (St Peter and St Paul) *Linc 20* **P** *Mercers' Co* **P-in-c** G MORGAN

KIRTON IN LINDSEY (St Andrew) w Manton *Linc 6* **P** *Bp* **OLM** J WILSON

KISLINGBURY (St Luke) *see* Bugbrooke, Harpole, Kislingbury etc *Pet*

KITT GREEN (St Francis of Assisi) *see* Pemberton St Fran Kitt Green *Liv*

KITTISFORD (St Nicholas) *see* Wellington and Distr *B & W*
KLIVE (Blessed Virgin Mary) *see* Quantock Coast *B & W*
KNAITH (St Mary) *see* Lea Gp *Linc*
KNAPHILL (Holy Trinity) w Brookwood *Guildf 12* **P** *CPAS*
V N D GREW, **OLM** J LEVETT
KNAPTON (St Peter) *see* Trunch *Nor*
KNAPWELL (All Saints) *see* Papworth *Ely*
KNARESBOROUGH (Holy Trinity) (St John the Baptist)
Ripon 1 **P** *Bp and Earl of Harewood (jt)* **TR** E J SEWELL,
TV E R FOSS, **C** D C HALL, **NSM** J R BULLAMORE, S J REILLY
KNARESDALE (St Jude) *see* Alston Moor *Newc*
**KNEBWORTH (St Martin) (St Mary the Virgin and St Thomas
of Canterbury)** *St Alb 20* **P** *Hon D A Fromanteel* **R** J T PYE
KNEESALL w Laxton and Wellow *S'well 3* **P** *DBP and Bp (jt)*
P-in-c C C LEVY
KNEETON (St Helen) *see* E Bridgford and Kneeton *S'well*
KNIGHTLEY (Christ Church) *see* Adbaston, High Offley,
Knightley, Norbury etc *Lich*
KNIGHTLEY PARISHES *see* Badby w Newham and
Charwelton w Fawsley etc *Pet*
KNIGHTON (St Mary Magdalene) (St Guthlac) *Leic 1* **P** *Bp*
C C A M THOMAS, **NSM** R J BONNEY
KNIGHTON (Village Hall) *see* Ashley and Mucklestone and
Broughton and Croxton *Lich*
KNIGHTON, WEST (St Peter) *see* Watercombe *Sarum*
KNIGHTON-ON-TEME (St Michael and All Angels)
see Teme Valley N *Worc*
KNIGHTS AND HOSPITALLERS PARISHES, The
Chelmsf 19 **P** *Hosp of St Jo of Jerusalem, Bp, and Earl of
Verulam (jt)* **V** *vacant* (01787) 463106
**KNIGHT'S ENHAM (St Michael and All Angels) (St Paul's
Church Centre) and Smannell w Enham Alamein** *Win 3*
P *Patr Bd* **TR** A W H ASHDOWN, **TV** T G WHARTON,
C E P A DINES, **NSM** M RITTMAN
KNIGHTSBRIDGE (St Paul) Wilton Place *see* Wilton Place
St Paul *Lon*
KNILL (St Michael and All Angels) *see* Presteigne w Discoed,
Kinsham, Lingen and Knill *Heref*
KNIPTON (All Saints) *see* High Framland Par *Leic*
KNIVETON (St Michael and All Angels) *see* Hulland, Atlow,
Kniveton, Bradley and Hognaston *Derby*
KNOCKHOLT (St Katharine) w Halstead *Roch 9* **P** *D&C*
R J P BENSON, **NSM** H V THOMAS
KNOCKIN (St Mary) *see* Kinnerley w Melverley and Knockin
w Maesbrook *Lich*
KNODISHALL (St Lawrence) *see* Whinlands *St E*
KNOOK (St Margaret) *see* Upper Wylye Valley *Sarum*
KNOSSINGTON (St Peter) *see* Whatborough Gp *Leic*
KNOTTINGLEY (St Botolph) and Kellington w Whitley
Wakef 10 **P** *Patr Bd* **TR** C A FLATTERS, **NSM** M J MARSH
KNOTTY ASH (St John) *Liv 2* **P** *R W Derby* **V** E R DORAN
KNOWBURY (St Paul) *see* Ludlow *Heref*
KNOWL HILL (St Peter) *see* Wargrave w Knowl Hill *Ox*
KNOWLE (Holy Nativity) *Bris 1* **P** *Bp* **V** *vacant* 0117-977
4260
KNOWLE (St Barnabas) *see* Filwood Park *Bris*
KNOWLE (St Boniface) *see* Crediton, Shobrooke and Sandford
etc *Ex*
KNOWLE (St John) *see* E Budleigh w Bicton and Otterton *Ex*
KNOWLE (St John the Baptist) (St Lawrence and St Anne)
Birm 11 **P** *Bp* **V** M J PARKER, **C** R J TRETHEWEY,
D M EDGERTON, **NSM** S C ASHTON
KNOWLE (St Martin) *Bris 1* **P** *Bp* **P-in-c** S A HAWKINS
KNOWLE, WEST (Holy Cross) *see* Filwood Park *Bris*
KNOWSLEY (St Mary) *Liv 2* **P** *Earl of Derby* **V** *vacant*
0151-546 4266
KNOWSTONE (St Peter) *see* Bishopsnympton, Rose Ash,
Mariansleigh etc *Ex*
KNOYLE, EAST (St Mary the Virgin) *see* St Bartholomew
Sarum
KNOYLE, WEST (St Mary the Virgin) *see* Mere w W Knoyle
and Maiden Bradley *Sarum*
KNUTSFORD (St Cross) Cross Town *Ches 12* **P** *Mrs J Singer*
V J E SHEPHERD
KNUTSFORD (St John the Baptist) and Toft *Ches 12* **P** *Bp*
(3 turns), Mrs L M Anderson (1 turn) **V** N T ATKINSON,
C D G H YOUNG
KNUTTON (St Mary) *Lich 9* **P** *Sir Beville Stanier Bt and
T H G Howard-Sneyd Esq (alt)* **NSM** L M A TIDESWELL
KNUZDEN (St Oswald) *Blackb 2* **P** *Bp* **V** M A MORRIS
KNYPERSLEY (St John the Evangelist) *see* Biddulph Moor
and Knypersley *Lich*
KYM VALLEY, The *Ely 10* **P** *Patr Bd* **R** S J BOWRING
KYME, NORTH (St Luke) *see* Carr Dyke Gp *Linc*
KYME, SOUTH (St Mary and All Saints) *see* Heckington Gp
Linc

KYNNERSLEY (St Chad) *see* Edgmond w Kynnersley and
Preston Wealdmoors *Lich*
KYRE WYARD (St Mary) *see* Teme Valley S *Worc*
LACEBY (St Margaret) and Ravendale Group, The *Linc 10*
P *D Parkinson Settled Estates, Ridley Hall Cam, and Earl of
Yarborough (jt), Bp, and Ld Chan (by turn)*
P-in-c P M TOMPKINS
LACEY GREEN (Church Hall) *see* Wilmslow *Ches*
LACEY GREEN (St John the Evangelist) *see* Risborough *Ox*
LACH DENNIS (All Saints) *see* Lostock Gralam *Ches*
LACHE (St Mark) cum Saltney *Ches 2* **P** *Bp*
V H E A JOHNSTON, **NSM** W A E STEADMAN
LACKFORD (St Lawrence) *see* Lark Valley *St E*
LACOCK (St Cyriac) *see* Gtr Corsham and Lacock *Bris*
LADBROKE (All Saints) *see* Harbury and Ladbroke *Cov*
LADBROKE GROVE (St Michael and All Angels) *see* Notting
Hill St Mich and Ch Ch *Lon*
LADDINGFORD (St Mary) *see* Yalding w Collier Street *Roch*
LADOCK (St Ladoca) *see* Probus, Ladock and Grampound w
Creed and St Erme *Truro*
LADY BAY (All Hallows) w Holme Pierrepont and Adbolton
S'well 9 **P** *Bp and DBP (jt)* **V** R W BRECKLES
LADYBARN (St Chad) *Man 6* **P** *Bp* **P-in-c** E J DAVIES
LADYBROOK (St Mary the Virgin) *see* Mansfield St Jo w St
Mary *S'well*
LADYWOOD (St John the Evangelist) (St Peter) *Birm 2*
P *Trustees* **V** I HARPER
LAFFORD, SOUTH *Linc 21* **P** *G Heathcote Esq, Bp,
J Wilson Esq, D&C, DBP, N Playne Esq, Sir Bruno Welby Bt,
and Lady Willoughby de Eresby (by turn)*
P-in-c C P ROBERTSON
LAINDON (St Martin of Tours) *see* Basildon St Martin
Chelmsf
LAINDON (St Nicholas) w Dunton *Chelmsf 6* **P** *Bp*
R D RICKETTS, **NSM** H A BRYAN
LAIRA (St Augustine) *see* Plymouth Em, St Paul Efford and
St Aug *Ex*
LAIRA (St Mary the Virgin) *see* Plymouth St Simon and St
Mary *Ex*
LAISTERDYKE St Mary *Bradf 3* **P** *Simeon's Trustees*
P-in-c J L TRENHOLME
LAITHKIRK (not known) *see* Romaldkirk w Laithkirk *Ripon*
LAKE (Good Shepherd) *Portsm 7* **P** *Bp* **P-in-c** J H DAVIES
LAKENHAM (St Alban) *see* Nor Lakenham St Alb and St
Mark *Nor*
LAKENHAM (St John the Baptist and All Saints) *see* Nor
Lakenham St Jo and All SS and Tuckswood *Nor*
LAKENHAM (St Mark) *see* Nor Lakenham St Alb and St
Mark *Nor*
LAKENHEATH (St Mary) *see* Brandon and Santon
Downham w Elveden etc *St E*
LALEHAM (All Saints) *Lon 13* **P** *Earl of Lucan*
V A SAVILLE, **C** A J BOWDEN, **NSM** I C SMAILES
LAMARSH (Holy Innocents) *see* N Hinckford *Chelmsf*
LAMBERHURST (St Mary) and Matfield *Roch 8* **P** *D&C and
V Brenchley (jt)* **P-in-c** A H CARR, **NSM** R J BISHOP
LAMBETH (St Andrew) *see* Waterloo St Jo w St Andr *S'wark*
LAMBETH (St John the Evangelist) *as above*
**LAMBETH, NORTH (St Anselm) (St Mary's Mission)
(St Peter)** *S'wark 11* **P** *The Crown (1 turn), Patr Bd (2 turns)*
TR A R AAGAARD, **TV** A M KENNEDY, **C** D J H LONGE, **Hon
C** R S STANIER, R F VICKERY, **NSM** M A K HILBORN
LAMBETH, SOUTH (St Anne and All Saints) *S'wark 11*
P *Abp and Bp* **OLM** O O OGBEDE
LAMBETH, SOUTH (St Stephen) *S'wark 11* **P** *CPAS*
V W A WILSON
LAMBFOLD Benefice, The *Pet 5* **P** *Bp, Hertf Coll Ox, Sons of
Clergy Corp, and S R de C Grant-Rennick Esq (alt)*
NSM C J M OLEY
LAMBLEY (Holy Trinity) *S'well 10* **P** *Revd W J Gull*
R *vacant* 0115-931 3531 *or* (01636) 814331
LAMBLEY (St Mary and St Patrick) *see* Alston Moor *Newc*
LAMBOURN (St Michael and All Angels) *Ox 14* **P** *Bp*
P-in-c A W CUMBERLIDGE
**LAMBOURNE (St Mary and All Saints) w Abridge and
Stapleford Abbotts** *Chelmsf 24* **P** *CCC Cam and
Ld Chan (alt)* **R** *vacant* (01992) 813424
LAMBROOK, EAST (St James) *see* Kingsbury Episcopi w
E Lambrook, Hambridge etc *B & W*
LAMERTON (St Peter) *see* Milton Abbot, Dunterton,
Lamerton etc *Ex*
LAMESLEY (St Andrew) *see* Harlow Green and Lamesley *Dur*
LAMMAS (St Andrew) *see* Bure Valley *Nor*
LAMORBEY (Holy Redeemer) *Roch 17* **P** *Bp* **V** *vacant* (020)
8300 1508

LAMORBEY (Holy Trinity) *Roch 17* **P** *Mrs H K L Whittow*
  V G W DAVIES
LAMORRAN (St Moran) *see* Tresillian and Lamorran w
  Merther *Truro*
LAMP *Ox 27* **P** *CPAS* **R** R A CADDELL,
  OLM H J LOWNDES
LAMPLUGH (St Michael) w Ennerdale *Carl 5* **P** *Trustees*
  NSM J H MARSHALL
LAMPORT (All Saints) *see* Maidwell w Draughton, Lamport w
  Faxton *Pet*
LAMYATT (St Mary and St John) *see* Bruton and Distr *B & W*
LANCASTER (Christ Church) (Christ Church Worship Centre)
  Blackb 11 **P** *V Lanc and Trustees (alt)* **V** P S HUDD,
  NSM B K HARDING
LANCASTER (St Chad) *see* Skerton St Chad *Blackb*
LANCASTER (St Luke) *see* Skerton St Luke *Blackb*
LANCASTER (St Mary) w St John and St Anne *Blackb 11*
  P *Trustees* **V** C W NEWLANDS, **C** J LOVE,
  NSM S MCMAHON
LANCASTER (St Paul) *see* Scotforth *Blackb*
LANCASTER (St Thomas) *Blackb 11* **P** *CPAS*
  P-in-c J L SCAMMAN, **C** V M L MUTHALALY
LANCHESTER (All Saints) *Dur 4* **P** *Ld Chan* **V** *vacant*
  (01207) 521170
LANCING (St James the Less) w Coombes *Chich 5* **P** *Bp Lon*
  R R G RUSSELL
LANCING (St Michael and All Angels) *Chich 5* **P** *Bp*
  V B G CARTER
LANDBEACH (All Saints) *Ely 6* **P** *CCC Cam*
  P-in-c L E CLELAND, **NSM** D M BAGULEY
LANDCROSS (Holy Trinity) *see* Bideford, Northam, Westward
  Ho!, Appledore etc *Ex*
LANDEWEDNACK (St Wynwallow) *see* St Ruan w St Grade
  and Landewednack *Truro*
LANDFORD (St Andrew) *see* Forest and Avon *Sarum*
LANDKEY (St Paul) *see* Swimbridge w W Buckland and
  Landkey *Ex*
LANDRAKE (St Michael) w St Erney and Botus Fleming
  Truro 11 **P** *Bp and MMCET (jt)* **V** M GRIFFITHS,
  OLM P C WILLIAMS
LANDSCOVE (St Matthew) *see* Broadhempston, Woodland,
  Staverton etc *Ex*
LANDULPH (St Leonard and St Dilpe) *see* St Dominic,
  Landulph and St Mellion w Pillaton *Truro*
LANDYWOOD (St Andrew) *see* Gt Wyrley *Lich*
LANE END (Holy Trinity) w Cadmore End *Ox 29* **P** *Bp*
  V R H JENNINGS
LANEAST (St Sidwell and St Gulvat) *see* Altarnon w Bolventor,
  Laneast and St Clether *Truro*
LANEHAM (St Peter) *see* Retford Area *S'well*
LANERCOST (St Mary Magdalene), Walton, Gilsland and
  Nether Denton *Carl 2* **P** *Bp, Adn, and the Hon*
  P C W Howard (jt) **R** R D ALLON-SMITH
LANESIDE (St Peter) *Blackb 1* **P** *V Haslingden St Jas*
  V S C BROWN, **NSM** D ALLSOP
LANGAR (St Andrew) *see* Cropwell Bishop w Colston Bassett,
  Granby etc *S'well*
LANGCLIFFE (St John the Evangelist) w Stainforth and
  Horton-in-Ribblesdale *Bradf 5* **P** *Bp, Adn Craven,*
  W R G Bell Esq, N Caton Esq, and Churchwardens of
  Horton-in-Ribblesdale (jt) **V** R G WOOD
LANGDALE (Holy Trinity) *see* Loughrigg *Carl*
LANGDALE, LITTLE (Mission Chapel) *as above*
LANGDALE END (St Peter) *see* Upper Derwent *York*
LANGDON, EAST (St Augustine) *see* St Margarets-at-Cliffe w
  Westcliffe etc *Cant*
LANGDON, WEST (St Mary the Virgin) *as above*
LANGDON HILLS (St Mary and All Saints) *Chelmsf 6*
  P *D&C St Paul's* **R** C E HOPKINSON, **C** S R SPENCER
LANGELEI *St Alb 2* **P** *Patr Bd* **TR** D M LAWSON,
  TV L J WILSON, **NSM** K L TURNER
LANGFORD (Blessed Virgin Mary) *see* Churchill and
  Langford *B & W*
LANGFORD (St Andrew) *see* Henlow and Langford *St Alb*
LANGFORD (St Bartholomew) *see* E Trent *S'well*
LANGFORD (St Giles) *see* Heybridge w Langford *Chelmsf*
LANGFORD (St Matthew) *see* Shill Valley and Broadshire *Ox*
LANGFORD, LITTLE (St Nicholas of Mira) *see* Wylye and
  Till Valley *Sarum*
LANGFORD BUDVILLE (St Peter) *see* Wellington and Distr
  B & W
LANGHAM (St George) *see* Stour Vale *Sarum*
LANGHAM (St Mary the Virgin) *see* Badwell and Walsham
  St E
LANGHAM (St Mary the Virgin) w Boxted *Chelmsf 17* **P** *Bp*
  and Duchy of Lanc (alt) **P-in-c** T M BULL

LANGHAM (St Peter and St Paul) *see* Oakham, Ashwell,
  Braunston, Brooke, Egleton etc *Pet*
LANGHAM EPISCOPI (St Andrew and St Mary) *see* Stiffkey
  and Bale *Nor*
LANGHAM PLACE (All Souls) *Lon 4* **P** *The Crown*
  R H PALMER, **C** M J H MEYNELL, M N PRENTICE, R I TICE
LANGHO BILLINGTON (St Leonard) *Blackb 7* **P** *V Blackb*
  V *vacant* (01254) 822246
LANGLEY (All Saints and Martyrs) *Man 14* **P** *Patr Bd*
  V P H MILLER, **C** J CALOW, **OLM** P E JONES
LANGLEY (St Francis) *see* Fawley *Win*
LANGLEY (St John) *see* Oldbury, Langley and Londonderry
  Birm
LANGLEY (St John the Evangelist) *see* Clavering and Langley
  w Arkesden etc *Chelmsf*
LANGLEY (St Mary) *see* Otham w Langley *Cant*
LANGLEY (St Mary the Virgin) *see* Wolverton w Norton
  Lindsey and Langley *Cov*
LANGLEY (St Michael) *see* Loddon, Sisland, Chedgrave,
  Hardley and Langley *Nor*
LANGLEY BURRELL (St Peter) *see* Chippenham St Paul w
  Hardenhuish etc *Bris*
LANGLEY GREEN (St Leonard) *see* Ifield *Chich*
LANGLEY MARISH (St Mary the Virgin) *Ox 23* **P** *Patr Bd*
  TR R J GRAYSON, **TV** C R HARTLEY, B H RUSSELL
LANGLEY MARSH (St Luke's Mission Church)
  see Wiveliscombe and the Hills *B & W*
LANGLEY MILL (St Andrew) *Derby 12* **P** *V Heanor*
  V *vacant* (01773) 712441
LANGLEY PARK (All Saints) *Dur 1* **P** *Prime Min*
  V M J PEERS
LANGLEY PARK (St Peter's Church Hall) *see* Beckenham
  St Barn *Roch*
LANGLEY STREET (Mission Room) *see* Derby St Barn
  Derby
LANGLEYBURY (St Paul) *St Alb 6* **P** *D W A Loyd Esq*
  P-in-c Y R PENTELOW
LANGNEY (St Richard of Chichester) *Chich 16* **P** *Bp*
  V D ASHTON, **NSM** M F WOODWARD
LANGOLD (St Luke) *see* Carlton-in-Lindrick and Langold w
  Oldcotes *S'well*
LANGPORT Area Churches, The *B & W 5* **P** *Patr Bd*
  TR H W ELLIS, **TV** R J TWITTY, **C** J PITMAN,
  NSM J M CUMMINGS
LANGRICK (St Margaret of Scotland) *see* Brothertoft Gp *Linc*
LANGRIDGE (St Mary Magdalene) *see* Bath Weston All SS w
  N Stoke and Langridge *B & W*
LANGRISH (St John the Evangelist) *Portsm 4* **P** *Bp*
  V T E LOUDEN
LANGSTONE (St Nicholas) *see* Havant *Portsm*
LANGTOFT (St Michael) *see* Ness Gp *Linc*
LANGTOFT (St Peter) w Foxholes, Butterwick, Cottam and
  Thwing *York 10* **P** *Abp and Keble Coll Ox (2 turns), Ld Chan*
  (1 turn) **NSM** C A ACONLEY, J A TONKIN
LANGTON (St Andrew) *see* W Buckrose *York*
LANGTON (St Margaret) *see* Woodhall Spa Gp *Linc*
LANGTON (St Peter) *as above*
LANGTON, GREAT (St Wilfrid) *see* Lower Swale *Ripon*
LANGTON, GREAT (The Good Shepherd) *as above*
LANGTON BY PARTNEY (St Peter and St Paul) *see* Partney
  Gp *Linc*
LANGTON-BY-WRAGBY (St Giles) *see* Wragby Gp *Linc*
LANGTON GREEN (All Saints) *Roch 12* **P** *R Speldhurst*
  V M J GENTRY, **NSM** S E FRANCIS
LANGTON HERRING (St Peter) *see* Abbotsbury, Portesham
  and Langton Herring *Sarum*
LANGTON LONG (All Saints) *see* Blandford Forum and
  Langton Long *Sarum*
LANGTON MATRAVERS (St George) *see* Kingston, Langton
  Matravers and Worth Matravers *Sarum*
LANGTON ON SWALE (St Wilfrid) *see* Lower Swale *Ripon*
LANGTREE *Ox 6* **P** *Patr Bd* **TR** K G DAVIES,
  TV L J SMITH, **NSM** A M LINTON, D J F ADDISON, C L ALCOCK
LANGTREE (All Saints) *see* Shebbear, Buckland Filleigh,
  Sheepwash etc *Ex*
LANGWATHBY (St Peter) *see* Cross Fell Gp *Carl*
LANGWITH, UPPER (Holy Cross) *see* E Scarsdale *Derby*
LANGWORTH (St Hugh) *see* Barlings *Linc*
LANHYDROCK (St Hydrock) *see* Bodmin w Lanhydrock and
  Lanivet *Truro*
LANIVET (St Ia) *as above*
LANLIVERY (St Brevita) *Truro 10* **P** *Bp (1 turn), Adn Bodmin*
  (1 turn), and DBP (2 turns) **P-in-c** P J CONWAY,
  C S DENYER
LANNER (Christ Church) *see* Redruth w Lanner and Treleigh
  Truro

LANREATH (St Marnarck), Pelynt and Bradoc *Truro 12*
P *A D G Fortescue Esq, J B Kitson Esq, and
H M Parker Esq (jt)* P-in-c M E GOODLAND, C S DENYER
LANSALLOS (St Ildierna) *Truro 12* P *DBP and
W Gundry-Mills Esq (alt)* P-in-c L A H COURTNEY
LANSDOWN (St Stephen) *see* Charlcombe w Bath St Steph
B & W
LANSDOWNE ROAD (St Mary the Virgin) *see* Tottenham St
Mary *Lon*
LANTEGLOS BY CAMELFORD (St Julitta) w Advent
Truro 10 P *Duchy of Cornwall* P-in-c M J W BENTON-EVANS,
C D A ROBERTS
LANTEGLOS BY FOWEY (St Wyllow) *Truro 12* P *D&C*
P-in-c L A H COURTNEY
LAPAL (St Peter) *see* Halas *Worc*
LAPFORD (St Thomas of Canterbury) *see* N Creedy *Ex*
LAPLEY (All Saints) *see* Watershed *Lich*
LAPWORTH (St Mary the Virgin) *Birm 6* P *Mert Coll Ox*
R P H GERARD
LARCHFIELD (St George) *see* Boyne Hill *Ox*
LARK VALLEY Benefice, The *St E 13* P *R W Gough Esq
(1 turn), Bp (2 turns)* R D P BURRELL
LARKFIELD (Holy Trinity) *Roch 7* P *DBP* V D J WALKER
LARLING (St Ethelbert) *see* E w W Harling, Bridgham w
Roudham, Larling etc *Nor*
LASBOROUGH (St Mary) *see* Boxwell, Leighterton,
Didmarton, Oldbury etc *Glouc*
LASHAM (St Mary) *see* Bentworth, Lasham, Medstead and
Shalden *Win*
LASHBROOK (Mission Room) *see* Shiplake w Dunsden and
Harpsden *Ox*
LASTINGHAM (St Mary) w Appleton-le-Moors, Rosedale and
Cropton *York 19* P *Abp (2 turns), Ld Chan (1 turn)*
V A S FERGUSON
LATCHFORD (Christ Church) *Ches 4* P *R Grappenhall*
V J L GOODE
LATCHFORD (St James) (St Hilda) *Ches 4* P *R Grappenhall*
V J T MCNAUGHTAN-OWEN, C J E HARRIES
LATCHINGDON (Christ Church) *see* Althorne and
Latchingdon w N Fambridge *Chelmsf*
LATHBURY (All Saints) *see* Newport Pagnell w Lathbury and
Moulsoe *Ox*
LATHOM PARK (St John) *see* Ormskirk *Liv*
LATIMER (St Mary Magdalene) *see* Chenies and Lt Chalfont,
Latimer and Flaunden *Ox*
LATTON (St John the Baptist) *see* Cricklade w Latton *Bris*
LAUGHTON (All Saints) *see* Corringham and Blyton Gp *Linc*
LAUGHTON (All Saints) w Ripe and Chalvington *Chich 18*
P *Bp (2 turns), Hertf Coll Ox (1 turn)* R *vacant* (01323)
811642
LAUGHTON (St Luke) *see* Foxton w Gumley and Laughton
Leic
LAUGHTON-EN-LE-MORTHEN (All Saints)
see Dinnington w Laughton and Throapham *Sheff*
LAUNCELLS (St Andrew and St Swithin) *see* Stratton and
Launcells *Truro*
LAUNCESTON (St Mary Magdalene) (St Thomas the Apostle)
(St Stephen) *Truro 9* P *Patr Bd* P-in-c D A E MICHAELS,
NSM M C WILLIAMSON
LAUNTON (Assumption of the Blessed Virgin Mary)
see Bicester w Bucknell, Caversfield and Launton *Ox*
LAVANT (St Mary) (St Nicholas) *Chich 3* P *Earl of March and
Kinrara* R D L PARKER
LAVENDER HILL (The Ascension) and Battersea St Philip w
St Bartholomew *S'wark 14* P *Bp and Keble Coll Ox (jt)*
P-in-c I C YOUNG
LAVENDON (St Michael) w Cold Brayfield, Clifton Reynes and
Newton Blossomville *Ox 27* P *T V Suthery Esq, The Revd
S F Hamill-Stewart, Exors M E Farrer Esq, and Bp (jt)*
R C E PUMFREY
LAVENHAM (St Peter and St Paul) w Preston *St E 10*
P *G&C Coll Cam, and Em Coll Cam (by turn)*
P-in-c S G F EARL
LAVENHAM (St Peter and St Paul) *see* Lavenham w Preston
St E
LAVER, HIGH (All Saints) w Magdalen Laver and Little Laver
and Matching *Chelmsf 26* P *Bp* P-in-c G A ANDERSON
LAVER, LITTLE (St Mary the Virgin) *see* High Laver w
Magdalen Laver and Lt Laver etc *Chelmsf*
LAVERSTOCK (St Andrew) *see* Salisbury St Martin and
Laverstock *Sarum*
LAVERSTOKE (St Mary) *see* Overton w Laverstoke and
Freefolk *Win*
LAVERTON (Blessed Virgin Mary) *see* Hardington Vale *B & W*
LAVINGTONS, Cheverells, and Easterton, The *Sarum 16* P *Bp
and Ch Ch Ox (jt)* R J M CAMPBELL, OLM A L COCKING

LAWFORD (St Mary) *Chelmsf 20* P *St Jo Coll Cam*
P-in-c S A HERON, NSM P W MANN
LAWHITTON (St Michael) *see* Three Rivers *Truro*
LAWLEY (St John the Evangelist) *see* Cen Telford *Lich*
LAWRENCE WESTON (St Peter) and Avonmouth *Bris 2* P *Bp*
P-in-c J A LOW
LAWRES Group, The SOUTH *Linc 3* P *D&C Linc, D&C Pet,
and Mercers' Co (jt)* P-in-c D P GREEN,
OLM S K BRADLEY, C BASON
LAWSHALL (All Saints) *see* St Edm Way *St E*
LAWTON (All Saints) *see* Church Lawton *Ches*
LAWTON MOOR (St Michael and All Angels) *Man 6* P *Bp*
P-in-c K L JUSTICE, OLM I V SMITH
LAXEY (Christ Church) *S & M 2* P *Bp* V J DUDLEY,
OLM J E GUILFORD
LAXFIELD (All Saints), Cratfield, Wilby and Brundish *St E 17*
P *Patr Bd* R F O NEWTON, NSM R T ORAMS
LAXTON (All Saints) *see* King's Cliffe, Bulwick and
Blatherwycke etc *Pet*
LAXTON (St Michael) *see* Kneesall w Laxton and Wellow
S'well
LAXTON (St Peter) *see* Howden *York*
LAYER BRETON (St Mary the Virgin) *see* Layer de la Haye
and Layer Breton w Birch etc *Chelmsf*
LAYER DE LA HAYE (St John the Baptist) and Layer Breton w
Birch and Layer Marney *Chelmsf 23* P *Bp, Col J G Round, and
N S Charrington Esq (by turn)* R M H CLARKE,
OLM J R RUSSELL GRANT
LAYER MARNEY (St Mary the Virgin) *see* Layer de la Haye
and Layer Breton w Birch etc *Chelmsf*
LAYHAM (St Andrew) *see* Hadleigh, Layham and Shelley *St E*
LAYSTON *see* Aspenden, Buntingford and Westmill *St Alb*
LAYTON (St Mark) *see* Blackpool St Mark *Blackb*
LAYTON, EAST (Christ Church) *see* Forcett and Aldbrough
and Melsonby *Ripon*
LAZONBY (St Nicholas) *see* Kirkoswald, Renwick, Gt Salkeld
and Lazonby *Carl*
LEA Group, The (St Helen) *Linc 2* P *Bp, DBP, and Exors Lt Col
J E W G Sandars (jt)* R P WAIN, NSM L Y LUCAS
LEA (St Christopher) (St Barnabas) *Blackb 13* P *Bp*
P-in-c F NAYLOR, NSM W I WALTERS
LEA (St Giles) *see* Garsdon, Lea and Cleverton and Charlton
Bris
LEA, THE (St John the Baptist) *see* Ariconium *Heref*
LEA AND HOLLOWAY (Christ Church) *see* Dethick, Lea and
Holloway *Derby*
LEA CROSS (St Anne) *see* Pontesbury I and II *Heref*
LEA HALL (St Richard) *Birm 9* P *Bp* V P M BRACHER,
NSM M S WALTON
LEA MARSTON (St John the Baptist) *see* The Whitacres, Lea
Marston, and Shustoke *Birm*
LEADEN RODING (St Michael) *see* S Rodings *Chelmsf*
LEADENHAM (St Swithin) *Linc 22* P *P R Reeve Esq*
R A J MEGAHEY
LEADGATE (St Ives) *see* Dipton and Leadgate *Dur*
LEAFIELD (St Michael and All Angels) *see* Forest Edge *Ox*
LEAGRAVE (St Luke) *St Alb 12* P *Bp* V S PURVIS,
C A E A BICKLEY, NSM L A JONES
LEAHOLM (St James's Chapel) *see* Middle Esk Moor *York*
LEAKE (St Mary) w Over and Nether Silton and Kepwick
York 18 P *Abp* V I D HOUGHTON, NSM T A LEWIS
LEAKE, EAST (St Mary), WEST (St Helena),
Stanford-on-Soar, Rempstone and Costock *S'well 9* P *Bp,
DBP, Lord Belper, and SS Coll Cam (jt)*
R G C HETHERINGTON
LEAKE, NEW (St Jude) *see* Stickney Gp *Linc*
LEAKE, OLD (St Mary) w Wrangle *Linc 20* P *Bp and DBP
(alt)* P-in-c F J M COTTON-BETTERIDGE, C N J BATES
LEAM LANE (St Andrew) *Dur 12* P *Bp* V A RAINE
LEAM VALLEY *Cov 6* P *Bp (2 turns), Mrs H M O Lodder
(1 turn)* P-in-c J CLOSE
LEAMINGTON, SOUTH (St John the Baptist) *Cov 11* P *Bp*
V D W LAWSON
LEAMINGTON HASTINGS (All Saints) *see* Leam Valley *Cov*
LEAMINGTON PRIORS (All Saints) *Cov 11* P *Bp*
P-in-c C H WILSON, NSM A MORRIS
LEAMINGTON PRIORS (St Mary) *Cov 11* P *Ch Patr Trust*
V *vacant* (01926) 425927
LEAMINGTON PRIORS (St Paul) *Cov 11* P *Ch Patr Trust*
V J N JEE, C S P WILLETTS, E L WOOLF
LEAMINGTON SPA (Holy Trinity) *Cov 11* P *Bp and
M Heber-Percy Esq (jt)* C C GALE, C H WILSON, G R COLES,
NSM F A SMITH, A MORRIS
LEAMINGTON SPA (St Mark) New Milverton *see* New
Milverton *Cov*

LEAMORE (St Aidan)   *see* Blakenall Heath *Lich*
LEASINGHAM (St Andrew) *Linc 21*   P *DBP*
P-in-c C PENNOCK
LEASOWE (St Chad) *Ches 7*   P *Bp*   P-in-c A P WATTS
LEATHERHEAD (All Saints) (St Mary and St Nicholas) and
Mickleham *Guildf 10*   P *Bp Guildf and D&C Roch (jt)*
R G D OSBORNE,   C K SATKUNANAYAGAM,
NSM D A IRELAND, C M STEWART
LEATHLEY (St Oswald)   *see* Washburn and Mid-Wharfe *Bradf*
LEATON (Holy Trinity) and Albrighton w Battlefield *Lich 20*
P *Mrs J M Jagger*   P-in-c C H DEAKIN,   Hon C R M PARSONS
LEAVELAND (St Laurence)   *see* Selling w Throwley, Sheldwich
w Badlesmere etc *Cant*
LEAVENHEATH (St Matthew)   *see* Stoke by Nayland w
Leavenheath and Polstead *St E*
LEAVENING (not known)   *see* W Buckrose *York*
LEAVESDEN (All Saints) *St Alb 6*   P *Bp*   P-in-c C M DAVEY,
C M M DU SAIRE,   NSM M W BROWN
LECHLADE (St Lawrence)   *see* Fairford Deanery *Glouc*
LECK (St Peter)   *see* E Lonsdale *Blackb*
LECKFORD (St Nicholas)   *see* Stockbridge and Longstock and
Leckford *Win*
LECKHAMPSTEAD (Assumption of the Blessed Virgin Mary)
see N Buckingham *Ox*
LECKHAMPSTEAD (St James)   *see* W Downland *Ox*
LECKHAMPTON (St Christopher)   *see* S Cheltenham *Glouc*
LECKHAMPTON (St Peter)   *as above*
LECKHAMPTON (St Philip and St James)   *as above*
LECONFIELD (St Catherine)   *see* Lockington and Lund and
Scorborough w Leconfield *York*
LEDBURY Team Ministry, The (St Michael and All Angels)
(St Katherine's Chapel *Heref 5*   P *Patr Bd*
TR P DUNTHORNE,   TV H J MAYELL, S STRUTT,   C F M ILIFFE,
NSM E C REED, E N SEABRIGHT, J G WATKINS,
OLM J L SCHOLEFIELD
LEDGEMOOR (Mission Room)   *see* Canon Pyon w King's
Pyon, Birley and Wellington *Heref*
LEDSHAM (All Saints) w Fairburn *York 4*   P *Lady Elizabeth
Hastings Estate Charity*   P-in-c A D ROBINSON
LEDSTON LUCK (Mission Church)   *see* Ledsham w Fairburn
York
LEE (Good Shepherd) (St Peter) *S'wark 4*   P *R Lee St Marg*
V R D BAINBRIDGE,   C A J CLARKE,   NSM B M KINGSTON
LEE (St Augustine) Grove Park *S'wark 4*   P *Bp*
V G A BERRIMAN
LEE (St Margaret) *S'wark 4*   P *Ld Chan*   R A RACE,
NSM J K BURKITT-GRAY
LEE (St Matthew)   *see* Ilfracombe, Lee, Woolacombe, Bittadon
etc *Ex*
LEE (St Mildred) Burnt Ash Hill *S'wark 4*   P *Bp*
V R J SHIMWELL,   NSM M BARBER
LEE (St Oswald)   *see* St Oswald in Lee w Bingfield *Newc*
LEE, THE (St John the Baptist) *Ox 28*   P *Bp*   V D J BURGESS
LEE BROCKHURST (St Peter) *Lich 22*   P *Lord Barnard*
P-in-c C S COOKE,   NSM T D SMITH
LEE MOOR (Mission Church)   *see* Bickleigh and Shaugh Prior
Ex
LEE-ON-THE-SOLENT (St Faith) *Portsm 3*   P *Bp*
V P A SUTTON,   C S A THREADGILL,   NSM B T WILLIAMS
LEEBOTWOOD (St Mary)   *see* Dorrington w Leebotwood,
Longnor, Stapleton etc *Heref*
LEEDS (All Hallows) *Ripon 7*   P *Bp and DBP (jt)*   V S SMITH,
Hon C D H RANDOLPH-HORN
LEEDS (All Saints) w Osmondthorpe *Ripon 8*   P *Bp*
P-in-c K L MARSHALL
LEEDS (All Souls) *Ripon 7*   P *V Leeds St Pet, Simeon's
Trustees, and DBP (jt)*   P-in-c A I G SNOWDEN
LEEDS Belle Isle (St John and St Barnabas) *Ripon 6*   P *Bp*
NSM D T HAYES
LEEDS (Emmanuel)   *see* Leeds St Geo *Ripon*
LEEDS Gipton (Church of the Epiphany) *Ripon 5*   P *Bp*
P-in-c P J PAYTON
LEEDS Halton (St Wilfrid) *Ripon 8*   P *Bp*   P-in-c D R MOORE
LEEDS (Parish Church)   *see* Leeds City *Ripon*
LEEDS Richmond Hill (St Saviour) *Ripon 5*   P *Bp and Keble
Coll Ox (jt)*   V A L TAYLOR
LEEDS (St Aidan) *Ripon 5*   P *V Leeds St Pet*   V A L TAYLOR,
NSM C T RAWLINS, D ZANKER
LEEDS (St Cyprian and St James) Harehills *Ripon 5*   P *Bp*
P-in-c A S KASIBANTE
LEEDS (St Edmund King and Martyr)   *see* Roundhay St Edm
Ripon
LEEDS (St George) *Ripon 7*   P *Simeon's Trustees*
TR J J CLARK,   TV J R PEARSON, M T POWLEY,   C J SWALES
LEEDS (St John the Evangelist)   *see* Roundhay St Jo *Ripon*

LEEDS (St Nicholas)   *see* Hollingbourne and Hucking w Leeds
and Broomfield *Cant*
LEEDS (St Paul)   *see* Ireland Wood *Ripon*
LEEDS (St Wilfrid) *Ripon 5*   P *Bp*   V J HILTON,
NSM T J BUCKINGHAM
LEEDS CITY (St Peter) (Holy Trinity) *Ripon 5*   P *DBP*
TR A F BUNDOCK,   TV S M WALLACE,   C D S FORD,
NSM S J ROBINSON
LEEDSTOWN (St James's Mission Church)   *see* Crowan and
Treslothan *Truro*
LEEK (All Saints) (St Edward the Confessor) (St John the
Evangelist) (St Luke) (St Paul) and Meerbrook *Lich 8*
P *Patr Bd*   TR M J PARKER,   TV C R PETERS, R A WOODS
LEEK WOOTTON (All Saints) *Cov 4*   P *Lord Leigh*   V *vacant*
(01926) 854832
LEEMING (St John the Baptist)   *see* Bedale and Leeming and
Thornton Watlass *Ripon*
LEEMING BAR (St Augustine)   *as above*
LEES HILL (Mission Hall)   *see* Lanercost, Walton, Gilsland and
Nether Denton *Carl*
LEESFIELD Knoll's Lane (St Agnes)   *see* Leesfield *Man*
LEESFIELD (St Thomas) *Man 15*   P *Bp*   OLM R FARRAR
LEFTWICH (Farm of the Good Shepherd)   *see* Davenham *Ches*
LEGBOURNE (All Saints) and Wold Marsh *Linc 12*
P *Ld Chan (1 turn), Bp, Viscountess Chaplin, Ch Trust Fund
Trust, D&C, and DBP (1 turn), Duchy of Lanc (1 turn)*
C L E TURNER
LEGBURTHWAITE (Mission Church)   *see* St
John's-in-the-Vale, Threlkeld and Wythburn *Carl*
LEGH, HIGH *Ches 12*   P *R H Cornwall-Legh Esq*
V J S CROFT
LEGSBY (St Thomas) *Linc 5*   P *Bp*   V M J CARTWRIGHT
LEICESTER (All Saints)   *see* Scraptoft *Leic*
LEICESTER (Church of the Nativity)   *see* Emmaus Par Team
Leic
LEICESTER Cornerstone   *see* Leic St Leon CD *Leic*
LEICESTER (Holy Apostles) (St Oswald) *Leic 1*   P *DBP and
Ridley Hall Cam (jt)*   P-in-c P R BERRY,   NSM T R DAY
LEICESTER (Holy Spirit) (St Andrew) (St Nicholas) *Leic 1*
P *Bp*   P-in-c J B NAYLOR
LEICESTER (Holy Trinity w St John the Divine) *Leic 1*
P *Peache Trustees*   V J C MCGINLEY,   C P C WHITE,
NSM E A SUTHERLAND
LEICESTER (Martyrs) *Leic 1*   P *Bp*   V R V WORSFOLD,
C M R CASTLE
LEICESTER Presentation of Christ (St Barnabas) (St Peter)
Leic 1   P *Bp*   P-in-c A J FULLER,   NSM B DAVIES
LEICESTER Resurrection (St Alban) *Leic 1*   P *Bp*
TR A A COSLETT,   TV S P J BURNHAM
LEICESTER (St Aidan) *Leic 1*   P *Bp*   V S LUMBY
LEICESTER (St Alban)   *see* Leic Resurr *Leic*
LEICESTER (St Anne) St Paul and St Augustine *Leic 1*   P *Bp*
V C R OXLEY,   NSM P J OXLEY, C A LACEY
LEICESTER (St Barnabas) Conventional District *Leic 1*
Min D H P BROWN
LEICESTER (St Chad) *Leic 1*   P *Bp*   P-in-c M J COURT,
C C M KING
LEICESTER St Christopher *Leic 1*   P *MMCET*
V A M ROCHE,   C R J LING
LEICESTER (St James the Greater) *Leic 1*   P *Bp*
V G RICHERBY,   NSM J M SHARP
LEICESTER (St John the Baptist)   *see* Emmaus Par Team *Leic*
LEICESTER St Leonard Conventional District *Leic 1*
P-in-c G W DUNSETH
LEICESTER (St Mary de Castro) *Leic 1*   P *Bp*
NSM S P WARD
LEICESTER (St Philip) *Leic 1*   P *Adn Leic, V Evington, V Leic
H Trin, G A Cooling Esq, and A S Price Esq (jt)*
P-in-c A RACE,   C S H J BROWN
LEICESTER (St Stephen)   *see* N Evington *Leic*
LEICESTER (St Theodore of Canterbury) *Leic 1*   P *Bp*
P-in-c E T SKINNER
LEICESTER, The Abbey (St Margaret and All Saints) *Leic 1*
P *Bp*   P-in-c J B NAYLOR,   NSM F M KNIGHT
LEICESTER FOREST EAST (St Andrew)   *see* Kirby Muxloe
Leic
LEIGH (All Saints)   *see* Ashton Keynes, Leigh and Minety *Bris*
LEIGH (All Saints)   *see* Uttoxeter Area *Lich*
LEIGH (All Saints' Mission)   *see* Bedford Leigh *Man*
LEIGH (Holy Saviour)   *see* White Horse *Sarum*
LEIGH or Wimborne (St John the Evangelist)   *see* New Borough
and Leigh *Sarum*
LEIGH (St Andrew)   *see* Wriggle Valley *Sarum*
LEIGH (St Bartholomew) *S'wark 26*   P *N J Charrington Esq*
P-in-c J M A WILLANS,   NSM F G LEHANEY

LEIGH (St Catherine) *see* Twigworth, Down Hatherley, Norton, The Leigh etc *Glouc*
LEIGH (St Clement) *Chelmsf 10* **P** *Bp* **R** K R HAVEY, **C** D J COSTER
LEIGH (St Edburga) *see* Worcs W *Worc*
LEIGH (St Mary) *Roch 11* **P** *Ch Trust Fund Trust* **V** L W G KEVIS
LEIGH (St Mary the Virgin) *Man 19* **P** *Bp* **P-in-c** K D CRINKS
LEIGH, LITTLE (St Michael and All Angels) *see* Antrobus, Aston by Sutton, Lt Leigh etc *Ches*
LEIGH, NORTH (St Mary) *Ox 8* **P** *Ld Chan* **V** A J SWEENEY, **C** A J D PRITCHARD, M F KEEN
LEIGH, SOUTH (St James the Great) *see* Cogges and S Leigh *Ox*
LEIGH, WEST (St Alban) *Portsm 5* **P** *Bp* **NSM** G A STEADMAN
LEIGH-ON-SEA (St Aidan) the Fairway *Chelmsf 10* **P** *Bp* **NSM** P FURBY
LEIGH-ON-SEA (St James) *Chelmsf 10* **P** *Bp* **V** W G BULLOCH
LEIGH-ON-SEA (St Margaret of Antioch) *Chelmsf 10* **P** *Bp* **V** I G BOOTH
LEIGH PARK (St Francis) *Portsm 5* **P** *Bp* **V** J G P JEFFERY, **C** S J TANCOCK
LEIGH UPON MENDIP (St Giles) w Stoke St Michael *B & W 3* **P** *DBP and V Doulting (jt)* **V** vacant (01373) 812559
LEIGH WOODS (St Mary the Virgin) *see* Abbots Leigh w Leigh Woods *Bris*
LEIGHLAND (St Giles) *see* Old Cleeve, Leighland and Treborough *B & W*
LEIGHS, GREAT (St Mary the Virgin) and LITTLE (St John) and Little Waltham *Chelmsf 8* **P** *Linc Coll Ox, Reformation Ch Trust, and Ex Coll Ox (jt)* **R** S J HOLMES
LEIGHTERTON (St Andrew) *see* Boxwell, Leighterton, Didmarton, Oldbury etc *Glouc*
LEIGHTON (Holy Trinity) *see* Trelystan *Heref*
LEIGHTON (St Mary) *see* Wrockwardine Deanery *Lich*
LEIGHTON BROMSWOLD (St Mary) *Ely 10* **P** *Bp* **V** vacant
LEIGHTON BUZZARD (All Saints) *see* Ouzel Valley *St Alb*
LEIGHTON-CUM-MINSHULL VERNON (St Peter) *Ches 15* **P** *Bp* **P-in-c** P F DE J GOGGIN
LEIGHTONSTONE, EAST *Ely 10* **P** *Bp (2 turns), Peterho Cam (1 turn)* **R** J P YOUNG
LEINTHALL EARLES (St Andrew) *see* Kingsland w Eardisland, Aymestrey etc *Heref*
LEINTHALL STARKES (St Mary Magdalene) *see* Wigmore Abbey *Heref*
LEINTWARDINE (St Andrew) Adforton *as above*
LEINTWARDINE (St Mary Magdalene) *as above*
LEIRE (St Peter) *see* Upper Soar *Leic*
LEISTON (St Margaret) *St E 19* **P** *Ch Hosp* **P-in-c** M E PERCIVAL, **OLM** R ELLIS
LELANT (St Uny) *see* Carbis Bay w Lelant *Truro*
LEMINGTON, LOWER (St Leonard) *see* Moreton-in-Marsh w Batsford, Todenham etc *Glouc*
LEMSFORD (St John the Evangelist) *see* Bp's Hatfield, Lemsford and N Mymms *St Alb*
LEN VALLEY, The *Cant 13* **P** *Abp, All So Coll Ox, Viscount Chilston, and Lord Cornwallis (jt)* **P-in-c** R F VENN, **OLM** M E HART
LENBOROUGH *Ox 22* **P** *Ch Ch Ox, Cam Univ, and New Coll Ox (2 turns), Ld Chan (1 turn)* **V** R M ROBERTS, **NSM** K M PECK, **OLM** J J SHIELDS
LENHAM (St Mary) *see* Len Valley *Cant*
LENTON (Holy Trinity) (Priory Church of St Anthony) *S'well 14* **P** *CPAS* **M** L KIRKBRIDE
LENTON (St Peter) *see* N Beltisloe Gp *Linc*
LENTON ABBEY (St Barnabas) *S'well 14* **P** *CPAS* **P-in-c** A R HOWE, **C** L P B O'BOYLE, **NSM** J M CORCORAN
LENWADE (All Saints) *see* Wensum Benefice *Nor*
LEOMINSTER (St Peter and St Paul) *Heref 6* **P** *Patr Bd* **TR** M J KNEEN, **TV** C E MUNDELL, S B THOMSON, **NSM** J H THEAKER, E M G BROWN, **OLM** P C REES, P SMITH, C P REES
LEONARD STANLEY (St Swithun) *see* The Stanleys *Glouc*
LEPTON (St John the Evangelist) *Wakef 1* **P** *R Kirkheaton* **P-in-c** A J RAGGETT
LESBURY (St Mary) w Alnmouth *Newc 6* **P** *Dioc Soc* **V** P J SUTCLIFFE
LESNEWTH (St Michael and All Angels) *see* Boscastle w Davidstow *Truro*
LESSINGHAM (All Saints) *see* Bacton, Happisburgh, Hempstead w Eccles etc *Nor*

LETCHWORTH (St Mary the Virgin) (St Michael) *St Alb 3* **P** *Guild of All So* **R** P BENNETT
LETCHWORTH (St Paul) w Willian *St Alb 3* **P** *Bp* **P-in-c** S Q MOORE, **C** P R KAY, M L MOORE, **NSM** M P DACK, A J FERRIS
LETCOMBE BASSETT (St Michael and All Angels) *see* Ridgeway *Ox*
LETCOMBE REGIS (St Andrew) *as above*
LETHERINGHAM (St Mary) *see* Mid Loes *St E*
LETHERINGSETT (St Andrew) *see* Blakeney w Cley, Wiveton, Glandford etc *Nor*
LETTON (St John the Baptist) w Staunton, Byford, Mansel Gamage and Monnington *Heref 4* **P** *Sir John Cotterell Bt (2 turns), Exors Mrs Dew (1 turn), Ch Ch Ox (3 turns), and DBP (1 turn)* **R** R D KING
LETWELL (St Peter) *see* Firbeck w Letwell *Sheff*
LEUSDON (St John the Baptist) *see* Ashburton, Bickington, Buckland in the Moor etc *Ex*
LEVEDALE (Mission Church) *see* Penkridge *Lich*
LEVEN (Holy Trinity) *see* Brandesburton and Leven w Catwick *York*
LEVEN VALLEY *Carl 11* **P** *Mrs C M Chaplin, V Colton, and Bp (jt)* **P-in-c** P N CALVERT
LEVENS (St John the Evangelist) *Carl 10* **P** *Trustees* **P-in-c** R J CROSSLEY, **Hon C** J C HANCOCK
LEVENSHULME (St Andrew) (St Mark) (St Peter) *Man 2* **P** *Bp and Trustees (jt)* **R** L S IRELAND, **C** L A IRELAND, **OLM** F G KERR
LEVER, GREAT (St Michael w St Bartholomew) *see* New Bury w Gt Lever *Man*
LEVER, LITTLE (St Matthew) *Man 7* **P** *V Bolton-le-Moors St Pet* **V** J WISEMAN, **NSM** I C ANTHONY
LEVER BRIDGE (St Stephen and All Martyrs) *see* Leverhulme *Man*
LEVERHULME *Man 12* **P** *Prime Min* **TV** S EDWARDS, **NSM** A PIERCE, **OLM** S P MCGREGOR
LEVERINGTON (St Leonard), Newton and Tydd St Giles *Ely 14* **P** *Bp* **R** S K GARDNER
LEVERSTOCK GREEN (Holy Trinity) *see* Langelei *St Alb*
LEVERTON (St Helena) *see* Freiston, Butterwick w Bennington, and Leverton *Linc*
LEVERTON, NORTH (St Martin) *see* Retford Area *S'well*
LEVERTON, SOUTH (All Saints) *as above*
LEVINGTON (St Peter) *see* Nacton and Levington w Bucklesham etc *St E*
LEVISHAM (St John the Baptist) *see* Pickering w Lockton and Levisham *York*
LEWANNICK (St Martin) *see* Three Rivers *Truro*
LEWES (St Anne) (St Michael) (St Thomas at Cliffe) w All Saints *Chich 18* **P** *Bp and SMF (1 turn), Ld Chan (1 turn)* **R** P R C HAMILTON-MANON, **NSM** P D YATES
LEWES (St John sub Castro) and South Malling *Chich 18* **P** *Bp and MMCET (jt)* **R** A D PICKERING
LEWES (St John the Baptist) *see* Southover *Chich*
LEWES (St Mary) *see* Lewes St Anne and St Mich and St Thos etc *Chich*
LEWISHAM (St Mary) *S'wark 4* **P** *Earl of Dartmouth* **V** P S ANDERSON
LEWISHAM (St Stephen) and St Mark *S'wark 4* **P** *Keble Coll Ox* **V** G KIRK, **Hon C** F D GARDOM, **NSM** P J HUDSON
LEWISHAM (St Swithun) Hither Green *S'wark 4* **P** *V Lewisham St Mary* **P-in-c** J L KUSTNER
LEWKNOR (St Margaret) *see* Thame *Ox*
LEWSEY (St Hugh) *see* Luton Lewsey St Hugh *St Alb*
LEWTRENCHARD (St Peter) *see* Lifton, Broadwoodwidger, Stowford etc *Ex*
LEXDEN (St Leonard) *Chelmsf 16* **P** *Bp* **P-in-c** T A J WYNNE, **NSM** R J ALLEN
LEXHAM, EAST (St Andrew) *see* Litcham w Kempston, E and W Lexham, Mileham etc *Nor*
LEXHAM, WEST (St Nicholas) *as above*
LEYBOURNE (St Peter and St Paul) *Roch 7* **P** *Major Sir David Hawley Bt* **P-in-c** M A J BUCHAN
LEYBURN (St Matthew) w Bellerby *Ripon 4* **P** *Lord Bolton and Mrs M E Scragg (alt)* **P-in-c** C M A HEPPER
LEYFIELDS (St Francis) *see* Tamworth *Lich*
LEYLAND (St Ambrose) *Blackb 5* **P** *V Leyland* **V** D J E CLARKE, **NSM** G E ASHWORTH
LEYLAND (St Andrew) *Blackb 5* **P** *CPAS* **V** D R A GIBB, **C** M L SIMPSON, K W CAMPBELL
LEYLAND (St James) *Blackb 5* **P** *Sir Henry Farington Bt* **P-in-c** I S MOSSLEY, **NSM** M H PENMAN
LEYLAND (St John) *Blackb 5* **P** *V Leyland St Andr and CPAS (jt)* **V** A MCHAFFIE, **NSM** B J WILSON, N J PROCTER
LEYSTERS (St Andrew) *see* Leominster *Heref*

LEYTON (All Saints) *Chelmsf 5*   **P** *V St Mary's Leyton*
V M I HOLMDEN
LEYTON (Christ Church) *Chelmsf 5*   **P** *Ch Trust Fund Trust*
V M E BURKILL,   **C** R J WOOD
LEYTON (Emmanuel) *Chelmsf 5*   **P** *Bp*   **V** A ADEMOLA,
NSM S M FERNANDES
LEYTON (St Catherine) (St Paul) *Chelmsf 5*
P *V Leyton St Mary w St Edw*   **C** P W BOWTELL,
NSM R C ASHLEY
LEYTON (St Mary w St Edward) and St Luke *Chelmsf 5*
P *Simeon's Trustees*   **V** C M RABLEN
LEYTONSTONE (Holy Trinity and St Augustine of Hippo)
Harrow Green *Chelmsf 5*   **P** *Bp*   **P-in-c** D J DALAIS
LEYTONSTONE (St Andrew) *Chelmsf 5*   **P** *Bp*
P-in-c D J DALAIS
LEYTONSTONE (St John the Baptist) *Chelmsf 5*   **P** *Bp*
V R J DRAPER,   **NSM** R A WHITE, K E ROBINSON
LEYTONSTONE (St Margaret w St Columba) *Chelmsf 5*
P *Bp*   **V** *vacant* (020) 8519 0813
LEZANT (St Briochus) *see* Three Rivers *Truro*
LEZAYRE (Holy Trinity) *S & M 3*   **P** *The Crown*
P-in-c B G EVANS-SMITH
LEZAYRE (St Olave) Ramsey *S & M 3*   **P** *The Crown and Bp*
(alt)   **V** *vacant*
LICHBOROUGH (St Martin) *see* Lambfold *Pet*
LICHFIELD (Christ Church) *Lich 1*   **P** *Bp*   **NSM** C J BAKER
LICHFIELD (St Chad) *Lich 1*   **P** *D&C*   **NSM** E A WALL
LICHFIELD (St John's Hospital) Proprietary Chapel *Lich 1*
P *Bp*   **Master** A A GORHAM
LICHFIELD (St Michael) (St Mary) and Wall St John *Lich 1*
P *D&C*   **R** D K BEEDON,   **C** D A DYSON, L K COLLINS,
NSM J ANKETELL, D YOUNGS
LICKEY, THE (Holy Trinity) *Birm 4*   **P** *V Bromsgrove*
V M E BRIGHTON
LIDEN (St Timothy) *see* Swindon Dorcan *Bris*
LIDGET GREEN (St Wilfrid) *see* Bradf St Wilfrid w St
Columba *Bradf*
LIFTON (St Mary), Broadwoodwidger, Stowford, Lewtrenchard,
Thrushelton and Kelly w Bradstone *Ex 25*   **P** *Bp,*
Mrs A M Baring-Gould Almond, W F Kelly Esq, and
J B Wollocombe Esq (jt)   **C** T C CURRY
LIGHTBOWNE (St Luke) *Man 4*   **P** *D&C*   **P-in-c** P A STAMP,
Hon C J G O'CONNOR
LIGHTCLIFFE (St Matthew) and Hove Edge *Wakef 2*   **P** *Bp*
and V Halifax (jt)   **V** K M BUCK
LIGHTHORNE (St Laurence) *Cov 8*   **P** *Lady Willoughby*
de Broke   **C** N S DUNLOP
LIGHTWATER (All Saints) *Guildf 6*   **P** *Ld Chan and Bp (alt)*
OLM R D BROWNING
LILBOURNE (All Saints) *see* Crick and Yelvertoft w Clay
Coton and Lilbourne *Pet*
LILLESHALL (St Michael and All Angels) and Muxton *Lich 16*
P *Bp*   **V** M C JONES,   **C** D A KICHENSIDE,   **OLM** J EVANS
LILLEY (St Peter) *see* King's Walden and Offley w Lilley *St Alb*
LILLINGSTONE DAYRELL (St Nicholas) *see* N Buckingham
Ox
LILLINGSTONE LOVELL (Assumption of the Blessed Virgin
Mary) *as above*
LILLINGTON (St Martin) *see* Sherborne w Castleton,
Lillington and Longburton *Sarum*
LILLINGTON (St Mary Magdalene) and Old Milverton *Cov 11*
P *Bp*   **P-in-c** C GALE,   **C** G R COLES,   **NSM** N J NIXON
LILLIPUT (Holy Angels) *Sarum 7*   **P** *Bp*
P-in-c C M LANGFORD
LIMBER, GREAT (St Peter) *see* Brocklesby Park *Linc*
LIMEHOUSE (St Anne) (St Peter) *Lon 7*   **P** *BNC Ox*
R G L WARREN,   **C** M C C NODDER, A J LATIMER
LIMESIDE (St Chad) *see* Hollinwood and Limeside *Man*
LIMINGTON (The Blessed Virgin Mary) *see* Ilchester w
Northover, Limington, Yeovilton etc *B & W*
LIMPENHOE (St Botolph) *see* Freethorpe, Wickhampton,
Halvergate etc *Nor*
LIMPLEY STOKE (St Mary) *see* Freshford, Limpley Stoke and
Hinton Charterhouse *B & W*
LIMPSFIELD (St Peter) and Tatsfield *S'wark 25*   **P** *Bp*
TR P J BROWN,   **TV** E L ELLIS,   **NSM** G P SOUTH,
A B COOPER
LIMPSFIELD CHART (St Andrew) Conventional District
S'wark 25   **C-in-c** A B COOPER
LINBY (St Michael) w Papplewick *S'well 4*
P *T W A Cundy Esq*   **R** K H TURNER
LINCH (St Luke) *see* Lynch w Iping Marsh and Milland *Chich*
LINCHMERE (St Peter) *see* Lynchmere and Camelsdale *Chich*
LINCOLN (All Saints) *Linc 15*   **P** *Bp*   **P-in-c** D EDGAR,
Hon C R G WILKINSON

LINCOLN Minster Group, The (St Mary Magdalene)
(St Michael on the Mount) (St Peter in Eastgate) *Linc 15*
P *Adn Linc, D&C, and Bp (by turn)*
P-in-c E M C BOWES-SMITH,   **C** N E ALEXANDER
LINCOLN (St Botolph by Bargate) *Linc 15*   **P** *Bp*
P-in-c J S CULLIMORE,   **C** E B JACKSON,   **Hon C** N BURGESS
LINCOLN (St Faith) (St Martin) (St Peter-at-Arches) *Linc 15*
P *Bp*   **P-in-c** A M PAVEY,   **Hon C** N BURGESS
LINCOLN (St George) Swallowbeck *Linc 15*   **P** *Bp and*
V Skellingthorpe (jt)   **V** I G SILK,   **NSM** D L FREEMAN,
OLM S A BROWN
LINCOLN (St Giles) *Linc 15*   **P** *Bp*   **V** M J O'CONNELL
LINCOLN (St John the Baptist) (St John the Evangelist) *Linc 15*
P *Bp*   **V** S A HOY,   **NSM** M J S JACKSON
LINCOLN (St Mary-le-Wigford) (St Benedict) (St Mark)
Linc 15   **P** *Bp*   **P-in-c** J S CULLIMORE,   **C** E B JACKSON,
Hon C N BURGESS
LINCOLN (St Nicholas) (St John) Newport *Linc 15*   **P** *Bp and*
D&C (alt)   **V** D W YABBACOME
LINCOLN (St Peter-at-Gowts) (St Andrew) *Linc 15*   **P** *Bp*
P-in-c J S CULLIMORE,   **C** E B JACKSON,   **Hon C** N BURGESS
LINCOLN (St Swithin) *Linc 15*   **P** *Bp*   **P-in-c** D EDGAR,
Hon C N BURGESS
LINDAL IN MARTON (St Peter) *see* Pennington and Lindal w
Marton and Bardsea *Carl*
LINDALE (St Paul) *see* Cartmel Peninsula *Carl*
LINDFIELD (All Saints) *Chich 6*   **P** *Ch Soc Trust*
V D J CLARKE,   **C** A O J PYMBLE
LINDLEY (St Stephen) *Wakef 5*   **P** *V Huddersfield*   **V** *vacant*
(01484) 650996
LINDOW (St John) *Ches 12*   **P** *Bp*   **V** S R GALES
LINDRIDGE (St Lawrence) *see* Teme Valley N *Worc*
LINDSELL (St Mary the Virgin) *see* Stebbing and Lindsell w Gt
and Lt Saling *Chelmsf*
LINDSEY (St Peter) *see* Bildeston w Wattisham and Lindsey,
Whatfield etc *St E*
LINFORD (St Francis) *see* E and W Tilbury and Linford
Chelmsf
LINFORD, GREAT (St Andrew) *see* Stantonbury and Willen
Ox
LINFORD, LITTLE (St Leonard) *see* Lamp *Ox*
LINGDALE (Mission Room) *see* Boosbeck and Lingdale *York*
LINGEN (St Michael and All Angels) *see* Presteigne w Discoed,
Kinsham, Lingen and Knill *Heref*
LINGFIELD (St Peter and St Paul) and Crowhurst *S'wark 25*
P *Bp*   **V** S M GENDALL,   **NSM** J A ATTWOOD
LINGWOOD (St Peter) *see* Burlingham St Edmund w
Lingwood, Strumpshaw etc *Nor*
LINKENHOLT (St Peter) *see* Hurstbourne Tarrant, Faccombe,
Vernham Dean etc *Win*
LINKINHORNE (St Mellor) *Truro 12*   **P** *DBP*
P-in-c P R SHARPE,   **C** M E ELLIOTT
LINSLADE (St Barnabas) *see* Ouzel Valley *St Alb*
LINSLADE (St Mary) *as above*
LINSTEAD PARVA (St Margaret) *see* Blyth Valley *St E*
LINTHORPE (St Barnabas) *York 17*   **P** *Abp*   **V** E WILSON,
C N J BARR-HAMILTON,   **NSM** R A MORRIS
LINTHWAITE (Christ Church) *see* Crosland Moor and
Linthwaite *Wakef*
LINTON (Christ Church) *see* Walton-on-Trent w Croxall,
Rosliston etc *Derby*
LINTON (St Aidan) *see* Ashington *Newc*
LINTON (St Mary) *Ely 5*   **P** *Patr Bd*   **TR** S M GRIFFITHS,
TV J M NORRIS,   **NSM** G E C RIDGWELL, M L GORE
LINTON (St Mary the Virgin) *see* Ariconium *Heref*
LINTON (St Nicholas) *see* Coxheath, E Farleigh, Hunton,
Linton etc *Roch*
LINTON IN CRAVEN (St Michael) *Bradf 7*   **P** *D&C*
R D MACHA,   **C** F JENKINS
LINWOOD (St Cornelius) *Linc 5*   **P** *MMCET*
R M J CARTWRIGHT
LIPHOOK (Church Centre) *see* Bramshott and Liphook
Portsm
LISCARD Resurrection (St Mary w St Columba) *Ches 7*   **P** *Bp*
V A J MANNINGS
LISCARD (St Thomas) *Ches 7*   **P** *Bp*   **P-in-c** R T NELSON
LISKEARD (St Martin) and St Keyne *Truro 12*   **P** *Simeon's*
Trustees   **P-in-c** A R INGLEBY,   **C** P P C SHARP, M A TUBBS
LISS (St Mary) (St Peter) (St Saviour) *Portsm 4*   **P** *Bp*
R C D WILLIAMS
LISSET (St James of Compostella) *see* Beeford w Frodingham
and Foston *York*
LISSINGTON (St John the Baptist) *see* Lissington *Linc*
LISSINGTON (St John the Baptist) *Linc 5*   **P** *D&C York*
V M J CARTWRIGHT

LISTON (not known) *see* N Hinckford *Chelmsf*

LITCHAM (All Saints) w Kempston, East and West Lexham, Mileham, Beeston-next-Mileham, Stanfield, Tittleshall and Godwick *Nor 14* **P** *Bp, Earl of Leic, Ch Soc Tr, DBP, Mrs E M Olesen, and N W D Foster Esq (jt)* **R** *vacant* (01328) 701011

LITCHFIELD (St James the Less) *see* Whitchurch w Tufton and Litchfield *Win*

LITHERLAND (St Andrew) *see* Bootle *Liv*

LITHERLAND (St John and St James) *see* Orrell Hey St Jo and St Jas *Liv*

LITHERLAND (St Paul) Hatton Hill *Liv 1* **P** *Bp*
V J W WHITLEY

LITHERLAND (St Philip) *Liv 1* **P** *Trustees*
P-in-c D A HAYES

LITLINGTON (St Catherine) *see* Shingay Gp *Ely*

LITLINGTON (St Michael the Archangel) *see* Alfriston w Lullington, Litlington and W Dean *Chich*

LITTLE *see also under substantive place name*

LITTLE BIRCH (St Mary) *see* Wormelow Hundred *Heref*

LITTLE COMMON *see* Bexhill St Mark *Chich*

LITTLE DART Team Ministry *see* Burrington, Chawleigh, Cheldon, Chulmleigh etc *Ex*

LITTLEBOROUGH (Holy Trinity) *Man 17* **P** *TR Rochdale*
P-in-c J MCGRATH, **Dss** K J OLIVER

LITTLEBOURNE (St Vincent) and Ickham w Wickhambreaux and Stodmarsh *Cant 1* **P** *Abp, D&C, Ch Trust Fund Trust, and Adn Cant (jt)* **NSM** C M WILKINSON

LITTLEBURY (Holy Trinity) *see* Saffron Walden w Wendens Ambo, Littlebury etc *Chelmsf*

LITTLEBURY GREEN (St Peter) *as above*

LITTLEDEAN (St Ethelbert) *see* Cinderford w Littledean *Glouc*

LITTLEHAM (St Margaret) w Exmouth *Ex 1* **P** *Patr Bd*
TR *vacant* (01395) 272227

LITTLEHAM (St Swithin) *see* Bideford, Northam, Westward Ho!, Appledore etc *Ex*

LITTLEHAMPTON (St James) (St Mary) and Wick *Chich 1*
P *Bp* **TR** R J CASWELL, **TV** J S A HUDSON, S R MERRIMAN,
NSM E A CARVER, P P SEDLMAYR

LITTLEHEMPSTON (St John the Baptist)
see Broadhempston, Woodland, Staverton etc *Ex*

LITTLEMOOR (St Francis of Assisi) *see* Preston w Sutton Poyntz and Osmington w Poxwell *Sarum*

LITTLEMORE (St Mary the Virgin and St Nicholas) *Ox 4*
P *Or Coll Ox* **P-in-c** M C M ARMITSTEAD,
NSM J B MUDDIMAN, T J MORGAN, H-A M HARTLEY

LITTLEOVER (St Peter) *Derby 10* **P** *PCC* **V** J A SEARLE,
NSM P M BAINBRIDGE

LITTLEPORT (St George) *Ely 8* **P** *Bp* **V** R H MASKELL,
NSM A BROXHAM

LITTLETHORPE (St Michael and All Angels) *see* Ripon Cathl *Ripon*

LITTLETON (St Catherine of Alexandria) *see* Downs Benefice *Win*

LITTLETON (St Mary Magdalene) *see* Shepperton and Littleton *Lon*

LITTLETON, HIGH (Holy Trinity) *see* Paulton w Farrington Gurney and High Littleton *B & W*

LITTLETON, NORTH (St Nicholas) *see* Cleeve Prior and The Littletons *Worc*

LITTLETON, SOUTH (St Michael the Archangel) *as above*

LITTLETON, WEST (St James) *see* Marshfield w Cold Ashton and Tormarton etc *Bris*

LITTLETON DREW (All Saints) *see* By Brook *Bris*

LITTLETON-ON-SEVERN (St Mary of Malmesbury)
see Alveston and Littleton-on-Severn w Elberton *Bris*

LITTLEWICK (St John the Evangelist) *see* Burchetts Green *Ox*

LITTLEWICK (St Thomas) *see* Horsell *Guildf*

LITTLEWORTH (Holy Ascension) *see* Cherbury w Gainfield *Ox*

LITTON (Christ Church) *see* Tideswell *Derby*

LITTON (St Mary the Virgin) *see* Chewton Mendip w Ston Easton, Litton etc *B & W*

LITTON CHENEY (St Mary) *see* Bride Valley *Sarum*

LIVERMERE, GREAT (St Peter) *see* Blackbourne *St E*

LIVERPOOL All Saints (St Mary) (St John the Divine) (St Philip w St David) *Liv 3* **P** *Patr Bd* **V** A W PORTER,
C M D COATES, **NSM** C E PORTER, A MURRAY, I D CASSIDY

LIVERPOOL (All Souls) Springwood *Liv 4* **P** *The Crown*
P-in-c P ELLIS

LIVERPOOL (Christ Church) Norris Green *Liv 8* **P** *Bp*
V H A EDWARDS, **C** J ANDERSON

LIVERPOOL (Our Lady and St Nicholas) *Liv 3* **P** *Sir William Gladstone Bt* **R** S D BROOKES, **C** J L WILLIAMS

LIVERPOOL (St Anne) *see* Stanley w Stoneycroft St Paul *Liv*

LIVERPOOL (St Christopher) Norris Green *Liv 8* **P** *Bp*
V P H BURMAN, **NSM** B A SMITH

LIVERPOOL (St James in the City) *Liv 6* **P** *Bp* **V** N R SHORT

LIVERPOOL (St Luke in the City) (St Bride w St Saviour)
(St Michael in the City) (St Stephen w St Catherine) *Liv 6*
P *Patr Bd* **TR** G C ELSMORE, **TV** M J FRY, **R V** STOCK

LIVERPOOL (St Philip w St David) *see* Liv All SS *Liv*

LIVERPOOL Stoneycroft (St Paul) *see* Stanley w Stoneycroft St Paul *Liv*

LIVERSEDGE (Christ Church) w Hightown *Wakef 8* **P** *Bp and V Birstall (jt)* **P-in-c** I BULLOCK, **NSM** S M HOLT,
P J DAWSON, **OLM** J C LEE

LIVERTON (St Michael) *see* Easington w Liverton *York*

LIVERTON MINES (St Hilda) *as above*

LIVESEY (St Andrew) *Blackb 2* **P** *Trustees*
P-in-c J P MILTON-THOMPSON

LLANCILLO (St Peter) *see* Ewyas Harold w Dulas, Kenderchurch etc *Heref*

LLANDINABO (St Junabius) *see* Wormelow Hundred *Heref*

LLANFAIR WATERDINE (St Mary) *see* Bucknell w Chapel Lawn, Llanfair Waterdine etc *Heref*

LLANGARRON (St Deinst) *see* Goodrich, Marstow, Welsh Bicknor, Llangarron etc *Heref*

LLANGROVE (Christ Church) *as above*

LLANGUA (St James) *see* Ewyas Harold w Dulas, Kenderchurch etc *Heref*

LLANVEYNOE (St Beuno and St Peter) *see* Clodock and Longtown w Craswall, Llanveynoe etc *Heref*

LLANWARNE (Christ Church) *see* Wormelow Hundred *Heref*

LLANYBLODWEL (St Michael), Llanymynech, Morton and Trefonen *Lich 19* **P** *Ld Chan (1 turn), Bp and Earl of Powis (2 turns)* **R** C W PENN

LLANYMYNECH (St Agatha) *see* Llanyblodwel, Llanymynech, Morton and Trefonen *Lich*

LOBLEY HILL (All Saints) *see* Hillside *Dur*

LOCKERLEY (St John) and East Dean w East and West Tytherley *Win 12* **P** *DBP (1 turn), H B G Dalgety Esq (2 turns)* **V** J M PITKIN

LOCKING (St Augustine) *see* Hutton and Locking *B & W*

LOCKING CASTLE (no church) Conventional District
B & W 10 *vacant* (01934) 515165

LOCKINGE (All Saints) *see* Wantage Downs *Ox*

LOCKINGE, WEST (All Souls) *as above*

LOCKINGTON (St Mary) and Lund and Scorborough w Leconfield *York 8* **P** *Abp* **P-in-c** E M MARSHMAN

LOCKINGTON (St Nicholas) *see* Castle Donington and Lockington cum Hemington *Leic*

LOCKLEAZE (St Mary Magdalene w St Francis) *see* Bris Lockleaze St Mary Magd w St Fran *Bris*

LOCKS HEATH (St John the Baptist) *Portsm 2* **P** *Bp*
V C E SUGDEN

LOCKTON (St Giles) *see* Pickering w Lockton and Levisham *York*

LODDINGTON (St Leonard) *see* Broughton w Loddington and Cransley etc *Pet*

LODDINGTON (St Michael and All Angels) *Leic 2* **P** *Bp*
P-in-c T J BLEWETT

LODDISWELL (St Michael and All Angels) *see* Modbury, Bigbury, Ringmore w Kingston etc *Ex*

LODDON (Holy Trinity), Sisland, Chedgrave, Hardley and Langley *Nor 8* **P** *Bp, E G Gilbert Esq, Gt Hosp, and Sir Christopher Beauchamp Bt (jt)* **V** W J STEWART,
C J L ODDY-BATES, **NSM** R M SEEL, **OLM** R M HOFFMANN

LODDON REACH *Ox 15* **P** *Patr Bd*
TR M C STANTON-SARINGER, **TV** B L PEARSON,
NSM C J LESLIE

LODE (St James) *see* Anglesey Gp *Ely*

LODERS (St Mary Magdalene) *see* Askerswell, Loders, Powerstock and Symondsbury *Sarum*

LODGE, THE (St John) *see* St Martins and Weston Rhyn *Lich*

LODGE MOOR (St Luke) *Sheff 4* **P** *CPAS* **V** *vacant* 0114-230 5271

LODSWORTH (St Peter) *see* Easebourne, Lodsworth and Selham *Chich*

LOFTHOUSE (Christ Church) *Ripon 8* **P** *DBP*
P-in-c A L RHODES

LOFTUS-IN-CLEVELAND (St Leonard) and Carlin How w Skinningrove *York 16* **P** *Ld Chan (2 turns), Abp (1 turn)*
R A GAUNT

LOLWORTH (All Saints) *see* Fen Drayton w Conington and Lolworth etc *Ely*

LONAN (All Saints) *S & M 2* **P** *The Crown* **V** J DUDLEY,
OLM J E GUILFORD

LONDESBOROUGH (All Saints) *see* Londesborough Wold *York*

LONDESBOROUGH WOLD York 5   **P** Abp (1 turn), Abp and Mrs P R Rowlands (1 turn)   **R** G HOLLINGSWORTH
LONDON, LITTLE (St Stephen)   see Bramley Win
LONDON CITY CHURCHES:
All Hallows Berkynchirche-by-the-Tower w St Dunstan-in-the-East Lon 1   **P** Abp   **V** B M D OLIVIER, Hon C G R DE MELLO,   **NSM** J M ROSENTHAL
St Andrew-by-the-Wardrobe w St Ann, Blackfriars Lon 1   **P** PCC and Mercers' Co (jt)   **P-in-c** G M TREWEEK, Hon C E R NORMAN
St Bartholomew the Great, Smithfield Lon 1   **P** D&C Westmr   **R** M R DUDLEY,   Hon C D W HIZA, P M FREEMAN, NSM C T OLADUJI
St Bartholomew the Less, Smithfield Gate Lon 1   **P** St Bart's Hosp   NSM N J GOULDING
St Botolph Aldgate w Holy Trinity Minories Lon 1   **P** Bp   V L J BURGESS,   NSM J PEIRCE
St Botolph without Bishopgate Lon 1   **P** D&C St Paul's   **P-in-c** A W MCCORMACK,   Hon C H J M TURNER
St Bride Fleet Street w Bridewell and Trinity Gough Square Lon 1   **P** D&C Westmr   **R** D G MEARA,   NSM G M PITCHER
St Clement Eastcheap w St Martin Orgar Lon 1   **P** D&C St Paul's   **P-in-c** J P WARNER
St Edmund the King and St Mary Woolnoth w St Nicholas Acons, All Hallows Lombard Street, St Benet Gracechurch, St Leonard Eastcheap, St Dionis Backchurch and St Mary Woolchurch, Haw Lon 1   **P** The Crown (3 turns), D&C Cant (1 turn), Bp (1 turn), and Abp (1 turn)   **R** vacant
St Giles Cripplegate w St Bartholomew Moor Lane and St Alphage London Wall and St Luke Old Street w St Mary Charterhouse and St Paul Clerkenwell Lon 1   **P** D&C St Paul's   **R** K M RUMENS
St Helen, Bishopsgate w St Andrew Undershaft and St Ethelburga, Bishopsgate and St Martin Outwich and St Mary Axe Lon 1   **P** Merchant Taylors' Co   **R** W T TAYLOR, C S D PEDLEY, A JONES, J O ROACH, M R ODONOGHUE, C W D SKRINE, M J FULLER, C D FISHLOCK, P W CLARKE, A SACH, D M LLOYD, T J NASH, A GLYN, J J CHILD
St James Garlickhythe w St Michael Queenhithe and Holy Trinity-the-Less Lon 1   **P** D&C St Paul's   **P-in-c** G M TREWEEK,   Hon C E R NORMAN
St Magnus the Martyr w St Margaret New Fish Street and St Michael Crooked Lane Lon 1   **P** DBP   **P-in-c** J P WARNER
St Margaret Lothbury and St Stephen Coleman Street w St Christopher-le-Stocks, St Bartholomew-by-the-Exchange, St Olave Old Jewry, St Martin Pomeroy, St Mildred Poultry and St Mary Colechurch Lon 1   **P** Simeon's Trustees   **R** W J H CROSSLEY
St Mary at Hill w St Andrew Hubbard, St George Botolph Lane and St Botolph by Billingsgate Lon 1   **P** Ball Coll Ox (2 turns), PCC (1 turn), and Abp (1 turn)   **P-in-c** F J L WINFIELD
St Mary le Bow w St Pancras Soper Lane, All Hallows Honey Lane, All Hallows Bread Street, St John the Evangelist Watling Street, St Augustine w St Faith under St Paul's and St Mildred Bread Street w St Margaret Moyses Lon 1   **P** Grocers' Co (1 turn), Abp (2 turns)   **R** G R BUSH
St Michael Cornhill w St Peter le Poer and St Benet Fink Lon 1   **P** Drapers' Co   **R** P J MULLEN
St Olave Hart Street w All Hallows Staining and St Catherine Coleman Lon 1   **P** Trustees   **R** O C M ROSS
St Peter Cornhill Lon 1   **P** City Corp   **R** W T TAYLOR
St Sepulchre w Christ Church Greyfriars and St Leonard Foster Lane Lon 1   **P** St Jo Coll Ox   **P-in-c** P J MULLEN
St Stephen Walbrook and St Swithun London Stone w St Benet Sherehog and St Mary Bothaw w St Laurence Pountney Lon 1   **P** Grocers' Co and Magd Coll Cam (alt)   **P-in-c** P A DELANEY
St Vedast w St Michael-le-Querne, St Matthew Friday Street, St Peter Cheap, St Alban Wood Street, St Olave Silver Street, St Michael Wood Street, St Mary Staining, St Anne and St Agnes and St John Zachary Gresham Street Lon 1   **P** D&C St Paul's   **P-in-c** A W MCCORMACK
LONDON COLNEY (St Peter) St Alb 5   **P** Bp   **V** L FAWNS
LONDON DOCKS (St Peter) w Wapping St John Lon 7   **P** Bp   **R** T E JONES
LONDON GUILD CHURCHES:
All Hallows London Wall Lon 1   **P** Ld Chan   **V** G B HEWITT, NSM C J ROSE, M C DONEY
St Andrew Holborn Lon 1   **P** Bp   **V** L DENNEN, C R M BASTABLE
St Benet Paul's Wharf Lon 1   **P** Bp   **V** vacant (020) 7723 3104 or 7489 8754
St Botolph without Aldersgate Lon 1   **P** Bp   **P-in-c** S M C DOWDY,   **C** R A BRAY
St Dunstan in the West Lon 1   **P** Abp   **V** W D F GULLIFORD
St Katharine Cree Lon 1   **P** Bp   **P-in-c** O C M ROSS

St Lawrence Jewry Lon 1   **P** City Corp   **V** D W PARROTT
St Margaret Pattens Lon 1   **P** Ld Chan   **V** vacant
St Martin Ludgate Lon 1   **P** D&C St Paul's   **P-in-c** S E GENT, NSM A J SMITH
St Mary Abchurch Lon 1   **P** CCC Cam   **P-in-c** J P WARNER
St Mary Aldermary Lon 1   **P** The Crown and Ld Chan (alt)   **P-in-c** D G MEARA,   **C** I J MOBSBY
St Michael Paternoster Royal Lon 1   **P** Bp   Hon C K PETERS
LONDONDERRY (St Mark)   see Oldbury, Langley and Londonderry Birm
LONDONTHORPE (St John the Baptist)   see Grantham, Harrowby w Londonthorpe Linc
LONG ASHTON (All Saints) w Barrow Gurney and Flax Bourton B & W 12   **P** Bp and Lady Virginia Gibbs (jt)   **R** A SARGENT,   NSM R Q GREATREX
LONG BENNINGTON (St Swithin)   see Saxonwell Linc
LONG BENTON (St Bartholomew) Newc 3   **P** Ball Coll Ox   **V** M P LEE,   **C** D M MCCARTHY,   NSM A M MCGIVERN
LONG BENTON (St Mary Magdalene) Newc 3   **P** Ball Coll Ox   **V** vacant 0191-266 2326
LONG BREDY (St Peter)   see Bride Valley Sarum
LONG BUCKBY (St Lawrence) w Watford and West Haddon w Winwick Pet 2   **P** Bp and DBP (1 turn), Ld Chan (1 turn)   **V** C R EVANS,   NSM T JORDAN
LONG BURTON (St James)   see Sherborne w Castleton, Lillington and Longburton Sarum
LONG CLAWSON (St Remigius)   see Vale of Belvoir Leic
LONG COMPTON (St Peter and St Paul)   see S Warks Seven Gp Cov
LONG CRENDON (St Mary the Virgin) w Chearsley and Nether Winchendon Ox 21   **P** Bp and R V Spencer-Bernard Esq (jt)   **V** J P B WYNBURNE
LONG DITTON (St Mary) Guildf 8   **P** Bp S'wark   **R** V E BURROWS,   NSM S P AYLING
LONG EATON (St John) Derby 13   **P** Bp   **V** P T WALLER, C R A HAWKINS
LONG EATON (St Laurence) Derby 13   **P** Bp   **V** vacant 0115-973 3154
LONG HANBOROUGH (Christ Church)   see Hanborough and Freeland Ox
LONG ITCHINGTON (Holy Trinity) and Marton Cov 10   **P** Bp   **P-in-c** J T H BRITTON,   **C** D R PATTERSON, OLM D J FORSTER
LONG LANE (Christ Church)   see Boylestone, Church Broughton, Dalbury, etc Derby
LONG LOAD (Christ Church)   see Langport Area B & W
LONG MARSTON (All Saints)   see Tring St Alb
LONG MARSTON (All Saints) York 1   **P** Col E C York   **P-in-c** P P ROBINSON,   NSM M R SHAW
LONG MARTON (St Margaret and St James)   see Heart of Eden Carl
LONG MELFORD (Holy Trinity)   see Chadbrook St E
LONG MELFORD (St Catherine)   as above
LONG NEWNTON (Holy Trinity)   see Tetbury, Beverston, Long Newnton etc Glouc
LONG PRESTON (St Mary the Virgin) w Tosside Bradf 5   **P** D&C Ch Ch Ox and V Gisburn (alt)   **P-in-c** M R RUSSELL-SMITH,   NSM R E WILSON
LONG RISTON (St Margaret)   see Skirlaugh w Long Riston, Rise and Swine York
LONG STANTON (All Saints) w St Michael Ely 6   **P** Magd Coll Cam and Bp (alt)   **P-in-c** M E RABY
LONG STANTON (St Michael and All Angels)   see Wenlock Heref
LONG STRATTON   see Stratton St Mary w Stratton St Michael etc Nor
LONG SUTTON (All Saints)   see N Hants Downs Win
LONG SUTTON (Holy Trinity)   see Langport Area B & W
LONG SUTTON (St Mary)   see Sutton St Mary Linc
LONG WHATTON (All Saints)   see Kegworth, Hathern, Long Whatton, Diseworth etc Leic
LONG WITTENHAM (St Mary the Virgin)   see Dorchester Ox
LONGBOROUGH (St James)   see Moreton-in-Marsh w Batsford, Todenham etc Glouc
LONGBRIDGE (St John the Baptist) Birm 4   **P** Bp   **V** C J CORKE
LONGBRIDGE DEVERILL (St Peter and St Paul)   see Cley Hill Villages Sarum
LONGCOT (St Mary the Virgin)   see Shrivenham and Ashbury Ox
LONGDEN (St Ruthen) and Annscroft w Pulverbatch Heref 12   **P** Bp and MMCET (jt)   **R** M G WHITTOCK, NSM C J WHITTOCK, L R BURNS, OLM O S DAWSON-CAMPBELL
LONGDON (St James) Lich 1   **P** Bp   **V** vacant (01543) 492871

LONGDON (St Mary), Castlemorton, Bushley, Queenhill w Holdfast *Worc 5* **P** *Bp, D&C Westmr, and Soc of the Faith (jt)* **V** C A MOSS

LONGDON-UPON-TERN (St Bartholomew) *see* Wrockwardine Deanery *Lich*

LONGFIELD (Mission Room) (St Mary Magdalene) *Roch 1* **P** *Ld Chan* **R** D G S JOHNSTON

LONGFLEET (St Mary) *Sarum 7* **P** *MMCET* **V** A N PERRY, **C** T F GOMM, J M TOMKINS

LONGFORD (St Chad) *see* Boylestone, Church Broughton, Dalbury, etc *Derby*

LONGFORD (St Thomas) *Cov 2* **P** *Bp* **V** *vacant* (024) 7636 4078

LONGFRAMLINGTON (St Mary the Virgin) w Brinkburn *Newc 6* **P** *Bp* **P-in-c** S J H WHITE

LONGHAM (St Andrew and St Peter) *see* Gressenhall w Longham w Wendling etc *Nor*

LONGHILL (St Margaret) *see* Sutton St Mich *York*

LONGHIRST (St John the Evangelist) *see* Bothal and Pegswood w Longhirst *Newc*

LONGHOPE (All Saints) *see* Huntley and Longhope, Churcham and Bulley *Glouc*

LONGHORSLEY (St Helen) *Newc 11* **P** *Ld Chan* **P-in-c** P S MCCONNELL

LONGHOUGHTON (St Peter and St Paul) (including Boulmer) w Howick *Newc 6* **P** *Duke of Northd and Bp (alt)* **V** P J SUTCLIFFE

LONGLEVENS (Holy Trinity) *see* Wotton St Mary *Glouc*

LONGNEWTON (St Mary) *see* Preston-on-Tees and Longnewton *Dur*

LONGNEY (St Lawrence) *see* Hardwicke and Elmore w Longney *Glouc*

LONGNOR (St Bartholomew), Quarnford and Sheen *Lich 5* **P** *Bp, V Alstonfield, and DBP (jt)* **V** J O FORRESTER

LONGNOR (St Mary) *see* Dorrington w Leebotwood, Longnor, Stapleton etc *Heref*

LONGPARISH (St Nicholas) *see* Hurstbourne Priors, Longparish etc *Win*

LONGRIDGE (St Lawrence) (St Paul) *Blackb 13* **P** *Trustees* **P-in-c** D L ANDERSON, **C** S C BELL

LONGSDON (St Chad) *see* Horton, Lonsdon and Rushton Spencer *Lich*

LONGSIGHT (St Anne) *see* Royton St Anne *Man*

LONGSIGHT (St Luke) *Man 1* **P** *D&C and Trustees (jt)* **R** P N CLARK

LONGSLEDDALE (St Mary) *see* Beacon *Carl*

LONGSOLE (Mission Room) *see* Barming *Roch*

LONGSTOCK (St Mary) *see* Stockbridge and Longstock and Leckford *Win*

LONGSTONE (St Giles), Curbar and Stony Middleton *Derby 2* **P** *V Bakewell etc and R Hathersage etc (jt)* **V** C H BENSON, **NSM** L E ELLSWORTH

LONGSTOWE (St Mary) *see* Papworth *Ely*

LONGTHORPE (St Botolph) *Pet 11* **P** *Sir Philip Naylor-Leyland Bt* **P-in-c** W S CROFT, **C** M R ALBERT

LONGTON (St Andrew) *Blackb 5* **P** A F Rawstorne Esq **V** A PARKINSON

LONGTON (St James and St John) *Lich 12* **P** *Bp* **R** S F JONES

LONGTON (St Mark) *see* Longton Hall *Lich*

LONGTON (St Mary and St Chad) *Lich 12* **P** *Bp* **V** P LOCKETT

LONGTON, NEW (All Saints) *Blackb 5* **P** *Bp* **V** D M ROGERS

LONGTON HALL *Lich 12* **P** *Prime Min* **P-in-c** P J MOCKFORD, **C** J ALESSI

LONGWELL GREEN (All Saints) *Bris 5* **P** *Bp* **V** D J A ADAMS

LONGWOOD (St Mark) *Wakef 5* **P** *V Huddersfield* **P-in-c** R M F CROMPTON

LONGWORTH (St Mary) *see* Cherbury w Gainfield *Ox*

LONSDALE, EAST *Blackb 14* **P** *Patr Bd* **P-in-c** M H CANNON, **Hon C** R HANNAFORD

LOOE, WEST (St Nicholas) *see* St Martin w Looe *Truro*

LOOSE (All Saints) *Cant 12* **P** *Abp* **P-in-c** S A PRICE, **NSM** C H THOM

LOPEN (All Saints) *see* Merriott w Hinton, Dinnington and Lopen *B & W*

LOPHAM NORTH (St Nicholas) *see* Upper Waveney *Nor*

LOPHAM SOUTH (St Andrew) *as above*

LOPPINGTON (St Michael and All Angels) w Newtown *Lich 22* **P** *Bp and R Wem (jt)* **P-in-c** P F BARNES, **OLM** A EVANS

LORDSBRIDGE Team, The *Ely 1* **P** *Ld Chan (1 turn), Patr Bd (2 turns)* **TR** M P M BOOKER, **TV** M R MATTHEWS, A M MYERS, **C** C M REDSELL, **NSM** J REISS

LORTON (St Cuthbert) and Loweswater w Buttermere *Carl 6* **P** *Bp and Earl of Lonsdale (alt)* **P-in-c** M JENKINSON

LOSCOE (St Luke) *Derby 12* **P** *Bp* **P-in-c** M G ALEXANDER, **NSM** R HOWORTH

LOSTOCK (St Thomas and St John) *Man 9* **P** *Bp and TR Deane St Mary the Virgin (jt)* **P-in-c** V ASHWORTH, **NSM** T ASHWORTH, **OLM** D J BARRETT

LOSTOCK GRALAM (St John the Evangelist) *Ches 6* **P** *V Witton* **P-in-c** B E SHARP

LOSTOCK HALL (St James) and Farington Moss *Blackb 5* **P** *Bp and V Penwortham (jt)* **P-in-c** M RIMMER

LOSTWITHIEL (St Bartholomew), St Winnow w St Nectan's Chapel, St Veep and Boconnoc *Truro 10* **P** *D&C and A D G Fortescue Esq (jt)* **P-in-c** P J CONWAY, **C** S DENYER, **Hon C** F E STUBBINGS

LOTHERSDALE (Christ Church) *see* Sutton w Cowling and Lothersdale *Bradf*

LOTHERTON (St James) *see* Aberford w Micklefield *York*

LOTTISHAM (The Blessed Virgin Mary) *see* Baltonsborough w Butleigh, W Bradley etc *B & W*

LOUDWATER (St Peter) *Ox 21* **P** *MMCET* **V** T G BUTLIN

LOUGHBOROUGH (All Saints) *see* Thorpe Acre w Dishley *Leic*

LOUGHBOROUGH (All Saints) w Holy Trinity *Leic 6* **P** *Bp and Em Coll Cam (jt)* **R** R A ROSS, **C** S R GAMBLE

LOUGHBOROUGH (Emmanuel) (St Mary in Charnwood) *Leic 6* **P** *Patr Bd* **TR** M J BROADLEY, **TV** S E FIELD, **NSM** J P DREW

LOUGHBOROUGH (Good Shepherd) *Leic 6* **P** *Bp* **V** E K WHITLEY, **NSM** R J WHITLEY

LOUGHRIGG Team Ministry, The *Carl 11* **P** *Patr Bd* **TR** T W BALL, **NSM** N F HALLAM, G G WRIGLEY

LOUGHTON (All Saints) *see* Watling Valley *Ox*

LOUGHTON (not known) *see* Ditton Priors w Neenton, Burwarton etc *Heref*

LOUGHTON (St John the Baptist) (St Gabriel) (St Nicholas) *Chelmsf 24* **P** *W W Maitland Esq* **R** G R SMITH, **C** R J FISHER, F G WAKELING, **NSM** P M TRAIN, M L BRADLEY

LOUGHTON (St Mary the Virgin) *Chelmsf 24* **P** *Bp* **V** M C MACDONALD, **C** S D POLLARD, **NSM** H N J TAYLOR

LOUGHTON (St Michael and All Angels) *Chelmsf 24* **P** *Bp* **V** N M COULTHARD

LOUND (St Anne) *see* Retford Area *S'well*

LOUND (St John the Baptist) *see* Somerleyton, Ashby, Fritton, Herringfleet etc *Nor*

LOUNDSLEY GREEN (Church of the Ascension) *Derby 5* **P** *Bp* **V** *vacant* (01246) 276805

LOUTH (Holy Trinity) (St James) (St Michael) *Linc 12* **P** *Patr Bd* **TR** S D HOLDAWAY, **TV** S J OLIVER, L E TURNER, **OLM** R W MANSFIELD

LOVERSALL (St Katherine) *see* Wadworth w Loversall *Sheff*

LOVINGTON (St Thomas à Becket) *see* Six Pilgrims *B & W*

LOW *see also under substantive place name*

LOW FELL (St Helen) *see* Gateshead St Helen *Dur*

LOW HAM (Chapel) *see* Langport Area *B & W*

LOW HILL (Good Shepherd) *see* Bushbury *Lich*

LOW MOOR (Holy Trinity) *see* Oakenshaw, Wyke and Low Moor *Bradf*

LOW VALLEY (St Matthew) *see* Darfield *Sheff*

LOWDHAM (St Mary the Virgin) w Caythorpe, and Gunthorpe *S'well 10* **P** *Bp* **V** C A TAINTON, **NSM** G R D EDLIN-WHITE

LOWER *see also under substantive place name*

LOWER MANOR (St Andrew) *see* Sheff Manor *Sheff*

LOWER MOOR (St Stephen and All Martyrs) *see* Coldhurst and Oldham St Steph *Man*

LOWESBY (All Saints) *see* Whatborough Gp *Leic*

LOWESTOFT (Christ Church) *Nor 9* **P** *CPAS* **V** M C PAYNE, **C** R J BURBIDGE

LOWESTOFT (Good Shepherd) *see* Lowestoft St Marg *Nor*

LOWESTOFT (St Andrew) *Nor 9* **P** *Ch Patr Tr* **V** M A MCCAGHREY

LOWESTOFT (St Margaret) *Nor 9* **P** *Bp, Adn Norfolk, and DBP (jt)* **R** M J ASQUITH, **NSM** G WILSON

LOWESWATER (St Bartholomew) *see* Lorton and Loweswater w Buttermere *Carl*

LOWGATE (St Mary) *see* Hexham *Newc*

LOWGATE (St Mary the Virgin) *see* Kingston upon Hull St Mary *York*

LOWICK (St John the Baptist) and Kyloe w Ancroft *Newc 12* **P** *D&C Dur (2 turns), Bp (1 turn)* **V** V T DICKINSON

LOWICK (St Luke) *see* Egton-cum-Newland and Lowick and Colton *Carl*

LOWICK (St Peter) *see* Brigstock w Stanion and Lowick and Sudborough *Pet*

LOWSONFORD (St Luke) *see* Hatton w Haseley, Rowington w Lowsonford etc *Cov*

LOWTHER (St Michael) and Askham and Clifton and Brougham *Carl 1* **P** *Earl of Lonsdale* **P-in-c** P J CLARKE

LOWTHORPE (St Martin)   see The Beacon York

LOWTON (St Luke) Liv 15   **P** Bp   **R** vacant (01942) 728434

LOWTON (St Mary) Liv 15   **P** Bp   **P-in-c** W J STALKER

LOXBEARE (St Michael and All Angels)   see Washfield, Stoodleigh, Withleigh etc Ex

LOXHORE (St Michael and All Angels)   see Shirwell, Loxhore, Kentisbury, Arlington, etc Ex

LOXLEY (St Nicholas)   see Hampton Lucy w Charlecote and Loxley Cov

LOXTON (St Andrew)   see Crook Peak B & W

LOXWOOD (St John the Baptist)   see Alfold and Loxwood Guildf

LOZELLS (St Paul and St Silas) Birm 3   **P** Aston Patr Trust   **P-in-c** J PRASADAM

LUBENHAM (All Saints)   see Market Harborough and The Transfiguration etc Leic

LUCCOMBE (The Blessed Virgin Mary)   see Porlock and Porlock Weir w Stoke Pero etc B & W

LUCKER (St Hilda)   see Belford and Lucker Newc

LUCKINGTON (St Mary)   see Sherston Magna, Easton Grey, Luckington etc Bris

LUDBOROUGH (St Mary)   see Fotherby Linc

LUDDENDEN (St Mary) w Luddenden Foot Wakef 3   **P** Bp and V Halifax (alt)   **P-in-c** J HARRIS

LUDDESDOWN (St Peter and St Paul)   see Cobham w Luddesdowne and Dode Roch

LUDDINGTON (All Saints)   see Stratford-upon-Avon, Luddington etc Cov

LUDDINGTON (St Margaret)   see Barnwell, Hemington, Luddington in the Brook etc Pet

LUDDINGTON (St Oswald)   see Crowle Gp Linc

LUDFORD (St Giles)   see Ludlow Heref

LUDFORD MAGNA (St Mary)   see Binbrook Gp Linc

LUDGERSHALL (St James)   see Tidworth, Ludgershall and Faberstown Sarum

LUDGERSHALL (St Mary the Virgin)   see Bernwode Ox

LUDGVAN (St Ludgvan and St Paul), Marazion, St Hilary and Perranuthnoe Truro 5   **P** D&C, Lord St Levan, and H M Parker Esq (jt)   **R** N G MARNS,   **C** D J F JONES,   **Hon C** F R N MICHELL,   **NSM** E A WHYTE

LUDHAM (St Catherine), Potter Heigham, Hickling and Catfield Nor 12   **P** Bp and G M H Mills Esq (jt)   **V** J M STRIDE,   **OLM** D M NICHOLSON

LUDLOW Team Minstry, The (St John) (St Laurence) Heref 11   **P** Patr Bd   **TR** C H WILLIAMS,   **TV** R A GREEN, M E WILSON,   **C** J S BEESLEY,   **NSM** S R JARVIS

LUFFENHAM, NORTH (St John the Baptist)   see Empingham, Edith Weston, Lyndon, Manton etc Pet

LUFFENHAM, SOUTH (St Mary the Virgin)   see Barrowden and Wakerley w S Luffenham etc Pet

LUFTON (St Peter and St Paul)   see Odcombe, Brympton, Lufton and Montacute B & W

LUGWARDINE (St Peter) w Bartestree, Weston Beggard and Dormington Heref 3   **P** D&C (3 turns), and A T Foley Esq (1 turn)   **V** vacant (01432) 850244

LULLINGSTONE (St Botolph)   see Eynsford w Farningham and Lullingstone Roch

LULLINGTON (All Saints)   see Beckington w Standerwick, Berkley, Rodden etc B & W

LULLINGTON (All Saints)   see Seale and Lullington w Coton in the Elms Derby

LULLINGTON (not known)   see Alfriston w Lullington, Litlington and W Dean Chich

LULWORTHS, (St Andrew) (Holy Trinity) Winfrith Newburgh and Chaldon, The Sarum 8   **P** Bp (3 turns), Col Sir Joseph Weld (1 turn)   **R** vacant (01929) 400550

LUMLEY (Christ Church) Dur 11   **P** Bp   **P-in-c** R A COLLINS

LUND (All Saints)   see Lockington and Lund and Scorborough w Leconfield York

LUND (St John the Evangelist) Blackb 10   **P** Ch Ch Ox   **V** G D ALLEN

LUNDWOOD (St Mary Magdalene) Wakef 7   **P** Bp   **P-in-c** K MADDY

LUNDY ISLAND (St Helen) Extra-Parochial Place Ex 15 vacant

LUPPITT (St Mary)   see Dunkeswell, Luppitt, Sheldon and Upottery Ex

LUPSET (St George) Wakef 11   **P** Bp   **V** vacant (01924) 373088

LUPTON (All Saints)   see Kirkby Lonsdale Carl

LURGASHALL (St Lawrence) Chich 11   **P** Lord Egremont   **V** vacant

LUSBY (St Peter)   see Marden Hill Gp Linc

LUSTLEIGH (St John the Baptist)   see Moretonhampstead, Manaton, N Bovey and Lustleigh Ex

LUTON (All Saints) (St Peter) St Alb 12   **P** Bp   **V** R C H FRANKLIN,   **C** I C IMAGE

LUTON (Christ Church) Roch 5   **P** R Chatham   **R** D J SUTTON

LUTON (Christ Church)   see Bushmead St Alb

LUTON (Holy Cross)   see Marsh Farm St Alb

LUTON Lewsey (St Hugh) St Alb 12   **P** Bp   **C** D E POULTNEY

LUTON Limbury (St Augustine of Canterbury) St Alb 12   **P** Bp   **P-in-c** J MACKENZIE,   **NSM** A M NEWTON

LUTON (St Andrew) St Alb 12   **P** Bp   **V** G A FINLAYSON

LUTON (St Andrew)   see Woodside St Alb

LUTON (St Anne) (St Christopher) Round Green St Alb 12   **P** Bp, V Luton St Mary, and Peache Trustees   **V** P C BUDGELL

LUTON (St Francis) St Alb 12   **P** Peache Trustees, Bp, and V Luton (jt)   **C** M SWIRES-HENNESSY

LUTON (St John)   see Teignmouth, Ideford w Luton, Ashcombe etc Ex

LUTON (St Mary) St Alb 12   **P** Peache Trustees   **V** N P J BELL,   **C** R P O'NEILL,   **NSM** C A MOSS

LUTON (St Matthew) High Town St Alb 12   **P** Ch Patr Trust   **V** M J PRITCHARD

LUTON (St Paul) St Alb 12   **P** Peache Trustees   **V** A SELLERS

LUTON (St Saviour) St Alb 12   **P** Bp   **NSM** D C ANDERSON

LUTTERWORTH (St Mary) w Cotesbach and Bitteswell Leic 7   **P** Prime Min (3 turns), Ld Chan (1 turn), and Ch Hosp (1 turn)   **R** M H W COUSSENS

LUTTON (St Nicholas) w Gedney Drove End, Dawsmere Linc 16   **P** The Crown, Ld Chan, and V Long Sutton (by turn)   **V** vacant (01406) 364199

LUTTON (St Peter)   see Barnwell, Hemington, Luddington in the Brook etc Pet

LUTTONS AMBO (St Mary)   see Weaverthorpe w Helperthorpe, Luttons Ambo etc York

LUXBOROUGH (Blessed Virgin Mary)   see Exton and Winsford and Cutcombe w Luxborough B & W

LUXULYAN (St Cyrus and St Julietta) Truro 1   **P** Bp (1 turn), Adn Cornwall (1 turn), and DBP (2 turns)   **P-in-c** F M BOWERS

LYDBROOK (Holy Jesus)   see Drybrook, Lydbrook and Ruardean Glouc

LYDBURY NORTH (St Michael and All Angels)   see Bishop's Castle w Mainstone, Lydbury N etc Heref

LYDD (All Saints) Cant 11   **P** Abp   **P-in-c** S R WILLIAMS,   **OLM** L P M TERRY

LYDDEN (St Mary the Virgin)   see Temple Ewell w Lydden Cant

LYDDINGTON (All Saints) and Wanborough and Bishopstone w Hinton Parva Bris 7   **P** Bp and Ld Chan (alt)   **V** J R CARDWELL

LYDDINGTON (St Andrew), Bisbrooke, Caldecott, Glaston, Harringworth, Seaton and Stoke Dry Pet 12   **P** Bp, G T G Conant Esq, Exors R E M Elborne Esq, Burghley Ho Preservation Trust, and Peterho Cam (jt)   **V** J E BAXTER

LYDEARD ST LAWRENCE (St Lawrence) and Combe Florey B & W 18   **P** W H J Hancock Esq (2 turns), Ld Chan (1 turn)   **R** vacant (01984) 667220

LYDFORD (St Petrock)   see Peter Tavy, Mary Tavy, Lydford and Brent Tor Ex

LYDFORD ON FOSSE (St Peter)   see Wheathill Priory Gp B & W

LYDGATE (St Anne)   see Saddleworth Man

LYDGATE (St Mary)   see Bansfield St E

LYDHAM (Holy Trinity)   see Wentnor w Ratlinghope, Myndtown, Norbury etc Heref

LYDIARD MILLICENT (All Saints)   see W Swindon and the Lydiards Bris

LYDIARD TREGOZE (St Mary)   as above

LYDIATE (St Thomas)   see Halsall, Lydiate and Downholland Liv

LYDLINCH (St Thomas à Beckett)   see Sturminster Newton, Hinton St Mary and Lydlinch Sarum

LYDNEY (St Mary the Virgin) Glouc 1   **P** Ld Chan   **P-in-c** S L FENBY,   **C** S UTTIN,   **NSM** P J COX

LYE, THE (Christchurch) and Stambermill Worc 12   **P** Bp and CPAS (alt)   **P-in-c** S M FALSHAW,   **NSM** C A KENT

LYFORD (St Mary)   see Cherbury w Gainfield Ox

LYME REGIS (St Michael the Archangel)   see Golden Cap Team Sarum

LYMINGE (St Mary and St Ethelburga) w Paddlesworth and Stanford w Postling and Radegund Cant 8   **P** Abp   **R** P N ASHMAN,   **NSM** V M ASHMAN,   **OLM** S G DOUGAL

LYMINGTON (St Thomas the Apostle) (All Saints) Win 11   **P** Bp   **V** P B C SALISBURY,   **C** A SMITH

LYMINSTER (St Mary Magdalene) Chich 1   **P** Eton Coll on nomination of BNC Ox   **P-in-c** J C QUIGLEY

LYMM (St Mary the Virgin) Ches 4   **P** Bp   **R** K MAUDSLEY

LYMPNE (St Stephen)   see Aldington w Bonnington and Bilsington etc Cant

LYMPSHAM (St Christopher) *see* Brent Knoll, E Brent and Lympsham *B & W*

LYMPSTONE (Nativity of the Blessed Virgin Mary) and Woodbury w Exton *Ex 1* **P** *SMF and D&C (jt)* **C** K P SPRAY, C S T CANT

LYNCH (St Luke) w Iping Marsh and Milland *Chich 10* **P** *Rathbone Trust Co, Cowdray Trust and Bp (jt)* **P-in-c** D W RENSHAW

LYNCHMERE (St Peter) and Camelsdale *Chich 10* **P** *Prime Min* **P-in-c** D TALKS

LYNCOMBE (St Bartholomew) *see* Bath St Bart *B & W*

LYNDHURST (St Michael) and Emery Down and Minstead *Win 11* **P** *Bp and P J P Green Esq (jt)* **V** J H BRUCE

LYNDON (St Martin) *see* Empingham, Edith Weston, Lyndon, Manton etc *Pet*

LYNEAL (St John the Evangelist) *see* Petton w Cockshutt, Welshampton and Lyneal etc *Lich*

LYNEHAM (St Michael) w Bradenstoke *Sarum 15* **P** *Ld Chan* **V** *vacant* (01249) 892475

LYNEMOUTH (St Aidan) *see* Cresswell and Lynemouth *Newc*

LYNESACK (St John the Evangelist) *Dur 7* **P** *Bp* **P-in-c** F J GRIEVE, **C** E L JOHNSON

LYNG (St Bartholomew) *see* Athelney *B & W*

LYNG (St Margaret), Sparham, Elsing, Bylaugh, Bawdeswell and Foxley *Nor 22* **P** *DBP, Sir Edward Evans-Lombe, and Bp (by turn)* **R** D N HEAD

LYNGFORD (St Peter) *see* Taunton Lyngford *B & W*

LYNMOUTH (St John the Baptist) *see* Combe Martin, Berrynarbor, Lynton, Brendon etc *Ex*

LYNN, NORTH (St Edmund) *see* King's Lynn St Marg w St Nic *Nor*

LYNN, SOUTH (All Saints) *Nor 20* **P** *Bp* **OLM** P J NORWOOD

LYNN, WEST (St Peter) *see* Clenchwarton and W Lynn *Ely*

LYNSTED (St Peter and St Paul) *see* Teynham w Lynsted and Kingsdown *Cant*

LYNTON (St Mary the Virgin) *see* Combe Martin, Berrynarbor, Lynton, Brendon etc *Ex*

LYONS (St Michael and All Angels) *see* Hetton-Lyons w Eppleton *Dur*

LYONSDOWN (Holy Trinity) *St Alb 14* **P** *Ch Patr Trust* **V** C W G DOBBIE

LYONSHALL (St Michael and All Angels) *see* Pembridge w Moor Court, Shobdon, Staunton etc *Heref*

LYSTON (not known) *see* N Hinckford *Chelmsf*

LYTCHETTS, The (not known) (St Mary the Virgin) and Upton *Sarum 7* **P** *Patr Bd* **TR** J H T DE GARIS, **TV** A MEPHAM, **C** A KERR, **NSM** J A ALEXANDER, **OLM** H D PAGE-CLARK

LYTHAM (St Cuthbert) *Blackb 10* **P** *DBP* **P-in-c** A CLITHEROW

LYTHAM (St John the Divine) *Blackb 10* **P** *J C Hilton Esq* **P-in-c** A CLITHEROW, **Hon C** J WIXON

LYTHAM ST ANNE (St Margaret of Antioch) *see* St Annes St Marg *Blackb*

LYTHAM ST ANNE (St Thomas) *see* St Annes St Thos *Blackb*

LYTHAM ST ANNES (St Anne) *see* St Annes St Anne *Blackb*

LYTHAM ST ANNES (St Paul) *see* Fairhaven *Blackb*

LYTHE (St Oswald) *see* Hinderwell, Roxby and Staithes etc *York*

MABE (St Laudus) *Truro 3* **P** *Bp* **P-in-c** J SAVAGE

MABLETHORPE (St Mary) w Trusthorpe *Linc 8* **P** *Bp Lon (2 turns), Bp Linc (1 turn)* **P-in-c** A C V HARVEY, **C** A P SMITH, **Hon C** C H LILLEY, **OLM** J TOMPKINS

MACCLESFIELD (Holy Trinity) *see* Hurdsfield *Ches*

MACCLESFIELD (St John the Evangelist) *Ches 13* **P** *Bp* **P-in-c** I SPARKS

MACCLESFIELD (St Paul) *Ches 13* **P** *Bp* **V** K M KIRBY

MACCLESFIELD Team Parish, The (All Saints) (Christ Church) (St Michael and All Angels) (St Peter) (St Barnabas) *Ches 13* **P** *Patr Bd* **TR** G C TURNER, **TV** D L MOCK, **NSM** D W L WIGHTMAN, R WARDLE

MACKWORTH (All Saints) *Derby 11* **P** *J M Clark-Maxwell Esq* **P-in-c** A P HARPER, **C** D A GLEN

MACKWORTH (St Francis) *Derby 9* **P** *Bp* **V** J R PHILLIPS

MADEHURST (St Mary Magdalene) *see* Slindon, Eartham and Madehurst *Chich*

MADELEY (All Saints) *Lich 9* **P** *J C Crewe Esq* **V** B F WILSON, **NSM** G A BAILEY

MADELEY (St Michael) *Heref 13* **P** *Patr Bd* **TR** H J MORRIS, **TV** M W LEFROY, **C** D I MOULDEN, **NSM** R FREEMAN

MADINGLEY (St Mary Magdalene) *Ely 6* **P** *Bp* **V** *vacant*

MADLEY (Nativity of the Blessed Virgin Mary) w Tyberton, Peterchurch, Vowchurch and Turnastone *Heref 1* **P** *Bp and D&C (jt)* **R** S D LOCKETT, **NSM** B A CHILLINGTON, J M DINNEN

MADRESFIELD (St Mary) *see* Powick and Guarlford and Madresfield w Newland *Worc*

MADRON (St Maddern) *see* Gulval and Madron *Truro*

MAER (St Peter) *see* Chapel Chorlton, Maer and Whitmore *Lich*

MAESBROOK (St John) *see* Kinnerley w Melverley and Knockin w Maesbrook *Lich*

MAESBURY (St John the Baptist) *Lich 19* **P** *Bp* **V** *vacant*

MAGDALEN LAVER (St Mary Magdalen) *see* High Laver w Magdalen Laver and Lt Laver etc *Chelmsf*

MAGHULL (St Andrew) (St James) (St Peter) and Melling *Liv 11* **P** *Patr Bd* **TR** N A WELLS, **TV** M S FOLLIN, S JONES, **C** A R CONANT, **NSM** G ARDERN

MAIDA VALE (St Peter) *see* Paddington St Mary Magd and St Pet *Lon*

MAIDA VALE (St Saviour) *see* Paddington St Sav *Lon*

MAIDEN BRADLEY (All Saints) *see* Mere w W Knoyle and Maiden Bradley *Sarum*

MAIDEN NEWTON (St Mary) *see* Melbury *Sarum*

MAIDENHEAD (All Saints) *see* Boyne Hill *Ox*

MAIDENHEAD (St Andrew and St Mary Magdalene) *Ox 13* **P** *Peache Trustees* **V** W M C STILEMAN, **C** A P KEARNS, S ALLBERRY, **Hon C** R P TAYLOR

MAIDENHEAD (St Luke) *Ox 13* **P** *Bp* **V** S M LYNCH, **NSM** T J ROBINSON

MAIDENHEAD (St Peter) *see* Furze Platt *Ox*

MAIDFORD (St Peter and St Paul) *see* Lambfold *Pet*

MAIDS MORETON (St Edmund) *see* N Buckingham *Ox*

MAIDSTONE (All Saints) (St Philip) w St Stephen Tovil *Cant 12* **P** *Abp* **V** C J MORGAN-JONES

MAIDSTONE Barming Heath (St Andrew) *see* Barming Heath *Cant*

MAIDSTONE (St Faith) *Cant 12* **P** *Abp* **P-in-c** J CRAY, **C** P J W SHELDRAKE

MAIDSTONE (St Luke the Evangelist) *Cant 12* **P** *Trustees* **V** E D DELVE, **OLM** R H WILLIAMSON

MAIDSTONE (St Martin) *Cant 12* **P** *Abp* **P-in-c** J R WALKER, **C** J H ADDISON, **NSM** J E GREEN

MAIDSTONE (St Michael and All Angels) *Cant 12* **P** *Abp* **V** P J GIBBONS

MAIDSTONE (St Paul) *Cant 12* **P** *Abp* **P-in-c** A W SEWELL, **C** I R PARRISH, **NSM** E S LANDER

MAIDWELL (St Mary) w Draughton and Lamport w Faxton *Pet 2* **P** *Bp (3 turns), Sir Ian Isham Bt (1 turn)* **R** M Y GARBUTT, **NSM** D SPENCELEY

MAINSTONE (St John the Baptist) *see* Bishop's Castle w Mainstone, Lydbury N etc *Heref*

MAISEMORE (St Giles) *see* Ashleworth, Corse, Hartpury, Hasfield etc *Glouc*

MAKER (St Mary and St Julian) w Rame *Truro 11* **P** *The Crown and Earl of Mount Edgcumbe (jt)* **R** *vacant* (01752) 822302

MALBOROUGH (All Saints) *see* Salcombe and Malborough w S Huish *Ex*

MALDEN (St James) *S'wark 15* **P** *Bp* **V** L M M FERNANDEZ-VICENTE, **OLM** C PIGGOTT

MALDEN (St John) *S'wark 15* **P** *Mert Coll Ox* **V** K W SCOTT, **NSM** M D BROOME

MALDEN, NEW (Christ Church) (St John the Divine) and Coombe *S'wark 15* **P** *CPAS* **P-in-c** S J KUHRT, **C** H M DURANT-STEVENSON, **NSM** H M HANCOCK, C G LUCAS

MALDON (All Saints w St Peter) *Chelmsf 11* **P** *Bp* **V** S CARTER, **C** J JONES

MALDON (St Mary) w Mundon *Chelmsf 11* **P** *D&C Westmr* **R** L P DARRANT

MALEW Ballasalla (St Mary the Virgin) *see* Malew *S & M*

MALEW (St Lupus) (St Mark) *S & M 1* **P** *The Crown* **V** *vacant* (01624) 822469

MALIN BRIDGE (St Polycarp) *Sheff 4* **P** *Bp* **V** P J COGHLAN

MALINS LEE (St Leonard) *see* Cen Telford *Lich*

MALLERSTANG (St Mary) *see* Kirkby Stephen w Mallerstang etc *Carl*

MALLING, EAST (St James), Wateringbury and Teston *Roch 7* **P** *D&C and Peache Trustees (jt)* **V** J D BROWN, **NSM** A M SEARLE, P R RINK

MALLING, SOUTH (St Michael the Archangel) *see* Lewes St Jo sub Castro and S Malling *Chich*

MALLING, WEST (St Mary) w Offham *Roch 7* **P** *Ld Chan and DBP (alt)* **P-in-c** D R J GREEN

MALMESBURY (St Peter and St Paul) w Westport and Brokenborough *Bris 6* **P** *Ch Trust Fund Trust* **P-in-c** N J ARCHER, **C** L BARNES, **Hon C** C E WINDLE, **NSM** M CHURCHER

MALPAS (St Andrew) *see* Truro St Paul and St Clem *Truro*

MALPAS (St Oswald) and Threapwood and Bickerton *Ches 5* **P** *Patr Bd* **R** I A DAVENPORT

MALTBY (St Bartholomew) (Ascension) (Venerable Bede) *Sheff 5* P *Bp* TR P J CRAIG-WILD, TV D E CRAIG-WILD, C J FRANKLIN

MALTON, NEW (St Michael) *York 6* P *Sir Philip Naylor-Leyland Bt* P-in-c P H BOWES, C I C ROBINSON, Q H WILSON, A D BOWDEN

MALTON, OLD (St Mary the Virgin) *York 6* P *Sir Philip Naylor-Leyland Bt* P-in-c Q H WILSON, C P H BOWES, A D BOWDEN

MALVERN (Holy Trinity) (St James) *Worc 2* P *Bp and D&C Westmr (jt)* V W D NICHOL, NSM R HERBERT, A C LANYON-HOGG

MALVERN (St Andrew) and Malvern Wells and Wyche *Worc 2* P *Bp* V P W FINCH, C S MARTIN, NSM A J GRAY

MALVERN, GREAT (Christchurch) *Worc 2* P *Bp* C C E GRIFFITHS

MALVERN, GREAT (St Mary and St Michael) *Worc 2* P *Bp* V M J A BARR, C P D EDWARDS, NSM M E BARR

MALVERN, LITTLE (St Giles) *Worc 2* P *Exors T M Berington Esq* P-in-c E G KNOWLES

MALVERN, WEST (St James) *see* Malvern H Trin and St Jas *Worc*

MALVERN LINK (Church of the Ascension) (St Matthias) w Cowleigh *Worc 2* P *Patr Bd* V P J KNIGHT, C J A WATSON, NSM M J NOBLES

MAMBLE (St John the Baptist) w Bayton, Rock w Heightington w Far Forest *Worc 4* P *Ld Chan and R Ribbesford w Bewdley etc (alt)* V S G F OWENS

MAMHEAD (St Thomas the Apostle) *see* Kenton, Mamhead, Powderham, Cofton and Starcross *Ex*

MANACCAN (St Manaccus and St Dunstan) *see* Meneage *Truro*

MANATON (St Winifred) *see* Moretonhampstead, Manaton, N Bovey and Lustleigh *Ex*

MANBY (St Mary) *see* Mid Marsh Gp *Linc*

MANCETTER (St Peter) *Cov 5* P *Ch Patr Trust* P-in-c A A TOOBY

MANCHESTER (Apostles) w Miles Platting *Man 1* P *DBP* R *vacant* 0161-220 7353

MANCHESTER (Church of the Resurrection) *see* Manchester Gd Shep and St Barn *Man*

MANCHESTER Clayton (St Cross w St Paul) *Man 1* P *Bp* P-in-c L T YOUNG

MANCHESTER Good Shepherd (St Barnabas) (Church of the Resurrection) *Man 1* P *Prime Min and Trustees (alt)* R T S R CHOW

MANCHESTER (St Ann) *Man 3* P *Bp* R J N ASHWORTH

MANCHESTER (St John Chrysostom) Victoria Park *Man 1* P *Bp* R I D GOMERSALL, C T CHARNOCK, Hon C K A C WASEY, OLM C N HARTLEY

MANCHESTER (St Werburgh) *see* Chorlton-cum-Hardy St Werburgh *Man*

MANEA (St Nicholas) *see* Christchurch and Manea and Welney *Ely*

MANEY (St Peter) *Birm 12* P *Bp* P-in-c M I RHODES

MANFIELD (All Saints) *see* E Richmond *Ripon*

MANGOTSFIELD (St James) *Bris 5* P *Peache Trustees* V *vacant* 0117-956 0510

MANLEY (St John the Evangelist) *see* Alvanley *Ches*

MANNINGFORD BRUCE (St Peter) *see* Vale of Pewsey *Sarum*

MANNINGHAM (St Paul and St Jude) *Bradf 1* P *Patr Bd* TV A A JOHN, C F J ROBERTSON

MANNINGS HEATH (Church of the Good Shepherd) *see* Nuthurst and Mannings Heath *Chich*

MANOR PARK (St Barnabas) *see* Lt Ilford St Barn *Chelmsf*

MANOR PARK (St John the Baptist) and Whitby Road *Ox 23* P *Eton Coll* V J S G COTMAN

MANOR PARK (St John the Evangelist) *see* Lt Ilford St Mich *Chelmsf*

MANOR PARK (St Mary the Virgin) *as above*

MANOR PARK (St Michael and All Angels) *as above*

MANOR PARK (William Temple) *see* Sheff Manor *Sheff*

MANSEL LACY (St Michael) *see* Credenhill w Brinsop and Wormsley etc *Heref*

MANSERGH (St Peter) *see* Kirkby Lonsdale *Carl*

MANSFIELD Oak Tree Lane *S'well 2* P *DBP* P-in-c P J STEAD

MANSFIELD (St Augustine) *S'well 2* P *Bp* P-in-c G E HOLLOWAY

MANSFIELD (St John the Evangelist) (St Mary) *S'well 2* P *Bp* V J M A ADAMS, C D N BERRY

MANSFIELD (St Lawrence) *S'well 2* P *Bp* V *vacant* (01623) 623698

MANSFIELD (St Mark) *S'well 2* P *Bp* V *vacant* (01623) 655548

MANSFIELD (St Peter and St Paul) *S'well 2* P *Bp* P-in-c D J FUDGER

MANSFIELD WOODHOUSE (St Edmund King and Martyr) *S'well 2* P *Bp* V R A SCRIVENER

MANSTON (St Catherine) *see* St Laur in Thanet *Cant*

MANSTON (St James) *Ripon 8* P *R Barwick in Elmet* NSM K G ELLIOTT

MANSTON (St Nicholas) *see* Okeford *Sarum*

MANTHORPE (St John the Evangelist) *see* Grantham, Manthorpe *Linc*

MANTON (St Mary the Virgin) *see* Empingham, Edith Weston, Lyndon, Manton etc *Pet*

MANUDEN (St Mary the Virgin) w Berden and Quendon w Rickling *Chelmsf 21* P *Bp, DBP and Ch Hosp (jt)* P-in-c C BISHOP

MAPERTON (St Peter and St Paul) *see* Camelot Par *B & W*

MAPLEBECK (St Radegund) *S'well 15* P *Sir Philip Naylor-Leyland Bt* P-in-c R D SEYMOUR-WHITELEY

MAPLEDURHAM (St Margaret) *see* Caversham Thameside and Mapledurham *Ox*

MAPLEDURWELL (St Mary) *see* N Hants Downs *Win*

MAPLESTEAD, GREAT (St Giles) *see* Knights and Hospitallers Par *Chelmsf*

MAPLESTEAD, LITTLE (St John) *as above*

MAPPERLEY (Holy Trinity) *see* W Hallam and Mapperley w Stanley *Derby*

MAPPERLEY (St Jude) *see* Nottingham St Jude *S'well*

MAPPLEBOROUGH GREEN (Holy Ascension) *see* Studley *Cov*

MAPPLETON (All Saints) *see* Aldbrough, Mappleton w Goxhill and Withernwick *York*

MAPPLETON (St Mary) *see* Ashbourne w Mapleton *Derby*

MAPPOWDER (St Peter and St Paul) *see* Hazelbury Bryan and the Hillside Par *Sarum*

MARAZION (All Saints) *see* Ludgvan, Marazion, St Hilary and Perranuthnoe *Truro*

MARBURY (St Michael) w Tushingham and Whitewell *Ches 5* P *MMCET and Bp (jt)* R S J WALTON

MARCH (St John) *Ely 11* P *Bp* P-in-c P BAXANDALL, Hon C D J ADDINGTON

MARCH (St Mary) *Ely 11* P *Bp* R A CHANDLER, NSM J R WEBB

MARCH (St Peter) *Ely 11* P *Bp* R A CHANDLER, NSM J R WEBB

MARCH (St Wendreda) *Ely 11* P *MMCET* R P BAXANDALL

MARCHAM (All Saints) w Garford *Ox 10* P *Ch Ch Ox* P-in-c R G ZAIR

MARCHINGTON (St Peter) *see* Uttoxeter Area *Lich*

MARCHINGTON WOODLANDS (St John) *as above*

MARCHWOOD (St John) *Win 11* P *Bp* R *vacant* (023) 8086 1496

MARCLE, LITTLE (St Michael and All Angels) *see* Ledbury *Heref*

MARCLE, MUCH (St Bartholomew) *as above*

MARDEN (All Saints) *see* Redhorn *Sarum*

MARDEN (St Hilda) w Preston Grange *Newc 5* P *Bp* V H C GREENWOOD

MARDEN (St Mary the Virgin) w Amberley and Wisteston *Heref 3* P *D&C* P-in-c H M SHORT

MARDEN (St Michael and All Angels) *Cant 10* P *Abp* V *vacant* (01622) 831379

MARDEN, EAST (St Peter) *see* Compton, the Mardens, Stoughton and Racton *Chich*

MARDEN, NORTH (St Mary) *as above*

MARDEN ASH (St James) *see* High Ongar w Norton Mandeville *Chelmsf*

MARDEN HILL Group, The *Linc 7* P *Various* R *vacant* (01790) 753534

MARDEN VALE *Sarum 15* P *Prime Min and Patr Bd (alt)* TR R A KENWAY, TV E A MASSEY, NSM M KIRBY

MAREHAM-LE-FEN (St Helen) *see* Fen and Hill Gp *Linc*

MAREHAM ON THE HILL (All Saints) *as above*

MARESFIELD (St Bartholomew) *Chich 21* P *Ch Trust Fund Trust* R J N A HOBBS

MARFLEET (St Giles) (St George) (St Hilda) (St Philip) *York 14* P *Patr Bd* TV A R GILCHRIST, R J W LONG

MARGARET MARSH (St Margaret) *see* Shaftesbury *Sarum*

MARGARET RODING (St Margaret) *see* High and Gd Easter w Margaret Roding *Chelmsf*

MARGARET STREET (All Saints) *see* St Marylebone All SS *Lon*

MARGARETTING (St Margaret) w Mountnessing and Buttsbury *Chelmsf 7* P *Bp* P-in-c J D HALLIDAY

MARGATE (All Saints) *Cant 5* P *Abp* P-in-c B P SHARP, Hon C D L CAWLEY

MARGATE (Holy Trinity) *Cant 5*   **P** *Ch Patr Trust*
  P-in-c J S RICHARDSON,   **C** N M GENDERS, M D TERRY
MARGATE (St John the Baptist in Thanet) *Cant 5*   **P** *Abp*
  V B P SHARP
MARGATE (St Paul)   *see* Cliftonville *Cant*
MARGATE (St Philip) Northdown Park *Cant 5*   **P** *Ch Patr Trust*   **V** S GAY
MARHAM (Holy Trinity) *Ely 9*   **P** *St Jo Coll Cam*
  P-in-c B L BURTON
MARHAMCHURCH (St Marwenne)   *see* Bude Haven and Marhamchurch *Truro*
MARHOLM (St Mary the Virgin)   *see* Castor w Sutton and Upton w Marholm *Pet*
MARIANSLEIGH (St Mary)   *see* Bishopsnympton, Rose Ash, Mariansleigh etc *Ex*
MARISHES, THE (St Francis)   *see* Pickering w Lockton and Levisham *York*
MARK (Holy Cross) w Allerton *B & W 1*   **P** *Bp and D&C (jt)*
  P-in-c G E C FENTON
MARK BEECH (Holy Trinity)   *see* Hever, Four Elms and Mark Beech *Roch*
MARK CROSS (St Mark)   *see* Rotherfield w Mark Cross *Chich*
MARKBY (St Peter)   *see* Hannah cum Hagnaby w Markby *Linc*
MARKET BOSWORTH (St Peter)   *see* Bosworth and Sheepy Gp *Leic*
MARKET DEEPING (St Guthlac) *Linc 13*   **P** *Ld Chan*
  R P BRENT,   **C** S I R HEARN
MARKET DRAYTON (St Mary)   *see* Drayton in Hales *Lich*
MARKET HARBOROUGH (St Dionysius) (The Transfiguration) - Little Bowden w Lubenham and Great Bowden *Leic 3*   **P** *Patr Bd*   **TR** H G BRAND,
  TV J D G SHAKESPEARE, A QUIGLEY,   **C** K K FORD,
  NSM J C DUDLEY
MARKET LAVINGTON (St Mary of the Assumption)   *see* The Lavingtons, Cheverells, and Easterton *Sarum*
MARKET OVERTON (St Peter and St Paul)   *see* Oakham, Ashwell, Braunston, Brooke, Egleton etc *Pet*
MARKET RASEN (St Thomas the Apostle) *Linc 5*   **P** *Ld Chan*
  V M J CARTWRIGHT
MARKET STAINTON (St Michael and All Angels)
  see Asterby Gp *Linc*
MARKET WEIGHTON (All Saints) *York 5*   **P** *Abp*
  V D J EVERETT
MARKET WESTON (St Mary)   *see* Stanton, Hopton, Market Weston, Barningham etc *St E*
MARKFIELD (St Michael), Thornton, Bagworth and Stanton under Bardon, and Copt Oak *Leic 9*   **P** *MMCET*
  R S J NICHOLLS
MARKHAM, EAST (St John the Baptist)   *see* Retford Area *S'well*
MARKHAM CLINTON (All Saints)   *see* Tuxford w Weston and Markham Clinton *S'well*
MARKINGTON (St Michael) w South Stainley and Bishop Thornton *Ripon 3*   **P** *Bp, D&C, Sir Thomas Ingilby Bt and N A Hudleston Esq (jt) (by turn)*   **P-in-c** G F BRAITHWAITE
MARKS GATE (St Mark) Chadwell Heath *Chelmsf 1*   **P** *Bp*
  V R K GAYLER
MARKS TEY (St Andrew) and Aldham *Chelmsf 17*   **P** *CPAS and MMCET (jt)*   **P-in-c** I M SCOTT-THOMPSON
MARKSBURY (St Peter)   *see* Farmborough, Marksbury and Stanton Prior *B & W*
MARKYATE STREET (St John the Baptist) *St Alb 7*   **P** *Bp*
  P-in-c J F H GREEN
MARLBOROUGH (St Mary the Virgin) *Sarum 18*   **P** *Patr Bd*
  TR A G STUDDERT-KENNEDY,   **TV** I C COOPER,   **C** T P SEAGO,
  OLM D P MAURICE
MARLBROOK (St Luke)   *see* Catshill and Dodford *Worc*
MARLBROOK Team Ministry, The   *see* Bath Twerton-on-Avon *B & W*
MARLDON (St John the Baptist)   *see* Totnes w Bridgetown, Berry Pomeroy etc *Ex*
MARLESFORD (St Andrew)   *see* Campsea Ashe w Marlesford, Parham and Hacheston *St E*
MARLEY HILL (St Cuthbert)   *see* Hillside *Dur*
MARLINGFORD (Assumption of the Blessed Virgin Mary)
  see Easton, Colton, Marlingford and Bawburgh *Nor*
MARLOW, GREAT (All Saints) w Marlow Bottom, Little Marlow and Bisham *Ox 29*   **P** *Patr Bd*   **TV** P F HINCKLEY,
  NSM G L C SMITH
MARLOW, LITTLE (St John the Baptist)   *see* Gt Marlow w Marlow Bottom, Lt Marlow and Bisham *Ox*
MARLOW BOTTOM (St Mary the Virgin)   *as above*
MARLPIT HILL (St Paulinus)   *see* Edenbridge *Roch*
MARLPOOL (All Saints) *Derby 12*   **P** *V Heanor*   **V** K PADLEY
MARLSTON (St Mary)   *see* Bucklebury w Marlston *Ox*

MARNHULL (St Gregory) *Sarum 5*   **P** *DBF*
  NSM S M W THOMAS
MAROWN (Old Parish Church) (St Runius) *S & M 2*
  P *The Crown*   **V** I DAVIES
MARPLE (All Saints) *Ches 16*   **P** *R Stockport St Mary*
  V I R PARKINSON,   **C** B A PERRIN,   **NSM** B J LOWE,
  C M BLODWELL, E A SHERCLIFF
MARPLE, LOW (St Martin) *Ches 16*   **P** *Keble Coll Ox*
  P-in-c E P MCKENNA
MARR (St Helen)   *see* Bilham *Sheff*
MARSDEN (St Bartholomew) *Wakef 5*   **P** *R Almondbury*
  P-in-c G M GARSIDE
MARSDEN, GREAT (St John's Church Centre) w Nelson St Philip *Blackb 6*   **P** *Prime Min and Bp (alt)*
  P-in-c L A HILLIARD
MARSDEN, LITTLE (St Paul) w Nelson St Mary and Nelson St Bede *Blackb 6*   **P** *Bp*   **V** P A KNOWLES
MARSH (St George)   *see* Lancaster St Mary w St John and St Anne *Blackb*
MARSH (St James Chapel)   *see* Huddersfield H Trin *Wakef*
MARSH BALDON (St Peter)   *see* Dorchester *Ox*
MARSH FARM (Holy Cross) *St Alb 12*   **P** *Bp*   **V** *vacant* (01582) 575757
MARSH GIBBON (St Mary the Virgin)   *see* The Claydons and Swan *Ox*
MARSH GREEN (St Barnabas) w Newtown *Liv 14*   **P** *Bp, Duke of Sutherland, and V Pemberton (jt)*   **V** M J DUERDEN,
  OLM M JENNINGS, S Y FULFORD, E TAULTY
MARSHALSWICK (St Mary)   *see* St Alb St Mary Marshalswick *St Alb*
MARSHAM (All Saints)   *see* Bure Valley *Nor*
MARSHCHAPEL (St Mary the Virgin)   *see* The North-Chapel Parishes *Linc*
MARSHFIELD (St Mary the Virgin) w Cold Ashton and Tormarton w West Littleton *Bris 4*   **P** *New Coll Ox and Bp (alt)*   **V** *vacant* (01225) 891850
MARSHLAND, The *Sheff 10*   **P** *Ld Chan and Bp (alt)*
  NSM K W SARGEANTSON
MARSHWOOD (St Mary)   *see* Golden Cap Team *Sarum*
MARSKE (St Edmund King and Martyr)   *see* Richmond w Hudswell and Downholme and Marske *Ripon*
MARSKE, NEW (St Thomas) *York 16*   **P** *Abp*
  V R E HARRISON
MARSKE IN CLEVELAND (St Mark) *York 16*   **P** *Trustees*
  P-in-c J H FIFE
MARSTON (St Alban)   *see* Stafford *Lich*
MARSTON (St Leonard)   *as above*
MARSTON (St Mary)   *see* Barkston and Hough Gp *Linc*
MARSTON (St Nicholas) w Elsfield *Ox 4*   **P** *Bp and D&C (jt)*
  V A R PRICE,   **NSM** A C HOLMES
MARSTON, NEW (St Michael and All Angels) *Ox 4*   **P** *Bp*
  V E B BARDWELL
MARSTON, NORTH (Assumption of the Blessed Virgin Mary)
  see Schorne *Ox*
MARSTON, SOUTH (St Mary Magdalene)   *see* Stratton St Margaret w S Marston etc *Bris*
MARSTON BIGOT (St Leonard)   *see* Nunney and Witham Friary, Marston Bigot etc *B & W*
MARSTON GREEN (St Leonard) *Birm 9*   **P** *Birm Dioc Trustees*   **V** R V ALLEN
MARSTON MAGNA (Blessed Virgin Mary)   *see* Chilton Cantelo, Ashington, Mudford, Rimpton etc *B & W*
MARSTON MEYSEY (St James)   *see* Fairford Deanery *Glouc*
MARSTON MONTGOMERY (St Giles)   *see* S Dales *Derby*
MARSTON MORTEYNE (St Mary the Virgin) w Lidlington *St Alb 9*   **P** *Bp and St Jo Coll Cam (alt)*   **P-in-c** G A WEBB
MARSTON ON DOVE (St Mary)   *see* Hilton w Marston-on-Dove *Derby*
MARSTON SICCA (St James the Great)   *see* Pebworth, Dorsington, Honeybourne etc *Glouc*
MARSTON ST LAWRENCE (St Lawrence)   *see* Chenderit *Pet*
MARSTON TRUSSELL (St Nicholas)   *see* Welford w Sibbertoft and Marston Trussell *Pet*
MARSTOW (St Matthew)   *see* Goodrich, Marstow, Welsh Bicknor, Llangarron etc *Heref*
MARSWORTH (All Saints)   *see* Ivinghoe w Pitstone and Slapton and Marsworth *Ox*
MARTHALL (All Saints) *Ches 12*   **P** *DBP*   **P-in-c** L J SWEET
MARTHAM (St Mary) and Repps with Bastwick, Thurne and Clippesby *Nor 6*   **P** *Bp, D&C, DBP and K Edw VI Gr Sch (jt)*
  V J A CRAFER,   **NSM** S H MITCHELL
MARTIN (All Saints)   *see* W Downland *Sarum*
MARTIN (Holy Trinity)   *see* Carr Dyke Gp *Linc*
MARTIN (St Michael)   *see* Horncastle Gp *Linc*
MARTIN HUSSINGTREE (St Michael)   *see* Salwarpe and Hindlip w Martin Hussingtree *Worc*

MARTINDALE (Old Church)   *see* Barton, Pooley Bridge and Martindale *Carl*
MARTINDALE (St Peter)   *as above*
MARTINHOE (St Martin)   *see* Combe Martin, Berrynarbor, Lynton, Brendon etc *Ex*
MARTLESHAM (St Mary the Virgin) w Brightwell *St E 2*   **P** *Bp*   **OLM** H L COOKE
MARTLESHAM HEATH (St Michael and All Angels)   *see* Martlesham w Brightwell *St E*
MARTLEY (St Peter)   *see* Worcs W *Worc*
MARTOCK (All Saints) w Ash *B & W 5*   **P** *Bp*   **P-in-c** D R GENT,   **NSM** M I MACCORMACK, J S ELLIS
MARTON (Room)   *see* Middleton, Newton and Sinnington *York*
MARTON (St Esprit)   *see* Long Itchington and Marton *Cov*
MARTON (St James), Siddington w Capesthorne, and Eaton w Hulme Walfield *Ches 11*   **P** *Bp and Sir W A B Davenport (jt)*   **V** *vacant* (01260) 224447
MARTON (St Margaret of Antioch)   *see* Lea Gp *Linc*
MARTON (St Mark) *Heref 12*   **P** *V Chirbury*   **P-in-c** R N LEACH
MARTON (St Mary)   *see* Forest of Galtres *York*
MARTON (St Paul) *Blackb 8*   **P** *V Poulton-le-Fylde*   **V** C J WREN,   **C** K A WREN
MARTON CUM GRAFTON (Christ Church)   *see* Gt and Lt Ouseburn w Marton cum Grafton etc *Ripon*
MARTON-IN-CHIRBURY (St Mark)   *see* Marton *Heref*
MARTON-IN-CLEVELAND (St Cuthbert) *York 17*   **P** *Abp*   **V** M J PROCTOR
MARTON IN CRAVEN (St Peter)   *see* Broughton, Marton and Thornton *Bradf*
MARTON MOSS (St Nicholas)   *see* Hawes Side and Marton Moss *Blackb*
MARTYR WORTHY (St Swithun)   *see* Itchen Valley *Win*
MARWOOD (St Michael and All Angels)   *see* Heanton Punchardon w Marwood *Ex*
MARY TAVY (St Mary)   *see* Peter Tavy, Mary Tavy, Lydford and Brent Tor *Ex*
MARYFIELD (St Philip and St James)   *see* Antony w Sheviock *Truro*
MARYLEBONE ROAD (St Marylebone)   *see* St Marylebone w H Trin *Lon*
MARYPORT (St Mary) (Christ Church), Netherton and Flimby *Carl 7*   **P** *Patr Bd*   **TR** G M HART,   **TV** S M MCKENDREY
MARYSTOWE (St Mary the Virgin)   *see* Milton Abbot, Dunterton, Lamerton etc *Ex*
MASBROUGH (St Paul) *Sheff 6*   **P** *Bp and Ld Chan (alt)*   **V** T H CASWELL
MASHAM (St Mary the Virgin) and Healey *Ripon 3*   **P** *Trin Coll Cam*   **V** D J CLEEVES,   **NSM** M SAUNDERS, M A WARNER
MASSINGHAM, GREAT (St Mary) and LITTLE (St Andrew), Harpley, Rougham, Weasenham and Wellingham *Nor 14*   **P** *Bp, Earl of Leicester, Mrs P M Brereton, T F North Esq, and DBP (jt)*   **R** M E THORNE
MATCHBOROUGH (Christ Church)   *see* Ipsley *Worc*
MATCHING (St Mary)   *see* High Laver w Magdalen Laver and Lt Laver etc *Chelmsf*
MATCHING GREEN (St Edmund)   *as above*
MATFEN (Holy Trinity)   *see* Stamfordham w Matfen *Newc*
MATFIELD (St Luke)   *see* Lamberhurst and Matfield *Roch*
MATHON (St John the Baptist)   *see* Cradley w Mathon and Storridge *Heref*
MATLASKE (St Peter)   *see* Barningham w Matlaske w Baconsthorpe etc *Nor*
MATLOCK (St Giles) (St John the Baptist) *Derby 7*   **P** *Bp*   **R** B M CROWTHER-ALWYN
MATLOCK BANK (All Saints) and Tansley *Derby 7*   **P** *Bp*   **V** R B READE,   **NSM** J D POSTON
MATLOCK BATH (Holy Trinity) and Cromford *Derby 7*   **P** *Ch Trust Fund Trust*   **P-in-c** P N W GRAYSHON,   **C** J BATTISON
MATSON (St Katharine) *Glouc 2*   **P** *D&C*   **R** J A PARSONS,   **C** K O HEBDEN
MATTERDALE (not known)   *see* Gd Shep TM *Carl*
MATTERSEY (All Saints)   *see* Everton, Mattersey, Clayworth and Gringley *S'well*
MATTINGLEY (not known)   *see* Whitewater *Win*
MATTISHALL (All Saints) and the Tudd Valley *Nor 17*   **P** *Bp, G&C Coll Cam, DBP, and J V Berney Esq (jt)*   **R** G R KEGG,   **C** G R ROOTHAM,   **NSM** G KEGG,   **OLM** S E THURGILL
MATTISHALL BURGH (St Peter)   *see* Mattishall and the Tudd Valley *Nor*
MAUGHOLD (St Maughold) *S & M 3*   **P** *The Crown*   **V** D J GREEN,   **NSM** I C FAULDS

MAULDEN (St Mary) *St Alb 8*   **P** *Bp*   **R** R C WINSLADE
MAUNBY (St Michael)   *see* Lower Swale *Ripon*
MAUTBY (St Peter and St Paul)   *see* S Trin Broads *Nor*
MAVESYN RIDWARE (St Nicholas)   *see* The Ridwares and Kings Bromley *Lich*
MAVIS ENDERBY (St Michael)   *see* Marden Hill Gp *Linc*
MAWDESLEY (St Peter) *Blackb 4*   **P** *R Croston*   **R** D J REYNOLDS
MAWNAN (St Mawnan) (St Michael) *Truro 3*   **P** *Bp*   **P-in-c** G K BENNETT,   **C** S G TURNER
MAXEY (St Peter)   *see* Etton w Helpston and Maxey *Pet*
MAXSTOKE (St Michael and All Angels) *Birm 9*   **P** *Lord Leigh*   **V** R N PARKER,   **C** K M LARKIN
MAY HILL (All Saints)   *see* Huntley and Longhope, Churcham and Bulley *Glouc*
MAYBRIDGE (St Richard) *Chich 5*   **P** *Bp*   **C** J K GAVIGAN
MAYBUSH Redbridge (All Saints)   *see* Maybush and Southampton St Jude *Win*
MAYBUSH (St Peter) and Southampton St Jude *Win 13*   **P** *Bp*   **V** R A HEMMINGS,   **C** D G OADES
MAYFAIR (Christ Church) extra-parochial place *Lon 3*   **P** *Bp*   **NSM** M BEEBY
MAYFIELD (St Dunstan) *Chich 19*   **P** *Keble Coll Ox*   **V** N J PRIOR,   **Hon C** J P CAPERON
MAYFIELD (St John the Baptist)   *see* Alton w Bradley-le-Moors and Denstone etc *Lich*
MAYFORD (Emmanuel)   *see* Woking St Jo *Guildf*
MAYLAND (St Barnabas) (St Barnabas Family Centre) *Chelmsf 11*   **P** *Bp*   **P-in-c** M R RYALL
MEANWOOD (Holy Trinity) *Ripon 7*   **P** *Bp*   **P-in-c** C M ORME
MEARE (Blessed Virgin Mary and All Saints)   *see* Glastonbury w Meare *B & W*
MEARS ASHBY (All Saints) and Hardwick and Sywell w Overstone *Pet 6*   **P** *Duchy of Cornwall (2 turns), Bracegirdle Trustees (1 turn), and Mrs C K Edmiston (1 turn)*   **P-in-c** D C BEET
MEASHAM (St Lawrence)   *see* Woodfield *Leic*
MEAVY (St Peter)   *see* Yelverton, Meavy, Sheepstor and Walkhampton *Ex*
MEDBOURNE (St Giles)   *see* Six Saints circa Holt *Leic*
MEDLOCK HEAD *Man 15*   **P** *Prime Min (2 turns), Patr Bd (1 turn)*   **TR** R W HAWKINS,   **TV** P M S MONK
MEDMENHAM (St Peter and St Paul)   *see* Hambleden Valley *Ox*
MEDOMSLEY (St Mary Magdalene) *Dur 4*   **P** *Bp*   **V** A D WHIPP
MEDSTEAD (St Andrew)   *see* Bentworth, Lasham, Medstead and Shalden *Win*
MEERBROOK (St Matthew)   *see* Leek and Meerbrook *Lich*
MEESDEN (St Mary)   *see* Hormead, Wyddial, Anstey, Brent Pelham etc *St Alb*
MEETH (St Michael and All Angels)   *see* Hatherleigh, Meeth, Exbourne and Jacobstowe *Ex*
MEIR (Holy Trinity) *Lich 6*   **P** *Bp*   **P-in-c** M M ALLBUTT
MEIR HEATH (St Francis of Assisi) and Normacot *Lich 12*   **P** *Bp and DBP (jt)*   **V** D W MCHARDY
MEIR PARK (St Clare)   *see* Meir Heath and Normacot *Lich*
MELBECKS (Holy Trinity)   *see* Swaledale *Ripon*
MELBOURN (All Saints) *Ely 7*   **P** *D&C*   **V** A D O'BRIEN,   **NSM** M L PRICE
MELBOURNE (St Michael), Ticknall, Smisby and Stanton by Bridge *Derby 15*   **P** *Bp*   **V** M POWELL,   **C** D J RAILTON,   **NSM** A J FLINTHAM
MELBOURNE (St Monica)   *see* Barmby Moor Gp *York*
MELBURY (St Mary the Virgin) (St Osmund) *Sarum 3*   **P** *Patr Bd*   **TR** G F PERRYMAN,   **TV** D P HARKNETT,   **OLM** L J WILCOCK
MELBURY ABBAS (St Thomas)   *see* Shaftesbury *Sarum*
MELBURY BUBB (St Mary the Virgin)   *see* Melbury *Sarum*
MELBURY OSMUND (St Osmund)   *as above*
MELCHBOURNE (St Mary Magdalene)   *see* The Stodden Churches *St Alb*
MELCOMBE HORSEY (St Andrew)   *see* Piddle Valley, Hilton, Cheselbourne etc *Sarum*
MELDON (St John the Evangelist)   *see* Bolam w Whalton and Hartburn w Meldon *Newc*
MELDRETH (Holy Trinity) *Ely 7*   **P** *D&C*   **V** A D O'BRIEN,   **NSM** M L PRICE
MELKSHAM (St Barnabas) (St Michael and All Angels) *Sarum 14*   **P** *DBP*   **TR** A E EVANS,   **TV** D J PARR,   **C** C E PARR, J PERRETT,   **NSM** J DARLING, H BEGLEY,   **OLM** A E WINTOUR, E A FIELDEN
MELKSHAM FOREST (St Andrew)   *see* Melksham *Sarum*
MELLING (St Thomas)   *see* Maghull and Melling *Liv*
MELLING (St Wilfrid)   *see* E Lonsdale *Blackb*

MELLIS (St Mary the Virgin)   *see* S Hartismere *St E*
MELLOR (St Mary) *Blackb 7*   P *V Blackb*   P-in-c P D ROLFE
MELLOR (St Thomas) *Ches 2*   P *Bp*   V P J JENNER
MELLS (St Andrew) w Buckland Dinham, Elm, Whatley, Vobster and Chantry *B & W 3*   P *DBP (2 turns), Bp (1 turns)*
P-in-c M E WEYMONT
MELMERBY (St John the Baptist)   *see* Cross Fell Gp *Carl*
MELPLASH (Christ Church)   *see* Beaminster Area *Sarum*
MELSONBY (St James the Great)   *see* Forcett and Aldbrough and Melsonby *Ripon*
MELTHAM Christ the King (St Bartholomew) (St James) *Wakef 1*   P Simeon's Trustees, R Almondbury w Farnley Tyas, and Bp (jt)   V M E READ,   NSM P ROLLS, D SHIELDS, OLM J H HELLIWELL, J F RADCLIFFE
MELTHAM (St Bartholomew)   *see* Meltham *Wakef*
MELTHAM MILLS (St James)   *as above*
MELTON (St Andrew) and Ufford *St E 7*   P *D&C Ely (3 turns), and T R E Blois-Brooke Esq (1 turn)*   R M J HATCHETT
MELTON, GREAT (All Saints)   *see* Hethersett w Canteloff w Lt and Gt Melton *Nor*
MELTON, HIGH (St James)   *see* Barnburgh w Melton on the Hill etc *Sheff*
MELTON, LITTLE (All Saints)   *see* Hethersett w Canteloff w Lt and Gt Melton *Nor*
MELTON, WEST (St Cuthbert)   *see* Brampton Bierlow *Sheff*
MELTON CONSTABLE (St Peter)   *see* Briston, Burgh Parva, Hindolveston etc *Nor*
MELTON MOWBRAY (St Mary) *Leic 2*   P *Patr Bd*
TR R F ADIDY,   TV 6 J CONETABLE,   C S M ROWLAND
MELTON ROSS (Ascension)   *see* Brocklesby Park *Linc*
MELVERLEY (St Peter)   *see* Kinnerley w Melverley and Knockin w Maesbrook *Lich*
MEMBURY (St John the Baptist)   *see* Axminster, Chardstock, All Saints etc *Ex*
MENDHAM (All Saints)   *see* Fressingfield, Mendham etc *St E*
MENDLESHAM (St Mary) *St E 6*   P *SMF*   V P T GRAY
MENEAGE (St Anthony) (St Martin) (St Mawgan) *Truro 4*
P *Ld Chan and Bp (alt)*   R L A WALKER,   NSM M L JEPP
MENHENIOT (St Lalluwy and St Antoninus) *Truro 12*
P *Ex Coll Ox*   V vacant (01579) 324705
MENITH WOOD (Chapel)   *see* Teme Valley N *Worc*
MENSTON (St John the Divine) w Woodhead *Bradf 4*   P *Bp*
V R J YEOMAN
MENTMORE (St Mary the Virgin)   *see* Cheddington w Mentmore *Ox*
MEOLE BRACE (Holy Trinity) *Lich 20*   P J K Bather Esq
V P J CANSDALE,   C C S MCBRIDE,   NSM V PITT,
OLM C RUXTON
MEOLS, GREAT (St John the Baptist) *Ches 8*   P *Bp*
V G A ROSSITER,   NSM J E BISSON
MEOLS, NORTH Team Ministry, The (St Cuthbert) *Liv 9*
P *Patr Bd*   TR P C GREEN,   TV J HILL
MEON, EAST (All Saints) *Portsm 4*   P *Ld Chan*
V T E LOUDEN
MEON, WEST (St John the Evangelist) and Warnford *Portsm 4*
P *Bp and DBP (alt)*   P-in-c C E SACKLEY
MEON BRIDGE *Portsm 1*   P *Bp*   R S H HOLT
MEONSTOKE (St Andrew)   *see* Meon Bridge *Portsm*
MEOPHAM (St John the Baptist) w Nurstead *Roch 1*   P *D&C and Lt-Col F B Edmeades (jt)*   R T G OLIVER,
C M A HARRIS,   NSM C D FORMAN
MEPAL (St Mary)   *see* Witcham w Mepal *Ely*
MEPPERSHALL (St Mary the Virgin) and Shefford *St Alb 8*
P *Bp and St Jo Coll Cam (alt)*   V J A HARPER
MERE (St Michael the Archangel) w West Knoyle and Maiden Bradley *Sarum 17*   P *Bp*   P-in-c P N BARNES
MERESIDE (St Wilfrid)   *see* Blackpool St Wilfrid *Blackb*
MEREVALE (St Mary the Virgin)   *see* Baxterley w Hurley and Wood End and Merevale etc *Birm*
MEREWORTH (St Lawrence) w West Peckham *Roch 7*
P *Viscount Falmouth and D&C (alt)*   R vacant (01622) 812214
MERIDEN (St Laurence) *Cov 4*   P *Chapter Cov Cathl*
R vacant (01676) 522719
MERRINGTON (St John the Evangelist) *Dur 6*   P *D&C*
P-in-c G NORMAN
MERRIOTT (All Saints) w Hinton, Dinnington and Lopen *B & W 14*   P *D&C Bris (2 turns), Bp (1 turn)*   R J R HICKS,
C R B HICKS
MERROW (St John the Evangelist) *Guildf 5*   P Earl of Onslow
R C J LUCKRAFT,   NSM R BROTHWELL,
OLM D E C MATTHEWS
MERRY HILL (St Joseph of Arimathea)   *see* Penn Fields *Lich*
MERRYMEET (St Mary)   *see* Menheniot *Truro*
MERSEA, WEST (St Peter and St Pau) w East (St Edmund), Peldon, Great and Little Wigborough *Chelmsf 16*
P *Prime Min (1 turn), Patr Bd (2 turns)*   R S C NORTON,
NSM J R PANTRY, A J ELMES

MERSHAM (St John the Baptist) w Hinxhill and Sellindge
Cant 6   P *Abp*   P-in-c R L LE ROSSIGNOL,   NSM S M COX
MERSTHAM (St Katharine) (Epiphany), South Merstham and Gatton *S'wark 26*   P *Patr Bd*   TR J E SMITH,
TV J P ASHTON,   NSM S M WEAKLEY,   OLM V J WILLIAMS
MERSTHAM, SOUTH (All Saints)   *see* Merstham, S Merstham and Gatton *S'wark*
MERTON (All Saints)   *see* Shebbear, Buckland Filleigh, Sheepwash etc *Ex*
MERTON (St James) *S'wark 13*   P *Bp and V Merton St Mary (jt)*   P-in-c J B EASTON-CROUCH
MERTON (St John the Divine)   *see* Merton Priory *S'wark*
MERTON (St Mary) *S'wark 13*   P *Bp*   V J A HAYWARD,
C K M CAMPION-SPALL
MERTON (St Peter)   *see* Caston, Griston, Merton, Thompson etc *Nor*
MERTON (St Swithun)   *see* Ray Valley *Ox*
MERTON PRIORY *S'wark 13*   P *Patr Bd*   TR C J I PALMER,
TV P G HAMBLING
MESHAW (St John)   *see* Burrington, Chawleigh, Cheldon, Chulmleigh etc *Ex*
MESSING (All Saints)   *see* Copford w Easthorpe and Messing w Inworth *Chelmsf*
MESSINGHAM (Holy Trinity) *Linc 4*   P *Bp*   V G D MASSEY
MESTY CROFT (St Luke)   *see* Wednesbury St Paul Wood Green *Lich*
METFIELD (St John the Baptist)   *see* Fressingfield, Mendham etc *St E*
METHERINGHAM (St Wilfred) w Blankney and Dunston
Linc 18   P *Bp (2 turns), Br Field Products Ltd (1 turn)*
C J S PARKIN
METHLEY (St Oswald) w Mickletown *Ripon 8*   P *Bp (3 turns), Duchy of Lanc (1 turn)*   P-in-c A J PEARSON
METHWOLD (St George)   *see* Grimshoe *Ely*
METTINGHAM (All Saints)   *see* Wainford *St E*
METTON (St Andrew)   *see* Roughton and Felbrigg, Metton, Sustead etc *Nor*
MEVAGISSEY (St Peter)   *see* St Mewan w Mevagissey and St Ewe *Truro*
MEXBOROUGH (St John the Baptist) *Sheff 12*   P *Adn York*
V D R WISE
MEYSEY HAMPTON (St Mary)   *see* Fairford Deanery *Glouc*
MICHAEL (St Michael and All Angels) *S & M 3*   P *The Crown*
V C D ROGERS,   C A M CONVERY
MICHAELCHURCH ESCLEY (St Michael)   *see* Clodock and Longtown w Craswall, Llanveynoe etc *Heref*
MICHAELSTOW (St Michael)   *see* St Tudy w St Mabyn and Michaelstow *Truro*
MICHELDEVER (St Mary)   *see* Upper Dever *Win*
MICHELMERSH (Our Lady) and Awbridge and Braishfield and Farley Chamberlayne and Timsbury *Win 12*   P *Bp*   R vacant (01794) 368335
MICKLEGATE (Holy Trinity)   *see* York H Trin Micklegate *York*
MICKLEHAM (St Michael)   *see* Leatherhead and Mickleham *Guildf*
MICKLEHURST (All Saints Institute) *Ches 14*   P *Bp*
P-in-c P J HIBBERT
MICKLEOVER (All Saints) *Derby 10*   P *MMCET*
NSM M P STAUNTON
MICKLEOVER (St John) *Derby 10*   P *Bp*
NSM M P STAUNTON
MICKLETON (St Lawrence), Willersey w Saintbury, Weston-sub-Edge and Aston-sub-Edge *Glouc 9*   P *Bp, Lt Col J H Gibbon, Viscount Sandon (1 turn), Ld Chan (1 turn)*
P-in-c F W DAWSON
MICKLEY (St George)   *see* Bywell and Mickley *Newc*
MICKLEY (St John the Evangelist)   *see* Fountains Gp *Ripon*
MID CHURNET   *see* Kingsley and Foxt-w-Whiston and Oakamoor etc *Lich*
MID LOES *St E 18*   P *Ld Chan (1 turn), MMCET, CPAS, Bp, and Wadh Coll Ox (1 turn)*   R S F BRIAN,
OLM J M CHENERY
MID MARSH Group, The *Linc 12*   P *A M D Hall Esq, Bp, D&C, and Lord Deramore (by turn)*   P-in-c C M TURNER,
OLM L W CARROLL, J R SELFE
MID TRENT *Lich 10*   P *Patr Bd*   TR P S DANIEL,
TV S J ABRAM,   NSM J P PHILLIPS
MID-WYEDEAN CHURCHES   *see* Coleford, Staunton, Newland, Redbrook etc *Glouc*
MIDDLE   *see also under substantive place name*
MIDDLE RASEN Group, The *Linc 5*   P *Bp, Charterhouse, and DBP (jt)*   R P C PATRICK,   C C R HARRINGTON
MIDDLEHAM (St Mary and St Alkelda) w Coverdale and East Witton and Thornton Steward *Ripon 4*   P *Bp,*

R Craven-Smith-Milnes Esq, and W R Burdon Esq (jt)
R B A GIBLIN, C Y S CALLAGHAN
MIDDLESBROUGH (All Saints) York 17 P Abp
V G HOLLAND, C P B ARCHIBALD
MIDDLESBROUGH (Ascension) York 17 P Abp
V D G HODGSON
MIDDLESBROUGH (Holy Trinity) see N Ormesby York
MIDDLESBROUGH (St Agnes) York 17 P Abp
P-in-c A M GRANGE, NSM M EDWARDS
MIDDLESBROUGH (St Barnabas) see Linthorpe York
MIDDLESBROUGH (St Columba w St Paul) York 17 P Abp
V S COOPER, C A HOWARD, NSM P M KRONBERGS
MIDDLESBROUGH (St John the Evangelist) York 17 P Abp
V S COOPER, C A HOWARD
MIDDLESBROUGH (St Martin of Tours) (St Cuthbert)
York 17 P Abp V D S WATSON, NSM J M COOK
MIDDLESBROUGH (St Oswald) (St Chad) York 17 P Abp
V S RICHARDSON
MIDDLESBROUGH (St Thomas) York 17 P Abp
V T M LEATHLEY
MIDDLESMOOR (St Chad) see Upper Nidderdale Ripon
MIDDLESTOWN (St Luke) Wakef 11 P R Thornhill
P-in-c L A MATTACKS
MIDDLETON (All Saints) see N Hinckford Chelmsf
MIDDLETON (Holy Ghost) see Kirkby Lonsdale Carl
MIDDLETON (Holy Trinity) see Ludlow Heref
MIDDLETON (Holy Trinity) Heref 12 P V Chirbury
P-in-c R N LEACH
MIDDLETON (Holy Trinity) see Yoxmere St E
MIDDLETON (St Andrew), Newton and Sinnington York 19
P Abp (2 turns), Simeon's Trustees (1 turn) R vacant (01751)
474858
MIDDLETON (St Cross) Ripon 6 P DBP
P-in-c A T C MYERS, NSM J H TURNER
MIDDLETON (St John the Baptist) see Curdworth, Middleton
and Wishaw Birm
MIDDLETON (St Leonard) (St Margaret) and Thornham
Man 14 P Bp R N J FEIST, OLM F JACKSON, S L SPENCER,
D E BROOKS, P J DEMAIN
MIDDLETON (St Mary) see W Winch w Setchey, N Runcton
and Middleton Nor
MIDDLETON (St Mary the Virgin) Ripon 6 P V Rothwell
P-in-c A T C MYERS
MIDDLETON (St Michael and All Angels) see Youlgreave,
Middleton, Stanton-in-Peak etc Derby
MIDDLETON (St Nicholas) Chich 1 P D&C
V W T MARSTON, NSM P G SWADLING
MIDDLETON-BY-WIRKSWORTH (Holy Trinity)
see Wirksworth Derby
MIDDLETON CHENEY (All Saints) see Chenderit Pet
MIDDLETON-IN-CHIRBY (Holy Trinity) see Middleton
Heref
**MIDDLETON-IN-TEESDALE (St Mary the Virgin) w Forest
and Frith** Dur 7 P Lord Barnard and The Crown (alt)
P-in-c C J ELLIOTT, NSM A E FREESTONE
MIDDLETON JUNCTION (St Gabriel) Man 14 P Bp
V vacant 0161-643 5064
MIDDLETON ON LEVEN (St Cuthbert) see Rudby in
Cleveland w Middleton York
MIDDLETON-ON-THE-HILL (St Mary the Virgin)
see Leominster Heref
MIDDLETON-ON-THE-WOLDS (St Andrew) see Woldsburn
York
MIDDLETON SCRIVEN (St John the Baptist) see Stottesdon
w Farlow, Cleeton St Mary etc Heref
MIDDLETON ST GEORGE (St George) (St Laurence) Dur 8
P Bp R P S D NEVILLE, C D TOLHURST
MIDDLETON STONEY (All Saints) see Akeman Ox
MIDDLETON TYAS (St Michael and All Angels) see E
Richmond Ripon
MIDDLETOWN (St John the Baptist) see Gt Wollaston Heref
MIDDLEWICH (St Michael and All Angels) w Byley Ches 6
P Bp V S M DREW, NSM E WOODE, C M HUGHES, L V REED
MIDDLEZOY (Holy Cross) and Othery and Moorlinch B & W 4
P Bp Worc (1 turn), Bp (2 turns) P-in-c J K L POWELL
MIDGHAM (St Matthew) see Aldermaston and Woolhampton
Ox
MIDHOPE (St James) see Penistone and Thurlstone Wakef
MIDHURST (St Mary Magdalene and St Denis) Chich 10
P Rathbone Trust Co and Cowdray Trust (jt)
V Q M RONCHETTI
MIDSOMER NORTON (St John the Baptist) w Clandown
B & W 11 P Ch Ch Ox V C G CHIPLIN
MIDVILLE (St Peter) see Stickney Gp Linc
MILBER (St Luke) Ex 10 P Bp V J E POTTER

MILBORNE (St Andrew) see Puddletown, Tolpuddle and
Milborne w Dewlish Sarum
**MILBORNE PORT (St John the Evangelist) w Goathill and
Charlton Horethorne w Stowell** B & W 2 P Bp and
J K Wingfield Digby Esq (jt) V G W HARTLEY
MILBORNE WICK (Mission Church) see Milborne Port w
Goathill etc B & W
MILBOURNE (Holy Saviour) see Ponteland Newc
MILBURN (St Cuthbert) see Heart of Eden Carl
MILCOMBE (St Laurence) see Bloxham w Milcombe and S
Newington Ox
MILDEN (St Peter) see Monks Eleigh w Chelsworth and Brent
Eleigh etc St E
MILDENHALL (St John the Baptist) see Marlborough Sarum
MILDENHALL (St Mary) St E 11 P Patr Bd (2 turns), Bp
(1 turn) TV R I MECHANIC, S M LEATHLEY, NSM S BARTON,
OLM H B MULLIN
MILDMAY GROVE (St Jude and St Paul) Lon 6 P Islington
Ch Trust V J A OMOYAJOWO
MILE CROSS (St Catherine) Nor 2 P Dr J P English, Canon
G F Bridger, the Revd K W Habershon, and the Revd
H Palmer (jt) V P D MACKAY
MILE END Old Town (St Paul) see Bow Common Lon
MILE OAK (The Good Shepherd) see Portslade Gd Shep Chich
MILEHAM (St John the Baptist) see Litcham w Kempston, E
and W Lexham, Mileham etc Nor
MILES PLATTING (St Cuthbert) see Man Apostles w Miles
Platting Man
MILFORD (Holy Trinity) see Hazelwood, Holbrook and
Milford Derby
MILFORD (St John the Evangelist) Guildf 4 P V Witley
V C G POTTER
MILFORD, SOUTH (St Mary the Virgin) see Monk Fryston
and S Milford York
MILFORD-ON-SEA (All Saints) Win 11 P Bp
V D J FURNESS
MILL END (St Peter) and Heronsgate w West Hyde St Alb 4
P Bp and V Rickmansworth P-in-c S G CUTMORE
MILL HILL (John Keble Church) Lon 15 P Bp
V C M CHIVERS, C S P YOUNG
MILL HILL (St Michael and All Angels) Lon 15 P Bp
P-in-c S P YOUNG, C C M CHIVERS
MILL HILL (St Paul) see Hendon St Paul Mill Hill Lon
MILLAND (St Luke) see Lynch w Iping Marsh and Milland
Chich
MILLBROOK (All Saints) see St John w Millbrook Truro
MILLBROOK (Christ the King) see Kettering Ch the King Pet
MILLBROOK (Holy Trinity) Win 13 P Bp
P-in-c W F P PERRY, NSM W WHITFIELD
MILLBROOK Regents Park (St Clement) see Millbrook Win
MILLBROOK (St James) Ches 14 P Bp, V Stalybridge St Paul,
and Mrs E Bissill (jt) P-in-c A M DI CHIARA
MILLBROOK (St Michael and All Angels) see Ampthill w
Millbrook and Steppingley St Alb
MILLERS DALE (St Anne) see Tideswell Derby
MILLFIELD (St Mark) and Pallion St Luke Dur 16 P Bp
P-in-c O L ERIKSSON
MILLFIELD (St Mary) Dur 16 P The Crown V B SKELTON,
NSM D RAINE
MILLHOUSES (Holy Trinity) Sheff 2 P Bp V P A INGRAM
MILLHOUSES (St Oswald) see Sheff St Pet and St Oswald
Sheff
MILLINGTON (St Margaret) see Pocklington Wold York
MILLOM Holburn Hill (Mission) see Millom Carl
MILLOM (Holy Trinity) (St George) Carl 9 P Bp and
Trustees (jt) V R K S BRACEGIRDLE
MILNROW (St James) Man 17 P TR Rochdale
V R R USHER, NSM S E WARD
MILNSHAW (St Mary Magdalen) see Accrington Ch the King
Blackb
MILNTHORPE (St Thomas) see Heversham and Milnthorpe
Carl
MILSON (St George) see Cleobury Mortimer w Hopton Wafers
etc Heref
MILSTED (St Mary and the Holy Cross) see Tunstall and
Bredgar Cant
MILSTON (St Mary) see Avon Valley Sarum
MILTON (All Saints) Ely 6 P K Coll Cam
R D J CHAMBERLIN, NSM D M BAGULEY
MILTON (St Blaise) see Steventon w Milton Ox
MILTON (St James) (St Andrew's Church Centre) (St Patrick)
Portsm 6 P V Portsea St Mary V vacant (023) 9273 2786
MILTON (St John the Evangelist) see Adderbury w Milton Ox
MILTON (St Mary Magdalene) Win 9 P V Milford
R A H BAILEY, C H C JEVONS, W A O'CONNELL

MILTON (St Peter) w St Jude and Kewstoke *B & W 10*
  P *Ld Chan* **V** G P EALES, **NSM** G PUTNAM
MILTON (St Philip and St James) *Lich 8* **P** *Bp*
  V B E STATHAM
MILTON (St Simon and St Jude) *see* Gillingham and
  Milton-on-Stour *Sarum*
MILTON, GREAT (St Mary the Virgin) w Little (St James) and
  Great Haseley *Ox 1* **P** *Bp and D&C Windsor (jt)*
  R V L STORY
MILTON, SOUTH (All Saints) *see* Thurlestone, S Milton, W
  Alvington etc *Ex*
MILTON ABBAS (St James the Great) *see* Winterborne Valley
  and Milton Abbas *Sarum*
MILTON ABBOT (St Constantine), Dunterton, Lamerton,
  Sydenham Damerel, Marystowe and Coryton *Ex 25* **P** *Bp,*
  Bedford Estates, J W Tremayne Esq, Mrs E J Bullock,
  P T L Newman Esq (jt) **V** G J STANTON
MILTON BRYAN (St Peter) *see* Woburn w Eversholt, Milton
  Bryan, Battlesden etc *St Alb*
MILTON CLEVEDON (St James) *see* Evercreech w
  Chesterblade and Milton Clevedon *B & W*
MILTON COMBE (Holy Spirit) *see* Buckland Monachorum
  Ex
MILTON DAMEREL (Holy Trinity) *see* Holsworthy w
  Hollacombe and Milton Damerel *Ex*
MILTON ERNEST (All Saints), Pavenham and Thurleigh
  St Alb 13 **P** *Bp (2 turns), Lord Luke (1 turn)*
  P-in-c F F INALL
MILTON KEYNES (Christ the Cornerstone) *Ox 25* **P** *Bp*
  P-in-c E LOZADA-UZURIAGA, **C** T NORWOOD,
  NSM K STRAUGHAN
MILTON KEYNES VILLAGE (All Saints) *see* Walton Milton
  Keynes *Ox*
MILTON LILBOURNE (St Peter) *see* Vale of Pewsey *Sarum*
MILTON MALSOR (Holy Cross) *see* Collingtree w
  Courteenhall and Milton Malsor *Pet*
MILTON NEXT GRAVESEND (Christ Church) *Roch 4* **P** *Bp*
  V S C BREWER, **C** J A DREW, **Hon C** A P WIBROE
MILTON NEXT GRAVESEND (St Peter and St Paul) w Denton
  Roch 4 **P** *Bp* **R** G V HERBERT
MILTON NEXT SITTINGBOURNE (Holy Trinity) *Cant 15*
  P *D&C* **P-in-c** L R DENNY
MILTON REGIS (Holy Trinity) *see* Milton next Sittingbourne
  Cant
MILTON REGIS (St Mary) *see* Sittingbourne St Mary and St
  Mich *Cant*
MILTON-UNDER-WYCHWOOD (St Simon and St Jude)
  see Shipton-under-Wychwood w Milton, Fifield etc *Ox*
MILVERTON (St Michael) w Halse, Fitzhead and Ash Priors
  B & W 18 **P** *Bp, Adn, R Wiveliscombe and the Hills, and*
  MMCET (jt) **R** H L STAINER
MILVERTON, NEW (St Mark) *Cov 11* **P** CPAS
  V P MANUEL
MILVERTON, OLD (St James) *see* Lillington and Old
  Milverton *Cov*
MILWICH (All Saints) *see* Mid Trent *Lich*
MIMMS *see also* MYMMS
MIMMS, SOUTH (Christ Church) *Lon 14* **P** *Ch Patr Trust*
  V N T W TAYLOR, **C** J E JAMES, **NSM** P W LIDDELOW
MINCHINHAMPTON (Holy Trinity) w Box and Amberley
  Glouc 4 **P** *Bp and DBP (jt)* **R** C P COLLINGWOOD,
  NSM A V M MORRIS, J WALDEN, S F EMERY
MINEHEAD (St Andrew) (St Michael) (St Peter) *B & W 15*
  P *Lt-Col G W F Luttrell and Bp (jt)* **V** P J DOBBIN
MINETY (St Leonard) *see* Ashton Keynes, Leigh and Minety
  Bris
MININGSBY WITH EAST KIRKBY (St Nicholas)
  see Marden Hill Gp *Linc*
MINLEY (St Andrew) *Guildf 1* **P** *Bp* **V** M W NEALE
MINNIS BAY (St Thomas) *see* Birchington w Acol and Minnis
  Bay *Cant*
MINSKIP (Mission Room) *see* Aldborough w Boroughbridge
  and Roecliffe *Ripon*
MINSTEAD (All Saints) *see* Lyndhurst and Emery Down and
  Minstead *Win*
MINSTER (St Mary the Virgin) w Monkton *Cant 5* **P** *Abp*
  P-in-c R R COLES, **OLM** J A BAKER
MINSTER (St Merteriana) *see* Boscastle w Davidstow *Truro*
MINSTER-IN-SHEPPEY (St Mary and St Sexburga) *Cant 15*
  P *Ch Patr Trust* **P-in-c** A J HOUSTON, **C** S J MARTIN, **Hon**
  C B I M DURKAN, C J SHIPLEY
MINSTER LOVELL (St Kenelm) *Ox 8* **P** *Eton Coll and*
  Ch Ch (jt) **V** A W D GABB-JONES
MINSTERLEY (Holy Trinity) *Heref 12* **P** *DBP and Bp (alt)*
  V A N TOOP, **NSM** M-L TOOP, P BICKLEY

MINSTERWORTH (St Peter) *see* Westbury-on-Severn w
  Flaxley, Blaisdon etc *Glouc*
MINTERNE MAGNA (St Andrew) *see* Buckland Newton,
  Cerne Abbas, Godmanstone etc *Sarum*
MINTING (St Andrew) *see* Bardney *Linc*
MIREHOUSE (St Andrew) *Carl 5* **P** *Bp* **P-in-c** C N CASEY
MIRFIELD (St Mary) *Wakef 9* **P** *Bp* **P-in-c** H C BAKER,
  C C A MACPHERSON, **NSM** H C BUTLER
MISERDEN (St Andrew) *see* Brimpsfield w Birdlip, Syde,
  Daglingworth etc *Glouc*
MISSENDEN, GREAT (St Peter and St Paul) w Ballinger and
  Little Hampden *Ox 28* **P** *Bp* **V** R E HARPER,
  NSM C BAILEY
MISSENDEN, LITTLE (St John the Baptist) *Ox 28*
  P *Earl Howe* **P-in-c** J V SIMPSON
MISSION (St John the Baptist) *see* Bawtry w Austerfield and
  Misson *S'well*
MISTERTON (All Saints) *see* Beckingham and Walkeringham
  and Misterton etc *S'well*
MISTERTON (St Leonard) *see* Wulfric Benefice *B & W*
MISTERTON (St Leonard) *see* Gilmorton, Peatling Parva,
  Kimcote etc *Leic*
MISTLEY (St Mary and St Michael) w Manningtree and
  Bradfield *Chelmsf 20* **P** *DBP and Bp (jt)* **P-in-c** C A HILLS,
  NSM J R BRIEN
MITCHAM (Ascension) Pollards Hill *S'wark 13* **P** *Bp*
  V J M THOMAS, **NSM** J E ROBERTS
MITCHAM (Christ Church) *see* Merton Priory *S'wark*
MITCHAM (St Barnabas) *S'wark 13* **P** *Bp*
  V J G CAVALCANTI, **Hon C** T PAYNE
MITCHAM (St Mark) *S'wark 13* **P** *Bp* **V** S H COULSON
MITCHAM (St Olave) *S'wark 13* **P** *The Crown* **V** P G ENSOR
MITCHAM (St Peter and St Paul) *S'wark 13* **P** *Keble Coll Ox*
  V J C ANSELL, **NSM** M J COCKFIELD
MITCHELDEAN (St Michael and All Angels) *see* Abenhall w
  Mitcheldean *Glouc*
MITFORD (St Mary Magdalene) and Hebron *Newc 11*
  P *Ld Chan and the Revd B W J Mitford (alt)*
  P-in-c J J L DOBSON, **OLM** J ROWLEY
MITHIAN (St Peter) *see* St Agnes and Mount Hawke w
  Mithian *Truro*
MITTON (All Hallows) *see* Hurst Green and Mitton *Bradf*
MIXBURY (All Saints) *see* Shelswell *Ox*
MIXENDEN (Holy Nativity) and Illingworth *Wakef 4* **P** *Bp*
  and V Halifax (jt) **V** D E FLETCHER
MOBBERLEY (St Wilfrid) *Ches 12* **P** *Bp* **R** I BLAY
MOCCAS (St Michael and All Angels) *see* Cusop w Blakemere,
  Bredwardine w Brobury etc *Heref*
MODBURY (St George), Bigbury, Ringmore w Kingston, Aveton
  Gifford, Woodleigh, Loddiswell and Allington, East *Ex 14*
  P *Patr Bd* **TR** N A BARKER, **TV** L J VALIANT
MODDERSHALL (All Saints) *see* Stone Ch Ch and Oulton
  Lich
MOGGERHANGER (St John the Evangelist) *see* Cople,
  Moggerhanger and Willington *St Alb*
MOLASH (St Peter) *see* Chilham w Challock and Molash *Cant*
MOLDGREEN (Christ Church) and Rawthorpe St James
  Wakef 1 **P** *R Kirkheaton and DBP (jt)*
  P-in-c H D ATKINSON
MOLESCROFT (St Leonard) *see* Beverley Minster *York*
MOLESEY, EAST (St Mary) (St Paul) *Guildf 8* **P** *Bp*
  V J P WEBB, **NSM** C S BOURNE, B C HUNT
MOLESEY, WEST (St Peter) *Guildf 8* **P** *Canon*
  W K Perry-Gore **V** P A TAILBY
MOLESWORTH (St Peter) *see* Brington w Molesworth and Old
  Weston *Ely*
MOLLAND (St Mary) *see* Bishopsnympton, Rose Ash,
  Mariansleigh etc *Ex*
MOLLINGTON (All Saints) *see* Shires' Edge *Ox*
MOLTON, NORTH (All Saints) *see* S Molton w Nymet
  St George, High Bray etc *Ex*
MOLTON, SOUTH (St Mary Magdalene) w Nymet St George,
  High Bray, Charles, Filleigh, East Buckland, Warkleigh,
  Satterleigh, Chittlehamholt, Kingsnympton, Romansleigh,
  North Molton, Twitchen and Chittlehampton *Ex 19* **P** *DBP*
  TV D W T RUDMAN, **C** C G ROBINSON, P J ATTWOOD,
  NSM C M G POUNCEY
MONEWDEN (St Mary) *see* Mid Loes *St E*
MONGEHAM, GREAT (St Martin) *see* Deal St Leon w
  St Rich and Sholden etc *Cant*
MONK BRETTON (St Paul) *Wakef 7* **P** *V Royston*
  V K MADDY, **OLM** J M CROSSLAND
MONK FRYSTON (St Wilfrid of Ripon) and South Milford
  York 4 **P** *Ld Chan and Abp (alt)* **R** J C HETHERINGTON
MONK SHERBORNE (All Saints) *see* The Sherbornes w
  Pamber *Win*

MONK SOHAM (St Peter) *see* Worlingworth, Southolt, Tannington, Bedfield etc *St E*

MONKEN HADLEY (St Mary the Virgin) *Lon 14* P *Bp* R *vacant* (020) 8449 2414

MONKHOPTON (St Peter) *see* Upton Cressett w Monk Hopton *Heref*

MONKLAND (All Saints) *see* Leominster *Heref*

MONKLEIGH (St George) *see* Bideford, Northam, Westward Ho!, Appledore etc *Ex*

MONKMOOR (St Peter) *see* Shrewsbury H Cross *Lich*

MONKOKEHAMPTON (All Saints) *Ex 20* P *Bp* P-in-c C A BRODRIBB

MONKS COPPENHALL (Christ Church) *see* Crewe Ch Ch *Ches*

MONKS ELEIGH (St Peter) w Chelsworth and Brent Eleigh w Milden and Kettlebaston *St E 10* P *Bp, Guild of All So, Ld Chan (2 turns), and M J Hawkins Esq* R B J FINDLAY

MONKS HILL (St Francis) *see* Selsdon St Fran CD *S'wark*

MONKS HORTON (St Peter) *see* Smeeth w Monks Horton and Stowting and Brabourne *Cant*

MONKS KIRBY (St Editha) *see* Revel Gp *Cov*

MONKS RISBOROUGH (St Dunstan) *see* Risborough *Ox*

MONKSEATON (St Mary) *Newc 5* P *Bp* V R P GREENWOOD, C B H CARTER, Hon C E J NOBLE

MONKSEATON (St Peter) *Newc 5* P *Bp* C P A CRAIGHEAD

MONKSILVER (All Saints) *see* Quantock Towers *B & W*

MONKTON (St Mary Magdalene) *see* Minster w Monkton *Cant*

MONKTON, WEST (St Augustine) w Kingston St Mary, Broomfield and Cheddon Fitzpaine *B & W 17* P *Bp and D&C (jt)* R G J BOUCHER, NSM S M HOUNSELL, A E FULTON

MONKTON COMBE (St Michael) *see* Combe Down w Monkton Combe and S Stoke *B & W*

MONKTON FARLEIGH (St Peter) *see* N Bradford on Avon and Villages *Sarum*

MONKTON WYLD (St Andrew) *see* Golden Cap Team *Sarum*

MONKWEARMOUTH (All Saints) (St Andrew) (St Peter) *Dur 16* P *Bp* TV T P GIBBONS, OLM P G A SMITHSON

MONKWOOD (Mission Church) *see* Bishop's Sutton and Ropley and W Tisted *Win*

MONNINGTON-ON-WYE (St Mary) *see* Letton w Staunton, Byford, Mansel Gamage etc *Heref*

MONTACUTE (St Catherine of Alexandria) *see* Odcombe, Brympton, Lufton and Montacute *B & W*

MONTFORD (St Chad) *see* Bicton, Montford w Shrawardine and Fitz *Lich*

MONTON (St Paul) *see* Eccles *Man*

MONXTON (St Mary) *see* Portway and Danebury *Win*

MONYASH (St Leonard) *see* Taddington, Chelmorton and Monyash etc *Derby*

MOOR (St Thomas) *see* Fladbury, Hill and Moor, Wyre Piddle etc *Worc*

MOOR ALLERTON (St John the Evangelist) (St Stephen) and Shadwell Team Ministry *Ripon 5* P *Patr Bd* TR C P DOBBIN, TV N D BEER, NSM D L LOFTHOUSE

MOOR COURT (St Mary) *see* Pembridge w Moor Court, Shobdon, Staunton etc *Heref*

MOOR GRANGE (St Andrew) *see* Abbeylands *Ripon*

MOOR MILNER (Church Institute) *see* Daresbury *Ches*

MOOR MONKTON (All Saints) *see* Rufforth w Moor Monkton and Hessay *York*

MOORBRIDGE LANE (St Luke) *see* Stapleford *S'well*

MOORCOURT (St Mary) *see* Pembridge w Moor Court, Shobdon, Staunton etc *Heref*

MOORDOWN (St John the Baptist) *Win 8* P *Bp* V S W MILLER, NSM J L WILLIAMS

MOORENDS (St Wilfrith) *Sheff 10* P *Bp* V *vacant* (01405) 741758

MOORHOUSE (Chantry Chapel) *see* Kneesall w Laxton and Wellow *S'well*

MOORHOUSES (St Lawrence) *see* Fen and Hill Gp *Linc*

MOORLAND TEAM *see* Ashburton, Bickington, Buckland in the Moor etc *Ex*

MOORLINCH (Blessed Virgin Mary) *see* Middlezoy and Othery and Moorlinch *B & W*

MOORSHOLM (St Mary) *York 21* P *Abp* V M J HAZELTON

MOORSIDE (St Thomas) *see* Oldham Moorside *Man*

MOORSIDE (St Wilfrid) *see* Doxford St Wilfrid *Dur*

MOORTOWN (St Stephen) *see* Moor Allerton and Shadwell *Ripon*

MORBORNE (All Saints) *see* Stilton w Denton and Caldecote etc *Ely*

MORCHARD BISHOP (St Mary) *see* N Creedy *Ex*

MORCOTT (St Mary the Virgin) *see* Barrowden and Wakerley w S Luffenham etc *Pet*

MORDEN (St Lawrence) (St George) (St Martin) (Emmanuel Church Hall) *S'wark 13* P *Patr Bd* TR R F SKINNER, TV D R H MCGOWAN, A L FLOWERDAY, L J WELLS, Hon C P S OMUKU, OLM J D GODDARD

MORDEN (St Mary) *see* Red Post *Sarum*

MORDIFORD (Holy Rood) *see* Fownhope w Mordiford, Brockhampton etc *Heref*

MORE (St Peter) *see* Wentnor w Ratlinghope, Myndtown, Norbury etc *Heref*

MOREBATH (St George) *see* Bampton, Morebath, Clayhanger, Petton etc *Ex*

MORECAMBE (Holy Trinity) *see* Poulton-le-Sands w Morecambe St Laur *Blackb*

MORECAMBE (St Andrew) *see* Heysham *Blackb*

MORECAMBE (St Barnabas) *Blackb 11* P *R Poulton-le-Sands* C T H DAVIS

MORECAMBE (St Christopher) *see* Bare *Blackb*

MORECAMBE (St James) *see* Heysham *Blackb*

MORECAMBE (St John) *see* Sandylands *Blackb*

MORECAMBE (St Peter) *see* Heysham *Blackb*

MORECAMBE (The Ascension) *see* Torrisholme *Blackb*

MORELEIGH (All Saints) *see* Diptford, N Huish, Harberton, Harbertonford etc *Ex*

MORESBY (St Bridget) *Carl 5* P *Earl of Lonsdale* P-in-c S R GRIFFITHS

MORESBY PARKS (Mission Church) *see* Moresby *Carl*

MORESTEAD (not known) *see* Twyford and Owslebury and Morestead etc *Win*

MORETON (Christ Church) *Ches 8* P *Simeon's Trustees* R G J COUSINS, C P C BOURKE

MORETON (St Mary) *see* Fyfield, Moreton w Bobbingworth etc *Chelmsf*

MORETON (St Mary) *see* Adbaston, High Offley, Knightley, Norbury etc *Lich*

MORETON (St Nicholas) and Woodsford w Tincleton *Sarum 1* P *Miss M B F Frampton* R J A BIRDSEYE

MORETON, NORTH (All Saints) *see* The Churn *Ox*

MORETON, SOUTH (St John the Baptist) *as above*

MORETON CORBET (St Bartholomew) *Lich 22* P C C *Corbet Esq* R D J HUMPHRIES

MORETON HALL (Christ Church) *see* Bury St Edmunds Ch Ch *St E*

MORETON-IN-MARSH (St David) w Batsford, Todenham, Lower Lemington and Longborough w Sezincote *Glouc 9* P *Bp and Lord Dulverton (1 turn), and Bp, Lord Dulverton, Lord Leigh, and Mrs S Peake (1 turn)* R S M WOOKEY

MORETON JEFFRIES (St Peter and St Paul) *see* Bromyard and Stoke Lacy *Heref*

MORETON MORRELL (Holy Cross) *see* Newbold Pacey w Moreton Morrell *Cov*

MORETON-ON-LUGG (St Andrew) *see* Pipe-cum-Lyde and Moreton-on-Lugg *Heref*

MORETON PINKNEY (St Mary the Virgin) *see* Culworth w Sulgrave and Thorpe Mandeville etc *Pet*

MORETON SAY (St Margaret of Antioch) *see* Adderley, Ash, Calverhall, Ightfield etc *Lich*

MORETON VALENCE (St Stephen) *see* Eastington, Frocester, Haresfield etc *Glouc*

MORETONHAMPSTEAD (St Andrew), Manaton, North Bovey and Lustleigh *Ex 9* P *Bp and DBP (jt)* R *vacant* (01647) 441098

MORGAN'S VALE (St Birinus) *see* Forest and Avon *Sarum*

MORLAND (St Lawrence), Thrimby, Gt Strickland and Cliburn *Carl 1* P *Lord Hothfield and D&C (jt)* P-in-c S J FYFE

MORLEY (St Botolph) *see* High Oak, Hingham and Scoulton w Wood Rising *Nor*

MORLEY (St Matthew) w Smalley and Horsley Woodhouse *Derby 12* P *Bp* C M G ALEXANDER, T J WILLIAMS, NSM R HOWORTH

MORLEY (St Peter) *see* High Oak, Hingham and Scoulton w Wood Rising *Nor*

MORLEY (St Peter) (St Paul) *Wakef 8* P *Patr Bd* TR M M DYE, TV M J GODFREY, C R SUTHERLAND, OLM K M DAVIS

MORNINGTHORPE (St John the Baptist) *see* Hempnall *Nor*

MORPETH (St James) (St Mary the Virgin) *Newc 11* P *Bp* R R H MCLEAN, C A G CURTIS, NSM M O CHESTER

MORRIS GREEN (St Bede) *see* Bolton St Bede *Man*

MORSTON (All Saints) *see* Stiffkey and Bale *Nor*

MORTEHOE (St Mary Magdalene) *see* Ilfracombe, Lee, Woolacombe, Bittadon etc *Ex*

MORTIMER COMMON (St John) *see* Stratfield Mortimer and Mortimer W End etc *Ox*

MORTIMER WEST END (St Saviour) *as above*

MORTLAKE (St Mary) w East Sheen *S'wark 16* P *Patr Bd* TR A L NICKSON, TV W S GRIFFITH, S G LEE, Hon C P D KING, OLM O J WILLIAMSON

MORTOMLEY (St Saviour) High Green *Sheff 3*   P *Bp*
V E MITCHELL

MORTON (Holy Cross) and Stonebroom w Shirland *Derby 1*
P *Bp, St Jo Coll Cam, Adn Chesterfield, and trustees (by turn)*
P-in-c M I JACQUES,   **NSM** J A S WOOD, C D WOOD, J A EPTON

MORTON (St Denis) *see* Rolleston w Fiskerton, Morton and Upton *S'well*

MORTON (St John the Baptist) *see* Ringstone in Aveland Gp *Linc*

MORTON (St Luke) *Bradf 8*   P *Bp*   **P-in-c** M C CANSDALE

MORTON (St Paul) *see* Gainsborough and Morton *Linc*

MORTON (St Philip and St James) *see* Llanyblodwel, Llanymynech, Morton and Trefonen *Lich*

MORTON, EAST *see* Morton St Luke *Bradf*

MORTON BAGOT (Holy Trinity) *see* Spernall, Morton Bagot and Oldberrow *Cov*

MORVAH (St Bridget of Sweden) *see* Pendeen w Morvah *Truro*

MORVAL (St Wenna) *see* Duloe, Herodsfoot, Morval and St Pinnock *Truro*

MORVILLE (St Gregory) w Aston Eyre *Heref 8*   P *DBP*
V S H CAWDELL,   **Hon C** H J PATTERSON

MORWENSTOW (St John the Baptist) *see* Kilkhampton w Morwenstow *Truro*

MOSBROUGH (St Mark) *Sheff 1*   P *Bp*   V S T STEWART

MOSELEY (St Agnes) *Birm 5*   P *V Moseley St Mary*
V P H ANSELL

MOSELEY (St Anne) (St Mary) *Birm 5*   P *Bp*
V J N J C DUSSEK,   **NSM** F J BERRY

MOSLEY COMMON (St John) *see* Astley, Tyldesley and Mosley Common *Man*

MOSS BANK (Mission Church) *see* Carr Mill *Liv*

MOSS SIDE (Christ Church) *Man 3*   P *Trustees*
R S D A KILLWICK

MOSS SIDE (St James w St Clement) *see* Whalley Range St Edm and Moss Side etc *Man*

MOSSER (St Michael's Chapel) *see* Clifton, Dean and Mosser *Carl*

MOSSER (St Philip) *as above*

MOSSLEY (Holy Trinity) *see* Congleton *Ches*

MOSSLEY (St George) *Man 13*   P *R Ashton-under-Lyne St Mich*   V R J LINDSAY,   **OLM** P PHILLIPS

MOSSLEY ESTATE (St Thomas Church) *see* Bloxwich *Lich*

MOSSLEY HILL (St Barnabas) (St Matthew and St James)
Liv 4   P *Patr Bd*   **TR** G J BUTLAND,   **TV** A KENNEDY,
OLM C NICHOLSON

MOSSWOOD (St Barnabas) *see* Cannock and Huntington *Lich*

MOSTERTON (St Mary) *see* Beaminster Area *Sarum*

MOSTON (St Chad) *Man 4*   P *Bp*   **OLM** I L SMITH

MOSTON (St John) Ashley Lane *Man 4*   P *Bp*   R *vacant*
0161-205 4967

MOSTON (St Luke) *see* Lightbowne *Man*

MOSTON (St Mary) *Man 4*   P *D&C*
P-in-c M R M CALLADINE,   **OLM** J E GRAYSON

MOTCOMBE (St Mary) *see* Shaftesbury *Sarum*

MOTSPUR PARK (Holy Cross) *S'wark 13*   P *Bp*
V R S TAYLOR

MOTTINGHAM (St Andrew) (St Alban Mission Church)
S'wark 3   P *Bp*   R I M WELCH,   **NSM** S P WARNER

MOTTINGHAM (St Edward the Confessor) *S'wark 3*   P *Bp*
V M J JACKSON

MOTTISFONT (St Andrew) *see* Broughton, Bossington, Houghton and Mottisfont *Win*

MOTTISTONE (St Peter and St Paul) *see* Brighstone and Brooke w Mottistone *Portsm*

MOTTRAM IN LONGDENDALE (St Michael) *Ches 14*   P *Bp*
V P G BURROWS

MOULSECOOMB (St Andrew) *Chich 2*   P *Bp*
P-in-c J C WALL,   **TV** R C GOULDTHORPE,   **C** W J WESSON,
NSM J W M COLLINS

MOULSFORD (St John the Baptist) *see* Cholsey and Moulsford *Ox*

MOULSHAM (St John the Evangelist) *Chelmsf 9*   P *Dean*
V K R MAGEE

MOULSHAM (St Luke) *Chelmsf 9*   P *Bp*   V C SMITH,
C M L BISHOP

MOULSOE (The Assumption of the Blessed Virgin Mary)
see Newport Pagnell w Lathbury and Moulsoe *Ox*

MOULTON (All Saints) (St James) (Mission Room) *Linc 17*
P *DBP*   **P-in-c** R J SEAL,   **NSM** E D CRUST

MOULTON (Mission Church) *see* E Richmond *Ripon*

MOULTON (St Peter) *see* Dalham, Gazeley, Higham, Kentford and Moulton *St E*

MOULTON (St Peter and St Paul) *Pet 4*   P *Ch Soc Trust*
V P H BRECKWOLDT,   **C** R A MILES

MOULTON (St Stephen the Martyr) *Ches 6*   P *R Davenham*
V *vacant* (01606) 593355

MOULTON, GREAT (St Michael) *see* Bunwell, Carleton Rode, Tibenham, Gt Moulton etc *Nor*

MOUNT BURES (St John) *see* Wormingford, Mt Bures and Lt Horkesley *Chelmsf*

MOUNT GOULD (St Simon) *see* Plymouth St Simon and St Mary *Ex*

MOUNT HAWKE (St John the Baptist) *see* St Agnes and Mount Hawke w Mithian *Truro*

MOUNT PELLON (Christ Church) *see* Halifax St Aug and Mount Pellon *Wakef*

MOUNTFIELD (All Saints) *see* Brightling, Dallington, Mountfield etc *Chich*

MOUNTNESSING (St Giles) *see* Margaretting w Mountnessing and Buttsbury *Chelmsf*

MOUNTSORREL (Christ Church) (St Peter) *Leic 6*   P *CPAS and Bp*   **P-in-c** K C EMMETT,   **NSM** M J BENNETT

MOW COP (St Luke's Mission Church) *see* Odd Rode *Ches*

MOW COP (St Thomas) *Lich 11*   P *Prime Min*   **C** C M CASE

MOWSLEY (St Nicholas) *see* Hexagon *Leic*

MOXLEY (All Saints) *Lich 26*   P *Prime Min*   V R E INGLESBY,
OLM A J DUCKWORTH

MUCH *see also under substantive place name*

MUCH BIRCH (St Mary and St Thomas à Becket)
see Wormelow Hundred *Heref*

MUCHELNEY (St Peter and St Paul) *see* Langport Area *B & W*

MUCKLESTONE (St Mary) *see* Ashley and Mucklestone and Broughton and Croxton *Lich*

MUDEFORD (All Saints) *Win 9*   P *Bp*   V H M GRIFFISS

MUDFORD (Blessed Virgin Mary) *see* Chilton Cantelo, Ashington, Mudford, Rimpton etc *B & W*

MUGGINTON (All Saints) and Kedleston *Derby 11*   P *Major J W Chandos-Pole*   **P-in-c** A P HARPER,   **C** D A GLEN

MUGGLESWICK (All Saints) *see* Blanchland w Hunstanworth and Edmundbyers etc *Newc*

MUKER (St Mary) *see* Swaledale *Ripon*

MULBARTON (St Mary Magdalene) w Bracon Ash, Hethel and Flordon *Nor 7*   P *R T Berney Esq (1 turn)*,
Mrs R M Watkinson (2 turns), DBP (1 turn), and Ld Chan (1 turn)   R J W STUBENBORD,   **OLM** D M DAVIDSON

MULLION (St Mellanus) *Truro 4*   P *Bp*   **P-in-c** S O GRIFFITHS

MUMBY (St Thomas of Canterbury) *see* Willoughby *Linc*

MUNCASTER (St Michael) *see* Eskdale, Irton, Muncaster and Waberthwaite *Carl*

MUNDEN, LITTLE (All Saints) *see* Standon and The Mundens w Sacombe *St Alb*

MUNDESLEY (All Saints) *see* Trunch *Nor*

MUNDFORD (St Leonard) w Lynford *Nor 13*   P *Ch Patr Trust*
R *vacant* (01842) 878220

MUNDHAM (St Peter) *see* Brooke, Kirstead, Mundham w Seething and Thwaite *Nor*

MUNDHAM, NORTH (St Stephen) w Hunston and Merston
Chich 3   P *St Jo Coll Cam*   **P-in-c** J A T RUSSELL,
C N G COLEMAN

MUNGRISDALE (St Kentigern) *see* Gd Shep TM *Carl*

MUNSLEY (St Bartholomew) *see* Ledbury *Heref*

MUNSLOW (St Michael) *see* Diddlebury w Munslow, Holdgate and Tugford *Heref*

MUNSTER SQUARE (Christ Church) (St Mary Magdalene)
Lon 17   P *Bp*   V M R POOLE

MUNSTONE (Church Room) *see* Holmer w Huntington *Heref*

MURCOTT (Mission Room) *see* Ray Valley *Ox*

MURROW (Corpus Christi) *see* Wisbech St Mary and Guyhirn w Ring's End etc *Ely*

MURSLEY (St Mary the Virgin) *see* Newton Longville, Mursley, Swanbourne etc *Ox*

MURSTON (All Saints) w Bapchild and Tonge *Cant 15*   P *Abp and St Jo Coll Cam (jt)*   **P-in-c** M MOSELEY

MURTON (Holy Trinity) *see* Hawthorn and Murton *Dur*

MURTON (St James) *see* Osbaldwick w Murton *York*

MURTON (St John the Baptist) *see* Heart of Eden *Carl*

MUSBURY (St Michael) *see* Colyton, Musbury, Southleigh and Branscombe *Ex*

MUSBURY (St Thomas) *Blackb 1*   P *The Crown*
P-in-c T R SMITH,   **NSM** J A BALKWELL, D ALLSOP

MUSGRAVE (St Theobald) *see* Brough w Stainmore, Musgrave and Warcop *Carl*

MUSKHAM, NORTH (St Wilfrid) and SOUTH (St Wilfrid)
S'well 3   P *Ld Chan*   V *vacant* (01636) 702655

MUSTON (All Saints) *see* Hunmanby w Muston *York*

MUSTON (St John the Baptist) *see* Vale of Belvoir *Leic*

MUSWELL HILL (St James) (St Matthew) *Lon 20*   P *Bp and CPAS (jt)*   V K S SWITHINBANK,   **C** G J DALY,
P DE ALMEIDA FEITAL,   **NSM** H C HENDRY

MUTFORD (St Andrew)   see Carlton Colville and Mutford Nor
MUXTON (St John the Evangelist)   see Lilleshall and Muxton
Lich
MYDDELTON SQUARE (St Mark)   see Clerkenwell St Mark
Lon
MYDDLE (St Peter) Lich 22   P Bp   P-in-c P F BARNES,
OLM A EVANS
MYLAND (St Michael)   see Colchester St Mich Myland
Chelmsf
MYLOR (St Mylor) w Flushing Truro 3   P Bp
P-in-c R F NICHOLLS,   NSM A J STEVENSON
MYLOR BRIDGE (All Saints)   see Mylor w Flushing Truro
MYMMS   see also MIMMS
MYMMS, NORTH (St Mary)   see Bp's Hatfield, Lemsford and
N Mymms St Alb
MYMMS, NORTH (St Michael)   as above
MYMMS, SOUTH (King Charles the Martyr)   see Potters Bar
K Chas St Alb
MYMMS, SOUTH (St Giles) and Ridge St Alb 14   P DBP
P-in-c B M TIPPING
MYNDTOWN (St John the Baptist)   see Wentnor w
Ratlinghope, Myndtown, Norbury etc Heref
MYTHOLMROYD (St Michael)   see Erringden Wakef
MYTON ON SWALE (St Mary)   see Brafferton w Pilmoor,
Myton-on-Swale etc York
NABB (Mission Church)   see Oakengates and Wrockwardine
Wood Lich
NABURN (St Matthew)   see Escrick and Stillingfleet w Naburn
York
NACKINGTON (St Mary)   see Bridge Cant
NACTON (St Martin) and Levington w Bucklesham and Foxhall
w Kirton and Falkenham St E 2   P Ld Chan and DBP (alt)
R G L GRANT,   NSM H M DAVY
NADDER VALLEY Sarum 11   P Patr Bd (4 turns), Ld Chan
(1 turn)   TV J D TAILBY, A STALEY,   Dss A SYMES
NAFFERTON (All Saints) w Wansford York 10   P Abp
P-in-c P J ARTLEY
NAILSEA (Christ Church) w Tickenham B & W 12   P CPAS
(3 turns), Ld Chan (1 turn)   R vacant (01275) 853187
NAILSEA (Holy Trinity) B & W 12   P MMCET
R C J TRICKEY,   C J S TILLEY, M J PARKMAN,   NSM T S DEAN
NAILSTONE (All Saints) and Carlton w Shackerstone Leic 10
P The Crown and DBP (alt)   P-in-c J F PLANT,
C J G HARGREAVES,   NSM A C HOLDSTOCK
NAILSWORTH (St George) w Shortwood, Horsley and
Newington Bapath w Kingscote Glouc 4   P Bp   V S J EARLEY
NANPANTAN (St Mary in Charnwood)   see Loughborough
Em and St Mary in Charnwood Leic
NANPEAN (St George)   see St Stephen in Brannel Truro
NANSTALLON (St Stephen's Mission Room)   see Bodmin w
Lanhydrock and Lanivet Truro
NANTWICH (St Mary) Ches 15   P Q H Crewe Esq and
J C Crewe Esq (jt)   R P T CHANTRY,   C T J WATSON
NAPTON-ON-THE-HILL (St Lawrence), Lower Shuckburgh
and Stockton Cov 10   P Ld Chan (2 turns), Sir Rupert
Shuckburgh Bt (1 turn), and New Coll Ox (2 turns)
P-in-c M L D GREIG,   C R D CLUCAS
NAR VALLEY, The Nor 13   P Bp (1 turn), Earl of Leicester,
H C Birkbeck Esq, and Bp (1 turn)   R S R NAIRN
NARBOROUGH (All Saints)   see Nar Valley Nor
NARBOROUGH (All Saints) and Huncote Leic 7   P SMF
R A J HAWKER
NARFORD (St Mary)   see Nar Valley Nor
NASEBY (All Saints)   see Clipston w Naseby and Haselbech w
Kelmarsh Pet
NASH (All Saints)   see Buckingham Ox
NASH (St John the Baptist)   see Tenbury Heref
NASSINGTON (St Mary the Virgin and All Saints) w Yarwell
and Woodnewton w Apethorpe Pet 10   P Bp and
Lord Brassey (jt)   P-in-c J R FLACK,   NSM P R MORRELL
NATELY SCURES (St Swithun)   see N Hants Downs Win
NATLAND (St Mark) Carl 10   P V Kendal H Trin
P-in-c A WHITTAKER,   NSM M P JAYNE
NAUGHTON (St Mary)   see Bildeston w Wattisham and
Lindsey, Whatfield etc St E
NAUNTON (St Andrew)   see The Guitings, Cutsdean, Farmcote
etc Glouc
NAUNTON BEAUCHAMP (St Bartholomew)   see Abberton,
The Flyfords, Naunton Beauchamp etc Worc
NAVENBY (St Peter)   see Graffoe Gp Linc
NAVESTOCK (St Thomas)   see Bentley Common, Kelvedon
Hatch and Navestock Chelmsf
NAWTON (St Hilda)   see Kirkdale w Harome, Nunnington and
Pockley York
NAYLAND (St James) w Wiston St E 3   P Ld Chan (2 turns)
and DBP (1 turn)   V vacant (01206) 262316

NAYLAND DRIVE (Church Centre)   see Clacton St Jas
Chelmsf
NAZEING (All Saints) (St Giles) Chelmsf 25   P Ld Chan
P-in-c C P PENNINGTON
NEASDEN (St Catherine w St Paul) Lon 21   P Bp and
D&C St Paul's (jt)   V E E GAUNT
NEATISHEAD (St Peter)   see Ashmanhaugh, Barton Turf etc
Nor
NECHELLS (St Matthew)   see Aston and Nechells Birm
NECTON (All Saints), Holme Hale w Pickenham, North and
South Nor 13   P Major-Gen R S Broke, Ch Soc Trust,
MMCET and S Pickenham Estate Co Ltd (jt)   R S L THORP
NEDGING (St Mary)   see Bildeston w Wattisham and Lindsey,
Whatfield etc St E
NEEDHAM (St Peter)   see Redenhall, Harleston, Wortwell and
Needham Nor
NEEDHAM MARKET (St John the Baptist) w Badley St E 1
P PCC   P-in-c D R WILLIAMS
NEEN SAVAGE (St Mary)   see Cleobury Mortimer w Hopton
Wafers etc Heref
NEEN SOLLARS (All Saints)   as above
NEENTON (All Saints)   see Ditton Priors w Neenton,
Burwarton etc Heref
NEITHROP (St Paul)   see Banbury St Paul Ox
NELSON (St Bede)   see Lt Marsden w Nelson St Mary and
Nelson St Bede Blackb
NELSON (St John the Evangelist)   see Gt Marsden w Nelson St
Phil Blackb
NELSON (St Mary)   see Lt Marsden w Nelson St Mary and
Nelson St Bede Blackb
NELSON (St Paul)   as above
NELSON (St Philip)   see Gt Marsden w Nelson St Phil Blackb
NEMPNETT THRUBWELL (Blessed Virgin Mary)   see Chew
Stoke w Nempnett Thrubwell B & W
NENTHEAD (St John)   see Alston Moor Newc
NESS Group, The Linc 13   P Ld Chan (1 turn), Bp and DBP
(2 turns)   V J M BEADLE,   OLM M J HOWARD
NESS, GREAT (St Andrew)   see Ruyton XI Towns w Gt and Lt
Ness Lich
NESS, LITTLE (St Martin)   as above
NESTON (St Mary and St Helen) Ches 9   P D&C
V R H N ROBB,   C A A HARRIS
NESTON (St Phillip and St James)   see Gtr Corsham and
Lacock Bris
NESTON, LITTLE (St Michael and All Angels)   see Neston
Ches
NETHER   see also under substantive place name
NETHER HALL (St Elizabeth)   see Scraptoft Leic
NETHERAVON (All Saints)   see Avon Valley Sarum
NETHERBURY (St Mary)   see Beaminster Area Sarum
NETHEREXE (St John the Baptist)   see Brampford Speke,
Cadbury, Newton St Cyres etc Ex
NETHERFIELD (St George) S'well 10   P DBP
P-in-c R B CHAPMAN
NETHERFIELD (St John the Baptist)   see Brightling,
Dallington, Mountfield etc Chich
NETHERHAMPTON (St Katherine)   see Wilton w
Netherhampton and Fugglestone Sarum
NETHERLEY (Christ Church)   see Gateacre Liv
NETHERSEAL (St Peter)   see Seale and Lullington w Coton n
the Elms Derby
NETHERTHONG (All Saints)   see Upper Holme Valley Wakef
NETHERTHORPE (St Bartholomew)   see Sheff St Bart Sheff
NETHERTHORPE (St Stephen) Sheff 4   P Ch Patr Trust and
Sheff Ch Burgesses Trust (jt)   V P J BATCHFORD,
C G L KALSI
NETHERTON (All Souls)   see Maryport, Netherton and
Flimby Carl
NETHERTON (St Andrew)   see Middlestown Wakef
NETHERTON (St Andrew) Worc 9   P Bp   V S H CARTER
NETHERTON (St Oswald) Liv 1   P Bp   P-in-c D H STATTER
NETHERWITTON (St Giles)   see Nether Witton Newc
NETLEY ABBEY   see Hound Win
NETLEY MARSH (St Matthew)   see Totton Win
NETTLEBED (St Bartholomew) w Bix, Highmoor, Pishill and
Rotherfield Greys Ox 6   P DBP, Earl of Macclesfield, Ch Patr
Trust, and Trin Coll Ox (jt)   R B J BAILEY,   OLM E F LAKEY
NETTLECOMBE (Blessed Virgin Mary)   see Quantock Towers
B & W
NETTLEDEN (Ashridge Chapel)   see Gt Berkhamsted, Gt and
Lt Gaddesden etc St Alb
NETTLEDEN (St Lawrence)   as above
NETTLEHAM (All Saints) Linc 3   P Bp   P-in-c J J E ROWLEY,
C M J RUSHTON,   NSM C A ZOTOV, J L HART, R O THORNTON
NETTLESTEAD (St Mary)   see Gt and Lt Blakenham w
Baylham and Nettlestead St E

NETTLESTEAD (St Mary the Virgin)   *see* E Peckham and
  Nettlestead *Roch*
NETTLETON (St John the Baptist)   *see* Swallow *Linc*
NETTLETON (St Mary)   *see* By Brook *Bris*
NEVENDON (St Peter)   *see* Pitsea w Nevendon *Chelmsf*
NEVILLE'S CROSS (St John)   *see* Dur St Marg and Neville's
  Cross St Jo *Dur*
NEW   *see also under substantive place name*
NEW BOROUGH and Leigh (St John the Evangelist) *Sarum 9*
  P *Ch Soc Trust*   **V** *vacant* (01202) 883490
NEW BUILDINGS (Beacon Church)   *see* Crediton, Shobrooke
  and Sandford etc *Ex*
NEW CROSS   *see* Hatcham St Jas *S'wark*
NEW FERRY (St Mark) *Ches 8*   **P** *R Bebington*
  V A Q GREENHOUGH,   **NSM** A D DRURY
NEW HAW (All Saints) *Guildf 11*   **P** *Bp*   **V** R J GOSTELOW
NEW MILL (Christ Church)   *see* Upper Holme Valley *Wakef*
NEW MILLS (St George) *Derby 6*   **P** *V Glossop*
  P-in-c J C BAINES
NEW PARKS (St Aidan)   *see* Leic St Aid *Leic*
NEW SPRINGS (St John the Baptist) and Whelley St Stephen
  Liv 14   **P** *Bp*   **P-in-c** S JONES
NEWALL GREEN (St Francis of Assisi)   *see* Wythenshawe
  Man
NEWARK-UPON-TRENT (St Mary Magdalene) (Christ
  Church) (St Leonard) w Coddington *S'well 3*   **P** *The Crown*
  TR V J ENEVER,   **TV** S J TREDWELL, D E ANDERTON,
  C J M POLLARD
NEWBALD (St Nicholas) *York 13*   **P** *Abp*   **P-in-c** M R BUSHBY
NEWBARNS (St Paul)   *see* Barrow St Paul *Carl*
NEWBIGGIN (St Edmund)   *see* Kirkby Thore w Temple
  Sowerby and Newbiggin *Carl*
NEWBIGGIN-BY-THE-SEA (St Bartholomew)
  see Woodhorn w Newbiggin *Newc*
NEWBIGGIN HALL (St Wilfrid) *Newc 4*   **P** *Bp*   **V** S L MILLER
NEWBOLD (St John the Evangelist) w Dunston *Derby 5*
  P *R Chesterfield*   **V** N V JOHNSON,   **C** K COCKING
NEWBOLD (St Peter)   *see* Deeplish and Newbold *Man*
NEWBOLD DE VERDUN (St James), Barlestone and Kirkby
  Mallory *Leic 10*   **P** *Bp and Trin Coll Ox (jt)*
  R T H C MEYRICK,   **C** L C TEMPERLEY-BARNES,
  NSM J A DOWNS
NEWBOLD ON AVON (St Botolph) *Cov 6*
  P H A F W Boughton Leigh Esq   **V** P M WILKINSON
NEWBOLD ON STOUR (St David)   *see* Stourdene Gp *Cov*
NEWBOLD PACEY (St George) w Moreton Morrell *Cov 8*
  P *Qu Coll Ox and Lt-Col J E Little (alt)*   **C** N S DUNLOP
NEWBOROUGH (All Saints)   *see* Hanbury, Newborough,
  Rangemore and Tutbury *Lich*
NEWBOROUGH (St Bartholomew) *Pet 11*   **P** *The Crown*
  P-in-c C HURST
NEWBOTTLE (St James)   *see* King's Sutton and Newbottle and
  Charlton *Pet*
NEWBOTTLE (St Matthew) *Dur 14*   **P** *Bp*   **V** E WILKINSON
NEWBOURN (St Mary)   *see* Waldringfield w Hemley and
  Newbourn *St E*
NEWBROUGH (St Peter)   *see* Warden w Newbrough *Newc*
NEWBURGH (Christ Church) w Westhead *Liv 11*   **P** *Bp and*
  V Ormskirk (jt)   **V** G A MILFORD,   **NSM** D M BURROWS,
  OLM J SEPHTON, C DRAPER
NEWBURN (St Michael and All Angels) *Newc 4*   **P** *MMCET*
  V J R SINCLAIR,   **OLM** M P LEDGER
NEWBURY (St John the Evangelist) (St Nicolas and St Mary)
  Ox 14   **P** *Bp*   **TR** W D HUNTER SMART,   **TV** M UDDIN,
  P H COWAN,   **C** S L ALEXANDER
NEWBY (St Mark) *York 15*   **P** *Abp*   **P-in-c** M J LEIGH
NEWCASTLE (Christ Church) (St Ann) *Newc 2*   **P** *Bp*
  P-in-c A W MARKS,   **C** A J FENTON
NEWCASTLE (St Andrew) (St Luke) *Newc 2*   **P** *Bp and*
  V Newcastle (jt)   **P-in-c** G EVANS,   **NSM** R C I WARD
NEWCASTLE (St John the Evangelist)   *see* Clun w
  Bettws-y-Crwyn and Newcastle *Heref*
NEWCASTLE (St Philip) and St Augustine and (St Matthew w
  St Mary) *Newc 4*   **P** *Bp*   **V** R G S DEADMAN
NEWCASTLE UNDER LYME (St George) *Lich 9*
  P *R Newcastle w Butterton*   **V** *vacant* (01782) 710056
NEWCASTLE UNDER LYME (St Giles) w Butterton *Lich 9*
  P *Simeon's Trustees*   **R** S M LEE,   **C** S A VINCENT,
  NSM P NISBECK,   **OLM** M A TAYLOR, J WARHAM
NEWCASTLE UNDER LYME (St Paul) *Lich 9*   **P** *Trustees*
  V D J LLOYD
NEWCASTLE UPON TYNE (Christ Church)   *see* Walker *Newc*
NEWCASTLE UPON TYNE Christ the King   *see* Ch the King
  Newc
NEWCASTLE UPON TYNE (Clayton Memorial Church)
  see Jesmond Clayton Memorial *Newc*

NEWCASTLE UPON TYNE (Holy Cross) *Newc 4*   **P** *Bp*
  V G WORT,   **C** J S PADDISON
NEWCASTLE UPON TYNE (Holy Trinity)   *see* Jesmond H
  Trin *Newc*
NEWCASTLE UPON TYNE (St Anthony)   *see* Byker St Ant
  Newc
NEWCASTLE UPON TYNE (St Barnabas and St Jude) *Newc 2*
  P *V Jesmond Clayton Memorial and CPAS (alt)*
  P-in-c M WROE,   **C** T SANDERSON
NEWCASTLE UPON TYNE (St Francis) High Heaton *Newc 3*
  P *Bp*   **V** P A JONES
NEWCASTLE UPON TYNE (St Gabriel) Heaton *Newc 3*
  P *Bp*   **V** S A WILSON
NEWCASTLE UPON TYNE (St George) (St Hilda) *Newc 2*
  P *Bp*   **V** N A CHAMBERLAIN,   **C** A J FORD,
  NSM P H PEARSON,   **OLM** C M CROMPTON
NEWCASTLE UPON TYNE (St James and St Basil)
  see Fenham St Jas and St Basil *Newc*
NEWCASTLE UPON TYNE (St John the Baptist) *Newc 2*
  P *V Newc*   **P-in-c** N WILSON
NEWCASTLE UPON TYNE (St Margaret)   *see* Scotswood
  Newc
NEWCASTLE UPON TYNE (St Martin)   *see* Byker St Martin
  Newc
NEWCASTLE UPON TYNE (St Michael w St Lawrence)
  see Byker St Mich w St Lawr *Newc*
NEWCASTLE UPON TYNE (St Oswald)   *see* Byker St Mark
  and Walkergate St Oswald *Newc*
NEWCASTLE UPON TYNE (St Paul)   *see* Elswick *Newc*
NEWCASTLE UPON TYNE (St Silas)   *see* Byker St Silas *Newc*
NEWCASTLE UPON TYNE (St Stephen)   *see* Elswick *Newc*
NEWCASTLE UPON TYNE (St Thomas) Proprietary Chapel
  Newc 2   **P** *Trustees of St Thos Chpl Charity*
  NSM J SKINNER, C M LACK
NEWCASTLE UPON TYNE, WEST Benwell   *see* Benwell
  Newc
NEWCHAPEL (St James the Apostle) *Lich 11*   **P** *CPAS*
  V W E SLATER,   **C** L R PLUMMER
NEWCHURCH (All Saints) *Portsm 7*   **P** *Bp*
  V J F O'SHAUGHNESSY
NEWCHURCH (not known) w Croft *Liv 15*   **P** *Bp*
  R C J STAFFORD,   **OLM** B SMART, B ALLDRED
NEWCHURCH (St Nicholas w St John)   *see* Rossendale Middle
  Valley *Man*
NEWCHURCH (St Peter and St Paul)   *see* Dymchurch w
  Burmarsh and Newchurch *Cant*
NEWCHURCH-IN-PENDLE (St Mary)   *see* Barrowford and
  Newchurch-in-Pendle *Blackb*
NEWDIGATE (St Peter)   *see* Surrey Weald *Guildf*
NEWENDEN (St Peter) and Rolvenden *Cant 16*   **P** *Abp*
  P-in-c J T M DESROSIERS
NEWENT (St Mary the Virgin) and Gorsley w Cliffords Mesne
  Glouc 3   **P** *Bp*   **P-in-c** S I V MASON,   **NSM** R G CHIVERS,
  K U MADDEN
NEWHALL (St John) *Derby 16*   **P** *Bp*   **V** R G HOLLINGS
NEWHAVEN (St Michael) *Chich 18*   **P** *Ch Patr Trust*
  R M M MILLER
NEWHEY (St Thomas) *Man 17*   **P** *Bp*   **P-in-c** G W LINDLEY,
  NSM S E WARD
NEWICK (St Mary) *Chich 21*   **P** *Ch Soc Trust*   **R** P P FRANCIS
NEWINGTON (St Christopher)   *see* St Laur in Thanet *Cant*
NEWINGTON (St Giles)   *see* Dorchester *Ox*
NEWINGTON (St John the Baptist) w Dairycoates St Mary and
  St Peter *York 14*   **P** *Abp*   **P-in-c** T A COTSON
NEWINGTON (St Martin)   *see* Hull St Martin w
  Transfiguration *York*
NEWINGTON (St Mary) *S'wark 10*   **P** *Bp*   **R** A P DODD,
  C R F HUNTE,   **Hon C** M E TODD
NEWINGTON (St Mary the Virgin) w Hartlip and Stockbury
  Cant 15   **P** *Abp*   **P-in-c** A J AMOS,   **C** H E NELSON,
  NSM E A COX
NEWINGTON (St Nicholas)   *see* Cheriton All So w Newington
  Cant
NEWINGTON (St Paul) *S'wark 10*   **P** *Bp*   **V** G D SHAW,
  NSM E BOGLE
NEWINGTON, SOUTH (St Peter ad Vincula)   *see* Bloxham w
  Milcombe and S Newington *Ox*
NEWLAND (All Saints)   *see* Coleford, Staunton, Newland,
  Redbrook etc *Glouc*
NEWLAND (St John)   *see* Hull St Jo Newland *York*
NEWLAND (St Lawrence)   *see* Bradwell on Sea and St
  Lawrence *Chelmsf*
NEWLANDS (not known)   *see* Upper Derwent *Carl*
NEWLAY LANE (St Margaret's Church Hall)   *see* Bramley
  Ripon

NEWLYN (St Newlyn) *Truro 5*   P *Bp*   P-in-c H L SAMSON
NEWLYN (St Peter) *Truro 5*   P *Bp*   V *vacant* (01736) 62678
NEWMARKET (All Saints) *St E 11*   P *Bp*   V M E OSBORNE
NEWMARKET (St Mary the Virgin) w Exning St Agnes *St E 11*
P *Bp and DBP (alt)*   R J C HARDY
NEWNHAM (St Mark)   *see* Cambridge St Mark *Ely*
NEWNHAM (St Michael and All Angels)   *see* Badby w
Newham and Charwelton w Fawsley etc *Pet*
NEWNHAM (St Nicholas)   *see* N Hants Downs *Win*
NEWNHAM (St Peter and St Paul)   *see* Doddington, Newnham
and Wychling *Cant*
NEWNHAM (St Peter) w Awre and Blakeney *Glouc 1*
P *Haberdashers' Co and Bp (alt)*   V J STEPHENSON
NEWNHAM (St Vincent)   *see* Ashwell w Hinxworth and
Newnham *St Alb*
NEWNTON, NORTH (St James)   *see* Vale of Pewsey *Sarum*
NEWPORT (St John the Baptist)   *see* Barnstaple *Ex*
NEWPORT (St John the Baptist) *Portsm 8*   P *Ch Patr Trust*
V K P ARKELL,   NSM R J WHATLEY, J K HALLAM
NEWPORT (St Mary the Virgin) and Widdington *Chelmsf 21*
P *Bp*   V *vacant* (01799) 540339
NEWPORT (St Nicholas) w Longford, and Chetwynd *Lich 16*
P *Bp*   V S MITCHELL,   NSM J ROPER
NEWPORT (St Stephen)   *see* Howden *York*
NEWPORT (St Thomas) *Portsm 8*   P *Bp*   V K P ARKELL,
NSM J K HALLAM
NEWPORT MINSTER   *see* Newport St Thos *Portsm*
NEWPORT PAGNELL (St Luke) w Lathbury and Moulsoe
Ox 27   P *Bp, Ch Ch Ox, and Lord Carrington (jt)*
R M GODFREY,   NSM K BROWNE,   OLM G M BELL
NEWQUAY (St Michael) *Truro 7*   P *Bp*   V M J ADAMS,
C S A BONE,   NSM P J KNEEBONE
NEWSHAM (St Bede) *Newc 1*   P *Bp*   V R J PRINGLE
NEWSHOLME (St John)   *see* Oakworth *Bradf*
NEWSOME (St John the Evangelist)   *see* Em TM *Wakef*
NEWSTEAD (St Mary the Virgin)   *see* Annesley w Newstead
S'well
NEWTIMBER (St John the Evangelist)   *see* Poynings w
Edburton, Newtimber and Pyecombe *Chich*
NEWTON (Church Hall)   *see* Blackwell w Tibshelf *Derby*
NEWTON (Good Shepherd)   *see* Clifton w Newton and
Brownsover *Cov*
NEWTON (Mission Church)   *see* Embleton w Rennington and
Rock *Newc*
NEWTON (St Botolph)   *see* S Lafford *Linc*
NEWTON (St John the Baptist)   *see* Clodock and Longtown w
Craswall, Llanveynoe etc *Heref*
NEWTON (St Luke)   *see* Bp's Hatfield, Lemsford and N
Mymms *St Alb*
NEWTON (St Margaret)   *see* Harston w Hauxton and Newton
Ely
NEWTON (St Michael and All Angels) *Ches 8*   P R W Kirby
St Bridget   V C J COVERLEY
NEWTON (St Oswald)   *see* Gt Ayton w Easby and Newton
under Roseberry *York*
NEWTON (St Petrock)   *see* Shebbear, Buckland Filleigh,
Sheepwash etc *Ex*
NEWTON Team, The (Emmanuel) (St Peter) *Liv 15*   P *Patr Bd*
TR J M MATTHEWS,   TV V E HUGHES,   C L A MONTGOMERY
NEWTON, NORTH (St Peter)   *see* Alfred Jewel *B & W*
NEWTON, OLD (St Mary)   *see* Bacton w Wyverstone, Cotton
and Old Newton etc *St E*
NEWTON, SOUTH (St Andrew)   *see* Wylye and Till Valley
Sarum
NEWTON, WEST (St Matthew)   *see* Solway Plain *Carl*
NEWTON, WEST (St Peter and St Paul)   *see* Sandringham w W
Newton and Appleton etc *Nor*
NEWTON ABBOT   *see* Highweek *Ex*
NEWTON ABBOT (St Michael)   *see* Wolborough and Ogwell
Ex
NEWTON ABBOT (St Paul)   *as above*
NEWTON ARLOSH (St John the Evangelist)
see Bowness-on-Solway, Kirkbride and Newton Arlosh *Carl*
NEWTON AYCLIFFE (St Clare)   *see* Gt Aycliffe *Dur*
NEWTON BLOSSOMVILLE (St Nicolas)   *see* Lavendon w
Cold Brayfield, Clifton Reynes etc *Ox*
NEWTON BROMSWOLD (St Peter)   *see* Rushden St Mary w
Newton Bromswold *Pet*
NEWTON-BY-CASTLE-ACRE (All Saints)   *see* Nar Valley
Nor
NEWTON BY TOFT (St Michael)   *see* Middle Rasen Gp *Linc*
NEWTON CAP (St Paul)   *see* Auckland St Andr and St Anne
Dur
NEWTON FERRERS (Holy Cross) w Revelstoke *Ex 21*   P *Bp*
and Comdr P E Yonge   C A C LEGGE

NEWTON FLOTMAN (St Mary the Virgin), Swainsthorpe,
Tasburgh, Tharston, Saxlingham Nethergate and Shotesham
Nor 5   P *Patr Bd*   TR S A GAZE,   TV A D MILLER,
C C E MARTIN,   OLM D L P SOCHON
NEWTON GREEN (All Saints)   *see* Boxford, Edwardstone,
Groton etc *St E*
NEWTON HALL (All Saints)   *see* Dur N *Dur*
NEWTON HARCOURT (St Luke)   *see* Wistow *Leic*
NEWTON HEATH (All Saints) *Man 4*   P *Prime Min and
D&C (alt)*   R A P WICKENS
NEWTON IN MAKERFIELD (Emmanuel)   *see* Newton *Liv*
NEWTON IN MAKERFIELD (St Peter)   *as above*
NEWTON IN MOTTRAM (St Mary) w Flowery Field *Ches 14*
P *V Mottram*   P-in-c R J LAMEY,   C A C WOODCOCK
NEWTON IN THE ISLE (St James)   *see* Leverington, Newton
and Tydd St Giles *Ely*
NEWTON-IN-WIRRAL (St Michael and All Angels)
see Newton *Ches*
NEWTON KYME (St Andrew)   *see* Tadcaster w Newton Kyme
York
NEWTON-LE-WILLOWS (All Saints) *Liv 15*   P *Bp*
V D HALL
NEWTON LINFORD (All Saints)   *see* Bradgate Team *Leic*
NEWTON LONGVILLE (St Faith), Mursley, Swanbourne,
Little Horwood and Drayton Parslow *Ox 26*   P *New Coll Ox,
Ch Soc Trust, Lord Cottesloe, Ch Patr Trust, and MMCET (jt)*
V L P R MEERING,   Hon C J M SAUNDERS,   OLM J K BROWN
NEWTON ON OUSE (All Saints)   *see* Skelton w Shipton and
Newton on Ouse *York*
NEWTON-ON-RAWCLIFFE (St John)   *see* Middleton,
Newton and Sinnington *York*
NEWTON-ON-TRENT (St Peter)   *see* Saxilby Gp *Linc*
NEWTON POPPLEFORD (St Luke)   *see* Ottery St Mary,
Alfington, W Hill, Tipton etc *Ex*
NEWTON PURCELL (St Michael)   *see* Shelswell *Ox*
NEWTON REGIS (St Mary)   *see* N Warks *Birm*
NEWTON REIGNY (St John)   *see* Penrith w Newton Reigny
and Plumpton Wall *Carl*
NEWTON SOLNEY (St Mary the Virgin)   *see* Foremark and
Repton w Newton Solney *Derby*
NEWTON ST CYRES (St Cyr and St Julitta)   *see* Brampford
Speke, Cadbury, Newton St Cyres etc *Ex*
NEWTON ST LOE (Holy Trinity)   *see* Saltford w Corston and
Newton St Loe *B & W*
NEWTON TONY (St Andrew)   *see* Bourne Valley *Sarum*
NEWTON TRACEY (St Thomas à Becket), Horwood,
Alverdiscott, Huntshaw, Yarnscombe, Tawstock, Atherington,
High Bickington, Roborough, St Giles in the Wood and Beaford
Ex 20   P *Ld Chan (1 turn), Patr Bd (3 turns)*
TR K D MATHERS,   TV M J CLARK,   C S R PATTERSON
NEWTON VALENCE (St Mary)   *see* Northanger *Win*
NEWTOWN   *see* Edgbaston St Geo *Birm*
NEWTOWN (Holy Spirit)   *see* Calbourne w Newtown *Portsm*
NEWTOWN (Holy Trinity)   *see* Soberton w Newtown *Portsm*
NEWTOWN (King Charles the Martyr)   *see* Loppington w
Newtown *Lich*
NEWTOWN (St George)   *see* Birm St Geo *Birm*
NEWTOWN (St Mark)   *see* Marsh Green w Newtown *Liv*
NEWTOWN (St Mary the Virgin)   *see* Hungerford and Denford
Ox
NEWTOWN (St Mary the Virgin and St John the Baptist)
see Burghclere w Newtown and Ecchinswell w Sydmonton *Win*
NEWTOWN (St Paul)   *see* Longnor, Quarnford and Sheen *Lich*
NIBLEY, NORTH (St Martin)   *see* Wotton-under-Edge w
Ozleworth, N Nibley etc *Glouc*
NICHOLFOREST (St Nicholas)   *see* Arthuret w
Kirkandrews-on-Esk and Nicholforest *Carl*
NIDD (St Paul and St Margaret) *Ripon 1*   P *Viscount
Mountgarret and R Knaresborough (alt)*   P-in-c E J SEWELL
NIDDERDALE, LOWER *Ripon 3*   P *Trustees K Bell Esq, DBP,
and C J Dent Esq (jt)*   R M P SPURGEON
NIDDERDALE, UPPER *Ripon 3*   P *D&C and V Masham and
Healey (jt)*   V P L DUNBAR
NINEBANKS (St Mark)   *see* Allendale w Whitfield *Newc*
NINEFIELDS (St Lawrence School Worship Centre)
see Waltham H Cross *Chelmsf*
NINFIELD (St Mary the Virgin) *Chich 14*   P *D&C Cant*
R S R EARL
NITON (St John the Baptist) *Portsm 7*   P *Qu Coll Ox*
R S E LLOYD
NOAK HILL (St Thomas)   *see* Harold Hill St Geo *Chelmsf*
NOCTON (All Saints)   *see* Branston w Nocton and
Potterhanworth *Linc*
NOEL PARK (St Mark) *Lon 19*   P *Bp*   P-in-c S P J CLARK
NOKE (St Giles)   *see* Ray Valley *Ox*

NONINGTON (St Mary the Virgin) w Wymynswold and Goodnestone w Chillenden and Knowlton *Cant 1* **P** *Abp and Lord Fitzwalter (jt)* **C** J V COLEMAN, S J A HARDY, **NSM** D N J HALE

NORBITON (St Peter) *S'work 15* **P** *V Kingston All SS* **V** P A HOLMES, **OLM** C A GROVES

NORBURY (All Saints) *see* Wentnor w Ratlinghope, Myndtown, Norbury etc *Heref*

NORBURY (St Mary and St Barlok) w Snelston *Derby 8* **P** *Mrs M F Stanton, L A Clowes Esq, and V Ashbourne (by turn)* **P-in-c** G P POND, **NSM** P A SHORT

NORBURY (St Oswald) *S'work 21* **P** *Bp* **V** C J MORGAN, **NSM** C MCARTHUR

NORBURY (St Peter) *see* Adbaston, High Offley, Knightley, Norbury etc *Lich*

NORBURY (St Philip) *S'work 21* **P** *Bp* **P-in-c** Y FRANCIS

NORBURY (St Stephen) and Thornton Heath *S'work 21* **P** *Bp* **P-in-c** G P THOMPSON, **OLM** J B FORBES

NORBURY (St Thomas) *Ches 16* **P** *Lord Newton* **V** R H LAWRY, **C** J E MAYO-LYTHALL, R H GREEN

NORDEN (St Paul) w Ashworth *Man 17* **P** *Bp* **V** *vacant* (01706) 641001

NORFOLK PARK (St Leonard) *see* Arbourthorne and Norfolk Park *Sheff*

NORHAM (St Cuthbert) and Duddo *Newc 12* **P** *D&C (1 turn), D&C Dur (2 turns)* **V** G R KELSEY

NORK (St Paul) *Guildf 9* **P** *The Crown* **P-in-c** J S CRESSWELL

NORLAND (St Luke) *Wakef 3* **P** *Bp* **P-in-c** M C CRABTREE, **NSM** L ENNIS

NORLANDS (St James) *see* Notting Dale St Clem w St Mark and St Jas *Lon*

NORLEY (St John the Evangelist), Crowton and Kingsley *Ches 3* **P** *Bp, V Frodsham, and V Weaverham (jt)* **P-in-c** P RUGEN, **C** G K STANNING

NORMACOT (Holy Evangelists) *see* Meir Heath and Normacot *Lich*

NORMANBY (St Andrew) *see* Kirby Misperton w Normanby, Edston and Salton *York*

NORMANBY (St George) *see* Eston w Normanby *York*

NORMANBY-LE-WOLD (St Peter) *see* Walesby *Linc*

NORMANTON (All Saints) *Wakef 11* **P** *Trin Coll Cam* **V** D M GILKES

NORMANTON (St Giles) *Derby 10* **P** *CPAS* **V** N A A BARBER, **C** A G P HUTCHINSON

NORMANTON, SOUTH (St Michael) *Derby 1* **P** *MMCET* **P-in-c** S M POTTER

NORMANTON-LE-HEATH (Holy Trinity) *see* Woodfield *Leic*

NORMANTON-ON-SOAR (St James) *see* Sutton Bonington w Normanton-on-Soar *S'well*

NORMANTON-ON-TRENT (St Matthew) *see* Sutton w Carlton and Normanton upon Trent etc *S'well*

NORRIS BANK (St Martin) *see* Heatons *Man*

NORRIS GREEN (Christ Church) *see* Liv Ch Ch Norris Green *Liv*

NORRIS GREEN (St Christopher) *see* Liv St Chris Norris Green *Liv*

NORRISTHORPE (All Souls) *see* Heckmondwike *Wakef*

NORTH *see also under substantive place name*

NORTH BLACKWATER *Chelmsf 23* **P** *Patr Bd* **V** G B T BAYLISS

NORTH BURY Team Ministry *see* Bury St Edmunds All SS w St Jo and St Geo *St E*

NORTH CAVE (All Saints) w Cliffe *York 13* **P** C H J Carver Esq **P-in-c** P G FAULKNER, **NSM** S J HUMPHRIES

NORTH-CHAPEL Parishes, The *Linc 10* **P** *The Revd J M Ashley, Mrs M F Davis, R H C Haigh Esq, and Trustees (1 turn), and Duchy of Lanc (1 turn)* **R** R K EMM

NORTH CHAPEL (St Michael) w Ebernoe *Chich 11* **P** *Lord Egremont* **P-in-c** M L PUDNEY

NORTH COVE (St Botolph) *see* Worlingham w Barnby and N Cove *St E*

NORTH DEVON COAST *see* Combe Martin, Berrynarbor, Lynton, Brendon etc *Ex*

NORTH END (Ascension) *see* Portsea Ascension *Portsm*

NORTH END (Chapel of Ease) *see* Burton Dassett *Cov*

NORTH END (St Francis) *see* Portsea N End St Mark *Portsm*

NORTH END (St Mark) *as above*

NORTH END (St Nicholas) *as above*

NORTH HAMPSHIRE DOWNS Benefice, The *Win 5* **P** *Bp, Qu Coll Ox, St Jo Coll Ox, N McNair Scott Esq, and J L Jervoise Esq (jt)* **R** P W DIXON, **C** A R A GRANT, G M W KEITH, **NSM** J E LEESE, K O'LOUGHLIN, M J EAST

NORTH HILL (St Torney) *see* Three Rivers *Truro*

NORTH SHIELDS (St Augustine) (Christ Church) *Newc 2* **P** *Patr Bd* **TR** A D KIRKWOOD, **NSM** K COCKBURN

NORTH SHORE (St Paul's Worship Centre) *see* Blackpool St Paul *Blackb*

NORTH WEALD BASSETT (St Andrew) *Chelmsf 26* **P** *Bp* **V** T C THORPE

NORTH WEST HAMPSHIRE Benefice, The *Win 6* **P** *Bp and Earl of Carnarvon (jt)* **R** C DALE, **NSM** A C PETTS

NORTHALLERTON (All Saints) w Kirby Sigston *York 18* **P** *D&C Dur* **V** H G SMITH, **C** A D WALKER

NORTHAM (St Margaret) *see* Bideford, Northam, Westward Ho!, Appledore etc *Ex*

NORTHAMPTON (All Saints w St Katharine) (St Peter) *Pet 4* **P** *Bp and R Foundn of St Kath (jt)* **R** *vacant* (01604) 621854 or 632194

NORTHAMPTON (Christ Church) *Pet 4* **P** *Bp* **P-in-c** D J WISEMAN, **NSM** A M MARCH

NORTHAMPTON (Emmanuel) *Pet 4* **P** *DBP* **TR** M A H JOHNSON, **NSM** P J R KING

NORTHAMPTON (Holy Sepulchre w St Andrew and St Lawrence) *Pet 4* **P** *Bp* **V** M W J HILLS, **NSM** A M MARCH

NORTHAMPTON (Holy Trinity) (St Paul) *Pet 4* **P** *Bp* **V** A C MCGOWAN, **NSM** A M MARCH

NORTHAMPTON (St Alban the Martyr) (Glorious Ascension) *Pet 4* **P** *Bp* **V** I R LOWELL

NORTHAMPTON (St Benedict) *Pet 4* **P** *Bp* **V** J R KIMBER, **C** M J PURNELL

NORTHAMPTON (St David) *see* Kingsthorpe w Northampton St Dav *Pet*

NORTHAMPTON (St Giles) *Pet 4* **P** *Simeon's Trustees* **V** D R BIRD, **C** M T GIBBS, A J B SYMES, **NSM** G J WATERS

NORTHAMPTON (St James) *Pet 4* **P** *Bp* **P-in-c** P E NIXON

NORTHAMPTON (St Mary the Virgin) *Pet 4* **P** *Bp* **V** I S HOLDSWORTH

NORTHAMPTON (St Matthew) *Pet 4* **P** *DBP* **V** N M SETTERFIELD, **C** P R ARMSTEAD, **NSM** G C RUMBOLD

NORTHAMPTON (St Michael and All Angels w St Edmund) *Pet 4* **P** *Bp* **V** M W J HILLS, **NSM** P D MUNCH, A M MARCH

NORTHAMPTON (St Peter) *see* Northampton All SS w St Kath and St Pet *Pet*

NORTHANGER Benefice, The *Win 2* **P** *Bp (1 turn), D&C (1 turn), Bp, Earl of Selborne and Sir James Scott Bt (1 turn)* **R** A J PEARS, **NSM** J ELLISON, L A LEON

NORTHAW (St Thomas of Canterbury) and Cuffley *St Alb 17* **P** *Mrs S Peasley* **P-in-c** R S PHILLIPS

NORTHBOROUGH (St Andrew) *see* Peakirk w Glinton and Northborough *Pet*

NORTHBOURNE (St Augustine) *see* Eastry and Northbourne w Tilmanstone etc *Cant*

NORTHCHURCH (St Mary) and Wigginton *St Alb 1* **P** *Duchy of Cornwall and Bp (alt)* **R** J A GORDON, **NSM** M J EGGLETON

NORTHCOURT (Christ Church) *see* Abingdon *Ox*

NORTHDOWN PARK (St Philip) *see* Margate St Phil *Cant*

NORTHENDEN (St Wilfrid) *Man 6* **P** *Bp* **R** G S FORSTER

NORTHFIELD (St Laurence) *Birm 4* **P** *Keble Coll Ox* **R** C A E LAWRENCE

NORTHFLEET (All Saints) *see* Perry Street *Roch*

NORTHFLEET (St Botolph) and Rosherville *Roch 4* **P** *Patr Bd and Prime Min (alt)* **TR** L P SMITH, **C** C S B ROUTLEDGE

NORTHGATE (St Elizabeth) *see* Crawley *Chich*

NORTHIAM (St Mary) *Chich 20* **P** *MMCET* **R** R H WHITE

NORTHILL (St Mary the Virgin) *see* Caldecote, Northill and Old Warden *St Alb*

NORTHINGTON (St John the Evangelist) *see* Farleigh, Candover and Wield *Win*

NORTHLEACH (St Peter and St Paul) w Hampnett and Farmington, Cold Aston w Notgrove and Turkdean, and Compton Abdale w Haselton *Glouc 9* **P** *Bp (2 turns), Ld Chan (1 turn)* **P-in-c** R W WOODGER, **Hon C** S J GOUNDREY-SMITH, **NSM** N FISHER

NORTHLEIGH (St Giles) *see* Offwell, Northleigh, Farway, Cotleigh etc *Ex*

NORTHLEW (St Thomas of Canterbury) *see* Okehampton w Inwardleigh, Bratton Clovelly etc *Ex*

NORTHMOOR (St Denys) *see* Lower Windrush *Ox*

NORTHMOOR GREEN (St Peter and St John) *see* Alfred Jewel *B & W*

NORTHOLT (St Joseph the Worker) (St Hugh) West End *Lon 22* **P** *DBP* **V** F A CALDECOURT, **C** D H CHAPMAN

NORTHOLT (St Mary) (St Richard) *Lon 22* **P** *BNC Ox* **R** G S THOMAS

NORTHOLT PARK (St Barnabas) *Lon 22* **P** *Bp* **V** P D HILLAS, **NSM** H M ASKWITH

NORTHORPE (St John the Baptist)   *see* Scotton w Northorpe *Linc*
NORTHOWRAM (St Matthew) *Wakef 2*   **P** *Bp*
  V P A HOLMES
NORTHREPPS (St Mary)   *see* Overstrand, Northrepps, Sidestrand etc *Nor*
NORTHUMBERLAND HEATH (St Paul)   *see* Erith St Paul *Roch*
NORTHWICH (St Helen)   *see* Witton *Ches*
NORTHWICH (St Luke) (Holy Trinity) *Ches 6*   **P** *Bp*
  V C S SEDDON
NORTHWOLD (St Andrew)   *see* Grimshoe *Ely*
NORTHWOOD (Emmanuel) *Lon 23*   **P** *Ch Trust Fund Trust*
  V D M TALBOT,   **C** H M WILKINSON, G H L WATTS,
  G A M ANSTIS,   **NSM** P D O GREENE, S A L WATTS
NORTHWOOD (Holy Trinity)   *see* Hanley H Ev *Lich*
NORTHWOOD (Holy Trinity) *Lon 23*   **P** *Trustees*
  V R C BARTLETT,   **NSM** A CLARRIDGE
NORTHWOOD Pinner Road (St Edmund the King)
  see Northwood Hills St Edm *Lon*
NORTHWOOD (St John the Baptist) *Portsm 8*   **P** *Bp*
  R L MCROSTIE,   **NSM** D M NETHERWAY
NORTHWOOD (St Mark)   *see* Kirkby *Liv*
NORTHWOOD GREEN (Mission Church)
  see Westbury-on-Severn w Flaxley, Blaisdon etc *Glouc*
NORTHWOOD HILLS (St Edmund the King) *Lon 23*   **P** *Bp*
  V P R BARNES
NORTON (All Saints)   *see* Hullavington, Norton and Stanton St Quintin *Bris*
NORTON (All Saints)   *see* Brington w Whilton and Norton etc *Pet*
NORTON (St Andrew)   *see* Pakenham w Norton and Tostock *St E*
NORTON (St Berteline and St Christopher) *Ches 3*   **P** *DBP*
  P-in-c J BEANEY
NORTON (St Egwin)   *see* Evesham w Norton and Lenchwick *Worc*
NORTON (St George) (St Nicholas) *St Alb 3*   **P** *Bp*
  P-in-c D V COLLINS
NORTON (St James) *Sheff 2*   **P** *CCC Cam*   **R** G B WHITE
NORTON (St James)   *see* Stoulton w Drake's Broughton and Pirton etc *Worc*
NORTON (St Mary) *Cant 14*   **P** *Ld Chan*
  P-in-c S H LILLICRAP
NORTON (St Mary)   *see* Twigworth, Down Hatherley, Norton, The Leigh etc *Glouc*
NORTON (St Mary the Virgin) *Dur 10*   **P** *Bp*   **V** N R SHAVE,
  C J NOBEL
NORTON (St Michael and All Angels) *Dur 10*   **P** *V Norton St Mary*   **P-in-c** D J BAGE
NORTON (St Michael and All Angels)   *see* Stourbridge St Mich Norton *Worc*
NORTON (St Peter)   *see* Norton juxta Malton *York*
NORTON, EAST (All Saints)   *see* Hallaton and Allexton, w Horninghold, Tugby etc *Leic*
NORTON, OVER (St James)   *see* Chipping Norton *Ox*
NORTON BAVANT (All Saints)   *see* Upper Wylye Valley *Sarum*
NORTON BRIDGE (St Luke)   *see* Chebsey, Creswell, Ellenhall, Ranton etc *Lich*
NORTON CANES (St James) *Lich 3*   **P** *Bp*   **R** N L HIBBINS
NORTON CANON (St Nicholas)   *see* Weobley w Sarnesfield and Norton Canon *Heref*
NORTON CUCKNEY (St Mary) *S'well 6*   **P** *Lady Alexandra Cavendish Bentinck*   **P-in-c** S A CASH
NORTON DISNEY (St Peter)   *see* Bassingham Gp *Linc*
NORTON FITZWARREN (All Saints)   *see* Staplegrove w Norton Fitzwarren *B & W*
NORTON IN HALES (St Chad)   *see* Woore and Norton in Hales *Lich*
NORTON IN THE MOORS (St Bartholomew) *Lich 8*
  P *Walsingham Coll Trust Assn*   **R** S J LORD,
  NSM A BALLARD
NORTON JUXTA MALTON (St Peter) *York 6*   **P** *Abp*
  V R A HIRST
NORTON JUXTA TWYCROSS (Holy Trinity)   *see* Woodfield *Leic*
NORTON LE MOORS   *see* Norton in the Moors *Lich*
NORTON LEES (St Paul) *Sheff 2*   **P** *R Norton*   **V** P M BROWN
NORTON LINDSEY (Holy Trinity)   *see* Wolverton w Norton Lindsey and Langley *Cov*
NORTON MALREWARD (Holy Trinity)   *see* Chew Magna w Dundry, Norton Malreward etc *B & W*
NORTON MANDEVILLE (All Saints)   *see* High Ongar w Norton Mandeville *Chelmsf*
NORTON ST PHILIP (St Philip and St James)   *see* Hardington Vale *B & W*

NORTON SUB HAMDON (Blessed Virgin Mary) w West Chinnock, Chiselborough and Middle Chinnock *B & W 5*
  P *Bp*   **P-in-c** P J THOMAS
NORTON SUBCOURSE (St Mary)   *see* Raveningham Gp *Nor*
NORTON WOODSEATS (St Chad)   *see* Woodseats St Chad *Sheff*
NORTON WOODSEATS (St Paul)   *see* Norton Lees St Paul *Sheff*
NORWELL (St Laurence), w Ossington, Cromwell and Caunton *S'well 3*   **P** *Bp, SMF, and Mrs P Goedhuis (jt)*   **V** *vacant* (01636) 636329
NORWICH (Christ Church)   *see* Eaton Ch Ch *Nor*
NORWICH (Christ Church)   *see* New Catton Ch Ch *Nor*
NORWICH Heartsease (St Francis) *Nor 1*   **P** *Bp*
  P-in-c P L HOWARD
NORWICH (Holy Trinity)   *see* Heigham H Trin *Nor*
NORWICH Lakenham (St Alban) (St Mark) *Nor 1*   **P** *D&C*
  V S E WEST-LINDELL,   **OLM** M A HIDER
NORWICH (St Andrew)   *see* Eaton St Andr *Nor*
NORWICH (St Andrew) *Nor 1*   **P** *PCC*   **P-in-c** M J YOUNG
NORWICH (St Anne)   *see* Earlham *Nor*
NORWICH (St Barnabas)   *see* Heigham St Barn w St Bart *Nor*
NORWICH (St Catherine)   *see* Mile Cross *Nor*
NORWICH (St Elizabeth)   *see* Earlham *Nor*
NORWICH (St Francis)   *see* Nor Heartsease St Fran *Nor*
NORWICH (St George) Colegate *Nor 1*   **P** *D&C*
  P-in-c P MCFADYEN
NORWICH (St George) Tombland *Nor 1*   **P** *Bp*
  P-in-c J C MINNS
NORWICH (St Giles) *Nor 1*   **P** *Ld Chan and Bp (alt)*
  P-in-c D T THORNTON
NORWICH (St Helen) *Nor 1*   **P** *Gt Hosp Nor*
  P-in-c J A WILSON
NORWICH (St John the Baptist) Timberhill w Norwich St Julian *Nor 1*   **P** *Bp, Guild of All So, and D&C (jt)*   **R** M D SMITH,
  C D E STEVENSON
NORWICH (St Julian)   *see* Nor St Jo w St Julian *Nor*
NORWICH (St Luke)   *see* New Catton St Luke w St Aug *Nor*
NORWICH (St Mary)   *see* Earlham *Nor*
NORWICH (St Mary in the Marsh) *Nor 1*   **P** *D&C*
  P-in-c R CAPPER
NORWICH (St Mary Magdalene) w St James *Nor 2*   **P** *D&C*
  V M R PALMER,   **OLM** J SPENCER
NORWICH (St Matthew)   *see* Thorpe St Matt *Nor*
NORWICH (St Michael)   *see* Bowthorpe *Nor*
NORWICH (St Peter Mancroft) (St John Maddermarket) *Nor 1*
  P *PCC*   **R** P W NOKES,   **C** J B WYER
NORWICH (St Stephen) *Nor 1*   **P** *D&C*   **P-in-c** M M LIGHT
NORWICH (St Thomas)   *see* Heigham St Thos *Nor*
NORWICH, Lakenham (St John the Baptist and All Saints) and Tuckswood St Paul *Nor 1*   **P** *Bp and D&C (jt)*   **V** P J FOX
NORWOOD (St Leonard)   *see* Sheff St Leon Norwood *Sheff*
NORWOOD (St Mary the Virgin) *Lon 22*   **P** *SMF*
  R J M PAYNE
NORWOOD, SOUTH (Holy Innocents) *S'wark 21*   **P** *Bp*
  P-in-c N J COLEMAN,   **C** A ELTRINGHAM
NORWOOD, SOUTH (St Alban the Martyr) *S'wark 21*   **P** *Bp*
  P-in-c R T LAWSON
NORWOOD, SOUTH (St Mark) *S'wark 21*   **P** *Bp*
  P-in-c T W HURCOMBE,   **NSM** S E WHEELER-KILEY
NORWOOD, UPPER (All Saints) *S'wark 21*   **P** *V Croydon*
  V L S A MARSH
NORWOOD, UPPER (St John) *S'wark 21*   **P** *Bp*
  V B A MASON
NORWOOD, WEST (St Luke) *S'wark 12*   **P** *Abp*   **V** D R DAVIS
NOTGROVE (St Bartholomew)   *see* Northleach w Hampnett and Farmington etc *Glouc*
NOTTING DALE (St Clement) (St Mark) and Norlands St James *Lon 12*   **P** *Bp*   **V** A N EVERETT,   **C** K G RIGLIN
NOTTING HILL (All Saints) (St Columb) *Lon 12*   **P** *SMF*
  V J K BROWNSELL
NOTTING HILL (St John) *Lon 12*   **P** *Bp*   **V** W H TAYLOR,
  NSM R HAWES, R DURWARD, B MAHILUM
NOTTING HILL (St Michael and All Angels) (Christ Church) (St Francis) *Lon 12*   **P** *Trustees*   **V** A B ANDREWS
NOTTING HILL (St Peter) *Lon 12*   **P** *Bp*   **V** M K HARGREAVES
NOTTINGHAM (All Saints) (St Mary the Virgin) (St Peter and St James) *S'well 13*   **P** *Bp*   **P-in-c** C D HARRISON,
  C S F MORRIS, C LITTLE, R H DAVEY
NOTTINGHAM (St Andrew) *S'well 13*   **P** *Peache Trustees*
  V R M CLARK
NOTTINGHAM (St Ann w Emmanuel) *S'well 13*   **P** *Trustees*
  P-in-c K S F ROOMS,   **C** E W KAMUYU
NOTTINGHAM (St George w St John the Baptist) *S'well 13*
  P *Bp*   **P-in-c** A L WAUDE

NOTTINGHAM (St Jude) *S'well 13* P *CPAS*
P-in-c G F HADFIELD
NOTTINGHAM (St Nicholas) *S'well 13* P *CPAS*
P-in-c S D SILVESTER, C N J HILL, NSM A R HASKEY
NOTTINGHAM (St Saviour) *S'well 13* P *CPAS*
P-in-c D G HAMMOND, NSM A R HASKEY
NOTTINGHAM (St Stephen) *see* Hyson Green and Forest
Fields *S'well*
NOWTON (St Peter) *see* St Edm Way *St E*
NUFFIELD (Holy Trinity) *Ox 6* P *MMCET*
P-in-c B J BAILEY
NUN MONKTON (St Mary) *see* Lower Nidderdale *Ripon*
NUNBURNHOLME (St James) *see* Pocklington Wold *York*
NUNEATON (St Mary) *Cov 5* P *V Nuneaton* V M LIDDELL
NUNEATON (St Nicolas) *Cov 5* P *The Crown* V D JONES,
C K A BETTERIDGE
NUNHEAD (St Antony) (St Silas) *S'wark 8* P *Bp*
P-in-c G C MASON, C D J OGUNYEMI, NSM S D LECK
NUNNEY (All Saints) and Witham Friary, Marston Bigot,
Wanstrow and Cloford *B & W 3* P *Bp, SMF, and*
C N Clarke Esq and Duke of Somerset *(jt)* R vacant (01373)
836732
NUNNINGTON (All Saints) *see* Kirkdale w Harome,
Nunnington and Pockley *York*
NUNTHORPE (St Mary the Virgin) (St Mary's Church Hall)
York 20 P *Abp* V S M EAST
NUNTON (St Andrew) *see* Chalke Valley *Sarum*
NURSLING (St Boniface) and Rownhams *Win 12* P *Bp*
R J T WILLIAMS
NURSTEAD (St Mildred) *see* Meopham w Nurstead *Roch*
NUTBOURNE (St Wilfrid) *see* Chidham *Chich*
NUTFIELD (St Peter and St Paul) *see* Bletchingley and
Nutfield *S'wark*
NUTFIELD, LOWER *see* S Nutfield w Outwood *S'wark*
NUTFIELD, SOUTH (Christ Church) w Outwood *S'wark 25*
P *Bp and Ch Patr Trust (jt)* V T G KEMP
NUTHALL (St Patrick) *S'well 7* P *Bp* P-in-c B M HOLBROOK
NUTHURST (St Andrew) and Mannings Heath *Chich 8*
P *Bp Lon* R vacant (01403) 891449
NUTHURST (St Thomas) *see* Packwood w Hockley Heath
Birm
NUTLEY (St James the Less) *Chich 21* P *R Maresfield*
V J N A HOBBS
NYMET (St George) *see* S Molton w Nymet St George, High
Bray etc *Ex*
NYMET ROWLAND (St Bartholomew) *see* N Creedy *Ex*
NYMET TRACEY (St Bartholomew) *see* Bow w Broad Nymet
Ex
NYMPSFIELD (St Bartholomew) *see* Uley w Owlpen and
Nympsfield *Glouc*
NYNEHEAD (All Saints) *see* Wellington and Distr *B & W*
OADBY (St Paul) (St Peter) *Leic 4* P *Bp* TR M F RUSK,
TV S A BAILEY, C B J EVANS-HILLS, P CLEMENT
OAKAMOOR (Holy Trinity) *see* Kingsley and Foxt-w-Whiston
and Oakamoor etc *Lich*
OAKDALE (St George) *see* N Poole Ecum Team *Sarum*
OAKE (St Bartholomew) *see* Deane Vale *B & W*
OAKENGATES (Holy Trinity) and Wrockwardine Wood *Lich 21*
P *Bp* R M C STAFFORD, C R J WALKER-HILL
OAKENROD (St George) and Bamford St Michael *Man 17*
P *Bp* C K L SMEETON, NSM P R ZUCCA
OAKENSHAW (Church of the Good Shepherd) *see* Willington
and Sunnybrow *Dur*
OAKENSHAW (St Andrew), Wyke and Low Moor (South
Bradford Benefice) *Bradf 2* P *Patr Bd* TV C E SHEDD,
Hon C M R M LYONS, NSM D P ELLIS
OAKFIELD (St John the Baptist) *Portsm 7* P *V St Helens*
V H E WRIGHT
OAKFORD (St Peter) *see* Washfield, Stoodleigh, Withleigh etc
Ex
OAKHAM (All Saints), Ashwell, Braunston, Brooke, Egleton,
Hambleton, Langham, Market Overton, Teigh and Whissendine
Pet 12 P *Patr Bd* TR L T FRANCIS-DEHQANI,
TV R J MACKRILL, NSM H A CROWTHER, S C PARSONS
OAKHANGER (St Luke's Mission Church) *see* Alsager Ch Ch
Ches
OAKHANGER (St Mary Magdalene) *see* Northanger *Win*
OAKHILL (All Saints) *see* Ashwick w Oakhill and Binegar
B & W
OAKHILL Eastwood View (shared church) *see* Clifton St Jas
Sheff
OAKINGTON (St Andrew) *Ely 6* P *Qu Coll Cam*
V J C ALEXANDER
OAKLEY (St Leonard) w Wootton St Lawrence *Win 4* P *Qu*
Coll Ox and D&C (alt) R C J M VAUGHAN,
NSM C A VAUGHAN

OAKLEY (St Mary) *see* Worminghall w Ickford, Oakley and
Shabbington *Ox*
OAKLEY (St Mary) *see* Bromham w Oakley and Stagsden
St Alb
OAKLEY (St Nicholas) *see* N Hartismere *St E*
OAKLEY, GREAT (All Saints) w Wix and Wrabness *Chelmsf 20*
P *Ld Chan, Ch Patr Trust, and St Jo Coll Cam (by turn)*
R vacant (01255) 880070
OAKLEY, GREAT (St Michael) and LITTLE (St Peter) *Pet 7*
P *H W G de Capell Brooke Esq and Boughton Estates Ltd (alt)*
P-in-c J M COLLINS
OAKLEY SQUARE (St Matthew) *see* Old St Pancras *Lon*
OAKMOOR *see* Bishopsnympton, Rose Ash, Mariansleigh etc
Ex
OAKRIDGE (St Bartholomew) *see* Bisley, Chalford, France
Lynch, and Oakridge *Glouc*
OAKS IN CHARNWOOD (St James the Greater) *see* Shepshed
and Oaks in Charnwood *Leic*
OAKSEY (All Saints) *see* Ashley, Crudwell, Hankerton and
Oaksey *Bris*
OAKWOOD (no dedication) *Derby 9* P *Bp and MMCET (jt)*
P-in-c C L HUGHES, C J L WHITEHEAD
OAKWOOD (St Thomas) *Lon 18* P *Bp* V C J P HOBBS
OAKWORTH (Christ Church) *Bradf 8* P *Bp* V J ROGERS,
NSM B G PARTRIDGE
OARE (Blessed Virgin Mary) w Culbone *B & W 15* P *Bp*
P-in-c C D BURKE
OARE (Holy Trinity) *see* Vale of Pewsey *Sarum*
OARE (St Bartholomew) *see* E Downland *Ox*
OARE (St Peter) *see* The Brents and Davington w Oare and
Luddenham *Cant*
OATLANDS (St Mary) *Guildf 8* P *Bp* V S BRUNN,
NSM M J HUSSEY, OLM L BOWDEN
OBORNE (St Cuthbert) *see* Queen Thorne *Sarum*
OCCOLD (St Michael) *see* Eye *St E*
OCKBROOK (All Saints) *Derby 13* P *Lt-Col T H Pares*
V T M SUMPTER, NSM V A BILLINGS
OCKENDON, NORTH (St Mary Magdalene) *Chelmsf 2* P *Bp*
P-in-c G BAISLEY
OCKENDON, SOUTH (St Nicholas) and Belhus Park
Chelmsf 14 P *Bp and Guild of All So (jt)*
R B G DUCKWORTH, C P D RABIN
OCKER HILL (St Mark) *Lich 26* P *Bp* V A J GWILLIM
OCKFORD RIDGE (St Mark) *see* Godalming *Guildf*
OCKHAM (All Saints) *see* E Horsley and Ockham w Hatchford
and Downside *Guildf*
OCKLEY (St Margaret), Okewood and Forest Green *Guildf 7*
P *Bp and J P M H Evelyn Esq (alt)*
P-in-c N A KNIGHTS JOHNSON, NSM J MARSH
OCLE PYCHARD (St James the Great) *see* Frome Valley *Heref*
ODCOMBE (St Peter and St Paul), Brympton, Lufton and
Montacute *B & W 6* P *Ch Ch (4 turns),*
C E B Clive-Ponsonby-Fane Esq *(1 turn)* R J F JENKINS
ODD DOWN (St Philip and St James) *see* Bath Odd Down w
Combe Hay *B & W*
ODD RODE (All Saints) *Ches 11* P *R Astbury*
R P S ATKINSON
ODDINGLEY (St James) *see* Bowbrook S *Worc*
ODDINGTON (Holy Ascension) *see* Broadwell, Evenlode,
Oddington, Adlestrop etc *Glouc*
ODDINGTON (St Andrew) *see* Ray Valley *Ox*
ODDINGTON (St Nicholas) *see* Broadwell, Evenlode,
Oddington, Adlestrop etc *Glouc*
ODELL (All Saints) *St Alb 13* P *Lord Luke*
P-in-c C M CLARK
ODIHAM (All Saints) *see* N Hants Downs *Win*
ODSTOCK (St Mary) *see* Chalke Valley *Sarum*
OFFCHURCH (St Gregory) *Cov 10* P *Bp*
P-in-c J T H BRITTON, C D R PATTERSON
OFFENHAM (St Mary and St Milburgh) *see* Badsey w
Aldington and Offenham and Bretforton *Worc*
OFFERTON (St Alban) (St John) *Ches 18* P *Bp* V J BATES,
NSM G M SELLORS
OFFHAM (Old St Peter) *see* Hamsey *Chich*
OFFHAM (St Michael) *see* W Malling w Offham *Roch*
OFFLEY (St Mary Magdalene) *see* King's Walden and Offley w
Lilley *St Alb*
OFFLEY, HIGH (St Mary the Virgin) *see* Adbaston, High
Offley, Knightley, Norbury etc *Lich*
OFFLEY HAY (Mission Church) *see* Eccleshall *Lich*
OFFORD D'ARCY w OFFORD CLUNY (All Saints)
see Buckden w the Offords *Ely*
OFFTON (St Mary) *see* Somersham w Flowton and Offton w
Willisham *St E*
OFFWELL (St Mary the Virgin), Northleigh, Farway, Cotleigh
and Widworthy *Ex 5* P *Trustees, R T Marker Esq, Cotleigh
PCC, and Bp (jt)* V vacant (01404) 831480

OGBOURNE (St Andrew)   *see* Ridgeway *Sarum*
OGBOURNE (St George)   *as above*
OGLEY HAY (St James) *Lich 1*   **P** *Bp*   **V** D BISHOP
OGWELL (St Bartholomew)   *see* Wolborough and Ogwell *Ex*
OKEFORD Benefice, The *Sarum 6*   **P** *G A L-F Pitt-Rivers Esq and DBP (alt)*   **C** W T RIDDING, D R R SEYMOUR, **NSM** S S MUFFETT,   **OLM** D J MARL
OKEFORD FITZPAINE (St Andrew)   *see* Okeford *Sarum*
OKEHAMPTON (All Saints) (St James) w Inwardleigh; Bratton Clovelly w Germansweek; Northlew w Ashbury; and Bridestowe and Sourton *Ex 11*   **P** *Patr Bd*   **TR** S W COOK, **TV** J DAVIES,   **C** D A ATALLAH, G D HARRIS
OKEWOOD (St John the Baptist)   *see* Ockley, Okewood and Forest Green *Guildf*
OLD   *see also under substantive place name*
OLD FORD (St Paul) (St Mark) *Lon 7*   **P** *Hyndman Trustees and CPAS (jt)*   **V** P J BOARDMAN
OLD HEATH (St Barnabas)   *see* Colchester St Barn *Chelmsf*
OLD HILL (Holy Trinity) *Worc 9*   **P** *Ch Soc Trust*   **V** J M HANCOCK
OLD LANE (Mission Church)   *see* Bloxwich *Lich*
OLD WIVES LEES (Mission Church)   *see* Chilham w Challock and Molash *Cant*
OLDBERROW (St Mary)   *see* Spernall, Morton Bagot and Oldberrow *Cov*
OLDBROOK (Community Church)   *see* Woughton *Ox*
OLDBURY *Sarum 15*   **P** *Bp, CPAS, Marquess of Lansdowne, and C E R Money-Kyrle Esq (jt)*   **R** P A BROMLEY
OLDBURY (Christ Church), Langley, and Londonderry *Birm 7*   **P** *Prime Min (1 turn), Bp (3 turns)*   **V** N P PELLING, **NSM** A E HANNY, P M EATON
OLDBURY (St Nicholas)   *see* Bridgnorth, Tasley, Astley Abbotts, etc *Heref*
OLDBURY-ON-SEVERN (St Arilda)   *see* Thornbury and Oldbury-on-Severn w Shepperdine *Glouc*
OLDCOTES (St Mark's Mission Church)
see Carlton-in-Lindrick and Langold w Oldcotes *S'well*
OLDHAM Moorside (St Thomas) *Man 15*   **P** *Trustees*   **P-in-c** B M MITCHELL
OLDHAM (St Barnabas)   *see* Medlock Head *Man*
OLDHAM (St Chad)   *see* Hollinwood and Limeside *Man*
OLDHAM (St James) (St Ambrose) *Man 15*   **P** *Bp and R Prestwich (jt)*   **V** P PLUMPTON
OLDHAM (St Mary w St Peter) *Man 16*   **P** *Patr Bd*   **V** D J PALMER,   **OLM** J M HURLSTON
OLDHAM (St Paul) *Man 16*   **P** *Bp*   **P-in-c** N J ANDREWES, **Hon C** D J QUARMBY
OLDHAM (St Stephen and All Martyrs)   *see* Coldhurst and Oldham St Steph *Man*
OLDHURST (St Peter)   *see* Somersham w Pidley and Oldhurst and Woodhurst *Ely*
OLDLAND (St Anne) *Bris 5*   **P** *Bp*   **V** A J M SPEAR, **C** P J P BRADLEY
OLDRIDGE (St Thomas)   *see* Tedburn St Mary, Cheriton Bishop, Whitestone etc *Ex*
OLDSWINFORD (St Mary)   *see* Old Swinford Stourbridge *Worc*
OLIVER'S BATTERY (St Mark)   *see* Stanmore *Win*
OLLERTON (St Giles) (St Paulinus) w Boughton *S'well 6*   **P** *Ld Chan and Bp (alt)*   **P-in-c** R GOODHAND, **C** C J PHILLIPS
OLNEY (St Peter and St Paul) *Ox 27*   **P** *Bp*   **R** C WOOD
OLTON (St Margaret) *Birm 11*   **P** *Bp and V Bickenhill (jt)*   **V** J M KNAPP,   **NSM** S M CHANDLER
OLVESTON (St Mary of Malmesbury)   *see* Almondsbury and Olveston *Bris*
OMBERSLEY (St Andrew) w Doverdale *Worc 8*   **P** *Bp and Lord Sandys (alt)*   **P-in-c** S P KERR,   **NSM** S L BARRETT
ONCHAN (St Peter) *S & M 2*   **P** *The Crown*   **V** C B BURGESS
ONECOTE (St Luke)   *see* Ipstones w Berkhamsytch and Onecote w Bradnop *Lich*
ONEHOUSE (St John the Baptist)   *see* Gt Finborough w Onehouse, Harleston, Buxhall etc *St E*
ONGAR, HIGH (St Mary the Virgin) w Norton Mandeville *Chelmsf 26*   **P** *Ch Soc Trust*   **P-in-c** M J PETERS
ONIBURY (St Michael and All Angels)   *see* Ludlow *Heref*
ONSLOW SQUARE (Holy Trinity) St Paul and South Kensington St Augustine *Lon 8*   **P** *Bp, MMCET, and Keble Coll Ox (jt)*   **V** N G P GUMBEL,   **C** N K LEE, P W COWLEY, J R HAITH, M R TOULMIN, T FLINT, T J MATTHEWS, D G WALKER, H L METTERS, I H DYBLE, J R O WYNNE, A D A FRANCE-WILLIAMS, J M FIELD, J DAVIES, P ALLERTON, H W J CAHUSAC, M P LAYZELL, E C CLIFFORD, C J B LEE,   **Hon C** J A K MILLAR
ONSLOW VILLAGE (All Saints)   *see* Guildf All SS *Guildf*

OPENSHAW (St Barnabas)   *see* Manchester Gd Shep and St Barn *Man*
OPENSHAW, HIGHER (St Clement) *Man 1*   **P** *Trustees*   **P-in-c** C J R HOWITZ
OPENWOODGATE (St Mark)   *see* Belper *Derby*
ORBY (All Saints)   *see* Burgh Gp *Linc*
ORCHARD (Community Centre)   *see* Egglescliffe *Dur*
ORCHARD PARK (St Michael and All Angels)   *see* N Hull St Mich *York*
ORCHARD PORTMAN (St Michael)   *see* Beercrocombe w Curry Mallet, Hatch Beauchamp etc *B & W*
ORCHARD WAY (St Barnabas)   *see* Cheltenham St Mark *Glouc*
ORCHARDLEIGH (Blessed Virgin Mary)   *see* Beckington w Standerwick, Berkley, Rodden etc *B & W*
ORCHESTON (St Mary)   *see* Wylye and Till Valley *Sarum*
ORCOP (St John the Baptist)   *see* St Weonards *Heref*
ORDSALL (All Hallows)   *see* Retford Area *S'well*
ORDSALL (St Clement) and Salford Quays *Man 20*   **P** *Bp*   **P-in-c** S KEARNEY
ORE (Christ Church) *Chich 17*   **P** *Simeon's Trustees*   **V** *vacant* (01424) 715193
ORE (St Helen) (St Barnabas) *Chich 17*   **P** *Simeon's Trustees*   **R** C H KEY,   **C** A M HAWKINS,   **NSM** A C WILLIAMS
ORESTON (Church of the Good Shepherd)   *see* Plymstock and Hooe *Ex*
ORFORD (St Andrew) *Liv 12*   **P** *Bp*   **V** M RAYNOR
ORFORD (St Bartholomew)   *see* Wilford Peninsula *St E*
ORFORD (St Margaret) *Liv 12*   **P** *Bp*   **P-in-c** S W BOYD, **NSM** A A C FAIRCLOUGH
ORLESTONE (St Mary) w Snave and Ruckinge w Warehorne and Kenardington *Cant 11*   **P** *Ld Chan and Abp (alt)*   **R** T R WHATELEY
ORLETON (St George)   *see* Leominster *Heref*
ORLINGBURY (St Mary)   *see* Gt w Lt Harrowden and Orlingbury and Isham etc *Pet*
ORMESBY (St Cuthbert) *York 17*   **P** *Abp*   **V** R BROWN
ORMESBY, NORTH (Holy Trinity) *York 17*   **P** *Abp*   **V** D P BLACK
ORMESBY ST MARGARET (St Margaret) w Scratby, Ormesby St Michael and Rollesby *Nor 6*   **P** *Bp, D&C, DBP and R J H Tacon Esq (jt)*   **V** N R SPENCER, **NSM** K J RAYNER
ORMESBY ST MICHAEL (St Michael)   *see* Ormesby St Marg w Scratby, Ormesby St Mich etc *Nor*
ORMSBY Group, The South (St Leonard) *Linc 7*   **P** *A J Massingberd-Mundy Esq, Sir Thomas Ingilby Bt, Mert Coll Ox, Bp, and DBP (jt)*   **P-in-c** C HILLIAM
ORMSGILL (St Francis)   *see* N Barrow *Carl*
ORMSIDE (St James)   *see* Heart of Eden *Carl*
ORMSKIRK (St Peter and St Paul) *Liv 11*   **P** *Earl of Derby*   **V** C H JONES,   **C** A R SHAW,   **NSM** S E HAYNES, **OLM** L CAMP
ORPINGTON (All Saints) *Roch 16*   **P** *D&C*   **V** B E MCHENRY
ORPINGTON (Christ Church) *Roch 16*   **P** *Ch Trust Fund Trust, Bp, and V Orpington (jt)*   **V** J P COLWILL
ORPINGTON (St Andrew) *Roch 16*   **P** *Bp*   **P-in-c** P F PRENTICE,   **Hon C** D HAMID
ORRELL (St Luke) *Liv 14*   **P** *Bp*   **V** P G WHITTINGTON, **OLM** F S FAIRBAIRN
ORRELL HEY (St John and St James) *Liv 1*   **P** *CPAS*   **P-in-c** C L DAWSON,   **OLM** A J FINCH
ORSETT (St Giles and All Saints) and Bulphan and Horndon on the Hill *Chelmsf 14*   **P** *Bp and D&C St Paul's (jt)*   **R** E W HANSON,   **NSM** S R BLAKE
ORSTON (St Mary)   *see* Whatton w Aslockton, Hawksworth, Scarrington etc *S'well*
ORTON (All Saints) and Tebay w Ravenstonedale and Newbiggin-on-Lune *Carl 1*   **P** *Bp and Ravenstonedale Trustees (1 turn), Resident Landowners (1 turn)*   **P-in-c** B LOCK
ORTON, GREAT (St Giles)   *see* Barony of Burgh *Carl*
ORTON GOLDHAY (St John)   *see* Orton Longueville w Bottlebridge *Ely*
ORTON LONGUEVILLE (Holy Trinity) w Bottlebridge *Ely 15*   **P** *Bp*   **NSM** J R PENN
ORTON MALBORNE (not known)   *see* Orton Longueville w Bottlebridge *Ely*
ORTON-ON-THE-HILL (St Edith of Polesworth)   *see* Bosworth and Sheepy Gp *Leic*
ORTON WATERVILLE (St Mary) *Ely 15*   **P** *Bp*   **V** R J HAMILTON
ORWELL Group, The (St Andrew) *Ely 7*   **P** *Bp, DBP, and Trin Coll Cam (jt)*   **R** F A COUCH
ORWELL Team Ministry   *see* Walton and Trimley *St E*
OSBALDWICK (St Thomas) w Murton *York 2*   **P** *Abp*   **V** A CLEMENTS

OSBOURNBY (St Peter and St Paul) *see* S Lafford *Linc*
OSCOTT, OLD (All Saints) *see* Kingstanding St Mark *Birm*
OSENEY CRESCENT (St Luke) *Lon 17* **P** *Bp* **V** J MARCH
OSGATHORPE (St Mary the Virgin) *see* Kegworth, Hathern, Long Whatton, Diseworth etc *Leic*
OSMASTON (St Martin) *see* Brailsford w Shirley, Osmaston w Edlaston etc *Derby*
OSMINGTON (St Osmond) *see* Preston w Sutton Poyntz and Osmington w Poxwell *Sarum*
OSMONDTHORPE (St Philip) *see* Leeds All SS w Osmondthorpe *Ripon*
OSMOTHERLEY (St Peter) w Harlsey and Ingleby Arncliffe *York 18* **P** J N Barnard Esq *(1 turn)*, Ld Chan *(2 turns)* **V** I D HOUGHTON, **NSM** T A LEWIS
OSMOTHERLY (St John) *see* Ulverston St Mary w H Trin *Carl*
OSNEY (St Frideswide) *Ox 7* **P** *Bp and Ch Ch Ox (jt)* **R** A C RUSTELL, **NSM** J M BROWN, R M HILL, M E HENIG
OSPRINGE (St Peter and St Paul) *see* Eastling w Ospringe and Stalisfield w Otterden *Cant*
OSSETT (Holy and Undivided Trinity) and Gawthorpe *Wakef 9* **P** *Bp and R Dewsbury (jt)* **V** P D MAYBURY, **OLM** A SHACKLETON
OSSETT, SOUTH (Christ Church) *Wakef 9* **P** *Bp* **V** D J ROBERTSON
OSSINGTON (Holy Rood) *see* Norwell w Ossington, Cromwell and Caunton *S'well*
OSTERLEY ROAD (St Mary) *see* Spring Grove St Mary *Lon*
OSWALDKIRK (St Oswald) *see* Ampleforth w Oswaldkirk, Gilling E etc *York*
OSWALDTWISTLE (Immanuel) (All Saints) *Blackb 1* **P** *Trustees* **P-in-c** J S HOLLAND
OSWALDTWISTLE (St Paul) *Blackb 1* **P** *Trustees* **P-in-c** J S HOLLAND, **NSM** C WILLIAMS
OSWESTRY (Holy Trinity) *Lich 19* **P** *Bp* **V** P T DARLINGTON
OSWESTRY (St Oswald) *Lich 19* **P** *Earl of Powis* **V** S G THORBURN
OTFORD (St Bartholomew) *Roch 10* **P** *D&C Westmr* **V** R M WORSSAM
OTFORD LANE (Mission Hall) *see* Knockholt w Halstead *Roch*
OTHAM (St Nicholas) w Langley *Cant 13* **P** *Abp and CPAS (jt)* **R** *vacant* (01622) 861470
OTHERY (St Michael) *see* Middlezoy and Othery and Moorlinch *B & W*
OTLEY (All Saints) *Bradf 4* **P** *Bp* **V** G C BUTTANSHAW, **NSM** J A PARKIN
OTLEY (St Mary) *see* Clopton w Otley, Swilland and Ashbocking *St E*
OTTER VALE *see* Ottery St Mary, Alfington, W Hill, Tipton etc *Ex*
OTTERBOURNE (St Matthew) *see* Compton, Hursley, and Otterbourne *Win*
OTTERBURN (St John the Evangelist) *see* N Tyne and Redesdale *Newc*
OTTERFORD (St Leonard) *see* Blackdown *B & W*
OTTERHAM (St Denis) *see* Boscastle w Davidstow *Truro*
OTTERINGTON, NORTH (St Michael and All Angels) *see* The Thorntons and The Otteringtons *York*
OTTERINGTON, SOUTH (St Andrew) *as above*
OTTERSHAW (Christ Church) *Guildf 11* **P** *Bp* **P-in-c** S C FACCINI, **OLM** J A M VICKERS, B A SEYMOUR
OTTERTON (St Michael) *see* E Budleigh w Bicton and Otterton *Ex*
OTTERY ST MARY (St Mary the Virgin), Alfington, West Hill, Tipton St John, Venn Ottery, Newton Poppleford, Harpford and Colaton Raleigh *Ex 7* **P** *Patr Bd* **TR** S G FRANKLIN, **TV** C E EDMONDS, M WARD, **C** T L V TREANOR, **Hon C** J G PANGBOURNE, A E H TURNER, **NSM** K J BRIMACOMBE, R J ALLEN, H D GOVIER, M G DICK
OTTRINGHAM (St Wilfrid) *see* Keyingham w Ottringham, Halsham and Sunk Is *York*
OUGHTIBRIDGE (Ascension) *Sheff 3* **P** *V Wadsley* **V** J F E MANN
OUGHTRINGTON (St Peter) and Warburton *Ches 10* **P** *Bp and Viscount Ashbrook (jt)* **R** E M BURGESS, **NSM** T R LEGGE
OULTON (St John the Evangelist) *see* Stone Ch Ch and Oulton *Lich*
OULTON (St John) w Woodlesford *Ripon 8* **P** *Bp* **P-in-c** A J PEARSON
OULTON (St Michael) *Nor 9* **P** *Ch Soc Trust* **R** A R PRITCHARD, **NSM** C S PRITCHARD
OULTON (St Peter and St Paul) *see* Lt Barningham, Blickling, Edgefield etc *Nor*

OULTON BROAD (St Mark) (St Luke the Evangelist) *Nor 9* **P** *Simeon's Trustees* **V** I R BENTLEY, **C** W N EVANS, **NSM** G POWELL, **OLM** M E ZIPFEL
OUNDLE (St Peter) w Ashton and Benefield w Glapthorn *Pet 10* **P** *Bp and Mrs G S Watts-Russell (jt)* **R** R J ORMSTON, **C** S J WEBSTER
OUSBY (St Luke) *see* Cross Fell Gp *Carl*
OUSDEN (St Peter) *see* Bansfield *St E*
OUSEBURN, GREAT (St Mary) and LITTLE (Holy Trinity) w Marton cum Grafton and Whixley w Green Hammerton *Ripon 3* **P** *Bp, R Knaresborough and DBP (3 turns), St Jo Coll Cam (1 turn)* **V** *vacant* (01423) 330928
OUT RAWCLIFFE (St John the Evangelist) *see* Waterside Par *Blackb*
OUTLANE (St Mary Magdalene) *see* Stainland w Outlane *Wakef*
OUTWELL (St Clement) *Ely 14* **P** *Bp* **R** A F JESSON
OUTWOOD (St John) *see* S Nutfield w Outwood *S'wark*
OUTWOOD (St Mary Magdalene) *Wakef 11* **P** *V Stanley* **V** J W BUTTERWORTH, **Hon Par Dn** G BUTTERWORTH
OUTWOOD COMMON (St John the Divine) *see* Billericay and Lt Burstead *Chelmsf*
OUZEL VALLEY, The *St Alb 11* **P** *Patr Bd* **TR** G FELLOWS, **TV** J M CAPPLEMAN, B J MINTON, **C** D C TEASDEL, **OLM** W JONES
OVAL WAY (All Saints) *see* Chalfont St Peter *Ox*
OVENDEN (St George) *Wakef 4* **P** *V Halifax* **NSM** P A PICKARD, G ROPER
OVENDEN (St John the Evangelist) *see* Bradshaw and Holmfield *Wakef*
OVER *see also under substantive place name*
OVER (St Chad) *Ches 6* **P** *Bp* **V** P F HARTOPP
OVER (St John the Evangelist) *Ches 6* **P** *Lord Delamere and W R Cullimore Esq (jt)* **V** G T CROWDER
OVER (St Mary) *Ely 6* **P** *Trin Coll Cam* **P-in-c** M E RABY
OVER WALLOP (St Peter) *see* Portway and Danebury *Win*
OVERBURY (St Faith) w Teddington, Alstone and Little Washbourne w Beckford and Ashton under Hill *Worc 4* **P** *D&C and MMCET (jt)* **P-in-c** M T C BAYNES, **C** T J HENDERSON, S K RENSHAW
OVERCHURCH (St Mary) *see* Upton (Overchurch) *Ches*
OVERPOOL (St Francis) *see* Ellesmere Port *Ches*
OVERSEAL (St Matthew) *see* Seale and Lullington w Coton in the Elms *Derby*
OVERSTONE (St Nicholas) *see* Mears Ashby and Hardwick and Sywell etc *Pet*
OVERSTRAND (St Martin), Northrepps, Sidestrand and Trimingham *Nor 21* **P** *Duchy of Lanc, DBP, and Bp (by turn)* **R** *vacant* (01263) 579350
OVERTON (St Helen) *Blackb 11* **P** *V Lanc* **Hon C** D G GODDARD
OVERTON (St Mary) w Laverstoke and Freefolk *Win 6* **P** *Bp* **P-in-c** I K SMALE, **C** S G WILSON
OVERTON (St Michael and All Angels) *see* Upper Kennet *Sarum*
OVING (All Saints) *see* Schorne *Ox*
OVING (St Andrew) *see* Tangmere and Oving *Chich*
OVINGDEAN (St Wulfran) *Chich 2* **P** *SMF* **P-in-c** P G WOLFENDEN
OVINGHAM (St Mary the Virgin) *Newc 9* **P** *Bp* **P-in-c** E LEWIS
OVINGTON (St John the Evangelist) *see* Ashill, Carbrooke, Ovington and Saham Toney *Nor*
OVINGTON (St Mary) *see* N Hinckford *Chelmsf*
OVINGTON (St Peter) *see* Arle Valley *Win*
OWERMOIGNE (St Michael) *see* Watercombe *Sarum*
OWERSBY, NORTH (St Martin) *see* Kelsey Gp *Linc*
OWLERTON (St John the Baptist) *Sheff 4* **P** *Ch Patr Trust* **V** N A DAWSON, **NSM** R W YOUNG
OWLPEN (Holy Cross) *see* Uley w Owlpen and Nympsfield *Glouc*
OWLSMOOR (St George) *Ox 16* **P** *Bp* **V** R G BURGESS
OWLSWICK (Chapel) *see* Risborough *Ox*
OWMBY Group, The (St Peter and St Paul) *Linc 3* **P** *Duchy of Lanc, Bp and D&C, Bp and Mrs S Hutton, and Mrs B K Cracroft-Eley (by turn)* **R** P D GODDEN, **NSM** R H CROSSLAND, **OLM** S E TURNBULL
OWSLEBURY (St Andrew) *see* Twyford and Owslebury and Morestead etc *Win*
OWSTON (All Saints) *Sheff 7* **P** *DBP* **V** M MOSSMAN
OWSTON (St Andrew) *see* Whatborough Gp *Leic*
OWSTON (St Martin) *Linc 1* **P** *The Crown* **P-in-c** J N GREEN
OWTHORNE (St Matthew) *see* Withernsea w Owthorne and Easington etc *York*
OWTHORPE (St Margaret) *S'well 8* **P** *Trustees Sir Rupert Bromley Bt* **P-in-c** P D S MASSEY

OWTON MANOR (St James) *Dur 3* P *Bp* V S J LOCKE
OXBOROUGH (St John the Evangelist) w Foulden and
Caldecote *Nor 13* P *G&C Coll Cam* C D J HANWELL
OXCLOSE (not known) *Dur 11* P *R Washington, TR Usworth,
and V Fatfield (jt)* P-in-c S M WHITE
OXENDON (St Helen) *see* Arthingworth, Harrington w
Oxendon and E Farndon *Pet*
OXENHALL (St Anne) *see* Redmarley D'Abitot,
Bromesberrow, Pauntley etc *Glouc*
OXENHOPE (St Mary the Virgin) *Bradf 8* P *Bp*
P-in-c P MAYO-SMITH, NSM N C J WRIGHT
OXENTON (St John the Baptist) *see* Bishop's Cleeve and
Woolstone w Gotherington etc *Glouc*
OXFORD Canning Crescent (St Luke) *see* Ox St Matt *Ox*
OXFORD (St Aldate) *Ox 7* P *Simeon's Trustees*
R C ST G CLEVERLY, C S C R PONSONBY, P J ATKINSON,
NSM C HOFREITER
OXFORD (St Andrew) *Ox 7* P *Trustees*
V A R WINGFIELD DIGBY, C P F SCAMMAN, P M WHITE,
NSM R M CUNNINGHAM, J MOBEY
OXFORD (St Barnabas and St Paul) *Ox 7* P *Keble Coll Ox*
P-in-c J W BESWICK, C M STAFFORD, NSM M E MAYLOR
OXFORD (St Clement) *Ox 4* P *Ox Ch Trust*
R J B GILLINGHAM, NSM J D BRANT
OXFORD (St Ebbe w Holy Trinity and St Peter-le-Bailey) *Ox 7*
P *Ox Ch Trust* R V E ROBERTS, C P D L WILKINSON,
P A JACK, Hon C S MENON, NSM D G REID
OXFORD (St Frideswide) *see* Osney *Ox*
OXFORD (St Giles) St Philip and St James (St Margaret) *Ox 7*
P *St Jo Coll Ox* V A W H BUNCH, C A E RAMSEY,
S A WELCH, Hon C B W SILVERMAN, J N A BRADBURY,
NSM P M CLIFFORD
OXFORD (St Mary Magdalene) *Ox 7* P *Ch Ch Ox*
P-in-c P J GROVES, C R J FRITH
OXFORD (St Mary the Virgin) (St Cross or Holywell) (St Peter
in the East) *Ox 7* P *Or Coll Ox and Mert Coll Ox (jt)*
V B W MOUNTFORD, C D A NEAUM, R E GREENE,
NSM C BANNISTER-PARKER
OXFORD (St Matthew) *Ox 7* P *Ox Ch Trust* R S J HELLYER,
NSM M J RAYNER, J SHERWOOD
OXFORD (St Michael at the North Gate w St Martin and All
Saints) *Ox 7* P *Linc Coll Ox* P-in-c R A WILKES, Hon
C G A D PLATTEN, NSM J MOFFETT-LEVY
OXFORD (St Thomas the Martyr) *Ox 7* P *Ch Ch Ox* Hon
C J M R BAKER
OXHEY (All Saints) *St Alb 6* P *Bp* V P M WISE,
C A SOWTON
OXHEY (St Matthew) *St Alb 6* P *DBP* V D M SHEPHERD
OXHILL (St Lawrence) *see* Tysoe w Oxhill and Whatcote *Cov*
OXLEY (Epiphany) *Lich 28* P *Bp* V P S HAWKINS,
NSM R MAXFIELD
OXNEAD (St Michael & all Angels) *see* Bure Valley *Nor*
OXSHOTT (St Andrew) *Guildf 10* P *Bp* V J P CRESSWELL,
C P M DICKIN, OLM M L L HAWRISH
OXSPRING (St Aidan) *see* Penistone and Thurlstone *Wakef*
OXTED (St Mary) and Tandridge *S'wark 25* P *Bp*
R A P RUMSEY, OLM D C WEIGHTMAN
OXTON (St Peter and St Paul) *see* Epperstone, Gonalston,
Oxton and Woodborough *S'well*
OXTON (St Saviour) *Ches 1* P *DBP* V J KENNEDY,
C G V LAUTENBACH, D E WATSON
PACKINGTON (Holy Rood) *see* Woodfield *Leic*
PACKWOOD (St Giles) w Hockley Heath *Birm 6* P *Bp and
M R Parkes Esq (alt)* V M CATLEY
PADBURY (St Mary the Virgin) *see* Lenborough *Ox*
PADDINGTON (Emmanuel) Harrow Road *Lon 2* P *Hyndman
Trustees* P-in-c A G THOM, C J F BARRY
PADDINGTON (St David's Welsh Church) Extra-Parochial
Place *Lon 2 vacant*
PADDINGTON (St James) *Lon 2* P *Bp* V P R THOMAS,
C G W MILLER, NSM R RAJ-SINGH
PADDINGTON (St John the Evangelist) (St Michael and All
Angels) *Lon 2* P *DBP* V S D MASON, C B Z GREEN, Hon
C M S PUDGE, NSM M LEGG
PADDINGTON (St Luke the Evangelist) *see* W Kilburn
St Luke w St Simon and St Jude *Lon*
PADDINGTON (St Mary) *Lon 2* P *Bp* P-in-c G S BRADLEY
PADDINGTON (St Mary Magdalene) (St Peter) *Lon 2*
P *Keble Coll Ox and Ch Patr Trust* V R H EVERETT,
NSM F W WARD
PADDINGTON (St Saviour) *Lon 2* P *Bp* V G S BRADLEY,
NSM F E BLACKMORE
PADDINGTON (St Stephen w St Luke) *Lon 2* P *Bp*
V J R ALLCOCK
PADDINGTON GREEN (St Mary) *see* Paddington St Mary
Lon

PADDLESWORTH (St Oswald) *see* Lyminge w Paddlesworth,
Stanford w Postling etc *Cant*
PADDOCK WOOD (St Andrew) *Roch 8* P *D&C Cant*
V B T KNAPP, C P S CALLWAY
PADGATE (Christ Church) *Liv 12* P *Bp, Adn, and
R Warrington (jt)* V S P ATTWATER
PADIHAM (St Leonard) w Hapton and Padiham Green *Blackb 3*
P *Bp* V M A JONES, C D J T RUSSELL
PADSTOW (St Petroc) *Truro 7* P *P J N Prideaux-Brune Esq*
V C M MALKINSON
PADWORTH (St John the Baptist) *see* Stratfield Mortimer and
Mortimer W End etc *Ox*
PAGANHILL (Holy Spirit) *see* Whiteshill and Randwick *Glouc*
PAGHAM (St Thomas à Becket) *Chich 1* P *Abp* V *vacant*
(01243) 262713
PAGLESHAM (St Peter) *see* Ashingdon w S Fambridge,
Canewdon and Paglesham *Chelmsf*
PAIGNTON (Christ Church) and Preston St Paul *Ex 12* P *Bp
and Peache Trustees (jt)* V D W WITCHELL
PAIGNTON (St John the Baptist) (St Andrew) (St Boniface)
Ex 12 P *DBP* V R J CARLTON, C R L BOYLE
PAILTON (St Denis) *see* Revel Gp *Cov*
PAINSWICK (St Mary the Virgin), Sheepscombe, Cranham,
The Edge, Pitchcombe, Harescombe and Brookthorpe *Glouc 4*
P *Bp, D&C, Mrs N Owen (1 turn), and Ld Chan (1 turn)*
V J LONGUET-HIGGINS, NSM J A JAMES, A J P LEACH,
OLM D W NEWELL, E J WARD
PAKEFIELD (All Saints and St Margaret) *Nor 9* P *Ch Patr
Trust* R R J K BAKER, C H Y WILCOX
PAKENHAM (St Mary) w Norton and Tostock *St E 9* P *Bp and
Peterho Cam (jt)* P-in-c K A VALENTINE
PALGRAVE (St Peter) *see* N Hartismere *St E*
PALLION (St Luke) *see* Millfield St Mark and Pallion St Luke
Dur
PALMARSH (Holy Cross) *see* Hythe *Cant*
PALMERS GREEN (St John the Evangelist) *Lon 18*
P *V Southgate Ch Ch* V J A CULLEN
PALTERTON (St Luke's Mission Room) *see* E Scarsdale *Derby*
PAMBER (St Mary and St John the Baptist) *see* The Sherbornes
w Pamber *Win*
PAMBER HEATH (St Luke) *see* Tadley S and Silchester *Win*
PAMPISFORD (St John the Baptist) *Ely 5*
P *Mrs B A Killander* V *vacant*
PANCRASWEEK (St Pancras) *see* Pyworthy, Pancrasweek and
Bridgerule *Ex*
PANFIELD (St Mary the Virgin) and Rayne *Chelmsf 15* P *Bp
and DBP (alt)* R J NELSON
PANGBOURNE (St James the Less) w Tidmarsh and Sulham
Ox 12 P *Bp, Ch Soc Trust, and Mrs I E Moon (jt)*
R H C W PARBURY
PANNAL (St Robert of Knaresborough) w Beckwithshaw *Ripon 1*
P *Bp and Peache Trustees (jt)* V N C SINCLAIR,
C C H WILSON
PANSHANGER (United Church) Conventional District
St Alb 6 vacant
PAPCASTLE (Mission Church) *see* Cockermouth Area *Carl*
PAPPLEWICK (St James) *see* Linby w Papplewick *S'well*
PAPWORTH (St Peter) *Ely 1* P *Patr Bd* TR J F WINDSOR,
TV S M DAY, C E ROTHWELL, NSM P GILDERSLEVE,
N H A PEARSON
PAR (St Mary the Virgin) (Good Shepherd) *Truro 1*
P *The Crown* P-in-c I M TUCKER
PARHAM (St Mary the Virgin) *see* Campsea Ashe w
Marlesford, Parham and Hacheston *St E*
PARHAM (St Peter) *see* Amberley w N Stoke and Parham,
Wiggonholt etc *Chich*
PARK BARN (St Clare) *see* Westborough *Guildf*
PARKEND (St Paul) and Viney Hill *Glouc 1* P *Bp and Univ Coll
Ox (jt)* V A BRUNT
PARKESTON (St Paul) *see* Harwich Peninsula *Chelmsf*
PARKFIELD (Holy Trinity) *see* Rhodes and Parkfield *Man*
PARKGATE (St Thomas) *see* Neston *Ches*
PARKHAM (St James), Alwington, Buckland Brewer, Hartland,
Welcombe, Clovelly, Woolfardisworthy West and Bucks Mills
Ex 16 P *Patr Bd (4 turns), Crown (1 turn)*
TV W M MITCHELL, S C HENDERSON, C F J R OTTO,
Hon C C W J HODGETTS, NSM D BAKER
PARKSTONE (Good Shepherd) *see* Heatherlands St Jo *Sarum*
PARKSTONE (St Barnabas) *see* Branksome St Clem *Sarum*
PARKSTONE (St Clement) *as above*
PARKSTONE (St John) *see* Heatherlands St Jo *Sarum*
PARKSTONE (St Luke) *Sarum 7* P *Ch Trust Fund Trust*
V C M STRAIN
PARKSTONE (St Peter) and St Osmund w Branksea St Mary
Sarum 7 P *Patr Bd* R N J C LLOYD, C J C GAFFIN,
NSM D J NEWMAN, B BARRETT, OLM P SOUTHGATE,
H S WRIGHT, Dss D J NEWMAN

PARKWOOD (Christ Church) Conventional District *Cant 15*
  C-in-c M A MCLAUGHLIN
PARKWOOD (St Paul) *see* S Gillingham *Roch*
PARLAUNT ROAD (Christ the Worker) *see* Langley Marish
  Ox
PARLEY, WEST (All Saints) (St Mark) *Sarum 9*
  P P E E Prideaux-Brune Esq R E C BOOTH
PARNDON, GREAT (St Mary) *Chelmsf 25* P *Patr Bd*
  TR M D BENNET, TV N R TAYLOR, NSM M J HILLIER
PARNDON, LITTLE (St Mary) *see* Harlow Town Cen w Lt
  Parndon *Chelmsf*
PARR (St Peter) (St Paul) (St Philip) (Holy Trinity) *Liv 10*
  P *Patr Bd* TR J L ROBERTS, TV N MCCATHIE, J E DRAYCOTT,
  C V C WHITWORTH, OLM A KIRKHAM, M E TAYLOR,
  H MCCANN
PARR MOUNT (Holy Trinity) *see* Parr *Liv*
PARRACOMBE (Christ Church) *see* Combe Martin,
  Berrynarbor, Lynton, Brendon etc *Ex*
PARSON CROSS (St Bernard of Clairvaux) *see* Southey Green
  St Bernard CD *Sheff*
PARSON CROSS (St Cecilia) *see* Sheff St Cecilia Parson Cross
  Sheff
PARSON'S GREEN (St Dionis) *see* Fulham St Dionis *Lon*
PARTINGTON (St Mary) and Carrington *Ches 10* P *Bp and*
  V Bowdon (alt) V P H GEDDES
PARTNEY Group, The (St Nicholas) *Linc 7* P *Bp and DBP,*
  Baroness Willoughby de Eresby, Mrs E M V Drake, and
  Mrs D F P Douglas (by turn) R R J BENSON
PARTRIDGE GREEN (St Michael and All Angels) *see* W
  Grinstead *Chich*
PARWICH (St Peter) *see* Fenny Bentley, Thorpe, Tissington,
  Parwich etc *Derby*
PASSENHAM (St Guthlac) *Pet 5* P *MMCET* R C J MURRAY
PASTON (All Saints) *Pet 11* P *Bp* R G M JESSOP,
  NSM S M ROLFE
PASTON (St Margaret) *see* Trunch *Nor*
PASTROW *Win 3* P *Bp, Qu Coll Ox, and St Mary's Coll*
  Win (jt) P-in-c J M BENTALL, NSM S HOBBINS
PATCHAM (All Saints) *Chich 2* P *MMCET*
  C A M BOUSFIELD, NSM M PHILIP
PATCHING (St John the Divine) *see* Findon w Clapham and
  Patching *Chich*
PATCHWAY (St Chad) *Bris 5* P *Trustees* V *vacant* 0117-969
  2935 *or* 979 3978
PATELEY BRIDGE (St Cuthbert) *see* Upper Nidderdale *Ripon*
PATRICK (Holy Trinity) *S & M 1* P *Bp* P-in-c N P GODFREY
PATRICK BROMPTON (St Patrick) and Hunton *Ripon 4*
  P *Bp* P-in-c B S DIXON, NSM J T OLDFIELD
PATRICROFT (Christ Church) *see* Eccles *Man*
PATRINGTON (St Patrick) w Hollym, Welwick and Winestead
  York 12 P *DBP, Ld Chan, and CPAS (by turn)*
  Hon C J A SHARP
PATRIXBOURNE (St Mary) *see* Bridge *Cant*
PATTERDALE (St Patrick) *see* Gd Shep TM *Carl*
PATTINGHAM (St Chad) w Patshull *Lich 24* P *Bp and Lady*
  Kwiatkowska (jt) P-in-c M P HOBBS
PATTISHALL (Holy Cross) w Cold Higham and Gayton w
  Tiffield *Pet 5* P *Bp, SS Coll Cam, and SMF (jt)* R *vacant*
  (01327) 830043
PAUL (St Pol de Lion) *Truro 5* P *Ld Chan* P-in-c T D HEANEY
PAULERSPURY (St James the Apostle) *see* Silverstone and
  Abthorpe w Slapton etc *Pet*
PAULL (St Andrew and St Mary) *see* Hedon w Paull *York*
PAULSGROVE (St Michael and All Angels) *Portsm 6* P *Bp*
  V I NEWTON
PAULTON (Holy Trinity) w Farrington Gurney and High
  Littleton *B & W 11* P *Bp and Hyndman Trustees (jt)*
  V J G EDWARDS
PAUNTLEY (St John the Evangelist) *see* Redmarley D'Abitot,
  Bromesberrow, Pauntley etc *Glouc*
PAVENHAM (St Peter) *see* Milton Ernest, Pavenham and
  Thurleigh *St Alb*
PAWLETT (St John the Baptist) *see* Puriton and Pawlett *B & W*
PAXFORD (Mission Church) *see* Blockley w Aston Magna and
  Bourton on the Hill *Glouc*
PAXTONS, The (Holy Trinity) (St James) w Diddington *Ely 13*
  P *D&C Linc (2 turns) and E G W Thornhill Esq (1 turn)*
  V A S REED
PAYHEMBURY (St Mary the Virgin) *see* Broadhembury,
  Payhembury and Plymtree *Ex*
PEACEHAVEN (Ascension) and Telscombe Cliffs *Chich 18*
  P *Bp* P-in-c I COOPER
PEAK DALE (Holy Trinity) *see* Tideswell *Derby*
PEAK FOREST (Charles the King and Martyr) and Dove Holes
  Derby 4 P *Bp and Duke of Devonshire (jt)* V *vacant* (01298)
  813344

PEAKIRK (St Pega) w Glinton and Northborough *Pet 11*
  P *D&C* P-in-c H P GEISOW
PEAR TREE (Jesus Chapel) *see* Southampton St Mary Extra
  Win
PEASE POTTAGE (Ascension) *see* Slaugham and Staplefield
  Common *Chich*
PEASEDOWN ST JOHN (St John the Baptist) w Wellow and
  Foxcote w Shoscombe *B & W 11* P *Bp* V M G STREET,
  Hon C R P FOTHERGILL
PEASEMORE (St Barnabas) *see* E Downland *Ox*
PEASENHALL (St Michael) *see* Yoxmere *St E*
PEASE'S WEST (St George) *see* Crook *Dur*
PEASLAKE (St Mark) *see* Shere, Albury and Chilworth *Guildf*
PEASLEY CROSS (Mission Hall) *see* Parr *Liv*
PEASMARSH (St Michael) *see* Shalford *Guildf*
PEASMARSH (St Peter and St Paul) *see* Beckley and
  Peasmarsh *Chich*
PEATLING MAGNA (All Saints) *see* Willoughby Waterleys,
  Peatling Magna etc *Leic*
PEATLING PARVA (St Andrew) *see* Gilmorton, Peatling
  Parva, Kimcote etc *Leic*
PEBMARSH (St John the Baptist) *see* Knights and Hospitallers
  Par *Chelmsf*
PEBWORTH (St Peter), Dorsington, Honeybourne and Marston
  Sicca *Glouc 9* P *Bp* P-in-c D J FORMAN
PECKHAM (St John w St Andrew) *S'wark 8* P *Bp*
  P-in-c P A PACKER, C S J HORNER
PECKHAM (St Luke) *see* Camberwell St Luke *S'wark*
PECKHAM (St Mary Magdalene) (St Paul) *S'wark 8*
  P *Ch Patr Soc* V O A ADAMS, NSM A O ADETAYO
PECKHAM (St Saviour) *S'wark 9* P *Bp*
  P-in-c D L GWILLIAMS, C P E COLLIER
PECKHAM, EAST (Holy Trinity) and Nettlestead *Roch 8*
  P *St Pet Coll Ox and D&C Cant (jt)* R A H CARR,
  NSM S M MORRELL
PECKHAM, WEST (St Dunstan) *see* Mereworth w
  W Peckham *Roch*
PECKLETON (St Mary Magdalene) *see* Desford and Peckleton
  w Tooley *Leic*
PEDLINGE (Estate Chapel) *see* Saltwood *Cant*
PEDMORE (St Peter) *Worc 12* P *Oldswinford Hosp*
  R A L HAZLEWOOD, C I R JENNINGS
PEEL (St Paul) *see* Walkden and Lt Hulton *Man*
PEEL GREEN (St Catherine) *see* Barton w Peel Green *Man*
PEEL GREEN (St Michael and All Angels) *as above*
PEGSWOOD (St Margaret) *see* Bothal and Pegswood w
  Longhirst *Newc*
PELDON (St Mary) *see* W w E Mersea, Peldon, Gt and Lt
  Wigborough *Chelmsf*
PELSALL (St Michael and All Angels) *Lich 25* P *Bp*
  V C A ST A RAMSAY, NSM A M MORRIS
PELTON (Holy Trinity) and West Pelton *Dur 11* P *Bp*
  V J LINTERN
PELTON, WEST (St Paul) *see* Pelton and W Pelton *Dur*
PELYNT (St Nun) *see* Lanreath, Pelynt and Bradoc *Truro*
PEMBERTON (St Francis of Assisi) Kitt Green *Liv 14*
  P *R Wigan and Bp (jt)* P-in-c R HARVEY
PEMBERTON (St John) *Liv 14* P *R Wigan* V *vacant* (01942)
  222237
PEMBERTON (St Mark) Newtown *see* Marsh Green w
  Newtown *Liv*
PEMBRIDGE (St Mary the Virgin) w Moor Court, Shobdon,
  Staunton-on-Arrow, Byton and Lyonshall *Heref 4* P *Ld Chan*
  (1 turn), Patr Bd (4 turns) R J M READ
PEMBURY (St Peter) *Roch 8* P *Ch Ch Ox* V D L ROBERTSON,
  NSM H A HUGHES
PEN SELWOOD (St Michael) *B & W 2* P *Bp*
  R N C M FEAVER
PENCOMBE (St John) *see* Bredenbury *Heref*
PENCOYD (St Denys) *see* St Weonards *Heref*
PENCOYS (St Andrew) *see* Redruth w Lanner and Treleigh
  Truro
PENDEEN (St John the Baptist) w Morvah *Truro 5*
  P *R A H Aitken Esq and C W M Aitken Esq (jt)* V A ROWELL
PENDEFORD (St Paul) *see* Tettenhall Regis *Lich*
PENDLEBURY (St Augustine) *see* Swinton and Pendlebury
  Man
PENDLEBURY (St John) *Man 20* P *Trustees* V S K TIMMINS,
  OLM V TYLDESLEY, J BRANDRETH
PENDLETON (All Saints) *see* Sabden and Pendleton *Blackb*
PENDLETON Claremont (Holy Angels) *see* Salford All SS
  Man
PENDLETON (St Thomas) *as above*
PENDOCK CROSS (Holy Redeemer) *see* Berrow w Pendock,
  Eldersfield, Hollybush etc *Worc*

PENDOMER (St Roch)   *see* W Coker w Hardington
Mandeville, E Chinnock etc *B & W*
PENGE (Christ Church w Holy Trinity)   *see* Anerley *Roch*
PENGE (St John the Evangelist) *Roch 13*   P *Simeon's Trustees*
V D MEDWAY
PENGE (St Paul)   *see* Anerley *Roch*
PENGE LANE (Holy Trinity) *Roch 13*   P *Bp*   V N G READ,
NSM M A WILKINSON
PENHILL *Ripon 4*   P *Trin Coll Cam and Lord Bolton (jt)*
R S C WHITEHOUSE,   NSM P S YEADON
PENHILL (St Peter) *Bris 7*   P *Bp*   P-in-c C A STONE
PENHURST (St Michael the Archangel)   *see* Ashburnham w
Penhurst *Chich*
PENISTONE (St John the Baptist) and Thurlstone *Wakef 7*
P *Bp*   TR D J HOPKIN,   OLM A P PARR
PENKETH (St Paul) *Liv 12*   P *Bp*   V P W HOCKLEY,
C D NYIRONGO
PENKEVIL (St Michael)   *see* St Michael Penkevil *Truro*
PENKHULL (St Thomas)   *see* Hartshill, Penkhull and Trent
Vale *Lich*
PENKRIDGE Team, The (St Michael and All Angels) *Lich 2*
P *Patr Bd*   TR G H YERBURY,   TV C M PLANT,
C J M TAYLOR,   OLM I NICHOLLS, V E D HOWARTH
PENN (Holy Trinity) and Tylers Green *Ox 20*   P *Earl Howe*
V M D BISSET,   OLM J R SMITH
PENN (St Bartholomew) (St Anne) *Lich 24*   P *Bp*
V B N WHITMORE,   C M HIRD
PENN FIELDS St Philip (St Aidan) *Lich 24*   P *Ch Trust Fund
Trust*   V J S OAKLEY,   C C N RUDD
PENN STREET (Holy Trinity) *Ox 20*   P *Earl Howe*
V W F MASON,   NSM C E L SMITH
PENNARD, EAST (All Saints)   *see* Fosse Trinity *B & W*
PENNARD, WEST (St Nicholas)   *see* Baltonsborough w
Butleigh, W Bradley etc *B & W*
PENNINGTON (Christ Church) *Man 19*   P *Trustees*
V A J BUTTERWORTH,   C C G ELMS, E J WHITE
PENNINGTON (St Mark) *Win 11*   P *V Milford*
P-in-c A B RUSSELL,   NSM E A ELLIOTT
PENNINGTON (St Michael and the Holy Angels) and Lindal w
Marton and Bardsea *Carl 9*   P *Bp and DBP (jt)*
P-in-c G A TUBBS
PENNY LANE (St Barnabas)   *see* Mossley Hill *Liv*
PENNYCROSS (St Pancras) *Ex 22*   P *CPAS*
P-in-c J J MARLOW
PENNYWELL (St Thomas)   *see* Sunderland St Thos and St
Oswald *Dur*
PENPONDS (Holy Trinity) *Truro 2*   P *The Crown*
P-in-c P DOUGLASS,   C M L PASCOE
PENRITH (Christ Church) (St Andrew) w Newton Reigny and
Plumpton Wall *Carl 4*   P *Bp*   TR D G SARGENT,
TV N G BYARD, R C PATTINSON,   C A M WALSH,
A M E OSMASTON
PENRUDDOCK (All Saints)   *see* Gd Shep TM *Carl*
PENSAX (St James the Great)   *see* Teme Valley N *Worc*
PENSBY (St Michael and All Angels)   *see* Barnston *Ches*
PENSHAW (All Saints)   *see* Herrington, Penshaw and Shiney
Row *Dur*
PENSHURST (St John the Baptist) and Fordcombe *Roch 12*
P *Viscount De L'Isle*   R T E HOLME
PENSILVA (St John)   *see* St Ive and Pensilva w Quethiock *Truro*
PENSNETT (St Mark) *Worc 10*   P *Bp*   V *vacant* (01384)
262666
PENTEWAN (All Saints)   *see* St Austell *Truro*
PENTLOW (St George and St Gregory)   *see* N Hinckford
Chelmsf
PENTNEY (St Mary Magdalene)   *see* Nar Valley *Nor*
PENTON MEWSEY (Holy Trinity)   *see* Pastrow *Win*
PENTONVILLE (St Silas w All Saints) (St James) *Lon 6*   P *Bp*
V R A WAKELING
PENTRICH (St Matthew)   *see* Swanwick and Pentrich *Derby*
PENTRIDGE (St Rumbold)   *see* Sixpenny Handley w Gussage
St Andrew etc *Sarum*
PENWERRIS (St Michael and All Angels) (Holy Spirit) *Truro 3*
P V *St Gluvias*   P-in-c M T MESLEY
PENWORTHAM (St Leonard) *Blackb 5*   P *Bp*
V J N MANSFIELD,   NSM S J BAINES
PENWORTHAM (St Mary) *Blackb 5*   P *Miss A M Rawstorne*
V C J NELSON
PENZANCE (St Mary) (St Paul) (St John the Baptist) *Truro 5*
P *Bp*   TR K R OWEN,   Hon C R H PESKETT,
NSM J COTTON
PEOPLETON (St Nicholas) and White Ladies Aston w Churchill
and Spetchley and Upton Snodsbury and Broughton Hackett
Worc 4   P *Bp, Croom Estate Trustees, and Major R J G Berkley
(1 turn), and Ld Chan (1 turn)*   P-in-c L M BUSFIELD,
C C A FAIRCLOUGH,   NSM S P JORDAN

PEOVER, OVER (St Lawrence) w Lower Peover (St Oswald)
Ches 12   P *DBP and Man Univ (jt)*   V P J LLOYD
PEPER HAROW (St Nicholas)   *see* Compton w Shackleford
and Peper Harow *Guildf*
PEPLOW (The Epiphany)   *see* Hodnet w Weston under
Redcastle *Lich*
PERIVALE (St Mary w St Nicholas) *Lon 22*   P *Trustees*
R A R CORSIE,   NSM V A AITKEN
PERLETHORPE (St John the Evangelist) *S'well 2*   P *Earl
Manvers' Trustees*   V *vacant*
PERRANARWORTHAL (St Piran)   *see* St Stythians w
Perranarworthal and Gwennap *Truro*
PERRANPORTH (St Michael's Mission Church)
see Perranzabuloe and Crantock w Cubert *Truro*
PERRANUTHNOE (St Michael and St Piran)   *see* Ludgvan,
Marazion, St Hilary and Perranuthnoe *Truro*
PERRANZABULOE (St Piran) and Crantock w Cubert *Truro 7*
P *Patr Bd*   V J C E ANDREW,   C S P ROBINSON,
NSM P M NIXON
PERROTT, NORTH (St Martin)   *see* Wulfric Benefice *B & W*
PERROTT, SOUTH (St Mary)   *see* Beaminster Area *Sarum*
PERRY BARR (St John the Evangelist) *Birm 3*   P *Bp and
trustees (jt)*   V C A PAILING,   C D T MACHIRIDZA
PERRY BEECHES (St Matthew) *Birm 3*   P *St Martin's
Trustees*   V S P M MACKENZIE,   C D T MACHIRIDZA
PERRY COMMON (St Martin)   *see* Erdington Ch the K *Birm*
PERRY GREEN (St Thomas)   *see* Albury, Braughing, Furneux
Pelham, Lt Hadham etc *St Alb*
PERRY HILL (St George) (Christ Church) (St Paul) *S'wark 5*
P *D&C and Earl of Dartmouth (1 turn), Bp and Earl of
Dartmouth (1 turn)*   V J R W ACKLAND,   C C J TUCKER,
NSM A D W DUPUY
PERRY STREET (All Saints) *Roch 4*   P *Bp*
V J PERUMBALATH
PERSHORE (Holy Cross) w Pinvin, Wick and Birlingham
Worc 4   P *Patr Bd*   V K I CRAWFORD
PERTENHALL (St Peter)   *see* The Stodden Churches *St Alb*
PETER TAVY (St Peter), Mary Tavy, Lydford and Brent Tor
Ex 25   P *Guild of All So and Bp (1 turn), Duchy of Cornwall
(1 turn)*   Hon C R D ORMSBY,   NSM J C HIGMAN
PETERBOROUGH (All Saints) *Pet 11*   P *Bp*
P-in-c P B DENTON
PETERBOROUGH (Christ the Carpenter) *Pet 11*   P *Bp*
V N E FRY
PETERBOROUGH (Holy Spirit) Bretton *Pet 11*   P *Bp*
P-in-c W S CROFT
PETERBOROUGH (St John the Baptist) (Mission Church)
Pet 11   P *Bp*   V G J STEELE
PETERBOROUGH (St Jude) *Pet 11*   P *Bp*   V G J KEATING
PETERBOROUGH (St Mark) and St Barnabas *Pet 11*   P *Bp*
V *vacant* (01733) 554516
PETERBOROUGH (St Mary) Boongate *Pet 11*   P *D&C*
M P J MOORE
PETERBOROUGH (St Paul) *Pet 11*   P *Bp*
P-in-c R F WATKINSON
PETERCHURCH (St Peter)   *see* Madley w Tyberton,
Peterchurch, Vowchurch etc *Heref*
PETERLEE (St Cuthbert) *Dur 2*   P *Bp*   V P M TEMPLEMAN
PETERSFIELD (St Peter) *Portsm 4*   P *Bp*   V W P M HUGHES,
C D J CLARKE
PETERSHAM (All Saints) (St Peter) *S'wark 16*   P *Bp*
V T J E MARWOOD,   NSM F M FORWARD
PETERSMARLAND (St Peter)   *see* Shebbear, Buckland
Filleigh, Sheepwash etc *Ex*
PETERSTOW (St Peter)   *see* Brampton *Heref*
PETHAM (All Saints)   *see* Stone Street Gp *Cant*
PETHERTON, NORTH (St Mary the Virgin)   *see* Alfred Jewel
B & W
PETHERTON, SOUTH (St Peter and St Paul) w the
Seavingtons *B & W 14*   P *D&C*   NSM D B FYFE
PETHERWIN, NORTH (St Paternus)   *see* Egloskerry, N
Petherwin, Tremaine, Tresmere etc *Truro*
PETHERWIN, SOUTH (St Paternus)   *see* Three Rivers *Truro*
PETROCKSTOWE (St Petrock)   *see* Shebbear, Buckland
Filleigh, Sheepwash etc *Ex*
PETT (St Mary and St Peter)   *see* Fairlight, Guestling and Pett
Chich
PETT LEVEL (St Nicholas)   *as above*
PETTAUGH (St Catherine)   *see* Debenham and Helmingham
St E
PETTISTREE (St Peter and St Paul)   *see* Wickham Market w
Pettistree *St E*
PETTON (not known) w Cockshutt, Welshampton and Lyneal w
Colemere *Lich 17*   P *Bp and R K Mainwaring Esq (jt)*
P-in-c D N ASH

PETTON (St Petrock)　*see* Bampton, Morebath, Clayhanger, Petton etc *Ex*
PETTS WOOD (St Francis) *Roch 16*　P *Bp*　V R D LANE
PETWORTH (St Mary) *Chich 11*　P *Lord Egremont*　P-in-c T J WRIGHT
PEVENSEY (St Nicholas) (St Wilfred) *Chich 16*　P *Bp*　V A C H CHRISTIAN
PEWSEY (St John the Baptist)　*see* Vale of Pewsey *Sarum*
PHEASEY (St Chad) *Lich 25*　P *DBP*　P-in-c D C WELLER
PHILADELPHIA (St Thomas) Extra-Parochial Place *Sheff 4*　NSM R J G HOPKINS, D J KERSHAW
PHILBEACH GARDENS (St Cuthbert)　*see* Earl's Court St Cuth w St Matthias *Lon*
PHILLACK (St Felicitas)　*see* Godrevy *Truro*
PHILLEIGH (St Philleigh)　*see* Gerrans w St Anthony-in-Roseland and Philleigh *Truro*
PICCADILLY (St James)　*see* Westmr St Jas *Lon*
PICKENHAM, NORTH (St Andrew)　*see* Necton, Holme Hale w N and S Pickenham *Nor*
PICKENHAM, SOUTH (All Saints)　*as above*
PICKERING (St Peter and St Paul) w Lockton and Levisham *York 19*　P *Abp*　P-in-c A M PRITCHETT,　NSM L GROVE
PICKHILL (All Saints)　*see* Kirklington w Burneston and Wath and Pickhill *Ripon*
PICKWELL (All Saints)　*see* Burrough Hill Pars *Leic*
PICKWORTH (All Saints)　*see* Gt and Lt Casterton w Pickworth and Tickencote *Pet*
PICKWORTH (St Andrew)　*see* S Lafford *Linc*
PICTON (St Hilary)　*see* Kirklevington w Picton, and High and Low Worsall *York*
PIDDINGHOE (St John) *Chich 18*　P *Bp and Gorham Trustees (jt)*　V *vacant*
PIDDINGTON (St John the Baptist)　*see* Hardingstone and Horton and Piddington *Pet*
PIDDINGTON (St Nicholas)　*see* Ray Valley *Ox*
PIDDLE, NORTH (St Michael)　*see* Abberton, The Flyfords, Naunton Beauchamp etc *Worc*
PIDDLE VALLEY, Hilton, Cheselbourne and Melcombe Horsey, The *Sarum 1*　P *Bp, Eton Coll, G A L-F Pitt-Rivers Esq, D&C Sarum, and D&C Win (by turn)*　V A J B MONDS,　NSM H J P EXON
PIDDLEHINTON (St Mary the Virgin)　*see* Piddle Valley, Hilton, Cheselbourne etc *Sarum*
PIDDLETRENTHIDE (All Saints)　*as above*
PIDLEY CUM FENTON (All Saints)　*see* Somersham w Pidley and Oldhurst and Woodhurst *Ely*
PIERCEBRIDGE (St Mary)　*see* Coniscliffe *Dur*
PILGRIM Benefice　*see* Bunwell, Carleton Rode, Tibenham, Gt Moulton etc *Nor*
PILHAM (All Saints)　*see* Corringham and Blyton Gp *Linc*
PILL (Christ Church), Portbury and Easton-in-Gordano *B & W 12*　P *Bp*　V R H M LEGG,　Hon C J N O WILLIAMS
PILLATON (St Modwen)　*see* Penkridge *Lich*
PILLATON (St Odolph)　*see* St Dominic, Landulph and St Mellion w Pillaton *Truro*
PILLERTON HERSEY (St Mary)　*see* Stourdene Gp *Cov*
PILLEY (Mission Church)　*see* Tankersley, Thurgoland and Wortley *Sheff*
PILLEY (St Nicholas)　*see* Boldre w S Baddesley *Win*
PILLING (St John the Baptist)　*see* Stalmine w Pilling *Blackb*
PILNING (St Peter) w Compton Greenfield *Bris 2*　P *Bp*　P-in-c P W ROWE,　C R J CREW
PILSLEY (St Mary the Virgin)　*see* N Wingfield, Clay Cross and Pilsley *Derby*
PILTON (All Saints)　*see* Aldwincle, Clopton, Pilton, Stoke Doyle etc *Pet*
PILTON (St John the Baptist) w Croscombe, North Wootton and Dinder *B & W 7*　P *Bp and Peache Trustees (jt)*　R D R OSBORNE,　C L D A AVERY
PILTON (St Mary the Virgin)　*see* Barnstaple *Ex*
PILTON (St Nicholas)　*see* Empingham, Edith Weston, Lyndon, Manton etc *Pet*
PIMLICO Bourne Street (St Mary)　*see* Pimlico St Mary Bourne Street *Lon*
PIMLICO (St Barnabas) *Lon 3*　P *Bp*　V D W CHERRY,　NSM A S MCGREGOR
PIMLICO (St Gabriel) *Lon 3*　P *Bp*　V L T IRVINE-CAPEL
PIMLICO (St James the Less)　*see* Westminster St Jas the Less *Lon*
PIMLICO (St Mary) Bourne Street *Lon 3*　P *Trustees*　V D W CHERRY,　NSM S N LEAMY, A S MCGREGOR
PIMLICO (St Peter) w Westminster Christ Church *Lon 3*　P *Bp*　V N C PAPADOPULOS,　C J E A MUSTARD,　Hon C C L MADDOCK,　NSM P M LOWTHER
PIMLICO (St Saviour) *Lon 3*　P *Bp*　V *vacant* (020) 7821 9865

PIMPERNE (St Peter), Stourpaine, Durweston and Bryanston *Sarum 6*　P *DBP (2 turns), D&C (1 turn)*　R S P COULTER,　NSM J W WHITTLE
PIN GREEN (All Saints)　*see* Stevenage All SS Pin Green *St Alb*
PINCHBECK (St Mary)　*see* Glen Gp *Linc*
PINCHBECK, WEST (St Bartholomew)　*as above*
PINHOE (St Michael and All Angels) (Hall) and Broadclyst *Ex 1*　P *Patr Bd*　TV J E GRIER,　P-in-c M J PARTRIDGE,　C S J DYSON
PINNER (St Anselm)　*see* Hatch End St Anselm *Lon*
PINNER (St John the Baptist) *Lon 23*　P *V Harrow*　V P C HULLYER,　C K N BLAKE
PINNER VIEW (St George)　*see* Headstone St Geo *Lon*
PINVIN (St Nicholas)　*see* Pershore w Pinvin, Wick and Birlingham *Worc*
PINXTON (St Helen) (Church Hall) *Derby 1*　P *Bp*　R L G C E HARRIS,　NSM P F GOODCHILD
PIPE-CUM-LYDE (St Peter) and Moreton-on-Lugg *Heref 3*　P *Bp, Soc of the Faith, and D&C (by turn)*　NSM E S V VERWEY, P A LITTLEWOOD
PIPEWELL (St Mary)　*see* Rothwell w Orton, Rushton w Glendon and Pipewell *Pet*
PIRBRIGHT (St Michael and All Angels) *Guildf 12*　P *Ld Chan*　P-in-c C MUSSER
PIRNOUGH (All Hallows)　*see* Ditchingham, Hedenham, Broome, Earsham etc *Nor*
PIRTON (St Mary)　*see* Holwell, Ickleford and Pirton *St Alb*
PIRTON (St Peter)　*see* Stoulton w Drake's Broughton and Pirton etc *Worc*
PISHILL (not known)　*see* Nettlebed w Bix, Highmoor, Pishill etc *Ox*
PITCHCOMBE (St John the Baptist)　*see* Painswick, Sheepscombe, Cranham, The Edge etc *Glouc*
PITCHFORD (St Michael and All Angels)　*see* Condover w Frodesley, Acton Burnell etc *Heref*
PITCOMBE (St Leonard)　*see* Bruton and Distr *B & W*
PITMINSTER (St Mary and St Andrew)　*see* Blackdown *B & W*
PITNEY (St John the Baptist)　*see* Langport Area *B & W*
PITSEA (St Gabriel) w Nevendon *Chelmsf 6*　P *Bp*　R S A LAW,　C N CHUMU MUTUKU, M J MARSHALL
PITSFORD (All Saints) w Boughton *Pet 2*　P *Bp*　R S TROTT
PITSMOOR (Christ Church) *Sheff 3*　P *Ch Patr Trust*　V P IRESON
PITTINGTON (St Laurence)　*see* Belmont and Pittington *Dur*
PITTON (St Peter)　*see* Clarendon *Sarum*
PITTVILLE (All Saints)　*see* N Cheltenham *Glouc*
PIXHAM (St Mary the Virgin)　*see* Dorking w Ranmore *Guildf*
PIXLEY (St Andrew)　*see* Ledbury *Heref*
PLAISTOW (Holy Trinity)　*see* Kirdford *Chich*
PLAISTOW (St Martin) (St Mary) (St Philip and St James) and North Canning Town *Chelmsf 3*　P *Patr Bd*　TR P J MOSSOP,　TV R J GANNEY,　Hon C P B KENNEDY
PLAISTOW (St Mary) *Roch 14*　P *Bp*　V A KEELER,　C G C BURNETT-CHETWYND
PLAISTOW The Divine Compassion　*see* Plaistow and N Canning Town *Chelmsf*
PLAITFORD (St Peter)　*see* Forest and Avon *Sarum*
PLAS NEWTON (St Michael) w Chester Christ Church *Ches 2*　P *Simeon's Trustees*　V R D PETERS,　C P CHABALA,　NSM R J KEMP
PLATT (Holy Trinity)　*see* Rusholme H Trin *Man*
PLATT (St Mary the Virgin) *Roch 10*　P *Bp*　P-in-c E M R WALKER
PLATT BRIDGE (St Nathaniel) *Liv 14*　P *Bp*　P-in-c L MCGREGOR
PLATT'S HEATH (St Edmund)　*see* Len Valley *Cant*
PLAXTOL (not known)　*see* Shipbourne w Plaxtol *Roch*
PLAYDEN (St Michael)　*see* Rye *Chich*
PLAYFORD (St Mary)　*see* Gt and Lt Bealings w Playford and Culpho *St E*
PLEASLEY (St Michael)　*see* E Scarsdale *Derby*
PLEASLEY HILL (St Barnabas) *S'well 2*　P *Bp*　P-in-c G E HOLLOWAY
PLEASLEY VALE (St Chad)　*see* Mansfield Woodhouse *S'well*
PLEMSTALL (St Peter) w Guilden Sutton *Ches 2*　P *Capt P Egerton Warburton*　V M HART
PLESHEY (Holy Trinity) *Chelmsf 8*　P *Bp*　P-in-c S F COUGHTREY,　NSM B M H MAIN
PLUCKLEY (St Mary) Bourne Street　*see* G7 Benefice *Cant*
PLUCKLEY (St Nicholas)　*as above*
PLUMBLAND (St Cuthbert)　*see* Binsey *Carl*
PLUMPTON (All Saints) (St Michael and All Angels) w East Chiltington cum Novington *Chich 18*　P *Ld Chan*　R G D BROSTER

PLUMPTON (St John the Baptist) *see* Astwell Gp *Pet*
PLUMPTON WALL (St John the Evangelist) *see* Penrith w
Newton Reigny and Plumpton Wall *Carl*
PLUMSTEAD (All Saints) Shooters Hill *S'wark 6* **P** *CPAS*
V H D OWEN
PLUMSTEAD (Ascension) *see* Plumstead Common *S'wark*
PLUMSTEAD (St John the Baptist) w St James and St Paul
S'wark 6 **P** *Simeon's Trustees and CPAS (alt)* **V** P J ROGERS,
C J E G MACY
PLUMSTEAD (St Mark and St Margaret) *see* Plumstead
Common *S'wark*
PLUMSTEAD (St Michael) *see* Barningham w Matlaske w
Baconsthorpe etc *Nor*
PLUMSTEAD (St Nicholas) *S'wark 6* **P** *V Plumstead St Mark*
w St Marg **V** A G STEVENS
PLUMSTEAD, GREAT (St Mary) and LITTLE (St Gervase
and Protase) w Thorpe End and Witton *Nor 4* **P** *Bp and*
D&C (jt) **R** C A GARROD
PLUMSTEAD COMMON *S'wark 6* **P** *Bp and DBP (jt)*
V C R WELHAM, **C** J A CONALTY
PLUMTREE (St Mary) *S'well 8* **P** *DBP* **P-in-c** T H KIRKMAN
PLUNGAR (St Helen) *see* Vale of Belvoir *Leic*
PLYMOUTH Crownhill (Ascension) *Ex 23* **P** *Bp* **V** *vacant*
(01752) 783617
PLYMOUTH (Emmanuel), St Paul Efford and St Augustine
Ex 24 **P** *Patr Bd* **TR** K F FREEMAN, **C** L P T SIM,
S G G TALBOT
PLYMOUTH (St Andrew) and St Paul Stonehouse *Ex 24*
P *Patr Bd* **TR** N H P MCKINNEL, **TV** J C MONEY,
C S R C NICHOLS
PLYMOUTH (St Augustine) *see* Plymouth Em, St Paul Efford
and St Aug *Ex*
PLYMOUTH (St Gabriel) Peverell *Ex 24* **P** *Bp* **V** *vacant*
(01752) 663938
PLYMOUTH (St John the Evangelist) *see* Sutton on Plym *Ex*
PLYMOUTH (St Jude) *Ex 24* **P** *Trustees* **P-in-c** T SMITH,
C I COOK
PLYMOUTH (St Mary the Virgin) *see* Plymouth St Simon and
St Mary *Ex*
PLYMOUTH (St Matthias) *see* Charles w Plymouth St
Matthias *Ex*
PLYMOUTH (St Pancras) *see* Pennycross *Ex*
PLYMOUTH (St Peter) and the Holy Apostles *Ex 22* **P** *Bp and*
Keble Coll Ox (jt) **P-in-c** S PHILPOTT
PLYMOUTH (St Simon) and St Mary Laira *Ex 24* **P** *Bp and*
St Simon Trustees (jt) **C** K F HAYDON
PLYMPTON (St Mary the Blessed Virgin) *Ex 23* **P** *Bp*
V M M CAMERON, **C** R W BECK, **NSM** M BRIMICOMBE,
J M COLLIS
PLYMPTON (St Maurice) *Ex 23* **P** *D&C Windsor*
P-in-c J P MASON, **NSM** J M FRENCH
PLYMSTOCK (St Mary and All Saints) and Hooe *Ex 24*
P *Patr Bd* **TR** D J WALLER, **TV** S M PAYNE,
NSM M P HINKS
PLYMTREE (St John the Baptist) *see* Broadhembury,
Payhembury and Plymtree *Ex*
POCKLEY (St John the Baptist) *see* Kirkdale w Harome,
Nunnington and Pockley *York*
POCKLINGTON (All Saints) *see* Pocklington Wold *York*
POCKLINGTON WOLD *York 5* **P** *Abp*
R G HOLLINGSWORTH, **C** R M HAUGHTY
PODIMORE (St Peter) *see* Ilchester w Northover, Limington,
Yeovilton etc *B & W*
PODINGTON (St Mary the Virgin) *see* Wymington w
Podington *St Alb*
POINT CLEAR (Mission) *see* St Osyth *Chelmsf*
POINTON (Christ Church) *see* Billingborough Gp *Linc*
POKESDOWN (All Saints) *Win 8* **P** *V Christchurch*
C J W E RODLEY
POKESDOWN (St James) *Win 8* **P** *Bp* **P-in-c** R L VERNON,
NSM P M SCHOLLAR, N J HOULTON
POLDENS, WEST *B & W 4* **P** *Bp* **P-in-c** P A OLLIVE
POLEBROOK (All Saints) *see* Barnwell, Hemington,
Luddington in the Brook etc *Pet*
POLEGATE (St John) *Chich 16* **P** *Bp* **V** C G SPINKS,
C G J BURROWS, **NSM** R A HERKES
POLEGATE (St Wilfrid) *see* Lower Willingdon St Wilfrid CD
Chich
POLESWORTH (St Editha) *Birm 10* **P** *Ld Chan*
V P A WELLS
POLING (St Nicholas) *Chich 1* **P** *Bp* **P-in-c** W R KILFORD
POLLINGTON (St John the Baptist) *see* Gt Snaith *Sheff*
POLPERRO (St John the Baptist) *see* Talland *Truro*
POLRUAN (St Saviour) *see* Lanteglos by Fowey *Truro*
POLSTEAD (St Mary) *see* Stoke by Nayland w Leavenheath
and Polstead *St E*

POLTIMORE (St Mary the Virgin) *see* Brampford Speke,
Cadbury, Newton St Cyres etc *Ex*
PONDERS END (St Matthew) *Lon 18* **P** *V Enfield*
P-in-c R C KNOWLING, **C** A C NEWCOMBE
PONDERSBRIDGE (St Thomas) *see* Whittlesey,
Pondersbridge and Coates *Ely*
PONSANOOTH (St Michael and All Angels) *see* Mabe *Truro*
PONSBOURNE (St Mary) *see* Lt Berkhamsted and Bayford,
Essendon etc *St Alb*
PONSONBY (not known) *see* Beckermet St Jo and St Bridget w
Ponsonby *Carl*
PONTEFRACT (All Saints) *Wakef 10* **P** *Bp*
P-in-c V IWANUSCHAK, **NSM** H MERRICK, W D PHILLIPS,
K B WARRENER
PONTEFRACT (St Giles) (St Mary) *Wakef 10* **P** *Bp*
V R G COOPER, **NSM** M J TAYLOR
PONTELAND (St Mary the Virgin) *Newc 4* **P** *Mert Coll Ox*
V P BARHAM, **NSM** C L BROWN
PONTESBURY First and Second Portions (St George) *Heref 12*
P *St Chad's Coll Dur* **P-in-c** M A JONES,
NSM C A CHADWICK, S M SMALL, C WRIGHT
PONTON, GREAT (Holy Cross) *see* Colsterworth Gp *Linc*
PONTON, LITTLE (St Guthlac) *as above*
POOL (St Wilfrid) *see* Lower Wharfedale *Ripon*
POOLBROOK (St Andrew) *see* Malvern St Andr and Malvern
Wells and Wyche *Worc*
POOLE (St James w St Paul) *Sarum 7* **P** *Ch Soc Trust and*
J H Cordle Esq (jt) **R** R H G MASON
POOLE, NORTH Ecumenical Team *Sarum 7* **P** *Bp*
TR A C MACROW-WOOD, **TV** J E AUDIBERT, P W GIBBS,
C B D BLACKFORD, C A BROOKS, J A STEPHENSON,
OLM T LOCK
POOLE KEYNES (St Michael and All Angels) *see* Kemble,
Poole Keynes, Somerford Keynes etc *Glouc*
POOLEY BRIDGE (St Paul) *see* Barton, Pooley Bridge and
Martindale *Carl*
POORTON, NORTH (St Mary Magdalene) *see* Askerswell,
Loders, Powerstock and Symondsbury *Sarum*
POPLAR (All Saints) *Lon 7* **P** *Patr Bd* **TR** A J WYNNE,
C J A C HODGES, **NSM** T J DUNCAN, J C SHELDON
POPPLETON, NETHER (St Everilda) w Upper (All Saints)
York 1 **P** *Abp* **V** J C E SYLVESTER, **NSM** M C S FOSSETT
POPPLETON ROAD (Mission Room) *see* York St Paul *York*
PORCHESTER (St James) *S'well 10* **P** *Bp* **V** P A WILLIAMS,
C D K DODD
PORINGLAND (All Saints) *Nor 8* **P** *Bp, BNC Ox,*
J D Alston Esq, and G H Hastings Esq (3 turns) and DBP
(1 turn) **R** R H PARSONAGE, **OLM** D J DRIVER
PORLOCK (St Dubricius) and Porlock Weir w Stoke Pero,
Selworthy and Luccombe *B & W 15* **P** *Ld Chan*
R W H M LEMMEY, **NSM** S R B HUMPHREYS
PORLOCK WEIR (St Nicholas) *see* Porlock and Porlock Weir
w Stoke Pero etc *B & W*
PORT ERIN (St Catherine) *see* Rushen *S & M*
PORT ISAAC (St Peter) *see* St Endellion w Port Isaac and
St Kew *Truro*
PORT ST MARY (St Mary) *see* Rushen *S & M*
PORTBURY (Blessed Virgin Mary) *see* Pill, Portbury and
Easton-in-Gordano *B & W*
PORTCHESTER (St Mary) *Portsm 2* **P** *J R Thistlethwaite Esq*
V C ALLEN, **C** C SHERMAN, **NSM** J A JONES
PORTESHAM (St Peter) *see* Abbotsbury, Portesham and
Langton Herring *Sarum*
PORTHILL (St Andrew) *see* Wolstanton *Lich*
PORTHLEVEN (St Bartholomew) w Sithney *Truro 4* **P** *Bp*
P-in-c H PUGH
PORTHPEAN (St Levan) *see* St Austell *Truro*
PORTINSCALE (Mission) *see* Crosthwaite Keswick *Carl*
PORTISHEAD (St Peter) *B & W 12* **P** *Patr Bd*
TR A W BRYANT, **TV** C A JUDSON, T E HODGETT,
C J J PUTNAM
PORTKELLIS (St Christopher) *see* Helston and Wendron
Truro
PORTLAND Team Minstry (All Saints) (St Andrew) (St John)
Sarum 4 **P** *Patr Bd* **TV** N A MCKINTY
PORTLEMOUTH, EAST (St Winwaloe Onocaus)
see Stokenham, Slapton, Charleton w Buckland etc *Ex*
PORTLOE (All Saints) *see* Veryan w Ruan Lanihorne *Truro*
PORTMAN SQUARE (St Paul) *see* Langham Place All So *Lon*
PORTON (St Nicholas) *see* Bourne Valley *Sarum*
PORTREATH (St Mary) *see* St Illogan *Truro*
PORTSDOWN (Christ Church) *Portsm 5* **P** *Simeon's Trustees*
V A M WILSON, **C** E R JESSIMAN, **NSM** S G PHILLIPS
PORTSEA (All Saints) *Portsm 6* **P** *V Portsea St Mary and*
Bp (jt) **V** M F PYE, **C** J A SWAINE, **NSM** M E TILLMAN

PORTSEA North End (St Mark) *Portsm 6*　**P** *DBP*
TR T P KENNAR,　**TV** C E KEAY,　**C** A W FORREST,
NSM L C DENNESS
PORTSEA (St Alban) *Portsm 6*　**P** *Bp*　**V** R P CALDER,
NSM M C DORRELL
PORTSEA (St Cuthbert) *Portsm 6*　**P** *Bp*　**V** D M POWER,
NSM J POWER, C G GULLY
PORTSEA (St George) *Portsm 6*　**P** *Bp*　**V** K B GREEN,
NSM S E WEST
PORTSEA (St Luke) *Portsm 6*　**P** *Ch Patr Trust*
P-in-c A J HUGHES,　**C** M N RODEL
PORTSEA (St Mary) (St Faith and St Barnabas) (St Wilfrid)
Portsm 6　**P** *Win Coll*　**V** R C WHITE,　**C** C E HETHERINGTON,
P W BOWDEN,　**NSM** S K WHITELOCK, E L A D´AETH
PORTSEA (St Saviour) *Portsm 6*　**P** *Bp*　**V** R P CALDER,
NSM M C DORRELL
PORTSEA (The Ascension) *Portsm 6*　**P** *Bp*
P-in-c M J R WHITING
PORTSLADE (Good Shepherd) *Chich 4*　**P** *Bp*
P-in-c D H HUMPHREY
PORTSLADE (St Nicolas) (St Andrew) *Chich 4*　**P** *Bp*
V R H RUSHFORTH
PORTSWOOD (Christ Church) *Win 13*　**P** *Bp*　**V** G J ARCHER,
NSM F M TYSON
PORTSWOOD (St Denys) *Win 13*　**P** *Bp*　**P-in-c** K J RANDALL
PORTWAY AND DANEBURY Benefice, The *Win 3*　**P** *Patr Bd*
TR C B RANKINE,　**TV** C F PETTET, V A COLE,
NSM J A TAYLOR
POSBURY (St Francis Proprietary Chapel) *see* Crediton,
Shobrooke and Sandford etc *Ex*
POSLINGFORD (St Mary) *see* Stour Valley *St E*
POSTBRIDGE (St Gabriel) *see* Ashburton, Bickington,
Buckland in the Moor etc *Ex*
POSTLEBURY *see* Nunney and Witham Friary, Marston Bigot
etc *B & W*
POSTLING (St Mary and St Radegund) *see* Lyminge w
Paddlesworth, Stanford w Postling etc *Cant*
POSTWICK (All Saints) *see* Brundall w Braydeston and
Postwick *Nor*
POTT SHRIGLEY (St Christopher) *Ches 13*　**P** *MMCET*
P-in-c J BUCKLEY
POTTEN END (Holy Trinity) *see* Gt Berkhamsted, Gt and Lt
Gaddesden etc *St Alb*
POTTER HEIGHAM (St Nicholas) *see* Ludham, Potter
Heigham, Hickling and Catfield *Nor*
POTTERHANWORTH (St Andrew) *see* Branston w Nocton
and Potterhanworth *Linc*
POTTERNE (St Mary the Virgin) w Worton and Marston
Sarum 16　**P** *Bp*　**V** D J HOWARD
POTTERNEWTON (St Martin) *Ripon 5*　**P** *Trustees*
P-in-c D L STEVENS,　**C** D E STEWART,　**NSM** S J DE GAY
POTTERS BAR (King Charles the Martyr) *St Alb 14*
P *Bp Lon*　**P-in-c** M J BURNS
POTTERS BAR (St Mary and All Saints) *St Alb 14*　**P** *Bp Lon*
V P J BEVAN
POTTERS GREEN (St Philip Deacon) *Cov 1*　**P** *Ld Chan*
V *vacant* (024) 7661 7568
POTTERS MARSTON (St Mary) *see* Barwell w Potters
Marston and Stapleton *Leic*
POTTERSPURY (St Nicholas) w Furtho and Yardley Gobion w
Cosgrove and Wicken *Pet 5*　**P** *D&C, Jes Coll Ox, and Soc*
Merchant Venturers Bris (jt)　**R** *vacant* (01908) 542428
POTTO (St Mary) *see* Whorlton w Carlton and Faceby *York*
POTTON (St Mary the Virgin) w Sutton and Cockayne Hatley
St Alb 10　**P** *The Crown (3 turns), St Jo Coll Ox (1 turn)*
P-in-c G SMITH,　**NSM** J L BUNDAY
POUGHILL (St Michael and All Angels) *see* N Creedy *Ex*
POUGHILL (St Olaf King and Martyr) *Truro 8*　**P** *Ch Soc*
Trust　**V** P A WHYBROW
POULNER (St John) *see* Ringwood *Win*
POULSHOT (St Peter) *see* Seend, Bulkington and Poulshot
Sarum
POULTON (St Luke) *Ches 7*　**P** *Bp*　**P-in-c** I HUGHES
POULTON (St Michael and All Angels) *see* Fairford Deanery
Glouc
POULTON CARLETON (St Chad) and Singleton *Blackb 12*
P *DBP and Exors R Dumbreck Esq (jt)*　**V** M P KEIGHLEY,
C J EVERITT
POULTON LANCELYN (Holy Trinity) *Ches 8*　**P** *R Bebington*
V R K WILES
POULTON-LE-FYLDE (St Chad) *see* Poulton Carleton and
Singleton *Blackb*
POULTON-LE-SANDS (Holy Trinity) w Morecambe
St Laurence *Blackb 11*　**P** *V Lanc*　**P-in-c** M R PEATMAN,
NSM A CUNLIFFE

POUND HILL (St Barnabas) *see* Worth, Pound Hill and
Maidenbower *Chich*
POUNDSBRIDGE (Chapel) *see* Penshurst and Fordcombe
Roch
POUNDSTOCK (St Winwaloe) *see* Week St Mary Circle of Par
Truro
POWDERHAM (St Clement Bishop and Martyr) *see* Kenton,
Mamhead, Powderham, Cofton and Starcross *Ex*
POWERSTOCK (St Mary the Virgin) *see* Askerswell, Loders,
Powerstock and Symondsbury *Sarum*
POWICK (St Peter) and Guarlford and Madresfield w Newland
Worc 2　**P** *Bp, Lady Rosalind Morrison, and Croome Estate*
Trustees (jt)　**R** S E IRWIN
POYNINGS (Holy Trinity) w Edburton, Newtimber and
Pyecombe *Chich 9*　**P** *Ld Chan (1 turn), Bp and Abp (1 turn)*
P-in-c C M CURRER
POYNTINGTON (All Saints) *see* Queen Thorne *Sarum*
POYNTON (St George) *Ches 17*　**P** *Bp*　**V** R I MCLAREN,
C P J CUMMING,　**NSM** A S LIVINGSTON
POYNTON, HIGHER (St Martin) *see* Poynton *Ches*
PRADOE (extra-parochial place) *Lich 19*　**C-in-c** O B PARRY
PRATTS BOTTOM (All Souls) *see* Green Street Green and
Pratts Bottom *Roch*
PREES (St Chad) *see* Edstaston, Fauls, Prees, Tilstock and
Whixall *Lich*
PREESALL (St Oswald) *see* Waterside Par *Blackb*
PRENTON (St Stephen) *Ches 1*　**P** *Bp*　**V** E W LAUTENBACH,
NSM H E BUCKLEY
PRENTON DELL (St Alban) *see* Prenton *Ches*
PRESCOT (St Mary) (St Paul) *Liv 2*　**P** *K Coll Cam*
V J A TAYLOR,　**C** J FLETCHER, P F SMYTH,　**NSM** P COWLEY,
OLM J D ROSE
PRESHUTE (St George) *see* Marlborough *Sarum*
PRESTBURY (St Mary) *see* N Cheltenham *Glouc*
PRESTBURY (St Nicholas) *as above*
PRESTBURY (St Peter) *Ches 13*　**P** *Ms C J C B Legh*
V P J M ANGIER,　**NSM** P HARDMAN, A S RAVENSCROFT,
S H CALLIS
PRESTEIGNE (St Andrew) w Discoed, Kinsham, Lingen and
Knill *Heref 4*　**P** *Patr Bd*　**R** S HOLLINGHURST
PRESTLEIGH (St James Mission Church) *see* Shepton Mallet
w Doulting *B & W*
PRESTOLEE (Holy Trinity) *see* Farnworth, Kearsley and
Stoneclough *Man*
PRESTON Acregate Lane (Mission) *see* Preston Risen Lord
Blackb
PRESTON (All Saints) *Blackb 13*　**P** *Trustees*
V D P AP G MEIRION-JONES,　**C** M J AYERS
PRESTON (All Saints) *see* S Cerney w Cerney Wick, Siddington
and Preston *Glouc*
PRESTON (All Saints) and Sproatley in Holderness *York 12*
P *Abp*　**P-in-c** P M BURDON
PRESTON (Church of the Ascension) *see* Wembley Park *Lon*
PRESTON (Emmanuel) *Blackb 13*　**P** *R Preston*　**V** S JOHNSON
PRESTON (Good Shepherd) *see* Brighton Gd Shep Preston
Chich
PRESTON (St Andrew) w Sutton Poyntz and Osmington w
Poxwell *Sarum 4*　**P** *Patr Bd*　**TR** T R WEST,
TV L S DOBBINS,　**C** D M WILSHERE,　**NSM** B E J ELLIS,
B A PORT
PRESTON (St Cuthbert) *Blackb 13*　**P** *Bp*　**V** C E HALLIWELL
PRESTON (St John) (St George the Martyr) (Christ the King
Chapel) *Blackb 13*　**P** *DBP*　**R** T W LIPSCOMB,
C A J TEATHER
PRESTON (St John the Baptist) *see* Redmarley D'Abitot,
Bromesberrow, Pauntley etc *Glouc*
PRESTON (St John) w Brighton St Augustine and St Saviour
Chich 2　**P** *Bp*　**V** A V BOWMAN
PRESTON (St Mark) *see* W Preston *Blackb*
PRESTON (St Martin) *see* St Paul's Walden *St Alb*
PRESTON (St Mary the Virgin) *see* Lavenham w Preston *St E*
PRESTON (St Matthias) *see* Brighton St Matthias *Chich*
PRESTON (St Mildred) *see* Wingham w Elmstone and Preston
w Stourmouth *Cant*
PRESTON (St Oswald) St Jude *Blackb 13*　**P** *Bp, Simeon's*
Trustees, and R Preston St Jo and St Geo (jt)
P-in-c G W NELSON
PRESTON (St Paul) *see* Paignton Ch Ch and Preston St Paul
Ex
PRESTON (St Peter and St Paul) *see* Empingham, Edith
Weston, Lyndon, Manton etc *Pet*
PRESTON (St Stephen) *Blackb 13*　**P** *Bp*　**V** M COOK
PRESTON The Risen Lord (St Matthew) (St Hilda) (St James's
church hall) *Blackb 13*　**P** *Patr Bd*　**P-in-c** P R NUNN,
C J T RICHARDSON

PRESTON, EAST (St Mary) w Kingston *Chich 1*   P *D&C*
V J H LYON
PRESTON, WEST *Blackb 13*   P *Patr Bd*
P-in-c D J RADCLIFFE,   C J D G NASH
PRESTON BAGOT (All Saints)   *see* Claverdon w Preston Bagot
Cov
PRESTON BISSET (St John the Baptist)   *see* The Claydons and
Swan *Ox*
PRESTON BROOK (St Faith)   *see* Daresbury *Ches*
PRESTON CAPES (St Peter and St Paul)   *see* Badby w Newham
and Charwelton w Fawsley etc *Pet*
PRESTON NEXT FAVERSHAM (St Catherine) w Goodnestone
and Graveney *Cant 14*   P *Abp*   V S C WILSON,
C A C OEHRING,   NSM N M ASH
PRESTON ON STOUR (St Mary)   *see* Ilmington w
Stretton-on-Fosse etc *Cov*
PRESTON-ON-TEES (All Saints) and Longnewton *Dur 10*
P *Bp*   P-in-c J C LAMBERT,   C S R GREEN,   OLM S WILSON
PRESTON-ON-WYE (St Lawrence)   *see* Cusop w Blakemere,
Bredwardine w Brobury etc *Heref*
PRESTON PATRICK (St Patrick)   *see* Kirkby Lonsdale *Carl*
PRESTON PLUCKNETT (St James the Great) (St Peter)
B & W 6   P *Bp (2 turns), Mrs S W Rawlins (1 turn)*
V A PERRIS,   C D M KEEN
PRESTON UNDER SCARR (St Margaret)   *see* Penhill *Ripon*
PRESTON WEALDMOORS (St Lawrence)   *see* Edgmond w
Kynnersley and Preston Wealdmoors *Lich*
PRESTON WYNNE (Holy Trinity)   *see* Bodenham, Felton and
Preston Wynne *Heref*
PRESTONVILLE (St Luke) *Chich 2*   P *CPAS*
P-in-c M B POOLE
PRESTWICH (St Gabriel) *Man 10*   P *Bp*
P-in-c S S WILLIAMS,   C B M HACKETT, D A PLUMMER,
NSM M TRIVASSE
PRESTWICH (St Hilda) *Man 10*   P *Trustees*   V *vacant*
0161-773 1642
PRESTWICH (St Margaret) (St George) *Man 10*
P *R Prestwich St Mary*   P-in-c D A PLUMMER,
C B M HACKETT, S S WILLIAMS, N C SHAVE
PRESTWICH (St Mary the Virgin) *Man 10*   P *Trustees*
P-in-c B M HACKETT,   C J M COOPER, S S WILLIAMS,
D A PLUMMER
PRESTWOLD (St Andrew)   *see* Wymeswold and Prestwold w
Hoton *Leic*
PRESTWOOD (Holy Trinity) and Great Hampden *Ox 28*
P *Bp and Hon I H Hope-Morley (jt)*
R D J O KEARLEY-HEYWOOD
PRICKWILLOW (St Peter)   *see* Ely *Ely*
PRIDDY (St Lawrence) *B & W 1*   P *Bp*   V *vacant*
PRIESTWOOD (St Andrew)   *see* Bracknell *Ox*
PRIMROSE HILL (Holy Trinity)   *see* Lydney *Glouc*
PRIMROSE HILL (St Mary the Virgin) w Avenue Road
(St Paul) *Lon 16*   P *Trustees*   V M J BROWN,
NSM L L DEAN, M J WAKEFIELD
PRINCE ALBERT ROAD (St Mark)   *see* Regent's Park St
Mark *Lon*
PRINCE CONSORT ROAD (Holy Trinity)   *see* S Kensington H
Trin w All SS *Lon*
PRINCE'S PARK (Christ the King) *Roch 5*   P *Bp*
P-in-c D E D'SOUZA
PRINCES RISBOROUGH (St Mary)   *see* Risborough *Ox*
PRINCETOWN (Church Hall)   *see* Ashburton, Bickington,
Buckland in the Moor etc *Ex*
PRIOR'S DEAN (not known)   *see* Greatham w Empshott and
Hawkley w Prior's Dean *Portsm*
PRIORS HARDWICK (St Mary the Virgin) w Priors Marston
and Wormleighton *Cov 10*   P *Earl Spencer*
P-in-c M L D GREIG,   C R D CLUCAS
PRIORS LEE (St Peter) (St Georges) *Lich 21*   P *Bp and*
V Shifnal (jt)   V P G F LAWLEY
PRIORS MARSTON (St Leonard)   *see* Priors Hardwick, Priors
Marston and Wormleighton *Cov*
PRIORS PARK (Mission Hall)   *see* Tewkesbury w Walton
Cardiff and Twyning *Glouc*
PRISTON (St Luke)   *see* Timsbury w Priston, Camerton and
Dunkerton *B & W*
PRITTLEWELL (All Saints)   *see* Southend *Chelmsf*
PRITTLEWELL (St Luke) *Chelmsf 13*   P *Bp*
V J T MCCLUSKEY
PRITTLEWELL (St Mary the Virgin) *Chelmsf 13*   P *Bp*
V S CONLON
PRITTLEWELL (St Peter) w Westcliff St Cedd and the Saints of
Essex *Chelmsf 13*   P *Bp*   V R H CADMAN,
NSM C ROBINSON
PRITTLEWELL (St Stephen) *Chelmsf 13*   P *Bp*
P-in-c C S BALDWIN,   NSM T J NUTTER

PROBUS (St Probus and St Grace), Ladock and Grampound w
Creed and St Erme *Truro 6*   P *DBP*   TR A J WADE,
C A E BROWN,   Hon C M E RICHARDS
PRUDHOE (St Mary Magdalene) *Newc 9*   P *Dioc Soc*
V C H HOPE
PSALTER LANE (St Andrew) *Sheff 2*   P *Trustees*
V N P A JOWETT
PUBLOW (All Saints) w Pensford, Compton Dando and
Chelwood *B & W 9*   P *Bp*   P-in-c J B SIMPSON,
NSM S M E STEVENS
PUCKINGTON (St Andrew)   *see* Winsmoor *B & W*
PUCKLECHURCH (St Thomas à Becket) and Abson *Bris 5*
P *D&C*   V S K YOUNG
PUDDINGTON (St Thomas à Becket)   *see* N Creedy *Ex*
PUDDLETOWN (St Mary the Virgin), Tolpuddle and Milborne
w Dewlish *Sarum 1*   P *Bp, Ch Ch Ox, Viscount Rothermere, and*
trustees (jt)   NSM S J GODFREY
PUDLESTON (St Peter)   *see* Leominster *Heref*
PUDSEY (St James the Great)   *see* Woodhall *Bradf*
PUDSEY (St Lawrence and St Paul) *Bradf 3*   P *Bp and*
V Calverley (jt)   V P N AYERS,   C P R ARNOLD
PULBOROUGH (St Mary) *Chich 12*   P *Lord Egremont*
R P B WELCH
PULFORD (St Mary the Virgin)   *see* Eccleston and Pulford *Ches*
PULHAM (St Thomas à Becket)   *see* Vale of White Hart *Sarum*
PULHAM MARKET (St Mary Magdalene)   *see* Dickleburgh
and The Pulhams *Nor*
PULHAM ST MARY (St Mary the Virgin)   *as above*
PULLOXHILL (St James the Apostle)   *see* Silsoe, Pulloxhill and
Flitton *St Alb*
PULVERBATCH (St Edith)   *see* Longden and Annscroft w
Pulverbatch *Heref*
PUNCKNOWLE (St Mary the Blessed Virgin)   *see* Bride Valley
Sarum
PUNNETS TOWN (St Peter)   *see* Heathfield *Chich*
PURBROOK (St John the Baptist) *Portsm 5*   P *Bp*
P-in-c P M AMEY,   Hon C C R ABBOTT
PUREWELL (St John)   *see* Christchurch *Win*
PURFLEET (St Stephen)   *see* Aveley and Purfleet *Chelmsf*
PURITON (St Michael and All Angels) and Pawlett *B & W 13*
P *Ld Chan (1 turn), D&C Windsor (2 turns)*
P-in-c D GODDARD,   NSM R A SELLERS
PURLEIGH (All Saints) *Chelmsf 11*   P *Oriel Coll Ox*
V *vacant*
PURLEY (Christ Church) *S'wark 22*   P *Bp*   V C R TREFUSIS,
C L C J DUCKETT,   OLM S P BISHOP
PURLEY (St Barnabas) *S'wark 22*   P *Bp*
P-in-c C G THOMSON,   NSM D C HADLEY
PURLEY (St Mark) Woodcote *S'wark 22*   P *Bp*
P-in-c F M LONG,   C K J PERCIVAL
PURLEY (St Mary the Virgin) *Ox 12*   P *Ld Chan*
R D J ARCHER,   NSM J ROTHERY, S A ROBERTSON,
OLM A MACKIE
PURLEY (St Swithun) *S'wark 22*   P *Bp*   P-in-c F M LONG,
C K J PERCIVAL
PURLWELL (St Andrew)   *see* Batley All SS and Purlwell *Wakef*
PURSE CAUNDLE (St Peter)   *see* Spire Hill *Sarum*
PURTON (St John)   *see* Sharpness, Purton, Brookend and
Slimbridge *Glouc*
PURTON (St Mary) *Bris 7*   P *Bp*   OLM J M WELLS
PUSEY (All Saints)   *see* Cherbury w Gainfield *Ox*
PUTFORD (St Stephen)   *see* Bradworthy, Sutcombe, Putford etc
Ex
PUTLEY (not known)   *see* Ledbury *Heref*
PUTNEY (St Margaret) *S'wark 18*   P *Bp*   P-in-c A BRODIE
PUTNEY (St Mary) (All Saints) *S'wark 18*   P *Patr Bd*
TR A B NEWBY,   TV C D EYDEN
PUTNEY, EAST (St Stephen)   *see* Wandsworth St Mich w
St Steph *S'wark*
PUTNOE HEIGHTS CHURCH CENTRE   *see* Bedf St Mark
St Alb
PUTTENHAM (St John the Baptist)   *see* Seale, Puttenham and
Wanborough *Guildf*
PUTTENHAM (St Mary)   *see* Tring *St Alb*
PYE NEST (St James)   *see* King Cross *Wakef*
PYECOMBE (Transfiguration)   *see* Poynings w Edburton,
Newtimber and Pyecombe *Chich*
PYLLE (St Thomas à Becket)   *see* Fosse Trinity *B & W*
PYPE HAYES (St Mary the Virgin)   *see* Erdington *Birm*
PYRFORD (Church of the Good Shepherd)   *see* Wisley w
Pyrford *Guildf*
PYRFORD (St Nicholas)   *as above*
PYRTON (St Mary)   *see* Icknield *Ox*
PYTCHLEY (All Saints)   *see* Gt w Lt Harrowden and
Orlingbury and Isham etc *Pet*

PYWORTHY (St Swithun), Pancrasweek and Bridgerule *Ex 17*
P *DBP* R *vacant* (01409) 254062
QUADRING (St Margaret) *see* Gosberton, Gosberton Clough
and Quadring *Linc*
QUAINTON (Holy Cross and St Mary) *see* Schorne *Ox*
QUANTOCK COAST Benefice, The *B & W 16* P *Bp, DBP,*
Eton Coll, and Lady Gass (jt) R *P J RAHILLY,*
NSM *D D BRIMSON, S L CAMPBELL, P CUFF, M HANCE*
QUANTOCK TOWERS, The *B & W 16* P *Bp, D&C Windsor,*
and D&C Wells (jt) R *V I D F PLUMB,* NSM *J G ROSE*
QUANTOXHEAD, EAST (Blessed Virgin Mary) *see* Quantock
Coast *B & W*
QUANTOXHEAD, WEST (St Ethelreda) *as above*
QUARLEY (St Michael and All Angels) *see* Portway and
Danebury *Win*
QUARNDON (St Paul) *Derby 11* P *Exors Viscount Scarsdale*
P-in-c *W F BATES,* NSM *J M NEEDLE*
QUARNFORD (St Paul) *see* Longnor, Quarnford and Sheen
Lich
QUARRENDON ESTATE (St Peter) *see* Aylesbury w Bierton
and Hulcott *Ox*
QUARRINGTON (St Botolph) w Old Sleaford *Linc 21* P *Bp*
P-in-c *S R BENHAM*
QUARRY BANK (Christ Church) *see* Brierley Hill *Worc*
QUARRY HILL (St Mary) *see* Leeds City *Ripon*
QUATFORD (St Mary Magdalene) *see* Bridgnorth, Tasley,
Astley Abbotts, etc *Heref*
QUATT (St Andrew) *see* Alveley and Quatt *Heref*
QUEDGELEY (St James) *Glouc 2* P *Bp* V *G J B STICKLAND*
QUEEN CAMEL (St Barnabas) *see* Cam Vale *B & W*
QUEEN CHARLTON (St Margaret) *see* Keynsham *B & W*
QUEEN THORNE *Sarum 3* P *Bp, The Revd J M P Goodden,*
J K Wingfield Digby Esq, and MMCET (jt) R *H G PEARSON*
QUEENBOROUGH (Holy Trinity) *Cant 15* P *Abp* V *vacant*
(01795) 662648
QUEENHILL (St Nicholas) *see* Longdon, Castlemorton,
Bushley, Queenhill etc *Worc*
QUEEN'S GATE (St Augustine) *see* Onslow Square and S
Kensington St Aug *Lon*
QUEEN'S PARK (St Barnabas) *see* Holdenhurst and Iford *Win*
QUEEN'S PARK (St Luke) *see* Brighton St Luke Queen's Park
Chich
QUEENSBURY (All Saints) *Lon 23* P *The Crown*
V *I M STONE*
QUEENSBURY (Holy Trinity) *Bradf 2* P *Bp*
P-in-c *S E W SHRINE*
QUENDON (St Simon and St Jude) *see* Manuden w Berden and
Quendon w Rickling *Chelmsf*
QUENIBOROUGH (St Mary) *see* Fosse *Leic*
QUENINGTON (St Swithun) *see* Fairford Deanery *Glouc*
QUERNMORE (St Peter) *see* Dolphinholme w Quernmore and
Over Wyresdale *Blackb*
QUETHIOCK (St Hugh) *see* St Ive and Pensilva w Quethiock
Truro
QUIDENHAM Group, The (St Andrew) *Nor 11* P *Ld Chan*
(1 turn), Bp, Sir Thomas Beevor Bt, Major E H C Garnier,
Trustees, and New Buckenham PCC (3 turns) R *D R HILL,*
OLM *D R A SHEPPARD*
QUINTET Group of Parishes *see* Cranborne w Boveridge,
Edmondsham etc *Sarum*
QUINTET GROUP *see* Aylmerton, Runton, Beeston Regis and
Gresham *Nor*
QUINTON and PRESTON DEANERY (St John the Baptist)
see Wootton w Quinton and Preston Deanery *Pet*
QUINTON (St Swithin) and Welford w Weston *Glouc 9* P *DBP*
and D&C Worc (jt) P-in-c *A M GRIGOR*
QUINTON, THE (Christ Church) *Birm 2* P *Bp*
R *C J S TURNER*
QUINTON ROAD WEST (St Boniface) *Birm 2* P *Bp*
V *R P YATES,* NSM *J M PLATT, J KNOX*
QUORN (St Bartholomew) *see* Quorndon *Leic*
QUORNDON (St Bartholomew) *Leic 6* P *Bp* V *D H BOWLER*
QUY (St Mary) *see* Anglesey Gp *Ely*
RACKENFORD (All Saints) *see* Washfield, Stoodleigh,
Withleigh etc *Ex*
RACKHEATH (Holy Trinity) and Salhouse *Nor 4* P *Bp*
P-in-c *L G ALLIES*
RACTON (St Peter) *see* Compton, the Mardens, Stoughton and
Racton *Chich*
RADBOURNE (St Andrew) *see* Boylestone, Church
Broughton, Dalbury, etc *Derby*
RADCLIFFE (St Andrew) Black Lane *Man 10* P *R Radcliffe*
St Mary P-in-c *A B WILLIAMS,* OLM *J VOST*
RADCLIFFE (St Mary) (St Thomas and St John) (St Philip
Mission Church) *Man 10* P *Patr Bd* TR *C C BROWN,*
TV *C T HAYDEN*

RADCLIFFE-ON-TRENT (St Mary) and Shelford *S'well 8*
P *DBP and Ld Chan (alt)* P-in-c *G E ANDERSON*
RADCLIVE (St John the Evangelist) *see* Buckingham *Ox*
RADDESLEY Group of Parishes, The *Ely 4* P *E H Vestey Esq,*
Mrs B O Killander, Mrs B A Taylor, Duke of Sutherland, Exors
C Thomas (5 turns), St Jo Coll Cam (1 turn) P-in-c *P A REID,*
NSM *K R BISHOP*
RADDINGTON (St Michael) *see* Wiveliscombe and the Hills
B & W
RADDON *see* Brampford Speke, Cadbury, Newton St Cyres etc
Ex
RADFORD (All Souls) (St Peter) *S'well 13* P *Bp*
Hon C *M T PHILLIPS,* NSM *J D LEEMING*
RADFORD (St Nicholas) *Cov 2* P *Bp* V *vacant* (024) 7659
8449
RADFORD, NORTH (St Francis of Assisi) *see* Cov St Fran N
Radford *Cov*
RADFORD SEMELE (St Nicholas) *Cov 10* P *Bp*
P-in-c *M C GREEN*
RADIPOLE (Emmanuel) (St Adhelm) (St Ann) and Melcombe
Regis *Sarum 4* P *Patr Bd* TR *K I HOBBS,*
TV *T J GREENSLADE, P J SALMON,* C *G R FOSTER,*
NSM *P E LEGG, G A HEBBERN*
RADLETT (Christ Church) *see* Aldenham, Radlett and Shenley
St Alb
RADLETT (St John) *as above*
RADLEY (St James the Great) and Sunningwell *Ox 10*
P *Radley Coll and DBP (by turn)* P-in-c *P J MCKELLEN,*
C *K J WRIGHT, E L COLEY,* OLM *G J BECKETT*
RADNAGE (St Mary) *see* W Wycombe w Bledlow Ridge,
Bradenham and Radnage *Ox*
RADNOR, OLD (St Stephen) *see* Kington w Huntington, Old
Radnor, Kinnerton etc *Heref*
RADSTOCK (St Nicholas) w Writhlington *B & W 11* P *Bp*
R *S K GREATOREX,* NSM *J A COLE*
RADSTONE (St Lawrence) *see* Astwell Gp *Pet*
RADWAY (St Peter) *see* Warmington w Shotteswell and
Radway w Ratley *Cov*
RADWELL (All Saints) *see* Stotfold and Radwell *St Alb*
RADWINTER (St Mary the Virgin) *see* The Sampfords and
Radwinter w Hempstead *Chelmsf*
RAGDALE (All Saints) *see* Upper Wreake *Leic*
RAINBOW HILL (St Barnabas) *see* Worc St Barn w Ch Ch
Worc
RAINFORD (All Saints) *Liv 11* P *V Prescot*
P-in-c *S W C GOUGH*
RAINHAM (St Helen and St Giles) w Wennington *Chelmsf 2*
P *MMCET* R *H PRADELLA,* C *G P DOWLING,*
NSM *K D NORRIS*
RAINHAM (St Margaret) *Roch 3* P *Bp* P-in-c *J HENNING*
RAINHILL (St Ann) *Liv 10* P *Trustees* V *N P ANDERSON,*
C *J DRUMMOND, M J LEYDEN*
RAINOW (Holy Trinity) w Saltersford and Forest *Ches 13* P *Bp*
V *S D RATHBONE*
RAINTON (not known) *see* Topcliffe, Baldersby w Dishforth,
Dalton etc *York*
RAINTON, EAST (St Cuthbert) *Dur 14* P *D&C*
P-in-c *M L BECK,* NSM *G M BECK, J M JEWSBURY*
RAINTON, WEST (St Mary) *Dur 14* P *Bp* P-in-c *M L BECK,*
NSM *G M BECK, J M JEWSBURY*
RAINWORTH (St Simon and St Jude) *see* Blidworth w
Rainworth *S'well*
RAITHBY (Holy Trinity) *see* Spilsby Gp *Linc*
RAITHBY (St Peter) *see* Legbourne and Wold Marsh *Linc*
RAME (St Germanus) *see* Maker w Rame *Truro*
RAMPISHAM (St Michael and All Angels) *see* Melbury *Sarum*
RAMPSIDE (St Michael) *see* Aldingham, Dendron, Rampside
and Urswick *Carl*
RAMPTON (All Saints) *Ely 6* P *Bp* P-in-c *K A HODGINS*
RAMPTON (All Saints) *see* Retford Area *S'well*
RAMSBOTTOM (St Andrew) (St John) (St Paul) and Edenfield
Man 8 P *Patr Bd (3 turns), Prime Min (1 turn)*
TR *A J LINDOP,* TV *A J BARNSHAW,* OLM *S J WOOD*
RAMSBURY (Holy Cross) *see* Whitton *Sarum*
RAMSDELL (Christ Church) *see* Baughurst, Ramsdell,
Wolverton w Ewhurst etc *Win*
RAMSDEN (Church of Unity) *see* Orpington All SS *Roch*
RAMSDEN (St James) *see* Forest Edge *Ox*
RAMSDEN BELLHOUSE (St Mary the Virgin) *see* Ramsden
Crays w Ramsden Bellhouse *Chelmsf*
RAMSDEN CRAYS w Ramsden Bellhouse *Chelmsf 6*
P *Reformation Ch Trust* R *vacant* (01268) 521043
RAMSDEN HEATH (St John) *see* Downham w S Hanningfield
Chelmsf
RAMSEY (St Michael) *see* Harwich Peninsula *Chelmsf*

RAMSEY, NORTH (St Olave) *see* Lezayre St Olave Ramsey *S & M*

RAMSEY, SOUTH (St Paul) *S & M 3* **P** *Bp*
V N D GREENWOOD

RAMSEY ST MARY'S (St Mary) *see* The Ramseys and Upwood *Ely*

RAMSEYS (St Thomas à Becket) (St Mary) and Upwood, The *Ely 12* **P** *Lord De Ramsey and Bp (jt)* **R** R A DARMODY, **C** G D BOND

RAMSGATE (Christ Church) *Cant 5* **P** *Ch Patr Trust*
V P F TIZZARD

RAMSGATE (Holy Trinity) (St George) *Cant 5* **P** *Abp*
R P A ADAMS

RAMSGATE (St Luke) *Cant 5* **P** *CPAS* **V** P R WORLEDGE

RAMSGATE (St Mark) *Cant 5* **P** *CPAS* **V** C G SKINGLEY

RAMSGILL (St Mary) *see* Upper Nidderdale *Ripon*

RAMSHOLT (All Saints) *see* Wilford Peninsula *St E*

RANBY (St German) *see* Asterby Gp *Linc*

RANBY (St Martin) *see* Retford Area *S'well*

RAND (St Oswald) *see* Wragby Gp *Linc*

RANDWICK (St John the Baptist) *see* Whiteshill and Randwick *Glouc*

RANGEMORE (All Saints) *see* Hanbury, Newborough, Rangemore and Tutbury *Lich*

RANGEWORTHY (Holy Trinity) *see* Charfield and Kingswood w Wickwar etc *Glouc*

RANMOOR (St John the Evangelist) *Sheff 4* **P** *Trustees*
P-in-c J C GRENFELL, **C** A WOODING

RANMORE (St Barnabas) *see* Dorking w Ranmore *Guildf*

RANSKILL (St Barnabas) *see* Blyth and Scrooby w Ranskill *S'well*

RANTON (All Saints) *see* Chebsey, Creswell, Ellenhall, Ranton etc *Lich*

RANWORTH (St Helen) w Panxworth, Woodbastwick, South Walsham and Upton *Nor 4* **P** *Bp, Qu Coll Cam, and J Cator Esq (jt)* **R** N J H GARRARD

RASEN, WEST (All Saints) *see* Middle Rasen Gp *Linc*

RASHCLIFFE (St Stephen) *see* Em TM *Wakef*

RASKELF (St Mary) *see* Easingwold w Raskelf *York*

RASTRICK (St John the Divine) (St Matthew) *Wakef 2* **P** *Bp and V Halifax (jt)* **V** M R POLLARD, **NSM** R S HANNAM

RATBY (St Philip and St James) *see* Bradgate Team *Leic*

RATCLIFFE CULEY (All Saints) *see* Bosworth and Sheepy Gp *Leic*

RATCLIFFE-ON-SOAR (Holy Trinity) *see* Kingston and Ratcliffe-on-Soar *S'well*

RATCLIFFE ON THE WREAKE (St Botolph) *see* Fosse *Leic*

RATHMELL (Holy Trinity) *see* Giggleswick and Rathmell w Wigglesworth *Bradf*

RATLEY (St Peter ad Vincula) *see* Warmington w Shotteswell and Radway w Ratley *Cov*

RATLINGHOPE (St Margaret) *see* Wentnor w Ratlinghope, Myndtown, Norbury etc *Heref*

RATTERY (Blessed Virgin Mary) *see* S Brent and Rattery *Ex*

RATTLESDEN (St Nicholas) w Thorpe Morieux, Brettenham and Hitcham *St E 10* **P** *Bp (3 turns), Ld Chan (1 turn)*
R E A LAW, **NSM** C MANSELL

RAUCEBY, NORTH (St Peter) *see* Ancaster Wilsford Gp *Linc*

RAUGHTON HEAD (All Saints) *see* Dalston w Cumdivock, Raughton Head and Wreay *Carl*

RAUNDS (St Peter), Hargrave, Ringstead and Stanwick *Pet 8*
P *Ld Chan (1 turn), Bp and L G Stopford-Sackville Esq (2 turns)* **R** S M BELL

RAVENDALE, EAST (St Martin) *see* Laceby and Ravendale Gp *Linc*

RAVENFIELD (St James), Hooton Roberts and Braithwell *Sheff 6* **P** *Bp and Sir Philip Naylor-Leyland Bt (jt)*
P-in-c J E BOLTON

RAVENGLASS (Mission Room) *see* Eskdale, Irton, Muncaster and Waberthwaite *Carl*

RAVENHEAD (St John) *see* Parr *Liv*

RAVENHEAD (St John the Evangelist) *see* Eccleston *Liv*

RAVENINGHAM Group, The (St Andrew) *Nor 8* **P** *Bp, Adn Nor, Sir Nicholas Bacon Bt, Major C A Boycott, D&C, K Coll Cam, and DBP (jt)* **R** N J WILL, **Hon C** A M R HOUSMAN

RAVENSBOURNE *see* Deptford St Jo w H Trin and Ascension *S'wark*

RAVENSCAR (St Hilda) *see* Cloughton and Burniston w Ravenscar etc *York*

RAVENSDEN (All Saints) *see* Wilden w Colmworth and Ravensden *St Alb*

RAVENSHEAD (St Peter) *S'well 4* **P** *Bp*
P-in-c C J RATTENBERRY, **NSM** Z BURTON

RAVENSTHORPE (St Denys) *see* Guilsborough and Hollowell and Cold Ashby etc *Pet*

RAVENSTHORPE (St Saviour) and Thornhill Lees w Savile Town *Wakef 9* **P** *Bp and V Mirfield (jt)* **V** R A P WARD

RAVENSTONE (All Saints) *see* Gayhurst w Ravenstone, Stoke Goldington etc *Ox*

RAVENSTONE (St Michael and All Angels) *see* Coalville w Bardon Hill and Ravenstone *Leic*

RAVENSTONEDALE (St Oswald) *see* Orton and Tebay w Ravenstonedale etc *Carl*

RAWCLIFFE (St James) *see* Airmyn, Hook and Rawcliffe *Sheff*

RAWCLIFFE (St Mark) *see* Clifton *York*

RAWCLIFFE BRIDGE (St Philip) *see* Airmyn, Hook and Rawcliffe *Sheff*

RAWDON (St Peter) *Bradf 4* **P** *Trustees* **P-in-c** C NORMAN

RAWMARSH (St Mary the Virgin) w Parkgate *Sheff 6*
P *Ld Chan* **R** J T BIRBECK

RAWMARSH (St Nicolas) *see* Ryecroft St Nic *Sheff*

RAWNSLEY (St Michael) *see* Hednesford *Lich*

RAWRETH (St Nicholas) *Chelmsf 12* **P** *Pemb Coll Cam*
P-in-c R W JORDAN

RAWTENSTALL (St Mary) *Man 11* **P** *CPAS*
P-in-c M R SHORT

RAWTHORPE (St James) *see* Moldgreen and Rawthorpe *Wakef*

RAY VALLEY, The *Ox 2* **P** *Canon E G A W Page-Turner, Ex Coll Ox, and Piddington PCC (1 Turn), D&C Westmr, Qu Coll Ox, and Walsingham Coll (1 turn)* **R** P T C MASHEDER, **NSM** D S WIPPELL, A G RYCRAFT

RAYDON (St Mary) *see* Higham, Holton St Mary, Raydon and Stratford *St E*

RAYLEIGH (Holy Trinity) (St Michael) *Chelmsf 12* **P** *Patr Bd* **TR** M J LODGE, **TV** N E ROWAN, **C** J E REILY

RAYNE (All Saints) *see* Panfield and Rayne *Chelmsf*

RAYNES PARK (St Saviour) and South Wimbledon All Saints *S'wark 13* **P** *Bp* **V** M O BLACKMAN, **NSM** C W NOKE

RAYNHAM, EAST (St Mary) *see* E w W Rudham, Helhoughton etc *Nor*

RAYNHAM, SOUTH (St Martin) *as above*

REACH (St Ethelreda and the Holy Trinity) *see* Burwell w Reach *Ely*

READ IN WHALLEY (St John the Evangelist) *Blackb 7*
P *V Whalley* **V** A SOWERBUTTS

READING (All Saints) *Ox 15* **P** *Bp* **V** N J CHEESEMAN, **C** G E LUNN

READING (Christ Church) *Ox 15* **P** *Bp* **V** D M WEST, **NSM** J B CROTON

READING Greyfriars (St James) *Ox 15* **P** *Ch Trust Fund Trust*
V J A DE B WILMOT, **C** C M MORRIS, D J HEYWARD

READING (Holy Trinity) *Ox 15* **P** *SMF* **V** *vacant* 0118-958 4842

READING (St Agnes w St Paul) (St Barnabas) *Ox 15* **P** *Bp*
R R V ORR, **C** L J COLLYER, **NSM** E J G ORME

READING (St Giles w St Saviour) *Ox 15* **P** *Bp* **R** D A HARRIS

READING (St John the Evangelist and St Stephen) *Ox 15*
P *Simeon's Trustees* **V** V L GARDNER, **NSM** S KNIGHT, A M MARSHALL, N H BENSON

READING (St Luke) (St Bartholomew) *Ox 15* **P** *Bp and V Reading St Giles (alt)* **V** N J HARDCASTLE, **C** R CHRISTOPHER, **NSM** C F BLACKMAN

READING (St Mark) *Ox 15* **P** *Bp* **C** G E LUNN

READING (St Mary the Virgin) (St Laurence) *Ox 15* **P** *Bp*
R B SHENTON, **C** C I RUSSELL

READING (St Matthew) *Ox 15* **P** *Bp* **P-in-c** M P DOLPHIN

REAPSMOOR (St John) *see* Longnor, Quarnford and Sheen *Lich*

REARSBY (St Michael and All Angels) *see* Fosse *Leic*

RECULVER (St Mary the Virgin) and Herne Bay St Bartholomew *Cant 4* **P** *Abp* **V** R L HAWKES, **NSM** E A HAWKES, **OLM** B R NICHOLSON, J L HADLOW

RED HOUSE (St Cuthbert) *see* N Wearside *Dur*

RED POST *Sarum 6* **P** *Mrs V M Chattey, H W Plunkett-Ernle-Erle-Drax Esq, and Bp (by turn)*
P-in-c J E WARING

REDBOURN (St Mary) *St Alb 7* **P** *Earl of Verulam*
V W J M GIBBS

REDBROOK (St Saviour) *see* Coleford, Staunton, Newland, Redbrook etc *Glouc*

REDCAR (St Peter) *York 16* **P** *Trustees* **NSM** J S WATSON

REDCLIFFE BAY (St Nicholas) *see* Portishead *B & W*

REDCLIFFE GARDENS (St Luke) *see* S Kensington St Luke *Lon*

REDCLIFFE WAY (St Mary the Virgin) *see* Bris St Mary Redcliffe w Temple etc *Bris*

REDDAL HILL (St Luke) *Worc 9* **P** *The Crown*
V H C HANKE

REDDISH (St Elisabeth) *Man 2* **P** *Bp* **P-in-c** A STANTON

REDDISH (St Mary)   see Heaton Reddish *Man*
REDDISH, NORTH (St Agnes) *Man 2*   **P** *The Crown*
   P-in-c C E LARSEN
REDDITCH Christ the King *Worc 7*   **P** *Patr Bd*
   TR M F BARTLETT,   **TV** M DEW,   **C** J C MUSSON
REDDITCH Holy Trinity *Worc 7*   **P** *Patr Bd*   **TR** D ROGERS,
   TV R M JOHNSON, P H WORRALL,   **C** J A HUMPHRIES
REDDITCH (St George)   see Redditch H Trin *Worc*
REDDITCH (St Peter)   see Ipsley *Worc*
REDDITCH (St Stephen)   see Redditch H Trin *Worc*
REDE (All Saints)   see Chevington w Hargrave, Chedburgh w
   Depden etc *St E*
REDENHALL (Assumption of the Blessed Virgin Mary),
   Harleston, Wortwell and Needham *Nor 10*   **P** *Bp*
   R D W JACKSON,   **OLM** C HUDSON
REDFIELD (St Leonard)   see E Bris St Ambrose and St Leon
   Bris
REDGRAVE cum Botesdale St Mary w Rickinghall *St E 16*
   P *P J H Wilson Esq*   **R** C R NORBURN
REDHILL (Christ Church)   see Wrington w Butcombe and
   Burrington *B & W*
REDHILL (Holy Trinity) *S'wark 26*   **P** *Simeon's Trustees*
   V G J JENKINS,   **C** A J SHUTTLEWORTH, L A IJAZ,
   OLM H J COWAN
REDHILL (St John the Evangelist) (Meadvale Hall) *S'wark 26*
   P *Bp*   **V** N J CALVER
REDHILL (St Matthew) *S'wark 26*   **P** *Bp*
   V A T CUNNINGTON,   **OLM** C R W WEBB
REDHORN *Sarum 16*   **P** *Patr Bd*   **P-in-c** W D LANG,
   NSM E P LORT-PHILLIPS
REDISHAM (St Peter)   see Wainford *St E*
REDLAND (not known) *Bris 3*   **P** *Ch Trust Fund Trust*
   P-in-c R P SYMMONS,   **C** M J TRENDALL,
   OLM A M ROWLANDS
REDLINGFIELD (St Andrew)   see Stradbroke, Horham,
   Athelington and Redlingfield *St E*
REDLYNCH (St Mary)   see Forest and Avon *Sarum*
REDLYNCH (St Peter)   see Bruton and Distr *B & W*
REDMARLEY D'ABITOT (St Bartholomew), Bromesberrow,
   Pauntley, Upleadon, Oxenhall, Dymock, Donnington, Kempley
   and Preston *Glouc 3*   **P** *Pemb Coll Ox, Bp, R D Marcon Esq,*
   and Miss C Daniel (jt)   **R** A D LOMAS,   **Hon C** M J BENNETT,
   NSM A W PERRY,   **OLM** V G CHESTER, J M BOND
REDMARSHALL (St Cuthbert) *Dur 10*   **P** *The Crown*
   R D M BROOKE,   **NSM** P CLAYTON
REDMILE (St Peter)   see Vale of Belvoir *Leic*
REDMIRE (St Mary)   see Penhill *Ripon*
REDNAL (St Stephen the Martyr) *Birm 4*   **P** *Bp*
   P-in-c M F SIBANDA
REDRUTH (St Andrew) (St Euny) w Lanner and Treleigh *Truro 2*
   P *DBP*   **TR** S P V CADE,   **TV** E C WOON, P W FELLOWS
REED (St Mary)   see Barkway, Reed and Buckland w Barley
   St Alb
REEDHAM (St John the Baptist)   see Freethorpe,
   Wickhampton, Halvergate etc *Nor*
REEPHAM (St Mary) and Hackford w Whitwell and Kerdiston,
   Thurning w Wood Dalling and Salle *Nor 22*   **P** *Bp, CCC Cam,*
   Pemb Coll Cam, Trin Coll Cam, and Ch Soc Trust (jt)
   R M H DEAN,   **NSM** T C P DEAN,   **OLM** G L WELLS
REEPHAM (St Peter and St Paul)   see S Lawres Gp *Linc*
REGENT'S PARK (Christ Church)   see Munster Square Ch Ch
   and St Mary Magd *Lon*
REGENT'S PARK (St Mark) *Lon 16*   **P** *D&C St Paul's*
   V P G BAKER,   **Hon C** R F MCLAREN
REGIL (St James Mission Church)   see Winford w Felton
   Common Hill *B & W*
REIGATE (St Luke) w Doversgreen St Peter *S'wark 26*   **P** *Bp*
   P-in-c A C COLPUS
REIGATE (St Mark) *S'wark 26*   **P** *Bp*   **V** M WRIGHT,
   NSM S E SMITH
REIGATE (St Mary Magdalene) *S'wark 26*   **P** *Trustees*
   V P J ANDREW,   **C** P M JACKSON, D T BULL,   **Hon**
   C M J H FOX,   **NSM** D G O ROBINSON
REIGATE (St Peter) Conventional District *S'wark 24 vacant*
REIGATE (St Philip) *S'wark 26*   **P** *Bp*   **P-in-c** J P SCOTT
REIGATE HEATH (not known)   see Reigate St Mary *S'wark*
REIGHTON (St Peter)   see Bempton w Flamborough, Reighton
   w Speeton *York*
REKENDYKE (St Jude) *Dur 15*   **P** *The Crown and D&C*
   V *vacant* 0191-455 2338
REMENHAM (St Nicholas)   see Henley w Remenham *Ox*
REMPSTONE (All Saints)   see E and W Leake,
   Stanford-on-Soar, Rempstone etc *S'well*
RENDCOMB (St Peter) *Glouc 7*   **P** *Major M T N H Wills*
   R *vacant* (01285) 831319

RENDHAM (St Michael)   see Upper Alde *St E*
RENDLESHAM (St Gregory the Great)   see Wilford Peninsula
   St E
RENHOLD (All Saints) *St Alb 9*   **P** *MMCET*
   P-in-c A S BURROW
RENISHAW (St Matthew)   see Barlborough and Renishaw
   Derby
RENNINGTON (All Saints)   see Embleton w Rennington and
   Rock *Newc*
RENWICK (All Saints)   see Kirkoswald, Renwick, Gt Salkeld
   and Lazonby *Carl*
REPPS (St Peter)   see Martham and Repps with Bastwick,
   Thurne etc *Nor*
REPTON (St Wystan)   see Foremark and Repton w Newton
   Solney *Derby*
RESTON, NORTH (St Edith)   see Legbourne and Wold Marsh
   Linc
RETFORD AREA Team Ministry, The (St Michael the
   Archangel) (St Saviour) (St Swithin) *S'well 5*   **P** *Patr Bd*
   TR A C ST J WALKER,   **TV** M J CANTRILL, S CADDY, S F WALES,
   J M JESSON, F E M FERRITER,   **C** C M S MOLONEY,
   NSM I CARTER, C A DUNK
RETTENDON (All Saints) and Hullbridge *Chelmsf 12*
   P *Ld Chan and Bp (alt)*   **V** W H REED,   **NSM** S ADAMS
REVEL GROUP, The *Cov 6*   **P** *Bp, Trin Coll Cam, and*
   H A F W Boughton-Leigh Esq (2 turns), Ld Chan (1 turn)
   R R J IRETON
REVELSTOKE (St Peter)   see Newton Ferrers w Revelstoke *Ex*
REVESBY (St Lawrence)   see Fen and Hill Gp *Linc*
REWE (St Mary the Virgin)   see Brampford Speke, Cadbury,
   Newton St Cyres etc *Ex*
REYDON (St Margaret)   see Sole Bay *St E*
REYMERSTON (St Peter)   see Barnham Broom and Upper
   Yare *Nor*
RHODES (All Saints) (St Thomas) *Man 14*   **P** *R Middleton*
   V *vacant* 0161-643 8701
RHODES and Parkfield *Man 14*   **P** *Patr Bd*   **V** M Z WALL
RHYDYCROESAU (Christ Church) *Lich 19*   **P** *Bp*
   R S G THORBURN
RIBBESFORD (St Leonard) w Bewdley and Dowles *Worc 11*
   P *E J Winnington-Ingram Esq*   **R** K N JAMES,
   C J A T HEATON,   **NSM** C L ALLEN
RIBBLETON (St Mary Magdalene) (St Anne's Church Centre)
   (Ascension) *Blackb 13*   **P** *Patr Bd*   **TR** N L STIMPSON,
   TV K J FENTON,   **Hon C** E A ALP
RIBBY CUM WREA (St Nicholas) and Weeton St Michael
   Blackb 10   **P** *V Kirkham*   **V** R W MARKS
RIBCHESTER (St Wilfred) w Stidd *Blackb 13*   **P** *Bp*
   R G K HENWOOD
RIBSTON, LITTLE (St Helen)   see Spofforth w Kirk Deighton
   Ripon
RIBY (St Edmund)   see Keelby Gp *Linc*
RICCALL (St Mary)   see Barlby w Riccall *York*
RICHARDS CASTLE (All Saints)   see Ludlow *Heref*
RICHMOND (Holy Trinity and Christ Church) *S'wark 16*
   P *CPAS*   **V** T H PATTERSON,   **C** D M R COOKE
RICHMOND (St Luke)   see Kew St Phil and All SS w St Luke
   S'wark
RICHMOND (St Mary Magdalene) (St Matthias) (St John the
   Divine) *S'wark 16*   **P** *K Coll Cam*   **TR** R J TITLEY,
   TV P J ASHWIN-SIEJKOWSKI,   **NSM** N T SUMMERS, A R SYKES
RICHMOND (St Mary w Holy Trinity) w Hudswell and
   Downholme and Marske *Ripon 2*   **P** *Bp*   **R** J R CHAMBERS,
   C A P KIRBY
RICHMOND, EAST *Ripon 2*   **P** *Patr Bd*   **TV** D T LEWIS,
   Hon C G O SPEDDING, S J GOLDING,   **NSM** L C THORIUS
RICHMOND HILL (All Saints)   see Leeds All SS w
   Osmondthorpe *Ripon*
RICHMOND HILL (St Hilda)   see Hunslet w Cross Green
   Ripon
RICHMOND HILL (St Saviour)   see Leeds Richmond Hill
   Ripon
RICKERSCOTE (St Peter) *Lich 10*   **P** *Bp and V Stafford*
   St Paul (jt)   **NSM** G P BOTT
RICKINGHALL (St Mary)   see Redgrave cum Botesdale w
   Rickinghall *St E*
RICKLING (All Saints)   see Manuden w Berden and Quendon
   w Rickling *Chelmsf*
RICKMANSWORTH (St Mary the Virgin) *St Alb 4*   **P** *Bp*
   P-in-c D J SNOWBALL
RIDDINGS (Holy Spirit)   see Bottesford w Ashby *Linc*
RIDDINGS (St James) and Ironville *Derby 1*   **P** *Wright Trustees*
   and V Alfreton (jt)   **P-in-c** F J C MERCURIO,   **C** J E MORRIS
RIDDLESDEN (St Mary the Virgin) *Bradf 8*   **P** *Bp*
   P-in-c M C CANSDALE

RIDDLESDOWN (St James) *S'wark 22* **P** *Bp*
  V C F SPURWAY
RIDDLESWORTH (St Peter) *see* Guiltcross *Nor*
RIDGE (St Margaret) *see* S Mymms and Ridge *St Alb*
RIDGE, The *see* Redditch H Trin *Worc*
RIDGEWAY *Ox 19* **P** *DBP, CCC Ox, and Qu Coll Ox (jt)*
  R *vacant* (01235) 763805
RIDGEWAY *Sarum 18* **P** *D&C Windsor and*
  Capt R C Langton (jt) **R** R R POWELL
RIDGEWAY Churches, The *see* Bishop's Castle w Mainstone,
  Lydbury N etc *Heref*
RIDGEWAY (St John the Evangelist) *see* Eckington and
  Ridgeway *Derby*
RIDGEWELL (St Laurence) w Ashen, Birdbrook and Sturmer
  Chelmsf 19 **P** *Duchy of Lanc, Bp, and DBP (by turn)*
  R M D HEWITT
RIDGMONT (All Saints) *see* Aspley Guise w Husborne
  Crawley and Ridgmont *St Alb*
RIDING MILL (St James) *Newc 9* **P** *Viscount Allendale*
  P-in-c A M WHITE, **OLM** G PROUD
RIDLEY (St Peter) *Roch 1* **P** *J R A B Scott Esq* **R** *vacant*
RIDLINGTON (St Mary Magdalene and St Andrew)
  see Empingham, Edith Weston, Lyndon, Manton etc *Pet*
RIDLINGTON (St Peter) *see* Bacton, Happisburgh,
  Hempstead w Eccles etc *Nor*
RIDWARES and Kings Bromley, The *Lich 1* **P** *Bp, Lord Leigh,*
  and D&C (jt) **R** T J LEYLAND, **NSM** D J SHERIDAN
RIEVAULX (St Mary) *see* Helmsley *York*
RIGSBY (St James) *see* Alford w Rigsby *Linc*
RIGTON, NORTH (St John) *see* Lower Wharfedale *Ripon*
RILLINGTON (St Andrew) *see* Buckrose Carrs *York*
RIMPTON (Blessed Virgin Mary) *see* Chilton Cantelo,
  Ashington, Mudford, Rimpton etc *B & W*
RINGLAND (St Peter) *see* Wensum Benefice *Nor*
RINGLEY (St Saviour) *see* Farnworth, Kearsley and
  Stoneclough *Man*
RINGMER (St Mary the Virgin) *Chich 18* **P** *Abp*
  V W R PRATT, **C** S A REEVE
RINGMORE (All Hallows) *see* Modbury, Bigbury, Ringmore
  w Kingston etc *Ex*
RINGSFIELD (All Saints) *see* Wainford *St E*
RINGSHALL (St Catherine) w Battisford, Barking w Darmsden
  and Great Bricett *St E 1* **P** *Bp, Ch Patr Trust, and J C W de la*
  Bere Esq (jt) **P-in-c** B F ROSE
RINGSTEAD (Nativity of the Blessed Virgin Mary)
  see Raunds, Hargrave, Ringstead and Stanwick *Pet*
RINGSTEAD (St Andrew) *see* Hunstanton St Edm w
  Ringstead *Nor*
RINGSTONE IN AVELAND Group, The *Linc 13* **P** *Bp*
  (2 turns), Baroness Willoughby de Eresby and Charterhouse
  (1 turn) **OLM** D J CREASEY
RINGWAY Hale Barns (All Saints) *see* Hale Barns w Ringway
  Ches
RINGWOOD (St Peter and St Paul) *Win 9* **P** *K Coll Cam*
  P-in-c D K MIELL
RINGWOULD (St Nicholas) w Kingsdown and Ripple w Sutton
  by Dover *Cant 9* **P** *Abp, Ch Patr Trust, and*
  S R Monins Esq (jt) **R** C M SIGRIST, **OLM** A J WINN
RIPE (St John the Baptist) *see* Laughton w Ripe and
  Chalvington *Chich*
RIPLEY (All Saints) *Derby 12* **P** *Wright Trustees*
  V J G KENNEDY, **C** N REUSS
RIPLEY (All Saints) w Burnt Yates *Ripon 3* **P** *Sir Thomas*
  Ingilby Bt **P-in-c** P R CRESSALL, **NSM** R HUDSPETH
RIPLEY (St Mary) *Guildf 12* **P** *Bp* **V** C J ELSON
RIPON (Holy Trinity) *Ripon 3* **P** *Simeon's Trustees*
  C I S LAWRENCE, **NSM** J A MONTGOMERY, W H GOWING,
  J S RUTTER
RIPPINGALE (St Andrew) *see* Ringstone in Aveland Gp *Linc*
RIPPLE (St Mary) *see* Upton-on-Severn, Ripple, Earls Croome
  etc *Worc*
RIPPLE (St Mary the Virgin) *see* Ringwould w Kingsdown and
  Ripple etc *Cant*
RIPPONDEN (St Bartholomew) *Wakef 4* **P** *Bp and*
  V Halifax (jt) **V** C WRAY, **NSM** C A HIRST
RISBOROUGH *Ox 21* **P** *Ld Chan (2 turns), Patr Bd (1 turn)*
  TR D G WILLIAMS, **TV** J A TOMKINS, D E CRITCHELL,
  C N J TAYLOR
RISBY (St Giles) *see* Barrow *St E*
RISE (All Saints) *see* Skirlaugh w Long Riston, Rise and Swine
  York
RISE PARK *see* Bestwood Park w Rise Park *S'well*
RISEHOLME (St Mary) *see* Nettleham *Linc*
RISELEY (All Saints) w Bletsoe *St Alb 13* **P** *MMCET*
  V M T BAILEY

RISHTON (St Peter and St Paul) *Blackb 7* **P** *Trustees*
  V M WOODS, **NSM** P G HUNT
RISHWORTH (St John) *see* Ripponden *Wakef*
RISLEY (All Saints) *see* Stanton-by-Dale w Dale Abbey and
  Risley *Derby*
RISSINGTON, GREAT (St John the Baptist)
  see Bourton-on-the-Water w Clapton etc *Glouc*
RISSINGTON, LITTLE (St Peter) *as above*
RITCHINGS PARK (St Leonard) *see* Iver *Ox*
RIVENHALL (St Mary the Virgin and All Saints) *Chelmsf 23*
  P *DBP* **R** *vacant* (01376) 511161
RIVER (St Peter and St Paul) *Cant 7* **P** *Abp*
  P-in-c A J BAWTREE
RIVERHEAD (St Mary) w Dunton Green *Roch 9*
  P *R Sevenoaks and Bp (jt)* **V** P E FRANCIS
RIVERS Team Ministry, The *Sheff 6* **P** *Patr Bd*
  TR D M BENT, **TV** J LEVERTON, **C** M BAKER
RIVERSMEET Benefice, The *St Alb 10* **P** *Prime Min, Trin Coll*
  Cam (2 turns), and Ball Coll Ox (by turn)
  P-in-c M E MARSHALL
RIVINGTON (not known) *see* Horwich and Rivington *Man*
ROADE (St Mary the Virgin) and Ashton w Hartwell *Pet 5*
  P *Ld Chan and Bp (alt)* **V** M J BURTON
ROADHEAD Kinkry Hill (Mission Room) *see* Bewcastle,
  Stapleton and Kirklinton etc *Carl*
ROADWATER (St Luke) *see* Old Cleeve, Leighland and
  Treborough *B & W*
ROBERTSBRIDGE (Mission Room) *see* Salehurst *Chich*
ROBERTTOWN (All Saints) w Hartshead *Wakef 8*
  P *V Birstall and TR Dewsbury (jt)* **P-in-c** E C R BURGE,
  NSM P J DAWSON, **OLM** J C LEE
ROBOROUGH *see* Bickleigh and Shaugh Prior *Ex*
ROBOROUGH (St Peter) *see* Newton Tracey, Horwood,
  Alverdiscott etc *Ex*
ROBY (St Bartholomew) *Liv 2* **P** *Bp* **V** T C GILL
ROCESTER (St Michael) and Croxden w Hollington *Lich 15*
  P *Bp and Trustees (jt)* **V** K R GOVAN
ROCHDALE (St Aidan) Sudden *see* Sudden and Heywood All
  So *Man*
ROCHDALE (St Chad) St Edmund (St John the Divine)
  (St Mary) *Man 17* **P** *Bp* **NSM** I G KAY
ROCHDALE (St George w St Alban) *see* Oakenrod and
  Bamford *Man*
ROCHE (St Gomonda of the Rock) and Withiel *Truro 1* **P** *Bp*
  and DBP (jt) **P-in-c** J A COOMBS, **NSM** E C DEELEY
ROCHESTER (St Justus) *Roch 5* **P** *Bp* **V** P T KERR,
  NSM P FOREMAN
ROCHESTER (St Margaret) (St Peter's Parish Centre) *Roch 5*
  P *Bp and D&C (jt)* **V** G S COLVILLE
ROCHESTER ROW (St Stephen) *see* Westmr St Steph w St Jo
  Lon
ROCHFORD (St Andrew) *Chelmsf 12* **P** *Bp* **R** *vacant* (01702)
  530621
ROCHFORD (St Michael) *see* Teme Valley S *Worc*
ROCK (St Peter and St Paul) *see* Mamble w Bayton, Rock w
  Heightington etc *Worc*
ROCK (St Philip and St James) *see* Embleton w Rennington and
  Rock *Newc*
ROCK FERRY (St Peter) *Ches 1* **P** *Bp* **V** P M FROGGATT,
  C C R SLATER
ROCKBEARE (St Mary w St Andrew) *see* Aylesbeare,
  Rockbeare, Farringdon etc *Ex*
ROCKBOURNE (St Andrew) *see* W Downland *Sarum*
ROCKCLIFFE (St Mary the Virgin) and Blackford *Carl 2*
  P *D&C* **P-in-c** J J VAN DEN BERG
ROCKHAMPTON (St Oswald) *see* Cromhall, Tortworth,
  Tytherington, Falfield etc *Glouc*
ROCKINGHAM (St Leonard) *see* Gretton w Rockingham and
  Cottingham w E Carlton *Pet*
ROCKLAND (All Saints) *see* Gt and Lt Ellingham, Rockland
  and Shropham etc *Nor*
ROCKLAND (St Peter) *as above*
ROCKLAND ST MARY (St Mary) with Hellington, Bramerton,
  Surlingham, Claxton, Carleton St Peter and Kirby Bedon w
  Whitlingham *Nor 8* **P** *Bp, Adn Nor, MMCET, and*
  BNC Ox (jt) **R** J B SHAW, **NSM** G D SAUNDERS,
  OLM A MANSELL
RODBOROUGH (St Mary Magdalene) *Glouc 4* **P** *Bp*
  P-in-c M M LUDLOW, **NSM** B P LUDLOW
RODBOURNE (Holy Rood) *see* Gt Somerford, Lt Somerford,
  Seagry, Corston etc *Bris*
RODBOURNE CHENEY (St Mary) *Bris 7* **P** *CPAS*
  R N D J LINES
RODDEN (All Saints) *see* Beckington w Standerwick, Berkley,
  Rodden etc *B & W*

RODE (St Lawrence)   *see* Hardington Vale *B & W*

RODE, NORTH (St Michael)   *see* Bosley and N Rode w Wincle and Wildboarclough *Ches*

RODE HEATH (Good Shepherd)   *see* Odd Rode *Ches*

RODHUISH (St Bartholomew)   *see* Dunster, Carhampton, Withycombe w Rodhuish etc *B & W*

RODING, HIGH (All Saints)   *see* Gt Canfield w High Roding and Aythorpe Roding *Chelmsf*

RODING, HIGH (Mission Hall)   *as above*

RODINGS, SOUTH *Chelmsf 18*   **P** *Ld Chan, Bp, and Viscount Gough (by turn)*   **P-in-c** M KITCHEN

RODINGTON (St George)   *see* Wrockwardine Deanery *Lich*

RODLEY (Ecumenical Centre)   *see* Bramley *Ripon*

RODLEY (Mission Church)   *see* Westbury-on-Severn w Flaxley, Blaisdon etc *Glouc*

RODMARTON (St Peter) **Conventional District** *Glouc 7 vacant*

RODMELL (St Peter)   *see* Iford w Kingston and Rodmell *Chich*

RODMERSHAM (St Nicholas)   *see* Tunstall and Bredgar *Cant*

RODNEY STOKE (St Leonard) **w Draycott** *B & W 1*   **P** *Bp*   **P-in-c** S M ROSE,   **C** C J BUTLER

ROEHAMPTON (Holy Trinity) *S'wark 18*   **P** *Bp*   **V** J A MCKINNEY

ROFFEY (All Saints)   *see* Roughey *Chich*

ROGATE (St Bartholomew) **w Terwick and Trotton w Chithurst** *Chich 10*   **P** *Ld Chan*   **R** E M DOYLE

ROGERS LANE (St Andrew's Chapel)   *see* Stoke Poges *Ox*

ROKER (St Aidan)   *see* Monkwearmouth *Dur*

ROLLESBY (St George)   *see* Ormesby St Marg w Scratby, Ormesby St Mich etc *Nor*

ROLLESTON (Holy Trinity) **w Fiskerton, Morton and Upton** *S'well 15*   **P** *Ld Chan*   **V** *vacant* (01636) 830131

ROLLESTON (St John the Baptist)   *see* Church Langton cum Tur Langton etc *Leic*

ROLLESTON (St Mary) *Lich 14*   **P** *MMCET*   **R** I R WHITEHEAD

ROLLRIGHT, GREAT (St Andrew)   *see* Hook Norton w Gt Rollright, Swerford etc *Ox*

ROLLRIGHT, LITTLE (St Phillip)   *see* Chipping Norton *Ox*

ROLVENDEN (St Mary the Virgin)   *see* Newenden and Rolvenden *Cant*

ROMALDKIRK (St Romald) **w Laithkirk** *Ripon 2*   **P** *Bp and Earl of Strathmore's Trustees (alt)*   **P-in-c** S A ADESANYA

ROMANBY (St James)   *see* Northallerton w Kirby Sigston *York*

ROMANSLEIGH (St Rumon)   *see* S Molton w Nymet St George, High Bray etc *Ex*

ROMFORD (Ascension) **Collier Row** *Chelmsf 2*   **P** *Trustees*   **P-in-c** B M HULL

ROMFORD (Good Shepherd) **Collier Row** *Chelmsf 2*   **P** *CPAS*   **P-in-c** D H HAGUE,   **C** R M SMART

ROMFORD (St Alban) *Chelmsf 2*   **P** *Bp*   **V** R S P HINGLEY

ROMFORD (St Andrew) **(St Agnes)** *Chelmsf 2*   **P** *New Coll Ox*   **R** R G FRIENDSHIP,   **Hon C** S J MAYES

ROMFORD (St Augustine) **Rush Green**   *see* Rush Green *Chelmsf*

ROMFORD (St Edward the Confessor) *Chelmsf 2*   **P** *New Coll Ox*   **V** D R ANDERSON

ROMFORD (St John the Divine) *Chelmsf 2*   **P** *Bp*   **V** *vacant* (01708) 742265

ROMILEY (St Chad) *Ches 16*   **P** *R Stockport St Mary*   **V** T D BARLOW,   **C** J PIENAAR

ROMNEY, NEW (St Nicholas) **w OLD (St Clement) and Midley** *Cant 11*   **P** *Abp*   **P-in-c** J L FIELD,   **NSM** P W S FIRTH

ROMSEY (St Mary and St Ethelflaeda) *Win 12*   **P** *Bp*   **V** T C K SLEDGE,   **C** J J MACHIN,   **NSM** D F WILLIAMS, B G TAPHOUSE

ROMSLEY (Mission Room)   *see* Halas *Worc*

ROMSLEY (St Kenelm)   *as above*

ROOKERY, THE (St Saviour)   *see* Mow Cop *Lich*

ROOKHOPE (St John the Evangelist)   *see* Upper Weardale *Dur*

ROOS (All Saints) **and Garton in Holderness w Tunstall, Grimston and Hilston** *York 12*   **P** *Abp (1 turn), SMF (2 turns)*   **P-in-c** A J BURDON,   **C** P M BURDON

ROOSE (St Perran)   *see* S Barrow *Carl*

ROPLEY (St Peter)   *see* Bishop's Sutton and Ropley and W Tisted *Win*

ROPSLEY (St Peter)   *see* N Beltisloe Gp *Linc*

ROSE ASH (St Peter)   *see* Bishopsnympton, Rose Ash, Mariansleigh etc *Ex*

ROSEDALE (St Lawrence)   *see* Lastingham w Appleton-le-Moors, Rosedale etc *York*

ROSHERVILLE (St Mark)   *see* Northfleet and Rosherville *Roch*

ROSLEY (Holy Trinity)   *see* Westward, Rosley-w-Woodside and Welton *Carl*

ROSLISTON (St Mary)   *see* Walton-on-Trent w Croxall, Rosliston etc *Derby*

ROSS (St Mary the Virgin) **w Walford** *Heref 7*   **P** *Bp (4 turns), Ld Chan (1 turn)*   **R** S J JONES

ROSSENDALE (St Anne) **(St Nicholas w St John) Middle Valley** *Man 11*   **P** *Patr Bd*   **TR** R BEVAN,   **TV** S A DAVIES, **OLM** S LYNCH

ROSSENDALE (St Peter)   *see* Laneside *Blackb*

ROSSENDALE (St Thomas)   *see* Musbury *Blackb*

ROSSINGTON (St Michael) *Sheff 9*   **P** *Bp*   **R** N R RAO

ROSSINGTON, NEW (St Luke) *Sheff 9*   **P** *Bp*   **V** *vacant* (01302) 868288

ROSTHERNE (St Mary) **w Bollington** *Ches 12*   **P** *C L S Cornwall-Legh Esq*   **P-in-c** P J ROBINSON

ROTHBURY (All Saints)   *see* Upper Coquetdale *Newc*

ROTHERBY (All Saints)   *see* Upper Wreake *Leic*

ROTHERFIELD (St Denys) **w Mark Cross** *Chich 19*   **P** *Bp, Adn Lewes and Hastings, and Ch Patr Trust (jt)*   **V** N F MASON

ROTHERFIELD GREYS (Holy Trinity)   *see* Henley H Trin *Ox*

ROTHERFIELD GREYS (St Nicholas)   *see* Nettlebed w Bix, Highmoor, Pishill etc *Ox*

ROTHERFIELD PEPPARD (All Saints) **and Kidmore End and Sonning Common** *Ox 6*   **P** *Bp and Jes Coll Ox (jt)*   **R** G D FOULIS BROWN,   **Hon C** A B OLSEN

ROTHERHAM (All Saints) *Sheff 6*   **P** *Bp*   **V** D C BLISS, **C** A NASCIMENTO COOK

ROTHERHAM (St Paul) **Ferham Park**   *see* Masbrough *Sheff*

ROTHERHITHE (Holy Trinity) *S'wark 7*   **P** *R Rotherhithe St Mary*   **V** A M DOYLE

ROTHERHITHE (St Katharine)   *see* Bermondsey St Kath w St Bart *S'wark*

ROTHERHITHE (St Mary) **w All Saints** *S'wark 7*   **P** *Clare Coll Cam*   **R** M R NICHOLLS,   **C** R J NORMAN

ROTHERSTHORPE (St Peter and St Paul)   *see* Bugbrooke, Harpole, Kislingbury etc *Pet*

ROTHERWICK (not known)   *see* Whitewater *Win*

ROTHLEY (St Mary the Virgin and St John the Baptist) *Leic 5*   **P** *MMCET*   **V** R M GLADSTONE,   **C** T ROUT

ROTHWELL (Holy Trinity) *Ripon 8*   **P** *Bp*   **P-in-c** J M TRIGG

ROTHWELL (Holy Trinity) **w Orton and Rushton w Glendon and Pipewell** *Pet 9*   **P** *Hosp of Jes (1 turn), Bp (2 turns), J Hipwell Esq (1 turn), and Mert Coll Ox (1 turn)*   **P-in-c** J R WESTWOOD,   **C** C H DOBSON

ROTHWELL (St Mary the Virgin)   *see* Swallow *Linc*

ROTTINGDEAN (St Margaret) *Chich 2*   **P** *Bp*   **V** M P MORGAN

ROUGH CLOSE (St Matthew)   *see* Meir Heath and Normacot *Lich*

ROUGH COMMON (St Gabriel)   *see* Harbledown *Cant*

ROUGH HAY (St Christopher)   *see* Darlaston St Lawr *Lich*

ROUGH HILLS (St Martin) *Lich 28*   **P** *Bp*   **P-in-c** S W POWELL

ROUGHAM (St Mary)   *see* Gt w Lt Massingham, Harpley, Rougham etc *Nor*

ROUGHAM (St Mary), **Beyton w Hessett and Rushbrooke** *St E 10*   **P** *Bp, MMCET (2 turns), and Ld Chan*   **R** N CUTLER

ROUGHEY or Roffey (All Saints) *Chich 8*   **P** *Bp*   **V** K R C AGNEW

ROUGHTON (St Margaret)   *see* Bain Valley Gp *Linc*

ROUGHTON (St Mary) **and Felbrigg, Metton, Suestad, Bessingham and Gunton w Hanworth** *Nor 21*   **P** *Bp and Exors G Whately Esq (jt)*   **P-in-c** J W SMITH

ROUGHTOWN (St John the Baptist) *Man 13*   **P** *Bp*   **P-in-c** C NIGHTINGALE

ROUNDHAY (St Edmund King and Martyr) *Ripon 5*   **P** *Bp*   **V** D G PATON-WILLIAMS,   **C** D M FLYNN

ROUNDHAY (St John the Evangelist) *Ripon 5*   **P** *DBF*   **P-in-c** C H CHEESEMAN

ROUNDS GREEN (St James) *Birm 7*   **P** *V Langley*   **V** *vacant* 0121-552 2822

ROUNDSHAW (St Paul)   *see* S Beddington and Roundshaw *S'wark*

ROUNDSWELL **Conventional District** *Ex 15 vacant*

ROUNTON, WEST (St Oswald) **and East (St Laurence) w Welbury** *York 18*   **P** *Ld Chan*   **R** J M E COOPER

ROUS LENCH (St Peter)   *see* Church Lench w Rous Lench and Abbots Morton etc *Worc*

ROUSHAM (St Leonard and St James) *Ox 2*   **P** *C Cottrell-Dormer Esq*   **P-in-c** R C SMAIL

ROUTH (All Saints) *York 8*   **P** *Ch Soc Trust and Reformation Ch Trust (jt)*   **P-in-c** J J FLETCHER

ROWBARTON (St Andrew)   *see* Taunton St Andr *B & W*

ROWBERROW (St Michael and All Angels)   *see* Axbridge w Shipham and Rowberrow *B & W*

ROWDE (St Matthew) **and Bromham** *Sarum 16*   **P** *DBP and S Spicer Esq (jt)*   **P-in-c** J N REES,   **NSM** N FERGUSSON

ROWENFIELD (Emmanuel)   *see* Cheltenham St Mark *Glouc*

ROWINGTON (St Lawrence)   *see* Hatton w Haseley, Rowington w Lowsonford etc *Cov*

ROWLAND LUBBOCK (Memorial Hall)   *see* E Horsley and Ockham w Hatchford and Downside *Guildf*

ROWLANDS CASTLE (St John the Baptist) *Portsm 5*   **P** *Bp*
NSM T M FILTNESS

ROWLANDS GILL (St Barnabas)   *see* High Spen and Rowlands Gill *Dur*

ROWLEDGE (St James) and Frensham *Guildf 3*   **P** *Adn Surrey and Ld Chan (alt)*   **V** C J RICHARDSON,   **NSM** S J CRABTREE, J L WALKER

ROWLESTONE (St Peter)   *see* Ewyas Harold w Dulas, Kenderchurch etc *Heref*

ROWLEY (St Peter) w Skidby *York 8*   **P** *Abp and N A C Hildyard Esq (jt)*   **R** A BAILEY,   **NSM** R K NEWTON

ROWLEY REGIS (St Giles) *Birm 7*   **P** *Ld Chan*
V I R SHELTON

ROWNER (St Mary the Virgin) *Portsm 3*
P *R J F Prideaux-Brune Esq*   **R** J W DRAPER

ROWNEY GREEN (Mission Chapel)   *see* Alvechurch *Worc*

ROWNHAMS (St John the Evangelist)   *see* Nursling and Rownhams *Win*

ROWSLEY (St Katherine)   *see* Bakewell, Ashford w Sheldon and Rowsley *Derby*

ROWSTON (St Clement)   *see* Digby Gp *Linc*

ROWTON (All Hallows)   *see* Wrockwardine Deanery *Lich*

ROXBOURNE (St Andrew) *Lon 23*   **P** *Bp*   **V** C M RABLEN

ROXBY (St Mary)   *see* Winterton Gp *Linc*

ROXBY (St Nicholas)   *see* Hinderwell, Roxby and Staithes etc *York*

ROXETH (Christ Church) *Lon 23*   **P** *Bp and Ch Patr Trust (jt)*
V M S PHILPS

ROXHOLME   *see* Leasingham *Linc*

ROXTON (St Mary Magdalene)   *see* Riversmeet *St Alb*

ROXWELL (St Michael and All Angels) *Chelmsf 8*
P *New Coll Ox*   **P-in-c** K B BEST

ROYDON (All Saints)   *see* Grimston, Congham and Roydon *Nor*

ROYDON (St Peter) *Chelmsf 25*   **P** *Earl Cowley*
P-in-c A M CANNELL

ROYDON (St Remigius)   *see* Upper Waveney *Nor*

ROYSTON (St John the Baptist) *St Alb 16*   **P** *Bp*
V L D HARMAN,   **NSM** J H FIDLER, T R WEEKS

ROYSTON (St John the Baptist) *Wakef 7*   **P** *Bp*
V M J BULLIMORE

ROYTON (St Anne) Longsight *Man 16*   **P** *Bp*
P-in-c J A READ,   **C** E J DEVALL,   **OLM** D J HALFORD, P A ROBINSON

ROYTON (St Paul) and Shaw *Man 16*   **P** *R Prestwich St Mary*
V P B MCEVITT

RUAN LANIHORNE (St Rumon)   *see* Veryan w Ruan Lanihorne *Truro*

RUAN MINOR (St Rumon)   *see* St Ruan w St Grade and Landewednack *Truro*

RUARDEAN (St John the Baptist)   *see* Drybrook, Lydbrook and Ruardean *Glouc*

RUBERY (St Chad) *Birm 4*   **P** *The Crown*   **P-in-c** D W JAMES

RUCKINGE (St Mary Magdalene)   *see* Orlestone w Snave and Ruckinge w Warehorne etc *Cant*

RUCKLAND (St Olave)   *see* S Ormsby Gp *Linc*

RUDBY IN CLEVELAND (All Saints) w Middleton *York 20*
P *Abp*   **V** P J SANDERS,   **Hon C** A J HUTCHINSON

RUDDINGTON (St Peter) *S'well 9*   **P** *Simeon's Trustees*
V A D BUCHANAN

RUDFORD (St Mary the Virgin)   *see* Highnam, Lassington, Rudford, Tibberton etc *Glouc*

RUDGWICK (Holy Trinity) *Chich 8*   **P** *Ld Chan*
V M P J KING

RUDHAM, EAST and WEST (St Mary), Helhoughton, Houghton-next-Harpley, The Raynhams, Tatterford, and Tattersett *Nor 15*   **P** *Bp, The Most Revd G D Hand, Marquess of Cholmondeley, and Marquess Townshend (jt)*
R E L BUNDOCK,   **C** A M THOMSON

RUDHEATH (Licensed Room)   *see* Witton *Ches*

RUDSTON (All Saints) w Boynton, Carnaby and Kilham *York 9*
P *Ld Chan (1 turn), Abp (3 turns)*   **V** G J OWEN

RUFFORD (St Mary the Virgin) and Tarleton *Blackb 5*   **P** *Bp and St Pet Coll Ox (jt)*   **P-in-c** N E DAVIS,   **Hon C** T TAYLOR

RUFFORTH (All Saints) w Moor Monkton and Hessay *York 1*
P *MMCET and Abp (alt)*   **P-in-c** P P ROBINSON,
NSM M R SHAW

RUGBY (Christ Church)   *see* Clifton w Newton and Brownsover *Cov*

RUGBY (St Andrew) (St George) (St John) (St Peter) *Cov 6*
P *Bp*   **TR** M H F BEACH,   **TV** J D PARKER,   **C** P J PRIVETT,
NSM R C ROGERS, H G IREDALE

RUGBY WEST (St Matthew) (St Oswald) *Cov 6*   **P** *Dioc Trustees and Ch Trust Fund Trust (jt)*   **V** M P SAXBY,
C T NORMAN, S M BRIDGE,   **OLM** A J CARTWRIGHT

RUGELEY (St Augustine)   *see* Brereton and Rugeley *Lich*

RUGELEY (The Good Shepherd)   *as above*

RUISHTON (St George)   *see* Creech St Michael and Ruishton w Thornfalcon *B & W*

RUISLIP (St Martin) *Lon 24*   **P** *D&C Windsor*   **V** S EVANS,
NSM M A BEDFORD, S C SIMPKINS

RUISLIP (St Mary) *Lon 24*   **P** *Bp*   **V** N G T WHEELER

RUISLIP MANOR (St Paul) *Lon 24*   **P** *Bp*
NSM B C PINNELL

RUMBURGH (St Michael and All Angels and St Felix)   *see* S Elmham and Ilketshall *St E*

RUNCORN (All Saints) (Holy Trinity) *Ches 3*   **P** *Bp and Ch Ch Ox (jt)*   **V** J H A HAYES,   **NSM** M A HAYES

RUNCORN (St John the Evangelist) Weston *Ches 3*   **P** *Bp*
V E M GARDNER

RUNCORN (St Michael and All Angels) *Ches 3*   **P** *Bp*
V V L SCHOFIELD

RUNCTON, NORTH (All Saints)   *see* W Winch w Setchey, N Runcton and Middleton *Nor*

RUNCTON, SOUTH (St Andrew)   *see* Holme Runcton w S Runcton and Wallington *Ely*

RUNCTON HOLME (St James)   *as above*

RUNHALL (All Saints)   *see* Barnham Broom and Upper Yare *Nor*

RUNHAM (St Peter and St Paul)   *see* S Trin Broads *Nor*

RUNNINGTON (St Peter and St Paul)   *see* Wellington and Distr *B & W*

RUNNYMEDE (St Jude)   *see* Englefield Green *Guildf*

RUNTON (Holy Trinity)   *see* Aylmerton, Runton, Beeston Regis and Gresham *Nor*

RUNTON, EAST (St Andrew)   *as above*

RUNWELL (St Mary)   *see* Wickford and Runwell *Chelmsf*

RUSCOMBE (St James the Great) and Twyford *Ox 16*   **P** *Bp*
P-in-c S C HOWARD,   **C** A C HARWOOD,   **Hon C** T J DAKIN,
NSM S DAKIN, G W PUGH

RUSH GREEN (St Augustine) Romford *Chelmsf 2*   **P** *Bp*
V M D HOWSE

RUSHALL (Christ the King) (St Michael the Archangel) *Lich 25*
P *Sir Andrew Buchanan Bt and H C S Buchanan Esq (jt)*
V C R SUCH

RUSHALL (St Mary)   *see* Dickleburgh and The Pulhams *Nor*

RUSHALL (St Matthew)   *see* Vale of Pewsey *Sarum*

RUSHBROOKE (St Nicholas)   *see* Rougham, Beyton w Hessett and Rushbrooke *St E*

RUSHBURY (St Peter) *Heref 10*   **P** *Bp Birm*   **P-in-c** J GROVES

RUSHDEN (St Mary)   *see* Sandon, Wallington and Rushden w Clothall *St Alb*

RUSHDEN (St Mary) w Newton Bromswold *Pet 8*   **P** *CPAS*
R S K PRIOR,   **C** M T TAYLOR

RUSHDEN (St Peter) *Pet 8*   **P** *CPAS*   **V** D J K WALLER

RUSHEN Christ Church (Holy Trinity) *S & M 1*   **P** *The Crown*
V *vacant* (01624) 832275

RUSHEY MEAD (St Theodore of Canterbury)   *see* Leic St Theodore *Leic*

RUSHFORD (St John the Evangelist)   *see* E w W Harling, Bridgham w Roudham, Larling etc *Nor*

RUSHLAKE GREEN (Little St Mary)   *see* Warbleton and Bodle Street Green *Chich*

RUSHMERE (St Andrew) *St E 4*   **P** *Bp*   **V** B WAKELING

RUSHMERE (St Michael)   *see* Kessingland, Gisleham and Rushmere *Nor*

RUSHMOOR (St Francis)   *see* Churt and Hindhead *Guildf*

RUSHOCK (St Michael)   *see* Elmley Lovett w Hampton Lovett and Elmbridge etc *Worc*

RUSHOLME (Holy Trinity) *Man 3*   **P** *CPAS*   **R** S L JAMES,
C P R HORLOCK, P M MATHOLE,   **NSM** P J GASKELL, P G JUMP

RUSHTON (All Saints)   *see* Rothwell w Orton, Rushton w Glendon and Pipewell *Pet*

RUSHTON SPENCER   *see* Horton, Lonsdon and Rushton Spencer *Lich*

RUSKIN PARK (St Saviour)   *see* Herne Hill *S'wark*

RUSKINGTON Group, The (All Saints) *Linc 21*   **P** *DBP*
P-in-c C PENNOCK,   **NSM** L M HUNTER, N R PANTING

RUSLAND (St Paul)   *see* Hawkshead and Low Wray w Sawrey and Rusland etc *Carl*

RUSPER (St Mary Magdalene) w Colgate *Chich 8*
P *Mrs E C Calvert and Bp (alt)*   **R** N A FLINT,
NSM M YOUNG

RUSTHALL (St Paul) (St Paul's Mission Church) *Roch 12*
P *R Speldhurst*   **V** R E N WILLIAMS

RUSTINGTON (St Peter and St Paul) *Chich 1*   **P** *Bp*
V Z E ALLEN

RUSTON, SOUTH   *see* Tunstead w Sco' Ruston *Nor*
RUSTON PARVA (St Nicholas)   *see* The Beacon *York*
RUSWARP (St Bartholomew)   *see* Whitby w Ruswarp *York*
RUYTON XI TOWNS (St John the Baptist) w Great Ness and
  Little Ness *Lich 17*   **P** *Bp and Guild of All So (jt) and Ld Chan
  (alt)*   **P-in-c** L FOSTER,   **OLM** J M BAKER
RYAL (All Saints)   *see* Stamfordham w Matfen *Newc*
RYARSH (St Martin)   *see* Birling, Addington, Ryarsh and
  Trottiscliffe *Roch*
RYBURGH, GREAT (St Andrew)   *see* Upper Wensum Village
  Gp *Nor*
RYDAL (St Mary) *Carl 11*   **P** *Bp*   **V** C J BUTLAND
RYDE (All Saints) *Portsm 7*   **P** *Bp*   **NSM** E W BUTCHER
RYDE (Holy Trinity) *Portsm 7*   **P** *Bp*   **V** vacant (01983) 562984
RYDE (St James) Proprietary Chapel *Portsm 7*   **P** *Ch Soc Trust*
  C-in-c J H A LEGGETT
RYDE (St John the Baptist)   *see* Oakfield St Jo *Portsm*
RYE (St Mary the Virgin) *Chich 20*   **P** *Patr Bd*   **TR** D R FROST,
  NSM J G DAVENPORT, G R ATFIELD
RYE HARBOUR (Holy Spirit)   *see* Rye *Chich*
RYE PARK (St Cuthbert) *St Alb 17*   **P** *DBP*   **V** vacant (01992)
  461856
RYECROFT (St Nicolas) *Rawmarsh Sheff 6*   **P** *Bp*   **V** vacant
  (01709) 522596
RYEDALE, UPPER *York 19*   **P** *Abp, Adn Cleveland, Sir Richard
  Beckett Bt, and Sir George Wombwell Bt (jt)*
  P-in-c T J ROBINSON,   **NSM** J B NICHOLSON, M D B SINCLAIR
RYHALL (St John the Evangelist) w Essendine and Carlby *Pet 12*
  P *Burghley Ho Preservation Trust*   **V** P J MCKEE
RYHILL (St James) *Wakef 11*   **P** *Bp*   **P-in-c** P A BOSTOCK
RYHOPE (St Paul) *Dur 16*   **P** *Bp*   **V** D E CHADWICK
RYLSTONE (St Peter)   *see* Burnsall w Rylstone *Bradf*
RYME INTRINSECA (St Hypolytus)   *see* Wriggle Valley
  Sarum
RYPE (St John the Baptist)   *see* Laughton w Ripe and
  Chalvington *Chich*
RYSTON (St Michael)   *see* Denver and Ryston w Roxham and
  W Dereham etc *Ely*
RYTHER (All Saints)   *see* Cawood w Ryther and Wistow *York*
RYTON (Holy Cross) *Dur 13*   **P** *Bp*   **R** T L JAMIESON
RYTON (Mission Chapel)   *see* Condover w Frodesley, Acton
  Burnell etc *Heref*
RYTON (St Andrew)   *see* Beckbury, Badger, Kemberton, Ryton,
  Stockton etc *Lich*
RYTON ON DUNSMORE (St Leonard)   *see* Baginton w
  Bubbenhall and Ryton-on-Dunsmore *Cov*
SABDEN (St Nicholas) and Pendleton-in-Whalley (All Saints)
  Blackb 7   **P** *Bp and Trustees (jt)*   **P-in-c** G M DYER
SACKLETON (St George the Martyr)   *see* The Street Par *York*
SACOMBE (St Catherine)   *see* Standon and The Mundens w
  Sacombe *St Alb*
SACRISTON (St Peter)   *see* Dur N *Dur*
SADBERGE (St Andrew) *Dur 8*   **P** *Bp*   **R** P S D NEVILLE
SADDINGTON (St Helen)   *see* Kibworth and Smeeton
  Westerby and Saddington *Leic*
SADDLEWORTH (St Chad) *Man 15*   **P** *Patr Bd*
  TR C N R HALLIDAY,   **TV** J R ROSEDALE,   **Hon**
  C H G SUTCLIFFE,   **OLM** B CHRISTOPHER
SAFFRON WALDEN (St Mary) w Wendens Ambo, Littlebury,
  Ashdon and Hadstock *Chelmsf 21*   **P** *Patr Bd*
  TR D R TOMLINSON,   **C** A M HOWSON,
  NSM J C TOMLINSON, W MOORE, P W L GRIFFITHS, A P WANT,
  T K HARDINGHAM
SAHAM TONEY (St George)   *see* Ashill, Carbrooke, Ovington
  and Saham Toney *Nor*
ST AGNES (St Agnes)   *see* Is of Scilly *Truro*
ST AGNES (St Agnes) and Mount Hawke w Mithian *Truro 6*
  P *Bp and D&C (alt)*   **V** A G BASHFORTH,   **C** J S J WILLIAMS,
  NSM J A MILLAR, D J WILLOUGHBY
ST ALBANS (Christ Church) *St Alb 5*   **P** *Trustees*
  V J M FOLLETT
ST ALBANS (St Luke) *St Alb 5*   **P** *DBP*   **V** M A SLATER
ST ALBANS (St Mary) Marshalswick *St Alb 5*   **P** *Bp*
  P-in-c G W A RUSSELL
ST ALBANS (St Michael) *St Alb 5*   **P** *Earl of Verulam*
  NSM J A HAYTON, M CROWLEY
ST ALBANS (St Paul) *St Alb 5*   **P** *V St Alb St Pet*
  V A R HURLE,   **C** J W D HASWELL,   **Hon C** G M ABBOTT,
  NSM L M HURLE
ST ALBANS (St Peter) *St Alb 5*   **P** *The Crown*
  V A E HOLLINGHURST,   **C** J C PERRIS
ST ALBANS (St Saviour) *St Alb 5*   **P** *Bp*   **V** P R WADSWORTH,
  NSM A N FERRAR
ST ALBANS (St Stephen) *St Alb 5*   **P** J N W Dudley Esq
  V D RIDGEWAY,   **NSM** G I KEIR, P J MADGWICK, C BAYNES

ST ALLEN (St Alleyne)   *see* Kenwyn w St Allen *Truro*
ST ANNES-ON-THE-SEA (St Anne) Heyhouses *Blackb 10*
  P J C Hilton Esq   **P-in-c** A D LYON
ST ANNES-ON-THE-SEA (St Margaret of Antioch) *Blackb 10*
  P *Bp*   **V** A R HODGSON
ST ANNES-ON-THE-SEA (St Thomas) *Blackb 10*
  P J C Hilton Esq   **V** P D LAW-JONES,   **C** N E GOODRICH
ST ANTHONY-IN-MENEAGE (St Anthony)   *see* Meneage
  Truro
ST AUSTELL (Holy Trinity) *Truro 1*   **P** *The Crown*
  V M D MARSHALL,   **C** H M MEARS, O H J MEARS
ST BEES (St Mary and St Bega) *Carl 5*   **P** *Trustees*
  P-in-c C R SWARTZ
ST BLAZEY (St Blaise) *Truro 1*   **P** *Bp*   **V** F M BOWERS
ST BREOKE (St Breoke) and Egloshayle in Wadebridge *Truro 10*
  P *Bp and DBP (jt)*   **P-in-c** W R STUART-WHITE,
  C D P WHITTING
ST BREWARD (St Breward)   *see* Blisland w St Breward *Truro*
ST BRIAVELS (St Mary the Virgin) w Hewelsfield *Glouc 1*
  P *D&C Heref*   **P-in-c** R J M GROSVENOR,   **Hon C** F E BUXTON
ST BUDEAUX   *see* Devonport St Budeaux *Ex*
ST BURYAN (St Buriana), St Levan and Sennen *Truro 5*
  P *Duchy of Cornwall*   **P-in-c** B J BERRIMAN,   **OLM** C M JAGO
ST CLEER (St Clarus) *Truro 12*   **P** *Ld Chan*
  P-in-c K LANYON JONES
ST CLEMENT (St Clement)   *see* Truro St Paul and St Clem
  Truro
ST CLEMENT DANES   *see* St Mary le Strand w St Clem
  Danes *Lon*
ST CLETHER (St Clederus)   *see* Altarnon w Bolventor, Laneast
  and St Clether *Truro*
ST COLAN (St Colan)   *see* St Columb Minor and St Colan
  Truro
ST COLUMB MAJOR (St Columba) w St Wenn *Truro 7*   **P** *Bp*
  NSM E C DEELEY
ST COLUMB MINOR (St Columba) and St Colan *Truro 7*
  P *Bp*   **P-in-c** C C MCQUILLEN-WRIGHT
ST DECUMANS   *see* Watchet and Williton *B & W*
ST DENNIS (St Denys) *Truro 1*   **P** *Bp*   **P-in-c** K P ARTHUR
ST DEVEREUX (St Dubricius)   *see* Ewyas Harold w Dulas,
  Kenderchurch etc *Heref*
ST DOMINIC (St Dominica), Landulph and St Mellion w
  Pillaton *Truro 11*   **P** *D&C and Trustees Major J Coryton,
  Duchy of Cornwall, and SMF (by turn)*   **R** P R J LAMB
ST EDMUND WAY *St E 10*   **P** *Bp, Mrs J Oakes, and
  Lord de Saumarez*   **R** J E BUCKLES,   **C** A D SHANNON,
  NSM J R LONGE
ST EDMUNDS Anchorage Lane Conventional District
  Sheff 7 vacant
ST ENDELLION (St Endelienta) w Port Isaac and St Kew
  Truro 10   **P** *Bp*   **P-in-c** J A C MAY,   **C** J R MOSEDALE,
  NSM J POLLINGER, A D E LEWIS
ST ENODER (St Enoder) *Truro 7*   **P** *Bp*   **P-in-c** H L SAMSON
ST ENODOC (St Enodoc)   *see* St Minver *Truro*
ST ERME (St Hermes)   *see* Probus, Ladock and Grampound w
  Creed and St Erme *Truro*
ST ERNEY (St Erney)   *see* Landrake w St Erney and Botus
  Fleming *Truro*
ST ERTH (St Erth)   *see* Godrevy *Truro*
ST ERVAN (St Ervan)   *see* St Mawgan w St Ervan and St Eval
  Truro
ST EVAL (St Uvelas)   *as above*
ST EWE (All Saints)   *see* St Mewan w Mevagissey and St Ewe
  Truro
ST GENNYS (St Gennys)   *see* Week St Mary Circle of Par *Truro*
ST GEORGE-IN-THE-EAST (St Mary) *Lon 7*   **P** *Bp*
  V P MCGEARY,   **Hon C** P WRIGHT
ST GEORGE-IN-THE-EAST w St Paul *Lon 7*   **P** *Bp*
  R M R AINSWORTH
ST GEORGES (St George)   *see* Priors Lee and St Georges *Lich*
ST GERMANS (St Germans of Auxerre) *Truro 11*   **P** *D&C*
  Windsor   **P-in-c** A I JOHNSTON,   **OLM** J M LOBB
ST GILES-IN-THE-FIELDS *Lon 3*   **P** *Bp*   **R** W M JACOB,
  C A C CARR
ST GILES-IN-THE-HEATH (St Giles)   *see* Boyton,
  N Tamerton, Werrington etc *Truro*
ST GILES IN THE WOOD (St Giles)   *see* Newton Tracey,
  Horwood, Alverdiscott etc *Ex*
ST GLUVIAS (St Gluvias) *Truro 3*   **P** *Bp*   **V** J HARRIS
ST GORAN (St Goranus) w Caerhays *Truro 1*   **P** *Bp*
  P-in-c E B L BROWNING,   **NSM** M MURFITT
ST HELENS (St Helen) (St Catherine by the Green) *Portsm 7*
  P *Bp*   **V** M M STRANGE
ST HELENS Town Centre (St Helen) (Barton Street Mission)
  (St Andrew) (St Mark) (St Thomas) *Liv 10*   **P** *Patr Bd*
  TR D D EASTWOOD,   **TV** C R SMITH, W J J MATTHEWS

ST HELIER (St Peter) (Bishop Andrewes Church) *S'wark 23*
  P *Bp* V H WONG, C K J LEWIS
ST HILARY (St Hilary) *see* Ludgvan, Marazion, St Hilary and
  Perranuthnoe *Truro*
ST ILLOGAN (St Illogan) *Truro 2* P *Ch Soc Trust*
  R M J KIPPAX, C S CLIFTON, NSM P I TREMELLING,
  R G SELBY-BOOTHROYD
ST IPPOLYTS (St Ippolyts) w Great and Little Wymondley
  St Alb 3 P *Bp and MMCET (jt)* R A E J POLLINGTON
ST ISSEY (St Issey) *see* St Merryn and St Issey w St Petroc
  Minor *Truro*
ST IVE (St Ive) and Pensilva w Quethiock *Truro 12* P *Bp*
  (1 turn), The Crown (2 turns) C P R SHARPE,
  K LANYON JONES
ST IVES (All Saints) *Ely 12* P *Guild of All So* V J M AMEY
ST IVES (St Ia the Virgin) *Truro 5* P *V Lelant*
  P-in-c A S GOUGH, C D GALANZINO
ST JOHN (St John the Baptist) w Millbrook *Truro 11* P *Bp and*
  Col Sir John Carew-Pole Bt (alt) P-in-c T E THOMAS
ST JOHN-AT-HACKNEY *Lon 5* P *Bp, Adn, and Lord Amherst*
  of Hackney (jt) R R J WICKHAM, NSM J M KING,
  S C EJIAKU, L HARVEY
ST JOHN IN BEDWARDINE (St John the Baptist) *Worc 3*
  P *D&C* P-in-c C J STUART
ST JOHN IN WEARDALE (St John the Baptist) *see* Upper
  Weardale *Dur*
ST JOHN LEE (St John of Beverley) *Newc 10* P *Viscount*
  Allendale R J J T THOMPSON
ST JOHN ON BETHNAL GREEN *Lon 7* P *Patr Bd*
  TR A J E GREEN, C F J GREEN, NSM R R R O'CALLAGHAN,
  S M LEE
ST JOHN'S-IN-THE-VALE (St John), St Mary's Threlkeld and
  Wythburn *Carl 6* P *Bp, Adn, V Crosthwaite, and Earl of*
  Lonsdale (jt) R B ROTHWELL
ST JOHN'S WOOD (St John) *Lon 4* P *Bp* V A K BERGQUIST,
  C O J DOBSON
ST JOHN'S WOOD (St Mark) *see* St Marylebone St Mark
  Hamilton Terrace *Lon*
ST JULIOT (St Julitta) *see* Boscastle w Davidstow *Truro*
ST JUST IN PENWITH (St Just) *Truro 5* P *Ld Chan*
  V S W LEACH
ST JUST-IN-ROSELAND (St Just) and St Mawes *Truro 6*
  P *A M J Galsworthy Esq* P-in-c K J BOULLIER
ST KEVERNE (St Keverne) *Truro 4* P *CPAS* V *vacant*
  (01326) 280227
ST KEW (St James the Great) *see* St Endellion w Port Isaac and
  St Kew *Truro*
ST KEYNE (St Keyna) *see* Liskeard and St Keyne *Truro*
ST LAURENCE in the Isle of Thanet (St Laurence) *Cant 5*
  P *Patr Bd* TR S IRELAND, TV O I AOKO, C L J W DEAN,
  NSM D VAN K VANNERLEY
ST LAWRENCE (Old Church) (St Lawrence) *Portsm 7* P *Bp*
  R *vacant*
ST LAWRENCE (St Lawrence) *see* Bradwell on Sea and St
  Lawrence *Chelmsf*
ST LEONARD (St Leonard) *see* Hawridge w Cholesbury and
  St Leonard *Ox*
ST LEONARDS and St Ives (All Saints) *Win 9* P *Bp*
  V J MORTON
ST LEONARDS (Christ Church and St Mary Magdalen)
  Chich 17 P *Bp and Trustees (jt)* R R A JUPP,
  NSM R G RALPH
ST LEONARDS, UPPER (St John the Evangelist) *Chich 17*
  P *Trustees* R A J PERRY, NSM J N HARTMAN
ST LEONARDS-ON-SEA (St Leonard) (St Ethelburga)
  Chich 17 P *Hyndman Trustees* R M J MILLS, Hon
  C E V WHEELER, W D BOULTON
ST LEONARDS-ON-SEA (St Matthew) *see* Silverhill St Matt
  Chich
ST LEONARDS-ON-SEA (St Peter and St Paul) *Chich 17*
  P *Bp* V *vacant* (01424) 445606
ST LEVAN (St Levan) *see* St Buryan, St Levan and Sennen
  Truro
ST MABYN (St Mabena) *see* St Tudy w St Mabyn and
  Michaelstow *Truro*
ST MARGARET'S (St Margaret) *see* Clodock and Longtown
  w Craswall, Llanveynoe etc *Heref*
ST MARGARETS-AT-CLIFFE (St Margaret of Antioch) w
  Westcliffe and East Langdon w West Langdon *Cant 7* P *Abp*
  Hon C D E FAWCETT
ST MARGARET'S-ON-THAMES (All Souls) *Lon 11* P *Bp*
  V R S FRANK, C C E C HUDSON, C O LINDSAY
ST MARTHA-ON-THE-HILL (St Martha) *see* Guildf Ch Ch
  w St Martha-on-the-Hill *Guildf*
ST MARTIN (St Martin) w Looe St Nicholas *Truro 12* P *Bp*
  and Revd W M M Picken (jt) R *vacant* (01503) 263070

ST MARTIN-IN-MENEAGE (St Martin) *see* Meneage *Truro*
ST MARTIN-IN-THE-FIELDS *Lon 3* P *Bp* C K HEDDERLY,
  R A CARTER, Hon C D R JACKSON, NSM W H MORRIS,
  P F HULLAH
ST MARTIN'S (St Martin) *see* Is of Scilly *Truro*
ST MARTINS (St Martin) and Weston Rhyn *Lich 19* P *Bp*
  (2 turns), Bp and Lord Trevor (1 turn) V S J JERMY
ST MARY ABBOTS *see* Kensington St Mary Abbots w Ch Ch
  and St Phil *Lon*
ST MARY-AT-LATTON Harlow *Chelmsf 25*
  P *J L H Arkwright Esq* V L S HURRY
ST MARY BOURNE (St Peter) *see* Hurstbourne Priors,
  Longparish etc *Win*
ST MARY CRAY and St Paul's (St Paulinus) Cray *Roch 16*
  P *Bp* V *vacant* (01689) 827697
ST MARY LE STRAND w St Clement Danes *Lon 3* P *Ld Chan*
  and Burley Ho Preservation Trust (alt) R *vacant* (020) 7405
  1929
ST MARYCHURCH (St Mary the Virgin) *Ex 12* P *D&C*
  C D L BRACEY
ST MARYLEBONE (All Saints) *Lon 4* P *Bp* V L A MOSES,
  C J A PRITCHARD
ST MARYLEBONE (All Souls) *see* Langham Place All So *Lon*
ST MARYLEBONE (Annunciation) Bryanston Street *Lon 4*
  P *Bp* P-in-c G C BEAUCHAMP, NSM S-H CHOI
ST MARYLEBONE (St Cyprian) *Lon 4* P *Bp*
  P-in-c G C BEAUCHAMP, NSM J BROWNING
ST MARYLEBONE (St Mark) Hamilton Terrace *Lon 4*
  P *The Crown* V A S G PLATTEN
ST MARYLEBONE (St Mark w St Luke) *see* Bryanston Square
  St Mary w St Marylebone St Mark *Lon*
ST MARYLEBONE (St Marylebone) (Holy Trinity) *Lon 4*
  P *The Crown* R S J EVANS, NSM R C D MACKENNA
ST MARYLEBONE (St Paul) *Lon 4* P *Prime Min*
  R G M BUCKLE, NSM M J REDMAN, D HART
ST MARYLEBONE (St Peter) *see* Langham Place All So *Lon*
ST MARY'S (St Mary) *see* Is of Scilly *Truro*
ST MARY'S BAY (All Saints) w St Mary-in-the-Marsh (St Mary
  the Virgin) and Ivychurch *Cant 11* P *Abp* V *vacant* (01797)
  362308
ST MARY'S ISLAND *see* Gillingham St Mark *Roch*
ST MAWES (St Mawes) *see* St Just-in-Roseland and St Mawes
  Truro
ST MAWGAN (St Mawgan) w St Ervan and St Eval *Truro 7*
  P *D&C and Bp (alt)* R *vacant* (01637) 860023
ST MAWGAN-IN-MENEAGE (St Mawgan) *see* Meneage
  Truro
ST MELLION (St Melanus) *see* St Dominic, Landulph and
  St Mellion w Pillaton *Truro*
ST MERRYN (St Merryn) and St Issey w St Petroc Minor
  Truro 7 P *Bp and Keble Coll Ox (jt)* R J M WILKINSON,
  C S E HOSKING
ST MEWAN (St Mewan) w Mevagissey and St Ewe *Truro 1*
  P *Bp, DBP, Penrice Ho (St Austell) Ltd, and*
  A M J Galsworthy Esq (jt) R M L BARRETT,
  NSM R H GRIGG
ST MICHAEL PENKEVIL (St Michael) *Truro 6* P *Viscount*
  Falmouth P-in-c A M YATES, NSM A L BUTCHER
ST MICHAEL ROCK (St Michael) *see* St Minver *Truro*
ST MICHAELCHURCH (St Michael) *see* Alfred Jewel *B & W*
ST MICHAELS-ON-WYRE (St Michael) *see* Garstang St
  Helen and St Michaels-on-Wyre *Blackb*
ST MINVER (St Menefreda) *Truro 10* P *DBP*
  P-in-c J A C MAY, C J R MOSEDALE, NSM J POLLINGER,
  A D E LEWIS
ST NECTAN (St Nectan) *see* Lostwithiel, St Winnow w
  St Nectan's Chpl etc *Truro*
ST NEOT (St Neot) and Warleggan w Cardynham *Truro 12*
  P *R G Grylls Esq (2 turns), J Coode Esq (1 turn), and DBP*
  (1 turn) R A C R BALFOUR
ST NEOTS (St Mary) *Ely 13* P *P W Rowley Esq*
  P-in-c P D ANDREWS, C S C GOWER
ST NEWLYN EAST (St Newlina) *see* Newlyn St Newlyn *Truro*
ST NICHOLAS (St Nicholas) *see* Shaldon, Stokeinteignhead,
  Combeinteignhead etc *Ex*
ST NICHOLAS AT WADE (St Nicholas) w Sarre and Chislet w
  Hoath *Cant 4* P *Abp* P-in-c R R COLES, NSM R D PLANT,
  A MCCALL, OLM J A BAKER
ST OSWALD IN LEE w Bingfield (St Mary) *Newc 8* P *Bp*
  P-in-c C F BULL
ST OSYTH (St Peter and St Paul) *Chelmsf 22* P *Bp*
  P-in-c S E A MILES
ST PANCRAS (Holy Cross) (St Jude) (St Peter) *Lon 17* P *Bp*
  P-in-c C W CAWRSE, NSM W NORWOOD
ST PANCRAS (Holy Trinity) *see* Kentish Town St Silas and H
  Trin w St Barn *Lon*

ST PANCRAS (Old Church) *Lon 17* **P** *Patr Bd*
TR P J NORTH, **TV** B BATSTONE, J F CASTER,
C G A COOPER, **NSM** J I ELSTON, M R DUCKETT, S J ATKINSON
ST PANCRAS (St Martin) *see* Kentish Town St Martin w
St Andr *Lon*
ST PANCRAS (St Pancras) (St James) (Christ Church) *Lon 17*
P *D&C St Paul's* **V** P H W HAWKINS, **C** J L WELSH
ST PAUL'S CRAY (St Barnabas) *Roch 16* **P** *CPAS*
V A E DAVIE, **Hon C** J E RAWLING
ST PAUL'S WALDEN (All Saints) *St Alb 3* **P** *D&C St Paul's*
P-in-c M A H RODEN, **NSM** E BUNKER
ST PETER in the Isle of Thanet (St Peter the Apostle) *Cant 5*
P *Abp* **V** J G CRUICKSHANK
ST PETER-UPON-CORNHILL *see* St Pet Cornhill *Lon*
ST PETER'S HOUSE (extra-parochial place) *Man 1* vacant
ST PETROC MINOR (St Petroc) *see* St Merryn and St Issey w
St Petroc Minor *Truro*
ST PINNOCK (St Pinnock) *see* Duloe, Herodsfoot, Morval and
St Pinnock *Truro*
ST RUAN w St Grade and Landewednack *Truro 4* **P** *CPAS and*
A F Vyvyan-Robinson Esq (jt) **R** vacant (01326) 291011
ST SAMPSON (St Sampson) *Truro 1* **P** *Bp*
P-in-c P DE GREY-WARTER
ST STEPHEN IN BRANNEL (not known) *Truro 1* **P** *Capt*
J D G Fortescue **P-in-c** E J WESTERMANN-CHILDS
ST STEPHENS (St Stephen) *see* Saltash *Truro*
ST STYTHIANS w Perranarworthal and Gwennap *Truro 2*
P *Viscount Falmouth (2 turns), D&C (1 turn)*
P-in-c P J KNIBBS, **C** A T NEAL, **Hon C** D R CARRIVICK,
NSM H V SPONG, N J POTTER, **OLM** L R T BARTER
ST TEATH (St Teatha) *Truro 10* **P** *Bp*
P-in-c M J W BENTON-EVANS, **C** D A ROBERTS
ST TUDY (St Tudy) w St Mabyn and Michaelstow *Truro 10*
P *Ch Ch Ox, Viscount Falmouth, and Duchy of Cornwall*
(by turn) **R** vacant (01208) 850374
ST VEEP (St Cyricius) *see* Lostwithiel, St Winnow w
St Nectan's Chpl etc *Truro*
ST WENN (St Wenna) *see* St Columb Major w St Wenn *Truro*
ST WEONARDS (St Weonard) *Heref 7* **P** *Bp, D&C, and*
MMCET (jt) **R** E C GODDARD
ST WINNOW (St Winnow) *see* Lostwithiel, St Winnow w
St Nectan's Chpl etc *Truro*
SALCOMBE (Holy Trinity) and Malborough w South Huish
Ex 14 **P** *Keble Coll Ox and D&C Sarum (jt)* **V** D A FRENCH,
Hon C E F CULLY, A K HAYE
SALCOMBE REGIS (St Mary and St Peter) *see* Sidmouth,
Woolbrook, Salcombe Regis, Sidbury etc *Ex*
SALCOT VIRLEY (St Mary the Virgin) *see* N Blackwater
Chelmsf
SALE (St Anne) (St Francis's Church Hall) *Ches 10* **P** *DBP*
V J R HEATON, **C** G G COHEN
SALE (St Paul) *Ches 10* **P** *Trustees* **V** vacant 0161-973 1042
SALE, WEST *see* Ashton-upon-Mersey St Mary Magd *Ches*
SALEBY (St Margaret) w Beesby and Maltby *Linc 8* **P** *Bp and*
DBP (jt) **R** vacant
SALEHURST (St Mary) *Chich 15* **P** *Bp* **V** J A LUSTED
SALESBURY (St Peter) *Blackb 7* **P** *V Blackb*
V J W HARTLEY, **NSM** A A MALCOLM
SALFORD All Saints *Man 20* **P** *Patr Bd* **TR** M N HAWORTH,
TV I C J GORTON, **C** J ELCOCK, **OLM** J I WHITTINGHAM
SALFORD (Sacred Trinity) (St Philip) *Man 20* **P** *D&C Man*
and Sir Josslyn Gore-Booth Bt (jt) **P-in-c** A I SALMON,
NSM R C CRAVEN
SALFORD (St Clement) Ordsall *see* Ordsall and Salford Quays
Man
SALFORD (St Ignatius and Stowell Memorial) *as above*
SALFORD (St Mary) *see* Chipping Norton *Ox*
SALFORD (St Mary) *see* Cranfield and Hulcote w Salford
St Alb
SALFORD (St Paul w Christ Church) *Man 20* **P** *The Crown*
and Trustees (alt) **R** D S C WYATT
SALFORD PRIORS (St Matthew) *Cov 7* **P** *Peache Trustees*
P-in-c P A WALKER, **C** R E WALKER, **NSM** L E DAVIES,
K GRUMBALL
SALFORDS (Christ the King) *S'wark 26* **P** *Bp* **V** P KEOWN
SALHOUSE (All Saints) *see* Rackheath and Salhouse *Nor*
SALING, GREAT (St James) *see* Stebbing and Lindsell w Gt
and Lt Saling *Chelmsf*
SALING, LITTLE (St Peter and St Paul) *as above*
SALISBURY (St Francis) and St Lawrence Stratford sub Castle
Sarum 12 **P** *Bp (3 turns), D&C (1 turn)* **V** P F D TAYLOR,
C G A HUNT, V S PERRETT, P A OSTLI-EAST, **Hon C** P A JOYCE,
NSM T G MANN
SALISBURY (St Mark) *Sarum 12* **P** *Bp* **P-in-c** J FINDLAY,
C M P CASTLETON, **NSM** T A FISHER, **OLM** J P OFFER

SALISBURY (St Martin) and Laverstock *Sarum 13* **P** *D&C*
and Bp (alt) **R** vacant (01722) 504813 *or* 503123
SALISBURY (St Paul) *see* Fisherton Anger *Sarum*
SALISBURY (St Thomas and St Edmund) *Sarum 12* **P** *Bp and*
D&C (alt) **P-in-c** D J J R LINAKER, **C** B J DAVIES,
NSM J PLOWS
SALKELD, GREAT (St Cuthbert) *see* Kirkoswald, Renwick,
Gt Salkeld and Lazonby *Carl*
SALLE (St Peter and St Paul) *see* Reepham, Hackford w
Whitwell, Kerdiston etc *Nor*
SALT (St James the Great) *see* Mid Trent *Lich*
SALTASH (St Nicholas and St Faith) *Truro 11* **P** *Patr Bd*
TR A BUTLER, **TV** M A J DAVIES, **NSM** P M SELLIX,
D BURROWS
SALTBURN-BY-THE-SEA (Emmanuel) *York 16* **P** *Abp, Adn*
Cleveland, Marquis of Zetland, Mrs M Brignall, and
Mrs S L Vernon (jt) **V** A M F REED
SALTBY (St Peter) *see* High Framland Par *Leic*
SALTDEAN (St Nicholas) *Chich 2* **P** *Bp*
V G J BUTTERWORTH
SALTER STREET (St Patrick) and Shirley *Birm 6* **P** *Patr Bd*
TR M G B C CADDY, **TV** S J HEIGHT, **C** K E STOWE
SALTERHEBBLE (All Saints) *see* Halifax All SS *Wakef*
SALTERSFORD (St John the Baptist) *see* Rainow w
Saltersford and Forest *Ches*
SALTFLEETBY (St Peter) *Linc 12* **P** *Or Coll Ox, Bp, and*
MMCET (jt) **P-in-c** C M TURNER
SALTFORD (Blessed Virgin Mary) w Corston and Newton
St Loe *B & W 9* **P** *DBP (2 turns), Duchy of Cornwall (1 turn)*
R G R W HALL, **C** C A SOURBUT
SALTHOUSE (St Nicholas) *see* Weybourne Gp *Nor*
SALTLEY (St Saviour) and Washwood Heath *Birm 13* **P** *Bp*
and Trustees (jt) **C** A THOMPSON
SALTNEY FERRY (St Matthew) *see* Lache cum Saltney *Ches*
SALTON (St John of Beverley) *see* Kirby Misperton w
Normanby, Edston and Salton *York*
SALTWOOD (St Peter and St Paul) *Cant 8* **P** *Abp*
P-in-c N COOPER, **NSM** P F HILL
SALVINGTON (St Peter) *see* Durrington *Chich*
SALWARPE (St Michael) and Hindlip w Martin Hussingtree
Worc 8 **P** *Bp, D&C, and Exors Lady Hindlip (by turn)*
P-in-c D C OWEN
SALWAY ASH (Holy Trinity) *see* Beaminster Area *Sarum*
SAMBOURNE (Mission Church) *see* Coughton *Cov*
SAMBROOK (St Luke) *see* Cheswardine, Childs Ercall, Hales,
Hinstock etc *Lich*
SAMFORD, NORTH *see* Sproughton w Burstall, Copdock w
Washbrook etc *St E*
SAMLESBURY (St Leonard the Less) *see* Walton-le-Dale
St Leon w Samlesbury St Leon *Blackb*
SAMPFORD, GREAT (St Michael) *see* The Sampfords and
Radwinter w Hempstead *Chelmsf*
SAMPFORD, LITTLE (St Mary) *as above*
SAMPFORD ARUNDEL (Holy Cross) *see* Wellington and
Distr *B & W*
SAMPFORD BRETT (St George) *see* Quantock Towers *B & W*
SAMPFORD COURTENAY (St Andrew) *see* N Tawton,
Bondleigh, Sampford Courtenay etc *Ex*
SAMPFORD PEVERELL (St John the Baptist), Uplowman,
Holcombe Rogus, Hockworthy, Burlescombe and Halberton w
Ash Thomas *Ex 4* **P** *Patr Bd* **TR** S J BLADE
SAMPFORD SPINEY (St Mary) w Horrabridge *Ex 25*
P *D&C Windsor* **R** vacant (01822) 855198
SAMPFORDS, The (St Michael) (St Mary) and Radwinter with
Hempstead *Chelmsf 21* **P** *Guild of All So, New Coll Ox, and*
Keble Coll Ox (jt) **P-in-c** G M MANN
SANCREED (St Creden) *Truro 5* **P** *D&C* **V** S W LEACH
SANCTON (All Saints) *York 5* **P** *Abp* **V** D J EVERETT
SAND HILL (Church of the Good Shepherd) *see* N
Farnborough *Guildf*
SAND HUTTON (St Leonard) *see* Thirsk *York*
SAND HUTTON (St Mary) *York 6* **P** *Abp and D&C Dur (jt)*
P-in-c I R HOWITT
SANDAL (St Catherine) *Wakef 11* **P** *V Sandal Magna*
P-in-c H M COLLINGS
SANDAL MAGNA (St Helen) *Wakef 11* **P** *Peache Trustees*
V R G MARTIN
SANDBACH (St Mary) *Ches 11* **P** *DBP* **V** T SHEPHERD
SANDBACH HEATH (St John the Evangelist) w Wheelock
Ches 11 **P** *V Sandbach* **V** J A BACON
SANDBANKS (St Nicolas) *see* Canford Cliffs and Sandbanks
Sarum
SANDERSTEAD (All Saints) (St Antony) (St Edmund the King
and Martyr) (St Mary) *S'wark 22* **P** *Bp* **TR** S BUTLER,
TV J F PERCIVAL, S F ATKINSON-JONES, **C** A M WATSON,
NSM R T FORD

SANDFORD (All Saints) *see* Winscombe and Sandford *B & W*
SANDFORD (St Martin) *see* Westcote Barton w Steeple Barton, Duns Tew etc *Ox*
SANDFORD (St Martin) *see* Wareham *Sarum*
SANDFORD (St Swithin) *see* Crediton, Shobrooke and Sandford etc *Ex*
SANDFORD-ON-THAMES (St Andrew) *Ox 4* **P** *DBP* **P-in-c** R C MORGAN
SANDFORD ORCAS (St Nicholas) *see* Queen Thorne *Sarum*
SANDGATE (St Paul) *see* Folkestone Trin *Cant*
SANDHURST (Mission Church) *see* Benenden and Sandhurst *Cant*
SANDHURST (St Lawrence) *see* Twigworth, Down Hatherley, Norton, The Leigh etc *Glouc*
SANDHURST (St Michael and All Angels) *Ox 16* **P** *Bp* **R** J A CASTLE
SANDHURST (St Nicholas) *see* Benenden and Sandhurst *Cant*
SANDHURST, LOWER (St Mary) *see* Sandhurst *Ox*
SANDHUTTON (St Leonard) *see* Thirsk *York*
SANDIACRE (St Giles) *Derby 13* **P** *Ld Chan* **NSM** K W G JOHNSON
SANDIWAY (St John the Evangelist) *Ches 6* **P** *Bp* **V** R J HUGHES
SANDLEHEATH (St Aldhelm) *see* Fordingbridge and Breamore and Hale etc *Win*
SANDON (All Saints) *see* Mid Trent *Lich*
SANDON (All Saints), Wallington and Rushden w Clothall *St Alb 16* **P** *Duchy of Lanc (1 turn), Marquess of Salisbury (1 turn), and Bp (2 turns)* **P-in-c** C KIMBERLEY, C S TETZLAFF
SANDON (St Andrew) *Chelmsf 9* **P** *Qu Coll Cam* **P-in-c** C A ASHLEY, P PENNELL
SANDOWN (Christ Church) *Portsm 7* **P** *Ch Patr Trust* **P-in-c** C M FEAK, C N J PORTER, NSM T B RICHARDS
SANDOWN, LOWER (St John the Evangelist) *Portsm 7* **P** *Bp* **P-in-c** C M FEAK, C N J PORTER, NSM T B RICHARDS
SANDRIDGE (St Leonard) *St Alb 7* **P** *Earl Spencer* **P-in-c** V G CATO, NSM J F HILLIER
SANDRINGHAM (St Mary Magdalene) w West Newton and Appleton, Wolferton w Babingley and Flitcham *Nor 16* **P** *The Crown* **R** J B V RIVIERE
SANDS (Church of the Good Shepherd) *see* Seale, Puttenham and Wanborough *Guildf*
SANDS (St Mary and St George) *see* High Wycombe *Ox*
SANDSEND (St Mary) *see* Hinderwell, Roxby and Staithes etc *York*
SANDSFIELD *see* Carl H Trin and St Barn *Carl*
SANDWELL (St Philip) *see* W Bromwich St Phil *Lich*
SANDWICH (St Clement) *Cant 9* **P** *Adn Cant* **R** J M A ROBERTS, NSM J C ROBERTS, R A BENDALL, OLM H T PASHLEY
SANDY (St Swithun) *St Alb 10* **P** *Lord Pym* **R** D G WILLIAMS
SANDY LANE (St Mary and St Nicholas) *see* Rowde and Bromham *Sarum*
SANDYLANDS (St John) *Blackb 11* **P** *Bp* **V** L MACLUSKIE
SANKEY, GREAT (St Mary) *Liv 12* **P** *Lord Lilford* **V** M BUCKLEY, NSM P J TURNER
SANTAN (St Sanctain) *S & M 1* **P** *The Crown* **V** P C ROBINSON
SANTON DOWNHAM (St Mary the Virgin) *see* Brandon and Santon Downham w Elveden etc *St E*
SAPCOTE (All Saints) and Sharnford w Wigston Parva *Leic 10* **P** *Ld Chan and DBP (alt)* **R** M J NORMAN
SAPEY, UPPER (St Michael) *see* Edvin Loach w Tedstone Delamere etc *Heref*
SAPPERTON (St Kenelm) *see* Kemble, Poole Keynes, Somerford Keynes etc *Glouc*
SAPPERTON (St Nicholas) *see* N Beltisloe Gp *Linc*
SARISBURY (St Paul) *Portsm 2* **P** *V Titchfield* **V** A J MATHESON
SARK (St Peter) *Win 14* **P** *Le Seigneur de Sercq* **P-in-c** K P MELLOR
SARN (Holy Trinity) *see* Churchstoke w Hyssington and Sarn *Heref*
SARNESFIELD (St Mary) *see* Weobley w Sarnesfield and Norton Canon *Heref*
SARRATT (Holy Cross) and Chipperfield *St Alb 4* **P** *Churchwardens and DBP (jt)* **R** J A STEVENS
SATLEY (St Cuthbert), Stanley and Tow Law *Dur 9* **P** *Bp, Ld Chan, and R Brancepeth (by turn)* **P-in-c** J P L WHALLEY, Hon C G H LAWES
SATTERTHWAITE (All Saints) *see* Hawkshead and Low Wray w Sawrey and Rusland etc *Carl*
SAUGHALL, GREAT (All Saints) *Ches 9* **P** *Bp* **P-in-c** J B HARRIS, NSM H M PANG

SAUL (St James the Great) *see* Frampton on Severn, Arlingham, Saul etc *Glouc*
SAUNDERTON (St Mary and St Nicholas) *see* Risborough *Ox*
SAUNTON (St Anne) *see* Braunton *Ex*
SAUSTHORPE (St Andrew) *see* Partney Gp *Linc*
SAVERNAKE (St Katharine) *Sarum 19* **P** *Patr Bd* **TR** N A LEIGH-HUNT, **TV** M EDWARDS, R L N HARRISON, NSM R A GRIST
SAW MILLS (St Mary) *see* Ambergate and Heage *Derby*
SAWBRIDGEWORTH (Great St Mary) *St Alb 15* **P** *Bp* **V** R F SIBSON, C R W WYNFORD-HARRIS
SAWLEY (All Saints) (St Mary) *Derby 13* **P** *D&C Lich* **R** A C M PETTY, C C E MCDONALD
SAWLEY (St Michael) *see* Fountains Gp *Ripon*
SAWREY (St Peter) *see* Hawkshead and Low Wray w Sawrey and Rusland etc *Carl*
SAWSTON (St Mary) *Ely 5* **P** *SMF* **P-in-c** A C PARTRIDGE
SAWTRY (All Saints) and Glatton *Ely 15* **P** *Duke of Devonshire* **R** vacant (01487) 830215
SAXBY (St Helen) *see* Owmby Gp *Linc*
SAXBY ALL SAINTS (All Saints) *Linc 6* **P** F C H H Barton Esq **R** D P ROWETT
SAXELBYE (St Peter) *see* Old Dalby, Nether Broughton, Saxelbye etc *Leic*
SAXHAM, GREAT (St Andrew) *see* Barrow *St E*
SAXHAM, LITTLE (St Nicholas) *as above*
SAXILBY Group, The (St Botolph) *Linc 2* **P** *Bp and DBP (jt)* **R** R PROSSER, C A B BARTON, NSM S PROSSER, OLM J A VICKERS
SAXLINGHAM (St Margaret) *see* Stiffkey and Bale *Nor*
SAXLINGHAM NETHERGATE (St Mary) *see* Newton Flotman, Swainsthorpe, Tasburgh, etc *Nor*
SAXMUNDHAM (St John the Baptist) w Kelsale cum Carlton *St E 19* **P** *Patr Bd* **R** A J WOLTON
SAXON SHORE *see* Hunstanton St Mary w Ringstead Parva etc *Nor*
SAXONWELL *Linc 22* **P** *Duchy of Lanc (2 turns), Ld Chan (1 turn)* **P-in-c** M E MASSEY
SAXTEAD (All Saints) *see* Framlingham w Saxtead *St E*
SAXTHORPE (St Andrew) *see* Lt Barningham, Blickling, Edgefield etc *Nor*
SAXTON (All Saints) *see* Sherburn in Elmet w Saxton *York*
SAYERS COMMON (Christ Church) *see* Albourne w Sayers Common and Twineham *Chich*
SCALBY (St Laurence) *York 15* **P** *Abp* **P-in-c** A J FERNELEY, NSM M J WRIGHT, D C PYNN
SCALDWELL (St Peter and St Paul) *see* Walgrave w Hannington and Wold and Scaldwell *Pet*
SCALEBY (All Saints) *see* Eden, Gelt and Irthing *Carl*
SCALFORD (St Egelwin) *see* Ironstone Villages *Leic*
SCAMMONDEN, WEST (St Bartholomew) *see* Barkisland w W Scammonden *Wakef*
SCAMPSTON (St Martin) *see* Buckrose Carrs *York*
SCAMPTON (St John the Baptist) *see* Spring Line Gp *Linc*
SCARBOROUGH (St Columba) *York 15* **P** *Abp* **P-in-c** K D JACKSON
SCARBOROUGH (St James w Holy Trinity) *York 15* **P** *Abp and CPAS (jt)* **P-in-c** P W WHITE, NSM L M HOLLIS
SCARBOROUGH (St Luke) *York 15* **P** *Abp* **P-in-c** A J FERNELEY, NSM D C PYNN
SCARBOROUGH (St Mark) *see* Newby *York*
SCARBOROUGH (St Martin) *York 15* **P** *Trustees* **P-in-c** D M DIXON, NSM R G C COSTIN
SCARBOROUGH (St Mary) w Christ Church and (Holy Apostles) *York 15* **P** *Abp* **V** M P DUNNING, C S WHITING, NSM P JENNINGS
SCARBOROUGH (St Saviour w All Saints) *York 15* **P** *Abp* **P-in-c** D M DIXON
SCARCLIFFE (St Leonard) *see* Ault Hucknall and Scarcliffe *Derby*
SCARISBRICK (St Mark) (Good Shepherd) *Liv 11* **P** *V Ormskirk* **P-in-c** E P TODD
SCARLE, NORTH (All Saints) *see* Swinderby *Linc*
SCARLE, SOUTH (St Helena) *see* E Trent *S'well*
SCARNING (St Peter and St Paul) *see* Dereham and Distr *Nor*
SCARRINGTON (St John of Beverley) *see* Whatton w Aslockton, Hawksworth, Scarrington etc *S'well*
SCARSDALE, EAST *Derby 3* **P** *Patr Bd* **TR** J W HARGREAVES, **TV** B DALE
SCARTHO (St Giles) St Matthew *Linc 9* **P** *Jes Coll Ox* **R** E J R MARTIN
SCAWBY (St Hybald), Redbourne and Hibaldstow *Linc 6* **P** T M S Nelthorpe Esq (2 turns), Bp (1 turn), and Duke of St Alb (1 turn) **V** vacant (01652) 652725
SCAWTHORPE (St Luke) *see* Doncaster St Leon and St Jude *Sheff*

SCAWTON (St Mary)   *see* Upper Ryedale *York*
SCAYNES HILL (St Augustine) *Chich 6*   **P** *Bp*
P-in-c L H BARNETT
SCHOLES (St Philip)   *see* Barwick in Elmet *Ripon*
SCHOLES (St Philip and St James) *Wakef 8*   **P** *Bp*
P-in-c E C R BURGE
SCHORNE *Ox 24*   **P** *Patr Bd (2 turns), Ld Chan (1 turn)*
TV V M CRUDDAS,   **P-in-c** D J MEAKIN,   **Hon C** P D MEARS,
OLM J BAYLY
SCILLY   *see* Is of Scilly *Truro*
SCISSETT (St Augustine)   *see* High Hoyland, Scissett and
Clayton W *Wakef*
SCOFTON (St John the Evangelist)   *see* Retford Area *S'well*
SCOLE (St Andrew) w Brockdish, Billingford, Thorpe Abbots and
Thorpe Parva *Nor 10*   **P** *Bp, Ex Coll Ox, MMCET, Adn
Norfolk, and Exors Lady Mann (jt)*   **P-in-c** T W RIESS
SCOPWICK (Holy Cross)   *see* Digby Gp *Linc*
SCORBOROUGH (St Leonard)   *see* Lockington and Lund and
Scorborough w Leconfield *York*
SCORTON (St Peter) and Barnacre All Saints and Calder Vale
St John the Evangelist *Blackb 9*   **P** *Bp, V Lanc St Mary w St Jo
and St Anne, and Mrs V O Shepherd-Cross (jt)*
P-in-c D V A BROWN
SCOT WILLOUGHBY (St Andrew)   *see* S Lafford *Linc*
SCOTBY (All Saints) and Cotehill w Cumwhinton *Carl 2*
P *Trustees (2 turns), Prime Min (1 turn)*   **V** G M CREGEEN,
C T D HERBERT,   **NSM** S HOLMES
SCOTFORTH (St Paul) *Blackb 11*   **P** *The Rt Revd J Nicholls*
V M A GISBOURNE,   **C** O TRELENBERG
SCOTHERN (St Germain)   *see* Welton and Dunholme w
Scothern *Linc*
SCOTSWOOD (St Margaret) *Newc 4*   **P** *Bp*   **V** *vacant*
0191-274 6322
SCOTTER (St Peter) w East Ferry *Linc 4*   **P** *Bp*   **R** *vacant*
(01724) 762951
SCOTTON (St Genewys) w Northorpe *Linc 4*   **P** *Ld Chan*
P-in-c M E BURSON-THOMAS,   **OLM** W KEAST, D L LANGFORD
SCOTTON (St Thomas)   *see* Walkingham Hill *Ripon*
SCOTTOW (All Saints)   *see* Worstead, Westwick, Sloley,
Swanton Abbot etc *Nor*
SCOULTON (Holy Trinity)   *see* High Oak, Hingham and
Scoulton w Wood Rising *Nor*
SCRAMBLESBY (St Martin)   *see* Asterby Gp *Linc*
SCRAPTOFT (All Saints) *Leic 1*   **P** *Bp, Dr M J A Sharp, and
DBP (jt)*   **V** M J COURT,   **NSM** A J POOLE
SCRAYINGHAM (St Peter and St Paul)   *see* Stamford Bridge
Gp *York*
SCREDINGTON (St Andrew)   *see* Helpringham w Hale *Linc*
SCREMBY (St Peter and St Paul)   *see* Partney Gp *Linc*
SCREMERSTON (St Peter) *Newc 12*   **P** *Bp*   **P-in-c** M S KNOX
SCREVETON (St Wilfrid)   *see* Car Colston w Screveton *S'well*
SCRIVELSBY (St Benedict)   *see* Fen and Hill Gp *Linc*
SCROOBY (St Wilfrid)   *see* Blyth and Scrooby w Ranskill *S'well*
SCROPTON (St Paul)   *see* S Dales *Derby*
SCRUTON (St Radegund)   *see* Lower Swale *Ripon*
SCULCOATES (St Mary)   *see* Hull St Mary Sculcoates *York*
SCULCOATES (St Paul) (St Stephen) *York 14*   **P** *Abp and
V Hull H Trin (1 turn), Ld Chan (1 turn)*   **P-in-c** M G CROOK
SCULTHORPE (St Mary and All Saints)   *see* N and S Creake w
Waterden, Syderstone etc *Nor*
SCUNTHORPE (All Saints)   *see* Brumby *Linc*
SCUNTHORPE (The Resurrection)   *see* Trentside E *Linc*
SEA MILLS (St Edyth) *Bris 2*   **P** *Bp*   **V** D A IZZARD,
C A A B PEREIRA,   **NSM** E C BEBB
SEA PALLING (St Margaret)   *see* Bacton, Happisburgh,
Hempstead w Eccles etc *Nor*
SEA VIEW (St Peter) *Portsm 7*   **P** *Bp*   **V** M M STRANGE
SEABOROUGH (St John)   *see* Beaminster Area *Sarum*
SEABROOK (Mission Hall)   *see* Cheriton St Martin *Cant*
SEACOMBE (St Paul) *Ches 7*   **P** *Trustees*   **P-in-c** I HUGHES
SEACROFT (St James) (Church of the Ascension) (St Richard)
Ripon 8   **P** *DBF*   **TR** M P BENWELL,
TV F J HARRISON-SMITH, C BANDAWE, R H JAMIESON
SEAFORD (St Leonard) w Sutton *Chich 18*   **P** *Ld Chan*
V P J OWEN,   **C** M A BLEWETT, C DOHERTY
SEAFORTH (St Thomas)   *see* Bootle *Liv*
SEAGRAVE (All Saints)   *see* Sileby, Cossington and Seagrave
Leic
SEAGRY (St Mary the Virgin)   *see* Gt Somerford, Lt Somerford,
Seagry, Corston etc *Bris*
SEAHAM (St Mary the Virgin) *Dur 2*   **P** *Bp*   **V** *vacant*
0191-581 3385
SEAHAM, NEW (Christ Church)   *see* Dalton le Dale and New
Seaham *Dur*
SEAHAM HARBOUR (St John) and Dawdon *Dur 2*   **P** *Bp*
V P TWISLETON

SEAL (St Lawrence) *Roch 9*   **P** *Bp*   **P-in-c** E C KITCHENER
SEAL (St Peter and St Paul) *Roch 9*   **P** *DBP*
P-in-c J A LE BAS,   **NSM** S T SNELLING
SEALE (St Lawrence), Puttenham and Wanborough *Guildf 4*
P *Adn Surrey, C R I Perkins Esq, and Ld Chan (by turn)*
P-in-c A G HARBIDGE
SEALE (St Peter) (St Matthew) and Lullington w Coton in the
Elms *Derby 16*   **P** *Bp, R D Nielson Esq, and
C W Worthington Esq (jt)*   **R** M A YATES
SEAMER (St Martin) w East Ayton *York 15*   **P** *Abp*
V L J MCWILLIAMS,   **NSM** S R DRURY
SEAMER IN CLEVELAND (St Martin)   *see* Stokesley w
Seamer *York*
SEARBY (St Nicholas)   *see* Caistor Gp *Linc*
SEASALTER (St Alphege)   *see* Whitstable *Cant*
SEASCALE (St Cuthbert) and Drigg *Carl 5*   **P** *DBP*
P-in-c J WOOLCOCK
SEATHWAITE (Holy Trinity)   *see* Broughton and Duddon *Carl*
SEATON (All Hallows)   *see* Lyddington, Bisbrooke, Caldecott,
Glaston etc *Pet*
SEATON (St Gregory) and Beer *Ex 5*   **P** *Lord Clinton and
D&C (jt)*   **V** J C TREW
SEATON (St Paul)   *see* Camerton, Seaton and W Seaton *Carl*
SEATON, WEST (Holy Trinity)   *as above*
SEATON CAREW (Holy Trinity) *Dur 3*   **P** *Bp*
P-in-c P T ALLINSON
SEATON HIRST (St John) (St Andrew) *Newc 11*   **P** *Bp*
R D P PALMER
SEATON ROSS (St Edmund)   *see* Holme and Seaton Ross Gp
York
SEATON SLUICE (St Paul)   *see* Delaval *Newc*
SEAVIEW   *see* Sea View *Portsm*
SEAVINGTON (St Michael and St Mary)   *see* S Petherton w the
Seavingtons *B & W*
SEBERGHAM (St Mary)   *see* Caldbeck, Castle Sowerby and
Sebergham *Carl*
SECKINGTON (All Saints)   *see* N Warks *Birm*
SEDBERGH (St Andrew), Cautley and Garsdale *Bradf 6*   **P** *Trin
Coll Cam*   **V** A W FELL,   **NSM** V J HOPKINS
SEDGEBERROW (St Mary the Virgin)   *see* Hampton w
Sedgeberrow and Hinton-on-the-Green *Worc*
SEDGEBROOK (St Lawrence)   *see* Saxonwell *Linc*
SEDGEFIELD (St Edmund)   *see* Upper Skerne *Dur*
SEDGEHILL (St Katherine)   *see* St Bartholomew *Sarum*
SEDGFORD (St Mary)   *see* Docking, the Birchams, Stanhoe
and Sedgeford *Nor*
SEDGLEY (All Saints)   *see* Gornal and Sedgley *Worc*
SEDGLEY (St Mary the Virgin) *Worc 10*   **P** *Bp and V Sedgley
All SS (jt)*   **P-in-c** S R BUCKLEY,   **NSM** T WESTWOOD
SEDLESCOMBE (St John the Baptist) w Whatlington *Chich 14*
P *Ld Chan and Bp (alt)*   **R** *vacant* (01424) 870233
SEEND (Holy Cross), Bulkington and Poulshot *Sarum 16*
P *D&C (2 turns), Bp (1 turn)*   **P-in-c** R Y COULSON
SEER GREEN (Holy Trinity) and Jordans *Ox 20*   **P** *Bp*
P-in-c G M HOCKEY
SEETHING (St Margaret)   *see* Brooke, Kirstead, Mundham w
Seething and Thwaite *Nor*
SEFTON (St Helen) and Thornton *Liv 5*   **P** *Bp*   **R** I C COWELL,
OLM E M HALBERT
SEFTON PARK (Christ Church)   *see* Toxteth Park Ch Ch and
St Mich w St Andr *Liv*
SEGHILL (Holy Trinity) *Newc 1*   **P** *The Crown*
V P G J HUGHES
SEIGHFORD (St Chad)   *see* Chebsey, Creswell, Ellenhall,
Ranton etc *Lich*
SELATTYN (St Mary) and Hengoed w Gobowen *Lich 19*   **P** *Bp
and Mrs A F Hamilton-Hill (jt)*   **P-in-c** A R BAILEY
SELBORNE (St Mary)   *see* Northanger *Win*
SELBY (St James the Apostle) *York 4*   **P** *Simeon's Trustees*
V C J REID
SELBY ABBEY (St Mary and St Germain) (St Richard) *York 4*
P *Abp*   **V** J C WEETMAN,   **NSM** R N WAINWRIGHT
SELHAM (St James)   *see* Easebourne, Lodsworth and Selham
Chich
SELLACK (St Tysilio)   *see* Wormelow Hundred *Heref*
SELLINDGE (St Mary the Virgin)   *see* Mersham w Hinxhill and
Sellindge *Cant*
SELLING (St Mary the Virgin) w Throwley and Sheldwich w
Badlesmere and Leaveland *Cant 14*   **P** *Abp and D&C (jt)*
P-in-c M G WEBB,   **NSM** M JOHNSON, D S WEBB
SELLY OAK (St Mary) *Birm 2*   **P** *Bp*   **V** J D R COX,
NSM S A IZZARD
SELLY PARK (Christ Church) *Birm 5*   **P** *Trustees*
V G P LANHAM
SELLY PARK (St Stephen) (St Wulstan) *Birm 5*   **P** *Trustees*
V C B HOBBS,   **C** R P LEADBEATER

SELMESTON (St Mary)　*see* Arlington, Berwick, Selmeston w Alciston etc *Chich*

SELSDON (St Francis) Conventional District *S'wark 20* Min　P C WYATT,　NSM　A ONYEKWELU

SELSDON (St John) (St Francis) *S'wark 19*　P *Bp* R　I S BROTHWOOD

SELSEY (St Peter) *Chich 3*　P *Bp*　R *vacant* (01243) 601984

SELSIDE (St Thomas)　*see* Beacon *Carl*

SELSLEY (All Saints)　*see* Cainscross w Selsley *Glouc*

SELSTON (St Helen) *S'well 4*　P *Wright Trustees* P-in-c　M F SHOULER,　NSM　P KEY

SELWORTHY (All Saints)　*see* Porlock and Porlock Weir w Stoke Pero etc *B & W*

SELWORTHY (Lynch Chapel)　*as above*

SEMER (All Saints)　*see* Bildeston w Wattisham and Lindsey, Whatfield etc *St E*

SEMINGTON (St George)　*see* Canalside Benefice *Sarum*

SEMLEY (St Leonard)　*see* St Bartholomew *Sarum*

SEMPRINGHAM (St Andrew)　*see* Billingborough Gp *Linc*

SEND (St Mary the Virgin) *Guildf 12*　P *Bp*　P-in-c　A J SHUTT

SENNEN (St Sennen)　*see* St Buryan, St Levan and Sennen *Truro*

SENNICOTTS (St Mary)　*see* Funtington and Sennicotts *Chich*

SESSAY (St Cuthbert) *York 18*　P *Viscountess Downe* P-in-c　N J CARNALL

SETCHEY (St Mary)　*see* W Winch w Setchey, N Runcton and Middleton *Nor*

SETMURTHY (St Barnabas)　*see* Binsey *Carl*

SETTLE (Holy Ascension) *Bradf 5*　P *Trustees*　V *vacant* (01729) 822288

SETTRINGTON (All Saints)　*see* W Buckrose *York*

SEVEN KINGS　*see* Gt Ilford St Jo *Chelmsf*

SEVEN TOWERS　*see* Twigworth, Down Hatherley, Norton, The Leigh etc *Glouc*

SEVENHAMPTON (St Andrew) w Charlton Abbots, Hawling and Whittington, Dowdeswell and Andoversford w The Shiptons and Cold Salperton, and Withington *Glouc 9*　P *Bp, MMCET, T W Bailey Esq, E M Bailey Esq, and Mrs J A Stringer (1 turn); Bp, MMCET, and Mrs L E Evans (1 turn)*　P-in-c　J A BECKETT, C　C L THOMAS

SEVENHAMPTON (St James)　*see* Highworth w Sevenhampton and Inglesham etc *Bris*

SEVENOAKS (St John the Baptist) *Roch 9*　P *Guild of All So* V *vacant* (01732) 451710

SEVENOAKS (St Luke) *Roch 9*　P *Bp*　V　M R GRIFFIN, NSM　A C BOURNE

SEVENOAKS (St Nicholas) *Roch 9*　P *Trustees* R　A M MACLEAY,　C　M ODEN,　Hon C　N N HENSHAW, J M DENT

SEVENOAKS WEALD (St George) *Roch 9*　P *R Sevenoaks* P-in-c　S L WILLOUGHBY

SEVERN BEACH (St Nicholas)　*see* Pilning w Compton Greenfield *Bris*

SEVERN STOKE (St Dennis)　*see* Kempsey and Severn Stoke w Croome d'Abitot *Worc*

SEVERNSIDE Group of Parishes, The　*see* Frampton on Severn, Arlingham, Saul etc *Glouc*

SEVINGTON (St Mary) *Cant 6*　P *Ch Soc Trust* P-in-c　J C N MACKENZIE

SEWARDS END (not known)　*see* Saffron Walden w Wendens Ambo, Littlebury etc *Chelmsf*

SEWERBY (St John)　*see* Bridlington H Trin and Sewerby w Marton *York*

SEWSTERN (Holy Trinity)　*see* S Framland *Leic*

SHABBINGTON (St Mary Magdalene)　*see* Worminghall w Ickford, Oakley and Shabbington *Ox*

SHACKERSTONE (St Peter)　*see* Nailstone and Carlton w Shackerstone *Leic*

SHACKLEFORD (St Mary the Virgin)　*see* Compton w Shackleford and Peper Harow *Guildf*

SHADFORTH (St Cuthbert)　*see* Shadforth and Sherburn *Dur*

SHADFORTH (St Cuthbert) and Sherburn *Dur 1*　P *D&C* P-in-c　A B BARTLETT,　C　J E CANDY,　NSM　E TARREN, D J WILSON, M THRUSH

SHADINGFIELD (St John the Baptist)　*see* Hundred River *St E*

SHADOXHURST (St Peter and St Paul)　*see* Kingsnorth and Shadoxhurst *Cant*

SHADWELL (St Paul)　*see* Moor Allerton and Shadwell *Ripon*

SHADWELL (St Paul) w Ratcliffe St James *Lon 7*　P *Bp* R　R C THORPE,　C　C I ROGERS, R GREEN, E J DIX

SHAFTESBURY (St James) (St Peter) *Sarum 5*　P *Patr Bd* TR　C A THOMAS,　TV　E C PEGLER, S P CHAMBERS, NSM　M E HARDING,　OLM　C J CROSSLEY

SHAFTON (St Hugh)　*see* Felkirk *Wakef*

SHALBOURNE (St Michael and All Angels)　*see* Savernake *Sarum*

SHALDEN (St Peter and St Paul)　*see* Bentworth, Lasham, Medstead and Shalden *Win*

SHALDON (St Nicholas) (St Peter), Stokeinteignhead, Combeinteignhead and Haccombe *Ex 10*　P *SMF and Sir Rivers Carew Bt (jt)*　R　G S RICHARDSON, C　A N WOODASON

SHALFLEET (St Michael the Archangel) *Portsm 8*　P *Ld Chan* V　D J BEVINGTON,　NSM　J C LEACH

SHALFORD (St Andrew)　*see* Finchingfield and Cornish Hall End etc *Chelmsf*

SHALFORD (St Mary the Virgin) *Guildf 5*　P *Ld Chan* V　J J CRUSE

SHALSTONE (St Edward the Confessor)　*see* W Buckingham *Ox*

SHAMLEY GREEN (Christ Church) *Guildf 2*　P *Bp* V　S J DAVIES

SHANGTON (St Nicholas)　*see* Church Langton cum Tur Langton etc *Leic*

SHANKLIN (St Blasius) *Portsm 7*　P *Bp*　P-in-c　V STANDING

SHANKLIN (St Paul)　*see* Gatten St Paul *Portsm*

SHANKLIN (St Saviour on the Cliff) *Portsm 7*　P *Bp* P-in-c　J H DAVIES

SHAP (St Michael) w Swindale and Bampton w Mardale *Carl 1* P *Earl of Lonsdale*　P-in-c　B LOCK,　NSM　M J DEW

SHAPWICK (Blessed Virgin Mary) w Ashcott and Burtle *B & W 4*　P *Lord Vestey (2 turns), Bp (1 turn)* P-in-c　P A OLLIVE

SHAPWICK (St Bartholomew)　*see* Bridge Par *Sarum*

SHARD END (All Saints) *Birm 9*　P *Keble Coll Ox* P-in-c　A J CLUCAS

SHARDLOW (St James)　*see* Aston on Trent, Elvaston, Weston on Trent etc *Derby*

SHARESHILL (St Luke and St Mary the Virgin) *Lich 2*　P *Bp* P-in-c　S BOWIE,　OLM　N E BELLAMY

SHARLSTON (St Luke) *Wakef 11*　P *Bp*　P-in-c　P A BOSTOCK

SHARNBROOK (St Peter), Felmersham and Knotting w Souldrop *St Alb 13*　P *Bp*　R　R A EVENS,　C　T W SANDER, NSM　D G MASON

SHARNFORD (St Helen)　*see* Sapcote and Sharnford w Wigston Parva *Leic*

SHAROW (St John the Evangelist)　*see* Ripon Cathl *Ripon*

SHARPNESS (St Andrew), Purton, Brookend and Slimbridge *Glouc 5*　P *Magd Coll Ox and Bp (alt)*　R　W J BOON, NSM　G M TUCKER

SHARRINGTON (All Saints)　*see* Stiffkey and Bale *Nor*

SHARROW (St Andrew)　*see* Psalter Lane St Andr *Sheff*

SHASTON　*see* Shaftesbury *Sarum*

SHAUGH PRIOR (St Edward)　*see* Bickleigh and Shaugh Prior *Ex*

SHAVINGTON (St Mark)　*see* Weston *Ches*

SHAW (Christchurch)　*see* Atworth w Shaw and Whitley *Sarum*

SHAW (Holy Trinity)　*see* W Swindon and the Lydiards *Bris*

SHAW (Holy Trinity)　*see* Royton St Paul and Shaw *Man*

SHAW (St Mary) cum Donnington *Ox 14*　P *DBP*　R　M WOOD

SHAWBURY (St Mary the Virgin) *Lich 22*　P *C C Corbet Esq* V　D J HUMPHRIES

SHAWELL (All Saints)　*see* Gilmorton, Peatling Parva, Kimcote etc *Leic*

SHEARSBY (St Mary Magdalene)　*see* Hexagon *Leic*

SHEBBEAR (St Michael), Buckland Filleigh, Sheepwash, Langtree, Newton St Petrock, Petrockstowe, Petersmarland, Merton and Huish *Ex 20*　P *Ld Chan (1 turn), Patr Bd (2 turns)*　P-in-c　M J WARREN

SHEDFIELD (St John the Baptist) and Wickham *Portsm 1* P *DBP and Sir Richard Rashleigh Bt (jt)*　R　B G DEANS, NSM　B R MCHUGH, E A GROVES

SHEEN (St Luke)　*see* Longnor, Quarnford and Sheen *Lich*

SHEEN, EAST (All Saints)　*see* Mortlake w E Sheen *S'wark*

SHEEN, EAST (Christ Church)　*as above*

SHEEPSCOMBE (St John the Evangelist)　*see* Painswick, Sheepscombe, Cranham, The Edge etc *Glouc*

SHEEPSTOR (St Leonard)　*see* Yelverton, Meavy, Sheepstor and Walkhampton *Ex*

SHEEPWASH (St Lawrence)　*see* Shebbear, Buckland Filleigh, Sheepwash etc *Ex*

SHEEPY (All Saints)　*see* Bosworth and Sheepy Gp *Leic*

SHEERING (St Mary the Virgin)　*see* Hatfield Heath and Sheering *Chelmsf*

SHEERNESS (Holy Trinity w St Paul) *Cant 15* P *V Minster-in-Sheppey*　V *vacant* (01795) 662589

SHEERWATER (St Michael and All Angels)　*see* Woodham *Guildf*

SHEET (St Mary Magdalene) *Portsm 4*　P *Bp* NSM　A J MARSH

SHEFFIELD (St Aidan w St Luke)　*see* Sheff Manor *Sheff*
SHEFFIELD (St Andrew)　*see* Psalter Lane St Andr *Sheff*
SHEFFIELD (St Bartholomew) *Sheff 4*　**P** *Ch Patr Trust and
Sheff Ch Burgesses Trust (jt)*　**P-in-c** P J BATCHFORD
SHEFFIELD (St Catherine of Siena) Richmond Road *Sheff 1*
P *The Crown*　**V** H LOXLEY
SHEFFIELD (St Cecilia) Parson Cross *Sheff 3*　**P** *Bp*
V K RYDER-WEST
SHEFFIELD (St Cuthbert) *Sheff 3*　**P** *Ch Burgesses*
V L R COLLINS,　**NSM** M R SUTTON
SHEFFIELD (St John the Evangelist) *Sheff 1*　**P** *Ch Burgesses*
V C H STEBBING
SHEFFIELD (St Leonard) Norwood *Sheff 3*　**P** *Bp*
V I K DUFFIELD,　**NSM** J H DALEY
SHEFFIELD (St Mark) Broomhill *Sheff 4*　**P** *Ch Burgesses*
V I G WALLIS,　**C** S HAMMERSLEY,　**NSM** S E RUSH
SHEFFIELD (St Mary) Bramall Lane *Sheff 2*　**P** *Ch Burgesses
and Dean (alt)*　**V** J C SULLIVAN,　**C** M J BAYLEY,
NSM G C D DUNCAN, K E CRIBB
SHEFFIELD (St Matthew) Carver Street *Sheff 2*　**P** *Bp and
Sheff Ch Burgess Trust (jt)*　**V** S M GRIFFITHS
SHEFFIELD (St Oswald) St Peter *Sheff 2*　**P** *Ch Burgesses*
V L M WELLS,　**Hon C** S A ST L HILLS
SHEFFIELD (St Paul)　*see* Arbourthorne and Norfolk Park
Sheff
SHEFFIELD (St Paul) Wordsworth Avenue *Sheff 3*　**P** *DBP*
P-in-c I SMITH,　**NSM** K J CROOKES
SHEFFIELD MANOR (St Swithun) *Sheff 1*　**P** *Patr Bd*
P-in-c J UPTON
SHEFFIELD PARK (St John the Evangelist)　*see* Sheff St Jo
Sheff
SHEFFORD (St Michael)　*see* Meppershall and Shefford *St Alb*
SHEFFORD, GREAT (St Mary)　*see* W Downland *Ox*
SHEINTON (St Peter and St Paul)　*see* Wenlock *Heref*
SHELDON (St Giles) *Birm 9*　**P** *J K Wingfield Digby Esq*
R B A L CAMP
SHELDON (St James the Greater)　*see* Dunkeswell, Luppitt,
Sheldon and Upottery *Ex*
SHELDON (St John)　*see* Shirley St Jo *S'wark*
SHELDON (St Michael and All Angels)　*see* Bakewell, Ashford
w Sheldon and Rowsley *Derby*
SHELDWICH (St James)　*see* Selling w Throwley, Sheldwich w
Badlesmere etc *Cant*
SHELF (St Michael and All Angels) w Buttershaw St Aidan
Bradf 2　**P** *Bp*　**TR** M I GASKELL,　**C** T J-L GUILLEMIN
SHELFANGER (All Saints)　*see* Winfarthing w Shelfanger w
Burston w Gissing etc *Nor*
SHELFIELD (St Mark) and High Heath *Lich 25*　**P** *R Walsall*
V R J FARMER,　**NSM** C SILVESTER
SHELFORD (St Peter and St Paul)　*see* Radcliffe-on-Trent and
Shelford *S'well*
SHELFORD, GREAT (St Mary) *Ely 5*　**P** *Bp*
NSM S G ANDERSON
SHELFORD, LITTLE (All Saints) *Ely 5*　**P** *Bp*　**R** S J SCOTT,
NSM T M CHAPMAN
SHELLAND (King Charles the Martyr)　*see* Gt Finborough w
Onehouse, Harleston, Buxhall etc *St E*
SHELLEY (All Saints)　*see* Hadleigh, Layham and Shelley *St E*
SHELLEY (Emmanuel) and Shepley *Wakef 6*　**P** *V Kirkburton*
P-in-c J R JONES,　**OLM** J M CRAVEN
SHELLEY (St Peter)　*see* Chipping Ongar w Shelley *Chelmsf*
SHELLINGFORD (St Faith)　*see* Uffington, Shellingford,
Woolstone and Baulking *Ox*
SHELSLEY BEAUCHAMP (All Saints)　*see* Worcs W *Worc*
SHELSLEY WALSH (St Andrew)　*as above*
SHELSWELL *Ox 2*　**P** *Ld Chan (1 turn) and Ch Ch Ox,
CCC Ox, Baroness von Maltzahn, and R J Vallings Esq (1 turn)*
R C M K HARGRAVES,　**NSM** M REYNOLDS
SHELTHORPE (Good Shepherd)　*see* Loughb Gd Shep *Leic*
SHELTON (Christ Church) and Oxon *Lich 20*　**P** *V Shrewsbury*
St Chad w St Mary　**P-in-c** D O'BRIEN,　**OLM** M I FEARNSIDE
SHELTON (St Mark)　*see* Hanley H Ev *Lich*
SHELTON (St Mary)　*see* Hempnall *Nor*
SHELTON (St Mary)　*see* The Stodden Churches *St Alb*
SHELTON (St Mary and All Saints) *S'well 3*　**P** *Bp*
P-in-c D HOLLIS
SHELVE (All Saints)　*see* Hope w Shelve *Heref*
SHENFIELD (St Mary the Virgin) *Chelmsf 7*　**P** *Personal Reps
R H Courage*　**R** D G THOMAS,　**NSM** E A LOCKHART
SHENINGTON (Holy Trinity)　*see* Ironstone *Ox*
SHENLEY (St Martin)　*see* Aldenham, Radlett and Shenley
St Alb
SHENLEY (St Mary)　*see* Watling Valley *Ox*
SHENLEY GREEN (St David) *Birm 4*　**P** *Bp*　**V** N A P EVANS,
NSM A R BEVAN

SHENSTONE (St John the Baptist) and Stonnall *Lich 1*
P *MMCET*　**V** D F OLNEY
SHENTON (St John the Evangelist)　*see* Bosworth and Sheepy
Gp *Leic*
SHEPHERD'S BUSH (St Luke) Uxbridge Road
see Hammersmith St Luke *Lon*
SHEPHERD'S BUSH (St Michael and St George) (St Stephen)
(St Thomas) *Lon 9*　**P** *Bp*　**V** R W MAYO,　**C** B P HUMPHRIES,
NSM J A COWLEY
SHEPHERD'S BUSH (St Simon)　*see* Hammersmith St Simon
Lon
SHEPLEY (St Paul)　*see* Shelley and Shepley *Wakef*
SHEPPERDINE (Chapel)　*see* Thornbury and
Oldbury-on-Severn w Shepperdine *Glouc*
SHEPPERTON (St Nicholas) and Littleton *Lon 13*　**P** *Bp and
C W L Barratt Esq (jt)*　**R** C J SWIFT,　**C** A J WATERS
SHEPRETH (All Saints)　*see* Fowlmere, Foxton, Shepreth and
Thriplow *Ely*
SHEPSHED (St Botolph) and Oaks in Charnwood *Leic 6*
P *DBP and Lord Crawshaw (jt)*　**V** C M HEBDEN,
C C D TAYLOR,　**NSM** J A BIRD
SHEPTON BEAUCHAMP (St Michael)　*see* Winsmoor *B & W*
SHEPTON MALLET (St Peter and St Paul) w Doulting
B & W 7　**P** *Duchy of Cornwall and Bp (alt)*　**C** T HANDY
SHEPTON MONTAGUE (St Peter)　*see* Bruton and Distr
B & W
SHEPWELL GREEN (St Matthias)　*see* Willenhall St Giles *Lich*
SHERBORNE (Abbey Church of St Mary) (All Souls) (St Paul)
w Castleton, Lillington and Longburton *Sarum 3*
P *J K Wingfield Digby Esq*　**V** E J WOODS,　**C** A C STEWART,
J E TREGALE, D R TREGALE,　**Hon C** J J RICHARDSON,
NSM R N F COLLINS, J A RENNIE, J M CRAW, L A MCCREADIE
SHERBORNE (St Mary Magdalene), Windrush, the Barringtons
and Aldsworth *Glouc 9*　**P** *C T R Wingfield Esq, Ch Ch Ox, and
DBP (by turn)*　**P-in-c** D M ACKERMAN,　**C** R W WOODGER,
Hon C S J GOUNDREY-SMITH
SHERBORNES (St Andrew) (Vyne Chapel) w Pamber, The
Win 4　**P** *Bp and Qu Coll Ox (jt)*　**R** J N HAMILTON
SHERBOURNE (All Saints)　*see* Barford w Wasperton and
Sherbourne *Cov*
SHERBURN (St Mary)　*see* Shadforth and Sherburn *Dur*
SHERBURN (St Hilda)　*see* Buckrose Carrs *York*
SHERBURN IN ELMET (All Saints) w Saxton *York 4*　**P** *Abp*
V C WILTON,　**NSM** M J OTTER
SHERE (St James), Albury and Chilworth *Guildf 2*　**P** *Bp,
Mrs H Bray, Duke of Northd, W F P Hugonin Esq, and the
Hon M W Ridley (jt)*　**R** N J WHITEHEAD,
C S M SOKOLOWSKI,　**NSM** S F HUTTON,　**OLM** D OAKDEN,
J A POTTER, A M PEARSON
SHEREFORD (St Nicholas)　*see* Upper Wensum Village Gp
Nor
SHERFIELD ENGLISH (St Leonard)　*see* E w W Wellow and
Sherfield English *Win*
SHERFIELD-ON-LODDON (St Leonard) and Stratfield Saye w
Hartley Wespall w Stratfield Turgis *Win 4*　**P** *Bp, Duke of
Wellington, and D&C Windsor (jt)*　**R** R W POLITT
SHERFORD (St Martin)　*see* Stokenham, Slapton, Charleton w
Buckland etc *Ex*
SHERIFF HUTTON (St Helen and the Holy Cross)　*see* Forest
of Galtres *York*
SHERIFFHALES (St Mary)　*see* Shifnal and Sheriffhales *Lich*
SHERINGHAM (St Peter) *Nor 21*　**P** *Bp*　**V** C J HEYCOCKS,
C L M CHAPMAN
SHERINGHAM, UPPER (All Saints)　*see* Weybourne Gp *Nor*
SHERINGTON (St Laud) w Chicheley, North Crawley, Astwood
and Hardmead *Ox 27*　**P** *Bp (2 turns), MMCET (1 turn), and
Major J G B Chester (1 turn)*　**R** A J MARRIOTT,
OLM P F FIELDING
SHERMANBURY (St Giles)　*see* Henfield w Shermanbury and
Woodmancote *Chich*
SHERNBOURNE (St Peter and St Paul)　*see* Dersingham w
Anmer and Shernborne *Nor*
SHERRARDS GREEN (St Mary the Virgin)　*see* Gt Malvern
Ch Ch *Worc*
SHERRINGTON (St Cosmo and St Damian)　*see* Upper Wylye
Valley *Sarum*
SHERSTON MAGNA (Holy Cross), Easton Grey, Luckington,
Alderton and Foxley w Bremilham *Bris 6*　**P** *D&C, Bp, Adn
Malmesbury and Lord Lilford (jt)*　**P-in-c** C P BRYAN,
Hon C M M MASLEN,　**NSM** S R EVANS,　**OLM** S E HARVEY
SHERWOOD (St Martin) *S'well 12*　**P** *Bp*　**V** S J GRIFFITHS,
NSM A RUSSELL
SHERWOOD PARK (St Philip)　*see* Tunbridge Wells St Phil
Roch
SHEVINGTON (St Anne) *Blackb 4*　**P** *R Standish*
V P I DENNISON

SHEVIOCK (Blessed Virgin Mary) *see* Antony w Sheviock *Truro*

SHIFFORD (St Mary) *see* Bampton w Clanfield *Ox*

SHIFNAL (St Andrew) and Sheriffhales *Lich 16* **P** *Bp and R I Legge Esq (jt)* **V** C D C THORPE, **C** S C LAWRENCE, **OLM** S A DAY

SHILBOTEL (St James) *see* Shilbottle *Newc*

SHILBOTTLE (St James) *Newc 6* **P** *Dioc Soc* **P-in-c** A J CAVANAGH, **OLM** P E RENNISON

SHILDON (St John) *Dur 6* **P** *Bp* **V** R KALUS, **C** D R TOMLINSON

SHILL VALLEY and Broadshire *Ox 8* **P** *J Heyworth Esq, Mrs P Allen, and Ch Ch Ox (1 turn), Ch Soc Tr, F R Goodenough Esq, and D F Goodenough Esq (1 turn)* **R** H C MACINNES, **C** P E WHEATON, **NSM** L N USHER-WILSON, E J JOHNSON

SHILLING OKEFORD (Holy Rood) *see* Okeford *Sarum*

SHILLINGFORD (St George) *see* Alphington, Shillingford St George and Ide *Ex*

SHILLINGSTONE (Holy Rood) *see* Okeford *Sarum*

SHILLINGTON (All Saints) *see* Gravenhurst, Shillington and Stondon *St Alb*

SHILTON (Holy Rood) *see* Shill Valley and Broadshire *Ox*

SHILTON (St Andrew) *see* Ansty and Shilton *Cov*

SHIMPLINGTHORNE (St George) *see* Chadbrook *St E*

SHINCLIFFE (St Mary the Virgin) *see* Dur St Oswald and Shincliffe *Dur*

SHINEY ROW (St Oswald) *see* Herrington, Penshaw and Shiney Row *Dur*

SHINFIELD (St Mary) *see* Loddon Reach *Ox*

SHINGAY Group of Parishes, The *Ely 7* **P** *Bp, Mrs E E Sclater, Ch Patr Trust, Down Coll Cam, New Coll Ox, and Jes Coll Cam (jt)* **R** S F C WILLIAMS, **NSM** P M SHARKEY

SHIPBOURNE (St Giles) w Plaxtol *Roch 10* **P** *Bp and Sir Edward Cazalet* **R** A D PROCTER

SHIPDHAM (All Saints) w East and West Bradenham *Nor 17* **P** *Bp* **P-in-c** A-L ALDER, **C** T A P WEATHERSTONE, **OLM** D FOTHERBY

SHIPHAM (St Leonard) *see* Axbridge w Shipham and Rowberrow *B & W*

SHIPHAY COLLATON (St John the Baptist) *Ex 12* **P** *Bp* **V** C E DEACON

SHIPLAKE (St Peter and St Paul) w Dunsden and Harpsden *Ox 6* **P** *All So Coll Ox, D&C Windsor, and DBP (jt)* **R** P E BRADISH, **OLM** M D SEYMOUR-JONES

SHIPLEY (St Mary the Virgin) *Chich 8* **P** *C R Burrell Esq* **P-in-c** P A SINTON

SHIPLEY (St Paul) *Bradf 1* **P** *Simeon's Trustees* **P-in-c** S HOPE, **C** S S GILL, **NSM** H LEALMAN

SHIPLEY (St Peter) *Bradf 1* **P** *V Shipley St Paul* **V** J C RAINER

SHIPPON (St Mary Magdalene) *Ox 10* **P** *Bp* **V** *vacant*

SHIPSTON-ON-STOUR (St Edmund) w Honington and Idlicote *Cov 9* **P** *Jes Coll Ox, D&C Worc, Bp (jt)* **R** D R THURBURN-HUELIN, **NSM** J TUCKER

SHIPTON (Holy Evangelist) *see* Skelton w Shipton and Newton on Ouse *York*

SHIPTON (St James) *see* Wenlock *Heref*

SHIPTON BELLINGER (St Peter) *see* Appleshaw, Kimpton, Thruxton, Fyfield etc *Win*

SHIPTON GORGE (St Martin) *see* Bride Valley *Sarum*

SHIPTON MOYNE (St John the Baptist) *see* Tetbury, Beverston, Long Newnton etc *Glouc*

SHIPTON OLIFFE (St Oswald) *see* Sevenhampton w Charlton Abbots, Hawling etc *Glouc*

SHIPTON ON CHERWELL (Holy Cross) *see* Blenheim *Ox*

SHIPTON-UNDER-WYCHWOOD (St Mary) w Milton-under-Wychwood, Fifield and Idbury *Ox 3* **P** *Bp* **V** K E STACEY, **OLM** A T HARTLEY

SHIPTONTHORPE (All Saints) *see* Londesborough Wold *York*

SHIREBROOK (Holy Trinity) *see* E Scarsdale *Derby*

SHIREGREEN (St James and St Christopher) *Sheff 3* **P** *Bp and Dean (alt)* **P-in-c** D F DEAN-REVILL

SHIREHAMPTON (St Mary) *Bris 2* **P** *Bp* **V** *vacant* 0117-985 5450

SHIREMOOR (St Mark) *Newc 5* **P** *Bp* **V** P M SCOTT

SHIREOAKS (St Luke) *S'well 6* **P** *Bp* **P-in-c** J L ALLEN

SHIRES' EDGE *Ox 5* **P** *Bp* **V** P FREETH, **OLM** L M ALCOCK

SHIRLAND (St Leonard) *see* Morton and Stonebroom w Shirland *Derby*

SHIRLEY (Christ the King) *see* Salter Street and Shirley *Birm*

SHIRLEY (St George) *S'wark 19* **P** *Bp* **V** D J FROST, **Hon C** H A FIFE, **OLM** C JONES

SHIRLEY (St James) (St John) *Win 13* **P** *Ch Patr Trust* **C** A D HARGREAVES

SHIRLEY (St James the Great) *see* Salter Street and Shirley *Birm*

SHIRLEY (St John) *S'wark 19* **P** *Bp* **V** S J KNOWERS, **Hon C** A C COLLIER, **NSM** B C GENTILELLA

SHIRLEY (St John the Divine) *see* Salter Street and Shirley *Birm*

SHIRLEY (St Luke) *as above*

SHIRLEY (St Mary Magdalene) *as above*

SHIRLEY (St Michael) *see* Brailsford w Shirley, Osmaston w Edlaston etc *Derby*

SHIRLEY WARREN (St Jude) *see* Maybush and Southampton St Jude *Win*

SHIRWELL (St Peter), Loxhore, Kentisbury, Arlington, East Down, Bratton Fleming, Challacombe and Stoke Rivers *Ex 18* **P** *Patr Bd* **TR** L E AUSTIN

SHOBDON (St John the Evangelist) *see* Pembridge w Moor Court, Shobdon, Staunton etc *Heref*

SHOBROOKE (St Swithin) *see* Crediton, Shobrooke and Sandford etc *Ex*

SHOCKLACH (St Edith) *see* Tilston and Shocklach *Ches*

SHOEBURY, NORTH (St Mary the Virgin) *Chelmsf 13* **P** *Ld Chan* **V** I ST J FISHER

SHOEBURY, SOUTH (St Andrew) (St Peter) *Chelmsf 13* **P** *Hyndman Trustees* **R** L M WILLIAMS

SHOLDEN (St Nicholas) *see* Deal St Leon w St Rich and Sholden etc *Cant*

SHOLING (St Francis of Assisi) (St Mary) *Win 13* **P** *Bp* **V** G K BAKKER, **C** J A OLIVER, **NSM** J J BAKKER

SHOOTERS HILL (All Saints) *see* Plumstead All SS *S'wark*

SHOOTERS HILL (Christ Church) *S'wark 6* **P** *Bp* **V** A R M VAN DEN HOF, **NSM** A S J HEALY

SHORE (St Barnabas) *Man 17* **P** *D&C* **P-in-c** J MCGRATH, **OLM** B WOODHEAD

SHOREDITCH (All Saints) Haggerston Road *see* Dalston H Trin w St Phil and Haggerston All SS *Lon*

SHOREDITCH (St Anne) Hoxton Street *see* Hoxton St Anne w St Columba *Lon*

SHOREDITCH (St Leonard) w St Michael *Lon 5* **P** *Bp and Adn (jt)* **V** P R TURP, **C** G E FOUHY

SHOREHAM (St Giles) *see* Kingston Buci *Chich*

SHOREHAM (St Peter and St Paul) *Roch 10* **P** *D&C Westmr* **P-in-c** R A FREEMAN

SHOREHAM, NEW (St Mary de Haura) *Chich 4* **P** *Bp* **V** V STANDING

SHOREHAM, OLD (St Nicolas) *Chich 4* **P** *Bp* **V** V STANDING

SHOREHAM BEACH (Good Shepherd) *Chich 4* **P** *Bp* **P-in-c** G C SOUPPOURIS

SHORELINE Benefice, The *St E 5* **P** *Ld Chan (1 turn), Bp (3 turns)* **R** L OOSTERHOF

SHORNE (St Peter and St Paul) *Roch 4* **P** *D&C* **P-in-c** G J ACKERLEY

SHORT HEATH (Holy Trinity) *see* Bentley Em and Willenhall H Trin *Lich*

SHORT HEATH (St Margaret) *see* Erdington Ch the K *Birm*

SHORTHAMPTON (All Saints) *see* Charlbury w Shorthampton *Ox*

SHORTLANDS (All Saints' Community Church) *see* Bromley SS Pet and Paul *Roch*

SHORTLANDS (St Mary) *Roch 13* **P** *Bp* **V** P MILLER, **NSM** J E PETERS

SHORWELL (St Peter) w Kingston *Portsm 8* **P** *Bp* **Hon C** D L DENNIS

SHOSCOMBE (St Julian) *see* Peasedown St John w Wellow and Foxcote etc *B & W*

SHOTESHAM (All Saints w St Mary) *see* Newton Flotman, Swainsthorpe, Tasburgh, etc *Nor*

SHOTLEY (St John) *Newc 9* **P** *Lord Crewe's Trustees* **NSM** D J WOOD

SHOTLEY (St Mary) *see* Shoreline *St E*

SHOTTERMILL (St Stephen) *Guildf 4* **P** *Adn Surrey* **V** D R P WIGNALL, **C** G M G CARPENTER

SHOTTERY (St Andrew) *Cov 8* **P** *Bp* **V** J R WARREN, **NSM** P EDMONDSON

SHOTTESBROOKE (St John the Baptist) *see* White Waltham w Shottesbrooke *Ox*

SHOTTESWELL (St Lawrence) *see* Warmington w Shotteswell and Radway w Ratley *Cov*

SHOTTISHAM (St Margaret) *see* Wilford Peninsula *St E*

SHOTTLE (St Lawrence) *see* Hazelwood, Holbrook and Milford *Derby*

SHOTTON (St Saviour) *see* Haswell, Shotton and Thornley *Dur*

SHOTWICK (St Michael) *see* Burton and Shotwick *Ches*

SHOULDHAM (All Saints) *Ely 9* **P** *Bp* **P-in-c** B L BURTON
SHOULDHAM THORPE (St Mary) *Ely 9* **P** *Bp*
  P-in-c B L BURTON
SHRAWARDINE (St Mary) *see* Bicton, Montford w
  Shrawardine and Fitz *Lich*
SHRAWLEY (St Mary), Witley, Astley and Abberley *Worc 13*
  P *Bp and Guild of All So (jt)* **R** *vacant* (01905) 620489
SHRED (Mission Church) *see* Slaithwaite w E Scammonden
  Wakef
SHREWSBURY (All Saints and St Michael) *Lich 20* **P** *Bp*
  P-in-c M FISH
SHREWSBURY (Christ Church) *see* Shelton and Oxon *Lich*
SHREWSBURY (Holy Cross) (St Peter) *Lich 20* **P** *Bp*
  V P G FIRMIN, **C** J E WILLIS
SHREWSBURY (Holy Trinity) (St Julian) *Lich 20* **P** *Bp and*
  Ch Patr Trust (jt) **V** R D SPENCER
SHREWSBURY (St Chad) St Mary (St Alkmund) *Lich 20*
  P *Bp* **V** M W THOMAS, **Hon C** C J D WALKER, R HAYES
SHREWSBURY (St George of Cappadocia) w Greenfields
  United Church *Lich 20* **P** *V Shrewsbury St Chad*
  V M MCBRIDE, **C** R W MCDONALD
SHREWSBURY (St Giles) w Sutton and Atcham *Lich 20* **P** *Bp*
  and R L Burton Esq (jt) **R** P J WILLIAMS
SHREWTON (St Mary) *see* Wylye and Till Valley *Sarum*
SHRIVENHAM (St Andrew) and Ashbury *Ox 17* **P** *Ld Chan*
  V R M A HANCOCK, **Hon C** E G CLEMENTS, **NSM** A E BELL
SHROPHAM (St Peter) *see* Gt and Lt Ellingham, Rockland and
  Shropham etc *Nor*
SHROTON (St Mary) *see* Iwerne Valley *Sarum*
SHRUB END (All Saints) (St Cedd) *Chelmsf 16* **P** *Bp*
  V N A W DAVIS
SHUCKBURGH, LOWER (St John the Baptist)
  see Napton-on-the-Hill, Lower Shuckburgh etc *Cov*
SHUDY CAMPS (St Mary) *see* Linton *Ely*
SHURDINGTON (St Paul) *see* Badgeworth, Shurdington and
  Witcombe w Bentham *Glouc*
SHUSTOKE (St Cuthbert) *see* The Whitacres, Lea Marston,
  and Shustoke *Birm*
SHUTE (St Michael) *see* Kilmington, Stockland, Dalwood,
  Yarcombe etc *Ex*
SHUTFORD (St Martin) *see* Wykeham *Ox*
SHUTTINGTON (St Matthew) *see* N Warks *Birm*
SHUTTLEWOOD (St Laurence Mission Church) *see* Bolsover
  Derby
SHUTTLEWORTH (St John) *see* Ramsbottom and Edenfield
  Man
SIBBERTOFT (St Helen) *see* Welford w Sibbertoft and Marston
  Trussell *Pet*
SIBERTSWOLD (St Andrew) *see* Eythorne and Elvington w
  Waldershare etc *Cant*
SIBFORD (Holy Trinity) *see* Wykeham *Ox*
SIBLE HEDINGHAM (St Peter) w Castle Hedingham
  Chelmsf 19 **P** *Bp, and Hon T R Lindsay (alt)* **P-in-c** L BOND
SIBSEY (St Margaret) w Frithville *Linc 20* **P** *Ld Chan*
  P-in-c R E TAYLOR, **NSM** J M MORTON
SIBSON (St Botolph) *see* Bosworth and Sheepy Gp *Leic*
SIBTHORPE (St Peter) *S'well 3* **P** *Bp* **P-in-c** D HOLLIS
SIBTON (St Peter) *see* Yoxmere *St E*
SICKLINGHALL (St Peter) *see* Lower Wharfedale *Ripon*
SID VALLEY *see* Sidmouth, Woolbrook, Salcombe Regis,
  Sidbury etc *Ex*
SIDBURY (Holy Trinity) *see* Stottesdon w Farlow, Cleeton
  St Mary etc *Heref*
SIDBURY (St Giles and St Peter) *see* Sidmouth, Woolbrook,
  Salcombe Regis, Sidbury etc *Ex*
SIDCUP (Christ Church) Longland *Roch 17* **P** *Ch Trust Fund*
  Trust **V** T J PARSONS
SIDCUP (St Andrew) *Roch 17* **P** *Bp* **V** R C A HANKEY
SIDCUP (St John the Evangelist) *Roch 17* **P** *D&C* **V** S SEALY,
  NSM S E TWYNAM
SIDDAL (St Mark) *Wakef 4* **P** *Ch Trust Fund Trust*
  P-in-c C MACDONALD
SIDDINGTON (All Saints) *see* Marton, Siddington w
  Capesthorne, and Eaton etc *Ches*
SIDDINGTON (St Peter) *see* S Cerney w Cerney Wick,
  Siddington and Preston *Glouc*
SIDESTRAND (St Michael) *see* Overstrand, Northrepps,
  Sidestrand etc *Nor*
SIDFORD (St Peter) *see* Sidmouth, Woolbrook, Salcombe
  Regis, Sidbury etc *Ex*
SIDLESHAM (St Mary the Virgin) *Chich 3* **P** *Bp*
  P-in-c S GUISE
SIDLEY (All Saints) *Chich 14* **P** *R Bexhill* **V** T G BUXTON
SIDLOW BRIDGE (Emmanuel) *S'wark 26* **P** *DBP*
  R W G CAMPEN

SIDMOUTH (St Nicholas w St Giles), Woolbrook, Salcombe
  Regis, Sidbury w Sidford, and All Saints Sidmouth *Ex 7*
  P *Patr Bd* **TR** D H JAMES, **TV** R G PECKHAM, R D TRUMPER,
  NSM E A M GAMMON
SIGGLESTHORNE (St Lawrence) w Nunkeeling and Bewholme
  York 11 **P** *Prime Min* **R** *vacant* (01964) 533033
SILCHESTER (St Mary) *see* Tadley S and Silchester *Win*
SILCHESTER COMMON (Mission Church) *as above*
SILEBY (St Mary), Cossington and Seagrave *Leic 5* **P** *Patr Bd*
  R R C J HOPKINS, **C** D J LOWER
SILK WILLOUGHBY (St Denis) *Linc 21* **P** *Sir Lyonel*
  Tollemache Bt **P-in-c** S R BENHAM
SILKSTONE (All Saints) *see* Hoylandswaine and Silkstone w
  Stainborough *Wakef*
SILKSTONE COMMON (Mission Room) *as above*
SILKSWORTH (St Matthew) *Dur 16* **P** *Bp*
  V R G E BRADSHAW, **C** S CLARK, **Hon C** J A BRADSHAW
SILLOTH (Christ Church) *see* Solway Plain *Carl*
SILSDEN (St James) *Bradf 8* **P** *Bp, Adn Craven, and*
  Trustees (jt) **V** D J GRIFFITHS, **C** D S J AUSTIN,
  S A GRIFFITHS, **NSM** P SMITH
SILSOE (St James), Pulloxhill and Flitton *St Alb 8* **P** *Ball Coll*
  Ox and Bp (alt) **V** S C HOLROYD
SILTON (St Nicholas) *Sarum 5* **P** *DBP* **R** *vacant*
SILTON, NETHER (All Saints) *see* Leake w Over and Nether
  Silton and Kepwick *York*
SILTON, OVER (St Mary) *as above*
SILVER END (St Francis) *see* Rivenhall *Chelmsf*
SILVERDALE (St John) *Blackb 14* **P** *V Warton*
  P-in-c P K WARREN
SILVERDALE (St Luke) *Lich 9* **P** *T H G Howard-Sneyd Esq*
  V *vacant* (01782) 723312
SILVERHILL (St Matthew) *Chich 17* **P** *Simeon's Trustees*
  R M S COE
SILVERSTONE (St Michael) and Abthorpe w Slapton and
  Whittlebury and Paulerspury *Pet 5*
  P *T L Langton-Lockton Esq, Leeson's Trustees, and New Coll*
  Ox (3 turns), Prime Min (2 turns) **R** P D MCLEOD,
  NSM G C BUCKLE
SILVERTON (St Mary), Butterleigh, Bickleigh and Cadeleigh
  Ex 8 **P** *Bp and Sir Rivers Carew Bt* **R** A H MACDONALD,
  NSM C JENKINS, R L MAUDSLEY
SILVINGTON (St Michael) *see* Stottesdon w Farlow, Cleeton
  St Mary etc *Heref*
SIMONBURN (St Mungo) *see* Humshaugh w Simonburn and
  Wark *Newc*
SIMONSTONE (St Peter) *see* Padiham w Hapton and Padiham
  Green *Blackb*
SIMPSON (St Thomas) *see* Woughton *Ox*
SINFIN (St Stephen) *Derby 10* **P** *CPAS* **V** P R SANDFORD
SINFIN MOOR (not known) *Derby 10* **P** *Bp* **V** *vacant* (01332)
  760016
SINGLETON (Blessed Virgin Mary) *see* E Dean, Singleton,
  and W Dean *Chich*
SINGLETON (St Anne) *see* Poulton Carleton and Singleton
  Blackb
SINNINGTON (All Saints) *see* Middleton, Newton and
  Sinnington *York*
SISLAND (St Mary) *see* Loddon, Sisland, Chedgrave, Hardley
  and Langley *Nor*
SISSINGHURST (Holy Trinity) w Frittenden *Cant 10* **P** *CPAS*
  V A E NORRIS
SITHNEY (St Sithney) *see* Porthleven w Sithney *Truro*
SITTINGBOURNE (Holy Trinity) w Bobbing *Cant 15* **P** *Abp*
  P-in-c M J RESCH, **OLM** S M SAMSON
SITTINGBOURNE (St Mary) (St Michael) *Cant 15* **P** *Abp*
  and D&C (jt) **V** *vacant* (01795) 472874
SITTINGBOURNE (St Peter and St Paul) *see* Borden *Cant*
SIX HILLS (Mission) *see* Old Dalby, Nether Broughton,
  Saxelbye etc *Leic*
SIX MILE BOTTOM (St George) *see* Lt Wilbraham *Ely*
SIX PILGRIMS, The *B & W 2* **P** *Ch Soc Trust, D&C, DBF, and*
  Bp (by turn) **R** *vacant*
SIX SAINTS circa Holt: Bringhurst, Great Easton, Medbourne
  cum Holt, Stockerston and Blaston *Leic 3* **P** *D&C Pet and*
  Adn Leic (2 turns), St Jo Coll Cam (2 turns) **R** S J BISHOP
SIXHILLS (All Saints) *see* Barkwith Gp *Linc*
SIXPENNY HANDLEY (St Mary) w Gussage St Andrew and
  Pentridge *Sarum 6* **P** *D&C Windsor and DBP (alt)*
  P-in-c M R B DURRANT, **C** M J FOSTER, **NSM** P A SKINNER,
  OLM P H SKINNER
SKEEBY (St Agatha's District Church) *see* Easby w Skeeby and
  Brompton on Swale etc *Ripon*
SKEFFINGTON (St Thomas à Beckett) *see* Church Langton
  cum Tur Langton etc *Leic*

SKEFFLING (St Helen)   *see* Withernsea w Owthorne and
Easington etc *York*
SKEGBY (St Andrew) w Teversal *S'well 4*   **P** *DBP and Ld Chan
(alt)*   **R** R KELLETT,   **C** K BOTTLEY
SKEGNESS Group, The (St Clement) (St Matthew) *Linc 8*
P *Bp and DBP (2 turns), and Ld Chan (1 turn)*
R C M FRANCE,   **C** J DONN, F A JEFFRIES,   **OLM** C ANDERSON
SKELBROOKE (St Michael and All Angels)
see Adwick-le-Street w Skelbrooke *Sheff*
SKELLINGTHORPE (St Lawrence) w Doddington *Linc 18*
P *MMCET*   **R** R G BILLINGHURST,   **OLM** F CLARKE
SKELLOW (St Michael and All Angels)   *see* Owston *Sheff*
SKELMANTHORPE (St Aidan) *Wakef 6*   **P** *Bp*
P-in-c P D REYNOLDS
SKELMERSDALE (Church at the Centre) *Liv 11*   **P** *Bp*
V *vacant* (01695) 728356
SKELMERSDALE (St Paul) *Liv 11*   **P** *V Ormskirk*
P-in-c C B SPITTLE
SKELSMERGH (St John the Baptist)   *see* Beacon *Carl*
SKELTON (All Saints) w Upleatham *York 16*   **P** *Abp*
P-in-c V E M-B HAYNES
SKELTON (St Giles) w Shipton and Newton on Ouse *York 3*
P *Abp*   **P-in-c** M H WAINWRIGHT
SKELTON (St Michael)   *see* Inglewood Gp *Carl*
SKELTON-CUM-NEWBY (St Helen's Old Church)
see Kirby-on-the-Moor, Cundall w Norton-le-Clay etc *Ripon*
SKENDLEBY (St Peter and St Paul)   *see* Partney Gp *Linc*
SKERNE (St Leonard)   *see* Hutton Cranswick w Skerne, Watton
and Beswick *York*
SKERNE, UPPER *Dur 5*   **P** *Ld Chan (1 turn), Patr Bd
(2 turns)*   **TR** M G T GOBBETT,   **TV** P L TAIT,
C A M RICHARDSON
SKERTON (St Chad) *Blackb 11*   **P** *Bp*   **P-in-c** N J HEALE
SKERTON (St Luke) *Blackb 11*   **P** *Trustees*   **V** G LEWIS
SKEYTON (All Saints)   *see* King's Beck *Nor*
SKIDBY (St Michael)   *see* Rowley w Skidby *York*
SKILGATE (St John the Baptist)   *see* Dulverton w Brushford,
Brompton Regis etc *B & W*
SKILLINGTON (St James)   *see* Colsterworth Gp *Linc*
SKIPSEA (All Saints) and Barmston w Fraisthorpe *York 9*
P *Abp and The Hon S E Cunliffe-Lister (jt)*
P-in-c C J MCCARTHY
SKIPTON (Christ Church) w Carleton St Mary *Bradf 7*
P *Ch Ch Ox and R Skipton H Trin (jt)*   **V** D N WILLIAMS,
C M E WINTER,   **NSM** V A LOWE
SKIPTON (Holy Trinity) *Bradf 7*   **P** *Ch Ch Ox*
R A P BOTWRIGHT,   **C** M E WINTER
SKIPTON ON SWALE (St John)   *see* Topcliffe, Baldersby w
Dishforth, Dalton etc *York*
SKIPWITH (St Helen)   *see* Bubwith w Skipwith *York*
SKIRBECK (Holy Trinity) *Linc 20*   **P** *Trustees*   **V** S P DOWSON
SKIRBECK (St Nicholas) *Linc 20*   **P** *DBP*   **R** P V NOBLE
SKIRBECK QUARTER (St Thomas)   *see* Boston *Linc*
SKIRLAUGH (St Augustine) w Long Riston, Rise and Swine
York 11   **P** *Abp, Abp and Baroness de Stempel, and Ld Chan
(by turn)*   **P-in-c** C J SIMMONS
SKIRPENBECK (St Mary)   *see* Garrowby Hill *York*
SKIRWITH (St John the Evangelist)   *see* Cross Fell Gp *Carl*
SLAD (Holy Trinity)   *see* Stroud and Uplands w Slad *Glouc*
SLADE GREEN (St Augustine) *Roch 15*   **P** *Bp*   **V** A J TARPER
SLAIDBURN (St Andrew) *Bradf 5*   **P** *Ch Soc Trust*
P-in-c M R RUSSELL-SMITH,   **NSM** R E WILSON
SLAITHWAITE (St James) w East Scammonden *Wakef 5*
P *V Huddersfield*   **V** C R TOWNSEND
SLALEY (St Mary the Virgin) *Newc 9*   **P** *Bp*
P-in-c D J IRVINE,   **NSM** J LYNCH
SLAPTON (Holy Cross)   *see* Ivinghoe w Pitstone and Slapton
and Marsworth *Ox*
SLAPTON (St Botolph)   *see* Silverstone and Abthorpe w
Slapton etc *Pet*
SLAPTON (St James the Great)   *see* Stokenham, Slapton,
Charleton w Buckland etc *Ex*
SLAUGHAM (St Mary) and Staplefield Common *Chich 6*
P *Mrs D M Irwin-Clark*   **R** G D SIMMONS,
C J W B WADDELL,   **Hon C** K W HABERSHON
SLAUGHTER, LOWER (St Mary)   *see* The Guitings,
Cutsdean, Farmcote etc *Glouc*
SLAUGHTER, UPPER (St Peter)   *as above*
SLAUGHTERFORD (St Nicholas)   *see* By Brook *Bris*
SLAWSTON (All Saints)   *see* Hallaton and Allexton, w
Horninghold, Tugby etc *Leic*
SLEAFORD, NEW (St Denys) *Linc 21*   **P** *Bp*
P-in-c J A PATRICK,   **C** J E TIMINGS
SLEDMERE (St Mary)   *see* Waggoners *York*
SLEEKBURN (St John)   *see* Cambois and Sleekburn *Newc*

SLEIGHTS (St John)   *see* Lower Esk *York*
SLIMBRIDGE (St John the Evangelist)   *see* Sharpness, Purton,
Brookend and Slimbridge *Glouc*
SLINDON (St Chad)   *see* Eccleshall *Lich*
SLINDON (St Mary), Eartham and Madehurst *Chich 1*   **P** *Bp,
D&C, and Mrs J Izard (jt)*   **P-in-c** M R CURTIS
SLINFOLD (St Peter)   *see* Itchingfield w Slinfold *Chich*
SLINGSBY (All Saints)   *see* The Street Par *York*
SLIPTON (St John the Baptist) *Pet 9*   **P** *L G Stopford
Sackville Esq*   **P-in-c** D H P FOOT
SLITTING MILL (St John the Baptist)   *see* Brereton and
Rugeley *Lich*
SLOANE STREET (Holy Trinity)   *see* Upper Chelsea H Trin
Lon
SLOLEY (St Bartholomew)   *see* Worstead, Westwick, Sloley,
Swanton Abbot etc *Nor*
SLOUGH (St Paul) (Christ Church) *Ox 23*   **P** *Trustees*
V M C COTTERELL
SLYNE W HEST (St Luke) and Halton St Wilfrid w Aughton
St Saviour *Blackb 14*   **P** *Bp and Exors R T Sanderson (jt)*
R P A BICKNELL
SMALL HEATH (All Saints) *Birm 13*   **P** *Patr Bd*   **V** O J COSS
SMALLBURGH (St Peter) w Dilham w Honing and Crostwight
Nor 12   **P** *Bp, T R Cubitt Esq, and J C Wickman Esq (jt)*
P-in-c B K FURNESS
SMALLEY (St John the Baptist)   *see* Morley w Smalley and
Horsley Woodhouse *Derby*
SMALLFIELD (Church Room)   *see* Burstow w Horne *S'wark*
SMALLHYTHE (St John the Baptist)   *see* Tenterden and
Smallhythe *Cant*
SMALLTHORNE (St Saviour) *Lich 11*   **P** *R Norton in the
Moors*   **V** R J S GRIGSON
SMALLWOOD (St John the Baptist)   *see* Astbury and
Smallwood *Ches*
SMANNELL (Christ Church)   *see* Knight's Enham and
Smannell w Enham Alamein *Win*
SMARDEN (St Michael)   *see* Biddenden and Smarden *Cant*
SMAWTHORPE (St Michael and All Angels) *Wakef 10*   **P** *Bp*
P-in-c M F WOOD,   **C** P W ATKINSON, C M WATKINS
SMEATON, GREAT (St Eloy)   *see* E Richmond *Ripon*
SMEETH (St Mary) w Monks Horton and Stowting and
Brabourne *Cant 6*   **P** *Abp*   **P-in-c** R L LE ROSSIGNOL,
NSM S M COX
SMEETON WESTERBY (Christ Church)   *see* Kibworth and
Smeeton Westerby and Saddington *Leic*
SMESTOW VALE TEAM *Lich 24*   **P** *Patr Bd*
TR A P BROWN,   **TV** J M HARTWELL, P A TAYLOR,
C E I ANDERTON,   **OLM** R A M COOK
SMETHCOTT (St Michael)   *see* Dorrington w Leebotwood,
Longnor, Stapleton etc *Heref*
SMETHWICK (Old Church) *Birm 7*   **P** *Dorothy Parkes Trustees*
V N J MASON
SMETHWICK (Resurrection) (St Stephen and St Michael)
Birm 7   **P** *Bp*   **V** D R GOULD,   **NSM** H M WHEELER
SMETHWICK (St Mary the Virgin)   *see* Bearwood *Birm*
SMETHWICK (St Matthew w St Chad) *Birm 7*   **P** *Bp and
V Smethwick (alt)*   **P-in-c** N J MASON
SMISBY (St James)   *see* Melbourne, Ticknall, Smisby and
Stanton *Derby*
SMITHILLS HALL (Chapel)   *see* Halliwell St Pet *Man*
SMORRALL LANE (St Andrew)   *see* Bedworth *Cov*
SNAILBEACH (St Luke)   *see* Minsterley *Heref*
SNAILWELL (St Peter)   *see* Three Rivers Gp *Ely*
SNAINTON (St Stephen)   *see* Upper Derwent *York*
SNAITH (St Laurence Priory)   *see* Gt Snaith *Sheff*
SNAITH, GREAT (Holy Trinity) (St John the Baptist) (St Paul)
Sheff 10   **P** *Bp*   **TR** C ROBERTS,   **NSM** P W HIBBS
SNAPE (St John the Baptist)   *see* Alde River *St E*
SNAPE CASTLE (Chapel of St Mary)   *see* W Tanfield and Well
w Snape and N Stainley *Ripon*
SNARESTONE (St Bartholomew)   *see* Woodfield *Leic*
SNARGATE (St Dunstan)   *see* Appledore w Brookland,
Fairfield, Brenzett etc *Cant*
SNEAD (St Mary the Virgin)   *see* Wentnor w Ratlinghope,
Myndtown, Norbury etc *Heref*
SNEATON (St Hilda)   *see* Lower Esk *York*
SNEINTON (St Christopher) w St Philip *S'well 13*   **P** *CPAS and
Trustees (alt)*   **P-in-c** S D SILVESTER,   **C** N J HILL,
NSM A R HASKEY
SNEINTON (St Cyprian) *S'well 13*   **P** *Bp*   **P-in-c** A L WAUDE
SNEINTON (St Stephen) w St Matthias *S'well 13*   **P** *Bp and
SMF (jt)*   **V** *vacant* 0115-924 1917
SNELLAND (All Saints)   *see* Wragby Gp *Linc*
SNELSTON (St Peter)   *see* Norbury w Snelston *Derby*
SNETTISHAM (St Mary) w Ingoldisthorpe and Fring *Nor 16*
P *Bp, CPAS, and D&C (jt)*   **R** G H SUART

SNEYD (Holy Trinity) *Lich 11* **P** *Bp* **V** B L WILLIAMS
SNEYD GREEN (St Andrew) *Lich 11* **P** *Bp* **V** G R DAVIES
SNITTERBY (St Nicholas) *see* Bishop Norton, Wadingham and Snitterby *Linc*
SNITTERFIELD (St James the Great) w Bearley *Cov 7* **P** *Bp and V Wootton Wawen* **P-in-c** R LIVINGSTON
SNODLAND (All Saints) (Christ Church) *Roch 1* **P** *Bp and CPAS (jt)* **R** H P C BROADBENT, **NSM** S M BROOKS
SNORING, GREAT (St Mary) *see* Barney, Fulmodeston w Croxton, Hindringham etc *Nor*
SNORING, LITTLE (St Andrew) *as above*
SNOWDEN HILL Chapel Farm (not known) *see* Penistone and Thurlstone *Wakef*
SNOWSHILL (St Barnabas) *see* Winchcombe *Glouc*
SOAR, UPPER *Leic 7* **P** *Prime Min (1 turn), Mrs A M Finn, Adn Loughb, and Ball Coll Ox (1 turn)* **R** C M BRENNAND
SOBERTON (St Peter) w Newtown *Portsm 1* **P** *Bp*
P-in-c S K BEAVIS
SOCKBURN (All Saints) *see* Dinsdale w Sockburn *Dur*
SODBURY, LITTLE (St Adeline) *see* Sodbury Vale *Glouc*
SODBURY, OLD (St John the Baptist) *as above*
SODBURY VALE Benefice, The *Glouc 5* **P** *D&C Worc, Duke of Beaufort, and CPAS (jt)* **R** J E B KENCHINGTON
SOHAM (St Andrew) and Wicken *Ely 4* **P** *Pemb Coll Cam (1 turn), Pemb Coll Cam and Ch Patr Trust (jt) (1 turn)*
V T M ALBAN JONES, **C** S F SIMPSON
SOHO (St Anne) (St Thomas) (St Peter) *Lon 3*
P *R Westmr St Jas* **NSM** R S F BUCKLEY
SOLE BAY *St E 15* **P** *Patr Bd* **TR** S J PITCHER,
TV J B LYON, R HENDERSON
SOLIHULL (Catherine de Barnes) (St Alphege) (St Helen) (St Michael) *Birm 11* **P** *Patr Bd* **TR** T W PILKINGTON,
TV P J TAYLOR, H T GREENHAM, S H MARSHALL, **C** G POWELL
SOLLARS HOPE (St Michael) *see* Brampton *Heref*
SOLWAY PLAIN *Carl 7* **P** *Patr Bd* **TR** B ROTHWELL,
TV D TEMBEY, **Hon C** P N HAYWARD,
NSM M I STUDHOLME
SOMBORNE w Ashley *Win 12* **P** *Bp* **P-in-c** R V STAPLETON
SOMERBY (All Saints) *see* Burrough Hill Pars *Leic*
SOMERBY (St Margaret) *see* N Wolds Gp *Linc*
SOMERBY, NEW (St Anne) *see* Grantham St Anne New Somerby and Spitalgate *Linc*
SOMERBY, OLD (St Mary Magdalene) *see* N Beltisloe Gp *Linc*
SOMERCOTES and Grainthorpe w Conisholme *Linc 12*
P *Duchy of Lanc (2 turns), Magd Coll Cam and Bp (1 turn)*
P-in-c S A ALLISON
SOMERCOTES (St Thomas) *Derby 1* **P** *Bp*
NSM T J HOLMES
SOMERCOTES, NORTH (St Mary) *see* Somercotes and Grainthorpe w Conisholme *Linc*
SOMERFORD (All Saints) *see* Astbury and Smallwood *Ches*
SOMERFORD (St Mary) *see* Christchurch *Win*
SOMERFORD, GREAT (St Peter and St Paul), Little Somerford, Seagry and Corston w Rodbourne *Bris 6* **P** *Bp, MMCET, and Ex Coll Ox (jt) (3 turns), Ld Chan (2 turns)*
P-in-c R K EAST, **C** L BARNES, N J ARCHER,
NSM M CHURCHER
SOMERFORD, LITTLE (St John the Baptist) *see* Gt Somerford, Lt Somerford, Seagry, Corston etc *Bris*
SOMERFORD KEYNES (All Saints) *see* Kemble, Poole Keynes, Somerford Keynes etc *Glouc*
SOMERLEYTON (St Mary), Ashby, Fritton, Herringfleet, Blundeston and Lound *Nor 9* **P** *Lord Somerleyton and SMF (jt)* **R** L R HOBBS
SOMERS TOWN (St Mary the Virgin) *see* Old St Pancras *Lon*
SOMERSAL HERBERT (St Peter) *see* S Dales *Derby*
SOMERSBY (St Margaret) *see* S Ormsby Gp *Linc*
SOMERSHAM (St John the Baptist) w Pidley and Oldhurst and Wooodhurst *Ely 12* **P** *Bp* **V** C S BARTER,
Hon C F J KILNER
SOMERSHAM (St Mary) w Flowton and Offton w Willisham *St E 1* **P** *Bp and MMCET (jt)* **P-in-c** B F ROSE
SOMERTON (St James) *see* Cherwell Valley *Ox*
SOMERTON (St Margaret) *see* Glemsford, Hartest w Boxted, Somerton etc *St E*
SOMERTON (St Michael and All Angels) w Compton Dundon, the Charltons and Kingsdon *B & W 5* **P** *Bp Lon (1 turn), Bp (2 turns), and DBP (1 turn)* **P-in-c** A J SYMONDS,
C B S FAULKNER, **NSM** W M GRIFFITH
SOMERTON, WEST (St Mary) *see* Flegg Coastal Benefice *Nor*
SOMPTING (St Mary the Virgin) (St Peter) *Chich 5* **P** OStJ
V E K HOWARD
SONNING (St Andrew) (St Patrick) *Ox 16* **P** *Bp*
V J A F TAYLOR, **Hon C** M D C FORRER
SONNING COMMON (Christ the King) *see* Rotherfield Peppard and Kidmore End etc *Ox*

SOOKHOLME (St Augustine) *see* Warsop *S'well*
SOOTHILL (St Luke) *see* Hanging Heaton *Wakef*
SOPLEY (St Michael and All Angels) *see* Burton and Sopley *Win*
SOPWORTH (St Mary the Virgin) *see* Boxwell, Leighterton, Didmarton, Oldbury etc *Glouc*
SOTHERTON (St Andrew) *see* Sole Bay *St E*
SOTTERLEY (St Margaret) *see* Hundred River *St E*
SOTWELL (St James) *see* Wallingford *Ox*
SOUDLEY (St Michael) *see* Cinderford w Littledean *Glouc*
SOULBURY (All Saints) *see* Stewkley w Soulbury *Ox*
SOULDERN (Annunciation of the Blessed Virgin Mary) *see* Cherwell Valley *Ox*
SOULDROP (All Saints) *see* Sharnbrook, Felmersham and Knotting w Souldrop *St Alb*
SOUNDWELL (St Stephen) *Bris 5* **P** *Bp* **V** I L WILLS,
NSM A J G COOPER, E A PERRY, **OLM** J C CHARD,
J M WILTSHIRE
SOURTON (St Thomas of Canterbury) *see* Okehampton w Inwardleigh, Bratton Clovelly etc *Ex*
SOUTH *see also under substantive place name*
SOUTH BANK (St John) *York 17* **P** *Abp* **V** T M LEATHLEY
SOUTH BARROW Team Ministry, The *Carl 8* **P** *Bp*
C I M HARVEY, L N CRONIN, **NSM** H GRAINGER
SOUTH CAVE (All Saints) and Ellerker w Broomfleet *York 13*
P *CPAS and D&C Dur (jt)* **V** P G FAULKNER,
NSM P R DRAPER
SOUTH COVE (St Lawrence) *see* Sole Bay *St E*
SOUTH DALES, The *Derby 14* **P** *Bp and Duke of Devonshire (jt)* **R** J J VICKERSTAFF, **C** A D WALKER,
NSM J M LEGH, P R JONES
SOUTH HILL (St Sampson) w Callington *Truro 11* **P** *PCC*
R P R SHARPE, **OLM** P A RAYNHAM
SOUTH MOOR (St George) *see* Ch the K *Dur*
SOUTH PARK (St Luke) *see* Reigate St Luke w Doversgreen *S'wark*
SOUTH POOL (St Nicholas and St Cyriac) *see* Stokenham, Slapton, Charleton w Buckland etc *Ex*
SOUTH SHIELDS (All Saints) (St Mary w St Martin) *Dur 15*
P *Patr Bd* **TR** M P THOMPSON, **TV** J C G POLLOCK
SOUTH SHIELDS St Aidan (St Stephen) The Lawe *Dur 15*
P *Bp and D&C* **P-in-c** P G STANNARD
SOUTH SHIELDS (St Hilda) w St Thomas *Dur 15* **P** *D&C*
P-in-c P G STANNARD
SOUTH SHIELDS (St Lawrence the Martyr) *see* Horsley Hill St Lawr *Dur*
SOUTH SHIELDS (St Simon) *Dur 15* **P** *The Crown*
P-in-c W E BRAVINER
SOUTH SHORE (Holy Trinity) *Blackb 8* **P** *J C Hilton Esq*
P-in-c T CHARNOCK
SOUTH SHORE (St Peter) *Blackb 8* **P** *Bp*
P-in-c T CHARNOCK
SOUTH TRINITY BROADS Benefice, The: Filby, Thrigby, Mautby, Stokesby, Runham and Burgh w Billockby *Nor 6*
P *Bp, Adn Nor, DBP, Mrs Z K Cognetti, R T Daniel Esq, and I F M Lucas Esq (jt)* **R** G R STEEL
SOUTH WARWICKSHIRE SEVEN Group, The *Cov 9* **P** *Bp, Mert Coll Ox, Ch Ch Ox, and Trin Coll Ox (jt)* **R** S P ALLEN,
Hon C G EVANS
SOUTHACRE (St George) *see* Nar Valley *Nor*
SOUTHALL (Christ the Redeemer) *Lon 22* **P** *Bp*
V N J ORCHARD
SOUTHALL (Emmanuel) *Lon 22* **P** *Bp and Ch Patr Trust (jt)*
V W E GILL
SOUTHALL (Holy Trinity) *Lon 22* **P** *Ch Patr Trust*
V M F BOLLEY
SOUTHALL (St George) *Lon 22* **P** *D&C St Paul's*
V C RAMSAY
SOUTHALL GREEN (St John) *Lon 22* **P** *Ch Patr Trust*
V A POULSON, **Hon C** D J C BOOKLESS,
NSM A L POULSON
SOUTHAM (Ascension) *see* Bishop's Cleeve and Woolstone w Gotherington etc *Glouc*
SOUTHAM (St James) *Cov 10* **P** *The Crown*
P-in-c J E ARMSTRONG
SOUTHAMPTON (Christ Church) Portswood *see* Portswood Ch Ch *Win*
SOUTHAMPTON City Centre (St Mary) (St Michael) *Win 13*
P *Bp* **TR** J E DAVIES, **TV** S P HALL, T E DAYKIN,
NSM P R HAND, R M ROBERTS
SOUTHAMPTON (Holy Trinity) *see* Weston *Win*
SOUTHAMPTON Lord's Hill and Lord's Wood *Win 13* **P** *Bp*
V R W SANDAY, **C** T OLIVER
SOUTHAMPTON (St Alban) *see* Swaythling *Win*
SOUTHAMPTON (St Barnabas) *Win 13* **P** *Bp* **V** B J FRY

SOUTHAMPTON (St Denys) Portswood   *see* Portswood St Denys *Win*

SOUTHAMPTON (St Jude)   *see* Maybush and Southampton St Jude *Win*

SOUTHAMPTON (St Mark) *Win 13*   **P** *Ch Patr Trust*   **P-in-c** D MAPES

SOUTHAMPTON (St Mary Extra) *Win 13*   **P** *Bp*   **P-in-c** M J A NEWTON

SOUTHAMPTON Thornhill (St Christopher) *Win 13*   **P** *Bp*   **C** D W JENNINGS,   **NSM** J B WALTERS

SOUTHAMPTON Winkle Street (St Julian)   *see* Southampton (City Cen) *Win*

SOUTHBERGH (St Andrew)   *see* Barnham Broom and Upper Yare *Nor*

SOUTHBOROUGH (St Peter) (Christ Church) (St Matthew) and Bidborough *Roch 12*   **P** *Patr Bd*   **TR** G E HOVENDEN,   **TV** C B WICKS, S A HILLS,   **C** M S A BARKER, P M WHITE,   **NSM** S G FAUCHON-JONES

SOUTHBOROUGH (St Thomas) *Roch 12*   **P** *Bp*   **P-in-c** J A WHEELER

SOUTHBOURNE (All Saints)   *see* Pokesdown All SS *Win*

SOUTHBOURNE (St Christopher) *Win 8*   **P** *Bp*   **P-in-c** A L MCPHERSON,   **NSM** N S LEGRAND

SOUTHBOURNE (St John the Evangelist) w West Thorney *Chich 13*   **P** *Bp*   **V** C R JENKINS,   **C** S C SILK,   **NSM** K J ROBINSON

SOUTHBOURNE (St Katharine) (St Nicholas) *Win 8*   **P** *Bp*   **V** J C WHITE,   **C** J M SHARP

SOUTHBROOM (St James) *Sarum 16*   **P** *D&C*   **V** J P TRIFFITT,   **C** J R G BRADBURY,   **NSM** S A IBBETSON,   **OLM** J A HAYNES

SOUTHCHURCH (Christ Church) *Chelmsf 13*   **P** *Bp*   **V** S N ROSCOE

SOUTHCHURCH (Holy Trinity) *Chelmsf 13*   **P** *Abp Cant*   **R** M A BALLARD

SOUTHCOATES (St Aidan)   *see* Kingston upon Hull St Aid Southcoates *York*

SOUTHCOURT (Good Shepherd) *Ox 21*   **P** *Ch Patr Trust*   **V** D A LAWTON

SOUTHDENE (St Martin)   *see* Kirkby *Liv*

SOUTHEA (Emmanuel)   *see* Wisbech St Mary and Guyhirn w Ring's End etc *Ely*

SOUTHEASE (St Peter) *Chich 18*   **P** *Bp and Gorham Trustees (jt)*   **V** vacant

SOUTHEND (St John the Baptist) (St Mark) (All Saints) (St Alban) *Chelmsf 13*   **P** *Patr Bd*   **TR** S M BURDETT,   **TV** W N PAXTON, P A ROBERTS,   **NSM** S SAYERS, P E OWEN

SOUTHEND (St Peter)   *see* Bradfield and Stanford Dingley *Ox*

SOUTHEND-ON-SEA (St Saviour) Westcliff *Chelmsf 13*   **P** *Bp, Adn Southend, and Churchwardens (jt)*   **V** L R MULLEN

SOUTHERY (St Mary) *Ely 9*   **P** *Guild of All So*   **R** D J EVANS

SOUTHEY GREEN (St Bernard of Clairvaux) Conventional District *Sheff 3 vacant*

SOUTHFIELDS (St Barnabas) *S'wark 18*   **P** *Bp*   **V** I S TATTUM,   **NSM** J G BOYCE

SOUTHFIELDS (St Michael and All Angels)   *see* Wandsworth St Mich w St Steph *S'wark*

SOUTHFLEET (St Nicholas) *Roch 4*   **P** *CPAS*   **R** D W J HOUSTON

SOUTHGATE (Christ Church) *Lon 18*   **P** *V Edmonton All SS*   **V** P J E JACKSON,   **NSM** H ROGERS

SOUTHGATE Local Ecumenical Partnership *St E 13 vacant*

SOUTHGATE (Shared Church)   *see* Grange St Andr *Ches*

SOUTHGATE (St Andrew) *Lon 18*   **P** *Bp*   **V** M L T MCGONIGLE

SOUTHGATE (St Mary) *Chich 7*   **P** *Patr Bd*   **TR** T J WILSON,   **TV** R E POOLE, R J EDWARDS,   **C** C HUTTON,   **NSM** G D M RICHARDS, N B JONES

SOUTHGATE, NEW (St Paul) *Lon 14*   **P** *V Southgate Ch Ch*   **V** M J S MCAULAY

SOUTHILL (All Saints)   *see* Clifton and Southill *St Alb*

SOUTHLAKE (St James) *Ox 15*   **P** *DBP*   **V** vacant 0118-954 5669

SOUTHLAKE (St James's Church Centre)   *see* Woodley *Ox*

SOUTHLEIGH (St Lawrence)   *see* Colyton, Musbury, Southleigh and Branscombe *Ex*

SOUTHMEAD (St Stephen) *Bris 2*   **P** *Bp*   **V** J C HALL

SOUTHMINSTER (St Leonard) *Chelmsf 11*   **P** *Govs Charterhouse*   **V** G S ANDERSON

SOUTHOE (St Leonard)   *see* Gt Staughton w Hail Weston w Southoe *Ely*

SOUTHOVER (St John the Baptist) *Chich 18*   **P** *CPAS*   **R** S J DAUGHTERY,   **C** D J GARRATT,   **NSM** J J BAMBER,   H L F GARRATT

SOUTHOWRAM (St Anne-in-the-Grove) and Claremount *Wakef 4*   **P** *V Halifax*   **V** G S JAMIESON

SOUTHPORT (All Saints) *Liv 9*   **P** *Trustees*   **C** A J EDWARDS

SOUTHPORT (Christ Church) *Liv 9*   **P** *Trustees*   **V** S T REID,   **NSM** S T MARSHALL, R MILTON

SOUTHPORT (Emmanuel) *Liv 9*   **P** *PCC*   **V** vacant (01704) 532743

SOUTHPORT (Holy Trinity) *Liv 9*   **P** *Trustees*   **V** R G GARNER

SOUTHPORT (St Luke) *Liv 9*   **P** *V Southport H Trin*   **V** vacant (01704) 513660

SOUTHPORT (St Philip) (St Paul) *Liv 9*   **P** *V Southport Ch Ch and Trustees (jt)*   **V** A J EDWARDS

SOUTHPORT (St Simon and St Jude) All Souls *Liv 9*   **P** *Trustees*   **P-in-c** D G WHITEHOUSE

SOUTHREPPS (St James)   *see* Trunch *Nor*

SOUTHREY (St John the Divine)   *see* Bardney *Linc*

SOUTHROP (St Peter)   *see* Fairford Deanery *Glouc*

SOUTHSEA (Holy Spirit) *Portsm 6*   **P** *Bp*   **V** vacant (023) 9287 3535

SOUTHSEA (St Jude) *Portsm 6*   **P** *Trustees*   **V** M I DUFF,   **C** S A THEOBALD,   **Hon C** N J BENNETT

SOUTHSEA (St Luke)   *see* Portsea St Luke *Portsm*

SOUTHSEA (St Peter) *Portsm 6*   **P** *Bp*   **P-in-c** A J HUGHES

SOUTHSEA (St Simon) *Portsm 6*   **P** *Ch Patr Trust*   **V** M F HOLLAND

SOUTHTOWN (St Mary)   *see* Gt Yarmouth *Nor*

SOUTHWARK (Christ Church) *S'wark 10*   **P** *Marshall's Charity*   **R** T C N SCOTT

SOUTHWARK (Holy Trinity w St Matthew) *S'wark 10*   **P** *Bp*   **R** N A MCKINNON

SOUTHWARK (St George the Martyr) (St Alphege) (St Jude) *S'wark 10*   **P** *Lon Corp (1 turn), Ld Chan (4 turns), Walsingham Coll Trust Assn (1 turn)*   **P-in-c** R C ANDREWS,   **Hon C** F Y-C HUNG, S MOUGHTIN-MUMBY,   **OLM** D PAPE

SOUTHWARK (St Hugh)   *see* Bermondsey St Hugh CD *S'wark*

SOUTHWATER (Holy Innocents) *Chich 8*   **P** *V Horsham*   **V** K F GODFREY

SOUTHWAY (Holy Spirit) *Ex 23*   **P** *Ld Chan*   **P-in-c** W P JACKSON,   **C** M L SIMMS, D B M GILL

SOUTHWELL (Holy Trinity) *S'well 15*   **P** *CPAS*   **V** M S TANNER,   **NSM** D L ROBBINS

SOUTHWELL (St Andrew)   *see* Portland *Sarum*

SOUTHWICK (Holy Trinity)   *see* N Wearside *Dur*

SOUTHWICK (St James) w Boarhunt *Portsm 1*   **P** *R Thistlewayte Esq*   **P-in-c** R L GREEN

SOUTHWICK (St Mary the Virgin)   *see* Warmington, Tansor and Cotterstock etc *Pet*

SOUTHWICK (St Michael and All Angels) (St Peter) *Chich 4*   **P** *Bp and Ld Chan (alt)*   **R** J D S FRENCH

SOUTHWICK (St Thomas)   *see* N Bradley, Southwick, Heywood and Steeple Ashton *Sarum*

SOUTHWOLD (St Edmund King and Martyr)   *see* Sole Bay *St E*

SOUTHWOOD (Mission Church)   *see* Evercreech w Chesterblade and Milton Clevedon *B & W*

SOWERBY (St Mary) (St Peter) *Wakef 3*   **P** *DBP*   **P-in-c** M C CRABTREE,   **NSM** L ENNIS

SOWERBY (St Oswald) *York 18*   **P** *Abp*   **P-in-c** N J CARNALL

SOWERBY BRIDGE (Christ Church) *Wakef 4*   **P** *V Halifax*   **P-in-c** A DICK

SOWTON (St Michael and All Angels)   *see* Aylesbeare, Rockbeare, Farringdon etc *Ex*

SPALDING (St John the Baptist) w Deeping St Nicholas *Linc 17*   **P** *Bp*   **V** P S J GARLAND

SPALDING (St Mary and St Nicolas) *Linc 17*   **P** *Feoffees*   **V** J D BENNETT,   **C** V POLLARD

SPALDING (St Paul) *Linc 17*   **P** *Bp and V Spalding (jt)*   **P-in-c** J D BENNETT,   **C** V POLLARD

SPALDWICK (St James)   *see* E Leightonstone *Ely*

SPARHAM (St Mary)   *see* Lyng, Sparham, Elsing, Bylaugh, Bawdeswell etc *Nor*

SPARKBROOK (Christ Church) *Birm 13*   **P** *Aston Trustees*   **P-in-c** S R SIMCOX,   **C** R J SUDWORTH

SPARKBROOK (St Agatha) w Balsall Heath St Barnabas *Birm 13*   **P** *Bp*   **V** J A HEWER

SPARKFORD (St Mary Magdalene)   *see* Cam Vale *B & W*

SPARKHILL (St John the Evangelist) *Birm 13*   **P** *Dioc Trustees and Aston Trustees (alt)*   **V** J A SELF,   **C** S G TAYLOR,   A I TAYLOR

SPARKWELL (All Saints) *Ex 21*   **P** *D&C Windsor*   **V** F G DENMAN

SPARROW HALL (St George)   *see* Fazakerley Em *Liv*

SPARSHOLT (Holy Cross)   *see* Ridgeway *Ox*

SPARSHOLT (St Stephen)   *see* Downs Benefice *Win*

SPAXTON (St Margaret)   *see* Aisholt, Enmore, Goathurst, Nether Stowey etc *B & W*

SPEEN (St Mary the Virgin)   *see* Newbury *Ox*

SPEETON (St Leonard)   *see* Bempton w Flamborough, Reighton w Speeton *York*

SPEKE (St Aidan) (All Saints) *Liv 4*   P *Bp*   TR C I KIDD, TV G PINNINGTON

SPELDHURST (St Mary the Virgin) w Groombridge and Ashurst *Roch 12*   P *DBP*   R D P WREN

SPELSBURY (All Saints)   *see* Chase *Ox*

SPEN, HIGH (St Patrick) and Rowlands Gill *Dur 13*   P *Bp* V *vacant* (01207) 542815

SPENCER BENEFICE   *see* Brington w Whilton and Norton etc *Pet*

SPENCER PERCIVAL MEMORIAL CHURCH   *see* Ealing All SS *Lon*

SPENCERS WOOD (St Michael and All Angels)   *see* Loddon Reach *Ox*

SPENNITHORNE (St Michael) w Finghall and Hauxwell *Ripon 4*   P R J Dalton Esq and M C A Wyvill Esq (alt) P-in-c W J HULSE

SPENNYMOOR (St Paul) and Whitworth *Dur 6*   P *D&C* V L E GOUGH

SPERNALL, Morton Bagot and Oldberrow *Cov 7*   P *Mrs J M Pinney and Bp (alt)*   NSM A W SHEARN

SPETISBURY (St John the Baptist) w Charlton Marshall and Blandford St Mary *Sarum 6*   P Worc Coll Ox (1 turn), Bp (2 turns)   R *vacant* (01258) 453153

SPEXHALL (St Peter)   *see* Blyth Valley *St E*

SPILSBY Group, The (St James) *Linc 7*   P Baroness Willoughby de Eresby (3 turns), Mrs J M Fox-Robinson (1 turn), and Bp (1 turn)   P-in-c P F COATES,   C M T FAULKNER

SPIRE HILL *Sarum 5*   P Bp, CCC Cam, and Mrs J C M Langmead (jt)   R W T RIDDING

SPITAL (St Agnes)   *see* New Windsor *Ox*

SPITAL (St Leonard's Mission Room)   *see* Chesterfield St Mary and All SS *Derby*

SPITALFIELDS (Christ Church w All Saints) *Lon 7* P MMCET   R A RIDER,   C J W D DOUGLAS

SPITALGATE (St John the Evangelist)   *see* Grantham St Anne New Somerby and Spitalgate *Linc*

SPITTAL (St John) *Newc 12*   P Bp and Mercers' Co (alt) P-in-c M S KNOX

SPIXWORTH (St Peter)   *see* Horsham St Faith, Spixworth and Crostwick *Nor*

SPOFFORTH (All Saints) w Kirk Deighton *Ripon 1*   P *Bp* Hon C M L SHACKLEY

SPONDON (St Werburgh) *Derby 9*   P Mrs L B Palmer V J F HOLLYWELL,   NSM E S BERRY

SPORLE (St Mary)   *see* Gt and Lt Dunham w Gt and Lt Fransham and Sporle *Nor*

SPOTLAND (St Clement) *Man 17*   P *Bp*   P-in-c K L SMEETON

SPRATTON (St Andrew)   *see* Guilsborough and Hollowell and Cold Ashby etc *Pet*

SPREYTON (St Michael)   *see* Chagford, Drewsteignton, Hittisleigh etc *Ex*

SPRIDLINGTON (St Hilary)   *see* Owmby Gp *Linc*

SPRIGG'S ALLEY (Mission Room)   *see* Chinnor, Sydenham, Aston Rowant and Crowell *Ox*

SPRING GROVE (St Mary) *Lon 11*   P Ch Patr Trust V R C HOAD,   Hon C M A WARMAN

SPRING LINE Group, The *Linc 3*   P Lord Monson, Ball Coll Ox, J M Wright Esq, Bp, and DBP (jt)   P-in-c P D GODDEN, NSM A H WILKINSON,   OLM W G WILLIAMS

SPRING PARK (All Saints) *S'wark 19*   P *Bp*   V Y V CLARKE

SPRINGFIELD (All Saints) *Chelmsf 8*   P Air Cdre N S Paynter R R J BROWN,   NSM C J MOORE

SPRINGFIELD (Holy Trinity) *Chelmsf 8*   P Simeon's Trustees V T W BALL,   C D V CHESNEY

SPRINGFIELD (St Christopher) *Birm 13*   P Trustees P-in-c T THOMAS

SPRINGFIELD Wallington   *see* Wallington Springfield Ch *S'wark*

SPRINGFIELD, EAST (Church of Our Saviour) (not known) *Chelmsf 8*   P *Bp*   P-in-c A MACKENZIE,   Hon C C A KOSLA, NSM M C HEWSON

SPRINGFIELD, NORTH (St Augustine of Canterbury) *Chelmsf 8*   P *Bp*   P-in-c J V ANDERSON

SPRINGFIELDS (St Stephen)   *see* Wolverhampton St Steph *Lich*

SPRINGTHORPE (St George and St Laurence) *see* Corringham and Blyton Gp *Linc*

SPRINGWELL (St Mary the Virgin)   *see* Sunderland St Mary and St Pet *Dur*

SPRINGWOOD (All Souls)   *see* Liv All So Springwood *Liv*

SPROATLEY (St Swithin)   *see* Preston and Sproatley in Holderness *York*

SPROTBROUGH (St Mary the Virgin) *Sheff 7*   P *Bp* R N A SOPHIANOU

SPROUGHTON (All Saints) w Burstall, Copdock w Washbrook and Belstead and Bentley w Tattingstone *St E 5*   P Patr Bd OLM D W MEHEN

SPROWSTON (St Cuthbert) (St Mary and St Margaret) w Beeston *Nor 2*   P *D&C*   R S C STOKES,   C A V WOODROW, D AKRILL,   NSM H M WRIGHT,   OLM P CHARLESWORTH

SPROXTON (St Bartholomew)   *see* High Framland Par *Leic*

SPROXTON (St Chad)   *see* Helmsley *York*

SQUIRRELS HEATH (All Saints) *Chelmsf 2*   P *Bp* V C W WRAGG

ST BARTHOLOMEW *Sarum 11*   P Ch Ch Ox, New Coll Ox, and DBP (by turn)   R S J MORGAN

STADHAMPTON (St John the Baptist)   *see* Dorchester *Ox*

STAFFHURST WOOD (St Silvan)   *see* Limpsfield and Tatsfield *S'wark*

STAFFORD (Christ Church) (St Chad) (St Mary) *Lich 10* P Patr Bd   TR G C FOWELL,   TV J E EVANS, C A F WALKER,   NSM M J FISHER, J J DAVIS, OLM A H HUTCHINSON, B BUTTERY

STAFFORD (St John the Baptist) and Tixall w Ingestre *Lich 10* P Bp and Earl of Shrewsbury and Talbot (jt)   V A G STONE, C A C T KELLY

STAFFORD (St Paul) Forebridge *Lich 10*   P V Castle Ch V P KELLY

STAFFORD (St Thomas and St Andrew) Doxey   *see* Castle Town *Lich*

STAFFORD, WEST (St Andrew)   *see* Dorchester *Sarum*

STAGSDEN (St Leonard)   *see* Bromham w Oakley and Stagsden *St Alb*

STAGSHAW CHAPEL (St Aidan)   *see* St John Lee *Newc*

STAINBY (St Peter)   *see* Witham Gp *Linc*

STAINCLIFFE (Christ Church) and Carlinghow *Wakef 9* P V Brownhill and V Batley (jt)   V A G HOWE, Hon C M G INMAN

STAINCROSS (St John the Evangelist) *Wakef 7*   P *Bp* V J K BUTTERWORTH,   NSM M SCHOLEY, OLM J M CROSSLAND

STAINDROP (St Mary) *Dur 7*   P Lord Barnard P-in-c K STEVENTON

STAINES (Christ Church) (St Mary) (St Peter) *Lon 13*   P *Bp* and Ld Chan (alt)   V R J COSH,   C G M A ROGERS, NSM S P WOOD

STAINFIELD (St Andrew)   *see* Bardney *Linc*

STAINFORTH (St Mary) *Sheff 10*   P *Bp*   V A W ALLINGTON, C E E M SIMPSON

STAINFORTH (St Peter)   *see* Langcliffe w Stainforth and Horton *Bradf*

STAINING (St Luke Mission Church)   *see* Blackpool St Mich *Blackb*

STAINLAND (St Andrew) w Outlane *Wakef 2*   P V Halifax V R A CHAPMAN,   C D BURROWS

STAINLEY, NORTH (St Mary the Virgin)   *see* W Tanfield and Well w Snape and N Stainley *Ripon*

STAINLEY, SOUTH (St Wilfrid)   *see* Markington w S Stainley and Bishop Thornton *Ripon*

STAINMORE (St Stephen)   *see* Brough w Stainmore, Musgrave and Warcop *Carl*

STAINTON (St Peter w St Paul) w Hilton *York 20*   P *Abp* (2 turns), DBP (1 turn)   P-in-c W J FORD, NSM W A DEWING

STAINTON (St Winifred)   *see* Tickhill w Stainton *Sheff*

STAINTON, GREAT (All Saints)   *see* Bishopton w Gt Stainton *Dur*

STAINTON BY LANGWORTH (St John the Baptist) *see* Barlings *Linc*

STAINTON DALE (St John the Baptist)   *see* Cloughton and Burniston w Ravenscar etc *York*

STAINTON LE VALE (St Andrew)   *see* Walesby *Linc*

STAITHES (St Peter)   *see* Hinderwell, Roxby and Staithes etc *York*

STAKEFORD (Holy Family)   *see* Choppington *Newc*

STALBRIDGE (St Mary)   *see* Spire Hill *Sarum*

STALHAM (St Mary), East Ruston, Brunstead, Sutton and Ingham *Nor 12*   P Bp, DBP and Mrs S F Baker (jt) R S P LAWRENCE,   C P-J B LEECH,   NSM R R F WASHFORD, OLM R H JACKSON

STALISFIELD (St Mary)   *see* Eastling w Ospringe and Stalisfield w Otterden *Cant*

STALLING BUSK (St Matthew)   *see* Askrigg w Stallingbusk *Ripon*

STALLINGBOROUGH (St Peter and St Paul)   *see* Keelby Gp *Linc*

STALMINE (St James) w Pilling St John the Baptist *Blackb 9* P Bp, V Lanc St Mary, Mrs C B Mason-Hornby, and H D H Elletson Esq (jt)   NSM D A DICKINSON

STALYBRIDGE (Holy Trinity and Christ Church) *Ches 14*
P *Trustees*   V T R PARKER
STALYBRIDGE (St George) *Man 13*   P *Lord Deramore and
R Ashton-under-Lyne St Mich (jt)*   **OLM** P BRIERLEY,
K M M STEWART
STALYBRIDGE (St Paul) *Ches 14*   P *Trustees*   V T ROBINSON
STAMBOURNE (St Peter and St Thomas Becket) *see* Upper
Colne *Chelmsf*
STAMBRIDGE (St Mary and All Saints) *Chelmsf 12*
P *Ld Chan (1 turn), Charterhouse (3 turns)*   R *vacant* (01702)
258272
STAMFORD (All Saints) w St John the Baptist *Linc 13*
P *Ld Chan and Burghley Ho Preservation Trust (alt)*
P-in-c M WARRICK,   **Hon C** D M BOND
STAMFORD (Christ Church) *Linc 13*   P *Bp*
P-in-c M A N TAYLOR
STAMFORD (St George) (St Paul) *Linc 13*   P *Burghley Ho
Preservation Trust*   R M A N TAYLOR,   C D A OXTOBY,
D C MAYLOR
STAMFORD (St Mary) (St Martin) *Linc 13*   P *Burghley Ho
Preservation Trust*   **P-in-c** M R RUFF
**STAMFORD BRIDGE Group of Parishes, The (St John the
Baptist)** *York 5*   P *Lord Egremont (2 turns), Prime
Min (1 turn)*   **P-in-c** A F WAKEFIELD
STAMFORD HILL (St Bartholomew) *Lon 5*   P *The Crown*
V C L CARD-REYNOLDS
STAMFORD HILL (St Thomas) *Lon 5*   P *R Hackney*
V W G CAMPBELL-TAYLOR,   **Hon C** I F VIBERT,
NSM M F E STEWART
STAMFORDHAM (St Mary the Virgin) w Matfen *Newc 9*
P *Ld Chan*   **P-in-c** M C V NASH-WILLIAMS
STAMSHAW (St Saviour) *see* Portsea St Sav *Portsm*
STANBRIDGE (St John the Baptist) *see* Totternhoe,
Stanbridge and Tilsworth *St Alb*
STANBURY (Mission Church) *see* Haworth *Bradf*
STAND (All Saints) *Man 10*   P *Earl of Wilton*   R A J HARDY,
NSM C D BINNS
STANDISH (St Nicholas) *see* Eastington, Frocester, Haresfield
etc *Glouc*
STANDISH (St Wilfrid) *Blackb 4*   P *Bp*   **NSM** G E WATSON
STANDLAKE (St Giles) *see* Lower Windrush *Ox*
STANDON (All Saints) *see* Cotes Heath and Standon and
Swynnerton etc *Lich*
STANDON (St Mary) and The Mundens w Sacombe *St Alb 15*
P *Ch Trust Fund Trust, K Coll Cam, and R Abel-Smith Esq
(1 turn), Ch Trust Fund Trust (1 turn)*   R D C PAYNE,
C L MOSS
STANFIELD (St Margaret) *see* Litcham w Kempston, E and W
Lexham, Mileham etc *Nor*
STANFORD (All Saints) *see* Lyminge w Paddlesworth,
Stanford w Postling etc *Cant*
STANFORD (All Saints) *Nor 13*   P *Bp*   V *vacant*
STANFORD (St Nicholas) *see* Gilmorton, Peatling Parva,
Kimcote etc *Leic*
STANFORD BISHOP (St James) *see* Frome Valley *Heref*
STANFORD DINGLEY (St Denys) *see* Bradfield and Stanford
Dingley *Ox*
STANFORD IN THE VALE (St Denys) w Goosey and Hatford
Ox 17   P *D&C Westmr (3 turns), Simeon's Trustees (2 turns)*
P-in-c T E F ROSE,   **NSM** A GOSDEN
STANFORD-LE-HOPE (St Margaret) w Mucking *Chelmsf 14*
P *MMCET*   R J A K GUEST,   C J WHITE
STANFORD-ON-SOAR (St John the Baptist) *see* E and W
Leake, Stanford-on-Soar, Rempstone etc *S'well*
STANFORD-ON-TEME (St Mary) *see* Teme Valley N *Worc*
STANFORD RIVERS (St Margaret)
see Greensted-juxta-Ongar w Stanford Rivers etc *Chelmsf*
**STANGROUND (St John the Baptist) (St Michael and All
Angels)** *Ely 15*   P *Em Coll Cam*   **P-in-c** S BETSON
STANHOE (All Saints) *see* Docking, the Birchams, Stanhoe
and Sedgeford *Nor*
STANHOPE (St Thomas) *see* Upper Weardale *Dur*
STANION (St Peter) *see* Brigstock w Stanion and Lowick and
Sudborough *Pet*
STANLEY (All Saints) *see* W Hallam and Mapperley w Stanley
Derby
STANLEY (St Agnes) *see* Bagnall w Endon *Lich*
STANLEY (St Andrew) *see* W Hallam and Mapperley w
Stanley *Derby*
STANLEY (St Andrew) *see* Ch the K *Dur*
STANLEY (St Anne) w Stoneycroft St Paul *Liv 8*   P *V W Derby
St Mary and St Chad's Coll Dur (jt)*   C E L WILLIAMS,
Hon C C WARRILOW
STANLEY (St Peter) *Wakef 11*   P *Dean*   V W E HENDERSON,
NSM J KILSBY

STANLEY (St Thomas) *see* Satley, Stanley and Tow Law *Dur*
STANLEY PONTLARGE (Chapel) *see* Winchcombe *Glouc*
STANLEYS, The *Glouc 4*   P *P Hollings Esq and Jes Coll
Cam (jt)*   V *vacant* (01453) 826698
STANMER w Falmer *Chich 2*   P *Bp*   **P-in-c** A N ROBINSON
STANMORE (St Luke) *Win 7*   P *Bp*   V M R GARDNER
STANMORE, GREAT (St John the Evangelist) *Lon 23*
P *R O Bernays Esq*   R A J CHRISTIAN
STANMORE, LITTLE (St Lawrence) *Lon 23*   P *Bp*
R P M REECE
STANNEY (St Andrew) *see* Ellesmere Port *Ches*
STANNINGFIELD (St Nicholas) *see* St Edm Way *St E*
STANNINGLEY (St Thomas) *Ripon 6*   P *V Leeds St Pet*
R R I M COUTTS
STANNINGTON (Christ Church) *Sheff 4*   P *Bp*   V P W WEST
STANNINGTON (St Mary the Virgin) *Newc 11*   P *Bp*
V *vacant* (01670) 789222
STANSFIELD (All Saints) *see* Bansfield *St E*
STANSTEAD (St James) *see* Glemsford, Hartest w Boxted,
Somerton etc *St E*
STANSTEAD ABBOTS (St Andrew) *see* Gt Amwell w
St Margaret's and Stanstead Abbots *St Alb*
STANSTEAD ST MARGARET (St Mary the Virgin) *as above*
STANSTED (St Mary) w Fairseat and Vigo *Roch 10*   P *Bp*
R C J L NOBLE
STANSTED (St Paul) (Christ Church) *Chich 13*   P *Stansted
Park Foundation*   **P-in-c** J D STRAIN
**STANSTED MOUNTFITCHET (St John) w Birchanger and
Farnham** *Chelmsf 18*   P *Bp, New Coll Ox, and
Mrs L A Murphy (jt)*   R P J WILKIN
**STANTON (All Saints), Hopton, Market Weston, Barningham
and Coney Weston** *St E 9*   P *Ld Chan (2 turns) and Bp
(1 turn)*   R D H MESSER,   C L DAWSON
STANTON (St Gabriel) *see* Golden Cap Team *Sarum*
STANTON (St Mary) *see* Alton w Bradley-le-Moors and
Denstone etc *Lich*
STANTON (St Mary and All Saints) *see* Markfield, Thornton,
Bagworth and Stanton etc *Leic*
STANTON (St Michael and All Angels) *see* Winchcombe *Glouc*
STANTON BY BRIDGE (St Michael) *see* Melbourne,
Ticknall, Smisby and Stanton *Derby*
**STANTON-BY-DALE (St Michael and All Angels) w Dale
Abbey and Risley** *Derby 13*   P *Bp*   R I E GOODING,
NSM G W DUNDAS
STANTON DREW (St Mary) *see* Chew Magna w Dundry,
Norton Malreward etc *B & W*
STANTON FITZWARREN (St Leonard) *see* Stratton
St Margaret w S Marston etc *Bris*
STANTON HARCOURT (St Michael) *see* Lower Windrush *Ox*
STANTON HILL (All Saints) *see* Skegby w Teversal *S'well*
STANTON-IN-PEAK (Holy Trinity) *see* Youlgreave,
Middleton, Stanton-in-Peak etc *Derby*
STANTON LACY (Hayton Bent Hall) *see* Ludlow *Heref*
STANTON LACY (St Peter) *as above*
STANTON ON HINE HEATH (St Andrew) *Lich 22*
P *Sir Beville Stanier Bt*   V D J HUMPHRIES
STANTON-ON-THE-WOLDS (All Saints) *see* Keyworth and
Stanton-on-the-Wolds and Bunny etc *S'well*
STANTON PRIOR (St Lawrence) *see* Farmborough,
Marksbury and Stanton Prior *B & W*
STANTON ST BERNARD (All Saints) *see* Vale of Pewsey
Sarum
STANTON ST JOHN (St John the Baptist) *see* Wheatley *Ox*
STANTON ST QUINTIN (St Giles) *see* Hullavington, Norton
and Stanton St Quintin *Bris*
STANTONBURY (Christ Church) and Willen *Ox 25*   P *Patr Bd*
TR P A SMITH,   **TV** A R B JOWITT, C E COLLINGE,
P S BALLANTINE,   **NSM** E M J M BAKER
STANWAY (St Albright) (St Andrew) *Chelmsf 17*
P *Magd Coll Ox*   R P R MCLAREN-COOK
STANWAY (St Peter) *see* Winchcombe *Glouc*
STANWELL (St Mary the Virgin) *Lon 13*   P *Ld Chan*
V W P STAFFORD-WHITTAKER
STANWICK (St Laurence) *see* Raunds, Hargrave, Ringstead
and Stanwick *Pet*
STANWIX (St Michael) *Carl 3*   P *Bp*   V B G PHILLIPS,
C C D BOLSTER
STAPEHILL (All Saints) *see* Hampreston *Sarum*
STAPENHILL (Immanuel) *Derby 16*   P *Ch Soc Trust*
P-in-c K WOOD
STAPENHILL (St Peter) w Cauldwell *Derby 16*   P *Ch Soc
Trust*   V M ANDREYEV,   **NSM** C R BICKNELL
STAPLE (St James) *see* Woodnesborough w Worth and Staple
Cant
STAPLE FITZPAINE (St Peter) *see* Beercrocombe w Curry
Mallet, Hatch Beauchamp etc *B & W*

STILTON (St Mary Magdalene) w Denton and Caldecote and Folkesworth w Morborne and Haddon *Ely 15*   **P** *MMCET and Bp, Ld Chan (alt)*   **R** R LONGFOOT

STINCHCOMBE (St Cyr)   *see Cam w Stinchcombe Glouc*

STINSFORD (St Michael)   *see Charminster and Stinsford Sarum*

STIRCHLEY (All Saints)   *see Cen Telford Lich*

STIRCHLEY (Ascension) *Birm 5*   **P** *R Kings Norton* **P-in-c** P A KAYE

STISTED (All Saints)   *see Cressing w Stisted and Bradwell etc Chelmsf*

STITHIANS (St Stythians)   *see St Stythians w Perranarworthal and Gwennap Truro*

STIXWOULD (St Peter)   *see Woodhall Spa Gp Linc*

STOAK (St Lawrence)   *see Ellesmere Port Ches*

STOCK (St Barnabas)   *see Spire Hill Sarum*

STOCK HARVARD (All Saints) *Chelmsf 9*   **P** *Guild of All So* **P-in-c** S W NEED

STOCKBRIDGE (Old St Peter) (St Peter) and Longstock and Leckford *Win 12*   **P** *Bp and St Jo Coll Ox (jt)* **P-in-c** J WATKINS

STOCKBRIDGE VILLAGE (St Jude) *Liv 2*   **P** *Bp and R W Derby (jt)*   **V** E D O'NEILL

STOCKBURY (St Mary Magdalene)   *see Newington w Hartlip and Stockbury Cant*

STOCKCROSS (St John)   *see E Downland Ox*

STOCKERSTON (St Peter)   *see Six Saints circa Holt Leic*

STOCKING FARM (St Luke) *Leic 1*   **P** *Bp* **P-in-c** A K FORD

STOCKING PELHAM (St Mary)   *see Albury, Braughing, Furneux Pelham, Lt Hadham etc St Alb*

STOCKINGFORD (St Paul) *Cov 5*   **P** *V Nuneaton* **V** M F VINCENT

STOCKLAND (St Mary Magdalene)   *see Cannington, Otterhampton, Combwich and Stockland B & W*

STOCKLAND (St Michael and All Angels)   *see Kilmington, Stockland, Dalwood, Yarcombe etc Ex*

STOCKLAND GREEN (St Mark) *Birm 8*   **P** *The Crown* **V** *vacant* 0121-373 0130

STOCKLEIGH ENGLISH (St Mary the Virgin)   *see N Creedy Ex*

STOCKLEIGH POMEROY (St Mary the Virgin)   *as above*

STOCKLINCH (St Mary Magdalene)   *see Winsmoor B & W*

STOCKPORT (St George) *Ches 18*   **P** *Trustees*   **V** A J BELL, **C** A S LYTHALL,   **NSM** H GRIFFITHS

STOCKPORT (St Mark)   *see Edgeley and Cheadle Heath Ches*

STOCKPORT (St Martin)   *see Heatons Man*

STOCKPORT (St Mary) *Ches 18*   **P** *G&C Coll Cam* **R** R P SCOONES

STOCKPORT (St Matthew)   *see Edgeley and Cheadle Heath Ches*

STOCKPORT (St Saviour) *Ches 18*   **P** *Trustees* **V** D V COOKSON

STOCKPORT (St Thomas) (St Peter) *Ches 18*   **P** *Bp and Soc of the Faith (jt)*   **R** K D N KENRICK,   **Hon C** K R BROOKES

STOCKSBRIDGE (St Matthias) *Sheff 3*   **P** *Bp* **P-in-c** C E BARNARD

STOCKSFIELD (St John)   *see Bywell and Mickley Newc*

STOCKTON (St Andrew)   *see Teme Valley N Worc*

STOCKTON (St Chad) *Dur 10*   **P** *Bp* **P-in-c** N R SHAVE, **C** J NOBEL,   **NSM** E WALKER

STOCKTON (St Chad)   *see Beckbury, Badger, Kemberton, Ryton, Stockton etc Lich*

STOCKTON (St John the Baptist)   *see Wylye and Till Valley Sarum*

STOCKTON (St Michael and All Angels)   *see Napton-on-the-Hill, Lower Shuckburgh etc Cov*

STOCKTON (St Michael and All Angels)   *see Gillingham w Geldeston, Stockton, Ellingham etc Nor*

STOCKTON HEATH (St Thomas) *Ches 4*   **P** P G Greenall Esq **V** M L RIDLEY,   **C** J E PROUDFOOT,   **Hon C** H S HOUSTON, **NSM** M A THOMSON

STOCKTON ON TEES (Holy Trinity) (St Mark) *Dur 10*   **P** *Bp* **P-in-c** S J GILES

STOCKTON-ON-TEES (St Chad)   *see Stockton St Chad Dur*

STOCKTON ON TEES (St James) *Dur 10*   **P** *Bp* **P-in-c** D J BELL

STOCKTON-ON-TEES (St John the Baptist) *Dur 10*   **P** *Bp* **P-in-c** D J BELL

STOCKTON-ON-TEES (St Paul) *Dur 10*   **P** *The Crown* **P-in-c** D W ROSAMOND

STOCKTON-ON-TEES (St Peter) *Dur 10*   **P** *Bp* **V** P D ASHDOWN

STOCKTON-ON-TEES (St Thomas) *Dur 10*   **P** *Bp* **P-in-c** A J FARISH,   **C** S R GREEN

STOCKTON-ON-THE-FOREST (Holy Trinity) w Holtby and Warthill *York 2*   **P** *Abp*   **P-in-c** N W R BIRD, **NSM** M E W WILLETTS

STOCKWELL (St Andrew) (St Michael) *S'wark 11*   **P** *Bp* **V** N C WHITTLE,   **OLM** I A BOWMAN

STOCKWITH, EAST (St Peter)   *see Corringham and Blyton Gp Linc*

STOCKWITH, WEST (St Mary the Virgin)   *see Beckingham and Walkeringham and Misterton etc S'well*

STOCKWOOD (Christ the Servant)   *see Bris Ch the Servant Stockwood Bris*

STODDEN Churches, The *St Alb 13*   **P** *MMCET and DBP (alt)*   **R** J C BROOKSHAW

STODMARSH (St Mary)   *see Littlebourne and Ickham w Wickhambreaux etc Cant*

STODY (St Mary)   *see Brinton, Briningham, Hunworth, Stody etc Nor*

STOGUMBER (Blessed Virgin Mary)   *see Quantock Towers B & W*

STOGURSEY (St Andrew)   *see Quantock Coast B & W*

STOKE (St Mary and St Andrew)   *see Colsterworth Gp Linc*

STOKE (St Michael)   *see Coventry Caludon Cov*

STOKE (St Peter and St Paul)   *see Grain w Stoke Roch*

STOKE, EAST (St Oswald) w Syerston *S'well 3*   **P** *Bp* **P-in-c** D HOLLIS

STOKE, NORTH (St Martin)   *see Bath Weston All SS w N Stoke and Langridge B & W*

STOKE, NORTH (St Mary the Virgin)   *see Langtree Ox*

STOKE, SOUTH (St Andrew)   *see Goring and Streatley w S Stoke Ox*

STOKE, SOUTH (St James the Great)   *see Combe Down w Monkton Combe and S Stoke B & W*

STOKE, SOUTH (St Leonard)   *see Arundel w Tortington and S Stoke Chich*

STOKE, WEST (St Andrew) *Chich 13*   **P** *Bp*   **R** *vacant*

STOKE ABBOTT (St Mary)   *see Beaminster Area Sarum*

STOKE ALBANY (St Botolph) w Wilbarston and Ashley w Weston-by-Welland and Sutton Bassett *Pet 7*   **P** *Comdr L M M Saunders-Watson (2 turns), Bp (1 turn), DBP (1 turn)* **P-in-c** S L HUGHES

STOKE ALDERMOOR (St Catherine)   *see Coventry Caludon Cov*

STOKE ASH (All Saints)   *see S Hartismere St E*

STOKE BARDOLPH (St Luke)   *see Burton Joyce w Bulcote and Stoke Bardolph S'well*

STOKE BISHOP (St Mary Magdalene) *Bris 2*   **P** *Bp* **V** D J R RITCHIE

STOKE BLISS (St Peter)   *see Teme Valley S Worc*

STOKE BRUERNE (St Mary the Virgin)   *see Blisworth and Stoke Bruerne w Grafton Regis etc Pet*

STOKE BY CLARE (St John the Baptist)   *see Stour Valley St E*

STOKE BY NAYLAND (St Mary) w Leavenheath and Polstead *St E 3*   **P** *Mrs S E F Holden and St Jo Coll Ox (alt)* **P-in-c** A S MASON,   **OLM** J A D SEPHTON, V ARMSTRONG

STOKE CANON (St Mary Magdalene)   *see Brampford Speke, Cadbury, Newton St Cyres etc Ex*

STOKE CHARITY (St Mary and St Michael)   *see Upper Dever Win*

STOKE CLIMSLAND (not known) *Truro 12*   **P** *Bp and Duchy of Cornwall (alt)*   **P-in-c** P R SHARPE,   **C** M E ELLIOTT

STOKE D'ABERNON (St Mary the Virgin)   *see Cobham and Stoke D'Abernon Guildf*

STOKE DAMEREL (St Andrew w St Luke) and Devonport St Aubyn *Ex 22*   **P** *Trustees Lord St Levan (2 turns), Prime Min (1 turn)*   **R** D J NIXON

STOKE DOYLE (St Rumbold)   *see Aldwincle, Clopton, Pilton, Stoke Doyle etc Pet*

STOKE DRY (St Andrew)   *see Lyddington, Bisbrooke, Caldecott, Glaston etc Pet*

STOKE EDITH (St Mary)   *see Ledbury Heref*

STOKE FLEMING (St Peter), Blackawton and Strete *Ex 14*   **P** *Bp and BDP (jt)*   **V** J H BELL

STOKE GABRIEL (St Gabriel) and Collaton *Ex 13*   **P** *Bp* **V** D A TREBY

STOKE GIFFORD (St Michael) *Bris 5*   **P** *Bp*   **TR** S JONES, **TV** T G E WEBBER,   **C** M L GORDON, S D DUNN, J A ROCKS, **Hon C** I J TOMKINS,   **NSM** J C BRADLEY, K E JONES

STOKE GOLDING (St Margaret)   *see Fenn Lanes Gp Leic*

STOKE GOLDINGTON (St Peter)   *see Gayhurst w Ravenstone, Stoke Goldington etc Ox*

STOKE HAMMOND (St Luke)   *see Brickhills and Stoke Hammond Ox*

STOKE HEATH (St Alban)   *see Cov E Cov*

STOKE HILL (St Peter) *Guildf 5*   **P** *Bp* **V** K L ROSSLYN-SMITH,   **OLM** B J RICH

STOKE HOLY CROSS (St Mary) w Dunston, Arminghall and Caistor St Edmunds w Markshall *Nor 8*   **P** *D&C and Mrs D Pott (jt)*   **R** *vacant* (01508) 492305

STOKE LACY (St Peter and St Paul) *see* Bromyard and Stoke Lacy *Heref*
STOKE LYNE (St Peter) *see* Shelswell *Ox*
STOKE MANDEVILLE (St Mary the Virgin) *see* Ellesborough, The Kimbles and Stoke Mandeville *Ox*
STOKE NEWINGTON (St Andrew) *Lon 5* P *Bp*
P-in-c V A ROBERTS
STOKE NEWINGTON St Faith (St Matthias) and All Saints *Lon 5* P *City Corp* V D J LAMBERT
STOKE NEWINGTON (St John the Evangelist) *see* Brownswood Park *Lon*
STOKE NEWINGTON (St Mary) (Old Parish Church) *Lon 5* P *Bp* R J D CLARK
STOKE NEWINGTON (St Olave) *Lon 5* P *Ld Chan*
V V A ROBERTS
STOKE NEWINGTON COMMON (St Michael and All Angels) *Lon 5* P *Bp* V J B LAWSON
STOKE-NEXT-GUILDFORD (St John the Evangelist) *Guildf 5* P *Simeon's Trustees* R M C WOODWARD, C F E SIMON
STOKE-ON-TRENT *see* Stoke-upon-Trent *Lich*
STOKE ORCHARD (St James the Great) *see* Deerhurst and Apperley w Forthampton etc *Glouc*
STOKE PARK (St Peter) *see* Ipswich St Mary at Stoke w St Pet and St Fran *St E*
STOKE PERO (not known) *see* Porlock and Porlock Weir w Stoke Pero etc *B & W*
STOKE POGES (St Giles) *Ox 23* P *Ch Ch Ox*
V H N L LATHAM
STOKE PRIOR (St Luke) *see* Leominster *Heref*
STOKE PRIOR (St Michael), Wychbold and Upton Warren *Worc 8* P *Bp and D&C (alt)* R R H ANTELL
STOKE RIVERS (St Bartholomew) *see* Shirwell, Loxhore, Kentisbury, Arlington, etc *Ex*
STOKE ROW (St John the Evangelist) *see* Langtree *Ox*
STOKE ST GREGORY (St Gregory) *see* Athelney *B & W*
STOKE ST MARY (St Mary) *see* Beercrocombe w Curry Mallet, Hatch Beauchamp etc *B & W*
STOKE ST MICHAEL (St Michael) *see* Leigh upon Mendip w Stoke St Michael *B & W*
STOKE ST MILBOROUGH (St Milburgha) *see* Ludlow *Heref*
STOKE SUB HAMDON (Blessed Virgin Mary) (All Saints Mission Room) *B & W 5* P *Ch Patr Trust* V vacant
STOKE TALMAGE (St Mary Magdalene) *see* Thame *Ox*
STOKE TRISTER (St Andrew) *see* Charlton Musgrove, Cucklington and Stoke Trister *B & W*
STOKE UPON TERN (St Peter) *see* Cheswardine, Childs Ercall, Hales, Hinstock etc *Lich*
STOKE-UPON-TRENT (St Peter-ad-Vincula) (St Paul) *Lich 12* P *Bp* TR D P LINGWOOD, C I MAITIN, OLM P M LOCKLEY
STOKEHAM (St Peter) *see* Retford Area *S'well*
STOKEINTEIGNHEAD (St Andrew) *see* Shaldon, Stokeinteignhead, Combeinteignhead etc *Ex*
STOKENCHURCH (St Peter and St Paul) and Ibstone *Ox 29* P *Bp* P-in-c R A FRANCE
STOKENHAM (St Michael and All Angels), Slapton, Charleton w Buckland-Tout-Saints, East Portlemouth, South Pool, and Chivelstone *Ex 14* P *Prime Min (1 turn), Bp, DBP, Sir Neil Jephcott Bt, and Ms S Tyler (1 turn), and Ld Chan (1 turn)* P-in-c A KEMP
STOKESAY (St Christopher) (St John the Baptist) *Heref 10* P *T P D La Touche Esq* P-in-c M L COPE, NSM M G WILLIAMS
STOKESBY (St Andrew) *see* S Trin Broads *Nor*
STOKESLEY (St Peter and St Paul) w Seamer *York 20* P *Abp* R A P HUTCHINSON, C P R HARFORD
STOLFORD (St Peter) *see* Quantock Coast *B & W*
STON EASTON (Blessed Virgin Mary) *see* Chewton Mendip w Ston Easton, Litton etc *B & W*
STONDON (All Saints) *see* Gravenhurst, Shillington and Stondon *St Alb*
STONDON MASSEY (St Peter and St Paul) *see* Blackmore and Stondon Massey *Chelmsf*
STONE (All Saints) *see* Berkeley w Wick, Breadstone, Newport, Stone etc *Glouc*
STONE (Christ Church) and Oulton-with-Moddershall *Lich 13* P *Simeon's Trustees* V P H C KINGMAN, C A D CRANSTON
STONE near Dartford (St Mary) *Roch 2* P *Bp* R K W CLARK
STONE (St John the Baptist) w Dinton and Hartwell *Ox 21* P *Bp and Grocers' Co (jt)* P-in-c P G RICH
STONE (St Mary the Virgin) *see* Chaddesley Corbett and Stone *Worc*
STONE (St Michael and St Wulfad) w Aston (St Saviour) *Lich 13* P *Bp* R I R CARDINAL, C S A SMITH
STONE CROSS (St Luke) w Langney, North *Chich 16* P *Bp* V J D VINE, NSM S A SHERIDAN

STONE-IN-OXNEY (St Mary the Virgin) *see* Wittersham w Stone and Ebony *Cant*
STONE QUARRY (St Luke) *see* E Grinstead St Swithun *Chich*
STONE STREET Group, The *Cant 2* P *Abp and Trustees Lord Tomlin (jt)* C L R ROGERS, Hon C M J STRONG
STONEBRIDGE (St Michael and All Angels) *Lon 21* P *Bp*
V R HERBERT
STONEBROOM (St Peter) *see* Morton and Stonebroom w Shirland *Derby*
STONEGATE (St Peter) *Chich 19* P *E J B Hardcastle Esq and Mrs C J J Reid (jt)* P-in-c J R JAMES, NSM R G ALFORD
STONEGRAVE (Holy Trinity) *see* Ampleforth w Oswaldkirk, Gilling E etc *York*
STONEHAM, NORTH (St Nicholas) (All Saints) and Bassett *Win 10* P *R H W Fleming Esq* P-in-c S HOLMES
STONEHAM, SOUTH (St Mary) *see* Swaythling *Win*
STONEHOUSE (St Cyr) *Glouc 4* P *The Crown*
P-in-c C S MINCHIN
STONEHOUSE (St Paul) *see* Plymouth St Andr and Stonehouse *Ex*
STONELEIGH (St John the Baptist) *Guildf 9* P *Bp*
V L M HELLMUTH
STONELEIGH (St Mary the Virgin) w Ashow *Cov 4* P *Lord Leigh and Bp (jt)* P-in-c J E PERRYMAN
STONESBY (St Peter) *see* Ironstone Villages *Leic*
STONESFIELD (St James the Great) w Combe Longa *Ox 9* P *Duke of Marlborough* P-in-c A R TURNER
STONEY MIDDLETON (St Martin) *see* Longstone, Curbar and Stony Middleton *Derby*
STONEY STANTON (St Michael) *see* Broughton Astley and Croft w Stoney Stanton *Leic*
STONEYCROFT (All Saints) *Liv 8* P *Bp* V R WILLIAMS, NSM S-A MASON
STONEYCROFT (St Paul) *see* Stanley w Stoneycroft St Paul *Liv*
STONEYDELPH (St Martin in the Delph) *see* Glascote and Stonydelph *Lich*
STONHAM ASPAL (St Mary and St Lambert) *see* Crowfield w Stonham Aspal and Mickfield *St E*
STONHAM PARVA (St Mary) *see* Creeting St Mary, Creeting St Peter etc *St E*
STONNALL (St Peter) *see* Shenstone and Stonnall *Lich*
STONTON WYVILLE (St Denys) *see* Welham, Glooston and Cranoe and Stonton Wyville *Leic*
STONY MIDDLETON (St Martin) *see* Longstone, Curbar and Stony Middleton *Derby*
STONY STRATFORD (St Mary and St Giles) *Ox 25* P *Bp*
V R NORTHING
STOODLEIGH (St Margaret) *see* Washfield, Stoodleigh, Withleigh etc *Ex*
STOPHAM (St Mary the Virgin) and Fittleworth *Chich 11* P *D&C and Col Sir Brian Barttelot Bt (jt)* P-in-c R D WYNN
STOPSLEY (St Thomas) *St Alb 12* P *Bp* V D G ALEXANDER
STORRIDGE (St John the Baptist) *see* Cradley w Mathon and Storridge *Heref*
STORRINGTON (St Mary) *Chich 12* P *Keble Coll Ox*
R J M ACHESON, NSM A R ROSS, R W TOOVEY
STORTH (All Saints Mission) *see* Arnside *Carl*
STOTFOLD (St Mary the Virgin) and Radwell *St Alb 3* P *Bp*
V P M QUINT
STOTTESDON (St Mary) w Farlow, Cleeton St Mary, Silvington, Sidbury and Middleton Scriven *Heref 8* P *Bp*
P-in-c C E RESCH
STOUGHTON (Emmanuel) *Guildf 5* P *Simeon's Trustees*
V F SCAMMELL, C P BUTLER, OLM R P F MASTERS
STOUGHTON (St Mary) *see* Compton, the Mardens, Stoughton and Racton *Chich*
STOUGHTON (St Mary and All Saints) *see* Thurnby w Stoughton *Leic*
STOULTON (St Edmund) w Drake's Broughton and Pirton and Norton *Worc 4* P *Croome Estate Trustees, D&C, and Bp (jt)*
R D G SLOGGETT
STOUR, EAST (Christ Church) *see* Stour Vale *Sarum*
STOUR, UPPER *Sarum 17* P *H C Hoare Esq (1 turn), Bp (2 turns), and Bourton Chpl Trustees (1 turn)*
R C A R MOORSOM
STOUR, WEST (St Mary) *see* Stour Vale *Sarum*
STOUR PROVOST (St Michael and All Angels) *as above*
STOUR ROW (All Saints) *as above*
STOUR VALE *Sarum 5* P *Bp* V vacant (01747) 838494
STOUR VALLEY, The *St E 8* P *DBP, Jes Coll Cam, Lady Loch, and Duchy of Lanc (by turn)* R S MITCHELL,
NSM G GREEN
STOURBRIDGE (St John the Evangelist) *see* Old Swinford Stourbridge *Worc*

STOURBRIDGE (St Mary)   *as above*
STOURBRIDGE (St Michael and All Angels) Norton *Worc 12*
   P *Bp*   **V** E BUTT
STOURBRIDGE (St Thomas) *Worc 12*   **P** *Bp*
   P-in-c R V CURTIS
STOURDENE Group, The *Cov 9*   **P** *SMF, Bp, Major and
   Mrs J E Shirley, Miss M L P Shirley, P E Shirley Esq, Ch Ch
   Ox, Jes Coll Ox,* and *Mr and Mrs G Howell*   **R** C M VICKERS,
   NSM J HORTON
STOURHEAD *St E 8*   **P** *E H Vestey Esq, St Chad's Coll Dur,
   Ridley Hall Cam,* and *Walsingham Coll Trust (jt)*   **V** *vacant*
   (01440) 712052
STOURPAINE (Holy Trinity)   *see* Pimperne, Stourpaine,
   Durweston and Bryanston *Sarum*
STOURPORT-ON-SEVERN (St Michael and All Angels) and
   Wilden *Worc 13*   **P** *Earl Baldwin of Bewdley and
   V Kidderminster St Mary and All SS (jt)*   **V** I E MCINTYRE
STOURTON (St Peter)   *see* Kinver and Enville *Lich*
STOURTON (St Peter)   *see* Upper Stour *Sarum*
STOURTON CAUNDLE (St Peter)   *see* Spire Hill *Sarum*
STOVEN (St Margaret)   *see* Hundred River *St E*
STOW Group, The (St Mary the Virgin) *Linc 2*   **P** *Bp and
   DBP (jt)*   **OLM** P I ROSE, J A VICKERS
STOW, WEST (St Mary)   *see* Lark Valley *St E*
STOW BARDOLPH (Holy Trinity)   *see* Wimbotsham w Stow
   Bardolph and Stow Bridge etc *Ely*
STOW BEDON (St Botolph)   *see* Caston, Griston, Merton,
   Thompson etc *Nor*
STOW BRIDGE Mission (St Peter)   *see* Wimbotsham w Stow
   Bardolph and Stow Bridge etc *Ely*
STOW LONGA (St Botolph)   *see* Kym Valley *Ely*
STOW MARIES (St Mary and St Margaret)   *see* Cold Norton w
   Stow Maries *Chelmsf*
STOW ON THE WOLD (St Edward), Condicote and The Swells
   Glouc 9   **P** *DBP and Ch Ch Ox (jt)*   **R** D C FRANCIS,
   NSM H J GARDNER, J A H FRANCIS
STOWE (Assumption of St Mary the Virgin) *Ox 22*
   P *Stowe Sch*   **P-in-c** R M BUNDOCK
STOWE (St Michael and All Angels)   *see* Bucknell w Chapel
   Lawn, Llanfair Waterdine etc *Heref*
STOWE, UPPER (St James)   *see* Heyford w Stowe Nine
   Churches and Flore etc *Pet*
STOWE BY CHARTLEY (St John the Baptist)   *see* Mid Trent
   Lich
STOWE NINE CHURCHES (St Michael)   *see* Heyford w Stowe
   Nine Churches and Flore etc *Pet*
STOWELL (St Leonard)   *see* Chedworth, Yanworth and Stowell,
   Coln Rogers etc *Glouc*
STOWELL (St Mary Magdalene)   *see* Milborne Port w Goathill
   etc *B & W*
STOWEY (St Nicholas and Blessed Virgin Mary)   *see* Clutton w
   Cameley, Bishop Sutton and Stowey *B & W*
STOWEY, NETHER (Blessed Virgin Mary)   *see* Aisholt,
   Enmore, Goathurst, Nether Stowey etc *B & W*
STOWEY, OVER (St Peter and St Paul)   *as above*
STOWFORD (St John)   *see* Lifton, Broadwoodwidger, Stowford
   etc *Ex*
STOWLANGTOFT (St George)   *see* Badwell and Walsham *St E*
STOWMARKET (St Peter and St Mary) *St E 6*   **P** *Ch Patr
   Trust*   **P-in-c** M W EDEN,   **OLM** R M STRETCH
STOWTING (St Mary the Virgin)   *see* Smeeth w Monks Horton
   and Stowting and Brabourne *Cant*
STOWUPLAND (Holy Trinity)   *see* Haughley w Wetherden and
   Stowupland *St E*
STRADBROKE (All Saints) w Horham, Athelington and
   Redlingfield *St E 17*   **P** *Bp (3 turns), Lt-Comdr G C Marshall
   (1 turn),* and *Dr G I Soden (1 turn)*   **R** D J STREETER
STRADISHALL (St Margaret)   *see* Bansfield *St E*
STRADSETT (St Mary)   *see* Downham Market and
   Crimplesham w Stradsett *Ely*
STRAGGLETHORPE (St Michael)   *see* Brant Broughton and
   Beckingham *Linc*
STRAITS, The (St Andrew)   *see* Gornal and Sedgley *Worc*
STRAMSHALL (St Michael and All Angels)   *see* Uttoxeter
   Area *Lich*
STRANTON (All Saints) *Dur 3*   **P** *St Jo Coll Dur*
   NSM A J CRAIG
STRATFIELD MORTIMER (St Mary) and Mortimer West End
   w Padworth *Ox 12*   **P** *Eton Coll, Ld Chan,* and *Englefield Estate
   Trust Corp (by turn)*   **V** P CHAPLIN
STRATFIELD SAYE (St Mary)   *see* Sherfield-on-Loddon and
   Stratfield Saye etc *Win*
STRATFORD (St John the Evangelist w Christ Church) and
   St James *Chelmsf 3*   **P** *V W Ham*   **V** D A RICHARDS,
   NSM J V MEADWAY

STRATFORD NEW TOWN (St Paul) *Chelmsf 3*   **P** *Ch Patr
   Trust*   **P-in-c** K F WOOLMER,   **Hon C** D M WEBB
STRATFORD ST MARY (St Mary)   *see* Higham, Holton
   St Mary, Raydon and Stratford *St E*
STRATFORD SUB CASTLE (St Lawrence)   *see* Salisbury
   St Fran and Stratford sub Castle *Sarum*
STRATFORD-UPON-AVON (Holy Trinity), Luddington and
   Clifford Chambers *Cov 8*   **P** *Bp*   **R** M C W GORICK,
   C D P BANBURY, S LABRAN,   NSM M A SWEET
STRATTON (St Andrew) and Launcells *Truro 8*   **P** *Duchy of
   Cornwall and CPAS (alt)*   **V** *vacant* (01288) 352318
STRATTON (St Mary) (St Michael) and Wacton *Nor 5*   **P** *G&C
   Coll Cam, DBP, and New Coll Ox (by turn)*   **R** H Y WILCOX,
   OLM E R SPRY, G M OSBORNE
STRATTON (St Mary the Virgin)   *see* Bradford Peverell,
   Stratton, Frampton etc *Sarum*
STRATTON (St Peter), North Cerney, Baunton and Bagendon
   Glouc 7   **P** *Mrs P M Chester Master, Jes Coll Ox, Univ Coll
   Ox (jt)*   **P-in-c** W G HEATHCOTE,   NSM D H S LEESON
STRATTON, EAST (All Saints)   *see* Upper Dever *Win*
STRATTON, UPPER (St Philip) *Bris 7*   **P** *Bp*   **V** C A STONE
STRATTON AUDLEY (St Mary and St Edburga)   *see* Shelswell
   Ox
STRATTON ON THE FOSSE (St Vigor)   *see* Chilcompton w
   Downside and Stratton on the Fosse *B & W*
STRATTON ST MARGARET (St Margaret) w South Marston
   and Stanton Fitzwarren *Bris 7*   **P** *Patr Bd*   **TV** V R FLEMING,
   Hon C R J BURSTON
STRATTON STRAWLESS (St Margaret)   *see* Coltishall w Gt
   Hautbois, Frettenham etc *Nor*
STREAT (not known)   *see* Ditchling, Streat and Westmeston
   Chich
STREATHAM (Christ Church) *S'wark 12*   **P** *Bp and
   R Streatham St Leon (jt)*   **V** S TRICKLEBANK
STREATHAM (Immanuel) (St Andrew) *S'wark 12*   **P** *Bp,
   Hyndman Trustees, and R Streatham St Leon (jt)*
   V E M SHEARCROFT
STREATHAM (St Leonard) *S'wark 12*   **P** *Bp*   **R** A J HODGSON
STREATHAM (St Paul) *S'wark 17*   **P** *Bp*
   P-in-c G G HOWARD,   NSM S E M CLARKE
STREATHAM (St Peter) *S'wark 12*   **P** *St Steph Ho Ox*
   V P D ANDREWS
STREATHAM (St Thomas)   *see* Telford Park *S'wark*
STREATHAM, WEST (St James) *S'wark 17*   **P** *CPAS*
   V G G HOWARD,   **C** D R BRITTON,   NSM S E M CLARKE,
   J ALLEN
STREATHAM HILL (St Margaret the Queen)   *see* Streatham
   Ch Ch *S'wark*
STREATHAM HILL (St Margaret the Queen) *S'wark 12*   **P** *Bp*
   V *vacant*
STREATHAM PARK (St Alban) *S'wark 17*   **P** *Ch Soc Trust*
   V M S RICHEUX
STREATHAM VALE (Holy Redeemer) *S'wark 12*   **P** *CPAS*
   V I H GILMOUR
STREATLEY (St Margaret) *St Alb 12*   **P** *Bp*
   P-in-c S P WOOD
STREATLEY (St Mary)   *see* Goring and Streatley w S Stoke *Ox*
STREET (Holy Trinity) (Mission Church) w Walton *B & W 4*
   P *DBP*   **R** S A WALKER,   **Hon C** D N HATREY
STREET Parishes, The *York 6*   **P** *Patr Bd*   **R** B S BOWES
STREETLY (All Saints) *Lich 25*   **P** *Bp*   **C** R E LIVESEY,
   OLM J W BLUNT
STRELLEY (All Saints)   *see* Bilborough w Strelley *S'well*
STRENSALL (St Mary the Virgin) *York 3*   **P** *Abp*
   V M HARRISON,   NSM J A PALMER
STRETE (St Michael)   *see* Stoke Fleming, Blackawton and
   Strete *Ex*
STRETFORD (All Saints) *Man 5*   **P** *Bp*   **P-in-c** M E SLACK,
   OLM H TOMLINSON
STRETFORD (St Bride)   *see* Old Trafford St Bride *Man*
STRETFORD (St Matthew) *Man 5*   **P** *D&C*
   P-in-c K L BURGESS
STRETFORD (St Peter)   *see* Firswood and Gorse Hill *Man*
STRETHALL (St Mary the Virgin)   *see* Icknield Way Villages
   Chelmsf
STRETHAM (St James)   *see* Ely *Ely*
STRETTON (St John)   *see* Penkridge *Lich*
STRETTON (St Mary) w Claymills *Lich 14*   **P** *Baroness Gretton*
   V K A THOMAS,   **C** S H VAZ,   NSM D V WARNER
STRETTON (St Matthew) and Appleton Thorn *Ches 4*
   P *Mrs P F du Bois Grantham and Dr S P L du Bois
   Davidson (jt)*   **V** E C HALL,   **C** G H BUCHAN
STRETTON (St Nicholas)   *see* Cottesmore and Burley,
   Clipsham, Exton etc *Pet*
STRETTON, LITTLE (All Saints)   *see* Church Stretton *Heref*

STRETTON GRANDISON (St Laurence) *see* Ledbury *Heref*
STRETTON MAGNA (St Giles) *see* Glen Magna cum Stretton Magna etc *Leic*
STRETTON ON DUNSMORE (All Saints) *see* Bourton w Frankton and Stretton on Dunsmore etc *Cov*
STRETTON ON DUNSMORE (Mission Church) *as above*
STRETTON ON FOSSE (St Peter) *see* Ilmington w Stretton-on-Fosse etc *Cov*
STRETTON PARVA (St John the Baptist) *see* Gaulby *Leic*
STRETTON SUGWAS (St Mary Magdalene) *Heref 3* **P** *DBP*
  NSM E S V VERWEY, P A LITTLEWOOD
STRICKLAND, GREAT (St Barnabas) *see* Morland, Thrimby, Gt Strickland and Cliburn *Carl*
STRINES (St Paul) *see* Marple All SS *Ches*
STRINGSTON (St Mary the Virgin) *see* Quantock Coast *B & W*
STRIXTON (St Romwald) *see* Wollaston w Strixton and Bozeat etc *Pet*
STROOD (St Francis) *Roch 6* **P** *Bp* **V** H DAUBNEY
STROOD (St Nicholas) w St Mary *Roch 6* **P** *Bp and D&C (jt)*
  V D W GREEN, **C** D L TURNER
STROUD (Holy Trinity) (St Alban Mission Church) *Glouc 4*
  P *Bp* **V** M J WITHEY
STROUD (Mission Church) *see* Steep and Froxfield w Privett *Portsm*
STROUD (St Laurence) and Uplands w Slad *Glouc 4* **P** *Bp*
  V B C E COKER
STROUD GREEN (Holy Trinity) *Lon 20* **P** *Bp*
  V P J HENDERSON, **C** I D PIKE, **NSM** P G ATHERTON
STROXTON (All Saints) *see* Harlaxton Gp *Linc*
STRUBBY (St Oswald) *see* Legbourne and Wold Marsh *Linc*
STRUMPSHAW (St Peter) *see* Burlingham St Edmund w Lingwood, Strumpshaw etc *Nor*
STUBBINGS (St James the Less) *see* Burchetts Green *Ox*
STUBBINGTON (St Edmund) *see* Crofton *Portsm*
STUBBINS (St Philip) *see* Ramsbottom and Edenfield *Man*
STUBBS CROSS (St Francis) *see* Kingsnorth and Shadoxhurst *Cant*
STUBSHAW CROSS (St Luke) *see* Ashton-in-Makerfield St Thos *Liv*
STUBTON (St Martin) *see* Claypole *Linc*
STUDHAM (St Mary the Virgin) *see* Kensworth, Studham and Whipsnade *St Alb*
STUDLAND (St Nicholas) *see* Swanage and Studland *Sarum*
STUDLEY (Nativity of the Blessed Virgin Mary) *Cov 7* **P** *DBP*
  NSM A W SHEARN, **OLM** J A STOTE
STUDLEY (St John the Evangelist) *Sarum 14* **P** R Trowbridge St Jas **P-in-c** S F DEACON, **C** S-A MCDOUGALL,
  NSM E A GIFFORD
STUKELEY, GREAT (St Bartholomew) *see* Huntingdon w the Stukeleys *Ely*
STUKELEY, LITTLE (St Martin) *as above*
STUKELEY MEADOWS Local Ecumenical Partnership
  Ely 12 vacant
STUNTNEY (Holy Cross) *see* Ely *Ely*
STURMER (St Mary) *see* Ridgewell w Ashen, Birdbrook and Sturmer *Chelmsf*
STURMINSTER MARSHALL (St Mary) *see* Bridge Par *Sarum*
STURMINSTER NEWTON (St Mary), Hinton St Mary and Lydlinch *Sarum 5* **P** Col J L Yeatman *(1 turn)*,
  G A L-F Pitt-Rivers Esq *(3 turns)*, V Iwerne Valley *(1 turn)*
  V D R R SEYMOUR, **OLM** R WYNN
STURRY (St Nicholas) w Fordwich and Westbere w Hersden
  Cant 3 **P** Abp, Ld Chan, and St Aug Foundn Cant *(by turn)*
  R P A CORNISH
STURTON (St Hugh) *see* Stow Gp *Linc*
STURTON, GREAT (All Saints) *see* Hemingby Gp *Linc*
STURTON-LE-STEEPLE (St Peter and St Paul) *see* Retford Area *S'well*
STUSTON (All Saints) *see* N Hartismere *St E*
STUTTON (St Aidan) *see* Tadcaster w Newton Kyme *York*
STUTTON (St Peter) *see* Holbrook, Stutton, Freston, Woolverstone etc *St E*
STYVECHALE (St James) *Cov 3* **P** Col A M H Gregory-Hood
  V J K MILLS, **OLM** C M NEWBORN, A PRETT
SUCKLEY (St John the Baptist) *see* Worcs W *Worc*
SUDBOROUGH (All Saints) *see* Brigstock w Stanion and Lowick and Sudborough *Pet*
SUDBOURNE (All Saints) *see* Wilford Peninsula *St E*
SUDBROOKE (St Edward) *see* Barlings *Linc*
SUDBURY (All Saints) *see* S Dales *Derby*
SUDBURY (All Saints) w Ballingdon and Brundon *St E 12*
  P Simeon's Trustees **P-in-c** S D GILL
SUDBURY (St Andrew) *Lon 21* **P** *Bp* **V** F M-L SCROGGIE,
  NSM L P NORTH

SUDBURY (St Gregory) St Peter and Chilton *St E 12* **P** *Bp*
  (3 turns), Ch Soc Trust *(1 turn)* **P-in-c** G J WEBB,
  NSM H M MITCHELL
SUDDEN (St Aidan) and Heywood All Souls *Man 14* **P** Patr Bd
  P-in-c M A READ, **OLM** I TAYLOR
SUDELEY MANOR (St Mary) *see* Winchcombe *Glouc*
SUFFIELD (St Margaret) *see* King's Beck *Nor*
SUFFIELD PARK (St Martin) *see* Cromer *Nor*
SUFFOLK HEIGHTS *see* Chevington w Hargrave, Chedburgh w Depden etc *St E*
SUGLEY (Holy Saviour) *Newc 4* **P** *Bp* **V** S T ROBSON
SULBY (St Stephen's Chapel) *see* Lezayre *S & M*
SULGRAVE (St James the Less) *see* Culworth w Sulgrave and Thorpe Mandeville etc *Pet*
SULHAM (St Nicholas) *see* Pangbourne w Tidmarsh and Sulham *Ox*
SULHAMSTEAD ABBOTS (St Mary) and Bannister w Ufton Nervet *Ox 12* **P** Qu Coll Ox and Or Coll Ox *(alt)*
  R G J LOVELL, **Hon C** P L DEWEY, **NSM** A J PEABODY
SULLINGTON (St Mary) and Thakeham w Warminghurst
  Chich 12 **P** *Bp and DBP (alt)* **P-in-c** D K SPENCER
SUMMERFIELD (Christ Church) (Cavendish Road Hall) *Birm 2*
  P R Birm St Martin w Bordesley **V** P D SAINSBURY,
  C W A BROWN
SUMMERFIELD (St John's Chapel) *see* Hartlebury *Worc*
SUMMERSDALE (St Michael) *see* Chich St Paul and Westhampnett *Chich*
SUMMERSTOWN (St Mary) *S'wark 17* **P** Ch Soc Trust
  V R J RYAN
SUMMERTOWN (St Michael and All Angels) *Ox 7* **P** St Jo Coll Ox **NSM** W L A PRYOR
SUNBURY, UPPER (St Saviour) *Lon 13* **P** V Sunbury
  P-in-c D R MCDOUGALL, **C** P OXLEY, T M ROSE
SUNBURY-ON-THAMES (St Mary) *Lon 13* **P** D&C St Paul's
  V P S DAVIES
SUNDERLAND (St Bede) Town End Farm *see* N Wearside *Dur*
SUNDERLAND (St Chad) *Dur 16* **P** *Bp* **V** J D CHADD,
  C B M EADON, **NSM** P THOMPSON
SUNDERLAND (St Cuthbert) Red House *see* N Wearside *Dur*
SUNDERLAND (St Ignatius) *see* Hendon *Dur*
SUNDERLAND (St Mary the Virgin) (St Peter) *Dur 16* **P** *Bp*
  P-in-c K J BAGNALL, **C** P F GARVIE
SUNDERLAND (St Michael) *see* Sunderland Minster *Dur*
SUNDERLAND (St Thomas) (St Oswald) *Dur 16* **P** *Bp*
  V D G JONES
SUNDERLAND, NORTH (St Paul) *Newc 7* **P** Lord Crewe's Trustees **V** E J WOOD
SUNDERLAND MINSTER Extra-Parochial Place *Dur 16*
  C-in-c S R TAYLOR, **Min** M E ANDERSON, S D HAZLETT
SUNDERLAND POINT (Mission Church) *see* Overton *Blackb*
SUNDON (St Mary) *St Alb 12* **P** *Bp* **P-in-c** Y M SMEJKAL
SUNDRIDGE (St Mary) w Ide Hill and Toys Hill *Roch 9*
  P Abp **R** D J E ATTWOOD, **NSM** A M BOYLE
SUNNINGDALE (Holy Trinity) *Ox 11* **P** *Bp*
  V H D UFFINDELL, **C** L A J TAYLOR
SUNNINGHILL (St Michael and All Angels) and South Ascot
  Ox 11 **P** St Jo Coll Cam **V** S A JOHNSON,
  NSM S M VAN BEVEREN, T L WILLIAMS
SUNNINGWELL (St Leonard) *see* Radley and Sunningwell *Ox*
SUNNYSIDE (St Barnabas) *see* E Grinstead St Swithun *Chich*
SUNNYSIDE (St Michael and All Angels) w Bourne End
  St Alb 1 **P** CPAS **V** D J ABBOTT, **C** H E GARDNER,
  NSM R CLARKSON
SURBITON (St Andrew) (St Mark) *S'wark 15* **P** *Bp*
  V D J HOUGHTON, **C** I J NAY, **NSM** E D LONGFELLOW
SURBITON (St Matthew) *S'wark 15* **P** Patr Bd
  TR S A HONES, **TV** C S LAKER
SURBITON HILL (Christ Church) *S'wark 15* **P** Ch Soc Trust and Trustees *(jt)* **V** J D BIRCHALL, **C** J B ERLEBACH,
  NSM A G FAIRBAIRN
SURFLEET (St Lawrence) *see* Glen Gp *Linc*
SURLINGHAM (St Mary) *see* Rockland St Mary w Hellington, Bramerton etc *Nor*
SURREY WEALD *Guildf 7* **P** Patr Bd *(1 turn)*, Ld Chan
  (2 turns) **TR** A D J COE, **TV** B STEADMAN-ALLEN,
  NSM V J SMITH, **OLM** S D EGERTON
SUSSEX GARDENS (St James) *see* Paddington St Jas *Lon*
SUSTEAD (St Peter and St Paul) *see* Roughton and Felbrigg, Metton, Sustead etc *Nor*
SUTCOMBE (St Andrew) *see* Bradworthy, Sutcombe, Putford etc *Ex*
SUTTERBY (not known) *see* Partney Gp *Linc*
SUTTERTON (St Mary) and Wigtoft *Linc 20* **P** Prime Min
  and Bp (alt) **P-in-c** D D S DE VERNY

SUTTON (All Saints) *see* Potton w Sutton and Cockayne Hatley *St Alb*

SUTTON (All Saints) *see* Wilford Peninsula *St E*

SUTTON (All Saints) w Shopland *Chelmsf 12* **P** *SMF* **R** *vacant* (01702) 544587

SUTTON (Christ Church) (St Barnabas) (St Nicholas) *S'wark 23* **P** *Patr Bd* **TR** S E MULLALLY, **TV** P M PULLINGER, **C** L K PHILBRICK, **NSM** B FRASER

SUTTON (Mission Room) *see* Felixkirk w Boltby *York*

SUTTON (St Andrew) *Ely 8* **P** *D&C* **P-in-c** M HANCOCK

SUTTON (St Barnabas' Mission Church) *see* Macclesfield Team *Ches*

SUTTON (St Clement), Huttoft and Anderby *Linc 8* **P** *Bp (2 turns), Magd Coll Cam (1 turn)* **P-in-c** A C V HARVEY, **Hon C** C H LILLEY, **OLM** J TOMPKINS

SUTTON (St James) *Ches 13* **P** *Trustees* **V** E W L DAVIES, **NSM** V B GISBY

SUTTON (St James) and Wawne *York 14* **P** *Patr Bd* **TV** C FISHER-BAILEY, D J CLUNE, S G SANDHAM

SUTTON (St John the Baptist) *see* Barlavington, Burton w Coates, Sutton and Bignor *Chich*

SUTTON (St Mary) *see* Calow and Sutton cum Duckmanton *Derby*

SUTTON (St Michael) *see* Stalham, E Ruston, Brunstead, Sutton and Ingham *Nor*

SUTTON (St Michael and All Angels) *see* Castor w Sutton and Upton w Marholm *Pet*

SUTTON (St Nicholas) (All Saints) (St Michael and All Angels) *Liv 10* **P** *Patr Bd* **TV** M J TAYLOR, **OLM** M A HARRISON

SUTTON (St Thomas) w Cowling and Lothersdale *Bradf 8* **P** *Ch Ch Ox and Bp (jt)* **V** M COWGILL, **Hon C** G L HALL, **NSM** T CALOW

SUTTON w Carlton and Normanton upon Trent and Marnham *S'well 3* **P** *Bp* **V** *vacant* (01636) 821797

SUTTON, EAST (St Peter and St Paul) *see* Headcorn and The Suttons *Cant*

SUTTON, GREAT (St John the Evangelist) *Ches 9* **P** *V Eastham* **V** D S FISHER, **NSM** C M Y JONES

SUTTON, NORTH *see* Plymouth Em, St Paul Efford and St Aug *Ex*

SUTTON AT HONE (St John the Baptist) *see* Horton Kirby and Sutton-at-Hone *Roch*

SUTTON BASSETT (All Saints) *see* Stoke Albany w Wilbarston and Ashley etc *Pet*

SUTTON BENGER (All Saints) *see* Draycot *Bris*

SUTTON BINGHAM (All Saints) *see* E Coker w Sutton Bingham and Closworth *B & W*

SUTTON BONINGTON (St Michael) (St Anne) w Normanton-on-Soar *S'well 9* **P** *Bp* **R** *vacant* (01509) 670757

SUTTON BRIDGE (St Matthew) *Linc 16* **P** *Bp* **P-in-c** J M DUNKLING

SUTTON BY DOVER (St Peter and St Paul) *see* Ringwould w Kingsdown and Ripple etc *Cant*

SUTTON CHENEY (St James) *see* Bosworth and Sheepy Gp *Leic*

SUTTON COLDFIELD (Holy Trinity) *Birm 12* **P** *Bp* **P-in-c** W J ROUTH, **NSM** P G DUCKERS

SUTTON COLDFIELD (St Chad) *Birm 12* **P** *Bp* **P-in-c** W J ROUTH, **C** E M WALLACE

SUTTON COLDFIELD (St Columba) *Birm 12* **P** *Bp* **V** R P TUCKER

SUTTON COURTENAY (All Saints) w Appleford *Ox 10* **P** *D&C Windsor* **P-in-c** H G KENDRICK

SUTTON-CUM-LOUND (St Bartholomew) *see* Retford Area *S'well*

SUTTON GREEN (All Souls) *see* Woking St Pet *Guildf*

SUTTON HILL (Pastoral Centre) *see* Madeley *Heref*

SUTTON IN ASHFIELD (St Mary Magdalene) *S'well 4* **P** *Bp* **C** A H DIGMAN

SUTTON IN ASHFIELD St Michael and All Angels *S'well 4* **P** *Bp* **P-in-c** T MITCHELL

SUTTON IN HOLDERNESS (St Michael) *York 14* **P** *Abp* **V** M A JEAVONS, **NSM** H M HOTCHIN

SUTTON LE MARSH (St Clement) *see* Sutton, Huttoft and Anderby *Linc*

SUTTON MADDOCK (St Mary) *see* Beckbury, Badger, Kemberton, Ryton, Stockton etc *Lich*

SUTTON MANDEVILLE (All Saints) *see* Fovant, Sutton Mandeville and Teffont Evias etc *Sarum*

SUTTON MONTIS (Holy Trinity) *see* Cam Vale *B & W*

SUTTON ON DERWENT (St Michael) *see* Derwent Ings *York*

SUTTON ON PLYM (St John the Evangelist) *Ex 24* **P** *Keble Coll Ox* **C** K F HAYDON

SUTTON-ON-SEA (St Clement) *see* Sutton, Huttoft and Anderby *Linc*

SUTTON ON THE FOREST (All Hallows) *see* Forest of Galtres *York*

SUTTON ON THE HILL (St Michael) *see* Boylestone, Church Broughton, Dalbury, etc *Derby*

SUTTON-ON-TRENT (All Saints) *see* Sutton w Carlton and Normanton upon Trent etc *S'well*

SUTTON PARK (St Andrew) *see* Sutton St Jas and Wawne *York*

SUTTON ST EDMUND (St Edmund King and Martyr) *see* The Suttons w Tydd *Linc*

SUTTON ST JAMES (St James) *as above*

SUTTON ST MARY (otherwise known as Long Sutton) (St Mary) *Linc 16* **P** *Bp* **P-in-c** J P E SIBLEY

SUTTON ST MICHAEL (St Michael) *see* Sutton St Nicholas w Sutton St Michael *Heref*

SUTTON ST NICHOLAS *see* Lutton w Gedney Drove End, Dawsmere *Linc*

SUTTON ST NICHOLAS (St Nicholas) w Sutton St Michael *Heref 3* **P** *Bp* **P-in-c** H M SHORT

SUTTON UNDER BRAILES (St Thomas à Becket) *Cov 9* **P** *Bp* **R** N J MORGAN, **NSM** J W ROLFE

SUTTON VALENCE (St Mary the Virgin) *see* Headcorn and The Suttons *Cant*

SUTTON VENY (St John the Evangelist) *see* Upper Wylye Valley *Sarum*

SUTTON WALDRON (St Bartholomew) *see* Iwerne Valley *Sarum*

SUTTONS w Tydd, The *Linc 16* **P** *Ld Chan (1 turn), V Long Sutton (2 turns)* **P-in-c** J M DUNKLING

SWABY (St Nicholas) *see* Legbourne and Wold Marsh *Linc*

SWADLINCOTE (Emmanuel) *Derby 16* **P** *V Gresley* **V** *vacant* (01283) 217756

SWAFFHAM (St Peter and St Paul) *Nor 13* **P** *Bp* **V** *vacant* (01760) 721373

SWAFFHAM BULBECK (St Mary) *see* Anglesey Gp *Ely*

SWAFFHAM PRIOR (St Mary) *as above*

SWAFIELD (St Nicholas) *see* Trunch *Nor*

SWAINSTHORPE (St Peter) *see* Newton Flotman, Swainsthorpe, Tasburgh, etc *Nor*

SWAINSWICK (Blessed Virgin Mary) *see* Bath St Sav w Swainswick and Woolley *B & W*

SWALCLIFFE (St Peter and St Paul) *see* Wykeham *Ox*

SWALE, LOWER *Ripon 4* **P** *D&C York, Duke of Northumberland, and Bp (jt)* **R** R J GLOVER, **Hon C** W H THACKRAY, **NSM** M TONGE

SWALECLIFFE (St John the Baptist) *see* Whitstable *Cant*

SWALEDALE *Ripon 2* **P** *Bp* **V** C J HEWLETT

SWALLOW (Holy Trinity) *Linc 5* **P** *The Revd J R H Thorold and J R Thorold Esq (jt), DBP, Bp, and Earl of Yarborough (by turn)* **R** *vacant* (01472) 371560

SWALLOWBECK (St George) *see* Linc St Geo Swallowbeck *Linc*

SWALLOWCLIFFE (St Peter) *see* Nadder Valley *Sarum*

SWALLOWFIELD (All Saints) *see* Loddon Reach *Ox*

SWALLOWNEST (Christ Church) *see* Aston cum Aughton w Swallownest and Ulley *Sheff*

SWALWELL (Holy Trinity) *see* Blaydon and Swalwell *Dur*

SWANAGE (All Saints) (St Mary the Virgin) and Studland *Sarum 8* **P** *Patr Bd* **TR** J S WOOD, **TV** A J CORKE, **C** C A GRAHAM, **NSM** W M FELLINGHAM, **OLM** A C HIGGINS

SWANBOURNE (St Swithun) *see* Newton Longville, Mursley, Swanbourne etc *Ox*

SWANLAND (St Barnabas) *York 14* **P** *H Trin Hull and Distr Ch Patr Soc Ltd* **V** F R SCOTT, **NSM** D KITCHING

SWANLEY (St Mary) *Roch 2* **P** *Guild of All So* **V** J E MOWBRAY

SWANLEY (St Paul) *Roch 2* **P** *Merchant Taylors' Co* **P-in-c** R C SAMME

SWANMORE (St Barnabas) *Portsm 1* **P** *DBP* **NSM** M J MORFILL

SWANMORE (St Michael and All Angels) *Portsm 7* **P** *SMF* **V** *vacant* (01983) 62984

SWANNINGTON (St George) *see* Whitwick, Thringstone and Swannington *Leic*

SWANNINGTON (St Margaret) *see* Wensum Benefice *Nor*

SWANSCOMBE (St Peter and St Paul) *Roch 4* **P** *DBP* **R** *vacant* (01322) 383160

SWANTON ABBOT (St Michael) *see* Worstead, Westwick, Sloley, Swanton Abbot etc *Nor*

SWANTON MORLEY (All Saints) *see* Dereham and Distr *Nor*

SWANTON NOVERS (St Edmund) *see* Brinton, Briningham, Hunworth, Stody etc *Nor*

SWANWICK (St Andrew) and Pentrich *Derby 1* **P** *Wright Trustees and Duke of Devonshire (alt)* **P-in-c** C B LLOYD

SWANWICK (St Barnabas)   *see* Sarisbury *Portsm*
SWARBY (St Mary and All Saints)   *see* S Lafford *Linc*
SWARCLIFFE (St Luke)   *see* Seacroft *Ripon*
SWARDESTON (St Mary the Virgin) w East Carleton, Intwood, Keswick and Ketteringham *Nor 7*   **P** *Bp, DBP, and Miss M B Unthank (jt)*   **R** P D BURR
SWARKESTONE (St James)   *see* Aston on Trent, Elvaston, Weston on Trent etc *Derby*
SWARTHMORE (Mission Church)   *see* Pennington and Lindal w Marton and Bardsea *Carl*
SWATON (St Michael)   *see* Helpringham w Hale *Linc*
SWAVESEY (St Andrew)   *see* Fen Drayton w Conington and Lolworth etc *Ely*
SWAY (St Luke) *Win 11*   **P** *Bp*   **P-in-c** J PAWSON, **NSM** R D C ELLIOTT
SWAYFIELD (St Nicholas)   *see* Corby Glen *Linc*
SWAYTHLING (St Mary South Stoneham w St Alban the Martyr) *Win 13*   **P** *Bp and TR Southn City Cen (jt)*   **V** G J PHILBRICK,   **C** S J WILLIAMS,   **NSM** C A DAY
SWEFFLING (St Mary)   *see* Upper Alde *St E*
SWELL (St Catherine)   *see* Curry Rivel w Fivehead and Swell *B & W*
SWELL, LOWER (St Mary)   *see* Stow on the Wold, Condicote and The Swells *Glouc*
SWELL, UPPER (St Mary)   *as above*
SWEPSTONE (St Peter)   *see* Woodfield *Leic*
SWERFORD (St Mary)   *see* Hook Norton w Gt Rollright, Swerford etc *Ox*
SWETTENHAM (St Peter)   *see* Goostrey w Swettenham *Ches*
SWILLAND (St Mary)   *see* Clopton w Otley, Swilland and Ashbocking *St E*
SWILLINGTON (St Mary) *Ripon 8*   **P** *Bp*   **P-in-c** L C PEARSON
SWIMBRIDGE (St James the Apostle) w West Buckland and Landkey *Ex 18*   **P** *Bp and Trustees Earl Fortescue (jt)*   **NSM** G F SQUIRE
SWINBROOK (St Mary)   *see* Burford w Fulbrook, Taynton, Asthall etc *Ox*
SWINDERBY (All Saints) *Linc 18*   **P** *Bp, Ld Chan, E M K Kirk Esq, and D&C (by turn)*   **V** G C GOALBY,   **NSM** J T ROOKE,   **OLM** P W WALKER
SWINDON (All Saints) (St Barnabas) *Bris 7*   **P** *Bp*   **V** A R STEVENSON,   **C** A M OVERTON-BENGE
SWINDON (Christ Church) (St Mary) *Bris 7*   **P** *Ld Chan*   **V** S M STEVENETTE,   **NSM** N E MCKEMEY, T A WIGLEY
SWINDON Dorcan *Bris 7*   **P** *Bp*   **TR** A B KNAPP,   **C** E C BROWN,   **OLM** S F FISHER
SWINDON New Town (St Mark) (St Adhelm) (St Luke) (St Saviour) *Bris 7*   **P** *Patr Bd*   **TR** D B MCCONKEY
SWINDON (St Andrew) (St John the Baptist) *Bris 7*   **P** *Ld Chan*   **TR** *vacant* (01793) 611473
SWINDON (St Augustine) *Bris 7*   **P** *Bp*   **C** A M OVERTON-BENGE
SWINDON (St John the Evangelist)   *see* Smestow Vale *Lich*
SWINDON (St Lawrence)   *see* N Cheltenham *Glouc*
SWINDON (St Peter)   *see* Penhill *Bris*
SWINDON, NORTH (St Andrew) *Bris 7*   **P** *Bp*   **V** *vacant* (01793) 701353
SWINDON, WEST and the Lydiards *Bris 7*   **P** *Patr Bd*   **TV** C D DEVERELL, T V ROBERTS,   **NSM** P F ROBERTS
SWINE (St Mary)   *see* Skirlaugh w Long Riston, Rise and Swine *York*
SWINEFLEET (St Margaret)   *see* The Marshland *Sheff*
SWINESHEAD (St Mary) *Linc 20*   **P** *Bp*   **P-in-c** D D S DE VERNY
SWINESHEAD (St Nicholas)   *see* The Stodden Churches *St Alb*
SWINFORD (All Saints)   *see* Gilmorton, Peatling Parva, Kimcote etc *Leic*
SWINFORD, OLD Stourbridge (St Mary) *Worc 12*   **P** *Bp*   **C** R I ATKINSON
SWINHOPE (St Helen)   *see* Binbrook Gp *Linc*
SWINNOW (Christ the Saviour)   *see* W Hampstead Trin *Lon*
SWINSTEAD (St Mary)   *see* Edenham w Witham on the Hill and Swinstead *Linc*
SWINTON (Holy Rood) *Man 18*   **P** *TR Swinton and Pendlebury*   **P-in-c** C J C HEWITT,   **OLM** D E FAIR
SWINTON (St Margaret) *Sheff 12*   **P** *Sir Philip Naylor-Leyland Bt*   **V** C J BARLEY,   **C** M T CHILDS
SWINTON (St Peter) and Pendlebury *Man 18*   **P** *Patr Bd*   **TR** J P SHEEHY,   **TV** P HUTCHINS
SWISS COTTAGE (Holy Trinity)   *see* W Hampstead Trin *Lon*
SWITHLAND (St Leonard)   *see* Woodhouse, Woodhouse Eaves and Swithland *Leic*
SWYNCOMBE (St Botolph)   *see* Icknield *Ox*
SWYNNERTON (St Mary)   *see* Cotes Heath and Standon w Swynnerton etc *Lich*

SWYRE (Holy Trinity)   *see* Bride Valley *Sarum*
SYDE (St Mary)   *see* Brimpsfield w Birdlip, Syde, Daglingworth etc *Glouc*
SYDENHAM (All Saints) *S'wark 5*   **P** *V Sydenham St Bart*   **P-in-c** P H SMITH
SYDENHAM (Holy Trinity) (St Augustine) *S'wark 5*   **P** *Bp and Simeon's Trustees (jt)*   **V** E J OLSWORTH-PETER,   **NSM** S R SCOTT, M BROOKS,   **OLM** V J SHIRLEY
SYDENHAM (St Bartholomew) *S'wark 5*   **P** *Earl of Dartmouth*   **V** M J KINGSTON,   **C** H A HUNTLEY
SYDENHAM (St Mary)   *see* Chinnor, Sydenham, Aston Rowant and Crowell *Ox*
SYDENHAM (St Philip) *S'wark 5*   **P** *V Sydenham St Bart*   **V** P W TIERNAN
SYDENHAM, LOWER (St Michael and All Angels) Bell Green *S'wark 5*   **P** *Bp*   **V** *vacant* (020) 8778 7196
SYDENHAM DAMEREL (St Mary)   *see* Milton Abbot, Dunterton, Lamerton etc *Ex*
SYDERSTONE (St Mary)   *see* N and S Creake w Waterden, Syderstone etc *Nor*
SYDLING ST NICHOLAS (St Nicholas)   *see* Bradford Peverell, Stratton, Frampton etc *Sarum*
SYERSTON (All Saints)   *see* E Stoke w Syerston *S'well*
SYKEHOUSE (Holy Trinity)   *see* Fishlake w Sykehouse and Kirk Bramwith etc *Sheff*
SYLEHAM (St Mary)   *see* Hoxne w Denham, Syleham and Wingfield *St E*
SYMONDS GREEN (Christ the King)   *see* Stevenage H Trin *St Alb*
SYMONDSBURY (St John the Baptist)   *see* Askerswell, Loders, Powerstock and Symondsbury *Sarum*
SYRESHAM (St James)   *see* Astwell Gp *Pet*
SYSTON (St Mary)   *see* Barkston and Hough Gp *Linc*
SYSTON (St Peter and St Paul)   *see* Fosse *Leic*
SYSTON (St Anne)   *see* Warmley, Syston and Bitton *Bris*
SYSTONBY (not known)   *see* Melton Mowbray *Leic*
SYWELL (St Peter and St Paul)   *see* Mears Ashby and Hardwick and Sywell etc *Pet*
TABLEY, OVER (St Paul) *Ches 12*   **P** *Bp*   **V** J S CROFT
TACKLEY (St Nicholas)   *see* Steeple Aston w N Aston and Tackley *Ox*
TACOLNESTON (All Saints)   *see* Ashwellthorpe, Forncett, Fundenhall, Hapton etc *Nor*
TADCASTER (St Mary) w Newton Kyme *York 1*   **P** *Abp*   **V** S SHERIFF,   **C** C L CULLINGWORTH
TADDINGTON (St Michael), Chelmorton and Monyash, Hartington, Biggin and Earl Sterndale *Derby 4*   **P** *Duke of Devonshire and V Bakewell (jt)*   **V** J O GOLDSMITH,   **NSM** M L GOLDSMITH, J S FOUNTAIN
TADDIPORT (St Mary Magdalene)   *see* Gt and Lt Torrington and Frithelstock *Ex*
TADLEY, NORTH (St Mary) *Win 4*   **P** *Bp*   **V** B J NORRIS
TADLEY SOUTH (St Peter) (St Paul) and Silchester *Win 4*   **P** *Duke of Wellington and Bp (alt)*   **R** P D COOPER,   **Hon C** K V BATT
TADLOW (St Giles)   *see* Shingay Gp *Ely*
TADMARTON (St Nicholas)   *see* Wykeham *Ox*
TADWORTH (Good Shepherd) *S'wark 5*   **P** *V Kingswood St Andr*   **V** M W ELFRED,   **OLM** A S BLAIN
TAKELEY (Holy Trinity) w Little Canfield *Chelmsf 18*   **P** *Bp and Ch Coll Cam*   **P-in-c** R J BURLES
TALATON (St James the Apostle)   *see* Whimple, Talaton and Clyst St Lawr *Ex*
TALBOT VILLAGE (St Mark) *Sarum 7*   **P** *Trustees*   **V** R A HIGGINS,   **OLM** P G C JONES
TALKE O' THE HILL (St Martin) *Lich 9*   **P** *V Audley*   **R** P D HOWARD
TALKIN (not known)   *see* Eden, Gelt and Irthing *Carl*
TALLAND (St Tallan) *Truro 12*   **P** *DBP and W Gundry-Mills Esq (alt)*   **P-in-c** L A H COURTNEY
TALLINGTON (St Laurence)   *see* Uffington Gp *Linc*
TAMERTON, NORTH (St Denis)   *see* Boyton, N Tamerton, Werrington etc *Truro*
TAMERTON FOLIOT (St Mary) *Ex 23*   **P** *Ld Chan*   **P-in-c** D B M GILL,   **C** W P JACKSON
TAMWORTH (St Editha) *Lich 4*   **P** *Bp*   **V** A BARRETT,   **C** R A KHAN, V M C VAN DEN BERGH,   **Hon C** A L WHEALE
TANDRIDGE (St Peter)   *see* Oxted and Tandridge *S'wark*
TANFIELD (St Margaret of Antioch)   *see* Ch the K *Dur*
TANFIELD, WEST (St Nicholas) and Well w Snape and North Stainley *Ripon 3*   **P** *Bp and Mrs M E Bourne-Arton (alt)*   **R** *vacant* (01677) 470321
TANGLEY (St Thomas of Canterbury)   *see* Pastrow *Win*
TANGMERE (St Andrew) and Oving *Chich 3*   **P** *Bp and Duke of Richmond (jt)*   **P-in-c** I C ROGERS

TANHOUSE The Oaks (Conventional District) *Liv 11*
Min W D PETTY
TANKERSLEY (St Peter), Thurgoland and Wortley *Sheff 11*
P *Dowager Countess of Wharncliffe, Sir Philip*
Naylor-Leyland Bt, and V Silkstone (jt) **R** K J E HALE
TANNINGTON (St Ethelbert) *see* Worlingworth, Southolt,
Tannington, Bedfield etc *St E*
TANSLEY (Holy Trinity) *see* Matlock Bank and Tansley *Derby*
TANSOR (St Mary) *see* Warmington, Tansor and Cotterstock
etc *Pet*
TANWORTH (St Mary Magdalene) *Birm 6* **P** *F D Muntz Esq*
V P E F CUDBY
TAPLOW (St Nicolas) and Dropmore *Ox 23* **P** *Eton Coll and*
DBP (jt) **V** A C DIBDEN
TARDEBIGGE (St Bartholomew) *see* Redditch H Trin *Worc*
TARLETON (Holy Trinity) *see* Rufford and Tarleton *Blackb*
TARLTON (St Osmund) *see* Rodmarton CD *Glouc*
TARPORLEY (St Helen) *Ches 5* **P** *Bp (4 turns), D&C*
(1 turn), and Sir John Grey Regerton Bt (1 turn) **R** K E HINE
TARRANT GUNVILLE (St Mary) *see* Chase *Sarum*
TARRANT HINTON (St Mary) *as above*
TARRANT KEYNSTON (All Saints) *as above*
TARRANT MONKTON (All Saints) *as above*
TARRANT RUSHTON (St Mary) *as above*
TARRING, WEST (St Andrew) *Chich 5* **P** *Abp* **R** W E JERVIS,
NSM G T SPENCER
TARRING NEVILLE (St Mary) *see* Denton w S Heighton and
Tarring Neville *Chich*
TARRINGTON (St Philip and St James) *see* Ledbury *Heref*
TARVIN (St Andrew) *Ches 2* **P** *Bp* **V** A L D FRIEND,
NSM M R MARR
TAS VALLEY *see* Newton Flotman, Swainsthorpe, Tasburgh,
etc *Nor*
TAS VALLEY, UPPER *see* Ashwellthorpe, Forncett,
Fundenhall, Hapton etc *Nor*
TASBURGH (St Mary) *see* Newton Flotman, Swainsthorpe,
Tasburgh, etc *Nor*
TASLEY (St Peter and St Paul) *see* Bridgnorth, Tasley, Astley
Abbotts, etc *Heref*
TATENHILL (St Michael and All Angels) *see* Barton under
Needwood w Dunstall and Tatenhill *Lich*
TATHAM (St James the Less) *see* E Lonsdale *Blackb*
TATHAM FELLS (Good Shepherd) *as above*
TATHWELL (St Vedast) *see* Legbourne and Wold Marsh *Linc*
TATSFIELD (St Mary) *see* Limpsfield and Tatsfield *S'wark*
TATTENHALL (St Alban) w Burwardsley and Handley *Ches 5*
P *Bp, Miss N C Barbour, and D&C (jt)* **R** L MUTETE
TATTENHAM CORNER (St Mark) *Guildf 9* **P** *Bp*
V D C WILLIAMSON
TATTENHOE (St Giles) *see* Watling Valley *Ox*
TATTERFORD (St Margaret) *see* E w W Rudham,
Helhoughton etc *Nor*
TATTERSETT (All Saints and St Andrew) *as above*
TATTERSHALL (Holy Trinity) *see* Bain Valley Gp *Linc*
TATTINGSTONE (St Mary) *see* Sproughton w Burstall,
Copdock w Washbrook etc *St E*
TATWORTH (St John the Evangelist) *see* Chaffcombe, Cricket
Malherbie etc *B & W*
TAUNTON (All Saints) *B & W 17* **P** *Bp* **V** D C W FAYLE
TAUNTON (Holy Trinity) *B & W 17* **P** *Bp*
V J B V LAURENCE, **Hon C** J J STRATTON
TAUNTON (St Andrew) *B & W 17* **P** *Bp* **V** R P LODGE
TAUNTON (St James) *B & W 17* **P** *Simeon's Trustees*
V T R N JONES, **NSM** D G AGER
TAUNTON (St John the Evangelist) *B & W 17* **P** *Bp*
P-in-c D ROBERTS, **Hon C** J R EASTELL
TAUNTON (St Mary Magdalene) *B & W 17* **P** *Ch Patr Trust*
V R G CORKE, **C** P B TULLETT, **Hon C** D E CAVAGHAN,
NSM S E MURRAY
TAUNTON (St Peter) Lyngford *B & W 17* **P** *Bp*
V I S MCFARLANE
TAVERHAM (St Edmund) *Nor 2* **P** *Bp* **R** P SEABROOK
TAVISTOCK (St Eustachius) and Gulworthy (St Paul) *Ex 25*
P *Bp* **P-in-c** M W BRIERLEY, **NSM** P RENNIE
TAW VALLEY *see* Barnstaple *Ex*
TAWSTOCK (St Peter) *see* Newton Tracey, Horwood,
Alverdiscott etc *Ex*
TAWTON, NORTH (St Peter), Bondleigh, Sampford Courtenay
and Honeychurch *Ex 11* **P** *MMCET, K Coll Cam, and*
D&C (jt) **P-in-c** N P WELDON, **NSM** R I BULLWORTHY
TAWTON, SOUTH (St Andrew) and Belstone *Ex 11* **P** *D&C*
Windsor and Bp (jt) **R** *vacant* (01837) 849048
TAYNTON (St John the Evangelist) *see* Burford w Fulbrook,
Taynton, Asthall etc *Ox*
TAYNTON (St Laurence) *see* Highnam, Lassington, Rudford,
Tibberton etc *Glouc*

TEALBY (All Saints) *see* Walesby *Linc*
TEAN, UPPER (Christ Church) *Lich 6* **P** *R Checkley*
P-in-c D C BICKERSTETH, **NSM** P A BECKETT
TEBAY (St James) *see* Orton and Tebay w Ravenstonedale etc
Carl
TEDBURN ST MARY (St Mary), Cheriton Bishop, Whitestone,
Oldridge and Holcombe Burnell *Ex 6* **P** *Bp, DBP, and Em Coll*
Cam (jt) **V** M R WOOD
TEDDINGTON (St Mark) and Hampton Wick *Lon 11* **P** *Bp*
V D P LUND
TEDDINGTON (St Mary) (St Alban the Martyr) *Lon 10* **P** *Bp*
V J B MOFFATT, **NSM** M E HAWES
TEDDINGTON (St Nicholas) *see* Overbury w Teddington,
Alstone etc *Worc*
TEDDINGTON (St Peter and St Paul) and Fulwell St Michael
and St George *Lon 10* **P** *Bp* **V** J W KNILL-JONES,
Hon C P R TOPHAM
TEDSTONE DELAMERE (St James) *see* Edvin Loach w
Tedstone Delamere etc *Heref*
TEDSTONE WAFER (St Mary) *as above*
TEFFONT EVIAS (St Michael) *see* Fovant, Sutton Mandeville
and Teffont Evias etc *Sarum*
TEFFONT MAGNA (St Edward) *as above*
TEIGH (Holy Trinity) *see* Oakham, Ashwell, Braunston,
Brooke, Egleton etc *Pet*
TEIGNGRACE (St Peter and St Paul) *see* Kingsteignton and
Teigngrace *Ex*
TEIGNMOUTH (St James) (St Michael the Archangel), Ideford
w Luton, Ashcombe and Bishopsteignton *Ex 6* **P** *Patr Bd*
TR J G STONES, **TV** S P WEST, **C** S ASTBURY
TELFORD, CENTRAL: Dawley, Lawley, Malinslee, Stirchley,
Brookside and Hollinswood *Lich 21* **P** *Patr Bd (3 turns),*
The Crown (1 turn) **TR** M A PETERS, **TV** G N CROWE,
K S EVANS, **C** B J JAMESON, S A KELLY, **NSM** E C PHILLIPS
TELFORD PARK (St Stephen) (St Thomas) *S'wark 12*
P *V Streatham and CPAS (jt)* **V** S P GATES,
C T D RAISTRICK
TELLISFORD (All Saints) *see* Hardington Vale *B & W*
TELSCOMBE VILLAGE (St Laurence) *Chich 18* **P** *Bp and*
Gorham Trustees (jt) **V** *vacant*
TEME VALLEY, LOWER *see* Worcs W *Worc*
TEME VALLEY NORTH: Knighton-on-Teme, Lindridge,
Pensax, Menith Wood, Stanford-on-Teme and Stockton
Worc 13 **P** *Bp and D&C (alt)* **R** L S GRACE, **NSM** S JONES
TEME VALLEY SOUTH: Eastham, Rochford, Stoke Bliss,
Hanley Child, Hanley William and Kyre Wyard *Worc 13*
P *Ld Chan, Bp, and Mrs M M Miles (by turn)*
P-in-c R M BARLOW
TEMPLE (St Catherine) *see* Blisland w St Breward *Truro*
TEMPLE BALSALL (St Mary) *Birm 11* **P** *Lady Leveson Hosp*
V K A M LLOYD ROBERTS
TEMPLE BRUER (St John the Baptist) *see* Graffoe Gp *Linc*
TEMPLE CLOUD (St Barnabas) *see* Clutton w Cameley,
Bishop Sutton and Stowey *B & W*
TEMPLE EWELL (St Peter and St Paul) w Lydden *Cant 7*
P *Abp* **R** P CHRISTIAN
TEMPLE GRAFTON (St Andrew) w Binton *Cov 7* **P** *Dioc*
Trustees **P-in-c** P A WALKER, **C** R E WALKER,
NSM L E DAVIES, K GRUMBALL
TEMPLE GUITING (St Mary) *see* The Guitings, Cutsdean,
Farmcote etc *Glouc*
TEMPLE HIRST (St John the Baptist) *see* Haddlesey w
Hambleton and Birkin *York*
TEMPLE NORMANTON (St James the Apostle) *Derby 5*
P *Bp* **V** M R AINSCOUGH
TEMPLE SOWERBY (St James) *see* Kirkby Thore w Temple
Sowerby and Newbiggin *Carl*
TEMPLECOMBE (Blessed Virgin Mary) *see* Abbas and
Templecombe, Henstridge and Horsington *B & W*
TEMPLETON (St Margaret) *see* Washfield, Stoodleigh,
Withleigh etc *Ex*
TEMPSFORD (St Peter) *see* Riversmeet *St Alb*
TEN MILE BANK (St Mark) *see* Hilgay *Ely*
TENBURY Team Minstry, The (St Mary) (St Michael and All
Angels) *Heref 11* **P** *Patr Bd* **TR** C A LORDING,
C C K W MOORE, **NSM** S FOSTER, H MORGAN
TENDRING (St Edmund King and Martyr) and Little Bentley w
Beaufort cum Moze *Chelmsf 20* **P** *Em Coll Cam, DBP, and*
Ball Coll Ox (by turn) **R** F R A MASON
TENTERDEN (St Mildred) (St Michael and All Angels) and
Smallhythe *Cant 16* **P** *Abp and D&C (jt)* **V** L J HAMMOND,
NSM M ROYLANCE
TERLING (All Saints) *see* Fairstead w Terling and White
Notley etc *Chelmsf*
TERRIERS (St Francis) *Ox 29* **P** *V High Wycombe*
V A W DICKINSON

TERRINGTON (All Saints) *see* Howardian Gp *York*
TERRINGTON ST CLEMENT (St Clement) *Ely 14*
  P *The Crown* **V** R J SLIPPER, **NSM** C G TINKER
TERRINGTON ST JOHN (St John) *see* E Marshland *Ely*
TERWICK (St Peter) *see* Rogate w Terwick and Trotton w
  Chithurst *Chich*
TESTON (St Peter and St Paul) *see* E Malling, Wateringbury
  and Teston *Roch*
TESTWOOD (St Winfrid) *see* Totton *Win*
TETBURY (St Mary the Virgin and St Mary Magdalen),
  Beverston, Long Newnton and Shipton Moyne *Glouc 7* **P** *DBP,*
  R Boggis-Rolfe Esq, and Mrs J C B Joynson (4 turns),
  Prime Min (1 turn) **R** A J WRIGHT, **C** L G HEWISH
TETCOTT (Holy Cross) *see* Ashwater, Halwill, Beaworthy,
  Clawton etc *Ex*
TETFORD (St Mary) *see* S Ormsby Gp *Linc*
TETNEY (St Peter and St Paul) *see* Holton-le-Clay, Tetney and
  N Cotes *Linc*
TETSWORTH (St Giles) *see* Thame *Ox*
TETTENHALL REGIS (St Michael and All Angels) *Lich 24*
  P *Patr Bd* **TR** R M REEVE, **TV** J M PERRY, E RATHBONE,
  C S A DOUGLAS, **NSM** A ROBERTS, **OLM** J F LLOYD
TETTENHALL WOOD (Christ Church) and Perton *Lich 24*
  P *Patr Bd* **C** P H J THORNEYCROFT, **OLM** C A HARLEY
TEVERSAL (St Katherine) *see* Skegby w Teversal *S'well*
TEVERSHAM (All Saints) *Ely 4* **P** *Bp* **P-in-c** M C BOWERS
TEW, GREAT (St Michael and All Angels) w Little (St John the
  Evangelist) *Ox 3* **P** *Bp and J M Johnston Esq (jt)*
  P-in-c P J SILVA
TEWIN (St Peter) *see* Welwyn *St Alb*
TEWKESBURY (Holy Trinity) *Glouc 10* **P** *Ch Soc Trust*
  V S M M WALKER
TEWKESBURY (St Mary the Virgin) w Walton Cardiff and
  Twyning *Glouc 10* **P** *Ld Chan (2 turns) and Ch Ch Ox*
  (1 turn) **V** P R WILLIAMS, **C** S L MILLER, T E CLAMMER,
  NSM C E WHITNEY, D J COULTON, W A RUFFLE
TEY, GREAT (St Barnabas) and LITTLE (St James the Less) w
  Wakes Colne and Chappel *Chelmsf 17* **P** *Bp, DBP,*
  PCC Chappel and Ch Patr Trust (jt) **R** J RICHARDSON
TEYNHAM (St Mary) (Primary School Worship Centre) w
  Lynsted and Kingsdown *Cant 14* **P** *Adn Cant*
  P-in-c S H LILLICRAP, **C** A H L PETTIT
THAKEHAM (St Mary) *see* Sullington and Thakeham w
  Warminghurst *Chich*
THAME (All Saints) (St Mary the Virgin) *Ox 1* **P** *Patr Bd*
  TR A W GARRATT, **TV** I D MOUNTFORD,
  C P M CHAMBERLAIN, **Hon C** K A A WESTON, J H FIELDSEND,
  S H BAYNES, R COPPING, **NSM** G C CHOLDCROFT,
  G P WATERSON
THAMES DITTON (St Nicholas) *Guildf 8* **P** *K Coll Cam*
  V J A SILK
THAMES VIEW (Christ Church) *see* Barking St Marg w St
  Patr *Chelmsf*
THAMESHEAD *see* Kemble, Poole Keynes, Somerford Keynes
  etc *Glouc*
THAMESMEAD (Church of the Cross) (St Paul's Ecumenical
  Centre) (William Temple) *S'wark 6* **P** *Bp*
  TR C H CLEMENTS, **TV** S R BOXALL, **C** A C MASSIAH
THANET (St Andrew) Conventional District *Cant*
  Min P MUSINDI
THANET (St Laurence) *see* St Laur in Thanet *Cant*
THANET (St Peter the Apostle) *see* St Peter-in-Thanet *Cant*
THANINGTON (St Nicholas) (St Faith's Mission Church)
  Cant 3 **P** *Abp* **P-in-c** C TODD
THARSTON (St Mary) *see* Newton Flotman, Swainsthorpe,
  Tasburgh, etc *Nor*
THATCHAM (St Mary) *Ox 14* **P** *Patr Bd* **TR** M D BENNET,
  TV P T JARVIS, **NSM** B HARLAND, **OLM** M E FONTAINE
THATTO HEATH (St Matthew) *see* Eccleston *Liv*
THAXTED (St John the Baptist, Our Lady and St Laurence)
  Chelmsf 21 **P** *Bp* **V** R M TAYLOR
THE *see under substantive place name*
THEALE (Christ Church) *see* Wedmore w Theale and
  Blackford *B & W*
THEALE (Holy Trinity) and Englefield *Ox 12* **P** *Magd Coll Ox*
  and Englefield Est Trust (jt) **P-in-c** A J TEMPLEMAN,
  Hon C B R SPENCE, P M TEMPLEMAN
THEBERTON (St Peter) *see* Yoxmere *St E*
THEDDINGWORTH (All Saints) *see* Hexagon *Leic*
THEDDLETHORPE (St Helen) *Linc 12* **P** *Baroness*
  Willoughby de Eresby (2 turns), Bp (1 turn)
  P-in-c C M TURNER
THELBRIDGE (St David) *see* Burrington, Chawleigh,
  Cheldon, Chulmleigh etc *Ex*
THELNETHAM (St Nicholas) *see* Hepworth, Hinderclay,
  Wattisfield and Thelnetham *St E*

THELVETON (St Andrew) *see* Dickleburgh and The Pulhams
  Nor
THELWALL (All Saints) *Ches 4* **P** *Keble Coll Ox*
  V D J BLACK
THEMELTHORPE (St Andrew) *see* Foulsham, Guestwick,
  Stibbard, Themelthorpe etc *Nor*
THENFORD (St Mary the Virgin) *see* Chenderit *Pet*
THERFIELD (St Mary the Virgin) w Kelshall *St Alb 16*
  P *Ld Chan and D&C St Paul's (alt)* **R** R M MORGAN
THETFORD (St Cuthbert) St Peter *Nor 11* **P** *Patr Bd*
  TV H L JARY, R M BAKER, R A HEYWOOD
THETFORD, LITTLE (St George) *see* Ely *Ely*
THEYDON BOIS (St Mary) and Theydon Garnon *Chelmsf 24*
  P *Bp* **P-in-c** S P WALKER
THEYDON GARNON (All Saints) *see* Theydon Bois and
  Theydon Garnon *Chelmsf*
THEYDON MOUNT (St Michael) *see* Greensted-juxta-Ongar
  w Stanford Rivers etc *Chelmsf*
THIMBLEBY (St Margaret) *see* Horncastle Gp *Linc*
THIRKLEBY (All Saints) w Kilburn and Bagby *York 18* **P** *Abp*
  V *vacant* (01347) 868234
THIRSK (St Mary) *York 18* **P** *Abp* **R** R F ROWLING,
  C G P BOWKETT
THISTLETON (St Nicholas) *see* Cottesmore and Burley,
  Clipsham, Exton etc *Pet*
THIXENDALE (St Mary) *see* Waggoners *York*
THOCKRINGTON (St Aidan) *see* Chollerton w Birtley and
  Thockrington *Newc*
THOMPSON (St Martin) *see* Caston, Griston, Merton,
  Thompson etc *Nor*
THONGSBRIDGE (St Andrew) *see* Upper Holme Valley
  Wakef
THORESBY, NORTH (St Helen) *see* The North-Chapel
  Parishes *Linc*
THORESBY, SOUTH (St Andrew) *see* Legbourne and Wold
  Marsh *Linc*
THORESWAY (St Mary) *see* Swallow *Linc*
THORGANBY (All Saints) *see* Binbrook Gp *Linc*
THORGANBY (St Helen) *see* Derwent Ings *York*
THORINGTON (St Peter) *see* Blyth Valley *St E*
THORLEY (St James the Great) *St Alb 15* **P** *Bp*
  R R H V PAYNE, **NSM** A K H PLATT
THORLEY (St Swithun) *Portsm 8* **P** *Bp* **V** J A YORKE
THORMANBY (St Mary Magdalene) *see* Brafferton w
  Pilmoor, Myton-on-Swale etc *York*
THORNABY, NORTH (St Luke) (St Paul) *York 17* **P** *Abp*
  V H C HOPKINS, **NSM** N PETTY
THORNABY, SOUTH (St Mark) (St Peter ad Vincula) *York 17*
  P *Abp* **V** M L CATHERALL
THORNAGE (All Saints) *see* Brinton, Briningham, Hunworth,
  Stody etc *Nor*
THORNBOROUGH (St Mary) *see* Buckingham *Ox*
THORNBURY (St Anna) *see* Bredenbury *Heref*
THORNBURY (St Margaret) *Bradf 3* **P** *Vs Bradf, Calverley,*
  and Laisterdyke (jt) **P-in-c** N CLEWS, **C** D J MUGHAL
THORNBURY (St Mary) (St Paul) and Oldbury-on-Severn w
  Shepperdine *Glouc 5* **P** *Ch Ch Ox* **V** J M SUDDARDS,
  C B W GOODWIN
THORNBURY (St Peter) *see* Black Torrington, Bradford w
  Cookbury etc *Ex*
THORNBY (St Helen) *see* Guilsborough and Hollowell and
  Cold Ashby etc *Pet*
THORNCOMBE (The Blessed Virgin Mary) *see* Chaffcombe,
  Cricket Malherbie etc *B & W*
THORNDON (All Saints) *see* S Hartismere *St E*
THORNE (St Nicholas) *Sheff 10* **P** *Bp* **P-in-c** D A GREEN
THORNE COFFIN (St Andrew) *see* Tintinhull w Chilthorne
  Domer, Yeovil Marsh etc *B & W*
THORNE ST MARGARET (St Margaret) *see* Wellington and
  Distr *B & W*
THORNER (St Peter) *Ripon 8* **P** *Earl of Mexborough*
  P-in-c A J NICHOLSON, **NSM** A B HAIGH
THORNES (St James) w Christ Church *Wakef 11* **P** *DBP*
  V *vacant* (01924) 299889
THORNEY (St Helen) *see* E Trent *S'well*
THORNEY, WEST (St Nicholas) *see* Southbourne w W
  Thorney *Chich*
THORNEY ABBEY (St Mary and St Botolph) *Ely 14* **P** *Bp*
  P-in-c C HURST
THORNEY CLOSE (St Peter) *see* Sunderland St Mary and
  St Pet *Dur*
THORNEY HILL (All Saints) *see* Bransgore and Hinton
  Admiral *Win*
THORNEYBURN (St Aidan) *see* N Tyne and Redesdale *Newc*
THORNFALCON (Holy Cross) *see* Creech St Michael and
  Ruishton w Thornfalcon *B & W*

THORNFORD (St Mary Magdalene)   *see* Gifle Valley *Sarum*
THORNGUMBALD (St Mary)   *see* Burstwick w Thorngumbald *York*
THORNHAM (All Saints)   *see* Hunstanton St Mary w Ringstead Parva etc *Nor*
THORNHAM (St James) *Man 16*   **P** *Bp*   **V** P N BARRATT
THORNHAM (St John)   *see* Middleton and Thornham *Man*
THORNHAM MAGNA (St Mary Magdalene)   *see* S Hartismere *St E*
THORNHAM PARVA (St Mary)   *as above*
THORNHAUGH (St Andrew) and Wansford *Pet 10*   **P** *Bp*   **P-in-c** T R CHRISTIE
THORNHILL (Mission Church)   *see* Beckermet St Jo and St Bridget w Ponsonby *Carl*
THORNHILL (St Christopher)   *see* Southampton Thornhill St Chris *Win*
THORNHILL (St Michael and All Angels) and Whitley Lower *Wakef 9*   **P** *Lord Savile*   **P-in-c** S C CLARKE
THORNHILL LEES (Holy Innocents w St Mary)   *see* Ravensthorpe and Thornhill Lees w Savile Town *Wakef*
THORNLEY (St Bartholomew)   *see* Wolsingham and Thornley *Dur*
THORNTHWAITE (St Mary the Virgin)   *see* Upper Derwent *Carl*
THORNTHWAITE (St Saviour)   *see* Dacre w Hartwith and Darley w Thornthwaite *Ripon*
THORNTON (St Frideswyde)   *see* Sefton and Thornton *Liv*
THORNTON (St James) *Bradf 1*   **P** *V Bradf*   **P-in-c** A J GREIFF,   **NSM** G HARDISTY
THORNTON (St Michael)   *see* Barmby Moor Gp *York*
THORNTON (St Peter)   *see* Markfield, Thornton, Bagworth and Stanton etc *Leic*
THORNTON (St Wilfrid)   *see* Horncastle Gp *Linc*
THORNTON, LITTLE (St John) *Blackb 12*   **P** *Bp*   **V** P R F CLEMENCE
THORNTON CURTIS (St Laurence)   *see* Ulceby Gp *Linc*
THORNTON DALE (All Saints) w Allerston, Ebberston, Ellerburn and Wilton *York 19*   **P** *A R Dudley-Smith Esq (1 turn), Abp (3 turns)*   **R** P J MOTHERSDALE
THORNTON HEATH (St Jude w St Aidan) *S'wark 21*   **P** *Bp*   **V** N K NTEGE
THORNTON HEATH (St Paul) *S'wark 21*   **P** *The Crown*   **V** *vacant* (020) 8653 2762
THORNTON HOUGH (All Saints) *Ches 9*   **P** *Simeon's Trustees*   **V** D J HOWARD
THORNTON IN CRAVEN (St Mary)   *see* Broughton, Marton and Thornton *Bradf*
THORNTON IN LONSDALE (St Oswald) w Burton in Lonsdale *Bradf 6*   **P** *Bp*   **P-in-c** J A SAVAGE
THORNTON LE FEN (St Peter)   *see* Brothertoft Gp *Linc*
THORNTON-LE-FYLDE (Christ Church) *Blackb 12*   **P** *Trustees*   **V** N SALT
THORNTON-LE-MOOR (All Saints)   *see* Kelsey Gp *Linc*
THORNTON-LE-MOORS (St Mary) w Ince and Elton *Ches 3*   **P** *Bp*   **V** M FLETCHER
THORNTON LE STREET (St Leonard)   *see* The Thorntons and The Otteringtons *York*
THORNTON RUST (Mission Room)   *see* Penhill *Ripon*
THORNTON STEWARD (St Oswald)   *see* Middleham w Coverdale and E Witton etc *Ripon*
THORNTON WATLASS (St Mary the Virgin)   *see* Bedale and Leeming and Thornton Watlass *Ripon*
THORNTONS and The Otteringtons, The *York 18*   **P** *Ch Ch Ox, Linc Coll Ox, and Abp (by turn)*   **R** S D RUDKIN
THOROTON (St Helena)   *see* Whatton w Aslockton, Hawksworth, Scarrington etc *S'well*
THORP ARCH (All Saints)   *see* Bramham *York*
THORPE (St Andrew) (Good Shepherd) *Nor 1*   **P** *Trustees W J Birkbeck Esq*   **R** B R OAKE,   **C** C D ELLIS
Thorpe (St Laurence)   *see* Farndon w Thorpe, Hawton and Cotham *S'well*
THORPE (St Leonard)   *see* Fenny Bentley, Thorpe, Tissington, Parwich etc *Derby*
THORPE (St Mary) *Guildf 11*   **P** *Keble Coll Ox*   **P-in-c** D S MILES
THORPE (St Matthew) *Nor 1*   **P** *R Thorpe St Andr*   **V** C D ELLIS
THORPE (St Peter)   *see* The Wainfleet Gp *Linc*
THORPE ABBOTS (All Saints)   *see* Scole, Brockdish, Billingford, Thorpe Abbots etc *Nor*
THORPE ACHURCH (St John the Baptist)   *see* Aldwincle, Clopton, Pilton, Stoke Doyle etc *Pet*
THORPE ACRE w Dishley (All Saints) *Leic 6*   **P** *Bp*   **V** K A ELLIOTT,   **NSM** R C ALEXANDER
THORPE ARNOLD (St Mary the Virgin)   *see* Melton Mowbray *Leic*

THORPE ASTLEY   *see* Braunstone Town *Leic*
THORPE AUDIN (Mission Room)   *see* Badsworth *Wakef*
THORPE BASSETT (All Saints)   *see* Buckrose Carrs *York*
THORPE BAY (St Augustine) *Chelmsf 13*   **P** *The Crown*   **V** J COLLIS
THORPE CONSTANTINE (St Constantine) *Lich 4*   **P** *Mrs E V G Inge-Innes*   **P-in-c** G J THOMPSON
THORPE EDGE (St John the Divine) *Bradf 3*   **P** *Vs Bradf, Calverley, and Idle (jt)*   **P-in-c** G S DARLISON
THORPE END (St David)   *see* Gt and Lt Plumstead w Thorpe End and Witton *Nor*
THORPE EPISCOPI (St Andrew)   *see* Thorpe St Andr *Nor*
THORPE HAMLET (St Matthew)   *see* Thorpe St Matt *Nor*
THORPE HESLEY (Holy Trinity) *Sheff 6*   **P** *Sir Philip Naylor-Leyland Bt*   **V** J F HARDY,   **NSM** L BROADHEAD
THORPE LANGTON (St Leonard)   *see* Church Langton cum Tur Langton etc *Leic*
THORPE-LE-SOKEN (St Michael) *Chelmsf 22*   **P** *Bp*   **P-in-c** J C DOWDING
THORPE MALSOR (All Saints)   *see* Broughton w Loddington and Cransley etc *Pet*
THORPE MANDEVILLE (St John the Baptist)   *see* Culworth w Sulgrave and Thorpe Mandeville etc *Pet*
THORPE MARKET (St Margaret)   *see* Trunch *Nor*
THORPE MORIEUX (St Mary the Virgin)   *see* Rattlesden w Thorpe Morieux, Brettenham etc *St E*
THORPE-NEXT-HADDISCOE (St Matthias)   *see* Raveningham Gp *Nor*
THORPE-ON-THE-HILL (St Michael)   *see* Swinderby *Linc*
THORPE SALVIN (St Peter)   *see* Harthill and Thorpe Salvin *Sheff*
THORPE SATCHVILLE (St Michael and All Angels)   *see* S Croxton Gp *Leic*
THORPE WILLOUGHBY (St Francis of Assisi)   *see* Brayton *York*
THORRINGTON (St Mary Magdalene)   *see* Alresford and Frating w Thorrington *Chelmsf*
THORVERTON (St Thomas of Canterbury)   *see* Brampford Speke, Cadbury, Newton St Cyres etc *Ex*
THRANDESTON (St Margaret)   *see* N Hartismere *St E*
THRAPSTON (St James), Denford and Islip *Pet 10*   **P** *Ld Chan (2 turns), L G Stopford-Sackville Esq (1 turn)*   **R** C D JEFFERSON
THREAPWOOD (St John)   *see* Malpas and Threapwood and Bickerton *Ches*
THRECKINGHAM (St Peter)   *see* S Lafford *Linc*
THREE LEGGED CROSS (All Saints)   *see* Verwood *Sarum*
THREE RIVERS Group, The *Ely 4*   **P** *Jes Coll Cam and Mrs D A Crawley (2 turns), Ld Chan (1 turn)*   **C** K R PEACOCK,   **NSM** P M DEBENHAM, M G BANYARD, J A GAGE
THREE RIVERS, The *Truro 9*   **P** *Ld Chan (1 turn), Ox Univ, Bp, and DBP (1 turn)*   **R** *vacant* (01566) 786976
THRELKELD (St Mary)   *see* St John's-in-the-Vale, Threlkeld and Wythburn *Carl*
THREXTON (All Saints)   *see* Gt and Lt Cressingham w Threxton *Nor*
THRIGBY (St Mary)   *see* S Trin Broads *Nor*
THRIMBY (St Mary)   *see* Morland, Thrimby, Gt Strickland and Cliburn *Carl*
THRINGSTONE (St Andrew)   *see* Whitwick, Thringstone and Swannington *Leic*
THRIPLOW (St George)   *see* Fowlmere, Foxton, Shepreth and Thriplow *Ely*
THROCKING (Holy Trinity)   *see* Cottered w Broadfield and Throcking *St Alb*
THROCKLEY (St Mary the Virgin)   *see* Newburn *Newc*
THROCKMORTON (Chapelry)   *see* Abberton, The Flyfords, Naunton Beauchamp etc *Worc*
THROOP (St Paul) *Win 8*   **P** *Ch Soc Trust*   **P-in-c** R K MODY
THROPTON (St Andrew)   *see* Upper Coquetdale *Newc*
THROWLEIGH (St Mary the Virgin)   *see* Chagford, Drewsteignton, Hittisleigh etc *Ex*
THROWLEY (St Michael and All Angels)   *see* Selling w Throwley, Sheldwich w Badlesmere etc *Cant*
THRUMPTON (All Saints) *S'well 9*   **P** *Mrs M Gottlieb*   **P-in-c** R I COLEMAN
THRUSCROSS (no dedication)   *see* Dacre w Hartwith and Darley w Thornthwaite *Ripon*
THRUSHELTON (St George)   *see* Lifton, Broadwoodwidger, Stowford etc *Ex*
THRUSSINGTON (Holy Trinity)   *see* Fosse *Leic*
THRUXTON (St Bartholomew)   *see* Cageboork *Heref*
THRUXTON (St Peter and St Paul)   *see* Appleshaw, Kimpton, Thruxton, Fyfield etc *Win*

THRYBERGH (St Leonard) *Sheff 6*　**P** *Mrs P N Fullerton*
　R *vacant* (01709) 850336
THUNDERSLEY (St Michael and All Angels) (St Peter)
　Chelmsf 10　**P** *Bp*　**R** M E STURROCK
THUNDERSLEY, NEW (St George) *Chelmsf 10*　**P** *Bp*
　V A J ROSE,　**NSM** P E C BEGLEY
THUNDRIDGE (St Mary) *St Alb 19*　**P** *Bp*　**V** B EBELING
THURCASTON (All Saints) *see* Anstey and Thurcaston w
　Cropston *Leic*
THURCROFT (St Simon and St Jude) *Sheff 5*　**P** *Bp*
　P-in-c P J CRAIG-WILD,　**C** J FRANKLIN, D E CRAIG-WILD
THURGARTON (St Peter) w Hoveringham and Bleasby w
　Halloughton *S'well 15*　**P** *Ld Chan and Trin Coll Cam (alt)*
　V *vacant* (01636) 830234
THURGOLAND (Holy Trinity) *see* Tankersley, Thurgoland
　and Wortley *Sheff*
THURLASTON (All Saints) *see* Enderby w Lubbesthorpe and
　Thurlaston *Leic*
THURLASTON (St Edmund) *see* Dunchurch *Cov*
THURLBY (St Firmin) *see* Ness Gp *Linc*
THURLBY (St Germain) *see* Bassingham Gp *Linc*
THURLEIGH (St Peter) *see* Milton Ernest, Pavenham and
　Thurleigh *St Alb*
THURLESTON (All Saints), South Milton, West Alvington and
　Churchstow *Ex 14*　**P** *Bp Ex and D&C Sarum (jt)*
　P-in-c P OSLER
THURLOW, GREAT (All Saints) *see* Stourhead *St E*
THURLOW, LITTLE (St Peter) *as above*
THURLOXTON (St Giles) *see* Alfred Jewel *B & W*
THURLSTONE (St Saviour) *see* Penistone and Thurlstone
　Wakef
THURLTON (All Saints) *see* Raveningham Gp *Nor*
THURMASTON (St Michael and All Angels) *see* Fosse *Leic*
THURNBY (St Luke) w Stoughton *Leic 4*　**P** *MMCET*
　V J M BARRETT,　**C** E R JEANS,　**NSM** H M BENCE
THURNBY LODGE (Christ Church) *see* Ascension TM *Leic*
THURNE (St Edmund) *see* Martham and Repps with
　Bastwick, Thurne etc *Nor*
THURNHAM (St Mary the Virgin) *see* Bearsted w Thurnham
　Cant
THURNING (St Andrew) *see* Reepham, Hackford w Whitwell,
　Kerdiston etc *Nor*
THURNING (St James the Great) *see* Barnwell, Hemington,
　Luddington in the Brook etc *Pet*
THURNSCOE (St Helen) (St Hilda) *Sheff 12*　**P** *Bp and*
　Sir Philip Naylor-Leyland Bt (jt)　**R** *vacant* (01709) 893259
THURROCK, LITTLE (St John the Evangelist) *see* Grays
　North *Chelmsf*
THURROCK, LITTLE (St Mary the Virgin) *see* Grays
　Thurrock *Chelmsf*
THURROCK, WEST (Church Centre) *as above*
THURSBY (St Andrew) *Carl 3*　**P** *D&C*　**P-in-c** G P RAVALDE
THURSFORD (St Andrew) *see* Barney, Fulmodeston w
　Croxton, Hindringham etc *Nor*
THURSLEY (St Michael and All Angels) *Guildf 4*　**P** *V Witley*
　V J J PAGE,　**OLM** P R J MUIR
THURSTASTON (St Bartholomew) *Ches 8*　**P** *D&C*
　R E J TURNER
THURSTON (St Peter) *St E 9*　**P** *Bp*　**V** D M B MATHERS
THURSTONLAND (St Thomas) *see* Upper Holme Valley
　Wakef
THURTON (St Ethelbert) w Ashby St Mary, Bergh Apton w
　Yelverton and Framingham Pigot *Nor 8*　**P** *Bp and Major*
　J H Thursby, Bp and MMCET, and Ld Chan (by turn)
　R P M KNIGHT,　**NSM** R J M COLLIER
THUXTON (St Paul) *see* Barnham Broom and Upper Yare *Nor*
THWAITE (All Saints) *see* Erpingham w Calthorpe, Ingworth,
　Aldborough etc *Nor*
THWAITE (St Mary) *see* Brooke, Kirstead, Mundham w
　Seething and Thwaite *Nor*
THWAITES (St Anne) *see* Millom *Carl*
THWAITES BROW (St Barnabas) *Bradf 8*　**P** *DBP*
　P-in-c J L PRITCHARD,　**Hon C** H M HODGSON
THWING (All Saints) *see* Langtoft w Foxholes, Butterwick,
　Cottam etc *York*
TIBBERTON (All Saints) w Bolas Magna and Waters Upton
　Lich 16　**P** *R Edgmond w Kynnersley etc, MMCET, and*
　A B Davies Esq (jt)　**P-in-c** W E WARD,
　NSM D N H STOKES-HARRISON
TIBBERTON (Holy Trinity) *see* Highnam, Lassington,
　Rudford, Tibberton etc *Glouc*
TIBBERTON (St Peter ad Vincula) *see* Bowbrook S *Worc*
TIBENHAM (All Saints) *see* Bunwell, Carleton Rode,
　Tibenham, Gt Moulton etc *Nor*
TIBSHELF (St John the Baptist) *see* Blackwell w Tibshelf *Derby*

TICEHURST (St Mary) and Flimwell *Chich 19*　**P** *Bp,*
　J A Sellick Esq, and K M H Millar Esq (jt)　**V** T J MILLS
TICHBORNE (St Andrew) *see* Upper Itchen *Win*
TICHMARSH (St Mary the Virgin) *see* Aldwincle, Clopton,
　Pilton, Stoke Doyle etc *Pet*
TICKENCOTE (St Peter) *see* Gt and Lt Casterton w Pickworth
　and Tickencote *Pet*
TICKENHAM (St Quiricus and St Julietta) *see* Nailsea Ch Ch
　w Tickenham *B & W*
TICKHILL (St Mary) w Stainton *Sheff 9*　**P** *Bp*　**V** *vacant*
　(01302) 742224
TICKNALL (St George) *see* Melbourne, Ticknall, Smisby and
　Stanton *Derby*
TICKTON (St Paul) *see* Beverley Minster *York*
TIDCOMBE (St Michael) *see* Savernake *Sarum*
TIDDINGTON *see* Wheatley *Ox*
TIDDINGTON (St Peter) *see* Alveston *Cov*
TIDEBROOK (St John the Baptist) *Chich 19*　**P** *V Wadhurst and*
　V Mayfield (alt)　**V** J R JAMES
TIDEFORD (St Luke) *see* St Germans *Truro*
TIDENHAM (St Mary) w Beachley and Lancaut *Glouc 1*　**P** *Bp*
　V R J M GROSVENOR
TIDENHAM CHASE (St Michael and All Angels)
　see Tidenham w Beachley and Lancaut *Glouc*
TIDESWELL (St John the Baptist) *Derby 4*　**P** *D&C Lich*
　V F E YATES
TIDMARSH (St Laurence) *see* Pangbourne w Tidmarsh and
　Sulham *Ox*
TIDMINGTON (not known) *see* Shipston-on-Stour w
　Honington and Idlicote *Cov*
TIDWORTH (Holy Trinity), Ludgershall and Faberstown
　Sarum 13　**P** *Ld Chan and DBP (alt)*　**R** M R FREEMAN,
　NSM P M POWELL
TIFFIELD (St John the Baptist) *see* Pattishall w Cold Higham
　and Gayton w Tiffield *Pet*
TILBROOK (All Saints) *see* Kym Valley *Ely*
TILBURY, EAST (St Katherine) and West Tilbury and Linford
　Chelmsf 14　**P** *Ld Chan*　**P-in-c** P L ROBINSON
TILBURY DOCKS (St John the Baptist) *Chelmsf 14*　**P** *Bp*
　V T M CODLING
TILBURY-JUXTA-CLARE (St Margaret) *see* Upper Colne
　Chelmsf
TILE CROSS (St Peter) *see* Garretts Green and Tile Cross *Birm*
TILE HILL (St Oswald) *Cov 3*　**P** *Bp*　**V** N W M LEGGETT
TILEHURST (St Catherine of Siena) and Calcot *Ox 15*
　P *Magd Coll Ox*　**V** D R SMITH,　**OLM** L D COLAM
TILEHURST (St George) *Ox 15*　**P** *Bp*　**V** A J CARLILL,
　NSM M J OKE, P G GROSSE
TILEHURST (St Mary Magdalen) *Ox 15*　**P** *Bp*
　P-in-c A J CARLILL,　**NSM** M J OKE, P G GROSSE
TILEHURST (St Michael) *Ox 15*　**P** *Magd Coll Ox*
　R J A ROGERS
TILFORD (All Saints) *see* The Bourne and Tilford *Guildf*
TILGATE (Holy Trinity) *see* Southgate *Chich*
TILLINGHAM (St Nicholas) *Chelmsf 11*　**P** *D&C St Paul's*
　P-in-c L R SMITH
TILLINGTON (All Hallows) *Chich 11*　**P** *Lord Egremont*
　P-in-c R M MITCHELL
TILMANSTONE (St Andrew) *see* Eastry and Northbourne w
　Tilmanstone etc *Cant*
TILNEY ALL SAINTS (All Saints) *see* E Marshland *Ely*
TILNEY ST LAWRENCE (St Lawrence) *as above*
TILSHEAD (St Thomas à Becket) *see* Wylye and Till Valley
　Sarum
TILSTOCK (Christ Church) *see* Edstaston, Fauls, Prees,
　Tilstock and Whixall *Lich*
TILSTON (St Mary) and Shocklach *Ches 5*　**P** *Bp*
　P-in-c J E STEPHENSON
TILSTONE FEARNALL (St Jude) *see* Bunbury and Tilstone
　Fearnall *Ches*
TILSWORTH (All Saints) *see* Totternhoe, Stanbridge and
　Tilsworth *St Alb*
TILTON ON THE HILL (St Peter) *see* Whatborough Gp *Leic*
TILTY (St Mary the Virgin) *see* Broxted w Chickney and Tilty
　etc *Chelmsf*
TIMBERHILL (St John the Baptist) *see* Nor St Jo w St Julian
　Nor
TIMBERLAND (St Andrew) *see* Carr Dyke Gp *Linc*
TIMBERSCOMBE (St Petroc) *see* Dunster, Carhampton,
　Withycombe w Rodhuish etc *B & W*
TIMPERLEY (Christ Church) (Holy Cross) *Ches 10*
　P *Trustees*　**V** J SUTTON,　**C** D A FROST,　**NSM** D R LAW
TIMSBURY (Blessed Virgin Mary) w Priston, Camerton and
　Dunkerton *B & W 11*　**P** *Bp, Ball Coll Ox, and*
　R W Lovegrove Esq (jt)　**R** C S HARE,　**NSM** G RIPLEY

TIMSBURY (St Andrew) *see* Michelmersh and Awbridge and Braishfield etc *Win*

TIMWORTH (St Andrew) *see* Lark Valley *St E*

TINCLETON (St John the Evangelist) *see* Moreton and Woodsford w Tincleton *Sarum*

TINDALE (Mission Church) *see* Lanercost, Walton, Gilsland and Nether Denton *Carl*

TINGEWICK (St Mary Magdalene) *see* W Buckingham *Ox*

TINGRITH (St Nicholas) *see* Westoning w Tingrith *St Alb*

TINSLEY (St Lawrence) *see* Rivers Team *Sheff*

TINTAGEL (St Materiana) *Truro 10* **P** *D&C Windsor* **NSM** J H BARFOOT

TINTINHULL (St Margaret) w Chilthorne Domer, Yeovil Marsh and Thorne Coffin *B & W 6* **P** *Guild of All So* **P-in-c** P M DOWN, **NSM** A J YOUNG

TINTWISTLE (Christ Church) *see* Hollingworth w Tintwistle *Ches*

TINWELL (All Saints) *see* Ketton, Collyweston, Easton-on-the-Hill etc *Pet*

TIPTOE (St Andrew) *see* Hordle *Win*

TIPTON Great Bridge (St Luke) *see* Tipton St Martin and St Paul *Lich*

TIPTON (St John) *see* Ottery St Mary, Alfington, W Hill, Tipton etc *Ex*

TIPTON (St John the Evangelist) *Lich 26* **P** *V W Bromwich St Jas* **V** *vacant* 0121-520 1584

TIPTON (St Mark) *see* Ocker Hill *Lich*

TIPTON (St Martin) (St Paul) *Lich 26* **P** *MMCET* **V** J F DUNN

TIPTON (St Matthew) *Lich 26* **P** *Simeon's Trustees* **V** C E HOWARD, **C** A BRYAN

TIPTREE (St Luke) *see* Tolleshunt Knights w Tiptree and Gt Braxted *Chelmsf*

TIRLEY (St Michael) *see* Ashleworth, Corse, Hartpury, Hasfield etc *Glouc*

TISBURY (St John the Baptist) *see* Nadder Valley *Sarum*

TISMANS COMMON (St John the Baptist) *see* Rudgwick *Chich*

TISSINGTON (St Mary) *see* Fenny Bentley, Thorpe, Tissington, Parwich etc *Derby*

TISTED, EAST w Colemore (St James) *see* Northanger *Win*

TISTED, WEST (St Mary Magdalene) *see* Bishop's Sutton and Ropley and W Tisted *Win*

TITCHFIELD (St Peter) *Portsm 2* **P** *D&C Win* **P-in-c** S ALLMAN

TITCHWELL (St Mary) *see* Hunstanton St Mary w Ringstead Parva etc *Nor*

TITLEY (St Peter) *see* Kington w Huntington, Old Radnor, Kinnerton etc *Heref*

TITTENSOR (St Luke) *see* Cotes Heath and Standon and Swynnerton etc *Lich*

TITTLESHALL (St Mary) *see* Litcham w Kempston, E and W Lexham, Mileham etc *Nor*

TIVERTON (St Andrew) *Ex 8* **P** *Bp* **V** *vacant* (01884) 257865 **OLM** G R WALLER

TIVERTON (St George) (St Paul) *Ex 8* **P** *MMCET and Peache Trustees (jt)* **P-in-c** B J DUGMORE, **C** C J ROUTLEDGE, **NSM** D A LYDDON

TIVERTON (St Peter) and Chevithorne w Cove *Ex 8* **P** *Peache Trustees (3 turns), Ld Chan (1 turn)* **P-in-c** R J GORDON

TIVETSHALL (St Mary and St Margaret) *see* Winfarthing w Shelfanger w Burston w Gissing etc *Nor*

TIVIDALE (St Michael the Archangel) (Holy Cross) (St Augustine) *Lich 26* **P** *Bp* **V** M M ENNIS

TIVINGTON (St Leonard) *see* Porlock and Porlock Weir w Stoke Pero etc *B & W*

TIXALL (St John the Baptist) *see* Stafford St Jo and Tixall w Ingestre *Lich*

TIXOVER (St Luke) *see* Barrowden and Wakerley w S Luffenham etc *Pet*

TOCKENHAM (St Giles) *see* Woodhill *Sarum*

TOCKHOLES (St Stephen) *see* Darwen St Cuth w Tockholes St Steph *Blackb*

TOCKWITH (Epiphany) and Bilton w Bickerton *York 1* **P** *Abp and D&C (jt)* **P-in-c** P P ROBINSON, **NSM** M R SHAW

TODBER (St Andrew) *see* Stour Vale *Sarum*

TODDINGTON (St Andrew) *see* Winchcombe *Glouc*

TODDINGTON (St George of England) and Chalgrave *St Alb 11* **P** *Bp and DBP (jt)* **R** A E CRAWFORD

TODENHAM (St Thomas of Canterbury) *see* Moreton-in-Marsh w Batsford, Todenham etc *Glouc*

TODMORDEN (St Mary) (Christ Church) *Wakef 3* **P** *Bp* **V** O R PAGE, **C** J ROBERTS, **NSM** N K WHITE, J L FLOOD

TODWICK (St Peter and St Paul) *Sheff 5* **P** *Bp* **R** *vacant* (01909) 770283

TOFT (St Andrew) *see* Lordsbridge *Ely*

TOFT (St John the Evangelist) *see* Knutsford St Jo and Toft *Ches*

TOFT MONKS (St Margaret) *see* Raveningham Gp *Nor*

TOFTREES (All Saints) *Nor 15* **P** *Marquess Townshend* **V** *vacant*

TOFTS, WEST and Buckenham Parva *Nor 13* **P** *Guild of All So* **R** *vacant*

TOKYNGTON (St Michael) *Lon 21* **P** *Bp* **V** P J HARNDEN

TOLLADINE (Christ Church) *see* Worc St Barn w Ch Ch *Worc*

TOLLAND (St John the Baptist) *see* Wiveliscombe and the Hills *B & W*

TOLLARD ROYAL (St Peter ad Vincula) *see* Chase *Sarum*

TOLLER FRATRUM (St Basil) *see* Melbury *Sarum*

TOLLER LANE St Chad *Bradf 1* **P** *Keble Coll Ox* **V** S R CROWE

TOLLER PORCORUM (St Andrew) *see* Beaminster Area *Sarum*

TOLLERTON (St Michael) *see* Alne *York*

TOLLERTON (St Peter) *S'well 8* **P** *Ld Chan* **P-in-c** M F PAYNE

TOLLESBURY (St Mary) *see* N Blackwater *Chelmsf*

TOLLESHUNT D'ARCY (St Nicholas) *as above*

TOLLESHUNT KNIGHTS w Tiptree and Great Braxted *Chelmsf 23* **P** *Bp (2 turns), Ld Chan (2 turns), and CCC Cam (1 turn)* **P-in-c** A-M L RENSHAW

TOLLESHUNT MAJOR (St Nicholas) *see* N Blackwater *Chelmsf*

TOLLINGTON (St Mark) *Lon 6* **P** *Patr Bd* **P-in-c** P J R BELLENGER, **C** S K WRIGHT, J A PRESTWOOD, **Hon C** E C M K JONES

TOLPUDDLE (St John the Evangelist) *see* Puddletown, Tolpuddle and Milborne w Dewlish *Sarum*

TOLWORTH (Emmanuel) *see* Surbiton Hill Ch Ch *S'wark*

TOLWORTH (St George) *see* Surbiton St Matt *S'wark*

TONBRIDGE (St Peter and St Paul) (St Andrew) (St Philip) (St Saviour) *Roch 11* **P** *Mabledon Trust* **V** M E BROWN, **C** P W GOODRIDGE

TONBRIDGE (St Stephen) (St Eanswythe Mission Church) *Roch 11* **P** *CPAS* **V** M BARKER, **NSM** S B PERKINS, J E PERKINS

TONG (St Bartholomew) *Lich 16* **P** *Bp* **C** J H K NORTON

TONG (St James) *Bradf 3* **P** *CR* **C** J L TRENHOLME, **NSM** M S BERNARD

TONGE (St Giles) *see* Murston w Bapchild and Tonge *Cant*

TONGE (St Michael) w Alkrington *Man 14* **P** *R Middleton St Leon* **V** M S THORP

TONGE FOLD (St Chad) *see* Leverhulme *Man*

TONGE MOOR (St Augustine) (St Aidan) *Man 12* **P** *Keble Coll Ox* **V** D A DAVIES

TONGHAM (St Paul) *Guildf 1* **P** *Adn Surrey* **P-in-c** N J WILLIAMS

TOOT BALDON (St Lawrence) *see* Dorchester *Ox*

TOOTING (All Saints) *S'wark 17* **P** *Bp* **V** S D METZNER, **OLM** G R WALLER

TOOTING, UPPER (Holy Trinity) (St Augustine) *S'wark 17* **P** *Bp and R Streatham St Leon (jt)* **NSM** B E NICHOLS, M J HANCOCK

TOOTING GRAVENEY (St Nicholas) *S'wark 17* **P** *MMCET* **R** C J DAVIS, **C** J J G FLETCHER

TOP VALLEY (St Philip) *see* Bestwood St Matt w St Phil *S'well*

TOPCLIFFE (St Columba), Baldersby w Dishforth, Dalton and Skipton on Swale *York 18* **P** *Abp, Viscountess Downe, and D&C (jt)* **P-in-c** R W DAVILL

TOPCROFT (St Margaret) *see* Hempnall *Nor*

TOPPESFIELD (St Margaret) *see* Upper Colne *Chelmsf*

TOPSHAM (St Margaret) *Ex 1* **P** *D&C* **P-in-c** R W C JEFFERY, **Hon C** M D A WILLIAMS, **NSM** J J HORWOOD

TORBRYAN (Holy Trinity) *see* Ipplepen, Torbryan and Denbury *Ex*

TORKSEY (St Peter) *see* Stow Gp *Linc*

TORMARTON (St Mary Magdalene) *see* Marshfield w Cold Ashton and Tormarton etc *Bris*

TORPENHOW (St Michael and all Angels) *see* Binsey *Carl*

TORPOINT (St James) *Truro 11* **P** *R Antony* **P-in-c** L PARKER

TORQUAY (St John) *Ex 12* **P** *Bp* **V** *vacant*

TORQUAY (St Luke) *Ex 12* **P** *D&C* **P-in-c** M R WESTALL, **NSM** E P LEWIS

TORQUAY (St Martin) Barton *Ex 12* **P** *V St Marychurch* **V** G CHAPMAN, **Hon C** G R EVANS

TORQUAY (St Mary Magdalene) *see* Upton *Ex*

TORQUAY (St Matthias) (St Mark) (Holy Trinity) *Ex 12* **P** *Ch Patr Trust, Bp and Torwood Trustees (jt)* **R** G R PERCY

TORRE (All Saints) *Ex 12* **P** *Bp* **P-in-c** R W SHAMBROOK

TORRIDGE ESTUARY   *see* Bideford, Northam, Westward Ho!, Appledore etc *Ex*

TORRINGTON, EAST (St Michael)   *see* Barkwith Gp *Linc*

TORRINGTON, GREAT (St Michael), Little Torrington and Frithelstock *Ex 20*   **P** *Ch Ch Ox (8 turns), Lord Clinton (1 turn), Prayer Book Soc (1 turn)*   **P-in-c** L A C MACLEAN

TORRINGTON, LITTLE (St Giles)   *see* Gt and Lt Torrington and Frithelstock *Ex*

TORRINGTON, WEST (St Michael)   *see* Barkwith Gp *Linc*

TORRISHOLME (Ascension) *Blackb 11*   **P** *Bp*   **V** P ENNION

TORTWORTH (St Leonard)   *see* Cromhall, Tortworth, Tytherington, Falfield etc *Glouc*

TORVER (St Luke) *Carl 9*   **P** *Peache Trustees*   **P-in-c** M R EAST

TOSELAND (St Michael)   *see* Papworth *Ely*

TOSSIDE (St Bartholomew)   *see* Long Preston w Tosside *Bradf*

TOSTOCK (St Andrew)   *see* Pakenham w Norton and Tostock *St E*

TOTHAM, GREAT (St Peter) and Little Totham w Goldhanger *Chelmsf 23*   **P** *Bp and Ld Chan (alt)*   **R** J PEARCE

TOTHAM, LITTLE (All Saints)   *see* Gt Totham and Lt Totham w Goldhanger *Chelmsf*

TOTLAND BAY (Christ Church) *Portsm 8*   **P** *Ch Patr Trust*   **V** J A YORKE

TOTLEY (All Saints) *Sheff 2*   **P** *Bp*   **V** vacant 0114-236 2322

TOTNES (St Mary) w Bridgetown, Berry Pomeroy, Dartington, Marldon, Ashprington and Cornworthy *Ex 13*   **P** *Patr Bd*   **TR** J C OULD,   **TV** D A PARSONS,   **NSM** J E LANKESTER

TOTON (St Peter) *S'well 7*   **P** *CPAS*   **P-in-c** C D BOURNE, C J L STEPHENS

TOTTENHAM (All Hallows) *Lon 19*   **P** *D&C St Paul's*   **V** R B PEARSON

TOTTENHAM (Holy Trinity) *Lon 19*   **P** *Bp*   **V** O A FAGBEMI

TOTTENHAM (St Bartholomew)   *see* Stamford Hill St Bart *Lon*

TOTTENHAM (St Benet Fink) *Lon 19*   **P** *D&C St Paul's*   **P-in-c** J A H HILL

TOTTENHAM (St Cuthbert)   *see* Chitts Hill St Cuth *Lon*

TOTTENHAM (St Mary the Virgin) *Lon 19*   **P** *Bp*   **C** S J MORRIS

TOTTENHAM (St Paul) *Lon 19*   **P** *V Tottenham All Hallows*   **C** C P TRUNDLE

TOTTENHAM (St Philip the Apostle) *Lon 19*   **P** *Bp*   **V** K EVANS

TOTTENHAM, SOUTH (St Ann) *Lon 19*   **P** *D&C St Paul's*   **V** J M WOOD,   **C** P T SANLON

TOTTENHILL (St Botolph) w Wormegay *Ely 9*   **P** *Bp*   **V** J C W NOLAN

TOTTERIDGE (St Andrew) *St Alb 14*   **P** *R Hatfield*   **V** vacant (020) 8445 6787

TOTTERNHOE (St Giles), Stanbridge and Tilsworth *St Alb 11*   **P** *Bp*   **V** D J R SPICER

TOTTINGTON (St Ann) *Man 8*   **P** *R Bury St Mary*   **V** H W BEARN

TOTTON *Win 11*   **P** *Bp*   **TR** M N PREVETT,   **TV** J K OLIVER, J R REEVE,   **C** A K NUTT,   **NSM** L M ROBERTSON

TOVE Benefice   *see* Towcester w Caldecote and Easton Neston etc *Pet*

TOW LAW (St Philip and St James)   *see* Satley, Stanley and Tow Law *Dur*

TOWCESTER (St Lawrence) w Caldecote and Easton Neston and Greens Norton and Bradden (The Tove Benefice) *Pet 5*   **P** *Prime Min (1 turn), Bp, Lord Hesketh, and J E Grant-Ives Esq (1 turn)*   **C** P J BOYLAND,   **NSM** E W PELLY

TOWEDNACK (St Tewinock) *Truro 5*   **P** *Bp*   **P-in-c** E V A FOOT

TOWER CHAPEL (St Nicholas)   *see* Whitehaven *Carl*

TOWERSEY (St Catherine)   *see* Thame *Ox*

TOWN END FARM (St Bede)   *see* N Wearside *Dur*

TOWNEND (St Paul)   *see* Morley *Wakef*

TOWNSTAL (St Clement)   *see* Dartmouth and Dittisham *Ex*

TOXTETH (St Bede) (St Clement) *Liv 6*   **P** *Simeon's Trustees and Trustees (jt)*   **V** J E WARHURST

TOXTETH (St Margaret) *Liv 6*   **P** *St Chad's Coll Dur*   **V** R GALLAGHER

TOXTETH (St Philemon) (St Gabriel) St Cleopas *Liv 6*   **P** *Patr Bd*   **TR** M R STANFORD,   **TV** D G GAVIN, R V STOCK,   **C** T WILSON

TOXTETH PARK (Christ Church) (St Michael-in-the-Hamlet) (St Andrew) *Liv 6*   **P** *Simeon's Trustees and Trustees (jt)*   **V** D A PARRY,   **C** L C MCIVER,   **NSM** M WATERS

TOXTETH PARK (St Agnes and St Pancras) *Liv 6*   **P** *St Chad's Coll Dur*   **V** J C D COOK

TOYNTON, HIGH (St John the Baptist)   *see* Horncastle Gp *Linc*

TOYNTON ALL SAINTS (All Saints)   *see* Marden Hill Gp *Linc*

TOYNTON ST PETER (St Peter)   *as above*

TOYS HILL (Hall)   *see* Hever, Four Elms and Mark Beech *Roch*

TRAFALGAR SQUARE (St Martin-in-the-Fields)   *see* St Martin-in-the-Fields *Lon*

TRAFFORD, OLD (St Bride) *Man 5*   **P** *Trustees*   **R** P J RAWLINGS,   **C** D A HOULTON,   **OLM** V M ECCLES, O H SAMUEL

TRAFFORD, OLD (St Hilda)   *see* Firswood and Gorse Hill *Man*

TRAFFORD, OLD (St John the Evangelist) *Man 5*   **P** *The Crown*   **P-in-c** J D HUGHES,   **C** E L TRIMBLE

TRANMERE (St Catherine) *Ches 1*   **P** *R Bebington*   **V** D L MOORE,   **C** C R SLATER

TRANMERE (St Paul w St Luke) *Ches 1*   **P** *Bp*   **V** K P ADDENBROOKE

TRANMERE PARK (St Peter's Hall)   *see* Guiseley w Esholt *Bradf*

TRAWDEN (St Mary the Virgin)   *see* Colne and Villages *Blackb*

TREALES (Christ Church)   *see* Wesham and Treales *Blackb*

TREBOROUGH (St Peter)   *see* Old Cleeve, Leighland and Treborough *B & W*

TREDINGTON (St Gregory) and Darlingscott *Cov 9*   **P** *Jes Coll Ox*   **P-in-c** C GOBLE,   **Hon C** G W KUHRT

TREDINGTON (St John the Baptist)   *see* Deerhurst and Apperley w Forthampton etc *Glouc*

TREETON (St Helen)   *see* Rivers Team *Sheff*

TREFONEN (All Saints)   *see* Llanyblodwel, Llanymynech, Morton and Trefonen *Lich*

TREGADILLET (St Mary's Mission)   *see* Launceston *Truro*

TREGONY (not known) w St Cuby and Cornelly *Truro 6*   **P** *Bp*   **P-in-c** S YATES,   **NSM** A L BUTCHER

TREKNOW (Holy Family)   *see* Tintagel *Truro*

TRELEIGH (St Stephen)   *see* Redruth w Lanner and Treleigh *Truro*

TRELYSTAN (St Mary the Virgin) *Heref 12*   **P** *Bp*   **P-in-c** R N LEACH

TREMAINE (St Winwalo)   *see* Egloskerry, N Petherwin, Tremaine, Tresmere etc *Truro*

TRENDLEWOOD   *see* Nailsea H Trin *B & W*

TRENEGLOS (St Gregory)   *see* Week St Mary Circle of Par *Truro*

TRENT (St Andrew)   *see* Queen Thorne *Sarum*

TRENT, EAST Group of Parishes, The *S'well 3*   **P** *Bp, Ld Chan, D&C Pet, and Keble Coll Ox (by turn)*   **V** vacant (01636) 892317

TRENT PARK (Christ Church)   *see* Enfield Ch Ch Trent Park *Lon*

TRENT VALE (St John the Evangelist)   *see* Hartshill, Penkhull and Trent Vale *Lich*

TRENTHAM (St Mary and All Saints) *Lich 13*   **P** *CPAS*   **V** E W MCLEOD,   **C** S A MORRIS

TRENTISHOE (St Peter)   *see* Combe Martin, Berrynarbor, Lynton, Brendon etc *Ex*

TRENTSIDE EAST *Linc 4*   **P** *Bp Linc (2 turns), Bp Lon (1 turn)*   **R** vacant (01724) 842196

TRESCO (St Nicholas)   *see* Is of Scilly *Truro*

TRESHAM (not known)   *see* Wotton-under-Edge w Ozleworth, N Nibley etc *Glouc*

TRESILLIAN (Holy Trinity) and Lamorran w Merther *Truro 6*   **P** *Viscount Falmouth*   **P-in-c** A M YATES,   **NSM** A L BUTCHER

TRESLOTHAN (St John the Evangelist)   *see* Crowan and Treslothan *Truro*

TRESMERE (St Nicholas)   *see* Egloskerry, N Petherwin, Tremaine, Tresmere etc *Truro*

TRESWELL (St John the Baptist)   *see* Retford Area *S'well*

TRETHEVY (St Piran)   *see* Tintagel *Truro*

TRETIRE (St Mary)   *see* St Weonards *Heref*

TREVALGA (St Petroc)   *see* Boscastle w Davidstow *Truro*

TREVENSON (St Illogan)   *see* St Illogan *Truro*

TREVERBYN (St Peter) *Truro 1*   **P** *The Crown*   **P-in-c** S D MICHAEL

TREVONE (St Saviour)   *see* Padstow *Truro*

TREWEN (St Michael)   *see* Egloskerry, N Petherwin, Tremaine, Tresmere etc *Truro*

TREYFORD CUM DIDLING (St Andrew)   *see* Harting w Elsted and Treyford cum Didling *Chich*

TRIANGLE (All Saints) (St Matthew) (Community Centre) Ipswich *St E 4*   **P** *Bp and Ld Chan (alt)*   **R** N S ATKINS,   **C** M P FIRTH,   **NSM** R H BEST, M J WALKER,   **OLM** H C DEAVES

TRIMDON (St Mary Magdalene)   *see* Upper Skerne *Dur*

TRIMDON GRANGE (St Alban)   *as above*

TRIMINGHAM (St John the Baptist)   *see* Overstrand, Northrepps, Sidestrand etc *Nor*

TRIMLEY (St Martin)   *see* Walton and Trimley *St E*

TRIMLEY (St Mary the Virgin)   *as above*
TRIMPLEY (Holy Trinity)   *see* Kidderminster St Mary and All SS w Trimpley etc *Worc*
TRING (St Martha) (St Peter and St Paul) (St Mary) *St Alb 1*   **P** *Bp*   **TR** H BELLIS,   **TV** J E J WETHERALL,   **NSM** J C BANISTER, D F JAQUET
TROSTON (St Mary the Virgin)   *see* Blackbourne *St E*
TROTTISCLIFFE (St Peter and St Paul)   *see* Birling, Addington, Ryarsh and Trottiscliffe *Roch*
TROTTON (St George)   *see* Rogate w Terwick and Trotton w Chithurst *Chich*
TROUTBECK (Jesus Church)   *see* Windermere St Mary and Troutbeck *Carl*
TROWBRIDGE (Holy Trinity)   *see* Trowbridge St Thos and W Ashton *Sarum*
TROWBRIDGE (St James) and Keevil *Sarum 14*   **P** *Ch Patr Trust and D&C (jt)*   **P-in-c** R G THOMAS
TROWBRIDGE (St Thomas) and West Ashton *Sarum 14*   **P** *CPAS*   **V** J A COUTTS
TROWELL (St Helen)   *see* Trowell, Awsworth and Cossall *S'well*
TROWELL (St Helen), Awsworth and Cossall *S'well 7*   **P** *Bp and Lord Middleton (jt)*   **R** A M LORD,   **C** M G STRANG,   **NSM** P C WHITEHEAD, B D BROWN
TROWSE (St Andrew) *Nor 1*   **P** *D&C*   **P-in-c** M D B LONG,   **NSM** R R BRABY
TRULL (All Saints) w Angersleigh *B & W 17*   **P** *DBP and M V Spurway Esq (jt)*   **R** A YOUINGS,   **C** S M GREEN,   M D WALLACE,   **Hon C** G C BOWYER
TRUMPINGTON (St Mary and St Michael) *Ely 3*   **P** *Trin Coll Cam*   **V** A J CHRICH,   **NSM** S M HARRIS
TRUNCH (St Botolph) *Nor 21*   **P** *Duchy of Lanc (3 turns), Patr Bd (1 turn)*   **TR** R C H KEY,   **TV** D W BARTLETT,   **NSM** R H MACPHEE, P A BAGGALEY, P J CHAPMAN
TRURO (St George the Martyr) (St John the Evangelist) *Truro 6*   **P** *Prime Min and V Kenwyn St Cuby (alt)*   **P-in-c** C D EPPS,   **NSM** A A HYDE
TRURO (St Mary's Cathedral and Parish Church) *Truro 6*   **P** *The Crown*   **R** C G HARDWICK
TRURO (St Paul) (St Clement) *Truro 6*   **P** *Bp*   **P-in-c** C D EPPS,   **NSM** A A HYDE
TRUSHAM (St Michael and All Angels)   *see* Chudleigh w Chudleigh Knighton and Trusham *Ex*
TRUSLEY (All Saints)   *see* Boylestone, Church Broughton, Dalbury, etc *Derby*
TRUSTHORPE (St Peter)   *see* Mablethorpe w Trusthorpe *Linc*
TRYSULL (All Saints)   *see* Smestow Vale *Lich*
TRYTHALL (Mission Church)   *see* Gulval and Madron *Truro*
TUBNEY (St Lawrence)   *see* Fyfield w Tubney and Kingston Bagpuize *Ox*
TUCKHILL (Holy Innocents)   *see* Claverley w Tuckhill *Heref*
TUCKINGMILL (All Saints) *Truro 2*   **P** *Bp*   **P-in-c** E C WOON
TUCKSWOOD (St Paul)   *see* Nor Lakenham St Jo and All SS and Tuckswood *Nor*
TUDDENHAM (St Martin)   *see* Westerfield and Tuddenham w Witnesham *St E*
TUDDENHAM (St Mary)   *see* Mildenhall *St E*
TUDDENHAM, EAST (All Saints)   *see* Mattishall and the Tudd Valley *Nor*
TUDDENHAM, NORTH (St Mary the Virgin)   *as above*
TUDELEY (All Saints) cum Capel w Five Oak Green *Roch 11*   **P** *Bp*   **P-in-c** J G A IVE,   **C** P F IVE
TUDHOE (St David)   *see* Croxdale and Tudhoe *Dur*
TUDHOE GRANGE (St Andrew) *Dur 6*   **P** *Bp*   **P-in-c** J LIVESLEY
TUEBROOK (St John)   *see* W Derby St Jo *Liv*
TUFFLEY (St Barnabas) *Glouc 2*   **P** *Bp*   **P-in-c** H M SAMMON,   **C** C M INGRAM,   **NSM** R F JEWELL
TUFNELL PARK (St George and All Saints) *Lon 6*   **P** *Trustees and CPAS (jt)*   **V** M L TOOGOOD
TUFNELL PARK (St Mary)   *see* Brookfield St Mary *Lon*
TUFTON (St Mary)   *see* Whitchurch w Tufton and Litchfield *Win*
TUGBY (St Thomas à Becket)   *see* Hallaton and Allexton, w Horninghold, Tugby etc *Leic*
TUGFORD (St Catherine)   *see* Diddlebury w Munslow, Holdgate and Tugford *Heref*
TULSE HILL (Holy Trinity and St Matthias) *S'wark 12*   **P** *Simeon's Trustees and Peache Trustees (jt)*   **V** R P DORMANDY,   **NSM** W W SHARPE
TUNBRIDGE WELLS (Holy Trinity w Christ Church) *Roch 12*   **P** *Mabledon Trust and CPAS (jt)*   **V** H M FLINT
TUNBRIDGE WELLS (King Charles the Martyr) *Roch 12*   **P** *Trustees*   **V** R E AVERY,   **NSM** S M PARTRIDGE
TUNBRIDGE WELLS (St Barnabas) *Roch 12*   **P** *Guild of All So*   **V** *vacant* (01892) 533826

TUNBRIDGE WELLS (St James) *Roch 12*   **P** *Ch Trust Fund Trust*   **V** J P STEWART,   **C** D J COMMANDER
TUNBRIDGE WELLS (St John) *Roch 12*   **P** *CPAS and V Tunbridge Wells H Trin (jt)*   **V** G R WALTER,   **C** R W FARR
TUNBRIDGE WELLS (St Luke) *Roch 12*   **P** *Five Trustees*   **V** C M GLASS
TUNBRIDGE WELLS (St Mark) Broadwater Down *Roch 12*   **P** *Bp*   **V** B C H FORTNUM,   **NSM** S J DIGGORY
TUNBRIDGE WELLS (St Peter) Windmill Fields *Roch 12*   **P** *Trustees and CPAS (jt)*   **V** M P WARREN
TUNBRIDGE WELLS (St Philip) *Roch 12*   **P** *Ch Trust Fund Trust*   **V** B S SENIOR
TUNSTALL (All Saints)   *see* Roos and Garton w Tunstall, Grimston and Hilston *York*
TUNSTALL (Christ Church)   *see* Goldenhill and Tunstall *Lich*
TUNSTALL (Holy Trinity)   *see* Catterick *Ripon*
TUNSTALL (St John the Baptist)   *see* E Lonsdale *Blackb*
TUNSTALL (St John the Baptist) and Bredgar *Cant 15*   **P** *Abp, D&C, O P Doubleday Esq, S G McCandlish Esq, Lord Kingsdown, and J Nightingale Esq (jt)*   **R** A K MCNICOL
TUNSTALL (St Michael and All Angels)   *see* Wilford Peninsula *St E*
TUNSTEAD (Holy Trinity)   *see* Bacup and Stacksteads *Man*
TUNSTEAD (St Mary) w Sco' Ruston *Nor 12*   **P** *Bp*   **P-in-c** A R LONG
TUNWORTH (All Saints)   *see* N Hants Downs *Win*
TUPSLEY (St Paul) w Hampton Bishop *Heref 3*   **P** *Bp*   **V** J C WATSON,   **C** A J WILLIAMS
TUPTON (St John)   *see* N Wingfield, Clay Cross and Pilsley *Derby*
TUR LANGTON (St Andrew)   *see* Church Langton cum Tur Langton etc *Leic*
TURKDEAN (All Saints)   *see* Northleach w Hampnett and Farmington etc *Glouc*
TURNASTONE (St Mary Magdalene)   *see* Madley w Tyberton, Peterchurch, Vowchurch etc *Heref*
TURNDITCH (All Saints)   *see* Belper Ch Ch w Turnditch *Derby*
TURNERS HILL (St Leonard) *Chich 7*   **P** *Bp*   **P-in-c** T F TREGUNNO
TURNFORD (St Clement)   *see* Cheshunt *St Alb*
TURNHAM GREEN (Christ Church) *Lon 11*   **P** *Bp*   **V** *vacant* (020) 8994 1617
TURNWORTH (St Mary)   *see* Winterborne Valley and Milton Abbas *Sarum*
TURTON MOORLAND MINISTRY (St Anne) (St James) *Man 12*   **P** *Patr Bd*   **TR** D M DUNN,   **TV** W BALDWIN,   **NSM** D R JONES, K THOMAS,   **OLM** A J HESLOP,   A M BULCOCK, S FOSTER
TURVEY (All Saints) *St Alb 13*   **P** *Mrs P K C Hanbury*   **P-in-c** P T MACKENZIE
TURVILLE (St Mary)   *see* Hambleden Valley *Ox*
TURWESTON (Assumption of the Blessed Virgin Mary)   *see* W Buckingham *Ox*
TUSHINGHAM (St Chad)   *see* Marbury w Tushingham and Whitewell *Ches*
TUTBURY (St Mary the Virgin)   *see* Hanbury, Newborough, Rangemore and Tutbury *Lich*
TUTSHILL (St Luke)   *see* Tidenham w Beachley and Lancaut *Glouc*
TUTTINGTON (St Peter and St Paul)   *see* King's Beck *Nor*
TUXFORD (St Nicholas) w Weston and Markham Clinton *S'well 3*   **P** *Ld Chan and Bp (alt)*   **P-in-c** C WALL
TWEEDMOUTH (St Bartholomew) *Newc 12*   **P** *D&C Dur*   **P-in-c** M S KNOX,   **OLM** K R COULTER
TWERTON-ON-AVON   *see* Bath Twerton-on-Avon *B & W*
TWICKENHAM (All Hallows) *Lon 10*   **P** *D&C St Paul's*   **V** N V STANLEY,   **NSM** A J WILLIAMS
TWICKENHAM (All Saints) *Lon 10*   **P** *Bp*   **V** *vacant* (020) 8894 3580
TWICKENHAM (St Mary the Virgin) *Lon 10*   **P** *D&C Windsor*   **V** R J H WILLIAMS,   **C** R J BARRIE,   **Hon C** D J ELLIOTT
TWICKENHAM, EAST (St Stephen) (St Paul) *Lon 10*   **P** *CPAS*   **V** J P B BARNES,   **C** D M EMERTON, A J SACHS,   E A ETHERINGTON
TWICKENHAM COMMON (Holy Trinity) *Lon 10*   **P** *Bp*   **V** T M GARRETT,   **Hon C** N R GARRETT
TWIGWORTH (St Matthew), Down Hatherley, Norton, The Leigh, Evington, Sandhurst and Staverton w Boddington *Glouc 3*   **P** *Ld Chan (1 turn), Bp Glouc and D&C Bris (1 turn)*   **V** M E THOMPSON
TWINEHAM (St Peter)   *see* Albourne w Sayers Common and Twineham *Chich*
TWINSTEAD (St John the Evangelist)   *see* N Hinckford *Chelmsf*
TWITCHEN (St Peter)   *see* S Molton w Nymet St George, High Bray etc *Ex*

TWO GATES (St Peter) *see* Wilnecote *Lich*
TWO MILE ASH (not known) *see* Watling Valley *Ox*
TWO MILE HILL (St Michael) *Bris 3* P *Prime Min*
NSM J F J GOODRIDGE
TWO RIVERS *see* Newton Tracey, Horwood, Alverdiscott etc
Ex
TWO RIVERS *see* Holbrook, Stutton, Freston, Woolverstone
etc *St E*
TWO SHIRES *see* Chaffcombe, Cricket Malherbie etc *B & W*
TWYCROSS (St James) *see* Bosworth and Sheepy Gp *Leic*
TWYDALL (Holy Trinity) *see* Gillingham H Trin *Roch*
TWYFORD (Assumption of the Blessed Virgin Mary) *see* The
Claydons and Swan *Ox*
TWYFORD (St Andrew) *see* Aston on Trent, Elvaston, Weston
on Trent etc *Derby*
TWYFORD (St Andrew) *see* S Croxton Gp *Leic*
TWYFORD (St Mary) and Owslebury and Morestead and
Colden Common *Win 7* P *Bp and Em Coll Cam (jt)*
V J P WATTS, NSM M I JACKSON
TWYFORD (St Mary the Virgin) *see* Ruscombe and Twyford
Ox
TWYFORD (St Nicholas) *see* N Elmham, Billingford, Bintree,
Guist etc *Nor*
TWYNING (St Mary Magdalene) *see* Tewkesbury w Walton
Cardiff and Twyning *Glouc*
TWYWELL (St Nicholas) *see* Cranford w Grafton Underwood
and Twywell *Pet*
TYBERTON (St Mary) *see* Madley w Tyberton, Peterchurch,
Vowchurch etc *Heref*
TYDD (St Mary) *see* The Suttons w Tydd *Linc*
TYDD ST GILES (St Giles) *see* Leverington, Newton and Tydd
St Giles *Ely*
TYE GREEN (St Barnabas) *see* Fairstead w Terling and White
Notley etc *Chelmsf*
TYE GREEN (St Stephen) w St Andrew Netteswell *Chelmsf 25*
P J L H *Arkwright Esq* R A V WATSON, NSM B L SURTEES
TYLDESLEY (St George) *see* Astley, Tyldesley and Mosley
Common *Man*
TYLER HILL (St Francis) *see* Hackington *Cant*
TYLERS GREEN (St Margaret) *see* Penn and Tylers Green *Ox*
TYLER'S HILL (St George) *see* Gt Chesham *Ox*
TYNE, NORTH and Redesdale Team *Newc 8* P *Patr Bd*
TR S M RAMSARAN, OLM R VIRDEN
TYNEMOUTH Balkwell (St Peter) *see* Balkwell *Newc*
TYNEMOUTH Cullercoats (St Paul) *Newc 5* P *Dioc Soc*
V G F GILCHRIST, C A R S FALUDY
TYNEMOUTH Shiremoor (St Mark) *see* Shiremoor *Newc*
TYNEMOUTH (St John Percy) *Newc 5* P *Dioc Soc*
P-in-c H B GILL
TYNEMOUTH PRIORY (Holy Saviour) *Newc 5* P *Dioc Soc*
P-in-c G A LOWSON, NSM D A ROBINSON
TYNINGS LANE (St Mary's Mission Church) *see* Aldridge
Lich
TYRINGHAM (St Peter) *see* Lamp *Ox*
TYRLEY (Mission Room) *see* Drayton in Hales *Lich*
TYSELEY (St Edmund) *Birm 13* P *The Crown* V S R SIMCOX,
C R J SUDWORTH
TYSOE (Assumption of the Blessed Virgin Mary) w Oxhill and
Whatcote *Cov 9* P *Marquess of Northampton and DBP (jt)*
P-in-c N J MORGAN, Hon C M J LEATON
TYTHBY (Holy Trinity) *see* Cropwell Bishop w Colston
Bassett, Granby etc *S'well*
TYTHERINGTON (St James) *see* Cromhall, Tortworth,
Tytherington, Falfield etc *Glouc*
TYTHERINGTON (St James) *see* Upper Wylye Valley *Sarum*
TYTHERLEY, EAST (St Peter) *see* Lockerley and E Dean w E
and W Tytherley *Win*
TYTHERLEY, WEST (St Peter) *as above*
TYTHERTON KELLAWAYS (St Giles) *see* Draycot *Bris*
TYTHERTON LUCAS (St Nicholas) *see* Chippenham St Andr
w Tytherton Lucas *Bris*
TYWARDREATH (St Andrew) w Tregaminion *Truro 1* P *DBP*
P-in-c F M BOWERS
UBLEY (St Bartholomew) *see* Blagdon w Compton Martin and
Ubley *B & W*
UCKFIELD (Holy Cross) (St Saviour) *Chich 21* P *Abp*
R B H WILCOX, C S J DATE, NSM C HOWARTH, H J TERRY
UDIMORE (St Mary) *see* Brede w Udimore *Chich*
UFFCULME (St Mary the Virgin) *see* Cullompton, Willand,
Uffculme, Kentisbeare etc *Ex*
UFFINGTON Group, The (St Michael and All Angels) *Linc 13*
P *Ld Chan (2 turns), Bp (2 turns), D&C (1 turn)*
R C R KENNEDY
UFFINGTON (Holy Trinity) *see* Wrockwardine Deanery *Lich*
UFFINGTON (St Mary), Shellingford, Woolstone and Baulking
Ox 17 P *Bp (2 turns), J J Twynam Esq (1 turn)*
P-in-c R S MARTIN

UFFORD (Assumption of the Blessed Virgin Mary) *see* Melton
and Ufford *St E*
UFTON (St Michael and All Angels) *Cov 10* P *Bp*
P-in-c J E ARMSTRONG
UGBOROUGH (St Peter) *see* Ermington and Ugborough *Ex*
UGGESHALL (St Mary) *see* Sole Bay *St E*
UGGLEBARNBY (All Saints) *see* Lower Esk *York*
UGLEY (St Peter) *see* Henham and Elsenham w Ugley *Chelmsf*
UGTHORPE (Christ Church) *see* Hinderwell, Roxby and
Staithes etc *York*
ULCEBY (All Saints) *see* Willoughby *Linc*
ULCEBY Group, The (St Nicholas) *Linc 6* P *Ld Chan*
V *vacant* (01469) 588239
ULCOMBE (All Saints) *see* Len Valley *Cant*
ULDALE (St James) *see* Binsey *Carl*
ULEY (St Giles) w Owlpen and Nympsfield *Glouc 5* P *Ld Chan*
P-in-c D E CROOK
ULGHAM (St John the Baptist) *Newc 11* P *Bp*
V H M BARTON
ULLENHALL (St Mary the Virgin) *see* Beaudesert and
Henley-in-Arden w Ullenhall *Cov*
ULLESKELFE (St Saviour) *see* Kirk Fenton w Kirkby Wharfe
and Ulleskelfe *York*
ULLEY (Holy Trinity) *see* Aston cum Aughton w Swallownest
and Ulley *Sheff*
ULLINGSWICK (St Luke) *see* Bredenbury *Heref*
ULPHA (St John) *see* Broughton and Duddon *Carl*
ULROME (St Andrew) *see* Bessingby *York*
ULTING (All Saints) *see* Hatfield Peverel w Ulting *Chelmsf*
ULVERSTON (St Mary w Holy Trinity) (St Jude) *Carl 9*
P *Peache Trustees* R A C BING, C A G BATCHELOR
UMBERLEIGH (Church of the Good Shepherd) *see* S Molton
w Nymet St George, High Bray etc *Ex*
UNDERBARROW (All Saints) *Carl 10* P *V Kendal H Trin*
P-in-c T J HARMER, NSM M L WOODCOCK, B J CROWE
UNDERRIVER (St Margaret) *Roch 9* P *Bp*
P-in-c E C KITCHENER
UNDERSKIDDAW (Parish Room) *see* Crosthwaite Keswick
Carl
UNDERWOOD (St Michael and All Angels) *see* Brinsley w
Underwood *S'well*
UNSTONE (St Mary) *see* Dronfield w Holmesfield *Derby*
UNSWORTH (St Andrew) *see* Hillock *Man*
UNSWORTH (St George) *Man 10* P *R Prestwich St Mary*
P-in-c D A WILLIAMS
UP HATHERLEY (St Philip and St James) *Glouc 6* P *Soc of
the Faith* P-in-c V R DUNSTAN-MEADOWS
UP MARDEN (St Michael) *see* Compton, the Mardens,
Stoughton and Racton *Chich*
UP NATELY (St Stephen) *see* N Hants Downs *Win*
UP WALTHAM (St Mary the Virgin) *Chich 11* P *Lord
Egremont* R *vacant*
UPAVON (St Mary the Virgin) *see* Vale of Pewsey *Sarum*
UPCHURCH (St Mary the Virgin) w Lower Halstow *Cant 15*
P *D&C* P-in-c A J AMOS, C H E NELSON,
NSM R W PARTRIDGE, OLM J DAVIS
UPHAM (All Saints) (Blessed Mary of Upham) *Portsm 1*
P *Ld Chan* R J C HUNT, NSM J BELOE
UPHILL (St Barnabas Mission Church)
see Weston-super-Mare St Nic w St Barn *B & W*
UPHILL (St Nicholas) *as above*
UPHOLLAND (St Thomas the Martyr) *Liv 11* P *Patr Bd*
TV J E HEIGHTON, C J A BALL
UPLANDS (All Saints) *see* Stroud and Uplands w Slad *Glouc*
UPLEADON (St Mary the Virgin) *see* Redmarley D'Abitot,
Bromesberrow, Pauntley etc *Glouc*
UPLOWMAN (St Peter) *see* Sampford Peverell, Uplowman,
Holcombe Rogus etc *Ex*
UPLYME (St Peter and St Paul) w Axmouth *Ex 5* P *CPAS and
Hyndman Trustees (jt)* P-in-c G A TYTE
UPMINSTER (St Laurence) *Chelmsf 2* P *W R Holden Esq*
R M J HORE, Hon C K J SKIPPON
UPNOR (St Philip and St James) *see* Frindsbury w Upnor and
Chattenden *Roch*
UPOTTERY (St Mary the Virgin) *see* Dunkeswell, Luppitt,
Sheldon and Upottery *Ex*
UPPER *see under substantive place name*
UPPERBY (St John the Baptist) *see* S Carl *Carl*
UPPERTHONG (St John the Evangelist) *see* Upper Holme
Valley *Wakef*
UPPINGHAM (St Peter and St Paul) w Ayston and Wardley w
Belton *Pet 12* P *Bp* R R D WATTS
UPPINGTON (Holy Trinity) *see* Wrockwardine Deanery *Lich*
UPSHIRE (St Thomas) *see* Waltham H Cross *Chelmsf*
UPTON (All Saints) *see* Lea Gp *Linc*
UPTON (Holy Ascension) *Ches 2* P *Duke of Westmr*
V P D SAYLE

UPTON (St Dunstan)   *see* The Lytchetts and Upton *Sarum*

UPTON (St James)   *see* Dulverton w Brushford, Brompton Regis etc *B & W*

UPTON (St John the Baptist)   *see* Castor w Sutton and Upton w Marholm *Pet*

UPTON (St Laurence)   *see* Upton cum Chalvey *Ox*

UPTON (St Margaret)   *see* Ranworth w Panxworth, Woodbastwick etc *Nor*

UPTON (St Margaret) and Copmanford *Ely 10*   **P** *Bp*
P-in-c M P JEPP

UPTON (St Mary) *Ches 8*   **P** *Simeon's Trustees*
V G J SKINNER,   **C** M J DALY, N J EASTWOOD,
NSM M MONTGOMERY

UPTON (St Mary Magdalene) *Ex 12*   **P** *Simeon's Trustees and Ch Patr Trust (alt)*   **C** M R SEARLE,   **NSM** J H GARNER

UPTON (St Mary the Virgin)   *see* The Churn *Ox*

UPTON (St Peter and St Paul)   *see* Rolleston w Fiskerton, Morton and Upton *S'well*

UPTON BISHOP (St John the Baptist)   *see* Ariconium *Heref*

UPTON CRESSETT w Monk Hopton *Heref 8*   **P** *DBP and Miss E A Bird (alt)*   **Hon C** H J PATTERSON

UPTON CROSS (St Paul)   *see* Linkinhorne *Truro*

UPTON CUM CHALVEY (St Mary) *Ox 23*   **P** *Bp*
TR A S ALLEN,   **TV** D E WEST

UPTON GREY (St Mary)   *see* N Hants Downs *Win*

UPTON HELLIONS (St Mary the Virgin)   *see* Crediton, Shobrooke and Sandford etc *Ex*

UPTON LOVELL (St Augustine of Canterbury)   *see* Upper Wylye Valley *Sarum*

UPTON MAGNA (St Lucia)   *see* Wrockwardine Deanery *Lich*

UPTON NOBLE (St Mary Magdalene)   *see* Bruton and Distr *B & W*

UPTON-ON-SEVERN (St Peter and St Paul), Ripple, Earls Croome w Hill Croome and Strensham *Worc 5*   **P** *Bp (2 turns), Mrs A J Hyde-Smith and Mrs A L Wynne (1 turn)*
P-in-c F A WOOKEY,   **NSM** J A FRASER, G R MOORE, G S CROSS

UPTON PARK (St Alban)   *see* E Ham w Upton Park *Chelmsf*

UPTON PRIORY (Church of the Resurrection) *Ches 13*   **P** *Bp*
V *vacant* (01625) 827761

UPTON PYNE (Our Lady)   *see* Brampford Speke, Cadbury, Newton St Cyres etc *Ex*

UPTON SCUDAMORE (St Mary the Virgin)   *see* Warminster St Denys and Upton Scudamore *Sarum*

UPTON SNODSBURY (St Kenelm)   *see* Peopleton and White Ladies Aston w Churchill etc *Worc*

UPTON ST LEONARDS (St Leonard) *Glouc 2*   **P** *Bp*
P-in-c P R LECKEY

UPTON WARREN (St Michael)   *see* Stoke Prior, Wychbold and Upton Warren *Worc*

UPWELL (St Peter) *Ely 14*   **P** *R T Townley Esq*   **R** A F JESSON

UPWELL CHRISTCHURCH (Christ Church)
see Christchurch and Manea and Welney *Ely*

UPWEY (St Laurence)   *see* Bincombe w Broadwey, Upwey and Buckland Ripers *Sarum*

UPWOOD (St Peter)   *see* The Ramseys and Upwood *Ely*

URCHFONT (St Michael and All Angels)   *see* Redhorn *Sarum*

URMSTON (St Clement) *Man 5*   **P** *Bp*   **OLM** C E FAULKNER

URSWICK (St Mary the Virgin and St Michael)
see Aldingham, Dendron, Rampside and Urswick *Carl*

USHAW MOOR (St Luke)   *see* Dur *Win*

USSELBY (St Margaret)   *see* Kelsey Gp *Linc*

USWORTH (Holy Trinity) (St Michael and All Angels) *Dur 11*
P *Bp*   **R** P GRUNDY

UTKINTON (St Paul)   *see* Tarporley *Ches*

UTLEY (St Mark) *Bradf 8*   **P** *Bp and R Keighley St Andr (jt)*
V D WALMSLEY,   **C** D TURLEY,   **NSM** J LONG

UTTERBY (St Andrew)   *see* Fotherby *Linc*

UTTOXETER AREA (St Mary the Virgin) *Lich 15*   **P** *Patr Bd*
TR E G WHITTAKER,   **TV** S WILLETTS, J C CANT,
NSM B WARREN,   **OLM** I M SMITH, C W DALE, C H BROWN,
J S LANDER

UXBRIDGE (St Andrew) (St Margaret) (St Peter) *Lon 24*
P *Bp*   **TR** A F SHEARD,   **TV** C W BOWMAN,
C J A HUGHMAN, J K ATKINS

UXBRIDGE (St John the Baptist)   *see* Hillingdon St Jo *Lon*

VALE OF BELVOIR Parishes *Leic 2*   **P** *Patr Bd (2 turns), Ld Chan (1 turn)*   **TV** F P R J CONNELL,   **P-in-c** M G SMITH

VALE OF PEWSEY *Sarum 19*   **P** *Patr Bd*   **TR** H G HOSKINS,
TV D F LARKEY, M T MCHUGH,   **OLM** G E R OSBORNE

VALE OF THE WHITE HART *Sarum 3*   **P** *D&C, DBP, N G Halsey Esq, and J K Wingfield Digby Esq (jt)*
R R G HART,   **NSM** A M BUDGELL

VALLEY END (St Saviour)   *see* Chobham w Valley End *Guildf*

VALLEY PARK (St Francis) *Win 10*   **P** *Bp*
V P F HUTCHINSON

VANGE (St Chad) *Chelmsf 6*   **P** *MMCET*   **R** D A O IBIAYO,
C I J E SWIFT,   **NSM** P CLARK

VAUXHALL (St Peter)   *see* N Lambeth *S'wark*

VENN OTTERY (St Gregory)   *see* Ottery St Mary, Alfington, W Hill, Tipton etc *Ex*

VENTA Group, The   *see* Stoke H Cross w Dunston, Arminghall etc *Nor*

VENTA GROUP   *see* Belton and Burgh Castle *Nor*

VENTNOR (Holy Trinity) *Portsm 7*   **P** *Bp*   **V** G E MORRIS,
NSM V M HEENAN

VENTNOR (St Alban)   *see* Godshill *Portsm*

VENTNOR (St Catherine) *Portsm 7*   **P** *Ch Patr Trust*
V G E MORRIS,   **NSM** V M HEENAN

VERNHAM DEAN (St Mary the Virgin)   *see* Hurstbourne Tarrant, Faccombe, Vernham Dean etc *Win*

VERWOOD (St Michael and All Angels) *Sarum 9*   **P** *Bp*
V A J M SINCLAIR,   **NSM** P E MILES, W S FRENCH,
OLM N F MOULAND

VERYAN (St Symphorian) w Ruan Lanihorne *Truro 6*   **P** *D&C and DBP (jt)*   **P-in-c** D G ROBINS

VICTORIA DOCKS (Ascension) *Chelmsf 3*   **P** *Bp*
V C HANSON

VICTORIA DOCKS (St Luke) *Chelmsf 3*   **P** *Ld Chan*
V D P WADE,   **Hon C** P E EJINKONYE,   **NSM** S M CHANDLER

VICTORIA PARK (St John Chrysostom)   *see* Man Victoria Park *Man*

VICTORIA PARK (St Mark)   *see* Old Ford St Paul and St Mark *Lon*

VIGO (Village Hall)   *see* Stansted w Fairseat and Vigo *Roch*

VINEY HILL (All Saints)   *see* Parkend and Viney Hill *Glouc*

VIRGINIA WATER (Christ Church) *Guildf 11*   **P** *Simeon's Trustees*   **V** S R SIZER,   **C** F C BLIGHT

VIRGINSTOW (St Bridget)   *see* Boyton, N Tamerton, Werrington etc *Truro*

VOWCHURCH (St Bartholomew)   *see* Madley w Tyberton, Peterchurch, Vowchurch etc *Heref*

WABERTHWAITE (St John)   *see* Eskdale, Irton, Muncaster and Waberthwaite *Carl*

WACTON (All Saints)   *see* Stratton St Mary w Stratton St Michael etc *Nor*

WADDESDON (St Michael and All Angels)   *see* Schorne *Ox*

WADDINGHAM (St Mary and St Peter)   *see* Bishop Norton, Wadingham and Snitterby *Linc*

WADDINGTON (St Helen) *Bradf 5*   **P** *E C Parker Esq*
P-in-c J R BROCKLEHURST,   **C** D W MEWIS,   **Hon C** G F MACK

WADDINGTON (St Michael) *Linc 18*   **P** *Linc Coll Ox*
R R J G PARKER

WADDON (St George)   *see* Croydon St Jo *S'wark*

WADEBRIDGE   *see* St Breoke and Egloshayle *Truro*

WADENHOE (St Michael and All Angels)   *see* Aldwincle, Clopton, Pilton, Stoke Doyle etc *Pet*

WADHURST (St Peter and St Paul) *Chich 19*
P *J M Hardcastle Esq and M R Toynbee Esq (jt)*   **V** J R JAMES,
C F A DAVIES,   **NSM** R G ALFORD

WADINGHAM (St Mary and St Peter)   *see* Bishop Norton, Wadingham and Snitterby *Linc*

WADSHELF (Mission Room)   *see* Old Brampton and Great Barlow *Derby*

WADSLEY (no dedication) *Sheff 4*   **P** *Ch Patr Trust*
V G J HUTCHISON

WADWORTH (St John the Baptist) w Loversall *Sheff 9*
P *V Doncaster and DBP (alt)*   **P-in-c** A PRICE

WAGGONERS *York 10*   **P** *Abp and Sir Tatton Sykes Bt, and Ld Chan (alt)*   **NSM** I D MACKARILL

WAINCLIFFE (St David)   *see* Beeston *Ripon*

WAINFLEET (All Saints)   *see* The Wainfleet Gp *Linc*

WAINFLEET Group, The (All Saints) (St Mary) (St Michael)
Linc 8   **P** *Ld Chan, Bp and T E Pitts Esq (alt)*
P-in-c B C BECHTOLLA

WAINFLEET (St Mary)   *see* The Wainfleet Gp *Linc*

WAINFLEET (St Michael)   *as above*

WAINFORD *St E 14*   **P** *Bp, Mrs B I T Suckling, CPAS, Magd Coll Cam, and Ch Soc Trust (jt)*   **C** P J NELSON, I B BYRNE,
OLM J E A MILLER

WAITHE (St Martin)   *see* The North-Chapel Parishes *Linc*

WAKEFIELD (St Andrew and St Mary) (St Swithun) *Wakef 11*
P *Peache Trustees*   **P-in-c** D INGHAM

WAKEFIELD (St John the Baptist) *Wakef 11*   **P** *Dean*
Hon C R B GRAINGER,   **NSM** P ELLIS

WAKEFIELD (St Mary) Chantry Bridge   *see* Wakef Cathl *Wakef*

WAKEFIELD (St Michael the Archangel)   *see* Westgate Common *Wakef*

WAKERING, GREAT (St Nicholas) w Foulness *Chelmsf 13*
P *Bp*   **P-in-c** A J HURD,   **NSM** T G A BROWN

WAKERING, LITTLE (St Mary the Virgin)   *see* Barling w Lt Wakering *Chelmsf*

WAKERLEY (St John the Baptist)   *see* Barrowden and Wakerley w S Luffenham etc *Pet*

WAKES COLNE (All Saints)   *see* Gt and Lt Tey w Wakes Colne and Chappel *Chelmsf*
WALBERSWICK (St Andrew)   *see* Sole Bay *St E*
WALBERTON (St Mary) w Binsted *Chich 21*   **P** *Bp*
V T J C WARD
WALBROOK Epiphany *Derby 10*   **P** *Patr Bd*   **TR** A J WARD
WALBURY BEACON Benefice, The *Ox 14*   **P** *Bp, D&C Windsor, DBP, and H M Henderson Esq (jt)*
R J F RAMSBOTTOM,   **NSM** C F ROBINSON, M J COOKSON,
M H YATES, J R COOK, C PYNN
WALCOT   *see* Bath Walcot *B & W*
WALCOT (All Saints)   *see* Bacton, Happisburgh, Hempstead w Eccles etc *Nor*
WALCOT (St Nicholas)   *see* S Lafford *Linc*
WALCOT (St Oswald)   *see* Carr Dyke Gp *Linc*
WALDEN, LITTLE (St John)   *see* Saffron Walden w Wendens Ambo, Littlebury etc *Chelmsf*
WALDERSLADE (St William)   *see* S Chatham H Trin *Roch*
WALDINGFIELD, GREAT (St Lawrence)   *see* Acton w Gt Waldingfield *St E*
WALDINGFIELD, LITTLE (St Lawrence)   *see* Boxford, Edwardstone, Groton etc *St E*
WALDITCH (St Mary)   *see* Bridport *Sarum*
WALDRINGFIELD (All Saints) w Hemley and Newbourn *St E 2*
P *The Revd Canon T Waller and the Revd A H N Waller, Ld Chan, and Mrs S E F Holden (by turn)*   **R** J P WALLER
WALDRON (All Saints) *Chich 15*   **P** *Ex Coll Ox*
P-in-c D G CHARLES
WALES (St John the Baptist) *Sheff 5*   **P** *Bp*   **V** G SCHOFIELD,
C V C CAMBER
WALESBY (St Edmund) *S'well 3*   **P** *DBP*   **V** C C LEVY
WALESBY (St Mary and All Saints) *Linc 5*   **P** *Bp, DBP, and C Drakes Esq (jt)*   **R** J H P CARR,   **C** J H MACKAY,
OLM E TURNER
WALFORD (St Michael and All Angels)   *see* Ross w Walford *Heref*
WALGRAVE (St Peter) w Hannington and Wold and Scaldwell *Pet 2*   **P** *Bp (2 turns), BNC Ox (1 turn)*
P-in-c K A I JONGMAN
WALHAM GREEN (St John) (St James) *Lon 9*   **P** *Bp*
P-in-c M W OSBORNE
WALKDEN (St Paul) and Little Hulton *Man 18*   **P** *Patr Bd*
OLM K HOPWOOD OWEN
WALKER (Christ Church) *Newc 3*   **P** *Bp*   **V** K HUNT,
C P J A MEDLEY
WALKERGATE (St Oswald)   *see* Byker St Mark and Walkergate St Oswald *Newc*
WALKERINGHAM (St Mary Magdalene)   *see* Beckingham and Walkeringham and Misterton etc *S'well*
WALKERN (St Mary the Virgin)   *see* Benington w Walkern *St Alb*
WALKHAMPTON (St Mary the Virgin)   *see* Yelverton, Meavy, Sheepstor and Walkhampton *Ex*
WALKINGHAM HILL *Ripon 1*   **P** *Bp, DBP, R Knaresborough, MMCET, and Major Sir Arthur Collins (jt)*   **R** P S MIDWOOD
WALKINGTON (All Hallows) *York 8*   **P** *Abp*   **V** A BAILEY
WALKLEY (St Mary) *Sheff 4*   **P** *Bp*   **V** M A FITZGERALD
WALL (St George)   *see* St Oswald in Lee w Bingfield *Newc*
WALL (St John the Baptist)   *see* Lich St Mich w St Mary and Wall *Lich*
WALL HEATH (Ascension)   *see* Kingswinford St Mary *Worc*
WALLASEY (St Hilary) *Ches 7*   **P** *Bp*   **R** A W WARD
WALLASEY (St Nicholas) All Saints *Ches 7*   **P** *Bp and DBP (jt)*   **V** J J STAPLES,   **NSM** P A ROSSITER, D A LAMB
WALLINGFORD (St Mary le More w All Hallows) (St Leonard) *Ox 18*   **P** *Bp*   **TR** D RICE,   **TV** J H GOULSTON,
Hon C J K SPENCE,   **NSM** J CHILTON
WALLINGTON (Holy Trinity) *S'wark 23*   **P** *Ch Soc Trust*
V S D COE,   **C** D M KING
WALLINGTON (Springfield Church) Extra-Parochial Place *S'wark 23*   **Min** W COOKSON,   **C** D J LAZENBY
WALLINGTON (St Mary)   *see* Sandon, Wallington and Rushden w Clothall *St Alb*
WALLINGTON (St Michael and All Angels)   *see* S Beddington and Roundshaw *S'wark*
WALLINGTON (St Patrick) *S'wark 23*   **P** *Ch Soc Trust*
V vacant (020) 8647 1026
WALLINGTON (St Paul)   *see* S Beddington and Roundshaw *S'wark*
WALLISDOWN (St Saviour)   *see* Talbot Village *Sarum*
WALLOP, NETHER (St Andrew)   *see* Portway and Danebury *Win*
WALLSEND (St John the Evangelist) *Newc 5*   **P** *Bp*
P-in-c C R BATES
WALLSEND (St Peter) (St Luke) *Newc 5*   **P** *Bp*   **R** vacant 0191-262 3723

WALMER (St Mary) (St Saviour) (Blessed Virgin Mary) *Cant 9*
P *Abp*   **V** S W COOPER
WALMERSLEY ROAD (Christ Church) (St John w St Mark) *Man 8*   **P** *R Bury St Mary and trustees (jt)*   **V** I J STAMP,
NSM D ALTHAM,   **OLM** P SANDERSON, J L LYSSEJKO,
E A BINNS
WALMGATE (St Denys)   *see* York St Denys *York*
WALMLEY (St John the Evangelist) *Birm 12*   **P** *Trustees*
V P S DOEL
WALMSLEY (Christ Church)   *see* Turton Moorland Min *Man*
WALNEY ISLAND (St Mary the Virgin) *Carl 8*
P *V Dalton-in-Furness*   **V** J D HODGKINSON
WALPOLE (St Mary the Virgin)   *see* Blyth Valley *St E*
WALPOLE ST PETER (St Peter and St Paul) w Walpole St Andrew *Ely 14*   **P** *The Crown and DBP (alt)*   **R** vacant (01945) 780252
WALSALL (Annunciation of Our Lady)   *see* Walsall St Gabr Fulbrook *Lich*
WALSALL (St Andrew) *Lich 25*   **P** *Bp*   **V** I M TEMPLETON
WALSALL (St Gabriel) Fulbrook *Lich 25*   **P** *Bp*
V R M MCINTYRE
WALSALL (St Luke) *Lich 25*   **P** *Bp*   **V** M R KINDER
WALSALL (St Martin) *Lich 25*   **P** *Bp*   **V** S C BICKERSTETH,
NSM P E BALL
WALSALL (St Matthew) *Lich 25*   **P** *Patr Bd*   **R** C T GIBSON,
C G S EVANS, E A CHAMBERLAIN,   **Hon C** G A FISHER,
NSM L F SAMUEL
WALSALL (St Michael and All Angels)   *see* Caldmore w Palfrey *Lich*
WALSALL St Paul *Lich 25*   **P** *R Walsall*   **V** M R KINDER,
C G S EVANS, S M LEACH, C T GIBSON,   **NSM** P J W LEES
WALSALL (St Peter) *Lich 25*   **P** *R Walsall*   **P-in-c** C R SUCH
WALSALL THE PLECK (St John) and Bescot *Lich 25*
P *V Walsall*   **V** G S EVANS,   **C** C T GIBSON, M R KINDER
WALSALL WOOD (St John) *Lich 25*   **P** *R Walsall*
V N J CARTER
WALSDEN (St Peter)   *see* Cornholme and Walsden *Wakef*
WALSGRAVE ON SOWE (St Mary) *Cov 1*   **P** *Ld Chan*
V M TYLER,   **C** S BAILEY,   **NSM** F E TYLER
WALSHAM, NORTH (St Nicholas) and Edingthorpe *Nor 12*
P *Bp (3 turns), Duchy of Lancaster (1 turn)*   **V** S D EARIS,
C K A F RENGERT, S M GUNNER,   **NSM** V A WATTS,
OLM N J M PATERSON
WALSHAM, SOUTH (St Mary)   *see* Ranworth w Panxworth, Woodbastwick etc *Nor*
WALSHAM LE WILLOWS (St Mary)   *see* Badwell and Walsham *St E*
WALSHAW (Christ Church) *Man 8*   **P** *Simeon's Trustees*
V S FOSTER
WALSINGHAM (St Mary and All Saints) (St Peter), Houghton and Barsham *Nor 15*   **P** *J Gurney Esq and Capt J D A Keith (jt)*   **P-in-c** N BANKS
WALSOKEN (All Saints) *Ely 14*   **P** *DBP*   **R** A R LANDALL
WALTERSTONE (St Mary)   *see* Ewyas Harold w Dulas, Kenderchurch etc *Heref*
WALTHAM (All Saints) *Linc 10*   **P** *The Crown*
NSM C E BUTLER
WALTHAM (Holy Cross) *Chelmsf 24*   **P** *Patr Bd*
TR P H SMITH,   **TV** G F HOPKINS,   **C** R A M REID,
NSM T I SCOTT, J M SMITH
WALTHAM (St Bartholomew)   *see* Stone Street Gp *Cant*
WALTHAM, GREAT (St Mary and St Lawrence) w Ford End *Chelmsf 8*   **P** *Trin Coll Ox*   **V** C I HAMPTON
WALTHAM, LITTLE (St Martin)   *see* Gt and Lt Leighs and Lt Waltham *Chelmsf*
WALTHAM, NEW (St Matthew) *Linc 10*   **P** *The Crown*
V vacant (01472) 589998
WALTHAM, NORTH (St Michael) and Steventon, Ashe and Deane *Win 6*   **P** *DBP*   **P-in-c** I K SMALE,
NSM C S READER, J FOSTER
WALTHAM ABBEY (Holy Cross)   *see* Waltham H Cross *Chelmsf*
WALTHAM CROSS (Christ Church)   *see* Cheshunt *St Alb*
WALTHAM ON THE WOLDS (St Mary Magdalene)
see Ironstone Villages *Leic*
WALTHAM ST LAWRENCE (St Lawrence) *Ox 13*   **P** *Lord Braybrooke*   **NSM** A J HARTROPP
WALTHAMSTOW (St Andrew) *Chelmsf 5*   **P** *Bp*
V A M E DOLLERY
WALTHAMSTOW (St Barnabas and St James the Great) *Chelmsf 5*   **P** *Bp*   **P-in-c** S M P SAXBY
WALTHAMSTOW (St Gabriel) St Luke (St Mary) (St Stephen) *Chelmsf 5*   **P** *Patr Bd*   **TR** S D HEATHFIELD,   **TV** N J ANSTEY,
J F SHOESMITH,   **C** K ASHTON, J V MOWBRAY,
NSM S C MOORE
WALTHAMSTOW (St John) *Chelmsf 5*   **P** *TR Walthamstow*
V A COMFORT

WALTHAMSTOW (St Michael and All Angels) *Chelmsf 5*
P *Bp*   V *vacant* (020) 8520 6328
WALTHAMSTOW (St Peter-in-the-Forest) *Chelmsf 5*   P *Bp*
Hon C E C M K JONES
WALTHAMSTOW (St Saviour) *Chelmsf 5*   P *Bp*
C W OBEDOZA
WALTON (Holy Trinity)   *see* Street w Walton *B & W*
WALTON (Holy Trinity) *Ox 21*   P *Ch Patr Trust*
V A K E BLYTH,   C R J LEGGE
WALTON Milton Keynes *Ox 25*   P *Patr Bd*   TR D LUNN,
TV S JACKSON,   NSM A J SMITH
WALTON (not known)   *see* Gilmorton, Peatling Parva, Kimcote
etc *Leic*
WALTON (St John)   *see* Brampton St Thos *Derby*
WALTON (St John) *Derby 5*   P *Bp*   V C S W VAN D´ARQUE,
C L SHEMILT, D P MOUNCER
WALTON (St John the Evangelist) *Ches 4*   P *P G Greenall Esq*
P-in-c J E HARRIES
WALTON (St Mary)   *see* Lanercost, Walton, Gilsland and
Nether Denton *Carl*
WALTON (St Mary) (St Philip) and Trimley *St E 2*   P *Patr Bd*
(2 turns), Ld Chan (1 turn)   TR N JOHN,   TV V J WHITE,
M G KICHENSIDE,   OLM W P SMITH, I W BARLEY
WALTON (St Paul)   *see* Sandal St Helen *Wakef*
WALTON (St Peter)   *see* Bramham *York*
WALTON (St Thomas)   *see* Baswich *Lich*
WALTON, EAST (St Mary)   *see* Gayton, Gayton Thorpe, E
Walton, E Winch etc *Nor*
WALTON, HIGHER (All Saints) *Blackb 5*   P *V Blackb*
V S J HUNT
WALTON, WEST (St Mary) *Ely 14*   P *Ld Chan*   R *vacant*
(01945) 61873
WALTON BRECK (Christ Church) (Holy Trinity) *Liv 3*
P *Simeon's Trustees*   P-in-c K BOLTON,   C A J BROWN,
T C STANFORD,   NSM J P ASQUITH
WALTON CLEVEDON (St Mary)   *see* E Clevedon w Clapton
in Gordano etc *B & W*
WALTON D'EIVILLE (St James) *Cov 8*   P *Sir Richard*
Hamilton Bt   P-in-c C E MIER
WALTON IN GORDANO (St Paul)   *see* E Clevedon w Clapton
in Gordano etc *B & W*
WALTON-LE-DALE (St Leonard) w Samlesbury St Leonard the
Less *Blackb 5*   P *V Blackb St Mary and St Paul*
P-in-c T R WEBBER,   NSM E BRIGGS
WALTON LE SOKEN (All Saints) (St George) *Chelmsf 22*
P *Bp*   V T J FLETCHER,   C R H GOODING
WALTON LE WOLDS (St Mary)   *see* Barrow upon Soar w
Walton le Wolds *Leic*
WALTON-ON-THAMES (St Mary) *Guildf 8*   P *Bp*
V C STEWART,   NSM K B E WRIGHT,   OLM J A RICHARDSON
WALTON ON THE HILL (St John) *Liv 7*   P *Bp, Adn, and*
R Walton (jt)   V S L WILLIAMS
WALTON ON THE HILL (St Luke) *Liv 7*   P *Bp*   V *vacant*
0151-523 5460
WALTON-ON-THE-HILL (St Mary) (St Aidan) *Liv 5*   P *Bp*
TR T M LATHAM,   TV C N PERRINS,   C I M GALLAGHER,
NSM J A FLOOD
WALTON-ON-THE-HILL (St Peter) *Guildf 9*   P *Bp*
P-in-c M E MARSH
WALTON-ON-TRENT (St Lawrence) w Croxall, Rosliston w
Linton and Castle Gresley *Derby 16*   P *Bp and*
R D Nielson Esq (jt)   R L A DE POMERAI,
NSM D I M DE POMERAI
WALTON STREET (St Saviour)   *see* Upper Chelsea St Sav and
St Simon *Lon*
WALWORTH (St Christopher) *S'wark 10*   P *Bp and Pemb Coll*
Miss   V D J J EVANS,   Hon C J M W SEDGWICK
WALWORTH (St John w the Lady Margaret) *S'wark 10*   P *Bp*
V J F WALKER,   Hon C G S ASKEY,   NSM O S CROWN
WALWORTH (St Peter) *S'wark 10*   P *Bp*
R A D P MOUGHTIN-MUMBY,   NSM S L SAUNDERS,
OLM A J WILD
WAMBROOK (Blessed Virgin Mary)   *see* Chard St Mary w
Combe St Nicholas, Wambrook etc *B & W*
WANBOROUGH (St Andrew)   *see* Lyddington and
Wanborough and Bishopstone etc *Bris*
WANBOROUGH (St Bartholomew)   *see* Seale, Puttenham and
Wanborough *Guildf*
WANDSWORTH (All Saints) (Holy Trinity) *S'wark 18*
P *Ch Soc Trust*   V G S PRIOR
WANDSWORTH (St Anne) (St Faith) *S'wark 18*   P *Bp*
V G P JEANES
WANDSWORTH (St Michael and All Angels) (St Stephen)
S'wark 18   P *CPAS and Ch Soc Trust (jt)*   V S MELLUISH,
C M PAVLOU,   NSM R J COLLINS
WANDSWORTH (St Paul) Wimbledon Park *S'wark 18*   P *Bp*
V H D TOLLER,   Hon C E M TOLLER

WANDSWORTH COMMON (St Mary Magdalene) *S'wark 17*
P *Bp*   V N J PEACOCK
WANDSWORTH COMMON (St Michael)   *see* Battersea
St Mich *S'wark*
WANGFORD (St Peter)   *see* Sole Bay *St E*
WANLIP (Our Lady and St Nicholas)   *see* Birstall and Wanlip
Leic
WANSFORD (St Mary)   *see* Nafferton w Wansford *York*
WANSFORD (St Mary the Virgin)   *see* Thornhaugh and
Wansford *Pet*
WANSTEAD (Holy Trinity) Hermon Hill *Chelmsf 4*   P *Bp*
V R E HAMPSON
WANSTEAD (St Mary) (Christ Church) *Chelmsf 4*   P *Bp*
R E HORWELL,   NSM R J WYBER
WANSTROW (Blessed Virgin Mary)   *see* Nunney and Witham
Friary, Marston Bigot etc *B & W*
WANTAGE (St Peter and St Paul) *Ox 19*   P *D&C Windsor*
V J L SALTER,   NSM M V BERRETT
WANTAGE DOWNS *Ox 19*   P *Bp, CCC Ox, and*
C L Lloyd Esq (jt)   R E A M BIRCH,   NSM D J PAGE
WANTISDEN (St John the Baptist)   *see* Wilford Peninsula *St E*
WANTSUM GROUP   *see* St Nicholas at Wade w Sarre and
Chislet w Hoath *Cant*
WAPLEY (St Peter)   *see* Yate New Town *Bris*
WAPPENBURY (St John the Baptist) w Weston under Wetherley
Cov 10   P *Bp*   P-in-c J T H BRITTON,   C D R PATTERSON
WAPPENHAM (St Mary the Virgin)   *see* Astwell Gp *Pet*
WARBLETON (St Mary) and Bodle Street Green *Chich 15*
P *Revd E S Havilund*   P-in-c M A LLOYD
WARBLINGTON (St Thomas à Becket) w Emsworth *Portsm 5*
P *Bp and J H Norris Esq (alt)*   R S P SAYERS,
C B C SARGENT
WARBOROUGH (St Lawrence) *Ox 1*   P *CCC Ox*
V S E BOOYS
WARBOYS (St Mary Magdalene) w Broughton and Bury w
Wistow *Ely 12*   P *Bp and Ch Soc Trust (jt)*   R P R DOWMAN
WARBSTOW (St Werburgh)   *see* Week St Mary Circle of Par
Truro
WARBURTON (St Werburgh)   *see* Oughtrington and
Warburton *Ches*
WARCOP (St Columba)   *see* Brough w Stainmore, Musgrave
and Warcop *Carl*
WARD END (Christ Church)   *see* Ward End w Bordesley Green
Birm
WARD END Holy Trinity (St Margaret) w Bordesley Green
Birm 13   P *Prime Min (1 turn), Bp and Aston Patr Trust*
(1 turn)   V P H SMITH,   C S J CARTWRIGHT, S K BARTER
WARDEN (St Michael and All Angels) w Newbrough *Newc 10*
P *Bp*   V J J T THOMPSON
WARDEN, OLD (St Leonard)   *see* Caldecote, Northill and Old
Warden *St Alb*
WARDINGTON (St Mary Magdalene)   *see* Shires' Edge *Ox*
WARDLE (no dedication) and Smallbridge *Man 17*   P *Bp*
P-in-c A J HOWELL
WARDLEWORTH (St Mary w St James)   *see* Rochdale *Man*
WARDLEY (All Saints)   *see* Swinton and Pendlebury *Man*
WARDLOW (Good Shepherd)   *see* Longstone, Curbar and
Stony Middleton *Derby*
WARE (Christ Church) *St Alb 19*   P *CPAS*   V J L W HOOKWAY
WARE (St Mary the Virgin) *St Alb 19*   P *Trin Coll Cam*
V D PEEL,   NSM M S E M BEAZLEY
WAREHAM (Lady Mary) (St Martin) *Sarum 8*   P *Patr Bd*
TV J MAW,   P-in-c A M BOWERMAN,   C S C ALLEN,
NSM M YOUNG
WAREHORNE (St Matthew)   *see* Orlestone w Snave and
Ruckinge w Warehorne etc *Cant*
WARESIDE (Holy Trinity)   *see* Hunsdon w Widford and
Wareside *St Alb*
WARESLEY (St James)   *see* Gt Gransden and Abbotsley and Lt
Gransden etc *Ely*
WARFIELD (St Michael the Archangel) (All Saints) (St Peter)
Ox 11   P *DBP*   P-in-c M GRIFFITHS,   C A BRADFORD,
Hon C J D PORTER,   NSM C M HILL
WARGRAVE (St Mary the Virgin) w Knowl Hill *Ox 16*   P *Lord*
Remnant   V J R M COOK,   NSM P A GORDON
WARHAM (All Saints)   *see* Holkham w Egmere w Warham,
Wells and Wighton *Nor*
WARK (St Michael)   *see* Humshaugh w Simonburn and Wark
Newc
WARKLEIGH (St John)   *see* S Molton w Nymet St George,
High Bray etc *Ex*
WARKTON (St Edmund King and Martyr)   *see* Barton
Seagrave w Warkton *Pet*
WARKWORTH (St Lawrence) and Acklington *Newc 6*   P *Bp*
and Duke of Northd (alt)   V J M BREARLEY,
NSM M E HOBROUGH,   OLM J BARRAS
WARKWORTH (St Mary the Virgin)   *see* Chenderit *Pet*

WARLEGGAN (St Bartholomew) *see* St Neot and Warleggan w Cardynham *Truro*

WARLEY (Christ Church) and Gt Warley St Mary *Chelmsf 7* **P** *Bp and Hon G C D Jeffreys (jt)* **V** C D GOLDSMITH, **NSM** E E GOLDSMITH

WARLEY (St John the Evangelist) *Wakef 4* **P** *V Halifax* **V** A J STREET, **NSM** J S BRADBERRY

WARLEY, GREAT (St Mary the Virgin) *see* Warley Ch Ch and Gt Warley St Mary *Chelmsf*

WARLEY, LITTLE (St Peter) *see* E and W Horndon w Lt Warley and Childerditch *Chelmsf*

WARLEY WOODS (St Hilda) *Birm 7* **P** *Bp* **V** P R G HINTON

WARLINGHAM (All Saints) w Chelsham and Farleigh *S'wark 24* **P** *Patr Bd* **TR** A D MIDDLETON, **TV** M K EDMONDS, **Hon C** J H STEVENS

WARMFIELD (St Peter) *Wakef 11* **P** *Oley Trustees Clare Coll Cam* **V** *vacant*

WARMINGHAM (St Leonard) *see* Elworth and Warmingham *Ches*

WARMINGTON (St Mary the Blessed Virgin), Tansor and Cotterstock and Fotheringhay and Southwick *Pet 10* **P** *Bp and D&C Linc (alt)* **V** B V ROGERS

WARMINGTON (St Michael) w Shotteswell and Radway w Ratley *Cov 8* **P** *Bp* **P-in-c** B J JACKSON, **C** R J COOKE

WARMINSTER (Christ Church) *Sarum 17* **P** *R Warminster St Denys etc* **P-in-c** P W HUNTER, **C** S G FAULKS, **NSM** P J FOY, **OLM** L A S MATHEW

WARMINSTER (St Denys) and Upton Scudamore *Sarum 17* **P** *Bp and Qu Coll Ox (jt)* **R** H L GIBBONS, **C** N J W BROWN, **NSM** C J OWEN

WARMLEY (St Barnabas), Syston and Bitton *Bris 5* **P** *Bp* **R** P H DENYER, **Hon C** J E NORMAN, **NSM** C A COSTER

WARMSWORTH (St Peter) *Sheff 9* **P** *Bp* **R** *vacant* (01302) 853324

WARMWELL (Holy Trinity) *see* Watercombe *Sarum*

WARNBOROUGH, SOUTH (St Andrew) *see* N Hants Downs *Win*

WARNDON (St Nicholas) *Worc 6* **P** *Bp* **P-in-c** D P RYAN, **NSM** S E POLLARD

WARNDON (St Wulstan) *see* Worc St Wulstan *Worc*

WARNERS END (St Alban) *see* Hemel Hempstead *St Alb*

WARNFORD (Our Lady) *see* W Meon and Warnford *Portsm*

WARNHAM (St Margaret) *Chich 8* **P** *J C Lucas Esq* **V** C H LOVELESS

WARNINGLID (St Andrew) *see* Slaugham and Staplefield Common *Chich*

WARREN PARK (St Clare) *Portsm 5* **P** *Bp* **V** J G P JEFFERY, **C** S J TANCOCK

WARREN ROW (St Paul) *see* Wargrave w Knowl Hill *Ox*

WARRINGTON (Holy Trinity) *Liv 12* **P** *R Warrington* **P-in-c** S R PARISH, **OLM** C E BATEY

WARRINGTON (St Ann) *see* Warrington St Ann *Liv*

WARRINGTON (St Ann) *Liv 12* **P** *Simeon's Trustees* **V** S R PARISH, **OLM** P LOVATT, M M MCDONNELL, J M WEAVER

WARRINGTON (St Barnabas) Bank Quay *Liv 12* **P** *R Warrington and Bp (jt)* **V** K L F TIMMIS

WARRINGTON (St Elphin) (St John) *Liv 12* **P** *Lord Lilford* **R** M S FINLAY

WARSLOW (St Lawrence) *see* Alstonfield, Butterton, Ilam etc *Lich*

WARSOP (St Peter and St Paul) *S'well 2* **P** *Trustees* **P-in-c** A FLETCHER, **C** P LAWLOR

WARTHILL (St Mary) *see* Stockton-on-the-Forest w Holtby and Warthill *York*

WARTLING (St Mary Magdalene) *see* Herstmonceux and Wartling *Chich*

WARTNABY (St Michael) *see* Old Dalby, Nether Broughton, Saxelbye etc *Leic*

WARTON (Holy Trinity) *see* N Warks *Birm*

WARTON (St Oswald or Holy Trinity) w Yealand Conyers *Blackb 14* **P** *Bp* **V** D M PORTER

WARTON (St Paul) *Blackb 10* **P** *Ch Ch Ox* **P-in-c** M L HARTLEY

WARWICK (St Leonard) *see* Holme Eden and Wetheral w Warwick *Carl*

WARWICK Team, The New (St Mary) (St Nicholas) (St Paul) *Cov 11* **P** *Ld Chan and Patr Bd (alt)* **TR** V S ROBERTS, **TV** L J DUCKERS, A W J FITZMAURICE, J HEARN

WARWICK SQUARE (St Michael) *see* Pimlico St Gabr *Lon*

WARWICKSHIRE, NORTH All Souls *Birm 10* **P** *Ld Chan (1 turn), V Polesworth, Birm Dioc Trustees and Mrs E V G Inge-Innes Lillington (1 turn)* **R** S J BANKS

WASDALE, NETHER (St Michael) *see* Gosforth w Nether Wasdale and Wasdale Head *Carl*

WASDALE HEAD (not known) *as above*

WASH COMMON (St George) *see* Newbury *Ox*

WASHBOURNE, GREAT (St Mary) *see* Winchcombe *Glouc*

WASHBURN and Mid-Wharfe *Bradf 4* **P** *Bp, G N le G Horton-Fawkes Esq, Lt Col H V Dawson and C Wyvill Esq (jt)* **P-in-c** S J WHARTON, **Hon C** M F CLEVERLEY, C A CAMPLING-DENTON, **NSM** T H BAXTER

WASHFIELD (St Mary the Virgin), Stoodleigh, Withleigh, Calverleigh, Oakford, Templeton, Loxbeare, Rackenford, and Cruwys Morchard *Ex 8* **P** *Patr Bd* **TR** S J GOODBODY, **C** R D BREWIS, **NSM** J C W ROBERTS

WASHFORD (St Mary) *see* Old Cleeve, Leighland and Treborough *B & W*

WASHFORD PYNE (St Peter) *see* N Creedy *Ex*

WASHINGBOROUGH (St John) w Heighington and Canwick *Linc 18* **P** *DBP and Mercers' Co (jt)* **R** S JONES-CRABTREE, **NSM** R E TREVELYAN

WASHINGTON (Holy Trinity) *Dur 11* **P** *Bp* **R** D C GLOVER

WASHINGTON (St Mary) *see* Ashington, Washington and Wiston w Buncton *Chich*

WASHWOOD HEATH (St Mark) *see* Saltley and Washwood Heath *Birm*

WASING (St Nicholas) *see* Aldermaston and Woolhampton *Ox*

WASKERLEY (St Andrew) *see* Blanchland w Hunstanworth and Edmundbyers etc *Newc*

WASPERTON (St John the Baptist) *see* Barford w Wasperton and Sherbourne *Cov*

WASS (St Thomas) *see* Coxwold and Husthwaite *York*

WATCHET (St Decuman) (Holy Cross Chapel) and Williton *B & W 16* **P** *Bp* **C** F M B GUTTRIDGE

WATCHFIELD (St Thomas's Chapel) *see* Shrivenham and Ashbury *Ox*

WATER EATON (St Frideswide) *Ox 25* **P** *Bp* **NSM** E L BREUILLY

WATER NEWTON (St Remigius) *see* Elton w Stibbington and Water Newton *Ely*

WATER ORTON (St Peter and St Paul) *Birm 9* **P** *Patr Bd* **V** S T MAYES

WATER STRATFORD (St Giles) *see* W Buckingham *Ox*

WATERBEACH (St John) *Ely 6* **P** *Bp* **P-in-c** L E CLELAND, **NSM** P M THORN, D M BAGULEY

WATERCOMBE *Sarum 1* **P** *M Cree Esq (1 turn), MMCET (2 turns), and Sir Robert Williams Bt (1 turn)* **R** J M COATES, **C** M J HARRISON, **OLM** W P A BUSH

WATERDEN (All Saints) *see* N and S Creake w Waterden, Syderstone etc *Nor*

WATERFALL (St James and St Bartholomew) *see* Calton, Cauldon, Grindon, Waterfall etc *Lich*

WATERFORD (St Michael and All Angels) *see* Bramfield, Stapleford, Waterford etc *St Alb*

WATERHEAD (Holy Trinity) *see* Medlock Head *Man*

WATERHOUSES (St Paul) *Dur 1* **P** *R Brancepeth Esq* **V** M J PEERS

WATERINGBURY (St John the Baptist) *see* E Malling, Wateringbury and Teston *Roch*

WATERLOO (Christ Church) St John *Liv 1* **P** *Trustees and Simeon's Trustees (jt)* **V** G J CUFF, **OLM** A L BROOKS

WATERLOO (St John the Evangelist) (St Andrew) *S'wark 11* **P** *Abp and CPAS (jt)* **P-in-c** G W GODDARD, **NSM** A M WARNER, **OLM** D PAPE, G S N KAZIRO

WATERLOO PARK (St Mary the Virgin) *see* Gt Crosby St Faith and Waterloo Park St Mary *Liv*

WATERLOOVILLE (St George the Martyr) *Portsm 5* **P** *Bp* **V** M J SHEFFIELD, **C** T B SINGH

WATERMILLOCK (All Saints) *see* Gd Shep TM *Carl*

WATERMOOR (Holy Trinity) *see* Cirencester *Glouc*

WATERPERRY (St Mary the Virgin) *see* Wheatley *Ox*

WATERS UPTON (St Michael) *see* Tibberton w Bolas Magna and Waters Upton *Lich*

WATERSHED *Lich 2* **P** *Keble Coll Ox and Earl of Bradford Trustees (jt)* **NSM** L BEECH, **OLM** G P ELLIS

WATERSIDE GROUP *see* Ludham, Potter Heigham, Hickling and Catfield *Nor*

WATERSIDE PARISHES of Hambleton, Out Rawcliffe and Preesall *Blackb 9* **P** *Bp, V Kirkham, and V Garstang St Helen etc (jt)* **NSM** D BANKS, **OLM** J A SQUIRES

WATERSTOCK (St Leonard) *see* Wheatley *Ox*

WATERTHORPE (Emmanuel) *see* Mosbrough *Sheff*

WATFORD (Christ Church) (St Mark) *St Alb 6* **P** *Bp, V Watford, and Churchwardens (jt)* **V** R C LEWIS

WATFORD (St Andrew) *St Alb 6* **P** *Bp and Churchwardens (jt)* **P-in-c** I C PANKHURST

WATFORD (St John) *St Alb 6* **P** *Bp* **V** *vacant* (01923) 236174

WATFORD (St Luke) *St Alb 6* **P** *Bp, Adn St Alb, V Watford, and Ch Trust Fund Trust (jt)* **P-in-c** D J MIDDLEBROOK, **C** G K N SENTAMU BAVERSTOCK, **NSM** S W MASSEY

WATFORD (St Mary) *St Alb 6* **P** *Ch Trust Fund Trust* **P-in-c** G K KNOTT

WATFORD (St Michael and All Angels) *St Alb 6* **P** *Bp* **P-in-c** G R CALVERT

WATFORD (St Peter) *St Alb 6*   **P** *Bp*   **V** C P COTTEE,
C R W YULE,   **NSM** A D T GORTON, A P PRIOR
WATFORD (St Peter and St Paul) *see* Long Buckby w Watford
and W Haddon w Winwick *Pet*
WATH (St Mary) *see* Kirklington w Burneston and Wath and
Pickhill *Ripon*
WATH BROW (Mission Church) *see* Crosslacon *Carl*
WATH-UPON-DEARNE (All Saints) *Sheff 12*   **P** *Ch Ch Ox*
V S E HOBLEY
WATLING VALLEY, Milton Keynes (not known) *Ox 25*
P *Patr Bd*   **TV** M J MORRIS, D B BELL,   **OLM** T HADDEN
WATLINGTON (St Leonard) *see* Icknield *Ox*
WATLINGTON (St Peter and St Paul) *Ely 9*   **P** *Bp*
R J C W NOLAN
WATTISFIELD (St Margaret) *see* Hepworth, Hinderclay,
Wattisfield and Thelnetham *St E*
WATTLESBOROUGH (St Margaret) *see* Alberbury w
Cardeston *Heref*
WATTON (St Mary) *Nor 13*   **P** *Ld Chan*   **V** G D GARRETT,
C S COOKE
WATTON (St Mary) *see* Hutton Cranswick w Skerne, Watton
and Beswick *York*
WATTON AT STONE (St Mary and St Andrew) *see* Bramfield,
Stapleford, Waterford etc *St Alb*
WAVENDON (Assumption of the Blessed Virgin Mary)
see Walton Milton Keynes *Ox*
WAVENEY Benefice, UPPER *Nor 10*   **P** *DBP, St Jo Coll Cam,
MMCET, and R D A Woode Esq (jt)*   **R** R J MELLOWSHIP
WAVERTON (Christ Church) *see* Solway Plain *Carl*
WAVERTON (St Peter) w Aldford and Bruera *Ches 5*   **P** *Bp,
D&C, and Duke of Westmr (jt)*   **R** J T P BEAUCHAMP,
C N T B DEANE
WAVERTREE (Holy Trinity) *Liv 6*   **P** *Bp*   **R** J EASTWOOD,
C B J STOBER,   **NSM** J PHILLIPS
WAVERTREE (St Bridget) (St Thomas) *Liv 6*   **P** *Simeon's
Trustees and R Wavertree H Trin (jt)*   **V** W J SANDERS
WAVERTREE (St Mary) *Liv 6*   **P** *Bp*
P-in-c M L CHAMBERLAIN,   **C** E JONES
WAWNE (St Peter) *see* Sutton St Jas and Wawne *York*
WAXHAM, GREAT (St John) *see* Bacton, Happisburgh,
Hempstead w Eccles etc *Nor*
WAYFORD (St Michael and All Angels) *see* Wulfric Benefice
B & W
WAYLAND Group, The *see* Caston, Griston, Merton,
Thompson etc *Nor*
WEALD (St George) *see* Sevenoaks Weald *Roch*
WEALD, SOUTH (St Peter) *Chelmsf 7*   **P** *Bp*   **V** I H JORYSZ
WEALDSTONE (Holy Trinity) *Lon 23*   **P** *Bp*
V T M MALONEY,   **NSM** F E MALONEY
WEAR (St Luke) *see* Countess Wear *Ex*
WEARDALE, UPPER *Dur 9*   **P** *Bp (5 turns), Duchy of
Lancaster (1 turn), and Ld Chan (1 turn)*   **R** S E KENT,
C A R M CROMARTY,   **NSM** B E BLOOMFIELD
WEARE (St Gregory) *see* Crook Peak *B & W*
WEARE GIFFARD (Holy Trinity) *see* Bideford, Northam,
Westward Ho!, Appledore etc *Ex*
WEARSIDE, NORTH *Dur 16*   **P** *Patr Bd*   **TV** S W ELSTOB
WEASENHAM (All Saints) *see* Gt w Lt Massingham, Harpley,
Rougham etc *Nor*
WEASENHAM (St Peter) *as above*
WEASTE (St Luke w All Saints) *see* Salford All SS *Man*
WEAVERHAM (St Mary the Virgin) *Ches 6*   **P** *Bp*
V A BROWN,   **C** J BROWN
**WEAVERTHORPE (St Andrew) w Helperthorpe, Luttons Ambo
and Kirby Grindalythe w Wharram** *York 6*   **P** *Abp and
D&C (jt)*   **P-in-c** A D BOWDEN,   **C** P H BOWES, Q H WILSON
WEBHEATH (St Philip) *see* Redditch H Trin *Worc*
WEDDINGTON (St James) and Caldecote *Cov 5*   **P** *Bp*
R *vacant* (024) 7635 3400
WEDMORE (St Mary) w Theale and Blackford *B & W 1*   **P** *Bp*
V R W NEILL,   **NSM** E R WILLS
WEDNESBURY (St Bartholomew) *Lich 26*   **P** *Bp*
V T R VASBY-BURNIE
WEDNESBURY (St James and St John) *Lich 26*   **P** *Trustees*
R K A PALMER,   **NSM** R C GILBERT
WEDNESBURY (St Paul) Wood Green *Lich 26*   **P** *Bp*
V D C NJUGUNA
WEDNESFIELD (St Gregory) *Lich 28*   **P** *Bp*
P-in-c S D MANSFIELD,   **NSM** J A LEACH
**WEDNESFIELD (St Thomas) (St Augustine and St Chad)
(St Alban)** *Lich 28*   **P** *Patr Bd*   **TR** N E WATSON,
C C E TURNER
WEDNESFIELD HEATH (Holy Trinity) *Lich 28*   **P** *CPAS*
V D A VESTERGAARD,   **C** P E V GOLDRING
WEEDON (School Chapel) *see* Schorne *Ox*
WEEDON BEC (St Peter and St Paul) w Everdon and Dodford
Pet 3   **P** *Bp*   **V** *vacant* (01327) 340359

WEEDON LOIS (St Mary and St Peter) *see* Astwell Gp *Pet*
WEEFORD (St Mary the Virgin) *see* Whittington w Weeford
Lich
WEEK ST MARY Circle of Parishes (St Mary the Virgin)
Truro 8   **P** *Bp, Walsingham Coll, Guild of All So, SS Coll Cam,
and Earl of St Germans (jt)*   **R** R C W DICKENSON
WEEKE *see* Win St Matt *Win*
WEEKLEY (St Mary the Virgin) *see* Geddington w Weekley *Pet*
WEELEY (St Andrew) and Little Clacton *Chelmsf 22*   **P** *Bp and
BNC Ox (alt)*   **R** D M NEWMAN
WEETHLEY (St James) *see* Alcester and Arrow w Oversley and
Weethley *Cov*
WEETING (St Mary) *see* Grimshoe *Ely*
WEETON (St Barnabas) *see* Lower Wharfedale *Ripon*
WEETON (St Michael) *see* Ribby cum Wrea and Weeton
Blackb
WEETSLADE (St Paul) *Newc 1*   **P** *Bp*   **V** A MAUGHAN
WELBORNE (All Saints) *see* Mattishall and the Tudd Valley
Nor
WELBOURN (St Chad) *Linc 22*   **P** *Hyndman Trustees*
R A J MEGAHEY
WELBURN (St John the Evangelist) *see* Howardian Gp *York*
WELBURY (St Leonard) *see* Rounton w Welbury *York*
WELBY (not known) *see* Melton Mowbray *Leic*
WELBY (St Bartholomew) *see* Ancaster Wilsford Gp *Linc*
WELCOMBE (St Nectan) *see* Parkham, Alwington, Buckland
Brewer etc *Ex*
WELDON (St Mary the Virgin) w Deene *Pet 7*   **P** *DBP and
E Brudenell Esq (jt)*   **P-in-c** C G SIMPSON
WELFORD (St Gregory) *see* W Downland *Ox*
**WELFORD (St Mary the Virgin) w Sibbertoft and Marston
Trussell** *Pet 2*   **P** *Bp*   **P-in-c** I W Y GEMMELL
WELFORD (St Peter) *see* Quinton and Welford w Weston
Glouc
**WELHAM (St Andrew), Glooston and Cranoe and Stonton
Wyville** *Leic 3*   **P** *Bp, E Brudenell Esq, and MMCET (jt)*
R *vacant* (01858) 462032
WELL (St Margaret) *Linc 8*   **P** *Bp*   **R** *vacant*
WELL (St Michael) *see* W Tanfield and Well w Snape and N
Stainley *Ripon*
WELL HILL (Mission) *see* Chelsfield *Roch*
WELLAND (St James) *see* Hanley Castle, Hanley Swan and
Welland *Worc*
WELLESBOURNE (St Peter) *Cov 8*   **P** *Ld Chan*
P-in-c C E MIER,   **OLM** W E BIDDINGTON
WELLING (St John the Evangelist) *Roch 15*   **P** *Bp*
V A J D FOOT,   **C** R M RADCLIFFE
WELLING (St Mary the Virgin) *S'wark 6*   **P** *Bp*   **V** K E ASTON,
NSM S E GREENWOOD
WELLINGBOROUGH (All Hallows) *Pet 6*   **P** *Exors Major
E C S Byng-Maddick*   **P-in-c** A M LYNETT,   **C** C M LOMAS
WELLINGBOROUGH (All Saints) *Pet 6*   **P** *V Wellingborough*
V A M LYNETT,   **C** C M LOMAS
WELLINGBOROUGH (St Andrew) *Pet 6*   **P** *Bp*   **V** *vacant*
(01933) 222692
WELLINGBOROUGH (St Barnabas) *Pet 6*   **P** *Bp*
V J P LEADER
WELLINGBOROUGH (St Mark) *Pet 6*   **P** *Bp*
V A CUTHBERTSON,   **NSM** G ALDERSON
WELLINGBOROUGH (St Mary the Virgin) *Pet 6*   **P** *Guild of
All So*   **V** R J T FARMER
WELLINGHAM (St Andrew) *see* Gt w Lt Massingham,
Harpley, Rougham etc *Nor*
WELLINGORE (All Saints) *see* Graffoe Gp *Linc*
WELLINGTON (All Saints) (St John the Baptist) and District
B & W 18   **P** *Patr Bd*   **TR** C M S RANDALL,
TV C F E ROWLEY,   **C** G H J CLAPHAM
WELLINGTON (All Saints) w Eyton (St Catherine) *Lich 21*
P *Ch Trust Fund Trust*   **V** M C IRELAND,   **C** G P RUTTER,
Hon C M A SMALLMAN
WELLINGTON (Christ Church) *see* Hadley and Wellington
Ch Ch *Lich*
WELLINGTON (St Margaret of Antioch) *see* Canon Pyon w
King's Pyon, Birley and Wellington *Heref*
WELLINGTON HEATH (Christ Church) *see* Ledbury *Heref*
WELLOW (St Julian the Hospitaller) *see* Peasedown St John w
Wellow and Foxcote etc *B & W*
WELLOW (St Swithin) *see* Kneesall w Laxton and Wellow
S'well
WELLOW, EAST w WEST (St Margaret) and Sherfield English
Win 12   **P** *Bp and CPAS (jt)*   **V** *vacant* (01794) 32356
WELLS (St Cuthbert) w Wookey Hole *B & W 7*   **P** *D&C*
V A Q H WHEELER,   **C** E S SIDWELL
WELLS (St Thomas) w Horrington *B & W 7*   **P** *D&C*
P-in-c T C OSMOND,   **NSM** A C HUNT, N T FRIDD
WELLS-NEXT-THE-SEA (St Nicholas) *see* Holkham w
Egmere w Warham, Wells and Wighton *Nor*

WELNEY (St Mary)　*see* Christchurch and Manea and Welney *Ely*

WELSH FRANKTON (St Andrew)　*see* Criftins w Dudleston and Welsh Frankton *Lich*

WELSH NEWTON (St Mary the Virgin)　*see* Goodrich, Marstow, Welsh Bicknor, Llangarron etc *Heref*

WELSH NEWTON COMMON (St Faith)　*see* St Weonards *Heref*

WELSHAMPTON (St Michael)　*see* Petton w Cockshutt, Welshampton and Lyneal etc *Lich*

WELTON (St Helen) w Melton *York 14*　P *DBP*
P-in-c　E E BIELBY,　NSM　A A V SCHRIMSHAW

WELTON (St James)　*see* Westward, Rosley-w-Woodside and Welton *Carl*

WELTON (St Martin)　*see* Daventry, Ashby St Ledgers, Braunston etc *Pet*

WELTON (St Mary) and Dunholme w Scothern *Linc 3*　P *Bp and DBP (jt)*　P-in-c　J J E ROWLEY

WELTON-LE-MARSH (St Martin)　*see* Burgh Gp *Linc*

WELTON-LE-WOLD (St Martin)　*see* Louth *Linc*

WELWICK (St Mary)　*see* Patrington w Hollym, Welwick and Winestead *York*

WELWYN Team Ministry, The (St Mary the Virgin) (St Michael) *St Alb 18*　P *Patr Bd*　TR　D L MUNCHIN,
C　D C WHITTAKER,　NSM　S L FIELDING

WELWYN GARDEN CITY (St Francis of Assisi) *St Alb 18*
P *Bp*　P-in-c　J E FENNELL,　C　J GRAY

WEM (St Peter and St Paul) *Lich 22*　P *Lord Barnard*
P-in-c　C S COOKE,　NSM　T D SMITH

WEMBDON (St George) *B & W 13*　P *Ch Soc Trust*
V　C D E MOLL,　C　D M HAKE

WEMBLEY (St Augustine)　*see* Wembley Park *Lon*

WEMBLEY (St John the Evangelist) *Lon 21*　P *Ch Patr Trust*
V　F ADU-BOACHIE

WEMBLEY, NORTH (St Cuthbert) *Lon 21*　P *Bp*
V　F G MCDERMOTT

WEMBLEY PARK (Church of the Ascension) (St Augustine) (Annunciation) *Lon 21*　P *Bp*　TR　M J CATTERICK,
TV　H L YOUNG,　Hon C　J M WARNER,　NSM　G E BEVAN

WEMBURY (St Werburgh) *Ex 21*　P *D&C Windsor*
P-in-c　M J HARMAN

WEMBWORTHY (St Michael)　*see* Burrington, Chawleigh, Cheldon, Chulmleigh etc *Ex*

WENDENS AMBO (St Mary the Virgin)　*see* Saffron Walden w Wendens Ambo, Littlebury etc *Chelmsf*

WENDLEBURY (St Giles)　*see* Akeman *Ox*

WENDLING (St Peter and St Paul)　*see* Gressenhall w Longham w Wendling etc *Nor*

WENDOVER (St Agnes's Chapel)　*see* Wendover and Halton *Ox*

WENDOVER (St Mary)　*as above*

WENDOVER (St Mary) (St Agnes's Chapel) and Halton *Ox 28*
P *Ld Chan*　R　M C DEARNLEY

WENDRON(St Wendron)　*see* Helston and Wendron *Truro*

WENDY (All Saints)　*see* Shingay Gp *Ely*

WENHAM, GREAT (St John)　*see* Capel St Mary w Lt and Gt Wenham *St E*

WENHASTON (St Peter)　*see* Blyth Valley *St E*

WENLOCK *Heref 10*　P *Patr Bd*　TR　S A LOWE,
TV　J DAVIES,　NSM　J A CUMBERLAND

WENLOCK, LITTLE (St Lawrence)　*see* Coalbrookdale, Iron-Bridge and Lt Wenlock *Heref*

WENLOCK, MUCH (Holy Trinity)　*see* Wenlock *Heref*

WENNINGTON (St Mary and St Peter)　*see* Rainham w Wennington *Chelmsf*

WENSUM Benefice, The *Nor 22*　P *New Coll Ox, Margaret Lady Prince-Smith, Bp, and D&C (jt)*　R　L S TILLETT

WENSUM VILLAGE Group, UPPER *Nor 15*
P *Marquess Townshend, the Revd C S P Douglas Lane, Ch Coll Cam, and DBP (jt)*　R　R D STAPLEFORD

WENT VALLEY *Wakef 10*　P *Bp, Earl of Rosse, and Sir Philip Naylor-Leyland Bt (jt)*　V　A T JUDD

WENTBRIDGE (St John)　*see* Went Valley *Wakef*

WENTNOR (St Michael and All Angels) w Ratlinghope, Myndtown, Norbury, More, Lydham and Snead *Heref 9*
P *Ch Ch Ox (4 turns) and J J C Coldwell Esq (1 turn)*
R　N F M MORRIS

WENTWORTH (Harley Mission Church) (Holy Trinity)
Sheff 12　P *Sir Philip Naylor-Leyland Bt*　V *vacant* (01226) 742274

WENTWORTH (St Peter)　*see* Witchford w Wentworth *Ely*

WEOBLEY (St Peter and St Paul) w Sarnesfield and Norton Canon *Heref 4*　P *Bp (2 turns), R A Marshall Esq (1 turn)*
R P D KING

WEOLEY CASTLE (St Gabriel) *Birm 2*　P *Bp*
P-in-c　A M DELMEGE

WEREHAM (St Margaret) *Ely 9*　P *Bp*　P-in-c　B L BURTON

WERNETH (St Paul) *Ches 16*　P *DBP*　V　L BOYLE,
NSM　W S ATKINSON

WERNETH (St Thomas) *Man 16*　P *Bp*
P-in-c　F A O D DAWSON

WERRINGTON (St John the Baptist w Emmanuel) *Pet 11*
P *Bp*　V　G H ROGERS,　C　S P KINDER,　NSM　S J FEAR

WERRINGTON (St Martin of Tours)　*see* Boyton, N Tamerton, Werrington etc *Truro*

WERRINGTON (St Philip) and Wetley Rocks *Lich 6*　P *Bp and V Caverswall and Weston Coyney w Dilhorne (jt)*
V　S E GOODWIN,　C　A MARCH,　OLM　S J PARKER,
I T COPELAND

WESHAM (Christ Church) and Treales *Blackb 10*
P *V Kirkham*　P-in-c　J D JONES

WESSINGTON (Christ Church)　*see* Ashover and Brackenfield w Wessington *Derby*

WEST　*see also under substantive place name*

WEST BAY (St John)　*see* Bridport *Sarum*

WEST DEAN (All Saints)　*see* Alfriston w Lullington, Litlington and W Dean *Chich*

WEST DEAN (St Andrew)　*see* E Dean, Singleton, and W Dean *Chich*

WEST DEAN (St Mary)　*see* Clarendon *Sarum*

WEST DOWN (St Calixtus)　*see* Ilfracombe SS Phil and Jas w W Down *Ex*

WEST DOWNLAND *Ox 14*　P *Bp, Sir Philip Wroughton, and D&C Westmr (jt)*　R　J P TOWNEND,　NSM　M A HARWOOD

WEST END　*see* Northolt St Jos *Lon*

WEST END (Holy Trinity)　*see* Bisley and W End *Guildf*

WEST END (St George)　*see* Esher *Guildf*

WEST END (St James) *Win 10*　P *Bp*　V　B L PICKETT,
NSM　J E PICKETT

WEST FELTON (St Michael)　*see* Whittington and W Felton w Haughton *Lich*

WEST GREEN (Christ Church w St Peter) *Lon 19*　P *Bp*
Hon C　M A R HAYNES

WEST GREEN (St Peter)　*see* Crawley *Chich*

WEST HAM (All Saints) *Chelmsf 3*　P *The Crown*
V　S R KIRBY

WEST HAM (St Matthew)　*see* Forest Gate St Sav w W Ham St Matt *Chelmsf*

WEST HEATH (St Anne) *Birm 4*　P *Bp*　V　S C L DIMES,
P-in-c　J G TSIPOURAS

WEST HILL (St Michael the Archangel)　*see* Ottery St Mary, Alfington, W Hill, Tipton etc *Ex*

WEST HYDE (St Thomas of Canterbury)　*see* Mill End and Heronsgate w W Hyde *St Alb*

WEST MOORS (St Mary the Virgin) *Sarum 9*　P *Bp*
V　A J W ROWLAND

WEST ORCHARD (St Luke)　*see* Shaftesbury *Sarum*

WEST ROW (St Peter)　*see* Mildenhall *St E*

WEST WINCH (St Mary) w Setchey, North Runcton and Middleton *Nor 20*　P *H N D Gurney Esq (1 turn) and Ld Chan (2 turns)*　R　J F RYAN

WEST WOODHAY (St Laurence)　*see* Walbury Beacon *Ox*

WESTACRE (All Saints)　*see* Nar Valley *Nor*

WESTBERE (All Saints)　*see* Sturry w Fordwich and Westbere w Hersden *Cant*

WESTBOROUGH (All Saints)　*see* Claypole *Linc*

WESTBOROUGH (St Clare) (St Francis) *Guildf 5*　P *Bp*
TR　S M HODGES,　TV　S POWNALL

WESTBOURNE (Christ Church) Chapel *Win 8*
Min　N R T HISCOCKS

WESTBOURNE (St John the Baptist) *Chich 13*　P *Bp*
R　F A WRIGHT

WESTBROOK (All Saints)　*see* Margate All SS *Cant*

WESTBROOK (St James) Hood Manor *Liv 12*　P *Bp, R Warrington, and V Gt Sankey (jt)*　P-in-c　M X THORPE

WESTBROOK (St Philip) Old Hall and Callands *Liv 12*　P *Bp and R Warrington (jt)*　V *vacant* (01925) 654400

WESTBURY (All Saints)　*see* White Horse *Sarum*

WESTBURY (St Augustine)　*see* W Buckingham *Ox*

WESTBURY (St Mary) *Heref 12*　P *Bp*　P-in-c　J P ROWE

WESTBURY-ON-SEVERN (St Peter and St Paul) w Flaxley, Blaisdon and Minsterworth *Glouc 3*　P *Bp, D&C Heref, and Sir Thomas Crawley-Boevey Bt (jt)*　P-in-c　I C GOBEY,
NSM　S L HOBBS

WESTBURY-ON-TRYM (Holy Trinity) *Bris 2*　P *SMF*
V　A H HART

WESTBURY-ON-TRYM (St Alban) *Bris 2*　P *Bp*
P-in-c　E L LANGLEY

WESTBURY PARK (Local Ecumenical Partnership) *Bris 2*
Min　E L LANGLEY,　NSM　M H JAMES

WESTBURY PARK (St Alban)　*see* Westbury-on-Trym St Alb *Bris*

WESTBURY SUB MENDIP (St Lawrence) w Easton *B & W 1* **P** *Bp* **P-in-c** P M HOLLINGSWORTH

WESTCLIFF (Church of Reconciliation) *see* Brumby *Linc*

WESTCLIFF (St Alban) *see* Southend *Chelmsf*

WESTCLIFF (St Andrew) *Chelmsf 13* **P** *Bp* **V** S F KIMBER

WESTCLIFF (St Cedd and the Saints of Essex) *see* Prittlewell St Pet w Westcliff St Cedd *Chelmsf*

WESTCLIFF (St Michael and All Angels) *Chelmsf 13* **P** *Bp* **V** P C NICHOLSON

WESTCLIFF (St Saviour) *see* Southend St Sav Westcliff *Chelmsf*

WESTCLIFFE (St Peter) *see* St Margarets-at-Cliffe w Westcliffe etc *Cant*

WESTCOMBE PARK (St George) *see* E Greenwich *S'wark*

WESTCOTE (St Mary the Virgin) *see* Broadwell, Evenlode, Oddington, Adlestrop etc *Glouc*

WESTCOTE BARTON (St Edward the Confessor) w Steeple Barton, Duns Tew and Sandford St Martin *Ox 9* **P** *Duke of Marlborough, Exors Mrs Rittson-Thomas, DBP, D C D Webb Esq, and Bp (jt)* **R** G R ARTHUR

WESTCOTT (Holy Trinity) *Guildf 7* **P** *Bp* **P-in-c** A C JONAS, **NSM** N E COE

WESTCOTT (St Mary) *see* Schorne *Ox*

WESTDENE (The Ascension) *see* Patcham *Chich*

WESTERDALE (Christ Church) *York 21* **P** *Abp* **V** M J HAZELTON

WESTERFIELD (St Mary Magdalene) and Tuddenham w Witnesham *St E 4* **P** *Bp, Peterho Cam, and DBP (alt)* **NSM** A W FORSDIKE, **OLM** C A FORSDIKE

WESTERHAM (St Mary the Virgin) *Roch 9* **P** *J St A Warde Esq* **V** P S MCVEAGH

WESTERLEIGH (St James the Great) *see* Yate New Town *Bris*

WESTERN DOWNLAND *Sarum 11* **P** *Hyndman Trustees, A N Hanbury Esq, and W J Purvis Esq (jt)* **R** L M PLAYER

WESTFIELD (St Andrew) *see* Barnham Broom and Upper Yare *Nor*

WESTFIELD (St John the Baptist) *Chich 20* **P** *Bp* **V** *vacant* (01424) 751029

WESTFIELD (St Mark) *see* Woking St Pet *Guildf*

WESTFIELD (St Mary) *Carl 7* **P** *Bp* **C** T COPELAND, **NSM** M T STILWELL

WESTFIELD (St Peter) *B & W 11* **P** *Bp* **P-in-c** E R H BUSH

WESTGATE (St Andrew) *see* Upper Weardale *Dur*

WESTGATE (St James) *Cant 5* **P** *Abp* **V** R T BASHFORD

WESTGATE (St Martin of Tours) *see* Torrisholme *Blackb*

WESTGATE COMMON (St Michael the Archangel) *Wakef 11* **P** *V Alverthorpe* **P-in-c** G A SYKES

WESTGATE-ON-SEA (St Saviour) *Cant 5* **P** *Abp* **P-in-c** T F BARNFATHER

WESTHALL (St Andrew) *see* Hundred River *St E*

WESTHAM (St Mary the Virgin) *Chich 16* **P** *Duke of Devonshire* **V** G J BARRETT

WESTHAMPNETT (St Peter) *see* Chich St Paul and Westhampnett *Chich*

WESTHEAD (St James) *see* Newburgh w Westhead *Liv*

WESTHIDE (St Bartholomew) *see* Withington w Westhide *Heref*

WESTHOPE (Mission Room) *see* Canon Pyon w King's Pyon, Birley and Wellington *Heref*

WESTHORPE (St Margaret) *see* Badwell and Walsham *St E*

WESTHOUGHTON (St Bartholomew) and Wingates *Man 9* **P** *Patr Bd* **TR** G A LAWSON, **C** J C BRADING, **OLM** V A RADFORD

WESTHOUGHTON (St James) *see* Daisy Hill *Man*

WESTHOUSES (St Saviour) *see* Blackwell w Tibshelf *Derby*

WESTLANDS (St Andrew) *Lich 9* **P** *Simeon's Trustees* **V** *vacant* (01782) 619594

WESTLEIGH (St Paul) *Man 19* **P** *V Leigh St Mary* **V** *vacant* (01942) 882883 *or* 672333

WESTLEIGH (St Peter) *see* Fremington, Instow and Westleigh *Ex*

WESTLEIGH (St Peter) *Man 19* **P** *Bp, Dioc Chan, and V Leigh St Mary (jt)* **NSM** D VICKERS

WESTLETON (St Peter) *see* Yoxmere *St E*

WESTLEY (St Mary) *see* Horringer *St E*

WESTLEY WATERLESS (St Mary the less) *see* Raddesley Gp *Ely*

WESTMEADS (St Michael and All Angels) *see* Aldwick *Chich*

WESTMESTON (St Martin) *see* Ditchling, Streat and Westmeston *Chich*

WESTMILL (St Mary the Virgin) *see* Aspenden, Buntingford and Westmill *St Alb*

WESTMINSTER Hanover Square (St George) *see* Hanover Square St Geo *Lon*

WESTMINSTER (St James) Piccadilly *Lon 3* **P** *Bp (2 turns), Ld Chan (1 turn)* **R** L C WINKETT, **C** J L MEADER, **NSM** H W J VALENTINE

WESTMINSTER (St James the Less) *Lon 3* **P** *D&C Westmr* **V** E A GODDARD, **NSM** W M CHOW

WESTMINSTER (St Mary le Strand) *see* St Mary le Strand w St Clem Danes *Lon*

WESTMINSTER (St Matthew) *Lon 3* **P** *D&C Westmr* **V** P A E CHESTER, **NSM** P L HANAWAY

WESTMINSTER (St Michael) *see* Ches Square St Mich w St Phil *Lon*

WESTMINSTER (St Saviour) *see* Pimlico St Sav *Lon*

WESTMINSTER (St Stephen) w St John *Lon 3* **P** *The Crown* **V** P P WELSH, **NSM** J M HICKS

WESTOE, SOUTH (St Michael and All Angels) *Dur 15* **P** *Bp* **P-in-c** P J A KENNEDY

WESTON (All Saints) *see* Bath Weston All SS w N Stoke and Langridge *B & W*

WESTON (All Saints) *see* Washburn and Mid-Wharfe *Bradf*

WESTON (All Saints) *Ches 15* **P** *Bp* **P-in-c** G M BREFFITT

WESTON (All Saints) *see* Quinton and Welford w Weston *Glouc*

WESTON (All Saints) *Guildf 8* **P** *Bp* **V** P T JOHNSON

WESTON (All Saints) *see* Tuxford w Weston and Markham Clinton *S'well*

WESTON (Emmanuel) *see* Bath Weston St Jo w Kelston *B & W*

WESTON (Holy Trinity) *see* Baldock w Bygrave and Weston *St Alb*

WESTON (Holy Trinity) *Win 13* **P** *Bp* **V** R A BURNINGHAM

WESTON (St John the Evangelist) *see* Bath Weston St Jo w Kelston *B & W*

WESTON (St John the Evangelist) *see* Runcorn St Jo Weston *Ches*

WESTON (St Mary) *see* Cowbit *Linc*

WESTON (St Peter) *see* Hundred River *St E*

WESTON, OLD (St Swithun) *see* Brington w Molesworth and Old Weston *Ely*

WESTON, SOUTH (St Lawrence) *see* Thame *Ox*

WESTON BAMPFYLDE (Holy Cross) *see* Cam Vale *B & W*

WESTON BEGGARD (St John the Baptist) *see* Lugwardine w Bartestree, Weston Beggard etc *Heref*

WESTON BY WELLAND (St Mary) *see* Stoke Albany w Wilbarston and Ashley etc *Pet*

WESTON COLVILLE (St Mary) *see* Balsham, Weston Colville, W Wickham etc *Ely*

WESTON COYNEY (St Andrew) *see* Caverswall and Weston Coyney w Dilhorne *Lich*

WESTON ESTATE CHURCH (not known) *see* Otley *Bradf*

WESTON FAVELL (St Peter) *Pet 4* **P** *DBP* **R** D G KIRBY, **C** M S COTTON

WESTON HILLS (St John the Evangelist) *see* Cowbit *Linc*

WESTON IN GORDANO (St Peter and St Paul) *see* E Clevedon w Clapton in Gordano etc *B & W*

WESTON LONGVILLE (All Saints) *see* Wensum Benefice *Nor*

WESTON LULLINGFIELD (Holy Trinity) *see* Baschurch and Weston Lullingfield w Hordley *Lich*

WESTON MILL (St Philip) *see* Devonport St Boniface and St Phil *Ex*

WESTON-ON-THE-GREEN (St Mary) *see* Akeman *Ox*

WESTON ON TRENT (St Mary the Virgin) *see* Aston on Trent, Elvaston, Weston on Trent etc *Derby*

WESTON PATRICK (St Lawrence) *see* N Hants Downs *Win*

WESTON POINT (Christ Church) *see* Runcorn St Jo Weston *Ches*

WESTON RHYN (St John) *see* St Martins and Weston Rhyn *Lich*

WESTON-SUB-EDGE (St Lawrence) *see* Mickleton, Willersey w Saintbury etc *Glouc*

WESTON SUPER MARE (All Saints) and St Saviour *B & W 10* **P** *Bp* **V** *vacant* (01934) 633910

WESTON SUPER MARE (Christ Church) (Emmanuel) *B & W 10* **P** *Trustees* **V** *vacant* (01934) 624376

WESTON-SUPER-MARE (St Andrew) Bournville *B & W 10* **P** *Bp* **P-in-c** P T STEVENS

WESTON SUPER MARE (St John the Baptist) *B & W 10* **P** *Bp and Trustees (jt)* **R** R J TAYLOR, **NSM** P L BERESFORD

WESTON-SUPER-MARE (St Nicholas) (St Barnabas) *B & W 10* **P** *Patr Bd* **R** *vacant* (01934) 620156

WESTON-SUPER-MARE (St Paul) *B & W 10* **P** *Bp* **V** A M ALDEN, **C** T P B YACOMENI

WESTON TURVILLE (St Mary the Virgin) *Ox 28* **P** *All So Coll Ox* **R** D N WALES, **NSM** S E FELLOWS

WESTON-UNDER-LIZARD (St Andrew) *see* Watershed *Lich*

WESTON-UNDER-PENYARD (St Lawrence) *see* Ariconium *Heref*

WESTON UNDER REDCASTLE (St Luke) *see* Hodnet w Weston under Redcastle *Lich*

WESTON UNDER WETHERLEY (St Michael) *see* Wappenbury w Weston under Wetherley *Cov*

WESTON UNDERWOOD (St Laurence) *see* Gayhurst w Ravenstone, Stoke Goldington etc *Ox*

WESTON UPON TRENT (St Andrew) *see* Mid Trent *Lich*
WESTON ZOYLAND (Blessed Virgin Mary) w Chedzoy
  B & W 13 **P** *Bp* **V** C D KEYS
WESTONING (St Mary Magdalene) w Tingrith *St Alb 8*
  P *Ld Chan* **P-in-c** N L WASHINGTON
WESTOW (St Mary) *see* W Buckrose *York*
WESTWARD (St Hilda), Rosley-with-Woodside and Welton
  Carl 3 **P** *D&C* **P-in-c** N L ROBINSON
WESTWARD HO! (Holy Trinity) *see* Bideford, Northam,
  Westward Ho!, Appledore etc *Ex*
WESTWAY (St Katherine) *see* N Hammersmith St Kath *Lon*
WESTWELL (St Mary) *see* G7 Benefice *Cant*
WESTWELL (St Mary) *see* Shill Valley and Broadshire *Ox*
WESTWICK (St Botolph) *see* Worstead, Westwick, Sloley,
  Swanton Abbot etc *Nor*
WESTWOOD (Mission Church) *see* Golcar *Wakef*
WESTWOOD (St John the Baptist) *Cov 3* **P** *Bp*
  V P FINDLEY, **C** A J DENNISS
WESTWOOD (St Mary) Jacksdale *see* Selston *S'well*
WESTWOOD (St Mary the Virgin) and Wingfield *Sarum 14*
  P *D&C Bris, CPAS, and Bp (jt)* **R** R M LOWRIE
WESTWOOD, LOW (Christ Church) *see* Ebchester *Dur*
WETHERAL (Holy Trinity and St Constantine) *see* Holme
  Eden and Wetheral w Warwick *Carl*
WETHERBY (St James) *Ripon 1* **P** *Bp* **V** *vacant* (01937)
  582423
WETHERDEN (St Mary the Virgin) *see* Haughley w
  Wetherden and Stowupland *St E*
WETHERINGSETT (All Saints) *see* S Hartismere *St E*
WETHERSFIELD (St Mary Magdalene) *see* Finchingfield and
  Cornish Hall End etc *Chelmsf*
WETLEY ROCKS (St John the Baptist) *see* Werrington and
  Wetley Rocks *Lich*
WETTENHALL (St David) *see* Acton and Worleston, Church
  Minshull etc *Ches*
WETTON (St Margaret) *see* Alstonfield, Butterton, Ilam etc
  Lich
WETWANG (St Nicholas) *see* Waggoners *York*
WEXHAM (St Mary) *Ox 23* **P** *Ld Chan*
  P-in-c R M DONOVAN, **NSM** J M LOCKE
WEYBOURNE (All Saints), Upper Sheringham, Kelling,
  Salthouse, Bodham and East and West Beckham (The
  Weybourne Group) *Nor 18* **P** *Bp (2 turns), Sir Charles
  Mott-Radclyffe (1 turn), D&C (1 turn), and Lord Walpole
  (1 turn)* **R** P G BLAMIRE, **OLM** F A CLARKE
WEYBREAD (St Andrew) *see* Fressingfield, Mendham etc *St E*
WEYBRIDGE (St James) *Guildf 8* **P** *Ld Chan*
  R B D PROTHERO, **C** B HENGIST, **NSM** J L MULDER
WEYHILL (St Michael and All Angels) *see* Pastrow *Win*
WEYMOUTH (Holy Trinity) (St Nicholas) *Sarum 4* **P** *Bp*
  V R H FRANKLIN, **C** D A'COURT, **OLM** A DUNN
WEYMOUTH (St Edmund) *see* Wyke Regis *Sarum*
WEYMOUTH (St John) *see* Radipole and Melcombe Regis
  Sarum
WEYMOUTH (St Mary) *as above*
WEYMOUTH (St Paul) *Sarum 4* **P** *Bp* **V** R M HARPER
WHADDON (St Margaret) *see* Glouc St Geo w Whaddon
  Glouc
WHADDON (St Mary) *Ely 7* **P** *D&C Windsor*
  P-in-c D C R MCFADYEN
WHADDON (St Mary) *see* Buckingham *Ox*
WHADDON (St Mary) *see* Clarendon *Sarum*
WHADDON (St Mary the Virgin) *see* Canalside Benefice
  Sarum
WHALEY BRIDGE (St James) *Ches 16* **P** *Bp and Bp Derby
  (alt)* **P-in-c** C L PINNER, **Hon C** J P PINNER
WHALEY THORNS (St Luke) *see* E Scarsdale *Derby*
WHALLEY (St Mary and All Saints) *Blackb 7* **P** *Hulme
  Trustees* **P-in-c** G M DYER, **NSM** J E HOLT
WHALLEY RANGE (St Edmund) and Moss Side St James w St
  Clement *Man 3* **P** *Bp and Simeon's Trustees (jt)*
  R S R BULLOCK
WHALLEY RANGE (St Margaret) *Man 3* **P** *Trustees*
  P-in-c R G BOULTER
WHALTON (St Mary Magdalene) *see* Bolam w Whalton and
  Hartburn w Meldon *Newc*
WHAPLODE (St Mary) *Linc 16* **P** *Ld Chan*
  P-in-c R J MORRISON
WHAPLODE DROVE (St John the Baptist) *Linc 16* **P** *Feoffees*
  V R J MORRISON
WHARFEDALE, LOWER *Ripon 1* **P** *Bp, V Otley, and
  W G C Sheepshanks Esq (jt)* **R** S W LEWIS
WHARNCLIFFE SIDE (not known) *see* Oughtibridge *Sheff*
WHARRAM (St Mary) *see* Weaverthorpe w Helperthorpe,
  Luttons Ambo etc *York*
WHARTON (Christ Church) *Ches 6* **P** *R Davenham*
  V T D HANSON, **C** T A WATTS

WHATBOROUGH Group of Parishes, The *Leic 3* **P** *Bp*
  V J D CURTIS
WHATCOTE (St Peter) *see* Tysoe w Oxhill and Whatcote *Cov*
WHATFIELD (St Margaret) *see* Bildeston w Wattisham and
  Lindsey, Whatfield etc *St E*
WHATLEY (St George) *see* Mells w Buckland Dinham, Elm,
  Whatley etc *B & W*
WHATLINGTON (St Mary Magdalene) *see* Sedlescombe w
  Whatlington *Chich*
WHATSTANDWELL (Mission Room) *see* Crich and S
  Wingfield *Derby*
WHATTON (St John of Beverley) w Aslockton, Hawksworth,
  Scarrington, Orston and Thoroton *S'well 8* **P** *Trustees*
  P-in-c K A PRZYWALA
WHEATACRE (All Saints) *see* Raveningham Gp *Nor*
WHEATCROFT (St Michael and All Angels) *see* Scarborough
  St Martin *York*
WHEATFIELD (St Andrew) *see* Thame *Ox*
WHEATHAMPSTEAD (St Helen) *St Alb 7* **P** *Bp*
  P-in-c R M BANHAM, **NSM** M H KING
WHEATHILL (Holy Trinity) w Ditton Priors w Neenton,
  Burwarton etc *Heref*
WHEATHILL PRIORY Group of Parishes, The *B & W 2*
  P *Ch Soc Trust and J H Cordle Esq (1 turn), A J Whitehead Esq
  (2 turns), Bp (1 turn), and Mrs E J Burden (1 turn)*
  P-in-c T R CRANSHAW
WHEATLEY (St Mary) *see* Doncaster St Mary and St Paul
  Sheff
WHEATLEY (St Mary the Virgin) *Ox 1* **P** *Patr Bd*
  TV E L PENNINGTON, S CROSS, **NSM** J EDMONDS-SEAL,
  C N KING, M D CHAPMAN
WHEATLEY, NORTH (St Peter and St Paul) *see* Retford Area
  S'well
WHEATLEY HILL (All Saints) and Wingate w Hutton Henry
  Dur 2 **P** *Bp* **P-in-c** R C DAVIES
WHEATLEY HILLS (St Aidan) *Sheff 8* **P** *Bp* **V** D J GOSS
WHEATLEY PARK (St Paul) *see* Doncaster St Mary and St
  Paul *Sheff*
WHEATON ASTON (St Mary) *see* Watershed *Lich*
WHEELOCK (Christ Church) *see* Sandbach Heath w
  Wheelock *Ches*
WHELDRAKE (St Helen) *see* Derwent Ings *York*
WHELFORD (St Anne) *see* Fairford Deanery *Glouc*
WHELLEY (St Stephen) *see* New Springs and Whelley *Liv*
WHELNETHAM, GREAT (St Thomas à Becket) *see* St Edm
  Way *St E*
WHELNETHAM, LITTLE (St Mary) *see* Bradfield St Clare,
  Bradfield St George etc *St E*
WHELPLEY HILL (St Michael and All Angels) *see* Gt
  Chesham *Ox*
WHENBY (St Martin) *see* Howardian Gp *York*
WHEPSTEAD (St Petronilla) *see* Horringer *St E*
WHERSTEAD (St Mary) *see* Holbrook, Stutton, Freston,
  Woolverstone etc *St E*
WHERWELL (St Peter and Holy Cross) *see* Downs Benefice
  Win
WHETSTONE (St John the Apostle) *Lon 14* **P** *Bp*
  P-in-c C KENT
WHETSTONE (St Peter) *see* Cosby and Whetstone *Leic*
WHICHAM (St Mary) *see* Bootle, Corney, Whicham and
  Whitbeck *Carl*
WHICHFORD (St Michael) *see* S Warks Seven Gp *Cov*
WHICKHAM (St Mary the Virgin) *Dur 13* **P** *Ld Chan*
  R B J ABBOTT, **C** J W BARRON
WHILTON (St Andrew) *see* Brington w Whilton and Norton
  etc *Pet*
WHIMPLE (St Mary), Talaton and Clyst St Lawrence *Ex 7*
  P *DBP, D&C and MMCET (jt)* **R** *vacant* (01404) 822521
WHINBURGH (St Mary) *see* Barnham Broom and Upper Yare
  Nor
WHINLANDS Benefice, The *St E 19* **P** *Mrs A C V Wentworth,
  Ch Patr Trust, and Ch Soc Trust (by turn)* **R** C E BROOKS,
  NSM S E HART
WHINMOOR (St Paul) *see* Seacroft *Ripon*
WHINNEY HILL (St Peter) *see* Thrybergh *Sheff*
WHIPPINGHAM (St Mildred) w East Cowes *Portsm 8*
  P *Ld Chan* **NSM** V J HARDS
WHIPSNADE (St Mary Magdalene) *see* Kensworth, Studham
  and Whipsnade *St Alb*
WHITON (St Boniface) *Ex 3* **P** *Bp* **P-in-c** J W BYATT
WHISSENDINE (St Andrew) *see* Oakham, Ashwell,
  Braunston, Brooke, Egleton etc *Pet*
WHISSONSETT (St Mary) *see* Upper Wensum Village Gp *Nor*
WHISTON (St Mary Magdalene) *Sheff 6* **P** *Bp* **R** N BOWLER
WHISTON (St Mary the Virgin) *see* Yardley Hastings, Denton
  and Grendon etc *Pet*

WHISTON (St Mildred) *see* Kingsley and Foxt-w-Whiston and Oakamoor etc *Lich*

WHISTON (St Nicholas) *Liv 2* **P** *V Prescot* **V** A J TELFER

WHITACRE, NETHER (St Giles) *see* The Whitacres, Lea Marston, and Shustoke *Birm*

WHITACRE, OVER (St Leonard) *as above*

WHITACRES, Lea Marston, and Shustoke, The *Birm 9* **P** J K Wingfield Digby Esq (1 turn), Bp (2 turns), and Ld Chan (1 turn) **R** D COUTURE

WHITBECK (St Mary) *see* Bootle, Corney, Whicham and Whitbeck *Carl*

WHITBOURNE (Bringsty Iron Church) *see* Edvin Loach w Tedstone Delamere etc *Heref*

WHITBOURNE (St John the Baptist) *as above*

WHITBURN (no dedication) *Dur 16* **P** *Bp* **R** K R SMITH

WHITBY (St Hilda) (St John) (St Mary) w Ruswarp *York 21* **P** *Abp* **TR** D W SMITH, **C** H N LAWRANCE

WHITBY (St Thomas) *see* Ellesmere Port *Ches*

WHITBY ROAD (St Michael) *see* Manor Park and Whitby Road *Ox*

WHITCHURCH (All Hallows) w Tufton and Litchfield *Win 6* **P** *Bp* **V** K J INGLIS

WHITCHURCH (St Alkmund) *Lich 22* **P** *Bp* **R** A R RIDLEY

WHITCHURCH (St Andrew) *Ex 25* **P** *Bp* **P-in-c** S A BRASSIL, **C** A J RYAN, **NSM** M L DONNE

WHITCHURCH (St Augustine) (St Nicholas) *Bris 1* **P** *Bp* **C** N J HAY

WHITCHURCH (St Dubricius) *see* Dixton, Wyesham, Bishopswood, Whitchurch etc *Heref*

WHITCHURCH (St John the Evangelist) *see* Schorne *Ox*

WHITCHURCH (St Lawrence) *see* Lt Stanmore St Lawr *Lon*

WHITCHURCH (St Mary the Virgin) *see* Ilmington w Stretton-on-Fosse etc *Cov*

WHITCHURCH (St Mary the Virgin) *see* Langtree *Ox*

WHITCHURCH CANONICORUM (St Candida and Holy Cross) *see* Golden Cap Team *Sarum*

WHITCHURCH HILL (St John the Baptist) *see* Langtree *Ox*

WHITE CITY ESTATE (St Michael and St George) *see* Shepherd's Bush St Steph w St Thos *Lon*

WHITE COLNE (St Andrew) *see* Halstead Area *Chelmsf*

WHITE HORSE, The *Sarum 17* **P** *Bp* **TR** J BURKE, **C** J C TOTNEY, **NSM** P J MCEUNE, S BAGGS

WHITE LADIES ASTON (St John) *see* Peopleton and White Ladies Aston w Churchill etc *Worc*

WHITE MOSS (St Mark) *see* Blackley St Mark White Moss Man

WHITE NOTLEY (St Etheldreda) *see* Fairstead w Terling and White Notley etc *Chelmsf*

WHITE RODING (St Martin) *see* S Rodings *Chelmsf*

WHITE WALTHAM (St Mary the Virgin) w Shottesbrooke *Ox 13* **P** *Sir John Smith* **P-in-c** D N ANDREW, **NSM** A J HARTROPP

WHITE WELL (St Mary) *see* St Paul's Walden *St Alb*

WHITECHAPEL (St James) *see* Fellside Team *Blackb*

WHITEFIELD (St Andrew) *see* Hillock Man

WHITEFRIARS (no dedication) *Rushden Pet 8* **P** CPAS **V** P R EVANS

WHITEGATE (St Mary) w Little Budworth *Ches 6* **P** *Bp, Lord Delamere and W R Cullimore Esq (alt)* **V** L P EDEN

WHITEHALL (St Ambrose) *see* E Bris St Ambrose and St Leon *Bris*

WHITEHALL PARK (St Andrew) *see* Upper Holloway *Lon*

WHITEHAVEN (St James) *Carl 5* **P** *Patr Bd* **TR** J L BANNISTER, **Hon C** J D KELLY

WHITEHAWK (St Cuthman) *Chich 2* **P** *Bp* **V** J D WRIGHT, **NSM** D R S PORTER

WHITEHILLS (St Mark) *see* Kingsthorpe w Northampton St Dav *Pet*

WHITELACKINGTON (Blessed Virgin Mary) *see* Ilminster and Whitelackington *B & W*

WHITELEAS (St Mary w St Martin) *see* S Shields All SS *Dur*

WHITELEY Conventional District *Portsm 2* **C-in-c** L E SNAPE, **NSM** G J S SNAPE

WHITEPARISH (All Saints) *see* Clarendon *Sarum*

WHITESHILL (St Paul) and Randwick *Glouc 4* **P** *Bp* **V** B WOOLLASTON

WHITESTAUNTON (St Andrew) *see* Chard St Mary w Combe St Nicholas, Wambrook etc *B & W*

WHITESTONE (St Catherine) *see* Tedburn St Mary, Cheriton Bishop, Whitestone etc *Ex*

WHITESTONE PATHFINDER (St John the Evangelist) *as above*

WHITEWATER Benefice, The *Win 5* **P** *Bp and New Coll Ox (alt)* **P** R F QUINNELL, **C** M I ASHTON, **NSM** P B HEWLETT-SMITH

WHITEWELL (St Mary) *see* Marbury w Tushingham and Whitewell *Ches*

WHITEWELL (St Michael) *see* Chipping and Whitewell *Blackb*

WHITFIELD (Holy Trinity) *see* Allendale w Whitfield *Newc*

WHITFIELD (St James) (St Luke) *Derby 6* **P** *Bp* **V** C COOPER, **C** B G MAGORRIAN, R A ENGLAND

WHITFIELD (St John) *see* Allendale w Whitfield *Newc*

WHITFIELD (St John the Evangelist) *see* Astwell Gp *Pet*

WHITFIELD (St Peter) w Guston *Cant 7* **P** *Abp and D&C (alt)* **V** vacant (01304) 829223

WHITFORD (St Mary at the Cross) *see* Kilmington, Stockland, Dalwood, Yarcombe etc *Ex*

WHITGIFT (St Mary Magdalene) *see* The Marshland *Sheff*

WHITGREAVE (St John the Evangelist) *see* Stafford *Lich*

WHITKIRK (St Mary) *Ripon 8* **P** *Meynell Trustees* **V** I C BLACK, **C** S EARLE, G J TRINDER

WHITLEIGH St Chad *Ex 23* **P** *Bp* **P-in-c** T THORP, **C** D R BAILEY

WHITLEY (Christ Church) *see* Reading Ch Ch *Ox*

WHITLEY (St Helen) *Newc 10* **P** *Bp* **V** A J PATTERSON

WHITLEY (St James) *Cov 1* **P** *Bp* **NSM** P A STOTE

WHITLEY, LOWER or NETHER (St Luke) *see* Antrobus, Aston by Sutton, Lt Leigh etc *Ches*

WHITLEY BRIDGE (All Saints) *see* Knottingley and Kellington w Whitley *Wakef*

WHITLEY LOWER (St Mary and St Michael) *see* Thornhill and Whitley Lower *Wakef*

WHITLINGHAM (St Andrew) *see* Rockland St Mary w Hellington, Bramerton etc *Nor*

WHITMINSTER (St Andrew) *see* Eastington, Frocester, Haresfield etc *Glouc*

WHITMORE (St Mary and All Saints) *see* Chapel Chorlton, Maer and Whitmore *Lich*

WHITNASH (St Margaret) *Cov 11* **P** *Lord Leigh* **R** R W S SUFFERN, **OLM** S D BATE

WHITNEY (St Peter and St Paul) *see* Eardisley w Bollingham, Willersley, Brilley etc *Heref*

WHITSBURY (St Leonard) *see* W Downland *Sarum*

WHITSTABLE (All Saints) (St Alphage) (St Andrew) (St Peter) *Cant 4* **P** *DBP* **TR** S J CONEYS, **TV** S C TILLOTSON, **R** C WEBBLEY, **C** A R BRADDY, **NSM** M A J GILLIBRAND

WHITSTONE (St Anne) *see* Week St Mary Circle of Par *Truro*

WHITTINGHAM (St Bartholomew) and Edlingham w Bolton Chapel *Newc 6* **P** *D&C Carl and D&C Dur (alt)* **V** J A ROBERTSON

WHITTINGTON (Christ Church) *see* Wretton w Stoke Ferry and Whittington *Ely*

WHITTINGTON (St Bartholomew) *Derby 5* **P** *Bp* **P-in-c** J B BABB

WHITTINGTON (St Bartholomew) *see* Sevenhampton w Charlton Abbots, Hawling etc *Glouc*

WHITTINGTON (St Giles) w Weeford *Lich 1* **P** *Bp* **V** F A HASKETT

WHITTINGTON (St John the Baptist) and West Felton w Haughton *Lich 19* **P** *Bp and Mrs A F Hamilton-Hill (jt)* **Hon C** A G SPARHAM

WHITTINGTON (St Michael the Archangel) *see* Hornby w Claughton and Whittington etc *Blackb*

WHITTINGTON (St Philip and St James) *see* Worc SE *Worc*

WHITTINGTON, NEW (St Barnabas) *Derby 5* **P** *Bp* **V** vacant (01246) 455830

WHITTLE-LE-WOODS (St John the Evangelist) *Blackb 4* **P** *V Leyland* **V** A L WINSTANLEY, **C** T A DONAGHEY

WHITTLEBURY (St Mary) *see* Silverstone and Abthorpe w Slapton etc *Pet*

WHITTLESEY (St Andrew) (St Mary), Pondersbridge and Coates *Ely 11* **P** *Ld Chan (2 turns), Patr Bd (1 turn)* **TR** N A WHITEHOUSE, **TV** G STEVENS, **NSM** M B JONES

WHITTLESFORD Local Ecumenical Partnership *Ely 7 vacant*

WHITTLESFORD (St Mary and St Andrew) *Ely 5* **P** *Jes Coll Cam* **V** vacant (01223) 833382

WHITTLEWOOD *see* Silverstone and Abthorpe w Slapton etc *Pet*

WHITTON *Sarum 18* **P** *Patr Bd* **TR** S A WEEDEN, **TV** C A MARCUS, **NSM** S E RODD

WHITTON (St Augustine of Canterbury) *Lon 10* **P** *Bp* **V** S M CAPLE

WHITTON (St John the Baptist) *see* Alkborough *Linc*

WHITTON (St Mary) *see* Thornton Steward

WHITTON (St Mary and St Botolph) and Thurleston w Akenham *St E 4* **P** *Bp (2 turns), Exors G K Drury Esq (1 turn)* **R** A S DOTCHIN

WHITTON (St Philip and St James) *Lon 10* **P** *V Twickenham St Mary* **NSM** V F FRAY

WHITTONSTALL (St Philip and St James) *Newc 9* **P** *D&C* **P-in-c** D J IRVINE, **NSM** J LYNCH

WHITWELL (St John the Evangelist) w Crambe and Foston *York 6* **P** *Abp* **P-in-c** I R HOWITT

WHITWELL (St Lawrence) *Derby 3* **P** *Bp* **P-in-c** A S G PIKE, NSM J A PALMER

WHITWELL (St Mary) *see* St Paul's Walden *St Alb*

WHITWELL (St Mary and St Rhadegunde) *Portsm 7* **P** *Bp* **V** S E LLOYD

WHITWELL (St Michael and All Angels) *see* Reepham, Hackford w Whitwell, Kerdiston etc *Nor*

WHITWELL (St Michael and All Angels) *see* Empingham, Edith Weston, Lyndon, Manton etc *Pet*

WHITWICK (St John the Baptist), Thringstone and Swannington *Leic 8* **P** *Duchy of Lanc (2 turns), Bp (1 turn)* **R** A J BURGESS

WHITWOOD (All Saints) *see* Castleford *Wakef*

WHITWORTH (not known) *see* Spennymoor and Whitworth *Dur*

WHITWORTH (not known) *see* St Pet Ho *Man*

WHITWORTH (St Bartholomew) w Facit *Man 17* **P** *Bp and Keble Coll Ox (jt)* **V** L E M WOODALL, OLM A P WALLBANK

WHIXALL (St Mary) *see* Edstaston, Fauls, Prees, Tilstock and Whixall *Lich*

WHIXLEY (Ascension) *see* Gt and Lt Ouseburn w Marton cum Grafton etc *Ripon*

WHORLTON (Holy Cross Old Church) w Carlton and Faceby *York 20* **P** *Mrs A P F Kynge* **V** L M SHIPP, NSM P J JOHNSON

WHORLTON (St John the Evangelist) *Newc 4* **P** *Bp* **V** J M GRIEVE, **C** R M PADDISON

WHORLTON (St Mary) *see* Barnard Castle w Whorlton *Dur*

WHYKE (St George) w Rumboldswhyke St Mary and Portfield All Saints *Chich 3* **P** *Bp* **R** S W CRADDUCK, **C** R L CANNON, Hon **C** J RHODES-WRIGLEY

WHYTELEAFE (St Luke) *see* Caterham *S'wark*

WIBTOFT (Assumption of Our Lady) *see* Upper Soar *Leic*

WICHENFORD (St Lawrence) *see* Worcs W *Worc*

WICK (All Saints) *see* Littlehampton and Wick *Chich*

WICK (St Bartholomew) w Doynton and Dyrham *Bris 5* **P** *Simeon's Trustees, Ld Chan, and M H W Blaythwayt Esq (by turn)* **P-in-c** T J K BELL

WICK (St Mary) *see* Pershore w Pinvin, Wick and Birlingham *Worc*

WICK ST LAWRENCE (St Lawrence) *see* Worle *B & W*

WICKEN (St John the Evangelist) *see* Potterspury w Furtho and Yardley Gobion etc *Pet*

WICKEN (St Laurence) *see* Soham and Wicken *Ely*

WICKEN BONHUNT (St Margaret) *see* Clavering and Langley w Arkesden etc *Chelmsf*

WICKENBY (St Peter and St Laurence) *see* Wragby Gp *Linc*

WICKERSLEY (St Alban) *Sheff 6* **P** *DBP* **R** P J HUGHES

WICKFORD (St Andrew) (St Catherine) and Runwell *Chelmsf 6* **P** *Patr Bd* **TR** J FREEMAN, **TV** J H DELFGOU

WICKHAM (St Nicholas) *see* Shedfield and Wickham *Portsm*

WICKHAM (St Swithun) *see* W Downland *Ox*

WICKHAM, EAST (St Michael the Archangel) *S'wark 6* **P** *D&C* **V** P ORGAN, NSM M W SMITH, OLM I J THOMAS

WICKHAM, WEST (St Francis) (St Mary of Nazareth) *S'wark 19* **P** *Bp* **V** M R MCKINNEY, **C** A G JUDGE

WICKHAM, WEST (St John) *S'wark 19* **P** *Bp* **V** J J H WARD, OLM K J D GAVED

WICKHAM, WEST (St Mary) *see* Balsham, Weston Colville, W Wickham etc *Ely*

WICKHAM BISHOPS (St Bartholomew) w Little Braxted *Chelmsf 23* **P** *Bp (3 turns), CCC Cam (1 turn)* **P-in-c** S W BATTEN, NSM I R BENDREY

WICKHAM MARKET (All Saints) w Pettistree *St E 18* **P** *Ch Trust Fund Trust and Ld Chan (alt)* **V** J F ELDRIDGE

WICKHAM SKEITH (St Andrew) *see* Bacton w Wyverstone, Cotton and Old Newton etc *St E*

WICKHAM ST PAUL (St Paul and All Saints) *see* N Hinckford *Chelmsf*

WICKHAMBREAUX (St Andrew) *see* Littlebourne and Ickham w Wickhambreaux etc *Cant*

WICKHAMBROOK (All Saints) *see* Bansfield *St E*

WICKHAMFORD (St John the Baptist) *see* Broadway w Wickhamford *Worc*

WICKHAMPTON (St Andrew) *see* Freethorpe, Wickhampton, Halvergate etc *Nor*

WICKLEWOOD (All Saints) *see* High Oak, Hingham and Scoulton w Wood Rising *Nor*

WICKMERE (St Andrew) *see* Lt Barningham, Blickling, Edgefield etc *Nor*

WICKWAR (Holy Trinity) *see* Charfield and Kingswood w Wickwar etc *Glouc*

WIDCOMBE *see* Bath Widcombe *B & W*

WIDDINGTON (St Mary) *see* Newport and Widdington *Chelmsf*

WIDDRINGTON (Holy Trinity) *Newc 11* **P** *Bp* **V** H M BARTON

WIDDRINGTON STATION (St Mary) *see* Ulgham *Newc*

WIDECOMBE-IN-THE-MOOR (St Pancras) *see* Ashburton, Bickington, Buckland in the Moor etc *Ex*

WIDEMOUTH BAY (Our Lady and St Anne) *see* Week St Mary Circle of Par *Truro*

WIDFORD (St John the Baptist) *see* Hunsdon w Widford and Wareside *St Alb*

WIDFORD (St Mary) (Holy Spirit) *Chelmsf 9* **P** *CPAS* **R** D R W ROBBINS

WIDFORD (St Oswald) *see* Burford w Fulbrook, Taynton, Asthall etc *Ox*

WIDMER END (Good Shepherd) *see* Hazlemere *Ox*

WIDMERPOOL (St Peter) *see* Willoughby-on-the-Wolds w Wysall and Widmerpool *S'well*

WIDNES (St Ambrose) *Liv 13* **P** *Trustees* **V** J P LEFFLER

WIDNES (St John) *Liv 13* **P** *Bp and V Farnworth (jt)* **V** D J GAIT

WIDNES, SOUTH (St Mary) (St Paul) *Liv 13* **P** *Patr Bd* **TR** J M COLLIER, **TV** J DUFF, **C** D M HARRISON

WIDWORTHY (St Cuthbert) *see* Offwell, Northleigh, Farway, Cotleigh etc *Ex*

WIELD (St James) *see* Farleigh, Candover and Wield *Win*

WIGAN (All Saints) (St George) *Liv 14* **P** *Bp* **R** R J HUTCHINSON, **C** J E HAWORTH

WIGAN (St Andrew) *Liv 14* **P** *R Wigan* **V** C HURST

WIGAN (St Anne) *Liv 14* **P** *Bp* **P-in-c** D J BURY

WIGAN (St Barnabas) Marsh Green *see* Marsh Green w Newtown *Liv*

WIGAN (St Catharine) *see* Ince Ch Ch w Wigan St Cath *Liv*

WIGAN (St James) (St Thomas) *Liv 14* **P** *R Wigan and Bp (jt)* **V** H A F YOUNG

WIGAN (St John the Baptist) New Springs *see* New Springs and Whelley *Liv*

WIGAN (St Michael and All Angels) *Liv 14* **P** *R Wigan* NSM S HIGGINSON

WIGAN (St Stephen) Whelley *see* New Springs and Whelley *Liv*

WIGBOROUGH, GREAT (St Stephen) *see* W w E Mersea, Peldon, Gt and Lt Wigborough *Chelmsf*

WIGBOROUGH, LITTLE (St Nicholas) *as above*

WIGGATON (St Edward the Confessor) *see* Ottery St Mary, Alfington, W Hill, Tipton etc *Ex*

WIGGENHALL ST GERMANS (St Mary the Virgin) *see* E Marshland *Ely*

WIGGENHALL ST MARY (St Mary Magdalene) *as above*

WIGGINTON (St Bartholomew) *see* Northchurch and Wigginton *St Alb*

WIGGINTON (St Giles) *see* Hook Norton w Gt Rollright, Swerford etc *Ox*

WIGGINTON (St Leonard) (St James) *Lich 4* **P** *V Tamworth* NSM R DAVIES

WIGGINTON (St Nicholas) *see* Haxby and Wigginton *York*

WIGGLESWORTH (School) *see* Giggleswick and Rathmell w Wigglesworth *Bradf*

WIGGONHOLT (not known) *see* Amberley w N Stoke and Parham, Wiggonholt etc *Chich*

WIGHILL (All Saints) *see* Healaugh w Wighill, Bilbrough and Askham Richard *York*

WIGHTON (All Saints) *see* Holkham w Egmere w Warham, Wells and Wighton *Nor*

WIGMORE (St James the Apostle) *see* Wigmore Abbey *Heref*

WIGMORE ABBEY *Heref 6* **P** *Trustees* **R** M D CATLING

WIGSLEY *see* E Trent *S'well*

WIGSTON, SOUTH (St Thomas) *see* Glen Parva and S Wigston *Leic*

WIGSTON MAGNA (All Saints) (St Wistan) *Leic 4* **P** *Haberdashers' Co* **P-in-c** L R CURTIS, **C** S D MONK

WIGSTON PARVA (St Mary the Virgin) *see* Sapcote and Sharnford w Wigston Parva *Leic*

WIGTOFT (St Peter and St Paul) *see* Sutterton and Wigtoft *Linc*

WIGTON (St Mary) *Carl 3* **P** *Bp* **V** G P RAVALDE

WIKE (School Room) *see* Bardsey *Ripon*

WILBARSTON (All Saints) *see* Stoke Albany w Wilbarston and Ashley etc *Pet*

WILBERFOSS (St John the Baptist) w Kexby *York 5* **P** *Viscount de Vesci and Lord Egremont (alt)*

WILBRAHAM, GREAT (St Nicholas) *Ely 4* **P** *DBP* **V** A A GOODMAN

WILBRAHAM, LITTLE (St John) *Ely 4* **P** *CCC Cam* **R** A A GOODMAN

WILBURTON (St Peter) *Ely 8* **P** *Adn Ely* **V** F E G BRAMPTON

WILBY (St Thomas) *St Alb 3* **P** *Bp* **V** B E C PATE

WILBY (All Saints) *see* Quidenham Gp *Nor*

WILBY (St Mary) *see* Laxfield, Cratfield, Wilby and Brundish *St E*

WILBY (St Mary the Virgin) *see* Gt Doddington and Wilby *Pet*

WILCOT (Holy Cross) *see* Vale of Pewsey *Sarum*

WILCOTE (St Peter) *see* Forest Edge *Ox*

WILDBOARCLOUGH (St Saviour) *see* Bosley and N Rode w Wincle and Wildboarclough *Ches*

WILDEN (All Saints) *see* Stourport and Wilden *Worc*

WILDEN (St Nicholas) w Colmworth and Ravensden *St Alb 13* **P** *Ld Chan, Bp, and DBP (by turn)* **R** S MORTON

WILFORD (St Wilfrid) *S'well 9* **P** *Lt Col Peter Clifton* **P-in-c** P E MARSH, **NSM** M R SMITH

WILFORD HILL (St Paul) *S'well 9* **P** *DBP* **P-in-c** C J HODDER

WILFORD PENINSULA, The *St E 7* **P** *Patr Bd* **TR** P J MURDOCH, **TV** J P LEAVER, J M ANDREWS, R M HATCHETT

WILKSBY (All Saints) *see* Fen and Hill Gp *Linc*

WILLAND (St Mary the Virgin) *see* Cullompton, Willand, Uffculme, Kentisbeare etc *Ex*

WILLASTON (Christ Church) *Ches 9* **P** *DBF* **V** R W DENT, **NSM** L R BANNON

WILLASTON (St Luke) *see* Wistaston *Ches*

WILLEN (St Mary Magdalene) *see* Stantonbury and Willen *Ox*

WILLENHALL (Holy Trinity) *see* Bentley Em and Willenhall H Trin *Lich*

WILLENHALL (St Anne) *Lich 28* **P** *Mrs L Grant-Wilson* **V** G A WELSBY

WILLENHALL (St Giles) *Lich 28* **P** *Trustees* **V** G A WELSBY

WILLENHALL (St John the Divine) *Cov 1* **P** *V Cov H Trin* **V** K R SCOTT, **NSM** N C A SCOTT

WILLENHALL (St Stephen) *Lich 28* **P** *Bp* **V** G E T BENNETT

WILLERBY (St Luke) *see* Kirk Ella and Willerby *York*

WILLERBY (St Peter) w Ganton and Folkton *York 15* **P** *N H T Wrigley Esq, MMCET, and the Revd C G Day (by turn)* **P-in-c** K G F HOLDING

WILLERSEY (St Peter) *see* Mickleton, Willersey w Saintbury etc *Glouc*

WILLESBOROUGH (St Mary the Virgin) *Cant 6* **P** *D&C* **P-in-c** J C N MACKENZIE

WILLESDEN (St Mark) *see* Kensal Rise St Mark *Lon*

WILLESDEN (St Martin) *see* Kensal Rise St Martin *Lon*

WILLESDEN (St Mary) *Lon 21* **P** *D&C St Paul's* **V** D C CLUES, **NSM** H R F O'GARRO

WILLESDEN (St Matthew) *Lon 21* **P** *Bp* **V** D R HUMPHREYS

WILLESDEN (St Michael and All Angels) *see* Stonebridge St Mich *Lon*

WILLESDEN GREEN (St Andrew) (St Francis of Assisi) *Lon 21* **P** *Bp* **V** C P M PATTERSON

WILLEY (St Leonard) *see* Revel Gp *Cov*

WILLIAN (All Saints) *see* Letchworth St Paul w Willian *St Alb*

WILLINGALE (St Christopher) *see* Fyfield, Moreton w Bobbingworth etc *Chelmsf*

WILLINGDON (St Mary the Virgin) *Chich 16* **P** *D&C* **V** M G ONIONS, **C** M J MAINE

WILLINGDON, LOWER (St Wilfrid) Conventional District *Chich 16* **C-in-c** A M TUCKER

WILLINGHAM (St Mary and All Saints) *Ely 6* **P** *Bp* **P-in-c** L S LIVERSIDGE

WILLINGHAM, NORTH (St Thomas) *see* Walesby *Linc*

WILLINGHAM, SOUTH (St Martin) *see* Barkwith Gp *Linc*

WILLINGHAM BY STOW (St Helen) *see* Stow Gp *Linc*

WILLINGTON (St Lawrence) *see* Cople, Moggerhanger and Willington *St Alb*

WILLINGTON (St Michael) *Derby 16* **P** *CPAS* **V** S A STARKEY

WILLINGTON (St Stephen) and Sunnybrow *Dur 9* **P** *R Brancepeth* **R** vacant (01388) 746242

WILLINGTON Team, The (Good Shepherd) (St Mary the Virgin) (St Paul) *Newc 5* **P** *Prime Min* **TR** R D HINDLEY, **TV** J E APPLEBY

WILLINGTON QUAY (St Paul) *see* Willington *Newc*

WILLISHAM (St Mary) *see* Somersham w Flowton and Offton w Willisham *St E*

WILLITON (St Peter) *see* Watchet and Williton *B & W*

WILLOUGHBY (St Helen) *Linc 8* **P** *Baroness Willoughby de Eresby, Ball Coll Ox, and Bp (jt)* **R** D C ROBINSON

WILLOUGHBY (St Nicholas) *see* Leam Valley *Cov*

WILLOUGHBY-ON-THE-WOLDS (St Mary and All Saints) w Wysall and Widmerpool *S'well 8* **P** *MMCET* **P-in-c** S D HIPPISLEY-COX

WILLOUGHBY WATERLEYS (St Mary), Peatling Magna and Ashby Magna *Leic 7* **P** *Bp* **R** vacant (01455) 209406

WILLOUGHTON (St Andrew) *see* Glentworth Gp *Linc*

WILMCOTE (St Andrew) *see* Aston Cantlow and Wilmcote w Billesley *Cov*

WILMINGTON (St Mary and St Peter) *see* Arlington, Berwick, Selmeston w Alciston etc *Chich*

WILMINGTON (St Michael) *Roch 2* **P** *D&C* **V** R ARDING, **Hon C** P J IVESON, **NSM** T WYATT

WILMSLOW (St Bartholomew) *Ches 12* **P** *Bp* **R** P A SMITH, **C** M M SMITH, **NSM** R A YATES, C J LEES

WILNE (St Chad) and Draycott w Breaston *Derby 13* **P** *Bp* **R** C J SMEDLEY, **NSM** M C PRZESLAWSKI

WILNECOTE (Holy Trinity) *Lich 4* **P** *V Tamworth* **V** O HARRISON, **OLM** C J ROBINSON

WILSDEN (St Matthew) *see* Harden and Wilsden *Bradf*

WILSFORD (St Mary) *see* Ancaster Wilsford Gp *Linc*

WILSFORD (St Michael) *see* Woodford Valley w Archers Gate *Sarum*

WILSFORD (St Nicholas) *see* Redhorn *Sarum*

WILSHAMSTEAD (All Saints) and Houghton Conquest *St Alb 9* **P** *St Jo Coll Cam and Bp (alt)* **V** S J TOZE

WILSHAW (St Mary) *see* Meltham *Wakef*

WILSILL (St Michael and All Angels) *see* Upper Nidderdale *Ripon*

WILSTHORPE (St Faith) *see* Uffington Gp *Linc*

WILSTONE (St Cross) *see* Tring *St Alb*

WILTON (St Cuthbert) *York 16* **P** *Abp* **V** R E HARRISON

WILTON (St George) *B & W 17* **P** *Mrs E C Cutbush* **NSM** J A JEFFERY

WILTON (St George) *see* Thornton Dale w Allerston, Ebberston etc *York*

WILTON (St Mary and St Nicholas) w Netherhampton and Fugglestone *Sarum 12* **P** *Earl of Pembroke* **P-in-c** M R WOOD, **C** J A BARNES, **NSM** S P J PORTER

WILTON PLACE (St Paul) *Lon 3* **P** *Bp* **V** A G GYLE, **C** S E YOUNG, **Hon C** N S MERCER

WIMBISH (All Saints) *see* Debden and Wimbish w Thunderley *Chelmsf*

WIMBLEDON (Emmanuel) Ridgway Proprietary Chapel *S'wark 13* **Min** J J M FLETCHER, **C** A T J BYFIELD, R H SHELLEY, **NSM** R J COEKIN, R A S THOMSON

WIMBLEDON (St Luke) *see* Wimbledon Park St Luke *S'wark*

WIMBLEDON (St Mary) (St Matthew) (St Mark) (St John the Baptist) *S'wark 13* **P** *Patr Bd* **TR** M E BIDE, **TV** H C ORCHARD, C B GARDNER, **C** M A BOOTH, B W RICKARDS, **NSM** C JACKSON

WIMBLEDON, SOUTH (All Saints) *see* Raynes Park St Sav and S Wimbledon All SS *S'wark*

WIMBLEDON, SOUTH (Holy Trinity and St Peter) *see* Merton Priory *S'wark*

WIMBLEDON, SOUTH (St Andrew) *S'wark 13* **P** *Bp* **V** A D WAKEFIELD

WIMBLEDON, WEST (Christ Church) *S'wark 13* **P** *TR Wimbledon* **V** R P LANE

WIMBLEDON PARK (St Luke) *S'wark 13* **P** *Simeon's Trustees* **V** R J R PAICE, **C** W J ROGERS

WIMBLEDON PARK (St Paul) *see* Wandsworth St Paul *S'wark*

WIMBLINGTON (St Peter) *see* Doddington w Benwick and Wimblington *Ely*

WIMBORNE (St John the Evangelist) *see* New Borough and Leigh *Sarum*

WIMBORNE MINSTER (St Cuthberga) *Sarum 9* **P** *Governors of Wimborne Minster* **C** D J TIGHE, **NSM** B GIBSON, T LOCKWOOD, E HARDING

WIMBORNE ST GILES (St Giles) *see* Cranborne w Boveridge, Edmondsham etc *Sarum*

WIMBOTSHAM (St Mary) w Stow Bardolph and Stow Bridge w Nordelph *Ely 9* **P** *Bp* **P-in-c** K BURNETT-HALL

WIMPOLE (St Andrew) *see* Orwell Gp *Ely*

WINCANTON (St Peter and St Paul) *B & W 2* **P** *D&C* **R** N C M FEAVER

WINCHAM (St Andrew) *see* Lostock Gralam *Ches*

WINCHCOMBE (St Peter) *Glouc 10* **P** *Patr Bd* **TR** P J PARTINGTON, **TV** J A NEWCOMBE, P M HAND, **NSM** N A CARTER, J A HOOK

WINCHELSEA (St Thomas) (St Richard) and Icklesham *Chich 20* **P** *Bp and Guild of All So (jt)* **R** H A S COCKS

WINCHENDON, NETHER (St Nicholas) *see* Long Crendon w Chearsley and Nether Winchendon *Ox*

WINCHENDON, OVER (St Mary Magdalene) *see* Schorne *Ox*

WINCHESTER (All Saints) *see* E Win *Win*

WINCHESTER (Christ Church) *Win 7* **P** *Simeon's Trustees* **V** D G WILLIAMS, **NSM** B R WAKELIN, D F FENTON

WINCHESTER (Holy Trinity) *Win 7* **P** *Bp* **P-in-c** M F JONES

WINCHESTER (St Barnabas) *Win 7* **P** *Bp* **V** vacant (01962) 882728

WINCHESTER (St Bartholomew) (St Lawrence) (St Swithun-upon-Kingsgate) *Win 7* **P** *Ld Chan* **R** C J BANNISTER, **NSM** A GOULDING

WINCHESTER (St Cross Hospital w St Faith) *Win 7* **P** *Bp,* **R** C SWEET **Hon C** S S M DAVIES

WINCHESTER (St John the Baptist w St Martin Winnall) *see* E
Win *Win*
WINCHESTER (St Luke) *see* Stanmore *Win*
WINCHESTER St Matthew (St Paul's Mission Church) *Win 7*
P *Bp* R N P SEAL, NSM N W BIRKETT
WINCHESTER, EAST P *Bp and Ld Chan (alt)*
R P A KENNEDY, C S J COLLIER
WINCHFIELD (St Mary the Virgin) *see* Hartley Wintney,
Elvetham, Winchfield etc *Win*
WINCHMORE HILL (Holy Trinity) *Lon 18* P *V Winchmore*
Hill St Paul P-in-c L J MILLER
WINCHMORE HILL (St Andrew) *see* Amersham *Ox*
WINCHMORE HILL (St Paul) *Lon 18* P *V Edmonton*
V W J ADAM, C M A WALKER
WINCLE (St Michael) *see* Bosley and N Rode w Wincle and
Wildboarclough *Ches*
WINCOBANK (St Thomas) *see* Brightside w Wincobank *Sheff*
WINDERMERE (St Martin) and St John *Carl 11* P *Bp and*
Trustees (jt) R J J RICHARDS, C C I JONES
WINDERMERE (St Mary) Applethwaite and Troutbeck *Carl 11*
P *Bp* V D M B WILMOT, C B T STREETER
WINDHILL (Christ Church) *Bradf 1* P *Bp*
NSM M J ALLISON
WINDLESHAM (St John the Baptist) *Guildf 6* P *Ld Chan*
R J HILLMAN, OLM J A LEWIS
WINDRUSH (St Peter) *see* Sherborne, Windrush, the
Barringtons etc *Glouc*
WINDRUSH, LOWER *Ox 8* P *Bp, DBP, St Jo Coll Ox,*
D&C Ex, and B Babington-Smith Esq (jt) R S E SHARP
WINDSOR, NEW (Holy Trinity) (St John the Baptist w All
Saints) *Ox 13* P *Ld Chan* P-in-c A L SWIFT,
C M J BARNES, Hon C D I DADSWELL, NSM M K BIRD,
OLM J M QUICK, J FAULKNER
WINDSOR, OLD (St Luke's Mission Room) (St Peter and
St Andrew) *Ox 13* P *Ld Chan* P-in-c M J BARNES,
OLM M CAMINER
WINDY NOOK (St Alban) *Dur 12* P *V Heworth St Mary*
V R A LUMLEY
WINESTEAD (St German) *see* Patrington w Hollym, Welwick
and Winestead *York*
WINFARTHING (St Mary) w Shelfanger w Burston w Gissing
and Tivetshall *Nor 10* P *Ld Chan, Bp, and DBP (jt), Hertf*
Coll Ox (alt) R D F MILLS
WINFORD (Blessed Virgin Mary and St Peter) w Felton
Common Hill *B & W 9* P *Worc Coll Ox and*
Mrs H D Pullman (jt) P-in-c P STEPHENS
WINFORTON (St Michael and All Angels) *see* Eardisley w
Bollingham, Willersley, Brilley etc *Heref*
WINFRITH NEWBURGH (St Christopher) *see* The
Lulworths, Winfrith Newburgh and Chaldon *Sarum*
WING (St Peter and St Paul) *see* Empingham, Edith Weston,
Lyndon, Manton etc *Pet*
WING w Grove (All Saints) *Ox 26* P *Bp*
P-in-c D W F WITCHELL, OLM S TUNNICLIFFE
WINGATE GRANGE (Holy Trinity) *see* Wheatley Hill and
Wingate w Hutton Henry *Dur*
WINGATES (St John the Evangelist) *see* Westhoughton and
Wingates *Man*
WINGERWORTH (All Saints) *Derby 5* P *Bp* R J M WHITE,
NSM J A WILLIS
WINGFIELD (St Andrew) *see* Hoxne w Denham, Syleham and
Wingfield *St E*
WINGFIELD (St Mary) *see* Westwood and Wingfield *Sarum*
WINGFIELD, NORTH (St Lawrence), Clay Cross and Pilsley
Derby 5 P *Bp* TV K E HAMBLIN, J R W BROOK,
C R G LAWRENCE, NSM M H BOWN
WINGFIELD, SOUTH (All Saints) *see* Crich and S Wingfield
Derby
WINGHAM (St Mary the Virgin) w Elmstone and Preston w
Stourmouth *Cant 1* P *Lord Fitzwalter and D&C (alt)*
P-in-c J SWEATMAN, C J A ROBERTSON
WINGRAVE (St Peter and St Paul) w Rowsham, Aston Abbotts
and Cublington *Ox 26* P *Bp and Linc Coll Ox (jt)*
P-in-c D W F WITCHELL, OLM S TUNNICLIFFE
WINKBURN (St John of Jerusalem) *S'well 15* P *Bp*
P-in-c R D SEYMOUR-WHITELEY
WINKFIELD (St Mary the Virgin) and Cranbourne *Ox 11*
P *Bp* V G W R HARPER
WINKLEBURY (Good Shepherd) and Worting *Win 4*
P *MMCET* R J A K WIGMORE
WINKLEIGH (All Saints) *Ex 20* P *D&C* V P J NORMAN
WINKSLEY (St Cuthbert and St Oswald) *see* Fountains Gp
Ripon
WINLATON (St Paul) *Dur 13* P *Bp* P-in-c G W R HARPER
WINMARLEIGH (St Luke) *see* Cockerham w Winmarleigh
and Glasson *Blackb*

WINNERSH (St Mary the Virgin) *see* Hurst *Ox*
WINSCOMBE (St James) and Sandford *B & W 10* P *D&C*
V *vacant* (01934) 843164
WINSFORD (St Mary Magdalene) *see* Exton and Winsford
and Cutcombe w Luxborough *B & W*
WINSHAM (St Stephen) *see* Chaffcombe, Cricket Malherbie
etc *B & W*
WINSHILL (St Mark) *Derby 16* P *Lady H M Gretton and*
Baroness Gretton (jt) V M M MOOKERJI
WINSLEY (St Nicholas) *see* N Bradford on Avon and Villages
Sarum
WINSLOW (St Laurence) w Great Horwood and Addington
Ox 24 P *Ld Chan (3 turns), New Coll Ox (2 turns), and DBP*
(1 turn) R B R SEARLE-BARNES, NSM G E BALL
WINSMOOR *B & W 14* P *Bp, D&C, CR, and*
P G H Speke Esq (jt) V G A WADE
WINSON (St Michael) *see* Fairford Deanery *Glouc*
WINSTER (Holy Trinity) *Carl 10* P *V Kendal H Trin*
P-in-c M D WOODCOCK, C M F J ALLEN,
NSM M L WOODCOCK, B J CROWE
WINSTER (St John the Baptist) *see* S Darley, Elton and Winster
Derby
WINSTON (St Andrew) *Dur 7* P *Bp* P-in-c M JACQUES
WINSTON (St Andrew) *see* Debenham and Helmingham *St E*
WINSTONE (St Bartholomew) *see* Brimpsfield w Birdlip, Syde,
Daglingworth etc *Glouc*
WINTERBORNE CLENSTON (St Nicholas) *see* Winterborne
Valley and Milton Abbas *Sarum*
WINTERBORNE HOUGHTON (St Andrew) *as above*
WINTERBORNE STICKLAND (St Mary) *as above*
WINTERBORNE VALLEY and Milton Abbas, The *Sarum 6*
P *Bp (3 turns) and P D H Chichester Esq (1 turn)*
V R N HUNGERFORD, NSM M C MILES, C M CHICHESTER
WINTERBORNE WHITECHURCH (St Mary)
see Winterborne Valley and Milton Abbas *Sarum*
WINTERBOURNE (St James) *see* E Downland *Ox*
WINTERBOURNE (St Michael the Archangel) *Bris 5*
P *St Jo Coll Ox* P-in-c M A CLACKER
WINTERBOURNE ABBAS (St Mary) *see* The Winterbournes
and Compton Valence *Sarum*
WINTERBOURNE BASSETT (St Katharine) *see* Upper
Kennet *Sarum*
WINTERBOURNE DOWN (All Saints) *see* Frenchay and
Winterbourne Down *Bris*
WINTERBOURNE EARLS (St Michael and All Angels)
see Bourne Valley *Sarum*
WINTERBOURNE GUNNER (St Mary) *as above*
WINTERBOURNE KINGSTON (St Nicholas) *see* Red Post
Sarum
WINTERBOURNE MONKTON (St Mary Magdalene)
see Upper Kennet *Sarum*
WINTERBOURNE MONKTON (St Simon and St Jude)
see Dorchester *Sarum*
WINTERBOURNE ST MARTIN (St Martin) *see* The
Winterbournes and Compton Valence *Sarum*
WINTERBOURNE STEEPLETON (St Michael) *as above*
WINTERBOURNE STOKE (St Peter) *see* Wylye and Till
Valley *Sarum*
WINTERBOURNE ZELSTONE (St Mary) *see* Red Post
Sarum
WINTERBOURNES and Compton Valence, The *Sarum 1*
P *Adn Sherborne, Linc Coll Ox, and Sir Robert Williams Bt*
(by turn) P-in-c H W B STEPHENS, Hon C J H GOOD
WINTERBURN (Chapel of Ease) *see* Gargrave w Coniston
Cold *Bradf*
WINTERINGHAM (All Saints) *see* Winterton Gp *Linc*
WINTERSLOW (All Saints) *see* Clarendon *Sarum*
WINTERSLOW (St John) *as above*
WINTERTON Group, The (All Saints) *Linc 4* P *Lord*
St Oswald, Exors Capt J G G P Elwes, and Em Coll Cam (jt)
V A C NUNN, OLM J J WHITEHEAD
WINTERTON (Holy Trinity and All Saints) *see* Flegg Coastal
Benefice *Nor*
WINTHORPE (All Saints) *see* E Trent *S'well*
WINTHORPE (St Mary) *see* Skegness Gp *Linc*
WINTON (St Mary Magdalene) *Man 18* P *Trustees*
P-in-c I A HALL
WINTRINGHAM (St Peter) *see* Buckrose Carrs *York*
WINWICK (All Saints) *Ely 10* P *Bp* P-in-c M P JEPP
WINWICK (St Michael and All Angels) *see* Long Buckby w
Watford and W Haddon w Winwick *Pet*
WINWICK (St Oswald) *Liv 15* P *Bp* P-in-c J L STEVENTON,
NSM M JONES, H GREENHALGH
WIRKSWORTH (St Mary) *Derby 7* P *Bp* TR D C TRUBY,
TV K K WERNER, C A TAYLOR-COOK, NSM K J ORFORD
WISBECH (St Augustine) *Ely 14* P *Bp* P-in-c N K GARDNER

WISBECH (St Peter and St Paul) *Ely 14*   **P** *Bp*
P-in-c P J WEST,   **C** N K GARDNER
WISBECH ST MARY (St Mary) and Guyhirn w Ring's End and Gorefield and Southea w Murrow and Parson Drove *Ely 14*
  P *Bp*   **V** M L BRADBURY,   **NSM** R D PARKINSON
WISBOROUGH GREEN (St Peter ad Vincula) *Chich 11*
  P *Bp Lon*   **V** P DIXON
WISHAW (St Chad) *see* Curdworth, Middleton and Wishaw *Birm*
WISHFORD, GREAT (St Giles) *see* Wylye and Till Valley *Sarum*
WISLEY (not known) w Pyrford *Guildf 12*   **P** *Bp*   **R** N J AIKEN,   **C** I M WALLACE,   **OLM** C D GIBSON
WISSETT (St Andrew) *see* Blyth Valley *St E*
WISSINGTON (St Mary the Virgin) *see* Nayland w Wiston *St E*
WISTANSTOW (Holy Trinity) *Heref 10*   **P** *Bp*
P-in-c M L COPE
WISTASTON (St Mary) *Ches 15*   **P** *Trustees*
R M F TURNBULL,   **NSM** K H SAMBROOK
WISTOW (All Saints) *see* Cawood w Ryther and Wistow *York*
WISTOW (St John the Baptist) *see* Warboys w Broughton and Bury w Wistow *Ely*
WISTOW (St Wistan) *Leic 4*   **P** *Bp and The Hon Ann Brooks (jt)*   **V** P J O'REILLY,   **C** A T FURSE
WITCHAM (St Martin) w Mepal *Ely 8*   **P** *D&C*
P-in-c M HANCOCK
WITCHAMPTON (St Mary and St Cuthberga and All Saints), Stanbridge and Long Crichel w Moor Crichel *Sarum 9*   **P** *DBP*
P-in-c A A GEE,   **NSM** L MORRIS
WITCHFORD (St Andrew) w Wentworth *Ely 8*   **P** *D&C*
P-in-c F E G BRAMPTON,   **NSM** T M DIXON
WITCHINGHAM GREAT (St Mary) *see* Wensum Benefice *Nor*
WITCOMBE, GREAT (St Mary) *see* Badgeworth, Shurdington and Witcombe w Bentham *Glouc*
WITHAM Group, The *Linc 14*   **P** *Sir Lyonel Tollemache Bt, The Revd J R H Thorold, J R Thorold Esq, and Bp (jt)*
P-in-c T W BROADBENT
WITHAM (St Nicholas) *Chelmsf 23*   **P** *Patr Bd*
TV S F GARWOOD,   **C** R J PATTEN
WITHAM, NORTH (St Mary) *see* Witham Gp *Linc*
WITHAM, SOUTH (St John the Baptist) *as above*
WITHAM FRIARY (Blessed Virgin Mary and St John the Baptist and All Saints) *see* Nunney and Witham Friary, Marston Bigot etc *B*
WITHAM-ON-THE-HILL (St Andrew) *see* Edenham w Witham on the Hill and Swinstead *Linc*
WITHAMSIDE United Group *see* Bassingham Gp *Linc*
WITHCALL (St Martin) *see* Legbourne and Wold Marsh *Linc*
WITHERIDGE (St John the Baptist) *see* Burrington, Chawleigh, Cheldon, Chulmleigh etc *Ex*
WITHERLEY (St Peter) *see* Fenn Lanes Gp *Leic*
WITHERNSEA (St Nicholas) w Owthorne and Easington w Skeffling and Holmpton *York 12*   **P** *Abp (1 turn), Ld Chan (2 turns)*   **R** S V COPE
WITHERNWICK (St Alban) *see* Aldbrough, Mappleton w Goxhill and Withernwick *York*
WITHERSDALE (St Mary Magdalene) *see* Fressingfield, Mendham etc *St E*
WITHERSFIELD (St Mary the Virgin) *see* Haverhill w Withersfield *St E*
WITHERSLACK (St Paul) *Carl 10*   **P** *DBP*
P-in-c M D WOODCOCK,   **C** M F J ALLEN,
NSM M L WOODCOCK, B J CROWE
WITHIEL (St Clement) *see* Roche and Withiel *Truro*
WITHIEL FLOREY (St Mary Magdalene) *see* Dulverton w Brushford, Brompton Regis etc *B & W*
WITHINGTON (St Christopher) *see* W Didsbury and Withington St Chris *Man*
WITHINGTON (St Crispin) *Man 3*   **P** *Bp*   **P-in-c** P C S DAVIES
WITHINGTON (St John the Baptist) *see* Wrockwardine Deanery *Lich*
WITHINGTON (St Michael and All Angels) *see* Sevenhampton w Charlton Abbots, Hawling etc *Glouc*
WITHINGTON (St Paul) *Man 6*   **P** *Trustees*   **R** G R RAINES,
OLM R A W SMITH
WITHINGTON (St Peter) w Westhide *Heref 3*   **P** *Bp*   **R** *vacant*
WITHINGTON, LOWER (St Peter) *see* Chelford w Lower Withington *Ches*
WITHLEIGH (St Catherine) *see* Washfield, Stoodleigh, Withleigh etc *Ex*
WITHNELL (St Paul) *see* Heapey and Withnell *Blackb*
WITHYBROOK (All Saints) *see* Wolvey w Burton Hastings, Copston Magna etc *Cov*
WITHYCOMBE (St Nicholas) *see* Dunster, Carhampton, Withycombe w Rodhuish etc *B & W*

WITHYCOMBE RALEIGH (St John the Evangelist) (St John in the Wilderness) (All Saints) *Ex 1*   **P** *Patr Bd*   **TR** R SELLERS, **TV** S J HOYLE, T C SMYTH
WITHYHAM (St John the Evangelist) *see* Crowborough St Jo *Chich*
WITHYHAM (St Michael and All Angels) *Chich 19*   **P** *Earl De la Warr*   **P-in-c** A S LEAK
WITHYPOOL (St Andrew) *see* Exford, Exmoor, Hawkridge and Withypool *B & W*
WITHYWOOD (shared church) *Bris 1*   **P** *Bp*
V J M CARPENTER
WITLEY (All Saints) *Guildf 4*   **P** *Bp*   **V** B M SHAND,
OLM E A FRASER
WITLEY, GREAT (St Michael) *see* Shrawley, Witley, Astley and Abberley *Worc*
WITLEY, LITTLE (St Michael) *as above*
WITNESHAM (St Mary) *see* Westerfield and Tuddenham w Witnesham *St E*
WITNEY (St Mary the Virgin) (Holy Trinity) *Ox 8*   **P** *Patr Bd*
TR T C WRIGHT,   **TV** E J THOMSON,   **Hon C** J H COOK,
S J WRIGHT,   **OLM** C TITCOMB
WITTENHAM, LITTLE (St Peter) *see* Dorchester *Ox*
WITTERING (All Saints) *see* Ketton, Collyweston, Easton-on-the-Hill etc *Pet*
WITTERING, EAST (St Anne) *see* Earnley and E Wittering *Chich*
WITTERING, WEST (St Peter and St Paul) and Birdham w Itchenor *Chich 3*   **P** *Bp*   **R** J B WILLIAMS,
Hon C C J HANKINS,   **NSM** B F HOLBEN, J M MOULD
WITTERSHAM (St John the Baptist) w Stone-in-Oxney and Ebony *Cant 11*   **P** *Abp*   **NSM** S M HALMSHAW, P L M FOGDEN
WITTON (St Helen) *Ches 6*   **P** *Bp*   **NSM** B W JOBBER
WITTON (St Margaret) *see* Bacton, Happisburgh, Hempstead w Eccles etc *Nor*
WITTON (St Margaret) *see* Gt and Lt Plumstead w Thorpe End and Witton *Nor*
WITTON (St Mark) *see* Blackb Christ the King *Blackb*
WITTON, EAST (St John the Evangelist) *see* Middleham w Coverdale and E Witton etc *Ripon*
WITTON, NETHER (St Giles) *Newc 11*   **P** *Ld Chan*
V M A G BRYCE,   **OLM** F J SAMPLE
WITTON, WEST (St Bartholomew) *see* Penhill *Ripon*
WITTON GILBERT (St Michael and All Angels) *see* Dur N *Dur*
WITTON LE WEAR (St Philip and St James) *see* Hamsterley and Witton-le-Wear *Dur*
WITTON PARK (St Paul) *Dur 6*   **P** *Bp*   **P-in-c** R W DEIMEL,
NSM M M DEIMEL
WIVELISCOMBE (St Andrew) and the Hills *B & W 18*   **P** *Bp and A H Trollope-Bellew Esq (4 turns), Ld Chan (1 turn)*
R D C R WIDDOWS
WIVELSFIELD (St Peter and St John the Baptist) *Chich 6*
  P *DBP*   **V** C R BREEDS
WIVENHOE (St Mary) *Chelmsf 16*   **P** *Bp*   **R** E B E LAMMENS
WIVERTON GROUP *see* Cropwell Bishop w Colston Bassett, Granby etc *S'well*
WIVETON (St Mary) *see* Blakeney w Cley, Wiveton, Glandford etc *Nor*
WIX (St Mary the Virgin) *see* Gt Oakley w Wix and Wrabness *Chelmsf*
WIXFORD (St Milburga) *see* Exhall w Wixford *Cov*
WIXOE (St Leonard) *see* Stour Valley *St E*
WOBURN (St Mary) w Eversholt, Milton Bryan, Battlesden and Pottesgrove *St Alb 8*   **P** *Bedf Estates Trustees*   **V** S W NUTH,
NSM L J WASHINGTON
WOBURN SANDS (St Michael) *St Alb 8*   **P** *Bp*
P-in-c C L D BEALES,   **NSM** N J PARKINSON
WOBURN SQUARE (Christ Church) *see* Bloomsbury St Geo w Woburn Square Ch Ch *Lon*
WOKING (Christ Church) *Guildf 12*   **P** *Ridley Hall Cam*
V P J HARWOOD,   **C** C J RYALLS, M F BALL,   **NSM** M S SMITH,
P A SIMPSON, A ETHERIDGE
WOKING (St John the Baptist) *Guildf 12*   **P** *V Woking St Pet*
V T A CANNON,   **OLM** R G BENNETT
WOKING (St Mary of Bethany) *Guildf 12*   **P** *V Woking Ch Ch*
V S R BEAK,   **C** G HOLLAND,   **OLM** D R MARKS
WOKING (St Paul) *Guildf 12*   **P** *Ridley Hall Cam*
P-in-c J L BLAIR,   **C** C J BLAIR
WOKING (St Peter) *Guildf 12*   **P** *Patr Bd*   **TR** B J GRIMSTER,
TV I D TWEEDIE-SMITH
WOKING, SOUTH Team Ministry *see* Woking St Pet *Guildf*
WOKINGHAM (All Saints) *Ox 16*   **P** *Bp*   **R** D P HODGSON,
C M R JOHNSON, C A KRAMER,   **NSM** C R JAMES,
H J CHARLTON
WOKINGHAM (St Paul) *Ox 16*   **P** *DBP*   **C** P A DAY,
NSM R G HOLMES

WOKINGHAM (St Sebastian) *Ox 16* **P** *Bp* **V** A P MARSDEN, **C** D L R MCLEOD, **NSM** E C FUDGE, **OLM** R I SEYMOUR

WOLBOROUGH (St Mary) and Ogwell *Ex 10* **P** *Earl of Devon and Bp (jt)* **R** R C CHAMBERLAIN, **C** A M WELLS

WOLD (St Andrew) *see* Walgrave w Hannington and Wold and Scaldwell *Pet*

WOLD NEWTON (All Saints) *see* Binbrook Gp *Linc*

WOLD NEWTON (All Saints) *see* Burton Fleming w Fordon, Grindale etc *York*

WOLDINGHAM (St Agatha) *see* Caterham *S'wark*

WOLDINGHAM (St Paul) *as above*

WOLDS, NORTH Group *Linc 6* **P** *Bp, DBP, and D&C (jt)* **V** M A BATTY

WOLDSBURN *York 10* **P** *Abp, St Jo Coll Ox, and A J Page Esq (1 turn), and Ld Chan (1 turn)* **NSM** R D WAITE

WOLFERTON (St Peter) *see* Sandringham w W Newton and Appleton etc *Nor*

WOLFORD (St Michael) *see* S Warks Seven Gp *Cov*

WOLLASTON (St James) *Worc 12* **P** *Bp* **P-in-c** A L HAZLEWOOD, **Hon C** D M FARMER

WOLLASTON (St Mary) w Strixton and Bozeat and Easton Maudit *Pet 6* **P** *Bp and Marquess of Northn (jt)* **V** A I MORTON

WOLLASTON, GREAT (All Saints) (St John the Baptist) *Heref 12* **P** *Bp* **P-in-c** V J TAIT, **OLM** M E NEAL

WOLLATON (St Leonard) *S'well 14* **P** *Lord Middleton* **R** J J LEPINE, **C** M A C GAYNOR, **NSM** P D C BROWN

WOLLATON PARK (St Mary) *S'well 14* **P** *CPAS* **P-in-c** J H CURRAN

WOLLESCOTE (St Andrew) *Worc 12* **P** *Bp* **V** R A BROADBENT

WOLSINGHAM (St Mary and St Stephen) and Thornley *Dur 9* **P** *Bp* **P-in-c** J P L WHALLEY

WOLSTANTON (St Margaret) *Lich 9* **P** *Bp* **TR** A R KNIGHT, **TV** P L DAVIS

WOLSTON (St Margaret) and Church Lawford *Cov 6* **P** *DBP (2 turns), Bp (1 turn)* **V** K J FLANAGAN, **Hon C** P A H SIMMONDS

WOLVERCOTE (St Peter) and Wytham *Ox 7* **P** *Ch Ch Ox and Mert Coll Ox (jt)* **V** M A BUTCHERS, **Hon C** J M CONEY, **NSM** V P BRIDGES, R J C GILBERT

WOLVERHAMPTON Pond Lane (Mission Hall) *see* Wolverhampton St Luke *Lich*

WOLVERHAMPTON (St Andrew) *Lich 28* **P** *Bp* **V** J L SMITH

WOLVERHAMPTON (St Jude) *Lich 28* **P** *CPAS* **V** P S ROBERTSON, **C** N L MOY, **OLM** I J SAUNDERS

WOLVERHAMPTON (St Luke) Blakenhall *Lich 28* **P** *Trustees* **V** R J ESPIN-BRADLEY, **C** J E T MARTIN

WOLVERHAMPTON (St Martin) *see* Rough Hills *Lich*

WOLVERHAMPTON (St Matthew) *Lich 28* **P** *Baldwin Pugh Trustees* **V** D GHOSH, **OLM** D G WATKIN

WOLVERHAMPTON (St Stephen) *Lich 28* **P** *Bp* **P-in-c** S W POWELL

WOLVERHAMPTON, CENTRAL (All Saints) (St Chad and St Mark) (St John in the Square) (St Peter) *Lich 28* **P** *Patr Bd* **TR** D W WRIGHT, **TV** S SCHOFIELD, H L DUCKETT, **C** P J L CODY, **OLM** E W BROOKES

WOLVERLEY (St John the Baptist) and Cookley *Worc 11* **P** *D&C and Bp (jt)* **V** G SHILVOCK

WOLVERTON (Holy Trinity) (St George the Martyr) *Ox 25* **P** *Bp* **C** P M DOCKREE, **Hon C** M T HURLEY

WOLVERTON (St Katherine) *see* Baughurst, Ramsdell, Wolverton w Ewhurst etc *Win*

WOLVERTON (St Mary the Virgin) w Norton Lindsey and Langley *Cov 7* **P** *Bp* **P-in-c** R LIVINGSTON

WOLVEY (St John the Baptist) w Burton Hastings, Copston Magna and Withybrook *Cov 5* **P** *Bp* **V** T J COLLING

WOLVISTON (St Peter) *see* Grindon, Stillington and Wolviston *Dur*

WOMBOURNE (St Benedict) *see* Smestow Vale *Lich*

WOMBRIDGE (St Mary and St Leonard) *Lich 21* **P** *W J Charlton Meyrick Esq* **P-in-c** K S EVANS

WOMBWELL (St Mary) (St George) *Sheff 12* **P** *Trin Coll Cam* **R** N H ELLIOTT

WOMERSLEY (St Martin) *see* Went Valley *Wakef*

WONERSH (St John the Baptist) w Blackheath *Guildf 2* **P** *Selw Coll Cam* **V** D M SELLIN, **OLM** K N BATESON, J M COOKE, E A TILLEY

WONSTON (Holy Trinity) *see* Upper Dever *Win*

WONSTON, SOUTH (St Margaret) *see* Lower Dever *Win*

WOOBURN (St Paul) *Ox 29* **P** *Bp* **V** M J WALLINGTON

WOOD DALLING (St Andrew) *see* Reepham, Hackford w Whitwell, Kerdiston etc *Nor*

WOOD DITTON (St Mary) w Saxon Street *Ely 4* **P** *Duke of Sutherland* **P-in-c** M A GURNER

WOOD END (St Chad) *Cov 1* **P** *Ld Chan* **V** *vacant* (024) 7661 2909

WOOD END (St Michael and All Angels) *see* Baxterley w Hurley and Wood End and Merevale etc *Birm*

WOOD GREEN (St Michael) w Bounds Green (St Gabriel) (St Michael-at-Bowes) *Lon 19* **P** *Patr Bd* **TR** C W COPPEN, **TV** R J WILKINSON, **NSM** D HARTLEY

WOOD GREEN (St Paul) *see* Wednesbury St Paul Wood Green *Lich*

WOOD NORTON (All Saints) *see* Foulsham, Guestwick, Stibbard, Themelthorpe etc *Nor*

WOOD STREET (St Alban) *see* Worplesdon *Guildf*

WOODBASTWICK (St Fabian and St Sebastian) *see* Ranworth w Panxworth, Woodbastwick etc *Nor*

WOODBERRY DOWN (St Olave) *see* Stoke Newington St Olave *Lon*

WOODBOROUGH (St Mary Magdalene) *see* Vale of Pewsey *Sarum*

WOODBOROUGH (St Swithun) *see* Epperstone, Gonalston, Oxton and Woodborough *S'well*

WOODBRIDGE (St John the Evangelist) and Bredfield *St E 7* **P** *Ch Patr Trust (3 turns), and Ld Chan (1 turn)* **V** D GARDNER, **C** P A M SHULER, **OLM** M M E ROBERTS

WOODBRIDGE (St Mary the Virgin) *St E 7* **P** *Bp* **R** K S MCCORMACK, **C** H E HUPFIELD, **NSM** M J HARE

WOODBURY (Holy Cross) *see* Axminster, Chardstock, All Saints etc *Ex*

WOODBURY (St Swithun) *see* Lympstone and Woodbury w Exton *Ex*

WOODBURY SALTERTON (Holy Trinity) *see* Clyst St Mary, Clyst St George etc *Ex*

WOODCHESTER (St Mary) and Brimscombe *Glouc 4* **P** *Simeon's Trustees* **R** S A BOWEN, **C** J M MAYNARD, **NSM** M G WRIGHT

WOODCHURCH (All Saints) *Cant 6* **P** *Abp* **C** P J WHITE

WOODCHURCH (Holy Cross) *Ches 1* **P** *DBP* **R** M A DAVIS, **NSM** J CALVERT

WOODCOTE (St Leonard) *see* Langtree *Ox*

WOODCOTE (St Mark) *see* Purley St Mark *S'wark*

WOODCOTE (St Peter) *see* Church Aston *Lich*

WOODCOTT (St James) *see* Hurstbourne Priors, Longparish etc *Win*

WOODDITTON (St Mary) *see* Wood Ditton w Saxon Street *Ely*

WOODEATON (Holy Rood) *see* Ray Valley *Ox*

WOODFIELD Team Benefice, The *Leic 8* **P** *Patr Bd (6 turns), Prime Min (1 turn), Ld Chan (1 turn)* **TR** V M ELPHICK, **TV** K R THOMAS, **C** H S WHITE, **NSM** L S BIRTWISTLE

WOODFORD (Christ Church) *Ches 12* **P** *W A B Davenport Esq* **P-in-c** J G KNOWLES, **NSM** F T COOKE

WOODFORD (St Barnabas) *Chelmsf 4* **P** *Bp* **V** *vacant* (020) 8504 8869

WOODFORD (St Mary the Virgin) *see* Gt w Lt Addington and Woodford *Pet*

WOODFORD (St Mary w St Philip and St James) *Chelmsf 4* **P** *Bp* **R** I D TARRANT, **C** A-M MCTIGHE

WOODFORD, SOUTH (Holy Trinity) *see* Wanstead H Trin Hermon Hill *Chelmsf*

WOODFORD BRIDGE (St Paul) *Chelmsf 4* **P** *R Woodford* **V** J H SPRINGBETT, **NSM** A F BOLDING

WOODFORD HALSE (St Mary the Virgin) *see* Aston-le-Walls, Byfield, Boddington, Eydon etc *Pet*

WOODFORD VALLEY (All Saints) w Archers Gate *Sarum 13* **P** *Bp* **P-in-c** A C PHILP, **C** I M R PRICE, **NSM** J M NAISH

WOODFORD WELLS (All Saints) (St Andrew) *Chelmsf 4* **P** *Trustees* **V** P G HARCOURT, **C** S MARSHALL, S P CLARKE, **NSM** D J BLACKLEDGE, M D PORTER

WOODGATE VALLEY Conventional District *Birm 2 vacant*

WOODGATE VALLEY (St Francis) *see* Bartley Green *Birm*

WOODGREEN (St Boniface) *see* Fordingbridge and Breamore and Hale etc *Win*

WOODHALL (St James the Great) *Bradf 3* **P** *Bp* **P-in-c** N CLEWS, **C** D J MUGHAL

WOODHALL, OLD *see* Woodhall Spa Gp *Linc*

WOODHALL SPA Group *Linc 11* **P** *Bp and DBP (jt)* **P-in-c** A C SMITH

WOODHAM (All Saints) *Guildf 12* **P** *Bp* **V** I W FORBES, **C** J A ROBINSON

WOODHAM (St Elizabeth of Hungary) *see* Gt Aycliffe *Dur*

WOODHAM FERRERS (St Mary) and Bicknacre *Chelmsf 9* **P** *Lord Fitzwalter* **R** *vacant* (01245) 320260

WOODHAM FERRERS, SOUTH (Holy Trinity) (St Mary) *Chelmsf 9* **P** *Bp* **P-in-c** P HAWORTH

WOODHAM MORTIMER (St Margaret) w Hazeleigh *Chelmsf 11* **P** *Bp* **P-in-c** S S STROEBEL

WOODHAM WALTER (St Michael) *Chelmsf 11* **P** *Ch Soc Trust* **P-in-c** S S STROEBEL

WOODHAY, EAST (St Martin) *see* NW Hants *Win*

WOODHILL *Sarum 15* **P** *Ld Chan, DBP, and Prime Min (by turns)* **R** A J WAY

WOODHORN w Newbiggin *Newc 11* **P** *Bp* **OLM** F WALTON

WOODHOUSE (Christ Church) *see* Birkby and Woodhouse *Wakef*

WOODHOUSE (St James) *Sheff 1* **P** *Bp* **P-in-c** D R GOUGH

WOODHOUSE (St Mark) and Wrangthorn *Ripon 7* **P** *DBP* **V** *vacant* 0113-245 4893

WOODHOUSE (St Mary in the Elms), Woodhouse Eaves and Swithland *Leic 6* **P** *Ld Chan and DBP (alt)* **R** R A HORTON

WOODHOUSE CLOSE (not known) *see* Bishop Auckland Woodhouse Close CD *Dur*

WOODHOUSE EAVES (St Paul) *see* Woodhouse, Woodhouse Eaves and Swithland *Leic*

WOODHOUSE MILL (St James) *see* Woodhouse St Jas *Sheff*

WOODHOUSE PARK (Wm Temple Church) *see* Wythenshawe *Man*

WOODHOUSES (not known) *see* Bardsley *Man*

WOODHOUSES (St John the Divine) *see* Dunham Massey St Marg and St Mark *Ches*

WOODHURST (St John the Baptist) *see* Somersham w Pidley and Oldhurst and Woodhurst *Ely*

WOODINGDEAN (Holy Cross) *Chich 2* **P** *Bp* **V** R A BROMFIELD

WOODKIRK (St Mary) *see* W Ardsley *Wakef*

WOODLAND (St John the Baptist) *see* Broadhempston, Woodland, Staverton etc *Ex*

WOODLAND (St John the Evangelist) *see* Broughton and Duddon *Carl*

WOODLAND (St Mary) *see* Lynesack *Dur*

WOODLANDS (All Saints) *Sheff 7* **P** *Bp* **V** S J GARDNER

WOODLANDS (Ascension) *see* Cranborne w Boveridge, Edmondsham etc *Sarum*

WOODLANDS (Mission Chapel) *see* W Meon and Warnford *Portsm*

WOODLANDS (St Katherine) *B & W 3* **P** *DBP* **V** C ALSBURY

WOODLANDS (St Mary) *see* Kemsing w Woodlands *Roch*

WOODLEIGH (St Mary the Virgin) *see* Modbury, Bigbury, Ringmore w Kingston etc *Ex*

WOODLEY (St John the Evangelist) *Ox 15* **P** *DBP* **V** E MARQUEZ, **C** S C RIORDAN

WOODMANCOTE (Mission Church) *see* Westbourne *Chich*

WOODMANCOTE (St James) *see* Upper Dever *Win*

WOODMANCOTE (St Mark) *see* Dursley *Glouc*

WOODMANCOTE (St Peter) *see* Henfield w Shermanbury and Woodmancote *Chich*

WOODMANSEY (St Peter) *see* Beverley Minster *York*

WOODMANSTERNE (St Peter) *S'wark 26* **P** *Ld Chan* **R** M J HOUGH, **NSM** A H BARRON

WOODNESBOROUGH (St Mary the Blessed Virgin) w Worth and Staple *Cant 9* **P** *Abp* **P-in-c** D D HARRISON, **C** J M A ROBERTS, **NSM** R STEVENSON

WOODNEWTON (St Mary) *see* Nassington w Yarwell and Woodnewton w Apethorpe *Pet*

WOODPLUMPTON (St Anne) *Blackb 9* **P** *V St Michael's-on-Wyre* **P-in-c** B WHITLEY

WOODRISING (St Nicholas) *see* High Oak, Hingham and Scoulton w Wood Rising *Nor*

WOODSEATS (St Chad) *Sheff 2* **P** *Bp* **V** T K HOLE

WOODSETTS (St George) *Sheff 5* **P** *Bp* **V** J TRICKETT

WOODSFORD (St John the Baptist) *see* Moreton and Woodsford w Tincleton *Sarum*

WOODSIDE (All Saints) *see* Lymington *Win*

WOODSIDE (St Andrew) *St Alb 12* **P** *D&C St Paul's* **P-in-c** C A PULLINGER

WOODSIDE (St James) *Ripon 7* **P** *Bp* **P-in-c** R J DIMERY

WOODSIDE (St Luke) *see* Croydon Woodside *S'wark*

WOODSIDE GREEN (St Andrew) *see* Gt Hallingbury and Lt Hallingbury *Chelmsf*

WOODSIDE PARK (St Barnabas) *Lon 14* **P** *Ch Patr Trust* **V** H D KENDAL, **C** C S BROOKES, H L SHANNON

WOODSTOCK (St Mary Magdalene) *see* Blenheim *Ox*

WOODSTON (St Augustine of Canterbury) (Mission Church) *Ely 15* **P** **R** W P L GAMMON

WOODTHORPE (St Mark) *S'well 10* **P** *Bp* **V** P J THOMAS

WOODTON (All Saints) *see* Hempnall *Nor*

WOODVILLE (St Stephen) *see* Blackfordby and Woodville *Leic*

WOOKEY (St Matthew) *see* Coxley w Godney, Henton and Wookey *B & W*

WOOKEY HOLE (St Mary Magdalene) *see* Wells St Cuth w Wookey Hole *B & W*

WOOL (Holy Rood) and East Stoke *Sarum 8* **P** *Bp (3 turns), Keble Coll Ox (1 turn)* **P-in-c** R C FLOATE, **OLM** J A HILL

WOOLACOMBE (St Sabinus) *see* Ilfracombe, Lee, Woolacombe, Bittadon etc *Ex*

WOOLASTON (St Andrew) w Alvington and Aylburton *Glouc 1* **P** *DBP and Ld Chan (by turn)* **P-in-c** S L FENBY, **NSM** A JONES

WOOLAVINGTON (Blessed Virgin Mary) w Cossington and Bawdrip *B & W 13* **P** *D&C Windsor and J A Church Esq (alt)* **V** W H H LANE

WOOLBEDING (All Hallows) *Chich 10* **P** *Rathbone Trust Co and Cowdray Trust (jt)* **R** *vacant*

WOOLBROOK (St Francis of Assisi) *see* Sidmouth, Woolbrook, Salcombe Regis, Sidbury etc *Ex*

WOOLER (St Mary) *see* Glendale Gp *Newc*

WOOLFARDISWORTHY (Holy Trinity) *see* Parkham, Alwington, Buckland Brewer etc *Ex*

WOOLFARDISWORTHY EAST (St Mary) *see* N Creedy *Ex*

WOOLFOLD (St James) *see* Kirklees Valley *Man*

WOOLHAMPTON (St Peter) *see* Aldermaston and Woolhampton *Ox*

WOOLHOPE (St George) *see* Fownhope w Mordiford, Brockhampton etc *Heref*

WOOLLAND (not known) *see* Hazelbury Bryan and the Hillside Par *Sarum*

WOOLLEY (All Saints) *see* Bath St Sav w Swainswick and Woolley *B & W*

WOOLLEY (St Mary) *see* E Leightonstone *Ely*

WOOLLEY (St Peter) *Wakef 11* **P** *Bp* **P-in-c** S P KELLY

WOOLMER GREEN (St Michael) *see* Welwyn *St Alb*

WOOLPIT (Blessed Virgin Mary) w Drinkstone *St E 10* **P** *Bp and A Harvie-Clark Esq (alt)* **R** M R FARRELL

WOOLSTASTON (St Michael and All Angels) *see* Dorrington w Leebotwood, Longnor, Stapleton etc *Heref*

WOOLSTHORPE (St James) *see* Harlaxton Gp *Linc*

WOOLSTON (Ascension) *Liv 12* **P** *Bp, Adn, and R Warrington (jt)* **V** *vacant* (01925) 813083

WOOLSTON (St Mark) *Win 13* **P** *Bp* **V** M J A NEWTON, **NSM** A R BEVIS

WOOLSTONE (All Saints) *see* Uffington, Shellingford, Woolstone and Baulking *Ox*

WOOLSTONE (not known) *see* Woughton *Ox*

WOOLSTONE (St Martin) *see* Bishop's Cleeve and Woolstone w Gotherington etc *Glouc*

WOOLTON, MUCH (St Peter) *Liv 4* **P** *Bp* **R** C J CROOKS, **C** P ANDREWS, R J A GEDGE

WOOLTON HILL (St Thomas) *see* NW Hants *Win*

WOOLVERSTONE (St Michael) *see* Holbrook, Stutton, Freston, Woolverstone etc *St E*

WOOLVERTON (St Lawrence) *see* Hardington Vale *B & W*

WOOLWICH (St Mary Magdelene and St Andrew) (St Michael and All Angels) *S'wark 1* **P** *Bp and Keble Coll Ox (jt)* **R** J VAN DER VALK

WOOLWICH (St Thomas) *see* Charlton *S'wark*

WOOLWICH, NORTH (St John) w Silvertown *Chelmsf 3* **P** *Bp and Lon Corp (alt)* **P-in-c** P M CAPRIELLO

WOONTON (Mission Room) *see* Eardisley w Bollingham, Willersley, Brilley etc *Heref*

WOORE (St Leonard) and Norton in Hales *Lich 18* **P** *Bp and CPAS (jt)* **P-in-c** D C NICOL

WOOSEHILL (Community Church) *see* Bearwood *Ox*

WOOTTON (St Andrew) *see* Ulceby Gp *Linc*

WOOTTON (St Edmund) *Portsm 8* **P** *DBP* **P-in-c** K F ABBOTT

WOOTTON (St George the Martyr) w Quinton and Preston Deanery *Pet 4* **P** *Ex Coll Ox and Bp (alt)* **P-in-c** J A PARKIN, **NSM** J E TEBBY

WOOTTON (St Martin) *see* Elham w Denton and Wootton *Cant*

WOOTTON (St Mary the Virgin) *St Alb 9* **P** *MMCET* **V** P M ACKROYD, **C** S E HAIGH

WOOTTON (St Mary) w Glympton and Kiddington *Ox 9* **P** *New Coll Ox (2 turns), Bp (1 turn), and Exors E W Towler Esq (1 turn)* **P-in-c** E E S JONES

WOOTTON (St Peter) and Dry Sandford *Ox 10* **P** *Bp and Ox Churches Trust (jt)* **P-in-c** J A WILLIAMS, **C** P N TOVEY, J R WILLIAMS, **Hon C** T R PERRY

WOOTTON, NORTH (All Saints) w SOUTH (St Mary) *Nor 20* **P** *Ld Chan and G Howard Esq (alt)* **R** J A NASH, **C** N R MCLEOD, **OLM** D TATE, L ASHBY

WOOTTON, NORTH (St Peter) *see* Pilton w Croscombe, N Wootton and Dinder *B & W*

WOOTTON BASSETT (St Bartholomew and All Saints) *Sarum 15* **P** *DBP* **V** T M B WOODHOUSE, **Hon C** B W HORLOCK

WOOTTON BRIDGE (St Mark) *see* Wootton *Portsm*

WOOTTON COURTENAY (All Saints) *see* Dunster, Carhampton, Withycombe w Rodhuish etc *B & W*

WOOTTON FITZPAINE (not known) *see* Golden Cap Team *Sarum*
WOOTTON RIVERS (St Andrew) *see* Vale of Pewsey *Sarum*
WOOTTON ST LAWRENCE (St Lawrence) *see* Oakley w Wootton St Lawrence *Win*
WOOTTON WAWEN (St Peter) *Cov 7* **P** *K Coll Cam* **P-in-c** T M MASON
WORCESTER Dines Green (St Michael), and Crown East, Rushwick *Worc 3* **P** *Bp and D&C (jt)* **V** R CHARLES
WORCESTER (St Barnabas) (Christ Church) *Worc 6* **P** *Bp* **TR** P G HADDLETON, **C** P E JONES, **NSM** A ORGAN, N S MURRAY-PETERS
WORCESTER (St Clement) and Lower Broadheath *Worc 3* **P** *Bp and D&C (jt)* **V** S L BLOOMER
WORCESTER (St John in Bedwardine) *see* St Jo in Bedwardine *Worc*
WORCESTER (St Martin in the Cornmarket) *see* Worc City *Worc*
WORCESTER (St Nicholas) *see* Warndon St Nic *Worc*
WORCESTER (St Stephen) *see* Barbourne *Worc*
WORCESTER (St Wulstan) *Worc 6* **P** *Bp* **V** vacant (01905) 456944
WORCESTER CITY (All Saints) (St George w St Mary Magdalene) (Old St Martin) *Worc 6* **P** *V Claines (1 turn), Bp and D&C (2 turns), Bp (1 turn)* **C** E HEASLIP, R W JOHNSON, **Hon C** R A H GREANY
WORCESTER PARK (Christ Church w St Philip) *S'wark 23* **P** *R Cheam* **V** C E ELVEY, **NSM** C A ROWLES
WORCESTER SOUTH EAST (St Martin w St Peter) (St Mark in the Cherry Orchard) (Holy Trinity w St Matthew) *Worc 6* **P** *Patr Bd* **TR** K A BOYCE, **TV** F M BINDING, **C** P J BRADFORD, **NSM** A M WHERRY
WORCESTERSHIRE WEST RURAL Team Ministry, The *Worc 3* **P** *Patr Bd (2 turns), Prime Min (1 turn)* **TR** D R SHERWIN, **TV** A B BULLOCK, **Hon C** J G SUMNER, **NSM** J M WHITTAKER
WORDSLEY (Holy Trinity) *Worc 10* **P** *Patr Bd* **TR** C S JONES, **C** E J STANFORD, **NSM** G HODGSON
WORFIELD (St Peter) *Heref 8* **P** *Trustees of the late J R S Greenshields Esq* **P-in-c** J H STOKES
WORKINGTON (St John) *Carl 7* **P** *R Workington* **V** J M COOK
WORKINGTON (St Michael) *Carl 7* **P** *Mrs E H S Thornely* **R** B ROWE
WORKSOP (Christ Church) *S'well 6* **P** *CPAS* **P-in-c** M C ALVEY
WORKSOP (St Anne) *S'well 6* **P** *Bp* **P-in-c** S A CASH, **C** P MACBAIN
WORKSOP (St John the Evangelist) *S'well 6* **P** *CPAS* **V** vacant (01909) 489868
WORKSOP (St Paul) *S'well 6* **P** *Bp* **V** B C B BROWN
WORKSOP PRIORY (St Mary and St Cuthbert) *S'well 6* **P** *St Steph Ho Ox* **P-in-c** N SPICER, **C** P P CORBETT
WORLABY (St Clement) *Linc 6* **P** *DBP* **V** G O MITCHELL
WORLDHAM, EAST (St Mary the Virgin) *see* Northanger *Win*
WORLDHAM, WEST (St Nicholas) *as above*
WORLE (St Martin) (St Mark's Church Centre) *B & W 10* **P** *Ld Chan* **TR** P R LARCOMBE, **TV** E C AMYES, A L FARMER, **NSM** G C BUNCE
WORLESTON (St Oswald) *see* Acton and Worleston, Church Minshull etc *Ches*
WORLINGHAM (All Saints) w Barnby and North Cove *St E 14* **P** *Ld Chan* **R** S M ELLIS, **NSM** C S LEE
WORLINGTON (All Saints) *see* Mildenhall *St E*
WORLINGTON, EAST (St Mary) *see* Burrington, Chawleigh, Cheldon, Chulmleigh etc *Ex*
WORLINGTON, WEST (St Mary) *as above*
WORLINGWORTH (St Mary) w Southolt, Tannington, Bedfield and Monk Soham *St E 17* **P** *Lord Henniker, R C Rous Esq and Bp, and DBP (by turn)* **R** vacant (01728) 768102
WORMBRIDGE (St Peter) *see* Ewyas Harold w Dulas, Kenderchurch etc *Heref*
WORMEGAY (St Michael and All Angels and Holy Cross) *see* Tottenhill w Wormegay *Ely*
WORMELOW HUNDRED *Heref 7* **P** *A W Twiston-Davies Esq (1 turn), Bp (3 turns), and Ld Chan (1 turn)* **R** M JOHNSON
WORMHILL (St Margaret) *see* Tideswell *Derby*
WORMINGFORD (St Andrew), Mount Bures and Little Horkesley *Chelmsf 17* **P** *J J Tufnell Esq, Mrs F Reynolds, and Keble Coll Ox (jt)* **P-in-c** H HEATH
WORMINGHALL (St Peter and St Paul) w Ickford, Oakley and Shabbington *Ox 21* **P** *Bp and Guild of All So (jt)* **R** D R KABOLEH
WORMINGTON (St Katharine) *see* Winchcombe *Glouc*

WORMLEIGHTON (St Peter) *see* Priors Hardwick, Priors Marston and Wormleighton *Cov*
WORMLEY (Church Room) *see* Broxbourne w Wormley *St Alb*
WORMLEY (St Laurence) *as above*
WORMSHILL (St Giles) *see* Tunstall and Bredgar *Cant*
WORPLESDON (St Mary the Virgin) *Guildf 5* **P** *Eton Coll* **R** H M GREAR, **OLM** A J WELCH
WORSALL, HIGH AND LOW (All Saints) *see* Kirklevington w Picton, and High and Low Worsall *York*
WORSBROUGH (St Mary) w Elsecar *Sheff 11* **P** *DBP and Sir Philip Naylor-Leyland Bt (alt)* **V** A LAMB
WORSBROUGH (St Thomas) *see* Worsbrough Common w Worsbrough St Thos *Sheff*
WORSBROUGH COMMON (St Luke) w Worsbrough St Thomas and St James *Sheff 11* **P** *Bp (2 turns), Prime Min (1 turn)* **V** T C KEIGHTLEY
WORSLEY (St Mark) *Man 18* **P** *Bp* **TR** G TURNER, **TV** K R CARMYLLIE
WORSLEY MESNES (not known) *see* Wigan St Jas w St Thos *Liv*
WORSTEAD (St Mary), Westwick, Sloley, Swanton Abbot and Scottow *Nor 12* **P** *DBP, J T D Shaw Esq, D&C, and Bp (by turn)* **R** A R LONG
WORSTHORNE (St John the Evangelist) *see* Holme-in-Cliviger w Worsthorne *Blackb*
WORTH (St Nicholas), Pound Hill and Maidenbower *Chich 7* **P** *DBP* **R** vacant (01293) 882229
WORTH (St Peter and St Paul) *see* Woodnesborough w Worth and Staple *Cant*
WORTH MATRAVERS (St Aldhelm) *see* Kingston, Langton Matravers and Worth Matravers *Sarum*
WORTH MATRAVERS (St Nicholas) *as above*
WORTHAM (St Mary the Virgin) *see* N Hartismere *St E*
WORTHEN (All Saints) *Heref 12* **P** *New Coll Ox (8 turns), J J C Coldwell Esq (1 turn), I Chirbury (1 turn)* **P-in-c** J P ROWE
WORTHING (Holy Trinity) (Christ Church) *Chich 5* **P** *R Broadwater, Bp and Bp Horsham, Ch Soc Trust, and CPAS (jt)* **C** H W SCHNAAR
WORTHING (St Andrew) *Chich 5* **P** *Keble Coll Ox* **P-in-c** C G H KASSELL
WORTHING (St George) (Emmanuel) *Chich 5* **P** *Ch Soc Trust* **V** B R PENFOLD, **NSM** C A CLARK
WORTHING (St Margaret) *see* N Elmham, Billingford, Bintree, Guist etc *Nor*
WORTHING (St Matthew) *Chich 5* **P** *R Broadwater, Bp and Bp Horsham, Ch Soc Trust, and CPAS (jt)* **V** E J CHITHAM, **NSM** M E PARISH
WORTHING, WEST (St John the Divine) *Chich 5* **P** *Bp* **V** J K T ELDRIDGE
WORTHINGTON (St Matthew) *see* Ashby-de-la-Zouch and Breedon on the Hill *Leic*
WORTING (St Thomas of Canterbury) *see* Winklebury and Worting *Win*
WORTLEY (St Leonard) *see* Tankersley, Thurgoland and Wortley *Sheff*
WORTLEY, NEW (St Mary's Parish Centre) *see* Armley w New Wortley *Ripon*
WORTLEY DE LEEDS (St John the Evangelist) *Ripon 6* **P** *Trustees* **V** K A P DOWLING, **C** A J COLLEDGE
WORTON (Christ Church) *see* Potterne w Worton and Marston *Sarum*
WORTON, NETHER (St James) *see* Over w Nether Worton *Ox*
WORTON, OVER (Holy Trinity) w Nether Worton *Ox 5* **P** *Exors J B Schuster Esq* **P-in-c** P J SILVA
WOTTON (St John the Evangelist) and Holmbury St Mary *Guildf 7* **P** *Bp and J P M H Evelyn Esq (jt)* **NSM** P J ROBSON
WOTTON ST MARY WITHOUT (Holy Trinity) *Glouc 2* **P** *Bp* **V** T J G NEWCOMBE, **C** S SKEPPER
WOTTON-UNDER-EDGE (St Mary the Virgin) w Ozleworth, N Nibley and Alderley *Glouc 5* **P** *Ch Ch Ox and Bp (jt)* **V** R H AXFORD, **C** V J BEXON, J F WARD, **NSM** P C E MARSH, C R AXFORD
WOTTON UNDERWOOD (All Saints) *see* Bernwode *Ox*
WOUGHTON *Ox 25* **P** *Patr Bd* **TV** C L WILLIAMS, **Hon C** I P S GOODING, **OLM** P NORRIS
WOUGHTON-ON-THE-GREEN (St Mary) *see* Woughton *Ox*
WOULDHAM (All Saints) *see* Burham and Wouldham *Roch*
WRABNESS (All Saints) *see* Gt Oakley w Wix and Wrabness *Chelmsf*
WRAGBY Group, The (All Saints) *Linc 11* **P** *Bp, MMCET, and DBP (jt)* **R** M N HOLDEN

WRAGBY (St Michael and Our Lady) *see* Kinsley w Wragby *Wakef*

WRAMPLINGHAM (St Peter and St Paul) *see* Barnham Broom and Upper Yare *Nor*

WRANGBROOK (St Michael) *see* Badsworth *Wakef*

WRANGLE (St Mary and St Nicholas) *see* Old Leake w Wrangle *Linc*

WRANGTHORN (St Augustine of Hippo) *see* Woodhouse and Wrangthorn *Ripon*

WRATTING, GREAT (St Mary) *see* Stourhead *St E*

WRATTING, LITTLE (St Mary) *as above*

WRATTING, WEST (St Andrew) *see* Balsham, Weston Colville, W Wickham etc *Ely*

WRAWBY (St Mary the Virgin) *see* Brigg, Wrawby and Cadney cum Howsham *Linc*

WRAXALL (All Saints) *B & W 12* P *Trustees* R R C LUNN, NSM F A TRICKEY

WRAXALL (St Mary) *see* Melbury *Sarum*

WRAXALL, NORTH (St James) *see* Colerne w N Wraxall *Bris*

WRAXALL, SOUTH (St James) *see* N Bradford on Avon and Villages *Sarum*

WRAY (Holy Trinity) *see* E Lonsdale *Blackb*

WRAYSBURY (St Andrew) *see* Horton and Wraysbury *Ox*

WREAKE, UPPER *Leic 2* P *Bp and DBP (jt)* P-in-c P G COLLINS

WREAY (St Mary) *see* Dalston w Cumdivock, Raughton Head and Wreay *Carl*

WRECCLESHAM (St Peter) *Guildf 3* P *Bp* V A E GELL, NSM S J CAVALIER, R C STURT

WRENBURY (St Margaret) *see* Baddiley and Wrenbury w Burleydam *Ches*

WRENINGHAM (All Saints) *see* Ashwellthorpe, Forncett, Fundenhall, Hapton etc *Nor*

WRENTHAM (St Nicholas), Covehithe w Benacre, Henstead w Hulver and Frostenden *St E 15* P *Susan Lady Gooch* P-in-c L J PAYNE

WRENTHORPE (St Anne) *Wakef 11* P *Bp* P-in-c R HARRIS

WRESSLE (St John of Beverly) *see* Howden *York*

WRESTLINGWORTH (St Peter) *see* Dunton w Wrestlingworth and Eyeworth *St Alb*

WRETHAM (St Ethelbert) *see* Thetford *Nor*

WRETTON (All Saints) w Stoke Ferry and Whittington *Ely 9* P *Ld Chan and Ch Patr Trust (alt)* V *vacant* (01366) 501075

WRIBBENHALL (All Saints) *Worc 11* P V *Kidderminster* P-in-c K N JAMES, NSM C L ALLEN

WRIGGLE VALLEY, The *Sarum 3* P *Duchy of Cornwall (1 turn), Bp (3 turns)* P-in-c S F L BRIGNALL

WRIGHTINGTON (St James the Great) *Blackb 4* P *Bp* V *vacant* (01257) 451332

WRINGTON (All Saints) w Butcombe and Burrington *B & W 10* P *Patr Bd* R N R MADDOCK, P-in-c J MALINS

WRITTLE (All Saints) w Highwood *Chelmsf 8* P *New Coll Ox* V D M JONES, NSM S M M ISKANDER

WROCKWARDINE, The Deanery of (St Peter) *Lich 23* P *Patr Bd* TR D F CHANTREY, TV P H CAWTHORNE, G S GOODWIN, C S E WILLIAMS

WROCKWARDINE WOOD (Holy Trinity) *see* Oakengates and Wrockwardine Wood *Lich*

WROOT (St Pancras) *see* Epworth Gp *Linc*

WROSE (St Cuthbert) *Bradf 3* P *The Crown* V P G WALKER

WROTHAM (St George) *Roch 10* P *D&C* P-in-c B E HURD

WROUGHTON (St John the Baptist and St Helen) *Bris 7* P *Bp* V M A JOHNSON, OLM B M ABREY

WROXALL (St John the Evangelist) *Portsm 7* P *Bp* P-in-c A E FAULKNER, K R ADLAM

WROXETER (St Mary) *see* Wrockwardine Deanery *Lich*

WROXHAM (St Mary) w Hoveton St John w Hoveton St Peter and Belaugh *Nor 12* P *Bp* R M A SEARS

WROXTON (All Saints) *see* Ironstone *Ox*

WULFRIC Benefice, The *B & W 14* P *Ld Chan (4 turns), Bp and H W F Hoskyns Esq (1 turn)* R M C GALLAGHER, C J R MORRIS

WYBERTON (St Leodegar) *Linc 20* P *DBP* P-in-c C W B SOWDEN

WYBUNBURY (St Chad) and Audlem w Doddington *Ches 15* P *Bp and Lady Rona Delves Broughton (jt)* V H F CHANTRY, C S J ARTUS

WYCH, HIGH (St James) and Gilston w Eastwick *St Alb 15* P V *Sawbridgeworth (2 turns), P T S Bowlby Esq (1 turn)* P-in-c A J GILES

WYCHBOLD (St Mary de Wyche) *see* Stoke Prior, Wychbold and Upton Warren *Worc*

WYCHE (All Saints) *see* Malvern St Andr and Malvern Wells and Wyche *Worc*

WYCHLING (St Margaret) *see* Doddington, Newnham and Wychling *Cant*

WYCHNOR (St Leonard) *Lich 1* P *Personal Reps W H Harrison Esq* V J W ALLAN, NSM P A L MADDOCK, A A LOW

WYCK RISSINGTON (St Laurence) *see* Bourton-on-the-Water w Clapton etc *Glouc*

WYCLIFFE (St Mary) *see* Barningham w Hutton Magna and Wycliffe *Ripon*

WYCOMBE, HIGH (All Saints) (St Andrew) (St Anne and St Peter) (St Birinus) (St James) (St Mary and St George) *Ox 29* P *Patr Bd* TR D A PICKEN, TV P WILLIS, S A WHITMORE, N R SKIPWORTH, Y L MURPHY, S P DUST, C J E KENNEDY, NSM P VINEY, OLM M A JACKSON, R M WOOSTER, J LOCK

WYCOMBE, WEST (St Laurence) (St Paul) w Bledlow Ridge, Bradenham and Radnage *Ox 29* P *Bp, DBP, Peache Trustees, and Sir Francis Dashwood Bt (jt)* R N J LACEY, NSM V J BEAUMONT, L J RICHARDSON

WYCOMBE AND CHADWELL (St Mary) *see* Ironstone Villages *Leic*

WYCOMBE LANE (St Mary) *see* Wooburn *Ox*

WYCOMBE MARSH (St Anne and St Peter) *see* High Wycombe *Ox*

WYDDIAL (St Giles) *see* Hormead, Wyddial, Anstey, Brent Pelham etc *St Alb*

WYE (St Gregory and St Martin) w Brook and Hastingleigh w Boughton Aluph and Eastwell *Cant 2* P *Abp* P-in-c R HOLY, OLM L A CROSS

WYE, SOUTH Team Ministry *see* Heref S Wye *Heref*

WYESHAM (St James) *see* Dixton, Wyesham, Bishopswood, Whitchurch etc *Heref*

WYFORDBY (St Mary) *see* S Framland *Leic*

WYKE *see* Win St Matt *Win*

WYKE (Holy Trinity) *see* Bruton and Distr *B & W*

WYKE (St Mark) *Guildf 5* P *Bp* V P A GODFREY, OLM M TAYLOR

WYKE (St Mary the Virgin) *see* Oakenshaw, Wyke and Low Moor *Bradf*

WYKE REGIS (All Saints) (St Edmund) *Sarum 4* P *D&C* R D J SMITH

WYKEHAM (All Saints) *see* Upper Derwent *York*

WYKEHAM: Broughton w North Newington, Epwell w Sibford, Shutford, Swalcliffe, and Tadmarton *Ox 5* P *New Coll, Worc Coll, and Lord Saye and Sele (jt)* R T WIMBUSH, NSM J H TATTERSALL

WYKEN (Church of Risen Christ) *see* Coventry Caludon *Cov*

WYKEN (Holy Cross) *as above*

WYKEN (St Mary Magdalene) *as above*

WYLAM (St Oswin) *Newc 9* P *Bp* V *vacant* (01661) 853254

WYLDE GREEN (Emmanuel) *Birm 12* P *Bp* V *vacant* 0121-373 8348

WYLYE (St Mary the Virgin) *see* Wylye and Till Valley *Sarum*

WYLYE AND TILL VALLEY *Sarum 13* P *Patr Bd (2 turns), Ld Chan (1 turn)* TV H R L BONSEY, OLM V M GARRARD, D A WALTERS

WYLYE VALLEY TEAM, UPPER *Sarum 17* P *Patr Bd (5 turns), Ld Chan (1 turn)* TR J H TOMLINSON, OLM A E BENNETT-SHAW, D M HAMMOND

WYMERING (St Peter and St Paul) *Portsm 6* P *Nugee Foundn* P-in-c J L STRAW, Hon C B R COOK

WYMESWOLD (St Mary) and Prestwold w Hoton *Leic 6* P *S J Packe-Drury-Lowe Esq and Bp (by turn)* P-in-c R M PADDISON, Hon C M R SAMUEL, NSM N J MCGINTY

WYMINGTON (St Lawrence) w Podington *St Alb 13* P *R M Orlebar Esq (1 turn), DBP (3 turns)* R *vacant* (01933) 313069

WYMONDHAM (St Mary and St Thomas) *Nor 7* P *Bp* V C J DAVIES, C D C OLDHAM

WYMONDHAM (St Peter) *see* S Framland *Leic*

WYMONDLEY, GREAT (St Mary the Virgin) *see* St Ippolyts w Gt and Lt Wymondley *St Alb*

WYMONDLEY, LITTLE (St Mary the Virgin) *as above*

WYMYNSWOLD (St Margaret) *see* Nonington w Wymynswold and Goodnestone etc *Cant*

WYNYARD PARK (Chapel) *see* Grindon, Stillington and Wolviston *Dur*

WYRE PIDDLE (St Anne) *see* Fladbury, Hill and Moor, Wyre Piddle etc *Worc*

WYRESDALE, OVER (Christ Church) *see* Dolphinholme w Quernmore and Over Wyresdale *Blackb*

WYRLEY, GREAT (St Mark) *Lich 3* P R *Cannock* V G HORNER, C M J HEATH, R A WESTWOOD, OLM M J PRICE

WYSALL (Holy Trinity) *see* Willoughby-on-the-Wolds w Wysall and Widmerpool *S'well*

WYTHALL (no church) *Birm 6* P R *Kings Norton* V *vacant* (01564) 823381

WYTHAM (All Saints) *see* Wolvercote and Wytham *Ox*
WYTHBURN (not known) *see* St John's-in-the-Vale, Threlkeld and Wythburn *Carl*
WYTHENSHAWE Lawton Moor (St Michael and All Angels) *see* Lawton Moor *Man*
WYTHENSHAWE (St Francis of Assisi) (St Luke) (St Martin) (St Richard of Chichester) (William Temple Church) *Man 6*
P *Patr Bd* TV K J STANTON, M J APPLEBY, J D DEVARAJ, NSM E J DISLEY, M E YOUNG, OLM G R MILLER
WYTHER (Venerable Bede) *Ripon 6* P *Bp* V B A A LAWAL
WYTHOP (St Margaret) *see* Cockermouth Area *Carl*
WYVERSTONE (St George) *see* Bacton w Wyverstone, Cotton and Old Newton etc *St E*
WYVILL (St Catherine) *see* Harlaxton Gp *Linc*
YAFFORTH (All Saints) *see* Lower Swale *Ripon*
YALDING (St Peter and St Paul) w Collier Street *Roch 8*
P *Ld Chan* V P J FILMER
YANWORTH (St Michael) *see* Chedworth, Yanworth and Stowell, Coln Rogers etc *Glouc*
YAPHAM (St Martin) *see* Barmby Moor Gp *York*
YAPTON (St Mary) *see* Clymping and Yapton w Ford *Chich*
YARCOMBE (St John the Baptist) *see* Kilmington, Stockland, Dalwood, Yarcombe etc *Ex*
YARDLEY (St Cyprian) Hay Mill *Birm 13* P *Bp* V *vacant*
0121-773 1278
YARDLEY (St Edburgha) *Birm 13* P *St Pet Coll Ox*
V W J SANDS, NSM R M MORTIMORE
YARDLEY (St Lawrence) *see* Ardeley *St Alb*
YARDLEY, SOUTH (St Michael and All Angels) *Birm 15*
P *Bp* V D A J MADDOX
YARDLEY GOBION (St Leonard) *see* Potterspury w Furtho and Yardley Gobion etc *Pet*
YARDLEY HASTINGS (St Andrew), Denton and Grendon w Castle Ashby and Whiston *Pet 6* P *Marquess of Northampton and Bp (alt)* R D L SPOKES, NSM J H CRAIG PECK
YARDLEY WOOD (Christ Church) *Birm 5* P *Bp*
V J G RICHARDS
YARKHILL (St John the Baptist) *see* Ledbury *Heref*
YARLINGTON (Blessed Virgin Mary) *see* Camelot Par *B & W*
YARM (St Mary Magdalene) *York 20* P *Abp* R *vacant*
(01642) 781115
YARMOUTH (St James) *Portsm 8* P *Keble Coll Ox*
R M E C WHATSON, C R STUART-BOURNE
YARMOUTH, GREAT (St John) (St Nicholas) (St Paul) (St Luke) (St Mary) *Nor 6* P *Patr Bd* TR C L TERRY, C A J AVERY, J W STEWART
YARNFIELD (Mission Room St Barnabas) *see* Cotes Heath and Standon and Swynnerton etc *Lich*
YARNSCOMBE (St Andrew) *see* Newton Tracey, Horwood, Alverdiscott etc *Ex*
YARNTON (St Bartholomew) *see* Blenheim *Ox*
YARPOLE (St Leonard) *see* Leominster *Heref*
YARWELL (St Mary Magdalene) *see* Nassington w Yarwell and Woodnewton w Apethorpe *Pet*
YATE New Town (St Mary) *Bris 5* P *Bp* TR D B HARREX, TV I P MACFARLANE, Hon C D C CHEDZEY
YATELEY (St Peter) *Win 5* P *Bp* R A C EDMUNDS
YATESBURY (All Saints) *see* Oldbury *Sarum*
YATTENDON (St Peter and St Paul) *see* Hermitage *Ox*
YATTON (All Saints) *see* Ledbury *Heref*
YATTON KEYNELL (St Margaret) *see* By Brook *Bris*
YATTON MOOR (St Mary the Virgin) *B & W 12* P *DBF*
TR I M HUBBARD, TV J C ANDREWS, NSM C R LLEWELYN-EVANS
YAVERLAND (St John the Baptist) *see* Brading w Yaverland *Portsm*
YAXHAM (St Peter) *see* Mattishall and the Tudd Valley *Nor*
YAXLEY (St Mary the Virgin) *see* S Hartismere *St E*
YAXLEY (St Peter) and Holme w Conington *Ely 15* P *Ld Chan (2 turns), J H B Heathcote Esq (1 turn)* V J A RANDALL
YEADON (St John the Evangelist) *Bradf 4* P *Bp and R Guiseley w Esholt (jt)* V R M WALKER, C S V KAYE
YEALAND CONYERS (St John the Evangelist) *see* Warton St Oswald w Yealand Conyers *Blackb*
YEALMPTON (St Bartholomew) and Brixton *Ex 21*
P *D&C Windsor and Bp (jt)* P-in-c D ARNOTT
YEARSLEY (Holy Trinity) *see* Crayke w Brandsby and Yearsley *York*
YEAVELEY (Holy Trinity) *see* Brailsford w Shirley, Osmaston w Edlaston etc *Derby*
YEDINGHAM (St John the Baptist) *see* Buckrose Carrs *York*
YELDEN (St Mary) *see* The Stodden Churches *St Alb*
YELDHAM, GREAT (St Andrew) *see* Upper Colne *Chelmsf*
YELDHAM, LITTLE (St John the Baptist) *as above*
YELFORD (St Nicholas and St Swithin) *see* Lower Windrush *Ox*

YELLING (Holy Cross) *see* Papworth *Ely*
YELVERTOFT (All Saints) *see* Crick and Yelvertoft w Clay Coton and Lilbourne *Pet*
YELVERTON (St Mary) *see* Thurton *Nor*
YELVERTON (St Paul), Meavy, Sheepstor and Walkhampton *Ex 25* P *Ld Chan (1 turn), Patr Bd (2 turns)* TV N M HUNT, NSM M SALMON, N S SHUTT
YEOFORD CHAPEL (Holy Trinity) *see* Crediton, Shobrooke and Sandford etc *Ex*
YEOVIL (Holy Trinity) w Barwick *B & W 6* P *Ms Y L Bennett and Ms R S Mullen (1 turn), The Crown (3 turns)*
R T J COOK, C P T MEAD
YEOVIL (St Andrew) (St John the Baptist) w Kingston Pitney *B & W 6* P *DBP* R J DUDLEY-SMITH, C T M P LEWIS
YEOVIL (St James the Great) *see* Preston Plucknett *B & W*
YEOVIL (St Michael and All Angels) *B & W 6* P *Bp*
V J R BAKER, C T J FARMILOE, NSM C Y JONES
YEOVIL (St Peter) *see* Preston Plucknett *B & W*
YEOVIL MARSH (All Saints) *see* Tintinhull w Chilthorne Domer, Yeovil Marsh etc *B & W*
YETMINSTER (St Andrew) *see* Wriggle Valley *Sarum*
YIEWSLEY (St Matthew) *Lon 24* P *V Hillingdon*
V R C YOUNG, C C S NEWBOLD
YOCKLETON (Holy Trinity) *Heref 12* P *Bp*
P-in-c J P ROWE
YORK Acomb (St Aidan) *see* Acomb St Steph *York*
YORK (All Saints) *see* Huntington *York*
YORK (All Saints) North Street *York 7* P *D&C*
P-in-c A A HUKSMAN
YORK (All Saints) Pavement w St Crux and St Michael Spurriergate *York 7* P *Abp* P-in-c E J NATTRASS, NSM A P HUGHES
YORK (Christ Church) *see* Heworth Ch Ch *York*
YORK (Holy Redeemer) *see* Acomb H Redeemer *York*
YORK (Holy Trinity) *see* Heworth H Trin and St Wulstan *York*
YORK (Holy Trinity) Micklegate *York 7* P *D&C*
R R M C SEED
YORK (James the Deacon) *see* Acomb Moor *York*
YORK (St Barnabas) *York 7* P *CPAS* P-in-c U L SIMPSON
YORK (St Chad) *York 7* P *Abp* P-in-c S R STANLEY
YORK (St Clement w St Mary) Bishophill *York 7* P *Abp and D&C (jt)* R A STOKER, NSM G J PETERS
YORK (St Denys) *York 7* P *Abp* P-in-c E J NATTRASS, NSM A P HUGHES
YORK (St Edward the Confessor) *see* Dringhouses *York*
YORK (St Helen) Stonegate w (St Martin) Coney Street *York 7* P *Abp* P-in-c E J NATTRASS
YORK (St Hilda) *York 7* P *Abp* P-in-c T L JONES, NSM M FAIREY, M H ELLISON
YORK (St Lawrence w St Nicholas) *York 7* P *D&C*
P-in-c T L JONES, NSM M H ELLISON
YORK (St Luke) *York 7* P *Abp* P-in-c S C BENFORD, NSM T M GANT, M E CARRINGTON
YORK (St Martin-cum-Gregory) *see* York H Trin Micklegate *York*
YORK (St Michael-le-Belfrey) (St Cuthbert) *York 7* P *Abp*
V M J PORTER, C A J RYCROFT, R W SIMPSON, NSM W J ROBERTS, C N SELVARATNAM, A T LINDLEY
YORK (St Olave w St Giles) *York 7* P *Abp*
P-in-c E J NATTRASS
YORK (St Oswald) *see* Fulford *York*
YORK (St Paul) Holgate Road *York 7* P *CPAS* R J M A LEE, NSM M J RUTTER
YORK (St Philip and St James) *see* Clifton *York*
YORK (St Stephen) *see* Acomb St Steph *York*
YORK (St Thomas w St Maurice) *York 7* P *Abp*
P-in-c P MOORE, OLM E A RANSFORD
YORK (St Wulstan) *see* Heworth H Trin and St Wulstan *York*
YORKLEY, LOWER (St Luke's Church Centre) *see* Parkend and Viney Hill *Glouc*
YORKTOWN (St Michael) *see* Camberley St Mich Yorktown *Guildf*
YOULGREAVE (All Saints), Middleton, Stanton-in-Peak and Birchover *Derby 2* P *Duke of Devonshire and N B B Davie-Thornhill Esq (jt)* V G C GRIFFITHS
YOXALL (St Peter) *Lich 1* P *Bp* P-in-c M H HAWKSWORTH, OLM M BINSLEY
YOXFORD (St Peter) *see* Yoxmere *St E*
YOXMERE Benefice, The *St E 19* P *Prime Min (1 turn), Ch Patr Trust, Lady Penelope Gilbey, Shadingfield Property, J K A Brooke Esq, CPAS, and Bp (2 turns)* V R J GINN, C C H REDGRAVE
ZEAL, SOUTH (St Mary) *see* S Tawton and Belstone *Ex*
ZEAL MONACHORUM (St Peter) *Ex 2* P *DBP* R *vacant*
ZEALS (St Martin) *see* Upper Stour *Sarum*
ZENNOR (St Senera) *Truro 5* P *Bp* P-in-c E V A FOOT

WELSH BENEFICES AND CHURCHES

An index of benefices of the Church in Wales (shown in bold type), together with entries for churches and other licensed places of worship. Where the church name is the same as the benefice (or the first place name in the benefice), the church entry is omitted. Church dedications are indicated in brackets.

The benefice entry gives the full legal name, followed by the diocese, its deanery number (p. 1015), and the name(s) and appointment(s) of the clergy serving there (if there are none, the telephone number of the parsonage house is given). The following are the main abbreviations used; for others see the full list of abbreviations.

C	Curate	P-in-c	Priest-in-charge
C-in-c	Curate-in-charge	Par Dn	Parish Deacon
Dn-in-c	Deacon-in-charge	R	Rector
Dss	Deaconess	TM	Team Minister
Hon C	Honorary Curate	TR	Team Rector
Hon Par Dn	Honorary Parish Deacon	TV	Team Vicar
NSM	Non-stipendiary Minister	V	Vicar

ABBEY CWMHIR (St Mary the Virgin)   *see* Lower Ithon Valley *S & B*

ABER (St Bodfan)   *see* Llanfairfechan w Aber *Ban*

ABERAERON (Holy Trinity)   *see* Henfynyw w Aberaeron and Llanddewi Aberarth etc *St D*

ABERAMAN (St Margaret) and Abercwmboi w Cwmaman *Llan 9*   **V**   D C WAY

ABERAVON (St Mary) (St Paul) (Holy Trinity) (St Agnes) *Llan 5*   **TR**   N CAHILL,   **TV**   M J H TRICK,   **C**   B T RABJOHNS,   **NSM**   J A SLENNETT

ABERBARGOED (St Peter)   *see* Bedwellty w New Tredegar *Mon*

ABERCANAID (St Peter)   *see* Merthyr Tydfil St Dav and Abercanaid *Llan*

ABERCARN and Cwmcarn *Mon 6*   **P-in-c**   A M BAKER,   **NSM**   M REDWOOD

ABERCRAF (St David)   *see* Cwmtawe Uchaf *S & B*

ABERCWMBOI   *see* Aberaman and Abercwmboi w Cwmaman *Llan*

ABERCYNON (St Donat) (St Gwynno) *Llan 9*   **V** *vacant* (01443) 740207

ABERDARE (St Fagan) *Llan 9*   **V**   K W LAKE

ABERDARE (St John the Baptist) (St Elvan) (St Matthew) (St John the Evangelist) *Llan 9*   **V**   R E DAVIES

ABERDARON (St Hywyn) and Llanfaelrhys *Ban 11*   **P-in-c**   J E COTTER

ABERDYFI (St Peter)   *see* Llanegryn w Aberdyfi w Tywyn *Ban*

ABEREDW (St Cewydd) w Llandeilo Graban and Llanbadarn-y-Garreg w Crickadarn and Gwenddwr *S & B 2*   **Hon C**   M K E MORGAN,   **NSM**   P J MORRIS

ABERERCH (St Cawrdaf)   *see* Denio w Abererch *Ban*

ABERFFRAW (St Beuno)   *see* Trefdraeth w Aberffraw, Llangadwaladr etc *Ban*

ABERGAVENNY (Holy Trinity) (Christ Church) *Mon 1*   **C**   B SIXTUS,   **OLM**   C R WALTERS

ABERGAVENNY (St Mary) (Christchurch) w Llanwenarth Citra *Mon 1*   **V**   J H WINSTON,   **C**   B SIXTUS

ABERGELE (St David) (St Michael) and St George *St As 6*   **V**   K A JOHNSON

ABERGORLECH (St David)   *see* Brechfa w Abergorlech etc *St D*

ABERGWILI (St David)   *see* E Carmarthen *St D*

ABERGWYNFI (St Thomas)   *see* Glyncorrwg and Upper Afan Valley *Llan*

ABERGWYNGREGYN (St Bodfan)   *see* Llanfairfechan w Aber *Ban*

ABERGYNOLWYN   *see* Llanegryn w Aberdyfi w Tywyn *Ban*

ABERHAFESP (St Gwynog)   *see* Llanllwchaiarn and Newtown w Aberhafesp *St As*

ABERKENFIG (St John)   *see* Llansantffraid, Bettws and Aberkenfig *Llan*

ABERNANT (St Lucia) *St D 10*   **P-in-c**   J GAINER

ABERNANT (St Matthew)   *see* Aberdare *Llan*

ABERPERGWM (St Cadoc)   *see* Vale of Neath *Llan*

ABERPORTH (St Cynwyl) w Tremain w Blaenporth and Betws Ifan *St D 5*   **V** *vacant* (01239) 810556

ABERSYCHAN (St Thomas)   *see* Blaenavon w Capel Newydd *Mon*

ABERTILLERY (St Michael) w Cwmtillery w Llanhilleth w Six Bells *Mon 9*   **V**   P F COLEMAN,   **C**   S K GILLARD-FAULKNER,   **Hon C**   M PARKER

ABERTYSSWG (St Paul)   *see* Bedwellty w New Tredegar *Mon*

ABERYSKIR (St Mary and St Cynidr)   *see* Dan yr Eppynt *S & B*

ABERYSTWYTH (St Michael) (Holy Trinity) (St Mary) (St Anne) *St D 9*   **TR**   S R BELL,   **TV**   A F HERRICK,   I J GIRLING,   **C**   J-D LAURENCE

AFAN VALE   *see* Glyncorrwg and Upper Afan Valley *Llan*

ALLTMAWR (St Mauritius)   *see* Builth and Llanddewi'r Cwm w Llangynog etc *S & B*

ALLTWEN (St John the Baptist)   *see* Cilybebyll *Llan*

AMBLESTON (St Mary)   *see* Spittal w Trefgarn and Ambleston w St Dogwells *St D*

AMLWCH (St Eleth) (St Peter) (St Gwenllwyfo) (St Eilian) *Ban 7*   **P-in-c**   H V JONES

AMMANFORD (All Saints)   *see* Betws w Ammanford *St D*

AMMANFORD (St Michael)   *as above*

AMROTH (St Elidyr)   *see* St Issell's and Amroth w Crunwere *St D*

ANGLE (St Mary)   *see* Monkton *St D*

ARTHOG (St Catherine) w Fairbourne w Llangelynnin w Rhoslefain *Ban 12*   **R** *vacant* (01341) 250919

BAGILLT (St Mary) (St Peter) *St As 4*   **V**   S F HILDRETH

BAGLAN (St Catherine) (St Baglan) *Llan 5*   **V**   P M WILLIAMS

BALA (Christ Church) *St As 17*   **R**   N W MORRIS

BANGOR (Cathedral of St Deiniol)   *see* Ban Cathl *Ban*

BANGOR (St David) (Eglwys y Groes) (St Mary) (St Peter) *Ban 5*   **TR**   J E PEARCE,   **C**   C S B ROBERTS,   **Hon C**   R M POWLEY

BANGOR MONACHORUM (St Dunawd), Worthenbury and Marchwiel *St As 11*   **R**   S BLAGDEN

BANGOR TEIFI (St David)   *see* Llandysul w Bangor Teifi w Henllan etc *St D*

BARGOED (St Gwladys) and Deri w Brithdir *Llan 8*   **V**   A P BOOKLESS

BARMOUTH   *see* Llanaber w Caerdeon *Ban*

BARRY (All Saints) (St John w St Baruc) *Llan 3*   **R**   A C BERRY,   **C**   E L REES

BARRY (St Paul)   *see* Merthyr Dyfan *Llan*

BASSALEG (St Basil) *Mon 5*   **TR**   J S WILLIAMS,   **TV**   C M L STONE,   **C**   H J LONG,   **NSM**   R P MULCAHY

BATTLE (St Cynog)   *see* Dan yr Eppynt *S & B*

BEAUFORT (St Andrew)   *see* Ebbw Vale *Mon*

BEAUFORT (St David)   *as above*

BEAUMARIS (St Mary and St Nicholas) (St Catherine) (St Seiriol) (St Cawrdaf) (St Michael) *Ban 6*   **R**   N FAIRLAMB

BEDDGELERT (St Mary)   *see* Penrhyndeudraeth and Llanfrothen w Maentwrog etc *Ban*

BEDLINOG (St Cadoc)   *see* Treharris, Trelewis and Bedlinog *Llan*

BEDLINOG (St Mary)   *as above*

BEDWAS (St Barrwg) w Machen w Rudry *Mon 5*   **R**   P D CROCKER,   **Par Dn**   D A WILLIAMS,   **NSM**   D E COLLINGBOURNE, G J COOMBES, M MOORE

BEDWELLTY (St Sannan) w New Tredegar *Mon 6*   **V**   R C DYMOND,   **C**   H-M DE GRUCHY,   **NSM**   J EVANS

BEGELLY (St Mary) w Ludchurch and East Williamston *St D 3*   **R**   S J GEACH

BEGUILDY (St Michael and All Angels) (St Peter) and Heyope and Llangynllo and Bleddfa *S & B 5*   **V**   A F PYE

BENLLECH (St Andrew)   *see* Llanfair Mathafarn Eithaf w Llanbedrgoch *Ban*

BERRIEW (St Beuno) *St As 10*   **V**   J B THELWELL

BERSE (Parish Church)   *see* Broughton and Berse Drelincourt *St As*

BERSHAM (St Mary)   *see* Wrexham *St As*

BETTISFIELD (St John the Baptist)   *see* Hanmer and Bronington and Bettisfield *St As*

BETTWS   *see* Dan yr Eppynt *S & B*

BETTWS (St David)   *see* Llansantffraid, Bettws and Aberkenfig *Llan*

BETTWS (St David) *Mon 8*   **P-in-c**   H J DAVIES

BETTWS CHAPEL   *see* Llantilio Pertholey w Bettws Chpl etc *Mon*

BETTWS DISSERTH (St Mary)   *see* Colwyn *S & B*
BETTWS NEWYDD (not known) w Trostrey and Kemeys Commander and Llanfihangel Gobion w Llanfair Kilgeddin   *Mon 4*   **R** T G CLEMENT
BETWS (Holy Trinity)   *see* Glasbury and Llowes w Clyro and Betws *S & B*
BETWS (St David) w Ammanford *St D 12*   **V** D BOWEN
BETWS BLEDRWS (St Bledrws or St Michael) *St D 8*   **R** *vacant*
BETWS CEDEWAIN (St Beuno) and Tregynon and Llanwyddelan *St As 7*   **Hon C** W T BRYAN
BETWS GARMON (St Garmon)   *see* Llanbeblig w Caernarfon and Betws Garmon etc *Ban*
BETWS GWERFUL GOCH (St Mary) w Llangwm w Llawrybetws *St As 17*   **P-in-c** S J ROBERTS
BETWS LEUCU (St Lucia)   *see* Bro Teifi Sarn Helen *St D*
BETWS-Y-COED (St Mary) and Capel Curig w Penmachno w Dolwyddelan *Ban 2*   **V** C R HILLMAN
BETWS-YN-RHOS (St Michael)   *see* Petryal and Betws yn Rhos *St As*
BEULAH   *see* Blaenau Irfon *S & B*
BIRCHGROVE (St John)   *see* Llansamlet *S & B*
BISHOPSTON (St Teilo) w Penmaen and Nicholaston *S & B 8*   **V** A J PEARCE
BISHTON (St Cadwaladr)   *see* Magor *Mon*
BISTRE (Emmanuel) (All Saints) (St Cecilia) *St As 13*   **V** M J BATCHELOR,   **C** A O MAYES,   **NSM** S BAIRD
BLACKWOOD (St Margaret) *Mon 6*   **P in e** M J TREGENZA
BLAENAU FFESTINIOG (St David)   *see* Llanffestiniog w Blaenau Ffestiniog etc *Ban*
BLAENAU IRFON *S & B 2*   **P-in-c** L ASHDOWN
BLAENAVON (St Peter) w Capel Newydd *Mon 9*   **V** J S BRAY,   **C** R A D LINDSAY
BLAENCELYN (St David)   *see* Llangrannog w Llandysiliogogo w Penbryn *St D*
BLAENGARW (St James)   *see* Llangeinor and the Garw Valley *Llan*
BLAENGWRACH (St Mary)   *see* Vale of Neath *Llan*
BLAENLLECHAU (St Thomas)   *see* Rhondda Fach Uchaf *Llan*
BLAENPENNAL (St David) *St D 8*   **V** P W DAVIES
BLAENPENNAL (St David)   *see* Bro Teifi Sarn Helen *St D*
BLAENPORTH (St David)   *see* Aberporth w Tremain w Blaenporth and Betws Ifan *St D*
BLAINA (St Peter) and Nantyglo *Mon 7*   **R** N C PERRY,   **Par Dn** C MORGAN,   **NSM** C I LEWIS
BLEDDFA (St Mary Magdalene)   *see* Beguildy and Heyope and Llangynllo and Bleddfa *S & B*
BLETHERSTON (St Mary)   *see* Llawhaden w Bletherston and Llanycefn *St D*
BODEDERN (St Edern) w Llanfaethlu *Ban 3*   **R** *vacant* (01407) 730241
BODELWYDDAN (St Margaret)   *see* Rhuddlan and Bodelwyddan *St As*
BODEWRYD (St Mary)   *see* Llanfechell w Bodewryd w Rhosbeirio etc *Ban*
BODFARI (St Stephen)   *see* Caerwys and Bodfari *St As*
BODWROG (St Twrog)   *see* Llandrygarn w Bodwrog and Heneglwys etc *Ban*
BONTDDU   *see* Llanaber w Caerdeon *Ban*
BONVILSTON (St Mary)   *see* St Nicholas w Bonvilston and St George-super-Ely *Llan*
BONYMAEN (St Margaret)   *see* Glantawe *S & B*
BORTH (St Matthew) and Eglwys-fach w Llangynfelyn *St D 9*   **V** M C CHARLES
BOSHERTON (St Michael)   *see* Monkton *St D*
BOTWNNOG (St Beuno) w Bryncroes w Llangwnnadl w Penllech *Ban 11*   **P-in-c** N M HAWKINS
BOUGHROOD (St Cynog)   *see* Llandefalle and Llyswen w Boughrood etc *S & B*
BOULSTON   *see* Slebech and Uzmaston w Boulston *St D*
BRAWDY (St David)   *see* Dewisland *St D*
BRECHFA (St Teilo) w Abergorlech and Llanfihangel Rhos-y-corn *St D 13*   **P-in-c** L CHAMBERS
BRECON (Cathedral of St John the Evangelist) (St Mary) w Llanddew *S & B 1*   **V** G O MARSHALL,   **P-in-c** M R D THOMAS
BRECON (St David) w Llanspyddid and Llanilltyd *S & B 1*   **V** T J WILLIAMS
BRIDELL (St David)   *see* Cilgerran w Bridell and Llantwyd and Eglwyswrw *St D*
BRIDGEND (St Illtud)   *see* Newcastle *Llan*
BRIDGEND (St Mary)   *see* Coity, Nolton and Brackla *Llan*
BRIGHTON, NEW (St James)   *see* Mold *St As*
BRITHDIR (St David)   *see* Bargoed and Deri w Brithdir *Llan*

BRITHDIR (St Mark)   *see* Dolgellau w Llanfachreth and Brithdir etc *Ban*
BRITHDIR (St Mary)   *see* Llanrhaeadr ym Mochnant etc *St As*
BRITON FERRY (St Clement)   *see* Llansawel, Briton Ferry *Llan*
BRO DDYFI UCHAF *Ban 10*   **NSM** R P BARNES, P N WARD
BRO FAUMA   *see* Cilcain, Gwernaffield, Llanferres etc *St As*
BRO TEIFI SARN HELEN *St D 8*   **NSM** W D JONES
BRONGWYN (St Mary)   *see* Newcastle Emlyn w Llandyfriog and Troedyraur etc *St D*
BRONINGTON (Holy Trinity)   *see* Hanmer and Bronington and Bettisfield *St As*
BRONLLYS (St Mary)   *see* Talgarth w Bronllys w Llanfilo *S & B*
BRONWYDD (St Celynnin)   *see* Llanpumsaint w Llanllawddog *St D*
BROUGHTON (St Mary)   *see* Hawarden *St As*
BROUGHTON (St Paul) (St Peter) and Berse Drelincourt *St As 15*   **V** J G AYLWARD
BRYMBO (St Alban) (St Mary), Southsea and Tanyfron *St As 15*   **P-in-c** N W CARTER
BRYN (St Tydfil)   *see* Llangynwyd w Maesteg *Llan*
BRYN Y MAEN (Christ Church)   *see* Brynymaen *St As*
BRYNAMAN (St Catherine) w Cwmllynfell *St D 12*   **V** A TEALE
BRYNCETHIN   *see* Llansantffraid, Bettws and Aberkenfig *Llan*
BRYNCOEDIFOR (St Paul)   *see* Dolgellau w Llanfachreth and Brithdir etc *Ban*
BRYNCROES (St Mary)   *see* Botwnnog w Bryncroes w Llangwnnadl w Penllech *Ban*
BRYNEGLWYS (St Tysilio) *St As 17*   **P-in-c** H FENTON
BRYNFORD (St Michael)   *see* Gorsedd w Brynford, Ysgeifiog and Whitford *St As*
BRYNGWRAN   *see* Valley w Llechylched and Caergeiliog *Ban*
BRYNGWYN (St Mary)   *see* Newcastle Emlyn w Llandyfriog and Troedyraur etc *St D*
BRYNGWYN (St Michael) and Newchurch and Llanbedr Painscastle and Llanddewi Fach *S & B 2*   **Hon C** M K E MORGAN
BRYNGWYN (St Peter)   *see* Raglan w Llandenny and Bryngwyn *Mon*
BRYNMAWR (St Mary the Virgin) *S & B 3*   **V** P M WINCHESTER
BRYNNA   *see* Llanharan w Peterston-super-Montem *Llan*
BRYNYMAEN (Christ Church) *St As*   **V** *vacant*
BUCKHOLT (St John the Baptist)   *see* Monmouth w Overmonnow etc *Mon*
BUCKLEY (St Matthew) (Good Shepherd) *St As 13*   **V** A M TILTMAN,   **NSM** P M OWENS
BUILTH (St Mary) and Llanddewi'r Cwm w Llangynog and Maesmynis and Llanynys and Alltmawr *S & B 2*   **NSM** C R HALL
BULWARK (St Christopher)   *see* Chepstow *Mon*
BURRY PORT (St Mary) and Pwll *St D 11*   **V** R P DAVIES,   **NSM** J E PHILLIPS, M R P WHEATLEY
BURTON (St Mary) and Rosemarket *St D 4*   **R** *vacant* (01646) 600275
BUTE TOWN (St Aidan)   *see* Pontlottyn w Fochriw *Llan*
BUTTINGTON (All Saints)   *see* Guilsfield w Buttington *St As*
BWLCH (All Saints)   *see* Llyn Safaddan *S & B*
BWLCHGWYN (Christ Church)   *see* Minera w Coedpoeth and Bwlchgwyn *St As*
BWLCHYCIBAU (Christ Church)   *see* Llanfyllin, Bwlchycibau and Llanwddyn *St As*
BYLCHAU (St Thomas)   *see* Henllan and Llannefydd and Bylchau *St As*
CADOXTON-JUXTA-BARRY (St Cadoc) (St Mary) *Llan 3*   **R** J M HUGHES
CADOXTON-JUXTA-NEATH (St Catwg) and Tonna *Llan 6*   **V** C A OWEN
CAERAU (St Cynfelin) (St Peter) *Llan 5*   **V** K ANDREWS
CAERAU w Ely (St David) (St Timothy) *Llan 2*   **V** J L SMITH
CAERDEON (St Philip)   *see* Llanaber w Caerdeon *Ban*
CAEREITHIN (St Teilo) *S & B 10*   **V** P F M GALLAGHER
CAERFALLWCH (St Paul)   *see* Halkyn w Caerfallwch w Rhesycae *St As*
CAERGEILIOG   *see* Valley w Llechylched and Caergeiliog *Ban*
CAERGYBI   *see* Holyhead *Ban*
CAERHUN (St Mary) and Llangelynnin and Llanbedr-y-Cennin *Ban 2*   **V** T BONNET
CAERLEON (St Cadoc) and Llanfrechfa Group, The *Mon 8*   **V** A J EDWARDS,   **NSM** M R JARMAN, E HILLS,   **OLM** F M A EVANS
CAERLEON-ULTRA-PONTEM (Holy Spirit)   *see* Newport Ch Ch *Mon*
CAERNARFON (St Mary)   *see* Llanbeblig w Caernarfon and Betws Garmon etc *Ban*

CAERPHILLY (St Martin) (St Catherine) (St Andrew) *Llan 8*
R R DONKIN, **C** S A ROGERS, **NSM** S G BROWN
CAERSWS (St Mary) *see* Llanwnnog and Caersws w Carno
Ban
**CAERWENT (St Stephen and St Tathan) w Dinham and Llanfair
Discoed and Shirenewton w Newchurch** *Mon 3*
P-in-c W C INGLE-GILLIS, **NSM** E N M DAVIES
CAERWYS (St Michael) and Bodfari *St As 2*
NSM G L HUGHES
CALDICOT (St Mary) *Mon 3* **TR** L HARRISON,
TV D RICHARDS, **C** D C BOUTFLOWER, A M CHURCH,
NSM H J DAVIES
CALLWEN (St John the Baptist) *see* Cwmtawe Uchaf *S & B*
CAMROSE (St Ishmael) *St D 4* **P-in-c** P BOYLE
CANTON Cardiff (St Luke) *Llan 1* **TR** M R PREECE,
TV M P COLTON
CANTON (St Catherine) *Llan 1* **V** *vacant* (029) 2038 2796
CANTON (St John) *Llan 1* **R** *vacant*
CANTREF (St Mary) *see* Llanfrynach and Cantref w
Llanhamlach *S & B*
CAPEL (Dewi Sant) *see* Llanwrda and
Manordeilo *St D*
CAPEL BANGOR (Church) *see* Elerch w Penrhyncoch w Capel
Bangor and Goginan *St D*
CAPEL COELBREN (Capel Coelbren) *see* Cwmtawe Uchaf
S & B
CAPEL COLMAN (St Colman) *see* Maenordeifi Gp *St D*
CAPEL CYNON (St Cynon) *see* Llanarth and Capel Cynon w
Talgarreg etc *St D*
CAPEL DEWI (St David) *see* Llanfihangel-ar-arth w Capel
Dewi *St D*
CAPEL GARMON *see* LLanrwst *St As*
CAPEL IFAN (St John the Baptist) *see* Gwendraeth Fawr *St D*
CAPEL LLANILLTERNE (St Ellteyrn) *see* Pentyrch w Capel
Llanillterne *Llan*
CAPEL MAIR *see* Llangeler w Pen-Boyr *St D*
CAPEL NEWYDD (St Paul) *see* Blaenavon w Capel Newydd
Mon
CAPEL TYGWYDD *see* Maenordeifi Gp *St D*
CAPEL-Y-FFIN (St Mary) *see* Hay w Llanigon and Capel-y-
Ffin *S & B*
CAPEL-Y-GROES *see* E Carmarthen *St D*
CARDIFF (Christ Church) Roath Park *Llan 1*
P-in-c R H SPENCER
CARDIFF City Parish (St John the Baptist) (St James the Great)
Llan 1 **V** E L GRIFFITHS
CARDIFF (Dewi Sant) *Llan 1* **V** D C LLOYD
CARDIFF (St Andrew and St Teilo) *see* Cathays *Llan*
CARDIFF (St Luke) *see* Canton Cardiff *Llan*
**CARDIFF (St Mary) (St Stephen) w Cardiff (St Dyfrig and
St Samson)** *Llan 1* **V** G J FRANCIS, **C** B ANDREWS
CARDIFF (St Michael and All Angels) *see* Cathays *Llan*
CARDIGAN (St Mary) w Mwnt and Y Ferwig w Llangoedmor
St D 5 **V** *vacant* (01239) 612722
CAREW (St Mary) *St D 3* **TR** N B THOMAS, **TV** T N BARBER,
S C RAYNER
CARMARTHEN (St David) (Christ Church) *St D 10*
V P H B THOMAS, **NSM** M K THORLEY
CARMARTHEN, EAST (St Peter) (St John the Evangelist)
St D 10 **TR** L L RICHARDSON, **C** W J GIBBONS
CARMEL (Eglwys Fair) *see* Gors-las *St D*
CARNHEDRYN *see* Dewisland *St D*
CARNO (St John) *see* Llanwnnog and Caersws w Carno *Ban*
CARROG (St Ffraid) *see* Corwen w Llangar, Glyndyfrdwy etc
St As
CASCOB (St Michael) *see* Knighton, Norton, Whitton, Pilleth
and Cascob *S & B*
CASTELL DWYRAN *see* Llanfallteg w Castell Dwyran *St D*
CASTELLAN *see* Maenordeifi Gp *St D*
CASTLE BYTHE *see* Letterston w Llanfair Nant-y-Gof etc
St D
CASTLE CAEREINION (St Garmon) *see* Welshpool, Castle
Caereinion and Pool Quay *St As*
CASTLEMARTIN (St Michael and All Angels) *see* Monkton
St D
CATHAYS (St Andrew and St Teilo) (St Michael and All Angels)
Llan 1 **P-in-c** C R DOWNS
CATHEDINE (St Michael) *see* Llyn Safaddan *S & B*
CATHEINIOG *St D 13* **V** W R HUGHES
CEFN (St Mary) (All Saints) w Trefnant w Tremeirchion *St As 2*
R C E MANSLEY, **NSM** P WYKES
CEFN COED (St John the Baptist) w Vaynor *S & B 1*
V B H JOHN
CEFN CRIBWR (St Colman) *see* Kenfig Hill *Llan*
CEFN FOREST (St Thomas) *see* Fleur-de-Lis *Mon*

CEFN HENGOED (St Anne) *see* Gelligaer *Llan*
CEFN PENNAR (St Illtyd) *see* Mountain Ash and Miskin *Llan*
CEFNLLYS (St Michael) *see* Llandrindod w Cefnllys and
Disserth *S & B*
CEIRCHIOG (St David) *see* Valley w Llechylched and
Caergeiliog *Ban*
CELLAN (All Saints) *see* Bro Teifi Sarn Helen *St D*
CEMAES *see* Llanfechell w Bodewryd w Rhosbeirio etc *Ban*
CEMAIS (St Tydecho) *see* Bro Ddyfi Uchaf *Ban*
CENARTH (St Llawddog) *see* Newcastle Emlyn w Llandyfriog
and Troedyraur etc *St D*
CERRIGCEINWEN (St Ceinwen) *see* Trefdraeth w Aberffraw,
Llangadwaladr etc *Ban*
**CERRIGYDRUDION (St Mary Magdalene) w Llanfihangel
Glyn Myfyr, Pentrefoelas and Ysbyty Ifan** *St As 17*
P-in-c R J PEARCE
CHEPSTOW (St Mary) *Mon 3* **V** C J BLANCHARD
CHERITON *see* Monkton *St D*
CHERITON (St Cadoc) *see* Llangennith w Llanmadoc and
Cheriton *S & B*
CHIRK (St Mary) *St As 14* **V** A J REES
**CIL-Y-CWM (St Michael) and Ystrad-ffin w Rhandirmwyn
Llanfair-ar-y-Bryn** *St D 13* **NSM** W FOULGER
**CILCAIN (St Mary), Gwernaffield, Llanferres, Rhyd-y-mwyn
and Nannerch** *St As 16* **R** A W A COPPING,
C P K BETTINSON, **NSM** J STEPHENS
CILCENNIN (Holy Trinity) *see* Llanfihangel Ystrad and
Cilcennin w Trefilan etc *St D*
CILFYNYDD (St Luke) *see* Pontypridd St Matt and Cilfynydd
w Llanwynno *Llan*
**CILGERRAN (St Llawddog) w Bridell and Llantwyd and
Eglwyswrw** *St D 5* **R** E L THOMAS
CILGWYN (St Mary) *see* Newport w Cilgwyn and Nevern and
Y Beifil etc *St D*
CILIAU AERON (St Michael) *see* Llanerch Aeron w Ciliau
Aeron and Dihewyd etc *St D*
CILYBEBYLL (St John the Evangelist) *Llan 6* **R** M PERRY
CLARBESTON (St Martin of Tours) *see* Wiston w Walton E
and Clarbeston *St D*
CLOCAENOG (St Foddhyd) and Gyffylliog *St As 3*
P-in-c R W CARTER
CLUNDERWEN (St David) *see* Whitland w Cyffig and Henllan
Amgoed etc *St D*
CLYDACH (St John the Evangelist) (St Mary) (St Michael)
S & B 7 **V** L J TAYLOR
CLYDACH VALE (St Thomas) *see* Tonypandy w Clydach Vale
Llan
CLYDAU (St Clydai) *see* Crymych Gp *St D*
CLYNNOG FAWR (St Beuno) *see* Llanaelhaearn w Clynnog
Fawr *Ban*
CLYRO (St Michael and All Angels) *see* Glasbury and Llowes w
Clyro and Betws *S & B*
CLYTHA *see* Llanddewi Rhydderch w Llangattock-juxta-Usk
etc *Mon*
COCKETT (St Peter) *see* Swansea St Pet *S & B*
COEDKERNEW *see* Marshfield and Peterstone Wentloog etc
Mon
COEDYPAEN (Christchurch) *see* Llangybi and Coedypaen w
Llanbadoc *Mon*
COETMOR *see* Glanogwen and Llanllechid w St Ann's and
Pentir *Ban*
COITY (St Mary), Nolton and Brackla *Llan 4* **R** M KOMOR,
C C J REES, **NSM** S J BEVERLY
COLVA (St David) *see* New Radnor and Llanfihangel
Nantmelan etc *S & B*
COLWINSTON (St Michael) *see* Colwinston, Llandow and
Llysworney *Llan*
COLWINSTON (St Michael), Llandow and Llysworney *Llan 7*
R P M LEONARD
COLWYN *S & B 2* **P-in-c** J R F KIRLEW
COLWYN (St Catherine) (St John the Baptist) and Llanelian
St As 6 **R** J P ATACK, **NSM** G COOPER
COLWYN BAY (St Paul) (St Andrew) (St David) w Brynymaen
St As 6 **V** N H WILLIAMS, **C** V A BURTON
COMINS COCH *see* Llanbadarn Fawr *St D*
CONNAH'S QUAY (St Mark) (St David's Mission Church)
St As 16 **V** P H VARAH, **C** R EVANS, **NSM** B P JONES
CONWY (St Mary and All Saints) w Gyffin *Ban 2* **V** P R JONES
CORRIS (Holy Trinity) *see* Pennal w Corris and Esgairgeiliog
Ban
**CORWEN (St Mael and St Sulien) w Llangar, Glyndyfrdwy and
Llansantffraid Glyn Dyfrdwy** *St As 17* **V** *vacant*
COSHESTON (St Michael) *see* Carew *St D*
COWBRIDGE (Holy Cross) *Llan 7* **TR** D G BELCHER,
NSM D R BOULT

COYCHURCH (St Crallo), Llangan and St Mary Hill *Llan 4*
P-in-c V HAMER
COYTREAHEN (St Thomas) *see* Llansantffraid, Bettws and Aberkenfig *Llan*
CRAI (St Ilid) *see* Defynnog, Llandilo'r Fan, Llanulid, Llywel etc *S & B*
CREGRINA (St David) *see* Colwyn *S & B*
CRIBYN (St Silin) *see* Llanfihangel Ystrad and Cilcennin w Trefilan etc *St D*
CRICCIETH (St Catherine) and Treflys w Llanystumdwy w Llangybi and Llanarmon *Ban 11*   R *vacant* (01766) 523183 *or* (01248) 354999
CRICKADARN (St Mary) *see* Aberedw w Llandeilo Graban and Llanbadarn etc *S & B*
CRICKHOWELL (St Edmund) w Cwmdu and Tretower *S & B 3*
V B LETSON
CRIGGION (St Michael) *see* Llandysilio and Penrhos and Llandrinio etc *St As*
CRINDAU (All Saints) *see* Newport All SS *Mon*
CRINOW (St Teilo) *see* Narberth w Mounton w Robeston Wathen etc *St D*
CROESCEILIOG (St Mary) *see* Cwmbran *Mon*
CROESERW (St Clare) *see* Glyncorrwg and Upper Afan Valley *Llan*
CROSS HANDS (St Anne) *see* Gors-las *St D*
CROSS INN (Holy Trinity) *see* Llanllwchaearn and Llanina *St D*
CROSS KEYS (St Catherine) *see* Risca *Mon*
CROSSGATES *see* Lower Ithon Valley *S & B*
CRUGYBYDDAR (St Peter) *see* Beguildy and Heyope and Llangynllo and Bleddfa *S & B*
CRUNWERE (St Elidyr) *see* St Issell's and Amroth w Crunwere *St D*
CRYMYCH Group, The *St D 14*   V J R THOMAS
CRYNANT (Chapel of Ease) *see* Dulais Valley *Llan*
CRYNANT (St Margaret) *as above*
CWM (St Mael and St Sulien) *see* Dyserth and Trelawnyd and Cwm *St As*
CWM (St Paul) *see* Ebbw Vale *Mon*
CWM-COCH (St Mark) *see* Llandybie *St D*
CWMAFAN (St Michael) *Llan 5*   P-in-c H M O'SHEA
CWMAMAN (Christ Church) *St D 12*   V A J MAUNDER
CWMAMAN (St Joseph) *see* Aberaman and Abercwmboi w Cwmaman *Llan*
CWMANN (St James) *see* Pencarreg and Llanycrwys *St D*
CWMAVON (St Michael) *see* Cwmafan *Llan*
CWMBACH (St Mary Magdalene) *Llan 9*   P-in-c C B W SMITH
CWMBACH LLECHRYD (St John the Divine) *see* Upper Wye *S & B*
CWMBRAN (St Gabriel) *Mon 9*   TR M J PHILLIPS, TV A J TURNER, R LANGTON, Hon C G W OPPERMAN
CWMBWRLA (St Luke) *see* Manselton and Cwmbwrla *S & B*
CWMCARN (St John the Evangelist) *see* Abercarn and Cwmcarn *Mon*
CWMCARVAN (St Clement) *see* Rockfield and Dingestow Gp *Mon*
CWMDARE (St Luke) *see* Aberdare St Fagan *Llan*
CWMDDAUDDWR (St Bride) *see* Gwastedyn *S & B*
CWMDDAUDDWR (St Winifred) *as above*
CWMDU (St Michael the Archangel) *see* Crickhowell w Cwmdu and Tretower *S & B*
CWMDUAD (St Alban) *see* Cynwyl Elfed w Newchurch and Trelech a'r Betws *St D*
CWMFFRWD (St Anne) *see* Llangunnor w Cwmffrwd *St D*
CWMFFRWDOER (All Saints) *see* Pontypool *Mon*
CWMLLYNFELL (St Margaret) *see* Brynaman w Cwmllynfell *St D*
CWMPARC (St George) *see* Pen Rhondda Fawr *Llan*
CWMTAWE UCHAF *S & B 7*   P-in-c A J BROOKFIELD
CWMTILLERY (St Paul) *see* Abertillery w Cwmtillery w Llanhilleth etc *Mon*
CWMYOY (St Martin) *see* Llanfihangel Crucorney w Oldcastle etc *Mon*
CWRT-HENRI (St Mary) *see* Catheiniog *St D*
CYDWELI (St Mary) (St Teilo) and Llandyfaelog *St D 11*
V J H A JAMES,   NSM A R MORLEY-JONES
CYFFIG (St Cyffig) *see* Whitland w Cyffig and Henllan Amgoed etc *St D*
CYMAU (All Saints) *see* Llanfynydd *St As*
CYMMER (St John the Evangelist) *see* Porth Newydd *Llan*
CYMMER AFAN (St John the Evangelist) *see* Glyncorrwg and Upper Afan Valley *Llan*
CYNCOED (All Saints) (St Edeyrn) *Mon 5*   TR S G WILLSON, TV S G CARBY, A TEMPLE-WILLIAMS
CYNWYL ELFED (St Cynwyl) w Newchurch and Trelech a'r Betws *St D 10*   C C J DAVIES

CYNWYL GAEO (St Cynwyl) w Llansawel and Talley *St D 13*
V *vacant*
DAFEN (St Michael and All Angels) *St D 11*   V G C POWELL
DALE (St James) and St Brides w Marloes *St D 4*
P-in-c L J EVANS
DAN YR EPPYNT *S & B 1*   V N HOOK
DAROWEN (St Tudur) *see* Bro Ddyfi Uchaf *Ban*
DEFYNNOG (St Cynog) and Llandilo'r Fan and Llanulid and Llywel and Traean-glas *S & B 1*   V M P WILDING
DEGANWY (All Saints) *see* Rhos-Cystennin *St As*
DENBIGH (St Mary) (St Marcella) (St David) *St As 2*
R J P SMITH
DENIO (St Peter) w Abererch *Ban 11*   V J E GOURDIE
DERI (St Peter) *see* Bargoed and Deri w Brithdir *Llan*
DERWEN (St Mary) *see* Llanfair DC, Derwen, Llanelidan and Efenechtyd *St As*
DEVAUDEN (St James) *see* St Arvans w Penterry, Itton, Devauden etc *Mon*
DEWISLAND (Cathedral of St David and St Andrew) *St D 2*
TR D J R LEAN,   TV J S BENNETT, D P DAVIES,   C G M REID, NSM M I PLANT
DIHEWYD (St Vitalis) *see* Llanerch Aeron w Ciliau Aeron and Dihewyd etc *St D*
DINAS (Mission) and Penygraig w Williamstown *Llan 12*
V C R LEWIS-JENKINS
DINAS (St Brynach) *see* Newport w Cilgwyn and Nevern and Y Beifil etc *St D*
DINGESTOW (St Dingad) *see* Rockfield and Dingestow Gp *Mon*
DINHAM *see* Caerwent w Dinham and Llanfair Discoed etc *Mon*
DINMAEL (St Catherine) *see* Betws Gwerful Goch w Llangwm w Llawrybetws *St As*
DISSERTH (St Cewydd) *see* Llandrindod w Cefnllys and Disserth *S & B*
DOLBENMAEN (St Mary) *see* Porthmadoc and Ynyscynhaearn and Dolbenmaen *Ban*
DOLFOR (St Paul) *see* Kerry, Llanmerewig, Dolfor and Mochdre *St As*
DOLGARROG (St Mary) *see* Caerhun and Llangelynnin and Llanbedr-y-Cennin *Ban*
DOLGELLAU (St Mary) w Llanfachreth and Brithdir and Bryncoedifor and Llanelltud *Ban 12*   R R B D REES, NSM M G JONES
DOLWYDDELAN (St Gwyddelan) *see* Betws-y-Coed and Capel Curig w Penmachno etc *Ban*
DOWLAIS (St John the Baptist) (Christ Church) and Penydarren *Llan 10*   R K J HARMAN
DULAIS VALLEY *Llan 6*   V S BARNES
DWYGYFYLCHI or Penmaenmawr (St Gwynin) (St Seiriol) (St David) *Ban 2*   V D M OUTRAM
DYFFRYN *see* Llanenddwyn w Llanddwywe, Llanbedr w Llandanwg *Ban*
DYFFRYN (St Matthew) *Llan 6*   V S J BODYCOMBE
DYFFRYN HONDDU (St Cynog) *see* Dan yr Eppynt *S & B*
DYSERTH (St Bridget) (St Michael) (St Mael and St Sulien) and Trelawnyd and Cwm *St As 1*   V R W ROWLAND
EBBW VALE (Christchurch) (St John the Baptist) *Mon 7*
TR G J WAGGETT,   TV P J ABBOTT,   NSM P V GRIFFITHS
EDERN (St Edern) *see* Nefyn w Tudweiliog w Llandudwen w Edern *Ban*
EFENECHTYD (St Michael) *see* Llanfair DC, Derwen, Llanelidan and Efenechtyd *St As*
EGLWYS-FACH (St Michael) *see* Borth and Eglwys-fach w Llangynfelyn *St D*
EGLWYS FAIR GLYN-TAF *see* Whitland w Cyffig and Henllan Amgoed etc *St D*
EGLWYS GYMYN (St Margaret) *see* Pendine w Llanmiloe and Eglwys Gymyn w Marros *St D*
EGLWYS NEWYDD *see* Grwp Bro Ystwyth a Mynach *St D*
EGLWYS OEN DUW *see* Blaenau Irfon *S & B*
EGLWYSFACH *see* Llansantffraid Glan Conwy and Eglwysbach *St As*
EGLWYSILAN (St Ilan) *Llan 8*   P-in-c S M REES
EGLWYSRHOS (St Eleri and St Mary) *see* Rhos-Cystennin *St As*
EGLWYSWEN *St D 5*   V *vacant*
EGLWYSWRW (St Cristiolus) *see* Cilgerran w Bridell and Llantwyd and Eglwyswrw *St D*
ELERCH (St Peter) w Penrhyncoch w Capel Bangor and Goginan *St D 9*   V J P LIVINGSTONE
ELY (St David) *see* Caerau w Ely *Llan*
ELY (St Timothy) *as above*
ERBISTOCK (St Hilary) *see* Overton and Erbistock and Penley *St As*

ESCLUSHAM (Holy Trinity)   *see* Wrexham *St As*
ESGAIRGEILIOG   *see* Pennal w Corris and Esgairgeiliog *Ban*
EVANCOYD (St Peter)   *see* New Radnor and Llanfihangel
   Nantmelan etc *S & B*
EWENNY (St Michael) w St Brides Major *Llan 4*
   P-in-c P G MORRIS,   **NSM** M J SPENCE
EYTON (St Deiniol)   *see* Bangor Monachorum, Worthenbury
   and Marchwiel *St As*
FAIRBOURNE (St Cynon)   *see* Arthog w Fairbourne w
   Llangelynnin w Rhoslefain *Ban*
FAIRHILL   *see* Cwmbran *Mon*
FAIRWATER (St Peter) *Llan 2*   **V** C P SUTTON
FAIRWATER (St Peter)   *see* Cwmbran *Mon*
FAWR   *see* Llandeilo Fawr and Taliaris *St D*
FELIN-FOEL (Holy Trinity)   *see* Llanelli *St D*
FELIN-GWM (St John)   *see* Llanegwad w Llanfihangel Uwch
   Gwili *St D*
FELINDRE (St Barnabas)   *see* Llangeler w Pen-Boyr *St D*
FERNDALE (St Dunstan)   *see* Rhondda Fach Uchaf *Llan*
FERRYSIDE (St Thomas)   *see* St Ishmael's w Llan-saint and
   Ferryside *St D*
FFESTINIOG (St Michael)   *see* Llanffestiniog w Blaenau
   Ffestiniog etc *Ban*
FFYNNONGROYW (All Saints)   *see* Llanasa and
   Ffynnongroew *St As*
**FISHGUARD (St Mary) w Llanychar and Pontfaen w Morfil and
   Llanychlwydog** *St D 2*   **V** D A T MACGREGOR,
   NSM J M ANNIS
FLEMINGSTON (St Michael)   *see* Cowbridge *Llan*
FLEUR-DE-LIS (St David) *Mon 6*   **P-in-c** T MORGAN
FLINT (St Mary) (St Thomas) (St David) *St As 4*   **R** B HARVEY
FOCHRIW (St Mary and St Andrew)   *see* Pontlottyn w Fochriw
   Llan
FORD (Church)   *see* Nolton w Roch and St Lawrence w Ford etc
   St D
FORDEN (St Michael)   *see* Montgomery and Forden and
   Llandyssil *St As*
FREYSTROP (St Justinian)   *see* Llangwm w Freystrop and
   Johnston *St D*
FRON (Mission Church)   *see* Berriew *St As*
FRONCYSYLLTE (St David)   *see* Chirk *St As*
FRONGOCH   *see* Bala *St As*
FURNACE (Mission Church)   *see* Llanelli *St D*
**GABALFA (St Mark) (Highfields Centre and Mynachdy
   Institute)** *Llan 1*   **V** R M CAPPER,   **C** J M WIDDESS,
   NSM R H ALDIS, G M DALLOW
GAERWEN   *see* Llanfihangel Ysgeifiog w Llangristiolus etc *Ban*
GARNDIFFAITH (St John the Evangelist)   *see* Blaenavon w
   Capel Newydd *Mon*
**GARTHBEIBIO (St Tydecho) w Llanerfyl w Llangadfan w
   Llanfihangel yn Nghwynfa w Llwydiarth** *St As 8*
   V D E B FRANCIS
GARTHBRENGY (St David)   *see* Dan yr Eppynt *S & B*
GARTHELI (St Gartheli)   *see* Bro Teifi Sarn Helen *St D*
GAUFRON (St David)   *see* Gwastedyn *S & B*
GELLIGAER (St Catwg) (St Margaret) (St Anne) *Llan 8*
   R A H STEVENS,   **NSM** S A STEVENS
GILESTON (St Giles)   *see* Llantwit Major *Llan*
GILFACH GOCH (St Barnabas)   *see* Tonyrefail w Gilfach Goch
   Llan
GILVACH (St Margaret)   *see* Gelligaer *Llan*
GLADWESTRY (St Mary)   *see* New Radnor and Llanfihangel
   Nantmelan etc *S & B*
GLAIS (St Paul)   *see* Llansamlet *S & B*
GLAN ELY (Resurrection) *Llan 2*   **P-in-c** J GOULD
GLANAMAN (St Margaret)   *see* Cwmaman *St D*
GLANGWRYNE (Mission Church)   *see* Llangenni and
   Llanbedr Ystrad Yw w Patricio *S & B*
**GLANOGWEN (Christ Church) and Llanllechid w St Ann's and
   Pentir** *Ban 5*   **V** N C WILLIAMS,   **C** J L HOOD,
   NSM C E MCCREA
GLANTAWE (St Margaret) (St Peter) *S & B 11*
   V C P G DICKSON
**GLASBURY (St Peter) (All Saints) and Llowes w Clyro and
   Betws** *S & B 4*   **V** D E THOMAS
GLASCOED (St Michael)   *see* Mamhilad w Monkswood and
   Glascoed Chapel *Mon*
GLASCOMBE (St David)   *see* Colwyn *S & B*
GLYN   *see* Brecon St David w Llanspyddid and Llanilltyd *S & B*
GLYNCOCH (All Saints' Church Centre)   *see* Pontypridd St
   Matt and Cilfynydd w Llanwynno *Llan*
**GLYNCORRWG (St John the Baptist) (St Clare) (St Thomas)
   and Upper Afan Valley** *Llan 5*   **V** *vacant* (01639) 851301
GLYNDYFRDWY (St Thomas)   *see* Corwen w Llangar,
   Glyndyfrdwy etc *St As*

GLYNTAFF (St Mary) *Llan 11*   **V** *vacant* (01443) 402535
GOETRE (St Peter) w Llanover *Mon 4*   **P-in-c** S N JAMES
GOGINAN (Church)   *see* Elerch w Penrhyncoch w Capel
   Bangor and Goginan *St D*
GOLDCLIFFE (St Mary Magdalen)   *see* Magor *Mon*
GOODWICK (St Peter)   *see* Llanwnda, Goodwick w
   Manorowen and Llanstinan *St D*
GORS-LAS (St Lleian) *St D 12*   **V** M L REES,   **NSM** J B JONES
GORSEDD (St Paul) w Brynford, Ysgeifiog and Whitford *St As 4*
   V G BECKETT,   **Par Dn** S M MORIARTY
GORSEINON (St Catherine) *S & B 9*   **V** M L COX,
   C D S DEMPSEY,   **NSM** A P DAVIES
GOVILON (Christchurch) w Llanfoist w Llanelen *Mon 1*
   P-in-c J H WINSTON,   **NSM** J L HUGHES
GOWER, SOUTH WEST *S & B 8*   **V** J W GRIFFIN,
   Hon C H M EVANS
GOWERTON (St John the Evangelist) *S & B 9*   **V** D ROBERTS
GRAIG (St John)   *see* Rhydyfelin w Graig *Llan*
GRANDSTON (St Catherine)   *see* Mathry w St Edren's and
   Grandston etc *St D*
GRANGETOWN (St Paul) *Llan 1*   **V** G J FRANCIS
GREENWAY (St Hilary)   *see* Rumney *Mon*
GRESFORD (All Saints)   *see* Holt and Gresford *St As*
GRIFFITHSTOWN (St Hilda) *Mon 9*   **V** P A GOLLEDGE,
   NSM N J TAYLOR
GROESWEN (St David)   *see* Pentyrch w Capel Llanillterne *Llan*
GRONANT (St Winifred)   *see* Llanasa and Ffynnongroew *St As*
**GROSMONT (St Nicholas) and Skenfrith and Llangattock
   Lingoed and Llanfair Chapel** *Mon 1*   **P-in-c** J PROSSER
**GRWP BRO YSTWYTH A MYNACH: Llanfihangel-y-
   Creuddyn w Llanafan-y-Trawscoed w Llanwnnws w Ysbyty
   Ystwyth w Ysbyty Cynfyn w Lantrisant w Eglwys Newydd**
   St D 9   **NSM** I E ROSE
GUILSFIELD (St Aelhaiarn) w Buttington *St As 10*
   V R A BIRD
GUMFRESTON (St Lawrence)   *see* Tenby *St D*
GWAENYSGOR   *see* Meliden and Gwaenysgor *St As*
GWASTEDYN *S & B 5*   **P-in-c** P BROOKS
GWAUN-CAE-GURWEN *St D 12*   **V** *vacant* (01269) 822430
GWEHELOG   *see* Usk and Gwehelog w Llantrisant w
   Llanllowell *Mon*
GWENDDWR (St Dubricius)   *see* Aberedw w Llandeilo
   Graban and Llanbadarn etc *S & B*
GWENDRAETH FAWR *St D 11*   **V** D R PAYNE
GWENLLI (St Mark)   *see* Llanarth and Capel Cynon w
   Talgarreg etc *St D*
GWERNAFFIELD (Holy Trinity)   *see* Cilcain, Gwernaffield,
   Llanferres etc *St As*
GWERNAMYNYDD (St Mark)   *see* Mold *St As*
GWERNESNEY (St Michael)   *see* Llangwm Uchaf and
   Llangwm Isaf w Gwernesney etc *Mon*
GWERNFFRWD (St David)   *see* Llanrhidian w Llanyrnewydd
   S & B
GWERSYLLT (Holy Trinity) *St As 12*   **V** S M HUYTON,
   C D J SWANN
GWYDDELWERN (St Beuno) *St As*   **P-in-c** H FENTON
GWYNFE (All Saints)   *see* Llangadog and Gwynfe w
   Llanddeusant *St D*
GWYTHERIN (St Winifred)   *see* Petryal and Betws yn Rhos
   St As
GYFFIN (St Benedict)   *see* Conwy w Gyffin *Ban*
GYFFYLLIOG (St Mary)   *see* Clocaenog and Gyffylliog *St As*
HAFOD (St John)   *see* Cen Swansea *S & B*
HAKIN (St Mary)   *see* Hubberston *St D*
HALKYN (St Mary the Virgin) w Caerfallwch w Rhesycae
   St As 4   **P-in-c** H N BURGESS
HANMER (St Chad) and Bronington and Bettisfield *St As 11*
   P-in-c C HUGHES
**HARLECH (St Tanwg) and Llanfair-juxta-Harlech w
   Llanfihangel-y-Traethau and Llandecwyn** *Ban 8*   **V** *vacant*
   (01766) 780383
HAROLDSTON ST ISSELLS (St Issell)   *see* Haverfordwest
   St D
HAROLDSTON WEST (St Madog)   *see* Walton W w Talbenny
   and Haroldston W *St D*
HAVERFORDWEST (St Martin) (St Mary) *St D 4*
   V P R MACKNESS,   **C** H A M WILLIAMS
HAWARDEN (St Deiniol) (Holy Spirit) *St As 13*
   TV P R-M DE G GOWER, I D FORSTER,   **C** G CHIGUMIRA
HAY (St Mary) (St John) w Llanigon and Capel-y-Ffin *S & B 4*
   V R D WILLIAMS
HAYSCASTLE (St Mary)   *see* Nolton w Roch and St Lawrence
   w Ford etc *St D*
HENDY (St David)   *see* Llangennech and Hendy *St D*
HENEGLWYS (St Llwydian)   *see* Llandrygarn w Bodwrog and
   Heneglwys etc *Ban*

HENFYNYW (St David) w Aberaeron and Llanddewi Aberarth w Llanbadarn Trefeglwys *St D 7* **V** J P LEWIS, **C** S D EDWARDS

HENLLAN (St David) *see* Llandysul w Bangor Teifi w Henllan etc *St D*

HENLLAN (St Sadwrn) and Llannefydd and Bylchau *St As 2* **R** J P P WILLIAMS

HENLLAN AMGOED (St David) *see* Whitland w Cyffig and Henllan Amgoed etc *St D*

HENLLYS (St Peter) *see* Cwmbran *Mon*

HENRY'S MOAT (St Bernard) *see* Maenclochog and New Moat etc *St D*

HEOL-Y-CYW (St Paul) *see* Llanilid w Pencoed *Llan*

HERBRANDSTON (St Mary) and Hasguard w St Ishmael's *St D 4* **P-in-c** L J EVANS

HEYOPE (St David) *see* Beguildy and Heyope and Llangynllo and Bleddfa *S & B*

HIGH CROSS (St Anne) *see* Bassaleg *Mon*

HIRWAUN (St Lleurwg) (St Winifred) *Llan 9* **V** B L JONES

HODGESTON (Church) *see* Monkton *St D*

HOLT (St Chad) and Gresford *St As 12* **V** J T HUGHES

HOLYHEAD (St Cybi) (Morawelon) (St Ffraid) (St Gwenfaen) *Ban 3* **R** C A LLEWELLYN, **TV** J R BAILEY

HOLYWELL (St James) (Holy Trinity) *St As 4* **V** J D P LOMAS

HOPE (Parish Church) *St As 13* **R** M K SNELLGROVE

HOWEY (St David) *see* Llandrindod w Cefnllys and Disserth *S & B*

HUBBERSTON (St David) (Holy Spirit) *St D 4* **R** *vacant*

HUNDLETON (St David) *see* Monkton *St D*

ILSTON (St Illtyd) w Pennard *S & B 8* **V** *vacant*

IRFON VALLEY *S & B 2* **P-in-c** L ASHDOWN

ISYCOED (St Paul) *see* Rossett and Isycoed *St As*

ITHON VALLEY, LOWER *S & B 5* **R** A G LOAT, **C** N FINLAY

ITHON VALLEY, UPPER *S & B 5* **V** A G LOAT, **C** N FINLAY

ITTON (St Deiniol) *see* St Arvans w Penterry, Itton, Devauden etc *Mon*

JAMESTON *see* Carew *St D*

JEFFREYSTON (St Jeffrey) w Reynoldston and Loveston and Martletwy w Lawrenny and Yerbeston *St D 3* **R** N P DAVIES

JOHNSTON (St Peter) *see* Llangwm w Freystrop and Johnston *St D*

JORDANSTON (St Cawrda) *see* Mathry w St Edren's and Grandston etc *St D*

KEMEYS COMMANDER (All Saints) *see* Bettws Newydd w Trostrey etc *Mon*

KENFIG *see* Pyle w Kenfig *Llan*

KENFIG HILL (St Theodore) (St Colman) *Llan 5* **P-in-c** J R H DURLEY

KERRY (St Michael), Llanmerewig, Dolfor and Mochdre *St As 7* **V** M W A CHADWICK

KILGETTY *see* Begelly w Ludchurch and E Williamston *St D*

KILGWRRWG (Holy Cross) *see* St Arvans w Penterry, Itton, Devauden etc *Mon*

KILLAY (St Hilary) (St Martin) *S & B 6* **V** T J WILLIAMS

KILVEY (All Saints) *see* Swansea St Thos and Kilvey *S & B*

KNELSTON *see* SW Gower *S & B*

KNIGHTON (St Edward) and Norton and Whitton and Pilleth and Cascob *S & B 5* **V** *vacant* (01547) 528566

LALESTON (St David) and Merthyr Mawr *Llan 4* **V** E J EVANS, **NSM** J M LEWIS

LAMBSTON (St Ishmael) *see* Haverfordwest *St D*

LAMPETER PONT STEFFAN (St Peter) *see* Bro Teifi Sarn Helen *St D*

LAMPETER VELFREY (St Peter) and Llanddewi Velfrey *St D 14* **P-in-c** D E HAMMON

LAMPHEY (St Faith and St Tyfei) *see* Monkton *St D*

LANDORE (St Paul) w Treboeth *S & B 10* **V** D JONES

LANGSTONE (not known) *see* Magor *Mon*

LAUGHARNE (St Martin) w Llansadwrnen and Llandawke *St D 14* **V** D L R BROWNRIDGE

LAVERNOCK (St Lawrence) *see* Penarth and Llandough *Llan*

LAWRENNY (St Caradog) *see* Jeffreyston w Reynoldston and Loveston etc *St D*

LECKWITH *see* Penarth and Llandough *Llan*

LETTERSTON (St Giles) w Llanfair Nant-y-Gof and Puncheston w Little Newcastle and Castle Bythe *St D 2* **R** R GRIFFITHS

LISVANE (St Denys) *Llan 1* **V** C E BURR

LISWERRY *see* Newport St Andr *Mon*

LITTLE NEWCASTLE (St Peter) *see* Letterston w Llanfair Nant-y-Gof etc *St D*

LLAN-GAN *see* Whitland w Cyffig and Henllan Amgoed etc *St D*

LLAN-LLWCH (St Mary) w Llangain and Llangynog *St D 10* **V** R I PROTHEROE

LLAN-NON (St Non) *see* Trisant *St D*

LLAN-SAINT (All Saints) *see* St Ishmael's w Llan-saint and Ferryside *St D*

LLAN-Y-BRI (Holy Trinity) *see* Llansteffan and Llan-y-bri etc *St D*

LLANABER (St Mary) (St John) (St David) w Caerdeon *Ban 8* **R** K G HORSWELL, **NSM** L R BAILY

LLANAELHAEARN (St Aelhaiarn) w Clynnog Fawr *Ban 1* **R** I THOMAS

LLANAFAN FAWR (St Afan) *see* Upper Wye *S & B*

LLANAFAN-Y-TRAWSCOED (St Afan) *see* Grwp Bro Ystwyth a Mynach *St D*

LLANALLGO (St Gallo) *see* Llaneugrad w Llanallgo and Penrhosllugwy etc *Ban*

LLANANNO (St Anno) *see* Upper Ithon Valley *S & B*

LLANARMON (St Garmon) *see* Criccieth and Treflys w Llanystumdwy etc *Ban*

LLANARMON DYFFRYN CEIRIOG (St Garmon) *see* Llansantffraid Glyn Ceirog and Llanarmon etc *St As*

LLANARMON MYNYD (St Garmon) *see* Llanrhaeadr ym Mochnant etc *St As*

LLANARMON YN IAL (St Garmon) *see* Llanbedr DC, Llangynhafal, Llanychan etc *St As*

LLANARTH (St David) (St Teilo) and Capel Cynon w Talgarreg and (St Mark) *St D 7* **V** C L BOLTON

LLANARTH (St Teilo) *see* Llanddewi Rhydderch w Llangattock-juxta-Usk etc *Mon*

LLANARTHNE (St David) and Llanddarog *St D 10* **P-in-c** A W EVANS

LLANASA (St Asaph and St Cyndeyrn) (St Winifred) and Ffynnongroew *St As 4* **V** S ELLIOTT

LLANBABO (St Pabo) *see* Valley w Llechylched and Caergeiliog *Ban*

LLANBADARN FAWR (St Padarn) *St D 9* **V** *vacant* (01970) 623368

LLANBADARN FAWR (St Padarn) *see* Lower Ithon Valley *S & B*

LLANBADARN FYNYDD (St Padarn) *see* Upper Ithon Valley *S & B*

LLANBADARN ODWYN (St Padarn) *see* Bro Teifi Sarn Helen *St D*

LLANBADARN TREFEGLWYS (St Padarn) *see* Henfynyw w Aberaeron and Llanddewi Aberarth etc *St D*

LLANBADARN-Y-GARREG (St Padarn) *see* Aberedw w Llandeilo Graban and Llanbadarn etc *S & B*

LLANBADOC (St Madog) *see* Llangybi and Coedypaen w Llanbadoc *Mon*

LLANBADRIG (St Padrig) *see* Llanfechell w Bodewryd w Rhosbeirio etc *Ban*

LLANBEBLIG (St Peblig) w Caernarfon and Betws Garmon w Waunfawr *Ban 1* **TR** R F DONALDSON, **TV** R J HUGHES

LLANBEDR (St Peter) *see* Llanenddwyn w Llanddwywe, Llanbedr w Llandanwg *Ban*

LLANBEDR DYFFRYN CLWYD (St Peter), Llangynhafal, Llanychan, Llanarmon yn Ial and Llanynys *St As 3* **R** P V F CHEW

LLANBEDR PAINSCASTLE (St Peter) *see* Bryngwyn and Newchurch and Llanbedr etc *S & B*

LLANBEDR PONT STEFFAN *see* Bro Teifi Sarn Helen *St D*

LLANBEDR-Y-CENNIN (St Peter) *see* Caerhun and Llangelynnin and Llanbedr-y-Cennin *Ban*

LLANBEDR YSTRAD YW (St Peter) *see* Llangenni and Llanbedr Ystrad Yw w Patricio *S & B*

LLANBEDRGOCH (St Peter) *see* Llanfair Mathafarn Eithaf w Llanbedrgoch *Ban*

LLANBEDROG (St Pedrog) w Llannor and Llangian *Ban 11* **R** A JONES

LLANBERIS (St Padarn) (St Peris), Llanrug and Llandinorwig *Ban 1* **R** *vacant* (01286) 873678

LLANBISTER (St Cynllo) *see* Upper Ithon Valley *S & B*

LLANBLETHIAN (St Blethian) *see* Cowbridge *Llan*

LLANBOIDY (St Brynach) *see* Meidrim and Llanboidy and Merthyr *St D*

LLANBRADACH (All Saints) *see* Ystrad Mynach w Llanbradach *Llan*

LLANBRYN-MAIR (St Mary) *see* Bro Ddyfi Uchaf *Ban*

LLANCARFAN (St Cadoc) *see* Penmark w Llancarfan w Llantrithyd *Llan*

LLANDAFF (Cathedral of St Peter and St Paul w St Dyfrig, St Teilo and St Euddogwy) *Llan 2* **V** J T LEWIS

LLANDAFF North (All Saints) *Llan 2* **P-in-c** S JENKYNS

LLANDANWG *see* Llanenddwyn w Llanddwywe, Llanbedr w Llandanwg *Ban*

LLANDAVENNY *see* Penhow, St Brides Netherwent w Llandavenny etc *Mon*

LLANDAWKE (St Odoceus) *see* Laugharne w Llansadwrnen and Llandawke *St D*

LLANDDANIEL-FAB (St Deiniolfab) *see* Llanfair-pwll and Llanddaniel-fab etc *Ban*

LLANDDAROG (St Twrog) *see* Llanarthne and Llanddarog *St D*

LLANDDEINIOL (St Deiniol) *see* Llansantffraed w Llanrhystud and Llanddeiniol *St D*

LLANDDEINIOLEN (St Deiniol) w Llanfair-is-gaer w Penisa'r-waun *Ban 1*   **V** J L JONES

LLANDDERFEL (St Derfel) *see* Llandrillo and Llandderfel *St As*

LLANDDEW (St David) *see* Brecon St Mary w Llanddew *S & B*

LLANDDEWI *see* Blaenau Irfon *S & B*

LLANDDEWI (St David) *see* SW Gower *S & B*

LLANDDEWI ABERARTH (St David) *see* Henfynyw w Aberaeron and Llanddewi Aberarth etc *St D*

LLANDDEWI FACH (St David) *see* Bryngwyn and Newchurch and Llanbedr etc *S & B*

LLANDDEWI RHONDDA (St Barnabas) *see* Pwllgwaun and Llanddewi Rhondda *Llan*

LLANDDEWI RHONDDA (St David) *as above*

LLANDDEWI RHYDDERCH (St David) w Llangattock-juxta-Usk and Llanarth w Clytha and Llansantffraed *Mon 1*   **P-in-c** L J DEROSAIRE

LLANDDEWI YSTRADENNI (St David) *see* Upper Ithon Valley *S & B*

LLANDDEWIBREFI (St David) *see* Bro Teifi Sarn Helen *St D*

LLANDDEWI'R CWM (St David) *see* Builth and Llanddewi'r Cwm w Llangynog etc *S & B*

LLANDDOGET (St Doged) *see* LLanrwst *St As*

LLANDDONA (St Dona) *see* Llansadwrn w Llanddona and Llaniestyn etc *Ban*

LLANDDOWROR (St Teilo) *see* St Clears w Llangynin and Llanddowror etc *St D*

LLANDDULAS (St Cynfryd) and Llysfaen *St As 6*   **R** M C PARRY

LLANDDWYWE (St Ddwywe) *see* Llanenddwyn w Llanddwywe, Llanbedr w Llandanwg *Ban*

LLANDDYFNAN (St Ddyfnan) *see* Llansadwrn w Llanddona and Llaniestyn etc *Ban*

LLANDDYFNAN (St Deiniol) *as above*

LLANDECWYN (St Tecwyn) *see* Harlech and Llanfair-juxta-Harlech etc *Ban*

LLANDEFAELOG-FACH (St Maelog) *see* Dan yr Eppynt *S & B*

LLANDEFALLE (St Matthew) and Llyswen w Boughrood and Llanstephen w Talachddu *S & B 4*   **R** I P CHARLESWORTH

LLANDEGFAN (St Tegfan) w Llandysilio *Ban 6*   **V** A WILLIAMS,   **C** S R LEYLAND

LLANDEGLA (St Tecla) *St As 17*   **R** S T GRIFFITHS

LLANDEGLEY (St Tecla) *see* Lower Ithon Valley *S & B*

LLANDEGVETH (St Tegfeth) *see* Caerleon and Llanfrechfa *Mon*

LLANDEILO *see* Maenclochog and New Moat etc *St D*

LLANDEILO ABERCYWYN *see* Llansteffan and Llan-y-bri etc *St D*

LLANDEILO FAWR (St Teilo) and Taliaris *St D 13*   **V** M S SADLER,   **NSM** P C A MANSEL LEWIS

LLANDEILO GRABAN (St Teilo) *see* Aberedw w Llandeilo Graban and Llanbadarn etc *S & B*

LLANDEILO TAL-Y-BONT (St Teilo) (St Michael) *S & B 9*   **V** J P H WALTERS

LLANDELOY (St Teilo) *see* Dewisland *St D*

LLANDENNY (St John the Apostle) *see* Raglan w Llandenny and Bryngwyn *Mon*

LLANDEUSSANT (St Simon and St Jude) *see* Llangadog and Gwynfe w Llanddeusant *St D*

LLANDEVAUD (St Peter) *see* Penhow, St Brides Netherwent w Llandavenny etc *Mon*

LLANDEWI FACH *see* Caerleon and Llanfrechfa *Mon*

LLANDEWI SKIRRID (St David) *see* Llantilio Pertholey w Bettws Chpl etc *Mon*

LLANDEWI VELFREY (St David) *see* Lampeter Velfrey and Llanddewi Velfrey *St D*

LLANDILO'R FAN (St Teilo) *see* Defynnog, Llandilo'r Fan, Llanulid, Llywel etc *S & B*

LLANDINAM (St Llonio) w Trefeglwys w Penstrowed *Ban 9*   **V** L B COWAN

LLANDINGAT (St Dingad) w Myddfai *St D 13*   **V** I H AVESON

LLANDINORWIG (Christ Church) *see* Llanberis, Llanrug and Llandinorwig *Ban*

LLANDINORWIG (St Mary) *as above*

LLANDOGO (St Oudoceus) w Whitebrook Chapel and Tintern Parva *Mon 2*   **NSM** J W DEARNLEY, N HILL

LLANDOUGH (St Dochdwy) *see* Penarth and Llandough *Llan*

LLANDOUGH (St Dochwy) *see* Cowbridge *Llan*

LLANDOVERY *see* Llandingat w Myddfai *St D*

LLANDOW (Holy Trinity) *see* Colwinston, Llandow and Llysworney *Llan*

LLANDRILLO (St Trilio) (St Derfel) and Llandderfel *St As 17*   **V** S J ROBERTS,   **NSM** M F WILKINSON

LLANDRILLO-YN-RHOS (St Trillo) (St George) *St As 6*   **V** D JACKS

LLANDRINDOD (Holy Trinity) (Old Parish Church) w Cefnllys and Disserth *S & B 5*   **R** I K REES,   **NSM** A TWEED, H REES

LLANDRINIO (St Trinio, St Peter and St Paul) *see* Llandysilio and Penrhos and Llandrinio etc *St As*

LLANDRYGARN (St Trygarn) w Bodwrog, Heneglwys, Trewalchmai and Llanerch-y-medd *Ban 4*   **NSM** E D JERMAN

LLANDUDNO (St George) (St Tudno) (Holy Trinity) (Our Saviour) *Ban 2*   **R** J E NICE

LLANDUDWEN (St Tudwen) *see* Nefyn w Tudweiliog w Llandudwen w Edern *Ban*

LLANDULAIS IN TIR ABAD (St David) *see* Blaenau Irfon *S & B*

LLANDWROG (St Twrog) and Llanwnda *Ban 1*   **P-in-c** R W TOWNSEND

LLANDYBIE (St Tybie) *St D 12*   **V** E A HOWELLS

LLANDYFAELOG (St Maelog) *see* Cydweli and Llandyfaelog *St D*

LLANDYFAN (Church) *see* Llandybie *St D*

LLANDYFODWG (St Tyfodwg) and Cwm Ogwr *Llan 4*   **P-in-c** J J JENKINS

LLANDYFRIOG (St Tyfriog) *see* Newcastle Emlyn w Llandyfriog and Troedyraur etc *St D*

LLANDYFRYDOG (St Tyfrydog) *see* Llandrygarn w Bodwrog and Heneglwys etc *Ban*

LLANDYGAI (St Ann) *see* Glanogwen and Llanllechid w St Ann's and Pentir *Ban*

LLANDYGAI (St Tegai) *see* Tregarth and Llandygai and Maes y Groes *Ban*

LLANDYGWYDD (St Tygwydd) *see* Maenordeifi Gp *St D*

LLANDYRNOG (St Tyrnog) (St Cwyfan) and Llangwyfan *St As 2*   **R** E B THOMAS

LLANDYRY (Church) *see* Pen-bre *St D*

LLANDYSILIO (St Tysilio) *see* Llandegfan w Llandysilio *Ban*

LLANDYSILIO (St Tysilio) *see* Whitland w Cyffig and Henllan Amgoed etc *St D*

LLANDYSILIO (St Tysilio) (St Mary) and Penrhos and Llandrinio w Criggion *St As 10*   **R** A G ELLACOTT

LLANDYSILIOGOGO (St Tysilio) *see* Llangrannog w Llandysiliogogo w Penbryn *St D*

LLANDYSSIL (St Tyssil) *see* Montgomery and Forden and Llandyssil *St As*

LLANDYSUL (St Tysul) w Bangor Teifi w Henllan and Llanfairorllwyn w Llangynllo *St D 6*   **V** vacant (01559) 362277

LLANEDEYRN (All Saints) *see* Cyncoed *Mon*

LLANEDI (St Edith) w Tycroes and Saron *St D 12*   **P-in-c** D A BAXTER

LLANEDWEN (St Edwen) *see* Llanfair-pwll and Llanddaniel-fab etc *Ban*

LLANEGRYN (St Mary and St Egryn) w Aberdyfi w Tywyn *Ban 12*   **C** A A WHITE,   **NSM** C C TEN WOLDE

LLANEGWAD (St Egwad) w Llanfihangel Uwch Gwili *St D 13*   **V** R J PATTINSON

LLANEILIAN (St Eilian) *see* Amlwch *Ban*

LLANELEN (St Helen) *see* Govilon w Llanfoist w Llanelen *Mon*

LLANELIAN (St Elian) *see* Colwyn and Llanelian *St As*

LLANELIDAN (St Elidan) *see* Llanfair DC, Derwen, Llanelidan and Efenechtyd *St As*

LLANELLI (St Elli) *S & B 3*   **C** C J BEVAN

LLANELLI (St Elli) (All Saints) (St Alban) (Christ Church) (St David) (St John) (St Peter) *St D 11*   **TR** S E JONES, **TV** R S WOOD

LLANELLTUD (St Illtyd) *see* Dolgellau w Llanfachreth and Brithdir etc *Ban*

LLANELWEDD (St Matthew) *see* Colwyn *S & B*

LLANENDDWYN (St Enddwyn) w Llanddwywe and Llanbedr w Llandanwg *Ban 8*   **R** S K N BEACON,   **C** S J JONES

LLANENGAN (St Engan) *see* Llanbedrog w Llannor and Llangian *Ban*

LLANERCH AERON (St Non) w Ciliau Aeron and Dihewyd and Mydroilyn *St D 7*   **P-in-c** R H E DAVIES

LLANERCH-Y-MEDD (Eglwys Crist) *see* Llandrygarn w Bodwrog and Heneglwys etc *Ban*

LLANERCH-Y-MEDD (St Mair) *as above*

LLANERFYL (St Erfyl) *see* Garthbeibio w Llanerfyl w Llangadfan etc *St As*

LLANEUGRAD (St Eugrad) w Llanallgo and Penrhosllugwy w Llanfihangel Tre'r Beirdd *Ban 7* **R** *vacant*
LLANFABON (St Mabon) (St John the Baptist) *Llan 8* **R** *vacant* (01443) 450355
LLANFACHRAETH (St Machraeth) *see* Bodedern w Llanfaethlu *Ban*
LLANFACHRETH (St Machreth) *see* Dolgellau w Llanfachreth and Brithdir etc *Ban*
LLANFAELOG (St Maelog) and Llangwyfan *Ban 3* **R** M M BRADY
LLANFAELRHYS (St Maelrhys) *see* Aberdaron and Llanfaelrhys *Ban*
LLANFAES *see* Brecon St David w Llanspyddid and Llanilltyd *S & B*
LLANFAETHLU (St Maethlu) *see* Bodedern w Llanfaethlu *Ban*
LLANFAGLAN (St Mary) *see* Llandwrog and Llanwnda *Ban*
LLANFAIR (Church) *see* Gwaun-cae-Gurwen *St D*
LLANFAIR (Church) *see* Llandingat w Myddfai *St D*
LLANFAIR (St Mary) *see* Grosmont and Skenfrith and Llangattock etc *Mon*
LLANFAIR-AR-Y-BRYN (St Mary) *see* Cil-y-Cwm and Ystrad-ffin w Rhandir-mwyn etc *St D*
LLANFAIR CAEREINION (St Mary), Llanllugan and Manafon *St As 8* **V** *vacant* (01938) 811335
LLANFAIR CLYDOGAU (St Mary) *see* Bro Teifi Sarn Helen *St D*
LLANFAIR DISCOED (St Mary) *see* Caerwent w Dinham and Llanfair Discoed etc *Mon*
LLANFAIR DYFFRYN CLWYD (St Cynfarch and St Mary) (Jesus Chapel) and Derwen and Llanelidan and Efenechtyd *St As 3* **P-in-c** R W CARTER
LLANFAIR-IS-GAER (Old Parish Church) *see* Llanddeiniolen w Llanfair-is-gaer etc *Ban*
LLANFAIR-IS-GAER (St Mary) *as above*
LLANFAIR-JUXTA-HARLECH (St Mary) *see* Harlech and Llanfair-juxta-Harlech etc *Ban*
LLANFAIR KILGEDDIN *see* Bettws Newydd w Trostrey etc *Mon*
LLANFAIR MATHAFARN EITHAF (St Mary) w Llanbedrgoch *Ban 6* **R** *vacant* (01248) 853744
LLANFAIR NANT-GWYN (St Mary) *see* Maenordeifi Gp *St D*
LLANFAIR NANT-Y-GOF (St Mary) *see* Letterston w Llanfair Nant-y-Gof etc *St D*
LLANFAIR-PWLL (St Mary) and Llanddaniel-fab w Penmynydd w Llanedwen *Ban 6* **R** P HUGHES, **Hon C** L J FRANCIS
LLANFAIR TALHAEARN (St Mary) *see* Petryal and Betws yn Rhos *St As*
LLANFAIR-YN-NEUBWLL *see* Valley w Llechylched and Caergeiliog *Ban*
LLANFAIR-YN-Y-CWMWD (St Mary) *see* Newborough w Llanidan w Llangeinwen etc *Ban*
LLANFAIR-YN-GHORNWY (St Mary) *see* Bodedern w Llanfaethlu *Ban*
LLANFAIRFECHAN (St Mary) (Christ Church) w Aber *Ban 2* **R** C M EVANS
LLANFAIRORLLWYN (St Mary) *see* Llandysul w Bangor Teifi w Henllan etc *St D*
LLANFAIRPWLLGWYNGYLLGOGERYCHWYRND-ROBWLL-LLANTISILIOGOGOGOCH (St Mary) *see* Llanfair-pwll and Llanddaniel-fab etc *Ban*
LLANFALLTEG (St Mallteg) w Castell Dwyran *St D 14* **V** *vacant*
LLANFAREDD (St Mary) *see* Colwyn *S & B*
LLANFECHAIN (St Garmon) *see* Llansantffraid-ym-Mechain and Llanfechain *St As*
LLANFECHAN (St Afan) *see* Irfon Valley *S & B*
LLANFECHELL (St Mechell) w Bodewryd w Rhosbeirio w Llanfflewin and Llanbadrig *Ban 7* **R** G W EDWARDS
LLANFERRES (St Berres) *see* Cilcain, Gwernaffield, Llanferres etc *St As*
LLANFEUGAN (St Meugan) w Llanthetty w Llansantffraed-juxta-Usk *S & B 3* **P-in-c** A S ROBINSON
LLANFFESTINIOG (St Michael) w Blaenau Ffestiniog w Trawsfynydd *Ban 8* **R** *vacant* (01766) 831536
LLANFFINAN (St Ffinan) *see* Llanfihangel Ysgeifiog w Llangristiolus etc *Ban*
LLANFFLEWIN (St Fflewin) *see* Llanfechell w Bodewryd w Rhosbeirio etc *Ban*
LLANFIHANGEL ABERCYWYN (St Michael) *see* St Clears w Llangynin and Llanddowror etc *St D*
LLANFIHANGEL ABERGWESSIN *see* Blaenau Irfon *S & B*
LLANFIHANGEL ABERYTHYCH (St Michael) *see* Catheiniog *St D*

LLANFIHANGEL-AR-ARTH (St Michael) w Capel Dewi *St D 6* **V** B D TIMOTHY
LLANFIHANGEL BRYNPABUAN (St Michael and All Angels) *see* Upper Wye *S & B*
LLANFIHANGEL CILFARGEN *see* Catheiniog *St D*
LLANFIHANGEL CRUCORNEY (St Michael) w Oldcastle and Cwmyoy and Llanthony *Mon 1* **V** D J YOUNG, **Hon Par Dn** D A LEE
LLANFIHANGEL FECHAN (St Michael) *see* Dan yr Eppynt *S & B*
LLANFIHANGEL GENAU'R-GLYN (St Michael) and Llangorwen *St D 9* **P-in-c** P O JONES
LLANFIHANGEL GLYN MYFYR (St Michael) *see* Cerrigydrudion w Llanfihangel Glyn Myfyr etc *St As*
LLANFIHANGEL GOBION (St Michael) *see* Bettws Newydd w Trostrey etc *Mon*
LLANFIHANGEL HELYGEN (St Michael) *see* Upper Wye *S & B*
LLANFIHANGEL LLEDROD (St Michael) *see* Llanilar w Rhostie and Llangwyryfon etc *St D*
LLANFIHANGEL NANTBRAN (St Michael) *see* Dan yr Eppynt *S & B*
LLANFIHANGEL NANTMELAN (St Michael) *see* New Radnor and Llanfihangel Nantmelan etc *S & B*
LLANFIHANGEL PENBEDW *see* Maenordeifi Gp *St D*
LLANFIHANGEL PONTYMOILE (St Michael) *see* Panteg w Llanfihangel Pontymoile *Mon*
LLANFIHANGEL RHOS Y CORN (St Michael) *see* Brechfa w Abergorlech etc *St D*
LLANFIHANGEL RHYDITHON (St Michael) *see* Lower Ithon Valley *S & B*
LLANFIHANGEL ROGIET *see* Caldicot *Mon*
LLANFIHANGEL TALYLLYN (St Michael) *see* Llyn Safaddan *S & B*
LLANFIHANGEL-TOR-Y-MYNYDD (St Michael) *see* Llanishen w Trellech Grange and Llanfihangel etc *Mon*
LLANFIHANGEL TRE'R BEIRDD (St Michael) *see* Llaneugrad w Llanallgo and Penrhosllugwy etc *Ban*
LLANFIHANGEL-UWCH-GWILI (St Michael) *see* Llanegwad w Llanfihangel Uwch Gwili *St D*
LLANFIHANGEL-Y-CREUDDYN (St Michael) *see* Grwp Bro Ystwyth a Mynach *St D*
LLANFIHANGEL-Y-PENNANT (St Michael) *see* Llanegryn w Aberdyfi w Tywyn *Ban*
LLANFIHANGEL-Y-TRAETHAU (St Michael) *see* Harlech and Llanfair-juxta-Harlech etc *Ban*
LLANFIHANGEL-YN-NHYWYN *see* Valley w Llechylched and Caergeiliog *Ban*
LLANFIHANGEL-YNG-NGHWYNFA (St Michael) *see* Garthbeibio w Llanerfyl w Llangadfan etc *St As*
LLANFIHANGEL YSGEIFIOG (St Michael) w Llangristiolus w Llanffinan w Llangaffo *Ban 4* **R** E C WILLIAMS, **NSM** E R ROBERTS
LLANFIHANGEL-YSTERN-LLEWERN (St Michael) *see* Rockfield and Dingestow Gp *Mon*
LLANFIHANGEL YSTRAD (St Michael) and Cilcennin w Trefilan and Nantcwnlle *St D 7* **V** *vacant* (01570) 471073
LLANFILO (St Bilo) *see* Talgarth w Bronllys w Llanfilo *S & B*
LLANFOIST (St Ffwyst) *see* Govilon w Llanfoist w Llanelen *Mon*
LLANFOR (St Mor and St Deiniol) w Rhosygwaliau *St As 17* **R** *vacant*
LLANFRECHFA (All Saints) *see* Caerleon and Llanfrechfa *Mon*
LLANFROTHEN (St Brothen) *see* Penrhyndeudraeth and Llanfrothen w Maentwrog etc *Ban*
LLANFRYNACH (St Brynach) *see* Cowbridge *Llan*
LLANFRYNACH (St Brynach) and Cantref w Llanhamlach *S & B 3* **P-in-c** A J R THOMAS
LLANFUGAIL (St Migail) *see* Valley w Llechylched and Caergeiliog *Ban*
LLANFWROG (St Mwrog and St Mary) *see* Ruthin w Llanrhydd and Llanfwrog *St As*
LLANFYLLIN (St Myllin), Bwlchycibau and Llanwddyn *St As 9* **R** *vacant*
LLANFYNYDD (St Egwad) *see* Catheiniog *St D*
LLANFYNYDD (St Michael) (All Saints) *St As 16* **R** *vacant* (01978) 760489
LLANFYRNACH (St Brynach) *see* Crymych Gp *St D*
LLANGADFAN (St Cadfan) *see* Garthbeibio w Llanerfyl w Llangadfan etc *St As*
LLANGADOG (St Cadog) and Gwynfe w Llanddeusant *St D 13* **V** K M D COTTAM
LLANGADWALADR (St Cadwaladr) *see* Llansilin w Llangadwaladr and Llangedwyn *St As*

LLANGADWALADR (St Cadwaladr)   *see* Trefdraeth w
Aberffraw, Llangadwaladr etc *Ban*
LLANGAFFO (St Caffo)   *see* Llanfihangel Ysgeifiog w
Llangristiolus etc *Ban*
LLANGAIN (St Cain)   *see* Llan-llwch w Llangain and
Llangynog *St D*
LLANGAMMARCH (St Cadmarch)   *see* Irfon Valley *S & B*
LLANGAN (St Canna)   *see* Coychurch, Llangan and St Mary
Hill *Llan*
LLANGANTEN (St Cannen)   *see* Irfon Valley *S & B*
LLANGAR (St John the Evangelist)   *see* Corwen w Llangar,
Glyndyfrdwy etc *St As*
LLANGASTY TALYLLYN (St Gastyn)   *see* Llyn Safaddan
S & B
LLANGATHEN (St Cathen)   *see* Catheiniog *St D*
LLANGATTOCK (St Cattwg) and Llangyndir *S & B 3*
R K RICHARDS
LLANGATTOCK-JUXTA-USK (St Cadoc)   *see* Llanddewi
Rhydderch w Llangattock-juxta-Usk etc *Mon*
LLANGATTOCK LINGOED (St Cadoc)   *see* Grosmont and
Skenfrith and Llangattock etc *Mon*
LLANGATTOCK-VIBON-AVEL (St Cadoc)   *see* Rockfield
and Dingestow Gp *Mon*
LLANGEDWYN (St Cedwyn)   *see* Llansilin w Llangadwaladr
and Llangedwyn *St As*
LLANGEFNI (St Cyngar) w Tregaean *Ban 4*   **R** P MCLEAN
LLANGEINOR (St Ceinor) and the Garw Valley *Llan 4*
P-in-c D J MORTIMORE
LLANGEINWEN (St Ceinwen)   *see* Newborough w Llanidan w
Llangeinwen etc *Ban*
LLANGEITHO (St Ceitho)   *see* Bro Teifi Sarn Helen *St D*
LLANGELER (St Celer) w Pen-Boyr *St D 6*   **V** J N GILLIBRAND
LLANGELYNIN (St Celynnin)   *see* Caerhun and Llangelynnin
and Llanbedr-y-Cennin *Ban*
LLANGELYNNIN (St Celynin)   *see* Arthog w Fairbourne w
Llangelynnin w Rhoslefain *Ban*
LLANGENNECH (St Gwynog) and Hendy *St D 11*
V P C JONES
LLANGENNI (St Cenau) and Llanbedr Ystrad Yw w Patricio
S & B 3   **R** C W BOWEN
LLANGENNITH (St Cenydd) w Llanmadoc and Cheriton
S & B 8   **R** P J WILLIAMS
LLANGERNYW (St Digain)   *see* Petryal and Betws yn Rhos
St As
LLANGEVIEW (St David)   *see* Llangwm Uchaf and Llangwm
Isaf w Gwernesney etc *Mon*
LLANGIAN (St Gian)   *see* Llanbedrog w Llannor and Llangian
Ban
LLANGIWG (St Ciwg) *S & B 7*   **V** G H GREEN
LLANGLYDWEN (St Cledwyn)   *see* Crymych Gp *St D*
LLANGOEDMOR (St Cynllo)   *see* Cardigan w Mwnt and Y
Ferwig w Llangoedmor *St D*
LLANGOLLEN (St Collen) (St John) w Trevor and Llantysilio
St As 14   **V** A C SULLY,   **C** N A KELLY
LLANGOLMAN (St Colman)   *see* Maenclochog and New
Moat etc *St D*
LLANGORSE (St Paulinus)   *see* Llyn Safaddan *S & B*
LLANGORWEN (All Saints)   *see* Llanfihangel Genau'r-glyn
and Llangorwen *St D*
LLANGOWER (St Cywair)   *see* Bala *St As*
LLANGRANNOG (St Carannog) w Llandysiliogogo w Penbryn
St D 7   **V** vacant (01239) 654943
LLANGRISTIOLUS (St Cristiolus)   *see* Llanfihangel Ysgeifiog
w Llangristiolus etc *Ban*
LLANGUNNOG   *see* Llanishen w Trellech Grange and
Llanfihangel etc *Mon*
LLANGUNNOR (St Ceinwr) w Cwmffrwd *St D 10*
V W D A GRIFFITHS,   **NSM** C M STEEL
LLANGURIG (St Curig)   *see* Llanidloes w Llangurig *Ban*
LLANGWLLOG (St Cwyllog)   *see* Llandrygarn w Bodwrog and
Heneglwys etc *Ban*
LLANGWLLONG (St Anau)   *as above*
LLANGWM (St Catherine)   *see* Betws Gwerful Goch w
Llangwm w Llawrybetws *St As*
LLANGWM (St Jerome) w Freystrop and Johnston *St D 4*
R J E GOUPILLON
LLANGWM ISAF (St John)   *see* Llangwm Uchaf and
Llangwm Isaf w Gwernesney etc *Mon*
LLANGWM UCHAF (St Jerome) and Llangwm Isaf w
Gwernesney and Llangeview w Wolvesnewton *Mon 4*
NSM K J HASLER
LLANGWNNADL (St Gwynhoedl)   *see* Botwnnog w
Bryncroes w Llangwnnadl w Penllech *Ban*
LLANGWYFAN   *see* Llandyrnog and Llangwyfan *St As*
LLANGWYFAN (St Cwyfan)   *see* Llanfaelog and Llangwyfan
Ban

LLANGWYFAN (St Cwyfan Old Church)   *as above*
LLANGWYRYFON (St Ursula)   *see* Llanilar w Rhostie and
Llangwyryfon etc *St D*
LLANGYBI (St Cybi)   *see* Criccieth and Treflys w
Llanystumdwy etc *Ban*
LLANGYBI (St Cybi)   *see* Bro Teifi Sarn Helen *St D*
LLANGYBI (St Cybi) and Coedypaen w Llanbadoc *Mon 4*
R A E MORTON
LLANGYFELACH (St David and St Cyfelach) (St Teilo-on-the-
Clase) *S & B 7*   **V** R J DAVIES-HANNEN
LLANGYNDEYRN (St Cyndeyrn)   *see* Trisant *St D*
LLANGYNDIR (St Cynidr and St Mary)   *see* Llangattock and
Llangyndir *S & B*
LLANGYNFELYN (St Cynfelyn)   *see* Borth and Eglwys-fach w
Llangynfelyn *St D*
LLANGYNHAFAL (St Cynhafal)   *see* Llanbedr DC,
Llangynhafal, Llanychan etc *St As*
LLANGYNIN (St Cynin)   *see* St Clears w Llangynin and
Llanddowror etc *St D*
LLANGYNLLO (St Cynllo)   *see* Llandysul w Bangor Teifi w
Henllan etc *St D*
LLANGYNLLO (St Cynllo)   *see* Beguildy and Heyope and
Llangynllo and Bleddfa *S & B*
LLANGYNOG   *see* Builth and Llanddewi'r Cwm w Llangynog
etc *S & B*
LLANGYNOG (St Cynog)   *see* Llanrhaeadr ym Mochnant etc
St As
LLANGYNOG (St Cynog)   *see* Llan-llwch w Llangain and
Llangynog *St D*
LLANGYNWYD (St Cynwyd) (St Stephen) (St Tydfil) w
Maesteg *Llan 4*   **V** G A BLYTH,   **NSM** B J REANEY
LLANGYNYW (St Cynyw)   *see* Meifod w Llangynyw w Pont
Robert w Pont Dolanog *St As*
LLANGYSTENNIN (St Cystenin)   *see* Rhos-Cystennin *St As*
LLANGYSTENNIN (St Katherine)   *as above*
LLANGYSTENNIN (St Mary)   *as above*
LLANGYSTENNIN (St Michael)   *as above*
LLANHAMLACH (St Peter and St Illtyd)   *see* Llanfrynach and
Cantref w Llanhamlach *S & B*
LLANHARAN (St Julius and St Aaron) w Peterston-super-
Montem *Llan 4*   **P-in-c** B A WOOD
LLANHARRY (St Illtud) *Llan 7*   **P-in-c** R T PITMAN
LLANHENNOCK (St John)   *see* Caerleon and Llanfrechfa
Mon
LLANHILLETH (Christ Church)   *see* Abertillery w Cwmtillery
w Llanhilleth etc *Mon*
LLANHILLETH (St Mark)   *as above*
LLANHYWEL (St Hywel)   *see* Dewisland *St D*
LLANIDAN (St Nidan)   *see* Newborough w Llanidan w
Llangeinwen etc *Ban*
LLANIDLOES (St Idloes) w Llangurig *Ban 9*   **V** M S STARKEY
LLANIESTYN (St Iestyn)   *see* Llansadwrn w Llanddona and
Llaniestyn etc *Ban*
LLANIESTYN (St Iestyn)   *see* Botwnnog w Bryncroes w
Llangwnnadl w Penllech *Ban*
LLANIGON (St Eigon)   *see* Hay w Llanigon and Capel-y-Ffin
S & B
LLANILAR (St Hilary) w Rhostie and Llangwyryfon w
Llanfihangel Lledrod *St D 9*   **V** vacant
LLANILID (St Illid and St Curig) w Pencoed *Llan 4*
R I M HODGES
LLANILLTYD (St John)   *see* Brecon St David w Llanspyddid
and Llanilltyd *S & B*
LLANINA (St Ina)   *see* Llanllwchaearn and Llanina *St D*
LLANISHEN (Christ Church)   *see* Cardiff Ch Ch Roath Park
Llan
LLANISHEN (St Dennis) w Trellech Grange and Llanfihangel
Tor-y-Mynydd w Llangunnog and Llansoy *Mon 2*
P-in-c D M OWEN
LLANISHEN (St Isan) (St Faith) *Llan 1*   **V** M D WITCOMBE
LLANLLAWDDOG (St Llawddog)   *see* Llanpumsaint w
Llanllawddog *St D*
LLANLLAWER   *see* Newport w Cilgwyn and Nevern and Y
Beifil etc *St D*
LLANLLECHID (St Cross)   *see* Tregarth and Llandygai and
Maes y Groes *Ban*
LLANLLECHID (St Llechid)   *see* Glanogwen and Llanllechid
w St Ann's and Pentir *Ban*
LLANLLEONFEL (Parish Church)   *see* Irfon Valley *S & B*
LLANLLOWELL (St Llywel)   *see* Usk and Gwehelog w
Llantrisant w Llanllowell *Mon*
LLANLLUGAN (St Mary)   *see* Llanfair Caereinion, Llanllugan
and Manafon *St As*
LLANLLWCHAEARN (St Llwchaiarn) and Llanina *St D 7*
P-in-c M F BAYNHAM

LLANYCHAR (Church)   *see* Fishguard w Llanychar and Pontfaen w Morfil etc *St D*
LLANYCHLWYDOG   *as above*
LLANYCIL (St Beuno)   *see* Bala *St As*
LLANYCRWYS (St David)   *see* Pencarreg and Llanycrwys *St D*
LLANYMAWDDWY (St Tydecho)   *see* Bro Ddyfi Uchaf *Ban*
LLANYNGHENEDL VALLEY (St Michael)   *see* Valley w Llechylched and Caergeiliog *Ban*
LLANYNYS   *see* Builth and Llanddewi'r Cwm w Llangynog etc *S & B*
LLANYNYS (St Saeran)   *see* Llanbedr DC, Llangynhafal, Llanychan etc *St As*
LLANYRE   *see* Upper Wye *S & B*
LLANYRNEWYDD (St Gwynour)   *see* Llanrhidian w Llanyrnewydd *S & B*
LLANYSTYMDWY (St John the Baptist)   *see* Criccieth and Treflys w Llanystumdwy etc *Ban*
LLANYWERN (St Mary the Virgin)   *see* Llyn Safaddan *S & B*
LLAWHADEN (St Aidan) w Bletherston and Llanycefn *St D 1*
V P H DAVIES
LLAWRYBETWS (St James)   *see* Betws Gwerful Goch w Llangwm w Llawrybetws *St As*
LLAY (St Martin) *St As 12*   **V** P A WALKER
LLECHGYNFARWY (St Cynfarwy)   *see* Bodedern w Llanfaethlu *Ban*
LLECHRYD (St Tydfil)   *see* Maenordeifi Gp *St D*
LLECHYLCHED (Holy Trinity)   *see* Valley w Llechylched and Caergeiliog *Ban*
LLISWERRY   *see* Newport St Andr *Mon*
LLOWES (St Meilig)   *see* Glasbury and Llowes w Clyro and Betws *S & B*
LLWYDCOED (St James)   *see* Aberdare St Fagan *Llan*
LLWYDIARTH (St Mary)   *see* Garthbeibio w Llanerfyl w Llangadfan etc *St As*
LLWYNCELLYN (St Luke)   *see* Porth Newydd *Llan*
LLWYNDERW (Holy Cross) (Clyne Chapel) *S & B 6*
V D B EVANS
LLWYNGWRIL   *see* Arthog w Fairbourne w Llangelynnin w Rhoslefain *Ban*
LLWYNHENDY (St David) *St D 11*   **V** A M GRAY
LLWYNYPIA   *see* Pont Rhondda *Llan*
LLYN SAFADDAN *S & B 4*   **V** A N JEVONS
LLYS-Y-FRAN (St Meilyr)   *see* Maenclochog and New Moat etc *St D*
LLYSFAEN (St Cynfran)   *see* Llanddulas and Llysfaen *St As*
LLYSWEN (St Gwendoline)   *see* Llandefalle and Llyswen w Boughrood etc *S & B*
LLYSWORNEY (St Tydfil)   *see* Colwinston, Llandow and Llysworney *Llan*
LLYWEL (St David)   *see* Defynnog, Llandilo'r Fan, Llanulid, Llywel etc *S & B*
LOUGHOR (St Michael) (St David) (St Paul) *S & B 9*
V G J TURNER,   **NSM** K MORGAN
LOVESTON (St Leonard)   *see* Jeffreyston w Reynoldston and Loveston etc *St D*
LUDCHURCH (St Elidyr)   *see* Begelly w Ludchurch and E Williamston *St D*
MACHEN (St John the Baptist)   *see* Bedwas w Machen w Rudry *Mon*
MACHEN (St Michael)   *as above*
MACHYNLLETH (St Peter) w Llanwrin and Penegoes *Ban 10*
P-in-c K A ROGERS
MAENCLOCHOG (St Mary) and Llandeilo w Henry's Moat w Mynachlogddu w Llangolman w New Moat w Llys y Fran *St D 1*   **V** R J DAVIES
MAENORDEIFI Group, The (St David) *St D 5*   **R** *vacant* (01239) 682830
MAENORDEIFI (Old Parish Church)   *see* Maenordeifi Gp *St D*
MAENTWROG (St Twrog)   *see* Penrhyndeudraeth and Llanfrothen w Maentwrog etc *Ban*
MAERDY (All Saints)   *see* Rhondda Fach Uchaf *Llan*
MAESGLAS and Duffryn *Mon 8*   **P-in-c** L C HALL,
NSM S L COLLINGBOURNE
MAESMYNIS AND LLANYNYS (St David)   *see* Builth and Llanddewi'r Cwm w Llangynog etc *S & B*
MAESTEG (St David)   *see* Llangynwyd w Maesteg *Llan*
MAESTEG (St Michael)   *as above*
MAESTEILO (St John)   *see* Llandeilo Fawr and Taliaris *St D*
MAESTIR (St Mary)   *see* Bro Teifi Sarn Helen *St D*
MAGOR (St Mary) *Mon 3*   **TR** C M LAWSON-JONES,
TV C L JONES, J D HARRIS,   **Par Dn** A M PRICE,
NSM N D HOWARD
MAINDEE NEWPORT (St John the Evangelist) (St Mary) (St Matthew) *Mon 8*   **V** D NEALE,   **NSM** J K BEARDMORE,
C H HOCKEY

MALLYWD (St Tydecho)   *see* Bro Ddyfi Uchaf *Ban*
MALPAS (St Mary) *Mon 8*   **V** D G PARFITT,   **NSM** M E DUNN
MAMHILAD (St Illtud) w Monkswood and Glascoed Chapel *Mon 4*   **P-in-c** R E PAIN
MANAFON (St Michael)   *see* Llanfair Caereinion, Llanllugan and Manafon *St As*
MANCOT (St Michael)   *see* Hawarden *St As*
MANORBIER (St James)   *see* Carew *St D*
MANORDEILO (St Paul)   *see* Llansadwrn w Llanwrda and Manordeilo *St D*
MANOROWEN (St Mary)   *see* Llanwnda, Goodwick w Manorowen and Llanstinan *St D*
MANSELTON (St Michael and All Angels) and Cwmbwrla *S & B 10*   **V** J B DAVIES
MARCHWIEL (St Marcella)   *see* Bangor Monachorum, Worthenbury and Marchwiel *St As*
MARCROSS (Holy Trinity)   *see* Llantwit Major *Llan*
MARGAM (St Mary) (St David) *Llan 5*   **V** T A DOHERTY
MARLOES (St Peter)   *see* Dale and St Brides w Marloes *St D*
MARROS (St Lawrence)   *see* Pendine w Llanmiloe and Eglwys Gymyn w Marros *St D*
MARSHFIELD (St Mary) and Peterstone Wentloog and Coedkernew w St Bride's Wentloog *Mon 5*   **V** D C MATTHEWS
MARTLETWY (St Marcellus)   *see* Jeffreyston w Reynoldston and Loveston etc *St D*
MATHERN (St Tewdric) and Mounton w St Pierre *Mon 3*
V J E L WHITE
MATHRY (Holy Martyrs) w St Edren's and Grandston w St Nicholas and Jordanston *St D 2*   **P-in-c** A C SALMON
MATTHEWSTOWN (All Saints)   *see* Penrhiwceiber, Matthewstown and Ynysboeth *Llan*
MAUDLAM (St Mary Magdalene)   *see* Pyle w Kenfig *Llan*
MEIDRIM (St David) and Llanboidy and Merthyr *St D 14*
V J GAINER
MEIFOD (St Tysilio and St Mary) w Llangynyw w Pont Robert w Pont Dolanog *St As 8*   **V** J L W WILLIAMS
MELIDEN (St Melyd) (St Mary Magdalene) and Gwaenysgor *St As 1*   **V** J C HARVEY
MELINE (St Dogmael) *St D 5*   **V** *vacant*
MENAI BRIDGE (St Mary)   *see* Llandegfan w Llandysilio *Ban*
MERLIN'S BRIDGE (St Mark)   *see* Haverfordwest *St D*
MERTHYR (St Martin)   *see* Meidrim and Llanboidy and Merthyr *St D*
MERTHYR CYNOG (St Cynog)   *see* Dan yr Eppynt *S & B*
MERTHYR DYFAN (St Dyfan and St Teilo) *Llan 3*
R R C PARRISH
MERTHYR MAWR (St Teilo)   *see* Laleston and Merthyr Mawr *Llan*
MERTHYR TYDFIL (Christ Church) (St Luke) *Llan 10*
V S S MORGAN
MERTHYR TYDFIL (St David) (St Tydfil's Well) and Abercanaid *Llan 10*   **R** M J DAVIES,   **C** D T MORRIS
MERTHYR VALE (St Mary and Holy Innocents)   *see* Troedyrhiw w Merthyr Vale *Llan*
MICHAELSTON-LE-PIT (St Michael and All Angels)   *see* St Andrews Major w Michaelston-le-Pit *Llan*
MICHAELSTON-SUPER-AVON   *see* Cwmafan *Llan*
MICHAELSTON-SUPER-ELY (St Michael)   *see* St Fagans w Michaelston-super-Ely *Llan*
MICHAELSTON-Y-FEDW (St Michael) *Mon 5*
P-in-c M C G LANE
MICHEL TROY (St Michael)   *see* Monmouth w Overmonnow etc *Mon*
MILFORD HAVEN (St Katherine) (St Peter) (St Thomas à Becket) *St D 4*   **V** *vacant*
MINERA (St Mary) (St Tudfil) w Coedpoeth and Bwlchgwyn *St As 15*   **V** J P HARRIS
MINWEAR (St Womar)   *see* Narberth w Mounton w Robeston Wathen etc *St D*
MISKIN (St John the Baptist)   *see* Mountain Ash and Miskin *Llan*
MOCHDRE (All Saints)   *see* Kerry, Llanmerewig, Dolfor and Mochdre *St As*
MOLD (St Mary) *St As 16*   **V** C I DAY
MONINGTON (St Nicholas)   *see* St Dogmael's w Moylgrove and Monington *St D*
MONKNASH (St Mary)   *see* Llantwit Major *Llan*
MONKSWOOD (St Matthew)   *see* Mamhilad w Monkswood and Glascoed Chapel *Mon*
MONKTON (St Nicholas and St John) *St D 3*   **TV** R JONES,
G P HOWELL
MONMOUTH (St Mary the Virgin) w Overmonnow w Wonastow w Michel Troy *Mon 2*   **V** D J MCGLADDERY,
C N J MUNDAY,   **NSM** A M GREEN, J M BOWEN
MONTGOMERY (St Nicholas) and Forden and Llandyssil *St As 10*   **R** T E BENNETT,   **NSM** R BRIGNELL

MORFIL   *see* Fishguard w Llanychar and Pontfaen w Morfil etc *St D*

MORRISTON (St David) (St John) *S & B 7*   V H M LERVY, C J M THOMAS

MOSTYN (Christ Church) *St As 4*   P-in-c S F HILDRETH

MOUNTAIN ASH (St Margaret) (St Illtyd) and Miskin *Llan 9*   V M K JONES

MOUNTON   *see* Narberth w Mounton w Robeston Wathen etc *St D*

MOUNTON (St Andoenus)   *see* Mathern and Mounton w St Pierre *Mon*

MOYLGROVE (St Mynno, St David and St Andrew)   *see* St Dogmael's w Moylgrove and Monington *St D*

MWNT (Holy Cross)   *see* Cardigan w Mwnt and Y Ferwig w Llangoedmor *St D*

MYDDFAI (St Michael)   *see* Llandingat w Myddfai *St D*

MYDROILYN (Holy Trinity)   *see* Llanerch Aeron w Ciliau Aeron and Dihewyd etc *St D*

MYNACHLOGDDU (St Dogmael)   *see* Maenclochog and New Moat etc *St D*

MYNYDD ISA   *see* Bistre *St As*

MYNYDDISLWYN (St Tudor) *Mon 6*   TR J HUMPHRIES, TV A S HUNT,   NSM B A SMITH,   OLM M BARGE

NANNERCH (St Michael)   *see* Cilcain, Gwernaffield, Llanferres etc *St As*

NANTCWNLLE (St Cynllo)   *see* Llanfihangel Ystrad and Cilcennin w Trefilan etc *St D*

NANTGLYN (St James)   *see* Llanrhaeadr-yng-Nghinmeirch and Prion w Nantglyn *St As*

NANTMEL (St Cynllo)   *see* Gwastedyn *S & B*

NANTYGLO (Holy Trinity and St Anne)   *see* Blaina and Nantyglo *Mon*

NARBERTH (St Andrew) w Mounton w Robeston Wathen and Crinow and Minwear w Templeton *St D 3*   R T P LEWIS

NASH (St Mary)   *see* Carew *St D*

NASH (St Mary)   *see* Magor *Mon*

NEATH (St Thomas) (St David) (St Catherine) (St Peter and St Paul) *Llan 6*   TR S J RYAN,   C D O JONES, NSM L E NEWMAN

NEBO (Dewi Sant)   *see* Llansantffraed w Llanrhystud and Llanddeiniol *St D*

NEFYN (St David) (St Mary) w Tudweiliog w Llandudwen w Edern *Ban 11*   V S M M WILLIAMS

NELSON (St John the Baptist)   *see* Llanfabon *Llan*

NERCWYS (St Mary)   *see* Treuddyn w Nercwys *St As*

NEVERN (St Brynach)   *see* Newport w Cilgwyn and Nevern and Y Beifil etc *St D*

NEW HEDGES (St Anne)   *see* Tenby *St D*

NEW MOAT (St Nicholas)   *see* Maenclochog and New Moat etc *St D*

NEW RADNOR (St Mary) and Llanfihangel Nantmelan and Evancoyd w Gladwestry and Colva *S & B 5* P-in-c M T BEATON

NEW TREDEGAR (St Dingat)   *see* Bedwellty w New Tredegar *Mon*

NEWBOROUGH (St Peter) (St Thomas) w Llanidan w Llangeinwen and Llanfair-yn-y-Cymwd *Ban 6* P-in-c E ROBERTS

NEWBRIDGE (St Paul) (St Peter) *Mon 6*   V M J JEFFORD, NSM V I HODGES

NEWBRIDGE-ON-WYE (All Saints)   *see* Upper Wye *S & B*

NEWCASTLE (St Illtyd) *Llan 4*   V D E C LLOYD

NEWCASTLE EMLYN (Holy Trinity) w Llandyfriog and Troedyraur w Brongwyn and Cenarth *St D 6*   V D J L ROBERTS

NEWCHURCH (St Mary)   *see* Cynwyl Elfed w Newchurch and Trelech a'r Betws *St D*

NEWCHURCH (St Mary)   *see* Bryngwyn and Newchurch and Llanbedr etc *S & B*

NEWCHURCH (St Michael)   *see* Cynwyl Elfed w Newchurch and Trelech a'r Betws *St D*

NEWCHURCH (St Peter)   *as above*

NEWCHURCH (St Peter)   *see* Caerwent w Dinham and Llanfair Discoed etc *Mon*

NEWMARKET   *see* Dyserth and Trelawnyd and Cwm *St As*

NEWPORT (All Saints) *Mon 8*   P-in-c M SOADY

NEWPORT (Cathedral of St Woolos) (St Martin) *Mon 8* V *vacant* (01633) 63338

NEWPORT (Christ Church) *Mon 8*   V I S DOULL

NEWPORT (St Andrew) (St Philip) *Mon 8* P-in-c H C P M HALL

NEWPORT (St John Baptist) *Mon 8*   P-in-c C D WESTBROOK

NEWPORT (St John the Evangelist)   *see* Maindee Newport *Mon*

NEWPORT (St Julian (St Julius and St Aaron) *Mon 8* P-in-c J R MATTHIAS

NEWPORT (St Mark) *Mon 8*   V A R WILLIE

NEWPORT (St Mary)   *see* Maindee Newport *Mon*

NEWPORT (St Mary) w Cilgwyn and Nevern and Y Beifil and Dinas w Llanllawer *St D 5*   V N A LLEWELLYN

NEWPORT (St Matthew)   *see* Maindee Newport *Mon*

NEWPORT St Paul *Mon 8*   P-in-c J S J GROVES

NEWPORT (St Stephen) and Holy Trinity *Mon 8* V E L MATHIAS-JONES

NEWPORT (St Teilo) *Mon 8*   P-in-c T H J PALMER

NEWQUAY (St Llwchaiarn)   *see* Llanllwchaearn and Llanina *St D*

NEWTON (St Peter) *S & B 6*   V G E BENNETT

NEWTON NORTH   *see* Slebech and Uzmaston w Boulston *St D*

NEWTON NOTTAGE (St John the Baptist) (All Saints) (St David) *Llan 5*   R P R MASSON,   C A M FLIPSE

NEWTOWN (St David)   *see* Llanllwchaiarn and Newtown w Aberhafesp *St As*

NEYLAND (St Clement)   *see* Llanstadwel *St D*

NICHOLASTON (St Nicholas)   *see* Bishopston w Penmaen and Nicholaston *S & B*

NOLTON (St Madog) w Roch and St Lawrence w Ford and Hayscastle *St D 4*   R M H ROWLANDS

NOLTON (St Mary)   *see* Coity, Nolton and Brackla *Llan*

NORTHOP (St Eurgain and St Peter) (St Mary) *St As 16* V R P BILLINGSLEY

NORTON (Mission Church)   *see* Oystermouth *S & B*

NORTON (St Andrew)   *see* Knighton, Norton, Whitton, Pilleth and Cascob *S & B*

NOTTAGE (St David)   *see* Newton Nottage *Llan*

OAKWOOD (St John)   *see* Neath *Llan*

OGMORE VALE (St David)   *see* Llandyfodwg and Cwm Ogwr *Llan*

OVERMONNOW (St Thomas)   *see* Monmouth w Overmonnow etc *Mon*

OVERTON (St Mary the Virgin) and Erbistock and Penley *St As 11*   R D T B LEWIS

OXWICH (St Illtyd)   *see* SW Gower *S & B*

OYSTERMOUTH (All Saints) *S & B 6*   V K EVANS

PANTEG (St Mary) w Llanfihangel Pontymoile *Mon 9* R J V MOLE,   Par Dn P R EVANS

PANTYFFRID (Mission Church)   *see* Berriew *St As*

PATRICIO (St Issui the Martyr)   *see* Llangenni and Llanbedr Ystrad Yw w Patricio *S & B*

PEMBROKE (St Daniel)   *see* Monkton *St D*

PEMBROKE (St Mary)   *as above*

PEMBROKE (St Michael)   *as above*

PEMBROKE DOCK (St John)   *see* Carew *St D*

PEMBROKE DOCK (St Patrick)   *as above*

PEMBROKE DOCK (St Teilo)   *as above*

PEN-BOYR (St Llawddog)   *see* Llangeler w Pen-Boyr *St D*

PEN-BRE (St Illtud) *St D 11*   V D G DAVIES

PEN RHONDDA FAWR *Llan 12*   V B TAYLOR

PENALLT (Old Church)   *see* Trellech and Penallt *Mon*

PENALLY (St Nicholas)   *see* Tenby *St D*

PENARTH (All Saints) (St Peter) (St Luke) *Llan 3*   V P A COX, C M J DIMOND

PENARTH (St Augustine) (Holy Nativity) and Llandough *Llan 3* R D R WILLIAMS,   C E F DOWLAND-OWEN, NSM R M GRIFFITHS

PENBRYN (St Michael)   *see* Llangrannog w Llandysiliogogo w Penbryn *St D*

PENCADER (St Mary)   *see* Llanfihangel-ar-arth w Capel Dewi *St D*

PENCARREG (St Patrick) and Llanycrwys *St D 8* V W A STRANGE

PENCLAWDD   *see* Llanrhidian w Llanyrnewydd *S & B*

PENCOED (St David)   *see* Llanilid w Pencoed *Llan*

PENCOED (St Paul)   *as above*

PENDERYN MELLTE (St Cynog) *S & B 1*   R J H SCOTT

PENDINE (St Margaret) w Llanmiloe and Eglwys Gymyn w Marros *St D 14*   R W P NASH

PENDOYLAN (St Cadoc) w Welsh St Donats *Llan 7* P-in-c R V C LEWIS

PENEGOES (St Cadfarch)   *see* Machynlleth w Llanwrin and Penegoes *Ban*

PENHOW (St John the Baptist) and St Brides Netherwent w Llandavenny and Llanvaches and Llandevaud *Mon 3* V J HEALES

PENISARWAEN (St Helen)   *see* Llanddeiniolen w Llanfair-is-gaer etc *Ban*

PENLEY (St Mary Magdalene)   *see* Overton and Erbistock and Penley *St As*

PENLLECH   *see* Botwnnog w Bryncroes w Llangwnnadl w Penllech *Ban*

PENLLERGAER (St David) *S & B 9*   V F A BAYES

PENLLWYN (St Mary the Virgin) *see* Mynyddislwyn *Mon*
PENLLYN (Chapel of Ease) *see* Cowbridge *Llan*
PENMAEN (St David) *see* Mynyddislwyn *Mon*
PENMAEN (St John the Baptist) *see* Bishopston w Penmaen and Nicholaston *S & B*
PENMAENMAWR *see* Dwygyfylchi *Ban*
PENMARK (St Mary) w Llancarfan w Llantrithyd *Llan 3* **P-in-c** F A JACKSON
PENMYNYDD (St Credifael) *see* Llanfair-pwll and Llanddaniel-fab etc *Ban*
PENNAL (St Peter ad Vincula) w Corris and Esgairgeiliog *Ban 10* **R** G AP IORWERTH
PENNANT (St Thomas) *see* Llanrhaeadr ym Mochnant etc *St As*
PENNANT MELANGELL (St Melangel) *as above*
PENNARD (St Mary) *see* Ilston w Pennard *S & B*
PENPONT (no dedication) *see* Dan yr Eppynt *S & B*
PENRHIWCEIBER (St Winifred), Matthewstown and Ynysboeth *Llan 9* **V** A K HOLMES
PENRHOS (Holy Trinity) *see* Llandysilio and Penrhos and Llandrinio etc *St As*
PENRHOS (St Cadoc) *see* Llantilio Crossenny w Penrhos, Llanvetherine etc *Mon*
PENRHOSLLUGWY (St Michael) *see* Llaneugrad w Llanallgo and Penrhosllugwy etc *Ban*
PENRHYDD *see* Maenordeifi Gp *St D*
PENRHYN-COCH (St John) *see* Elerch w Penrhyncoch w Capel Bangor and Goginan *St D*
PENRHYNDEUDRAETH (Holy Trinity) and Llanfrothen w Maentwrog and Beddgelert *Ban 8* **P-in-c** B BAILEY
PENRHYNSIDE BAY (St David) *see* Rhos-Cystennin *St As*
PENRICE (St Andrew) *see* SW Gower *S & B*
PENSARN (St David) *see* Abergele and St George *St As*
PENSTROWED (St Gwrhai) *see* Llandinam w Trefeglwys w Penstrowed *Ban*
PENTERRY (St Mary) *see* St Arvans w Penterry, Itton, Devauden etc *Mon*
PENTIR (St Cedol) *see* Glanogwen and Llanllechid w St Ann's and Pentir *Ban*
PENTRAETH (St Mary) *see* Llansadwrn w Llanddona and Llaniestyn etc *Ban*
PENTRE (St Peter) *see* Ystradyfodwg *Llan*
PENTRECHWYTH (St Peter) *see* Glantawe *S & B*
PENTREFOELAS (Parish Church) *see* Cerrigydrudion w Llanfihangel Glyn Myfyr etc *St As*
PENTROBIN (St John) *see* Hawarden *St As*
PENTWYN (St David) *see* Cyncoed *Mon*
PENTYRCH (St Cadwg) w Capel Llanillterne *Llan 2* **V** J W BINNY
PENYBONTFAWR *see* Llanrhaeadr ym Mochnant etc *St As*
PENYCAE (St Thomas) *see* Rhosymedre w Penycae *St As*
PENYCLAWDD (St Martin) *see* Rockfield and Dingestow Gp *Mon*
PENYDARREN (St John the Baptist) *see* Dowlais and Penydarren *Llan*
PENYFAI (All Saints) *Llan 4* **P-in-c** E S HARRIS
PENYFFORDD (Emmanuel) *see* Hope *St As*
PENYGRAIG (St Barnabas) *see* Dinas and Penygraig w Williamstown *Llan*
PENYWAUN (St Winifred) *see* Hirwaun *Llan*
PETERSTON-SUPER-ELY (St Peter) w St Brides-super-Ely *Llan 7* **P-in-c** R V C LEWIS
PETERSTON-SUPER-MONTEM (St Peter) *see* Llanharan w Peterston-super-Montem *Llan*
PETERSTONE WENTLOOG (St Peter) *see* Marshfield and Peterstone Wentloog etc *Mon*
PETRYAL and Betws yn Rhos *St As 6* **R** S J ROGERS
PILLETH (Our Lady of Pilleth) *see* Knighton, Norton, Whitton, Pilleth and Cascob *S & B*
PISTYLL (St Beuno) *see* Nefyn w Tudweiliog w Llandudwen w Edern *Ban*
PONT AMAN (St Thomas) *see* Betws w Ammanford *St D*
PONT DOLANOG (St John the Evangelist) *see* Meifod w Llangynyw w Pont Robert w Pont Dolanog *St As*
PONT-IETS (St Mary) *see* Gwendraeth Fawr *St D*
PONT RHONDDA *Llan 12* **V** P S GALE
PONT ROBERT (St John the Evangelist) *see* Meifod w Llangynyw w Pont Robert w Pont Dolanog *St As*
PONTARDAWE (All Saints) *see* Llangiwg *S & B*
PONTARDAWE (St Peter) *as above*
PONTARDDULAIS *see* Llandeilo Tal-y-bont *S & B*
PONTARFYNACH *see* Grwp Bro Ystwyth a Mynach *St D*
PONTARGOTHI (Holy Trinity) *see* Llanegwad w Llanfihangel Uwch Gwili *St D*
PONTBLYDDYN (Christ Church) *St As 16* **P-in-c** C M POOLMAN

PONTERWYD *see* Grwp Bro Ystwyth a Mynach *St D*
PONTFADOG (St John) *see* Llansantffraid Glyn Ceirog and Llanarmon etc *St As*
PONTFAEN (St Brynach) *see* Fishguard w Llanychar and Pontfaen w Morfil etc *St D*
PONTLLANFRAITH (St Augustine) *see* Mynyddislwyn *Mon*
PONTLLIW (St Anne) *see* Penllergaer *S & B*
PONTLOTTYN (St Tyfaelog) (St Michael) (St Aidan) w Fochriw *Llan 8* **V** P A DEROY-JONES
PONTNEATHVAUGHAN (St John) *see* Penderyn Mellte *S & B*
PONTNEWYDD (Holy Trinity) *Mon 9* **V** D J DUNN, **Par Dn** H D THOMAS, **OLM** D L THOMAS
PONTNEWYNYDD (All Saints) *see* Pontypool *Mon*
PONTRHYDFENDIGAID (St David) *see* Tregaron w Ystrad Meurig and Strata Florida *St D*
PONTSIAN (St John) *see* Llandysul w Bangor Teifi w Henllan etc *St D*
PONTYATES (St Mary) *see* Gwendraeth Fawr *St D*
PONTYBEREM (St John) *as above*
PONTYCLUN (St Paul) w Talygarn *Llan 7* **V** G P KARAMURA
PONTYCYMMER (St David) *see* Llangeinor and the Garw Valley *Llan*
PONTYGWAITH (St Mary Magdalene) *see* Rhondda Fach Uchaf *Llan*
PONTYMISTER (St Margaret) *see* Risca *Mon*
PONTYPOOL (St James) (St Matthew) *Mon 9* **R** B R PIPPEN, **TV** M C WARREN
PONTYPRIDD (St Catherine) *Llan 11* **V** vacant (01443) 402021
PONTYPRIDD St Matthew and Cilfynydd w Llanwynno *Llan 11* **P-in-c** E EVANS
POOL QUAY (St John the Evangelist) *see* Welshpool, Castle Caereinion and Pool Quay *St As*
PORT EYNON (St Cattwg) *see* SW Gower *S & B*
PORT TALBOT (St Agnes) *see* Aberavon *Llan*
PORT TALBOT (St David) *see* Margam *Llan*
PORT TALBOT (St Theodore) (Holy Cross) (St Peter) *Llan 5* **V** C J AMOS
PORTH NEWYDD (St Paul) *Llan 12* **P-in-c** C W COLES
PORTHCAWL (All Saints) *see* Newton Nottage *Llan*
PORTHKERRY (St Curig) and Rhoose *Llan 3* **P-in-c** D O TREHARNE
PORTHMADOC (St John) (St Cyngar) and Ynyscynhaearn and Dolbenmaen *Ban 11* **P-in-c** K V WILLIAMS, D J WILLIAMS
PORTSKEWETT (St Mary) *see* Caldicot *Mon*
PRENDERGAST (St David) w Rudbaxton *St D 1* **R** G D GWYTHER
PRESTATYN (Christ Church) (Church of Holy Spirit) *St As 1* **V** D Q BELLAMY
PRINCES GATE (St Catherine) *see* Lampeter Velfrey and Llanddewi Velfrey *St D*
PRION (St James) *see* Llanrhaeadr-yng-Nghinmeirch and Prion w Nantglyn *St As*
PUNCHESTON (St Mary) *see* Letterston w Llanfair Nant-y-Gof etc *St D*
PUNCHSTON *see* Fishguard w Llanychar and Pontfaen w Morfil etc *St D*
PWLL (Holy Trinity) *see* Burry Port and Pwll *St D*
PWLLCROCHAN *see* Monkton *St D*
PWLLGWAUN (St Mark) and Llanddewi Rhondda *Llan 11* **P-in-c** D K SHEEN
PWLLHELI *see* Denio w Abererch *Ban*
PYLE (St James) (St Mary Magdalene) w Kenfig *Llan 5* **V** D A WALKER
QUAR, THE (St Tydfil's Well) *see* Merthyr Tydfil St Dav and Abercanaid *Llan*
QUEENSFERRY (St Andrew) *see* Shotton *St As*
RADNOR (St Mary) *see* New Radnor and Llanfihangel Nantmelan etc *S & B*
RADNOR, EAST *see* Knighton, Norton, Whitton, Pilleth and Cascob *S & B*
RADYR (St John the Baptist) (Christ Church) *Llan 2* **R** J WIGLEY,   **NSM** C A COLTON
RAGLAN (St Cadoc) w Llandenny and Bryngwyn *Mon 4* **P-in-c** J WAKELING
REDBERTH (Church) *see* Carew *St D*
REDWICK (St Thomas) *see* Magor *Mon*
RESOLVEN (St David) *see* Vale of Neath *Llan*
REYNOLDSTON (Church) *see* Jeffreyston w Reynoldston and Loveston etc *St D*
REYNOLDSTON (St George) *see* SW Gower *S & B*
RHANDIRMWYN (St Barnabas) *see* Cil-y-Cwm and Ystradffin w Rhandir-mwyn etc *St D*
RHAYADER (St Clement) *see* Gwastedyn *S & B*

STRATA FLORIDA (St Mary)   *see* Tregaron w Ystrad Meurig and Strata Florida *St D*

SULLY (St John the Baptist) *Llan 3*   **R** E B DOWDING

SWANSEA (St Barnabas) *S & B 11*   **V** *vacant* (01792) 298601

SWANSEA (St Gabriel) *S & B 6*   **V** D M GRIFFITHS

SWANSEA (St James) *S & B 11*   **V** *vacant* (01792) 470532

SWANSEA (St Jude) (St Nicholas-on-the-Hill) *S & B 11*   **V** H V PARSELL

SWANSEA (St Luke)   *see* Manselton and Cwmbwrla *S & B*

SWANSEA (St Peter) *S & B 10*   **V** H M WILLIAMS

SWANSEA (St Thomas) (St Stephen) and Kilvey *S & B 11*   **V** A J M MEREDITH,   **NSM** J W WEDGBURY

SWANSEA, CENTRAL (St Mary) (Holy Trinity) (Christ Church) (St Matthew) (St Mark) (St John) *S & B 11*   **TV** C L WILLIAMS, S M KNIGHT,   **C** I DREW-JONES,   **NSM** A JONES

TAI'RGWAITH (St David)   *see* Gwaun-cae-Gurwen *St D*

TAL-Y-LLYN (St David)   *see* Llanegryn w Aberdyfi w Tywyn *Ban*

TALACHDDU (St Mary)   *see* Llandefalle and Llyswen w Boughrood etc *S & B*

TALBENNY (St Mary)   *see* Walton W w Talbenny and Haroldston W *St D*

TALGARREG (St David)   *see* Llanarth and Capel Cynon w Talgarreg etc *St D*

TALGARTH (St Gwendoline) w Bronllys w Llanfilo *S & B 4*   **V** R T EDWARDS

TALIARIS (Holy Trinity)   *see* Llandeilo Fawr and Taliaris *St D*

TALLARN GREEN (St Mary Magdalene)   *see* Hanmer and Bronington and Bettisfield *St As*

TALLEY (St Michael)   *see* Cynwyl Gaeo w Llansawel and Talley *St D*

TALYBONT (St Cross)   *see* Tregarth and Llandygai and Maes y Groes *Ban*

TALYBONT (St David)   *see* Llanfihangel Genau'r-glyn and Llangorwen *St D*

TALYGARN (St Anne)   *see* Pontyclun w Talygarn *Llan*

TALYLLYN   *see* Pennal w Corris and Esgairgeiliog *Ban*

TALYLLYN (St Mary)   *see* Llanegryn w Aberdyfi w Tywyn *Ban*

TEMPLETON (St John)   *see* Narberth w Mounton w Robeston Wathen etc *St D*

TENBY (St Mary) (St Julian's Chapel) *St D 3*   **TR** A J DAVIES,   **TV** S M JOHN,   **C** M L OSBORNE

TINTERN (St Michael)   *see* Llandogo w Whitebrook Chpl and Tintern Parva *Mon*

TIRABAD (St David)   *see* Blaenau Irfon *S & B*

TIRTHIL (St Michael)   *see* Pontlottyn w Fochriw *Llan*

TON PENTRE   *see* Ystradyfodwg *Llan*

TON-YR-YWEN (School)   *see* Llanishen *Llan*

TONDU (St John)   *see* Llansantffraid, Bettws and Aberkenfig *Llan*

TONDU (St Thomas)   *as above*

TONGWYNLAIS (St Michael) (St James) *Llan 2*   **V** *vacant* (029) 2081 0437

TONMAWR (St Teilo)   *see* Neath *Llan*

TONNA (St Anne)   *see* Cadoxton-juxta-Neath and Tonna *Llan*

TONYPANDY (St Andrew) w Clydach Vale *Llan 12*   **V** P A LEYSHON

TONYREFAIL (St David) (St Alban) w Gilfach Goch *Llan 12*   **V** R E MOVERLEY,   **NSM** J SHAW

TOWNHILL   *see* Swansea St Jude w St Nic *S & B*

TOWYN (St Mary) *St As 1*   **V** *vacant*

TRAEAN-GLAS (St Mary)   *see* Defynnog, Llandilo'r Fan, Llanulid, Llywel etc *S & B*

TRALLWNG (St David)   *see* Dan yr Eppynt *S & B*

TRAWSFYNYDD (St Madryn)   *see* Llanffestiniog w Blaenau Ffestiniog etc *Ban*

TRE-GROES (St Ffraid)   *see* Llandysul w Bangor Teifi w Henllan etc *St D*

TRE-LECH A'R BETWS (St Teilo)   *see* Cynwyl Elfed w Newchurch and Trelech a'r Betws *St D*

TREALAW (All Saints)   *see* Pont Rhondda *Llan*

TREBANOS (St Michael)   *see* Clydach *S & B*

TREBOETH (Penlan Church)   *see* Landore w Treboeth *S & B*

TREBOETH (St Alban)   *as above*

TREDEGAR (St George) (St James) *Mon 6*   **V** J G DAVIS,   **C** V L ASHLEY

TREDUNNOC (St Andrew) *Mon 4*   **V** *vacant*

TREFDRAETH (St Beuno) (Eglwys Crist y Brenin) w Aberffraw w Llangadwaladr w Cerrigceinwen *Ban 4*   **R** *vacant* (01407) 840190

TREFEGLWYS (St Michael)   *see* Llandinam w Trefeglwys w Penstrowed *Ban*

TREFGARN (St Michael)   *see* Spittal w Trefgarn and Ambleston w St Dogwells *St D*

TREFILAN (St Hilary)   *see* Llanfihangel Ystrad and Cilcennin w Trefilan etc *St D*

TREFLYS (St Michael)   *see* Criccieth and Treflys w Llanystumdwy etc *Ban*

TREFNANT (Holy Trinity)   *see* Cefn w Trefnant w Tremeirchion *St As*

TREFOR (St George)   *see* Llanaelhaearn w Clynnog Fawr *Ban*

TREFRIW (St Mary)   *see* Caerhun and Llangelynnin and Llanbedr-y-Cennin *Ban*

TREGAEAN (St Caian)   *see* Llangefni w Tregaean *Ban*

TREGAER (St Mary)   *see* Rockfield and Dingestow Gp *Mon*

TREGARON (St Caron) w Ystrad Meurig and Strata Florida *St D 8*   **V** P W DAVIES

TREGARTH (St Mair) and Llandygai and Maes y Groes *Ban 5*   **P-in-c** J G MATTHEWS

TREGYNON (St Cynon)   *see* Betws Cedewain and Tregynon and Llanwyddelan *St As*

TREHARRIS (St Matthias), Trelewis and Bedlinog *Llan 10*   **P-in-c** M GIBBON

TREHERBERT (St Alban)   *see* Pen Rhondda Fawr *Llan*

TREHERBERT (St Mary Communion Centre)   *as above*

TRELAWNYD (St Michael)   *see* Dyserth and Trelawnyd and Cwm *St As*

TRELLECH (St Nicholas) and Penallt *Mon 3*   **V** S J HOWELLS

TRELLECH GRANGE (not known)   *see* Llanishen w Trellech Grange and Llanfihangel etc *Mon*

TREMAIN (St Michael)   *see* Aberporth w Tremain w Blaenporth and Betws Ifan *St D*

TREMEIRCHION (Corpus Christi)   *see* Cefn w Trefnant w Tremeirchion *St As*

TREMORFA (St Philip) Conventional District *Llan 3*   **P-in-c** R M CAPPER

TREORCHY (St Matthew)   *see* Pen Rhondda Fawr *Llan*

TRETHOMAS (St Thomas)   *see* Bedwas w Machen w Rudry *Mon*

TRETOWER (St John the Evangelist)   *see* Crickhowell w Cwmdu and Tretower *S & B*

TREUDDYN (St Mary) w Nercwys *St As 16*   **V** J B JONES

TREVETHIN (St Cadoc)   *see* Pontypool *Mon*

TREVETHIN (St John the Divine)   *as above*

TREVOR (Church)   *see* Llangollen w Trevor and Llantysilio *St As*

TREWALCHMAI (St Morhaiarn)   *see* Llandrygarn w Bodwrog and Heneglwys etc *Ban*

TRISANT *St D 11*   **TR** M A ROWLANDS

TROED-YR-AUR (St Michael)   *see* Newcastle Emlyn w Llandyfriog and Troedyraur etc *St D*

TROEDRHIWGARTH (St Mary the Virgin) *Llan 5*   **V** C T REANEY

TROEDYRHIW (St John) w Merthyr Vale *Llan 10*   **V** S J BARNES

TROSTEY (St David)   *see* Bettws Newydd w Trostrey etc *Mon*

TROWBRIDGE MAWR (St Hilary)   *see* Rumney *Mon*

TUDWEILIOG (St Cwyfan)   *see* Nefyn w Tudweiliog w Llandudwen w Edern *Ban*

TUMBLE (Dewi Sant)   *see* Trisant *St D*

TY SIGN (St David)   *see* Risca *Mon*

TYCOCH (All Souls) *S & B 6*   **V** P J GWYNN

TYCROES (St Edmund)   *see* Llanedi w Tycroes and Saron *St D*

TYLORSTOWN (Holy Trinity)   *see* Rhondda Fach Uchaf *Llan*

TYNANT (Mission Church)   *see* Penrhyndeudraeth and Llanfrothen w Maentwrog etc *Ban*

TYWYN (St Cadfan)   *see* Llanegryn w Aberdyfi w Tywyn *Ban*

TYWYN (St Matthew)   *as above*

UNDY (St Mary)   *see* Magor *Mon*

UPPER WYE, The *S & B 2*   **V** B L T GRIFFITH

USK (St Mary) and Gwehelog w Llantrisant w Llanllowell *Mon 4*   **V** J F GRAY

UZMASTON (St Ismael)   *see* Slebech and Uzmaston w Boulston *St D*

VALE OF NEATH *Llan 6*   **V** P A LEWIS

VALLEY (St Michael) w Llechylched and Caergeiliog *Ban 3*   **R** N A RIDINGS

VAYNOR (St Gwynno)   *see* Cefn Coed w Vaynor *S & B*

WALTON EAST (St Mary)   *see* Wiston w Walton E and Clarbeston *St D*

WALTON WEST (All Saints) w Talbenny and Haroldston West *St D 4*   **R** A P JOHNSON

WALWYN'S CASTLE (St James the Great) w Robeston West *St D 4*   **P-in-c** R M M JOHNSON

WATERSTON   *see* Llanstadwel *St D*

WATTSTOWN (St Thomas)   *see* Ynyshir *Llan*

WAUNARLLWYDD (St Barnabas) *S & B 9*   **V** I DAVIES

WAUNFAWR (St John the Evangelist)   *see* Llanbeblig w Caernarfon and Betws Garmon etc *Ban*

WAUNFELIN (St John the Divine)   *see* Pontypool *Mon*

WAUNWEN (St Mark) *see* Cen Swansea *S & B*
WELSH ST DONATS (St Donat) *see* Pendoylan w Welsh St Donats *Llan*
WELSHPOOL (St Mary), Castle Caereinion and Pool Quay *St As 10* **NSM** E M POWELL
WENVOE (St Mary) and St Lythans *Llan 3* **R** E B DOWDING
WHISTON (not known) *see* Magor *Mon*
WHITCHURCH (St David) *see* Dewisland *St D*
WHITCHURCH (St Mary) (St Thomas) (All Saints) *Llan 2* **TR** J H L ROWLANDS, **TV** A P JAMES, **Hon C** H G LEWIS, **NSM** P A MORTIMER
WHITEBROOK (Holy Trinity) *see* Llandogo w Whitebrook Chpl and Tintern Parva *Mon*
WHITECHURCH IN KEMES *see* Eglwyswen *St D*
WHITFORD (St Mary and St Beuno) *see* Gorsedd w Brynford, Ysgeifiog and Whitford *St As*
WHITLAND (St Mary) w Cyffig and Henllan Amgoed and Llangan w Llandysilio and Clunderwen *St D 14* **V** K G TAYLOR
WHITTON (St David) *see* Knighton, Norton, Whitton, Pilleth and Cascob *S & B*
WICK (St James) *see* Llantwit Major *Llan*
WILCRICK (St Mary) *see* Magor *Mon*
WILLIAMSTON, EAST (Church) *see* Begelly w Ludchurch and E Williamston *St D*
WILLIAMSTOWN (St Illtud) *see* Dinas and Penygraig w Williamstown *Llan*
WISTON (St Mary Magdalene) w Walton East and Clarbeston *St D 1* **V** N CALE
WOLVESNEWTON (St Thomas à Becket) *see* Llangwm Uchaf and Llangwm Isaf w Gwernesney etc *Mon*
WONASTOW (St Wonnow) *see* Monmouth w Overmonnow etc *Mon*
WORTHENBURY (St Deiniol) *see* Bangor Monachorum, Worthenbury and Marchwiel *St As*
WREXHAM (St Giles's Parish Church) (St David) (St Mark) (St Mary) (All Saints) (St Margaret) (St James) (St John) *St As 18* **TR** M F WEST, **TV** R J HAINSWORTH, S ERRINGTON, E OWEN, M BURNS, **P-in-c** G WINDON, **C** A ANTHAPURUSHA, K J TILTMAN

WYNDHAM (St David) *see* Llandyfodwg and Cwm Ogwr *Llan*
Y BEIFIL (St Andrew) *see* Newport w Cilgwyn and Nevern and Y Beifil etc *St D*
Y FERWIG (St Pedrog) *see* Cardigan w Mwnt and Y Ferwig w Llangoedmor *St D*
YERBESTON *see* Jeffreyston w Reynoldston and Loveston etc *St D*
YNYSBOETH *see* Penrhiwceiber, Matthewstown and Ynysboeth *Llan*
YNYSCYHAEARN (Mission Church) *see* Porthmadoc and Ynyscynhaearn and Dolbenmaen *Ban*
YNYSCYHAEARN (St Cynhaearn) *as above*
YNYSCYNON (St Cynon) *see* Pont Rhondda *Llan*
YNYSDDU (St Theodore) *see* Mynyddislwyn *Mon*
YNYSHIR (St Thomas) *Llan 12* **V** G P BIGMORE
YNYSMEUDW (St Mary) *see* Llangiwg *S & B*
YSBYTY CYNFYN (St John the Baptist) *see* Grwp Bro Ystwyth a Mynach *St D*
YSBYTY IFAN (St John the Baptist) *see* Cerrigydrudion w Llanfihangel Glyn Myfyr etc *St As*
YSBYTY YSTWYTH (St John the Baptist) *see* Grwp Bro Ystwyth a Mynach *St D*
YSFA (St Mark) *see* Gwastedyn *S & B*
YSGEIFIOG (St Mary) *see* Gorsedd w Brynford, Ysgeifiog and Whitford *St As*
YSTALYFERA (St David) *S & B 7* **V** T J HEWITT
YSTRAD-FFIN (St Paulinus) *see* Cil-y-Cwm and Ystrad-ffin w Rhandir-mwyn etc *St D*
YSTRAD MEURIG (St John the Baptist) *see* Tregaron w Ystrad Meurig and Strata Florida *St D*
YSTRAD MYNACH (Holy Trinity) w Llanbradach *Llan 8* **V** S P KIRK
YSTRAD RHONDDA (St Stephen) *see* Pont Rhondda *Llan*
YSTRAD ROAD (St Illtyd) *see* Swansea St Pet *S & B*
YSTRADFELLTE (St Mary) *see* Penderyn Mellte *S & B*
YSTRADGYNLAIS (St Cynog) *S & B 7* **R** D I DAVIES
YSTRADOWEN (St Owain) *see* Cowbridge *Llan*
YSTRADYFODWG (St John the Baptist) *Llan 12* **V** H H ENGLAND-SIMON

SCOTTISH INCUMBENCIES

An index of incumbencies of the Scottish Episcopal Church. The incumbency entry gives the full legal name, followed by the diocese and the name(s) and appointment(s) of the clergy serving there (if there are none, the telephone number of the parsonage house is given where known). Church dedications are indicated in brackets. The following are the main abbreviations used; for others see the full list of abbreviations.

C	Curate	**NSM**	Non-stipendiary Minister
Dss	Deaconess	**P-in-c**	Priest-in-charge
Hon C	Honorary Curate	**R**	Rector

ABERCHIRDER (St Marnan) *Mor* **R** *vacant*
ABERDEEN (Cathedral of St Andrew) *Ab* **R** R E KILGOUR
ABERDEEN (St Clement) *Ab* **NSM** N O EGBE
ABERDEEN (St James) *Ab* **P-in-c** S M PATERSON,
NSM R B EDWARDS
ABERDEEN (St John the Evangelist) *Ab* **R** I M POOBALAN
ABERDEEN (St Margaret of Scotland) *Ab* **R** A E NIMMO,
Hon C D H WRIGHT
ABERDEEN (St Mary) *Ab* **R** G S TAYLOR, **C** J M HOBBS
ABERDEEN (St Ninian) *Ab* **P-in-c** R E KILGOUR,
S J FERGUSON
ABERDEEN (St Peter) *Ab* **P-in-c** I M POOBALAN
ABERDOUR (St Columba) - West Fife Team Ministry *St And*
R V A NELLIST, **NSM** M A STIRZAKER
ABERFOYLE (St Mary) *St And* **R** R W GROSSE
ABERLOUR (St Margaret of Scotland) *Mor* **NSM** N C MILNE
ABOYNE (St Peter) *Ab* **R** J S CURRY
AIRDRIE (St Paul) *Glas* **R** *vacant* (01236) 763402
ALEXANDRIA (St Mungo) *Glas* **P-in-c** S H B GORTON
ALFORD (St Andrew) *Ab* **P-in-c** A L JAMES,
NSM J BURCHILL
ALLOA (St John the Evangelist) *St And* **C** V A WALKER,
NSM E FORGAN
ALYTH (St Ninian) *St And* **R** K W RATHBAND,
NSM D A CAMERON, M LEGGATT
ANNAN (St John the Evangelist) *Glas* **P-in-c** M P CALLAGHAN,
Hon C J L HIGGINS
APPIN *see* W Highland Region *Arg*
ARBROATH (St Mary) *Bre* **R** J CUTHBERT, **C** J M MUMFORD
ARDBRECKNISH (St James) *Arg* **R** N D MACCALLUM
ARDCHATTAN (Holy Spirit) *Arg* **R** N D MACCALLUM
ARDROSSAN (St Andrew) *Glas* **NSM** A MONTGOMERIE
ARPAFEELIE (St John the Evangelist) *Mor* **R** M O LANGILLE
ARRAN, ISLE OF *Arg* **R** *vacant*
AUCHENBLAE *see* Drumtochty *Bre*
AUCHINDOIR (St Mary) *Ab* **R** J WALKER, **C** D ATKINSON,
NSM J BURCHILL
AUCHMITHIE (St Peter) *Bre* **R** J CUTHBERT,
C J M MUMFORD
AUCHTERARDER (St Kessog) *St And* **R** A E BARTON
AYR (Holy Trinity) *Glas* **R** I MEREDITH, **C** N COX,
NSM P S NEIL
BAILLIESTON (St John) *see* Glas E End *Glas*
BALERNO (St Mungo) *Edin* **R** M J H ROUND
BALLACHULISH (St John) *Arg* **R** *vacant*
BALLATER (St Kentigern) *Ab* **R** J S CURRY
BANCHORY (St Ternan) *Ab* **R** L K EUNSON
BANFF (St Andrew) *Ab* **P-in-c** J M PAISEY
BARROWFIELD (St John the Baptist) *Glas* **R** *vacant*
BATHGATE (St Columba) *Edin* **P-in-c** P V P BLACKLEDGE,
NSM P F KIRK
BEARSDEN (All Saints) w Milngavie *Glas* **TR** *vacant*
BELLS WYND *see* Douglas *Glas*
BIELDSIDE (St Devenick) *Ab* **R** P R WATSON,
Dss J E MACCORMACK
BIRNAM *see* Dunkeld *St And*
BISHOPBRIGGS (St James-the-Less) *Glas* **R** S A MARSH
BLAIR ATHOLL *see* Kilmaveonaig *St And*
BLAIRGOWRIE (St Catherine) *St And* **R** K W RATHBAND,
NSM D A CAMERON, M LEGGATT
BO'NESS (St Catharine) *Edin* **P-in-c** D R BUNYAN
BRAEMAR (St Margaret) *Ab* **R** J S CURRY
BRECHIN (St Andrew) *Bre* **R** D C MUMFORD,
NSM U R SHONE, J NELSON
BRIDGE OF ALLAN (St Saviour) *St And* **R** D M IND
BRIDGE OF WEIR (St Mary) *Glas*
P-in-c P J C MCGRANAGHAN
BRIDGEND *see* Islay *Arg*
BRORA (St Columba) *Mor* **R** *vacant*
BROUGHTY FERRY (St Mary) *Bre* **R** *vacant*
BUCKIE (All Saints) *Ab* **P-in-c** J M PAISEY
BUCKSBURN (St Machar) *Ab* **P-in-c** D HEDDLE
BUCKSTONE (St Fillan) *see* Edin St Fillan *Edin*
BURNSIDE *see* Moffat *Glas*

BURNTISLAND (St Serf) - West Fife Team Ministry *St And*
R V A NELLIST, **NSM** M A STIRZAKER
BURRAVOE (St Colman) *Ab* **NSM** E H MCNAB
CALLANDER (St Andrew) *St And* **R** R W GROSSE
CAMBUSLANG (St Cuthbert) *Glas* **R** S L LILLIE
CAMPBELTOWN (St Kiaran) *Arg* **R** *vacant* (01586) 53846
CARNOUSTIE (Holy Rood) *Bre* **R** A M HUGHES,
Hon C J B HARDIE
CASTLE DOUGLAS (St Ninian) *Glas* **P-in-c** D W BAYNE
CATHEDRAL OF THE ISLES *see* Cumbrae (or Millport) *Arg*
CATTERLINE (St Philip) *Bre* **P-in-c** M E JACKSON
CENTRAL BUCHAN *Ab* **R** *vacant*
CHALLOCH (All Saints) *Glas* **P-in-c** C MYLNE
CHAPELHILL *see* Cruden Bay *Ab*
CLARKSTON (St Aidan) *Glas* **R** N H TAYLOR,
NSM C CURTIS
CLERMISTON *see* Edin Clermiston Em *Edin*
CLYDEBANK (St Columba) *Glas* **R** *vacant*
COATBRIDGE (St John the Evangelist) *Glas* **R** *vacant*
COLDSTREAM (St Mary and All Souls) *Edin*
P-in-c C H KNIGHTS, **Hon C** J L EVANS
COLINTON *see* Edin St Cuth *Edin*
COMRIE (St Serf) *St And* **R** P LEWER ALLEN
COUPAR ANGUS (St Anne) *St And* **R** K W RATHBAND,
NSM D A CAMERON, M LEGGATT
COURTHILL Chapel *see* Kishorn *Mor*
COVE BAY (St Mary) *Ab* **R** *vacant* (01224) 895033
CRAIGHALL *see* Ellon *Ab*
CRIEFF (St Columba) *St And* **R** P LEWER ALLEN
CROACHY *see* Strathnairn St Paul *Mor*
CROMARTY (St Regulus) *Mor* **R** M O LANGILLE
CRUDEN BAY (St James the Less) *Ab* **R** P J MANDER,
NSM G P WHALLEY
CULLODEN (St Mary-in-the-Fields) *Mor*
P-in-c A A SINCLAIR
CUMBERNAULD (Holy Name) *Glas* **P-in-c** B A OGUGUO
CUMBRAE (Cathedral of The Isles and Collegiate Church of the
Holy Spirit) *Arg* **R** *vacant* (01475) 530353
CUMINESTOWN (St Luke) *see* Cen Buchan *Ab*
CUPAR (St James the Great) *St And* **R** A HASELHURST,
C J B BLACK
DALBEATTIE (Christ Church) *Glas* **R** K G STEPHEN,
Hon C R W STEPHENS, **NSM** B M SCOTT
DALKEITH (St Mary) *Edin* **R** P S HARRIS, **NSM** M E JONES,
E S JONES, J O GODFREY
DALMAHOY (St Mary) *Edin* **R** D L COLLINGWOOD,
NSM J DYER
DALRY (St Peter) *Glas* **R** *vacant*
DENNISTOUN (St Kentigern) *see* Glas E End *Glas*
DINGWALL (St James the Great) *Mor* **P-in-c** I N PALLETT,
NSM R FLOCKHART, V C SAUNDERS
DOLLAR (St James the Great) *St And* **R** A R FREARSON,
NSM F A M LAWRY, H I SOGA
DORNOCH (St Finnbarr) *Mor* **R** *vacant*
DOUGLAS (Sancta Sophia) *Glas* **R** *vacant* (01555) 663065
DOUNE (St Modoc) *St And* **NSM** S M COATES
DRUMLITHIE (St John the Baptist) *Bre* **R** M J R TURNER
DRUMTOCHTY (St Palladius) *Bre* **R** M J R TURNER
DUFFTOWN (St Michael and All Angels) *Mor*
NSM N C MILNE
DUMBARTON (St Augustine) *Glas* **R** K L MACAULAY
DUMFRIES (St John the Evangelist) *Glas* **R** S R PAISLEY,
Hon C A M SHUKMAN
DUNBAR (St Anne) *Edin* **P-in-c** S H M CAMERON
DUNBLANE (St Mary) *St And* **R** K BOHAN
DUNDEE (Cathedral of St Paul) *Bre* **R** *vacant*
DUNDEE (St John the Baptist) *Bre* **R** H A JONES
DUNDEE (St Luke) *Bre* **P-in-c** E H CAMPBELL
DUNDEE (St Margaret) *Bre* **R** H A JONES, **Hon C** A WALLER
DUNDEE (St Martin) *Bre* **R** H A JONES, **P-in-c** D ELDER
DUNDEE (St Mary Magdalene) *Bre* **R** D SHEPHERD
DUNDEE (St Ninian) *Bre* **P-in-c** E M LAMONT
DUNDEE (St Salvador) *Bre* **P-in-c** C H CLAPSON,
Hon C G M GREIG

DUNFERMLINE (Holy Trinity) - West Fife Team Ministry
  St And   **R** T P BENNISON,   **C** V A WALKER,
  Hon C R K KENNEDY
DUNKELD (St Mary) w Birnam *St And*   **R** D F BROOKE,
  NSM I ATKINSON
DUNOON (Holy Trinity) *Arg*   **P-in-c** A C SWIFT
DUNS (Christ Church) *Edin*   **P-in-c** K G WEBB
DUROR (St Adamnan)   *see* W Highland Region *Arg*
EAST END   *see* Glas S E End *Glas*
EAST KILBRIDE (St Mark) *Glas*   **P-in-c** K H FREEMAN
EASTGATE (St Peter)   *see* Peebles *Edin*
EASTRIGGS (St John the Evangelist) *Glas*
  P-in-c M P CALLAGHAN
EDINBURGH (Cathedral of St Mary) *Edin*   **R** G J T FORBES,
  C N MCNELLY,   **NSM** G P FOSTER
EDINBURGH (Christ Church) *Edin*   **R** S E MACDONALD,
  C A D L BAKER,   **NSM** J WILLIAMS, M H RAVEN
EDINBURGH (Emmanuel) *Edin*   **R** *vacant*
EDINBURGH (Good Shepherd) *Edin*   **R** D J B FOSTEKEW,
  C N MOLL,   **NSM** B M JOHNSON
EDINBURGH (Holy Cross) *Edin*   **R** W D KORNAHRENS
EDINBURGH (Old St Paul) *Edin*   **R** I J PATON,   **C** S J TIBBS,
  Hon C C S DAVIES-COLE,   **NSM** C NAISMITH
EDINBURGH (St Andrew and St Aidan) *Edin*   **R** *vacant*
EDINBURGH (St Barnabas) *Edin*   **P-in-c** P D DIXON,
  NSM A C ANDERSON
EDINBURGH (St Columba) *Edin*   **TV** R O GOULD,
  J B RICHARDSON, J D R WHITLEY,   **C** A C W WAGSTAFF
EDINBURGH (St Cuthbert) *Edin*   **R** E A LENNON
EDINBURGH (St David of Scotland) *Edin*   **P-in-c** D J DURIE
EDINBURGH (St Fillan) *Edin*   **R** M D ROBSON,
  Hon C M C REED
EDINBURGH (St Hilda) *Edin*   **R** *vacant*
EDINBURGH (St James the Less) *Edin*   **R** D A S MACLAREN,
  NSM M S NORTHCOTT, J P MITCHELL, J L MACLAREN
EDINBURGH (St John the Evangelist) *Edin*   **R** J A ARMES,
  C D REID,   **NSM** P J BRAND, C A HUME, F E ALEXANDER
EDINBURGH (St Luke)   *see* Wester Hailes St Luke *Edin*
EDINBURGH (St Margaret of Scotland) *Edin*
  P-in-c G R HART
EDINBURGH (St Mark) *Edin*   **R** *vacant*
EDINBURGH (St Martin of Tours) *Edin*   **R** J A CONWAY,
  C S B MARRIAGE,   **NSM** S KILBEY, D J WARNES
EDINBURGH (St Michael and All Saints) *Edin*
  R D C STANDEN,   **Hon C** M F CHATTERLEY
EDINBURGH (St Ninian) *Edin*   **R** F S BURBERRY
EDINBURGH (St Paul and St George) *Edin*   **R** D G RICHARDS,
  C D L NORBY, R J CORNFIELD, V C PARR
EDINBURGH (St Peter) *Edin*   **R** F W TOMLINSON,
  C R GREEN
EDINBURGH (St Philip and St James) *Edin*   **R** T N RONGONG
EDINBURGH (St Salvador) *Edin*   **C** N MOLL
EDINBURGH (St Thomas) Private Chapel *Edin*
  R I R HOPKINS
EDINBURGH (St Vincent) Private Chapel *Edin*
  P-in-c R A GRANT
ELGIN (Holy Trinity) w Lossiemouth (St Margaret) *Mor*
  NSM R E TAIT, J SCLATER, N C MILNE
ELIE AND EARLSFERRY (St Michael and All Angels) *St And*
  R I M DOWLEN
ELLON (St Mary on the Rock) *Ab*   **R** P J MANDER,
  NSM G P WHALLEY, C A FOX
EORROPAIDH (St Moluag) *Arg*   **NSM** B A MORRISON,
  C P A LOCKHART
ERSKINE   *see* Renfrew *Glas*
EYEMOUTH (St Ebba) *Edin*   **NSM** F D J SMOUT
FALKIRK (Christ Church) *Edin*   **R** J B PENMAN, R INNES,
  Hon C T NJUGUNA
FASQUE (St Andrew) *Bre*   **R** M J R TURNER
FETTERCAIRN   *see* Fasque *Bre*
FOCHABERS Gordon Chapel *Mor*   **R** *vacant* (01343) 820337
FORFAR (St John the Evangelist) *St And*   **R** W A MCCAFFERTY
FORRES (St John the Evangelist) *Mor*   **P-in-c** C J PIPER
FORT WILLIAM (St Andrew) *Arg*   **R** G A GUINNESS
FORTROSE (St Andrew) *Mor*   **R** M O LANGILLE
FRASERBURGH (St Peter) *Ab*   **R** *vacant* (01346) 23541
FYVIE (All Saints) *Ab*   **R** *vacant*
GALASHIELS (St Peter) *Edin*   **R** D I MCCOSH
GALLOWGATE   *see* Aberdeen St Marg *Ab*
GARTCOSH (St Andrew) *Glas*   **R** *vacant*
GATEHOUSE OF FLEET (St Mary) *Glas*   **R** R C CUTLER
GIRVAN (St John) *Glas*   **R** I MEREDITH,   **C** N COX
GLASGOW (All Saints) *Glas*   **R** *vacant* 0141-959 3730
GLASGOW (Cathedral of St Mary the Virgin) *Glas*
  R K HOLDSWORTH,   **NSM** C A MCKILLOP

GLASGOW East End (St John) (St Kentigern) (St Serf) *Glas*
  P-in-c A E J RICHARDSON
GLASGOW (Good Shepherd and Ascension) *Glas*
  P-in-c C OKEKE
GLASGOW (Holy Cross) *Glas*   **NSM** D D KEEBLE
GLASGOW (St Bride) *Glas*   **R** J H MILNE,
  Hon C S M P MAITLAND,   **NSM** I T DRAPER
GLASGOW (St Gabriel) *Glas*   **R** *vacant*
GLASGOW (St George) *Glas*   **R** *vacant*
GLASGOW (St Margaret) *Glas*   **R** S ROBERTSON,
  NSM P ROMANO
GLASGOW (St Matthew) *Glas*   **P-in-c** D K WOSTENHOLM
GLASGOW (St Ninian) *Glas*   **NSM** E J RODGERS
GLASGOW (St Oswald) *Glas*   **R** U J GERRY
GLASGOW (St Silas) Private Chapel *Glas*   **R** D W MCCARTHY
GLENCARSE (All Saints) *Bre*   **R** *vacant* (01738) 860386
GLENCOE (St Mary) *Arg*   **R** *vacant* (01855) 811335
GLENROTHES (St Luke the Evangelist) - Central Fife Team
  Ministry *St And*   **TV** J D MARTIN
GLENURQUHART (St Ninian) *Mor*   **R** *vacant* (01456) 476264
GOUROCK (St Bartholomew) *Glas*   **P-in-c** A R SHERIDAN
GOVAN   *see* Glas St Gabr *Glas*
GRANGEMOUTH (St Mary) *Edin*   **R** D R BUNYAN
GRANTOWN-ON-SPEY (St Columba) *Mor*
  P-in-c P A THOMPSON
GREENOCK (St John the Evangelist) *Glas*   **R** A R SHERIDAN
GRETNA (All Saints) *Glas*   **P-in-c** M P CALLAGHAN
GREYFRIARS   *see* Kirkcudbright *Glas*
GRULINE (St Columba)   *see* W Highland Region *Arg*
GULLANE (St Adrian) *Edin*   **R** J C LINDSAY
HADDINGTON (Holy Trinity) *Edin*   **R** A C DYER,
  NSM J WOOD
HAMILTON (St Mary the Virgin) *Glas*   **R** I D BARCROFT,
  NSM J B M MACLEOD, D JASPER
HARRIS, ISLE OF   *see* Leverburgh *Arg*
HARRIS, ISLE OF (Christ Church) *Arg*   **P-in-c** J D L DAVIES
HAWICK (St Cuthbert) *Edin*   **R** *vacant* (01450) 372043
HAY DRIVE   *see* Edin St Andr and St Aid *Edin*
HELENSBURGH (St Michael and All Angels) *Glas*
  P-in-c D A COOK
HUNTLY (Christ Church) *Mor*   **R** *vacant*
HYNDLAND (St Bride)   *see* Glas St Bride *Glas*
INNERLEITHEN (St Andrew) *Edin*   **NSM** C B AITCHISON,
  C CHAPLIN
INSCH (St Drostan) *Ab*   **R** *vacant*
INVERARAY (All Saints) *Arg*   **R** *vacant*
INVERBERVIE (St David) *Bre*   **R** S T COLLIS
INVERGORDON (St Ninian) *Mor*   **R** *vacant* (01349) 852392
INVERGOWRIE (All Souls) *Bre*   **C** A W CUMMINS
INVERKEITHING (St Peter) - West Fife Team Ministry *St And*
  R V A NELLIST,   **NSM** M A STIRZAKER
INVERNESS (Cathedral of St Andrew) *Mor*   **R** *vacant*
INVERNESS (St John the Evangelist) *Mor*
  P-in-c A A SINCLAIR
INVERNESS (St Michael and All Angels) *Mor*   **R** *vacant*
  (01463) 233797 or 224433
INVERURIE (St Mary) *Ab*   **R** J WALKER,   **C** D ATKINSON,
  NSM J BURCHILL
IONA (St Columba) *Arg*   **R** *vacant*
IRVINE (St Andrew) Local Ecumenical Partnership *Glas*
  NSM A MONTGOMERIE
ISLAY (St Columba) *Arg*   **R** *vacant*
ISLE OF HARRIS   *see* Harris Ch Ch *Arg*
JEDBURGH (St John the Evangelist) *Edin*   **Hon C** W J GROVER
JOHNSTONE (St John) *Glas*   **P-in-c** D M ORR
JORDANHILL (All Saints)   *see* Glas All SS *Glas*
KEITH (Holy Trinity) *Mor*   **R** *vacant*
KELSO (St Andrew) *Edin*   **R** C H KNIGHTS,   **Hon C** J L EVANS
KEMNAY (St Anne) *Ab*   **P-in-c** J WALKER,   **C** D ATKINSON,
  NSM J BURCHILL
KENTALLEN (St Moluag)   *see* W Highland Region *Arg*
KESSOCK-TORE   *see* Arpafeelie *Mor*
KILLIN (St Fillan) *St And*   **Hon C** J L L FAGERSON
KILMACOLM (St Fillan) *Glas*   **P-in-c** P J C MCGRANAGHAN
KILMARNOCK (Holy Trinity) *Glas*   **P-in-c** P M DOUGLAS
KILMARTIN (St Columba) *Arg*   **R** *vacant*
KILMAVEONAIG (St Adamnan) *St And*   **R** *vacant*
KINCARDINE O'NEIL (Christ Church) *Ab*   **R** L K EUNSON
KINGHORN (St Mary and St Leonard) *St And*
  NSM G N BENSON
KINLOCH RANNOCH (All Saints) *St And*   **R** *vacant*
KINLOCHLEVEN (St Paul)   *see* W Highland Region *Arg*
KINLOCHMOIDART (St Finian) *Arg*   **P-in-c** C G TONGUE
KINROSS (St Paul) *St And*   **R** *vacant*
KIRKCALDY (St Peter) *St And*   **NSM** G N BENSON

KIRKCUDBRIGHT (St Francis of Assisi) *Glas*   R R C CUTLER
KIRKWALL (St Olaf) *Ab*   NSM D DAWSON
KIRRIEMUIR (St Mary) *St And*   P-in-c R P HARLEY
KISHORN Chapel *Mor*   NSM H S WIDDOWS
KNIGHTSWOOD (Holy Cross)   *see* Glas H Cross *Glas*
LADYBANK (St Mary) *St And*   R A HASELHURST
LADYCROFT   *see* Balerno *Edin*
LANARK (Christ Church) *Glas*   R *vacant* (01555) 663065
LANGHOLM (All Saints) *Glas*   R *vacant* (01461) 38268
LARGS (St Columba) *Glas*   R G B FYFE
LASSWADE (St Leonard) *Edin*   R P S HARRIS,
  NSM M E JONES, E S JONES, J O GODFREY
LAURENCEKIRK (St Laurence) *Bre*   R M J R TURNER
LEITH (St James the Less)   *see* Edin St Jas *Edin*
LENZIE (St Cyprian) *Glas*   P-in-c G E W SCOBIE,
  C M E JAMIESON
LERWICK (St Magnus) *Ab*   NSM E H MCNAB
LEVEN (St Margaret) - Central Fife Team Ministry *St And*
  TV J D MARTIN
LEVERBURGH *Arg*   R *vacant*
LEWIS, ISLE OF   *see* Stornoway *Arg*
LINLITHGOW (St Peter) *Edin*   P-in-c P V P BLACKLEDGE
LIVINGSTON Local Ecumenical Partnership *Edin*
  Min E C THOMPSON
LOCHALSH (St Donnan) *Mor*   R *vacant*
LOCHBUIE (St Kilda) *Arg*   R *vacant*
LOCHEARNHEAD (St Angus) *St And*   R P LEWER ALLEN
LOCHEE (St Margaret)   *see* Dundee St Marg *Bre*
LOCHGELLY (St Finnian) - Central Fife Team Ministry *St And*
  TV J D MARTIN
LOCHGILPHEAD (Christ Church) *Arg*   R *vacant*
LOCHINVER (St Gilbert) *Mor*   R *vacant*
LOCKERBIE (All Saints) *Glas*   P-in-c M P CALLAGHAN,
  C L M BANDS
LONGSIDE (St John)   *see* Cen Buchan *Ab*
LOSSIEMOUTH (St Margaret)   *see* Elgin w Lossiemouth *Mor*
LUNAN HEAD (St Margaret) *St And*   R W A MCCAFFERTY
MARYGATE   *see* Pittenweem *St And*
MAYBOLE (St Oswald) *Glas*   R I MEREDITH,   C N COX
MELROSE (Holy Trinity) *Edin*   R M I HOUSTON,
  NSM D W WOOD, D J DALGLISH
MILLPORT   *see* Cumbrae (or Millport) *Arg*
MILNGAVIE (St Andrew)   *see* Bearsden w Milngavie *Glas*
MOFFAT (St John the Evangelist) *Glas*
  P-in-c M P CALLAGHAN,   C L M BANDS
MONIFIETH (Holy Trinity) *Bre*   R A M HUGHES
MONKLANDS   *see* Airdrie *Glas*
MONKSTOWN   *see* Ladybank *St And*
MONTROSE (St Mary and St Peter) *Bre*   R S T COLLIS
MOTHERWELL (Holy Trinity) *Glas*   P-in-c A WYLIE
MUCHALLS (St Ternan) *Bre*   R *vacant* (01569) 730625
MULL, ISLE OF   *see* Lochbuie *Arg*
MULL, ISLE OF   *see* W Highland Region *Arg*
MURRAYFIELD (Good Shepherd)   *see* Edin Gd Shep *Edin*
MUSSELBURGH (St Peter) *Edin*   R A F C KEULEMANS,
  Hon C L A MORTIS,   NSM D J S MUNRO
MUTHILL (St James) *St And*   R A E BARTON
NAIRN (St Columba) *Mor*   R A J SIMPSON
NETHER LOCHABER (St Bride) *Arg*   R *vacant*
NEW GALLOWAY (St Margaret of Scotland) *Glas*
  P-in-c J R REPATH
NEW PITSLIGO (St John the Evangelist)   *see* Cen Buchan *Ab*
NEWBURGH (St Katherine) *St And*   R *vacant*
NEWPORT-ON-TAY (St Mary) *St And*   R D B H HERBERT
NEWTON STEWART   *see* Challoch *Glas*
NORTH BALLACHULISH   *see* Onich *Arg*
NORTH BERWICK (St Baldred) *Edin*   R J C LINDSAY
NORTH MEARNS   *see* Stonehaven *Bre*
OBAN (Cathedral of St John) *Arg*   R N D MACCALLUM
OLD DEER (St Drostan)   *see* Cen Buchan *Ab*
OLDMELDRUM (St Matthew) *Ab*   P-in-c R SPENCER
ONICH (St Bride) *Arg*   R *vacant*
OXGANGS (St Hilda)   *see* Edin St Hilda *Edin*
PAISLEY (Holy Trinity) *Glas*   C J PAGE
PAISLEY (St Barnabas) *Glas*   C J PAGE
PEEBLES (St Peter) *Edin*   NSM C B AITCHISON, C CHAPLIN
PENICUIK (St James the Less) *Edin*   R R J WARREN,
  Hon C G P C CROSFIELD,   NSM N F SUTTLE, T A BRAMLEY
PERTH (Cathedral of St Ninian) *St And*   NSM R F SAUNDERS
PERTH (St John the Baptist) *St And*   R P I D GRANT,
  Hon C R H DARROCH

PETERHEAD (St Peter) *Ab*   P-in-c R N O'SULLIVAN
PILTON (St David)   *see* Edin St Dav *Edin*
PINMORE *Glas* *vacant*
PITLOCHRY (Holy Trinity) *St And*   R *vacant* (01796) 472539
PITTENWEEM (St John the Evangelist) *St And*
  R I M DOWLEN
POLLOCKSHIELDS (St Ninian)   *see* Glas St Ninian *Glas*
POLTALLOCH   *see* Kilmartin *Arg*
POOLEWE (St Maelrubha) *Mor*   NSM H S WIDDOWS
PORT GLASGOW (St Mary the Virgin) *Glas*
  R A H MCMICHAEL
PORTNACROIS (Holy Cross)   *see* W Highland Region *Arg*
PORTPATRICK (St Ninian) *Glas*   P-in-c E A TUGWELL
PORTREE (St Columba) *Arg*   P-in-c R W BREADEN
PORTSOY (St John the Baptist) *Ab*   P-in-c J M PAISEY
PRESTONPANS (St Andrew) *Edin*   R A F C KEULEMANS,
  Hon C L A MORTIS,   NSM D J S MUNRO
PRESTWICK (St Ninian) *Glas*   R *vacant* (01292) 77108
RENFREW (St Margaret) w Erskine *Glas*   P-in-c D M ORR
ROSLIN (Collegiate Church of St Matthew) *Edin*
  P-in-c J E ROULSTON,   C W L F MOUNSEY
ROTHESAY (St Paul) *Arg*   P-in-c A C SWIFT
ROTHIEMURCHUS (St John the Baptist) *Mor*
  NSM P M LOCKHART
ST ANDREWS (All Saints) *St And*   R J P MASON,
  C M-L MOFFETT,   Hon C G D WHITE, D W DAY, M C ALDCROFT
ST ANDREWS (St Andrew) *St And*   R D WILSON,
  C P B ROBERTSON,   NSM D A BEADLE, R T EVANS, T A HART,
  N A WILKINS
ST FILLANS (Church of the Holy Spirit) *St And*   R *vacant*
SANDYLOAN   *see* Gullane *Edin*
SELKIRK (St John the Evangelist) *Edin*   P-in-c D D SCEATS
SHETTLESTON (St Serf)   *see* Glas E End *Glas*
SKYE, ISLE OF   *see* Portree *Arg*
SOUTH QUEENSFERRY (Priory Church St Mary of Mount
  Carmel) *Edin*   P-in-c T J HARKIN,   NSM J MACROBERT
STANLEY (St Columba) *St And*   NSM R F SAUNDERS
STIRLING (Holy Trinity) *St And*   R A M PEDEN
STONEHAVEN (St James) *Bre*   R M E JACKSON
STORNOWAY (St Peter) *Arg*   R *vacant*
STRANRAER (St John the Evangelist) *Glas*
  P-in-c E A TUGWELL
STRATHNAIRN (St Paul) *Mor*   R *vacant*
STRATHPEFFER (St Anne) *Mor*   P-in-c I N PALLETT,
  NSM R FLOCKHART, V C SAUNDERS
STRATHTAY (St Andrew) *St And*   R D F BROOKE
STRICHEN (All Saints)   *see* Cen Buchan *Ab*
STROMNESS (St Mary) *Ab*   NSM I S T C COSBY
STRONTIAN *Arg*   P-in-c C G TONGUE
TAIN (St Andrew) *Mor*   R *vacant*
TARFSIDE (St Drostan) *Bre*   R D C MUMFORD,
  NSM J NELSON
TAYPORT (St Margaret of Scotland) *St And*   R C A BARCLAY,
  P-in-c R G SOMMERVILLE
TEINDHILLGREEN   *see* Duns *Edin*
THURSO (St Peter and Holy Rood) *Mor*   P-in-c W G KNOTT,
  Hon C F E DAVIES
TIGHNABRUAICH *Arg*   P-in-c A C SWIFT
TOFTS   *see* Dalry *Glas*
TORRY   *see* Aberdeen St Pet *Ab*
TROON (St Ninian) *Glas*   R T C O MONTGOMERY
TURRIFF (St Congan) *Ab*   Hon C P J LEES,
  NSM R M HAINES
UDDINGSTON (St Andrew) *Glas*   R S L LILLIE
ULLAPOOL (St Mary the Virgin) *Mor*   R *vacant*
  (01854) 612143
WEST FIFE Team Ministry - *see* ABERDOUR;
  BURNTISLAND; DUNFERMLINE; INVERKEITHING
  and LOCHGELLY *St And*   TR *vacant*
WEST HIGHLAND Region *Arg*   R S A FALLOWS,
  C D DAVIDSON
WEST LINTON (St Mungo) *Edin*   P-in-c R J WARREN,
  Hon C G P C CROSFIELD,   NSM T A BRAMLEY
WESTGATE   *see* Dunbar *Edin*
WESTHILL (Trinity) *Ab*   R I J FERGUSON
WHITERASHES (All Saints) *Ab*   R *vacant*
WHITING BAY   *see* Is of Arran *Arg*
WICK (St John the Evangelist) *Mor*   R W G KNOTT,
  Hon C F E DAVIES
WISHAW (St Andrew) *Glas*   P-in-c A WYLIE
WOODHEAD OF FETTERLETTER   *see* Fyvie *Ab*
YELL   *see* Burravoe *Ab*

IRISH BENEFICES AND CHURCHES

An index of benefices of the Church of Ireland (shown in bold type), together with entries for churches and other licensed places of worship. Where the church name is the same as that of the benefice (or the first place name in the benefice), the church entry is omitted. Church dedications are indicated in brackets.

The benefice entry gives the full legal name, together with the diocese and the name(s) and appointment(s) of clergy serving there (if there are none, the telephone number of the parsonage house is given). The following are the main abbreviations used; for others see the full list of abbreviations.

Bp's C	Bishop's Curate	**I**	Incumbent (includes Rector or Vicar)
C	Curate	**NSM**	Non-stipendiary Minister
C-in-c	Curate-in-charge	**P-in-c**	Priest-in-charge
Hon C	Honorary Curate		

AASLEAGH (St John the Baptist) *see* Tuam w Cong and Aasleagh *T, K & A*

ABBEYLEIX (St Michael and All Angels) w Ballyroan, Ballinakill, Killermogh, Aughmacart, Durrow and Attanagh *C & O* **I** P A HARVEY, **NSM** A WALLACE, A PURSER

ABBEYSTREWRY (no dedication) w Creagh, Tullagh, Castlehaven and Caheragh *C, C & R* **I** B J HAYES

ABINGDON (no dedication) *see* Killaloe w Stradbally *L & K*

ACHILL (Holy Trinity) *see* Aughaval w Achill, Knappagh, Dugort etc *T, K & A*

ACTON (no dedication) and Drumbanagher *Arm* **Bp's C** D W R DUNN

ADARE (St Nicholas) and Kilmallock w Kilpeacon, Croom, Kilflynn, Kilfinane, Knockaney, Bruff and Caherconlish *L & K* **I** *vacant* (00353) (61) 396227

AGHABOG (no dedication) *see* Ematris w Rockcorry, Aghabog and Aughnamullan *Clogh*

AGHADE (All Saints) *see* Fenagh w Myshall, Aghade and Ardoyne *C & O*

AGHADERG (St Mellan) w Donaghmore and Scarva *D & D* **I** P D THORNBURY

AGHADOE *see* Killarney w Aghadoe and Muckross *L & K*

AGHADOWEY (St Guaire) w Kilrea *D & R* **I** L D A CRAWFORD-MCCAFFERTY

AGHADOWN (Church Cross) *see* Ballydehob w Aghadown *C, C & R*

AGHADOWN (St Matthew) *as above*

AGHADRUMSEE (no dedication) w Clogh and Drumsnatt *Clogh* **I** *vacant*

AGHALEE (Holy Trinity) *D & D* **I** R C MCCARTNEY

AGHALURCHER (no dedication) w Tattykeeran, Cooneen and Mullaghfad *Clogh* **Bp's C** E G MCM THOMPSON

AGHANAGH (no dedication) *see* Boyle and Elphin w Aghanagh, Kilbryan etc *K, E & A*

AGHANCON (no dedication) *see* Shinrone w Aghancon etc *L & K*

AGHANLOO (St Lugha) *see* Tamlaghtard w Aghanloo *D & R*

AGHAVEA (no dedication) *Clogh* **I** G MCMURRAY

AGHAVILLY (St Mary) *see* Tynan w Middletown and Aghavilly *Arm*

AGHAVOE (no dedication) *see* Rathdowney w Castlefleming, Donaghmore etc *C & O*

AGHER (no dedication) *see* Dunboyne and Rathmolyon *M & K*

AGHERTON (St John the Baptist) *Conn* **I** S A FIELDING, **C** J M NIBLOCK

AGHOLD (no dedication) *see* Tullow w Shillelagh, Aghold and Mullinacuff *C & O*

AGHOUR (St Lachtan) *see* Kilkenny w Aghour and Kilmanagh *C & O*

AHASCRAGH *see* Aughrim w Ballinasloe etc *L & K*

AHERLA *see* Moviddy Union *C, C & R*

AHOGHILL (St Colmanell) w Portglenone *Conn* **I** M W J LONEY

ALDERGROVE *see* Killead w Gartree *Conn*

ALMORITIA (St Nicholas) *see* Mullingar, Portnashangan, Moyliscar, Kilbixy etc *M & K*

ALTEDESERT (no dedication) *see* Kildress w Altedesert *Arm*

ANNACLONE (Christ Church) *see* Magherally w Annaclone *D & D*

ANNADUFF (St Ann) *see* Kiltoghart w Drumshambo, Annaduff and Kilronan *K, E & A*

ANNAGH (St Andrew) w Drumaloor, Cloverhill and Drumlane *K, E & A* **I** S K CLARK, **NSM** T J WOODS

ANNAGHMORE (St Francis) *Arm* **I** D S MCVEIGH

ANNAHILT (Ascension) w Magherahamlet *D & D* **I** J R HOWARD

ANNALONG (no dedication) *D & D* **I** W J PRESS

ANNESTOWN *see* Waterford w Killea, Drumcannon and Dunhill *C & O*

ANTRIM (All Saints) *Conn* **I** S R MCBRIDE, **NSM** A R HALLIGAN

ANTRIM (St Patrick) *see* Connor w Antrim St Patr *Conn*

ARBOE (no dedication) *see* Ballinderry, Tamlaght and Arboe *Arm*

ARDAGH (St Patrick) w Tashinny, Shrule and Kilcommick *K, E & A* **Bp's C** A W KINGSTON

ARDAMINE (St John the Evangelist) w Kiltennel, Glascarrig, Kilnamanagh, Kilmuckridge and Monamolin *C & O* **I** R J GRAY

ARDARA (St Connall) w Glencolumbkille, Inniskeel, Glenties and Lettermacaward *D & R* **Bp's C** J DEANE, **NSM** M C CLASSON

ARDCARNE (no dedication) *see* Boyle and Elphin w Aghanagh, Kilbryan etc *K, E & A*

ARDCLINIS (St Mary) and Tickmacrevan w Layde and Cushendun *Conn* **I** *vacant*

ARDCOLM (no dedication) *see* Wexford and Kilscoran Union *C & O*

ARDEE (St Mary) *see* Drogheda w Ardee, Collon and Termonfeckin *Arm*

ARDGLASS (St Nicholas) *see* Lecale Gp *D & D*

ARDKEEN (Christ Church) *see* Ballyhalbert w Ardkeen *D & D*

ARDMORE (no dedication) w Craigavon *D & D* **I** *vacant* (028) 3834 0357

ARDMORE (St Paul) *see* Youghal Union *C, C & R*

ARDNAGEEHY (no dedication) *see* Fermoy Union *C, C & R*

ARDOYNE (Holy Trinity) *see* Fenagh w Myshall, Aghade and Ardoyne *C & O*

ARDOYNE (Immanuel) *see* Belfast H Trin and St Silas *Conn*

ARDQUIN (no dedication) *see* Ballyphilip w Ardquin *D & D*

ARDRAHAN *see* Aughrim w Ballinasloe etc *L & K*

ARDSTRAW (St Eugene) w Baronscourt, Badoney Lower and Badoney Upper and Greenan *D & R* **I** *vacant*

ARDTREA (St Andrew) w Desertcreat *Arm* **I** D J BELL

ARKLOW (St Saviour) w Inch and Kilbride *D & G* **I** N J W SHERWOOD

ARMAGH (St Mark) *Arm* **I** J W MCKEGNEY, **C** J R MCLOUGHLIN

ARMAGHBREAGUE (no dedication) *see* Keady w Armaghbreague and Derrynoose *Arm*

ARMOY (St Patrick) w Loughguile and Drumtullagh *Conn* **I** F M BACH

ARVAGH (no dedication) w Carrigallen, Gowna and Columbkille *K, E & A* **P-in-c** H R HICKS

ASHFIELD (no dedication) *see* Drumgoon *K, E & A*

ASKEATON (St Mary) *see* Rathkeale w Askeaton, Kilcornan and Kilnaughtin *L & K*

ATHBOY (St James) *see* Trim and Athboy Gp *M & K*

ATHLONE (St Mary) w Benown, Kiltoom and Forgney *M & K* **I** G T DOYLE

ATHY (St Michael) w Kilberry, Fontstown and Kilkea *D & G* **I** C P JEFFERS

AUGHANUNSHIN *see* Conwal Union w Gartan *D & R*

AUGHAVAL (no dedication) w Achill, Knappagh, Dugort, Castlebar and Turlough *T, K & A* **I** V H ROGERS

AUGHAVAS (no dedication) *see* Mohill w Farnaught, Aughavas, Oughteragh etc *K, E & A*

AUGHER (no dedication) w Newtownsaville and Eskrahoole *Clogh* **I** *vacant*

AUGHMACART (St Tighernagh) *see* Abbeyleix w Ballyroan etc *C & O*

AUGHNACLIFFE *see* Arvagh w Carrigallen, Gowna and Columbkille *K, E & A*

AUGHNACLOY *see* Carnteel and Crilly *Arm*

AUGHNAMULLAN (Christ Church) *see* Ematris w Rockcorry, Aghabog and Aughnamullan *Clogh*

AUGHRIM (Holy Trinity) w Ballinasloe, Clontuskert, Ahascragh, Woodlawn, Kilmacduagh and Ardrahan *L & K* **I** A V G FLYNN

AUGHRIM (St John the Evangelist) *see* Castlemacadam w Ballinaclash, Aughrim etc *D & G*
BADONEY LOWER (St Patrick) *see* Ardstraw w Baronscourt, Badoney Lower etc *D & R*
BADONEY UPPER (St Aichen) *as above*
BAGENALSTOWN *see* Dunleckney w Nurney, Lorum and Kiltennel *C & O*
BAILIEBOROUGH (no dedication) w Knockbride, Shercock and Mullagh *K, E & A* I F E J RANKIN
BALBRIGGAN (St George) *see* Holmpatrick w Balbriggan and Kenure *D & G*
BALGRIFFIN (St Doulagh) *see* Malahide w Balgriffin *D & G*
BALLAGHTOBIN (no dedication) *see* Kells Gp *C & O*
BALLEE (no dedication) *see* Bright w Ballee and Killough *D & D*
BALLIGAN *see* Ballywalter w Inishargie *D & D*
BALLINA *see* Killala w Dunfeeny, Crossmolina, Kilmoremoy etc *T, K & A*
BALLINACLASH (no dedication) *see* Castlemacadam w Ballinaclash, Aughrim etc *D & G*
BALLINADEE (no dedication) *see* Bandon Union *C, C & R*
BALLINAFAD *see* Boyle and Elphin w Aghanagh, Kilbryan etc *K, E & A*
BALLINAKILL (All Saints) *see* Abbeyleix w Ballyroan etc *C & O*
BALLINALEA *see* Mostrim w Granard, Clonbroney, Killoe etc *K, E & A*
BALLINALECK *see* Cleenish w Mullaghdun *Clogh*
BALLINAMALLARD *see* Magheracross *Clogh*
BALLINAMORE *see* Mohill w Farnaught, Aughavas, Oughteragh etc *K, E & A*
BALLINASLOE (St John the Evangelist) *see* Aughrim w Ballinasloe etc *L & K*
BALLINATONE *see* Castlemacadam w Ballinaclash, Aughrim etc *D & G*
BALLINDERRY (no dedication) *Conn* I *vacant*
BALLINDERRY (St John), Tamlaght and Arboe *Arm*
I W B PAINE
BALLINEEN *see* Kinneigh Union *C, C & R*
BALLINGARRY (no dedication) *see* Cloughjordan w Borrisokane etc *L & K*
BALLINLOUGH *see* Roscommon w Donamon, Rathcline, Kilkeevin etc *K, E & A*
BALLINROBE (St Mary) *see* Tuam w Cong and Aasleagh *T, K & A*
BALLINTEMPLE (no dedication) *see* Kilmore w Ballintemple *K, E & A*
BALLINTEMPLE (St Mary) *see* Cashel w Magorban, Tipperary, Clonbeg etc *C & O*
BALLINTOGHER *see* Taunagh w Kilmactranny, Ballysumaghan etc *K, E & A*
BALLINTOY (no dedication) w Rathlin and Dunseverick *Conn*
I P M BARTON
BALLINTUBBERT (St Brigid) *see* Stradbally w Ballintubbert, Coraclone etc *C & O*
BALLISODARE (Holy Trinity) w Collooney and Emlaghfad *T, K & A* I A W PULLEN
BALLIVOR *see* Trim and Athboy Gp *M & K*
BALLNACARGY *see* Mullingar, Portnashangan, Moyliscar, Kilbixy etc *M & K*
BALLYBAY (Christ Church) w Mucknoe and Clontibret *Clogh*
I *vacant* (00353) (42) 974 1102
BALLYBEEN (St Mary) *D & D* I J M HARVEY
BALLYBRACK (St Matthias) *see* Killiney Ballybrack *D & G*
BALLYBUNNION *see* Tralee w Kilmoyley, Ballymacelligott etc *L & K*
BALLYCANEW (no dedication) *see* Gorey w Kilnahue, Leskinfere and Ballycanew *C & O*
BALLYCARNEY (no dedication) *see* Ferns w Kilbride, Toombe, Kilcormack etc *C & O*
BALLYCARRY *see* Kilroot and Templecorran *Conn*
BALLYCASTLE (Holy Trinity) *see* Ramoan w Ballycastle and Culfeightrin *Conn*
BALLYCLARE *see* Ballynure and Ballyeaston *Conn*
BALLYCLOG (St Patrick) *see* Brackaville w Donaghendry and Ballyclog *Arm*
BALLYCLUG (St Patrick) *see* Ballymena w Ballyclug *Conn*
BALLYCOMMON *see* Geashill w Killeigh and Ballycommon *M & K*
BALLYCONNELL *see* Kildallon and Swanlinbar *K, E & A*
BALLYCOTTON *see* Youghal Union *C, C & R*
BALLYCULTER (Christ Church) *see* Lecale Gp *D & D*
BALLYDEHOB (St Matthias) w Aghadown *C, C & R*
I S T MCCANN
BALLYEASTON (St John the Evangelist) *see* Ballynure and Ballyeaston *Conn*

BALLYEGLISH (St Matthias) *see* Desertlyn w Ballyeglish *Arm*
BALLYFIN (no dedication) *see* Maryborough w Dysart Enos and Ballyfin *C & O*
BALLYGAWLEY (no dedication) *see* Errigle Keerogue w Ballygawley and Killeshil *Arm*
BALLYHAISE *see* Drung w Castleterra, Larah and Lavey etc *K, E & A*
BALLYHALBERT (St Andrew) w Ardkeen *D & D*
I J J HEMPHILL
BALLYHOLME (St Columbanus) *D & D* I S E DOOGAN, C W R S SMYTH
BALLYHOOLEY (no dedication) *see* Fermoy Union *C, C & R*
BALLYJAMESDUFF (no dedication) *see* Kildrumferton w Ballymachugh and Ballyjamesduff *K, E & A*
BALLYKELLY *see* Tamlaghtfinlagan w Myroe *D & R*
BALLYLESSON *see* Drumbo *D & D*
BALLYMACARRETT (St Patrick) (St Christopher) (St Martin) *D & D* I J J CUNNINGHAM, NSM I M FRAZER, S P HOOPER
BALLYMACASH (St Mark) *Conn* I W G IRWIN, NSM K W GAMBLE
BALLYMACELLIGOTT (no dedication) *see* Tralee w Kilmoyley, Ballymacelligott etc *L & K*
BALLYMACHUGH (St Paul) *see* Kildrumferton w Ballymachugh and Ballyjamesduff *K, E & A*
BALLYMACKEY (St Michael) *see* Nenagh *L & K*
BALLYMACORMACK (no dedication) *see* Templemichael w Clongish, Clooncumber etc *K, E & A*
BALLYMAGLASSON *see* Dunboyne and Rathmolyon *M & K*
BALLYMAHON *see* Ardagh w Tashinny, Shrule and Kilcommick *K, E & A*
BALLYMARTLE (no dedication) *see* Kinsale Union *C, C & R*
BALLYMASCANLAN (St Mary) w Creggan and Rathcor *Arm*
I S A PRAGNELL, NSM R W R MOORE
BALLYMENA (St Patrick) w Ballyclug *Conn* I S G E LLOYD, C A D IRWIN, C B LACEY
BALLYMONEY *see* Kinneigh Union *C, C & R*
BALLYMONEY (St Patrick) w Finvoy and Rasharkin *Conn*
NSM W J HOLMES, B M HOWE
BALLYMORE *see* Clondehorkey w Cashel *D & R*
BALLYMORE (St Mark) *Arm* I T S FORSTER
BALLYMORE EUSTACE (St John) *see* Blessington w Kilbride, Ballymore Eustace etc *D & G*
BALLYMOTE *see* Ballisodare w Collooney and Emlaghfad *T, K & A*
BALLYMOYER (St Luke) *see* Newtownhamilton w Ballymoyer and Belleck *Arm*
BALLYNAFEIGH (St Jude) *D & D* I N JARDINE
BALLYNAHINCH *see* Magheradroll *D & D*
BALLYNAKILL (St Thomas) *see* Omey w Ballynakill, Errislannan and Roundstone *T, K & A*
BALLYNASCREEN *see* Kilcronaghan w Draperstown and Sixtowns *D & R*
BALLYNURE (Ascension) *see* Baltinglass w Ballynure etc *C & O*
BALLYNURE (Christ Church) and Ballyeaston *Conn*
I R M MCCONNELL
BALLYPHILIP (no dedication) w Ardquin *D & D* I *vacant*
BALLYRASHANE (St John the Baptist) w Kildollagh *Conn*
I A E ADAMS
BALLYROAN (no dedication) *see* Abbeyleix w Ballyroan etc *C & O*
BALLYSALLY (St Andrew) *see* Coleraine *Conn*
BALLYSCULLION (no dedication) *see* Drummaul w Duneane and Ballyscullion *Conn*
BALLYSCULLION (St Tida) *D & R* P-in-c E R LAVERY
BALLYSEEDY (no dedication) *see* Tralee w Kilmoyley, Ballymacelligott etc *L & K*
BALLYSHANNON *see* Kilbarron w Rossnowlagh and Drumholm *D & R*
BALLYSILLAN *see* Belfast St Mark *Conn*
BALLYSUMAGHAN (no dedication) *see* Taunagh w Kilmactranny, Ballysumaghan etc *K, E & A*
BALLYWALTER (Holy Trinity) w Inishargie *D & D*
I J R L BOWLEY
BALLYWARD *see* Drumgath w Drumgooland and Clonduff *D & D*
BALLYWILLAN (Holy Trinity) *Conn* I P K MCDOWELL, NSM D J STEELE, R J SIMPSON
BALRATHBOYNE *see* Kells Union *M & K*
BALTEAGH (St Canice) w Carrick *D & R* I E DINSMORE
BALTIMORE *see* Abbeystrewry Union *C, C & R*
BALTINGLASS (St Mary) w Ballynure, Stratford-on-Slaney and Rathvilly *C & O* I M A MCCULLAGH
BANAGHER (St Moresuis) *see* Cumber Lower w Banagher *D & R*

BANAGHER (St Paul) *see* Clonfert Gp *L & K*
BANBRIDGE *see* Seapatrick *D & D*
BANDON (St Peter) w Rathclaren, Innishannon, Ballinadee and Brinny *C, C & R* I D F A MACCARTHY, NSM E C M FERGUSON
BANGOR Primacy (Christ Church) *D & D* Bp's C F G RUTLEDGE
BANGOR (St Columbanus) *see* Ballyholme *D & D*
BANGOR (St Comgall) *D & D* I N H PARKER
BANGOR ABBEY (Bangor Abbey) *D & D* I R NESBITT, C A R MCLAUGHLIN
BANNOW (no dedication) *see* Taghmon w Horetown and Bannow *C & O*
BANTRY *see* Kilmocomogue *C, C & R*
BARONSCOURT (no dedication) *see* Ardstraw w Baronscourt, Badoney Lower etc *D & R*
BARR (no dedication) *see* Donacavey w Barr *Clogh*
BEARA (St Peter) *see* Kilmocomogue *C, C & R*
BECTIVE *see* Trim and Athboy Gp *M & K*
BELFAST (All Saints) *Conn* I B A FOLLIS
BELFAST (Cathedral of St Anne) *Conn* I J O MANN, C J T P TWOMEY
BELFAST (Christ Church) *Conn* I *vacant*
BELFAST (Holy Trinity) (St Silas) *Conn* I R M M CREIGHTON
BELFAST Malone (St John) *Conn* I *vacant*
BELFAST (St Aidan) *Conn* I T P KERR
BELFAST (St Andrew) *Conn* NSM S K HOUSTON
BELFAST (St Bartholomew) *Conn* I R ELSDON
BELFAST (St Brendan) *D & D* I F MCCREA, C J HARRIS
BELFAST (St Christopher) *see* Ballymacarrett *D & D*
BELFAST (St Clement) *D & D* I S D LOGAN
BELFAST (St Donard) *D & D* I K H HIGGINS
BELFAST (St George) *Conn* I B STEWART
BELFAST (St Jude) *see* Ballynafeigh St Jude *D & D*
BELFAST (St Katharine) *Conn* I W J TAGGART
BELFAST (St Mark) *Conn* I R H MOORE
BELFAST (St Martin) *see* Ballymacarrett *D & D*
BELFAST (St Mary) (Holy Redeemer) *Conn* I J P WALKER
BELFAST (St Mary Magdalene) *Conn* I *vacant* (028) 9066 7516
BELFAST (St Matthew) *Conn* I G J O DUNSTAN
BELFAST (St Michael) *Conn* I N B DODDS, C J MCCLURE
BELFAST (St Nicholas) *Conn* I E HANNA
BELFAST (St Ninian) *Conn* I *vacant*
BELFAST (St Patrick) *see* Ballymacarrett *D & D*
BELFAST (St Paul) (St Barnabas) *Conn* I G MILLAR
BELFAST (St Peter) (St James) *Conn* I A T W DORRIAN
BELFAST (St Simon) (St Philip) *Conn* I P JACK
BELFAST (St Stephen) (St Luke) *Conn* I E QUIREY
BELFAST (St Thomas) *Conn* I W A LEWIS, C T MCROBERTS, NSM J M ELSDON
BELFAST Titanic Quarter *D & D* Bp's C C I BENNETT
BELFAST Upper Falls (St John the Baptist) *Conn* I T CLELAND
BELFAST Upper Malone (Epiphany) *Conn* I *vacant*
BELFAST Whiterock (St Columba) *Conn* P-in-c C R A EASTON
BELLAGHY *see* Ballyscullion *D & R*
BELLEEK (no dedication) *see* Garrison w Slavin and Belleek *Clogh*
BELLEEK (St Luke) *see* Newtownhamilton w Ballymoyer and Belleck *Arm*
BELLERENA *see* Tamlaghtard w Aghanloo *D & R*
BELMONT (St Peter) *see* Londonderry Ch Ch, Culmore, Muff and Belmont *D & R*
BELTURBET *see* Annagh w Drumaloor, Cloverhill and Drumlane *K, E & A*
BELVOIR (Transfiguration) *D & D* I T KEIGHTLEY, C J MOULD, A A MCCARTNEY
BENOWN (no dedication) *see* Athlone w Benown, Kiltoom and Forgney *M & K*
BILBOA (no dedication) *see* Castlecomer w Colliery Ch, Mothel and Bilboa *C & O*
BILLIS (no dedication) *see* Lurgan w Billis, Killinkere and Munterconnaught *K, E & A*
BILLY (no dedication) w Derrykeighan *Conn* I J R ANDERSON, NSM G H NEVIN
BIRR (St Brendan) w Eglish, Lorrha, Dorrha and Lockeen *L & K* I R W CARNEY, NSM R M GILL
BLACKLION *see* Killinagh w Kiltyclogher and Innismagrath *K, E & A*
BLACKROCK (All Saints) *see* Stillorgan w Blackrock *D & G*
BLACKROCK (St Michael) *see* Douglas Union w Frankfield *C, C & R*
BLARNEY *see* Carrigrohane Union *C, C & R*
BLESSINGTON (St Mary) w Kilbride, Ballymore Eustace and Holywood *D & G* I L W RUDDOCK

BOHO (no dedication) *see* Devenish w Boho *Clogh*
BOOTERSTOWN (St Philip and St James) *see* Dublin Booterstown *D & G*
BORNACOOLA *see* Templemichael w Clongish, Clooncumber etc *K, E & A*
BORRIS Clonagoose *see* Leighlin w Grange Sylvae, Shankill etc *C & O*
BORRIS Littleton *see* Kilcooley w Littleon, Crohane and Fertagh *C & O*
BORRIS-IN-OSSORY (no dedication) *see* Clonenagh w Offerlane, Borris-in-Ossory etc *C & O*
BORRISNAFARNEY (no dedication) *see* Cloughjordan w Borrisokane etc *L & K*
BORRISOKANE (no dedication) *as above*
BOURNEY (St Burchin) *see* Roscrea w Kyle, Bourney and Corbally *L & K*
BOVEVAGH (St Eugenius) *see* Dungiven w Bovevagh *D & R*
BOYLE (no dedication) and Elphin w Aghanagh, Kilbryan, Ardcarne and Croghan *K, E & A* I R S J BOURKE
BRACKAVILLE (Holy Trinity) w Donaghendry and Ballyclog *Arm* NSM A MCWILLIAMS
BRANTRY (Holy Trinity) *see* Caledon w Brantry *Arm*
BRAY (Christ Church) *D & G* I B T STANLEY
BRIGHT (no dedication) w Ballee and Killough *D & D* I J EWART
BRIGOWN (St George) *see* Fermoy Union *C, C & R*
BRINNY (no dedication) *see* Bandon Union *C, C & R*
BROOKEBOROUGH *see* Aghavea *Clogh*
BROOMHEDGE (St Matthew) *Conn* I P J GALDRAITH
BROUGHSHANE *see* Skerry w Rathcavan and Newtowncrommelin *Conn*
BRYANSFORD *see* Castlewellan w Kilcoo *D & D*
BUNBEG *see* Gweedore, Carrickfin and Templecrone *D & R*
BUNCLODY (St Mary) w Kildavin, Clonegal and Kilrush *C & O* I K L J HOMFRAY, NSM I DUNGAN
BUNCRANA *see* Fahan Lower and Upper *D & R*
BUNDORAN *see* Cloonclare w Killasnett, Lurganboy and Drumlease *K, E & A*
BUSH *see* Ballymascanlan w Creggan and Rathcor *Arm*
BUSHMILLS *see* Dunluce *Conn*
CAHERAGH (St Mary) *see* Abbeystrewry Union *C, C & R*
CAHERCONLISH (St Ailbe) *see* Adare and Kilmallock w Kilpeacon, Croom etc *L & K*
CAHIR (St Paul) *see* Clonmel w Innislounagh, Tullaghmelan etc *C & O*
CAIRNCASTLE (St Patrick) *see* Kilwaughter w Cairncastle and Craigy Hill *Conn*
CALARY (no dedication) *see* Newcastle w Newtownmountkennedy and Calary *D & G*
CALEDON (St John) w Brantry *Arm* I *vacant*
CALRY (no dedication) *K, E & A* I P H BAMBER
CAMLOUGH (Christ the Redeemer) w Mullaglass *Arm* I R G HOEY, C W J MCCRACKEN
CAMP *see* Dingle w Killiney and Kilgobbin *L & K*
CAMUS-JUXTA-BANN (St Mary) *D & R* I M P ROEMMELE
CAMUS-JUXTA-MOURNE (Christ Church) *D & R* I G S A WILSON
CAPPAGH (St Eugene) w Lislimnaghan *D & R* I D J QUINN
CAPPOQUIN (St Anne) *see* Lismore w Cappoquin, Kilwatermoy, Dungarvan etc *C & O*
CARBURY (no dedication) *see* Clonsast w Rathangan, Thomastown etc *M & K*
CARLOW (St Mary) w Urglin and Staplestown *C & O* I O H WILLIAMS, Hon C N G GILLESPIE
CARNALEA (St Gall) *D & D* I M A PARKER
CARNALWAY (St Patrick) *see* Newbridge w Carnalway and Kilcullen *M & K*
CARNDONAGH *see* Moville w Greencastle, Donagh, Cloncha etc *D & R*
CARNEW (All Saints) *see* Crosspatrick Gp *C & O*
CARNLOUGH *see* Ardclinis and Tickmacrevan w Layde and Cushendun *Conn*
CARNMONEY (Holy Evangelists) *Conn* I M A MALCOLM, NSM C R HARVEY
CARNTEEL (St James) and Crilly *Arm* I W T LONG
CARRICK (no dedication) *see* Balteagh w Carrick *D & R*
CARRICK-ON-SHANNON *see* Kiltoghart w Drumshambo, Annaduff and Kilronan *K, E & A*
CARRICKFERGUS (St Nicholas) *Conn* I G T W DAVISON, C P A FERGUSON
CARRICKFIN (St Andrew) *see* Gweedore, Carrickfin and Templecrone *D & R*
CARRICKMACROSS (St Fin Barre) w Magheracloone *Clogh* I R G KINGSTON
CARRIGALINE (St Mary) w Killanully and Monkstown *C, C & R* NSM H E A MINION

CARRIGALLEN (no dedication) *see* Arvagh w Carrigallen, Gowna and Columbkille *K, E & A*

CARRIGANS *see* Taughboyne, Craigadooish, Newtowncunningham etc *D & R*

CARRIGART *see* Mevagh w Glenalla *D & R*

CARRIGROHANE (St Peter) w Garrycloyne, Inniscarra and Magourney *C, C & R* **I** I R JONAS

CARRIGTWOHILL (St David) *see* Rathcooney Union *C, C & R*

CARROWDORE (Christ Church) w Millisle *D & D* **I** C A J DAVIS

CARRYDUFF (St Ignatius) *see* Killaney w Carryduff *D & D*

CASHEL (Cathedral of St John the Baptist) w Magorban, Tipperary, Clonbeg and Ballintemple *C & O* **I** P J KNOWLES

CASHEL (no dedication) *see* Clondehorkey w Cashel *D & R*

CASTLEARCHDALE (St Patrick) *see* Derryvullen N w Castlearchdale *Clogh*

CASTLEBAR (Christ Church) *see* Aughaval w Achill, Knappagh, Dugort etc *T, K & A*

CASTLEBLAYNEY *see* Ballybay w Mucknoe and Clontibret *Clogh*

CASTLECOMER (St Mary) w the Colliery Church, Mothel and Bilboa *C & O* **I** T A SHERLOCK, **NSM** I H Y COULTER

CASTLECONNELL *see* Killaloe w Stradbally *L & K*

CASTLECONNOR (no dedication) *see* Killala w Dunfeeny, Crossmolina, Kilmoremoy etc *T, K & A*

CASTLEDAWSON (Christ Church) *D & R* **I** D S MCLEAN

CASTLEDERG *see* Derg w Termonamongan *D & R*

CASTLEDERMOT (St James) *see* Narraghmore and Timolin w Castledermot etc *D & G*

CASTLEFLEMING (no dedication) *see* Rathdowney w Castlefleming, Donaghmore etc *C & O*

CASTLEGREGORY *see* Dingle w Killiney and Kilgobbin *L & K*

CASTLEHAVEN (no dedication) *see* Abbeystrewry Union *C, C & R*

CASTLEKNOCK (St Brigid) and Mulhuddart w Clonsilla *D & G* **I** W P HOUSTON, **C** V R A FITZPATRICK

CASTLELOST *see* Mullingar, Portnashangan, Moyliscar, Kilbixy etc *M & K*

CASTLEMACADAM (Holy Trinity) w Ballinaclash, Aughrim and Macreddin *D & G* **I** G W BUTLER

CASTLEMAINE *see* Kilcolman w Kiltallagh, Killorglin, Knockane etc *L & K*

CASTLEMARTYR (St Anne) *see* Youghal Union *C, C & R*

CASTLEPOLLARD (St Michael) and Oldcastle w Loughcrew, Mount Nugent, Mayne and Drumcree *M & K* **I** D G O'CATHAIN

CASTLEREA *see* Roscommon w Donamon, Rathcline, Kilkeevin etc *K, E & A*

CASTLERICKARD *see* Dunboyne and Rathmolyon *M & K*

CASTLEROCK (Christ Church) w Dunboe and Fermoyle *D & R* **I** D M MATCHETT, **NSM** A QUIGLEY

CASTLETERRA (no dedication) *see* Drung w Castleterra, Larah and Lavey etc *K, E & A*

CASTLETOWN *see* Killeshin w Cloydagh and Killabban *C & O*

CASTLETOWN *see* Rathkeale w Askeaton, Kilcornan and Kilnaughtin *L & K*

CASTLETOWN *see* Kells Union *M & K*

CASTLETOWNBERE (St Peter) *see* Kilmocomogue *C, C & R*

CASTLETOWNROCHE (no dedication) *see* Mallow Union *C, C & R*

CASTLETOWNSEND *see* Abbeystrewry Union *C, C & R*

CASTLEVENTRY (no dedication) *see* Ross Union *C, C & R*

CASTLEWELLAN (St Paul) w Kilcoo *D & D* **I** B S CADDEN

CAVAN *see* Urney w Denn and Derryheen *K, E & A*

CELBRIDGE (Christ Church) w Straffan and Newcastle-Lyons *D & G* **I** S L HALES, **NSM** R W LAWSON

CHAPELIZOD (St Laurence) *see* Dublin Crumlin w Chapelizod *D & G*

CHARLEMONT (no dedication) *see* Moy w Charlemont *Arm*

CLABBY (St Margaret) *see* Tempo and Clabby *Clogh*

CLANABOGAN (no dedication) *see* Edenderry w Clanabogan *D & R*

CLANE (St Michael and All Angels) w Donadea and Coolcarrigan *M & K* **Bp's C** K M RONNÉ

CLARA (St Brigid) w Liss, Moate and Clonmacnoise *M & K* **I** vacant (00353) (506) 31406

CLARE (no dedication) *see* Loughgilly w Clare *Arm*

CLAUDY *see* Cumber Upper w Learmount *D & R*

CLEENISH (no dedication) *see* Mullaghdun *Clogh* **I** G P BRIDLE

CLIFDEN *see* Omey w Ballynakill, Errislannan and Roundstone *T, K & A*

CLOGH (Holy Trinity) *see* Aghadrumsee w Clogh and Drumsnatt *Clogh*

CLOGHER (Cathedral of St Macartan) w Errigal Portclare *Clogh* **NSM** M B PRINGLE

CLOGHERNY (St Patrick) w Seskinore and Drumnakilly *Arm* **R** vacant (028) 8075 8219

CLONAGOOSE (St Moling) *see* Leighlin w Grange Sylvae, Shankill etc *C & O*

CLONAKILTY *see* Kilgariffe Union *C, C & R*

CLONALLON (no dedication) w Warrenpoint *D & D* **I** vacant (028) 3077 2267

CLONARD *see* Mullingar, Portnashangan, Moyliscar, Kilbixy etc *M & K*

CLONASLEE *see* Mountmellick w Coolbanagher, Rosenallis etc *M & K*

CLONBEG (St Sedna) *see* Cashel w Magorban, Tipperary, Clonbeg etc *C & O*

CLONBRONEY (St John) *see* Mostrim w Granard, Clonbroney, Killoe etc *K, E & A*

CLONBULLOGUE *see* Clonsast w Rathangan, Thomastown etc *M & K*

CLONCHA (no dedication) *see* Moville w Greencastle, Donagh, Cloncha etc *D & R*

CLONDALKIN (St John) w Rathcoole *D & G* **I** A J RUFLI, **NSM** O BOOTHMAN, A A SHINE

CLONDEHORKEY (St John) w Cashel *D & R* **I** C D PIERCE

CLONDEVADDOCK (Christ the Redeemer) w Portsalon and Leatbeg *D & R* **P-in-c** W P QUILL

CLONDUFF (St John) *see* Drumgath w Drumgooland and Clonduff *D & D*

CLONE (St Paul) *see* Enniscorthy w Clone, Clonmore, Monart etc *C & O*

CLONEGAL (no dedication) *see* Bunclody w Kildavin, Clonegal and Kilrush *C & O*

CLONEGAM (Holy Trinity) *see* Fiddown w Clonegam, Guilcagh and Kilmeaden *C & O*

CLONENAGH (no dedication) w Offerlane, Borris-in-Ossory, Seirkieran and Roskelton *C & O* **I** I P POULTON

CLONES (St Tighernach) w Killeevan *Clogh* **I** H STEED

CLONEYHURKE (no dedication) *see* Portarlington w Cloneyhurke, Lea etc *M & K*

CLONFADFORAN *see* Tullamore w Durrow, Newtownfertullagh, Rahan etc *M & K*

CLONFEACLE (St Patrick) w Derrygortreavy *Arm* **I** vacant

CLONFERT (Cathedral of St Brendan) w Donanaughta, Banagher and Lickmolassy *L & K* **I** A J NEVIN

CLONGISH (St Paul) *see* Templemichael w Clongish, Clooncumber etc *K, E & A*

CLONLARA *see* Killaloe w Stradbally *L & K*

CLONLEIGH (St Lugadius) *see* Raphoe w Raymochy and Clonleigh *D & R*

CLONMACNOISE (St Kieran) *see* Clara w Liss, Moate and Clonmacnoise *M & K*

CLONMEL (St Mary) w Innislounagh, Tullaghmelan, Fethard, Kilvemnon and Cahir *C & O* **I** B Y FRYDAY, **C** A E CARTER

CLONMEL UNION (Christ Church) *C, C & R* **I** vacant (00353) (21) 811790

CLONMELLON *see* Trim and Athboy Gp *M & K*

CLONMORE (St John) *see* Enniscorthy w Clone, Clonmore, Monart etc *C & O*

CLONMORE (St John) *see* Kiltegan w Hacketstown, Clonmore and Moyne *C & O*

CLONOE (St Michael) *see* Tullaniskin w Clonoe *Arm*

CLONSAST (no dedication) w Rathangan, Thomastown, Monasteroris, Carbury and Rahan *M & K* **I** L E A PEILOW

CLONSILLA (St Mary) *see* Castleknock and Mulhuddart w Clonsilla *D & G*

CLONTARF *see* Dublin Clontarf *D & G*

CLONTIBRET (St Colman) *see* Ballybay w Mucknoe and Clontibret *Clogh*

CLONTUSKERT (St Matthew) *see* Aughrim w Ballinasloe etc *L & K*

CLOONCLARE (no dedication) w Killasnett, Lurganboy and Drumlease *K, E & A* **Bp's C** C J STEVENSON

CLOONCUMBER (no dedication) *see* Templemichael w Clongish, Clooncumber etc *K, E & A*

CLOONEY (All Saints) w Strathfoyle *D & R* **I** M R K FERRY, **NSM** M T E PEOPLES

CLOUGH *see* Craigs w Dunaghy and Killagan *Conn*

CLOUGHFERN (Ascension) *Conn* **I** D LOCKHART, **C** A E STEWART

CLOUGHJORDAN (St Kieran) w Borrisokane, Ballingary, Borrisnafarney and Templeharry *L & K* **I** S M NEILL

CLOUGHMILLS *see* Craigs w Dunaghy and Killagan *Conn*

CLOVERHILL (St John) *see* Annagh w Drumaloor, Cloverhill and Drumlane *K, E & A*

CLOYDAGH (no dedication) *see* Killeshin w Cloydagh and Killabban *C & O*

DONAGHEADY (St James) *D & R*   I D H J FERRY,
NSM J MCGAFFIN
DONAGHENDRY (St Patrick)   *see* Brackaville w Donaghendry
and Ballyclog *Arm*
DONAGHMORE (no dedication)   *see* Rathdowney w
Castlefleming, Donaghmore etc *C & O*
DONAGHMORE (St Bartholomew)   *see* Aghaderg w
Donaghmore and Scarva *D & R*
DONAGHMORE (St Michael) w Upper Donaghmore *Arm*
I P A THOMPSON
DONAGHMORE (St Patrick)   *see* Convoy w Monellan and
Donaghmore *D & R*
DONAGHMORE, UPPER (St Patrick)   *see* Donaghmore w
Upper Donaghmore *Arm*
DONAGHPATRICK (St Patrick)   *see* Kells Union *M & K*
DONAMON (no dedication)   *see* Roscommon w Donamon,
Rathcline, Kilkeevin etc *K, E & A*
DONANAUGHTA (St John the Baptist)   *see* Clonfert Gp *L & K*
DONARD (no dedication)   *see* Donoughmore and Donard w
Dunlavin *D & G*
DONEGAL (no dedication) w Killymard, Lough Eske and Laghey
D & R   I D I HUSS
DONEGORE (St John)   *see* Templepatrick w Donegore *Conn*
DONEMANA   *see* Donagheady *D & R*
DONERAILE (St Mary)   *see* Mallow Union *C, C & R*
DONNYBROOK (St Mary)   *see* Dublin Irishtown w
Donnybrook *D & G*
DONOUGHMORE (no dedication) and Donard w Dunlavin
D & G   I G D B SMITH
DORRHA (no dedication)   *see* Birr w Lorrha, Dorrha and
Lockeen *L & K*
DOUGLAS (St Luke) w Blackrock, Frankfield and Marmullane
C, C & R   I A M WILKINSON,   C P BURKE,
NSM P T HANNA
DOWN (Cathedral of the Holy and Undivided Trinity) *D & D*
I *vacant*
DOWN (St Margaret) w Hollymount *D & D*   I S S BURNS
DOWNPATRICK   *see* Down H Trin w Hollymount *D & D*
DOWNPATRICK   *see* Down Cathl *D & D*
DRAPERSTOWN (St Columb)   *see* Kilcronaghan w
Draperstown and Sixtowns *D & R*
DREW MEMORIAL   *see* Belfast St Simon w St Phil *Conn*
DRIMOLEAGUE (St Matthew)   *see* Fanlobbus Union
C, C & R
DRINAGH (Christ Church)   *as above*
DROGHEDA (St Mary)   *see* Julianstown and Colpe w
Drogheda and Duleek *M & K*
DROGHEDA (St Peter) w Ardee, Collon and Termonfeckin *Arm*
I M GRAHAM,   NSM J MOORE
DROMAHAIR   *see* Cloonclare w Killasnett, Lurganboy and
Drumlease *K, E & A*
DROMARA (St John) w Garvaghy *D & D*   I C B LEEKE
DROMARD (Christ Church)   *see* Skreen w Kilmacshalgan and
Dromard *T, K & A*
DROMOD (St Michael and All Angels)   *see* Kenmare w Sneem,
Waterville etc *L & K*
DROMORE (Cathedral of Christ the Redeemer) *D & D*
I S H LOWRY,   NSM T J MCKEOWN
DROMORE (Holy Trinity) *Clogh*   I W J BOYD
DRUM (no dedication)   *see* Currin w Drum and Newbliss *Clogh*
DRUMACHOSE (Christ Church) *D & R*   I S MCVEIGH,
C J W KERNOHAN
DRUMALOOR (St Andrew)   *see* Annagh w Drumaloor,
Cloverhill and Drumlane *K, E & A*
DRUMANY (Christ Church)   *see* Kinawley w H Trin *K, E & A*
DRUMBANAGHER (St Mary)   *see* Acton and Drumbanagher
Arm
DRUMBEG (St Patrick) *D & D*   I R R W DEVENNEY
DRUMBO (Holy Trinity) *D & D*   I R C NEILL
DRUMCANNON (Christ Church)   *see* Waterford w Killea,
Drumcannon and Dunhill *C & O*
DRUMCAR   *see* Kilsaran w Drumcar, Dunleer and Dunany
Arm
DRUMCLAMPH (no dedication) w Lower Langfield and Upper
Langfield *D & R*   I R G KEOGH
DRUMCLIFFE (St Columba) w Kilrush, Kilfenora, Kilfarboy,
Kilnasoolagh, Shannon and Kilferagh *L & K*   I R C HANNA,
NSM P E HANNA
DRUMCLIFFE (St Columba) w Lissadell and Munninane
K, E & A   I B I LINTON
DRUMCONDRA   *see* Dublin Drumcondra w N Strand *D & G*
DRUMCONRATH (St Peter)   *see* Kingscourt w Syddan *M & K*
DRUMCREE (Ascension) *Arm*   I G F GALWAY
DRUMCREE (St John)   *see* Castlepollard and Oldcastle w
Loughcrew etc *M & K*

DRUMGATH (St John) w Drumgooland and Clonduff *D & D*
I D SOMERVILLE
DRUMGLASS (St Anne) w Moygashel *Arm*   I A J FORSTER,
NSM M E M STEVENSON
DRUMGOOLAND (no dedication)   *see* Drumgath w
Drumgooland and Clonduff *D & D*
DRUMGOON (All Saints)   *see* Drumgoon *K, E & A*
DRUMGOON (All Saints) w Ashfield, Killesherdoney and
Dernakesh *K, E & A*   P-in-c R W STAFFORD
DRUMHOLM (no dedication)   *see* Kilbarron w Rossnowlagh
and Drumholm *D & R*
DRUMINISKILL (Chapel of Ease)   *see* Killesher *K, E & A*
DRUMKEERAN   *see* Killinagh w Kiltyclogher and
Innismagrath *K, E & A*
DRUMKEERAN (no dedication) w Templecarne and Muckross
Clogh   P-in-c C T PRINGLE
DRUMLANE (no dedication)   *see* Annagh w Drumaloor,
Cloverhill and Drumlane *K, E & A*
DRUMLEASE (no dedication)   *see* Cloonclare w Killasnett,
Lurganboy and Drumlease *K, E & A*
DRUMMAUL (St Brigid) w Duneane and Ballyscullion *Conn*
I D P KERR
DRUMMULLY (no dedication)   *see* Galloon w Drummully and
Sallaghy *Clogh*
DRUMNAKILLY (Holy Trinity)   *see* Clogherny w Seskinore
and Drumnakilly *Arm*
DRUMQUIN   *see* Drumclamph w Lower and Upper Langfield
D & R
DRUMRAGH (St Columba) w Mountfield *D & R*
I W A SEALE,   C L A CAPPER
DRUMREILLY (no dedication)   *see* Mohill w Farnaught,
Aughavas, Oughteragh etc *K, E & A*
DRUMSHAMBO (St John)   *see* Kiltoghart w Drumshambo,
Annaduff and Kilronan *K, E & A*
DRUMSNATT (St Molua)   *see* Aghadrumsee w Clogh and
Drumsnatt *Clogh*
DRUMTALLAGH (no dedication)   *see* Armoy w Loughguile
and Drumtullagh *Conn*
DRUNG (no dedication) w Castleterra, Larah and Lavey and
Killoughter *K, E & A*   I *vacant*
DUBLIN Booterstown (St Philip and St James) *D & G*
I G V WHARTON,   NSM S S HARRIS
DUBLIN (Christ Church Cathedral) Group: (St Andrew)
(St Werburgh) (St Michan) and Grangegorman *D & G*
V D A PIERPOINT,   C D A MCDONNELL
DUBLIN Clontarf (St John the Baptist) *D & G*   I D C SARGENT
DUBLIN Crumlin (St Mary) w Chapelizod *D & G*
I A GALLIGAN
DUBLIN Drumcondra (no dedication) w North Strand *D & G*
I R H BYRNE
DUBLIN (Irish Church Missions) and St Thomas *D & G*
Supt E J COULTER
DUBLIN Irishtown (St Matthew) w Donnybrook *D & G*
I E G ARDIS
DUBLIN Mount Merrion (St Thomas) *D & G*   I G V WHARTON
DUBLIN Rathfarnham (no dedication) *D & G*   I E C J WOODS,
C A E TAYLOR
DUBLIN Rathmines (Holy Trinity) w Harold's Cross *D & G*
I N G MCENDOO,   TV R D JONES
DUBLIN Sandford (no dedication) w Milltown *D & G*
I S O GYLES,   NSM A M O'FARRELL
DUBLIN Sandymount (St John the Evangelist) *D & G*   I *vacant*
DUBLIN Santry (St Pappan) w Glasnevin and Finglas *D & G*
I D W OXLEY
DUBLIN (St Ann) (St Stephen) *D & G*   I D I GILLESPIE
DUBLIN (St Bartholomew) w Leeson Park *D & G*
I A M MCCROSKERY
DUBLIN (St George and St Thomas) *D & G*
Bp's C O C ULOGWARA
DUBLIN (St Patrick's Cathedral) Group: (St Catherine and
St James) (St Audoen) *D & G*   I M D GARDNER,
NSM C E BAKER
DUBLIN Whitechurch (no dedication) *D & G*
I A H N MCKINLEY,   NSM P COMERFORD
DUBLIN (Zion Church) *D & G*   I S A FARRELL
DUGORT (St Thomas)   *see* Aughaval w Achill, Knappagh,
Dugort etc *T, K & A*
DULEEK   *see* Julianstown and Colpe w Drogheda and Duleek
M & K
DUN LAOGHAIRE (Christ Church) *D & G*   I V G STACEY
DUNAGHY (St James)   *see* Craigs w Dunaghy and Killagan
Conn
DUNANY   *see* Kilsaran w Drumcar, Dunleer and Dunany *Arm*
DUNBOE (St Paul)   *see* Castlerock w Dunboe and Fermoyle
D & R

DUNBOYNE (St Peter and St Paul) w Rathmolyon, Dunshaughlin, Maynooth, Agher and Rathcore *M & K* I J H AITON, **C** P D BOGLE, **NSM** A V STEWART
DUNDALK (St Nicholas) w Heynestown *Arm* I S A PRAGNELL, **NSM** R W R MOORE
DUNDELA (St Mark) *D & D* **C** L M GIBSON
DUNDONALD (St Elizabeth) *D & D* I T G ANDERSON
DUNDRUM *see* Cashel w Magorban, Tipperary, Clonbeg etc *C & O*
DUNDRUM (St Donard) *see* Kilmegan w Maghera *D & D*
DUNEANE (no dedication) *see* Drummaul w Duneane and Ballyscullion *Conn*
DUNFANAGHY (Holy Trinity), Raymunterdoney and Tullaghbegley *D & R* I M S HARTE
DUNFEENY (no dedication) *see* Killala w Dunfeeny, Crossmolina, Kilmoremoy etc *T, K & A*
DUNGANNON *see* Drumglass w Moygashel *Arm*
DUNGANSTOWN (St Kevin) w Redcross and Conary *D & G* I J R HEANEY
DUNGARVAN (St Mary) *see* Lismore w Cappoquin, Kilwatermoy, Dungarvan etc *C & O*
DUNGIVEN (no dedication) w Bovevagh *D & R* I D R MCBETH
DUNGLOE *see* Gweedore, Carrickfin and Templecrone *D & R*
DUNHILL (St John the Baptist) *see* Waterford w Killea, Drumcannon and Dunhill *C & O*
DUNKERRIN (no dedication) *see* Shinrone w Aghancon etc *L & K*
DUNLAVIN (St Nicholas) *see* Donoughmore and Donard w Dunlavin *D & G*
DUNLECKNEY (St Mary) w Nurney, Lorum and Kiltennel *C & O* I C J MCCOLLUM, **NSM** H M OXLEY
DUNLEER (no dedication) *see* Kilsaran w Drumcar, Dunleer and Dunany *Arm*
DUNLUCE (St John the Baptist) *Conn* I G E GRAHAM
DUNMANWAY *see* Fanlobbus Union *C, C & R*
DUNMORE EAST *see* Waterford w Killea, Drumcannon and Dunhill *C & O*
DUNMURRY (St Colman) *Conn* I D M ACHESON
DUNNALONG (St John) *see* Leckpatrick w Dunnalong *D & R*
DUNSEVERICK (no dedication) *see* Ballintoy w Rathlin and Dunseverick *Conn*
DUNSFORD (St Mary) *see* Lecale Gp *D & D*
DUNSHAUGHLIN (St Seachnal) *see* Dunboyne w Rathmolyon *M & K*
DURROW (St Columba) *see* Tullamore w Durrow, Newtownfertullagh, Rahan etc *M & K*
DURROW (St Fintan) *see* Abbeyleix w Ballyroan etc *C & O*
DURRUS (St James the Apostle) *see* Kilmocomogue *C, C & R*
DYSART ENOS (Holy Trinity) *see* Maryborough w Dysart Enos and Ballyfin *C & O*
EASKEY (St Anne) *see* Killala w Dunfeeny, Crossmolina, Kilmoremoy etc *T, K & A*
EDENDERRY *see* Clonsast w Rathangan, Thomastown etc *M & K*
EDENDERRY (no dedication) w Clanabogan *D & R* I R W CLARKE
EDGEWORTHSTOWN *see* Mostrim w Granard, Clonbroney, Killoe etc *K, E & A*
EGLANTINE (All Saints) *Conn* I *vacant*
EGLINTON *see* Faughanvale *D & R*
EGLISH (Holy Trinity) w Killylea *Arm* I *vacant*
ELPHIN (no dedication) *see* Boyle and Elphin w Aghanagh, Kilbryan etc *K, E & A*
EMATRIS (St John the Evangelist) w Rockcorry, Aghabog and Aughnamullan *Clogh* **NSM** D G BEATTIE
EMLAGHFAD (no dedication) *see* Ballisodare w Collooney and Emlaghfad *T, K & A*
ENNIS *see* Drumcliffe w Kilnasoolagh *L & K*
ENNISCORTHY (St Mary) w Clone, Clonmore, Monart and Templescobin *C & O* I C W LONG, **NSM** R J STOTESBURY
ENNISKEEN *see* Kingscourt w Syddan *M & K*
ENNISKERRY *see* Powerscourt w Kilbride *D & G*
ENNISKILLEN *see* Rossorry *Clogh*
ENNISKILLEN (Cathedral of St Macartin) *Clogh* I K R J HALL
ENNISNAG (St Peter) *see* Kells Gp *C & O*
ERRIGAL (St Paul) w Garvagh *D & R* I K P WHITTAKER
ERRIGAL PORTCLARE (no dedication) *see* Clogh w Errigal Portclare *Clogh*
ERRIGAL TRUAGH (St Muadhan) *see* Donagh w Tyholland and Errigal Truagh *Clogh*
ERRIGLE KEEROGUE (no dedication) w Ballygawley and Killeshil *Arm* I *vacant*
ERRISLANNNAN (no dedication) *see* Omey w Ballynakill, Errislannan and Roundstone *T, K & A*

ESKRAHOOLE (no dedication) *see* Augher w Newtownsaville and Eskrahoole *Clogh*
EYRECOURT *see* Clonfert Gp *L & K*
FAHAN LOWER (Christ Church) and UPPER (St Mura) *D & R* **Bp's C** S D BARTON
FALLS, LOWER (St Luke) *see* Belfast St Steph w St Luke *Conn*
FALLS, UPPER *see* Belfast Upper Falls *Conn*
FANLOBBUS (St Mary) w Drimoleague, Drinagh and Coolkellure *C, C & R* I W NESBITT
FARNAUGHT (no dedication) *see* Mohill w Farnaught, Aughavas, Oughteragh etc *K, E & A*
FAUGHANVALE (St Canice) *D & R* I J W BLAIR, **NSM** B J HASSAN
FENAGH (All Saints) w Myshall, Aghade and Ardoyne *C & O* I L D D SCOTT
FERMOY (Christ Church) w Ballyhooley, Knockmourne, Ardnageehy and Brigown *C, C & R* I E V CREMIN, **NSM** A P MORAN
FERMOYLE (no dedication) *see* Castlerock w Dunboe and Fermoyle *D & R*
FERNS (Cathedral of St Edan) w Kilbride, Toombe, Kilcormack and Ballycarney *C & O* I P G MOONEY, **NSM** M SYKES
FERRY, EAST *see* Cloyne Union *C, C & R*
FERTAGH (no dedication) *see* Kilcooley w Littleon, Crohane and Fertagh *C & O*
FETHARD (Holy Trinity) *see* Clonmel w Innislounagh, Tullaghmelan etc *C & O*
FETHARD (St Mogue) *see* New w Old Ross, Whitechurch, Fethard etc *C & O*
FIDDOWN (no dedication) w Clonegam, Guilcagh and Kilmeaden *C & O* I C G CLIFFE
FINAGHY (St Polycarp) *Conn* I A L STEWART, **C** E HENDERSON
FINGLAS (St Canice) *see* Dublin Santry w Glasnevin and Finglas *D & G*
FINNER (Christ Church) *see* Killinagh w Kiltyclogher and Innismagrath *K, E & A*
FINTONA *see* Donacavey w Barr *Clogh*
FINVOY (no dedication) *see* Ballymoney w Finvoy and Rasharkin *Conn*
FIVEMILETOWN (St John) *Clogh* I T K HANLON
FLORENCECOURT *see* Killesher *K, E & A*
FONTSTOWN (St John the Evangelist) *see* Athy w Kilberry, Fontstown and Kilkea *D & G*
FORGNEY (St Munis) *see* Athlone w Benown, Kiltoom and Forgney *M & K*
FOUNTAINS *see* Lismore w Cappoquin, Kilwatermoy, Dungarvan etc *C & O*
FOXFORD *see* Straid *T, K & A*
FOYNES *see* Rathkeale w Askeaton, Kilcornan and Kilnaughtin *L & K*
FRANKFIELD (Holy Trinity) *see* Douglas Union w Frankfield *C, C & R*
FRENCH CHURCH *see* Portarlington w Cloneyhurke, Lea etc *M & K*
FRENCHPARK *see* Roscommon w Donamon, Rathcline, Kilkeevin etc *K, E & A*
GALLOON (St Comgall) w Drummully and Sallaghy *Clogh* I *vacant*
GALWAY (St Nicholas) w Kilcummin *T, K & A* I G L HASTINGS
GARRISON (no dedication) w Slavin and Belleek *Clogh* **P-in-c** N H L REGAN
GARRYCLOYNE (no dedication) *see* Carrigrohane Union *C, C & R*
GARTAN (St Columba) *see* Conwal Union w Gartan *D & R*
GARTREE (no dedication) *see* Killead w Gartree *Conn*
GARVAGH *see* Errigal w Garvagh *D & R*
GARVAGHY (no dedication) *see* Dromara w Garvaghy *D & D*
GARVARY (Holy Trinity) *see* Derryvullen S w Garvary *Clogh*
GEASHILL (St Mary) w Killeigh and Ballycommon *M & K* **P-in-c** D HUTTON-BURY
GILFORD *see* Tullylish *D & D*
GILFORD (St Paul) *D & D* I D I CADDOO
GILNAHIRK (St Dorothea) *D & D* I N D J KIRKPATRICK
GLANDORE *see* Ross Union *C, C & R*
GLANMIRE *see* Rathcooney Union *C, C & R*
GLASCARRIG (no dedication) *see* Ardamine w Kiltennel, Glascarrig etc *C & O*
GLASLOUGH *see* Donagh w Tyholland and Errigal Truagh *Clogh*
GLASNEVIN (St Mobhi) *see* Dublin Santry w Glasnevin and Finglas *D & G*
GLENAGEARY (St Paul) *D & G* I G G DOWD, **C** P I ARBUTHNOT
GLENALLA (St Columbkille) *see* Mevagh w Glenalla *D & R*

KILDALLON (no dedication) w Newtowngore and Corrawallen and Swanlinbar w Kinawley, Templeport and Tomregan K, E & A   I vacant
KILDARE (Cathedral of St Brigid) w Kilmeague and Curragh Garrison Church M & K   I J J MARSDEN
KILDARTON (no dedication)   see Lisnadill w Kildarton Arm
KILDAVIN (St Paul)   see Bunclody w Kildavin, Clonegal and Kilrush C & O
KILDOLLAGH (St Paul)   see Ballyrashane w Kildollagh Conn
KILDRESS (St Patrick) w Altedesert Arm   I B J A CRUISE
KILDRUMFERTON (St Patrick) w Ballymachugh and Ballyjamesduff K, E & A   I vacant
KILFANE (no dedication)   see Kells Gp C & O
KILFARBOY (Christ Church)   see Drumcliffe w Kilnasoolagh L & K
KILFAUGHNABEG (Christ Church)   see Ross Union C, C & R
KILFENORA (Cathedral of St Fachan)   see Drumcliffe w Kilnasoolagh L & K
KILFERAGH (no dedication)   as above
KILFINANE (St Andrew)   see Adare and Kilmallock w Kilpeacon, Croom etc L & K
KILFITHMONE (no dedication)   see Templemore w Thurles and Kilfithmone C & O
KILFLYNN (no dedication)   see Adare and Kilmallock w Kilpeacon, Croom etc L & K
KILGARIFFE (no dedication) w Kilmalooda, Kilnagross, Timoleague and Courtmacsherry C, C & R   I D J OWEN
KILGLASS (no dedication)   see Killala w Dunfeeny, Crossmolina, Kilmoremoy etc T, K & A
KILGLASS (St Anne)   see Mostrim w Granard, Clonbroney, Killoe etc K, E & A
KILGOBBIN (no dedication)   see Dingle w Killiney and Kilgobbin L & K
KILHORNE   see Annalong D & D
KILKEA (no dedication)   see Athy w Kilberry, Fontstown and Kilkea D & G
KILKEE   see Drumcliffe w Kilnasoolagh L & K
KILKEEL (Christ Church) D & D   I K D MCGRATH, NSM S J K TEGGARTY
KILKEEVIN (Holy Trinity)   see Roscommon w Donamon, Rathcline, Kilkeevin etc K, E & A
KILKENNY (Cathedral of St Canice) (St John), Aghour and Kilmanagh C & O   I K M POULTON,   C E M E MURRAY
KILKENNY WEST   see Athlone w Benown, Kiltoom and Forgney M & K
KILL (no dedication) D & G   I S F GLENFIELD
KILL (St John)   see Naas w Kill and Rathmore M & K
KILL O' THE GRANGE   see Kill D & G
KILLABBAN (no dedication)   see Killeshin w Cloydagh and Killabban C & O
KILLADEAS (Priory Church)   see Trory w Killadeas Clogh
KILLAGAN (no dedication)   see Craigs w Dunaghy and Killagan Conn
KILLAGHTEE (St Peter)   see Inver w Mountcharles, Killaghtee and Killybegs D & R
KILLALA (Cathedral of St Patrick) w Dunfeeny, Crossmolina, Kilmoremoy, Castleconnor, Easkey and Kilglass T, K & A   I W M CALLAN,   Bp's C N J O'RAW,   NSM D T S CLEMENTS, A WILLS
KILLALLON (St John)   see Trim and Athboy Gp M & K
KILLALOE (Cathedral of St Flannan) w Stradbally, Clonlara, Mountshannon, Abingdon and Tuomgraney L & K   NSM L J GREEN
KILLANEY (St Andrew) w Carryduff D & D   I W S NIXON
KILLANNE (St Anne) w Killegney, Rossdroit and Templeshanbo C & O   I R J HARMSWORTH
KILLANULLY   see Carrigaline Union C, C & R
KILLARGUE (no dedication)   see Killinagh w Kiltyclogher and Innismagrath K, E & A
KILLARNEY (St Mary) w Aghadoe and Muckross L & K   P-in-c S M WATTERSON
KILLASHEE (St Paul)   see Templemichael w Clongish, Clooncumber etc K, E & A
KILLASNETT (no dedication)   see Cloonclare w Killasnett, Lurganboy and Drumlease K, E & A
KILLCONNELL   see Aughrim w Ballinasloe etc L & K
KILLEA (St Andrew)   see Waterford w Killea, Drumcannon and Dunhill C & O
KILLEA (St Fiach)   see Taughboyne, Craigadooish, Newtowncunningham etc D & R
KILLEAD (St Catherine) w Gartree Conn   I W J C ORR
KILLEDMOND   see Dunleckney w Nurney, Lorum and Kiltennel C & O
KILLEEVAN (no dedication)   see Clones w Killeevan Clogh
KILLEGAR (no dedication)   see Killeshandra w Killegar and Derrylane K, E & A

KILLEGNEY (no dedication)   see Killanne w Killegney, Rossdroit and Templeshanbo C & O
KILLEIGH (no dedication)   see Geashill w Killeigh and Ballycommon M & K
KILLELAGH (no dedication)   see Maghera w Killelagh D & R
KILLENAULE (no dedication)   see Kilcooley w Littleon, Crohane and Fertagh C & O
KILLERMOGH (no dedication)   see Abbeyleix w Ballyroan etc C & O
KILLERY   see Taunagh w Kilmactranny, Ballysumaghan etc K, E & A
KILLESHANDRA (no dedication) w Killegar and Derrylane K, E & A   C A CALVIN
KILLESHER (St John) K, E & A   I I J RUITERS
KILLESHERDONEY (St Mark)   see Drumgoon K, E & A
KILLESHIL (St Paul)   see Errigle Keerogue w Ballygawley and Killeshil Arm
KILLESHIN (no dedication) w Cloydagh and Killabban C & O   I vacant
KILLESK (All Saints)   see New w Old Ross, Whitechurch, Fethard etc C & O
KILLETER   see Derg w Termonamongan D & R
KILLINAGH (no dedication) w Kiltyclogher and Innismagrath K, E & A   I vacant
KILLINCHY (no dedication) w Kilmood and Tullynakill D & D   I A S DELAMERE
KILLINEY Ballybrack (St Matthias) D & G   I W P OLHAUSEN, NSM N STRATFORD
KILLINEY (Holy Trinity) D & G   I vacant
KILLINEY (St Brendan)   see Dingle w Killiney and Kilgobbin L & K
KILLINICK (no dedication)   see Wexford and Kilscoran Union C & O
KILLINKERE (no dedication)   see Lurgan w Billis, Killinkere and Munterconnaught K, E & A
KILLISKEY (no dedication)   see Wicklow w Killiskey D & G
KILLODIERNAN (no dedication)   see Nenagh L & K
KILLOE (St Catherine)   see Mostrim w Granard, Clonbroney, Killoe etc K, E & A
KILLORAN (no dedication)   see Tubbercurry w Killoran T, K & A
KILLORGLIN (no dedication)   see Kilcolman w Kiltallagh, Killorglin, Knockane etc L & K
KILLOUGH (St Anne)   see Bright w Ballee and Killough D & D
KILLOUGHTER (no dedication)   see Drung w Castleterra, Larah and Lavey etc K, E & A
KILLOUGHY   see Tullamore w Durrow, Newtownfertullagh, Rahan etc M & K
KILLOWEN   see Kinneigh Union C, C & R
KILLOWEN (St John) D & R   I D M COLLINS, C S J CAMPBELL
KILLSALLAGHAN (St David)   see Swords w Donabate and Kilsallaghan D & G
KILLUCAN (St Etchen)   see Mullingar, Portnashangan, Moyliscar, Kilbixy etc M & K
KILLURIN (no dedication)   see Wexford and Kilscoran Union C & O
KILLYBEGS (no dedication)   see Inver w Mountcharles, Killaghtee and Killybegs D & R
KILLYGARVAN (St Columb)   see Tullyaughnish w Kilmacrennan and Killygarvan D & R
KILLYLEA (St Mark)   see Eglish w Killylea Arm
KILLYLEAGH (St John the Evangelist) D & D   I J C MUNYANGAJU
KILLYMAN (St Andrew) Arm   I S R T BOYD
KILLYMARD (no dedication)   see Donegal w Killymard, Lough Eske and Laghey D & R
KILMACABEA (no dedication)   see Ross Union C, C & R
KILMACDUAGH (no dedication)   see Aughrim w Ballinasloe etc L & K
KILMACRENNAN (St Finnian and St Mark)   see Tullyaughnish w Kilmacrennan and Killygarvan D & R
KILMACSHALGAN (St Mary)   see Skreen w Kilmacshalgan and Dromard T, K & A
KILMACTHOMAS (no dedication)   see Lismore w Cappoquin, Kilwatermoy, Dungarvan etc C & O
KILMACTRANNY (no dedication)   see Taunagh w Kilmactranny, Ballysumaghan etc K, E & A
KILMAINHAMWOOD   see Kingscourt w Syddan M & K
KILMAKEE (St Hilda) Conn   I D H BOYLAND
KILMALLOCK (St Peter and St Paul)   see Adare and Kilmallock w Kilpeacon, Croom etc L & K
KILMALOODA (All Saints)   see Kilgariffe Union C, C & R
KILMANAGH (no dedication)   see Kilkenny w Aghour and Kilmanagh C & O

KILMEADEN (St Mary)   see Fiddown w Clonegam, Guilcagh and Kilmeaden C & O

KILMEAGUE (no dedication)   see Kildare w Kilmeague and Curragh M & K

KILMEEN (Christ Church)   see Kinneigh Union C, C & R

KILMEGAN (no dedication) w Maghera D & D   I C J CARSON

KILMOCOMOGUE (St Brendan the Navigator) w Castletownbere and Durrus C, C & R   I P M WILLOUGHBY, NSM A M SKUSE

KILMOE (no dedication) w Teampol-na-mbocht, Schull and Crookhaven C, C & R   I T R LESTER

KILMOGANNY (St Matthew)   see Kells Gp C & O

KILMOOD (St Mary)   see Killinchy w Kilmood and Tullynakill D & D

KILMORE (Cathedral of St Fethlimidh) w Ballintemple K, E & A   I W R FERGUSON

KILMORE (Christ Church) and Inch D & D   I vacant

KILMORE (no dedication)   see Monaghan w Tydavnet and Kilmore Clogh

KILMORE (no dedication)   see Kiltoghart w Drumshambo, Annaduff and Kilronan K, E & A

KILMORE (St Aidan) (St Saviour) Arm   I M T KINGSTON

KILMOREMOY (St Michael)   see Killala w Dunfeeny, Crossmolina, Kilmoremoy etc T, K & A

KILMOYLEY   see Tralee w Kilmoyley, Ballymacelligott etc L & K

KILMUCKRIDGE (no dedication)   see Ardamine w Kiltennel, Glascarrig etc C & O

KILMURRY (St Andrew)   see Moviddy Union C, C & R

KILNAGROSS (no dedication)   see Kilgariffe Union C, C & R

KILNAHUE (St John the Evangelist)   see Gorey w Kilnahue, Leskinfere and Ballycanew C & O

KILNALECK   see Kildrumferton w Ballymachugh and Ballyjamesduff K, E & A

KILNAMANAGH (St John)   see Ardamine w Kiltennel, Glascarrig etc C & O

KILNASOOLAGH (no dedication)   see Drumcliffe w Kilnasoolagh L & K

KILNAUGHTIN (St Brendan)   see Rathkeale w Askeaton, Kilcornan and Kilnaughtin L & K

KILPEACON (St Beacon)   see Adare and Kilmallock w Kilpeacon, Croom etc L & K

KILPIPE (no dedication)   see Crosspatrick Gp C & O

KILREA (St Patrick)   see Aghadowey w Kilrea D & R

KILRONAN (St Thomas)   see Kiltoghart w Drumshambo, Annaduff and Kilronan K, E & A

KILROOT (St Colman) and Templecorran Conn
I M J MCCANN,   NSM W STEWART

KILROSSANTY (no dedication)   see Lismore w Cappoquin, Kilwatermoy, Dungarvan etc C & O

KILRUSH   see Drumcliffe w Kilnasoolagh L & K

KILRUSH (St Brigid)   see Bunclody w Kildavin, Clonegal and Kilrush C & O

KILSARAN (St Mary) w Drumcar, Dunleer and Dunany Arm
I M GRAHAM

KILSCORAN (no dedication)   see Wexford and Kilscoran Union C & O

KILSKEERY (no dedication) w Trillick Clogh   I R C LOGUE

KILTALLAGH (St Carthage)   see Kilcolman w Kiltallagh, Killorglin, Knockane etc L & K

KILTEEVOGUE (St John)   see Stranorlar w Meenglas and Kilteevogue D & R

KILTEGAN (St Peter) w Hacketstown, Clonmore and Moyne C & O   I S E B DURAND

KILTENNEL (no dedication)   see Ardamine w Kiltennel, Glascarrig etc C & O

KILTENNEL (St Peter)   see Dunleckney w Nurney, Lorum and Kiltennel C & O

KILTERNAN (St Kiernan) D & G   I D G MOYNAN,
NSM R I T LILBURN

KILTINANLEA (no dedication)   see Killaloe w Stradbally L & K

KILTOGHART (St George) w Drumshambo, Anaduff and Kilronan K, E & A   I vacant (00353) (61) 20053

KILTOOM   see Athlone w Benown, Kiltoom and Forgney M & K

KILTUBRIDE (St Brigid)   see Mohill w Farnaught, Aughavas, Oughteragh etc K, E & A

KILTULLAGH (no dedication)   see Roscommon w Donamon, Rathcline, Kilkeevin etc K, E & A

KILTYCLOGHER (no dedication)   see Killinagh w Kiltyclogher and Innismagrath K, E & A

KILVEMNON (St Hugh)   see Clonmel w Innislounagh, Tullaghmelan etc C & O

KILWARLIN UPPER (St John) w LOWER (St James) D & D
I T D B PIERCE

KILWATERMOY (St Mary)   see Lismore w Cappoquin, Kilwatermoy, Dungarvan etc C & O

KILWAUGHTER (no dedication) w Cairncastle and Craigy Hill Conn   I R Q THOMPSON

KINAWLEY (no dedication) w Holy Trinity K, E & A
I A T E QUILL

KINAWLEY (St Paul)   see Kildallon and Swanlinbar K, E & A

KINGSCOURT (St Ernan) w Drumconrath, Syddan and Moybologue M & K   I W L STEACY

KINLOUGH   see Killinagh w Kiltyclogher and Innismagrath K, E & A

KINNEAGH (no dedication)   see Narraghmore and Timolin w Castledermot etc D & G

KINNEIGH (St Bartholomew) w Ballymoney, Kilmeen, Desertserges, Killowen and Murragh C, C & R   I S F JONES

KINNITTY (St Trinnian)   see Shinrone w Aghancon etc L & K

KINSALE (St Multose) w Runcurran, Ballymartle and Templetrine C, C & R   I D H WILLIAMS

KIRCONRIOLA   see Ballymena w Ballyclug Conn

KIRCUBBIN (Holy Trinity)   see Grey Abbey w Kircubbin D & D

KNAPPAGH (St Thomas)   see Aughaval w Achill, Knappagh, Dugort etc T, K & A

KNOCK (St Columba) D & D   I J R AUCHMUTY,   C R J FERRIS

KNOCKANE (no dedication)   see Kilcolman w Kiltallagh, Killorglin, Knockane etc L & K

KNOCKANEY (St John)   see Adare and Kilmallock w Kilpeacon, Croom etc L & K

KNOCKBREDA (no dedication) D & D   I P F PATTERSON,
C S T R GAMBLE

KNOCKBRIDE (no dedication)   see Bailieborough w Knockbride, Shercock and Mullagh K, E & A

KNOCKLOUGHRIM   see Desertmartin w Termoneeny D & R

KNOCKMOURNE (no dedication)   see Fermoy Union C, C & R

KNOCKNAGONEY (Annunciation) D & D
Bp's C D L BROWN

KNOCKNAMUCKLEY (St Matthias) D & D
I D J MCCARTNEY

KNOCKNAREA (St Anne)   see Sligo w Knocknarea and Rosses Pt K, E & A

KYLE (no dedication)   see Roscrea w Kyle, Bourney and Corbally L & K

LACK (no dedication) Clogh   I vacant (028) 6863 1360

LAGHEY (no dedication)   see Donegal w Killymard, Lough Eske and Laghey D & R

LAMBEG (no dedication) Conn   I K A MCREYNOLDS

LANESBOROUGH   see Roscommon w Donamon, Rathcline, Kilkeevin etc K, E & A

LANGFIELD, LOWER (no dedication)   see Drumclamph w Lower and Upper Langfield D & R

LANGFIELD, UPPER (no dedication)   as above

LARAGH (St John)   see Rathdrum w Glenealy, Derralossary and Laragh D & G

LARAH AND LAVEY (no dedication)   see Drung w Castleterra, Larah and Lavey etc K, E & A

LARNE AND INVER (St Cedma) Conn   I S B FORDE,
NSM R A KER, H SHARP

LAVEY   see Drung w Castleterra, Larah and Lavey etc K, E & A

LAYDE (no dedication)   see Ardclinis and Tickmacrevan w Layde and Cushendun Conn

LEA (no dedication)   see Portarlington w Cloneyhurke, Lea etc M & K

LEAP   see Ross Union C, C & R

LEARMOUNT (no dedication)   see Cumber Upper w Learmount D & R

LEATBEG (no dedication)   see Clondevaddock w Portsalon and Leatbeg D & R

LECALE Group: Saul, Ardglass, Dunsford, Ballyculter and Kilclief D & D   I T H HULL,   NSM G J SAVAGE

LECKPATRICK (St Patrick) w Dunnalong D & R
I N I LYTTLE

LEESON PARK (Christ Church)   see Dublin St Bart w Leeson Park D & G

LEIGHLIN (Cathedral of St Laserian) w Grange Sylvae, Shankill, Clonagoose and Gowran C & O   I T W GORDON

LEIXLIP (St Mary)   see Lucan w Leixlip D & G

LESKINFERE (no dedication)   see Gorey w Kilnahue, Leskinfere and Ballycanew C & O

LETTERKENNY   see Conwal Union w Gartan D & R

LETTERMACAWARD (no dedication)   see Ardara w Glencolumbkille, Inniskeel etc D & R

LICKMOLASSY   see Clonfert Gp L & K

LIFFORD   see Raphoe w Raymochy and Clonleigh D & R

LIMAVADY   see Drumachose D & R

LIMAVADY *see* Tamlaghtfinlagan w Myroe *D & R*
LIMERICK CITY (Cathedral of St Mary) (St Michael) *L & K*
I *vacant*
LISBELLAW (no dedication) *Clogh* I B T KERR
LISBURN (Christ Church) *Conn* I E P DUNDAS
LISBURN (Christ Church Cathedral) *Conn* I W S WRIGHT,
C S A GENOE
LISBURN (St Paul) *Conn* I J I CARSON
LISLIMNAGHAN (Holy Trinity) *see* Cappagh w Lislimnaghan
D & R
**LISMORE (Cathedral of St Carthage) w Cappoquin,
Kilwatermoy, Dungarvan, Kilrossanty, Stradbally and
Kilmacthomas** *C & O* I P R DRAPER, C J G MULHALL,
NSM C O'DOWD SMYTH
LISNADILL (St John) w Kildarton *Arm* I M C KENNEDY
LISNASKEA (Holy Trinity) *Clogh* I W A CAPPER
LISS (no dedication) *see* Clara w Liss, Moate and Clonmacnoise
M & K
LISSADELL (no dedication) *see* Drumcliffe w Lissadell and
Munninane *K, E & A*
LISSAN (no dedication) *Arm* I T A CROSS
LISTOWEL *see* Tralee w Kilmoyley, Ballymacelligott etc *L & K*
LITTLE ISLAND (St Lappan) *see* Rathcooney Union
C, C & R
LITTLETON (no dedication) *see* Kilcooley w Littleon,
Crohane and Fertagh *C & O*
LOCKEEN (no dedication) *see* Birr w Lorrha, Dorrha and
Lockeen *L & K*
LONDONDERRY *see* Templemore *D & R*
LONDONDERRY (Christ Church), Culmore, Muff and Belmont
D & R I R S MILLER, NSM K M MCATEER
LONDONDERRY (St Augustine) *D & R* I P L STOREY
LONGFORD *see* Templemichael w Clongish, Clooncumber etc
K, E & A
LORRHA (St Ruadhan) *see* Birr w Lorrha, Dorrha and
Lockeen *L & K*
LORUM (no dedication) *see* Dunleckney w Nurney, Lorum and
Kiltennel *C & O*
LOUGH ESKE (Christ Church) *see* Donegal w Killymard,
Lough Eske and Laghey *D & R*
LOUGHBRICKLAND *see* Aghaderg w Donaghmore and
Scarva *D & D*
LOUGHCREW *see* Castlepollard and Oldcastle w Loughcrew
etc *M & K*
LOUGHGALL (St Luke) w Grange *Arm* I G P MCADAM
LOUGHGILLY (St Patrick) w Clare *Arm* I *vacant*
LOUGHGUILE (All Saints) *see* Armoy w Loughguile and
Drumtullagh *Conn*
LOUGHINISLAND (no dedication) *D & D* I *vacant*
LUCAN (St Andrew) w Leixlip *D & G* I J S PEOPLES
LUGGACURREN (Resurrection) *see* Stradbally w
Ballintubbert, Coraclone etc *C & O*
LURGAN (Christ the Redeemer) (St Andrew) *D & D*
I S G WILSON, C C S COONEY
**LURGAN (no dedication) w Billis, Killinkere and
Munterconnaught** *K, E & A* I C W L MCCAULEY
LURGAN (St John the Evangelist) *D & D* I J M WHITE
LURGANBOY (Chapel of Ease) *see* Cloonclare w Killasnett,
Lurganboy and Drumlease *K, E & A*
MACOSQUIN *see* Camus-juxta-Bann *D & R*
MACREDDIN *see* Castlemacadam w Ballinaclash, Aughrim
etc *D & G*
MACROOM *see* Moviddy Union *C, C & R*
MAGHABERRY (Methodist church) *D & D* NSM C E BAXTER
MAGHERA (no dedication) *see* Kilmegan w Maghera *D & D*
MAGHERA (St Lurach) w Killelagh *D & R* I I J HANNA,
NSM M LENNOX
MAGHERACLOONE (St Molua) *see* Carrickmacross w
Magheracloone *Clogh*
MAGHERACROSS (no dedication) *Clogh* I C J MATCHETT,
NSM C G EAMES
MAGHERACULMONEY (St Mary) *Clogh* I W H BLAIR
MAGHERADROLL (no dedication) *D & D* I W W RUSSELL
MAGHERAFELT (St Swithin) *Arm* I T SCOTT
MAGHERAGALL (no dedication) *Conn* I N J DARK
MAGHERAHAMLET (no dedication) *see* Annahilt w
Magherahamlet *D & D*
MAGHERALIN (Holy and Undivided Trinity) w Dollingstown
D & D I G A HARRON
MAGHERALLY (St John the Evangelist) w Annaclone *D & D*
I D M PALMER
MAGORBAN (no dedication) *see* Cashel w Magorban,
Tipperary, Clonbeg etc *C & O*
MAGOURNEY *see* Carrigrohane Union *C, C & R*
MAGUIRESBRIDGE (Christ Church) w Derrybrusk *Clogh*
I D SKUCE

MALAHIDE (St Andrew) w Balgriffin *D & G* I N E C GAMBLE,
NSM K H SHERWOOD
MALIN *see* Moville w Greencastle, Donagh, Cloncha etc *D & R*
MALLOW (St James) w Doneraile and Castletownroche
C, C & R I E E M LYNCH
MALLUSK (St Brigid) *Conn* I W A BOYCE
MALONE *see* Belfast Malone St Jo *Conn*
MALONE, UPPER *see* Belfast Upper Malone (Epiphany)
Conn
MANORCUNNINGHAM *see* Raphoe w Raymochy and
Clonleigh *D & R*
MANORHAMILTON *see* Cloonclare w Killasnett, Lurganboy
and Drumlease *K, E & A*
MARKETHILL (no dedication) *see* Mullabrack w Markethill
and Kilcluney *Arm*
MARMULLANE (St Mary) *see* Douglas Union w Frankfield
C, C & R
MARYBOROUGH (St Peter) w Dysart Enos and Ballyfin
C & O I W S MONKHOUSE
MAYNE *see* Castlepollard and Oldcastle w Loughcrew etc
M & K
MAYNOOTH (St Mary) *see* Dunboyne and Rathmolyon
M & K
MAYO (no dedication) *see* Killeshin w Cloydagh and Killabban
C & O
MEALIFFE *see* Templemore w Thurles and Kilfithmone *C & O*
MEENGLASS (Ascension) *see* Stranorlar w Meenglas and
Kilteevogue *D & R*
MEVAGH (Holy Trinity) w Glenalla *D & R* I *vacant*
MIDDLE CHURCH (no dedication) *see* Ballinderry *Conn*
MIDDLETOWN (St John) *see* Tynan w Middletown and
Aghavilly *Arm*
MIDLETON (St John the Baptist) *see* Cloyne Union *C, C & R*
MILLISLE (St Patrick) *see* Carrowdore w Millisle *D & D*
MILLTOWN *see* Kilcolman w Kiltallagh, Killorglin, Knockane
etc *L & K*
MILLTOWN (St Andrew) *Arm* I G W MACARTNEY
MILLTOWN (St Philip) *see* Dublin Sandford w Milltown
D & G
MILLTOWN MALBAY *see* Drumcliffe w Kilnasoolagh *L & K*
MITCHELSTOWN *see* Fermoy Union *C, C & R*
MOATE (St Mary) *see* Clara w Liss, Moate and Clonmacnoise
M & K
**MOHILL (St Mary) w Farnaught, Aughavas, Oughteragh,
Kiltubride and Drumreilly** *K, E & A* I F W ATKINS
MOIRA (St John) *D & D* I T R WEST, C J M MEGARRELL
MONAGHAN (St Patrick) w Tydavnet and Kilmore *Clogh*
I I T H BERRY
MONAMOLIN (St Molig) *see* Ardamine w Kiltennel,
Glascarrig etc *C & O*
MONART (St Peter) *see* Enniscorthy w Clone, Clonmore,
Monart etc *C & O*
MONASTEREVAN (St John the Evangelist) *see* Portarlington
w Cloneyhurke, Lea etc *M & K*
MONASTERORIS (no dedication) *see* Clonsast w Rathangan,
Thomastown etc *M & K*
MONELLAN (St Anne) *see* Convoy w Monellan and
Donaghmore *D & R*
MONEYMORE *see* Desertlyn w Ballyeglish *Arm*
MONEYREAGH (no dedication) *see* Orangefield w
Moneyreagh *D & D*
MONKSTOWN (Good Shepherd) *Conn* P-in-c A MOORE
MONKSTOWN (no dedication) *D & G* I P H A LAWRENCE
MONKSTOWN (St John) *see* Carrigaline Union *C, C & R*
MOSSLEY (Holy Spirit) *Conn* I N R CUTCLIFFE
**MOSTRIM (St John) w Granard, Clonbroney, Killoe,
Rathaspeck and Streete** *K, E & A* P-in-c J M CATTERALL
MOTHEL (no dedication) *see* Castlecomer w Colliery Ch,
Mothel and Bilboa *C & O*
MOUNT MERRION (Pentecost) *D & D* P-in-c D A MCCLAY
MOUNT MERRION (St Thomas) *see* Dublin Mt Merrion
D & G
MOUNT NUGENT (St Bride) *see* Castlepollard and Oldcastle
w Loughcrew etc *M & K*
MOUNTCHARLES (Christ Church) *see* Inver w
Mountcharles, Killaghtee and Killybegs *D & R*
MOUNTFIELD (no dedication) *see* Drumragh w Mountfield
D & R
**MOUNTMELLICK (St Paul) w Coolbanagher, Rosenallis and
Clonaslee** *M & K* I R E JACKSON
MOUNTRATH *see* Clonenagh w Offerlane, Borris-in-Ossory
etc *C & O*
MOUNTSHANNON *see* Killaloe w Stradbally *L & K*
**MOVIDDY (no dedication), Kilbonane, Kilmurry, Templemartin
and Macroom** *C, C & R* I R E B WHITE, NSM P J GEARY

MOVILLA (no dedication) *D & D*   I T K D GRAHAM

MOVILLE (St Columb) w Greencastle, Donagh, Cloncha and Culdaff *D & R*   I *vacant*

MOY (St James) w Charlemont *Arm*   I A W A MAYES

MOYBOLOGUE *see* Kingscourt w Syddan *M & K*

MOYDOW (no dedication) *see* Ardagh w Tashinny, Shrule and Kilcommick *K, E & A*

MOYGASHEL (no dedication) *see* Drumglass w Moygashel *Arm*

MOYGLARE (All Saints) *see* Dunboyne and Rathmolyon *M & K*

MOYLISCAR *see* Mullingar, Portnashangan, Moyliscar, Kilbixy etc *M & K*

MOYNALTY (St Mary) *see* Kells Union *M & K*

MOYNE (St John) *see* Kiltegan w Hacketstown, Clonmore and Moyne *C & O*

MOYNTAGHS *see* Ardmore w Craigavon *D & D*

MOYRUS *see* Omey w Ballynakill, Errislannan and Roundstone *T, K & A*

MUCKAMORE (St Jude) (St Matthias) *Conn*   I W J C ORR

MUCKNOE (St Maeldoid) *see* Ballybay w Mucknoe and Clontibret *Clogh*

MUCKROSS (Holy Trinity) *see* Killarney w Aghadoe and Muckross *L & K*

MUCKROSS (St John) *see* Drumkeeran w Templecarne and Muckross *Clogh*

MUFF (no dedication) *see* Londonderry Ch Ch, Culmore, Muff and Belmont *D & R*

MULHUDDART (St Thomas) *see* Castleknock and Mulhuddart w Clonsilla *D & G*

MULLABRACK (no dedication) w Markethill and Kilcluney *Arm*   I N J HUGHES

MULLAGH (no dedication) *see* Bailieborough w Knockbride, Shercock and Mullagh *K, E & A*

MULLAGHDUN (no dedication) *see* Cleenish w Mullaghdun *Clogh*

MULLAGHFAD (All Saints) *see* Aghalurcher w Tattykeeran, Cooneen etc *Clogh*

MULLAGLASS (St Luke) *see* Camlough w Mullaglass *Arm*

MULLAVILLY (no dedication) *Arm*   I B J HARPER

MULLINACUFF (no dedication) *see* Tullow w Shillelagh, Aghold and Mullinacuff *C & O*

MULLINGAR (All Saints) w Portnashangan, Moyliscar, Kilbixy, Almoritia, Killucan, Clonard and Castlelost *M & K*   I M A GRAHAM,   NSM H M SCULLY

MULRANKIN (St David) *see* Wexford and Kilscoran Union *C & O*

MUNNINANE (St Kevin) *see* Drumcliffe w Lissadell and Munninane *K, E & A*

MUNTERCONNAUGHT (no dedication) *see* Lurgan w Billis, Killinkere and Munterconnaught *K, E & A*

MURRAGH (no dedication) *see* Kinneigh Union *C, C & R*

MYROE (St John) *see* Tamlaghtfinlagan w Myroe *D & R*

MYROSS *see* Ross Union *C, C & R*

MYSHALL (Christ the Redeemer) *see* Fenagh w Myshall, Aghade and Ardoyne *C & O*

NAAS (St David) w Kill and Rathmore *M & K*   I P G HEAK

NARRAGHMORE (Holy Saviour) and Timolin w Castledermot and Kinneagh *D & G*   I G DELAMERE,   NSM T ALCOCK

NAVAN (St Mary) w Kentstown, Tara, Slane, Painestown and Stackallen *M & K*   I J D M CLARKE

NENAGH (St Mary) w Ballymackey, Templederry and Killodiernan *L & K*   I M G ROWLEY-BROOKE,   NSM P E HANNA

NEWBLISS (no dedication) *see* Currin w Drum and Newbliss *Clogh*

NEWBRIDGE (St Patrick) w Carnalway and Kilcullen *M & K*   I J J MARSDEN

NEWCASTLE (no dedication) w Newtownmountkennedy and Calary *D & G*   I W L BENNETT

NEWCASTLE (St John) *D & D*   I I M ELLIS,   NSM M S WALSHE

NEWCASTLE-LYONS (no dedication) *see* Celbridge w Straffan and Newcastle-Lyons *D & G*

NEWCESTOWN *see* Kinneigh Union *C, C & R*

NEWMARKET-ON-FERGUS *see* Drumcliffe w Kilnasoolagh *L & K*

NEWRY (St Mary) (St Patrick) *D & D*   I K E SUTTON

NEWTOWNARDS (St Mark) *D & D*   I *vacant*

NEWTOWNBARRY *see* Bunclody w Kildavin, Clonegal and Kilrush *C & O*

NEWTOWNBUTLER *see* Galloon w Drummully and Sallaghy *Clogh*

NEWTOWNCROMMELIN (no dedication) *see* Skerry w Rathcavan and Newtowncrommelin *Conn*

NEWTOWNCUNNINGHAM (All Saints) *see* Taughboyne, Craigadooish, Newtowncunningham etc *D & R*

NEWTOWNFERTULLAGH *see* Tullamore w Durrow, Newtownfertullagh, Rahan etc *M & K*

NEWTOWNFORBES *see* Templemichael w Clongish, Clooncumber etc *K, E & A*

NEWTOWNGORE (no dedication) *see* Kildallon and Swanlinbar *K, E & A*

NEWTOWNHAMILTON (St John) w Ballymoyer and Belleck *Arm*   I *vacant*

NEWTOWNMOUNTKENNEDY (St Matthew) *see* Newcastle w Newtownmountkennedy and Calary *D & G*

NEWTOWNSAVILLE (no dedication) *see* Augher w Newtownsaville and Eskrahoole *Clogh*

NEWTOWNSTEWART *see* Ardstraw w Baronscourt, Badoney Lower etc *D & R*

NOHOVAL (no dedication) *see* Templebreedy w Tracton and Nohoval *C, C & R*

NURNEY (no dedication) *see* Portarlington w Cloneyhurke, Lea etc *M & K*

NURNEY (St John) *see* Dunleckney w Nurney, Lorum and Kiltennel *C & O*

OFFERLANE (no dedication) *see* Clonenagh w Offerlane, Borris-in-Ossory etc *C & O*

OLD LEIGHLIN *see* Leighlin w Grange Sylvae, Shankill etc *C & O*

OLDCASTLE (St Bride) *see* Castlepollard and Oldcastle w Loughcrew etc *M & K*

OMAGH *see* Drumragh w Mountfield *D & R*

OMEY (Christ Church) w Ballynakill, Errislannan and Roundstone *T, K & A*   I D L SANDES

ORANGEFIELD (St John the Evangelist) w Moneyreagh *D & D*   I W J R LAVERTY,   NSM R A B MOLLAN

OSSORY *see* Kilcooley w Littleon, Crohane and Fertagh *C & O*

OUGHTERAGH (no dedication) *see* Mohill w Farnaught, Aughavas, Oughteragh etc *K, E & A*

OUGHTERARD *see* Galway w Kilcummin *T, K & A*

PACKANE *see* Nenagh *L & K*

PAINESTOWN *see* Navan w Kentstown, Tara, Slane, Painestown etc *M & K*

PALLASKENRY *see* Rathkeale w Askeaton, Kilcornan and Kilnaughtin *L & K*

PASSAGE WEST *see* Douglas Union w Frankfield *C, C & R*

PAULSTOWN *see* Leighlin w Grange Sylvae, Shankill etc *C & O*

PETTIGO *see* Drumkeeran w Templecarne and Muckross *Clogh*

PILTOWN *see* Fiddown w Clonegam, Guilcagh and Kilmeaden *C & O*

POMEROY (no dedication) *Arm*   NSM W J A DAWSON

PORT LAOIS *see* Maryborough w Dysart Enos and Ballyfin *C & O*

PORTADOWN (St Columba) *Arm*   I W M ADAIR,   C D E CAIRNS

PORTADOWN (St Mark) *Arm*   I J N T CAMPBELL,   C C M HAYES

PORTAFERRY *see* Ballyphilip w Ardquin *D & D*

PORTARLINGTON (St Paul) w Cloneyhurke, Lea, Monasterevin, Nurney and Rathdaire *M & K*   I L T C STEVENSON

PORTGLENONE (no dedication) *see* Ahoghill w Portglenone *Conn*

PORTLAOISE *see* Maryborough w Dysart Enos and Ballyfin *C & O*

PORTLAW *see* Fiddown w Clonegam, Guilcagh and Kilmeaden *C & O*

PORTNASHANGAN *see* Mullingar, Portnashangan, Moyliscar, Kilbixy etc *M & K*

PORTRUSH *see* Ballywillan *Conn*

PORTSALON (All Saints) *see* Clondevaddock w Portsalon and Leatbeg *D & R*

PORTSTEWART *see* Agherton *Conn*

PORTUMNA (Christ Church) *see* Clonfert Gp *L & K*

POWERSCOURT (St Patrick) w Kilbride *D & G*   I R B ROUNTREE,   NSM H E A LEW, J B MARCHANT, K RUE

PREBAN (St John) *see* Crosspatrick Gp *C & O*

RAHAN *see* Clonsast w Rathangan, Thomastown etc *M & K*

RAHAN (St Carthach) *see* Tullamore w Durrow, Newtownfertullagh, Rahan etc *M & K*

RAHENY (All Saints) w Coolock *D & G*   I J T CARROLL,   NSM M WALLER

RALOO (no dedication) *see* Glynn w Raloo *Conn*

RAMELTON *see* Tullyaughnish w Kilmacrennan and Killygarvan *D & R*

RAMOAN (St James) w Ballycastle and Culfeightrin *Conn*   I D E FERGUSON

STRADBALLY (St Patrick) w Ballintubbert, Coraclone, Timogue and Luggacurren *C & O* **P-in-c** O M R DONOHOE

STRAFFAN (no dedication) *see* Celbridge w Straffan and Newcastle-Lyons *D & G*

STRAID (no dedication) *T, K & A* **I** *vacant*

STRAND, NORTH (no dedication) *see* Dublin Drumcondra w N Strand *D & G*

STRANGFORD *see* Lecale Gp *D & D*

STRANORLAR (no dedication) w Meenglas and Kilteevogue *D & R* **I** A S ADAMSON

STRATFORD-ON-SLANEY (St John the Baptist) *see* Baltinglass w Ballynure etc *C & O*

STRATHFOYLE (no dedication) *see* Clooney w Strathfoyle *D & R*

STREETE (no dedication) *see* Mostrim w Granard, Clonbroney, Killoe etc *K, E & A*

SUMMER COVE *see* Kinsale Union *C, C & R*

SWANLINBAR (St Augustine) *see* Kildallon and Swanlinbar *K, E & A*

SWATRAGH *see* Maghera w Killelagh *D & R*

SWORDS (St Columba) w Donabate and Kilsallaghan *D & G*
I R W DEANE, **NSM** K E LONG

SYDDAN (St David) *see* Kingscourt w Syddan *M & K*

SYDENHAM *see* Belfast St Brendan *D & D*

TAGHMON (St Munn) w Horetown and Bannow *C & O*
I *vacant*

TALLAGHT (St Maelruain) *D & G* **I** W R H DEVERELL, **NSM** A E J BENNETT

TAMLAGHT *see* Derryvullen S w Garvary *Clogh*

TAMLAGHT (St Luke) *see* Ballinderry, Tamlaght and Arboe *Arm*

TAMLAGHT O'CRILLY UPPER (no dedication) w LOWER (no dedication) *D & R* **I** R J STEWART

TAMLAGHTARD (St Gedanus) w Aghanloo *D & R*
I I E DINSMORE

TAMLAGHTFINLAGAN (St Findlunganus) w Myroe *D & R*

TANEY (Christ Church) (St Nahi) *D & G* **I** W D SINNAMON, **C** N J SLOANE

TARA *see* Navan w Kentstown, Tara, Slane, Painestown etc *M & K*

TARBERT *see* Tralee w Kilmoyley, Ballymacelligott etc *L & K*

TARTARAGHAN (St Paul) w Diamond *Arm* **I** D HILLIARD

TASHINNY (no dedication) *see* Ardagh w Tashinny, Shrule and Kilcommick *K, E & A*

TATTYKEERAN (no dedication) *see* Aghalurcher w Tattykeeran, Cooneen etc *Clogh*

TAUGHBOYNE (St Baithan) w Craigadooish, Newtowncunningham and Killea *D & R* **I** D W T CROOKS

TAUNAGH (no dedication) w Kilmactranny, Ballysumaghan and Killery *K, E & A* **I** *vacant* (00350) (71) 65368

TEAMPOL-NA-MBOCHT (Altar) *see* Kilmoe Union *C, C & R*

TEMPLEBREEDY (Holy Trinity) w Tracton and Nohoval *C, C & R* **I** I M JACKSON

TEMPLECARNE (no dedication) *see* Drumkeeran w Templecarne and Muckross *Clogh*

TEMPLECORRAN (St John) *see* Kilroot and Templecorran *Conn*

TEMPLECRONE (St Crone) *see* Gweedore, Carrickfin and Templecrone *D & R*

TEMPLEDERRY (no dedication) *see* Nenagh *L & K*

TEMPLEHARRY (no dedication) *see* Cloughjordan w Borrisokane etc *L & K*

TEMPLEMARTIN (St Martin) *see* Moviddy Union *C, C & R*

TEMPLEMICHAEL (St John) w Clongish, Clooncumber, Killashee and Ballymacormack *K, E & A* **I** D A CATTERALL

TEMPLEMORE Londonderry (Cathedral of St Columb) *D & R*
I W W MORTON

TEMPLEMORE (St Mary) w Thurles and Kilfithmore *C & O*
I P M COLE-BAKER

TEMPLEPATRICK (St Patrick) w Donegore *Conn*
I J K MCWHIRTER

TEMPLEPORT (St Peter) *see* Kildallon and Swanlinbar *K, E & A*

TEMPLESCOBIN (St Paul) *see* Enniscorthy w Clone, Clonmore, Monart etc *C & O*

TEMPLESHANBO (St Colman) *see* Killanne w Killegney, Rossdroit and Templeshanbo *C & O*

TEMPLETRINE (no dedication) *see* Kinsale Union *C, C & R*

TEMPO (no dedication) and Clabby *Clogh* **I** M A ARMSTRONG

TERMONAMONGAN (St Bestius) *see* Derg w Termonamongan *D & R*

TERMONEENY (no dedication) *see* Desertmartin w Termoneeny *D & R*

TERMONFECKIN (St Feckin) *see* Drogheda w Ardee, Collon and Termonfeckin *Arm*

TERMONMAGUIRKE (St Columbkille) *see* Sixmilecross w Termonmaguirke *Arm*

THOMASTOWN (no dedication) *see* Clonsast w Rathangan, Thomastown etc *M & K*

THURLES (no dedication) *see* Templemore w Thurles and Kilfithmone *C & O*

TICKMACREVAN (St Patrick) *see* Ardclinis and Tickmacrevan w Layde and Cushendun *Conn*

TIMOGUE (St Mogue) *see* Stradbally w Ballintubbert, Coraclone etc *C & O*

TIMOLEAGUE (Ascension) *see* Kilgariffe Union *C, C & R*

TIMOLIN (St Mullin) *see* Narraghmore and Timolin w Castledermot etc *D & G*

TINTERN (St Mary) *see* New w Old Ross, Whitechurch, Fethard etc *C & O*

TIPPERARY (St Mary) *see* Cashel w Magorban, Tipperary, Clonbeg etc *C & O*

TOBERMORE *see* Kilcronaghan w Draperstown and Sixtowns *D & R*

TOMREGAN (no dedication) *see* Kildallon and Swanlinbar *K, E & A*

TOOMBE (St Catherine) *see* Ferns w Kilbride, Toombe, Kilcormack etc *C & O*

TOOMNA (no dedication) *see* Kiltoghart w Drumshambo, Annaduff and Kilronan *K, E & A*

TOORMORE *see* Kilmoe Union *C, C & R*

TRACTON *see* Templebreedy w Tracton and Nohoval *C, C & R*

TRALEE (St John the Evangelist) w Kilmoyley, Ballymacelligott, Ballyseedy, Listowel and Ballybunnion *L & K* **I** R WARREN, **C** J HARDY

TRAMORE *see* Waterford w Killea, Drumcannon and Dunhill *C & O*

TRILLICK (Christ Church) *see* Kilskeery w Trillick *Clogh*

TRIM (Cathedral of St Patrick) and Athboy Group, The *M & K*
I R W JONES

TRORY (St Michael) w Killadeas *Clogh* **I** G M S WATSON

TUAM (Cathedral of St Mary) w Cong and Aasleagh *T, K & A*
I A J GRIMASON, **C** M RYAN

TUAMGRANEY (St Cronan) *see* Killaloe w Stradbally *L & K*

TUBBERCURRY (St George) w Killoran *T, K & A*
I K R TRIMBY

TUBRID *see* Drumkeeran w Templecarne and Muckross *Clogh*

TULLAGH (no dedication) *see* Abbeystrewry Union *C, C & R*

TULLAGHBEGLEY (St Ann) *see* Dunfanaghy, Raymunterdoney and Tullaghbegley *D & R*

TULLAGHMELAN (no dedication) *see* Clonmel w Innislounagh, Tullaghmelan etc *C & O*

TULLAMORE (St Catherine) w Durrow, Newtownfertullagh, Rahan, Tyrellspass and Killoughy *M & K* **I** G G FIELD

TULLANISKIN (Holy Trinity) w Clonoe *Arm*
C W ANDERSON

TULLOW (no dedication) *D & G* **I** L J TANNER

TULLOW (St Columba) w Shillelagh, Aghold and Mullinacuff *C & O* **I** A D H ORR

TULLYAUGHNISH (St Paul) w Kilmacrennan and Killygarvan *D & R* **I** H GILMORE

TULLYLISH (All Saints) *D & D* **I** A YOUNG

TULLYNAKILL (no dedication) *see* Killinchy w Kilmood and Tullynakill *D & D*

TUNNY (St Andrew) *see* Glenavy w Tunny and Crumlin *Conn*

TURLOUGH (no dedication) *see* Aughaval w Achill, Knappagh, Dugort etc *T, K & A*

TYBOHINE (no dedication) *see* Roscommon w Donamon, Rathcline, Kilkeevin etc *K, E & A*

TYDAVNET (St Davnet) *see* Monaghan w Tydavnet and Kilmore *Clogh*

TYHOLLAND (St Sillian) *see* Donagh w Tyholland and Errigal Truagh *Clogh*

TYNAN (St Vindic) w Middletown and Aghavilly *Arm*
P-in-c M H HAGAN

TYRELLA (St John) *see* Rathmullan w Tyrella *D & D*

TYRELLSPASS (St Sinian) *see* Tullamore w Durrow, Newtownfertullagh, Rahan etc *M & K*

UPPER DONAGHMORE (St Patrick) *see* Donaghmore w Upper Donaghmore *Arm*

URGLIN (no dedication) *see* Carlow w Urglin and Staplestown *C & O*

URNEY (Christ Church) w Sion Mills *D & R* **I** *vacant*

URNEY (no dedication) w Denn and Derryheen *K, E & A*
I M R LIDWILL

VALENTIA (St John the Baptist) *see* Kenmare w Sneem, Waterville etc *L & K*

VIRGINIA   *see* Lurgan w Billis, Killinkere and
  Munterconnaught *K, E & A*
WARINGSTOWN (Holy Trinity)   *see* Donaghcloney w
  Waringstown *D & D*
WARRENPOINT (no dedication)   *see* Clonallon w Warrenpoint
  D & D
**WATERFORD (Christ Church Cathedral) w Killea, Drumcannon
  and Dunhill** *C & O*   **C** R J WEST
WATERVILLE   *see* Kenmare w Sneem, Waterville etc *L & K*
WESTPORT   *see* Aughaval w Achill, Knappagh, Dugort etc
  T, K & A
WEXFORD (St Iberius) and Kilscoran Union *C & O*
  I M P JANSSON,   **NSM** P A NEILAND
WHITECHURCH   *see* Dublin Whitechurch *D & G*
WHITECHURCH (no dedication)   *see* New w Old Ross,
  Whitechurch, Fethard etc *C & O*

WHITEGATE   *see* Cloyne Union *C, C & R*
WHITEHEAD (St Patrick) and Islandmagee *Conn*
  I M F TAYLOR
WHITEHOUSE (St John) *Conn*   **I** E O'BRIEN
WHITEROCK   *see* Belfast Whiterock *Conn*
WICKLOW (no dedication) w Killiskey *D & G*   **I** J P CLARKE
WILLOWFIELD (no dedication) *D & D*   **I** D A MCCLAY,
  NSM A P GREEN, N GORDON
WOODBURN (Holy Trinity) *Conn*   **I** T A G MCCANN
WOODLAWN (no dedication)   *see* Aughrim w Ballinasloe etc
  L & K
WOODSCHAPEL (St John) w Gracefield *Arm*   **I** E R MURRAY
**YOUGHAL (St Mary's Collegiate) w Ardmore, Castlemartyr
  and Ballycotton** *C, C & R*   **I** W P HEWITT
ZION   *see* Dublin Zion Ch *D & G*

THE DIOCESE IN EUROPE

Diocesan Office, 14 Tufton Street, London SW1P 3QZ
Tel (020) 7898 1155   Fax 7898 1166
E-mail diocesan.office@europe.churchofengland.org
Web site www.europe.anglican.org

ARCHDEACONS

1. Eastern   P M S CURRAN
2. France   K J LETTS
3. Gibraltar   C D SUTCH
4. Italy and Malta   J BOARDMAN
5. North West Europe   J DE WIT
6. Germany and Northern Europe   J W LLOYD
7. Switzerland   P M POTTER

Further information may be obtained from the appropriate archdeacon (the archdeaconry number is given after the name of each country), and a detailed leaflet is obtainable from the diocesan office. Mission to Seafarers chaplaincies are listed separately at the end of the section.

Andorra 3
Served from Barcelona (Spain)

Armenia 1
YEREVAN   *vacant*

Austria 1
VIENNA (Christ Church)   **Chapl** P M S CURRAN,
 Asst Chapl J D KOCH

Azerbaijan 1
BAKU   *vacant*

Belgium 5
ANTWERP (St Boniface)   **Chapl** A R WAGSTAFF, **C** A E BABB
BRUSSELS (Pro-Cathedral of the Holy Trinity)
 Sen Chapl R N INNES, **Asst Chapl** G I WILTON, J M DAY,
 A U NWAEKWE
CHARLEROI   *vacant*
GHENT (St John)   **P-in-c** S MURRAY
KNOKKE (St George)   **P-in-c** S MURRAY
LEUVEN   *vacant*
LIÈGE   **P-in-c** P M YIEND
MONS   Served by Sen CF UK Support Unit Supreme
 Headquarters Allied Powers Europe
OSTEND   **P-in-c** P C OWEN
TERVUREN   **Chapl** C EDWARDS, **Asst Chapl** G L WILTON,
 J C NEWCOMBE
YPRES (St George)   **P-in-c** B M LLEWELLYN

Bosnia and Herzegovina 1
Served from Belgrade (Serbia)

Bulgaria 1
Served from Bucharest (Romania)

Croatia 1
Served from Vienna (Austria)

Czech Republic 1
PRAGUE   **P-in-c** W J YATES

Denmark 6
COPENHAGEN (St Alban) w Aarhus   **Chapl** J W LLOYD

Estonia 6
TALLINN (St Timothy and St Titus)   **P-in-c** G PIIR

Finland 6
HELSINKI w Tampere   **Chapl** R R J MORETON,
 Asst Chapl M K T PAJUNEN, **C** T MÄKIPÄÄ, A MANGA,
 NSM D L OLIVER

France 2
AIX-EN-PROVENCE   *see* Marseille w Aix-en-Provence
AMBERNAC   *see* Poitou-Charentes
AQUITAINE (Bertric Burée, Bordeaux, Limeuil, Monteton,
 Périgueux-Chancelade, Sorges and Ste Nathalène)
 Chapl P D VROLIJK, **Asst Chapl** C GORDON-WALKER,
 G L STRACHAN, B A BEARCROFT, A B DAVIES, **C** E A MORRIS
ARRAS   *see* Nord Pas de Calais
BARBEZIEUX ST HILAIRE   *see* Poitou-Charentes
BEAULIEU-SUR-MER (St Michael)   **P-in-c** P L BUSTIN
BORDEAUX   *see* Aquitaine
BOULOGNE-SUR-MER   *see* Nord Pas de Calais
BRITTANY (Ploërmel, Huelgoat and Rostrene)   *vacant*
CAEN   *see* Paris St George
CAHORS   *see* Midi-Pyrénées and Aude
CALAIS   *see* Nord Pas de Calais
CANNES (Holy Trinity)   G P WILLIAMS
CAYLUS   *see* Midi-Pyrénées and Aude
CHANTILLY (St Peter)   **Chapl** N J CLARKE
CHEF BOUTONNE   *see* Poitou-Charentes
CHEVRY   *see* Versailles w Chevry
CIVRAY   *see* Poitou-Charentes
DINARD (St Bartholomew)   **P-in-c** G J RANDALL
FONTAINEBLEAU   **Chapl** J A WILKINSON
GIF SUR YVETTE   *see* Versailles
GRATOT HOMÉEL (Christ Church)   **Chapl** P J HALES
GRENOBLE   **Chapl** S COFFIN
HESDIN   *see* Nord Pas de Calais
HUELGOAT   *see* Brittany
JARNAC   *see* Poitou-Charentes
LA ROCHEFOUCAULD   *see* Poitou-Charentes
LE GARD   **P-in-c** J DEVERILL
LILLE (Christ Church)   **P-in-c** D M R FLACH
LIMEUIL   *see* Aquitaine
LIMOUX   *see* Midi-Pyrénées and Aude
LORGUES   *see* St Raphaël
LYON   **Chapl** C J MARTIN
MAGNÉ   *see* Poitou-Charentes
MAISONS-LAFFITTE (Holy Trinity)   **Chapl** T WHITFIELD
MARSEILLE (All Saints) w Aix-en-Provence
 P-in-c G J AMAT-TORREGROSA
MENTON (St John)   *vacant*
MIDI-PYRÉNÉES and Aude (Cahors, Caylus, Limoux, Tarn,
 Toulouse and Valence d'Agen)   **Chapl** A R HAWKEN,
 Asst Chapl A H JEWISS, M J HUTCHINSON
MONTAUROUX   Served by the Community of the
 Glorious Ascension
MONTETON   *see* Aquitaine
NANTES   *see* Vendée
NICE (Holy Trinity) w Vence   **Chapl** K J LETTS
NORD PAS DE CALAIS (Arras, Boulogne-sur-Mer, Calais
 and Hesdin)   **P-in-c** S A A MACVANE
PARIS (St George)   **Chapl** M H HARRISON,
 Asst Chapl R M FERMER
PARIS (St Michael)   **Chapl** P I MOUNSTEPHEN, **C** J MOORE
PARTHENAY   *see* Poitou-Charentes
PAU (St Andrew)   **P-in-c** I F NAYLOR
PÉRIGUEUX-CHANCELADE   *see* Aquitaine
PLOËRMEL   *see* Brittany
POITOU-CHARENTES (Christ the Good Shepherd) w
 Ambernac, Barbézieux St Hilaire, Chef Boutonne, Civray,
 Jarnac, La Rochefoucauld, Magné, Parthenay,
 St Jean d'Angély, Verteuil and Villejésus
 Asst Chapl H L DOOR

PORT GRIMAUD *see* St Raphaël
ROSTRENEN *see* Brittany
ST JEAN D'ANGÉLY *see* Poitou-Charentes
ST RAPHAËL (St John the Evangelist) w Lorgues, Port Grimaud and Sellians P-in-c K M BRETEL
STE NATHALÈNE *see* Aquitaine
SELLIANS *see* St Raphaël
SORGES *see* Aquitaine
STRASBOURG P-in-c H J NAHABEDIAN, C C L BLOOMFIELD
TARN *see* Midi-Pyrénées and Aude
TOULOUSE *see* Midi-Pyrénées and Aude
VALENCE D'AGEN *see* Midi-Pyrénées and Aude
VENCE (St Hugh) *see* Nice w Vence
VENDÉE (Puy de Serre, La Chapelle Archard and La Chapelle Palluau) *vacant*
VERSAILLES (St Mark) w Chevry Asst Chapl E O LABOUREL
VERTEUIL *see* Poitou-Charentes
VILLEJÉSUS *see* Poitou-Charentes

Georgia 1

TBILISI *vacant*

Germany 6

BERLIN (St George) Chapl O W JAGE BOWLER, Asst Chapl I K E AHRENS
BONN w Cologne *vacant*
DRESDEN *see* Berlin
DÜSSELDORF (Christ Church) Chapl S J G SEAMER
FREIBURG-IM-BREISGAU P-in-c R P STOCKITT
HAMBURG (St Thomas à Becket) Chapl M B JONES, Asst Chapl E G ANDERS
HEIDELBERG *vacant*
LEIPZIG Chapl G M REAKES-WILLIAMS
STUTTGART P-in-c K R DIMMICK

Gibraltar 3

GIBRALTAR (Cathedral of the Holy Trinity) Chapl J A B PADDOCK (Dean)

Greece 1

ATHENS, GREATER Sen Chapl M M BRADSHAW, Asst Chapl T G WILCOCK, C A R LANE, Hon C W J BURKE
CORFU (Holy Trinity) P-in-c J R GULLAND

Hungary 1

BUDAPEST P-in-c F M HEGEDUS

Italy 4

AVIANO *see* Venice
BARI *see* Naples
BOLOGNA *see* Florence
BORDIGHERA *see* Genova
CADENABBIA *see* Milan and Varese
CAPRI *see* Naples
FLORENCE (St Mark) w Siena (St Peter) and Bologna *vacant*
GENOVA (The Holy Ghost) and Bordighera *vacant*
MACERATA *see* Rome
MILAN (All Saints) and Varese P-in-c J P PAYNE
NAPLES (Christ Church) w Sorrento, Capri and Bari Chapl K R JOYCE
PADOVA *see* Venice
PALERMO (Holy Cross) *see* Sicily
ROME (All Saints) w Macerata Chapl J BOARDMAN
SICILY P-in-c D G PHILLIPS
SIENA *see* Florence
SORRENTO *see* Naples
TAORMINA (St George) *see* Sicily
TRIESTE *see* Venice
VARESE *see* Milan
VENICE (St George) w Trieste P-in-c H LEVETT, C S C AJUKA
VINCENZA Served by US Army Base

Latvia 6

RIGA (St Saviour) Chapl J CALITIS

Luxembourg 5

LUXEMBOURG Chapl C D LYON

Malta and Gozo 4

VALLETTA (Pro-Cathedral of St Paul) w Sliema (Holy Trinity) Sen Chapl S H M GODFREY, Chapl J WILLIAMS

Monaco 2

MONTE CARLO (St Paul) Chapl W RAYMOND

Morocco 3

CASABLANCA (St John the Evangelist) P-in-c M CREGAN
TANGIER (St Andrew) *vacant*

The Netherlands 5

AMSTERDAM (Christ Church) w Heiloo Chapl M P C COLLINSON, Asst Chapl J R ALBERS, J R BALL, A R MACDONALD, C E FLORENTINUS
ARNHEM *see* East Netherlands
EAST NETHERLANDS *vacant*
EINDHOVEN Chapl F P NOORDANUS
HAARLEM *vacant*
HAGUE, THE (St John and St Philip) Chapl A R G ROAKE, Asst Chapl R K PRICE
NIJMEGEN *see* East Netherlands
ROTTERDAM (St Mary) Chapl S G AXTELL
TWENTE (St Mary) *see* East Netherlands
UTRECHT (Holy Trinity) w Zwolle Chapl J DE WIT, C C A NICHOLLS
VOORSCHOTEN Chapl A P ISON
ZWOLLE *see* Utrecht

Norway 6

OSLO (St Edmund) w Bergen, Trondheim , Stavanger, Drammen, Moss, Sandefjord, Tromsö and Kristiansand Chapl J HEIL, Asst Chapl P R HOGARTH, NSM M STRØMMEN

Poland 1

WARSAW w Gdansk *vacant*

Portugal 3

ALGARVE (St Vincent) Sen Chapl H Q HUBBARD, Chapl R J BATES
ALMANCIL *see* Algarve
ESTORIL *see* Lisbon
GORJÕES *see* Algarve
LISBON (St George) w Estoril (St Paul) Chapl M BULLOCK
MADEIRA (Holy Trinity) P-in-c N DAWSON
PORTO (*or* OPORTO) (St James) P-in-c M SUMARES
PRAIA DA LUZ *see* Algarve

Romania 1

BUCHAREST (The Resurrection) P A IRWIN

Russian Federation 1

MOSCOW (St Andrew) w Vladivostock Chapl S E STEPHENS
ST PETERSBURG *vacant*

Serbia 1

BELGRADE Chapl J R FOX

Slovakia

Served from Vienna (Austria)

Slovenia

Served from Vienna (Austria)

Spain 3

ALCOCEBRE *see* Costa Azahar
ALBOX *see* Costa Almeria and Costa Calida
ALHAURÍN EL GRANDE *see* Costa del Sol East
ALMUÑÉCAR *see* Nerja and Almuñécar
BARCELONA (St George) **Chapl** A C M TWEEDY
BENALMADENA COSTA *see* Costa del Sol East
BENIDORM *see* Costa Blanca
CALA BONA *see* Palma de Mallorca
CALA D'OR *see* Palma de Mallorca
CALAHONDA *see* Costa del Sol East
CALPE *see* Costa Blanca
CAMPOVERDE *see* Torrevieja
CAYO SALVAJ *see* Tenerife Sur
COIN *see* Costa del Sol East
CÓMPETA *see* Málaga
CORRALEJO *see* Lanzarote
COSTA ALMERIA **P-in-c** H D BROAD,
  Asst Chapl A W BENNETT
COSTA AZAHAR **P-in-c** P R NEEDLE
COSTA BLANCA **Sen Chapl** P C EDWARDS,
  Chapl R CARTER
COSTA CALIDA *see* Costa Almeria
COSTA DEL SOL EAST **Chapl** C D SUTCH
COSTA DEL SOL WEST **P-in-c** A MAUDE
COSTA TEGUISE *see* Lanzarote
COSTACABANA *see* Costa Almeria and Costa Calida
DENIA *see* Costa Blanca
EL CAMPELLO *see* Costa Blanca
EL HIERRO *see* Tenerife Sur
FORMENTERA *see* Ibiza
FUENGIROLA (St Andrew) *see* Costa del Sol East
FUERTEVENTURA *see* Lanzarote
GANDIA *see* Costa Blanca
GOLF DEL SUR *see* Tenerife Sur
IBIZA **P-in-c** R L SHORT
JÁVEA *see* Costa Blanca
LA GOMERA *see* Tenerife Sur
LA MANGA *see* Torrevieja
LA MARINA *see* Torrevieja
LA PALMA *see* Puerto de la Cruz
LA SIESTA *see* Torrevieja
LAGO JARDIN *see* Torrevieja
LANZAROTE *vacant*
LAS PALMAS (Holy Trinity) **P-in-c** P FORD
LOS BALCONES *see* Torrevieja
LOS GIGANTES *see* Tenerife Sur
MADRID (St George) **Chapl** I C HUTCHINSON CERVANTES,
  C N C THOMAS
MÁLAGA (St George) **Chapl** J-H D BOWDEN
MALLORCA *see* Palma de Mallorca
MENORCA **Chapl** M J BUNCE
MOJÁCAR *see* Costa Almeria
MORALEDA DE ZAFAYONA *see* Málaga
NAZARET *see* Lanzarote
NERJA and Almuñécar **P-in-c** G S JOHNSTON
ORBA *see* Costa Blanca
PALMA DE MALLORCA (St Philip and St James)
  Chapl R A ELLIS, **Asst Chapl** W M SMITH
PLAYA BLANCA *see* Lanzarote
PLAYA DE LAS AMERICAS *see* Tenerife Sur
PLAYA DEL INGLES *see* Las Palmas
PUERTO DE LA CRUZ Tenerife (All Saints)
  Chapl M R G SMITH, C J K ELLIOTT DE RIVEROL
PUERTO DEL CARMEN *see* Lanzarote
PUERTO POLLENSA *see* Palma de Mallorca
PUERTO SOLLER *see* Palma de Mallorca

ROQUETAS DE MAR *see* Costa Almeria and
  Costa Calida
SAN ANTONIO *see* Ibiza
SAN PEDRO *see* Costa del Sol West
SAN RAFAEL *see* Ibiza
SANTA EULALIA *see* Ibiza
SOTOGRANDE *see* Costa del Sol West
TENERIFE SUR (St Eugenio) **P-in-c** K A GORDON
TEULADA *see* Costa Blanca
TORRE DEL MAR *see* Málaga
TORREMOLINOS *see* Málaga
TORREVIEJA **Chapl** C M SCARGILL
VILLENUEVA DE TAPIS *see* Málaga
VINAROS *see* Costa Azahar

Sweden 6

GOTHENBURG (St Andrew) w Halmstad, Jönköping and
  Uddevalla **Chapl** B P MOSS
MALMÖ Served from Copenhagen (Denmark)
STOCKHOLM (St Peter and St Sigfrid) w Gävle and
  Västerås **Chapl** N S HOWE

Switzerland 7

ANZERE *see* Montreux
BADEN *see* Zürich
BASLE **Chapl** G P READ, **Asst Chapl** R STOCKITT,
  R B HILLIARD, **NSM** A L LOWEN
BERNE (St Ursula) w Neuchâtel **Chapl** P M POTTER,
  Asst Chapl L D BISIG
GENEVA (Holy Trinity) **Chapl** R TAYLOR
GSTAAD *see* Montreuz
LA CÔTE **Chapl** C J COOKE, C J CHAMBEYRON
LAUSANNE (Christ Church) **P-in-c** A KELHAM
LUGANO (St Edward the Confessor) **P-in-c** A J HORLOCK
MONTHEY *see* Montreux
MONTREUX (St John) w Anzere, Gstaad and Monthey
  P-in-c D P DALZELL
NEUCHÂTEL *see* Berne
ST GALLEN *see* Zürich
VEVEY (All Saints) w Château d'Oex **Chapl** C J ATKINSON
VILLARS *see* Montreux
ZUG *see* Zürich
ZÜRICH (St Andrew) w Baden, St Gallen and Zug
  Chapl J K NEWSOME, **Asst Chapl** D R MORROW

Turkey 1

ANKARA (St Nicholas) *vacant*
ISTANBUL (Christ Church) (Chapel of St Helena)
  w Moda (All Saints) **Chapl** I W L SHERWOOD
IZMIR (SMYRNA) (St John the Evangelist) w Bornova
  (St Mary Magdalene) **Chapl** R W EVANS

Turkmenistan 1

Served from Moscow (Russian Federation)

Ukraine 1

KIEV (Christ Church) *vacant*

Uzbekistan 1

Served from Moscow (Russian Federation)

MISSION TO SEAFARERS CHAPLAINCIES

Belgium 5
ANTWERP *Lay Chapl*
GHENT **Chapl** S MURRAY

France 2
DUNKERQUE **Chapl** P W BENNETT

The Netherlands 5
ROTTERDAM and Schiedam **Chapl** S G AXTELL
VLISSINGEN **Chapl** R ROBINSON

CHAPLAINS TO HER MAJESTY'S SERVICES

ROYAL NAVY

Chaplain of the Fleet and Archdeacon for the Royal Navy
Director General Naval Chaplaincy Service
The Ven J GREEN CB
Royal Naval Chaplaincy Service, Mail Point 1–2, Leach Building, Whale Island, Portsmouth PO2 8BY
Tel (023) 9262 5055   Fax 9262 5134

Chaplains RN

M D ALLSOPP	A J DUFF	A G PHILLIPS
P R ANDREW	M L EVANS	M G POLL
J R BACKHOUSE	J S FRANCIS	A RAWDING
R W BARBER	M F GODFREY	K A ROBUS
N A BEARDSLEY	M J GOUGH	P J D S SCOTT
S A R BEVERIDGE	S P HALLAM	D J SIMPSON
J M BRIDGES	A HILLIER	S P SPRINGETT
K C BROMAGE	M H JACKSON	J H TABOR
M BROTHERTON	N J KELLY	M WAGSTAFF
A M CALLON	A J F MANSFIELD	I J WHEATLEY
B R CLARKE	J O MORRIS	D V WYLIE
A S CORNESS		

ARMY

Chaplain-General HM Land Forces
The Revd J Wodehouse
(The present Chaplain General is a Baptist Minister)

Archdeacon for the Army
The Ven P A EAGLES
*Ministry of Defence, Chaplains (Army), HQ Land Forces, 2nd Floor Zone 6,
Ramillies Building, Marlborough Lines, Monxton Road, Andover SP11 8HJ*
Tel (01264) 381841 Fax 381824

Chaplains to the Forces

D J ADAMS	P T FRANCIS	D T MORGAN
W G ASHTON	S A FRANKLIN	M P MORTON
K G BARRY	L F GANDIYA	F E MYATT
T J BATESON	J R B GOUGH	R OLLIFF
A R F BATTEY	S E GRIFFITH	T R PLACE
C D BELL	C J GROOCOCK	R PLUCK
K D BELL	R A B HALL	R M PRIEST
A S F BENNETT	A B HARDING	M E REYNOLDS
S F BLOXAM-ROSE	L T J HILLARY	S A RICHARDS
P R BOSHER	G J HUMPHRYES	R J RICHARDSON
C S T BRODDLE	A W INGHAM	A ROACHE
C S BUTLER	M V JONES	G C SMITH
M R CHRISTIAN	P W S KING	M W SPEEKS
J S CLARKE	N P KINSELLA	A C STEELE
T A R COLE	C M LANGSTON	M R N STEVENSON
D P CONNING	A M LATIFA	S B THATCHER
N L COOK	W B LISTER	N S TODD
A J COOPER	S H LODWICK	C A TOME DA SILVA
D P CREES	J M LOVEDAY	A J TOTTEN
A I DALTON	S T J MCCAULAY	P VICKERS
D W DAVIES	J A MCWHIRTER	D E VINCE
R J DOWNES	K D MENTZEL	J L VINCENT
S J H DUNWOODY	D J MERCERON	B WALTON
W J N DURANT	P J MILLS	H WANLISS
P A EAGLES	B D MILLSON	D C WEAVER
H D EVANS	J S MOESEL	P S WRIGHT
A J FELTHAM-WHITE		

ROYAL AIR FORCE

Chaplain-in-Chief and Archdeacon for the RAF
The Ven R J PENTLAND QHC
Chaplaincy Services, Valiant Block, HQ Air Command, RAF High Wycombe HP14 4UE
Tel (01494) 496800   Fax 496343

Chaplains RAF

N B P BARRY	A J D GILBERT	S J RADLEY
J M BEACH	R V HAKE	P A RENNIE
K S CAPELIN-JONES	N P HERON	D RICHARDSON
J P M CHAFFEY	A D HEWETT	S J SHAW
S J CHAPMAN	J A HOBSON	M D SHELDON
M F CHATFIELD	J M S HOLLAND	L E SPICER
R P CLEMENT	I A JONES	M STEVENS
A T COATES	M P D KENNARD	J W K TAYLOR
G L COLLINGWOOD	S P LAMOND	A J TURNER
P M COLLINS	C D LAWRENCE	A W WAKEHAM-DAWSON
A L DYER	G L LEGOOD	I S WARD
M J ELLIOTT	A B MCMULLON	G WILLIAMS
J R ELLIS	C A MITCHELL	G E WITHERS
G D FIRTH	D J NORFIELD	T WRIGHT
L FLEWKER-BARKER	C J O'DELL	E L WYNN
A C GATRILL	D T OSBORN	

PRISON CHAPLAINS
HM PRISON SERVICE
(England and Wales)

Chaplain General to HM Prisons
The Ven W A NOBLETT
Anglican Adviser Canon M L KAVANAGH

Chaplaincy HQ, Post Point 3.08, 3rd Floor Red Zone, Clive House, 70 Petty France, London SW1H 9HD
Tel 03000-475186   Fax 03000-476822/3

Prisons

Acklington   M D TETLEY
Altcourse   K A CANTY
Ashfield   E A PERRY
Askham Grange   R A CLEGG
Bedford   S C GRENHAM-TOZE
Belmarsh   T G JACQUET
Birmingham   J R A SAMPSON
Blundeston   W I SALMON
Bristol   D J H POWE
Brixton   O O SOTONWA, P T J CHADDER
Buckley Hall   R W A REECE
Bullingdon   A J FORAN
Bullwood Hall   S J MAYES
Bure   A V HEDGES
Canterbury   C I HITCHENS
Cardiff   M C JOHN, M J UNDERDOWN
Channings Wood   N R MARTIN
Chelmsford   J S RIDGE
Coldingley   M E BRAIN
Dartmoor   L H COOPER, W H BIRDWOOD
Dorchester   T A M SANKEY
Dovegate   R W BAILEY
Drake Hall   D J HOWARD
Durham   B K COOPER
Eastwood Park   J M PHILLIPS
Elmley   J K M NJOROGE
Everthorpe   C R DUXBURY
Exeter   M D MILLER
Ford   P J WALKER
Forest Bank   S D HARROP
Foston Hall   F V G BALLENTYNE, H THAKE
Frankland   P G E TYLER
Full Sutton   S JUKES
Gartree   I L JOHNSON
Gloucester   K A L DENNIS, C RAWLINSON
Grendon and Spring Hill   M B WHITAKER
Guys Marsh   M J RIDGEWELL
Haverigg   G JONES, R P SPRATT
Hewell   M A SCHUTTE
Highpoint (north)   E R BELL
Highpoint (south)   A L FOWLER
Hindley   N G JONES
Hollesley Bay   J T PERRY, R B THOMPSON, M R RENNARD
Holloway   K WILKIN
Holme House   K M BROOKE, T A MCCARTHY, J N GREENWOOD
Hull   N J WHETTON
Isis   S A SIMPSON
Isle of Wight   R A DEEDES
Kennet   D W GOODWIN
Kingston (Portsmouth)   P A NEWMAN, R J PRESTON

Kirkham   B J MAYNE, D NOBLET
Lancaster Castle   A PIERCE-JONES
Latchmere House   C R WOOD
Leeds   K F A GABBADON
Leicester   H E DEARNLEY
Lewes   D E KENDRICK, G R HOCKEN
Leyhill   C F TODD
Lincoln   A J ROBERTS
Lindholme   N LEFROY-OWEN
Littlehey   D J KINDER, L LLEWELLYN-MACDUFF
Liverpool   N G SHAW
Long Lartin   J K HAYWARD
Lowdham Grange   C KNIGHT
Maidstone   G L LONG
Manchester   H R F MARTIN, N G JONES, D VICKERS
Moorland   C D LETHBRIDGE, G PITT
Morton Hall   A SEYMOUR-WHITELEY, C C MUNN
Mount, The   P J ABREY
New Hall   C J TRUMAN
North Sea Camp   P D STELL
Onley   J A FOX
Parc (Bridgend)   D C TILT
Peterborough   T C HARLING
Preston   B A EATON
Reading   D J LITTLE
Rye Hill   N I JONES
Send   L J MASON
Shepton Mallet   P C BROWNE
Shrewsbury   D S FARLEY, R M WILTSHIRE
Stafford   J D BIRD
Standford Hill   S H DUNN
Styal   M THOMPSON
Sudbury   F V G BALLENTYNE
Swaleside   J H WAITE
Swansea   L HOPKINS
Swinfen Hall   M J NEWSOME, R C PAYNE
Usk and Prescoed   N R SANDFORD
Verne, The   G A HEBBERN
Wakefield   A R ROWE
Wandsworth   S C LUCAS, T A BRYAN
Warren Hill   J T PERRY, R B THOMPSON
Wayland   S R TAN
Wealstun   T M BAYFORD
Wellingborough   S NTOYIMONDO
Whatton   J C HONOUR
Winchester   T LANE
Wolds, The   G F COOKE
Woodhill   A P HODGETTS
Wormwood Scrubs   W A WHITCOMBE
Wymott   P N TYERS**

Young Offender Institutions

Aylesbury M L HUNTER
Castington E P BOSSWARD
Deerbolt A J MARTIN, G KIRTLEY
Feltham M J BOYES, P FOSTER
Glen Parva A M ADAMS
Huntercombe and Finnamore Wood I D THACKER

Isle of Man N D GREENWOOD
Lancaster Farms A PIERCE-JONES
Portland P THOMPSON
Stoke Heath S J MORRIS
Thorn Cross S G VERHEY, M P MARTIN
Wetherby D E HERTH, I G THOMPSON

Immigration Centres

Campsfield House S K R PARKINSON
Dover P A CLARK

Haslar N G STARTIN

CHANNEL ISLANDS PRISON SERVICE

Guernsey K C NORTHOVER

Jersey S M WHITE

SCOTTISH PRISON SERVICE

Scottish Prison Service, Calton House, 5 Redheughs Rigg, Edinburgh E12 9HW
Tel (0131) 556 8400   Fax 244 8774

Edinburgh M C REED

Kilmarnock J W GEEN

NORTHERN IRELAND PRISON SERVICE

Northern Ireland Office, Dundonald House, Upper Newtownards Road, Belfast BT4 3SU
Tel (028) 9052 0700   Fax 9052 5327

Belfast N B DODDS
Maghaberry J R HOWARD

Maze, The W A MURPHY

IRISH PRISON SERVICE

Department of Justice, 72–76 St Stephen's Green, Dublin 2, Republic of Ireland
Tel (00353) (1) 678 9711   Fax 676 4718

Limerick J M G SIRR

Midlands and Portlaoise H A DUNGAN

HOSPITAL CHAPLAINS

An index of whole-time and part-time hospital chaplains

Hospital Chaplaincies Council
Church House, Great Smith Street, London SW1P 3AZ
Tel (020) 7898 1894   Fax 7898 1891

At institutions with more than one chaplain the names are listed in order of senority.

ABERDARE   *see* N Glam NHS Trust
ABERDEEN ROYAL INFIRMARY   *see* Grampian Univ Hosp NHS Trust
ABINGDON   *see* SW Oxon Primary Care Trust
ABRAHAM COWLEY UNIT Chertsey   *see* Surrey and Borders Partnership NHS Trust
ADDENBROOKE'S Cambridge   *see* Cam Univ Hosps NHS Foundn Trust
ADELAIDE AND MEATH Dublin   M A J WILSON, T ALCOCK
AIREDALE GENERAL   *see* Airedale NHS Trust
AIREDALE NHS TRUST   D P HALLIDAY, D J GRIFFITHS, J P SMITH
ALDEBURGH AND DISTRICT COMMUNITY   *see* Suffolk Coastal Primary Care Trust
ALDER HEY CHILDREN'S Liverpool   *see* R Liverpool Children's NHS Trust
ALEXANDRA Redditch   *see* Worcs Acute Hosps NHS Trust
ALL SAINTS Eastbourne   *see* E Sussex Hosps NHS Trust
ALNWICK INFIRMARY   *see* Northumbria Healthcare NHS Trust
ALPHA Woking   J A ROBINSON
ALTRINCHAM GENERAL   *see* Trafford Healthcare NHS Trust
AMBERSTONE Hailsham   *see* E Sussex Co Healthcare NHS Trust
AMERSHAM   *see* Bucks Hosps NHS Trust
ANDOVER DISTRICT COMMUNITY HEALTH CARE NHS TRUST   D F KING
ANDOVER WAR MEMORIAL COMMUNITY HOSPITAL   *see* Andover District Community Health Care NHS Trust
ARCHERY HOUSE Dartford   *see* Kent & Medway NHS and Soc Care Partnership Trust
ARGYLL AND CLYDE   S H B GORTON
ARMAGH AND DUNGANNON HEALTH AND SOCIAL SERVICES TRUST   C W M ROLSTON
ASHFIELD COMMUNITY Kirkby-in-Ashfield   *see* Sherwood Forest Hosps NHS Trust
ASHFORD   *see* E Kent Hosps NHS Trust
ASHFORD   *see* Surrey and Borders Partnership NHS Trust
ASHINGTON   *see* Northumbria Healthcare NHS Trust
ASHWORTH Maghull   C J MOON
ATKINSON MORLEY   *see* SW Lon and St George's Mental Health NHS Trust
BARKING, HAVERING AND REDBRIDGE UNIVERSITY HOSPITALS NHS TRUST   T COLEMAN, R A E LAMBERT
BARNES   *see* SW Lon and St George's Mental Health NHS Trust
BARNET   *see* Barnet and Chase Farm Hosps NHS Trust
BARNET, ENFIELD AND HARINGEY MENTAL HEALTH TRUST   T M BARON
BARNET AND CHASE FARM HOSPITALS NHS TRUST   T M BARON, T R BONIWELL
BARTLET Felixstowe   *see* Suffolk Coastal Primary Care Trust
BARTS AND THE LONDON NHS TRUST   D W RUSHTON
BASILDON   *see* S Essex Mental Health & Community Care NHS Trust
BASILDON AND THURROCK UNIVERSITY HOSPITALS NHS FOUNDATION TRUST   L G PEALL
BASINGSTOKE AND NORTH HAMPSHIRE NHS FOUNDATION TRUST   D L GRACE
BASSETLAW DISTRICT GENERAL Worksop   *see* Doncaster and Bassetlaw Hosps NHS Trust
BATH AND WEST COMMUNITY NHS TRUST   H ANDREWES UTHWATT, M JOYCE
BATTLE Reading   *see* R Berks NHS Foundn Trust
BEBINGTON   M B KELLY
BECKENHAM   *see* S Lon Healthcare NHS Trust
BEIGHTON HOSPITAL Sheffield   *see* Sheff Care Trust
BELFAST CITY   *see* Belfast Health and Soc Care Trust
BELFAST HEALTH AND SOCIAL CARE TRUST   J K MCWHIRTER, D G BEATTIE, D W GAMBLE
BENNION CENTRE Leicester   *see* Leics Partnership NHS Trust
BENSHAM Gateshead   *see* Gateshead Health NHS Trust

BERWICK INFIRMARY   *see* Northumbria Healthcare NHS Trust
BETHLEM ROYAL Beckenham   *see* S Lon and Maudsley NHS Foundn Trust
BEXHILL   *see* E Sussex Co Healthcare NHS Trust
BIDEFORD   *see* N Devon Healthcare NHS Trust
BILLINGE   *see* Wrightington Wigan and Leigh NHS Trust
BIRCH HILL   *see* Pennine Acute Hosps NHS Trust
BIRMINGHAM AND SOLIHULL MENTAL HEALTH TRUST   R J FARMAN
BIRMINGHAM CHILDREN'S HOSPITAL NHS TRUST   E BLAIR-CHAPPELL, P NASH
BIRMINGHAM CITY   *see* Sandwell and W Birm Hosps NHS Trust
BIRMINGHAM HEARTLANDS AND SOLIHULL NHS TRUST   A M BOYD
BIRMINGHAM SKIN   *see* Sandwell and W Birm Hosps NHS Trust
BIRMINGHAM SPECIALIST COMMUNITY HEALTH NHS TRUST   L M MORRIS
BISHOP AUCKLAND GENERAL   *see* Co Durham and Darlington NHS Foundn Trust
BLACKBERRY HILL Bristol   *see* N Bris NHS Trust
BLACKBURN ROYAL INFIRMARY   *see* E Lancs Hosps NHS Trust
BLACKPOOL, FYLDE AND WYRE HOSPITALS NHS TRUST   C G LORD
BLYTH COMMUNITY   *see* Northumbria Healthcare NHS Trust
BODMIN   *see* Cornwall and Is of Scilly Primary Care Trust *and* Cornwall Partnership NHS Trust
BOLTON GENERAL   *see* Bolton Hosps NHS Trust
BOLTON HOSPITALS NHS TRUST   N K GRAY, G F WEIR, S FOSTER
BOOTH HALL CHILDREN'S Manchester   *see* Cen Man/Man Children's Hosp NHS Trust
BOOTHAM PARK   *see* York Hosps NHS Foundn Trust
BOURNEMOUTH, ROYAL GENERAL   *see* R Bournemouth and Christchurch Hosps NHS Trust
BOWNESS UNIT Prestwich   *see* Gtr Man W Mental Health NHS Foundn Trust
BRADFORD HOSPITALS NHS TRUST   C P JOHNSON
BRADGATE MENTAL HEALTH UNIT Leicester   *see* Leics Partnership NHS Trust
BRADWELL Chesterton   *see* Newcastle-under-Lyme Primary Care Trust
BRAMCOTE Nuneaton   *see* N Warks NHS Trust
BRANDON MENTAL HEALTH UNIT Leicester   *see* Leics Partnership NHS Trust
BRIDGWATER COMMUNITY   *see* Somerset Primary Care Trust
BRIDLINGTON AND DISTRICT   *see* Scarborough and NE Yorks Healthcare NHS Trust
BRIDPORT COMMUNITY   *see* SW Dorset Primary Care Trust
BRIGHTON AND SUSSEX UNIVERSITY HOSPITALS NHS TRUST   R J ST C HARLOW-TRIGG, P R WELLS, S UNDERDOWN
BRIGHTON GENERAL   *see* Brighton and Sussex Univ Hosps NHS Trust
BRISTOL GENERAL   *see* Univ Hosps Bris NHS Foundn Trust
BRISTOL ROYAL HOSPITAL FOR CHILDREN   *as above*
BRISTOL ROYAL INFIRMARY   *as above*
BROADGREEN Liverpool   *see* R Liverpool and Broadgreen Univ Hosps NHS Trust
BROADMOOR Crowthorne   *see* W Lon Mental Health NHS Trust
BROADOAK Mental Health Unit   *see* Mersey Care NHS Trust
BRONGLAIS GENERAL   *see* Hywel Dda Health Bd
BROOKLANDS Marston Green   *see* N Warks NHS Trust
BROOMFIELD Chelmsford   *see* Mid-Essex Hosp Services NHS Trust
BRYN Y NEUADD Llanfairfechan   *see* NW Wales NHS Trust
BUCKINGHAMSHIRE HOSPITALS NHS TRUST   D R ELLIOTT

BUCKLAND Dover *see* E Kent Hosps NHS Trust
BURNLEY GENERAL *see* E Lancs Hosps NHS Trust
BURTON HOSPITALS NHS TRUST C P BARRETT,
G J CROSSLEY
CAERPHILLY DISTRICT MINERS' *see* Gwent Healthcare
NHS Trust
CALDERDALE AND HUDDERSFIELD NHS TRUST
M W PARROTT, S V BROOKS, M D ELLERTON
CAMBOURNE/REDRUTH COMMUNITY *see* Cornwall
and Is of Scilly Primary Care Trust
CAMBRIDGE UNIVERSITY HOSPITALS NHS
FOUNDATION TRUST D P FORD, A L ALDRIDGE,
S D GRIFFITHS, K C MORRISON
CAMBRIDGESHIRE AND PETERBOROUGH NHS
FOUNDATION TRUST J P NICHOLSON, M R BASS
CAMDEN AND ISLINGTON COMMUNITY HEALTH
SERVICES NHS TRUST B BATSTONE
CANNOCK CHASE *see* Mid Staffs NHS Foundn Trust
CANTERBURY St Martin's *see* Kent & Medway NHS and Soc
Care Partnership Trust
CARDIFF AND VALE NHS TRUST C ARGLES, E J BURKE
CARDIFF COMMUNITY HEALTHCARE NHS TRUST
J H L ROWLANDS
CARDIFF ROYAL INFIRMARY *see* Cardiff and Vale NHS
Trust
CASSEL Richmond *see* W Lon Mental Health NHS Trust
CASTEL *see* States of Guernsey Bd of Health
CASTLE HILL Cottingham *see* Hull and E Yorks Hosps NHS
Trust
CASTLEFORD NORMANTON AND DISTRICT *see* Mid
Yorks Hosps NHS Trust
CATERHAM *see* Surrey and Sussex Healthcare NHS Trust
CAWSTON PARK T W HARRIS
CEFN COED Swansea *see* Swansea NHS Trust
CENTRAL MANCHESTER/MANCHESTER CHILDREN'S
UNIVERSITY HOSPITAL NHS TRUST S TURNER,
J S A LAW
CENTRAL MIDDLESEX NHS TRUST M D MOORHEAD
CHAPEL ALLERTON Leeds *see* Leeds Teaching Hosps NHS
Trust
CHARING CROSS Pilot Wing *see* W Lon Mental Health NHS
Trust
CHARLTON LANE CENTRE Leckhampton *see* Glos Hosps
NHS Foundn Trust
CHASE FARM Enfield *see* Barnet and Chase Farm Hosps
NHS Trust
CHELMSFORD Broomfield *see* Mid-Essex Hosp Services
NHS Trust
CHELSEA AND WESTMINSTER HOSPITAL NHS
FOUNDATION TRUST S M CONNELL, C BEARDSLEY
CHELTENHAM GENERAL *see* Glos Hosps NHS Foundn
Trust
CHEPSTOW COMMUNITY *see* Gwent Healthcare NHS
Trust
CHERRY KNOWLE Sunderland *see* Northumberland, Tyne
and Wear NHS Foundn Trust
CHERRY TREE Stockport *see* Stockport NHS Trust
CHESHIRE AND WIRRAL PARTNERSHIPS NHS TRUST
A SCAIFE, G L HODKINSON, D R NUGENT
CHESTERFIELD AND NORTH DERBYSHIRE NHS
TRUST J K BUTTERFIELD
CHESTERTON Cambridge *see* Cam Univ Hosps NHS Foundn
Trust
CHICHESTER St Richard's *see* R W Sussex NHS Trust
CHIPPENHAM COMMUNITY *see* Wilts and Swindon
Healthcare NHS Trust
CHRISTCHURCH *see* R Bournemouth and Christchurch
Hosps NHS Trust
CHRISTIE HOSPITAL NHS TRUST Manchester K L DUNN
CHURCHILL, THE Oxford *see* Ox Radcliffe Hosps NHS Trust
CIRENCESTER *see* Glos Primary Care Trust
CIRENCESTER *see* Glos Hosps NHS Foundn Trust
CITY Birmingham *see* Sandwell and W Birm Hosps NHS Trust
CITY HOSPITAL York *see* York Hosps NHS Foundn Trust
CITY HOSPITALS SUNDERLAND NHS TRUST P H WEBB,
M WARNER
CLACTON GENERAL *see* Colchester Hosp Univ NHS
Foundn Trust
CLATTERBRIDGE Wirral *see* Cheshire and Wirral
Partnerships NHS Trust
CLAYTON Wakefield *see* Mid Yorks Hosps NHS Trust
CLEVELAND, SOUTH Middlesbrough *see* S Tees Hosps NHS
Trust
CLIFTON Lytham St Annes *see* Blackpool, Fylde and Wyre
Hosps NHS Trust

COLCHESTER GENERAL *see* Colchester Hosp Univ NHS
Foundn Trust
COLCHESTER HOSPITAL UNIVERSITY NHS
FOUNDATION TRUST M W THOMPSON, H A N PLATTS
COLCHESTER MATERNITY *see* Colchester Hosp Univ
NHS Foundn Trust
COLINDALE *see* Enfield Primary Care Trust
COLMAN Norwich *see* Norfolk Primary Care Trust
CONQUEST St Leonards-on-Sea *see* E Sussex Hosps NHS
Trust
COOKRIDGE Leeds *see* Leeds Teaching Hosps NHS Trust
CORK UNIVERSITY D R NUZUM
CORNWALL AND ISLES OF SCILLY PRIMARY CARE
TRUST R OAKES
CORNWALL HEALTHCARE NHS TRUST J T MCCABE
CORNWALL PARTNERSHIP NHS TRUST C D NEWELL
COUNTESS MOUNTBATTEN HOSPICE Southampton *see*
Southn Univ Hosps NHS Trust
COUNTESS OF CHESTER HOSPITAL NHS FOUNDATION
TRUST G M HIBBERT, G L HODKINSON
COUNTY DURHAM AND DARLINGTON NHS
FOUNDATION TRUST B SELMES, K S TROMANS, T P GIBBONS
COUNTY DURHAM AND DARLINGTON PRIORITY
SERVICES NHS TRUST C JAY
COVENTRY AND WARWICKSHIRE *see* Univ Hosps Cov
and Warks NHS Trust
CROMER *see* Norfolk and Nor Univ Hosp NHS Trust
CROMER AND DISTRICT *see* Norfolk Primary Care Trust
CROSSLANE Newby *see* Tees and NE Yorks NHS Trust
CROWBOROUGH WAR MEMORIAL *see* Sussex Downs and
Weald Primary Care Trust
CROYDON MENTAL HEALTH SERVICES Warlingham *see*
S Lon and Maudsley NHS Foundn Trust
CUMBERLAND INFIRMARY *see* N Cumbria Univ Hosps
NHS Trust
DARLINGTON MEMORIAL *see* Co Durham and
Darlington NHS Foundn Trust
DARTFORD AND GRAVESHAM NHS TRUST M H KELLY
DELANCEY Leckhampton *see* Glos Hosps NHS Foundn
Trust
DELLWOOD Reading *see* R Berks NHS Foundn Trust
DERBY HOSPITALS NHS FOUNDATION TRUST
D W ASHTON, M HARGREAVES, H P JONES, S C NEAL, P A SHORT
DERBYSHIRE CHILDREN'S *see* Derby Hosps NHS Foundn
Trust
DERBYSHIRE ROYAL INFIRMARY *as above*
DEREHAM *see* Norfolk Primary Care Trust
DERRIFORD *see* Plymouth Hosps NHS Trust
DEVIZES COMMUNITY *see* Wilts and Swindon Healthcare
NHS Trust
DEVONSHIRE ROAD Blackpool *see* Blackpool, Fylde and
Wyre Hosps NHS Trust
DEWI SANT Pontypridd *see* Pontypridd and Rhondda NHS
Trust
DEWSBURY AND DISTRICT *see* Mid Yorks Hosps NHS
Trust
DIANA, PRINCESS OF WALES Grimsby *see* N Lincs and
Goole Hosps NHS Trust
DILKE MEMORIAL Cinderford *see* Glos Primary Care Trust
DONCASTER AND BASSETLAW HOSPITALS NHS TRUST
C L SMITH
DONCASTER ROYAL INFIRMARY *see* Doncaster and
Bassetlaw Hosps NHS Trust
DONCASTER ROYAL INFIRMARY PSYCHIATRIC UNIT
see Rotherham, Doncaster and S Humber NHS Trust
DORKING *see* Surrey and Sussex Healthcare NHS Trust
DOWN LISBURN HEALTH AND SOCIAL SERVICES
TRUST E HENDERSON
DUCHESS OF KENT HOUSE St Andrews *see* States of
Guernsey Bd of Health
DUCHY Truro H C T OLIVEY
DUNSTON HILL Gateshead *see* Gateshead Health NHS Trust
DURHAM AND DARLINGTON NHS FOUNDATION
TRUST *see* Co Durham and Darlington NHS Foundn Trust
DURHAM AND DARLINGTON PRIORITY SERVICES
NHS TRUST *see* Co Dur & Darlington Priority Services NHS
Trust
EALING HOSPITAL NHS TRUST M K DAVIDGE-SMITH,
E J WALLER
EARLS HOUSE Durham *see* Co Dur & Darlington Priority
Services NHS Trust
EAST AND NORTH HERTFORDSHIRE NHS TRUST
A J FERRIS, S V BECK, J E HATTON, L E SUMMERS
EAST CHESHIRE NHS TRUST J BUCKLEY
EAST HAM MEMORIAL *see* E Lon NHS Foundation Trust

EAST HAMPSHIRE PRIMARY CARE TRUST   J E HAIR,
C R PRESTIDGE
EAST KENT HOSPITALS NHS TRUST   P F HILL, P M KIRBY,
K FAZZANI
EAST LANCASHIRE HOSPITALS NHS TRUST
A S HORSFALL, D ALTHAM
EAST LONDON NHS FOUNDATION TRUST   N J COPSEY
EAST SOMERSET NHS TRUST   E J ROTHWELL
EAST SURREY PRIORITY CARE NHS TRUST   N J COPSEY
EAST SUSSEX COUNTY HEALTHCARE NHS TRUST
M J ELWIS
EAST SUSSEX HOSPITALS NHS TRUST   G J A COOK,
C I WOODWARD, C R GORING, J G DAVENPORT
EASTBOURNE GENERAL   see E Sussex Hosps NHS Trust
and E Sussex Co Healthcare NHS Trust
EASTERN AND COASTAL KENT PRIMARY CARE TRUST
P M KIRBY
EDGWARE COMMUNITY   see Barnet and Chase Farm
Hosps NHS Trust
EDITH CAVELL Peterborough   see Pet Hosps NHS Trust
ELIZABETH GARRETT ANDERSON OBSTETRIC London
see Univ Coll Lon Hosps NHS Foundn Trust
ELLESMERE PORT   see Cheshire and Wirral Partnerships
NHS Trust
ELY Cardiff   see Cardiff and Vale NHS Trust
ELY Cardiff   see Cardiff Community Healthcare NHS Trust
ENFIELD PRIMARY CARE TRUST   T M BARON
EPSOM St Ebba's   see Surrey and Borders Partnership NHS
Trust
EPSOM AND ST HELIER UNIVERSITY HOSPITALS NHS
TRUST   S J ELLISON, S F SEWELL
EPSOM GENERAL   see Epsom and St Helier Univ Hosps NHS
Trust
ESSEX COUNTY   see Colchester Hosp Univ NHS Foundn
Trust
EVESHAM COMMUNITY   see Worcs Community and
Mental Health Trust
FAIRFIELD GENERAL   see Pennine Acute Hosps NHS Trust
FALMOUTH   see Cornwall and Is of Scilly Primary Care Trust
FARNHAM   see Surrey and Borders Partnership NHS Trust
FARNHAM ROAD Guildford   as above
FIELDHEAD Wakefield   see SW Yorks Mental Health NHS
Trust
FINCHLEY MEMORIAL   see Enfield Primary Care Trust
FOREST LODGE Sheffield   see Sheff Care Trust
FORSTER GREEN   see Belfast Health and Soc Care Trust
FREEMAN Newcastle   see Newcastle upon Tyne Hosps NHS
Foundn Trust
FRENCHAY Bristol   see N Bris NHS Trust
FRIMLEY PARK HOSPITAL NHS FOUNDATION TRUST
B D BURBIDGE, J H A HATTAWAY
FULBOURN Cambridge   see Cam Univ Hosps NHS Foundn
Trust
FURNESS GENERAL Barrow-in-Furness   see Univ Hosps of
Morecambe Bay NHS Trust
GATESHEAD HEALTH NHS TRUST   J R PERRY
GEORGE ELIOT HOSPITAL NHS TRUST Nuneaton
E C POGMORE, S P MOULT, P DODDS
GLANGWILI GENERAL   see Hywel Dda Health Bd
GLENFIELD Bennion Centre   see Leics Partnership NHS Trust
GLENFIELD Bradgate Mental Health Unit   as above
GLENFIELD Leicester   see Univ Hosps Leic NHS Trust
GLOUCESTERSHIRE HOSPITALS NHS FOUNDATION
TRUST   W B IRVINE, M S RILEY, C A MCCLURE
GLOUCESTERSHIRE PARTNERSHIP TRUST   M J WITHEY
GLOUCESTERSHIRE PRIMARY CARE TRUST   G L BURN,
M J WITHEY, C CARTER
GLOUCESTERSHIRE ROYAL   see Glos Hosps NHS Foundn
Trust
GOOD HOPE HOSPITAL NHS TRUST Sutton Coldfield
A T BALL, D A MURPHY
GOOLE AND DISTRICT   see N Lincs and Goole Hosps NHS
Trust
GORSE HILL Leicester   see Leics Partnership NHS Trust
GOSPORT WAR MEMORIAL   see E Hants Primary Care
Trust
GRAMPIAN HEALTHCARE NHS TRUST   J DUTHIE
GRAMPIAN UNIVERSITY HOSPITAL NHS
TRUST   S SPENCER
GREAT ORMOND STREET HOSPITAL FOR CHILDREN
NHS TRUST   J D LINTHICUM, P J SHERRINGTON
GREATER MANCHESTER WEST MENTAL HEALTH NHS
FOUNDATION TRUST   D R SUTTON
GREENACRES Dartford   see Kent & Medway NHS and Soc
Care Partnership Trust

GRIMSBY   see N Lincs and Goole Hosps NHS Trust
GUILDFORD St Luke's   see R Surrey Co Hosp NHS Trust
GUY'S AND ST THOMAS' NHS FOUNDATION TRUST
London   M A K HILBORN, N J K TEGALLY, A H BARRON,
O O SOTONWA, C B HALL, W W SHARPE, J M WATTS
GWENT COUNTY Griffithstown   see Gwent Healthcare NHS
Trust
GWENT HEALTHCARE NHS TRUST   A W TYLER,
M J MARSDEN, D C ROBERTS, M C G LANE
HALSTEAD COMMUNITY   see Colchester Hosp Univ NHS
Foundn Trust
HALTON GENERAL   see N Cheshire Hosps NHS Trust
HAM GREEN Bristol   see N Bris NHS Trust
HAMPSHIRE PARTNERSHIP NHS TRUST   J E HAIR,
V J LAWRENCE, D L GRACE, G M K MORGAN
HAROLD WOOD   see Barking Havering and Redbridge Hosps
NHS Trust
HARROGATE AND DISTRICT NHS FOUNDATION
TRUST   K COUCHMAN
HARROW   see NW Lon Hosp NHS Trust
HARROW AND HILLINGDON HEALTHCARE NHS
TRUST   D P BYRNE
HARTLEPOOL GENERAL   see N Tees and Hartlepool NHS
Trust and Tees and NE Yorks NHS Trust
HARTSHILL ORTHOPAEDIC   see N Staffs Hosp NHS Trust
HARWICH COMMUNITY   see Colchester Hosp Univ NHS
Foundn Trust
HASLAR   see Portsm Hosps NHS Trust
HEART HOSPITAL London   see Univ Coll Lon Hosps NHS
Foundn Trust
HEART OF ENGLAND NHS FOUNDATION TRUST
M MACLACHLAN
HEATHERWOOD AND WEXHAM PARK HOSPITAL NHS
TRUST   C E L SMITH, R A CHEEK
HELLESDON Norfolk   see Norfolk & Waveney Mental Health
NHS Foundn Trust
HEMEL HEMPSTEAD GENERAL   see W Herts Hosps NHS
Trust
HEREFORD HOSPITALS NHS TRUST   P A ROBERTS,
L C RHODES
HERGEST UNIT Ysbyty Gwynedd   see NW Wales NHS Trust
HERTFORDSHIRE AND ESSEX COMMUNITY NHS
TRUST   K I GOSS
HERTFORDSHIRE PARTNERSHIP NHS FOUNDATION
TRUST   V M HARVEY
HEXHAM   see Northumbria Healthcare NHS Trust
HIGHBURY Bulwell   see Notts Healthcare NHS Trust
HILL HOUSE Swansea   see Swansea NHS Trust
HILLINGDON HOSPITAL NHS TRUST   S J LAFFORD
HINCHINGBROOKE HEALTH CARE NHS TRUST
S A WATTS, P M DUFFETT-SMITH, S GRIFFITH, C M FURLONG
HITCHIN   see E and N Herts NHS Trust
HITHER GREEN London   see Lewisham Healthcare NHS
Trust
HOPE Salford   see Salford R Hosps NHS Foundn Trust
HORSHAM   see W Sussex Health and Soc Care NHS Trust
HUDDERSFIELD ROYAL INFIRMARY   see Calderdale and
Huddersfield NHS Trust
HULL AND EAST YORKSHIRE HOSPITALS NHS TRUST
P J NELSON, J A SHARP, A M LAIRD, R MARSDEN
HULL MATERNITY   see Hull and E Yorks Hosps NHS Trust
HULL ROYAL INFIRMARY   as above
HUMBER MENTAL HEALTH TEACHING NHS TRUST
E ROSE
HURSTWOOD PARK Haywards Heath   see Brighton and
Sussex Univ Hosps NHS Trust
HYWEL DDA HEALTH BOARD   E HOWELLS
IDA DARWIN Cambridge   see Cam Univ Hosps NHS Foundn
Trust
IMPERIAL COLLEGE HEALTHCARE NHS TRUST
C P GUINNESS, S J FLATT, J G S MORGAN,
A P R KYRIAKIDES-YELDHAM
INVICTA COMMUNITY CARE NHS TRUST
S A J MITCHELL
IPSWICH St Clements   see Local Health Partnerships NHS
Trust
IPSWICH HOSPITAL NHS TRUST   G T MELVIN, S J RAINE
ISLE OF MAN DEPARTMENT OF HEALTH AND SOCIAL
SECURITY   P S FREAR
ISLE OF WIGHT NHS PRIMARY CARE TRUST
G J CLIFTON-SMITH, D L DENNIS, M D H JOHNSTON,
D M NETHERWAY
JAMES COOK UNIVERSITY Middlesbrough   see S Tees
Hosps NHS Trust
JERSEY GENERAL St Helier   see Jersey Gp of Hosps

JERSEY GROUP M TURNER, S M WHITE
JESSOP WOMEN'S Sheffield see Sheff Teaching Hosps NHS Foundn Trust
JOHN CONOLLY WING Southall see W Lon Mental Health NHS Trust
JOHN RADCLIFFE Oxford see Ox Radcliffe Hosps NHS Trust
KELLING Holt see Norfolk Primary Care Trust
KENT AND CANTERBURY see E Kent Hosps NHS Trust
KENT AND MEDWAY NHS AND SOCIAL CARE PARTNERSHIP TRUST P J RICHMOND, R A BIERBAUM, M CLEEVE
KENT AND SUSSEX Tunbridge Wells see Maidstone and Tunbridge Wells NHS Trust
KETTERING GENERAL HOSPITAL NHS TRUST C H WALKER, R G BROWN
KEYCOL Kent see Thames Gateway NHS Trust
KIDDERMINSTER see Worcs Acute Hosps NHS Trust
KIDDERMINSTER GENERAL see Worcs Community and Mental Health Trust
KING EDWARD VII Castel see States of Guernsey Bd of Health
KING EDWARD VII Midhurst D B WELSMAN
KING GEORGE Redbridge see Barking Havering and Redbridge Hosps NHS Trust
KING'S COLLEGE HOSPITAL NHS TRUST B RHODES, S NJOKA
KING'S LYNN AND WISBECH HOSPITALS NHS TRUST A M DAVIES
KINGS MILL Sutton-in-Ashfield see Sherwood Forest Hosps NHS Trust
KING'S WOOD CENTRE Colchester see N Essex Partnership NHS Foundn Trust
KINGSTON HOSPITAL NHS TRUST Surrey G W HOLMES
KNEESWORTH HOUSE Royston N TAYLOR
LAGAN VALLEY see Down Lisburn Health and Soc Services Trust
LAKESIDE MENTAL HEALTH UNIT Isleworth see W Lon Mental Health NHS Trust
LANSDOWNE see Cardiff and Vale NHS Trust
LEA CASTLE Wolverley see N Warks NHS Trust
LEEDS St Mary's see Leeds Mental Health Teaching NHS Trust
LEEDS GENERAL INFIRMARY see Leeds Teaching Hosps NHS Trust
LEEDS MENTAL HEALTH TEACHING NHS TRUST M I KIMBALL
LEEDS TEACHING HOSPITALS NHS TRUST C J SWIFT, I WILLIAMS, A CLAYTON
LEICESTER GENERAL see Univ Hosps Leic NHS Trust
LEICESTER GENERAL Brandon Mental Health Unit see Leics Partnership NHS Trust
LEICESTER ROYAL INFIRMARY see Univ Hosps Leic NHS Trust
LEICESTERSHIRE PARTNERSHIP NHS TRUST T H GIRLING
LEIGH INFIRMARY see Wrightington Wigan and Leigh NHS Trust
LEIGHTON Crewe see Cheshire and Wirral Partnerships NHS Trust
LEIGHTON Crewe see Mid Cheshire Hosps Trust
LEWISHAM HEALTHCARE NHS TRUST M J HANCOCK
LIBERTON Edinburgh see Lothian Univ Hosps NHS Trust
LIFECARE Caterham see Surrey and Borders Partnership NHS Trust
LIMES, THE Southall see W Lon Mental Health NHS Trust
LINCOLN St Barnabas' Hospice see Linc Distr Health Services and Hosps NHS Trust
LINCOLN St George's as above
LINCOLN COUNTY see Lincs Partnership NHS Foundn Trust
LINCOLN COUNTY see United Lincs Hosps NHS Trust
LINCOLN DISTRICT HEALTH SERVICES NHS TRUST AND LINCOLN HOSPITALS NHS TRUST W G WILLIAMS
LINCOLNSHIRE PARTNERSHIP NHS FOUNDATION TRUST H G SMART, J K WILSON, A M PAVEY
LINCOLNSHIRE TEACHING PRIMARY CARE TRUST P S J GARLAND
LINDEN CENTRE Broomfield see N Essex Partnership NHS Foundn Trust
LISKEARD COMMUNITY see Cornwall and Is of Scilly Primary Care Trust
LISTER Stevenage see E and N Herts NHS Trust
LITTLE BROMWICH CENTRE FOR ELDERLY MENTAL HEALTH Small Heath see Birm and Solihull Mental Health Trust

LITTLE PLUMSTEAD see Norfolk Primary Care Trust
LITTLEMORE Oxford see Oxon & Bucks Mental Health Partnership NHS Trust
LIVERPOOL CARDIOTHORACIC CENTRE see R Liverpool and Broadgreen Univ Hosps NHS Trust
LLANDOUGH see Cardiff and Vale NHS Trust
LLANDUDNO GENERAL see NW Wales NHS Trust
LLANFRECHFA GRANGE Cwmbran see Gwent Healthcare NHS Trust
LLANTRISANT Royal Glamorgan see Pontypridd and Rhondda NHS Trust
LLWYNYPIA as above
LOCAL HEALTH PARTNERSHIPS NHS TRUST Suffolk G T MELVIN
LONDON AND SURREY see R Marsden NHS Foundn Trust
LONDON CHEST see Barts and The Lon NHS Trust
LONGLEY CENTRE Sheffield see Sheff Care Trust
LOTHIAN UNIVERSITY HOSPITALS NHS TRUST C T UPTON
LOUTH COUNTY see United Lincs Hosps NHS Trust
LOVERSALL Doncaster see Rotherham, Doncaster and S Humber NHS Trust
LUDLOW see Shropshire Co Primary Care Trust
LUTON AND DUNSTABLE HOSPITAL NHS TRUST E A BRADLEY
MACCLESFIELD DISTRICT GENERAL see Cheshire and Wirral Partnerships NHS Trust
MACCLESFIELD DISTRICT GENERAL see E Cheshire NHS Trust
MAIDSTONE AND TUNBRIDGE WELLS NHS TRUST N J MITRA
MAINDIFF COURT Abergavenny see Gwent Healthcare NHS Trust
MANCHESTER see also Greater Manchester
MANCHESTER AND SALFORD SKIN see Salford R Hosps NHS Foundn Trust
MANCHESTER ROYAL EYE see Cen Man/Man Children's Univ Hosp NHS Trust
MANCHESTER ROYAL INFIRMARY as above
MANOR Walsall see Walsall Hosps NHS Trust
MANSFIELD COMMUNITY see Sherwood Forest Hosps NHS Trust
MANSFIELD DISTRICT PRIMARY CARE TRUST P BENTLEY
MATER see Belfast Health and Soc Care Trust
MAUDSLEY Denmark Hill see S Lon and Maudsley NHS Foundn Trust
MAYDAY HEALTHCARE NHS TRUST Thornton Heath H A FIFE
MAYDAY UNIVERSITY see Mayday Healthcare NHS Trust Thornton Heath
MEADOWBROOK UNIT Salford see Gtr Man W Mental Health NHS Foundn Trust
MEADOWFIELD Worthing see W Sussex Health and Soc Care NHS Trust
MEANWOOD PARK Leeds see Leeds Mental Health Teaching NHS Trust
MEDWAY Gillingham see Thames Gateway NHS Trust
MEDWAY MARITIME Gillingham see Kent & Medway NHS and Soc Care Partnership Trust
MEDWAY NHS FOUNDATION TRUST S C SPENCER, D V GOWER
MELKSHAM COMMUNITY see Wilts and Swindon Healthcare NHS Trust
MERSEY CARE NHS TRUST R D FIELDING
MERTHYR TYDFIL see N Glam NHS Trust
MICHAEL CARLISLE CENTRE Sheffield see Sheff Care Trust
MID CHESHIRE HOSPITALS TRUST D MARSH, C J SANDERSON
MID-ESSEX HOSPITAL SERVICES NHS TRUST J SHEFFIELD, S M SOUTHEE
MID STAFFORDSHIRE NHS FOUNDATION TRUST P J GRAYSMITH, M J COULTER
MID YORKSHIRE HOSPITALS NHS TRUST R J BAILES
MIDDLESBROUGH GENERAL see S Tees Hosps NHS Trust
MIDDLESEX see Univ Coll Lon Hosps NHS Foundn Trust
MILDMAY MISSION M F SCHLEGER
MILLBROOK MENTAL HEALTH UNIT Sutton-in-Ashfield see Notts Healthcare NHS Trust
MONKWEARMOUTH Sunderland see Northumberland, Tyne and Wear NHS Foundn Trust
MONTAGU Mexborough see Doncaster and Bassetlaw Hosps NHS Trust
MOORFIELDS EYE HOSPITAL NHS TRUST D E ALLEN

MOORGREEN West End Southampton *see* Chapl Hants Partnership NHS Trust
MORPETH COTTAGE *see* Northumbria Healthcare NHS Trust
MORRISTON Swansea *see* Swansea NHS Trust
MOSELEY HALL Birmingham *see* Birm Specialist Community Health NHS Trust
MOSSLEY HILL Liverpool *see* Mersey Care NHS Trust
MUSGRAVE PARK *see* Belfast Health and Soc Care Trust
MUSGROVE PARK Taunton *see* Taunton and Somerset NHS Trust
NAPSBURY St Albans *see* Enfield Primary Care Trust
NATIONAL HOSPITAL FOR NEUROLOGY AND NEUROSURGERY London *see* Univ Coll Lon Hosps NHS Foundn Trust
NEVILL HALL Abergavenny *see* Gwent Healthcare NHS Trust
NEW CRAIGS Inverness *see* NHS Highland
NEW CROSS Wolverhampton *see* R Wolv Hosps NHS Trust
NEWARK *see* Sherwood Forest Hosps NHS Trust
NEWCASTLE Freeman *see* Newcastle upon Tyne Hosps NHS Foundn Trust
NEWCASTLE Royal Victoria Infirmary *as above*
NEWCASTLE St Nicholas *see* Northumberland, Tyne and Wear NHS Foundn Trust
NEWCASTLE GENERAL *see* Newcastle upon Tyne Hosps NHS Foundn Trust
NEWCASTLE MENTAL HEALTH UNIT A E MARR
NEWCASTLE-UNDER-LYME PRIMARY CARE TRUST P D HOWARD
NEWCASTLE UPON TYNE HOSPITALS NHS FOUNDATION TRUST M J SHIPTON, K L JONES, K J FRANCIS
NEWHAM PRIMARY CARE TRUST N J COPSEY
NEWHAVEN DOWNS *see* Sussex Downs and Weald Primary Care Trust
NEWTON ABBOT *see* S Devon Healthcare NHS Foundn Trust
NEWTOWN Worcester *see* Worcs Community and Mental Health Trust
NHS DUMFRIES AND GALLOWAY S R PAISLEY
NHS HIGHLAND M F HICKFORD
NORFOLK AND NORWICH UNIVERSITY HOSPITAL NHS TRUST S L GREEN, J L NURSEY, E S LANGAN, J M STEWART
NORFOLK AND WAVENEY MENTAL HEALTH NHS FOUNDATION TRUST W F BAZELY
NORFOLK PRIMARY CARE TRUST P A ATKINSON, M J TALBOT
NORTH BRISTOL NHS TRUST S J ORAM, D C DAVIES, N A HECTOR, A J PARKER, C A G LEGGATE, A M BUCKNALL, A R GOOD
NORTH CAMBRIDGESHIRE Wisbech *see* King's Lynn and Wisbech Hosps NHS Trust
NORTH CHESHIRE HOSPITALS NHS TRUST J E DUFFIELD
NORTH CUMBRIA UNIVERSITY HOSPITALS NHS TRUST A M ROBERTS, J A EVANS, M C DANKS-FLOWER
NORTH DEVON DISTRICT Barnstaple *see* N Devon Healthcare NHS Trust
NORTH EAST LONDON MENTAL HEALTH TRUST M O PRITCHARD, G F JENKINS
NORTH EAST WALES NHS TRUST K B COLLINS
NORTH ESSEX PARTNERSHIP NHS FOUNDATION TRUST C A HAWKINS, R A LANE
NORTH GLAMORGAN NHS TRUST E A POWELL
NORTH MANCHESTER GENERAL *see* Pennine Acute Hosps NHS Trust
NORTH MIDDLESEX HOSPITAL NHS TRUST B D FENTON, P C ATHERTON
NORTH STAFFORDSHIRE HOSPITAL NHS TRUST J M AUSTERBERRY, L B VARQUEZ, T B BLOOR
NORTH SURREY PRIMARY CARE TRUST J M ALLFORD
NORTH TEES AND HARTLEPOOL NHS TRUST L PURVIS
NORTH TEES GENERAL *see* Tees and NE Yorks NHS Trust
NORTH TYNESIDE GENERAL North Shields *see* Northumbria Healthcare NHS Trust
NORTH WARWICKSHIRE NHS TRUST S P MOULT
NORTH WEST LONDON HOSPITALS NHS TRUST D P BYRNE
NORTH WEST WALES NHS TRUST W ROBERTS, R H GRIFFITHS
NORTHAMPTON GENERAL HOSPITAL NHS TRUST G A SARMEZEY, R G MORTON
NORTHAMPTONSHIRE HEALTHCARE NHS TRUST C R GOODLEY, R J T FARMER
NORTHCROFT Erdington *see* Birm and Solihull Mental Health Trust
NORTHERN DEVON HEALTHCARE NHS TRUST K E W MATHERS, R M REYNOLDS

NORTHERN GENERAL Sheffield *see* Sheff Teaching Hosps NHS Foundn Trust
NORTHERN LINCOLNSHIRE AND GOOLE HOSPITALS NHS TRUST A R BARBER
NORTHGATE Morpeth *see* Northgate and Prudhoe NHS Trust
NORTHGATE AND PRUDHOE NHS TRUST D E BOWLER
NORTHUMBERLAND, TYNE AND WEAR NHS FOUNDATION TRUST C J WORSFOLD, D E BOWLER, F B ALLEN
NORTHUMBERLAND MENTAL HEALTH NHS TRUST S D MASON
NORTHUMBRIA HEALTHCARE NHS TRUST D MACNAUGHTON, G HARWOOD, J L J COOPER, J WAIYAKI
NORWICH, WEST *see* Norfolk and Nor Univ Hosp NHS Trust
NORWICH COMMUNITY *see* Norfolk Primary Care Trust
NOTTINGHAMSHIRE HEALTHCARE NHS TRUST K R EVANS, J L ALLEN
NUFFIELD Brighton R A BROMFIELD
NUFFIELD ORTHOPAEDIC CENTRE NHS TRUST J E COCKE
NUNNERY FIELDS Canterbury *see* E Kent Hosps NHS Trust
OLDCHURCH Romford *see* Barking Havering and Redbridge Hosps NHS Trust
ORPINGTON *see* S Lon Healthcare NHS Trust
ORSETT *see* Basildon & Thurrock Univ Hosps NHS Foundn Trust
OVERDALE St Helier *see* Jersey Gp of Hosps
OXFORD RADCLIFFE HOSPITALS NHS TRUST J M TURNER, P F SUTTON, H L ADEY HUISH
OXFORDSHIRE AND BUCKINGHAMSHIRE MENTAL HEALTH PARTNERSHIP NHS TRUST S L BUSHELL, A F RABLEN
OXTED *see* Surrey and Sussex Healthcare NHS Trust
PAIGNTON *see* S Devon Healthcare NHS Foundn Trust
PAPWORTH HOSPITAL NHS FOUNDATION TRUST G R ROWLANDS
PARKLANDS Basingstoke *see* Chapl Hants Partnership NHS Trust
PEMBURY Tunbridge Wells *see* Maidstone and Tunbridge Wells NHS Trust
PEMBURY Tunbridge Wells *see* Kent & Medway NHS and Soc Care Partnership Trust
PENDERED CENTRE Northampton *see* Northants Healthcare NHS Trust
PENDLE COMMUNITY Nelson *see* E Lancs Hosps NHS Trust
PENNINE ACUTE HOSPITALS NHS TRUST, THE R R WATSON, S A PURVIS
PETERBOROUGH AND STAMFORD HOSPITALS NHS FOUNDATION TRUST M P M STEWART, J J PRICE
PETERBOROUGH HOSPITALS NHS TRUST R E HIGGINS
PETERSFIELD COMMUNITY *see* E Hants Primary Care Trust
PIERREMONT UNIT Darlington *see* Co Dur & Darlington Priority Services NHS Trust
PILGRIM Boston *see* United Lincs Hosps NHS Trust
PINDERFIELDS GENERAL Wakefield *see* Mid Yorks Hosps NHS Trust
PLAISTOW *see* Newham Primary Care Trust
PLYMOUTH HOSPITALS NHS TRUST S J PEARCE, R D BAXENDALE, M B BROWN
PONTEFRACT GENERAL INFIRMARY *see* Mid Yorks Hosps NHS Trust
PONTYPRIDD AND RHONDDA NHS TRUST R T PITMAN
POOLE HOSPITAL NHS TRUST E J LLOYD, I R PEARCE
PORTSMOUTH HOSPITALS NHS TRUST B R SMITH, N P FENNEMORE, C A SMITH, M J A LINDSAY, C J HEADLEY, J POWER
PRINCE CHARLES Merthyr Tydfil *see* N Glam NHS Trust
PRINCESS ALEXANDRA Harlow *see* N Essex Partnership NHS Foundn Trust
PRINCESS ALEXANDRA HOSPITAL NHS TRUST Harlow T R WEEKS
PRINCESS ANNE Southampton *see* Southn Univ Hosps NHS Trust
PRINCESS ELIZABETH St Martin *see* States of Guernsey Bd of Health
PRINCESS MARGARET ROSE ORTHOPAEDIC Edinburgh *see* Lothian Univ Hosps NHS Trust
PRINCESS MARINA Northampton *see* Northants Healthcare NHS Trust
PRINCESS OF WALES COMMUNITY Bromsgrove *see* Worcs Community and Mental Health Trust
PRINCESS ROYAL Haywards Heath *see* Brighton and Sussex Univ Hosps NHS Trust

PRINCESS ROYAL Hull   see Hull and E Yorks Hosps NHS Trust

PRINCESS ROYAL UNIVERSITY Orpington   see S Lon Healthcare NHS Trust

PRIORITY HOUSE Maidstone   see Kent & Medway NHS and Soc Care Partnership Trust

PRIORY Birmingham   J A GRIFFIN

PROSPECT PARK Reading   R S WADEY

QUEEN ALEXANDRA Portsmouth   see Portsm Hosps NHS Trust

QUEEN ELIZABETH Birmingham   see Univ Hosp Birm NHS Foundn Trust

QUEEN ELIZABETH Gateshead   see Gateshead Health NHS Trust

QUEEN ELIZABETH King's Lynn   see King's Lynn and Wisbech Hosps NHS Trust

QUEEN ELIZABETH Woolwich   see S Lon Healthcare NHS Trust

QUEEN ELIZABETH HOSPITAL KING'S LYNN NHS TRUST   H R BRIDGER

QUEEN ELIZABETH II Welwyn Garden City   see E and N Herts NHS Trust

QUEEN ELIZABETH PSYCHIATRIC Birmingham   see Birm and Solihull Mental Health Trust

QUEEN ELIZABETH THE QUEEN MOTHER Margate   see E Kent Hosps NHS Trust

QUEEN MARY'S Sidcup   see S Lon Healthcare NHS Trust

QUEEN MARY'S UNIVERSITY Roehampton Lane   see Wandsworth Primary Care Trust

QUEEN VICTORIA Morecambe   see Univ Hosps of Morecambe Bay NHS Trust

QUEEN VICTORIA HOSPITAL NHS TRUST East Grinstead   C EVERETT-ALLEN

QUEEN VICTORIA MEMORIAL Welwyn   see E and N Herts NHS Trust

QUEEN'S Burton-on-Trent   see Burton Hosps NHS Trust

QUEEN'S Romford   see Barking Havering and Redbridge Hosps NHS Trust

QUEEN'S MEDICAL CENTRE NOTTINGHAM UNIVERSITY HOSPITAL NHS TRUST   J HEMSTOCK, G SPENCER, C T DOLBY, A M BROOKS, P S WEEDING

QUEEN'S MEDICAL CENTRE UNIVERSITY HOSPITAL Nottingham, Department of Psychiatry and Psychiatric Medicine   see Notts Healthcare NHS Trust

QUEEN'S PARK Blackburn   see E Lancs Hosps NHS Trust

RADCLIFFE INFIRMARY Oxford   see Ox Radcliffe Hosps NHS Trust

RAIGMORE HOSPITAL NHS TRUST Inverness   A A SINCLAIR

RAMPTON Retford   see Notts Healthcare NHS Trust

RAMSGATE GENERAL   see E Kent Hosps NHS Trust

RATHBONE Liverpool   see Mersey Care NHS Trust

REASIDE CLINIC Rednal   see Birm and Solihull Mental Health Trust

REDBRIDGE King George   see Barking Havering and Redbridge Hosps NHS Trust

RICHMOND AND TWICKENHAM PRIMARY CARE TRUST   J W KNILL-JONES

RIDGEWOOD CENTRE Frimley   see Surrey and Borders Partnership NHS Trust

ROBERT JONES/AGNES HUNT ORTHOPAEDIC HOSPITAL NHS TRUST Oswestry   A R BAILEY

ROCHDALE INFIRMARY   see Pennine Acute Hosps NHS Trust

ROCHFORD   see S Essex Mental Health & Community Care NHS Trust

ROEHAMPTON LANE Queen Mary's University   see Wandsworth Primary Care Trust

ROOKWOOD Llandaff   see Cardiff and Vale NHS Trust

ROTHERAM NHS FOUNDATION TRUST   H FERGUSSON-STUART

ROTHERHAM, DONCASTER AND SOUTH HUMBER MENTAL HEALTH NHS TRUST   C M J THODY, A I MCCORMICK

ROTHERHAM GENERAL HOSPITALS NHS TRUST   J E ASHTON

ROWLEY REGIS Warley   see Sandwell and W Birm Hosps NHS Trust

ROYAL ALBERT EDWARD INFIRMARY   see Wrightington Wigan and Leigh NHS Trust

ROYAL ALEXANDRA CHILDREN'S Brighton   see Brighton and Sussex Univ Hosps NHS Trust

ROYAL BELFAST HOSPITAL FOR SICK CHILDREN see Belfast Health and Soc Care Trust and R Group of Hosps Health and Soc Services Trust

ROYAL BERKSHIRE NHS FOUNDATION TRUST   R J SIMMONDS, F M G HALL

ROYAL BOLTON HOSPITAL NHS FOUNDATION TRUST   B S GASKELL

ROYAL BOURNEMOUTH AND CHRISTCHURCH HOSPITALS NHS TRUST   B WILLIAMS, A SESSFORD

ROYAL BROMPTON AND HAREFIELD NHS TRUST   R G THOMPSON, N K LEE, T HANDLEY MACMATH

ROYAL CHELSEA, R H WHITTINGTON

ROYAL CORNWALL HOSPITALS TRUST   A D WEST, J K P S ROBERTSHAW, J A MILLAR

ROYAL DERBY   see Derby Hosps NHS Foundn Trust

ROYAL DEVON AND EXETER NHS FOUNDATION TRUST   S R SWARBRICK

ROYAL FREE HAMPSTEAD NHS TRUST   R H MITCHELL, P D CONRAD

ROYAL GLAMORGAN Llantrisant   see Pontypridd and Rhondda NHS Trust

ROYAL GROUP OF HOSPITALS AND DENTAL HOSPITALS HEALTH AND SOCIAL SERVICES TRUST Belfast   A MALLON

ROYAL GWENT Newport   see Gwent Healthcare NHS Trust

ROYAL HALLAMSHIRE Sheffield   see Sheff Teaching Hosps NHS Foundn Trust

ROYAL HOSPITAL FOR SICK CHILDREN Edinburgh   see Lothian Univ Hosps NHS Trust

ROYAL HOSPITAL HASLAR   see Portsm Hosps NHS Trust

ROYAL INFIRMARY OF EDINBURGH   see Lothian Univ Hosps NHS Trust

ROYAL JUBILEE MATERNITY SERVICE   see Belfast Health and Soc Care Trust

ROYAL LANCASTER INFIRMARY   see Univ Hosps of Morecambe Bay NHS Trust

ROYAL LIVERPOOL AND BROADGREEN UNIVERSITY HOSPITALS NHS TRUST   G A PERERA, C J PETER

ROYAL LIVERPOOL CHILDREN'S NHS TRUST   D J WILLIAMS

ROYAL LONDON   see Barts and The Lon NHS Trust

ROYAL MANCHESTER CHILDREN'S   see Cen Man/Man Children's Univ Hosp NHS Trust

ROYAL MARSDEN NHS FOUNDATION TRUST London and Surrey   A J MCCULLOCH, J M MCLUCKIE

ROYAL MATERNITY Belfast   see R Group of Hosps Health and Soc Services Trust

ROYAL NATIONAL ORTHOPAEDIC HOSPITAL NHS TRUST   W A BROOKER

ROYAL OLDHAM   see Pennine Acute Hosps NHS Trust

ROYAL SHREWSBURY   see Shrewsbury and Telford NHS Trust

ROYAL SOUTH HAMPSHIRE   see Southn Univ Hosps NHS Trust

ROYAL SURREY COUNTY HOSPITAL NHS TRUST   D N HOBDEN, J S MCARTHUR-EDWARDS

ROYAL SUSSEX COUNTY Brighton   see Brighton and Sussex Univ Hosps NHS Trust

ROYAL UNITED HOSPITAL BATH NHS TRUST   A J DAVIES, S M E STEVENS

ROYAL VICTORIA Belfast   see Belfast Health and Soc Care Trust and R Group of Hosps Health and Soc Services Trust

ROYAL VICTORIA Edinburgh   see Lothian Univ Hosps NHS Trust

ROYAL VICTORIA Folkestone   see E Kent Hosps NHS Trust

ROYAL VICTORIA INFIRMARY Newcastle   see Newcastle upon Tyne Hosps NHS Foundn Trust

ROYAL WEST SUSSEX NHS TRUST   J P COOPER, J V EMERSON

ROYAL WOLVERHAMPTON HOSPITALS NHS TRUST   C W FULLARD, C SILVESTER

RUNWELL   see S Essex Mental Health & Community Care NHS Trust

ST Monica Trust Sandford Station, J M H SIMS

ST ALBANS Napsbury   see Enfield Primary Care Trust

ST ALBANS CITY   see W Herts Hosps NHS Trust

ST ANDREW'S Northampton   J M BOWERS, N PURVEY-TYRER

ST ANDREW'S HEALTHCARE Birmingham, Essex, Northampton, Nottinghamshire   K J SKIPPON, C D WOOD, D I A BRAZELL, R M HETHERINGTON

ST ANNE'S CENTRE St Leonards-on-Sea   see E Sussex Co Healthcare NHS Trust

ST ANN'S Tottenham   see Barnet, Enfield and Haringey Mental Health Trust

ST AUSTELL COMMUNITY   see Cornwall and Is of Scilly Primary Care Trust

ST BARNABAS Saltash   see Cornwall Healthcare NHS Trust

ST BARNABAS' HOSPICE Lincoln   see Linc Distr Health Services and Hosps NHS Trust
ST BARTHOLOMEW'S London   see Barts and The Lon NHS Trust
ST BARTHOLOMEW'S Rochester   see Kent and Medway NHS and Social Care Partnership Trust and Medway NHS Foundn Trust
ST CADOC'S Caerleon   see Gwent Healthcare NHS Trust
ST CATHERINE'S Doncaster   see Rotherham, Doncaster and S Humber NHS Trust
ST CLEMENT'S London   see E Lon NHS Foundation Trust
ST CROSS Rugby   see Univ Hosps Cov and Warks NHS Trust
ST EBBA'S Epsom   see Surrey and Borders Partnership NHS Trust
ST EDMUND'S Northampton   see Northn Gen Hosp NHS Trust
ST GEORGE'S Lincoln   see Linc Distr Health Services and Hosps NHS Trust
ST GEORGE'S Morpeth   see Northd Mental Health NHS Trust
ST GEORGE'S Stafford   see S Staffs Healthcare NHS Trust
ST GEORGE'S HEALTHCARE NHS TRUST London   H A JOHNSON, R W WALL, C J CARTER
ST HELENS AND KNOWSLEY HOSPITALS NHS TRUST   M JONES
ST HELIER Carshalton   see Epsom and St Helier Univ Hosps NHS Trust
ST JAMES'S UNIVERSITY Leeds   see Leeds Mental Health Teaching NHS Trust and Leeds Teaching Hosps NHS Trust
ST LUKE'S Armagh   see Armagh and Dungannon Health and Soc Services
ST LUKE'S Bradford   see Bradf Hosps NHS Trust
ST LUKE'S Middlesbrough   see Tees and NE Yorks NHS Trust
ST MARTIN'S Bath   see Bath and West Community NHS Trust
ST MARTIN'S Canterbury   see Kent & Medway NHS and Soc Care Partnership Trust
ST MARY'S Armley   see Leeds Mental Health Teaching NHS Trust
ST MARY'S Kettering   see Northants Healthcare NHS Trust
ST MARY'S Portsmouth   see Portsm Hosps NHS Trust
ST MARY'S HOSPITAL FOR WOMEN AND CHILDREN Manchester   see Cen Man/Man Children's Univ Hosp NHS Trust
ST MICHAEL'S Aylsham   see Norfolk Primary Care Trust
ST MICHAEL'S Bristol   see Univ Hosps Bris NHS Foundn Trust
ST MICHAEL'S Warwick   see S Warks Combined Care NHS Trust
ST NICHOLAS Canterbury   M A MORRIS
ST NICHOLAS Newcastle   see Northumberland, Tyne and Wear NHS Foundn Trust
ST PANCRAS   see Camden and Islington Community Health NHS Trust
ST PETER'S Chertsey   see N Surrey Primary Care Trust
ST RICHARD'S Chichester   see R W Sussex NHS Trust
ST SAVIOUR   see Jersey Gp of Hosps
ST THOMAS' London   see Guy's and St Thos' NHS Foundn Trust
ST THOMAS Stockport   see Stockport NHS Trust
ST TYDFIL'S Merthyr Tydfil   see N Glam NHS Trust
ST WOOLOS Newport   see Gwent Healthcare NHS Trust
SALFORD ROYAL HOSPITALS NHS FOUNDATION TRUST   I S CARTER, L H LEE
SALISBURY NHS FOUNDATION TRUST   C RENYARD, K S M STEPHENS, F E CANHAM, A SYMES
SALKELD DAY Chepstow   see Gwent Healthcare NHS Trust
SALVINGTON LODGE Worthing   see W Sussex Health and Soc Care NHS Trust
SANDWELL AND WEST BIRMINGHAM HOSPITALS NHS TRUST   K A DUCKETT, D H GARNER, M FARR
SANDWELL GENERAL West Bromwich   see Sandwell and W Birm Hosps NHS Trust
SANDWELL MENTAL HEALTH NHS AND SOCIAL CARE TRUST   E C LOUIS, A E HANNY
SAVERNAKE Marlborough   see Wilts and Swindon Healthcare NHS Trust
SCARBOROUGH AND NORTH EAST YORKSHIRE HEALTHCARE NHS TRUST   M C DOE, L M HOLLIS
SCARBOROUGH GENERAL   see Scarborough and NE Yorks Healthcare NHS Trust
SCUNTHORPE GENERAL   see N Lincs and Goole Hosps NHS Trust
SEACROFT Leeds   see Leeds Teaching Hosps NHS Trust
SELBY WAR MEMORIAL   see York Hosps NHS Foundn Trust

SELLY OAK   see Univ Hosp Birm NHS Foundn Trust
SEVENOAKS   see Invicta Community Care NHS Trust
SEVERALLS HOUSE Colchester   see N Essex Partnership NHS Foundn Trust
SHEFFIELD CARE TRUST   S H ROSS, J P RAFFAY
SHEFFIELD TEACHING HOSPITALS NHS FOUNDATION TRUST   J H DALEY, M R COBB, K G LOWE, M J KERRY, M J NEWITT
SHELTON Bicton Heath   see Shropshire Co Primary Care Trust
SHEPPEY COMMUNITY Minster-on-Sea   see Thames Gateway NHS Trust
SHEPTON MALLET COMMUNITY   see Somerset Primary Care Trust
SHERWOOD FOREST HOSPITALS NHS TRUST   J A S WOOD
SHOTLEY BRIDGE GENERAL Consett   see Co Durham and Darlington NHS Foundn Trust
SHREWSBURY AND TELFORD NHS TRUST   P HRYZIUK, M G WILLIAMS, M I FEARNSIDE
SHREWSBURY ROYAL INFIRMARY   see Shrewsbury and Telford NHS Trust
SHROPSHIRE COUNTY PRIMARY CARE TRUST   M E POTTER, R A GREEN
SIMPSON MEMORIAL MATERNITY PAVILION Edinburgh   see Lothian Univ Hosps NHS Trust
SINGLETON Swansea   see Swansea NHS Trust
SIR ROBERT PEEL Tamworth   see S Staffs Healthcare NHS Trust
SOBELL HOUSE Oxford   see Ox Radcliffe Hosps NHS Trust
SOLIHULL   see Birm Heartlands and Solihull NHS Trust
SOMERSET PRIMARY CARE TRUST   G M KIRK
SOUTH DEVON HEALTHCARE NHS FOUNDATION TRUST   J H GARNER
SOUTH DOWNS HEALTH NHS TRUST   D L I PERKS
SOUTH ESSEX MENTAL HEALTH AND COMMUNITY CARE NHS TRUST   J H DELFGOU
SOUTH LONDON AND MAUDSLEY NHS FOUNDATION TRUST   I N FISHWICK, R B REYNOLDS, R RATCLIFFE, J SAXTON
SOUTH LONDON HEALTHCARE NHS TRUST   D COUTTS, T J MERCER, D M FLAGG, T N ALEXANDER-WATTS, G M HESKINS
SOUTH MANCHESTER UNIVERSITY HOSPITALS NHS TRUST   S GROSSCURTH, P BUTLER
SOUTH SHORE Blackpool   see Blackpool, Fylde and Wyre Hosps NHS Trust
SOUTH STAFFORDSHIRE HEALTHCARE NHS TRUST   K A SHAW, H J BAKER
SOUTH TEES HOSPITALS NHS TRUST   M MASTERMAN, A M GRANGE
SOUTH WARWICKSHIRE COMBINED CARE NHS TRUST   J A CARTWRIGHT
SOUTH WARWICKSHIRE GENERAL HOSPITALS NHS TRUST   F E TYLER, H F COCKELL
SOUTH WEST DORSET PRIMARY CARE TRUST   E J WOODS
SOUTH WEST LONDON AND ST GEORGE'S MENTAL HEALTH NHS TRUST   C WILES, C CARSON, R J S ALLEN
SOUTH WEST OXFORDSHIRE PRIMARY CARE TRUST   L HODGES
SOUTH WEST YORKSHIRE MENTAL HEALTH NHS TRUST   C M GARTLAND
SOUTHAMPTON CITY PRIMARY CARE TRUST   A R BEVIS
SOUTHAMPTON GENERAL   see Southn Univ Hosps NHS Trust
SOUTHAMPTON UNIVERSITY HOSPITALS NHS TRUST   P A BOGGUST, R O L LOWNDES, J V PERCIVAL, K A MACKINNON, S M PITKIN
SOUTHEND HEALTH CARE NHS TRUST   G L CROOK
SOUTHLANDS Shoreham-by-Sea   see Worthing and Southlands Hosps NHS Trust
SOUTHMEAD Bristol   see N Bris NHS Trust
SOUTHPORT AND ORMSKIRK NHS TRUST   P TARLETON
SPRINGFIELD UNIVERSITY   see SW Lon and St George's Mental Health NHS Trust
STAFFORD DISTRICT GENERAL   see Mid Staffs NHS Foundn Trust
STAMFORD AND RUTLAND   see Pet Hosps NHS Trust
STANDISH Stonehouse   see Glos Hosps NHS Foundn Trust
STATES OF GUERNSEY BOARD OF HEALTH   P J CARRINGTON, J LE BILLON, J E D LUFF
STEPPING HILL Stockport   see Stockport NHS Trust
STOCKPORT NHS TRUST   B J LOWE
STOKE MANDEVILLE Aylesbury   see Bucks Hosps NHS Trust
STROUD GENERAL   see Glos Primary Care Trust
SUFFOLK COASTAL PRIMARY CARE TRUST   N J WINTER

WORCESTERSHIRE PRIMARY CARE TRUST
S ROSENTHAL
WORTHING AND SOUTHLANDS HOSPITALS NHS
TRUST R E BENNETT
WORTHING PRIORITY CARE NHS TRUST R J CASWELL
WREXHAM MAELOR *see* NE Wales NHS Trust
WRIGHTINGTON WIGAN AND LEIGH NHS TRUST
R J HUTCHINSON, A J HESLOP, G E WATSON, A J EDWARDS
WYCOMBE *see* Bucks Hosps NHS Trust
WYTHENSHAWE Manchester *see* S Man Univ Hosps NHS
Trust

YEOVIL DISTRICT *see* E Somerset NHS Trust
YEOVIL DISTRICT HOSPITAL NHS FOUNDATION
TRUST J M CUMMINGS
YORK HOSPITALS NHS FOUNDATION TRUST S PETTY
YSBYTY GEORGE THOMAS Treorchy *see* Pontypridd and
Rhondda NHS Trust
YSBYTY GWYNEDD Penrhosgarnedd *see* NW Wales NHS
Trust
YSBYTY PENRHOS STANLEY Holyhead *as above*
YSTRAD MYNACH Hengoed *see* Gwent Healthcare NHS
Trust

HOSPICE CHAPLAINS

BOLTON   M O BRACKLEY
CHESTNUT TREE HOUSE Arundel   S J GURR
CHILDREN'S SOUTH WEST Fremington   G C PHILLIPS
COMPTON Wolverhampton   B A I SMART
CRANSLEY   L S MCCORMACK
DOROTHY HOUSE Winsley   R WARHURST
DOUGLAS MACMILLAN Blurton   S GOODWIN
DOVE HOUSE Hull   R A LENS VAN RIJN
EXETER HOSPISCARE, D J WALFORD
FARLEIGH Chelmsford   K L HACKER HUGHES
GARDEN HOUSE Letchworth   M L MOORE
GREENWICH AND BEXLEY COTTAGE   A C WILLIAMSON
HEART OF KENT   M J HAYES
HELEN AND DOUGLAS HOUSE Oxford   R S S WEIR
ISLE OF MAN   L BRADY
JERSEY   G J HOUGHTON
JOHN TAYLOR Birmingham   N E D SCHIBILD
KATHARINE HOUSE Banbury   T A WARD
KATHARINE HOUSE Stafford   P J GRAYSMITH
KEMP Kidderminster   S FOSTER
KIRKWOOD Huddersfield   M E WOOD
LOROS   H M NEWMAN
MARIE CURIE Glasgow   R F JONES
MARIE CURIE Solihull   D R L WHITE
MARY ANN EVANS Nuneaton   G HANCOCK
MYTON HAMLET Warwick   W S GRAHAM
NIGHTINGALE HOUSE Wrexham   G WINDON
NORFOLK, THE Snettisham   G H SUART
NORTH DEVON   B P LUCK
OAKHAVEN TRUST   J E L ALEXANDER
OVERGATE Elland   D BURROWS
PHYLLIS TUCKWELL Farnham   J L WALKER
PILGRIMS Canterbury   E A CHAPMAN
PRIMROSE Bromsgrove   D R L WHITE
ROWCROFT Torquay   G STILL
ST ANDREW'S Airdrie   M S PATERSON
ST ANDREW'S Grimsby   T STOTT
ST ANN'S Manchester   J F AMBROSE
ST BARNABAS HOUSE Worthing   S J GURR

ST CATHERINE'S Crawley   J M NEVILL
ST CATHERINE'S Preston   I J J DEWAR
ST CATHERINE'S Scarborough   K D JACKSON
ST CLARE Hastingwood   J M SMITH
ST FRANCIS Berkhamsted   E J HUGHES
ST GILES Lichfield   D J SHERIDAN,   P L HOLLIDAY
ST JOHN'S Moggerhanger   C E HOUGH
ST JOHN'S Wirral   P B PRITCHARD
ST JOSEPH'S Hackney   S M HARTLEY
ST LEONARD'S York   C W M BALDOCK
ST LUKE'S Plymouth   T A SMITH
ST LUKE'S Sheffield   M W P REEDER
ST MARY'S Birmingham   R J FARMAN
ST MICHAEL'S Basingstoke   A EDMEADS
ST MICHAEL'S Harrogate (Crimple House)   C HENSON,   J J BOWER
ST MICHAEL'S Hereford   S E HARRIS
ST MICHAEL'S St Leonards-on-Sea   G L DRIVER
ST NICHOLAS' Bury St Edmunds   S M NUTT
ST OSWALD'S Newcastle upon Tyne   C L BROWN
ST PETER AND ST JAMES North Chailey   G R HOCKEN,   S C M MCLARNON
ST RICHARD'S Worcester   D A KNIGHT,   S ROSENTHAL
ST ROCCO'S Warrington   H S HOUSTON
ST WILFRID'S Chichester   B M WATERS
ST WILFRID'S Eastbourne   C R BEARD
SAM BEARE Weybridge   B D PROTHERO
SEVERN Shrewsbury   E C PHILLIPS, P M FREEMAN, H J EDWARDS
SHAKESPEARE Stratford-upon-Avon   S L GOBLE
STRATHCARRON Denny   S M COATES
SUSSEX BEACON Brighton   J K T ELDRIDGE
THORPE HALL Peterborough   A-L K GARVIE
TRINITY London   C A CLARKE
TRINITY IN THE FYLDE Blackpool   J E DENNETT
TYNEDALE Hexham, J L JACKSON
WAKEFIELD   A D WOOD,   G BUTTERWORTH
WILLEN Milton Keynes   S W BARNES
WILLOWBROOK Prescot, H C BLACKBURN
WOKING   P J HARWOOD

EDUCATIONAL CHAPLAINS

This index only lists deans and chaplains, and does not aim to provide a comprehensive list of clergy serving at educational institutions. Those institutions which do not currently have Anglican chaplains are not recorded.

UNIVERSITIES

ABERDEEN   D HEDDLE
ABERTAY   D SHEPHERD
ANGLIA RUSKIN   A D CANT, N S COOPER
ASTON   A D RAMBLE
BANGOR   K P J PADLEY
BATH   A V I BERNERS-WILSON, B F CHAPMAN
BATH SPA   J P KNOTT
BEDFORDSHIRE   A F M GOODMAN
BIRMINGHAM   A J JOYCE, N LO POLITO
BOLTON   P G EDWARDS
BOURNEMOUTH   B MERRINGTON
BRADFORD   S J C CORLEY
BRIGHTON   C R LAWLOR
BRISTOL   E G A DAVIS
BRUNEL Uxbridge Campus   N P MORROW
BUCKINGHAMSHIRE NEW   A W DICKINSON, T A STACEY
CAMBRIDGE
   Churchill   J RAWLINSON
   Clare   G J SEACH
   Corpus Christi   J A D BUXTON
   Downing   K J EYEONS
   Emmanuel   R M MACKLEY
   Fitzwilliam   T J K CONLIN
   Girton   A M GUITE
   Gonville and Caius   C J-B HAMMOND, D H JONES
   Jesus   J M D HUGHES
   King's   R E LLOYD MORGAN, J N MORRIS
   Magdalene   S BARRINGTON-WARD, P P HOBDAY
   Newnham   H D SHILSON-THOMAS
   Pembroke   J T D GARDOM
   Peterhouse   S W P HAMPTON
   Queens'   J M HOLMES
   Robinson   M E DAWN
   Selwyn   B C GRAY, H D SHILSON-THOMAS
   St Catharine's   A M MOORE
   St John's   E ADEKUNLE, D J DORMOR
   Trinity   C B STOLTZ
CANTERBURY CHRIST CHURCH   J T LAW, D A STROUD,
   S A WOMERSLEY
CARDIFF   T O HUGHES
CENTRAL LANCASHIRE   S JOHNSON
CHESTER   I M ARCH, E M BURGESS, I M DELINGER
CHICHESTER   J W DANE
CORK University College   J K ARDIS
COVENTRY   D M H RICHARDS
CRANFIELD   H K SYMES-THOMPSON
CREATIVE ARTS   S J TALBOTT
CUMBRIA   M A GISBOURNE
DE MONTFORT   D J CUNDILL
DERBY   R M C LEIGH
DUBLIN CITY   J B MARCHANT
DUBLIN Trinity College   D M MCCALLIG
DUNDEE   A WALLER
DURHAM
   Hatfield   A BASH
   John Snow   D J BAGE
   St Chad's   A P WILSON
   St Cuthbert's Society   D B GODSELL
   St Hild and St Bede   J H LAWSON
   St John's   K S BRUCE
   St Mary's   J L MOBERLY
   Trevelyan   P J REGAN
   University   M THRELFALL-HOLMES
   Van Mildert   P J REGAN
EAST ANGLIA   D T THORNTON
EAST LONDON   J DRUMMOND, J A RAMSAY, A W M RITCHIE
EDINBURGH   F S BURBERRY, H A HARRIS, D P WILLIAMS
ESSEX   T F P YAP
EXETER   C G GRAHAM, J W F THEODOSIUS
GLOUCESTERSHIRE   T L R MERCHANT
GREENWICH   C P BAKER, J J FROST
HUDDERSFIELD   A J RAGGETT
HULL   J C COWAN
KEELE   C C CLAPHAM

KENT   S C E LAIRD
KINGSTON   D BUCKLEY
LANCASTER   K J HUGGETT
LEEDS   M A J WARD
LEICESTER   S A FOSTER
LINCOLN   L C ACKLAM
LIVERPOOL   J HARDING, R G LEWIS
LIVERPOOL HOPE   P G ANDERSON, S SHAKESPEARE,
   I C STUART
LIVERPOOL JOHN MOORES   J HARDING, R G LEWIS
LONDON
   Central Chaplaincies   S G WILLIAMS
   Goldsmiths' College   A C REES
   Imperial College of Science, Technology and Medicine
      A W WILLSON
   King's   R A BURRIDGE (Dean), T F DITCHFIELD,
      A J M MACHAM, J E SPECK
   London School of Economics and Political Science   J A WALTERS
   Queen Mary and Westfield   J E PETERSEN
   Royal Free and University College Medical School   P A TURNER
   Royal Holloway and Bedford New   C F IRVINE
   Royal Veterinary College   P A TURNER
   University   J L WELSH
LONDON METROPOLITAN   C J F BARBER, F M WEAVER
LOUGHBOROUGH   J O AJAEFOBI, S J RICHARDSON, S M STEVENS
MANCHESTER   T E BIDDINGTON
MANCHESTER METROPOLITAN   T E BIDDINGTON,
   I D GOMERSALL
NEWCASTLE   C M LACK
NORTHAMPTON   S N MOUSIR-HARRISON
NORTHUMBRIA AT NEWCASTLE   A P BOWSHER
NOTTINGHAM   J W BENTHAM, J H CURRAN
NOTTINGHAM TRENT   R H DAVEY
OXFORD
   All Souls   J H DRURY
   Balliol   J M BROWN, H D DUPREE
   Brasenose   G J RICHARDSON
   Christ Church   R J WILLIAMSON
   Christ Church (Dean)   C A LEWIS
   Corpus Christi   J D MALTBY
   Jesus   M I J DAFFERN
   Lady Margaret Hall   A G DOIG
   Lincoln   G A D PLATTEN
   Magdalen   S M ALKIRE, M J PIRET, A W M RITCHIE
   Mansfield   J B MUDDIMAN
   Merton   P B ANTHONY, S M JONES
   New   L TONGE
   Oriel   R B TOBIN
   Pembroke   A R TEAL
   Queen's   M F LLOYD
   St Hilda's   B W MOUNTFORD
   St Hugh's   S C HENSON
   St John's   E D H CARMICHAEL, E C MACFARLANE
   St Peter's   M P WARD
   Trinity   E M PERCY
   University   A F GREGORY
   Wadham   J J HERAPATH
   Worcester   J A ARNOLD
OXFORD BROOKES   A J MARKEY
PORTSMOUTH   A S MARSHALL
QUEEN'S Belfast   B G FORDE
READING   M D LAYNESMITH
ROYAL COLLEGE OF ART   A W WILLSON
ST ANDREWS   J P MASON
SALFORD   D F MYERS
SHEFFIELD   J M S CLINES
SOUTH BANK   H J WORSLEY
SOUTHAMPTON   C A DAY
STAFFORDSHIRE   B H CAMBRIDGE, M WILLIAMS
STIRLING   D M IND
STRATHCLYDE   C OKEKE
SURREY Roehampton   D J ESHUN
SUSSEX   G R P ASHENDEN, A N ROBINSON
TEESSIDE   A HOWARD

ULSTER   J E G BACH
UNIVERSITY OF THE ARTS *Chelsea College of Art and Design*   J HOGAN, A D NORWOOD
WALES
Aberystwyth   S R BELL
Swansea   N JOHN
Trinity St David   J M A GRIFFITHS, M A R HILL

WARWICK   A J KIRK
WEST LONDON   D M AYRES
WINCHESTER   P J DYKES
WORCESTER   S L BLOOMER, F H HAWORTH
YORK   R C WILLIAMS
YORK ST JOHN   L NJENGA

COLLEGES OF HIGHER EDUCATION

This index only includes those establishments known to have Anglican chaplains. It is not intended to be comprehensive.

BISHOP GROSSETESTE *Lincoln*   C A JAMES
GUILDFORD   M C WOODWARD
HARPER ADAMS UNIVERSITY COLLEGE *Newport*
   W E WARD
NORWICH CITY   C J BLACKMAN
ROSE BRUFORD *Sidcup*   G W DAVIES

ROYAL NAVAL *Greenwich*   J J FROST
ST MARK AND ST JOHN *Plymouth*   P N THOMPSON
SANDWELL *West Bromwich*   J A LEACH, K S NJENGA
TRINITY AND ALL SAINTS COLLEGE *Leeds*   R G BOULTER
TRINITY COLLEGE OF MUSIC   J J FROST
WESLEY *Bristol*   P M L PHILLIPS

COLLEGES OF FURTHER EDUCATION

This index only includes those establishments known to have Anglican chaplains. It is not intended to be comprehensive.

ALTON   T C L HELLINGS
BISHOP BURTON COLLEGE OF AGRICULTURE *York*
   M J WESTBY
CANNINGTON   P MARTIN
CITY OF BATH   A R HAWKINS
COLEG GWENT   A E MORTON
FARNBOROUGH COLLEGE OF TECHNOLOGY
   G P H NEWTON
MIDDLESBROUGH   P B ARCHIBALD
NEW *Swindon*   D ORMSTON

NORTH EAST LONDON   S P J CLARK
NORTH LINDSEY *Scunthorpe*   S J WALKER
NORTH WARWICKSHIRE AND HINCKLEY   N J NIXON
NORTH WEST LONDON   F B CAPIE
NORTHUMBERLAND   D P PALMER
NORTON RADSTOCK   E R H BUSH
ROYAL ACADEMY OF MUSIC   P R THOMAS
SOMERSET COLLEGE OF ARTS AND TECHNOLOGY
   P J HUGHES

SIXTH-FORM COLLEGES

This index only includes those colleges known to have Anglican chaplains. It is not intended to be comprehensive.

FARNBOROUGH   R M BENNETTS
ST VINCENT *Gosport*   C J L J THOMPSON

STRODE'S *Egham*   T M SUDWORTH

SCHOOLS

This index only includes those schools known to have Anglican chaplains. It is not intended to be comprehensive.

ABBEY GRANGE HIGH D S FORD
ABBOTS BROMLEY P G GREEN
ABINGDON P D B GOODING, H L KIRK
ALDENHAM *Hertfordshire* D M BOND
ALL SAINTS ACADEMY *Dunstable* A C COLES
ALL SAINTS COLLEGE *Newcastle upon Tyne* J M GRIEVE
ALLEYN'S *Dulwich* A G BUCKLEY
ARCHBISHOP SENTAMU ACADEMY *Hull* J V TAYLOR
ARCHBISHOP TENISON'S *Kennington* R S STANIER
ARDINGLY COLLEGE *Haywards Heath*
  D L LAWRENCE-MARCH
BACON'S COLLEGE *Rotherhithe* R J HALL
BANCROFT'S *Woodford Green* I MOORE
BARNARD CASTLE S J RIDLEY
BEARWOOD COLLEGE *Wokingham* S J KING
BEDFORD A S ATKINS
BEESTON *Norfolk* M L BANKS
BENNETT MEMORIAL DIOCESAN *Tunbridge Wells*
  R A KNAPP
BETHANY *Goudhurst* P J BENTHAM
BISHOP BELL *Eastbourne* V L FLANAGAN
BISHOP HENDERSON *Taunton* J A JEFFERY
BISHOP JUSTUS CHURCH OF ENGLAND *Bromley*
  J A DONNELLY
BISHOP LUFFA *Chichester* P M GILBERT
BISHOP OF LLANDAFF HIGH G W WILLIAMS
BISHOP OF WINCHESTER COMPREHENSIVE
  Bournemouth J NIGHTINGALE
BISHOP WAND *Sunbury-on-Thames* S E LEESON
BISHOP WORDSWORTH *Salisbury* J A BERSWEDEN
BISHOP'S BLUE COAT CHURCH OF ENGLAND HIGH
  Chester I J HUTCHINGS
BISHOPS' COLLEGE *Gloucester* C J H BLOCKLEY
BLACKHEATH BLUECOAT CHURCH OF ENGLAND
  E A NEWMAN
BLOXHAM M G PRICE
BLUECOAT *Nottingham* K W G JOHNSON
BLUNDELL'S *Tiverton* T C HUNT
BOX HILL D A IRELAND
BRADFIELD COLLEGE *Berkshire* R G HILLIARD
BRADFORD ACADEMY R I TAYLOR
BRENTWOOD *Essex* D J GILCHRIST
BRIDGEMARY COMMUNITY SPORTS COLLEGE
  R J PRESTON
BRIGHTON COLLEGE R P S EASTON
BROMSGROVE P S J HEDWORTH
BRYANSTON *Dorset* A M J HAVILAND
CANFORD *Wimborne* C JERVIS, J A STEPHENSON
CHARTERHOUSE *Godalming* C A CASE, S J HARKER
CHELTENHAM COLLEGE A J DUNNING
CHELTENHAM LADIES' COLLEGE D T MERRY,
  H R WOOD
CHIGWELL *Essex* S N PAUL
CHRIST'S COLLEGE *Brecon* R M LLEWELLYN
CHRIST'S HOSPITAL *Horsham* I R COLSON, S GOLDING
CITY OF LONDON FREEMEN'S *Ashtead*
  D F P RUTHERFORD
CLAYESMORE *Blandford* J C E POTTINGER
CLIFTON COLLEGE *Bristol* K TAPLIN
COKETHORPE *Witney* R J HUMPHREYS
COTHILL HOUSE *Abingdon* T R PERRY
COVENTRY BLUE COAT CHURCH OF ENGLAND
  P J MESSAM
CRANLEIGH *Surrey* P V PARKER
CULFORD *Bury St Edmunds* S C BATTERSBY
DAUNTSEY'S *Devizes* D R JOHNSON
DEAN CLOSE *Cheltenham* E L TALBOT
DEANERY CHURCH OF ENGLAND HIGH *Wigan*
  D J BURY
DENSTONE COLLEGE *Uttoxeter* R C M JARVIS
DERBY HIGH R J A BARRETT
DUKE OF YORK'S ROYAL MILITARY *Dover*
  A D T RICHARDS
DULWICH PREPARATORY *Cranbrook* M S BENNETT
DURHAM HIGH B P S VALLIS
EASTBOURNE COLLEGE C K MACDONALD
ELIZABETH COLLEGE *Guernsey* R G HARNISH
ELLESMERE COLLEGE *Shropshire* D A SLIM
ELMHURST SCHOOL FOR DANCE *Birmingham* A J JOYCE
EMANUEL *Wandsworth* P M HUNT

ENTERPRISE SOUTH LIVERPOOL ACADEMY
  A J COLMER
EPSOM COLLEGE P THOMPSON
ETON COLLEGE *Berkshire* R E R DEMERY, P A HESS, C M JONES,
  K H WILKINSON
FELSTED *Essex* J A W BRICE
FETTES COLLEGE *Edinburgh* D CAMPBELL
GIGGLESWICK J E BAVINGTON
GLENALMOND COLLEGE G W DOVE
GODOLPHIN *Salisbury* J BALL
GORDON'S *Woking* D H ROBINSON
GOSDEN HOUSE J N E BUNDOCK
GREIG CITY ACADEMY P J HENDERSON
GRESHAM'S *Holt* B R ROBERTS
GRYPHON *Sherborne* D R TREGALE
HABERDASHERS' ASKE'S *Elstree* J GOODAIR
HAILEYBURY COLLEGE *Hertfordshire* C R BRIGGS
HARROW J E POWER
HEADINGTON *Oxford* D M WHEATLEY
HEREFORD CATHEDRAL P A ROW
HIGHGATE *London* P J J KNIGHT
IMMANUEL COLLEGE CHURCH OF ENGLAND *Bradford*
  S P HACKING
IPSWICH A C WINTER
JCB ACADEMY K R GOVAN
KELLY COLLEGE *Tavistock* K LANYON JONES
KENT COLLEGE *Pembury* H J MATTHEWS
KING EDWARD VI *Southampton* J G POPPLETON
KING EDWARD'S *Bath* C L O´NEILL
KING EDWARD'S *Birmingham* D H RAYNOR
KING HENRY VIII *Coventry* R STEPHEN
KING WILLIAM'S COLLEGE *Isle of Man* T H MORDECAI
KING'S *Bruton* N H WILSON-BROWN
KING'S COLLEGE SCHOOL *Wimbledon* J W CROSSLEY
KING'S COLLEGE *Taunton* M A SMITH
KING'S HOSPITAL *Dublin* P R CAMPION
KING'S *Rochester* J A THACKRAY
KING'S *Tynemouth* C J CLINCH
KING'S *Wolverhampton* L K COLLINS
KING'S *Worcester* M R DORSETT
KING'S, THE *Canterbury* C F ARVIDSSON, M C ROBBINS
KING'S, THE *Ely* T P HUMPHRY
KINGHAM HILL *Oxfordshire* A M SAVAGE
LANCING COLLEGE R K HARRISON
LICHFIELD CATHEDRAL J M MCHALE
LORD WANDSWORTH COLLEGE *Basingstoke* S LEYSHON
MAGDALEN COLLEGE SCHOOL *Oxford*
  T H N KUIN LAWTON
MALVERN COLLEGE A P LAW
MANOR *York* M A HAND
MARLBOROUGH COLLEGE D J DALES
MATTHEW HUMBERSTON *Grimsby* T STOTT
MELKSHAM OAK COMMUNITY J PERRETT
MERCHANT TAYLORS' *Crosby* D A SMITH
MERCHANT TAYLORS' *Northwood* R D E BOLTON
MILL HILL *London* R J WARDEN
MILLFIELD *Somerset* P C A HARBRIDGE
MILTON ABBEY *Dorset* R W B THOMSON
MONKTON COMBE *Bath* M P R DIETZ
MONMOUTH G R KNIGHT, D J MCGLADDERY
MORETON HALL A B STRATFORD
NORWICH N TIVEY
OAKHAM A C V ALDOUS, J P TAYLOR
OLD BUCKENHAM HALL *Ipswich* J V J G WATSON
OLD SWINFORD HOSPITAL *Stourbridge* M W SOAR
OSWESTRY J G PARRY
OUNDLE *Peterborough* I C BROWNE, B J CUNNINGHAM,
  D M REES-JONES
PANGBOURNE COLLEGE *Berkshire* N G T JEFFERS
PETER SYMONDS COLLEGE *Winchester* N P SEAL
PETERBOROUGH T J WHITWELL
PIPERS CORNER M S GURR
PITSFORD *Northamptonshire* S TROTT
POCKLINGTON *York* W J ROBERTS
PORTSMOUTH GRAMMAR A K BURTT
PREBENDAL *Chichester* T D NASON
PRIOR'S FIELD J M FELLOWS
QUEEN ANNE'S *Caversham* H C BENSON
QUEEN ELIZABETH *Wimborne* A J H EDWARDS
QUEEN ELIZABETH'S *Mansfield* A M SMYTHE

QUEEN MARGARET'S *York*   R L OWEN
QUEENSWOOD *Herts*   G J A WRIGHT
RADLEY COLLEGE *Oxfordshire*   T J E FERNYHOUGH,
   T D MULLINS
RANBY HOUSE *Retford*   P FINLINSON
RAVENSCLIFFE HIGH *Halifax*   A MAUDE
REED'S *Cobham*   A J CLARKE
REPTON *Derby*   A J M WATKINSON
REPTON PREPARATORY *Foremarke Hall*   N A BAILEY
RIDDLESWORTH HALL *Norwich*   K A HAWKES
RIPLEY ST THOMAS CHURCH OF ENGLAND HIGH
   Lancaster   S IRVINE
RISHWORTH *Ripponden*   J S BRADBERRY
ROEDEAN *Brighton*   G N RAINEY
ROYAL RUSSELL *Croydon*   S J PADFIELD
RUGBY   R M HORNER
ST ALBANS   C D PINES
ST ALBANS HIGH SCHOOL FOR GIRLS
   D C FITZGERALD CLARK
ST AUGUSTINE ACADEMY *Maidstone*   K GRANT
ST BEDE'S ECUMENICAL *Reigate*   J P SCOTT
ST BEDE'S INTER-CHURCH SECONDARY *Cambridge*
   H J CROMPTON-BATTERSBY
ST BEES *Cumbria*   C R SWARTZ
ST CATHERINE'S *Bramley*   C DE F TICKNER
ST CECILIA'S WANDSWORTH CHURCH OF ENGLAND
   P A KURK
ST COLUMBA'S *Dublin*   N N CROSSEY
ST DAVID'S COLLEGE *Llandudno*   T R HALL
ST EDMUND'S *Canterbury*   M-A B TISDALE
ST EDWARD'S *Oxford*   E C KERR
ST FRANCIS XAVIER *Richmond*   P J MATTHEWS
ST GEORGE'S *Ascot*   J J SISTIG
ST GEORGE'S *Harpenden*   A P MANNING
ST GEORGE'S *Windsor*   A S ZIHNI
ST HELEN'S AND ST KATHARINE'S *Abingdon*   J A TAFT
ST HILDA'S *Whitby*   M R STANFORD
ST JOHN'S *Leatherhead*   S E BRYANT
ST LAWRENCE COLLEGE *Ramsgate*   P R RUSSELL
ST MARK'S CHURCH OF ENGLAND ACADEMY *Mitcham*
   R A BURGE-THOMAS
ST MARY MAGDALENE ACADEMY *London*   A I KEECH
ST MARY'S *Calne*   P M O GILES
ST MARY'S HALL *Brighton*   D J BIGGS,
   A H MANSON-BRAILSFORD
ST MARY'S *Twickenham*   R J BARRIE
ST MARY'S *Westbrook*   B D R WOOD
ST OLAVE'S GRAMMAR *Orpington*   A D MCCLELLAN
ST PAUL'S *Barnes*   P L F ALLSOP
ST PAUL'S GIRLS' *Hammersmith*   V L BARON
ST PETER'S CHURCH OF ENGLAND AIDED *Exeter*
   K D N CHANDRA

ST PETER'S COLLEGIATE *Wolverhampton*   L K COLLINS
ST PETER'S *York*   D A JONES
ST SAVIOUR'S AND ST OLAVE'S *Newington*   K GRANT
ST SWITHUN'S *Winchester*   K M DYKES
SALFORD CITY ACADEMY   A E KAY
SEAFORD COLLEGE *Petworth*   S J N GRAY
SEDBERGH   P L SWEETING
SEVENOAKS   N N HENSHAW
SHERBORNE   L R F COLLINS
SHIPLAKE *Henley-on-Thames*   S M COUSINS
SHREWSBURY   G W DOBBIE
SIR JAMES SMITH'S COMMUNITY *Camelford*
   M J W BENTON-EVANS
SIR ROBERT WOODARD ACADEMY *Lancing*
   W DALRYMPLE
SIR THOMAS BOTELER HIGH *Warrington*
   J E HARRIES
SMALLWOOD MANOR PREPARATORY *Uttoxeter*
   C J CANN
SOLIHULL   A C HUTCHINSON
STAMFORD   M A S GOODMAN
STOCKPORT ACADEMY   S MAYO
STOCKPORT GRAMMAR   L E J LEAVER
STOWE *Buckingham*   R B JACKSON
STRATHALLAN *Perth*   R A M T QUICK
ST MARY REDCLIFFE AND TEMPLE *Bristol*
   W L HOUGH
SUTTON VALENCE *Kent*   P A KISH
TALBOT HEATH *Bournemouth*   C M LANGFORD
TAVERHAM HALL *Norwich*   R W B MASSINGBERD-MUNDY
TONBRIDGE   T D PAGE, D A PETERS
TRELOAR COLLEGE *Alton*   M R BIRCH
TRINITY ACADEMY *Halifax*   M RUSSELL
TRINITY *Lewisham*   M E TODD
TUDOR HALL *Banbury*   J F JACKSON
UPPINGHAM *Leicestershire*   J B J SAUNDERS
WADHAM *Crewkerne*   A J LEGG
WARMINSTER   A G WATTS
WARWICK   A W GOUGH
WELLINGBOROUGH   M J WALKER
WELLINGTON COLLEGE *Berkshire*   T W G NOVIS
WELLINGTON *Somerset*   J P HELLIER
WELLS CATHEDRAL   J M HULME
WEST BUCKLAND *Barnstaple*   A M KETTLE
WESTMINSTER   G J WILLIAMS
WESTONBIRT   P DIXON
WINCHESTER COLLEGE   P A BURT, J M WHITE
WOODBRIDGE   I A WILSON
WORKSOP COLLEGE *Nottinghamshire*   P FINLINSON
WREN ACADEMY *London*   S T KIRBY
WYCOMBE ABBEY *High Wycombe*   J F CHAFFEY
WYMONDHAM COLLEGE   I JONES

THEOLOGICAL COLLEGES AND COURSES

This index includes the name of the principal or warden and the names of staff members who are Anglican clergy and whose appointments are at least half-time.

Theological Colleges

Church of Ireland Theological College
Braemor Park, Dublin 14, Irish Republic
Tel (00353) (1) 492 3506 Fax 492 3082
E-mail admin@theologicalinstitute.ie
PRIN M J ELLIOTT, TUTOR/LECT P G MCGLINCHEY, P COMERFORD

College of the Resurrection
Stocks Bank Road, Mirfield WF14 0BW
Tel (01924) 490441 Fax 492738   E-mail hscott@mirfield.org.uk
PRIN P G ALLAN CR, TUTOR/LECT B N GORDON-TAYLOR,
J E COOPER

Cranmer Hall
St John's College, 3 South Bailey, Durham DH1 3RJ
Tel 0191–334 3894 Fax 334 3501
E-mail enquiries@cranmerhall.com
PRIN S D WILKINSON[1] WARDEN M S A TANNER
DIR MISS AND PIONEER MIN M J VOLLAND
DIR MINI PRACTICE D I GOODHEW
TUTOR/LECT C C H COOK, H M THORP

Oak Hill College
Chase Side, London N14 4PS
Tel (020) 8449 0467 Fax 8441 5996
PRIN M J OVEY, VICE-PRIN C M GREEN
TUTOR/LECT R J PORTER, G M N RAIKES, M T SLEEMAN,
P T SANLON

The Queen's Foundation
Somerset Road, Edgbaston, Birmingham B15 2QH
Tel 0121–454 1527 Fax 454 8171 E-mail enquire@queens.ac.uk
PRIN D J P HEWLETT, TUTOR/LECT M R EAREY, R G GASTON

Ridley Hall
Ridley Hall Road, Cambridge CB3 9HG
Tel (01223) 746580 Fax 746581 E-mail ridley-pa@lists.cam.ac.uk
PRIN A R NORMAN, VICE-PRIN M B THOMPSON
DIR PAST STUDIES R A HIGGINSON, TUTOR/LECT P P JENSON,
P D A WESTON, J E KEILLER, D E MALE, A C WALTON, A F CHATFIELD,
G CHATFIELD

Ripon College
Cuddesdon, Oxford OX44 9EX
Tel (01865) 874404 Fax 875431
E-mail enquiries@ripon-cuddesdon.ac.uk
PRIN M W PERCY, VICE-PRIN AND LECT M D CHAPMAN
SEN TUTOR M J WHIPP, TUTOR/LECT D S HEYWOOD, A R TEAL,
P N TOVEY, H-A M HARTLEY, H M BURN, J R COLLICUTT MCGRATH,
G D BAYLISS

St John's College
Chilwell Lane, Bramcote, Nottingham NG9 3DS
Tel 0115–925 1114 Fax 943 6438
E-mail enquiries@stjohns-nottm.ac.uk
PRIN D H K HILBORN, DEAN N M LADD, DEAN STUDIES I B PAUL
TUTOR/LECT S D DYAS, P NASH, T D HULL, A P BOWSHER,
D C RUNCORN, A R ANGEL

St Michael's College
54 Cardiff Road, Llandaff, Cardiff CF5 2YJ
Tel (029) 2056 3379 Fax 2083 8008 E-mail info@stmichaels.ac.uk
PRIN P H SEDGWICK, VICE-PRIN S B ROBERTS
DEAN MIN STUDIES S P ADAMS, DEAN CHAPL STUDIES A J TODD

St Stephen's House
16 Marston Street, Oxford OX4 1JX
Tel (01865) 613500 Fax 613513 E-mail enquiries@ssho.ox.ac.uk
PRIN R WARD, VICE-PRIN D P A FEENEY

Theological Institute of the Scottish Episcopal Church
21 Grosvenor Crescent, Edinburgh EH12 5EE
Tel 0131–225 6357 Fax 346 7247
E-mail tisec@scotland.anglican.org
PRIN M J FULLER

Trinity College
Stoke Hill, Bristol BS9 1JP
Tel 0117–968 2803 Fax 968 7470
E-mail principal@trinity-bris.ac.uk
PRIN G I KOVOOR, VICE-PRIN AND SEN TUTOR D WENHAM
DIR PART-TIME COURSES W D MACDOUGALL
TUTOR/LECT J CORRIE, J SEARS, N A D SCOTLAND, E G INESON,
S M ARNOLD, J L NOLLAND, P J ROBERTS

Westcott House
Jesus Lane, Cambridge CB5 8BP
Tel (01223) 741000 Fax 741002
E-mail general-enquiries@westcott.cam.ac.uk
PRIN M A SEELEY, VICE-PRIN W R S LAMB
DIR STUDIES V E RAYMER, TUTOR J A D BUXTON, A P DAVISON,
T J K CONLIN

Wycliffe Hall
54 Banbury Road, Oxford OX2 6PW
Tel (01865) 274200 Fax 274215
E-mail enquiries@wycliffe.ox.ac.uk
PRIN R D TURNBULL, VICE-PRIN S D N VIBERT
DIR CH LEADERSHIP W R DONALDSON,
DIR DEVELOPMENT P W L WALKER
TUTOR J R WILLIAMS, E A HOARE, A C ATHERSTONE, J E ROBSON

Regional Courses

Eastern Region Ministry Course
Wesley House, Jesus Lane, Cambridge CB5 8BJ
Tel (01223) 741026 E-mail secretary@ermc.cam.ac.uk
PRIN I M MCINTOSH, DIR PAST STUDIES E C CARDALE
TUTOR R M MORGAN

Lancashire and Cumbria Theological Partnership
Church House, West Walls, Carlisle CA3 8UE
Tel (01228) 815405 Fax 815400 E-mail admin@lctp.org.uk
PRIN T D HERBERT, VICE-PRIN R A LATHAM, S J WILLIAMS

Lincoln School of Theology
Chad Varah House, Wordsworth Street, Lincoln LN1 3BS
Tel (01522) 895127 E-mail lradcliffe@lincoln.ac.uk
PRIN M D HOCKNULL, DIR STUDIES S A MYERS

Lindisfarne Regional Training Partnership
Church House, St John's Terrace, North Shields, NE29 6HS
Tel 0191–270 4100 E-mail enquiries@lindisfarnertp.org
PRIN C ROWLING, DIR STUDIES D J BRYAN, DIR IME R L SIMPSON
TUTOR M L BECK

Oxford Ministry Course
Ripon College, Cuddesdon, Oxford OX44 9EX
Tel (01865) 874404 Fax 875431
E-mail enquiries@ripon-cuddesdon.ac.uk
PRIN M W PERCY, VICE-PRIN M D CHAPMAN, DEAN T J N NAISH

The Queen's Foundation (Course)
Somerset Road, Edgbaston, Birmingham B15 2QH
Tel 0121–454 1527 Fax 454 8171 E-mail enquire@queens.ac.uk
PRIN D J P HEWLETT, TUTOR/LECT M R EAREY, R G GASTON

St Mellitus College
St Paul's Church, Onslow Square, London SW7 3NX
Tel (020) 7052 0575 E-mail info@stmellitus.org
DEAN G S TOMLIN, ASST-DEAN A N EMERTON, TUTOR M F LLOYD,
L HARVEY, A V COLEMAN, S W DOHERTY

The South East Institute for Theological Education
Ground Floor, Sun Pier House, Medway Street,
Chatham ME4 4HF
Tel (01634) 846683 Fax 819347
E-mail administrator@seite.co.uk
PRIN J F WORTHEN, VICE-PRIN J P H ALLAIN CHAPMAN
TUTOR S P STOCKS

[1] Dr Wilkinson is a Methodist.

Southern North West Training Partnership
Aiken Hall, University of Chester, Crab Lane, Fernhead,
Warrington WA2 0BD
Tel (01925) 534373 E-mail snwtp@chester.ac.uk
PRIN THE VEN J APPLEGATE, DEAN STUDIES M P ADAMS

Southern Theological Education and Training Scheme
19 The Close, Salisbury SP1 2EE
Tel (01722) 424820 Fax 424811 E-mail ayoung@stets.ac.uk
PRIN D A HOLGATE, TUTOR P OVEREND, D P LLOYD

South West Ministry Training Course
Amory Building, University of Exeter, Rennes Drive, Exeter
EX4 4RJ
Tel (01392) 264403 E-mail admin@swmtc.org.uk
PRIN D G MOSS, DIR READER TR J W F THEODOSIUS
TUTOR S SHEPPARD, P J SOUBUT

West of England Ministerial Training Course
12 College Green, Gloucester GL1 2LX
Tel (01452) 874969 E-mail office@wemtc.org.uk
PRIN M W S PARSONS, VICE-PRIN R F DABORN, TUTOR H M BURN

Yorkshire Ministry Course
Mirfield Centre, Stocks Bank Road, Mirfield WF14 0BW
Tel (01924) 481925 Fax 481922 E-mail office@ymc.org.uk
PRIN C GORE, DIR PAST STUDIES T S EVANS, TUTOR S C SPENCER

Ordained Local Ministry Schemes

Guildford Diocesan Ministry Course
Diocesan House, Quarry Street, Guildford GU1 3XG
Tel (01483) 790319 E-mail steve.summers@cofeguildford.org.uk
DIR S B SUMMERS

Lichfield OLM Scheme
St Mary's House, The Close, Lichfield WS13 7LD
Tel (01543) 306222
E-mail pauline.shelton@lichfield.anglican.org
DIR P M SHELTON

Oxford OLM Scheme
Oxford Ministry Course, Diocesan Church House, North
Hinksey Lane, Botley, Oxford OX2 0NB
Tel (01865) 208258 E-mail beren.hartless@oxford.anglican.org
PRIN B I de la T HARTLESS

BISHOPS OF ANGLICAN DIOCESES OVERSEAS

AUSTRALIA

PROVINCE OF NEW SOUTH WALES

Armidale — Peter Robert Brain
Anglican Diocesan Registry, PO Box 198,
Armidale, NSW, Australia 2350
Tel (0061) (2) 6772 4491
Fax (0061) (2) 6772 9261
E-mail office@armidaleanglicandiocese.com

Bathurst — Richard Warwick Hurford OAM
PO Box 23, Bathurst, NSW, Australia 2795
Tel (0061) (2) 6331 1722
Fax (0061) (2) 6332 2772
E-mail
registrar@bathurstanglican.org.au

(Assistant) — John Stead
PO Box 619, Dubbo, NSW, Australia 2830
Tel (0061) (2) 6882 2670
Fax (0061) (2) 6881 6740
E-mail mdo@bathurstanglican.org

Canberra and — Stuart Peter Robinson
Goulburn — GPO Box 1981, Canberra,
ACT, Australia 2601
Tel (0061) (2) 2650
Fax (0061) (2) 6247 6829
E-mail stuart.robinson@anglicancg.org.au

(Assistants) — Allan Bowers Ewing
GPO Box 8605, Wagga Wagga
NSW Australia 2650
Tel (0061) (2) 6926 4226
Fax as telephone
E-mail allan.ewing@anglicancg.org.au

Trevor William Edwards
28 McBryde Crescent, Wanniassa, ACT 2903
Tel (0061) (2) 6248 0811
Fax (0061) (2) 6247 6829
E-mail trevor.edwards@anglicancg.org

Grafton — Keith Francis Slater
Bishopsholme, PO Box 4,
Grafton, NSW, Australia 2460
Tel (0061) (2) 6643 4122
Fax (0061) (2) 6643 1814
E-mail angdiog@nor.com.au

Newcastle — Brian George Farran
The Bishop's Registry, PO Box 817,
Newcastle, NSW, Australia 2300
Tel (0061) (2) 4926 3733
Fax (0061) (2) 4936 1968
E-mail bishop@angdon.com

(Assistant) — Peter Derrick James Stuart
PO Box 817,
Newcastle, NSW, Australia 2300
Tel (0061) (2) 4926 3733
Fax (0061) (2) 4926 1968
E-mail bishoppeter@angdon.com

Riverina — Douglas Robert Stephens
PO Box 10, Narrandera,
NSW, Australia 2700
Tel (0061) (2) 6959 1648
Fax (0061) (2) 6959 2903
E-mail rivdio@dragnet.com.au

Sydney — Peter Frederick Jensen
(Archbishop — PO Box Q190, Queen Victoria Buildings,
and — Sydney, NSW, Australia 1230
Metropolitan) — Tel (0061) (2) 9265 1555
Fax (0061) (2) 9261 1170
E-mail registry@sydney.anglican.asn.au

(Liverpool) — *Vacant*

(North — Glenn Naunton Davies
Sydney) — *address as above*
Tel (0061) (2) 9265 1533
Fax (0061) (2) 9265 1543
E-mail gdavies@sydney.anglican.asn.au

(Western — Ivan Yin Lee
Sydney, — PO Box 129, Parramatta,
formerly — NSW, Australia 2124
Parramatta) — Tel (0061) (2) 8023 6700
Fax (0061) (2) 9689 3636
E-mail ilee@westernsydney.anglican.asn.au

(South — Robert Charles Forsyth
Sydney) — PO Box Q190, Queen Victoria Buildings,
Sydney, NSW, Australia 1230
Tel (0061) (2) 9265 1501
Fax (0061) (2) 9265 1543
E-mail robforsyth@sydney.anglican.asn.au

(Wollongong) — P L Hayward
74 Church Street, Wollongong,
NSW, Australia 2500
Tel (0061) (2) 4201 1800
Fax (0061) (2) 4228 4296
E-mail phaywood@wollongong.anglican.asn.au

PROVINCE OF QUEENSLAND

Brisbane — Phillip John Aspinall
(Archbishop — PO Box 421, Brisbane, Qld, Australia 4001
and Primate) — Tel (0061) (7) 3835 2222
Fax (0061) (7) 3831 1170
E-mail archbishop@anglicanbrisbane.org.au

(Northern — Jonathan Charles Holland
Region) — *address as above*
Tel (0061) (7) 3835 2213
Fax (0061) (7) 3832 5030
E-mail jholland@anglicanbrisbane.org.au

(Southern — Geoffrey Martyn Smith
Region) — *address as above*
Tel (0061) (7) 3835 2213
Fax (0061) (7) 3832 5030

(Western — Robert William Nolan
Region) — PO Box 2600, Toowomba, Qld, Australia 4350
Tel (0061) (7) 4639 1875
Fax (0061) (7) 4632 6882
E-mail rnolan@anglicanbrisbane.org.au

North — William James Ray
Queensland — PO Box 1244, Townsville, Qld, Australia 4810
Tel (0061) (7) 4771 4175
Fax (0061) (7) 4721 1756
E-mail bishopnq@anglicannq.org

(Torres Strait — Saibo Mabo
Islander — PO Box 338, Thursday Island, Qld, Australia
Bishop) — 4875
Tel (0061) (7) 4069 2747
Fax (0061) (7) 4069 1960
E-mail bishopti@anglicannq.org

(National — James Randolph Leftwich
Aboriginal — 14 Village Terrace, Redlynch, Qld, Australia 4870
Tel (0061) (7) 4051 1055
Bishop) — Fax (0061) (7) 4051 1033
E-mail bishopleftwich@gmail.com

Northern — Gregory Edwin Thompson
Territory, The — PO Box 2950, Darwin, NT, Australia
0801
Tel (0061) (8) 8941 7440
Fax (0061) (8) 8941 7446 *or* 8941 7227
E-mail ntdiocese@internode.on.net

Rockhampton — Godfrey Charles Fryar
PO Box 710, Central Queensland Mail Centre,
Rockhampton, Qld, Australia 4702
Tel (0061) (7) 4927 3188
Fax (0061) (7) 4922 4562
E-mail bishop@anglicanrock.org.au

PROVINCE OF SOUTH AUSTRALIA

Adelaide — Jeffrey William Driver
(Archbishop — 18 King William Road,
and — North Adelaide, S Australia 5006
Metropolitan) — Tel (0061) (8) 8305 9350
Fax (0061) (8) 8305 9399
E-mail archbishop@adelaide.anglican.com.au

(Assistant) Stephen Kim Pickard
address, tel and fax as above
E-mail spickard@adelaide.anglican.com.au

The Murray *Vacant*

Willochra Garry John Weatherill
PO Box 96, Gladstone,
S Australia 5473
Tel (0061) (8) 8662 2249
Fax (0061) (8) 8662 2027
E-mail bishop@diowillochra.org.au

PROVINCE OF VICTORIA

Ballarat *vacant*

Bendigo Andrew William Curnow
PO Box 2, Bendigo, Vic, Australia 3552
Tel (0061) (3) 5443 4711
Fax (0061) (3) 5441 2173
E-mail bishop@bendigoanglican.org.au

Gippsland John Charles McIntyre
PO Box 928, Sale, Vic, Australia 3853
Tel (0061) (3) 5144 2044
Fax (0061) (3) 5144 7183
E-mail bishop@gippsanglican.org.au

Melbourne Philip Leslie Freier
(Archbishop) The Anglican Centre, 209 Flinders Lane,
Melbourne, Vic, Australia 3000
Tel (0061) (3) 9653 4220
Fax (0061) (3) 9653 4268
E-mail archbishopsoffice
@melbourne.anglican.com.au

(Eastern Barbara Darling
Region) *address, tel and fax as above*
E-mail estregion@melbourne.anglican.com.au

(North- Philip James Huggins
western *address, tel and fax as above*
Region) E-mail phuggins@melbourne.anglican.com.au

(Southern Paul Raymond White
Region) *address and tel as above*
Fax (0061) (3) 9653 4268
E-mail sthregbishop@melbourne.anglican.au

Wangaratta Anthony John Parkes
Bishop's Registry, PO Box 457,
Wangaratta, Vic, Australia 3676
Tel (0061) (3) 5721 3484
Fax (0061) (3) 5722 1427
E-mail bishop@wangaratta.anglican.org

PROVINCE OF WESTERN AUSTRALIA

Bunbury Allan Bowers Ewing
Bishopscourt, PO Box 15,
Bunbury, W Australia 6231
Tel (0061) (8) 9721 2100
Fax (0061) (8) 9791 2300
E-mail bishop@bunbury.org.au

North West David Gray Mulready
Australia PO Box 2783, Geraldton, W Australia 6531
Tel (0061) (8) 9921 7277
Fax (0061) (8) 9964 2220
E-mail bishop@anglicandnwa.org

Perth Roger Adrian Herft
(Archbishop GPO Box W2067, Perth, W Australia 6001
and Tel (0061) (8) 9325 7455
Metropolitan) Fax (0061) (8) 9221 4118
E-mail archbishop@perth.anglican.org

(Assistant Kay Maree Goldsworthy
Bishops) *address, tel and fax as above*
E-mail kgoldsworthy@perth.anglican.org

Tom Wilmot
address, tel and fax as above
E-mail twilmot@perth.anglican.org

EXTRA-PROVINCIAL DIOCESES

Defence Force Leonard Sidney Eacott AM
(and Bishop Department of Defence,
Assistant to DSG-Duntroon, ACT, Australia 2600
the Primate) Tel (0061) (2) 9265 9935
Fax (0061) (2) 9265 9959
E-mail dfc@anglican.org.au

Tasmania John Douglas Harrower
GPO Box 748, Hobart, Tas, 7001
Tel (0061) (3) 6220 2015
Fax (0061) (3) 6223 8968
E-mail bishop@anglicantas.org.au

BRAZIL

Amazon Saulo Mauricio de Barros
Av. Sezerdelo Correia, 514, Batista Campos,
66025–240, Belem, PA, Brazil
Tel: (0055) (91) 3241 9720
fax as telephone
E-mail saulomauricio@gmail.com

Brasilia Maurício José Araújo de Andrade
(Primate) SCHS 309–310, conjunta A, 1. andar – Asa Sul,
Caixa Postal 093, 70362–4, Brasilia, Brazil
Tel (0055) (61) 443 4305
Fax (0055) (61) 443 4337
E-mail mandrade@ieab.org.br

Curitiba Naudal Alves Gomes
Rua Sete de Setembro, 3927 – Centro,
80250–010 Curitiba, PR, Brazil
Tel (0055) (41) 3079 9992
E-mail naudal@yahoo.com.br

Pelotas Renato da Cruz Raatz
Rua Felix da Cunha, 425 – Centro, Caixa Postal
Caixa Postal 791, 96001–970 Pelotas, RS, Brazil
Tel (0055) (53) 3302 8618
fax as telephone
E-mail renato.raatz@terra.com.br

Recife Sebastião Armando Gameleira Soares
Rua Virgílio Mota, 70, Parnamirim, 52060–582,
Recife, PE, Brazil
Tel (0055) (81) 3421 1684
E-mail sgameleira@gmail.com

Rio de Janeiro Filadelfo Oliveira Neto
Rua Fonseca Guimarães, 12 Sta.Teresa,
20240–260, Rio de Janeiro, RJ, Brazil
Tel (0055) (21) 2220 2148
Fax (0055) (21) 2252 9686
E-mail oliveira.ieab@gmail.com

São Paulo Roger Douglas Bird
Rua Borges Lagoa 172 Vila Clementino
04038–020,
São Paulo, SP, Brazil
Tel (0055) (11) 5549 9086
E-mail rogerbird@uol.com.br

South Western Francisco de Assis Silva
Brazil Av. Rio Branco, 880 / Sub-solo – Centro, Caixa
Postal 116, Santa Maria,
RS, Brazil
Tel (0055) (55) 3223 4328
fax as telephone
E-mail fassis@ieab.org.br

Southern Brazil Orlando Santos de Oliveira
Av. Eng. Ludolfo Boehl, 278,
Teresópolis, 91720–150, Porto Alegre,
RS, Brazil
Tel (0055) (51) 318 6199
fax as telephone
E-mail dmbispo@terra.com.br

BURMA *see* MYANMAR

BURUNDI

Bujumbura Pie Ntukamazina
BP 1300, Bujumbura, Burundi
Tel (00257) (22) 222 641
Fax (00257) (22) 227 495
E-mail mgrpie@cbinf.com *or*
bishoppie@yahoo.com

Buye Sixbert Macumi
Eglise Episcopale du Burundi,
BP 94, Ngozi, Burundi
Tel (00257) (22) 302 210
Fax (00257) (22) 302 317
E-mail buyedioc@yahoo.fr

Gitega   Jean W Nduwayo
BP 23, Gitega, Burundi
Tel (00257) (22) 402 247
E-mail eebgitega@cbinf.com

Makamba   Martin Blaise Nyaboho
BP 96, Makamba, Burundi
Tel (00257) (22) 508 080
Fax (00257) (22) 229 129
E-mail eabdiocmak@yahoo.fr

Matana
(Archbishop)   Bernard Ntahoturi
BP 447, Bujumbura, Burundi
Tel (00257) (22) 924 595
Fax (00257) (22) 229 129
E-mail ntahober@cbinf.com

Muyinga   Eraste Bigirimana
BP 55, Muyinga, Burundi
Tel (00257) (22) 306 019
Fax (00257) (22) 306 152
E-mail bigirimanaerast@yahoo.fr

CANADA

Primate of
Canada   Fred J Hiltz
80 Hayden Street, Toronto ON,
Canada, M4Y 3G2
Tel (001) (416) 924 9192
Fax (001) (416) 924 0211
E-mail primate@national.anglican.ca

PROVINCE OF BRITISH COLUMBIA AND YUKON

British Columbia   James A J Cowan
900 Vancouver Street,
Victoria BC, Canada, V8V 3V7
Tel (001) (250) 386 7781
Fax (001) (250) 386 4013
E-mail synod@bc.anglican.ca

Caledonia   William J Anderson
201-4716 Lazelle Ave,
Terrace, BC, Canada, V8V 3V7
Tel (001) (250) 635 6016
Fax (001) (250) 635 6026
E-mail caledonia@telus.net

Anglican
Parishes of the
Central Interior   Barbara J Andrews
c/o St. Paul's Cathedral, 360 Nicola
St, Kamloops, BC, Canada, V2C 2P5
Tel (001) (250) 819 5753
E-mail apci@shaw.ca

Kootenay
(Metropolitan)   John E Privett
1876 Richter Street,
Kelowna BC, Canada, V1Y 2M9
Tel (001) (250) 762 3306
Fax (001) (250) 762 4150
E-mail diocese_of_kootenay@telus.net

New
Westminster   Michael C Ingham
580, 401 W Georgia Street,
Vancouver BC, Canada, V6B 5A1
Tel (001) (604) 684 6306
Fax (001) (604) 684 7017
E-mail bishop@vancouver.anglican.ca

Yukon   Larry D Robertson
PO Box 31136, Whitehorse YT,
Canada, Y1A 3T3
Tel (001) (867) 667 7746
Fax (001) (867) 667 6125
E-mail synodoffice@klondiker.com

PROVINCE OF CANADA

Central
Newfoundland   F David Torraville
34 Fraser Road, Gander NL,
Canada, A1V 2E8
Tel (001) (709) 256 2372
Fax (001) (709) 256 2396
E-mail bishopcentral@nfld.net

Eastern
Newfoundland
and Labrador   Cyrus C J Pitman
19 King's Bridge Road,
St John's NL, Canada, A1C 3K4
Tel (001) (709) 576 6697
Fax (001) (709) 576 7122
E-mail cpitman@anglicanenl.nf.net

Fredericton
(Metropolitan)   Claude E W Miller
115 Church Street,
Fredericton NB, Canada, E3B 4C8
Tel (001) (506) 459 1801
Fax (001) (506) 460 0520
E-mail diocese@anglican.nb.ca

Montreal   Barry B Clarke
1444 Union Avenue,
Montreal QC, Canada, H3A 2B8
Tel (001) (514) 843 6577
Fax (001) (514) 843 3221
E-mail bishops.office@montreal.anglican.org

Nova Scotia
and Prince
Edward Island   Susan Moxley
6017 Quinpool Road
Halifax NS, Canada, B3K 5J6
Tel (001) (902) 420 0717
Fax (001) (902) 425 0717
E-mail office@nspeidiocese.ca

Quebec   Dennis P Drainville
31 rue des Jardins,
Quebec QC, Canada, G1R 4L6
Tel (001) (418) 692 3858
Fax (001) (418) 692 3876
E-mail synodoffice@quebec.anglican.ca

Western
Newfoundland   Percy D Coffin
25 Main Street, Corner Brook NF,
Canada, A2H 1C2
Tel (001) (709) 639 8712
Fax (001) (709) 639 1636
E-mail dsown@nf.aibn.ca

PROVINCE OF ONTARIO

Algoma   Stephen Andrews,
PO Box 1168, Sault Ste Marie ON,
Canada, P6A 5N7
Tel (001) (705) 256 5061
Fax (001) (705) 946 1860
E-mail bishop@dioceseofalgoma.com

Huron   Robert F Bennett,
190 Queens Avenue,
London ON, Canada, N6A 6H7
Tel (001) (519) 434 6893
Fax (001) (519) 673 4151
E-mail bishops@huron.anglican.org

(Suffragan)   Terrance A Dance
address etc as above

Moosonee   Thomas A Corston
435 Hemlock Ave, Timmins, ON,
Canada, P4N 6T0
Tel (001) (705) 360 1129
Fax (001) (705) 360 1120
E-mail dmoose@domaa.ca

Niagara   Michael A Bird
Cathedral Place, 252 James Street N,
Hamilton ON, Canada, L8R 2L3
Tel (001) (905) 527 1316
Fax (001) (905) 527 1281
E-mail bishop@niagara.anglican.ca

Ontario   Michael D Oulton
90 Johnson Street,
Kingston ON, Canada, K7L 1X7
Tel (001) (613) 544 4774
Fax (001) (613) 547 3745
E-mail moulton@ontario.anglican.ca

Ottawa   John H Chapman
71 Bronson Avenue,
Ottawa ON, Canada, K1R 6G6
Tel (001) (613) 232 7124 *or* 233 7741 ext 223
Fax (001) (613) 232 3955
E-mail admin@ottawa.anglican.ca

Toronto
(Archbishop
and
Metropolitan)   Colin R Johnson
135 Adelaide Street East,
Toronto ON, Canada, M5C 1L8
Tel (001) (416) 363 6021
Fax (001) (416) 363 3683
E-mail cjohnson@toronto.anglican.ca *or*
diocese@toronto.anglican.ca

(York-Simcoe) George Elliott
2174 King Rd, Suite 2, King City ON,
Canada, L7B 1L6
Tel (001) (905) 833 8327
Fax (001) (905) 833 8329
E-mail ysimcoe@neptune.on.ca

(York
Credit Valley) M Philip Poole
135 Adelaide St East
Toronto ON, Canada M5C 1L8
Tel (001) (416) 363 6021
Fax (001) (416) 363 3683
E-mail ppoole@toronto.anglican.ca

(Trent-Durham) Linda Nicholls
965 Dundas St West, Suite 207, Whitby, ON,
Canada L1P 1G8
Tel (001) (905) 668 1558
Fax (001) (905) 668 8216
E-mail lnicholls@toronto.anglican.ca

(York-
Scarborough) Patrick T Yu
135 Adelaide St East,
Scarborough ON, Canada, M5C 1L8
Tel (001) (416) 363 6021
Fax (001) (416) 363 3683
E-mail patyu@toronto.anglican.ca

PROVINCE OF RUPERT'S LAND

The Arctic Andrew P Atagotaaluk
PO Box 190,
Yellowknife NT, Canada, X1A 2N2
Tel (001) (867) 873 5432
Fax (001) (867) 837 8478
E-mail diocese@arcticnet.org

Athabasca Fraser W Lawton
Box 6868, Peace River AB,
Canada, T8S 1S6
Tel (001) (780) 624 2767
Fax (001) (780) 624 2365
E-mail bpath@telusplanet.net

Brandon James D. Njegovan
PO Box 21009, WEPO,
Brandon MB, Canada, R7B 3W8
Tel (001) (204) 727 7550
Fax (001) (204) 727 4135
E-mail bishopbdn@mts.net

Calgary Derek B E Hoskin
180–1209 59th Avenue SE
Calgary AB, Canada, T2H 2P6
Tel (001) (403) 243 3673
Fax (001) (403) 243 2182
E-mail synod@calgary.anglican.ca

Edmonton Jane Alexander
10035–103 Street,
Edmonton AB, Canada, T5J 0X5
Tel (001) (403) 439 7344
Fax (001) (403) 439 6549
E-mail bishopv@edmonton.anglican.ca

Keewatin David N Ashdown
(Archbishop 915 Ottawa Street, PO Box 567
and Keewatin ON, Canada, P0X 1C0
Metropolitan) Tel (001) (807) 547 3353
Fax (001) (807) 547 3356
E-mail dioceseofkeewatin@shaw.ca

Northern Lydia Mamakwa
Ontario PO Box 65
Kingfisher Lake, ON, Canada, P0X 1C0
Tel (001) (807) 547 3353
Fax (001) (807) 547 3356
E-mail lydia@kingfisherlake.ca

Qu'Appelle Gregory K Kerr-Wilson
1501 College Avenue, Regina SK,
Canada, S4P 1B8
Tel (001) (306) 522 1608
Fax (001) (306) 352 6808
E-mail quappelle@sasktel.net

Rupert's Land Donald D Phillips
935 Nesbitt Bay, Winnipeg MB,
Canada, R3T 1W6
Tel (001) (204) 922 4200
Fax (001) (204) 922 4219
E-mail general@rupertsland.ca

Saskatchewan Michael W Hawkins
1308 Fifth Avenue East,
Prince Albert SK, Canada, S6V 2H7
Tel (001) (306) 763 2455
Fax (001) (306) 764 5172
E-mail synod@sasktel.net

Saskatoon David M Irving
PO Box 1965, Saskatoon SK
Canada, S7K 3S5
Tel (001) (306) 244 5651 or 242 0837
Fax (001) (306) 933 4606
E-mail anglicansynod@sasktel.net

CENTRAL AFRICA

Botswana Trevor Mwamba
PO Box 679, Gaborone, Botswana
Tel (00267) 395 3779
Fax (00267) 391 3015
E-mail angli_diocese@info.bw

Central Zambia Derek Gary Kamukwanba
PO Box 70172, Ndola, Zambia
Tel (00260) (2) 612431
Fax (00260) (2) 615954
E-mail adcznla@zamnet.zm

Central Ishmael Mukuwanda
Zimbabwe PO Box 25, Gweru, Zimbabwe
Tel (00263) (54) 21030
Fax (00263) (54) 21097
E-mail diocent@telconet.co.zw

Eastern Zambia William Muchombo
PO Box 510154, Chipata, Zambia
Tel (00260) (62) 21294
fax as telephone
E-mail dioeastzm@zamnet.zm

Harare Chad Nicholas Gandiya
Monmouth Road,
Avondale, Harare, Zimbabwe
Tel (00263) (4) 308042
E-mail diohrecpca@ecoweb.co.zw

Lake Malawi Francis Kaulanda
PO Box 30349, Lilongwe 3, Malawi
Tel (00265) 797858
Fax (00265) 731966 or 731895

Luapula Robert Mumbi
PO Box 70210, Mansa, Luapula, Zambia

Lusaka David Njovu
Bishop's Lodge, PO Box 30183
Lusaka, Zambia
Tel (00260) (1) 264515
Fax (00260) (1) 262379
E-mail dnjovu@zamnet.zm

Manicaland Julius Makoni
115 Herbert Chitepo Street
Mutare, Zimbabwe
Tel (00263) (20) 64194
Fax (00262) (20) 63076
E-mail diomani@syscom.co.zw

Masvingo Godfrey Tawonezvi
PO 1421, Masvingo, Zambia
Tel (00263) (39) 362 536
E-mail anglicandiomsv@comone.co.zw

Matabeleland Wilson Sitshebo
PO Box 2422, Bulawayo, Zimbabwe
Tel (00263) (9) 61370
Fax (00263) (9) 68353
E-mail angdiomat@telconet.co.zw

Northern Leslie Mtekateka
Malawi PO Box 120, Mzuzu, Malawi
Tel (00265) 331486
Fax (00265) 333805

Northern Albert Chama
Zambia PO Box 20798, Kitwe, Zambia
Tel (00260) (2) 223 264
Fax (00260) (2) 224 778
E-mail dionorth@zamnet.zm

Southern Malawi	James Tengatenga PO Box 30220, Chichiri, Blantyre, 3, Malawi Tel (00265) (1) 641 218 Fax (00265) (1) 641 235 E-mail angsoma@sdnp.org.mw or jtengatenga@unima.wn.apc.org
Southern Malawi – Upper Shire (Archbishop)	Brighton Vitta Masala Private Bag 1, Chilema, Zomba, Malawi Tel (00260) (1) 539 514 fax as telephone E-mail dionorth@zamnet.zm

CENTRAL AMERICA

Costa Rica	Hector Monterroso Iglesia Episcopal Costarricense, Apt 10520, 1000 San Jose, Costa Rica Tel (00506) 225 0209 or 253 0790 Fax (00506) 253 8331 E-mail anglicancr@racsa.co.cr or iarca@amnet.co.cr
El Salvador (Primate)	Martin de Jesus Barahona 47 Avenida Sur, 723 Col Flor Blanca, Apt Postal (01), 274 San Salvador, El Salvador Tel (00503) 2 223 2252 Fax (00503) 2 223 7952 E-mail anglican.sal@integra.com.sv
Guatemala	Armando Roman Guerra-Soria Apartado 58A, Guatemala City, Guatemala Tel (00502) 2472 0852 Fax (00502) 2472 0764 E-mail diocesis@terra.com.gt or diocesis@infovia.com.gt
Nicaragua	Sturdie Downs Apartado 1207, Managua, Nicaragua Tel (00505) (2) 225174 Fax (00505) (2) 226701 E-mail episcnic@cablenet.com.ni or episcnic@tmx.com.ni
Panama	Julio Murray Box R, Balboa, Republic of Panama Tel (00507) 212 0062 Fax (00507) 262 2097 E-mail iepan@cwpanama.net or anglipan@sinfo.net

CEYLON (SRI LANKA)

Colombo	Dhiloraj R Canagasabey 368/3A Bauddhaloka Mawatha, Colombo 7, Sri Lanka Tel (0094) (1) 684810 Fax (0094) (1) 684811 E-mail anglican@sltnet.lk
Kurunegala	Shantha Francis Bishop's House, Cathedral Close, Kurunegala, Sri Lanka Tel (0094) (37) 222 2191 Fax (0094) (37) 222 6806 E-mail bishopkg@sltnet.lk

CONGO (formerly ZAÏRE)

Aru	Georges Titre Ande PO Box 226 Aura, Uganda Tel (00243) 81 039 30 71 E-mail revdande@yahoo.co.uk
Boga	William Bahemuka Mugenyi PO Box 25586, Kampala, Uganda Tel (00243) 99 0668639 E-mail mugenyiwilliam@yahoo.com
Bukavu	Sylvestre Bahati Bali-Busane BP 134, Cyangugu, Rwanda Mobile (00243) 99 401 3647 E-mail bhati_bali@yahoo.fr
Kasais	Marcel Kapinga Kayibabu wa Ilunga PO Box 16482, Kinshasa 1, DR Congo Tel (00243) 993570080 Email anglicanekasai@yahoo.fr

Katanga (formerly Shaba)	Corneille Kasima Muno PO Box 22037, Kitwe, Zambia Tel (00243) 99 587 3629 Fax (00243) 81 475 6075 Email kasimamc@yahoo.fr
Kindu	Zacharie Masimango Katanda PO Box 5, Gisenyi, Rwanda Tel (243) 99 891 6258 Mobile (243) 813 286 255 E-mail angkindu@yahoo.fr or angkindu@antenna.nl
Kinshasa (Archbishop)	Henri Isingoma Kahwa PO Box 16482, DR Congo Tel (00243) 99 333 30908 E-mail peac_isingoma@yahoo.fr
(Assistant)	Jean Molanga Botola address as above Tel (00243) 99 471 3802 E-mail molanga2k@yahoo.co.uk
Kisangani	Lambert Funga Botolome PO Box 25586, Kampala, Uganda Tel (00243) 997 252 868 E-mail lambertfunga@hotmail.com
Nord Kivu	Adoply Muihindo Isesomo PO Box 25586, Kampala, Uganda Tel (00243) 99 854 8601 E-mail revd_isesomo@yahoo.fr

HONG KONG

Eastern Kowloon	Louis Tsan-sang Tsui Diocesan Office, 4/F Holy Trinity Bradbury Centre, 139 Ma Tau Chung Road, Kowloon, Hong Kong, China Tel (00852) 2713 9983 Fax (00852) 2711 1609 E-mail ekoffice@ekhkskh.org.hk
Hong Kong Island (Archbishop)	Paul Kwong 25/F Wyndham Place, 40–44, Wyndham Street, Central Hong Kong SAR, China Tel (00852) 2526 5355 Fax (00852) 2525 3344 E-mail do.dhk@hkskh.org
Western Kowloon	Thomas Yee-po Soo 15/F Ultragrace Commercial Building, 5 Jordan Road, Kowloon, Hong Kong, China Tel (00852) 2783 0811 Fax (00852) 2783 0799 E-mail hkskhdwk@netvigator.com

INDIAN OCEAN

Antananarivo	Samoela Jaona Ranarivelo Evêché Anglican, Lot VK57 ter, Ambohimanoro, 101 Antananarivo, Madagascar Tel (00261) (20) 222 0827 Fax (00261) (20) 226 1331 E-mail eemdanta@dts.mg
(Assistant)	Todd McGregor address as above
Antsiranana	Roger Chung Po Chuen Evêché Anglican, BP 278, 201 Antsiranana, Madagascar Tel (00261) (20) 822 2650 fax as telephone
Fianarantsoa	Gilbert Rateloson Rakotondravelo Évêché Anglican, Manantsara, BP 1418, Madagascar
Mahajanga	Jean-Claude Andrianjafimanana BP 570, Mahajanga 401, Madagascar E-mail eemdmaha@dts.mg or revmctod@dts.mg
Mauritius (Archbishop)	Ian Ernest Bishop's House, Nallelamby Road, Phoenix, Mauritius Tel (00230) 686 5158 Fax (00230) 697 1096 E-mail dioang@intnet.mu

Seychelles James Richard Wong Yin Song
Bishop's House, PO Box 44, Victoria,
Seychelles
Tel (00248) 321 977
Fax (00248) 323 879
E-mail angdio@seychelles.net

Toamasina Jean Paul Solo
Evêché Anglican, Rue James Seth, BP 531,
Toamasina 501, Madagascar
Tel (00261) (20) 533 1663
Fax (00261) (20) 533 1689
E-mail eemtoam@wanadoo.mg

JAPAN

Chubu Francis Toshiaki Mori
28–1 Meigetsu-cho, 2 chome,
Showa-ku, Nagoya 466–0034, Japan
Tel (0081) (52) 858 1007
Fax (0081) (52) 858 1008
E-mail office.chubu@nskk.org

Hokkaido Nathaniel Makoto Uematsu
(Primate) Kita 15 jo, Nishi 5–20,
Kita-ku, Sapporo 001–0015, Japan
Tel (0081) (11) 717 8181
Fax (0081) (11) 736 8377
E-mail hokkaido@nskk.org or
bishop.hok@nskk.org

Kita Kanto Zerubbabel Katsuichi Hirota
2–172 Sakuragi-cho, Omiya-ku, Saitama-shi,
331–0852, Japan
Tel (0081) (48) 642 2680
Fax (0081) (48) 648 0358 or 476 7484
E-mail kitakanto@nskk.org

Kobe Andrew Yutaka Nakamura, 5–11–1
Yamatedori, Chuo-ku, Kobe-shi 650–0011,
Japan
Tel (0081) (78) 351 5469
Fax (0081) (78) 382 1095
E-mail aao52850@syd.odn.ne.jp

Kyoto Stephen Takashi Kochi
380 Okakuencho, Shimotachiuri-agaru,
Karasumadori, Kamikyo-ku, Kyoto 602–8011,
Japan
Tel (0081) (75) 431 7204
Fax (0081) (75) 441 4238 or 432 6723
E-mail nskk-kyoto@mse.biglobe.ne.jp

Kyushu Gabriel Shoji Igarashi
2–9–22 Kusakae, Chuo-ku,
Fukuoka 810–0045, Japan
Tel (0081) (92) 771 2050
Fax (0081) (92) 771 9857
E-mail d-kyushu@try-net.or.jp

Okinawa David Shoji Tani
3–5–5 Meada, Urasoe-shi,
Okinawa 910–2102, Japan
Tel (0081) (98) 942 1101
Fax (0081) (98) 942 1102
E-mail office.okinawa@nskk.org

Osaka Samuel Osamu Onishi
2–1–8 Matsuzaki-cho, Abeno-ku,
Osaka 545–0053, Japan
Tel (0081) (6) 621 2179
Fax (0081) (6) 621 3097 or 6219148
E-mail office.osaka@nskk.org

Tohoku John Hiromichi Kato
2–13–15 Kokobun-cho, Aoba-ku,
Sendai 980–0803, Japan
Tel (0081) (22) 223 2349
Fax (0081) (22) 223 2387
E-mail hayashi.tohoku@nskk.org

Tokyo Peter Jintaro Ueda
3–6–18 Shiba Koen, Minato-ku,
Tokyo 105–0011, Japan
Tel (0081) (3) 3433 0987 or 3433 2417
Fax (0081) (3) 3433 8678
E-mail office.tko@nskk.org

Yokohama Laurence Yutaka Minabe
14–57 Mitsuzawa Shimo-cho,
Kanagawa-ku, Yokohama 221–0852, Japan
Tel (0081) (45) 321 4988
Fax (0081) (45) 321 4978
E-mail yokohama.kyouku@nskk.org

JERUSALEM AND THE MIDDLE EAST

Cyprus and Michael Augustine Owen Lewis,
the Gulf PO Box 22075, CY 1517–Nicosia, Cyprus
(Bishop in) Tel (00357) (22) 671220
Fax (00357) (22) 674553
E-mail bishop@spidernet.com.cy or
georgia@spidernet.com.cy

Egypt Mouneer Hanna Anis
(Bishop in) Diocesan Office, PO Box 87,
(President) Zamalek Distribution, 11211, Cairo, Egypt
Tel (0020) (2) 738 0829
Fax (0020) (2) 735 8941
E-mail bishopmouneer@gmail.com

(Suffragan) Andrew Proud
(Horn of address etc as above
Africa)
(North Africa) Bill Musk
address etc as above
E-mail billamusk@googlemail.com

Iran (Episcopal Azad Marshall
Vicar General) St Thomas Center, Raiwind Road, PO
Box 688, Lohore, Punjab, 54000, Pakistan
Tel (0092) (42) 542 0452
E-mail bishop@saintthomascenter.org

Jerusalem Suheil Dawani
(Bishop in) St George's Close, PO Box 9122,
20 Nablus Rd, Jerusalem 91 191, Israel
Tel (00972) (2) 627 1670
Fax (00972) (2) 627 3847
E-mail bishop@j-diocese.com

KENYA

All Saints Eliud Wabukala
Cathedral PO Box 40502, 00100 Nairobi, Kenya
(Archbishop) Tel (00254) (20) 714 755
Fax (00254) (20) 718 442/714 750
E-mail archoffice@swiftkenya.com

Bondo Johannes Otieno Angela
PO Box 240, 40601 Bondo, Kenya
Tel (00254) (335) 20415
E-mail ackbondo@swiftkenya.com

Bungoma Vacant
PO Box 2392, 50200 Bungoma, Kenya
Tel (00254) (337) 30481
fax as telephone
E-mail ackbungoma@swiftkenya.com

Butere Michael Sande
PO Box 54, 50101 Butere, Kenya
Tel (00254) (56) 620 412
Fax (00254) (56) 620 038
E-mail ackbutere@swiftkenya.com

Eldoret Thomas Kogo
PO Box 3404, 30100 Eldoret, Kenya
Tel (00254) (321) 62785
E-mail ackeldoret@africaonline.co.ke

Embu Henry Tiras Nyaga Kathii,
PO Box 189, Embu, Kenya
Tel (00254) (68) 30614
Fax (00254) (68) 30468
E-mail ackembu@maf.org.ke or
ackembu@swiftkenya.com

Kajiado Jeremiah John Mutua Taama
PO Box 203, 01100 Kajiado, Kenya
Tel (00254) (301) 21201
Fax (00254) (301) 21106
E-mail ackajiado@swiftkenya.com

Katakwa Zakayo Iteba Epusi
PO Box 68, 50244 Amagoro, Kenya
Tel (00254) (55) 54079
E-mail ackatakwa@swiftkenya.com

Kericho   Jackson Ole Sapit
c/o PO Box 181, Kericho

Kirinyaga   Daniel Munene Ngoru
PO Box 95, 10304 Kutus, Kenya
Tel (00254) (163) 44221 or 44028
Fax (00254) (163) 44020
E-mail ackirinyaga@swiftkenya.com

Kitale   Stephen Kewasis Nyorsok
PO Box 4176, 30200 Kitale, Kenya
Tel (00254) (325) 31631
Fax (00254) (325) 31387
E-mail ack.ktl@africaonline.co.ke

Kitui   Josephat Mule
PO Box 1054, 90200 Kitui, Kenya
Tel (00254) (141) 22682
Fax (00254) (141) 22119
E-mail ackitui@swiftkenya.com

Machakos   Joseph Mutie Kanuku
PO Box 282, 90100 Machakos, Kenya
Tel (00254) (145) 21379
Fax (00254) (145) 20178
E-mail ackmachakos@swiftkenya.com

Maseno North   Simon Mutingole Oketch
PO Box 416, 50100 Kakemega, Kenya
Tel (00254) (331) 30729
Fax (00254) (331) 30752
E-mail ackmnorth@swiftkenya.com

Maseno South   Francis Mwayi Abiero
PO Box 114, 40100 Kisumu, Kenya
Tel (00254) (35) 21297
Fax (00254) (35) 21009
E-mail ackmsouth@swiftkenya.com

Maseno West   Joseph Otieno Wasonga
PO Box 793, 40600 Siaya, Kenya
Tel (00254) (334) 21483
Fax (00254) (334) 21483
E-mail ackmwest@swiftkenya.com

Mbeere   Moses Masambe Nthuka
PO Box 122, 60104 Siakago, Kenya
Tel (00254) (162) 21261
Fax (00254) (162) 21083
E-mail ackmbeere@swiftkenya.com

Meru   Charles Ndiga Mwendwa
PO Box 427, 60200 Meru, Kenya
Tel (00254) (64) 30719
E-mail ackmeru@swiftkenya.com or
ackmeru@plansonline.net

Mombasa   Julius Robert Katoi Kalu
Ukumbusho House, Nkrumah Road,
PO Box 80072, 80100 Mombasa, Kenya
Tel (00254) (41) 231 1105
Fax (00254) (41) 231 6361
E-mail ackmsa@swiftmombasa.com

(Assistant)   Lawrence Dena
address etc as above

Mt Kenya Central   Isaac Maina Ng'ang'a
PO Box 121, 10200 Murang'a, Kenya
Tel (00254) (60) 30560 or 30559
Fax (00254) (60) 30148
E-mail ackmkcentral@wananchi.com

(Assistant)   Allan Waithaka
address etc as above

Mt Kenya South   Timothy Ranji
PO Box 886, 00900 Kiambu, Kenya
Tel (00254) (66) 22997 or 22521
Fax (00254) (66) 22408
E-mail ackmtksouth@swiftkenya.com

Mt Kenya West   Joseph M Kagunda
PO Box 229, 10100 Nyeri, Kenya
Tel (00254) (61) 203 2281
E-mail ackmtkwest@africaonline.co.ke

Mumias   Beneah Justin Okumu Salalah
PO Box 213, 50102 Mumias, Kenya
Tel: (00254) (333) 41476
Fax (00254) (333) 41232
E-mail ackmumias@swiftkenya.com

Nairobi   Peter Njagi Njoka
PO Box 72846, 00200 Nairobi, Kenya
Tel (00254) (2) 714 755
Fax (00254) (2) 226 259
E-mail acknairobi@swiftkenya.com

Nakuru   Stephen Njihia Mwangi
PO Box 56, (Moi Road), 20100 Nakuru, Kenya
Tel (00254) (37) 212155 or 212151
Fax (00254) (37) 44379
E-mail acknkudioc@net2000ke.com

Nambale   Josiah Makhandia Were
PO Box 4, 50409 Nambale, Kenya
Tel (00254) (336) 24040
fax as telephone
E-mail acknambale@swiftkenya.com

Nyahururu   Charles Gaikia Gaita
PO Box 926, 20300 Nyahururu, Kenya
Tel (00254) (365) 32179
E-mail nyahu_dc@africaonline.co.ke

Southern Nyanza   James Kenneth Ochiel
PO Box 65, 40300 Homa Bay, Kenya
Tel (00254) (385) 22127
Fax (00254) (385) 22056
E-mail acksnyanza@swiftkenya.com

Taita Taveta   Samson Mwakitawa Mwaluda
PO Box 75, 80300 Voi, Kenya
Tel (00254) (147) 30096
Fax (00254) (147) 30364 or 31387
E-mail acktaita@swiftmombasa.com

Thika   Gideon Gichuhi Githiga
PO Box 214, 01000 Thika, Kenya
Tel (00254) (151) 21735 or 31654
Fax (00254) (151) 31544
E-mail ackthika@swiftkenya.com

KOREA

Pusan (Primate)   Solomon Jong Mo Yoon
18 Daechengdong-2ga, Chung-Ku,
Pusan 600–092,
Republic of Korea
Tel (0082) (51) 463 5742
Fax (0082) (51) 463 5957
E-mail yoonsjm@hanmail.net

Seoul   Paul Keun Sang Kim
3 Chong-Dong, Chung-Ku,
Seoul 100–120, Republic of Korea
Tel (0082) (2) 735 6157 or 738 6597
Fax (0082) (2) 723 2640
E-mail 44kyung@hanmail.net

Taejon (Acting)   Michael Hi Yeon Kwon
87–6 Sunwha 2don, Chung-Ku,
Taejon 302–823, Republic of Korea
Tel (0082) (42) 256 9987
Fax (0082) (42) 255 8918
E-mail tdio@unitel.co.kr

MELANESIA

Banks and Torres (formerly North Vanuatu)   Nathan Tome
c/o PO Box 19, Sola, Vanualava,
Torba Province, Vanuatu
Tel (00678) 38520
fax as telephone

Central Melanesia (Archbishop)   David Vunagi
Church of Melanesia, PO Box 19,
Honiara, Solomon Islands
Tel (00677) 26601
Fax (00677) 21435
E-mail dvunagi@comphq.org.sb

Central Solomons   Charles Koete
Church of Melanesia, PO Box 52,
Tulagi, CIP, Solomon Islands
Tel (00677) 32006
Fax (00677) 32119

Hanuato'o   Alfred Karibongi
c/o Post Office, Kira Kira,
Makira Province, Solomon Islands
Tel (00677) 50012
E-mail episcopal@solomon.com.sb

Malaita	Samuel Sahu Bishop's House, PO Box 7, Auki Malaita, Solomon Islands Tel (0066) 11 4512 1071 Fax (00677) 40027 *or* (00872) (762) 822444 E-mail domauki@solomon.com.sb	Yangon (Archbishop)	Stephen Than Myint Oo PO Box 11191, 140 Pyidaungsu-Yeiktha Rd, Dagon, Yangon, Myanmar Tel (0095) (1) 395350 Fax (0095) (1) 251 405
Temotu	George Angus Takeli Bishop's House, Lluesalo, Lata, Santa Cruz, Temotu Province, Solomon Islands Tel (00677) 53080	(Assistant)	Samuel Htan Oak 44 Pyi Road, Dagon, Yangon, Myanmar Tel (0095) (1) 372 300
Vanuatu	James Marvin Ligo Bishop's House, PO Box 238, Luganville, Santo, Vanuatu Tel (00678) 37065 *or* 36631 Fax (00678) 36631 E-mail diocese_of_vanuatu@ecunet.org		

NEW ZEALAND
(AOTEAROA, NEW ZEALAND AND POLYNESIA)

Ysabel	Richard Naramana PO Box 6, Buala, Jejevo, Ysabel Province, Solomon Islands Tel (00677) 35124 E-mail episcopal@solomon.com.sb	(Primate/ Archbishop and Bishop of Aotearoa and te Tairawhiti	William Brown Turei PO Box 568, Gisborne 4040, New Zealand Tel (0064) (6) 868 7028 Fax (0064) (6) 867 8859 E-mail browntmihi@xtra.co.nz

MEXICO

		(Primate/ Archbishop and Bishop of Polynesia)	Winston Halapua PO Box 35, Suva, Fiji Islands Tel (0067) (9) 330 4716 Fax (0067) (9) 330 2152 E-mail episcopus@connect.com.fj
Cuernavaca	James H Ottley Calle Minerva No 1, Col. Delicas, CP 62330 Cuernavaca, Morelos, Mexico Tel (0052) (777) 315 2870 *or* 322 2259 E-mail diocesisdecuernavaca@hotmail.com	(Primate/ Archbishop and Bishop of Waikato)	David John Moxon PO Box 21, Hamilton 3240 New Zealand Tel (0064) (7) 857 0020 Fax (0064) (7) 856 9975 E-mail bishop@hn-ang.org. .nz
Mexico (Archbishop)	Carlos Touché-Porter Ave San Jeronimo 117, Col S Angel, Deleg A Obregon, 01000, Mexico Tel (0052) (55) 5616 3193 Tel (0052) (55) 5616 2205 E-mail diomex@netvoice.com.mx *or* diomex@adetel.net.mx	(Bishop of Te Manawa O Te Wheke)	Ngarahu Katene P O Box 146, Rotorua, New Zealand Tel (0064) (7) 348 4043 Fax (0064) (7) 348 4053 E-mail bishop@motw.org.nz
Northern Mexico	Francisco Moreno Simón Bolivar 2005 Norte, Col. Mitras Centro CP 64460, Monterrey NL, Mexico Tel (0052) (81) 8333 0992 Fax (0052) (81) 8348 7362 E-mail diocesisdelnorte@att.net.mx	(Bishop of Te Tai Tokerau)	Te Kitohi Wiremu Pikaahu PO Box 59301, Mangere Bridge, Manukau 2151, New Zealand Tel (0064) (9) 278 2527 Fax (0064) (9) 278 2524 E-mail tkwp@xtra.co.nz
Southeastern Mexico	Benito Juárez-Martinez Avenida de Las Americas #73, Col Aguacatal 91130 Xalapa, Veracruz, Mexico Tel (0052) (228) 814 6951 Fax (0052) (228) 814 4387 E-mail dioste99@aol.com	(Bishop of Te Waipounamu)	John Robert Kuru Gray PO Box 10086, Phillipstown, Christchurch 8145, New Zealand Tel (0064) (3) 389 1683 Fax (0064) (3) 389 0912 E-mail bishopgray@hawaipounamu.co.nz
Western Mexico	Lino Rodríguez-Amaro Fco. Javier Gamboa #255, Col. Sector Juarez 44100 Guadalajara, Jalisco, Mexico Tel (0052) (33) 3560 4726 Fax (0052) (33) 3616 4413 E-mail iamoccidente@prodigy.net.mx	(Bishop of Te Upoko O Te Ika)	Muru Walters 14 Amesbury Drive, Churton,, Wellington 6037, New Zealand Tel (0064) (4) 478 3549 Fax (0064) (4) 472 8863 E-mail muruwalters@xtra.co.nz
		Auckland	Ross Graham Bay PO Box 37242, Parnell, Auckland 1151, New Zealand Tel (0064) (9) 302 7201 Fax (0064) (9) 302 7217

MYANMAR (BURMA)

Hpa-an	Saw Stylo No (4) Block, Bishop Gone, Diocesan Office, Hpa-an, Kayin State , Myanmar Tel (0095) (58) 21696 Fax (0095) (1) 77512	(Assistant) ‘	James White *address etc as above*
Mandalay	Noel Nay Lin Bishopscourt, 22nd Street, 'C' Road (between 85–86 Road), Mandalay, Myanmar Tel (0095) (2) 34110	Christchurch	Victoria Matthews PO Box 4438, Christchurch 8140, New Zealand Tel (0064) (3) 379 5950 Fax (0064) (3) 379 5954 E-mail bishop@anglicanlife.org.nz
Mytikyina	David Than Lwin Diocesan Office, Tha Kin Nat Pe Road, Thida Ya, Myitkyina, Kachin State, Myanmar Tel (0095) (74) 23104	Dunedin	Kelvin Peter Wright PO Box 13170, Green Island, Dunedin 9052, New Zealand Tel (0064) (3) 488 0820 Fax (0064) (3) 488 2038 E-mail bishop@dn.anglican.org.nz
Sittwe	James Min Dein St John's Church, Paletwa, Southern Chin State, via Sittwe, Myanmar	Nelson	Richard Victor Ellena PO Box l00, Nelson, New Zealand Tel (0064) (3) 548 3124 Fax (0064) (3) 548 2125 E-mail bprichard@nelsonanglican.org.nz
Toungoo	Saw John Wilme Diocesan Office, Nat-shin-Naung Road, Toungoo, Myanmar Tel (0095) (54) 23519		

Waiapu | David Cappel Rice
PO Box 227, Napier, New Zealand
Tel (0064) (6) 835 8230
Fax (0064) (6) 835 0680
E-mail bishop@waiapu.com

Taranaki | Philip Richardson
PO Box 547, Taranaki Mail Centre,
New Plymouth, 4340, New Zealand
Tel (0064) (6) 759 1178
Fax (0064) (6) 759 1180
E-mail bishop@taranakianglican.org.nz

Wellington | Thomas John Brown
PO Box 12046, Wellington 6144, New Zealand
Tel (0064) (4) 472 1057
Fax (0064) (4) 449 1360
E-mail bishoptom@paradise.net.nz

Vanua Levu and Taveuni | Apimeleki Nadoki Qiliho
PO Box 29, Labasa, Fiji Islands
Tel (0067) (9) 881 1420
E-mail minoff@connect.com.fj

Viti Levu West | Gabriel Mahesh Prasad Sharma
P O Box 117, Lautoka, Fiji Islands
Tel (0067 (9) 666 0124
fax as telephone
E-mail gabsharma@yahoo.com

NIGERIA

A large number of new dioceses have been created in the Church of Nigeria. At the time of going to press, some details were unavailable, and so this list is incomplete.

PROVINCE OF ABUJA

Abuja (Archbishop and Primate) | Peter Jasper Akinola
Archbishop's Palace, PO Box 212, ADCP,
Abuja, Nigeria
Tel (00234) (9) 524 0496
E-mail primate@anglican-nig.org

Bida | Jonah Kolo
c/o PO Box 2469, Minna, Nigeria
Tel (00234) (66) 460 178
E-mail bida@anglican-nig.org

Gwagwalada | Tanimu Samari Aduda
Diocesan Headquarters, Secretariat Road, PO
Box 287, Gwagwalada, FCT, Abuja, Nigeria
Tel (00234) (9) 882 2083
E-mail gwagwalada@anglican-nig.org

Idah | Joseph N Musa
Bishop's Lodge, PO Box 25, Idah, Kogi State,
Nigeria
Mobile (00234) 804 334 0189
E-mail idah@anglican-nig.org *or*
jilmusa@yahoo.com

Kafanchan | William Weh Diya
Bishopscourt, 5B Jemma'a Street,
PO Box 29, Kafanchan, Kaduna State, Nigeria
Tel (00234) (61) 20634

Kubwa | Duke Akamisoko
Bishopscourt, PO Box 67, Kubwa FCT, Nigeria
Tel (00234) (9) 670 7094
E-mail kubwa@anglican-nig.org

Lafia | Miller Kangdim Maza
PO Box 560, Lafia, Nasarawa State, Nigeria
Tel (00234) (47) 221 329

Lokoja | Emmanuel Egbunu
PO Box 11, Lokoja, Kogi State, Nigeria
Tel (00234) (58) 220 588
Fax (00234) (58) 221 788
E-mail lokoja@anglican-nig.org

Makurdi | Nathaniel Nyitar Inyom
Bishopscourt, PO Box 1, Makurdi, Benue State,
Nigeria
Tel (00234) (44) 533 349
E-mail makurdi@anglican-nig. org

Minna | Nathaniel Yisa
Bishopscourt, Dutsen Kura,
PO Box 2469, Minna, Niger State, Nigeria
Tel (00234) (66) 220 035 (Office) *or* 220 514
(Home)

Otukpo | David K Bello
St John's Cathedral, Sgt Ugbade Ave,
PO Box 360, Otukpo, Benue State, Nigeria
Tel (00234) (44) 662 212
E-mail otukpo@anglican-nig.org *or*
bishopdkbello@yahoo.com

Zonkwa (Missionary diocese) | Praise Omole-Ekun
Bishop's Residence, PO Box 21,
Zonkwa, Kaduna State 802002, Nigeria
E-mail zonkwa@anglican-nig.org

PROVINCE OF BENDEL

Asaba (Archbishop) | Nicholas D Okoh
Bishopscourt, Cable Point,
PO Box 216, Asaba, Delta State, Nigeria
Tel (00234) (46) 280 682 or 280043
E-mail asaba@anglican-nig.org

Benin | P O J Imasuen
Bishopscourt, PO Box 82,
Benin City, Edo State, Nigeria
Mobile (00234) 803 079 9560
E-mail benin@anglican-nig.org *or*
petglad2002@yahoo.com

Esan | Friday John Imakhai
Bishopscourt, Ujoelen, PO Box 921, Ekpoma,
Edo State, Nigeria
Tel (00234) (55) 981 29
E-mail bishopfriday@hotmail.com

Ika | Peter Onekpe
Bishopscourt, c/o PO Box 5,
Agbor, Delta State, Nigeria
Tel (00234) (55) 25014
E-mail ika@anglican-nig.org *or*
bishoppeter@yahoo.com

Oleh | Jonathan Francis Ekokotu Edewor
PO Box 8, Oleh, Delta State, Nigeria
Mobile (00234) 803 549 4215
E-mail oleh@anglican-nig.org *or*
angoleh2000@yahoo.com

Sabongidda-Ora | John Akao
Bishopscourt, PO Box 13,
Sabongidda-Ora, Edo State, Nigeria
Tel (00234) (57) 54049
E-mail akao@cashette.com

Ughelli | Vincent O Muoghereh
Bishopscourt, Ovurodawanre,
PO Box 760, Ughelli, Delta State, Nigeria
Tel (00234) (53) 258 307
Fax (00234) (53) 250 091

Warri | Christian Ideh
Bishopscourt, 17 Mabiaku Road, GRA, PO
Box 4571, Warri, Nigeria
Tel (00234) (53) 255 857
E-mail warri@anglican-nig.org

Western Izon (Missionary diocese) | Edafe Emamezi, Bishopscourt
PO Box 56, Sagbama, River State, Nigeria
Mobile (00234) 806 357 2263
E-mail anglizon@yahoo.co.uk

PROVINCE OF IBADAN

Ajayi Crowther | Olukemi Oduntan, Bishopscourt, Iseyin,
PO Box 430, Iseyin, Oyo State
Mobile (00234) (837) 198 182
email: ajayicrowtherdiocese@yahoo.com

Ibadan (Archbishop) | Joseph Akinfenwa
Bishopscourt, PO Box 3075,
Mapo, Ibadan, Nigeria
Tel (00234) (2) 810 1400
Fax (00234) (2) 810 1413
E-mail ibadan@anglican-nig.org *or*
bishop@skannet.com

Ibadan North | Segun Okubadejo
Bishopscourt, Moyede, PO Box 28961, Agodi,
Ibadan, Nigeria
Tel (00234) (2) 8107 482
E-mail angibn@skannet.com *or*
segtal52@yahoo.co.uk

Ibadan South   Jacob Ademola Ajetunmobi
Bishopscourt, PO Box 166,
Dugbe, Ibadan, Nigeria
Tel (00234) (2) 231 6464
fax as telephone
E-mail ibadan-south@anglican-nig.org *or*
jacajet@skannet.com

Ife   Oluranti Odubogun
Bishopscourt, PO Box 312,
Ife-Ife, Osun State, Nigeria
Tel (00234) (36) 232 255
E-mail stphilipscathayetoroife@yahoo.com

Igbomina   Michael Oluwakayode Akinyemi
Bishopscourt, Esie, PO Box 102, Oro P.A,
Kwara State, Nigeria
Tel (00234) (31) 700 0025

Ilesa   Olubayo Samuel Sowale
Bishopscourt, Oke-Ooye, PO Box 237, Ilesa,
Nigeria
Tel (00234) (36) 461 153
E-mail ilesha@anglican-nig.org *or*
bishop-solwale@yahoo.com

Kwara   Olusegun Adeyemi
Bishopscourt, Fate Road, PO Box 1884, Ilorin,
Kwara State, Nigeria
Tel (00234) (31) 220879
F-mail kwara@anglican.skannet.com.ng

Offa   Gabriel Akinbolarin Akinbiyi
PO Box 21, Offa, Kwara State, Nigeria
Tel (00234) (31) 801011
E-mail offa@anglican-nig.org

Ogbomoso   Matthew Osunade
(Missionary   Bishop's House, PO Box 1909, Ogbomoso,
diocese)   Osun State, Nigeria
Mobile (00234) 803 524 4606
E-mail ogbomoso@anglican-nig.org *or*
maaosunade@yahoo.com

Oke-Osun   Nathaniel Fasogbon
Bishopscourt, PO Box 251,
Gbongan, Osun State, Nigeria
Mobile: (00234) 803 356 9384

Osun   James Afolabi Popoola
Bishopscourt, Isale-Aro,
PO Box 285, Osogbo, Nigeria
Tel (00234) (35) 240 036
Mobile (00234) 803 356 1628
E-mail osun@anglican-nig.org

Oyo   Jacob Ola Fasipe
Bishopscourt, PO Box 23, Oyo, Nigeria
Mobile (00234) 803 380 2530
E-mail oyo@anglican-nig.org

PROVINCE OF JOS

Bauchi   Musa Tula
Bishop's House, 2 Hospital Road,
PO Box 2450, Bauchi, Nigeria
Tel (00234) (77) 543 460
E-mail bauchi@anglican-nig.org

Damaturu   Abiodun Ogunyemi
PO Box 312, Damaturu, Yobe State, Nigeria
Tel (00234) (74) 522 142
E-mail damaturu@anglican-nig.org

Gombe   Henry Chukwudum Ndukuba
St Peter's Cathedral, PO Box 39, Gombe,
Nigeria
Tel (00234) (72) 220489 or 221212
Fax (00234) (72) 221141
E-mail gombe@anglican-nig.org *or*
ndukuba@yahoo.com

Jalingo   Timothy Yahaya
PO Box 4, Jalingo, Taraba State, Nigeria
Tel (00234) (79) 23312
fax as telephone
E-mail jalingo@anglican-nig.org

Jos   Benjamin Argak Kwashi
(Archbishop)   Bishopscourt, PO Box 6283,
Jos, Plateau State, Nigeria
Tel (00234) (73) 464 325
Mobile (00234) 803 701 7928
E-mail jos@anglican-nig.org

Maiduguri   Emmanuel K Mani
Bishopscourt, Off Lagos Street,
GRA PO Box 1693,
Maiduguri, Borno State, Nigeria
Tel (00234) (76) 234010
fax as telephone
E-mail maiduguri@anglican-nig.org

Yola   Markus A Ibrahim
PO Box 601, Jemeta-Yola, Adamawa State,
Nigeria
Tel (00234) (75) 624303
E-mail yola@anglican-nig.org

PROVINCE OF KADUNA

Dutse   Yusuf Ibrahim Lumu
PO Box 15, Dutse, Jigawa State, Nigeria
Tel (00234) (64) 721 379
E-mail dutse@anglican-nig.org

Gusau   John G Danbinta
PO Box 64, Gusau, Zamfara State, Nigeria
Tel (00234) (63) 204 747
E-mail gusau@anglican-nig.org

Kaduna   Josiah Idowu-Fearon
PO Box 72, Kaduna, Nigeria
Tel (00234) (62) 240 085
Fax (00234) (62) 244 408
E-mail kaduna@anglican-nig.org

Kano   Zakka Lalle Nyam
Bishopscourt, PO Box 362, Kano, Nigeria
Tel (00234) (64) 647 816
fax as telephone
E-mail kano@anglican-nig.org *or*
kano@anglican.skannet.com.ng

Katsina   Jonathan Bamaiyi
Bishop's Lodge, PO Box 904, Katsina, Nigeria
Tel (00234) (65) 432718
E-mail katsina@anglican-nig.org *or*
bpjonathanbamaiyi@yahoo.co.uk

Kebbi   Edmund Efoyikeye Akanya
(Archbishop)   PO Box 701, Birnin Kebbi, Kebbi State, Nigeria
Tel (00234) (68) 321 179
fax as telephone
E-mail kebbi@anglican.skannet.com

Sokoto   Augustine Omole
Bishop's Lodge, 68 Shuni Road,
PO Box 3489, Sokoto, Nigeria
Tel (00234) (60) 234 639
Fax (00234) (60) 232 323
E-mail sokoto@anglican-nig.org

Wusasa   Ali Buba Lamido
Box 28, Wusasa Zaria, Nigeria
Tel (00234) (69) 334 594
E-mail wusasa@anglican-nig.org *or*
wusasa@anglican.skannet.com.ng

PROVINCE OF LAGOS

Badagry   Babatunde J. Adeyemi
(Missionary   Bishopscourt, PO Box 7, Badagry, Lagos State,
diocese)   Nigeria
Tel (00234) (1) 773 5546
Mobile (00234) 803 306 4601
E-mail badagry@anglican-nig.org

Egba   Matthew Oluremi Owadayo
Bishopscourt, Onikolobo, PO Box 267, Ibara,
Abeokuta, Nigeria
Tel (00234) (39) 240 933
fax as telephone
E-mail egba@anglican-nig.org *or*
mowadayo@yahoo.com

Ijebu   Ezekiel Awosoga
Bishopscourt, Ejirin Road,
PO Box 112, Ijebu-Ode, Nigeria
Tel (00234) (37) 431 801
E-mail ijebu@anglican-nig.org *or*
bishop@ang-ijebudiocese.com

Ijebu North   Solomon Kuponu
Bishopscourt, PO Box 2, Ijebu-Igbo, Ogun
State, Nigeria
Mobile (00234) 803 741 9372
E-mail dioceseofijebunorth@yahoo.com

Lagos
(Archbishop)
Ephraim Adebola Ademowo
Archbishop's Palace, 29 Marina,
PO Box 13, Lagos, Nigeria
Tel and fax (00234) (1) 263 6026
Fax (00234) (1) 263 6536
E-mail lagos@anglican.skannet.com.ng or
diocesan@dioceseoflagos.org

Lagos
Mainland
Adebayo Akinde
PO Box 45, Ebute-Metta, Lagos, Nigeria

Lagos West
Peter A Adebiyi
Vining House (2nd Floor), Archbishop Vining
Memorial Cathedral, Oba Akinjobi Road,
G.R.A. Ikeja, Nigeria
Tel (00234) (1) 493 7333
Fax (00234) (1) 493 7337
E-mail lagoswest@anglican-nig.org or
dioceseoflagoswest@yahoo.com

On the Coast
Joshua Ogunele
Bishopscourt, Ikoya Rd, P. M. B. 3, Ilutitun
Osooro, Ondo State, Nigeria
Mobile (00234) 8056 345 496

Remo
Michael O. Fape
Bishopscourt, Ewusi Street, PO Box 522,
Sagamu, Ogun State, Nigeria
Tel (00234) (37) 640 598
E-mail remo@anglican nig.org or
mofape@skannet.com

Yewa
Simeon O M Adebola
Bishopscourt, PO Box 484,
Ilaro, Ogun State, Nigeria
Tel (00234) (1) 792 696

PROVINCE OF THE NIGER

Abakaliki
Benson C B Onyeibor
All Saints' Cathedral, PO Box 112,
Abakaliki, Ebonyi State, Nigeria
Tel (00234) (43) 220 762
Mobile (00234) 803 501 3083
E-mail abakaliki@anglican-nig.org

Aguata
Christian Ogochukwo Efobi
Bishopscourt, PO Box 1128, Ekwulobia,
Anambra State, Nigeria
Mobile (00234) 803 750 1077

Awka
(Archbishop)
Maxwell Samuel Chike Anikwenwa
Bishopscourt, Ifite Road, PO Box 130, Awka,
Anambra State, Nigeria
Tel (00234) (48) 550 058 or 553 516
E-mail awka@anglican-nig.org or
anglawka@infoweb.abs.net or
provoftheniger@infoweb.abs.net

Enugu
Emmanuel O Chukwuma
Bishop's House, PO Box 418, Enugu, Enugu
State, Nigeria
Tel (00234) (42) 435 804
Fax (00234) (42) 259 808
E-mail enugu@anglican-nig.org

Nnewi
Godwin Izundu Nmezinwa Okpala
c/o Bishopscourt,
PO Box 2630, Uruagu-Nnewi, Anambra State,
Nigeria
Mobile (00234) 803 348 5741
E-mail nnewi@anglican-nig.org

Nsukka
Alloysius Agbo
PO Box 516, Nsukka, Enugu State, Nigeria
E-mail nsukka@anglican-nig.org

Oji River
Amos Amankechinelo Madu
PO Box 213, Oji River,
Enugu State, Nigeria
Tel (00234) (48) 882 219
Mobile (00234) 804 611 0117
E-mail ojiriver@anglican-nig.org

The Niger
(Bishop on)
Ken Okeke
PO Box 42, Onitsha, Anambra State,
Nigeria
Tel (00234) (46) 210 337
E-mail niger@anglican-nig.org or
kengoziokeke@yahoo.com

PROVINCE OF THE NIGER DELTA

Aba
(Archbishop)
Ugochuckwu U. Ezuoke
Bishopscourt, 70/72 St Michael's Road,
PO Box 212, Aba, Nigeria
Tel (00234) (82) 220 231
E-mail aba@anglican-nig.org

Aba Ngwa
North
Nathan C. Kanu
Bishopscourt, PO Box 43, Aba, Abia State
Tel (00234) 803 822 4623
E-mail odinathnfe@sbcglobal.net

Ahoada
Clement Nathan Ekpeye
Bishopscourt, St Paul's Cathedral, PO Box 4,
Ahoada,
Ahoada East L.G.A., Rivers State, Nigeria
Mobile (00234) 803 542 2847
E-mail ahoada@anglican-nig.org

Arochukwu-
Ohafia
(Missionary
diocese)
Johnson C. Onuoha,
Bishopscourt, PO Box 193, Arochukwu,
Abia State, Nigeria
Mobile (00234) 802 538 6407
E-mail: aroohafia@anglican-nig.org or
johnchiobishop@yahoo.com

Calabar
Tunde Adeleye
Bishopscourt, PO Box 74, Calabar,
Cross River State, Nigeria
Tel (00234) (98) 232 812
Mobile (00234) 803 337 3120
E-mail calabar@anglican-nig.org or
bishoptunde@yahoo.com

Etche
Okechukwu Precious Nwala
Bishopscourt, PO Box 89, Okehi,
Etche Rivers State
Mobile (00234) 807 525 2842
E-mail etchediocese@yahoo.com or
precious_model5@yahoo.com

Ikwerre
Blessing Enyindah
Bishopscourt, PO Box 14229, Port Harcourt,
Rivers State
Mobile (00234) 802 321 2824
E-mail blessingenyindah@yahoo.com

Ikwuano
(Missionary
diocese)
Chigozirim Onyegbule
Bishopscourt, PO Box 5, Oloko, Ikwuano,
Abia State, Nigeria
Mobile (00234) 803 085 9310
E-mail ikwuano@anglican-nig.org

Isiala Ngwa
Owen N. Azubuike
Bishopscourt, St George's Cathedral
Compound, Umuomainta Mbawsi P.M.B.,
Mbawsi, Abia State
Mobile (00234) 805 467 0528
E-mail bpowenazubuike@yahoo.com

Isiala Ngwa
South
Isaac Nwaobia
St Peter's Cathedral, PO Box 15,
Owerrinta, Abia State
Mobile (00234) 805 787 1100
E-mail bishopisaacnwaobia@priest.com

Isiukwuato
(Missionary
diocese)
Samuel C. Chukuka
Bishop's House, PO Box 350, Ovim
Abia State, Nigeria
Mobile (00234) 803 338 6221
E-mail isiukwuato@anglican-nig.org or
rootedword@yahoo.com

The Niger
Delta
Gabriel H Pepple
Bishopcourt, 4 Harley St, Old G.R.A./ Forces
Ave, Port Harcourt, Rivers State, Nigeria
Tel (00234) (84) 233308
E-mail nigerdelta@anglican-nig.org

Niger Delta
North
Ignatius Kattey
PO Box 53, Diobu, Port Harcourt,
Rivers State, Nigeria
Tel (00234) (84) 231 338
E-mail niger-delta-north@anglican-nig.org or
bishopicokattey@yahoo.com

Niger Delta
West
Adoluphus Amabebe
Bishopscourt, PO Box 10,
Yenagoa, Bayelsa, Nigeria
Tel (00234) (84) 490 010
E-mail niger-delta-west@anglican-nig.org

Ogoni
(Missionary
diocese)
Solomon S Gberegbara
Bishopscourt, PO Box 73, Bori-Ogoni,
Rivers State, Nigeria
Mobile (00234) 803 339 2545
E-mail ogoni@anglican-nig.org *or*
ogoniangdiocese@yahoo.com

Okrika
Tubokosemie Abere
Bishopscourt, PO Box 11, Okrika, Rivers State,
Nigeria
Tel (00234) (84) 575 003
E-mail dioceseofokrika@yahoo.com

Ukwa
Samuel Kelechi Eze
PO Box 20468, Aba, Nigeria
Mobile (00234) 803 789 2431
E-mail ukwa@anglican-nig.org

Umuahia
Ikechi N Nwosu
St Stephen's Cathedral Church Compound,
PO Box 96, Umuahia, Abia State, Nigeria
Tel (00234) (88) 220 311
E-mail umuahia@anglican-nig.org

Uyo
(Archbishop)
Isaac Orama
Bishopscourt, PO Box 70, Uyo,
Akwa Ibom State, Nigeria
Tel (00234) (85) 204142
E-mail uyo@anglican-nig.org

PROVINCE OF ONDO

Akoko
Gabriel Akinbiyi
PO Box 572, Ikare-Akoko,
Ondo State, Nigeria
Tel (00234) (50) 670 668
akoko@anglican.skannet.com.ng

Akure
Michael Ipinmoye
Bishopscourt, PO Box 1622, Akure, Nigeria
Tel (00234) (34) 241 572
fax as telephone
E-mail angdak@gannetcity.net

Ekiti
(Archbishop)
Samuel Adedayo Abe
Bishopscourt, PO Box 12,
Okesa Street, Ado-Ekiti, Nigeria
Tel (00234) (30) 250 305
Mobile (00234) 802 225 9389
E-mail ekiti@anglican.skannet.com.ng *or*
ekiti@anglican-nig.org

Ekiti-Oke
Isaac Olatunde Olubowale
Bishopscourt, Temidire St, P.M.B. 207, Usi-
Ekiti, Ekiti State, Nigeria
Mobile (00234) 803 600 9582
E-mail ekitioke@anglican-nig.org

Ekiti West
Samuel Oludare Oke
Bishop's Residence, 6 Ifaki Street,
PO Box 477, Ijero-Ekiti, Nigeria
Tel (00234) (30) 850 314
Mobile (00234) 803 429 2823

Kabba
Samuel O Olayanju
Bishopscourt, Obaro Way, PO Box 62, Kabba,
Kogi State, Nigeria
Tel (00234) (58) 300 633
Mobile (00234) 803 653 0180

Ondo
George L Lasebikan
Bishopscourt, College Road,
PO Box 265, Ondo, Nigeria
Tel (00234) (34) 610 718
Mobile (00234) 803 472 1813
E-mail ondo@anglican-nig.org *or*
angondo@skannet.com

Owo
James Adedayo Oladunjoye
Bishopscourt, PO Box 472,
Owo, Ondo State, Nigeria
Tel (00234) (51) 241 463
Mobile (00234) 803 475 3291
E-mail owo@anglican-nig.org

PROVINCE OF OWERRI

Egbu
Emmanuel Uchechukwu Iheagwam
All Saints' Cathedral, Diocese of Egbu, PO Box
1967, Owerri, Imo State, Nigeria
Tel (00234) (83) 231 797
Mobile (00234) 803 491 1090
E-mail egbu@anglican-nig.org

Ideato
Caleb A Maduoma
Bishopscourt, PO Box 2, Arondizuogu, Ideato
North L.G.A., Imo State, Nigeria
Mobile (00234) 803 745 4503
E-mail ideato@anglican-nig.org *or*
bpomacal@hotmail.com

Mbaise
Bright Joseph Egemasi Ogu
Bishopscourt, PO Box 10, Ife,
Ezinihitte Mbaise, Imo State, Nigeria
Tel (00234) (83) 441 483
Mobile (00234) 803 553 4762
E-mail mbaise@anglican-nig.org *or*
bjeogu@yahoo.com

Okigwe North
Godson Ukanwa
PO Box 156, Okigwe,
Imo State, Nigeria
Tel (00234) (42) 420 124
Mobile (00234) 804 507 5592
E-mail okigwenorth@anglican-nig.org

Okigwe South
David Onuoha
Bishopscourt, Ezeoke Nsu,
PO Box 235, Nsu, Ehime Mbano LGA, Imo
State, Nigeria
Mobile (00234) 803 745 4510
E-mail okigwe-south@anglican-nig.org *or*
okisouth@yahoo.com

Orlu
(Archbishop)
Bennett C I Okoro
Bishopscourt, PO Box 260,
Nkwerre, Imo State, Nigeria
Tel (00234) (82) 440 538
Mobile (00234) 803 671 1271

Owerri
Cyril Chukwunonyerem Okorocha
No. 1 Mission Crescent, PMB 1063,
Owerri, Imo State, Nigeria
Tel (00234) (83) 230 417
Mobile (00234) 803 338 9344
Fax (00234) (82) 440 183
E-mail owerri@anglican-nig.org *or*
adowe@phca.linkserve.com

PAPUA NEW GUINEA

Aipo Rongo
(Archbishop)
James Simon Ayong
PO Box 893, Mount Hagen,
Western Highlands Province,
Papua New Guinea
Tel (00675) 542 1131 *or* 3727
Fax (00675) 542 1181
E-mail acpngair@global.net.pg *or*
archbishopjayong@hotmail.com

(Suffragans)
Nathan Ingen
address, etc. as above

Denys Ririka
PO Box 1178, Goroka, Eastern Highlands
Province, Papua New Guinea

Dogura
Clyde Igara
PO Box 19, Dogura, MBP,
Papua New Guinea
Tel (00675) 641 1530
Fax (00675) 641 1129

New Guinea
Islands, The
Allan Migi
Bishop's House, PO Box 806,
Kimbe, Papua New Guinea
Tel (00675) 983 5120
fax as telephone
E-mail acpngngi@global.net.pg *or*
acpngngibishop@global.net.pg

Popondota
Joe Kopapa
Anglican Diocese of Popondota, PO Box 26,
Popondetta, Oro Province,
Papua New Guinea
Tel (00675) 329 7194
Fax (00675) 329 7476
E-mail acpngpop@online.net.pg

Port Moresby
Peter Ramsden
PO Box 6491, Boroko, NCD
Port Moresby, Papua New Guinea
Tel (00675) 323 2489
Fax (00675) 323 2493
E-mail acpngpom@global.net.pg *or*
psramsden.pomanglican@gmail.com

THE PHILIPPINES

Prime Bishop	Ignacio Capuyan Soliba PO Box 10321, Broadway Centrum 1112 Quezon City, Philippines *or* 275 E Rodriguez Sr Avenue 1102 Quezon City, Philippines Tel (0063) (2) 722 8478, 722 8481 *or* 722 9459 Fax (0063) (2) 721 1923 E-mail isoliba@hotmail.com
Central Philippines	Dixie C Taclobao 281 E. Rodriguez Sr. Avenue, 1102 Quezon City, Philippines Tel (0063) (2) 412 8561 Fax (0063) (2) 724 2143 E-mail central@i-next.net
North Central Philippines	Joel A Pachao 358 Magsaysay Avenue, Baguio City 2600, Philippines Tel (0063) (74) 443 7705 Fax (0063) (74) 442 2432 E-mail edncp@digitelone.com
Northern Luzon	Renato M Abibico Bulanao, 3800 Tabuk, Kalinga, Philippines Tel (0063) (74) 872 2295 Mobile (0063) 9921 687 1933 Fax (0063) (74) 872 2013
Northern Philippines	Edward Pacyaya Malecdan Diocesan Center, 2616 Bontoc, Mountain Province, Philippines Tel (0063) (74) 602 1026 *fax as telephone* E-mail ednpvic@hotmail.com
Santiago	Alexander A Wandag Sr Episcopal Diocese of Santiago, Divisoria, 3311 Santiago City, Isabela, Philippines Tel (0063) (78) 682 3756 Fax (0063) (78) 682 1256 E-mail alexwandageds@yahoo.com
Southern Philippines	Danilo Labacanacruz 186 Sinsuat Avenue, Rosario Heights, Cotabato City 9600, Philippines Tel (0063) (64) 421 2960 Fax (0063) (64) 421 1703 E-mail edsp_ecp@cotabato.mozcom.com

RWANDA

Butare	Nathan Gasatura BP 255, Butare, Rwanda Tel (00250) 530 504 *fax as telephone* E-mail rusodilo@yahoo.fr
Byumba	Onesphore Rwaje BP 17, Byumba, Rwanda Tel (00250) 64242 *fax as telephone* E-mail eer@rwanda1.com
Cyangugu	Geoffrey Rwubusisi PO Box 52, Cyangugu, Rwanda Tel (00250) 53 7878 *fax as telephone* E-mail bishoprwubusisi@yahoo.co.uk
Gahini	Alexis Bilindabagabo BP 22, Kigali, Rwanda Tel (00250) 567 422
Kibungo	Josias Sendegaya EER Kibungo Diocese, BP 719, Kibungo, Rwanda Tel (00250) 566 194 *fax as telephone* E-mail bpjosias@yahoo.fr
Kigali (Archbishop)	Emmanuel Musaba Kolini EER/DK, BP 61, Kigali, Rwanda Tel (00250) 573 213 *fax as telephone* E-mail ek@terracom.rw
Kigeme	Augustin Mvunabandi BP 67, Gikongoro, Rwanda Tel (00250) 535 086 *or* 088 *or* 087 E-mail dkigeme@rwanda1.com

Kivu	Augustin Ahimana BP 166 Gisenyi Tel (00250) 788 350 119
Shyira	John Rucyahana Kabango EER – Shyira Diocese, BP 26, Ruhengeri, Rwanda Tel (00250) 546 449 *fax as telephone* E-mail bpjohnr@rwanda1.com
Shyogwe	Jéred Karimba BP 27, Gitarama, Rwanda Tel (00250) 562 469 *fax as telephone* E-mail dsgwegit@yahoo.com

SOUTH EAST ASIA

Kuching	Bolly Anak Lapok Bishop's House, PO Box 347, 93704 Kuching, Sarawak, Malaysia Tel (0060) (82) 240 187 *or* 240 188 Fax (0060) (82) 426 488 E-mail bishopk@streamyx.com
Sabah	Albert Vun Cheong Fui PO Box 10811, 88809 Kota Kinabalu, Sabah, Malaysia Tel (0060) (88) 245 846 Fax (0060) (88) 245 942 E-mail dosabah@streamyx.com
Singapore (Archbishop)	John Chew Hiang Chea 4 Bishopsgate, Singapore 249970 Tel (0065) 6288 7585 Fax (0065) 6288 5574 E-mail bpoffice@anglican.org.sg
(Assistant)	Rennis Poniah St John's and St Margaret's Church, 30 Dover Avenue, Singapore 139790, Singapore Tel (0065) 6773 9415 Fax (0065) 6778 6624 E-mail rennis@sjsm.org.sg
West Malaysia	Ng Moon Hing No.16 Jalan Pudu Lama, 50200 Kuala Lumpur, Malaysia Tel (0060) (3) 2031 2728 Fax (0060) (3) 2031 3225 E-mail anglican@streamyx.com

SOUTHERN AFRICA

Angola (Missionary diocese)	Andre Soares Av Lenini, Travessa D Antonia, Saldanha N 134, CP 10 1498, Angola Tel (00244) (2) 395 792 Fax: (00244) (2) 396 794 E-mail anglicana@ebonet.net *or* bispo-Soares@hotmail.com
Cape Town (Archbishop)	Winston Hugh Njongonkulu Ndungane 16–20 Bishopscourt, Claremont 7708, South Africa Tel (0027) (21) 761 2531 Fax (0027) (21) 797 1298 *or* 761 4193 E-mail archpa@anglicanchurchsa.org.za
(Table Bay)	Garth Counsell PO Box 1932, Cape Town 8000, South Africa Tel (0027) (21) 465 1557 Fax (0027) (21) 465 1571 E-mail tablebay@ctdiocese.org.za
Christ the King	Peter John Lee PO Box 1653, Rosettenville 2130, South Africa Tel (0027) (11) 435 0097 Fax (0027) (11) 435 2868 E-mail dckpeter@corpdial.co.za
False Bay	Merwyn Edwin Castle PO Box 2804, Somerset West 7129 South Africa Tel (0027) (21) 852 5243 Fax (0027) (21) 852 9430 E-mail bishopm@falsebaydiocese.org.za
George	Donald Frederick Harker PO Box 227, George 6530, South Africa Tel (0027) (44) 873 5680 *fax as telephone* E-mail dharker@intekom.co.za *or* glynis@george.diocese.co.za

Grahamstown	Ebenezer St Mark Ntlali PO Box 181, Grahamstown 6140, South Africa Tel (0027) (46) 636 1996 Fax (0027) (46) 622 5231 E-mail bpgtn@intekom.co.za	(Suffragan)	Mazwi Ernest Tisani 348 General Beyers St, PO Box 16425, Pretoria North 0116, South Africa Tel (00264) (12) 546 6253 E-mail bishopmazwi@mweb.co.za
Highveld	David Hugh Bannerman PO Box 17462, Benoni West 1503, South Africa Tel (0027) (11) 422 2231 Fax (0027) (11) 420 1336 E-mail bishophveld@iafrica.com	Saldanha Bay	Raphael Bernard Viburt Hess PO Box 420, Malmesbury 7299, South Africa Tel (0027) (22) 487 3885 Fax (0027) (22) 487 3886 E-mail bishop@dioceseofsaldanhabay.org.za
Johannesburg	Brian Charles Germond PO Box 1131, Johannesburg 2000, South Africa Tel (0027) (11) 336 8724 Fax (0027) (11) 333 3053 E-mail bgermond@cpsajoburg.org.za	St Helena	John William Salt Bishopsholme, PO Box 62, St Helena, South Atlantic Ocean Tel (00290) 4471 Fax (00290) 4728 E-mail bishop@helanta.sh
Kimberley and Kuruman	Oswald Peter Patrick Swartz PO Box 45, Kimberley 8300, South Africa Tel (0027) (53) 833 2433 Fax (0027) (53) 831 2730 E-mail oppswartz@onetel.com	St Mark the Evangelist	Martin Andre Breytenbach PO Box 643, Polokwane 0700, South Africa Tel (0027) (15) 297 3297 Mobile (0027) 82 441 2568 Fax (0027) (15) 297 0408 E-mail martin@stmark.co.za
Lebombo	Dinis Salomâo Sengulane CP 120, Maputo, Mozambique Tel (00258) (1) 405 364 or 404 885 Fax (00258) (1) 401 093 E-mail bispo_sengulane@virconn.com	Swaziland	Meshack Boy Mabuza PO Box 118, Mbabane, Swaziland Tel (00268) 404 3624 Fax (00268) 404 6759 E-mail bishopmabuza@africaonline.co.sz
Lesotho	Adam Andrease Mallane Taaso PO Box 87, Maseru 100, Lesotho Tel (00266) (22) 311 974 Fax (00266) (22) 310 161 E-mail diocese@ilesotho.com	The Free State	Elistan Patrick Glover PO Box 411, Bloemfontein 9300, South Africa Tel (0027) (51) 447 6053 Fax (0027) (51) 447 5874 E-mail bishoppatrick@dsc.co.za
Matlosane	Stephen Molopi Diseko PO Box 11417, Klerksdorp, 2570 South Africa Tel (0027) (18) 462 5530 or 464 2260 Fax (0027) (18) 462 4939 E-mail diocesematlosane@telkomsa.net	Umzimvubu	Mlibo Mteteleli Ngewu PO Box 644, Kokstad 4700, South Africa Tel (0027) (39) 727 4117 *fax as telephone* E-mail mzimvubu@futurenet.co.za
Mpumalanga	Leslie Walker PO Box 4327, White River 1240, South Africa Tel (0027) (13) 751 1960 Fax (0027) (13) 751 3638 E-mail bishoples@telkomsa.net	Zululand	Dino Gabriel PO Box 147, Eshowe, Zululand, 3815 South Africa Tel (0027) (354) 742047 *fax as telephone* E-mail bishopdino@netactive.co.za
Mthatha	Sitembele Tobela Mzamane PO Box 25, Umtata, Transkei 5100, South Africa Tel (0027) (47) 532 4450 Fax (0027) (47) 532 4191 E-mail anglicbspmthatha@intekom.co.za		
Namibia	Nathaniel Ndxuma Nakwatumbah PO Box 57, Windhoek 9000, Namibia Tel (00264) (61) 238 920 Fax (00264) (61) 225 903 E-mail bishop@anglicanchurchnamibia.com		**SOUTHERN CONE OF AMERICA**
Natal	Rubin Phillip PO Box 47439, Greyville 4023, South Africa Tel (0027) (31) 309 2066 Fax (0027) (31) 308 9316 E-mail bishop@dionatal.org.za	Argentina (Presiding Bishop)	Gregory Venables Rioja 2995 (1636), Olivos, Provincia de Buenos Aires, Argentina Tel (0054) (11) 4342 4618 Fax (0054) (11) 4331 0234 E-mail bpgreg@ciudad.com.ar
(South)	Hummingfield Charles Nkosinathi Ndwandwe *address as above* Tel (0027) (33) 394 1560 E-mail bishopndwandwe@dionatal.org.za	Bolivia	Frank Lyons Iglesia Anglicana Episcopal de Bolivia, Casilla 848, Cochabamba, Bolivia Tel (00591) (4) 440 1168 *fax as telephone* E-mail BpFrank@sams-usa.org
(North-West)	Funginkosi Mbhele PO Box 123, Estcort 3310, South Africa Tel (0027) (36) 352 2893 Fax (0027) (36) 352 2810 E-mail bishopmbhele@dionatal.org.za	Chile	Héctor Zavala Muñoz Casilla 50675, Correo Central, Santiago, Chile Tel (0056) (2) 638 3009 or 639 1509 Fax (0056) (2) 639 4581 E-mail tzavala@iach.cl
Niassa	Mark van Koevering Diocese do Niassa, CP 264, Lichinga, Niassa, Mozambique Tel (00258) 712 0735 *fax as telephone* E-mail bishop.niassa@gmail.com	(Assistant)	Abelino Manuel Apeleo Casilla de Correo 26-D, Temuco, Chile Tel (0056) (45) 910 484 *fax as telephone* E-mail aapeleo@iach.cl
Port Elizabeth	Nceba Bethlehem Nopece PO Box 7109, Newton Park 6055, South Africa Tel (0027) (41) 365 1387 Fax (0027) (41) 365 2049 E-mail pebishop@iafrica.com	Northern Argentina	Gregory James Venables (Bishop of Argentina) *address etc as above*
Pretoria	Johannes T Seoka PO Box 1032, Pretoria, 0001 South Africa Tel (0027) (12) 322 2218 Fax (0027) (12) 322 9411 E-mail ptabish@cpsa.org.za	(Assistant)	Nicholas Drayson Casilla 19, CP 3636 Ingeniero Juárez, FCNGB Formosa, Argentina Tel (0054) (387) 431 1718 Fal (0054) (387) 431 2622 E-mail diana.epi@salnet.com.ar

Paraguay	Peter Bartlett Iglesia Anglicana de Paraguya, Casilla de Correo 1124, Asunción, Paraguay Tel (00595) (21) 200 933 Fax (00595) (21) 214 328 E-mail jellison@pla.net.py
Peru	Harold William Godfrey Calle Alcalá 336, Urb. la Castellana, Santiago de Surco, Lima 33, Peru Tel (0051) (1) 422 9160 Fax (0051) (1) 440 8540 E-mail diocesisperu@anglicanperu.org or wgodfrey@amauta.rcp.net.pe
Uruguay	Miguel Tamayo Casilla de Correos 6108, 11000 Montevideo, Uruguay Tel (00598) (2) 915 9627 Fax (00598) (2) 916 2519 E-mail mtamayo@netgate.com.uy
(Suffragan)	Gilberto Obdulio Porcal Martinez Reconquista 522, CC 6108, 11000 Montevideo, Uruguay Tel (00598) (2) 915 9627 Fax (00598) (2) 916 2519 E-mail anglican@netgate.com.uy

SUDAN

A number of new dioceses have been created in the Church of the Province of Sudan. At the time of going to press, some details were unavailable, and so this list is incomplete.

Akot	Isaac Dhieu Ater c/o CMS Office, PO Box 40360, Nairobi, Kenya
Bor	Nathaniel Garang Anyieth c/o NSCC, PO Box 52802, Nairobi, Kenya Tel (00254) (733) 855 521 or 855 675 E-mail ecs_dioceseofbor@yahoo.co.uk
(Assistant)	Ezekel Diing Malaangdit c/o NSPCC, PO Box 52802, Nairobi, Kenya
Cueibet	Reuben Maciir Makoi c/o CEAS, PO Box 40870, Nairobi, Kenya Fax (00254) (2) 570807 E-mail eapo@cms-africa.org
El-Obeid	Ismail Abudigan Gibreil Kawo PO Box 211, El Obeid, Sudan Mobile (00249) 9122 53459 E-mail ecsprovince@hotmail.com
Ezo	John Zawo c/o ECS Support Office, PO Box 7576, Kampala, Uganda Tel (00256) (41) 343 497 E-mail kereborojohn@yahoo.com
Ibba	Wilson Elisa Kamani c/o ECS, PO Box 7576, Kampala, Uganda Tel (00256) (41) 343 497 fax as telephone E-mail ecs_ibbadiocese@hotmail.com or ecs-kpa@africaonline.co.ug
Juba (Archbishop)	Daniel Deng Bul PO Box 604, Khartoum, Sudan Tel (00249) (811) 820 065 E-mail dioceseofjuba@yahoo.com
(Assistant)	Joseph Makor Atot c/o CMS, PO Box 40360, Nairobi, Kenya
Kadugli and Nuba Mountains	Andudu Adam Elnail PO Box 35, Kadugli, Sudan Tel (00249) (631) 822898 E-mail bishandudu@yahoo.com or kadudiocese@hotmail.com
Kajo-Keji	Anthony Poggo c/o ECS Support Office, PO Box 7576, Kampala, Uganda Tel (00254) (41) 343 497 E-mail bishopkk@gmail.com
Khartoum	Ezekiel Kondo PO Box 65, Omdurman, 35 Khartoum, Sudan Tel (00249) (187) 556931 E-mail ecs_bishop_Khartoum@kastanet.org

Lainya	Peter Amidi c/o ECS Support Office, PO Box 7576, Kampala, Uganda Tel (00256) (77) 658 753 fax as telephone E-mail petamidi@yahoo.com
Lui	Bullen A Dolli PO Box 60837, Nairobi, Kenya Tel (00254) (2) 720 037 or 720 056 Fax (00249) (2) 714 420 E-mail bishop@luidiocese.org or cms-nbi@maf.org.ke
Malakal	Hilary Garang Aweer PO Box 604, Khartoum, Sudan E-mail ecsprovince@hotmail.com
Maridi	Justin Badi Arama c/o ECS, PO Box 7576, Kampala, Uganda Tel (00256) (41) 343 497 fax as telephone E-mail ecsmaridi@hotmail.com
Mundri	Bismark Monday Avokaya c/o ECS, PO Box 7576, Kampala, Uganda Tel (00256) (41) 343 497 fax as telephone E-mail ecsmundri@yahoo.com
Pacong	Joseph Maker E-mail ecs.pacongdiocese@yahoo.com
Port Sudan	Yousif Abdalla Kuku PO Box 278, Port Sudan, Sudan Tel (00249) (311) 821 224 E-mail ecsprovince@hotmail.com
Rejaf	Michael Sokiri Lugör PO Box 110, Juba, Sudan Tel (00249) 1290 76288 E-mail rejafdioceseecs@yahoo.com
Renk	Joseph Garang Atem PO Box 1532, Khartoum North, Sudan Mobile (00249) 122 99275 fax as telephone E-mail ecs_renk@hotmail.com
Rokon	Francis Loyo PO Box 6702, Nairobi 00100 APO, Kenya Tel (00254) (2) 568 541 or 568 539 Fax (00254) (2) 560 864 E-mail bployo@yahoo.co.uk
Rumbek	Alapayo Manyang Kuctiel c/o CMS Nairobi, PO Box 56, Nakuro, Kenya Tel (00254) (37) 43186 E-mail kuctiel@yahoo.com
(Assistants)	Isaac Dhieu Ater c/o CMS. PO Box 40360, Nairobi, Kenya Micah Dawidi, PO Box 111, Juba, Sudan
Terekeka	Micah Dawidi c/o CMS Nairobi, PO Box 56, Nakuro, Kenya
Torit	Bernard Oringa Balmoi c/o ECS Support Office, PO Box 7576, Kampala, Uganda Tel (00256) (41) 343 497 E-mail ecs_bishop_torit@kastanet.org
Wau	Henry Cuir Riak c/o CMS Nairobi, PO Box 56, Nakuru, Kenya Tel (00254) (37) 43186 E-mail riakcuir@yahoo.com or wauvtc@yahoo.com
Yambio	Peter Munde Yacoub c/o ECS, PO Box 7576, Kampala, Uganda Tel (00256) (41) 343 497 Mobile (00256) 77 622367 fax as telephone E-mail yambio2002@yahoo.com or ecs-kpa@africaonline.co.ug
Yei	Hilary Luate Adeba PO Box 588, Arua, Uganda Tel (00256) (756) 561 175 E-mail hill_sherpherd@yahoo.com or 72wca@techserve.org
Yirol	Benjamin Mangar Mamur c/o St Matthew's Church, PO Box 39, Eldoret, Kenya E-mail mamurmangar@yahoo.com or cms-nbi@maf.or.ke

TANZANIA

Central Tanganyika — Godfrey Mdimi Mhogolo
Makay House, PO Box 15, Dodoma, Tanzania
Tel (00255) (26) 232 1714
Fax (00255) (26) 232 4518
E-mail bishop@dct-tz.org or
mhogolo@pnc.com.au

(Assistant) — Ainea Kusenha
address, tel and fax as above
E-mail ngombe2004@kicheko.com

Dar-es-Salaam (Archbishop) — Valentino Mokiwa
PO Box 25016, Ilala, Dar-es-Salaam, Tanzania
Tel (00255) (22) 286 4426
E-mail mokiwa_valentine@hotmail.com

Kagera — Aaron Kijanjali
PO Box 18, Ngara, Tanzania
Tel (00255) (28) 222 3624
Fax (00255) (28) 222 2518
E-mail act-kagera@africaonline.co.tz

Kiteto — Isaiah Chambala
PO Box 74, Kibaya, Tanzania
Tel (00255) (27) 255 2106
E-mail dkiteto@iwayafrica.com

Kondoa — Yohana Zakaria Mkavu
PO Box 7, Kondoa, Tanzania
Tel (00255) (26) 236 0312
Fax: (00255) (26) 236 0304 or 0324
E-mail d_kondoa@ do.ucc.co.tz

Lweru — Jackton Yeremiah Lugumira
PO Box 12, Muleba, Tanzania
Tel (00255) (713) 274 085
E-mail jlugumira2@juno.com

Mara — Hilkiah Deya Omindo Deya
PO Box 131, Musoma, Tanzania
Tel (00255) (28) 262 2376
Fax (00255) (28) 262 2414
E-mail actmara@juasun.net

Masasi — Patrick Mwachiko
Private Bag, PO Masasi, Mtwara Region, Tanzania
Tel (00255) (23) 251 0016
Fax (00255) (23) 251 0351
E-mail actmasasi@africaonline.co.tz

Morogoro — Dudley Mageni
PO Box 320, Morogoro, Tanzania
Tel (00255) (23) 260 4602
fax as telephone
E-mail act-morogoro@africaonline.co.tz

Mount Kilimanjaro — Simon Elilekia Makundi
PO Box 1057, Arusha, Tanzania
Tel (00255) (27) 254 8396
Fax (00255) (27) 254 4187
E-mail dmk@habari.co.tz

Mpwapwa — Jacob Chimeledya
PO Box 2, Mpwapwa, Tanzania
Tel (00255) (26) 232 0017 or 0825
Fax (00255) (26) 232 0063
E-mail dmp@do.ucc.co.tz

Newala — Oscar Mnunga
c/o Bishop of Masasi

Rift Valley — John Lupaa
PO Box 16, Manyoni, Tanzania
Tel (00255) (26) 254 0013
Fax (00255) (26) 250 3014
E-mail act-drv@maf.or.tz

Ruaha — Donald Leo Mtetemela
Box 1028, Iringa, Tanzania
Tel (00255) (26) 270 1211
Fax (00225) (26) 270 2479
E-mail ruaha@anglican.or.tz

Ruvuma — Maternus K Kapinga
PO Box 1357, Songea, Ruvuma, Tanzania
Tel (00255) (25) 260 0090
Fax (00255) (25) 260 2987
E-mail mkkapinga@yahoo.com

Shinyanga — Ngusa Charles Kija
PO Box 421, Shinyanga, Tanzania
Tel (00255) (28) 276 3584
E-mail ckngusa@yahoo.com

Southern Highlands — John Mwela
PO Box 198, Mbeya, Tanzania
Tel (00255) (25) 250 0216
E-mail dsh-dev@atma.co.tz

South West Tanganyika — vacant
Bishop's House, PO Box 32, Njombe, Tanzania
Tel (00255) (26) 278 2010
Fax (00255) (26) 278 2403
E-mail dswt@africaonline.co.tz

Tabora — Sadock Makaya
PO Box 1408, Tabora, Tanzania
Tel (00255) (26) 260 4124
Fax (00255) (26) 260 4899
E-mail dtdevtb@taboraonline.com or
smakaya1@yahoo.co.uk

Tanga — Philip D Baji
PO Box 35, Korogwe, Tanga, Tanzania
Tel (00255) (27) 264 0522
Fax (00255) (27) 264 0631
E-mail bajipp@anglican.or.tz

Victoria Nyanza — Boniface Kwangu
PO Box 278, Mwanza, Tanzania
Tel (00255) (28) 250 0627
Fax (00255) (28) 250 0676
E-mail revkahene1@yahoo.com

Western Tanganyika — Gerard E Mpango
PO Box 13, Kasulu, Tanzania
Tel (00255) (28) 281 0321
Fax (00255) (28) 281 0706
E-mail askofugm@yahoo.com

(Lake Zone, Kigoma) — Naftali Bikaka
PO Box 1378, Kigoma, Tanzania
Tel (00255) (28) 280 3407
E-mail bpwbikaka@yahoo.co.uk

(Southern Zone, Rukwa in Sumbawanga) — Mark Badeleya
PO Box 226, Sumbawanga, Tanzania
Tel (00255) (25) 280 0287
E-mail bpbadeleya@yahoo.co.uk

Zanzibar — vacant
PO Box 5, Mkunazini, Zanzibar, Tanzania
Tel (00255) (24) 223 5348
Fax (00255) (24) 223 6772
E-mail secactznz@zanlink.com

UGANDA

Ankole — George Tibeesigwa
PO Box 14, Mbarara, Ankole, Uganda
Tel (00256) (485) 20290
Mobile (00256) 772 542 164

Bukedi — Nicodemus Engwalas-Okille
PO Box 170, Tororo, Uganda
Mobile (00256) 772 542 164

Bunyoro-Kitara — Nathan Kyamanywa
PO Box 20, Hoima, Uganda
Tel (00256) (465) 40128
Mobile (00256) 772 648 232
E-mail bkdioces@infocom.co.ug

Busoga — Michael Kyomya
PO Box 1658, Jinja, Uganda
Mobile (00256) 752 649 102

Central Buganda — Jackson Matovu
PO Box 1200, Kinoni-Gomba, Mpigi, Uganda
Mobile (00256) 772 475 640
E-mail bishopmatovu@yahoo.com

Kampala (Archbishop) — Henry Luke Orombi
PO Box 335, Kampala, Uganda
Tel (00256) (414) 279 218
Mobile (00256) 772 450 178
Fax (00256) (414) 251 925
E-mail kdcou@africaonline.co.ug

(Assistant) — Zac Niringiye
PO Box 335, Kampala, Uganda
Tel (00256) (414) 290 231
Fax (00256) (414) 342 601

Karamoja — Joseph Abura
PO Box 44, Moroto, Uganda
Tel (00256) 782 658 502

Kigezi
George Katwesigye
PO Box 3, Kabale, Uganda
Tel (00256) (486) 22003
Mobile (00256) 772 446 954

Kinkizi
John Ntegyereize
PO Box 77, Karuhinda, Rukungiri, Uganda
Tel (00873) (761) 604794 or 604795
Fax (00873) (761) 604796 or 604797
Mobile (00256) 772 507 163

Kitgum
Benjamin Ojwang
PO Box 187, Kitgum, Uganda
Mobile (00256) 772 959 924
E-mail benojwang2004@yahoo.co.uk

Kumi
Thomas Edison Irigei
PO Box 18, Kumi, Uganda
Mobile (00256) 772 659 460
E-mail coukumidiocese@yahoo.com

Lango
John Charles Odurkami
PO Box 6, Lira, Uganda
Mobile (00256) 772 614 000
E-mail bishoplango@yahoo.com

Luwero
Evans Mukasa Kisekka
PO Box 125, Luwero, Uganda
Tel (00256) (41) 610 070 or 610 048
Fax (00256) (41) 610 132 or 610 070
Mobile (00256) 772 421 220
E-mail kiromas@yahoo.co.uk

Madi and West Nile
Joel Obetia
PO Box 370, Arua, Uganda
Mobile (00256) 752 625 414
E-mail jobetia@ucu.ac.ug

Masindi-Kitari
Stanley Ntagali
PO Box 515, Masindi, Uganda
Tel (00256) (41) 270 218
Fax (00256) (41) 251 925
E-mail bishopntagali@yahoo.com

Mbale
Samwiri Namakhetsa Khaemba Wabulakha
Bishop's House, PO Box 473, Mbale, Uganda
Tel (00256) (45) 33533
Mobile (00256) 772 512 051
E-mail wabulakhasa@yahoo.com

Mityana
Stephen Samuel Kaziimba
PO Box 102, Mityana, Uganda
Tel (00256) (46) 2017
E-mail mtndiocese@hotmail.com

Muhabura
Cranmer Mugisha
Church of Uganda, PO Box 22, Kisoro, Uganda
Tel (00256) (486) 30014 or 30058
Fax (00256) (486) 30059
Mobile (00256) 712 195 891

Mukono
Elia Paul Luzinda
PO Box 39, Mukono, Uganda
Tel (00256) (41) 290 229
Mobile (00256) 772 603 348
E-mail mukodise@utlonline.co.ug

Namirembe
Samuel Balagadde Ssekkadde
PO Box 14297, Kampala, Uganda
Tel (00256) (41) 271682 or 244347
Mobile (00256) 772 500 494
E-mail namid@infocom.co.ug

Nebbi
Alphonse Watho-kudi
PO Box 27, Nebbi, Uganda
Mobile (00256) 772 650 032
E-mail bpalphonse@ekk.org

North Ankole
John Muhanguzi
c/o PO Box 14, Rushere Mbarara, Ankole, Uganda
Mobile (00256) 772 369 947
E-mail northankole@gmail.com

North Karamoja
James Nasak
PO Box 26, Kotido, Uganda
Mobile (00256) 772 660 228

North Kigezi
Edward Muhima
PO Box 23, Rukungiri, Uganda
Tel (00256) (486) 42433
Mobile (00256) 772 709 387
E-mail northkigezi@infocom.co.ug

North Mbale
Daniel Gimadu
PO Box 1837, Mbale, Uganda
Fax (00256) (41) 254 576
E-mail northmbalediocese@yahoo.com or petgim2000@yahoo.com

Northern Uganda
Nelson Onono-Onweng
PO Box 232, Gulu, Uganda
Mobile (00256) 772 838 193
E-mail ononobp@yahoo.co.uk

Ruwenzori
Benezeri Kisembo
PO Box 37, Fort Portal, Uganda
Mobile (00256) 772 470 671
E-mail bishop@biznas.com

Sebei
Augusto Arapyona Salimo
PO Box 23, Kapchorwa, Uganda
Tel (00256) (45) 51072 or 51008
Mobile (00256) 772 550 520
E-Mail augustinesalimo@yahoo.co.uk

Soroti
Charles Bernard Obaikol-Ebitu
PO Box 107, Soroti, Uganda
Tel (00256) (45) 61795
Mobile (00256) 772 557 909
E-mail couteddo@infocom.co.ug

South Ruwenzori
Jackson T Nzerebende
PO Box 42, Kasese, Uganda
Mobile (00256) 772 713 736
Fax (00256) (483) 444450
E-mail bpbende@yahoo.com

West Ankole
Yonah Katoneene
PO Box 140, Bushenyi, Uganda
Tel (00256) 752 377 193
E-mail wad@westankolediocese.org

West Buganda
Samuel Kefa Kamya
PO Box 242, Masaka, Uganda
Mobile (00256) 772 413 400
E-mail wesbug@infocom.co.ug

UNITED STATES OF AMERICA

The roman numerals indicate to which of the nine provinces of ECUSA the diocese belongs

Presiding Bishop
Katharine Jefferts Schori
Episcopal Church Center,
815 Second Avenue,
New York, NY 10017, USA
Tel (001) (212) 716 6000
E-mail pboffice@episcopalchurch.org

(Office of Pastoral Development)
Thomas Ferguson
8100 Three Chopt Road, Suite 102,
Richmond, VA 23229, USA
Tel (001) (804) 282 6007
Fax (001) (804) 282 6008
E-mail cmatthews@episcopalchurch.org

(Bishop Suffragan for Chaplaincies and Bishop in Charge of Micronesia)
James B Magness
111 Maryland Avenue NE
203 Washington DC 20002
Tel (001) (2020) 459 9998
E-mail jmagness@episcopalchurch.org

Alabama (IV)
Henry Nutt Parsley
521 North 20th Street, Birmingham, AL 35203–2611, USA
Tel (001) (205) 715 2060
Fax (001) (205) 715 2066
E-mail Hparsley@dioala.org

(Suffragan)
John McKee Sloan
address etc as above

Alaska (VIII)
Mark Lattime
1205 Denali Way, Fairbanks, AK 99701–4137, USA
Tel (001) (907) 452 3040
Fax (001) (907) 456 6552
E-mail mlattime@gci.net

Albany (II)
William Howard Love
68 South Swan Street, Albany, NY 12210, USA
Tel (001) (518) 465 4737
Fax (001) (518) 436 1182
E-mail *via* www.albanyepiscopaldiocese.org

Arizona (VIII)	Kirk Stevan Smith 114 West Roosevelt Street, Phoenix, AZ 85003–1406, USA Tel (001) (602) 254 0976 Fax (001) (602) 495 6603 Email bishop@azdiocese.org
Arkansas (VII)	Larry R Benfield Cathedral House, PO Box 164668, Little Rock, AR 72216–4668, USA Tel (001) (501) 372 2168 Fax (001) (501) 372 2147 E-mail bishopbenfield@mac.com
Atlanta (IV)	John Neil Alexander 2744 Peachtree Road NW, Atlanta, GA 30363–0701, USA Tel (001) (404) 601 5320 Fax (001) (404) 601 5330 E-mail bishop@episcopalatlanta.org
(Assistant)	Keith Bernard Whitmore E-mail bishopkeith@episcopalatlanta.org
Bethlehem (III)	Paul Victor Marshall 333 Wyandotte Street, Bethlehem, PA 18015–1527, USA Tel (001) (610) 691 5655 or 691 5656 Fax (001) (610) 691 1682 E-mail bpoffice@diobeth.org
(Assistant)	John P Croneberger address, etc. as above E-mail bishopjpc@epix.net
California (VIII)	Marc Handley Andrus 1055 Taylor Street, San Francisco, CA 94108, USA Tel (001) (415) 673 5015 Fax (001) (415) 673 9268 E-mail bishopmarc@diocal.org
Central Ecuador (IX)	Luis Fernando Ruíz Ofcinas Diocesanas, Francico Sarmiento N 39–54 Portete, sector el Batán, Quito, Ecuador Tel (002) 254 1735 Fax (002) 227 1627 E-mail obisporuiz@gmail.com
Central Florida (IV)	John Wadsworth Howe Diocesan Office, 1017 E Robinson Street, Orlando, FL 32801–2023, USA Tel (001) (407) 423 3567 Fax (001) (407) 872 0006 E-mail jhowe@cfdiocese.net
Central Gulf Coast (IV)	Philip Menzie Duncan II 201 Mo Baylen (BX13330), Pensacola, FL 32591–3330, USA Tel (001) (850) 434 7337 Fax (001) (850) 434 8577 E-mail bishopduncan@diocgc.org
Central New York (II)	Gladstone Bailey 'Skip' Adams 310 Montgomery Street, Suite 200, Syracuse, NY 13202–2093, USA Tel (001) (315) 474 6596 Fax (001) (315) 478 1632 E-mail kmcdaniel@cny.anglican.org
Central Pennsylvania (III)	Nathan Dwight Baxter Box 11937, Harrisburg, PA 17108–1937, USA Tel (001) (717) 236 5959 Fax (001) (717) 236 6448 E-mail via www.diocesecpa.org
Chicago (V)	Jeffrey Dean Lee 65 East Huron Street, Chicago, IL 60611, USA Tel (001) (312) 751 4200 or 751 4217 E-mail bishop@episcopalchicago.org
(Assistant)	Victor Alfonso Scantlebury address and fax as above Tel (001) (312) 751 4216 E-mail vscantlebury@episcopalchicago.org
Colombia (IX)	Francisco Jose Duque-Gómez Centro Diocesano, Cra 6 No 49–85 Piso 2, Bogotá DC, Colombia Tel (0057) (1) 288 3187 or 288 3167 Fax (0057) (1) 288 3248 E-mail iec@iglesiaepiscopal.org.co
Colorado (VI)	Robert John O'Neill 1300 Washington Street, Denver, CO 80203–2008, USA Tel (001) (303) 837 1173 Fax (001) (303) 837 1311 E-mail bishoponeill@coloradodiocese.org
Connecticut (I)	Ian T Douglas 1335 Asylum Avenue, Hartford, CT 06105–2295, USA Tel (001) (860) 233 4481 E-mail itdouglas@ctdiocese.org
(Suffragans)	James Elliott Curry address etc as above E-mail jcurry@ctdiocese.org
	Laura Ahrens address etc as above E-mail lahrens@ctdiocese.org
Dallas (VII)	James Monte Stanton 1630 North Garrett Street, Dallas, TX 75206, USA Tel (001) (214) 826 8310 Fax (001) (214) 826 5968 E-mail jmsdallas@dod.org
(Suffragan)	Paul E Lambert address etc as above E-mail plambert@episcopal-dallas.org
Delaware (III)	Wayne Parker Wright 2020 Tatnall Street, Wilmington, DE 19802, USA Tel (001) (302) 656 5441 Fax (001) (302) 656 7342 E-mail bishop@dioceseofdelaware.net
Dominican Republic (IX)	Julio Cesar Holguin Apartado 764, Calle Santiago No 114, Gazcue, DR 764, Dominican Republic Tel (001) (809) 686 6014 Fax (001) (809) 686 6364 E-mail iglepidom@verizon.net.do
East Carolina (IV)	Clifton Daniel Box 1336, Kinston, NC 27803, USA Tel (001) (252) 522 0885 Fax (001) (252) 523 5272 E-mail cdaniel@diocese-eastcarolina.org
(Suffragan)	Santosh Marray address etc as above E-mail smarray@diocese-eastcarolina.org
East Tennessee (IV)	George Dibrell Young III 401 Cumberland Avenue, Knoxville, TN 37902–2302, USA Tel (001) (865) 966 2110 Fax (001) (865) 966 2535 E-mail gyoung@etdiocese.net
Eastern Michigan (V)	Steven Todd Ousley Diocesan Office, 924 N Niagara Street, Saginaw, MI 48602, USA Tel (001) (989) 752 6020 Fax (001) (989) 752 6120 E-mail tousely@eastmich.org
Eastern Oregon (VIII)	Bavi Edna 'Nedi' Rivera PO Box 1548, The Dalles, OR 97058, USA Tel (001) (541) 298 4477 Fax (001) (541) 296 0939 E-mail nrivera@episdioeo.org
Easton (III)	James Joseph Shand 314 North St, Easton, MD 21601–3684, USA Tel (001) (410) 822 1919 E-mail bishopshand@dioceseofeaston.org
Eau Claire (V)	Edwin M Leidel 510 South Farwell Street, Eau Claire, WI 54701, USA Tel (001) (715) 835 3331 Fax (001) (715) 835 9212 E-mail edleidel@anglicancoach.com
El Camino Real (VIII)	Mary Gray-Reeves PO Box 1903, Monterey, CA 93942, USA Tel (001) (831) 394 4466 Fax (001) (831) 394 7133 E-mail bishopmary@edecr.org

Europe, Convocation of American Churches in (VII)   Pierre Welté Whalon
American Cathedral of the Holy Trinity,
23 Avenue George V, 75008 Paris, France
Tel (0033) (1) 53 23 84 06
Fax (0033) (1) 49 52 96 85
E-mail bishop@tec-europe.org

Florida (IV)   Samuel Johnson Howard
325 Market Street, Jacksonville,
FL 32202–2796, USA
Tel (001) (904) 356 1328
Fax (001) (904) 355 1934
E-mail jhoward@diocesefl.org

Fond du Lac (V)   Russell Edward Jacobus
1051 N. Lynndale Dr., Suite 1B, Appleton, WI
54914, USA
Tel (001) (920) 830 8866
Fax (001) (920) 830 8761
E-mail rjacobus@diofdl.org

Fort Worth (VII)   Jack Leo Iker
2900 Alemeda Street, Fort Worth, TX 76116,
USA
Tel (001) (817) 244 2885
Fax (001) (817) 244 3363
E-mail jliker@fwepiscopal.org

Georgia (IV)   Scott Anson Benhase
611 East Bay Street, Savannah, GA
31401–1296, USA
Tel (001) (912) 236 4279
Fax (001) (912) 236 2007
E-mail bishop@gaepiscopal.org

Haiti (II)   Jean Zache Duracin
Eglise Episcopale d'Haiti,
BP 1309, Port-au-Prince, Haiti
Tel (00509) 257 1624
Fax (00509) 257 3412
E-mail epihaiti@hotmail.com

Hawaii (VIII)   Robert LeRoy Fitzpatrick
Diocesan Office, 229 Queen Emma Square,
Honolulu, HI 96813–2304, USA
Tel (001) (808) 536 7776
Fax (001) (808) 538 7194
E-mail rlfitzpatrick@episcopalhawaii.org

Honduras (IX)   Lloyd Emmanuel Allen
Colonia Trejo, 23 Ave, 21 Calle Colonia, San
Pedro Sula, Honduras, Central America
Tel (00504) 566 6155 or 556 6268
Fax (00504) 556 6467
E-mail obispoallen@yahoo.com

Idaho (VIII)   Brian James Thom
1858 W. Judith Lane, Boise, ID 83705, USA
Tel (001) (208) 345 4440
Fax (001) (208) 345 9735
E-mail bthom@idahodiocese.org

Indianapolis (V)   Catherine Elizabeth Maples
Waynick
1100 West 42nd Street,
Indianapolis, IN 46208, USA
Tel (001) (317) 926 5454
Fax (001) (317) 926 5456
E-mail bishop@indydio.org

Iowa (VI)   Alan Scarfe
225 37th Street, Des Moines,
IA 50312–4399, USA
Tel (001) (515) 277 6165
Fax (001) (515) 277 0273
E-mail Ascarfe@iowaepiscopal.org

Kansas (VII)   Dean Elliott Wolfe
Bethany Place, 833–35 Polk Street,
Topeka, KS 66612, USA
Tel (001) (785) 235 9255
Fax (001) (785) 235 2449
E-mail dwolfe@episcopal-ks.org

Kentucky (IV)   Terry Allen
425 South Second Street,
Louisville, KY 40202–1417, USA
Tel (001) (502) 584 7148
Fax (001) (502) 587 8123
E-mail bishopwhite@episcopalky.org

Lexington (IV)   *Vacant*
PO Box 610, Lexington, KY, 40586, USA
Tel (001) (859) 252 6527
Fax (001) (859) 231 9077
E-mail *via website* www.diolex.org

Litoral Diocese of Ecuador (IX)   Alfredo Ulloa Morante España
Box 0901–5250,
Amarilis Fuentes entre V Trujillo,
y La 'D', Guayaquil, Ecuador
Tel (00593) (4) 443 050
Fax (00593) (4) 443 088
E-mail bishopmorante@hotmail.com *or*
iedl@gu.pro.ec

Long Island (II)   Laurence C Provenzano
36 Cathedral Avenue,
Garden City, NY 11530, USA
Tel (001) (516) 248 4800
Fax (001) (516) 248 1616
E-mail lprovenzano@dioceseli.org

Los Angeles (VIII)   Joseph Jon Bruno
Box 512164, Los Angeles, CA 90051–0164,
USA
Tel (001) (213) 482 2040 ext 236
Fax (001) (213) 482 5304
E-mail bishop@ladiocese.org

(Suffragans)   Diane M Jardine Bruce
address etc as above
E-mail djbsuffragan@ladiocese.org

Mary Douglas Glasspool
address etc as above
E-mail dmdgsuffragan@ladiocese.org

Louisiana (IV)   Morris K Thompson
1PO Box 5026 Baton Rouge,
LA 70821–5026
Tel (001) (504) 895 6634 *or*
(001) (225) 706 6634
E-mail mthompson@edola.org

Maine (I)   Stephen Taylor Lane
Loring House, 143 State Street,
Portland, ME 04101, USA
Tel (001) (207) 772 1953
E-mail slane@episcopalmaine.org

Maryland (III)   Eugene Taylor Sutton
4 East University Parkway,
Baltimore, MD 21218–2437, USA
Tel (001) (800) 443 1399 *or* (410) 467 1399
Fax (001) (410) 554 6387
E-mail esutton@ang-md.org

(Assistant)   Joe Goodwin Burnett
address etc as above
E-mail jburnett@ang-md.org

Massachusetts (I)   Marvil Thomas Shaw
Society of St John the Evangelist,
138 Tremont St, Boston, MA 02111, USA
Tel (001) (617) 482 5800
E-mail jdrameau@diomass.org

(Suffragans)   Roy Frederick Cederholm
address etc as above
E-mail dianep@diomass.org

Gayle Elizabeth Harris
address etc as above
E-mail SHP@diomass.org

Michigan (V)   Wendell Nathaniel Gibbs
4800 Woodward Avenue,
Detroit, MI 48201, USA
Tel (001) (313) 832 4435
Fax (001) (313) 831 2155
E-mail wgibbs@edomi.org

Milwaukee (V)   Steven Andrew Miller
804 East Juneau Street,
Milwaukee, WI 53202, USA
Tel (001) (414) 272 3028
Fax (001) (414) 272 7790
E-mail bishop11@diomil.org

Minnesota (VI)   Brian N Prior
1730 Clifton Place, Suite 201,
Minneapolis, MN 55403, USA
Tel (001) (612) 871 5311
Fax (001) (612) 871 0552
E-mail episcopal.centre@episcopalmn.org

Mississippi (IV)	Duncan Montgomery Gray III PO Box 23107, Jackson, MS 39225–3107, USA Tel (001) (601) 948 5954 Fax (001) (601) 354 3401 E-mail pjones@dioms.org	North Dakota (VI)	Michael Gene Smith 3600 25th St S, Fargo, ND 58104–6861, USA Tel (001) (701) 235 6688 Fax (001) (701) 232 3077 E-mail BpNodak@aol.com
Missouri (V)	George Wayne Smith 1210 Locust Street, St Louis, MO 63103, USA Tel (001) (314) 231 1220 Fax (001) (314) 231 3373 E-mail bishop@diocesemo.org	Northern California (VIII)	Barry Leigh Beisner 350 University Avenue, Suite 280, Sacramento, CA 95825, USA Tel (001) (916) 442 6918 Fax (001) (916) 442 6927 E-mail barry@norcalepiscopal.org
Montana (VI)	Charles Franklin Brookhart, Jr 515 North Park Avenue, Helena, MT 59601, USA Tel (001) (406) 422 2230 Fax (001) (406) 442 2238 E-mail cfbmt@qwestoffice.net	Northern Indiana (V)	Edward Stuart Little II 117 North Lafayette Boulevard, South Bend, IN 46601, USA Tel (001) (574) 233 6489 Fax (001) (574) 287 7914 E-mail bishop@ednin.org
Navajoland Area Mission (VIII)	David Earle Bailey PO Box 720, Farmington, NM 87499–0720, USA Tel (001) (505) 327 7549 Fax (001) (505) 327 6904 E-mail dbaileyecn@cox.net	Northern Michigan (V)	Rayford J Ray 131 East Ridge Street, Marquette, MI 49855, USA Tel (001) (906) 228 7160 Fax (001) (906) 228 7171 E-mail diocese@upepiscopal.org
Nebraska (VIII)	*Vacant* 109 North 18th Street, Omaha, NE 68102–4903, USA Tel (001) (402) 341 5373 Fax (001) (402) 341 8683 E-mail kbaxley@episcopal-ne.org	Northwest Texas (VII)	James Scott Mayer The Hulsey Episcopal Church Center, 1802 Broadway, Lubbock, TX 79401, USA Tel (001) (806) 763 1370 Fax (001) (804) 472 0641 E-mail diocese@nwt.org
Nevada (VIII)	Dan Thomas Edwards 6135 Harrison Drive, Suite 236, Las Vegas, NV 89120–4076, USA Tel (001) (702) 737 9190 Fax (001) (702) 737 6488 E-mail bishop@nvdiocese.org	Northwestern Pennsylvania (III)	Sean W Rowe 145 West 6th Street, Erie, PA 16501, USA Tel (001) (814) 456 4203 *or* (800) 643 2351 Fax (001) (814) 454 8703 E-mail seanrowe@dionwpa.org
New Hampshire (I)	*Vacant* 63 Green Street, Concord, NH 03301, USA Tel (001) (603) 224 1914 Fax (001) (603) 225 7884 E-mail info@nhepiscopal.org	Ohio (V)	Mark Hollingsworth Jr. 2230 Euclid Avenue, Cleveland, OH 44115–2499, USA Tel (001) (216) 771 4815 Fax (001) (216) 623 0735 E-mail mh@dohio.org
		(Assisting)	David C Bowman Wiliam D Persell *address etc as above*
New Jersey (II)	George Edward Councell 808 West State Street, Trenton, NJ 08618, USA Tel (001) (609) 394 5281 Fax (001) (609) 394 9546 E-mail gcouncell@newjersey.anglican.org	Oklahoma (VII)	Edward Joseph Konieczny 924 North Robinson, Oklahoma City, OK 73102, USA Tel (001) (405) 232 4820 Fax (001) (405) 232 4912 E-mail bishoped@epiok.org
New York (II)	Mark Sean Sisk Synod House, 1047 Amsterdam Avenue, New York, NY 10025, USA Tel (001) (212) 316 7400 Fax (001) (212) 316 7405 E-mail *via website* www.dioceseny.org	Olympia (VIII)	Gregory H Rickel PO Box 12126, Seattle, WA 98102, USA Tel (001) (206) 325 4200 Fax (001) (206) 325 4631 E-mail grickel@ecww.org
(Suffragan)	Catherine Scimeca Roskam Region Two Office, 55 Cedar St, Dobbs Ferry, NY 10522, USA Tel (001) 914 693 3848 Fax (001) 914 693 0407 E-mail bproskam@dioceseny.org	Oregon (VIII)	Michael Hanley 11800 S.W. Military Lane, Portland, OR 97219, USA Tel (001) (503) 636 5613 Fax (001) (503) 636 5616 E-mail bishop@episcopaldioceseoregon.org
Newark (II)	Mark Beckwith 31 Mulberry Street, Newark, NJ 07102, USA Tel (001) (973) 622 4306 Fax (001) (973) 622 3503 E-mail mbeckwith@dioceseofnewark.org	(Assistant)	Sanford ('Sandy') Hampton William D Persell
		Pennsylvania (III)	Charles Ellesworth Bennison 240 South Fourth Street, Philadelphia, PA 19106, USA Tel (001) (215) 627 6434 ext 112 *or* 131 Fax (001) (215) 627 7750 E-mail charlesb@diopa.org
North Carolina (IV)	Michael Bruce Curry 200 West Morgan St., Suite 300, Raleigh, NC 27601, USA Tel (001) (919) 834 7474 Fax (001) (919) 834 7546 E-mail michael.curry@episdionc.org	Pittsburgh (III)	Kenneth L Price 4099 William Penn Hwy, suite 502, Monroeville, PA 151416 Pittsburgh, PA 15222–2467, USA Tel (001) (412) 281 6131 Fax (001) (412) 471 5591 E-mail info@episcopall.org
(Assistant)	William B Gregg 115 West 7th St, Charlotte, NC 2802 Tel (001) (740) 332 7746 E-mail william.gregg@episdionic.org		
(Assisting)	Alfred 'Chip' Marble 1901 W Market St, Greensboro NC 27403 Tel (001) (273) 5700 E-mail chip.marble@episdionic.org	Puerto Rico	David Andres Alvarez PO Box 902, St Just, PR 00978, Puerto Rico Tel (001) (787) 761 9800 Fax (001) (787) 761 0320 E-mail david@coqui.net

Quincy (V)	Juan Alberto Morale 3601 N North Street, Peoria, IL 61604–1599, USA Tel (001) (309) 688 8221 Fax (001) (309) 688 8229 *or* 692 2421 E-mail bishop@dioceseofquincy.org	Spokane (VIII)	James Edward Waggoner 245 East 13th Avenue, Spokane, WA 99202–1114, USA Tel (001) (509) 624 3191 Fax (001) (509) 747 0049 E-mail jimw@spokanediocese.org
(Assistant)	Wesley L Nolden *address, etc. as above* E-mail nolden01@msn.com	Springfield (VIII)	Daniel H Martins 821 South 2nd Street, Springfield, IL 62704–2694, USA Tel (001) (217) 525 1876
Rhode Island (I)	Geralyn Wolf 275 North Main Street, Providence, RI 02903–1298, USA Tel (001) (401) 274 4500 Fax (001) (401) 331 9430 E-mail bishop@episcopalri.org		Fax (001) (217) 525 1877 E-mail diocese@episcopalspringfield.org *or* phbxebs@midwest.net
		Taiwan (VIII)	David J H Lai Hangzhoue South Rd, Taipei City 105, Lane no. 7, Taiwan, Republic of China
Rio Grande (VII)	Michael Louis Vono 4304 Carlisle Boulevard North East, Albuquerque, NM 87107–4811, USA Tel (001) (505) 881 0636 Fax (001) (505) 883 9048 E-mail bpmichael@dioceserg.org		Tel (00886) (2) 2341 1265 Fax (00886) (2) 2396 2014 E-mail skh.tpe@msa.hinet.net
		Tennessee (IV)	John Crawford Bauerschmidt 50 Vantage Way, Suite 107, Nashville, TN 37228–1504, USA
Rochester (II)	Prince G Singh 935 East Avenue, Rochester, NY 14607, USA Tel (001) (585) 473 2977 E-mail prince@episcopaldioceseofrochester.org		Tel (001) (615) 251 3322 Fax (001) (615) 251 8010 E-mail info@episcopaldiocese-tn.org
San Diego (VIII)	James Robert Mathes 2728 Sixth Avenue, San Diego, CA 92103–6397, USA Tel (001) (619) 291 5947 Fax (001) (619) 291 8362 E-mail bishopmathes@edsd.org	Texas (VII)	Charles Andrew Doyle 1225 Texas Ave, Houston, TX 77002, USA Tel (001) (713) 353 2100 Fax (001) (713) 520 5723 E-mail adoyle@epicenter.org
San Joaquin (VIII)	Chester L Tatton 4159 East Dakota Avenue, Fresno, CA 93726, USA Tel (001) (559) 576 0104 Fax (001) (559) 576 0114 E-mail bishop@diosanjoaquin.org	(Suffragan)	Dena A Harrison *address etc as above* E-mail dharrison@episcenter.org
		Upper South Carolina (IV)	W Andrew Waldo 1115 Marion Street, Columbia, SC 29201, USA Tel (001) (803) 771 7800 Fax (001) (803) 799 5119 E-mail bishopwaldo@edusc.org
South Carolina (IV)	Edward Lloyd Salmon Box 20127, Charleston, SC 29413–0127, USA Tel (001) (843) 722 4075 Fax (001) (843) 723 7628 E-mail elsalmon@dioceseofsc.org	Utah (VIII)	Scott B Hayashi 80 South 300 East Street, PO Box 3090, Salt Lake City, UT 84110–3090, USA Tel (001) (801) 322 4131 Fax (001) (801) 322 5096 E-mail shayashi@episcopal-ut.org
South Dakota (VI)	John Thomas Tarrant 500 South Main Street, Sioux Falls, SD 57104–6814, USA Tel (001) (605) 338 9751 Fax (001) (605) 336 6243 E-mail bishope.diocese@midconetwork.com	Venezuela (IX)	Orlando Guerrero Torres Apartado 49–143, Avenida Caroni 100, Colinas de Bello Monte, Caracas 1042 A, Venezuela Tel (0058) (212) 753 0723 Fax (0058) (212) 751 3180 E-mail obispoguerrero@iglesianglicanavzla.org
Southeast Florida (IV)	Leopold Frade 525 North East 15th Street, Miami, FL 33132, USA Tel (001) (305) 373 0881 Fax (001) (305) 375 8054 E-mail bishopfrade@aol.com	Vermont (I)	Thomas Clark Ely Diocesan House, 5 Rock Point Road, Burlington, VT 05401–2735, USA Tel (001) (802) 863 3431 Fax (001) (802) 860 1562 E-mail tely@dioceseofvermont.org
Southern Ohio (V)	Thomas Edward Breidenthal 412 Sycamore Street, Cincinnati, OH 45202–4179, USA Tel (001) (513) 421 0311 Fax (001) (513) 421 0315 E-mail breidenthal@diosohio.org	Virgin Islands (II)	Edward Ambrose Gumbs PO Box 7488, St Thomas, VI 00801, USA Tel (001) (340) 776 1797 Fax (001) (809) 777 8485 E-mail bpambrosegumbs@yahoo.com
Southern Virginia (III)	Herman 'Holly' Hollerith 600 Talbot Hall Road, Norfolk, VA 23505–4361, USA Tel (001) (757) 423 8287 Fax (001) (757) 440 5354 E-mail 600@diosova.org	Virginia (III)	Shannon Sherwood Johnston 110 West Franklin Street, Richmond, VA 23220, USA Tel (001) (804) 643 8451 Fax (001) (804) 644 6928 E-mail sjohnston@thediocese.net
Southwest Florida (IV)	Dabney T Smith 7313 Merchant Ct, Sarasota, FL 34240–8437, USA Tel (001) (941) 556 0315 Fax (001) (941) 556 0321 E-mail dsmith@episcopalswfla.org	(Suffragan)	David Colin Jones Northern Virginia Office, Goodwin House, 4800 Fillmore Avenue, Alexandria, VA 22311, USA Tel (001) (703) 824 1325 Fax (001) (703) 824 1348 E-mail djones@thediocese.net
Southwestern Virginia (III)	*Vacant* PO Box 2279, Roanoke, VA 24009–2279, USA Tel (001) (540) 342 6797 Fax (001) (540) 343 9114 E-mail info@dioswva.org	Washington (III)	John Bryson Chane Episcopal Church House, Mount St Alban, Washington, DC 20016, USA Tel (001) (202) 537 6555 Tel (001) (202) 364 6605 E-mail jchane@edow.org

West Missouri (VII)
Martin S Field
PO Box 413227, Kansas City,
MO 64141–3227, USA
Tel (001) (816) 471 6161
Fax (001) (816) 471 0379
E-mail bishopfield@episwtn.org

West Tennessee (IV)
Don Edward Johnson
692 Poplar Avenue,
Memphis, TN 38105, USA
Tel (001) (901) 526 0023
Fax (001) (901) 526 1555
E-mail bishopjohnston@episwtn.org

West Texas (VII)
Gary Richard Lillibridge
PO Box 6885, San Antonio, TX 78209, USA
Tel (001) (210) 824 5387
Fax (001) (210) 824 2164
E-mail general.mail@dwtx.org

(Suffragan)
David Reed
address etc as above

West Virginia (III)
William Michie Klusmeyer
PO Box 5400, Charleston,
WV 25361–5400, USA
Tel (001) (304) 344 3597
Fax (001) (304) 343 3295
E-mail mklusmeyer@wvdiocese.org

Western Kansas (VII)
Michael Milliken
2 Hyde Park, Hutchinson, KS 67502
Tel (001) (620) 662 0011
Fax as telephone
E-mail tec.wks2011@gmail.com

Western Louisiana (VII)
David Bruce MacPherson
PO Box 2031, Alexandria, LA 71309,
USA
Tel (001) (318) 442 1304
Fax (001) (318) 442 8712
E-mail dbm3wla@aol.com

Western Massachusetts (I)
Gordon Paul Scruton
37 Chestnut Street,
Springfield, MA 01103, USA
Tel (001) (413) 737 4786
Fax (001) (413) 746 9873
E-mail *via* www.diocesewma.org

Western Michigan (V)
Robert R Gepert
Episcopal Center, 535 Burdick St,
Suite 1, Kalamazoo, MI49007, USA
Tel (001) (296) 381 2710
E-mail diowestmi@edwm.org *or*
edwmorg@edwm.org

Western New York (II)
William Franklin
1064 Brighton Road, Tonawanda,
NY 14150, USA
Tel (001) (716) 881 0660
Fax (001) (716) 881 1724
E-mail rwfranklin@episcopalwny.org

Western North Carolina (IV)
Granville Porter Taylor
900B CenterPark Drive, Asheville,
NC 28805, USA
Tel (001) (828) 225 6656
Fax (001) (828) 225 6657
E-mail bishop@diocesewnc.org

Wyoming (VI)
John S Smylie
123 S Durbin St,
Casper, WY 82601, USA
Tel (001) (307) 265 5200
E-mail bishopsmylie@wyoming.diocese.org

WEST AFRICA

Accra (Archbishop)
Justice Ofei Akrofi
Bishopscourt, PO Box 8, Accra, Ghana
Tel (00233) (21) 662 292 *or* 663 595
Fax (00233) (21) 668 822
E-mail cwpa@4u.com.gh *or*
bishopakrofi@yahoo.com

Bo
Emmanuel Josie Samuel Tucker
1 A MacRobert Street, PO Box 21, Bo,
Southern Province, Sierra Leone
Tel (00232) (32) 648
Fax (00233) (32) 605
Email bomission@justice.com *or*
ejstucker@gmail.com

Cameroon
Thomas-Babyngton Elango Dibo
BP 15705, New Bell, Duala, Cameroon
Tel (00237) 755 58276
E-mail camanglica-church@camnet.cm *or*
agneslabep@yahoo.com

Cape Coast
Daniel S A Allotey
Bishopscourt, PO Box A233,
Adisadel Estates, Cape Coast, Ghana
Tel (00233) (42) 32 502
Fax (00233) (42) 32 637
E-mail danallotey@priest.com

Dunkwa-on-Offin
Edmund K. Dawson-Ahmoah
PO Box DW 42, Dunkwa-on-Offin, Ghana
Mobile (00233) (24) 464 4764

Freetown
Julius Olotu Prince Lynch
Bishop's Court, PO Box 537,
Freetown, Sierra Leone
Tel (00232) (22) 251 307
Mobile (00232) 76 620 690
E-mail bertajuls@yahoo.co.uk

The Gambia
Solomon Tilewa E W Johnson
Bishopscourt, PO Box 51,
Banjul, The Gambia
Tel (00220) 228 405
Mobile (00220) 905 227
E-mail stilewaj@hotmail.com

Guinea
Albert D Gomez
BP 187, Conakry, Guinea
Tel (00224) 451 323
E-mail galbertdgomez@yahoo.fr

Ho
Matthias K Mededues-Badohu
Bishopslodge, PO Box MA 300, Ho, Volta
Region, Ghana
Tel (00233) (91) 26644 *or* 26806
Mobile (00233) 208 162 246
E-mail matthoda@ucomgh.com *or*
matthiaskwab@googlemail.com

Koforidua
Francis B Quashie
PO Box 980, Koforidua, Ghana
Tel (00233) (81) 22 329
Fax (00233) (81) 22 060
E-mail fbquashie@yahoo.com

Kumasi
Daniel Yinka Sarfo
St Cyprian's Avenue,
PO Box 144, Kumasi, Ghana
Tel (00233) (51) 24 117
Mobile (00233) 277 890 411
fax as telephone
E-mail anglicandioceseofkumasi@yahoo.com
or dysarfo2000@yahoo.co.uk

(Suffragan)
Cyril K Ben-Smith
address as above
Tel (00233) 247 4308

Liberia
Jonathan B B Hart
PO Box 10–0277, 1000 Monrovia 10, Liberia
Tel (00231) 224 760
Mobile (00231) 651 4343
Fax (00231) 227 519
E-mail jbbhart@yahoo.com *or*
bishopec112@yahoo.com

Sekondi
John Kwamina Otoo
PO Box 85, Sekondi, Ghana
Tel (00233) 3120 46832
Mobile (00233) 208 200887
E-mail angdiosek@yahoo.com

Sunyani
Festus Yeboah-Asuamah
PO Box 23, Sunyani, Ghana
Tel (00233) (61) 23213
Mobile (00233) 208 121 670
Fax (00233) (61) 712300
E-mail fyasuamah@yahoo.com

Tamale
Emmanuel Anyindana Arongo
PO Box 110, Tamale NR, Ghana
Tel (00233) (71) 26639
Mobile (00233) 277 890 878
Fax (00233) (71) 22906
E-mail bishopea2000@yahoo.com

(Coadjutor)
Jacob Kofi Ayeebo
Mobile (00233) 243 419 864

Wiawso
Abraham Kobina Ackah
PO Box 4, Sefwi, Wiawso, Ghana
E-mail bishopackah@yahoo.com

WEST INDIES

The Bahamas and the Turks and Caicos Islands
Laish Zane Bogd
Church House, PO Box N-7107,
Nassau, Bahamas
Tel (001242) 322 3015
Fax (001242) 322 7943
E-mail primate@batelnet.bs

(New Providence)
Drexel Wellington Gomez
address etc as above

Barbados (Archbishop)
John Walder Dunlop Holder
Mandeville House, Collymore Rock,
St Michael, Barbados
Tel (001246) 426 2762
Fax (001246) 426 0871
E-mail jwdh@sunbeach.net

Belize
Philip S Wright
25 Bishopsthorpe, Southern Foreshore,
PO Box 535, Belize City, Belize
Tel (00501) (2) 73029
Fax (00501) (2) 76898
E-mail bzediocese@btl.net

Guyana
Cornell Moss
The Diocesan Office, PO Box 10949,
49 Barrack Street, Georgetown, Guyana
Tel (00592) (22) 64 775
Fax (00592) (22) 76 091
E-mail dioofguy@networksgy.com

Jamaica and the Cayman Islands
Alfred Charles Reid
2 Caledonia Avenue, Kingston 5, Jamaica
Tel (001876) 920 2712
Fax (001876) 960 1774
E-mail bishopja@anglicandiocese.com

(Kingston)
Robert McLean Thompson
14 Ottawa Avenue, Kingston 6, Jamaica
Tel (001876) 926 6692
Fax (001876) 960 8463
E-mail bishop.kingston@anglican.diocese.com

(Mandeville)
Harold Benjamin Daniel
Bishop's Residence, 3 Cotton Tree Road, PO Box 84, Mandeville, Jamaica
Tel (001876) 625 6817
Fax (001876) 625 6819
E-mail hbdaniel@cwjamaica.com

(Montego Bay)
Howard Gregory
PO Box 346, Montego Bay, Jamaica
Tel (001876) 952 4963
Fax (001876) 971 8838
E-mail hkagregory@hotmail.com

North Eastern Caribbean and Aruba
Leroy Errol Brooks
St Mary's Rectory, PO Box 180,
The Valley, Anguilla
Tel (001264) 497 2235
Fax (001264) 497 8555
E-mail brookx@anguillanet.com

Trinidad and Tobago
Calvin Wendell Bess
Hayes Court, 21 Maraval Road,
Port of Spain, Trinidad
Tel (001868) 622 7387
Fax (001868) 628 1319
E-mail bessc@tstt.net.tt

Windward Islands
C. Leopold Friday,
Bishop's Court, Montrose, PO Box 502,
St Vincent and the Grenadines
Tel (001784) 456 1895
Fax (001784) 456 2591
E-mail diocesewi@vincysurf.com

EXTRA-PROVINCIAL DIOCESES

Bermuda (Canterbury)
Vacant
Diocesan Office, PO Box HM 769,
Hamilton HM CX, Bermuda
Tel (001441) 293 1787
E-mail bishopratteray@ibl.bm or
dioooff@ibl.bm

§Cuba
Griselda Delgado Del Carpio
Calle 6 No 273, Vedado,
Havana 4, 10400 Cuba
Tel (0053) (7) 321120
Fax (0053) (7) 333293
E-mail griselda@enet.cu

Lusitanian Church (Canterbury)
Fernando da Luz Soares
Secretaria Diocesana, Apartado 392,
P-4430 Vila Nova de Gaia, Portugal
Tel (00351) (22) 375 4018
Fax (00351) (22) 375 2016
E-mail centrodiocesano@igreja-lusitana.org

Spanish Reformed Episcopal Church (Canterbury)
Carlos López Lozano
Calle Beneficencia 18, 28004 Madrid, Spain
Tel (0034) (91) 445 2560
Fax (0034) (91) 594 4572
E-mail eclesiae@arrakis.es

§ Under a Metropolitan Council of the Primate of Canada, the Archbishop of the West Indies and the President-Bishop of the Episcopal Church's Province IX.

BISHOPS OF CHURCHES WHERE ANGLICANS HAVE UNITED WITH CHRISTIANS OF OTHER TRADITIONS

NORTH INDIA

Agra
Samuel R Cutting
Bishop's House,
St Paul's Church Compound,
4/116-B Church Road, Civil Lines,
Agra, UP, 282 002, India
Tel (0091) (562) 285 4845
Fax (0091) (562) 252 0074
E-mail doacni@sancharnet.in

Amritsar
Pradeep Kumar Samantaroy
26 R B Prakash Chand Road, opp Police Ground,
Amritsar, Punjab, 143 001, India
Tel (0091) (183) 222 2910
fax as telephone
E-mail bunu13@rediffmail.com

Andaman and Car Nicobar Islands
Christopher Paul
Bishop's House, 21 Church Lane, Goal Ghar,
Port Blair 744 101, Andaman and Nicobar Islands, India
Tel (0091) (3192) 231 362
fax as telephone

Barrackpore (Deputy Moderator)
Brojen Malakar
Bishop's Lodge, 86 Middle Road,
Barrackpore, Kolkata 700120, West Bengal, India
Tel (0091) (33) 2592 0147
Fax (0091) (33) 2561 1852

Bhopal
Laxman L Maida
Bishop's House, 57, Residency Area,
Behind Narmada Water Tank, Indore 452 001,
MP, India
Tel (0091) (731) 270 0232
Mobile (0091) 98270 34737
E-mail bhopal_diocese@rediffmail.com

Chandigarh (Moderator)
Joel Vidyasagar Mal
Bishop's House, Mission Compound,
Brown Road, Ludhiana,
Punjab, 141 001, India
Tel (0091) (161) 222 5707
fax as telephone
E-mail bishopdoc@yahoo.com or
joelvmal@yahoo.com

Chotanagpur	B. B. Baskey Bishop's Lodge, PO Box 1, Church Road, Ranchi, Bihar, 834 001, India Tel (0091) (651) 235 1184 *Fax as telephone* E-mail rch_cndta@sancharnet.in	North East India (Deputy Moderator)	Purely Lyngdoh Bishop's Kuti, Shillong 1, Meghalaya, 793 001, India Tel (0091) (364) 2223 155 Fax (0091) (364) 2501 178 E-mail bishopnei15@hotmail.com
Cuttack	Samson Das Bishop's House, Mission Road, Cuttack, Orissa, 753 001, India Tel (0091) (671) 230 0102 E-mail diocese@vsnl.net	Patna	Philip Phembuar Marandih Bishop's House, Christ Church Compound, Bhagalpur, Bihar, 812 001, India Tel (0091) (641) 2300 714 *fax as telephone* E-mail cnipatna@rediffmail.com
Delhi	Sunil Singh Bishop's House, 1 Church Lane, off North Avenue, New Delhi, 110 001, India Tel (0091) (11) 2371 7471 E-mail stmartin@dels.vsnl.net.in	Phulbani	Bijay Kumar Nayak Bishop's House, Gudripori, Gudaigiri, Phulbani, Kandhamal, Orissa, 762 001, India Tel (0091) (6847) 260569 E-mail bp.bkn@rediffmail.com
Durgapur	Probal Kanto Dutta St Michael's Church Compound, Aldrin Path, Bidhan Nagar, Dugapur 713 212, India Tel (0091) (343) 253 4552 E-mail probal_dutta@yahoo.com	Pune	Vijay Bapurao Sathe 1A Steveley Road (General Bhagat Marg), Pune, MS, 411 001, India Tel (0091) (20) 2633 4374 E-mail punediocese@yahoo.co.in
Eastern Himalaya	Naresh Ambala Bishop's Lodge, PO Box 4, Darjeeling, West Bengal, 734 101, India Tel (0091) (354) 225 8183 E-mail bpambala@yahoo.com	Rajasthan	Collin Theodore 2/10 CNI Social Centre, Civil Lines, Opp. Bus Stand, Jaipur Rd, Ajmer 305 001, India Tel (0091) (145) 2420 633 Fax (0091) (145) 2621 627
Gujarat	Vinod Kumar Mathushellah Malaviya Bishop's House, Ellis Bridge, Ahmedabad, Gujarat State, 380 006, India Tel (0091) (79) 2656 1950 *fax as telephone* E-mail gujdio@yahoo.co.in	Sambalpur	Christ Kiron Das Mission Compound, Bolangir, Orissa, 767 001, India Tel (0091) (665) 2230 625 *fax as telephone* E-mail bishop–ckdas@rediffmail.com
Jabalpur	Prem Chand Singh Bishop's House, 2131 Napier Town, Jabalpur, MP, 482 001, India Tel (0091) (761) 2622 109 E-mail bishoppcsingh@yahoo.co.in		

SOUTH INDIA

Kolhapur	Bathuel Ramchandra Tiwade Bishop's House, EP School Compound, Kolhapur, Maharashtra, 416 001, India Tel (0091) (231) 2654 832 *fax as telephone* E-mail kdccni@vsnl.com	Chennai	V Devasahayam Diocesan Office, PO Box 4914, Chennai, TN, 600 086, India Tel (0091) (44) 2811 3929 Fax (0091) (44) 2811 0608 Email bishopdeva@hotmail.com
Kolkata	Ashok Biwas Bishop's House, 51 Chowringhee Road, Calcutta, WB, 700 071, India Tel (0091) (33) 6534 7770 Fax (0091) (33) 282 6340 E-mail samrajubh@vsnl.net	Coimbatore	M Dorai Bishop's House, 256 Race Course Road, Coimbatore, TN1, 641018, India Tel (0091) (422) 213 605 Fax (0091) (442) 200 400 Email bishopdorai@presidency.com
Lucknow	Anil R Stephen Bishop's House, 25 Mahatma Gandhi Marg, Allahabad, UP, 211 001, India Tel (0091) (532) 242 7053 Fax (0091) (532) 256 0713	Dornakal	B S Devamani Bishop's House, Cathedral Compound, Dornakal, Andhra Pradesh 506 381, India Tel (0091) (8719) 227 752 E-mail bshpindk@yahoo.co.in
Marathwada	M. U. Kasab, Bungalow 28/A, Mission Compound, Cantonment, Aurangabad 431 002, MS, India Tel (0091) (240) 237 3136 *fax as telephone* E-mail revmukasab@yahoo.co.in	East Kerala	K G Daniel Bishop's House, Melukavumattom, Kottayam, Kerala State, 686 652, India Tel (0091) (482) 291 044 *fax as telephone* Email bishopkgdaniel@rediffmail.com
Mumbai	Prakash Dinkar Patole 19 Hazarimal Somani Marg, Fort Mumbai 400 001, India Tel (0091) (22) 2206 0248 E-mail bishopbomcni@rediffmail.com	Jaffna	Daniel S Thiagarajah Bishop's Office in Colombo, 36 5/2 Sinsapa Road, Colombo, Sri Lanka Tel (0094) (60) 21495 0795 Fax (0094) (11) 250 5805 Email dsthiagarajah@yahoo.com
Nagpur	Paul Dupare Cathedral House, Sadar, Nagpur, MS, 440 001, India Tel (0091) (712) 562 1737 Fax (0091) (712) 309 7310 E-mail bishop@nagpur.dot.org.in	Kanyakumari	G. Devakadasham CSI Diocesan Office, 71A Dennis Street, Nagercoil, 629 001, India Tel (0091) (4652) 231 539 Fax (0091) (4652) 226 560 Email csikkd@vsnl.in
Nasik	Kamble Lemuel Pradip Bishop's House, Tarakur, 1 Outram Road, Ahmednagar, Maharashtra, 414 001, India Tel (0091) (241) 241 1806 Fax (0091) (241) 242 2314 E-mail bishopofnasik@rediffmail.com	Karimnagar	P Surya Prakas Bishop's House, PO Box 40, Mukarampura Post, Karimnagar, Andhra Pradesh, 505 001, India Tel (0091) (878) 226 2229 Email suryaprakash@yahoo.com

Karnataka Central
S Vasanthkumar
Diocesan Office, 20 Third Cross,
CSI Compound, Bangalore,
Karnataka, 560 027, India
Tel (0091) (80) 222 3766
Email csikcd@vsnl.com

Karnataka North
J Prabhakara Rao,
Bishop's House, All Saints Church Compound,
Dharwad, Karnataka State, 580 008, India
Tel (0091) (836) 244 7733
Fax (0091) (836) 274 5461
Email bishopprabhakar@yahoo.co.in

Karnataka South
Devaraj Bangera
Bishop's House, Balmatta,
Mangalore, Karnataka, 575 001, India
Tel (0091) (824) 243 2657
Fax (0091) (824) 242 1802
Email bishopbangera@rediffmail.com

Krishna-Godavari
G Dyvasirvadam
CSI St Andrew's Cathedral Campus, Main Rd,
Machilipatnam 521 002, AP, India
Tel (0091) (8672) 220 623
E-mail bishopkrishna@yahoo.com

Madhya Kerala
Thomas Samuel
CSI Bishop's House, Cathedral Road,
Kottayam, Kerala State, 686 018, India
Tel (0091) (481) 2566 536
Fax (0091) (481) 2566 531
E-mail csimkdbishop@sancharnet.in

Madurai-Ramnad (Deputy Moderator)
Christopher Asir
CSI Diocesan Office, 5 Bhulabai Desai Rd,
Chockikulam, Madurai District,
Tamil Nadu, 625 002, India
Tel (0091) (452) 732 0541
Fax (0091) (452) 256 0864
Email bishop@csidmr.net

Medak
Kanak Prasad
Bishop's Annexe, 145 MacIntyre Road,
Secunderabad, Andhra Pradesh, 500 003, India
Tel (0091) (40) 2783 3151
Fax (0091) (40) 2784 4215

Nandyal
P J Lawrence
Bishop's House, Nandyal RS, Kurnool District,
Andhra Pradesh, 518 502, India
Tel (0091) (8514) 222 477
Fax (0091) (8514) 242 255

North Kerala
K P Kuruvilla
PO Box 104, Shoranur,
Kerala State, 679 121, India
Tel (0091) (466) 222 4454
Fax (0091) (466) 222 2545
Email csinkd@md5.vsnl.net

Rayalaseema
K B Yesuvaraprasad
Bishop's House, CSI Compound,
Gooty, Ananthapur District,
Andhra Pradesh, 515 401, India
Tel (0091) (866) 232 5320
Fax (0091) (856) 227 5200

South Kerala (Moderator)
John Wilson Gladstone
Bishop's House, LMS Compound,
Trivandrum 695 033, Kerala State, India
Tel (0091) (471) 231 5490
Fax (0091) (471) 231 6439
E-mail bishopgladstone@yahoo.com

Thoothukudi-Nazareth
J A D Jebachdran
Bishop's House, 111/32T, Polpettai Extension,
State Bank Colony, Thoothukudi 628 002 TN,
India
Tel (0091) (461) 234 5430
Fax (0091) (431) 234 6911
Email bishoptnd@dataone.in

Tirunelveli
Jeyapaul David
Bishopstowe, PO Box 118, Tirunelveli, Tamil
Nadu, 627 002, India
Tel (0091) (462) 257 8744
Fax (0019) (462) 257 4525
E-mail bishop@csitirunelveli.org

Trichy-Tanjore
G P Vasanthakumar
PO Box 31, 17 VOC Road,
Tiruchirapalli, Tamil Nadu, 620 017, India
Tel (0091) (431) 771254
Fax (0091) (431) 418485
E-mail csittd@tr.net.in

Vellore
Yesurathnam William
CSI Diocesan Office, 1/A Officer's Lane,
Vellore, North Arcot District, 632 001, India
Tel (0091) (416) 2232 160
Fax (0091) (416) 2223 835
Email bishopwilliam@sify.com

BANGLADESH

Dhaka
Michael S Baroi
St Thomas's Church, 54 Johnson Road,
Dhaka-1100, Bangladesh
Tel (00880) (2) 711 6546
Fax (00880) (2) 712 1632
E-mail cbdacdio@bangla.net

Kushtia (Moderator)
Paul S Sarkar
94 NS Road, Thanapara, Kushtia, Bangladesh
Tel (00880) (71) 61892
fax as telephone
E-mail cob@citechco.net

PAKISTAN

The Arabian Gulf (Bishop for) (Area Bishop within the Diocese of Cyprus)
Azad Marshall
PO Box 688, Lahore,
Punjab, 54660, Pakistan
Tel (0092) (42) 542 0452
E-mail bishop@saintthomascenter.org

Faisalabad
John Samuel
Bishop's House, PO Box 27, Mission Road,
Gojra, Distt Toba Tek Sing, Faisalabad,
Pakistan
Tel (0092) (46) 351 4689
Mobile (0092) 300 655 0074
E-mail jsamuel@brain.net.pk

Hyderabad
Raffique Masih
27 Liaquat Road, Civil Lines,
Hyderabad, Sind, 71000, Pakistan
Tel (0092) (22) 2780 221
Fax (0092) (22) 2285 879
E-mail dohcop@yahoo.com

Karachi (Deputy Moderator)
Saddiq Daniel
Holy Trinity Cathedral, Fatima Jinnah Rd,
Karachi 75530, Pakistan
Tel (0092) (21) 521 6843
E-mail sadiqdaniel@hotmail.com

Lahore (Moderator)
Alexander John Malik
Bishopsbourne, Cathedral Close,
The Mall, Lahore, 54000, Pakistan
Tel (0092) (42) 723 3560
Fax (0092) (42) 722 1270
E-mail bishop_Lahore@hotmail.com

Multan
Leo Rodrick Paul
113 Qasim Road, PO Box 204,
Multan Cantt, Pakistan
Tel (0092) (61) 458 3694
E-mail bishop_mdcap@bain.net.pk

Peshawar
Humphrey Sarfaraz Peters
Diocesan Centre, 1 Sir-Syed Road,
Peshawar, NWFP, 25000, Pakistan
Tel (0092) (91) 527 9094
Fax (0092) (91) 527 749
E-mail bishopdop@hotmail.com

Raiwind (Moderator)
Samuel Robert Azariah
17 Warris Road, PO Box 2319,
Lahore 54000, Pakistan
Tel (0092) (42) 758 8950
Fax (0092) (42) 757 7255
E-mail sammyazariah49@yahoo.com

Sialkot
Samuel Robert Pervez
Lal Kothi, Barah Patthar,
Sialkot 2, Punjab, Pakistan
Tel (0092) (432) 264 895
Fax (0092) (432) 264 828
E-mail chs_sialkot@yahoo.com

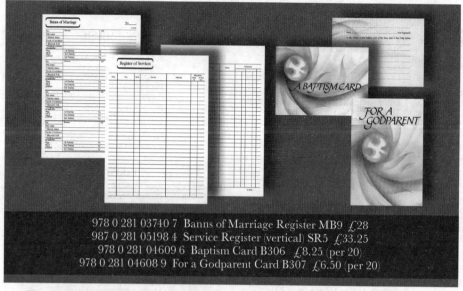

PROVINCIAL OFFICES

From which further information may be sought.

Anglican Communion Office   St Andrew's House, 16 Tavistock Crescent, Westbourne Park, London W11 1AP, UK
Tel (020) 7313 3900   E-mail aco@anglicancommunion.org

Australia   Suite 2, Level 9, 51 Druitt Street, Sydney NSW 2000, Australia
Fax (0061) (2) 8267 2727   E-mail gsoffice@anglican.org.au

Bangladesh   St Thomas's Church, 54 Johnson Road, Dhaka 1100, Bangladesh
Fax (00880) (2) 712 1632   E-mail cbdacdio@bangla.net

Brazil   Praça Olavo Bilac 63, Campos Eliseos, CEP 01201–050, São Paulo, SP, Brazil
Fax (0055) (11) 3667 8161   E-mail acavalcante@ieab.org.br

Burundi   BP 2098, Bujumbura, Burundi
Fax (00257) 22 229 129   E-mail peab@cbinf.com

Canada   80 Hayden Street, Toronto ON M4Y 3G2, Canada
Fax (001) (416) 968 7983   E-mail general.secretary@national.anglican.ca

Central Africa   PO Box 22317, Kitwe, Zambia (00260) 267 351 668

Central America   Iglesia Episcopal Costarricense, Apartado 10502, 1000 San José, Costa Rica
Fax (00506) 253 8331   E-mail anglicancr@racsa.co.cr

Ceylon   Bishop's House, 368/3A Bauddhaloka Mawatha, Colombo 7, Sri Lanka
Fax (0094) (1) 684811   E-mail sec.diocese.tr@gmail.com

Congo   PO Box 16482, Kinshasa 1, DR Congo
Tel (00243) 99 471 3802   E-mail molanga2k@yahoo.co.uk

England   Church House, Great Smith Street, London SW1P 3NZ, UK
Tel (020) 7898 1000   Fax (020) 7898 1001   E-mail feedback@churchofengland.org

Hong Kong   1 Lower Albert Road, Hong Kong, China
Fax (00852) 2521 2199   E-mail office1@hkskh.org

Indian Ocean   Evêché Anglican, 12 rue Rabezavana, Ambodifilao, 101TNR Antananarivo, Madagascar
Fax (00261) (20) 226 1331   E-mail eemdanta@dts.mg or eemtma@hotmail.com

Ireland   Church of Ireland House, Church Avenue, Rathmines, Dublin 6, Republic of Ireland
Fax (00353) (1) 497 8821   E-mail office@rcbdub.org

Japan   65-3 Yarai-cho, Shinjuku-ku,Tokyo 162–0805, Japan
Fax (0081) (3) 5228 3175   E-mail province@nskk.org

Jerusalem and the Middle East   PO Box 3, Doha, Qatar
Fax (00974) 442 4329   E-mail tianyoung@hotmail.com

Kenya   PO Box 40502, 00100 Nairobi, Kenya
Fax (00254) (2) 718 442   E-mail archoffice@swiftkenya.com

Korea   3 Chong-dong, Chung-ku, Seoul 100–120, Korea
Fax (0082) (2) 737 4210   E-mail yoonsjm@hanmail.net

Melanesia   Provincial Headquarters, PO Box 19, Honiara, Solomon Islands
Fax (0067) 21 890   E-mail kiriau_g@comphq.org.sb

Mexico   Calle La Otra Banda 40, Col. San Angel, Delegación Alvaro Obregón, 01000 México, DF, Mexico
Fax (0052) (55) 5616 4063   E-mail ofipam@att.net.mx or habacuc-mx@yahoo.es

Myanmar (Burma)   PO Box 11191, 140 Pyidaungsu Yeiktha Road, Dagon, Yangon, Myanmar
Fax (0095) (1) 39 5350   E-mail cpm.140@mptmail.net.mm

New Zealand (Aotearoa, New Zealand and Polynesia)   PO Box 87188, Meadowbank, Auckland 1742, New Zealand
Fax (0064) (9) 521 4490   E-mail gensec@ang.org.nz

Nigeria   Episcopal House, PO Box 212, AD CP, Abuja, Nigeria
E-mail abuja@anglican.skannet.com.ng

North India   CNI, 16 Pandit Pant Marg, New Delhi 110001, India
Fax (0091) (11) 2371 6901   E-mail gscni@ndb.vsnl.net.in

Pakistan   St John's Cathedral, 1 Sir Syed Road, Peshawar Cantt 2500, Pakistan
Fax (0092) (91) 277 499   E-mail bishopdop@hotmail.com

Papua New Guinea   Box 673, Lae, MP, Papua New Guinea
Fax (00675) 472 1852   E-mail acpnggensec@global.net.pg

Philippines   PO Box 10321, Broadway Centrum, 1112 Quezon City, Philippines
Fax (0063) (2) 721 1923   E-mail ecpnational@yahoo.com.ph

Rwanda   BP 2487, Kigali, Rwanda
Fax (00250) 516 162   E-mail egapeer@yahoo.com

Scotland   21 Grosvenor Crescent, Edinburgh EH12 5EE, UK
Tel 0131-255 6357   Fax 0131-346 7247   E-mail secgen@scotland.anglican.org

South East Asia   16 Jalan Pudu Lama, 50200 Kuala Lumpur, Malaysia
Fax (0060) (3) 2031 3225   E-mail anglican@streamyx.com

South India   CSI Centre, 5 Whites Road, Royapettah, Chennai 600 041, India
E-mail csi@vsnl.com

Southern Africa   20 Bishopscourt Drive, Bishopscourt, Claremont, 7708 South Africa
Fax (0027) (21) 797 1329   E-mail peo@anglicanchurchsa.org.za

South America   A. Gallinal 1852, Montevideo, Uruguay
E-mail lego@adinet.co.uy

Sudan   PO Box 604, Khartoum, Sudan
E-mail ecsprovince@hotmail.com

Tanzania   PO Box 899, Dodoma, Tanzania
Tel (00255) (26) 232 4565   E-mail akiri@anglican.or.tz

Uganda   PO Box 14123, Kampala, Uganda
Fax (00256) (41) 251 925   E-mail provinceuganda@yahoo.com

USA   Episcopal Church Center, 815 Second Avenue, New York NY 10017, USA
Fax (001) (212) 490 3298   E-mail pboffice@episcopalchurch.org

Wales   39 Cathedral Road, Cardiff CF11 9XF, UK
Tel (029) 2034 8200   Fax (029) 2038 7835   E-mail: information@churchinwales.org.uk

West Africa   PO Box Lt 226, Lartebiokorshie, Accra, Ghana
E-mail cpwa@4u.com.gh *or* morkelwuley@gmail.com

West Indies   Provincial Secretariat, Bamford House, Society Hill, St John, Barbados, West Indies
Fax (001) (246) 426 0871   E-mail bamford@sunbeach.net

DIRECTORIES OF THE ANGLICAN PROVINCES

Many provinces in the Anglican Communion now maintain online directories of their clergy. The web site addresses given below are for the home pages of the provinces concerned. From the home page, follow links either to the online church or clergy directory, or to the pages for individual dioceses and, where available, to the information for individual parishes. The 'Tour' web page on the Anglican Communion Office website (www.anglicancommunion.org/tour/index.cfm) also lists information about Anglican provinces (bishops, provinicial secretary, provincial treasurer), and gives links to online provincial information where this is available.

Where a province is known to publish a printed directory, details are given below. For the provinces not listed here, information should be sought from the provincial secretary or from dioceses.

Australia www.anglican.org.au

Canada www.anglican.ca; *Anglican Church Directory*, published annually by Anglican Book Centre, 80 Hayden Street, Toronto ON M4Y 3G2, Canada, Tel (001) (416) 924 1332 Fax (001) (416) 924 2760 E-mail info@afcanada.com

Ireland www.ireland.anglican.org;

Japan www.nskk.org; *Seikokai Yearbook*, published annually (in Japanese) by Nippon Sei Ko Kai Provincial Office, 65 Yarai-cho, Shinjuku, Tokyo 162–0805, Japan

Jerusalem and the Middle East *A Provincial Directory*, published by Provincial Office, Box 1248, 20 Nablus Road, Jerusalem

New Zealand www.anglican.org.nz; *Clerical Directory*, published annually by General Synod Office, PO Box 11061, Ellerslie, New Zealand, Tel (0064) (9) 525 1380, Fax (0064) (9) 525 1664 E-mail sales@churchstores.co.nz

Nigeria www.anglican-nig.org

Scotland www.scotland.anglican.org

Southern Africa www.anglicanchurchsa.org; *Clerical Directory*, published by CPSA, PO Box 61394, Marshalltown 2107, South Africa Tel (0027) (11) 836 5825 Fax (0027) (11) 836 5782 E-mail publish@mail.ngo.za

Southern Cone of America *Directorio Provincial*, published every three years: Casilla 50675, Correo Central, Santiago, Chile

United States of America www.episcopalchurch.org is the main website for ECUSA; the main online directory is to be found at www.redbook.org; *Episcopal Clerical Directory*, published every two years by Episcopal Books and Resources, 815 Second Avenue, NY 100017, USA Tel (001) (212) 716 6117 Fax (001) (212) 716 6206 E-mail bookstore@episcopalchurch.org

The **Diocese of Jamaica** (fax (001) (876) 968 0618) publishes a *Clerical Directory*.

Close links with many overseas provinces are maintained by the following missionary organizations:

Church Mission Society Watlington Road, Oxford OX4 6BZ Tel 0845-620 1799 *or* (01865) 787400 Fax (01865) 776375 E-mail info@cms-uk.org

Crosslinks (formerly the Bible Churchmen's Missionary Society) 251 Lewisham Way, London SE4 1XF Tel (020) 8691 6111 Fax (020) 8694 8023 E-mail *via website* www.crosslinks.org (link to Headquarters staff at the foot of the Contact page)

Mission to Seafarers (formerly The Missions to Seamen) St Michael Paternoster Royal, College Hill, London EC4R 2RL Tel (020) 7248 5202 Fax (020) 7248 4761 E-mail depsecgen@missiontoseafarers.org

Mothers' Union Mary Sumner House, 24 Tufton Street, London SW1P 3RB Tel (020) 7222 5533 Fax (020) 7222 1591 E-mail mu@themothersunion.org

Society for Promoting Christian Knowledge 36 Causton Street, London SW1P 4ST Tel (020) 7592 3900 Fax (020) 7592 3939 E-mail spck@spck.org.uk

South American Mission Society Allen Gardiner Cottage, Pembury Road, Tunbridge Wells, TN2 3QU Tel (01892) 538647 Fax (01892) 525797 E-mail finsec@samsgb.org

United Society for the Propagation of the Gospel 200 Great Dover Street, London SE1 4YB Tel 0845-273 1701 *or* (020) 7378 5678 Fax (020) 7378 5650 E-mail enquiries@uspg.org.uk

ADDRESSES UNKNOWN

The following are clergy whose addresses are currently unknown. Fuller details are contained in the biographical section. We should be grateful for any information to help us complete our records in respect of these clergy.

ABRAHAM, Estelle Pamela. b 46. d 04. Canada from 11
ADAMS, Godfrey Bernard. b 47. d 93. Perm to Offic *Man* 09-10
ADENEKAN, Latiff Aremu. b 38. d 04. Perm to Offic *S'wark* 08-09
ANDREWS, Frances. b 24. d 87. rtd 95
APPLEBY, Miss Janet Mohr. b 32. d 91. Perm to Offic *Ox* 02-07
ASHDOWN, Barry Frederick. b 42. d 68. C Southwick St Mich *Chich* 91-93
ATKINS, Peter. b 29. d 54. Asst Dir Soc Services E Sussex from 83
AVES, Peter Colin. b 57. d 88. TV Beaminster Area *Sarum* 03-07
BAKER, Peter Graham. b 55. d 82. rtd 11
BAKER, Sarah Jane. b 59. d 02. Perm to Offic *Wakef* from 07
BALLARD, Peter James. b 55. d 87. Dioc Dir of Educn *Blackb* 98-10
BAMBERG, Robert William. b 43. d 01. Perm to Offic *Ex* 08-10
BARNSLEY, Mrs Angela Vera. b 47. d 93. NSM Codicote *St Alb* 93-94
BARRON, Kurt Karl. b 60. d 92. P-in-c Mansfield St Lawr *S'well* 01-08
BEEBY, Matthew. b 57. d 11. NSM Mayfair Ch Ch *Lon* from 11
BELL, Andrew Thomas. b 58. d 95. TV Schorne *Ox* 98-10
BENNETT, Nigel John. b 47. d 71. rtd 08; Hon C Southsea St Jude *Portsm* from 09
BENNETT, Paul Jonathan. b 61. d 87. V German St Jo *S & M* 96-00
BERRY-DAVIES, Charles William Keith. b 48. d 83. Chapl RAF 86-09
BLAY, Kenneth Neil. b 72. d 07. C Dearnley *Man* 08-10
BLOCK, Robert Allen. b 62. d 88. P-in-c Hammersmith St Luke *Lon* 96-02
BOLSTER, David Richard. b 50. d 84. V Edmonton St Aldhelm *Lon* 01-10
BOND, Alan Richard. b 49. d 83. NSM Westbourne *Chich* 83-86
BRACE, Stuart. b 49. d 74. rtd 11; Perm to Offic *Worc* from 95
BRADDICK-SOUTHGATE, Charles Anthony Michael. b 70. d 94. Perm to Offic *S'wark* from 11
BRENTNALL, David John. b 53. d 86. V St Alb St Pet *St Alb* 96-09
BURKE, Michael Robert. b 61. d 89. V Hucclecote *Glouc* 00-09
CABLE, Kevin John. b 74. d 08. C Bromley Common St Aug *Roch* 08-11
CALDER, David Ainsley. b 60. d 96. V Woodhouse and Wrangthorn *Ripon* 00-10
CALLAGHAN, Michael James. b 63. d 97. NSM Blackheath Park St Mich *S'wark* 97-08
CHRISTIE, David James. b 58. d 91. V Patrick Brompton and Hunton *Ripon* 95-09; V Hornby 95-09; V Crakehall 95-09
CHURCHER, Ms Mandy. b 54. d 99. NSM Malmesbury w Westport and Brokenborough *Bris* from 11; NSM Gt Somerford, Lt Somerford, Seagry, Corston etc from 11
CLARK, Andrew James. b 50. d 94. NSM Walbrook Epiphany *Derby* 03-05
CLARK, Antony. b 61. d 88. C Bletchley *Ox* 98-00
CLARK, Brian John. b 48. d 00. Perm to Offic *Portsm* 02-06
COLLINS, Bruce Churton. b 47. d 83. Perm to Offic *St D* from 07
COOKE, Mrs Carolyn Jane. b 65. d 02. Chapl La Côte *Eur* from 10
COWELL, Peter James. b 58. d 82. New Zealand from 09
COX, The Very Revd Albert Horace Montague. b 26. d 86. Perm to Offic *Cant* from 10
CRAVEN, Miss Alison Ruth Miranda. b 63. d 07. C Chelsea St Luke and Ch Ch *Lon* 07-11
DAVID, William John. b 57. d 04. NSM Eltham St Barn *S'wark* from 11
DAVIES, Christopher. b 51. d 02. NSM Peckham St Sav *S'wark* 02-07
DAVIES, Mrs Margaret Adelaide. b 45. d 95. rtd 11
DAVIES, Neil Anthony Bowen. b 52. d 78. Perm to Offic *Ox* 99-02
DAVIES, Stephen John. b 65. d 97. P-in-c Enderby w Lubbesthorpe and Thurlaston *Leic* 01-09
DAVIS, Trevor Lorenzo. b 45. d 94. NSM Upper Norwood St Jo *S'wark* 94-00
DAVIS, Mrs Yvonne Annie. b 30. d 96. Perm to Offic *S'wark* from 00
de la BAT SMIT, Reynaud. b 50. d 82. rtd 11
DEAN, Stuart Peter. b 75. d 06. C Lindfield *Chich* 06-10
DEUCHAR, Canon Andrew Gilchrist. b 55. d 84. Hon Prov Can Cant Cathl *Cant* from 95; Dioc Audit Officer *Mor* from 08
DIAZ BUTRON, Marcos Máximo. b 72. d 08. C Wantage *Ox* 08-10
DICKIE, James Graham Wallace. b 50. d 81. rtd 10

DINES, The Very Revd Philip Joseph (Griff). b 59. d 86. Lic to Offic *Glas* 05-08
DORANS, Robert Marshall. b 47. d 01. NSM Longhorsley and Hebron *Newc* 01-05
DOWIE, Canon Winifred Brenda McIntosh. b 57. d 92. Hon Can Bris Cathl *Bris* from 02
DOWNER, Barry Michael. b 58. d 02. NSM Oakfield St Jo *Portsm* 09-10
DOWNES, Gregory Charles. b 69. d 96. Chapl Ox Pastorate 05-06
DOYE, Andrew Peter Charles. b 64. d 93. R Wheathampstead *St Alb* 00-09
DUCKWORTH, Mrs Angela Denise. b 58. d 07. Perm to Offic *Roch* from 10
DUNGAN, Hilary Anne. b 46. d 00. rtd 11
DUNGAN, Ivan. d 09. NSM Bunclody w Kildavin, Clonegal and Kilrush *C & O* from 09
EADES, David Julian John. b 74. d 00. Chapl Essex Univ *Chelmsf* 04-06
EATON, Mrs Margaret Anne. b 44. d 86. C Elgin w Lossiemouth *Mor* 06-09; C Aberlour 06-09; C Dufftown 06-09
ECHOLS, Mrs Janet Lyn Roberts. b 58. d 95. Dn-in-c Stapleford *Ely* 02-07
ECKHARD, Robert Leo Michael. b 60. d 05. C Hounslow H Trin w St Paul *Lon* 08-10
EDWARDSON, David Roger Hately. b 54. d 91. Asst Chapl Oundle Sch 98-09
EGGERT, Max Alexander. b 43. d 67. NSM Haywards Heath St Rich *Chich* 78-93
ELMES, Sister Evelyn Sandra. b 61. d 97. CA from 89
FACEY, Andrew John. b 57. d 92. V Epsom Common Ch Ch *Guildf* 02-10; Dioc Inter Faith Adv 96-10
FORMAN, Alastair Gordon. b 48. d 80. P-in-c Jersey Millbrook St Matt *Win* 95-01; P-in-c Jersey St Lawr 95-01
FOSTER-CLARK, Mrs Sarah Hazel. b 75. d 00. Perm to Offic *Man* 07-08
FOULDS, John Stuart. b 64. d 91. P-in-c Meir *Lich* 99-07
FRANZ, Kevin Gerhard. b 53. d 79. Gen Sec Action of Churches Together in Scotland 99-07
FRAY, Bernard Herbert. b 44. d 03. rtd 11; Perm to Offic *York* and *Eur* from 11
GIBSON, Nigel Stephen David. b 53. d 87. Milan w Cadenabbia and Varese *Eur* 04-10
GILCHRIST, Spencer. b 66. d 91. I Connor w Antrim St Patr *Conn* 97-09
GILMORE, David Samuel. b 70. d 03. R Soho St Anne w St Thos and St Pet *Lon* 08-10
GILPIN, Jeremy David. b 59. d 88. Chapl St Hugh's Coll Ox 97-07
GOLLEDGE, Christopher John. b 66. d 92. Perm to Offic *Chich* 95-00
✠GOMEZ, The Rt Revd Drexel Wellington. b 37. d 59. rtd 09
GOODHEW, Mrs Lindsey Jane Ellin. b 66. d 93. Hon C Fulford *York* 07-08
GRAHAM, Ronald Fleming. b 33. d 69. rtd 89
GREEN, Lucinda Jane. d 09. NSM Killaloe w Stradbally *L & K* from 09
GREEN, Mrs Maureen. b 49. d 98. NSM Ipswich St Jo *St E* 98-10
GREY, Richard Thomas. b 50. d 75. V Brynmawr *S & B* 02-09
HAGGER, Jonathan Paul. b 59. d 95. C Newc St Fran *Newc* 02-10
HARFORD, Timothy William. b 58. d 89. Perm to Offic *Bradf* from 04
HAWKINS, John Colin. b 50. d 00. P-in-c Burwash Weald *Chich* 04-11
HAY, Miss Lesley Jean Hamilton. b 48. d 06. C Bethany USA 08; Asst R Hamden from 08
HELM, Nicholas. b 57. d 88. Continuing Minl Development Officer *Heref* from 10
HERBERT, Jonathan Patrick. b 62. d 88. Pilsdon Community 96-10
HILLMAN, Peter. b 69. d 07. C Rayleigh *Chelmsf* 07-11
HINTON, Nigel Keith. b 49. d 92. Perm to Offic *Lon* from 03
HIRST, Malcolm. b 62. d 00. C Farnborough *Roch* 03-08
HOBBS, Simon John. b 59. d 83. Bonn w Cologne *Eur* 08-11
HOLDAWAY, Simon Douglas. b 47. d 81. NSM Gleadless *Sheff* from 81; Tutor Sheff Univ from 81
HOLDSWORTH, Michael Andrew. b 65. d 93. TV Sheff Manor *Sheff* 97-99; Tutor Ripon Coll Cuddesdon 97-99
HOLLINGTON, David Mark. b 61. d 94. C Cannock *Lich* 95-96
HORTON, Cathy Lynne Bosworth. b 62. d 99. USA 03-07

HOUGHTON, Timothy John. b 56. d 97. C Normanton *Derby* 97-03

HOWARTH, Mrs Henriette. b 66. d 04. Perm to Offic *Birm* from 09

HULT, Mrs Anna Eva Hildegard. b 73. Sweden from 08

HUMPHRIES, Miss Dorothy Maud. b 22. d 87. Perm to Offic *Worc* 98-09

HUMPHRYS, Laura Frances. b 53. d 03. Perm to Offic *Portsm* from 07

HURLEY, Robert. b 64. d 90 R Oldbury *Sarum* 02-04

HUTCHENS, Holly Blair. b 42. d 88. Dn-in-c Glenurquhart *Mor* 05-11

HUTTON, Susan Elizabeth. b 70. d 95. Dn-in-c Trowbridge H Trin *Sarum* 05-09

HUXLEY, Edward Jonathan. b 74. d 05. C Sea Mills *Bris* 05-08

HYETT, Derek Walter. b 79. d 05. C Edmonton St Alphege *Lon* 05-08; C Ponders End St Matt 05-08

IRVINE, Simon Timothy. b 74. d 03. C Dublin Sandymount *D & G* 06-11

JACOB, Neville Peter. b 60. d 96. Perm to Offic *Win* from 11

JENKINS, John Howard David. b 51. d 74. rtd 10

JEPSON, Joanna Elizabeth. b 76. d 03. Chapl Lon Coll of Fashion *Lon* 06-11

JOHNSON, Margaret Joan (Meg). b 41. d 95. NSM Sanderstead St Mary *S'wark* 95-04

JOHNSON, Miss Susan Elaine. b 44. d 03. rtd 11

JOHNSTON, Mrs Carole Ann. b 58. d 06. TM Turton Moorland Min *Man* 09-11

JONES, John Howard. b 48. d 77. rtd 08

JONES, Mrs Katie Ann. d 99. Perm to Offic *Cant* 04-11

JONES, Matthew Christopher Howell. b 74. d 01. V Southgate St Andr *Lon* 05-10

JUDGE, Mark Rollo. b 60. d 92. Asst Chapl Barking Havering and Redbridge Hosps NHS Trust 01-08

KELK, Michael Anthony. b 48. d 83. P-in-c Llangarron w Llangrove, Whitchurch and Ganarew *Heref* 02-08

KENNEDY, John Frederick. b 42. d 06. NSM Edgbaston St Geo *Birm* 06-10

KIMBERLEY, John Harry. b 49. d 76. Chapl Eastbourne Hosps NHS Trust 95-06

KING, David Charles. b 52. d 78. V Middle Esk Moor *York* 00-07

KINGDON, Mrs Margaret Victoria. b 44. d 98. NSM Wokingham St Sebastian *Ox* 98-03

KISSELL, Jonathan Mark Barrington. b 66. d 01. C Dublin St Patr Cathl Gp *D & G* 05-11

KOLOGARAS, Mrs Linda Audrey. b 48. d 95. Australia 03-07

KYEI-BAFFOUR, Jacob Owusu. b 62. d 93. Hon C Willesden Green St Andr and St Fran *Lon* 06-09

LAMB, Graeme William. b 68. d 01. P-in-c Whaley Bridge *Ches* 06-09

LANCHANTIN, Mrs Eveline. b 51. d 07. C Ashford *Cant* 07-10

LANE, Bernard Charles. b 59. d 01. C Sittingbourne St Mary and St Mich *Cant* 01-05

LAWRENCE, Mrs Judith Patricia. b 53. d 04. C Glastonbury w Meare *B & W* 04-09

LAWRENCE (*née* FOREMAN), Mrs Vanessa Jane. b 73. d 00. NSM Ampfield, Chilworth and N Baddesley *Win* from 10; Chapl Hants Partnership NHS Trust from 09

LEE, Robert David. b 53. d 77. rtd 11

LENNOX, Mark. d 09. NSM Maghera w Killelagh *D & R* from 09

LENTON, John Robert. b 46. d 00. NSM Bramley *Win* from 10

LIDDLE, Stephen John. b 60. d 91. P-in-c Billingham St Aid *Dur* 05-10

LING, Timothy Charles. b 61. d 92. V Bathford *B & W* 00-09

LISTER (*née* AISBITT), Mrs Joanne. b 69. d 93. NSM Mill End and Heronsgate w W Hyde *St Alb* 93-96

LYALL, Richard Keith. b 70. d 02. Canada 08-09

LYNAS, Canon Norman Noel. b 55. d 79. Can Res Bermuda from 09

LYNCH, Mrs Victoria. d 09. Lic to Offic *L & K* from 09

MACAULAY (*née* BRAYBROOKS), Mrs Bridget Ann. b 63. d 98. Coracle Trust from 01

MACAULAY, Kenneth Russell. b 63. d 98. Coracle Trust from 01

McCLOSKEY, Robert Johnson. b 42. d 67. rtd 01

McGAFFIN, Judi. d 09. NSM Donagheady *D & R* from 09

MacGILLIVRAY, Canon Alexander Buchan. b 33. d 57. rtd 07

McGIRR, Canon William Eric. b 43. d 71. rtd 10

MACHELL, Leigh Douglas. b 64. d 03. P-in-c Churchill and Langford *B & W* 07-10

MACKIE, Kenneth Johnston. b 20. d 47. Perm to Offic *Roch* 97-08

MACKRILL, Mrs Deirdre Anne. b 49. d 05. NSM Hemel Hempstead *St Alb* 05-09

McLEOD, Ms Susan Margaret. b 48. d 95. NSM Charlesworth and Dinting Vale *Derby* 95-02; Chapl Asst S Man Univ Hosps NHS Trust 97-02

McWILLIAMS, Amelia. d 09. NSM Brackaville w Donaghendry and Ballyclog *Arm* from 09

MAKIN, Valerie Diana. d 88. Perm to Offic *Lon* 95-97 and *Guildf* 95-05

✠MALANGO, The Rt Revd Bernard Amos. b 43. d 71. Malawi from 02; rtd 07

MANN, Lt Comdr Anthony James. b 34. d 88. rtd 01

MARQUIS-FAULKES, Edmund. b 62. d 91. R Bieldside *Ab* 02-07

MARTIN, Peter. b 66. d 92. Chapl Lancs Teaching Hosps NHS Trust 06-08

MAYBURY, Paul. b 31. d 88. Perm to Offic *Ches* 01-08

MEEHAN, Cyril Frederick. b 52. d 80. Chapl Northumbria Healthcare NHS Trust 03-04

MELDRUM, David Peter John. b 73. d 01. S Africa from 10

MOORHOUSE, Christine Susan. b 49. d 87. Perm to Offic *Worc* 02-07

MORGAN, Christopher. b 66. d 04. R Reepham, Hackford w Whitwell, Kerdiston etc *Nor* 07-10

MORGAN, David Farnon Charles. b 43. d 70. V Adlington *Blackb* 86-11

MORGAN, Peter Neville. b 36. d 98. rtd 09

MORROW, Daniel Ross. b 77. d 07. USA from 11

MORTON, Michelle. b 67. d 02. Dn-in-c Stewkley w Soulbury and Drayton Parslow *Ox* 05-09

MOSS, Canon Denis. b 32. d 74. Chapl Budapest *Eur* 92-10

MOY, Mrs Joy Patricia. b 35. d 90. Perm to Offic *Win* 96-02

MOYNAGH, Michael Digby. b 50. d 85. Tomorrow Project from 04

MOYO, Edmore Illingworth. b 71. d 02. NSM Luton St Mary St Alb 06-08

MPUNZI, Nduna Ananias. b 46. d 71. TV Worc St Barn w Ch Ch *Worc* 04-08

MUKHOLI, Eshuchi Patrick. b 60. d 98. NSM Blackbird Leys *Ox* 02-08

NEWMAN, Kevin Richard. b 74. d 06. C Crowborough *Chich* 06-10

NICHOLS, Mark Steven. b 68. d 97. C Balham Hill Ascension *S'wark* 97-99

O'DOWD SMYTH, Christine. d 09. NSM Lismore w Cappoquin, Kilwatermoy, Dungarvan etc *C & O* from 09

O'DWYER, John Francis Joseph. b 61. d 03. P-in-c Bury St Pet *Man* 06-10

ODEWOLE, Israel Oluwagbemiga Omoniyi. b 68. d 97. Perm to Offic *Man* from 06

OGSTON, Russell James. b 71. d 98. Egypt from 10

ORMROD, Jonathan. d 11. C Llantrisant *Llan* from 11

OWEN-MOORE, Ms Petra Davine. b 65. d 98. TM N Wingfield, Clay Cross and Pilsley *Derby* 08-09

PAINE DAVEY, Nathan Paul. b 64. d 92. Perm to Offic *Lon* 01-05

PAINTER, Christopher Mark. b 65. d 00. TV Eccles *Man* 03-07

PANTER MARSHALL, Canon Susan Lesley. b 49. d 91. rtd 10

PARFITT, Canon Keith John. b 44. d 70. Dir Is of Wight Rural Community Coun from 97

PASCOE, Mrs Caroline Elizabeth Alice. d 08. Lay Development Officer *Heref* from 10

PAYNE, Elizabeth. b 50. d 98. TM Cyncoed *Mon* 03-04

PERRICONE, Vincent James. b 50. d 90. Asst Chapl Florence w Siena *Eur* 08-09

PHILLIPSON, Hugh Brian. b 41. d 96. NSM Ox St Mary V w St Cross and St Pet *Ox* 06-08

PIGGOT, Alan Robert Lennox. b 62. d 02. P-in-c Hackney Wick St Mary of Eton w St Aug *Lon* 05-10

PITKETHLY (*née* CHEVILL), Elizabeth Jane. b 65. d 08. C Blackheath St Jo *S'wark* 08-11

PITT, Mrs Valerie. b 55. d 05. NSM Meole Brace *Lich* from 09

✠POGO, The Most Revd Sir Ellison Leslie. b 47. d 79. Solomon Is from 81; rtd 08

PRICE, Mrs Jean Amelia. b 44. d 02. rtd 11

PRITCHARD, Miss Kathryn Anne. b 60. d 87. Product Development Manager Ch Ho Publishing 01-09

QUIGLEY, Donna Maree. d 01. I Derryvolgie *Conn* 04-09

RANCE, Eleanor Jane. b 72. d 96. Perm to Offic *Blackb* from 10

RANKIN, John Cooper. b 24. d 50. rtd 84

RAWLINGS, Gayle Ann Mary. b 53. d 03. Canada from 09

REDKNAP, Clive Douglas. b 53. d 95. V Hollington St Jo *Chich* 05-10

RIGBY, Francis Michael. b 29. d 90. Perm to Offic *Heref* 00-07

RIVERS, John Arthur. b 21. d 81. Perm to Offic *Nor* 87-06

ROBINSON, Jennifer Elizabeth. b 53. d 04. Perm to Offic *Sheff* from 08

ROMER, William Miller. b 35. d 60. rtd 08

ROSS (*née* YOUNG), Mrs Karen Heather. b 66. d 05. Hon C Ravenshead *S'well* 07-09; Chapl Notts Healthcare NHS Trust 08-09

SAGOVSKY, Canon Nicholas. b 47. **d** 74. rtd 11
SANDERS, Diana Louise. b 59. **d** 98. NSM Clarendon *Sarum* 01-08
SANDERS, Roderick David Scott. b 58. **d** 88. NSM Guildf Ch Ch w St Martha-on-the-Hill *Guildf* 03-10
SANDERS (*née* COLLINGRIDGE), Mrs Susan Rachel. b 61. **d** 88. V Guildf Ch Ch w St Martha-on-the-Hill *Guildf* 03-11
SANDOM, Miss Carolyn Elizabeth. b 63. **d** 94. C Cambridge H Sepulchre *Ely* 96-05
SANKEY, Julian. b 52. **d** 86. Chapl St Luke's Hospice Sheff 94-07
SAUNDERS, Moira Ruth Forbes. b 76. **d** 04. C Welling *Roch* 04-08
SCALES, Barbara Marion. b 24. **d** 87. rtd 95
SCOTT, William John. b 46. **d** 71. rtd 11
SKINNER, Arthur. b 38. **d** 97. rtd 08; Perm to Offic *Cant* from 08
SMITH, David Leonard. b 37. **d** 91. NSM Potton w Sutton and Cockayne Hatley *St Alb* 91-09
SMITH (*née* SAMPSON), Ms Gail Sampson. b 49. **d** 93. USA from 07
SMITH, Ms Vivienne Ruth. b 57. **d** 00. TM Dewsbury *Wakef* 03-06
✠SOLIBA, The Most Revd Ignacio Capuyan. b 44. **d** 73. rtd 09
STAFFORD, Mark Anthony. b 64. **d** 98. TV Retford *S'well* 02-09; P-in-c Babworth w Sutton-cum-Lound and Scofton etc 08-09
STEVEN, Richard John. b 54. **d** 99. Australia from 09
STEWART-SYKES, Teresa Melanie. b 64. **d** 89. USA 98-01
STOKES, David Francis Robert. b 53. **d** 03. Perm to Offic *Sarum* from 08
STRATFORD, Niall. **d** 09. NSM Killiney Ballybrack *D & G* from 09
SUTHERLAND, Mark Robert. b 55. **d** 85. USA from 10
SWIFT, Sarah Jane. b 65. **d** 06. C Wealdstone H Trin *Lon* 06-10
SWINNEY, Shawn Douglas. b 76. **d** 09. NSM Gerrards Cross and Fulmer *Ox* from 09
TAYLOR, John. b 58. **d** 98. Australia from 09
TAYLOR, Peter John. b 60. **d** 87. R Gatehouse of Fleet *Glas* 97-07
✠TEROM, The Rt Revd Zechariah James. b 41. **d** 71. rtd 09
THOMAS, Andrew Peter. **d** 08. C Llanishen *Llan* 08-10
THOMAS, Graham Wallace. b 51. **d** 75. Chapl RN 84-07
THOMAS, John Arun. b 47. **d** 88. India from 04
THOMPSON-VEAR, John Arthur. b 76. **d** 03. TV Harrogate St Wilfred *Ripon* 08-11

TOMLIN, Keith Michael. b 53. **d** 80. Louthesk Deanery Chapl *Linc* 06-10
TREASURE, Mrs Joy Elvira. b 23. **d** 87. rtd 92
TWOMEY, Jeremiah Thomas Paul. b 46. **d** 87. C Belfast St Anne *Conn* from 08
UDAL, Canon Joanna Elizabeth Margaret. b 64. **d** 97. Abp's Sec for Angl Communion Affairs *Cant* 09
VAN DEN BOS (*née* MUMFORD), Mrs Clare. b 74. **d** 07. C N Shields *Newc* 08-10
WALKER, Richard David. b 45. **d** 95. Hon C Cromhall, Tortworth, Tytherington, Falfield etc *Glouc* 04-07
WARD, Ronald Albert. b 29. **d** 03. rtd 07
WATKINS, Michael John. b 61. **d** 05. TV Chippenham St Paul w Hardenhuish etc *Bris* 09-10; TV Kington St Michael 09-10
WAUDBY, Miss Christine. b 45. **d** 90. rtd 10
WHEELER, Nicholas Paul. b 60. **d** 87. Brazil from 08
WHETTLETON, Timothy John. b 53. **d** 99. P-in-c Gowerton *S & B* 01-05
WHITE (*née* DUNCOMBE), Mrs Maureen Barbara. b 42. **d** 89. rtd 07
WILKIE, Michael John David. b 65. **d** 00. NSM Combe Martin, Berrynarbor, Lynton, Brendon etc *Ex* 00-05
WILKINSON, Matthew John George. b 81. **d** 06. C Wrexham *St As* 06-11
WILLIAMS, Bryan George. b 37. **d** 01. rtd 05
WILLIAMS, Mary Elizabeth. b 72. **d** 06. C Birstall and Wanlip *Leic* 06-09
WILLIAMS, Paul Robert. b 66. **d** 99. Mongolia from 09
WILLIAMS, Robert Edward. b 50. **d** 74. Chapl Ellesmere Coll 05-08
WILSON, David Brian. b 47. **d** 71. rtd 11
WILSON, George Thomas. b 47. **d** 00. NSM Cartmel Peninsula *Carl* from 10
WOODCOCK, Canon Carolyn. b 47. **d** 98. rtd 10; Perm to Offic *Blackb* from 10
WRIGHT, Christopher Joseph Herbert. b 47. **d** 77. Prin All Nations Chr Coll Ware 93-04
WRIGHT, Miss Pamela Jean. b 38. **d** 03. NSM Harrow Weald St Mich *Lon* 05-08
YALLOP, John. b 47. **d** 79. P-in-c Cliftonville *Cant* 94-99
YONG, Sok Han. b 61. **d** 10. NSM Abingdon *Ox* from 11

CLERGY WHO HAVE DIED SINCE THE LAST EDITION

A list of clergy who have died since 5 August 2009, when the compilation of the 2010–2011 edition was completed. The month and year of death (if known) are recorded with each entry.

ABSOLON, Michael John 12/10
ADAM, Michael MacIntosh 04/10
ADENEY, Harold Walter 04/10
ADNETT, Roy Gumley 12/10
ALDER, Eric Reginald Alfred 05/10
ALLANDER, William Edward Morgell Kidd 06/11
ALLCHIN, Arthur Macdonald (Donald) 12/10
ALLEN, John Michael 06/11
ALLEN, Michael Edward Gerald 12/09
ALLEN, Patrick Charles Benedict 04/11
ANSELL, Stuart Adrian 02/11
APPLETON, Ronald Percival 07/11
APPS, Anthony Howard 12/10
APTED, Peter John 01/10
ASHLEY, John Michael 12/10
ASKEW, Dennis 03/11
ASPDEN, Peter George 06/11
ASTIN, Alfred Ronald 10/09
ATKINSON, Albert Edward 05/10
AYERST, Edward Richard 10/09
BAILEY, Anthony 09/10
BAINES, John Edmund 01/11
BAKER, Gerald Stothert 01/11
BAKER, Harry Hallas 03/10
BALL, George Raymond 09/10
BARFF, John Robert 05/11
BARKER, Arundel Charles 03/10
BARKER, Hugh Remington 12/09
BARNES, Bryan Peter 05/11
BARNES, Charles Peter Kentish 01/11
BARNES, Donald Edward 06/11
BARNETT, Norman 09/09
BARNSLEY, Valerie Anne (Anna) 11/09
BARR, William Norman Cochrane 10/10
BARRALL, John Henry 05/10
BARRATT, Anthony John 01/10
BARRATT, Peter 08/09
BASTOCK, Kenneth William 01/10
BAXTER, Brian Raymond 01/11
BAYLEY, John Benson 09/09
BEAL, Malcolm 01/11
BEARDSMORE, John 11/09
BEDFORD, Colin Michael 12/09
BEDWELL, Stanley Frederick 02/11
BEEK, Michael Peter 02/10
BELCHER, Frederick William 12/09
BELL, Philip Harold 04/10
BENNETT, Peter Hugh 05/11
BEVAN, Charles Joseph Godfrey 11/10
BEVAN, Gordon Richard 04/10
BIBBY, Frank 07/10
BIRCH, Janet Ann 05/11
BIRD, Colin Richard Bateman 06/10
BIRD, Geoffrey Neville 06/11
BISHOP, David Harold 09/10
BLACKFORD, David Walker 09/09
BLACKWELL, Geoffrey David 04/11
BLAIR-FISH, John Christopher 09/10
BLAKELEY, Robert Daniel 02/10
BLANT, Edgar 09/10
BLENKIN, Hugh Linton 12/10
BLISS, Neil Humberstone 06/10
BLOWERS, Ralph Barrie 08/10

BOND, Douglas Gregory 03/11
BOND-THOMAS, David Harradence 10/09
BOULT, Anthony Christopher 08/09
BOWDEN, John Stephen 12/10
BOWEN, Vincent Paul 02/11
BOWERS, Stanley Percival 09/10
BOWLES, Ronald Leonard 09/10
BOWYER, Frank 10/09
BOX, David Norman 11/09
BOYS, Margaret Ann 08/10
BRADBURY, Herbert Cedric 01/11
BRADDOCK, Arthur Derek 03/11
BRADLEY, John Owen 08/09
BRAND, Frank Ronald Walter 08/09
BRANT, Leslie Harold 10/10
BRAY, Richard 04/10
BREED, Kenneth Wilfred 08/09
BRENCHLEY, Royston Harry Peter 09/10
BRIERLEY, David James 08/09
BRIGGS, Derek 12/10
BRITTON, John Anthony 10/10
BROOKS, Roger John 07/11
BROWN, Frank Seymour 09/10
BROWN, James Michael 04/10
BROWN, John William Etheridge 09/09
BROWN, Richard Lessey 08/09
BROWNRIGG, Ronald Allen 01/11
BRYAN, Nigel Arthur 10/10
BRYAN, Percival John Milward 05/10
BRYANS, Joseph 03/11
BUCHANAN, George Rowland 10/10
BUCKETT, James Frederick 10/10
BUDD, John Victor 12/10
BURBERY, Ian Edward 03/11
BURDON, Edward Arthur 01/11
BURLTON, William Frank 08/09
BURROUGHS, Edward Graham 09/09
BURT, Leslie Reginald 09/10
BUTLER, Alan John 01/11
BUTTERWORTH, Derek 11/09
BYFORD, David Charles 11/09
CAMERON, William James 04/11
CAMP, Frederick Walter 06/11
CAMPBELL, Frederick David Gordon 06/10
CARD, Thomas Ian 01/11
CARDEN, John Brumfitt 07/11
CARTER, Eric 09/09
CATON, David Arthur 12/10
CATT, Douglas Gordon 10/10
CHALK, John Edward 04/11
CHAPMAN, Edwin Thomas 10/10
CHAPMAN, Eric Ronald 06/11
CHARLTON, Arthur David 02/10
CHEESMAN, Ashley Frederick Bruce 10/10
CHERRILL, John Oliver 10/10
CHERRIMAN, Colin Wilfred (Brother Colin Wilfred) 08/11
CHITTY, Philip Crofts 07/10
CHIVERTON, Dennis Lionel Dunbar 06/11
CLARE, Lionel Philip 02/10
CLARK, Roland Mark Allison 07/10
CLARKE, Peter 09/09
CLAWSON, Derek George 06/10
CLAYTON, Norman James 09/10
CLEGG, Herbert 05/11

COATES, Kenneth Will 12/09
COBB, Peter George 05/10
COCHRANE, Kenneth Wilbur 12/09
COLE, Elizabeth Marie 07/11
COLEMAN, Beverley Warren 07/10
COLES, Geoffrey Herbert 03/11
COLLARD, John Cedric 12/10
COLLIE, John Norman 06/11
COLLINGS, Neil 06/10
COLLINS, Frederick Spencer 01/10
COLLINSON, Ernest John 04/10
CONEY, Peter Norman Harvey 07/10
CONNOR, Ellis Jones 05/11
COOKE, Hereward Roger Gresham 12/09
COOMBES, Derek Fennessey 01/11
COOPER, Barry Jack 01/10
COOPER, Wallace Peter 11/10
COPLAND, Charles McAlester 12/09
CORE, Edward 12/09
CORKE, John Harry 08/10
CORKER, Ronald 01/10
CORRY, Caroline Anne 09/10
CORSTORPHINE, Margaret 10/10
COTGROVE, Edwin John 02/11
COUCH, Andrew Nigel 12/09
COUSLAND, Andrew Oliver 08/10
COWDREY, Herbert Edward John 11/09
CRADDOCK, Brian Arthur 06/11
CRAWFORD, Peter 05/10
CROWE, Norman Charles 11/10
DALE, Olive Sylvia 11/09
DANIEL, Arthur Guy St John 06/10
DARVILL, Geoffrey 10/09
DAVEY, Frederick Hutley David 07/10
DAVIES, Alun Edwards 08/10
DAVIES, David Arthur Guy Hampton 12/10
DAVIES, Dennis William 12/09
DAVIES, Geoffrey Lovat 02/10
✠DAVIES, Howell Haydn 11/09
DAVIES, Stephen Walter 03/11
DAVIS, Edwin John Charles 10/09
DAY, John Alfred 10/10
DAY, Sheila Imogen 05/11
de BURGH-THOMAS, George Albert 12/10
de CHAZAL, Nancy Elizabeth 04/10
de la MARE, Benedick James Hobart 10/09
DEAN, Raymond Charles 01/10
DENNY, Peter Bond 12/09
DESPARD, Eric Herbert 06/11
DISS, Ronald George 12/10
DOBB, Arthur Joseph 11/09
DODD, James Henry Birchenough 12/10
DODD, John Dudley 07/10
DODDS, Neil Sutherland 04/11
DORMER, Christopher Robert 03/10
DOWDING, Stanley Frederick 09/09
DOWSE, Edgar 09/09
DOWSON, Roger Christopher 11/10
DOYLE, Alan Holland 06/10
DREWETT, Mervyn Henry 09/10
DUCK, Jacqueline 10/10
DUDDING, Edward Leslie (Father Gregory) 08/09
DUNCAN, Peter Harold Furlong 04/10

DURNFORD, Peter Jeffrey 02/10
DYKES, Michael David Allan 02/11
EASON, Cyril Edward 10/10
EDDISON, Robert John Buchanan 05/11
EDGE, John Francis 10/10
EDWARDS, Thomas Erwyd Pryse 03/11
ELBOURNE, Raymond Nigel Wilson 09/10
ELLIOTT, George Evan 10/10
EMBLETON, Harold 06/11
EMSON, Stanley George 11/09
ESCRITT, Michael William 01/11
EVANS, Gareth Milton 08/10
EVANS, Gerald Arthur 03/10
EVANS, John Barrie 11/09
EVANS, Richard Edward Victor 03/10
EVANS, Thomas Norman 12/09
EVEREST, Graham Robert 07/10
FANE, Clifford Charles 11/09
FARGUS, Maxwell Stuart 10/09
FARRANT, John Frederick Ames 11/09
FAWCETT, Frederick William 04/11
FENN, Roy William Dearnley 07/10
FIELD, William Jenkin 05/11
FIENNES, Oliver William 06/11
FILBY, William Charles Leonard 12/09
FINNIE, Robert 08/10
FISHER, Diana Margaret 11/10
FLATT, Roy Francis Ferguson 03/11
FOOKES, Roger Mortimer 12/09
FORD, Eric Copeland 06/11
FORRYAN, John Edward 07/11
FORSTER, Victor Henry 11/09
FOSDIKE, Lewis Bertram 08/10
FOSTER, Thomas Arthur 02/10
FOULGER, Bernard Darwin 11/09
FOX, Cynthia 04/10
FRASER, Alister Douglas 01/10
FREEMAN, Douglas James 05/10
FRICKER, David Duncan 03/10
FRY, Roger Owen 05/10
FULLER, Robert Peter 06/11
FURNESS, John Alfred 11/10
GALLETLY, Thomas 11/10
GARNETT, James Arthur 01/11
GARRETT, John Watkins 05/10
GATHERCOLE, John Robert 10/10
GEAKE, Peter Henry 01/11
GEDDES, Gordon David 01/11
GELLING, John Drury 03/11
GEORGE, Charles Roy 10/09
GEORGE, Penelope (formerly COMPTON), 08/10
GILBERT, John Edwin 09/09
GILBERT, Margaret Ann 06/11
GILL, Thomas 10/10
GILLETT, Victor Henry John 02/11
GILLING, John Reginald 03/10
GILLMOR, Samuel Frederick 11/09
GILMAN, Michael 04/11
GLASS, Kenneth William 02/11
GLEDHILL, James William 07/11
GODDARD, Sydney Thomas 11/09
GODFREY, Edward Colin 12/10
GOLBOURNE, Winston George 04/11
GOLDSMITH, Malcolm Clive 07/11
GOOD, George Fitzgerald 03/10
GOOD, Robert Stanley 12/09
GOODMAN, Sidney William 08/09
GOODRUM, Alice 11/10
GORDON, John Michael 01/11
GOULDER, Michael Douglas 01/10
GOURLEY, William Robert Joseph 05/10
GRACE, Wilfrid Windsor 11/09

GRAHAM, Marion McKenzie 03/11
GRAHAM, Peter Bartlemy 10/09
GRAHAM, Robert John 11/09
GRAY, Alan Eric 10/10
GREEN, Derek George Wilson 04/10
GREEN, John Herbert Gardner-Waterman 02/10
GREEN, Joseph Hudson 08/09
✠GREEN, Mark 08/09
GREEN, Peter Edwin 01/11
GREENACRE, Roger Tagent 07/11
GREENHALGH, Eric 03/11
GREENWAY, Margaret Hester 01/10
GRIBBLE, Howard Frank 09/09
GRIFFITH, Hugh Emrys 07/10
GRIFFITHS, Arthur Evan 02/10
GRIFFITHS, Russell Howard 12/10
GRIFFITHS, Thomas 08/10
GRIFFITHS, Vyrnach Morgan 06/10
GRIGG, William John Frank 04/11
GRIGGS, Frederick John 12/09
GRINHAM, Garth Clews 02/11
GROUNDSELL, Melanie Anne 06/10
GUSH, Laurence Langley 01/11
HALE, John Frederick 04/10
HALL, Charles John 01/11
HALL, Harold Henry Stanley Lawson 01/10
HALL, Stephen Clarence 01/11
HALLETT, Jacqueline Victoria (Lyn) 06/10
HAMBLIN, John Talbot 11/09
HAMEY, Geoffrey Allan 07/10
HAMILTON, Gerald Murray Percival 04/10
HAMILTON, James Davy 02/11
HAMMERSLEY, Peter 06/11
HAMNETT, Herbert Arnold 06/11
HANSON, John Westland 04/11
HARBOTTLE, Anthony Hall Harrison 12/09
HARDAKER, Ian Alexander 11/10
✠HARE, Thomas Richard 07/10
HARPER, Geoffrey 12/09
HARPER, John Hugh 05/10
HARPER, Michael Claude 01/10
HARRIS, John Peter 06/11
HARRISON, Francis Russell 08/10
HART, David Leonard 10/09
HARTLAND, David Robson 09/09
HARTLEY, Graham William Harrington 03/11
HARTLEY, Herbert 03/10
HARVEY, Trevor John 08/10
HASSELL, John Charles 03/11
HATCHLEY, Walter John 12/10
HATCHMAN, Hugh Alleyne 12/10
HATHERLEY, Victor Charles 11/10
HAWKINS, Ian Clinton 11/09
HAWKINS, John Arthur 08/10
HAWKINS, John Charles Lacey 02/11
HAWKINS, William Arthur 03/11
HAYNES, Leonard Thomas 03/10
HAYWARD, John Derek Risdon 04/10
HEAL, Guy Martin 08/09
HEBDEN, Peter 11/09
HEFFERNAN, May Olive 02/11
HEGARTY, Gerald 06/11
HEIDT, John Harrison 10/09
HENCHER, John Bredon 04/11
HIGGINS, Frank Roylance 02/11
HIGGINS, Geoffrey Minta 06/10
HILL, John 06/10
HILL, Michael 11/09
HJORTH, Rolf Gunnar Leer 01/10
HOBBS, Antony Ewan Talbot 10/10
HOLBROOKE-JONES, Stanley Charles 03/10

HOLDEN, Geoffrey Ralph 02/11
HOLLINGSHURST, Robert Peter 11/09
HOLLOWAY, Roger Graham 10/10
HOMFRAY, John Bax Tayler 03/10
HONNER, Robert Ralph 01/11
HOOD, Leslie 03/11
HOOKER, Richard Malcolm Neil 05/11
HOUGHTON, John Caswell 09/09
HUDSON, Gerald Ernest 02/10
HUDSON, John Cecil 06/11
HUDSPITH, Ernest 10/10
HUGHES, Bertram Arthur Edwin 01/10
HUGHES, Elfed 06/11
HUGHES, Hugh 01/11
HUMPHREYS, William Alfred 04/11
HUNKIN, Oliver John Wellington 01/11
HURRELL, John William 07/10
HURST, Antony 03/11
HUTT, Colin Villette 01/10
HUXTABLE, Michael George 07/11
ILOTT, Philip Edwin 03/10
INGLESBY, Eric Vredenburg (Paul) 05/10
IRVINE, John Graham Gerard Charles 01/11
IRWIN, Albert Samuel 05/10
ISITT, David Edgar Reid 08/09
IVIN, Maureen 04/10
JACK, Alexander Richard 04/11
JACK, Henry Graham 03/11
JACKSON, Arthur Malcolm 05/10
JAGGER, Peter John 10/09
✠JAMES, Colin Clement Walter 12/09
JAMES, Herbert Royston Joseph 12/09
JARDIN, Kenneth 10/09
JARVIS, Geoffrey Thomas Henry 11/09
JENNINGS, Barry Randall 06/10
JENNINGS, Harold Andrew 07/11
JESSUP, William Roy 01/11
JEWELL, Charles John 06/10
JOHNSON, Anthony Trevor 11/09
JOHNSON, David Clark 07/11
JOHNSON, John Cecil 02/10
JOHNSTON-HUBBOLD, Clifford Johnston 02/10
JONES, Albert 11/10
JONES, Brian 01/10
JONES, Christopher John Stark 04/11
JONES, David Frederick Donald 01/10
JONES, David Robert 09/09
JONES, Eric Vernon 04/11
JONES, Gordon Howlett 03/11
JONES, Griffith Walter Hywyn 03/10
JONES, John Francis Williams 04/10
✠JONES, Noël Debroy 08/09
JONES, Robert 12/10
JONES, Victor Harvey 04/10
JONES, William Edward Benjamin 10/10
JORDAN, Ronald Henry 03/10
KEARNS, Philip Gillin 05/10
KEEGAN, Donald Leslie 04/10
KEIGHTLEY, Peter Edward 07/11
KELLAND, Kenneth William Jerome 08/09
✠KEMP, Eric Waldram 11/09
KENNEDY, James Ernest Campbell 08/10
KENNEDY, William Edmund 08/10
KERR, George Cecil 08/10
KERRISON, Anne Edmonstone 11/10

KETTLE, David John 03/11
KEYTE, Douglas Joseph Henry 01/11
KIDD, Timothy 06/11
KING, Donald 04/11
KING, Lawrence Norman 04/10
KIRK, George 02/11
KITCHING, Paul 05/10
KITTERINGHAM, Ian 01/10
KNICKERBOCKER, Driss Richard 02/10
LAMB, Peter Francis Charles 02/11
LANCASTER, Norman 05/10
LAST, Harold Wilfred 02/11
LAVERACK, John Justin 01/11
LAW, Gordon Peter 12/10
LECKEY, Hamilton 10/09
LEE, Henry 11/09
LEE WARNER, Theodore John 04/10
LEES-SMITH, Christopher John (Brother Edward) 02/10
LENNOX, James 03/10
LENNOX, William Ernest Michael 12/10
LEWIS, Arthur Roland 01/10
LEWIS, Eric 07/10
LEWIS, John Percival 12/10
LIKEMAN, Martin Kaye 07/11
LINDLEY, Geoffrey 11/10
LINDO, Leithland Oscar 07/10
LISTER, Anthony Galen 05/11
LITTLEWOOD, John Richard 07/10
LLEWELYN, John Dilwyn 02/10
LLOYD, Herbert James 07/10
LOCKHART, Robert Joseph Norman 05/10
LOCKYER, Desmond Edward Weston 10/10
LONGFORD, Edward de Toesny Wingfield 07/10
LONGRIDGE, Richard Nevile 09/09
LOWRY, Robert Harold 02/11
LUNNEY, Henry 12/10
LUNT, Derek 01/10
LUTHER THOMAS, Ilar Roy 06/11
LYNE, Roger Howard 01/10
LYON, Donald Robert 02/11
McCANN, David Terence 09/09
McCREADY, Marcus Diarmuid Julian 07/10
McDONALD, John Richard Burleigh 05/11
MacDONALD, Trevor John 12/10
McGOWN, Robert Jackson 06/11
McKAY, John Andrew 07/10
McKECHNIE, John Gregg 01/11
McKEON, James Ernest 10/10
McLAREN, Ronald 10/10
McLELLAN, Eric Macpherson Thompson 10/10
McNAMEE, William Graham 03/11
McNAUGHTON-JORDAN, Lindy 01/10
MACQUIBAN, Gordon Alexander 06/10
McSPARRON, Cecil 03/10
MADDOX, Goronwy Owen 06/10
MALINS, Peter 11/09
MANHIRE, Ashley Lewin 06/11
MANT, Frances Joy 05/11
✠MANTLE, John Ambrose Cyril 11/10
MARR, Joan Mary 04/11
MARSHALL, Timothy John 09/10
MARTIN, John Stuart 03/10
MASHEDER, Richard 02/11
MATCHETT, Alan William 04/10
MAXWELL, Ralph 05/10
MAYERSON, Paul Strom 02/11
MAYHEW, Charles 04/10

MAYNARD, Raymond 12/09
MEREDITH, Robert 09/09
MEREDITH-JONES, Richard 02/10
METHUEN, John Alan Robert 07/10
MICHELL, Douglas Reginald 03/11
MIDDLEMISS, Jeffrey Thomas 12/09
MILLAM, Peter John 06/10
MILLAR, Alan Askwith 07/11
MILLER, James Ivimey 01/10
MILLETT, William Hugh 03/11
MILLINGTON, Robert William Ernest 08/09
MILLWARD, Pauline Freda 06/10
MILLYARD, Alexander John 10/10
MILROY, Ethel Doreen 04/10
MILVERTON, Frederic Jack 08/09
MITCHELL, William Blanchard 05/11
MOORGAS, Geoffrey Gordon 03/11
MORRELL, Robin Mark George 03/10
MORRIS, Edward 03/11
MORRIS, Edwin Alfred 07/11
MORRIS, Frank Leo 10/10
MORRIS, Peter Arthur William 02/11
MORRIS, Peter Michael Keighley 01/10
MORRIS, Raymond John Walton 03/11
MORTIMER, Charles Philip 01/10
MORTON, William Derek 10/10
MOWAT, Robert Alexander Laird (Sandy) 08/09
MURRAY, Thomas Brian 08/09
MYNETT, Colin 04/10
NAYLOR, John Watson 10/10
NEECH, Alan Summons 07/11
NEELY, William George 12/09
NEILL, James Purdon 01/10
NEWMAN, Alan George 08/10
NEWMAN, Geoffrey Maurice 01/11
NEWTON, John Richard 07/11
NICOL, Ernest 07/10
NORTHWOOD, Michael Alan 09/09
NORTON, Lesley Gillian 07/10
OGDEN, Eric 01/11
O'GORMAN, Paul Anthony 12/09
ONSLOW, Denzil Octavia 04/11
ORCHARD, Harry Frank 04/10
ORLAND, Ernest George 01/11
OTTAWAY, Michael John 09/10
OWEN, Stanley Alfred George 02/10
PAICE, Alan 04/11
PALMER, David Roderick 06/11
PARKER, Alfred 08/09
PARKINSON, George Stanley 03/11
PARNELL-HOPKINSON, Clive 10/09
PARRETT, Stanley Frederick Donald 04/10
PARSONS, Bernard 02/11
PARSONS, Laurie 04/11
PATERSON, Gordon Ronald (Ron) 12/09
PATON, George Hemsell 04/10
PATTISON, Anthony 05/10
PAUL, John Douglas 09/09
PAWSEY, Jack Edward 02/10
PAYNE, Warwick Martin 05/10
PEAKE, Robert Ernest 05/11
PEARCE, Eustace Kenneth Victor 08/10
PEARSON, Edgar 10/10
PEERS, John Edward 05/10
PEET, John Michael 04/11
PENN, Clive Llewellyn 01/10
PENNINGTON, Frederick William 08/09
PENNINGTON, John Michael 01/11
PERCIVAL, Geoffrey 08/09

PERKIN, David Arthur 01/11
PERRENS, Everard George 03/10
PERRINS, Harold 09/09
PERROTT, John Alastair Croome 03/10
PERRY, Anthony Robert 06/10
PERRY, Colin Charles 11/10
PERRY, Robert Anthony 01/11
PETTITT, Simon 12/09
PHILLIPS, John William Burbridge 03/11
PHILLIPS, Patrick Noble Stowell 08/09
PICK, William Harry 03/11
PICKERING, Fred 01/10
PIERCE, Neil David 04/10
PIGOTT, John Drummond 02/11
PILDITCH, Patricia Desiree 11/09
PILKINGTON OF OXENFORD, (Peter) 02/11
✠PILLAR, Kenneth Harold 02/11
PIPER, John Howard 02/11
PIPER, Kenneth John 12/10
PITTARD, Roger Frederick 05/11
POIL, Ronald Wickens 10/09
POLLAK, Peter Henry 11/10
POLLOCK, Hugh Gillespie 05/10
POPE, Colin 09/09
PORTER, Arthur William 08/10
POWELL, Llewellyn 01/11
PREBBLE, Albert Ernest 06/10
PRESTON-THOMAS, Colin Barnabas Rashleigh 04/11
PRICE, Philip 10/10
PRICHARD, Thomas John 10/10
PRIEST, Helen Elizabeth 08/10
PRIME, Geoffrey Daniel 03/11
PRIOR, John Gilman Leathes 09/09
PRIOR, Kenneth George William 10/09
PRITCHARD, Donald Oliver 12/10
PYM, Francis Victor 12/09
QUINE, Ernest Kendrick Leigh 05/11
RAINBOW, Gerald Anton Hayward 03/10
RAINSBERRY, Edward John 02/11
RANDELL, John Harrison 08/10
RANSOME, Arthur 12/10
RANSON, George Sidney 08/09
✠RAWCLIFFE, Derek Alec 02/11
REEDE, Samuel William 10/10
REES, Gruffydd Nicholas 07/10
REEVE, Kenneth Robert 10/09
✠REEVES, The Rt Revd Sir Paul Alfred 08/11
RENSHAW, Peter Selwyn Kay 11/09
REYNOLDS, John Stewart 08/09
RHAM, John Theodore 11/10
RICHARDS, John Stanley 06/11
RICHARDSON, James Horner 05/10
RICHARDSON, John William 10/09
RICHARDSON, Kathleen Beatrice 05/10
RICHENS, Geoffrey Roger 01/10
RIDYARD, Malcolm Charles 10/09
RIGGS, Sidney James 03/11
RIMMER, John Clive 09/09
RIVERS, Arthur 04/10
ROBERTS, Bernard John 09/09
ROBERTS, Kenneth William Alfred 11/09
ROBERTS, Matthew Garnant 09/10
ROBERTS, Peter Gwilym 06/10
ROBERTS, Phillip 12/09
ROBERTS, Richard 09/09
ROBERTSON, Edward Macallan 04/11
ROBERTSON, Thomas John (David) 08/10
ROBINSON, Neil 10/09

ROBINSON, Thomas Fisher 07/11
ROE, Robin 07/10
ROSS, Frederick 09/09
ROWE, Peter Farquharson 12/09
ROWSTON, Geoffrey 05/10
ROYDS, John Caress 03/11
RUDD, Julian Douglas Raymond 12/09
RUFFLE, Peter Cousins 09/09
RUSSELL, Ralph Geoffrey Major 07/11
✠RUSTON, John Harry Gerald 04/10
RYE, David Ralph 07/10
SAGE, John Arthur 07/11
SANDERSON, Peter Richard Fallowfield 07/11
SAVILE, Ian Keith Wrey 04/10
SAVILLE, Jeremy David 08/09
SAWLE, Ralph Burford 02/10
SCATTERGOOD, William Henry 11/09
SCHOFIELD, Edward Denis 12/10
SCHOLEY, Donald 01/10
SCHOLFIELD, Peter 10/10
SCOTT, Walter David Craig 12/09
SCOTT, William 01/10
SCRUBY, Ronald Victor 01/11
SEABROOK, Geoffrey Barry 01/11
SEAL, Ronald Frederick 04/11
SEAMAN, Arthur Roland Mostyn 04/11
SELLORS, Michael Harry 01/10
SHAIL, William Frederick 03/11
SHANNON, Brian James 12/10
SHARE, David James 09/09
SHARMAN, Hilary John 03/11
SHARPLES, John Charles 07/11
SHAW, Colin Clement Gordon 11/09
SHAW, Geoffrey Norman 02/11
SHEPHERD, John Donald 03/10
SHERWOOD, Gordon Frederick 02/10
SHIRE, William Stanley 11/09
SIDES, James Robert 12/09
SIMCOCK, Michael Pennington 04/11
SIMMONS, Joan Yvonne 06/11
SIMPKINS, Frank Charles 06/11
SIMS, Peter George Russell 11/10
SKELTON, Henry John Nugent 03/10
SKINNER, David Malcolm 01/10
SLADDEN, Duncan Julius Edward 04/11
SLADDEN, John Cyril 03/11
SLATER, John Albert 03/11
SLATOR, Edward Douglas Humphreys 05/10
SLEE, Colin Bruce 11/10
SMART, Malcolm Graham 07/10
SMITH, Charles David 01/10
SMITH, Derek Arthur Douglas 02/10
SMITH, Eric Frederick James 06/10
SMITH, Peter William 01/11
SMITH, Richard 07/11
SMITH, William Joseph Thomas 05/10
✠SMITHSON, Alan 06/10
SMYTH, Francis George 04/10
SOLOMON, Arthur Creagh 04/11
SOMERVELL, Katherine Mary 02/11
SOUTHWELL, Roy 07/11
SPAFFORD, Christopher Garnett Howsin 04/11
SPELLMAN, John 12/09
SPENCE, Walter Cyril 11/09
SPENCER, Peter Cecil 05/11
SPILLER, Edward William 08/10
SPINK, George Arthur Peter 11/10
SPIVEY, Peter 03/11
SQUIRE, Clenyg 10/10

STAPLES, Terence Malcolm 06/11
STEDDON, Peter James Raymond 01/11
STEPHENSON, Nicolas William 12/09
STEVENS, David Charles 11/10
STEVENS, Sylvia Joyce 11/10
✠STEVENSON, Kenneth William 01/11
STOCKBRIDGE, Nelson William 12/09
STOKES, Terence Ronald 10/09
STOTT, John Robert Walmsley 07/11
STRANGE, Brian 06/10
STRONG, Jack 10/09
STYLES, Clive William John 09/10
SULLIVAN, Adrian Michael 04/11
TAILBY, Mark Kevan 04/10
TASSELL, Dudley Arnold 11/09
TAYLOR, Brian Valentine 05/11
TAYLOR, Clive Cavanagh 09/09
TAYLOR, Dennis James 03/11
TAYLOR, Neil Hamish 08/11
TAYLOR, Thomas Ronald Bennett 04/10
TEBBUTT, Simon Albert 10/09
TEDMAN, Alfred 10/09
THACKER, Roger Ailwyn Mackintosh 09/10
THEOBALD, Henry Charles 01/10
THOMAS, Colin Norman 01/10
THOMAS, David Geoffrey 01/11
THOMAS, David William 08/10
THOMAS, Eileen Anne Harwood 11/10
THOMAS, Owen James 12/10
THOMAS, William Kenneth 01/10
THOMPSON, Giles Derwent 07/11
THOMPSON, Ian Malcolm 09/09
THOMSON, Peter Ashley 01/10
THOMSON, Ronald Arthur 11/09
THORNETT, Frederick Charles 09/10
THOROLD, John Robert Hayford 01/10
THRALL, Margaret Eleanor 10/10
TIMBERLAKE, Neil Christopher 04/11
TINKER, Eric Franklin 07/11
TOLLERSON, Peter Joseph Moncrieff 07/10
TOZER, Frank William 09/10
TOZER, Reginald Ernest 06/11
TUBBS, Christopher Norman 04/10
TUDBALL, Arthur James 09/10
TUFFEL, Kennedy Joseph 10/09
TUNBRIDGE, John Stephen 02/11
TURNER, Beryl Rose 01/10
TURNER, William Edward 05/10
TURTON, Arthur Bickerstaffe 04/10
TYDEMAN, Richard 04/11
TYLER, Leonard George 09/10
URWIN, Roger Talbot 06/10
VANDERSTOCK, Alan 09/10
VAUGHAN, John 04/11
VAUGHAN-JONES, John Paschal 04/10
✠VERNEY, Stephen Edmund 11/09
VICK, Richard Arthur 12/09
VINCENT, George William Walter 12/10
VINE, Michael Derek 02/11
VODEN, Raymond William Lang 10/10
WADDY, Lawrence Heber 03/10
WALKER, Albert William John 11/09
✠WALKER, Peter Knight 12/10
✠WALL, Eric St Quintin 04/11

WALLACE, Richard Samuel 04/10
WALLS, Roland Charles 04/11
WARBURTON, Walter George 11/09
WARCHUS, Michael Edward George 04/11
WARD, David Conisbee 07/11
WARD, Frank Neal 11/10
WARD, John Raymond 03/11
WARD, Michael Anthony 11/09
WATSON, John Davidson 11/09
WATSON, John Robertson Thomas 06/11
WATTS, Geoffrey Frederick 01/11
WAUCHOPE, George Mpapa 05/11
WEALE, Colin Alexander 03/11
WEATHERHEAD, Thomas Leslie 01/11
WEAVER, Arthur Kenneth (Ken) 04/11
WEBER, Douglas John Craig 11/10
WEBSTER, David Edward 08/09
WEBSTER, Sheila Mary 07/11
WELCH, Harold Gerald 10/10
WELLING, Anthony Wyndham 07/10
WELLS, Edward Arthur 07/11
WELTON, Peter Abercrombie 09/10
WERNER, David Robert Edmund 03/11
WEST, Eric Edward 09/10
WEST, Harold Reginald 11/09
WETHERELL, Philip Anthony 07/10
WHARTON, Thomas Anthony 01/11
WHEELER, Anthony William 01/10
WHIFFEN, William Timothy 07/10
WHITE, Frederick William Hartland 09/10
WHITEHORN, Arthur Basil 03/10
WHITTA, Rex Alfred Rought 04/10
WHITTAKER, James Rawstron 11/09
WHITWELL, Martin Corbett 12/09
WHYMAN, Oliver 11/10
WIDDECOMBE, Malcolm Murray 10/10
WILBOURNE, Geoffrey Owen 05/10
WILESMITH, Mary Adelaide 01/11
WILKINSON, David James 02/11
WILKINSON, Wilfred Badger 02/10
WILLCOX, Sydney Harold 03/11
WILLETTS, Alfred 02/10
WILLIAMS, Anthony Francis 06/11
WILLIAMS, Benjamin Clive 04/11
WILLIAMS, David 08/09
WILLIAMS, John James 04/11
WILLIAMS, Malcolm Clive 04/10
WILLIAMS, Vincent Handley 12/09
WILLOUGHBY, George Charles 04/10
WILSON, James Phillip Maclean 07/10
WILSON, Robert Brian 02/11
WILSON, Ronald 09/09
WINDER, John William 12/10
WINTER, Raymond McMahon 09/10
WOOD, Frederick Leonard 12/09
WOODHOUSE, Hugh Frederic 10/10
WOODWARD, Richard Tharby 09/10
WRIGHT, Charles Frederick Peter 08/09
WRIGHT, Thomas Stephen 06/10
WYNN-EVANS, James Naylor 08/10
WYNNE, Trefor 01/10
YATES-ROUND, Joseph Laurence John 07/11
YIN, Roy Henry Bowyer 12/10

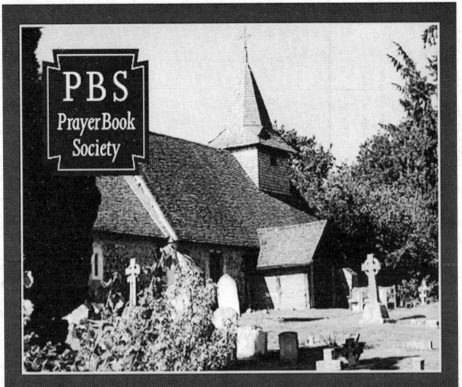

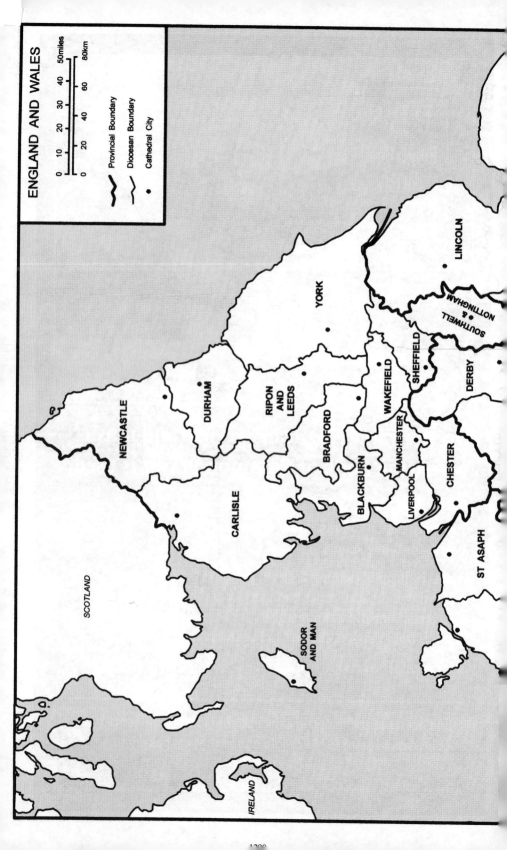

NORWICH

ST EDMUNDSBURY AND IPSWICH

CANTERBURY

CHELMSFORD

ELY

ROCHESTER

SOUTHWARK

LONDON

ST ALBANS

CHICHESTER

GUILDFORD

PETERBOROUGH

LEICESTER

OXFORD

WINCHESTER

PORTSMOUTH

COVENTRY

BIRMINGHAM

WORCESTER

BRISTOL

GLOUCESTER

SALISBURY

LICHFIELD

HEREFORD

BATH AND WELLS

MONMOUTH

SWANSEA AND BRECON

LLANDAFF

BANGOR

EXETER

ST DAVIDS

TRURO

The Channel Islands are annexed to the Diocese of Winchester

The Isles of Scilly are included in the Diocese of Truro

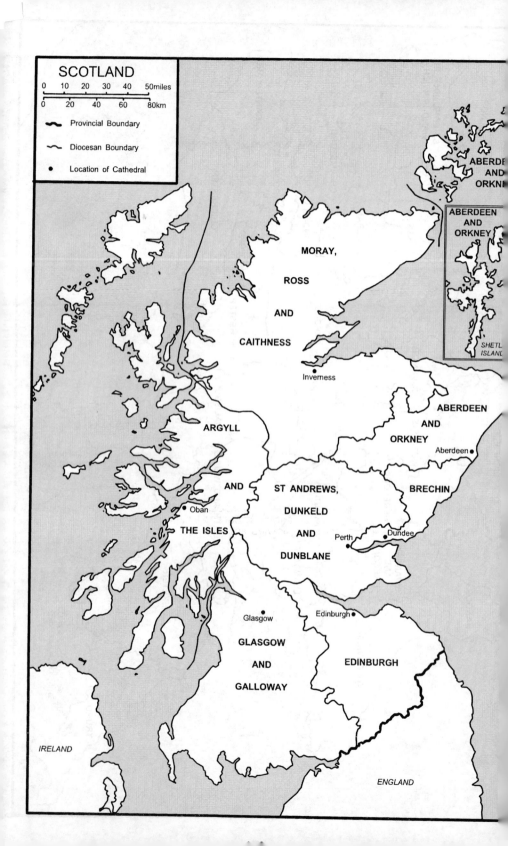

SCOTLAND

0 10 20 30 40 50miles

0   20   40   60   80km

~~~ Provincial Boundary

~~ Diocesan Boundary

● Location of Cathedral

MORAY,

ROSS

AND

CAITHNESS

● Inverness

ARGYLL

AND

● Oban

THE ISLES

ST ANDREWS,

DUNKELD

AND

● Perth

DUNBLANE

ABERDEEN

AND

ORKNEY

● Aberdeen

BRECHIN

● Dundee

ABERDEEN
AND
ORKNEY

SHETLAND
ISLANDS

ABERDE
AND
ORKNE

GLASGOW

AND

GALLOWAY

● Glasgow

Edinburgh ●

EDINBURGH

IRELAND

ENGLAND

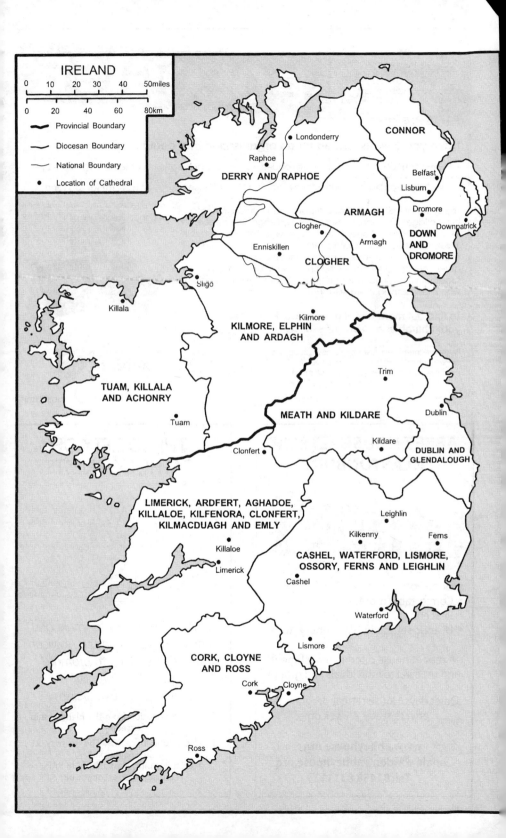